2025

Harris

North Carolina

Manufacturers Directory

MERGENT

Exclusive Provider of
Dun & Bradstreet Library Solutions

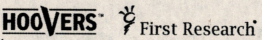

dun & bradstreet

HOOVERS™

First Research·

HARRIS
INFOSOURCE™

Published May 2025 next update May 2026

Publisher

Mergent Inc.
444 Madison Ave
New York, NY 10022

©Mergent Inc All Rights Reserved
2025 Mergent Business Press
ISSN 1080-2614
ISBN 978-1-63053-053-2

MERGENT
BUSINESS PRESS
by FTSE Russell

TABLE OF CONTENTS

SUMMARY OF CONTENTS

Number of Companies 13,531
Number of Decision Makers 20,395
Minimum Number of Employees 4

EXPLANATORY NOTES

How to Cross-Reference in This Directory

Sequential Entry Numbers. Each establishment in the Geographic Section is numbered sequentially (G-0000). The number assigned to each establishment is referred to as its "entry number." To make cross-referencing easier, each listing in the Geographic, SIC, Alphabetic and Product Sections includes the establishment's entry number. To facilitate locating an entry in the Geographic Section, the entry numbers for the first listing on the left page and the last listing on the right page are printed at the top of the page next to the city name.

Source Suggestions Welcome

Although all known sources were used to compile this directory, it is possible that companies were inadvertently omitted. Your assistance in calling attention to such omissions would be greatly appreciated. A special form on the facing page will help you in the reporting process.

Analysis

Every effort has been made to contact all firms to verify their information. The one exception to this rule is the annual sales figure, which is considered by many companies to be confidential information. Therefore, estimated sales have been calculated by multiplying the nationwide average sales per employee for the firm's major SIC/NAICS code by the firm's number of employees. Nationwide averages for sales per employee by SIC/NAICS codes are provided by the U.S. Department of Commerce and are updated annually. All sales—sales (est)—have been estimated by this method. The exceptions are parent companies (PA), division headquarters (DH) and headquarter locations (HQ) which may include an actual corporate sales figure—sales (corporate-wide) if available.

Types of Companies

Descriptive and statistical data are included for companies in the entire state. These comprise manufacturers, machine shops, fabricators, assemblers and printers. Also identified are corporate offices in the state.

Employment Data

This directory contains companies with 4 or more employees. The employment figure shown in the Geographic Section includes male and female employees and embraces all levels of the company: administrative, clerical, sales and maintenance. This figure is for the facility listed and does not include other plants or offices. It should be recognized that these figures represent an approximate year-round average. These employment figures are broken into codes A through G and used in the Product and SIC Sections to further help you in qualifying a company. Be sure to check the footnotes on the bottom of pages for the code breakdowns.

Standard Industrial Classification (SIC)

The Standard Industrial Classification (SIC) system used in this directory was developed by the federal government for use in classifying establishments by the type of activity they are engaged in. The SIC classifications used in this directory are from the 1987 edition published by the U.S. Government's Office of Management and Budget. The SIC system separates all activities into broad industrial divisions (e.g., manufacturing, mining, retail trade). It further subdivides each division. The range of manufacturing industry classes extends from two-digit codes (major industry group) to four-digit codes (product).

For example:

Industry Breakdown	Code	Industry, Product, etc.
*Major industry group	20	Food and kindred products
Industry group	203	Canned and frozen foods
*Industry	2033	Fruits and vegetables, etc.

*Classifications used in this directory

Only two-digit and four-digit codes are used in this directory.

Arrangement

1. The **Geographic Section** contains complete in-depth corporate data. This section is sorted by cities listed in alphabetical order and companies listed alphabetically within each city. A County/City Index for referencing cities within counties precedes this section.

IMPORTANT NOTICE: It is a violation of both federal and state law to transmit an unsolicited advertisement to a facsimile machine. Any user of this product that violates such laws may be subject to civil and criminal penalties, which may exceed $500 for each transmission of an unsolicited facsimile. Mergent Inc. provides fax numbers for lawful purposes only and expressly forbids the use of these numbers in any unlawful manner.

2. The **Standard Industrial Classification (SIC) Section** lists companies under approximately 500 four-digit SIC codes. An alphabetical and a numerical index precedes this section. A company can be listed under several codes. The codes are in numerical order with companies listed alphabetically under each code.

3. The **Alphabetic Section** lists all companies with their full physical or mailing addresses and telephone number.

4. The **Product Section** lists companies under unique Harris categories. An index preceding this section lists all product categories in alphabetical order. Companies can be listed under several categories.

USER'S GUIDE TO LISTINGS

GEOGRAPHIC SECTION

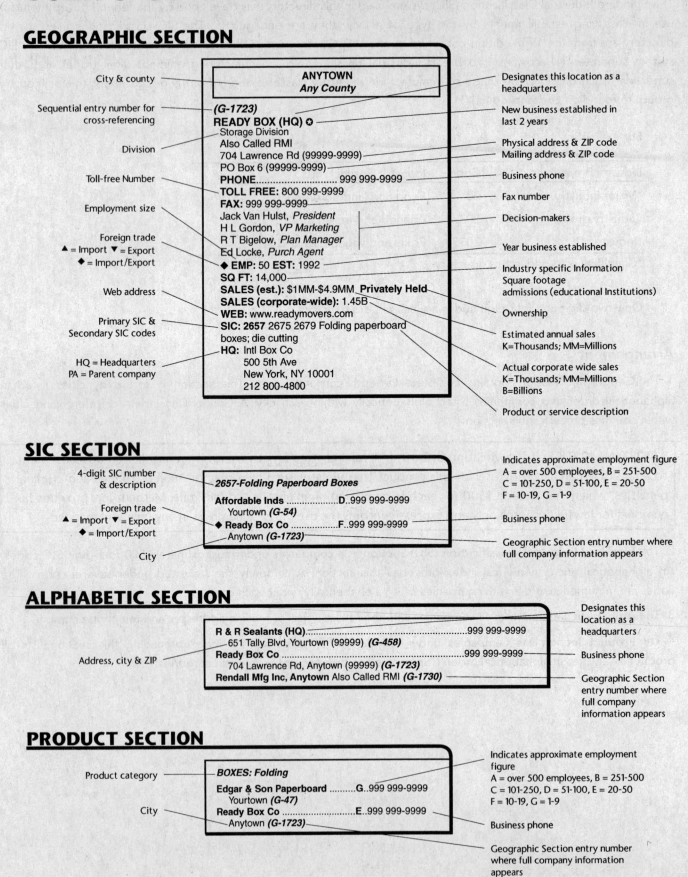

City & county

Sequential entry number for cross-referencing

Division

Toll-free Number

Employment size

Foreign trade
▲ = Import ▼ = Export
◆ = Import/Export

Web address

Primary SIC & Secondary SIC codes

HQ = Headquarters
PA = Parent company

ANYTOWN
Any County

(G-1723)
READY BOX (HQ) ✪
Storage Division
Also Called RMI
704 Lawrence Rd (99999-9999)
PO Box 6 (99999-9999)
PHONE............................ 999 999-9999
TOLL FREE: 800 999-9999
FAX: 999 999-9999
Jack Van Hulst, *President*
H L Gordon, *VP Marketing*
R T Bigelow, *Plan Manager*
Ed Locke, *Purch Agent*
◆ **EMP:** 50 **EST:** 1992
SQ FT: 14,000
SALES (est.): $1MM-$4.9MM **Privately Held**
SALES (corporate-wide): 1.45B
WEB: www.readymovers.com
SIC: 2657 2675 2679 Folding paperboard boxes; die cutting
HQ: Intl Box Co
500 5th Ave
New York, NY 10001
212 800-4800

Designates this location as a headquarters

New business established in last 2 years

Physical address & ZIP code
Mailing address & ZIP code

Business phone

Fax number

Decision-makers

Year business established

Industry specific Information
Square footage
admissions (educational Institutions)

Ownership

Estimated annual sales
K=Thousands; MM=Millions

Actual corporate wide sales
K=Thousands; MM=Millions
B=Billions

Product or service description

SIC SECTION

4-digit SIC number & description

Foreign trade
▲ = Import ▼ = Export
◆ = Import/Export

City

2657-Folding Paperboard Boxes

Affordable Inds ....D..999 999-9999
Yourtown *(G-54)*
◆ **Ready Box Co** ....F..999 999-9999
Anytown *(G-1723)*

Indicates approximate employment figure
A = over 500 employees, B = 251-500
C = 101-250, D = 51-100, E = 20-50
F = 10-19, G = 1-9

Business phone

Geographic Section entry number where full company information appears

ALPHABETIC SECTION

Address, city & ZIP

R & R Sealants (HQ)............................999 999-9999
651 Tally Blvd, Yourtown (99999) *(G-458)*
Ready Box Co 999 999-9999
704 Lawrence Rd, Anytown (99999) *(G-1723)*
Rendall Mfg Inc, Anytown Also Called RMI *(G-1730)*

Designates this location as a headquarters

Business phone

Geographic Section entry number where full company information appears

PRODUCT SECTION

Product category

City

BOXES: Folding

Edgar & Son Paperboard ....G..999 999-9999
Yourtown *(G-47)*
Ready Box Co ....E..999 999-9999
Anytown *(G-1723)*

Indicates approximate employment figure
A = over 500 employees, B = 251-500
C = 101-250, D = 51-100, E = 20-50
F = 10-19, G = 1-9

Business phone

Geographic Section entry number where full company information appears

GEOGRAPHIC SECTION

Companies sorted by city in alphabetical order
In-depth company data listed

STANDARD INDUSTRIAL CLASSIFICATIONS

Alphabetical index of classification descriptions
Numerical index of classification descriptions
Companies sorted by SIC product groupings

ALPHABETIC SECTION

Company listings in alphabetical order

PRODUCT INDEX

Product categories listed in alphabetical order

PRODUCT SECTION

Companies sorted by product and manufacturing service classifications

GEOGRAPHIC

SIC

ALPHABETIC

PRDT INDEX

PRODUCT

COUNTY/CITY CROSS-REFERENCE INDEX

ENTRY #	ENTRY #	ENTRY #	ENTRY #	ENTRY #

Mc Leansville .... (G-8218)
Oak Ridge .... (G-9569)
Pleasant Garden .... (G-9792)
Stokesdale .... (G-11810)
Summerfield .... (G-11834)
Whitsett .... (G-12599)

Halifax

Enfield .... (G-4481)
Halifax .... (G-6046)
Littleton .... (G-7883)
Roanoke Rapids ...... (G-10729)
Scotland Neck .... (G-11263)
Weldon .... (G-12518)

Harnett

Angier .... (G-110)
Bunnlevel .... (G-1015)
Cameron .... (G-1214)
Coats .... (G-3261)
Dunn .... (G-3839)
Erwin .... (G-4491)
Lillington .... (G-7788)

Haywood

Canton .... (G-1242)
Clyde .... (G-3255)
Maggie Valley .... (G-8005)
Waynesville .... (G-12450)

Henderson

Dana .... (G-3694)
East Flat Rock .... (G-4328)
Etowah .... (G-4495)
Flat Rock .... (G-4703)
Fletcher .... (G-4716)
Hendersonville .... (G-6183)
Horse Shoe .... (G-6929)
Mills River .... (G-8309)
Mountain Home .... (G-9274)
Zirconia .... (G-13528)

Hertford

Ahoskie .... (G-41)
Cofield .... (G-3266)
Harrellsville .... (G-6104)
Murfreesboro .... (G-9281)
Winton .... (G-13427)

Hoke

Raeford .... (G-9832)

Hyde

Swanquarter .... (G-11880)

Iredell

Harmony .... (G-6097)
Mooresville .... (G-8588)
Olin .... (G-9598)
Statesville .... (G-11641)
Troutman .... (G-12128)
Union Grove .... (G-12184)

Jackson

Cashiers .... (G-1490)
Dillsboro .... (G-3819)
Sylva .... (G-11890)
Whittier .... (G-12624)

Johnston

Benson .... (G-783)

Clayton .... (G-3129)
Four Oaks .... (G-4807)
Kenly .... (G-7228)
Pine Level .... (G-9678)
Princeton .... (G-9823)
Selma .... (G-11282)
Smithfield .... (G-11433)

Jones

Maysville .... (G-8210)
Pollocksville .... (G-9816)
Trenton .... (G-12109)

Lee

Broadway .... (G-986)
Sanford .... (G-11144)

Lenoir

Deep Run .... (G-3732)
Kinston .... (G-7391)
La Grange .... (G-7465)
Pink Hill .... (G-9764)

Lincoln

Crouse .... (G-3659)
Denver .... (G-3767)
Iron Station .... (G-7106)
Lincolnton .... (G-7806)
Vale .... (G-12207)

Macon

Franklin .... (G-4818)
Highlands .... (G-6842)
Otto .... (G-9606)

Madison

Hot Springs .... (G-6932)
Mars Hill .... (G-8076)
Marshall .... (G-8079)

Martin

Everetts .... (G-4497)
Hamilton .... (G-6048)
Jamesville .... (G-7182)
Robersonville .... (G-10765)
Williamston .... (G-12667)

Mcdowell

Little Switzerland .... (G-7882)
Marion .... (G-8029)
Nebo .... (G-9327)
Old Fort .... (G-9589)

Mecklenburg

Charlotte .... (G-1600)
Cornelius .... (G-3582)
Davidson .... (G-3696)
Huntersville .... (G-6962)
Matthews .... (G-8098)
Mint Hill .... (G-8329)
Paw Creek .... (G-9649)
Pineville .... (G-9712)

Mitchell

Bakersville .... (G-675)
Spruce Pine .... (G-11565)

Montgomery

Biscoe .... (G-846)
Candor .... (G-1237)
Ether .... (G-4494)

Mount Gilead .... (G-9198)
Star .... (G-11627)
Troy .... (G-12156)

Moore

Aberdeen .... (G-1)
Carthage .... (G-1275)
Eagle Springs .... (G-4319)
Pinebluff .... (G-9684)
Pinehurst .... (G-9688)
Robbins .... (G-10751)
Southern Pines .... (G-11494)
Vass .... (G-12227)
West End .... (G-12555)

Nash

Bailey .... (G-668)
Castalia .... (G-1492)
Middlesex .... (G-8272)
Nashville .... (G-9308)
Rocky Mount .... (G-10821)
Sharpsburg .... (G-11307)
Spring Hope .... (G-11552)
Whitakers .... (G-12574)

New Hanover

Carolina Beach .... (G-1257)
Castle Hayne .... (G-1493)
Kure Beach .... (G-7463)
Wilmington .... (G-12684)
Wrightsville Beach .. (G-13431)

Northampton

Conway .... (G-3578)
Garysburg .... (G-4977)
Gaston .... (G-4978)
Pendleton .... (G-9661)
Pleasant Hill .... (G-9797)
Potecasi .... (G-9819)
Seaboard .... (G-11269)
Severn .... (G-11298)

Onslow

Holly Ridge .... (G-6886)
Hubert .... (G-6935)
Jacksonville .... (G-7112)
Richlands .... (G-10720)
Sneads Ferry .... (G-11472)
Surf City .... (G-11862)
Swansboro .... (G-11882)

Orange

Carrboro .... (G-1265)
Cedar Grove .... (G-1516)
Chapel Hill .... (G-1521)
Efland .... (G-4374)
Hillsborough .... (G-6857)

Pamlico

Arapahoe .... (G-208)
Bayboro .... (G-711)
Grantsboro .... (G-5329)
Lowland .... (G-7936)
Merritt .... (G-8267)
Oriental .... (G-9599)
Vandemere .... (G-12226)

Pasquotank

Elizabeth City .... (G-4377)

Pender

Burgaw .... (G-1018)
Hampstead .... (G-6066)
Maple Hill .... (G-8025)
Rocky Point .... (G-10877)
Willard .... (G-12665)

Perquimans

Belvidere .... (G-778)
Hertford .... (G-6251)

Person

Roxboro .... (G-10917)
Semora .... (G-11295)
Timberlake .... (G-12099)

Pitt

Ayden .... (G-652)
Bethel .... (G-839)
Farmville .... (G-4525)
Fountain .... (G-4806)
Greenville .... (G-5934)
Grifton .... (G-6034)
Grimesland .... (G-6040)
Winterville .... (G-13414)

Polk

Columbus .... (G-3300)
Mill Spring .... (G-8300)
Saluda .... (G-11139)
Tryon .... (G-12172)

Randolph

Asheboro .... (G-323)
Cedar Falls .... (G-1515)
Franklinville .... (G-4855)
Liberty .... (G-7759)
Ramseur .... (G-10625)
Randleman .... (G-10634)
Seagrove .... (G-11273)
Sophia .... (G-11486)
Staley .... (G-11592)
Trinity .... (G-12113)

Richmond

Cordova .... (G-3580)
Ellerbe .... (G-4462)
Hamlet .... (G-6050)
Hoffman .... (G-6885)
Rockingham .... (G-10768)

Robeson

Fairmont .... (G-4500)
Lumber Bridge .... (G-7939)
Lumberton .... (G-7942)
Maxton .... (G-8199)
Orrum .... (G-9604)
Pembroke .... (G-9656)
Red Springs .... (G-10664)
Rowland .... (G-10915)
Saint Pauls .... (G-11004)

Rockingham

Eden .... (G-4339)
Madison .... (G-7983)
Mayodan .... (G-8206)
Reidsville .... (G-10671)
Stoneville .... (G-11819)

Rowan

China Grove .... (G-3072)
Cleveland .... (G-3209)

Faith .... (G-4520)
Gold Hill .... (G-5190)
Granite Quarry .... (G-5326)
Landis .... (G-7473)
Mount Ulla .... (G-9267)
Rockwell .... (G-10793)
Salisbury .... (G-11010)
Woodleaf .... (G-13429)

Rutherford

Bostic .... (G-960)
Cliffside .... (G-3225)
Ellenboro .... (G-4456)
Forest City .... (G-4783)
Rutherfordton .... (G-10972)
Spindale .... (G-11543)
Union Mills .... (G-12187)

Sampson

Autryville .... (G-647)
Clinton .... (G-3228)
Garland .... (G-4908)
Godwin .... (G-5186)
Harrells .... (G-6100)
Ivanhoe .... (G-7109)
Newton Grove .... (G-9514)
Roseboro .... (G-10911)
Turkey .... (G-12181)

Scotland

Gibson .... (G-5175)
Laurel Hill .... (G-7482)
Laurinburg .... (G-7492)
Wagram .... (G-12254)

Stanly

Albemarle .... (G-57)
Badin .... (G-665)
Locust .... (G-7889)
New London .... (G-9413)
Norwood .... (G-9553)
Oakboro .... (G-9575)
Richfield .... (G-10719)
Stanfield .... (G-11602)

Stokes

Danbury .... (G-3695)
Germanton .... (G-5173)
King .... (G-7321)
Lawsonville .... (G-7519)
Pine Hall .... (G-9677)
Pinnacle .... (G-9767)
Sandy Ridge .... (G-11141)
Walnut Cove .... (G-12326)

Surry

Ararat .... (G-209)
Dobson .... (G-3820)
Elkin .... (G-4438)
Mount Airy .... (G-9095)
Pilot Mountain .... (G-9670)
State Road .... (G-11636)
Westfield .... (G-12572)

Swain

Bryson City .... (G-1007)
Cherokee .... (G-3050)

Transylvania

Brevard .... (G-967)
Penrose .... (G-9662)

ENTRY #	ENTRY #	ENTRY #	ENTRY #	ENTRY #

Pisgah Forest .... (G-9769)
Rosman .... (G-10913)
Sapphire .... (G-11258)

Tyrrell

Columbia .... (G-3294)

Union

Indian Trail .... (G-7065)
Marshville .... (G-8085)
Matthews .... (G-8158)
Mineral Springs .... (G-8327)
Monroe .... (G-8414)
Stallings .... (G-11600)
Waxhaw .... (G-12422)
Wingate .... (G-13062)

Vance

Henderson .... (G-6146)

Kittrell .... (G-7438)
Manson .... (G-8022)
Middleburg .... (G-8271)

Wake

Apex ....(G-132)
Cary .... (G-1282)
Fuquay Varina .... (G-4864)
Garner ....(G-4911)
Holly Springs .... (G-6892)
Knightdale .... (G-7448)
Morrisville .... (G-8913)
New Hill .... (G-9409)
Raleigh .... (G-9857)
Rolesville .... (G-10889)
Wake Forest .... (G-12258)
Wendell ....(G-12529)
Willow Spring .... (G-12678)
Zebulon .... (G-13500)

Warren

Macon ....(G-7982)
Norlina .... (G-9520)
Warrenton .... (G-12349)

Washington

Plymouth .... (G-9798)
Roper .... (G-10899)

Watauga

Blowing Rock .... (G-880)
Boone .... (G-894)
Deep Gap ....(G-3727)
Vilas .... (G-12230)
Zionville .... (G-13527)

Wayne

Dudley .... (G-3834)
Fremont ....(G-4859)

Goldsboro .... (G-5196)
Mount Olive .... (G-9246)
Pikeville .... (G-9666)
Seven Springs .... (G-11297)

Wilkes

Boomer .... (G-890)
Hays ....(G-6145)
Mc Grady .... (G-8217)
Millers Creek .... (G-8304)
Moravian Falls .... (G-8807)
North Wilkesboro ...... (G-9521)
Purlear .... (G-9831)
Roaring River .... (G-10749)
Ronda .... (G-10893)
Thurmond .... (G-12097)
Traphill .... (G-12106)
Wilkesboro .... (G-12626)

Wilson

Elm City .... (G-4464)
Lucama .... (G-7937)
Saratoga .... (G-11261)
Sims .... (G-11428)
Stantonsburg .... (G-11626)
Wilson .... (G-12959)

Yadkin

Boonville .... (G-956)
East Bend .... (G-4322)
Hamptonville .... (G-6081)
Jonesville .... (G-7194)
Yadkinville .... (G-13434)

Yancey

Burnsville .... (G-1181)
Micaville .... (G-8270)

GEOGRAPHIC SECTION

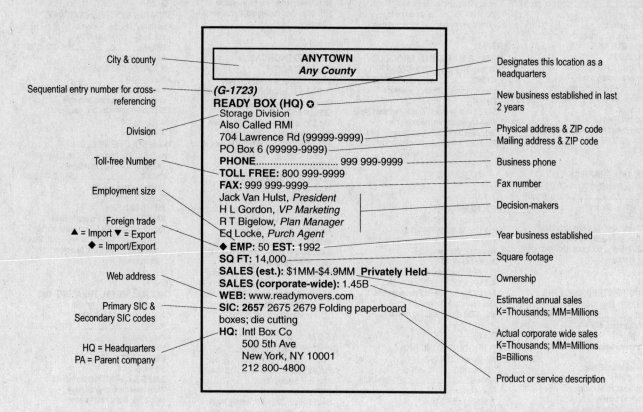

City & county

Sequential entry number for cross-referencing

Division

Toll-free Number

Employment size

Foreign trade
▲ = Import ▼ = Export
◆ = Import/Export

Web address

Primary SIC &
Secondary SIC codes

HQ = Headquarters
PA = Parent company

ANYTOWN
Any County

(G-1723)
READY BOX (HQ) ✪
Storage Division
Also Called RMI
704 Lawrence Rd (99999-9999)
PO Box 6 (99999-9999)
PHONE.............................. 999 999-9999
TOLL FREE: 800 999-9999
FAX: 999 999-9999
Jack Van Hulst, *President*
H L Gordon, *VP Marketing*
R T Bigelow, *Plan Manager*
Ed Locke, *Purch Agent*
◆ **EMP:** 50 **EST:** 1992
SQ FT: 14,000
SALES (est.): $1MM-$4.9MM **Privately Held**
SALES (corporate-wide): 1.45B
WEB: www.readymovers.com
SIC: 2657 2675 2679 Folding paperboard
boxes; die cutting
HQ: Intl Box Co
500 5th Ave
New York, NY 10001
212 800-4800

Designates this location as a headquarters

New business established in last 2 years

Physical address & ZIP code
Mailing address & ZIP code

Business phone

Fax number

Decision-makers

Year business established

Square footage

Ownership

Estimated annual sales
K=Thousands; MM=Millions

Actual corporate wide sales
K=Thousands; MM=Millions
B=Billions

Product or service description

See footnotes for symbols and codes identification.
- This section is in alphabetical order by city.
- Companies are sorted alphabetically under their respective cities.
- To locate cities within a county refer to the County/City Cross Reference Index.

IMPORTANT NOTICE: It is a violation of both federal and state law to transmit an unsolicited advertisement to a facsimile machine. Any user of this product that violates such laws may be subject to civil and criminal penalties which may exceed $500 for each transmission of an unsolicited facsimile. Harris InfoSource provides fax numbers for lawful purposes only and expressly forbids the use of these numbers in any unlawful manner.

Aberdeen
Moore County

(G-1)
ABERDEEN COCA-COLA BTLG CO INC
203 W South St (28315-2709)
P.O. Box 518 (28315-0518)
PHONE..............................910 944-2305
Gary Alan Moon, *Pr*
Doris B Moon, *VP*
EMP: 16 **EST:** 1913
SQ FT: 4,800
SALES (est) 1.91MM **Privately Held**
Web: www.aberdeencocacola.com
SIC: 2086 Bottled and canned soft drinks

(G-2)
BUILDERS FRSTSRCE - STHAST GRO
Also Called: Pbc of Aberdeen
900 Pinehurst Dr (28315-2023)
P.O. Box 8 (28315-0008)
PHONE..............................910 944-2516
Paul Portfilio, *Genl Mgr*
EMP: 109

SALES (corp-wide): 16.4B **Publicly Held**
Web: www.bldr.com
SIC: 5211 2431 Lumber products; Doors, wood
HQ: Builders Firstsource - Southeast Group, Llc
6031 Connection Dr # 400
Irving TX 75039
844 487-8625

(G-3)
CALCO ENTERPRISES INC (PA)
Also Called: Calco Sheet Metal Works
240 Crestline Ln (28315-7797)
P.O. Box 142 (28315-0142)
PHONE..............................910 695-0089
Mark Francis, *Pr*
Joel Francis, *Treas*
Jonathon Francis, *Sec*
Timothy Buie, *VP*
EMP: 15 **EST:** 1991
SQ FT: 12,000
SALES (est): 1.62MM **Privately Held**
Web: www.francis-steel.com
SIC: 3545 3444 Machine tool accessories; Sheet metalwork

(G-4)
ERICO INTERNATIONAL CORP
188 Carolina Rd (28315-4754)
PHONE..............................910 944-3355
Jarvis Daniel, *Mgr*
EMP: 5
Web: www.nvent.com
SIC: 3643 Current-carrying wiring services
HQ: Erico International Corporation
1665 Utica Ave Ste 700
Saint Louis Park MN 55416
440 349-2630

(G-5)
GREAT PRODUCTS INC
Us Hwy 15 501 (28315)
P.O. Box 546 (28315-0546)
PHONE..............................910 944-2020
William Marts, *Pr*
Sandy Marts, *VP*
Bruce Medlin, *Stockholder*
◆ **EMP:** 7 **EST:** 1989
SQ FT: 7,500
SALES (est): 171.38K **Privately Held**
SIC: 3589 5085 Coffee brewing equipment; Filters, industrial

(G-6)
HAMPTON CAPITAL PARTNERS LLC
Also Called: Gullistan Carpet
3140 Nc Highway 5 (28315-8700)
P.O. Box 1059 (24151-8059)
▲ **EMP:** 700
SIC: 2273 Carpets and rugs

(G-7)
INDUSTRIAL MTAL PDTS ABRDEEN I
Also Called: Wire Form
461 Carolina Rd (28315-4733)
PHONE..............................910 944-8110
Samuel Kenworthy, *Pr*
Barbara Kenworthy, *Sec*
EMP: 15 **EST:** 1988
SQ FT: 15,000
SALES (est): 2.66MM **Privately Held**
SIC: 3441 3429 3559 3599 Building components, structural steel; Hardware, nec ; Brick making machinery; Machine and other job shop work

(G-8)
INTERNTNAL TRAY PADS PACKG INC
3299 Nc Highway 5 (28315)
P.O. Box 307 (28315-0307)

PHONE..............910 944-1800
Robert J Knorr, *Pr*
Shaen Kirkpatrick, *
Wilma Hogan, *Stockholder**
▲ EMP: 6 EST: 1988
SQ FT: 100,000
SALES (est): 2.36MM **Publicly Held**
Web: www.traypads.com
SIC: 2671 5199 Paper; coated and laminated packaging; Packaging materials
HQ: Pactiv Llc
   1900 W Field Ct
   Lake Forest IL 60045
   847 482-2000

(G-9)
J SIGNS AND GRAPHICS LLC
1345 N Sandhills Blvd Ste 1 (28315-2211)
PHONE..............910 315-2657
Jeremy White, *Owner*
▲ EMP: 4 EST: 2005
SALES (est): 262.38K **Privately Held**
Web: www.jsignsandgraphics.com
SIC: 3993 Signs, not made in custom sign painting shops

(G-10)
KOLCRAFT ENTERPRISES INC
10832 Nc 211 Hwy (28315-4722)
PHONE..............910 944-9345
Dave Schuchard, *Mgr*
EMP: 169
SALES (corp-wide): 22.96MM **Privately Held**
Web: www.kolcraft.com
SIC: 2512 2511 Juvenile furniture: upholstered on wood frames; Wood household furniture
PA: Kolcraft Enterprises, Inc.
   1100 W Monroe St
   Chicago IL 60607
   312 361-6315

(G-11)
LONGWORTH INDUSTRIES INC
3140 Nc 5 Hwy (28315-8700)
PHONE..............910 673-5290
EMP: 50
SALES (corp-wide): 99.5MM **Privately Held**
SIC: 2341 2322 Women's and children's undergarments; Underwear, men's and boys': made from purchased materials
HQ: Longworth Industries, Inc.
   565 Air Tool Dr Ste K
   Southern Pines NC 28387

(G-12)
MCMURRAY FABRICS INC (PA)
105 Vann Pl (Sandhills Industrial Park) (28315)
PHONE..............910 944-2128
Brian L Mcmurray, *Pr*
Connie Mcmurray, *VP*
◆ EMP: 150 EST: 1968
SALES (est): 48.46MM
SALES (corp-wide): 48.46MM **Privately Held**
Web: www.mcmurrayfabrics.com
SIC: 2257 Weft knit fabric mills

(G-13)
MERIDIAN ZERO DEGREES LLC (PA)
Also Called: Meridian Kiosks
312 S Pine St (28315-2608)
PHONE..............866 454-6757
Christopher Gilder, *Pr*
◆ EMP: 43 EST: 2005
SQ FT: 63,000
SALES (est): 22.54MM
SALES (corp-wide): 22.54MM **Privately Held**

Web: www.meridiankiosks.com
SIC: 2851 7373 Coating, air curing; Computer systems analysis and design

(G-14)
METAL & MATERIALS PROC LLC
3250 Nc Highway 5 (28315-8618)
PHONE..............260 438-8901
Markus Novosel Dirdof, *Operations*
EMP: 6
SALES (corp-wide): 90.58K **Privately Held**
Web: www.metalandmaterials.com
SIC: 2899 3356 Anti-glare material; Nickel
PA: Metal & Materials Processing, L.L.C.
   1513 W Dallas St Ste 200
   Houston TX 77019
   713 664-0050

(G-15)
METCHEM INC
106 Jordan Pl (28315-8613)
P.O. Box 3879 (28374-3879)
PHONE..............910 944-1405
Thomas V Cirigliano, *CEO*
Robert Morris, *CFO*
Elizabeth Cirigliano, *Sec*
▲ EMP: 6 EST: 1990
SALES (est): 1.75MM **Privately Held**
Web: www.cobalt-nickel.com
SIC: 3339 Cobalt refining (primary)

(G-16)
MFI PRODUCTS INC (HQ)
105 Vann Pl (28315-8612)
P.O. Box 950 (28315-0950)
PHONE..............910 944-2128
Brian Mcmurray, *Pr*
▼ EMP: 15 EST: 1999
SQ FT: 20,000
SALES (est): 4.01MM
SALES (corp-wide): 48.46MM **Privately Held**
SIC: 5013 2211 Automotive hardware; Apparel and outerwear fabrics, cotton
PA: Mcmurray Fabrics, Inc.
   105 Vann Pl
   Aberdeen NC 28315
   910 944-2128

(G-17)
NAFSHI ENTERPRISES LLC ✪
14796 Us Highway 15 501 (28315-5512)
PHONE..............910 986-9888
EMP: 9 EST: 2023
SALES (est): 356.22K **Privately Held**
SIC: 2099 7389 Food preparations, nec; Business Activities at Non-Commercial Site

(G-18)
PACTIV LLC
3299 Nc Hwy 5 (28315)
P.O. Box 307 (28315-0307)
PHONE..............910 944-1800
EMP: 6
Web: www.pactivevergreen.com
SIC: 2657 5199 Folding paperboard boxes; Packaging materials
HQ: Pactiv Llc
   1900 W Field Ct
   Lake Forest IL 60045
   847 482-2000

(G-19)
PINNACLE FURNISHINGS INC
10570 Nc Highway 211 E Ste G (28315-4813)
PHONE..............910 944-0908
Jack Berggren, *Pr*
▲ EMP: 38 EST: 1996
SQ FT: 45,000
SALES (est): 2.24MM **Privately Held**

Web: www.pinnaclefurnishings.com
SIC: 2599 Bar, restaurant and cafeteria furniture

(G-20)
QUANTICO TACTICAL INCORPORATED
9796 Aberdeen Rd (28315-7742)
PHONE..............910 944-5800
David Hensley, *CEO*
EMP: 30 EST: 2017
SALES (est): 991.78K **Privately Held**
Web: www.quanticotactical.com
SIC: 2499 Picture and mirror frames, wood

(G-21)
RELIANCE PACKAGING LLC
175 Anderson St (28315-2141)
P.O. Box 808 (07071-0808)
PHONE..............910 944-2561
Satish Sharma, *Managing Member*
Alfred Teo, *Managing Member**
▲ EMP: 50 EST: 2014
SALES (est): 24.62MM **Privately Held**
Web: www.reliancepkg.com
SIC: 5199 2672 Packaging materials; Adhesive backed films, foams and foils
PA: Alpha Industries Management, Inc.
   2919 Center Port Cir
   Pompano Beach FL 33064

(G-22)
ROSITAS TORTILLAS INC
1317 N Sandhills Blvd (28315-2211)
PHONE..............910 944-0577
Aguirre A Jessie, *Prin*
EMP: 4 EST: 2013
SALES (est): 322.4K **Privately Held**
Web: www.aberdeengrocerystore.com
SIC: 2099 Tortillas, fresh or refrigerated

(G-23)
ROSTRA PRECISION CONTROLS INC
Also Called: Marmon Powertrain Controls
3056 Nc Hwy 5 (28315-8673)
PHONE..............910 291-2502
Jim Pineau, *CEO*
Pete Kallgren, *
▲ EMP: 100 EST: 1987
SQ FT: 80,000
SALES (est): 22.89MM
SALES (corp-wide): 22.89MM **Privately Held**
Web: www.rostra.com
SIC: 3714 3679 Acceleration equipment, motor vehicle; Solenoids for electronic applications
PA: Aftermarket Controls Corp.
   2519 Dana Dr
   Laurinburg NC 28352
   910 291-2500

(G-24)
SOUTHEASTERN TOOL & DIE INC
105 Taylor St (28315-2026)
PHONE..............910 944-7677
Jimmy Thompson, *Pr*
Lynne C Thompson, *
Samuel Watson, *
Darlene Roberts, *
Peggy Kumm, *
◆ EMP: 85 EST: 1984
SQ FT: 105,000
SALES (est): 1.11MM **Privately Held**
Web: www.setoolinc.com
SIC: 3441 3544 3599 Fabricated structural metal; Special dies, tools, jigs, and fixtures; Machine shop, jobbing and repair

(G-25)
SPIRITUS SYSTEMS COMPANY
Also Called: Spiritus Systems
112 Bud Pl (28315-8617)
PHONE..............910 637-0196
Adam Holroyd, *Admn*
▼ EMP: 50 EST: 2015
SQ FT: 10,000
SALES (est): 4.97MM **Privately Held**
Web: www.spiritussystems.com
SIC: 2389 Uniforms and vestments

(G-26)
TFAM SOLUTIONS LLC
Also Called: Decorative Def Con Coatings
134 Aqua Shed Ct (28315-8685)
PHONE..............910 637-0266
Judith Thompson, *CEO*
Timothy Thompson, *Pr*
EMP: 8 EST: 2014
SALES (est): 843K **Privately Held**
SIC: 5075 3444 3545 Compressors, air conditioning; Casings, sheet metal; Chucks: drill, lathe, or magnetic (machine tool accessories)

(G-27)
THERMAL METAL TREATING INC
9546 Hwy 211 East (28315)
P.O. Box 367 (28315-0367)
PHONE..............910 944-3636
Jerry Ritter, *Pr*
Mark A Scott, *
EMP: 24 EST: 1988
SQ FT: 60,000
SALES (est): 4MM **Privately Held**
Web: www.thermalmetal.com
SIC: 3398 Metal heat treating

(G-28)
TRAVIS ALFREY WOODWORKING INC
9988 Aberdeen Rd (28315-7740)
PHONE..............910 639-3553
Travis Alfrey, *Pr*
EMP: 4 EST: 2008
SALES (est): 167.83K **Privately Held**
SIC: 2434 Wood kitchen cabinets

(G-29)
VA COMPOSITES INC
707 S Pinehurst St Ste D (28315-1844)
PHONE..............844 474-2387
Victor Afable, *Pr*
Heather Afable, *Prin*
EMP: 5 EST: 2016
SALES (est): 254.98K **Privately Held**
Web: www.vashafts.com
SIC: 3949 Shafts, golf club

(G-30)
VINYL WINDOWS & DOORS CORP
165 Taylor St (28315-2026)
PHONE..............910 944-2100
Carol Barbera, *Pr*
Mike Barbera Senior, *Sec*
EMP: 14 EST: 1985
SQ FT: 62,000
SALES (est): 1.62MM **Privately Held**
Web: www.vwdcorp.com
SIC: 3442 5031 5033 1761 Storm doors or windows, metal; Windows; Siding, except wood; Siding contractor

▲ = Import ▼ = Export
◆ = Import/Export

Advance
Davie County

(G-31)
ASHLEY FURNITURE INDS LLC
Also Called: Ashley Furniture
333 Ashley Furniture Way (27006-8005)
PHONE...................................336 998-1066
EMP: 46
SALES (corp-wide): 4.17B Privately Held
Web: www.ashleyfurniture.com
SIC: 4225 5021 2511 General warehousing
and storage; Furniture; Bed frames, except
water bed frames: wood
PA: Ashley Furniture Industries, Llc
1 Ashley Way
Arcadia WI 54612
608 323-3377

(G-32)
FRISBY TECHNOLOGIES INC (PA)
136 Medical Dr (27006-6651)
PHONE...................................336 998-6652
Duncan R Russell, Pr
Douglas J Mccrosson, Sec
Mark Gillis, CRO
EMP: 10 EST: 1989
SQ FT: 20,000
SALES (est): 674.2K Privately Held
SIC: 3086 Plastics foam products

(G-33)
INDAUX USA INC
548 Nc Highway 801 N (27006-7949)
PHONE...................................336 861-0740
Mikel Arzallus, Pr
EMP: 5 EST: 2015
SALES (est): 570.28K Privately Held
SIC: 3599 Industrial machinery, nec

(G-34)
IQ BRANDS INC (HQ)
129 Nc Highway 801 S (27006-7645)
PHONE...................................336 751-0040
John Robinson, CEO
Jeff Arnold, *
James Clegg, *
Teresa Bridges, *
Tom Bowlds, *
▲ EMP: 10 EST: 1999
SQ FT: 6,340
SALES (est): 7.73MM
SALES (corp-wide): 51.17K Privately Held
Web: www.iqbrands.net
SIC: 2252 Men's, boys', and girls' hosiery
PA: Huron Capital Partners Llc
500 Griswold Ste 2700
Detroit MI 48226
313 962-5800

(G-35)
MARY KAY INC
685 Redland Rd (27006-6724)
PHONE...................................336 998-1663
Hellen Bennett, Owner
EMP: 4 EST: 2018
SALES (est): 176.09K Privately Held
Web: www.marykay.com
SIC: 3599 Industrial machinery, nec

(G-36)
N2 PUBLISHING
161 Shallowbrook Dr (27006-6731)
PHONE...................................336 293-3845
Leslie Mccraw, Prin
EMP: 4 EST: 2017
SALES (est): 102.69K Privately Held
Web: www.strollmag.com

SIC: 2741 Miscellaneous publishing

(G-37)
PRO TOOL COMPANY INC
1765 Peoples Creek Rd (27006-7453)
P.O. Box 2253 (27006-2253)
PHONE...................................336 998-9212
Andrew L Mossman, Pr
Jace Hougland, VP
EMP: 19 EST: 1998
SQ FT: 19,000
SALES (est): 5.02MM Privately Held
Web: www.protoolcompany.com
SIC: 3599 Machine shop, jobbing and repair

(G-38)
SALEM PROFESSIONAL ANESTHESIA
128 Peachtree Ln Ste B (27006-6783)
PHONE...................................336 998-3396
Jim Nitz, Owner
EMP: 7 EST: 2006
SALES (est): 1.32MM Privately Held
Web: www.salemanesthesia.com
SIC: 3841 Anesthesia apparatus

(G-39)
SPARTAN SYSTEMS LLC
Also Called: Spartan Tower
106 York Way Ste 101 (27006-7665)
PHONE...................................336 946-1244
Doyle Freeman, Managing Member
EMP: 19 EST: 2022
SALES (est): 21MM Privately Held
SIC: 3585 5075 Refrigeration and heating
equipment; Warm air heating and air
conditioning

(G-40)
TWG INC
Also Called: Simply Stitching
652 Nc Highway 801 S (27006-7633)
PHONE...................................336 998-9731
Lori L Walker, Pr
EMP: 4 EST: 2000
SALES (est): 248.62K Privately Held
Web: www.simplystitching.com
SIC: 2395 Embroidery products, except
Schiffli machine

Ahoskie
Hertford County

(G-41)
ALBEMRLE ORTHOTICS PROSTHETICS (PA)
103 Nc Highway 42 W (27910-9725)
PHONE...................................252 332-4334
Scott Truesdale, Pr
Kim Williamson, VP
EMP: 4 EST: 1998
SALES (est): 876.8K
SALES (corp-wide): 876.8K Privately Held
Web: www.albemarleop.com
SIC: 3842 3845 Orthopedic appliances;
Electromedical equipment

(G-42)
BERRY GLOBAL INC
Also Called: Berry Plastics
228 Johnny Mitchell Rd (27910-9461)
PHONE...................................252 332-7270
EMP: 27
Web: www.berryglobal.com
SIC: 3089 Plastics containers, except foam
HQ: Berry Global, Inc.
101 Oakley St
Evansville IN 47710

(G-43)
BOONE NEWSPAPERS INC
Also Called: Gates County Index Shopper
801 Parker Ave E Ste 803 (27910-3641)
P.O. Box 1325 (27910-1325)
PHONE...................................252 332-2123
David Sullens, Brnch Mgr
EMP: 25
SALES (corp-wide): 19.94MM Privately
Held
Web: www.boonenewsmedia.com
SIC: 2711 Job printing and newspaper
publishing combined
PA: Boone Newsmedia, Inc.
3933 Rice Mine Rd Ne
Tuscaloosa AL 35406
205 330-4100

(G-44)
BRITTENHAMS REBUILDING SERVICE
2314 Us Hway13 S (27910-9483)
P.O. Box 40 (27910-0040)
PHONE...................................252 332-3181
Thomas Earl Brittenham, Pr
Cumin Brittenham, VP
Lorraine Harrell, Sec
EMP: 6 EST: 1965
SQ FT: 10,000
SALES (est): 364.96K Privately Held
Web: www.brittenhams.com
SIC: 7694 Electric motor repair

(G-45)
COMMERCIAL READY MIX PDTS INC
Also Called: Crmp
100 Hayes St E (27910-3125)
PHONE...................................252 332-3590
Bill Ballance, Mgr
EMP: 7
SALES (corp-wide): 48.13MM Privately
Held
Web: www.crmpinc.com
SIC: 1771 3273 Concrete work; Ready-
mixed concrete
PA: Commercial Ready Mix Products, Inc.
115 Hwy 158 W
Winton NC 27986
252 358-5461

(G-46)
D T BRACY LOGGING INC
520 Kiwanis St (27910-3618)
PHONE...................................252 332-8332
Darrell Bracy, Owner
EMP: 5 EST: 1981
SALES (est): 64.94K Privately Held
SIC: 2411 Logging camps and contractors

(G-47)
DARRELL T BRACY
Also Called: Barcy, D T Logging
520 Kiwanis St (27910-3618)
PHONE...................................252 358-1432
Darrell T Bracy, Owner
EMP: 5 EST: 1983
SALES (est): 68.49K Privately Held
SIC: 2411 Logging camps and contractors

(G-48)
ELECTRIC MOTOR SVC AHOSKIE INC
2103 Us Highway 13 S (27910-9481)
P.O. Box 711 (27910-0711)
PHONE...................................252 332-4364
Ernest Venable, Pr
EMP: 7 EST: 2008
SALES (est): 2.3MM Privately Held
Web: www.ahoskienc.gov

SIC: 5063 7694 Motors, electric; Electric
motor repair

(G-49)
ENVIVA PELLETS AHOSKIE LLC
142 Nc Highway 561 W (27910-9741)
PHONE...................................301 657-5560
EMP: 60 EST: 2010
SALES (est): 8.23MM
SALES (corp-wide): 1.18MM Privately
Held
Web: www.envivabiomass.com
SIC: 2421 Wood chips, produced at mill
PA: Enviva, Llc
7500 Old Grgtown Rd Ste 1
Bethesda MD 20814
301 657-5560

(G-50)
H T JONES LUMBER COMPANY
Also Called: Down East Molding Company
204 Catherine Creek Rd N (27910-3404)
P.O. Box 608 (27910-0608)
PHONE...................................252 332-4135
M C Jones Iii, Pr
W Frank Jones, VP
W E Jones, Sec
EMP: 5 EST: 1966
SQ FT: 60,000
SALES (est): 150.64K Privately Held
SIC: 2431 2426 Moldings, wood: unfinished
and prefinished; Hardwood dimension and
flooring mills

(G-51)
PERDUE FARMS INC
Also Called: PERDUE FARMS INC.
2108 Us Highway 13 S (27910-9481)
PHONE...................................252 348-4287
Randy Mclawhorn, Brnch Mgr
EMP: 34
SALES (corp-wide): 1.24B Privately Held
Web: www.perdue.com
SIC: 2015 Chicken, processed: fresh
PA: Perdue Farms Incorporated
31149 Old Ocean City Rd
Salisbury MD 21804
800 473-7383

(G-52)
ROANOKE CHOWAN READY MIX INC
108 Williford Rd (27910-9646)
P.O. Box 146 (27967-0146)
PHONE...................................252 332-7995
Rhedda Waters, Pr
Gerald Waters, Sec
EMP: 5 EST: 2000
SQ FT: 192
SALES (est): 616.04K Privately Held
SIC: 3273 Ready-mixed concrete

(G-53)
STANLEY E DIXON JR INC
Also Called: Stitch Count
113 Rail Road St (27910-3331)
PHONE...................................252 332-5004
Stanley Dixon, Pr
Pat Dixon, Sec
EMP: 5 EST: 1988
SQ FT: 5,500
SALES (est): 286.11K Privately Held
SIC: 2395 Embroidery and art needlework

(G-54)
TOWN OF AHOSKIE
208 Johnny Mitchell Rd (27910-9461)
P.O. Box 767 (27910-0767)
PHONE...................................252 332-3840
Stewart White, Brnch Mgr
EMP: 5

Web: www.ahoskienc.gov
SIC: 3589 Sewage and water treatment
equipment
PA: Town Of Ahoskie
201 Main St W
Ahoskie NC 27910
252 332-5146

Alamance
Alamance County

(G-55)
CONTINENTAL TICKING CORP AMER (PA)
Also Called: CT Nassau Mat Tape & Ticking
4101 South Nc Hwy 62 (27201)
P.O. Box 39 (27201-0039)
PHONE.............................336 570-0091
Rudolf Schriner, *Pr*
Ernie Farley, *
John Bauman, *
◆ **EMP:** 75 **EST:** 1995
SALES (est): 30.15MM
SALES (corp-wide): 30.15MM **Privately Held**
Web: www.ctnassau.com
SIC: 2241 5131 Narrow fabric mills; Piece
goods and notions

(G-56)
CT-NASSAU TAPE LLC
Also Called: Nassau Tape
4101 S N Carolina Hwy 62 (27201)
P.O. Box 39 (27201-0039)
PHONE...............................336 570-0091
Rudolph Schreiner, *Managing Member*
Rudolph Schreiner, *Managing Member*
◆ **EMP:** 100 **EST:** 1959
SQ FT: 100,000
SALES (est): 24.82MM
SALES (corp-wide): 30.15MM **Privately Held**
Web: www.ctnassau.com
SIC: 2241 Narrow fabric mills
PA: Continental Ticking Corporation Of
America
4101 South Nc Hwy 62
Alamance NC 27201
336 570-0091

Albemarle
Stanly County

(G-57)
A AND H MILLWORK INC
509 Old Charlotte Rd (28001-5749)
PHONE...............................704 983-2402
Edward Harris, *Pr*
Hazel Harris, *VP*
EMP: 10 **EST:** 1979
SQ FT: 15,500
SALES (est): 162.44K **Privately Held**
SIC: 2431 Interior and ornamental woodwork
and trim

(G-58)
ALBEMARLE GLASS COMPANY INC
Also Called: Albemarle Glass and Stone
1217 Pee Dee Ave (28001-5142)
PHONE...............................704 982-3323
Pat Banakes, *Pr*
Dean Banakes, *VP*
Phyllis Coley, *Sec*
EMP: 6 **EST:** 1974
SQ FT: 20,000
SALES (est): 494.46K **Privately Held**
Web: www.albemarleglassinc.com

SIC: 1793 3231 Glass and glazing work;
Products of purchased glass

(G-59)
ALBEMARLE TIRE RETREADING INC
542 W Main St (28001-4644)
PHONE...............................704 982-4113
Kent Cook, *Pr*
Sandra Cook, *VP*
Wade Jones, *Mgr*
EMP: 6 **EST:** 1935
SQ FT: 7,500
SALES (est): 842.06K **Privately Held**
SIC: 5531 7534 Automotive tires; Rebuilding
and retreading tires

(G-60)
ALBEMARLE WOOD PRSV PLANT INC
1509 Snuggs Park Rd (28001)
P.O. Box 181 (28002-0181)
PHONE...............................704 982-2516
Thomas S Griffin, *Pr*
Cirrie W Kendall, *Sec*
Stephen Griffin, *VP*
EMP: 4 **EST:** 1961
SQ FT: 1,300
SALES (est): 1.99MM **Privately Held**
Web: primary.forestproductslocator.org
SIC: 2491 Structural lumber and timber,
treated wood

(G-61)
AMERICAN FIBER & FINISHING INC (PA)
Also Called: AF&f
225 N Depot St (28001)
PHONE...............................704 984-9256
Paul Robichaud, *Pr*
Marcus Weibel, *
▲ **EMP:** 28 **EST:** 1986
SQ FT: 450,000
SALES (est): 11.46MM
SALES (corp-wide): 11.46MM **Privately Held**
Web: www.affinc.com
SIC: 3842 2844 2392 2211 Surgical
appliances and supplies; Perfumes,
cosmetics and other toilet preparations;
Household furnishings, nec; Basket weave
fabrics, cotton

(G-62)
AURIA ALBEMARLE LLC
313 Bethany Rd (28001-8520)
P.O. Box 580 (28002-0580)
PHONE...............................704 983-5166
EMP: 285
SALES (corp-wide): 19K **Privately Held**
Web: www.auriasolutions.com
SIC: 3714 Motor vehicle parts and
accessories
HQ: Auria Albemarle, Llc
26999 Centrl Pk Blvd # 30
Southfield MI 48076
248 728-8000

(G-63)
BROOMES POULTRY INC
24816 Austin Rd (28001-8385)
PHONE...............................704 983-0965
Randy Honeycutt, *Owner*
Randy Huneycutt, *Owner*
EMP: 4 **EST:** 1996
SALES (est): 248.75K **Privately Held**
SIC: 2015 Poultry slaughtering and
processing

(G-64)
BROTHERS PRECISION TOOL CO
310 S Broome St (28001-4715)
PHONE...............................704 982-5667
Joe S Brooks, *Owner*
Robert Brooks, *Pt*
John M Brooks, *Pt*
EMP: 7 **EST:** 1974
SQ FT: 4,000
SALES (est): 700.81K **Privately Held**
Web: www.brotherstool.com
SIC: 3544 Special dies and tools

(G-65)
BROWNS WOODWORKING LLC
210 Charter St (28001-8702)
PHONE...............................704 983-5917
EMP: 5 **EST:** 2001
SALES (est): 347.89K **Privately Held**
SIC: 2431 5712 Woodwork, interior and
ornamental, nec; Customized furniture and
cabinets

(G-66)
CTX BUILDERS SUPPLY
2100 Sterling Dr (28001-5390)
PHONE...............................704 983-6748
Chris Borrego, *Mgr*
Chris Borrego, *Prin*
EMP: 4 **EST:** 2004
SALES (est): 294.73K **Privately Held**
SIC: 3555 Printing trades machinery

(G-67)
CUSTOM DOORS INCORPORATED
800 Laton Rd (28001-8607)
PHONE...............................704 982-2885
Michael P Laton Senior, *Pr*
Michael P Laton Junior, *VP*
Brooke E Laton, *Sec*
▲ **EMP:** 10 **EST:** 1967
SQ FT: 15,200
SALES (est): 443.11K **Privately Held**
Web: www.customdoorsinc.com
SIC: 2431 7521 Garage doors, overhead,
wood; Parking garage

(G-68)
D & M PACKING COMPANY
687 Morgan Rd (28001-5653)
PHONE...............................704 982-3716
Gary H Langford, *Owner*
EMP: 4 **EST:** 1962
SQ FT: 10,000
SALES (est): 483.81K **Privately Held**
SIC: 2011 Meat packing plants

(G-69)
DEAN S READY MIXED INC
517 Old Charlotte Rd (28001-5750)
PHONE...............................704 982-5520
Dusty West, *Pr*
Jessy Hayes, *VP*
Vicki Burleson, *Sec*
Wanda Hayes, *Stockholder*
EMP: 7 **EST:** 1951
SQ FT: 700
SALES (est): 861.03K **Privately Held**
Web: www.atlanticairinc.com
SIC: 3273 Ready-mixed concrete

(G-70)
DENNIS VINEYARDS INC
24043 Endy Rd (28001-9041)
PHONE...............................704 982-6090
Sandon Dennis, *Pr*
Amy Dennis, *Sec*
EMP: 8 **EST:** 1997
SALES (est): 222.86K **Privately Held**
Web: www.dennisvineyards.com

SIC: 2084 Wines

(G-71)
ENFORGE LLC
1600 Woodhurst Ln (28001-5374)
PHONE...............................704 983-4146
EMP: 49 **EST:** 2009
SQ FT: 100,000
SALES (est): 8.1MM **Privately Held**
Web: www.enforgellc.com
SIC: 3559 Automotive related machinery
HQ: Angstrom Usa Llc
26980 Trolley Indus Dr
Taylor MI 48180
313 295-0100

(G-72)
FABRICATED SOLUTIONS LLC
1210 Poplar St (28001-3130)
P.O. Box 429 (28002-0429)
PHONE...............................704 982-7789
Danny Storm, *Managing Member*
EMP: 4 **EST:** 2006
SALES (est): 3.03MM **Privately Held**
Web: www.fabsolutionsnc.com
SIC: 3441 Fabricated structural metal

(G-73)
FLEET FIXERS INC
927a Concord Rd (28001-8332)
P.O. Box 958 (28002-0958)
PHONE...............................704 986-0066
Henry Kiefer, *Pr*
Annette Kiefer, *Sec*
EMP: 4 **EST:** 2003
SALES (est): 473.55K **Privately Held**
Web: www.fleetfitters.net
SIC: 3537 Trucks, tractors, loaders, carriers,
and similar equipment

(G-74)
GENTRY MILLS INC
2035 Kingsley Dr (28001-4473)
PHONE...............................704 983-5555
Jan Berkovic, *Pr*
Alvaro Kraizel, *
Emilio Kraizel, *
Paula Corne, *
▲ **EMP:** 60 **EST:** 1992
SQ FT: 175,000
SALES (est): 9.57MM **Privately Held**
Web: www.gentrymills.com
SIC: 5131 3999 Textiles, woven, nec;
Atomizers, toiletry

(G-75)
GMD LOGGING INC
44100 Dennis Rd (28001-7662)
PHONE...............................704 985-5460
Gregory Mark Dennis, *Pr*
EMP: 5 **EST:** 2016
SALES (est): 542.27K **Privately Held**
SIC: 2411 Logging

(G-76)
GREENCROSS INC
241 W North St (28001-3923)
P.O. Box 896 (28002-0896)
PHONE...............................704 984-6700
Mark Andrew, *Pr*
EMP: 4 **EST:** 1988
SALES (est): 159.18K **Privately Held**
Web: www.greencrossinc.biz
SIC: 2752 Offset printing

(G-77)
HAMMOND ELECTRIC MOTOR COMPANY
811 Concord Rd (28001-8331)
PHONE...............................704 983-3178

▲ = Import ▼ = Export
◆ = Import/Export

Wayne Hoffman, *Pr*
Steven Hoffman, *VP*
EMP: 13 **EST:** 1960
SQ FT: 6,250
SALES (est): 1.83MM **Privately Held**
Web: www.hammondelectricmotors.com
SIC: 7694 5063 Electric motor repair;
  Motors, electric

(G-78)
HUNTPACK INC
320 Anderson Rd (28001-8103)
PHONE..............................704 986-0684
Marc Hunt, *Pr*
Rick Armstrong, *VP*
Jennifer Michelle, *Sec*
EMP: 5 **EST:** 1997
SQ FT: 12,000
SALES (est): 230.68K **Privately Held**
Web: www.phoenixflexographic.com
SIC: 2752 2754 Tag, ticket, and schedule
  printing: lithographic; Labels: gravure
  printing

(G-79)
KRAFTSMAN TACTICAL INC
1650 Woodhurst Ln (28001-5374)
PHONE..............................336 465-3576
Michael Kaufman, *Pr*
EMP: 5 **EST:** 2017
SALES (est): 423.8K **Privately Held**
Web: www.kraftsmantrailers.com
SIC: 2759 Promotional printing

(G-80)
M & R FORESTRY SERVICE INC
24062 Sam Rd (28001-9032)
P.O. Box 2012 (28002-2012)
PHONE..............................980 439-1261
Lelis Mejia, *Pr*
Lelis Noel Mejia, *Owner*
EMP: 4 **EST:** 2011
SALES (est): 998.79K **Privately Held**
SIC: 0851 3448 Forestry services; Carports,
  prefabricated metal

(G-81)
MARTIN SPROCKET & GEAR INC
306 Bethany Rd (28001-8520)
PHONE..............................817 258-3000
Jimmy Mcswain, *Mgr*
EMP: 12
SALES (corp-wide): 292.47MM **Privately
Held**
Web: www.martinsprocket.com
SIC: 3566 3568 Gears, power transmission,
  except auto; Power transmission
  equipment, nec
PA: Martin Sprocket & Gear, Inc.
  3100 Sprocket Dr
  Arlington TX 76015
  817 258-3000

(G-82)
NABELL USA CORPORATION
208 Charter St (28001-8702)
PHONE..............................704 986-2455
Don Stewart, *Pr*
▲ **EMP:** 20 **EST:** 1998
SQ FT: 6,000
SALES (est): 5.39MM **Privately Held**
Web: www.nabell.com
SIC: 3599 3861 Bellows, industrial: metal;
  Sensitized film, cloth, and paper

(G-83)
OLD SCHOOL MILL INC
28113 Nc 24 27 Hwy (28001-7413)
PHONE..............................704 781-5451
Robin Hinson, *Pr*
Parker D Hinson, *VP*

Virginia H Sedhom, *Sec*
EMP: 6 **EST:** 1995
SALES (est): 561.49K **Privately Held**
Web: www.oldschool.com
SIC: 2041 Corn grits and flakes, for brewers'
  use

(G-84)
PREFORMED LINE PRODUCTS CO
1700 Woodhurst Ln (28001-5376)
P.O. Box 818 (28002-0818)
PHONE..............................704 983-6161
John Ziebarth, *Mgr*
EMP: 168
SQ FT: 277,547
SALES (corp-wide): 593.71MM **Publicly
Held**
Web: www.plp.com
SIC: 3644 3496 3229 3643 Pole line
  hardware; Miscellaneous fabricated wire
  products; Pressed and blown glass, nec;
  Current-carrying wiring services
PA: Preformed Line Products Company
  660 Beta Dr
  Mayfield Village OH 44143
  440 461-5200

(G-85)
QUALITY HOME FASHIONS INC
28569 Flint Ridge Rd (28001-8004)
PHONE..............................704 983-5906
Tony Hill, *Pr*
EMP: 5 **EST:** 1995
SQ FT: 50,000
SALES (est): 148.99K **Privately Held**
SIC: 2392 Sheets, fabric: made from
  purchased materials

(G-86)
R & S PRECISION CUSTOMS LLC
338 E Main St (28001-4922)
PHONE..............................704 984-3480
EMP: 4 **EST:** 2015
SALES (est): 77.71K **Privately Held**
SIC: 3482 Small arms ammunition

(G-87)
RAM INDUSTRIES INC
Also Called: Martin Industries
1135 Montgomery Ave (28001-4328)
P.O. Box 2252 (28002-2252)
PHONE..............................704 982-4015
Roger Martin, *Pr*
Gina Martin, *
▲ **EMP:** 4 **EST:** 1981
SQ FT: 95,000
SALES (est): 651.42K **Privately Held**
SIC: 3083 Plastics finished products,
  laminated

(G-88)
SECURE CANOPY LLC
1215 Pineview St (28001-3048)
P.O. Box 833 (28002-0833)
PHONE..............................980 322-0590
EMP: 5 **EST:** 2013
SQ FT: 2,000
SALES (est): 302.28K **Privately Held**
Web: www.securecanopy.com
SIC: 3651 Video camera-audio recorders,
  household use

(G-89)
SMITH NOVELTY COMPANY INC
2120 W Main St (28001-5424)
PHONE..............................704 982-7413
Janet Swaringen, *Treas*
EMP: 7 **EST:** 1942
SQ FT: 20,000
SALES (est): 128.42K **Privately Held**
Web: www.smithnovelty.com

SIC: 2512 Chairs: upholstered on wood
  frames

(G-90)
SOUTH CENTRAL OIL AND PRPN INC
2121 W Main St (28001-5423)
PHONE..............................704 982-2173
Garrison J Banks, *Prin*
EMP: 7 **EST:** 2016
SALES (est): 5.05MM
SALES (corp-wide): 5.05MM **Privately
Held**
Web: www.southcentraloil.com
SIC: 5172 1321 Petroleum products, nec;
  Propane (natural) production
PA: South Central Oil Co., Inc.
  2121 W Main St
  Albemarle NC 28001
  704 982-2173

(G-91)
SOUTHERN MARBLE CO LLC
2033 W Main St (28001-5421)
PHONE..............................704 982-4142
Donald Fincher, *Managing Member*
EMP: 6 **EST:** 1990
SQ FT: 12,000
SALES (est): 183.42K **Privately Held**
SIC: 3281 5719 5032 Marble, building: cut
  and shaped; Bath accessories; Marble
  building stone

(G-92)
SOUTHERN PIPE INC
445 N 4th St (28001-4021)
PHONE..............................704 550-5935
Bryan Mitchell, *Brnch Mgr*
EMP: 16
SALES (corp-wide): 14.87MM **Privately
Held**
Web: www.southern-pipe.com
SIC: 3084 Plastics pipe
PA: Southern Pipe, Inc.
  135 Random Dr
  New London NC 28127
  704 463-5202

(G-93)
STONY GAP WHOLESALE CO INC
40616c Stony Gap Rd Ste C (28001-8151)
P.O. Box 1016 (28002-1016)
PHONE..............................704 982-5360
John Lowder, *Pr*
Vicky Audy, *Mgr*
EMP: 7 **EST:** 1970
SALES (est): 110.37K **Privately Held**
SIC: 2099 5149 Cole slaw, in bulk; Groceries
  and related products, nec

(G-94)
SURE TRIP INC (PA)
703a Concord Rd (28001-9301)
PHONE..............................704 983-4651
Bill Penniston, *Pr*
Joel Henson, *VP*
EMP: 11 **EST:** 1996
SALES (est): 1.32MM
SALES (corp-wide): 1.32MM **Privately
Held**
Web: www.suretrip.com
SIC: 3625 Industrial controls: push button,
  selector switches, pilot

(G-95)
TRITON GLASS LLC
232 S 1st St (28001-4809)
PHONE..............................704 982-4333
Hemant Patel, *Managing Member*
EMP: 6 **EST:** 2014
SALES (est): 1.5MM **Privately Held**
Web: www.tritonglassllc.com

SIC: 3231 Tempered glass: made from
  purchased glass

(G-96)
WALTER PRINTING COMPANY INC
Also Called: Walter Tape & Label Co
130 Anderson Rd (28001-8114)
P.O. Box 10 (28002-0010)
PHONE..............................704 982-8899
Donald A Walter, *Pr*
Lillian Walter, *Sec*
EMP: 8 **EST:** 1957
SQ FT: 2,600
SALES (est): 1.33MM **Privately Held**
Web: www.walterprinting.net
SIC: 2752 Offset printing

(G-97)
**WENDYS EMBRDRED SPC SCREEN
PRT**
308 Concord Rd (28001-3606)
PHONE..............................704 982-5978
Wendy Lingerfelt, *Owner*
Randy Lingerfelt, *Pr*
EMP: 10 **EST:** 1991
SQ FT: 2,800
SALES (est): 328.61K **Privately Held**
Web: www.embroideredspecialties.com
SIC: 2395 Embroidery products, except
  Schiffli machine

Albertson
Duplin County

(G-98)
BAY VALLEY FOODS LLC
2953 N Nc 111 903 Hwy (28508-9635)
PHONE..............................715 366-4511
Dwight Jepson, *Brnch Mgr*
EMP: 100
SALES (corp-wide): 3.35B **Publicly Held**
Web: www.bayvalleyfoods.com
SIC: 2099 Food preparations, nec
HQ: Bay Valley Foods, Llc
  3200 Riverside Dr Ste A
  Green Bay WI 54301
  800 236-1119

(G-99)
EAST COAST LOG & TIMBER INC
305 Kator Dunn Rd (28508-9629)
PHONE..............................252 568-4344
Nicholas Sholar, *Prin*
EMP: 6 **EST:** 2018
SALES (est): 452.91K **Privately Held**
SIC: 2411 Logging

Alexander
Buncombe County

(G-100)
G A LANKFORD CONSTRUCTION
Also Called: Hayfield Auto Sales
333 Old Nc 20 Hwy (28701-9113)
PHONE..............................828 254-2467
Gary A Lankford, *Pr*
Diane Lankford, *Sec*
EMP: 4 **EST:** 1979
SALES (est): 122.49K **Privately Held**
SIC: 1521 2511 5521 New construction,
  single-family houses; Wood household
  furniture; Automobiles, used cars only

(G-101)
SOUTHERN CLASSIC STAIRS INC
24 Carl Roberts Rd (28701-9118)
PHONE..............................828 285-9828

GEOGRAPHIC

Louis E Coker Junior, *Pr*
EMP: 8 EST: 1992
SQ FT: 3,500
SALES (est): 212.21K **Privately Held**
SIC: 2431 Staircases, stairs and railings

Alexis
Gaston County

(G-102)
ALLOY FABRICATORS INC
334 Alexis High Shoals Rd (28006)
P.O. Box 779 (28164-0779)
PHONE..............................704 263-2281
Jeffrey R Fisher, *Pr*
Donnie Fisher, *
Michael D Fisher, *
Donald K Fisher, *
EMP: 35 EST: 1966
SQ FT: 15,000
SALES (est): 5.46MM **Privately Held**
Web: www.alloyfab.net
SIC: 3443 7692 3444 3429 Metal parts;
Welding repair; Sheet metalwork;
Hardware, nec

Altamahaw
Alamance County

(G-103)
GLEN RAVEN INC
Also Called: Glen Touch Division
3726 Altamahaw Union Ridge Rd (27202)
P.O. Box 8 (27202-0008)
PHONE..............................336 227-6211
Charlie Edgerton, *Bmch Mgr*
EMP: 15
SALES (corp-wide): 878.83M **Privately Held**
Web: www.glenraven.com
SIC: 2251 2282 Women's hosiery, except socks; Throwing and winding mills
PA: Glen Raven, Inc.
192 Glen Raven Rd
Burlington NC 27217
336 227-6211

Andrews
Cherokee County

(G-104)
ACCENT AWNINGS INC (PA)
91 Morgan Rd (28901-0739)
P.O. Box 1950 (28901-1950)
PHONE..............................828 321-4517
J A Rodeck, *Pr*
EMP: 10 EST: 1986
SQ FT: 8,000
SALES (est): 842.13K **Privately Held**
Web: www.accentawningsinc.com
SIC: 2394 1799 Awnings, fabric: made from purchased materials; Awning installation

(G-105)
ANDREWS TRUSS INC
47 Mcclelland Creek Rd (28901-7310)
P.O. Box 1429 (28901-1429)
PHONE..............................828 321-3105
Jonathan Chapman, *Pr*
Holly Chapman, *Sec*
EMP: 21 EST: 1990
SQ FT: 14,000
SALES (est): 4.74MM **Privately Held**
Web: www.andrewstruss.com
SIC: 2439 Trusses, wooden roof

(G-106)
CREATIVE PRINTERS & BRKS INC
Also Called: Creative Printers
980 Main St (28901-7087)
P.O. Box 757 (28901-0757)
PHONE..............................828 321-4663
William K Moore, *Pr*
Sherry Moore, *Sec*
Virginia Moore, *Treas*
Thomas Moore, *VP*
EMP: 6 EST: 1967
SALES (est): 113.88K **Privately Held**
Web:
www.creativeprintersandbrokers.com
SIC: 2752 7389 Offset printing; Printing broker

(G-107)
INDUSTRIAL OPPORTUNITIES INC
Also Called: ELASTIC PRODUCTS
2586 Business 19 (28901-8044)
P.O. Box 1649 (28901-1649)
PHONE..............................828 321-4754
EMP: 345 EST: 1974
SALES (est): 4.53MM **Privately Held**
Web: www.industrialopportunities.com
SIC: 2211 2395 8331 Elastic fabrics, cotton; Looping: for the trade; Job training and related services

(G-108)
JUNALUSKA MILL ENGINEERING
181 Gipp Creek Rd (28901-7200)
P.O. Box 2625 (28901-2625)
PHONE..............................828 321-3693
EMP: 5 EST: 1967
SQ FT: 5,000
SALES (est): 380K **Privately Held**
SIC: 3532 Mining machinery

(G-109)
TEAM INDUSTRIES INC
3750 Airport Rd (28901-7493)
PHONE..............................828 837-5377
David W Ricke, *Bmch Mgr*
EMP: 70
Web: www.team-ind.com
SIC: 8711 3599 Engineering services; Machine shop, jobbing and repair
HQ: Team Industries, Inc.
105 Park Ave Nw
Bagley MN 56621
218 694-3550

Angier
Harnett County

(G-110)
ADVANCE SIGNS & SERVICE INC
596 W Church St (27501-6052)
P.O. Box 1090 (27501-1090)
PHONE..............................919 639-4666
Scott Brown, *Pr*
Marcel Brown Junior, *VP*
EMP: 20 EST: 1990
SQ FT: 15,000
SALES (est): 2.38MM **Privately Held**
Web: www.advancesignservice.net
SIC: 1799 3993 Sign installation and maintenance; Signs and advertising specialties

(G-111)
ARS EXTREME CONSTRUCTION INC
175 Medical Dr (27501-6029)
P.O. Box 959 (27501-0959)
PHONE..............................919 331-8024
Sherry Harvey, *Pr*
Roger Harvey, *VP*

EMP: 10 EST: 2006
SALES (est): 845.34K **Privately Held**
Web: www.arsextreme.com
SIC: 1761 3441 Roofing contractor; Fabricated structural metal

(G-112)
BLACK RIVER WOODWORK LLC
574 N Broad St E (27501-8953)
PHONE..............................919 757-4559
Robert M Jusnes Senior, *Admn*
EMP: 5 EST: 2013
SALES (est): 1.16MM **Privately Held**
SIC: 2431 Millwork

(G-113)
BRICK & MORTAR GRILL
8 N Broad St E Ste 200 (27501-5638)
PHONE..............................919 639-9700
EMP: 4 EST: 2014
SALES (est): 126.2K **Privately Held**
Web: www.brickandmortargrill.com
SIC: 2024 5812 Ice cream and frozen deserts
; Grills (eating places)

(G-114)
BULLDOG HOSE COMPANY LLC
141 Junny Rd (27501-8625)
PHONE..............................919 639-6151
EMP: 20 EST: 2018
SALES (est): 5.76MM **Privately Held**
Web: www.puck.com
SIC: 3492 Hose and tube couplings, hydraulic/pneumatic

(G-115)
C & D FABRICATIONS INC
199 Fabrication Ln (27501-7201)
P.O. Box 1778 (27501-1778)
PHONE..............................919 639-2489
Donny Hawley, *Pr*
Ricky Armentrout, *VP*
Sharon Broadwell, *Sec*
EMP: 5 EST: 1988
SQ FT: 5,600
SALES (est): 712.82K **Privately Held**
SIC: 3499 Machine bases, metal

(G-116)
CAROLINA SIGN SVC
174 Kinnis Creek Dr (27501-9591)
P.O. Box 127 (27501-0127)
PHONE..............................919 247-0927
Jaimie Parker, *Pr*
EMP: 4 EST: 2018
SALES (est): 1.18MM **Privately Held**
Web: www.carolinasignandservice.com
SIC: 3993 Signs and advertising specialties

(G-117)
CHEROKEE INSTRUMENTS INC (PA)
Also Called: Amp-Cherokee Envmtl Solutions
100 Logan Ct (27501-8579)
P.O. Box 2017 (27501)
PHONE..............................919 552-0554
Timothy Zapf, *Pr*
John Kelley, *VP*
Reginald Stroupe, *Ch Bd*
Donna Moore, *Sec*
EMP: 18 EST: 1995
SQ FT: 20,000
SALES (est): 7.05MM **Privately Held**
Web: www.ampcherokee.com
SIC: 7359 3829 7699 Equipment rental and leasing, nec; Measuring and controlling devices, nec; Scientific equipment repair service

(G-118)
CUSTOM SMILES INC
Also Called: Joy Dental Lab
123 Fish Dr Ste 101 (27501-9479)
PHONE..............................919 331-2090
Michael Creech, *Pr*
EMP: 13 EST: 2005
SQ FT: 6,200
SALES (est): 1.82MM **Privately Held**
Web: www.customsmilesinc.com
SIC: 3843 Dental equipment and supplies

(G-119)
GREGORY VINEYARDS
275 Bowling Spring Dr (27501-9052)
PHONE..............................919 427-9409
EMP: 4 EST: 2018
SALES (est): 141.33K **Privately Held**
Web: www.gregoryvineyards.com
SIC: 2084 Wines

(G-120)
HEATMASTER LLC (PA)
3625 Benson Rd (27501-7380)
PHONE..............................919 639-4568
Scott Michaels, *Pr*
▲ **EMP: 44 EST:** 1974
SQ FT: 100,000
SALES (est): 6.06MM
SALES (corp-wide): 6.06MM **Privately Held**
Web: www.heatmaster.com
SIC: 3317 Conduit: welded, lock joint, or heavy riveted

(G-121)
INNOVATIVE DESIGN TECH LLC
Also Called: Rhinoshelf.com
475 S Raleigh St (27501-8256)
P.O. Box 2296 (27501-2296)
PHONE..............................919 331-0204
EMP: 7 EST: 2010
SALES (est): 2.05MM **Privately Held**
Web: www.rhinoshelf.com
SIC: 5046 2542 Shelving, commercial and industrial; Shelving, office and store, except wood

(G-122)
J &D CONTRACTOR SERVICE INC
246 Scotts Ln (27501-7078)
PHONE..............................919 427-0218
Lee Johnson, *Pr*
Lee Scott Johnson, *Pr*
Dustin Lee Johnson, *VP*
Julie Bolton, *Sec*
EMP: 5 EST: 2017
SALES (est): 504.13K **Privately Held**
SIC: 7389 1521 1799 1389 Business Activities at Non-Commercial Site; Single-family housing construction; Construction site cleanup; Construction, repair, and dismantling services

(G-123)
L L C BATTERIES OF N C
101 Medical Dr (27501-6029)
P.O. Box 1969 (27546-1969)
PHONE..............................919 331-0241
Lonnie D Scott Junior, *Managing Member*
Ruth Scott, *Prin*
EMP: 5 EST: 2003
SALES (est): 7.1MM **Privately Held**
Web: www.batteriesofnc.com
SIC: 5063 5531 3692 Batteries; Auto and home supply stores; Primary batteries, dry and wet

(G-124)
LA ESTRELLA INC
61 W Williams St (27501-7277)
PHONE..............................919 639-6559
Fortino Rios, *Owner*
EMP: 4 **EST:** 1994
SALES (est): 246.94K **Privately Held**
Web: la-estrella.edan.io
SIC: 2051 Bread, cake, and related products

(G-125)
NATIONAL FOAM INC
Also Called: Angus Fire
141 Junny Rd (27501-8625)
PHONE..............................919 639-6151
Willy Brown, *Mgr*
EMP: 117
SALES (corp-wide): 35.56MM **Privately Held**
Web: www.nationalfoam.com
SIC: 5087 3052 3494 2241 Service establishment equipment; Rubber and plastics hose and beltings; Valves and pipe fittings, nec; Narrow fabric mills
PA: National Foam, Inc.
141 Junny Rd
Angier NC 27501
919 639-6100

(G-126)
NATIONAL FOAM INC (PA)
Also Called: Angus Fire
141 Junny Rd (27501-8625)
PHONE..............................919 639-6100
Paul Williams, *CEO*
Hank Shaefer, *VP*
◆ **EMP:** 20 **EST:** 2013
SALES (est): 35.56MM
SALES (corp-wide): 35.56MM **Privately Held**
Web: www.nationalfoam.com
SIC: 3569 2899 5012 Firefighting and related equipment; Foam charge mixtures; Fire trucks

(G-127)
R L LASATER PRINTING
32 E Depot St (27501-6017)
PHONE..............................919 639-6662
R L Lasater, *Prin*
EMP: 4 **EST:** 2004
SALES (est): 178.32K **Privately Held**
SIC: 2752 Commercial printing, lithographic

(G-128)
TRIMSTERS INC
150 West Rd (27501-6968)
PHONE..............................919 639-3126
Shawn Ogni, *Pr*
John F Ogni, *VP*
EMP: 7 **EST:** 1999
SQ FT: 5,000
SALES (est): 2.07MM **Privately Held**
Web: www.trimstersinc.com
SIC: 2431 Woodwork, interior and ornamental, nec

Ansonville
Anson County

(G-129)
ANSONVILLE PIPING & FABG INC
122 Ansonville Polkton Rd (28007)
P.O. Box 394 (28007-0394)
PHONE..............................704 826-8403
Kenneth Wayne Pope, *Pr*
William Martin, *VP*
Brandon Pope, *VP*
EMP: 4 **EST:** 1975

SQ FT: 9,000
SALES (est): 160.62K **Privately Held**
SIC: 1711 7692 1791 Process piping contractor; Welding repair; Structural steel erection

(G-130)
NAT BLACK LOGGING INC
Mcbride Rd (28007)
P.O. Box 779 (28007-0779)
PHONE..............................704 826-8834
James Nathaniel Black, *Pr*
Carol P Black, *Sec*
Barry James, *VP*
EMP: 6 **EST:** 1976
SALES (est): 579.75K **Privately Held**
SIC: 2411 Logging camps and contractors

(G-131)
PREMIERE FIBERS LLC
10056 Hwy 52 N (28007)
PHONE..............................704 826-8321
John T Amirtharaj, *Pr*
Jeff Johnson, *
R Marcus Ammen, *
◆ **EMP:** 160 **EST:** 1999
SQ FT: 1,500
SALES (est): 11.08MM
SALES (corp-wide): 84.87MM **Privately Held**
Web: www.premierefibers.com
SIC: 2282 Throwing and winding mills
PA: Universal Fiber Systems, Llc
14401 Industrial Park Rd
Bristol VA 24202
276 669-1161

Apex
Wake County

(G-132)
ACCU-TOOL LLC
2490 Reliance Ave (27539-6331)
PHONE..............................919 363-2600
EMP: 15 **EST:** 1982
SQ FT: 12,000
SALES (est): 5.8MM **Privately Held**
Web: www.accutool.net
SIC: 3599 Machine shop, jobbing and repair

(G-133)
AIRCRAFT PARTS SOLUTIONS LLC
3378 Apex Peakway (27502-6310)
P.O. Box 3511 (29910-3511)
PHONE..............................843 300-1725
Todd Chambers, *Managing Member*
EMP: 4 **EST:** 2019
SALES (est): 1.24MM **Privately Held**
Web: www.aps.parts
SIC: 3728 Aircraft parts and equipment, nec

(G-134)
AMERICAN PHYSCL SEC GROUP LLC
1030 Goodworth Dr (27539-3869)
PHONE..............................919 363-1894
Kristen Mckenna, *Admn*
EMP: 4 **EST:** 2008
SQ FT: 10,000
SALES (est): 565.31K **Privately Held**
Web: www.americanpsg.com
SIC: 7382 3699 8712 Protective devices, security; Security control equipment and systems; Architectural engineering

(G-135)
APEX EMBROIDERY INC
996 Ambergate Sta (27502-2431)
PHONE..............................919 793-6083

Seth Matkowsky, *Owner*
EMP: 7 **EST:** 2009
SALES (est): 99.7K **Privately Held**
Web: www.apexembdesigns.com
SIC: 2395 Embroidery products, except Schiffli machine

(G-136)
APEX PRINTING COMPANY
514 E Williams St (27502-2183)
P.O. Box 1357 (27502-3357)
PHONE..............................919 362-9856
Hayden Woodard, *Owner*
EMP: 4 **EST:** 1977
SQ FT: 5,200
SALES (est): 234.15K **Privately Held**
Web: www.zebraprintsolutions.com
SIC: 2752 Offset printing

(G-137)
APEX SALSA COMPANY
912 N York Ct (27502-4647)
PHONE..............................919 363-1486
EMP: 4 **EST:** 2010
SALES (est): 195.67K **Privately Held**
Web: www.apexsalsa.com
SIC: 2099 Dips, except cheese and sour cream based

(G-138)
APEX TOOL GROUP LLC
Also Called: Apex Facility and Dist Ctr
1000 Lufkin Rd (27539-8160)
PHONE..............................919 387-0099
Mike Cox, *Ex Dir*
EMP: 128
SALES (corp-wide): 2.81B **Privately Held**
Web: www.apextoolgroup.com
SIC: 3546 Power-driven handtools
HQ: Apex Tool Group, Llc
910 Ridgebrook Rd Ste 200
Sparks Glencoe MD 21152

(G-139)
ARISAKA LLC
Also Called: Arisaka
1600 Olive Chapel Rd Ste 260 (27502-6764)
PHONE..............................919 601-5625
EMP: 12 **EST:** 2014
SALES (est): 2.35MM **Privately Held**
Web: www.arisakadefense.com
SIC: 3484 7389 Guns (firearms) or gun parts, 30 mm. and below; Business Activities at Non-Commercial Site

(G-140)
ASCO POWER TECHNOLOGIES LP
3412 Apex Peakway (27502-5756)
PHONE..............................919 460-5200
EMP: 105
SALES (corp-wide): 1.09K **Privately Held**
Web: www.ascopower.com
SIC: 3699 Electrical equipment and supplies, nec
HQ: Asco Power Technologies, L.P.
160 Park Ave
Florham Park NJ 07932

(G-141)
ATI INDUSTRIAL AUTOMATION INC (DH)
1031 Goodworth Dr (27539)
PHONE..............................919 772-0115
Jason Laud, *Pr*
Keith A Morris, *
Dwayne M Perry, *
EMP: 100 **EST:** 1989
SQ FT: 8,000
SALES (est): 42.96MM **Publicly Held**
Web: www.ati-ia.com

SIC: 3823 3674 Process control instruments; Semiconductors and related devices
HQ: Novanta Corporation
125 Middlesex Tpke
Bedford MA 01730
781 266-5700

(G-142)
AUTOSMART INC
510 Fairview Rd (27502-1306)
PHONE..............................919 210-7936
Thomas W Lewis, *Pr*
EMP: 6 **EST:** 2006
SQ FT: 5,500
SALES (est): 165.27K **Privately Held**
Web: www.driveautosmart.com
SIC: 7534 Tire repair shop

(G-143)
AXCCELLUS LLC
2501 Schieffelin Rd (27502-4431)
PHONE..............................919 589-9800
EMP: 10 **EST:** 2015
SALES (est): 2.1MM **Privately Held**
Web: www.axccellus.com
SIC: 3599 3444 Custom machinery; Machine guards, sheet metal

(G-144)
BARNES PRECISION MACHINE INC
1434 Farrington Rd Ste 300 (27523-5728)
PHONE..............................919 362-6805
Andrew S Barnes, *Pr*
EMP: 18 **EST:** 1992
SQ FT: 11,000
SALES (est): 1.24MM **Privately Held**
Web: www.usamade-ar15parts.com
SIC: 3599 Machine shop, jobbing and repair

(G-145)
BIORESOURCE INTERNATIONAL INC
Also Called: Apex Manufacturing Facility
2000 N Salem St (27523-8206)
PHONE..............................919 267-3758
EMP: 5 **EST:** 2017
SALES (est): 493.34K **Privately Held**
Web: www.briworldwide.com
SIC: 2834 Pharmaceutical preparations

(G-146)
BLUE GAS MARINE INC
2528 Schieffelin Rd (27502-7000)
PHONE..............................919 238-3427
Miguel Guerreiro, *CEO*
EMP: 10 **EST:** 2012
SALES (est): 2.44MM **Privately Held**
Web: www.bluegasmarine.com
SIC: 3519 4924 Internal combustion engines, nec; Natural gas distribution

(G-147)
BUILDERS FRSTSRCE - RLEIGH LLC
23 Red Cedar Way (27502)
PHONE..............................919 363-4956
Dennis Darling, *Mgr*
EMP: 55
SALES (corp-wide): 16.4B **Publicly Held**
Web: www.bldr.com
SIC: 2439 5211 Trusses, wooden roof; Lumber and other building materials
HQ: Builders Firstsource - Raleigh, Llc.
401 Valley Forge Rd
Hillsborough NC 27278
919 644-1231

(G-148)
COMPUTATIONAL ENGRG INTL INC (HQ)
Also Called: C E I
2166 N Salem St Ste 101 (27523-6456)

PHONE.................919 363-0883
Anders Grimsrud, *Pr*
EMP: 26 **EST:** 1994
SQ FT: 4,200
SALES (est): 4.62MM
SALES (corp-wide): 2.54B **Publicly Held**
Web: nexusdemo.ensight.com
SIC: 7372 7371 Prepackaged software;
Computer software development and
applications
PA: Ansys, Inc.
2600 Ansys Dr
Canonsburg PA 15317
844 462-6797

(G-149)
CONMECH INDUSTRIES LLC
117 Beaver Creek Rd (27502-8011)
PHONE.................919 306-6228
Jason Stephenson, *Prin*
EMP: 4 **EST:** 2016
SALES (est): 415.93K **Privately Held**
Web: www.conmechindustries.com
SIC: 3999 Manufacturing industries, nec

(G-150)
DESIGNED FOR JOY
2408 Merion Creek Dr (27539-6300)
PHONE.................919 395-2884
Cary Heise, *Prin*
EMP: 19 **EST:** 2017
SALES (est): 349.24K **Privately Held**
Web: www.designedforjoy.com
SIC: 7389 3171 Design services; Handbags,
women's

(G-151)
DUTCHMAN CREEK SELF-STORAGE
8712 Holly Springs Rd (27539-9120)
PHONE.................919 363-8878
Paul Brewer, *Pt*
Joe Thompson, *Pt*
Webb White, *Pt*
Randy Miller, *Pt*
Laura Thompson, *Pt*
EMP: 5 **EST:** 2001
SALES (est): 203.27K **Privately Held**
Web: www.dcselfstorage.com
SIC: 7692 7513 Welding repair; Truck rental
and leasing, no drivers

(G-152)
EAGLE ROCK CONCRETE LLC
Also Called: Apex Plant
500 Pristine Water Dr (27539-7206)
PHONE.................919 596-7077
EMP: 44
SALES (corp-wide): 22.7MM **Privately
Held**
Web: www.eaglerockconcrete.com
SIC: 3273 Ready-mixed concrete
PA: Eagle Rock Concrete Llc
8310 Bandford Way
Raleigh NC 27615
919 781-3744

(G-153)
ECODYST INC
Also Called: Ecodyst
1010 Goodworth Dr (27539-3869)
PHONE.................919 599-4963
George Adjabeng, *Pr*
Kwabena Williams, *VP*
EMP: 6 **EST:** 2014
SALES (est): 3.19MM **Privately Held**
Web: www.ecodyst.com
SIC: 3821 Distilling apparatus, laboratory
type

(G-154)
EJ USA INC
Also Called: Ej
1006 Investment Blvd (27502-1954)
P.O. Box 186 (27502-0186)
PHONE.................919 362-7744
Gordon Wells, *Mgr*
EMP: 6
Web: www.ejco.com
SIC: 3321 Gray and ductile iron foundries
HQ: Ej Usa, Inc.
301 Spring St
East Jordan MI 49727
800 874-4100

(G-155)
FERNEL THERAPEUTICS INC
408 Gablefield Ln (27502-1358)
PHONE.................919 614-2375
Matthew Fraiser, *Pr*
EMP: 4 **EST:** 2021
SALES (est): 149.26K **Privately Held**
SIC: 3845 Electromedical apparatus

(G-156)
FORBES CUSTOM CABINETS LLC
Also Called: Forbes Fixtures
2025 Production Dr (27539-6349)
PHONE.................919 362-4277
EMP: 28
SIC: 2542 Cabinets: show, display, or
storage: except wood

(G-157)
GEOTRAK INCORPORATED
2521 Schieffelin Rd Ste 136 (27502-4400)
P.O. Box 190 (27502)
PHONE.................919 303-1467
Keith Lesage, *COO*
Donald Lesage, *CEO*
Judith Ann Lesage, *Pr*
Ann Evans, *Stockholder*
Margaret Schlereth, *Stockholder*
EMP: 12 **EST:** 1999
SALES (est): 1.26MM **Privately Held**
Web: www.geotrakinc.com
SIC: 3679 Electronic circuits

(G-158)
GINGER SUPREME INC
4925 Lett Rd (27539-6629)
P.O. Box 1292 (27502-3292)
PHONE.................919 812-8986
Randolph Duncan, *Pr*
Wendy Duncan, *Sec*
EMP: 4 **EST:** 2003
SALES (est): 132.89K **Privately Held**
Web: gingersupremedrinks.square.site
SIC: 2086 Soft drinks: packaged in cans,
bottles, etc.

(G-159)
GOEMBEL INC
Also Called: The Design Center
7303 Vanclaybon Rd (27523-4110)
PHONE.................919 303-0485
Patrick Goembel, *Pr*
Dina Goembel, *VP*
EMP: 10 **EST:** 1994
SQ FT: 3,000
SALES (est): 201.29K **Privately Held**
SIC: 1521 2434 Single-family home
remodeling, additions, and repairs; Wood
kitchen cabinets

(G-160)
GRAPHIX SOLUTION INC
Also Called: Gxs Wraps
1094 Classic Rd (27539-4401)
PHONE.................919 213-0371

EMP: 12 **EST:** 2018
SALES (est): 1.16MM **Privately Held**
Web: www.graphixsolutionnc.com
SIC: 3993 Signs and advertising specialties

(G-161)
GRIFFIN MOTION LLC
1040 Classic Rd (27539-4401)
P.O. Box 1298 (27540-1298)
PHONE.................919 577-6333
▲ **EMP:** 15 **EST:** 2005
SQ FT: 2,500
SALES (est): 4.88MM **Privately Held**
Web: www.griffinmotion.com
SIC: 3625 Motor controls and accessories

(G-162)
HARRISON FENCE INC
1680 E Williams St (27539-7703)
P.O. Box 828 (27502-0828)
PHONE.................919 244-6908
Rob Harrison, *Pr*
Shauna Harrison, *CFO*
EMP: 8 **EST:** 2004
SQ FT: 1,000
SALES (est): 3.23MM **Privately Held**
Web: www.harrisonfence.com
SIC: 1799 3315 Fence construction; Chain
link fencing

(G-163)
HBB GLOBAL LLC
8324 Covington Hill Way (27539-7939)
PHONE.................615 306-1270
Hong Baker, *Prin*
EMP: 4 **EST:** 2014
SALES (est): 96.79K **Privately Held**
SIC: 2323 Men's and boy's neckwear

(G-164)
HEMA ONLINE INDIAN BTQ LLC
1954 Rothesay Dr (27502-2524)
PHONE.................919 771-4374
EMP: 4
SALES (est): 334.19K **Privately Held**
SIC: 7389 3577 Business Activities at Non-
Commercial Site; Computer peripheral
equipment, nec

(G-165)
HIMCEN BATTERY INC
Also Called: Himcen Battery
2313 Blue Cedar Ct (27523-7155)
PHONE.................408 828-8744
Soon Duck Kim, *CEO*
Chang Kyum Kim, *Pr*
EMP: 9 **EST:** 2019
SALES (est): 499.43K **Privately Held**
Web: www.himcenbattery.com
SIC: 3692 Dry cell batteries, single or
multiple cell

(G-166)
IFANATIC LLC (PA)
105 Shalon Ct (27502-9019)
PHONE.................919 387-6062
▲ **EMP:** 5 **EST:** 2006
SALES (est): 626.53K **Privately Held**
Web: www.i-fanatic.com
SIC: 3629 Electronic generation equipment

(G-167)
IMAGINATION FABRICATION
810 Center St (27502-2567)
PHONE.................919 280-4430
Nicholas Spring, *CEO*
Nick String, *Owner*
▼ **EMP:** 6 **EST:** 2009
SALES (est): 1.23MM **Privately Held**
Web: www.ncimaginationfabrication.com

SIC: 7692 Welding repair

(G-168)
INDUSTRIAL MOTIONS INC
1401 Boxwood Ln (27502-1505)
PHONE.................734 284-8944
Frank Murray, *Owner*
EMP: 6 **EST:** 1961
SALES (est): 92.3K **Privately Held**
Web: www.industrial-motions.com
SIC: 2752 Commercial printing, lithographic

(G-169)
INNOVA-CON INCORPORATED
2521 Schieffelin Rd Ste 136 (27502-4400)
PHONE.................919 303-1467
Keith Lesage, *Brnch Mgr*
EMP: 6
SALES (corp-wide): 222.89K **Privately
Held**
SIC: 3679 Electronic circuits
PA: Innova-Con, Incorporated
8501 Potobac Shores Rd
Port Tobacco MD 20677
301 934-0481

(G-170)
INNOVATIVE MFG SOLUTIONS INC
675 Wooded Lake Dr (27523-6017)
PHONE.................919 219-2424
EMP: 4 **EST:** 2017
SALES (est): 267.13K **Privately Held**
Web: www.imsigroup.com
SIC: 3469 Metal stampings, nec

(G-171)
JBT MAREL CORPORATION
2000 Lufkin Rd (27539-7068)
PHONE.................919 362-8811
EMP: 7
Web: www.jbtc.com
SIC: 3556 Food products machinery
PA: Jbt Marel Corporation
70 W Madison St Ste 4400
Chicago IL 60602

(G-172)
JM WILLIAMS TIMBER COMPANY
4525 Green Level West Rd (27523-7301)
PHONE.................919 362-1333
J Macon Williams, *Pr*
J M Williams Junior, *VP*
Eliza C Williams, *Sec*
EMP: 4 **EST:** 1995
SALES (est): 1.04MM **Privately Held**
SIC: 1629 2411 Timber removal; Timber, cut
at logging camp

(G-173)
JUSTNEEM LLC
Also Called: Justneem Body Care
2416 Maxton Crest Dr (27539-7485)
PHONE.................919 414-8826
◆ **EMP:** 5 **EST:** 2007
SALES (est): 348.24K **Privately Held**
Web: www.justneem.com
SIC: 3999 Chairs, hydraulic, barber and
beauty shop

(G-174)
KLIERSOLUTIONS
4041 Brook Cross Dr (27539-8870)
PHONE.................919 806-1287
Korey Klier, *Prin*
EMP: 4 **EST:** 2017
SALES (est): 894.91K **Privately Held**
Web: www.kleinertfamily.com
SIC: 3861 Photographic equipment and
supplies

(G-175)
KORBER PHARMA INC (DH)
2243 Energy Dr (27502-4353)
PHONE..................................727 538-4644
Stephen Lundeen, *Prin*
Stephen Lundeen, *Sec*
Jorg Tafelmaier, *
Jrn Gosse, *
Kerry Fillmore, *
▲ **EMP:** 90 **EST:** 1994
SQ FT: 45,000
SALES (est): 47.65MM
SALES (corp-wide): 54.57MM **Privately Held**
Web: www.koerber-pharma.com
SIC: 3565 Packaging machinery
HQ: Korber Ag
    Anckelmannsplatz 1
    Hamburg HH 20537
    402110701

(G-176)
LARRY BISSETTE INC
8012 Dirt Rd (27539-6849)
P.O. Box 232 (27526-0232)
PHONE..................................919 773-2140
Larry Bissette, *Pr*
Larry Bissette Junior, *VP*
EMP: 12 **EST:** 1972
SALES (est): 659.79K **Privately Held**
SIC: 1761 3444 Roofing contractor; Sheet metalwork

(G-177)
MADERN USA INC
1010 Burma Dr (27539-5021)
PHONE..................................919 363-4248
Jean H R Madern, *Pr*
▲ **EMP:** 40 **EST:** 1997
SQ FT: 45,000
SALES (est): 9.66MM **Privately Held**
Web: www.madern.com
SIC: 3544 Special dies and tools

(G-178)
MC PRECAST CONCRETE INC
520 Pristine Water Dr (27539-7206)
P.O. Box 189 (27502-0189)
PHONE..................................919 367-3636
Raymond Duchaine, *Pr*
Chantale Duchaine, *
EMP: 9 **EST:** 1996
SQ FT: 30,000
SALES (est): 682.99K **Privately Held**
SIC: 3272 Concrete products, precast, nec

(G-179)
MELLINEUM PRINTING
2015 Production Dr (27539-6349)
PHONE..................................919 267-5752
Charles E Norton, *Pr*
Lorraine C Norton, *VP*
EMP: 10 **EST:** 1973
SQ FT: 5,000
SALES (est): 279.49K **Privately Held**
SIC: 2752 Offset printing

(G-180)
MERCURY SIGNS INC
Also Called: Custom Sgns - Dsign Mnfcture I
7306 Vanclaybon Rd (27523-4110)
PHONE..................................919 808-1205
Hamid Lalani, *CEO*
EMP: 6 **EST:** 2019
SALES (est): 342.52K **Privately Held**
Web: www.mercurysignsinc.com
SIC: 3993 Signs and advertising specialties

(G-181)
MIL3 INC
500 Upchurch St (27502-1872)
PHONE..................................919 362-1217
Pam Cleland, *Ex VP*
John Cleland, *Pr*
EMP: 4 **EST:** 1993
SQ FT: 3,200
SALES (est): 905.87K **Privately Held**
Web: www.pexcrimpusa.com
SIC: 3423 Plumbers' hand tools

(G-182)
MONO PLATE INC
2404 Pilsley Rd (27539-9048)
PHONE..................................631 643-3100
Michael Bader, *Pr*
Harvey Bader, *VP*
EMP: 8 **EST:** 1965
SALES (est): 372.66K **Privately Held**
SIC: 3559 Rubber working machinery, including tires

(G-183)
ON-SITE HOSE INC
1001 Goodworth Dr (27539-3802)
P.O. Box 2216 (27502-2238)
PHONE..................................919 303-3840
Andrew Brumsey, *Pr*
EMP: 5 **EST:** 2005
SALES (est): 2.62MM **Privately Held**
Web: www.on-sitehose.com
SIC: 3492 Hose and tube couplings, hydraulic/pneumatic

(G-184)
PARHELION INCORPORATED
Also Called: Stripelight
126 N Salem St Ste 200 (27502-1476)
P.O. Box 5456 (27512-5456)
PHONE..................................866 409-1839
James Redpath, *CEO*
Richard Redpath, *Pr*
Larry Switzer, *Dir*
EMP: 14 **EST:** 2010
SQ FT: 12,000
SALES (est): 832.33K **Privately Held**
Web: www.parhelion.com
SIC: 3648 Lighting equipment, nec

(G-185)
PEAK STEEL LLC
1610 N Salem St (27523-9498)
PHONE..................................919 362-5955
EMP: 17 **EST:** 2005
SALES (est): 2.54MM **Privately Held**
Web: www.peaksteel.com
SIC: 3441 Building components, structural steel

(G-186)
POLYZEN LLC
Also Called: Polyzen, Inc.
1041 Classic Rd (27539-4402)
P.O. Box 1299 (27502-3299)
PHONE..................................919 319-9599
EMP: 65 **EST:** 1997
SQ FT: 32,000
SALES (est): 15.56MM
SALES (corp-wide): 28.22MM **Privately Held**
Web: www.polyzen.com
SIC: 3841 Diagnostic apparatus, medical
PA: The Secant Group Llc
    551 E Church Ave
    Telford PA 18969
    877 774-2835

(G-187)
PROGRESSIVE INDUSTRIES INC
1020 Goodworth Dr (27539-3869)
PHONE..................................919 267-6948
EMP: 5 **EST:** 2018
SALES (est): 133.53K **Privately Held**
Web: www.progressiveindustries.net
SIC: 3999 Manufacturing industries, nec

(G-188)
PROPANE TRUCKS & TANKS INC (PA)
1600 E Williams St (27539-7703)
P.O. Box 340 (27502-0340)
PHONE..................................919 362-5000
Paul Harris, *CEO*
Laura Kedzierzawski, *CFO*
John S Jay Wooten Iii, *Sec*
EMP: 12 **EST:** 1969
SQ FT: 5,000
SALES (est): 3.39MM
SALES (corp-wide): 3.39MM **Privately Held**
Web: www.propanetrucksandtanks.com
SIC: 3713 3711 3537 Truck bodies (motor vehicles); Motor vehicles and car bodies; Industrial trucks and tractors

(G-189)
PSNC ENERGY
2451 Schieffelin Rd (27502-6330)
PHONE..................................919 367-2735
Gary Burney, *Mgr*
EMP: 6 **EST:** 2008
SALES (est): 183.42K **Privately Held**
Web: www.dominionenergy.com
SIC: 5722 5064 3639 Electric household appliances, major; Electrical appliances, major; Major kitchen appliances, except refrigerators and stoves

(G-190)
QUARRIES PETROLEUM
2540 Schieffelin Rd (27502-7000)
PHONE..................................919 387-0986
EMP: 4 **EST:** 2007
SALES (est): 83.07K **Privately Held**
SIC: 1422 Crushed and broken limestone

(G-191)
R & J MECHANICAL & WELDING LLC
Also Called: R&J Custom Exhaust
554 E Williams St (27502-2151)
PHONE..................................919 362-6630
Robert Lowery, *Managing Member*
EMP: 7 **EST:** 1985
SQ FT: 3,200
SALES (est): 249.76K **Privately Held**
SIC: 7538 7692 General automotive repair shops; Welding repair

(G-192)
S T WOOTEN CORPORATION
Also Called: Apex/Pittsboro Concrete Plant
51 Red Cedar Way (27523-8401)
PHONE..................................919 363-3141
Scott Wooten, *Pr*
EMP: 22
SALES (corp-wide): 319.83MM **Privately Held**
Web: www.stwcorp.com
SIC: 3531 Concrete plants
PA: S. T. Wooten Corporation
    3801 Black Creek Rd Se
    Wilson NC 27894
    252 291-5165

(G-193)
SCIEPHARM LLC (PA)
Also Called: CRS Laboratories

(G-194)
2201 Candun Dr Ste 102 (27523-6413)
PHONE..................................307 352-9559
Estela Molini, *Managing Member*
EMP: 6 **EST:** 2018
SALES (est): 9.67MM
SALES (corp-wide): 9.67MM **Privately Held**
SIC: 2819 Chemicals, high purity: refined from technical grade

(G-194)
SIGN SHOP OF THE TRIANGLE INC
4001 Midstream Ct (27539-6319)
PHONE..................................919 363-3930
Nicole C Rowe, *Pr*
EMP: 5 **EST:** 2005
SALES (est): 181.92K **Privately Held**
Web: www.gosignshop.com
SIC: 3993 7389 Signs and advertising specialties; Business Activities at Non-Commercial Site

(G-195)
SPRANTO AMERICA INC
1870 Lazio Ln (27502-4753)
PHONE..................................919 741-5095
Simon Horne, *Prin*
Xiaoke Chen, *Prin*
EMP: 5 **EST:** 2012
SALES (est): 250.48K **Privately Held**
Web: www.spranto.com
SIC: 7372 Application computer software

(G-196)
STEVENSON WOODWORKING
300 Hickory View Ln (27502-6599)
PHONE..................................919 362-9121
Gregory Stevenson, *Prin*
EMP: 5 **EST:** 2005
SALES (est): 125.11K **Privately Held**
SIC: 2431 Millwork

(G-197)
TIGERSWAN LLC
3453 Apex Peakway (27502-5757)
PHONE..................................919 439-7110
James Reese, *Ch*
Michael Biglin, *
Niki Taylor, *
Scott Cullather, *
Zachary Venegas, *
EMP: 120 **EST:** 2005
SALES (est): 20.42MM **Privately Held**
Web: www.tigerswan.com
SIC: 1542 3728 Nonresidential construction, nec; Military aircraft equipment and armament

(G-198)
TIPPER TIE INC (HQ)
2000 Lufkin Rd (27539-7068)
PHONE..................................919 362-8811
Charlie Rogers, *
◆ **EMP:** 105 **EST:** 1980
SQ FT: 130,000
SALES (est): 25.88MM **Publicly Held**
Web: www.jbtc.com
SIC: 3556 Meat processing machinery
PA: Jbt Marel Corporation
    70 W Madison St Ste 4400
    Chicago IL 60602

(G-199)
TRAUMTIC DRECT TRNSFSION DVCS
1007 Woodbriar St (27502-1371)
PHONE..................................423 364-5828
Michael Stout, *Mgr*
EMP: 4 **EST:** 2018
SALES (est): 103.91K **Privately Held**

SIC: **3841** Surgical and medical instruments

(G-200)
TRIANGLE CUSTOM CABINETS INC
807 Center St (27502-1713)
P.O. Box 1327 (27502-3327)
PHONE.................................919 387-1133
Jack P Truelove, *Pr*
Mark Hearn, *VP*
EMP: 7 EST: 1989
SQ FT: 3,700
SALES (est): 173.48K **Privately Held**
SIC: **2541** Cabinets, lockers, and shelving

(G-201)
TRIANGLE INSTALLATION SVC INC
2445 Reliance Ave (27539-7012)
PHONE.................................919 363-7637
John D Abood, *Pr*
Marilyn Abood, *Sec*
EMP: 8 EST: 1975
SQ FT: 7,000
SALES (est): 881.14K **Privately Held**
Web: www.carygutters.com
SIC: **3444** 1761 Gutters, sheet metal; Gutter
   and downspout contractor

(G-202)
VINTAGE SOUTH INC
1100 Chimney Hill Dr (27502-8824)
P.O. Box 7 (27502-0007)
PHONE.................................919 362-4079
Vic Lloyd, *Pr*
EMP: 5 EST: 1997
SALES (est): 88.68K **Privately Held**
SIC: **5149** 2099 Condiments; Food
   preparations, nec

(G-203)
VISION TECHNOLOGIES INC
8509 Smith Rd (27539-8169)
PHONE.................................919 387-7878
Davis Chamblee, *Pr*
EMP: 10 EST: 1994
SALES (est): 993.35K **Privately Held**
Web: www.vision-technologies.com
SIC: **3643** Lightning arrestors and coils

(G-204)
VISITECH SYSTEMS INC
1012 Napa Pl (27502-7125)
PHONE.................................919 387-0524
James P Rogers Iii, *Pr*
John Rogers, *VP*
EMP: 4 EST: 1994
SALES (est): 650.95K **Privately Held**
Web: www.visitechsystems.com
SIC: **3841** Surgical and medical instruments

(G-205)
VITTRO SIGN STUDIO
1106 Cameron Woods Dr (27523-3721)
PHONE.................................917 698-1594
Sharon Munoz, *Prin*
EMP: 4 EST: 2014
SALES (est): 81.63K **Privately Held**
Web: www.vittroglass.com
SIC: **3993** Signs and advertising specialties

(G-206)
WEIDENMILLER CO
1010 Burma Dr (27539-5021)
PHONE.................................630 250-2500
▲ **EMP: 16 EST:** 2022
SALES (est): 2.5MM **Privately Held**
Web: www.weidenmiller.com
SIC: **3556** Biscuit cutting dies

(G-207)
XTRA LIGHT MANUFACTURING
1301 Davis Dr (27523-8229)
PHONE.................................919 422-7281
Allen Kirk, *Prin*
EMP: 5 EST: 2011
SALES (est): 219.92K **Privately Held**
Web: www.xtralight.com
SIC: **3999** Manufacturing industries, nec

Arapahoe
Pamlico County

(G-208)
**WILLIAMS SEAFOOD ARAPAHOE
INC**
2383 Don Lee Rd (28510-9534)
PHONE.................................252 249-0594
Sherri Midyette, *Pr*
Jerry Midyette, *
EMP: 55 EST: 1980
SALES (est): 402.76K **Privately Held**
SIC: **2092** Seafoods, fresh: prepared

Ararat
Surry County

(G-209)
C & B SALVAGE COMPANY INC
2882 Ararat Rd (27007-8324)
PHONE.................................336 374-3946
Brent Simpson, *Pr*
EMP: 6 EST: 1976
SALES (est): 974.29K **Privately Held**
SIC: **5051** 3599 Steel; Machine shop,
   jobbing and repair

(G-210)
CALVIN C MOONEY POULTRY
4167 Nc 268 (27007-8129)
PHONE.................................336 374-6690
EMP: 6 EST: 2019
SALES (est): 84.29K **Privately Held**
SIC: **2015** Poultry slaughtering and
   processing

Archdale
Guilford County

(G-211)
**ARCHDALE FURNITURE
DISTRIBUTOR**
112 Englewood Dr (27263-2814)
PHONE.................................336 431-1081
John Hicks, *Owner*
EMP: 8 EST: 2003
SQ FT: 9,000
SALES (est): 247.48K **Privately Held**
SIC: **2512** Upholstered household furniture

(G-212)
ARCHDALE MILLWORKS INC
1204 Corporation Dr (27263-1649)
PHONE.................................336 431-9019
John White, *Pr*
EMP: 6 EST: 2001
SALES (est): 446.18K **Privately Held**
Web: www.millworkin.com
SIC: **2499** 2431 Decorative wood and
   woodwork; Millwork

(G-213)
**BOBBY LABONTE ENTERPRISES
INC**
403 Interstate Dr (27263-3162)

P.O. Box 607 (27370-0607)
PHONE.................................336 434-1800
Bobby Labonte, *Owner*
EMP: 10 EST: 1989
SQ FT: 7,680
SALES (est): 972.01K **Privately Held**
Web: www.bobbylabonte.com
SIC: **3711** Automobile assembly, including
   specialty automobiles

(G-214)
BROOKLINE FURNITURE CO INC
Also Called: Brookline Furniture
4015 Cheyenne Dr (27263-3240)
PHONE.................................336 841-8503
David Sowinski, *Pr*
Kenneth R Brooks, *Managing Member**
Dave Sowinski, *Managing Member**
Patricia P Brooks, *
EMP: 85 EST: 1999
SQ FT: 79,000
SALES (est): 22.17MM **Privately Held**
Web: www.brooklinefurniture.com
SIC: **5021** 2512 Furniture; Chairs:
   upholstered on wood frames

(G-215)
BURROUGH FURNITURE
1302 Kersey Valley Rd (27263-9439)
PHONE.................................336 841-3129
Stanton Edward Yarborough, *Owner*
EMP: 7 EST: 1981
SQ FT: 3,000
SALES (est): 78.07K **Privately Held**
SIC: **2512** 5712 Upholstered household
   furniture; Furniture stores

(G-216)
CENTRAL MACHINE COMPANY
2509 Surrett Dr (27263-8500)
PHONE.................................336 855-0022
Charles Harris, *Prin*
EMP: 5 EST: 2007
SALES (est): 718.25K **Privately Held**
Web: www.cmiperformance.com
SIC: **3599** Machine shop, jobbing and repair

(G-217)
CLARK SIGN CORPORATION
11530 N Main St (27263-2899)
PHONE.................................336 431-4944
Glen E Clark, *Pr*
EMP: 4 EST: 1993
SALES (est): 484.24K **Privately Held**
Web: www.clarksigncorp.com
SIC: **3993** Signs, not made in custom sign
   painting shops

(G-218)
COVENANTMADE LLC
2509 Surrett Dr (27263-8500)
PHONE.................................336 434-4725
EMP: 6 EST: 2012
SALES (est): 450.79K **Privately Held**
SIC: **2434** Wood kitchen cabinets

(G-219)
**CRANFORD SILK SCREEN PRCESS
IN**
7066 Mendenhall Rd (27263-3909)
P.O. Box 7321 (27264-7321)
PHONE.................................336 434-6544
Robert Leonard, *Pr*
Tanya Leonard, *VP*
EMP: 10 EST: 1976
SQ FT: 20,000
SALES (est): 468.36K **Privately Held**
Web: www.cranfordimaging.com
SIC: **2759** Screen printing

(G-220)
FAIRMONT METAL FINISHING INC
1301 Corporation Dr (27263-1652)
P.O. Box 7366 (27264-7366)
PHONE.................................336 434-4188
Luther Moore, *Pr*
Paul Moore, *VP*
EMP: 8 EST: 1983
SQ FT: 9,600
SALES (est): 129.45K **Privately Held**
SIC: **3471** Electroplating of metals or formed
   products

(G-221)
FAST ARCH OF CAROLINAS INC
617 Eden Ter Ste B (27263-2698)
P.O. Box 577 (27370-0577)
PHONE.................................336 431-2724
Mat Hawley, *Pr*
EMP: 5 EST: 2005
SALES (est): 330.56K **Privately Held**
SIC: **2439** Arches, laminated lumber

(G-222)
FIXXUS INDUS HOLDINGS CO LLC
6116 Old Mendenhall Rd (27263-3937)
PHONE.................................336 674-3088
EMP: 40 EST: 2016
SALES (est): 2.96MM **Privately Held**
Web: www.gosuperior.com
SIC: **2851** Lacquers, varnishes, enamels,
   and other coatings

(G-223)
FUTURE FOAM INC
3803 Comanche Rd (27263-3167)
PHONE.................................336 861-8095
John Cane, *Brnch Mgr*
EMP: 44
SALES (corp-wide): 495.02MM **Privately
Held**
Web: www.futurefoam.com
SIC: **3086** Plastics foam products
PA: Future Foam, Inc.
   1610 Ave N
   Council Bluffs IA 51501
   712 323-9122

(G-224)
HAFELE AMERICA CO (HQ)
3901 Cheyenne Dr (27263-3157)
P.O. Box 4000 (27263-4000)
PHONE.................................800 423-3531
Paul K Smith, *Pr*
Ursula Hafele, *
Gary A Crysel, *
◆ **EMP: 210 EST:** 1996
SQ FT: 500,000
SALES (est): 84.03MM
SALES (corp-wide): 1.86B **Privately Held**
Web: www.hafele.com
SIC: **5072** 3429 4225 Furniture hardware,
   nec; Furniture hardware; General
   warehousing and storage
PA: Hafele Se & Co Kg
   Adolf-Hafele-Str. 1
   Nagold BW 72202
   7452950

(G-225)
HARRIS HOUSE FURN INDS INC
104 Seminole Dr (27263-3253)
PHONE.................................336 431-2802
Otis E Harris Senior, *Pr*
Otis E Harris Junior, *VP*
Kevin Harris, *
Amber Harris, *
EMP: 50 EST: 1981
SQ FT: 33,000
SALES (est): 4.33MM **Privately Held**
Web: www.habitat.org

SIC: **2531** 2521 Public building and related furniture; Wood office furniture

(G-226)
HUBBELL INDUSTRIAL CONTRLS INC (HQ)
Also Called: Femco Radio Controls
4301 Cheyenne Dr (27263-3246)
PHONE.............................336 434-2800
Timothy H Powers, *Ch Bd*
David G Nord, *
James H Biggart Junior, *VP*
Gary N Amato, *
Gerben W Bakker, *
◆ **EMP:** 200 **EST:** 1985
SQ FT: 80,000
SALES (est): 97.08MM
SALES (corp-wide): 5.63B **Publicly Held**
Web: www.hubbell.com
SIC: **5063** 3625 Electrical apparatus and equipment; Motor controls, electric
PA: Hubbell Incorporated
   40 Waterview Dr
   Shelton CT 06484
   800 626-0005

(G-227)
IE FURNITURE INC (PA)
1121 Corporation Dr (27263-1648)
P.O. Box 5861 (27262)
PHONE.............................336 475-5050
Tommy Mathena, *Pr*
Randy Woolard, *
EMP: 50 **EST:** 2014
SALES (est): 5.57MM
SALES (corp-wide): 5.57MM **Privately Held**
Web: www.iefurniture.com
SIC: **1799** 2521 5021 Office furniture installation; Wood office furniture; Office and public building furniture

(G-228)
INNOVATIVE CUSHIONS LLC
4010 Cheyenne Dr (27263-3239)
PHONE.............................336 861-2060
Trela R Hendrix Junior, *Managing Member*
EMP: 4 **EST:** 2010
SALES (est): 217.4K **Privately Held**
SIC: **2392** Cushions and pillows

(G-229)
IV-S METAL STAMPING INC
2400 Shore St (27263-2514)
PHONE.............................336 861-2100
Jerri Smith, *Pr*
Nelson Smith, *
David Willard, *
David Ernest, *
EMP: 35 **EST:** 1988
SQ FT: 100,000
SALES (est): 3.86MM **Privately Held**
Web: www.us-metalcrafters.com
SIC: **3469** 3499 2599 7692 Stamping metal for the trade; Strapping, metal; Hotel furniture; Welding repair

(G-230)
J & J MACHINE WORKS INC
1300 Corporation Dr (27263-1651)
P.O. Box 360 (27374-0360)
PHONE.............................336 434-4081
Jerry Ledwell, *Pr*
EMP: 7 **EST:** 1974
SQ FT: 15,000
SALES (est): 364.11K **Privately Held**
Web: www.jjmachineworks.com
SIC: **3599** Machine shop, jobbing and repair

(G-231)
JOWAT CORPORATION
5637 Evelyn View Dr (27263-3863)
PHONE.............................336 434-9356
EMP: 5
SALES (corp-wide): 440.85MM **Privately Held**
Web: www.jowat.com
SIC: **2891** Adhesives
HQ: Jowat Corporation
   5608 Uwharrie Rd
   Archdale NC 27263
   336 434-9000

(G-232)
JOWAT CORPORATION
5265 Surrett Dr (27263-4045)
PHONE.............................336 442-5834
EMP: 64
SALES (corp-wide): 440.85MM **Privately Held**
Web: www.jowat.com
SIC: **2891** Adhesives
HQ: Jowat Corporation
   5608 Uwharrie Rd
   Archdale NC 27263
   336 434-9000

(G-233)
JOWAT CORPORATION (HQ)
Also Called: Jowat Adhesives
5608 Uwharrie Rd (27263-4167)
P.O. Box 1368 (27261)
PHONE.............................336 434-9000
Rainhard Kramme, *Pr*
Gerhard Haas, *
Jerry Crouse, *
◆ **EMP:** 26 **EST:** 1979
SQ FT: 120,000
SALES (est): 55.02MM
SALES (corp-wide): 440.85MM **Privately Held**
Web: www.jowat.com
SIC: **2891** 5169 Adhesives; Adhesives, chemical
PA: Jowat Se
   Ernst-Hilker-Str. 10-14
   Detmold NW 32758
   52317490

(G-234)
JOWAT INTERNATIONAL CORP
5608 Uwharrie Rd (27263-4167)
P.O. Box 1368 (27261-1368)
PHONE.............................336 434-9000
Rainhard Kramme, *Pr*
EMP: 21 **EST:** 1979
SALES (est): 460.4K
SALES (corp-wide): 440.85MM **Privately Held**
Web: www.jowat.com
SIC: **2891** 5169 Adhesives; Adhesives, chemical
PA: Jowat Se
   Ernst-Hilker-Str. 10-14
   Detmold NW 32758
   52317490

(G-235)
JOWAT PROPERTIES CORP
5608 Uwharrie Rd (27263-4167)
P.O. Box 1368 (27261-1368)
PHONE.............................336 434-9000
EMP: 6 **EST:** 2018
SALES (est): 478.9K
SALES (corp-wide): 440.85MM **Privately Held**
Web: www.jowat.com
SIC: **2891** Adhesives
PA: Jowat Se
   Ernst-Hilker-Str. 10-14

Detmold NW 32758
52317490

(G-236)
KING TEXTILES LLC
400 Interstate Dr (27263-3161)
PHONE.............................336 861-3257
Matthew H Underwood, *Managing Member*
◆ **EMP:** 14 **EST:** 2000
SQ FT: 60,000
SALES (est): 1.14MM **Privately Held**
Web: www.kingtextilesllc.com
SIC: **2221** Textile mills, broadwoven: silk and manmade, also glass

(G-237)
LEITZ TOOLING SYSTEMS LP
Also Called: Leitz Tooling Demp's Div.
401 Interstate Dr (27263-3162)
P.O. Box 4129 (27263-4129)
PHONE.............................336 861-3367
Bill Johnsone, *Mgr*
EMP: 7
SQ FT: 25,660
SALES (corp-wide): 14.78MM **Privately Held**
Web: www.leitz.org
SIC: **3553** 3546 3425 Woodworking machinery; Power-driven handtools; Saw blades and handsaws
HQ: Leitz Tooling Systems Lp
   4301 East Paris Ave Se
   Grand Rapids MI 49512
   800 253-6070

(G-238)
LOWDER STEEL INC
2450 Coltrane Mill Rd (27263-8907)
P.O. Box 4158 (27263-4158)
PHONE.............................336 431-9000
J Dean Lowder, *Pr*
EMP: 24 **EST:** 2015
SALES (est): 4.58MM **Privately Held**
Web: www.lowdersteel.net
SIC: **1521** 3449 New construction, single-family houses; Bars, concrete reinforcing: fabricated steel

(G-239)
O HENRY HOUSE LTD
308 Greenoak Dr (27263-2344)
P.O. Box 7463 (27264-7463)
PHONE.............................336 431-5350
Richard Pulliam, *Pr*
John Sutton, *
EMP: 32 **EST:** 1988
SQ FT: 28,500
SALES (est): 2.55MM **Privately Held**
Web: www.ohenryhouseltd.com
SIC: **2512** 5712 Upholstered household furniture; Furniture stores

(G-240)
ORNAMENTAL MOULDINGS LLC (DH)
Also Called: Ornamental
3804 Comanche Rd (27263-3166)
PHONE.............................336 431-9120
Dennis Berry, *Managing Member*
▲ **EMP:** 18 **EST:** 1993
SQ FT: 100,000
SALES (est): 11.74MM
SALES (corp-wide): 198.3MM **Privately Held**
Web: www.ornamental.com
SIC: **2431** 5031 Moldings and baseboards, ornamental and trim; Molding, all materials
HQ: Fletcher Wood Solutions, Inc.
   200 Westgate Cir Ste 402
   Annapolis MD 21401

(G-241)
RELIABLE BEDDING COMPANY
7147 Mendenhall Rd (27263-3910)
PHONE.............................336 883-0648
Robert W Parris, *Pr*
Kember Parris, *Sec*
Dustin Rebert, *VP*
EMP: 12 **EST:** 1967
SALES (est): 937.34K **Privately Held**
Web: www.reliablebeddingcompany.com
SIC: **2515** 5712 Mattresses, innerspring or box spring; Mattresses

(G-242)
SALUTE INDUSTRIES INC
105 Apache Dr (27263-3153)
PHONE.............................844 937-2588
Malek Lahmar, *Pr*
EMP: 6 **EST:** 2013
SQ FT: 40,000
SALES (est): 522.02K **Privately Held**
Web: www.uniforms-4u.com
SIC: **2337** 2311 2329 Women's and misses' suits and coats; Firemen's uniforms: made from purchased materials; Shirt and slack suits: men's, youths', and boys'

(G-243)
STAMPER SHEET METAL INC
357 Bud Kanoy Rd (27263)
PHONE.............................336 476-5145
Thomas Stamper, *Pr*
EMP: 6 **EST:** 1994
SQ FT: 6,300
SALES (est): 692.08K **Privately Held**
Web: www.cameroncanine.com
SIC: **3444** 1799 Sheet metalwork; Welding on site

(G-244)
STEELCITY LLC (PA)
Also Called: Harts Striping
505 Aztec Dr (27263-3248)
PHONE.............................336 434-7000
EMP: 27 **EST:** 2018
SALES (est): 9.8MM
SALES (corp-wide): 9.8MM **Privately Held**
SIC: **2395** Quilting and quilting supplies

(G-245)
US METAL CRAFTERS LLC
Also Called: Raptor Attachments
2400 Shore St (27263-2514)
PHONE.............................336 861-2100
EMP: 50 **EST:** 2018
SALES (est): 9.68MM **Privately Held**
Web: www.us-metalcrafters.com
SIC: **3599** 3444 3441 Machine and other job shop work; Sheet metalwork; Fabricated structural metal

(G-246)
WAYNE INDUSTRIES INC
4107 Cheyenne Dr (27263-3242)
P.O. Box 4130 (27263-4130)
PHONE.............................336 434-5017
Wayne Smith, *Pr*
Doug Connor, *
▲ **EMP:** 29 **EST:** 1980
SQ FT: 36,000
SALES (est): 4.37MM **Privately Held**
SIC: **2392** Cushions and pillows

Arden
Buncombe County

(G-247)
A-1 CONCRETE & CNSTR LLC
42 Avery Creek Rd (28704-8726)

GEOGRAPHIC

PHONE.................828 712-1160
Tim Reeves, *Mgr*
EMP: 4 **EST:** 2010
SALES (est): 173.73K **Privately Held**
SIC: 3531 Finishers, concrete and
　bituminous: powered

(G-248)
ADVANTAGE PRINTING INC
1848 Brevard Rd (28704-9488)
PHONE.................828 252-7667
Judy Montcastle, *Pr*
John P Montcastle, *VP*
EMP: 13 **EST:** 1981
SQ FT: 7,000
SALES (est): 3.52MM **Privately Held**
Web: www.buyadvantageprinting.com
SIC: 2752 Offset printing

(G-249)
AKURATEMP LLC
170 Bradley Branch Rd Ste 7 (28704-9216)
PHONE.................828 708-7178
Andreas Reinhart, *CEO*
EMP: 13 **EST:** 2020
SALES (est): 1.28MM **Privately Held**
Web: www.akuratemp.com
SIC: 2899 7389 2819 Chemical
　preparations, nec; Packaging and labeling
　services; Industrial inorganic chemicals, nec

(G-250)
ALTECH-ECO CORPORATION
101 Fair Oaks Rd (28704-9702)
PHONE.................828 654-8300
Alexander Kovalchuk, *Pr*
Miles George, *VP*
EMP: 13 **EST:** 2006
SALES (est): 4.53MM **Privately Held**
Web: www.transecoenergy.com
SIC: 2869 Fuels

(G-251)
ANGELS PATH VENTURES INC
21 Commerce Way (28704-9712)
PHONE.................828 654-9530
David Coates, *Pr*
Mellanie Coates, *Sec*
EMP: 8 **EST:** 1985
SQ FT: 5,000
SALES (est): 2.77MM **Privately Held**
SIC: 3599 3451 Custom machinery; Screw
　machine products

(G-252)
ARCADIA BEVERAGE LLC (PA)
Also Called: Arcadia Beverage
34 Arcadia Farms Rd (28704-0015)
PHONE.................828 684-3556
David Johnston, *CFO*
Dan Nifong, *VP Opers*
EMP: 5 **EST:** 2017
SALES (est): 10.98MM
SALES (corp-wide): 10.98MM **Privately
Held**
Web: www.arcadiabev.com
SIC: 2033 Fruit juices: packaged in cans,
　jars, etc.

(G-253)
ARCADIA FARMS LLC
34 Arcadia Farms Rd (28704-0015)
PHONE.................828 684-3556
Tom Moore, *Pr*
Steve Decorte, *
David Johnston, *
Dan Nifong, *
Michael Audet, *
EMP: 80 **EST:** 1940
SQ FT: 2,000
SALES (est): 18.6MM

SALES (corp-wide): 484.47MM **Privately
Held**
Web: www.arcadiabev.com
SIC: 2033 Fruit juices: packaged in cans,
　jars, etc.
PA: Investors Management Corporation
　801 N. West St
　Raleigh NC 27612
　919 653-7499

(G-254)
**ASHEVILLE MAINTENANCE AND
CONSTRUCTION INC**
Also Called: AMC
150 Glenn Bridge Rd (28704-8502)
P.O. Box 1348 (28704-1348)
PHONE.................828 687-8110
EMP: 50
Web: www.amcincorp.com
SIC: 1796 7349 3441 1791 Millwright;
　Building maintenance, except repairs;
　Building components, structural steel;
　Structural steel erection

(G-255)
ATLAS PRECISION INC
170 Clayton Rd (28704-8708)
PHONE.................828 687-9900
EMP: 104 **EST:** 1987
SALES (est): 11MM **Privately Held**
Web: www.atlas-plastics.com
SIC: 3089 Injection molding of plastics

(G-256)
BORGWARNER ARDEN LLC
1849 Brevard Rd (28704-9488)
PHONE.................248 754-9200
Brady Ericson, *Pr*
EMP: 10 **EST:** 2018
SALES (est): 4.7MM
SALES (corp-wide): 14.09B **Publicly Held**
Web: www.phinia.com
SIC: 3714 Motor vehicle parts and
　accessories
PA: Borgwarner Inc.
　3850 Hamlin Rd
　Auburn Hills MI 48326
　248 754-9200

(G-257)
BORGWARNER INC
1849 Brevard Rd (28704-9488)
P.O. Box 15075 (28813-0509)
PHONE.................828 684-4000
Nancy Payne, *Mgr*
EMP: 30
SALES (corp-wide): 14.09B **Publicly Held**
Web: www.borgwarner.com
SIC: 3714 Transmissions, motor vehicle
PA: Borgwarner Inc.
　3850 Hamlin Rd
　Auburn Hills MI 48326
　248 754-9200

(G-258)
**BORGWARNER TURBO SYSTEMS
LLC (DH)**
1849 Brevard Rd (28704)
P.O. Box 15075 (28813)
PHONE.................828 684-4000
Joseph F Fadool, *Pr*
Craig Aaron, *
Tonit M Calaway, *CAO*
Paul Farrell, *CSO*
Tania Wingfield, *Chief Human Resource
Officer*
▲ **EMP:** 89 **EST:** 1989
SALES (est): 62.14MM
SALES (corp-wide): 14.09B **Publicly Held**
Web: www.borgwarner.com

SIC: 3089 3465 Automotive parts, plastic;
　Body parts, automobile: stamped metal
HQ: Bwa Turbo Systems Holding Llc
　3850 Hamlin Rd
　Auburn Hills MI

(G-259)
CAM CRAFT LLC
54 Atrium Trl (28704-9141)
PHONE.................828 681-5183
Charles Reichard, *CEO*
Harriett Reichard, *VP*
EMP: 4 **EST:** 2008
SALES (est): 552.81K **Privately Held**
Web: www.camcraftcams.com
SIC: 3714 5015 Camshafts, motor vehicle;
　Automotive supplies, used: wholesale and
　retail

(G-260)
CCBCC OPERATIONS LLC
Also Called: Coca-Cola
36 Clayton Rd (28704-8707)
PHONE.................828 687-1300
Gary Beard, *Mgr*
EMP: 51
SALES (corp-wide): 6.9B **Publicly Held**
Web: www.coca-cola.com
SIC: 2086 Bottled and canned soft drinks
HQ: Ccbcc Operations, Llc
　4100 Coca-Cola Plz
　Charlotte NC 28211
　704 364-8728

(G-261)
CELTIC OCEAN INTERNATIONAL INC
Also Called: Selina Naturally
4 Celtic Dr (28704-9157)
PHONE.................828 299-9005
Selina Delangre, *Pr*
▲ **EMP:** 31 **EST:** 1968
SQ FT: 19,000
SALES (est): 5.42MM **Privately Held**
Web: www.selinanaturally.com
SIC: 5961 2731 5153 5149 Catalog and mail-
　order houses; Books, publishing only;
　Grains; Natural and organic foods

(G-262)
CJE CONSTRUCTION INC
3869 Sweeten Creek Rd (28704-3135)
P.O. Box 311 (28704)
PHONE.................828 650-6600
Juan Carlos Borges, *Prin*
EMP: 4 **EST:** 2010
SALES (est): 252.95K **Privately Held**
SIC: 3299 Stucco

(G-263)
CONSOLIDATED METCO INC
90 Christ School Rd (28704-9556)
PHONE.................360 828-2689
EMP: 32
SALES (corp-wide): 3.96B **Privately Held**
Web: www.conmet.com
SIC: 3089 Injection molding of plastics
HQ: Consolidated Metco, Inc.
　5701 Se Columbia Way
　Vancouver WA 98661
　360 828-2599

(G-264)
CUSTOM PACKAGING INC
Also Called: Custom Packaging of Asheville
20 Beale Rd (28704-9235)
PHONE.................828 684-5060
Jeff West, *Genl Mgr*
EMP: 165 **EST:** 1970
SALES (est): 8.2MM
SALES (corp-wide): 18.23MM **Privately
Held**

Web: www.hoodcontainer.com
SIC: 5113 2653 Corrugated and solid fiber
　boxes; Corrugated and solid fiber boxes
PA: Custom Packaging, Lp
　1315 W Baddour Pkwy
　Lebanon TN 37087
　615 444-6025

(G-265)
DIAMOND DOG TOOLS INC
Also Called: Stf Precision
75 Old Shoals Rd (28704-9401)
PHONE.................828 687-3686
Jason Ford, *Pr*
David Novak, *
◆ **EMP:** 52 **EST:** 1992
SQ FT: 15,000
SALES (est): 4.58MM **Privately Held**
Web: www.gwstoolgroup.com
SIC: 3545 5049 Precision tools, machinists';
　Precision tools

(G-266)
EATON CORPORATION
221 Heywood Rd (28704-2655)
PHONE.................828 684-2381
Winston Stanton, *Mgr*
EMP: 500
SQ FT: 250,953
Web: www.dix-eaton.com
SIC: 3625 3613 3621 3612 Motor controls,
　electric; Switchgear and switchgear
　accessories, nec; Motors and generators;
　Transformers, except electric
HQ: Eaton Corporation
　1000 Eaton Blvd
　Cleveland OH 44122
　440 523-5000

(G-267)
ETBF LLC ⊙
Also Called: SECURE RESTORATION
3863 Sweeten Creek Rd (28704-3135)
PHONE.................937 543-2223
Robert Franks, *Managing Member*
EMP: 13 **EST:** 2023
SALES (est): 3.48MM **Privately Held**
Web: www.securerestoration.com
SIC: 1389 Construction, repair, and
　dismantling services

(G-268)
FILMON PROCESS CORP
100 Baldwin Rd (28704-8573)
P.O. Box 869 (28704-0869)
PHONE.................828 684-1360
Robert Ploeger, *Mgr*
Carl Ploeger, *Product Vice President*
EMP: 4 **EST:** 1961
SQ FT: 3,000
SALES (est): 271.52K **Privately Held**
Web: www.filmonploeger.com
SIC: 3955 Ribbons, inked: typewriter, adding
　machine, register, etc.

(G-269)
FLINT GROUP INC
Also Called: Flint Group Flexographic Pdts
25 Old Shoals Rd (28704-9010)
PHONE.................828 687-4363
William B Miller, *Pr*
Paul R Carnarvon, *CFO*
Michelle A Domas, *Treas*
Peter M Schreck, *Sec*
EMP: 24 **EST:** 2016
SALES (est): 3.56MM **Privately Held**
Web: www.flint-group.com
SIC: 2893 Printing ink

▲ = Import ▼ = Export
◆ = Import/Export

(G-270)
FLINT GROUP US LLC
Also Called: Flint Group Print Media N Amer
95 Glenn Bridge Rd (28704-9414)
PHONE................................828 687-4309
EMP: 5
SALES (corp-wide): 1.91B **Privately Held**
Web: www.flintgrp.com
SIC: 2893 Printing ink
PA: Flint Group Us Llc
    17177 N Lrel Pk Dr Ste 30
    Livonia MI 48152
    734 781-4600

(G-271)
FLINT GROUP US LLC
25 Old Shoals Rd (28704-9010)
PHONE................................828 687-4291
Amy Dill, *Brnch Mgr*
EMP: 5
SALES (corp-wide): 1.91B **Privately Held**
Web: www.flintgrp.com
SIC: 2893 Printing ink
PA: Flint Group Us Llc
    17177 N Lrel Pk Dr Ste 30
    Livonia MI 48152
    734 781-4600

(G-272)
FLINT GROUP US LLC
Also Called: Day International Prtg Pdts
95 Glenn Bridge Rd (28704-9414)
PHONE................................828 687-2485
John Hodges, *Brnch Mgr*
EMP: 11
SALES (corp-wide): 1.91B **Privately Held**
Web: www.flintgrp.com
SIC: 2759 3069 Commercial printing, nec;
    Molded rubber products
PA: Flint Group Us Llc
    17177 N Lrel Pk Dr Ste 30
    Livonia MI 48152
    734 781-4600

(G-273)
HEALTH CHOICE PHARMACY
2690 Hendersonville Rd (28704-8576)
PHONE................................281 741-8358
Felicia R Young, *Prin*
EMP: 6 EST: 2010
SALES (est): 544.36K **Privately Held**
SIC: 2834 Pharmaceutical preparations

(G-274)
HUBBELL INCORPORATED
Also Called: Hubbell Premise Wiring
20 Glenn Bridge Rd (28704-9450)
PHONE................................828 687-8505
Norman Vint, *Brnch Mgr*
EMP: 20
SALES (corp-wide): 5.63B **Publicly Held**
Web: www.hubbell.com
SIC: 3643 Current-carrying wiring services
PA: Hubbell Incorporated
    40 Waterview Dr
    Shelton CT 06484
    800 626-0005

(G-275)
INDUSTRIAL SHEET METAL WORKS
149 Old Shoals Rd (28704-5501)
PHONE................................828 654-9655
Perry Bartsch, *Prin*
EMP: 4 EST: 2015
SALES (est): 620.71K **Privately Held**
SIC: 3444 Sheet metalwork

(G-276)
**INJECTION TECHNOLOGY
CORPORATION**

Also Called: Itech
199 Airport Rd (28704-8516)
P.O. Box 1107 (28704-1107)
PHONE................................828 684-1362
EMP: 105
SIC: 3089 Injection molding of plastics

(G-277)
ISM INC
149 Old Shoals Rd (28704-5501)
EMP: 22 EST: 1977
SQ FT: 28,000
SALES (est): 3.78MM **Privately Held**
Web: www.ism-nc.com
SIC: 3444 3446 3499 3535 Sheet metalwork
    ; Architectural metalwork; Aerosol valves,
    metal; Conveyors and conveying equipment

(G-278)
JABIL INC
100 Vista Blvd (28704-9457)
PHONE................................828 684-3141
EMP: 43
SALES (corp-wide): 28.88B **Publicly Held**
Web: www.jabil.com
SIC: 3672 Printed circuit boards
PA: Jabil Inc.
    10800 Roosevelt Blvd N
    Saint Petersburg FL 33716
    727 577-9749

(G-279)
JAYSON CONCEPTS INC
115 Vista Blvd (28704-9457)
PHONE................................828 654-8900
Jay Stingel, *Pr*
Janet Stingel, *
John Stingel, *
▲ EMP: 7 EST: 1981
SQ FT: 50,000
SALES (est): 900.21K **Privately Held**
Web: www.vertique.com
SIC: 3535 Conveyors and conveying
    equipment

(G-280)
LE BLEU CORPORATION
212 Baldwin Rd (28704-8568)
P.O. Box 8127 (28814-8127)
PHONE................................828 254-5105
Andy Scotchie, *Brnch Mgr*
EMP: 5
Web: www.lebleu.com
SIC: 2086 Water, natural: packaged in cans,
    bottles, etc.
PA: Le Bleu Corporation
    3134 Cornatzer Rd
    Advance NC 27006

(G-281)
**LEGACY AEROSPACE AND DEF LLC
(PA)**

Also Called: Legacy Aerospace & Defense
150 Glenn Bridge Rd (28704-8502)
PHONE................................828 398-0981
Thomas Kane, *Ex Dir*
EMP: 4 EST: 2013
SQ FT: 10,000
SALES (est): 3.54MM
SALES (corp-wide): 3.54MM **Privately
Held**
Web: www.legacy-aerospace.com
SIC: 3728 Aircraft parts and equipment, nec

(G-282)
LEGEND-TEES
37 Loop Rd (28704-8401)
PHONE................................828 585-2066
EMP: 4 EST: 2019
SALES (est): 73.28K **Privately Held**
Web: www.legend-tees.com

SIC: 2759 Screen printing

(G-283)
LINAMAR NORTH CAROLINA INC
2169 Hendersonville Rd (28704-9742)
PHONE................................828 348-5343
Linda Hasenfratz, *CEO*
Jim Jarrell, *COO*
▲ EMP: 11 EST: 2011
SQ FT: 400,000
SALES (est): 18.49MM
SALES (corp-wide): 5.89B **Privately Held**
SIC: 3545 Precision measuring tools
HQ: Linamar Holding Nevada, Inc.
    32233 8 Mile Rd
    Livonia MI 48152
    248 477-6240

(G-284)
**MEDICAL ACTION INDUSTRIES INC
(HQ)**

Also Called: Medical Action
25 Heywood Rd (28704-9302)
PHONE................................631 404-3700
Ed Pesicka, *CEO*
Paul Chapman, *
◆ EMP: 86 EST: 1987
SQ FT: 28,200
SALES (est): 82.85MM **Publicly Held**
Web: www.medical-action.com
SIC: 3842 Applicators, cotton tipped
PA: Owens & Minor, Inc.
    10900 Nuckols Rd Ste 400
    Glen Allen VA 23060

(G-285)
MILLAR INDUSTRIES INC
20 Loop Rd (28704-8401)
P.O. Box 1259 (28704-1259)
PHONE................................828 687-0639
Fred Millar, *CEO*
Brett Millar, *Pr*
Marilyn Millar, *Sec*
EMP: 21 EST: 1989
SQ FT: 27,000
SALES (est): 4.8MM **Privately Held**
Web:
a-mtool-
com.securec95biz.ezhostingserver.com
SIC: 3089 3544 Injection molding of plastics;
    Special dies, tools, jigs, and fixtures

(G-286)
MILLER GLASS
72 Bradley Branch Rd (28704-9303)
PHONE................................828 681-8083
Cindy Miller, *Pr*
Jamie Zullo, *VP*
EMP: 5 EST: 2005
SALES (est): 1.74MM **Privately Held**
Web: www.millerglass.biz
SIC: 3231 Products of purchased glass

(G-287)
MOUNTAIN LEISURE HOT TUBS LLC
40 Business Park Cir Ste 60 (28704-8649)
PHONE................................828 649-7727
EMP: 6 EST: 2019
SALES (est): 2.36MM **Privately Held**
Web: www.mountainleisurehottubs.com
SIC: 3999 Hot tubs

(G-288)
NEW PECO INC
10 Walden Dr (28704-3314)
PHONE................................828 684-1234
Peter Cook, *Pr*
▲ EMP: 21 EST: 2009
SALES (est): 2.92MM **Privately Held**
Web: www.lawnvac.com

SIC: 3524 3444 Grass catchers, lawn mower
    ; Sheet metal specialties, not stamped

(G-289)
**NORTH CAROLINA DEPARTMENT
OF A**

Also Called: Western Anmal Dsase Dgnstc
Lab
785 Airport Rd (28704)
P.O. Box 279 (28704-0279)
PHONE................................828 684-8188
Richard Oliver, *Mgr*
EMP: 6
SALES (corp-wide): 74.26B **Privately Held**
Web: www.ncagr.gov
SIC: 2835 9512 Veterinary diagnostic
    substances; Land, mineral, and wildlife
    conservation, State government
HQ: North Carolina Department Of
    Agriculture & Consumer Services
    2 W Edenton St
    Raleigh NC 27601

(G-290)
NOVA ENTERPRISES INC (PA)
Also Called: Nova Kitchen & Bath
305 Airport Rd (28704-8402)
P.O. Box 1167 (28704-1167)
PHONE................................828 687-8770
Bill Purdue, *Pr*
Renee Purdue, *
Ken Dinkins, *
EMP: 48 EST: 1969
SQ FT: 7,000
SALES (est): 9.79MM
SALES (corp-wide): 9.79MM **Privately
Held**
Web: www.novakitchen.com
SIC: 5031 3281 1799 Kitchen cabinets;
    Table tops, marble; Kitchen and bathroom
    remodeling

(G-291)
NYPRO ASHEVILLE INC
Also Called: Nypro
100 Vista Blvd (28704-9457)
PHONE................................828 684-3141
▲ EMP: 200
SIC: 3089 Injection molding of plastics

(G-292)
NYPRO OREGON INC
100 Vista Blvd (28704-9457)
PHONE................................541 753-4700
Theodore E Lapres I, *Pr*
▲ EMP: 361 EST: 1994
SQ FT: 94,000
SALES (est): 5.04MM
SALES (corp-wide): 28.88B **Publicly Held**
SIC: 3089 Molding primary plastics
HQ: Nypro Inc.
    101 Union St
    Clinton MA 01510
    978 365-9721

(G-293)
PARKWAY PRODUCTS LLC
Also Called: Parkway Asheville
199 Airport Rd (28704-8516)
PHONE................................828 684-1362
EMP: 105
SALES (corp-wide): 177.91K **Privately
Held**
Web: www.parkwayproducts.com
SIC: 3089 Injection molding of plastics
HQ: Parkway Products, Llc
    3 Research Dr Ste 135
    Greenville SC 29607
    864 484-8700

G
E
O
G
R
A
P
H
I
C

(G-294)
PARKWAY PRODUCTS LLC
199 Airport Rd (28704-8516)
PHONE..............................828 684-1362
EMP: 200 **EST:** 2013
SALES (est): 5.32MM **Privately Held**
Web: www.parkwayproducts.com
SIC: 2821 3677 Molding compounds, plastics
; Transformers power supply, electronic type

(G-295)
PARTS AND SYSTEMS COMPANY INC
Also Called: Pasco
44 Buck Shoals Rd Ste D2 (28704-3380)
P.O. Box 5468 (28813-5468)
PHONE..............................828 684-7070
John M Crook, *Pr*
Joy C Crook, *VP*
▲ **EMP:** 10 **EST:** 1987
SQ FT: 4,800
SALES (est): 1.44MM **Privately Held**
Web: www.pascorolls.com
SIC: 3552 Textile machinery

(G-296)
PECO INC
Also Called: Peco
100 Airport Rd (28704-8516)
PHONE..............................828 684-1234
EMP: 22
SIC: 3524 3531 3553 3563 Blowers and
vacuums, lawn; Chippers: brush, limb, and
log; Woodworking machinery; Air and gas
compressors

(G-297)
POWDERTEK
6 Bagwell Mill Rd (28704-8553)
PHONE..............................828 225-3250
Bryan Street, *Prin*
EMP: 4 **EST:** 2009
SALES (est): 968.92K **Privately Held**
Web: www.powdertekswannanoa.com
SIC: 3479 Coating of metals and formed
products

(G-298)
PRECEPT MEDICAL PRODUCTS INC (DH)
Also Called: Precept
370 Airport Rd (28704-9202)
PHONE..............................828 681-0209
John Sopcisak, *CEO*
▲ **EMP:** 16 **EST:** 1960
SQ FT: 25,000
SALES (est): 9.52MM
SALES (corp-wide): 142.17MM **Privately Held**
SIC: 3842 2389 Clothing, fire resistant and
protective; Disposable garments and
accessories
HQ: Aspen Surgical Products, Inc.
6945 Southbelt Dr Se
Caledonia MI 49316
888 364-7004

(G-299)
PRECISION PDTS ASHEVILLE INC (PA)
118 Glenn Bridge Rd (28704-8502)
P.O. Box 1047 (28704-1047)
PHONE..............................828 684-4207
Shannon Herren, *Pr*
Julie Herren, *VP*
EMP: 21 **EST:** 1962
SQ FT: 20,000
SALES (est): 9.74MM
SALES (corp-wide): 9.74MM **Privately Held**

Web: www.ppofa.com
SIC: 3599 Machine shop, jobbing and repair

(G-300)
PRECISION PDTS PRFMCE CTR INC
191 Airport Rd (28704-8516)
P.O. Box 1229 (28704-1229)
PHONE..............................828 684-8569
Leo Jackson, *Pr*
Debra Jackson, *Sec*
EMP: 10 **EST:** 1985
SQ FT: 30,000
SALES (est): 3.06MM **Privately Held**
Web: www.pppcenter.com
SIC: 3714 Motor vehicle parts and
accessories

(G-301)
PRECISION TOOL DYE AND MOLD
69 Bagwell Mill Rd (28704-8553)
P.O. Box 727 (28704-0727)
PHONE..............................828 687-2990
Vollie Whitaker, *Pr*
Keith Whitaker, *VP*
EMP: 10 **EST:** 1995
SQ FT: 3,000
SALES (est): 1.62MM **Privately Held**
SIC: 3544 3599 Special dies and tools;
Machine shop, jobbing and repair

(G-302)
PRODUCTION WLDG FBRICATION INC
1791 Brevard Rd (28704-9659)
P.O. Box 726 (28728-0726)
PHONE..............................828 687-7466
Michael Philips, *Pr*
Elaine Phillips, *VP*
Michael Phillips, *Pr*
EMP: 8 **EST:** 1983
SQ FT: 6,000
SALES (est): 2.73MM **Privately Held**
SIC: 3599 3441 Custom machinery;
Fabricated structural metal

(G-303)
REICH LLC
140 Vista Blvd (28704-9457)
PHONE..............................828 651-9019
Andre Reich, *Managing Member*
◆ **EMP:** 120 **EST:** 2010
SQ FT: 40,000
SALES (est): 24.84MM **Privately Held**
Web: www.reich-llc.com
SIC: 3562 Ball bearings and parts

(G-304)
RGEES LLC
170 Bradley Branch Rd Ste 6&7
(28704-9216)
PHONE..............................828 708-7178
Harshul Gupta, *CEO*
▲ **EMP:** 6 **EST:** 2009
SALES (est): 423.82K **Privately Held**
Web: www.rgees.com
SIC: 2679 2671 2673 Crepe paper or crepe
paper products: purchased material; Paper;
coated and laminated packaging; Bags:
plastic, laminated, and coated

(G-305)
SARE GRANITE & TILE
Also Called: Sare Kitchen and Bed
128 Greene Rd (28704-9582)
PHONE..............................828 676-2666
Ray Koruk, *Pr*
EMP: 8 **EST:** 2012
SALES (est): 490.98K **Privately Held**
Web: www.saregranite.com

SIC: 1743 1799 2541 Tile installation,
ceramic; Kitchen cabinet installation;
Counter and sink tops

(G-306)
SIMPLYHOME LLC
48 Fisk Dr (28704-9469)
P.O. Box 1155 (28704-1155)
PHONE..............................828 684-8441
Jason Ray, *CEO*
Allen Ray, *Managing Member*
EMP: 19 **EST:** 2009
SQ FT: 2,000
SALES (est): 3.66MM **Privately Held**
Web: www.simply-home.com
SIC: 3669 Visual communication systems

(G-307)
SMITH & FOX INC
Also Called: Imagesmith
19 Walden Dr (28704-3314)
PHONE..............................828 684-4512
Mary Smith, *Pr*
David Smith, *Prin*
EMP: 10 **EST:** 1983
SQ FT: 21,000
SALES (est): 973.58K **Privately Held**
Web: www.imagesmith.com
SIC: 2752 Offset printing

(G-308)
SOUTHERN CONCRETE MTLS INC
Hendersonville Rd (28704)
P.O. Box 5395 (28813-5395)
PHONE..............................828 684-3636
Jeffery Linderman, *Mgr*
EMP: 20
SALES (corp-wide): 238.17MM **Privately Held**
Web: www.scmusa.com
SIC: 3273 Ready-mixed concrete
HQ: Southern Concrete Materials, Inc.
35 Meadow Rd
Asheville NC 28803
828 253-6421

(G-309)
SPECIALITY COX MFG LLC
25 Commerce Way (28704-9712)
PHONE..............................828 684-5762
Hoyt L Cox, *Managing Member*
EMP: 5 **EST:** 1986
SQ FT: 3,200
SALES (est): 599.41K **Privately Held**
SIC: 3544 Forms (molds), for foundry and
plastics working machinery

(G-310)
THRILLS HAULING LLC
173 New Rockwood Rd (28704-9492)
PHONE..............................407 383-3483
EMP: 10 **EST:** 2021
SALES (est): 814.89K **Privately Held**
SIC: 1442 Construction sand and gravel

(G-311)
TRANSECO ENERGY CORPORATION
101 Fair Oaks Rd (28704-9702)
PHONE..............................828 684-6400
Alexander Kovalchuk, *CEO*
Miles George, *VP*
Mark Oleskiewicz, *CFO*
EMP: 7 **EST:** 2007
SALES (est): 608.03K **Privately Held**
Web: www.transecoenergy.com
SIC: 2869 Fuels

(G-312)
TREG TOOL INC
10 Summer Meadow Rd (28704-7601)

PHONE..............................828 676-0035
Gert Lykke, *Prin*
EMP: 5 **EST:** 2016
SALES (est): 81.71K **Privately Held**
SIC: 3089 Injection molding of plastics

(G-313)
TRIUMPH TOOL NC INC
44 Buck Shoals Rd Ste B3 (28704-3384)
PHONE..............................828 676-3677
John Duffy, *Pr*
Patrick Duffy, *
EMP: 50 **EST:** 2011
SALES (est): 2.03MM **Privately Held**
Web: www.triumphtool.com
SIC: 3599 Machine shop, jobbing and repair

(G-314)
TUTCO INC
Farnam Custom Products
30 Legend Dr (28704-6203)
PHONE..............................828 654-1665
Neil Farnum, *Genl Mgr*
EMP: 54
SALES (corp-wide): 3.97B **Privately Held**
Web: www.tutco.com
SIC: 3567 Heating units and devices,
industrial: electric
HQ: Tutco, Llc
500 Gould Dr
Cookeville TN 38506
931 432-4141

(G-315)
TUTCU-FARNAM CUSTOM PRODUCTS
30 Legend Dr (28704-6203)
PHONE..............................828 684-3766
Greg Canada, *Prin*
EMP: 30 **EST:** 2011
SALES (est): 2.08MM **Privately Held**
Web: www.farnam-custom.com
SIC: 2819 Elements

(G-316)
VIKTORS GRAN MBL KIT CNTER TOP
28 Beale Rd (28704-9235)
PHONE..............................828 681-0713
Viktor Polishchuk, *Prin*
EMP: 10 **EST:** 2004
SALES (est): 1.67MM **Privately Held**
Web: www.vgmwnc.com
SIC: 1799 3253 5032 5211 Kitchen and
bathroom remodeling; Ceramic wall and
floor tile; Ceramic wall and floor tile, nec;
Counter tops

(G-317)
VISTA HORTICULTURAL GROUP INC
Also Called: Eden Brothers
2099 Brevard Rd (28704)
PHONE..............................828 633-6338
Sabine Randon, *Pr*
EMP: 19 **EST:** 2011
SALES (est): 3.67MM **Privately Held**
Web: www.edenbrothers.com
SIC: 2099 Food preparations, nec

(G-318)
WILLIAMS PLATING COMPANY INC
6 Industrial Dr (28704-7712)
P.O. Box 3042 (28802-3042)
PHONE..............................828 681-0301
Michael Williams, *Pr*
Deborah Williams, *Sec*
EMP: 10 **EST:** 1982
SQ FT: 10,000
SALES (est): 977.68K **Privately Held**
Web: www.williamsplating.com

SIC: 3471 Electroplating of metals or formed products

(G-319)
WPH VENTURES INC
Also Called: Hickman
4 Commerce Way (28704-9712)
P.O. Box 15005 (28813-0005)
PHONE..............................828 676-1700
▼ EMP: 28
SIC: 3444 Metal roofing and roof drainage equipment

(G-320)
XSYS NORTH AMERICA CORPORATION
Also Called: Xsys Global
95 Glenn Bridge Rd (28704-9414)
PHONE..............................828 654-6805
EMP: 32
SALES (corp-wide): 857.59K **Privately Held**
Web: www.xsysglobal.com
SIC: 2796 Platemaking services
HQ: Xsys North America Corporation
2915 Whthall Pk Dr Ste 60
Charlotte NC 28273
704 504-2626

(G-321)
XSYS NORTH AMERICA CORPORATION
25 Old Shoals Rd (28704-9010)
PHONE..............................828 687-2485
Joe Bauer, *Mgr*
EMP: 32
SALES (corp-wide): 857.59K **Privately Held**
Web: www.xsysglobal.com
SIC: 2893 Printing ink
HQ: Xsys North America Corporation
2915 Whthall Pk Dr Ste 60
Charlotte NC 28273
704 504-2626

Ash
Brunswick County

(G-322)
SIMMONS LOGGING & TRUCKING INC
5923 Simmons Rd Nw (28420-3835)
PHONE..............................910 287-6344
Lathion Simmons, *Pr*
Betty Simmons, *VP*
EMP: 5 EST: 1967
SALES (est): 248.92K **Privately Held**
SIC: 2411 Logging camps and contractors

Asheboro
Randolph County

(G-323)
ACME-MCCRARY CORPORATION
159 North St (27203-5411)
PHONE..............................336 625-2161
Horace Luther, *Brnch Mgr*
EMP: 124
Web: www.acme-mccrary.com
SIC: 2251 Women's hosiery, except socks
HQ: Acme-Mccrary Corporation
162 N Cherry St
Asheboro NC 27203
336 625-2161

(G-324)
ACME-MCCRARY CORPORATION (DH)
162 N Cherry St (27203-5310)
PHONE..............................336 625-2161
Charles W Mc Crary Junior, *Ch Bd*
John O H Toledano Senior, *V Ch Bd*
Neal Anderson, *
Donnie White, *
Bruce T Patram, *
◆ EMP: 350 EST: 1909
SQ FT: 200,000
SALES (est): 18.02MM **Privately Held**
Web: www.acme-mccrary.com
SIC: 2251 Panty hose
HQ: Mas Us Holdings, Inc.
162 N Cherry St
Asheboro NC 27203
336 625-2161

(G-325)
ALLEN MCH & FABRICATION LLC
420 Industrial Park Ave (27205-7330)
P.O. Box 309 (27204-0309)
PHONE..............................336 521-4409
Todd Allen, *Pr*
EMP: 13 EST: 2016
SALES (est): 4.19MM **Privately Held**
Web: www.allenmaf.com
SIC: 3599 Machine shop, jobbing and repair

(G-326)
ANA MUF CORPORATION
1046 Briles Dr (27205-2012)
PHONE..............................336 653-3509
Miguel Uribe, *Pr*
Javier Uribe, *Contrlr*
EMP: 8 EST: 2021
SALES (est): 478.23K **Privately Held**
SIC: 2426 Frames for upholstered furniture, wood

(G-327)
ASHEBORO ELASTICS CORP (PA)
Also Called: AEC Narrow Fabrics
150 N Park St (27203-5455)
P.O. Box 1143 (27204-1143)
PHONE..............................336 629-2626
Larry Himes, *CEO*
Robert B Lawson, *
John K Crisco Junior, *VP*
Jeff Crisco, *
Jane Crisco, *
◆ EMP: 60 EST: 1985
SQ FT: 60,000
SALES (est): 10.9MM
SALES (corp-wide): 10.9MM **Privately Held**
Web: www.aecnarrowfabrics.com
SIC: 2221 2241 Broadwoven fabric mills, manmade; Elastic narrow fabrics, woven or braided

(G-328)
ASHEBORO ELASTICS CORP
Also Called: AEC Narrow Fabrics
1947 N Fayetteville St (27203-3269)
PHONE..............................336 629-2626
EMP: 4
SALES (corp-wide): 10.9MM **Privately Held**
Web: www.aecnarrowfabrics.com
SIC: 2241 2221 Elastic narrow fabrics, woven or braided; Broadwoven fabric mills, manmade
PA: Asheboro Elastics Corp.
150 N Park St
Asheboro NC 27203
336 629-2626

(G-329)
ASHEBORO MACHINE SHOP INC
3027 Us Business 220 S (27204)
P.O. Box 361 (27204-0361)
PHONE..............................336 625-6322
Ronnie Hussey, *Pr*
Ricky Moore, *VP*
EMP: 8 EST: 1980
SQ FT: 7,425
SALES (est): 1.82MM **Privately Held**
Web: www.randolphmachine.com
SIC: 3599 Machine shop, jobbing and repair

(G-330)
ASHEBORO READY-MIX INC
524 W Bailey St (27203-3610)
P.O. Box 984 (27204-0984)
PHONE..............................336 672-0957
Todd Richardson, *Pr*
EMP: 8 EST: 1979
SQ FT: 7,000
SALES (est): 857.97K **Privately Held**
SIC: 3273 Ready-mixed concrete

(G-331)
BEANE SIGNS INC
218 Vista Pkwy (27205-5064)
PHONE..............................336 629-6748
William Beane, *Pr*
EMP: 4 EST: 1971
SQ FT: 600
SALES (est): 185.28K **Privately Held**
Web: www.beanesignsinc.com
SIC: 3993 Signs and advertising specialties

(G-332)
BOSSONG CORPORATION
840 W Salisbury St (27203-4327)
P.O. Box 789 (27204-0789)
PHONE..............................336 625-2175
F Huntley Bossong, *Pr*
Charles J Bossong, *VP*
EMP: 7 EST: 2011
SQ FT: 140,000
SALES (est): 97.31K **Privately Held**
Web: www.bossonghosiery.com
SIC: 2251 Women's hosiery, except socks

(G-333)
BOSSONG HOSIERY MILLS INC (PA)
840 W Salisbury St (27204)
P.O. Box 789 (27204-0789)
PHONE..............................336 625-2175
Huntley Bossong, *CEO*
F Bossong, *
Charles J Bossong, *
Joseph C Bossong, *
▲ EMP: 220 EST: 1927
SQ FT: 140,000
SALES (est): 23.92MM
SALES (corp-wide): 23.92MM **Privately Held**
Web: www.bossonghosiery.com
SIC: 2252 Socks

(G-334)
BURROW FAMILY CORPORATION (PA)
5346 Nc Highway 49 S (27205-1974)
P.O. Box 2683 (27261-2683)
PHONE..............................336 887-3173
Gary Burrow, *Pr*
Douglas Burrow, *VP*
EMP: 40 EST: 1941
SQ FT: 100,000
SALES (est): 5.69MM
SALES (corp-wide): 5.69MM **Privately Held**
SIC: 2752 Offset printing

(G-335)
CAROLINA PRECISION PLASTICS L (HQ)
Also Called: Cpp Global
405 Commerce Pl (27203-0553)
PHONE..............................336 498-2654
◆ EMP: 178 EST: 1984
SQ FT: 95,000
SALES (est): 54.13MM
SALES (corp-wide): 500.49MM **Privately Held**
Web: www.cppglobal.com
SIC: 3089 Injection molding of plastics
PA: Westfall Technik, Llc
9280 S Kyrene Rd
Tempe AZ 85284
702 659-9898

(G-336)
CENTRAL CAROLINA PRINTING LLC
464 Cheshire Pl (27205-8229)
PHONE..............................910 572-3344
Troy Danner, *Managing Member*
EMP: 9 EST: 2001
SALES (est): 294.08K **Privately Held**
Web: www.ccprintandmail.com
SIC: 2752 Offset printing

(G-337)
CHANDLER CONCRETE INC
Also Called: Central Concrete
205 W Academy St (27203-5650)
PHONE..............................336 625-1070
Ronnie Faulkmer, *Brnch Mgr*
EMP: 10
Web: www.chandlerconcrete.com
SIC: 3273 Ready-mixed concrete
PA: Chandler Concrete Co., Inc.
1006 S Church Street
Burlington NC 27215

(G-338)
CHRIS ISOM INC
Also Called: Carolina Frames
1228 Green Farm Rd (27205-2346)
PHONE..............................336 629-0240
Chris Isom, *Prin*
EMP: 15 EST: 2001
SALES (est): 2.23MM **Privately Held**
SIC: 2511 2426 Wood household furniture; Hardwood dimension and flooring mills

(G-339)
CHROMA COLOR CORPORATION
Also Called: Plastics Color
1134 Nc Highway 49 S (27205-9584)
PHONE..............................336 629-9184
Arely Palomino, *Prin*
EMP: 96
SALES (corp-wide): 78.23MM **Privately Held**
Web: www.chromacolors.com
SIC: 2821 Plastics materials and resins
PA: Chroma Color Corporation
3900 W Dayton St
Mc Henry IL 60050
877 385-8777

(G-340)
COMM-KAB INC
1865 Spero Rd (27205-0501)
PHONE..............................336 873-8787
Nelson Rowland, *Pr*
Kentie Rowland, *VP*
EMP: 11 EST: 1988
SALES (est): 275.7K **Privately Held**
SIC: 5712 1751 2521 2434 Cabinet work, custom; Cabinet and finish carpentry; Wood office furniture; Wood kitchen cabinets

GEOGRAPHIC

(G-341)
CORNER STONE PLASTICS INC
1027 Luck Rd (27205-7864)
PHONE..............................336 629-1828
Virgil F Hill, *Pr*
Virgil F Hill, *Pr*
Gaye Hill, *VP*
EMP: 4 **EST:** 1983
SQ FT: 5,000
SALES (est): 672.98K **Privately Held**
SIC: 3089 Plastics hardware and building
products

(G-342)
COX PRECISION SPRINGS INC
3162 Spoons Chapel Rd (27205-8129)
P.O. Box 1417 (27204-1417)
PHONE..............................336 629-8500
Gary Cox, *Pr*
Judy Cox, *Sec*
Todd Schwarz, *VP*
Jennifer Schwarz, *Treas*
▲ **EMP:** 10 **EST:** 2002
SQ FT: 6,000
SALES (est): 660K **Privately Held**
Web: www.coxprecisionspring.com
SIC: 3495 Precision springs

(G-343)
CUSTOM EXTRUSION INC
2971 Taylor Dr (27203-0554)
PHONE..............................336 495-7070
Gralen Cranford, *Mgr*
EMP: 7
SALES (corp-wide): 295.68MM **Privately
Held**
Web: www.pexco.com
SIC: 3089 5162 Injection molding of plastics;
Plastics sheets and rods
HQ: Custom Extrusion, Inc.
34 Home Road
Sheffield MA 01257
413 229-8748

(G-344)
DALIAH PLASTICS CORP
134 W Wainman Ave (27205-5639)
P.O. Box 27 (27204-0027)
PHONE..............................336 629-0551
Charles Gans, *Pr*
Daliah Gans, *
Al Holland, *
EMP: 50 **EST:** 1981
SQ FT: 25,000
SALES (est): 11.79MM **Privately Held**
Web: www.daliahplastics.com
SIC: 3081 Polyethylene film

(G-345)
DATAMARK GRAPHICS INC
603 W Bailey St (27203-3611)
PHONE..............................336 629-0267
Don Byers, *CEO*
Elizabeth Byers, *
Eric Mcpherson, *Genl Mgr*
EMP: 25 **EST:** 1984
SQ FT: 16,000
SALES (est): 2.85MM **Privately Held**
Web: www.datamarkgraphics.com
SIC: 2759 2672 2671 2241 Labels and
seals: printing, nsk; Paper; coated and
laminated, nec; Paper; coated and
laminated packaging; Narrow fabric mills

(G-346)
DONALD HENLEY & SONS SAWMILL
Also Called: Henley Sawmill
2351 Old Cedar Falls Rd (27203-8356)
PHONE..............................336 625-5665
EMP: 5
SALES (est): 478.54K **Privately Held**

SIC: 2421 Sawmills and planing mills,
general

(G-347)
EDGEWELL PER CARE BRANDS LLC
2331 Carl Dr (27203)
P.O. Box 849 (27204-0849)
PHONE..............................336 672-4500
Jake Casper, *Brnch Mgr*
EMP: 21
SALES (corp-wide): 2.25B **Publicly Held**
Web: www.edgewell.com
SIC: 3421 Razor blades and razors
HQ: Edgewell Personal Care Brands, Llc
6 Research Dr
Shelton CT 06484
203 944-5500

(G-348)
EDGEWELL PER CARE BRANDS LLC
800 Albemarle Rd (27203-6263)
PHONE..............................336 629-1581
Reggie Rodman, *Brnch Mgr*
EMP: 22
SALES (corp-wide): 2.25B **Publicly Held**
Web: www.edgewell.com
SIC: 3421 Razor blades and razors
HQ: Edgewell Personal Care Brands, Llc
6 Research Dr
Shelton CT 06484
203 944-5500

(G-349)
EDGEWELL PER CARE BRANDS LLC
419 Art Bryan Dr (27203-3089)
PHONE..............................336 672-4500
Joe Tisone, *Brnch Mgr*
EMP: 9
SALES (corp-wide): 2.25B **Publicly Held**
Web: www.edgewell.com
SIC: 3421 3692 5063 Razor blades and
razors; Primary batteries, dry and wet;
Batteries, dry cell
HQ: Edgewell Personal Care Brands, Llc
6 Research Dr
Shelton CT 06484
203 944-5500

(G-350)
ELASTIC THERAPY LLC
718 Industrial Park Ave (27205-7336)
P.O. Box 4068 (27204-4068)
PHONE..............................336 625-0529
◆ **EMP:** 25 **EST:** 1989
SQ FT: 125,000
SALES (est): 8.62MM
SALES (corp-wide): 2.11B **Publicly Held**
Web: www.elastictherapy.com
SIC: 3842 Elastic hosiery, orthopedic
(support)
HQ: Djo, Llc
5919 Sea Otter Pl Ste 200
Carlsbad CA 92010
800 321-9549

(G-351)
ENERGIZER BATTERY MFG
419 Art Bryan Dr (27203-3089)
PHONE..............................336 736-7936
EMP: 6 **EST:** 2019
SALES (est): 2.06MM **Privately Held**
SIC: 3999 Manufacturing industries, nec

(G-352)
ENERGIZER HOLDINGS INC
800 Albemarle Rd (27203-6263)
PHONE..............................336 672-3526
EMP: 174
SALES (corp-wide): 2.89B **Publicly Held**
Web: www.energizer.com

SIC: 3691 3648 Storage batteries; Flashlights
PA: Energizer Holdings, Inc.
8235 Forsyth Blvd Ste 100
Saint Louis MO 63105
314 985-2000

(G-353)
EXLON EXTRUSION INC
2971 Taylor Dr (27203-0554)
PHONE..............................336 621-1295
Dennis Swink, *Pr*
Viola Fay Swink, *Sec*
EMP: 11 **EST:** 1984
SALES (est): 1.11MM
SALES (corp-wide): 295.68MM **Privately
Held**
Web: www.pexco.com
SIC: 3089 Injection molding of plastics
PA: Pexco Llc
3440 Preston Ridge Rd
Alpharetta GA 30005
678 990-1523

(G-354)
FARR KNITTING COMPANY INC
171 Boyd Ave (27205-7405)
PHONE..............................336 625-5561
Billy Farr, *Pr*
Tim Farr, *VP*
EMP: 6 **EST:** 1991
SQ FT: 1,700
SALES (est): 475.22K **Privately Held**
SIC: 2252 Socks

(G-355)
FIBER CUSHIONING INC (PA)
4454 Us Highway 220 Bus S (27205-0837)
PHONE..............................336 629-8442
W E Mcgee, *Pr*
▲ **EMP:** 18 **EST:** 1988
SQ FT: 62,500
SALES (est): 3.1MM
SALES (corp-wide): 3.1MM **Privately Held**
Web: www.fibercushioning.com
SIC: 2392 Cushions and pillows

(G-356)
FINE LINE HOSIERY INC
2012 Sunny Ln (27205-7256)
P.O. Box 4606 (27204-4606)
PHONE..............................336 498-8022
John C Luffman, *Pr*
Lisa Elliott, *VP*
Bryan Luffman, *Sec*
◆ **EMP:** 5 **EST:** 1995
SQ FT: 20,000
SALES (est): 255.08K **Privately Held**
Web: www.finelinehosiery.com
SIC: 2251 5632 2843 Women's hosiery,
except socks; Hosiery; Finishing agents

(G-357)
FOX APPAREL INC
100 Industrial Park Ave (27205-7324)
PHONE..............................336 629-7641
Wallace Thompson, *Pr*
John Thompson, *
Dolores Thompson, *
EMP: 135 **EST:** 1966
SQ FT: 167,000
SALES (est): 4.17MM **Privately Held**
Web: www.foxapparel.net
SIC: 2325 2329 2337 2339 Jeans: men's,
youths', and boys'; Jackets (suede,
leatherette, etc.), sport: men's and boys';
Jackets and vests, except fur and leather:
women's; Jeans: women's, misses', and
juniors'

(G-358)
G-4 ELECTRIC INC
4635 Us Highway 220 Bus N (27203-3331)
PHONE..............................336 495-0500
Thomas M Saunders, *Pr*
Sue W Saunders, *VP*
EMP: 12 **EST:** 1970
SQ FT: 26,000
SALES (est): 3.45MM **Privately Held**
Web: www.piedmontelectricmotor.com
SIC: 7694 5063 Rewinding services; Motors,
electric

(G-359)
**GALLIMORE FMLY INVESTMENTS
INC**
Also Called: Gallimore Body Shop
1431 E Salisbury St (27203-5053)
PHONE..............................336 625-5138
Kenneth Gallimore, *Pr*
Bridget Gallimore, *VP*
EMP: 18 **EST:** 2012
SALES (est): 1.28MM **Privately Held**
Web: www.gallimorebodyshop.com
SIC: 3999 Atomizers, toiletry

(G-360)
GATEHOUSE MEDIA LLC
Also Called: Asheboro Courier Tribune
500 Sunset Ave (27203-5330)
P.O. Box 340 (27204-0340)
PHONE..............................336 626-6103
Dave Renfro, *Mgr*
EMP: 44
SALES (corp-wide): 2.51B **Publicly Held**
Web: www.gannett.com
SIC: 2711 7313 Newspapers: publishing
only, not printed on site; Newspaper
advertising representative
HQ: Gatehouse Media, Llc
175 Sllys Trl Fl 3 Corp C
Pittsford NY 14534
585 598-0030

(G-361)
GEORGIA-PACIFIC LLC
Also Called: Georgia-Pacific
200 Mcdowell Rd (27205-7357)
PHONE..............................336 629-2151
Beverly L Franks, *Brnch Mgr*
EMP: 83
SQ FT: 200,000
SALES (corp-wide): 64.44B **Privately Held**
Web: www.gp.com
SIC: 2653 5113 Boxes, corrugated: made
from purchased materials; Corrugated and
solid fiber boxes
HQ: Georgia-Pacific Llc
133 Peachtree St Ne
Atlanta GA 30303
404 652-4000

(G-362)
HS HYOSUNG USA INC
890 Pineview Rd (27203)
PHONE..............................336 495-2202
Roslyn Byrd, *Brnch Mgr*
EMP: 119
Web: www.hyosungusa.com
SIC: 2221 2296 Broadwoven fabric mills,
manmade; Cord for reinforcing rubber tires
HQ: Hs Hyosung Usa, Inc.
15801 Brxham Hl Ave Ste 5
Charlotte NC 28277
704 790-6100

(G-363)
HUNSUCKER PRINTING CO INC
522 N Fayetteville St (27203-4729)
P.O. Box 219 (27204-0219)
PHONE..............................336 629-9125

▲ = Import ▼ = Export
◆ = Import/Export

James T Russell Senior, *Pr*
Terry L Russell, *Sec*
Joe Russell, *VP*
EMP: 7 **EST:** 1946
SQ FT: 7,800
SALES (est): 377.92K **Privately Held**
Web: www.hunsuckerprinting.com
SIC: 2752 2759 Offset printing; Letterpress
printing

(G-364)
INDIAN TFF-TANK GREENSBORO INC
2491 Mountain Lake Rd (27205-4433)
PHONE...................336 625-2629
Mike Chewning Senior, *Pr*
Jackie Chewning, *Sec*
EMP: 8 **EST:** 1968
SQ FT: 10,000
SALES (est): 262.29K **Privately Held**
SIC: 3559 Chemical machinery and
equipment

(G-365)
INK N STITCHES LLC
2739 Us Highway 220 Bus S (27205-0820)
PHONE...................336 633-3898
Penny York, *Pt*
Michael Wheless, *Pt*
Faye Wheless, *Pt*
EMP: 4 **EST:** 1999
SQ FT: 3,000
SALES (est): 134.52K **Privately Held**
Web: www.inknstitches.com
SIC: 2759 2395 5199 Screen printing;
Embroidery and art needlework; Advertising
specialties

(G-366)
INNOVATIVE BUSINESS GROWTH LLC
1157 S Cox St (27203-6952)
PHONE...................888 334-4367
EMP: 22
SALES (est): 871.5K **Privately Held**
SIC: 2068 Seeds: dried, dehydrated, salted
or roasted

(G-367)
INTERRS-EXTERIORS ASHEBORO INC
Also Called: Carpet One
2013 S Fayetteville St (27203)
PHONE...................336 629-2148
Ken W Cornwell, *Pr*
Sally Cornwell, *Sec*
EMP: 5 **EST:** 1970
SQ FT: 18,000
SALES (est): 378.15K **Privately Held**
Web: www.magnusanderson.com
SIC: 5713 5211 2211 5719 Carpets; Lumber
and other building materials; Draperies and
drapery fabrics, cotton; Lighting fixtures

(G-368)
JAECO PRECISION INC
721 Jaeco Caudill Dr (27205-9678)
P.O. Box 726 (27204-0726)
PHONE...................336 633-1025
Eric Lambeth, *Pr*
Jeff Callicutt, *Sec*
EMP: 6 **EST:** 1998
SQ FT: 4,000
SALES (est): 2.48MM **Privately Held**
Web: www.jaecoprecision.com
SIC: 3599 Machine shop, jobbing and repair

(G-369)
KEANI FURNITURE INC
1546 N Fayetteville St (27203-3854)

PHONE...................336 303-5484
Eric Racosta, *Pr*
EMP: 20 **EST:** 2013
SALES (est): 600K **Privately Held**
SIC: 2512 5712 2326 5047 Chairs:
upholstered on wood frames; Furniture
stores; Medical and hospital uniforms,
men's; Medical equipment and supplies

(G-370)
KENNAMETAL INC
201 Yzex St (27203-3280)
PHONE...................336 672-3313
Earl Leonard, *Mgr*
EMP: 61
SQ FT: 116,644
SALES (corp-wide): 2.05B **Publicly Held**
Web: www.kennametal.com
SIC: 3545 Cutting tools for machine tools
PA: Kennametal Inc.
525 Wlliam Penn Pl Ste 33
Pittsburgh PA 15219
412 248-8000

(G-371)
LABEL LINE LTD
5356 Nc Highway 49 S (27205-1974)
PHONE...................336 857-3115
EMP: 95 **EST:** 1985
SALES (est): 1.83MM **Privately Held**
SIC: 2679 2672 2671 Labels, paper: made
from purchased material; Labels
(unprinted), gummed: made from
purchased materials; Paper; coated and
laminated packaging

(G-372)
LAMBETH DIMENSION INC
443 Mount Shepherd Road Ext
(27205-2891)
PHONE...................336 629-3838
Roger C Lambeth, *Pr*
Donna Lambeth, *VP*
▲ **EMP:** 15 **EST:** 1992
SALES (est): 3.98MM **Privately Held**
SIC: 2426 Frames for upholstered furniture,
wood

(G-373)
LEONARD ELECTRIC MTR REPR INC
531 N Fayetteville St (27203-4728)
P.O. Box 292 (27204-0292)
PHONE...................336 625-2375
Paul Comer, *Pr*
Ronnie Kinney, *VP*
EMP: 4 **EST:** 1952
SQ FT: 10,000
SALES (est): 257.34K **Privately Held**
SIC: 7694 Rewinding stators

(G-374)
LONGS MACHINE & TOOL INC
Also Called: G Force South
2224 S Fayetteville St (27205-7312)
PHONE...................336 625-3844
Roger Chilton, *Brnch Mgr*
EMP: 25
Web: www.longsmachinetool.com
SIC: 3714 Air conditioner parts, motor vehicle
PA: Longs Machine & Tool Inc
150 N Grant St
Cleona PA 17042

(G-375)
MAGNET GUYS
720 Industrial Park Ave (27205-7336)
PHONE...................855 624-4897
Blesson George, *Owner*
EMP: 4 **EST:** 2017
SALES (est): 380.48K **Privately Held**
Web: www.themagnetguys.com

SIC: 2759 Promotional printing

(G-376)
MAS ACME USA
159 North St (27205-5411)
PHONE...................336 625-2161
EMP: 4 **EST:** 2017
SALES (est): 155.74K **Privately Held**
Web: www.acme-mccrary.com
SIC: 2251 Women's hosiery, except socks

(G-377)
MATLAB INC (PA)
1112 Nc Highway 49 S (27205-9584)
P.O. Box 2046 (27204-2046)
PHONE...................336 629-4161
Gayle F Peddycord Kurdian, *Pr*
Bill Kurdian, *VP*
William Kurdian, *Prin*
▲ **EMP:** 14 **EST:** 1979
SQ FT: 135,000
SALES (est): 9.34MM
SALES (corp-wide): 9.34MM **Privately Held**
Web: www.matlabinc.com
SIC: 2851 Paints and allied products

(G-378)
MID TOWN DIXIE EXPRESS FUEL
455 W Salisbury St (27203-5443)
PHONE...................336 318-1200
Lee Davidson, *Genl Mgr*
EMP: 6 **EST:** 2010
SALES (est): 586K **Privately Held**
SIC: 2869 Fuels

(G-379)
MRREFINISH LLC
1804 Winchester Heights Dr (27205-8179)
PHONE...................336 625-2400
Joel Dixon, *Managing Member*
EMP: 10 **EST:** 2004
SALES (est): 393.13K **Privately Held**
SIC: 1752 3069 Floor laying and floor work,
nec; Rubber floorcoverings/mats and
wallcoverings

(G-380)
OLIVER RUBBER COMPANY LLC
408 Telephone Ave (27205-6800)
PHONE...................336 629-1436
Alan Blanton, *Mgr*
EMP: 394
SALES (corp-wide): 1.95B **Privately Held**
Web: www.oliverrubber.com
SIC: 3011 3061 Tires and inner tubes;
Mechanical rubber goods
HQ: Oliver Rubber Company, Llc
1 Parkway S
Greenville SC 29615
866 464-2580

(G-381)
PEMMCO MANUFACTURING INC
631 Veterans Loop Rd (27205-0818)
PHONE...................336 625-1122
EMP: 51 **EST:** 1980
SALES (est): 10.43MM **Privately Held**
Web: www.pemmcomfg.com
SIC: 3599 Machine shop, jobbing and repair

(G-382)
PEXCO LLC
2971 Taylor Dr (27203-0554)
PHONE...................336 493-7500
EMP: 54
SALES (corp-wide): 295.68MM **Privately Held**
Web: www.pexco.com

SIC: 3354 Aluminum extruded products
PA: Pexco Llc
3440 Preston Ridge Rd
Alpharetta GA 30005
678 990-1523

(G-383)
PIEDMONT CUSTOM MEATS INC
430 Nc Highway 49 S (27205-9561)
PHONE...................336 628-4949
Donna Moore, *Pr*
EMP: 35 **EST:** 2014
SQ FT: 20,000
SALES (est): 7.35MM **Privately Held**
Web: www.piedmontcustommeats.com
SIC: 2011 Meat packing plants

(G-384)
POST CONSUMER BRANDS LLC
Also Called: Asheboro Maltomeal
2525 Bank St (27203-3087)
PHONE...................336 672-0124
Dale Ducommun, *Brnch Mgr*
EMP: 19
Web: www.postconsumerbrands.com
SIC: 2043 Oatmeal: prepared as cereal
breakfast food
HQ: Post Consumer Brands, Llc
20802 Kensington Blvd
Lakeville MN 55044
952 322-8000

(G-385)
PREMIER POWDER COATING INC
1948 N Fayetteville St (27203-3270)
PHONE...................336 672-3828
Jerry Raines, *Pr*
Karen Raines, *Sec*
EMP: 7 **EST:** 1994
SQ FT: 21,000
SALES (est): 986.93K **Privately Held**
Web: www.prempowdcoat.com
SIC: 3479 Coating of metals and formed
products

(G-386)
PRESTIGE FABRICATORS INC
905 Nc Highway 49 S (27205-9566)
P.O. Box 816 (27204-0816)
PHONE...................336 626-4595
Joseph R Wingfield, *Pr*
Hans Klaussner, *
J B Davis, *
Scott Kauffman, *
David O Bryant, *
EMP: 270 **EST:** 1993
SQ FT: 402,000
SALES (est): 23.19MM **Privately Held**
Web: www.vpcgroup.com
SIC: 3086 Insulation or cushioning material,
foamed plastics

(G-387)
PRINTLOGIC INC
Also Called: Tiedmont Printing
2753 Us Highway 220 Bus S (27205-0820)
P.O. Box 430 (27204-0430)
PHONE...................336 626-6680
Bob Williams, *Managing Member*
Terry A Huskey, *
Robert V Williams, *
EMP: 25 **EST:** 2011
SALES (est): 2.22MM **Privately Held**
Web: www.printlogicllc.com
SIC: 2752 Offset printing

(G-388)
RAMSEUR INTER-LOCK KNITTING CO
2409 Old Lexington Rd (27205-2578)
PHONE...................336 824-2427

(PA)=Parent Co (HQ)=Headquarters
✪ = New Business established in last 2 years

Samuel A Rankin Junior, *Pr*
Jane Rankin Slaughter, *Stockholder*
▲ **EMP:** 4 **EST:** 1946
SQ FT: 225,000
SALES (est): 97.23K **Privately Held**
SIC: 2257 2241 Weft knit fabric mills;
Trimmings, textile

(G-389)
RANDOLPH MACHINE INC (PA)
1206 Uwharrie St (27203-7671)
P.O. Box 147 (27204-0147)
PHONE.................................336 625-0411
Steve Coleman, *Pr*
EMP: 5 **EST:** 1989
SQ FT: 3,200
SALES (est): 863.28K **Privately Held**
Web: www.randolphmachine.com
SIC: 3599 Machine shop, jobbing and repair

(G-390)
RANDOLPH PACKING COMPANY
403 W Balfour Ave (27203-3247)
PHONE.................................336 672-1470
C Donald Hamlet, *Pr*
Rebecca T Hamlet, *
D Craig Hamlet, *
Rex A Hamlet, *
EMP: 87 **EST:** 1947
SQ FT: 25,000
SALES (est): 4.04MM **Privately Held**
Web: www.randpacknc.com
SIC: 2011 Meat packing plants

(G-391)
RODNEY TYLER
530 Albemarle Rd (27203-6257)
PHONE.................................336 629-0951
Rodney Tyler, *Prin*
EMP: 4 **EST:** 2017
SALES (est): 147.25K **Privately Held**
SIC: 2752 Commercial printing, lithographic

(G-392)
SAPONA MANUFACTURING CO INC
Also Called: Sapona Plastics
7039 Us Highway 220 S (27205-1581)
PHONE.................................336 873-8700
Dean Lail, *Mgr*
EMP: 205
SALES (corp-wide): 22.97MM **Privately Held**
Web: www.saponamfg.com
SIC: 2282 3089 Throwing and winding mills;
Injection molding of plastics
PA: Sapona Manufacturing Company,
Incorporated
2478 Cedar Falls Rd
Cedar Falls NC 27230
336 625-2727

(G-393)
SAPONA MANUFACTURING CO INC
159 North St (27203-5411)
PHONE.................................336 625-2161
Kevin Flenniken, *Prin*
EMP: 6 **EST:** 2009
SALES (est): 185.45K **Privately Held**
SIC: 3999 Manufacturing industries, nec

(G-394)
SAPONA PLASTICS LLC
7039 Us Highway 220 S (27205-1581)
PHONE.................................336 873-8700
Jack Lail, *Managing Member*
▲ **EMP:** 72 **EST:** 2004
SQ FT: 52,000
SALES (est): 8.98MM **Privately Held**
Web: www.saponaplastics.com
SIC: 3089 Injection molding of plastics

(G-395)
SEDIA SYSTEMS INC
335 Commerce Pl (27203-0552)
PHONE.................................336 887-3818
EMP: 10
Web: www.sediasystems.com
SIC: 2531 Public building and related
furniture
PA: Sedia Systems, Inc.
1820 W Hubbard St Ste 300
Chicago IL 60622

(G-396)
SOUTHCORR LLC
Also Called: Ds Smith Packaging
3021 Taylor Dr (27203-0555)
PHONE.................................336 498-1700
Jeff Mcneill, *Genl Mgr*
▲ **EMP:** 60 **EST:** 1994
SQ FT: 125,000
SALES (est): 7.17MM **Privately Held**
Web: www.southcorr.com
SIC: 2631 Corrugating medium

(G-397)
SOUTHERN STATES COOP INC
Also Called: S S C 7516-7
504 E Dixie Dr (27203-7035)
PHONE.................................336 629-3977
Frank Thompson, *Mgr*
EMP: 9
SALES (corp-wide): 1.71B **Privately Held**
Web: www.southernstates.com
SIC: 5999 2048 Feed and farm supply;
Prepared feeds, nec
PA: Southern States Cooperative,
Incorporated
6606 W Broad St Ste B
Richmond VA 23230
804 281-1000

(G-398)
STARPET INC
801 Pineview Rd (27203-3192)
PHONE.................................336 672-0101
Stephen C Edwards, *Pr*
Muthukumer Paramasivam, *
Hussam Awad, *
Yashwant Awasthi, *
Sachin Agarwalla, *
▲ **EMP:** 105 **EST:** 2000
SALES (est): 6.42MM **Privately Held**
SIC: 2821 Polyethylene resins
HQ: Indorama Ventures Public Company
Limited
75/102 Soi Sukhumvit 19 (Vadhana),
Asok Road
Vadhana 10110

(G-399)
STEEL SUPPLY AND ERECTION CO
1237 N Fayetteville St (27203-4563)
P.O. Box 607 (27204-0607)
PHONE.................................336 625-4830
Eric D Newton, *Pr*
Jonathan Newton, *Sec*
EMP: 18 **EST:** 1946
SQ FT: 6,400
SALES (est): 2.95MM **Privately Held**
Web: www.steelsupplycompany.com
SIC: 1791 7389 7692 Structural steel
erection; Crane and aerial lift service;
Welding repair

(G-400)
SWATCH WORKS INC
453 Oakhurst Rd (27205-0996)
PHONE.................................336 626-9971
EMP: 4 **EST:** 2020
SALES (est): 827.19K **Privately Held**
Web: www.theswatchworks.com

SIC: 2211 Broadwoven fabric mills, cotton

(G-401)
SWATCHWORKS INC
730 Industrial Park Ave (27205-7336)
P.O. Box 369 (27204-0369)
PHONE.................................336 626-9971
James N Davis, *Pr*
EMP: 5 **EST:** 1989
SALES (est): 621.41K **Privately Held**
Web: www.theswatchworks.com
SIC: 2211 2782 Upholstery fabrics, cotton;
Blankbooks and looseleaf binders

(G-402)
TECHNIMARK LLC
4509 Us Highway 220 Bus N (27203-3362)
P.O. Box 2068 (27204-2068)
PHONE.................................336 498-4171
Chris Clark, *Brnch Mgr*
EMP: 6
SALES (corp-wide): 652.4MM **Privately
Held**
Web: www.technimark.com
SIC: 3089 Injection molding of plastics
HQ: Technimark Llc
180 Commerce Pl
Asheboro NC 27203
336 498-4171

(G-403)
TECHNIMARK LLC
2536 Bank St (27203-3086)
P.O. Box 2068 (27204-2068)
PHONE.................................336 498-4171
Keith Mullin, *Brnch Mgr*
EMP: 32
SALES (corp-wide): 652.4MM **Privately
Held**
Web: www.technimark.com
SIC: 3089 Injection molding of plastics
HQ: Technimark Llc
180 Commerce Pl
Asheboro NC 27203
336 498-4171

(G-404)
TECHNIMARK LLC (HQ)
180 Commerce Pl (27203-0515)
P.O. Box 2068 (27204-2068)
PHONE.................................336 498-4171
Brad Wellington, *CEO*
◆ **EMP:** 162 **EST:** 1983
SQ FT: 700,000
SALES (est): 469.09MM
SALES (corp-wide): 652.4MM **Privately
Held**
Web: www.technimark.com
SIC: 3089 Injection molding of plastics
PA: Technimark Holdings Llc
180 Commerce Pl
Asheboro NC 27203
336 498-4171

(G-405)
TECHNIMARK REYNOSA LLC
2510 Bank St (27203-3086)
PHONE.................................336 498-4171
EMP: 5
SALES (corp-wide): 652.4MM **Privately
Held**
Web: www.technimark.com
SIC: 3089 Injection molding of plastics
HQ: Technimark Reynosa Llc
180 Commerce Pl
Asheboro NC 27203

(G-406)
TECHNIMARK REYNOSA LLC (DH)
180 Commerce Pl (27203-0515)
P.O. Box 2068 (27204-2068)

PHONE.................................336 498-4171
Donald F Wellington, *Managing Member*
Robert Burkhart, *
▲ **EMP:** 475 **EST:** 2007
SQ FT: 67,000
SALES (est): 19.23MM
SALES (corp-wide): 652.4MM **Privately
Held**
Web: www.technimark.com
SIC: 3089 Injection molding of plastics
HQ: Technimark Llc
180 Commerce Pl
Asheboro NC 27203
336 498-4171

(G-407)
**TELEFLEX MEDICAL
INCORPORATED**
312 Commerce Pl (27203-0552)
PHONE.................................336 498-4153
Ryan Payne, *Brnch Mgr*
EMP: 7
SALES (corp-wide): 3.05B **Publicly Held**
Web: www.teleflex.com
SIC: 3841 Surgical and medical instruments
HQ: Teleflex Medical Incorporated
3015 Carrington Mill Blvd
Morrisville NC 27560
919 544-8000

(G-408)
THERMACO INCORPORATED
Also Called: Big Dipper
646 Greensboro St (27203-4739)
P.O. Box 2548 (27204-2548)
PHONE.................................336 629-4651
William C Batten, *Pr*
Susan Thomson Batten, *VP*
EMP: 9 **EST:** 1983
SQ FT: 15,000
SALES (est): 2.76MM **Privately Held**
Web: www.thermaco.com
SIC: 3823 Industrial process control
instruments

(G-409)
THOMAS BROTHERS FOODS LLC
Also Called: Thomas Brothers Ham Company
1852 Gold Hill Rd (27203-4291)
PHONE.................................336 672-0337
H Franklin Thomas Junior, *Managing
Member*
EMP: 10 **EST:** 2009
SQ FT: 25,000
SALES (est): 3.53MM **Privately Held**
Web: www.thomasbrothersham.com
SIC: 5147 5142 2013 Meats, cured or
smoked; Packaged frozen goods;
Sausages and other prepared meats

(G-410)
TREJO SOCCER ACADEMY LLC
Also Called: Piedmont Printing
2753 Us Highway 220 Bus S (27205-0820)
P.O. Box 430 (27204-0430)
PHONE.................................336 899-7910
Larry Presnell, *Pr*
Betty Presnell, *
EMP: 4 **EST:** 1986
SQ FT: 6,000
SALES (est): 150.58K **Privately Held**
Web: www.piedmontprinting.com
SIC: 2752 2791 2789 Offset printing;
Typesetting; Bookbinding and related work

(G-411)
**TRIAD CORRUGATED METAL INC
(PA)**
208 Luck Rd (27205-7856)
P.O. Box 4907 (27204-4907)
PHONE.................................336 625-9727

▲ = Import ▼ = Export
◆ = Import/Export

Garrett Eugene Smith, *CEO*
Patrick Smith, *
Jeannie K Smith, *
EMP: 35 **EST:** 2000
SALES (est): 23.91MM
SALES (corp-wide): 23.91MM **Privately Held**
Web: www.triadcorrugatedmetal.com
SIC: 2952 5211 5033 3444 Roofing materials ; Roofing material; Roofing and siding materials; Sheet metalwork

(G-412)
TRIAD CUTTING TOOLS INC
5527 Us Highway 220 S (27205-1568)
P.O. Box 60 (27341-0060)
PHONE................................336 873-8708
James R Cain Junior, *Pr*
James R Cain Senior, *VP*
EMP: 6 **EST:** 1990
SQ FT: 6,000
SALES (est): 995.94K **Privately Held**
Web: www.tctoolz.com
SIC: 5251 7699 3541 Tools; Knife, saw and tool sharpening and repair; Machine tools, metal cutting type

(G-413)
TROTTERS SEWING COMPANY INC
321 Industrial Park Ave (27205-7327)
P.O. Box 1145 (27204-1145)
PHONE................................336 629-4550
Barbara J Trotter, *Pr*
Jerry L Trotter, *
EMP: 55 **EST:** 1992
SQ FT: 47,000
SALES (est): 5.48MM **Privately Held**
Web: www.trotterssewing.com
SIC: 2311 Men's and boy's suits and coats

(G-414)
UNITED WOOD PRODUCTS INC
451 Railroad St (27203-4322)
P.O. Box 1083 (27204-1083)
PHONE................................336 626-2281
David Smith, *Pr*
Roger C Chriscoe, *VP*
EMP: 8 **EST:** 1997
SQ FT: 10,000
SALES (est): 497.02K **Privately Held**
Web: www.unitedwoodproductsinc.com
SIC: 2431 Millwork

(G-415)
UNIVERSAL FIBERS INC
749 Pineview Rd (27203-3191)
P.O. Box 438 (28007-0438)
PHONE................................336 672-2600
Deepak Khopkar, *Mgr*
EMP: 110
SQ FT: 166,584
SALES (corp-wide): 84.87MM **Privately Held**
Web: www.universalfibers.com
SIC: 2281 Polyester yarn, spun: made from purchased staple
HQ: Universal Fibers, Inc.
14401 Industrial Park Rd
Bristol VA 24202
276 669-1161

(G-416)
UWHARRIE FRAMES MFG LLC
247 Leo Cranford Rd (27205-1060)
PHONE................................336 626-6649
EMP: 30 **EST:** 2007
SALES (est): 2.34MM **Privately Held**
SIC: 2426 Frames for upholstered furniture, wood

(G-417)
VILLAGE PRINTING CO
530 Albemarle Rd (27203-6257)
PHONE................................336 629-0951
Rodney Tyler, *Owner*
EMP: 16 **EST:** 1969
SQ FT: 10,000
SALES (est): 2.46MM **Privately Held**
Web: www.villageprinting.com
SIC: 2752 Offset printing

(G-418)
VPC FOAM USA INC
2206 Dumont St (27203-2909)
PHONE................................336 626-4595
EMP: 38
SALES (corp-wide): 6.46MM **Privately Held**
SIC: 3086 Plastics foam products
PA: Vpc Foam Usa Inc.
1820 Evans St Ne
Conover NC 28613
704 622-0552

(G-419)
WAYNE TRADEMARK PRTG PACKG LLC
Also Called: Wayne Trademark International
5346 Nc Highway 49 S (27205-1974)
P.O. Box 2683 (27260)
PHONE................................800 327-1290
Daniel S Meader, *CEO*
William L Burke, *
EMP: 35
SALES (est): 1.63MM
SALES (corp-wide): 5.69MM **Privately Held**
Web: www.waynetrademark.com
SIC: 2752 Offset printing
PA: Burrow Family Corporation
5346 Nc Hwy 49 S
Asheboro NC 27205
336 887-3173

(G-420)
WELLS HOSIERY MILLS INC (PA)
Also Called: Asheboro Activewear
1758 S Fayetteville St (27205-7356)
P.O. Box 1566 (27204-1566)
PHONE................................336 633-4881
Theodore Cooley, *CEO*
Rodney Debusk, *
Janet L Nance, *
Paul Avato, *
◆ **EMP:** 200 **EST:** 1951
SALES (est): 14.44MM
SALES (corp-wide): 14.44MM **Privately Held**
Web: www.wellshosiery.com
SIC: 2252 Socks

(G-421)
WILLIAM BOSTIC
3854 Us Highway 64 E (27203-8462)
PHONE................................336 629-5243
William Bostic, *Owner*
EMP: 4 **EST:** 2014
SALES (est): 186.98K **Privately Held**
SIC: 2899 Flares

Asheville
Buncombe County

(G-422)
A STITCH IN TIME
Also Called: A Balloon For You
1259 Sweeten Creek Rd 25a (28803-1865)
PHONE................................828 274-5193
Elaine Mcpherson, *Owner*

EMP: 4 **EST:** 1962
SQ FT: 7,000
SALES (est): 250.25K **Privately Held**
Web: www.astitchintimenc.com
SIC: 7219 5947 3942 7389 Tailor shop, except custom or merchant tailor; Gift shop; Stuffed toys, including animals; Balloons, novelty and toy

(G-423)
ADORATHERAPY INC
31 Mount Vernon Cir (28804-2440)
PHONE................................917 297-8904
Laura Ramsey, *CEO*
Dorothy Winquist, *Pr*
EMP: 10 **EST:** 2013
SALES (est): 960.21K **Privately Held**
Web: www.adoratherapy.com
SIC: 2844 7389 Perfumes, cosmetics and other toilet preparations; Business services, nec

(G-424)
AFFORDABLE BEDDING INC
996 Patton Ave Ste A (28806-3662)
PHONE................................828 254-5555
Patrick Mcmahon, *Pr*
Rebecca Banner, *VP*
EMP: 5 **EST:** 2000
SQ FT: 3,000
SALES (est): 243.34K **Privately Held**
Web: www.affordablebedding.com
SIC: 5021 2515 Mattresses; Mattresses and bedsprings

(G-425)
AMCOR TOB PACKG AMERICAS INC
3055 Sweeten Creek Rd (28803-2114)
PHONE................................828 274-1611
Michael Schmitt, *Pr*
Eileen Burns Lerum, *VP*
Robert Mosesian, *VP*
◆ **EMP:** 94 **EST:** 2009
SALES (est): 2.11MM
SALES (corp-wide): 14.69B **Privately Held**
SIC: 3089 Molding primary plastics
HQ: Amcor Flexibles Llc
3 Parkway N Ste 300
Deerfield IL 60015
224 313-7000

(G-426)
ANDY-OXY CO INC (PA)
27 Heritage Dr (28806-1914)
P.O. Box 6389 (28816-6389)
PHONE................................828 258-0271
EMP: 26 **EST:** 1975
SALES (est): 22.39MM
SALES (corp-wide): 22.39MM **Privately Held**
Web: www.andyoxy.com
SIC: 5084 2813 Welding machinery and equipment; Acetylene

(G-427)
APPALACHIAN TECHNOLOGY LLC
Also Called: Appalachian Technology
187 Elk Mountain Rd (28804-2045)
PHONE................................828 210-8888
Astrid Schneider, *Pr*
Charles Billy Beck, *
Alfred Lewis Jackson Junior, *Treas*
Al Jackson, *
▲ **EMP:** 42 **EST:** 2001
SQ FT: 16,500
SALES (est): 5.71MM **Privately Held**
Web: www.appalachiantech.com
SIC: 3678 3429 Electronic connectors; Locks or lock sets

(G-428)
APPALACHIAN STOVE FBRCATORS INC
Also Called: ASC Distribution
329 Emma Rd (28806-3809)
PHONE................................828 253-0164
James S Rice, *Pr*
Thomas A Bryson, *
▲ **EMP:** 5 **EST:** 1976
SQ FT: 60,000
SALES (est): 432.99K **Privately Held**
Web: www.appalachianstove.com
SIC: 3433 5023 5075 3429 Stoves, wood and coal burning; Fireplace equipment and accessories; Warm air heating equipment and supplies; Hardware, nec

(G-429)
APROTECH POWERTRAIN LLC
31 Adams Hill Rd (28806-3822)
PHONE................................828 253-1350
Karyl Kyser, *Mgr*
EMP: 30
Web: www.aprotechgroup.com
SIC: 3612 Transformers, except electric
PA: Aprotech Powertrain, Llc
2150 Butterfield Dr
Troy MI 48084

(G-430)
AQUAPRO SOLUTIONS LLC
46 New Leicester Hwy Ste 102 (28806-2719)
P.O. Box 160 (28778-0160)
PHONE................................828 255-0772
EMP: 6 **EST:** 2006
SQ FT: 2,500
SALES (est): 492.61K **Privately Held**
Web: www.aquaprosolutions.com
SIC: 3589 Water purification equipment, household type

(G-431)
ART ENTERPRISES INC
Also Called: Mountain Graphics
1156 Sweeten Creek Rd (28803-1728)
P.O. Box 9585 (28815-0585)
PHONE................................828 277-1211
Alan Mojonnier, *Pr*
EMP: 5 **EST:** 1984
SQ FT: 5,200
SALES (est): 180.97K **Privately Held**
SIC: 2759 Screen printing

(G-432)
ASHE HAMS INC
707 Merrimon Ave (28804-6628)
PHONE................................828 259-9426
Carolyn Slider, *Mgr*
EMP: 5
SIC: 2013 5421 Ham, smoked: from purchased meat; Meat and fish markets
PA: Ashe Hams Inc
78 Forest Rd
Asheville NC 28803

(G-433)
ASHEVILLE BIT & STEEL COMPANY
111 Edgewood Rd S (28803-1816)
P.O. Box 5913 (28813-5913)
PHONE................................828 274-3766
James V Stafford, *Pr*
Vicki S Stafford, *VP*
▲ **EMP:** 14 **EST:** 1968
SQ FT: 12,500
SALES (est): 2.54MM **Privately Held**
Web: www.ashevillebit.com
SIC: 3423 5051 Edge tools for woodworking: augers, bits, gimlets, etc.; Iron and steel (ferrous) products

(G-434)
ASHEVILLE CITIZEN-TIMES
Also Called: Tegna
14 Ohenry Ave (28803-9106)
P.O. Box 2090 (28802-0716)
PHONE...................................828 252-5611
Jeffrey P Green, Pr
Randy Hammer, *
Virgil L Smith, *
EMP: 10 EST: 1990
SALES (est): 1.53MM
SALES (corp-wide): 3.1B Publicly Held
Web: www.citizen-times.com
SIC: 2711 Newspapers, publishing and
printing
PA: Tegna Inc.
8350 Broad St Ste 2000
Tysons VA 22102
703 873-6600

(G-435)
ASHEVILLE COLOR & IMAGING INC
611 Tunnel Rd Ste E (28805-1973)
PHONE...................................828 774-5040
Jeffrey Jones, Pr
EMP: 6 EST: 2013
SALES (est): 445.57K Privately Held
Web: www.goaciprint.com
SIC: 2759 7389 Commercial printing, nec;
Design services

(G-436)
ASHEVILLE DISTILLING COMPANY
45 S French Broad Ave (28801-3364)
PHONE...................................828 575-2000
Albert L Sneed Junior, Prin
EMP: 6 EST: 2012
SALES (est): 113.97K Privately Held
Web: www.ashevilledistilling.com
SIC: 2085 Bourbon whiskey

(G-437)
ASHEVILLE GLOBAL REPORT
20 Battery Park Ave (28801-2720)
PHONE...................................828 236-3103
Shawn Gaynor, Prin
EMP: 7 EST: 2009
SALES (est): 120.75K Privately Held
Web: www.mountainx.com
SIC: 2711 Newspapers, publishing and
printing

(G-438)
ASHEVILLE MEADERY LLC
Also Called: Fae Nectar
155 Johnston Blvd (28806-1820)
PHONE...................................828 454-6188
Tom Halladay Iii, Pr
EMP: 5 EST: 2020
SALES (est): 64.64K Privately Held
Web: www.faenectar.com
SIC: 2084 Wines

(G-439)
ASHEVILLE METAL FINISHING INC
178 Clingman Ave (28801-3240)
P.O. Box 16237 (28816-0237)
PHONE...................................828 253-1476
Thomas L Finger, Pr
Kay C Finger, *
EMP: 35 EST: 1988
SQ FT: 19,000
SALES (est): 2.57MM
SALES (corp-wide): 13.14MM Privately
Held
Web: www.ashevillemetalfinishing.com
SIC: 3471 Electroplating of metals or formed
products
PA: T L F Inc
280 Cane Creek Rd.
Fletcher NC 28732

828 681-5343

(G-440)
ASHEVILLE PRINT SHOP
740 Haywood Rd (28806-3136)
PHONE...................................828 214-5286
EMP: 4 EST: 2019
SALES (est): 94.55K Privately Held
Web: www.ashevillescreenprinting.com
SIC: 2752 Offset printing

(G-441)
ASHEVILLE PROMO LLC
202 Asheland Ave (28801-4016)
P.O. Box 18704 (28814-0704)
PHONE...................................828 575-2767
Clarence Raymond Greiner, Admn
EMP: 4 EST: 2014
SALES (est): 406.04K Privately Held
Web: www.ashevillepromo.com
SIC: 2759 Screen printing

(G-442)
**ASHEVLLE PRCSION MCH RBLDING
I**
51 Haywood Rd (28806-4521)
PHONE...................................828 254-0884
Jackie Queen, Pr
Hubert Queen, VP
Brenda Queen, Sec
EMP: 4 EST: 1997
SQ FT: 6,000
SALES (est): 264.92K Privately Held
Web: www.ppofa.com
SIC: 7699 7692 Industrial machinery and
equipment repair; Welding repair

(G-443)
ASHVILLE POSTAGE EXPRESS
22 New Leicester Hwy Ste C (28806-2753)
PHONE...................................828 255-9250
Terry Simmons, Owner
EMP: 4 EST: 2005
SALES (est): 228.4K Privately Held
SIC: 2741 Miscellaneous publishing

(G-444)
ASHVILLE WRECKER SERVICE INC
80 Weaverville Rd (28804-1360)
PHONE...................................828 252-2388
Edward Peek, Pr
EMP: 9 EST: 1980
SQ FT: 1,287
SALES (est): 422.75K Privately Held
SIC: 3711 Wreckers (tow truck), assembly of

(G-445)
ASTRAL BUOYANCY COMPANY
Also Called: Astral Designs
347 Depot St # 201 (28801-4310)
P.O. Box 2 (28802-0002)
PHONE...................................828 255-2638
Philip G Curry, Pr
▲ EMP: 9 EST: 2002
SALES (est): 3.21MM Privately Held
Web: www.astraldesigns.com
SIC: 3842 Life preservers, except cork and
inflatable

(G-446)
ATELIER MAISON AND CO LLC
121 Sweeten Creek Rd Ste 50
(28803-1526)
PHONE...................................828 277-7202
EMP: 15 EST: 2017
SALES (est): 3.96MM Privately Held
Web: www.ateliermaisonco.com
SIC: 2599 Furniture and fixtures, nec

(G-447)
AVADIM HOLDINGS INC
600a Centrepark Dr (28805-1276)
P.O. Box 457 (28778)
PHONE...................................877 677-2723
EMP: 30
SALES (corp-wide): 24.62MM Privately
Held
Web: www.avadimhealth.com
SIC: 2834 Pharmaceutical preparations
PA: Avadim Holdings, Inc.
4 Old Patton Cove Rd
Swannanoa NC 28778
877 677-2723

(G-448)
AVL CUSTOM FABRICATION
250 Baird Cove Rd (28804-9706)
PHONE...................................828 713-0333
Coffey Robert Sean, Owner
EMP: 5 EST: 2014
SALES (est): 105.67K Privately Held
SIC: 3499 Novelties and giftware, including
trophies

(G-449)
AVL TECHNOLOGIES INC
Also Called: Avl Technologies
15 N Merrimon Ave (28804-1367)
PHONE...................................828 250-9950
Jim Oliver, Pr
Esther O Cartwright, *
Jerry Ivester, Chief Commercial Officer*
▲ EMP: 100 EST: 1994
SALES (est): 22.9MM Privately Held
Web: www.avltech.com
SIC: 3663 Space satellite communications
equipment

(G-450)
B V HEDRICK GRAVEL & SAND CO
15 Yorkshire St (28803-7783)
PHONE...................................336 337-0706
EMP: 4
SALES (corp-wide): 332.33MM Privately
Held
SIC: 1442 Construction sand and gravel
PA: B. V. Hedrick Gravel & Sand Company
120 1/2 N Church St
Salisbury NC 28144
704 633-5982

(G-451)
BALL PHOTO SUPPLY INC
Also Called: Ball Photo
569 Merrimon Ave (28804-3421)
P.O. Box 1146 (28802-1146)
PHONE...................................828 252-2443
Laura Ball, Pr
Daniel Palmer, Genl Mgr
EMP: 6 EST: 1892
SALES (est): 265.55K Privately Held
Web: www.ballphotosupply.com
SIC: 5946 3861 Cameras; Trays,
photographic printing and processing

(G-452)
BAY TECH LABEL INC
36 Old Charlotte Hwy (28803-9404)
PHONE...................................828 296-8900
TOLL FREE: 800
Julie Goding, Mgr
EMP: 5
SALES (corp-wide): 9.38MM Privately
Held
Web: www.baytechlabel.com
SIC: 2672 2679 Labels (unprinted),
gummed: made from purchased materials;
Labels, paper: made from purchased
material
PA: Bay Tech Label, Inc.

12177 28th St N
Saint Petersburg FL 33716
727 572-9311

(G-453)
BETWEEN TWO WORLDS LLC
Also Called: Eurisko Beer Company
255 Short Coxe Ave (28801-4143)
PHONE...................................828 774-5055
Zac Harris, CEO
EMP: 6 EST: 2018
SALES (est): 360.68K Privately Held
SIC: 2082 Beer (alcoholic beverage)

(G-454)
BILTMORE ESTATE WINE CO LLC
1 N Pack Sq Ste 400 (28801-3409)
PHONE...................................828 225-6776
William A V Cecil Junior, Pr
Richard Pressley, Sr VP
Steve Miller, Sr VP
Mary Ryan, VP
John Stevens, Sec
▲ EMP: 120 EST: 1970
SQ FT: 95,000
SALES (est): 6.03MM Privately Held
Web: www.biltmore.com
SIC: 2084 Wines

(G-455)
BLUE RIDGE ELC MTR REPR INC
Also Called: Wnc Starter
629 Emma Rd (28806-2839)
P.O. Box 16557 (28816-0557)
PHONE...................................828 258-0800
Rustin D Rice, Pr
Sharon Rice, Sec
EMP: 4 EST: 1987
SQ FT: 8,000
SALES (est): 241.66K Privately Held
SIC: 7694 5063 5999 Electric motor repair;
Motors, electric; Motors, electric

(G-456)
BLUE RIDGE GLOBAL INC
128 Bingham Rd (28806-3884)
PHONE...................................828 252-5225
Alex Williams, Pr
EMP: 4 EST: 2005
SALES (est): 681.66K Privately Held
Web: www.blueridgeglobal.com
SIC: 3429 Motor vehicle hardware

(G-457)
BLUE RIDGE PRINTING CO INC
544 Haywood Rd (28806-3556)
PHONE...................................828 254-1000
Bruce Fowler, Pr
EMP: 67 EST: 1974
SQ FT: 14,000
SALES (est): 5.45MM Privately Held
Web: www.blueridgeprinting.com
SIC: 2752 Offset printing

(G-458)
BLUE-HEN INC
Also Called: Fireproof Office Files
60 N Market St Ste C200 (28801-8124)
PHONE...................................407 322-2262
Henry Dieckhaus, Pr
Edith Dieckhaus, Sec
EMP: 8 EST: 1923
SQ FT: 7,000
SALES (est): 1.08MM Privately Held
Web: www.bluehen.com
SIC: 2522 5712 Office cabinets and filing
drawers, except wood; Office furniture

▲ = Import ▼ = Export
◆ = Import/Export

(G-459)
BOGGS COLLECTIVE INC
239 Amboy Rd (28806-4331)
PHONE..................828 398-9701
Brian P Boggs, *Prin*
▲ **EMP:** 4 **EST:** 2010
SALES (est): 155.67K **Privately Held**
Web: www.brianboggschairmakers.com
SIC: 2511 Wood household furniture

(G-460)
BP SOLUTIONS GROUP INC
24 Wilmington St (28806-4227)
P.O. Box 6250 (28816-6250)
PHONE..................828 252-4476
Robert W Williams, *Pr*
Barry Kempson, *
Scott Cotten, *
Carl Connelly, *
EMP: 40 **EST:** 1931
SQ FT: 40,000
SALES (est): 6.42MM **Privately Held**
Web: www.bpsg.us
SIC: 2752 2791 2789 Offset printing;
Typesetting; Bookbinding and related work

(G-461)
BRAIFORM ENTERPRISES INC
Also Called: Plasti-Form
12 Gerber Rd Ste B (28803-2497)
PHONE..................828 277-6420
◆ **EMP:** 220
SIC: 3089 Clothes hangers, plastics

(G-462)
BROOKSHIRE WOODWORKING INC (PA)
Also Called: Brookshire Buiulders
355 Haywood Rd (28806-4231)
PHONE..................828 779-2119
Jeremy Brookshire, *Prin*
EMP: 6 **EST:** 2007
SALES (est): 1.3MM
SALES (corp-wide): 1.3MM **Privately Held**
SIC: 2431 Millwork

(G-463)
BURCO INTERNATIONAL INC
1900 Hendersonville Rd Ste 10
(28803-7769)
PHONE..................828 252-4481
James Burleson, *Pr*
Leslie Burleson, *Sec*
EMP: 9 **EST:** 1972
SQ FT: 36,000
SALES (est): 116.45K **Privately Held**
Web: www.goburco.com
SIC: 2752 Offset printing

(G-464)
C & C CHEMICAL COMPANY INC
119 Haywood Rd (28806-4523)
P.O. Box 6634 (28816-6634)
PHONE..................828 255-7639
William D Creasman, *Pr*
Joan Creasman, *Sec*
John W Creasman, *VP*
Nikki Herron, *Off Mgr*
EMP: 9 **EST:** 1972
SQ FT: 15,000
SALES (est): 1.94MM **Privately Held**
SIC: 2841 Soap and other detergents

(G-465)
CALDWELLS WATER CONDITIONING
22 Country Spring Dr (28804-9710)
P.O. Box 6937 (28816-6937)
PHONE..................828 253-6605
Mike Byerly, *Owner*
EMP: 6 **EST:** 1981

SALES (est): 201.59K **Privately Held**
Web: www.caldwellsh2o.com
SIC: 3589 Swimming pool filter and water
conditioning systems

(G-466)
CANNON & DAUGHTERS INC
2000 Riverside Dr Ste 9 (28804-2061)
PHONE..................828 254-9236
Becky Cannon, *Pr*
Memi Kubota, *
▲ **EMP:** 55 **EST:** 1982
SQ FT: 45,000
SALES (est): 9.85MM **Privately Held**
Web: www.greensprouts.com
SIC: 3944 2361 5641 Games, toys, and
children's vehicles; Girl's and children's
dresses, blouses; Children's and infants'
wear stores

(G-467)
CARBON MARKET EXCHANGE LLC
28 Schenck Pkwy Ste 200 (28803-5088)
PHONE..................828 545-0140
Shenna Fortner, *Managing Member*
EMP: 5 **EST:** 2021
SALES (est): 177.63K **Privately Held**
SIC: 2299 Carbonizing of wool, mohair, and
similar fibers

(G-468)
CAROLINA 1926 LLC
40 Interstate Blvd (28806-2261)
PHONE..................828 251-2500
EMP: 6
SALES (corp-wide): 638.71MM **Privately Held**
Web: www.carolinacat.com
SIC: 7692 Welding repair
HQ: Carolina 1926 Llc
9000 Statesville Rd
Charlotte NC 28269
704 596-6700

(G-469)
CAROLINA CUSTOM EXTERIORS INC
211 Amboy Rd (28806-4331)
PHONE..................828 232-0402
Mike Presley, *Owner*
EMP: 10 **EST:** 1995
SQ FT: 12,000
SALES (est): 987.85K **Privately Held**
Web:
www.carolinacustomexteriorsinc.com
SIC: 1761 2439 Roofing contractor; Trusses,
wooden roof

(G-470)
CAROLINA METALS INC
1398 Brevard Rd (28806-8511)
PHONE..................828 667-0876
Alan Wagner, *CEO*
Steve Cathcart, *
Tonya Bush, *
EMP: 12 **EST:** 1985
SQ FT: 23,000
SALES (est): 1.99MM **Privately Held**
Web: www.carolinametals.com
SIC: 3728 3769 3677 3469 Aircraft parts and
equipment, nec; Space vehicle equipment,
nec; Electronic coils and transformers;
Metal stampings, nec

(G-471)
CAROLINA SOLAR STRUCTURES INC
1007 Tunnel Rd (28805-2013)
P.O. Box 905 (28704-0905)
PHONE..................828 684-9900
TOLL FREE: 800
Robert A Thompson, *Pr*

EMP: 10 **EST:** 1967
SQ FT: 13,575
SALES (est): 967.73K **Privately Held**
Web: www.carolinasolar.com
SIC: 3448 1799 Screen enclosures;
Swimming pool construction

(G-472)
CECO PUBLISHING INC (PA)
Also Called: Ceco Publishing
208 Elk Park Dr (28804-2063)
P.O. Box 1380 (28787-1380)
PHONE..................828 253-2047
Steve Cooper, *Pr*
EMP: 8 **EST:** 1985
SALES (est): 107.27K **Privately Held**
Web: www.expiredwixdomain.com
SIC: 2721 Magazines: publishing only, not
printed on site

(G-473)
CFS PRESS SLIM RAY
8 Pelham Rd (28803-2550)
PHONE..................828 505-1030
Fred Ray, *Prin*
EMP: 6 **EST:** 2011
SALES (est): 142.47K **Privately Held**
Web: www.cfspress.com
SIC: 2741 Miscellaneous publishing

(G-474)
CHIRON PUBLICATIONS LLC
451 Beaucatcher Rd (28805-1710)
PHONE..................828 285-0838
Steven Buser, *Prin*
EMP: 7 **EST:** 2020
SALES (est): 177.21K **Privately Held**
Web: www.chironpublications.com
SIC: 2741 Miscellaneous publishing

(G-475)
CHOCOLATE FETISH LLC
36 Haywood St (28801-2832)
PHONE..................828 258-2353
EMP: 5 **EST:** 1986
SQ FT: 800
SALES (est): 541.93K **Privately Held**
Web: www.chocolatefetish.com
SIC: 2066 5441 5149 2064 Chocolate candy,
solid; Confectionery produced for direct
sale on the premises; Chocolate; Candy
and other confectionery products

(G-476)
CINTOMS INC
3080 Sweeten Creek Rd (28803-2114)
PHONE..................828 684-1317
Thomas Barkei, *Pr*
Sandra Barkei, *Treas*
EMP: 8 **EST:** 2002
SQ FT: 2,458
SALES (est): 172.68K **Privately Held**
SIC: 2024 5812 Ice cream and frozen deserts
; Eating places

(G-477)
CLARKS PRINTING SERVICE INC
Also Called: Clark Communications
2 Westside Dr (28806-2845)
PHONE..................828 254-1432
Thomas A Clark, *Pr*
David E Diehn, *
Rebecca L Clark, *
Jane Altizer, *
Mary K Clark, *
EMP: 35 **EST:** 1973
SQ FT: 8,000
SALES (est): 4.45MM **Privately Held**
Web: www.oneclearchoice.com
SIC: 2752 7311 Offset printing; Advertising
agencies

(G-478)
CLASSICAL ELEMENTS
9 Sweeten Creek Xing (28803-2543)
PHONE..................828 575-9145
Sean Catinella, *Prin*
EMP: 6 **EST:** 2016
SALES (est): 31.84K **Privately Held**
Web: www.classicalelements.com
SIC: 5736 5131 2221 Musical instrument
stores; Upholstery fabrics, woven;
Manmade and synthetic broadwoven fabrics

(G-479)
COLD MOUNTAIN CAPITAL LLC (PA)
2 Town Square Blvd (28803-5022)
PHONE..................828 210-8129
Horace Jennings, *Mgr*
Bernard Stanek Junior, *Mgr*
Anthony Bergen, *CFO*
EMP: 12 **EST:** 2011
SALES (est): 10.86MM
SALES (corp-wide): 10.86MM **Privately Held**
SIC: 3324 3792 Aerospace investment
castings, ferrous; Tent-type camping trailers

(G-480)
CROSS CANVAS COMPANY INC
63 Glendale Ave (28803-1438)
P.O. Box 15024 (28813-0024)
PHONE..................828 252-0440
Glenn Russell, *Pr*
Paul Wayne Heflin, *VP*
EMP: 20 **EST:** 1986
SQ FT: 20,000
SALES (est): 2.49MM **Privately Held**
Web: www.crosscanvas.com
SIC: 2393 3161 2394 Duffle bags, canvas:
made from purchased materials; Luggage;
Canvas and related products

(G-481)
CSIT GROUP
205 Newstock Rd (28804-8749)
PHONE..................828 233-5750
Chuck Salerno, *Owner*
EMP: 4 **EST:** 2014
SALES (est): 1.65MM **Privately Held**
SIC: 7372 Prepackaged software

(G-482)
D C CRSMAN MFR FINE JWLY INC
Also Called: Creasman D C Mfrs Fine Jewe
269 Tunnel Rd (28805-1832)
PHONE..................828 252-9891
David Creasman, *Pr*
Ramona Creasman, *Sec*
EMP: 7 **EST:** 1979
SQ FT: 1,500
SALES (est): 417.36K **Privately Held**
Web: www.dccreasmanjewelers.com
SIC: 3911 5944 7631 Jewel settings and
mountings, precious metal; Jewelry,
precious stones and precious metals;
Jewelry repair services

(G-483)
DANIELS BUSINESS SERVICES INC (PA)
Also Called: Daniels Graphics
131 Sweeten Creek Rd 25a (28803-1526)
P.O. Box 40 (28802-0040)
PHONE..................828 277-8250
James W Daniels, *Pr*
Tim Bryant, *
James Cannon, *
Jeff Howell, *
Jami Daniels, *
EMP: 42 **EST:** 1948
SQ FT: 60,000
SALES (est): 4.86MM

SALES (corp-wide): 4.86MM **Privately Held**
Web: www.allegramarketingprint.com
SIC: 2752 7389 2759 Offset printing; Telephone answering service; Commercial printing, nec

(G-484)
DAVE STEEL COMPANY INC (PA)
40 Meadow Rd (28803)
P.O. Box 2630 (28802)
PHONE.....................828 252-2771
Jeffrey Dave, *
Timothy Heffner, *VP*
Babette Freund, *Ex VP*
Mark Buff, *
Chris Crosby, *VP*
EMP: 54 **EST:** 1929
SQ FT: 90,000
SALES (est): 40.93MM
SALES (corp-wide): 40.93MM **Privately Held**
Web: www.davesteel.com
SIC: 5051 3449 3441 3471 Steel; Miscellaneous metalwork; Fabricated structural metal; Plating and polishing

(G-485)
DELKOTE MACHINE FINISHING INC
69 Bingham Rd (28806-3824)
PHONE.....................828 253-1023
David Gutierrez, *Mgr*
EMP: 5 **EST:** 2005
SALES (est): 169.36K **Privately Held**
Web: www.deltechomes.com
SIC: 1742 3822 Insulation, buildings; Building services monitoring controls, automatic

(G-486)
DELTEC HOMES INC (PA)
69 Bingham Rd (28806-3824)
PHONE.....................828 253-0483
Robert C Kinser, *Ch Bd*
Steve Linton, *
John Nicholson, *
Joseph Schlenk, *
Matt Oblinsky, *
▼ **EMP:** 42 **EST:** 1955
SQ FT: 110,000
SALES (est): 13.22MM **Privately Held**
Web: www.deltechomes.com
SIC: 5271 2452 Mobile home dealers; Prefabricated wood buildings

(G-487)
DEVERGER SYSTEMS INC
Also Called: DSI Blackpages
87 Downing St (28806-3523)
PHONE.....................919 201-5146
Derrick A Deverger, *Pr*
Cynthia A Deverger, *VP*
EMP: 5 **EST:** 1986
SALES (est): 378.96K **Privately Held**
Web: www.dsiblackpages.com
SIC: 7371 2741 Custom computer programming services; Directories, nec: publishing and printing

(G-488)
DOREL ECOMMERCE INC
37 Haywood St Ste 300 (28801-2708)
PHONE.....................828 378-0092
Martin Schwartz, *Pr*
Jeffrey Schwartz, *Ex VP*
EMP: 7 **EST:** 2007
SALES (est): 300.05K
SALES (corp-wide): 1.39B **Privately Held**
Web: www.dorel.com
SIC: 2514 Household furniture: upholstered on metal frames

PA: Les Industries Dorel Inc.
1255 Av Greene Bureau 300
Westmount QC H3Z 2
514 934-3034

(G-489)
DOTSON METAL FINISHING INC
Also Called: Asheville Paint & Powder Coat
16 Old Charlotte Hwy (28803-9404)
P.O. Box 5814 (28813-5814)
PHONE.....................828 298-9844
Thomas L Finger, *Pr*
Kay C Finger, *Sec*
EMP: 19 **EST:** 1975
SQ FT: 12,500
SALES (est): 2.89MM
SALES (corp-wide): 13.14MM **Privately Held**
Web: www.ashevillepowdercoat.com
SIC: 3479 Coating of metals and formed products
PA: T L F Inc
280 Cane Creek Rd.
Fletcher NC 28732
828 681-5343

(G-490)
EAST COAST OXYGEN INC
310 Elk Park Dr (28804-2066)
P.O. Box 18727 (28814-0727)
PHONE.....................828 252-7770
Clayborn Carroll, *Pr*
Wade Dahlberg, *VP*
EMP: 8 **EST:** 2010
SALES (est): 582.89K **Privately Held**
SIC: 2813 Industrial gases

(G-491)
EAST FORK POTTERY LLC
144 Caribou Rd Ste 70 (28803-1522)
PHONE.....................828 237-7200
EMP: 8
SALES (corp-wide): 13.44MM **Privately Held**
Web: www.eastfork.com
SIC: 3269 Stoneware pottery products
PA: East Fork Pottery, Llc
531 Short Mcdowell St
Asheville NC 28803
828 237-7200

(G-492)
EAST FORK POTTERY LLC (PA)
Also Called: East Fork
531 Short Mcdowell St (28803)
PHONE.....................828 237-7200
Alex Matisse, *CEO*
EMP: 9 **EST:** 2017
SALES (est): 13.44MM
SALES (corp-wide): 13.44MM **Privately Held**
Web: www.eastfork.com
SIC: 3269 Stoneware pottery products

(G-493)
EAST FORK POTTERY LLC
15 W Walnut St # A (28801-8102)
PHONE.....................828 575-2150
Alex Matisse, *CEO*
EMP: 8
SALES (corp-wide): 13.44MM **Privately Held**
Web: www.eastfork.com
SIC: 3271 Concrete block and brick
PA: East Fork Pottery, Llc
531 Short Mcdowell St
Asheville NC 28803
828 237-7200

(G-494)
ENPLAS LIFE TECH INC
230 Sardis Rd (28806-8504)
PHONE.....................828 633-2250
Joe Malasky, *Pr*
Leonore Andreae, *Contrlr*
EMP: 8 **EST:** 1995
SQ FT: 45,000
SALES (est): 6.64MM **Privately Held**
Web: en.enplas.com
SIC: 3544 3559 Forms (molds), for foundry and plastics working machinery; Plastics working machinery

(G-495)
FIBERLINK INC
122 Deerlake Dr (28803-3171)
PHONE.....................828 274-5629
Andrew T Piatek, *Pr*
Stephanie F Cooper, *Sr VP*
Joseph C Harrison, *Genl Mgr*
EMP: 5 **EST:** 1999
SQ FT: 200
SALES (est): 521.73K **Privately Held**
SIC: 3661 Fiber optics communications equipment

(G-496)
FIRST COAST ENERGY LLP
301 Smokey Park Hwy (28806-1026)
PHONE.....................828 667-0625
EMP: 8
Web: www.firstcoastenergy.com
SIC: 1311 Crude petroleum and natural gas
PA: First Coast Energy, L.L.P.
6867 Southpoint Dr N
Jacksonville FL 32216

(G-497)
FIRSTREPORT SOFTWARE INC
369 London Rd (28803-2805)
PHONE.....................828 441-0404
John Gellman, *Pr*
John Gallman, *Pr*
EMP: 4 **EST:** 1996
SALES (est): 197.81K **Privately Held**
Web: www.firstrecords.com
SIC: 7372 7371 Business oriented computer software; Custom computer programming services

(G-498)
FISHER SCIENTIFIC COMPANY LLC
275 Aiken Rd (28804-8740)
PHONE.....................800 252-7100
Robert Hundley, *VP*
EMP: 63
SALES (corp-wide): 42.86B **Publicly Held**
Web: www.fishersci.com
SIC: 3821 5049 3829 3826 Clinical laboratory instruments, except medical and dental; Scientific instruments; Measuring and controlling devices, nec; Analytical instruments
HQ: Fisher Scientific Company Llc
300 Industry Dr
Pittsburgh PA 15275
800 766-7000

(G-499)
FOREST MILLWORK INC
93 Thompson St (28803-2330)
PHONE.....................828 251-5264
EMP: 16 **EST:** 1991
SALES (est): 893.09K **Privately Held**
Web: www.forestmillwork.com
SIC: 2431 Millwork

(G-500)
FOUR CORNERS HOME INC (PA)
1 Page Ave Ste 112I (28801-2389)
PHONE.....................828 398-4187
William Griffin, *Pr*
Melissa Ness, *Prin*
Taylor Brandt, *Prin*
Joe Pawlus, *Prin*
EMP: 5 **EST:** 2008
SALES (est): 440.93K
SALES (corp-wide): 440.93K **Privately Held**
Web: www.fourcornershome.com
SIC: 2514 Household furniture: upholstered on metal frames

(G-501)
FOX FACTORY INC
1240 Brevard Rd (28806-9547)
PHONE.....................828 633-6840
EMP: 5 **EST:** 2016
SALES (est): 559.05K **Privately Held**
SIC: 3714 Shock absorbers, motor vehicle

(G-502)
FRENCH BROAD CHOCOLATES LLC
821 Riverside Dr (28801-0281)
PHONE.....................828 252-4181
Daniel Rattigan, *Managing Member*
EMP: 7 **EST:** 2006
SALES (est): 5.36MM **Privately Held**
Web: www.frenchbroadchocolates.com
SIC: 5441 2064 Candy; Candy bars, including chocolate covered bars

(G-503)
GALLO LEA ORGANICS LLC
Also Called: Gallolea Pizza Kits
9 Inglewood Rd (28804-1633)
PHONE.....................828 337-1037
EMP: 6 **EST:** 2010
SALES (est): 245.29K **Privately Held**
Web: www.gallolea.com
SIC: 2099 Food preparations, nec

(G-504)
GE AVIATION SYSTEMS LLC
Also Called: GE Aviation
502 Sweeten Creek Industrial Park
(28803-1730)
PHONE.....................828 210-5076
EMP: 107
SALES (corp-wide): 38.7B **Publicly Held**
Web: www.geaerospace.com
SIC: 3728 Aircraft parts and equipment, nec
HQ: Ge Aviation Systems Llc
1 Neumann Way
Cincinnati OH 45215
937 898-9600

(G-505)
GENELECT SERVICES INC
Also Called: Generac Distributors
50 Glendale Ave (28803-1463)
P.O. Box 3155 (28802-3155)
PHONE.....................828 255-7999
Gerald Wagstaff, *Pr*
EMP: 10 **EST:** 1994
SALES (est): 815.44K **Privately Held**
Web: www.genelectservices.com
SIC: 3621 7629 Motors and generators; Generator repair

(G-506)
GINGERS REVENGE LLC
829 Riverside Dr Ste 100 (28801-0228)
PHONE.....................828 505-2462
EMP: 14 **EST:** 2015
SALES (est): 2.76MM **Privately Held**
Web: www.gingersrevenge.com

SIC: 2082 Beer (alcoholic beverage)

(G-507)
GINKGO PRINT STUDIO LLC
1 Grace Ave (28804-2503)
PHONE.....................................828 275-6300
Whitney Ponder, *Prin*
EMP: 4 **EST:** 2010
SALES (est): 180.88K **Privately Held**
Web: www.ginkgoprintstudio.com
SIC: 2752 Commercial printing, lithographic

(G-508)
**GOLF ASSOCIATES ADVERTISING
CO**
Also Called: Golf Associates Score Card Co
91 Westside Dr (28806-2846)
P.O. Box 6917 (28816-6917)
PHONE.....................................828 252-6544
Edward S Pinkston Senior, *Pr*
Edward S Pinkston Junior, *VP*
Faye Pinkston, *
◆ **EMP:** 24 **EST:** 1972
SQ FT: 18,000
SALES (est): 1.66MM **Privately Held**
Web: www.golfassociates.com
SIC: 2752 7311 2761 2759 Offset printing;
 Advertising consultant; Manifold business
 forms; Commercial printing, nec

(G-509)
GRATEFUL STEPS FOUNDATION
119 Buffalo Trl (28805-9761)
PHONE.....................................828 277-0998
Nicke Cavennes, *CEO*
Micki Cabaniss, *Ex Dir*
Jon Elliston, *Ch Bd*
EMP: 5 **EST:** 2011
SQ FT: 1,400
SALES (est): 194.34K **Privately Held**
Web: www.gratefulsteps.org
SIC: 5942 2731 Book stores; Book publishing

(G-510)
GRATEFUL UNION FAMILY INC (PA)
Also Called: Earth Guild
33 Haywood St (28801-2835)
PHONE.....................................828 622-3258
Marshall B Crawford, *Pr*
B J Crawford, *VP*
Barbara Hernden Field, *Sec*
Esther Holsen, *Treas*
EMP: 12 **EST:** 1976
SQ FT: 34,000
SALES (est): 2.06MM
SALES (corp-wide): 2.06MM **Privately
Held**
Web: www.earthguild.com
SIC: 2331 5961 5945 5092 Women's and
 misses' blouses and shirts; Mail order
 house, nec; Arts and crafts supplies; Arts
 and crafts equipment and supplies

(G-511)
GREAT EASTERN SUN TRDG CO INC
Also Called: Great Eastern Sun
 92 Mcintosh Rd (28806-1406)
PHONE.....................................828 665-7790
Barry E Evans, *CEO*
Janet Paige, *Pr*
Yoshihiro Kato, *VP*
Leila Bakkum, *VP*
Kenny Green, *Sec*
▲ **EMP:** 18 **EST:** 1982
SQ FT: 11,000
SALES (est): 12.02MM **Privately Held**
Web: www.great-eastern-sun.com
SIC: 2099 5149 2087 Food preparations, nec
 ; Health foods; Flavoring extracts and
 syrups, nec

(G-512)
GREEN LINE MEDIA INC
Also Called: Mountain Xpress
 2 Wall St Ste 214 (28801-2756)
 P.O. Box 144 (28802-0144)
PHONE.....................................828 251-1333
Jeff Fobes, *Owner*
EMP: 46 **EST:** 1994
SALES (est): 1.83MM **Privately Held**
Web: www.mountainx.com
SIC: 2741 2711 Newsletter publishing;
 Newspapers

(G-513)
GREYBEARD PRINTING INC
Also Called: American Speedy Printing
 1304c Patton Ave Ste C (28806-2604)
PHONE.....................................828 252-3082
Peter Boggs, *Pr*
EMP: 6 **EST:** 1979
SQ FT: 3,000
SALES (est): 176.07K **Privately Held**
Web: www.americanspeedy.com
SIC: 2752 Offset printing

(G-514)
H&H DISTILLERY LLC
Also Called: Cultivated Cocktails
 204 Charlotte Hwy Ste D (28803-8681)
PHONE.....................................828 338-9779
EMP: 5 **EST:** 2012
SALES (est): 764.68K **Privately Held**
Web: www.cultivated-cocktails.com
SIC: 2085 Distilled and blended liquors

(G-515)
HAMILTON INDUS GRINDING INC
Also Called: Carolina Knife Company
 273 Kimberly Ave (28804-3518)
PHONE.....................................828 253-6796
Walter Ashbrook, *Mgr*
EMP: 21
SALES (corp-wide): 4.63MM **Privately
Held**
Web: www.carolinaknife.com
SIC: 5085 7699 3541 3423 Knives, industrial
 ; Knife, saw and tool sharpening and repair;
 Machine tools, metal cutting type; Hand
 and edge tools, nec
PA: Hamilton Industrial Grinding, Inc.
 240 N B St
 Hamilton OH 45013
 513 863-1221

(G-516)
HARRINS SAND & GRAVEL INC
195 Amboy Rd (28806-4330)
 P.O. Box 51 (28748)
PHONE.....................................828 254-2744
Danny Rice, *Pr*
Jeff Rice, *VP*
EMP: 4 **EST:** 1966
SQ FT: 6,000
SALES (est): 910.2K **Privately Held**
Web: www.harrinssandgravel.com
SIC: 1442 Construction sand and gravel

(G-517)
HIGHLAND BREWING COMPANY INC
Also Called: Highland
 12 Old Charlotte Hwy Ste H (28803-9419)
PHONE.....................................828 299-3370
Oscar Wong, *Pr*
John M Lyda, *VP*
▲ **EMP:** 18 **EST:** 1994
SALES (est): 8.42MM **Privately Held**
Web: www.highlandbrewing.com
SIC: 2082 5813 Ale (alcoholic beverage);
 Bars and lounges

(G-518)
HIS GLASSWORKS INC
2000 Riverside Dr Ste 19 (28804-2099)
PHONE.....................................828 254-2559
Robert W Stephan, *Pr*
Margaret Stephan, *VP*
Mark Bolick, *COO*
▼ **EMP:** 6 **EST:** 1980
SQ FT: 3,100
SALES (est): 2.25MM **Privately Held**
Web: www.hisglassworks.com
SIC: 5084 3291 3541 Industrial machinery
 and equipment; Abrasive stones, except
 grinding stones: ground or whole; Buffing
 and polishing machines

(G-519)
HYDRAULICS EXPRESS
40 Interstate Blvd (28806-2261)
 P.O. Box 5637 (28813-5637)
PHONE.....................................828 251-2500
Robert Bugg, *Prin*
EMP: 7 **EST:** 2016
SALES (est): 202.31K **Privately Held**
Web: www.hydraulicsexpress.com
SIC: 3599 Machine shop, jobbing and repair

(G-520)
ICON SIGN SYSTEMS INC
23 Villemagne Dr (28804-6109)
PHONE.....................................828 253-4266
Scott Villemagne, *Pr*
Craig Garrett, *VP*
EMP: 4 **EST:** 1999
SALES (est): 133.97K **Privately Held**
Web: www.signsystemsnc.com
SIC: 3993 Signs and advertising specialties

(G-521)
ILUMIVU INC
1200 Ridgefield Blvd Ste 170 (28806-2286)
PHONE.....................................410 570-8846
Susan Steinmann, *Contrlr*
EMP: 8 **EST:** 2021
SALES (est): 3.65MM **Privately Held**
Web: www.ilumivu.com
SIC: 7372 Prepackaged software

(G-522)
IN BLUE HANDMADE INC
20 Westside Dr (28806-2845)
PHONE.....................................828 774-5094
EMP: 7 **EST:** 2015
SALES (est): 148.77K **Privately Held**
Web: www.inbluehandmade.com
SIC: 3199 Leather goods, nec

(G-523)
INDUSTRY NINE LLC
21 Old County Home Rd (28806-9713)
 P.O. Box 16309 (28816-0309)
PHONE.....................................828 210-5113
▲ **EMP:** 7 **EST:** 2008
SALES (est): 1.56MM **Privately Held**
Web: www.industrynine.com
SIC: 3751 Bicycles and related parts

(G-524)
INGRAM MACHINE & BALANCING
Also Called: Ingram Racing Engines
 48 Ben Lippen Rd (28806-2028)
PHONE.....................................828 254-3420
David Ingram, *Owner*
EMP: 6 **EST:** 1964
SQ FT: 10,000
SALES (est): 494.17K **Privately Held**
Web:
ingram-machine-balancing.usautos.repair
SIC: 3599 Machine shop, jobbing and repair

(G-525)
ITS A SNAP
66 Asheland Ave (28801-3246)
PHONE.....................................828 254-3456
Mike Rangel, *Prin*
EMP: 5 **EST:** 2009
SALES (est): 291.72K **Privately Held**
SIC: 3544 Special dies and tools

(G-526)
J & K TOOLS LLC
490 Upper Grassy Br Rd (28805-9233)
PHONE.....................................828 299-0589
Joseph Higdon, *Prin*
EMP: 6 **EST:** 2016
SALES (est): 98.61K **Privately Held**
SIC: 3599 Industrial machinery, nec

(G-527)
JAG GRAPHICS INC
Also Called: Sir Speedy
 231 Biltmore Ave (28801-4107)
PHONE.....................................828 259-9020
Gary Forbes, *Pr*
EMP: 5 **EST:** 1994
SQ FT: 2,500
SALES (est): 214.71K **Privately Held**
Web: www.sirspeedy.com
SIC: 2752 2791 2789 Commercial printing,
 lithographic; Typesetting; Bookbinding and
 related work

(G-528)
JOHNSON CONTROLS INC
Also Called: Johnson Controls
 905 Riverside Dr (28804-3114)
PHONE.....................................828 225-3200
John Ogden, *Mgr*
EMP: 19
Web: www.johnsoncontrols.com
SIC: 2531 Seats, automobile
HQ: Johnson Controls, Inc.
 5757 N Green Bay Ave
 Milwaukee WI 53209
 866 496-1999

(G-529)
KING BIO INC
150 Westside Dr (28806-2847)
PHONE.....................................828 398-6058
EMP: 46
Web: www.drkings.com
SIC: 3221 Medicine bottles, glass
PA: King Bio, Inc.
 3 Westside Dr
 Asheville NC 28806

(G-530)
KING BIO INC (PA)
Also Called: Safe Care Rx
 3 Westside Dr (28806-2846)
PHONE.....................................828 255-0201
Frank J King Junior, *Pr*
Suzie King, *
EMP: 54 **EST:** 1989
SQ FT: 150,000
SALES (est): 4.73MM **Privately Held**
Web: www.drkings.com
SIC: 5912 2834 5122 Proprietary (non-
 prescription medicine) stores;
 Pharmaceutical preparations;
 Pharmaceuticals

(G-531)
KKB BILTMORE INC
479 Hendersonville Rd (28803-2750)
 P.O. Box 3243 (28717-3243)
PHONE.....................................828 274-6711
Paul Bradham, *Prin*
EMP: 4 **EST:** 2011

GEOGRAPHIC

SALES (est): 317.63K **Privately Held**
Web: www.keystonekb.com
SIC: 2434 Wood kitchen cabinets

(G-532)
L F T INC
123 Lyman St (28801-4371)
PHONE..............................828 253-6830
Tom Finger, *Prin*
EMP: 5
SALES (est): 606.27K **Privately Held**
Web: www.t-fab.com
SIC: 3471 Electroplating of metals or formed products

(G-533)
LAUREL OF ASHEVILLE LLC
Also Called: Laurel of Asheville, The
110 Executive Park (28801-2426)
P.O. Box 2059 (28802-2059)
PHONE..............................828 670-7503
EMP: 14 **EST:** 2006
SALES (est): 940.62K **Privately Held**
Web: www.thelaurelofasheville.com
SIC: 2759 Publication printing

(G-534)
LEVI STRAUSS INTERNATIONAL
800 Brevard Rd (28806-2251)
PHONE..............................828 665-2417
EMP: 5
SALES (corp-wide): 6.36B **Publicly Held**
Web: www.levi.com
SIC: 2329 2339 Men's and boys' sportswear and athletic clothing; Women's and misses' outerwear, nec
HQ: Levi Strauss International
1155 Battery St
San Francisco CA 94111
415 501-6000

(G-535)
LIGHTFORM INC
403 Shelwood Cir Apt H (28804-8238)
PHONE..............................908 281-9098
Jeremy Lerner, *Pr*
EMP: 4 **EST:** 1996
SALES (est): 160.58K **Privately Held**
Web: www.lightforminc.com
SIC: 3827 Optical instruments and apparatus

(G-536)
LIGHTNING BOLT INK LLC
100 N Lexington Ave (28801-2815)
PHONE..............................828 281-1274
EMP: 4 **EST:** 2019
SALES (est): 1.45MM **Privately Held**
Web: www.lightningboltink.com
SIC: 3452 Bolts, nuts, rivets, and washers

(G-537)
LINTER NORTH AMERICA CORP (DH)
48 Patton Ave (28801-3321)
PHONE..............................828 645-4261
Alberto Moratiel, *Pr*
C Roy Mendenhall, *VP*
Ramon Noblejas, *Sec*
EMP: 8 **EST:** 2009
SQ FT: 127,000
SALES (est): 25.2MM **Privately Held**
Web: www.balcrank.com
SIC: 3569 Lubricating equipment
HQ: Linter Investments Sl
Calle Gandia, 8 - Local 13
Madrid M 28007

(G-538)
LUCKY MAN INC (HQ)
160 Broadway St (28801-2305)
PHONE..............................828 251-0090

▲ **EMP:** 25 **EST:** 1978
SALES (est): 12.08MM
SALES (corp-wide): 21.58MM **Privately Held**
Web: www.moogmusic.com
SIC: 3931 Musical instruments
PA: Inmusic Brands, Inc.
200 Scnic View Dr Ste 201
Cumberland RI 02864
401 658-3131

(G-539)
LUSTAR DYEING AND FINSHG INC
144 Caribou Rd (28803-1521)
PHONE..............................828 274-2440
Gerald Lubin, *Prin*
EMP: 4 **EST:** 2007
SQ FT: 121,140
SALES (est): 160.07K **Privately Held**
SIC: 2231 Broadwoven fabric mills, wool

(G-540)
LUSTY MONK LLC
29 Canoe Ln (28804-8612)
PHONE..............................828 645-5056
Kelly Davis, *Pt*
EMP: 4 **EST:** 2008
SALES (est): 467.14K **Privately Held**
Web: www.lustymonk.com
SIC: 2035 Mustard, prepared (wet)

(G-541)
MAIL MANAGEMENT SERVICES LLC
Also Called: Allegra Marketing
88 Roberts St (28801-3149)
P.O. Box 7557 (28802-7557)
PHONE..............................828 236-0076
David Campbell, *Managing Member*
EMP: 19 **EST:** 1998
SQ FT: 10,000
SALES (est): 5.63MM **Privately Held**
Web: www.allegramarketingprint.com
SIC: 2752 Offset printing

(G-542)
MAKE SOLUTIONS INC
23 Tacoma St (28801-1621)
PHONE..............................623 444-0098
Patti Marshall, *CEO*
Brian Kottenstette, *CFO*
Paul Marshall, *Sec*
EMP: 15 **EST:** 2012
SALES (est): 1.79MM **Privately Held**
Web: www.makesolutionsinc.com
SIC: 7372 8742 7389 Prepackaged software ; Management consulting services; Business services, nec

(G-543)
MARINE SYSTEMS INC
7 Westside Dr (28806-2846)
PHONE..............................828 254-5354
Edward Riester, *Pr*
Sylvia Riester, *Sec*
EMP: 10 **EST:** 1977
SQ FT: 24,250
SALES (est): 1.33MM **Privately Held**
Web: www.airmsi.com
SIC: 3446 3544 Grillwork, ornamental metal; Forms (molds), for foundry and plastics working machinery

(G-544)
MATHIS ELEC SLS & SVC INC
Also Called: Mathis Electronics
102a Caribou Rd (28803-1523)
P.O. Box 5871 (28813-5871)
PHONE..............................828 274-5925
Edmond Mathis, *Pr*
EMP: 14 **EST:** 1980
SQ FT: 5,000

SALES (est): 4.14MM **Privately Held**
Web: www.mathiselectronics.com
SIC: 3672 Circuit boards, television and radio printed

(G-545)
MB MARKETING & MFG INC
Also Called: Mbm
128 Bingham Rd Ste 400 (28806-3893)
P.O. Box 2296 (28802-2296)
PHONE..............................828 285-0882
John Mc Leod, *Pr*
▲ **EMP:** 7 **EST:** 1984
SALES (est): 3.53MM **Privately Held**
Web: www.mbmbrakes.com
SIC: 3714 Motor vehicle parts and accessories

(G-546)
MH LIBMAN WOODTURNING
191 Lyman St (28801-4371)
PHONE..............................828 360-5530
M H Libman, *Prin*
EMP: 4 **EST:** 2012
SALES (est): 175.1K **Privately Held**
Web: www.marlowelfrey.com
SIC: 2431 Millwork

(G-547)
MILKCO INC
Also Called: Milkco
220 Deaverview Rd (28806-1710)
P.O. Box 16160 (28816-0160)
PHONE..............................828 254-8428
Keith Collins, *Pr*
EMP: 265 **EST:** 1982
SQ FT: 120,000
SALES (est): 49.2MM
SALES (corp-wide): 5.64B **Publicly Held**
Web: www.milkco.com
SIC: 2026 2037 2086 Milk processing (pasteurizing, homogenizing, bottling); Fruit juices; Mineral water, carbonated: packaged in cans, bottles, etc.
PA: Ingles Markets, Incorporated
2913 Us Highway 70
Black Mountain NC 28711
828 669-2941

(G-548)
MILLS MANUFACTURING CORP (PA)
22 Mills Pl (28804-1216)
P.O. Box 8100 (28814-8100)
PHONE..............................828 645-3061
James W Turner, *CEO*
Pamela M Turner, *
John Oswald, *
EMP: 149 **EST:** 1934
SQ FT: 172,000
SALES (est): 11.06MM
SALES (corp-wide): 11.06MM **Privately Held**
Web: www.millsmanufacturing.com
SIC: 2399 2298 Parachutes; Twine, cord and cordage

(G-549)
MONOGRAM ASHEVILLE
Also Called: Celesta's
800 Brevard Rd Ste 812 (28806-2297)
PHONE..............................828 707-8110
Jennifer Mariko Walker, *Managing Member*
EMP: 6 **EST:** 2018
SALES (est): 525.54K **Privately Held**
Web: www.monogramasheville.com
SIC: 2395 Embroidery and art needlework

(G-550)
MORRISON MILL WORK
51 Thompson St (28803-2367)
PHONE..............................828 774-5415

EMP: 7 **EST:** 2013
SALES (est): 91.72K **Privately Held**
Web: www.morrisonmillwork.com
SIC: 2431 Millwork

(G-551)
MOSS SIGN COMPANY INC
526 Swannanoa River Rd (28805-2429)
P.O. Box 5099 (28813-5099)
PHONE..............................828 299-7766
Ronnie Moss, *Pr*
EMP: 11 **EST:** 1996
SALES (est): 858.38K **Privately Held**
Web: www.mosssigncompany.com
SIC: 3993 1731 Electric signs; Electrical work

(G-552)
MOUNTAIN AREA INFO NETWRK
Also Called: M A I N
34 Wall St Ste 407 (28801-2713)
PHONE..............................828 255-0182
Wally Bowen, *Ex Dir*
EMP: 10 **EST:** 1995
SALES (est): 789.91K **Privately Held**
Web: www.main.nc.us
SIC: 4813 2711 Internet host services; Newspapers

(G-553)
NACHOS & BEER LLC
230 Charlotte Hwy (28803-8628)
PHONE..............................828 298-2280
Merle Butterick, *Prin*
EMP: 4 **EST:** 2009
SALES (est): 229.49K **Privately Held**
SIC: 2082 Beer (alcoholic beverage)

(G-554)
NARAYANA INC
247 Old Weaverville Rd (28804-8733)
PHONE..............................828 708-0954
Wally Zeman, *CEO*
EMP: 8 **EST:** 2004
SALES (est): 508.84K **Privately Held**
Web: www.narayanainc.com
SIC: 2844 Cosmetic preparations

(G-555)
NATURES PHARMACY INC
752 Biltmore Ave (28803-2558)
PHONE..............................828 251-0094
Mike Rogers, *Pr*
Bill Cheek, *VP*
EMP: 5 **EST:** 1996
SQ FT: 2,000
SALES (est): 141.64K **Privately Held**
SIC: 2834 5912 5499 Druggists' preparations (pharmaceuticals); Drug stores ; Spices and herbs

(G-556)
NEURAMETRIX INC
18 Lookout Rd (28804-3238)
PHONE..............................408 507-2366
Jan Samzelius, *CEO*
Christian Olsson, *VP*
EMP: 4 **EST:** 2016
SALES (est): 189.9K **Privately Held**
Web: www.neurametrix.com
SIC: 8731 8071 7372 7389 Biotechnical research, commercial; Neurological laboratory; Application computer software; Business services, nec

(G-557)
OAK & GRIST DISTILLING CO LLC
40 West St (28801-1124)
PHONE..............................914 450-0589
EMP: 5
SALES (est): 64.7K **Privately Held**

▲ = Import ▼ = Export
◆ = Import/Export

Web: www.oakandgrist.com
SIC: 2085 Distilled and blended liquors

(G-558)
OCEAN 10 SECURITY LLC
329 Gashes Creek Rd (28803-9405)
PHONE..............................828 484-1481
EMP: 14 EST: 2015
SALES (est): 2.46MM **Privately Held**
Web: www.ocean10security.com
SIC: 3651 Video camera-audio recorders,
household use

(G-559)
OLD WOOD COMPANY
Also Called: Old Wood Co
99 Riverside Dr (28801-3134)
PHONE..............................828 259-9663
Darren Green, *Pr*
EMP: 6 EST: 2010
SALES (est): 245.5K **Privately Held**
Web: www.theoldwoodco.com
SIC: 2511 Wood household furniture

(G-560)
ON DEMAND PRINTING & DESI
200 Patton Ave (28801-2606)
PHONE..............................828 252-0965
Micah Crosson, *Prin*
EMP: 4 EST: 2006
SALES (est): 247.21K **Privately Held**
Web: www.ondemandink.com
SIC: 2752 Offset printing

(G-561)
ORIGAMI INK LLC
6 Boston Way Ste 10 (28803-2996)
PHONE..............................828 225-2300
EMP: 4 EST: 2008
SALES (est): 536.85K **Privately Held**
Web: www.origamiink.com
SIC: 3423 Engravers' tools, hand

(G-562)
**ORTHOPEDIC APPLIANCE
COMPANY**
75 Victoria Rd (28801-4487)
PHONE..............................828 254-6305
TOLL FREE: 800
William R Aycock Senior, *Pr*
William R Aycock Junior, *VP*
Owen E Aycock, *Sec*
EMP: 56 EST: 1960
SQ FT: 8,000
SALES (est): 3.71MM **Privately Held**
Web: www.orthopedicapplianceco.com
SIC: 3842 Orthopedic appliances

(G-563)
OTIS ELEVATOR COMPANY
203 Elk Park Dr (28804-2063)
PHONE..............................828 251-1248
Mary Green, *Mgr*
EMP: 6
SALES (corp-wide): 14.26B **Publicly Held**
Web: www.otis.com
SIC: 5084 1796 3534 Elevators; Installing
building equipment; Dumbwaiters
HQ: Otis Elevator Company
1 Carrier Pl
Farmington CT 06032
860 674-3000

(G-564)
PALLET WORLD USA INC
124 Sondley Pkwy (28805-1149)
PHONE..............................828 298-7270
Robert Jolly, *Prin*
EMP: 6 EST: 2016
SALES (est): 162.55K **Privately Held**

SIC: 2448 Pallets, wood

(G-565)
PALMER INSTRUMENTS INC
Also Called: Palmer Wahl Instrmnttion Group
234 Old Weaverville Rd (28804-1260)
PHONE..............................828 658-3131
Stephen J Santangelo, *Pr*
Jack J Santangelo, *
Richard J Santangelo, *
Sky Tilly, *
▲ EMP: 50 EST: 1918
SQ FT: 50,000
SALES (est): 3.21MM **Privately Held**
Web: www.palmerwahl.com
SIC: 3823 3829 3825 Differential pressure
instruments, industrial process type;
Measuring and controlling devices, nec;
Instruments to measure electricity

(G-566)
PALMER WAHL INSTRUMENTS INC
Also Called: Palmer Wahl Instrmnttion Group
234 Old Weaverville Rd (28804-1260)
PHONE..............................828 658-3131
Stephen J Santangelo, *Pr*
Richard Santangelo, *
▲ EMP: 35 EST: 1953
SQ FT: 20,000
SALES (est): 8.75MM **Privately Held**
Web: www.palmerwahl.com
SIC: 5084 3823 Industrial machinery and
equipment; Temperature instruments:
industrial process type

(G-567)
PARKER OIL INC
290 Depot St (28801-3998)
PHONE..............................828 253-7265
Tom Nuckolls, *Pr*
EMP: 4 EST: 2007
SALES (est): 168.89K **Privately Held**
SIC: 1389 Oil and gas field services, nec

(G-568)
PAYMENT COLLECT LLC
70 Charlotte St (28801-2434)
PHONE..............................828 214-5550
EMP: 5 EST: 2011
SALES (est): 443.6K **Privately Held**
Web: www.paymentcollect.com
SIC: 7372 Business oriented computer
software

(G-569)
PEABERRY PRESS LLC
Also Called: Peaberry
802 Fairview Rd Ste 800 (28803-7773)
PHONE..............................828 773-1489
Brittony Miller, *Prin*
EMP: 4 EST: 2014
SALES (est): 215.02K **Privately Held**
Web: www.peaberrypress.com
SIC: 2741 Miscellaneous publishing

(G-570)
PERFECTION GEAR INC (DH)
9 N Bear Creek Rd (28806-1731)
PHONE..............................828 253-0000
Randy Gredly, *CEO*
Robert Sirak, *
▲ EMP: 60 EST: 1982
SQ FT: 65,000
SALES (est): 9.59MM
SALES (corp-wide): 241.4MM **Privately
Held**
Web: www.perfectiongear.com
SIC: 3566 Reduction gears and gear units
for turbines, except auto
HQ: Peerless-Winsmith, Inc.
5200 Upper Mtro Pl Ste 11

Dublin OH 43017
614 526-7000

(G-571)
**PHARMACEUTICAL EQUIPMENT
SVCS**
15 Magnolia Hill Ct (28806-8485)
PHONE..............................239 699-9120
Barbara Hosack, *Prin*
EMP: 4 EST: 2014
SALES (est): 91.1K **Privately Held**
SIC: 5084 2834 Industrial machinery and
equipment; Pharmaceutical preparations

(G-572)
PHOTON ENERGY CORP
1095 Hendersonville Rd (28803-1891)
PHONE..............................888 336-8128
Craig Sherman, *CFO*
Ashley Campbell, *Mgr*
EMP: 6 EST: 2017
SALES (est): 474.84K **Privately Held**
Web: www.photonenergy.com
SIC: 3661 Fiber optics communications
equipment

(G-573)
PIEDMONT MEDIAWORKS INC
Also Called: Sign-A-Rama
5a Hedgerose Ct (28805-1986)
PHONE..............................828 575-2250
Arlene Sullivan, *Pr*
Edward Sullivan, *Prin*
Graham Mew, *Prin*
EMP: 10 EST: 2011
SALES (est): 1.67MM **Privately Held**
Web: www.signarama.com
SIC: 3993 Signs and advertising specialties

(G-574)
PIEDMONT TRUCK TIRES INC
125 Sweeten Creek Rd (28803-1526)
PHONE..............................828 277-1549
Michael Taylor, *Brnch Mgr*
EMP: 13
SALES (corp-wide): 636MM **Privately
Held**
Web: www.piedmonttrucktires.com
SIC: 5014 5531 7534 Truck tires and tubes;
Auto and home supply stores; Rebuilding
and retreading tires
HQ: Piedmont Truck Tires, Inc.
312 S Regional Rd
Greensboro NC 27409
336 668-0091

(G-575)
PINKSTON PROPERTIES LLC
Also Called: Golf Associates
91 Westside Dr (28806-2846)
P.O. Box 6917 (28816-6917)
PHONE..............................828 252-9867
EMP: 7 EST: 1995
SALES (est): 427.46K **Privately Held**
Web: www.golfassociates.com
SIC: 6733 2759 Private estate, personal
investment and vacation fund trusts; Card
printing and engraving, except greeting

(G-576)
PLASTICARD PRODUCTS INC
99 Pond Rd (28806-2250)
PHONE..............................828 665-7774
Mark Goldberg, *Prin*
EMP: 18 EST: 2006
SALES (est): 809.16K **Privately Held**
Web: www.plicards.com
SIC: 2759 Commercial printing, nec

(G-577)
PLAYRACE INC
Also Called: Fastsigns
1202 Patton Ave (28806-2708)
PHONE..............................828 251-2211
Ric Davenport, *Pr*
Carla Heatherly, *VP*
EMP: 20 EST: 2007
SQ FT: 4,940
SALES (est): 2.35MM **Privately Held**
Web: www.fastsigns.com
SIC: 3993 Signs and advertising specialties

(G-578)
PLEB URBAN WINERY
289 Lyman St (28801-4741)
PHONE..............................828 767-6445
EMP: 5 EST: 2019
SALES (est): 135.25K **Privately Held**
Web: www.pleburbanwinery.com
SIC: 2084 Wines

(G-579)
PLUM PRINT INC
45 S French Broad Ave Ste 100
(28801-0187)
PHONE..............................828 633-5535
EMP: 18 EST: 2015
SALES (est): 480.02K **Privately Held**
Web: www.plumprint.com
SIC: 2752 Offset printing

(G-580)
POPE PRINTING & DESIGN INC
Also Called: Kwik Kopy Printing
485 Hendersonville Rd Ste 7 (28803-2765)
PHONE..............................828 274-5945
Larry Pope, *Pr*
Brad Pope, *VP*
EMP: 4 EST: 1983
SQ FT: 1,540
SALES (est): 192.5K **Privately Held**
Web: www.kwikkopy.com
SIC: 2752 Offset printing

(G-581)
**POPPY HANDCRAFTED POPCORN
INC (PA)**
12 Gerber Rd (28803-2496)
P.O. Box 18448 (28814-0448)
PHONE..............................828 552-3149
Ginger Frank, *Managing Member*
EMP: 10 EST: 2014
SALES (est): 6.62MM
SALES (corp-wide): 6.62MM **Privately
Held**
Web:
www.poppyhandcraftedpopcorn.com
SIC: 2099 Food preparations, nec

(G-582)
POWELL INK INC
Also Called: Allegra Print & Imaging
191 Charlotte St (28801-1989)
PHONE..............................828 253-6886
Mike Powell, *Pr*
Debbie Powell, *VP*
EMP: 10 EST: 1986
SQ FT: 2,400
SALES (est): 576.82K **Privately Held**
Web: www.allegramarketingprint.com
SIC: 2752 2789 2791 Offset printing;
Bookbinding and related work; Typesetting

(G-583)
PRATT & WHITNEY ENG SVCS INC
330 Pratt And Whitney Blvd (28806-0490)
PHONE..............................860 565-4321
EMP: 1842
SALES (corp-wide): 80.74B **Publicly Held**

Web: www.prattwhitney.com
SIC: 3724 Airfoils, aircraft engine
HQ: Pratt & Whitney Engine Services, Inc.
1525 Midway Park Rd
Bridgeport WV 26330
304 842-5421

(G-584)
PRESLEY GROUP LTD (DH)
Also Called: Hayes & Lunsford Elec Contrs
739 Dogwood Rd (28806-0366)
P.O. Box 973 (28802-0973)
PHONE.................................828 254-9971
TOLL FREE: 800
Eugene L Presley, *Pr*
Richard H Presley, *
Ralph P Presley, *
Eugene L Presley, *Stockholder*
EMP: 100 EST: 1926
SQ FT: 40,000
SALES (est): 8.73MM
SALES (corp-wide): 7.03B **Publicly Held**
SIC: 1731 7694 7629 General electrical
contractor; Electric motor repair; Electrical
repair shops
HQ: Starr Electric Company Incorporated
6 Battleground Ct
Greensboro NC 27408
336 275-0241

(G-585)
PRINTING PRESS
16 Pleasant Ridge Dr (28805-2623)
PHONE.................................828 299-1234
Sandra Lawrence, *Pr*
George Lawrence, *VP*
EMP: 4 EST: 1985
SALES (est): 84.92K **Privately Held**
Web: www.blueridgeprinting.com
SIC: 2752 5943 5112 2782 Offset printing;
Office forms and supplies; Envelopes;
Checkbooks

(G-586)
PROCESS AUTOMATION TECH INC
3113 Sweeten Creek Rd (28803-2115)
PHONE.................................828 298-1055
Bruce J Campbell, *Pr*
Bruce Campbell, *Pr*
EMP: 4 EST: 2001
SQ FT: 30,000
SALES (est): 761.24K **Privately Held**
SIC: 3535 Conveyors and conveying
equipment

(G-587)
R&H MACHINING FABRICATION INC
329 Emma Rd (28806-3809)
PHONE.................................828 253-8930
Sean Gould, *Pr*
EMP: 5 EST: 2000
SQ FT: 640
SALES (est): 471.38K **Privately Held**
SIC: 3599 Machine shop, jobbing and repair

(G-588)
RCLGH INC
Also Called: Logangate Homes Timber
Homes
69 Bingham Rd (28806-3824)
P.O. Box 1922 (28730-1922)
PHONE.................................828 707-4383
Robert Cole, *Pr*
Carissa Cole, *Sec*
EMP: 5 EST: 1958
SQ FT: 30,000
SALES (est): 500.07K **Privately Held**
Web: www.deltechomes.com
SIC: 2452 Modular homes, prefabricated,
wood

(G-589)
RED SKY SHELTERS LLC
2002 Riverside Dr Ste 42h (28804-2052)
PHONE.................................828 258-8417
Peter Belt, *Owner*
EMP: 4 EST: 1995
SALES (est): 263.66K **Privately Held**
Web: www.redskyshelters.com
SIC: 2394 Tents: made from purchased
materials

(G-590)
RHINO NETWORKS LLC
1025 Brevard Rd Ste 8 (28806-8563)
PHONE.................................855 462-9434
Todd Carriker, *Mgr*
EMP: 24 EST: 2013
SALES (est): 9.57MM **Privately Held**
Web: www.rhinonetworks.com
SIC: 3674 Integrated circuits, semiconductor
networks, etc.

(G-591)
RM LIQUIDATION INC (PA)
81 Thompson St (28803-2329)
PHONE.................................828 274-7996
Charlie Owen Iii, *Ch*
David Fann, *Pr*
Scott Pasquith, *Sec*
EMP: 64 EST: 2015
SALES (est): 12.15MM
SALES (corp-wide): 12.15MM **Privately
Held**
Web: www.relioninc.com
SIC: 3841 5047 5999 Surgical and medical
instruments; Medical equipment and
supplies; Medical apparatus and supplies

(G-592)
ROARING LION PUBLISHING
47 Stone River Dr (28804-4408)
PHONE.................................828 350-1454
Tony Balistreri, *Prin*
EMP: 5 EST: 2006
SALES (est): 241.79K **Privately Held**
Web: www.roaringlionpublishing.com
SIC: 2741 Miscellaneous publishing

(G-593)
ROCKGEIST LLC
2000 Riverside Dr Ste 33 (28804-2081)
PHONE.................................518 461-2009
EMP: 4 EST: 2017
SALES (est): 109.89K **Privately Held**
Web: www.rockgeist.com
SIC: 7389 3999 5941 Design services;
Manufacturing industries, nec; Backpacking
equipment

(G-594)
RUG & HOME INC
Also Called: Rug & Home
5 Rocky Ridge Rd (28806-2263)
PHONE.................................828 785-4480
EMP: 30 EST: 2009
SALES (est): 517.46K **Privately Held**
Web: www.rugandhome.com
SIC: 2273 Floor coverings, textile fiber

(G-595)
SAUNDRA D HALL
Also Called: Liberty Street Baggage
237 S Liberty St (28801-2334)
PHONE.................................828 251-9859
Saundra D Hall, *Owner*
EMP: 7 EST: 1991
SALES (est): 93.85K **Privately Held**
SIC: 3161 Luggage

(G-596)
SBFI-NORTH AMERICA INC (DH)
123 Lyman St (28801-4371)
P.O. Box 5677 (28813-5677)
PHONE.................................828 236-3993
Tom Finger, *Pr*
▲ EMP: 17 EST: 2005
SQ FT: 80,000
SALES (est): 24.09MM
SALES (corp-wide): 18.96MM **Privately
Held**
Web: www.sbfi-na.com
SIC: 2521 2522 Wood office furniture; Office
furniture, except wood
HQ: Sbfi Group Limited
International House
London E1W 1

(G-597)
SCIOLYTIX INC
Also Called: Digitalchalk
2 Town Square Blvd Ste 330 (28803-5035)
PHONE.................................877 321-2451
Richard Rawson, *Ch*
Richard G Rawson, *
John D Garr, *
Troy Tolle, *
Tony Mccune, *Marketing*
EMP: 40 EST: 2007
SALES (est): 2.05MM **Privately Held**
Web: www.digitalchalk.com
SIC: 7372 Application computer software

(G-598)
SHEP BERRYHILL WOODWORKING
197 Deaverview Rd (28806-1707)
PHONE.................................828 242-3227
Shep Berryhill, *Prin*
EMP: 4 EST: 2001
SALES (est): 129.09K **Privately Held**
SIC: 2431 Millwork

(G-599)
SILVER-LINE PLASTICS LLC (DH)
900 Riverside Dr (28804)
PHONE.................................828 252-8755
Ricky C Silver, *Pr*
William H Beard, *
Treena Cooper, *
◆ EMP: 121 EST: 1962
SQ FT: 98,000
SALES (est): 49.88MM
SALES (corp-wide): 8.01MM **Privately
Held**
Web: www.slpipe.com
SIC: 3084 Plastics pipe
HQ: Ipex Usa Llc
10100 Rodney Blvd
Pineville NC 28134

(G-600)
SIMPLESHOT INC
2000 Riverside Dr Ste 5a (28804-2061)
PHONE.................................888 202-7475
Nathan Masters, *CEO*
Nathan Wade Masters, *Pr*
EMP: 6 EST: 2012
SQ FT: 1,800
SALES (est): 440.63K **Privately Held**
Web: www.simple-shot.com
SIC: 3949 Archery equipment, general

(G-601)
SJR INCORPORATED
Also Called: Kitchens Unlimited Asheville
120 New Leicester Hwy (28806-1918)
PHONE.................................828 254-8966
James C Ramsey, *Pr*
Joy J Ramsey, *VP*
EMP: 14 EST: 1977
SQ FT: 6,000

SALES (est): 2.16MM **Privately Held**
Web: www.kitchensunlimitednc.com
SIC: 2434 Wood kitchen cabinets

(G-602)
**SMOKEY MOUNTAIN LUMBER INC
(PA)**
19 Lower Grassy Branch Rd (28805-1618)
P.O. Box 9207 (28815-0207)
PHONE.................................828 298-3958
Lynn L Fidler, *Pr*
Lynn C Fidler, *VP*
EMP: 5 EST: 1987
SQ FT: 10,000
SALES (est): 601.78K
SALES (corp-wide): 601.78K **Privately
Held**
Web:
www.smokeymountainlumberinc.com
SIC: 2431 5211 2439 Moldings, wood:
unfinished and prefinished; Millwork and
lumber; Structural wood members, nec

(G-603)
SMOKY MOUNTAIN MACHINING INC
80 Mcintosh Rd (28806-1406)
P.O. Box 6173 (28816-6173)
PHONE.................................828 665-1193
Paul Mckinney, *CEO*
Bryan Mckinney, *Pr*
Phil Skidmore, *
EMP: 65 EST: 1978
SQ FT: 30,000
SALES (est): 8.48MM **Privately Held**
Web: www.smmasheville.com
SIC: 3599 5571 Machine shop, jobbing and
repair; Motorcycle parts and accessories

(G-604)
SNYDER PAPER CORPORATION
85 Thompson St (28803-2329)
PHONE.................................800 222-8562
Craig Faircloth, *Brnch Mgr*
EMP: 6
SALES (corp-wide): 41.68MM **Privately
Held**
Web: www.snydersolutions.com
SIC: 2621 Text paper
PA: Snyder Paper Corporation
250 26th Street Dr Se
Hickory NC 28602
828 328-2501

(G-605)
SOULKU LLC (PA)
45 S French Broad Ave Ste 180
(28801-0188)
PHONE.................................828 273-4278
EMP: 16 EST: 2011
SALES (est): 2.05MM
SALES (corp-wide): 2.05MM **Privately
Held**
Web: www.soulku.com
SIC: 3911 5094 Jewelry, precious metal;
Jewelry

(G-606)
SOUP MAVEN LLC
Also Called: 18 Chestnuts
825 Merrimon Ave Ste C (28804-2467)
PHONE.................................727 919-5242
Ilona Kossoff, *CEO*
EMP: 6 EST: 2021
SALES (est): 605.26K **Privately Held**
SIC: 2032 Soups and broths, canned, jarred,
etc.

(G-607)
SOUTHBRIDGE INC
Also Called: Artful Shelter
2000 Riverside Dr Ste 5 (28804-2061)

P.O. Box 19539 (28815-1539)
PHONE.................................828 350-9112
Roger Roundtree, Pr
▲ EMP: 4 EST: 1990
SALES (est): 229.24K Privately Held
Web: www.artfulshelter.com
SIC: 2394 Tents: made from purchased
materials

(G-608)
**SOUTHERN CONCRETE MATERIALS
INC (HQ)**
35 Meadow Rd (28803)
P.O. Box 5395 (28813)
PHONE.................................828 253-6421
EMP: 120 EST: 1958
SALES (est): 83.49MM
SALES (corp-wide): 238.17MM Privately
Held
Web: www.scmusa.com
SIC: 3273 5211 Ready-mixed concrete;
Electrical construction materials
PA: B. V. Hedrick Gravel & Sand Company
120 1/2 Church St
Salisbury NC 28144
704 633-5982

(G-609)
SOUTHERN CONCRETE MTLS INC
80 Pond Rd (28806-2221)
P.O. Box 2569 (28806)
PHONE.................................828 670-6450
Matt Parrett, Mgr
EMP: 19
SALES (corp-wide): 238.17MM Privately
Held
Web: www.scmusa.com
SIC: 3273 Ready-mixed concrete
HQ: Southern Concrete Materials, Inc.
35 Meadow Rd
Asheville NC 28803
828 253-6421

(G-610)
SQUARE PEG CONSTRUCTION INC
28 London Rd (28803-2706)
PHONE.................................828 277-5164
Leslie Humphrey, Pr
EMP: 4 EST: 1999
SALES (est): 473.86K Privately Held
Web: www.squarepeginc.net
SIC: 2499 Decorative wood and woodwork

(G-611)
STAR FLEET COMMUNICATIONS INC
Also Called: Asheville Daily Planet, The
224 Broadway St (28801-2347)
P.O. Box 8081 (28814-8081)
PHONE.................................828 252-6565
John North, Pr
EMP: 8 EST: 2004
SALES (est): 162.51K Privately Held
Web: www.ashevilledailyplanet.com
SIC: 2711 Commercial printing and
newspaper publishing combined

(G-612)
SUNRISE SAWMILL INC
68 W Chapel Rd (28803-9694)
PHONE.................................828 277-0120
Don Shuford, Pr
Michelle Shuford, Sec
EMP: 4 EST: 1980
SQ FT: 2,720
SALES (est): 187.82K Privately Held
Web: www.sunrisesawmill.com
SIC: 2421 Lumber: rough, sawed, or planed

(G-613)
T PRECISION MACHINING INC
Also Called: T-Fab Precision Machining
123 Lyman St (28801-4371)
PHONE.................................828 250-0993
Tom Finger, Pr
▲ EMP: 14 EST: 1998
SALES (est): 1.32MM Privately Held
Web: www.t-fab.com
SIC: 3599 Machine shop, jobbing and repair

(G-614)
TA LOST PINES WOODWORK
24 Rose Hill Rd (28803-9586)
PHONE.................................828 367-7517
EMP: 6 EST: 2015
SALES (est): 79.37K Privately Held
SIC: 2431 Millwork

(G-615)
**THERMO ELCTRON SCNTFIC
INSTRS**
Also Called: Thermo Electron
501 Elk Park Dr (28804-2065)
PHONE.................................828 281-2651
EMP: 5
SALES (corp-wide): 42.86B Publicly Held
SIC: 3826 Analytical instruments
HQ: Thermo Electron Scientific Instruments
Llc
5225 Verona Rd
Madison WI 53711
608 276-6100

(G-616)
**THERMO FSHER SCNTFIC ASHVLLE
L (HQ)**
Also Called: Thermo Fisher Scientific
275 Aiken Rd (28804)
PHONE.................................828 658-2711
Bill Mcmahon, Pr
▲ EMP: 260 EST: 1996
SALES (est): 386.75MM
SALES (corp-wide): 42.86B Publicly Held
Web: www.marysittonteam.com
SIC: 3826 3821 3829 Analytical instruments;
Laboratory apparatus and furniture;
Measuring and controlling devices, nec
PA: Thermo Fisher Scientific Inc.
168 3rd Ave
Waltham MA 02451
781 622-1000

(G-617)
THROWIN STONES LLC
825c Merrimon Ave Ste 123 (28804-2404)
PHONE.................................828 280-7870
Rusty James, Mgr
EMP: 5 EST: 2015
SALES (est): 1.73MM Privately Held
Web: www.throwinstones.com
SIC: 1499 Semiprecious stones mining, nec

(G-618)
THUNDER EAGLE ENTERPRISES INC
165 Coleman Ave Apt 15d (28801-1381)
PHONE.................................828 242-0267
Erik Nordsell, CEO
EMP: 4 EST: 2013
SALES (est): 240.52K Privately Held
SIC: 2899 Oil treating compounds

(G-619)
TIARA INC
Also Called: Babeegreens
2002 Riverside Dr Ste 42k (28804-2052)
PHONE.................................828 484-8236
Rachel Friel, VP
EMP: 5 EST: 2010
SALES (est): 77.85K Privately Held

Web: www.babeegreens.com
SIC: 2361 5137 Girl's and children's
dresses, blouses; Infants' wear

(G-620)
TOMPKINS INDUSTRIES INC
Also Called: Philip Products
150 Westside Dr (28806-2847)
PHONE.................................828 254-2351
Dan Dippel, Mgr
EMP: 150
SALES (corp-wide): 48.56MM Privately
Held
Web: www.tompkinsind.com
SIC: 5031 3442 Windows; Metal doors,
sash, and trim
PA: Tompkins Industries, Inc.
1651 E Kansas City Rd
Olathe KS 66061
913 764-8088

(G-621)
TOURIST BASEBALL INC
Also Called: Asheville Tourist Baseball
30 Buchanan Pl (28801-4243)
PHONE.................................828 258-0428
Shawn Henry, Pr
Mike Bower, Ex Dir
EMP: 38 EST: 1976
SALES (est): 440.75K Privately Held
Web: www.theashevilletourists.com
SIC: 7941 2721 Baseball club, professional
and semi-professional; Periodicals

(G-622)
TRACYS GOURMET LLC
Also Called: Tracy's Gourmet
315 Old Haw Creek Rd (28805-1401)
PHONE.................................919 672-1731
EMP: 5 EST: 2013
SALES (est): 150.96K Privately Held
Web: www.tracysgourmet.com
SIC: 5149 2035 Salad dressing; Pickles,
sauces, and salad dressings

(G-623)
TRANE US INC
Also Called: Trane
168 Sweeten Creek Rd (28803-1526)
PHONE.................................828 277-8664
Marianne Mace, Mgr
EMP: 7
Web: www.trane.com
SIC: 3585 Refrigeration and heating
equipment
HQ: Trane U.S. Inc.
800-E Beaty St
Davidson NC 28036
704 655-4000

(G-624)
TRIBUNE PAPERS INC
P.O. Box 5005 (28813-5005)
PHONE.................................828 606-5050
Rich C Bradham Iii, Pr
EMP: 4 EST: 2019
SALES (est): 113.33K Privately Held
Web: www.tribpapers.com
SIC: 2711 Newspapers, publishing and
printing

(G-625)
TRVE-AVL LLC
255 Short Coxe Ave (28801-4143)
PHONE.................................303 909-1956
EMP: 4
SALES (est): 292K Privately Held
SIC: 2082 Malt beverages

(G-626)
TURNAMICS INC
25 Old County Home Rd (28806-9713)
PHONE.................................828 254-1059
Harvey Spiegel, Pr
Clint Spiegel, *
EMP: 42 EST: 1969
SALES (est): 11.48MM Privately Held
Web: www.turnamics.com
SIC: 3599 Custom machinery

(G-627)
UNISON ENGINE COMPONENTS INC
401 Sweeten Creek Industrial Park
(28803-1729)
PHONE.................................828 274-4540
Mike Grunza, Pr
◆ EMP: 380 EST: 1981
SQ FT: 20,000
SALES (est): 27.42MM
SALES (corp-wide): 38.7B Publicly Held
SIC: 3728 Aircraft parts and equipment, nec
PA: General Electric Company
1 Aviation Way
Cincinnati OH 45215
617 443-3000

(G-628)
URBAN ORCHARD CIDER COMPANY
24 Buxton Ave (28801-4020)
PHONE.................................252 904-5135
Thomas Hilliard Miller, Pr
EMP: 10 EST: 2021
SALES (est): 2.33MM Privately Held
Web: www.urbanorchardcider.com
SIC: 2084 Wines, brandy, and brandy spirits

(G-629)
US FILTER
1129 Sweeten Creek Rd (28803-1728)
PHONE.................................828 274-8282
Maurice Shuford, Prin
EMP: 4 EST: 1999
SALES (est): 219.78K Privately Held
SIC: 3569 Filters

(G-630)
VARIFORM INC
12 Gerber Rd Ste A (28803-2497)
PHONE.................................828 277-6420
EMP: 85
SALES (corp-wide): 5.58B Privately Held
SIC: 3089 Siding, plastics
HQ: Variform, Inc.
303 W Major St
Kearney MO 64060
919 677-3900

(G-631)
VENTURE PRODUCTS INTL INC
Also Called: Venture Products
27 Mulvaney St (28803-1457)
P.O. Box 1687 (28802-1687)
PHONE.................................828 285-0495
Stephen Mcleod, Pr
John W Mcleod Junior, Pr
▲ EMP: 9 EST: 1989
SQ FT: 43,000
SALES (est): 933.2K Privately Held
Web: www.ventureproducts.com
SIC: 3321 5013 Gray iron castings, nec;
Truck parts and accessories

(G-632)
WEDGE BREWING CO
125b Roberts St (28801-3128)
PHONE.................................828 505-2792
Timothy Paul Schaller, Prin
EMP: 8 EST: 2008
SALES (est): 1.15MM Privately Held

Web: www.wedgebrewing.com
SIC: 2082 Beer (alcoholic beverage)

(G-633)
WELLCO TWO INC
1835 Old Haywood Rd (28806-1129)
PHONE..................................828 667-4662
Timothy J Wells, *Prin*
EMP: 6 EST: 2005
SALES (est): 86.73K **Privately Held**
SIC: 2822 Synthetic rubber

(G-634)
WHITE KNGHT ENGNEERED PDTS INC
Also Called: White Knight Engineered
Products, Inc.
9 Sw Pack Sq Ste 201 (28801-3526)
PHONE..................................828 687-0940
EMP: 42
SALES (corp-wide): 23.16MM **Privately Held**
Web: www.wkep.com
SIC: 2326 Service apparel (baker, barber, lab, etc.), washable: men's
PA: Criticore, Inc.
9525 Monroe Rd Ste 150
Charlotte NC 28270
704 542-6876

(G-635)
WHITENER SALES COMPANY
91 Carter Cove Rd (28804-1743)
PHONE..................................828 253-0518
Pat Whitener, *Pr*
EMP: 4 EST: 1990
SALES (est): 117.85K **Privately Held**
SIC: 2411 Mine timbers, hewn

(G-636)
WILDWOOD STUDIOS INC
2163 Riceville Rd (28805-8709)
PHONE..................................828 299-8696
Carl Giesenschlag, *Pr*
Virginia Giesenschlag, *Sec*
EMP: 5 EST: 1984
SQ FT: 4,000
SALES (est): 484.24K **Privately Held**
Web: www.wildwdstudios.com
SIC: 2541 1751 5712 Cabinets, lockers, and shelving; Carpentry work; Customized furniture and cabinets

(G-637)
ZEAL INDUSTRIES LLC
101 Bee Ridge Rd (28803-9423)
PHONE..................................828 575-9894
EMP: 5 EST: 2013
SALES (est): 109.48K **Privately Held**
SIC: 3999 Manufacturing industries, nec

Atlantic
Carteret County

(G-638)
NORTHROP GRUMMAN SYSTEMS CORP
Also Called: Northrop Grmman Technical Svcs
Bldg 7029 (28511)
P.O. Box 99 (28511-0099)
PHONE..................................252 225-0911
Duke Savage, *Brnch Mgr*
EMP: 51
Web: www.northropgrumman.com
SIC: 3812 7374 7378 Search and navigation equipment; Computer processing services; Computer maintenance and repair

HQ: Northrop Grumman Systems
Corporation
2980 Fairview Park Dr
Falls Church VA 22042
703 280-2900

Atlantic Beach
Carteret County

(G-639)
EASTERN OFFSET PRINTING CO
410 W Fort Macon Rd (28512)
P.O. Box 1091 (28512)
PHONE..................................252 247-6791
Rebecca Mcmillan, *Owner*
EMP: 4 EST: 1984
SQ FT: 2,500
SALES (est): 219.41K **Privately Held**
Web: easternoffset.blogspot.com
SIC: 2752 Offset printing

Aulander
Bertie County

(G-640)
HOG SLAT INCORPORATED
440 Nc Highway 561 W (27805-9219)
PHONE..................................252 209-0092
Bridget Askew, *Mgr*
EMP: 12
SALES (corp-wide): 451.86MM **Privately Held**
Web: www.hogslat.com
SIC: 3523 Farm machinery and equipment
PA: Hog Slat, Incorporated
206 Fayetteville St
Newton Grove NC 28366
800 949-4647

Aurora
Beaufort County

(G-641)
AURORA PACKING CO INC
655 Second St (27806)
P.O. Box 354 (27806-0354)
PHONE..................................252 322-5232
Glenn Williamson, *Pr*
EMP: 4 EST: 1945
SQ FT: 6,200
SALES (est): 100.17K **Privately Held**
SIC: 2092 Crab meat, fresh: packaged in nonsealed containers

(G-642)
GLADSONS LOGGING LLC
8902 Nc Highway 306 S (27806-9184)
PHONE..................................252 670-8813
Gilbert A Gladson, *Prin*
EMP: 5 EST: 2014
SALES (est): 717.04K **Privately Held**
SIC: 2411 Logging camps and contractors

(G-643)
M F C INC
Hwy 33 (27806)
P.O. Box 309 (27806-0309)
PHONE..................................252 322-5004
John C Hooker Junior, *Pr*
John C Hooker Senior, *VP*
EMP: 48 EST: 1979
SQ FT: 16,000
SALES (est): 4.82MM **Privately Held**
SIC: 1542 3441 Commercial and office building, new construction; Fabricated structural metal

(G-644)
NUTRIEN AG SOLUTIONS INC
Also Called: Nutrien Phosphate
1530 Nc Highway 306 S (27806-9245)
PHONE..................................252 322-4111
William Ponton, *Brnch Mgr*
EMP: 950
SALES (corp-wide): 29.06B **Privately Held**
Web: www.nutrienagsolutions.com
SIC: 2873 Fertilizers: natural (organic), except compost
HQ: Nutrien Ag Solutions, Inc.
3005 Rocky Mountain Ave
Loveland CO 80538
970 685-3300

(G-645)
PCS PHOSPHATE COMPANY INC
P.O. Box 48 (27806-0048)
PHONE..................................252 322-4111
EMP: 30
SALES (corp-wide): 29.06B **Privately Held**
SIC: 1475 1474 2874 2819 Phosphate rock; Potash mining; Phosphatic fertilizers; Phosphates, except fertilizers: defluorinated and ammoniated
HQ: Pcs Phosphate Company, Inc.
1101 Skokie Blvd Ste 400
Northbrook IL 60062
847 849-4200

(G-646)
POTASH CORP SASKATCHEWAN INC
1530 Hwy 306 S (27806)
PHONE..................................252 322-4111
Mark Johnson, *Genl Mgr*
EMP: 44
SALES (corp-wide): 29.06B **Privately Held**
Web: www.nutrien.com
SIC: 2874 Phosphates
HQ: Potash Corporation Of Saskatchewan Inc
1700-211 19 St E
Saskatoon SK S7K 5
306 933-8500

Autryville
Sampson County

(G-647)
C & R BUILDING SUPPLY INC
2300 Ernest Williams Rd (28318-7954)
PHONE..................................910 567-6293
Charlie D Williams Junior, *Pr*
Regina Williams, *
EMP: 6 EST: 1970
SQ FT: 6,000
SALES (est): 1.34MM **Privately Held**
SIC: 2439 5211 Trusses, wooden roof; Lumber and other building materials

(G-648)
HONEYCUTT CUSTOM CABINETS INC
1068 Baptist Chapel Rd (28318-8220)
PHONE..................................910 567-6766
Joe Honeycutt, *Pt*
Greg Honeycutt, *Pt*
EMP: 22 EST: 1995
SALES (est): 1.84MM **Privately Held**
SIC: 2434 Wood kitchen cabinets

(G-649)
MAC GRADING CO
971 Leroy Autry Rd (28318-7053)
P.O. Box 376 (28318-0376)
PHONE..................................910 531-4642
Melissa Amos, *Pr*

Christopher Hales, *
EMP: 5 EST: 1998
SALES (est): 236.14K **Privately Held**
SIC: 5031 7699 2448 Pallets, wood; Pallet repair; Pallets, wood

Avon
Dare County

(G-650)
AVON SEAFOOD
Harbor Rd (27915)
P.O. Box 251 (27915-0251)
PHONE..................................252 995-4553
Tillman Gray, *Owner*
EMP: 6 EST: 1989
SALES (est): 218.76K **Privately Held**
Web: www.sunriseseafood.net
SIC: 2091 Fish, canned and cured

(G-651)
NORTH SPORTS INC
Also Called: Windsurfing Hatteras
Waterside Shops Hwy 45 (27915)
PHONE..................................252 995-4970
Brian Klouser, *Mgr*
EMP: 7
Web: www.oceanairsports.com
SIC: 3949 Windsurfing boards (sailboards) and equipment
PA: North Sports, Inc.
1345 Nw Wall St Ste 100
Bend OR 97703

Ayden
Pitt County

(G-652)
ANDERSON TRUSS COMPANY INC
4825 Anderson Truss Rd (28513-8635)
PHONE..................................252 746-7726
Greg Anderson, *Pr*
EMP: 12 EST: 1995
SALES (est): 2.84MM **Privately Held**
Web: www.andersontrussnc.com
SIC: 2439 Trusses, wooden roof

(G-653)
BABCO INC
639 Sumrell Rd (28513-8717)
PHONE..................................888 376-5083
David Orren Babcock, *Pr*
EMP: 9 EST: 2003
SALES (est): 281.34K **Privately Held**
SIC: 3499 Welding tips, heat resistant: metal

(G-654)
CLASSIC SEAFOOD GROUP INC
7178 Nc 11 S (28513-8404)
P.O. Box 10 (28513-0010)
PHONE..................................252 746-2818
Robert A Mayo, *Pr*
◆ EMP: 120 EST: 1985
SQ FT: 11,500
SALES (est): 7.15MM **Privately Held**
Web: www.classicseafoodgroup.com
SIC: 5146 2091 Seafoods; Fish, filleted (boneless)

(G-655)
CMI PLASTICS INC
222 Pepsi Way (28513-7609)
PHONE..................................252 746-2171
Steven Hasselbach, *CEO*
EMP: 26 EST: 2007
SALES (est): 4.96MM **Privately Held**
Web: www.cmiplastics.com

SIC: 3089 Injection molding of plastics

(G-656)
CONSOLIDATED MODELS INC
Also Called: CMI Plastics
222 Pepsi Way (28513-7609)
PHONE.................................252 746-2171
Stephen D Hasselbach, *CEO*
Steven A Hasselbach, *
Mark D Hasselbach, *
EMP: 50 **EST:** 1939
SQ FT: 70,000
SALES (est): 2.89MM **Privately Held**
Web: www.cmiplastics.com
SIC: 3089 Injection molding of plastics

(G-657)
FREE WILL BPTST PRESS FNDTION (PA)
Also Called: Cross & Crown
3928 Lee St (28513-3026)
P.O. Box 159 (28513-0159)
PHONE.................................252 746-6128
Rick Watson, *Pr*
Mike Scott, *Ch Bd*
Darren Davenport, *VP*
Mellinda Edwards, *Sec*
EMP: 10 **EST:** 1876
SQ FT: 20,000
SALES (est): 488.71K
SALES (corp-wide): 488.71K **Privately Held**
Web: www.mycrossandcrown.com
SIC: 5999 2741 5942 2791 Religious goods; Miscellaneous publishing; Book stores; Typesetting

(G-658)
QUILT LIZZY
4260 Lee St (28513-7178)
PHONE.................................252 257-3800
Susan Harris, *Prin*
EMP: 7 **EST:** 2011
SALES (est): 467.89K **Privately Held**
Web: www.quiltlizzy.com
SIC: 2395 Quilting and quilting supplies

(G-659)
READY MIXED CONCRETE
Also Called: Southern Equipment Company
3928 Jolly Rd (28513-8767)
P.O. Box 877 (27835-0877)
PHONE.................................252 758-1181
George C Turner, *S*
EMP: 7 **EST:** 2002
SQ FT: 1,200
SALES (est): 125.39K **Privately Held**
Web: www.dpdconcrete.com
SIC: 3273 Ready-mixed concrete

(G-660)
SIEBER INDUSTRIAL INC
221 Pepsi Way (28513-7609)
PHONE.................................252 746-2003
EMP: 10 **EST:** 2006
SQ FT: 17,000
SALES (est): 2.37MM **Privately Held**
Web: www.sieberindustrial.com
SIC: 3441 Fabricated structural metal

(G-661)
SIGNATURE SEASONINGS LLC
3254 Nc 102 E (28513-8566)
P.O. Box 56438 (23456-9438)
PHONE.................................252 746-1001
Chris Anderson, *Managing Member*
EMP: 8 **EST:** 2006
SQ FT: 9,500
SALES (est): 1.88MM **Privately Held**
Web: www.signatureseasonings.com

SIC: 2099 Seasonings and spices

(G-662)
SIMPLE & SENTIMENTAL LLC
6248 Nc 11 S (28513-8801)
PHONE.................................252 320-9458
Taylor Walden, *Managing Member*
EMP: 8 **EST:** 2017
SALES (est): 595.21K **Privately Held**
Web: www.simplesentimental.com
SIC: 2396 2752 5961 5947 Fabric printing and stamping; Commercial printing, lithographic; Electronic shopping; Gifts and novelties

(G-663)
SIMPLY NATURAL CREAMERY LLC
1265 Carson Edwards Rd (28513-2173)
PHONE.................................252 746-3334
Robert N Moye, *Mgr*
EMP: 20 **EST:** 2014
SALES (est): 2.32MM **Privately Held**
Web: www.simplynaturalcreamery.com
SIC: 2024 Ice cream and ice milk

(G-664)
SPM MACHINE WORKS INC
4721 Old Nc 11 (28513-8400)
P.O. Box 778 (28513-0778)
PHONE.................................252 321-2134
Yan Lin, *Prin*
Clint Sanders, *Prin*
EMP: 5 **EST:** 2006
SALES (est): 1.33MM **Privately Held**
Web: www.spmmachineworks.com
SIC: 3599 Machine shop, jobbing and repair

Badin
Stanly County

(G-665)
ALCOA POWER GENERATING INC
Also Called: Alcoa Badin Works
293 Nc Hwy 740 (28009)
P.O. Box 576 (28009-0576)
PHONE.................................704 422-5691
Larry E Tate, *Brnch Mgr*
EMP: 35
SALES (corp-wide): 11.89B **Publicly Held**
Web: www.alcoa.com
SIC: 3334 Primary aluminum
HQ: Alcoa Power Generating Inc.
201 Isabella St
Pittsburgh PA 15212
412 553-4545

Bahama
Durham County

(G-666)
LOUD LEMON BEVERAGE LLC
8512 Meadow View Ln (27503-8402)
PHONE.................................919 949-7649
William Jeffrey Outlaw, *Managing Member*
EMP: 4 **EST:** 2019
SALES (est): 223.57K **Privately Held**
Web: www.loudlemon.com
SIC: 2085 Cocktails, alcoholic

(G-667)
TERRY LOGGING COMPANY
7917 S Lowell Rd (27503-8746)
PHONE.................................919 477-9170
Davis Terry, *Owner*
EMP: 6 **EST:** 2000
SALES (est): 473.69K **Privately Held**

SIC: 2411 Logging camps and contractors

Bailey
Nash County

(G-668)
B & Y MACHINING CO INC
4495 Us Highway 264a (27807-9192)
PHONE.................................252 235-2180
Teresa Renfrow, *Pr*
Michael Renfrow, *Sec*
EMP: 4 **EST:** 1976
SQ FT: 10,000
SALES (est): 667.46K **Privately Held**
SIC: 3451 Screw machine products

(G-669)
DEAN ST PROCESSING LLC
5645 Deans St (27807-8642)
PHONE.................................252 235-0401
Barrett Twitty, *Pr*
EMP: 7 **EST:** 2014
SALES (est): 456.39K **Privately Held**
Web: www.deanstreetprocessing.com
SIC: 3556 Meat processing machinery

(G-670)
HEIDELBERG MTLS STHAST AGG LLC
P.O. Box 458 (27807-0458)
PHONE.................................252 235-4162
Chris White, *Mgr*
EMP: 10
SALES (corp-wide): 23.02B **Privately Held**
Web: www.hansonbiz.com
SIC: 1429 Trap rock, crushed and broken-quarrying
HQ: Heidelberg Materials Southeast Agg Llc
3237 Satellite Blvd # 30
Duluth GA 30096
770 491-2756

(G-671)
IMAGE DESIGNS INK LLC
12687 Sanford St (27807-9623)
P.O. Box 277 (27807-0277)
PHONE.................................252 235-1964
Amy Pearson, *Managing Member*
EMP: 9 **EST:** 2013
SALES (est): 303.59K **Privately Held**
Web: www.imagedesignsink.com
SIC: 2759 Screen printing

(G-672)
NUTRIEN AG SOLUTIONS INC
9702 Global Rd (27807)
P.O. Box 577 (27807-0577)
PHONE.................................252 235-4161
Larry Boyant, *Mgr*
EMP: 4
SALES (corp-wide): 29.06B **Privately Held**
Web: www.nutrienagsolutions.com
SIC: 2873 Nitrogenous fertilizers
HQ: Nutrien Ag Solutions, Inc.
3005 Rocky Mountain Ave
Loveland CO 80538
970 685-3300

(G-673)
PBS VENTURES INC
5469 Us Highway 264a (27807-9002)
PHONE.................................252 235-2001
EMP: 5
SALES (corp-wide): 1.9MM **Privately Held**
SIC: 3089 Injection molding of plastics
PA: Pbs Ventures, Inc.
131 Johnston Pkwy
Kenly NC 27542
919 284-9001

(G-674)
WOODWORKING UNLIMITED
6378 Vance St (27807-9609)
PHONE.................................252 235-5285
Isaac Glenn Perry, *Owner*
EMP: 4 **EST:** 1985
SALES (est): 208.03K **Privately Held**
Web: www.expiredwixdomain.com
SIC: 2434 Wood kitchen cabinets

Bakersville
Mitchell County

(G-675)
BETTER PUBLISHING INC
467 Byrd Rd (28705-7854)
PHONE.................................828 688-9188
Doug Harrell, *CEO*
EMP: 4 **EST:** 2004
SALES (est): 184.36K **Privately Held**
SIC: 2741 Miscellaneous publishing

(G-676)
COVIA HOLDINGS CORPORATION
Also Called: COVIA HOLDINGS CORPORATION
2241 Nc 197 (28705-7899)
PHONE.................................828 688-2169
EMP: 5
SALES (corp-wide): 1.47B **Privately Held**
Web: www.coviacorp.com
SIC: 1446 Industrial sand
PA: Covia Holdings Llc
3 Summit Park Dr Ste 700
Independence OH 44131
800 243-9004

(G-677)
COVIA HOLDINGS LLC
Red Hill Iota Plant (28705)
PHONE.................................828 688-2169
EMP: 4
SALES (corp-wide): 1.47B **Privately Held**
Web: www.coviacorp.com
SIC: 1446 Industrial sand
PA: Covia Holdings Llc
3 Summit Park Dr Ste 700
Independence OH 44131
800 243-9004

(G-678)
JAMES W MCMANUS INC
Also Called: McManus Microwave
2419 Beans Creek Rd (28705-7747)
PHONE.................................828 688-2560
James W Mcmanus, *Pr*
EMP: 9 **EST:** 1981
SALES (est): 1.09MM **Privately Held**
Web: www.mcmanusmicrowave.com
SIC: 3679 3812 Microwave components; Search and navigation equipment

(G-679)
LEDGER HARDWARE INC
Also Called: Ace Hardware
5489 S 226 Hwy (28705-7329)
PHONE.................................828 688-4798
James P Webb, *Pr*
Charles S Webb, *Sec*
EMP: 8 **EST:** 1987
SQ FT: 12,000
SALES (est): 399.88K **Privately Held**
Web: www.acehardware.com
SIC: 5251 5231 5084 3546 Hardware stores; Paint; Engines, gasoline; Saws and sawing equipment

G E O G R A P H I C

(G-680)
PERKINS FABRICATIONS INC
5632 Nc 261 (28705-7709)
PHONE..............................828 688-3157
Kay Perkins, *Prin*
EMP: 4 **EST:** 2010
SALES (est): 91.37K **Privately Held**
SIC: 7692 Welding repair

(G-681)
TOE RIVER SERVICE STATION LLC
4928 S 226 Hwy (28705-7256)
PHONE..............................828 688-6385
Daniel Pitman, *Owner*
Daniel Pitman, *Managing Member*
EMP: 4 **EST:** 1999
SALES (est): 223.1K **Privately Held**
SIC: 7534 Tire repair shop

Banner Elk
Avery County

(G-682)
BANNER ELK WINERY INC
Also Called: Winery At The Blueberry Farm
135 Deer Run Ln (28604-6529)
PHONE..............................828 898-9090
Richard Arlen Wolfe, *Brnch Mgr*
EMP: 4
SALES (corp-wide): 271.99K **Privately Held**
Web: www.bannerelkwinery.com
SIC: 2084 Wines
PA: Banner Elk Winery Inc
　　60 Deer Run Ln
　　Banner Elk NC 28604
　　828 260-1790

(G-683)
DARK MOON DISTILERIES LLC
60 Deer Run, Banner Elk (28604)
P.O. Box 30 (28168-0030)
PHONE..............................704 222-8063
Anthony Pruitt, *Managing Member*
EMP: 9 **EST:** 2021
SALES (est): 241.56K **Privately Held**
SIC: 2085 Distilled and blended liquors

(G-684)
DEWOOLFSON DOWN INTL INC (PA)
Also Called: Dewoolfson Down
9452 Nc Highway 105 S (28604-8646)
PHONE..............................828 963-2750
Richard B Schaffer, *Pr*
Marsha Turner, *Sec*
▲ **EMP:** 7 **EST:** 1983
SQ FT: 3,300
SALES (est): 965.81K
SALES (corp-wide): 965.81K **Privately Held**
Web: www.dewoolfsonlinens.com
SIC: 2392 5719 Comforters and quilts: made from purchased materials; Beddings and linens

(G-685)
GRANDFATHER VINYRD WINERY LLC
225 Vineyard Ln (28604-8053)
PHONE..............................828 963-2400
Dylan Tatum, *Mgr*
EMP: 9 **EST:** 2017
SALES (est): 641.31K **Privately Held**
Web: www.grandfathervineyard.com
SIC: 2084 Wines

(G-686)
HIGH CNTRY CBNETS BNNER ELK IN
2850 Tynecastle Hwy (28604-9716)
P.O. Box 2243 (28604-2243)
PHONE..............................828 898-3435
John Page, *Pr*
EMP: 5 **EST:** 2006
SQ FT: 800
SALES (est): 474.31K **Privately Held**
Web: www.highcountrycabinets.com
SIC: 2434 Wood kitchen cabinets

(G-687)
MASTER TESH STONE WORKS
Also Called: Master Tesh Stone Works The
1921 Tynecastle Hwy (28604-9709)
P.O. Box 733 (28604-0733)
PHONE..............................828 898-8333
Michael Tesh, *Owner*
EMP: 6 **EST:** 2002
SALES (est): 147.88K **Privately Held**
Web:
www.masterstouchstoneworks.com
SIC: 3281 5211 Granite, cut and shaped; Counter tops

(G-688)
MITERS TOUCH INC
Also Called: Miters Touch
591 Old Hartley Rd (28604-9142)
PHONE..............................828 963-4445
Denise R Grohs, *Pr*
Marshall J Stein, *VP*
EMP: 5 **EST:** 1982
SALES (est): 98.98K **Privately Held**
SIC: 2431 5712 2434 Woodwork, interior and ornamental, nec; Furniture stores; Wood kitchen cabinets

(G-689)
TATUM GALLERIES INC
5320 Nc Highway 105 S (28604-8726)
PHONE..............................828 963-6466
Stephen Tatum, *Pr*
Sally Tatum, *Sec*
EMP: 8 **EST:** 1983
SQ FT: 8,000
SALES (est): 674.2K **Privately Held**
Web: www.tatumgalleries.com
SIC: 5712 2511 7389 Furniture stores; Wood household furniture; Interior design services

(G-690)
VAUGHN WOODWORKING INC
442 Aldridge Rd (28604-9002)
PHONE..............................828 963-6858
Henry Vaughn, *Pr*
EMP: 6 **EST:** 1981
SALES (est): 235.88K **Privately Held**
Web: www.vaughnwoodworking.com
SIC: 1751 2499 Cabinet and finish carpentry; Carved and turned wood

Barnardsville
Buncombe County

(G-691)
DOMCO TECHNOLOGY LLC
1342 Barnardsville Hwy Ste A
(28709-9709)
PHONE..............................888 834-8541
Quincey Brock, *Managing Member*
EMP: 4 **EST:** 2013
SALES (est): 80.38K **Privately Held**
Web: www.domco.us
SIC: 2741 Internet publishing and broadcasting

(G-692)
HARLEY S WOODWORKS INC
917 N Fork Rd (28709-9760)
PHONE..............................828 776-0120
Harley Stewart, *Prin*
EMP: 4 **EST:** 2008
SALES (est): 239.92K **Privately Held**
Web: www.washluberepair.com
SIC: 2431 Millwork

(G-693)
OHIO ELECTRIC MOTORS INC
30 Paint Fork Rd (28709)
P.O. Box 172 (28787)
PHONE..............................828 626-2901
Randy L Greely, *Prin*
Mark R Dyll, *
Michael T Clancey, *
Robert A Sirak, *
◆ **EMP:** 63 **EST:** 1979
SQ FT: 80,000
SALES (est): 9.92MM
SALES (corp-wide): 241.4MM **Privately Held**
Web: www.ohioelectricmotors.com
SIC: 3621 Motors, electric
HQ: Peerless-Winsmith, Inc.
　　5200 Upper Mtro Pl Ste 11
　　Dublin OH 43017
　　614 526-7000

(G-694)
SMILING HARA LLC
Also Called: Smiling Hara Tempeh
735 N Fork Rd (28709-8711)
P.O. Box 570 (28709-0570)
PHONE..............................828 545-4150
Sarah Yancey, *Managing Member*
EMP: 4 **EST:** 2011
SALES (est): 373.38K **Privately Held**
Web: www.eathempeh.com
SIC: 2099 Food preparations, nec

Battleboro
Edgecombe County

(G-695)
BERRY GLOBAL INC
6941 Corporation Pkwy (27809-9274)
PHONE..............................252 984-4100
EMP: 4
Web: www.berryglobal.com
SIC: 3089 Plastics containers, except foam
HQ: Berry Global, Inc.
　　101 Oakley St
　　Evansville IN 47710

(G-696)
DELIZZA LLC
6610 Corporation Pkwy (27809-9804)
PHONE..............................252 442-0270
Raymond Laruelle, *CEO*
Frans Castelein, *Pr*
Delizza Pattiserie, *Sec*
Brian Hill, *VP*
▲ **EMP:** 10 **EST:** 1999
SQ FT: 6,000
SALES (est): 704.48K **Privately Held**
Web: www.delizza.us
SIC: 2024 Dairy based frozen desserts

(G-697)
FLOW X RAY CORPORATION
Also Called: Flow Dental
133 Wolf Rd (27809-7502)
PHONE..............................631 242-9729
Carolyn Camiola, *CEO*
Martin B Wolf, *
Howard Wolf, *
Arlene Wolf, *
Carolyn Price, *
▲ **EMP:** 72 **EST:** 1974
SALES (est): 2.49MM **Privately Held**
Web: www.flowdental.com
SIC: 3844 X-ray apparatus and tubes

(G-698)
HANOR CO INC
6717 Nc 97 W (27809-8956)
PHONE..............................252 977-0035
EMP: 7 **EST:** 1993
SALES (est): 541.52K **Privately Held**
Web: www.hanorcompany.com
SIC: 2099 Food preparations, nec

(G-699)
HOSPIRA INC
6551 N Us Highway 301 (27809-9778)
PHONE..............................252 977-5111
Terry Chavis, *Prin*
EMP: 28
SALES (corp-wide): 63.63B **Publicly Held**
Web: www.pfizerhospitalus.com
SIC: 2834 Pharmaceutical preparations
HQ: Hospira, Inc.
　　275 N Field Dr
　　Lake Forest IL 60045
　　224 212-2000

(G-700)
LANE LAND & TIMBER INC
5631 Hart Farm Rd (27809-9171)
PHONE..............................252 443-1151
Ralph H Lane, *Pr*
Ray Jordan, *Sec*
EMP: 5 **EST:** 1968
SALES (est): 506.28K **Privately Held**
SIC: 2411 0811 Logging camps and contractors; Timber tracts

(G-701)
LOG CABIN HOMES LTD
7677 N Halifax Rd (27809-9601)
PHONE..............................252 454-1548
Barbara Muller, *Mgr*
EMP: 8
SALES (corp-wide): 7.91MM **Privately Held**
Web: www.logcabinhomes.com
SIC: 2452 Log cabins, prefabricated, wood
PA: Log Cabin Homes Ltd.
　　513 Keen St 515
　　Rocky Mount NC 27804
　　252 454-1500

(G-702)
MONSANTO COMPANY
Also Called: MONSANTO COMPANY
5746 Pearsall St (27809-9184)
PHONE..............................252 212-5421
EMP: 6
SALES (corp-wide): 49.29B **Privately Held**
Web: www.monsanto.com
SIC: 2879 Agricultural chemicals, nec
HQ: Monsanto Technology Llc.
　　800 North Lindbergh Blvd
　　Saint Louis MO 63167
　　314 694-1000

(G-703)
NUTKAO USA INC
7044 Nc 48 (27809-9561)
PHONE..............................252 595-1000
Luca Benedetto, *CEO*
Davide Braida, *
◆ **EMP:** 42 **EST:** 2013
SQ FT: 100,000
SALES (est): 11.91MM
SALES (corp-wide): 29.76MM **Privately Held**

Web: www.nutkao.com
SIC: 2066 Chocolate
HQ: Nutkao Srl
Via Alcide De Gasperi 2/Rstu
Govone CN 12040
017 362-1211

(G-704)
OSSID LLC (DH)
4000 College Rd (27809-8500)
P.O. Box 1968 (27802-1968)
PHONE..............................252 446-6177
Bud Lane, *Managing Member*
Kim Brewer, *
Jimmy Hemric, *
▲ EMP: 78 EST: 1981
SQ FT: 80,000
SALES (est): 24.34MM Privately Held
Web: www.ossid.com
SIC: 3565 Packaging machinery
HQ: Pro Mach, Inc.
50 E Rvrcnter Blvd Ste 18
Covington KY 41011
513 831-8778

(G-705)
PFIZER INC
6563 N Us Highway 301 (27809-9778)
PHONE..............................252 382-3309
EMP: 5
SALES (corp-wide): 63.63B Publicly Held
Web: www.pfizer.com
SIC: 2834 Pharmaceutical preparations
PA: Pfizer Inc.
66 Hudson Blvd E
New York NY 10001
212 733-2323

(G-706)
PHOENIX ASSEMBLY NC LLC
7101 N Us Highway 301 (27809-9651)
PHONE..............................252 801-4250
Brian Cousins, *Mgr*
EMP: 8 EST: 2010
SALES (est): 898.03K Privately Held
SIC: 3569 4225 4731 8741 Assembly
machines, non-metalworking; General
warehousing; Freight transportation
arrangement; Industrial management
HQ: Phoenix Assembly, Llc
164 S Park Blvd
Greenwood IN 46143
317 884-3600

(G-707)
POPPIES INTERNATIONAL I INC
6610 Corporation Pkwy (27809-9804)
PHONE..............................252 442-4016
Frans Castelein, *Pr*
Raymond Laruelle, *
Bobby Davis, *
Anthony Popelier, *
▲ EMP: 70 EST: 1999
SALES (est): 22.21MM
SALES (corp-wide): 7.75MM Privately
Held
Web: www.poppiesbakeries.com
SIC: 2038 Frozen specialties, nec
HQ: Poppies Bakeries
Kasteelstraat 29
Zonnebeke VWV 8980
57460200

(G-708)
WAKE STONE CORP
7379 N Halifax Rd (27809-9569)
PHONE..............................252 985-4411
Chris Puns, *Superintnt*
EMP: 6 EST: 1990
SALES (est): 1.14MM Privately Held
Web: www.wakestonecorp.com

SIC: 1429 1423 Grits mining (crushed stone)
; Crushed and broken granite

(G-709)
WEBB S MAINT & PIPING INC
217 Daniels Ave (27809-7509)
P.O. Box 928 (27809-0928)
PHONE..............................252 972-2616
James Dustin Webb, *Pr*
Ramsey Webb, *Sec*
EMP: 18 EST: 1991
SQ FT: 15,000
SALES (est): 904.91K Privately Held
SIC: 7692 Welding repair

(G-710)
WOLF X-RAY CORPORATION
133 Wolf Rd (27809-7502)
PHONE..............................631 242-9729
Carolyn Camiola, *CEO*
Martin Wolf, *
▲ EMP: 68 EST: 1931
SALES (est): 1.92MM Privately Held
Web: www.wolfxray.com
SIC: 3844 X-ray apparatus and tubes

Bayboro
Pamlico County

(G-711)
HARDISON TIRE CO INC
13504 Nc Highway 55 (28515-9106)
PHONE..............................252 745-4561
Elmo Hardison, *Pr*
Barry Hardison, *VP*
EMP: 10 EST: 1974
SALES (est): 89.28K Privately Held
Web: www.hardisontire.com
SIC: 7534 5541 Tire repair shop; Gasoline
service stations

Bear Creek
Chatham County

(G-712)
BEAR CREEK FABRICATION LLC
1930 Campbell Rd (27207-9484)
PHONE..............................919 837-2444
Allen Johnson, *CEO*
EMP: 14 EST: 2008
SALES (est): 5.15MM Privately Held
Web: www.bearcreekfabrication.com
SIC: 3441 Fabricated structural metal

(G-713)
CENTRAL CAROLINA BTLG CO INC
1506 Mays Chapel Rd (27207-8219)
PHONE..............................919 542-3226
Staffany Smith, *Pr*
EMP: 4 EST: 1998
SALES (est): 191.65K Privately Held
Web: www.grandsprings.com
SIC: 2086 Carbonated soft drinks, bottled
and canned

(G-714)
GARY TUCKER
Also Called: Tucker Welding
12988 Nc 902 Hwy (27207-9293)
PHONE..............................919 837-5724
Gary Tucker, *Owner*
EMP: 4 EST: 1977
SQ FT: 1,600
SALES (est): 504.05K Privately Held
SIC: 7692 Welding repair

(G-715)
LILAS TRUNK
145 Cc Routh Rd (27207-9120)
PHONE..............................919 548-0784
Shelly Joyce, *Prin*
EMP: 5 EST: 2011
SALES (est): 148.98K Privately Held
SIC: 3161 Trunks

(G-716)
MOORE S WELDING SERVICE INC
142 Elmer Moore Rd (27207-9341)
PHONE..............................919 837-5769
Lewis D Moore Senior, *Pr*
Lewis D Moore Junior, *VP*
Ann Moore, *Sec*
EMP: 7 EST: 1970
SQ FT: 12,250
SALES (est): 389.36K Privately Held
Web:
www.mooresweldingandcraneservice.com
SIC: 7692 3452 7389 Welding repair; Bolts,
metal; Crane and aerial lift service

(G-717)
**MOORES MCH CO FAYETTEVILLE
INC (PA)**
13120 Nc 902 Hwy (27207-9295)
PHONE..............................919 837-5354
E Eugene Moore, *Pr*
Ruby Moore, *
▲ EMP: 100 EST: 1971
SQ FT: 22,500
SALES (est): 1.22MM
SALES (corp-wide): 1.22MM Privately
Held
SIC: 3542 3469 7692 3714 Rebuilt machine
tools, metal forming types; Machine parts,
stamped or pressed metal; Welding repair;
Motor vehicle parts and accessories

(G-718)
SCOTTS & ASSOCIATES INC
Also Called: Southern Supreme Fruit Cakes
1699 Hoyt Scott Rd (27207-8727)
PHONE..............................336 581-3141
Hoyt Scott, *Pt*
Berta Scott, *Pt*
Lisa Scott, *Pt*
Belinda Jordan, *Pt*
Wayne Jordan, *Pt*
▲ EMP: 12 EST: 1985
SQ FT: 7,400
SALES (est): 2.91MM Privately Held
Web: www.southernsupreme.com
SIC: 2051 2052 2099 Cakes, bakery: except
frozen; Cookies; Food preparations, nec

Beaufort
Carteret County

(G-719)
**ATLANTIC VENEER COMPANY LLC
(HQ)**
Also Called: Moehring-Group
2457 Lennoxville Rd (28516-7899)
P.O. Box 660 (28516)
PHONE..............................252 728-3169
Christian Weygoldp, *CEO*
Mike Kraszeski, *
John Varner, *
▼ EMP: 145 EST: 1964
SQ FT: 750,000
SALES (est): 23.89MM
SALES (corp-wide): 23.89MM Privately
Held
Web: www.moehring-group.com
SIC: 2435 Plywood, hardwood or hardwood
faced

PA: Moehring Group Holding, Llc
2457 Lennoxville Rd
Beaufort NC 28516
252 728-3169

(G-720)
**BARBOUR S MARINE SUPPLY CO
INC**
410 Hedrick St (28516-2019)
P.O. Box 248 (28516-0248)
PHONE..............................252 728-2136
Nelson B Gillikin Ii, *Pr*
Harold Booth Iii, *VP*
EMP: 4 EST: 1919
SQ FT: 5,000
SALES (est): 894.14K Privately Held
Web: www.mooresmarine.com
SIC: 5088 5551 3599 Marine supplies;
Marine supplies, nec; Machine shop,
jobbing and repair

(G-721)
BEAUFORT COMPOSITE TECH INC
Also Called: Composites.com
111 Safrit Dr (28516-9017)
PHONE..............................252 728-1547
Phil Herting, *Pr*
EMP: 9 EST: 1995
SQ FT: 11,000
SALES (est): 988.96K Privately Held
Web: www.composites.com
SIC: 3089 Molding primary plastics

(G-722)
CCBS & SIGN SHOP INC
1626 Live Oak St (28516-1532)
PHONE..............................252 728-4866
Kimberly Beasley, *Pr*
Joseph Beasley, *VP*
EMP: 7 EST: 2007
SQ FT: 4,500
SALES (est): 328.96K Privately Held
Web: www.ccbsandsignshop.com
SIC: 3993 Signs and advertising specialties

(G-723)
COASTAL CANVAS MFG INC
Also Called: Coastal Canvas
1403 Harkers Island Rd (28516-7226)
PHONE..............................252 728-4946
Michael Sasser, *Pr*
Joyce Sasser, *Off Mgr*
EMP: 4 EST: 1985
SQ FT: 2,000
SALES (est): 239.35K Privately Held
Web: www.coastalcanvasmfg.com
SIC: 2394 Awnings, fabric: made from
purchased materials

(G-724)
**CONWAY ENTPS CARTERET CNTY
LLC**
313 Laurel Rd (28516-6553)
PHONE..............................252 504-3518
Bruce Conway, *Prin*
EMP: 4 EST: 2011
SALES (est): 203.76K Privately Held
Web: www.conway-enterprises.com
SIC: 2451 Mobile buildings: for commercial
use

(G-725)
CURRIER WOODWORKS INC
1622 Live Oak St (28516-1532)
PHONE..............................252 725-4233
Donald H Currier, *Pr*
Judith Currier, *Treas*
EMP: 4 EST: 1993
SALES (est): 240.76K Privately Held
Web: www.currierwoodworks.com

SIC: 2431 Millwork

(G-726)
FISHERMAN CREATIONS INC
1175 Hwy 70 Otway (28516-7206)
P.O. Box 118 (28512-0118)
PHONE.....................................252 725-0138
Donald Acree, *Pr*
George Brearey, *VP*
Loretta Acree, *Sec*
EMP: 20 **EST:** 2009
SQ FT: 2,400
SALES (est): 447.15K **Privately Held**
Web: www.crabpottrees.com
SIC: 3999 5093 Christmas trees, artificial;
  Scrap and waste materials

(G-727)
FRONT STREET VLG MSTR ASSN
INC
2450 Lennoxville Rd (28516-7898)
PHONE.....................................252 838-1524
Oliver Charles Ii, *Prin*
EMP: 5 **EST:** 2010
SALES (est): 316.32K **Privately Held**
Web: www.boathousemarinanc.com
SIC: 2335 Wedding gowns and dresses

(G-728)
GILLIKIN MARINE RAILWAYS INC
Also Called: Morgan Creek Seafood
195 Morgan Rd (28516-8656)
P.O. Box 533 (28516-0533)
PHONE.....................................252 726-7284
James Gillikin, *Pr*
Jeannette Josey, *Sec*
EMP: 9 **EST:** 1971
SQ FT: 9,120
SALES (est): 368.04K **Privately Held**
SIC: 3732 5146 Boatbuilding and repairing;
  Seafoods

(G-729)
HANCOCK & GRANDSON INC
971 Harkers Island Rd (28516-7290)
PHONE.....................................252 728-2416
Deena Lynk, *Pr*
Lisa Guthrie, *Sec*
EMP: 5 **EST:** 1989
SALES (est): 1.26MM **Privately Held**
SIC: 3599 7692 Machine shop, jobbing and
  repair; Welding repair

(G-730)
HARDING ENTERPRISE INC
Also Called: Carolina Yachts
1110 Spartina Dr (28516-7760)
PHONE.....................................252 725-9785
William Harding, *Pr*
Tracy Harding, *VP*
EMP: 8 **EST:** 2011
SALES (est): 153.91K **Privately Held**
Web: www.carolinayachtsnc.com
SIC: 3732 Boatbuilding and repairing

(G-731)
OLIVE BEAUFORT OIL COMPANY
300 Front St Ste 4 (28516)
PHONE.....................................252 504-2474
Merrell Clarke, *Prin*
EMP: 4 **EST:** 2014
SALES (est): 175.47K **Privately Held**
Web: www.beaufortoliveoil.com
SIC: 2079 Olive oil

(G-732)
ONE HUNDRED TEN PERCENT
SCREEN
150 Lake Rd (28516-7546)
PHONE.....................................252 728-3848

Carlos Sanderson, *Owner*
EMP: 4 **EST:** 1991
SALES (est): 161.48K **Privately Held**
SIC: 2261 Screen printing of cotton
  broadwoven fabrics

(G-733)
PARKER MARINE ENTERPRISES INC
2570 Nc Highway 101 (28516-7751)
P.O. Box 2129 (28516-5129)
PHONE.....................................252 728-5621
E Linwood Parker Iii, *Pr*
Trudy G Parker, *
▼ **EMP:** 62 **EST:** 1960
SQ FT: 100,000
SALES (est): 5.17MM **Privately Held**
Web: www.parkerboats.com
SIC: 3732 Boats, fiberglass: building and
  repairing

(G-734)
SOL-REX MINIATURE LAMP WORKS
802 Mulberry St (28516-1936)
PHONE.....................................845 292-1510
Charles Perrenod Junior, *Owner*
EMP: 4 **EST:** 1931
SALES (est): 232.25K **Privately Held**
SIC: 3641 Lamps, incandescent filament,
  electric

(G-735)
STARFLITE COMPANIES INC (PA)
530 Sensation Weigh (28516-7672)
PHONE.....................................252 728-2690
▼ **EMP:** 123 **EST:** 1986
SALES (est): 9.19MM **Privately Held**
Web: www.jarrettbay.com
SIC: 3732 5983 5947 Boatbuilding and
  repairing; Fuel oil dealers; Gift shop

(G-736)
TRITON MARINE SERVICES INC
1050 Sensation Weigh (28516-7759)
P.O. Box 486 (28516-0486)
PHONE.....................................252 728-9958
Angela Mcmahon, *Pr*
Croy Mcmahon, *VP*
EMP: 5 **EST:** 2001
SQ FT: 60,000
SALES (est): 787.9K **Privately Held**
Web: www.triton-marine.net
SIC: 1629 3663 7699 Marine construction;
  Marine radio communications equipment;
  Marine engine repair

(G-737)
WOOD SURGEON
1403 Lennoxville Rd (28516-9023)
PHONE.....................................252 728-5767
Kemp Guthrie, *Owner*
EMP: 7 **EST:** 1989
SALES (est): 162.77K **Privately Held**
SIC: 2431 Millwork

Beech Mountain
Avery County

(G-738)
MORETZ SIGNS INC
Also Called: Signs By Tomorrow
125 Staghorn Hollow Rd (28604-8218)
PHONE.....................................828 387-4600
Dorothy Moretz, *Pr*
Michael Moretz, *VP*
EMP: 6 **EST:** 1997
SQ FT: 1,660
SALES (est): 95.48K **Privately Held**
Web: www.signsbytomorrow.com

SIC: 3993 Signs and advertising specialties

Belews Creek
Forsyth County

(G-739)
TITAN AMERICA LLC
3193 Pine Hall Rd (27009-9157)
PHONE.....................................336 754-0143
Eric Poitras, *Pr*
EMP: 5
SALES (corp-wide): 8.01MM **Privately**
Held
Web: www.titanamerica.com
SIC: 3273 Ready-mixed concrete
HQ: Titan America Llc
  5700 Lk Wright Dr Ste 300
  Norfolk VA 23502
  757 858-6500

Belmont
Gaston County

(G-740)
ALAMO DISTRIBUTION LLC (DH)
Also Called: Alamo Iron Works
2100 Oaks Pkwy (28012-5141)
PHONE.....................................704 398-5600
Frances Shey, *Pr*
James C Melton, *
▼ **EMP:** 113 **EST:** 2010
SALES (est): 25.67MM **Privately Held**
SIC: 5051 3441 3443 3444 Steel; Fabricated
  structural metal; Fabricated plate work
  (boiler shop); Sheet metalwork
HQ: Vallen Distribution, Inc.
  2100 The Oaks Pkwy
  Belmont NC 28012

(G-741)
CARUS LLC
181 Woodlawn St (28012-2149)
PHONE.....................................704 822-1441
Craig Mazzucca, *Brnch Mgr*
EMP: 24
SALES (corp-wide): 117.4MM **Privately**
Held
Web: www.carusllc.com
SIC: 2819 Industrial inorganic chemicals, nec
HQ: Carus Llc
  315 5th St
  Peru IL 61354
  815 223-1500

(G-742)
CERTIFIED LAWNMOWER INC
124 Hubbard St (28012-2951)
PHONE.....................................704 527-2765
Carlos Romeros, *Pr*
Graciela Romeros, *Sec*
EMP: 7 **EST:** 1977
SALES (est): 279.94K **Privately Held**
Web: www.certifiedlawnmowers.com
SIC: 7699 3524 5261 Lawn mower repair
  shop; Lawn and garden equipment; Garden
  tractors and tillers

(G-743)
CHAMPIONX LLC
2000 Oaks Pkwy (28012-5133)
PHONE.....................................704 506-4830
EMP: 5
SALES (corp-wide): 3.63B **Publicly Held**
Web: www.championx.com
SIC: 2899 Chemical preparations, nec
HQ: Championx Llc
  2445 Tech Frest Blvd Bldg
  The Woodlands TX 77381
  281 632-6500

(G-744)
CUSTOM INDUSTRIES INC
Also Called: Contract Manufacturing Div
111 Hubbard St (28012-2947)
P.O. Box 785 (28012-0785)
PHONE.....................................704 825-3346
Paul Heffner, *Mgr*
EMP: 13
SALES (corp-wide): 2.26MM **Privately**
Held
Web: www.customindustries.com
SIC: 3552 3599 Textile machinery; Machine
  and other job shop work
PA: Custom Industries, Inc.
  215 Aloe Rd
  Greensboro NC 27409
  336 299-2885

(G-745)
DELLINGER ENTERPRISES LTD
759 Cason St (28012-2219)
P.O. Box 627 (28012-0627)
PHONE.....................................704 825-9687
Gregory Dellinger, *Pr*
Larry D Dellinger, *
EMP: 28 **EST:** 1979
SQ FT: 24,000
SALES (est): 9.99MM **Privately Held**
Web: www.dellingerenterprises.com
SIC: 3569 3599 Assembly machines, non-
  metalworking; Machine shop, jobbing and
  repair

(G-746)
DEPALO FOODS INC
2010 Oaks Pkwy (28012-5133)
PHONE.....................................704 827-0245
Enrico Diraino, *Pr*
Enrico Piraino, *
Gianni Piraino, *
EMP: 35 **EST:** 2003
SALES (est): 13.06MM **Privately Held**
Web: www.depalofoods.com
SIC: 2051 Bakery: wholesale or wholesale/
  retail combined

(G-747)
DISPLAY OPTIONS WOODWORK INC
205 Colonial Dr (28012-9531)
PHONE.....................................704 599-6525
Alberto Macchivello, *Pr*
EMP: 4 **EST:** 1995
SALES (est): 446.58K **Privately Held**
SIC: 2541 Display fixtures, wood

(G-748)
DIVERSIFIED SPECIALTIES INC
10 Airline Ave (28012-3854)
P.O. Box 1003 (28012-1003)
PHONE.....................................704 825-3671
Douglas B Phifer, *Pr*
William J Phifer, *
Dorothy Phifer, *
EMP: 38 **EST:** 1974
SQ FT: 40,000
SALES (est): 6.85MM **Privately Held**
Web: www.div-spec.com
SIC: 3599 Machine shop, jobbing and repair

(G-749)
EQUIPMENT PARTS INC (PA)
Also Called: Carolina Machine Works
795 Cason St (28012-2219)
P.O. Box 1156 (28012-1156)
PHONE.....................................704 827-7545
William L Jarchow, *Pr*
Karen S Jarchow, *
EMP: 35 **EST:** 1956
SQ FT: 25,000
SALES (est): 5.98MM
SALES (corp-wide): 5.98MM **Privately**
Held

▲ = Import ▼ = Export
◆ = Import/Export

Web: www.mfgsolutionsinc.com
SIC: **3599** Machine shop, jobbing and repair

(G-750)
FEINBERG ENTERPRISES INC
3 Caldwell Dr (28012-2750)
PHONE..............................704 822-2400
Aaron Feinberg, *Pr*
Adam Feinberg, *VP*
▲ **EMP:** 12 **EST:** 1996
SQ FT: 42,500
SALES (est): 6.6MM **Privately Held**
Web: www.textum.com
SIC: **2221** Glass and fiberglass broadwoven fabrics

(G-751)
FERGUSON DESIGN INC
236 Hawthorne Park Ave (28012-4152)
PHONE..............................704 394-0120
Mike Ferguson, *Pr*
Suzanne Ferguson, *Sec*
EMP: 20 **EST:** 1998
SALES (est): 914.87K **Privately Held**
Web: www.fergusondesign.com
SIC: **3993** Signs and advertising specialties

(G-752)
FIREHOUSE CABINETS
715 Brook Forest Dr (28012-9656)
PHONE..............................704 689-5243
Al Briggs, *Prin*
EMP: 5 **EST:** 2010
SALES (est): 164K **Privately Held**
Web: www.firehousecabinets.com
SIC: **2434** Wood kitchen cabinets

(G-753)
GASTON PRINTING AND SIGNS LLC
720 Wood Lily Dr (28012-6542)
PHONE..............................702 267-5633
EMP: 9 **EST:** 2018
SALES (est): 766.64K **Privately Held**
Web: www.gastonprintingandsigns.com
SIC: **2752** Offset printing

(G-754)
GLOBAL SENSORS LLC
63 Mcadenville Rd (28012-2434)
P.O. Box 750 (28012-0750)
PHONE..............................704 827-4331
David K Caskey, *Pr*
◆ **EMP:** 6 **EST:** 2004
SALES (est): 1.06MM **Privately Held**
Web: www.global-sensors.com
SIC: **3823** Process control instruments

(G-755)
JO-MAR GROUP LLC
Also Called: Jo-Mar Spinning
701 Plum St (28012-3423)
EMP: 38 **EST:** 2010
SALES (est): 1.69MM **Privately Held**
SIC: **3523** Balers, farm: hay, straw, cotton, etc.

(G-756)
NC FILTRATION OF FLORIDA LLC
Also Called: Ssnc LLC Pba NC Filtration
1 Miller St (28012-2162)
PHONE..............................704 822-4444
Eli Kershaw, *Managing Member*
Jeffrey Kershaw, *
EMP: 85 **EST:** 2010
SQ FT: 2,000
SALES (est): 1.63MM **Privately Held**
Web: www.ncfiltration.com
SIC: **3564** Blowers and fans

(G-757)
NUNN PROBST INSTALLATIONS INC
6428 W Wilkinson Blvd (28012-2858)
P.O. Box 549 (28098-0549)
PHONE..............................704 822-9443
Jason L Nunn, *Pr*
EMP: 9 **EST:** 2000
SALES (est): 1.2MM **Privately Held**
SIC: **3535** Conveyors and conveying equipment

(G-758)
PARKDALE MILLS INCORPORATED
Also Called: Plant 15
103 E Woodrow Ave (28012-3164)
PHONE..............................704 825-5324
Bernard Harvey, *Mgr*
EMP: 45
SALES (corp-wide): 1.44B **Privately Held**
Web: www.parkdalemills.com
SIC: **2281** Cotton yarn, spun
HQ: Parkdale Mills, Incorporated
531 Cotton Blossom Cir
Gastonia NC 28054
704 874-5000

(G-759)
PARKDALE MILLS INCORPORATED
Also Called: Plant 17
1000 Parkdale Dr (28012-3574)
P.O. Box 856 (28012-0856)
PHONE..............................704 913-3917
Shane Trull, *Mgr*
EMP: 63
SALES (corp-wide): 1.44B **Privately Held**
Web: www.parkdalemills.com
SIC: **2281** Cotton yarn, spun
HQ: Parkdale Mills, Incorporated
531 Cotton Blossom Cir
Gastonia NC 28054
704 874-5000

(G-760)
PARKDALE MILLS INCORPORATED
501 10th St (28012)
PHONE..............................704 825-2529
Danny Huntley, *Brnch Mgr*
EMP: 14
SALES (corp-wide): 1.44B **Privately Held**
Web: www.parkdalemills.com
SIC: **4225 2282 2281 4953** General warehousing and storage; Throwing and winding mills; Yarn spinning mills; Refuse systems
HQ: Parkdale Mills, Incorporated
531 Cotton Blossom Cir
Gastonia NC 28054
704 874-5000

(G-761)
PIEDMONT LITHIUM CAROLINAS INC (HQ)
42 E Catawba St (28012-3349)
PHONE..............................434 664-7643
Keith Phillips, *Pr*
Jeff Armstrong, *Ch Bd*
EMP: 18 **EST:** 2019
SALES (corp-wide): 99.88MM **Privately Held**
Web: www.piedmontlithium.com
SIC: **2819** Industrial inorganic chemicals, nec
PA: Piedmont Lithium Inc.
42 E Catawba St
Belmont NC 28012
704 461-8000

(G-762)
PIEDMONT LITHIUM INC (PA)
42 E Catawba St (28012)
PHONE..............................704 461-8000
Keith Phillips, *Pr*

Jeff Armstrong, *Ch Bd*
Patrick Brindle, *Ex VP*
Michael White, *Ex VP*
Austin Devaney, *CCO*
EMP: 15 **EST:** 1983
SALES (est): 99.88MM
SALES (corp-wide): 99.88MM **Privately Held**
Web: www.piedmontlithium.com
SIC: **1479** Lithium mineral mining

(G-763)
RAMSEY INDUSTRIES INC
Also Called: Carolina Custom Windows
816 Woodlawn St (28012-2134)
PHONE..............................704 827-3560
Charles W Ramsey, *Pr*
Lavon Ramsey, *Sec*
EMP: 11 **EST:** 1980
SQ FT: 8,500
SALES (est): 1.41MM **Privately Held**
Web: www.ramseywinch.com
SIC: **3089 6162 1761 3442** Windows, plastics ; Mortgage brokers, using own money; Roofing, siding, and sheetmetal work; Storm doors or windows, metal

(G-764)
RAMSEY PRODUCTS CORPORATION
135 Performance Dr (28012-2446)
P.O. Box 668827 (28266-8827)
PHONE..............................704 394-0322
Mark Taylor, *CEO*
David Holcomb, *
Grier N Killough, *
◆ **EMP:** 84 **EST:** 1923
SQ FT: 80,000
SALES (est): 10.34MM
SALES (corp-wide): 167.14K **Privately Held**
Web: www.ramseychain.com
SIC: **3499** Ice cream freezers, household, nonelectric: metal
PA: Rondot International
9 Rue Jean-Elysee Dupuy
Champagne-Au-Mont-D'or ARA

(G-765)
SHORT RUN PRO LLC
710 E Catawba St Ste A (28012-3504)
PHONE..............................704 825-1599
Bruce Toal, *Prin*
Victoria Breeedlove, *Opers*
▼ **EMP:** 12 **EST:** 2006
SALES (est): 1.84MM **Privately Held**
Web: www.shortrunpro.com
SIC: **3471** Plating of metals or formed products

(G-766)
SOLVERE LLC
69 Mcadenville Rd (28012-2434)
PHONE..............................704 829-1015
Barry Stringer, *Managing Member*
EMP: 27 **EST:** 2003
SQ FT: 12,000
SALES (est): 7.65MM **Privately Held**
Web: www.solvere.net
SIC: **3625** Relays and industrial controls

(G-767)
SPARTAN DYERS INC
217 Sterling St (28012-3218)
P.O. Box 790 (28012-0790)
PHONE..............................704 829-0467
Alphonse G Kelada, *Prin*
George Kelada, *
Nabila R Kelada, *
▲ **EMP:** 53 **EST:** 1988
SQ FT: 150,000
SALES (est): 9.85MM **Privately Held**

Web: www.spartandyers.com
SIC: **2269** Dyeing: raw stock, yarn, and narrow fabrics

(G-768)
STEEL SPECIALTY CO BELMONT INC (PA)
Also Called: Ssi
5907 W Wilkinson Blvd (28012-4802)
P.O. Box 985 (28012-0985)
PHONE..............................704 825-4745
Farrell W Mauldin, *CEO*
Jason S Mauldin, *
Jason Mauldin, *Prin*
Victor Scott, *
Edward H Reese, *
EMP: 45 **EST:** 1971
SQ FT: 60,000
SALES (est): 1.69MM
SALES (corp-wide): 1.69MM **Privately Held**
Web: www.steel-specialty.com
SIC: **3441 3446** Building components, structural steel; Stairs, staircases, stair treads: prefabricated metal

(G-769)
SYNCOT PLASTICS LLC
350 Eastwood Dr (28012-3754)
P.O. Box 1350 (28012-1350)
PHONE..............................704 967-0010
Charles Bing, *CEO*
Darren Bing, *
Sharon Bing, *
▲ **EMP:** 75 **EST:** 1995
SALES (est): 2.1MM **Privately Held**
Web: www.syncot.com
SIC: **2821** Plastics materials and resins

(G-770)
T T S D PRODUCTIONS LLC
Also Called: T Toppers
27 E Woodrow Ave (28012-3142)
PHONE..............................704 829-6666
EMP: 7 **EST:** 1997
SALES (est): 102.95K **Privately Held**
SIC: **2759 2396** Screen printing; Automotive and apparel trimmings

(G-771)
TASTEBUDS LLC
Also Called: Tastebuds Popcorn
208 N Main St (28012-3125)
PHONE..............................704 461-8755
EMP: 4 **EST:** 2011
SQ FT: 1,000
SALES (est): 182.77K **Privately Held**
Web: www.tastebudspopcorn.com
SIC: **5441 2064 5145** Popcorn, including caramel corn; Popcorn balls or other treated popcorn products; Popcorn and supplies

(G-772)
TECWORKS INC
4041 S Cove Ln (28012-9586)
PHONE..............................704 829-9700
P Craig Helton, *Prin*
EMP: 5 **EST:** 2006
SALES (est): 846.84K **Privately Held**
SIC: **3679** Antennas, receiving

(G-773)
TEXTUM OPCO LLC
3 Caldwell Dr (28012-2750)
PHONE..............................704 822-2400
Aaron Feinberg, *Managing Member*
Kerstin Hunicke, *Acctg Mgr*
Chris Maynard, *Dir Opers*
EMP: 36 **EST:** 2020
SALES (est): 8.77MM **Privately Held**

Web: www.textum.com
SIC: 2211 Broadwoven fabric mills, cotton

(G-774)
US COTTON LLC
1000 Parkdale Dr Ste 1 (28012-3574)
PHONE..............................704 874-5000
Nelson Everhart, *Mgr*
EMP: 85
SALES (corp-wide): 1.44B **Privately Held**
Web: www.uscotton.com
SIC: 2844 2241 Perfumes, cosmetics and
   other toilet preparations; Cotton narrow
   fabrics
HQ: U.S. Cotton, Llc
   531 Cotton Blossom Cir
   Gastonia NC 28054
   216 676-6400

(G-775)
WILBERT INC (HQ)
Also Called: Wilbert Plastic Services
100 N Main St Ste 200 (28012-3104)
PHONE..............................704 247-3850
Greg Botner, *Pr*
▲ EMP: 20 EST: 2012
SALES (est): 218.2MM
SALES (corp-wide): 218.2MM **Privately
Held**
Web: www.wilbertplastics.com
SIC: 3089 Injection molding of plastics
PA: Piedmont Manufacturing Group, Llc
   1411 Broadway Fl 34
   New York NY 10018
   212 752-1356

(G-776)
WILBERT PLASTIC SERVICES INC
100 N Main St Ste 200 (28012-3104)
PHONE..............................866 273-1810
EMP: 5 EST: 2006
SALES (est): 244.98K **Privately Held**
Web: www.wilbertplastics.com
SIC: 3089 Injection molding of plastics

(G-777)
**WILBERT PLSTIC SVCS ACQSTION
L (DH)**
Also Called: Wilbert Plastic Services
1000 Oaks Pkwy (28012-5139)
PHONE..............................704 822-1423
Greg M Botner, *Pr*
▲ EMP: 103 EST: 2010
SALES (est): 48.1MM
SALES (corp-wide): 218.2MM **Privately
Held**
Web: www.wilbertplastics.com
SIC: 3089 Injection molding of plastics
HQ: Wilbert, Inc.
   100 N Main St Ste 200
   Belmont NC 28012
   704 247-3850

Belvidere
Perquimans County

(G-778)
CJ STALLINGS LOGGING INC
1307 Acorn Hill Rd (27919-9802)
PHONE..............................252 297-2272
Clifton J Stallings, *Pr*
EMP: 10 EST: 1990
SALES (est): 116.15K **Privately Held**
SIC: 2411 Logging camps and contractors

Belville
Brunswick County

(G-779)
CURTI USA CORPORATION
161 Poole Rd (28451-9962)
PHONE..............................910 769-1977
EMP: 9 EST: 2020
SALES (est): 5.3MM
SALES (corp-wide): 116.43MM **Privately
Held**
Web: www.curti.com
SIC: 3599 Custom machinery
PA: Curti Costruzioni Meccaniche Spa
   Via Emilia Ponente 750
   Castel Bolognese RA 48014
   054 665-5911

(G-780)
PSA INCORPORATED
150 Backhoe Rd Ne (28451-8506)
PHONE..............................910 371-1115
Bert Moody, *Pr*
EMP: 4 EST: 1998
SALES (est): 151.86K **Privately Held**
SIC: 2891 Adhesives

(G-781)
QUALITY BEVERAGE LLC
157 Poole Rd (28451-9508)
PHONE..............................910 371-3596
Danny Curtis, *Genl Mgr*
EMP: 21
SALES (corp-wide): 10.39MM **Privately
Held**
Web: www.cheerwine.com
SIC: 2086 Soft drinks: packaged in cans,
   bottles, etc.
PA: Quality Beverage, L.L.C.
   1413 Jake Alxander Blvd S
   Salisbury NC 28146
   704 637-5881

Bennett
Chatham County

(G-782)
PHILIP BRADY
Also Called: Airloom Furnishing
185 Charlie Garner Rd (27208-9374)
PHONE..............................336 581-3999
Philip Brady, *Owner*
EMP: 5 EST: 1993
SQ FT: 30,120
SALES (est): 191.68K **Privately Held**
SIC: 2511 2517 Wood bedroom furniture;
   Home entertainment unit cabinets, wood

Benson
Johnston County

(G-783)
**ACME GENERAL DESIGN GROUP
LLC**
101 N Market St (27504-1514)
PHONE..............................843 466-6000
EMP: 4 EST: 2019
SALES (est): 139.88K **Privately Held**
SIC: 3911 Jewelry, precious metal

(G-784)
AMWARE PALLET SERVICES LLC
1700 Chicopee Rd (27504-2147)
PHONE..............................919 207-2403
Jaime Loney, *Mgr*
EMP: 9

SALES (corp-wide): 11.81MM **Privately
Held**
SIC: 2448 Pallets, wood
PA: Amware Pallet Services, Llc
   216 Main St Unit 100
   Edwards CO 81632
   970 337-7070

(G-785)
BERRY GLOBAL INC
1203 Chicopee Rd (27504-2121)
PHONE..............................919 207-3202
EMP: 26
Web: www.berryglobal.com
SIC: 3089 Bottle caps, molded plastics
HQ: Berry Global, Inc.
   101 Oakley St
   Evansville IN 47710

(G-786)
CHICOPEE INC
Also Called: Polymer Group
1203 Chicopee Rd (27504-2121)
P.O. Box 308 (27504-0308)
PHONE..............................919 894-4111
John Mortoen, *Mgr*
EMP: 4
Web: www.chicopee.com
SIC: 7389 2297 Personal service agents,
   brokers, and bureaus; Nonwoven fabrics
HQ: Chicopee, Inc.
   9335 Hrris Crners Pkwy St
   Charlotte NC 28269

(G-787)
COUNTY PRESS INC
Also Called: Four Oks/Benson News In
Review
113 S Market St (27504-1520)
P.O. Box 9 (27504-0009)
PHONE..............................919 894-2112
Norman Delano, *Pr*
EMP: 8 EST: 1951
SQ FT: 5,000
SALES (est): 334K **Privately Held**
Web: www.bensonfouroaksnews.com
SIC: 2711 Newspapers, publishing and
   printing

(G-788)
EASTERN READY MIX LLC
3170 Federal Rd (27504-5009)
PHONE..............................919 207-2722
Timothy Eldridge, *Managing Member*
EMP: 18 EST: 2020
SALES (est): 3.02MM **Privately Held**
SIC: 3273 Ready-mixed concrete

(G-789)
ELITE MARINE LLC
Also Called: Savannah Boats
554 Old Roberts Rd (27504-6902)
PHONE..............................919 495-6388
EMP: 37 EST: 2019
SALES (est): 4.15MM **Privately Held**
Web: www.savannahboats.com
SIC: 3732 Boatbuilding and repairing

(G-790)
GRAPHIC PRODUCTS INC
Also Called: Benton Card
105 S Wall St (27504-1327)
P.O. Box 369 (27504-0369)
PHONE..............................919 894-3661
Suzanne Benton Cook, *Pr*
EMP: 6 EST: 1980
SQ FT: 12,000
SALES (est): 1.12MM **Privately Held**
Web: www.bentonprint.com
SIC: 2752 Offset printing

(G-791)
**HAMLIN SHEET METAL COMPANY
INC**
200 N Walton Ave (27504-6697)
P.O. Box 249 (27504-0249)
PHONE..............................919 894-2224
Paul Turner, *Mgr*
EMP: 100
SALES (corp-wide): 13.19MM **Privately
Held**
Web: www.hamlincos.com
SIC: 3444 Awnings and canopies
PA: Hamlin Sheet Metal Company,
   Incorporated
   1411 W Garner Rd
   Garner NC 27529
   919 772-8780

(G-792)
HARRIS REBAR INC
803 S Market St (27504-2111)
PHONE..............................919 528-8333
Harris Rebar, *Owner*
EMP: 7 EST: 2015
SALES (est): 667.93K **Privately Held**
Web: www.harrisrebar.com
SIC: 5051 3325 3441 Steel; Steel foundries,
   nec; Fabricated structural metal

(G-793)
JPS CUPCAKERY LLC
111 S Railroad St (27504-1325)
PHONE..............................919 894-5000
Joseph Parker, *Admn*
EMP: 16 EST: 2014
SALES (est): 852.88K **Privately Held**
Web: www.jpspastry.com
SIC: 2051 Bread, cake, and related products

(G-794)
MARTIN MARIETTA MATERIALS INC
Also Called: Martin Marietta Aggregates
13661 Raleigh Rd (27504-6819)
P.O. Box 365 (27504-0365)
PHONE..............................919 894-2003
Arlen Carpenter, *Mgr*
EMP: 5
Web: www.martinmarietta.com
SIC: 1422 Crushed and broken limestone
PA: Martin Marietta Materials Inc
   4123 Parklake Ave
   Raleigh NC 27612

(G-795)
NEWS AND OBSERVER PUBG CO
Gold Leaf Publishers
611 Chicopee Rd (27504-1943)
P.O. Box 130 (27504-0130)
PHONE..............................919 894-4170
Colen Davis, *Brnch Mgr*
EMP: 43
SALES (corp-wide): 1.39B **Privately Held**
SIC: 2711 Newspapers, publishing and
   printing
HQ: The News And Observer Publishing
   Company
   421 Fayetteville St # 104
   Raleigh NC 27601
   919 829-4500

(G-796)
PRECISION METALS LLC
589 Old Roberts Rd (27504-6903)
PHONE..............................919 762-7481
EMP: 6 EST: 2017
SALES (est): 2.26MM **Privately Held**
SIC: 3724 Aircraft engines and engine parts

▲ = Import ▼ = Export
◆ = Import/Export

(G-797)
TAYLOR MADE CASES INC
107 Last Cast Dr (27504-8043)
PHONE..............................919 209-0555
Diane Perry, *Pr*
Greg Perry, *VP*
Jason Miles, *Sec*
EMP: 18 **EST:** 2003
SQ FT: 4,000
SALES (est): 484.35K **Privately Held**
Web: www.taylormadecases.com
SIC: 3199 Holsters, leather

(G-798)
TWIN TROLLER BOATS INC
Also Called: Carolina Electric Boats
501 S Wall St Ste A (27504-1856)
PHONE..............................919 207-2622
Frank Jones, *Pr*
EMP: 5 **EST:** 2005
SQ FT: 20,000
SALES (est): 94.98K **Privately Held**
Web: www.freedomelectricmarine.com
SIC: 3732 Tenders (small motor craft),
building and repairing

(G-799)
ULTRATECH INDUSTRIES INC
200 Hamlin Rd (27504)
P.O. Box 465 (27529-0465)
PHONE..............................919 779-2004
William F Hamlin Junior, *Pr*
Christine H Hamlin, *Sec*
EMP: 7 **EST:** 1980
SQ FT: 2,000
SALES (est): 729.15K **Privately Held**
SIC: 3822 Pneumatic relays, air-conditioning
type

(G-800)
**XTREME POSTCARD PROFITS
SYSTEM**
22 Boardwalk Ave (27504-7848)
PHONE..............................919 894-8886
Emerson Jordan, *Prin*
EMP: 4 **EST:** 2016
SALES (est): 165.95K **Privately Held**
SIC: 2752 Commercial printing, lithographic

Bessemer City
Gaston County

(G-801)
ACORN PRINTING
4122 Kings Mountain Hwy (28016-7525)
P.O. Box 244 (28016-0244)
PHONE..............................704 868-4522
Tony Green, *Prin*
EMP: 5 **EST:** 2008
SALES (est): 89.04K **Privately Held**
Web: www.acornprints.com
SIC: 5699 2759 Miscellaneous apparel and
accessory stores; Screen printing

(G-802)
ADVANCED DRAINAGE SYSTEMS
333 Southridge Pkwy (28016-7805)
PHONE..............................704 629-4151
EMP: 17
SALES (est): 3.18MM **Privately Held**
SIC: 3089 Plastics products, nec

(G-803)
**ADVANCED DRAINAGE SYSTEMS
INC**
Also Called: ADS
902 E Maine Ave (28016-7805)
P.O. Box 9 (28016-0009)
PHONE..............................704 629-4151

Doug Attit, *Rgnl Mgr*
EMP: 62
SALES (corp-wide): 2.87B **Publicly Held**
Web: www.adspipe.com
SIC: 3084 5051 Plastics pipe; Pipe and
tubing, steel
PA: Advanced Drainage Systems, Inc.
4640 Trueman Blvd
Hilliard OH 43026
614 658-0050

(G-804)
ALCO METAL FABRICATO
1111 Oates Rd (28016-7574)
PHONE..............................704 739-1168
EMP: 7 **EST:** 2019
SALES (est): 2.69MM **Privately Held**
Web: www.alcometalfabricatorsinc.com
SIC: 3499 Fabricated metal products, nec

(G-805)
ARC STEEL FABRICATION LLC
649 Bess Town Rd (28016-7544)
P.O. Box 545 (28021-0545)
PHONE..............................980 533-8302
Ira Brewster Senior, *Pr*
EMP: 10 **EST:** 2015
SALES (est): 2.84MM **Privately Held**
Web: www.arcsteelfab.com
SIC: 3499 Metal household articles

(G-806)
**BESSEMER CITY MACHINE SHOP
INC**
Also Called: Bessemer City Machinery Sales
524 Bess Town Rd (28016-7543)
P.O. Box 305 (28016-0305)
PHONE..............................704 629-4111
Steven E Bowen, *Pr*
Janet Haynes, *Sec*
▲ **EMP:** 9 **EST:** 1963
SQ FT: 16,000
SALES (est): 2.28MM **Privately Held**
Web: www.bessemercity.com
SIC: 5051 3312 3599 Steel; Blast furnaces
and steel mills; Machine shop, jobbing and
repair

(G-807)
C & B WELDING & FAB INC
2070 Mauney Rd (28016-9643)
PHONE..............................704 435-6942
Thomas J Carpender, *Pr*
EMP: 6 **EST:** 2008
SQ FT: 21,000
SALES (est): 239.94K **Privately Held**
SIC: 7692 Welding repair

(G-808)
CARO-POLYMERS INC (PA)
611 Bess Town Rd (28016-7544)
P.O. Box 755 (28016-0755)
PHONE..............................704 629-5319
Todd Boyter, *Pr*
W Curtis Boyter, *VP*
Myrna Boyter, *Sec*
EMP: 10 **EST:** 1984
SQ FT: 24,500
SALES (est): 1.6MM
SALES (corp-wide): 1.6MM **Privately Held**
SIC: 3089 Plastics hardware and building
products

(G-809)
**CONNER BROTHERS MACHINE CO
INC**
Also Called: Cbm
3200 Bessemer City Rd (28016-9774)
PHONE..............................704 864-6084
Bobby Conner, *Pr*

Cathy Conner, *
EMP: 95 **EST:** 1990
SQ FT: 200,000
SALES (est): 9.62MM **Privately Held**
Web: www.cbmprecisionparts.com
SIC: 3599 3451 Machine shop, jobbing and
repair; Screw machine products

(G-810)
CRC MACHINE & FABRICATION INC
4375 Dallas Cherryville Hwy (28016-7729)
P.O. Box 1001 (28016-1001)
PHONE..............................980 522-1361
David Halk, *Pr*
Kelly Halk, *Pr*
EMP: 16 **EST:** 2013
SALES (est): 1.94MM **Privately Held**
Web: www.crc-incorp.com
SIC: 3599 Machine shop, jobbing and repair

(G-811)
CUSTOM MACHINE COMPANY INC
221 White Jenkins Rd (28016-9559)
P.O. Box 625 (28016-0625)
PHONE..............................704 629-5326
Thomas M Jones, *Pr*
EMP: 11 **EST:** 1980
SQ FT: 7,300
SALES (est): 1.06MM **Privately Held**
Web: www.cmtco.com
SIC: 3599 5084 7692 Machine shop, jobbing
and repair; Textile machinery and equipment
; Welding repair

(G-812)
DALLAS FABRICATION
1346 Ramseur Rd (28016-7636)
PHONE..............................704 629-4000
EMP: 6 **EST:** 2015
SALES (est): 510.05K **Privately Held**
Web: www.spgear.com
SIC: 3312 Ammonia and liquor, from
chemical recovery coke ovens

(G-813)
DALLAS MACHINE AND
Also Called: Dallas Machine Company
1326 Ramseur Rd (28016-7636)
P.O. Box 1340 (28016-1340)
PHONE..............................704 629-5611
Richard Easler, *Off Mgr*
EMP: 5 **EST:** 2010
SALES (est): 1.99MM **Privately Held**
SIC: 3599 Machine shop, jobbing and repair

(G-814)
DHOLLANDIA US LLC (HQ)
270 Southridge Pkwy (28016-7801)
P.O. Box 310794 (92331-0794)
PHONE..............................909 251-7979
Jan Dhollander, *Managing Member*
Nancy Dhollander, *Managing Member*
Melissa Cash, *Managing Member*
Lieve Dehertogh, *Managing Member*
EMP: 6 **EST:** 2014
SALES (est): 9.2MM
SALES (corp-wide): 41.3MM **Privately
Held**
Web: www.dhollandia.be
SIC: 3714 Motor vehicle parts and
accessories
PA: Dhollandia Service
Zoomstraat 9
Lokeren VOV 9160
93490692

(G-815)
FARMER MACHINE GROUP LLC
308 White Jenkins Rd (28016-7753)
P.O. Box 711 (28016-0711)
PHONE..............................704 629-5133

Rodney Farmer, *Pt*
Robert Woodall, *Pt*
EMP: 10 **EST:** 1996
SQ FT: 10,000
SALES (est): 950.33K **Privately Held**
SIC: 3599 Machine shop, jobbing and repair

(G-816)
FARRIS FAB & MACHINE INC
Also Called: Farris Fab & Machine, Inc.
1941 Bess Town Rd (28016-6813)
PHONE..............................704 629-4879
Greg Farris, *VP*
EMP: 9
SALES (corp-wide): 21.1MM **Privately
Held**
Web: www.farrisgrp.com
SIC: 3441 3599 Fabricated structural metal;
Machine shop, jobbing and repair
PA: Farris Fab & Machine, Inc.
1006 West Academy St
Cherryville NC 28021
704 629-4879

(G-817)
FARRIS FAB & MACHINE INC
Also Called: FARRIS FAB. & MACHINE, INC.
522 Bess Town Rd (28016-7543)
PHONE..............................704 629-4879
Kevin Wheeler, *Brnch Mgr*
EMP: 137
SALES (corp-wide): 21.1MM **Privately
Held**
Web: www.farrisgrp.com
SIC: 3441 3599 Fabricated structural metal;
Machine shop, jobbing and repair
PA: Farris Fab & Machine, Inc.
1006 West Academy St
Cherryville NC 28021
704 629-4879

(G-818)
FMC CORPORATION
F M C Lithium Division
161 Kings Mtn Hwy (28016)
P.O. Box 795 (28016-0795)
PHONE..............................704 868-5300
Robert Haire, *Brnch Mgr*
EMP: 53
SALES (corp-wide): 4.25B **Publicly Held**
Web: www.fmc.com
SIC: 2819 2899 Lithium compounds,
inorganic; Chemical preparations, nec
PA: Fmc Corporation
2929 Walnut St
Philadelphia PA 19104
215 299-6000

(G-819)
FMC CORPORATION
Also Called: FMC Lithium Division
1115 Bessemer City Kings Mtn Hwy
(28016-9640)
PHONE..............................704 426-5336
EMP: 272
SALES (corp-wide): 4.25B **Publicly Held**
Web: www.fmc.com
SIC: 2819 2899 Lithium compounds,
inorganic; Chemical preparations, nec
PA: Fmc Corporation
2929 Walnut St
Philadelphia PA 19104
215 299-6000

(G-820)
GASTON INDUS MACHINING LLC
125 Robinsons Park Dr (28016-7792)
P.O. Box 785 (28012-0785)
PHONE..............................704 825-3346
EMP: 4 **EST:** 2018
SALES (est): 652.64K **Privately Held**

Web: www.gastonindustrialmachining.com
SIC: **3599** Machine shop, jobbing and repair

(G-821)
HEART ELECTRIC MOTOR SERVICE
Also Called: Heart Electric
Rt 1 Costner School Rd (28016)
PHONE..............................704 922-4720
Thomas R Doss, *Owner*
EMP: 6 **EST:** 1991
SQ FT: 10,000
SALES (est): 299.74K **Privately Held**
SIC: **7694 5999** Rewinding services; Motors, electric

(G-822)
HUNTER DOUGLAS INC
201 Southridge Pkwy (28016-7801)
PHONE..............................704 629-6500
EMP: 118
Web: www.hunterdouglas.com
SIC: **2591 3444 5084** Window blinds; Sheet metalwork; Industrial machinery and equipment
HQ: Hunter Douglas Inc.
　　55 W 46th St 27th Fl
　　New York NY 10036
　　845 664-7000

(G-823)
IMPERIAL MACHINE COMPANY INC
Also Called: Imperial Machine Co
4429 Kings Mountain Hwy (28016-7528)
P.O. Box 12506 (28052-0021)
PHONE..............................704 739-8038
Tommy A Russell, *Pr*
EMP: 35 **EST:** 1958
SALES (est): 2.51MM **Privately Held**
Web: www.imperialmachineco.com
SIC: **3599 3552** Machine shop, jobbing and repair; Textile machinery

(G-824)
JOE AND KITTY BROWN INC
1312 Ramseur Rd (28016-7636)
P.O. Box 15 (28053-0015)
PHONE..............................704 629-4327
Tim Carter, *Pr*
EMP: 6 **EST:** 1954
SQ FT: 25,500
SALES (est): 1.32MM **Privately Held**
Web: www.spgear.com
SIC: **3566** Speed changers, drives, and gears

(G-825)
M S I PRECISION MACHINE INC
725 E Maine Ave (28016-2186)
PHONE..............................704 629-9375
Kenneth M Kirby, *Pr*
EMP: 4 **EST:** 2003
SALES (est): 489.93K **Privately Held**
SIC: **3599** Machine shop, jobbing and repair

(G-826)
MANUFACTURING SERVICES INC
Also Called: MSI
725 E Maine Ave (28016-2186)
PHONE..............................704 629-4163
Ron Grenier, *Pr*
William Blalock Junior, *VP*
Kenneth Kirby, *
EMP: 45 **EST:** 1970
SQ FT: 31,700
SALES (est): 10.95MM **Privately Held**
Web: www.msicarolina.com
SIC: **3089 3451 3599** Plastics hardware and building products; Screw machine products; Machine and other job shop work

(G-827)
METSO USA INC
3200 Bessemer City Rd (28016-9774)
PHONE..............................877 677-2005
EMP: 51
SIC: **3554** Paper industries machinery
HQ: Metso Usa Inc.
　　2715 Pleasant Valley Rd
　　York PA 17402

(G-828)
OLD MILL PRECISION GUN WORKS &
323 Old Mill Rd (28016-7686)
PHONE..............................704 284-2832
EMP: 4 **EST:** 2013
SALES (est): 100K **Privately Held**
SIC: **2431** Millwork

(G-829)
PATRICIA HALL
Also Called: Hull's Wall Covering
128 Terrace Dr (28016-2855)
PHONE..............................704 729-6133
Michael Hull, *Owner*
EMP: 4 **EST:** 2010
SALES (est): 149.78K **Privately Held**
SIC: **1721 2221** Wallcovering contractors; Wall covering fabrics, manmade fiber and silk

(G-830)
PLASTIC PRODUCTS INC (PA)
1413 Bessemer City Kings Mtn Hwy (28016-6654)
P.O. Box 69 (28086-0069)
PHONE..............................704 739-7463
Jay Raxter, *Pr*
Karen Fore, *
EMP: 24 **EST:** 1968
SQ FT: 20,000
SALES (est): 10.26MM
SALES (corp-wide): 10.26MM **Privately Held**
Web: www.plastic-products.com
SIC: **2821** Plastics materials and resins

(G-831)
PRECISION DRIVE SYSTEMS LLC (PA)
4367 Dallas Cherryville Hwy (28016-7729)
P.O. Box 461 (28034-0461)
PHONE..............................704 922-1206
Robert Turk, *Pr*
▲ **EMP:** 9 **EST:** 1997
SQ FT: 10,000
SALES (est): 4.84MM
SALES (corp-wide): 4.84MM **Privately Held**
Web: www.spindlerepair.com
SIC: **3699** Electrical equipment and supplies, nec

(G-832)
ROSS WOODWORKING INC
Also Called: Pallets & Such
125 L E Perry Rd (28016-9705)
PHONE..............................704 629-4551
EMP: 8
SALES (corp-wide): 615.23K **Privately Held**
SIC: **2448** Pallets, wood and wood with metal
PA: Ross Woodworking Inc
　　1004 Dameron Rd
　　Bessemer City NC 28016
　　704 629-4551

(G-833)
ROSS WOODWORKING INC (PA)
Also Called: Pallets & Such

1004 Dameron Rd (28016-8793)
PHONE..............................704 629-4551
EMP: 8
SALES (est): 615.23K
SALES (corp-wide): 615.23K **Privately Held**
Web: www.rosswoodworking.com
SIC: **2448** Pallets, wood and wood with metal

(G-834)
STINE GEAR & MACHINE COMPANY
2015 Hephzibah Church Rd (28016-7673)
P.O. Box 1157 (28034-1157)
PHONE..............................704 445-1245
Brian Harper, *Pr*
Martha Harker, *VP*
EMP: 11 **EST:** 1970
SQ FT: 3,200
SALES (est): 1.03MM **Privately Held**
Web: www.stinegear.com
SIC: **3599** Machine shop, jobbing and repair

(G-835)
TIM CONNER ENTERPRISES INC
Also Called: Spencer-Pettus Machine Co
1312 Ramseur Rd (28016-7636)
PHONE..............................704 629-4327
Timothy Dean Conner, *Pr*
◆ **EMP:** 20 **EST:** 2004
SALES (est): 6.04MM **Privately Held**
Web: www.spgear.com
SIC: **3462** Gears, forged steel

(G-836)
TOSAF INC
132 W Virginia Ave (28016-2373)
P.O. Box 758 (28016-0758)
PHONE..............................704 396-7097
EMP: 9
SALES (corp-wide): 4.58K **Privately Held**
SIC: **2821** Plastics materials and resins
HQ: Tosaf, Inc.
　　330 Southridge Pkwy
　　Bessemer City NC 28016
　　980 533-3000

(G-837)
TOSAF INC (DH)
Also Called: Tosaf USA
330 Southridge Pkwy (28016)
PHONE..............................980 533-3000
Amos Megides, *Pr*
Eldad Tveria, *
◆ **EMP:** 19 **EST:** 2014
SALES (est): 49.9MM **Privately Held**
Web: www.tosaf.com
SIC: **2821 2891 3089** Plasticizer/additive based plastic materials; Sealing compounds, synthetic rubber or plastic; Coloring and finishing of plastics products
HQ: Tosaf Compounds Ltd.
　　Tnuvot Industrial Zone
　　Kfar Yona

(G-838)
TOSAF AW INC
330 Southridge Pkwy (28016-7805)
PHONE..............................980 533-3000
EMP: 75 **EST:** 2022
SALES (est): 1.17MM **Privately Held**
Web: www.tosaf.com
SIC: **2295** Resin or plastic coated fabrics
HQ: Tosaf, Inc.
　　330 Southridge Pkwy
　　Bessemer City NC 28016
　　980 533-3000

Bethel
Pitt County

(G-839)
BLOUNT PRECISION MACHINING INC
155 Railroad St W (27812-9303)
P.O. Box 201 (27812-0201)
PHONE..............................252 825-3701
Jordan Blount, *Pr*
EMP: 4 **EST:** 2009
SALES (est): 1.13MM **Privately Held**
Web: www.blountprecisionmachining.com
SIC: **3599** Machine shop, jobbing and repair

(G-840)
PACKAGE CRAFT LLC (DH)
146 Package Craft Rd (27812-9541)
P.O. Box 430 (27812-0430)
PHONE..............................252 825-0111
Craig Roberts, *Managing Member*
EMP: 28 **EST:** 1960
SQ FT: 54,000
SALES (est): 9.84MM
SALES (corp-wide): 653.03MM **Privately Held**
Web: www.packagecraft.com
SIC: **2653** Boxes, corrugated: made from purchased materials
HQ: Schwarz Partners Packaging, Llc
　　10 W Carmel Dr Ste 300 In
　　Carmel IN 46032
　　317 290-1140

Beulaville
Duplin County

(G-841)
DAPHNE LAWSON ESPINO
Also Called: East Cast Emrgncy Response Svc
413 N Railroad Ave (28518-8742)
PHONE..............................910 290-2762
Daphne Lawson, *Owner*
EMP: 5
SALES (est): 211.92K **Privately Held**
SIC: **3524** Lawn and garden equipment

(G-842)
ENSALES ELECTRICAL ASSOC INC
140 E Park Dr Unit B (28518-6925)
PHONE..............................910 298-3305
Barry Jones, *Pr*
Fred Murray, *CEO*
EMP: 10 **EST:** 1994
SALES (est): 3.44MM **Privately Held**
Web: www.ensales.com
SIC: **3629** Rectifiers (electrical apparatus)

(G-843)
MILLER S UTILITY MGT INC
163 Jackson Store Rd (28518-6801)
PHONE..............................910 298-3847
Stanley Miller, *Pr*
Thad Miller, *VP*
Angie Miller, *Sec*
EMP: 4 **EST:** 1994
SALES (est): 245.48K **Privately Held**
SIC: **3589** Water treatment equipment, industrial

(G-844)
NATIONAL SPINNING CO INC
326 Lyman Rd (28518-7618)
P.O. Box 191 (27889-0191)
PHONE..............................910 298-3131
Jesse Sumner, *Brnch Mgr*

▲ = Import ▼ = Export
◆ = Import/Export

EMP: 115
SALES (corp-wide): 40.55MM **Privately Held**
Web: www.natspin.com
SIC: 2282 2231 2281 Wool yarn: twisting, winding, or spooling; Wool broadwoven fabrics; Yarn spinning mills
PA: National Spinning Co., Inc.
1481 W 2nd St
Washington NC 27889
252 975-7111

(G-845)
S DUFF FABRICATING INC
228 N Nc 41 Hwy (28518-8632)
PHONE..............................910 298-3060
Sheral Murphy, *Pr*
Sonya Hall, *Sec*
EMP: 6 EST: 1988
SQ FT: 6,000
SALES (est): 473.39K **Privately Held**
SIC: 3462 3524 3444 3423 Anchors, forged; Lawn and garden equipment; Sheet metalwork; Hand and edge tools, nec

---

Biscoe
Montgomery County

(G-846)
ARAUCO - NA
157 Atc Dr (27209-9669)
PHONE..............................910 569-7020
Pamela Daggett, *Prin*
EMP: 8 EST: 2015
SALES (est): 1.84MM **Privately Held**
Web: na.arauco.com
SIC: 2493 2411 2611 2621 Particleboard products; Timber, cut at logging camp; Pulp mills; Paper mills

(G-847)
BELEVATION LLC
207 Shady Oak Dr (27209-9574)
P.O. Box 1554 (27209-1554)
PHONE..............................803 517-9030
Thomas Miles, *CEO*
EMP: 10 EST: 2008
SALES (est): 437.79K **Privately Held**
Web: www.belevation.com
SIC: 2253 5621 Basque shirts, knit; Maternity wear

(G-848)
CAROLINA DAIRY LLC
116 Industrial Park (27209-8096)
PHONE..............................910 569-7070
EMP: 10 EST: 2019
SALES (est): 2.67MM
SALES (corp-wide): 11.8B **Privately Held**
SIC: 2026 Yogurt
PA: Saputo Inc
6869 Boul Metropolitain E
Saint-Leonard QC H3B 4
514 328-3869

(G-849)
CENTRAL CAROLINA HOSIERY INC (PA)
211 Shady Oak Dr (27209-9574)
P.O. Box 99 (27209-0099)
PHONE..............................910 428-9688
Serge Babayan, *Pr*
▲ EMP: 48 EST: 1997
SALES (est): 2.2MM
SALES (corp-wide): 2.2MM **Privately Held**
Web: www.cchosiery.com
SIC: 2251 2252 Women's hosiery, except socks; Tights, except women's

(G-850)
CHANDLER CONCRETE CO INC
Also Called: Chandler Concrete
1517 Us Highway 220 Alt S (27209)
P.O. Box 460 (27209-0460)
PHONE..............................910 974-4744
Tom Dunn, *Mgr*
EMP: 5
Web: www.chandlerconcrete.com
SIC: 3273 Ready-mixed concrete
PA: Chandler Concrete Co., Inc.
1006 S Church Street
Burlington NC 27215

(G-851)
COMFORT TECH INC
Also Called: Comfort Seals
Hwy 2427 (27209)
P.O. Box 768 (27209-0768)
PHONE..............................910 428-1779
Randy Deese, *Pr*
Ray Phillips, *VP*
EMP: 6 EST: 1996
SQ FT: 20,000
SALES (est): 1.41MM **Privately Held**
Web: www.comforttechdocks.com
SIC: 3069 Weather strip, sponge rubber

(G-852)
GREDE II LLC
Also Called: Biscoe Foundry
530 E Main St (27209-9779)
PHONE..............................910 428-2111
Ed Buker, *Brnch Mgr*
EMP: 430
SALES (corp-wide): 668.55MM **Privately Held**
Web: www.grede.com
SIC: 3714 Motor vehicle parts and accessories
HQ: Grede Ii Llc
20750 Cvic Ctr Dr Ste 100
Southfield MI 48076
248 440-9500

(G-853)
HOME CITY LTD (PA)
2086 Hwy 2427 W (27209)
P.O. Box 99 (27356-0099)
PHONE..............................910 428-2196
Mike Allen, *Owner*
EMP: 6 EST: 1956
SALES (est): 610.29K
SALES (corp-wide): 610.29K **Privately Held**
SIC: 2451 5271 Mobile homes; Mobile home dealers

(G-854)
JORDAN INNVTIVE FBRICATION LLC
275 Sedberry Rd (27209-9688)
PHONE..............................910 428-2368
EMP: 15 EST: 2021
SALES (est): 5.97MM **Privately Held**
SIC: 3441 Fabricated structural metal for bridges

(G-855)
K-M MACHINE COMPANY INC
275 Sedberry Rd (27209-9688)
PHONE..............................910 428-2368
Leslie Kellam, *Pr*
Kelly Kellam, *
Robert Kellam, *
Bobby Kellam, *
Dale Newman, *
▲ EMP: 72 EST: 1969
SQ FT: 37,450
SALES (est): 4.84MM **Privately Held**
Web: www.kmmachineco.com

SIC: 3599 7389 Machine shop, jobbing and repair; Crane and aerial lift service

(G-856)
SAPUTO CHEESE USA INC
116 Industrial Park (27209-8096)
PHONE..............................910 569-7070
Lino A Saputo Junior, *Brnch Mgr*
EMP: 10
SALES (corp-wide): 3.79B **Privately Held**
Web: www.saputousafoodservice.com
SIC: 2026 Yogurt
HQ: Saputo Cheese Usa Inc.
10700 W Res Dr Ste 400
Milwaukee WI 53226

(G-857)
SELECT FRAME SHOP INC
138 Coggins Rd (27209-9699)
P.O. Box 216 (27247-0216)
PHONE..............................910 428-1225
David Joyce, *Pr*
Renee W Bingham, *
Donna S Joyce, *
EMP: 56 EST: 1994
SQ FT: 75,000
SALES (est): 6.35MM **Privately Held**
Web: www.select-frames.com
SIC: 2426 Furniture stock and parts, hardwood

(G-858)
UFP BISCOE LLC
402 Capel St (27209-8054)
PHONE..............................910 294-8179
EMP: 10 EST: 2017
SALES (est): 2.07MM
SALES (corp-wide): 9.63B **Publicly Held**
SIC: 2491 Millwork, treated wood
PA: Ufp Industries, Inc.
2801 E Beltline Ave Ne
Grand Rapids MI 49525
616 364-6161

Black Mountain
Buncombe County

(G-859)
A E NESBITT WOODWORK
40 Bald Mountain Church Rd (28711-9592)
P.O. Box 276 (28710-0276)
PHONE..............................828 625-2428
Arnold E Nesbitt, *Owner*
EMP: 4 EST: 1982
SALES (est): 173.13K **Privately Held**
Web: www.blueridgeonline.com
SIC: 2511 Wood household furniture

(G-860)
ASHLEYS KIT BATH DSIGN STDIO L
2950 Us 70 Hwy (28711-9103)
PHONE..............................828 669-5281
Ashley Mcelreath, *Owner*
EMP: 10 EST: 2011
SALES (est): 1.28MM **Privately Held**
Web: www.ashleyskb.com
SIC: 2434 Wood kitchen cabinets

(G-861)
BLACK MOUNTAIN NEWS INC
111 Richardson Blvd (28711-3526)
PHONE..............................828 669-8727
Jennifer Fitzgerald, *Genl Mgr*
EMP: 8 EST: 1986
SALES (est): 444.04K
SALES (corp-wide): 2.51B **Publicly Held**
Web: www.blackmountainnews.com
SIC: 2711 Newspapers, publishing and printing

HQ: Gannett Media Corp.
7950 Jones Branch Dr
Mclean VA 22102
703 854-6000

(G-862)
BLACK MTN MCH FABRICATION INC
Also Called: Black Mountain Machine & Tool
2988 Us 70 Hwy (28711-9103)
P.O. Box 1106 (28711-1106)
PHONE..............................828 669-9557
James F Tolley, *Pr*
Samuel C Tolley, *
EMP: 30 EST: 1985
SQ FT: 10,500
SALES (est): 5.66MM **Privately Held**
Web: www.blackmtnmachine.com
SIC: 3451 3599 3499 Screw machine products; Machine and other job shop work; Machine bases, metal

(G-863)
CELCORE INC
3148 Us Highway 70 W (28711-5526)
PHONE..............................828 669-4875
Matt Hilton, *Mgr*
EMP: 5
SALES (corp-wide): 799.73K **Privately Held**
Web: www.celcoreinc.com
SIC: 2899 Foam charge mixtures
PA: Celcore Inc
7850 Freeway Cir Ste 100
Cleveland OH 44130
440 234-7888

(G-864)
EYE GLASS LADY LLC
Also Called: Pack Your Wings
411 Tomahawk Ave (28711-2848)
PHONE..............................828 669-2154
Kimberly Barber, *CEO*
EMP: 15 EST: 2013
SALES (est): 1.25MM **Privately Held**
SIC: 3841 3851 Eye examining instruments and apparatus; Frames, lenses, and parts, eyeglass and spectacle

(G-865)
GRACE APPAREL COMPANY INC ❂
19 Timber Park Dr (28711-9460)
PHONE..............................828 242-8172
Shane Lee Lunsford, *CEO*
EMP: 5 EST: 2023
SALES (est): 859.31K **Privately Held**
Web: www.graceapparel.co
SIC: 5621 2396 2395 Ready-to-wear apparel, women's; Screen printing on fabric articles; Embroidery and art needlework

(G-866)
HUSO INC
6 Mountain Farm Ln (28711-8812)
PHONE..............................845 553-0100
EMP: 5 EST: 2015
SALES (est): 96.52K **Privately Held**
Web: www.thisishuso.com
SIC: 3651 Audio electronic systems

(G-867)
IMAGINE THAT CREATIONS LLC
104 Eastside Dr (28711-8208)
PHONE..............................480 528-6775
T Paige Jackson, *Prin*
EMP: 4 EST: 2008
SALES (est): 241.04K **Privately Held**
SIC: 3272 Concrete products, nec

GEOGRAPHIC

(G-868)
KEARFOTT CORPORATION
2858 Us 70 Hwy (28711-9111)
PHONE..............................828 350-5300
Mac Mccormic, *Genl Mgr*
EMP: 405
SALES (corp-wide): 471.74MM **Privately Held**
Web: www.kearfott.com
SIC: 3728 3812 3769 3643 Aircraft parts and equipment, nec; Search and navigation equipment; Space vehicle equipment, nec; Current-carrying wiring services
HQ: Kearfott Corporation
19 Chapin Rd Bldg C
Pine Brook NJ 07058
973 785-6000

(G-869)
OAK & GRIST DISTILLING CO LLC
1556 Grovestone Rd (28711-8722)
PHONE..............................828 357-5750
Russell Dodson, *Pr*
EMP: 6 **EST:** 2017
SALES (est): 254.62K **Privately Held**
Web: www.oakandgrist.com
SIC: 2085 Distilled and blended liquors

(G-870)
PARAMETER GENERATION CTRL INC
1054 Old Us Hwy 70 W (28711-2518)
P.O. Box 129 (28711-0129)
PHONE..............................828 669-8717
Clay Hile, *Pr*
Randy Wilson, *
Ross Hile, *
▼ **EMP:** 49 **EST:** 1977
SQ FT: 13,000
SALES (est): 6.6MM **Privately Held**
Web: www.humiditycontrol.com
SIC: 3822 3821 3585 Humidity controls, air-conditioning types; Laboratory apparatus and furniture; Refrigeration and heating equipment

(G-871)
SONG OF WOOD LTD
203 W State St (28711-3408)
P.O. Box 19112 (28815-1112)
PHONE..............................828 669-7675
Jerry R Smith, *Owner*
Jo Ann Smith, *Sec*
EMP: 6 **EST:** 1975
SQ FT: 1,000
SALES (est): 239.25K **Privately Held**
Web: www.songofthewood.com
SIC: 3931 5736 5735 5099 String instruments and parts; String instruments; Audio tapes, prerecorded; Tapes and cassettes, prerecorded

(G-872)
WESTERN CRLINA CSTM CSWORK INC
2952 Us 70 Hwy (28711-9103)
P.O. Box 1281 (28711-1281)
PHONE..............................828 669-0459
Allen Burpeau, *Owner*
EMP: 10 **EST:** 2010
SALES (est): 977.49K **Privately Held**
SIC: 2431 Millwork

Bladenboro
Bladen County

(G-873)
AUTHENTIC IRON LLC
17838 Nc 131 Hwy (28320-6008)

PHONE..............................910 648-6989
Kelly Barnhill, *Owner*
EMP: 6 **EST:** 1995
SALES (est): 523.9K **Privately Held**
SIC: 3462 5211 Iron and steel forgings; Lumber and other building materials

(G-874)
BLADEN FABRICATORS LLC
2646 Old Hwy 41 (28320-7880)
PHONE..............................910 866-5225
EMP: 5 **EST:** 2009
SALES (est): 480.35K **Privately Held**
SIC: 7692 Welding repair

(G-875)
COLUMBUS INDUSTRIES LLC (PA)
Also Called: Gene Franklin Brisson
941 Cabbage Rd (28320-9055)
P.O. Box 65 (28320-0065)
PHONE..............................910 872-1625
EMP: 15 **EST:** 2008
SALES (est): 2.48MM **Privately Held**
SIC: 3589 3441 Water purification equipment, household type; Fabricated structural metal

(G-876)
DYMETROL COMPANY INC (PA)
1305 W Seaboard St (28320)
P.O. Box 250 (28320-0250)
PHONE..............................866 964-8632
◆ **EMP:** 11 **EST:** 1993
SALES (est): 2.75MM **Privately Held**
Web: www.dymetrol.com
SIC: 3081 3559 Packing materials, plastics sheet; Plastics working machinery

(G-877)
INTEGRA FOODS LLC
476 Industrial Dr (28320-6419)
PHONE..............................910 984-2007
EMP: 15 **EST:** 2019
SALES (est): 14.71MM **Privately Held**
Web: www.integrafoods.net
SIC: 2015 Poultry, processed: cooked

(G-878)
K L BUTLER LOGGING INC
12237 Nc 41 Hwy W (28320-7831)
PHONE..............................910 648-6016
Kirby Lee Butler, *Pr*
Tolmy Butler, *Sec*
EMP: 4 **EST:** 1972
SQ FT: 1,700
SALES (est): 104.47K **Privately Held**
SIC: 2411 Logging camps and contractors

Blanch
Caswell County

(G-879)
WATER-REVOLUTION LLC
2246 Nc Highway 62 N (27212-9203)
PHONE..............................336 525-1015
▲ **EMP:** 6 **EST:** 2014
SALES (est): 2.33MM **Privately Held**
Web: www.water-revolution.com
SIC: 3589 Water filters and softeners, household type

Blowing Rock
Watauga County

(G-880)
BILCAT INC (PA)
Also Called: Kilwins Chocolate & Ice Cream

1103 Main St (28605)
P.O. Box 682 (28605)
PHONE..............................828 295-3088
Bill Williamson, *Pr*
Catherine Williamson, *
EMP: 30 **EST:** 1990
SALES (est): 2.33MM **Privately Held**
SIC: 2064 2024 5812 5441 Candy and other confectionery products; Ice cream and frozen deserts; Ice cream stands or dairy bars; Candy

(G-881)
CCO HOLDINGS LLC
278 Shoppes On The Parkway Rd (28605-8340)
PHONE..............................828 414-4238
EMP: 168
SALES (corp-wide): 55.09MM **Publicly Held**
SIC: 4841 3663 3651 Cable television services; Radio and t.v. communications equipment; Household audio and video equipment
HQ: Cco Holdings, Llc
400 Atlantic St
Stamford CT 06901
203 905-7801

(G-882)
WILDFLWERS BTQ OF BLOWING ROCK
Also Called: High Country Candles
Old Martin House On Main Street (28605)
P.O. Box 374 (28605-0374)
PHONE..............................828 295-9655
Larry Ziegler, *Pr*
EMP: 6 **EST:** 1992
SALES (est): 277.49K **Privately Held**
Web: www.highcountrycandles.net
SIC: 3999 5999 Candles; Candle shops

Boiling Springs
Cleveland County

(G-883)
BT AMERICA INC
415 S Main St (28017)
P.O. Box 818 (28017-0818)
PHONE..............................704 434-8072
Atacushi Deyaman, *Pr*
▲ **EMP:** 5 **EST:** 1996
SALES (est): 577.35K **Privately Held**
SIC: 3714 Motor vehicle parts and accessories

(G-884)
HAMRICK FENCE COMPANY
407 E College Ave (28017)
P.O. Box 1195 (28017-1195)
PHONE..............................704 434-5011
Wesley Hamrick, *Owner*
EMP: 10 **EST:** 1985
SQ FT: 400
SALES (est): 343.05K **Privately Held**
SIC: 1799 3699 1521 Fence construction; Security devices; Single-family home remodeling, additions, and repairs

(G-885)
INGLES MARKETS INCORPORATED
Also Called: Ingles
214 N Main St (28017)
P.O. Box 878 (28017-0878)
PHONE..............................704 434-0096
James King, *Mgr*
EMP: 75
SALES (corp-wide): 5.64B **Publicly Held**
Web: www.ingles-markets.com

SIC: 5411 5461 2051 Supermarkets, chain; Retail bakeries; Bread, cake, and related products
PA: Ingles Markets, Incorporated
2913 Us Highway 70
Black Mountain NC 28711
828 669-2941

Bolivia
Brunswick County

(G-886)
MUD DUCK OPERATIONS
Also Called: Mud Duck Construction
1470 Old Lennon Rd Se (28422-8285)
P.O. Box 192 (28462-0192)
PHONE..............................910 253-7669
L Dean Hewitt, *Owner*
EMP: 8 **EST:** 1972
SALES (est): 77.19K **Privately Held**
Web: www.customspecialist.com
SIC: 2411 Logging camps and contractors

(G-887)
THATS A GOOD SIGN INC
Also Called: Sign-A-Rama
1802 Urchin Ln Se (28422-8978)
PHONE..............................301 870-0299
Craig Hickerson, *Pr*
Shaila Hickerson, *Treas*
EMP: 4 **EST:** 1995
SALES (est): 388.71K **Privately Held**
Web: www.signarama.com
SIC: 3993 7532 Signs and advertising specialties; Truck painting and lettering

Bolton
Columbus County

(G-888)
APPLIED PLASTIC SERVICES INC
5932 Old Lake Rd (28423-8914)
P.O. Box 99 (28423-0099)
PHONE..............................910 655-2156
Stefan M Jacobs, *Pr*
EMP: 22 **EST:** 2004
SALES (est): 3.25MM **Privately Held**
Web: www.appliedplasticservices.com
SIC: 3089 Injection molding of plastics

(G-889)
T CS SERVICES INC
286 Jacobs Rd (28423-8936)
PHONE..............................910 655-2796
Travis Jacobs, *Pr*
EMP: 6 **EST:** 2014
SALES (est): 633.91K **Privately Held**
SIC: 3441 Fabricated structural metal

Boomer
Wilkes County

(G-890)
EDMISTON HYDRLIC SWMILL EQP IN
8540 W Nc Highway 268 (28606-9236)
P.O. Box 428 (28624-0428)
PHONE..............................336 921-2304
William H Edmiston, *Pr*
Johnny J Edmiston, *Sec*
EMP: 6 **EST:** 1969
SQ FT: 11,000
SALES (est): 2.24MM **Privately Held**
SIC: 3553 Sawmill machines

(G-891)
GREEN PASTURES LAWN CARE
5920 Hollow Springs Cir (28606-9651)
PHONE..............................828 758-9265
William Pope Senior, *Owner*
EMP: 6 **EST:** 2011
SALES (est): 237.33K **Privately Held**
SIC: 3524 Lawn and garden equipment

(G-892)
HARTLEY BROTHERS SAWMILL INC
8507 West North Carolina Hwy 268
(28606-9236)
P.O. Box 992 (28697-0992)
PHONE..............................336 921-2955
Gene Hartley, *Pr*
James Hartley, *Treas*
EMP: 4
SALES (est): 466.81K **Privately Held**
SIC: 2421 Sawmills and planing mills,
general

(G-893)
RONNIE ANDREWS
Also Called: Ronnie Andrews Logging
5077 Beaver Creek Rd (28606-8209)
PHONE..............................336 921-4017
Ronnie Andrews, *Owner*
EMP: 4 **EST:** 1997
SALES (est): 227.78K **Privately Held**
SIC: 2411 Logging camps and contractors

Boone
Watauga County

(G-894)
**ADVERTISING DESIGN SYSTEMS
INC**
Also Called: ADS Graphic Design
269 Grand Blvd (28607-3617)
PHONE..............................828 264-8060
Dana Willett, *Pr*
EMP: 6 **EST:** 1975
SQ FT: 2,500
SALES (est): 96.38K **Privately Held**
SIC: 7335 7336 2791 7311 Photographic
studio, commercial; Graphic arts and
related design; Typesetting; Advertising
agencies

(G-895)
APPALACHIAN STATE UNIVERSITY
Also Called: The Physics Teacher Magazine
525 Rivers St Rm 221 (28608-0001)
P.O. Box 32142 (28608-2142)
PHONE..............................828 262-7497
Karl Mamola, *Editor*
EMP: 5
SALES (corp-wide): 5.82MM **Privately
Held**
Web: www.appstate.edu
SIC: 2754 8221 Magazines: gravure printing,
not published on site; University
HQ: Appalachian State University Inc
438 Academy St Rm 340
Boone NC 28608
828 262-2000

(G-896)
APPALACHIAN STATE UNIVERSITY
Also Called: Office of Printing
169 Air Ln (28608-0001)
PHONE..............................828 262-2047
Joyce Mahaffay, *Dir*
EMP: 10
SALES (corp-wide): 5.82MM **Privately
Held**
Web: www.appstate.edu

SIC: 2741 2791 2789 2759 Miscellaneous
publishing; Typesetting; Bookbinding and
related work; Commercial printing, nec
HQ: Appalachian State University Inc
438 Academy St Rm 340
Boone NC 28608
828 262-2000

(G-897)
**BETTYS DRAPERY DESIGN
WORKROOM**
Also Called: Custom Win Trtments Dctr Items
3207 Nc Highway 105 S (28607-7310)
PHONE..............................828 264-2392
Betty S Hayes, *Owner*
Rebekah Hayes, *Asstg*
EMP: 7 **EST:** 1979
SALES (est): 90.9K **Privately Held**
SIC: 2221 5714 Draperies and drapery
fabrics, manmade fiber and silk; Draperies

(G-898)
BLUE RIDGE SILVER INC
173 Marsh Lndg (28607-7583)
PHONE..............................828 729-8610
Steven Griffin, *Pr*
EMP: 4 **EST:** 2013
SALES (est): 94.67K **Privately Held**
Web: www.blueridgesilver.com
SIC: 2023 Dietary supplements, dairy and
non-dairy based

(G-899)
BOLES HOLDING INC
2165 Highway 105 (28607-7812)
PHONE..............................828 264-4200
Todd Bingahn, *Mgr*
EMP: 7
SALES (corp-wide): 2.08MM **Privately
Held**
SIC: 3585 5075 Air conditioning equipment,
complete; Air conditioning equipment,
except room units, nec
PA: Boles Holding, Inc.
2748 Swan Creek Rd
Jonesville NC 28642
910 424-0319

(G-900)
BOONE IRON WORKS INC
Also Called: Boone Ironworks
253 Ray Brown Rd (28607-9023)
P.O. Box 449 (28607-0449)
PHONE..............................828 264-5284
John Councill Junior, *Pr*
John Councill Senior, *VP*
EMP: 4 **EST:** 1980
SALES (est): 139.91K **Privately Held**
SIC: 3599 Machine shop, jobbing and repair

(G-901)
BOONESHINE BREWING CO INC
465 Industrial Park Dr (28607-3942)
PHONE..............................828 263-4305
Tim Herdjlotb, *Pr*
EMP: 5 **EST:** 2015
SALES (est): 1.55MM **Privately Held**
Web: www.booneshine.beer
SIC: 5813 3556 5812 Bars and lounges;
Brewers' and maltsters' machinery;
American restaurant

(G-902)
BP OIL CORP DISTRIBUTORS
Also Called: Tarheel Oil
585 E King St (28607-4177)
P.O. Box 428 (28607-0428)
PHONE..............................828 264-8516
Ted Hall, *Pr*
Arthur Lankford, *Mgr*
EMP: 6 **EST:** 2001

SALES (est): 251.5K **Privately Held**
SIC: 1382 Oil and gas exploration services

(G-903)
CANVAS BEAUTY BAR LLC
181 Meadowview Dr (28607-5213)
PHONE..............................828 355-9688
Romiah Zimmerman, *Admn*
EMP: 11 **EST:** 2014
SALES (est): 397K **Privately Held**
Web: www.canvasboone.com
SIC: 2211 Canvas

(G-904)
CARROLL COMPANIES INC (PA)
1640 Old 421 S (28607-6291)
P.O. Box 1549 (28607-1549)
PHONE..............................828 264-2521
Sterling C Carroll, *Pr*
Royce A Carroll, *VP*
Jo Evelyn Miller, *Sec*
◆ **EMP:** 50 **EST:** 1950
SQ FT: 36,500
SALES (est): 22.6MM
SALES (corp-wide): 22.6MM **Privately
Held**
Web: www.clgco.com
SIC: 5199 3199 Leather goods, except
footwear, gloves, luggage, belting;
Equestrian related leather articles

(G-905)
CCBCC OPERATIONS LLC
Also Called: Coca-Cola
795 Nc Highway 105 Byp (28607-7605)
PHONE..............................828 297-2141
Allen Shelton, *Brnch Mgr*
EMP: 38
SALES (corp-wide): 6.9B **Publicly Held**
Web: www.coca-cola.com
SIC: 2086 Bottled and canned soft drinks
HQ: Ccbcc Operations, Llc
4100 Coca-Cola Plz
Charlotte NC 28211
704 364-8728

(G-906)
CCO HOLDINGS LLC
531 W King St (28607-3536)
PHONE..............................828 355-4149
EMP: 112
SALES (corp-wide): 55.09MM **Publicly
Held**
SIC: 4841 3663 3651 Cable television
services; Radio and t.v. communications
equipment; Household audio and video
equipment
HQ: Cco Holdings, Llc
400 Atlantic St
Stamford CT 06901
203 905-7801

(G-907)
CHANDLER CONCRETE HIGH CO
805 State Farm Rd Ste 203 (28607-4914)
PHONE..............................828 264-8694
Ted Greene, *Prin*
EMP: 4 **EST:** 2009
SALES (est): 481.59K **Privately Held**
Web: www.chandlerconcrete.com
SIC: 3273 Ready-mixed concrete

(G-908)
CRAFT BREW ALLIANCE INC
Also Called: Appalachian Mountain Brewery
163 Boone Creek Dr (28607-7911)
PHONE..............................828 263-1111
EMP: 9
SALES (corp-wide): 788.94MM **Privately
Held**
Web: www.amb.beer

SIC: 2082 Beer (alcoholic beverage)
HQ: Craft Brew Alliance, Inc.
1 Busch Pl
Saint Louis MO 63118
314 577-4608

(G-909)
CREATIVE PRINTING INC
1738 Nc Highway 105 Byp (28607-7613)
P.O. Box 2202 (28607-2202)
PHONE..............................828 265-2800
Mark Curry, *Pr*
Lee Q Mcmillian, *Pr*
Donna Carter, *VP*
EMP: 7 **EST:** 1993
SALES (est): 163.79K **Privately Held**
Web: www.creative-printing.com
SIC: 2791 3555 Typesetting; Printing trades
machinery

(G-910)
CREATIVE PRTG INTRNET SVCS LLC
1738 Nc Highway 105 Byp (28607-7613)
PHONE..............................828 265-2800
EMP: 5 **EST:** 2022
SALES (est): 76.29K **Privately Held**
Web: www.creative-printing.com
SIC: 2752 Offset printing

(G-911)
**DANIEL WINKLER KNIFEMAKER
LLC**
Also Called: Winkler Knives
141 Leigh Ln (28607-9484)
P.O. Box 2166 (28605-2166)
PHONE..............................828 262-3691
Daniel Winkler, *Managing Member*
EMP: 9 **EST:** 1994
SALES (est): 1.14MM **Privately Held**
Web: www.winklerknives.com
SIC: 3421 Knife blades and blanks

(G-912)
DIVERSIFIED ENERGY LLC
148 Highway 105 Ext Ste 202
(28607-5847)
P.O. Box 130 (28692-0130)
PHONE..............................828 266-9800
Kirk Bailey, *Brnch Mgr*
EMP: 5
SALES (corp-wide): 2.41MM **Privately
Held**
Web: www.sharpenergy.com
SIC: 1321 5084 Propane (natural) production
; Propane conversion equipment
PA: Diversified Energy, Llc
148 Highway 105 Ext # 202
Boone NC 28607
480 507-0297

(G-913)
ECOATM LLC
200 Village Dr (28607)
PHONE..............................858 324-4111
EMP: 24
SALES (corp-wide): 26.11B **Publicly Held**
Web: www.ecoatm.com
SIC: 3671 Electron tubes
HQ: Ecoatm, Llc
10121 Barnes Canyon Rd
San Diego CA 92121

(G-914)
**ECR SOFTWARE CORPORATION
(PA)**
Also Called: Ecrs
277 Howard St (28607-4011)
PHONE..............................828 265-2907
◆ **EMP:** 50 **EST:** 1989
SALES (est): 17.11MM **Privately Held**

Web: www.ecrs.com
SIC: 7372 Prepackaged software

(G-915)
EDCO PRODUCTS INC
643 Greenway Rd Ste J5 (28607-5304)
P.O. Box 2028 (28607-2028)
PHONE..............................828 264-1490
John Edmisten, *Pr*
EMP: 10 EST: 2008
SALES (est): 197.86K **Privately Held**
Web: www.edcoproducts.com
SIC: 3433 Heating equipment, except electric

(G-916)
GEORGE F WLSON WLDG FBRICATION
1777 Nc Highway 194 N (28607-7702)
PHONE..............................828 262-1668
Grayson Gordon, *Prin*
EMP: 4 EST: 2009
SALES (est): 129.12K **Privately Held**
Web: www.weldingfabricationboone.com
SIC: 7692 Welding repair

(G-917)
GO POSTAL IN BOONE INC
207 New Market Ctr (28607-3993)
PHONE..............................828 262-0027
Christy Gottfried, *Pr*
EMP: 11 EST: 2008
SALES (est): 708.56K **Privately Held**
Web: www.gopostalprinting.com
SIC: 4215 2759 Package delivery, vehicular;
    Commercial printing, nec

(G-918)
GOODNIGHT BROTHERS PROD CO INC (PA)
Also Called: Watauga County Country Hams
372 Industrial Park Dr (28607-3977)
P.O. Box 287 (28607-0287)
PHONE..............................828 264-8892
Bill Goodnight, *Pr*
James C Goodnight Junior, *Sec*
EMP: 26 EST: 1933
SALES (est): 8.95MM
SALES (corp-wide): 8.95MM **Privately Held**
Web: www.goodnightbrothers.com
SIC: 5147 5191 2013 Meats, cured or
    smoked; Seeds: field, garden, and flower;
    Sausages and other prepared meats

(G-919)
GREENE PRECISION PRODUCTS INC
4016 Nc Highway 194 N (28607-7293)
PHONE..............................828 262-0116
John F Greene Junior, *Pr*
John Greene Iii, *Mgr*
EMP: 4 EST: 1987
SQ FT: 4,800
SALES (est): 209.49K **Privately Held**
Web: www.greenemachinearchery.com
SIC: 3312 3949 Tool and die steel and alloys
    ; Sporting and athletic goods, nec

(G-920)
H & T CHAIR CO INC
1598 Meat Camp Rd (28607-7259)
PHONE..............................828 264-7742
Richard Todd Junior, *CEO*
Mary Jane Todd, *Sec*
EMP: 7 EST: 1968
SQ FT: 10,000
SALES (est): 517.8K **Privately Held**
SIC: 2531 Chairs, portable folding

(G-921)
HIGH CNTRY TMBRFRAME GLLERY WD
689 George Wilson Rd (28607-8613)
P.O. Box 1858 (28607-1858)
PHONE..............................828 264-8971
Tom M Owens, *Pr*
EMP: 8 EST: 1997
SALES (est): 305.21K **Privately Held**
Web: www.highcountrytimberframe.com
SIC: 1521 2439 New construction, single-
    family houses; Arches, laminated lumber

(G-922)
HIGH COUNTRY NEWS INC
1600 Highway 105 (28607-8731)
P.O. Box 152 (28607-0152)
PHONE..............................828 264-2262
Ken Ketchie, *Pr*
EMP: 5 EST: 2005
SALES (est): 295.02K **Privately Held**
Web: www.hcpress.com
SIC: 2711 Commercial printing and
    newspaper publishing combined

(G-923)
HIGHLAND INTERNATIONAL
160b Den-Mac Dr (28607-6543)
PHONE..............................828 265-2513
EMP: 12 EST: 2020
SALES (est): 175.34K **Privately Held**
Web: www.highland-international.com
SIC: 2819 Industrial inorganic chemicals, nec

(G-924)
HIGHLAND INTERNATIONAL LLC
465 Industrial Park Dr (28607-3942)
P.O. Box 3564 (28607-0864)
PHONE..............................828 265-2513
EMP: 10
Web: www.highland-international.com
SIC: 5198 2851 Paints; Paints and paint
    additives

(G-925)
HOSPITALITY MINTS LLC
996 George Wilson Rd (28607-8616)
PHONE..............................828 262-0950
William Wacaster, *Brnch Mgr*
EMP: 40
SALES (corp-wide): 269.24MM **Privately Held**
Web: www.hospitalitymints.com
SIC: 2064 Candy and other confectionery
    products
HQ: Hospitality Mints Llc
    1800 Northwestern Dr
    El Paso TX 79912
    828 264-3045

(G-926)
INOVATIVE VAPES OF BOONE
244 Shadowline Dr (28607-4921)
PHONE..............................828 386-1041
EMP: 5
SALES (est): 103.34K **Privately Held**
SIC: 3999 Cigar and cigarette holders

(G-927)
JARED MUNDAY ELECTRIC INC
123 Tarheel Ln (28607-5489)
P.O. Box 2077 (28607-2077)
PHONE..............................828 355-9024
Jared Munday, *Owner*
EMP: 4 EST: 2010
SALES (est): 757.83K **Privately Held**
Web: www.mundayelectric.com
SIC: 3699 1731 Electrical equipment and
    supplies, nec; Electrical work

(G-928)
JONES MEDIA
Also Called: Blowing Rocket
474 Industrial Park Dr (28607-3937)
PHONE..............................828 264-3612
Greg Jones, *Pr*
EMP: 5 EST: 1994
SALES (est): 235.38K **Privately Held**
Web: www.wataugademocrat.com
SIC: 2711 2752 2796 2791 Newspapers,
    publishing and printing; Commercial
    printing, lithographic; Platemaking services;
    Typesetting

(G-929)
LEGACY VULCAN LLC
Mideast Division
3869 Hwy 105 S (28607)
P.O. Box 2995 (28607-2995)
PHONE..............................828 963-7100
Ronnie Godman, *Mgr*
EMP: 4
Web: www.vulcanmaterials.com
SIC: 3273 Ready-mixed concrete
HQ: Legacy Vulcan, Llc
    1200 Urban Center Dr
    Birmingham AL 35242
    205 298-3000

(G-930)
LOVEN READY MIX LLC
1996 Us Highway 421 N (28607-7646)
PHONE..............................828 265-4671
Richard Greer, *Mgr*
EMP: 8
SALES (corp-wide): 62.82MM **Privately Held**
Web: www.lovenreadymix.com
SIC: 3273 Ready-mixed concrete
HQ: Loven Ready Mix, Llc
    1995 Roan Creek Rd
    Mountain City TN 37683
    423 727-2000

(G-931)
M-PRINTS INC
713 W King St (28607-3423)
P.O. Box 506 (28607-0506)
PHONE..............................828 265-4929
Stuart Mangum, *Pr*
Kim Havelos, *Sec*
EMP: 9 EST: 1992
SQ FT: 7,500
SALES (est): 110.36K **Privately Held**
Web: www.mprintsinc.com
SIC: 2396 2759 2395 Screen printing on
    fabric articles; Commercial printing, nec;
    Embroidery products, except Schiffli
    machine

(G-932)
MAST GENERAL STORE INC
Also Called: Mast General Store CPC
996 George Wilson Rd (28607-8616)
PHONE..............................423 895-1632
David Cliett, *Pr*
EMP: 9
SALES (corp-wide): 56.7MM **Privately Held**
Web: www.mastgeneralstore.com
SIC: 2064 Candy and other confectionery
    products
PA: The Mast General Store Inc
    Hwy 194
    Valle Crucis NC 28691
    828 963-6511

(G-933)
MAX B SMITH JR
Also Called: Red Gremlin Design Studio
1055 Blowing Rock Rd (28607-6132)

PHONE..............................828 434-0238
Max Smith Junior, *Owner*
EMP: 4 EST: 2014
SALES (est): 81.85K **Privately Held**
SIC: 2759 7336 Screen printing; Chart and
    graph design

(G-934)
MILLENNIUM MFG STRUCTURES LLC
353 Industrial Park Dr (28607-3978)
PHONE..............................828 265-3737
▼ EMP: 6 EST: 1987
SQ FT: 2,500
SALES (est): 450.69K **Privately Held**
SIC: 1541 3448 3441 Steel building
    construction; Prefabricated metal buildings
    and components; Fabricated structural
    metal

(G-935)
MOLECULAR TOXICOLOGY INC
Also Called: Moltox
157 Industrial Park Dr (28607-3974)
P.O. Box 1189 (28607-1189)
PHONE..............................828 264-9099
Ray Cameron, *Pr*
Heather R Cameron, *VP*
Raymond S Cameron, *VP*
EMP: 10 EST: 1987
SQ FT: 6,000
SALES (est): 5.76MM **Privately Held**
Web: www.moltox.com
SIC: 2836 2899 2835 Biological products,
    except diagnostic; Chemical preparations,
    nec; Diagnostic substances

(G-936)
MR TIRE INC
Also Called: Clark Tire & Auto Service
1563 Blowing Rock Rd (28607-6143)
PHONE..............................828 262-3555
Travis Reese, *Brnch Mgr*
EMP: 6
SALES (corp-wide): 1.28B **Publicly Held**
Web: locations.mrtire.com
SIC: 5941 5531 7538 7534 Bicycle and
    bicycle parts; Automotive tires; General
    automotive repair shops; Tire recapping
HQ: Mr. Tire Inc.
    2078 New York Ave Unit 2
    Huntington Station NY 11746
    631 499-3700

(G-937)
PACE SCIENTIFIC INC
112 Paul Critcher Dr (28607-7932)
P.O. Box 2263 (28607-2263)
PHONE..............................704 799-0688
Joseph Dobson, *Pr*
Gayle Dobson, *Sec*
EMP: 8 EST: 1990
SQ FT: 2,000
SALES (est): 843.64K **Privately Held**
Web: www.pace-sci.com
SIC: 3829 Measuring and controlling
    devices, nec

(G-938)
PRECISION CABINETS INC
1324 Old 421 S (28607-6288)
PHONE..............................828 262-5080
Ken Murray, *Pr*
EMP: 7 EST: 1980
SQ FT: 5,000
SALES (est): 241.15K **Privately Held**
Web: www.precisioncabinetinc.com
SIC: 2434 5211 Wood kitchen cabinets;
    Cabinets, kitchen

(G-939)
RADFORD QUARRIES INC (PA)
5605 Bamboo Rd (28607-9678)
P.O. Box 2071 (28607-2071)
PHONE...............................828 264-7008
Danny J Cecile Junior, *Prin*
Danny J Cecile, *Pr*
Raymond S Cecile, *VP*
EMP: 19 **EST:** 1992
SQ FT: 1,300
SALES (est): 1.87MM **Privately Held**
SIC: 1422 5032 Crushed and broken limestone; Stone, crushed or broken

(G-940)
RADON CONTROL INC
P.O. Box 2873 (28607-2873)
PHONE...............................828 265-9534
EMP: 5 **EST:** 2001
SALES (est): 158.87K **Privately Held**
Web: www.focusbusinesssolutions.com
SIC: 3825 Radar testing instruments, electric

(G-941)
RIBBON ENTERPRISES INC
1640 Old 421 S (28607-6291)
PHONE...............................828 264-6444
Thurman Johnson, *Owner*
EMP: 4 **EST:** 2001
SALES (est): 102.77K **Privately Held**
SIC: 2211 Broadwoven fabric mills, cotton

(G-942)
SOHA HOLDINGS LLC
Also Called: Harmony Timberworks
645 Roby Greene Rd (28607-9152)
PHONE...............................828 264-2314
Tommy Sofield, *Managing Member*
EMP: 25 **EST:** 2009
SALES (est): 2.19MM **Privately Held**
Web: www.harmonytimberworks.com
SIC: 2491 Structural lumber and timber, treated wood

(G-943)
SOUTHERN AG INSECTICIDES INC
Also Called: Southern AG Insecticides
395 Brook Hollow Rd (28607-8528)
P.O. Box 85 (28607-0085)
PHONE...............................828 264-8843
Mike Presnell, *Mgr*
EMP: 25
SALES (corp-wide): 22.18MM **Privately Held**
Web: www.southernag.com
SIC: 5191 2879 Insecticides; Agricultural chemicals, nec
PA: Southern Agricultural Insecticides Inc.
7500 Bayshore Rd
Palmetto FL 34221
941 722-3285

(G-944)
STACKHOUSE PUBLISHING INC
299 Blackberry Rd (28607-7023)
PHONE...............................203 699-6571
Timothy Prickett-morgan, *Ch*
EMP: 4 **EST:** 2017
SALES (est): 208.29K **Privately Held**
Web: www.nextplatform.com
SIC: 2741 Miscellaneous publishing

(G-945)
SURELIFT INC
151 H O Aldridge Rd Unit B (28607-7825)
P.O. Box 3442 (28607-0742)
PHONE...............................828 963-6899
William Miller, *Pr*
EMP: 5 **EST:** 2013
SALES (est): 373.44K **Privately Held**
Web: www.sureliftinc.com
SIC: 4785 3569 Highway bridge operation; Bridge or gate machinery, hydraulic

(G-946)
TRESCO
Also Called: I R C
736 Greenway Rd (28607-4830)
P.O. Box 1860 (28607-1860)
PHONE...............................361 985-3154
▲ **EMP:** 200 **EST:** 2005
SALES (est): 3.07MM **Privately Held**
SIC: 3679 Electronic circuits

(G-947)
TRIPLETT & COFFEY INC
204 Jefferson Rd (28607-8811)
P.O. Box 1640 (28607-1640)
PHONE...............................828 263-0561
Bill Triplett, *Pr*
Kent W Coffey, *VP*
EMP: 10 **EST:** 1976
SQ FT: 6,000
SALES (est): 745.8K **Privately Held**
Web: www.triplettandcoffey.com
SIC: 3599 7692 Machine shop, jobbing and repair; Welding repair

(G-948)
TY BROWN
Also Called: Homes & Land Mag of High S
126 Iris Ln Apt 4 (28607-3664)
PHONE...............................828 264-6865
Ty Brown, *Owner*
Ty Brown, *Pr*
EMP: 4 **EST:** 1992
SALES (est): 160K **Privately Held**
SIC: 2721 Magazines: publishing only, not printed on site

(G-949)
US BUILDINGS LLC (PA)
Also Called: Millennium Mfg or US Chem
355 Industrial Park Dr (28607-3978)
PHONE...............................828 264-6198
▼ **EMP:** 99 **EST:** 1987
SALES (est): 2.5MM
SALES (corp-wide): 2.5MM **Privately Held**
Web: www.us-buildings-support.com
SIC: 3441 Fabricated structural metal

(G-950)
VULCAN MATERIALS COMPANY
3869 Nc Highway 105 S (28607-3326)
PHONE...............................828 963-7100
Brad Allison, *Brnch Mgr*
EMP: 4
Web: www.vulcanmaterials.com
SIC: 3273 Ready-mixed concrete
PA: Vulcan Materials Company
1200 Urban Center Dr
Birmingham AL 35242

(G-951)
WATAUGA OPPORTUNITIES INC (PA)
642 Greenway Rd (28607-4812)
P.O. Box 2330 (28607-2330)
PHONE...............................828 264-5009
Michael Maybee, *Pr*
EMP: 32 **EST:** 1974
SQ FT: 22,000
SALES (est): 6.82MM
SALES (corp-wide): 6.82MM **Privately Held**
Web: www.woiworks.org
SIC: 3086 8331 8361 Packaging and shipping materials, foamed plastics; Vocational rehabilitation agency; Mentally handicapped home

(G-952)
WATAUGA READY MIXED
525 George Wilson Rd (28607-8612)
PHONE...............................336 246-6441
David Hardin, *Prin*
EMP: 7 **EST:** 1984
SALES (est): 193.55K **Privately Held**
SIC: 3273 Ready-mixed concrete

(G-953)
WINDOW MOTOR WORLD INC
779 Ball Branch Rd (28607-8209)
PHONE...............................800 252-2649
Ernest Bonham, *Owner*
EMP: 7 **EST:** 2005
SALES (est): 248.32K **Privately Held**
Web: www.windowmotorworld.net
SIC: 3694 5511 Voltage regulators, automotive; New and used car dealers

(G-954)
WINE TO WATER
689 George Wilson Rd (28607-8613)
P.O. Box 2567 (28607-2567)
PHONE...............................828 355-9655
Doc Hendley, *Pr*
Tina Owen, *
Dickson Hendley, *
EMP: 30 **EST:** 2007
SALES (est): 7.3MM **Privately Held**
Web: www.wtw.org
SIC: 3589 Water filters and softeners, household type

(G-955)
XP CLIMATE CONTROL LLC
643 Greenway Rd Ste P (28607-4840)
P.O. Box 432 (28605-0432)
PHONE...............................828 266-2006
Will Knight, *Managing Member*
EMP: 8 **EST:** 2012
SQ FT: 6,000
SALES (est): 1.22MM **Privately Held**
Web: www.xpclimate.com
SIC: 3585 Heating and air conditioning combination units

Boonville
Yadkin County

(G-956)
A PLUS CARPORTS
6833 Us Highway 601 (27011-7944)
P.O. Box 1448 (27041-1448)
PHONE...............................336 367-1261
Chelsa Adkins, *Prin*
EMP: 6 **EST:** 2013
SALES (est): 300.81K **Privately Held**
Web: www.aplussuperstore.com
SIC: 3448 3444 Carports, prefabricated metal ; Bins, prefabricated sheet metal

(G-957)
BOONVILLE FLOUR FEED MILL INC
203 S Carolina Ave (27011-9065)
P.O. Box 337 (27011-0337)
PHONE...............................336 367-7541
Eugene Phillips, *Pr*
Marcus E Phillips, *VP*
Donna Phillips, *Sec*
EMP: 8 **EST:** 1898
SQ FT: 5,000
SALES (est): 469.27K **Privately Held**
Web: www.boonvillemill.com
SIC: 2048 5999 2041 Prepared feeds, nec; Feed and farm supply; Pizza dough, prepared

(G-958)
SANDERS RIDGE INC (PA)
Also Called: Sanders Ridge Vinyrd & Winery
3200 Round Hill Rd (27011-8444)
PHONE...............................336 677-1700
Neil Shore, *Pr*
EMP: 4 **EST:** 2007
SALES (est): 440.71K
SALES (corp-wide): 440.71K **Privately Held**
Web: www.sandersridge.com
SIC: 2084 5921 0762 Wines; Wine; Vineyard management and maintenance services

(G-959)
VIKING STEEL STRUCTURES LLC
113 W Main St Nc (27011-9125)
PHONE...............................877 623-7549
Alberto Ochoa, *Prin*
EMP: 7 **EST:** 2017
SALES (est): 5.13MM **Privately Held**
Web: www.vikingsteelstructures.com
SIC: 3448 Prefabricated metal buildings and components

Bostic
Rutherford County

(G-960)
AMERICAN COIL INC
157 N Main St (28018-6744)
PHONE...............................310 515-1215
Jeff Aiello, *CEO*
▲ **EMP:** 4 **EST:** 2013
SQ FT: 23,000
SALES (est): 462.25K **Privately Held**
Web: www.american-coil.com
SIC: 3585 Heating and air conditioning combination units

(G-961)
BLUE RIDGE DISTILLING CO INC
228 Redbud Ln (28018-6611)
PHONE...............................828 245-2041
Tim Serris, *Pr*
EMP: 5 **EST:** 2011
SALES (est): 443.72K **Privately Held**
Web: www.defiantwhisky.com
SIC: 2085 Distiller's dried grains and solubles, and alcohol

(G-962)
ERIC MARTIN JERMEY
Also Called: Martin Logging
1815 Salem Church Rd (28018-7569)
PHONE...............................704 692-0389
Jeremy Eric Martin, *Prin*
EMP: 6 **EST:** 2012
SALES (est): 165.42K **Privately Held**
SIC: 2411 Logging

(G-963)
MILLIKEN & COMPANY
Also Called: Golden Valley Mfg Plant Div
2080 Nc Highway 226 (28018-7659)
PHONE...............................828 247-4300
EMP: 18
SALES (corp-wide): 1.69B **Privately Held**
Web: www.milliken.com
SIC: 2231 2211 2281 Broadwoven fabric mills, wool; Broadwoven fabric mills, cotton; Yarn spinning mills
PA: Milliken & Company
920 Milliken Rd
Spartanburg SC 29303
864 503-2020

GEOGRAPHIC

Brasstown
Clay County

(G-964)
KELHORN CORPORATION
Also Called: Kelishek Workshop
199 Waldroup Rd (28902-8114)
PHONE............................828 837-5833
Michael Kelischek, *Pr*
George Kelischek, *Prin*
Rose Marie Kelischek, *Sec*
EMP: 7 **EST:** 1960
SQ FT: 5,000
SALES (est): 223.78K **Privately Held**
Web: www.susato.com
SIC: 3931 5736 Guitars and parts, electric
and nonelectric; Musical instrument stores

(G-965)
LONG BRANCH PARTNERS LLC
1960 Brasstown Rd (28902-8002)
PHONE............................828 837-1400
Steve Whitmire, *Prin*
EMP: 6 **EST:** 2008
SALES (est): 253.46K **Privately Held**
SIC: 1442 Construction sand and gravel

(G-966)
PEACHTREE LUMBER COMPANY INC
Also Called: Buckhorn Lumber and Wood
Pdts
6926 Highway 64 W (28902-8081)
P.O. Box 100 (28902-0100)
PHONE............................828 837-0118
Brian T Smith, *Pr*
EMP: 20 **EST:** 1993
SQ FT: 12,000
SALES (est): 3MM **Privately Held**
Web: www.peachtreelumber.com
SIC: 2421 Sawmills and planing mills,
general

Brevard
Transylvania County

(G-967)
ALLENS ENVIRONMENTAL CNSTR LLC
84 Greenfield Cir (28712-0149)
PHONE............................407 774-7100
EMP: 8 **EST:** 2004
SALES (est): 562.51K **Privately Held**
Web: www.allensenvironmental.com
SIC: 3589 1799 Sewage and water
treatment equipment; Protective lining
installation, underground (sewage, etc.)

(G-968)
BLUE RIDGE QUICK PRINT INC
Also Called: Quick Print
82 E French Broad St (28712-4751)
PHONE............................828 883-2420
Carol L Mathews, *Pr*
EMP: 5 **EST:** 1978
SALES (est): 246.77K **Privately Held**
Web: www.blueridgequickprint.com
SIC: 2752 8742 7389 5999 Offset printing;
Marketing consulting services; Finishing
services; Banners, flags, decals, and
posters

(G-969)
DMARCIAN (PA)
43 S Broad St Ste 203 (28712-3985)
P.O. Box 1007 (28712-1007)
PHONE............................828 767-7588
Shannon Draegen, *CEO*
EMP: 27 **EST:** 2016
SALES (est): 2.32MM
SALES (corp-wide): 2.32MM **Privately
Held**
Web: www.dmarcian.com
SIC: 3861 Photographic equipment and
supplies

(G-970)
GREY HOLDINGS INC
Also Called: Genie Products
283 Old Rosman Hwy (28712-8329)
P.O. Box 1028 (28772-1028)
PHONE............................828 862-4772
▼ **EMP:** 21
SIC: 3542 Plasma jet spray metal forming
machines

(G-971)
HEAVEN & EARTH WORKS
102 College Station Dr (28712-3194)
PHONE............................845 797-0902
Teresa Cox, *Prin*
EMP: 6 **EST:** 2015
SALES (est): 109.32K **Privately Held**
Web: www.terahcox.com
SIC: 2741 Miscellaneous publishing

(G-972)
HERBS GAIA INC (PA)
101 Gaia Herbs Rd (28712-8930)
PHONE............................828 884-4242
Ric Scalzo, *CEO*
Etson Brandenburg, *
Angela Mcelwee, *Pr*
▲ **EMP:** 89 **EST:** 1992
SQ FT: 30,000
SALES (est): 23.69MM **Privately Held**
Web: www.gaiaherbs.com
SIC: 2079 8011 2833 Edible oil products,
except corn oil; Offices and clinics of
medical doctors; Medicinals and botanicals

(G-973)
JACKSON WINE
183 King St (28712-3376)
P.O. Box 1649 (28712-1649)
PHONE............................828 508-9292
Jackson Wine, *Admn*
EMP: 6 **EST:** 2019
SALES (est): 267.83K **Privately Held**
SIC: 2084 Wines

(G-974)
LINDE ADVANCED MTL TECH INC
Praxair
283 Old Rosman Hwy (28712-8329)
P.O. Box B1028 (28772)
PHONE............................828 862-4772
Brad Walsh, *Mgr*
EMP: 107
Web: www.linde-amt.com
SIC: 3542 Plasma jet spray metal forming
machines
HQ: Linde Advanced Material Technologies
Inc.
1500 Polco St
Indianapolis IN 46222
317 240-2500

(G-975)
MEGA MEDIA CONCEPTS LTD LBLTY
101 Old Hendersonville Hwy (28712-4420)
PHONE............................973 919-5661
Anthony Senatora, *VP*
▼ **EMP:** 4 **EST:** 2000
SALES (est): 460.64K **Privately Held**
Web: www.megamediaconcepts.com

SIC: 3993 2759 8412 Signs and advertising
specialties; Commercial printing, nec;
Museums and art galleries

(G-976)
MONSTER BREWING COMPANY LLC
342 Mountain Industrial Dr (28712-5122)
PHONE............................828 883-2337
EMP: 82
SALES (corp-wide): 7.49B **Publicly Held**
Web: www.canarchy.beer
SIC: 2082 Beer (alcoholic beverage)
HQ: Monster Brewing Company Llc
1800 Pike Rd Unit B
Longmont CO 80501
303 776-1914

(G-977)
MOUNTAIN CABINETRY CLOSETS LLC
309 S Country Club Rd (28712-7822)
PHONE............................828 966-9000
Robert Grieves, *Pr*
Cindy Grieves, *VP*
EMP: 6 **EST:** 2020
SALES (est): 790.8K **Privately Held**
Web: www.legacync.us
SIC: 2434 Wood kitchen cabinets

(G-978)
MOUNTAIN INTERNATIONAL LLC
1345 Old Hendersonville Hwy
(28712-9359)
P.O. Box 394 (28787-0394)
PHONE............................828 606-0194
Jerry Gaddy, *Managing Member*
Bruce W Rau, *
EMP: 25 **EST:** 2004
SALES (est): 5.16MM **Privately Held**
Web: www.mountainintl.com
SIC: 2393 2297 Textile bags; Nonwoven
fabrics

(G-979)
PHARMAGRA HOLDING COMPANY LLC
158 Mclean Rd (28712-9432)
PHONE............................828 884-8656
Peter Newsome, *Pr*
EMP: 5 **EST:** 1998
SALES (est): 872.02K **Privately Held**
Web: www.raybow.com
SIC: 2834 8731 Druggists' preparations
(pharmaceuticals); Commercial physical
research
HQ: Zhejiang Raybow Pharmaceutical Co.,
Ltd.
No. 18, Nanyangsan Road, Linhai,
Taizhou ZJ 31701

(G-980)
RAYBOW USA INC
158 Mclean Rd (28712-9432)
PHONE............................828 884-8656
Peter Newsome, *Pr*
EMP: 12 **EST:** 1999
SQ FT: 11,400
SALES (est): 9.96MM **Privately Held**
Web: www.raybow.com
SIC: 2834 8731 Druggists' preparations
(pharmaceuticals); Commercial physical
research
HQ: Zhejiang Raybow Pharmaceutical Co.,
Ltd.
No. 18, Nanyangsan Road, Linhai,
Taizhou ZJ 31701

(G-981)
RITEWAY EXPRESS INC OF NC
1106 Rosman Hwy (28712-4173)

PHONE............................828 966-4822
Larry E Morgan, *Prin*
EMP: 5 **EST:** 2006
SALES (est): 214.38K **Privately Held**
SIC: 2741 Miscellaneous publishing

(G-982)
SMITH SYSTEMS INC
Also Called: S S I
6 Mill Creek Ctr (28712-0236)
P.O. Box 667 (28712)
PHONE............................828 884-3490
Claire Smith, *Pr*
William Smith, *
EMP: 40 **EST:** 1982
SQ FT: 6,500
SALES (est): 8.34MM **Privately Held**
Web: www.smith-systems-inc.com
SIC: 3679 Transducers, electrical

(G-983)
TRANSYLVNIA VCATIONAL SVCS INC (PA)
Also Called: T V S
11 Mountain Industrial Dr (28712-6723)
PHONE............................828 884-3195
Jamie Brandenburg, *CEO*
Nancy Stricker, *
Rilla Hughart, *
EMP: 125 **EST:** 1967
SQ FT: 60,000
SALES (est): 27.47MM
SALES (corp-wide): 27.47MM **Privately
Held**
Web: www.tvsinc.org
SIC: 8093 8331 2652 Rehabilitation center,
outpatient treatment; Job training and
related services; Setup paperboard boxes

Bridgeton
Craven County

(G-984)
FRIT CAR INC
Hwy 17 N Ste 2012 (28519)
P.O. Box 569 (28519-0569)
PHONE............................252 638-2675
Gary Barnes, *Mgr*
EMP: 25
Web: www.fritcar.com
SIC: 3743 Railroad equipment
HQ: Frit Car, Inc.
1965 South Blvd
Brewton AL 36426
251 867-7752

(G-985)
PHILLIPS PLATING CO INC
1617 Hwy 17 N Ste 1617 (28519)
P.O. Box 336 (28519-0336)
PHONE............................252 637-2695
George E Phillips, *Pr*
Mark Phillips, *VP*
EMP: 6 **EST:** 1956
SALES (est): 192.97K **Privately Held**
Web: www.phillipselectroplating.com
SIC: 3471 Electroplating of metals or formed
products

Broadway
Lee County

(G-986)
FOO MACHINE & TOOL PRECISION
311 W Harrington Ave (27505-9543)
PHONE............................919 258-5099
Steve Cran, *Owner*
EMP: 10 **EST:** 1997

SALES (est): 411.47K **Privately Held**
Web: www.foosprecision.com
SIC: 3599 Machine shop, jobbing and repair

(G-987)
SOUTHERN CONCRETE INCORPORATED
3560 Mcarthur Rd (27505-9210)
P.O. Box 875 (27505-0875)
PHONE.................................919 906-4069
Steve Thomas, *Pr*
EMP: 18 EST: 1994
SALES (est): 2.46MM **Privately Held**
SIC: 3273 Ready-mixed concrete

Browns Summit
Guilford County

(G-988)
ABCO AUTOMATION INC
6202 Technology Dr (27214-9702)
PHONE.................................336 375-6400
W Graham Ricks, *Ch Bd*
Brad Kemmerer, *
EMP: 155 EST: 1977
SQ FT: 135,000
SALES (est): 34.9MM **Privately Held**
Web: www.goabco.com
SIC: 3569 3599 8711 3625 Liquid automation machinery and equipment; Machine shop, jobbing and repair; Consulting engineer; Relays and industrial controls

(G-989)
AIM INDUSTRIES INC
391 Brann Rd (27214-9585)
PHONE.................................336 656-9990
Duval Dumas, *Prin*
EMP: 4 EST: 2014
SALES (est): 260.08K **Privately Held**
SIC: 3999 Manufacturing industries, nec

(G-990)
BANKNOTE CORP AMERICA INC
6109 Corporate Park Dr (27214-9700)
PHONE.................................336 375-1134
Sandra Lane, *Pr*
▲ EMP: 150 EST: 1989
SQ FT: 9,000
SALES (est): 39.78MM
SALES (corp-wide): 4.84B **Privately Held**
Web: www.banknote.com
SIC: 2759 Bank notes: engraved
PA: Ccl Industries Inc
111 Gordon Baker Rd Suite 801
Toronto ON M2H 3
416 756-8500

(G-991)
BONSET AMERICA CORPORATION (PA)
6107 Corporate Park Dr (27214-8301)
PHONE.................................336 375-0234
Shinji Takahashi, *CEO*
◆ EMP: 106 EST: 1989
SQ FT: 148,000
SALES (est): 21.58MM **Privately Held**
Web: www.bonset.com
SIC: 3081 Packing materials, plastics sheet

(G-992)
FMP EQUIPMENT CORP
6204 Technology Dr (27214-9702)
PHONE.................................336 621-2882
Jennifer Friedrich, *Pr*
Laura Bargebuhr, *VP*
Robert Friedrich, *Treas*
EMP: 4 EST: 1985

SQ FT: 30,000
SALES (est): 294.46K **Privately Held**
Web: browns-summit-nc.north-carolina-pages.com
SIC: 3556 Food products machinery

(G-993)
FRIEDRICH METAL PDTS CO INC
6204 Technology Dr (27214-9702)
PHONE.................................336 375-3067
Laura Friedrich-bargebuhr, *Owner*
Jennifer Friedrich, *VP*
Robert Friedrich, *Asst VP*
▼ EMP: 20 EST: 1950
SQ FT: 30,000
SALES (est): 3.86MM **Privately Held**
Web: www.nu-meat.com
SIC: 3443 2542 3469 3556 Tanks, lined: metal plate; Cabinets: show, display, or storage: except wood; Electronic enclosures, stamped or pressed metal; Smokers, food processing equipment

(G-994)
FUJI FOODS INC
6205 Corporate Park Dr (27214-9745)
PHONE.................................336 897-3373
Joshua Walker, *Mgr*
EMP: 20
Web: www.fujifoodsusa.com
SIC: 2087 Extracts, flavoring
HQ: Fuji Foods Inc.
6206 Corporate Park Dr
Browns Summit NC 27214
336 375-3111

(G-995)
FUJI FOODS INC (DH)
6206 Corporate Park Dr (27214-8302)
PHONE.................................336 375-3111
Hiroaki Nagatomi, *Pr*
Yasushi Muranaka, *
▲ EMP: 35 EST: 1982
SQ FT: 20,000
SALES (est): 3.88MM **Privately Held**
Web: www.fujifoodsusa.com
SIC: 2087 2099 Extracts, flavoring; Food preparations, nec
HQ: Fuji Foods Corporation
94, Mamedocho, Kohoku-Ku
Yokohama KNG 222-0

(G-996)
GOLD REFINERY
2177 Scott Rd (27214-9608)
PHONE.................................336 501-2977
Donna Beasley, *Prin*
EMP: 5 EST: 2010
SALES (est): 65.87K **Privately Held**
SIC: 3559 Refinery, chemical processing, and similar machinery

(G-997)
H T WADE ENTERPRISES INC
5838 Rudd Station Rd (27214-9708)
P.O. Box 13644 (27415-3644)
PHONE.................................336 375-8900
Harold T Wade, *Pr*
Harold T Wade, *Pr*
Gretchen Carden, *Sec*
EMP: 12 EST: 1992
SALES (est): 976.23K **Privately Held**
SIC: 3441 Building components, structural steel

(G-998)
HOPKINS POULTRY COMPANY
7741 Doggett Rd (27214-9875)
P.O. Box 595 (27214-0595)
PHONE.................................336 656-3361
Jerry R Hopkins, *Pr*

Jeff Hopkins Senior, *VP*
Phyllis Pascal, *Treas*
EMP: 10 EST: 1932
SQ FT: 1,800
SALES (est): 4.16MM **Privately Held**
Web: www.hopkinspoultry.com
SIC: 2015 Chicken slaughtering and processing

(G-999)
JAMES MOORE & SON LOGGING
7435 Friendship Church Rd (27214-9756)
PHONE.................................336 656-9858
James Moore, *Pr*
EMP: 6 EST: 1974
SALES (est): 68.02K **Privately Held**
SIC: 2411 Logging camps and contractors

(G-1000)
JLY INVSTMNTS INC FKA NWMAN MC (HQ)
Also Called: Newman-Whitney
2949 Lees Chapel Rd (27214-9765)
P.O. Box 5467 (27435-0467)
PHONE.................................336 273-8261
Frank W York, *CEO*
James Laster, *Ex VP*
Jane L Stadler, *Sec*
◆ EMP: 45 EST: 1837
SQ FT: 150,000
SALES (est): 1.97MM
SALES (corp-wide): 35.91MM **Privately Held**
Web: www.newmanmachine.com
SIC: 3553 7699 Woodworking machinery; Industrial equipment services
PA: Incompass, Inc.
3500 Viking Ln N Ste 174
Minneapolis MN 55447
651 379-1200

(G-1001)
JOHN JENKINS COMPANY
5949 Summit Ave (27214-9704)
P.O. Box 346 (27214-0346)
PHONE.................................336 375-3717
John M Jenkins Junior, *Pr*
Kelly Jenkins, *Ch Bd*
Perry Jenkins, *VP*
Carolyn Jenkins, *VP*
Terrie Boyd, *Sec*
EMP: 20 EST: 1962
SQ FT: 24,080
SALES (est): 3.15MM **Privately Held**
SIC: 3713 3441 3444 Truck beds; Fabricated structural metal; Sheet metalwork

(G-1002)
MDSI INC
3505 Lake Herman Dr Bldg A (27214-9874)
PHONE.................................919 783-8730
Milton R Peele, *CEO*
Derrick Caul, *Pr*
Matt Roughgarden, *Treas*
Jim Schlosser, *VP*
EMP: 5 EST: 1992
SQ FT: 3,200
SALES (est): 305.56K **Privately Held**
Web: www.mdsi-mfg.net
SIC: 5162 3559 Plastics products, nec; Plastics working machinery

(G-1003)
PRECAST SOLUTIONS INC
7121 Choctaw Ct (27214-6000)
P.O. Box 127 (27214-0127)
PHONE.................................336 656-7991
Chad Harrell, *Pr*
Roy Poitras, *VP*
▲ EMP: 15 EST: 2008

SALES (est): 2.99MM **Privately Held**
Web: www.precast-solutions.com
SIC: 3272 Concrete products, nec

(G-1004)
PROCTER & GAMBLE MFG CO
Also Called: Procter & Gamble
6200 Bryan Park Rd (27214-9755)
PHONE.................................336 954-0000
A R Hilton, *Brnch Mgr*
EMP: 446
SQ FT: 20,000
SALES (corp-wide): 84.04B **Publicly Held**
Web: us.pg.com
SIC: 2844 Hair preparations, including shampoos
HQ: The Procter & Gamble Manufacturing Company
1 Procter And Gamble Plz
Cincinnati OH 45202
513 983-1100

(G-1005)
SENNETT SECURITY PRODUCTS LLC
Also Called: Banknote Corporation America
6109 Corporate Park Dr (27214-9700)
PHONE.................................336 375-1134
David Canon, *Brnch Mgr*
EMP: 60
SALES (corp-wide): 9.9MM **Privately Held**
Web: www.sspsecure.com
SIC: 2752 Commercial printing, lithographic
PA: Sennett Security Products Llc
21 Beech Ridge Ct
Greensboro NC 27455
336 404-3284

(G-1006)
TREFENA WELDS
8408 Exmoor Trce (27214-9879)
PHONE.................................203 551-1370
EMP: 4 EST: 2018
SALES (est): 25.09K **Privately Held**
SIC: 7692 Welding repair

Bryson City
Swain County

(G-1007)
B & B WOOD SHOP & BLDG CONTRS
Also Called: B&B Wood Shop Showroom
4829 Highway 19 W (28713-8575)
PHONE.................................828 488-2078
Thurmond Breedlove, *Owner*
EMP: 8 EST: 1979
SQ FT: 7,500
SALES (est): 114.44K **Privately Held**
SIC: 5712 2431 Cabinet work, custom; Doors, wood

(G-1008)
BEASLEY FLOORING PRODUCTS INC
77 Industrial Park Rd (28713)
PHONE.................................828 524-3248
EMP: 35
SALES (corp-wide): 92.42MM **Privately Held**
Web: www.beasleyflooring.com
SIC: 2421 Flooring (dressed lumber), softwood
HQ: Beasley Flooring Products, Inc.
770 Uvalda Hwy
Hazlehurst GA 31539

GEOGRAPHIC

(G-1009)
CCBCC OPERATIONS LLC
Also Called: Coca-Cola
441 Industrial Park Rd (28713-9424)
PHONE..............................828 488-2874
Gary Gray, *Brnch Mgr*
EMP: 37
SALES (corp-wide): 6.9B **Publicly Held**
Web: www.cokeconsolidated.com
SIC: 2086 Bottled and canned soft drinks
HQ: Ccbcc Operations, Llc
4100 Coca-Cola Plz
Charlotte NC 28211
704 364-8728

(G-1010)
CONSOLIDATED METCO INC
1821 Hwy 19 (28713)
P.O. Box 1457 (28713-1457)
PHONE..............................828 488-5126
Nate Vingus, *Brnch Mgr*
EMP: 83
SALES (corp-wide): 3.96B **Privately Held**
Web: www.conmet.com
SIC: 3714 Motor vehicle parts and
accessories
HQ: Consolidated Metco, Inc.
5701 Se Columbia Way
Vancouver WA 98661
360 828-2599

(G-1011)
SMOKY MOUNTAIN JET BOATS LLC
414 Black Hill Rd (28713-9722)
PHONE..............................828 488-0522
Bryan Nicholas Williams, *Managing Member*
EMP: 12 **EST:** 2002
SQ FT: 2,000
SALES (est): 372.4K **Privately Held**
Web: www.smokymountainjetboats.com
SIC: 3732 Motorboats, inboard or outboard:
building and repairing

Bullock
Granville County

(G-1012)
ACTION GRAPHICS AND SIGNS INC
8694b Us Highway 15 (27507-9618)
P.O. Box 277 (27507-0277)
PHONE..............................919 690-1260
Kenny Forbes, *Owner*
EMP: 4 **EST:** 1997
SALES (est): 156.34K **Privately Held**
SIC: 3993 Signs and advertising specialties

Bunn
Franklin County

(G-1013)
**AROUND HOUSE IMPROVEMENT
LLC**
75 Gus Mcghee Rd (27508-7683)
PHONE..............................919 496-7029
EMP: 6 **EST:** 2003
SALES (est): 118.94K **Privately Held**
SIC: 2431 1521 Doors and door parts and
trim, wood; General remodeling, single-
family houses

(G-1014)
INTERNATIONAL INSTRUMENTATION
382 N Carolina 98 Hwy W (27508-7218)
PHONE..............................919 496-4208
Thomas Lancaster, *Genl Mgr*
EMP: 4 **EST:** 2001
SALES (est): 166.93K **Privately Held**

SIC: 3825 Measuring instruments and
meters, electric

Bunnlevel
Harnett County

(G-1015)
B & B BUILDING MAINTENANCE LLC
5318 Hwy 210 S (28323)
PHONE..............................910 494-2715
Bennie Bryant, *Pr*
EMP: 4 **EST:** 2012
SALES (est): 793.98K **Privately Held**
SIC: 3432 Plastic plumbing fixture fittings,
assembly

(G-1016)
**HEIDELBERG MTLS STHAST AGG
LLC**
3155 Nc 210 S (28323-8993)
PHONE..............................910 893-8308
Chris Ward, *Mgr*
EMP: 40
SALES (corp-wide): 23.02B **Privately Held**
Web: www.hansonbiz.com
SIC: 3281 5032 1423 Slate products; Stone,
crushed or broken; Crushed and broken
granite
HQ: Heidelberg Materials Southeast Agg Llc
3237 Satellite Blvd # 30
Duluth GA 30096
770 491-2756

(G-1017)
STRICKLAND BACKHOE
3216 Nc 210 S (28323-8994)
PHONE..............................910 893-5274
Sarah Strickland, *Prin*
EMP: 4 **EST:** 2017
SALES (est): 72.86K **Privately Held**
SIC: 3531 Backhoes

Burgaw
Pender County

(G-1018)
AMERICAN SKIN FOOD GROUP LLC
140 Industrial Dr (28425-5081)
PHONE..............................910 259-2232
Neil Blake, *Managing Member*
EMP: 25 **EST:** 2005
SALES (est): 9.93MM **Publicly Held**
Web: www.asfg.com
SIC: 2013 2096 Sausages and other
prepared meats; Pork rinds
HQ: Smithfield Foods, Inc.
200 Commerce St
Smithfield VA 23430
757 365-3000

(G-1019)
ATLANTIC CORP WILMINGTON INC
Also Called: Prestige Label
151 Industrial Dr (28425-5080)
PHONE..............................910 259-3600
Tim Kegan, *Manager*
EMP: 50
SALES (corp-wide): 483.78MM **Privately
Held**
Web: www.atlanticpkg.com
SIC: 5113 2621 2679 Industrial and personal
service paper; Paper mills; Paper products,
converted, nec
PA: Atlantic Corporation Of Wilmington Inc.
806 N 23rd St
Wilmington NC 28405
800 722-5841

(G-1020)
CARDINAL FOODS LLC
201 Progress Dr (28425-4619)
P.O. Box 990 (28425)
PHONE..............................910 259-9407
David Ross, *Managing Member*
Cory Barnhill, *Managing Member*
EMP: 38 **EST:** 2017
SALES (est): 744.31K **Privately Held**
Web: www.cardinalfoodsllc.com
SIC: 5411 2033 Grocery stores; Apple
sauce: packaged in cans, jars, etc.

(G-1021)
CARDINAL METALWORKS LLC
1090 E Wilmington Street Ext (28425-3800)
P.O. Box 580 (28425-0580)
PHONE..............................910 259-9990
Max Valentine, *Pr*
Larry Isaacson, *General Vice President**
Thomas Rankin, *
▲ **EMP:** 65 **EST:** 2002
SQ FT: 27,000
SALES (est): 13.31MM **Privately Held**
Web: www.cardinalmetalworks.com
SIC: 3441 Fabricated structural metal

(G-1022)
EDGE-WORKS MANUFACTURING CO
Also Called: Edgeworks
272 W Stag Park Service Rd (28425-4437)
PHONE..............................910 455-9834
Scott Evans, *Pr*
Dave Pomeroy, *VP*
EMP: 9 **EST:** 1992
SQ FT: 4,500
SALES (est): 3.16MM **Privately Held**
Web: www.tacticalholsters.com
SIC: 3421 Cutlery

(G-1023)
**HARE ASIAN TRADING COMPANY
LLC**
49 International Rd (28425-4434)
PHONE..............................910 524-4667
Tiong Chen, *Pr*
EMP: 28 **EST:** 2021
SALES (est): 3.57MM **Privately Held**
SIC: 2092 5149 Fresh or frozen fish or
seafood chowders, soups, and stews;
Canned goods: fruit, vegetables, seafood,
meats, etc.

(G-1024)
INTERNATIONAL PAPER COMPANY
Also Called: International Paper
3870 Highsmith Rd (28425-4736)
P.O. Box 710 (28456-0710)
PHONE..............................910 259-1723
Gary Beacher, *Brnch Mgr*
EMP: 5
SALES (corp-wide): 18.62B **Publicly Held**
Web: www.internationalpaper.com
SIC: 2621 Paper mills
PA: International Paper Company
6400 Poplar Ave
Memphis TN 38197
901 419-7000

(G-1025)
JOFRA GRAPHICS INC
Also Called: Bee Line Printing
401 Us Highway 117 S (28425-7742)
PHONE..............................910 259-1717
John Rau, *Pr*
EMP: 4 **EST:** 1970
SQ FT: 3,000
SALES (est): 294.46K **Privately Held**
SIC: 2752 5943 Offset printing; Office forms
and supplies

(G-1026)
KILN-DIRECTCOM
200a Progress Dr (28425-4618)
P.O. Box 159 (28425-0159)
PHONE..............................910 259-9794
EMP: 5 **EST:** 2016
SALES (est): 163.48K **Privately Held**
Web: www.kiln-direct.com
SIC: 2421 Sawmills and planing mills,
general

(G-1027)
M&S ENTERPRISES INC
784 New Rd (28425-3128)
PHONE..............................910 259-1763
Mattie Boston, *Pr*
Mack Smith, *Ch Bd*
EMP: 9 **EST:** 1994
SALES (est): 126.63K **Privately Held**
SIC: 1389 Construction, repair, and
dismantling services

(G-1028)
NIELS JORGENSEN COMPANY INC
200 Progress Dr (28425-4618)
P.O. Box 159 (28425-0159)
PHONE..............................910 259-1624
Neils Jorgensen, *Pr*
EMP: 5 **EST:** 1994
SQ FT: 5,000
SALES (est): 906.47K **Privately Held**
Web: www.kiln-direct.com
SIC: 3535 Conveyors and conveying
equipment

(G-1029)
PHOENIX TECHNOLOGY LTD
2 Progress Dr (28425)
P.O. Box 249 (28425-0249)
PHONE..............................910 259-6804
Zeljko Vesligaj, *Pr*
Veronica Veslijaq, *
Brenda Vesligaj, *
▲ **EMP:** 25 **EST:** 1982
SQ FT: 20,000
SALES (est): 2.38MM **Privately Held**
Web: www.kicklitestocks.com
SIC: 3089 Injection molding of plastics

(G-1030)
**ROGERS MANUFACTURING
COMPANY (PA)**
Also Called: Rogers Portable Buildings
505 W Wilmington St (28425-5577)
P.O. Box 1403 (28425-1403)
PHONE..............................910 259-9898
Aubrey A Rogers Iii, *Pr*
Joy C Rogers, *Sec*
EMP: 5 **EST:** 1975
SQ FT: 6,000
SALES (est): 540K
SALES (corp-wide): 540K **Privately Held**
SIC: 3448 1521 Buildings, portable:
prefabricated metal; Patio and deck
construction and repair

(G-1031)
SKIN BOYS LLC
Also Called: American Skin
140 Industrial Dr (28425-5081)
PHONE..............................910 259-2232
Neil Blake, *Managing Member*
EMP: 17 **EST:** 1998
SQ FT: 40,000
SALES (est): 2.55MM **Privately Held**
SIC: 2096 2013 Pork rinds; Sausages and
other prepared meats

(G-1032)
SOLO FOODS LLC
201w Progress Dr (28425-4619)
P.O. Box 990 (28425-0990)
PHONE..............910 259-9407
Willie R Moore, *Managing Member*
EMP: 23 **EST:** 2001
SQ FT: 30,000
SALES (est): 208.5K
SALES (corp-wide): 8.45MM **Privately Held**
Web: www.solofoods.com
SIC: 2099 Food preparations, nec
HQ: Saco Foods, Llc
1845 Deming Way
Middleton WI 53562
608 662-2662

(G-1033)
SOUTHERN PRINTING COMPANY INC
203 S Dudley St (28425-5542)
P.O. Box 833 (28425-0833)
PHONE..............910 259-4807
Benjamin R Pusey, *Pr*
Benjamin J Pusey, *Pr*
Matt Pusey, *VP*
EMP: 4 **EST:** 1962
SQ FT: 3,000
SALES (est): 237.26K **Privately Held**
Web: southernprinting.webs.com
SIC: 5731 2752 5943 Radio, television, and electronic stores; Offset printing; Office forms and supplies

(G-1034)
TEHAN COMPANY INC
Also Called: Tehan Distributing
2620 Stag Park Rd (28425-3360)
PHONE..............800 283-7290
Harry Tehan, *CEO*
Colleen Bannerman, *Treas*
Tom Cox, *Svc Ex*
EMP: 5 **EST:** 1957
SALES (est): 383.71K **Privately Held**
SIC: 3861 Photographic equipment and supplies

(G-1035)
VACS AMERICA INC
3490 Stag Park Rd (28425-3370)
PHONE..............910 259-9854
Clyde Harrelson Iii, *Pr*
Buddy Harrelson, *VP*
EMP: 7 **EST:** 1995
SQ FT: 2,900
SALES (est): 218.71K **Privately Held**
SIC: 3589 8731 Vacuum cleaners and sweepers, electric: industrial; Commercial physical research

(G-1036)
W R RAYSON EXPORT LTD
720 S Dickerson St (28425-4904)
PHONE..............910 686-5802
Michael Di Martino, *Pr*
Jean Swanson, *
▲ **EMP:** 6 **EST:** 1978
SALES (est): 366.71K **Privately Held**
Web: www.wrraysonexport.com
SIC: 2679 Paper products, converted, nec

(G-1037)
WALKER PALLET COMPANY INC
3802 New Savannah Rd (28425-4126)
PHONE..............910 259-2235
Harold Walker, *Pr*
EMP: 14 **EST:** 1987
SQ FT: 10,000
SALES (est): 988K **Privately Held**
SIC: 2448 Pallets, wood

(G-1038)
WELLS PORK AND BEEF PDTS INC
750 Croomsbridge Rd (28425-7964)
PHONE..............910 259-2523
Teresa Swinson, *Pr*
EMP: 12 **EST:** 2008
SALES (est): 346.28K **Privately Held**
Web: www.wellsporkandbeef.com
SIC: 2011 Pork products, from pork slaughtered on site

(G-1039)
WILMINGTON BOX COMPANY
101 Industrial Dr (28425-5080)
P.O. Box 2106 (28402-2106)
PHONE..............910 259-0402
Mark Williams, *Pr*
EMP: 23 **EST:** 1986
SQ FT: 29,000
SALES (est): 4.94MM **Privately Held**
Web: www.wilmingtonbusinessdevelopment.com
SIC: 2653 Boxes, corrugated: made from purchased materials

(G-1040)
WINDSOR FIBERGLASS INC
301 Progress Dr (28425-3280)
P.O. Box 597 (28425-0597)
PHONE..............910 259-0057
Robert I Handler, *Pr*
Curtis Howard, *VP*
David Riebe, *VP*
EMP: 9 **EST:** 1990
SALES (est): 2.24MM **Privately Held**
Web: www.windsorfiberglass.com
SIC: 2221 Fiberglass fabrics

(G-1041)
WR RAYSON CO INC
Also Called: Raylabcon
720 S Dickerson St (28425-4904)
PHONE..............910 259-8100
Michael Di Martino, *Pr*
Jean Swanson, *
◆ **EMP:** 35 **EST:** 1969
SQ FT: 45,000
SALES (est): 6.08MM **Privately Held**
Web: www.wrrayson.com
SIC: 2621 Paper mills

Burlington
Alamance County

(G-1042)
ABEE CUSTOM SIGNS INC
544 Chapel Hill Rd (27215-6449)
P.O. Box 2514 (27216-2514)
PHONE..............336 229-1554
Kyle Abee, *Pr*
EMP: 7 **EST:** 1997
SALES (est): 494.12K **Privately Held**
Web: www.abeecustomsigns.com
SIC: 3993 Signs, not made in custom sign painting shops

(G-1043)
ALAMANCE FOODS INC (PA)
Also Called: Triton Water
840 Plantation Dr (27215)
PHONE..............336 226-6392
William C Scott Senior, *Ch*
Bill Scott, *
▼ **EMP:** 160 **EST:** 1959
SQ FT: 40,000
SALES (est): 71.4MM
SALES (corp-wide): 71.4MM **Privately Held**
Web: www.alamancefoods.com

SIC: 2026 2899 2024 2086 Milk and cream, except fermented, cultured, and flavored; Distilled water; Ice cream and frozen deserts; Fruit drinks (less than 100% juice): packaged in cans, etc.

(G-1044)
ALAMANCE KAFFEE WERKS LLC
3105 Midland Ct (27215-9148)
PHONE..............662 617-4573
Daniel Krenzer, *Managing Member*
EMP: 8 **EST:** 2016
SALES (est): 247.76K **Privately Held**
Web: www.visitalamance.com
SIC: 5812 2095 Coffee shop; Roasted coffee

(G-1045)
AMERICAN MULTIMEDIA INC (PA)
Also Called: American Media International
2609 Tucker St (27215-8857)
PHONE..............336 229-7101
Bill B Brit, *Pr*
Richard Clark, *Pr*
Peggy Britt, *Sec*
Jay Jones, *CFO*
Dave Embler, *Sr VP*
EMP: 85 **EST:** 1978
SQ FT: 180,000
SALES (est): 610.63K
SALES (corp-wide): 610.63K **Privately Held**
SIC: 7819 2752 3652 2791 Video tape or disk reproduction; Offset printing; Magnetic tape (audio): prerecorded; Typesetting

(G-1046)
AMERICAN YARN LLC
1305 Graham St (27217-6148)
P.O. Box 1410 (27253-1410)
PHONE..............919 614-1542
Pierre Willy Simmen, *Admn*
EMP: 5 **EST:** 2006
SQ FT: 200,000
SALES (est): 1.03MM **Privately Held**
Web: www.american-yarn.com
SIC: 2221 Textile warping, on a contract basis

(G-1047)
APOLLO CHEMICAL CORP
2001 Willow Spring Ln (27215-8854)
P.O. Box 2176 (27216)
PHONE..............336 226-1161
Dexter R Barbee Senior, *Ch Bd*
Rocky Butler, *CEO*
James Brown, *CFO*
◆ **EMP:** 89 **EST:** 1977
SQ FT: 50,000
SALES (est): 9.73MM
SALES (corp-wide): 450.19MM **Privately Held**
Web: www.apollochemical.com
SIC: 2819 Industrial inorganic chemicals, nec
HQ: Mount Vernon Mills, Inc.
503 S Main St
Mauldin SC 29662
864 688-7100

(G-1048)
ATLANTIC SIGN MEDIA INC
111 Trail One Ste 101 (27215-5672)
P.O. Box 4205 (27215-0902)
PHONE..............336 584-1375
Richard Orcutt, *VP*
EMP: 6 **EST:** 2001
SALES (est): 799.92K **Privately Held**
Web: www.atlanticsignmedia.com
SIC: 3993 Signs, not made in custom sign painting shops

(G-1049)
ATLAS LIGHTING PRODUCTS INC
Also Called: Atlas American Lighting
1406 S Mebane St (27215-6443)
PHONE..............336 222-9258
James Clark, *CEO*
James Galeese, *Treas*
◆ **EMP:** 137 **EST:** 1992
SQ FT: 300,000
SALES (est): 19.96MM
SALES (corp-wide): 469.64MM **Publicly Held**
Web: www.atlaslightingproducts.com
SIC: 3645 3646 Residential lighting fixtures; Commercial lighting fixtures
PA: Lsi Industries Inc.
10000 Alliance Rd
Cincinnati OH 45242
513 793-3200

(G-1050)
AUTOSOUND 2000 INC
2557 Faucette Ln (27217-8913)
PHONE..............336 227-3434
Richard Clark, *Pr*
Dave Navone, *VP*
Wanda Hicks, *Off Mgr*
EMP: 4 **EST:** 1991
SALES (est): 56.29K **Privately Held**
Web: www.autosound2000.com
SIC: 2741 Newsletter publishing

(G-1051)
BARNHILL CONTRACTING COMPANY
APAC
1858 Huffman Mill Rd (27215-8898)
P.O. Box 1782 (27216-1782)
PHONE..............336 584-1306
Leonard Conway, *Mgr*
EMP: 17
SQ FT: 700
SALES (corp-wide): 490.43MM **Privately Held**
Web: www.barnhillcontracting.com
SIC: 2951 1771 Asphalt and asphaltic paving mixtures (not from refineries); Blacktop (asphalt) work
PA: Barnhill Contracting Company Inc
800 Tiffany Blvd Ste 200
Rocky Mount NC 27804
252 823-1021

(G-1052)
BNNANO INC
2119 W Webb Ave (27217-1065)
PHONE..............844 926-6266
Steve Wilcenski, *CEO*
EMP: 12 **EST:** 2016
SALES (est): 993.4K **Privately Held**
Web: www.bnnano.com
SIC: 2899 Chemical preparations, nec

(G-1053)
BONAVENTURE CO LLC
Also Called: Peaches 'n Cream
1147 Saint Marks Church Rd Ste G (27215-9825)
PHONE..............336 584-7530
EMP: 15 **EST:** 1998
SQ FT: 2,700
SALES (est): 2.17MM **Privately Held**
Web: www.properprincess.com
SIC: 2369 Children's snowsuits, coats, and jackets

(G-1054)
BROOKS MFG SOLUTIONS INC
418 N Main St (27217-3908)
PHONE..............336 438-1280
Troy Brooks, *CEO*

Nancy Brooks, *Prin*
EMP: 15 **EST:** 2010
SALES (est): 714.43K **Privately Held**
Web: www.manufacturednc.com
SIC: 3613 Control panels, electric

(G-1055)
BUILT BY BEN WOODWORKS LLC
2232 Eric Ln (27215-5470)
PHONE..................................336 438-1159
EMP: 4 **EST:** 2016
SQ FT: 12,000
SALES (est): 1.62MM **Privately Held**
Web: www.builtbybenwoodworks.com
SIC: 2431 Millwork

(G-1056)
BURLINGTON MACHINE SERVICE
632 Chapel Hill Rd (27215-6664)
P.O. Box 1374 (27216-1374)
PHONE..................................336 228-6758
R Mike Bryan, *Owner*
EMP: 5 **EST:** 1970
SQ FT: 1,800
SALES (est): 404.53K **Privately Held**
SIC: 3599 Custom machinery

(G-1057)
BURTON GLOBAL LOGISTICS LLC
Also Called: Bw Trailer
1603 Anthony Rd (27215-8979)
P.O. Box 2083 (27216-2083)
PHONE..................................336 663-6449
Jack Burton, *Managing Member*
Nathan Burton, *
EMP: 50 **EST:** 2016
SALES (est): 5.24MM **Privately Held**
Web: www.bblogistics.company
SIC: 3537 4225 Trucks: freight, baggage, etc.: industrial, except mining; General warehousing and storage

(G-1058)
C S AMERICA INC (HQ)
1305 Graham St (27216-6148)
PHONE..................................336 578-0110
Soo Bong Joo, *Pr*
Chilsung Textile Co Stckhdlr, *Prin*
◆ **EMP:** 90 **EST:** 1997
SALES (est): 20.44MM **Privately Held**
SIC: 2282 Throwing and winding mills
PA: Chil Sung Textiles Co., Ltd.
　　80 Busong 1-Gil, Jiksan-Eup, Seobuk-Gu
　　Cheonan 31038

(G-1059)
CARAUSTAR BRLNGTON RGID BOX IN
Also Called: Burlington Rigid Box Plant
322 Fonville St (27217-2626)
P.O. Box 240 (27216-0240)
PHONE..................................336 226-1616
Peggy Tew, *Sec*
Johnny Coffee, *
EMP: 5 **EST:** 1908
SQ FT: 125,000
SALES (est): 2.32MM
SALES (corp-wide): 5.45B **Publicly Held**
SIC: 2657 2653 2631 Folding paperboard boxes; Corrugated and solid fiber boxes; Paperboard mills
HQ: Caraustar Industries, Inc.
　　5000 Astell Pwdr Sprng Rd
　　Austell GA 30106
　　770 948-3101

(G-1060)
CAROLINA BIOLOGICAL SUPPLY COMPANY (PA)

2700 York Rd (27215-3398)
PHONE..................................336 584-0381
◆ **EMP:** 220 **EST:** 1927
SALES (est): 29.35MM
SALES (corp-wide): 29.35MM **Privately Held**
Web: www.carolina.com
SIC: 5049 2836 3829 3826 Laboratory equipment, except medical or dental; Biological products, except diagnostic; Measuring and controlling devices, nec; Analytical instruments

(G-1061)
CAROLINA DYEING AND FINSHG LLC
220 Elmira St (27217-1322)
PHONE..................................336 227-2770
Ashok Dhingra, *Executive President*
EMP: 50 **EST:** 2015
SALES (est): 348.03K **Privately Held**
Web: carolinadyeingandfinishing.squarespace.com
SIC: 2269 Linen fabrics: dyeing, finishing, and printing
PA: Stanek Netting Co. Inc.
　　111 Orange St
　　Bloomfield NJ 07003

(G-1062)
CAROLINA HOSIERY MILLS INC
710 Koury Dr (27215-6721)
PHONE..................................336 226-5581
EMP: 7
SALES (corp-wide): 22.87MM **Privately Held**
Web: www.carolinahosiery.com
SIC: 2252 Hosiery, nec
PA: Carolina Hosiery Mills, Inc.
　　2316 Tucker St
　　Burlington NC 27215
　　336 570-2129

(G-1063)
CAROLINA HOSIERY MILLS INC
735 Koury Dr (27215-6720)
P.O. Box 850 (27216-0850)
PHONE..................................336 226-5581
Drew Dunn, *Brnch Mgr*
EMP: 8
SALES (corp-wide): 22.87MM **Privately Held**
Web: www.carolinahosiery.com
SIC: 2252 Hosiery, nec
PA: Carolina Hosiery Mills, Inc.
　　2316 Tucker St
　　Burlington NC 27215
　　336 570-2129

(G-1064)
CAROLINA HOSIERY MILLS INC (PA)
2316 Tucker St. Extension (27215-6741)
P.O. Box 850 (27216-0850)
PHONE..................................336 570-2129
Maurice J Koury, *Pr*
Ernest A Koury Senior, *VP*
Ernest A Koury Junior, *VP*
Miltom E Petty, *
▲ **EMP:** 40 **EST:** 1946
SQ FT: 90,000
SALES (est): 22.87MM
SALES (corp-wide): 22.87MM **Privately Held**
Web: www.carolinahosiery.com
SIC: 2252 Hosiery, nec

(G-1065)
CARY KEISLER INC
1372 Tiki Ln (27215-8241)
PHONE..................................336 586-9333
Cary Keisler, *Mgr*

EMP: 4 **EST:** 2016
SALES (est): 264.39K **Privately Held**
SIC: 2099 Food preparations, nec

(G-1066)
CDP INC
4014 Forbes Way (27215-9439)
PHONE..................................336 270-6151
EMP: 8 **EST:** 2011
SALES (est): 98.39K **Privately Held**
Web: www.cdp-inc.com
SIC: 7372 Prepackaged software

(G-1067)
CEDARLANE LABORATORIES USA
Also Called: Cedarlane
1210 Turrentine St (27215-6836)
PHONE..................................336 513-5135
Cindy Greer, *Pr*
John Course, *VP*
EMP: 23 **EST:** 2005
SALES (est): 1.65MM **Privately Held**
Web: www.cedarlanelabs.com
SIC: 2836 8731 Biological products, except diagnostic; Biotechnical research, commercial

(G-1068)
CENTRAL CAROLINA PRODUCTS INC
2804 Troxler Rd (27215-8534)
PHONE..................................336 226-1449
Diego Diaz, *Brnch Mgr*
EMP: 110
Web: www.centralcarolinaproducts.com
SIC: 3089 Automotive parts, plastic
PA: Central Carolina Products, Inc.
　　250 W Old Glencoe Rd
　　Burlington NC 27217

(G-1069)
CENTRAL CAROLINA PRODUCTS INC (PA)
250 W Old Glencoe Rd (27217-8293)
PHONE..................................336 226-0005
Carlos Diaz, *Pr*
EMP: 60 **EST:** 1993
SQ FT: 112,000
SALES (est): 27.92MM **Privately Held**
Web: www.centralcarolinaproducts.com
SIC: 3089 3599 Automotive parts, plastic; Machine and other job shop work

(G-1070)
CHANDLER CON PDTS OF CHRSTNBER
1006 S Church St (27215-5046)
P.O. Box 131 (27216-0131)
PHONE..................................336 226-1181
Rich Gabrielli, *Brnch Mgr*
EMP: 7
SALES (corp-wide): 9.34MM **Privately Held**
Web: www.chandlerconcrete.com
SIC: 3273 Ready-mixed concrete
PA: Chandler Concrete Products Of Christianberg Inc
　　700 Block Ln
　　Christiansburg VA 24073
　　540 382-1734

(G-1071)
CHANDLER CONCRETE CO INC (PA)
Also Called: Blue Stone Block Supermarket
1006 S Church St (27215-5046)
P.O. Box 131 (27216)
PHONE..................................336 272-6127
Ted Chandler, *Pr*
Thomas Chandler, *
Robert Chandler, *

Madeline Chandler, *
EMP: 75 **EST:** 1974
SALES (est): 97.31MM **Privately Held**
Web: www.chandlerconcrete.com
SIC: 3273 Ready-mixed concrete

(G-1072)
COBB SIGN COMPANY INCORPORATED
528 Elmira St (27217-1328)
P.O. Box 5030 (27216-5030)
PHONE..................................336 227-0181
Kenneth Speagle, *Pr*
EMP: 6 **EST:** 1924
SQ FT: 35,000
SALES (est): 626.09K **Privately Held**
Web: www.cobbsign.com
SIC: 3993 Signs and advertising specialties

(G-1073)
COMMERCIAL METALS COMPANY
Park Road (27216)
PHONE..................................336 584-0333
EMP: 4
SALES (corp-wide): 7.93B **Publicly Held**
Web: www.cmcrecycling.com
SIC: 3312 Blast furnaces and steel mills
PA: Commercial Metals Company
　　6565 N Mcrthur Blvd Ste 8
　　Irving TX 75039
　　214 689-4300

(G-1074)
COMMERCIAL SPCLTY TRCK HLDNGS
1425 Brittney Ln (27215-9155)
PHONE..................................859 234-1100
EMP: 199
SALES (corp-wide): 52.72MM **Privately Held**
Web: www.ezpacktrucks.com
SIC: 3273 Ready-mixed concrete
PA: Commercial Specialty Truck Holdings, Llc
　　200 Ladish Road
　　Cynthiana KY 41031
　　859 234-1100

(G-1075)
COPLAND FABRICS INC
Also Called: Copland
1714 Carolina Mill Rd (27217-7837)
P.O. Box 1208 (27216-1208)
PHONE..................................336 226-0272
EMP: 300
Web: www.coplandfabrics.com
SIC: 2221 Manmade and synthetic broadwoven fabrics

(G-1076)
COPLAND INDUSTRIES INC
1714 Carolina Mill Rd (27217-7837)
P.O. Box 1208 (27216-1208)
PHONE..................................336 226-0272
◆ **EMP:** 355
SIC: 5131 2221 2211 Piece goods and other fabrics; Broadwoven fabric mills, manmade; Pocketing twill, cotton

(G-1077)
CROSS MANUFACTURING LLC
2505 Parrish St (27215-4423)
PHONE..................................336 269-6542
John Agner, *Owner*
EMP: 4 **EST:** 2016
SALES (est): 1.86MM **Privately Held**
SIC: 3999 Manufacturing industries, nec

(G-1078)
CS CAROLINA INC
1305 Graham St (27217-6148)
PHONE....................336 578-0110
Intae Joo, *Pr*
◆ **EMP: 5 EST:** 2008
SALES (est): 4.87MM **Privately Held**
SIC: 2281 Yarn spinning mills
HQ: C S America, Inc.
    1305 Graham St
    Burlington NC 27217
    336 578-0110

(G-1079)
CT-NASSAU TICKING LLC
1504 Anthony Rd (27215-8978)
P.O. Box 160 (27201-0160)
PHONE....................336 570-0091
Ernie Farley, *
Carl Carpenter, *
John Bauman, *
◆ **EMP: 27 EST:** 2000
SQ FT: 45,400
SALES (est): 5.28MM
SALES (corp-wide): 30.15MM **Privately Held**
Web: www.ctnassau.com
SIC: 2221 2211 Broadwoven fabric mills, manmade; Tickings
PA: Continental Ticking Corporation Of America
    4101 South Nc Hwy 62
    Alamance NC 27201
    336 570-0091

(G-1080)
CULP INC
Also Called: Culp of Mississippi
2742 Tucker St # A (27215-8860)
PHONE....................662 844-7144
Tanya Scott, *Mgr*
EMP: 38
SALES (corp-wide): 225.33MM **Publicly Held**
Web: www.culp.com
SIC: 2211 5131 Upholstery fabrics, cotton; Piece goods and notions
PA: Culp, Inc.
    1823 Eastchester Dr
    High Point NC 27265
    336 889-5161

(G-1081)
CUSTOM ENTERPRISES INC
129 E Ruffin St (27217-3959)
P.O. Box 1406 (27216-1406)
PHONE....................336 226-8296
Brian J Kelly, *Pr*
Sarah Sykes, *Sec*
▲ **EMP: 7 EST:** 1978
SQ FT: 40,000
SALES (est): 2.7MM **Privately Held**
Web: www.customenterprisesinc.com
SIC: 3552 3441 3498 7692 Textile machinery ; Fabricated structural metal; Tube fabricating (contract bending and shaping); Welding repair

(G-1082)
DEXCO MCHINING FABRICATION LLC
326 Macarthur Ln (27217-8739)
PHONE....................336 584-0260
Shannon Huffman, *CEO*
EMP: 40 EST: 2017
SALES (est): 3.04MM **Privately Held**
Web: www.dexcoinc.com
SIC: 3599 Machine shop, jobbing and repair

(G-1083)
DICKSON ELBERTON MILL INC
1831 N Park Ave (27217-1137)
PHONE....................336 226-3556
Allen E Gant, *Pr*
Allen Gant, *Pr*
Carl Wallace, *VP*
EMP: 4 EST: 2005
SALES (est): 107.22K **Privately Held**
SIC: 2399 Military insignia, textile

(G-1084)
DISRUPTIVE ENTERPRISES LLC (PA)
Also Called: Primaforce
1452 Industry Dr (27215-8951)
PHONE....................336 567-0104
EMP: 8 EST: 2017
SALES (est): 662.78K
SALES (corp-wide): 662.78K **Privately Held**
Web: www.disruptive-enterprises.com
SIC: 2023 Dietary supplements, dairy and non-dairy based

(G-1085)
DODSON DEFENSE LLC
4756 Blanchard Rd (27217-6741)
PHONE....................336 421-9649
EMP: 5 EST: 2017
SALES (est): 92.84K **Privately Held**
SIC: 3812 Defense systems and equipment

(G-1086)
ELDER HOSIERY MILLS INC
139 Homewood Ave (27217-2835)
P.O. Box 2377 (27216-2377)
PHONE....................336 226-0673
Delos M Elder, *Pr*
John F Elder, *
EMP: 5 EST: 1931
SQ FT: 50,000
SALES (est): 267.52K **Privately Held**
Web: www.elderhosiery.com
SIC: 2252 Socks

(G-1087)
ELEVATE TEXTILES INC
906 N Anthony St (27217-6663)
PHONE....................336 379-6220
Brandon Crawley, *Brnch Mgr*
EMP: 6
SALES (corp-wide): 1.98B **Privately Held**
Web: www.elevatetextiles.com
SIC: 5023 2221 Homefurnishings; Broadwoven fabric mills, manmade
HQ: Elevate Textiles, Inc.
    121 W Trade St Ste 1700
    Charlotte NC 28202

(G-1088)
ENGINEERED CONTROLS INTL LLC
Also Called: Rego
3181 Lear Dr (27215-8817)
P.O. Box 247 (27244-0247)
PHONE....................336 226-3244
Ken Meyers, *Genl Mgr*
EMP: 229
SALES (corp-wide): 7.75B **Publicly Held**
Web: www.regoproducts.com
SIC: 3491 3494 Industrial valves; Valves and pipe fittings, nec
HQ: Engineered Controls International, Llc
    100 Rego Dr
    Elon NC 27244

(G-1089)
FALCON INDUSTRIES LLC
2834 Bedford St (27215-4673)
PHONE....................336 229-1048

EMP: 5 EST: 2019
SALES (est): 77.49K **Privately Held**
SIC: 3599 Machine shop, jobbing and repair

(G-1090)
FLYNT/AMTEX INC (PA)
Also Called: Tex Care Medical
2908 Alamance Rd (27215-5462)
PHONE....................336 226-0621
Ray Baynard, *CEO*
Robert Gibb, *
Jim Adams, *
Captain Ross Bryson, *Prin*
Chuck Flynt, *
◆ **EMP: 49 EST:** 1990
SQ FT: 120,000
SALES (est): 9.24MM
SALES (corp-wide): 9.24MM **Privately Held**
Web: www.carriff.com
SIC: 2221 Manmade and synthetic broadwoven fabrics

(G-1091)
FUJI FOODS INC
363 W Old Glencoe Rd (27217-8294)
PHONE....................336 226-8817
Maria Keating, *Pr*
EMP: 5
SQ FT: 10,394
Web: www.fujifoodsusa.com
SIC: 2087 2099 Flavoring extracts and syrups, nec; Food preparations, nec
HQ: Fuji Foods Inc.
    6206 Corporate Park Dr
    Browns Summit NC 27214
    336 375-3111

(G-1092)
FULLER SPECIALTY COMPANY INC
Also Called: Clay Creek Athletics
804 Bradley St (27215-6806)
P.O. Box 947 (27216-0947)
PHONE....................336 226-3446
Mark Fuller, *Pr*
Steve Wall, *VP*
Debbie Fuller, *Sec*
EMP: 5 EST: 1944
SQ FT: 10,000
SALES (est): 829.24K **Privately Held**
Web: www.claycreek.com
SIC: 3496 2393 Miscellaneous fabricated wire products; Textile bags

(G-1093)
G S MATERIALS INC
1521 Huffman Mill Rd (27215-8815)
P.O. Box 1335 (27216-1335)
PHONE....................336 584-1745
Ronald Kirkpatrick Senior, *Pr*
Karen Hilliard, *
EMP: 37 EST: 1984
SQ FT: 2,500
SALES (est): 10.35MM **Privately Held**
SIC: 1442 Sand mining

(G-1094)
GENERAL MCH WLDG OF BURLINGTON
3304 Maple Ave (27215-7005)
PHONE....................336 227-5400
Thomas P Gathings, *Pr*
Lynda Gathings, *Sec*
EMP: 8 EST: 1971
SQ FT: 10,000
SALES (est): 474.35K **Privately Held**
Web: www.e-gmw.com
SIC: 3599 7692 Machine shop, jobbing and repair; Welding repair

(G-1095)
GENEVIEVE M BROWNLEE
Also Called: Ravenox Rope
2824 Anthony Rd (27215-8985)
P.O. Box 3588 (98273-0378)
PHONE....................336 226-5260
Genevieve M Brownlee, *Owner*
Genevieve Brownlee, *Prin*
EMP: 4 EST: 2018
SALES (est): 162.76K **Privately Held**
Web: www.ravenox.com
SIC: 5085 2298 Industrial supplies; Binder and baler twine

(G-1096)
GERRINGER ENTERPRISES
180 Spoon Dr (27217-3279)
PHONE....................336 227-6535
Glenn R Gerringer, *Owner*
EMP: 4 EST: 1988
SALES (est): 180.77K **Privately Held**
SIC: 3549 Metalworking machinery, nec

(G-1097)
GIBSON ACCUMULATOR LLC
2208 Airpark Rd (27215-8824)
P.O. Box 44 (27249-0044)
PHONE....................336 449-4753
EMP: 15 EST: 2004
SALES (est): 7.49MM **Privately Held**
SIC: 3569 Assembly machines, non-metalworking

(G-1098)
GLEN RAVEN INC (PA)
Also Called: Glenraven.com
192 Glen Raven Rd (27217)
PHONE....................336 227-6211
◆ **EMP: 150 EST:** 1880
SALES (est): 878.83MM
SALES (corp-wide): 878.83MM **Privately Held**
Web: www.glenraven.com
SIC: 2221 2281 2261 2211 Manmade and synthetic broadwoven fabrics; Manmade and synthetic fiber yarns, spun; Finishing plants, cotton; Broadwoven fabric mills, cotton

(G-1099)
GLEN RVEN TCHNICAL FABRICS LLC (HQ)
Also Called: Glenraven.com
1831 N Park Ave (27217-1137)
PHONE....................336 227-6211
Harold W Hill Junior, *Pr*
EMP: 39 EST: 1999
SALES (est): 19.06MM
SALES (corp-wide): 878.83MM **Privately Held**
Web: www.glenraven.com
SIC: 2221 Broadwoven fabric mills, manmade
PA: Glen Raven, Inc.
    192 Glen Raven Rd
    Burlington NC 27217
    336 227-6211

(G-1100)
GLEN RVEN TCHNICAL FABRICS LLC
Also Called: Park Ave Division
1821 N Park Ave (27217-1137)
PHONE....................336 229-5576
Ricky Michael, *Brnch Mgr*
EMP: 111
SALES (corp-wide): 878.83MM **Privately Held**
Web: www.glenraven.com

SIC: 2281 2221 2269 2261 Manmade and synthetic fiber yarns, spun; Manmade and synthetic broadwoven fabrics; Finishing plants, nec; Finishing plants, cotton
HQ: Glen Raven Technical Fabrics Llc
1831 N Park Ave
Burlington NC 27217
336 227-6211

(G-1101)
GRAHAM DYEING & FINISHING INC
240 Hawkins St (27217-3926)
P.O. Box 2857 (27216-2857)
PHONE..............................336 228-9981
Greg Gravitte, *Pr*
Angela Gravitte, *
◆ **EMP:** 75 **EST:** 1987
SQ FT: 40,000
SALES (est): 8.05MM **Privately Held**
SIC: 2252 Socks

(G-1102)
HAAND INC
Also Called: Haand Hospitality
413 Tucker St (27215-5961)
PHONE..............................336 350-7597
Christopher Pence, *Pr*
Christopher Pence, *Prin*
Mark Warren, *Prin*
EMP: 16 **EST:** 2013
SALES (est): 1.02MM **Privately Held**
Web: www.haand.us
SIC: 3269 Cookware: stoneware, coarse earthenware, and pottery

(G-1103)
HOLT HOSIERY MILLS INC
733 Koury Dr (27215-6720)
P.O. Box 1757 (27216-1757)
PHONE..............................336 227-1431
◆ **EMP:** 200
Web: www.holthosiery.com
SIC: 2252 Hosiery, nec

(G-1104)
HOLT SUBLIMATION PRINTING & PRODUCTS INC
2208 Airpark Rd (27215-8824)
P.O. Box 2017 (27216-2017)
PHONE..............................336 222-3600
◆ **EMP:** 5
Web: www.holtsublimation.com
SIC: 2261 2262 2789 Printing of cotton broadwoven fabrics; Printing, manmade fiber and silk broadwoven fabrics; Bookbinding and related work

(G-1105)
HONDA AERO LLC (HQ)
2989 Tucker Street Ext (27215)
PHONE..............................336 226-2376
Atsukuni Waragai, *Pr*
EMP: 100 **EST:** 2004
SQ FT: 130,000
SALES (est): 25.75MM **Privately Held**
Web: www.honda.com
SIC: 3724 Aircraft engines and engine parts
PA: Honda Motor Co., Ltd.
2-1-1, Minamiaoyama
Minato-Ku TKY 107-0

(G-1106)
HUFFMAN SALES AND SERVICE LLC
326 Macarthur Ln (27217-8739)
PHONE..............................828 234-0693
Shannon Huffman, *Managing Member*
EMP: 6 **EST:** 2009
SALES (est): 499.54K **Privately Held**

SIC: 2011 Meat by-products, from meat slaughtered on site

(G-1107)
HYDRO EXTRUSION USA LLC
1512 Industry Dr (27215-8910)
PHONE..............................336 227-8826
Jerry Nies, *VP*
EMP: 63
Web: www.hydro.com
SIC: 3354 3644 Aluminum extruded products ; Noncurrent-carrying wiring devices
HQ: Hydro Extrusion Usa, Llc
6250 N River Rd Ste 5000
Rosemont IL 60018

(G-1108)
INDIE SERVICES
205 E Davis St (27215-5987)
PHONE..............................336 524-6966
EMP: 5 **EST:** 2016
SALES (est): 101.67K **Privately Held**
SIC: 2741 Miscellaneous publishing

(G-1109)
INDTOOL INC
766 Koury Dr (27215-6721)
PHONE..............................336 226-4923
David Phillips, *Pr*
EMP: 22 **EST:** 1986
SALES (est): 4.38MM **Privately Held**
Web: www.indtoolinc.com
SIC: 3599 Machine shop, jobbing and repair

(G-1110)
INNOVATIVE KNITTING LLC
3720 S Church St (27215-9107)
P.O. Box 2717 (27216-2717)
PHONE..............................336 350-8122
William Bo Foster Iii, *Managing Member*
EMP: 25 **EST:** 2017
SALES (est): 2.06MM **Privately Held**
SIC: 2257 Weft knit fabric mills

(G-1111)
JB II PRINTING LLC
Also Called: PIP Printing
825 S Main St (27215-5740)
PHONE..............................336 222-0717
Jimmy Brumley, *CEO*
Jimmy Brumley, *Managing Member*
EMP: 22 **EST:** 1983
SALES (est): 2.18MM **Privately Held**
Web: www.pip.com
SIC: 2752 3993 7311 Offset printing; Signs and advertising specialties; Advertising agencies

(G-1112)
JEFFERIES SOCKS LLC
2203 Tucker St (27215-6738)
P.O. Box 850 (27216-0850)
PHONE..............................336 226-7316
▲ **EMP:** 18 **EST:** 1937
SQ FT: 28,000
SALES (est): 1.97MM **Privately Held**
Web: www.jefferiessocks.com
SIC: 2252 Socks

(G-1113)
JOE AND LA INC
326 Macarthur Ln (27217-8739)
P.O. Box 1516 (27216-1516)
PHONE..............................336 585-0313
John R Michael, *Ch Bd*
Joseph R Michael, *Pr*
EMP: 18 **EST:** 1963
SQ FT: 24,800
SALES (est): 2.38MM **Privately Held**
Web: www.dexcoinc.com

SIC: 3599 3444 3549 Machine shop, jobbing and repair; Sheet metalwork; Metalworking machinery, nec

(G-1114)
KCK HOLDING CORP
Also Called: TEC Tran Brake
2215 Airpark Rd (27215-8824)
PHONE..............................336 513-0002
▲ **EMP:** 23
Web: www.wabteccorp.com
SIC: 5088 3714 3743 Railroad equipment and supplies; Motor vehicle parts and accessories; Brakes, air and vacuum: railway

(G-1115)
KNIT-WEAR FABRICS INC
145 N Cobb Ave (27217-2824)
P.O. Box 790 (27216-0790)
PHONE..............................336 226-4342
Flavius D Hornaday Iii, *Pr*
David Hornaday, *VP*
EMP: 20 **EST:** 1967
SQ FT: 13,000
SALES (est): 2.48MM **Privately Held**
SIC: 2258 2257 Lace and warp knit fabric mills; Weft knit fabric mills

(G-1116)
L & K MACHINING INC
Also Called: Machine Shop, Job Shop
1312 Whitsett St (27215-6977)
P.O. Box 1312 (27253-1312)
PHONE..............................336 222-9444
Ronnie Miles, *Pr*
EMP: 10 **EST:** 1997
SQ FT: 11,000
SALES (est): 904.95K **Privately Held**
Web: www.landkmachining.com
SIC: 3599 Machine shop, jobbing and repair

(G-1117)
LABELS TAGS & INSERTS INC
2302 Airpark Rd (27215-8818)
P.O. Box 2137 (27216-2137)
PHONE..............................336 227-8485
Rhonda Baker, *Pr*
A Leroy Baker, *VP*
Rhonda Baker-capps, *Pr*
Leoma Baker, *Treas*
EMP: 18 **EST:** 1996
SQ FT: 17,000
SALES (est): 3.81MM **Privately Held**
Web: www.labelstagsandinserts.com
SIC: 2759 Commercial printing, nec

(G-1118)
LEESONA CORP
2050b Willow Spring Ln (27215-8854)
PHONE..............................336 226-5511
Matthew Clark, *CEO*
Sanjay Gupta, *
EMP: 36 **EST:** 2019
SALES (est): 10.69MM **Privately Held**
SIC: 3469 Machine parts, stamped or pressed metal

(G-1119)
LEONARD ALUM UTLITY BLDNGS INC
Also Called: Leonard Building and Truck ACC
2602 Alamance Rd (27215-6256)
PHONE..............................336 226-9410
Johanathon Hobbs, *Brnch Mgr*
EMP: 4
SALES (corp-wide): 98.91MM **Privately Held**
Web: www.leonardusa.com

SIC: 5531 3448 Truck equipment and parts; Prefabricated metal buildings
PA: Leonard Aluminum Utility Buildings, Inc.
630 W Indpndnce Blvd
Mount Airy NC 27030
336 789-5018

(G-1120)
LIGNA MACHINERY INC
315 Macarthur Ln (27217-8739)
PHONE..............................336 584-0030
H E Wilson Junior, *Pr*
H Ed Wilson Iii, *Sec*
▲ **EMP:** 6 **EST:** 1986
SQ FT: 5,000
SALES (est): 809.93K **Privately Held**
Web: www.lignamachineryinc.com
SIC: 3553 5084 Sawmill machines; Industrial machinery and equipment

(G-1121)
LONG J E & SONS GRADING INC (PA)
Also Called: Long, J E Sand & Stone
3218 Foy Jane Trl (27217-7125)
PHONE..............................336 228-9706
Anthony E Long, *Pr*
William S Long, *Treas*
EMP: 14 **EST:** 1971
SQ FT: 500
SALES (est): 2.23MM
SALES (corp-wide): 2.23MM **Privately Held**
SIC: 1442 Construction sand and gravel

(G-1122)
MARKELL PUBLISHING COMPANY INC
Also Called: Markell Printing and Prom Pdts
718 E Davis St (27215-5924)
P.O. Box 668 (27216-0668)
PHONE..............................336 226-7148
Robert A Forrester, *Pr*
Mark Forrester, *VP*
EMP: 4 **EST:** 1964
SALES (est): 146.45K **Privately Held**
Web: www.markellprinting.com
SIC: 2752 5199 Offset printing; Advertising specialties

(G-1123)
MARTIN MARIETTA MATERIALS INC
Also Called: Martin Marietta Aggregates
1671 Huffman Mill Rd (27215-9211)
PHONE..............................336 584-8875
Tommy Jenkins, *Owner*
EMP: 7
Web: www.martinmarietta.com
SIC: 1422 1423 Crushed and broken limestone; Crushed and broken granite
PA: Martin Marietta Materials Inc
4123 Parklake Ave
Raleigh NC 27612

(G-1124)
MARVEL-SCHBLER ARCFT CRBRTORS
2208 Airpark Rd (27215-8824)
P.O. Box 44 (27249-0044)
PHONE..............................336 446-0002
EMP: 7 **EST:** 2008
SALES (est): 2.06MM **Privately Held**
Web: www.msacarbs.com
SIC: 3592 Carburetors

(G-1125)
MASSEY READY-MIX CONCRETE INC
1421 Railroad St (27217-7054)
P.O. Box 1983 (27216-1983)

PHONE..................336 221-8100
Randy Massey, *Pr*
EMP: 8 **EST:** 1998
SALES (est): 970.71K **Privately Held**
SIC: 3273 Ready-mixed concrete

(G-1126)
MCCOMB INDUSTRIES LLLP
Also Called: Alexander Fabrics
1311 Industry Dr (27215-8950)
P.O. Box 147 (27216-0147)
PHONE..................336 229-9139
Todd Whitley, *Pt*
▼ **EMP:** 80 **EST:** 2002
SQ FT: 100,000
SALES (est): 5.49MM **Privately Held**
Web: www.mccombind.com
SIC: 2258 Dyeing and finishing lace goods
and warp knit fabric

(G-1127)
MCMICHAEL MILLS INC
2050 Willow Spring Ln (27215-8854)
PHONE..................336 584-0134
Dalton L Mcmichael Junior, *Brnch Mgr*
EMP: 40
Web: www.mcmichaelmills.com
SIC: 2241 Rubber and elastic yarns and
fabrics
PA: Mcmichael Mills, Inc.
130 Shakey Rd
Mayodan NC 27027

(G-1128)
MEREDITH - WEBB PRTG CO INC
334 N Main St (27217-3906)
P.O. Box 2196 (27216-2196)
PHONE..................336 228-8378
Travers G Webb, *Pr*
George T Webb Ii, *Ch*
Betty N Webb, *
H Cooper Walker, *Stockholder*
EMP: 73 **EST:** 1952
SQ FT: 40,000
SALES (est): 23.1MM **Privately Held**
Web: www.meredithwebb.com
SIC: 7331 2752 Direct mail advertising
services; Commercial printing, lithographic

(G-1129)
MIDWAY BLIND & AWNING CO INC
1836 E Webb Ave (27217-7418)
P.O. Box 1761 (27216-1761)
PHONE..................336 226-4532
Randy Minor, *Pr*
Ricky Minor, *VP*
Hazel Minor, *Sec*
EMP: 4 **EST:** 1951
SQ FT: 4,000
SALES (est): 114.68K **Privately Held**
SIC: 1761 1521 3444 Siding contractor;
General remodeling, single-family houses;
Awnings, sheet metal

(G-1130)
MONGOOSE LLC
Also Called: Noa Living
423 Lakeside Ave (27217-2329)
PHONE..................919 400-0772
Sam Mehme, *CEO*
Sam Mehme, *Managing Member*
EMP: 12 **EST:** 2018
SALES (est): 1.79MM **Privately Held**
Web: www.noaliving.com
SIC: 5023 5021 5713 3281 Rugs; Household
furniture; Rugs; Altars, cut stone

(G-1131)
MOUNT VERNON CHEMICALS LLC
Apollo Chemical
2001 Willow Spring Ln (27215-8854)

PHONE..................336 226-1161
Randy Smith, *Brnch Mgr*
EMP: 98
SALES (corp-wide): 450.19MM **Privately
Held**
Web: www.apollochemical.com
SIC: 2819 Industrial inorganic chemicals, nec
HQ: Mount Vernon Chemicals Llc
2001 Willow Spring Ln
Burlington NC 27215

(G-1132)
MOUNT VERNON MILLS INC
Apollo Chemical Div
2001 Willow Spring Ln (27215-8854)
PHONE..................336 226-1161
Ed Fish, *Div Pres*
EMP: 554
SALES (corp-wide): 450.19MM **Privately
Held**
Web: www.mvmills.com
SIC: 2819 Industrial inorganic chemicals, nec
HQ: Mount Vernon Mills, Inc.
503 S Main St
Mauldin SC 29662
864 688-7100

(G-1133)
MTS HOLDINGS CORP INC
2900 Tucker St (27215-9575)
PHONE..................336 227-0151
Michael L Scoggins, *Pr*
Tommy G Scoggins, *
Michael Paul Spierer, *
▲ **EMP:** 35 **EST:** 1965
SQ FT: 60,000
SALES (est): 981.32K **Privately Held**
Web: www.psmachine.com
SIC: 7692 3444 3441 Welding repair; Sheet
metalwork; Fabricated structural metal

(G-1134)
NATEL INC
Also Called: Sir Speedy
1257 S Church St (27215-5049)
PHONE..................336 227-1227
Deva Reece, *Pr*
Tim Clark, *VP*
EMP: 5 **EST:** 2010
SALES (est): 488.12K **Privately Held**
Web: www.sirspeedy.com
SIC: 2752 Commercial printing, lithographic

(G-1135)
NATIONAL SPINNING CO INC
226 Glen Raven Rd (27217-1026)
PHONE..................336 226-0141
Ed Atkins, *Mgr*
EMP: 115
SALES (corp-wide): 40.55MM **Privately
Held**
Web: www.natspin.com
SIC: 2281 Wool yarn, spun
PA: National Spinning Co., Inc.
1481 W 2nd St
Washington NC 27889
252 975-7111

(G-1136)
**NC MOTOR VHCL LCNSE PLATE
AGCY**
Also Called: N C Mtor Vhcl Lcnse Plate Agcy
2668 Ramada Rd (27215-5469)
PHONE..................336 228-7152
Julia Miller, *Pt*
Julia Miller, *Mgr*
Marry Newsome, *Pt*
EMP: 7 **EST:** 1950
SALES (est): 511.36K **Privately Held**
SIC: 3469 Automobile license tags, stamped
metal

(G-1137)
P&S MACHINING FABRICATION LLC
2900 Tucker St (27215-9575)
PHONE..................336 227-0151
Michael Paul Spierer, *Managing Member*
EMP: 45 **EST:** 2022
SALES (est): 5.14MM **Privately Held**
Web: www.psmachine.com
SIC: 3444 Sheet metalwork

(G-1138)
PARADISE PRINTERS
3651 Alamance Rd (27215-9130)
PHONE..................336 570-2922
Jeffrey Baldwin, *Pr*
Georgia Baldwin, *VP*
EMP: 4 **EST:** 1981
SQ FT: 3,000
SALES (est): 139.46K **Privately Held**
Web: www.paradiseprinters.com
SIC: 2759 Screen printing

(G-1139)
PICKETT HOSIERY MILLS INC
707 S Main St (27215-5844)
P.O. Box 877 (27216-0877)
PHONE..................336 227-2716
Larry Small, *CEO*
J Nimrod Harris Junior, *Pr*
Amy Harris Deal, *
Christine Harris, *
EMP: 50 **EST:** 1927
SALES (est): 6.29MM **Privately Held**
Web: www.picketthosiery.com
SIC: 2252 Socks

(G-1140)
**PIEDMONT METALS BURLINGTON
INC**
215 Macarthur Ln (27217-8738)
PHONE..................336 584-7742
Jeremy Troxler, *Pr*
EMP: 23
SALES (est): 3MM **Privately Held**
SIC: 3441 Fabricated structural metal

(G-1141)
PIP PRINTING & DOCUMENT SERVIC
Also Called: PIP Printing
717 Chapel Hill Rd (27215-6452)
PHONE..................336 222-0717
Judy Brumley, *Prin*
EMP: 4 **EST:** 2008
SALES (est): 19.86K **Privately Held**
Web: www.pip.com
SIC: 2752 Offset printing

(G-1142)
POSTAL INSTANT PRESS
Also Called: PIP Printing
825 S Main St (27215-5740)
PHONE..................336 222-0717
Jimmy Burmley, *Owner*
EMP: 6 **EST:** 1983
SALES (est): 256.52K **Privately Held**
Web: www.pip.com
SIC: 2752 2789 Offset printing; Bookbinding
and related work

(G-1143)
**QUALITY MECHANICAL CONTRS
LLC**
3032a Rock Hill Rd (27215-8623)
PHONE..................336 228-0638
Barbara Newsome, *
EMP: 75 **EST:** 1985
SQ FT: 3,500
SALES (est): 15.8MM **Privately Held**
Web:
www.qualitymechanicalcontractors.com

SIC: 3312 Stainless steel

(G-1144)
**RACE TECH RACE CARS CMPNNTS
IN**
403 Macarthur Ln (27217-8740)
PHONE..................336 538-4941
Russ Farmer, *Pr*
Donna Farmer Srec, *Treas*
EMP: 9 **EST:** 1988
SQ FT: 25,000
SALES (est): 889.69K **Privately Held**
Web: www.racetechracecars.com
SIC: 3711 Automobile assembly, including
specialty automobiles

(G-1145)
RESOLUTE ELEVATOR LLC
2309 Airpark Rd (27215-8818)
PHONE..................919 903-0189
Jonathan Fox, *Managing Member*
EMP: 25 **EST:** 2015
SALES (est): 5.98MM **Privately Held**
Web: www.resoluteelevator.com
SIC: 3534 Elevators and equipment

(G-1146)
RG CONVERGENCE TECH LLC
Also Called: Convergence Technologies
1325 N Church St B (27217-2803)
P.O. Box 1490 (27302-1490)
PHONE..................336 953-2796
EMP: 5 **EST:** 2006
SQ FT: 10,000
SALES (est): 1.34MM **Privately Held**
Web: www.convergenceusa.com
SIC: 3829 Measuring and controlling
devices, nec

(G-1147)
RIDDLE & COMPANY LLC
Also Called: Riddle Home & Gift
1214 Turrentine St (27215-6836)
PHONE..................336 229-1856
▼ **EMP:** 6 **EST:** 1991
SQ FT: 68,600
SALES (est): 211.52K **Privately Held**
Web: www.rciwoven.com
SIC: 2211 2392 Blankets and blanketings,
cotton; Household furnishings, nec

(G-1148)
RIVERVIEW CABINET & SUPPLY INC
1111 N Riverview Dr (27217-8735)
PHONE..................336 228-1486
Tommy Murray, *Pr*
Harold Fogleman, *VP*
Barney Jordan, *Sec*
EMP: 4 **EST:** 1979
SQ FT: 3,000
SALES (est): 165.22K **Privately Held**
Web: www.riverviewcabinet.com
SIC: 2511 2434 Novelty furniture: wood;
Vanities, bathroom: wood

(G-1149)
ROSE REPROGRAPHICS
2030 S Church St (27215-5326)
PHONE..................336 222-0727
Todd Rose, *Pr*
EMP: 8 **EST:** 2006
SALES (est): 101.28K **Privately Held**
SIC: 2732 Book printing

(G-1150)
ROTO-PLATE INC
2025 Cesnna Dr (27215-8447)
P.O. Box 1559 (27216-1559)
PHONE..................336 226-4965
James Freeman Junior, *Pr*

James W Freeman Junior, *Pr*
Alison Mary Freeman, *VP Mktg*
Tracy Alcorn, *CFO*
EMP: 8 **EST:** 1974
SQ FT: 15,000
SALES (est): 526.41K **Privately Held**
Web: www.roto-plate.com
SIC: 2796　Platemaking services

(G-1151)
RUSSELL PRINTING INC
2589 Deep Creek Church Rd (27217-7814)
PHONE....................404 366-0552
Douglas Russell, *Pr*
Jeff Lindler, *VP*
EMP: 5 **EST:** 1977
SALES (est): 116.81K **Privately Held**
Web: www.russellprinting.com
SIC: 2752 2759　Offset printing; Visiting
　cards (including business): printing, nsk

(G-1152)
RYDER INTEGRATED LOGISTICS INC
1603 Anthony Rd (27215-8979)
P.O. Box 2628 (27216-2628)
PHONE....................336 227-1130
EMP: 8
SALES (corp-wide): 12.64B **Publicly Held**
Web: www.impactfs.com
SIC: 3999　Advertising display products
HQ: Ryder Integrated Logistics, Inc.
　2333 Ponce De Leon Blvd
　Miami FL 33134
　786 247-1987

(G-1153)
RYDER INTEGRATED LOGISTICS INC
1361 Anthony Rd (27215-8937)
P.O. Box 2628 (27216-2628)
PHONE....................336 227-1130
EMP: 16
SALES (corp-wide): 12.64B **Publicly Held**
Web: www.impactfs.com
SIC: 3999　Advertising display products
HQ: Ryder Integrated Logistics, Inc.
　2333 Ponce De Leon Blvd
　Miami FL 33134
　786 247-1987

(G-1154)
SAUERESSIG NORTH AMERICA INC
2056 Willow Spring Ln (27215-8854)
PHONE....................336 395-6200
Robert L Frost, *Pr*
Carla Frost, *VP*
▲ **EMP:** 20 **EST:** 2004
SQ FT: 300
SALES (est): 8.57MM
SALES (corp-wide): 1.8B **Publicly Held**
Web: www.saueressig.com
SIC: 3366　Bronze foundry, nec
PA: Matthews International Corporation
　2 N Shore Ctr
　Pittsburgh PA 15212
　412 442-8200

(G-1155)
SHAWMUT CORPORATION
Also Called: Shawmut Corporation
1821 N Park Ave (27217-1137)
PHONE....................336 229-5576
EMP: 12
SALES (corp-wide): 152.55MM **Privately
Held**
Web: www.shawmutcorporation.com
SIC: 2295　Coated fabrics, not rubberized
PA: Shawmut Llc
　208 Manley St
　West Bridgewater MA 02379
　508 588-3300

(G-1156)
SHOFFNER INDUSTRIES INC
5631 S Nc Highway 62 (27215-9025)
PHONE....................336 226-9356
Butch Matthews, *Prin*
EMP: 6 **EST:** 2009
SALES (est): 157.83K **Privately Held**
Web: www.ufpi.com
SIC: 3999　Manufacturing industries, nec

(G-1157)
SIGN WORXPRESS
2529 S Church St (27215-5203)
P.O. Box 4038 (27215-0901)
PHONE....................336 437-9889
FAX: 336 437-1229
EMP: 4
SALES (est): 250.23K **Privately Held**
SIC: 3993　Signs and advertising specialties

(G-1158)
SMITH DRAPERIES INC
Also Called: Stevenso Vestal
2347 W Hanford Rd (27215-6765)
PHONE....................336 226-2183
David Stevenson, *Pr*
William Vestel, *Sec*
EMP: 16 **EST:** 1962
SQ FT: 30,000
SALES (est): 1.43MM **Privately Held**
Web: www.stevensonvestal.com
SIC: 2391 2392　Draperies, plastic and
　textile: from purchased materials;
　Bedspreads and bed sets: made from
　purchased materials

(G-1159)
SOUTHERN WOODWORKING INC
418 Hawthorne Ln (27215-2050)
PHONE....................336 693-5892
EMP: 4 **EST:** 2018
SALES (est): 72.62K **Privately Held**
SIC: 2431　Millwork

(G-1160)
SOUTHLAND ELECTRICAL SUP LLC
147 N Main St (27217-3901)
P.O. Box 1329 (27216)
PHONE....................336 227-1486
James H Griggs, *Pr*
Michael Griggs, *
Virginia Griggs, *
▲ **EMP:** 115 **EST:** 1983
SQ FT: 100,000
SALES (est): 24.97MM **Privately Held**
Web: www.southlandelectrical.com
SIC: 5211 5063 3678　Electrical construction
　materials; Electrical supplies, nec;
　Electronic connectors

(G-1161)
SPECIAL T HOSIERY MILLS INC
1102 N Anthony St (27217-7013)
P.O. Box 1439 (27216-1439)
PHONE....................336 227-2858
Jerry Richardson, *Pr*
Jody Richardson, *
Wendy Davis, *
EMP: 5 **EST:** 1977
SQ FT: 50,000
SALES (est): 316.19K **Privately Held**
SIC: 2252 2251　Socks; Women's hosiery,
　except socks

(G-1162)
SPLAWN BELTING INC
1758 Anthony Rd (27215-8980)
P.O. Box 1299 (27216-1299)
PHONE....................336 227-4277
Stephen Splawn, *Pr*

J Michael Splawn, *
Dan R Bird, *
◆ **EMP:** 35 **EST:** 1939
SQ FT: 42,000
SALES (est): 4.71MM **Privately Held**
Web: www.splawnbelting.com
SIC: 5085 3052 3199　Hose, belting, and
　packing; Rubber and plastics hose and
　beltings; Belting for machinery: solid,
　twisted, flat, etc.: leather

(G-1163)
STANS QUALITY FOODS INC
1503 N Graham Hopedale Rd
(27217-1819)
P.O. Box 477 (27216-0477)
PHONE....................336 570-2572
Sherriee Tapp, *Owner*
EMP: 5 **EST:** 1952
SQ FT: 4,000
SALES (est): 87.44K **Privately Held**
SIC: 2022　Cheese; natural and processed

(G-1164)
STAR FOOD PRODUCTS INC (PA)
727 S Spring St (27215-5870)
PHONE....................336 227-4079
George Bradford, *CEO*
Norman Mabry, *
▼ **EMP:** 57 **EST:** 1953
SQ FT: 15,000
SALES (est): 22.64MM
SALES (corp-wide): 22.64MM **Privately
Held**
Web: www.starfoodproducts.com
SIC: 5147 2099　Meats and meat products;
　Ready-to-eat meals, salads, and
　sandwiches

(G-1165)
STILLWOOD AMMUN SYSTEMS LLC
Also Called: Stillwood
642 E Webb Ave (27217-5970)
PHONE....................919 721-9096
Joshua Kratky, *Managing Member*
▲ **EMP:** 7 **EST:** 2012
SQ FT: 30,000
SALES (est): 200.35K **Privately Held**
Web: www.stillwoodammo.com
SIC: 3331 3482　Refined primary copper
　products; Small arms ammunition

(G-1166)
SYNTECH OF BURLINGTON INC
1825 Frank Holt Dr (27215-8946)
P.O. Box 168 (27216-0168)
PHONE....................336 570-2035
Brad Harmon, *CEO*
A J Harmon, *Ch*
Bonnie Harmon, *VP*
EMP: 12 **EST:** 1992
SQ FT: 20,000
SALES (est): 2.3MM **Privately Held**
Web: www.syntechsigns.com
SIC: 3993 3949　Signs, not made in custom
　sign painting shops; Racket sports
　equipment

(G-1167)
T S DESIGNS INCORPORATED
2053 Willow Spring Ln (27215-8854)
PHONE....................336 226-5694
Thomas G Sineath, *CEO*
Eric Henry, *
EMP: 45 **EST:** 1977
SQ FT: 20,000
SALES (est): 1.24MM **Privately Held**
Web: www.tsdesigns.com
SIC: 2759　Screen printing

(G-1168)
**TIMES NEWS PUBLISHING
COMPANY**
Also Called: Times-News
707 S Main St (27215-5844)
P.O. Box 481 (27216-0481)
PHONE....................336 226-4414
Jonathan Segal, *Pr*
▲ **EMP:** 10 **EST:** 2008
SALES (est): 827.94K **Privately Held**
Web: www.thetimesnews.com
SIC: 2711　Commercial printing and
　newspaper publishing combined

(G-1169)
TRIAD ENGINES PARTS & SVCS INC
3439 S Aviation Dr (27215-9241)
PHONE....................800 334-6437
Bonnie Blough Managing, *Prin*
Janet Moore, *Prin*
EMP: 5 **EST:** 2014
SALES (est): 364.63K **Privately Held**
Web: www.hhtriad.com
SIC: 3724　Research and development on
　aircraft engines and parts

(G-1170)
TRIPATH IMAGING INC (HQ)
Also Called: Bd Diagnostics Tripath
780 Plantation Dr (27215-6723)
PHONE....................336 222-9707
Edward Ludwij, *CEO*
Stephen P Hall, *
Ray W Swanson, *Senior Vice President
Commercial*
◆ **EMP:** 100 **EST:** 1996
SQ FT: 70,000
SALES (est): 16.24MM
SALES (corp-wide): 20.18B **Publicly Held**
SIC: 2835 3841 5047　Diagnostic substances
　; Diagnostic apparatus, medical; Diagnostic
　equipment, medical
PA: Becton, Dickinson And Company
　1 Becton Dr
　Franklin Lakes NJ 07417
　201 847-6800

(G-1171)
TRIVANTAGE LLC (HQ)
1831 N Park Ave (27217-1137)
PHONE....................800 786-1876
Steve Ellington, *Pr*
Gary Smith, *
Derek Steed, *
◆ **EMP:** 90 **EST:** 1876
SQ FT: 100,000
SALES (est): 44.61MM
SALES (corp-wide): 878.83MM **Privately
Held**
Web: www.trivantage.com
SIC: 5199 5088 5099 5091　Canvas products
　; Marine supplies; Signs, except electric;
　Camping equipment and supplies
PA: Glen Raven, Inc.
　192 Glen Raven Rd
　Burlington NC 27217
　336 227-6211

(G-1172)
TWO BROTHERS NC LLC
1601 Anthony Rd (27215-8979)
PHONE....................336 516-5181
John Porterfield, *Prin*
EMP: 4 **EST:** 2012
SALES (est): 151.8K **Privately Held**
SIC: 2451　Mobile homes, industrial or
　commercial use

▲ = Import ▼ = Export
◆ = Import/Export

(G-1173)
VANCE INDUSTRIAL ELEC INC
1208 Belmont St (27215-6933)
P.O. Box 1150 (27253-1150)
PHONE..................................336 570-1992
John B Vance, *Pr*
Jeanne Vance, *Sec*
EMP: 9 **EST:** 1994
SQ FT: 6,000
SALES (est): 3.04MM **Privately Held**
Web: www.vanceelectronics.com
SIC: 3625 Relays and industrial controls

(G-1174)
VISION DIRECTIONAL DRILLING
3462 Nc Highway 62 E (27215-9216)
P.O. Box 514 (27201-0514)
PHONE..................................336 570-4621
Mark Hall, *Pr*
Gale Fernandes, *Acctg Mgr*
EMP: 9 **EST:** 2006
SALES (est): 4.06MM **Privately Held**
Web: www.visiondirectionaldrilling.com
SIC: 1381 1623 Directional drilling oil and gas wells; Telephone and communication line construction

(G-1175)
VITAFLEX LLC
Also Called: Vitaflex USA
1305 Graham St (27217-6148)
P.O. Box 585 (27216-0585)
PHONE..................................888 616-8848
De-sheng Tsai, *Mgr*
Charles A Blalock, *CEO*
▲ **EMP:** 10 **EST:** 2009
SQ FT: 20,000
SALES (est): 418.02K **Privately Held**
Web: www.vitaflexusastore.com
SIC: 2297 Nonwoven fabrics

(G-1176)
WEAPON WORKS LLC (PA)
1110 Vaughn Rd (27217-2734)
PHONE..................................800 556-9498
David Z Harward, *Managing Member*
EMP: 5 **EST:** 2013
SALES (est): 1.11MM
SALES (corp-wide): 1.11MM **Privately Held**
Web: www.weaponworksllc.com
SIC: 3479 3484 Painting of metal products; Small arms

(G-1177)
WEAPON WORKS LLC
1433 University Dr Ste 102 (27215-8335)
PHONE..................................800 556-9498
EMP: 5
SALES (corp-wide): 1.11MM **Privately Held**
SIC: 3479 3484 Painting of metal products; Small arms
PA: Weapon Works Llc
1110 Vaughn Rd
Burlington NC 27217
800 556-9498

(G-1178)
WELCOME INDUSTRIAL CORP
717 N Park Ave (27217-2343)
PHONE..................................336 329-9640
Anthony Lin, *CEO*
EMP: 71
SALES (corp-wide): 4.66MM **Privately Held**
Web: www.welcomeind.com
SIC: 1799 3261 5021 Window treatment installation; Bathroom accessories/fittings, vitreous china or earthenware; Beds and bedding

PA: Welcome Industrial Corp.
261 5th Ave Rm 410
New York NY 10016
212 481-7112

(G-1179)
WEST HLLCREST DDA GROUP HM LLC ✪
925 S Church St (27215-3845)
PHONE..................................336 478-7444
Esther Korway Richards, *CEO*
Tolulope O Roberts, *COO*
EMP: 10 **EST:** 2023
SALES (est): 390.61K **Privately Held**
SIC: 2326 8099 Medical and hospital uniforms, men's; Health screening service

(G-1180)
WILSON BROWN INC
Also Called: Pro Feet
2220 Anthony Rd (27215-8982)
P.O. Box 2720 (27216-2720)
PHONE..................................336 226-0237
Taylor L Wilson, *Pr*
W Callum Brown, *VP*
Russell R Wilson, *Sec*
▲ **EMP:** 15 **EST:** 1979
SQ FT: 45,000
SALES (est): 3.33MM **Privately Held**
Web: www.wilsonbrownsocks.com
SIC: 2252 Socks

Burnsville
Yancey County

(G-1181)
ALTEC INDUSTRIES INC
150 Altec Rd (28714)
PHONE..................................828 678-5500
Jeff Mooney, *Brnch Mgr*
EMP: 58
SALES (corp-wide): 1.21B **Privately Held**
Web: www.altec.com
SIC: 3531 Construction machinery
HQ: Altec Industries, Inc.
210 Inverness Center Drv
Birmingham AL 35242
205 991-7733

(G-1182)
AMY SMITH
Also Called: Embroidery Authority
100 Club Dr Ste 270 (28714-3112)
PHONE..................................828 352-1001
Amy Smith, *Owner*
Thomas M Smith, *Owner*
EMP: 5 **EST:** 2004
SALES (est): 243.39K **Privately Held**
Web: www.embroideryauthority.com
SIC: 2395 7389 2396 Embroidery and art needlework; Advertising, promotional, and trade show services; Screen printing on fabric articles

(G-1183)
ARTISAN AROMATICS
517 Jim Creek Rd (28714-6100)
PHONE..................................800 456-6675
EMP: 4
SALES (est): 114.03K **Privately Held**
Web: www.artisanaromatics.com
SIC: 2844 Perfumes, cosmetics and other toilet preparations

(G-1184)
BWI ETN LLC
Also Called: Blue Wtr Indstries-Yancey Quar
19 Crushing Rd (28714-7084)
PHONE..................................828 682-2645

Jeff Ferrell, *Brnch Mgr*
EMP: 14
SALES (corp-wide): 99.08MM **Privately Held**
Web: www.bluewaterindustries.com
SIC: 1422 Crushed and broken limestone
HQ: Bwi Etn Llc
9509 Diggs Gap Rd
Heiskell TN 37754
865 573-7625

(G-1185)
GLEN RAVEN MTL SOLUTIONS LLC
Also Called: Filament Fabrics
73 E Us Highway 19e (28714-0087)
P.O. Box 100 (28714-0100)
PHONE..................................828 682-2142
Randy Blackston, *Brnch Mgr*
EMP: 150
SALES (corp-wide): 878.83MM **Privately Held**
Web: www.glenraven.com
SIC: 2221 5961 Polyester broadwoven fabrics; Catalog and mail-order houses
HQ: Glen Raven Material Solutions, Llc
1831 N Park Ave
Burlington NC 27217
336 227-6211

(G-1186)
GOUGE LOGGING
360 Rock Creek Rd (28714-6509)
PHONE..................................828 675-9216
Rex Gouge, *Owner*
EMP: 6 **EST:** 1978
SALES (est): 269.78K **Privately Held**
SIC: 2411 Logging camps and contractors

(G-1187)
HOWLING MOON DISTILLERY INC
361 Bradford Rd (28714-6223)
P.O. Box 18724 (28814-0724)
PHONE..................................828 208-1469
EMP: 4 **EST:** 2019
SALES (est): 186.09K **Privately Held**
Web: www.howlingmoonshine.com
SIC: 2085 Distilled and blended liquors

(G-1188)
IENTERTAINMENT NETWORK INC (PA)
100 Club Dr Ste 203 (28714-1728)
P.O. Box 3897 (27519-3897)
PHONE..................................919 238-4090
John W Stealey, *CEO*
David Terry, *CFO*
EMP: 5 **EST:** 1994
SALES (est): 955.95K **Publicly Held**
Web: www.corporate-ient.com
SIC: 7372 Home entertainment computer software

(G-1189)
PHIL S TIRE SERVICE INC
617 W Main St (28714-2737)
PHONE..................................828 682-2421
Phillip C Harris, *Pr*
Mildred Harris, *Sec*
EMP: 4 **EST:** 1952
SQ FT: 5,000
SALES (est): 286.76K **Privately Held**
Web: www.philstireservice.com
SIC: 5531 7534 Automotive tires; Tire recapping

(G-1190)
RIPTIDE PUBLISHING LLC
128 Academy St (28714-2904)
PHONE..................................908 295-4517
Rachel Haimowitz, *Prin*
EMP: 4 **EST:** 2011

SALES (est): 236.36K **Privately Held**
Web: www.riptidepublishing.com
SIC: 2741 Miscellaneous publishing

(G-1191)
SOUTHERN CONCRETE MTLS INC
129 Depot St (28714-3401)
PHONE..................................828 682-2298
Kevin Martin, *Mgr*
EMP: 8
SQ FT: 2,000
SALES (corp-wide): 238.17MM **Privately Held**
Web: www.scmusa.com
SIC: 3273 Ready-mixed concrete
HQ: Southern Concrete Materials, Inc.
35 Meadow Rd
Asheville NC 28803
828 253-6421

(G-1192)
STONE SUPPLY INC
159 Depot St (28714-3401)
PHONE..................................828 678-9966
Greg Bryant, *Prin*
EMP: 8 **EST:** 2005
SALES (est): 489.51K **Privately Held**
Web: www.bodyharmony.me
SIC: 3532 4212 1611 3531 Rock crushing machinery, stationary; Local trucking, without storage; General contractor, highway and street construction; Graders, road (construction machinery)

(G-1193)
TIMES JOURNAL INC
Also Called: Yancey Common Times Journal
22 N Main St (28714-2925)
P.O. Box 280 (28714-0280)
PHONE..................................828 682-4067
Bob Tribble, *Pr*
EMP: 6 **EST:** 1971
SALES (est): 85.37K **Privately Held**
Web: www.yanceytimesjournal.com
SIC: 2711 Newspapers, publishing and printing

(G-1194)
YANCEY STONE INC
19 Crushing Rd (28714-7084)
PHONE..................................828 682-2645
William M Mccrary, *Pr*
Charles Patrick Mccrary, *VP*
Sally Young, *Sec*
EMP: 4 **EST:** 1956
SQ FT: 480
SALES (est): 479.5K **Privately Held**
SIC: 1429 Igneus rock, crushed and broken-quarrying

(G-1195)
YANCY COMMON TIMES JOURNAL
Also Called: Yancy County Common Times
22 N Main St (28714-2925)
P.O. Box 280 (28714-0280)
PHONE..................................828 682-2120
Bob Tribble, *Pr*
Pat Randolph, *Genl Mgr*
EMP: 5 **EST:** 1994
SALES (est): 78.08K **Privately Held**
Web: www.yanceytimesjournal.com
SIC: 2711 Newspapers, publishing and printing

(G-1196)
YOUNG & MCQUEEN GRADING CO INC
25 Crest View Rd (28714-8400)
PHONE..................................828 682-7714
Sam Young, *Pr*
Kim Young, *Sec*

Earl Tipton, *VP*
Jim Mcqueen Shkhldr, *Prin*
Earl Young Shkhldr, *Prin*
EMP: 100 **EST:** 1986
SQ FT: 9,000
SALES (est): 22.76MM **Privately Held**
Web: www.youngmcqueen.com
SIC: 1794 1611 8711 1771 Excavation and grading, building construction; Highway and street paving contractor; Construction and civil engineering; Concrete work

Butner
Granville County

(G-1197)
ATHOL MANUFACTURING CORP
100 22nd St (27509-2441)
P.O. Box 105 (27509-0105)
PHONE..............................919 575-6523
John Givens, *Ch Bd*
▲ **EMP:** 6 **EST:** 1915
SQ FT: 210,000
SALES (est): 167.47K **Privately Held**
SIC: 2295 Coated fabrics, not rubberized

(G-1198)
AXIS CORRUGATED CONTAINER LLC (HQ)
201 Industrial Dr (27509-2511)
P.O. Box 299 (27509-0299)
PHONE..............................919 575-0500
Edward Casson, *Managing Member*
EMP: 19 **EST:** 2008
SQ FT: 74,000
SALES (est): 16.28MM
SALES (corp-wide): 21.72MM **Privately Held**
Web: www.accbox.com
SIC: 2653 Boxes, corrugated: made from purchased materials
PA: Southern Lithoplate Inc.
　　105 Jeffrey Way
　　Youngsville NC 27596
　　919 556-9400

(G-1199)
BFS INDUSTRIES LLC
200 Industrial Dr (27509-2500)
PHONE..............................919 575-6711
Thomas Garbarino, *Managing Member*
◆ **EMP:** 30 **EST:** 1945
SQ FT: 25,000
SALES (est): 5.09MM **Privately Held**
Web: www.bfs-ind.com
SIC: 3561 3443 Pumps and pumping equipment; Fabricated plate work (boiler shop)

(G-1200)
CAROLINA SUNROCK LLC (HQ)
1001 W B St (27509-1821)
P.O. Box 25 (27509-0025)
PHONE..............................919 575-4502
▲ **EMP:** 50 **EST:** 1984
SQ FT: 3,600
SALES (est): 49.26MM
SALES (corp-wide): 51.02MM **Privately Held**
Web: www.thesunrockgroup.com
SIC: 1429 3273 2951 1411 Trap rock, crushed and broken-quarrying; Ready-mixed concrete; Asphalt paving mixtures and blocks; Dimension stone
PA: Sunrock Group Holdings Corporation
　　200 Horizon Dr Ste 100
　　Raleigh NC 27615
　　919 747-6400

(G-1201)
FCC BUTNER
P.O. Box 1600 (27509-4600)
PHONE..............................919 575-3900
Greg Jaenicke, *Prin*
EMP: 6 **EST:** 2010
SALES (est): 390.25K **Privately Held**
Web: www.butnernc.org
SIC: 2869 Industrial organic chemicals, nec

(G-1202)
MASONITE INTERNATIONAL CORP
1712 E D St (27509-2543)
PHONE..............................919 575-3700
Don Greene, *Brnch Mgr*
EMP: 30
Web: www.masonite.com
SIC: 2431 Doors, wood
HQ: Masonite International Corporation
　　1242 E 5th Ave
　　Tampa FL 33605
　　813 877-2726

(G-1203)
NEWTON INSTRUMENT COMPANY (PA)
111 E A St (27509-2426)
P.O. Box 536915 (30353-6915)
PHONE..............................919 575-6426
▲ **EMP:** 140 **EST:** 1949
SALES (est): 24.73MM
SALES (corp-wide): 24.73MM **Privately Held**
Web: www.enewton.com
SIC: 3661 Telephone and telegraph apparatus

(G-1204)
PALLETONE NORTH CAROLINA INC
10 26th St (27509-2556)
PHONE..............................919 575-6491
Tony Fogleman, *Brnch Mgr*
EMP: 87
SALES (corp-wide): 6.65B **Publicly Held**
Web: www.palletone.com
SIC: 2448 Pallets, wood
HQ: Palletone Of North Carolina, Inc.
　　2340 Ike Brooks Rd
　　Siler City NC 27344
　　704 462-1882

(G-1205)
PREFERRED COMMUNICATION INC
410 Central Ave (27509-1916)
PHONE..............................919 575-4600
Bob Meeker, *CEO*
EMP: 20 **EST:** 2014
SALES (est): 1.43MM **Privately Held**
Web: www.satstar.com
SIC: 3669 Communications equipment, nec

(G-1206)
RICEWRAP FOODS CORPORATION
300 Business Park Dr (27509-2477)
PHONE..............................919 614-1179
Richard Cronk, *Pr*
Kyle Cronk, *Sec*
EMP: 13 **EST:** 2011
SALES (est): 3.39MM **Privately Held**
Web: www.ricewrapsushi.com
SIC: 2092 2038 Seafoods, frozen: prepared; Ethnic foods, nec, frozen

(G-1207)
TRIANGLE STAINLESS INC
200 20th St (27509-2443)
PHONE..............................919 596-1335
Mel Phillips, *Pr*
EMP: 5 **EST:** 1999
SALES (est): 853.98K **Privately Held**

Web: www.trianglestainless.com
SIC: 3444 Sheet metal specialties, not stamped

(G-1208)
UNITED LUMBER INC
10 26th St (27509-2556)
P.O. Box 510 (27509-0510)
PHONE..............................919 575-6491
Anthony C Fogleman, *Prin*
EMP: 4 **EST:** 2010
SALES (est): 143.43K **Privately Held**
SIC: 2448 Pallets, wood

Calabash
Brunswick County

(G-1209)
COLONIAL CABINETS LLC
259 Koolabrew Dr Nw (28467-1937)
P.O. Box 1747 (29566-1747)
PHONE..............................910 579-2954
EMP: 4 **EST:** 2011
SALES (est): 258.81K **Privately Held**
SIC: 2434 Wood kitchen cabinets

Camden
Camden County

(G-1210)
AMBROSE SIGNS INC
123 Sawyers Creek Rd (27921-7507)
P.O. Box 56 (27921-0056)
PHONE..............................252 338-8522
Roger Ambrose, *Pr*
Gary Ambrose, *VP*
EMP: 8 **EST:** 1945
SALES (est): 265.15K **Privately Held**
Web: www.ambrosesigns.com
SIC: 2759 Commercial printing, nec

(G-1211)
DUNAVANTS WELDING & STEEL INC
207 Us Highway 158 E (27921-7524)
P.O. Box 28 (27921-0028)
PHONE..............................252 338-6533
David Dunavant, *Pr*
Sharon Dunavant, *Sec*
EMP: 8 **EST:** 1988
SQ FT: 2,400
SALES (est): 1.34MM **Privately Held**
SIC: 3441 5051 7692 3444 Fabricated structural metal; Steel; Welding repair; Sheet metalwork

(G-1212)
PAULS CSTM FBRICATION MCH LLC
166 Us Highway 158 W (27921-9020)
PHONE..............................757 746-2743
Paul Justin Cohen, *Owner*
EMP: 4 **EST:** 2016
SALES (est): 828.64K **Privately Held**
SIC: 3499 Novelties and giftware, including trophies

(G-1213)
TARHEEL MATS INC
654 Nc Highway 343 N (27921-8311)
PHONE..............................252 325-1903
Gary Sawyer, *Pt*
EMP: 4 **EST:** 2004
SALES (est): 190.84K **Privately Held**
SIC: 3996 Hard surface floor coverings, nec

Cameron
Harnett County

(G-1214)
BRISK TRANSPORT 910 LLC
232 Old Montague Way (28326-4403)
PHONE..............................910 527-7398
Andre Dawkins, *Pr*
EMP: 4 **EST:** 2020
SALES (est): 1.59MM **Privately Held**
SIC: 3799 Transportation equipment, nec

(G-1215)
PROTEK SERVICES LLC
905 Cranes Creek Rd (28326-8117)
PHONE..............................910 556-4121
Jonathan Floyd, *Managing Member*
EMP: 4 **EST:** 2019
SALES (est): 829.63K **Privately Held**
Web: www.protek-svcs.com
SIC: 4959 2899 Environmental cleanup services; Acid resist for etching

Candler
Buncombe County

(G-1216)
ADVANCED MFG SOLUTIONS NC INC
53 Rutherford Rd (28715-9204)
P.O. Box 1390 (28715-1390)
PHONE..............................828 633-2633
Bjorn Robert Johannessen, *Pr*
Carolyn Johannessen, *
EMP: 15 **EST:** 2010
SALES (est): 4.25MM **Privately Held**
Web: www.amsncinc.com
SIC: 3444 7373 Sheet metal specialties, not stamped; Computer-aided manufacturing (CAM) systems service

(G-1217)
ASHEVILLE CONTRACTING CO INC
Also Called: Asheville Fence
1270 Smoky Park Hwy (28715-9248)
P.O. Box 1540 (28715)
PHONE..............................828 665-8900
Carla H Maddux, *Pr*
Michael Maddux, *
EMP: 32 **EST:** 1993
SQ FT: 6,000
SALES (est): 7.02MM **Privately Held**
Web: www.ashevillefence.com
SIC: 1799 1611 5039 2411 Fence construction; Highway signs and guardrails; Wire fence, gates, and accessories; Rails, fence: round or split

(G-1218)
ASHEVILLE VAULT SERVICE INC (PA)
Also Called: Asheville Wilbert Vault Svc
2239 Smoky Park Hwy (28715-9717)
PHONE..............................828 665-6799
Taylor Sword, *Pr*
Sally Sword, *
EMP: 31 **EST:** 1950
SQ FT: 38,000
SALES (est): 2.59MM
SALES (corp-wide): 2.59MM **Privately Held**
Web: www.ashevillewilbert.com
SIC: 3272 5087 Burial vaults, concrete or precast terrazzo; Caskets

(G-1219)
BALL S MACHINE & MFG CO INC
Also Called: Ball S Machine

▲ = Import ▼ = Export
◆ = Import/Export

2120 Smoky Park Hwy (28715-9702)
P.O. Box 267 (28715-0267)
PHONE................................828 667-0411
FAX: 828 665-4764
EMP: 15
SQ FT: 18,150
SALES (est): 2.66MM **Privately Held**
Web: www.ballsmachine.com
SIC: 3599 Machine shop, jobbing and repair

(G-1220)
CHARLES HILL ENTERPRISES
Also Called: Trugreen Chemlawn
145 Brooks Cove Rd (28715-9485)
P.O. Box 566 (28728-0566)
PHONE................................828 665-2116
Charles Hill, *Pr*
Tammy Smith, *Mgr*
EMP: 10 EST: 1982
SQ FT: 5,000
SALES (est): 198.67K **Privately Held**
SIC: 2875 Fertilizers, mixing only

(G-1221)
CLAYTON HOMES INC
651 Smokey Park Hwy (28715-9638)
PHONE................................828 667-8701
Ken Meyers, *Mgr*
EMP: 9
SALES (corp-wide): 424.23B **Publicly Held**
Web: www.claytonhomesofasheville.com
SIC: 2451 Mobile homes
HQ: Clayton Homes, Inc.
5000 Clayton Rd.
Maryville TN 37802
865 380-3000

(G-1222)
CS SYSTEMS COMPANY INC
Also Called: Milspec Plastics
1465 Sand Hill Rd Ste 2050 (28715-8984)
P.O. Box 1455 (28730-1455)
PHONE................................800 525-9878
Robert Harrington, *Pr*
EMP: 11 EST: 1999
SALES (est): 1.08MM **Privately Held**
Web: www.milspecplastics.com
SIC: 2821 Plastics materials and resins

(G-1223)
DANLEY SOUND LABS INC
204 Dogwood Rd (28715-8434)
PHONE................................877 419-5805
EMP: 5
Web: www.danleysoundlabs.com
SIC: 3651 Speaker systems
PA: Danley Sound Labs, Inc.
2196 Hilton Dr Ste A
Gainesville GA 30501

(G-1224)
DIVERSFIED MCHNING CNCEPTS INC
5 Sagefield Dr (28715-9477)
P.O. Box 2349 (28715-2349)
PHONE................................828 665-2465
Jim Clontz, *Pr*
Kenneth Pike, *VP*
Dennis Edwards, *Treas*
EMP: 5 EST: 1995
SQ FT: 7,000
SALES (est): 663.1K **Privately Held**
SIC: 3599 Chemical milling job shop

(G-1225)
FREUDENBERG PRFMCE MTLS LP
Also Called: Freudenberg Performance Materials L.P.
1301 Sand Hill Rd (28715-4508)
PHONE................................828 665-5000

Bruce Olson, *CEO*
EMP: 226
SALES (corp-wide): 12.96B **Privately Held**
Web: www.colbacksolutions.com
SIC: 5199 3296 2899 2297 Yarns, nec; Mineral wool; Chemical preparations, nec; Nonwoven fabrics
HQ: Freudenberg Performance Materials L.P.
3500 Industrial Dr
Durham NC 27704
919 479-7443

(G-1226)
GLATFELTER INDS ASHEVILLE INC
1265 Sand Hill Rd (28715-6907)
PHONE................................828 670-0041
Patricia Sargeant, *Pr*
Poul M Mikkelsen, *
Jill L Urey, *
▲ EMP: 89 EST: 2004
SQ FT: 200,000
SALES (est): 34.01MM
SALES (corp-wide): 1.39B **Publicly Held**
Web: www.glatfelter.com
SIC: 2297 Bonded-fiber fabrics, except felt
HQ: Glatfelter Denmark A/S
Alexandriagade 8
Nordhavn
59258500

(G-1227)
INVISIBLE FENCING OF MTN REG
176 Pete Luther Rd (28715-9499)
PHONE................................828 667-8847
Bill Jamison, *Pr*
Janice Jamison, *VP*
EMP: 4 EST: 1989
SALES (est): 448.12K **Privately Held**
Web: www.theusi.com
SIC: 3676 1799 Electronic resistors; Fence construction

(G-1228)
KAYNE & SON CUSTOM HDWR INC
Also Called: Kayne & Son Hardware
100 Daniel Ridge Rd (28715-5557)
PHONE................................828 665-1988
Shirley Kayne, *Pr*
David Kayne, *VP*
▲ EMP: 4 EST: 1957
SQ FT: 7,000
SALES (est): 517.06K **Privately Held**
Web: www.blacksmithsdepot.com
SIC: 7699 3366 3471 Blacksmith shop; Castings (except die), nec, bronze; Finishing, metals or formed products

(G-1229)
LENNOX INTERNATIONAL INC
Also Called: Lennox Store Asheville
1251 Sand Hill Rd (28715-6907)
PHONE................................828 633-4805
EMP: 172
SALES (corp-wide): 5.34B **Publicly Held**
Web: www.lennox.com
SIC: 3621 3585 Coils, for electric motors or generators; Furnaces, warm air: electric
PA: Lennox International Inc.
2140 Lake Park Blvd
Richardson TX 75080
972 497-5000

(G-1230)
OOWEE INCORPORATED
2194 Smoky Park Hwy Ste 100 (28715-1109)
PHONE................................828 633-0289
William G Hargett, *Pr*
EMP: 12 EST: 2011
SQ FT: 8,500

SALES (est): 827.92K **Privately Held**
Web: www.ooweeproducts.com
SIC: 5722 3111 3199 Kitchens, complete (sinks, cabinets, etc.); Accessory products, leather; Leather goods, nec

(G-1231)
QUALITY MUSICAL SYSTEMS INC
Also Called: Q M S
204 Dogwood Rd (28715-8434)
P.O. Box 850 (28715-0850)
PHONE................................828 667-5719
Daniel Stuart Wilson, *Pr*
Hubert Jackson Wilson Ii, *VP*
▲ EMP: 30 EST: 1984
SQ FT: 19,000
SALES (est): 5.24MM **Privately Held**
Web: www.qualitymusicalsystems.com
SIC: 3651 3444 2517 Loudspeakers, electrodynamic or magnetic; Sheet metalwork; Wood television and radio cabinets

(G-1232)
ROAD KING TRAILERS INC
2240 Smoky Park Hwy (28715-9717)
PHONE................................828 670-8012
Larry Hamm, *Pr*
Steve Soule, *
Phyllis Hamm, *
EMP: 50 EST: 2002
SQ FT: 15,000
SALES (est): 1.87MM **Privately Held**
Web: www.roadkingtrailers.com
SIC: 5599 3715 Utility trailers; Bus trailers, tractor type

(G-1233)
SOUTHERN ORGAN SERVICES LTD
Also Called: Phil Parkey & Associates
3 English Pl (28715-9632)
PHONE................................828 667-8230
Philip Parkey, *Pt*
EMP: 9 EST: 1987
SALES (est): 158.14K **Privately Held**
SIC: 3931 Blowers, pipe organ

(G-1234)
TGR ENTERPRISES INCORPORATED
26 Charity Ln (28715-8545)
P.O. Box 1030 (28715-1030)
PHONE................................828 665-4427
Terry Rutherford, *Pr*
Brian Rutherford, *VP*
Jerrie Rutherford, *Sec*
EMP: 4 EST: 1989
SQ FT: 5,000
SALES (est): 498.31K **Privately Held**
Web: www.tgrenterprises.com
SIC: 3544 Special dies and tools

(G-1235)
W N C PALLET FOREST PDTS INC
1414 Smoky Park Hwy (28715-8237)
PHONE................................828 667-5426
Dale Tharsh, *Pr*
Gary L Robinson, *
Thomas B Orr, *
EMP: 15 EST: 1959
SQ FT: 9,360
SALES (est): 1.77MM **Privately Held**
SIC: 2448 5031 2421 Pallets, wood; Lumber: rough, dressed, and finished; Sawmills and planing mills, general

(G-1236)
WNC BLUE RIDGE FD VENTURES LLC
1461 Sand Hill Rd (28715-8907)

PHONE................................828 348-0130
Michael Mcdonald, *Mgr*
EMP: 11 EST: 2015
SALES (est): 1.01MM **Privately Held**
Web: www.blueridgefoodventures.org
SIC: 3589 Service industry machinery, nec

Candor
Montgomery County

(G-1237)
JL HOSIERY LLC
130 S Main St (27229-9092)
P.O. Box 725 (27229-0725)
PHONE................................910 974-7156
John Lamonds, *Pr*
▲ EMP: 14 EST: 1982
SALES (est): 841.2K **Privately Held**
SIC: 2252 Socks

(G-1238)
LONGWORTH INDUSTRIES INC
480 E Main St (27229-9095)
P.O. Box 520 (27229-0520)
PHONE................................910 974-3068
Mittie Longworth, *Brnch Mgr*
EMP: 50
SALES (corp-wide): 99.5MM **Privately Held**
Web: www.proxgo.com
SIC: 2341 2322 Women's and children's undergarments; Underwear, men's and boys': made from purchased materials
HQ: Longworth Industries, Inc.
565 Air Tool Dr Ste K
Southern Pines NC 28387

(G-1239)
MOUNTAIRE FARMS LLC
Also Called: Mountaire Farms North Carolina
203 Morris Farm Rd (27229-8090)
P.O. Box 129 (27229-0129)
PHONE................................910 974-3232
Carol Tucker, *Mgr*
EMP: 276
SALES (corp-wide): 2.07B **Privately Held**
Web: www.mountaire.com
SIC: 2048 5191 Chicken feeds, prepared; Animal feeds
HQ: Mountaire Farms Inc.
1901 Napa Valley Dr
Little Rock AR 72212
501 372-6524

(G-1240)
PERDUE FARMS INC
Also Called: Perdue Farms
Hwy 211 S (27229)
P.O. Box 657 (27229-0657)
PHONE................................910 673-4148
Ronald Mcfayden, *Mgr*
EMP: 112
SALES (corp-wide): 1.24B **Privately Held**
Web: www.perdue.com
SIC: 2015 Poultry slaughtering and processing
PA: Perdue Farms Incorporated
31149 Old Ocean City Rd
Salisbury MD 21804
800 473-7383

(G-1241)
RUSS KNITS INC
520 E Main St (27229-9111)
PHONE................................910 974-4114
John B Martin, *Pr*
David Martin, *
EMP: 18 EST: 1971
SQ FT: 97,000

SALES (est): 230.53K **Privately Held**
Web: www.russknits.com
SIC: 2257 Pile fabrics, circular knit

Canton
Haywood County

(G-1242)
BEARWATERS BREWING COMPANY
101 Park St (28716-5013)
PHONE..............................828 237-4200
Kevin Sandefur, *CEO*
Arthur Oneil, *COO*
Melanie Sandefur, *Treas*
Josphine Heart, *Dir*
EMP: 16 **EST:** 2011
SALES (est): 1.05MM **Privately Held**
Web: www.bearwatersbrewing.com
SIC: 5813 2082 Bars and lounges; Malt beverages

(G-1243)
BLUE RIDGE CONTRACTING LLC
14 New Clyde Hwy (28716-4210)
PHONE..............................828 400-5194
EMP: 4 **EST:** 2018
SALES (est): 2.58MM **Privately Held**
SIC: 1389 Construction, repair, and dismantling services

(G-1244)
BLUE RIDGE PAPER PRODUCTS LLC (DH)
Also Called: Evergreen Packaging
41 Main St (28716-4331)
PHONE..............................828 454-0676
John Rooney, *Pr*
John Wadsworth, *
Phillip Bowen, *
Terry Huskey, *
Robert Shanahan, *
◆ **EMP:** 80 **EST:** 1999
SALES (est): 123.14MM **Publicly Held**
Web: www.pactiveevergreen.com
SIC: 2621 Fine paper
HQ: Pactiv Evergreen Inc.
1900 W Field Ct
Lake Forest IL 60045
800 879-5067

(G-1245)
BLUE RIDGE PAPER PRODUCTS LLC
Also Called: Evergreen Packaging
119 Park St (28716-4319)
PHONE..............................828 235-3023
Albert Darlington, *Brnch Mgr*
EMP: 171
Web: www.pactiveevergreen.com
SIC: 2621 Fine paper
HQ: Blue Ridge Paper Products Llc
41 Main St
Canton NC 28716
828 454-0676

(G-1246)
BRIGMAN ELECTRIC MOTORS INC
6110 Old Clyde Rd (28716-3256)
P.O. Box 1047 (28716-1047)
PHONE..............................828 492-0568
Jack Guinn, *Pr*
Kathleen Guinn, *VP*
EMP: 7 **EST:** 1949
SQ FT: 8,000
SALES (est): 472.76K **Privately Held**
SIC: 7694 5999 Electric motor repair; Motors, electric

(G-1247)
CANTON HARDWOOD COMPANY
5373 Thickety Rd (28716-8702)
PHONE..............................828 492-0715
James T Powell Junior, *Pr*
James T Powell Iii, *VP*
J N Sam Powell Junior, *Sec*
EMP: 4 **EST:** 1950
SQ FT: 15,000
SALES (est): 469.92K **Privately Held**
Web: www.cantonsawmill.com
SIC: 2421 Sawmills and planing mills, general

(G-1248)
CAROLINA CONVEYING INC
162 Great Oak Dr (28716-8715)
PHONE..............................828 235-1005
Liam Mccauley, *Pr*
▲ **EMP:** 5 **EST:** 1999
SALES (est): 3.17MM **Privately Held**
Web: www.carolinaconveying.com
SIC: 3491 Industrial valves

(G-1249)
COAST LAMP MANUFACTURING INC
Also Called: Lam Factory, The
35 Church St (28716-4431)
P.O. Box 887 (28716-0887)
PHONE..............................828 648-7876
K Marshall Gann, *Pr*
Candy Smith, *Sec*
◆ **EMP:** 9 **EST:** 1955
SQ FT: 22,000
SALES (est): 500.3K **Privately Held**
Web: www.coastlampmfg.com
SIC: 3645 Table lamps

(G-1250)
CONSOLIDATED METCO INC
Also Called: Con Met
171 Great Oak Dr (28716-8715)
PHONE..............................828 488-5114
Scott Yeager, *Brnch Mgr*
EMP: 200
SALES (corp-wide): 3.96B **Privately Held**
Web: www.conmet.com
SIC: 3714 Motor vehicle parts and accessories
HQ: Consolidated Metco, Inc.
5701 Se Columbia Way
Vancouver WA 98661
360 828-2599

(G-1251)
D & M LOGGING OF WNC LLC
1936 Beaverdam Rd (28716-7095)
P.O. Box 233 (28716-0233)
PHONE..............................828 648-4366
Daniel Worley, *Prin*
EMP: 4 **EST:** 2016
SALES (est): 218.15K **Privately Held**
SIC: 2411 Logging camps and contractors

(G-1252)
EVERGREEN PACKAGING LLC
Also Called: Canton Mill
175 Main St (28716-4401)
PHONE..............................828 454-0676
Larry Shutzberg, *Brnch Mgr*
EMP: 1008
Web: www.pactiveevergreen.com
SIC: 2621 Absorbent paper
HQ: Evergreen Packaging Llc
1900 W Field Ct
Lake Forest IL 60045

(G-1253)
FRED WINFIELD LUMBER CO INC
Dutch Cove Rd (28716)

P.O. Box 1258 (28716-1258)
PHONE..............................828 648-3414
John Plemmons, *Pr*
EMP: 10 **EST:** 1940
SQ FT: 500
SALES (est): 320.67K **Privately Held**
SIC: 2421 Sawmills and planing mills, general

(G-1254)
IMERYS CLAYS INC
125 N Main St (28716-3939)
P.O. Box 1008 (28716-1008)
PHONE..............................828 648-2668
Peter O'rouke, *Mgr*
EMP: 9
SALES (corp-wide): 5.36MM **Privately Held**
Web: www.imerys.com
SIC: 3295 Minerals, ground or treated
HQ: Imerys Clays, Inc.
100 Mansell Ct E Ste 300
Roswell GA 30076
770 594-0660

(G-1255)
ROGERS EXPRESS LUBE LLC
167 Pisgah Dr (28716-1456)
PHONE..............................828 648-7772
EMP: 4 **EST:** 2005
SALES (est): 554.86K **Privately Held**
Web: www.rogersexpresslubeandtire.com
SIC: 2741 Miscellaneous publishing

(G-1256)
SONOCO PRODUCTS COMPANY
6175 Pigeon Rd (28716-6511)
PHONE..............................828 648-1987
EMP: 5
SALES (corp-wide): 5.31B **Publicly Held**
Web: www.sonoco.com
SIC: 2631 Paperboard mills
PA: Sonoco Products Company
1 N 2nd St
Hartsville SC 29550
843 383-7000

Carolina Beach
New Hanover County

(G-1257)
CANVAS GICLEE PRINTING
1018 Lake Park Blvd N Ste 19
(28428-4162)
PHONE..............................910 458-4229
EMP: 4 **EST:** 2019
SALES (est): 235.01K **Privately Held**
Web: www.canvasgicleeprinting.com
SIC: 2752 Commercial printing, lithographic

(G-1258)
CAROLINA COAST VINEYARD
1328 Lake Park Blvd N (28428-3935)
PHONE..............................910 707-1777
EMP: 5 **EST:** 2016
SALES (est): 72.95K **Privately Held**
Web: www.carolinacoast-vc.org
SIC: 2084 Wines

(G-1259)
CISCO SYSTEMS INC
Also Called: Cisco Systems
1004 North Carolina Ave (28428-5631)
PHONE..............................910 707-1052
EMP: 5
SALES (corp-wide): 53.8B **Publicly Held**
Web: www.cisco.com

SIC: 3577 Data conversion equipment, media-to-media: computer
PA: Cisco Systems, Inc.
170 W Tasman Dr
San Jose CA 95134
408 526-4000

(G-1260)
CMS TOOL AND DIE INC
1331 Bridge Barrier Rd (28428-3996)
P.O. Box 819 (28428-0819)
PHONE..............................910 458-3322
Nick Chambliss, *Pr*
Lynne Willis, *Sec*
EMP: 11 **EST:** 1988
SQ FT: 5,000
SALES (est): 2.74MM **Privately Held**
Web: www.cmsmachineshop.com
SIC: 3599 3469 Machine shop, jobbing and repair; Machine parts, stamped or pressed metal

(G-1261)
FUDGEBOAT INC
920 Riptide Ln (28428-4643)
PHONE..............................910 617-9793
EMP: 4 **EST:** 2018
SALES (est): 80.38K **Privately Held**
Web: www.fudgeboat.com
SIC: 2064 Fudge (candy)

(G-1262)
LIGHT-BEAMS PUBLISHING
111 Island Palms Dr (28428-4331)
PHONE..............................603 659-1300
Barry Kane, *Prin*
▲ **EMP:** 10 **EST:** 1997
SALES (est): 71.92K **Privately Held**
Web: www.fairyhouses.com
SIC: 2731 Books, publishing only

(G-1263)
PROMOGRAPHIX INC
Also Called: Proforma Promographix
406 Fayetteville Ave (28428-5009)
PHONE..............................919 846-1379
Kevin Dovel, *Pr*
Don Titka, *VP*
▲ **EMP:** 10 **EST:** 1996
SALES (est): 2.2MM **Privately Held**
Web: www.promographixinc.com
SIC: 7389 2752 3993 Advertising, promotional, and trade show services; Commercial printing, lithographic; Advertising novelties

(G-1264)
SEASIDE PRESS CO INC
Also Called: Island Gazette Newspaper, The
1003 Bennet Ln Ste F (28428-5770)
P.O. Box 183 (28428-0183)
PHONE..............................910 458-8156
Roger Mckee, *Pr*
Beattie Mckee, *VP*
EMP: 7 **EST:** 1975
SALES (est): 95.69K **Privately Held**
SIC: 2752 2711 Offset printing; Newspapers, publishing and printing

Carrboro
Orange County

(G-1265)
ARGOS USA LLC
219 Guthrie Ave (27510)
PHONE..............................919 942-0381
James Walters, *Mgr*
EMP: 7
Web: www.argos-us.com

▲ = Import ▼ = Export
◆ = Import/Export

SIC: **3241** Cement, hydraulic
HQ: Argos Usa Llc
3015 Windward Plz Ste 300
Alpharetta GA 30005
678 368-4300

(G-1266)
BACKSTREETS PUBLISHING
200 N Greensboro St Ste D (27510-1838)
PHONE..............................919 968-9466
Christopher Phillips, *Owner*
EMP: 4 EST: 2005
SALES (est): 221.36K **Privately Held**
Web: www.backstreets.com
SIC: **2741** Miscellaneous publishing

(G-1267)
CORTICAL METRICS LLC
209 Lloyd St Ste 360 (27510-1858)
PHONE..............................919 903-9943
EMP: 8 EST: 2019
SALES (est): 966.63K **Privately Held**
Web: www.corticalmetrics.com
SIC: **3699** Electrical equipment and supplies, nec

(G-1268)
DALLAS L PRIDGEN INC
Also Called: Dallas L Pridgen Jewelry
104 Morningside Dr (27510-1253)
PHONE..............................919 732-4422
Dallas L Pridgen, *Pr*
EMP: 4 EST: 1989
SQ FT: 800
SALES (est): 129.22K **Privately Held**
Web: www.dallaspridgenjewelry.com
SIC: **5961 3911** Jewelry, mail order; Jewelry, precious metal

(G-1269)
HTX TECHNOLOGIES LLC
Also Called: Htx Imaging
610 Jones Ferry Rd Ste 207 (27510-6113)
P.O. Box 16007 (27516-6007)
PHONE..............................919 928-5688
EMP: 10 EST: 2010
SALES (est): 1.2MM **Privately Held**
Web: www.htximaging.com
SIC: **3826** Analytical instruments

(G-1270)
MIDDLE OF NOWHERE MUSIC LLC
112 Nc 54 Apt B8 (27510-1567)
PHONE..............................301 237-7290
EMP: 5 EST: 2018
SALES (est): 48K **Privately Held**
SIC: **2741** Miscellaneous publishing

(G-1271)
RAPP PRODUCTIONS INC
Also Called: Furniture Lab
103 W Weaver St (27510-6003)
PHONE..............................919 913-0270
Gregory Rapp, *Pr*
Bryna Rapp, *VP*
EMP: 13 EST: 1988
SQ FT: 5,000
SALES (est): 2.98MM **Privately Held**
Web: www.furniturelab.com
SIC: **2599 7336** Restaurant furniture, wood or metal; Silk screen design

(G-1272)
RICE S GLASS COMPANY INC
107 Lloyd St (27510-1819)
P.O. Box 40 (27510-0040)
PHONE..............................919 967-9214
Alton Rice, *Pr*
Sara Rice, *
EMP: 32 EST: 1973

SQ FT: 25,000
SALES (est): 9.55MM **Privately Held**
Web: www.ricesglasscompany.com
SIC: **1793** 7536 3442 Glass and glazing work
; Automotive glass replacement shops;
Metal doors, sash, and trim

(G-1273)
RINGS TRUE LLC
200 N Greensboro St Ste B9 (27510-1867)
PHONE..............................919 265-7600
EMP: 6 EST: 2016
SALES (est): 191.66K **Privately Held**
Web: www.thisringtrue.com
SIC: **3732** Boatbuilding and repairing

(G-1274)
TECHNICA EDITORIAL SERVICES
205 W Main St Ste 206 (27510-2087)
PHONE..............................919 918-3991
Jack Nestor, *Pt*
Arlene Furnon, *Pt*
EMP: 4 EST: 1990
SALES (est): 470.75K **Privately Held**
Web: www.technicaeditorial.com
SIC: **2731** Books, publishing only

Carthage
Moore County

(G-1275)
ASHWORTH LOGGING
249 Hunter Ridge Ln (28327-7415)
PHONE..............................910 464-2136
Kester Ashworth, *Owner*
EMP: 7 EST: 1992
SALES (est): 117.49K **Privately Held**
SIC: **2411** Logging camps and contractors

(G-1276)
BIG VAC
551 Priest Hill Rd (28327-7823)
PHONE..............................910 947-3654
J R Cardona, *Owner*
Kathy Cardona, *Owner*
EMP: 5 EST: 1987
SALES (est): 658.79K **Privately Held**
SIC: **4959 3639** Sweeping service: road, airport, parking lot, etc.; Major kitchen appliances, except refrigerators and stoves

(G-1277)
BLACK ROCK LANDSCAPING LLC
6652 Us 15 501 Hwy (28327-9154)
PHONE..............................910 295-4470
Ronnie Swilliams, *Admn*
EMP: 5 EST: 2007
SALES (est): 494.82K **Privately Held**
SIC: **2084** Wines

(G-1278)
PUZZLE PIECE LLC
2287 Underwood Rd (28327-8819)
PHONE..............................910 688-7119
Brian Garton, *Owner*
EMP: 4 EST: 2011
SALES (est): 203.24K **Privately Held**
Web: www.thepuzzlepieceshop.com
SIC: **3944** Puzzles

(G-1279)
REEL SOLUTIONS INC
1341 Red Branch Rd (28327-9780)
P.O. Box 128 (28394-0128)
PHONE..............................910 947-3117
Mike Wilson, *CEO*
EMP: 6 EST: 1997
SQ FT: 22,500
SALES (est): 102.37K **Privately Held**

SIC: **2499** Spools, reels, and pulleys: wood

(G-1280)
SPEER CONCRETE INC
4221 Us 15 501 Hwy (28327-6798)
P.O. Box 280 (28327-0280)
PHONE..............................910 947-3144
Clayton Speer, *Pr*
Jeanette Speer, *Sec*
Mike Gatti, *VP*
EMP: 22 EST: 1978
SQ FT: 540
SALES (est): 3.69MM **Privately Held**
SIC: **5032 3273 3272** Concrete mixtures;
Ready-mixed concrete; Concrete products, nec

(G-1281)
STEVENS LIGHTING INC (PA)
Also Called: Nolarec
488 Bibey Rd (28327-7230)
PHONE..............................910 944-7187
Charles H Stevens, *Pr*
EMP: 12 EST: 1973
SQ FT: 40,000
SALES (est): 692.09K
SALES (corp-wide): 692.09K **Privately Held**
SIC: **3645 3646** Residential lighting fixtures;
Commercial lighting fixtures

Cary
Wake County

(G-1282)
360 BALLISTICS LLC
Also Called: Amidon Ballistic Concrete
206 High House Rd Ste 102 (27513-8496)
PHONE..............................919 883-8338
Mark Buchmann, *Managing Member*
EMP: 5 EST: 2010
SALES (est): 117.98K **Privately Held**
SIC: **3272** Concrete products, nec

(G-1283)
A4 HEALTH SYSTEMS INC
5501 Dillard Dr (27518-9233)
PHONE..............................919 851-6177
Lee A Shapiro, *Pr*
David Bond, *
EMP: 400 EST: 1970
SQ FT: 55,000
SALES (est): 2.41MM
SALES (corp-wide): 1.5B **Publicly Held**
Web: www.a4healthsys.com
SIC: **7372 7379** Prepackaged software;
Computer related consulting services
PA: Veradigm Inc.
222 Mrchndise Mart Plz St
Chicago IL 60654
800 334-8534

(G-1284)
ABB HOLDINGS INC (DH)
305 Gregson Dr (27511-6496)
PHONE..............................919 856-2360
Enrique Santacana, *Pr*
David Onuscheck, *Sr VP*
John Brett, *VP*
Michael Gray Senior, *Tax Vice President*
Daniel Hagmann, *Sr VP*
▲ **EMP: 92 EST:** 1998
SALES (est): 2.81B **Privately Held**
Web: www.abb.com
SIC: **3612** Transformers, except electric
HQ: Abb Asea Brown Boveri Ltd
Affolternstrasse 44
Zurich ZH 8050

(G-1285)
ABB INC (DH)
305 Gregson Dr (27511)
P.O. Box 90502 (27675)
PHONE..............................919 856-2360
Michael Gray, *Pr*
Michael Gray, *Prin*
Greg Scheu, *
Jan Allde, *
John Brett, *
◆ **EMP: 200 EST:** 1980
SQ FT: 10,000
SALES (est): 1.74B **Privately Held**
Web: www.abb.com
SIC: **8711 3612 3511 5063** Engineering services; Transformers, except electric;
Steam turbine generator set units, complete
; Electrical apparatus and equipment
HQ: Abb Holdings Inc.
305 Gregson Dr
Cary NC 27511
919 856-2360

(G-1286)
ADMISSIONPROS LLC
800 Pinner Weald Way Ste 101
(27513-2607)
P.O. Box 1492 (27512-1492)
PHONE..............................919 256-3889
Jeffrey Hilts, *Pr*
EMP: 10 EST: 2004
SALES (est): 2.19MM **Privately Held**
Web: www.admissionpros.com
SIC: **7372** Prepackaged software

(G-1287)
AGILE MICROWAVE TECHNOLOGY INC
Also Called: Agile Mwt
701 Cascade Pointe Ln Ste 101
(27513-5799)
PHONE..............................984 228-8001
Sanjay Chudasama, *Genl Mgr*
Ants Rimm, *Engr*
EMP: 6 EST: 2011
SQ FT: 5,000
SALES (est): 422.43K **Privately Held**
Web: www.agilemwt.com
SIC: **3674** Integrated circuits, semiconductor networks, etc.

(G-1288)
AMIKA LLC
5000 Centre Green Way (27513-5817)
PHONE..............................984 664-9804
Randall Canady, *Managing Member*
EMP: 4 EST: 2014
SALES (est): 1.16MM
SALES (corp-wide): 496.86MM **Privately Held**
Web: www.loveamika.com
SIC: **2879** Insecticides, agricultural or household
HQ: Manna Pro Products, Llc
707 Sprit 40 Pk Dr Ste 15
Chesterfield MO 63005
636 681-1700

(G-1289)
AMRYT PHARMACEUTICALS INC
175 Regency Woods Pl (27518-6001)
PHONE..............................877 764-3131
Joe Wiley, *CEO*
Gregory Perry, *CFO*
John Orloff, *Ex VP*
Remi Menes, *CMO*
EMP: 12 EST: 2005
SALES (est): 7.57MM
SALES (corp-wide): 3.29B **Privately Held**
Web: www.amrytpharma.com

SIC: 2834 Pharmaceutical preparations
HQ: Amryt Pharma Limited
C/O Corporation Service Company
(Uk) Ltd
London E14 5
160 454-9952

(G-1290)
ANDERS NATURAL SOAP CO INC
1943 Evans Rd (27513-2041)
PHONE.................................919 678-9393
Michael Anderson, *Pr*
Patricia Anderson, *VP*
Jennifer Holmes, *Sec*
Jon Anderson, *Treas*
EMP: 4 EST: 1999
SQ FT: 1,600
SALES (est): 423.34K **Privately Held**
Web: www.andersnaturalsoap.com
SIC: 2841 Soap and other detergents

(G-1291)
ANTHONY DEMARIA LABS INC
122 Windbyrne Dr (27513-2830)
PHONE.................................845 255-4695
Anthony Demaria, *Pr*
EMP: 15 EST: 1989
SALES (est): 596.56K **Privately Held**
SIC: 3651 Household audio and video
equipment

(G-1292)
APEX WAVES LLC
1624 Old Apex Rd (27513-5719)
PHONE.................................919 809-5227
EMP: 4 EST: 2016
SALES (est): 3.37MM **Privately Held**
Web: www.apexwaves.com
SIC: 3826 5961 Analytical instruments;
Computers and peripheral equipment, mail
order

(G-1293)
APPSENSE INCORPORATED
Also Called: Appsense
1100 Crescent Green Ste 206
(27518-8110)
PHONE.................................919 666-0080
EMP: 120
SIC: 7372 Application computer software

(G-1294)
ARKEMA INC
Also Called: Arkema Coating Resins
410 Gregson Dr (27511-6445)
PHONE.................................919 469-6700
EMP: 82
SALES (corp-wide): 134.78MM **Privately
Held**
Web: www.arkema.com
SIC: 2819 Industrial inorganic chemicals, nec
HQ: Arkema Inc.
900 1st Ave
King Of Prussia PA 19406
610 205-7000

(G-1295)
ARYSTA LIFESCIENCE INC
15401 Weston Pkwy Ste 150 (27513-8640)
P.O. Box 12219 (27709-2219)
PHONE.................................919 678-4900
Mark Gibbens, *Treas*
EMP: 50 EST: 2001
SALES (est): 8.83MM **Privately Held**
Web: www.arystalifescience.com
SIC: 2879 Agricultural chemicals, nec
HQ: Upl Corporation Limited
Harbour Front Building Suite 157b,
President John Kennedy Street
Port Louis 11324

(G-1296)
ARYSTA LIFESCIENCE N AMER LLC
(HQ)
15401 Weston Pkwy Ste 150 (27513-8640)
P.O. Box 12219 (27709-2219)
PHONE.................................919 678-4900
Rico Christensen, *Pr*
Stuart Kippelman, *
Flavio Prezzi, *
Tom Smith, *
Diego Lopez Casanello, *
▲ EMP: 50 EST: 1995
SALES (est): 17.66MM **Privately Held**
Web:
www.caryeconomicdevelopment.com
SIC: 2879 Agricultural chemicals, nec
PA: Upl Limited
Upl House, 610 B/2, Bandra Village,
Mumbai MH 40005

(G-1297)
ASCO LP
111 Corning Rd Ste 120 (27518-9236)
PHONE.................................919 460-5200
Matt Rogers, *Mgr*
EMP: 7
SALES (corp-wide): 17.49B **Publicly Held**
Web: www.emerson.com
SIC: 3823 Process control instruments
HQ: Asco, L.P.
160 Park Ave
Florham Park NJ 07932
800 972-2726

(G-1298)
ATMOSPHRIC PLSMA SOLUTIONS
INC
Also Called: AP Solutions
11301 Penny Rd Ste D (27518-2433)
PHONE.................................919 341-8325
Peter Yancey, *Pr*
Jerome Cuomo, *VP*
EMP: 4 EST: 2005
SALES (est): 2.1MM **Privately Held**
Web: www.apsplasma.com
SIC: 3559 Electronic component making
machinery

(G-1299)
ATTICUS LLC
940 Nw Cary Pkwy Ste 200 (27513-2792)
PHONE.................................984 465-4754
Randy Canady, *CEO*
EMP: 25 EST: 2014
SQ FT: 6,900
SALES (est): 23.27MM
SALES (corp-wide): 49MM **Privately Held**
Web: www.atticusllc.com
SIC: 2879 6719 Agricultural chemicals, nec;
Investment holding companies, except
banks
PA: Cse Life Science Holdings, Llc
5000 Centre Green Way # 10
Cary NC 27513
984 465-4754

(G-1300)
AURUM CAPITAL VENTURES INC
Also Called: Miningstore
270 Cornerstone Dr Ste 101c (27519-8400)
PHONE.................................877 467-7780
Jp Baric, *Prin*
EMP: 12 EST: 2018
SALES (est): 4.16MM **Privately Held**
SIC: 1241 Mining services, nec: anthracite

(G-1301)
AUTOMOTIVE MGT SOLUTIONS
301 Birdwood Ct (27519-9719)
PHONE.................................919 481-2439
Terry Hubbard, *Pr*

EMP: 9 EST: 1994
SALES (est): 924.77K **Privately Held**
Web: www.protractorsoftware.com
SIC: 7372 Application computer software

(G-1302)
AVCON INC
101 Triangle Trade Dr Ste 101 (27513)
P.O. Box 4793 (27519)
PHONE.................................919 388-0203
Frank B Yarborough, *Pr*
Nick Senert, *
EMP: 27 EST: 1997
SQ FT: 4,500
SALES (est): 7MM **Privately Held**
Web: www.avconusa.com
SIC: 7812 3646 Audio-visual program
production; Commercial lighting fixtures

(G-1303)
AVIOR INC
Also Called: Avior Bio
221 James Jackson Ave (27513-3166)
PHONE.................................919 234-0068
Niraj Vasisht, *CEO*
Mani Vasisht, *Pr*
Samarth Vasisht, *VP*
Siddharth Vasisht, *Sec*
EMP: 4 EST: 2017
SQ FT: 500
SALES (est): 423.39K **Privately Held**
Web: www.aviorbio.com
SIC: 2834 Proprietary drug products

(G-1304)
AWC HOLDING COMPANY
5020 Weston Pkwy Ste 400 (27513-2322)
PHONE.................................919 677-3900
EMP: 15 EST: 2010
SALES (est): 3.43MM
SALES (corp-wide): 5.58B **Privately Held**
SIC: 3089 Plastics products, nec
HQ: Ply Gem Holdings, Inc.
5020 Weston Pkwy Ste 400
Cary NC 27513
919 677-3900

(G-1305)
BE PHARMACEUTICALS INC
203 New Edition Ct (27511-4452)
PHONE.................................704 560-1444
William Hill, *Pr*
▲ EMP: 4 EST: 2018
SQ FT: 2,200
SALES (est): 482.67K **Privately Held**
Web: www.be-pharmaceuticals.com
SIC: 2834 Pharmaceutical preparations

(G-1306)
BIOFLUIDICA INC
100 Conway Ct (27513-9400)
PHONE.................................858 535-6493
Rolf Muller, *CEO*
Samuel Tetlow, *Ch Bd*
David Claypool, *COO*
Mateusz Hupert, *Research & Development*
EMP: 8 EST: 2007
SQ FT: 523
SALES (est): 2.18MM **Privately Held**
Web: www.biofluidica.com
SIC: 3826 Analytical instruments

(G-1307)
BIOLOGIX OF THE TRIANGLE INC
103 Hidden Rock Ct (27513-8309)
PHONE.................................919 696-4544
Van Kloempken, *Pr*
Gretel Kloempken, *VP*
EMP: 6 EST: 2000
SALES (est): 69.99K **Privately Held**
Web: biologics.mckesson.com

SIC: 2836 Biological products, except
diagnostic

(G-1308)
BLACQUELADI STYLES LLC
5000 Centre Green Way Ste 500
(27513-5821)
PHONE.................................877 977-7798
Lula Jackson, *CEO*
EMP: 5 EST: 2022
SALES (est): 223.34K **Privately Held**
Web: blacqueladi-styles.myshopify.com
SIC: 3911 2339 3171 Jewelry apparel;
Women's and misses' accessories;
Women's handbags and purses

(G-1309)
BLOOM AI INC
101 S Devimy Ct (27511-6389)
PHONE.................................704 620-2886
Amit Shanker, *Pr*
EMP: 8 EST: 2021
SALES (est): 703.08K **Privately Held**
SIC: 7372 7389 Business oriented computer
software; Business Activities at Non-
Commercial Site

(G-1310)
BLUE STONE INDUSTRIES LTD
10030 Green Level Church Rd
(27519-8194)
PHONE.................................919 379-3986
Scott Olive, *Pr*
EMP: 6 EST: 1996
SALES (est): 244.04K **Privately Held**
Web: www.bluestoneind.com
SIC: 5199 2448 3086 Packaging materials;
Cargo containers, wood; Packaging and
shipping materials, foamed plastics

(G-1311)
BLUESKY POLYMERS LLC
100 Woodsage Way (27518-8996)
PHONE.................................919 522-4374
EMP: 5 EST: 2020
SALES (est): 383.11K **Privately Held**
SIC: 2821 Plastics materials and resins

(G-1312)
BLUR DEVELOPMENT GROUP LLC
Also Called: Blur Product Development
170 Weston Oaks Ct (27513-2256)
PHONE.................................919 701-4213
EMP: 54 EST: 2019
SALES (est): 5.03MM **Privately Held**
Web: www.blurpd.com
SIC: 3999 Advertising curtains

(G-1313)
BMG LABTECH INC
13000 Weston Pkwy Ste 109 (27513-2250)
PHONE.................................919 678-1633
Ronald Earp, *Prin*
EMP: 10 EST: 1995
SQ FT: 3,500
SALES (est): 2.81MM
SALES (corp-wide): 50.82MM **Privately
Held**
Web: www.bmglabtech.com
SIC: 3826 Analytical instruments
PA: Bmg Labtech Gmbh
Allmendgrun 8
Ortenberg BW 77799
781969680

(G-1314)
BRICK CITY GAMING INC
80 Hamilton Hedge Pl (27519-9102)
PHONE.................................919 297-2081
Michael Robinson, *CEO*

▲ = Import ▼ = Export
◆ = Import/Export

EMP: 11 EST: 2022
SALES (est): 449.1K **Privately Held**
Web: www.brickcitygaming.net
SIC: 7372 Educational computer software

(G-1315)
BRIGHTLY SOFTWARE INC (HQ)
Also Called: Schooldude.com
11000 Regency Pkwy Ste 110
(27518-8518)
P.O. Box 200236 (15251)
PHONE................................919 816-8237
Don Kurelich, *CEO*
Lee Prevost, *
Michael Beierwaltes, *
Erikka Buracchio, *
EMP: 213 EST: 1999
SQ FT: 50,000
SALES (est): 46.52MM
SALES (corp-wide): 84.78B **Privately Held**
Web: www.brightlysoftware.com
SIC: 8748 7372 Educational consultant;
   Prepackaged software
PA: Siemens Ag
   Werner-Von-Siemens-Str. 1
   Munchen BY 80333
   893 803-5491

(G-1316)
BUHLER INC
100 Aeroglide Dr (27511-6900)
PHONE................................800 722-7483
Andreas Kratzer, *Mgr*
EMP: 208
Web: www.buhlergroup.com
SIC: 3556 3585 3567 Food products
   machinery; Refrigeration and heating
   equipment; Industrial furnaces and ovens
HQ: Buhler Inc.
   13105 12th Ave N
   Plymouth MN 55441
   763 847-9900

(G-1317)
**BURLINGTON COAT FCTRY WHSE
COR**
Also Called: Burlington Coat Factory
1741 Walnut St (27511-5930)
PHONE................................919 468-9312
EMP: 48
SALES (corp-wide): 9.73B **Publicly Held**
Web: www.burlington.com
SIC: 5311 5137 5136 2389 Department
   stores; Women's and children's clothing;
   Men's and boy's clothing; Apparel for
   handicapped
HQ: Burlington Coat Factory Warehouse
   Corporation
   1830 Rte 130 N
   Burlington NJ 08016
   609 387-7800

(G-1318)
C W LAWLEY INCORPORATED
Also Called: Transit & Level Clinic
201 Towerview Ct (27513-3592)
PHONE................................919 467-7782
Charles Lawley, *Pr*
EMP: 6 EST: 1988
SALES (est): 3.96MM **Privately Held**
Web: www.transitandlevel.com
SIC: 3829 Measuring and controlling
   devices, nec

(G-1319)
CADENCE DESIGN SYSTEMS INC
11000 Regency Pkwy Ste 401
(27518-8518)
PHONE................................919 380-3900
Rick Cole, *Mgr*
EMP: 8

SALES (corp-wide): 4.64B **Publicly Held**
Web: www.cadence.com
SIC: 7372 Application computer software
PA: Cadence Design Systems, Inc.
   2655 Seely Ave Bldg 5
   San Jose CA 95134
   408 943-1234

(G-1320)
**CAMELOT RTURN INTRMDATE
HLDNGS (PA)**
5020 Weston Pkwy Ste 400 (27513)
PHONE................................866 419-0042
Rose Lee, *Pr*
EMP: 93 EST: 2022
SALES (est): 5.58B
SALES (corp-wide): 5.58B **Privately Held**
SIC: 3448 Buildings, portable: prefabricated
   metal

(G-1321)
CAROLINA
8204 Tryon Woods Dr (27518-7163)
PHONE................................919 851-0906
Qing Lin, *Prin*
EMP: 4 EST: 2015
SALES (est): 109.93K **Privately Held**
Web: www.visitraleigh.com
SIC: 7539 3599 Automotive repair shops, nec
   ; Machine shop, jobbing and repair

(G-1322)
CAROLINA CAB SPECIALIST LLC
311 Ashville Ave Ste K (27518-6668)
PHONE................................919 818-4375
EMP: 7 EST: 2014
SALES (est): 59.16K **Privately Held**
Web: www.carolinacabinetspecialist.com
SIC: 2434 5211 2541 Wood kitchen cabinets
   ; Cabinets, kitchen; Cabinets, lockers, and
   shelving

(G-1323)
CAROLINA PRINT MILL
527 E Chatham St (27511-6933)
PHONE................................919 607-9452
EMP: 5 EST: 2010
SALES (est): 106.61K **Privately Held**
Web: www.carolinaprintmill.com
SIC: 2752 Offset printing

(G-1324)
CELPLOR LLC
115 Centrewest Ct Ste B (27513-2015)
PHONE................................919 961-1961
Simon Cooper, *Bd of Dir*
EMP: 5 EST: 2010
SALES (est): 192.04K **Privately Held**
Web: www.celplor.com
SIC: 2835 Microbiology and virology
   diagnostic products

(G-1325)
CENERX BIOPHARMA INC
270 Cornerstone Dr Ste 103 (27519-8400)
PHONE................................919 234-4072
Daniel Burch, *Chief Medical Officer*
Paola Pagano, *Dir*
EMP: 6 EST: 2006
SALES (est): 214.29K **Privately Held**
Web: www.cenerx.com
SIC: 2834 Pharmaceutical preparations

(G-1326)
CHEROKEE PUBLISHING CO INC
Also Called: Smith & Associates
301 Cascade Pointe Ln (27513-5778)
PHONE................................919 674-6020
Ronald H Smith, *Pr*
EMP: 10 EST: 1990

SQ FT: 1,500
SALES (est): 451.25K **Privately Held**
Web: www.sacommunications.com
SIC: 2721 Magazines: publishing only, not
   printed on site

(G-1327)
CHOCOLATE SMILES VILLAGE LLC
312 W Chatham St Ste 101 (27511-3291)
PHONE................................919 469-5282
Sandra Horton, *Managing Member*
EMP: 6 EST: 1982
SQ FT: 2,000
SALES (est): 484.5K **Privately Held**
Web: www.chocolatesmiles.com
SIC: 2066 5441 5149 Chocolate candy, solid
   ; Candy; Chocolate

(G-1328)
CICERO INC (PA)
2500 Regency Pkwy (27518-8549)
PHONE................................919 380-5000
John Broderick, *CEO*
John L Steffens, *Ch Bd*
Todd Sherin, *CRO*
EMP: 7 EST: 1988
SALES (est): 1.54MM **Privately Held**
Web: www.ciceroinc.com
SIC: 7373 7372 Computer integrated
   systems design; Prepackaged software

(G-1329)
CIVENTICHEM USA LLC
329 Matilda Pl (27513-9677)
PHONE................................919 672-8865
Bhaskar Venepalli, *Prin*
EMP: 5 EST: 2019
SALES (est): 76.38K **Privately Held**
Web: www.civentichem.com
SIC: 2834 Pharmaceutical preparations

(G-1330)
COIL INNOVATION USA INC
125 Edinburgh South Dr Ste 201
(27511-6484)
PHONE................................919 659-0300
Richard Kimball, *Pr*
EMP: 4 EST: 2013
SALES (est): 947.72K **Privately Held**
Web: www.coilinnovation.com
SIC: 3677 Electronic coils and transformers

(G-1331)
**COMMSCOPE HOLDING COMPANY
INC**
101 Stamford Dr (27513-9503)
PHONE................................919 677-2422
EMP: 12
Web: www.commscope.com
SIC: 3663 4899 Radio and t.v.
   communications equipment;
   Communication signal enhancement
   network services
PA: Commscope Holding Company, Inc.
   3642 E Us Hwy 70
   Claremont NC 28610

(G-1332)
CONNEXION TECHNOLOGIES
111 Corning Rd Ste 250 (27518-9238)
PHONE................................919 674-0036
Peter Ley, *Prin*
EMP: 10 EST: 2013
SALES (est): 2.42MM **Privately Held**
SIC: 3229 Fiber optics strands

(G-1333)
CONTAINER GRAPHICS CORP (PA)
Also Called: C G C
114 Edinburgh South Dr Ste 104
(27511-6480)

PHONE................................919 481-4200
▲ **EMP: 16 EST:** 1975
SALES (est): 3.99MM
SALES (corp-wide): 3.99MM **Privately
Held**
Web: www.containergraphics.com
SIC: 3544 3555 5084 Special dies and tools;
   Printing plates; Printing trades machinery,
   equipment, and supplies

(G-1334)
CONVERSANT PRODUCTS INC
120 Preston Executive Dr Ste 200
(27513-8445)
PHONE................................919 465-3456
Mike Sullivan, *Pr*
Robert Scherle, *VP*
◆ **EMP: 4 EST:** 2003
SALES (est): 412.56K **Privately Held**
Web: www.conversantproducts.com
SIC: 3661 7629 Telephone and telegraph
   apparatus; Telephone set repair

(G-1335)
CORNERSTONE BIOPHARMA INC
175 Regency Woods Pl Ste 600
(27518-6001)
PHONE................................919 678-6507
Craig Collard, *CEO*
Alastair Mcewan, *CFO*
EMP: 11 EST: 2004
SALES (est): 5.32MM **Privately Held**
Web: www.chiesiusa.com
SIC: 2834 Proprietary drug products

(G-1336)
**CORNERSTONE BLDG BRANDS INC
(HQ)**
Also Called: Cornerstone Building Brands
5020 Weston Pkwy (27513-2321)
PHONE................................281 897-7788
Rose Lee, *Pr*
Jeffrey S Lee, *Ex VP*
Katy K Theroux, *Chief Human Resources
Officer*
James F Keppler, *Ofcr*
Alena S Brenner, *Corporate Secretary*
▲ **EMP: 400 EST:** 1991
SALES (est): 5.4B
SALES (corp-wide): 5.58B **Privately Held**
Web:
www.cornerstonebuildingbrands.com
SIC: 3448 3444 3442 1542 Buildings,
   portable: prefabricated metal; Metal roofing
   and roof drainage equipment; Rolling doors
   for industrial buildings or warehouses, metal
   ; Nonresidential construction, nec
PA: Camelot Return Intermediate Holdings,
   Llc
   5020 Weston Pkwy Ste 400
   Cary NC 27513
   866 419-0042

(G-1337)
CREATIVE IMAGES INC
226 E Chatham St (27511-3459)
PHONE................................919 467-2188
Adita J Marshall, *Pr*
Paul G Marshall, *VP*
Chack J Cooke, *Sec*
EMP: 5 EST: 1983
SALES (est): 149.77K **Privately Held**
Web: www.creativeimagesnc.com
SIC: 3993 Signs and advertising specialties

(G-1338)
CREATIVE SCREENING
303 E Durham Rd Ste C (27513-4047)
PHONE................................919 467-5081
Bing M Creasy, *Owner*
EMP: 6 EST: 1977

SQ FT: 8,000
SALES (est): 198.57K **Privately Held**
Web: www.creativescreening.com
SIC: 2759 Screen printing

(G-1339)
CRM A LLC
8000 Weston Pkwy Ste 100 (27513-2123)
PHONE..............................888 600-7567
Mathew B Rank, *Managing Member*
EMP: 10 EST: 2018
SALES (est): 3.82MM **Privately Held**
Web: www.crma.com
SIC: 7372 Application computer software

(G-1340)
CROWDGUARD INC
12218 Bradford Green Sq Ste 151
(27519-9228)
PHONE..............................919 605-1948
Herbert Ubbens, *Pr*
EMP: 4
SALES (est): 586.67K **Privately Held**
Web: www.crowdguard.co.uk
SIC: 3699 Security devices

(G-1341)
CURLEE MACHINERY COMPANY
412 Field St (27513-4129)
P.O. Box 552 (27512-0552)
PHONE..............................919 467-9311
Greg Duke, *Pr*
EMP: 9 EST: 1947
SQ FT: 7,200
SALES (est): 1.31MM **Privately Held**
Web: www.curleemachinery.com
SIC: 3648 Street lighting fixtures

(G-1342)
CYMBAL LLC
2500 Regency Pkwy (27518-8549)
PHONE..............................877 365-9622
Nathan Brinson, *CEO*
EMP: 7 EST: 2021
SALES (est): 462.9K **Privately Held**
SIC: 4789 7349 1799 5039 Transportation
   services, nec; Janitorial service, contract
   basis; Construction site cleanup;
   Construction materials, nec

(G-1343)
DEFINITIVE MEDIA CORP (PA)
Also Called: Thread
2000 Centre Green Way Ste 300
(27513-5756)
PHONE..............................714 730-4958
Jeff Fazier, *CEO*
EMP: 11 EST: 2008
SALES (est): 9.03MM
SALES (corp-wide): 9.03MM **Privately
Held**
Web: www.threadresearch.com
SIC: 7372 Business oriented computer
   software

(G-1344)
**DELTA MSRMENT CMBSTN CNTRLS
LL**
207 Kettlebridge Dr (27511-6344)
PHONE..............................919 623-7133
Richard A Nowak, *Pr*
EMP: 30 EST: 2007
SALES (est): 4.08MM **Privately Held**
Web: www.deltameasurement.com
SIC: 3823 3825 Combustion control
   instruments; Internal combustion engine
   analyzers, to test electronics
PA: Environmental Energy Services, Inc.
   5 Turnberry Ln
   Sandy Hook CT 06482

(G-1345)
DELZER CONSTRUCTION
632 Northwoods Dr (27513-3818)
PHONE..............................919 625-0755
Jeff Delzer, *Admn*
EMP: 6 EST: 1993
SALES (est): 81.16K **Privately Held**
SIC: 2421 Siding (dressed lumber)

(G-1346)
DEWILL INC
951 High House Rd (27513-3510)
PHONE..............................919 426-9550
William Brown, *Pr*
EMP: 7 EST: 2014
SALES (est): 270.26K **Privately Held**
SIC: 2842 Laundry cleaning preparations

(G-1347)
DEX MEDIA EAST LLC
1001 Winstead Dr Ste 1 (27513-2154)
PHONE..............................919 297-1600
Brenda Davis, *Prin*
EMP: 17 EST: 2003
SALES (est): 2.42MM
SALES (corp-wide): 824.16MM **Publicly
Held**
SIC: 2731 Book publishing
HQ: Thryv, Inc.
   2200 W Airfield Dr
   Dfw Airport TX 75261
   972 453-7000

(G-1348)
DEX ONE CORPORATION
1001 Winstead Dr (27513-2117)
PHONE..............................919 297-1600
EMP: 2300
SIC: 2741 8732 Directories, telephone:
   publishing only, not printed on site; Market
   analysis or research

(G-1349)
DG MATRIX INC
809 Montvale Ridge Dr (27519-1022)
PHONE..............................724 877-7773
Haroon Inam, *Prin*
EMP: 6
SALES (est): 899.89K **Privately Held**
SIC: 3613 7389 Power switching equipment;
   Business Activities at Non-Commercial Site

(G-1350)
E&C MEDICAL INTELLIGENCE INC
Also Called: Perigen
100 Regency Forest Dr Ste 200
(27518-8597)
PHONE..............................609 228-7898
Matthew Sappern, *CEO*
John Coats, *
Thomas J Garite, *CCO*
Rebecca Cypher, *
EMP: 38 EST: 1999
SQ FT: 7,800
SALES (est): 1.41MM **Privately Held**
SIC: 7372 Prepackaged software

(G-1351)
**EDUCATED DESIGN &
DEVELOPMENT INCORPORATED**
Also Called: ED&d
901 Sheldon Dr (27513-2014)
PHONE..............................919 469-9434
EMP: 30 EST: 1988
SALES (est): 4.02MM **Privately Held**
Web: www.productsafet.com
SIC: 3825 8734 3829 Instruments to
   measure electricity; Product testing
   laboratory, safety or performance;
   Measuring and controlling devices, nec

(G-1352)
EMATH360 LLC
302 Parish House Rd (27513-1676)
PHONE..............................919 744-4944
Jawahar Lal, *Pr*
Raj Marota, *Dir*
EMP: 10 EST: 2010
SALES (est): 199.07K **Privately Held**
Web: www.emath360.com
SIC: 8299 8748 7372 8742 Tutoring school;
   Testing service, educational or personnel;
   Educational computer software; Business
   planning and organizing services

(G-1353)
EMPLOYUS INC
122 E Chatham St Ste 300 (27511-3360)
PHONE..............................919 706-4008
Ryan O'donnell, *CEO*
Francis Stocks, *Ch Bd*
EMP: 10 EST: 2014
SALES (est): 971.87K **Privately Held**
Web: www.hireology.com
SIC: 7372 Business oriented computer
   software

(G-1354)
**ENVIRONMENTAL SCIENCE US LLC
(HQ)**
Also Called: Bayer Cropscience
5000 Centre Green Way Ste 400 (27513)
PHONE..............................800 331-2867
Gilles Galliou, *CEO*
Jonathan Margolis, *Sr VP*
Ashish Malik, *VP*
Joel R Jung, *CFO*
Michael Mille, *COO*
▲ EMP: 18 EST: 1995
SQ FT: 28,000
SALES (est): 106.88MM
SALES (corp-wide): 344.15MM **Privately
Held**
Web: us.envu.com
SIC: 2834 Pharmaceutical preparations
PA: Cinven Limited
   21 St. James's Square
   London SW1Y
   207 661-3333

(G-1355)
ERLECLAIR INC
Also Called: AlphaGraphics
301 Ashville Ave Ste 121 (27518-6131)
PHONE..............................919 233-7710
Edwrad Erleclair, *Pr*
Carol Leclair, *VP*
EMP: 22 EST: 2007
SQ FT: 6,500
SALES (est): 3.15MM **Privately Held**
Web: www.alphagraphics.com
SIC: 2752 Commercial printing, lithographic

(G-1356)
ETHICON INC
Also Called: Ethicon Endo - Surgery
125 Edinburgh South Dr Ste 201
(27511-6484)
PHONE..............................919 234-2124
Greg Casale, *Mgr*
EMP: 6
SALES (corp-wide): 88.82B **Publicly Held**
SIC: 3842 Surgical appliances and supplies
HQ: Ethicon Inc.
   1000 Route 202
   Raritan NJ 08869
   800 384-4266

(G-1357)
EXPERSIS SOFTWARE INC
1060 Kennicott Ave (27513-8450)
PHONE..............................919 874-0608

Manoj Patwardhan, *Pr*
EMP: 4 EST: 2010
SALES (est): 148.97K **Privately Held**
Web: www.expersis.com
SIC: 7372 Prepackaged software

(G-1358)
EZBREW INC
1006 Sw Maynard Rd (27511-4385)
PHONE..............................833 233-2739
Andrew Baker, *Prin*
EMP: 4 EST: 2019
SALES (est): 371.2K **Privately Held**
Web: www.ezbrew.beer
SIC: 3556 Brewers' and maltsters' machinery

(G-1359)
FABCO INDUSTRIES
312 N Dixon Ave (27513-4427)
PHONE..............................919 481-3010
Marty Garmon, *Owner*
EMP: 5 EST: 1985
SQ FT: 3,200
SALES (est): 460.48K **Privately Held**
Web: www.fabco-industries.com
SIC: 3441 Fabricated structural metal

(G-1360)
FACILITYDUDECOM INC
11000 Regency Pkwy Ste 200
(27518-8518)
PHONE..............................919 459-6430
Kent Hudson, *Ch Bd*
Tom Knox, *
Brian Bell, *Strategy Vice President**
Joan Maddox, *Client Services Vice
President**
EMP: 6 EST: 2006
SALES (est): 325.83K **Privately Held**
Web: www.brightlysoftware.com
SIC: 7372 Business oriented computer
   software

(G-1361)
FAIR PRODUCTS INC
806 Reedy Creek Rd (27513-3307)
P.O. Box 386 (27512-0386)
PHONE..............................919 467-1599
H Frank Grainger, *Pr*
EMP: 7 EST: 1978
SALES (est): 4.12MM **Privately Held**
Web: www.fairproductsinc.com
SIC: 2879 Agricultural chemicals, nec

(G-1362)
FATHOM HOLDINGS INC (PA)
Also Called: Intelliagent
2000 Regency Pkwy Ste 300 (27518-8508)
PHONE..............................888 455-6040
Marco Fregenal, *Pr*
Scott Flanders, *
Jon Gwin, *CRO*
Joanne Zach, *CFO*
Samantha Giuggio, *COO*
EMP: 38 EST: 2010
SQ FT: 28,700
SALES (est): 345.23MM
SALES (corp-wide): 345.23MM **Publicly
Held**
Web: www.fathomrealty.com
SIC: 6531 7372 Real estate listing services;
   Prepackaged software

(G-1363)
GALVIX INC
1036 Canyon Shadows Ct (27519-1003)
PHONE..............................925 434-6243
Piyush Agrawal, *CEO*
EMP: 6
SALES (est): 373.25K **Privately Held**

▲ = Import ▼ = Export
◆ = Import/Export

SIC: **7389** 7372 Business Activities at Non-Commercial Site; Prepackaged software

(G-1364)
GARMIN INTERNATIONAL INC
100 Regency Forest Dr (27518-8597)
PHONE.....................919 337-0116
EMP: 729
Web: www.garmin.com
SIC: **3812** Navigational systems and instruments
HQ: Garmin International, Inc.
1200 E 151st St
Olathe KS 66062

(G-1365)
GEM ASSET ACQUISITION LLC
Also Called: Gemseal Pvments Pdts - Raleigh
200 Travis Park (27511-6908)
PHONE.....................919 851-0799
EMP: 4
SALES (corp-wide): 10.35MM **Privately Held**
Web: www.sealmaster.net
SIC: **2951** Asphalt paving mixtures and blocks
PA: Gem Asset Acquisition Llc
1855 Lindbergh St Ste 500
Charlotte NC 28208
704 225-3321

(G-1366)
GLOBAL FORMING TECH LTD
801 Cascade Pointe Ln Ste 102
(27513-5823)
PHONE.....................919 234-1384
Erich Dominik, *Managing Member*
▲ EMP: 4 EST: 2001
SALES (est): 568.1K **Privately Held**
Web: www.globalforming.us
SIC: **3317** Tubing, mechanical or hypodermic sizes: cold drawn stainless

(G-1367)
GLOVES-ONLINE INC
Also Called: Go Gloves
231 E Johnson St Ste K (27513-4010)
P.O. Box 4468 (27519-4468)
PHONE.....................919 468-4244
Joseph Mcgarry, *Pr*
▲ EMP: 6 EST: 1998
SALES (est): 374.96K **Privately Held**
Web: www.gloves-online.com
SIC: **2259** 3089 3151 3842 Work gloves, knit ; Work gloves, plastics; Welders' gloves; Gloves, safety

(G-1368)
GREEN APPLE STUDIO
590 E Chatham St (27511-6955)
PHONE.....................919 377-2239
Jing Wang, *Admn*
EMP: 4 EST: 2015
SALES (est): 451.89K **Privately Held**
Web: green-apple-studio.hub.biz
SIC: **3571** Electronic computers

(G-1369)
GREENLIGHTS LLC
1211 Walnut St (27511-4730)
PHONE.....................919 766-8900
Alan D King, *Brnch Mgr*
EMP: 20
SALES (corp-wide): 49.6K **Privately Held**
Web: www.greenlighthealth.com
SIC: **3641** Electric lamps
PA: Greenlights Llc
221 Brook Manor Ct
Cary NC

(G-1370)
HELIUM BRANDS LLC
109 Granby Ct (27511-6702)
PHONE.....................561 350-1328
EMP: 4
SALES (corp-wide): 579.47K **Privately Held**
SIC: **2813** Helium
PA: Helium Brands Llc
3201 Edwards Mill Rd # 1
Raleigh NC

(G-1371)
HERON THERAPEUTICS INC (PA)
Also Called: Heron Therapeutics
100 Regency Forest Dr Ste 300 (27518)
PHONE.....................858 251-4400
Craig Collard, *CEO*
Adam Morgan, *Ch Bd*
Ira Duarte, *Ex VP*
William Forbes, *CDO*
Brett Fleshman, *Chief Business Officer*
EMP: 122 EST: 1983
SQ FT: 52,148
SALES (est): 144.28MM
SALES (corp-wide): 144.28MM **Publicly Held**
Web: www.herontx.com
SIC: **2834** Pharmaceutical preparations

(G-1372)
HILL-ROM INC
1225 Crescent Green Ste 300
(27518-8119)
PHONE.....................919 854-3600
Mark Hesner, *Mgr*
EMP: 31
SALES (corp-wide): 10.64B **Publicly Held**
Web: www.hillrom.com
SIC: **2515** Sleep furniture
HQ: Hill-Rom, Inc.
1069 State Rte 46 E
Batesville IN 47006
812 934-7777

(G-1373)
IN PINK
112 Swiss Stone Ct (27513-4753)
PHONE.....................919 380-1487
Linda Pink, *Prin*
EMP: 6 EST: 2006
SALES (est): 121.55K **Privately Held**
Web: www.prettyinpinkfoundation.org
SIC: **2342** Bras, girdles, and allied garments

(G-1374)
INDUSTRIAL CNNCTONS SLTONS LLC (DH)
305 Gregson Dr (27511-6496)
PHONE.....................203 229-3932
Michael D Gray, *Managing Member*
Michael Plaster, *Managing Member*
Bridget Smith, *Managing Member*
EMP: 34 EST: 2017
SALES (est): 5.89MM **Privately Held**
SIC: **3613** Control panels, electric
HQ: Abb Inc.
305 Gregson Dr
Cary NC 27511

(G-1375)
INFORMTION RTRVAL CMPANIES INC
Also Called: Irc
3500 Regency Pkwy Ste 140 (27511)
PHONE.....................919 460-7447
Tony Colle, *Brnch Mgr*
EMP: 35
SALES (corp-wide): 598.67K **Privately Held**

SIC: **7372** 7379 Application computer software; Computer related consulting services
PA: Information Retrieval Companies, Inc.
225 W Wacker Dr Ste 2200
Chicago IL 60606
312 726-7587

(G-1376)
INN-FLOW LLC
Also Called: Inn-Flow Hotel Software
5640 Dillard Dr Ste 300 (27518-7174)
PHONE.....................919 277-9027
John Erhart, *Pr*
EMP: 20 EST: 2012
SQ FT: 2,000
SALES (est): 1.68MM **Privately Held**
Web: www.inn-flow.com
SIC: **7372** Application computer software

(G-1377)
JAGUAR GENE THERAPY LLC
203 Mackenan Dr (27511-6498)
PHONE.....................919 465-6400
EMP: 18
SALES (corp-wide): 9.69MM **Privately Held**
Web: wwwjaguargenetherapy.com
SIC: **5047** 3841 Therapy equipment; Surgical and medical instruments
PA: Jaguar Gene Therapy, Llc
150 N Field Dr
Lake Forest IL

(G-1378)
JMP STATISTICAL DISCOVERY LLC
920 Sas Campus Dr (27513-2087)
PHONE.....................877 594-6567
Patricia L Brown, *Managing Member*
EMP: 10 EST: 2021
SALES (est): 3.76MM
SALES (corp-wide): 1.35B **Privately Held**
Web: www.jmp.com
SIC: **7372** Operating systems computer software
PA: Sas Institute Inc.
100 Sas Campus Dr
Cary NC 27513
919 677-8000

(G-1379)
JOBS MAGAZINE LLC
1240 Se Maynard Rd Ste 104 (27511-6929)
PHONE.....................919 319-6816
EMP: 7 EST: 1995
SALES (est): 479.14K **Privately Held**
SIC: **2721** Periodicals
PA: Prism Publishing, Inc.
1240 Se Mynard Rd Ste 104
Cary NC 27511

(G-1380)
JOHN DEERE CONSUMER PDTS INC (HQ)
Also Called: John Deere
2000 John Deere Run (27513-2789)
P.O. Box 8808 (61266-8808)
PHONE.....................919 804-2000
Curt Hoppestad, *Pr*
Randy Rulin, *
EMP: 170 EST: 1987
SALES (est): 174.23MM
SALES (corp-wide): 8.51B **Publicly Held**
Web: www.deere.com
SIC: **3546** 8711 3524 Chain saws, portable; Engineering services; Lawn and garden equipment
PA: Deere & Company
1 John Deere Pl
Moline IL 61265
309 765-8000

(G-1381)
JOURNAL VACUUM SCIENCE & TECH
Also Called: Jvst
51 Kilmayne Dr Ste 104 (27511-7719)
P.O. Box 13994 (27709-3994)
PHONE.....................919 361-2787
Yvonne Towse, *Dir*
EMP: 5 EST: 1990
SALES (est): 48.59K **Privately Held**
SIC: **2711** Newspapers, publishing and printing

(G-1382)
JUSTI LLC
109 Oxyard Way (27519-7327)
PHONE.....................919 434-5002
Selva Mohan, *CEO*
EMP: 11 EST: 2017
SALES (est): 574.74K **Privately Held**
SIC: **7372** Utility computer software

(G-1383)
KING PHRMCEUTICALS RES DEV LLC
Also Called: King Pharmaceutical R & D
4000 Centre Green Way Ste 300
(27513-5758)
P.O. Box 13886 (27709-3886)
PHONE.....................919 653-7001
Bryan Markinson, *Pr*
King Jolly, *Ex VP*
EMP: 205 EST: 1978
SQ FT: 11,900
SALES (est): 910.29K
SALES (corp-wide): 63.63B **Publicly Held**
SIC: **8733** 8731 2834 Medical research; Commercial physical research; Pharmaceutical preparations
HQ: King Pharmaceuticals Llc
501 5th St
Bristol TN 37620

(G-1384)
KORBER PHARMA INC
8000 Regency Pkwy Ste 403 (27518-8514)
PHONE.....................727 538-4644
Kerry Fillmore, *Brnch Mgr*
EMP: 37
SALES (corp-wide): 54.57MM **Privately Held**
Web: www.koerber-pharma.com
SIC: **3565** Packaging machinery
HQ: Korber Pharma, Inc.
2243 Energy Dr
Apex NC 27502
727 538-4644

(G-1385)
LA FARM INC
Also Called: La Farm Bakery
220 W Chatham St (27511-3244)
PHONE.....................919 657-0657
Elisabeth Vatinet, *Pr*
Lionel Vatinet, *Sec*
EMP: 20 EST: 1999
SALES (est): 3.58MM **Privately Held**
Web: www.lafarmbakery.com
SIC: **2051** Bread, cake, and related products

(G-1386)
LARRY SHACKELFORD
309 Dunhagan Pl (27511-5611)
PHONE.....................919 467-8817
Larry Shackelford, *Prin*
EMP: 4 EST: 2001
SALES (est): 291.02K **Privately Held**
SIC: **3674** Semiconductors and related devices

GEOGRAPHIC

(G-1387)
LASER RECHARGE CAROLINA INC
Also Called: Lrc
2474 Walnut St (27518-9212)
PHONE....................................919 467-5902
Sam Robinson, *Pr*
Robert Wood, *VP*
EMP: 10 EST: 1989
SQ FT: 2,500
SALES (est): 1.6MM Privately Held
Web: www.go-lrc.com
SIC: 3861 7372 5112 Toners, prepared
photographic (not made in chemical plants);
Business oriented computer software;
Laser printer supplies

(G-1388)
LIGHTHOUSE PRESS INC
102 Eagle Meadow Ct (27519-5070)
PHONE....................................919 371-8640
Scott C Wagner, *Prin*
EMP: 20 EST: 2005
SALES (est): 676.6K Privately Held
SIC: 2741 Miscellaneous publishing

(G-1389)
LINDE GAS & EQUIPMENT INC
Also Called: Linde Gas North America
1120 W Chatham St (27511-6230)
PHONE....................................919 380-7411
Robert Farrell, *Mgr*
EMP: 13
Web: www.lindedirect.com
SIC: 2813 Nitrogen
HQ: Linde Gas & Equipment Inc.
10 Riverview Dr
Danbury CT 06810
844 445-4633

(G-1390)
LIQUIDEHR INC
1939 High House Rd Ste 107 (27519-8452)
PHONE....................................866 618-1531
Gabie Lambrechtse, *Prin*
EMP: 25 EST: 2013
SALES (est): 981.15K Privately Held
Web: www.liquidehr.com
SIC: 7372 Prepackaged software

(G-1391)
LIVING INTNTIONALLY FOR EXCELL
Also Called: Life
200 Commonwealth Ct Ste 200
(27511-2431)
PHONE....................................810 600-3425
Robert Hallstrand, *Mng Pt*
Rob Hallstrand, *Mng Pt*
EMP: 33 EST: 2011
SALES (est): 995.94K Privately Held
SIC: 2759 Publication printing

(G-1392)
LOPAREX LLC (DH)
Also Called: Easy Mask
1255 Crescent Green Ste 400
(27518-8132)
PHONE....................................919 678-7700
Michael Apperson, *
Jack Taylor, *
◆ EMP: 96 EST: 2001
SQ FT: 24,000
SALES (est): 456.82MM Privately Held
Web: www.loparex.com
SIC: 2672 Coated paper, except
photographic, carbon, or abrasive
HQ: Loparex Holding B.V.
Laan Van Westenenk 45
Apeldoorn GE
555276999

(G-1393)
LORD CORPORATION
Also Called: Materials Division
406 Gregson Dr (27511-6445)
PHONE....................................919 342-3380
Gerald Estes, *VP*
EMP: 84
SQ FT: 35,835
SALES (corp-wide): 19.93B Publicly Held
Web: www.lord.com
SIC: 3593 2992 3714 2899 Fluid power
actuators, hydraulic or pneumatic; Brake
fluid (hydraulic): made from purchased
materials; Shock absorbers, motor vehicle;
Magnetic inspection oil or powder
HQ: Lord Corporation
111 Lord Dr
Cary NC 27511
919 468-5979

(G-1394)
LORD CORPORATION (HQ)
Also Called: Parker-Lord
111 Lord Dr (27511)
P.O. Box 8012 (27512)
PHONE....................................919 468-5979
◆ EMP: 391 EST: 1940
SALES (est): 794.78MM
SALES (corp-wide): 19.93B Publicly Held
Web: www.lord.com
SIC: 2891 3724 3728 2851 Adhesives;
Engine mount parts, aircraft; Aircraft parts
and equipment, nec; Polyurethane coatings
PA: Parker-Hannifin Corporation
6035 Parkland Blvd
Cleveland OH 44124
216 896-3000

(G-1395)
LORD CORPORATION
Stellar Technology
110 Lord Dr (27511-7917)
PHONE....................................919 469-2500
David G Thomas, *Brnch Mgr*
EMP: 80
SALES (corp-wide): 19.93B Publicly Held
Web: www.lord.com
SIC: 2891 8731 Adhesives; Commercial
physical research
HQ: Lord Corporation
111 Lord Dr
Cary NC 27511
919 468-5979

(G-1396)
LORD CORPORATION
200 Lord Dr Nc (27511-7924)
PHONE....................................877 275-5673
EMP: 6 EST: 1981
SALES (est): 2.68MM Privately Held
Web: www.lord.com
SIC: 3829 Measuring and controlling
devices, nec

(G-1397)
LORD FAR EAST INC
111 Lord Dr (27511-7923)
PHONE....................................919 468-5979
EMP: 5 EST: 1969
SALES (est): 447.56K
SALES (corp-wide): 19.93B Publicly Held
SIC: 2891 3724 3728 2851 Adhesives;
Engine mount parts, aircraft; Aircraft parts
and equipment, nec; Polyurethane coatings
HQ: Lord Corporation
111 Lord Dr
Cary NC 27511
919 468-5979

(G-1398)
LUCERNO DYNAMICS LLC
140 Towerview Ct (27513-3595)
PHONE....................................317 294-1395
EMP: 5 EST: 2011
SALES (est): 2.07MM Privately Held
Web: www.lucerno.com
SIC: 3841 7389 Surgical and medical
instruments; Business Activities at Non-
Commercial Site

(G-1399)
MASTIC HOME EXTERIORS INC (DH)
Also Called: Kroy Building Products
5020 Weston Pkwy Ste 400 (27513-2322)
PHONE....................................816 426-8200
Rose Lee, *Pr*
▲ EMP: 25 EST: 1928
SQ FT: 25,000
SALES (est): 113.48MM
SALES (corp-wide): 5.58B Privately Held
Web: www.plygem.com
SIC: 3081 3089 Plastics film and sheet;
Siding, plastics
HQ: Ply Gem Industries, Inc.
5020 Weston Pkwy Ste 400
Cary NC 27513
919 677-3900

(G-1400)
MCGILL CORPORATION
1220 Se Maynard Rd (27511-6944)
PHONE....................................919 467-1993
Todd Stine, *Brnch Mgr*
EMP: 11
SALES (corp-wide): 67.2MM Privately
Held
Web: www.unitedmcgill.com
SIC: 3444 Ducts, sheet metal
PA: The Mcgill Corporation
One Mission Park
Groveport OH 43125
614 829-1200

(G-1401)
MEDTRNIC SOFAMOR DANEK USA INC
Also Called: Medtronic
2000 Regency Pkwy Ste 270 (27518-8509)
PHONE....................................919 457-9982
EMP: 8
Web: www.medtronic.com
SIC: 5047 3842 Hospital equipment and
furniture; Implants, surgical
HQ: Medtronic Sofamor Danek Usa, Inc.
4340 Swinnea Rd
Memphis TN 38118
901 396-3133

(G-1402)
MOON AUDIO
1157 Executive Cir Ste 101 (27511-4665)
PHONE....................................919 649-5018
Drew Baird, *Owner*
EMP: 5 EST: 2008
SALES (est): 1.38MM Privately Held
Web: www.moon-audio.com
SIC: 5999 3651 2298 Audio-visual
equipment and supplies; Audio electronic
systems; Ropes and fiber cables

(G-1403)
MTS SYSTEMS CORPORATION
Also Called: MTS Sensors Division
3001 Sheldon Dr (27513-2006)
PHONE....................................919 677-2352
Joachim Hellwig, *Mgr*
EMP: 200
SQ FT: 55,835
SALES (corp-wide): 16.11B Publicly Held
Web: www.mts.com

SIC: 3679 3825 3823 Transducers, electrical
; Test equipment for electronic and electric
measurement; Process control instruments
HQ: Mts Systems Corporation
14000 Technology Dr
Eden Prairie MN 55344
952 937-4000

(G-1404)
MW MANUFACTURERS INC
Also Called: Cascade Windows
5020 Weston Pkwy Ste 400 (27513-2322)
P.O. Box 3647 (27513)
PHONE....................................919 677-3900
EMP: 29
SALES (corp-wide): 5.58B Privately Held
SIC: 2431 Window frames, wood
HQ: Mw Manufacturers Inc.
433 N Main St
Rocky Mount VA 24151
540 483-0211

(G-1405)
NCI GROUP INC (DH)
Also Called: M B C I
5020 Weston Pkwy (27513)
P.O. Box 692055 (77269)
PHONE....................................281 897-7788
Joel Viechnicki, *Pr*
Mark E Johnson, *
Eric J Brown, *
Katy K Theroux, *
◆ EMP: 294 EST: 1993
SQ FT: 261,250
SALES (est): 553.19MM
SALES (corp-wide): 5.58B Privately Held
Web:
www.bluescopecoatedproducts.com
SIC: 3448 3446 Buildings, portable:
prefabricated metal; Architectural metalwork
HQ: Cornerstone Building Brands, Inc.
5020 Weston Pkwy
Cary NC 27513
281 897-7788

(G-1406)
NCR VOYIX CORPORATION
Also Called: NCR
115 Centrewest Ct (27513-2015)
PHONE....................................937 445-5000
Bo Holmgreen, *Brnch Mgr*
EMP: 5
SALES (corp-wide): 2.83B Publicly Held
Web: www.ncr.com
SIC: 3575 3578 3577 7379 Computer
terminals; Point-of-sale devices; Magnetic
ink and optical scanning devices; Computer
related maintenance services
PA: Ncr Voyix Corporation
864 Spring St Nw
Atlanta GA 30308
917 821-9817

(G-1407)
NIRAS INC
1000 Centre Green Way Ste 200
(27513-2282)
PHONE....................................919 439-4562
Henrik Linnemann, *Pr*
EMP: 4 EST: 2016
SALES (est): 449.06K Privately Held
Web: www.niras.com
SIC: 2834 Druggists' preparations
(pharmaceuticals)

(G-1408)
NKT INC
Also Called: Nkt Cables
1255 Crescent Green (27518-8123)
PHONE....................................919 601-1970
Andreas Berthou, *Pr*

Mikael Wenneberg, *VP*
EMP: 5 **EST:** 2017
SALES (est): 28.21MM
SALES (corp-wide): 2.79B **Privately Held**
Web: www.nkt.com
SIC: 1731 3355 Fiber optic cable installation; Aluminum wire and cable
PA: Nkt A/S
　　Vibeholms Alle 20
　　Brondby
　　43482000

(G-1409)
NORTHWEST AG PRODUCT
1001 Winstead Dr Ste 480 (27513-2117)
PHONE.................................509 547-8234
David Bergevin, *Pr*
EMP: 6 **EST:** 2015
SALES (est): 309.55K **Privately Held**
SIC: 2875 Fertilizers, mixing only

(G-1410)
NXP USA INC
Also Called: Philips Semiconductors
113 Fieldbrook Ct (27519-7914)
PHONE.................................919 468-3251
Bradley Loisel, *Brnch Mgr*
EMP: 7
SALES (corp-wide): 13.28B **Privately Held**
Web: www.nxp.com
SIC: 3674 Semiconductors and related devices
HQ: Nxp Usa, Inc.
　　6501 W William Cannon Dr
　　Austin TX 78735
　　512 933-8214

(G-1411)
OASYS MOBILE INC
Also Called: Summus
8000 Regency Pkwy Ste 285 (27518-0004)
P.O. Box 519 (27540-0519)
PHONE.................................919 807-5600
Douglas B Dyer, *CEO*
Tracy T Jackson, *CFO*
Donald T Locke, *Executive Corporate Development Vice President*
EMP: 7 **EST:** 1984
SQ FT: 7,339
SALES (est): 988.41K **Privately Held**
Web: www.oasysmobile.com
SIC: 7372 Application computer software

(G-1412)
OXFORD UNIVERSITY PRESS LLC
Chancllor Msters Schlars of Th
4000 Centre Green Way (27513-5758)
PHONE.................................919 677-0977
Giles Kerr, *Dir Fin*
EMP: 75
SALES (corp-wide): 3.69B **Privately Held**
Web: corp.oup.com
SIC: 8721 5192 2741 Accounting services, except auditing; Books, periodicals, and newspapers; Miscellaneous publishing
HQ: Oxford University Press, Llc
　　198 Madison Ave
　　New York NY 10016
　　212 726-6000

(G-1413)
OXFORD UNIVERSITY PRESS LLC
Also Called: Customer Service Department
4000 Centre Green Way (27513-2010)
PHONE.................................919 677-0977
TOLL FREE: 800
Thomas Mccarty, *Mgr*
EMP: 300
SALES (corp-wide): 3.69B **Privately Held**
Web: corp.oup.com

SIC: 8721 5192 2741 Accounting services, except auditing; Books, periodicals, and newspapers; Miscellaneous publishing
HQ: Oxford University Press, Llc
　　198 Madison Ave
　　New York NY 10016
　　212 726-6000

(G-1414)
PASSPORT HEALTH TRIANGLE
8450 Chapel Hill Rd Ste 205 (27513-4577)
PHONE.................................919 781-0053
Melissa Wagers, *Pr*
EMP: 4 **EST:** 2007
SALES (est): 1.66MM **Privately Held**
Web: www.passporthealthusa.com
SIC: 2836 Vaccines and other immunizing products

(G-1415)
PAYLOAD MEDIA INC
129 Parkcrest Dr (27519-6609)
PHONE.................................919 367-2969
Neil Smyth, *CEO*
EMP: 5 **EST:** 2016
SALES (est): 90.78K **Privately Held**
Web: www.payloadbooks.com
SIC: 5734 2731 Software, business and non-game; Books, publishing only

(G-1416)
PCI OF NORTH CAROLINA LLC
Also Called: Syracuse Plastics
100 Falcone Pkwy (27511-6712)
P.O. Box 1067 (27512-1067)
PHONE.................................919 467-5151
EMP: 50 **EST:** 2019
SALES (est): 10.02MM **Privately Held**
Web: www.rosti.com
SIC: 3089 Injection molding of plastics

(G-1417)
PENTAIR WATER POOL AND SPA INC
400 Regency Forest Dr Ste 300 (27518-7702)
PHONE.................................919 463-4640
EMP: 75
Web: www.pentairpool.com
SIC: 3589 3561 3569 3648 Swimming pool filter and water conditioning systems; Pumps, domestic: water or sump; Heaters, swimming pool: electric; Underwater lighting fixtures
HQ: Pentair Water Pool And Spa, Inc.
　　1620 Hawkins Ave
　　Sanford NC 27330
　　919 566-8000

(G-1418)
PEPSI BOTTLING VENTURES LLC
Also Called: Call Center
500 Gregson Dr (27511-6461)
PHONE.................................800 879-8884
EMP: 45
Web: www.pepsibottlingventures.com
SIC: 2086 Carbonated soft drinks, bottled and canned
HQ: Pepsi Bottling Ventures Llc
　　4141 Parklake Ave
　　Raleigh NC 27612
　　919 865-2300

(G-1419)
PERFECT 10 BRANDS LLC
129 Glenmore Rd (27519-6152)
PHONE.................................702 738-0183
Rajeev Prasad, *Pr*
EMP: 4 **EST:** 2017
SALES (est): 842.24K **Privately Held**
Web: www.p10mm.com

SIC: 2844 Shampoos, rinses, conditioners: hair

(G-1420)
PHOENIX ST CLAIRE PUBG LLC
Also Called: Cornell Lab Publishing Gropu
321 Glen Echo Ln Apt C (27518-9676)
PHONE.................................919 303-3223
Brian Scott Sockin, *CEO*
EMP: 4 **EST:** 2013
SALES (est): 190.93K **Privately Held**
SIC: 2731 Books, publishing only

(G-1421)
PLY GEM HOLDINGS INC (DH)
Also Called: Ply Gem
5020 Weston Pkwy Ste 400 (27513-2322)
PHONE.................................919 677-3900
Gary E Robinette, *Pr*
Shawn K Poe, *
John C Wayne, *
Bryan Boyle, *Chief Accounting Officer**
EMP: 54 **EST:** 2004
SQ FT: 38,000
SALES (est): 2.06B
SALES (corp-wide): 5.58B **Privately Held**
Web: www.plygem.com
SIC: 2431 2952 Millwork; Siding materials
HQ: Ply Gem Midco, Llc
　　5020 Weston Pkwy Ste 400
　　Cary NC 27513
　　919 677-3900

(G-1422)
PLY GEM INDUSTRIES INC (DH)
Also Called: Ply Gem Industries
5020 Weston Pkwy Ste 400 (27513)
PHONE.................................919 677-3900
Gary E Robinette, *Pr*
Shawn K Poe, *
EMP: 100 **EST:** 1987
SALES (est): 1.98B
SALES (corp-wide): 5.58B **Privately Held**
Web: www.plygem.com
SIC: 2431 Windows, wood
HQ: Ply Gem Holdings, Inc.
　　5020 Weston Pkwy Ste 400
　　Cary NC 27513
　　919 677-3900

(G-1423)
POLYZEN INC
115 Woodwinds Industrial Ct (27511-6240)
PHONE.................................919 319-9599
Lisa Bozinovic, *CFO*
EMP: 8 **EST:** 2010
SALES (est): 764.66K **Privately Held**
Web: www.polyzen.com
SIC: 3841 Surgical and medical instruments

(G-1424)
PORTABLE DISPLAYS LLC
Also Called: Godfrey Group
5640 Dillard Dr Ste 301 (27518-7199)
P.O. Box 788 (44087-0788)
PHONE.................................919 544-6504
◆ **EMP:** 48
Web: www.godfreygroup.com
SIC: 2522 8742 3993 Panel systems and partitions, office: except wood; Marketing consulting services; Signs and advertising specialties

(G-1425)
PPG INDUSTRIES INC
Also Called: PPG 4650
210 Nottingham Dr (27511-4915)
PHONE.................................919 319-0113
Ronald Pegeus, *Mgr*
EMP: 4
SALES (corp-wide): 17.65B **Publicly Held**

Web: www.ppgpaints.com
SIC: 2851 Paints and allied products
PA: Ppg Industries, Inc.
　　1 Ppg Pl
　　Pittsburgh PA 15272
　　412 434-3131

(G-1426)
PRAMANA LLC
709 Dennison Ln (27519-8854)
PHONE.................................910 233-5118
Robert Corey Patton, *Managing Member*
EMP: 4 **EST:** 2018
SALES (est): 1.45MM **Privately Held**
SIC: 7372 7389 Application computer software; Business services, nec

(G-1427)
PRISM PRINTING & DESIGN INC
109 Loch Haven Ln (27518-8409)
PHONE.................................919 706-5977
William F Metcalfe, *Pr*
EMP: 5 **EST:** 1986
SQ FT: 3,200
SALES (est): 68.91K **Privately Held**
SIC: 2752 Offset printing

(G-1428)
PRISM PUBLISHING INC (PA)
Also Called: Job Finder USA
1240 Se Maynard Rd Ste 104 (27511-6946)
P.O. Box 4844 (27519)
PHONE.................................919 319-6816
John Beavans, *Pr*
EMP: 10 **EST:** 1995
SQ FT: 2,000
SALES (est): 541.61K **Privately Held**
SIC: 2721 7336 Periodicals, publishing and printing; Commercial art and graphic design

(G-1429)
PROFESSIONAL LAMINATING LLC
107 Turnberry Ln (27518-9772)
PHONE.................................919 465-0400
EMP: 5
SALES (est): 144.83K **Privately Held**
Web: www.prorecognition.com
SIC: 2752 Commercial printing, lithographic

(G-1430)
PROFESSIONAL LAMINATING LLC
Also Called: Professional Laminating
233 E Johnson St Ste M (27513-4046)
PHONE.................................919 465-0400
EMP: 7 **EST:** 2007
SALES (est): 1.34MM **Privately Held**
Web: www.prolamsolutions.com
SIC: 3999 2759 3479 7331 Plaques, picture, laminated; Invitation and stationery printing and engraving; Etching and engraving; Direct mail advertising services

(G-1431)
PROPHYSICS INNOVATIONS INC
1911 Evans Rd (27513-2041)
PHONE.................................919 245-0406
William Deforest, *Owner*
William Defrost, *Owner*
Lani De Forest, *Point of Contact*
EMP: 5 **EST:** 1997
SALES (est): 983.26K
SALES (corp-wide): 6.23B **Publicly Held**
Web: www.landauer.com
SIC: 3842 8999 Radiation shielding aprons, gloves, sheeting, etc.; Scientific consulting
PA: Fortive Corporation
　　6920 Seaway Blvd
　　Everett WA 98203
　　425 446-5000

(G-1432)
QC LLC (DH)
1001 Winstead Dr Ste 480 (27513-2117)
PHONE................................800 883-0010ˇ
Jason Gordon, *Pr*
Eric Hyatt, *COO*
◆ **EMP:** 37 **EST:** 1981
SALES (est): 22.82MM
SALES (corp-wide): 4.71B **Privately Held**
SIC: 2819 Iron (ferric/ferrous) compounds or
    salts
HQ: Verdesian Life Sciences, Llc
    1001 Winstead Dr Ste 480
    Cary NC 27513
    919 825-1901

(G-1433)
RAPIDFORM INC
1001 Winstead Dr Ste 400 (27513-2117)
PHONE................................408 856-6200
Calvin Hur, *CEO*
Martin Chader, *VP*
Thomas Charron, *COO*
EMP: 7 **EST:** 2005
SQ FT: 3,000
SALES (est): 102.28K **Privately Held**
SIC: 7372 Prepackaged software

(G-1434)
RBW LLC
105 Graywick Way (27513-1610)
PHONE................................919 319-1289
Patricia W Wheeley, *Prin*
EMP: 5 **EST:** 2018
SALES (est): 86.96K **Privately Held**
SIC: 3599 Machine shop, jobbing and repair

(G-1435)
RENNASENTIENT INC
Also Called: AlphaGraphics
301 Ashville Ave (27518-6131)
PHONE................................919 233-7710
Eric J Webb, *Prin*
Eric James Webb, *Prin*
EMP: 8 **EST:** 2017
SALES (est): 1.51MM **Privately Held**
Web: www.alphagraphics.com
SIC: 8742 2711 Marketing consulting
    services; Commercial printing and
    newspaper publishing combined

(G-1436)
**RESEARCH TRIANGLE SOFTWARE
INC**
109 Lochview Dr (27518-9619)
PHONE................................919 233-8796
Jeffrey W Lerose, *Prin*
EMP: 6 **EST:** 2011
SALES (est): 94.15K **Privately Held**
SIC: 2741 Miscellaneous publishing

(G-1437)
RHD SERVICE LLC
1001 Winstead Dr Ste 1 (27513-2154)
PHONE................................919 297-1600
EMP: 28
SALES (est): 141.04K **Privately Held**
SIC: 2741 Directories, telephone: publishing
    only, not printed on site

(G-1438)
RITAS ONE INC
208 Dowington Ln (27519-6382)
PHONE................................919 650-2415
Lena Sitzler, *Prin*
EMP: 5 **EST:** 2009
SALES (est): 193.35K **Privately Held**
SIC: 2032 Canned specialties

(G-1439)
**ROBERTSON-CECO II
CORPORATION (DH)**
Also Called: Ceco Building Systems
5020 Weston Pkwy (27513)
PHONE................................281 897-7788
Norman C Chambers, *Pr*
Mark E Johnson, *
Todd R Moore, *
▼ **EMP:** 126 **EST:** 2006
SALES (est): 80.23MM
SALES (corp-wide): 5.58B **Privately Held**
Web: robertson-cecoii.mfgpages.com
SIC: 3448 Buildings, portable: prefabricated
    metal
HQ: Cornerstone Building Brands, Inc.
    5020 Weston Pkwy
    Cary NC 27513
    281 897-7788

(G-1440)
ROCKWELL AUTOMATION INC
113 Edinburgh South Dr Ste 200
(27511-6456)
PHONE................................919 804-0200
Bill Feuerstein, *Mgr*
EMP: 6
Web: www.rockwellautomation.com
SIC: 3625 Control equipment, electric
PA: Rockwell Automation, Inc.
    1201 S 2nd St
    Milwaukee WI 53204

(G-1441)
RONAK LLC
2302 Skye Ln (27518-9334)
PHONE................................781 589-1973
Raghav K Iyengar, *Prin*
EMP: 5 **EST:** 2012
SALES (est): 143.17K **Privately Held**
SIC: 7372 Prepackaged software

(G-1442)
RUCKUS WIRELESS LLC
Also Called: Telewire Supply
101 Stamford Dr (27513-9503)
PHONE................................919 677-0571
Jerry Obrian, *Brnch Mgr*
EMP: 311
SALES (corp-wide): 15.22B **Publicly Held**
Web: www.commscope.com
SIC: 3663 Radio and t.v. communications
    equipment
HQ: Ruckus Wireless Llc
    350 W Java Dr
    Sunnyvale CA 94089

(G-1443)
S & A CHEROKEE LLC
Also Called: S & A Cherokee Publishing
301 Cascade Pointe Ln Ste 101
(27513-5778)
PHONE................................919 674-6020
EMP: 40 **EST:** 2004
SALES (est): 4.98MM **Privately Held**
Web: www.sacommunications.com
SIC: 2741 7374 8741 8743 Miscellaneous
    publishing; Computer graphics service;
    Management services; Public relations
    services

(G-1444)
S C I A INC
Also Called: Security Ultraviolet
204 Dundalk Way (27511-5056)
PHONE................................919 387-7000
Dale A Dutcher Junior, *Pr*
EMP: 5 **EST:** 1969
SQ FT: 3,000
SALES (est): 121.7K **Privately Held**

SIC: 7373 7389 3648 7371 Computer
    integrated systems design; Fund raising
    organizations; Lighting equipment, nec;
    Computer software development

(G-1445)
SAMSUNG SEMICONDUCTOR INC
8000 Regency Pkwy Ste 585 (27518-8589)
PHONE................................919 380-8483
Matthew Allen, *Mgr*
EMP: 6
Web: www.samsung.com
SIC: 3674 Semiconductors and related
    devices
HQ: Samsung Semiconductor, Inc.
    3655 N 1st St
    San Jose CA 95134
    408 544-4000

(G-1446)
SAS FEDERAL LLC
100 Sas Campus Dr (27513-8617)
PHONE................................919 531-7505
Jim Goodnight, *Prin*
EMP: 9 **EST:** 2009
SALES (est): 393.9K **Privately Held**
SIC: 7372 Application computer software

(G-1447)
SAS INSTITUTE INC
940 Nw Cary Pkwy (27513-2792)
PHONE................................954 494-8189
Marcelo Gavazzi, *Brnch Mgr*
EMP: 4
SALES (corp-wide): 1.35B **Privately Held**
Web: www.sas.com
SIC: 7372 Application computer software
PA: Sas Institute Inc.
    100 Sas Campus Dr
    Cary NC 27513
    919 677-8000

(G-1448)
SAS INSTITUTE INC
P.O. Box 610 (27512-0610)
PHONE................................919 677-8000
EMP: 5
SALES (corp-wide): 1.35B **Privately Held**
Web: www.sas.com
SIC: 7372 Application computer software
PA: Sas Institute Inc.
    100 Sas Campus Dr
    Cary NC 27513
    919 677-8000

(G-1449)
SAS INSTITUTE INC
820 Sas Campus Dr # C (27513-2086)
PHONE................................919 531-4153
Ethan Ekkens, *Brnch Mgr*
EMP: 7
SALES (corp-wide): 1.35B **Privately Held**
Web: www.sas.com
SIC: 7372 Application computer software
PA: Sas Institute Inc.
    100 Sas Campus Dr
    Cary NC 27513
    919 677-8000

(G-1450)
SAS INSTITUTE INC (PA)
100 Sas Campus Dr (27513-8617)
PHONE................................919 677-8000
▲ **EMP:** 217 **EST:** 1976
SALES (est): 1.35B
SALES (corp-wide): 1.35B **Privately Held**
Web: www.sas.com
SIC: 7372 7371 Application computer
    software; Custom computer programming
    services

(G-1451)
SENSUS
113 Gorecki Pl (27513-9619)
PHONE................................919 376-2617
Carolina Cely, *Prin*
EMP: 20 **EST:** 2018
SALES (est): 466.66K **Privately Held**
Web: www.sensus.com
SIC: 3824 Fluid meters and counting devices

(G-1452)
SIEMENS CORPORATION
3333 Regency Pkwy (27518-7705)
PHONE................................919 465-1287
EMP: 10
SALES (corp-wide): 84.78B **Privately Held**
Web: www.siemens.com
SIC: 3661 Telephone and telegraph
    apparatus
HQ: Siemens Corporation
    300 New Jrsey Ave Ste 100
    Washington DC 20001
    202 434-4800

(G-1453)
SIEMENS MED SOLUTIONS USA INC
Also Called: Clinical Workflow Consulting
221 Gregson Dr (27511-6495)
PHONE................................919 468-7400
EMP: 34
SALES (corp-wide): 84.78B **Privately Held**
Web: new.siemens.com
SIC: 3621 Armatures, industrial
HQ: Siemens Medical Solutions Usa, Inc.
    40 Liberty Blvd
    Malvern PA 19355
    888 826-9702

(G-1454)
**SIEMENS POWER TRANSMISSION &
DISTRIBUTION INC**
110 Macalyson Ct (27511-7912)
PHONE................................919 463-8702
▲ **EMP:** 2100
SIC: 3613 3625 Switches, electric power
    except snap, push button, etc.; Relays and
    industrial controls

(G-1455)
SIGNALSCAPE INC
200 Regency Forest Dr Ste 310
(27518-8695)
PHONE................................919 859-4565
Jhan Vannatta, *CEO*
Jhan Vannatta, *Pr*
Ed Allen, *
Barbara Mcnamara, *Dir*
Robert Kinney, *
EMP: 45 **EST:** 2000
SQ FT: 56,506
SALES (est): 6.21MM **Privately Held**
Web: www.signalscape.com
SIC: 8731 7371 3823 Commercial physical
    research; Custom computer programming
    services; Process control instruments

(G-1456)
SIMONTON WINDOWS & DOORS INC
5020 Weston Pkwy Ste 300 (27513-2322)
PHONE................................919 677-3938
EMP: 12 **EST:** 1946
SALES (est): 4.49MM
SALES (corp-wide): 5.58B **Privately Held**
Web: www.simonton.com
SIC: 3448 Buildings, portable: prefabricated
    metal
HQ: Cornerstone Building Brands, Inc.
    5020 Weston Pkwy
    Cary NC 27513
    281 897-7788

(G-1457)
SIMPLECERTIFIEDMAILCOM LLC
111 Commonwealth Ct Ste 103
(27511-4447)
PHONE..................................888 462-1750
Charles W Crutchfield, *Prin*
EMP: 6 EST: 2012
SALES (est): 240.83K **Privately Held**
Web: www.simplecertifiedmail.com
SIC: 7372 Prepackaged software

(G-1458)
SIMPLICTI SFTWR SOLUTIONS INC
Also Called: Simplicti
1255 Crescent Green Ste 145
(27518-8123)
PHONE..................................919 858-8898
Wen-kai Ho, *CEO*
Bruce Calhoon, *
EMP: 6 EST: 1997
SQ FT: 14,000
SALES (est): 749.53K **Privately Held**
Web: www.onec1.com
SIC: 7372 Prepackaged software

(G-1459)
SIZE STREAM LLC
Also Called: Formcut 3d
223 Commonwealth Ct (27511-4474)
PHONE..................................919 355-5708
David Bruner, *Managing Member*
EMP: 9 EST: 2012
SQ FT: 5,000
SALES (est): 1.34MM **Privately Held**
Web: www.sizestream.com
SIC: 3845 Ultrasonic scanning devices,
medical

(G-1460)
SLICKEDIT INC
408 Bathgate Ln (27513-5582)
P.O. Box 1953 (27528-1953)
PHONE..................................919 473-0070
Jill L Maurer, *Ch*
Donald L Reppert, *
William F Denman Junior, *Prin*
Joseph Clark Maurer, *
Howard H Lewis, *
EMP: 25 EST: 1988
SALES (est): 3.58MM **Privately Held**
Web: www.slickedit.com
SIC: 7372 Business oriented computer
software

(G-1461)
SMALLHD LLC (DH)
301 Gregson Dr (27511-6496)
PHONE..................................919 439-2166
Wes Phillips, *CEO*
▲ **EMP: 15 EST:** 2014
SQ FT: 5,400
SALES (est): 23.44MM
SALES (corp-wide): 383.4MM **Privately
Held**
Web: www.smallhd.com
SIC: 3679 3861 Liquid crystal displays (LCD)
; Lens shades, camera
HQ: Videndum Production Solutions Inc.
14 Progress Dr
Shelton CT 06484
203 929-1100

(G-1462)
SMARTLINK MOBILE SYSTEMS LLC
1000 Centre Green Way Ste 250
(27513-2284)
PHONE..................................919 674-8400
Alex Tse, *Chief Medical Officer*
EMP: 20 EST: 2015
SALES (est): 2.18MM **Privately Held**
Web: www.smartlinkhealth.com

SIC: 7372 Application computer software

(G-1463)
SMARTWARE GROUP INC
11000 Regency Pkwy Ste 110
(27518-8518)
PHONE..................................866 858-7800
Paul Lachance, *CEO*
Marc Bromberg, *VP*
David Peelstrom, *CFO*
EMP: 5 EST: 2002
SALES (est): 276.37K **Privately Held**
SIC: 7372 Business oriented computer
software

(G-1464)
SPATIAL LIGHT LLC
1017 Pueblo Ridge Pl (27519-0832)
P.O. Box 12658 (27709-2658)
PHONE..................................617 213-0314
Willie Johnpadilla, *CEO*
Willie Padilla, *CEO*
EMP: 4 EST: 2015
SALES (est): 442.7K **Privately Held**
SIC: 3812 Infrared object detection
equipment

(G-1465)
**SPECTRASITE COMMUNICATIONS
LLC (HQ)**
400 Regency Forest Dr Ste 300
(27518-7703)
PHONE..................................919 468-0112
Stephen Clark, *Pr*
David Tomick, *
Dan Hunt, *
Richard Byrne, *WIRELESS TOWER
GROUP*
Timothy Biltz, *
▲ **EMP: 35 EST:** 1997
SQ FT: 150,000
SALES (est): 3.62MM **Publicly Held**
Web: www.spectrasite.com
SIC: 8748 1623 3661 4813 Business
consulting, nec; Transmitting tower
(telecommunication) construction;
Telephone and telegraph apparatus;
Telephone communication, except radio
PA: American Tower Corporation
116 Huntington Ave Fl 11
Boston MA 02116

(G-1466)
SPNC ASSOCIATES INC
Also Called: Rosti Cary NC
100 Falcone Pkwy (27511-6712)
P.O. Box 1067 (27512-1067)
PHONE..................................919 467-5151
Thomas R Falcone, *CEO*
Joseph R Falcone, *VP*
▲ **EMP: 54 EST:** 1981
SQ FT: 35,000
SALES (est): 23.3MM
SALES (corp-wide): 6.85MM **Privately
Held**
Web: www.rosti.com
SIC: 3089 3544 Injection molding of plastics;
Special dies, tools, jigs, and fixtures
HQ: Plastic Components, Inc.
N 116 W 18271 Morse Dr
Germantown WI 53022

(G-1467)
STERLING PHARMA USA LLC
Also Called: Sterling Pharma USA
1001 Sheldon Dr Ste 101 (27513-2079)
P.O. Box 12041 (27709-2041)
PHONE..................................919 678-0702
Mathew Minardi, *Managing Member*
Tushar Bahadur, *
EMP: 36 EST: 2019

SQ FT: 6,000
SALES (est): 6.21MM **Privately Held**
Web: www.sterlingpharmasolutions.com
SIC: 2834 Pharmaceutical preparations
HQ: Sterling Pharma Solutions Limited
Sterling Place Dudley
Cramlington NORTHD NE23
191 250-0471

(G-1468)
**STONEHAVEN JEWELRY GALLERY
LTD**
111 Adams St (27513-4527)
PHONE..................................919 462-8888
Billy Webster, *Pr*
Ron Lodholz, *VP*
EMP: 5 EST: 1996
SALES (est): 202.49K **Privately Held**
Web: www.stonehavenjewelry.com
SIC: 3915 7631 Jewelers' materials and
lapidary work; Jewelry repair services

(G-1469)
TEMPOSONICS LLC
3001 Sheldon Dr (27513-2006)
PHONE..................................470 380-5103
David Hore, *Pr*
Michael Ivas, *VP*
Craig Lampo, *CFO*
Lance D'amico, *Sec*
EMP: 5 EST: 2021
SALES (est): 8.46MM
SALES (corp-wide): 15.22B **Publicly Held**
Web: www.temposonics.com
SIC: 3823 Primary elements for process flow
measurement
PA: Amphenol Corporation
358 Hall Ave
Wallingford CT 06492
203 265-8900

(G-1470)
THINKING MAPS INC (PA)
401 Cascade Pointe Ln (27513-5780)
PHONE..................................919 678-8778
Shirwin Suddreth, *Pr*
EMP: 5 EST: 1990
SALES (est): 2.09MM
SALES (corp-wide): 2.09MM **Privately
Held**
Web: www.thinkingmaps.com
SIC: 8748 2741 Educational consultant;
Miscellaneous publishing

(G-1471)
THORCO LLC
301 Birdwood Ct (27519-9719)
PHONE..................................919 363-6234
Richard C Stephenson, *Managing Member*
EMP: 10 EST: 2012
SALES (est): 730.71K **Privately Held**
SIC: 7379 7372 Computer related services,
nec; Utility computer software

(G-1472)
TOWERCO LLC
5000 Valleystone Dr Ste 200 (27519-8434)
PHONE..................................919 653-5700
Daniel Hunt, *CFO*
EMP: 18 EST: 2004
SQ FT: 2,500
SALES (est): 3.07MM **Privately Held**
Web: www.towerco.com
SIC: 3441 Tower sections, radio and
television transmission

(G-1473)
TRIANGLE SOLUTIONS INC
Also Called: PIP Printing
1074 W Chatham St (27511-6201)
PHONE..................................919 481-1235

Dave Callaghan, *Pr*
Charles Wolff, *VP*
EMP: 5 EST: 1990
SQ FT: 2,700
SALES (est): 505.32K **Privately Held**
Web: www.trianglesolutions.com
SIC: 2752 7334 7336 3993 Offset printing;
Photocopying and duplicating services;
Commercial art and graphic design; Signs
and advertising specialties

(G-1474)
TRIGGERMESH INC
109 Harmony Hill Ln (27513-8306)
PHONE..................................919 228-8049
Mark Hinkle, *Owner*
EMP: 4 EST: 2020
SALES (est): 3.32MM **Privately Held**
Web: www.triggermesh.com
SIC: 7372 Prepackaged software

(G-1475)
TRUSS BUILDINGS LLC
1512 Wackena Rd (27519-9547)
PHONE..................................919 377-0217
John Ottaway, *Prin*
EMP: 4 EST: 2015
SALES (est): 1.27MM **Privately Held**
Web: www.tbllcnc.com
SIC: 2439 Trusses, wooden roof

(G-1476)
UPL NA INC (HQ)
Also Called: Upi
15401 Weston Pkwy Ste 170 (27513-8637)
PHONE..................................800 358-7642
David Elser, *CEO*
Kevin Meitzler, *
William Herbert, *
Joao Esteves, *
▲ **EMP: 30 EST:** 1996
SQ FT: 2,100
SALES (est): 91.15MM **Privately Held**
Web: www.upl-ltd.com
SIC: 5191 2879 Chemicals, agricultural;
Agricultural chemicals, nec
PA: Upl Limited
Upl House, 610 B/2, Bandra Village,
Mumbai MH 40005

(G-1477)
VALUE PRINTING INC
604 E Chatham St Ste D (27511-6926)
PHONE..................................919 380-9883
Margaret Kehoe, *Pr*
Steven Kehoe, *Sec*
EMP: 8 EST: 2009
SQ FT: 1,200
SALES (est): 274.28K **Privately Held**
Web: www.valueprinting.com
SIC: 2752 Offset printing

(G-1478)
**VERDESIAN LIFE SCIENCE US LLC
(DH)**
Also Called: Verdesian Life Sciences
1001 Winstead Dr Ste 480 (27513-2117)
PHONE..................................919 825-1901
Francis Pirozzi, *Governor*
EMP: 37 EST: 2014
SALES (est): 22.82MM
SALES (corp-wide): 4.71B **Privately Held**
Web: www.vlsci.com
SIC: 1479 Fertilizer mineral mining
HQ: Verdesian Life Sciences, Llc
1001 Winstead Dr Ste 480
Cary NC 27513
919 825-1901

(G-1479)
VIDENDUM PROD SOLUTIONS INC
215 Trimble Ave (27511-6209)
PHONE..............................919 244-0760
Dale Backus, *Brnch Mgr*
EMP: 5
SALES (corp-wide): 383.4MM **Privately Held**
Web: www.antonbauer.com
SIC: 3861 Lens shades, camera
HQ: Videndum Production Solutions Inc.
14 Progress Dr
Shelton CT 06484
203 929-1100

(G-1480)
VIRTUS ENTERTAINMENT INC
114 Mackenan Dr Ste 100 (27511-7920)
PHONE..............................919 467-9700
Mark Baric, *Ch Bd*
David A Smith, *
James H Hayne, *CFO*
EMP: 41 EST: 1990
SQ FT: 16,000
SALES (est): 581.43K **Privately Held**
SIC: 7372 Prepackaged software

(G-1481)
WAKE STONE CORPORATION
Also Called: Triangel Quarry
222 Star Ln (27513-2114)
PHONE..............................919 677-0050
Paul Pierce, *Mgr*
EMP: 25
SQ FT: 9,129
SALES (corp-wide): 23.51MM **Privately Held**
Web: www.wakestonecorp.com
SIC: 3281 Stone, quarrying and processing of own stone products
PA: Wake Stone Corporation
6821 Knightdale Blvd
Knightdale NC 27545
919 266-1100

(G-1482)
WESTSTAR PRECISION INC
Also Called: Weststar
101 Fern Bluff Way (27518-8973)
PHONE..............................919 557-2820
▲ EMP: 24
Web: www.weststarprecision.com
SIC: 3728 R and D by manuf., aircraft parts and auxiliary equipment

(G-1483)
WISDOM FOR HEART
2703 Jones Franklin Rd Ste 105 (27518-7172)
P.O. Box 37297 (27627-7297)
PHONE..............................866 482-4253
Stephen Davey, *Pr*
Pastor Stephen Davey, *Prin*
Scott Wsylie, *Ex Dir*
EMP: 10 EST: 2005
SALES (est): 2.02MM **Privately Held**
Web: www.wisdomonline.org
SIC: 2731 Books, publishing only

(G-1484)
WISPRY INC
4001 Weston Pkwy St 200 (27513-2311)
PHONE..............................919 854-7500
EMP: 7 EST: 2002
SALES (est): 2.53MM
SALES (corp-wide): 14.91B **Publicly Held**
Web: www.wispry.com
SIC: 7372 3559 Prepackaged software; Electronic component making machinery
HQ: Coventor, Inc.
4650 Cushing Pkwy

Fremont CA 94538

(G-1485)
WIT & WHISTLE
929 Manchester Dr (27511-4716)
PHONE..............................919 609-5309
Amanda Wright, *Admn*
EMP: 4 EST: 2015
SALES (est): 111.62K **Privately Held**
SIC: 2771 5112 5947 Greeting cards; Social stationery and greeting cards; Greeting cards

(G-1486)
WORKCOM INC
1001 Winstead Dr (27513-2155)
PHONE..............................310 586-4000
Mark W Hianik, *Sr VP*
EMP: 43 EST: 2009
SALES (est): 700.8K **Privately Held**
SIC: 2741 Directories, telephone: publishing only, not printed on site

(G-1487)
XEROX CORPORATION
11000 Weston Pkwy (27513-2261)
PHONE..............................919 428-9718
EMP: 27
SALES (corp-wide): 6.22B **Publicly Held**
Web: www.xerox.com
SIC: 3577 Computer peripheral equipment, nec
HQ: Xerox Corporation
201 Merritt 7
Norwalk CT 06851
203 849-5216

Casar
Cleveland County

(G-1488)
FISH GETTER LURE CO LLC
254 Hull Rd (28020-8757)
PHONE..............................704 538-9863
Richard Smith, *Owner*
EMP: 5 EST: 1969
SALES (est): 194.93K **Privately Held**
SIC: 3949 Lures, fishing: artificial

(G-1489)
M O DEVINEY LUMBER CO INC (PA)
Also Called: Deviney Lumber & Salvage
838 Moriah School Rd (28020-7701)
PHONE..............................704 538-9071
James Deviney, *Pr*
James O Deviney, *Pr*
Robert M Deviney, *VP*
Max D Deviney, *Sec*
EMP: 5 EST: 1936
SQ FT: 10,000
SALES (est): 2.4MM
SALES (corp-wide): 2.4MM **Privately Held**
Web: www.beckercustomseating.com
SIC: 5031 5211 2449 Lumber, plywood, and millwork; Lumber and other building materials; Rectangular boxes and crates, wood

Cashiers
Jackson County

(G-1490)
COMMUNITY NEWSPAPERS INC
Also Called: Cashiers Crossroads Chronicles
426 Nc 107 S (28717)
P.O. Box 1040 (28717-1040)
PHONE..............................828 743-5101
Michael Henry, *Mgr*

EMP: 6
SALES (corp-wide): 40.95MM **Privately Held**
Web: www.cninewspapers.com
SIC: 2711 Newspapers, publishing and printing
PA: Community Newspapers, Inc.
2365 Prince Ave # A
Athens GA 30606
706 548-0010

(G-1491)
TOXAWAY CONCRETE INC
Hwy 64 E (28717)
P.O. Box 40 (28774-0040)
PHONE..............................828 966-4270
Randy Dillard, *Mgr*
EMP: 10
SALES (corp-wide): 1.24MM **Privately Held**
Web: www.mcneelycompanies.com
SIC: 3273 Ready-mixed concrete
PA: Toxaway Concrete Inc
Off Hwy 281 N Hwy 64 E
Lake Toxaway NC 28747
828 966-4270

Castalia
Nash County

(G-1492)
EAGLE ASSEMBLY UNLIMITED INC
8928 Main St (27816-9262)
PHONE..............................252 462-0408
EMP: 8 EST: 2000
SALES (est): 180.14K **Privately Held**
SIC: 3492 Hose and tube fittings and assemblies, hydraulic/pneumatic

Castle Hayne
New Hanover County

(G-1493)
AC VALOR REYES LLC
Also Called: Glam Gal
4610 College Rd N (28429-5664)
P.O. Box 11237 (28404-1237)
PHONE..............................910 431-3256
EMP: 4 EST: 2005
SQ FT: 3,000
SALES (est): 204.31K **Privately Held**
SIC: 2759 5137 3199 Screen printing; Women's and children's accessories; Dog furnishings: collars, leashes, muzzles, etc.: leather

(G-1494)
AMERICAN CHROME & CHEM NA INC
5408 Holly Shelter Rd (28429-6350)
PHONE..............................910 675-7200
EMP: 18
Web: www.elementischromium.com
SIC: 5169 2899 Chemicals and allied products, nec; Chemical preparations, nec
HQ: American Chrome & Chemicals N.A. Inc.
3800 Buddy Lawrence Dr
Corpus Christi TX
361 883-6421

(G-1495)
ARGOS USA LLC
Also Called: Redi-Mix Concrete
5225 Holly Shelter Rd (28429-6358)
PHONE..............................910 675-1262
James Walters, *Mgr*
EMP: 31

Web: www.argos-us.com
SIC: 3273 Ready-mixed concrete
HQ: Argos Usa Llc
3015 Windward Plz Ste 300
Alpharetta GA 30005
678 368-4300

(G-1496)
BURTON STEEL COMPANY (PA)
102b Ritter Dr (28429-5449)
P.O. Box 265 (28402-0265)
PHONE..............................910 675-9241
Paul Burton, *Pr*
Robert W Johnson, *Sec*
EMP: 18 EST: 1975
SQ FT: 35,000
SALES (est): 589.28K
SALES (corp-wide): 589.28K **Privately Held**
SIC: 1791 3441 Structural steel erection; Fabricated structural metal

(G-1497)
CASTLE HAYNE HARDWARE LLC
Also Called: Hudson's Hardware
6301 Castle Hayne Rd (28429-5013)
PHONE..............................910 675-9205
Doug Reeves, *Managing Member*
EMP: 5 EST: 2009
SQ FT: 16,000
SALES (est): 751.37K **Privately Held**
Web: www.castlehayneboatandrvstorage.com
SIC: 5251 2329 Builders' hardware; Athletic clothing, except uniforms: men's, youths' and boys'

(G-1498)
EXLEY CUSTOM WOODWORK INC
2921 Castle Hayne Rd (28429-5430)
PHONE..............................910 763-5445
Michael Exley, *Pr*
Marsha Exley, *Sec*
EMP: 4 EST: 1990
SQ FT: 3,825
SALES (est): 198.01K **Privately Held**
Web: www.ceotnc.org
SIC: 2431 Interior and ornamental woodwork and trim

(G-1499)
FORGED CSTM MET FBRICATION LLC
6804 Holly Shelter Rd (28429-6374)
PHONE..............................910 274-8300
Pete Pucella, *Prin*
EMP: 6 EST: 2018
SALES (est): 3.21MM **Privately Held**
Web: www.forgedcustommetal.com
SIC: 3441 Fabricated structural metal

(G-1500)
GE-HITCHI NCLEAR ENRGY AMRCAS (HQ)
3901 Castle Hayne Rd (28429)
P.O. Box 780 (28402)
PHONE..............................910 819-5000
Jay Wileman, *Managing Member*
Angela Thornhill, *
Mike Ford, *
◆ EMP: 2000 EST: 2007
SALES (est): 69.71MM
SALES (corp-wide): 34.94B **Publicly Held**
Web: nuclear.gepower.com
SIC: 2819 Nuclear fuel and cores, inorganic
PA: Ge Vernova Inc.
58 Charles St
Cambridge MA 02141
617 433-7555

▲ = Import ▼ = Export
◆ = Import/Export

(G-1501)
GLOBAL NUCLEAR FUEL-AMERICAS LLC (HQ)
3901 Castle Hayne Rd (28429-6546)
P.O. Box 780 (28402-0780)
PHONE...............................910 819-5950
◆ **EMP:** 37 **EST:** 1999
SALES (est): 38.41MM
SALES (corp-wide): 34.94B **Publicly Held**
SIC: 2819 Nuclear fuel and cores, inorganic
PA: Ge Vernova Inc.
58 Charles St
Cambridge MA 02141
617 433-7555

(G-1502)
HOLLINGSWRTH CBNETS INTRORS LL
2913 Castle Hayne Rd (28429-5430)
PHONE...............................910 251-1490
Robert M Hollingsworth, *Pr*
EMP: 12 **EST:** 1994
SQ FT: 6,000
SALES (est): 2.65MM **Privately Held**
Web: www.hollingsworthcabinetry.com
SIC: 2541 2511 2434 Cabinets, except refrigerated: show, display, etc.: wood; Wood household furniture; Wood kitchen cabinets

(G-1503)
IDEA OVEN LLC
Also Called: Inshore Technology Associates
3507 Marathon Ave (28429-5152)
PHONE...............................910 343-5280
John Philips, *Managing Member*
John Philips, *Owner*
EMP: 4 **EST:** 2004
SQ FT: 950
SALES (est): 611.97K **Privately Held**
SIC: 2231 5159 Alpacas, mohair: woven; Farm animals

(G-1504)
LABORIE SONS CSTM WODWORKS LLC
Also Called: Ls Woodworks
301 Chesterfield Rd (28429-5858)
PHONE...............................910 769-2524
David E Laborie, *Managing Member*
EMP: 6 **EST:** 2014
SALES (est): 572.52K **Privately Held**
SIC: 2431 2434 Millwork; Wood kitchen cabinets

(G-1505)
MARTIN MARIETTA MATERIALS INC
Also Called: Martin Marietta Aggregates
5408 Holly Shelter Rd (28429-6350)
P.O. Box 398 (28429-0398)
PHONE...............................910 675-2283
Butch Barnhardt, *Brnch Mgr*
EMP: 6
Web: www.martinmarietta.com
SIC: 1422 Crushed and broken limestone
PA: Martin Marietta Materials Inc
4123 Parklake Ave
Raleigh NC 27612

(G-1506)
MARTIN MARIETTA MATERIALS INC
Also Called: Castle Hayne Yard
5635 Holly Shelter Rd (28429-6362)
PHONE...............................910 602-6058
Marietta Martin, *Mgr*
EMP: 4
Web: www.martinmarietta.com
SIC: 3273 Ready-mixed concrete
PA: Martin Marietta Materials Inc
4123 Parklake Ave

Raleigh NC 27612

(G-1507)
MASTER MACHINING INC
410 Hermitage Rd (28429-5832)
PHONE...............................910 675-3660
James Carter, *Pr*
Marilyn Carter, *Sec*
Jonathan Carter, *VP*
EMP: 20 **EST:** 1982
SQ FT: 6,000
SALES (est): 1.01MM **Privately Held**
Web: www.mastermachininginc.com
SIC: 3599 Machine shop, jobbing and repair

(G-1508)
OCCIDENTAL CHEMICAL CORP
5408 Holly Shelter Rd (28429-6350)
P.O. Box 368 (28429-0368)
PHONE...............................910 675-7200
Robert E Running, *Prin*
EMP: 10
SALES (corp-wide): 26.88B **Publicly Held**
Web: www.oxy.com
SIC: 2812 Alkalies and chlorine
HQ: Occidental Chemical Corporation
14555 Dallas Pkwy Ste 400
Dallas TX 75254
972 404-3800

(G-1509)
PORT CITY ELEVATOR INC
5704 Nixon Ln (28429-5652)
PHONE...............................910 790-9300
Robert Page, *Pr*
Seth Newman, *VP*
EMP: 26 **EST:** 2012
SALES (est): 5.11MM **Privately Held**
Web: www.portcityelevator.com
SIC: 5084 3534 3537 Elevators; Dumbwaiters; Lift trucks, industrial: fork, platform, straddle, etc.

(G-1510)
VISIONAIR INC
5601 Barbados Blvd (28429-5655)
PHONE...............................910 675-9117
Mike Lyons, *Pr*
Gary Bunyard, *
Samuel T Hensley, *
Scott Macdonald, *CPO*
EMP: 560 **EST:** 1989
SQ FT: 22,500
SALES (est): 979.58K
SALES (corp-wide): 272.32MM **Privately Held**
Web: www.visionair.com
SIC: 7372 Application computer software
HQ: Tritech Software Systems, Inc.
1000 Business Center Dr
Lake Mary FL 32746
858 799-7000

Catawba
Catawba County

(G-1511)
DAGENHART PALLET INC
2088 Mathis Church Rd (28609-7936)
PHONE...............................828 241-2374
Wayne Dagenhart, *Pr*
G Michael Dagenhart, *
EMP: 6 **EST:** 1952
SQ FT: 7,200
SALES (est): 856.68K **Privately Held**
SIC: 1629 2421 2448 Land clearing contractor; Sawmills and planing mills, general; Pallets, wood

(G-1512)
JENKINS SERVICES GROUP LLC
5577 Little Mountain Rd (28609-8220)
PHONE...............................704 881-3210
Marya Jenkins, *Pr*
EMP: 7 **EST:** 2014
SALES (est): 1.03MM **Privately Held**
SIC: 1711 3585 7389 Heating and air conditioning contractors; Heating equipment, complete; Business Activities at Non-Commercial Site

(G-1513)
ROWES
7546 Long Island Rd (28609-8923)
PHONE...............................828 241-2609
Nick Rowe, *Owner*
EMP: 4 **EST:** 1996
SALES (est): 157.29K **Privately Held**
SIC: 2512 Upholstered household furniture

(G-1514)
SMITH SETZER AND SONS INC
4708 E Nc 10 Hwy (28609-8115)
P.O. Box 250 (28609-0250)
PHONE...............................828 241-3161
Jerry Setzer, *Pr*
Michael N Setzer, *
Mitchell Setzer, *
EMP: 48 **EST:** 1949
SQ FT: 15,000
SALES (est): 5.8MM **Privately Held**
SIC: 3545 Boring machine attachments (machine tool accessories)

Cedar Falls
Randolph County

(G-1515)
SAPONA MANUFACTURING CO INC (PA)
2478 Cedar Falls Rd (27230)
PHONE...............................336 625-2727
Steele Redding, *Pr*
John O Toledano Senior, *Sec*
C W Mc Crary Junior, *Ch Bd*
Bruce Patram, *
William H Redding Junior, *Treas*
◆ **EMP:** 50 **EST:** 1916
SQ FT: 4,000
SALES (est): 22.97MM
SALES (corp-wide): 22.97MM **Privately Held**
Web: www.saponayarns.com
SIC: 2282 Throwing and winding mills

Cedar Grove
Orange County

(G-1516)
BOTANIST AND BARREL
105 Persimmon Hill Ln (27231-8807)
PHONE...............................919 644-7777
EMP: 8 **EST:** 2019
SALES (est): 389.3K **Privately Held**
Web: www.botanistandbarrel.com
SIC: 2084 Wines

(G-1517)
JAMES COTTER IRONWORKS
5102 Eno Cemetery Rd (27231-9756)
PHONE...............................919 644-2664
James Cotter, *Owner*
EMP: 10 **EST:** 1990
SALES (est): 204.77K **Privately Held**
SIC: 3446 Architectural metalwork

(G-1518)
TIN CAN VENTURES LLC
Also Called: Boxcarr Handmade Cheese
2207 Carr Store Rd (27231-9214)
PHONE...............................919 732-9078
Austin Genke, *Prin*
Samantha Genke, *Prin*
EMP: 6 **EST:** 2013
SQ FT: 2,900
SALES (est): 1.2MM **Privately Held**
Web: www.boxcarrhandmadecheese.com
SIC: 3411 2022 Tin cans; Cheese: natural and processed

Chadbourn
Columbus County

(G-1519)
FULL THROTTLE FABRICATION LLC
1047 Old Cribbtown Rd (28431-9319)
PHONE...............................910 770-1180
Ryan Stephens, *Prin*
EMP: 4 **EST:** 2015
SALES (est): 350.64K **Privately Held**
Web: www.fullthrottlefabrication.com
SIC: 7692 Welding repair

(G-1520)
IDAHO TIMBER NC LLC
1844 Joe Brown Hwy S (28431-8502)
P.O. Box 365 (28431-0365)
PHONE...............................910 654-5555
Jim Bowen, *Genl Mgr*
EMP: 38
SALES (corp-wide): 308.2MM **Privately Held**
Web: www.idahotimber.com
SIC: 2421 Sawmills and planing mills, general
HQ: Idaho Timber Of North Carolina Llc
1431 Nicholas St
Henderson NC 27536
252 430-0030

Chapel Hill
Orange County

(G-1521)
/N SOFTWARE INC (PA)
101 Europa Dr Ste 150 (27517-2380)
PHONE...............................919 544-7070
Gent Hito, *CEO*
EMP: 24 **EST:** 1994
SALES (est): 3.03MM
SALES (corp-wide): 3.03MM **Privately Held**
Web: www.nsoftware.com
SIC: 7372 Prepackaged software

(G-1522)
2U NC
1210 Environ Way (27517-4426)
PHONE...............................919 525-5075
EMP: 16 **EST:** 2019
SALES (est): 507.89K **Privately Held**
Web: www.2u.com
SIC: 7372 Prepackaged software

(G-1523)
ABCOR SUPPLY INC (PA)
Also Called: Carolina Coating Solutions
811 Oxfordshire Ln (27517-6218)
PHONE...............................919 468-0856
Jeanna Mccraw, *Pr*
Kenneth Mccraw, *VP*
EMP: 16 **EST:** 1999
SALES (est): 2.19MM
SALES (corp-wide): 2.19MM **Privately Held**

Web: www.carolinacoatingsolutions.com
SIC: 3479 Coating of metals and formed
products

(G-1524)
ALLOTROPICA TECHNOLOGIES INC
601 W Rosemary St Unit 503 (27516-2353)
PHONE..............................919 522-4374
Edward Samulski, *CEO*
EMP: 6 EST: 2008
SALES (est): 242.69K **Privately Held**
SIC: 8082 2821 Home health care services;
Plastics materials and resins

(G-1525)
AMERICAN STONE COMPANY
1807 Nc Highway 54 W (27516-8801)
P.O. Box 1288 (27510-3288)
PHONE..............................919 929-7131
Bill Allgood, *Prin*
EMP: 5 EST: 1969
SALES (est): 468.8K **Publicly Held**
Web: www.rockquarryfarm.com
SIC: 3281 Stone, quarrying and processing
of own stone products
PA: Martin Marietta Materials Inc
4123 Parklake Ave
Raleigh NC 27612

(G-1526)
ANELLEO INC
519 Dairy Glen Rd (27516-4386)
PHONE..............................919 448-4008
Rahima Benhabbour, *Ex Dir*
EMP: 4
SALES (est): 151.75K **Privately Held**
Web: www.anelleo.com
SIC: 2834 Proprietary drug products

(G-1527)
ARETEIA THERAPEUTICS INC
101 Glen Lennox Dr (27517-4086)
PHONE..............................973 985-0597
Frank Bosley, *Prin*
EMP: 14 EST: 2022
SALES (est): 5.99MM **Privately Held**
Web: www.areteiatx.com
SIC: 2834 Pharmaceutical preparations

(G-1528)
ARMACELL LLC (HQ)
55 Vilcom Center Dr Ste 200 (27514)
PHONE..............................919 913-0555
Patrick Mathieu, *CEO*
Max Padberg, *
Thomas Himmel, *
Karl Paetz-lauter, *VP*
Roberto Mengoli, *
◆ EMP: 195 EST: 1999
SALES (est): 84.16MM **Privately Held**
Web: www.armacell.us
SIC: 3086 Plastics foam products
PA: Insulation United States Holdings, Llc
7600 Oakwood St
Mebane NC 27302

(G-1529)
**ARTESIAN FUTURE TECHNOLOGY
LLC**
Also Called: Artesian Builds
5801 Cascade Dr (27514-9692)
PHONE..............................919 904-4940
Noah Katz, *Managing Member*
EMP: 6 EST: 2018
SALES (est): 629.87K **Privately Held**
Web: www.artesianfuturetechnology.com
SIC: 2752 7378 Commercial printing,
lithographic; Computer and data processing
equipment repair/maintenance

(G-1530)
BLIND NAIL AND COMPANY INC
Also Called: Alf Sjoberg
3027 Blueberry Ln (27516-5711)
P.O. Box 157 (27510-0157)
PHONE..............................919 967-0388
Alf Sjoberg, *Pr*
EMP: 4 EST: 1980
SALES (est): 98.4K **Privately Held**
SIC: 2499 Decorative wood and woodwork

(G-1531)
**BREAD & BUTTER CUSTOM SCRN
PRT**
Also Called: Bread N Butter Screenprinting
1201 Raleigh Rd Ste 100 (27517-4047)
PHONE..............................919 942-3198
Melanie Wall, *Pr*
Anne Page-watson, *Treas*
EMP: 4 EST: 1977
SQ FT: 1,000
SALES (est): 118.21K **Privately Held**
Web: www.bread-butter.com
SIC: 2261 Screen printing of cotton
broadwoven fabrics

(G-1532)
C M M
2114 Damascus Church Rd (27516-8033)
P.O. Box 4472 (27515-4472)
PHONE..............................919 619-1716
Joe Currin, *Owner*
EMP: 6 EST: 2017
SALES (est): 46.4K **Privately Held**
Web: www.zeiss.com
SIC: 3827 Optical instruments and lenses

(G-1533)
**CARBON CONVERSION SYSTEMS
LLC**
95 Wood Laurel Ln (27517-7471)
PHONE..............................919 883-4238
EMP: 5 EST: 2015
SALES (est): 87.47K **Privately Held**
SIC: 2869 High purity grade chemicals,
organic

(G-1534)
**CARDIOXYL PHARMACEUTICALS
INC**
1450 Raleigh Rd Ste 212 (27517-8833)
PHONE..............................919 869-8586
Christopher A Kroeger, *Pr*
Doug Cowart, *Ex VP*
EMP: 7 EST: 2005
SALES (est): 854.64K
SALES (corp-wide): 48.3B **Publicly Held**
SIC: 2834 Druggists' preparations
(pharmaceuticals)
PA: Bristol-Myers Squibb Company
Route 206/Prvince Line Rd
Princeton NJ 08540
609 252-4621

(G-1535)
CDATA SOFTWARE INC (PA)
101 Europa Dr Ste 110 (27517-2380)
PHONE..............................919 928-5214
Amit Sharma, *CEO*
Will Davis, *CMO*
EMP: 14 EST: 2014
SALES (est): 14.53MM
SALES (corp-wide): 14.53MM **Privately
Held**
Web: www.cdata.com
SIC: 7372 Application computer software

(G-1536)
CEM-102 PHARMACEUTICALS INC
6320 Quadrangle Dr Ste 360 (27517-7815)

PHONE..............................919 576-2306
EMP: 11 EST: 2010
SALES (est): 792.26K
SALES (corp-wide): 30.6MM **Privately
Held**
SIC: 2834 Pharmaceutical preparations
PA: Melinta Therapeutics, Llc
389 Intrspace Pkwy Ste 45
Parsippany NJ 07054
908 617-1300

(G-1537)
CEMPRA PHARMACEUTICALS INC
6320 Quadrangle Dr Ste 360 (27517-7815)
PHONE..............................919 803-6882
Mark W Hahn, *Ex VP*
Kong Garheng, *Ch Bd*
Carl T Foster, *VP*
EMP: 15 EST: 2005
SQ FT: 6,300
SALES (est): 2.19MM
SALES (corp-wide): 30.6MM **Privately
Held**
SIC: 2834 Pharmaceutical preparations
PA: Melinta Therapeutics, Llc
389 Intrspace Pkwy Ste 45
Parsippany NJ 07054
908 617-1300

(G-1538)
CLOUD SOFTWARE GROUP INC
200 W Franklin St Ste 250 (27516-2559)
PHONE..............................919 969-6500
Naresh Bala, *Brnch Mgr*
EMP: 6
SALES (corp-wide): 4.38B **Privately Held**
Web: www.tibco.com
SIC: 7372 Prepackaged software
HQ: Cloud Software Group, Inc.
851 W Cypress Creek Rd
Fort Lauderdale FL 33309

(G-1539)
CONSERVATION STATION INC
Also Called: C S I
60 Sun Forest Way (27517-9105)
PHONE..............................919 932-9201
Doreen Michaud, *Pr*
EMP: 5 EST: 1994
SQ FT: 1,800
SALES (est): 229.57K **Privately Held**
Web: www.conservationstation.net
SIC: 5063 3646 Lighting fixtures;
Commercial lighting fixtures

(G-1540)
COOKE COMPANIES INTL
Also Called: Cooke Training
105 York Pl (27517-6521)
P.O. Box 810 (27514-0810)
PHONE..............................919 968-0848
William Cooke, *Owner*
EMP: 10 EST: 1972
SALES (est): 219.94K **Privately Held**
SIC: 3826 3822 Environmental testing
equipment; Environmental controls

(G-1541)
DTH PUBLISHING INC
Also Called: Daily Tarheel
151 E Rosemary St Ste 101 (27514-3539)
P.O. Box 3257 (27515-3257)
PHONE..............................919 962-1163
Kevin Scawarz, *Mgr*
EMP: 7 EST: 1893
SQ FT: 5,500
SALES (est): 465.94K **Privately Held**
Web: www.dailytarheel.com
SIC: 2711 Commercial printing and
newspaper publishing combined

(G-1542)
EATCLUB INC
114 Saint Ayers Way (27517-2362)
PHONE..............................609 578-7942
EMP: 5 EST: 2018
SALES (est): 263.16K **Privately Held**
SIC: 7372 7389 Application computer
software; Business Activities at Non-
Commercial Site

(G-1543)
EFFIPHARMA INC
2018 N Lakeshore Dr (27514-2024)
PHONE..............................919 338-2628
Alan L Dow, *Pr*
EMP: 4 EST: 2007
SALES (est): 260.94K **Privately Held**
Web: www.effipharma.com
SIC: 2834 Pharmaceutical preparations

(G-1544)
ENERGY AND ENTROPY INC
301 Palafox Dr (27516-1181)
PHONE..............................919 933-1365
Weitao Yang, *Prin*
EMP: 4 EST: 2008
SALES (est): 275.26K **Privately Held**
SIC: 1382 Oil and gas exploration services

(G-1545)
ENG SOLUTIONS INC
1109 Pinehurst Dr (27517-5662)
PHONE..............................919 831-1830
Mark Enyedi, *Pr*
Martin Gentil, *Sec*
Michael Nativi, *Treas*
Julie Sandford, *Prin*
EMP: 22 EST: 1999
SALES (est): 1.3MM **Privately Held**
SIC: 3823 Industrial process control
instruments

(G-1546)
ENTEX TECHNOLOGIES INC
1340 Environ Way (27517-4430)
PHONE..............................919 933-1380
Wayne Flournoy, *Pr*
Richard Pehrson, *VP*
Robert Freudenberg, *VP*
D Ick Pehrson, *Ex VP*
◆ EMP: 12 EST: 2004
SALES (est): 2.27MM **Privately Held**
Web: www.entexinc.com
SIC: 3589 Water treatment equipment,
industrial

(G-1547)
FINES AND CARRIEL INC
Also Called: Signs Now
1322 Fordham Blvd Ste 5 (27514-5879)
PHONE..............................919 929-0702
Wayne Fines, *Pr*
Elizabeth Carriel, *VP*
EMP: 4 EST: 1980
SQ FT: 2,700
SALES (est): 201.76K **Privately Held**
Web: www.signsnow.com
SIC: 3993 7389 5999 2395 Signs and
advertising specialties; Engraving service;
Rubber stamps; Embroidery products,
except Schiffli machine

(G-1548)
GREEN BEAN COUNTERS LLC
587 Old Farrington Rd (27517-8724)
P.O. Box 1852 (27312-1852)
PHONE..............................919 545-2324
Tracy Kondracki, *Prin*
EMP: 6 EST: 2012
SALES (est): 366K **Privately Held**

Web: www.greenbeancounters.com
SIC: 3131 Counters

(G-1549)
HOPE RENOVATIONS
3 Bolin Hts (27514-5739)
PHONE..........................919 960-1957
Nora Spencer, *CEO*
EMP: 10 EST: 2017
SALES (est): 1.02MM **Privately Held**
Web: www.hoperenovations.org
SIC: 2452 8331 1521 8249 Chicken coops,
prefabricated, wood; Vocational training
agency; General remodeling, single-family
houses; Trade school

(G-1550)
JOURNALISTIC INC
Also Called: Dine America
101 Europa Dr Ste 150 (27517-2380)
PHONE..........................919 945-0700
Webb C Howell Iii, *Pr*
EMP: 29 EST: 1992
SQ FT: 2,000
SALES (est): 3.4MM **Privately Held**
Web: www.finebooksmagazine.com
SIC: 2741 Miscellaneous publishing

(G-1551)
KRENITSKY PHARMACEUTICALS INC
2516 Homestead Rd (27516-9086)
PHONE..........................919 493-4631
Thomas Krenitsky Ph.d., *Pr*
Wayne Eberhardt, *VP*
Sylvia Stanat, *Treas*
Joseph Sica, *Dir*
EMP: 6 EST: 1996
SQ FT: 800
SALES (est): 482.02K **Privately Held**
Web: www.kpi-pharma.com
SIC: 2834 Pharmaceutical preparations

(G-1552)
LEO GAEV METALWORKS INC
616 Nc Highway 54 W (27516-7911)
PHONE..........................919 883-4666
Leo Gaev, *Prin*
EMP: 7 EST: 2009
SALES (est): 1.15MM **Privately Held**
Web: www.leogaevmetalworks.com
SIC: 3446 Acoustical suspension systems,
metal

(G-1553)
LONGLEAF SERVICES INC
116 S Boundary St (27514-3808)
PHONE..........................800 848-6224
Jami Clay, *Dir*
▼ EMP: 10 EST: 2005
SALES (est): 4.13MM **Privately Held**
Web: www.longleafservices.org
SIC: 2731 Book publishing

(G-1554)
MARTIN MARIETTA MATERIALS INC
Martin Marietta Aggregates
1807 Hwy 54 W (27516)
P.O. Box 1288 (27510-3288)
PHONE..........................919 929-7131
Roger Ramey, *Mgr*
EMP: 5
Web: www.martinmarietta.com
SIC: 3273 Ready-mixed concrete
PA: Martin Marietta Materials Inc
4123 Parklake Ave
Raleigh NC 27612

(G-1555)
MELINTA THERAPEUTICS LLC
6340 Quadrangle Dr Ste 36 (27517-8077)
PHONE..........................919 313-6601
EMP: 11
SALES (corp-wide): 30.6MM **Privately Held**
Web: www.melinta.com
SIC: 2834 Pharmaceutical preparations
PA: Melinta Therapeutics, Llc
389 Intrspace Pkwy Ste 45
Parsippany NJ 07054
908 617-1300

(G-1556)
MERGE MEDIA LTD
Also Called: Merge Records
104 S Christopher Rd (27514-4466)
P.O. Box 1235 (27514-1235)
PHONE..........................919 688-9969
Ralph Mccaughan, *Prin*
Laura Ballance, *VP*
EMP: 15 EST: 1989
SQ FT: 2,500
SALES (est): 204.82K **Privately Held**
Web: www.merge-records.com
SIC: 3652 Master records or tapes,
preparation of

(G-1557)
MEY CORPORATION (PA)
121 S Estes Dr Ste 101 (27514-2868)
PHONE..........................919 932-5800
Antoine A Puech, *CEO*
Larry Hodges, *Dir*
Kathy Martyn, *VP Fin*
◆ EMP: 4 EST: 1993
SALES (est): 7.78MM
SALES (corp-wide): 7.78MM **Privately Held**
Web: www.meycorp.com
SIC: 2879 Insecticides, agricultural or
household

(G-1558)
MINIPRO LLC
1289 Fordham Blvd Ste 263 (27514-6110)
PHONE..........................844 517-4776
Jose M Mendez, *Prin*
EMP: 5 EST: 2017
SALES (est): 346.2K **Privately Held**
Web: www.minipro.com
SIC: 3825 Test equipment for electronic and
electric measurement

(G-1559)
NEW PARADIGM THERAPEUTICS INC
8024 Burnette Womack 100 Dental Cir
(27599-0001)
PHONE..........................919 259-0026
David Clemmons, *CEO*
EMP: 5
SQ FT: 400
SALES (est): 247.45K **Privately Held**
SIC: 2834 Druggists' preparations
(pharmaceuticals)

(G-1560)
NOBSCOT CONSTRUCTION CO INC
Also Called: Hill Country Woodworks
2113 Old Greensboro Rd (27516-0515)
PHONE..........................919 929-2075
Robert Bacon, *Pr*
EMP: 7 EST: 1976
SQ FT: 2,000
SALES (est): 164.09K **Privately Held**
Web: www.hillcountrywoodworks.com

SIC: 5712 2511 2512 1521 Customized
furniture and cabinets; Wood household
furniture; Upholstered household furniture;
New construction, single-family houses

(G-1561)
OCUTECH INC
105 Conner Dr Ste 2105 (27514-7126)
PHONE..........................919 967-6460
Henry Greene, *Pr*
◆ EMP: 8 EST: 1984
SQ FT: 700
SALES (est): 867.3K **Privately Held**
Web: www.ocutech.com
SIC: 3851 Ophthalmic goods

(G-1562)
ORTHORX INC
Also Called: Carolina Brace Systems
400 Meadowmont Village Cir # 425
(27517-7505)
PHONE..........................919 929-5550
Tammy Wood, *Prin*
EMP: 5
Web: www.breg.com
SIC: 3842 Orthopedic appliances
HQ: Orthorx, Inc.
5204 Tennyson Pkwy # 100
Plano TX 75024
214 501-0180

(G-1563)
PREGNANCY SUPPORT SERVICES
1777 Fordham Blvd Ste 203 (27514-5885)
P.O. Box 52599 (27717-2599)
PHONE..........................919 490-0203
Ruby Peters, *Ex Dir*
EMP: 7 EST: 1984
SALES (est): 466.7K **Privately Held**
Web:
www.pregnancysupportservices.org
SIC: 8699 2835 8071 Charitable organization
; Pregnancy test kits; Ultrasound laboratory

(G-1564)
QUICK COLOR SOLUTIONS INC
Also Called: Cooper Thomas & Benton
1801 E Franklin St Ste 208b (27514-5855)
P.O. Box 2515 (27515-2515)
PHONE..........................336 282-3900
S Glenn Benton Junior, *Pr*
Mary Glenn Benton, *VP*
EMP: 5 EST: 1998
SQ FT: 1,000
SALES (est): 393.41K **Privately Held**
Web: www.quickcolorsolutions.com
SIC: 2752 Color lithography

(G-1565)
QUINSITE LLC FKA MILE 5 ANLYTI
1818 Martin Luther King Jr Blvd Pmb 185
(27514-7415)
PHONE..........................317 313-5152
Jeff Maze, *CEO*
EMP: 10 EST: 2017
SALES (est): 1.76MM **Privately Held**
Web: www.quinsite.com
SIC: 7374 7375 7372 Data processing
service; Data base information retrieval;
Business oriented computer software

(G-1566)
RAMBUS INC
512 E Franklin St Ste 200 (27514-3708)
PHONE..........................919 960-6600
Fred Heaton, *Mgr*
EMP: 14
Web: www.rambus.com
SIC: 3674 Semiconductors and related
devices
PA: Rambus Inc.

4453 N 1st St Ste 100
San Jose CA 95134

(G-1567)
RETROJECT INC
1125 Pinehurst Dr (27517-5662)
PHONE..........................919 619-3042
Molly Walsh, *CEO*
Stuart Mckinnon, *Pr*
David Epstein, *Sec*
EMP: 4 EST: 2012
SALES (est): 200.43K **Privately Held**
SIC: 3841 7389 Surgical and medical
instruments; Business services, nec

(G-1568)
RSSBUS INC
490 Sun Forest Way (27517-7717)
PHONE..........................919 969-7675
Gent Hito, *Pr*
EMP: 8 EST: 2010
SALES (est): 531.84K **Privately Held**
Web: arc.cdata.com
SIC: 7372 Prepackaged software

(G-1569)
RUTLAND FIRE CLAY COMPANY
1430 Environ Way (27517-4433)
PHONE..........................802 775-5519
EMP: 8 EST: 2013
SALES (est): 1.18MM **Privately Held**
Web: www.rutland.com
SIC: 2891 Adhesives

(G-1570)
SHANNON MEDIA INC
Also Called: Chapel Hill Magazine
1777 Fordham Blvd Ste 105 (27514-5810)
PHONE..........................919 933-1551
Daniel Shannon, *Prin*
EMP: 11 EST: 2010
SALES (est): 2.48MM **Privately Held**
Web: www.chapelhillmagazine.com
SIC: 2721 7311 Magazines: publishing and
printing; Advertising agencies

(G-1571)
SIGNSATIONS LTD
104 Concord Dr (27516-3216)
PHONE..........................571 340-3330
Judith L Birchfield, *Prin*
EMP: 6 EST: 2010
SALES (est): 117.03K **Privately Held**
Web: www.signsationsrc.com
SIC: 3993 Signs and advertising specialties

(G-1572)
SITZER & SPURIA INC
Also Called: Sitzer Spuria Studios
601 W Rosemary St Unit 111 (27516-2353)
PHONE..........................919 929-0299
Cindy Spuria, *Pr*
Joseph Spuria, *VP*
EMP: 8 EST: 1987
SQ FT: 750
SALES (est): 1.04MM **Privately Held**
Web: www.sitzerspuria.com
SIC: 8711 3993 7389 Industrial engineers;
Displays and cutouts, window and lobby;
Design, commercial and industrial

(G-1573)
STEVE HENRY WOODCRAFT LLC
Also Called: Sukkah Project, The
4 Pine Tree Ln (27514-9587)
PHONE..........................919 489-7325
Steve Herman, *Owner*
▲ EMP: 4 EST: 1996
SALES (est): 237.74K **Privately Held**
Web: www.sukkot.com

SIC: 2844 Home permanent kits

(G-1574)
STORYBOOK FARM METAL SHOP INC
Also Called: Storybook Metal Shop
231 Storybook Farm Ln (27516-9160)
PHONE..................................919 967-9491
George W Barrett Junior, *Pr*
Kathleen Andrews, *VP*
EMP: 4 EST: 1980
SQ FT: 3,500
SALES (est): 250.7K Privately Held
Web: www.storybookmetals.com
SIC: 7699 7692 Blacksmith shop; Welding repair

(G-1575)
SUN PUBLISHING COMPANY
107 N Roberson St (27516-2332)
PHONE..................................919 942-5282
Sy Safransky, *Pr*
EMP: 11 EST: 1974
SQ FT: 1,500
SALES (est): 2.76MM Privately Held
Web: www.thesunmagazine.org
SIC: 2741 Miscellaneous publishing

(G-1576)
SYNERECA PHARMACEUTICALS INC
Also Called: Synereca
39519 Glenn Glade (27517-8584)
PHONE..................................919 966-3929
Scott Singleton, *Prin*
Elaine Hamm, *Dir*
EMP: 4 EST: 2009
SALES (est): 324.17K Privately Held
Web: www.synereca.com
SIC: 2834 Pharmaceutical preparations

(G-1577)
TPT COATING INC
150 Providence Rd (27514-2208)
PHONE..................................919 479-0758
Vernon Tyson, *Pr*
EMP: 5 EST: 1997
SALES (est): 162.48K Privately Held
Web: www.tptcoatinginc.com
SIC: 3479 Coating of metals and formed products

(G-1578)
TRAILMATE INC
912 Pinehurst Dr (27517-3432)
PHONE..................................941 739-5743
Harry Bakker, *Pr*
▲ EMP: 7 EST: 1977
SALES (est): 1.22MM Privately Held
Web: www.trailmate.com
SIC: 3524 3751 Lawnmowers, residential: hand or power; Bicycles and related parts

(G-1579)
TRIANGLE CHEMICAL COMPANY
7100 Old Greensboro Rd (27516-8539)
PHONE..................................919 942-3237
Thomas E Braxton, *Owner*
EMP: 4 EST: 1976
SQ FT: 3,000
SALES (est): 100.7K Privately Held
Web: www.trianglecc.com
SIC: 2869 Industrial organic chemicals, nec

(G-1580)
TRIANGLE POINTER INC
Also Called: Triangle Pointer Magazine
88 Vilcom Center Dr (27514-1660)
PHONE..................................919 968-4801
Sue Chen Reeder, *Publisher*

EMP: 8 EST: 1997
SALES (est): 264.74K Privately Held
SIC: 2741 Atlas, map, and guide publishing
PA: The Stamford Capital Group Inc
1266 East Main St
Stamford CT 06902

(G-1581)
TRIANGLE SYSTEMS INC (PA)
882 Pinehurst Dr (27517-6532)
P.O. Box 3260 (27515-3260)
PHONE..................................919 544-0090
James W Ott, *Pr*
Sara Virginia Ott, *Sec*
EMP: 6 EST: 1981
SALES (est): 1.03MM
SALES (corp-wide): 1.03MM Privately Held
Web: www.triangle-systems.com
SIC: 7372 Educational computer software

(G-1582)
TURNSMITH LLC
710 Market St (27516-9358)
PHONE..................................919 667-9804
EMP: 4 EST: 2019
SALES (est): 308.4K Privately Held
Web: www.turnsmith.com
SIC: 3652 Prerecorded records and tapes

(G-1583)
ULTRALOOP TECHNOLOGIES INC
1289 Fordham Blvd (27514-6110)
PHONE..................................919 636-2842
Aditya Bhatt, *Ch*
Tom Morioka, *Ofcr*
Jared Porter, *COO*
EMP: 4 EST: 2021
SALES (est): 580.95K Privately Held
SIC: 3559 Special industry machinery, nec

(G-1584)
UNC CAMPUS HEALTH SERVICES
320 Emergency Room Dr (27599-5035)
PHONE..................................919 966-2281
Kim Pittman, *Ex Dir*
Kim Pittman, *Dir*
EMP: 90 EST: 1980
SALES (est): 725.5K Privately Held
Web: www.unc.edu
SIC: 8742 7372 Hospital and health services consultant; Application computer software

(G-1585)
UNIVERSITY NC AT CHAPEL HL
Also Called: University NC Press
116 S Boundary St (27514-3808)
P.O. Box 2288 (27515-2288)
PHONE..................................919 962-0369
Kate Torrey, *Dir*
EMP: 8
SALES (corp-wide): 5.82MM Privately Held
Web: www.unc.edu
SIC: 2731 8221 Book publishing; University
HQ: University Of North Carolina At Chapel Hill
104 Airport Dr
Chapel Hill NC 27599
919 962-1370

(G-1586)
UNIVERSITY NC PRESS INC
Also Called: UNIVERSITY OF NORTH CAROLINA P
116 S Boundary St (27514-3808)
PHONE..................................919 966-3561
Jami Clay, *Dir*
John Sherer, *
Vicky Wells, *
Joanna Ruth Marsland, *

▲ EMP: 50 EST: 1922
SALES (est): 7.35MM Privately Held
Web: www.uncpress.org
SIC: 2731 Book publishing

(G-1587)
USAT LLC
Also Called: U S A T
104 S Estes Dr Ste 204 (27514-2866)
P.O. Box 9334 (27515-9334)
PHONE..................................919 942-4214
Keith Mcrae, *CEO*
Beverly Mcrae, *Pr*
Tyler Larkin, *
EMP: 50 EST: 1992
SALES (est): 3.92MM Privately Held
Web: www.usatcorp.com
SIC: 7372 7379 3829 3812 Prepackaged software; Computer related consulting services; Measuring and controlling devices, nec; Search and navigation equipment

(G-1588)
VASCULAR PHARMACEUTICALS INC
116 Manning Dr (27599-6117)
PHONE..................................919 345-7933
Kenneth E Eheman, *Prin*
EMP: 4 EST: 2013
SALES (est): 225.7K Privately Held
Web: www.vascularpharma.com
SIC: 2834 Pharmaceutical preparations

(G-1589)
VERITY AMERICA LLC
1340 Environ Way (27517-4430)
PHONE..................................347 960-4198
Markus Waibel, *Pr*
Richard Stockmans, *Treas*
EMP: 4 EST: 2020
SALES (est): 719.08K Privately Held
SIC: 3569 Robots, assembly line: industrial and commercial

(G-1590)
VIIV HEALTHCARE COMPANY
Also Called: Genetic Medicine Building
120 Mason Farm Rd (27514-4617)
PHONE..................................919 445-2770
EMP: 4
SALES (est): 415.67K Privately Held
Web: www.viivhealthcare.com
SIC: 2834 Pharmaceutical preparations

(G-1591)
VILLAGE INSTANT PRINTING INC
Also Called: VIP Printing and Signs Express
2204 Damascus Church Rd (27516-8035)
PHONE..................................919 968-0000
Kenneth Cash, *Pr*
Kenneth Cash, *Prin*
Donna Cash, *Treas*
EMP: 4 EST: 1980
SQ FT: 3,000
SALES (est): 285.2K Privately Held
SIC: 2752 7334 Offset printing; Photocopying and duplicating services

(G-1592)
VOLTAGE LLC
1450 Raleigh Rd Ste 208 (27517-8833)
PHONE..................................919 391-9405
EMP: 13 EST: 2016
SALES (est): 5.4MM Privately Held
Web: www.voltage-llc.com
SIC: 3496 3199 Cable, uninsulated wire: made from purchased wire; Harness or harness parts

(G-1593)
WILLIAM TRAVIS JEWELRY LTD
1819 Fordham Blvd (27514-2200)
PHONE..................................919 968-0011
William Kukovich, *Prin*
EMP: 4 EST: 2006
SALES (est): 186.94K Privately Held
Web: www.williamtravisjewelry.com
SIC: 3911 5944 Jewelry, precious metal; Jewelry stores

(G-1594)
WISDOM HOUSE BOOKS INC
209 Kousa Trl (27516-4669)
PHONE..................................919 883-4669
Ted Ruybal, *Prin*
EMP: 5 EST: 2016
SALES (est): 226.25K Privately Held
Web: www.wisdomhousebooks.com
SIC: 5192 2731 Books; Books, publishing only

(G-1595)
WOOD DONE RIGHT INC
525 Colony Woods Dr (27517-7906)
PHONE..................................919 623-4557
EMP: 4 EST: 2011
SALES (est): 129.31K Privately Held
Web: wooddoneright.houzzsite.com
SIC: 2434 Wood kitchen cabinets

(G-1596)
XINRAY SYSTEMS INC
312 Silver Creek Trl (27514-1840)
PHONE..................................919 701-4100
Moritz Beckmann, *CEO*
Michael Poe, *CFO*
EMP: 11 EST: 2007
SALES (est): 2.18MM Privately Held
SIC: 3844 X-ray apparatus and tubes

(G-1597)
XINTEK INC
312 Silver Creek Trl (27514-1840)
PHONE..................................919 449-5799
Otto Zhou, *Ch*
Doctor Shan Bai, *CEO*
EMP: 4 EST: 2001
SALES (est): 1.04MM Privately Held
Web: www.xintek.com
SIC: 3671 Cathode ray tubes, including rebuilt

(G-1598)
YACKETY YACK PUBLISHING INC
P.O. Box 958 (27514-0958)
PHONE..................................919 843-5092
Kelly Young, *Dir*
EMP: 5
SALES (est): 65.12K Privately Held
Web: heellife.unc.edu
SIC: 2741 Miscellaneous publishing

(G-1599)
ZYSENSE LLC
6701 Glen Forrest Dr (27517-8647)
PHONE..................................215 485-1955
Jeffrey Garwood, *Mgr*
Jeff Garwood, *Managing Member*
EMP: 4 EST: 2016
SALES (est): 418.06K Privately Held
Web: www.zysense.com
SIC: 3826 7389 Infrared analytical instruments; Business Activities at Non-Commercial Site

Charlotte
Mecklenburg County

(G-1600)
2TOPIA CYCLES INC
1512 Southwood Ave (28203-4445)
PHONE..............................704 778-7849
EMP: 5 EST: 2012
SALES (est): 56.33K **Privately Held**
Web: www.2topiacycles.com
SIC: 3732 Boatbuilding and repairing

(G-1601)
3M COMPANY
Also Called: 3M
13840 S Lakes Dr (28273-6738)
PHONE..............................704 588-4782
EMP: 8
SALES (corp-wide): 32.68B **Publicly Held**
Web: www.3m.com
SIC: 3841 3291 2842 Surgical and medical
  instruments; Abrasive products; Polishes
  and sanitation goods
PA: 3m Company
  3m Center
  Saint Paul MN 55144
  651 733-1110

(G-1602)
3NINE USA INC
Also Called: M Grill
8325 Arrowridge Blvd Ste E (28273)
P.O. Box 186 (28134)
PHONE..............................512 210-4005
James Pate, Pr
Christian Grill, Pr
Cliff Betty, Dir
Leonard Pate, Dir
▲ EMP: 13 EST: 2009
SQ FT: 2,000
SALES (est): 3.16MM
SALES (corp-wide): 2.27MM **Privately
Held**
Web: www.3nine.us
SIC: 3564 5084 Air cleaning systems;
  Industrial machinery and equipment
HQ: Grimaldi Development Ab
  Cylindervagen 12
  Nacka Strand

(G-1603)
3RD PHAZE BDY OILS URBAN LNKS
3300 N Graham St (28206-1934)
PHONE..............................704 344-1138
Gary Gray, CEO
▲ EMP: 5 EST: 2005
SALES (est): 852.29K **Privately Held**
Web: www.3rdphazebodyoils.com
SIC: 2844 Face creams or lotions

(G-1604)
A & W ELECTRIC INC
127 W 28th St (28206-2652)
P.O. Box 561898 (28256-1898)
PHONE..............................704 333-4986
Holly Hebert, Pr
Tim Hebert, *
EMP: 30 EST: 1987
SQ FT: 4,000
SALES (est): 1.15MM **Privately Held**
Web: www.aandwelectric.com
SIC: 7694 7629 Electric motor repair;
  Electrical repair shops

(G-1605)
A N E SERVICES LLC
1716 Garette Rd (28218)
PHONE..............................704 882-1117
Betty Morales, Managing Member

EMP: 6 EST: 2002
SALES (est): 354.33K **Privately Held**
SIC: 2519 Lawn and garden furniture, except
  wood and metal

(G-1606)
A O SMITH WATER PRODUCTS CO
4302 Raleigh St (28213-6904)
PHONE..............................704 597-8910
Violet Carter Per, Ofcr
EMP: 16 EST: 2017
SALES (est): 6.6MM **Privately Held**
Web: www.hotwater.com
SIC: 3443 Fabricated plate work (boiler shop)

(G-1607)
A+ PRO TRANSPORT INC
6201 Fairview Rd (28210-3297)
PHONE..............................980 215-8694
Michael Daniel, Pr
EMP: 5 EST: 2019
SALES (est): 1.68MM **Privately Held**
SIC: 3537 Trucks, tractors, loaders, carriers,
  and similar equipment

(G-1608)
**AALBERTS INTEGRATED PIPING
SYSTEMS AMERICAS INC (HQ)**
Also Called: Apollo Valves
10715 Sikes Pl Ste 200 (28277)
P.O. Box 247 (28106)
PHONE..............................704 841-6000
◆ EMP: 48 EST: 1982
SALES (est): 465.94MM
SALES (corp-wide): 3.35B **Privately Held**
Web: www.aalberts-ips.us
SIC: 3625 3494 Actuators, industrial; Valves
  and pipe fittings, nec
PA: Aalberts N.V.
  Stadsplateau 18
  Utrecht UT
  303079300

(G-1609)
ABB INC
12037 Goodrich Dr (28273-6511)
PHONE..............................704 587-1362
Andrew Headley, Brnch Mgr
EMP: 24
Web: www.abb.com
SIC: 3625 5063 3612 3613 Relays and
  industrial controls; Electrical apparatus and
  equipment; Transformers, except electric;
  Switchgear and switchboard apparatus
HQ: Abb Inc.
  305 Gregson Dr
  Cary NC 27511

(G-1610)
ABCO CONTROLS AND EQP INC
4110 Monroe Rd (28205-7708)
P.O. Box 221918 (28222-1918)
PHONE..............................704 394-2424
William Simmons, Pr
Derek Mulder, VP
EMP: 4 EST: 1998
SALES (est): 311.79K **Privately Held**
SIC: 3625 Control equipment, electric

(G-1611)
ABLE METAL FABRICATORS INC
3441 Reno Ave (28216-4111)
PHONE..............................704 394-8972
Horace Strickland, Pr
Shelly Ford, Sec
EMP: 6 EST: 1981
SQ FT: 22,000
SALES (est): 1.74MM **Privately Held**
SIC: 3444 Sheet metal specialties, not
  stamped

(G-1612)
**ABUNDANT POWER SOLUTIONS
LLC**
222 S Church St Ste 401 (28202-3247)
PHONE..............................704 271-9890
Shannon Smith, CEO
Francis Pinckney, COO
Greg Montgomery, CFO
Dank Pinckney, COO
EMP: 7 EST: 2009
SALES (est): 710.72K **Privately Held**
Web: www.abundantpower.com
SIC: 3612 Voltage regulating transformers,
  electric power

(G-1613)
**ABX INNVTIVE PCKG SLUTIONS
LLC (PA)**
2015 Ayrsley Town Blvd Ste 202 (28273)
PHONE..............................980 443-1100
Jason Santamaria, CEO
Eric Tan, CFO
Jeff Godsey, COO
EMP: 95 EST: 2005
SALES (est): 121.96MM
SALES (corp-wide): 121.96MM **Privately
Held**
Web: www.abxpackaging.com
SIC: 3081 2671 2679 Plastics film and sheet
  ; Paper; coated and laminated packaging;
  Tags and labels, paper

(G-1614)
ACCENT COMFORT SERVICES LLC
8421 Old Statesville Rd Ste 17
(28269-1808)
PHONE..............................704 509-1200
Daniel L Mills, Managing Member
EMP: 27 EST: 2004
SALES (est): 4.76MM **Privately Held**
Web: www.accentcomfortservices.com
SIC: 1711 3088 Warm air heating and air
  conditioning contractor; Plastics plumbing
  fixtures

(G-1615)
ACE PLASTICS INC
Also Called: Ace Plastics
5130 Hovis Rd Ste A (28208-1208)
PHONE..............................704 527-5752
Ray Dlugos, Pr
Mary Dlugos, Sec
Nikki Smalls, Off Mgr
▲ EMP: 5 EST: 1994
SALES (est): 5.9MM **Privately Held**
Web: www.aceframes.com
SIC: 5162 3089 Plastics materials and basic
  shapes; Air mattresses, plastics

(G-1616)
ACEYUS INC
11111 Carmel Commons Blvd Ste 210
(28226-4075)
PHONE..............................704 443-7900
Mike Ary, Pr
EMP: 41 EST: 2002
SALES (est): 6.52MM **Privately Held**
Web: www.aceyus.com
SIC: 7372 8748 Business oriented computer
  software; Systems engineering consultant,
  ex. computer or professional

(G-1617)
ACHILLI USA INC
8610 Air Park West Dr Ste 100
(28214-8519)
PHONE..............................704 940-0115
George Hallak, CFO
EMP: 6 EST: 2018
SALES (est): 1.22MM **Privately Held**

Web: www.achilliusa.com
SIC: 3541 Grinding machines, metalworking

(G-1618)
ACME AEROFAB LLC
1907 Scott Futrell Dr (28208-2704)
PHONE..............................704 806-3582
Matthew Mcswain, COO
Matthew Mcswain, Pr
Eric Robinson, COO
EMP: 8 EST: 2013
SALES (est): 521.66K **Privately Held**
SIC: 3469 3728 Appliance parts, porcelain
  enameled; Aircraft parts and equipment, nec

(G-1619)
ACQUIONICS INC
4215 Stuart Andrew Blvd Ste E
(28217-4616)
PHONE..............................980 256-5700
EMP: 4 EST: 2018
SALES (est): 953.62K
SALES (corp-wide): 2.58B **Privately Held**
SIC: 3641 Ultraviolet lamps
PA: Halma Public Limited Company
  Misbourne Court
  Amersham BUCKS HP7 0
  149 472-1111

(G-1620)
ACSM INC
113 Freeland Ln (28217-1617)
PHONE..............................704 910-0243
Glen Nocik, Pr
EMP: 7 EST: 2012
SALES (est): 1.06MM **Privately Held**
Web: www.acsminc.com
SIC: 3993 Signs and advertising specialties

(G-1621)
AD-ART SIGNS INC
2613 Lucena St (28206-2109)
PHONE..............................704 377-5369
Coleman M Hambley, Pr
Mary Sullivan, Sec
EMP: 4 EST: 1973
SQ FT: 3,775
SALES (est): 113.16K **Privately Held**
SIC: 3993 Electric signs

(G-1622)
ADAMS BEVERAGES NC LLC (PA)
7505 Statesville Rd (28269-3704)
PHONE..............................704 509-3000
Clay Adams, Pr
EMP: 18 EST: 2012
SALES (est): 8.55MM
SALES (corp-wide): 8.55MM **Privately
Held**
Web: www.adamsbeverages.net
SIC: 2084 Wine coolers (beverages)

(G-1623)
ADAMS OLDCASTLE
9968 Metromont Industrial Blvd
(28269-7608)
PHONE..............................980 229-7678
EMP: 6 EST: 2019
SALES (est): 228.02K **Privately Held**
Web: www.adamsproducts.com
SIC: 3273 Ready-mixed concrete

(G-1624)
ADKINS TRUCK EQUIPMENT CO
11300 Reames Rd (28269-7674)
P.O. Box 1515 (28070-1515)
PHONE..............................704 596-2299
Eddie Adkins, Pr
Judy Adkins, *
Chifen Parker, *

GEOGRAPHIC

EMP: 48 **EST:** 1979
SQ FT: 34,000
SALES (est): 17.1MM **Privately Held**
Web: www.adkinste.com
SIC: 3713 Utility truck bodies

(G-1625)
ADVANCED TEO CORP
5707 Hornet Dr (28216-2309)
P.O. Box 961330 (33296-1330)
PHONE..............................305 278-4474
Walter Rodriguez, *Prin*
EMP: 6 **EST:** 2013
SALES (est): 248.63K **Privately Held**
SIC: 2752 Offset printing

(G-1626)
AEL SERVICES LLC
Also Called: United Printing Company
8200 Arrowridge Blvd Ste A (28273-5673)
PHONE..............................704 525-3710
Daniel Marshall, *Pr*
EMP: 20 **EST:** 1996
SALES (est): 3.28MM **Privately Held**
Web: www.unitedprintingnc.com
SIC: 2752 2754 2759 Commercial printing,
lithographic; Business form and card
printing, gravure; Commercial printing, nec

(G-1627)
AFSC LLC
Also Called: American Fence & Supply
3605 S Tryon St (28217-1629)
PHONE..............................704 523-4936
EMP: 51 **EST:** 1968
SALES (est): 4.07MM
SALES (corp-wide): 27.34MM **Privately Held**
SIC: 3446 2411 5039 1799 Fences, gates,
posts, and flagpoles; Rails, fence: round or
split; Wire fence, gates, and accessories;
Fence construction
PA: Oxco, Llc
547 Kings Ridge Dr Ste H
Fort Mill SC 29708
704 333-7514

(G-1628)
**AGAINST GRAIN WOODWORKING
INC**
1015 Seigle Ave (28205-2746)
PHONE..............................704 309-5750
Ian Ratcliffe, *Pr*
EMP: 4 **EST:** 2018
SALES (est): 119.25K **Privately Held**
Web: www.againstthegrainnc.com
SIC: 2431 Millwork

(G-1629)
AGINGO CORPORATION
Also Called: Agingo
1401 W Morehead St Ste 150
(28208-5605)
PHONE..............................888 298-0777
Paul Hall, *Pr*
Christopher Vizas, *Ch*
EMP: 7 **EST:** 2009
SQ FT: 500
SALES (est): 244.63K **Privately Held**
Web: www.agingo.com
SIC: 7372 7299 7379 7371 Prepackaged
software; Personal document and
information services; Computer related
consulting services; Computer software
systems analysis and design, custom

(G-1630)
AIM MOLDING & DOOR LLC
5431 Starflower Dr (28215-7574)
PHONE..............................704 913-7211
Michael Archie, *Prin*

EMP: 6 **EST:** 2013
SALES (est): 230.1K **Privately Held**
SIC: 3089 Molding primary plastics

(G-1631)
AIR & GAS SOLUTIONS LLC
Also Called: Nano-Purification Solutions
5509 David Cox Rd (28269-0324)
PHONE..............................704 897-2182
EMP: 50 **EST:** 2020
SALES (est): 7.14MM **Privately Held**
Web: www.nano-purification.com
SIC: 3563 5169 Air and gas compressors;
Industrial gases
PA: Atlas Copco Ab
Sickla Industrivag 19
Nacka 131 5
87438000

(G-1632)
AIRGAS USA LLC
5311 77 Center Dr (28217-2724)
PHONE..............................704 333-5475
EMP: 17
SALES (corp-wide): 114.13MM **Privately
Held**
Web: www.airgas.com
SIC: 2813 5084 Acetylene; Welding
machinery and equipment
HQ: Airgas Usa, Llc
259 N Rdnor Chster Rd Ste
Radnor PA 19087
216 642-6600

(G-1633)
AIRGAS USA LLC
Also Called: Airgas National Carbonation
3101 Stafford Dr (28208-3572)
PHONE..............................704 394-1420
Russell Jewett, *Brnch Mgr*
EMP: 8
SALES (corp-wide): 114.13MM **Privately
Held**
Web:
www.airgasnationalcarbonation.com
SIC: 5169 5084 5085 2813 Industrial gases;
Welding machinery and equipment;
Welding supplies; Industrial gases
HQ: Airgas Usa, Llc
259 N Rdnor Chster Rd Ste
Radnor PA 19087
216 642-6600

(G-1634)
AJ & RAINE SCRUBS & MORE LLC
Also Called: Upshinemedical
657 Fielding Rd (28214-1230)
PHONE..............................646 374-5198
Sydell Chewitt, *Managing Member*
EMP: 5 **EST:** 2020
SALES (est): 218.44K **Privately Held**
SIC: 5047 2326 7389 Medical equipment
and supplies; Medical and hospital
uniforms, men's; Business services, nec

(G-1635)
AKZO NOBEL COATINGS INC
7506 E Independence Blvd (28227-9471)
PHONE..............................704 366-8435
Ton Buchner, *CEO*
EMP: 16
SALES (corp-wide): 11.6B **Privately Held**
SIC: 2851 Paints: oil or alkyd vehicle or
water thinned
HQ: Akzo Nobel Coatings Inc.
535 Marriott Dr Ste 500
Nashville TN 37214
440 297-5100

(G-1636)
ALAN R WILLIAMS INC (HQ)
Also Called: Electro-Motion Agency
2318 Arty Ave (28208-5104)
P.O. Box 34549 (28234-4549)
PHONE..............................704 372-8281
EMP: 26 **EST:** 1954
SALES (est): 16.13MM
SALES (corp-wide): 26.88MM **Privately
Held**
SIC: 5085 3625 Power transmission
equipment and apparatus; Relays and
industrial controls
PA: Motor City Fasteners Llc
1600 E 10 Mile Rd
Hazel Park MI 48030
248 399-2830

(G-1637)
ALBEMARLE AMENDMENTS LLC
4250 Congress St (28209-4860)
PHONE..............................800 535-3030
EMP: 15
Web: www.albemarle.com
SIC: 2819 Bromine, elemental
HQ: Albemarle Amendments, Llc
1664 Highland Rd Ste 3
Twinsburg OH 44087
330 425-2354

(G-1638)
ALBEMARLE CORPORATION (PA)
Also Called: ALBEMARLE
4250 Congress St Ste 900 (28209)
PHONE..............................980 299-5700
J Kent Masters Junior, *Ch Bd*
Neal Sheorey, *Ex VP*
Melissa Anderson, *Chief Human Resources
Officer*
Cynthia Lima, *EXTERNAL AFFAIRS
COMMS*
Donald J Labauve Junior, *CAO*
▼ **EMP:** 530 **EST:** 1993
SALES (est): 5.38B **Publicly Held**
Web: www.albemarle.com
SIC: 2821 2834 2819 2899 Plastics
materials and resins; Pharmaceutical
preparations; Bromine, elemental; Fire
retardant chemicals

(G-1639)
ALBEMARLE US INC
4250 Congress St Ste 900 (28209-0044)
PHONE..............................980 299-5700
Kent Masters, *CEO*
Neal Sheorey, *CFO*
EMP: 8
SALES (est): 1.28MM **Privately Held**
SIC: 1479 Chemical and fertilizer mining

(G-1640)
ALEX AND ANI LLC
4400 Sharon Rd Ste 201 (28211-3608)
PHONE..............................704 366-6029
EMP: 8
SALES (corp-wide): 17.51MM **Privately
Held**
Web: www.alexandani.com
SIC: 3915 3911 Jewelers' materials and
lapidary work; Jewelry, precious metal
HQ: Alex And Ani, Llc
10 Briggs Dr
East Greenwich RI 02818

(G-1641)
ALL SOURCE SECURITY CONT CAL
1500 Continental Blvd Ste K (28273-6376)
PHONE..............................704 504-9908
Martha Busch, *Pr*
▼ **EMP:** 5 **EST:** 2007
SALES (est): 718.65K **Privately Held**

SIC: 3089 Garbage containers, plastics

(G-1642)
ALL-STATE INDUSTRIES INC
Also Called: All State Belting
1400 Westinghouse Blvd Ste 100
(28273-6325)
PHONE..............................704 588-4081
Jay Mcneary, *Mgr*
EMP: 9
SQ FT: 3,500
SALES (corp-wide): 99.48MM **Privately
Held**
Web: www.all-stateind.com
SIC: 2399 Belting and belt products
HQ: All-State Industries, Inc.
500 S 18th St
West Des Moines IA 50265
515 223-5843

(G-1643)
ALLBIRDS INC
100 W Worthington Ave (28203-6813)
PHONE..............................980 296-0006
EMP: 17
SALES (corp-wide): 254.06MM **Publicly
Held**
Web: www.allbirds.com
SIC: 3143 Men's footwear, except athletic
PA: Allbirds Inc.
730 Montgomery St
San Francisco CA 94111
628 225-4848

(G-1644)
ALLIED METAL FINISHING INC
2525 Lucena St (28206-2107)
PHONE..............................704 347-1477
Steve Turner, *Pr*
Hilda Turner, *VP*
Bruce Turner, *Sec*
EMP: 5 **EST:** 1986
SQ FT: 25,000
SALES (est): 471.38K **Privately Held**
Web: www.alliedmetalfinishing.com
SIC: 3471 Electroplating of metals or formed
products

(G-1645)
ALLIED SHEET METAL WORKS INC
612 Charles Ave (28205-1040)
PHONE..............................704 376-8469
Michael D Herndon, *Pr*
EMP: 10 **EST:** 1952
SQ FT: 28,000
SALES (est): 2.62MM **Privately Held**
Web: www.alliedsheetmetalworks.com
SIC: 3444 Sheet metal specialties, not
stamped

(G-1646)
**ALLISON GLOBL MNUFACTURING
INC**
3900 Sam Wilson Rd (28214-9599)
PHONE..............................704 392-7883
James Allison, *Pr*
EMP: 6 **EST:** 2004
SQ FT: 2,503
SALES (est): 357.16K **Privately Held**
SIC: 3792 Trailer coaches, automobile

(G-1647)
ALPEK POLYESTER MISS INC (DH)
7621 Little Ave Ste 500 (28226-8370)
PHONE..............................228 533-4000
Jorge Young, *Pr*
EMP: 160 **EST:** 1996
SALES (est): 972.76MM **Privately Held**
Web: www.alpek.com

SIC: 2821 Plastics materials and resins
HQ: Alpek, S.A.B. De C.V.
Av. Gomez Morin No. 1111 Sur
San Pedro Garza Garcia NLE 66254

(G-1648)
ALPEK POLYESTER USA LLC (DH)
7621 Little Ave Ste 500 (28226-8370)
P.O. Box 470408 (28247-0408)
PHONE...............................704 940-7500
Jorge P Young Cerecedo, *CEO*
Carlos Garcia, *
Antonio Garza, *
Alejandro Gutierrez, *
Jonathan Mcnaull, *VP*
◆ EMP: 60 EST: 2001
SALES (est): 972.76MM **Privately Held**
Web: www.alpekpolyester.com
SIC: 2821 Thermoplastic materials
HQ: Alpek Polyester Mississippi, Inc.
7621 Little Ave Ste 500
Charlotte NC 28226
228 533-4000

(G-1649)
ALPHA 3D LLC
1141 Homestead Glen Blvd (28214-8710)
P.O. Box 1278 (28012-1278)
PHONE...............................704 277-6300
Harry Ellingwood, *Managing Member*
EMP: 4 EST: 2014
SALES (est): 988.87K **Privately Held**
SIC: 1796 3599 Machinery installation;
Machine shop, jobbing and repair

(G-1650)
ALPHA CANVAS AND AWNING CO INC
411 E 13th St (28206-3310)
PHONE...............................704 333-1581
Eric Riggins, *Pr*
Brian Regans, *VP*
Angie Riggins, *Sec*
EMP: 15 EST: 1983
SQ FT: 2,800
SALES (est): 847.59K **Privately Held**
Web: www.alphacanvas.com
SIC: 2394 Awnings, fabric: made from
purchased materials

(G-1651)
ALPHA THEORY LLC
2201 Coronation Blvd Ste 140
(28227-7764)
PHONE...............................704 844-1018
EMP: 4
Web: www.alphatheory.com
SIC: 7372 Prepackaged software
PA: Alpha Theory, Llc
5701 Westpark Dr Ste 105
Charlotte NC 28217

(G-1652)
ALPHA THEORY LLC
3537 Keithcastle Ct (28210-7008)
PHONE...............................212 235-2180
Cameron Hight, *Managing Member*
EMP: 4
Web: www.alphatheory.com
SIC: 7372 8748 Prepackaged software;
Business consulting, nec
PA: Alpha Theory, Llc
5701 Westpark Dr Ste 105
Charlotte NC 28217

(G-1653)
ALPHA THEORY LLC (PA)
5701 Westpark Dr Ste 105 (28217-3525)
PHONE...............................212 235-2180
Cameron Hight, *CEO*
EMP: 8 EST: 2005

SALES (est): 4.15MM **Privately Held**
Web: www.alphatheory.com
SIC: 7372 8748 Prepackaged software;
Business consulting, nec

(G-1654)
ALPHAGRAPHICS
13850 Ballantyne Corporate Pl Ste 500
(28277-2829)
PHONE...............................704 887-3430
EMP: 12 EST: 2018
SALES (est): 83.91K **Privately Held**
Web:
www.alphagraphicssouthcharlotte.com
SIC: 2752 Commercial printing, lithographic

(G-1655)
ALPHAGRAPHICS PINEVILLE
Also Called: AlphaGraphics
10100 Park Cedar Dr Ste 178
(28210-8932)
PHONE...............................704 541-3678
Mike Brown, *Owner*
EMP: 6 EST: 2006
SALES (est): 300.7K **Privately Held**
Web: www.alphagraphics.com
SIC: 2752 7389 Commercial printing,
lithographic; Lettering and sign painting
services

(G-1656)
ALPITRONIC AMERICAS INC
5815 Westpark Dr (28217-3554)
PHONE...............................704 997-4201
Mike Doucleff, *CEO*
Avner Penchas, *CFO*
EMP: 40 EST: 2022
SALES (est): 2.55MM **Privately Held**
SIC: 3699 Electrical equipment and supplies,
nec

(G-1657)
ALTRA INDUSTRIAL MOTION CORP
Boston Gear
701 N I-85 Service Rd (28216)
PHONE...............................704 588-5610
Ed Novotny, *Brnch Mgr*
EMP: 101
SALES (corp-wide): 6.03B **Publicly Held**
Web: www.altramotion.com
SIC: 3714 3462 Power transmission
equipment, motor vehicle; Iron and steel
forgings
HQ: Altra Industrial Motion Corp.
300 Granite St Ste 201
Braintree MA 02184
781 917-0600

(G-1658)
ALTRA INDUSTRIAL MOTION CORP
Also Called: Boston Gear
701 Carrier Dr (28216-3445)
PHONE...............................704 588-5610
EMP: 13
SALES (corp-wide): 6.03B **Publicly Held**
Web: www.altramotion.com
SIC: 3568 5085 Power transmission
equipment, nec; Power transmission
equipment and apparatus
HQ: Altra Industrial Motion Corp.
300 Granite St Ste 201
Braintree MA 02184
781 917-0600

(G-1659)
ALVEOLUS INC
9013 Perimeter Woods Dr Ste B
(28216-0042)
P.O. Box 31247 (28231-1247)
PHONE...............................704 921-2215
Eric Mangiardi, *Pr*

Tony Alexander, *
EMP: 30 EST: 2001
SQ FT: 3,000
SALES (est): 1.41MM
SALES (corp-wide): 1.36B **Publicly Held**
Web: www.merit.com
SIC: 3841 Surgical and medical instruments
PA: Merit Medical Systems, Inc.
1600 W Merit Pkwy
South Jordan UT 84095
801 253-1600

(G-1660)
AMANN GIRRBACH NORTH AMER LP
Also Called: Amann Girrbach North America
13900 S Lakes Dr Ste D (28273-7119)
PHONE...............................704 837-1404
Kathleen Dunham, *Dir*
Carol Smith, *Mgr*
◆ EMP: 12 EST: 2012
SALES (est): 5.77MM
SALES (corp-wide): 355.83K **Privately Held**
Web: www.amanngirrbach.com
SIC: 3843 Dental equipment and supplies
HQ: Amann Girrbach Ag
GewerbestraBe 10
MAder 6841
552 362-3330

(G-1661)
AMARR COMPANY
Also Called: Amarr Garage Doors
2801 Hutchison Mcdonald Rd (28269-4203)
PHONE...............................704 599-5858
Trey Varn, *Mgr*
EMP: 6
Web: www.amarr.com
SIC: 2431 3442 Garage doors, overhead,
wood; Garage doors, overhead: metal
HQ: Amarr Company
165 Carriage Ct
Winston Salem NC 27105
336 744-5100

(G-1662)
AMBRA LE ROY LLC
Also Called: Ambra Leroy Medical Products
8541 Crown Crescent Ct (28227-7733)
PHONE...............................704 392-7080
▲ EMP: 4 EST: 2001
SALES (est): 1.8MM **Privately Held**
Web: www.ambraleroy.com
SIC: 3842 5122 Bandages and dressings;
Bandages

(G-1663)
AMERICAN CIRCUITS INC
10100 Sardis Crossing Dr (28270-2412)
PHONE...............................704 376-2800
Vic Gondha, *Pr*
Jayant D Gondha, *
EMP: 25 EST: 1990
SALES (est): 8.56MM **Privately Held**
Web: www.americancircuits.com
SIC: 3672 Circuit boards, television and
radio printed

(G-1664)
AMERICAN CITY BUS JOURNALS INC (HQ)
Also Called: South Florida Business Journal
120 W Morehead St Ste 400 (28202-1874)
PHONE...............................704 973-1000
Whitney R Shaw, *Pr*
Mike Olivieri, *
George B Guthinger, *
S I Newhouse Junior, *VP*
▲ EMP: 45 EST: 1985
SQ FT: 77,000

SALES (est): 63.54MM
SALES (corp-wide): 2.88B **Privately Held**
Web: www.acbj.com
SIC: 2711 2721 Newspapers: publishing
only, not printed on site; Magazines:
publishing only, not printed on site
PA: Advance Publications, Inc.
1 World Trade Ctr Fl 43
New York NY 10007
718 981-1234

(G-1665)
AMERICAN CITY BUS JOURNALS INC
Also Called: Charlotte Business Journal
120 W Morehead St (28202-1800)
PHONE...............................704 973-1100
EMP: 5
SALES (corp-wide): 2.88B **Privately Held**
Web: www.acbj.com
SIC: 2721 Periodicals
HQ: American City Business Journals, Inc.
120 W Morehead St Ste 400
Charlotte NC 28202
704 973-1000

(G-1666)
AMERICAN RIPENER LLC
803 Pressley Rd Ste 106 (28217-0971)
PHONE...............................704 527-8813
Ann H Wilson, *Sec*
▼ EMP: 4 EST: 1987
SQ FT: 5,000
SALES (est): 725.57K **Privately Held**
Web: www.ripening.com
SIC: 2819 Catalysts, chemical

(G-1667)
AMERICAN SCALE COMPANY LLC
7231 Covecreek Dr (28215-1854)
PHONE...............................704 921-4556
C Hartman, *Managing Member*
EMP: 19 EST: 2018
SALES (est): 4.21MM **Privately Held**
Web: www.americanscaleus.com
SIC: 3596 Truck (motor vehicle) scales

(G-1668)
AMERICAN SIGN SHOP INC
Also Called: American Sign Shop
2440 Whitehall Park Dr Ste 100
(28273-3553)
PHONE...............................704 527-6100
Walton Aldrend, *Pr*
EMP: 4 EST: 1985
SQ FT: 1,280
SALES (est): 249.77K **Privately Held**
Web: www.theamericansignshop.com
SIC: 3993 Signs and advertising specialties

(G-1669)
AMERICAN TRUTZSCHLER INC
5315 Heavy Equipment School Rd
(28214-9497)
PHONE...............................704 399-4521
Pamela Harrelson, *Prin*
EMP: 20
SALES (corp-wide): 12.57MM **Privately Held**
Web: www.am-truetzschler.com
SIC: 3441 Fabricated structural metal
PA: American Trutzschler, Inc.
12300 Moores Chapel Rd
Charlotte NC 28214
704 399-4521

(G-1670)
AMERICAN TRUTZSCHLER INC (PA)
Also Called: American Truetzschler
12300 Moores Chapel Rd (28214-8928)
P.O. Box 669228 (28266-9228)

PHONE.................704 399-4521
Kurt Scholler, *CEO*
Detlef Jaekel, *
Stefan Engel, *
James R Short, *
Michael Schuerenkramer, *
▲ EMP: 60 EST: 1969
SQ FT: 140,000
SALES (est): 12.57MM
SALES (corp-wide): 12.57MM **Privately Held**
Web: www.am-truetzschler.com
SIC: 3552 5084 Textile machinery; Textile machinery and equipment

(G-1671)
AMERICH CORPORATION
10700 John Price Rd (28273-4529)
PHONE.................704 588-3075
Dino Pacifi, *Brnch Mgr*
EMP: 80
SALES (corp-wide): 9.85MM **Privately Held**
Web: www.americh.com
SIC: 3431 Bathtubs: enameled iron, cast iron, or pressed metal
PA: Americh Corporation
    13222 Saticoy St
    North Hollywood CA 91605
    818 982-1711

(G-1672)
AMPLATE INC
7820 Tyner St (28262-3329)
PHONE.................704 607-0191
David French, *Pr*
Kim Payseur, *CFO*
EMP: 21 EST: 1972
SQ FT: 17,000
SALES (est): 256.06K **Privately Held**
Web: www.pro-phx.com
SIC: 3471 Electroplating and plating

(G-1673)
AMR SYSTEMS LLC
13850 Balntyn Corp Pl # 500 (28277-2829)
PHONE.................704 980-9072
EMP: 4
SALES (est): 950K **Privately Held**
SIC: 3822 Environmental controls

(G-1674)
AMREP INC (DH)
6525 Morrison Blvd Ste 300 (28211-3561)
PHONE.................909 923-0430
Gabriel Ghibaudo, *CEO*
Eric Mattson, *VP*
Vivian Ford, *Sec*
EMP: 47 EST: 1976
SQ FT: 40,000
SALES (est): 20.65MM **Privately Held**
Web: www.amrepproducts.com
SIC: 3713 Truck bodies (motor vehicles)
HQ: Wastequip, Llc
    6525 Crnegie Blvd Ste 300
    Charlotte NC 28211

(G-1675)
AMT DATASOUTH CORP
5033 Sirona Dr Ste 800 (28273-3960)
P.O. Box 240947 (28224-0947)
PHONE.................704 523-8500
Chris Biggers, *Genl Mgr*
EMP: 20
SALES (corp-wide): 2.2MM **Privately Held**
Web: www.amtdatasouth.com
SIC: 3577 5045 Printers, computer; Printers, computer
PA: Amt Datasouth Corp.
    3222 Corte Malpaso
    Camarillo CA 93012

805 388-5799

(G-1676)
ANAV YOFI INC
1501 Majestic Meadow Dr (28216-9920)
PHONE.................828 217-7746
Amanda Linder, *Prin*
EMP: 4 EST: 2019
SALES (est): 83.91K **Privately Held**
SIC: 2752 Commercial printing, lithographic

(G-1677)
ANHEUSER-BUSCH LLC
Also Called: Anheuser-Busch
11325 N Community House Rd (28277-1978)
PHONE.................704 321-9319
Pat Harrison, *Mgr*
EMP: 13
SALES (corp-wide): 1.7B **Privately Held**
Web: www.budweisertours.com
SIC: 2082 Beer (alcoholic beverage)
HQ: Anheuser-Busch, Llc
    1 Busch Pl
    Saint Louis MO 63118
    800 342-5283

(G-1678)
ANILOX ROLL COMPANY INC (PA)
Also Called: ARC West
10955 Withers Cove Park Dr (28278-0020)
PHONE.................704 588-1809
Michael Foran, *Pr*
Robert Perfetto, *Sec*
▲ EMP: 5 EST: 1984
SQ FT: 65,000
SALES (est): 7.07MM **Privately Held**
Web: www.arcinternational.com
SIC: 2759 3555 Engraving, nec; Printing trades machinery

(G-1679)
ANSGAR INDUSTRIAL LLC (PA)
6000 Fairview Rd Ste 1200 (28210-2252)
PHONE.................866 284-1931
Michael Edward Faulkner, *Pr*
Greg Boben, *Dir*
EMP: 1784 EST: 2016
SALES (est): 82.02MM
SALES (corp-wide): 82.02MM **Privately Held**
Web: www.ansgarindustrial.com
SIC: 1541 3498 Industrial buildings, new construction, nec; Pipe sections, fabricated from purchased pipe

(G-1680)
AO SMITH CHATLOTTE
4302 Raleigh St (28213-6904)
PHONE.................704 597-8910
EMP: 6 EST: 2011
SALES (est): 1.54MM **Privately Held**
Web: www.hotwater.com
SIC: 3621 Motors and generators

(G-1681)
APB WRECKER SERVICE LLC
114 E 28th St (28206-2718)
PHONE.................704 400-0857
Alan Brown, *Managing Member*
EMP: 4 EST: 2012
SALES (est): 1.37MM **Privately Held**
Web: www.selljunkcarcharlottenc.com
SIC: 3559 7549 Recycling machinery; Towing services

(G-1682)
APEX PACKAGING CORPORATION LLC
Also Called: United Packaging

15105 John J Delaney Dr (28277-2847)
PHONE.................704 847-7274
▲ EMP: 25
Web: www.apexconverting.com
SIC: 5085 3086 Packing, industrial; Packaging and shipping materials, foamed plastics

(G-1683)
APLIX INC (DH)
12300 Steele Creek Rd (28273-3738)
P.O. Box 7505 (28241-7505)
PHONE.................704 588-1920
Sandrine Billarant, *CEO*
Wes Barnes, *Pr*
Richard Little, *VP*
John Rinaldi, *Treas*
Quresh Sachee, *VP*
◆ EMP: 292 EST: 1978
SQ FT: 127,000
SALES (est): 35.13MM **Privately Held**
Web: www.aplix.com
SIC: 3965 Fasteners, hooks and eyes
HQ: Sa Aplix
    Rd 723
    Le Cellier PDL 44850
    228220000

(G-1684)
APPALACHIAN PIPE DISTRS LLC
Also Called: APD
828 East Blvd (28203-5116)
P.O. Box 5217 (25361-0217)
PHONE.................704 688-5703
Michael Fox, *Managing Member*
EMP: 9 EST: 2013
SALES (est): 3.38MM **Privately Held**
Web: www.apdpipe.com
SIC: 3317 3494 7389 Steel pipe and tubes; Pipe fittings; Pipeline and power line inspection service

(G-1685)
APPERSON INC
2908 Stewart Creek Blvd (28216-3592)
P.O. Box 480309 (28269-5338)
PHONE.................704 399-2571
Paul Apperson, *Brnch Mgr*
EMP: 50
SQ FT: 600
SALES (corp-wide): 9.86MM **Privately Held**
Web: www.apperson.com
SIC: 2761 Manifold business forms
PA: Apperson, Inc.
    17315 Studebaker Rd # 209
    Cerritos CA 90703
    562 356-3333

(G-1686)
APPLIED DRIVES INC
11016 Tara Oaks Dr (28227-5489)
P.O. Box 690245 (28227-7004)
PHONE.................704 573-2324
Dennis Hayes, *Pr*
Julie Hayes, *Sec*
EMP: 6 EST: 2001
SQ FT: 2,000
SALES (est): 1.32MM **Privately Held**
Web: www.applieddrives.com
SIC: 3679 5999 7629 Electronic switches; Electronic parts and equipment; Electronic equipment repair

(G-1687)
APPLIED ROLLER TECHNOLOGY INC
8800 Statesville Rd (28269-7638)
P.O. Box 26825 (28221-6825)
PHONE.................704 598-9500
Don Bigham, *Pr*

Ron Mullis, *VP*
Nancy Bigham, *Sec*
EMP: 15 EST: 1986
SQ FT: 20,000
SALES (est): 3.61MM **Privately Held**
Web: www.appliedroller.com
SIC: 3829 Measuring and controlling devices, nec

(G-1688)
APPLIED STRATEGIES INC
1515 Mockingbird Ln Ste 700 (28209-3236)
PHONE.................704 525-4478
James F Matthews, *Pr*
EMP: 5 EST: 1992
SALES (est): 488.92K **Privately Held**
Web: www.appstratinc.com
SIC: 7372 7371 8243 Prepackaged software ; Computer software systems analysis and design, custom; Data processing schools

(G-1689)
APT INDUSTRIES INC
601 E Sugar Creek Rd (28213-6916)
P.O. Box 7486 (28241-7486)
PHONE.................704 598-9100
Roger D Blackwell, *Pr*
Greg Blackwell, *Sec*
EMP: 10 EST: 1979
SQ FT: 27,000
SALES (est): 2.05MM **Privately Held**
Web: www.aptair.com
SIC: 3444 Ducts, sheet metal

(G-1690)
ARBON EQUIPMENT CORPORATION
14100 S Lakes Dr (28273-7110)
PHONE.................414 355-2600
Tom Burrill, *Mgr*
EMP: 15
SALES (corp-wide): 798.11MM **Privately Held**
Web: arbon.ritehite.com
SIC: 3537 5084 5031 Loading docks: portable, adjustable, and hydraulic; Industrial machinery and equipment; Lumber, plywood, and millwork
HQ: Arbon Equipment Corporation
    195 S Rite Hite Way
    Milwaukee WI 53204
    414 355-2600

(G-1691)
ARCHER-DANIELS-MIDLAND COMPANY
Also Called: ADM
620 W 10th St (28202-1430)
P.O. Box 31155 (28231-1155)
PHONE.................704 332-3165
Dennis Tucker, *Brnch Mgr*
EMP: 22
SALES (corp-wide): 85.53B **Publicly Held**
Web: www.adm.com
SIC: 2041 Flour and other grain mill products
PA: Archer-Daniels-Midland Company
    77 W Wacker Dr Ste 4600
    Chicago IL 60601
    312 634-8100

(G-1692)
ARCHROMA US INC (DH)
Also Called: Archroma
5435 77 Center Dr Ste 10 (28217-0750)
P.O. Box 696523 (78249)
PHONE.................704 353-4100
Bryan Dill, *Pr*
Roland Waibel, *
Robin Mccann, *Sec*
Bas Coolen, *
Mark Delevie, *
◆ EMP: 50 EST: 2013

SALES (est): 115.98MM
SALES (corp-wide): 2.67MM **Privately Held**
Web: www.archroma.com
SIC: 2819 Industrial inorganic chemicals, nec
HQ: Archroma Paper Gmbh
Hardstrasse 1
Pratteln BL 4133

(G-1693)
ARCUS MEDICAL LLC
4400 Stuart Andrew Blvd Ste A
(28217-1591)
PHONE..............................704 332-3424
EMP: 5 EST: 2002
SALES (est): 934.79K **Privately Held**
Web: www.arcusmedical.com
SIC: 3841 Diagnostic apparatus, medical

(G-1694)
ARDEN ENGRAVING US INC
100 Forsyth Hall Dr (28273-5727)
PHONE..............................704 547-4581
Andrew Hall, CFO
EMP: 6 EST: 2013
SALES (est): 106.24K **Privately Held**
Web: www.ardenengraving.com
SIC: 2759 Engraving, nec

(G-1695)
ARGOS USA LLC
325 E Hebron St (28273-5974)
PHONE..............................704 679-9431
Willie Hyes, Mgr
EMP: 5
Web: www.argos-us.com
SIC: 3273 Ready-mixed concrete
HQ: Argos Usa Llc
3015 Windward Plz Ste 300
Alpharetta GA 30005
678 368-4300

(G-1696)
ARGUS FIRE CONTROL-PF&S INC
Also Called: Argus Fire Control
2723 Interstate St (28208)
PHONE..............................704 372-1228
Bob Duncan, Pr
Frances K Duncan, *
▲ EMP: 26 EST: 1982
SQ FT: 5,300
SALES (est): 3.73MM **Privately Held**
Web: www.argusfirecontrol.com
SIC: 3669 Fire detection systems, electric

(G-1697)
ARIBEX INC
11727 Fruehauf Dr (28273-6507)
P.O. Box 7800 (28241-7800)
PHONE..............................866 340-5522
EMP: 48
Web: www.dexis.com
SIC: 3843 Ultrasonic dental equipment

(G-1698)
ARROW EQUIPMENT LLC (PA)
Also Called: Caterpillar Authorized Dealer
9000 Statesville Rd (28269-7680)
PHONE..............................803 765-2040
Kevin Franklin, Prin
EMP: 5 EST: 2004
SALES (est): 1.42MM **Privately Held**
Web: www.arrowequipinc.com
SIC: 3531 Construction machinery

(G-1699)
ARTISTIC IMAGES INC
Also Called: Gallery G
900 Remount Rd 920 (28203-5553)
P.O. Box 470043 (28247-0043)

PHONE..............................704 332-6225
Charles G Williams, Pr
EMP: 4 EST: 1985
SALES (est): 319.32K **Privately Held**
Web: www.artisticimages.net
SIC: 3993 Signs and advertising specialties

(G-1700)
ARTISTIC SOUTHERN INC
Also Called: Southern Staircase
1108 Continental Blvd (28273-6385)
PHONE..............................919 861-4695
Caleb Stewart, Brnch Mgr
EMP: 18
SALES (corp-wide): 3.1MM **Privately Held**
Web: www.southernstaircase.com
SIC: 1751 Carpentry work; Staircases,
stairs and railings
PA: Artistic Southern, Inc.
6025 Shiloh Rd Ste E
Alpharetta GA 30005
770 888-7333

(G-1701)
ARVA LLC
Also Called: Hylite Led
1327 Wood Branch Dr Ste E (28273-7280)
PHONE..............................803 336-2230
▲ EMP: 5 EST: 2010
SALES (est): 919.35K **Privately Held**
Web: www.hyliteledlighting.com
SIC: 3646 3641 3674 Commercial lighting
fixtures; Electric lamps and parts for
generalized applications; Semiconductors
and related devices

(G-1702)
ARZBERGER ENGRAVERS INC
2518 Dunavant St (28203-5034)
PHONE..............................704 376-1151
Luther Dudley, Pr
EMP: 20 EST: 1953
SQ FT: 6,000
SALES (est): 2.88MM **Privately Held**
SIC: 2754 2789 2759 2752 Commercial
printing, gravure; Bookbinding and related
work; Commercial printing, nec;
Commercial printing, lithographic

(G-1703)
AS AMERICA INC
4500 Morris Field Dr (28208-5837)
PHONE..............................704 398-4602
Michael Tran, Mgr
EMP: 17
Web: www.americanstandard-us.com
SIC: 3261 Vitreous plumbing fixtures
HQ: As America, Inc.
30 Knghtsbrdge Rd Ste 301
Piscataway NJ 08854

(G-1704)
ASHLEY SLING INC
Also Called: ASHLEY SLING, INC.
2401 N Graham St (28206-2507)
PHONE..............................704 347-0071
Tomy Ellis, Brnch Mgr
EMP: 42
Web: www.ashleysling.com
SIC: 3496 Mesh, made from purchased wire
PA: Ashley Sling, Llc
7929 Troon Cir Sw
Austell GA 30168

(G-1705)
ASIAN (KOREAN) HERALD INC
1300 Baxter St Ste 155 (28204-0064)
PHONE..............................704 332-5656
Ki-hyun Chun, Owner
EMP: 6 EST: 2001
SALES (est): 209.7K **Privately Held**

Web: www.asianlibrary.org
SIC: 2711 Commercial printing and
newspaper publishing combined

(G-1706)
ASSEMBLY TECHNOLOGIES INC
Also Called: ATI
6716 Orr Rd (28213-6439)
P.O. Box 560623 (28256-0623)
PHONE..............................704 596-3903
Rohit Savani, Pr
▲ EMP: 16 EST: 1990
SQ FT: 12,000
SALES (est): 8.18MM **Privately Held**
Web: www.assemblytechinc.com
SIC: 3672 Printed circuit boards

(G-1707)
AT YOUR SERVICE EXPRESS LLC
101 N Tryon St Ste 112 (28246-0104)
PHONE..............................704 270-9918
EMP: 27 EST: 2019
SALES (est): 2.9MM **Privately Held**
SIC: 3537 4789 5088 Trucks, tractors,
loaders, carriers, and similar equipment;
Transportation services, nec;
Transportation equipment and supplies

(G-1708)
ATCOM INC
Also Called: Atcom Bus Telecom Solutions
3330 Oak Lake Blvd (28208-7707)
P.O. Box 13476 (27709-3476)
PHONE..............................704 357-7900
Rhonda Morgan, Brnch Mgr
EMP: 15
SALES (corp-wide): 8.81MM **Privately Held**
Web: www.atcombts.com
SIC: 3661 1731 Telephones and telephone
apparatus; Computer installation
PA: Atcom Inc.
4920 S Alston Ave
Durham NC 27713
919 544-5751

(G-1709)
ATLANTIC COMMERCIAL CASEWORKS
4700 Rozzelles Ferry Rd (28216-3341)
P.O. Box 35067 (28235-5067)
PHONE..............................704 393-9500
Nathaniel Gatewood, Owner
EMP: 4 EST: 2011
SALES (est): 2.98MM **Privately Held**
Web: www.atlanticcaseworks.com
SIC: 3553 Cabinet makers' machinery

(G-1710)
ATLANTIC CORP WILMINGTON INC
Atlantic Packaging
12200 Steele Creek Rd (28273-3736)
P.O. Box 7006 (28241-7006)
PHONE..............................704 588-1400
Eric Farmer, Brnch Mgr
EMP: 75
SALES (corp-wide): 483.78MM **Privately Held**
Web: www.atlanticpkg.com
SIC: 5199 2679 2621 Packaging materials;
Corrugated paper: made from purchased
material; Wrapping and packaging papers
PA: Atlantic Corporation Of Wilmington Inc.
806 N 23rd St
Wilmington NC 28405
800 722-5841

(G-1711)
ATLANTIC TRADING LLC
307 Ridgewood Ave (28209-1633)
EMP: 10 EST: 2004

SALES (est): 499.77K **Privately Held**
Web: www.onelittlebox.com
SIC: 5331 2211 2389 Variety stores;
Alpacas, cotton; Academic vestments (caps
and gowns)

(G-1712)
ATLANTIC WINDOW COVERINGS INC
Also Called: AWC
6150 Brookshire Blvd Ste D (28216-2444)
PHONE..............................704 392-0043
Rob Mitchell, Pr
Margaret Mitchell, VP
EMP: 20 EST: 1963
SQ FT: 8,000
SALES (est): 4.7MM **Privately Held**
Web: www.awcproducts.com
SIC: 5023 2391 Window covering parts and
accessories; Draperies, plastic and textile:
from purchased materials

(G-1713)
ATLANTIC WOOD & TIMBER LLC
2200 Border Dr (28208-4061)
PHONE..............................704 390-7479
EMP: 15 EST: 2014
SALES (est): 7.26MM **Privately Held**
Web: www.atlanticwt.com
SIC: 2491 Wood preserving

(G-1714)
ATLAS COPCO COMPRESSORS LLC
Also Called: Woodward Compressor Sales
2101 Westinghouse Blvd # D (28273-6310)
PHONE..............................704 525-0124
EMP: 15
Web: www.atlascopco.us
SIC: 3563 Air and gas compressors
HQ: Atlas Copco Compressors Llc
300 Tchnlogy Ctr Way Ste
Rock Hill SC 29730
866 472-1015

(G-1715)
ATMOX INC
10612d Providence Rd Ste 229
(28277-0459)
PHONE..............................704 248-2858
Myriam Breedlove, Pr
EMP: 12 EST: 2008
SALES (est): 2.08MM **Privately Held**
Web: www.atmox.com
SIC: 1389 Oil consultants

(G-1716)
ATTUS TECHNOLOGIES INC
13860 Ballantyne Corporate Pl Ste 200
(28277-2467)
PHONE..............................704 341-5750
Trey Sullivan, Pr
EMP: 20 EST: 1998
SALES (est): 2.35MM
SALES (corp-wide): 316.65MM **Privately Held**
SIC: 7372 Prepackaged software
PA: Computer Services, Inc.
3901 Technology Dr
Paducah KY 42001
800 545-4274

(G-1717)
AURIGA POLYMERS INC (DH)
4235 Southstream Blvd Ste 450
(28217-0143)
PHONE..............................864 579-5570
Tom Brekovsky, Pr
Avnish Madan, *
Hitendra Mathur, *
Hunter Stamey, *
◆ EMP: 200 EST: 2010
SALES (est): 52.49MM **Privately Held**

Web: www.indoramaventures.com
SIC: 2821 2824 Plastics materials and resins
; Polyester fibers
HQ: Indorama Ventures Public Company
Limited
75/102 Soi Sukhumvit 19 (Vadhana),
Asok Road
Vadhana 10110

(G-1718)
AUTOPARK LOGISTICS LLC
2703 Madison Oaks Ct (28226-7672)
PHONE..............................704 365-3544
Peter Anderes, *Managing Member*
▲ EMP: 4 EST: 2013
SALES (est): 938.32K Privately Held
Web: www.autoparkinc.com
SIC: 3559 Parking facility equipment and
supplies

(G-1719)
AUTRY CON PDTS & BLDRS SUP CO
Also Called: Autry Con Pdts & Septic Svcs
8918 Byrum Dr (28217-2368)
PHONE..............................704 504-8830
Steve Autry, *Pr*
Carol Autry, *Sec*
EMP: 6 EST: 1929
SQ FT: 4,000
SALES (est): 255.41K Privately Held
SIC: 3272 7699 Pipe, concrete or lined with
concrete; Septic tank cleaning service

(G-1720)
AVADIM HOLDINGS INC
4944 Parkway Plaza Blvd Ste 480
(28217-1972)
PHONE..............................877 677-2723
EMP: 30
SALES (corp-wide): 24.62MM Privately
Held
Web: www.avadimhealth.com
SIC: 2834 Pharmaceutical preparations
PA: Avadim Holdings, Inc.
4 Old Patton Cove Rd
Swannanoa NC 28778
877 677-2723

(G-1721)
AVIATION METALS NC INC
Also Called: Aviation Metals
1810 W Pointe Dr Ste D (28214-9293)
PHONE..............................704 264-1647
James Contes, *CEO*
Charles F Contes, *Pr*
Ames Contes, *Sec*
▲ EMP: 15 EST: 1976
SQ FT: 30,000
SALES (est): 11.44MM Privately Held
Web: www.aviationmetals.com
SIC: 5051 3354 3353 3356 Steel; Aluminum
extruded products; Aluminum sheet, plate,
and foil; Nickel and nickel alloy pipe, plates,
sheets, etc.

(G-1722)
AVIDXCHANGE HOLDINGS INC (PA)
Also Called: AVIDXCHANGE
1210 Avid Xchange Ln (28206)
PHONE..............................800 560-9305
Michael Praeger, *Ch Bd*
Daniel Drees, *Pr*
Joel Wilhite, *Sr VP*
Ryan Stahl, *Sr VP*
Angelic Gibson, *CIO*
EMP: 24 EST: 2000
SQ FT: 201,000
SALES (est): 438.94MM
SALES (corp-wide): 438.94MM Publicly
Held
Web: www.avidxchange.com

SIC: 7372 Prepackaged software

(G-1723)
AVIENT COLORANTS USA LLC
Reedspectrum Division
4000 Monroe Rd (28205-7706)
PHONE..............................704 331-7000
Phil Strassle, *Managing Member*
EMP: 99
SQ FT: 63,320
Web: www.avient.com
SIC: 3087 2816 Custom compound
purchased resins; Inorganic pigments
HQ: Avient Colorants Usa Llc
85 Industrial Dr
Holden MA 01520
877 546-2885

(G-1724)
AVINTIV INC (HQ)
9335 Harris Corners Pkwy Ste 300
(28269-3817)
PHONE..............................704 697-5100
J Joel Hackney Junior, *Pr*
◆ EMP: 43 EST: 2010
SALES (est): 4.72MM Publicly Held
SIC: 2297 Nonwoven fabrics
PA: Berry Global Group, Inc.
101 Oakley St
Evansville IN 47710

(G-1725)
AVINTIV SPECIALTY MTLS INC (HQ)
9335 Harris Corners Pkwy Ste 300
(28269-3817)
PHONE..............................704 697-5100
J Joel Hackney Junior, *Pr*
Dennis Norman, *
Daniel L Rikard, *
Daniel Guerrero Senior, *Strategy Vice
President*
Mary Tomasello Senior, *Vice-President
Global Human Resources*
◆ EMP: 2000 EST: 1994
SALES (est): 450.25MM Publicly Held
Web: www.berryglobal.com
SIC: 2297 2392 Nonwoven fabrics; Towels,
dishcloths and dust cloths
PA: Berry Global Group, Inc.
101 Oakley St
Evansville IN 47710

(G-1726)
AXTRA3D INC
Also Called: Axtra3d
5510 77 Center Dr Ste 150 (28217-3044)
PHONE..............................888 315-5103
Praveen Tummala, *COO*
EMP: 20 EST: 2022
SALES (est): 2.96MM Privately Held
Web: www.axtra3d.com
SIC: 3571 Electronic computers

(G-1727)
AZURE SKYE BEVERAGES INC
5253 Old Dowd Rd Unit 3 (28208-2162)
P.O. Box 668132 (28266-8132)
PHONE..............................704 909-7394
John Johnson, *Pr*
◆ EMP: 4 EST: 2010
SQ FT: 1,300
SALES (est): 236.9K Privately Held
Web: www.myazureskye.com
SIC: 2085 5149 Rum (alcoholic beverage);
Flavorings and fragrances

(G-1728)
B & B LEATHER CO INC
5518 Nevin Rd (28269-7359)
PHONE..............................704 598-9080
Alan Blaentine, *Pr*

Rebecca Balentine, *Treas*
Robert H Balentine, *Sec*
EMP: 10 EST: 1961
SQ FT: 6,000
SALES (est): 72.57K Privately Held
Web: www.bbleather.com
SIC: 3199 5199 Harness or harness parts;
Pet supplies

(G-1729)
B ROBERTS FOODS LLC
Also Called: B. Robert's Prepared Foods
2700 Westinghouse Blvd Ste A
(28273-0114)
PHONE..............................704 522-1977
EMP: 40
Web: www.brobertsfoods.com
SIC: 2038 Frozen specialties, nec

(G-1730)
B S R-HESS RACE CARS INC
7701 N Tryon St (28262-3498)
PHONE..............................704 547-0901
Harold Stevens, *Pr*
EMP: 20 EST: 1986
SALES (est): 337.18K Privately Held
SIC: 3711 7539 Automobile assembly,
including specialty automobiles; Automotive
repair shops, nec

(G-1731)
B/E AEROSPACE INC (DH)
Also Called: Rockwell Collins
2730 W Tyvola Rd (28217)
PHONE..............................704 423-7000
Troy Brunk, *Pr*
Tatum Buse, *Finance**
▲ EMP: 30 EST: 1987
SQ FT: 31,300
SALES (est): 1.67B
SALES (corp-wide): 80.74B Publicly Held
Web: www.collinsaerospace.com
SIC: 3647 3728 2531 Aircraft lighting fixtures
; Aircraft body and wing assemblies and
parts; Seats, aircraft
HQ: Rockwell Collins, Inc.
400 Collins Rd Ne
Cedar Rapids IA 52498

(G-1732)
BAAC BUSINESS SOLUTIONS INC
Also Called: Sign-A-Rama
1701 South Blvd (28203-4727)
PHONE..............................704 333-4321
William Cruz, *Dir*
EMP: 9 EST: 2016
SALES (est): 1.43MM Privately Held
Web: www.signarama.com
SIC: 3993 Signs and advertising specialties

(G-1733)
**BABCOCK WLCOX EQITY
INVSTMNTS**
13024 Ballantyne Corporate Pl Ste 700
(28277-2113)
PHONE..............................704 625-4900
EMP: 8 EST: 2018
SALES (est): 3.55MM
SALES (corp-wide): 999.35MM Publicly
Held
Web: www.babcock.com
SIC: 3511 Turbines and turbine generator
sets
PA: Babcock & Wilcox Enterprises, Inc.
1200 E Market St Ste 650
Akron OH 44305
330 753-4511

(G-1734)
**BABCOCK WLCOX INTL SLS SVC
COR**
13024 Ballantyne Corporate Pl Ste 700
(28277-2113)
PHONE..............................704 625-4900
EMP: 5 EST: 2017
SALES (est): 2.22MM
SALES (corp-wide): 999.35MM Publicly
Held
Web: www.babcock.com
SIC: 3511 Turbines and turbine generator
sets
PA: Babcock & Wilcox Enterprises, Inc.
1200 E Market St Ste 650
Akron OH 44305
330 753-4511

(G-1735)
BABUSCI CRTIVE PRTG IMGING LLC
Also Called: Minuteman Press
4115 Rose Lake Dr Ste A (28217-2870)
PHONE..............................704 423-9864
EMP: 4 EST: 2011
SALES (est): 179.48K Privately Held
Web: airport.intlminutepress.com
SIC: 2752 Offset printing

(G-1736)
BACCI AMERICA INC
1704 East Blvd Ste 101 (28203-5888)
PHONE..............................704 375-5044
Claudio Carpano, *Pr*
▲ EMP: 10 EST: 2014
SALES (est): 1.11MM Privately Held
Web: www.bacci.com
SIC: 3553 Bandsaws, woodworking

(G-1737)
BACE LLC
322 W 32nd St (28206-4256)
PHONE..............................704 394-2230
Fred Waite, *CEO*
Drew Sigmund Junior, *Sr VP*
Gregory J Leon, *Sr VP*
Randy Sossamon, *Sr VP*
EMP: 15 EST: 2006
SQ FT: 90,000
SALES (est): 13.51MM
SALES (corp-wide): 99.92MM Privately
Held
Web: www.bacecorp.com
SIC: 3599 Machine and other job shop work
PA: Komar Industries, Llc
4425 Marketing Pl
Groveport OH 43125
614 836-2368

(G-1738)
BAE SYSTEMS INC
11215 Rushmore Dr (28277-3439)
PHONE..............................855 223-8363
Robert Eggleston, *Brnch Mgr*
EMP: 72
SALES (corp-wide): 28.77B Privately Held
Web: www.baesystems.com
SIC: 3812 Search and navigation equipment
HQ: Bae Systems, Inc.
2941 Frview Pk Dr Ste 100
Falls Church VA 22042

(G-1739)
BAGCRAFTPAPERCON III LLC (DH)
3436 Toringdon Way Ste 100 (28277-2449)
PHONE..............................800 845-6051
Gaby Ajram, *Pr*
Patrick T Chambliss, *CFO*
Mike Klaes, *VP*
▲ EMP: 99 EST: 2006
SALES (est): 46.53MM
SALES (corp-wide): 26.11B Publicly Held

▲ = Import ▼ = Export
◆ = Import/Export

SIC: 2671 5199 Paper, coated or laminated for packaging; Packaging materials
HQ: Gmg International Inc.
   3436 Tringdon Way Ste 100
   Charlotte NC 28277

(G-1740)
BAHAKEL COMMUNICATIONS LTD LLC
Also Called: Wcc Television
701 Television Pl (28205-1061)
P.O. Box 32488 (28232-2488)
PHONE.................................704 372-4434
Beverly Poston, *Owner*
EMP: 350 EST: 1992
SALES (est): 2.05MM **Privately Held**
Web: www.bahakelsports.com
SIC: 3663 Television broadcasting and communications equipment

(G-1741)
BAIKOWSKI INTERNATIONAL CORP (HQ)
6601 Northpark Blvd Ste H (28216-0092)
PHONE.................................704 587-7100
Claude Djolollan, *Pr*
▲ EMP: 10 EST: 1979
SQ FT: 19,335
SALES (est): 16.51MM
SALES (corp-wide): 31.68MM **Privately Held**
Web: www.baikowski.com
SIC: 2819 Industrial inorganic chemicals, nec
PA: Baikowski
   1046 Rte De Chaumontet
   Poisy ARA 74330
   450226902

(G-1742)
BAILY ENTERPRISES LLC
Also Called: Special Service Plastic
12016 Steele Creek Rd (28273-3734)
PHONE.................................704 587-0109
Richard Baily, *Pr*
EMP: 18 EST: 2018
SALES (est): 5.83MM **Privately Held**
Web: www.specialserviceplastic.com
SIC: 3089 Injection molding of plastics

(G-1743)
BAKESHOT PRTG & GRAPHICS LLC
121 Greenwich Rd Ste 101 (28211-2343)
PHONE.................................704 532-9326
EMP: 4 EST: 2004
SALES (est): 233.79K **Privately Held**
Web: www.bakeshotprinting.com
SIC: 2752 Offset printing

(G-1744)
BAKKAVOR FOODS USA INC
10220 Western Ridge Rd Ste P (28273-7264)
PHONE.................................704 522-1977
EMP: 189
SALES (corp-wide): 2.91B **Privately Held**
Web: www.bakkavor.com
SIC: 2051 Breads, rolls, and buns
HQ: Bakkavor Foods Usa, Inc.
   2700 Westinghouse Blvd
   Charlotte NC 28273
   704 522-1977

(G-1745)
BAKKAVOR FOODS USA INC (DH)
2700 Westinghouse Blvd (28273-0113)
PHONE.................................704 522-1977
Kamran Lodi, *CEO*
Michael Gold, *
▲ EMP: 150 EST: 1985
SQ FT: 97,000

SALES (est): 313.83MM
SALES (corp-wide): 2.91B **Privately Held**
Web: www.bakkavor.com
SIC: 2051 2013 2092 Bread, all types (white, wheat, rye, etc); fresh or frozen; Spreads, sandwich: meat, from purchased meat; Fresh or frozen fish or seafood chowders, soups, and stews
HQ: Bakkavor Usa Limited
   5th Floor
   London
   177 566-3800

(G-1746)
BALANCED HEALTH PLUS LLC
7804 Fairview Rd Box 275 (28226-4998)
PHONE.................................704 604-9524
Ronald Hunt, *Pr*
Richard Rauh, *Treas*
EMP: 10 EST: 2014
SALES (est): 221.1K **Privately Held**
Web: www.aromaidclips.com
SIC: 2911 Aromatic chemical products

(G-1747)
BALLANTYNE ONE
15720 Brixham Hill Ave Ste 300 (28277-4651)
PHONE.................................704 926-7009
EMP: 4 EST: 2018
SALES (est): 344.37K **Privately Held**
Web: www.goballantyne.com
SIC: 2752 Commercial printing, lithographic

(G-1748)
BAMAL CORPORATION (HQ)
Also Called: Bamal Fastener
13725 S Point Blvd (28207)
P.O. Box 7809 (28241)
PHONE.................................980 225-7700
Mikel D Miller, *Pr*
Kevin Miller, *Sr VP*
Kyle Miller, *Ofcr*
Marilyn Goodrich, *CFO*
▲ EMP: 15 EST: 1953
SQ FT: 20,000
SALES (est): 16.29MM **Privately Held**
Web: www.bamal.com
SIC: 5072 3565 7389 Bolts; Bottling machinery: filling, capping, labeling; Labeling bottles, cans, cartons, etc.
PA: Pacific Components De Mexico, S. De R.L. De C.V.
   Juarez No. 1102 Oficina 3204
   Monterrey NLE 64000

(G-1749)
BARBARAS CANINE CATERING INC
Also Called: Canine Cafe
1447 S Tryon St Ste 101 (28203-4259)
PHONE.................................704 588-3647
Barbara Burg, *Pr*
EMP: 6 EST: 1995
SQ FT: 1,000
SALES (est): 110.38K **Privately Held**
Web: www.caninecafe.net
SIC: 2047 Dog food

(G-1750)
BARCOVISION LLC
4420 Taggart Creek Rd (28208-5412)
PHONE.................................704 392-9371
Steve Altman, *VP*
EMP: 7 EST: 2010
SALES (est): 771.66K **Privately Held**
Web: www.bmsvision.com
SIC: 3823 Process control instruments

(G-1751)
BARCOVVSION LLC (PA)
4420 Taggart Creek Rd Ste 110 (28208-5412)
PHONE.................................704 392-9371
Steve Altman, *VP*
Steve Mccullough, *Sec*
Ann Watkins, *Asst Tr*
EMP: 16 EST: 2000
SALES (est): 1.56MM **Privately Held**
SIC: 2221 3571 Textile mills, broadwoven: silk and manmade, also glass; Electronic computers

(G-1752)
BARIATRIC PARTNERS INC
7401 Carmel Executive Park Dr (28226-8275)
P.O. Box 470176 (28247-0176)
PHONE.................................704 542-2256
Edmund C Bujalski, *Pr*
Stephen R Puckett, *Ch Bd*
EMP: 7 EST: 2005
SALES (est): 797.42K **Privately Held**
SIC: 3841 Surgical and medical instruments

(G-1753)
BARKER INDUSTRIES INC (PA)
220 Crompton St (28273-6204)
PHONE.................................704 391-1023
Robert F Settin, *Pr*
Marc F Settin, *Ex VP*
▲ EMP: 8 EST: 1973
SQ FT: 115,000
SALES (est): 3.21MM
SALES (corp-wide): 3.21MM **Privately Held**
Web: www.barkerind.com
SIC: 2899 Salt

(G-1754)
BARNHARDT MANUFACTURING CO
1300 Hawthorne Ln (28205-2922)
PHONE.................................704 331-0657
Mark Dobbins, *Mgr*
EMP: 200
SALES (corp-wide): 268.75MM **Privately Held**
Web: www.barnhardt.net
SIC: 0131 3086 Cotton; Plastics foam products
PA: Barnhardt Manufacturing Company
   1100 Hawthorne Ln
   Charlotte NC 28205
   800 277-0377

(G-1755)
BARNHARDT MANUFACTURING COMPANY (PA)
Also Called: Richmond Dental and Medical
1100 Hawthorne Ln (28205)
P.O. Box 34276 (28234)
PHONE.................................800 277-0377
◆ EMP: 250 EST: 1900
SALES (est): 268.75MM
SALES (corp-wide): 268.75MM **Privately Held**
Web: www.barnhardt.net
SIC: 3086 2299 2211 Plastics foam products ; Quilt fillings: curled hair, cotton waste, moss, hemp tow; Sheets, bedding and table cloths: cotton

(G-1756)
BARRDAY CORP (HQ)
Also Called: Barrday Protective Solutions
1450 W Pointe Dr Ste C (28214-9291)
PHONE.................................704 395-0311
Michael Buckstein, *CEO*
Andrew Galbraith, *VP*
Anne Verstraete, *CFO*

▲ EMP: 9 EST: 2000
SALES (est): 52.63MM
SALES (corp-wide): 18.34MM **Privately Held**
Web: www.barrday.com
SIC: 2231 Broadwoven fabric mills, wool
PA: Barrday, Inc
   201e-181 Groh Ave
   Cambridge ON N3C 1
   519 621-3620

(G-1757)
BARRON LEGACY MGMT GROUP LLC
1737 Arbor Vista Dr (28262-2531)
PHONE.................................301 367-4735
Keith Barron, *Managing Member*
EMP: 4 EST: 2019
SALES (est): 119.33K **Privately Held**
SIC: 2261 7336 8742 Screen printing of cotton broadwoven fabrics; Commercial art and graphic design; Marketing consulting services

(G-1758)
BASF CORPORATION
Also Called: B A S F Colors & Colorants
11501 Steele Creek Rd (28273-3730)
PHONE.................................704 588-5280
Klaus Loeffler, *VP*
EMP: 240
SQ FT: 43,252
SALES (corp-wide): 74.89B **Privately Held**
Web: www.basf.com
SIC: 2869 Industrial organic chemicals, nec
HQ: Basf Corporation
   100 Park Ave
   Florham Park NJ 07932
   800 962-7831

(G-1759)
BASOFIL FIBERS LLC
4824 Parkway Plaza Blvd Ste 250 (28217-1970)
P.O. Box 1238 (28728-1238)
PHONE.................................828 304-2307
Bogdan Ewendt, *Managing Member*
▼ EMP: 24 EST: 1995
SALES (est): 609K **Privately Held**
Web: www.basofil.com
SIC: 2824 Organic fibers, noncellulosic

(G-1760)
BAYER CORP
2332 Croydon Rd (28207-2704)
PHONE.................................704 373-0991
Shanna Simpson, *Marketing Executive*
EMP: 10 EST: 2017
SALES (est): 169.27K **Privately Held**
SIC: 2834 Pharmaceutical preparations

(G-1761)
BCP EAST LAND LLC
13860 Ballantyne Corporate Pl (28277-2467)
PHONE.................................704 248-2000
EMP: 4 EST: 2012
SALES (est): 1.49MM **Privately Held**
SIC: 1389 Construction, repair, and dismantling services

(G-1762)
BEACON INDUSTRIAL MFG LLC
4404a Chesapeake Dr (28216-3413)
PHONE.................................704 399-7441
▼ EMP: 1242 EST: 2000
SALES (est): 2.14MM **Privately Held**
SIC: 3569 Filters, general line: industrial

HQ: Environmental Filtration Technologies
Llc
4404a Chesapeake Dr
Charlotte NC 28216
704 399-7441

(G-1763)
BEACON ROOFING SUPPLY INC
Also Called: Lyf-Tym Building Products
1836 Equitable Pl (28213-6500)
PHONE.................................704 886-1555
EMP: 4
SALES (corp-wide): 9.76B **Publicly Held**
Web: www.lyftym.com
SIC: 5031 3444 3089 Lumber, plywood, and
millwork; Gutters, sheet metal; Windows,
plastics
PA: Beacon Roofing Supply, Inc.
505 Huntmar Pk Dr Ste 300
Herndon VA 20170
571 323-3939

(G-1764)
BEARDOWADAMS INC
3034 Horseshoe Ln (28208-6435)
PHONE.................................704 359-8443
Bob Adams, *Ch*
Thomas Semans, *Pr*
Mark Rowland, *Dir*
Nick Beardow, *Dir*
▲ EMP: 12 EST: 2012
SALES (est): 21.64MM
SALES (corp-wide): 3.57B **Publicly Held**
Web: www.beardowadams.com
SIC: 2891 Adhesives
HQ: H.B. Fuller U.K. Production Ltd
32 Blundells Road
Milton Keynes BUCKS MK13
190 857-4000

(G-1765)
BEATY CORPORATION
Also Called: Fastsigns
7407 N Tryon St (28262-5051)
PHONE.................................704 599-4949
EMP: 4 EST: 2020
SALES (est): 662.36K **Privately Held**
Web: www.fastsigns.com
SIC: 3993 Signs and advertising specialties

(G-1766)
BEAUTY 4 LOVE LLC
1819 Sardis Rd N Ste 350 (28270-2471)
PHONE.................................704 802-2844
EMP: 4
SALES (est): 305.71K **Privately Held**
SIC: 2844 Depilatories (cosmetic)

(G-1767)
BECO HOLDING COMPANY INC (PA)
Also Called: Brooks Equipment
10926 David Taylor Dr Ste 300 (28262)
P.O. Box 481888 (28269)
PHONE.................................800 826-3473
Eric Smith, *Pr*
Richard Fairclough, *
EMP: 115 EST: 1998
SQ FT: 30,000
SALES (est): 132.17MM **Privately Held**
Web: www.brooksequipment.com
SIC: 5099 5087 3569 Fire extinguishers;
Firefighting equipment; Firefighting and
related equipment

(G-1768)
BELHAM MANAGEMENT IND LLC
9307 Monroe Rd Ste A (28270-1484)
PHONE.................................704 815-4246
Ben Green, *Mgr*
EMP: 8 EST: 1980
SQ FT: 2,100

SALES (est): 492.54K **Privately Held**
Web: www.bmienergy.com
SIC: 8711 1731 3822 Energy conservation
engineering; Energy management controls;
Air conditioning and refrigeration controls

(G-1769)
BELK DEPARTMENT STORES LP
2801 W Tyvola Rd (28217-4525)
PHONE.................................704 357-4000
Belk Mckay, *Mng Pt*
William R Langley, *Pt*
EMP: 35 EST: 2002
SALES (est): 4.65MM **Publicly Held**
SIC: 2211 5311 Dress fabrics, cotton;
Department stores
HQ: Belk, Inc.
2801 W Tyvola Rd
Charlotte NC 28217
704 357-1000

(G-1770)
BELLAIRE DYNAMIK LLC
4714 Stockholm Ct (28273-5900)
PHONE.................................704 779-3755
Sergio Koppany, *Managing Member*
▲ EMP: 4 EST: 2012
SALES (est): 4MM **Privately Held**
Web: www.b-dynamik.com
SIC: 2273 Carpets and rugs

(G-1771)
**BENDEL TANK HEAT EXCHANGER
LLC**
4823 N Graham St (28269-4822)
PHONE.................................704 596-5112
Bill Beaver, *Pr*
Mark Oleskiewicz, *CFO*
EMP: 24 EST: 2020
SALES (est): 1.48MM **Privately Held**
Web: www.bendel.com
SIC: 3443 Tanks, standard or custom
fabricated: metal plate

(G-1772)
BERLIN PACKAGING LLC
8008 Corporate Center Dr Ste 208
(28226-4489)
PHONE.................................704 612-4500
EMP: 6
SALES (corp-wide): 545.85MM **Privately
Held**
Web: www.berlinpackaging.com
SIC: 5199 2631 3086 4783 Packaging
materials; Container, packaging, and
boxboard; Packaging and shipping
materials, foamed plastics; Containerization
of goods for shipping
HQ: Berlin Packaging L.L.C.
525 W Monroe St
Chicago IL 60661
312 876-9292

(G-1773)
BERRY GLOBAL INC
Also Called: Berry Plastics
9335 Harris Corners Pkwy Ste 300
(28269-3818)
PHONE.................................704 697-5100
EMP: 560
Web: www.berryglobal.com
SIC: 2297 2392 Spunbonded fabrics; Slip
covers and pads
HQ: Berry Global, Inc.
101 Oakley St
Evansville IN 47710

(G-1774)
BESTDRIVE LLC (DH)
9827 Mount Holly Rd (28214-9214)
PHONE.................................800 450-3187

Jochen Etzel, *Managing Member*
EMP: 26 EST: 2015
SALES (est): 74.12MM
SALES (corp-wide): 45.02B **Privately Held**
Web: www.bestdrivetire.com
SIC: 5014 3011 Tires and tubes; Tires and
inner tubes
HQ: Continental Tire The Americas, Llc
1830 Macmillan Park Dr
Fort Mill SC 29707
800 847-3349

(G-1775)
BETEK TOOLS INC
8325 Arrowridge Blvd Ste A (28273-5603)
PHONE.................................980 498-2523
Hannes Redman, *CEO*
▲ EMP: 11 EST: 2015
SALES (est): 3.08MM
SALES (corp-wide): 1.96B **Privately Held**
Web: www.betek.de
SIC: 3541 3313 Electrolytic metal cutting
machine tools; Tungsten carbide powder
HQ: Betek Gmbh & Co. Kg
Sulgener Str. 21-23
Aichhalden BW 78733
74225650

(G-1776)
BEVANS STEEL FABRICATION INC
4017 Hargrove Ave (28208-5503)
PHONE.................................704 395-0200
Paul Bevans, *Pr*
Irene Bevans, *VP*
EMP: 13 EST: 2004
SALES (est): 2.09MM **Privately Held**
Web: www.bevanssteel.com
SIC: 3441 Fabricated structural metal

(G-1777)
BEVS & BITES LLC
Also Called: Bruce Julian Heritage Foods
2913 Selwyn Ave (28209-1734)
PHONE.................................704 247-7573
Bruce Julian, *Managing Member*
EMP: 5 EST: 2014
SALES (est): 498.56K **Privately Held**
SIC: 2033 2035 Tomato cocktails: packaged
in cans, jars, etc.; Vegetables, pickled

(G-1778)
BI COUNTY GAS PRODUCERS LLC
10600 Nations Ford Rd (28273-5762)
PHONE.................................704 844-8990
William Brinker, *Owner*
EMP: 7 EST: 2009
SALES (est): 1.49MM **Privately Held**
Web: www.landfillgroup.com
SIC: 1321 Natural gas liquids

(G-1779)
BIC CORPORATION
5900 Long Creek Park Dr (28269-3737)
PHONE.................................704 598-7700
Tod Adams, *Mgr*
EMP: 99
SALES (corp-wide): 844.79MM **Privately
Held**
Web: corporate.bic.com
SIC: 3951 3421 5091 5112 Pens and
mechanical pencils; Cutlery; Sporting and
recreation goods; Stationery and office
supplies
HQ: Bic Corporation
1 Bic Way Ste 1
Shelton CT 06484
203 783-2000

(G-1780)
BIESSE AMERICA INC
Intermac Glass and Stone Div
4110 Meadow Oak Dr (28208-7721)
PHONE.................................704 357-3131
EMP: 10
SQ FT: 36,000
Web: www.intermac.com
SIC: 3559 Glass making machinery: blowing,
molding, forming, etc.
HQ: Biesse America, Inc.
4110 Meadow Oak Dr
Charlotte NC 28208

(G-1781)
BILGE MASTERS INC
6239 River Cabin Ln (28278-6574)
PHONE.................................704 995-4293
EMP: 6
SALES (est): 105.86K **Privately Held**
Web: www.clippinslawncare.com
SIC: 3732 Boatbuilding and repairing

(G-1782)
BILL TRUITT WOOD WORKS INC
3124 W Trade St # B (28208-3386)
PHONE.................................704 398-8499
Bill Truitt, *Pr*
EMP: 6 EST: 1974
SQ FT: 6,500
SALES (est): 240.29K **Privately Held**
Web: www.btwoodworks.com
SIC: 2434 Wood kitchen cabinets

(G-1783)
BINDERS INCORPORATED
1303 Upper Asbury Ave (28206-1527)
PHONE.................................704 377-9704
TOLL FREE: 800
Ronald Lee, *Pr*
EMP: 13 EST: 1981
SQ FT: 14,000
SALES (est): 2.32MM **Privately Held**
Web: www.bindersinc.com
SIC: 2782 Looseleaf binders and devices

(G-1784)
BIOSELECT INC
4740 Dwight Evans Rd (28217-0982)
P.O. Box 221216 (28222-1216)
PHONE.................................704 521-8585
Kathi Levine, *Pr*
▲ EMP: 6 EST: 2008
SALES (est): 240.26K **Privately Held**
Web: www.bioselect.com
SIC: 2673 3089 Food storage and frozen
food bags, plastic; Cups, plastics, except
foam

(G-1785)
BIOTAGE LLC (HQ)
10430 Harris Oak Blvd Ste C (28269)
PHONE.................................704 654-4900
Torben Jorgensen, *CEO*
Ed Connell, *Treas*
▲ EMP: 90 EST: 2001
SQ FT: 51,000
SALES (est): 45.4MM **Privately Held**
Web: www.biotage.com
SIC: 3829 Chronometers, electronic
PA: Biotage Ab
Uppsala

(G-1786)
BIOVIND LLC
2219 Vail Ave (28207-1529)
PHONE.................................512 217-3077
Ehinomen Iyoha-nwani, *CEO*
EMP: 4 EST: 2021
SALES (est): 95.66K **Privately Held**

SIC: 3821 Laboratory apparatus, except heating and measuring

(G-1787)
BJMF INC
8200 South Blvd (28273-6916)
PHONE...............................704 554-6333
EMP: 40
SIC: 2515 5712 Mattresses and bedsprings; Mattresses

(G-1788)
BLACK & DECKER CORPORATION
Also Called: Black & Decker
15040 Choate Cir (28273-6947)
PHONE...............................803 396-3700
John Petza, *Brnch Mgr*
EMP: 6
SALES (corp-wide): 15.78B **Publicly Held**
Web: www.blackanddecker.com
SIC: 3546 Power-driven handtools
HQ: The Black & Decker Corporation
701 E Joppa Rd
Towson MD 21286
410 716-3900

(G-1789)
BLAZING FOODS LLC
1520 West Blvd (28208-7070)
PHONE...............................336 865-2933
David Foy, *Managing Member*
EMP: 6 EST: 2018
SALES (est): 415.34K **Privately Held**
Web: www.blazingfoods2.com
SIC: 5499 2096 Gourmet food stores; Potato chips and similar snacks

(G-1790)
BLUE HORSESHOE
13024 Ballantyne Corporate Pl (28277-2113)
PHONE...............................980 312-8202
EMP: 6 EST: 2016
SALES (est): 726.54K **Privately Held**
SIC: 3462 Horseshoes

(G-1791)
BLUESKYE AUTOMATION LLC
440 E Westinghouse Blvd (28273-5769)
PHONE...............................404 998-1320
EMP: 50 EST: 2019
SALES (est): 4.68MM **Privately Held**
Web: www.blueskye.com
SIC: 3569 Liquid automation machinery and equipment

(G-1792)
BLUMENTHAL HOLDINGS LLC (PA)
1355 Greenwood Clfs Ste 200 (28204-2982)
PHONE...............................704 688-2302
Alan Blumenthal, *Managing Member*
EMP: 6 EST: 2010
SALES (est): 11.95MM
SALES (corp-wide): 11.95MM **Privately Held**
Web: www.gunk.com
SIC: 2992 Lubricating oils and greases

(G-1793)
BLYTHE CONSTRUCTION INC (DH)
2911 N Graham St (28206-3535)
P.O. Box 31635 (28231-1635)
PHONE...............................704 375-8474
Bill Carphardt, *Pr*
Alan Cahill, *
J Mcbryde, *VP*
Fred Odea, *
▲ EMP: 300 EST: 1949
SQ FT: 18,500

SALES (est): 159.07MM
SALES (corp-wide): 21.74MM **Privately Held**
Web: www.blytheconstruction.com
SIC: 1611 1622 2951 Highway and street paving contractor; Bridge construction; Asphalt and asphaltic paving mixtures (not from refineries)
HQ: The Hubbard Group Inc
1936 Lee Rd Ste 101
Winter Park FL 32789
407 645-5500

(G-1794)
BMA AMERICA INC
2020 Starita Rd Ste E (28206-1298)
PHONE...............................970 353-3770
Dennis Brice, *Pr*
◆ EMP: 15 EST: 1926
SALES (est): 3.87MM
SALES (corp-wide): 136.17MM **Privately Held**
Web: www.bma-america.us
SIC: 3441 3443 Fabricated structural metal; Fabricated plate work (boiler shop)
HQ: Bma Braunschweigische Maschinenbauanstalt Gmbh
Am Alten Bahnhof 5
Braunschweig NI 38122
5318040

(G-1795)
BOB TRAILERS INC
13501 S Ridge Dr (28273-6741)
PHONE...............................208 375-5171
EMP: 25
SIC: 3799 Trailers and trailer equipment

(G-1796)
BOEING COMPANY
Also Called: Boeing
4930 Minuteman Way (28208-3866)
PHONE...............................704 572-8280
EMP: 6 EST: 2018
SALES (est): 1.7MM **Privately Held**
Web: jobs.boeing.com
SIC: 3721 Aircraft

(G-1797)
BOINGO GRAPHICS INC
656 Michael Wylie Dr (28217-1545)
PHONE...............................704 527-4963
Edward Nowokunski, *Ch*
Scott Nowokunski, *
Carolyn Nowokunski, *
Linda Kirby, *
EMP: 37 EST: 1979
SQ FT: 24,000
SALES (est): 8.46MM **Privately Held**
Web: www.boingographics.com
SIC: 2752 2791 2789 2675 Offset printing; Typesetting; Bookbinding and related work; Die-cut paper and board

(G-1798)
BONOMI NORTH AMERICA INC
306 Forsyth Hall Dr (28273-5817)
PHONE...............................704 412-9031
Aldo Bonomi, *Pr*
Alberto Malaguti, *Genl Mgr*
▲ EMP: 17 EST: 2005
SALES (est): 8.44MM
SALES (corp-wide): 365.34MM **Privately Held**
Web: www.bonominorthamerica.com
SIC: 5085 3593 3491 3494 Valves and fittings; Fluid power actuators, hydraulic or pneumatic; Industrial valves; Plumbing and heating valves
PA: Bonomi Group Spa
Via Massimo Bonomi 1

Gussago BS 25064
030 825-0011

(G-1799)
BONSAL AMERICAN INC (DH)
625 Griffith Rd Ste 100 (28217-3576)
PHONE...............................704 525-1621
David J Maske, *Pr*
Robert D Quinn, *
Barry Hirsch, *
Marsha Lewis, *
Gil Seco, *
◆ EMP: 60 EST: 1895
SQ FT: 20,000
SALES (est): 95.68MM
SALES (corp-wide): 34.95B **Privately Held**
SIC: 3272 1442 3253 2899 Dry mixture concrete; Construction sand and gravel; Ceramic wall and floor tile; Chemical preparations, nec
HQ: Crh Americas, Inc.
900 Ashwood Pkwy Ste 600
Atlanta GA 30338
770 804-3363

(G-1800)
BORDER CONCEPTS INC (PA)
Also Called: B C I
15720 Brixham Hill Ave Ste 120 (28277)
PHONE...............................704 541-5509
Neil R Miller, *Pr*
Tony Ferguson, *VP*
Anthony J Fergusonf, *VP*
David Larr, *Dir*
Sandy Peterson, *Contrlr*
◆ EMP: 7 EST: 1990
SALES (est): 21.99MM **Privately Held**
Web: www.borderconcepts.com
SIC: 3317 3446 3269 Steel pipe and tubes; Architectural metalwork; Art and ornamental ware, pottery

(G-1801)
BOSCH REXROTH CORPORATION (DH)
Also Called: Indramat Div
14001 S Lakes Dr South Point Business Park (28273)
P.O. Box 3264 (48333)
PHONE...............................704 583-4338
Paul Cooke, *Pr*
Ken Hank, *
Steve Roberts, *
▲ EMP: 40 EST: 1967
SALES (est): 564.89MM
SALES (corp-wide): 391.51MM **Privately Held**
Web: www.boschrexroth-us.com
SIC: 5084 3714 Hydraulic systems equipment and supplies; Acceleration equipment, motor vehicle
HQ: Bosch Rexroth Ag
Zum EisengieBer 1
Lohr A. Main BY 97816
9352180

(G-1802)
BOSTON GEAR LLC
701 Carrier Dr (28216-3445)
PHONE...............................704 588-5610
EMP: 270 EST: 2004
SALES (est): 36.63MM
SALES (corp-wide): 6.03B **Publicly Held**
Web: www.bostongear.com
SIC: 3568 5085 Power transmission equipment, nec; Power transmission equipment and apparatus
HQ: Altra Industrial Motion Corp.
300 Granite St Ste 201
Braintree MA 02184
781 917-0600

(G-1803)
BOTTOMLINE MEDICAL
5200 Milford Rd (28210-2846)
P.O. Box 12214 (28220-2214)
PHONE...............................704 527-0919
EMP: 8 EST: 2006
SALES (est): 160K **Privately Held**
Web: www.bottomline.com
SIC: 7372 Business oriented computer software

(G-1804)
BOUGIEJONES
5212 Galway Dr (28215-3131)
PHONE...............................704 492-3029
Cassandra Jones, *CEO*
EMP: 4 EST: 2021
SALES (est): 41.02K **Privately Held**
SIC: 3944 Craft and hobby kits and sets

(G-1805)
BOWMAN-HOLLIS MANUFACTURING CO (PA)
2925 Old Steele Creek Rd (28208-6726)
P.O. Box 19249 (28219-9249)
PHONE...............................704 374-1500
Tom Bowman, *Pr*
Russ Bowman, *
Debbie Price, *
Ann Bowman, *
▲ EMP: 35 EST: 1956
SQ FT: 20,000
SALES (est): 9.08MM
SALES (corp-wide): 9.08MM **Privately Held**
Web: www.bowmanhollis.com
SIC: 3552 7699 Textile machinery; Industrial machinery and equipment repair

(G-1806)
BRANDEL LLC
2909 Rockbrook Dr (28211-2641)
PHONE...............................704 525-4548
Prescott Little, *Prin*
EMP: 4 EST: 2011
SALES (est): 453.97K **Privately Held**
Web: www.brandel.com
SIC: 3841 Surgical and medical instruments

(G-1807)
BRANDRPM LLC
Also Called: Brandrpm
9555 Monroe Rd (28270-1446)
PHONE...............................704 225-1800
Vivienne Anderson, *Managing Member*
Vivienne S Anderson, *Managing Member*
EMP: 96 EST: 1998
SQ FT: 40,000
SALES (est): 18.42MM **Privately Held**
Web: www.brandrpm.com
SIC: 2396 5941 Screen printing on fabric articles; Team sports equipment

(G-1808)
BREEZEPLAY LLC
8045 Corporate Center Dr (28226-4555)
PHONE...............................980 297-0885
Rick Sabath, *CEO*
EMP: 18 EST: 2008
SQ FT: 2,500
SALES (est): 459.65K **Privately Held**
SIC: 3825 Energy measuring equipment, electrical

(G-1809)
BREEZER HOLDINGS LLC
Also Called: Breezer Mobile Cooling
4835 Sirona Dr Ste 400 (28273-3245)
PHONE...............................844 233-5673
Brian Street, *Pr*

Zena Clarke, *
Joe Fairleigh, *
Ofir Baharav, *
◆ **EMP: 85 EST:** 2010
SALES (est): 24.68MM **Privately Held**
Web: www.powerbreezer.com
SIC: 3564 Blowers and fans

(G-1810)
BREW PUBLIK INCORPORATED
312 W Park Ave (28203-4441)
PHONE..............................704 231-2703
Charles Vincent Mulligan, *Prin*
EMP: 5 **EST:** 2015
SALES (est): 203.15K **Privately Held**
Web: www.brewpublik.beer
SIC: 2082 Malt beverages

(G-1811)
BREWITT & DREENKUPP INC
Also Called: Tea Rex Teahouse
4321 Stuart Andrew Blvd Ste I
(28217-4625)
PHONE..............................704 525-3366
Wayne Powers, *Prin*
EMP: 4 **EST:** 1997
SALES (est): 176.08K **Privately Held**
Web: www.tearex.com
SIC: 2086 5812 Tea, iced: packaged in cans,
bottles, etc.; Coffee shop

(G-1812)
BRISTOL-MYERS SQUIBB COMPANY
Also Called: Bristol-Myers Squibb
P.O. Box 751095 (28275)
PHONE..............................800 321-1335
EMP: 4
SALES (corp-wide): 48.3B **Publicly Held**
Web: www.bms.com
SIC: 2834 Pharmaceutical preparations
PA: Bristol-Myers Squibb Company
Route 206/Prvince Line Rd
Princeton NJ 08540
609 252-4621

(G-1813)
BROWN MITCHELL HODGES LLC
Also Called: Playerz Haul
4111 Rose Lake Dr Ste E Pmb 678
(28217-2864)
PHONE..............................800 477-8982
Latonya Brown, *Managing Member*
Kathy Brown, *Prin*
Dana Brown, *Prin*
Tracey Brown, *Prin*
Linda Fleet, *Prin*
EMP: 5 **EST:** 2020
SALES (est): 90.11K **Privately Held**
Web: www.playerzhaul.com
SIC: 7929 7993 3711 Entertainment service;
Video game arcade; Mobile lounges (motor
vehicle), assembly of

(G-1814)
BROWN PRINTING INC
Also Called: AlphaGraphics
9129 Monroe Rd Ste 160 (28270-2431)
P.O. Box 279 (28106-0279)
PHONE..............................704 849-9292
Kedar Brown, *Pr*
EMP: 8 **EST:** 2009
SALES (est): 345.85K **Privately Held**
Web: www.alphagraphics.com
SIC: 2752 Commercial printing, lithographic

(G-1815)
BSN MEDICAL INC (DH)
5825 Carnegie Blvd (28209-4633)
PHONE..............................704 554-9933
Darrell Jenkins, *Pr*
Steve Brown, *

Shawn Fry, *
◆ **EMP:** 110 **EST:** 2000
SQ FT: 12,000
SALES (est): 44.59MM
SALES (corp-wide): 14B **Privately Held**
Web: medical.essityusa.com
SIC: 3842 Orthopedic appliances
HQ: Bsn Medical Gmbh
Schutzenstr. 1-3
Hamburg HH 22761
40593612100

(G-1816)
BTHEC INC
4823 N Graham St (28269-4822)
PHONE..............................704 596-5112
EMP: 36
Web: www.bendelcorp.com
SIC: 3443 Tanks, standard or custom
fabricated: metal plate

(G-1817)
BUCKEYE INTERNATIONAL INC
Also Called: Buckeye Cleaning Center
4123 Revolution Park Dr Ste A
(28217-1522)
PHONE..............................704 523-9400
Brian Morabito, *Brnch Mgr*
EMP: 5
SALES (corp-wide): 93.17MM **Privately
Held**
Web: www.buckeyeinternational.com
SIC: 2842 2841 2899 2812 Specialty
cleaning; Detergents, synthetic organic or
inorganic alkaline; Chemical preparations,
nec; Alkalies and chlorine
PA: Buckeye International, Inc.
2700 Wagner Pl
Maryland Heights MO 63043
314 291-1900

(G-1818)
**BULL ENGINEERED PRODUCTS INC
(PA)**
Also Called: Bull
12001 Steele Creek Rd (28273)
P.O. Box 39170 (28278)
PHONE..............................704 504-0300
Gary Dickison, *Pr*
▲ **EMP:** 37 **EST:** 2001
SALES (est): 9.86MM
SALES (corp-wide): 9.86MM **Privately
Held**
Web: www.bullep.com
SIC: 3089 Molding primary plastics

(G-1819)
**BURROWS PAPER CORPORATION
(DH)**
3436 Toringdon Way Ste 100 (28277-2449)
P.O. Box 987 (13365-0987)
PHONE..............................800 272-7122
◆ **EMP:** 200 **EST:** 1919
SALES (est): 41.38MM
SALES (corp-wide): 26.11B **Publicly Held**
Web: www.burrowspaper.com
SIC: 2621 2671 2611 2679 Tissue paper;
Waxed paper: made from purchased
material; Pulp manufactured from waste or
recycled paper; Food dishes and utensils,
from pressed and molded pulp
HQ: Novolex Holdings, Llc
3436 Tringdon Way Ste 100
Charlotte NC 28277
800 845-6051

(G-1820)
BUSINESS JOURNALS (DH)
120 W Morehead St Ste 420 (28202-1874)
PHONE..............................704 371-3248
Mike Olivieri, *Pr*

Tina Carusillo, *
EMP: 9 **EST:** 1986
SALES (est): 5.95MM
SALES (corp-wide): 2.88B **Privately Held**
Web: www.sportsbusinessjournal.com
SIC: 2711 Newspapers, publishing and
printing
HQ: American City Business Journals, Inc.
120 W Morehead St Ste 400
Charlotte NC 28202
704 973-1000

(G-1821)
BUSINESS SYSTEMS OF AMERICA
3020 Prosperity Church Rd (28269-7197)
PHONE..............................704 766-2755
Eric S Martin, *Prin*
EMP: 4 **EST:** 2015
SALES (est): 482.29K **Privately Held**
Web: www.ordersplus.com
SIC: 7372 Prepackaged software

(G-1822)
BUSINESS WISE INC
615 S College St Ste 810 (28202-3355)
PHONE..............................704 554-4112
Lee Martin, *Brnch Mgr*
EMP: 5
SALES (corp-wide): 2.42MM **Privately
Held**
Web: www.businesswise.com
SIC: 2754 Commercial printing, gravure
PA: Business Wise Inc
5641 Bahia Mar Cir
Stone Mountain GA 30087
770 956-1955

(G-1823)
BWX TECHNOLOGIES INC
11525 N Community House Rd Ste 600
(28277-0770)
PHONE..............................980 365-4000
Peyton S Baker, *Brnch Mgr*
EMP: 97
Web: www.bwxt.com
SIC: 3621 Power generators
PA: Bwx Technologies, Inc.
800 Main St Fl 4
Lynchburg VA 24504

(G-1824)
BWXT INVESTMENT COMPANY (HQ)
Also Called: B&W
13024 Ballantyne Corporate Pl Ste 700
(28277-0496)
PHONE..............................704 625-4900
Peyton Baker, *Pr*
EMP: 21 **EST:** 1990
SALES (est): 1.38B **Publicly Held**
Web: www.babcock.com
SIC: 3511 3564 1629 1541 Turbines and
turbine generator set units, complete;
Purification and dust collection equipment;
Industrial plant construction; Industrial
buildings, new construction, nec
PA: Bwx Technologies, Inc.
800 Main St Fl 4
Lynchburg VA 24504

(G-1825)
BWXT MPOWER INC
11525 N Community House Rd Ste 600
(28277-3609)
PHONE..............................980 365-4000
William Fox, *Pr*
Jason Kerr, *
David Black, *
EMP: 11 **EST:** 2012
SALES (est): 2.44MM **Publicly Held**
Web: www.bwxt.com

SIC: 3443 Fabricated plate work (boiler shop)
PA: Bwx Technologies, Inc.
800 Main St Fl 4
Lynchburg VA 24504

(G-1826)
BYMONETCROCHET
8536 Caden Lee Way Apt 2208
(28273-8026)
PHONE..............................443 613-1736
EMP: 4 **EST:** 2016
SALES (est): 106.7K **Privately Held**
Web: www.bymonetcrochet.com
SIC: 2399 Hand woven and crocheted
products

(G-1827)
C D STAMPLEY ENTERPRISES INC
6100 Orr Rd (28213-6326)
P.O. Box 33172 (28233-3172)
PHONE..............................704 333-6631
Crews Walden, *Pr*
Sam C Walden, *VP*
Zella Stampley, *VP*
◆ **EMP:** 10 **EST:** 1940
SQ FT: 13,082
SALES (est): 811.45K **Privately Held**
Web: www.stampley.com
SIC: 2731 Books, publishing only

(G-1828)
CABINETS PLUS INC
8431 Old Statesville Rd (28269-1852)
PHONE..............................718 213-3300
EMP: 5 **EST:** 2012
SALES (est): 134.82K **Privately Held**
SIC: 2434 Wood kitchen cabinets

(G-1829)
CABINETWORKS GROUP MICH LLC
1200 Westinghouse Blvd Ste O
(28273-6313)
PHONE..............................803 984-2285
Ken Spangler, *Brnch Mgr*
EMP: 20
SALES (corp-wide): 486.01MM **Privately
Held**
Web: www.cabinetworksgroup.com
SIC: 2434 Wood kitchen cabinets
PA: Cabinetworks Group Michigan, Llc
20000 Victor Pkwy
Livonia MI 48152
734 205-4600

(G-1830)
CABLE DEVICES INCORPORATED
10736 Nations Ford Rd (28273-5773)
PHONE..............................704 588-0859
Joseph R Hynes, *Brnch Mgr*
EMP: 10
Web: www.commscope.com
SIC: 3663 Radio and t.v. communications
equipment
HQ: Cable Devices Incorporated
3642 E Us Highway 70
Hickory NC 28602
714 554-4370

(G-1831)
CAESARSTONE TECH USA INC (HQ)
1401 W Morehead St Ste 100
(28208-5261)
PHONE..............................818 779-0999
Yos Shiran, *Pr*
Alexios Vorissis, *CFO*
▲ **EMP:** 7 **EST:** 2012
SQ FT: 23,800
SALES (est): 16.23MM **Privately Held**
Web: www.caesarstoneus.com
SIC: 3281 Marble, building: cut and shaped
PA: Caesarstone Ltd

▲ = Import　▼ = Export
◆ = Import/Export

M.P. Menashe
Sdot Yam 37804

(G-1832)

CAMELOT COMPUTERS INC

Also Called: Camelot Software Consulting
10020 Park Cedar Dr Ste 205
(28210-8912)
PHONE......................704 554-1670
Randy Stephenson, *Pr*
EMP: 10 **EST:** 1985
SQ FT: 2,204
SALES (est): 489.48K **Privately Held**
Web: www.3plsoftware.com
SIC: 7371 7372 Computer software systems analysis and design, custom; Prepackaged software

(G-1833)

CAMSTAR SYSTEMS INC

13024 Ballantyne Corporate Pl
(28277-2113)
PHONE......................704 227-6600
EMP: 110
SIC: 7372 8748 8742 8243 Educational computer software; Systems engineering consultant, ex. computer or professional; Training and development consultant; Software training, computer

(G-1834)

CAN-AM CUSTOM TRUCKS INC

1734 University Commercial Pl
(28213-6444)
PHONE......................704 334-0322
Terry Potts, *Pr*
Tammy Potts-mcelreath, *VP*
EMP: 8 **EST:** 1998
SALES (est): 1.47MM **Privately Held**
Web: www.canamcustomtrucks.com
SIC: 3711 3713 3714 Truck and tractor truck assembly; Truck bodies and parts; Motor vehicle body components and frame

(G-1835)

CANDIES ITALIAN ICEE LLC

3428 Nevin Brook Rd Ste 101
(28269-2917)
PHONE......................980 475-7429
EMP: 5 **EST:** 2020
SALES (est): 119.5K **Privately Held**
SIC: 2656 Frozen food and ice cream containers

(G-1836)

CANVAS SX LLC (HQ)

6325 Ardrey Kell Rd Ste 400 (28277-4967)
PHONE......................980 474-3700
Eugene J Lowe Iii, *Pr*
Patrick J O'leary, *Ch Bd*
Mark A Carano, *VP*
Natausha H White, *Chief Human Resources Officer*
John W Nurkin, *VP*
◆ **EMP:** 200 **EST:** 2022
SALES (est): 1.22B
SALES (corp-wide): 1.83B **Privately Held**
Web: www.spx.com
SIC: 3829 3443 3599 3559 Measuring and controlling devices, nec; Heat exchangers, condensers, and components; Air intake filters, internal combustion engine, except auto; Automotive related machinery
PA: Canvas Holdco, Llc
    7401 W 129th St
    Overland Park KS

(G-1837)

CAPTIVE-AIRE SYSTEMS INC

6303 Carmel Rd Ste 105 (28226-8281)
PHONE......................704 844-9088

Avery Grant, *Brnch Mgr*
EMP: 9
SALES (corp-wide): 485.13MM **Privately Held**
Web: www.captiveaire.com
SIC: 3444 Sheet metalwork
PA: Captive-Aire Systems, Inc.
    4641 Pragon Pk Rd Ste 104
    Raleigh NC 27616
    919 882-2410

(G-1838)

CARAUSTAR INDUSTRIES INC

Also Called: Charlotte Recycling Plant
4915 Hovis Rd (28208-1512)
PHONE......................704 333-5488
Joe Cippletti, *Genl Mgr*
EMP: 16
SALES (corp-wide): 5.45B **Publicly Held**
Web: www.greif.com
SIC: 2631 Paperboard mills
HQ: Caraustar Industries, Inc.
    5000 Astell Pwdr Sprng Rd
    Austell GA 30106
    770 948-3101

(G-1839)

CARAUSTAR INDUSTRIES INC

Also Called: Carolina Carton Plant
8800 Crump Rd (28273-7243)
P.O. Box 32816 (28232-2816)
PHONE......................704 554-5796
Jimmy Hendrix, *Mgr*
EMP: 19
SQ FT: 112,570
SALES (corp-wide): 5.45B **Publicly Held**
Web: www.greif.com
SIC: 2631 Paperboard mills
HQ: Caraustar Industries, Inc.
    5000 Astell Pwdr Sprng Rd
    Austell GA 30106
    770 948-3101

(G-1840)

CARDINAL HEALTH 414 LLC

Also Called: Cardinal Health 414
3845 Shopton Rd Ste 18a (28217-3027)
PHONE......................704 644-7989
James Smith, *Prin*
EMP: 9
SALES (corp-wide): 226.83B **Publicly Held**
SIC: 2834 2835 Pharmaceutical preparations; Radioactive diagnostic substances
HQ: Cardinal Health, Llc
    7000 Cardinal Pl
    Dublin OH 43017
    614 757-5000

(G-1841)

CARGILL INCORPORATED

Also Called: Cargill
5000 South Blvd (28217-2700)
PHONE......................704 523-0414
Jerry Zajecek, *BD*
EMP: 94
SALES (corp-wide): 159.59B **Privately Held**
Web: www.cargill.com
SIC: 2048 Prepared feeds, nec
PA: Cargill, Incorporated
    15407 Mcginty Rd W
    Wayzata MN 55391
    800 227-4455

(G-1842)

CARLISLE CORPORATION

Also Called: Carlisle Syntec Systems A Div
11605 N Community House Rd
(28277-4797)
PHONE......................704 501-1100

Stephen P Munn, *CEO*
David A Roberts, *
Dennis J Hall, *Vice Chairman**
John S Barsanti, *
Steven J Ford, *Secretary General**
◆ **EMP:** 6973 **EST:** 1968
SQ FT: 15,500
SALES (est): 23.51MM
SALES (corp-wide): 5B **Publicly Held**
Web: www.carlisle.com
SIC: 2952 2899 3011 2295 Roofing materials; Waterproofing compounds; Industrial tires, pneumatic; Tape, varnished: plastic, and other coated (except magnetic)
PA: Carlisle Companies Incorporated
    16430 N Scttsdale Rd Ste
    Scottsdale AZ 85254
    480 781-5000

(G-1843)

CAROCRAFT CABINETS INC

1932 Statesville Ave (28206-3059)
P.O. Box 11739 (28220-1739)
PHONE......................704 376-0022
Larry Stroud, *Pr*
Michael L Stroud, *
EMP: 37 **EST:** 1976
SQ FT: 30,000
SALES (est): 2.49MM **Privately Held**
Web: www.carocraftcabinets.com
SIC: 2434 Wood kitchen cabinets

(G-1844)

CAROLINA CARTRIDGE SYSTEMS INC

Also Called: Carolina Cartridge
516 E Hebron St (28273-5989)
P.O. Box 7304 (28241-7304)
PHONE......................704 347-2447
Sharon Summers, *CEO*
Jim Gammill, *VP*
John E Summers, *Dir*
Mark Summers, *Sec*
EMP: 20 **EST:** 1991
SQ FT: 20,000
SALES (est): 2.49MM **Privately Held**
Web: www.ccsinside.com
SIC: 3861 7378 Toners, prepared photographic (not made in chemical plants); Computer maintenance and repair

(G-1845)

CAROLINA CONCRETE INC

11509 Reames Rd (28269-7676)
PHONE......................704 596-6511
Danny Mcclain, *Mgr*
EMP: 15
SALES (corp-wide): 1.79MM **Privately Held**
Web: www.carolinaconcrete.net
SIC: 3273 Ready-mixed concrete
PA: Carolina Concrete, Inc.
    1316 Waxhaw Rd
    Matthews NC 28105
    704 821-7645

(G-1846)

CAROLINA FOODS LLC (PA)

1807 S Tryon St (28203-4471)
P.O. Box 896454 (28289)
PHONE......................704 333-9812
Dan Myers, *CEO*
Paul R Scarborough, *Pr*
Sallie Scarborough, *VP*
Kathryn Scarborough, *CFO*
▲ **EMP:** 325 **EST:** 1934
SQ FT: 250,000
SALES (est): 85.24MM
SALES (corp-wide): 85.24MM **Privately Held**
Web: www.carolinafoodsinc.com

SIC: 2051 Pastries, e.g. danish: except frozen

(G-1847)

CAROLINA FOUNDRY INC

228 W Tremont Ave (28203-4944)
PHONE......................704 376-3145
James L Griffin, *Pr*
EMP: 4 **EST:** 1946
SALES (est): 193.34K **Privately Held**
SIC: 3363 3364 Aluminum die-castings; Brass and bronze die-castings

(G-1848)

CAROLINA GOLFCO INC

209 E Exmore St (28217-1803)
PHONE......................704 525-7846
Ellen Dooley, *Pr*
William Dooley, *VP*
EMP: 5 **EST:** 1992
SQ FT: 3,000
SALES (est): 432.68K **Privately Held**
SIC: 2999 3523 0711 Waxes, petroleum: not produced in petroleum refineries; Turf and grounds equipment; Soil preparation services

(G-1849)

CAROLINA LAWNSCAPE INC

Also Called: Landscape Design & Lawn Maint
13105 Greencreek Dr (28273-6972)
PHONE......................803 230-5570
Octavius Watkins, *Pr*
EMP: 7 **EST:** 1993
SALES (est): 240.16K **Privately Held**
SIC: 0782 0781 3271 Lawn care services; Landscape services; Blocks, concrete: landscape or retaining wall

(G-1850)

CAROLINA MARBLE & GRANITE

1924 Dilworth Rd W (28203-5730)
PHONE......................704 523-2112
Terrell Fridell, *Pt*
EMP: 6 **EST:** 1907
SQ FT: 1,203
SALES (est): 284.25K **Privately Held**
Web: www.integrativehealth.com
SIC: 3281 1799 Monuments, cut stone (not finishing or lettering only); Sandblasting of building exteriors

(G-1851)

CAROLINA MOLDINGS INC

4601 Macie St (28217-1810)
P.O. Box 11324 (28220)
PHONE......................704 523-7471
Jack S Crouch Senior, *Pr*
EMP: 10 **EST:** 1975
SQ FT: 15,000
SALES (est): 2.14MM **Privately Held**
Web: www.carolinamoldings.com
SIC: 3089 5084 Injection molding of plastics; Meters, consumption registering

(G-1852)

CAROLINA PAPER GUYS LLC

5800 Brookshire Blvd (28216-3384)
P.O. Box 31543 (28231-1543)
PHONE......................704 980-3112
Freddy Grodino, *CEO*
Matthew Gragop, *Pr*
EMP: 4 **EST:** 2012
SALES (est): 320.52K **Privately Held**
Web: www.carolinapaperguys.com
SIC: 2621 Towels, tissues and napkins; paper and stock

(G-1853)
CAROLINA PARENTING INC (PA)
Also Called: Charlotte Parent
214 W Tremont Ave Ste 302 (28203-5161)
PHONE.................................704 344-1980
Mark Ethridge, *Pr*
Mary Kate Cline, *Mgr*
EMP: 15 EST: 1990
SALES (est): 362.86K **Privately Held**
Web: www.charlotteparent.com
SIC: 2721 Magazines: publishing only, not
printed on site

(G-1854)
CAROLINA PRODUCTS INC
Also Called: Honeywell Authorized Dealer
1132 Pro Am Dr (28211-1100)
PHONE.................................704 364-9029
John G Blackmon, *Pr*
William S Blackmon, .*
EMP: 36 EST: 1969
SALES (est): 5.14MM **Privately Held**
Web: www.cpipanels.com
SIC: 3613 3644 3585 3443 Switchgear and
switchboard apparatus; Electric outlet,
switch, and fuse boxes; Refrigeration and
heating equipment; Fabricated plate work
(boiler shop)

(G-1855)
CAROLINA SIGN CO INC
2925 Beatties Ford Rd (28216-3713)
PHONE.................................704 399-3995
Ruth Singleton, *Pr*
Bob Singleton, *VP*
EMP: 5 EST: 1984
SALES (est): 402.13K **Privately Held**
Web: www.carolinarealtysigns.com
SIC: 3993 Signs and advertising specialties

(G-1856)
**CAROLINA SIGNS AND WONDERS
INC**
Also Called: Provizion Led
1700 University Commercial Pl
(28213-6444)
PHONE.................................704 286-1343
Jacquelyn M Golbus, *CEO*
Jacquelyn M Golbus, *Pr*
Todd A Golbus, *COO*
EMP: 12 EST: 2020
SALES (est): 4.05MM **Privately Held**
Web: www.carolinasignage.com
SIC: 3993 Signs and advertising specialties

(G-1857)
CAROLINA SPECIALTIES INC
4230 Barringer Dr (28217-1512)
PHONE.................................704 525-9599
Richard Ealy, *Dir*
EMP: 4
Web: www.carospec.com
SIC: 3299 Stucco
PA: Carolina Specialties, Inc.
4706 Kirk Rd
Winston Salem NC 27103

(G-1858)
**CAROLINA SPRAL DUCT FBRCTION
L**
11524 Wilmar Blvd (28273-6448)
PHONE.................................704 395-3289
Hunter Edwards, *CEO*
Michael James, *Ex VP*
Jeff Tettambel, *VP*
Steve Mcdonald, *VP*
Wes Dunaway, *VP*
EMP: 6 EST: 2016
SALES (est): 1.93MM **Privately Held**

SIC: 3444 Sheet metalwork

(G-1859)
**CAROLINA TIME EQUIPMENT CO
INC (PA)**
Also Called: Carolina Time
1801 Norland Rd (28205-5707)
P.O. Box 18158 (28218-0158)
PHONE.................................704 536-2700
Henry Allen, *Pr*
Debra Jones, *
Alfred Tate, *
EMP: 24 EST: 1962
SQ FT: 26,000
SALES (est): 9.29MM
SALES (corp-wide): 9.29MM **Privately
Held**
Web: www.carolinatime.net
SIC: 3446 1731 3579 5063 Fences, gates,
posts, and flagpoles; Access control
systems specialization; Time clocks and
time recording devices; Service entrance
equipment, electrical

(G-1860)
CAROLINA TRAFFIC DEVICES INC
11900 Goodrich Dr (28278)
P.O. Box 38220 (28278)
PHONE.................................704 588-7055
William Curtin, *Pr*
EMP: 10 EST: 2002
SQ FT: 2,000
SALES (est): 2.47MM **Privately Held**
Web: www.carolinatraffic.com
SIC: 5082 3272 Road construction
equipment; Concrete products used to
facilitate drainage

(G-1861)
CAROLINA YORK LLC
1235 East Blvd Ste E Pmb 248
(28203-5876)
PHONE.................................704 237-0873
EMP: 10 EST: 2016
SALES (est): 641.68K **Privately Held**
Web: www.carolinayork.com
SIC: 3229 Candlesticks, glass

(G-1862)
**CAROLNAS TOP SHELF CSTM
CBNETS**
Also Called: Carolnas Top Shelf Cstm Cbnets
519 Armour Dr (28206)
PHONE.................................704 376-5844
Sherry Upchurch, *Managing Member*
EMP: 4 EST: 2014
SALES (est): 542.11K **Privately Held**
Web: www.ctscustom.com
SIC: 2541 2434 Cabinets, lockers, and
shelving; Wood kitchen cabinets

(G-1863)
CARRIER CORPORATION
Also Called: Carrier Chiller Op
9701 Old Statesville Rd (28269-7630)
PHONE.................................704 921-3800
Mike Mckee, *Mgr*
EMP: 200
SQ FT: 260,794
SALES (corp-wide): 22.49B **Publicly Held**
Web: www.carrier.com
SIC: 3585 Air conditioning equipment,
complete
HQ: Carrier Corporation
13995 Pasteur Blvd
Palm Beach Gardens FL 33418
561 365-2000

(G-1864)
**CARY MANUFACTURING
CORPORATION**
10815 John Price Rd Ste E (28273-4633)
PHONE.................................704 527-4402
Jim Kehoe, *Pr*
Lisa Kehoe, *Treas*
▲ EMP: 6 EST: 1978
SALES (est): 1.8MM **Privately Held**
Web: www.carymfg.com
SIC: 3589 3555 Vacuum cleaners and
sweepers, electric: industrial; Printing
trades machinery

(G-1865)
**CATAMOUNT ENERGY
CORPORATION (DH)**
550 S Tryon St (28202-4200)
PHONE.................................802 773-6684
James J Moore Junior, *CEO*
Joseph E Cofelice, *Pr*
Robert H Young, *Ch Bd*
Robert J Charlebois, *Sr VP*
EMP: 18 EST: 1986
SQ FT: 2,500
SALES (est): 5.75MM
SALES (corp-wide): 180.97MM **Publicly
Held**
SIC: 3569 Generators: steam, liquid oxygen,
or nitrogen
HQ: Degs Wind I, Llc
2801 Via Fortuna Ste 100
Austin TX 78746

(G-1866)
**CATES MECHANICAL
CORPORATION**
3901 Corporation Cir (28216-3420)
P.O. Box 550488 (28055-0488)
PHONE.................................704 458-5163
John Cates, *Pr*
John T Cates, *Pr*
EMP: 4 EST: 1969
SQ FT: 18,000
SALES (est): 407.93K **Privately Held**
Web: www.catesmechanical.com
SIC: 3565 3556 Packaging machinery; Food
products machinery

(G-1867)
CATHOLIC NEWS AND HERALD
Also Called: Cathedral Publishing
1123 S Church St (28203-4003)
PHONE.................................704 370-3333
Kevin Murray, *Supervisor*
EMP: 5 EST: 2000
SALES (est): 122.52K **Privately Held**
Web: www.catholicnewsherald.com
SIC: 2711 Newspapers, publishing and
printing

(G-1868)
CAUSA LLC
9303 Monroe Rd (28270-1472)
PHONE.................................866 695-7022
William Cameron, *Managing Member*
J Hayward Morgan, *Managing Member*
▲ EMP: 6 EST: 2011
SQ FT: 1,500
SALES (est): 284.59K **Privately Held**
Web: www.causadirect.in
SIC: 2326 Work apparel, except uniforms

(G-1869)
CBDMD INC (PA)
Also Called: Cbdmd
2101 Westinghouse Blvd Ste A (28273)
PHONE.................................704 445-3060
T Ronan Kennedy, *CFO*
Scott G Stephen, *Ch Bd*

Kevin Macdermott, *Pr*
Brad Whitford, *CAO*
EMP: 19 EST: 2015
SQ FT: 80,000
SALES (est): 19.48MM
SALES (corp-wide): 19.48MM **Publicly
Held**
Web: www.cbdmd.com
SIC: 2833 5961 2844 Medicinals and
botanicals; Catalog and mail-order houses;
Perfumes, cosmetics and other toilet
preparations

(G-1870)
CBS RADIO HOLDINGS INC
Also Called: W F N Z Radio Station
1520 South Blvd Ste 300 (28203-3701)
PHONE.................................704 319-9369
Bill Schoening, *Genl Mgr*
EMP: 40 EST: 2001
SALES (est): 239.57K **Privately Held**
Web: www.audacyinc.com
SIC: 7389 3663 Radio broadcasting music
checkers; Radio broadcasting and
communications equipment

(G-1871)
CCBCC INC
4115 Coca Cola Plz (28211-3400)
PHONE.................................704 557-4000
Hank W Flint, *Pr*
Umesh M Kasbekar, *
Clifford M Deal Iii, *VP*
EMP: 410 EST: 1994
SALES (est): 7.55MM
SALES (corp-wide): 6.9B **Publicly Held**
SIC: 2086 Bottled and canned soft drinks
PA: Coca-Cola Consolidated, Inc.
4100 Coca-Cola Plz
Charlotte NC 28211
980 392-8298

(G-1872)
CCBCC OPERATIONS LLC
Also Called: Coca-Cola
4115 Coca Cola Plz (28211-3400)
P.O. Box 31487 (28231-1487)
PHONE.................................704 557-4038
R Jack Hawkins, *Brnch Mgr*
EMP: 44
SALES (corp-wide): 6.9B **Publicly Held**
Web: www.cokeconsolidated.com
SIC: 2086 Bottled and canned soft drinks
HQ: Ccbcc Operations, Llc
4100 Coca-Cola Plz
Charlotte NC 28211
704 364-8728

(G-1873)
CCBCC OPERATIONS LLC
Also Called: Coca-Cola
4690 First Flight Dr (28208-5770)
PHONE.................................704 359-5600
Mark Chaney, *Brnch Mgr*
EMP: 10
SALES (corp-wide): 6.9B **Publicly Held**
Web: www.cokeconsolidated.com
SIC: 2086 Bottled and canned soft drinks
HQ: Ccbcc Operations, Llc
4100 Coca-Cola Plz
Charlotte NC 28211
704 364-8728

(G-1874)
CCBCC OPERATIONS LLC (HQ)
Also Called: Coca-Cola
4100 Coca Cola Plz (28211-3588)
P.O. Box 31487 (28231-1487)
PHONE.................................704 364-8728
J Frank Harrison Iii, *CEO*
EMP: 40 EST: 2003

SALES (est): 992.43MM
SALES (corp-wide): 6.9B Publicly Held
Web: www.cokeconsolidated.com
SIC: 2086 Bottled and canned soft drinks
PA: Coca-Cola Consolidated, Inc.
    4100 Coca-Cola Plz
    Charlotte NC 28211
    980 392-8298

(G-1875)
CCBCC OPERATIONS LLC
Also Called: Coca-Cola
801 Black Satchel Rd (28216-3453)
PHONE..................................704 399-6043
Guy Tarrance, *Mgr*
EMP: 42
SALES (corp-wide): 6.9B Publicly Held
Web: www.cokeconsolidated.com
SIC: 2086 Bottled and canned soft drinks
HQ: Ccbcc Operations, Llc
    4100 Coca-Cola Plz
    Charlotte NC 28211
    704 364-8728

(G-1876)
CCBCC OPERATIONS LLC
Also Called: Coca-Cola
920 Black Satchel Rd (28216)
PHONE..................................980 321-3226
Daniel Williams, *Brnch Mgr*
EMP: 129
SALES (corp-wide): 6.9B Publicly Held
Web: www.cokeconsolidated.com
SIC: 2086 Bottled and canned soft drinks
HQ: Ccbcc Operations, Llc
    4100 Coca-Cola Plz
    Charlotte NC 28211
    704 364-8728

(G-1877)
CCL LABEL INC
Also Called: Robbinsville Plant
4000 Westinghouse Blvd (28273-4518)
PHONE..................................704 714-4800
Geoff Martin, *Pr*
EMP: 146
SALES (corp-wide): 4.84B Privately Held
Web: www.cclind.com
SIC: 2759 Labels and seals: printing, nsk
HQ: Ccl Label, Inc.
    161 Worcester Rd Ste 603
    Framingham MA 01701
    508 872-4511

(G-1878)
CD DICKIE & ASSOCIATES INC
Also Called: Fastsigns
3400 S Tryon St Ste D (28217-1326)
PHONE..................................704 527-9102
Barbara Dickie, *Pr*
EMP: 11 EST: 1999
SALES (est): 597.52K Privately Held
Web: www.fastsigns.com
SIC: 7389 7336 3993 Lettering and sign
    painting services; Commercial art and
    graphic design; Signs and advertising
    specialties

(G-1879)
CDA INC
8500 S Tryon St (28273-3312)
▲ EMP: 186 EST: 2000
SQ FT: 60,000
SALES (est): 9.27MM Privately Held
Web: www.cdaenvironmental.com
SIC: 5099 3652 Compact discs; Prerecorded
    records and tapes

(G-1880)
CEAST USA INC
4816 Sirus Ln (28208-6391)
PHONE..................................704 423-0081
Mario Grosso, *Prin*
EMP: 4 EST: 2016
SALES (est): 422.73K Privately Held
SIC: 3829 Measuring and controlling
    devices, nec

(G-1881)
CEFLA DENTAL GROUP AMERICA
6125 Harris Technology Blvd (28269-3731)
PHONE..................................704 731-5293
Vittorio Belus, *VP*
▲ EMP: 7 EST: 2010
SALES (est): 762.57K Privately Held
Web: www.ceflamedicalna.com
SIC: 3843 Dental equipment and supplies

(G-1882)
CEFLA NORTH AMERICA INC
6125 Harris Technology Blvd (28269-3731)
PHONE..................................704 598-0020
Recardo Quattrini, *Pr*
Walter Favruzzo, *
Vittorio Belluz, *
▲ EMP: 39 EST: 1987
SQ FT: 8,500
SALES (est): 25.04MM
SALES (corp-wide): 744.49MM Privately
Held
Web: www.ceflafinishing.com
SIC: 5084 3553 Woodworking machinery;
    Furniture makers machinery, woodworking
PA: Cefla Soc Coop
    Via Bicocca 14/C
    Imola BO 40026
    054 265-4344

(G-1883)
CELEROS FLOW TECHNOLOGY LLC (PA)
14045 Ballantyne Corporate Pl Ste 300
(28277)
PHONE..................................704 752-3100
Jose Larios, *Managing Member*
EMP: 116 EST: 2019
SALES (est): 632.31MM
SALES (corp-wide): 632.31MM Privately
Held
Web: www.celerosft.com
SIC: 3491 Industrial valves

(G-1884)
CELGARD LLC
13800 S Lakes Dr (28273-6738)
PHONE..................................704 588-5310
EMP: 80
Web: www.celgard.com
SIC: 2821 Plastics materials and resins
HQ: Celgard, Llc
    11430 N Cmnity Hse Rd
    Charlotte NC 28277
    800 235-4273

(G-1885)
CELGARD LLC (HQ)
11430 N Community House Rd Ste 350
(28277-1591)
PHONE..................................800 235-4273
Lie Shi, *Pr*
◆ EMP: 71 EST: 1999
SALES (est): 48.92MM Privately Held
Web: www.celgard.com
SIC: 2821 3081 Plastics materials and resins
    ; Unsupported plastics film and sheet
PA: Asahi Kasei Corporation
    1-1-2, Yurakucho
    Chiyoda-Ku TKY 100-0

(G-1886)
CEMCO ELECTRIC INC
Also Called: Cemco Systems
10913 Office Park Dr (28273-6549)
P.O. Box 38100 (28278-1001)
PHONE..................................704 504-0294
Cliff Morgan, *Pr*
Cheryl Morgan, *VP*
EMP: 10 EST: 1984
SQ FT: 800
SALES (est): 1.81MM Privately Held
Web: www.cemcosystemsinc.com
SIC: 1731 5063 3569 General electrical
    contractor; Generators; Firefighting and
    related equipment

(G-1887)
CENTRIA INC
10801 Johnston Rd Ste 226 (28226-7856)
PHONE..................................704 341-0202
Gary Cooper, *Brnch Mgr*
EMP: 6
SALES (corp-wide): 30.73B Publicly Held
Web: www.centria.com
SIC: 3444 Metal flooring and siding
HQ: Centria, Inc.
    1550 Corpls Hts Rd # 500
    Moon Township PA 15108
    412 299-8000

(G-1888)
CENTURY PLACE II LLC
Also Called: Century Place Apparel
10220 Western Ridge Rd Ste A
(28273-7264)
P.O. Box 668 (28145-0668)
PHONE..................................704 790-0970
Jeffrey Smith, *Pr*
Mike Carter, *
Tom Pepper, *
Juan Sanchez, *
◆ EMP: 48 EST: 2000
SQ FT: 45,000
SALES (est): 5MM Privately Held
Web: www.centuryplace.com
SIC: 2321 Polo shirts, men's and boys':
    made from purchased materials

(G-1889)
CERAMCO INCORPORATED
Also Called: Printech
11009 Carpet St (28273-6232)
P.O. Box 7265 (28241-7265)
PHONE..................................704 588-4814
Terry Link, *Pr*
Jan Link, *
Steve Luther, *
◆ EMP: 40 EST: 1971
SQ FT: 20,000
SALES (est): 5.61MM Privately Held
Web: www.ceramcoprintech.com
SIC: 3469 Machine parts, stamped or
    pressed metal

(G-1890)
CHAMPION LLC
Also Called: Champion
8844 Mount Holly Rd (28214-8350)
PHONE..................................704 392-1038
EMP: 15 EST: 1983
SQ FT: 11,600
SALES (est): 2.32MM Privately Held
Web: www.championcu.com
SIC: 3531 Graders, road (construction
    machinery)

(G-1891)
CHAMPION WIN CO OF CHARLOTTE
Also Called: Champion Wndows Sding Ptio
Rom
9100 Perimeter Woods Dr Ste C
(28216-2262)

PHONE..................................704 398-0085
TOLL FREE: 800
Robert Fleischer, *Pr*
EMP: 7 EST: 1999
SALES (est): 1.46MM Privately Held
Web: www.championwindow.com
SIC: 3442 3444 Storm doors or windows,
    metal; Awnings, sheet metal

(G-1892)
CHARAH LLC
4235 Southstream Blvd Ste 180
(28217-0142)
PHONE..................................704 731-2300
EMP: 138
SALES (corp-wide): 293.17MM Publicly
Held
Web: www.charah.com
SIC: 1081 Metal mining exploration and
    development services
HQ: Charah, Llc
    12601 Plantside Dr
    Louisville KY 40299

(G-1893)
CHARGE ONSITE LLC
1015 East Blvd (28203-5713)
PHONE..................................888 343-2688
Jim Swain, *Managing Member*
EMP: 5
SALES (est): 1.01MM Privately Held
SIC: 7372 Application computer software

(G-1894)
CHARLOTTE INSTYLE INC
801 Pressley Rd Ste 1071 (28217-0981)
PHONE..................................704 665-8880
Lennart Wiktorin, *Pr*
▲ EMP: 30 EST: 1995
SQ FT: 40,000
SALES (est): 2.35MM Privately Held
Web: www.instylecharlotte.com
SIC: 1423 Crushed and broken granite

(G-1895)
CHARLOTTE MAGAZINE
214 W Tremont Ave Ste 303 (28203-5161)
PHONE..................................980 207-5124
EMP: 9 EST: 2017
SALES (est): 234.06K Privately Held
Web: www.charlottemagazine.com
SIC: 2721 Magazines: publishing only, not
    printed on site

(G-1896)
CHARLOTTE OBSERVER
550 S Caldwell St Ste 1010 (28202-2633)
PHONE..................................704 358-5000
EMP: 72 EST: 2014
SALES (est): 1.73MM Privately Held
Web: www.charlotteobserver.com
SIC: 2711 Newspapers, publishing and
    printing

(G-1897)
CHARLOTTE OBSERVER PUBG CO
9140 Research Dr Ste C1 (28262-8544)
P.O. Box Cornelius (28031)
PHONE..................................704 987-3660
Bill Hutters, *Mgr*
EMP: 47
SALES (corp-wide): 1.39B Privately Held
Web: www.carpet-cleaning-charlotte.com
SIC: 2711 Newspapers, publishing and
    printing
HQ: The Charlotte Observer Publishing
    Company
    550 S Caldwell St Fl 10
    Charlotte NC 28202
    704 358-5000

(G-1898)
CHARLOTTE OBSERVER PUBG CO
Also Called: Charlotte Observer
724 Montana Dr (28216)
PHONE..............................704 572-0747
Al Shelley, *Genl Mgr*
EMP: 47
SALES (corp-wide): 1.39B **Privately Held**
Web: www.carpet-cleaning-charlotte.com
SIC: 2711 Newspapers, publishing and
printing
HQ: The Charlotte Observer Publishing
Company
550 S Caldwell St Fl 10
Charlotte NC 28202
704 358-5000

(G-1899)
**CHARLOTTE OBSERVER PUBG CO
(DH)**
Also Called: Charlotte Observer
550 S Caldwell St Ste 1010 (28202-2633)
PHONE..............................704 358-5000
TOLL FREE: 800
Ann Coulkins, *Pr*
Victor Fields, *
Jim Lamm, *
Kelly Mirt, *
Ken Riddick, *
EMP: 600 EST: 1955
SALES (est): 16.46MM
SALES (corp-wide): 1.39B **Privately Held**
Web: www.carpet-cleaning-charlotte.com
SIC: 2711 4813 Commercial printing and
newspaper publishing combined; Internet
connectivity services
HQ: Jck Legacy Company
1601 Alhmbra Blvd Ste 100
Sacramento CA 95816
916 321-1844

(G-1900)
**CHARLOTTE PIPE AND FOUNDRY
CO (PA)**
2109 Randolph Rd (28207)
P.O. Box 35430 (28235)
PHONE..............................800 438-6091
W Frank Dowd Iv, *CEO*
Roddey Dowd Junior, *Pr*
J Alan Biggers, *
Mark E Black, *
William R Hutaff Iii, *VP Fin*
◆ EMP: 110 EST: 1901
SQ FT: 27,000
SALES (est): 841.88MM
SALES (corp-wide): 841.88MM **Privately
Held**
Web: www.charlottepipe.com
SIC: 3312 3089 3321 Pipes and tubes;
Fittings for pipe, plastics; Soil pipe and
fittings: cast iron

(G-1901)
**CHARLOTTE PIPE AND FOUNDRY
CO**
Also Called: Cast Iron Division
1335 S Clarkson St (28208-5315)
PHONE..............................704 348-5416
Marshall Coble, *Mgr*
EMP: 450
SALES (corp-wide): 841.88MM **Privately
Held**
Web: www.charlottepipe.com
SIC: 3084 3498 3312 Plastics pipe;
Fabricated pipe and fittings; Blast furnaces
and steel mills
PA: Charlotte Pipe And Foundry Company
2109 Randolph Rd
Charlotte NC 28207
800 438-6091

(G-1902)
**CHARLOTTE PIPE AND FOUNDRY
COM**
2109 Randolph Rd (28207-1521)
PHONE..............................704 379-0700
EMP: 18
SALES (est): 2.1MM **Privately Held**
Web: www.charlottepipe.com
SIC: 3084 Plastics pipe

(G-1903)
CHARLOTTE PLATING INC
8421 Kirchenbaum Dr (28210-5856)
PHONE..............................704 552-2100
W Todd Osmolski, *Pr*
David H Osmolski, *Treas*
Susan Osmolski, *VP*
EMP: 8 EST: 1989
SALES (est): 328.32K **Privately Held**
Web: www.charlotteplating.com
SIC: 3471 Electroplating of metals or formed
products

(G-1904)
CHARLOTTE POST PUBG CO INC
Also Called: CHARLOTTE POST
5118 Princess St (28269-4861)
P.O. Box 30144 (28230)
PHONE..............................704 376-0496
Gerald Johnson, *Pr*
Robert Johnson, *VP*
EMP: 15 EST: 1971
SQ FT: 4,500
SALES (est): 146.39K **Privately Held**
Web: www.thecharlottepost.com
SIC: 2711 Newspapers, publishing and
printing

(G-1905)
**CHARLOTTE TRIMMING COMPANY
INC (PA)**
900 Pressley Rd (28217-0974)
PHONE..............................704 529-8427
Antonio Lopez Ibanez Junior, *Pr*
Antonio Lopez Ibanez Junior, *Pr*
Juan Lopez Ibanez, *Treas*
Raul Lopez Ibanez, *Sec*
◆ EMP: 20 EST: 1961
SQ FT: 75,000
SALES (est): 1.55MM
SALES (corp-wide): 1.55MM **Privately
Held**
SIC: 2253 2396 Collar and cuff sets, knit;
Trimming, fabric, nsk

(G-1906)
**CHARLTTE MCKLNBURG DREAM
CTR I**
129 W Trade St (28202-2143)
P.O. Box 30877 (28230-0877)
PHONE..............................704 421-4440
Kim Shaftner, *Admn*
EMP: 6 EST: 2017
SALES (est): 195.88K **Privately Held**
Web: www.charlotteballet.org
SIC: 2711 Newspapers

(G-1907)
CHARTER JET TRANSPORT INC
5400 Airport Dr (28208-5734)
P.O. Box 19333 (28219-9333)
PHONE..............................704 359-8833
Harold Singleton, *Pr*
Richard Keffer, *CEO*
EMP: 6 EST: 1997
SQ FT: 250
SALES (est): 1.04MM **Privately Held**
Web: www.flycjt.com

SIC: 4512 3721 Air passenger carrier,
scheduled; Airplanes, fixed or rotary wing

(G-1908)
**CHELSEA THERAPEUTICS
INTERNATIONAL LTD**
3530 Toringdon Way Ste 200 (28277-3436)
PHONE..............................704 341-1516
EMP: 18
Web: www.chelsearx.com
SIC: 2836 Biological products, except
diagnostic

(G-1909)
**CHEMRING SNSORS ELCTRNIC
SYSTE**
Also Called: Chemring Detection Systems
4205 Westinghouse Commons Dr
(28273-3958)
PHONE..............................980 235-2200
EMP: 6
SALES (corp-wide): 684.37MM **Privately
Held**
Web: www.chemringds.com
SIC: 3812 Search and detection systems
and instruments
HQ: Chemring Sensors And Electronic
Systems, Inc.
14401 Penrose Pl Ste 130
Chantilly VA 20151

(G-1910)
**CHEMTRADE LOGISTICS (US) INC
(HQ)**
814 Tyvola Rd Ste 126 (28217-3539)
PHONE..............................773 646-2500
Mark Davis, *Pr*
EMP: 9 EST: 2001
SALES (est): 18.47MM
SALES (corp-wide): 1.34B **Privately Held**
SIC: 2819 Industrial inorganic chemicals, nec
PA: Chemtrade Logistics Income Fund
300-155 Gordon Baker Rd
North York ON M2H 3
416 496-5856

(G-1911)
CHF INDUSTRIES INC
Also Called: Joanna Co
8710 Red Oak Blvd (28217-3957)
PHONE..............................704 522-5000
Fred Nichols, *Pr*
EMP: 81
SALES (corp-wide): 32.37MM **Privately
Held**
Web: www.chfindustries.com
SIC: 2591 Venetian blinds
PA: Chf Industries, Inc.
1 Bridge St Ste 130
Irvington NY 10533
212 951-7800

(G-1912)
CHF INDUSTRIES INC
Also Called: Cameo Curtains Div
9741 Southern Pine Blvd Ste A
(28273-5541)
PHONE..............................212 951-7800
Frank Foley, *Brnch Mgr*
EMP: 31
SALES (corp-wide): 32.37MM **Privately
Held**
Web: www.chfindustries.com
SIC: 5023 2511 2392 2391 Curtains; Wood
household furniture; Household furnishings,
nec; Curtains and draperies
PA: Chf Industries, Inc.
1 Bridge St Ste 130
Irvington NY 10533
212 951-7800

(G-1913)
CHICAGO PNEUMATIC TOOL CO LLC
11313 Steele Creek Rd (28273-3713)
PHONE..............................704 504-6937
John Cleveland, *Brnch Mgr*
EMP: 18
Web: www.cp.com
SIC: 3546 Power-driven handtools
HQ: Chicago Pneumatic Tool Company Llc
1815 Clubhouse Dr
Rock Hill SC 29730
803 817-7100

(G-1914)
CHICOPEE INC (DH)
Also Called: Pgi Nonwovens
9335 Harris Corners Pkwy Ste 300
(28269-3817)
PHONE..............................704 697-5100
Veronica M Hagen, *CEO*
Robert Kocourek, *CAO*
Michael W Hale, *VP*
Dan Rikerd, *Sec*
◆ EMP: 20 EST: 1995
SQ FT: 8,000
SALES (est): 30.28MM **Publicly Held**
Web: www.chicopee.com
SIC: 2297 Spunbonded fabrics
HQ: Avintiv Specialty Materials Inc.
9335 Hrris Crners Pkwy St
Charlotte NC 28269

(G-1915)
CHIEF CORPORATION
10926 David Taylor Dr Ste 300
(28262-1293)
PHONE..............................704 916-4521
Jeff Tousa, *Pr*
EMP: 5 EST: 2005
SALES (est): 119.03K **Privately Held**
SIC: 2741 Catalogs: publishing and printing

(G-1916)
CHIRON AMERICA INC (DH)
10950 Withers Cove Park Dr (28278-0020)
PHONE..............................704 587-9526
Steve Morris, *Pr*
Morsey Tsiukes, *
▲ EMP: 60 EST: 1993
SQ FT: 76,000
SALES (est): 23.91MM
SALES (corp-wide): 804.13MM **Privately
Held**
Web: www.chiron-group.com
SIC: 5084 7539 3599 Machine tools and
accessories; Machine shop, automotive;
Machine and other job shop work
HQ: Chiron Group Se
Kreuzstr. 75
Tuttlingen BW 78532
74619400

(G-1917)
CHT R BEITLICH CORPORATION
5046 Old Pineville Rd (28217-3032)
P.O. Box 240497 (28224-0497)
PHONE..............................704 523-4242
Theodore Dickson, *CEO*
◆ EMP: 34 EST: 1971
SQ FT: 65,000
SALES (est): 4.24MM
SALES (corp-wide): 144.19K **Privately
Held**
Web: www.cht.com
SIC: 2843 Surface active agents
HQ: Cht Germany Gmbh
Bismarckstr. 102
Tubingen BW 72072
70711540

2025 Harris North Carolina
Manufacturers Directory

▲ = Import ▼ = Export
◆ = Import/Export

(G-1918)
CISCO SYSTEMS INC
Also Called: Cisco Systems
1900 South Blvd Ste 200 (28203-0067)
P.O. Box 2063 (48090-2063)
PHONE...............................704 338-7350
EMP: 5
SALES (corp-wide): 53.8B Publicly Held
Web: www.cisco.com
SIC: 3577 Data conversion equipment,
media-to-media: computer
PA: Cisco Systems, Inc.
170 W Tasman Dr
San Jose CA 95134
408 526-4000

(G-1919)
CITILIFT COMPANY
Also Called: Elevators & Conveyors
4732 West Blvd Ste D (28208-6398)
PHONE...............................704 241-6477
Carl Sturdivant, Pr
EMP: 5 EST: 2010
SQ FT: 2,000
SALES (est): 419.15K Privately Held
Web: www.citilift.com
SIC: 3534 Elevators and moving stairways

(G-1920)
**CITY COMPRESSOR REBUILDERS
(PA)**
9750 Twin Lakes Pkwy (28269-7650)
PHONE...............................704 947-1811
Dwayne Moreland, Pr
Sandra Moreland, Sec
EMP: 20 EST: 1938
SQ FT: 40,000
SALES (est): 2.39MM
SALES (corp-wide): 2.39MM Privately
Held
Web: www.citycompressor.com
SIC: 3585 Refrigeration and heating
equipment

(G-1921)
CITY COMPRESSOR REBUILDERS
9750 Twin Lakes Pkwy (28269-7650)
PHONE...............................704 947-1811
Dwayne Moreland, Mgr
EMP: 8
SALES (corp-wide): 2.39MM Privately
Held
Web: www.citycompressor.com
SIC: 3585 Compressors for refrigeration and
air conditioning equipment
PA: City Compressor Rebuilders Inc
9750 Twin Lakes Pkwy
Charlotte NC 28269
704 947-1811

(G-1922)
CITY OF CHARLOTTE-ATANDO
1031 Atando Ave (28206-2252)
PHONE...............................704 336-2722
Gene White, Owner
EMP: 4 EST: 2018
SALES (est): 901.29K Privately Held
SIC: 3714 Motor vehicle parts and
accessories

(G-1923)
CLARIANT CORPORATION
4331 Chesapeake Dr (28216-3410)
PHONE...............................704 331-7000
John Schofield, Mgr
EMP: 58
SQ FT: 51,364
Web: www.clariant.com
SIC: 2865 2899 Dyes and pigments;
Chemical preparations, nec
HQ: Clariant Corporation

500 E Morehead St Ste 400
Charlotte NC 28202
704 331-7000

(G-1924)
CLARIANT CORPORATION
Also Called: Mt Holly Plant
11701 Mount Holly Rd (28214-9229)
PHONE...............................704 371-3272
Nick Altman, Mgr
EMP: 83
Web: www.clariant.com
SIC: 2869 Industrial organic chemicals, nec
HQ: Clariant Corporation
500 E Morehead St Ste 400
Charlotte NC 28202
704 331-7000

(G-1925)
CLARIANT CORPORATION (HQ)
Also Called: Clariant
500 E Morehead St Ste 400 (28202-2744)
PHONE...............................704 331-7000
Scott A Wood, Pr
Gene Mueller, *
Akin Butuner, *
◆ EMP: 55 EST: 1983
SQ FT: 240,000
SALES (est): 1.01B Privately Held
Web: www.clariant.com
SIC: 2819 2869 8641 2899 Catalysts,
chemical; High purity grade chemicals,
organic; Environmental protection
organization; Fire retardant chemicals
PA: Clariant Ag
Rothausstrasse 61
Muttenz BL 4132

(G-1926)
CLARIOS LLC
Also Called: Controls Group
9844 Southern Pine Blvd (28273-5502)
P.O. Box 905240 (28290-5240)
PHONE...............................866 589-8883
Jim Beam, Mgr
EMP: 48
SALES (corp-wide): 69.83B Privately Held
Web: www.clarios.com
SIC: 2531 Seats, automobile
HQ: Clarios, Llc
5757 N Green Bay Ave Flor
Glendale WI 53209

(G-1927)
CLAUSEN CRAFTWORKS LLC
900 Pressley Rd Ste C (28217-0974)
PHONE...............................704 252-5048
EMP: 5
SALES (est): 309.06K Privately Held
SIC: 2499 Wood products, nec

(G-1928)
CLEAN CATCH FISH MARKET LLC
2820 Selwyn Ave Ste 150 (28209-1786)
PHONE...............................704 333-1212
EMP: 7 EST: 2009
SALES (est): 1.34MM Privately Held
Web: www.cleancatchfish.com
SIC: 2099 5411 5421 Food preparations, nec
; Grocery stores; Fish markets

(G-1929)
CLINE PRINTING INC
3445 Carolina Ave Ste A (28208-5896)
PHONE...............................704 394-8144
Ben Cline Junior, Pr
Danny Lanier, VP
EMP: 4 EST: 1968
SQ FT: 5,000
SALES (est): 35.64K Privately Held

SIC: 2752 2721 Offset printing; Periodicals,
publishing and printing

(G-1930)
CLINICIANS ADVOCACY GROUP INC
1433 Emerywood Dr Ste A (28210-4591)
PHONE...............................704 751-9515
Steven Crawford, Pr
EMP: 7 EST: 2020
SALES (est): 317.38K Privately Held
Web: www.carolinaadvocacygroup.com
SIC: 3821 Clinical laboratory instruments,
except medical and dental

(G-1931)
CLOSETS BY DESIGN
1108 Continental Blvd Ste A (28273-6385)
PHONE...............................704 361-6424
Laura Vansickle, Owner
EMP: 72 EST: 2008
SALES (est): 13MM Privately Held
Web: www.closetsbydesign.com
SIC: 1799 2511 Closet organizers,
installation and design; Bed frames, except
water bed frames: wood

(G-1932)
CLOUDGENERA INC
1824 Statesville Ave Ste 103 (28206-3564)
PHONE...............................980 332-4040
Brian Kelly, CEO
EMP: 20 EST: 2012
SALES (est): 2.1MM Privately Held
Web: go.cloudgenera.com
SIC: 7372 Application computer software

(G-1933)
CLT 2016 INC
1836 Equitable Pl (28213-6500)
PHONE...............................704 886-1555
EMP: 59
SIC: 5031 3444 3089 Lumber, plywood, and
millwork; Gutters, sheet metal; Windows,
plastics

(G-1934)
CLYDE UNION (US) INC (HQ)
Also Called: Clydeunion Pumps
14045 Ballantyne Corporate Pl Ste 300
(28277-0099)
PHONE...............................704 808-3000
◆ EMP: 225 EST: 2008
SALES (est): 39.78MM
SALES (corp-wide): 632.31MM Privately
Held
Web: www.celerosft.com
SIC: 3561 5084 Industrial pumps and parts;
Pumps and pumping equipment, nec
PA: Celeros Flow Technology, Llc
14045 Bllntyne Corp Pl St
Charlotte NC 28277
704 752-3100

(G-1935)
CLYDESDLE ACQ HLD INC (HQ) ✪
Also Called: Novolex
3436 Toringdon Way Ste 100 (28277-2449)
PHONE...............................843 857-4800
EMP: 61 EST: 2023
SALES (est): 46.11B
SALES (corp-wide): 26.11B Publicly Held
SIC: 3089 Plastics kitchenware, tableware,
and houseware
PA: Apollo Global Management, Inc.
9 W 57th St Fl 42
New York NY 10019
212 515-3200

(G-1936)
CLYDEUNION PUMPS INC
Also Called: SPX
13320 Ballantyne Corporate Pl
(28277-3607)
PHONE...............................704 808-3848
Jeremy Smeltser, Pr
EMP: 35 EST: 2009
SALES (est): 5.91MM
SALES (corp-wide): 1.78B Privately Held
Web: www.celerosft.com
SIC: 3561 Pumps and pumping equipment
HQ: Spx Flow, Inc.
13320 Ballantyne Corp Pl
Charlotte NC 28277
704 752-4400

(G-1937)
CMISOLUTIONS INC
7520 E Independence Blvd Ste 400
(28227-9441)
PHONE...............................704 759-9950
Dwight Mc Knight, CEO
Don Robinson, VP
Gregg Peele, Pr
EMP: 29 EST: 1995
SQ FT: 8,128
SALES (est): 3.8MM Privately Held
Web: www.cmisolutions.com
SIC: 7371 7372 Computer software
development; Prepackaged software

(G-1938)
CNC PERFORMANCE ENG LLC
11125 Metromont Pkwy (28269-7510)
P.O. Box 3025 (28070-3025)
PHONE...............................704 599-2555
Chris Nachtmann, Pr
EMP: 8 EST: 2010
SALES (est): 781.8K Privately Held
Web: www.cncpe.com
SIC: 8711 3599 Consulting engineer;
Machine shop, jobbing and repair

(G-1939)
CNC-KE INC
1340 Amble Dr (28206-1308)
P.O. Box 625 (37148)
PHONE...............................704 333-0145
Ken Best Junior, Pr
Vince Haynes, *
EMP: 90 EST: 1969
SQ FT: 25,000
SALES (est): 3.39MM
SALES (corp-wide): 20.22MM Privately
Held
Web: www.cncke.com
SIC: 3679 Electronic circuits
PA: Kentucky Electronics, Inc.
222 Riggs Ave
Portland TN 37148
615 325-4127

(G-1940)
COALOGIX INC
11707 Steele Creek Rd (28273-3718)
PHONE...............................704 827-8933
EMP: 133
Web: www.cormetech.com
SIC: 8711 2819 Pollution control engineering
; Catalysts, chemical

(G-1941)
COATING CONCEPTS INC
8154 Westbourne Dr (28216-1141)
PHONE...............................704 391-0499
Melanie K Paul, Pr
EMP: 5 EST: 1995
SALES (est): 506.02K Privately Held
SIC: 3479 Coating of metals with plastic or
resins

(G-1942)
COATS & CLARK INC (HQ)
Also Called: Coats N Amer De Rpblica
Dmncan
2550 W Tyvola Rd Ste 150 (28217)
PHONE..............................888 368-8401
Maxwell Perks, *Pr*
Donna L Armstrong, *
Ryan Newell, *
◆ **EMP:** 65 **EST:** 1937
SALES (est): 33.39MM
SALES (corp-wide): 973.96K **Privately Held**
Web: www.makeitcoats.com
SIC: 2284 2281 3364 3089 Cotton thread;
Cotton yarn, spun; Zinc and zinc-base alloy
die-castings; Molding primary plastics
PA: Spinrite Inc
320 Livingstone Ave S
Listowel ON N4W 3
519 929-4146

(G-1943)
COATS AMERICAN INC (HQ)
Also Called: Coats North America
14120 Ballantyne Corporate Pl Ste 300
(28277)
P.O. Box 1847 (28086)
PHONE..............................800 242-8095
Soundar Rajan, *Pr*
Michael Schofer, *
Rajiv Sharma, *
Simon Boddie, *
Ronan Cox, *
▲ **EMP:** 200 **EST:** 1898
SALES (est): 157.16MM
SALES (corp-wide): 1.39B **Privately Held**
SIC: 2284 Cotton thread
PA: Coats Group Plc
4th Floor
London EC2V
208 210-5010

(G-1944)
COATS HP INC (DH)
14120 Ballantyne Corporate Pl Ste 300
(28277-3169)
PHONE..............................704 329-5800
Rajiv Sharma, *CEO*
EMP: 27 **EST:** 2019
SALES (est): 9.03MM
SALES (corp-wide): 1.39B **Privately Held**
SIC: 2281 2282 2824 Manmade and
synthetic fiber yarns, spun; Manmade and
synthetic fiber yarns, twisting, winding, etc.;
Acrylic fibers
HQ: Coats American, Inc.
14120 Bllntyne Corp Pl St
Charlotte NC 28277
800 242-8095

(G-1945)
**COATS N AMER DE RPBLICA
DMNCAN (HQ)**
14120 Ballantyne Corporate Pl Ste 300
(28277-3169)
PHONE..............................800 242-8095
Soundar Jan, *Pr*
Shawna Blomkvist, *
Julian Urquidi, *
▲ **EMP:** 175 **EST:** 1981
SQ FT: 34,000
SALES (est): 24.38MM
SALES (corp-wide): 1.39B **Privately Held**
SIC: 2284 3089 3364 2281 Cotton thread;
Molding primary plastics; Zinc and zinc-
base alloy die-castings; Cotton yarn, spun
PA: Coats Group Plc
4th Floor
London EC2V
208 210-5010

(G-1946)
COCA COLA BOTTLING CO
5020 W W T Harris Blvd (28269-1861)
PHONE..............................704 509-1812
EMP: 6 **EST:** 2022
SALES (est): 2.11MM **Privately Held**
Web: www.coca-cola.com
SIC: 5149 2086 Cooking oils and shortenings
; Bottled and canned soft drinks

(G-1947)
COCA-COLA CONSOLIDATED INC
Also Called: Coca-Cola
801 Black Satchel Rd (28216-3453)
PHONE..............................704 398-2252
Guy Tarrance, *Mgr*
EMP: 5
SALES (corp-wide): 6.9B **Publicly Held**
Web: www.cokeconsolidated.com
SIC: 2086 Bottled and canned soft drinks
PA: Coca-Cola Consolidated, Inc.
4100 Coca-Cola Plz
Charlotte NC 28211
980 392-8298

(G-1948)
COCA-COLA CONSOLIDATED INC
Also Called: Coca-Cola
5001 Chesapeake Dr (28216-2936)
PHONE..............................980 321-3001
Dave Hopkins, *Genl Mgr*
EMP: 72
SALES (corp-wide): 6.9B **Publicly Held**
Web: www.cokeconsolidated.com
SIC: 2086 Bottled and canned soft drinks
PA: Coca-Cola Consolidated, Inc.
4100 Coca-Cola Plz
Charlotte NC 28211
980 392-8298

(G-1949)
**COCA-COLA CONSOLIDATED INC
(PA)**
Also Called: Coca-Cola
4100 Coca Cola Plz Ste 100 (28211)
P.O. Box 31487 (28231)
PHONE..............................980 392-8298
J Frank Harrison Iii, *Ch Bd*
Morgan H Everett, *
Umesh M Kasbekar, *Non-Executive Vice
Chairman of the Board*
David M Katz, *
F Scott Anthony, *Ex VP*
▲ **EMP:** 554 **EST:** 1902
SQ FT: 172,000
SALES (est): 6.9B
SALES (corp-wide): 6.9B **Publicly Held**
Web: www.cokeconsolidated.com
SIC: 2086 Bottled and canned soft drinks

(G-1950)
COCO LUMBER COMPANY LLC
2101 Sardis Rd N Ste 201 (28227-6785)
PHONE..............................336 906-3754
◆ **EMP:** 4 **EST:** 2007
SALES (est): 653.19K **Privately Held**
Web: www.cocolumber.com
SIC: 2421 Sawmills and planing mills,
general

(G-1951)
CODER FOUNDRY
8430 University Exec Park Dr (28262-1350)
PHONE..............................704 910-3077
EMP: 8 **EST:** 2015
SALES (est): 1.14MM **Privately Held**
Web: www.coderfoundry.com
SIC: 3325 Steel foundries, nec

(G-1952)
COLEFIELDS PUBLISHING INC
Also Called: Real Estate Book, The
2626 Hampton Ave (28207-2522)
PHONE..............................704 661-1599
William F Medearis Iii, *Pr*
Bill Medearis, *Pr*
Polly Medearis, *Sec*
EMP: 8 **EST:** 1991
SALES (est): 78.81K **Privately Held**
Web: www.realestatebook.net
SIC: 2721 Magazines: publishing only, not
printed on site

(G-1953)
COLLINS & AIKMAN EUROPE INC
701 Mccullough Dr (28262)
PHONE..............................704 548-2350
EMP: 25 **EST:** 2007
SALES (est): 397.03K **Privately Held**
SIC: 2221 Automotive fabrics, manmade fiber

(G-1954)
COLLINS & AIKMAN INTERIORS
701 Mccullough Dr (28262)
PHONE..............................704 548-2350
EMP: 45 **EST:** 2007
SALES (est): 832.18K **Privately Held**
SIC: 2221 Automotive fabrics, manmade fiber

(G-1955)
**COLLINS & AIKMAN
INTERNATIONAL**
701 Mccullough Dr (28262)
PHONE..............................704 548-2350
EMP: 30 **EST:** 2007
SALES (est): 318.65K **Privately Held**
SIC: 2221 Automotive fabrics, manmade fiber

(G-1956)
COLLINS & AIKMAN PRPTS INC
701 Mccullough Dr (28262)
PHONE..............................704 548-2350
EMP: 50 **EST:** 2007
SALES (est): 856.35K **Privately Held**
SIC: 2221 Automotive fabrics, manmade fiber

(G-1957)
COLLINS AEROSPACE
2730 W Tyvola Rd (28217-4527)
PHONE..............................704 423-7000
EMP: 11 **EST:** 2020
SALES (est): 5.07MM **Privately Held**
Web: www.collinsaerospace.com
SIC: 3728 8711 Bodies, aircraft; Aviation and/
or aeronautical engineering

(G-1958)
**COLLINS AKMAN CANADA DOM
HOLDG**
701 Mccullough Dr (28262)
PHONE..............................704 548-2350
EMP: 45 **EST:** 2007
SALES (est): 769.2K **Privately Held**
SIC: 2221 Automotive fabrics, manmade fiber

(G-1959)
COLQUIMICA ADHESIVES INC
2205 Beltway Blvd Ste 200 (28214)
PHONE..............................704 318-4750
Joao Pedro Koehler, *Ch*
Joao Pedro Koehler, *Ch*
Sofia Koehler, *Ch*
Pedro Goncalves, *COO*
EMP: 50 **EST:** 2019
SALES (est): 3.51MM **Privately Held**
Web: www.colquimica.com
SIC: 2891 Adhesives

HQ: ColquImica - IndUstria Nacional De
Colas, S.A.
Rua Das Lousas, 885
Valongo 4440-

(G-1960)
COLSENKEANE LEATHER LLC
1707 E 7th St (28204-2413)
PHONE..............................704 750-9887
EMP: 4 **EST:** 2017
SALES (est): 201.18K **Privately Held**
Web: www.colsenkeane.com
SIC: 3199 Leather goods, nec

(G-1961)
COLTEC INDUSTRIES INC
Also Called: Garlock Bearings
5605 Carnegie Blvd Ste 500 (28209-4642)
PHONE..............................704 731-1500
▲ **EMP:** 1700
SIC: 3053 3519 3089 Gaskets and sealing
devices; Engines, diesel and semi-diesel or
dual-fuel; Plastics containers, except foam

(G-1962)
**COLUMBUS MCKINNON
CORPORATION (PA)**
Also Called: Columbus McKinnon
13320 Ballantyne Corporate Pl Ste D
(28277)
PHONE..............................716 689-5400
David J Wilson, *Pr*
Gerald G Colella, *
Gregory P Rustowicz, *VP Fin*
Alan S Korman, *Sr VP*
Adrienne Williams, *Chief Human
Resources Officer*
◆ **EMP:** 145 **EST:** 1875
SALES (est): 1.01B
SALES (corp-wide): 1.01B **Publicly Held**
Web: www.columbusmckinnon.com
SIC: 3536 3496 3535 3537 Hoists; Chain,
welded; Conveyors and conveying
equipment; Tables, lift: hydraulic

(G-1963)
COMMERCIAL METALS COMPANY
419 Atando Ave (28206-1909)
PHONE..............................704 375-5937
Trevor Bokor, *Manager*
EMP: 22
SALES (corp-wide): 7.93B **Publicly Held**
Web: www.cmc.com
SIC: 3441 Fabricated structural metal
PA: Commercial Metals Company
6565 N Mcrthur Blvd Ste 8
Irving TX 75039
214 689-4300

(G-1964)
COMMERCIAL METALS COMPANY
Ameristeel Chrltte Fab Rnfrcin
301 Black Satchel Rd (28216-2941)
PHONE..............................704 399-9020
Van Taylor, *Mgr*
EMP: 32
SALES (corp-wide): 7.93B **Publicly Held**
Web: www.cmc.com
SIC: 3441 Fabricated structural metal
PA: Commercial Metals Company
6565 N Mcrthur Blvd Ste 8
Irving TX 75039
214 689-4300

(G-1965)
COMPASS GROUP USA INC
Canteen Vending Services
3112 Horseshoe Ln (28208-6457)
P.O. Box 698 (28001)
PHONE..............................704 398-6515
Bob Mangiafico, *Owner*

EMP: 1748
SALES (corp-wide): 42B **Privately Held**
Web: www.canteen.com
SIC: 5962 2099 Merchandising machine
operators; Food preparations, nec
HQ: Compass Group Usa, Inc.
2400 Yorkmont Rd
Charlotte NC 28217

(G-1966)
COMPASS PRECISION LLC (PA)
4600 Westinghouse Blvd (28273-9619)
PHONE..............................704 790-6764
Gary Holcomb, *Pr*
Paul Wilhelm, *VP*
Jim Miller, *VP Sls*
EMP: 11 **EST:** 2019
SALES (est): 12.01MM
SALES (corp-wide): 12.01MM **Privately
Held**
Web: www.compassprecision.com
SIC: 3599 Machine shop, jobbing and repair

(G-1967)
COMPONENT SOURCING INTL LLC
Also Called: Csi
1301 Westinghouse Blvd Ste 1
(28273-6393)
PHONE..............................704 843-9292
James Glasscock, *CEO*
Eric Llorey, *VP Fin*
EMP: 20 **EST:** 1982
SALES (est): 4.53MM
SALES (corp-wide): 9.8MM **Privately Held**
Web: www.componentsourcing.com
SIC: 3448 1629 5051 3469 Prefabricated
metal components; Dams, waterways,
docks, and other marine construction;
Castings, rough: iron or steel; Stamping
metal for the trade
PA: Cpc Llc
1511 Bltimore Ave Ste 500
Kansas City MO 64108
816 756-2225

(G-1968)
**COMPONENT TECHNOLOGY INTL
INC**
1000 Upper Asbury Ave (28206-1509)
PHONE..............................704 331-0888
Chad Mcellee, *Brnch Mgr*
EMP: 5
SIC: 3599 3568 Machine shop, jobbing and
repair; Power transmission equipment, nec
PA: Component Technology International,
Inc.
2229 S 54th St
Milwaukee WI 53219

(G-1969)
CONCIERGE TRANSIT LLC
Also Called: Concierge Consulting - Itsm
1623 Swan Dr (28216-5915)
PHONE..............................704 778-0755
EMP: 5 **EST:** 2016
SQ FT: 500
SALES (est): 575K **Privately Held**
Web: www.conciergetransit.com
SIC: 4111 3499 4513 Local and suburban
transit; Stabilizing bars (cargo), metal; Air
courier services

(G-1970)
CONCRETE SUPPLY CO LLC (HQ)
3823 Raleigh St (28206-2042)
P.O. Box 5247 (28299-5247)
PHONE..............................864 517-4055
EMP: 6 **EST:** 2013
SALES (est): 19.02MM
SALES (corp-wide): 149.62MM **Privately
Held**

Web: www.concretesupplyco.com
SIC: 3273 Ready-mixed concrete
PA: Concrete Supply Holdings, Inc.
3823 Raleigh St
Charlotte NC 28206
704 372-2930

(G-1971)
CONCRETE SUPPLY CO LLC (HQ)
Also Called: Concrete Supply Co
3823 Raleigh St (28206-2042)
P.O. Box 5247 (28299)
PHONE..............................704 372-2930
EMP: 21 **EST:** 2013
SALES (est): 26.22MM
SALES (corp-wide): 149.62MM **Privately
Held**
Web: www.concretesupplyco.com
SIC: 3273 Ready-mixed concrete
PA: Concrete Supply Holdings, Inc.
3823 Raleigh St
Charlotte NC 28206
704 372-2930

(G-1972)
**CONCRETE SUPPLY HOLDINGS INC
(PA)**
3823 Raleigh St (28206-2042)
P.O. Box 5247 (28299-5247)
PHONE..............................704 372-2930
EMP: 352 **EST:** 1958
SALES (est): 149.62MM
SALES (corp-wide): 149.62MM **Privately
Held**
Web: www.concretesupplyco.com
SIC: 3273 Ready-mixed concrete

(G-1973)
CONFAB MANUFACTURING CO LLC
6525 Morrison Blvd Ste 300 (28211-3561)
PHONE..............................704 366-7140
EMP: 11 **EST:** 2019
SALES (est): 5.19MM **Privately Held**
Web: www.con-fab.com
SIC: 3441 Fabricated structural metal
HQ: Wastequip, Llc
6525 Crnegie Blvd Ste 300
Charlotte NC 28211

(G-1974)
CONJET INC
3400 International Airport Dr Ste 100
(28208-4788)
PHONE..............................636 485-4724
Jonah Lindh, *CEO*
EMP: 4 **EST:** 2021
SALES (est): 515.03K **Privately Held**
Web: www.conjet.com
SIC: 3531 Construction machinery

(G-1975)
CONSOLIDATED PRESS INC
Also Called: Consolidated Press Charlotte
3900 Greensboro St (28206-2036)
PHONE..............................704 372-6785
Tim Mullaney, *Pr*
▼ **EMP:** 8 **EST:** 1966
SQ FT: 10,500
SALES (est): 486.42K **Privately Held**
Web: www.consolidatedpress.net
SIC: 2752 5112 Offset printing; Business
forms

(G-1976)
CONSULTANTS IN DATA PROC INC
Also Called: Cdp
6911 Shannon Willow Rd Ste 100
(28226-1346)
P.O. Box 472046 (28247-2046)
PHONE..............................704 542-6339
Paul Riefenberg, *Pr*

EMP: 5 **EST:** 1981
SALES (est): 2.58MM **Privately Held**
Web: www.cdp-inc.com
SIC: 7372 7374 7379 Prepackaged software
; Data processing service; Computer
related consulting services

(G-1977)
CONTAGIOUS GRAPHICS INC
5901 Orr Rd (28213-6321)
P.O. Box 560825 (28256-0825)
PHONE..............................704 529-5600
William Vasil, *Pr*
Steve Munsell, *
EMP: 38 **EST:** 1995
SQ FT: 15,000
SALES (est): 724.61K **Privately Held**
Web: www.contagiousgraphics.com
SIC: 2759 3993 2396 Screen printing; Signs
and advertising specialties; Automotive and
apparel trimmings

(G-1978)
**CONTECH ENGNERED SOLUTIONS
LLC**
4242 Raleigh St (28213-6902)
PHONE..............................704 596-4226
Aaron Johnson, *Mgr*
EMP: 23
SQ FT: 25,355
Web: www.conteches.com
SIC: 3443 Fabricated plate work (boiler shop)
HQ: Contech Engineered Solutions Llc
9025 Centre Pointe Dr # 400
West Chester OH 45069
513 645-7000

(G-1979)
CONVERGENT INTEGRATION INC
10205 Foxhall Dr (28210-7848)
PHONE..............................704 516-5922
Trevor D Petruk, *Prin*
EMP: 4 **EST:** 2008
SALES (est): 367.18K **Privately Held**
SIC: 3674 Semiconductors and related
devices

(G-1980)
CONXIT TECHNOLOGY GROUP INC
9101 Southern Pine Blvd Ste 250
(28273-5529)
PHONE..............................877 998-4227
Shawn Glenn Miller, *CEO*
EMP: 6 **EST:** 2007
SALES (est): 467.56K **Privately Held**
SIC: 7372 Educational computer software

(G-1981)
COOPER B-LINE INC
3810 Ayscough Rd (28211-3206)
PHONE..............................704 522-6272
EMP: 84
Web: www.eaton.com
SIC: 3441 Fabricated structural metal
HQ: Cooper B-Line, Inc.
509 W Monroe St
Highland IL 62249
618 654-2184

(G-1982)
COPY CAT INSTANT PRTG CHRLTTE
4612 South Blvd Ste B (28209-2864)
PHONE..............................704 529-6606
Diane Gilbert, *Pr*
EMP: 5 **EST:** 1987
SALES (est): 179.89K **Privately Held**
Web: www.copycatsouth.com
SIC: 2752 Offset printing

(G-1983)
COPY EXPRESS CHARLOTTE INC
4004 South Blvd Ste A (28209-2054)
PHONE..............................704 527-1750
Bennett Z Travis, *Pr*
Sandy Travis, *VP*
EMP: 7 **EST:** 1986
SQ FT: 4,000
SALES (est): 567.36K **Privately Held**
Web: www.mycopyexpress.com
SIC: 2752 Offset printing

(G-1984)
CORDEX INSTRUMENTS INC
5309 Monroe Rd (28205-7829)
PHONE..............................877 836-0764
Gary Copeland, *Prin*
EMP: 6 **EST:** 2010
SALES (est): 377.11K **Privately Held**
SIC: 3823 Process control instruments

(G-1985)
CORMETECH INC (HQ)
11707 Steele Creek Rd (28273-3718)
PHONE..............................704 827-8933
Patricia Martinez, *Pr*
Mike Mattes, *
Matt Leimieux, *
Scott Daugherty, *
Mark Vasco, *
◆ **EMP:** 176 **EST:** 1989
SQ FT: 90,000
SALES (est): 99.92MM
SALES (corp-wide): 106.43MM **Privately
Held**
Web: www.cormetech.com
SIC: 3295 2819 Filtering clays, treated;
Catalysts, chemical
PA: Steag Scr-Tech, Inc.
11707 Steele Creek Rd
Charlotte NC 28273
704 827-8933

(G-1986)
**CORNING OPTCAL CMMNCATIONS
LLC (HQ)**
4200 Corning Pl (28216)
PHONE..............................828 901-5000
Giovanni N Cortazzo, *
Steven Morris, *
◆ **EMP:** 510 **EST:** 1977
SALES (est): 581.2MM
SALES (corp-wide): 13.12B **Publicly Held**
Web: www.corning.com
SIC: 3661 Telephone and telegraph
apparatus
PA: Corning Incorporated
1 Riverfront Plz
Corning NY 14831
607 974-9000

(G-1987)
**CORNING OPTCAL CMMNCATIONS
LLC**
Also Called: Corning
4200 Corning Pl (28216-1298)
PHONE..............................828 901-5000
EMP: 517
SALES (corp-wide): 13.12B **Publicly Held**
Web: www.corning.com
SIC: 3661 Fiber optics communications
equipment
HQ: Corning Optical Communications Llc
4200 Corning Pl
Charlotte NC 28216
828 901-5000

(G-1988)
COROB NORTH AMERICA INC
Also Called: Cpscolor

4901 Gibbon Rd A (28269-8531)
PHONE.............................704 588-8408
Tero Telaranta, *CEO*
◆ **EMP: 17 EST:** 1994
SALES (est): 4.47MM
SALES (corp-wide): 2.11B **Publicly Held**
SIC: 3559 Paint making machinery
HQ: Corob Spa
　　Via Dell'agricoltura 103
　　San Felice Sul Panaro MO 41038

(G-1989)
CORPORATE PLACE LLC
13320 Ballantyne Corporate Pl
(28277-3607)
PHONE.............................704 808-3848
Marc Michael, *Pr*
David Kowalski, *Global Manufacturing
Operations President*
EMP: 7 EST: 2015
SALES (est): 4.47MM
SALES (corp-wide): 1.78B **Privately Held**
Web: www.goballantyne.com
SIC: 3556 3559 Dairy and milk machinery;
　　Pharmaceutical machinery
HQ: Spx Flow, Inc.
　　13320 Ballantyne Corp Pl
　　Charlotte NC 28277
　　704 752-4400

(G-1990)
COSMOPROS
1001 E W T Harris Blvd (28213-4104)
PHONE.............................704 717-7420
Lisa Oldham, *Mgr*
EMP: 4 EST: 2007
SALES (est): 200.96K **Privately Held**
SIC: 3999 5087 Barber and beauty shop
　　equipment; Beauty salon and barber shop
　　equipment and supplies

(G-1991)
COUNTRY LOTUS SOAPS LLC
2313 Ginger Ln Apt H (28213-6567)
PHONE.............................786 384-4174
Iris Gutierrez, *CEO*
EMP: 4 EST: 2020
SALES (est): 126.85K **Privately Held**
SIC: 2841 Soap and other detergents

(G-1992)
CP LIQUIDATION INC
5104 N Graham St (28269-4829)
PHONE.............................704 921-1100
EMP: 85
SIC: 2448 Pallets, wood

(G-1993)
CRACKLE HOLDINGS LP
1800 Continental Blvd Ste 200c
(28273-6388)
PHONE.............................704 927-7620
John Heyman, *CEO*
EMP: 1302 EST: 2017
SQ FT: 69,953
SALES (est): 4.45MM **Privately Held**
SIC: 3679 Electronic circuits

(G-1994)
CRAFT REVOLUTION LLC (PA)
Also Called: Artisanal Brewing Ventures
4001 Yancey Rd Ste A (28217-1772)
PHONE.............................347 924-7540
EMP: 10 EST: 2016
SALES (est): 10.75MM
SALES (corp-wide): 10.75MM **Privately
Held**
SIC: 2082 Malt beverage products

(G-1995)
CRANE SOUTH LLC
2905 Westinghouse Blvd Ste 300
(28273-6498)
PHONE.............................980 422-5874
EMP: 5
SALES (est): 1.4MM **Privately Held**
SIC: 3536 Hoists, cranes, and monorails

(G-1996)
CRITICORE INC (PA)
9525 Monroe Rd Ste 150 (28270-2451)
PHONE.............................704 542-6876
Scott Banks, *Pr*
Greg Winn, *VP*
Michael Dawid, *CFO*
▲ **EMP: 10 EST:** 1998
SALES (est): 23.16MM
SALES (corp-wide): 23.16MM **Privately
Held**
Web: www.criticoreinc.com
SIC: 2326 Service apparel (baker, barber,
　　lab, etc.), washable: men's

(G-1997)
CROFT PRECISION TOOLS INC
4424 Taggart Creek Rd Ste 108
(28208-5494)
PHONE.............................704 399-4124
Derek T Goring, *Pr*
EMP: 6 EST: 1982
SALES (est): 483.48K **Privately Held**
Web: www.crofttools.com
SIC: 3545 Diamond cutting tools for turning,
　　boring, burnishing, etc.

(G-1998)
CROWN CASE CO
801 Atando Ave Ste C (28206-1949)
PHONE.............................704 453-1542
Fred Floye, *Pr*
EMP: 6 EST: 2010
SALES (est): 157.35K **Privately Held**
SIC: 3443 Containers, shipping (bombs,
　　etc.): metal plate

(G-1999)
CRYOVAC LLC (HQ)
2415 Cascade Pointe Blvd (28208-6899)
PHONE.............................980 430-7000
▲ **EMP: 600 EST:** 1981
SALES (est): 446.97MM
SALES (corp-wide): 5.39B **Publicly Held**
Web: www.sealedair.com
SIC: 3086 Packaging and shipping
　　materials, foamed plastics
PA: Sealed Air Corporation
　　2415 Cascade Pointe Blvd
　　Charlotte NC 28208
　　980 221-3235

(G-2000)
CRYOVAC INTL HOLDINGS INC (HQ)
2415 Cascade Pointe Blvd (28208-6899)
PHONE.............................980 430-7000
EMP: 48 EST: 1997
SALES (est): 13.98MM
SALES (corp-wide): 5.39B **Publicly Held**
Web: www.sealedair.com
SIC: 3086 Packaging and shipping
　　materials, foamed plastics
PA: Sealed Air Corporation
　　2415 Cascade Pointe Blvd
　　Charlotte NC 28208
　　980 221-3235

(G-2001)
CRYOVAC LEASING CORPORATION
2415 Cascade Pointe Blvd (28208-6899)
PHONE.............................980 430-7000

EMP: 7 EST: 2001
SALES (est): 2MM
SALES (corp-wide): 5.39B **Publicly Held**
SIC: 2673 Bags: plastic, laminated, and
　　coated
PA: Sealed Air Corporation
　　2415 Cascade Pointe Blvd
　　Charlotte NC 28208
　　980 221-3235

(G-2002)
CSM LOGISTICS LLC
4835 Sirona Dr Ste 300 (28273-3965)
PHONE.............................980 800-2621
EMP: 4 EST: 2018
SALES (est): 355.13K **Privately Held**
SIC: 3537 Containers (metal), air cargo

(G-2003)
CUMMINS INC
Also Called: Cummins
3700 Jeff Adams Dr (28206-1288)
PHONE.............................704 596-7690
Jeff Johnson, *Mgr*
EMP: 15
SALES (corp-wide): 34.1B **Publicly Held**
Web: www.cummins.com
SIC: 5063 7538 5084 3519 Generators;
　　Diesel engine repair: automotive; Industrial
　　machinery and equipment; Internal
　　combustion engines, nec
PA: Cummins Inc.
　　500 Jackson St
　　Columbus IN 47201
　　812 377-5000

(G-2004)
CUMULUS FIBRES INC
1101 Tar Heel Rd (28208-1524)
P.O. Box 669609 (28266-9609)
PHONE.............................704 394-2111
Darrell C Steagall, *Pr*
EMP: 258 EST: 1981
SQ FT: 59,276
SALES (est): 718.07K
SALES (corp-wide): 32.76MM **Privately
Held**
Web: www.cumulusfibres.com
SIC: 2297 2299 Nonwoven fabrics; Apparel
　　filling: cotton waste, kapok, and related
　　material
PA: Empire Investment Holdings, Llc
　　1220 Malaga Ave
　　Coral Gables FL 33134
　　305 403-1111

(G-2005)
**CURTISS-WRIGHT CONTROLS INC
(HQ)**
15801 Brixham Hill Ave Ste 200
(28277-4792)
PHONE.............................704 869-4600
Tom Quinly, *Pr*
Brian Freeman, *
Allan E Symonds, *
▲ **EMP: 24 EST:** 1945
SQ FT: 1,260
SALES (est): 844.03MM
SALES (corp-wide): 3.12B **Publicly Held**
Web: www.curtisswright.com
SIC: 3728 Aircraft assemblies,
　　subassemblies, and parts, nec
PA: Curtiss-Wright Corporation
　　130 Harbour Pl Dr Ste 300
　　Davidson NC 28036
　　704 869-4600

(G-2006)
CURTISS-WRIGHT CORPORATION
13925 Ballantyne Corporate Pl
(28277-2704)

PHONE.............................973 541-3700
EMP: 4
SALES (corp-wide): 3.12B **Publicly Held**
Web: www.curtisswright.com
SIC: 3491 Industrial valves
PA: Curtiss-Wright Corporation
　　130 Harbour Pl Dr Ste 300
　　Davidson NC 28036
　　704 869-4600

(G-2007)
CURTISS-WRIGHT CORPORATION
500 Springbrook Rd (28217-2147)
PHONE.............................704 869-4675
EMP: 5
SALES (corp-wide): 3.12B **Publicly Held**
Web: www.curtisswright.com
SIC: 3491 Industrial valves
PA: Curtiss-Wright Corporation
　　130 Harbour Pl Dr Ste 300
　　Davidson NC 28036
　　704 869-4600

(G-2008)
CUSTOM CORRUGATED CNTRS INC
5024 Westinghouse Blvd (28273-9641)
P.O. Box 38899 (28278-1015)
PHONE.............................704 588-0371
W Wayne Forbis, *Pr*
Dean Forbis, *
EMP: 38 EST: 1972
SQ FT: 65,000
SALES (est): 2.48MM **Privately Held**
Web: www.customcorr.com
SIC: 2653 Boxes, corrugated: made from
　　purchased materials

(G-2009)
CUSTOM GLASS WORKS INC
2000 W Morehead St Ste F (28208-5175)
PHONE.............................704 597-0290
Georgia Droppelman, *Pr*
EMP: 9 EST: 1988
SQ FT: 5,000
SALES (est): 286.57K **Privately Held**
Web: www.customglassofnc.com
SIC: 3231 Leaded glass

(G-2010)
CUSTOM NEON & GRAPHICS INC
1722 Toal St (28206-1524)
PHONE.............................704 344-1715
Cynthia Wilcox, *Pr*
Mike Wilcox, *Sec*
EMP: 6 EST: 1997
SQ FT: 10,000
SALES (est): 179.11K **Privately Held**
SIC: 5046 3993 Neon signs; Neon signs

(G-2011)
CUSTOM POLYMERS INC (PA)
Also Called: Custom Polymers
831 E Morehead St Ste 840 (28202)
PHONE.............................704 332-6070
Philip F Howerton Iii, *Pr*
John N Calhoun Ii, *VP*
◆ **EMP: 10 EST:** 1996
SQ FT: 42,000
SALES (est): 43.39MM **Privately Held**
Web: www.custompolymers.com
SIC: 4953 2821 2822 Recycling, waste
　　materials; Plastics materials and resins;
　　Ethylene-propylene rubbers, EPDM
　　polymers

(G-2012)
CUSTOM POLYMERS PET LLC (PA)
831 E Morehead St Ste 840 (28202-2726)
PHONE.............................866 717-0716
Byron Geiger, *Pr*
▲ **EMP: 68 EST:** 2008

SALES (est): 15.95MM **Privately Held**
Web: www.custompolymerspet.com
SIC: 2821 Plastics materials and resins

(G-2013)
D&E FREIGHT LLC
Also Called: Freight Company
4427 Knollcrest Dr (28208-1424)
PHONE..............................704 977-4847
Eric Mitchell, *Managing Member*
EMP: 10 EST: 2021
SALES (est): 265.74K **Privately Held**
Web: www.dandefreight.com
SIC: 4789 3537 Transportation services, nec
; Trucks: freight, baggage, etc.: industrial,
except mining

(G-2014)
DAIKIN APPLIED AMERICAS INC
13504 S Point Blvd Ste G (28273-6763)
PHONE..............................704 588-0087
Dimitris Alexand, *Mgr*
EMP: 8
Web: www.daikinapplied.com
SIC: 3585 7623 Air conditioning units,
complete: domestic or industrial;
Refrigeration service and repair
HQ: Daikin Applied Americas Inc.
13600 Industrial Pk Blvd
Minneapolis MN 55441
763 553-5330

(G-2015)
DAILY LIVING SOLUTIONS INC
9711 Stewart Spring Ln (28216-1857)
PHONE..............................704 614-0977
Wilson Ford, *Prin*
EMP: 4 EST: 2010
SALES (est): 245.75K **Privately Held**
SIC: 2711 Newspapers, publishing and
printing

(G-2016)
DAISY PINK CO
10335 Worsley Ln (28269-8163)
PHONE..............................704 907-3526
Sutrina Benge, *Prin*
EMP: 6 EST: 2013
SALES (est): 87.88K **Privately Held**
Web: www.pinkdaisyco.com
SIC: 3999 Candles

(G-2017)
DALE REYNOLDS CABINETS INC
301 Kimmswick Rd (28214-1247)
PHONE..............................704 890-5962
EMP: 5 EST: 2017
SALES (est): 249.14K **Privately Held**
SIC: 3999 2541 Manufacturing industries,
nec; Cabinets, lockers, and shelving

(G-2018)
DARAMIC LLC (DH)
11430 N Community House Rd Ste 350
(28277-0454)
PHONE..............................704 587-8599
Hiroyoshi Matsuyama, *CEO*
Tucker Roe, *VP Sls*
◆ EMP: 100 EST: 1994
SALES (est): 46.22MM **Privately Held**
Web: www.daramic.com
SIC: 3069 2499 3269 Roofing, membrane
rubber; Battery separators, wood; Filtering
media, pottery
HQ: Polypore International, Lp
13800 S Lakes Dr
Charlotte NC 28273
704 587-8409

(G-2019)
DATAWISE LLC ✪
9111 Kristen Lake Ct (28270-0022)
PHONE..............................704 293-1482
Elizabeth I Johnson, *Managing Member*
EMP: 4 EST: 2024
SALES (est): 1.1MM **Privately Held**
SIC: 7372 Prepackaged software

(G-2020)
DAVID YURMAN ENTERPRISES LLC
4400 Sharon Rd Ste 177 (28211-3612)
PHONE..............................704 366-7259
Glen T Senk, *CEO*
EMP: 9
SALES (corp-wide): 171.21MM **Privately
Held**
Web: www.davidyurman.com
SIC: 3911 Jewelry, precious metal
PA: David Yurman Enterprises Llc
24 Vestry St
New York NY 10013
212 896-1550

(G-2021)
DAVIS EQUIPMENT HANDLERS INC
3860 Abiliene Rd (28205)
PHONE..............................704 792-9176
Jonathan Davis, *Pr*
Laura Davis, *Sec*
EMP: 4 EST: 1991
SALES (est): 198.59K **Privately Held**
SIC: 3312 Stainless steel

(G-2022)
DAVIS VOGLER ENTERPRISES LLC
5316 Camilla Dr (28226-6769)
PHONE..............................402 257-7188
Scott P Vgler, *Prin*
EMP: 4 EST: 2016
SALES (est): 304.05K **Privately Held**
Web: vogler-davis-enterprises.hub.biz
SIC: 2759 Screen printing

(G-2023)
DBT HOLDINGS LLC
Also Called: Deutsche Beverage
6030 Airport Dr (28208)
PHONE..............................704 900-6606
Cameron J Cane, *Pr*
Sheila R Cane, *
▲ EMP: 57 EST: 2007
SALES (est): 9.21MM
SALES (corp-wide): 3.88B **Publicly Held**
Web: www.deutscheequipment.com
SIC: 3556 5084 Beverage machinery;
Brewery products manufacturing
machinery, commercial
PA: The Middleby Corporation
1400 Toastmaster Dr
Elgin IL 60120
847 741-3300

(G-2024)
DEBMED USA LLC
2815 Coliseum Centre Dr # 6 (28217-1452)
PHONE..............................704 263-4240
Dawn Huston, *Mktg Mgr*
EMP: 7 EST: 2013
SALES (est): 933.89K
SALES (corp-wide): 1.11B **Privately Held**
Web: www.scjp.com
SIC: 2834 Medicines, capsuled or ampuled
PA: S. C. Johnson & Son, Inc.
1525 Howe St
Racine WI 53403
262 260-2000

(G-2025)
DECIMA CORPORATION LLC
2201 South Blvd (28203-0076)
PHONE..............................734 516-1535
Arto Diamond, *CEO*
EMP: 30 EST: 2019
SALES (est): 3.14MM **Privately Held**
SIC: 2434 5099 Wood kitchen cabinets;
Wood and wood by-products

(G-2026)
DECOLUX USA
6024 Shining Oak Ln (28269-0001)
PHONE..............................704 340-3532
Monica Vasquez, *Admn*
EMP: 5
SALES (est): 67.62K **Privately Held**
Web: www.decoluxusa.com
SIC: 2591 7389 Blinds vertical; Business
services, nec

(G-2027)
DELANEY HOLDINGS CO
13320 Ballantyne Corporate Pl
(28277-3607)
PHONE..............................704 808-3848
Marc Michael, *Pr*
David Kowalski, *Global Manufacturing
Operations President*
EMP: 6 EST: 2011
SALES (est): 2.42MM
SALES (corp-wide): 1.78B **Privately Held**
SIC: 3556 3559 Dairy and milk machinery;
Pharmaceutical machinery
HQ: Spx Flow, Inc.
13320 Ballantyne Corp Pl
Charlotte NC 28277
704 752-4400

(G-2028)
DELLNER INC
Also Called: Dellner Brakes
4016 Shutterfly Rd Ste 100 (28217-3078)
PHONE..............................704 527-2121
Jeron Cain, *Pr*
David Pagels, *
Tom Sharp, *
▲ EMP: 37 EST: 1960
SQ FT: 10,000
SALES (est): 8.43MM
SALES (corp-wide): 209.33MM **Privately
Held**
Web: www.dellner.com
SIC: 3743 Railroad locomotives and parts,
electric or nonelectric
HQ: Dellner Couplers Ab
Vikavagen 144
Falun 791 9
23765407

(G-2029)
DELTA MOLD INC
9415 Stockport Pl (28273-4564)
PHONE..............................704 588-6600
Eric Mozer, *CEO*
Jim Quinn, *
◆ EMP: 90 EST: 1978
SQ FT: 50,000
SALES (est): 21.45MM **Privately Held**
Web: www.deltamold.com
SIC: 3089 Injection molding of plastics

(G-2030)
DENTAL EQUIPMENT LLC
Also Called: Marus Dental
11727 Fruehauf Dr (28273-6507)
P.O. Box 7800 (28241-7800)
PHONE..............................704 588-2126
John Regan, *
Vicente Reynal, *
▲ EMP: 500 EST: 2005

SQ FT: 137,438
SALES (est): 7.77MM
SALES (corp-wide): 23.88B **Publicly Held**
Web:
www.henryscheinequipmentcatalog.com
SIC: 3843 Dental equipment and supplies
PA: Danaher Corporation
2200 Pa Ave Nw Ste 800w
Washington DC 20037
202 828-0850

(G-2031)
DENTSPLY NORTH AMERICA LLC
13320 Ballantyne Corporate Pl
(28277-3645)
PHONE..............................844 848-0137
Mark A Thierer, *CEO*
EMP: 8 EST: 2000
SALES (est): 3.07MM
SALES (corp-wide): 3.79B **Publicly Held**
SIC: 3843 Dental equipment and supplies
PA: Dentsply Sirona Inc.
13320 Ballantyne Corp Pl
Charlotte NC 28277
844 848-0137

(G-2032)
DENTSPLY SIRONA INC (PA)
Also Called: DENTSPLY SIRONA
13320 Ballantyne Corporate Pl (28277)
PHONE..............................844 848-0137
Simon D Campion, *Pr*
Gregory T Lucier, *Non-Executive Chairman
of the Board*
Andrea L Frohning, *Chief Human
Resources Officer*
Robert A Johnson Senior, *Co-Vice President*
Richard C Rosenzweig, *Ex VP*
◆ EMP: 600 EST: 1877
SALES (est): 3.79B
SALES (corp-wide): 3.79B **Publicly Held**
Web: www.dentsplysirona.com
SIC: 3843 Dental equipment and supplies

(G-2033)
DENVER GLOBAL PRODUCTS INC
6420 Rea Rd Ste A1 (28277-0771)
PHONE..............................704 665-1800
David Agee, *CFO*
Keith Piercy, *CFO*
Jeanne Hendrix, *COO*
◆ EMP: 52 EST: 2010
SQ FT: 5,500
SALES (est): 9.29MM **Privately Held**
SIC: 3546 Power-driven handtools
PA: Chongqing Runtong Holding (Group)
Co., Ltd.
No.99, Jiujiang Ave, Area B, Shuangfu
Industrial Park, Jiangjin
Chongqing CQ 40224

(G-2034)
DERITA PRECISION MCH CO INC
605 Toddville Rd (28214-1835)
P.O. Box 645 (28130-0645)
PHONE..............................704 392-7285
Dennis L Butts Senior, *Pr*
Dennis L Butts Junior, *VP*
EMP: 10 EST: 1955
SQ FT: 12,000
SALES (est): 1.52MM **Privately Held**
Web: www.derita.com
SIC: 3469 3452 Machine parts, stamped or
pressed metal; Bolts, metal

(G-2035)
DESIGNLINE CORPORATION
Also Called: Designline Intl Holdings
2309 Nevada Blvd (28273-6430)
PHONE..............................704 494-7800
▲ EMP: 250

GEOGRAPHIC

Web: www.transteq.com
SIC: 3711 Buses, all types, assembly of

(G-2036)
DESIGNLINE USA LLC
2309 Nevada Blvd (28273-6430)
P.O. Box 7405 (28241-7405)
PHONE....................704 494-7800
G Michael Floyd, *Ex VP*
Joshua Anderson, *Ex VP*
Andy Maunder, *CFO*
Michael Floyd, *Ex VP*
EMP: 11 EST: 2008
SQ FT: 172,039
SALES (est): 1.42MM **Privately Held**
Web: www.designlineusa.com
SIC: 3711 3713 Bus and other large
   specialty vehicle assembly; Truck and bus
   bodies

(G-2037)
DEUROTECH AMERICA INC
4526 Westinghouse Blvd Ste A
(28273-9602)
PHONE....................980 272-6827
Brett Davis, *Prin*
EMP: 8 EST: 2016
SALES (est): 2.86MM **Privately Held**
Web: america.deurotechgroup.com
SIC: 3569 5084 General industrial
   machinery, nec; Industrial machinery and
   equipment

(G-2038)
DFA DAIRY BRANDS FLUID LLC
3540 Toringdon Way Ste 200 (28277-4650)
PHONE....................704 341-2794
Anita Sasser, *Brnch Mgr*
EMP: 8
SALES (corp-wide): 21.72B **Privately Held**
Web: www.dfamilk.com
SIC: 2033 2097 5143 5149 Fruit juices:
   packaged in cans, jars, etc.; Manufactured
   ice; Ice cream and ices; Coffee, green or
   roasted
HQ: Dfa Dairy Brands Fluid, Llc
   1405 N 98th St
   Kansas City KS 66111
   816 801-6455

(G-2039)
DIAGNOSTIC DEVICES
2701 Hutchison Mcdonald Rd Ste A
(28269-4217)
PHONE....................704 599-5908
Stephanie Cranford, *Mgr*
EMP: 8 EST: 2018
SALES (est): 886.03K **Privately Held**
SIC: 2834 Pharmaceutical preparations

(G-2040)
DIAMOND POWER INTL LLC
13024 Ballantyne Corporate Pl Ste 700
(28277-2113)
PHONE....................704 625-4900
EMP: 4 EST: 2018
SALES (est): 1.78MM
SALES (corp-wide): 999.35MM **Publicly
Held**
Web: www.babcock.com
SIC: 3511 Turbines and turbine generator
   sets
PA: Babcock & Wilcox Enterprises, Inc.
   1200 E Market St Ste 650
   Akron OH 44305
   330 753-4511

(G-2041)
DIAMOND PWR EQITY INVSTMNTS IN
13024 Ballantyne Corporate Pl Ste 700
(28277-2113)

PHONE....................704 625-4900
EMP: 4 EST: 2017
SALES (est): 1.78MM
SALES (corp-wide): 999.35MM **Publicly
Held**
SIC: 3511 Turbines and turbine generator
   sets
PA: Babcock & Wilcox Enterprises, Inc.
   1200 E Market St Ste 650
   Akron OH 44305
   330 753-4511

(G-2042)
DICKERSON GROUP INC (PA)
1111 Metropolitan Ave Ste 1090
(28204-3439)
P.O. Box 5011 (28111)
PHONE....................704 289-3111
John Joyner, *Pr*
EMP: 5 EST: 1945
SALES (est): 47.01MM
SALES (corp-wide): 47.01MM **Privately
Held**
Web: www.dickersoninc.com
SIC: 1611 2951 Highway and street paving
   contractor; Asphalt paving mixtures and
   blocks

(G-2043)
DICKIE CD & ASSOCIATES INC
Also Called: Fastsigns
4612 South Blvd Ste A (28209-2864)
PHONE....................704 527-9102
Carl Dickey, *Pr*
Barbara Dickey, *VP*
EMP: 10 EST: 1995
SALES (est): 108.23K **Privately Held**
Web: www.fastsigns.com
SIC: 3993 Signs and advertising specialties

(G-2044)
DIEBOLD NIXDORF INCORPORATED
5900 Northwoods Business Pkwy Ste K
(28269-5747)
PHONE....................704 599-3100
Bud Hancock, *Mgr*
EMP: 26
SALES (corp-wide): 3.75B **Publicly Held**
Web: www.dieboldnixdorf.com
SIC: 5049 1731 7382 7381 Bank equipment
   and supplies; Banking machine installation
   and service; Security systems services;
   Detective and armored car services
PA: Diebold Nixdorf, Incorporated
   350 Orchard Ave Ne
   North Canton OH 44720
   330 490-4000

(G-2045)
DIGITAL AP PRTG DBA F4MILY MTT
3623 Latrobe Dr (28211-4864)
PHONE....................980 939-8066
Samir Hamid, *CEO*
EMP: 5 EST: 2012
SALES (est): 590.76K **Privately Held**
Web: www.f4milymatters.com
SIC: 2752 Commercial printing, lithographic

(G-2046)
DIGITAL DESIGNS INC
3540 Toringdon Way Ste 200 (28277-4650)
P.O. Box 5011 (28111-5011)
PHONE....................704 790-7100
John C Queen, *Pr*
Sue Ratliff, *
Jeff Buckner, *
EMP: 25 EST: 1980
SALES (est): 4.15MM **Privately Held**
Web: www.ddilink.com

SIC: 7371 7379 7372 Custom computer
   programming services; Computer related
   consulting services; Prepackaged software

(G-2047)
**DIGITAL PRINTING SYSTEMS INC
(PA)**
Also Called: Visual Impressions
606 E Hebron St (28273-5991)
P.O. Box 470666 (28247-0666)
PHONE....................704 525-0190
John Forgach, *Pr*
Brian Mckenna, *VP*
Roger Cox, *Contrlr*
EMP: 20 EST: 1994
SQ FT: 25,000
SALES (est): 6.45MM **Privately Held**
Web: www.visualimpressions.net
SIC: 3993 5712 7372 2759 Signs and
   advertising specialties; Cabinet work,
   custom; Application computer software;
   Posters, including billboards: printing, nsk

(G-2048)
DILWORTH CUSTOM FRAMING
125 Remount Rd Ste C2 (28203-6459)
PHONE....................704 370-7660
EMP: 4 EST: 2017
SALES (est): 90.53K **Privately Held**
Web: www.dilworthcustomframing.com
SIC: 2499 Picture frame molding, finished

(G-2049)
**DILWORTH MATTRESS COMPANY
INC (PA)**
211 W Worthington Ave (28203-4419)
PHONE....................704 333-6564
Alan Hirsch, *Pr*
Deborah Hirsch, *Sec*
EMP: 4 EST: 1931
SQ FT: 15,000
SALES (est): 121.27K
SALES (corp-wide): 121.27K **Privately
Held**
Web: www.dilworthmattressfactory.com
SIC: 2515 5712 Mattresses, innerspring or
   box spring; Mattresses

(G-2050)
DIRECT CHASSISLINK INC (PA)
Also Called: Dcli
3525 Whitehall Park Dr Ste 400 (28273)
PHONE....................704 594-3800
Bill Shea, *CEO*
Lee Newitt, *
◆ EMP: 25 EST: 1974
SQ FT: 147,000
SALES (est): 116.43MM
SALES (corp-wide): 116.43MM **Privately
Held**
Web: www.dcli.com
SIC: 3711 Chassis, motor vehicle

(G-2051)
DIRECT DIGITAL LLC (PA)
Also Called: Adaptive Health
615 S College St Ste 1300 (28202-0144)
PHONE....................704 557-0987
Michael Amburgey, *Managing Member*
EMP: 15 EST: 2009
SALES (est): 71.99MM **Privately Held**
Web: www.adaptivehealth.com
SIC: 2833 Medicinals and botanicals

(G-2052)
DISCOUNT PRINTING INC
2914 Crosby Rd (28211-2815)
PHONE....................704 365-3665
Paul Snyder, *Pr*
Connie Snyder, *Sec*

EMP: 5 EST: 1983
SQ FT: 2,000
SALES (est): 66.86K **Privately Held**
SIC: 2752 Offset printing

(G-2053)
DISTINCTIVE CABINETS INC
319 Old Hebron Rd Ste A (28273-5709)
PHONE....................704 529-6234
Steve Young, *CEO*
Jenny Smith, *Sec*
EMP: 12 EST: 1995
SQ FT: 12,500
SALES (est): 2.05MM **Privately Held**
Web: www.distinctivecabinets.com
SIC: 1751 2517 2434 Cabinet building and
   installation; Wood television and radio
   cabinets; Wood kitchen cabinets

(G-2054)
DISTINCTIVE SOUL CREATIONS LLC
214 Oakton Glen Ct (28262-1756)
PHONE....................704 299-3269
Tameeka Ford, *Managing Member*
EMP: 5 EST: 2020
SALES (est): 150K **Privately Held**
Web: www.dsccatering.com
SIC: 2599 Food wagons, restaurant

(G-2055)
DIVERSFIED PRTG TECHNIQUES INC
Also Called: Franklin Investments
13336 S Ridge Dr (28273-4738)
P.O. Box 411409 (28241-1409)
PHONE....................704 583-9433
Tony F Chaney Senior, *Pr*
Judy W Chaney, *Sec*
Tony F Chaney Junior, *VP*
▲ EMP: 20 EST: 1983
SQ FT: 8,694
SALES (est): 4.9MM **Privately Held**
Web: www.diverprint.com
SIC: 5084 3555 Printing trades machinery,
   equipment, and supplies; Printing trades
   machinery

(G-2056)
DIVERSIFIED SIGNS GRAPHICS INC
5245 Old Dowd Rd (28208-2163)
PHONE....................704 392-8165
EMP: 10
SALES (corp-wide): 3.81MM **Privately
Held**
Web: www.diversified-signs.com
SIC: 3993 Signs and advertising specialties
PA: Diversified Signs & Graphics Inc.
   1123 James Harvey Rd
   York SC 29745
   803 628-1121

(G-2057)
DIXIE ELECTRO MECH SVCS INC
2115 Freedom Dr (28208-5153)
P.O. Box 668944 (28266-8944)
PHONE....................704 332-1116
Peggy Hunnicutt, *Pr*
Daryl Hunnicutt, *VP*
EMP: 16 EST: 1958
SQ FT: 35,000
SALES (est): 2.75MM **Privately Held**
Web: www.dixieemsi.com
SIC: 7694 5063 5999 Electric motor repair;
   Motors, electric; Motors, electric

(G-2058)
DLM SALES INC
Also Called: Charlotte Tent & Awning Co
5901 N Hill Cir (28213-6237)
PHONE....................704 399-2776
Travis Jenkins, *CEO*
EMP: 14 EST: 1994

SALES (est): 2.14MM **Privately Held**
Web: www.charlottetentandawning.com
SIC: **5999** 2394 Awnings; Canvas and
related products

(G-2059)
DMA INC
3123 May St (28217-1337)
PHONE..............................704 527-0992
Richard M Shanklin, *Pr*
Edward M Shanklin, *CEO*
Ronald Tucker, *VP*
EMP: 6 EST: 1972
SQ FT: 10,900
SALES (est): 1.86MM **Privately Held**
Web: www.dmainc.net
SIC: **3599** Machine shop, jobbing and repair

(G-2060)
DOC PORTERS DISTILLERY LLC
1010 Lexington Ave (28203-4831)
PHONE..............................704 266-1399
Andrew Porter, *Prin*
EMP: 6 EST: 2018
SALES (est): 175.86K **Privately Held**
Web: www.docporters.com
SIC: **2085** Distilled and blended liquors

(G-2061)
DOLE FOOD COMPANY INC (DH)
Also Called: Dole Food
200 S Tryon St Ste 600 (28202)
P.O. Box 5700 (91359)
PHONE..............................818 874-4000
David Murdock, *CEO*
Johan Linden, *
Charlene Mims, *
Yoon Hugh, *
Jay Esban, *
◆ **EMP: 26 EST:** 1851
SALES (est): 1.01B **Privately Held**
Web: www.dole.com
SIC: **5148** 2033 0175 0161 Fruits; Fruit
juices: fresh; Deciduous tree fruits; Lettuce
farm
HQ: Total Produce Limited
1 Beresford Street
Dublin

(G-2062)
DONALD HAACK DIAMONDS INC
Also Called: Donald Hack Diamonds Fine
Gems
3900 Colony Rd Ste E (28211-5022)
PHONE..............................704 365-4400
Julie Haack, *Pr*
Janet Haack, *Sec*
EMP: 9 EST: 1980
SQ FT: 2,200
SALES (est): 944.27K **Privately Held**
Web: www.donaldhaack.com
SIC: **7631** 3911 6411 5944 Jewelry repair
services; Jewel settings and mountings,
precious metal; Loss prevention services,
insurance; Jewelry, precious stones and
precious metals

(G-2063)
DOT BLUE READI-MIX LLC
1022 Exchange St (28208-1220)
PHONE..............................704 391-3000
Donnie Presson, *Manager*
EMP: 27
SALES (corp-wide): 23.52MM **Privately
Held**
Web: www.bluedotreadimix.com
SIC: **3273** Ready-mixed concrete
PA: Blue Dot Readi-Mix, Llc
11330 Bain School Rd
Mint Hill NC 28227
704 971-7676

(G-2064)
DOT BLUE SERVICES INC
Also Called: Envirnmental Svcs of Charlotte
11819 Reames Rd (28269-7639)
PHONE..............................704 342-2970
James Brannen, *VP*
EMP: 5 EST: 1985
SALES (est): 200.86K **Privately Held**
SIC: **3444** Sheet metalwork

(G-2065)
DRIVECO INC
13519 Norlington Ct (28273-6784)
PHONE..............................704 615-2111
Tomeka Lynch-purcel, *CEO*
Tomeka Purcell, *Prin*
EMP: 4 EST: 2020
SALES (est): 436.05K **Privately Held**
SIC: **3537** Trucks, tractors, loaders, carriers,
and similar equipment

(G-2066)
DRONESCAPE PLLC
9716 Rea Rd Ste B (28277-6790)
PHONE..............................704 953-3798
EMP: 5 EST: 2015
SQ FT: 2,000
SALES (est): 1.37MM **Privately Held**
Web: www.dronescape.com
SIC: **3728** 7389 8711 Target drones; Pipeline
and power line inspection service;
Engineering services

(G-2067)
DURABLE WOOD PRESERVERS INC
7901 Pence Rd (28215-4325)
P.O. Box 25825 (28229)
PHONE..............................704 537-3113
Beverly E Barksdale Iii, *Pr*
B D Barksdale, *Sec*
EMP: 7 EST: 1939
SQ FT: 8,000
SALES (est): 113.56K **Privately Held**
Web: www.durablewood.com
SIC: **2491** 5031 Wood preserving; Lumber,
plywood, and millwork

(G-2068)
DURAMAX HOLDINGS LLC
Also Called: Otto Environmental Systems
12700 General Dr (28273-6415)
PHONE..............................704 588-9191
Bryan Coll, *Managing Member*
EMP: 215 EST: 2021
SALES (est): 48.05MM
SALES (corp-wide): 48.05MM **Privately
Held**
Web: www.otto-usa.com
SIC: **4953** 3089 Recycling, waste materials;
Garbage containers, plastics
PA: Duramax Solutions Llc
1660 W 2nd St Ste 1100
Cleveland OH 44113
704 588-9191

(G-2069)
DURO HILEX POLY LLC (DH)
Also Called: Duro
3436 Toringdon Way Ste 100 (28277-2449)
PHONE..............................800 845-6051
Stan Bikulege, *Managing Member*
EMP: 99 EST: 2014
SALES (est): 213.62MM
SALES (corp-wide): 26.11B **Publicly Held**
Web: www.novolex.com
SIC: **2674** Paper bags: made from
purchased materials
HQ: Novolex Holdings, Llc
3436 Tringdon Way Ste 100
Charlotte NC 28277
800 845-6051

(G-2070)
DUTCH MILLER CHARLOTTE INC
Also Called: Dutch Miller Auto Group
7725 South Blvd (28273-5941)
PHONE..............................704 522-8422
Chris Miller, *Pr*
Matt Miller, *
Sam Miller, *
EMP: 15 EST: 2016
SALES (est): 1.3MM **Privately Held**
Web: www.dutchmillerclt.com
SIC: **5511** 3465 Automobiles, new and used;
Body parts, automobile: stamped metal

(G-2071)
DWM INTERNATIONAL INC
Also Called: Society Awards
2151 Hawkins St Ste 1225 (28203-4981)
PHONE..............................646 290-7448
David Moritz, *Pr*
◆ **EMP: 44 EST:** 2007
SQ FT: 3,000
SALES (est): 475.12K **Privately Held**
Web: www.societyawards.com
SIC: **3914** 7336 Trophies, nsk; Art design
services

(G-2072)
DYNACAST LLC (DH)
Also Called: Dynacast
11325 N Community House Rd Ste 300
(28277-1978)
PHONE..............................704 927-2790
Simon Newman, *Pr*
Adrian Murphy, *
David J Angell, *
Josef Ungerhofer, *
Sheriff Babu, *
▲ **EMP: 28 EST:** 1988
SQ FT: 75,000
SALES (est): 15.46MM
SALES (corp-wide): 1.08B **Privately Held**
Web: www.dynacast.com
SIC: **3364** 3363 3089 3365 Nonferrous die-
castings except aluminum; Aluminum die-
castings; Molding primary plastics;
Aluminum foundries
HQ: Dynacast Us Holdings, Inc.
14045 Balntyn Corp Pl
Charlotte NC 28277
704 927-2790

(G-2073)
**DYNACAST INTERNATIONAL LLC
(HQ)**
14045 Ballantyne Corporate Pl (28277)
PHONE..............................704 927-2790
EMP: 7 EST: 2011
SALES (est): 108.12MM
SALES (corp-wide): 1.08B **Privately Held**
Web: www.dynacast.com
SIC: **3369** 3364 3363 White metal castings
(lead, tin, antimony), except die; Nonferrous
die-castings except aluminum; Aluminum
die-castings
PA: Form Technologies, Inc.
11325 N Cmnty Hse Rd Ste
Charlotte NC 28277
704 927-2790

(G-2074)
DYNACAST US HOLDINGS INC
Dynacast Indus Prdcts-Fsteners
14045 Ballantyne Corporate Pl Ste 300
(28277-0099)
PHONE..............................704 927-2786
Simon Newman, *Brnch Mgr*
EMP: 10
SALES (corp-wide): 1.08B **Privately Held**
Web: www.dynacast.com

SIC: **3364** Nonferrous die-castings except
aluminum
HQ: Dynacast Us Holdings, Inc.
14045 Balntyn Corp Pl
Charlotte NC 28277
704 927-2790

(G-2075)
DYNACAST US HOLDINGS INC (DH)
Also Called: Dynacast
14045 Ballantyne Corporate Pl Ste 400
(28277-0099)
PHONE..............................704 927-2790
Simon Newman, *CEO*
Adrian Murphy, *CFO*
David Angell, *Prin*
Josef Ungerhofer, *Ex VP*
Herv Mallet, *Ex VP*
▲ **EMP: 9 EST:** 1999
SALES (est): 92.29MM
SALES (corp-wide): 1.08B **Privately Held**
Web: www.dynacast.com
SIC: **3544** Dies and die holders for metal
cutting, forming, die casting
HQ: Dynacast International Llc
14045 Ballantyne Corp Pl
Charlotte NC 28277

(G-2076)
**DYSTAR AMERICAS HOLDING CORP
(PA)**
9844 Southern Pine Blvd Ste A
(28273-5503)
PHONE..............................704 561-3000
Steve M Hennen, *Pr*
EMP: 9 EST: 2004
SALES (est): 5.19MM **Privately Held**
SIC: **2865** Dyes: azine, azo, azoic

(G-2077)
**DYSTAR CAROLINA CHEMICAL
CORP**
8309 Wilkinson Blvd (28214-9052)
PHONE..............................704 391-6322
Ron Tedemonte, *CEO*
EMP: 100 EST: 2006
SALES (est): 4.96MM **Privately Held**
SIC: **2865** Dyes: azine, azo, azoic
PA: Dystar Americas Holding Corporation
9844 A Southern Pine Blvd
Charlotte NC 28273

(G-2078)
DYSTAR LP (DH)
9844 Southern Pine Blvd Ste A (28273)
PHONE..............................704 561-3000
Ron Pedemonte, *Pr*
Steve Hennen, *CFO*
◆ **EMP: 25 EST:** 1995
SQ FT: 40,000
SALES (est): 85.13MM **Privately Held**
Web: www.dystar.com
SIC: **2819** 2869 2865 Industrial inorganic
chemicals, nec; Industrial organic
chemicals, nec; Cyclic crudes and
intermediates
HQ: Dystar Global Holdings (Singapore)
Pte. Ltd.
1a International Business Park
Singapore 60993

(G-2079)
E AND J PUBLISHING LLC
3502 Lukes Dr (28216-7665)
PHONE..............................877 882-2138
Latravis E Blanton, *CEO*
EMP: 5 EST: 2022
SALES (est): 130.5K **Privately Held**
SIC: **2741** Miscellaneous publishing

G
E
O
G
R
A
P
H
I
C

(G-2080)
E CACHE & CO LLC
6316 Old Sugar Creek Rd Ste E
(28269-7010)
PHONE.............................919 590-0779
EMP: 10 EST: 2019
SALES (est): 569.42K Privately Held
Web: www.expiredwixdomain.com
SIC: 3999 Hair and hair-based products

(G-2081)
E2M KITCHEN LLC
1907 Gateway Blvd (28208-2748)
PHONE.............................704 731-5070
Jeffrey Witherspoon, CEO
James Barbee, Pr
EMP: 19 EST: 2022
SALES (est): 2.68MM Privately Held
Web: www.e2mkitchen.com
SIC: 2099 Ready-to-eat meals, salads, and
sandwiches

(G-2082)
EASTERN PLASTICS COMPANY
10724 Carmel Commons Blvd Ste 580
(28226-0919)
P.O. Box 470115 (28247-0115)
PHONE.............................704 542-7786
Andrew R Ball, Pr
Stephen S Ball, VP
Joann Ball, Sec
▲ EMP: 5 EST: 1976
SQ FT: 600
SALES (est): 4.74MM Privately Held
SIC: 2821 Plastics materials and resins

(G-2083)
**EASTERN SUN COMMUNICATIONS
INC**
4019 Sheridan Dr (28205-5651)
PHONE.............................704 408-7668
Ryan Knick, Pr
Michelle Faulkenberry, Sec
EMP: 5 EST: 2004
SALES (est): 297.87K Privately Held
Web: www.easternsuncom.com
SIC: 3651 Audio electronic systems

(G-2084)
EASTONSWEB MULTIMEDIA
4111 Nicole Eileen Ln (28216-6750)
PHONE.............................704 607-0941
EMP: 4 EST: 2017
SALES (est): 69.74K Privately Held
Web: www.eastonsweb.com
SIC: 2741 Miscellaneous publishing

(G-2085)
EASY STONES CORP
1440 Westinghouse Blvd Ste A
(28273-6421)
PHONE.............................980 201-9506
Sreekanth Manam, CEO
EMP: 5 EST: 2018
SALES (est): 993.05K Privately Held
Web: www.easystones.com
SIC: 3272 Floor slabs and tiles, precast
concrete

(G-2086)
EASYKEYSCOM INC
Also Called: Quickshipkeys.com
11407 Granite St (28273-6678)
PHONE.............................877 839-5397
Robert Maczka, CEO
Greg Martisauski, Pr
Cindy Cox, VP
EMP: 11 EST: 2008
SQ FT: 2,500
SALES (est): 3.43MM Privately Held

Web: www.easykeys.com
SIC: 3429 Keys and key blanks

(G-2087)
EATON-SCHULTZ INC
3800 Woodpark Blvd Ste I (28206-4247)
P.O. Box 30874 (28230-0874)
PHONE.............................704 331-8004
Phil Eaton, Pr
David Schultz, VP
Christopher Price, Prin
EMP: 10 EST: 1998
SALES (est): 961.37K Privately Held
Web: www.steeltechus.com
SIC: 3446 Architectural metalwork

(G-2088)
ECOLAB INC
9335 Harris Corners Pkwy Ste 100
(28269-3819)
PHONE.............................704 527-5912
Wayne Landerth, Brnch Mgr
EMP: 4
SALES (corp-wide): 15.32B Publicly Held
Web: www.ecolab.com
SIC: 2842 Polishes and sanitation goods
PA: Ecolab Inc.
1 Ecolab Pl
Saint Paul MN 55102
800 232-6522

(G-2089)
**ECONOMY GRINDING
STRAIGHTENING**
Also Called: Economy Grinding
432 Springbrook Rd (28217-2145)
P.O. Box 3634 (28117-3634)
PHONE.............................704 400-2500
David Rembowski, Pr
Marc Stankovich, VP
EMP: 6 EST: 1987
SQ FT: 30,000
SALES (est): 722.47K Privately Held
Web: www.economygrinding.com
SIC: 3599 Machine shop, jobbing and repair

(G-2090)
ECOVEHICLE ENTERPRISES INC
15022 Ballantyne Country Club Dr
(28277-2719)
PHONE.............................704 544-9907
John Dabels, Pr
EMP: 6 EST: 2004
SALES (est): 201.21K Privately Held
SIC: 3715 3711 Truck trailer chassis; Motor
vehicles and car bodies

(G-2091)
EDMAC COMPRESSOR PARTS ✪
Also Called: Edmac
2101 Westinghouse Blvd Ste D
(28273-6310)
PHONE.............................800 866-2959
EMP: 26 EST: 2024
SALES (est): 3.62MM Privately Held
SIC: 3563 Air and gas compressors

(G-2092)
EFCO USA INC
11600 Goodrich Dr (28273-6510)
P.O. Box 38839 (28278-1014)
PHONE.............................800 332-6872
Thomas Wiget, CEO
▲ EMP: 6 EST: 2009
SALES (est): 1.64MM Privately Held
Web: www.efcousa.com
SIC: 3546 3549 3541 3829 Power-driven
handtools; Metalworking machinery, nec;
Flange facing machines; Physical property
testing equipment

(G-2093)
EGI ASSOCIATES INC
417 Minuet Ln Ste A (28217-2702)
P.O. Box 240993 (28224-0993)
PHONE.............................704 561-3337
David Lock, Owner
EMP: 13 EST: 2007
SALES (est): 2.58MM Privately Held
Web: www.teamlighting.com
SIC: 3645 5063 Residential lighting fixtures;
Lighting fixtures

(G-2094)
ELAN TRADING INC
Also Called: Southern Resources
3826 Raleigh St (28206-2043)
P.O. Box 3247 (28106-3247)
PHONE.............................704 342-1696
Mark Clackum, CEO
Samuel Waldman, *
Elisa Clackum, *
◆ EMP: 28 EST: 1992
SQ FT: 40,000
SALES (est): 828.54K Privately Held
Web: www.southernresources.com
SIC: 5093 4953 3341 Ferrous metal scrap
and waste; Recycling, waste materials;
Secondary nonferrous metals

(G-2095)
ELECTRONIC IMAGING SVCS INC
Also Called: Vestcom Retail Solutions
1500 Continental Blvd (28273-6376)
PHONE.............................704 587-3323
Claudia Wallace, Mgr
EMP: 11
SALES (corp-wide): 8.76B Publicly Held
SIC: 8742 2759 Marketing consulting
services; Commercial printing, nec
HQ: Electronic Imaging Services, Inc.
2800 Cantrell Rd Ste 400
Little Rock AR 72202
501 663-0100

(G-2096)
ELEMENT DESIGNS INC
Also Called: Element Designs
235 Crompton St (28273-6204)
P.O. Box 10 (29716-0010)
PHONE.............................704 332-3114
Heinz Uerbersax, Pr
Nelson Wills, *
R N Wills Junior, VP
Kevin Creedon, *
Beata Klecha, *
▲ EMP: 58 EST: 2002
SQ FT: 65,000
SALES (est): 13.73MM Privately Held
Web: www.element-designs.com
SIC: 2521 Cabinets, office: wood

(G-2097)
ELEMENTS BRANDS LLC
Also Called: Elements Brands
1515 Mockingbird Ln Ste 400 (28209-3298)
PHONE.............................503 230-8008
William Dalessandero, CEO
EMP: 10
SALES (corp-wide): 11.02MM Privately
Held
Web: www.elementsbrands.com
SIC: 2819 Industrial inorganic chemicals, nec
PA: Elements Brands, Llc
2202 Hawkins St
Charlotte NC 28203
704 661-2244

(G-2098)
ELEVATE TEXTILES INC (HQ)
121 W Trade St Ste 1700 (28202-1154)
P.O. Box 26540 (27408)

PHONE.............................336 379-6220
Per-olof Loof, Pr
Gail A Kuczkowski, Ex VP
Neil W Koonce, VP
Craig J Hart, VP
Robert E Garren, Chief Human Resources
Officer
◆ EMP: 10 EST: 1994
SALES (est): 1.61B
SALES (corp-wide): 1.98B Privately Held
Web: www.elevatetextiles.com
SIC: 2211 2231 2221 2273 Denims; Worsted
fabrics, broadwoven; Polyester broadwoven
fabrics; Carpets and rugs
PA: Elevate Textiles Holding Corporation
121 W Trade St Ste 1700
Charlotte NC 28202
336 379-6220

(G-2099)
**ELEVATE TEXTILES HOLDING CORP
(PA)**
121 W Trade St Ste 1700 (28202-1154)
PHONE.............................336 379-6220
Per-olof Loof, Pr
EMP: 61 EST: 2016
SALES (est): 1.98B
SALES (corp-wide): 1.98B Privately Held
SIC: 2211 2231 2221 2273 Denims; Worsted
fabrics, broadwoven; Polyester broadwoven
fabrics; Carpets and rugs

(G-2100)
ELGI COMPRESSORS USA INC (HQ)
4610 Entrance Dr Ste A (28273)
PHONE.............................704 943-7966
Brian Pahl, CEO
Mani Kumar, *
John Patton, *
▲ EMP: 8 EST: 2012
SALES (est): 59.87MM Privately Held
Web: www.elgi.com
SIC: 3563 Air and gas compressors
including vacuum pumps
PA: Elgi Equipments Limited
Elgi Industrial Complex Iii,
Coimbatore TN 64100

(G-2101)
ELLA B CANDLES LLC
9517 Monroe Rd Ste C (28270-1489)
PHONE.............................980 339-8898
Christopher Tassy, Prin
Julie Tassy, Prin
EMP: 22 EST: 2016
SALES (est): 2.73MM Privately Held
Web: www.ellabcandles.com
SIC: 3999 Candles

(G-2102)
ELLISON COMPANY INC
Specialty Mfg
13501 S Ridge Dr (28273-6741)
P.O. Box 240122 (28224-0122)
PHONE.............................704 889-7518
John Peace, VP Sls
EMP: 120
SALES (corp-wide): 1.65MM Privately
Held
SIC: 3199 Safety belts, leather
PA: The Ellison Company Inc
706 Green Valley Rd # 206
Greensboro NC 27408
336 275-8565

(G-2103)
ELLISON TECHNOLOGIES INC
9724 Southern Pine Blvd (28273-5539)
PHONE.............................704 545-7362
Robert Johnson, Mgr
EMP: 60

▲ = Import ▼ = Export
◆ = Import/Export

Web: www.ellisontechnologies.com
SIC: 3451 5084 Screw machine products;
  Metalworking machinery
HQ: Ellison Technologies, Inc.
  9828 Arlee Ave
  Santa Fe Springs CA 90670
  562 949-8311

(G-2104)
**ELSTER AMERICAN METER
COMPANY LLC (HQ)**
855 S Mint St (28202-1517)
PHONE.............................402 873-8200
◆ EMP: 15 EST: 1836
SALES (est): 198.19MM
SALES (corp-wide): 38.5B Publicly Held
Web: automation.honeywell.com
SIC: 3824 3613 Gasmeters, domestic and
  large capacity: industrial; Regulators, power
PA: Honeywell International Inc.
  855 S Mint St
  Charlotte NC 28202
  704 627-6200

(G-2105)
ELXSI CORPORATION
6325 Ardrey Kell Rd Ste 400 (28277-4966)
PHONE.............................407 849-1090
Alexander Milley, Pr
Farrokh K Kavarana, *
Denis M O'donnell, Dir
EMP: 317 EST: 1986
SALES (est): 507.73K
SALES (corp-wide): 1.83B Privately Held
SIC: 5812 3569 5046 Restaurant, family:
  chain; Filters and strainers, pipeline;
  Restaurant equipment and supplies, nec
HQ: Canvas Sx, Llc
  6325 Ardrey Kell Rd Ste 4
  Charlotte NC 28277
  980 474-3700

(G-2106)
EMAGE MEDICAL LLC
7515 Robin Crest Rd (28226-3703)
PHONE.............................704 904-1873
Lonnie Wallace, Pr
Lonnie Roy Wallace, Managing Member
EMP: 5 EST: 2008
SALES (est): 633.23K Privately Held
Web: www.emagemedical.com
SIC: 2844 Cosmetic preparations

(G-2107)
EMBROID IT
16324 York Rd (28278-5824)
PHONE.............................704 617-0357
EMP: 5 EST: 2015
SALES (est): 44.49K Privately Held
Web: www.embroidit.net
SIC: 2395 Embroidery and art needlework

(G-2108)
EMC CORPORATION
10815 David Taylor Dr Ste 200
(28262-1047)
PHONE.............................720 341-3274
Steven Elliott, Mgr
EMP: 6
Web: www.autoemc.net
SIC: 3572 7372 5045 Computer storage
  devices; Prepackaged software;
  Computers, peripherals, and software
HQ: Emc Corporation
  176 S St
  Hopkinton MA 01748
  508 435-1000

(G-2109)
**EMERALD CAROLINA CHEMICAL
LLC**
8309 Wilkinson Blvd (28214-9052)
PHONE.............................704 393-0089
Sean Stack, *
EMP: 19 EST: 2001
SALES (est): 2.24MM Privately Held
Web: www.emeralddist.com
SIC: 2899 Chemical preparations, nec
HQ: Dystar L.P.
  9844 A Southern Pine Blvd
  Charlotte NC 28273

(G-2110)
**EMERSON PRCESS MGT PWR WTR
SLT**
6135 Lakeview Rd (28269-2615)
PHONE.............................704 357-0294
Thomas Smith, Brnch Mgr
EMP: 15
SALES (corp-wide): 17.49B Publicly Held
Web: www.emerson.com
SIC: 3823 Process control instruments
HQ: Emerson Process Management Power
  & Water Solutions, Inc.
  2507 Lovi Rd
  Freedom PA 15042
  412 963-4000

(G-2111)
EMPIRE CARPET & BLINDS INC
10500 Mcmullen Creek Pkwy (28226-1632)
PHONE.............................704 541-3988
EMP: 5 EST: 1996
SALES (est): 133.07K Privately Held
Web: www.carpetone.com
SIC: 2591 Window blinds

(G-2112)
END CAMP NORTH
300 Camp Rd (28206-4005)
PHONE.............................980 337-4600
EMP: 10 EST: 2017
SALES (est): 2.18MM Privately Held
Web: www.camp.nc
SIC: 3761 Guided missiles and space
  vehicles

(G-2113)
ENDGRAIN WOODWORKS LLC
301 Queens Rd Apt 302 (28204-3288)
PHONE.............................980 237-2612
EMP: 4 EST: 2018
SALES (est): 74.98K Privately Held
SIC: 2431 Millwork

(G-2114)
**ENGINEERED RECYCLING
COMPANY LLC**
Also Called: ERC
1011 Woodward Ave 1101 (28206-2461)
P.O. Box 790973 (28206-7915)
PHONE.............................704 358-6700
▲ EMP: 35
SIC: 2295 Resin or plastic coated fabrics

(G-2115)
ENPRO INC (PA)
Also Called: Enpro
5605 Carnegie Blvd Ste 500 (28209)
PHONE.............................704 731-1500
Eric A Vaillancourt, Pr
David L Hauser, *
J Milton Childress Ii, Ex VP
Robert S Mclean, Ex VP
Steven R Bower, CAO
◆ EMP: 217 EST: 2002
SALES (est): 1.05B
SALES (corp-wide): 1.05B Publicly Held

Web: www.enproindustries.com
SIC: 3053 3519 3089 Gaskets and sealing
  devices; Engines, diesel and semi-diesel or
  dual-fuel; Bearings, plastics

(G-2116)
ENRG BRAND LLC
1235 East Blvd Ste E2168 (28203-5870)
PHONE.............................980 298-8519
EMP: 5 EST: 2021
SALES (est): 90K Privately Held
SIC: 1389 Construction, repair, and
  dismantling services

(G-2117)
ENRICHED ABUNDANCE ENTP LLC
15316 Trickling Water Ct (28273)
PHONE.............................704 369-6363
EMP: 10 EST: 2021
SALES (est): 133.53K Privately Held
SIC: 2621 Book paper

(G-2118)
**ENVIRNMENTAL WIN SOLUTIONS
LLC**
Also Called: Climate Seal
1401 Morningside Dr (28205-5328)
PHONE.............................704 200-2001
EMP: 4 EST: 2008
SALES (est): 318.13K Privately Held
Web: www.climateseal.com
SIC: 3442 Storm doors or windows, metal

(G-2119)
ENVIRNMTAL SYSTEMS RES INST I
Also Called: Esri
3325 Springbank Ln Ste 200 (28226-3365)
PHONE.............................704 541-9810
Christian Carlson, Prin
EMP: 39
SALES (corp-wide): 872.47MM Privately
Held
Web: www.esri.com
SIC: 5045 7372 Computer software;
  Prepackaged software
PA: Environmental Systems Research
  Institute, Inc.
  380 New York St
  Redlands CA 92373
  909 793-2853

(G-2120)
ENVIROTEK WORLDWIDE LLC
Also Called: Sterimed
2701 Hutchison Mcdonald Rd Ste A
(28269-4276)
PHONE.............................704 285-6400
Richard Admani, CEO
EMP: 10 EST: 2015
SALES (est): 246.34K Privately Held
SIC: 3559 Chemical machinery and
  equipment

(G-2121)
EP NISBET COMPANY
1818 Baxter St (28204-3118)
P.O. Box 35367 (28235-5367)
PHONE.............................704 332-7755
Heather Stroupe, Prin
EMP: 4 EST: 2003
SALES (est): 614.44K Privately Held
Web: www.nisbetoil.com
SIC: 1382 Oil and gas exploration services

(G-2122)
EPI CENTRE SUNDRIES
210 E Trade St (28202-2404)
PHONE.............................704 650-9575
Keum Kim, Prin
EMP: 6 EST: 2008

SALES (est): 221.33K Privately Held
Web: www.epicentrenc.com
SIC: 3931 Musical instruments

(G-2123)
EPIC APPAREL
8118 Statesville Rd (28269-3829)
PHONE.............................980 335-0463
Christopher Pham, Prin
EMP: 7 EST: 2013
SALES (est): 97.68K Privately Held
Web: www.4brandedproducts.com
SIC: 2759 Screen printing

(G-2124)
EPV CORPORATION
2309 Nevada Blvd (28273-6430)
PHONE.............................704 494-7800
Tony Luo, Pr
Marla Teague, *
Joshua Anderson, *
Ruowen Chen, *
EMP: 51 EST: 2014
SQ FT: 100,000
SALES (est): 1.45MM Privately Held
SIC: 3711 3713 Motor buses, except
  trackless trolleys, assembly of; Truck and
  bus bodies

(G-2125)
EQUINOM ENTERPRISES LLC
16310 Magnolia Woods Ln (28277-3400)
PHONE.............................704 817-8489
EMP: 4 EST: 2019
SALES (est): 30.77K Privately Held
Web: www.equi-nom.com
SIC: 2099 Food preparations, nec

(G-2126)
**ERDLE PERFORATING HOLDINGS
INC**
Erdle Perforating Carolina Div
1100 Culp Rd # A (28241)
P.O. Box 411292 (28241-1292)
PHONE.............................704 588-4380
Lou Ely, Prin
EMP: 15
SALES (corp-wide): 92.55MM Privately
Held
Web: www.erdle.com
SIC: 3469 3569 3444 3498 Perforated metal,
  stamped; Filters, general line: industrial;
  Sheet metalwork; Fabricated pipe and
  fittings
HQ: Erdle Perforating Holdings, Inc.
  100 Pixley Indus Pkwy
  Rochester NY 14624
  585 247-4700

(G-2127)
ESSEX GROUP INC
3300 Woodpark Blvd (28206-4213)
PHONE.............................704 921-9605
EMP: 5
SALES (corp-wide): 70.43MM Privately
Held
SIC: 3357 3644 3496 3351 Building wire and
  cable, nonferrous; Insulators and insulation
  materials, electrical; Miscellaneous
  fabricated wire products; Copper rolling and
  drawing
HQ: Essex Group, Inc.
  1601 Wall St
  Fort Wayne IN 30327
  260 461-4000

(G-2128)
ETIMEX USA INC
9405 D Ducks Ln Ste A (28273-4513)
PHONE.............................704 583-0002
Marc Vogt, Pr

H Ross, *
▲ EMP: 53 EST: 1997
SQ FT: 38,000
SALES (est): 14.22MM
SALES (corp-wide): 81.01K Privately Held
Web: www.etimex.global
SIC: 3089 Injection molding of plastics
HQ: Etimex Technical Components Gmbh
Ehinger Str. 30
Rottenacker BW 89616
7393520

(G-2129)
EUCLID INNOVATIONS INC (PA)
101 S Tryon St Ste 2410 (28280-0006)
PHONE...............................877 382-5431
Satyavani Rayankula, Pr
Suresh Karusala, VP
EMP: 16 EST: 2009
SALES (est): 2.4MM
SALES (corp-wide): 2.4MM Privately Held
Web: www.euclidinnovations.com
SIC: 7372 Business oriented computer
software

(G-2130)
EV FLEET INC
11701 Mount Holly Rd Bldg 32
(28214-9229)
PHONE...............................704 425-6272
EMP: 7 EST: 2014
SQ FT: 3,600
SALES (est): 116.81K Privately Held
Web: www.brooksagnew.blog
SIC: 3711 Cars, electric, assembly of

(G-2131)
EVERYDAY EDISONS LLC
Also Called: Bouncing Brain Productions
520 Elliot St Ste 200 (28202-1363)
PHONE...............................704 369-7333
Louis Foreman, CEO
▲ EMP: 4 EST: 2005
SALES (est): 711.53K
SALES (corp-wide): 9.79MM Publicly
Held
SIC: 3949 Sporting and athletic goods, nec
HQ: Edison Nation Holdings, Llc
24 Aspen Park Blvd
East Syracuse NY 13057

(G-2132)
EVOLUTION OF STYLE LLC
2901 N Davidson St Unit 170 (28205-1078)
PHONE...............................914 329-3078
EMP: 8 EST: 2017
SALES (est): 80.32K Privately Held
SIC: 7389 2329 Design services; Athletic
clothing, except uniforms: men's, youths'
and boys'

(G-2133)
EW2 ENVIRONMENTAL INC (PA)
7245 Pineville Matthews Rd Ste 100
(28226-6164)
P.O. Box 470503 (28247-0503)
PHONE...............................704 542-2444
Lewis D Eckley, Pr
Gail Kellar, Sec
EMP: 6 EST: 1991
SQ FT: 2,000
SALES (est): 2.49MM Privately Held
Web: www.ew2.net
SIC: 3589 Water treatment equipment,
industrial

(G-2134)
EXIDE
3308 Oak Lake Blvd Ste A (28208-7701)
PHONE...............................704 357-9845
EMP: 5 EST: 2011

SALES (est): 434.92K Privately Held
Web: www.exide.com
SIC: 3691 Storage batteries

(G-2135)
EXIDE TECHNOLOGIES LLC
Also Called: Exide Battery
648 Griffith Rd Ste G (28217-3573)
PHONE...............................704 521-8016
Tommy Tice, Mgr
EMP: 5
SALES (corp-wide): 482.75MM Privately
Held
Web: www.exide.com
SIC: 5063 3629 Electrical apparatus and
equipment; Battery chargers, rectifying or
nonrotating
PA: Exide Technologies, Llc
13000 Drfeld Pkwy Bldg 20
Milton GA 30004
678 566-9000

(G-2136)
EXPRESS WIRE SERVICES INC
2947 Interstate St (28208-3607)
PHONE...............................704 393-5156
Nick Huzzlla, Pr
Scott Ramsey, VP
Wayne Searcy, VP
EMP: 4 EST: 2000
SQ FT: 14,000
SALES (est): 982.66K Privately Held
Web: www.expresswireservices.com
SIC: 3496 Miscellaneous fabricated wire
products

(G-2137)
EYE DIALOGUE
412 N Crigler St (28216-3914)
PHONE...............................704 567-7789
Jack Kelly, Prin
EMP: 4 EST: 2010
SALES (est): 1.81MM Privately Held
Web: www.eyedialogue.com
SIC: 3648 Stage lighting equipment

(G-2138)
EYE TRAX INC
4200 Performance Rd (28214-7000)
PHONE...............................800 594-4157
Jerome Mcsorley, Pr
Brie Dixson, Off Mgr
EMP: 6 EST: 2007
SQ FT: 4,000
SALES (est): 713.98K Privately Held
Web: www.eyetrax.net
SIC: 3651 Video camera-audio recorders,
household use

(G-2139)
F & C REPAIR AND SALES LLC
Also Called: A Foodtruckqueen
4720 Brookshire Blvd (28216-3818)
PHONE...............................704 907-2461
Charlene Steele, Managing Member
EMP: 12 EST: 2017
SALES (est): 611.84K Privately Held
SIC: 7538 3715 General automotive repair
shops; Truck trailers

(G-2140)
FABRICATION ASSOCIATES INC
7950 Pence Rd (28215-4326)
P.O. Box 25326 (28229-5326)
PHONE...............................704 535-8050
William Heath Little, Pr
EMP: 52 EST: 1996
SALES (est): 4.14MM Privately Held
Web: www.fai6.com

SIC: 3443 7692 3444 3441 Fabricated plate
work (boiler shop); Welding repair; Sheet
metalwork; Fabricated structural metal

(G-2141)
FABRIX INC
231 Foster Ave Ste A (28203-5462)
P.O. Box 33686 (28233-3686)
PHONE...............................704 953-1239
Scott Donovan, Pr
EMP: 4 EST: 2002
SQ FT: 5,850
SALES (est): 56.74K Privately Held
Web: www.fabrixdigital.com
SIC: 2759 Commercial printing, nec

(G-2142)
FAGUS GRECON INC
648 Griffith Rd Ste A (28217-3573)
PHONE...............................503 641-7731
Eric Peterson, CEO
EMP: 20 EST: 2017
SALES (est): 5.5MM Privately Held
Web: www.fagus-grecon.com
SIC: 3569 Firefighting and related equipment

(G-2143)
FARRIS BELT & SAW COMPANY
235 Foster Ave (28203-5421)
PHONE...............................704 527-6166
Bill Garris, Pr
▲ EMP: 13 EST: 1942
SQ FT: 14,000
SALES (est): 1.65MM Privately Held
Web: www.farrisbelt.com
SIC: 3291 3553 Abrasive products;
Bandsaws, woodworking

(G-2144)
FASTLIFE TRANSPORT LLC (PA)
7710 Holliswood Ct (28217-3098)
PHONE...............................484 350-6754
EMP: 5 EST: 2018
SALES (est): 2.09MM
SALES (corp-wide): 2.09MM Privately
Held
SIC: 3537 Trucks, tractors, loaders, carriers,
and similar equipment

(G-2145)
FEREBEE CORPORATION (HQ)
Also Called: Ferebee Asphalt
10045 Metromont Industrial Blvd
(28269-7611)
P.O. Box 480066 (28269-5300)
PHONE...............................704 509-2586
James Ferebee, Pr
James C Ferebee, *
Joseph B Ferebee, *
David Ferebee, *
Tiffany Ferebee, *
EMP: 117 EST: 1985
SQ FT: 13,000
SALES (est): 43.91MM
SALES (corp-wide): 1.82B Publicly Held
Web: www.ferebee.com
SIC: 1611 1623 1771 3531 General
contractor, highway and street construction;
Water, sewer, and utility lines; Blacktop
(asphalt) work; Asphalt plant, including
gravel-mix type
PA: Construction Partners, Inc.
290 Healthwest Dr Ste 2
Dothan AL 36303
334 673-9763

(G-2146)
FERGUSON & COMPANY LLC
201 S Tryon St (28202-3212)
PHONE...............................704 332-4396
Ian Ferguson, Prin

EMP: 4 EST: 2010
SALES (est): 1.4MM Privately Held
Web: www.fergusonbox.com
SIC: 2653 Boxes, corrugated: made from
purchased materials

(G-2147)
FERGUSON BOX
10820 Quality Dr (28278-7702)
PHONE...............................704 597-0310
Pat Garvey, Pr
EMP: 43 EST: 2017
SALES (est): 10.26MM Privately Held
Web: www.fergusonbox.com
SIC: 2653 Boxes, corrugated: made from
purchased materials

(G-2148)
**FERGUSON SUPPLY AND BOX MFG
CO (PA)**
10820 Quality Dr (28278-7702)
PHONE...............................704 597-0310
Paige F Burgess, Pr
Charles L Ferguson Junior, Ex VP
Chip Ferguson, *
Janice Rappleyea, *
EMP: 85 EST: 1959
SQ FT: 60,000
SALES (est): 19.75MM
SALES (corp-wide): 19.75MM Privately
Held
Web: www.fergusonbox.com
SIC: 2653 5113 Boxes, corrugated: made
from purchased materials; Corrugated and
solid fiber boxes

(G-2149)
FFI HOLDINGS III CORP (PA)
Also Called: Flow Control Group
3915 Shopton Rd (28217)
PHONE...............................800 690-3650
David Patterson, CEO
Hans Van Der Meulen, CFO
EMP: 27 EST: 2015
SALES (est): 724.03MM
SALES (corp-wide): 724.03MM Privately
Held
Web: www.flowcontrolgroup.com
SIC: 3564 3569 5075 5074 Air purification
equipment; Filters; Air filters; Water
purification equipment

(G-2150)
FIBRIX LLC
Also Called: Cumulus Fibres - Charlotte
1101 Tar Heel Rd (28208-1524)
PHONE...............................704 394-2111
Garry Furr, Brnch Mgr
EMP: 22
SALES (corp-wide): 46.63MM Privately
Held
Web: www.fibrix.com
SIC: 2299 2297 Batting, wadding, padding
and fillings; Nonwoven fabrics
HQ: Fibrix, Llc
1820 Evans St Ne
Conover NC 28613

(G-2151)
FICS AMERICA INC
2815 Coliseum Centre Dr Ste 300
(28217-1452)
PHONE...............................704 329-7391
Chip Mahn, CEO
Matthew Hale, Pr
Fred Dumas, VP
Terri Horton, Admn
EMP: 55 EST: 1996
SALES (est): 998.98K Publicly Held

▲ = Import ▼ = Export
◆ = Import/Export

GEOGRAPHIC

SIC: **7372** 7371 Prepackaged software;
Custom computer programming services
HQ: S1 Corporation
705 Westech Dr
Norcross GA 30092
678 966-9499

(G-2152)
FILTER SRVCNG OF CHRLTTE 135
6608 Woodmont Pl (28211-5647)
PHONE.................................704 619-3768
Steven D Akins, *Admn*
EMP: 4 EST: 2014
SALES (est): 1.22MM **Privately Held**
SIC: **1389** Roustabout service

(G-2153)
FINISHING PARTNERS INC
1301 Westinghouse Blvd Ste E
(28273-6475)
P.O. Box 410347 (28241-0347)
PHONE.................................704 583-7322
Teresa C Reidy, *Pr*
▲ EMP: 5 EST: 1998
SALES (est): 483.56K **Privately Held**
Web: www.finishingpartners.com
SIC: **2231** Fabric finishing: wool, mohair, or
similar fibers

(G-2154)
FIRM ASCEND LLC
Also Called: Truventure Logistics
224 Westinghouse Blvd Ste 602
(28273-6228)
PHONE.................................704 464-3024
Bianca Payne, *Managing Member*
EMP: 5 EST: 2018
SALES (est): 357.97K **Privately Held**
Web: www.quovius.com
SIC: **4213** 7389 2621 Trucking, except local;
Notary publics; Printing paper

(G-2155)
FIRST ALANCE LOGISTICS MGT LLC
14120 Ballantyne Corporate Pl
(28277-2640)
PHONE.................................704 522-0233
Glenn Merritt, *Pt*
Glenn Merritt, *CEO*
EMP: 10 EST: 1995
SALES (est): 4.25MM **Privately Held**
Web: www.falm.com
SIC: **2448** Pallets, wood

(G-2156)
FIRST IMPRESSIONS LTD
8500 Monroe Rd (28212-7514)
PHONE.................................704 536-3622
Treva Mason, *Pr*
Keith Mason, *Sec*
EMP: 15 EST: 1981
SQ FT: 11,500
SALES (est): 1.93MM **Privately Held**
Web: www.firstimpressionsltd.com
SIC: **2759** Screen printing

(G-2157)
FIRST NOODLE CO INC
333 Oakdale Rd (28216-2959)
PHONE.................................704 393-3238
Ying Yu Kan, *Pr*
Derren L Kan, *Treas*
Dennis V Leong, *Sec*
▲ EMP: 5 EST: 1988
SQ FT: 10,000
SALES (est): 441.26K **Privately Held**
Web: www.firstnoodleco.com
SIC: **2098** Noodles (e.g. egg, plain, and
water), dry

(G-2158)
FLA ORTHOPEDICS INC (DH)
5825 Carnegie Blvd (28209-4633)
PHONE.................................800 327-4110
Rex Niles, *Pr*
George Blews, *
Carl Partridge, *
Rhonda Newman, *
EMP: 100 EST: 1975
SALES (est): 9.33MM
SALES (corp-wide): 14B **Privately Held**
SIC: **3842** 5047 Supports: abdominal, ankle,
arch, kneecap, etc.; Medical and hospital
equipment
HQ: Bsn Medical, Inc.
5825 Carnegie Blvd
Charlotte NC 28209
704 554-9933

(G-2159)
FLASH PRINTING COMPANY INC
Also Called: Metrographics Printing
1003 Louise Ave Ste A (28205-2726)
P.O. Box 18427 (28218)
PHONE.................................704 375-2474
Jason Almes, *Pr*
Dana Almes, *VP*
EMP: 22 EST: 1970
SQ FT: 18,000
SALES (est): 4.32MM **Privately Held**
Web: www.metrographicsprinters.com
SIC: **2752** 2791 2789 Offset printing;
Typesetting; Bookbinding and related work

(G-2160)
FLASH TECHNOLOGY LLC
6325 Ardrey Kell Rd Ste 400 (28277-4967)
PHONE.................................980 474-3700
EMP: 5 EST: 2022
SALES (est): 1.85MM
SALES (corp-wide): 1.83B **Privately Held**
Web: www.flashtechnology.com
SIC: **3569** General industrial machinery, nec
HQ: Canvas Sx, Llc
6325 Ardrey Kell Rd Ste 4
Charlotte NC 28277
980 474-3700

(G-2161)
FLAT WATER CORP
800 Clanton Rd Ste R (28217-1373)
PHONE.................................704 584-7764
Jason Otte, *Pr*
EMP: 4
SALES (est): 1.74MM **Privately Held**
SIC: **3669** Visual communication systems

(G-2162)
FLEX FINISHING INC
4811 Worth Pl (28216-3321)
PHONE.................................704 342-3600
Craig J Hobbs, *Pr*
J Craig Hobbs, *Pr*
EMP: 9 EST: 1999
SQ FT: 7,000
SALES (est): 173.89K **Privately Held**
SIC: **2789** Binding only: books, pamphlets,
magazines, etc.

(G-2163)
FLEXI NORTH AMERICA LLC
2405 Center Park Dr (28217-3257)
PHONE.................................704 588-0785
Dennis Dubblemen, *VP Sls*
EMP: 4 EST: 2013
SALES (est): 2.26MM
SALES (corp-wide): 39.72MM **Privately
Held**
Web: www.flexi-northamerica.com
SIC: **2399** Pet collars, leashes, etc.: non-
leather

PA: Flexi-Bogdahn International Gmbh &
Co. Kg
Carl-Benz-Weg 13
Bargteheide SH 22941
453240440

(G-2164)
FLEXTRONICS CORPORATION
6800 Solectron Dr (28262-2492)
PHONE.................................704 598-3300
EMP: 7
SALES (corp-wide): 24.42B **Privately Held**
SIC: **3672** Printed circuit boards
HQ: Flextronics Corporation
6201 America Center Dr
Alviso CA 95002
803 936-5200

(G-2165)
FLEXTRONICS INTL USA INC
6800 Solectron Dr (28262)
P.O. Box 562148 (28256)
PHONE.................................704 509-8700
Richard Haywood, *Brnch Mgr*
EMP: 319
Web: www.flex.com
SIC: **3672** Printed circuit boards
HQ: Flextronics International Usa, Inc.
12455 Research Blvd
Austin TX 78759

(G-2166)
FLINT GROUP US LLC
2915 Whitehall Park Dr Ste 600
(28273-3579)
PHONE.................................704 504-2626
Joe Bauer, *Mgr*
EMP: 7
SALES (corp-wide): 1.91B **Privately Held**
Web: www.flintgrp.com
SIC: **2893** Printing ink
PA: Flint Group Us Llc
17177 N Lrel Pk Dr Ste 30
Livonia MI 48152
734 781-4600

(G-2167)
FLOW RHYTHM INC
1520 Mockingbird Ln (28209-0063)
PHONE.................................704 737-2178
Adetutu Jacobs, *CEO*
EMP: 8
SALES (est): 330.92K **Privately Held**
SIC: **7372** Prepackaged software

(G-2168)
FLOWSERVE CORPORATION
Flowserve
2801 Hutchison Mcdonald Rd Ste T
(28269-4275)
PHONE.................................704 494-0497
Christopher Robinson, *Off Mgr*
EMP: 27
SALES (corp-wide): 4.56B **Publicly Held**
Web: www.flowserve.com
SIC: **3561** Pumps and pumping equipment
PA: Flowserve Corporation
5215 N Ocnnor Blvd Ste 70
Irving TX 75039
972 443-6500

(G-2169)
**FONTAINE MODIFICATION
COMPANY (DH)**
9827 Mount Holly Rd (28214-9214)
P.O. Box 565 (28120-0565)
PHONE.................................704 392-8502
EMP: 17 EST: 1985
SALES (est): 32.2MM
SALES (corp-wide): 424.23B **Publicly
Held**

Web: www.fontainemodification.com
SIC: **3713** 5013 Truck bodies and parts;
Truck parts and accessories
HQ: Marmon Group Llc
181 W Madison St Ste 3900
Chicago IL 60602
312 372-9500

(G-2170)
FOOT TO DIE FOR
2545 Valleyview Dr (28212-8306)
PHONE.................................704 577-2822
Melissa Myer, *Pr*
EMP: 6 EST: 2010
SALES (est): 104.59K **Privately Held**
SIC: **3544** Special dies and tools

(G-2171)
FORBO MOVEMENT SYSTEMS
Also Called: Transtex Belting
10125 S Tryon St (28273-6509)
PHONE.................................704 334-5353
This E Schneider, *Ch Bd*
This E Schneider, *Ch Bd*
◆ EMP: 22 EST: 2008
SALES (est): 4.5MM **Privately Held**
Web: www.forbo.com
SIC: **3496** 3535 Conveyor belts; Conveyors
and conveying equipment

(G-2172)
**FORM TECH CONCRETE FORMS
INC**
Also Called: Charlotte Branch
1000 Thomasboro Dr (28208-2312)
PHONE.................................704 395-9910
Jim Upton, *Mgr*
EMP: 21
SALES (corp-wide): 7.35B **Privately Held**
Web: www.formtechinc.com
SIC: **7359** 3444 Rental store, general;
Concrete forms, sheet metal
HQ: Form Tech Concrete Forms, Inc.
975 Ladd Rd
Walled Lake MI 48390
248 344-8260

(G-2173)
FORM TECHNOLOGIES INC (PA)
11325 N Community House Rd Ste 300
(28277)
PHONE.................................704 927-2790
David Angell, *CEO*
Zack Mccorkle, *CFO*
Veronica Isban, *
EMP: 27 EST: 2011
SALES (est): 1.08B
SALES (corp-wide): 1.08B **Privately Held**
Web: www.formtechnologies.com
SIC: **3364** Zinc and zinc-base alloy die-
castings

(G-2174)
FORTECH INC
2124 Wilkinson Blvd (28208-5642)
PHONE.................................704 333-0621
Jon R Forrest, *Pr*
Nancy Forrest, *VP*
EMP: 10 EST: 1984
SQ FT: 6,500
SALES (est): 2.48MM **Privately Held**
Web: www.fortech.us
SIC: **3625** Control equipment, electric

(G-2175)
FORTERRA BRICK LLC
Also Called: Hanson Brick
7400 Carmel Executive Park Dr Ste 200
(28226-8400)
P.O. Box 842481 (75284-2481)
PHONE.................................704 341-8750

▲ **EMP: 234**
SIC: 3251 Structural brick and blocks

(G-2176)
FOUNDRY COMMERCIAL
101 N Tryon St Ste 1000 (28246-0108)
PHONE..................704 348-6875
EMP: 8 EST: 2018
SALES (est): 2.06MM Privately Held
Web: www.foundrycommercial.com
SIC: 3366 Copper foundries

(G-2177)
FREEDOM ENTERPRISE LLC
Also Called: Weathersby Guild Louisville
1235 East Blvd Ste E Pmb 2238
(28203-5876)
PHONE..................502 510-7296
Jeffrey Walton, *Pt*
Doug Roye, *Pt*
EMP: 6 EST: 2014
SALES (est): 138.01K Privately Held
Web: www.weathersbyguild.com
SIC: 2431 2441 7641 Moldings, wood:
  unfinished and prefinished; Chests and
  trunks, wood; Office furniture repair and
  maintenance

(G-2178)
FREEDOM METALS INC
2014 Vanderbilt Rd (28206-2495)
P.O. Box 26397 (28221)
PHONE..................704 333-1214
TOLL FREE: 800
Bobby L Reitzel, *Pr*
Betty Reitzel, *VP*
EMP: 12 EST: 1982
SQ FT: 100,000
SALES (est): 6.39MM Privately Held
Web: www.freedommetalsinc.com
SIC: 5051 3441 Steel; Fabricated structural
  metal

(G-2179)
FREEMAN SCREEN PRINTERS INC
4442 South Blvd Ste B (28209-2739)
PHONE..................704 521-9148
Joseph F Joe Freeman, *Pr*
Leroy F Roy Freeman, *VP*
Carol Freeman, *Sec*
EMP: 8 EST: 1989
SQ FT: 11,000
SALES (est): 248.9K Privately Held
Web: www.freemanscreenprinters.com
SIC: 2396 2395 Screen printing on fabric
  articles; Pleating and stitching

(G-2180)
FRESH-N-MOBILE LLC
8640 University City Blvd Ste 135
(28213-3501)
PHONE..................704 251-4643
Madison Anderson, *Mng Pt*
EMP: 6 EST: 2021
SALES (est): 125.33K Privately Held
Web: www.freshnmobile.com
SIC: 2842 4212 Laundry cleaning
  preparations; Delivery service, vehicular

(G-2181)
FRITO-LAY NORTH AMERICA INC
Also Called: Frito-Lay
2911 Nevada Blvd (28273-6434)
PHONE..................704 588-4150
Tony Mattie, *Mgr*
EMP: 167
SALES (corp-wide): 91.47B Publicly Held
Web: www.fritolay.com
SIC: 2096 2099 Corn chips and other corn-
  based snacks; Food preparations, nec
HQ: Frito-Lay North America, Inc.

7701 Legacy Dr
Plano TX 75024

(G-2182)
FSC THERAPEUTICS LLC
6100 Fairview Rd Ste 300 (28210-4262)
PHONE..................704 941-2500
EMP: 15
SQ FT: 5,000
SALES (est): 1.1MM Privately Held
SIC: 2834 Solutions, pharmaceutical

(G-2183)
G & E INVESTMENTS INC
Also Called: Diamond Finish Car Wash
601 S Kings Dr (28204-3089)
PHONE..................704 395-2155
George Rhyne, *Pr*
EMP: 10 EST: 1997
SALES (est): 919.44K Privately Held
Web: www.diamondclt.com
SIC: 3559 Automotive maintenance
  equipment

(G-2184)
GALAXY ELECTRONICS INC
4233 Trailer Dr (28269-4731)
PHONE..................704 343-9881
Kwabena T Ekuban, *Pr*
EMP: 10 EST: 1993
SALES (est): 3.26MM Privately Held
Web: www.galaxyelectronicsinc.com
SIC: 3672 3674 Printed circuit boards;
  Integrated circuits, semiconductor
  networks, etc.

(G-2185)
GALE PACIFIC USA INC (HQ)
Also Called: Gale Pacific
5311 77 Center Dr Ste 150 (28217-2724)
PHONE..................407 772-7900
Nicholas Pritchard, *CEO*
Peter Mcdonald, *CEO*
Martin Denney, *
James Douglas White, *
Jeff Cox, *
▲ **EMP: 11 EST:** 1998
SQ FT: 25,000
SALES (est): 7.12MM Privately Held
Web: www.galepacific.com
SIC: 2221 Polypropylene broadwoven fabrics
PA: Gale Pacific Limited
  145 Woodlands Dr
  Braeside VIC 3195

(G-2186)
GALLOREECOM
6211 Moss Bank Ct (28262-4230)
PHONE..................704 644-0978
Stephen Mckillip, *Pr*
EMP: 5 EST: 2017
SALES (est): 156.25K Privately Held
Web: www.galloree.com
SIC: 2759 Screen printing

(G-2187)
GAMBLE ASSOCIATES INC
Also Called: Gamble Pallet & Whse Eqp Co
701 Johnson Rd (28206-1634)
P.O. Box 217034 (28221-0034)
PHONE..................704 375-9301
Cheryl A Gamble, *Pr*
John F Gamble Junior, *Sec*
EMP: 15 EST: 1980
SQ FT: 20,000
SALES (est): 1.49MM Privately Held
SIC: 7699 2448 Pallet repair; Pallets, wood

(G-2188)
GARAGE GUYS
4820 N Graham St (28269-4823)
PHONE..................704 494-8841
Vin Bang, *Prin*
EMP: 4 EST: 2007
SALES (est): 446.84K Privately Held
Web:
www.autoinspectioncharlottenc.com
SIC: 3312 Blast furnaces and steel mills

(G-2189)
**GARDNER MACHINERY
CORPORATION**
700 N Summit Ave (28216-5561)
P.O. Box 33818 (28233-3818)
PHONE..................704 372-3890
Richard W Gardner, *Pr*
Ramona T Gardner, *Corporate Secretary*
EMP: 13 EST: 1947
SQ FT: 40,000
SALES (est): 2.18MM Privately Held
Web: www.gardnermachinery.com
SIC: 3535 5087 3559 Conveyors and
  conveying equipment; Laundry equipment
  and supplies; Petroleum refinery equipment

(G-2190)
GAS-FIRED PRODUCTS INC (PA)
Also Called: Space-Ray
1700 Parker Dr (28208)
P.O. Box 36485 (28236)
PHONE..................704 372-3485
◆ **EMP: 56 EST:** 1949
SALES (est): 18.94MM
**SALES (corp-wide): 18.94MM Privately
Held**
Web: www.gasfiredproducts.com
SIC: 3523 3433 Tobacco curers; Heating
  equipment, except electric

(G-2191)
GASTON SCREEN PRINTING INC
8620 Wilkinson Blvd (28214-8059)
P.O. Box 227 (28012-0227)
PHONE..................704 399-0459
Kurt R Rawald, *Pr*
James C Poag Junior, *VP*
Larry L Martin Junior, *Sec*
EMP: 9 EST: 1975
SALES (est): 1MM Privately Held
Web: www.gastonprint.com
SIC: 2262 2261 2396 2395 Screen printing:
  manmade fiber and silk broadwoven fabrics
  ; Screen printing of cotton broadwoven
  fabrics; Automotive and apparel trimmings;
  Pleating and stitching

(G-2192)
GAYLORD INC
Also Called: Medical Specialist Mfg
4600 Lebanon Rd Ste K (28227-8252)
P.O. Box 977 (28170)
PHONE..................704 694-2434
John F Gaylord Junior, *Pr*
Lewis H Parham Junior, *Sec*
Rick Gaylord, *
Scott Gaylord, *
EMP: 89 EST: 1967
SQ FT: 40,000
SALES (est): 4.76MM Privately Held
Web: www.medspec.com
SIC: 3086 3081 Plastics foam products;
  Unsupported plastics film and sheet

(G-2193)
GBC DISTRIBUTION LLC
10123 Park Rd (28210-7826)
PHONE..................704 341-8473
Michael Griffin, *Prin*
EMP: 5 EST: 2014

SALES (est): 585.54K Privately Held
SIC: 2653 Corrugated and solid fiber boxes

(G-2194)
GE VERNOVA INTERNATIONAL LLC
Also Called: GE
12037 Goodrich Dr (28273-6511)
PHONE..................704 587-1300
Andrew Headley, *Brnch Mgr*
EMP: 28
SQ FT: 37,960
SALES (corp-wide): 34.94B Publicly Held
Web: www.ge.com
SIC: 7699 7694 7629 3621 Industrial
  equipment services; Armature rewinding
  shops; Electrical repair shops; Motors and
  generators
HQ: Ge Vernova International Llc
  58 Charles St
  Cambridge MA 02141
  617 443-3000

(G-2195)
GEFRAN INC
4209 Stuart Andrew Blvd Ste C
(28217-4623)
PHONE..................501 442-1521
Bob Vivier, *Brnch Mgr*
EMP: 10
Web: www.gefran.com
SIC: 3566 Speed changers, drives, and
  gears
HQ: Gefran, Inc.
  400 Willow St
  North Andover MA 01845
  781 729-5249

(G-2196)
GEM ASSET ACQUISITION LLC (PA)
Also Called: Gemseal
1855 Lindbergh St Ste 500 (28208-3769)
PHONE..................704 225-3321
Jeff Lax, *Managing Member*
EMP: 5 EST: 2015
SALES (est): 10.35MM
**SALES (corp-wide): 10.35MM Privately
Held**
Web: www.sealmaster.net
SIC: 2951 Asphalt paving mixtures and
  blocks

(G-2197)
GEM ASSET ACQUISITION LLC
Also Called: Gemseal Pvmnts Pdts - Chrlotte
1955 Scott Futrell Dr (28208-2704)
PHONE..................704 697-9577
EMP: 5
**SALES (corp-wide): 10.35MM Privately
Held**
Web: www.sealmaster.net
SIC: 2951 Asphalt paving mixtures and
  blocks
PA: Gem Asset Acquisition Llc
  1855 Lindbergh St Ste 500
  Charlotte NC 28208
  704 225-3321

(G-2198)
**GEMSEAL PAVEMENT PRODUCTS
(PA)**
3700 Arco Corporate Dr Ste 425
(28273-7155)
PHONE..................866 264-8273
Jeff Lax, *CEO*
EMP: 9 EST: 2016
SALES (est): 4.88MM
**SALES (corp-wide): 4.88MM Privately
Held**
Web: www.gemsealproducts.com
SIC: 1721 2952 Pavement marking
  contractor; Asphalt felts and coatings

(G-2199)
GENERAL CONTROL EQUIPMENT CO
Also Called: Gc Valves
456 Crompton St (28273-6215)
P.O. Box 7066 (28241-7066)
PHONE..............................704 588-0484
William B Young Junior, *Pr*
Beth Young, *Sec*
▲ **EMP:** 10 **EST:** 1964
SQ FT: 7,000
SALES (est): 1.62MM **Privately Held**
Web: www.gcvalves.com
SIC: 3491 Industrial valves

(G-2200)
GENERAL ELECTRIC COMPANY
Also Called: GE
4601 Park Rd Ste 400 (28209-3239)
PHONE..............................704 561-5700
Annet Davis, *Mgr*
EMP: 4
SALES (corp-wide): 38.7B **Publicly Held**
Web: www.ge.com
SIC: 3613 Switchgear and switchboard apparatus
PA: General Electric Company
1 Aviation Way
Cincinnati OH 45215
617 443-3000

(G-2201)
GENERAL STEEL DRUM LLC (PA)
Also Called: North Coast Container
4500 South Blvd (28209-2841)
P.O. Box 513840 (90051-3840)
PHONE..............................704 525-7160
Kyle Stavig, *Managing Member*
Christian Stavig, *
Cody Stavig, *
EMP: 10 **EST:** 2010
SALES (est): 32.94MM
SALES (corp-wide): 32.94MM **Privately Held**
Web: www.northcoastcontainer.com
SIC: 3412 Drums, shipping: metal

(G-2202)
GENERICS BIDCO II LLC
Also Called: Prinston Laboratories
3700 Woodpark Blvd Ste A (28206-4251)
PHONE..............................980 389-2501
Jeff Green, *Brnch Mgr*
EMP: 105
SQ FT: 16,000
SIC: 2834 Cough medicines
HQ: Generics Bidco Ii, Llc
3241 Woodpark Blvd
Charlotte NC 28206
704 612-8830

(G-2203)
GENERICS BIDCO II LLC (DH)
Also Called: Prinston Laboratories
3241 Woodpark Blvd (28206-4212)
PHONE..............................704 612-8830
◆ **EMP:** 55 **EST:** 1985
SALES (est): 27.34MM **Privately Held**
SIC: 2834 Cough medicines
HQ: Prinston Pharmaceutical Inc.
700 Atrium Dr
Somerset NJ 08873

(G-2204)
GENESIS WATER TECHNOLOGIES INC
10130 Perimeter Pkwy Ste 200 (28216-2447)
PHONE..............................704 360-5165
Nick Nicholas, *Brnch Mgr*

EMP: 40
Web: www.genesiswatertech.com
SIC: 5074 3569 Plumbing and hydronic heating supplies; Assembly machines, non-metalworking
PA: Genesis Water Technologies, Inc.
555 Winderley Pl Ste 300
Maitland FL 32751

(G-2205)
GENPAK INDUSTRIES INC
10601 Westlake Dr (28273-3930)
PHONE..............................518 798-9511
Jim Riley, *Pr*
EMP: 50 **EST:** 2018
SALES (est): 10.46MM
SALES (corp-wide): 28.29B **Privately Held**
Web: www.genpak.com
SIC: 3089 Plastics containers, except foam
HQ: Great Pacific Enterprises (U.S.) Inc.
10601 Westlake Dr
Charlotte NC 28273
980 256-7729

(G-2206)
GENPAK LLC (DH)
Also Called: Genpak
10601 Westlake Dr (28273)
PHONE..............................800 626-6695
Jeff Hebert, *Pr*
◆ **EMP:** 45 **EST:** 1969
SQ FT: 30,000
SALES (est): 104.58MM **Privately Held**
Web: www.genpak.com
SIC: 3089 Plastics containers, except foam
HQ: C. P. Converters, Inc.
15 Grumbacher Rd
York PA 17406
717 764-1193

(G-2207)
GENPAK LLC
1001 Westinghouse Blvd (28273-6323)
P.O. Box 7846 (28241-7846)
PHONE..............................704 588-6202
Bruce Eveans, *Mgr*
EMP: 100
SQ FT: 22,428
Web: www.genpak.com
SIC: 5113 2821 Sanitary food containers; Plastics materials and resins
HQ: Genpak Llc
10601 Westlake Dr
Charlotte NC 28273
800 626-6695

(G-2208)
GEO PLASTICS
3801 Westinghouse Commons Dr (28273-3864)
PHONE..............................704 588-8585
Michael Morris, *CEO*
▲ **EMP:** 10 **EST:** 1992
SALES (est): 2.48MM **Privately Held**
Web: www.geoplastics.com
SIC: 3089 Injection molding of plastics

(G-2209)
GEOGRAPHICS SCREENPRINTING INC
3622 Green Park Cir (28217-2866)
PHONE..............................704 357-3300
James Mcnally, *Pr*
Josephine Mcnally, *Pr*
Susan Workley, *VP*
EMP: 7 **EST:** 1970
SQ FT: 5,815
SALES (est): 326.38K **Privately Held**
Web: www.geographicsprinting.com
SIC: 2759 Screen printing

(G-2210)
GERDAU AMERISTEEL US INC
Ameristeel Chrltte Stl Mill Di
6601 Lakeview Rd (28269-2604)
P.O. Box 481980 (28269-5331)
PHONE..............................704 596-0361
Anthony Read, *Mgr*
EMP: 165
SALES (corp-wide): 1.56B **Privately Held**
Web: gerdau.com
SIC: 3312 Blast furnaces and steel mills
HQ: Gerdau Ameristeel Us Inc.
4221 W Boy Scout Blvd Ste
Tampa FL 33607
813 286-8383

(G-2211)
GINGRAS SLEEP MEDICINE PA
6207 Park South Dr Ste 101 (28210-3653)
PHONE..............................704 944-0562
Jeannine Louise Gingras Md, *Prin*
EMP: 4 **EST:** 2010
SALES (est): 240.55K **Privately Held**
Web: www.gingrassleepmedicine.com
SIC: 2834 Medicines, capsuled or ampuled

(G-2212)
GINKGO STONE LLC
5340 Camilla Dr (28226-6769)
PHONE..............................704 451-8678
Collin Ladue, *Pr*
EMP: 6 **EST:** 2018
SALES (est): 637.08K **Privately Held**
Web: www.ginkgores.com
SIC: 3281 Cut stone and stone products

(G-2213)
GLATFLTER SNTARA OLD HCKRY INC (DH)
4350 Congress St Ste 600 (28209-4953)
PHONE..............................615 526-2100
Martin Mikkelsen, *CEO*
EMP: 14 **EST:** 2014
SALES (est): 36.03MM
SALES (corp-wide): 1.39B **Publicly Held**
Web: www.sontara.com
SIC: 2297 Nonwoven fabrics
HQ: Glatfelter Holding (Switzerland) Ag
Aeschenvorstadt 67
Basel BS

(G-2214)
GLOBAL PLASMA SOLUTIONS INC
3101 Yorkmont Rd Ste 400 (28208-0034)
PHONE..............................980 279-5622
Glenn Brinckman, *CEO*
▲ **EMP:** 20 **EST:** 2018
SALES (est): 7.9MM **Privately Held**
Web: www.gpsair.com
SIC: 3564 Air purification equipment

(G-2215)
GLOBAL PRODUCTS & MFG SVCS INC
Also Called: Gpms
6000 Fairview Rd Ste 1200 (28210-2252)
PHONE..............................360 870-9876
Cynthea Williams, *Pr*
EMP: 6 **EST:** 2007
SALES (est): 390.7K **Privately Held**
SIC: 2299 8711 5699 5734 Textile goods, nec ; Engineering services; Customized clothing and apparel; Computer peripheral equipment

(G-2216)
GLS PRODUCTS LLC (PA)
Also Called: Power Adhesives
1209 Lilac Rd (28209-1418)
PHONE..............................704 334-2425

Lee Stegall, *Pr*
EMP: 6 **EST:** 2004
SQ FT: 3,000
SALES (est): 1.38MM
SALES (corp-wide): 1.38MM **Privately Held**
Web: www.glsproducts.com
SIC: 2891 Adhesives

(G-2217)
GMG INTERNATIONAL INC (DH)
3436 Toringdon Way Ste 100 (28277-2449)
PHONE..............................800 845-6051
Stanley Bikulege, *CEO*
Lori B Goldin, *Sec*
Dennis E Norman, *CFO*
EMP: 7 **EST:** 1968
SQ FT: 100,000
SALES (est): 46.53MM
SALES (corp-wide): 26.11B **Publicly Held**
SIC: 2371 Glazing furs
HQ: Papercon Canada Holding Corp
200 Av Marien
Montreal-Est QC H1B 4
514 645-4571

(G-2218)
GNB VENTURES LLC
Also Called: Sisco Safety
1800 Associates Ln (28217-2801)
PHONE..............................704 488-4468
Naomi Reale, *CEO*
EMP: 18 **EST:** 2003
SALES (est): 898.25K **Privately Held**
Web: www.siscosafety.com
SIC: 5099 3999 5047 5999 Fire extinguishers ; Fire extinguishers, portable; Industrial safety devices: first aid kits and masks; Fire extinguishers

(G-2219)
GNH PHARMACEUTICALS USA LLC
1235 East Blvd Ste E499 (28203-5870)
PHONE..............................704 585-8769
EMP: 6 **EST:** 2019
SALES (est): 257.79K **Privately Held**
Web: www.gnhindia.com
SIC: 2834 Pharmaceutical preparations

(G-2220)
GO EV AND GO GREEN CORP ✪
9711 David Taylor Dr Apt 106 (28262-2366)
PHONE..............................704 327-9040
Edwin D Daniel, *CEO*
Edwin D Daniel, *Ex Dir*
Chandell Daniel, *COO*
EMP: 4 **EST:** 2023
SALES (est): 133.5K **Privately Held**
Web: www.goevandgogreen.org
SIC: 3647 4911 7534 Vehicular lighting equipment; Tire repair shop

(G-2221)
GO FOR GREEN FLEET SVCS LLC
1911 Greymouth Rd Apt 305 (28262-8233)
PHONE..............................803 306-3683
Michael Green, *Managing Member*
EMP: 4 **EST:** 2022
SALES (est): 692.04K **Privately Held**
SIC: 3537 7389 Trucks: freight, baggage, etc.: industrial, except mining; Business Activities at Non-Commercial Site

(G-2222)
GOFFSTAR INC
Also Called: Lake Printing & Design
5015 W W T Harris Blvd Ste F (28269-3756)
PHONE..............................704 895-3878
Timothy Goff, *Pr*
EMP: 7 **EST:** 2006

SQ FT: 3,000
SALES (est): 1.72MM **Privately Held**
Web: www.lakeprinting.biz
SIC: 2752 Offset printing

(G-2223)
GOLD BOND BUILDING PDTS LLC
(HQ)
Also Called: National Gypsum
2001 Rexford Rd (28211-3498)
PHONE..............................704 365-7300
Thomas Nelson, *Managing Member*
EMP: 7 **EST:** 2020
SALES (est): 96.43MM
SALES (corp-wide): 96.43MM **Privately Held**
Web: www.nationalgypsum.com
SIC: 2621 Building and roofing paper, felts and insulation siding
PA: Ng Operations, Llc
    2001 Rexford Rd
    Charlotte NC 28211
    704 365-7300

(G-2224)
GOLDEN POP SHOP LLC ✪
9805 Statesville Rd Ste 6012 (28269-7647)
PHONE..............................704 236-9455
EMP: 5 **EST:** 2023
SALES (est): 222.74K **Privately Held**
SIC: 2096 Potato chips and other potato-based snacks

(G-2225)
GOLDMINE SOFTWARE
Also Called: Willis Consulting
10130 Mallard Creek Rd Ste 300
(28262-6000)
PHONE..............................704 944-3579
Greg Willis, *Pr*
EMP: 5 **EST:** 2001
SALES (est): 953.31K **Privately Held**
SIC: 7372 7371 Prepackaged software; Custom computer programming services

(G-2226)
GOOD WILL CATHOLIC MEDIA LLC
Also Called: Saint Benedict Press, LLC
13315 Carowinds Blvd Ste 2 (28273)
P.O. Box 269 (28053)
PHONE..............................704 731-0651
Conor Galgher, *Managing Member*
▲ **EMP:** 30 **EST:** 2009
SALES (est): 2.41MM
SALES (corp-wide): 12.64MM **Privately Held**
Web: www.tanbooks.com
SIC: 2741 Miscellaneous publishing
PA: Good Will Publishers, Inc.
    1520 S York Rd
    Gastonia NC 28052
    704 853-3237

(G-2227)
GOODRICH CORPORATION (HQ)
Also Called: Collins Aerospace
2730 W Tyvola Rd (28217)
PHONE..............................704 423-7000
David Gitlin, *Pr*
Jennifer Pollino, *Sr VP*
Christopher T Calio, *Sec*
Richard S Caswell, *Treas*
Scott E Kuechle, *CFO*
◆ **EMP:** 120 **EST:** 1912
SQ FT: 120,000
SALES (est): 3.63B
SALES (corp-wide): 80.74B **Publicly Held**
Web: www.collinsaerospace.com
SIC: 7372 3724 3728 Prepackaged software ; Aircraft engines and engine parts; Aircraft parts and equipment, nec

PA: Rtx Corporation
    1000 Wilson Blvd
    Arlington VA 22209
    781 522-3000

(G-2228)
GOUGH ECON INC
9400 N Lakebrook Rd (28214-9008)
PHONE..............................704 399-4501
David P Risley, *Pr*
Don Calvert Junior, *VP*
▲ **EMP:** 38 **EST:** 1974
SQ FT: 42,000
SALES (est): 9.55MM **Privately Held**
Web: www.goughecon.com
SIC: 3535 Conveyors and conveying equipment

(G-2229)
GRACE COMMUNION INTERNATIONAL (PA)
3120 Whitehall Park Dr (28273-3335)
PHONE..............................626 650-2300
Joseph Tkach, *Pr*
Michael Feazell, *
Mathew Morgan, *
EMP: 32 **EST:** 1947
SQ FT: 54,000
SALES (est): 1.15MM
SALES (corp-wide): 1.15MM **Privately Held**
Web: www.gci.org
SIC: 2721 8661 Magazines: publishing only, not printed on site; Church of God

(G-2230)
GRANCREATIONS INC
3400 N Graham St (28206-1936)
P.O. Box 562880 (28256-2880)
PHONE..............................704 332-7625
Augusto P Septimio, *Pr*
Cristina Septimio, *Sec*
▲ **EMP:** 7 **EST:** 2007
SALES (est): 365.75K **Privately Held**
Web: www.grancreations.com
SIC: 1743 1799 5722 3281 Terrazzo, tile, marble and mosaic work; Counter top installation; Kitchens, complete (sinks, cabinets, etc.); Curbing, granite or stone

(G-2231)
GRAND ENCORE CHARLOTTE LLC
Also Called: Encore Label & Packaging
3700 Rose Lake Dr (28217-2814)
PHONE..............................513 482-7500
Travis Potter, *Managing Member*
EMP: 25 **EST:** 2020
SALES (est): 1.02MM **Privately Held**
Web: www.encorelp.com
SIC: 2679 Labels, paper: made from purchased material

(G-2232)
GRAPHIC IMPRESSIONS INC
7910 District Dr (28213-6557)
PHONE..............................704 596-4921
W L Galloway Junior, *Pr*
W L Galloway Iii, *VP*
Kevin L Galloway, *
Bill Gallowa, *
EMP: 27 **EST:** 1975
SQ FT: 22,000
SALES (est): 4.7MM **Privately Held**
Web: www.giprinters.com
SIC: 2752 Offset printing

(G-2233)
GRAVEOKE INC
Also Called: National Textile Engravers
1814 Bradenton Dr (28206)
PHONE..............................704 534-3480

Andrew Graven, *Pr*
Philip Okey, *
EMP: 25 **EST:** 1972
SQ FT: 15,000
SALES (est): 1.55MM **Privately Held**
SIC: 2759 Textile printing rolls: engraving

(G-2234)
GRAY MANUFACTURING CO
8548 Highland Glen Dr (28269-6112)
P.O. Box 90363 (37209-0363)
PHONE..............................615 841-3066
William Gray, *Owner*
EMP: 7 **EST:** 1958
SQ FT: 2,500
SALES (est): 388.49K **Privately Held**
Web: www.grayusa.com
SIC: 3499 Metal household articles

(G-2235)
GREAT PACIFIC ENTPS US INC (DH)
Also Called: Genpak
10601 Westlake Dr (28273-3930)
PHONE..............................980 256-7729
James Pattison, *Ch Bd*
Michael Korenberg, *CEO*
Nick Geer, *VP*
James Reilly, *Ch*
▲ **EMP:** 23 **EST:** 1978
SQ FT: 36,000
SALES (est): 17.91MM
SALES (corp-wide): 28.29B **Privately Held**
Web: www.genpak.com
SIC: 3089 Plastics containers, except foam
HQ: Great Pacific Enterprises Inc
    1800-1067 Cordova St W
    Vancouver BC V6C 1
    604 278-4841

(G-2236)
GREAT WAGON ROAD DISTLG CO LLC
227 Southside Dr Ste B (28217-1727)
PHONE..............................704 469-9330
John Marrino, *Pr*
EMP: 16 **EST:** 2017
SALES (est): 240.16K **Privately Held**
Web: www.gwrdistilling.com
SIC: 2085 Distilled and blended liquors

(G-2237)
GRECON INC (HQ)
648 Griffith Rd Ste A (28217-3573)
PHONE..............................503 641-7731
Hermann Staats, *Ex VP*
Cary Jentzsch, *Treas*
▲ **EMP:** 18 **EST:** 1989
SQ FT: 10,000
SALES (est): 3.85MM
SALES (corp-wide): 90.86MM **Privately Held**
Web: www.fagus-grecon.com
SIC: 5084 3825 3613 Instruments and control equipment; Instruments to measure electricity; Switchgear and switchboard apparatus
PA: Fagus-Grecon Greten Gmbh Und Co Kg
    Hannoversche Str. 58
    Alfeld (Leine) NI 31061
    5181790

(G-2238)
GREEN POWER PRODUCERS
10600 Nations Ford Rd # 150 (28273-5762)
PHONE..............................704 844-8990
William Brinker, *Prin*
EMP: 6 **EST:** 2009
SALES (est): 679.14K **Privately Held**
SIC: 1321 Natural gas liquids

(G-2239)
GREEN WASTE MANAGEMENT LLC
101 N Tryon St Ste 112 (28246-0104)
PHONE..............................704 289-0720
EMP: 6 **EST:** 2018
SALES (est): 38.97K **Privately Held**
SIC: 7349 6531 3589 Janitorial service, contract basis; Real estate brokers and agents; Commercial cleaning equipment

(G-2240)
GREENLINE CORPORATION
200 Forsyth Hall Dr Ste E (28273-5815)
PHONE..............................704 333-3377
Donald Patterson, *Prin*
EMP: 6 **EST:** 2007
SALES (est): 1.64MM **Privately Held**
Web: www.greenlinepoultryparts.com
SIC: 3535 Conveyors and conveying equipment

(G-2241)
GREIF INC
900 Westinghouse Blvd (28273-6306)
P.O. Box 7026 (28241-7026)
PHONE..............................704 588-3895
Khalias Rahman, *Mgr*
EMP: 80
SALES (corp-wide): 5.45B **Publicly Held**
Web: www.greif.com
SIC: 2655 3412 Drums, fiber: made from purchased material; Metal barrels, drums, and pails
PA: Greif, Inc.
    425 Winter Rd
    Delaware OH 43015
    740 549-6000

(G-2242)
GRICE SHOWCASE DISPLAY MFG INC
5001 White Oak Rd (28210-2326)
PHONE..............................704 423-8888
Keely A Grice Iii, *Pr*
Keely Grice Iii, *Pr*
EMP: 8 **EST:** 1984
SALES (est): 385.14K **Privately Held**
Web: www.griceshowcase.com
SIC: 2541 2542 Display fixtures, wood; Office and store showcases and display fixtures

(G-2243)
GRONINGER USA LLC
14045 S Lakes Dr (28273-6791)
PHONE..............................704 588-3873
Horst Groeninger, *Pr*
Juergen Riedel, *Managing Member*
Ana Pryor, *
EMP: 37 **EST:** 1996
SQ FT: 2,800
SALES (est): 11.91MM
SALES (corp-wide): 2.14MM **Privately Held**
Web: www.groningerusa.com
SIC: 3565 Packaging machinery
PA: Groninger Gmbh &Co. Kg
    Alte Str. 9
    Aichtal BW 72631
    712750495

(G-2244)
H & B TOOL & DIE SUPPLY CO
5005 W Wt Harris Blvd Ste A (28269)
PHONE..............................704 376-8531
David Black, *Pr*
EMP: 9 **EST:** 1963
SQ FT: 3,500
SALES (est): 1.16MM **Privately Held**
Web: www.handbtool.com

SIC: 3599 Machine shop, jobbing and repair

(G-2245)
H & H POLISHING INC
4256 Golf Acres Dr (28208-5863)
PHONE...............................704 393-8728
Don G Hurst, *Pr*
Myrna Hurst, *Sec*
EMP: 10 **EST:** 1987
SQ FT: 24,000
SALES (est): 962.15K **Privately Held**
Web: www.hhpolishinginc.com
SIC: 3471 Plating of metals or formed
products

(G-2246)
H & H REPRESENTATIVES INC
Also Called: H & H REPRESENTATIVES, INC
University Parkway (28229)
PHONE...............................704 596-6950
Scott Sansberry, *Brnch Mgr*
EMP: 4
SALES (corp-wide): 2.26MM **Privately
Held**
Web: www.hhreps.com
SIC: 3432 Plastic plumbing fixture fittings,
assembly
PA: H & H Representatives, Inc.
1708 University Coml Pl
Charlotte NC 28213
704 596-6950

(G-2247)
H + M USA MANAGEMENT CO INC
Also Called: Hinderer & Muehlich
3200 Woodpark Blvd (28206-4211)
PHONE...............................704 599-9325
Faust Muehlich, *Pr*
▲ **EMP:** 6 **EST:** 1997
SALES (est): 757.74K **Privately Held**
SIC: 3544 Special dies and tools

(G-2248)
H F KINNEY CO INC
Also Called: Kinneys Stamp & Engraving
13852 Ballantyne Meadows Dr
(28277-3726)
PHONE...............................704 540-9367
Harold Fred Kinney Ii, *Pr*
Grace Kinney, *
Ron Kinney, *
EMP: 27 **EST:** 1962
SQ FT: 10,000
SALES (est): 172.33K **Privately Held**
SIC: 3953 3555 3993 Postmark stamps,
hand: rubber or metal; Printing trades
machinery; Signs and advertising specialties

(G-2249)
H-T-L PERMA USA LTD PARTNR (PA)
10333 Westlake Dr (28273-3785)
PHONE...............................704 377-3100
Kevin Keating, *Pt*
▲ **EMP:** 20 **EST:** 1964
SQ FT: 1,000
SALES (est): 9.82MM
SALES (corp-wide): 9.82MM **Privately
Held**
Web: www.permausa.com
SIC: 5085 3949 Industrial supplies;
Ammunition belts, sporting type

(G-2250)
HACKEDU INC (PA)
Also Called: Security Journey
1235 East Blvd Ste E Pmb 5073
(28203-5876)
PHONE...............................804 742-2533
Dan Newton, *CEO*
Joseph Ferrara, *CEO*
Jared Ablon, *CFO*

Matthew Koskela, *Prin*
EMP: 66 **EST:** 2017
SALES (est): 10.59MM
SALES (corp-wide): 10.59MM **Privately
Held**
Web: www.securityjourney.com
SIC: 7372 Prepackaged software

(G-2251)
HAIS KOOKIES & MORE
600 Hartford Ave (28209-1931)
PHONE...............................980 819-8256
EMP: 7
SALES (est): 631.97K **Privately Held**
SIC: 2053 Cakes, bakery: frozen

(G-2252)
HAMILTON SUNDSTRAND CORP
Also Called: UTC Aerospace Systems
2730 W Tyvola Rd (28217-4527)
PHONE...............................860 654-6000
EMP: 582
SALES (corp-wide): 80.74B **Publicly Held**
Web: www.collinsaerospace.com
SIC: 3714 Motor vehicle parts and
accessories
HQ: Hamilton Sundstrand Corporation
1 Hamilton Rd
Windsor Locks CT 06096
619 714-9442

(G-2253)
**HAMMOCK PHARMACEUTICALS
INC**
Also Called: Hammock Consumer
11922 General Dr Unit C (28273-7176)
PHONE...............................704 727-7926
William Maichle, *CEO*
Terence Novak, *COO*
Frank Stokes, *CFO*
EMP: 5 **EST:** 2016
SALES (est): 495.48K **Privately Held**
SIC: 2834 Pharmaceutical preparations

(G-2254)
HANS KRUG
4310 Sharon Rd Ste U01 (28211-0033)
PHONE...............................704 370-0809
Hans Krug, *Prin*
EMP: 14 **EST:** 2016
SALES (est): 148.89K **Privately Held**
Web: www.hanskrug.com
SIC: 2434 Wood kitchen cabinets

(G-2255)
HARBISONWALKER INTL INC
6600 Northpark Blvd Ste E (28216-0083)
PHONE...............................704 599-6540
Carol Jackson, *CEO*
EMP: 4
SALES (corp-wide): 1.58B **Privately Held**
Web: www.thinkhwi.com
SIC: 3255 5085 Clay refractories; Refractory
material
HQ: Harbisonwalker International, Inc.
2000 Park Ln Ste 400
Pittsburgh PA 15275

(G-2256)
HARDCOATINGS INC
Also Called: Hardcoatings
2601 Lucena St (28206-2109)
P.O. Box 596 (28164-0596)
PHONE...............................704 377-2996
Greg Stowe, *Pr*
Sharon Stowe, *VP*
EMP: 10 **EST:** 1964
SQ FT: 2,592
SALES (est): 933.59K **Privately Held**
Web: www.hardcoatingsinc.com

SIC: 3471 3353 Anodizing (plating) of metals
or formed products; Aluminum sheet, plate,
and foil

(G-2257)
HARDWOOD PUBLISHING CO INC
Also Called: Hardwood Review Export
6400 Bannington Rd (28226-1327)
PHONE...............................704 543-4408
George Barrett, *Pr*
Mike Barrett, *VP*
EMP: 9 **EST:** 1985
SALES (est): 579.27K **Privately Held**
Web: www.hardwoodreview.com
SIC: 2741 Newsletter publishing

(G-2258)
HARPER COMPANIES INTL INC
11625 Steele Creek Rd (28273-3731)
PHONE...............................800 438-3111
Ronald H Harper, *Pr*
EMP: 6 **EST:** 2017
SALES (est): 789.68K **Privately Held**
Web: www.harperimage.com
SIC: 3555 Printing trades machinery

(G-2259)
**HARPER CORPORATION OF
AMERICA (PA)**
11625 Steele Creek Rd (28273-3731)
P.O. Box 38490 (28278-1008)
PHONE...............................704 588-3371
Margaret Harper Kluttz, *Pr*
Ronald H Kluttz, *
Katherine Harper, *
Ronald James Harper, *
Eckehard Mecklenburg, *
◆ **EMP:** 125 **EST:** 1971
SQ FT: 12,000
SALES (est): 14.1MM
SALES (corp-wide): 14.1MM **Privately
Held**
Web: www.harperimage.com
SIC: 3555 2842 Printing trades machinery;
Cleaning or polishing preparations, nec

(G-2260)
**HARPER-LOVE ADHESIVES CORP
(HQ)**
11101 Westlake Dr (28273-3783)
P.O. Box 410408 (28241-0408)
PHONE...............................704 588-4395
Allan Clark, *CEO*
Thomas Evans, *
◆ **EMP:** 70 **EST:** 1978
SQ FT: 86,000
SALES (est): 24.56MM
SALES (corp-wide): 559.81MM **Privately
Held**
Web: www.harperlove.com
SIC: 2891 Glue
PA: Hbm Holdings Company
101 S Hanley Rd Ste 1050
Saint Louis MO 63105
314 376-2522

(G-2261)
HARSCO METRO RAIL LLC
3440 Toringdon Way Ste 100 (28277-3191)
PHONE...............................980 960-2624
EMP: 4 **EST:** 2016
SALES (est): 360.53K
SALES (corp-wide): 2.34B **Publicly Held**
Web: www.harscorail.com
SIC: 3531 Railroad related equipment
PA: Enviri Corporation
100-120 N 18th St # 17
Philadelphia PA 19103
267 857-8715

(G-2262)
HARSCO RAIL LLC (HQ)
3440 Toringdon Way Ste 100 (28277-3191)
PHONE...............................980 960-2624
Nicholas Grasberger Iii, *Managing Member*
EMP: 4 **EST:** 2016
SALES (est): 29.02MM
SALES (corp-wide): 2.34B **Publicly Held**
Web: www.harscorail.com
SIC: 3531 5088 1629 4789 Railway track
equipment; Railroad equipment and
supplies; Railroad and railway roadbed
construction; Railroad maintenance and
repair services
PA: Enviri Corporation
100-120 N 18th St # 17
Philadelphia PA 19103
267 857-8715

(G-2263)
HAYWARD HOLDINGS INC (PA)
Also Called: Hayward
1415 Vantage Park Dr Ste 400 (28203)
PHONE...............................704 837-8002
Kevin Holleran, *Pr*
Stephen Felice, *Ch Bd*
Eifion Jones, *Sr VP*
Susan Canning, *CLO*
John Collins, *CCO*
EMP: 119 **EST:** 2017
SALES (est): 1.05B
SALES (corp-wide): 1.05B **Publicly Held**
Web: hayward.com
SIC: 3569 3589 3648 Heaters, swimming
pool: electric; Swimming pool filter and
water conditioning systems; Swimming pool
lighting fixtures

(G-2264)
**HAYWARD INDUSTRIAL PRODUCTS
(DH)**
Also Called: Hayward Plastic Products Div
1415 Vantage Park Dr Ste 400 (28203)
P.O. Box 18 (07207)
PHONE...............................704 837-8002
Robert Davis, *CEO*
Oscar Davis, *CEO*
Robert Davis, *Pr*
◆ **EMP:** 250 **EST:** 1980
SALES (corp-wide): 1.05B **Publicly Held**
Web: hayward.com
SIC: 3089 3492 3491 3494 Plastics
hardware and building products; Control
valves, fluid power: hydraulic and pneumatic
; Pressure valves and regulators, industrial;
Line strainers, for use in piping systems
HQ: Hayward Industries, Inc.
1415 Vntage Pk Dr Ste 400
Charlotte NC 28203
704 837-8002

(G-2265)
HAYWARD INDUSTRIES INC (HQ)
Also Called: Haywood Pool Products
1415 Vantage Park Dr Ste 400 (28203)
PHONE...............................704 837-8002
Kevin Holleran, *CEO*
Oscar Davis, *
Eifion Jones, *
◆ **EMP:** 350 **EST:** 1925
SALES (est): 752.64MM
SALES (corp-wide): 1.05B **Publicly Held**
Web: hayward.com
SIC: 3589 3561 3423 3494 Swimming pool
filter and water conditioning systems;
Pumps and pumping equipment; Leaf
skimmers or swimming pool rakes; Valves
and pipe fittings, nec
PA: Hayward Holdings, Inc.
1415 Vntage Pk Dr Ste 400

Charlotte NC 28203
704 837-8002

(G-2266)
HC FORKLIFT AMERICA CORP
Also Called: Hangcha America
1338 Hundred Oaks Dr Ste Dd
(28217-3920)
PHONE.............................980 888-8335
Ning Zhang, *CEO*
Jimmy Zhang, *VP Opers*
EMP: 15 EST: 2017
SALES (est): 1.32MM **Privately Held**
Web: www.hcforkliftamerica.com
SIC: 3537 Forklift trucks

(G-2267)
HEALTH AT HOME INC
1321 Cavendish Ct (28211-3937)
PHONE.............................850 543-4482
Robert Murray, *CEO*
EMP: 10 EST: 2010
SALES (est): 582.65K **Privately Held**
Web: www.healthathomeinc.com
SIC: 8099 3999 Health and allied services,
nec; Manufacturing industries, nec

(G-2268)
HEARST CORPORATION
Also Called: Hearst Service Center
3540 Toringdon Way Ste 700 # 7
(28277-4969)
PHONE.............................704 348-8000
EMP: 10
SALES (corp-wide): 4.29B **Privately Held**
Web: www.hearst.com
SIC: 2721 Magazines: publishing only, not
printed on site
PA: The Hearst Corporation
300 W 57th St
New York NY 10019
212 649-2000

(G-2269)
HEARST CORPORATION
Also Called: King Features Syndicate
3540 Toringdon Way Ste 700 # 7
(28277-4969)
PHONE.............................704 348-8000
Teri Walding, *Asst Cont*
EMP: 17
SALES (corp-wide): 4.29B **Privately Held**
Web: www.hearst.com
SIC: 2721 Comic books: publishing and
printing
PA: The Hearst Corporation
300 W 57th St
New York NY 10019
212 649-2000

(G-2270)
HEIST BREWING COMPANY LLC
Also Called: Heist Brewery
525 Oakland Ave Apt 1 (28204-2355)
PHONE.............................603 969-8012
Kurt Hogan, *Managing Member*
EMP: 6 EST: 2011
SQ FT: 6,500
SALES (est): 429.29K **Privately Held**
SIC: 2082 Ale (alcoholic beverage)

(G-2271)
HERFF JONES LLC
9525 Monroe Rd Ste 150 (28270-2451)
PHONE.............................704 845-3355
Tom Reef, *Brnch Mgr*
EMP: 5
SQ FT: 160,152
SALES (corp-wide): 8.23B **Privately Held**
Web: www.yearbookdiscoveries.com

SIC: 2741 2732 Yearbooks: publishing and
printing; Book printing
HQ: Herff Jones, Llc
4501 W 62nd St
Indianapolis IN 46268
317 297-3741

(G-2272)
HERFF JONES LLC
Also Called: Herff Jones
14931 Santa Lucia Dr (28277-3382)
P.O. Box 568 (28173-1000)
PHONE.............................704 962-1483
Deborah Forrest, *Brnch Mgr*
EMP: 4
SALES (corp-wide): 8.23B **Privately Held**
Web: www.yearbookdiscoveries.com
SIC: 3911 Rings, finger: precious metal
HQ: Herff Jones, Llc
4501 W 62nd St
Indianapolis IN 46268
317 297-3741

(G-2273)
HERITAGE CUSTOM SIGNS & DISP
2731 Interstate St (28208-3603)
PHONE.............................704 655-1465
EMP: 50 EST: 2017
SALES (est): 674.11K **Privately Held**
Web: www.bluefiresigns.com
SIC: 3993 Signs and advertising specialties

(G-2274)
HERITAGE PRTG & GRAPHICS INC
2739 Interstate St (28208-3603)
PHONE.............................704 551-0700
Joseph Gass, *Pr*
EMP: 9
SQ FT: 6,300
SALES (corp-wide): 5.11MM **Privately
Held**
Web: www.heritageprinting.com
SIC: 2752 5131 5199 5999 Offset printing;
Flags and banners; Posters and decals;
Banners, flags, decals, and posters
PA: Heritage Printing & Graphics, Inc.
2854 Old Washington Rd
Waldorf MD 20601
301 843-1997

(G-2275)
HERRIN BROS COAL & ICE CO
315 E 36th St (28206-2021)
P.O. Box 5291 (28299-5291)
PHONE.............................704 332-2193
Marshall L Herrin, *Pr*
Marshall L Herrin, *Pr*
Merl Lee Herrin, *General Vice President*
EMP: 5 EST: 1929
SQ FT: 700
SALES (est): 246.83K **Privately Held**
Web: www.herrinice.com
SIC: 5983 5172 2097 5989 Fuel oil dealers;
Gasoline; Manufactured ice; Coal

(G-2276)
HEUBACH COLORANTS USA LLC
5500 77 Center Dr (28217-3072)
PHONE.............................408 686-2935
Alex Baron, *Managing Member*
EMP: 30 EST: 2019
SALES (est): 5.17MM **Privately Held**
SIC: 2865 Color pigments, organic

(G-2277)
HIATUS INC
Also Called: Hiatus
1515 Mockingbird Ln Ste 400 (28209)
PHONE.............................844 572-6185
James D Callis, *CEO*
EMP: 20 EST: 2019

SALES (est): 3.11MM **Privately Held**
Web: www.hiatusapp.com
SIC: 7372 Prepackaged software

(G-2278)
HIGH GROUND INCORPORATED
2209 Park Rd Ste 1 (28203-6096)
PHONE.............................704 372-6620
Stephen Hofstatter, *Dir*
EMP: 4 EST: 2010
SALES (est): 91.51K **Privately Held**
Web: www.nspworldwide.com
SIC: 2326 Men's and boy's work clothing

(G-2279)
HIGH TEMPERATURE TECH INC
4324 Revolution Park Dr Ste 106 (28203)
PHONE.............................704 375-2111
Jennifer Gelorme, *Pr*
Tom Rush, *VP*
Karen Rush, *Sec*
EMP: 15 EST: 1998
SALES (est): 1.89MM **Privately Held**
Web: www.isomembrane.com
SIC: 8611 3259 Contractors' association;
Adobe brick

(G-2280)
HILEX POLY CO LLC (DH)
Also Called: Novolex
3436 Toringdon Way Ste 100 (28277-2449)
◆ EMP: 100 EST: 2003
SQ FT: 30,000
SALES (est): 966.79MM
SALES (corp-wide): 26.11B **Publicly Held**
Web: www.novolex.com
SIC: 2674 2673 Paper bags: made from
purchased materials; Plastic bags: made
from purchased materials
HQ: Novolex Holdings, Llc
3436 Tringdon Way Ste 100
Charlotte NC 28277
800 845-6051

(G-2281)
HOLMAN & MOODY INC
9119 Forsyth Park Dr (28273-3882)
PHONE.............................704 394-4141
Lee F Holman, *Pr*
Zona Holman, *Ch*
Tomoo Furusaka, *VP*
Jolana Holman, *Sec*
▲ EMP: 6 EST: 1955
SQ FT: 74,000
SALES (est): 578.35K **Privately Held**
Web: www.holmanmoody.com
SIC: 3714 3599 3519 Motor vehicle parts
and accessories; Machine and other job
shop work; Internal combustion engines,
nec

(G-2282)
HOLMAN AUTOMOTIVE INC
9119 Forsyth Park Dr (28273-3882)
P.O. Box 669351 (28266)
PHONE.............................704 583-2888
Lee Holman, *Pr*
Libby Holman, *Sec*
EMP: 4 EST: 1983
SQ FT: 8,500
SALES (est): 420.35K **Privately Held**
Web: www.holmanmoody.com
SIC: 3714 3519 3711 Motor vehicle engines
and parts; Gas engine rebuilding; Motor
vehicles and car bodies

(G-2283)
HOLY COW PUBLICATIONS LLC
811 Queens Rd Apt 1 (28207-1639)
PHONE.............................704 900-5779
Charles Bennett, *Prin*

EMP: 5 EST: 2011
SALES (est): 89.64K **Privately Held**
SIC: 2741 Miscellaneous publishing

(G-2284)
HOME T LLC
652 Griffith Rd Ste I (28217-3563)
PHONE.............................646 797-4768
Ryan Shell, *CEO*
EMP: 10 EST: 2012
SQ FT: 500
SALES (est): 1.58MM **Privately Held**
Web: www.thehomet.com
SIC: 5136 2326 Sweaters, men's and boys';
Men's and boy's work clothing

(G-2285)
HONEYWELL
13509 S Point Blvd Ste 150 (28273-7900)
PHONE.............................734 942-5823
EMP: 26 EST: 2019
SALES (est): 2.24MM **Privately Held**
Web: www.honeywell.com
SIC: 3724 Aircraft engines and engine parts

(G-2286)
HONEYWELL INTERNATIONAL INC
(PA)
Also Called: Honeywell
855 S Mint St (28202)
PHONE.............................704 627-6200
Vimal Kapur, *Ch Bd*
Greg Lewis, *Sr VP*
Karen Mattimore, *Chief Human Resource
Officer*
Anne T Madden, *Sr VP*
◆ EMP: 2855 EST: 1885
SALES (est): 38.5B
SALES (corp-wide): 38.5B **Publicly Held**
Web: www.honeywell.com
SIC: 3724 Aircraft engines and engine parts

(G-2287)
HORMEL FOODS CORP SVCS LLC
Also Called: Hormel
3420 Toringdon Way (28277-4433)
PHONE.............................704 527-1535
Clyde Maddux, *Prin*
EMP: 15
SALES (corp-wide): 11.92B **Publicly Held**
Web: www.hormelfoods.com
SIC: 2013 Sausages and other prepared
meats
HQ: Hormel Foods Corporate Services, Llc
1 Hormel Pl
Austin MN 55912

(G-2288)
HOSPIRA INC
2815 Coliseum Centre Dr Ste 250
(28217-0137)
PHONE.............................704 335-1300
Shade Mecum, *Mgr*
EMP: 12
SALES (corp-wide): 63.63B **Publicly Held**
Web: www.pfizerhospitalus.com
SIC: 2834 Druggists' preparations
(pharmaceuticals)
HQ: Hospira, Inc.
275 N Field Dr
Lake Forest IL 60045
224 212-2000

(G-2289)
HOT BOX POWER COATING INC
1033 Berryhill Rd (28208-4117)
PHONE.............................704 398-8224
Sean Boudreaux, *Pr*
EMP: 4 EST: 2006
SALES (est): 176.55K **Privately Held**
Web: www.hotboxusa.com

SIC: 3479 Coating of metals and formed products

(G-2290)
HOWMET AEROSPACE INC
Also Called: Howmet Aerospace Inc
301 N Smith St (28202-1445)
PHONE.................................704 334-7276
EMP: 135
SALES (corp-wide): 7.43B Publicly Held
Web: www.howmet.com
SIC: 3353 Aluminum sheet and strip
PA: Howmet Aerospace Inc.
201 Isabella St Ste 200
Pittsburgh PA 15212
412 553-1950

(G-2291)
HP INC
Also Called: HP
4035 South Blvd (28209-2616)
PHONE.................................704 523-3548
Bruce Chandler, Mgr
EMP: 5
SALES (corp-wide): 53.56B Publicly Held
Web: www.hp.com
SIC: 3571 Personal computers
(microcomputers)
PA: Hp Inc.
1501 Page Mill Rd
Palo Alto CA 94304
650 857-1501

(G-2292)
HS HYOSUNG USA INC (DH)
15801 Brixham Hill Ave Ste 575 (28277)
PHONE.................................704 790-6100
Jong Bock Lee, CEO
Bong Kwan Choi, *
◆ EMP: 30 EST: 1993
SALES (est): 96.5MM Privately Held
Web: www.hyosungusa.com
SIC: 2221 2296 5199 Broadwoven fabric
mills, manmade; Cord for reinforcing rubber
tires; Fabrics, yarns, and knit goods
HQ: Hs Hyosung Usa Holdings, Inc.
15801 Brxham Hl Ave Ste 5
Charlotte NC 28277
704 790-6134

(G-2293)
**HS HYOSUNG USA HOLDINGS INC
(HQ)**
15801 Brixham Hill Ave Ste 575 (28277)
PHONE.................................704 790-6134
Terry Swanner, Pr
Hyeong Seob Jeong, CFO
▲ EMP: 8 EST: 2008
SALES (est): 472.09MM Privately Held
Web: www.hyosungusa.com
SIC: 2221 2296 5199 Broadwoven fabric
mills, manmade; Cord for reinforcing rubber
tires; Fabrics, yarns, and knit goods
PA: Hyosung Corporation
119 Mapo-Daero, Mapo-Gu
Seoul 04144

(G-2294)
HSI LEGACY INC
3528 N Graham St (28206-1625)
PHONE.................................704 376-9631
James Howard, Pr
EMP: 7 EST: 1982
SQ FT: 25,000
SALES (est): 5.25MM Privately Held
Web: www.howardsteelinc.com
SIC: 5051 3441 Steel; Fabricated structural
metal

(G-2295)
HUBER + SUHNER INC (DH)
3540 Toringdon Way Ste 560 (28277-3867)
PHONE.................................704 790-7300
Andy Hollywood, Managing Member
Andy Hollywood, Pr
Yvonne Barney, *
Sean Thomas, *
Joshua Wittensoldner, Finance*
▲ EMP: 40 EST: 1986
SQ FT: 35,000
SALES (est): 24.84MM Privately Held
Web: www.hubersuhner.com
SIC: 3679 3678 3357 5065 Microwave
components; Electronic connectors;
Nonferrous wiredrawing and insulating;
Electronic parts and equipment, nec
HQ: Huber + Suhner (North America)
Corporation
3540 Toringdon Way
Charlotte NC 28277

(G-2296)
**HUBER + SUHNER NORTH AMER
CORP (HQ)**
Also Called: Hubersuhner
3540 Toringdon Way (28277-3867)
PHONE.................................704 790-7300
Ian Shergold, Pr
Drew Nixon, *
Guy Petignat, *
▲ EMP: 98 EST: 1988
SALES (est): 58.32MM Privately Held
Web: www.hubersuhner.com
SIC: 3357 5065 Nonferrous wiredrawing and
insulating; Electronic parts
PA: Huber+Suhner Ag
Degersheimerstrasse 14
Herisau AR 9100

(G-2297)
**HUBER ENGINEERED WOODS LLC
(HQ)**
10925 David Taylor Dr Ste 300
(28262-1041)
PHONE.................................800 933-9220
Brian Carlson, Pr
Kirk Blanchette, *
Charles Lewis, *
Andrew Verrinder, *
◆ EMP: 50 EST: 2003
SQ FT: 21,000
SALES (est): 140.77MM
SALES (corp-wide): 1.24B Privately Held
Web: www.huberwood.com
SIC: 2493 Reconstituted wood products
PA: J.M. Huber Corporation
3100 Cmbrland Blvd Ste 60
Atlanta GA 30339
678 247-7300

(G-2298)
HUNTSMAN CORPORATION
3400 Westinghouse Blvd (28273-4541)
PHONE.................................706 272-4020
Kay Moore, Brnch Mgr
EMP: 10
SALES (corp-wide): 6.04B Publicly Held
Web: www.huntsman.com
SIC: 2821 Polystyrene resins
PA: Huntsman Corporation
10003 Woodloch Forest Dr
The Woodlands TX 77380
281 719-6000

(G-2299)
HUNTSMAN INTERNATIONAL LLC
3400 Westinghouse Blvd (28273-4541)
PHONE.................................704 588-6082
Monte Edlund, Mgr
EMP: 29

SALES (corp-wide): 6.04B Publicly Held
Web: www.huntsman.com
SIC: 2821 Polystyrene resins
HQ: Huntsman International Llc
10003 Woodloch Forest Dr
The Woodlands TX 77380
281 719-6000

(G-2300)
HUNTSMAN TEXTILE EFFECTS
3400 Westinghouse Blvd (28273-4541)
PHONE.................................704 587-5000
Carol Walker, Prin
▲ EMP: 30 EST: 2009
SALES (est): 1.75MM Privately Held
Web: www.huntsman.com
SIC: 2821 Plastics materials and resins

(G-2301)
**HUSQVRNA CNSMR OUTDOOR PDTS
NA (HQ)**
Also Called: Husqvarna Forest & Garden
9335 Harris Corners Pkwy Ste 500
(28269-3830)
PHONE.................................704 597-5000
Henric Andersson, CEO
Jill Jacobson, *
◆ EMP: 95 EST: 2005
SQ FT: 37,000
SALES (est): 457.22MM
SALES (corp-wide): 2.23B Privately Held
SIC: 3524 Lawn and garden equipment
PA: Husqvarna Ab
Drottninggatan 2
Huskvarna 561 3
36146500

(G-2302)
**HUSQVRNA CNSMR OUTDOOR PDTS
NA**
Also Called: Husqvarna Prof Outdoor Pdts
7349 Statesville Rd (28269-3702)
PHONE.................................704 597-5000
David Heinz, Crdt Mgr
EMP: 1342
SALES (corp-wide): 2.23B Privately Held
SIC: 3524 Lawn and garden equipment
HQ: Husqvarna Consumer Outdoor
Products N.A., Inc.
9335 Hrris Crners Pkwy St
Charlotte NC 28269

(G-2303)
**HUSQVRNA CNSMR OUTDOOR PDTS
NA**
8825 Statesville Rd (28269-7638)
PHONE.................................704 494-4810
EMP: 1123
SALES (corp-wide): 2.23B Privately Held
SIC: 3524 Lawn and garden tractors and
equipment
HQ: Husqvarna Consumer Outdoor
Products N.A., Inc.
9335 Hrris Crners Pkwy St
Charlotte NC 28269

(G-2304)
HYDE PARK PARTNERS INC (PA)
Also Called: Livingston & Haven
11529 Wilmar Blvd (28273-6448)
P.O. Box 7207 (28241-7207)
PHONE.................................704 587-4819
Anne Q Woody Prea, Treas
Anne Q Woody, Pr
Clifton B Vann Iii, Ch
Clifton B Vann Iv, Pr
James T Skinner Iii, Sec
▲ EMP: 95 EST: 1947
SQ FT: 50,000
SALES (est): 98.44MM
SALES (corp-wide): 98.44MM Privately
Held

Web: www.hydeparkpartners.us
SIC: 5084 3594 Hydraulic systems
equipment and supplies; Fluid power
pumps and motors

(G-2305)
**HYDRALIC ENGNERED PDTS SVC
INC**
Also Called: Hepsco
803 Pressley Rd Ste 101 (28217-0771)
P.O. Box 1528 (28070-1528)
PHONE.................................704 374-1306
Kenneth Jahns Senior, CEO
Kenneth Jahns Junior, Pr
Terry Treadwell, Sec
EMP: 4 EST: 1991
SQ FT: 5,000
SALES (est): 214.92K Privately Held
Web: www.hepsco.com
SIC: 5084 3594 Hydraulic systems
equipment and supplies; Fluid power
pumps and motors

(G-2306)
HYDRECO INC
1500 Continental Blvd Ste Z (28273-6376)
PHONE.................................704 295-7575
James Hill, Prin
EMP: 18 EST: 2008
SALES (est): 613.64K Privately Held
Web: www.hydreco.com
SIC: 3566 Speed changers, drives, and
gears

(G-2307)
HYPERNOVA INC
Also Called: Hypernova Solutions
1228 Archdale Dr Apt E (28217-4355)
PHONE.................................704 360-0096
Matthew Cauthen, Pr
EMP: 8 EST: 2018
SALES (est): 548.15K Privately Held
SIC: 3571 Electronic computers

(G-2308)
ICEE COMPANY
1901 Associates Ln Ste A (28217-2874)
PHONE.................................704 357-6865
Kurt Ritzel, Prin
EMP: 4
SALES (corp-wide): 1.57B Publicly Held
Web: www.icee.com
SIC: 2086 Bottled and canned soft drinks
HQ: The Icee Company
265 Mason Rd
La Vergne TN 37086
800 426-4233

(G-2309)
ID IMAGES LLC
2311 Distribution Center Dr Ste A
(28269-4288)
PHONE.................................704 494-0444
Robert Miller, Pr
EMP: 4 EST: 2016
SALES (est): 224.81K Privately Held
Web: www.idimages.com
SIC: 2759 Commercial printing, nec

(G-2310)
IGH ENTERPRISES INC
Also Called: Mitchum Quality Snack
2001 W Morehead St (28208-5139)
PHONE.................................704 372-6744
John Wilson, Pr
Bonnie Tirvette, *
Cheri Shipley, *
Henry D Pully, *
▲ EMP: 16 EST: 2004
SQ FT: 170,000
SALES (est): 928.15K Privately Held

SIC: **2096** 2099 Potato chips and other potato-based snacks; Food preparations, nec

(G-2311)
IGM RESINS USA INC (DH)
Also Called: I G M
8700 Red Oak Blvd Ste M (28217)
PHONE.....................704 588-2500
Wilfrid Gambade, *CEO*
Jan Averes, *
◆ **EMP:** 59 **EST:** 2010
SALES (est): 22.47MM **Privately Held**
Web: www.igmresins.com
SIC: **2851** Coating, air curing
HQ: Igm Specialties Holding, Inc.
　　3300 Westinghouse Blvd
　　Charlotte NC 28273
　　704 945-8702

(G-2312)
IGM SPECIALTIES HOLDING INC (DH)
3300 Westinghouse Blvd (28273-6521)
PHONE.....................704 945-8702
Gerald Walker, *Prin*
Hohn Huiberts, *Prin*
EMP: 12 **EST:** 2012
SALES (est): 22.73MM **Privately Held**
Web: www.igmresins.com
SIC: **6799** 2851 Investors, nec; Coating, air curing
HQ: I.G.M. Resins B.V.
　　Gompenstraat 49
　　Waalwijk NB 5145

(G-2313)
ILSEMANN CORP
2555 Westinghouse Blvd (28273-7509)
PHONE.....................610 323-4143
Stephan Ilsemann, *Pr*
▲ **EMP:** 4 **EST:** 2013
SALES (est): 955.25K **Privately Held**
Web: www.ilsemann.com
SIC: **3559** Robots, molding and forming plastics

(G-2314)
IM8 (US) LLC ✪
11401 Granite St (28273)
PHONE.....................862 485-8325
David Beckham, *Managing Member*
EMP: 9 **EST:** 2024
SALES (est): 332.84K **Privately Held**
SIC: **2023** Dietary supplements, dairy and non-dairy based

(G-2315)
IMPERIAL FALCON GROUP INC
3440 Toringdon Way Ste 205 (28277-3190)
PHONE.....................646 717-1128
Wael Elias, *CEO*
EMP: 5 **EST:** 2014
SALES (est): 1.8MM **Privately Held**
SIC: **2052** 3944 2869 7389 Biscuits, dry; Automobiles and trucks, toy; Industrial organic chemicals, nec; Business Activities at Non-Commercial Site

(G-2316)
IMPERIAL USA LTD
Also Called: Global Door Controls
1535 Elizabeth Ave Ste 201 (28204-2502)
PHONE.....................704 596-2444
Antoune E Battah Junior, *Pr*
◆ **EMP:** 30 **EST:** 1994
SALES (est): 6.96MM **Privately Held**
Web: www.impusa.com
SIC: **3429** 5072 Furniture hardware; Hardware

(G-2317)
IMPRINTING SYSTEMS SPCALTY INC
803 Pressley Rd Ste 104 (28217-0971)
PHONE.....................704 527-4545
Glenn Randolph, *Pr*
Lois Randolph, *VP*
Mark Kessler, *VP*
Cindy Kessler, *Sec*
EMP: 6 **EST:** 1979
SQ FT: 8,000
SALES (est): 241.69K **Privately Held**
Web: www.imprintinginc.com
SIC: **2759** Labels and seals: printing, nsk

(G-2318)
IMR HOLDINGS LLC
10028 Highlands Crossing Dr (28277-1779)
PHONE.....................980 287-8139
EMP: 5
SALES (est): 341.83K **Privately Held**
SIC: **7389** 7372 Business Activities at Non-Commercial Site; Application computer software

(G-2319)
INCANTARE ART BY MARILYN LLC
15701 Pedlar Mills Rd (28278-7686)
PHONE.....................704 713-8846
Marilyn Marte, *CEO*
EMP: 12 **EST:** 2020
SALES (est): 127.72K **Privately Held**
SIC: **8999** 3229 Artist; Art, decorative and novelty glassware

(G-2320)
INDEPENDENT BEVERAGE CO LLC (PA)
3936 Corporation Cir (28216-3421)
PHONE.....................704 399-2504
Jeff Rogers, *Pr*
David Barker, *Sec*
◆ **EMP:** 10 **EST:** 1992
SQ FT: 105,000
SALES (est): 37.46MM **Privately Held**
Web: www.independentbeverage.com
SIC: **2086** Bottled and canned soft drinks

(G-2321)
INDIAN HEAD INDUSTRIES INC (PA)
Also Called: MGM Brakes
6200 Harris Technology Blvd (28269-3732)
PHONE.....................704 547-7411
Ron Parker, *CEO*
Jeffrey Parker, *
Susan Pfeiffr, *
◆ **EMP:** 45 **EST:** 1984
SQ FT: 15,000
SALES (est): 30.92MM
SALES (corp-wide): 30.92MM **Privately Held**
Web: www.mgmbrakes.com
SIC: **3593** 3714 Fluid power cylinders and actuators; Motor vehicle brake systems and parts

(G-2322)
INDUSTRIAL MECHATRONICS INC
117 Freeland Ln (28217-1617)
P.O. Box 620457 (28262-0107)
PHONE.....................704 900-2407
David Lewis, *Pr*
EMP: 5 **EST:** 2005
SALES (est): 767.89K **Privately Held**
SIC: **3441** Fabricated structural metal

(G-2323)
INDUSTRIAL PIPING INC
212 S Tryon St Ste 1050 (28281-0003)
P.O. Box Po Box 518 (28281)
PHONE.....................704 588-1100

▲ **EMP:** 650
Web: www.usindustrialpiping.com
SIC: **3599** 3569 Machine shop, jobbing and repair; Sprinkler systems, fire: automatic

(G-2324)
INDUSTRIAL SIGN & GRAPHICS INC (PA)
4227 N Graham St (28206-1214)
P.O. Box 35565 (28235-5565)
PHONE.....................704 371-4985
Larry M Lee, *Pr*
Alan Pressley, *VP*
▲ **EMP:** 21 **EST:** 1990
SQ FT: 20,000
SALES (est): 2.86MM **Privately Held**
Web: www.industrialsign.com
SIC: **3993** 2752 Signs and advertising specialties; Commercial printing, lithographic

(G-2325)
INDUSTRIAL TECH SVCS AMRCAS IN (DH)
Also Called: SPX Flow Technology Usa, Inc.
13320 Ballantyne Corporate Pl (28277-3607)
PHONE.....................704 808-3848
Marc Michael, *Pr*
David Kowalski, *Global Manufacturing Operations President*
EMP: 58 **EST:** 1992
SALES (est): 13.07MM
SALES (corp-wide): 1.78B **Privately Held**
Web: www.spx.com
SIC: **3556** 3559 Dairy and milk machinery; Pharmaceutical machinery
HQ: Spx Flow, Inc.
　　13320 Ballantyne Corp Pl
　　Charlotte NC 28277
　　704 752-4400

(G-2326)
INDUSTRIAL TIMBER LLC (PA)
6441 Hendry Rd Ste B (28269-3848)
PHONE.....................704 919-1215
Michael Ruch, *Mgr*
▲ **EMP:** 75 **EST:** 2017
SALES (est): 37.25MM
SALES (corp-wide): 37.25MM **Privately Held**
Web: www.thesmartplay.com
SIC: **2493** 5031 Reconstituted wood products ; Lumber, plywood, and millwork

(G-2327)
INFINITE SOFTWARE RESORCES LLC (PA)
3020 Prosperity Church Rd 1 (28269-7197)
PHONE.....................704 509-0031
EMP: 9 **EST:** 1998
SQ FT: 1,500
SALES (est): 776.52K
SALES (corp-wide): 776.52K **Privately Held**
SIC: **8748** 7372 Systems analysis and engineering consulting services; Prepackaged software

(G-2328)
INFINITY S END INC (PA)
Also Called: Infinity Signs and Screen Prtg
7804 Fairview Rd Ste C (28226-4999)
PHONE.....................704 900-8355
Frank Pietras, *Pr*
John Pietras, *Sec*
Patricia Ann Manning, *Prin*
EMP: 11 **EST:** 1970
SQ FT: 5,500
SALES (est): 2.43MM
SALES (corp-wide): 2.43MM **Privately Held**

Web: www.infinitysend.com
SIC: **5331** 5999 2759 3993 Variety stores; Art and architectural supplies; Screen printing; Signs and advertising specialties

(G-2329)
INFISOFT SOFTWARE
7422 Carmel Executive Park Dr (28226-8273)
PHONE.....................704 307-2619
Jeff Barefoot, *Prin*
EMP: 5 **EST:** 2009
SALES (est): 526.86K **Privately Held**
Web: www.infisoft.com
SIC: **7372** 7371 5734 Prepackaged software ; Computer software development; Computer software and accessories

(G-2330)
INFO-GEL LLC (PA)
2311 Distribution Center Dr Ste F (28269-4294)
PHONE.....................704 599-5770
Quint Barefoot, *Managing Member*
James Olesinski, *Owner*
▲ **EMP:** 7 **EST:** 2007
SQ FT: 1,000
SALES (est): 7.1MM **Privately Held**
Web: www.info-gel.com
SIC: **2899** Gelatin: edible, technical, photographic, or pharmaceutical

(G-2331)
INFOBELT LLC (PA)
4100 Beresford Rd (28211-3810)
PHONE.....................980 223-4000
Srinivas Mannava, *Managing Member*
EMP: 11 **EST:** 2011
SQ FT: 2,500
SALES (est): 2.3MM
SALES (corp-wide): 2.3MM **Privately Held**
Web: www.infobelt.com
SIC: **7373** 7374 7372 7376 Computer integrated systems design; Data processing service; Business oriented computer software; Computer facilities management

(G-2332)
INFORMATION AGE PUBLISHING INC
11600 N Community House Rd # R (28277-1887)
P.O. Box 79049 (28271-7047)
PHONE.....................704 752-9125
George Johnson, *Prin*
EMP: 9 **EST:** 2007
SALES (est): 946.27K **Privately Held**
Web: www.infoagepub.com
SIC: **2741** Miscellaneous publishing

(G-2333)
INFOSENSE INC
2102 Cambridge Beltway Dr Ste D1 (28273)
PHONE.....................704 644-1164
George Alexander Churchill, *CEO*
EMP: 7
SIC: **3679** Electronic circuits
PA: Infosense, Inc.
　　8116 S Tryon St Ste B3-20
　　Charlotte NC 28273

(G-2334)
INFOSENSE INC (PA)
8116 S Tryon St Ste B3-203 (28273)
PHONE.....................704 644-1164
George Alexander Churchill, *CEO*
EMP: 8 **EST:** 2007
SALES (est): 3.51MM **Privately Held**
Web: www.infosense.com
SIC: **3679** Electronic circuits

▲ = Import ▼ = Export
◆ = Import/Export

(G-2335)
INGERSOLL RAND INC
6000 General Commerce Dr (28213-6394)
PHONE..............................704 774-4290
EMP: 50
SALES (corp-wide): 7.24B **Publicly Held**
Web: www.irco.com
SIC: 3563 Air and gas compressors
PA: Ingersoll Rand Inc.
525 Harbor Pl Dr Ste 600
Davidson NC 28036
704 896-4000

(G-2336)
INGERSOLL-RAND COMPANY
Also Called: Ingersoll-Rand
10000 Twin Lakes Pkwy (28269-7653)
PHONE..............................704 655-4836
EMP: 84
SIC: 3561 Pumps and pumping equipment
HQ: Ingersoll-Rand Company
800 Beaty St Ste B
Davidson NC 28036
704 655-4000

(G-2337)
INNAIT INC
Also Called: Innait
5524 Joyce Dr (28215-2417)
PHONE..............................406 241-5245
Roger Mukai, *CEO*
Roger Mukai, *Prin*
Jonathon Robin, *Prin*
Alan Anderson, *Prin*
Lee Speers, *Prin*
EMP: 6 EST: 2020
SALES (est): 240.74K **Privately Held**
SIC: 7371 7378 7372 7374 Software
programming applications; Computer and
data processing equipment repair/
maintenance; Operating systems computer
software; Data processing service

(G-2338)
INPLAC NORTH AMERICA INC
10926 S Tryon St Ste F (28273-4154)
PHONE..............................704 587-1151
Fernando Marcondes, *Pr*
▲ EMP: 4 EST: 2003
SALES (est): 1.04MM **Privately Held**
Web: www.inplacna.com
SIC: 3089 5113 Plastics processing; Bags,
paper and disposable plastic

(G-2339)
INSTA COPY SHOP LTD
Also Called: ICI Copy Forms & Printing
4311 South Blvd Ste D (28209-2624)
PHONE..............................704 376-1350
Don Lloyd, *Pr*
Rick Lloyd, *VP*
EMP: 14 EST: 1982
SQ FT: 6,000
SALES (est): 998.67K **Privately Held**
Web: www.iciprint.com
SIC: 2752 Offset printing

(G-2340)
INTEPLAST GROUP CORPORATION
10701 S Commerce Blvd Ste A
(28273-5300)
PHONE..............................704 504-3200
Kim Knapik, *Off Mgr*
EMP: 26
Web: www.inteplast.com
SIC: 3081 Polyethylene film
PA: Inteplast Group Corporation
9 Peach Tree Hill Rd
Livingston NJ 07039

(G-2341)
INTER-CONTINENTAL GEAR & BRAKE (PA)
6431 Reames Rd (28216-5280)
PHONE..............................704 599-3420
Dave Morgan, *Mgr*
▲ EMP: 8 EST: 2007
SALES (est): 4.28MM
SALES (corp-wide): 4.28MM **Privately Held**
Web: www.icgb.ca
SIC: 3714 Motor vehicle parts and
accessories

(G-2342)
INTERIOR TRIM CREATIONS INC
11912 Erwin Ridge Ave (28213-2137)
PHONE..............................704 821-1470
Antonio Valdez, *Pr*
Lynn Valdez, *Sec*
EMP: 6 EST: 1986
SALES (est): 125.26K **Privately Held**
SIC: 1751 2431 Finish and trim carpentry;
Millwork

(G-2343)
INTERNATIONAL FOAM PDTS INC (PA)
10530 Westlake Dr (28273-3788)
PHONE..............................704 588-0080
Steve Sklow, *Pr*
EMP: 5 EST: 1963
SQ FT: 65,000
SALES (est): 2.72MM
SALES (corp-wide): 2.72MM **Privately Held**
Web: www.internationalfoam.com
SIC: 2396 5199 Bindings, bias: made from
purchased materials; Foam rubber

(G-2344)
INTERNATIONAL MOTORS LLC
Navistar
3325 Rotary Dr (28269-4494)
PHONE..............................704 596-3860
Rebecca Jordan, *Owner*
EMP: 7
SALES (corp-wide): 343.33B **Privately Held**
Web: www.internationaltrucks.com
SIC: 3711 Motor vehicles and car bodies
HQ: International Motors, Llc
2701 Navistar Dr
Lisle IL 60532
331 332-5000

(G-2345)
INTERNATIONAL PAPER COMPANY
Also Called: International Paper
11020 David Taylor Dr (28262-1101)
PHONE..............................704 393-8210
EMP: 5
SALES (corp-wide): 18.62B **Publicly Held**
Web: www.internationalpaper.com
SIC: 2621 Paper mills
PA: International Paper Company
6400 Poplar Ave
Memphis TN 38197
901 419-7000

(G-2346)
INTERNATIONAL PAPER COMPANY
International Paper
10601 Westlake Dr (28273-3930)
PHONE..............................704 588-8522
Keith Miller, *Brnch Mgr*
EMP: 7
SALES (corp-wide): 18.62B **Publicly Held**
Web: www.internationalpaper.com
SIC: 2621 Paper mills

PA: International Paper Company
6400 Poplar Ave
Memphis TN 38197
901 419-7000

(G-2347)
INTERNATIONAL PAPER COMPANY
Also Called: International Paper
5419 Hovis Rd (28208-1241)
PHONE..............................704 398-8354
Jim Atkins, *Brnch Mgr*
EMP: 150
SALES (corp-wide): 18.62B **Publicly Held**
Web: www.internationalpaper.com
SIC: 2621 Paper mills
PA: International Paper Company
6400 Poplar Ave
Memphis TN 38197
901 419-7000

(G-2348)
INTERNATIONAL PAPER COMPANY
Also Called: International Paper
201 E 28th St (28206-2720)
PHONE..............................704 334-5222
Jack Docell, *Mgr*
EMP: 6
SQ FT: 62,950
SALES (corp-wide): 18.62B **Publicly Held**
Web: www.internationalpaper.com
SIC: 2621 2611 Pulp; Pulp
manufactured from waste or recycled paper
PA: International Paper Company
6400 Poplar Ave
Memphis TN 38197
901 419-7000

(G-2349)
INTERNATIONAL PAPER COMPANY
Also Called: International Paper
3700 Display Dr (28273-4133)
PHONE..............................704 588-8522
EMP: 5
SALES (corp-wide): 18.62B **Publicly Held**
Web: www.internationalpaper.com
SIC: 2653 Boxes, corrugated: made from
purchased materials
PA: International Paper Company
6400 Poplar Ave
Memphis TN 38197
901 419-7000

(G-2350)
INTERNATIONAL THERMODYNE INC
3120 Latrobe Dr Ste 110 (28211-2190)
PHONE..............................704 579-8218
Greg Hackworth, *Admn*
EMP: 4 EST: 2013
SQ FT: 500
SALES (est): 964.81K **Privately Held**
Web: www.opal.us
SIC: 3699 Electrical equipment and supplies,
nec

(G-2351)
INVENTIVE GRAPHICS INC
Also Called: AlphaGraphics
9129 Monroe Rd Ste 160 (28270-2431)
P.O. Box 279 (28106-0279)
PHONE..............................704 814-4900
Gary Grefrath, *Prin*
EMP: 6 EST: 2005
SALES (est): 311.42K **Privately Held**
Web: www.alphagraphics.com
SIC: 2752 Commercial printing, lithographic

(G-2352)
INX INTERNATIONAL INK CO
Also Called: INX International
10820 Withers Cove Park Dr (28278-6928)
PHONE..............................704 372-2080

Al Baird, *Mgr*
EMP: 31
Web: www.inxinternational.com
SIC: 2893 Printing ink
HQ: Inx International Ink Co.
150 N Mrtngale Rd Ste 700
Schaumburg IL 60173
630 382-1800

(G-2353)
IPERIONX CRITICAL MINERALS LLC
129 W Trade St Ste 1405 (28202-2143)
PHONE..............................980 237-8900
Anastasios Arima, *Managing Member*
EMP: 35 EST: 2020
SALES (est): 5.1MM **Privately Held**
SIC: 1081 Metal mining exploration and
development services

(G-2354)
IPERIONX LIMITED
129 W Trade St Ste 1405 (28202-2143)
PHONE..............................980 237-8900
Anastasios Arima, *CEO*
Todd W Hannigan, *Ex Ch Bd*
Gregory D Swan, *VP*
Dominic Allen, *CCO*
Jeanne Mcmullin, *CLO*
EMP: 20 EST: 2017
SALES (est): 5.62MM **Privately Held**
Web: www.iperionx.com
SIC: 1099 3295 Titanium and zirconium ores
mining; Minerals, ground or treated

(G-2355)
IPERIONX TECHNOLOGY LLC
129 W Trade St Ste 1405 (28202-2143)
PHONE..............................980 237-8900
Kayla Luther, *
EMP: 35 EST: 2021
SALES (est): 5.39MM **Privately Held**
SIC: 1081 Metal mining exploration and
development services

(G-2356)
IPI ACQUISITION LLC
13504 S Point Blvd Ste M (28273-6763)
P.O. Box 518 (28134-0518)
PHONE..............................704 588-1100
Michael L Jones, *Pr*
Blair A Swogger, *
EMP: 650 EST: 2008
SIC: 6719 3599 3569 Investment holding
companies, except banks; Machine shop,
jobbing and repair; Sprinkler systems, fire:
automatic

(G-2357)
ITT LLC
4828 Parkway Plaza Blvd # 200
(28217-1038)
PHONE..............................704 716-7600
Jim Dartez, *Brnch Mgr*
EMP: 11
SALES (corp-wide): 3.63B **Publicly Held**
Web: www.itt.com
SIC: 3625 Control equipment, electric
HQ: Itt Llc
1133 Westchester Ave
White Plains NY 10604
914 641-2000

(G-2358)
IVM CHEMICALS INC
Also Called: Milesi Wood Coatings
301 Mccullough Dr Fl 4 (28262-3310)
PHONE..............................407 506-4913
Jeffrey Takac, *Pr*
EMP: 50 EST: 2015
SALES (est): 3.44MM **Privately Held**
Web: www.ivmchemicals.com

SIC: 2899 Chemical preparations, nec

(G-2359)
IVY BRAND LLC
106 Foster Ave (28203-5420)
PHONE.............................980 225-7866
Lisa M Thompson, *CEO*
EMP: 4 EST: 2014
SALES (est): 264.28K **Privately Held**
SIC: 2231 2211 2221 Apparel and outerwear broadwoven fabrics; Apparel and outerwear fabrics, cotton; Apparel and outerwear fabric, manmade fiber or silk

(G-2360)
J L SMITH & CO INC (PA)
901 Blairhill Rd Ste 400 (28217-1578)
PHONE.............................704 521-1088
Jeff L Smith, *Pr*
Cathy Phillips, *Dir*
EMP: 15 EST: 1990
SQ FT: 8,575
SALES (est): 4.76MM **Privately Held**
Web: www.jlsmithco.com
SIC: 5736 3931 5099 Musical instrument stores; Musical instruments; Musical instruments

(G-2361)
J R COLE INDUSTRIES INC (PA)
435 Minuet Ln (28217-2718)
PHONE.............................704 523-6622
Joseph Robert Cole Senior, *Ch Bd*
Donald W Griffin, *VP*
EMP: 19 EST: 1984
SQ FT: 8,500
SALES (est): 24.59MM
SALES (corp-wide): 24.59MM **Privately Held**
Web: www.jrcole.com
SIC: 2752 Commercial printing, lithographic

(G-2362)
J R COLE INDUSTRIES INC
Labeltec
10708 Granite St (28273-6379)
PHONE.............................704 523-6622
Ken Thunder, *Brnch Mgr*
EMP: 90
SALES (corp-wide): 24.59MM **Privately Held**
Web: www.jrcole.com
SIC: 7389 2679 Packaging and labeling services; Labels, paper: made from purchased material
PA: J. R. Cole Industries, Inc.
435 Minuet Ln
Charlotte NC 28217
704 523-6622

(G-2363)
JCI JONES CHEMICALS INC
1500 Tar Heel Rd (28208-1533)
PHONE.............................704 392-9767
Lynn Martin, *Mgr*
EMP: 16
SALES (corp-wide): 105.12MM **Privately Held**
Web: www.jcichem.com
SIC: 2812 5169 2899 2842 Chlorine, compressed or liquefied; Chemicals and allied products, nec; Chemical preparations, nec; Polishes and sanitation goods
PA: Jci Jones Chemicals, Inc.
1765 Ringling Blvd
Sarasota FL 34236
941 330-1537

(G-2364)
JCTM LLC
Also Called: Jctm
16710 Tulloch Rd (28278-8905)
PHONE.............................252 571-8678
Audie Cooper, *Mgr*
EMP: 60 EST: 2015
SALES (est): 8.28MM **Privately Held**
Web: www.jctm.us
SIC: 7371 7372 Computer software systems analysis and design, custom; Application computer software

(G-2365)
JDH CAPITAL LLC (PA)
3735 Beam Rd Unit B (28217-8800)
PHONE.............................704 357-1220
Gary J Davies, *Managing Member*
David P Hill, *Managing Member*
EMP: 13 EST: 1999
SALES (est): 187.63MM
SALES (corp-wide): 187.63MM **Privately Held**
SIC: 6531 2011 Real estate agents and managers; Meat packing plants

(G-2366)
JELD-WEN INC (HQ)
Also Called: Jeld Wen International Supply
2645 Silver Crescent Dr (28273)
PHONE.............................800 535-3936
William Christensen, *CEO*
Jas Hayes, *Ex VP*
Samantha L Stoddard, *Ex VP*
◆ EMP: 263 EST: 1960
SQ FT: 12,000
SALES (est): 1.76B **Publicly Held**
Web: www.jeld-wen.ca
SIC: 3442 5031 2421 Shutters, door or window: metal; Doors, combination, screen-storm; Building and structural materials, wood
PA: Jeld-Wen Holding, Inc.
2645 Silver Crescent Dr
Charlotte NC 28273

(G-2367)
JELD-WEN HOLDING INC (PA)
Also Called: JELD-WEN
2645 Silver Crescent Dr (28273)
PHONE.............................704 378-5700
William Christensen, *CEO*
David G Nord, *Ch Bd*
Samantha Stoddard, *Ex VP*
Wendy Livingston, *Chief Human Resources Officer*
Matthew Meier, *DIGITAL*
▲ EMP: 388 EST: 1960
SALES (est): 3.78B **Publicly Held**
Web: www.jeld-wen.com
SIC: 2431 3442 Millwork; Metal doors, sash, and trim

(G-2368)
JENKINS ELECTRIC COMPANY
Also Called: Jenkins
5933 Brookshire Blvd (28216-3386)
P.O. Box 32127 (28232-2127)
PHONE.............................800 438-3003
Iain Jenkins, *Pr*
Edward Jenkins Junior, *Ch*
Wayne L Hall, *
◆ EMP: 74 EST: 1907
SQ FT: 50,000
SALES (est): 19.94MM **Privately Held**
Web: www.jenkinselectric.com
SIC: 3699 7694 5063 Electrical equipment and supplies, nec; Electric motor repair; Electrical apparatus and equipment

(G-2369)
JENKINS ELECTRIC II LLC
5933 Brookshire Blvd (28216-3386)
PHONE.............................704 392-7371
Brian Esque, *Pr*
Wayne Hall, *
Iain Jenkins, *
Diane Geddes, *
EMP: 25 EST: 2006
SALES (est): 5.62MM **Privately Held**
Web: www.jenkinselectric.com
SIC: 3699 7694 Electrical equipment and supplies, nec; Armature rewinding shops

(G-2370)
JIM MYERS & SONS INC
5120 Westinghouse Blvd (28273)
P.O. Box 38778 (28278)
PHONE.............................704 554-8397
David L Myers, *Pr*
James B Myers Iii, *VP*
EMP: 55 EST: 1962
SQ FT: 50,000
SALES (est): 23.25MM **Privately Held**
Web: www.jmsequipment.com
SIC: 3589 Water treatment equipment, industrial

(G-2371)
JM GRAPHICS INC
3400 International Airport Dr Ste 950 (28208-4787)
PHONE.............................704 375-1147
James Marek, *Pr*
EMP: 7 EST: 1974
SALES (est): 539K **Privately Held**
Web: www.jmgraphics.org
SIC: 2752 Offset printing

(G-2372)
JOERNS HEALTHCARE PARENT LLC (PA)
2430 Whitehall Park Dr Ste 100 (28273-3948)
PHONE.............................800 966-6662
EMP: 275 EST: 2006
SALES (est): 259.82MM
SALES (corp-wide): 259.82MM **Privately Held**
Web: www.joerns.com
SIC: 5047 2512 Medical equipment and supplies; Recliners: upholstered on wood frames

(G-2373)
JOHN J MORTON COMPANY INC (PA)
2211 W Morehead St (28208-5143)
P.O. Box 32773 (28232-2773)
PHONE.............................704 332-6633
William R Standish Ii, *Pr*
Frank Morfit, *VP*
William R Standish, *Stockholder*
Betty E Standish, *Stockholder*
EMP: 17 EST: 1920
SQ FT: 29,000
SALES (est): 1.3MM
SALES (corp-wide): 1.3MM **Privately Held**
SIC: 3281 1741 Cut stone and stone products; Marble masonry, exterior construction

(G-2374)
JOHNSON CONTROLS
9826 Southern Pine Blvd (28273-5561)
PHONE.............................704 501-0500
Barry Wells, *Brnch Mgr*
EMP: 200
SIC: 3669 Emergency alarms
HQ: Johnson Controls Fire Protection Lp
6600 Congress Ave
Boca Raton FL 33487
561 988-7200

(G-2375)
JOHNSON CONTROLS INC
Also Called: Johnson Controls
9844 Southern Pine Blvd Ste B (28273-5502)
PHONE.............................704 521-8889
Ernest Ray Thompson, *Genl Mgr*
EMP: 53
Web: www.johnsoncontrols.com
SIC: 3822 5075 5074 5063 Thermostats, except built-in; Warm air heating and air conditioning; Plumbing and hydronic heating supplies; Electrical apparatus and equipment
HQ: Johnson Controls, Inc.
5757 N Green Bay Ave
Milwaukee WI 53209
866 496-1999

(G-2376)
JOHNSON CONTROLS INC
Also Called: Johnson Controls
9844 Southern Pine Blvd (28273-5502)
PHONE.............................704 521-8889
EMP: 20
Web: www.johnsoncontrols.com
SIC: 2531 Seats, automobile
HQ: Johnson Controls, Inc.
5757 N Green Bay Ave
Milwaukee WI 53209
866 496-1999

(G-2377)
JOHNSON GLOBAL CMPLNCE CONTRLS
13950 Ballantyne Corporate Pl (28277-3159)
PHONE.............................704 552-1119
James Burke, *CEO*
EMP: 4 EST: 2011
SALES (est): 3.79MM
SALES (corp-wide): 1.99B **Privately Held**
Web: www.navex.com
SIC: 3822 Appliance regulators
PA: Vista Equity Partners Management, Llc
401 Congress Ave Ste 3100
Austin TX 78701
512 730-2400

(G-2378)
JORDAN GROUP CORPORATION
7007 Berolina Ln Apt 1613 (28226-8687)
PHONE.............................803 309-9988
Robert Jordan, *Pr*
EMP: 4 EST: 2006
SALES (est): 235.73K **Privately Held**
SIC: 2499 Wood products, nec

(G-2379)
JOSEPH F DECKER
Also Called: Decker Advanced Fabrication
341 Dalton Ave (28206-3117)
PHONE.............................704 335-0021
Joseph F Decker, *Pr*
Margie Decker, *VP*
EMP: 8 EST: 1996
SQ FT: 13,000
SALES (est): 764.32K **Privately Held**
SIC: 3446 3444 Architectural metalwork; Sheet metalwork

(G-2380)
JRG TECHNOLOGIES CORP
9300 Harris Corners Pkwy Ste 450 (28269-3814)
PHONE.............................850 362-4310
Joseph R Gregory, *Prin*
David Haadsma, *Prin*
William E Loran Iii, *Prin*
Andrew K Stull, *Prin*
EMP: 57 EST: 2007

▲ = Import ▼ = Export
◆ = Import/Export

SALES (est): 2.42MM **Privately Held**
SIC: 7372 Application computer software
HQ: Avg Technologies Usa, Inc.
   2100 Powell St
   Emeryville CA 94608

(G-2381)
JRS CUSTOM FRAMING
7604 Waterford Lakes Dr (28210-6491)
P.O. Box 5202 (28299-5202)
PHONE..............................704 449-2830
EMP: 4 EST: 2018
SALES (est): 46.85K **Privately Held**
Web: www.dilworthcustomframing.com
SIC: 2499 Picture frame molding, finished

(G-2382)
JS ROYAL HOME USA INC
13451 S Point Blvd (28273-2701)
PHONE..............................704 542-2304
Kathy O Dayvault, *CEO*
Kathy O Dayvault, *Pr*
Lei Huang, *
▲ EMP: 45 EST: 2007
SQ FT: 80,000
SALES (est): 65.61MM **Privately Held**
Web: www.jsroyalhome.com
SIC: 5023 2392 Homefurnishings; Blankets,
   comforters and beddings

(G-2383)
JUST N TYME TRUCKING LLC
6015 Lake Forest Rd E (28227-0910)
PHONE..............................704 804-9519
Enola Murchison-ottley, *Managing Member*
EMP: 4
SALES (est): 587.18K **Privately Held**
SIC: 3537 7389 Trucks, tractors, loaders,
   carriers, and similar equipment; Business
   services, nec

(G-2384)
JUST SHRIMP HOLDINGS US INC
2820 Selwyn Ave Ste 420 (28209-1790)
PHONE..............................805 832-1828
Harkeet Chadha, *CEO*
EMP: 5
SALES (est): 298.68K **Privately Held**
SIC: 2092 Shrimp, frozen: prepared

(G-2385)
K&K HOLDINGS INC
Also Called: Signs Now
1310 S Church St (28203-4112)
PHONE..............................704 341-5567
Cathy Habluetzel, *CEO*
Randy Habluetzel, *VP*
Cathy Habluetzel, *Pr*
EMP: 8 EST: 2003
SALES (est): 677.95K **Privately Held**
Web: www.signsnow.com
SIC: 3993 7389 6719 Signs and advertising
   specialties; Lettering and sign painting
   services; Investment holding companies,
   except banks

(G-2386)
K2 SCIENTIFIC LLC
3029 Horseshoe Ln Ste D (28208-6434)
PHONE..............................800 218-7613
Thomas Baugh, *Managing Member*
Dee Jetton, *COO*
Art Henson, *Dir*
Venitra White-dean, *Contrlr*
William Papathanassiou, *Mgr*
EMP: 10 EST: 2016
SALES (est): 5.04MM **Privately Held**
Web: www.k2sci.com
SIC: 3632 Household refrigerators and
   freezers

(G-2387)
KA-EX LLC
125 Remount Rd Ste C1 Pmb 2002
(28203-6459)
PHONE..............................704 343-5143
Pedro Schmidt, *Managing Member*
EMP: 8 EST: 2022
SALES (est): 258.06K **Privately Held**
Web: www.ka-ex.ch
SIC: 2023 Dietary supplements, dairy and
   non-dairy based

(G-2388)
KASK AMERICA INC
301 W Summit Ave (28203-4452)
PHONE..............................704 960-4851
Kask Angelo Gotti, *CEO*
EMP: 29 EST: 2010
SALES (est): 6.47MM **Privately Held**
Web: www.kask.com
SIC: 3949 Helmets, athletic

(G-2389)
KAVO KERR GROUP
11727 Fruehauf Dr (28273-6507)
PHONE..............................704 927-0617
EMP: 13 EST: 2016
SALES (est): 5.64MM **Privately Held**
Web: www.kavo.com
SIC: 3843 Dental equipment and supplies

(G-2390)
KEE AUTO TOP MANUFACTURING
CO
3018 Stewart Creek Blvd (28216-3594)
PHONE..............................704 332-8213
Erman J Evans, *Pr*
EMP: 40 EST: 1964
SQ FT: 21,000
SALES (est): 4.87MM **Privately Held**
Web: www.keeautotop.com
SIC: 3714 Tops, motor vehicle

(G-2391)
KEIM MINERAL COATINGS AMER
INC
3935 Perimeter West Dr Ste 100
(28214-0110)
PHONE..............................704 588-4811
John C Bogert, *CEO*
◆ EMP: 10 EST: 2006
SALES (est): 2.26MM **Privately Held**
Web: www.keim.com
SIC: 2851 5198 Paints and paint additives;
   Paints, varnishes, and supplies

(G-2392)
KEM-WOVE INC (PA)
Also Called: K W
10530 Westlake Dr (28273-3788)
P.O. Box 3871 (08756-3871)
PHONE..............................704 588-0080
Steven Sklow, *Pr*
Jennifer Sklow, *
EMP: 20 EST: 1962
SQ FT: 55,000
SALES (est): 2.2MM
SALES (corp-wide): 2.2MM **Privately Held**
Web: www.kemwove.com
SIC: 2299 2297 Batts and batting: cotton mill
   waste and related material; Nonwoven
   fabrics

(G-2393)
KENNAMETAL INC
8910 Lenox Pointe Dr Ste F (28273-3431)
PHONE..............................704 588-4777
Suzanne Gillenwater, *Prin*
EMP: 11
SALES (corp-wide): 2.05B **Publicly Held**

Web: www.kennametal.com
SIC: 3545 Cutting tools for machine tools
PA: Kennametal Inc.
   525 Wlliam Penn Pl Ste 33
   Pittsburgh PA 15219
   412 248-8000

(G-2394)
KEYMAC USA LLC
8301 Arrowridge Blvd Ste I (28273-5772)
PHONE..............................704 877-5137
Michael C A Bradley, *Mgr*
▲ EMP: 8 EST: 2010
SALES (est): 5.2MM **Privately Held**
Web: www.keymac.co.uk
SIC: 3565 Packaging machinery

(G-2395)
KIDS PLAYHOUSE LLC
10823 John Price Rd (28273-4510)
PHONE..............................704 299-4449
Roxie S Carter, *Prin*
EMP: 4 EST: 2022
SQ FT: 1,300
SALES (est): 104.14K **Privately Held**
Web: www.kidsplayhousellc.com
SIC: 7359 2299 Party supplies rental
   services; Bagging, jute

(G-2396)
KIMBERLY GORDON STUDIOS INC
525 N Tryon St (28202-0202)
PHONE..............................980 287-6420
Kimberly Mix, *CEO*
EMP: 22
SALES (est): 1.47MM **Privately Held**
SIC: 2678 Stationery products

(G-2397)
KINCOL INDUSTRIES
INCORPORATED
Also Called: Kci
1721 Toal St (28206-1523)
P.O. Box 26614 (28221-6614)
PHONE..............................704 372-8435
Robert Collins, *Pr*
James S King, *Ch Bd*
▲ EMP: 9 EST: 1981
SQ FT: 10,000
SALES (est): 5.2MM **Privately Held**
Web: www.kciincorporated.com
SIC: 5169 3548 Chemicals, industrial and
   heavy; Gas welding equipment

(G-2398)
KING STONE INNOVATION LLC
7313 Mossborough Ct (28227-1244)
PHONE..............................704 352-1134
Sergio Gonzalez Rios, *Pr*
EMP: 5 EST: 2017
SALES (est): 937.67K **Privately Held**
SIC: 3281 1791 1799 Granite, cut and
   shaped; Structural steel erection; Welding
   on site

(G-2399)
KLAZZY MAGAZINE INC
Also Called: Klazzy.com The Magazine
100 N Tryon St Ste B220-127 (28202-4000)
PHONE..............................704 293-8321
Bobby Bowden, *CEO*
Stacy Moye, *Pr*
EMP: 8 EST: 2004
SQ FT: 1,500
SALES (est): 431.16K **Privately Held**
SIC: 2741 Art copy and poster publishing

(G-2400)
KNA
Also Called: Charlotte T Shirt Authority

9535 Monroe Rd Ste 150 (28270-2452)
PHONE..............................704 847-4280
Keith Abrams, *Pr*
EMP: 7 EST: 2002
SALES (est): 492.93K **Privately Held**
Web: www.tshirtauthority.com
SIC: 2759 Screen printing

(G-2401)
KRAFT HEINZ FOODS COMPANY
Also Called: Kraft Foods
2815 Coliseum Centre Dr Ste 100
(28217-0137)
PHONE..............................704 565-5500
Joe Polite, *Brnch Mgr*
EMP: 4
SALES (corp-wide): 25.85B **Publicly Held**
Web: www.kraftheinz.com
SIC: 2033 Canned fruits and specialties
HQ: Kraft Heinz Foods Company
   1 Ppg Pl Ste 3400
   Pittsburgh PA 15222
   412 456-5700

(G-2402)
KRISPY KREME DOUGHNUT CORP
(DH)
2116 Hawkins St Ste 102 (28203-4477)
P.O. Box 83 (27102)
PHONE..............................980 270-7117
Josh Charlesworth, *Pr*
J Paul Breitbach, *
John Mc Aleer, *
John Tate, *CSO*
James Morgan, *
◆ EMP: 150 EST: 1933
SALES (est): 463.39MM
SALES (corp-wide): 1.69B **Publicly Held**
Web: www.krispykreme.com
SIC: 5461 2051 Doughnuts; Doughnuts,
   except frozen
HQ: Krispy Kreme Doughnuts, Inc.
   370 Knollwood St
   Winston Salem NC 27103
   336 725-2981

(G-2403)
KUEBLER INC
10430 Harris Oak Blvd Ste J (28269-7521)
PHONE..............................704 705-4711
John Stanczuk, *VP*
EMP: 12 EST: 2013
SALES (est): 7.67MM **Privately Held**
Web: www.kuebler.com
SIC: 5065 3699 Electronic parts; Electrical
   equipment and supplies, nec

(G-2404)
L & S AUTOMOTIVE INC
Also Called: L & S Custom Trailer Service
1214 Caldwell Williams Rd (28216-2414)
PHONE..............................704 391-7657
Lawrence Martin, *Pr*
Sandra M Martin, *VP*
EMP: 6 EST: 1986
SQ FT: 6,000
SALES (est): 350.2K **Privately Held**
Web: www.ls-automotive.com
SIC: 3715 7538 Truck trailers; General
   automotive repair shops

(G-2405)
L3HARRIS TECHNOLOGIES INC
Also Called: Harris Repair Service
8406 Mcalpine Dr (28217-5330)
PHONE..............................704 588-7126
Douglas Harris, *Pr*
EMP: 6
SALES (corp-wide): 21.32B **Publicly Held**
Web: www.l3harris.com

SIC: **3699** Electrical equipment and supplies, nec
PA: L3harris Technologies, Inc.
1025 W Nasa Blvd
Melbourne FL 32919
321 727-9100

(G-2406)
LA NOTICIA INC
Also Called: La Noticia Foundation
5936 Monroe Rd (28212-6106)
PHONE.....................704 568-6966
Hilda Gurdian, *CEO*
Hilda Gurdian, *Pr*
Alvaro Gurdian, *VP*
EMP: 18 EST: 1992
SQ FT: 3,500
SALES (est): 2.07MM **Privately Held**
Web: www.lanoticia.com
SIC: **2711 2721 7319** Newspapers, publishing and printing; Periodicals, publishing and printing; Media buying service

(G-2407)
LADY MAY SWETS CONFECTIONS INC
14301 S Lakes Dr Ste C (28273-0017)
PHONE.....................704 749-9258
EMP: 4
SALES (corp-wide): 736.04K **Privately Held**
SIC: **2064** Candy and other confectionery products
PA: Lady May Sweets & Confections, Inc.
515 Madison Ave Rm 2316
New York NY 10022
516 818-6649

(G-2408)
LANDFILL GAS PRODUCERS
10600 Nations Ford Rd # 150 (28273-5762)
PHONE.....................704 844-8990
William Brinker, *Prin*
Peter Kamel, *Mgr*
EMP: 9 EST: 2009
SALES (est): 1.73MM **Privately Held**
Web: www.landfillgroup.com
SIC: **1321** Natural gas liquids

(G-2409)
LATINO COMMUNICATIONS INC
Also Called: Que Pasa Charlotte
7508 E Independence Blvd Ste 109 (28227-9473)
PHONE.....................704 319-5044
Julio Suarez, *Brnch Mgr*
EMP: 10
SALES (corp-wide): 1.2MM **Privately Held**
Web: www.quepasamedia.com
SIC: **4832 2711** Radio broadcasting stations; Newspapers
PA: Latino Communications, Inc.
3067 Waughtown St
Winston Salem NC 27107
336 714-2823

(G-2410)
LCI CORPORATION INTERNATIONAL
4404b Chesapeake Dr (28216-3413)
PHONE.....................704 399-7441
EMP: 4 EST: 1992
SALES (est): 390.95K **Privately Held**
Web: www.lcicorp.com
SIC: **3559** Special industry machinery, nec

(G-2411)
LCI CORPORATION INTERNATIONAL
Also Called: LCI
4433 Chesapeake Dr (28216-3412)
P.O. Box 16348 (28297-6348)

PHONE.....................704 399-7441
Tomas Hagstrom, *CEO*
John Fields, *VP*
◆ **EMP: 20 EST:** 1992
SQ FT: 12,000
SALES (est): 9.09MM **Privately Held**
Web: www.lcicorp.com
SIC: **3559 5084 2899 2099** Refinery, chemical processing, and similar machinery; Chemical process equipment; Chemical preparations, nec; Food preparations, nec
HQ: Nederman Corporation
4404a Chesapeake Dr
Charlotte NC 28216
704 399-7441

(G-2412)
LEAPFROG DOCUMENT SERVICES INC
4651 Charlotte Park Dr Ste 230 (28217-1956)
PHONE.....................704 372-1078
Amy L Parris, *Pr*
Debbie Laflamme, *VP*
EMP: 15 **EST:** 2001
SALES (est): 634.06K **Privately Held**
Web: www.leapfrogllc.com
SIC: **2621 5943** Parchment, securities, and bank note papers; Notary and corporate seals

(G-2413)
LEAR ENTERPRISES INC
8145 Ardrey Kell Rd (28277-5720)
PHONE.....................704 321-0027
EMP: 9 EST: 2018
SALES (est): 2.06MM **Privately Held**
Web: www.lear.com
SIC: **3714** Motor vehicle parts and accessories

(G-2414)
LEARNINGSTATIONCOM INC (PA)
8022 Providence Rd Ste 500 (28277-9719)
PHONE.....................704 926-5400
James Kirchner, *Pr*
Bart Temperville, *Treas*
Steven Kirchner, *VP*
EMP: 10 EST: 1997
SQ FT: 2,548
SALES (est): 1.08MM
SALES (corp-wide): 1.08MM **Privately Held**
Web: www.learningstation.com
SIC: **7372** Application computer software

(G-2415)
LEES PRESS AND PUBG CO LLC
3515 David Cox Rd (28269-2571)
P.O. Box 2031 (27323)
PHONE.....................833 440-0770
William Lee, *CEO*
EMP: 4 EST: 2011
SALES (est): 44.01K **Privately Held**
Web: www.leespress.net
SIC: **2731** Book publishing

(G-2416)
LEGACY COMMERCIAL SERVICE LLC
13921 Allison Forest Trl (28278-7758)
PHONE.....................757 831-5291
EMP: 4 EST: 2019
SALES (est): 269.05K **Privately Held**
SIC: **3589** Commercial cleaning equipment

(G-2417)
LEGACY MANUFACTURING LLC
Also Called: Production Tool and Die
537 Scholtz Rd (28217-2138)

PHONE.....................704 525-0498
Ronald Smith, *Prin*
Michelle Smith, *Prin*
EMP: 6 EST: 2017
SALES (est): 2.12MM **Privately Held**
Web: www.ptdmachining.com
SIC: **3599** Machine shop, jobbing and repair

(G-2418)
LEIGHDEUX LLC
355 Eastover Rd (28207-2349)
PHONE.....................704 965-4889
Leigh Goodwyn, *Managing Member*
EMP: 6 EST: 2015
SALES (est): 237.8K **Privately Held**
Web: www.leighdeux.com
SIC: **2299 5719** Linen fabrics; Beddings and linens

(G-2419)
LIFESPAN INCORPORATED (PA)
1511 Shopton Rd Ste A (28217-3240)
PHONE.....................704 944-5100
Davan Claniger, *CEO*
Ralph Adams, *Treas*
Holly Newinski, *Corporate Secretary*
EMP: 20 EST: 1973
SQ FT: 75,000
SALES (est): 19.26MM
SALES (corp-wide): 19.26MM **Privately Held**
Web: www.lifespanservices.org
SIC: **8211 8361 3842** School for retarded, nec; Self-help group home; Surgical appliances and supplies

(G-2420)
LIGHT SOURCE USA INC
3935 Westinghouse Blvd (28273-4517)
PHONE.....................704 504-8399
Eric V Fange, *Pr*
Joy Von Fange, *
EMP: 35 EST: 2007
SQ FT: 67,000
SALES (est): 16.82MM **Privately Held**
Web: www.thelightsource.com
SIC: **3648** Decorative area lighting fixtures

(G-2421)
LIGHTNING X PRODUCTS INC
Also Called: Fire & Safety Outfitters
2365 Tipton Dr (28206-1060)
PHONE.....................704 295-0299
John Spivey, *Pr*
Andy Spivey, *VP*
EMP: 7 EST: 2006
SALES (est): 4.8MM **Privately Held**
Web: www.gearbags.com
SIC: **5087 3569** Firefighting equipment; Firefighting and related equipment

(G-2422)
LIGNATERRA GLOBAL LLC
Also Called: World By Wood
6000 Fairview Rd Ste 1200 (28210-2252)
PHONE.....................970 481-6952
Ralf Meier, *Prin*
Nick Holgorsen, *Prin*
EMP: 4 EST: 2014
SALES (est): 1.14MM **Privately Held**
Web: www.lignaterra.com
SIC: **2439** Timbers, structural: laminated lumber

(G-2423)
LIKEABLE PRESS LLC
227 W 4th St (28202-1545)
PHONE.....................844 882-8340
EMP: 4 EST: 2018
SALES (est): 135.75K **Privately Held**
Web: www.likeablepress.com

SIC: **2741** Miscellaneous publishing

(G-2424)
LINDE GAS & EQUIPMENT INC
Also Called: Linde Gas North America
3810 Shutterfly Rd Ste 100 (28217-3070)
PHONE.....................704 587-7096
Mark Kimel, *Brnch Mgr*
EMP: 10
Web: www.lindeus.com
SIC: **2813** Nitrogen
HQ: Linde Gas & Equipment Inc.
10 Riverview Dr
Danbury CT 06810
844 445-4633

(G-2425)
LIONS SERVICES INC
4600 N Tryon St Ste A (28213-7058)
P.O. Box 561987 (28256)
PHONE.....................704 921-1527
Jim Cranford, *CEO*
Philip Murph, *
EMP: 302 EST: 1935
SQ FT: 58,000
SALES (est): 16.46MM **Privately Held**
Web: www.lionsservices.org
SIC: **2392 7389 8331** Mops, floor and dust; Packaging and labeling services; Job training and related services

(G-2426)
LIQUI-BOX CORPORATION (HQ)
2415 Cascade Pointe Blvd (28208)
PHONE.....................804 325-1400
Ken Swanson, *Pr*
Lou Marmo, *
Andrew Mcleland, *COO*
Diana Smith, *
◆ **EMP: 65 EST:** 1963
SALES (est): 370.16MM
SALES (corp-wide): 5.39B **Publicly Held**
Web: www.liquibox.com
SIC: **2673 3585 3089 3081** Plastic bags: made from purchased materials; Soda fountain and beverage dispensing equipment and parts; Plastics containers, except foam; Plastics film and sheet
PA: Sealed Air Corporation
2415 Cascade Pointe Blvd
Charlotte NC 28208
980 221-3235

(G-2427)
LIVE IT BOUTIQUE LLC
Also Called: Retail
509 Old Vine Ct (28214-0032)
PHONE.....................704 492-2402
Oleta Harris, *CEO*
EMP: 5 EST: 2021
SALES (est): 117.24K **Privately Held**
SIC: **5621 2339** Women's clothing stores; Women's and misses' accessories

(G-2428)
LIVINGSTON & HAVEN LLC (HQ)
Also Called: AEG International
11529 Wilmar Blvd (28273-6448)
P.O. Box 7207 (28241-7207)
PHONE.....................704 588-3670
Clifton B Vann Iii, *Ch*
Clifton B Vann Iv, *Pr*
James T Skinner Iii, *Sec*
Anne Q Woody, *
Bruce Mckay, *Dir*
EMP: 140 EST: 1947
SQ FT: 50,000
SALES (est): 21.82MM
SALES (corp-wide): 98.44MM **Privately Held**
Web: www.livhaven.com

▲ = Import ▼ = Export
◆ = Import/Export

SIC: **5084** 3594 4911 7389 Hydraulic systems equipment and supplies; Fluid power pumps and motors; Business services, nec
PA: Park Hyde Partners Inc
11529 Wilmar Blvd
Charlotte NC 28273
704 587-4819

(G-2429)
LMB CORP
Also Called: Dairy Queen
3020 Prosperity Church Rd Ste D (28269-8100)
PHONE..............................704 547-8886
Lisa Battaglia, *Pr*
Stephanie Wicherstoon, *Mgr*
EMP: 8 **EST:** 2010
SALES (est): 220.33K **Privately Held**
Web: www.dairyqueen.com
SIC: **5812** 2013 Ice cream stands or dairy bars; Sausages and other prepared meats

(G-2430)
LOCKWOOD IDENTITY INC
Also Called: Sign Art
6225 Old Concord Rd (28213-6311)
P.O. Box 560648 (28213)
PHONE..............................704 597-9801
Randy Souther, *Pr*
Larry Johnson, *
EMP: 104 **EST:** 2002
SALES (est): 6.75MM **Privately Held**
Web: www.signartsign.com
SIC: **3993** 1799 Electric signs; Sign installation and maintenance

(G-2431)
LOFTIN & COMPANY INC
Also Called: Loftin & Company Printers
1908 Gateway Blvd (28208-2746)
P.O. Box 669407 (28266-9407)
PHONE..............................704 393-9393
William E Loftin Junior, *Pr*
EMP: 25 **EST:** 1898
SQ FT: 20,000
SALES (est): 4.03MM **Privately Held**
Web: www.loftinco.com
SIC: **2752** 2789 2791 Offset printing; Bookbinding and related work; Typesetting

(G-2432)
LONDON LUXURY LLC ✪
3540 Toringdon Way Ste 200 (28277-3867)
PHONE..............................980 819-1966
EMP: 7 **EST:** 2023
SALES (est): 1.32MM **Privately Held**
SIC: **7372** Prepackaged software

(G-2433)
LONE STAR CONTAINER SALES CORP
Also Called: Dixie Reel & Box Co
10901 Carpet St (28273-6206)
P.O. Box 7791 (28241-7791)
PHONE..............................704 588-1737
William Harkey, *Brnch Mgr*
EMP: 56
SALES (corp-wide): 12.83MM **Privately Held**
Web: www.lonestarbox.com
SIC: **2653** Boxes, corrugated: made from purchased materials
PA: Lone Star Container Sales Corporation
700 N Wildwood Dr
Irving TX 75061
972 579-1551

(G-2434)
LOOKWHATQMADE LLC
101 N Tryon St Ste 112 (28246-0100)
PHONE..............................980 330-1995
EMP: 5
SALES (est): 170.89K **Privately Held**
SIC: **2741** Internet publishing and broadcasting

(G-2435)
LOS VIENTOS WINDPOWER IB LLC
526 S Church St (28202-1802)
PHONE..............................704 594-6200
B Keith Trent, *CEO*
EMP: 6 **EST:** 2011
SALES (est): 1.13MM
SALES (corp-wide): 30.36B **Publicly Held**
SIC: **3829** Wind direction indicators
PA: Duke Energy Corporation
525 S Tryon St
Charlotte NC 28202
704 382-3853

(G-2436)
LTD INDUSTRIES LLC (PA)
5509 David Cox Rd (28269-0324)
P.O. Box 481930 (28269-5319)
PHONE..............................704 897-2182
▲ **EMP:** 48 **EST:** 2011
SALES (est): 9.24MM **Privately Held**
Web: www.nano-purification.com
SIC: **3569** 5085 Filters; Filters, industrial

(G-2437)
LUBRIZOL ADVANCED MTLS INC
11425 Granite St (28273-6429)
PHONE..............................704 587-5583
EMP: 33
SALES (corp-wide): 424.23B **Publicly Held**
SIC: **2899** Chemical preparations, nec
HQ: Lubrizol Advanced Materials, Inc.
9911 Brecksville Rd
Brecksville OH 44141
216 447-5000

(G-2438)
LUCAS CONCRETE PRODUCTS INC
401 Rountree Rd (28217-2130)
PHONE..............................704 525-9622
John R L Johnson Iii, *Pr*
Evelyn Johnson, *
EMP: 33 **EST:** 1971
SQ FT: 8,140
SALES (est): 4.99MM **Privately Held**
Web: www.lucasconcrete.com
SIC: **3272** Concrete products, precast, nec

(G-2439)
LUCKY LANDPORTS
Also Called: C Y Yard
6510 Rozzelles Ferry Rd (28214-1881)
PHONE..............................704 399-9880
Dim Feimster, *Owner*
EMP: 4 **EST:** 2000
SALES (est): 192.14K **Privately Held**
SIC: **2448** Cargo containers, wood and wood with metal

(G-2440)
LULLICOIN LLC
3540 Toringdon Way (28277-3867)
PHONE..............................336 955-1159
EMP: 5 **EST:** 2021
SALES (est): 714K **Privately Held**
SIC: **3674** Diodes, solid state (germanium, silicon, etc.)

(G-2441)
LUNAR INTERNATIONAL TECH LLC
338 S Sharon Amity Rd (28211-2806)
PHONE..............................800 975-7153
Omer Ford, *Pr*
Omer Ford, *Managing Member*
EMP: 12 **EST:** 2020
SALES (est): 457.25K **Privately Held**
Web: www.lunarinternationaltech.com
SIC: **4214** 7382 1711 3663 Local trucking with storage; Security systems services; Solar energy contractor; Satellites, communications

(G-2442)
LUTZE INC
13330 S Ridge Dr (28273-4738)
PHONE..............................704 504-0222
Friedrich Lutze, *Sec*
Udo Lutze, *
▲ **EMP:** 26 **EST:** 1989
SQ FT: 24,000
SALES (est): 10.92MM
SALES (corp-wide): 15.22B **Publicly Held**
Web: www.lutze.com
SIC: **5063** 5065 3679 Electronic wire and cable; Electronic parts and equipment, nec; Harness assemblies, for electronic use: wire or cable
HQ: Friedrich Lutze Gmbh
Bruckwiesenstr. 17-19
Weinstadt BW 71384
715160530

(G-2443)
LYNN LADDER SCAFFOLDING CO INC
3801 Corporation Cir (28216-3418)
PHONE..............................301 336-4700
TOLL FREE: 800
Eric Yates, *Mgr*
EMP: 4
SALES (corp-wide): 32.59MM **Privately Held**
Web: www.lynnladder.com
SIC: **5082** 2499 7359 Ladders; Ladders, wood; Equipment rental and leasing, nec
HQ: Lynn Ladder And Scaffolding Co., Inc.
20 Boston St 24
Lynn MA 01904
781 598-6010

(G-2444)
M AND R INC
Also Called: Eden Dry Cleaners
820 E 7th St Ste C (28202-3050)
PHONE..............................704 332-5999
Inhonthi Lee, *Pr*
EMP: 4 **EST:** 2015
SALES (est): 275.98K **Privately Held**
Web: www.mrlandscapinggroup.com
SIC: **2842** Laundry cleaning preparations

(G-2445)
MAAG REDUCTION INC (HQ)
9401 Southern Pine Blvd Ste Q (28273-5598)
PHONE..............................704 716-9000
▲ **EMP:** 48 **EST:** 1991
SALES (est): 17.71MM
SALES (corp-wide): 7.75B **Publicly Held**
Web: www.maag.com
SIC: **3561** 5084 Pumps and pumping equipment; Pumps and pumping equipment, nec
PA: Dover Corporation
3005 Hghland Pkwy Ste 200
Downers Grove IL 60515
630 541-1540

(G-2446)
MACLEOD CONSTRUCTION INC (PA)
Also Called: Concrete Pumping By Macleod
4304 Northpointe Industrial Blvd (28216-6303)
P.O. Box 320 (28037)
PHONE..............................704 483-3580
Robert Macleod, *Pr*
Lorne Macleod, *
Judith Macleod, *
EMP: 101 **EST:** 1987
SALES (est): 6.93MM **Privately Held**
Web: www.macleodnc.com
SIC: **3273** 1611 Ready-mixed concrete; Grading

(G-2447)
MADE BY CUSTOM LLC
3206 N Davidson St (28205-1034)
PHONE..............................704 980-9840
EMP: 4 **EST:** 2013
SALES (est): 202.15K **Privately Held**
Web: www.customjewelrylab.com
SIC: **3479** 5094 5944 7631 Engraving jewelry, silverware, or metal; Jewelry and precious stones; Jewelry stores; Jewelry repair services

(G-2448)
MAGNERA CORPORATION (PA)
9335 Harris Corners Pkwy Ste 300 (28269)
PHONE..............................866 744-7380
Curtis L Begle, *Pr*
Curtis L Begle, *CEO*
Kevin M Fogarty, *Non-Executive Chairman of the Board*
James Till, *Ex VP*
Tarun Manroa, *Ex VP*
EMP: 1100 **EST:** 1864
SALES (est): 1.39B
SALES (corp-wide): 1.39B **Publicly Held**
Web: www.glatfelter.com
SIC: **2621** Book paper

(G-2449)
MAKEMINE INC
805 Pressley Rd Ste 109 (28217)
PHONE..............................704 906-7164
Rick Tate, *Pr*
EMP: 5 **EST:** 2018
SALES (est): 800.73K **Privately Held**
Web: www.makemine.com
SIC: **7371** 2211 Computer software development; Apparel and outerwear fabrics, cotton

(G-2450)
MALLARD CREEK POLYMERS LLC
14800 Mallard Creek Rd (28262-4000)
PHONE..............................704 547-0622
Bo Brown, *Prin*
EMP: 8
Web: www.mcpolymers.com
SIC: **2821** Plastics materials and resins
PA: Mallard Creek Polymers, Llc
8901 Research Dr
Charlotte NC 28262

(G-2451)
MALLARD CREEK POLYMERS LLC (PA)
Also Called: Mallard Creek Polymers
8901 Research Dr (28262-8541)
PHONE..............................704 547-0622
Aaron Parekh, *Pr*
Dan Neri, *VP*
◆ **EMP:** 20 **EST:** 1994
SALES (est): 48.03MM **Privately Held**
Web: www.mcpolymers.com

SIC: **2821** Plastics materials and resins

(G-2452)
MALLARD CREEK POLYMERS LLC
2800 Morehead Rd (28262-0430)
PHONE..............................877 240-0171
EMP: 9
Web: www.mcpolymers.com
SIC: 2821 Elastomers, nonvulcanizable
(plastics)
PA: Mallard Creek Polymers, Llc
8901 Research Dr
Charlotte NC 28262

(G-2453)
MANTISSA CORPORATION
Also Called: Mantissa Material Handling
616 Pressley Rd (28217-4610)
PHONE..............................704 525-1749
J David Fortenbery, *Pr*
Megan Mccormick, *VP*
▲ **EMP:** 42 **EST:** 1973
SQ FT: 28,300
SALES (est): 13.56MM **Privately Held**
Web: www.mantissacorporation.com
SIC: 1796 3535 Machinery installation;
Conveyors and conveying equipment

(G-2454)
MAP SHOP LLC
3421 St Vardell Ln Ste H (28217-0086)
PHONE..............................704 332-5557
Anthony Rodono, *Mgr*
EMP: 9 **EST:** 2016
SALES (est): 956.29K **Privately Held**
Web: www.mapshop.com
SIC: 2741 2752 Maps: publishing and
printing; Maps, lithographed

(G-2455)
MARBACH AMERICA INC
100 Forsyth Hall Dr Ste B (28273-5726)
P.O. Box 935 (28134-0935)
PHONE..............................704 644-4900
Jan Brunner, *Pr*
Fernando Tires, *
▲ **EMP:** 31 **EST:** 2011
SALES (est): 5.22MM
SALES (corp-wide): 153.12MM **Privately**
Held
Web: www.marbach.com
SIC: 3423 Cutting dies, except metal cutting
PA: Karl Marbach Gmbh & Co. Kg
Karl-Marbach-Str. 1
Heilbronn BW 74080
71319180

(G-2456)
MARIETTA MARTIN MATERIALS INC
Also Called: Martin Marietta Aggregates
8701 Red Oak Blvd Ste 540 (28217-2960)
P.O. Box 30013 (27622-0013)
PHONE..............................704 525-7740
James Thompson, *VP*
EMP: 24
Web: www.martinmarietta.com
SIC: 1422 Crushed and broken limestone
PA: Martin Marietta Materials Inc
4123 Parklake Ave
Raleigh NC 27612

(G-2457)
MARKETING ONE SPORTSWEAR
INC
3101 Yorkmont Rd Ste 1100 (28208-7375)
PHONE..............................704 334-9333
Bo Rhinehardt, *Pr*
EMP: 5 **EST:** 1992
SALES (est): 487.6K **Privately Held**

SIC: **7389** 2396 5136 5137 Embroidery
advertising; Screen printing on fabric articles
; Sportswear, men's and boys'; Sportswear,
women's and children's

(G-2458)
MARLATEX CORPORATION
8425 Winged Bourne (28210-5930)
PHONE..............................704 829-7797
Barnabas Martonffy, *Pr*
▲ **EMP:** 25 **EST:** 1982
SALES (est): 894.48K **Privately Held**
Web: www.perfectdomain.com
SIC: 2211 Upholstery fabrics, cotton

(G-2459)
MARLEY COMPANY LLC (DH)
Also Called: S P X
13515 Ballantyne Corporate Pl
(28277-2706)
PHONE..............................704 752-4400
Steve Zeller, *CEO*
Christopher J Kearney, *
Patrick J O'leary, *VP Fin*
Robert B Foreman, *
▲ **EMP:** 200 **EST:** 1922
SALES (est): 106.34MM
SALES (corp-wide): 1.83B **Privately Held**
Web: www.spx.com
SIC: 3443 3433 3586 3561 Cooling towers,
metal plate; Heating equipment, except
electric; Measuring and dispensing pumps;
Pumps and pumping equipment
HQ: Canvas Sx, Llc
6325 Ardrey Kell Rd Ste 4
Charlotte NC 28277
980 474-3700

(G-2460)
MARSHALL AIR SYSTEMS INC
419 Peachtree Dr S (28217-2098)
PHONE..............................704 525-6230
Deborah B Stuck, *CEO*
Robert M Stuck, *
Ron B Reynders, *
▼ **EMP:** 100 **EST:** 1976
SQ FT: 85,000
SALES (est): 15.6MM **Privately Held**
Web: www.marshallair.com
SIC: 3589 Commercial cooking and
foodwarming equipment

(G-2461)
MARTIN MARIETTA MATERIALS INC
Also Called: Martin Marietta Aggregates
575 E Mallard Creek Church Rd
(28262-0809)
P.O. Box 621238 (28262-0120)
PHONE..............................704 547-9775
John Sherrill, *Mgr*
EMP: 6
Web: www.martinmarietta.com
SIC: 1422 Crushed and broken limestone
PA: Martin Marietta Materials Inc
4123 Parklake Ave
Raleigh NC 27612

(G-2462)
MARTIN MARIETTA MATERIALS INC
Also Called: Martin Marietta Aggregates
11325 Texland Blvd (28273)
P.O. Box 7121 (28241-7121)
PHONE..............................704 588-1471
John Smith, *Mgr*
EMP: 7
Web: www.martinmarietta.com
SIC: 1422 Crushed and broken limestone
PA: Martin Marietta Materials Inc
4123 Parklake Ave
Raleigh NC 27612

(G-2463)
MARTIN MARIETTA MATERIALS INC
Also Called: Martin Marietta Aggregates
4551 Beatties Ford Rd (28216-2849)
P.O. Box 680698 (28216-0012)
PHONE..............................704 392-1333
Jerry Moss, *Brnch Mgr*
EMP: 4
Web: www.martinmarietta.com
SIC: 3273 Ready-mixed concrete
PA: Martin Marietta Materials Inc
4123 Parklake Ave
Raleigh NC 27612

(G-2464)
MARTIN SPROCKET & GEAR INC
3901 Scott Futrell Dr (28208-3548)
PHONE..............................704 394-9111
David Sills, *Mgr*
EMP: 31
SALES (corp-wide): 292.47MM **Privately**
Held
Web: www.martinsprocket.com
SIC: 3566 Gears, power transmission,
except auto
PA: Martin Sprocket & Gear, Inc.
3100 Sprocket Dr
Arlington TX 76015
817 258-3000

(G-2465)
MARTINS FMOUS PSTRY SHOPPE
INC
1933 Scott Futrell Dr (28208-2704)
PHONE..............................800 548-1200
EMP: 5
SALES (corp-wide): 149.7MM **Privately**
Held
Web: www.potatorolls.com
SIC: 2051 Bread, cake, and related products
PA: Martin's Famous Pastry Shoppe, Inc.
1000 Potato Roll Ln
Chambersburg PA 17202
800 548-1200

(G-2466)
MASONITE CORPORATION
7300 Reames Rd (28216-2228)
PHONE..............................704 599-0235
Steve Stafstrom, *Brnch Mgr*
EMP: 547
Web: www.masonite.com
SIC: 3423 3546 3429 3315 Hand and edge
tools, nec; Power-driven handtools;
Builders' hardware; Nails, steel: wire or cut
HQ: Masonite Corporation
1242 E 5th Ave
Tampa FL 33605
800 663-3667

(G-2467)
MASONRY REINFORCING CORP
AMER (PA)
Also Called: Wire-Bond
400 Rountree Rd (28217-2131)
P.O. Box 240988 (28224-0988)
PHONE..............................704 525-5554
Ralph O Johnson Junior, *Ch Bd*
Ralph O Johnson Iii, *Pr*
Gary Tyler, *
Kathryn J Tyler, *
Mark Mcclure, *CFO*
▲ **EMP:** 130 **EST:** 1975
SQ FT: 111,200
SALES (est): 44.98MM
SALES (corp-wide): 44.98MM **Privately**
Held
Web: www.wirebond.com
SIC: 3496 Concrete reinforcing mesh and
wire

(G-2468)
MATHISEN VENTURES INC
Also Called: Cruise Industry News
17343 Meadow Bottom Rd (28277-6588)
PHONE..............................212 986-1025
Oivind Mathisen, *Pr*
EMP: 6 **EST:** 1978
SALES (est): 200.03K **Privately Held**
Web: www.cruiseindustrynews.com
SIC: 2731 2721 2741 Book publishing;
Periodicals, publishing only; Newsletter
publishing

(G-2469)
MATSUSADA PRECISION INC
5960 Fairview Rd Ste 400 (28210-3119)
PHONE..............................704 496-2644
Sadayoshi Matsuda, *Pr*
▲ **EMP:** 6 **EST:** 2004
SALES (est): 707.74K **Privately Held**
Web: www.matsusada.com
SIC: 3679 Power supplies, all types: static

(G-2470)
MATTHEW WARREN INC (PA)
Also Called: Paragon Medical - Southington
3426 Toringdon Way Ste 400 (28277)
EMP: 30 **EST:** 1995
SALES (est): 400.43MM
SALES (corp-wide): 400.43MM **Privately**
Held
Web: www.mwcomponents.com
SIC: 3493 Coiled flat springs

(G-2471)
MAUSER USA LLC
1209 Tar Heel Rd (28208-1526)
PHONE..............................704 398-2325
Paul Wehmer, *Brnch Mgr*
EMP: 42
SALES (corp-wide): 3.82B **Privately Held**
Web: www.mauserpackaging.com
SIC: 3412 Metal barrels, drums, and pails
HQ: Mauser Usa, Llc
1515 W 22nd St Ste 1100
Oak Brook IL 60523

(G-2472)
MAUSER USA LLC
701 Lawton Rd (28216-3438)
PHONE..............................704 625-0737
EMP: 151
SALES (corp-wide): 3.82B **Privately Held**
Web: www.mauserpackaging.com
SIC: 3412 2655 Barrels, shipping: metal;
Fiber cans, drums, and containers
HQ: Mauser Usa, Llc
1515 W 22nd St Ste 1100
Oak Brook IL 60523

(G-2473)
MAXIME KNITTING INTERNATIONAL
4925 Sirona Dr Ste 200 (28273-4201)
PHONE..............................803 627-2768
Denis Th Riault, *CEO*
▲ **EMP:** 9 **EST:** 2015
SALES (est): 1.21MM **Privately Held**
Web: www.bekaertdeslee.com
SIC: 3069 Mattresses, pneumatic: fabric
coated with rubber

(G-2474)
MAXTRONIC TECHNOLOGIES LLC
9545 Greyson Ridge Dr (28277-0659)
PHONE..............................704 756-5354
EMP: 7 **EST:** 2004
SALES (est): 1.54MM **Privately Held**
Web: www.maxtronictech.com
SIC: 3674 Solid state electronic devices, nec

▲ = Import ▼ = Export
◆ = Import/Export

(G-2475)
MC CULLOUGH AUTO ELC & ASSOC
3219 N Davidson St (28205-1033)
PHONE..................................704 376-5388
George W Mc Cullough Iii, *Owner*
EMP: 7 **EST:** 1970
SQ FT: 4,500
SALES (est): 161.17K **Privately Held**
Web:
auto-electrical-repair-services.cmac.ws
SIC: 5013 3694 7539 Automotive supplies
and parts; Automotive electrical equipment,
nec; Electrical services

(G-2476)
MCDONALD SERVICES INC
1734 University Commercial Pl
(28213-6444)
P.O. Box 561238 (28256-1238)
PHONE..................................704 597-0590
James Mcdold, *Mgr*
EMP: 30
SALES (corp-wide): 4.54MM **Privately
Held**
Web: www.msibalers.com
SIC: 3559 Recycling machinery
PA: Mcdonald Services, Inc.
7427 Price Tucker Rd
Monroe NC 28110
704 753-9669

(G-2477)
MCGILL ADVSORY PBLICATIONS INC
8816 Red Oak Blvd Ste 240 (28217-5516)
PHONE..................................866 727-6100
Brian Mcgillicuddy, *Dir*
EMP: 6 **EST:** 2019
SALES (est): 180.46K **Privately Held**
Web: www.corient.com
SIC: 2741 Miscellaneous publishing

(G-2478)
**MCGRANN PAPER CORPORATION
(PA)**
Also Called: McGrann Digital Imaging
13400 Sage Thrasher Ln (28278-6861)
PHONE..................................800 240-9455
Adam Mcgrann, *Pr*
Karl Mcgrann, *Pr*
◆ **EMP:** 40 **EST:** 1974
SALES (est): 4.56MM
SALES (corp-wide): 4.56MM **Privately
Held**
Web: www.gouldpaper.com
SIC: 5111 2752 Fine paper; Advertising
posters, lithographed

(G-2479)
MCKELVEY FULKS
1432 Center Park Dr (28217-2909)
PHONE..................................704 357-1550
EMP: 5 **EST:** 2005
SALES (est): 330.23K **Privately Held**
SIC: 3571 5045 Electronic computers;
Computers, peripherals, and software

(G-2480)
MCLAMB GROUP INC
1003 Louise Ave Apt B (28205-3257)
P.O. Box 36369 (28236-6369)
PHONE..................................704 333-1171
Ed Mclamb, *Pr*
Steve Langdon, *Sec*
EMP: 7 **EST:** 2000
SQ FT: 14,000
SALES (est): 861.39K **Privately Held**
Web: www.themclambgroup.com
SIC: 2759 Promotional printing

(G-2481)
MCSHAN INC
Also Called: Wireless Communications NC
16607 Riverstone Way Ste 200
(28277-5749)
PHONE..................................980 355-9790
Anthony Mcshan, *Pr*
EMP: 4 **EST:** 1999
SALES (est): 208.17K **Privately Held**
SIC: 3663 4812 Satellites, communications;
Paging services

(G-2482)
MDB INVESTORS LLC
Also Called: Bilt USA Manufacturing
4000 Sam Wilson Rd (28214-8996)
P.O. Box 2905 (28070-2905)
PHONE..................................704 507-6850
Richard Mikels, *Mng Pt*
EMP: 10 **EST:** 2011
SALES (est): 317.91K **Privately Held**
SIC: 3713 Truck and bus bodies

(G-2483)
MDKSCRUBS LLC
8401 Parkland Cir Apt 102 (28227-2203)
PHONE..................................980 250-4708
Mary Mackins, *Managing Member*
EMP: 7 **EST:** 2021
SALES (est): 75.08K **Privately Held**
SIC: 2211 7389 Scrub cloths; Business
services, nec

(G-2484)
MEASUREMENT CONTROLS INC
6131 Old Concord Rd (28213)
P.O. Box 27 (29726)
PHONE..................................704 921-1101
Paresh Patel, *Pr*
Ila Patel, *VP*
▲ **EMP:** 10 **EST:** 1977
SQ FT: 20,000
SALES (est): 1.56MM **Privately Held**
Web: www.measurementcontrolsllc.com
SIC: 7699 5085 3824 Professional
instrument repair services; Gas equipment,
parts and supplies; Fluid meters and
counting devices

(G-2485)
MEDICAL DEVICE BUS SVCS INC
900 Center Park Dr Ste Bc (28217-2961)
PHONE..................................704 423-0033
Mark Hawkins, *Brnch Mgr*
EMP: 15
SALES (corp-wide): 88.82B **Publicly Held**
SIC: 3842 Surgical appliances and supplies
HQ: Medical Device Business Services, Inc.
700 Orthopaedic Dr
Warsaw IN 46582

(G-2486)
MEDICOR IMAGING INC
1927 S Tryon St Ste 200 (28203-4688)
PHONE..................................704 332-5532
Richard G Little, *Pr*
EMP: 6 **EST:** 2009
SALES (est): 244.01K **Privately Held**
Web: www.medicorimaging.com
SIC: 5045 7371 7372 7373 Computer
software; Computer software systems
analysis and design, custom; Prepackaged
software; Systems software development
services

(G-2487)
MEGTEC INDIA HOLDINGS LLC
13024 Ballantyne Corporate Pl Ste 700
(28277-2113)
PHONE..................................704 625-4900

EMP: 4 **EST:** 2017
SALES (est): 1.78MM
SALES (corp-wide): 999.35MM **Publicly
Held**
SIC: 3511 Turbines and turbine generator
sets
PA: Babcock & Wilcox Enterprises, Inc.
1200 E Market St Ste 650
Akron OH 44305
330 753-4511

(G-2488)
MEGTEC TURBOSONIC TECH INC
13024 Ballantyne Corporate Pl Ste 700
(28277-2113)
PHONE..................................704 625-4900
EMP: 5 **EST:** 2017
SALES (est): 2.22MM
SALES (corp-wide): 999.35MM **Publicly
Held**
SIC: 3511 Turbines and turbine generator
sets
PA: Babcock & Wilcox Enterprises, Inc.
1200 E Market St Ste 650
Akron OH 44305
330 753-4511

(G-2489)
MELATEX INCORPORATED
3818 Northmore St (28205-1308)
P.O. Box 5127 (28299-5127)
PHONE..................................704 332-5046
Kevin Corley, *Pr*
Patrick Lawrence, *Pr*
Warren Boone, *Ch*
John Shuler, *VP*
▲ **EMP:** 10 **EST:** 1995
SQ FT: 21,000
SALES (est): 2.49MM **Privately Held**
Web: www.melatex.com
SIC: 2865 5169 Cyclic crudes and
intermediates; Dyestuffs

(G-2490)
MERCHANT CASH SYSTEMS LLC
301 S Mcdowell St Ste 125 (28204-0031)
PHONE..................................336 499-9937
Steven Graham, *CEO*
EMP: 7 **EST:** 2020
SALES (est): 340K **Privately Held**
SIC: 7372 Application computer software

(G-2491)
MERCHANTS METALS INC
Also Called: Meadow Burke Products
3401 Woodpark Blvd Ste A (28206-4249)
PHONE..................................704 921-9192
Baxter Ellis, *Mgr*
EMP: 4
SALES (corp-wide): 1.09B **Privately Held**
Web: www.merchantsmetals.com
SIC: 5032 3272 Concrete building products;
Concrete products, nec
HQ: Merchants Metals Llc
3 Ravinia Dr Ste 1750
Atlanta GA 30346
770 741-0300

(G-2492)
MERCK & CO INC
Also Called: Merck
10301 David Taylor Dr (28262-2334)
PHONE..................................908 423-3000
John Canan, *Pr*
EMP: 47
SALES (corp-wide): 64.17B **Publicly Held**
Web: www.merck.com
SIC: 2834 Pharmaceutical preparations
PA: Merck & Co., Inc.
126 E Lincoln Ave
Rahway NJ 07065

908 740-4000

(G-2493)
MERIDIAN PRFMCE SYSTEMS INC
2018 Dilworth Rd E (28203-5726)
PHONE..................................706 905-5637
Joshua Kohn, *CEO*
EMP: 4
SALES (est): 334.19K **Privately Held**
SIC: 7389 7372 Business Activities at Non-
Commercial Site; Prepackaged software

(G-2494)
MESSER LLC
2820 Nevada Blvd (28273-6433)
PHONE..................................704 583-0313
Jay Navel, *Brnch Mgr*
EMP: 5
SALES (corp-wide): 2.29B **Privately Held**
Web: www.messeramericas.com
SIC: 2813 Oxygen, compressed or liquefied
HQ: Messer Llc
200 Smrset Corp Blvd Ste
Bridgewater NJ 08807
800 755-9277

(G-2495)
**METAL IMPROVEMENT COMPANY
LLC**
500 Springbrook Rd (28217-2147)
PHONE..................................704 525-3818
Tom Barden, *Mgr*
EMP: 88
SALES (corp-wide): 3.12B **Publicly Held**
Web: www.imrtest.com
SIC: 3398 Shot peening (treating steel to
reduce fatigue)
HQ: Metal Improvement Company, Llc
80 Route 4 E Ste 310
Paramus NJ 07652
201 843-7800

(G-2496)
METRO WOODCRAFTER OF NC INC
Also Called: Metro Woodcrafter
3710 Performance Rd (28214-8095)
P.O. Box 669488 (28266-9488)
PHONE..................................704 394-9622
Barry Rigby, *Pr*
Nicole Filion-ashline, *CFO*
EMP: 21 **EST:** 2015
SQ FT: 18,000
SALES (est): 4.27MM **Privately Held**
Web: www.metrowoodcrafter.com
SIC: 2434 Wood kitchen cabinets

(G-2497)
METROTECH CHEMICALS INC
2101 Wilkinson Blvd (28208-5646)
PHONE..................................704 343-9315
Joseph H Gigler, *Pr*
Thomas Karrenstein, *
EMP: 52 **EST:** 1987
SQ FT: 12,000
SALES (est): 11.4MM **Privately Held**
Web: www.metrotechauto.com
SIC: 2842 2841 Cleaning or polishing
preparations, nec; Soap and other
detergents

(G-2498)
MIAS INC
Also Called: Mias Group
14240 S Lakes Dr (28273-6793)
PHONE..................................704 665-1098
Manfred Klug, *CEO*
Albert E Guarnieri, *Prin*
Nils Fleig, *CFO*
Doctor Cornelius Uhl, *Dir Opers*
Tracey Robins, *Off Mgr*
▲ **EMP:** 5 **EST:** 2006

GEOGRAPHIC

SALES (est): 4.9MM
SALES (corp-wide): 2.67MM **Privately Held**
Web: www.mias-group.com
SIC: 3536 Hoists, cranes, and monorails
HQ: Mias Gmbh
　　　Dieselstr. 12
　　　Eching BY 85386
　　　816570310

(G-2499)
MICROSOFT CORPORATION
Also Called: Microsoft
8055 Microsoft Way (28273-8106)
PHONE............................704 527-2987
Keith Schifferli, *Brnch Mgr*
EMP: 2000
SALES (corp-wide): 245.12B **Publicly Held**
Web: www.microsoft.com
SIC: 7372 Application computer software
PA: Microsoft Corporation
　　　1 Microsoft Way
　　　Redmond WA 98052
　　　425 882-8080

(G-2500)
MIGN INC
301 Camp Rd Ste 105 (28206-3577)
PHONE............................609 304-1617
Lisa Tweardy, *CEO*
Fredrik Meyer, *Prin*
Marcus Engman, *Prin*
EMP: 9 **EST:** 2019
SALES (est): 1.55MM **Privately Held**
Web: www.mign.design
SIC: 3842 Surgical appliances and supplies

(G-2501)
MIKROPOR AMERICA INC
10512 Kilmory Ter (28210-8350)
◆ **EMP:** 10 **EST:** 2005
SALES (est): 136.18K **Privately Held**
Web: www.mikroporamerica.com
SIC: 3564 3589 Air purification equipment; Water purification equipment, household type

(G-2502)
MIKROPUL LLC
4500 Chesapeake Dr (28216-3415)
PHONE............................704 998-2600
Richard Bearse, *Managing Member*
EMP: 5 **EST:** 2014
SALES (est): 197.81K **Privately Held**
Web: www.nedermanmikropul.com
SIC: 3564 Purification and dust collection equipment

(G-2503)
MILLENNIUM PHARMACEUTICALS INC
10430 Harris Oak Blvd Ste 1 (28269-7521)
PHONE............................866 466-7779
Zack Freese, *Brnch Mgr*
EMP: 54
Web: www.takedaoncology.com
SIC: 2834 Pharmaceutical preparations
HQ: Millennium Pharmaceuticals, Inc.
　　　40 Landsdowne St
　　　Cambridge MA 02139

(G-2504)
MILLER DUMPSTER SERVICE LLC
16450 Shallow Pond Rd (28278-8722)
PHONE............................704 504-9300
Shannon Miller, *Prin*
EMP: 4 **EST:** 2017
SALES (est): 1.66MM **Privately Held**
Web: www.millercarolina.com

SIC: 3443 Dumpsters, garbage

(G-2505)
MILLER PRODUCTS INC
Also Called: M P I Lable Systems Carolina
4100 Turtle Creek Ln (28273-3742)
PHONE............................704 587-1870
Stephen Offits, *Mgr*
EMP: 36
SALES (corp-wide): 70.41MM **Privately Held**
Web: www.mpilabels.com
SIC: 2759 Labels and seals: printing, nsk
PA: Miller Products, Inc.
　　　450 Courtney Rd
　　　Sebring OH 44672
　　　330 938-2134

(G-2506)
MILLWOOD INC
Also Called: Millwood
5950 Fairview Rd Ste 250 (28210-0093)
PHONE............................704 817-7541
EMP: 15
Web: www.millwoodinc.com
SIC: 2448 Pallets, wood
PA: Millwood, Inc.
　　　3708 International Blvd
　　　Vienna OH 44473

(G-2507)
MINNEWAWA INC
10612 Providence Rd Ste D (28277-9561)
PHONE............................865 522-8103
EMP: 8 **EST:** 2020
SALES (est): 249.44K **Privately Held**
Web: www.minnewawa.com
SIC: 3999 Manufacturing industries, nec

(G-2508)
MIRRORMATE LLC
9317 Monroe Rd Ste A (28270-1476)
PHONE............................704 390-7377
EMP: 16 **EST:** 2003
SALES (est): 2.4MM **Privately Held**
Web: www.mirrormate.com
SIC: 5999 2499 Picture frames, ready made; Picture and mirror frames, wood

(G-2509)
MITSUBISHI CHEMICAL AMER INC (DH)
Also Called: Mitsubishi Chem Methacrylates
9115 Harris Corners Pkwy Ste 300 (28269)
PHONE............................980 580-2839
Jean-marc Gilson, *CEO*
Randy Queen, *
◆ **EMP:** 53 **EST:** 1981
SALES (est): 1.28B **Privately Held**
Web: www.mitsubishichemicalholdings.com
SIC: 3355 3444 3443 2893 Aluminum rolling and drawing, nec; Sheet metalwork; Fabricated plate work (boiler shop); Printing ink
HQ: Mitsubishi Chemical Corporation
　　　1-1-1, Marunouchi
　　　Chiyoda-Ku TKY 100-8

(G-2510)
MJT US INC
Also Called: Dataforce
6801 Northpark Blvd Ste A (28216-0080)
P.O. Box 680490 (28216-0009)
PHONE............................704 826-7828
Mechelle Timmons, *Pr*
Daniel Hoover, *Sec*
John Timmons, *Dir Opers*
EMP: 7 **EST:** 2017
SQ FT: 25,000
SALES (est): 766.33K **Privately Held**

Web: www.dataforceresearch.com
SIC: 7389 7374 2752 7331 Printing broker; Data processing and preparation; Commercial printing, lithographic; Mailing service

(G-2511)
MK GLOBAL HOLDINGS LLC (DH)
Also Called: Mountain Khakis
5101 Terminal St (28208-1247)
PHONE............................704 334-1904
Ross Saldarini, *Managing Member*
EMP: 20 **EST:** 2003
SALES (est): 2.38MM
SALES (corp-wide): 175.58MM **Privately Held**
SIC: 2329 7999 2329 Men's and boys' sportswear and athletic clothing; Agricultural fair; Sportswear, women's
HQ: Mk Acquisition Llc
　　　5101 Terminal St
　　　Charlotte NC 28208
　　　866 686-7778

(G-2512)
MMB ONE INC (PA)
4629 Dwight Evans Rd (28217-0907)
P.O. Box 30636 (28230-0636)
PHONE............................704 523-8163
Marvin Bruce Junior, *Pr*
Thomas Walker, *VP*
▲ **EMP:** 17 **EST:** 1963
SQ FT: 25,000
SALES (est): 3.29MM
SALES (corp-wide): 3.29MM **Privately Held**
Web: www.catawbarubber.com
SIC: 3052 5085 Automobile hose, rubber; Rubber goods, mechanical

(G-2513)
MOBIUS IMAGING LLC
Also Called: Mobius Imaging
1723 Beverly Dr (28207-2513)
PHONE............................704 773-7652
EMP: 30
SIC: 3845 CAT scanner (computerized axial tomography) apparatus

(G-2514)
MOMENTIVE PERFORMANCE MTLS INC
9129 Southern Pine Blvd (28273-5548)
PHONE............................704 805-6252
EMP: 167
Web: www.momentive.com
SIC: 2869 Silicones
HQ: Momentive Performance Materials Inc.
　　　2750 Balltown Rd
　　　Niskayuna NY 12309

(G-2515)
MONARCH COLOR CORPORATION (PA)
5327 Brookshire Blvd (28216)
PHONE............................704 394-4626
Gregory S West, *Pr*
Ian West, *
Ralph Petros, *
◆ **EMP:** 50 **EST:** 1977
SQ FT: 30,000
SALES (est): 15.64MM
SALES (corp-wide): 15.64MM **Privately Held**
Web: www.monarchcolor.com
SIC: 2893 Letterpress or offset ink

(G-2516)
MONARCH MEDICAL TECH LLC
112 S Tryon St Ste 800 (28284-2106)

PHONE............................704 335-1300
Bruce Lisanti, *Pr*
Stuart Long, *CEO*
Sharai Lavoie, *CFO*
Laurel Fuqua, *CCO*
EMP: 11 **EST:** 2012
SALES (est): 2.26MM **Privately Held**
Web: www.monarchmedtech.com
SIC: 7372 Application computer software

(G-2517)
MONARCH PRINTERS
3900 Greensboro St (28206-2036)
PHONE............................704 376-1533
Ira Kennedy, *Prin*
EMP: 5 **EST:** 2010
SALES (est): 100.51K **Privately Held**
SIC: 2752 Offset printing

(G-2518)
MOON N SEA NC LLC
Also Called: Kgi Trading NC
12810 Virkler Dr (28273-4253)
PHONE............................704 588-1963
EMP: 4 **EST:** 2018
SALES (est): 2.65MM **Privately Held**
SIC: 3537 Trucks, tractors, loaders, carriers, and similar equipment

(G-2519)
MORRIS FAMILY THEATRICAL INC (PA)
Also Called: Morris East
6900 Morris Estate Dr (28262-4259)
PHONE............................704 332-3304
Scott Morris, *Pr*
Teri Bate, *VP*
Philip Morris Smith, *Sec*
Amy Morris Smith, *Treas*
▲ **EMP:** 20 **EST:** 1967
SQ FT: 300,000
SALES (est): 2.34MM
SALES (corp-wide): 2.34MM **Privately Held**
Web: www.morriscostumes.com
SIC: 2389 5632 5699 Costumes; Dancewear ; Costumes, masquerade or theatrical

(G-2520)
MORRIS SOUTH LLC
Also Called: Morris South M T S
8530 Steele Creek Place Dr Ste H (28273)
PHONE............................704 523-6008
Rich Hussey, *Mgr*
Rich Hussey, *Pr*
EMP: 81 **EST:** 1980
SQ FT: 16,000
SALES (est): 3.68MM **Privately Held**
Web: www.gotomorris.com
SIC: 3599 Machine shop, jobbing and repair

(G-2521)
MOSS SUPPLY COMPANY (PA)
Also Called: Old Dominion Win Door Hanover
5001 N Graham St (28269-4826)
P.O. Box 26338 (28221-6338)
PHONE............................704 596-8717
Robert Moss Senior, *CEO*
Robert Moss Junior, *VP*
Cassandra Nott, *
Juanita Moss, *Stockholder*
Gregory Smith, *
EMP: 250 **EST:** 1961
SQ FT: 225,000
SALES (est): 20.3MM
SALES (corp-wide): 20.3MM **Privately Held**
Web: www.mosssupply.com
SIC: 3442 Storm doors or windows, metal

(G-2522)

MOULDING MILLWORK LLC
11445 Granite St Unit C (28273-7174)
PHONE...............................704 504-9880
Robert Wright, *Prin*
▲ **EMP:** 4 **EST:** 2005
SALES (est): 194.09K **Privately Held**
Web: www.cmouldings.com
SIC: 2431 Millwork

(G-2523)

MOUNT HOPE MACHINERY CO
2000 Donald Ross Rd (28208-6123)
P.O. Box 250 (22645-0250)
▲ **EMP:** 11 **EST:** 1954
SALES (est): 814.88K **Privately Held**
Web: www.andritz.com
SIC: 3552 3312 3069 5084 Textile machinery
; Blast furnaces and steel mills; Medical
and laboratory rubber sundries and related
products; Plastic products machinery

(G-2524)

MOVERS AND SHAKERS LLC
Also Called: Pink Zebra Moving Charlotte NC
1016 W Craighead Rd (28206-1613)
PHONE...............................980 771-0505
EMP: 7 **EST:** 2022
SALES (est): 818.13K **Privately Held**
SIC: 7372 Prepackaged software

(G-2525)

MUDGEAR LLC
2522 Handley Pl (28226-4946)
PHONE...............................347 674-9102
Alex Thrasher, *Prin*
EMP: 4 **EST:** 2017
SALES (est): 534.11K **Privately Held**
Web: www.mudgear.com
SIC: 2323 Men's and boy's neckwear

(G-2526)

MUELLER DIE CUT SOLUTIONS INC
(HQ)
10415 Westlake Dr (28273-3784)
P.O. Box 7503 (28241-7503)
PHONE...............................704 588-3900
Ken Stober, *Pr*
Donald Stober, *
Brian Stober, *
Carl Stober, *
James Brazas, *
◆ **EMP:** 24 **EST:** 1940
SQ FT: 44,000
SALES (est): 25.54MM
SALES (corp-wide): 82.97MM **Privately
Held**
Web: www.muellercustomcut.com
SIC: 3053 5084 2675 Gaskets, all materials;
Conveyor systems; Die-cut paper and board
PA: Sur-Seal, Llc
6156 Wesselman Rd
Cincinnati OH 45248
513 574-8500

(G-2527)

MULLEN PUBLICATIONS INC
9301 Forsyth Park Dr Ste A (28273-3957)
P.O. Box 7746 (28241)
PHONE...............................704 527-5111
Mason W Smith Iii, *Pr*
EMP: 15 **EST:** 1945
SALES (est): 1.21MM **Privately Held**
Web: www.mullenpublications.com
SIC: 2711 Newspapers, publishing and
printing

(G-2528)

MULTI-SHIFTER INC
11110 Park Charlotte Blvd (28273-8859)

P.O. Box 38310 (28278-1005)
PHONE...............................704 588-9611
Dale Williams, *Pr*
Kelly Minchener, *CFO*
▼ **EMP:** 15 **EST:** 1983
SQ FT: 24,000
SALES (est): 4.18MM **Privately Held**
Web: www.multi-shifter.com
SIC: 3537 Lift trucks, industrial: fork,
platform, straddle, etc.

(G-2529)

MULTISITE LED LLC
6715 Fairview Rd (28210-3355)
PHONE...............................650 823-7247
EMP: 4
SALES (corp-wide): 341.76K **Privately
Held**
SIC: 3674 Light emitting diodes
PA: Multisite Led, Llc
540 University Ave # 300
Palo Alto CA 94301
650 823-7247

(G-2530)

MULTITRODE INC
14125 S Bridge Cir (28273-6747)
PHONE...............................561 994-8090
Craig Parkinson, *Ch Bd*
Craig Parkinson, *Ch*
Aaron Parkinson, *Bd of Dir*
David Doin, *Pr*
▲ **EMP:** 7 **EST:** 1986
SQ FT: 7,700
SALES (est): 2.53MM **Publicly Held**
Web: www.xylem.com
SIC: 3825 Instruments to measure electricity
PA: Xylem Inc.
301 Water St Se Ste 200
Washington DC 20003

(G-2531)

MUNDO UNIFORMES LLC
10806 Reames Rd Ste W (28269-3766)
PHONE...............................704 287-1527
Juan Pablo Rojas, *Managing Member*
EMP: 5 **EST:** 2010
SALES (est): 163.65K **Privately Held**
Web: www.mundotees.com
SIC: 2759 Screen printing

(G-2532)

MURATA MACHINERY USA INC (DH)
Also Called: Muratec
2120 Queen City Dr (28208-2709)
P.O. Box 667609 (28266-7609)
PHONE...............................704 875-9280
Masahiko Hattori, *Pr*
Dale R Mitchell, *
Dan Luithle, *
◆ **EMP:** 120 **EST:** 1989
SQ FT: 97,000
SALES (est): 39.73MM **Privately Held**
Web: www.muratec-usa.com
SIC: 5084 5085 3542 Textile and leather
machinery; Clean room supplies; Punching
and shearing machines
HQ: Murata Machinery Usa Holdings, Inc.
2120 Queen City Dr
Charlotte NC 28266
704 394-8331

(G-2533)

MURATA MCHY USA HOLDINGS INC
(HQ)
Also Called: Muratatec
2120 Queen City Dr (28266)
P.O. Box 667609 (28266-7609)
PHONE...............................704 394-8331
Masazumi Fukushima, *Pr*
Chris Cobb, *

◆ **EMP:** 15 **EST:** 2002
SQ FT: 100,000
SALES (est): 51.45MM **Privately Held**
Web: www.muratec-usa.com
SIC: 3542 3552 5065 Punching and
shearing machines; Textile machinery;
Facsimile equipment
PA: Murata Machinery, Ltd.
136, Takedamukaishirocho, Fushimi-Ku
Kyoto KYO 612-8

(G-2534)

MURRAY INC
4508 Westinghouse Blvd Ste B
(28273-9602)
PHONE...............................704 329-0400
Tanner Hargens, *Prin*
EMP: 27
Web: www.medicalmurray.com
SIC: 3841 Surgical and medical instruments
PA: Murray, Inc.
400 N Rand Rd
Barrington IL 60010

(G-2535)

MURRAY INC
Also Called: Medical Murray
8531 Steele Creek Place Dr Unit D
(28273-4270)
PHONE...............................847 620-7990
EMP: 28
Web: www.medicalmurray.com
SIC: 3841 Surgical and medical instruments
PA: Murray, Inc.
400 N Rand Rd
Barrington IL 60010

(G-2536)

MUSA GOLD LLC
8425 Cleve Brown Rd (28269-0969)
PHONE...............................704 579-7894
Alinda Mitchell, *CEO*
EMP: 10 **EST:** 2021
SALES (est): 100.02K **Privately Held**
SIC: 2834 Pharmaceutical preparations

(G-2537)

MVA LEATHERWOOD LLC
4530 Park Rd (28209-3716)
PHONE...............................704 519-4200
Lat W Purser Iii, *Admn*
EMP: 4 **EST:** 2005
SALES (est): 56.8K **Privately Held**
SIC: 3199 Leather goods, nec

(G-2538)

MW INDUSTRIES INC (PA)
Also Called: Mw Components
3426 Toringdon Way Ste 100 (28277-3497)
PHONE...............................704 837-0331
Simon Newman, *CEO*
Kyle O'meara *Cfb, Prin*
EMP: 27 **EST:** 1975
SQ FT: 40,000
SALES (est): 406.38MM
SALES (corp-wide): 406.38MM **Privately
Held**
Web: www.mwcomponents.com
SIC: 3451 3444 Screw machine products;
Sheet metalwork

(G-2539)

N3XT INC ✪
8022 Providence Rd Ste 500-130 (28277)
PHONE...............................704 905-2209
Jeffrey Wallis, *CEO*
Jesseson Michael, *Dir*
Scott Shay, *Dir*
EMP: 5 **EST:** 2023
SALES (est): 927.45K **Privately Held**

SIC: 7372 7389 Prepackaged software;
Business Activities at Non-Commercial Site

(G-2540)

NAARVA
614 Chipley Ave (28205-7002)
PHONE...............................704 333-3070
Elbert Smith, *Prin*
EMP: 4 **EST:** 2007
SALES (est): 340.72K **Privately Held**
Web: www.naarva.com
SIC: 3799 Recreational vehicles

(G-2541)

NAKOS PAPER PRODUCTS INC
Also Called: Blp Paper
2020 Starita Rd Ste G (28206-1298)
P.O. Box 77181 (28271-7004)
PHONE...............................704 238-0717
Chris Nakos, *Pr*
Nick Nakos, *VP*
EMP: 7 **EST:** 2003
SALES (est): 700K **Privately Held**
SIC: 2621 Napkin stock, paper

(G-2542)

NAPOLEON JAMES
Also Called: Tshirtskings
6113 Delta Landing Rd (28227-1123)
PHONE...............................413 331-9560
Napoleon James, *Owner*
EMP: 4 **EST:** 2021
SALES (est): 130.28K **Privately Held**
SIC: 2759 Commercial printing, nec

(G-2543)

NASCENT TECHNOLOGY LLC
Also Called: Nascent
2744 Yorkmont Rd (28208-7324)
PHONE...............................704 654-3035
Ray West, *Pr*
Michael Bratt, *CFO*
Julie Corrado Ctrl, *Prin*
▲ **EMP:** 17 **EST:** 1996
SQ FT: 2,000
SALES (est): 6.2MM
SALES (corp-wide): 36.41MM **Privately
Held**
Web: www.nascent.com
SIC: 3822 Building services monitoring
controls, automatic
PA: System Development Resources Inc.
1 International Blvd
Mahwah NJ 07495
201 995-9060

(G-2544)

NATIONAL CONTAINER GROUP LLC
1209c Tar Heel Rd (28208-1526)
PHONE...............................704 393-9050
Eric Perez, *Mgr*
EMP: 7
Web: www.mauserpackaging.com
SIC: 7699 5085 3999 4953 Plastics products
repair; Drums, new or reconditioned;
Grinding and pulverizing of materials, nec;
Refuse collection and disposal services
PA: National Container Group, Llc
3620 W 38th St
Chicago IL 60632

(G-2545)

**NATIONAL CONVEYORS COMPANY
INC**
4404a Chesapeake Dr (28216-3413)
P.O. Box 530176 (30353-0176)
PHONE...............................860 325-4011
Tomas Hagstrom, *CEO*
Arnold Serenkin, *Pr*
Melissa Garrity, *Sec*
Brian Smith, *VP Engg*

James Dumaine-savage, *FOR ELCTL AND FIELD SERVICE*
▲ **EMP:** 4 **EST:** 1933
SQ FT: 17,500
SALES (est): 2.28MM **Privately Held**
Web: www.nationalconveyors.com
SIC: 3535 Conveyors and conveying equipment
HQ: Nederman Corporation
　　4404a Chesapeake Dr
　　Charlotte NC 28216
　　704 399-7441

(G-2546)
NATIONAL GYPS RECEIVABLES LLC
Also Called: Ngc Receivables
2001 Rexford Rd (28211-3498)
PHONE.................................704 365-7300
Thomas C Nelson, *Pr*
EMP: 7 **EST:** 2015
SALES (est): 2.24MM
SALES (corp-wide): 795.88MM **Privately Held**
Web: www.nationalgypsum.com
SIC: 2679 Wallboard, decorated: made from purchased material
HQ: Proform Finishing Products, Llc
　　2001 Rexford Rd
　　Charlotte NC 28211

(G-2547)
NATIONAL GYPSUM SERVICES CO
2001 Rexford Rd (28211-3498)
PHONE.................................704 365-7300
Tom Nelson, *Pr*
Cd Spangler Junior, *Pr*
EMP: 16 **EST:** 2003
SQ FT: 20,448
SALES (est): 6.22MM
SALES (corp-wide): 795.88MM **Privately Held**
Web: www.nationalgypsum.com
SIC: 1499 Gypsum and calcite mining
HQ: Proform Finishing Products, Llc
　　2001 Rexford Rd
　　Charlotte NC 28211

(G-2548)
NATIONAL TANK MONITOR INC
9801 Ferguson Rd (28227-6497)
PHONE.................................704 335-8265
Rick Hardy, *Pr*
EMP: 10 **EST:** 1996
SALES (est): 736.56K **Privately Held**
SIC: 1389 Testing, measuring, surveying, and analysis services

(G-2549)
NAVEX GLOBAL INC
13950 Ballantyne Corporate Pl Ste 300 (28277-3193)
P.O. Box 60941 (28260-0941)
PHONE.................................866 297-0224
EMP: 8
SALES (corp-wide): 1.99B **Privately Held**
Web: www.navex.com
SIC: 7372 Prepackaged software
HQ: Navex Global, Inc.
　　5885 Meadows Rd Ste 500
　　Lake Oswego OR 97035
　　971 250-4100

(G-2550)
ND SOUTHEASTERN FASTENER
2220 Center Park Dr Ste C (28217-2994)
PHONE.................................704 329-0033
EMP: 8 **EST:** 2019
SALES (est): 375.71K **Privately Held**
Web: www.ndindustries.com
SIC: 3965 Fasteners

(G-2551)
NEAL S PALLET COMPANY INC
8808 Wilkinson Blvd (28214-8061)
P.O. Box 992 (28012-0992)
PHONE.................................704 393-8568
Phillip Neal Sparrow, *Pr*
William Hawley, *
EMP: 42 **EST:** 1981
SQ FT: 11,250
SALES (est): 4.3MM **Privately Held**
Web: www.nealspalletcompany.com
SIC: 2448 7699 Pallets, wood; Pallet repair

(G-2552)
NEDERMAN MANUFACTURING
4500 Chesapeake Dr (28216-3415)
PHONE.................................704 898-7945
EMP: 7 **EST:** 2016
SALES (est): 2.27MM **Privately Held**
Web: www.nederman.com
SIC: 3999 Barber and beauty shop equipment

(G-2553)
NEDERMAN MIKROPUL LLC (DH)
4404a Chesapeake Dr (28216-3413)
PHONE.................................704 998-2600
Lacy Hayes Iii, *Pr*
Jonas Fogelberg, *CFO*
EMP: 30 **EST:** 2013
SALES (est): 23.93MM **Privately Held**
Web: www.nedermanmikropul.com
SIC: 5075 3564 Air filters; Air cleaning systems
HQ: Nederman Mikropul Holding Inc.
　　4404a Chesapeake Dr
　　Charlotte NC 28216
　　701 399-7441

(G-2554)
NEDERMAN MIKROPUL CANADA INC (DH)
4404a Chesapeake Dr (28216-3413)
P.O. Box 16348 (28297-6348)
PHONE.................................704 998-2606
Lacy Hayes Iii, *Pr*
Sam Lavin, *VP*
◆ **EMP:** 7 **EST:** 1999
SALES (est): 4.47MM **Privately Held**
Web: www.nedermanmikropul.com
SIC: 3677 Filtration devices, electronic
HQ: Nederman Mikropul, Llc
　　4404a Chesapeake Dr
　　Charlotte NC 28216
　　704 998-2600

(G-2555)
NEW BEGINNINGS TRNSP LLC
5904 Johnnette Dr (28212-2365)
PHONE.................................704 293-0493
EMP: 5
SALES (est): 1.15MM **Privately Held**
SIC: 3799 Transportation equipment, nec

(G-2556)
NEW DRECTIONS SCREEN PRTRS INC
241 I K Beatty St (28214-1646)
PHONE.................................704 393-1769
Wanda P Mauch, *Pr*
Curtis Phillips, *VP*
Harvey F Phillips, *Sec*
EMP: 4 **EST:** 1977
SQ FT: 2,000
SALES (est): 211.05K **Privately Held**
Web: www.newdirectionsco.com
SIC: 2759 Screen printing

(G-2557)
NEW ELEMENT
1021 Polk St (28206-2933)
PHONE.................................704 890-7292
William Himes, *Prin*
EMP: 4 **EST:** 2010
SALES (est): 17.03K **Privately Held**
SIC: 2819 Elements

(G-2558)
NEW VISION MOMENTUM ENTP LLC
4456 The Plaza Ste E (28215-2176)
PHONE.................................800 575-1244
EMP: 6 **EST:** 2019
SALES (est): 1.41MM **Privately Held**
SIC: 3537 Trucks, tractors, loaders, carriers, and similar equipment

(G-2559)
NEWS 14 CAROLINA
316 E Morehead St Ste 316 (28202-2308)
PHONE.................................704 973-5700
Ronald Miller, *Prin*
EMP: 5 **EST:** 2008
SALES (est): 248.35K **Privately Held**
Web: www.news14.com
SIC: 4833 2711 Television broadcasting stations; Newspapers, publishing and printing

(G-2560)
NEWTON MACHINE CO INC
1120 N Hoskins Rd (28216-3599)
PHONE.................................704 394-2099
James E Newton Iii, *Pr*
William A Newton, *VP*
▲ **EMP:** 15 **EST:** 1948
SQ FT: 35,000
SALES (est): 1.55MM **Privately Held**
Web: www.newtonmachine.com
SIC: 3599 Machine shop, jobbing and repair

(G-2561)
NEXJEN SYSTEMS LLC
5933 Brookshire Blvd (28216-3386)
P.O. Box 29622 (27626-0622)
PHONE.................................704 969-7070
Darren Lingafeldt, *Pr*
EMP: 22 **EST:** 2006
SQ FT: 10,850
SALES (est): 2.25MM
SALES (corp-wide): 25.35MM **Privately Held**
Web: www.thenexjen.com
SIC: 3823 3625 3825 Process control instruments; Relays and industrial controls; Instruments to measure electricity
PA: Averna Technologies Inc.
　　1001 Rue Lenoir Bureau A400
　　Montreal QC H4C 2
　　514 842-7577

(G-2562)
NEXXT LEVEL TRUCKING LLC
627 Minuet Ln (28217-2768)
PHONE.................................980 205-4425
Aaron Simmons, *CEO*
Aaron C Simmons, *Prin*
EMP: 5 **EST:** 2008
SALES (est): 250.19K **Privately Held**
SIC: 8742 3537 Transportation consultant; Trucks: freight, baggage, etc.: industrial, except mining

(G-2563)
NEXXUS LIGHTING INC
124 Floyd Smith Office Park Dr Ste 300 (28262-1684)
PHONE.................................704 405-0416
Michael Bauer, *Pr*

Gary Langford, *Treas*
EMP: 10 **EST:** 2014
SALES (est): 3.06MM **Privately Held**
Web: www.nexxuslighting.com
SIC: 3648 Lighting equipment, nec

(G-2564)
NG CORPORATE LLC
2001 Rexford Rd (28211-3415)
PHONE.................................704 365-7300
EMP: 33
SALES (est): 6.06MM **Privately Held**
SIC: 2679 Wallboard, decorated: made from purchased material

(G-2565)
NG OPERATIONS LLC (PA)
2001 Rexford Rd (28211)
PHONE.................................704 365-7300
EMP: 8 **EST:** 2020
SALES (est): 96.43MM
SALES (corp-wide): 96.43MM **Privately Held**
SIC: 2679 Wallboard, decorated: made from purchased material

(G-2566)
NG OPERATIONS LLC
Also Called: NG OPERATIONS, LLC
5901 Carnegie Blvd (28209-4635)
P.O. Box 221799 (28222-1799)
PHONE.................................704 916-2082
EMP: 92
SALES (corp-wide): 795.88MM **Privately Held**
Web: www.nationalgypsum.com
SIC: 3275 Gypsum products
HQ: Proform Finishing Products, Llc
　　2001 Rexford Rd
　　Charlotte NC 28211

(G-2567)
NIC NAC WELDING CO
550 W 32nd St (28206-2215)
PHONE.................................704 502-5178
Marc Maddox, *Prin*
EMP: 4 **EST:** 2012
SALES (est): 125.99K **Privately Held**
SIC: 7692 Welding repair

(G-2568)
NITE CRAWLERS LLC
301 S Mcdowell St Ste 125-1898 (28204)
PHONE.................................980 229-8706
Dejavu Mclean, *Managing Member*
EMP: 6 **EST:** 2022
SALES (est): 896.41K **Privately Held**
SIC: 7372 Prepackaged software

(G-2569)
NN INC (PA)
Also Called: NN
6210 Ardrey Kell Rd Ste 120 (28277)
PHONE.................................980 264-4300
Harold C Bevis, *Pr*
Jeri J Harman, *Non-Executive Chairman of the Board*
Timothy French, *Sr VP*
Christopher H Bohnert, *Sr VP*
D Gail Nixon, *Chief Human Resource Officer*
▲ **EMP:** 6 **EST:** 1980
SALES (est): 464.29MM
SALES (corp-wide): 464.29MM **Publicly Held**
Web: www.nninc.com
SIC: 3562 Ball bearings and parts

▲ = Import ▼ = Export
◆ = Import/Export

(G-2570)
NOAHS INC
Also Called: Biotechnology
7289 Meeting St (28210-7296)
PHONE..................704 718-2354
R William Brinkely Iii, *Pr*
EMP: 10 **EST:** 2015
SALES (est): 127.17K **Privately Held**
SIC: 4939 2813 3569 8748 Combination utilities, nec; Industrial gases; General industrial machinery, nec; Business consulting, nec

(G-2571)
NORD GEAR CORPORATION
300 Forsyth Hall Dr (28273-5842)
PHONE..................888 314-6673
Mike Vouchon, *Mgr*
EMP: 8
SALES (corp-wide): 1.18MM **Privately Held**
Web: www.nord.com
SIC: 3566 Gears, power transmission, except auto
HQ: Nord Gear Corporation
800 Nord Dr
Waunakee WI 53597
608 849-7300

(G-2572)
NORDFAB DUCTING
4404 Chesapeake Dr (28216-3413)
P.O. Box 16348 (28297-6348)
PHONE..................336 821-0840
EMP: 6 **EST:** 2015
SALES (est): 4.32MM **Privately Held**
Web: www.nordfab.com
SIC: 3444 Sheet metalwork

(G-2573)
NORSAN MEDIA LLC
8655 Crown Crescent Ct (28227-6783)
PHONE..................704 494-7181
EMP: 25 **EST:** 2012
SALES (est): 3.83MM **Privately Held**
Web: www.norsanmedia.com
SIC: 2741 Internet publishing and broadcasting

(G-2574)
NORTH STAR FBRICATION REPR INC
124 Carothers St (28216-3820)
P.O. Box 742 (28130-0742)
PHONE..................704 393-5243
Chris Kashino, *Pr*
Susan Kashino, *Sec*
EMP: 5 **EST:** 1984
SQ FT: 20,000
SALES (est): 614.23K **Privately Held**
SIC: 3499 3498 Fire- or burglary-resistive products; Tube fabricating (contract bending and shaping)

(G-2575)
NORTHROP GRMMAN GDNCE ELEC INC
Northrop Grumman Synoptics
1201 Continental Blvd (28273-6320)
PHONE..................704 588-2340
Scott Griffin, *Mgr*
EMP: 30
Web: www.northropgrumman.com
SIC: 3812 3674 Search and navigation equipment; Infrared sensors, solid state
HQ: Northrop Grumman Guidance And Electronics Company, Inc.
2980 Fairview Park Dr
Falls Church VA 22042

(G-2576)
NOTEPAD ENTERPRISES LLC
Also Called: International
901 N Tryon St Ste G (28206-3294)
PHONE..................704 377-3467
EMP: 5 **EST:** 2018
SALES (est): 56.46K **Privately Held**
SIC: 2752 Commercial printing, lithographic

(G-2577)
NOVA MOBILITY SYSTEMS INC
8604 Cliff Cameron Dr Ste 152 (28269-8526)
PHONE..................800 797-9861
George Ecker, *CEO*
EMP: 4 **EST:** 2012
SALES (est): 483.24K **Privately Held**
SIC: 3429 Hardware, nec

(G-2578)
NOVAERUS US INC (PA)
3540 Toringdon Way Ste 200 (28277-4650)
PHONE..................813 304-2468
Kevin Maughan, *Pr*
Eric Murphy, *Sec*
EMP: 4 **EST:** 2013
SALES (est): 2.4MM
SALES (corp-wide): 2.4MM **Privately Held**
Web: www.novaerus.com
SIC: 3564 Air cleaning systems

(G-2579)
NOVAS BAKERY INC (PA)
1800 Odessa Ln (28216-1440)
PHONE..................704 333-5566
Vlado Novakovic, *Pr*
Sladjana Novakovic, *
EMP: 15 **EST:** 1996
SALES (est): 1.68MM
SALES (corp-wide): 1.68MM **Privately Held**
Web: www.novasbakery.com
SIC: 5149 5461 2051 Bakery products; Retail bakeries; Bread, cake, and related products

(G-2580)
NOVEM INDUSTRIES INC
1801 Cottonwood St (28206-1280)
P.O. Box 1272 (28031-1272)
PHONE..................704 660-6460
Allen Reyen, *Prin*
EMP: 6 **EST:** 2008
SALES (est): 787.89K **Privately Held**
Web: www.novemindustries.com
SIC: 3999 Manufacturing industries, nec

(G-2581)
NOVOLEX BAGCRAFT INC (DH)
3436 Toringdon Way Ste 100 (28227)
PHONE..................800 845-6051
Stanley B Bikulege, *Ch Bd*
EMP: 77 **EST:** 2006
SALES (est): 180.19MM
SALES (corp-wide): 26.11B **Publicly Held**
Web: www.novolex.com
SIC: 3086 Packaging and shipping materials, foamed plastics
HQ: Novolex Holdings, Llc
3436 Tringdon Way Ste 100
Charlotte NC 28277
800 845-6051

(G-2582)
NOVOLEX HERITAGE BAG LLC (DH)
Also Called: Novolex
3436 Toringdon Way Ste 100 (28277)
PHONE..................800 845-6051
▲ **EMP:** 183 **EST:** 1973
SALES (est): 232.21MM

SALES (corp-wide): 26.11B **Publicly Held**
Web: www.heritage-bag.com
SIC: 2673 Plastic bags: made from purchased materials
HQ: Novolex Holdings, Llc
3436 Tringdon Way Ste 100
Charlotte NC 28277
800 845-6051

(G-2583)
NOVOLEX HOLDINGS LLC (DH)
Also Called: Novolex
3436 Toringdon Way Ste 100 (28277)
PHONE..................800 845-6051
Stanley B Bikulege, *Ch Bd*
Dennis Norman, *
Daniel L Rikard, *
▲ **EMP:** 32 **EST:** 2009
SQ FT: 30,000
SALES (est): 3.76B
SALES (corp-wide): 26.11B **Publicly Held**
Web: www.novolex.com
SIC: 3089 Plastics kitchenware, tableware, and houseware
HQ: Clydesdale Acquisition Holdings, Inc.
3436 Tringdon Way Ste 100
Charlotte NC 28277
843 857-4800

(G-2584)
NOVOLEX SHIELDS LLC (DH)
3436 Toringdon Way Ste 100 (28277-2449)
P.O. Box 9848 (98909-0848)
PHONE..................800 845-6051
Stanley Bikulege, *Pr*
Paul Palmisano, *Sec*
EMP: 480 **EST:** 2017
SQ FT: 400,000
SALES (est): 42.64MM
SALES (corp-wide): 26.11B **Publicly Held**
Web: www.novolex.com
SIC: 3081 Plastics film and sheet
HQ: Novolex Holdings, Llc
3436 Tringdon Way Ste 100
Charlotte NC 28277
800 845-6051

(G-2585)
NUCOR CASTRIP ARKANSAS LLC
1915 Rexford Rd (28211-3465)
PHONE..................704 366-7000
Scott Andrews, *Pr*
EMP: 5 **EST:** 2014
SALES (est): 443.21K
SALES (corp-wide): 30.73B **Publicly Held**
Web: www.nucor.com
SIC: 3312 Blast furnaces and steel mills
PA: Nucor Corporation
1915 Rexford Rd
Charlotte NC 28211
704 366-7000

(G-2586)
NUCOR CORPORATION (PA)
Also Called: NUCOR
1915 Rexford Rd Ste 400 (28211)
PHONE..................704 366-7000
Leon J Topalian, *Ch Bd*
David A Sumoski, *COO*
Stephen D Laxton, *Ex VP*
Douglas J Jellison, *Executive Strategy Vice President*
Gregory J Murphy, *Ex VP*
◆ **EMP:** 200 **EST:** 1905
SALES (est): 30.73B
SALES (corp-wide): 30.73B **Publicly Held**
Web: www.nucor.com
SIC: 3312 3441 3448 Blast furnaces and steel mills; Building components, structural steel; Prefabricated metal buildings

(G-2587)
NUCOR ENERGY HOLDINGS INC
1915 Rexford Rd (28211-3465)
PHONE..................704 366-7000
John J Ferriola, *CEO*
EMP: 9 **EST:** 2012
SALES (est): 417.08K
SALES (corp-wide): 30.73B **Publicly Held**
Web: www.nucor.com
SIC: 3312 Blast furnaces and steel mills
PA: Nucor Corporation
1915 Rexford Rd
Charlotte NC 28211
704 366-7000

(G-2588)
NUCOR STEEL SALES CORPORATION
1915 Rexford Rd (28211-3465)
PHONE..................302 622-4066
Mark Ferucci, *Pr*
EMP: 10 **EST:** 1997
SALES (est): 2.61MM
SALES (corp-wide): 30.73B **Publicly Held**
Web: www.nucor.com
SIC: 3312 Blast furnaces and steel mills
PA: Nucor Corporation
1915 Rexford Rd
Charlotte NC 28211
704 366-7000

(G-2589)
NUFABRX LLC ✪
1515 Mockingbird Ln Ste 400 (28209-3236)
PHONE..................888 683-2279
Glenn Normoyle Junior, *CEO*
Glenn Normoyle Junior, *Managing Member*
EMP: 9 **EST:** 2023
SALES (est): 1.66MM **Privately Held**
SIC: 3842 Surgical appliances and supplies

(G-2590)
NUTROTONIC LLC
5031 W W T Harris Blvd Ste H (28269-3761)
PHONE..................855 948-0008
Hamed Khalili, *CEO*
Hamed Kahlili, *Managing Member*
EMP: 10 **EST:** 2021
SALES (est): 2.1MM **Privately Held**
Web: www.nutrotonic.com
SIC: 2048 5961 7389 5499 Feed supplements; Electronic shopping; Business services, nec; Health and dietetic food stores

(G-2591)
ODIN TECHNOLOGIES LLC
4810 Ashley Park Ln Unit C1-1307 (28210-3835)
PHONE..................408 309-1925
EMP: 4 **EST:** 2018
SALES (est): 202.23K **Privately Held**
Web: www.odinhealthtech.com
SIC: 3845 3841 Electromedical equipment; Diagnostic apparatus, medical

(G-2592)
OKAYA SHINNICHI CORP AMERICA
Also Called: Osa
300 Crompton St (28273-6214)
P.O. Box 7027 (28241-7027)
PHONE..................704 588-3131
Yoshio Kinoshita, *Pr*
Mikiya Nakamura, *
Akio Ichikawa, *
Masahide Yamazaki, *
Harry Kato, *
▲ **EMP:** 40 **EST:** 1990
SQ FT: 25,100
SALES (est): 3.09MM **Privately Held**

Web: www.osa-usa.com
SIC: 3312 Pipes, iron and steel
PA: Okaya & Co.,Ltd.
   2-4-18, Sakae, Naka-Ku
   Nagoya AIC 460-0

(G-2593)
OKUMA AMERICA CORPORATION
11900 Westhall Dr (28278-7127)
P.O. Box 7866 (28241-7866)
PHONE...............................704 588-7000
▲ EMP: 200 EST: 1978
SALES (est): 41.61MM **Privately Held**
Web: www.okuma.com
SIC: 5084 3541 Machine tools and
   accessories; Machine tools, metal cutting
   type
PA: Okuma Corporation
   5-25-1, Shimooguchi, Oguchicho
   Niwa-Gun AIC 480-0

(G-2594)
OLDCASTLE RETAIL INC (DH)
625 Griffith Rd Ste 100 (28217-3576)
PHONE...............................704 525-1621
David Maske, *Pr*
◆ EMP: 17 EST: 2006
SALES (est): 19.77MM
SALES (corp-wide): 34.95B **Privately Held**
SIC: 3272 Concrete products, precast, nec
HQ: Bonsal American, Inc.
   625 Griffith Rd Ste 100
   Charlotte NC 28217
   704 525-1621

(G-2595)
OLE MEXICAN FOODS INC
Also Called: Ole-Charlotte Distribution Ctr
11001a S Commerce Blvd (28273-6354)
PHONE...............................704 587-1763
Eduardo Moreno, *Pr*
EMP: 23
Web: www.olemex.com
SIC: 2099 Tortillas, fresh or refrigerated
PA: Ole' Mexican Foods, Inc.
   6585 Crescent Dr
   Norcross GA 30071

(G-2596)
OMEGA MANUFACTURING CORP
1800 Industrial Center Cir (28213-4301)
P.O. Box 560338 (28256-0338)
PHONE...............................704 597-0418
Ron C Hunte, *Pr*
▲ EMP: 12 EST: 1997
SQ FT: 5,000
SALES (est): 4.94MM **Privately Held**
Web: www.omega-mfg.com
SIC: 3599 Machine shop, jobbing and repair

(G-2597)
ON POINT MOBILE DETAILING LLC
10906 Featherbrook Rd Apt 1b
(28262-7757)
PHONE...............................404 593-8882
EMP: 5
SALES (est): 335.72K **Privately Held**
SIC: 3714 7389 Cleaners, air, motor vehicle;
   Business services, nec

(G-2598)
ONE LIBRARY AT A TIME INC
4107 Crossgate Rd (28226-7010)
PHONE...............................704 578-1812
EMP: 4 EST: 2018
SALES (est): 38.54K **Privately Held**
Web: www.onelibraryatatime.com
SIC: 2731 Book publishing

(G-2599)
ONEAKA DANCE COMPANY
4430 The Plaza # 13 (28215-2034)
PHONE...............................704 299-7432
Oneaka Mack, *Prin*
EMP: 5 EST: 2013
SALES (est): 177.34K **Privately Held**
SIC: 7922 8322 3931 7929 Performing arts
   center production; Child guidance agency;
   Drums, parts, and accessories (musical
   instruments); Popular music groups or
   artists

(G-2600)
**ONSITE WOODWORK
CORPORATION**
645 Pressley Rd Ste E (28217-4600)
PHONE...............................704 523-1380
Richard Greene, *Brnch Mgr*
EMP: 10
SALES (corp-wide): 20.83MM **Privately
Held**
Web: www.osw.io
SIC: 2431 Woodwork, interior and
   ornamental, nec
PA: Onsite Woodwork Corporation
   4100 Rock Valley Pkwy
   Loves Park IL 61111
   815 633-6400

(G-2601)
OSPREA LOGISTICS USA LLC
Also Called: Osprea Logistics USA
11108 Quality Dr (28273-7714)
PHONE...............................704 504-1677
Michael Chamberlain, *
Raynard Mack, *
EMP: 40 EST: 2015
SQ FT: 1,000
SALES (est): 7.77MM
SALES (corp-wide): 14.85MM **Privately
Held**
Web: www.osprea.com
SIC: 3713 Truck bodies and parts
HQ: Osprea Logistics Sa (Pty) Ltd
   2 Warblers Rd
   Cape Town WC 7806

(G-2602)
OTIS ELEVATOR COMPANY
9625 Southern Pine Blvd Ste G
(28273-5506)
PHONE...............................704 519-0100
Jeff Duggan, *Rgnl Mgr*
EMP: 190
SALES (corp-wide): 14.26B **Publicly Held**
Web: www.otis.com
SIC: 3534 1796 5084 Elevators and
   equipment; Installing building equipment;
   Elevators
HQ: Otis Elevator Company
   1 Carrier Pl
   Farmington CT 06032
   860 674-3000

(G-2603)
OTTO ENVMTL SYSTEMS NC LLC
12700 Gen Dr (28273)
P.O. Box 410251 (28241-0251)
PHONE...............................800 227-5885
David Piejak, *CEO*
EMP: 300 EST: 2003
SALES (est): 3.66MM **Privately Held**
SIC: 3537 Industrial trucks and tractors

(G-2604)
OVER RAINBOW INC
Also Called: Uptown Catering Company, The
1431 Bryant St (28208-5201)
PHONE...............................704 332-5521
Mike Ingersoll, *Pr*

EMP: 7 EST: 2003
SALES (est): 433.97K **Privately Held**
Web: www.uptowncateringco.com
SIC: 5812 5963 2099 Caterers; Food
   services, direct sales; Food preparations,
   nec

(G-2605)
PAI SERVICES LLC
Also Called: Sage Payroll Services
11215 N Community House Rd Ste 800
(28277-4961)
PHONE...............................856 231-4667
EMP: 28
SALES (corp-wide): 3.09B **Privately Held**
SIC: 7371 7372 Computer software
   development; Business oriented computer
   software
HQ: Pai Services, Llc
   11215 N Cmnty Hse Rd Ste
   Charlotte NC 28277
   856 231-0195

(G-2606)
PALMER SENN
Also Called: Mvi Productions
3113 Airlie St (28205-3244)
PHONE...............................704 451-3971
Palmer Senn, *Owner*
EMP: 5 EST: 1999
SALES (est): 236.8K **Privately Held**
SIC: 3544 7812 3651 Special dies and tools;
   Video tape production; Household audio
   and video equipment

(G-2607)
PANENERGY CORP (DH)
526 S Church St (28202-1802)
P.O. Box 1642 (77251-1642)
PHONE...............................704 594-6200
James E Rogers, *CEO*
EMP: 15 EST: 1997
SALES (est): 22.43MM
SALES (corp-wide): 30.36B **Publicly Held**
SIC: 4922 1321 2813 5172 Pipelines, natural
   gas; Natural gas liquids production; Helium;
   Gases
HQ: Duke Energy Registration Services,
   Inc.
   526 S Church St
   Charlotte NC 28202
   704 594-6200

(G-2608)
PAPERWORKS
3040 Parker Green Trl (28269-1490)
PHONE...............................704 548-9057
EMP: 6 EST: 2010
SALES (est): 150.94K **Privately Held**
Web: www.onepaperworks.com
SIC: 2679 Wallpaper

(G-2609)
PARKER ATHLETIC PRODUCTS LLC
2401 Distribution St (28203-5377)
PHONE...............................704 370-0400
Bruce Parker, *Managing Member*
EMP: 8 EST: 1986
SQ FT: 7,500
SALES (est): 248.17K **Privately Held**
Web: www.parkermedicalassociates.com
SIC: 3949 Team sports equipment

(G-2610)
**PARKER MEDICAL ASSOCIATES
LLC**
2400 Distribution St (28203-5026)
PHONE...............................704 344-9998
▲ EMP: 11 EST: 1986
SQ FT: 5,000
SALES (est): 256.26K **Privately Held**

Web: www.parkermedicalassociates.com
SIC: 3949 2295 Protective sporting
   equipment; Varnished glass and coated
   fiberglass fabrics

(G-2611)
**PARKER MEDICAL ASSOCIATES
LLC (PA)**
Also Called: Ultrascope
2400 Distribution St (28203-5026)
PHONE...............................704 344-9998
Bruce Parker, *CEO*
▲ EMP: 19 EST: 1981
SQ FT: 5,000
SALES (est): 2.44MM
SALES (corp-wide): 2.44MM **Privately
Held**
Web: www.parkermedicalassociates.com
SIC: 3841 Stethoscopes and stethographs

(G-2612)
PARKER-HANNIFIN CORPORATION
Ssd Drives Division
9225 Forsyth Park Dr (28273-3884)
PHONE...............................704 588-3246
Jim Budnar, *Brnch Mgr*
EMP: 113
SALES (corp-wide): 19.93B **Publicly Held**
Web: www.parker.com
SIC: 3679 3566 Electronic loads and power
   supplies; Speed changers, drives, and
   gears
PA: Parker-Hannifin Corporation
   6035 Parkland Blvd
   Cleveland OH 44124
   216 896-3000

(G-2613)
PARMER INTERNATIONAL INC
Also Called: Fluid Power Technology
1225 Graphic Ct Ste D (28206-1526)
PHONE...............................704 374-0066
Carl L Parmer, *Pr*
Dolores Parmer, *Sec*
EMP: 6 EST: 1983
SQ FT: 7,950
SALES (est): 793.33K **Privately Held**
Web: www.fluidpowertech.com
SIC: 3593 Fluid power actuators, hydraulic
   or pneumatic

(G-2614)
PARRISH TIRE COMPANY
Also Called: Bandag
300 E 36th St (28206)
PHONE...............................704 372-2013
TOLL FREE: 800
Val Brusso, *Mgr*
EMP: 43
SALES (corp-wide): 378.88MM **Privately
Held**
Web: www.parrishtire.com
SIC: 5014 5531 7534 Truck tires and tubes;
   Automotive tires; Tire retreading and repair
   shops
PA: Parrish Tire Company
   5130 Indiana Ave
   Winston Salem NC 27106
   800 849-8473

(G-2615)
PATRICE BRENT ○
Also Called: Melt ME
8606 Panglemont Dr (28269-2294)
PHONE...............................980 999-7217
Patrice Brent, *Owner*
EMP: 6 EST: 2024
SALES (est): 1.12MM **Privately Held**
SIC: 3999 7389 Candles; Business Activities
   at Non-Commercial Site

▲ = Import ▼ = Export
◆ = Import/Export

(G-2616)
PATTERN BOX
8325 Nathanael Greene Ln (28227-0659)
PHONE...............................704 535-8743
Anita Wheeless, *Prin*
EMP: 5 **EST:** 2008
SALES (est): 113.14K **Privately Held**
SIC: 3543 Industrial patterns

(G-2617)
PATTONS MEDICAL LLC
Also Called: Pattons Medical
4610 Entrance Dr Ste H (28273-4389)
PHONE...............................704 529-5442
▲ **EMP:** 26 **EST:** 2008
SALES (est): 11.27MM **Privately Held**
Web: www.pattonsmedical.com
SIC: 3563 3841 Air and gas compressors;
Surgical and medical instruments
HQ: Patton's Inc.
3201 South Blvd
Charlotte NC 28209
704 523-4122

(G-2618)
PAUL NORMAN COMPANY INC
8700 Wilkinson Blvd (28214-8060)
P.O. Box 25118 (28229-5118)
PHONE...............................704 399-4221
Suzanne Norman, *Pr*
Jean Norman, *Treas*
EMP: 7 **EST:** 1965
SQ FT: 18,000
SALES (est): 506.64K **Privately Held**
SIC: 3599 Custom machinery

(G-2619)
PAVCO INC
9401 Nations Ford Rd (28273-5739)
PHONE...............................704 496-6800
▲ **EMP:** 49 **EST:** 1953
SALES (est): 9.07MM **Privately Held**
Web: www.pavco.com
SIC: 5084 5169 5051 2899 Industrial
machinery and equipment; Chemicals and
allied products, nec; Metals service centers
and offices; Chemical preparations, nec

(G-2620)
PAYZER LLC
11111 Carmel Commons Blvd Ste 400
(28226-0008)
PHONE...............................866 488-6525
Joseph Giordano, *CEO*
EMP: 10 **EST:** 2012
SALES (est): 5.37MM **Privately Held**
Web: www.payzer.com
SIC: 7372 Prepackaged software

(G-2621)
**PBI PERFORMANCE PRODUCTS
INC (PA)**
9800 Southern Pine Blvd Ste D
(28273-5522)
PHONE...............................704 554-3378
Bill Lawson, *Pr*
◆ **EMP:** 80 **EST:** 2002
SALES (est): 11.59MM
SALES (corp-wide): 11.59MM **Privately
Held**
Web: www.pbi-int.com
SIC: 3624 2824 Carbon and graphite
products; Organic fibers, noncellulosic

(G-2622)
PCAI INC
Also Called: Cummins
11101 Nations Ford Rd (28206)
PHONE...............................704 588-1240
Mike Grace, *Ch Bd*

Steve Jordan, *VP*
EMP: 75 **EST:** 1970
SQ FT: 42,000
SALES (est): 8.68MM
SALES (corp-wide): 34.1B **Publicly Held**
SIC: 5084 5063 3519 Engines and parts;
diesel; Generators; Internal combustion
engines, nec
PA: Cummins Inc.
500 Jackson St
Columbus IN 47201
812 377-5000

(G-2623)
PELTON & CRANE COMPANY
11727 Fruehauf Dr (28273-6507)
PHONE...............................704 588-2126
Donald W Lochman, *Pr*
▲ **EMP:** 350 **EST:** 1900
SQ FT: 1,611,719
SALES (est): 5.15MM
SALES (corp-wide): 23.88B **Publicly Held**
Web: www.peltonandcrane.com
SIC: 3843 3841 Dental equipment; Surgical
instruments and apparatus
PA: Danaher Corporation
2200 Pa Ave Nw Ste 800w
Washington DC 20037
202 828-0850

(G-2624)
PENDULUM INC
6128 Brookshire Blvd Ste A (28216-2423)
PHONE...............................704 491-6320
Willam Krause, *Pr*
EMP: 4 **EST:** 1996
SQ FT: 2,000
SALES (est): 154.44K **Privately Held**
SIC: 3577 Data conversion equipment,
media-to-media: computer

(G-2625)
PEPSI COLA CO
Also Called: Pepsico
3530 Toringdon Way Ste 400 (28277-3431)
PHONE...............................704 357-9166
Tom Tansey, *Prin*
EMP: 5 **EST:** 2008
SALES (est): 383.12K **Privately Held**
Web: www.pepsistore.com
SIC: 2086 Carbonated soft drinks, bottled
and canned

(G-2626)
PEPSI-COLA METRO BTLG CO INC
Also Called: Pepsico
2820 South Blvd (28209-1802)
PHONE...............................980 581-1099
Barksdale Halton, *Brnch Mgr*
EMP: 9
SALES (corp-wide): 91.47B **Publicly Held**
Web: www.pepsico.com
SIC: 2086 Carbonated soft drinks, bottled
and canned
HQ: Pepsi-Cola Metropolitan Bottling
Company, Inc.
700 Anderson Hill Rd
Purchase NY 10577
914 767-6000

(G-2627)
PERFECT FIT INDUSTRIES LLC
8501 Tower Point Dr Ste C (28227-7868)
PHONE...............................800 864-7618
▲ **EMP:** 125
SIC: 2392 2211 5712 Cushions and pillows;
Yarn-dyed fabrics, cotton; Beds and
accessories

(G-2628)
PERFORMANCE GOODS LLC
5825 Mctaggart Ln (28269-5217)
PHONE...............................704 361-8600
EMP: 6 **EST:** 2010
SALES (est): 186.05K **Privately Held**
SIC: 2299 Insulating felts

(G-2629)
PERLMAN INC
Also Called: Action Graphics
5312 Wingedfoot Rd (28226-7966)
PHONE...............................704 332-1164
Jackie J Perlman, *Pr*
David H Perlman, *VP*
EMP: 13 **EST:** 1982
SALES (est): 1.03MM **Privately Held**
SIC: 2752 Offset printing

(G-2630)
PF2 EIS LLC
10735 David Taylor Dr Ste 100
(28262-1060)
PHONE...............................704 549-6931
Annette Morris, *Asstg*
EMP: 154
SALES (corp-wide): 1.5B **Publicly Held**
SIC: 7372 Prepackaged software
HQ: Pf2 Eis Llc
5995 Windward Pkwy Fl 3
Alpharetta GA 30005
404 338-6000

(G-2631)
PFAFF MOLDS LTD PARTNERSHIP
11825 Westhall Dr (28278-7119)
PHONE...............................704 423-9484
Werkzeug Formenbau, *Mng Pt*
Michael Birkle, *Pt*
▲ **EMP:** 17 **EST:** 1998
SQ FT: 38,000
SALES (est): 4.81MM **Privately Held**
Web: www.pfaff-mold.de
SIC: 5013 3053 Automotive supplies and
parts; Gaskets and sealing devices

(G-2632)
PFC GROUP LLC
Also Called: Plastex Fabricators
5900 Old Mount Holly Rd (28208-1131)
PHONE...............................704 393-4040
John Thompson, *Managing Member*
James Michael Lippard, *
Y Put Mloduondu, *
Hayes Lutz, *
Donald E Crumpton, *
EMP: 65 **EST:** 1968
SQ FT: 56,000
SALES (est): 2.89MM **Privately Held**
Web: www.plastexfab.com
SIC: 3993 Electric signs

(G-2633)
PGI POLYMER INC
Also Called: Chicopee
9335 Harris Corners Pkwy Ste 300
(28269-3818)
PHONE...............................704 697-5100
◆ **EMP:** 560
SIC: 2297 2392 Spunbonded fabrics; Slip
covers and pads

(G-2634)
PHILPOTT MOTORS LTD
5401 E Independence Blvd (28212-0503)
PHONE...............................704 566-2400
Linda Rew, *Prin*
EMP: 10 **EST:** 2013
SALES (est): 964.01K **Privately Held**
Web: www.philpottmotors.net

SIC: 3612 Transformers, except electric

(G-2635)
PHOENIX TAPES USA LLC
10900 S Commerce Blvd (28273-6672)
PHONE...............................704 588-3090
◆ **EMP:** 4 **EST:** 2010
SALES (est): 8.04MM **Privately Held**
Web: www.phoenixtapes.com
SIC: 2891 Adhesives

(G-2636)
PIEDMONT PLASTICS INC (PA)
5010 W W T Harris Blvd (28269-1861)
P.O. Box 26006 (28221)
PHONE...............................704 597-8200
Owen H Whitfield Junior, *Pr*
Tyler Booth, *
Greg Young, *
William Barth, *CSO*
Marc Klinger, *CIO*
◆ **EMP:** 100 **EST:** 1968
SQ FT: 73,000
SALES (est): 201.65MM
SALES (corp-wide): 201.65MM **Privately
Held**
Web: www.piedmontplastics.com
SIC: 3081 3082 5162 Plastics film and sheet
; Rods, unsupported plastics; Plastics
sheets and rods

(G-2637)
PIEDMONT STAIRWORKS LLC (PA)
2246 Old Steele Creek Rd (28208-6031)
PHONE...............................704 697-0259
Jack Watson, *Prin*
Jack Watson, *Managing Member*
EMP: 8 **EST:** 2009
SALES (est): 2.23MM
SALES (corp-wide): 2.23MM **Privately
Held**
Web: www.piedmontstairworks.com
SIC: 2431 Railings, stair: wood

(G-2638)
PIEDMONT TECHNICAL SERVICES
9127 Arbor Glen Ln (28210-7988)
PHONE...............................770 530-8313
Robert Stone, *Pr*
EMP: 4 **EST:** 2018
SALES (est): 147.79K **Privately Held**
Web: www.ptecdaf.com
SIC: 3599 Industrial machinery, nec

(G-2639)
PIRANHA INDUSTRIES INC
2515 Allen Rd S (28269-4603)
PHONE...............................704 248-7843
Richard J Kuehler, *Prin*
EMP: 5 **EST:** 1995
SALES (est): 397.48K **Privately Held**
Web: www.piranhapackaging.com
SIC: 7389 7336 3993 3086 Packaging and
labeling services; Package design; Displays
and cutouts, window and lobby; Packaging
and shipping materials, foamed plastics

(G-2640)
PLASKOLITE LLC
Also Called: Plazit-Polygal
1100 Bond St (28208-1212)
PHONE...............................704 588-3800
Ryan Schroeder, *CEO*
EMP: 117
SALES (corp-wide): 542.25MM **Privately
Held**
Web: www.plaskolite.com
SIC: 2821 Plastics materials and resins
PA: Plaskolite, Llc
400 W Ntnwide Blvd Ste 40
Columbus OH 43215

614 294-3281

SIC: 2752 Commercial printing, lithographic

▲ EMP: 18 EST: 2000
SALES (est): 3.78MM
SALES (corp-wide): 241.4MM Privately Held
Web: www.powertecmotors.com
SIC: 3621 Motors, electric
HQ: Peerless-Winsmith, Inc.
5200 Upper Mtro Pl Ste 11
Dublin OH 43017
614 526-7000

706 746-4012

(G-2641)
**PLASKOLITE NORTH CAROLINA
LLC (HQ)**
1100 Bond St (28208-1212)
PHONE.....................704 588-3800
Michael Gilbert, *CEO*
◆ EMP: 12 EST: 2003
SQ FT: 36,000
SALES (est): 34.54MM Privately Held
Web: www.plaskolite.com
SIC: 2821 Plastics materials and resins
PA: Plaskolite Israel Ltd
Kibbutz
Gazit 19340

(G-2647)
POTEET PRINTING SYSTEMS LLC
9103 Forsyth Park Dr (28273-3882)
PHONE.....................704 588-0005
Carey Cannon, *
EMP: 60 EST: 1998
SQ FT: 36,000
SALES (est): 9.7MM
SALES (corp-wide): 1.91B Privately Held
Web: www.poteetsystems.com
SIC: 2759 Screen printing
PA: Flint Group Us Llc
17177 N Lrel Pk Dr Ste 30
Livonia MI 48152
734 781-4600

(G-2653)
PPG INDUSTRIES INC
Also Called: PPG 4670
10701 Park Rd (28210-8492)
PHONE.....................704 542-8880
Joe Corbin, *Mgr*
EMP: 4
SALES (corp-wide): 17.65B Publicly Held
Web: www.ppg.com
SIC: 2851 Paints and allied products
PA: Ppg Industries, Inc.
1 Ppg Pl
Pittsburgh PA 15272
412 434-3131

(G-2658)
PRECISION PARTNERS LLC
Also Called: Stampsource
1830 Statesville Ave Ste C (28206-3231)
P.O. Box 32333 (28232-2333)
PHONE.....................800 545-3121
Luke Faulstick, *Managing Member*
Steve Hollis, *
Jim Murray, *
EMP: 40 EST: 2013
SQ FT: 18,000
SALES (est): 3.61MM Privately Held
SIC: 3469 3544 3599 Stamping metal for the
trade; Special dies and tools; Machine
shop, jobbing and repair
PA: Phoenix Stamping Group, Llc
6100 Emmanuel Dr Sw
Atlanta GA 30336

(G-2642)
PLASTICS FAMILY HOLDINGS INC
Also Called: Calsak Plastics
3000 Crosspoint Center Ln Ste A
(28269-4274)
PHONE.....................704 597-8555
Gaston Penalba, *Brnch Mgr*
EMP: 37
Web: www.calsakplastics.com
SIC: 3089 Windows, plastics
HQ: Plastics Family Holdings, Inc.
5800 Cmpus Cir Dr E Ste 1
Irving TX 75063
469 299-7000

(G-2648)
POWER ADHESIVES LTD
1209 Lilac Rd (28209-1418)
PHONE.....................704 578-9984
Lee Stegall, *Pr*
EMP: 4
SQ FT: 6,000
SALES (corp-wide): 34.96MM Privately
Held
Web: www.poweradhesives.com
SIC: 2891 Adhesives
HQ: Power Adhesives Limited
1 Lords Way
Basildon SS13
126 888-5800

(G-2654)
PPG INDUSTRIES INC
Also Called: PPG 4668
3022 Griffith St (28203-5432)
PHONE.....................704 523-0888
David Mcmillan, *Brnch Mgr*
EMP: 4
SALES (corp-wide): 17.65B Publicly Held
Web: www.ppgpaints.com
SIC: 2851 Paints and allied products
PA: Ppg Industries, Inc.
1 Ppg Pl
Pittsburgh PA 15272
412 434-3131

(G-2659)
PRECISION WLDG MCH CHARLOTTE
4701 Beam Rd (28217-9421)
PHONE.....................704 357-1288
Russell R Furr, *Owner*
EMP: 7 EST: 1969
SQ FT: 6,000
SALES (est): 512.25K Privately Held
Web:
www.carolinaprecisioncontractors.com
SIC: 3599 Machine shop, jobbing and repair

(G-2643)
PLASTIEXPORTS TN LLC
9405 D Ducks Ln Ste A (28273-4513)
PHONE.....................423 735-2207
EMP: 27
Web: www.plastiexportsusa.com
SIC: 2821 Molding compounds, plastics
HQ: Plastiexports Tn Llc
1000 S Industrial Dr
Erwin TN 37650
423 735-2316

(G-2649)
POWER AND CTRL SOLUTIONS LLC
6205 Boykin Spaniel Rd (28277-8744)
PHONE.....................704 609-9623
James Keane Busker, *Pr*
EMP: 5 EST: 2009
SALES (est): 1.56MM Privately Held
Web: www.pcssupply.com
SIC: 3699 7389 Electrical equipment and
supplies, nec; Business Activities at Non-
Commercial Site

(G-2655)
**PRACTICEPRO SFTWR SYSTEMS
INC**
Also Called: Quick Practice
14225 Plantation Park Blvd (28277-2275)
P.O. Box 620220 (28262-0103)
PHONE.....................212 244-2100
Gary Balsamo, *CEO*
EMP: 7 EST: 2010
SALES (est): 401.58K Privately Held
SIC: 7372 Prepackaged software

(G-2660)
PREM CORP
Also Called: Austin Tarp & Cargo Control
2901 Stewart Creek Blvd (28216-3593)
PHONE.....................704 921-1799
David Albertson, *Pr*
David Jacobson, *
Bellita Winger, *
Josh Albertson, *
▲ EMP: 48 EST: 1981
SALES (est): 3.98MM Privately Held
Web: www.austincanvas.com
SIC: 5999 2394 5531 7699 Canvas products
; Canvas and related products; Auto and
truck equipment and parts; Miscellaneous
automotive repair services

(G-2644)
POLYPORE INC
11430 N Community House Rd Ste 350
(28277-0454)
PHONE.....................704 587-8409
Robert B Toth, *CEO*
EMP: 73 EST: 1994
SALES (est): 3.65MM Privately Held
Web: www.polypore.com
SIC: 3629 Battery chargers, rectifying or
nonrotating

(G-2650)
POWER COMPONENTS INC
10837 Coachman Cir (28277-9148)
P.O. Box 472221 (28247-2221)
PHONE.....................704 321-9481
Rick Mc Daniel, *Pr*
EMP: 6 EST: 1985
SALES (est): 155.33K Privately Held
Web: www.powercomponentsusa.com
SIC: 3559 Semiconductor manufacturing
machinery

(G-2656)
PRECISE TECHNOLOGY INC
4201 Congress St Ste 340 (28209-4640)
PHONE.....................704 576-9527
Dave Outlaw, *Brnch Mgr*
EMP: 8
SALES (corp-wide): 11.79B Publicly Held
Web: www.ball.com
SIC: 3089 3082 Injection molded finished
plastics products, nec; Unsupported
plastics profile shapes
HQ: Rexam Limited
100 Capability Green
Luton BEDS LU1 3

(G-2661)
PRESS GANEY ASSOCIATES INC
700 E Morehead St Ste 100 (28202-2789)
PHONE.....................800 232-8032
EMP: 5 EST: 2019
SALES (est): 456.06K Privately Held
Web: www.pressganey.com
SIC: 2741 Miscellaneous publishing

(G-2645)
**POLYPORE INTERNATIONAL LP
(HQ)**
13800 S Lakes Dr (28273-6738)
PHONE.....................704 587-8409
Shgeki Takayama, *Pr*
Hiroyoshi Matsuyama, *COO*
EMP: 99 EST: 2004
SALES (est): 72.67MM Privately Held
Web: www.polypore.net
SIC: 3691 Lead acid batteries (storage
batteries)
PA: Asahi Kasei Corporation
1-1-2, Yurakucho
Chiyoda-Ku TKY 100-0

(G-2651)
**POWER-UTILITY PRODUCTS
COMPANY (PA)**
Also Called: Pupco
8710 Air Park West Dr Ste 100
(28214-8686)
PHONE.....................704 375-0776
George C Todd Iii, *CEO*
EMP: 16 EST: 1973
SALES (est): 2.3MM
SALES (corp-wide): 2.3MM Privately Held
Web: www.pupco.com
SIC: 5063 3446 Electrical supplies, nec;
Channels, furring

(G-2657)
PRECISION PARTNERS LLC
Also Called: Stampsource
1830 Statesville Ave (28206-3229)
PHONE.....................704 560-6442
Stephen Taggart, *Mgr*
EMP: 7
SALES (corp-wide): 1.13MM Privately
Held
SIC: 3499 Chair frames, metal
PA: Precision Partners, L.L.C.
400 Kellys Creek Rd # 10
Rabun Gap GA 30568

(G-2662)
**PRESTIGE CLEANING
INCORPORATED**
13903 Ballantyne Meadows Dr
(28277-3727)
PHONE.....................704 752-7747
Margo Young, *Pr*
EMP: 10 EST: 2008
SALES (est): 1.58MM Privately Held
Web: www.prestigecleaning-inc.com
SIC: 7349 1389 1711 Janitorial service,
contract basis; Construction, repair, and
dismantling services; Plumbing contractors

(G-2646)
POLYPRINT USA INC
1704 East Blvd (28203-5888)
PHONE.....................888 389-8618
EMP: 5 EST: 2010
SALES (est): 180.68K Privately Held
Web: www.polyprintdtg.com

(G-2652)
**POWERTEC INDUSTRIAL MOTORS
INC**
13509 S Point Blvd Ste 190 (28273-6897)
PHONE.....................704 227-1580
Cecil Thomas, *Pr*
Robert Lordo, *VP*

(G-2663)
PRESTRESS OF CAROLINAS LLC
11630 Texland Blvd (28273-6220)
P.O. Box 339 (28134-0339)
PHONE.....................704 587-4273
Bob Alger, *Managing Member*
EMP: 5 EST: 1998
SALES (est): 813K Privately Held

Web: www.prestressotc.com
SIC: 3272 Concrete products, precast, nec

(G-2664)
PRETORIA TRANSIT INTERIORS INC
Also Called: Specialty Manufacturing
13501 S Ridge Dr (28273-6741)
PHONE..................................615 867-8515
Greg Plate, *Manager*
▲ EMP: 64 EST: 1995
SALES (est): 889.56K **Privately Held**
SIC: 3829 Transits, surveyors'
HQ: Specialty Manufacturing, Inc.
    13501 S Ridge Dr
    Charlotte NC 28273
    704 247-9300

(G-2665)
PRIDE COMMUNICATIONS INC
Also Called: Pride Magazine
8401 University Exec Park Dr Ste 122
(28262-4357)
P.O. Box 30113 (28230-0113)
PHONE..................................704 375-9553
Dee Dixon, *Pr*
EMP: 5 EST: 2000
SALES (est): 489.81K **Privately Held**
Web: www.pridemagazineonline.com
SIC: 2721 Magazines: publishing only, not
    printed on site

(G-2666)
PRIDE PUBLISHING & TYPSG INC
920 Central Ave (28204-2028)
P.O. Box 221841 (28222-1841)
PHONE..................................704 531-9988
James Yarbrough, *Pr*
EMP: 5 EST: 1984
SQ FT: 2,200
SALES (est): 407.71K **Privately Held**
Web: www.qnotescarolinas.com
SIC: 2711 Newspapers, publishing and
    printing

(G-2667)
PRIMAX USA INC
Also Called: Primax Pumps
11000 S Commerce Blvd Ste A
(28273-6373)
PHONE..................................704 587-3377
Doug Bartholomew, *Pr*
▲ EMP: 9 EST: 2009
SQ FT: 5,500
SALES (est): 3.15MM **Privately Held**
Web: www.primaxproperties.com
SIC: 3561 Industrial pumps and parts

(G-2668)
PRINCETON INFORMATION
201 S College St (28244-0002)
PHONE..................................980 224-7114
EMP: 4 EST: 2018
SALES (est): 83.96K **Privately Held**
SIC: 2741 Miscellaneous publishing

(G-2669)
PRINT MANAGEMENT GROUP LLC
425 E Arrowhead Dr (28213-6378)
PHONE..................................704 821-0114
Matthew Wilson, *Managing Member*
EMP: 15 EST: 2001
SALES (est): 4.2MM **Privately Held**
Web: www.printmgt.biz
SIC: 2752 3993 5943 5084 Offset printing;
    Signs and advertising specialties; Office
    forms and supplies; Printing trades
    machinery, equipment, and supplies

(G-2670)
PRINT MEDIA ASSOCIATES INC
Also Called: South City Print
834 Tyvola Rd Ste 110 (28217-3542)
PHONE..................................704 529-0555
Lee Clement Huffman, *Pr*
Jacquelyn Huffman, *VP*
EMP: 8 EST: 1988
SQ FT: 5,100
SALES (est): 991.5K **Privately Held**
Web: www.southcityprint.com
SIC: 2752 Offset printing

(G-2671)
PRINTFUL INC (PA)
Also Called: Behappy.me
11025 Westlake Dr (28273-3782)
PHONE..................................818 351-7181
Alexander C Saltonstall, *CEO*
Baiba Orbidane, *
Lauris Liberts, *
EMP: 15 EST: 2013
SQ FT: 85,767
SALES (est): 86.03MM
SALES (corp-wide): 86.03MM **Privately
Held**
Web: www.printful.com
SIC: 2759 Commercial printing, nec

(G-2672)
PRODUCTION TOOL AND DIE CO INC
Also Called: PT&D
537 Scholtz Rd (28217-2138)
P.O. Box 11034 (28220-1034)
PHONE..................................704 525-0498
FAX: 704 525-3596
EMP: 10 EST: 1959
SQ FT: 12,000
SALES (est): 1MM **Privately Held**
Web: www.productiontool-die.com
SIC: 3545 Machine tool attachments and
    accessories

(G-2673)
PROFESSIONAL BUS SYSTEMS INC
201 E Cama St (28217-1701)
PHONE..................................704 333-2444
W T Hopkins, *Pr*
EMP: 4 EST: 1985
SALES (est): 330.43K **Privately Held**
Web: www.2pbsinc.com
SIC: 3993 2752 Signs and advertising
    specialties; Commercial printing,
    lithographic

(G-2674)
**PROFORM FINISHING PRODUCTS
LLC (DH)**
Also Called: National Gypsum Company
2001 Rexford Rd (28211-3415)
P.O. Box 221799 (28222-1799)
PHONE..................................704 365-7300
Thomas C Nelson, *Pr*
John Mixson, *VP*
Craig Robertson, *VP*
Dennis Merriam, *VP*
Laura Budzichowski, *Sec*
◆ EMP: 275 EST: 1993
SQ FT: 40,000
SALES (est): 780.04MM
SALES (corp-wide): 795.88MM **Privately
Held**
Web: www.nationalgypsum.com
SIC: 2679 3275 Wallboard, decorated: made
    from purchased material; Gypsum products
HQ: Delcor, Incorporated
    834 Rivit St
    Greenville NC 27834

(G-2675)
PROPLASTIC DESIGNS INC
Also Called: Clickfold Plastics
2900 Westinghouse Blvd Ste 118
(28273-5517)
PHONE..................................866 649-8665
Patrick Oltmanns, *Pr*
EMP: 15 EST: 2000
SQ FT: 5,000
SALES (est): 4.45MM **Privately Held**
Web: www.clickfoldplastics.com
SIC: 3089 Injection molding of plastics

(G-2676)
PSI CONTROL SOLUTIONS LLC (PA)
Also Called: PSI Power & Controls
9900 Twin Lakes Pkwy (28269-7614)
P.O. Box 2247 (28031)
PHONE..................................704 596-5617
Mark Todd, *Pr*
Natalie Phillips, *
EMP: 35 EST: 1993
SQ FT: 10,000
SALES (est): 24.47MM
SALES (corp-wide): 24.47MM **Privately
Held**
Web: www.psicontrolsolutions.com
SIC: 3613 Control panels, electric

(G-2677)
PUMPKIN PACIFIC LLC
10206 Pineshadow Dr Apt 107
(28262-1180)
PHONE..................................704 226-4176
Kevin Perkins, *Managing Member*
EMP: 8 EST: 2021
SALES (est): 150K **Privately Held**
Web: www.pumpkinpacific.com
SIC: 7549 7539 7534 Towing services;
    Automotive repair shops, nec; Tire repair
    shop

(G-2678)
QASIOUN LLC
Also Called: Fastsigns
4845 E Independence Blvd Unit B
(28212-5407)
PHONE..................................704 531-8000
EMP: 10 EST: 2018
SALES (est): 562.3K **Privately Held**
Web: www.fastsigns.com
SIC: 3993 Signs and advertising specialties

(G-2679)
QMAX INDUSTRIES LLC
Also Called: QMAX Industries
11000 S Commerce Blvd (28273)
P.O. Box 470924 (28247)
PHONE..................................704 643-7299
EMP: 8 EST: 2010
SALES (est): 4MM **Privately Held**
Web: www.qmaxindustries.com
SIC: 3823 Industrial process measurement
    equipment

(G-2680)
QUAD/GRAPHICS INC
Also Called: QUAD/GRAPHICS INC.
10911 Granite St (28273-6316)
PHONE..................................706 648-5456
Tom Palmer, *Mgr*
EMP: 49
SALES (corp-wide): 2.67B **Publicly Held**
Web: www.quad.com
SIC: 2752 Offset printing
PA: Quad/Graphics, Inc.
    N61 W23044 Harry's Way
    Sussex WI 53089
    414 566-6000

(G-2681)
QUAIL DRY CLEANING
5818 Prosperity Church Rd (28269-2298)
PHONE..................................704 947-7335
EMP: 6
SALES (corp-wide): 763.2K **Privately Held**
SIC: 2842 Laundry cleaning preparations
PA: Quail Dry Cleaning
    6420 Rea Rd
    Charlotte NC 28277
    704 541-6199

(G-2682)
QUALISEAL TECHNOLOGY LLC
5605 Carnegie Blvd Ste 500 (28209-4642)
PHONE..................................704 731-1522
EMP: 4
SALES (est): 897.11K
SALES (corp-wide): 1.05B **Publicly Held**
SIC: 3053 Gaskets; packing and sealing
    devices
PA: Enpro Inc.
    5605 Crnegie Blvd Ste 500
    Charlotte NC 28209
    704 731-1500

(G-2683)
QUALITROL COMPANY LLC
3030 Whitehall Park Dr (28273-3334)
PHONE..................................704 587-9267
Roy Pelkey, *Brnch Mgr*
EMP: 7
SALES (corp-wide): 6.23B **Publicly Held**
Web: www.qualitrolcorp.com
SIC: 3829 Measuring and controlling
    devices, nec
HQ: Qualitrol Company Llc
    1385 Fairport Rd
    Fairport NY 14450
    585 586-1515

(G-2684)
**QUALITY PRODUCTS & MACHINE
LLC**
4600 Westinghouse Blvd (28273-9619)
PHONE..................................704 504-3330
Brent Zelnak, *Managing Member*
Stephen Zelnak, *
Julius A Schachner Iv, *Managing Member*
EMP: 41 EST: 1962
SQ FT: 43,000
SALES (est): 3.77MM **Privately Held**
Web: www.qprod.com
SIC: 3599 Machine shop, jobbing and repair

(G-2685)
QUEEN CITY SCREEN PRINTERS
1907 Bobolink Ln (28226-5700)
PHONE..................................980 335-2334
EMP: 6 EST: 2019
SALES (est): 87.92K **Privately Held**
Web: www.queencityscreenprinters.com
SIC: 2759 Screen printing

(G-2686)
R J YELLER DISTRIBUTION INC
Also Called: Biz On Wheels
1835 Lindbergh St (28208-3768)
PHONE..................................800 944-2589
Ron Yeller, *Pr*
EMP: 4 EST: 2007
SALES (est): 1.44MM **Privately Held**
Web: www.foodtrucks4sale.com
SIC: 3713 Beverage truck bodies

(G-2687)
R T BARBEE COMPANY INC
724 Montana Dr Ste F (28216-3997)
P.O. Box 37246 (28237-7246)
PHONE..................................704 375-4421

David Schrum, *Managing Member*
John L Schrum Iii, *Pr*
Ramsy Schrum, *VP*
EMP: 14 EST: 1932
SQ FT: 5,000
SALES (est): 3.5MM Privately Held
Web: www.barbeetickets.com
SIC: 2752 2672 Forms, business: lithographed; Paper; coated and laminated, nec

(G-2688)
RANDALL-REILLY LLC
Also Called: Real Time Content
1509 Orchard Lake Dr Ste E (28270-1473)
PHONE.................................704 814-1390
David Schwartz, *Brnch Mgr*
EMP: 125
Web: www.randallreilly.com
SIC: 2721 7331 Magazines: publishing and printing; Mailing list compilers
HQ: Randall-Reilly, Llc
    1460 Nrthbank Pkwy Ste 10
    Tuscaloosa AL 35406
    855 288-3783

(G-2689)
RAPID RESPONSE INC
Also Called: Label Store, The
218 Westinghouse Blvd (28273-6242)
PHONE.................................704 588-8890
Harris E Clark Junior, *Pr*
Carolyn Clark, *VP*
EMP: 4 EST: 1988
SALES (est): 223.96K Privately Held
Web: www.rapidresponselabels.com
SIC: 2679 5084 Labels, paper: made from purchased material; Printing trades machinery, equipment, and supplies

(G-2690)
RAPID RUN TRANSPORT LLC
12430 Clackwyck Ln (28262-1628)
PHONE.................................704 615-3458
Jonathon Lilley, *CEO*
Ankh Alli, *Managing Member*
EMP: 10 EST: 2018
SALES (est): 431.72K Privately Held
Web: www.rapidruntransportllc.com
SIC: 4215 4731 3537 Courier services, except by air; Freight forwarding; Trucks, tractors, loaders, carriers, and similar equipment

(G-2691)
RASIN HAITIAN RESTAURANT LLC ✪
10104 Bellhaven Blvd (28214)
PHONE.................................704 780-5129
EMP: 5 EST: 2023
SALES (est): 222.74K Privately Held
SIC: 2599 Bar, restaurant and cafeteria furniture

(G-2692)
RAY ROOFING COMPANY INC
2921 N Tryon St (28206-2762)
P.O. Box 19150 (28219-9150)
PHONE.................................704 372-0100
Michael W Wilkinson, *Pr*
John W Wilkinson, *
James R Bradley, *
EMP: 24 EST: 1904
SQ FT: 20,000
SALES (est): 4.54MM Privately Held
Web: www.raycompany.com
SIC: 3444 1761 Sheet metalwork; Roofing contractor

(G-2693)
RE SHADS GROUP LLC
5819 Creola Rd (28270-5223)
PHONE.................................704 299-8972
EMP: 4 EST: 2019
SALES (est): 60K Privately Held
SIC: 1389 Construction, repair, and dismantling services

(G-2694)
REACT INNOVATIONS LLC
1809 Browning Ave (28205-3549)
PHONE.................................704 773-1276
EMP: 4 EST: 2015
SALES (est): 611.64K Privately Held
Web: www.reactinnovations.com
SIC: 3841 Surgical and medical instruments

(G-2695)
REAGENTS HOLDINGS LLC (HQ)
3825 Parrott Dr (28214-9001)
P.O. Box 788 (28012-0788)
PHONE.................................800 732-8484
Nate Meyer, *Pr*
Frank Vrtis, *VP Sls*
EMP: 28 EST: 2009
SALES (est): 25.39MM
SALES (corp-wide): 25.39MM Privately Held
Web: www.reagents.com
SIC: 5169 2819 2869 Chemicals and allied products, nec; Chemicals, reagent grade: refined from technical grade; Industrial organic chemicals, nec
PA: Tcp Analytical, Llc
    300 Parkway View Dr
    Pittsburgh PA 15205
    800 637-6074

(G-2696)
REC PLUS INC
1101 Central Ave (28204-2198)
PHONE.................................704 375-9098
Roy L Smith, *Ch*
Linda M Smith, *
Leigh Ann Neely, *
Jamie Neely, *
EMP: 42 EST: 1984
SQ FT: 20,000
SALES (est): 2.4MM Privately Held
Web: www.recognitionplus.net
SIC: 5999 3993 5699 Trophies and plaques; Signs and advertising specialties; Sports apparel

(G-2697)
RECOUPL INC
16430 Redstone Mountain Ln (28277-2994)
PHONE.................................704 544-0202
Richard L Smith, *Pr*
Rl Smith, *Pr*
Barbara Smith, *VP*
Barbara Smith, *Prin*
EMP: 5 EST: 1996
SALES (est): 178.5K Privately Held
SIC: 3569 Firehose equipment: driers, rack, and reels

(G-2698)
RED HAND MEDIA LLC (PA)
Also Called: Business North Carolina
1230 W Morehead St Ste 308 (28208-5205)
PHONE.................................704 523-6987
David Kinney, *Managing Member*
EMP: 13 EST: 1981
SQ FT: 5,000
SALES (est): 1.45MM
SALES (corp-wide): 1.45MM Privately Held
Web: www.businessnc.com

SIC: 2721 Magazines: publishing and printing

(G-2699)
REDI-MIX LP
Also Called: Ready Mix
11509 Reames Rd (28269-7676)
PHONE.................................704 596-6511
Dan Montgomony, *Brnch Mgr*
EMP: 53
SIC: 3531 Construction machinery
HQ: Redi-Mix Lp
    1445 Mac Arthur Dr Ste 13
    Carrollton TX 75007
    972 242-4550

(G-2700)
REDTRUC LLC ✪
5131 Gorham Dr (28226-6405)
PHONE.................................704 968-7888
Afshin Ghazi, *Managing Member*
EMP: 4 EST: 2024
SALES (est): 1.1MM Privately Held
SIC: 7372 7389 Application computer software; Business Activities at Non-Commercial Site

(G-2701)
REEDY INTERNATIONAL CORP (PA)
Also Called: Reedy Chem Foam Spclty Addtves
9301 Forsyth Park Dr Ste A (28273-3957)
P.O. Box 38486 (28278-1008)
PHONE.................................980 819-6930
Peter Schroeck, *Pr*
Elena Miller, *Ex VP*
Anne Marie Reedy, *CFO*
Kristen Reedy, *VP*
▼ **EMP: 11 EST: 1989**
SALES (est): 2.52MM Privately Held
Web: www.reedyintl.com
SIC: 3086 5169 Carpet and rug cushions, foamed plastics; Chemicals and allied products, nec

(G-2702)
REEL-SCOUT INC
1900 Abbott St Ste 100 (28203-4497)
PHONE.................................704 348-1484
Ed Henegar, *Pr*
EMP: 15 EST: 2001
SALES (est): 211.61K Privately Held
Web: www.reel-scout.com
SIC: 3652 Prerecorded records and tapes

(G-2703)
REGAL REXNORD CORPORATION
701 Carrier Dr (28216-3445)
PHONE.................................800 825-6544
EMP: 7
SALES (corp-wide): 6.03B Publicly Held
Web: www.regalrexnord.com
SIC: 3621 3566 Motors and generators; Speed changers, drives, and gears
PA: Regal Rexnord Corporation
    111 W Michigan St
    Milwaukee WI 53203
    608 364-8800

(G-2704)
REGINALD DWAYNE DILLARD
Also Called: Global Dominion Enterprise
13026 Planters Row Dr (28278-0010)
PHONE.................................980 254-5505
Reginald D'wayne Dillard, *Owner*
EMP: 5 EST: 2022
SALES (est): 1.06MM Privately Held
SIC: 3537 Trucks, tractors, loaders, carriers, and similar equipment

(G-2705)
REMAN TECHNOLOGIES INC
11421 Reames Rd (28269-7675)
PHONE.................................704 921-2293
Carl Keller, *Pr*
▲ **EMP: 9 EST: 2004**
SALES (est): 3.9MM Privately Held
Web: remantechnologies.lbu.com
SIC: 3694 Engine electrical equipment

(G-2706)
REMEDIOS LLC
Also Called: Component Sourcing Intl
1301 Westinghouse Blvd Ste I (28273-6475)
PHONE.................................203 453-6000
▲ **EMP: 5 EST: 2003**
SALES (est): 573.52K Privately Held
SIC: 3448 Prefabricated metal components

(G-2707)
REMINGTON 1816 FOUNDATION
Also Called: 1816
1435 W Morehead St Ste 120 (28208-5208)
P.O. Box 700 (27025-0700)
PHONE.................................866 686-7778
Jason Watson, *Prin*
EMP: 4 EST: 2008
SALES (est): 99.5K Privately Held
SIC: 2342 2389 Corset accessories: clasps, stays, etc.; Uniforms and vestments

(G-2708)
REMODEEZ LLC
1920 Abbott St Ste 303 (28203-5194)
P.O. Box 301 (28106-0301)
PHONE.................................704 428-9050
Jason Jacobs, *CEO*
EMP: 10 EST: 2014
SQ FT: 1,700
SALES (est): 329.07K Privately Held
Web: www.remodeez.com
SIC: 2842 Deodorants, nonpersonal

(G-2709)
RENEWABLE POWER PRODUCERS LLC
10600 Nations Ford Rd # 150 (28273-5762)
PHONE.................................704 844-8990
EMP: 7 EST: 2009
SALES (est): 2.1MM Privately Held
Web: www.landfillgroup.com
SIC: 1321 Natural gas liquids

(G-2710)
RENEWBLE ENRGY INTGRTION GROUP
9115 Old Statesville Rd Ste A (28269-6605)
PHONE.................................704 596-6186
EMP: 8 EST: 2016
SQ FT: 3,500
SALES (est): 1.78MM Privately Held
Web: www.reig-us.com
SIC: 3825 Instruments to measure electricity

(G-2711)
RENNER USA CORP
651 Michael Wylie Dr (28217-1546)
P.O. Box 7172 (27264-7172)
PHONE.................................704 527-9261
Marcelo Cenacchi, *Pr*
Leo Migoto, *Dir*
▲ **EMP: 5 EST: 2003**
SALES (est): 7.81MM Privately Held
Web: rennerwoodcoatings.a2web1.srv.br
SIC: 2499 Decorative wood and woodwork
HQ: Renner Sayerlack S/A
    Av. Jordano Mendes 1500
    Cajamar SP 07776

▲ = Import ▼ = Export
◆ = Import/Export

(G-2712)
RENNER WOOD COMPANIES
651 Michael Wylie Dr (28217-1546)
PHONE.....................704 527-9261
EMP: 11 EST: 2020
SALES (est): 2.39MM Privately Held
Web: rennerwoodcoatings.a2web1.srv.br
SIC: 2851 Epoxy coatings

(G-2713)
RESERVOIR GROUP LLC
9219 Heritage Woods Pl (28269-0300)
PHONE.....................610 764-0269
EMP: 5 EST: 2017
SALES (est): 472.46K Privately Held
Web: www.reservoirgroup.com
SIC: 1389 Oil field services, nec

(G-2714)
RESIDENT CULTURE BREWING LLC
2101 Central Ave (28205-5203)
P.O. Box 36369 (28236-6369)
PHONE.....................704 333-1862
Phillip Mclamb, CEO
EMP: 22 EST: 2016
SALES (est): 2.38MM Privately Held
Web: www.residentculturebrewing.com
SIC: 5813 2082 Bars and lounges; Beer
(alcoholic beverage)

(G-2715)
RESIDEO LLC
Also Called: ADI Global Distribution
800 Clanton Rd Ste F (28217-1324)
PHONE.....................704 525-8899
Dan Denton, Mgr
EMP: 7
SALES (corp-wide): 6.76B Publicly Held
Web: www.adiglobaldistribution.us
SIC: 5063 3669 Electrical apparatus and
equipment; Emergency alarms
HQ: Resideo Llc
275 Bradhollow Rd Ste 400
Melville NY 11747
631 692-1000

(G-2716)
REVLOC RECLAMATION SERVICE INC
13024 Ballantyne Corporate Pl Ste 700
(28277-2113)
PHONE.....................704 625-4900
EMP: 5 EST: 2017
SALES (est): 2.22MM
SALES (corp-wide): 999.35MM Publicly
Held
SIC: 3511 Turbines and turbine generator
sets
PA: Babcock & Wilcox Enterprises, Inc.
1200 E Market St Ste 650
Akron OH 44305
330 753-4511

(G-2717)
REVMAX PERFORMANCE LLC
4400 Westinghouse Blvd 2 (28273-9620)
PHONE.....................877 780-4334
EMP: 10 EST: 2017
SALES (est): 5.25MM Privately Held
Web: www.revmaxconverters.com
SIC: 3465 Body parts, automobile: stamped
metal

(G-2718)
REXAM BEAUTY AND CLOSURES INC
Also Called: Rexam Cosmetic Packaging
4201 Congress St Ste 340 (28209-4640)
PHONE.....................704 551-1500
▲ EMP: 540

SIC: 3089 Injection molding of plastics

(G-2719)
REYNAERS INC
9347 D Ducks Ln (28273-4553)
PHONE.....................480 272-9688
EMP: 25
SALES (corp-wide): 409.32MM Privately
Held
Web: www.reynaers.us
SIC: 3442 Metal doors, sash, and trim
HQ: Reynaers Inc.
21430 N 15th Ln Ste 100
Phoenix AZ 85027
480 272-9688

(G-2720)
REYNOLDS ADVANCED MTLS INC
10725a John Price Rd (28273-4529)
PHONE.....................704 357-0600
Fal Bianco, Brnch Mgr
EMP: 4
SALES (corp-wide): 3.4MM Privately Held
Web: www.reynoldsam.com
SIC: 3442 5051 Molding, trim, and stripping;
Castings, rough: iron or steel
PA: Reynolds Advanced Materials, Inc.
13700 Diplomat Dr
Farmers Branch TX 75234
800 421-4378

(G-2721)
REYNOLDS AND REYNOLDS COMPANY
Also Called: Reynolds & Reynolds
6000 Monroe Rd Ste 340 (28212-6178)
PHONE.....................321 287-3939
Jim Riggs, Mgr
EMP: 6
SALES (corp-wide): 1.54B Privately Held
Web: www.reyrey.com
SIC: 2761 5045 7372 Manifold business
forms; Computers, nec; Application
computer software
HQ: The Reynolds And Reynolds Company
1 Reynolds Way
Kettering OH 45430
937 485-2000

(G-2722)
RF DAS SYSTEMS INC
Also Called: Emergency Responder Systems
8230 Trail View Dr (28226-4672)
P.O. Box 471309 (28247-1309)
PHONE.....................980 279-2388
John Bone, Prin
EMP: 9 EST: 2018
SALES (est): 972.96K Privately Held
Web: www.rfdassystems.com
SIC: 3663 Antennas, transmitting and
communications

(G-2723)
RGA ENTERPRISES INC (PA)
4001 Performance Rd (28214-8090)
PHONE.....................704 398-0487
Will Fidler, CEO
Julie Miller, *
EMP: 100 EST: 1977
SQ FT: 67,000
SALES (est): 25.67MM
SALES (corp-wide): 25.67MM Privately
Held
Web: www.rgaenterprises.com
SIC: 2842 Specialty cleaning

(G-2724)
RICHA INC
231 E Tremont Ave (28203-5021)
PHONE.....................704 944-0230
Katherine Gerbanni, Mgr

EMP: 4
SALES (corp-wide): 7.13MM Privately
Held
Web: www.richa.com
SIC: 7374 7334 5199 2752 Computer
graphics service; Blueprinting service;
Architects' supplies (non-durable); Offset
printing
PA: Richa, Inc.
800 N College St
Charlotte NC 28206
704 331-9744

(G-2725)
RICHA INC (PA)
Also Called: RICHA GRAPHICS
800 N College St (28206-3227)
PHONE.....................704 331-9744
Rita Vyas, Pr
Suresh Vyas, VP
EMP: 14 EST: 1985
SQ FT: 11,500
SALES (est): 7.13MM
SALES (corp-wide): 7.13MM Privately
Held
Web: www.richa.com
SIC: 7374 7334 5199 2752 Computer
graphics service; Blueprinting service;
Architects' supplies (non-durable); Offset
printing

(G-2726)
RICHARD E PAGE
8500 Andrew Carnegie Blvd (28262-8500)
PHONE.....................704 988-7090
Richard Page, Owner
EMP: 4 EST: 2017
SALES (est): 129.64K Privately Held
SIC: 2261 Finishing plants, cotton

(G-2727)
RIPARI AUTOMOTIVE LLC
2910 Patishall Ln (28214-5610)
PHONE.....................585 267-0228
Sabina Dixon, Managing Member
EMP: 7 EST: 2020
SALES (est): 701.31K Privately Held
Web: www.ripari-automotive.com
SIC: 3714 Motor vehicle parts and
accessories

(G-2728)
RNS INTERNATIONAL INC
5001 Sirus Ln (28208-6397)
P.O. Box 19867 (28219-0867)
PHONE.....................704 329-0444
Hans Nocher, Pr
EMP: 33 EST: 1983
SQ FT: 5,664
SALES (est): 1.54MM Privately Held
Web: www.rns-usa.com
SIC: 5013 3829 3825 Testing equipment,
engine; Measuring and controlling devices,
nec; Instruments to measure electricity

(G-2729)
ROADACTIVE SUSPENSION INC
2705 Whitehall Park Dr (28273-3350)
PHONE.....................704 523-2646
Clive Schewitz, Pr
Andrea Schewitz, VP
▲ EMP: 8 EST: 1997
SALES (est): 1.02MM Privately Held
Web: www.activesuspension.com
SIC: 3714 Motor vehicle parts and
accessories

(G-2730)
ROBERTS POLYPRO INC
5416 Wyoming Ave (28273-8861)
PHONE.....................704 588-1794

John W Paxton, CEO
Allan Sutherland, *
Jack H Aguero, *
◆ EMP: 41 EST: 1978
SQ FT: 80,000
SALES (est): 9.1MM Privately Held
Web: www.robertspolypro.com
SIC: 3565 Packaging machinery
HQ: Pro Mach, Inc.
50 E Rvrcnter Blvd Ste 18
Covington KY 41011
513 831-8778

(G-2731)
ROCKWELL AUTOMATION INC
9401 Southern Pine Blvd Ste E
(28273-5596)
PHONE.....................704 665-6000
Michael Carbone, Mgr
EMP: 47
Web: www.rockwellautomation.com
SIC: 3625 Control equipment, electric
PA: Rockwell Automation, Inc.
1201 S 2nd St
Milwaukee WI 53204

(G-2732)
ROLF KOERNER LLC
Also Called: Rolf Koerner
514 Springbrook Rd Ste B (28217-2170)
PHONE.....................704 714-8866
Philip Lail, Managing Member
◆ EMP: 5 EST: 2005
SALES (est): 875.22K Privately Held
Web: www.rolfkoerner.com
SIC: 3496 Miscellaneous fabricated wire
products

(G-2733)
ROYAL BATHS MANUFACTURING CO
Also Called: Royal Manufacturing
4525 Reagan Dr # A (28206-3192)
PHONE.....................704 837-1701
EMP: 42
SALES (corp-wide): 43.25MM Privately
Held
Web: www.royal-mfg.com
SIC: 3842 3949 3432 3281 Whirlpool baths,
hydrotherapy equipment; Sporting and
athletic goods, nec; Plumbing fixture fittings
and trim; Cut stone and stone products
PA: Royal Baths Manufacturing Company
14635 Chrisman Rd
Houston TX 77039
281 442-3400

(G-2734)
ROYAL CUP INC
3010 Hutchison Mcdonald Rd Ste F
(28269-4280)
PHONE.....................704 597-5756
Scottie Kimble, Mgr
EMP: 18
SALES (corp-wide): 243.1MM Privately
Held
Web: www.royalcupcoffee.com
SIC: 2095 5149 Roasted coffee; Coffee,
green or roasted
PA: Royal Cup Inc.
160 Cleage Dr
Birmingham AL 35217
205 849-5836

(G-2735)
ROYAL TEXTILE PRODUCTS SW LLC
2918 Caldwell Ridge Pkwy (28213-5888)
PHONE.....................602 276-4598
Julie Henkel, Mgr
Kristian Henkel, Mgr
EMP: 5 EST: 2017

SALES (est): 171.17K **Privately Held**
Web: www.royaltextileproductssw.com
SIC: 2591 5023 7389 Window blinds;
   Window covering parts and accessories;
   Business Activities at Non-Commercial Site

(G-2736)
ROYAL WIRE PRODUCTS INC
7500 Grier Rd (28213-6536)
PHONE.................................704 596-2110
Rudy Maschke Junior, *Mgr*
EMP: 20
SQ FT: 17,520
SALES (corp-wide): 9.01MM **Privately Held**
Web: www.royalwire.com
SIC: 3496 Miscellaneous fabricated wire products
PA: Royal Wire Products, Inc.
   13450 York Delta Dr
   North Royalton OH 44133
   440 237-8787

(G-2737)
RSC BIO SOLUTIONS LLC (HQ)
Also Called: Terresolve
2318 Arty Ave (28208-5104)
PHONE.................................800 661-3558
Mark Miller, *CEO*
Curtis R Scharf, *Pr*
James M Pertas, *Ch Bd*
James D Ireland Iii, *Ltd Pt*
Mike Guggenheimer, *Dir*
EMP: 5 EST: 1996
SALES (est): 11.95MM
SALES (corp-wide): 11.95MM **Privately Held**
Web: www.rscbio.com
SIC: 2899 Chemical preparations, nec
PA: Blumenthal Holdings, Llc
   1355 Greenwood Clfs # 200
   Charlotte NC 28204
   704 688-2302

(G-2738)
RSI LEASING INC NS TBT
2820 Nevada Blvd (28273-6433)
PHONE.................................704 587-9300
James Davis, *Prin*
EMP: 4 EST: 2012
SALES (est): 116.19K **Privately Held**
SIC: 4213 3535 3537 Trucking, except local;
   Bulk handling conveyor systems; Trucks,
   tractors, loaders, carriers, and similar
   equipment

(G-2739)
RSTACK SOLUTIONS LLC
3540 Toringdon Way Ste 200 (28277-3867)
PHONE.................................980 337-1295
EMP: 10
SALES (est): 842.35K **Privately Held**
Web: www.rstacksolutions.com
SIC: 7372 Prepackaged software

(G-2740)
RTX CORPORATION
Also Called: Goodrich Fuel Utility Systems
2730 W Tyvola Rd (28217-4527)
PHONE.................................704 423-7000
EMP: 7
SALES (corp-wide): 80.74B **Publicly Held**
Web: www.rtx.com
SIC: 3728 Aircraft parts and equipment, nec
PA: Rtx Corporation
   1000 Wilson Blvd
   Arlington VA 22209
   781 522-3000

(G-2741)
RUCKER INTRGRTED LOGISTICS LLC
15519 Rathangan Dr (28273-7012)
PHONE.................................704 352-2018
EMP: 4 EST: 2021
SALES (est): 547.78K **Privately Held**
SIC: 3537 7389 Trucks: freight, baggage,
   etc.: industrial, except mining; Business
   Activities at Non-Commercial Site

(G-2742)
RUDDICK OPERATING COMPANY LLC
301 S Tryon St Ste 1800 (28282-1905)
PHONE.................................704 372-5404
EMP: 20000
SIC: 5411 2284 Supermarkets, chain; Cotton thread

(G-2743)
RUSSELL T BUNDY ASSOCIATES INC
Also Called: Pan Glo, Charlotte
3400 Pelton St (28217-1320)
PHONE.................................704 523-6132
Robert Sloan, *Mgr*
EMP: 13
SALES (corp-wide): 46.03MM **Privately Held**
Web: www.bundybakingsolutions.com
SIC: 3479 Pan glazing
PA: Russell T. Bundy Associates, Inc.
   417 E Water St
   Urbana OH 43078
   937 652-2151

(G-2744)
RUTLAND GROUP INC
13827 Carowinds Blvd Ste A (28273-5007)
PHONE.................................704 553-0046
Jimmy Reed, *Brnch Mgr*
EMP: 5
Web: www.avientspecialtyinks.com
SIC: 2893 Printing ink
HQ: Rutland Group, Inc.
   10021 Rodney St
   Pineville NC 28134

(G-2745)
S TRI INC
Also Called: Hi-Tech Signs
10110 Johnston Rd Ste 12 (28210-9202)
PHONE.................................704 542-8186
Art Sullivan, *Pr*
Tommie Sullivan, *Mgr*
EMP: 6 EST: 1988
SQ FT: 1,200
SALES (est): 117.02K **Privately Held**
SIC: 3993 Signs, not made in custom sign
   painting shops

(G-2746)
S&A MARKETING INC
Also Called: M & M Graphics
2526 S Tyron St (28203-4966)
P.O. Box 36633 (28236-6633)
PHONE.................................704 376-0938
Matthre Christopher Kinser, *Pr*
EMP: 4 EST: 2018
SALES (est): 340.42K **Privately Held**
Web: www.allegramarketingprint.com
SIC: 2752 Offset printing

(G-2747)
S-L SNACKS NATIONAL LLC (DH)
13024 Balntyn Corp Pl (28277-2113)
P.O. Box 32368 (28232-2368)
PHONE.................................704 554-1421
▼ EMP: 31 EST: 2010

SALES (est): 357.68MM
SALES (corp-wide): 8.56B **Publicly Held**
Web: www.lance.com
SIC: 2052 Cookies
HQ: Snyder's-Lance, Inc.
   13515 Balntyn Corp Pl
   Charlotte NC 08103
   704 554-1421

(G-2748)
S-L SNACKS PA LLC
13024 Balntyn Corp Pl (28277-2113)
P.O. Box 32368 (28232-2368)
PHONE.................................704 554-1421
EMP: 123 EST: 2011
SQ FT: 357,193
SALES (est): 9.15MM
SALES (corp-wide): 8.56B **Publicly Held**
SIC: 2052 2096 Cookies and crackers;
   Potato chips and similar snacks
HQ: S-L Snacks National, Llc
   13024 Balntyn Corp Pl
   Charlotte NC 28277

(G-2749)
SALICE AMERICA INC (DH)
Also Called: Salice
2123 Crown Centre Dr (28227-7701)
PHONE.................................704 841-7810
Luciano Salice, *CEO*
Matteo Fregosi, *
Massimo Salice, *
Sergio Salice, *
Lori Miller, *
◆ EMP: 23 EST: 1989
SQ FT: 100,000
SALES (est): 17.95MM
SALES (corp-wide): 2.67MM **Privately Held**
Web: www.salice.com
SIC: 5072 3822 3545 Furniture hardware,
   nec; Damper operators: pneumatic,
   thermostatic, electric; Machine tool
   accessories
HQ: Arturo Salice Spa
   Via Provinciale Novedratese 10
   Novedrate CO 22060
   031790424

(G-2750)
SALONEXCLUSIVE BEAUTY LLC
3015 Kraus Glen Dr (28214-8918)
PHONE.................................704 488-3909
EMP: 8 EST: 2022
SALES (est): 80.13K **Privately Held**
SIC: 2844 7389 Hair preparations, including
   shampoos; Business services, nec

(G-2751)
SALUD LLC
Also Called: Brewpub
3306 N Davidson St (28205-1036)
PHONE.................................980 495-6612
Jason Scott Glunt, *Mgr*
EMP: 24 EST: 2012
SALES (est): 2.14MM **Privately Held**
Web: www.saludbeershop.com
SIC: 2082 Beer (alcoholic beverage)

(G-2752)
SALVIN DENTAL SPECIALTIES LLC
3450 Latrobe Dr (28211-4847)
PHONE.................................704 442-5400
Robert H Salvin, *CEO*
William Simmons, *Pr*
Greg Slayton, *VP*
◆ EMP: 60 EST: 1981
SQ FT: 12,500
SALES (est): 8.18MM
SALES (corp-wide): 191.04MM **Privately Held**

Web: www.salvin.com
SIC: 3843 Dental equipment and supplies
PA: Young Innovations, Inc.
   2260 Wendt St
   Algonquin IL 60102
   847 458-5400

(G-2753)
SAM M BUTLER INC
Also Called: Service Thread Co
447 S Sharon Amity Rd Ste 125
   (28211-2877)
P.O. Box 673 (28353-0673)
PHONE.................................704 364-8647
Jim Myers, *Mgr*
EMP: 45
SALES (corp-wide): 12.55MM **Privately Held**
Web: www.servicethread.com
SIC: 5131 2284 2282 Piece goods and
   notions; Thread mills; Throwing and
   winding mills
PA: Sam M. Butler, Inc.
   17900 Dana Dr
   Laurinburg NC 28352
   910 277-7456

(G-2754)
SANHER STUCCO & LATHER INC
1101 Tyvola Rd Ste 110 (28217-3515)
PHONE.................................704 241-8517
Carlos Desantiago, *Pr*
EMP: 10 EST: 2008
SALES (est): 1.43MM **Privately Held**
SIC: 3299 Stucco

(G-2755)
SAS INSTITUTE INC
2200 Interstate North Dr (28280)
PHONE.................................704 831-5595
EMP: 5
SALES (corp-wide): 1.35B **Privately Held**
Web: www.sas.com
SIC: 7372 Application computer software
PA: Sas Institute Inc.
   100 Sas Campus Dr
   Cary NC 27513
   919 677-8000

(G-2756)
SAS INSTITUTE INC
525 N Tryon St Ste 1600 (28202-0213)
PHONE.................................704 331-3956
Marcus Hassen, *Brnch Mgr*
EMP: 6
SALES (corp-wide): 1.35B **Privately Held**
Web: www.sas.com
SIC: 7372 Application computer software
PA: Sas Institute Inc.
   100 Sas Campus Dr
   Cary NC 27513
   919 677-8000

(G-2757)
SATO AMERICA LLC (HQ)
Also Called: Sato America
14125 S Bridge Cir (28273-6747)
PHONE.................................704 644-1650
Goro Yumiba, *CEO*
Tim Cook, *
Rick Rumler, *
▲ EMP: 150 EST: 2002
SALES (est): 46.94MM **Privately Held**
Web: www.satoamerica.com
SIC: 5045 7372 Printers, computer;
   Prepackaged software
PA: Sato Holdings Corporation
   3-1-1, Shibaura
   Minato-Ku TKY 108-0

(G-2758)
SATO GLOBAL SOLUTIONS INC
10350 Nations Ford Rd Ste A (28273-5824)
PHONE......................954 261-3279
Yumiba Goro, *CEO*
EMP: 6 EST: 2014
SALES (est): 1.03MM **Privately Held**
Web: www.sato-global.com
SIC: 3577 7373 7371 3955 Bar code (magnetic ink) printers; Computer-aided manufacturing (CAM) systems service; Software programming applications; Print cartridges for laser and other computer printers
PA: Sato Holdings Corporation
    3-1-1, Shibaura
    Minato-Ku TKY 108-0

(G-2759)
SAVE-A-LOAD INC
327 W Tremont Ave Ste A (28203-4980)
PHONE......................704 650-4947
EMP: 8 EST: 2018
SALES (est): 634.44K **Privately Held**
Web: hd.tramec.com
SIC: 3714 Motor vehicle parts and accessories

(G-2760)
SC JOHNSON PROF USA INC (DH)
2815 Coliseum Centre Dr Ste 600
(28217-0144)
PHONE......................443 521-1606
Michael Slagg, *Pr*
Stephen Havala, *
◆ EMP: 114 EST: 1989
SQ FT: 75,000
SALES (est): 49.49MM **Privately Held**
Web: www.scjp.com
SIC: 2844 Face creams or lotions
HQ: Sc Johnson Professional Group Limited
    Denby Hall Way
    Ripley DE5 8

(G-2761)
SCALTROL INC
2010 Sterling Rd (28209-1612)
P.O. Box 3288 (30024-0990)
PHONE......................678 990-0858
Chris Hansen, *Pr*
EMP: 6 EST: 1994
SALES (est): 477.11K **Privately Held**
Web: www.scaltrolinc.com
SIC: 3589 5074 5999 Water purification equipment, household type; Water purification equipment; Water purification equipment

(G-2762)
**SCENTAIR TECHNOLOGIES LLC
(PA)**
3810 Shutterfly Rd Ste 900 (28217-3071)
PHONE......................704 504-2320
Andrew Kindfuller, *CEO*
Brian Edwards, *CRO*
Daniel Behrendt, *
▲ EMP: 105 EST: 2004
SQ FT: 33,000
SALES (est): 46.97MM
SALES (corp-wide): 46.97MM **Privately Held**
Web: www.scentair.com
SIC: 8731 2844 2821 Commercial physical research; Perfumes, natural or synthetic; Plastics materials and resins

(G-2763)
**SCHAEFER SYSTEMS
INTERNATIONAL INC (HQ)**
Also Called: S S I

5032 Sirona Dr Ste 100 (28273)
PHONE......................704 944-4500
◆ EMP: 250 EST: 1968
SALES (est): 208.08MM
SALES (corp-wide): 1.88B **Privately Held**
Web: www.ssi-schaefer.com
SIC: 5084 7372 5046 5099 Industrial machinery and equipment; Business oriented computer software; Shelving, commercial and industrial; Containers: glass, metal or plastic
PA: Ssi Schafer Gmbh & Co Kg
    Fritz-Schafer-Str. 20
    Neunkirchen NW 57290
    2735701

(G-2764)
SCHAEFER SYSTEMS INTL INC
Also Called: Schaefer Shelving
10125 Westlake Dr Bldg 3 (28273-3786)
PHONE......................704 944-4500
EMP: 6
SALES (corp-wide): 1.88B **Privately Held**
Web: www.schaefershelving.com
SIC: 3089 Garbage containers, plastics
HQ: Schaefer Systems International, Inc.
    5032 Sirona Dr Ste 100
    Charlotte NC 28273
    704 944-4500

(G-2765)
SCHAEFER SYSTEMS INTL INC
10124 Westlake Dr (28273-3739)
PHONE......................704 944-4550
Arnold J Heuzen, *Brnch Mgr*
EMP: 5
SALES (corp-wide): 1.88B **Privately Held**
Web: www.ssi-schaefer.com
SIC: 3089 5046 5099 5084 Garbage containers, plastics; Shelving, commercial and industrial; Containers: glass, metal or plastic; Industrial machinery and equipment
HQ: Schaefer Systems International, Inc.
    5032 Sirona Dr Ste 100
    Charlotte NC 28273
    704 944-4500

(G-2766)
SCHLEICH USA INC
10000 Twin Lakes Pkwy Ste A
(28269-7653)
PHONE......................704 659-7997
Michael Keaton, *Pr*
▲ EMP: 9 EST: 2009
SALES (est): 7.52MM **Privately Held**
Web: us.schleich-s.com
SIC: 3944 Games, toys, and children's vehicles
HQ: Schleich Gmbh
    St.-Martin-Str. 102
    Munchen BY 81669
    717180010

(G-2767)
SCHLETTER NA INC
11529 Wilmar Blvd (28273-6448)
PHONE......................704 595-4200
Adrian Noronho, *Pr*
EMP: 14 EST: 2018
SALES (est): 1.06MM **Privately Held**
Web: www.schletter-group.com
SIC: 3564 Air purification equipment

(G-2768)
SCHOOL DIRECTOREASE LLC
1213 W Morehead St (28208-5581)
PHONE......................240 206-6273
EMP: 4 EST: 2009
SALES (est): 244.65K **Privately Held**
Web: www.atozconnect.com

SIC: 2741 7371 Telephone and other directory publishing; Software programming applications

(G-2769)
SCIENTIGO INC (PA)
6701 Carmel Rd Ste 205 (28226-0210)
PHONE......................704 837-0500
Stuart J Yarbrough, *Ch Bd*
Harry Pettit, *CEO*
Paul Odom Senior, *Software Vice President*
Clifford A Clark, *CFO*
EMP: 6 EST: 1995
SQ FT: 5,000
SALES (est): 2.61MM
SALES (corp-wide): 2.61MM **Privately Held**
SIC: 7372 Business oriented computer software

(G-2770)
SCORPIO ACQUISITION CORP
9335 Harris Corners Pkwy Ste 300
(28269-3817)
PHONE......................704 697-5100
J Joel Hackney Junior, *Pr*
◆ EMP: 5 EST: 2010
SALES (est): 838.68K **Publicly Held**
SIC: 2297 Nonwoven fabrics
HQ: Avintiv Inc.
    9335 Hrris Crners Pkwy St
    Charlotte NC 28269
    704 697-5100

(G-2771)
SCOTT SYSTEMS INTL INC (DH)
Also Called: Scott Automation
2205 Beltway Blvd Ste 100 (28214)
PHONE......................704 362-1115
Stacey Mcgill, *Prin*
Greg Chiles, *CFO*
EMP: 16 EST: 2014
SALES (est): 9.87MM **Publicly Held**
SIC: 3549 8742 Assembly machines, including robotic; Automation and robotics consultant
HQ: Scott Technology Limited
    630 Kaikorai Valley Rd
    Dunedin OTA 9011

(G-2772)
SCR-TECH LLC
11707 Steele Creek Rd (28273-3718)
PHONE......................704 504-0191
EMP: 131
Web: www.cormetech.com
SIC: 3564 8734 7389 Air purification equipment; Testing laboratories; Industrial and commercial equipment inspection service

(G-2773)
SE CO-BRAND VENTURES LLC
Also Called: Auntie Anne's
6801 Northlake Mall Dr Ste 188
(28216-0749)
PHONE......................704 598-9322
Rick Belcher, *Brnch Mgr*
EMP: 8
SALES (corp-wide): 9.44MM **Privately Held**
Web: www.auntieannes.com
SIC: 5461 2052 Pretzels; Pretzels
PA: Se Co-Brand Ventures Llc
    12 Deer Moss Ct
    Pawleys Island SC

(G-2774)
SEACON CORP
525 N Tryon St Ste 1600 (28202-0213)
PHONE......................704 331-3920

EMP: 9 EST: 2018
SALES (est): 296.21K **Privately Held**
Web: www.seaconcorp.com
SIC: 2869 Industrial organic chemicals, nec

(G-2775)
SEACON CORPORATION (PA)
1917 John Crosland Jr Dr (28208-5554)
PHONE......................704 333-6000
Sean E Condren, *Pr*
▲ EMP: 14 EST: 2002
SQ FT: 22,000
SALES (est): 9.29MM
SALES (corp-wide): 9.29MM **Privately Held**
Web: www.seaconcorp.com
SIC: 2899 Chemical preparations, nec

(G-2776)
SEALED AIR CORPORATION (PA)
Also Called: Sealed Air
2415 Cascade Pointe Blvd (28208)
PHONE......................980 221-3235
Dustin J Semach, *Pr*
Henry R Keizer, *
Emile Z Chammas, *Sr VP*
Sergio Pupkin Senior, *Chief Growth Vice President*
Veronika Johnson, *Interim Chief Financial Officer*
EMP: 1500 EST: 1960
SALES (est): 5.39B
SALES (corp-wide): 5.39B **Publicly Held**
Web: www.sealedair.com
SIC: 2821 Plastics materials and resins

(G-2777)
SEALED AIR CORPORATION (US)
2415 Cascade Pointe Blvd (28208-6899)
PHONE......................201 791-7600
Jerome Peribere, *Pr*
David H Kelsey, *
Robert A Pesci, *
H Katherine White, *
Tod Christie, *
EMP: 7500 EST: 1969
SALES (est): 67.79MM
SALES (corp-wide): 5.39B **Publicly Held**
Web: www.sealedair.com
SIC: 2673 2671 3087 3086 Plastic and pliofilm bags; Paper; coated and laminated packaging; Custom compound purchased resins; Plastics foam products
PA: Sealed Air Corporation
    2415 Cascade Pointe Blvd
    Charlotte NC 28208
    980 221-3235

(G-2778)
SEALED AIR INTL HOLDINGS LLC
2415 Cascade Pointe Blvd (28208-6899)
PHONE......................980 221-3235
EMP: 54 EST: 2017
SALES (est): 24.62MM
SALES (corp-wide): 5.39B **Publicly Held**
Web: www.sealedair.com
SIC: 3086 Packaging and shipping materials, foamed plastics
PA: Sealed Air Corporation
    2415 Cascade Pointe Blvd
    Charlotte NC 28208
    980 221-3235

(G-2779)
SEALED AIR LLC ✪
2415 Cascade Pointe Blvd (28208-6899)
PHONE......................980 430-7000
EMP: 10 EST: 2023
SALES (est): 5.04MM
SALES (corp-wide): 5.39B **Publicly Held**
Web: www.sealedair.com

SIC: **2673** Plastic and pliofilm bags
PA: Sealed Air Corporation
2415 Cascade Pointe Blvd
Charlotte NC 28208
980 221-3235

(G-2780)
SEANS TRANSPORTATION LLC
Also Called: Shawn Trucking and Towing
6826 Centerline Dr (28278-7398)
PHONE.............................646 603-8128
Travis Forde, *CEO*
EMP: 4 EST: 2019
SALES (est): 585.67K **Privately Held**
SIC: **3799** Transportation equipment, nec

(G-2781)
SECRET CHOCOLATIER LLC
2935 Providence Rd Ste 104 (28211-2762)
PHONE.............................704 323-8178
Richard Ciordia, *Prin*
EMP: 4 EST: 2009
SALES (est): 290.84K **Privately Held**
Web: www.homemadechocolategifts.com
SIC: **5441** 2066 Candy; Baking chocolate

(G-2782)
SECURITY CONSULT INC
1318 Beechdale Dr (28212-6804)
P.O. Box 12611 (28220-2611)
PHONE.............................704 531-8399
Julius L Ulanday, *Ofcr*
EMP: 4 EST: 2010
SALES (est): 457.69K **Privately Held**
Web: www.securityconsult411.com
SIC: **8748** 3699 7382 Business consulting,
nec; Security control equipment and
systems; Security systems services

(G-2783)
SELECT STAINLESS PRODUCTS
LLC
7621 Little Ave Ste 212 (28226-8402)
PHONE.............................888 843-2345
▲ **EMP: 7 EST:** 2012
SALES (est): 1.26MM **Privately Held**
Web: www.selectstainless.com
SIC: **3431** 3469 5078 2431 Metal sanitary
ware; Kitchen fixtures and equipment;
metal, except cast aluminum; Refrigerators,
commercial (reach-in and walk-in); Millwork

(G-2784)
SELECTIVE ENTERPRISES INC (PA)
Also Called: United Supply Company
10701 Texland Blvd (28273-6202)
P.O. Box 410149 (28241-0149)
PHONE.............................704 588-3310
John J Hawkins Junior, *Pr*
◆ **EMP: 103 EST:** 1962
SQ FT: 65,000
SALES (est): 22.94MM
SALES (corp-wide): 22.94MM **Privately
Held**
Web: www.unitedsupplyco.com
SIC: **5131** 5023 2591 Drapery material,
woven; Window covering parts and
accessories; Window blinds

(G-2785)
SELF MADE CLT
Also Called: Construction
9111 Olmsted Dr (28262-5466)
PHONE.............................704 249-5263
Octavious Elmore, *Owner*
EMP: 12 EST: 2019
SALES (est): 60.41K **Privately Held**
Web: www.selfmadeclt.com

SIC: **1389** 1522 Construction, repair, and
dismantling services; Remodeling, multi-
family dwellings

(G-2786)
SENOX CORPORATION
3500 Woodpark Blvd (28206-4243)
PHONE.............................704 371-5043
Patrick Wiley, *Mgr*
EMP: 47
SALES (corp-wide): 99.49MM **Privately
Held**
Web: www.senox.com
SIC: **3089** (glass fiber reinforced),
fiberglass or plastics
PA: Senox Corporation
15409 Long Vista Dr
Austin TX 78728
512 251-3333

(G-2787)
SENSATIONAL SIGNS
2100 N Davidson St (28205-1828)
P.O. Box 142 (28037-0142)
PHONE.............................704 358-1099
Sharlene Green, *Owner*
EMP: 4 EST: 2000
SALES (est): 333.97K **Privately Held**
Web: www.yoursignneeds.com
SIC: **3993** Electric signs

(G-2788)
SENTINEL DOOR CONTROLS LLC
3020 Hutchison Mcdonald Rd Ste D
(28269-4289)
PHONE.............................704 921-4627
David Maroon, *Managing Member*
▲ **EMP: 12 EST:** 1997
SALES (est): 4.48MM **Privately Held**
Web: www.sentineldoor.com
SIC: **5072** 3429 3699 Builders' hardware, nec
; Door opening and closing devices, except
electrical; Door opening and closing
devices, electrical

(G-2789)
SERRA WIRELESS INC
2431 Tallet Trce (28216-1309)
PHONE.............................980 318-0873
Fahaad Sayed, *CEO*
EMP: 6 EST: 2022
SALES (est): 8.59MM **Privately Held**
SIC: **5065** 3663 5731 3571 Mobile telephone
equipment; Cellular radio telephone;
Consumer electronic equipment, nec;
Electronic computers

(G-2790)
SESMFG LLC
1705 Orr Industrial Ct Ste C (28213-6464)
PHONE.............................803 917-3248
Samuel Lattimore, *Pr*
EMP: 6 EST: 2015
SALES (est): 271.91K **Privately Held**
Web: www.sesmfg.com
SIC: **3999** Manufacturing industries, nec

(G-2791)
SEVEN CAST
901 N Church St (28206-3220)
PHONE.............................704 335-0692
William Ruettgers, *Pr*
Cheryl Ruettgers, *VP*
EMP: 8 EST: 1997
SALES (est): 91.88K **Privately Held**
SIC: **3325** Steel foundries, nec

(G-2792)
SGL CARBON LLC (DH)
10715 David Taylor Dr Ste 460
(28262-1770)

PHONE.............................704 593-5100
◆ **EMP: 42 EST:** 1939
SALES (est): 308.86MM
SALES (corp-wide): 1.18B **Privately Held**
Web: www.sglcarbon.com
SIC: **3624** Carbon and graphite products
HQ: Sgl Carbon Beteiligung Gmbh
Sohnleinstr. 8
Wiesbaden HE 65201
61160290

(G-2793)
SGL COMPOSITES INC
10715 David Taylor Dr Ste 460
(28262-1283)
PHONE.............................704 593-5100
EMP: 17 EST: 2018
SALES (est): 2.69MM **Privately Held**
Web: www.sglcarbon.com
SIC: **3624** Carbon and graphite products

(G-2794)
SGL TECHNOLOGIES LLC
10715 David Taylor Dr Ste 460
(28262-1283)
PHONE.............................704 593-5100
Andreas Wuellner, *Pr*
Steve Swanson, *VP Opers*
Benoit Labelle, *VP Fin*
Jeffrey Schade, *VP Sls*
Anna Blackwelder, *Sec*
EMP: 5 EST: 1992
SALES (est): 1.54MM
SALES (corp-wide): 1.18B **Privately Held**
Web: www.sglcarbon.com
SIC: **3624** Fibers, carbon and graphite
HQ: Sgl Carbon, Llc
10715 Dvid Tylor Dr Ste 4
Charlotte NC 28262
704 593-5100

(G-2795)
SHAW INDUSTRIES GROUP INC
Also Called: Salem Carpet Mills
10901 Texland Blvd (28273-6237)
PHONE.............................877 996-5942
David Moore, *Mgr*
EMP: 4
SALES (corp-wide): 424.23B **Publicly
Held**
Web: www.shawfloors.com
SIC: **2273** Carpets and rugs
HQ: Shaw Industries Group, Inc.
616 E Walnut Ave
Dalton GA 30722
706 278-3812

(G-2796)
SHAW INDUSTRIES GROUP INC
Carpet Plant Division 25
10901 Texland Blvd (28273-6237)
PHONE.............................877 996-5942
Robert Belden, *Mgr*
EMP: 49
SQ FT: 102,203
SALES (corp-wide): 424.23B **Publicly
Held**
Web: www.shawfloors.com
SIC: **3086** 2273 Carpet and rug cushions,
foamed plastics; Carpets and rugs
HQ: Shaw Industries Group, Inc.
616 E Walnut Ave
Dalton GA 30722
706 278-3812

(G-2797)
SHED BRAND INC (PA)
216 Iverson Way Ste A (28203-5617)
PHONE.............................704 523-0096
Marvin Knight, *Pr*
Ellie Knight, *VP*

EMP: 9 EST: 1966
SQ FT: 2,250
SALES (est): 938.19K
SALES (corp-wide): 938.19K **Privately
Held**
Web: www.shedbrandstudios.com
SIC: **3231** 3269 Stained glass: made from
purchased glass; Art and ornamental ware,
pottery

(G-2798)
SHERWIN-WILLIAMS COMPANY
Also Called: Sherwin-Williams
10300 Claude Freeman Dr (28262-2339)
PHONE.............................704 548-2820
John Mccracken, *Brnch Mgr*
EMP: 85
SALES (corp-wide): 23.1B **Publicly Held**
Web: www.sherwin-williams.com
SIC: **2851** Paints and paint additives
PA: The Sherwin-Williams Company
101 W Prospect Ave
Cleveland OH 44115
216 566-2000

(G-2799)
SHOWER ME WITH LOVE LLC
4845 Ashley Park Ln Ste H (28210-3341)
PHONE.............................704 302-1555
Emily Shallal, *Managing Member*
EMP: 10 EST: 2006
SALES (est): 2MM **Privately Held**
Web: www.showermewithlove.com
SIC: **2676** Infant and baby paper products

(G-2800)
SHURTAPE TECHNOLOGIES LLC
4725 Piedmont Row Dr Ste 210
(28210-4279)
PHONE.............................704 553-9441
EMP: 5
SALES (corp-wide): 787.56MM **Privately
Held**
Web: www.shursealsecure.com
SIC: **2672** Tape, pressure sensitive: made
from purchased materials
HQ: Shurtape Technologies, Llc
1712 8th St Dr Se
Hickory NC 28602

(G-2801)
SIEMENS AIRPORT
5601 Wilkinson Blvd (28208-3557)
PHONE.............................704 359-5551
EMP: 4 EST: 2018
SALES (est): 1.43MM **Privately Held**
Web: www.cltairport.com
SIC: **3661** Telephones and telephone
apparatus

(G-2802)
SIEMENS ENERGY INC
5101 Westinghouse Blvd (28273-9601)
P.O. Box 4356 (97208-4356)
PHONE.............................704 551-5100
Len Sharpe, *Mgr*
EMP: 200
SALES (corp-wide): 38.48B **Privately Held**
Web: www.siemens.com
SIC: **3511** Turbines and turbine generator
sets
HQ: Siemens Energy, Inc.
4400 N Alafaya Trl
Orlando FL 32826
407 736-2000

(G-2803)
SIEMENS INDUSTRY SOFTWARE INC
Also Called: Siemens PLM Software
13024 Ballantyne Corporate Pl
(28277-2113)

▲ = Import ▼ = Export
◆ = Import/Export

PHONE.............704 227-6600
EMP: 13
SALES (corp-wide): 84.78B Privately Held
Web: www.siemens.com
SIC: 7372 Prepackaged software
HQ: Siemens Industry Software Inc.
5800 Granite Pkwy Ste 600
Plano TX 75024
972 987-3000

(G-2804)
SIENA PLASTICS LLC
839 Exchange St (28208-1205)
PHONE.............704 323-5252
Peter Suttoni, *Pr*
Michael Chorpash, *VP*
EMP: 11 EST: 2019
SALES (est): 6.31MM Privately Held
Web: www.sienaplastics.com
SIC: 3089 Injection molding of plastics

(G-2805)
SIGHTTECH LLC
9421 Perimeter Station Dr Apt 101
(28216-4425)
PHONE.............855 997-4448
EMP: 6 EST: 2011
SALES (est): 213.68K Privately Held
Web: www.sighttech.us
SIC: 8331 8732 7379 5045 Job training and
related services; Commercial sociological
and educational research; Computer
related maintenance services; Computers,
peripherals, and software

(G-2806)
SIGN WORLD INC
200 Foster Ave (28203-5422)
P.O. Box 2784 (28070-2784)
PHONE.............704 529-4440
Jerry L Mc Kenzie, *Pr*
Debra Henson, *Mgr*
Debra Mckenzie, *Sec*
EMP: 6 EST: 1975
SQ FT: 6,000
SALES (est): 327.9K Privately Held
Web: www.signworldamerica.com
SIC: 3993 1799 Electric signs; Sign
installation and maintenance

(G-2807)
SIGNS BY TOMORROW
2440 Whitehall Park Dr Ste 100
(28273-3552)
PHONE.............704 527-6100
EMP: 4 EST: 2015
SALES (est): 83.08K Privately Held
Web: www.signsbytomorrow.com
SIC: 3993 Signs and advertising specialties

(G-2808)
SIGNS ETC OF CHARLOTTE (PA)
4941 Chastain Ave (28217-2115)
PHONE.............704 522-8860
Spencer Brower, *Prin*
EMP: 15 EST: 2010
SALES (est): 2.24MM
SALES (corp-wide): 2.24MM **Privately Held**
Web: www.signsetcofcharlotte.com
SIC: 3993 Electric signs

(G-2809)
SIGNS ETC OF CHARLOTTE
Also Called: Signs Etc
4044 South Blvd (28209-2746)
PHONE.............704 522-8860
Spencer Brower, *Brnch Mgr*
EMP: 35
SALES (corp-wide): 653.88K **Privately Held**

Web: www.signsetcofcharlotte.com
SIC: 3993 Signs, not made in custom sign
painting shops
PA: Signs Etc Of Charlotte
4941 Chastain Ave
Charlotte NC 28217
704 522-8860

(G-2810)
**SINGLE TEMPERATURE CONTRLS
INC**
14201 S Lakes Dr Ste B (28273-7708)
PHONE.............704 504-4800
Fred Hatberg, *VP*
Michael Bloomhuff, *Pr*
▲ EMP: 6 EST: 2008
SALES (est): 4.31MM Privately Held
Web: www.single-temp.com
SIC: 3559 Plastics working machinery
HQ: Single Temperiertechnik Gmbh
Ostring 17-19
Hochdorf BW 73269
715330090

(G-2811)
SKIN SO SOFT SPA INC
4456 The Plaza Ste 5e (28215-2175)
PHONE.............800 674-7554
Sheleana Brown, *Prin*
EMP: 6 EST: 2021
SALES (est): 481.61K Privately Held
SIC: 2844 Perfumes, cosmetics and other
toilet preparations

(G-2812)
SKYVIEW COMMERCIAL CLEANING
Also Called: Building Stars of Charlotte
5725 Carnegie Blvd (28209-4867)
PHONE.............704 858-0134
Antonio Norman, *CEO*
EMP: 8 EST: 2022
SALES (est): 364.19K Privately Held
SIC: 3589 7389 Commercial cleaning
equipment; Business services, nec

(G-2813)
SL - LASER SYSTEMS LLC
4920 Larkmoore Ct (28208-6305)
PHONE.............704 561-9990
EMP: 5 EST: 2019
SALES (est): 2.63MM Privately Held
Web: www.sl-laser.com
SIC: 3559 Special industry machinery, nec

(G-2814)
SL LASER SYSTEMS LP
8107 Arrowridge Blvd Ste Q (28273-5613)
PHONE.............704 561-9990
Andria Russ, *Pt*
EMP: 7 EST: 2003
SQ FT: 7,200
SALES (est): 2.35MM Privately Held
Web: www.sl-laser.com
SIC: 3699 Laser systems and equipment

(G-2815)
SLS BAKING COMPANY
15720 Brixham Hill Ave (28277-4651)
PHONE.............704 421-2763
EMP: 4 EST: 2015
SALES (est): 378.43K Privately Held
SIC: 2051 Bread, cake, and related products

(G-2816)
SLUM DOG HEAD GEAR LLC
9912 Jeanette Cir (28213-2129)
PHONE.............704 713-8125
EMP: 10 EST: 2020
SALES (est): 143.78K Privately Held

SIC: 2253 Hats and headwear, knit

(G-2817)
SMARTWAY OF CAROLINAS LLC
Also Called: Smart Way
3304 Eastway Dr (28205-5649)
PHONE.............704 900-7877
Benjamin Bost, *Pr*
EMP: 9 EST: 2012
SALES (est): 2.39MM Privately Held
Web: www.gosmartwaync.net
SIC: 5712 3639 5045 Furniture stores; Major
kitchen appliances, except refrigerators and
stoves; Computers, nec

(G-2818)
SNAP ONE LLC (DH)
Also Called: Snapav
1800 Continental Blvd Ste 200
(28273-6388)
PHONE.............704 927-7620
Jay Geldmacher, *CEO*
Craig Craze, *
Adam Levy, *
Brad Redmond, *
Carlos Catalahana, *
▲ EMP: 350 EST: 2000
SQ FT: 69,953
SALES (est): 412.11MM
SALES (corp-wide): 6.76B **Publicly Held**
Web: www.snapav.com
SIC: 3679 Electronic circuits
HQ: Snap One Holdings Corp.
1800 Contntl Blvd Ste 200
Charlotte NC 28273
704 927-7620

(G-2819)
SNAP ONE HOLDINGS CORP (HQ)
Also Called: Snap One
1800 Continental Blvd Ste 200 (28273)
PHONE.............704 927-7620
Rob Aarnes, *Pr*
EMP: 33 EST: 2017
SQ FT: 69,953
SALES (est): 1.06B
SALES (corp-wide): 6.76B **Publicly Held**
Web: www.snapav.com
SIC: 3679 Electronic circuits
PA: Resideo Technologies, Inc.
16100 N 71st St Ste 550
Scottsdale AZ 85254
480 573-5340

(G-2820)
SNIDER TIRE INC
900 Atando Ave (28206-1507)
PHONE.............704 373-2910
Matt Creswell, *Mgr*
EMP: 70
SALES (corp-wide): 501.16MM **Privately
Held**
Web: www.sniderfleet.com
SIC: 5531 7534 Automotive tires; Tire
recapping
PA: Snider Tire, Inc.
1081 Red Ventures Dr
Fort Mill SC 29707
800 528-2840

(G-2821)
SNYDERS-LANCE INC
1900 Continental Blvd (28273-6390)
PHONE.............704 557-8013
◆ EMP: 9
SALES (corp-wide): 9.64B **Publicly Held**
Web: www.campbellsoupcompany.com
SIC: 2052 Cookies
HQ: Snyder's-Lance, Inc.
1 Campbell Pl
Camden NJ 08103
704 554-1421

(G-2822)
SOCIALTOPIAS LLC
1415 S Church St Ste C (28203-4158)
PHONE.............704 910-1713
Timothy Gruber, *CEO*
EMP: 14 EST: 2015
SALES (est): 901.07K Privately Held
Web: www.socialtopias.com
SIC: 7372 Application computer software

(G-2823)
SOCK INC
1908 Belvedere Ave (28205-3010)
PHONE.............561 254-2223
Steven Heinecke, *Pr*
EMP: 5 EST: 2013
SALES (est): 109.44K Privately Held
Web: www.customsocklab.com
SIC: 2252 Socks

(G-2824)
SOCKS AND OTHER THINGS LLC
4413 Mickleton Rd (28226-5549)
PHONE.............704 904-2472
EMP: 7 EST: 2017
SALES (est): 224.71K Privately Held
Web: www.socksthings.com
SIC: 2252 Socks

(G-2825)
SOLID HOLDINGS LLC
3820 Rose Lake Dr (28217-2833)
PHONE.............704 423-0260
Phil Calabritto, *Pr*
EMP: 18 EST: 2014
SALES (est): 1MM Privately Held
Web: www.solidcare.com
SIC: 8712 2952 1771 Architectural services;
Roofing felts, cements, or coatings, nec;
Stucco, gunite, and grouting contractors

(G-2826)
SONABLATE CORP (PA)
10130 Perimeter Pkwy Ste 410
(28216-2447)
PHONE.............888 874-4384
Richard Yang, *CEO*
Richard Yang, *Pr*
Stephen R Puckett, *
EMP: 26 EST: 2004
SALES (est): 24.87MM Privately Held
Web: www.sonablate.com
SIC: 3841 Surgical and medical instruments

(G-2827)
SONOCO PRODUCTS COMPANY
12000 Vance Davis Dr (28269-7696)
PHONE.............704 875-2685
Phillip Pimlott, *Brnch Mgr*
EMP: 23
SALES (corp-wide): 5.31B **Publicly Held**
Web: www.sonoco.com
SIC: 2653 Corrugated and solid fiber boxes
PA: Sonoco Products Company
1 N 2nd St
Hartsville SC 29550
843 383-7000

(G-2828)
SOTO INDUSTRIES LLC
6201 Fairview Rd Ste 200 (28210-3297)
PHONE.............706 643-5011
Farnsworth Coleman, *Managing Member*
EMP: 8 EST: 1991
SALES (est): 873.18K Privately Held
SIC: 2861 2899 Gum and wood chemicals;
Chemical preparations, nec

(G-2829)
SOUTH BOULEVARD ASSOCIATES INC
186 Cherokee Rd (28207-1904)
PHONE....................704 525-7160
Kyle Stavig, *CEO*
Christian Stavig, *Pr*
EMP: 90 EST: 1985
SALES (est): 969.84K **Privately Held**
SIC: 3412 Metal barrels, drums, and pails

(G-2830)
SOUTH POINT HOSPITALITY INC
13451 S Point Blvd (28273-2701)
PHONE....................704 542-2304
Kathy Dayvault, *CEO*
EMP: 10 EST: 2020
SALES (est): 200K **Privately Held**
Web: www.southpointhospitality.com
SIC: 2299 Textile goods, nec

(G-2831)
SOUTHEASTERN CORRUGATED LLC (PA)
10901 Carpet St (28273-6206)
PHONE....................980 224-9551
James Tolbert, *Managing Member*
EMP: 9 EST: 2019
SALES (est): 1.86MM
SALES (corp-wide): 1.86MM **Privately Held**
Web: www.southeasterncorrugated.com
SIC: 2631 Container, packaging, and boxboard

(G-2832)
SOUTHEASTERN ENTERPRISES (HQ)
3545 Asbury Ave (28206-1505)
PHONE....................704 373-1750
Fred Miltz, *Pr*
Eric Miltz, *VP*
EMP: 15 EST: 1997
SALES (est): 4.5MM
SALES (corp-wide): 18.69MM **Privately Held**
SIC: 3599 Machine shop, jobbing and repair
PA: Container Products Corporation
   112 N College Rd
   Wilmington NC 28405
   910 392-6100

(G-2833)
SOUTHERN CAST INC
901 N Church St (28206-3220)
P.O. Box 9427 (28299-9427)
PHONE....................704 335-0692
William Ruettgers, *Pr*
Cheryl Ruettgers, *
William J Ruettgers, *
David P Ruettgers, *
EMP: 25 EST: 1983
SQ FT: 55,000
SALES (est): 5.89MM **Privately Held**
Web: www.southerncastinc.com
SIC: 3321 Gray iron castings, nec

(G-2834)
SOUTHERN CONCRETE MTLS INC
11609 Texland Blvd (28273-6221)
PHONE....................704 394-2346
Tom Hawthorne, *VP*
EMP: 17
SALES (corp-wide): 238.17MM **Privately Held**
Web: www.scmusa.com
SIC: 3273 Ready-mixed concrete
HQ: Southern Concrete Materials, Inc.
   35 Meadow Rd
   Asheville NC 28803
   828 253-6421

(G-2835)
SOUTHERN CONCRETE MTLS INC
715 State St (28208-4147)
P.O. Box 33038 (28233-3038)
PHONE....................704 394-2344
Tom Hawthorne, *Brnch Mgr*
EMP: 48
SQ FT: 14,040
SALES (corp-wide): 238.17MM **Privately Held**
Web: www.scmusa.com
SIC: 3273 Ready-mixed concrete
HQ: Southern Concrete Materials, Inc.
   35 Meadow Rd
   Asheville NC 28803
   828 253-6421

(G-2836)
SOUTHERN ELECTRICAL EQP CO INC (PA)
4045 Hargrove Ave (28208-5503)
P.O. Box 668547 (28266-8547)
PHONE....................704 392-1396
Barry Thomas, *Pr*
Craig Thomas, *
Andrew Panto, *
◆ EMP: 41 EST: 1920
SQ FT: 20,000
SALES (est): 10.18MM
SALES (corp-wide): 10.18MM **Privately Held**
Web: www.seecoswitch.com
SIC: 3625 Relays and industrial controls

(G-2837)
SOUTHERN METALS COMPANY
2200 Donald Ross Rd (28208-6127)
P.O. Box 668923 (28266-8923)
PHONE....................704 394-3161
Robert I Helbein, *Pr*
Marc Helbein, *
Michael Helbein, *
Mary Anne Davis, *
EMP: 50 EST: 1938
SQ FT: 55,000
SALES (est): 8.97MM **Privately Held**
Web: www.southernmetalscompany.com
SIC: 3356 3316 Nonferrous rolling and drawing, nec; Cold finishing of steel shapes

(G-2838)
SOUTHERN PRECISION SPRING INC
2200 Old Steele Creek Rd (28208-6031)
P.O. Box 668186 (28266-8186)
PHONE....................704 392-4393
Hugh M Duncan Junior, *Pr*
Thomas T Duncan, *
▲ EMP: 29 EST: 1956
SQ FT: 55,000
SALES (est): 9.2MM **Privately Held**
Web: www.spspring.com
SIC: 3495 Wire springs

(G-2839)
SOUTHERN STAIRCASE INC
Also Called: Southern Staircase
1108 Continental Blvd Ste O (28273-6485)
PHONE....................704 357-1221
Diane Newport, *Mgr*
EMP: 81
SALES (corp-wide): 13.75MM **Privately Held**
Web: www.southernstaircase.com
SIC: 5031 3446 2431 Building materials, interior; Architectural metalwork; Millwork
PA: Southern Staircase, Inc.
   6025 Shiloh Rd Ste E
   Alpharetta GA 30005
   770 888-7333

(G-2840)
SOUTHERN STAIRCASE INC
1108 Continental Blvd Ste O (28273-6485)
PHONE....................704 363-2123
Billy Baker, *Off Mgr*
EMP: 5
SALES (corp-wide): 13.75MM **Privately Held**
Web: www.artisticstairs-us.com
SIC: 2431 Staircases and stairs, wood
PA: Southern Staircase, Inc.
   6025 Shiloh Rd Ste E
   Alpharetta GA 30005
   770 888-7333

(G-2841)
SPECIALTY MANUFACTURING INC (HQ)
Also Called: SMI
13501 S Ridge Dr (28273-6741)
PHONE....................704 247-9300
Joseph Uebbing, *CEO*
Richard Ayre, *
◆ EMP: 96 EST: 1965
SQ FT: 90,000
SALES (est): 19.51MM **Privately Held**
Web: www.safefleet.net
SIC: 3648 3641 3444 3441 Lighting equipment, nec; Electric lamps; Sheet metalwork; Building components, structural steel
PA: The Sterling Group L P
   9 Greenway Plz Ste 2400
   Houston TX 77046

(G-2842)
SPECTRUM BRANDS INC
15040 Choate Cir (28273-6947)
PHONE....................800 854-3151
EMP: 5
SALES (corp-wide): 2.96B **Publicly Held**
Web: www.spectrumbrands.com
SIC: 3692 Primary batteries, dry and wet
HQ: Spectrum Brands, Inc.
   3001 Deming Way
   Middleton WI 53562
   608 275-3340

(G-2843)
SPEEDPRO IMAGING
2301 Crownpoint Executive Dr (28227-7824)
PHONE....................704 321-1200
David Amo, *Prin*
EMP: 4 EST: 2011
SALES (est): 246.61K **Privately Held**
Web: www.speedpro.com
SIC: 3993 Signs and advertising specialties

(G-2844)
SPGPRINTS AMERICA INC (DH)
Also Called: Spg Prints
2121 Distribution Center Dr Ste E (28269-4228)
P.O. Box 26458 (28221-6458)
PHONE....................704 598-7171
▲ EMP: 60 EST: 1968
SALES (est): 6.55MM **Privately Held**
Web: www.spgprints.com
SIC: 3552 3555 Printing machinery, textile; Printing trades machinery
HQ: Spgprints B.V.
   Raamstraat 3
   Boxmeer NB 5831
   485599555

(G-2845)
SPRAYING SYSTEMS CO
5727 Westpark Dr Ste 204 (28217-3651)
PHONE....................704 357-6499
John Weir, *Owner*

EMP: 4
SALES (corp-wide): 434.45MM **Privately Held**
Web: www.spray.com
SIC: 3499 Nozzles, spray: aerosol, paint, or insecticide
PA: Spraying Systems Co.
   200 W North Ave
   Glendale Heights IL 60139
   630 665-5000

(G-2846)
SPX COOLING TECH LLC
Also Called: SPX Cooling Tech, LLC
13515 Ballantyne Corporate Pl (28277-2706)
PHONE....................630 881-9777
Michael Reilly, *Brnch Mgr*
EMP: 18
SALES (corp-wide): 1.83B **Privately Held**
Web: www.spxcooling.com
SIC: 3443 Cooling towers, metal plate
HQ: Canvas Ct, Llc
   7401 W 129th St
   Overland Park KS 66213
   913 664-7400

(G-2847)
SPX FLOW INC (HQ)
Also Called: SPX Flow
13320 Ballantyne Corporate Pl (28277-3607)
PHONE....................704 752-4400
Marcus G Michael, *Pr*
Robert F Hull Junior, *Non-Executive Chairman of the Board*
Jaime M Easley, *VP*
Kevin J Eamigh, *CIO*
Tyrone Jeffers V, *President Global Manufacturing*
EMP: 127 EST: 2015
SALES (est): 1.35B
SALES (corp-wide): 1.78B **Privately Held**
Web: www.spxflow.com
SIC: 3556 3561 3491 Food products machinery; Pumps and pumping equipment ; Industrial valves
PA: Lsf11 Redwood Acquisitions, Llc
   2711 N Hskell Ave Ste 170
   Dallas TX 75204
   214 754-8300

(G-2848)
SPX FLOW HOLDINGS INC
13320 Ballantyne Corporate Pl (28277-3607)
PHONE....................704 808-3848
Marc Michael, *Pr*
David Kowalski, *Global Manufacturing Operations President*
EMP: 9 EST: 1997
SALES (est): 2.13MM
SALES (corp-wide): 1.78B **Privately Held**
Web: www.spxflow.com
SIC: 3556 3559 Dairy and milk machinery; Pharmaceutical machinery
HQ: Spx Flow, Inc.
   13320 Ballantyne Corp Pl
   Charlotte NC 28277
   704 752-4400

(G-2849)
SPX FLOW TECH SYSTEMS INC
13320 Ballantyne Corporate Pl (28277-3607)
PHONE....................704 752-4400
EMP: 920
SALES (corp-wide): 1.78B **Privately Held**
Web: www.spxflow.com
SIC: 3556 Food products machinery
HQ: Spx Flow Technology Systems, Inc.

105 Crosspoint Pkwy
Getzville NY 14068
716 692-3000

(G-2850)
SPX LATIN AMERICA CORPORATION
13320 Ballantyne Corporate Pl
(28277-3607)
PHONE.............................704 808-3848
Marc Michael, *Pr*
David Kowalski, *Global Manufacturing Operations President*
EMP: 8 **EST:** 2007
SALES (est): 2.09MM
SALES (corp-wide): 1.78B **Privately Held**
Web: www.spxflow.com
SIC: 3556 3559 Dairy and milk machinery; Pharmaceutical machinery
HQ: Spx Flow, Inc.
13320 Ballantyne Corp Pl
Charlotte NC 28277
704 752-4400

(G-2851)
SPX TECHNOLOGIES INC (PA)
6325 Ardrey Kell Rd Ste 400 (28277)
PHONE.............................980 474-3700
Eugene J Lowe Iii, *Pr*
Patrick O'leary, *Ch Bd*
Mark A Carano, *VP*
John W Nurkin, *VP*
Wayne M Mclaren, *CAO*
EMP: 91 **EST:** 1912
SQ FT: 100,000
SALES (est): 1.98B
SALES (corp-wide): 1.98B **Publicly Held**
Web: www.spx.com
SIC: 3443 3599 3829 3559 Heat exchangers, condensers, and components; Air intake filters, internal combustion engine, except auto; Measuring and controlling devices, nec; Automotive related machinery

(G-2852)
SRNG-T&W LLC
Also Called: Sustain Rng
1942 E 7th St (28204-2418)
PHONE.............................704 271-9889
Rick Wilcox, *Managing Member*
EMP: 6 **EST:** 2020
SALES (est): 5.38MM **Privately Held**
SIC: 1311 Natural gas production

(G-2853)
SSB MANUFACTURING COMPANY
Also Called: Simmons
5100r E W T Harris Blvd (28269-2157)
PHONE.............................704 596-4935
Bill Wagner, *Brnch Mgr*
EMP: 111
SALES (corp-wide): 4.59B **Privately Held**
Web: www.sertasimmons.com
SIC: 2515 Mattresses, innerspring or box spring
HQ: Ssb Manufacturing Company
2451 Industry Ave
Doraville GA 30360
404 534-5000

(G-2854)
SSD DESIGNS LLC (PA)
9935d Rea Rd # 433 (28277-6710)
PHONE.............................980 245-2988
Sara Samuelson, *Pr*
Sara Samuelson, *Managing Member*
EMP: 18 **EST:** 2017
SQ FT: 5,000
SALES (est): 2.08MM
SALES (corp-wide): 2.08MM **Privately Held**

Web: www.ssd-designs.com
SIC: 2821 Plastics materials and resins

(G-2855)
SSPC INC
12016 Steele Creek Rd (28273-3734)
P.O. Box 38040 (28278-1000)
▲ **EMP:** 24 **EST:** 1992
SQ FT: 24,000
SALES (est): 2.8MM **Privately Held**
Web: www.specialserviceplastic.com
SIC: 3089 Injection molding of plastics

(G-2856)
ST INVESTORS INC
Also Called: Source Technolgies Holdings
4064 Colony Rd Ste 150 (28211-5033)
PHONE.............................704 969-7500
Miles T Busby, *Pr*
John R Spencer Junior, *Ex VP*
Gordon W Friedrich, *Finance Treasurer**
Rodger B Morrison, *
Michael E Bailey, *
EMP: 87 **EST:** 1986
SQ FT: 58,000
SALES (est): 2.11MM **Privately Held**
SIC: 3577 7373 5045 7378 Printers, computer; Computer integrated systems design; Printers, computer; Computer peripheral equipment repair and maintenance

(G-2857)
STAINLESS & NICKEL ALLOYS LLC
1700 W Pointe Dr Ste E (28214-7901)
P.O. Box 12446 (28220-2446)
PHONE.............................704 201-2898
Tom Lockhart, *Managing Member*
▲ **EMP:** 4 **EST:** 2010
SQ FT: 1,000
SALES (est): 276.94K **Privately Held**
SIC: 3356 Nickel

(G-2858)
STANLEY BLACK & DECKER INC
9115 Old Statesville Rd Ste E (28269-6605)
PHONE.............................704 509-0844
Dick Verwyane, *Brnch Mgr*
EMP: 7
SALES (corp-wide): 15.78B **Publicly Held**
Web: www.stanleyblackanddecker.com
SIC: 3429 Builders' hardware
PA: Stanley Black & Decker, Inc.
1000 Stanley Dr
New Britain CT 06053
860 225-5111

(G-2859)
STANZA MACHINERY INC
6801 Northpark Blvd Ste B (28216-0080)
PHONE.............................704 599-0623
James L Desarno, *Pr*
▲ **EMP:** 50 **EST:** 2005
SALES (est): 4.35MM **Privately Held**
Web: www.stanzamachinery.com
SIC: 5084 3556 Machine tools and accessories; Bakery machinery

(G-2860)
STARCKE ABRASIVES USA INC
Also Called: Abrasive Resource
9109 Forsyth Park Dr (28273-3882)
PHONE.............................704 583-3338
Robert Steve Kelly, *Pr*
Paul W Burzynski, *
▲ **EMP:** 30 **EST:** 2003
SQ FT: 10,000
SALES (est): 4.79MM
SALES (corp-wide): 65.12MM **Privately Held**
Web: www.starckeusa.com

SIC: 3291 Abrasive products
PA: Starcke Gmbh & Co. Kg
Markt 10
Melle NI 49324
54229660

(G-2861)
STARNES PALLET SERVICE INC (PA)
4000 Jeff Adams Dr (28206-1237)
P.O. Box 5484 (28299)
PHONE.............................704 596-9006
Tommy Starnes Junior, *Pr*
Tommy Starnes Senior, *VP*
EMP: 36 **EST:** 1994
SQ FT: 7,500
SALES (est): 5.52MM **Privately Held**
Web: www.starnespalletservice.com
SIC: 2448 Pallets, wood

(G-2862)
STATE INDUSTRIES INC
STATE INDUSTRIES, INC.
4302 Raleigh St (28213-6927)
PHONE.............................704 597-8910
Roy Jones, *Brnch Mgr*
EMP: 8
SQ FT: 93,014
SALES (corp-wide): 3.82B **Publicly Held**
Web: www.statewaterheaters.com
SIC: 3639 Hot water heaters, household
HQ: State Industries, Llc
500 Tennessee Waltz Pkwy
Ashland City TN 37015
615 244-7040

(G-2863)
STEAG SCR-TECH INC (PA)
Also Called: Cormetech
11707 Steele Creek Rd (28273-3718)
PHONE.............................704 827-8933
Mike Mattes, *CEO*
Dave Morris, *
Thies Hoffmann, *
EMP: 30 **EST:** 2016
SALES (est): 106.43MM
SALES (corp-wide): 106.43MM **Privately Held**
Web: www.cormetech.com
SIC: 2819 Fuel propellants, solid: inorganic

(G-2864)
STEELFAB INC (PA)
3025 Westport Rd (28208-3688)
P.O. Box 19289 (28219-9289)
PHONE.............................704 394-5376
EMP: 365 **EST:** 1955
SALES (est): 408.94MM
SALES (corp-wide): 408.94MM **Privately Held**
Web: www.steelfab-inc.com
SIC: 3441 3449 Building components, structural steel; Miscellaneous metalwork

(G-2865)
STEFANO FOODS INC
4825 Hovis Rd (28208-1510)
PHONE.............................704 399-3935
▼ **EMP:** 150
Web: www.stefanofoods.com
SIC: 2099 2053 2038 Ready-to-eat meals, salads, and sandwiches; Frozen bakery products, except bread; Frozen specialties, nec

(G-2866)
STEIN FIBERS LTD
Also Called: Stein Fibers, Ltd.
10130 Mallard Creek Rd (28262-6000)
PHONE.............................704 599-2804
Marcus Dellinger, *Of Development*
EMP: 69

SALES (corp-wide): 63.42MM **Privately Held**
Web: www.steinfibers.com
SIC: 2824 Polyester fibers
PA: Stein Fibers, Llc
4 Computer Dr W
Albany NY 12205
518 489-5700

(G-2867)
STEPHANIES MATTRESS LLC
5920 N Tryon St (28213-7811)
PHONE.............................704 763-0705
Ramon A Mercedes, *CEO*
EMP: 5 **EST:** 2017
SALES (est): 1.02MM **Privately Held**
Web: www.stephaniesmattressclt.com
SIC: 5712 2519 Mattresses; Furniture, household: glass, fiberglass, and plastic

(G-2868)
STI TURF EQUIPMENT LLC
4355 Golf Acres Dr (28208-5874)
PHONE.............................704 393-8873
Wayne Smith, *Prin*
EMP: 49 **EST:** 2001
SALES (est): 1.99MM
SALES (corp-wide): 116.89MM **Privately Held**
SIC: 3523 Turf equipment, commercial
PA: Smith Turf & Irrigation Llc
4355 Golf Acres Dr
Charlotte NC 28208
704 393-8873

(G-2869)
STOCKHOLM CORPORATION
4729 Stockholm Ct (28273-5995)
P.O. Box 240360 (28224)
PHONE.............................704 552-9314
Charles H Wunner, *Pr*
Barbara J Wunner, *
▲ **EMP:** 28 **EST:** 1982
SQ FT: 10,000
SALES (est): 7.16MM **Privately Held**
Web: www.vooner.com
SIC: 3561 Industrial pumps and parts

(G-2870)
STORK UNITED CORPORATION
3201 Rotary Dr (28269-4493)
P.O. Box 26458 (28221-6458)
PHONE.............................704 598-7171
▲ **EMP:** 713
SIC: 5084 3552 3556 Food product manufacturing machinery; Printing machinery, textile; Poultry processing machinery

(G-2871)
STRATEGY
525 N Tryon St Ste 1705 (28202)
PHONE.............................704 331-6521
Tim Gunter, *Mgr*
EMP: 10
Web: www.microstrategy.com
SIC: 7372 Application computer software
PA: Strategy
1850 Towers Crescent Plz
Tysons Corner VA 22182

(G-2872)
STRONG GLOBAL ENTRMT INC (PA)
5960 Fairview Rd Ste 275 (28210-3102)
PHONE.............................704 994-8279
Mark D Roberson, *CEO*
D Kyle Cerminara, *Ch Bd*
Ray F Boegner, *Pr*
Todd R Major, *CFO*
EMP: 175 **EST:** 2021
SALES (est): 42.62MM

SALES (corp-wide): 42.62MM **Privately Held**
SIC: **3861** Photographic equipment and supplies

(G-2873)
STROUP MACHINE & MFG INC
2019 W Laporte Dr (28216-6114)
PHONE..................................704 394-0023
Robert Stroup, *Pr*
Matthew Stroup, *VP*
EMP: 7 EST: 2010
SQ FT: 6,600
SALES (est): 563.07K **Privately Held**
SIC: **3469** Machine parts, stamped or pressed metal

(G-2874)
STS PACKAGING CHARLOTTE LLC
1201 Westinghouse Blvd (28273-6489)
PHONE..................................980 259-2290
Lauren Mikos, *Pr*
EMP: 82 EST: 2022
SALES (est): 8.12MM **Privately Held**
SIC: **2621** Paper mills

(G-2875)
STUMP AND GRIND LLC
7420 Ponders End Ln (28213-5752)
PHONE..................................704 488-2271
T Tillman, *Owner*
EMP: 4 EST: 2013
SALES (est): 140.03K **Privately Held**
Web: www.charlottestumpgrinding.com
SIC: **3599** Grinding castings for the trade

(G-2876)
SUAREZ BAKERY INC
4245 Park Rd (28209-2231)
PHONE..................................704 525-0145
Carlos A Suarez, *Pr*
EMP: 10 EST: 1962
SQ FT: 3,000
SALES (est): 939.95K **Privately Held**
Web: www.suarezbakery.com
SIC: **2051** Bakery: wholesale or wholesale/retail combined

(G-2877)
SUBARU FOLGER AUTOMOTIVE
Also Called: Daewoo-Folger Automotive
5701 E Independence Blvd (28212-0513)
PHONE..................................704 531-8888
Ward Williams, *Pr*
Glenn Moore, *
EMP: 17 EST: 1937
SQ FT: 70,000
SALES (est): 227.83K **Privately Held**
Web: www.williamssubaru.com
SIC: **5511** 7539 3711 Automobiles, new and used; Machine shop, automotive; Motor vehicles and car bodies

(G-2878)
SUGAR CREEK BREWING CO LLC
215 Southside Dr (28217-1727)
PHONE..................................704 521-3333
Joseph Vogelbacher, *Managing Member*
EMP: 22 EST: 2014
SQ FT: 30,000
SALES (est): 5MM **Privately Held**
Web: www.sugarcreekbrewing.com
SIC: **2082** 5813 5812 Beer (alcoholic beverage); Beer garden (drinking places); Cafe

(G-2879)
SUMPTERS JWLY & COLLECTIBLES
3501 Wilkinson Blvd (28208-5536)
PHONE..................................704 399-5348

Hal R Sumpter, *Pr*
EMP: 4 EST: 1991
SQ FT: 10,000
SALES (est): 213.81K **Privately Held**
Web: www.sumptersjewelry.com
SIC: **3911** 5094 7631 5932 Jewelry, precious metal; Precious stones and metals; Jewelry repair services; Pawnshop

(G-2880)
SUN CHEMICAL CORPORATION
General Printing Ink Division
1701 Westinghouse Blvd (28273-6383)
P.O. Box 7087 (28241-7087)
PHONE..................................704 587-4531
Scott Smith, *Brnch Mgr*
EMP: 52
SQ FT: 81,744
Web: www.sunchemical.com
SIC: **2893** Printing ink
HQ: Sun Chemical Corporation
35 Waterview Blvd
Parsippany NJ 07054
973 404-6000

(G-2881)
SUNCO POWDER SYSTEMS INC
3230 Valentine Ln (28270-0685)
PHONE..................................704 545-3922
Ivan Wilson, *Pr*
EMP: 20 EST: 1982
SALES (est): 954.79K **Privately Held**
Web: www.suncoblowers.com
SIC: **3535** 3564 Pneumatic tube conveyor systems; Filters, air: furnaces, air conditioning equipment, etc.

(G-2882)
SUNNEX INC
Also Called: Sunnex
8001 Tower Point Dr (28227-7726)
PHONE..................................800 445-7869
John Herbert, *Pr*
Lena Melton, *VP*
◆ EMP: 11 EST: 1974
SQ FT: 58,300
SALES (est): 4.05MM
SALES (corp-wide): 138.87MM **Privately Held**
Web: www.sunnex.com
SIC: **3648** 3641 3645 Lighting equipment, nec; Electric lamps; Table lamps
HQ: Sunnex Equipment Ab
Korkarlsvagen 4
Karlstad 653 4
54555160

(G-2883)
SUNSTAR HEATING PRODUCTS INC
305 Doggett St (28203-4923)
P.O. Box 36485 (28236-6485)
PHONE..................................704 372-3486
Frank L Horne, *Pr*
EMP: 7 EST: 1987
SALES (est): 416.37K
SALES (corp-wide): 18.94MM **Privately Held**
Web: www.sunstarheaters.com
SIC: **3433** Gas infrared heating units
PA: Gas-Fired Products, Inc.
1700 Parker Dr
Charlotte NC 28208
704 372-3485

(G-2884)
SUPPLIERS TO WHOLESALERS INC
1816 W Pointe Dr Ste A (28214-0100)
PHONE..................................704 375-7406
C N Witherspoon, *Pr*
Marcus E Yandle, *
Mike Eppley, *

Lois Yandle, *
EMP: 6 EST: 1963
SALES (est): 1.68MM **Privately Held**
SIC: **3444** Ducts, sheet metal

(G-2885)
SUPREME SWEEPERS LLC
6135 Park South Dr Ste 510 (28210-3272)
PHONE..................................888 698-9996
EMP: 4 EST: 2011
SALES (est): 2.06MM **Privately Held**
SIC: **3589** 3569 Commercial cleaning equipment; Blast cleaning equipment, dustless

(G-2886)
SWEATNET LLC
310 Arlington Ave Unit 229 (28203-4289)
PHONE..................................847 331-7287
EMP: 6 EST: 2017
SALES (est): 624.86K **Privately Held**
Web: www.sweatnet.com
SIC: **7372** 7312 Application computer software; Outdoor advertising services

(G-2887)
SWEEP 24 LLC
301 S Mcdowell St (28204-2623)
PHONE..................................980 428-5624
EMP: 10
SALES (est): 1.12MM **Privately Held**
SIC: **3589** Commercial cleaning equipment

(G-2888)
SWING KURVE LOGISTIC TRCKG LLC
2428 Freedom Dr (28208-4045)
PHONE..................................704 506-7371
EMP: 4 EST: 2022
SALES (est): 465.81K **Privately Held**
SIC: **3537** Trucks: freight, baggage, etc.: industrial, except mining

(G-2889)
SWIRL OAKHURST LLC
Also Called: Cakes
1640 Oakhurst Commons Dr Ste 103 (28205-6299)
PHONE..................................704 258-1209
Curtis Stone, *CEO*
EMP: 7 EST: 2019
SALES (est): 771.96K **Privately Held**
Web: www.swirldessertbar.com
SIC: **2051** 5812 5461 Cakes, pies, and pastries; Ice cream, soft drink and soda fountain stands; Cookies

(G-2890)
SWISS MADE BRANDS USA INC
Also Called: Swiss Diamond
200 Forsyth Hall Dr Ste H (28273-5815)
PHONE..................................704 900-6622
Amir Alon, *Pr*
▲ EMP: 7 EST: 2012
SALES (est): 1.75MM **Privately Held**
Web: www.swissdiamond.com
SIC: **3263** Cookware, fine earthenware

(G-2891)
SYCAMORE BREWING LLC
401 W 24th St (28206-2664)
PHONE..................................704 910-3821
Sarah T Brigham, *Owner*
EMP: 47 EST: 2013
SALES (est): 5.46MM **Privately Held**
Web: www.sycamorebrew.com
SIC: **2082** 5813 Beer (alcoholic beverage); Beer garden (drinking places)

(G-2892)
SYNQ MARKETING GROUP LLC
338 S Sharon Amity Rd (28211-2806)
PHONE..................................800 380-6360
John W Keith, *Mgr*
Mark M Williams, *Mgr*
EMP: 10 EST: 2018
SALES (est): 753.14K **Privately Held**
Web: www.gosynq.com
SIC: **2782** Account books

(G-2893)
SYNTECH ABRASIVES INC
8325 Arrowridge Blvd Ste H (28273-6128)
PHONE..................................704 525-8030
Fred Rodgers, *Pr*
William Tonuci, *Contrlr*
EMP: 10 EST: 1986
SQ FT: 8,500
SALES (est): 641.21K
SALES (corp-wide): 21.57MM **Privately Held**
SIC: **3291** Abrasive products
HQ: Jassco Corp.
9400 State Rd
Philadelphia PA 19114
215 824-0401

(G-2894)
T - SQUARE ENTERPRISES INC
8318 Pineville Matthews Rd (28226-4753)
PHONE..................................704 846-8233
Thomas G Duffy, *Pr*
▲ EMP: 5 EST: 1995
SQ FT: 4,000
SALES (est): 505.11K **Privately Held**
SIC: **5169** 2672 Industrial chemicals; Adhesive papers, labels, or tapes: from purchased material

(G-2895)
T AIR INC (PA)
Also Called: Airt
11020 David Taylor Dr Ste 350 (28262)
PHONE..................................980 595-2840
Nicholas Swenson, *Ch Bd*
Tracy Kennedy, *CFO*
EMP: 70 EST: 1980
SQ FT: 4,900
SALES (est): 286.83MM
SALES (corp-wide): 286.83MM **Publicly Held**
Web: www.airt.net
SIC: **4513** 4512 3728 7699 Air courier services; Air cargo carrier, scheduled; Aircraft parts and equipment, nec; Aircraft flight instrument repair

(G-2896)
T-METRICS INC
4430 Stuart Andrew Blvd (28217-1543)
PHONE..................................704 523-9583
Ronald Kahn, *Pr*
Roger Pohl, *
EMP: 27 EST: 1989
SQ FT: 850
SALES (est): 4.83MM **Privately Held**
Web: www.tmetrics.com
SIC: **3663** Radio broadcasting and communications equipment

(G-2897)
TAFFORD UNIFORMS LLC
Also Called: Tafford
2121 Distribution Center Dr Ste E (28269-4228)
PHONE..................................888 823-3673
EMP: 60
Web: www.uniformadvantage.com
SIC: **2326** 5632 Medical and hospital uniforms, men's; Apparel accessories

▲ = Import ▼ = Export
◆ = Import/Export

(G-2898)
TAN BOOKS AND PUBLISHERS INC (PA)
13315 Carowinds Blvd Ste Q (28273-7700)
P.O. Box 269 (28053)
PHONE.............................704 731-0651
Thomas A Nelson, *Pr*
Mary F Lester, *Sec*
▲ **EMP:** 8 **EST:** 1967
SQ FT: 354,000
SALES (est): 956.21K
SALES (corp-wide): 956.21K **Privately Held**
Web: www.tanbooks.com
SIC: 2731 2732 Books, publishing and printing; Books, printing and binding

(G-2899)
TAT TECHNOLOGIES GROUP
Also Called: Tat Technologies
9335 Harris Corners Pkwy Ste 26 (28269-3818)
PHONE.............................704 910-2215
Igal Zamir, *Brnch Mgr*
EMP: 600
Web: www.tat-technologies.com
SIC: 3724 Aircraft engines and engine parts
PA: Tat Technologies Ltd.
4 Habonim
Kiryat Gat 82582

(G-2900)
TAWNICO LLC
11612 James Jack Ln (28277-3747)
PHONE.............................704 606-2345
Tawanna Turner, *Managing Member*
EMP: 5 **EST:** 2021
SALES (est): 436.38K **Privately Held**
SIC: 3553 7389 Furniture makers machinery, woodworking; Business Activities at Non-Commercial Site

(G-2901)
TAYLOR INTERIORS LLC
2818 Queen City Dr (28208-3682)
P.O. Box 561035 (28256-1035)
PHONE.............................980 207-3160
Tarris Arnold, *Managing Member*
EMP: 18 **EST:** 2007
SALES (est): 7.57MM **Privately Held**
Web: www.taylorinteriorsllc.com
SIC: 7389 1742 2295 Interior design services ; Insulation, buildings; Waterproofing fabrics, except rubberizing

(G-2902)
TB WOODS INCORPORATED
Also Called: Boston Gear
701 Carrier Dr (28216-3445)
PHONE.............................704 588-5610
Ed Nevotne, *Brnch Mgr*
EMP: 57
SALES (corp-wide): 6.03B **Publicly Held**
Web: www.tbwoods.com
SIC: 3568 Power transmission equipment, nec
HQ: Tb Wood's Incorporated
440 N 5th Ave
Chambersburg PA 17201
717 264-7161

(G-2903)
TEC COAT
14030 S Lakes Dr (28273-6791)
PHONE.............................412 215-0152
David Kelley, *Managing Member*
▲ **EMP:** 35 **EST:** 2012
SALES (est): 1.89MM **Privately Held**
Web: www.teccoat-usa.com

SIC: 3479 Coating of metals and formed products

(G-2904)
TECHNOLOGY PARTNERS LLC (PA)
Also Called: Imaginesoftware
8757 Red Oak Blvd 2f (28217-3983)
PHONE.............................704 553-1004
Sam Khashman, *Pr*
Charles Kauffman, *
EMP: 100 **EST:** 2000
SQ FT: 8,000
SALES (est): 22.45MM
SALES (corp-wide): 22.45MM **Privately Held**
Web: www.imagineteam.com
SIC: 7372 3577 Application computer software; Computer peripheral equipment, nec

(G-2905)
TECNOFIRMA AMERICA INC
2030 Airport Flex Dr (28208)
PHONE.............................704 674-1296
Francisco Goi, *Pr*
Dario Geraci, *VP*
EMP: 6 **EST:** 2022
SALES (est): 150.15K
SALES (corp-wide): 1.06MM **Privately Held**
SIC: 3547 Rolling mill machinery
HQ: Tecnofirma Spa
Viale Elvezia 35
Monza MB 20900

(G-2906)
TEGUAR CORPORATION (PA)
Also Called: Teguar Computers
2920 Whitehall Park Dr (28273-3333)
PHONE.............................704 960-1761
Jonathan Staub, *Pr*
▲ **EMP:** 37 **EST:** 2010
SQ FT: 5,000
SALES (est): 4.55MM
SALES (corp-wide): 4.55MM **Privately Held**
Web: www.teguar.com
SIC: 3571 5045 Electronic computers; Computers, peripherals, and software

(G-2907)
TEKTRONIX INC
Also Called: Tektronix
4400 Stuart Andrew Blvd Ste O (28217-4626)
PHONE.............................704 527-5000
Beverly Peters, *Admn*
EMP: 5
SALES (corp-wide): 6.23B **Publicly Held**
Web: www.tek.com
SIC: 3825 Instruments to measure electricity
HQ: Tektronix, Inc.
14150 Sw Karl Braun Dr
Beaverton OR 97077
800 833-9200

(G-2908)
TENNESSEE NEDGRAPHICS INC
1809 Cross Beam Dr Ste E (28217-2891)
PHONE.............................704 414-4224
Robbert Ausems, *Dir*
EMP: 10
SALES (corp-wide): 144.82MM **Privately Held**
Web: www.nedgraphics.com
SIC: 2759 Commercial printing, nec
HQ: Nedgraphics Of Tennessee, Inc.
855 Abutment Rd Ste 6
Dalton GA 30721

(G-2909)
TEXTILE PRINTING INC
2431 Thornridge Rd (28226-6450)
P.O. Box 337 (28042-0337)
PHONE.............................704 521-8099
Robert Dale Dixon, *Pr*
Jane Dixon, *
▲ **EMP:** 5 **EST:** 1987
SALES (est): 471.81K **Privately Held**
Web: www.fishertextiles.com
SIC: 2396 Screen printing on fabric articles

(G-2910)
TFS MANAGEMENT GROUP LLC
Also Called: New Wave Acrylics
4331 Chesapeake Dr (28216-3410)
PHONE.............................704 399-3999
EMP: 8 **EST:** 2005
SALES (est): 1.17MM **Privately Held**
Web: www.newwaveacrylics.com
SIC: 3089 Injection molding of plastics

(G-2911)
THOMAS CONCRETE CAROLINA INC
3701 N Graham St (28206-1628)
P.O. Box 790105 (28206-7901)
PHONE.............................704 333-0390
Donny Senter, *Brnch Mgr*
EMP: 10
SALES (corp-wide): 1.15B **Privately Held**
Web: www.thomasconcrete.com
SIC: 3273 Ready-mixed concrete
HQ: Thomas Concrete Of Carolina, Inc.
1131 Nw Street
Raleigh NC 27603
919 832-0451

(G-2912)
THOMAS GOLF INC
9716 Rea Rd Ste B # 170 (28277-6663)
PHONE.............................704 461-1342
Thomas Sacco, *CEO*
EMP: 6 **EST:** 1995
SALES (est): 239.4K **Privately Held**
Web: www.thomasgolf.com
SIC: 3949 5091 Shafts, golf club; Golf equipment

(G-2913)
THOMAS M BROWN INC
Also Called: Tmb Cranes
1311 Amble Dr (28206-1307)
P.O. Box 26612 (28221-6612)
PHONE.............................704 597-0246
EMP: 15 **EST:** 1970
SALES (est): 2.03MM **Privately Held**
Web: www.tmbcranes.com
SIC: 3536 5084 1796 Hoists, cranes, and monorails; Cranes, industrial; Installing building equipment

(G-2914)
THREADLINE PRODUCTS INC
3346 Pelton St (28217-1318)
P.O. Box 11650 (28220-1650)
PHONE.............................704 527-9052
Jennifer Z Miller, *Pr*
Joshua Miller, *VP*
EMP: 10 **EST:** 1984
SQ FT: 10,000
SALES (est): 4.2MM **Privately Held**
Web: www.threadlineproducts.com
SIC: 3441 Fabricated structural metal

(G-2915)
THREATSWITCH INC
300 W Summit Ave Ste 110 (28203-4476)
PHONE.............................877 449-3220
John Dillard, *CEO*

EMP: 20 **EST:** 2016
SALES (est): 1.06MM **Privately Held**
Web: www.signincompliance.com
SIC: 7372 Application computer software

(G-2916)
THREE LADIES AND A MALE LLC
3515 Arsenal Ct Apt 103 (28273-3997)
PHONE.............................704 287-1584
EMP: 5 **EST:** 2021
SALES (est): 405.7K **Privately Held**
SIC: 3537 7389 Trucks: freight, baggage, etc.: industrial, except mining; Business services, nec

(G-2917)
THREE TREES BINDERY
1600 Burtonwood Cir (28212-7019)
PHONE.............................704 724-9409
Michelle Skiba-smith, *Owner*
EMP: 5 **EST:** 2015
SALES (est): 113.04K **Privately Held**
SIC: 2789 Bookbinding and related work

(G-2918)
THURSTON GENOMICS LLC
7806 Springs Village Ln (28226-3350)
PHONE.............................980 237-7547
Virginia Thurston, *Prin*
EMP: 5 **EST:** 2017
SALES (est): 97.34K **Privately Held**
SIC: 2835 Microbiology and virology diagnostic products

(G-2919)
TIMBER WOLF WOOD CREATIONS INC
2008 Starbrook Dr (28210-6007)
PHONE.............................704 309-5118
Ken Nahas, *Ofcr*
EMP: 4 **EST:** 2001
SALES (est): 274.95K **Privately Held**
SIC: 2431 Millwork

(G-2920)
TIMEPLANNER CALENDARS INC
Also Called: Journalbooks
1010 Timeplanner Dr (28206-1951)
P.O. Box 536400 (30353-6400)
PHONE.............................704 377-0024
▲ **EMP:** 110 **EST:** 1971
SALES (est): 9.74MM **Privately Held**
Web: www.journalbooks.com
SIC: 2759 Calendars: printing, nsk
HQ: Polyconcept North America, Inc.
400 Hunt Valley Rd
New Kensington PA 15068

(G-2921)
TITEFLEX CORPORATION
P.O. Box 905743 (28290-5743)
PHONE.............................647 638-7160
EMP: 71
SALES (corp-wide): 3.97B **Privately Held**
Web: www.titeflex.com
SIC: 3052 3599 Plastic hose; Hose, flexible metallic
HQ: Titeflex Corporation
603 Hendee St
Springfield MA 01104
413 739-5631

(G-2922)
TLV CORPORATION
Also Called: T L V
13901 S Lakes Dr (28273-6790)
PHONE.............................704 597-9070
James Risko, *Pr*
Trevor Dubroff, *
▲ **EMP:** 30 **EST:** 1985

SQ FT: 25,000
SALES (est): 6.19MM **Privately Held**
SIC: 3494 Steam fittings and specialties

(G-2923)
TMS INTERNATIONAL LLC
6601 Lakeview Rd (28269-2604)
PHONE.............................704 604-0287
EMP: 11
Web: www.tmsinternational.com
SIC: 3312 Blast furnaces and steel mills
HQ: Tms International, Llc
    2835 East Carson Street
    Pittsburgh PA 15203
    412 678-6141

(G-2924)
TOBACCO OUTLET PRODUCTS LLC
Also Called: Tobacco Outlet Products
6401 Carmel Rd Ste 204 (28226-8299)
P.O. Box 669 (28103)
PHONE.............................704 341-9388
Jennifer Lown, *Mgr*
Paul Walsh, *Prin*
EMP: 5 EST: 1997
SQ FT: 1,800
SALES (est): 339.68K **Privately Held**
Web: www.smokeodorsolution.com
SIC: 3999 5199 Candles; Candles

(G-2925)
TODAYS CHARLOTTE WOMAN
5200 Park Rd Ste 126 (28209-3675)
PHONE.............................704 521-6872
Cama Mcnamara, *Owner*
EMP: 6 EST: 2004
SALES (est): 113.9K **Privately Held**
Web: www.charlotteseen.com
SIC: 2721 Magazines: publishing and printing

(G-2926)
TODAYTEC LLC
6701 Northpark Blvd Ste K (28216-0081)
PHONE.............................704 790-2440
Paggy Zhou, *Pr*
Jack Liu, *VP*
Keith Furr, *VP*
▲ EMP: 32 EST: 2010
SQ FT: 12,160
SALES (est): 5.14MM
SALES (corp-wide): 90.06MM **Privately Held**
Web: www.todaytecllc.com
SIC: 3825 Analog-digital converters, electronic instrumentation type
PA: Hangzhou Todaytec Digital Co., Ltd
    No. 600 Kangxin Road, Donghu Street, Linping District
    Hangzhou ZJ 31110
    57186358910

(G-2927)
TOKAI CARBON GE LLC (DH)
6210 Ardrey Kell Rd Ste 270 (28277-4945)
PHONE.............................980 260-1130
Scott Carlton, *Pr*
EMP: 21 EST: 2015
SQ FT: 10,000
SALES (est): 26.44MM **Privately Held**
Web: www.tokaicarbonusa.com
SIC: 3624 Carbon and graphite products
HQ: Tokai Carbon Ge Holding Llc
    6210 Ardrey Kell Rd Ste 2
    Charlotte NC 28277
    704 593-5100

(G-2928)
TOM ROCHESTER & ASSOCIATES INC (PA)
Also Called: Southstern Archtctural Systems
9325 Forsyth Park Dr (28273-3885)

PHONE.............................704 896-5805
Tom Rochester, *Pr*
Cindy Rochester, *Treas*
EMP: 4 EST: 1989
SALES (est): 4.22MM **Privately Held**
Web: www.seas-tr.com
SIC: 3531 Construction machinery

(G-2929)
TONYAS CROCHETED CREATIONS
7535 Marlbrook Dr (28212-4769)
PHONE.............................704 421-2143
Guatonya Reese, *Prin*
EMP: 4 EST: 2011
SALES (est): 104.44K **Privately Held**
SIC: 2399 Hand woven and crocheted products

(G-2930)
TOPGOLF
8024 Savoy Corporate Dr (28273-6267)
PHONE.............................704 612-4745
EMP: 51 EST: 2017
SALES (est): 7.09MM **Privately Held**
Web: www.topgolf.com
SIC: 3949 Sporting and athletic goods, nec

(G-2931)
TOTER LLC
6525 Morrison Blvd Ste 300 (28211-3561)
PHONE.............................704 936-5610
EMP: 52
Web: www.toter.com
SIC: 3089 Garbage containers, plastics
HQ: Toter, Llc
    841 Meacham Rd
    Statesville NC 28677
    800 424-0422

(G-2932)
TRAFAG INC
8848 Red Oak Blvd Ste I (28217-5517)
PHONE.............................704 343-6339
Robert Kinkopf, *Mgr*
EMP: 5 EST: 2013
SQ FT: 2,357
SALES (est): 1.82MM **Privately Held**
Web: www.trafag.com
SIC: 3829 5049 3823 Thermometers and temperature sensors; Precision tools; Pressure measurement instruments, industrial
HQ: Trafag Ag
    Industriestrasse 11
    Bubikon ZH 8608

(G-2933)
TRANE COMPANY (DH)
4500 Morris Field Dr (28208-5837)
PHONE.............................704 398-4600
Michael Truan, *Prin*
▲ EMP: 34 EST: 1973
SALES (est): 23.13MM **Privately Held**
Web: www.trane.com
SIC: 3585 Air conditioning equipment, complete
HQ: Trane Technologies International Limited
    Units 170/175 Lake View Drive
    Swords

(G-2934)
TRANE US INC
Also Called: Trane
4501 S Tryon St (28217-1843)
P.O. Box 240605 (28224-0605)
PHONE.............................704 525-9600
Mark Cresitello, *Prin*
EMP: 128
Web: www.trane.com

SIC: 3585 Refrigeration and heating equipment
HQ: Trane U.S. Inc.
    800-E Beaty St
    Davidson NC 28036
    704 655-4000

(G-2935)
TRANE US INC
Also Called: Trane
8610 Air Park West Dr Ste C (28214-8519)
PHONE.............................704 697-9006
Jon White, *Brnch Mgr*
EMP: 11
Web: www.trane.com
SIC: 3585 1711 Refrigeration and heating equipment; Septic system construction
HQ: Trane U.S. Inc.
    800-E Beaty St
    Davidson NC 28036
    704 655-4000

(G-2936)
TRANSBOTICS CORPORATION
3400 Latrobe Dr (28211-4847)
PHONE.............................704 362-1115
▲ EMP: 30
Web: www.scottautomation.com
SIC: 3535 7372 Conveyors and conveying equipment; Prepackaged software

(G-2937)
TRANSTEX BELTING
10125 S Tryon St (28273-6509)
PHONE.............................704 334-5353
Peter Nikolich, *Mgr*
EMP: 6 EST: 2010
SALES (est): 591.44K **Privately Held**
Web: www.forbo.com
SIC: 3052 Rubber and plastics hose and beltings

(G-2938)
TRAXON TECHNOLOGIES LLC
2915 Whitehall Park Dr (28273-3383)
PHONE.............................201 508-1570
Terry H Oneal, *Pr*
EMP: 7 EST: 2016
SALES (est): 2.25MM **Privately Held**
Web: www.traxon-ecue.com
SIC: 3641 Electric lamps

(G-2939)
TRESATA INC (PA)
1616 Candem Rd Ste 300 (28203)
PHONE.............................980 224-2097
Abhishek Mehta, *CEO*
Richard Morris, *
Elizabeth Sterling, *
Michael Dulin, *CMO**
EMP: 22 EST: 2011
SQ FT: 10,000
SALES (est): 5.23MM
SALES (corp-wide): 5.23MM **Privately Held**
Web: www.tresata.ai
SIC: 7372 Application computer software

(G-2940)
TRI-CITY CONCRETE LLC
3823 Raleigh St (28206-2042)
PHONE.............................704 372-2930
Michael J Wenig, *Prin*
EMP: 4 EST: 2011
SALES (est): 124.97K **Privately Held**
SIC: 3273 Ready-mixed concrete

(G-2941)
TRI-TEC IND INC
200 Peachtree Dr S (28217-2066)

PHONE.............................704 424-5995
Michael Davidson, *Pr*
Raymond Motley, *Sec*
Richard Loyd, *Sec*
EMP: 8 EST: 1997
SQ FT: 6,000
SALES (est): 928.94K **Privately Held**
Web: www.tritecindustries.com
SIC: 3599 Machine shop, jobbing and repair

(G-2942)
TRIANGLE INDUS SUP HLDINGS LLC (PA)
228 Westinghouse Blvd Ste 104 (28273-6230)
PHONE.............................704 395-0600
EMP: 5 EST: 2001
SALES (est): 6.87MM **Privately Held**
Web: www.hughesindustrial.com
SIC: 5085 3052 5072 Industrial supplies; Rubber and plastics hose and beltings; Hardware

(G-2943)
TRICK TANK INC
2250 Toomey Ave (28203-4635)
PHONE.............................980 406-3200
Bob Gilbertson, *Pr*
▲ EMP: 6 EST: 2000
SALES (est): 378.83K **Privately Held**
Web: www.tricktank.com
SIC: 3634 Air purifiers, portable

(G-2944)
TRIMECH SOLUTIONS LLC
201 Mccullough Dr Ste 300 (28262-1367)
PHONE.............................704 503-6644
Mike Voll, *Mgr*
EMP: 6
SALES (corp-wide): 30.06MM **Privately Held**
Web: www.trimech.com
SIC: 7372 7373 Prepackaged software; Value-added resellers, computer systems
PA: Trimech Solutions, Llc
    3060 Williams Dr Ste 300
    Fairfax VA 22031
    443 824-3052

(G-2945)
TRIPLE C BREWING COMPANY LLC
Also Called: Triple C Brewing Co
2900 Griffith St (28203-5430)
PHONE.............................704 372-3212
Christopher J Harker, *Managing Member*
▲ EMP: 17 EST: 2011
SALES (est): 1.1MM **Privately Held**
Web: www.triplecbrewing.com
SIC: 5813 2082 Bars and lounges; Beer (alcoholic beverage)

(G-2946)
TRIPLE CROWN INTERNATIONAL LLC
Also Called: T C I
12205 Parks Farm Ln (28277-5621)
P.O. Box 79313 (28271-7063)
PHONE.............................704 846-4983
Thomas J Mcalpine Senior, *Managing Member*
◆ EMP: 5 EST: 2008
SALES (est): 553.63K **Privately Held**
SIC: 3554 8742 7389 Paper industries machinery; Distribution channels consultant ; Business Activities at Non-Commercial Site

(G-2947)
TROPICAL NUT & FRUIT CO (PA)
Also Called: Truly Good Foods

▲ = Import ▼ = Export
◆ = Import/Export

1100 Continental Blvd (28273)
P.O. Box 7507 (28241)
PHONE..................800 438-4470
TOLL FREE: 800
John R Bauer, *Pr*
Carolyn Y Bennett, *
Angela Bauer, *
Michael R P York, *
Betty Lee York, *
◆ EMP: 101 EST: 1977
SALES (est): 100.82MM
SALES (corp-wide): 100.82MM **Privately Held**
Web: www.trulygoodfoods.com
SIC: 5149 5145 2099 2068 Specialty food items; Nuts, salted or roasted; Food preparations, nec; Salted and roasted nuts and seeds

(G-2948)
TRUCK PARTS INC
707 Kennedy St (28206-1939)
PHONE..................704 332-7909
Robert K Sims, *Pr*
EMP: 12 EST: 1966
SQ FT: 14,750
SALES (est): 1.83MM **Privately Held**
Web: www.truckpartsinc.com
SIC: 5013 3714 Truck parts and accessories; Rebuilding engines and transmissions, factory basis

(G-2949)
TSG2 INC
1235 East Blvd Ste E (28203-5876)
PHONE..................704 347-4484
Deborah Starne, *CEO*
Beborah Starne, *CEO*
EMP: 4 EST: 2009
SALES (est): 513.14K **Privately Held**
SIC: 2674 Shipping and shopping bags or sacks

(G-2950)
TTI FLOOR CARE NORTH AMER INC
Also Called: Techtronic Industries
8405 Ibm Dr (28262-4331)
PHONE..................440 996-2000
EMP: 100
Web: www.ttifloorcare.com
SIC: 5722 3634 Vacuum cleaners; Air purifiers, portable
HQ: Tti Floor Care North America, Inc.
8405 Ibm Dr
Charlotte NC 28262

(G-2951)
TTI FLOOR CARE NORTH AMER INC (DH)
Also Called: Royal Appliance Manufacturing
8405 Ibm Dr (28262)
PHONE..................888 321-1134
Chris Gurreri, *Pr*
◆ EMP: 350 EST: 2007
SQ FT: 450,000
SALES (est): 48.1MM **Privately Held**
Web: www.ttifloorcare.com
SIC: 3825 5072 Power measuring equipment, electrical; Power tools and accessories
HQ: Royal Appliance Mfg. Co.
8405 Ibm Dr
Charlotte NC 28262
888 321-1134

(G-2952)
TUCKERS FARM INC
201 W 31st St (28206-2205)
P.O. Box 790008 (28206-7900)
PHONE..................704 375-8199
Mike Kelly, *Pr*

EMP: 7 EST: 1995
SQ FT: 9,000
SALES (est): 841.16K **Privately Held**
Web: www.millworkon31st.com
SIC: 2431 Millwork

(G-2953)
TUMI STORE - CHRLTTE DGLAS INT
5501 Josh Birmingham Pkwy Unit 21a (28208-5750)
PHONE..................704 359-8771
EMP: 16 EST: 2018
SALES (est): 126.83K
SALES (corp-wide): 8.01MM **Privately Held**
Web: www.cltairport.com
SIC: 3161 Luggage
PA: Samsonite Group S.A.
Avenue De La Liberte 13-15
Luxembourg 1931

(G-2954)
TURMAR MARBLE INC
Also Called: Turmar
914 Richland Dr (28211-1250)
PHONE..................704 391-1800
Aydin Yoruk, *Pr*
▲ EMP: 4 EST: 2006
SALES (est): 225.18K **Privately Held**
Web: www.turmar.com
SIC: 3281 Marble, building: cut and shaped

(G-2955)
TWO OF A KIND PUBLISHING LLC
8239 Romana Red Ln (28213-5328)
PHONE..................704 497-2879
Al Bogur, *COO*
EMP: 4 EST: 2003
SALES (est): 230.67K **Privately Held**
SIC: 2731 Books, publishing and printing

(G-2956)
TWORK TECHNOLOGY INC
3536 N Davidson St (28205-1125)
PHONE..................704 218-9675
Keith Minder, *Pr*
EMP: 4 EST: 2002
SALES (est): 662.94K **Privately Held**
Web: www.tworktechnology.com
SIC: 7372 7373 7379 7371 Business oriented computer software; Systems software development services; Online services technology consultants; Computer software systems analysis and design, custom

(G-2957)
U S BOTTLERS MCHY CO INC
11911 Steele Creek Rd (28273-3773)
P.O. Box 7203 (28241-7203)
PHONE..................704 588-4750
Tom Risser, *Pr*
Anthony J Triana, *
L Cameron Caudle, *
▲ EMP: 75 EST: 1912
SQ FT: 61,000
SALES (est): 24.6MM **Privately Held**
Web: www.usbottlers.com
SIC: 3565 5084 Bottling machinery: filling, capping, labeling; Recapping machinery, for tires

(G-2958)
UKG KRONOS SYSTEMS LLC
8801 J M Keynes Dr Ste 240 (28262-8436)
PHONE..................800 225-1561
Janet Mcguirt, *Mgr*
EMP: 8
SALES (corp-wide): 1.85B **Privately Held**
Web: www.ukg.com

SIC: 7372 Business oriented computer software
HQ: Ukg Kronos Systems, Llc
900 Chelmsford St
Lowell MA 01851
978 250-9800

(G-2959)
ULLMAN GROUP LLC
10925 Westlake Dr (28273-3740)
P.O. Box 430 (28173-1047)
PHONE..................704 246-7333
Luke Ullman, *Prin*
EMP: 17 EST: 2010
SQ FT: 10,000
SALES (est): 2.79MM **Privately Held**
Web: www.theullmangroup.com
SIC: 1751 2541 Cabinet and finish carpentry; Wood partitions and fixtures

(G-2960)
ULTIMATE FLOOR CLEANING
9625 Commons East Dr Apt L (28277-1717)
PHONE..................704 912-8978
Eric Chisholm, *VP*
Anthony Ceasar, *VP*
EMP: 4 EST: 2014
SALES (est): 179.79K **Privately Held**
SIC: 3645 7359 7699 7389 Floor lamps; Floor maintenance equipment rental; Cleaning services; Business services, nec

(G-2961)
UNITED AIR FILTER COMPANY CORP
Also Called: Clear-Flo Air Filters
1000 W Palmer St (28208-5344)
P.O. Box 34215 (28234-4215)
PHONE..................704 334-5311
William Kinney Iii, *Pr*
E Allen Miller, *
EMP: 25 EST: 1968
SQ FT: 40,000
SALES (est): 4.6MM **Privately Held**
Web: www.unitedairfilter.com
SIC: 3564 3585 Filters, air: furnaces, air conditioning equipment, etc.; Refrigeration and heating equipment

(G-2962)
UNITED SERVICES GROUP LLC (PA)
2505 Hutchison Mcdonald Rd (28269)
PHONE..................980 237-1335
Joshua Armstrong, *CEO*
Stephen Gillman, *COO*
EMP: 5 EST: 2013
SQ FT: 5,000
SALES (est): 10.3MM
SALES (corp-wide): 10.3MM **Privately Held**
Web: www.united-services.com
SIC: 7692 Automotive welding

(G-2963)
UNITED TECHNICAL SERVICES LLC
2505 Hutchison Mcdonald Rd (28269-4254)
PHONE..................980 237-1335
Joshua Armstrong, *CEO*
Stephen Gillman, *COO*
Kerrie Holden, *Off Mgr*
EMP: 10 EST: 2013
SALES (est): 440.5K
SALES (corp-wide): 10.3MM **Privately Held**
Web: www.united-services.com
SIC: 7692 3599 Welding repair; Machine shop, jobbing and repair
PA: United Services Group, Llc
2505 Htchison Mcdonald Rd
Charlotte NC 28269
980 237-1335

(G-2964)
UNITY HLTHCARE LAB BILLING LLP
Also Called: Health Services
7508 E Independence Blvd Ste 109 (28227-9473)
PHONE..................980 209-0402
Tanya Diaz, *Pt*
EMP: 7 EST: 2007
SALES (est): 214.9K **Privately Held**
SIC: 8099 8093 8734 3999 Health screening service; Mental health clinic, outpatient; Testing laboratories

(G-2965)
UNIVERSAL AIR PRODUCTS CORP
4715 Stockholm Ct (28273-5995)
PHONE..................704 374-0600
John Haslam, *Brnch Mgr*
EMP: 6
SALES (corp-wide): 14.11MM **Privately Held**
Web: www.uapc.com
SIC: 3563 3564 Air and gas compressors; Blowers and fans
PA: Universal Air Products Corporation
1140 Kingwood Ave
Norfolk VA 23502
757 461-0077

(G-2966)
UPCHURCH MACHINE CO INC
11633 Fruehauf Dr (28273-5510)
P.O. Box 7792 (28241-7792)
PHONE..................704 588-2895
Fred D Upchurch, *Pr*
Martha Upchurch, *Sec*
EMP: 9 EST: 1974
SQ FT: 16,000
SALES (est): 1.04MM **Privately Held**
Web: www.upchurchmachine.com
SIC: 3599 Machine shop, jobbing and repair

(G-2967)
UPTOWN PUBLISHING INC
8037 Corporate Center Dr (28226-4545)
PHONE..................704 543-0690
Todd C Brockmann, *Prin*
EMP: 4 EST: 2008
SALES (est): 213.42K **Privately Held**
SIC: 2741 Miscellaneous publishing

(G-2968)
URBAN SPICED LLC
15720 Brixham Hill Ave Ste 300 (28277-4651)
PHONE..................704 741-1174
EMP: 5 EST: 2020
SALES (est): 254.23K **Privately Held**
SIC: 2099 Spices, including grinding

(G-2969)
USRX LLC
Also Called: Urban Skin Rx
8604 Cliff Cameron Dr Ste 175 (28269-8511)
PHONE..................980 221-1200
Victoria Payne, *CEO*
Lindsey Fore, *
Cheryl Moss, *
▼ EMP: 50 EST: 2015
SALES (est): 10.37MM **Privately Held**
Web: www.urbanskinrx.com
SIC: 2844 5122 5999 Cosmetic preparations; Cosmetics; Cosmetics

(G-2970)
VALD GROUP INC
2108 South Blvd Ste 115 (28203-5098)
PHONE..................704 345-5145
Christopher Rowe, *Pr*

EMP: 7 EST: 2018
SALES (est): 2.25MM **Privately Held**
Web: www.valdperformance.com
SIC: 3845 Electromedical apparatus

(G-2971)
VALMET INC
3440 Toringdon Way Ste 300 (28277-3190)
PHONE..........................803 289-4900
Jim Longwith, *Mgr*
EMP: 6
SALES (corp-wide): 6.01B **Privately Held**
Web: www.valmet.com
SIC: 3554 Pulp mill machinery
HQ: Valmet, Inc.
   3720 Davinci Ct Ste 300
   Norcross GA 30092
   770 263-7863

(G-2972)
VALMET INC
Also Called: Metso Power USA
3430 Toringdon Way (28277-2446)
PHONE..........................704 541-1453
Calderone Vito, *Brnch Mgr*
EMP: 219
SALES (corp-wide): 6.01B **Privately Held**
Web: www.valmet.com
SIC: 3544 Special dies, tools, jigs, and
   fixtures
HQ: Valmet, Inc.
   3720 Davinci Ct Ste 300
   Norcross GA 30092
   770 263-7863

(G-2973)
VANS INC
4400 Sharon Rd Ste 159 (28211-3674)
PHONE..........................704 364-3811
Christine Quimby, *Brnch Mgr*
EMP: 6
SALES (corp-wide): 10.45B **Publicly Held**
Web: www.vans.com
SIC: 3021 Canvas shoes, rubber soled
HQ: Vans, Inc.
   1588 S Coast Dr
   Costa Mesa CA 92626
   714 755-4000

(G-2974)
VAV PLASTICS NC LLC
8710 Air Park West Dr Ste 200
(28214-8686)
PHONE..........................704 325-9332
EMP: 8 **EST:** 2020
SALES (est): 3.11MM **Privately Held**
SIC: 3085 Plastics bottles

(G-2975)
VERBATIM AMERICAS LLC
7300 Reames Rd (28216-2228)
PHONE..........................704 547-6551
EMP: 5
Web: www.verbatim.com
SIC: 3572 Computer storage devices
PA: Verbatim Americas Llc
   8210 Univ Exec Pk Dr Ste
   Charlotte NC 28262

(G-2976)
VERBATIM AMERICAS LLC (PA)
8210 University Exec Park Dr Ste 300
(28262-3595)
PHONE..........................704 547-6500
▲ **EMP:** 91 **EST:** 2007
SALES (est): 23.91MM **Privately Held**
Web: www.verbatim.com
SIC: 3572 Computer storage devices

(G-2977)
VERBATIM CORPORATION
8210 University Exec Park Dr Ste 300
(28262-3368)
PHONE..........................704 547-6500
◆ **EMP:** 62
Web: www.verbatim.com.sg
SIC: 3572 Computer storage devices

(G-2978)
VERMEER MANUFACTURING
COMPANY
10900 Carpet St (28273-6205)
PHONE..........................410 285-0200
EMP: 10
SALES (corp-wide): 885.68MM **Privately**
Held
Web: www.vermeerma.com
SIC: 3531 Construction machinery
PA: Vermeer Manufacturing Company
   1210 E Vermeer Rd
   Pella IA 50219
   641 628-3141

(G-2979)
VERONA CABINETS & SURFACES
LLC
6700 South Blvd (28217-4379)
PHONE..........................704 755-5259
EMP: 4 **EST:** 2017
SALES (est): 94.34K **Privately Held**
SIC: 2434 Wood kitchen cabinets

(G-2980)
VESTIGE GROUP LLC
2459 Wilkinson Blvd Ste 205 (28208-5675)
P.O. Box 1107 (28173)
PHONE..........................704 321-4960
Matthew Lyons, *CEO*
EMP: 50 **EST:** 2013
SALES (est): 4.37MM **Privately Held**
Web: www.vestigeview.com
SIC: 7372 Application computer software

(G-2981)
VESUVIUS PENN CORPORATION
(HQ)
5510 77 Center Dr Ste 100 (28217-3108)
PHONE..........................724 535-4374
Cedric Woindrich, *Pr*
EMP: 22 **EST:** 2021
SALES (est): 45.74MM
SALES (corp-wide): 2.41B **Privately Held**
SIC: 3255 Castable refractories: clay
PA: Vesuvius Plc
   165 Fleet Street
   London EC4A
   207 822-0000

(G-2982)
VESUVIUS USA CORPORATION
5510 77 Center Dr # 100 (28217-3108)
PHONE..........................412 429-1800
Glenn Cowie, *Pr*
Luis Alberto Ordaz, *
Steven Delcotto, *
Glenn Cowie, *Treas*
◆ **EMP:** 75 **EST:** 1989
SALES (est): 4.28MM
SALES (corp-wide): 2.41B **Privately Held**
SIC: 3297 Nonclay refractories
PA: Vesuvius Plc
   165 Fleet Street
   London EC4A
   207 822-0000

(G-2983)
VIBRATION SOLUTIONS LLC
5900 Harris Technology Blvd Ste G
(28269-3808)

PHONE..........................704 896-7535
Allan Hansen, *Managing Member*
EMP: 8 **EST:** 2003
SQ FT: 20,000
SALES (est): 1.01MM **Privately Held**
Web: www.vibration-solutions.com
SIC: 3465 Automotive stampings

(G-2984)
VIGOR LLC
1209 S College St Apt 1130 (28203-4368)
PHONE..........................980 474-1124
EMP: 4 **EST:** 2016
SALES (est): 98.95K **Privately Held**
SIC: 3731 Shipbuilding and repairing

(G-2985)
VINEYARD BLUFFTON LLC
1001 Morehead Square Dr Ste 320
(28203-4253)
PHONE..........................704 307-2737
Sean Pesek, *Owner*
EMP: 6 **EST:** 2018
SALES (est): 193.93K **Privately Held**
Web: www.vineyardseniorliving.com
SIC: 2084 Wines

(G-2986)
VISION ENVELOPE INC
Also Called: Vision Print Solutions
2451 Executive St (28208-3635)
PHONE..........................704 392-9090
Susan Zerona, *CEO*
Mark Zerona, *Pr*
EMP: 16 **EST:** 1990
SQ FT: 16,400
SALES (est): 941.1K **Privately Held**
Web: www.visionenvelope.com
SIC: 2759 Envelopes: printing, nsk

(G-2987)
VISUAL COMFORT
2137 South Blvd Ste 100 (28203-5189)
PHONE..........................980 666-4120
EMP: 6
SALES (est): 390.85K **Privately Held**
SIC: 3645 Residential lighting fixtures

(G-2988)
VMOD FIBER LLC
811 Pressley Rd (28217-0970)
PHONE..........................704 525-6851
William Younts, *Pr*
Michael Alexander, *CFO*
◆ **EMP:** 10 **EST:** 2004
SALES (est): 489.36K
SALES (corp-wide): 13.72MM **Privately**
Held
SIC: 2299 5023 Fibers, textile: recovery from
   textile mill waste and rags; Sheets, textile
PA: Rsm Co.
   811 Pressley Rd
   Charlotte NC 28217
   704 525-6851

(G-2989)
VOCOLLECT INC
855 S Mint St (28202-1517)
PHONE..........................980 279-4119
EMP: 25
SALES (corp-wide): 38.5B **Publicly Held**
SIC: 3577 Encoders, computer peripheral
   equipment
HQ: Vocollect, Inc.
   2555 Smallman St Ste 200
   Pittsburgh PA 15222
   412 829-8145

(G-2990)
VOLVO MOTOR GRADERS INC
8844 Mount Holly Rd (28214-8350)
PHONE..........................704 609-3604
Andres Larsson, *Pr*
Patrick Olnery, *
EMP: 5 **EST:** 1993
SQ FT: 14,562
SALES (est): 985.43K
SALES (corp-wide): 52.58B **Privately Held**
SIC: 3462 Construction or mining equipment
   forgings, ferrous
HQ: Vna Holding Inc.
   7825 National Service Rd
   Greensboro NC 27409
   336 393-4890

(G-2991)
VULCAN MATERIALS COMPANY
11020 David Taylor Dr Ste 105
(28262-1101)
PHONE..........................704 549-1540
Dave Ford, *Mgr*
EMP: 4
Web: www.vulcanmaterials.com
SIC: 3273 Ready-mixed concrete
PA: Vulcan Materials Company
   1200 Urban Center Dr
   Birmingham AL 35242

(G-2992)
VULCAN MATERIALS COMPANY
11435 Brooks Mill Rd (28227-8005)
PHONE..........................704 545-5687
John Basso, *Mgr*
EMP: 4
Web: www.vulcanmaterials.com
SIC: 3273 2951 Ready-mixed concrete;
   Asphalt paving mixtures and blocks
PA: Vulcan Materials Company
   1200 Urban Center Dr
   Birmingham AL 35242

(G-2993)
VULCRAFT CARRIER CORP
2100 Rexford Rd (28211-3589)
PHONE..........................704 367-8674
EMP: 12 **EST:** 2014
SALES (est): 692.82K **Privately Held**
Web: www.vulcraft.com
SIC: 3312 Blast furnaces and steel mills

(G-2994)
W B MASON CO INC
10800 Withers Cove Park Dr (28278-6928)
PHONE..........................888 926-2766
EMP: 35
SALES (corp-wide): 1.01B **Privately Held**
Web: www.wbmason.com
SIC: 5943 5712 2752 Office forms and
   supplies; Office furniture; Commercial
   printing, lithographic
PA: W. B. Mason Co., Inc.
   59 Centre St
   Brockton MA 02301
   508 586-3434

(G-2995)
W H RGERS SHTMTL IR WRKS INC
837 Toddville Rd (28214-1839)
PHONE..........................704 394-2191
Robert Canipe, *Pr*
Wendell Canipe, *
EMP: 23 **EST:** 1963
SQ FT: 46,000
SALES (est): 2.97MM **Privately Held**
Web: www.whrogers.com
SIC: 3599 3444 Machine shop, jobbing and
   repair; Sheet metalwork

▲ = Import ▼ = Export
◆ = Import/Export

(G-2996)
W M PLASTICS INC
Also Called: National Textile Supply
5301 Terminal St (28208-1254)
PHONE.....................704 599-0511
William Mackinnon, *Pr*
Joyce Brown, *Sec*
▲ EMP: 16 EST: 1983
SQ FT: 30,000
SALES (est): 7.54MM Privately Held
Web: www.wmplasticsinc.com
SIC: 2821 Polyvinyl chloride resins, PVC

(G-2997)
WADDINGTON GROUP INC (DH)
Also Called: Wna
3436 Toringdon Way Ste 100 (28277-2449)
PHONE.....................800 845-6051
Stan Bikulege, *CEO*
Dennis Norman, *
EMP: 41 EST: 2014
SALES (est): 83.35MM
SALES (corp-wide): 26.11B Publicly Held
Web: www.novolex.com
SIC: 3089 2656 Injection molding of plastics;
Sanitary food containers
HQ: Novolex Holdings, Llc
3436 Tringdon Way Ste 100
Charlotte NC 28277
800 845-6051

(G-2998)
WADDINGTON NORTH AMERICA INC (DH)
Also Called: Novolex Covington
3436 Toringdon Way Ste 100 (28277-2449)
PHONE.....................800 845-6051
Stanley Bikulege, *Pr*
Ryan Stephens, *Sec*
◆ EMP: 13 EST: 1985
SQ FT: 5,000
SALES (est): 452.73MM
SALES (corp-wide): 26.11B Publicly Held
Web: www.novolex.com
SIC: 3089 Plastics kitchenware, tableware,
and houseware
HQ: Novolex Holdings, Llc
3436 Tringdon Way Ste 100
Charlotte NC 28277
800 845-6051

(G-2999)
WALDENWOOD GROUP INC
Also Called: Steel Tech
3800 Woodpark Blvd Ste I (28206-4247)
PHONE.....................704 313-8004
EMP: 10 EST: 1998
SALES (est): 768.41K Privately Held
Web: www.steeltechus.com
SIC: 3441 1799 Bridge sections,
prefabricated, railway; Welding on site

(G-3000)
WALDENWOOD GROUP LLC
Also Called: Steel Tech
3800 Woodpark Blvd Ste I (28206-4247)
PHONE.....................704 331-8004
EMP: 10 EST: 2020
SALES (est): 1.07MM Privately Held
SIC: 3441 Fabricated structural metal

(G-3001)
WALGREEN CO
Also Called: Walgreens
2215 W Arrowood Rd (28217-7939)
PHONE.....................704 525-2628
EMP: 8
SALES (corp-wide): 147.66B Publicly
Held
Web: www.walgreens.com

SIC: 5912 5999 2771 2759 Drug stores;
Alarm and safety equipment stores;
Greeting cards; Commercial printing, nec
HQ: Walgreen Co.
200 Wilmot Rd
Deerfield IL 60015
800 925-4733

(G-3002)
WAMBAM FENCE INC
6935 Reames Rd Ste K (28216-2408)
PHONE.....................877 778-5733
Linda Lachance, *Pr*
EMP: 6 EST: 2009
SALES (est): 2.49MM Privately Held
Web: www.wambamfence.com
SIC: 3089 Fences, gates, and accessories:
plastics

(G-3003)
WANDFLUH OF AMERICA INC
8200 Arrowridge Blvd (28273-5673)
PHONE.....................847 566-5700
James R Brooks, *Pr*
Hansrudolph Wandfluh, *VP*
Bruno Dollar, *Asst Tr*
Robert C Knuetfer, *Sec*
▲ EMP: 15 EST: 1984
SALES (est): 3.48MM Privately Held
Web: www.wandfluh-us.com
SIC: 3492 1799 Control valves, fluid power:
hydraulic and pneumatic; Hydraulic
equipment, installation and service

(G-3004)
WARD VESSEL AND EXCHANGER CORP (PA)
Also Called: Equipment Enterprises Division
6835 E W T Harris Blvd (28215-4141)
P.O. Box 44568 (28215)
PHONE.....................704 568-3001
Jon Ward, *Prin*
Bob Besh, *
Tim Ramsey, *
▲ EMP: 60 EST: 1982
SALES (est): 24.49MM
SALES (corp-wide): 24.49MM Privately
Held
Web:
www.wardvesselandexchanger.com
SIC: 3443 Tanks, standard or custom
fabricated: metal plate

(G-3005)
WASTEQUIP LLC (DH)
Also Called: Wastequip
6525 Carnegie Blvd Ste 300 (28211-0500)
PHONE.....................704 366-7140
Marty Bryant, *CEO*
Steven Klueg, *CFO*
Mike Marchetti, *CIO*
Nick Wiseman, *Chief Human Resource
Officer*
◆ EMP: 18 EST: 1988
SQ FT: 1,000
SALES (est): 576.59MM Privately Held
Web: www.wastequip.com
SIC: 3443 3537 Dumpsters, garbage;
Industrial trucks and tractors
HQ: H.I.G. Capital, L.L.C.
1450 Brickell Ave Fl 31
Miami FL 33131
305 379-2322

(G-3006)
WASTEQUIP MANUFACTURING CO LLC (DH)
6525 Carnegie Blvd Ste 300 (28211-0500)
PHONE.....................704 366-7140
Robert Rasmussen, *Pr*
◆ EMP: 5 EST: 1992

SQ FT: 2,500
SALES (est): 408.58MM Privately Held
Web: www.wastequip.com
SIC: 3443 Dumpsters, garbage
HQ: Wastequip, Llc
6525 Crnegie Blvd Ste 300
Charlotte NC 28211

(G-3007)
WATER-GEN INC
Also Called: Watergen Americas
10709 Granite St (28273-6353)
PHONE.....................888 492-8370
Dan Clifford, *Pr*
Joel Townsend, *Dir*
EMP: 5 EST: 2017
SALES (est): 667.11K Privately Held
Web: www.watergen.com
SIC: 5078 3589 5074 Drinking water coolers,
mechanical; Water purification equipment,
household type; Water purification
equipment

(G-3008)
WAXHAW CANDLE COMPANY LLC
9830 Rea Rd Ste G (28277-0793)
PHONE.....................980 245-2827
Rebecca Walter, *Pr*
EMP: 4 EST: 2015
SALES (est): 244.26K Privately Held
Web: www.waxhawcandlecompany.com
SIC: 3999 Candles

(G-3009)
WEB-DON INCORPORATED (PA)
Also Called: Web-Don
1400 Ameron Dr (28206-1604)
P.O. Box 26367 (28221-6367)
PHONE.....................800 532-0434
▲ EMP: 30 EST: 1972
SALES (est): 30.08MM
SALES (corp-wide): 30.08MM Privately
Held
Web: www.web-don.com
SIC: 2891 5722 2452 3281 Adhesives;
Kitchens, complete (sinks, cabinets, etc.);
Panels and sections, prefabricated, wood;
Table tops, marble

(G-3010)
WEDECO UV TECHNOLOGIES INC
Also Called: Xylem
4828 Parkway Plaza Blvd Ste 200
(28217-1038)
PHONE.....................704 716-7600
John Marrino, *Pr*
Jesse Rodriguez, *
▲ EMP: 79 EST: 1975
SALES (est): 9.64MM Publicly Held
SIC: 3589 Water treatment equipment,
industrial
PA: Xylem Inc.
301 Water St Se Ste 200
Washington DC 20003

(G-3011)
WELL DOCTOR LLC
9607 Autumn Applause Dr (28277-1696)
P.O. Box 1420 (28124-1420)
PHONE.....................704 909-9258
EMP: 4 EST: 2017
SALES (est): 1.74MM Privately Held
Web: www.welldoctor.biz
SIC: 1389 Pumping of oil and gas wells

(G-3012)
WENKER INC (PA)
112 S Tryon St Ste 1130 (28284-2109)
PHONE.....................704 333-7790
EMP: 8 EST: 2016
SALES (est): 5.08MM

SALES (corp-wide): 5.08MM Privately
Held
Web: www.wenker.de
SIC: 3714 Motor vehicle parts and
accessories

(G-3013)
WEPAK CORPORATION
601 Gulf Dr (28208-1311)
P.O. Box 36803 (28236-6803)
PHONE.....................704 334-5781
Robert Poffenbarger Junior, *Pr*
Charles Gage, *VP*
EMP: 20 EST: 1976
SQ FT: 45,000
SALES (est): 2.34MM Privately Held
Web: www.wepakonline.com
SIC: 2841 2842 Soap and other detergents;
Polishes and sanitation goods

(G-3014)
WEWOKA GAS PRODUCERS LLC
10600 Nations Ford Rd (28273-5762)
PHONE.....................704 844-8990
Robin Keziah, *Prin*
EMP: 5 EST: 2010
SALES (est): 588.25K Privately Held
Web: www.landfillgroup.com
SIC: 1389 Building oil and gas well
foundations on site

(G-3015)
WEYERHAEUSER COMPANY
10601 Westlake Dr (28273-3930)
PHONE.....................253 924-2345
David Bowen, *Branch*
EMP: 9
SALES (corp-wide): 7.12B Publicly Held
Web: www.weyerhaeuser.com
SIC: 2653 Boxes, corrugated: made from
purchased materials
PA: Weyerhaeuser Company
220 Occidental Ave S
Seattle WA 98104
206 539-3000

(G-3016)
WHALEY FOODSERVICE LLC
8334 Arrowridge Blvd Ste K (28273-5611)
PHONE.....................704 529-6242
Woody Adkins, *Brnch Mgr*
EMP: 54
SALES (corp-wide): 1.14B Privately Held
Web: www.whaleyfoodservice.com
SIC: 3631 7699 Household cooking
equipment; Restaurant equipment repair
HQ: Whaley Foodservice, Llc
137 Cedar Rd
Lexington SC 29073
803 996-9900

(G-3017)
WHITE CAP LP
5900 W Wt Harris Blvd (28269)
PHONE.....................704 921-4420
Paul Harris, *Brnch Mgr*
EMP: 7
SALES (corp-wide): 7.35B Privately Held
Web: www.hdsupply.com
SIC: 3273 Ready-mixed concrete
HQ: White Cap, L.P.
6250 Brook Hollow Pkwy
Norcross GA 30071
800 944-8322

(G-3018)
WICKES MANUFACTURING COMPANY
701 Mccullough Dr (28262)
PHONE.....................704 548-2350
EMP: 50 EST: 2007

SALES (est): 912.62K **Privately Held**
SIC: 2221 Automotive fabrics, manmade fiber

(G-3019)
WIKOFF COLOR CORPORATION
Also Called: Wikoff Color
2828 Interstate St (28208-3606)
PHONE.................................704 392-4657
Check Walters, *Mgr*
EMP: 40
SALES (corp-wide): 156.45MM **Privately Held**
Web: www.wikoff.com
SIC: 2893 Printing ink
PA: Wikoff Color Corporation
　　1886 Merrit Rd
　　Fort Mill SC 29715
　　803 548-2210

(G-3020)
WILBERT YATES VAULT CO INC
2839 Rosemont St (28208-5512)
P.O. Box 669343 (28266-9343)
PHONE.................................704 399-8453
Dan G Yates Junior, *Pr*
Robert Yates, *
EMP: 15 **EST:** 1952
SQ FT: 29,900
SALES (est): 2.34MM **Privately Held**
Web: www.yateswilbert.com
SIC: 3272 Burial vaults, concrete or precast
　　terrazzo

(G-3021)
WILLOWCROFT
15301 Marvin Rd (28277-1928)
PHONE.................................704 540-0367
Kevin J Hall, *Prin*
EMP: 10 **EST:** 2008
SALES (est): 334.83K **Privately Held**
SIC: 2084 Wines

(G-3022)
WINSO DSGNS SCREENPRINTING
LLC
7027 Orr Rd Ste F (28213-6460)
PHONE.................................704 967-5776
EMP: 4 **EST:** 2019
SALES (est): 83.72K **Privately Held**
SIC: 2759 Screen printing

(G-3023)
WINTON PRODUCTS COMPANY
2500 West Blvd Ste B (28208-6759)
P.O. Box 36332 (28236-6332)
PHONE.................................704 399-5151
Jack Mc Creary, *Pr*
W Michael Mc Creary, *VP*
EMP: 10 **EST:** 1950
SQ FT: 15,000
SALES (est): 2.04MM **Privately Held**
Web: www.wintonproducts.com
SIC: 2899 Chemical preparations, nec

(G-3024)
WOODTECH/INTERIORS INC
2228 N Brevard St (28206-3454)
PHONE.................................704 332-7215
Bob Binner, *Pr*
EMP: 8 **EST:** 1983
SQ FT: 7,500
SALES (est): 650K **Privately Held**
SIC: 2431 Millwork

(G-3025)
WORKING WIDGET TECHNOLOGY
LLC
7920 Alexander Rd (28270-0860)
PHONE.................................704 684-6277
Matt Bradford, *Owner*

EMP: 5 **EST:** 2012
SALES (est): 99.68K **Privately Held**
SIC: 2499 Wood products, nec

(G-3026)
WORLD STONE FABRICATORS INC
4908 Hovis Rd (28208-1513)
PHONE.................................704 372-9968
Robert Gambill, *Pr*
David Eller, *Stockholder**
Mark Pegram, *Stockholder**
EMP: 35 **EST:** 1996
SALES (est): 4.87MM **Privately Held**
Web: www.worldstonefabricators.com
SIC: 3281 Cut stone and stone products

(G-3027)
WORLDWIDE ENTRMT MLTIMEDIA
LLC
11511 Sidney Crest Ave (28213-4873)
PHONE.................................704 208-6113
EMP: 5 **EST:** 2021
SALES (est): 100K **Privately Held**
SIC: 3651 Music distribution apparatus

(G-3028)
WTO INC
9210 Porters View Dr (28273-0329)
PHONE.................................704 714-7765
Sascha Tschiggfrei, *Pr*
EMP: 12 **EST:** 1993
SALES (est): 8.58MM
SALES (corp-wide): 68.24MM **Privately**
Held
Web: www.wto-tools.com
SIC: 3546 Drills and drilling tools
PA: Wto Werkzeug - Einrichtungen Gmbh
　　Neuer Hohdammweg 1
　　Ohlsbach BW 77797
　　780393920

(G-3029)
WYDA PACKAGING CORP ✪
3301 Woodpark Blvd (28206-4205)
PHONE.................................980 403-3346
Daniel Mendes, *Mgr*
EMP: 12 **EST:** 2023
SALES (est): 1.3MM **Privately Held**
SIC: 3353 Foil, aluminum

(G-3030)
XELERA INC
10806 Reames Rd Ste Y (28269-3766)
PHONE.................................855 493-5372
Rafael Gonzalez, *Pr*
Rafael Gonzalez Junior, *VP*
Cheri T Gonzalez, *Sec*
Kirsten Y Swanson, *Treas*
EMP: 4 **EST:** 1998
SALES (est): 989.94K **Privately Held**
SIC: 2899 Water treating compounds

(G-3031)
XEROXDATA CENTER
1400 Cross Beam Dr (28217-2803)
PHONE.................................704 329-7245
EMP: 4 **EST:** 2013
SALES (est): 411.58K **Privately Held**
SIC: 3577 Computer peripheral equipment,
　　nec

(G-3032)
XSPORT GLOBAL INC
1800 Camden Rd # 107-196 (28203-4690)
PHONE.................................212 541-6222
Ray Mariorenzi, *Pr*
Maurice E Durschlag, *Ch Bd*
EMP: 13 **EST:** 2012
SALES (est): 367.62K **Privately Held**
Web: www.xsportglobal.com

SIC: 7371 7372 Computer software systems
　　analysis and design, custom; Application
　　computer software

(G-3033)
XSYS NORTH AMERICA
CORPORATION (DH)
2915 Whitehall Park Dr Ste 600
(28273-3579)
PHONE.................................704 504-2626
Dagmar Schmidt, *CEO*
EMP: 17 **EST:** 2020
SALES (est): 31.74MM
SALES (corp-wide): 857.59K **Privately**
Held
Web: www.xsysglobal.com
SIC: 2796 Platemaking services
HQ: Xsys Germany Gmbh
　　Industriestr. 1
　　Willstatt BW 77731
　　78529340

(G-3034)
XTINGUISH LLC
3021 N Myers St (28205-1558)
PHONE.................................704 868-9500
Wim Debaudringhein, *Pr*
Dirk Duymelinck, *
Peter Duymelinck, *
▲ **EMP:** 5 **EST:** 2004
SQ FT: 30,000
SALES (est): 452.73K **Privately Held**
SIC: 2253 2261 2231 Knit outerwear mills;
　　Finishing plants, cotton; Broadwoven fabric
　　mills, wool

(G-3035)
XYLEM LNC (DH)
Also Called: Ultra Violet Systems Division
4828 Parkway Plaza Blvd # 200
(28217-1957)
P.O. Box 7107 (28241)
PHONE.................................704 409-9700
Ronald Port, *Pr*
Scott Miller, *VP*
Werner Klink, *Ch Bd*
William Carr, *Treas*
James Anderson, *Sec*
▲ **EMP:** 26 **EST:** 1969
SALES (est): 20.84MM
SALES (corp-wide): 3.63B **Publicly Held**
SIC: 3621 3613 3674 3511 Power generators
　　; Control panels, electric; Semiconductors
　　and related devices; Turbines and turbine
　　generator sets
HQ: Itt Llc
　　1133 Westchester Ave
　　White Plains NY 10604
　　914 641-2000

(G-3036)
XYLEM WATER SOLUTIONS USA
INC (HQ)
4828 Parkway Plaza Blvd Ste 200
(28217-3781)
PHONE.................................704 409-9700
Patrick Decker, *CEO*
▲ **EMP:** 75 **EST:** 2011
SALES (est): 119MM **Publicly Held**
Web: www.xylem.com
SIC: 3561 Pumps and pumping equipment
PA: Xylem Inc.
　　301 Water St Se Ste 200
　　Washington DC 20003

(G-3037)
XYLEM WATER SOLUTIONS USA INC
Also Called: Wedeco
14125 S Bridge Cir (28273-6747)
PHONE.................................704 409-9700
EMP: 53

Web: www.xylem.com
SIC: 2899 Water treating compounds
HQ: Xylem Water Solutions U.S.A., Inc.
　　4828 Parkway Plz Blvd 200
　　Charlotte NC 28217

(G-3038)
YALE INDUSTRIAL PRODUCTS INC
(HQ)
Also Called: Duff-Norton Company, Inc.
13320 Ballantyne Corporate Pl Ste D
(28277)
P.O. Box 7010 (28241)
PHONE.................................704 588-4610
David J Wilson, *Pr*
Appal Chintapalli, *
Yan Wei, *Dir Fin*
◆ **EMP:** 27 **EST:** 1983
SALES (est): 18.62MM
SALES (corp-wide): 1.01B **Publicly Held**
Web: www.cmco.com
SIC: 3569 3625 3536 3593 Jack screws;
　　Actuators, industrial; Hoists; Fluid power
　　cylinders and actuators
PA: Columbus Mckinnon Corporation
　　13320 Bllntyne Corp Pl St
　　Charlotte NC 28277
　　716 689-5400

(G-3039)
YANG MING AMERICA
CORPORATION
Also Called: Yang Mine Lines
11124 Ascoli Pl (28277-4121)
PHONE.................................704 357-3817
Steve Bullock, *Mgr*
EMP: 5
SIC: 3731 Cargo vessels, building and
　　repairing
HQ: Ming Yang America Corporation
　　1085 Raymond Blvd 9th Fl
　　Newark NJ 07102
　　201 222-8899

(G-3040)
YG-1 AMERICA INC
11001 Park Charlotte Blvd (28273-8860)
PHONE.................................980 318-5348
Don Hun Ham, *Pr*
▲ **EMP:** 25 **EST:** 2014
SQ FT: 60,000
SALES (est): 5.28MM **Privately Held**
SIC: 3545 Diamond cutting tools for turning,
　　boring, burnishing, etc.
PA: Yg-1 Co., Ltd.
　　13-40 Songdogwahak-Ro 16beon-Gil,
　　Yeonsu-Gu
　　Incheon 21984

(G-3041)
YOUR SOURCE FOR PRINTING
8116 S Tryon St (28273-4300)
PHONE.................................704 957-5922
EMP: 4 **EST:** 2017
SALES (est): 114.77K **Privately Held**
Web: www.heritageprintingcharlotte.com
SIC: 2752 Commercial printing, lithographic

(G-3042)
YP ADVRTISING PUBG LLC NOT LLC
Also Called: BellSouth
9144 Arrowpoint Blvd Ste 150
(28273-8133)
PHONE.................................704 522-5500
Jerry Furr, *Mgr*
EMP: 144
SALES (corp-wide): 824.16MM **Publicly**
Held

SIC: **2741** 7311 7331 7313 Directories, telephone: publishing only, not printed on site; Advertising agencies; Direct mail advertising services; Radio, television, publisher representatives
HQ: Yp Advertising & Publishing Llc (Not Llc)
2247 Northlake Pkwy
Tucker GA 30084

(G-3043)
YUMITOS CORPORATION
3540 Toringdon Way Ste 200 (28277-4650)
PHONE.................................786 952-6202
Charlie Green, *CEO*
EMP: **40 EST:** 2022
SALES (est): 1.08MM **Privately Held**
Web: www.yumitos.com
SIC: **7372** 4215 Application computer software; Package delivery, vehicular

(G-3044)
ZARGES INC
1440 Center Park Dr (28217-2909)
P.O. Box 19768 (28219-9768)
PHONE.................................704 357-6285
Olaf Klutke, *Ex Dir*
Carsten Rethmeier, *Pr*
◆ EMP: **10 EST:** 2007
SQ FT: 10,000
SALES (est): 4.95MM
SALES (corp-wide): 479.35K **Privately Held**
Web: www.zargesusa.com
SIC: **3441** Fabricated structural metal
PA: Zarges Gmbh
Markt 16-18
Frankfurt Am Main HE
69299030

(G-3045)
ZEBRA TECHNOLOGIES CORPORATION
Also Called: Zebra Technologies
9075 Meadowmont View Dr (28269-6194)
PHONE.................................704 517-5271
EMP: 5
SALES (corp-wide): 4.98B **Publicly Held**
Web: www.zebra.com
SIC: **3577** Bar code (magnetic ink) printers
PA: Zebra Technologies Corporation
3 Overlook Pt
Lincolnshire IL 60069
847 634-6700

(G-3046)
ZELAYA BROS LLC
3525 Ritch Ave (28206-2013)
PHONE.................................980 833-0099
EMP: **5 EST:** 2020
SALES (est): 187.81K **Privately Held**
Web: www.zelayabros.com
SIC: **3571** 7389 Electronic computers; Business services, nec

(G-3047)
ZEPSA INDUSTRIES INC
Also Called: Zepsa Stairs
1501 Westinghouse Blvd (28273-6329)
PHONE.................................704 583-9220
Edward Zepsa, *Pr*
Maripat Zepsa, *
▲ EMP: **90 EST:** 1981
SQ FT: 20,000
SALES (est): 12.05MM **Privately Held**
Web: www.zepsa.com
SIC: **2431** Millwork

(G-3048)
ZINGERLE GROUP USA INC
Also Called: Mastertent
6965 Northpark Blvd (28216-2321)
PHONE.................................704 312-1600
Justin Russell, *CEO*
Russell Justin, *CEO*
EMP: **20 EST:** 2017
SALES (est): 1.34MM **Privately Held**
Web: www.mastertent.com
SIC: **5999** 5099 2599 2211 Tents; Durable goods, nec; Furniture and fixtures, nec; Tentage

(G-3049)
ZIPPY ICE INC (PA)
5701 N Graham St (28269-4838)
PHONE.................................980 355-9851
Christine Mackie, *Pr*
EMP: **24 EST:** 2006
SALES (est): 5.55MM **Privately Held**
Web: www.zippyicecompany.com
SIC: **2097** Block ice

Cherokee
Swain County

(G-3050)
C B C PRINTING
149 Childrens Home Rd (28719-8605)
P.O. Box 507 (28719-0507)
PHONE.................................828 497-5510
Skooter Maccoy, *Genl Mgr*
Ray Kinsland, *Mgr*
EMP: **6 EST:** 1984
SALES (est): 145.32K **Privately Held**
Web: www.cherokeeboysclub.com
SIC: **2752** Offset printing

(G-3051)
CHEROKEE PUBLICATIONS
Also Called: Native Amercn Collections Xii
66 Luftee Lake Rd (28719)
P.O. Box 430 (28719-0430)
PHONE.................................828 627-2424
Ed Sharpe, *Owner*
EMP: **5 EST:** 1970
SQ FT: 2,000
SALES (est): 162.85K **Privately Held**
SIC: **5192** 2731 5961 Books; Pamphlets: publishing only, not printed on site; Book club, mail order

(G-3052)
CHEROKEE TRANSFER STATION
Aloveit Church Rdd (28719)
PHONE.................................828 497-4519
Bill Reid, *Mgr*
EMP: **5 EST:** 2001
SALES (est): 289.32K **Privately Held**
SIC: **3443** Trash racks, metal plate

(G-3053)
EASTERN BAND CHEROKEE INDIANS
Also Called: Waste Water Treatment Plant
2000 Old #4 Rd (28719)
P.O. Box 547 (28719-0547)
PHONE.................................828 497-6824
Larry Hornbuckle, *Mgr*
EMP: 47
Web: www.cherokeegamingcommission.com
SIC: **3231** Products of purchased glass
PA: Eastern Band Of Cherokee Indians
88 Council House Loop
Cherokee NC 28719
828 497-2771

Cherry Point
Craven County

(G-3054)
NORTHROP GRUMMAN SYSTEMS CORP
Bldg 4280 (28533)
PHONE.................................252 447-7557
EMP: 68
Web: www.northropgrumman.com
SIC: **3812** Search and navigation equipment
HQ: Northrop Grumman Systems Corporation
2980 Fairview Park Dr
Falls Church VA 22042
703 280-2900

(G-3055)
UNITED STATES DEPT OF NAVY
Also Called: Naval Air Warfare
Av 8b Psc Box 8019 (28533)
PHONE.................................252 466-4514
John Truet, *Mgr*
EMP: 5
Web: www.navy.mil
SIC: **3812** 9711 Aircraft/aerospace flight instruments and guidance systems; Navy
HQ: United States Department Of The Navy
1200 Navy Pentagon
Washington DC 20350

(G-3056)
UNITED STATES DEPT OF NAVY
Also Called: Air Force Fleet Readiness Ctr
Bldg 137 A St (28533)
PHONE.................................252 464-7228
Mary Beth Fennell, *Brnch Mgr*
EMP: 5
Web: www.navy.mil
SIC: **3721** 9711 Aircraft; Navy
HQ: United States Department Of The Navy
1200 Navy Pentagon
Washington DC 20350

(G-3057)
UNITED STATES DEPT OF NAVY
Also Called: Fleet Readiness Center East
Cunningham Bldg 159 (28533)
PHONE.................................252 466-4415
Kathy Rogers, *Brnch Mgr*
EMP: 30
Web: www.navy.mil
SIC: **3728** Aircraft parts and equipment, nec
HQ: United States Department Of The Navy
1200 Navy Pentagon
Washington DC 20350

Cherryville
Gaston County

(G-3058)
1ST CHOICE SERVICE INC
3661 Eaker Rd (28021-9692)
PHONE.................................704 913-7685
Jonathan Watts, *Owner*
EMP: **8 EST:** 2009
SALES (est): 902.36K **Privately Held**
Web: www.stanleyenviro.com
SIC: **5039** 1623 3561 Septic tanks; Sewer line construction; Industrial pumps and parts

(G-3059)
BRADINGTON-YOUNG LLC
Bradington-Young
941 Tot Dellinger Rd (28021-9246)
P.O. Box 9080 (28603-9080)
PHONE.................................276 656-3335

Ding Scronce, *Brnch Mgr*
EMP: 200
SALES (corp-wide): 433.23MM **Publicly Held**
Web: www.bradington-young.com
SIC: **2512** 2511 Upholstered household furniture; Wood household furniture
HQ: Bradington-Young Llc
4040 10th Avenue Dr Sw
Hickory NC 28602
704 435-5881

(G-3060)
CHERRYVILLE DISTRG CO INC
322 E Main St (28021-3411)
P.O. Box 250 (28021-0250)
PHONE.................................704 435-9692
Matthew H Dellinger, *Pr*
Linn Bowen, *Sec*
EMP: **6 EST:** 1955
SQ FT: 60,000
SALES (est): 991.33K **Privately Held**
Web: www.cherryvilledistributing.com
SIC: **5087** 2842 Janitors' supplies; Cleaning or polishing preparations, nec

(G-3061)
CUSTOM HYDRAULICS & DESIGN (PA)
Also Called: Chd
242 Dick Beam Rd (28021)
PHONE.................................704 347-0023
Kelly D Watkins, *Pr*
Kelly D Watkins, *CEO*
Adam Watkins, *
Sherry Watkins, *
▲ EMP: **12 EST:** 1981
SQ FT: 5,500
SALES (est): 10.4MM
SALES (corp-wide): 10.4MM **Privately Held**
Web: www.customhydraulicsdesign.com
SIC: **5084** 5085 3492 Hydraulic systems equipment and supplies; Industrial supplies; Hose and tube fittings and assemblies, hydraulic/pneumatic

(G-3062)
CUSTOM METAL FINISHING
617 E Main St # B (28021-3416)
PHONE.................................704 445-1710
Rick Mullinax, *Owner*
EMP: **4 EST:** 1992
SALES (est): 208.04K **Privately Held**
SIC: **3471** Electroplating of metals or formed products

(G-3063)
CVC EQUIPMENT COMPANY
Also Called: Cvc & Equipment
316 Old Stubbs Rd Ste 1 (28021-9395)
PHONE.................................704 300-6242
Kerry Vess, *Pr*
Walter Vess, *VP*
Dena Vess, *Treas*
EMP: **6 EST:** 1989
SALES (est): 534.42K **Privately Held**
Web: cvcequipment.wordpress.com
SIC: **3559** 7389 Chemical machinery and equipment; Crane and aerial lift service

(G-3064)
FARRIS FAB & MACHINE INC (PA)
1006 W Academy St (28021-3004)
PHONE.................................704 629-4879
Bryan Farris, *Pr*
Greg Farris, *
Corwin E Farris, *Stockholder**
▲ EMP: **78 EST:** 1979
SQ FT: 110,000
SALES (est): 21.1MM

SALES (corp-wide): 21.1MM **Privately Held**
Web: www.farrisgrp.com
SIC: 3441 3599 Fabricated structural metal; Machine shop, jobbing and repair

(G-3065)
KEYSTONE POWDERED METAL CO
100 Commerce Dr (28021-8905)
P.O. Box 189 (28021-0189)
PHONE......................704 435-4036
Randy Dacanal, *Mgr*
EMP: 54
SQ FT: 35,000
Web: www.keystonepm.com
SIC: 3399 3568 Paste, metal; Power transmission equipment, nec
HQ: Keystone Powdered Metal Co
　251 State St
　Saint Marys PA 15857
　814 781-1591

(G-3066)
LNS TURBO NORTH AMERICA
242 Dick Beam Rd (28021-8943)
PHONE......................704 435-6376
Terry Dunn, *Pr*
EMP: 4 **EST:** 2015
SALES (est): 248.3K **Privately Held**
SIC: 3545 Machine tool accessories

(G-3067)
MODERN POLYMERS INC
901 W Academy St (28021-3045)
P.O. Box 398 (28021-0398)
PHONE......................704 435-5825
W Richard Hilliard Senior, *Pr*
Ann Hilliard, *
Jon E Hilliard, *
W R Hilliard Ii, *VP*
Joyce Paysour, *
▼ **EMP:** 35 **EST:** 1970
SQ FT: 67,000
SALES (est): 11.43MM **Privately Held**
Web: www.modernpolymers.com
SIC: 2821 Plastics materials and resins

(G-3068)
PEPSI-COLA METRO BTLG CO INC
Also Called: Pepsi-Cola
152 Commerce Dr (28021-8905)
PHONE......................704 736-2640
Ernest Pharr, *Mgr*
EMP: 53
SQ FT: 44,216
SALES (corp-wide): 91.47B **Publicly Held**
Web: www.pepsico.com
SIC: 2086 Carbonated beverages, nonalcoholic: pkged. in cans, bottles
HQ: Pepsi-Cola Metropolitan Bottling Company, Inc.
　700 Anderson Hill Rd
　Purchase NY 10577
　914 767-6000

(G-3069)
POCONO COATED PRODUCTS LLC
100 Sweetree St (28021-3066)
P.O. Box 303 (08867-0303)
PHONE......................704 445-7891
Susan Myer, *Managing Member*
▼ **EMP:** 6 **EST:** 2004
SQ FT: 15,000
SALES (est): 3.82MM **Privately Held**
Web: www.poconoctd.com
SIC: 2672 Adhesive backed films, foams and foils

(G-3070)
TAR HEEL CUISINE INC
1009 N Mountain St (28021-2020)
PHONE......................704 435-6979
Charles K Beam, *Prin*
EMP: 6 **EST:** 2008
SALES (est): 155.31K **Privately Held**
SIC: 2865 Tar

(G-3071)
WRIGHT ELECTRIC INC
3114 Tryon Courthouse Rd (28021-8934)
P.O. Box 815 (28016-0815)
PHONE......................704 435-6988
Jerry Wright, *Pr*
Brandon Wright, *VP*
Deanna Walker, *Sec*
EMP: 5 **EST:** 1974
SALES (est): 465.33K **Privately Held**
Web: www.weflywright.com
SIC: 3643 Current-carrying wiring services

China Grove
Rowan County

(G-3072)
CAROLINA SITEWORKS INC
300 Wade Dr (28023-8464)
P.O. Box 280 (28023-0280)
PHONE......................704 855-7483
John D Shell, *Pr*
John J Reilly, *
EMP: 25 **EST:** 1999
SQ FT: 1,000
SALES (est): 4.78MM **Privately Held**
Web: www.carolinasiteworksinc.com
SIC: 1389 Construction, repair, and dismantling services

(G-3073)
DNJ ENGINE COMP ONENTS
1450 N Main St (28023-6433)
PHONE......................704 855-5505
EMP: 4 **EST:** 2015
SALES (est): 96.82K **Privately Held**
SIC: 3714 Motor vehicle parts and accessories

(G-3074)
HARWOOD SIGNS
112 Chippewa Trl (28023-9700)
PHONE......................704 857-6203
N Harwood, *Prin*
EMP: 4 **EST:** 2008
SALES (est): 121.99K **Privately Held**
SIC: 3993 Signs, not made in custom sign painting shops

(G-3075)
HOGAN CABINETRY AND MLLWK LLC
1720 S Main St (28023-8632)
PHONE......................704 856-0425
EMP: 4 **EST:** 2020
SALES (est): 2.11MM **Privately Held**
SIC: 2431 Millwork

(G-3076)
MARTIN MARIETTA MATERIALS INC
Also Called: Martin Marietta Aggregates
2270 China Grove Rd (28023-6629)
PHONE......................704 932-4377
Ronald Borum, *Brnch Mgr*
EMP: 5
Web: www.martinmarietta.com
SIC: 1422 Crushed and broken limestone
PA: Martin Marietta Materials Inc
　4123 Parklake Ave
　Raleigh NC 27612

(G-3077)
OLD TOWN SOAP CO
104 S Main St (28023-2448)
PHONE......................704 796-8775
Brent Engelhardt, *Managing Member*
EMP: 16 **EST:** 2010
SALES (est): 2.26MM **Privately Held**
Web: www.oldtownsoapco.com
SIC: 5122 2841 Toilet soap; Detergents, synthetic organic or inorganic alkaline

(G-3078)
PROTERIAL NORTH CAROLINA LTD
Also Called: Hitachi Metals NC Ltd
1 Hitachi Metals Dr (28023-9461)
PHONE......................704 855-2800
Luke Koizumi, *Pr*
Mark Stockwell, *Sec*
◆ **EMP:** 150 **EST:** 1989
SQ FT: 480,000
SALES (est): 24.79MM **Privately Held**
SIC: 3264 Magnets, permanent: ceramic or ferrite
HQ: Proterial America, Ltd.
　4 Manhttnville Rd Ste 205
　Purchase NY 10577
　914 694-9200

(G-3079)
ROWAN CUSTOM CABINETS INC
2515 S Us 29 Hwy (28023-9644)
PHONE......................704 855-4778
Jacob C Speck, *Pr*
Judy Speck, *Sec*
Darrell Esrid, *VP*
EMP: 6 **EST:** 2002
SALES (est): 118.12K **Privately Held**
Web: www.rowancustomcabinets.com
SIC: 2434 Wood kitchen cabinets

(G-3080)
WIGGINS KART SHOP INC
4010 Nc 152 W (28023-6775)
PHONE......................704 855-3165
Harrill Wiggins Junior, *Pr*
Staci Wiggins, *Sec*
▲ **EMP:** 10 **EST:** 1987
SALES (est): 883.95K **Privately Held**
Web: www.phantomchassis.com
SIC: 3799 Go-carts, except children's

Chinquapin
Duplin County

(G-3081)
A3-USA INC
1674 Fountaintown Rd (28521-8700)
PHONE......................724 871-7170
Jens Sonntag, *VP*
EMP: 4 **EST:** 2009
SALES (est): 1.74MM **Privately Held**
Web: www.a3-usa.com
SIC: 3589 Water treatment equipment, industrial

(G-3082)
DONALDS WELDING INC
1806 S Nc 111 Hwy (28521-8554)
PHONE......................910 298-5234
Donald G Chase, *Pr*
Brenda Chase, *Sec*
EMP: 10 **EST:** 1980
SALES (est): 959.38K **Privately Held**
SIC: 7692 Welding repair

Chocowinity
Beaufort County

(G-3083)
ICONIC MARINE GROUP LLC
1653 Whichards Beach Rd (27817-9076)
P.O. Box 457 (27889-0457)
PHONE......................252 975-2000
Tom Klontz, *CFO*
Jeff Harris, *
EMP: 370 **EST:** 2016
SQ FT: 248,000
SALES (est): 23.42MM **Privately Held**
Web: www.bajamarine.com
SIC: 3732 5091 Boatbuilding and repairing; Boat accessories and parts

(G-3084)
OBI MACHINE & TOOL INC
411 Patrick Ln (27817)
P.O. Box 326 (27817-0326)
PHONE......................252 946-1580
J C Jenkins, *Owner*
EMP: 9 **EST:** 2000
SALES (est): 165.96K **Privately Held**
SIC: 3549 Metalworking machinery, nec

(G-3085)
TAYLOR TIMBER TRANSPORT INC
1977 Old New Bern Rd (27817-8393)
PHONE......................252 943-1550
Barbara Taylor, *Pr*
James G Taylor, *VP*
EMP: 9 **EST:** 1977
SQ FT: 2,400
SALES (est): 930.29K **Privately Held**
SIC: 1446 Industrial sand

Claremont
Catawba County

(G-3086)
A KLEIN & CO INC
1 Heart Dr (28610)
P.O. Box 670 (28610-0670)
PHONE......................828 459-9261
FAX: 828 459-9608
EMP: 145
SQ FT: 180,000
SALES (est): 16.97MM **Privately Held**
SIC: 2652 2657 Setup paperboard boxes; Folding paperboard boxes

(G-3087)
ADVANCEPIERRE FOODS INC
Also Called: Pierre Foods
3437 E Main St (28610-8672)
P.O. Box 399 (28610-0399)
PHONE......................828 459-7626
Ted Karre, *Brnch Mgr*
EMP: 1427
SALES (corp-wide): 53.31B **Publicly Held**
Web: www.tysonfoodservice.com
SIC: 2011 2013 2015 2099 Meat packing plants; Frozen meats, from purchased meat ; Poultry, processed: frozen; Sandwiches, assembled and packaged: for wholesale market
HQ: Advancepierre Foods, Inc.
　9990 Prnceton Glendale Rd
　West Chester OH 45246
　513 874-8741

(G-3088)
ARRIS SOLUTIONS LLC (DH)
Also Called: Arris
3642 E Us Highway 70 (28610)
PHONE......................678 473-2000

▲ = Import ▼ = Export
◆ = Import/Export

Charles L Treadway, *CEO*
James Douglas Moore Junior, *CFO*
Patrick W Macken, *
◆ **EMP: 600 EST:** 2007
SALES (est): 690.44MM
SALES (corp-wide): 15.22B **Publicly Held**
Web: www.commscope.com
SIC: 3661 3663 3357 Telephone and
   telegraph apparatus; Radio and t.v.
   communications equipment; Fiber optic
   cable (insulated)
HQ: Ruckus Wireless Llc
   350 W Java Dr
   Sunnyvale CA 94089

(G-3089)
ARRIS TECHNOLOGY INC (DH)
3642 E Us Highway 70 (28610)
PHONE.................................828 324-2200
Charles L Treadway, *CEO*
Kyle D Lorentzen, *
Justin C Choi, *
◆ **EMP: 60 EST:** 1997
SALES (est): 119.46MM
SALES (corp-wide): 15.22B **Publicly Held**
Web: www.commscope.com
SIC: 7372 3825 Application computer
   software; Network analyzers
HQ: Arris Solutions Llc
   3642 E Us Highway 70
   Claremont NC 28610

(G-3090)
**CAROLINA HOUSE FURNITURE INC
(PA)**
Also Called: Riverbend Frameworks
5485 Herman Rd (28610-9485)
PHONE.................................828 459-7400
Dennis Abernathy, *Pr*
Donna Abernathy, *
▲ **EMP: 24 EST:** 1975
SQ FT: 22,000
SALES (est): 776.95K
SALES (corp-wide): 776.95K **Privately
Held**
Web: www.carolinahousefurniture.com
SIC: 2521 Chairs, office: padded,
   upholstered, or plain: wood

(G-3091)
CATAWBA FRAMES INC
4827 S Depot St (28610-8549)
P.O. Box 302 (28610-0302)
PHONE.................................828 459-7717
John A Bolick, *Pr*
Mark Bolick, *VP*
Shirley Bolick, *Sec*
EMP: 5 EST: 1968
SQ FT: 12,000
SALES (est): 244.81K **Privately Held**
SIC: 2426 Frames for upholstered furniture,
   wood

(G-3092)
CENTRO INC
2725 Kelly Blvd (28610-7451)
PHONE.................................319 626-3200
Brian Olesen, *Brnch Mgr*
EMP: 65
SALES (corp-wide): 89.48MM **Privately
Held**
Web: www.centroinc.com
SIC: 3089 Molding primary plastics
PA: Centro, Inc.
   One Centro Way
   North Liberty IA 52317
   319 626-3200

(G-3093)
CERTAINTEED LLC
2651 Penny Rd (28610-8635)
P.O. Box 760 (28610-0760)
PHONE.................................828 459-0556
Denny Riffel, *Brnch Mgr*
EMP: 99
SALES (corp-wide): 402.18MM **Privately
Held**
Web: www.certainteed.com
SIC: 3089 Siding, plastics
HQ: Certainteed Llc
   20 Moores Rd
   Malvern PA 19355
   610 893-5000

(G-3094)
**COMMSCOPE INC NORTH
CAROLINA**
Also Called: Comm Scope Network
3642 E Us Highway 70 (28610-8583)
PHONE.................................828 459-5000
Mike Kelley, *Prin*
EMP: 800
Web: www.commscope.com
SIC: 3357 1731 Communication wire; Cable
   television installation
HQ: Commscope, Inc. Of North Carolina
   3642 E Us Highway 70
   Claremont NC 28610
   828 324-2200

(G-3095)
**COMMSCOPE INC NORTH
CAROLINA**
3565 Centennial Blvd (28610)
PHONE.................................828 459-5001
EMP: 14
Web: www.commscope.com
SIC: 3663 Microwave communication
   equipment
HQ: Commscope, Inc. Of North Carolina
   3642 E Us Highway 70
   Claremont NC 28610
   828 324-2200

(G-3096)
**COMMSCOPE INC NORTH
CAROLINA (DH)**
Also Called: Commscope
3642 E Us Highway 70 (28610)
P.O. Box 1729 (28603)
PHONE.................................828 324-2200
Charles L Treadway, *Pr*
Mark Olson, *
Randall Crenshaw, *
Robert Suffern, *
Morgan Kurk, *
◆ **EMP: 43 EST:** 1977
SQ FT: 84,000
SALES (est): 3.92B **Publicly Held**
Web: www.commscope.com
SIC: 3663 3357 3679 3812 Microwave
   communication equipment; Communication
   wire; Waveguides and fittings; Search and
   navigation equipment
HQ: Commscope, Llc
   3642 E Us Highway 70
   Claremont NC 28610
   828 324-2200

(G-3097)
COMMSCOPE LLC (HQ)
3642 E Us Highway 70 (28610)
PHONE.................................828 324-2200
Charles L Treadway, *Pr*
EMP: 129 EST: 1997
SALES (est): 3.92B **Publicly Held**
Web: www.commscope.com

SIC: 3663 4899 Radio and t.v.
   communications equipment;
   Communication signal enhancement
   network services
PA: Commscope Holding Company, Inc.
   3642 E Us Hwy 70
   Claremont NC 28610

(G-3098)
**COMMSCOPE CONNECTIVITY LLC
(HQ)**
3642 E Us Highway 70 (28610-8530)
PHONE.................................828 324-2200
EMP: 50 EST: 1953
SALES (est): 210.13MM **Publicly Held**
Web: www.commscope.com
SIC: 3663 Radio and t.v. communications
   equipment
PA: Commscope Holding Company, Inc.
   3642 E Us Hwy 70
   Claremont NC 28610

(G-3099)
COMMSCOPE DSL SYSTEMS LLC
3642 E Us Highway 70 (28610-8530)
P.O. Box 69035 (17106-9035)
PHONE.................................828 324-2200
Suzan M Campbell, *VP*
EMP: 11 EST: 1988
SALES (est): 2.42MM
SALES (corp-wide): 15.22B **Publicly Held**
Web: www.commscope.com
SIC: 3663 Radio and t.v. communications
   equipment
HQ: Commscope Technologies Llc
   3642 E Us Highway 70
   Claremont NC 28610
   828 324-2200

(G-3100)
**COMMSCOPE HOLDING COMPANY
INC (PA)**
Also Called: Commscope
3642 E Us Highway 70 (28610)
PHONE.................................828 459-5000
Charles L Treadway, *Pr*
Randy Crenshaw, *COO*
Kyle D Lorentzen, *Ex VP*
Jennifer L Crawford, *CAO*
Justin C Choi, *CLO*
EMP: 541 EST: 2010
SALES (est): 4.21B **Publicly Held**
Web: www.commscope.com
SIC: 3663 4899 Radio and t.v.
   communications equipment;
   Communication signal enhancement
   network services

(G-3101)
COMMSCOPE INTL HOLDINGS LLC
3642 E Us Highway 70 (28610-8583)
PHONE.................................828 324-2200
Brian D Garrett, *Pr*
EMP: 11 EST: 2010
SALES (est): 1.3MM **Publicly Held**
Web: www.commscope.com
SIC: 3663 Radio and t.v. communications
   equipment
HQ: Commscope, Inc. Of North Carolina
   3642 E Us Highway 70
   Claremont NC 28610
   828 324-2200

(G-3102)
**COMMSCOPE SOLUTIONS INTL INC
(HQ)**
3642 E Us Highway 70 (28610-8530)
PHONE.................................828 324-2200
Marvin S Edwards, *CEO*
EMP: 21 EST: 2003
SALES (est): 1.97MM **Publicly Held**

Web: www.commscope.com
SIC: 3663 Radio and t.v. communications
   equipment
PA: Commscope Holding Company, Inc.
   3642 E Us Hwy 70
   Claremont NC 28610

(G-3103)
**COMMSCOPE TECHNOLOGIES FIN
LLC**
3642 E Us Highway 70 (28610-8530)
PHONE.................................828 323-4970
EMP: 9 EST: 2015
SALES (est): 1.6MM **Privately Held**
Web: www.commscope.com
SIC: 3663 Radio and t.v. communications
   equipment

(G-3104)
**COMMSCOPE TECHNOLOGIES LLC
(HQ)**
Also Called: Andrew
3642 E Us Highway 70 (28610)
PHONE.................................828 324-2200
R Adam Norwitt, *CEO*
◆ **EMP: 1200 EST:** 1986
SALES (est): 2.24B
SALES (corp-wide): 15.22B **Publicly Held**
Web: www.commscope.com
SIC: 3663 3357 3679 3812 Microwave
   communication equipment; Communication
   wire; Waveguides and fittings; Search and
   navigation equipment
PA: Amphenol Corporation
   358 Hall Ave
   Wallingford CT 06492
   203 265-8900

(G-3105)
**CRWW SPECIALTY COMPOSITES
INC**
2678 Heart Dr Bldg B (28610-8715)
P.O. Box 1087 (28610-1087)
PHONE.................................828 548-5002
Craig Girdwood, *Pr*
EMP: 15 EST: 2018
SQ FT: 20,000
SALES (est): 1.92MM **Privately Held**
Web: www.crwwassociates.com
SIC: 3357 Fiber optic cable (insulated)

(G-3106)
DEXTER INC
Also Called: Livin' Rooms
5718 Oxford School Rd (28610-9437)
PHONE.................................828 459-7904
Gene Setzer, *Mgr*
EMP: 5
SALES (corp-wide): 960.65K **Privately
Held**
Web: www.dexterfurniture.com
SIC: 2512 Upholstered household furniture
PA: Dexter, Inc.
   8411 Glenwood Ave Ste 101
   Raleigh NC 27612
   919 510-5050

(G-3107)
DIMENSION WOOD PRODUCTS INC
2885 Kelly Blvd (28610-7473)
P.O. Box 70 (28610-0070)
PHONE.................................828 459-9891
David Wayne-reinhardt, *Pr*
David Wayne Reinhardt, *
Karen Reinhardt, *
EMP: 12 EST: 1981
SQ FT: 20,000
SALES (est): 1.98MM **Privately Held**
Web: www.dimensionwoodproducts.com

SIC: 2426　Carvings, furniture: wood

(G-3108)
DRAKA COMMUNICATIONS AMERICAS INC
Also Called: Draka Communication
2512 Penny Rd　(28610-8634)
P.O. Box 39　(28610-0039)
PHONE..............................828 459-8456
▲ EMP: 500
SIC: 3357　Coaxial cable, nonferrous

(G-3109)
DRAKA HOLDINGS USA INC
Also Called: Prysmian Cables & Systems USA
2512 Penny Rd　(28610-8634)
PHONE..............................828 383-0020
▲ EMP: 1130
SIC: 3357　Communication wire

(G-3110)
DRAKA TRANSPORT USA LLC
2512 Penny Rd　(28610-8634)
PHONE..............................828 459-8895
EMP: 4 EST: 2007
SALES (est): 957.19K Privately Held
SIC: 3357　Automotive wire and cable, except ignition sets: nonferrous
HQ: Prysmian Cables And Systems Usa, Llc
　4 Tesseneer Dr
　Highland Heights KY 41076
　859 572-8000

(G-3111)
DRAKA USA INC
2512 Penny Rd　(28610-8634)
PHONE..............................828 459-9787
Gary R Wilbur, Prin
EMP: 13 EST: 2011
SALES (est): 418.5K Privately Held
SIC: 3357　Nonferrous wiredrawing and insulating

(G-3112)
DYNAMIC AIR ENGINEERING INC
Also Called: Dae Systems
2421 Bga Dr　(28610-9253)
PHONE..............................714 540-1000
Sharon C Morrison, CEO
Jeremy I Morrison, *
EMP: 43 EST: 1942
SQ FT: 45,000
SALES (est): 5.64MM Privately Held
Web: www.dynamic-air.co.uk
SIC: 3564 3585　Blowers and fans; Air conditioning units, complete: domestic or industrial

(G-3113)
FROSTIE BOTTOM TREE STAND LLC
Also Called: Frostie Bottom At Doors
3280 Yount Rd　(28610-9524)
PHONE..............................828 466-1708
Shon Kale, CEO
Kisha Morrison, Pr
EMP: 7 EST: 2012
SALES (est): 121.99K Privately Held
Web: www.frostiebottom.com
SIC: 3949 7389　Hunting equipment; Business Activities at Non-Commercial Site

(G-3114)
GRAM FURNITURE
4513 Nc Highway 10 E　(28610-8241)
PHONE..............................828 241-2836
EMP: 8
SALES (est): 90K Privately Held

SIC: 2531 2511　Church furniture; Wood bedroom furniture

(G-3115)
MCKINLEY LEATHER HICKORY INC
3131 W Main St　(28610-9609)
P.O. Box 1030　(28610-1030)
PHONE..............................828 459-2884
Lewis Mitchell, Pr
Denise Mitchell, *
Lori M Shadowski, *
◆ EMP: 24 EST: 1989
SQ FT: 38,785
SALES (est): 2.28MM Privately Held
Web: www.mckinleyleatherfurniture.com
SIC: 3172 2512　Personal leather goods, nec ; Upholstered household furniture

(G-3116)
POPPELMANN PLASTICS USA LLC
2180 Heart Dr　(28610)
P.O. Box 459　(28610)
PHONE..............................828 466-9500
Jack Dempsey Shelton, Managing Member
Thomas Orr, *
◆ EMP: 35 EST: 2004
SALES (est): 24.98MM
SALES (corp-wide): 355.83K Privately Held
Web: www.poeppelmann.com
SIC: 2821　Plastics materials and resins
HQ: Poppelmann Gmbh & Co. Kg
　Kunststoffwerk-Werkzeugbau
　Bakumer Str. 73
　Lohne (Oldenburg) NI 49393
　44429820

(G-3117)
POPPELMANN PROPERTIES USA LLC
2180 Heart Dr　(28610-8708)
PHONE..............................828 466-9500
Guido Schmidt, Managing Member
▲ EMP: 4 EST: 2004
SALES (est): 1.93MM Privately Held
SIC: 3089　Air mattresses, plastics

(G-3118)
PROGRESSIVE FURNITURE INC
2555 Penny Rd　(28610-8634)
P.O. Box 729　(28610-0729)
PHONE..............................828 459-2151
Ban Kendrick, Prin
EMP: 175
SALES (corp-wide): 543.69MM Privately Held
Web: www.progressivefurniture.com
SIC: 2511　Tables, household: wood
HQ: Progressive Furniture, Inc.
　502 Middle St
　Archbold OH 43502
　419 446-4500

(G-3119)
REGENCY FIBERS LLC
2788 S Oxford St　(28610)
PHONE..............................828 459-7645
James Julius Bush Junior, Managing Member
EMP: 36 EST: 2019
SALES (est): 6.36MM Privately Held
Web: www.regencyfibers.com
SIC: 2299　Batting, wadding, padding and fillings

(G-3120)
RESTAURANT FURNITURE INC
2688 E Us Highway 70　(28610-8674)
PHONE..............................828 459-9992
Ernest Baldwin, Pr
EMP: 10 EST: 1994

SQ FT: 20,000
SALES (est): 245.65K Privately Held
Web:
www.restaurantfurnitureindustries.com
SIC: 2599 5046 2512　Restaurant furniture, wood or metal; Commercial cooking and food service equipment; Upholstered household furniture

(G-3121)
RUCKUS WIRELESS LLC
Also Called: Arris Group
3642 E Us Highway 70　(28610-8530)
PHONE..............................503 495-9240
Janet Douglas, Mgr
EMP: 622
SALES (corp-wide): 15.22B Publicly Held
Web: www.commscope.com
SIC: 3661 3663 3357　Fiber optics communications equipment; Radio and t.v. communications equipment; Nonferrous wiredrawing and insulating
HQ: Ruckus Wireless Llc
　350 W Java Dr
　Sunnyvale CA 94089

(G-3122)
SUBSTANCE INCORPORATED
3000 Frazier Dr　(28610-8631)
PHONE..............................800 985-9485
EMP: 6 EST: 2012
SALES (est): 1.01MM Privately Held
Web: www.substance.com
SIC: 2759　Commercial printing, nec

(G-3123)
UNIVERSAL FURNITURE INTL INC
Also Called: Catawba Plant
4436 Old Catawba Rd　(28610)
P.O. Box 160　(28610-0160)
PHONE..............................828 241-3191
Ron Young, Mgr
EMP: 5
Web: www.universalfurniture.com
SIC: 2511 2512　Wood household furniture; Upholstered household furniture
HQ: Universal Furniture International Inc.
　2575 Penny Rd
　High Point NC 27265
　336 822-8425

(G-3124)
WESTROCK COMPANY
2690 Kelly Blvd　(28610-7427)
PHONE..............................470 484-1183
EMP: 12
Web: www.westrock.com
SIC: 2653　Boxes, corrugated: made from purchased materials
HQ: Westrock Company
　1000 Abernathy Rd Ne
　Atlanta GA 30328
　770 448-2193

(G-3125)
WESTROCK RKT LLC
2690 Kelly Blvd　(28610-7427)
PHONE..............................828 459-8006
Martin Szalay, Mgr
EMP: 98
Web: www.westrock.com
SIC: 2657 2652　Folding paperboard boxes; Setup paperboard boxes
HQ: Westrock Rkt, Llc
　1000 Abernathy Rd Ste 125
　Atlanta GA 30328
　770 448-2193

(G-3126)
WHITESIDE MCH & REPR CO INC
Also Called: Whiteside Machine Co
4506 Shook Rd　(28610-8612)
PHONE..............................828 459-2141
William Whiteside, Pr
Mike Whiteside, *
Lark Whiteside, *
Barbara Whiteside, *
Lori W Garrett, *
▼ EMP: 45 EST: 1970
SQ FT: 44,000
SALES (est): 5.53MM Privately Held
Web: www.whitesiderouterbits.com
SIC: 3541　Machine tools, metal cutting type

Clarendon
Columbus County

(G-3127)
GTG ENGINEERING INC (PA)
Also Called: Gtg Engineering
766 Furnie Hammond Rd　(28432-9017)
P.O. Box 11182　(28461-1182)
PHONE..............................877 569-8572
Michael Leblanc, Pr
◆ EMP: 5 EST: 2001
SALES (est): 901.19K
SALES (corp-wide): 901.19K Privately Held
Web: www.gtgengineering.com
SIC: 2899　Insulating compounds

Clarkton
Bladen County

(G-3128)
SACHS PEANUTS LLC
9323 Hwy 70　(28433)
P.O. Box 7　(28433)
PHONE..............................910 647-4711
EMP: 25 EST: 2010
SALES (est): 7.38MM Privately Held
Web: www.sachspeanuts.com
SIC: 5441 2068　Nuts; Nuts: dried, dehydrated, salted or roasted

Clayton
Johnston County

(G-3129)
A PLUS FIVE STAR TRNSP LLC
301 Mccarthy Dr　(27527-5795)
PHONE..............................919 771-4820
Charles Burroughs, Pr
EMP: 6 EST: 2015
SALES (est): 243.41K Privately Held
SIC: 3999 4212　Manufacturing industries, nec; Dump truck haulage

(G-3130)
ADC INDUSTRIES INC
Also Called: Automated Entrances
106 N Lombard St　(27520-2544)
PHONE..............................919 550-9515
Ken Fisher, Mgr
EMP: 6
SALES (corp-wide): 2.25MM Privately Held
Web: www.airlockdoor.com
SIC: 3491　Valves, automatic control
PA: Adc Industries Inc.
　181a E Jamaica Ave
　Valley Stream NY 11580
　516 596-1304

▲ = Import　▼ = Export
◆ = Import/Export

(G-3131)
AP GRANITE INSTALLATION LLC
2213 Stephanie Ln (27520-8407)
PHONE..................919 215-1795
Abel Salas Perea, *Pr*
EMP: 8 **EST:** 2016
SALES (est): 265.27K **Privately Held**
SIC: 1799 2541 Counter top installation;
Counter and sink tops

(G-3132)
ASHBRAN LLC
700 Parkridge Dr (27527-5304)
PHONE..................919 215-3567
▲ **EMP:** 5 **EST:** 2009
SALES (est): 256.84K **Privately Held**
Web: www.ashbran.com
SIC: 3679 3621 Commutators, electronic;
Sliprings, for motors or generators

(G-3133)
BAKER THERMAL SOLUTIONS LLC
Also Called: Turkington
8182 Us 70 Bus Hwy W (27520-9463)
PHONE..................919 674-3750
Eric Cruse, *Pr*
John Rollins, *VP Fin*
▲ **EMP:** 50 **EST:** 2012
SALES (est): 17.5MM
SALES (corp-wide): 3.88B **Publicly Held**
Web: www.bakerthermal.com
SIC: 3556 Bakery machinery
PA: The Middleby Corporation
1400 Toastmaster Dr
Elgin IL 60120
847 741-3300

(G-3134)
BATISTA GRADING INC
710 E Main St (27520-2626)
PHONE..................919 359-3449
Carlos Batista Junior, *Pr*
Carlos Batista, *Pr*
Connie Batista, *Sec*
EMP: 15 **EST:** 2001
SALES (est): 4.78MM **Privately Held**
Web: www.bgsus.com
SIC: 1611 1795 3532 1623 Surfacing and
paving; Demolition, buildings and other
structures; Crushing, pulverizing, and
screening equipment; Underground utilities
contractor

(G-3135)
BLACKLEYS PRINTING CO
Also Called: Blackleys Printing & Sign Shop
229 E Main St (27520-2449)
PHONE..................919 553-6813
Joyce Blackley, *Owner*
EMP: 5 **EST:** 1974
SALES (est): 423.76K **Privately Held**
Web: www.blackleysprinting.com
SIC: 2752 Offset printing

(G-3136)
CARPATHIAN WOODWORKS INC
46 Albemarle Dr (27527-4210)
PHONE..................919 669-7546
Paul Mcdonald, *Owner*
EMP: 5 **EST:** 2011
SALES (est): 231.69K **Privately Held**
Web: www.carpathianwoodworks.com
SIC: 2431 Millwork

(G-3137)
CATERPILLAR INC
Also Called: Caterpillar
954 Nc Highway 42 E (27527-8078)
PHONE..................919 550-1100
John Carpenter, *Brnch Mgr*

EMP: 59
SALES (corp-wide): 64.81B **Publicly Held**
Web: www.caterpillar.com
SIC: 3531 3594 3553 Loaders, shovel: self-
propelled; Fluid power pumps and motors;
Woodworking machinery
PA: Caterpillar Inc.
5205 N Ocnnor Blvd Ste 10
Irving TX 75039
972 891-7700

(G-3138)
CCBCC OPERATIONS LLC
Also Called: Coca-Cola
977 Shotwell Rd Ste 104 (27520-5126)
PHONE..................919 359-2966
Tim Kelley, *Mgr*
EMP: 67
SQ FT: 62,500
SALES (corp-wide): 6.9B **Publicly Held**
Web: www.coca-cola.com
SIC: 2086 Bottled and canned soft drinks
HQ: Ccbcc Operations, Llc
4100 Coca-Cola Plz
Charlotte NC 28211
704 364-8728

(G-3139)
**CENTER FOR ORTHOTIC &
PROSTHET**
166 Springbrook Ave Ste 203 (27520-8520)
PHONE..................919 585-4173
Donald Dixon, *CEO*
EMP: 70
SALES (corp-wide): 1.12B **Privately Held**
Web: www.centeropcare.com
SIC: 3842 Limbs, artificial
HQ: Center For Orthotic & Prosthetic Care
Of North Carolina, Inc.
4702 Creekstone Dr
Durham NC 27703
919 797-1230

(G-3140)
CITGO QUIK LUBE OF CLAYTON
11133 Us 70 Business Hwy W
(27520-2369)
PHONE..................919 550-0935
Tim Matthews, *Pr*
EMP: 9 **EST:** 1996
SALES (est): 325.13K **Privately Held**
SIC: 2992 Lubricating oils

(G-3141)
COCA-COLA CONSOLIDATED INC
Also Called: Coca-Cola
977 Shotwell Rd Ste 104 (27520-5126)
PHONE..................919 550-0611
Cola Coca, *Brnch Mgr*
EMP: 205
SALES (corp-wide): 6.9B **Publicly Held**
Web: www.cokeconsolidated.com
SIC: 5962 5149 2086 Merchandising
machine operators; Beverages, except
coffee and tea; Bottled and canned soft
drinks
PA: Coca-Cola Consolidated, Inc.
4100 Coca-Cola Plz
Charlotte NC 28211
980 392-8298

(G-3142)
DAMSEL IN DEFENSE
109 Lake Point Dr (27527-5217)
PHONE..................919 744-8776
EMP: 4 **EST:** 2014
SALES (est): 557.36K **Privately Held**
Web: www.damselindefense.net
SIC: 3812 Defense systems and equipment

(G-3143)
DAYCO MANUFACTURING INC
6116 Us 70 W (27520-6312)
PHONE..................919 989-1820
Mitch Day, *Prin*
EMP: 14 **EST:** 2007
SALES (est): 2.49MM **Privately Held**
Web: www.daycomanufacturing.com
SIC: 3599 Machine shop, jobbing and repair

(G-3144)
DEW GROUP ENTERPRISES INC
Also Called: C G P
501 Atkinson St (27520-2155)
P.O. Box 129 (27528-0129)
PHONE..................919 585-0100
▼ **EMP:** 25 **EST:** 1988
SALES (est): 1.71MM **Privately Held**
Web: www.cgplabels.com
SIC: 2752 Offset printing
HQ: Sml (Hong Kong) Limited
6/F C-Bons Intl Ctr
Kwun Tong KLN

(G-3145)
EDGE PROMO TEAM LLC
7868 Us 70 Bus Hwy W Ste B
(27520-5008)
PHONE..................919 946-4218
Theodore Ormsby, *Admn*
EMP: 24 **EST:** 2014
SALES (est): 4.76MM **Privately Held**
Web: www.edgepromoteam.com
SIC: 2759 Screen printing

(G-3146)
**EDWARDS ELECTRONIC SYSTEMS
INC (HQ)**
3821 Powhatan Rd (27520-9235)
P.O. Box 39 (27528-0039)
PHONE..................919 359-2239
Jim Devries, *CEO*
EMP: 30 **EST:** 1997
SQ FT: 6,500
SALES (est): 5.45MM
SALES (corp-wide): 713.15MM **Privately
Held**
Web: www.everonsolutions.com
SIC: 1731 1711 5065 5063 Sound
equipment specialization; Fire sprinkler
system installation; Security control
equipment and systems; Fire alarm systems
PA: Everon, Llc
1501 W Yamato Rd
Boca Raton FL 33431
844 538-3766

(G-3147)
EXIDE TECHNOLOGIES LLC
104 N Tech Dr (27520-5002)
PHONE..................919 553-3578
Kim Parrish, *Mgr*
EMP: 5
SALES (corp-wide): 482.75MM **Privately
Held**
Web: www.exide.com
SIC: 5063 3629 Batteries; Battery chargers,
rectifying or nonrotating
PA: Exide Technologies, Llc
13000 Drfeld Pkwy Bldg 20
Milton GA 30004
678 566-9000

(G-3148)
FRAZIER HOLDINGS LLC
2009 Pope Ct (27520-8217)
PHONE..................919 868-8651
EMP: 4 **EST:** 2008
SQ FT: 2,000
SALES (est): 133.58K **Privately Held**

SIC: 2522 Office furniture, except wood

(G-3149)
GENERAL PRECISION SVC
321 E Main St (27520-2463)
P.O. Box 746 (27528-0746)
PHONE..................919 553-2604
Larry E Belvin, *Owner*
Judy Belvin, *Mgr*
EMP: 4 **EST:** 1980
SQ FT: 6,000
SALES (est): 590.32K **Privately Held**
SIC: 3599 Machine shop, jobbing and repair

(G-3150)
GRIFOLS INC
8368 Us 70 Bus Hwy W (27520-9464)
PHONE..................919 553-5011
Gregory Gene Rich, *CEO*
David Bell, *
EMP: 44 **EST:** 2003
SALES (est): 8.53MM **Privately Held**
Web: www.gamunex-c.com
SIC: 2834 Pharmaceutical preparations

(G-3151)
GRIFOLS THERAPEUTICS LLC
Also Called: Grifols
9257 Us 70 Bus Hwy W Ste B-302
(27520-9461)
PHONE..................919 359-7069
Gregory Rich, *Managing Member*
EMP: 99
Web: www.discovertheplasma.com
SIC: 2834 Pharmaceutical preparations
HQ: Grifols Therapeutics Llc
79 Tw Alexander Dr
Research Triangle Pa NC 27709

(G-3152)
GRIFOLS THERAPEUTICS LLC
8368 Clayton Blvd (27520)
PHONE..................919 553-0172
Rich Gregory, *Brnch Mgr*
EMP: 155
Web: www.discovertheplasma.com
SIC: 2834 Pharmaceutical preparations
HQ: Grifols Therapeutics Llc
79 Tw Alexander Dr
Research Triangle Pa NC 27709

(G-3153)
HEALTH EDUCATOR PUBLICATIONS
476 Shotwell Rd Ste 102 (27520-3506)
PHONE..................919 243-1299
Dana F Oakes, *Prin*
EMP: 7 **EST:** 2016
SALES (est): 109.62K **Privately Held**
SIC: 2741 Miscellaneous publishing

(G-3154)
HOSPIRA INC
8484 Us 70 Bus Hwy W (27520-9465)
PHONE..................919 553-3831
Tom Ludke, *Mgr*
EMP: 331
SALES (corp-wide): 63.63B **Publicly Held**
Web: www.pfizerhospitalus.com
SIC: 2869 2899 2834 Amines, acids, salts,
esters; Chemical preparations, nec;
Pharmaceutical preparations
HQ: Hospira, Inc.
275 N Field Dr
Lake Forest IL 60045
224 212-2000

(G-3155)
J & D THORPE ENTERPRISES INC
Also Called: Sign-A-Rama
116 Shady Meadow Ln (27520-6404)

PHONE...................919 553-0918
James L Thorpe, *Pr*
Dolores A Thorpe, *VP*
EMP: 5 **EST:** 2011
SQ FT: 2,600
SALES (est): 232.42K **Privately Held**
Web: www.signarama.com
SIC: 3993 5999 Signs and advertising
specialties; Banners, flags, decals, and
posters

(G-3156)
LASH OUT INC
117 Georgetowne Dr (27520-1846)
PHONE...................919 342-0221
Amy Lynn Rhoden, *Prin*
EMP: 5 **EST:** 2012
SALES (est): 65.48K **Privately Held**
Web: www.lashoutpro.com
SIC: 2844 Face creams or lotions

(G-3157)
LEWIS BROTHERS TIRE & ALGNMT
451 E Main St (27520-2528)
PHONE...................919 359-9050
Michael Lewis, *Owner*
EMP: 6 **EST:** 2004
SALES (est): 195.4K **Privately Held**
SIC: 7538 7534 General automotive repair
shops; Tire repair shop

(G-3158)
M D PREVATT INC
338 Winding Oak Way (27520-8025)
PHONE...................919 796-4944
Michael Prevatt, *Pr*
EMP: 10 **EST:** 2000
SALES (est): 757.38K **Privately Held**
SIC: 1389 Construction, repair, and
dismantling services

(G-3159)
MAGNEVOLT INC
5335 Us 70 Bus Hwy W (27520-6812)
P.O. Box 58099 (27658-8099)
PHONE...................919 553-2202
William Davidson, *Ch Bd*
EMP: 10 **EST:** 1985
SQ FT: 5,600
SALES (est): 887.1K **Privately Held**
Web: www.magnevolt.com
SIC: 3691 Storage batteries

(G-3160)
MM CLAYTON LLC
Also Called: Essentra Packaging
1000 Ccc Dr (27520-8015)
PHONE...................919 553-4113
John Cullen, *Pr*
Sparky Cullen, *
William Karstenson, *
EMP: 324 **EST:** 1979
SQ FT: 70,000
SALES (est): 24.65MM
SALES (corp-wide): 4.53B **Privately Held**
Web: www.3cpackaging.com
SIC: 5199 2655 Packaging materials;
Ammunition cans or tubes, board laminated
with metal foil
HQ: Mm Packaging Us Inc.
Two Westbrook Corp Ctr
Westchester IL 60154

(G-3161)
MULTI TECHNICAL SERVICES INC
Also Called: MTS Communication Products
950 Nc Highway 42 W (27520-7434)
PHONE...................919 553-2995
Lnywood A Williams, *Pr*
Lynwood A Williams, *Pr*
▲ **EMP:** 7 **EST:** 1988

SQ FT: 15,000
SALES (est): 368.63K **Privately Held**
SIC: 3663 8711 3823 3651 Radio and t.v.
communications equipment; Engineering
services; Process control instruments;
Household audio and video equipment

(G-3162)
NOBLE WHOLESALERS INC
Also Called: Youshirt
356 Trenburg Pl (27520-9241)
PHONE...................409 739-3803
Ugur Soylu, *Pr*
EMP: 4 **EST:** 2013
SALES (est): 56.36K **Privately Held**
SIC: 2253 T-shirts and tops, knit

(G-3163)
NORTHEAST FOODS INC
68 Harvest Mill Ln (27520-4849)
PHONE...................919 585-5178
Bill Paterakis, *Prin*
EMP: 6 **EST:** 2010
SALES (est): 243.4K **Privately Held**
Web: www.nefoods.com
SIC: 2051 Bakery: wholesale or wholesale/
retail combined

(G-3164)
NOVO NORDISK PHRM INDS LP
646 Glp Oneway (27527)
PHONE...................919 820-9985
EMP: 67
SALES (corp-wide): 39.23B **Privately Held**
Web: www.novonordisk-us.com
SIC: 2834 Pharmaceutical preparations
HQ: Novo Nordisk Pharmaceutical
Industries, Lp
3612 Powhatan Rd
Clayton NC 27527

(G-3165)
NOVO NORDISK PHRM INDS LP
3611 Powhatan Rd (27527-6058)
PHONE...................919 820-9985
Elliot Zieglmeier, *Prin*
EMP: 134 **EST:** 2020
SALES (est): 11.47MM **Privately Held**
Web: www.novonordisk-us.com
SIC: 2834 Pharmaceutical preparations

(G-3166)
PAINTING BY COLORS LLC
562 Rock Pillar Rd (27520-6876)
PHONE...................919 963-2300
EMP: 5 **EST:** 2013
SALES (est): 277.04K **Privately Held**
SIC: 1721 3589 Residential painting; High
pressure cleaning equipment

(G-3167)
RAY HOUSES MACHINE SHOP
110 N Tech Dr (27520-5002)
P.O. Box 1104 (27528-1104)
PHONE...................919 553-1249
EMP: 7
SQ FT: 6,250
SALES (est): 586.87K **Privately Held**
SIC: 3599 Machine shop, jobbing and repair

(G-3168)
RENEW RECYCLING LLC
440 S Tech Park Ln (27520-5016)
PHONE...................919 550-8012
Gary Taylor, *Pr*
EMP: 65 **EST:** 2020
SALES (est): 4.75MM **Privately Held**
Web: www.renewrecycling.com

SIC: 5093 3341 Ferrous metal scrap and
waste; Recovery and refining of nonferrous
metals

(G-3169)
SMISSONS INC
425 Swann Trl (27527-6506)
PHONE...................660 537-3219
Ramani Morales, *CEO*
Benino Morales, *Ch Bd*
EMP: 5 **EST:** 2020
SALES (est): 156.72K **Privately Held**
Web: www.smissonsmedicalsupply.com
SIC: 7389 6221 5047 2326 Business
Activities at Non-Commercial Site;
Commodity contracts brokers, dealers;
Medical laboratory equipment; Medical and
hospital uniforms, men's

(G-3170)
SML RALEIGH LLC
501 Atkinson St (27520-2155)
P.O. Box 129 (27528-0129)
PHONE...................919 585-0100
Tommy Dew, *Pr*
Beverly Dew, *VP*
EMP: 7 **EST:** 2012
SALES (est): 1.41MM **Privately Held**
Web: www.sml.com
SIC: 2741 2759 5131 Miscellaneous
publishing; Commercial printing, nec; Labels
PA: Sml Usa Inc.
1 Harmon Plz # 6fl
Secaucus NJ 07094

(G-3171)
**STRUCTURAL STEEL PRODUCTS
CORP**
8027 Us 70 Bus Hwy W (27520-4807)
PHONE...................919 359-2811
Trudy Hales, *Pr*
Ray Hales, *
Rick Brown, *
EMP: 80 **EST:** 1981
SQ FT: 53,000
SALES (est): 5.18MM **Privately Held**
Web: www.structuralcoatingsinc.com
SIC: 3441 Building components, structural
steel

(G-3172)
STUDIO TK LLC
3940 Us 70 Hwy Business (27520)
P.O. Box 1529 (27528-1529)
PHONE...................919 464-2920
Charlie Bell, *Pr*
▲ **EMP:** 45 **EST:** 2012
SQ FT: 75,000
SALES (est): 14.29MM
SALES (corp-wide): 109.98MM **Privately
Held**
Web: www.studiotk.com
SIC: 2522 Office furniture, except wood
HQ: Teknion Limited
1150 Flint Rd
North York ON M3J 2
416 661-1577

(G-3173)
TARHEEL PUBLISHING CO
120 N Tech Dr Ste 102 (27520-5084)
PHONE...................919 553-9042
Hayes Jeff, *Owner*
EMP: 16 **EST:** 1998
SQ FT: 4,000
SALES (est): 958.11K **Privately Held**
Web: www.tmsdigi.com
SIC: 2741 Telephone and other directory
publishing

(G-3174)
TEKNI-PLEX INC
Also Called: Natvar
8720 Us 70 Bus Hwy W (27520-4808)
P.O. Box 658 (27528-0658)
PHONE...................919 553-4151
George Coggins, *Mgr*
EMP: 61
SQ FT: 50,000
SALES (corp-wide): 996.3MM **Privately
Held**
Web: www.tekni-plex.com
SIC: 5999 3069 3083 Medical apparatus and
supplies; Tubing, rubber; Laminated
plastics plate and sheet
PA: Tekni-Plex, Inc.
460 E Swdsford Rd Ste 300
Wayne PA 19087
484 690-1520

(G-3175)
TURNER & REEVES FENCE CO LLC
2016 Pope Ct (27520-8813)
PHONE...................910 671-8851
EMP: 4 **EST:** 2012
SALES (est): 340.26K **Privately Held**
SIC: 3315 Chain link fencing

Clemmons
Forsyth County

(G-3176)
1ST TIME CONTRACTING
104 Western Villa Dr (27012-8277)
PHONE...................774 289-3321
EMP: 4 **EST:** 2020
SALES (est): 151.96K **Privately Held**
SIC: 2499 Fencing, docks, and other outdoor
wood structural products

(G-3177)
ATLANTIS FOODS INC
Also Called: Atlantis Food Service
4525 Hampton Rd (27012-9456)
PHONE...................336 768-6101
Vasileios Tsiaras, *Pr*
EMP: 30 **EST:** 1999
SQ FT: 125,000
SALES (est): 7.62MM **Privately Held**
Web: www.atlantisfoodsinc.com
SIC: 5146 2032 Fish and seafoods; Italian
foods, nec: packaged in cans, jars, etc.

(G-3178)
BAHNSON HOLDINGS INC (HQ)
4731 Commercial Park Ct (27012-8700)
PHONE...................336 760-3111
Timothy J Whitener, *Pr*
James P Hutcherson, *Sec*
Lisa J Cunningham, *Treas*
EMP: 79 **EST:** 1915
SALES (est): 156.06MM
SALES (corp-wide): 14.57B **Publicly Held**
Web: www.bahnson.com
SIC: 8711 1711 3585 3564 Heating and
ventilation engineering; Warm air heating
and air conditioning contractor; Heating
equipment, complete; Blowers and fans
PA: Emcor Group, Inc.
301 Merritt 7
Norwalk CT 06851
203 849-7800

(G-3179)
BATTERY WATERING SYSTEMS LLC
6645 Holder Rd (27012-9287)
PHONE...................336 714-0448
Scott D Elliott, *Managing Member*
EMP: 6 **EST:** 2010

SALES (est): 982.98K **Privately Held**
Web: www.batterywatering.com
SIC: **2834** Chlorination tablets and kits (water purification)

(G-3180)
CLEMMONS PALLET SKID WORKS INC
3449 Hwy 158 E (27012)
P.O. Box 745 (27012-0745)
PHONE............................336 766-5462
Dewey B Edwards, *Pr*
Frances D Edwards, *VP*
EMP: 20 EST: 1971
SQ FT: 7,500
SALES (est): 3.12MM **Privately Held**
Web: www.clemmonspallet.com
SIC: **2448** 2441 Pallets, wood; Nailed wood boxes and shook

(G-3181)
DONS FINE JEWELRY INC
2503 Lewisville Clemmons Rd (27012-8712)
P.O. Box 1544 (27012-1544)
PHONE............................336 724-7826
Don Pope, *Pr*
Chris Pope, *VP*
Danny Wingo, *Mgr*
EMP: 6 EST: 1984
SALES (est): 144.27K **Privately Held**
Web: www.wingosfinejewelry.com
SIC: **5944** 7631 3911 Jewelry, precious stones and precious metals; Jewelry repair services; Jewelry, precious metal

(G-3182)
DYNAMIC MACHINE WORKS LLC
2655 Knob Hill Dr (27012-8831)
PHONE............................336 462-7370
Michael Kruth, *Prin*
EMP: 4 EST: 2015
SALES (est): 1.48MM **Privately Held**
SIC: **3599** Amusement park equipment

(G-3183)
FORSYTH FAMILY MAGAZINE INC
6255 Towncenter Dr (27012-9376)
PHONE............................336 782-0331
Kim Beane, *Prin*
EMP: 5 EST: 2010
SALES (est): 448.24K **Privately Held**
Web: www.forsythfamilymagazine.com
SIC: **2721** Magazines: publishing only, not printed on site

(G-3184)
FOURSHARE LLC
Also Called: Battery Watering Technology
6645 Holder Rd (27012-9287)
PHONE............................336 714-0448
Scott Elliott, *Pr*
EMP: 17 EST: 2011
SQ FT: 9,300
SALES (est): 3.53MM **Privately Held**
Web: www.batterywatering.com
SIC: **3089** Battery cases, plastics or plastics combination

(G-3185)
FRISBY AEROSPACE INC
4520 Hampton Rd (27012-9456)
PHONE............................336 712-8004
Michael Rife, *Engr*
EMP: 4 EST: 2017
SALES (est): 1.6MM **Privately Held**
Web: www.frisbyaerospace.com
SIC: **3728** Aircraft parts and equipment, nec

(G-3186)
G & G ENTERPRISES
210 Industrial Dr Ste 2 (27012-6872)
PHONE............................336 764-2493
Ann Beeson, *Owner*
EMP: 4 EST: 1983
SQ FT: 4,000
SALES (est): 248.34K **Privately Held**
SIC: **2396** 5621 Screen printing on fabric articles; Women's sportswear

(G-3187)
GROUPE LACASSE LLC
Also Called: Neocase
2235 Lewisville Clemmons Rd Ste D (27012-7406)
P.O. Box 129 (27012-0129)
PHONE............................336 778-2098
Sylvain Garneau, *Pr*
Rene Frechette, *
Guy Lacasse, *
Robin Lacasse, *
Benjamin Wagenmaker, *
EMP: 8 EST: 2015
SALES (est): 415.45K **Privately Held**
Web: www.groupelacasse.com
SIC: **2521** Desks, office: wood

(G-3188)
HAYWARD INDUSTRIES INC
1 Hayward Industrial Dr (27012)
P.O. Box 5100 (27012)
PHONE............................336 712-9900
Terry Payne, *Brnch Mgr*
EMP: 51
SALES (corp-wide): 1.05B **Publicly Held**
Web: hayward.com
SIC: **3589** 3561 3423 3494 Swimming pool filter and water conditioning systems; Pumps and pumping equipment; Leaf skimmers or swimming pool rakes; Valves and pipe fittings, nec
HQ: Hayward Industries, Inc.
1415 Vntage Pk Dr Ste 400
Charlotte NC 28203
704 837-8002

(G-3189)
HAYWARD INDUSTRIES INC
Hayward Pool Products
1 Hayward Industrial Dr (27012)
P.O. Box 5100 (27012)
PHONE............................336 712-9900
Don Alcorn, *Mgr*
EMP: 700
SALES (corp-wide): 1.05B **Publicly Held**
Web: hayward.com
SIC: **3589** 3561 3563 Swimming pool filter and water conditioning systems; Pumps and pumping equipment; Air and gas compressors
HQ: Hayward Industries, Inc.
1415 Vntage Pk Dr Ste 400
Charlotte NC 28203
704 837-8002

(G-3190)
HORIZON HOME IMPORTS INC
6211 Clementine Dr (27012-9477)
P.O. Box 11742 (28220-1742)
PHONE............................704 859-5133
Nash Smith, *Managing Member*
EMP: 8
SIC: **2273** Carpets and rugs
PA: Horizon Home Imports Inc.
4943 Park Rd Unit 506
Charlotte NC 28209

(G-3191)
IMAGE MATTERS INC
1808 Ramhurst Dr (27012-9201)
PHONE............................336 940-3000
Roger K Laudy, *Pr*
Diane Laudy, *Sec*
EMP: 5 EST: 1991
SQ FT: 60,000
SALES (est): 479.38K **Privately Held**
Web: www.imagemattersinc.com
SIC: **3993** 2392 2796 Advertising novelties; Pads and padding, table: except asbestos, felt, or rattan; Platemaking services

(G-3192)
INTELLIGENT ENDOSCOPY LLC
4740 Commercial Park Ct Ste 1 (27012-9786)
PHONE............................336 608-4375
EMP: 20 EST: 2014
SALES (est): 2.43MM **Privately Held**
SIC: **3841** Surgical and medical instruments

(G-3193)
J R CRAVER & ASSOCIATES INC
Also Called: Salem Collection, The
265 Ashbourne Lake Ct (27012-7907)
PHONE............................336 769-3330
J Richard Craver, *Pr*
EMP: 5 EST: 1983
SQ FT: 88,000
SALES (est): 401.23K **Privately Held**
SIC: **2493** 5199 3993 Reconstituted wood products; Christmas trees, including artificial ; Signs and advertising specialties

(G-3194)
JRM INC
8491 N Nc Hwy 150 (27012-6843)
PHONE............................888 576-7007
James R Merritt, *Pr*
Jennifer Merritt, *
Chester Clark, *
EMP: 49 EST: 1992
SQ FT: 10,000
SALES (est): 9.03MM **Privately Held**
Web: www.jrmonline.com
SIC: **3524** Lawn and garden mowers and accessories

(G-3195)
K9 INSTALLS INC
6255 Towncenter Dr Ste 875 (27012-9376)
PHONE............................743 207-1507
Staceyn Linster, *CEO*
EMP: 5 EST: 2022
SALES (est): 934.38K **Privately Held**
SIC: **1389** Construction, repair, and dismantling services

(G-3196)
KALAJDZIC INC
Also Called: My Kolors
1415 River Ridge Dr (27012-8355)
PHONE............................855 465-4225
Dragoslav Kalajdzic, *Pr*
▲ EMP: 10 EST: 2008
SQ FT: 300,000
SALES (est): 304.94K **Privately Held**
Web: www.ink4cakes.com
SIC: **2759** Business forms: printing, nsk

(G-3197)
MUSCADINE NATURALS INC
6332 Cephis Dr (27012-9230)
PHONE............................888 628-5898
Robert Dalton, *Pr*
Linn Davis, *CFO*
EMP: 6 EST: 2001
SALES (est): 131.77K **Privately Held**

Web: www.muscadinenaturals.com
SIC: **2023** Dietary supplements, dairy and non-dairy based

(G-3198)
PAINT COMPANY OF NC
Also Called: Johnson's Industrial Coatings
10436 N Nc Hwy 150 (27012-6863)
PHONE............................336 764-1648
Jay Mehta, *Pr*
Jennifer Kinosh, *Off Mgr*
EMP: 7 EST: 1989
SQ FT: 14,000
SALES (est): 347.21K **Privately Held**
Web: www.johnsoncoating.com
SIC: **2851** Paints and paint additives

(G-3199)
PRINT EXPRESS ENTERPRISES INC
Also Called: Nu Expression
6255 Towncenter Dr (27012-9376)
PHONE............................336 765-5505
Jan Allison, *Pr*
Brian Leimone, *VP*
Craig Phillips, *Sec*
EMP: 6 EST: 2008
SALES (est): 1MM **Privately Held**
Web: www.nuagency.com
SIC: **2752** Offset printing

(G-3200)
QUALCOMM INCORPORATED
Also Called: Qualcomm
6209 Ramada Dr Ste A (27012-9733)
PHONE............................336 323-3300
Mark Dole, *Dir*
EMP: 12
SALES (corp-wide): 38.96B **Publicly Held**
Web: www.qualcomm.com
SIC: **3663** Space satellite communications equipment
PA: Qualcomm Incorporated
5775 Morehouse Dr
San Diego CA 92121
858 587-1121

(G-3201)
QUARTER TURN LLC
8340 Holler Farm Rd (27012-8084)
PHONE............................336 712-0811
Grace C Jones, *Prin*
EMP: 4 EST: 2008
SALES (est): 148.22K **Privately Held**
SIC: **3131** Footwear cut stock

(G-3202)
ROADRNNER MTRCYCLE TURING TRVL
2245 Lewisville Clemmons Rd Ste D (27012-7461)
PHONE............................336 765-7780
Christa Neuheuser, *Pr*
▲ EMP: 4 EST: 2005
SALES (est): 150.74K **Privately Held**
Web: www.roadrunner.travel
SIC: **2741** Miscellaneous publishing

(G-3203)
STANFORD MANUFACTURING LLC
3720 Stanford Way (27012-8842)
PHONE............................336 999-8799
Scott D Elliott, *Managing Member*
EMP: 11 EST: 2016
SALES (est): 5.63MM **Privately Held**
Web: www.stanfordmanufacturing.com
SIC: **3089** Injection molding of plastics

(G-3204)
TOPSIDER BUILDING SYSTEMS INC
3710 Dillon Industrial Dr (27012-8571)

P.O. Box 1490 (27012-1490)
PHONE..............................336 766-9300
Sheldon J Storer, *Pr*
J Joseph Kruse, *
Peter F Anthony, *
▼ **EMP:** 40 **EST:** 1968
SQ FT: 105,000
SALES (est): 8.29MM **Privately Held**
Web: www.topsiderhomes.com
SIC: 2452 Modular homes, prefabricated, wood

(G-3205)
TRIAD WELDING CONTRACTORS INC
146 Silkwind Ct (27012-7271)
PHONE..............................336 882-3902
Daryl Hartsell, *Owner*
EMP: 4 **EST:** 1997
SALES (est): 1.32MM **Privately Held**
SIC: 3444 Booths, spray: prefabricated sheet metal

(G-3206)
TRIUMPH ACTUATION SYSTEMS LLC (HQ)
Also Called: Triumph Acttion Systms-Clmmons
4520 Hampton Rd (27012-9456)
PHONE..............................336 766-9036
John B Wright Ii, *Mgr*
M David Kornblatt, *
Richard Reed, *
▲ **EMP:** 220 **EST:** 2003
SALES (est): 34.41MM **Publicly Held**
Web:
www.triumphactuationsystems.com
SIC: 3593 3728 Fluid power cylinders and actuators; Aircraft parts and equipment, nec
PA: Triumph Group, Inc.
     555 E Lncster Ave Ste 400
     Radnor PA 19087

(G-3207)
UNITED MOBILE IMAGING INC
2554 Lewisville Clemmons Rd Ste 201
(27012-8749)
P.O. Box 11 (27012-0011)
PHONE..............................800 983-9840
Paul Smith Junior, *CEO*
EMP: 5 **EST:** 2006
SALES (est): 165.18K **Privately Held**
SIC: 5047 5999 3845 Medical equipment and supplies; Medical apparatus and supplies; Electromedical equipment

(G-3208)
VELOCITA INC
383 Grant Rd (27012-7049)
PHONE..............................336 764-8513
Bradley Smith, *Pr*
EMP: 5 **EST:** 2015
SALES (est): 164.21K **Privately Held**
Web: www.velocita-usa.com
SIC: 3999 Manufacturing industries, nec

Cleveland
Rowan County

(G-3209)
BARBER FURNITURE & SUPPLY
590 Mountain Rd (27013-9707)
PHONE..............................704 278-9367
Charles P Barber, *Owner*
EMP: 10 **EST:** 1976
SQ FT: 4,600
SALES (est): 397.3K **Privately Held**
Web: www.barberwood.com

SIC: 2511 2434 2431 5211 Wood household furniture; Wood kitchen cabinets; Doors and door parts and trim, wood; Lumber and other building materials

(G-3210)
CARGILL INCORPORATED
Also Called: Cargill
9150 Statesville Blvd (27013-9022)
PHONE..............................704 278-2941
Mark Whitaker, *Mgr*
EMP: 9
SALES (corp-wide): 159.59B **Privately Held**
Web: www.cargill.com
SIC: 2048 Prepared feeds, nec
PA: Cargill, Incorporated
     15407 Mcginty Rd W
     Wayzata MN 55391
     800 227-4455

(G-3211)
CLESTERS AUTO RUBBER SEALS LLC
5415 Statesville Blvd (27013)
PHONE..............................704 637-9979
Robert Clester, *Owner*
EMP: 15 **EST:** 1997
SALES (est): 288.17K **Privately Held**
Web: www.clestersauto.com
SIC: 2891 Sealing compounds, synthetic rubber or plastic

(G-3212)
CLEVELAND FREIGHTLINER TRUCK
11550 Statesville Blvd (27013-8114)
P.O. Box 399 (27013-0399)
PHONE..............................704 645-5000
John Stevenson, *Mgr*
▲ **EMP:** 12 **EST:** 2002
SALES (est): 1.29MM **Privately Held**
Web: www.freightliner.com
SIC: 3711 Truck and tractor truck assembly

(G-3213)
DAIMLER TRUCK NORTH AMER LLC
Also Called: Chrysler Freight Liner
11550 Statesville Blvd (27013-8114)
P.O. Box 399 (27013-0399)
PHONE..............................704 645-5000
Mike Mccurry, *Mgr*
EMP: 1200
SALES (corp-wide): 60.75B **Privately Held**
Web: northamerica.daimlertruck.com
SIC: 5511 3715 3711 3537 Automobiles, new and used; Truck trailers; Motor vehicles and car bodies; Industrial trucks and tractors
HQ: Daimler Truck North America Llc
     4555 N Channel Ave
     Portland OR 97217
     503 745-8000

(G-3214)
HERSEY METERS CO LLC
10210 Statesville Blvd (27013-8103)
PHONE..............................704 278-2221
Charles Riney, *Manager*
EMP: 7 **EST:** 2006
SALES (est): 3.21MM
SALES (corp-wide): 1.31B **Publicly Held**
Web: www.muellersystems.com
SIC: 3491 Industrial valves
PA: Mueller Water Products, Inc.
     1200 Abrnthy Rd Ne Ste 12
     Atlanta GA 30328
     770 206-4200

(G-3215)
JIM FAB OF NORTH CAROLINA INC
10230 Statesville Blvd (27013-8103)
PHONE..............................704 278-1000
Robert Moss, *Pr*
EMP: 50 **EST:** 2010
SALES (est): 1.52MM **Privately Held**
SIC: 3498 5074 5993 Fabricated pipe and fittings; Pipes and fittings, plastic; Pipe store
PA: Miles Moss Of New York, Inc.
     586 Commercial Ave
     Garden City NY 11530

(G-3216)
MUELLER SYSTEMS LLC
Also Called: Hersey Meters Division
10210 Statesville Blvd (27013-8103)
P.O. Box 128 (27013-0128)
PHONE..............................704 278-2221
Hassan Ali, *
Thomas Butler, *
Tom Cullinan, *
Lowell Rust, *
▲ **EMP:** 156 **EST:** 1999
SALES (est): 45.06MM
SALES (corp-wide): 1.31B **Publicly Held**
Web: www.muellersystems.com
SIC: 3824 Water meters
PA: Mueller Water Products, Inc.
     1200 Abrnthy Rd Ne Ste 12
     Atlanta GA 30328
     770 206-4200

(G-3217)
MYERS FOREST PRODUCTS INC
Also Called: C & M Sawmill
355 Barber Junction Rd (27013-9775)
P.O. Box 38 (27013-0038)
PHONE..............................704 278-4532
Craig Myers, *Pr*
Gilbert Myers Senior, *VP*
Gilbert Myers Junior, *Treas*
Leanna Myers, *
EMP: 8 **EST:** 1981
SQ FT: 7,500
SALES (est): 477.81K **Privately Held**
SIC: 2421 2448 Sawmills and planing mills, general; Pallets, wood

(G-3218)
PERDUE FARMS INC
Also Called: Perdue Grain Market
9150 Statesville Blvd (27013-9022)
PHONE..............................704 278-2228
Frank Perdue, *Pr*
EMP: 34
SALES (corp-wide): 1.24B **Privately Held**
Web: www.perdue.com
SIC: 2015 Poultry slaughtering and processing
PA: Perdue Farms Incorporated
     31149 Old Ocean City Rd
     Salisbury MD 21804
     800 473-7383

(G-3219)
PHELPS WOOD PRODUCTS LLC
12010 Statesville Blvd (27013-9422)
PHONE..............................336 284-2149
James W Phelps, *Pr*
EMP: 5 **EST:** 2001
SALES (est): 457.19K **Privately Held**
SIC: 2499 Fencing, docks, and other outdoor wood structural products

(G-3220)
RDH TIRE AND RETREAD COMPANY
1315 Redmon Rd (27013-8058)
P.O. Box 187 (27013-0187)
PHONE..............................980 368-4576
Bradly Ragan Junior, *Pr*

Homer Huskins, *
▲ **EMP:** 76 **EST:** 1987
SQ FT: 38,500
SALES (est): 9.86MM **Privately Held**
Web: www.rdhtire.com
SIC: 7534 Rebuilding and retreading tires

(G-3221)
SHAVER WOOD PRODUCTS INC
14440 Statesville Blvd (27013-8791)
PHONE..............................704 278-1482
Richard Shaver, *Pr*
Chad Shaver, *
EMP: 60 **EST:** 1973
SQ FT: 15,600
SALES (est): 11.26MM **Privately Held**
Web: www.lilshavers.com
SIC: 2426 2421 Hardwood dimension and flooring mills; Chipper mill

(G-3222)
SOUTHERN ROOTS MONOGRAMMING
148 Cotton Wood Rd (27013-8938)
PHONE..............................706 599-5383
Erika Scott, *Prin*
EMP: 5 **EST:** 2018
SALES (est): 76.27K **Privately Held**
SIC: 2395 Embroidery and art needlework

(G-3223)
TAR HEEL MATERIALS & HDLG LLC
725 Kesler Rd (27013-9459)
PHONE..............................704 659-5143
Tim Ladowski, *Prin*
EMP: 4 **EST:** 2017
SALES (est): 461.75K **Privately Held**
Web: www.tarheelmaterials.com
SIC: 2865 Cyclic crudes and intermediates

(G-3224)
VISUAL IMPACT PRFMCE SYSTEMS L
2720 Amity Hill Rd (27013-9251)
PHONE..............................704 278-3552
EMP: 5 **EST:** 2010
SALES (est): 243.34K **Privately Held**
Web:
www.visualimpactperformancesystems.com
SIC: 3714 Motor vehicle parts and accessories

Cliffside
Rutherford County

(G-3225)
CRYPTON MILLS LLC
3400 Hwy 221a (28024)
PHONE..............................828 202-5875
John G Regan, *CEO*
EMP: 21 **EST:** 2019
SALES (est): 2.73MM
SALES (corp-wide): 13.64B **Publicly Held**
Web: www.cryptonmills.com
SIC: 7389 2221 Textile and apparel services; Acetate broadwoven fabrics
PA: W. R. Berkley Corporation
     475 Steamboat Rd
     Greenwich CT 06830
     203 629-3000

Climax
Guilford County

(G-3226)
INDUSTRIAL WOOD PRODUCTS INC (PA)

▲ = Import ▼ = Export
◆ = Import/Export

9205 Hwy 22 S (27233)
P.O. Box 206 (27233-0206)
PHONE..............................336 333-5959
Johnny Hall, *CEO*
Ryan Hilsinger, *
Wendy Showalter, *
▲ **EMP: 49 EST:** 1979
SQ FT: 1,000
SALES (est): 10.82MM
SALES (corp-wide): 10.82MM **Privately Held**
Web: www.industrialwood.com
SIC: 2421 Lumber: rough, sawed, or planed

(G-3227)
MECHANICAL MAINTENANCE INC
6028 Liberty Rd (27233-8009)
PHONE..............................336 676-7133
Valarie Webb, *Pr*
Robert Webb, *VP*
EMP: 13 **EST:** 2003
SQ FT: 17,000
SALES (est): 2.28MM **Privately Held**
Web:
www.mechanicalmaintenanceinc.com
SIC: 1711 7692 1799 Mechanical contractor; Welding repair; Welding on site

Clinton
Sampson County

(G-3228)
ARGOS USA LLC
Also Called: Ready Mixed Concrete
3095 Turkey Hwy (28328-0742)
PHONE..............................910 299-5046
EMP: 22
Web: www.argos-us.com
SIC: 3273 Ready-mixed concrete
HQ: Argos Usa Llc
3015 Windward Plz Ste 300
Alpharetta GA 30005
678 368-4300

(G-3229)
CCL METAL SCIENCE LLC
520 E Railroad St (28328-4304)
PHONE..............................910 299-0911
▲ **EMP:** 58 **EST:** 2014
SALES (est): 18.95MM
SALES (corp-wide): 4.84B **Privately Held**
SIC: 3354 Aluminum extruded products
PA: Ccl Industries Inc
111 Gordon Baker Rd Suite 801
Toronto ON M2H 3
416 756-8500

(G-3230)
COMMERCIAL ENTERPRISES NC INC
Also Called: International Minute Press
103 E Morisey Blvd (28328-4122)
PHONE..............................910 592-8163
Windy Schulte, *Pr*
David Schulte, *Pr*
EMP: 5 **EST:** 2005
SQ FT: 6,000
SALES (est): 203.61K **Privately Held**
Web: www.impclinton.com
SIC: 2752 Offset printing

(G-3231)
COMMERCIAL PRTG CO OF CLINTON
Also Called: Minuteman Press
103 E Morisey Blvd (28328-4122)
P.O. Box 878 (28329-0878)
PHONE..............................910 592-8163
Lynwood Daughtry, *Pr*
EMP: 8 **EST:** 1949

SQ FT: 6,000
SALES (est): 194.91K **Privately Held**
Web: www.impclinton.com
SIC: 2752 Offset printing

(G-3232)
DUBOSE STRAPPING INC (PA)
Also Called: Guardian Strapping
906 Industrial Dr (28328-8068)
P.O. Box 819 (28329-0819)
PHONE..............................910 590-1020
Charles Dubose Junior, *Pr*
Paul Ruddock, *
Charles Dubose Iii, *VP*
Larry Johansen, *
◆ **EMP:** 80 **EST:** 1990
SQ FT: 13,000
SALES (est): 53.5MM **Privately Held**
Web: www.dubosestrapping.com
SIC: 2671 3499 Paper; coated and laminated packaging; Strapping, metal

(G-3233)
F L TURLINGTON LUMBER CO INC
229 E Railroad St (28328-4134)
P.O. Box 288 (28329-0288)
PHONE..............................910 592-7197
William Turlington, *Pr*
Thomas E Turlington Junior, *VP*
Jean Turlington, *
Lyenette Willaims, *
EMP: 34 **EST:** 1918
SQ FT: 15,000
SALES (est): 2.8MM **Privately Held**
Web: www.turlingtonlbr.com
SIC: 2421 2426 Sawmills and planing mills, general; Hardwood dimension and flooring mills

(G-3234)
MARY MACKS INC
Also Called: Hawaiian Shaved Ice
214 Armory Dr (28328-9731)
P.O. Box 10 (28366-0010)
PHONE..............................770 234-6333
Gary Herring, *Managing Member*
Gary Mac Herring Junior, *Managing Member*
Carli Herring, *Sec*
▲ **EMP:** 4 **EST:** 1995
SQ FT: 3,000
SALES (est): 5.35MM **Privately Held**
Web: www.marymacks.com
SIC: 2087 Flavoring extracts and syrups, nec

(G-3235)
MILLER CTRL MFG INC CLINTON NC
1008 Southwest Blvd (28328-4624)
P.O. Box 1065 (28329-1065)
PHONE..............................910 592-5112
William L Miller Junior, *Pr*
EMP: 6 **EST:** 1986
SQ FT: 13,000
SALES (est): 1.02MM **Privately Held**
SIC: 3564 3625 3613 3822 Ventilating fans: industrial or commercial; Relays and industrial controls; Switchgear and switchboard apparatus; Environmental controls

(G-3236)
MOORE MACHINE PRODUCTS INC
919 Rowan Rd (28328-0872)
PHONE..............................910 592-2718
Terry Moore, *Pr*
EMP: 6 **EST:** 1994
SQ FT: 5,000
SALES (est): 577.66K **Privately Held**
Web: www.mooremachine.com
SIC: 3599 Machine shop, jobbing and repair

(G-3237)
PARKER BROTHERS INCORPORATED
825 Kitty Fork Rd (28329-8211)
P.O. Box 1045 (28329-1045)
PHONE..............................910 564-4132
Richard Wynn Parker, *Pr*
EMP: 8 **EST:** 1940
SALES (est): 295.75K **Privately Held**
SIC: 2542 Partitions and fixtures, except wood

(G-3238)
PARKER GAS COMPANY INC (PA)
Also Called: Rapid Exchange
1504 Sunset Ave (28328-3828)
P.O. Box 159 (28366-0159)
PHONE..............................800 354-7250
Ethel Parker, *Pr*
Daren Parker, *Treas*
David Parker, *Sec*
▲ **EMP:** 10 **EST:** 1959
SQ FT: 1,500
SALES (est): 39.76MM
SALES (corp-wide): 39.76MM **Privately Held**
Web: www.parkergas.com
SIC: 5984 5983 2911 3714 Propane gas, bottled; Fuel oil dealers; Liquefied petroleum gases, LPG; Propane conversion equipment, motor vehicle

(G-3239)
PRECISION TOOL & STAMPING INC
800 Warsaw Rd (28328-3716)
P.O. Box 615 (28329-0615)
PHONE..............................910 592-0174
Tart Lee, *Pr*
Sue Lee, *
EMP: 45 **EST:** 1980
SQ FT: 55,000
SALES (est): 8.78MM **Privately Held**
Web: www.precisiontool.com
SIC: 3469 3544 Metal stampings, nec; Special dies and tools

(G-3240)
ROBINSON & SON MACHINE INC
446 Faison Hwy (28328-3645)
PHONE..............................910 592-4779
Walter T Robinson, *Pr*
Doris Robinson, *Treas*
Patricia Hering, *Sec*
Ellen R Jones, *VP*
EMP: 9 **EST:** 1975
SQ FT: 7,200
SALES (est): 2.24MM **Privately Held**
SIC: 3599 Machine shop, jobbing and repair

(G-3241)
S & W READY MIX CON CO LLC
1395 Turkey Hwy (28328-3731)
PHONE..............................910 592-2191
Danny Bordeaux, *VP*
EMP: 16
SALES (corp-wide): 8.01MM **Privately Held**
Web: www.snwreadymix.com
SIC: 3273 Ready-mixed concrete
HQ: S & W Ready Mix Concrete Company Llc
217 Lisbon St
Clinton NC 28329
910 592-1733

(G-3242)
S & W READY MIX CON CO LLC (DH)
217 Lisbon St (28329)
P.O. Box 872 (28328)
PHONE..............................910 592-1733
Bill West, *VP*

Earl Wells, *Pr*
EMP: 16 **EST:** 1986
SQ FT: 10,000
SALES (est): 37.05MM
SALES (corp-wide): 8.01MM **Privately Held**
Web: www.snwreadymix.com
SIC: 3273 Ready-mixed concrete
HQ: Titan America Llc
5700 Lk Wright Dr Ste 300
Norfolk VA 23502
757 858-6500

(G-3243)
S KIVETT INC
711 Southwest Blvd (28328-4636)
P.O. Box 590 (28329-0590)
PHONE..............................910 592-0161
R Jerol Kivett, *Pr*
Christine Kivett, *
John Weaks, *
◆ **EMP:** 16 **EST:** 1958
SQ FT: 55,000
SALES (est): 2.73MM **Privately Held**
Web: www.kivetts.com
SIC: 1799 2531 7641 5031 Fiberglass work; Public building and related furniture; Reupholstery and furniture repair; Lumber, plywood, and millwork

(G-3244)
SAFE TIRE & AUTOS LLC
Also Called: Safe Tire & Auto Services
1308 Hobbton Hwy (28328-1958)
PHONE..............................910 590-3101
Patricia Martines, *Pr*
Sipriano Batista, *VP*
Chris Sherbert, *Executive Manager*
EMP: 6 **EST:** 2017
SALES (est): 152.55K **Privately Held**
SIC: 7534 Tire repair shop

(G-3245)
SCHINDLER ELEVATOR CORPORATION
Also Called: Schindler 9749
821 Industrial Dr (28328-9749)
PHONE..............................910 590-5590
Charles Spell, *Genl Mgr*
EMP: 12
Web: www.schindler.com
SIC: 7699 3534 Elevators: inspection, service, and repair; Automobile elevators
HQ: Schindler Elevator Corporation
20 Whippany Rd
Morristown NJ 07960
973 397-6500

(G-3246)
SMITHFIELD FOODS INC
424 E Railroad St (28328-4360)
P.O. Box 49 (28329-0049)
PHONE..............................910 299-3009
John Allis, *Brnch Mgr*
EMP: 118
Web: www.smithfieldfoods.com
SIC: 2011 2013 Meat packing plants; Sausages and other prepared meats
HQ: Smithfield Foods, Inc.
200 Commerce St
Smithfield VA 23430
757 365-3000

(G-3247)
SMITHFIELD PACKING COMPANY INC
424 E Railroad St (28328-4360)
PHONE..............................910 592-2104
EMP: 31 **EST:** 2017
SALES (est): 12.43MM **Privately Held**
Web: www.smithfieldfoods.com

SIC: 2011 Meat packing plants

(G-3248)
STEEL TECHNOLOGIES LLC
Also Called: Steel Technologies Carolinas
112 Sycamore St (28328-3948)
PHONE.................................910 592-1266
EMP: 10 EST: 1989
SQ FT: 63,000
SALES (est): 1.97MM **Privately Held**
Web: www.steeltechnologies.com
SIC: 3312 Blast furnaces and steel mills
HQ: Steel Technologies Llc
　　700 N Hrstbrne Pkwy Ste 4
　　Louisville KY 40222
　　502 245-2110

(G-3249)
TIRES INCORPORATED OF CLINTON
Also Called: Bandag
317 Southeast Blvd (28328)
PHONE.................................910 592-4741
Boyd A Mattocks, *Pr*
Trixie Mattocks, *Sec*
Boyed A Mattocks, *Pr*
EMP: 10 EST: 1978
SQ FT: 9,000
SALES (est): 1.93MM **Privately Held**
Web: www.tireincofclinton.com
SIC: 7534 5531 Tire recapping; Automotive
　　tires

(G-3250)
TONYS CABINETS
Also Called: Tony's Custom Cabinets
671 Cartertown Rd (28328-7439)
PHONE.................................910 592-2028
Tony Rackley, *Owner*
EMP: 6 EST: 1984
SALES (est): 166.76K **Privately Held**
SIC: 2434 Wood kitchen cabinets

(G-3251)
TRI-W FARMS INC
4671 Faison Hwy (28328-6141)
PHONE.................................910 533-3596
Wayne Wilson, *Pr*
Anthony G Wilson, *VP*
Daniel A Wilson, *Cnslt*
EMP: 6 EST: 1952
SALES (est): 215.48K **Privately Held**
SIC: 3523 Planting, haying, harvesting, and
　　processing machinery

(G-3252)
UFP SITE BUILT LLC
Also Called: Ufp Mid-Atlantic
254 Superior Dr (28328-1828)
PHONE.................................910 590-3220
Patrick Benton, *VP*
EMP: 16
SALES (corp-wide): 6.65B **Publicly Held**
Web: www.ufpsitebuilt.com
SIC: 5211 2426 Lumber products; Blanks,
　　wood: bowling pins, handles, etc.
HQ: Ufp Site Built, Llc
　　2801 E Beltline Ave Ne
　　Grand Rapids MI 49525
　　616 634-6161

(G-3253)
WILLIAMSON GREENHOUSES INC
Also Called: BJ Williamson
1469 Beulah Rd (28328-9773)
PHONE.................................910 592-7072
Burl Williamson, *CEO*
Trip Williamson, *Genl Mgr*
▲ EMP: 6 EST: 2003
SALES (est): 1.13MM **Privately Held**
Web: www.williamsongreenhouses.com

SIC: 3448 Greenhouses, prefabricated metal

(G-3254)
WOOD N THINGS
139 Buckhorn Creek Ln (28328-7451)
PHONE.................................910 990-4448
EMP: 5 EST: 2013
SALES (est): 69.27K **Privately Held**
SIC: 2511 Wood household furniture

Clyde
Haywood County

(G-3255)
AISTHESIS PRODUCTS INC
70 Brigadoon Dr (28721-8751)
PHONE.................................828 627-6555
Finch Dudley, *CEO*
Heidi Haehlen, *Sec*
EMP: 5 EST: 2015
SALES (est): 615.57K **Privately Held**
Web: www.aisthesis-products.com
SIC: 3821 Laboratory measuring apparatus

(G-3256)
CHEROKEE PUBLICATIONS INC
186 Bobcat Trl (28721-9443)
PHONE.................................828 627-2424
Travis Crisp, *Owner*
EMP: 4 EST: 2010
SALES (est): 249.44K **Privately Held**
SIC: 2741 Miscellaneous publishing

(G-3257)
CUSTOM CNC LLC
6989 Carolina Blvd (28721-7085)
P.O. Box 622 (28716-0622)
PHONE.................................828 734-8293
EMP: 4 EST: 2012
SALES (est): 1.08MM **Privately Held**
Web: www.customcnc622.com
SIC: 3499 Machine bases, metal

(G-3258)
DAYDREAM EDUCATION LLC
21 Listening Cv (28721-6471)
P.O. Box 639 (28715-0639)
PHONE.................................800 591-6150
▲ EMP: 4 EST: 2007
SALES (est): 233.3K **Privately Held**
Web: www.daydreameducation.com
SIC: 3999 Education aids, devices and
　　supplies

(G-3259)
E Z STOP NUMBER TWO
8721 Carolina Blvd (28721-8025)
PHONE.................................828 627-9081
David Pace, *Owner*
EMP: 5 EST: 1994
SALES (est): 176.27K **Privately Held**
SIC: 5541 2411 Gasoline Stations with
　　convenience stores; Poles, posts, and
　　pilings: untreated wood

(G-3260)
MUSICLAND EXPRESS
500 Jones Cove Rd (28721-6400)
PHONE.................................828 627-9431
Robert Dany, *Pr*
EMP: 6 EST: 2005
SQ FT: 7,200
SALES (est): 106.01K **Privately Held**
SIC: 2741 Miscellaneous publishing

Coats
Harnett County

(G-3261)
ECONOMY CLRS LILLINGTON LLC
235 Skeet Range Rd (27521-9506)
PHONE.................................910 893-3927
EMP: 8 EST: 2021
SALES (est): 114.43K **Privately Held**
SIC: 2842 Drycleaning preparations

(G-3262)
GRAY FLEX SYSTEMS INC (PA)
232 N Ida St (27521-8626)
P.O. Box 1326 (27521-1326)
PHONE.................................910 897-3539
William R Gray, *Pr*
Carrie Gray, *
EMP: 81 EST: 1997
SQ FT: 195,000
SALES (est): 7.26MM **Privately Held**
Web: www.grayflex.com
SIC: 3444 Ducts, sheet metal

(G-3263)
JMK TOOL & DIE INC
3482 Nc 27 E (27521-8509)
P.O. Box 828 (27521-0828)
PHONE.................................910 897-6373
Jeffrey Kulijof, *Pr*
EMP: 5 EST: 1996
SQ FT: 4,000
SALES (est): 909.77K **Privately Held**
Web: www.jmktoolanddie.com
SIC: 3544 Special dies and tools

(G-3264)
LIGHTS-LIGHTS LLC
1206 Bill Avery Rd (27521-9209)
P.O. Box 547 (27521-0547)
PHONE.................................919 798-2317
EMP: 4 EST: 2018
SALES (est): 890.86K **Privately Held**
SIC: 3993 Signs and advertising specialties

(G-3265)
**SNAP RITE MANUFACTURING INC
(PA)**
232 N Ida St (27521-8626)
P.O. Box 577 (27521-0577)
PHONE.................................910 897-4080
William R Gray, *Prin*
EMP: 20 EST: 1998
SQ FT: 155,000
SALES (est): 4.91MM
SALES (corp-wide): 4.91MM **Privately
Held**
Web: www.snaprite.com
SIC: 3433 3585 Heating equipment, except
　　electric; Air conditioning equipment,
　　complete

Cofield
Hertford County

(G-3266)
GILLAM & MASON INC
1835 Nc 45 Highway N (27922)
P.O. Box 387 (27942-0387)
PHONE.................................252 356-2874
Wiley B Gillam Iii, *Pr*
Carolyn Gillam, *Sec*
Wiley B Gillam Iv, *VP*
EMP: 7 EST: 1971
SQ FT: 9,350
SALES (est): 960.96K **Privately Held**
Web: www.gillammason.com

SIC: 5999 1623 2875 1731 Farm machinery,
　　nec; Water and sewer line construction;
　　Fertilizers, mixing only; General electrical
　　contractor

(G-3267)
HYDRAULIC HOSE DEPOT INC
1520c River Rd (27922-9502)
PHONE.................................252 356-1862
Edmund M Waters, *Pr*
Merrill Waters, *Sec*
EMP: 5 EST: 2002
SQ FT: 5,400
SALES (est): 1.04MM **Privately Held**
SIC: 3492 Hose and tube fittings and
　　assemblies, hydraulic/pneumatic

(G-3268)
NUCOR CORPORATION
Nucor Plate Mill
1505 River Rd (27922-9502)
P.O. Box 279 (27986-0279)
PHONE.................................252 356-3700
Giffin Daughtridge, *Brnch Mgr*
EMP: 102
SALES (corp-wide): 30.73B **Publicly Held**
Web: www.nucor.com
SIC: 3325 3312 Steel foundries, nec; Blast
　　furnaces and steel mills
PA: Nucor Corporation
　　1915 Rexford Rd
　　Charlotte NC 28211
　　704 366-7000

(G-3269)
PERDUE FARMS INC
Also Called: Perdue Agribusiness
242 Perdue Rd (27922-9505)
PHONE.................................252 358-8245
Bill Mizelle, *Mgr*
EMP: 504
SALES (corp-wide): 1.24B **Privately Held**
Web: www.perdue.com
SIC: 2015 Poultry slaughtering and
　　processing
PA: Perdue Farms Incorporated
　　31149 Old Ocean City Rd
　　Salisbury MD 21804
　　800 473-7383

(G-3270)
**STRUCTRAL CATINGS HERTFORD
LLC**
930 River Rd (27922-9577)
PHONE.................................919 553-3034
Edwin Hales, *Managing Member*
Tamara Bryan, *CFO*
EMP: 15 EST: 2012
SALES (est): 1.86MM **Privately Held**
Web: www.structuralcoatingshertford.net
SIC: 3479 Coating of metals and formed
　　products

Colerain
Bertie County

(G-3271)
PDF AND ASSOCIATES
116 Luther Brown Rd (27924-9418)
PHONE.................................252 332-7749
Patricia Ferguson, *Pr*
Steven Ferguson, *Prin*
EMP: 5 EST: 2001
SQ FT: 12,000
SALES (est): 115.72K **Privately Held**
SIC: 8299 5651 2741 Public speaking school
　　; Family clothing stores; Miscellaneous
　　publishing

▲ = Import ▼ = Export
◆ = Import/Export

(G-3272)
ROSS PHELPS LOGGING CO INC
1548 Wakelon Rd (27924-8987)
PHONE...............................252 356-2560
Ross Phelps, *Pr*
Sandra Phelps, *Treas*
Vonda Hardin, *VP*
Marcie Todd, *Sec*
EMP: 10 **EST:** 1988
SALES (est): 104.2K **Privately Held**
SIC: 2411 2426 2421 Logging camps and
contractors; Hardwood dimension and
flooring mills; Sawmills and planing mills,
general

Colfax
Guilford County

(G-3273)
BALTEK INC (DH)
5240 National Center Dr (27235-9719)
P.O. Box 16148 (27261-6148)
PHONE...............................336 398-1900
Roman Thomassin, *CEO*
Georg Reif, *
◆ **EMP:** 174 **EST:** 1927
SQ FT: 85,000
SALES (est): 4.29MM **Privately Held**
Web: www.3acomposites.com
SIC: 2436 Softwood veneer and plywood
HQ: 3a Composites Usa Inc.
3480 Taylorsville Hwy
Statesville NC 28625
704 872-8974

(G-3274)
BURCHETTE SIGN COMPANY INC
Also Called: A & B Signs
8705 Triad Dr (27235-9440)
P.O. Box 56 (27235-0056)
PHONE...............................336 996-6501
Tim Burchette, *Pr*
Wendy Burchette, *VP*
EMP: 13 **EST:** 1960
SQ FT: 2,880
SALES (est): 2.48MM **Privately Held**
Web: www.burchettesign.com
SIC: 1799 3993 Sign installation and
maintenance; Signs and advertising
specialties

(G-3275)
COLFAX TRAILER & REPAIR LLC
8426a Norcross Rd (27235-9754)
P.O. Box 448 (27235-0448)
PHONE...............................336 993-8511
EMP: 6 **EST:** 2006
SALES (est): 2.48MM **Privately Held**
Web: www.colfaxtrailer.com
SIC: 3799 7539 Trailers and trailer
equipment; Trailer repair

(G-3276)
CREATIVE METAL AND WOOD INC
8512 Blackstone Dr (27235-9774)
PHONE...............................336 475-9400
Sean Farrell, *Pr*
John S Farrell, *VP*
EMP: 4 **EST:** 1954
SALES (est): 295.39K **Privately Held**
Web: www.creativemetalwood.com
SIC: 2514 2519 Metal household furniture;
Household furniture, except wood or metal:
upholstered

(G-3277)
CROWN EQUIPMENT CORPORATION
Also Called: Crown Lift Trucks
8220 Tyner Rd (27235-9763)

PHONE...............................336 291-2500
Ron Winner, *Brnch Mgr*
EMP: 48
SALES (corp-wide): 7.12B **Privately Held**
Web: www.crown.com
SIC: 3537 5084 Lift trucks, industrial: fork,
platform, straddle, etc.; Materials handling
machinery
PA: Crown Equipment Corporation
44 S Washington St
New Bremen OH 45869
419 629-2311

(G-3278)
CSC FAMILY HOLDINGS INC
9035 Us Hwy 421 (27235)
PHONE...............................336 993-2680
Ernie Duggins, *Brnch Mgr*
EMP: 7
SALES (corp-wide): 17.66MM **Privately
Held**
SIC: 3441 3429 Fabricated structural metal;
Hardware, nec
PA: Csc Family Holdings, Inc.
101 Centreport Dr Ste 400
Greensboro NC 27409
336 275-9711

(G-3279)
ENDURA PRODUCTS LLC (DH)
8817 W Market St (27235-9419)
PHONE...............................336 668-2472
▲ **EMP:** 300 **EST:** 1954
SALES (est): 88.23MM **Publicly Held**
Web: www.enduraproducts.com
SIC: 3429 Builders' hardware
HQ: Masonite International Corporation
1242 E 5th Ave
Tampa FL 33605
813 877-2726

(G-3280)
**HORIZON FOREST PRODUCTS CO
LP**
9050 W Market St (27235-9705)
PHONE...............................336 993-9663
Jd Ziegelhoser, *Prin*
EMP: 7
SALES (corp-wide): 595.03MM **Privately
Held**
Web: www.horizonforest.com
SIC: 5031 2426 Lumber: rough, dressed,
and finished; Flooring, hardwood
HQ: Horizon Forest Products Company, L.P.
4115 Commodity Pkwy
Raleigh NC 27610

(G-3281)
ITT LLC
8511 Norcross Rd (27235-8703)
PHONE...............................336 662-0113
Al Bader, *Brnch Mgr*
EMP: 8
SALES (corp-wide): 3.63B **Publicly Held**
Web: www.itt.com
SIC: 3625 Control equipment, electric
HQ: Itt Llc
1133 Westchester Ave
White Plains NY 10604
914 641-2000

(G-3282)
LC AMERICA INC
8221 Tyner Rd (27235-9763)
PHONE...............................336 676-5129
Cristoforo Riva, *Pr*
▲ **EMP:** 13 **EST:** 2011
SALES (est): 23.86MM **Privately Held**
Web: www.lcamerica.com
SIC: 5145 2096 Snack foods; Cheese curls
and puffs

PA: Le Caselle Spa
Via Enrico Mattei 2
Pontevico BS 25026

(G-3283)
M&N CONSTRUCTION SUPPLY INC
Also Called: M & N Equipment Rental
8431 Norcross Rd (27235-9754)
PHONE...............................336 996-7740
Ghris Greiner, *Brnch Mgr*
EMP: 6
SALES (corp-wide): 1.92MM **Privately
Held**
Web: www.mnconstructionsupply.com
SIC: 7359 5082 3444 Tool rental;
Contractor's materials; Concrete forms,
sheet metal
PA: M&N Construction Supply, Inc.
323 Eastwood Rd
Wilmington NC 28403
910 791-0908

(G-3284)
NATIONAL PIPE & PLASTICS INC
9609 W Market St (27235-9615)
PHONE...............................336 996-2711
Robert Nappier, *Brnch Mgr*
EMP: 110
SALES (corp-wide): 34.95B **Privately Held**
Web: www.nationalpipe.com
SIC: 3084 Plastics pipe
HQ: National Pipe & Plastics, Inc.
1 N Page Ave
Endicott NY 13760

(G-3285)
OLDCASTLE ADAMS
3415 Sandy Ridge Rd (27235-9610)
PHONE...............................336 310-0542
EMP: 6 **EST:** 2013
SALES (est): 716.25K **Privately Held**
Web: www.adamsproducts.com
SIC: 3271 Concrete block and brick

(G-3286)
PHILLIPS CORPORATION
Also Called: Jeffreys Division
8500 Triad Dr (27235-9403)
PHONE...............................336 665-1080
Brooks Barwick, *Pr*
Larry Hubbard, *
Kim Debruhl, *
EMP: 25 **EST:** 2000
SALES (est): 9.87MM **Privately Held**
Web: www.phillipscorp.com
SIC: 5084 3999 Machine tools and
accessories; Atomizers, toiletry

(G-3287)
**PIEDMONT CHEERWINE BOTTLING
CO**
Also Called: Piedmont Cheerwine Bottling
2913 Sandy Ridge Rd (27235-9691)
PHONE...............................336 993-7733
John Tallant, *Mgr*
EMP: 83
SALES (corp-wide): 9.32MM **Privately
Held**
Web: www.cheerwine.com
SIC: 2086 Bottled and canned soft drinks
PA: Piedmont Cheerwine Bottling Co Inc
1413 Jake Alxander Blvd S
Salisbury NC
704 636-2191

(G-3288)
QUANTUM MATERIALS LLC (HQ)
5280 National Center Dr (27235-9719)
PHONE...............................336 605-9002
Robert R Benko, *Pr*
Barbara Page, *

▲ **EMP:** 26 **EST:** 1985
SQ FT: 143,000
SALES (est): 24.99MM
SALES (corp-wide): 92.7MM **Privately
Held**
Web: www.quantum5280.com
SIC: 2221 Broadwoven fabric mills,
manmade
PA: Twitchell Technical Products, Llc
4031 Ross Clark Cir
Dothan AL 36304
334 792-0002

(G-3289)
RAMCO FABRICATORS LLC
9501 W Market St (27235-9616)
PHONE...............................336 996-6073
Robert Simmons, *Managing Member*
EMP: 15 **EST:** 2021
SALES (est): 2.6MM **Privately Held**
Web: www.ramcofabricators.com
SIC: 3441 Fabricated structural metal

(G-3290)
SECOND GREEN HOLDINGS INC
9501 W Market St (27235-9616)
P.O. Box 549 (27235)
PHONE...............................336 996-6073
EMP: 18 **EST:** 1987
SALES (est): 2.41MM **Privately Held**
Web: www.ramcofabricators.com
SIC: 3443 Fabricated plate work (boiler shop)

(G-3291)
TENN-TEX PLASTICS INC
8011 National Service Rd (27235-9762)
P.O. Box 550 (27235-0550)
PHONE...............................336 931-1100
Richard Marsh, *Pr*
Robert Hightower, *
EMP: 27 **EST:** 1986
SQ FT: 40,000
SALES (est): 5.07MM **Privately Held**
Web: www.tenntex.com
SIC: 3089 Plastics hardware and building
products

(G-3292)
VISIGRAPHIX INC
8911 Cedar Spring Dr (27235-9605)
PHONE...............................336 882-1935
Tom Livengood, *Pr*
Jean S Livengood, *Sec*
EMP: 5 **EST:** 1988
SQ FT: 4,500
SALES (est): 69.56K **Privately Held**
Web: www.visigraphix.com
SIC: 2262 2759 Screen printing: manmade
fiber and silk broadwoven fabrics;
Commercial printing, nec

(G-3293)
W&W-AFCO STEEL LLC
Also Called: 079948726
9035 W Market St (27235-9620)
PHONE...............................336 993-2680
EMP: 74
SALES (corp-wide): 424.23B **Publicly
Held**
Web: www.wwafcosteel.com
SIC: 3441 Fabricated structural metal
HQ: W&W-Afco Steel Llc
1730 W Reno Ave
Oklahoma City OK 73106
405 235-3621

Columbia
Tyrrell County

(G-3294)
CAPT CHARLIES SEAFOOD INC
Also Called: Captain Charlie's Seafood
508 N Road St (27925-8949)
PHONE.............................252 796-7278
Phillip Carawan, Pr
Melony Carawan, *
EMP: 41 EST: 1998
SQ FT: 12,000
SALES (est): 1.14MM Privately Held
Web: www.captcharliesdaughter.com
SIC: 5146 2092 Seafoods; Fresh or frozen
  packaged fish

(G-3295)
CAPT NEILLS SEAFOOD INC
508 N Road St (27925-8949)
P.O. Box 164 (27925-0164)
PHONE.............................252 796-0795
Phillip R Carawan, Pr
Melony S Carawan, *
EMP: 138 EST: 1982
SALES (est): 2.73MM Privately Held
SIC: 2092 2091 Crab meat, fresh: packaged
  in nonsealed containers; Canned and cured
  fish and seafoods

(G-3296)
ROSE WELDING & CRANE SERVICE I
1060 S Gum Neck Rd (27925-9491)
PHONE.............................252 796-9171
Hank Rose, Pr
Sue Rose, VP
EMP: 5 EST: 2004
SALES (est): 3.84MM Privately Held
SIC: 5084 7692 Cranes, industrial; Welding
  repair

(G-3297)
STILETTO MANUFACTURING INC
107 S Water St (27925)
PHONE.............................252 564-4877
Jay Phillips, CEO
Margaret Phillips, VP
EMP: 8 EST: 2015
SALES (est): 238.19K Privately Held
Web: www.sailstiletto.com
SIC: 3999 Boat models, except toy

(G-3298)
TYRRELL READY MIX INC
1280 Hwy 94 North (27925)
P.O. Box 300 (27925-0300)
PHONE.............................252 796-0265
Roger Hudson, Pr
Connie Hudson, VP
EMP: 5 EST: 1977
SQ FT: 5,000
SALES (est): 164.83K Privately Held
SIC: 3273 Ready-mixed concrete

(G-3299)
VINEYARDS ON SCUPPERNONG LLC
1894 Nc Highway 94 N (27925-9611)
PHONE.............................252 796-4727
EMP: 7 EST: 2008
SALES (est): 439.58K Privately Held
Web:
www.vineyardsonthescuppernong.com
SIC: 2084 Wines

Columbus
Polk County

(G-3300)
BUFFER ZONE CERAMICS
655 John Weaver Rd (28722-9610)
PHONE.............................828 863-2000
Charlotte Morris Costa, Owner
EMP: 5 EST: 2009
SALES (est): 78.61K Privately Held
Web: www.bufferzoneceramics.com
SIC: 3269 Pottery products, nec

(G-3301)
ENERGY MANAGEMENT INSULATION
Also Called: EMI
P.O. Box 125 (28722-0125)
PHONE.............................828 894-3635
Joyce Hart, Pr
Johnathan Hart, VP
EMP: 10 EST: 1984
SQ FT: 9,000
SALES (est): 164.62K Privately Held
SIC: 2298 Insulator pads, cordage

(G-3302)
LOOKING GLASS CREAMERY LLC
115 Harmon Dairy Ln (28722-8505)
PHONE.............................828 458-0088
▲ EMP: 7 EST: 2007
SALES (est): 228.9K Privately Held
Web: www.lookingglasscreamery.com
SIC: 2022 Natural cheese

(G-3303)
METALLUS INC
205 Industrial Park Dr (28722-7740)
PHONE.............................330 471-6293
Rhonda Digue, Opers Mgr
EMP: 76
SALES (corp-wide): 1.08B Publicly Held
Web: www.metallus.com
SIC: 3312 Blast furnaces and steel mills
PA: Metallus Inc.
  1835 Dueber Ave Sw
  Canton OH 44706
  330 471-7000

(G-3304)
RONNIE GARRETT LOGGING
4625 Landrum Rd (28722-6460)
PHONE.............................828 894-8413
Ronnie M Garrett, Owner
Ronnie Garrett, Owner
EMP: 6 EST: 1970
SALES (est): 73.4K Privately Held
SIC: 2411 Logging camps and contractors

(G-3305)
WOODLANE ENVMTL TECH INC
Also Called: Condar Company
111 Kangaroo Dr (28722-6828)
P.O. Box 250 (28722-0250)
PHONE.............................828 894-8383
Michael Mccue, Pr
Timothy R Pope, VP
◆ EMP: 9 EST: 1975
SQ FT: 17,000
SALES (est): 3.95MM Privately Held
Web: www.condar.com
SIC: 3823 3429 Resistance thermometers
  and bulbs, industrial process type;
  Fireplace equipment, hardware: andirons,
  grates, screens

Concord
Cabarrus County

(G-3306)
26 INDUSTRIES INC
337 Sunnyside Dr Se (28025-3638)
P.O. Box 912 (28026-0912)
PHONE.............................704 839-3218
Ron Peterson, Owner
EMP: 4 EST: 2015
SALES (est): 735.78K Privately Held
SIC: 3999 Manufacturing industries, nec

(G-3307)
A A LOGO GEAR
310 Church St N (28025-4515)
PHONE.............................704 795-7100
Alex Mills, Prin
EMP: 6 EST: 2011
SALES (est): 185.65K Privately Held
SIC: 2759 Screen printing

(G-3308)
ABL ELECTRONICS SUPPLY INC
1032 Central Dr Nw Ste A (28027-4344)
PHONE.............................704 784-4225
Robert Diorio, Pr
Dena Diorio, Sec
EMP: 5 EST: 1975
SQ FT: 8,500
SALES (est): 3.23MM Privately Held
Web: www.ablewire-cable.com
SIC: 5063 3357 Wire and cable; Building
  wire and cable, nonferrous

(G-3309)
ALLEGION ACCESS TECH LLC
Stanley Block and Decker
1000 Stanley Dr (28027-7679)
PHONE.............................704 789-7000
Bruce Watson, Mgr
EMP: 32
Web: www.stanleyaccess.com
SIC: 3423 5072 Hand and edge tools, nec;
  Hardware
HQ: Allegion Access Technologies Llc
  65 Scott Swamp Rd
  Farmington CT 06032

(G-3310)
ALLIED/CARTER MACHINING INC
540 Lake Lynn Rd (28025-9648)
PHONE.............................704 784-1253
Jeff Carter, Pr
Teresa Carter, Sec
EMP: 5 EST: 2006
SQ FT: 2,500
SALES (est): 260.9K Privately Held
SIC: 3561 Industrial pumps and parts

(G-3311)
AMERICHEM INC
723 Commerce Dr (28025-7746)
PHONE.............................704 782-6411
James Cook, Mgr
EMP: 37
SALES (corp-wide): 188.64MM Privately
Held
Web: www.americhem.com
SIC: 2865 2851 2816 Color pigments,
  organic; Paints and allied products;
  Inorganic pigments
PA: Americhem, Inc.
  2000 Americhem Way
  Cuyahoga Falls OH 44221
  330 929-4213

(G-3312)
ARTESIAS SWETS BNGED BY DIOR
L
208 Church St Ne Ste 1 (28025-4766)
PHONE.............................704 794-3792
EMP: 4
SALES (est): 116.15K Privately Held
SIC: 2051 Bakery, for home service delivery

(G-3313)
ARTISAN LLC
8620 Westmoreland Dr Nw (28027-7963)
PHONE.............................855 582-3539
Robert Bender, CEO
EMP: 4 EST: 2021
SALES (est): 493.35K Privately Held
Web: www.venueflex.com
SIC: 2531 Stadium furniture

(G-3314)
ATLAS SIGN INDUSTRIES NC LLC
Also Called: Atlas Sign Industries
707 Commerce Dr (28025-7746)
PHONE.............................704 788-3733
Jeffery Adinolfe, Managing Member
James Adinolfe, *
Jill Adinolfe, *
EMP: 50 EST: 2005
SALES (est): 4.93MM Privately Held
Web: www.atlasbtw.com
SIC: 3993 Signs, not made in custom sign
  painting shops

(G-3315)
AXALTA COATING SYSTEMS LLC
5388 Stowe Ln (28027-6029)
PHONE.............................855 629-2582
EMP: 8
SALES (corp-wide): 5.28B Publicly Held
Web: www.axalta.com
SIC: 2851 Polyurethane coatings
HQ: Axalta Coating Systems, Llc
  50 Applied Bnk Blvd Ste 3
  Glen Mills PA 19342
  855 547-1461

(G-3316)
AXLE HOLDINGS LLC
Also Called: Rv One Superstores Charlotte
5051 Davidson Hwy (28027-8413)
PHONE.............................800 895-3276
TOLL FREE: 800
Don Strollo, Pr
▼ EMP: 42 EST: 1994
SALES (est): 2.35MM
SALES (corp-wide): 70.24MM Privately
Held
Web: rvonecharlotte.rvone.com
SIC: 5511 5012 3714 Trucks, tractors, and
  trailers: new and used; Trailers for trucks,
  new and used; Acceleration equipment,
  motor vehicle
PA: Blue Compass Rv, Llc
  301 E Las Olas Blvd Ste 7
  Fort Lauderdale FL 33301
  954 908-3645

(G-3317)
BARNHILL CONTRACTING COMPANY
Also Called: APAC
725 Derita Rd (28027-3343)
PHONE.............................704 721-7500
John Taylor, Brnch Mgr
EMP: 5
SALES (corp-wide): 490.43MM Privately
Held
Web: www.barnhillcontracting.com

▲ = Import ▼ = Export
◆ = Import/Export

SIC: 1611 2951 Highway and street paving contractor; Asphalt paving mixtures and blocks
PA: Barnhill Contracting Company Inc
800 Tiffany Blvd Ste 200
Rocky Mount NC 27804
252 823-1021

(G-3318)
BASSETT FURNITURE DIRECT INC
Also Called: Bassett Furniture Direct
7830 Lyles Ln Nw (28027-7193)
PHONE.............................704 979-5700
Carla Voss, *Mgr*
EMP: 12
SALES (corp-wide): 3.78MM **Privately Held**
Web: www.bassettfurniture.com
SIC: 2511 Wood household furniture
PA: Bassett Furniture Direct, Inc.
15305 Katy Fwy
Houston TX 77094
281 616-5409

(G-3319)
BAYATRONICS LLC
7089 Weddington Rd Nw (28027-3411)
PHONE.............................980 432-0438
Samir Patel, *Prin*
EMP: 26 **EST:** 2021
SALES (est): 1.19MM **Privately Held**
SIC: 3559 Semiconductor manufacturing machinery

(G-3320)
BEVERAGE INNOVATION CORP
1858 Kannapolis Pkwy (28027-8550)
PHONE.............................425 222-4900
Stephanie Meier, *Prin*
EMP: 10
SALES (corp-wide): 1.45MM **Privately Held**
SIC: 2082 Beer (alcoholic beverage)
PA: Beverage Innovation Corp.
30520 Se 84th St
Preston WA 98050
425 222-4900

(G-3321)
BLANKET AERO LLC
9300 Aviation Blvd Nw Ste A (28027-7232)
PHONE.............................704 591-2878
Donald Noarman, *Pr*
Donald Noarman, *Pr*
Tamara Noarman, *VP*
EMP: 5 **EST:** 2014
SALES (est): 1.91MM **Privately Held**
SIC: 3728 Aircraft assemblies, subassemblies, and parts, nec

(G-3322)
BLYTHE CONSTRUCTION INC
Also Called: Blythe Construction
7450 Poplar Tent Rd (28027-7591)
PHONE.............................704 788-9733
Allen Hendricks, *VP*
EMP: 6
SALES (corp-wide): 21.74MM **Privately Held**
Web: www.blytheconstruction.com
SIC: 2951 Asphalt paving mixtures and blocks
HQ: Blythe Construction, Inc.
2911 N Graham St
Charlotte NC 28206
704 375-8474

(G-3323)
BONITZ INC
4539 Enterprise Dr Nw (28027-6437)
PHONE.............................803 799-0181

EMP: 79
SALES (corp-wide): 425MM **Privately Held**
Web: www.bonitz.com
SIC: 3448 Panels for prefabricated metal buildings
PA: Bonitz, Inc.
645 Rosewood Dr
Columbia SC 29201
803 799-0181

(G-3324)
BREMBO NORTH AMERICA INC
Also Called: Bremeo North America
7275 Westwinds Blvd Nw (28027-3310)
PHONE.............................704 799-0530
Jim Contje, *Mgr*
EMP: 9
SALES (corp-wide): 4.18B **Privately Held**
Web: www.brembo.com
SIC: 3714 Motor vehicle parts and accessories
HQ: Brembo North America, Inc.
47765 Halyard Dr
Plymouth MI 48170

(G-3325)
BROOME SIGN COMPANY
348 Spring St Nw (28025-4542)
PHONE.............................704 782-0422
Raymond Ned Blackwelder Junior, *Pr*
R Ned Blackwelder Junior, *Pr*
Leonard Franklin Turner Iii, *Sec*
EMP: 4 **EST:** 1927
SQ FT: 4,000
SALES (est): 244.97K **Privately Held**
Web: www.broomesignco.com
SIC: 7389 2396 Sign painting and lettering shop; Fabric printing and stamping

(G-3326)
CABARRUS BREWING COMPANY LLC
Also Called: Gibson Mill Ciderworks
329 Mcgill Ave Nw (28027-6149)
PHONE.............................704 490-4487
EMP: 21 **EST:** 2016
SQ FT: 15,000
SALES (est): 3.98MM **Privately Held**
Web: www.cabarrusbrewing.com
SIC: 2082 5813 5812 Beer (alcoholic beverage); Beer garden (drinking places); Cafe

(G-3327)
CABARRUS CONCRETE CO (PA)
2807 Armentrout Dr (28025-5866)
PHONE.............................704 788-3000
Rusty Shealy Junior, *Pr*
William W Jory, *VP*
M L Williams, *Marketing*
Joanne Johnson, *Sec*
Jane Arnold, *Treas*
EMP: 18 **EST:** 1998
SQ FT: 3,200
SALES (est): 620.81K
SALES (corp-wide): 620.81K **Privately Held**
SIC: 3273 Ready-mixed concrete

(G-3328)
CABARRUS PLASTICS INC
2845 Armentrout Dr (28025-5866)
PHONE.............................704 784-2100
Ru Hayes, *Pr*
EMP: 200 **EST:** 1988
SQ FT: 150,000
SALES (est): 7.05MM
SALES (corp-wide): 994.68MM **Publicly Held**
Web: www.cvgrp.com

SIC: 3089 3713 Injection molding of plastics; Truck bodies and parts
PA: Commercial Vehicle Group, Inc.
7800 Walton Pkwy
New Albany OH 43054
614 289-5360

(G-3329)
CAPNOSTICS LLC
9724 Colts Neck Ln (28027-2873)
PHONE.............................610 442-1363
EMP: 4 **EST:** 2017
SALES (est): 319.18K
SALES (corp-wide): 2.45MM **Publicly Held**
Web: www.pavmed.com
SIC: 2834 Pharmaceutical preparations
PA: Pavmed Inc.
360 Madison Ave Fl 25
New York NY 10117
917 813-1828

(G-3330)
CARBOTECH USA INC
4031 Dearborn Pl Nw (28027-4624)
P.O. Box 2907 (28151-2907)
PHONE.............................704 481-8500
Lawrence D Narcus, *Pr*
Deborah Narcus, *VP*
EMP: 6 **EST:** 2002
SALES (est): 478.95K **Privately Held**
Web: www.ctbrakes.com
SIC: 3714 Motor vehicle parts and accessories

(G-3331)
CARPENTER INDUSTRIES INC
Also Called: Carpenter Dnnis Rprdctns-Frd-C
21 Carpenter Ct Nw (28027-4627)
PHONE.............................704 786-8139
Daniel Carpenter, *Pr*
Sylvia Wright, *
▲ **EMP:** 100 **EST:** 1965
SALES (est): 23.34MM **Privately Held**
Web: www.dennis-carpenter.com
SIC: 5531 3714 Automotive parts; Acceleration equipment, motor vehicle

(G-3332)
CARTERS MACHINE COMPANY INC
540 Lake Lynn Rd (28025-9648)
PHONE.............................704 784-3106
Jeff W Carter, *Pr*
EMP: 5 **EST:** 1985
SQ FT: 4,200
SALES (est): 2.03MM **Privately Held**
SIC: 3599 Machine shop, jobbing and repair

(G-3333)
CASCO SIGNS INC
199 Wilshire Ave Sw (28025-5633)
PHONE.............................704 788-9055
Cheryl Crutchfield, *CEO*
Cheryl Trutthsield, *
EMP: 40 **EST:** 1998
SALES (est): 4.89MM **Privately Held**
Web: www.cascosigns.com
SIC: 3993 Signs and advertising specialties

(G-3334)
CHARLOTTE PRINTING COMPANY INC (PA)
Also Called: Evangelistic Press
3751 Dakeita Cir (28025-9262)
PHONE.............................704 888-5181
James Martin, *Pr*
Greg Thorton, *VP*
Tommie S Burris, *Sec*
EMP: 13 **EST:** 1964
SQ FT: 15,000
SALES (est): 356.85K

SALES (corp-wide): 356.85K **Privately Held**
Web: www.charlotteprinting.com
SIC: 2752 Offset printing

(G-3335)
CHEM-TEX LABORATORIES INC
180 Gee Rd (28025)
P.O. Box 5228 (28027-1503)
PHONE.............................706 602-8600
Michael Smith, *Pr*
David Bilbro, *
▲ **EMP:** 26 **EST:** 1973
SQ FT: 1,000
SALES (est): 2.23MM **Privately Held**
Web: www.chemtexlaboratories.com
SIC: 2899 5169 Chemical preparations, nec; Chemicals and allied products, nec

(G-3336)
CLIENT CARE WEB INC
Also Called: Ccw
4078 Morris Burn Dr Sw (28027-9411)
P.O. Box 503 (28075-0503)
PHONE.............................704 787-9901
William Copeland, *CEO*
EMP: 34 **EST:** 2004
SALES (est): 404.63K **Privately Held**
Web: www.clientcareweb.com
SIC: 7372 Business oriented computer software

(G-3337)
CMC INDUSTRIAL SERVICES LLC
7160 Weddington Rd Nw Ste 136 (28027-3676)
PHONE.............................980 565-5224
Mike Coleman, *Mgr*
EMP: 10 **EST:** 2020
SALES (est): 10.59MM **Privately Held**
Web: www.cmcindustrialservices.com
SIC: 2813 Dry ice, carbon dioxide (solid)

(G-3338)
COMFORT PUBLISHING SVCS LLC
Also Called: Cabarrus Business Magazine
8890 Brandon Cir (28025-8112)
P.O. Box 6265 (28027-1521)
PHONE.............................704 907-7848
EMP: 5 **EST:** 2000
SALES (est): 244.35K **Privately Held**
Web: www.comfortpublishing.com
SIC: 5192 2731 Magazines; Book publishing

(G-3339)
COMMDOOR INC
5555 Yorke St Nw (28027-5333)
PHONE.............................800 565-1851
Larry Canipe, *Prin*
EMP: 5 **EST:** 2008
SALES (est): 109.33K **Privately Held**
Web: www.commdooraluminum.com
SIC: 3999 Manufacturing industries, nec

(G-3340)
COMMERCIAL VEHICLE GROUP INC
2845 Armentrout Dr (28025-5866)
PHONE.............................704 886-6407
EMP: 38
SALES (corp-wide): 994.68MM **Publicly Held**
Web: www.cvgrp.com
SIC: 3714 Motor vehicle parts and accessories
PA: Commercial Vehicle Group, Inc.
7800 Walton Pkwy
New Albany OH 43054
614 289-5360

(G-3341)
CONCORD CUSTOM CABINETS
4530 Cochran Farm Rd Sw (28027-9210)
PHONE..............................704 773-0081
EMP: 4 EST: 2011
SALES (est): 78.85K Privately Held
SIC: 2434 Wood kitchen cabinets

(G-3342)
CONCORD PRINTING COMPANY INC
660 Abington Dr Ne (28025-2568)
PHONE..............................704 786-3717
Ben Palmer, Pr
Pat Palmer, *
EMP: 5 EST: 1971
SALES (est): 427.69K Privately Held
Web: www.concordprint.com
SIC: 2752 2759 Offset printing; Letterpress
printing

(G-3343)
CONCORD TRADING INC
225 Wilshire Ave Sw (28025-5631)
PHONE..............................704 375-3333
Sam Kapland, Pr
Lake Elrod, CNTR*
EMP: 27 EST: 2017
SQ FT: 70,000
SALES (est): 673.2K Privately Held
SIC: 2251 2252 Panty hose; Socks

(G-3344)
CONTROLS INSTRUMENTATION INC
Also Called: CIC
272 International Dr Nw (28027-9406)
PHONE..............................704 786-1700
Joseph Krause, Pr
Bill Will, VP
EMP: 10 EST: 1985
SALES (est): 3.29MM Privately Held
Web: www.cicpro.com
SIC: 3825 Instruments to measure electricity

(G-3345)
COSATRON
640 Church St N (28025-4320)
PHONE..............................704 785-8145
Eric Bratton, Pr
Doug Crooks, Prin
Larry Green, Prin
Hugh Bradley, Prin
EMP: 6 EST: 2014
SALES (est): 956.84K Privately Held
Web: www.cosatron.com
SIC: 3564 Air cleaning systems

(G-3346)
COUGAR RUN WINERY
215 Union St S (28025-5050)
PHONE..............................704 788-2746
John Boardson, Bd of Dir
EMP: 7 EST: 2012
SALES (est): 214.88K Privately Held
Web: www.cougarrunwinery.com
SIC: 2084 Wines

(G-3347)
CPM OF NC INC
4222 Barfield St (28027-9608)
PHONE..............................704 467-5819
EMP: 4 EST: 2011
SALES (est): 307.14K Privately Held
SIC: 1389 0721 Construction, repair, and
dismantling services; Weed control
services, after planting

(G-3348)
CROWN EQUIPMENT CORPORATION
Crown Lift Trucks
8401 Westmoreland Dr Nw (28027-7596)

PHONE..............................704 721-4000
Alan Rudolph, Brnch Mgr
EMP: 54
SALES (corp-wide): 7.12B Privately Held
Web: www.crown.com
SIC: 3537 Lift trucks, industrial: fork,
platform, straddle, etc.
PA: Crown Equipment Corporation
44 S Washington St
New Bremen OH 45869
419 629-2311

(G-3349)
CROWN TOWN INDUSTRIES LLC
813 Hydrangea Cir Nw (28027-7259)
PHONE..............................704 579-0387
Kenneth Baltes, Managing Member
EMP: 5 EST: 2015
SALES (est): 143.47K Privately Held
SIC: 3999 Manufacturing industries, nec

(G-3350)
CUSTOM ELECTRIC MFG LLC
Also Called: Kanthal
180 International Dr Nw (28027-9443)
PHONE..............................248 305-7700
Bob Edwards, Pr
EMP: 20 EST: 2018
SALES (est): 5MM
SALES (corp-wide): 2.28MM Privately
Held
Web: www.custom-electric.com
SIC: 3567 Heating units and devices,
industrial: electric
HQ: Kanthal Ab
Sorkvarnsvagen 3
Hallstahammar 734 4
22021101

(G-3351)
CZECHMATE ENTERPRISES LLC
6101 Zion Church Rd (28025-7058)
PHONE..............................704 784-6547
EMP: 5 EST: 1994
SQ FT: 1,000
SALES (est): 250.16K Privately Held
Web: www.czech-mate.com
SIC: 7371 3823 Software programming
applications; Data loggers, industrial
process type

(G-3352)
DBW PRINT & PROMO
6012 Bayfield Pkwy (28027-7597)
PHONE..............................704 906-8551
Dianne Walker, Prin
EMP: 4 EST: 2013
SALES (est): 169.91K Privately Held
SIC: 2752 Commercial printing, lithographic

(G-3353)
DEB MANUFACTURING INC
4040 Dearborn Pl Nw (28027-4624)
PHONE..............................704 703-6618
Daniel Miller, Pr
Hollis Mueller, Treas
EMP: 8 EST: 1989
SALES (est): 1.83MM Privately Held
Web: www.debmfg.com
SIC: 3544 3728 Industrial molds; Aircraft
parts and equipment, nec

(G-3354)
DESIGNER FABRICS INC
Also Called: Minky Botique The
412 Action Dr Nw (28027-4128)
PHONE..............................704 305-4144
Denise Cline, Pr
EMP: 6 EST: 2012
SALES (est): 240.08K Privately Held
Web: www.modern-fabrics.com

SIC: 5949 5023 5719 2211 Fabric stores
piece goods; Blankets; Bedding (sheets,
blankets, spreads, and pillows); Blankets
and blanketings, cotton

(G-3355)
DMC LLC (PA)
1319 Lily Green Ct Nw (28027-2304)
PHONE..............................980 352-9806
Airelle Mcneal, CEO
EMP: 50 EST: 2019
SALES (est): 1.8MM
SALES (corp-wide): 1.8MM Privately Held
SIC: 8742 Marketing consulting
services; Scrubbers for CATV systems;
Cable television installation

(G-3356)
DNP IMAGINGCOMM AMERICA CORP (DH)
Also Called: Dnp Photo Imaging
4524 Enterprise Dr Nw (28027-6437)
PHONE..............................704 784-8100
Katsyuki Oshima, CEO
Kojie Kuzusako, *
Yamashita Shinichi, *
▲ EMP: 355 EST: 1994
SQ FT: 270,000
SALES (est): 143.7MM Privately Held
Web: www.dnpphoto.com
SIC: 3955 Ribbons, inked: typewriter, adding
machine, register, etc.
HQ: Dnp Corporation Usa
780 3rd Ave Ste 1000
New York NY 10017

(G-3357)
DOUBLE O PLASTICS INC
981 Biscayne Dr (28027-8424)
PHONE..............................704 788-8517
EMP: 48 EST: 1990
SALES (est): 4.99MM Privately Held
Web: www.doubleoplastics.net
SIC: 3089 Injection molding of plastics

(G-3358)
EAST COAST DOOR & HARDWARE INC
464 Action Dr Nw (28027-4128)
PHONE..............................704 791-4128
Deanna Smith, Pr
EMP: 4 EST: 2016
SALES (est): 245.5K Privately Held
SIC: 2431 Doors and door parts and trim,
wood

(G-3359)
ELOMI INC
Also Called: Piedmont Machine & Mfg
22 Carpenter Ct Nw (28027-4627)
PHONE..............................904 591-0095
Neil Lansing, Pr
EMP: 20 EST: 2016
SALES (est): 4MM Privately Held
Web: www.piedmontmachine.com
SIC: 3599 Machine shop, jobbing and repair

(G-3360)
FABRICATION AUTOMATION LLC
2772 Concord Pkwy S (28027-9046)
PHONE..............................704 785-2120
Randal Stewart, Genl Mgr
EMP: 5 EST: 1997
SALES (est): 4.43MM Privately Held
Web: www.fabricationautomation.com
SIC: 3441 Fabricated structural metal

(G-3361)
FAITH PRSTHTC-RTHOTIC SVCS INC (DH)

1025 Concord Pkwy N (28026)
P.O. Box 792 (28026-0792)
PHONE..............................704 782-0908
Jim Price, Pr
Ida L Price, Treas
Steve Overcash, VP
Carol Lynn Price Rorie, Sec
EMP: 11 EST: 1960
SALES (est): 1.86MM
SALES (corp-wide): 1.12B Privately Held
Web: www.opiesoftware.com
SIC: 3842 5999 Limbs, artificial; Orthopedic
and prosthesis applications
HQ: Hanger Prosthetics & Orthotics, Inc.
10910 Domain Dr Ste 300
Austin TX 78758
512 777-3800

(G-3362)
FIBERON
411 International Dr Nw (28027-9408)
PHONE..............................704 463-2955
EMP: 6 EST: 2022
SALES (est): 598.79K Privately Held
SIC: 2491 Wood preserving

(G-3363)
FINE SHEER INDUSTRIES INC
Also Called: Highland Mills
225 Wilshire Ave Sw (28025-5631)
P.O. Box 5043 (28027-1500)
PHONE..............................704 375-3333
EMP: 257
SALES (corp-wide): 2.45MM Privately
Held
Web: www.finesheer.com
SIC: 2251 2252 Panty hose; Socks
PA: Fine Sheer Industries, Inc.
350 5th Ave Ste 4710
New York NY 10118
212 594-4224

(G-3364)
FLAWTECH INC
4486 Raceway Dr Sw (28027-8979)
PHONE..............................704 795-4401
Aaron Pherigo, CEO
George Pherigo, Ch
Jean Pherigo, Sec
John Turner, Pr
Tina Rock Offf, Mgr
EMP: 21 EST: 1982
SQ FT: 5,000
SALES (est): 3.74MM Privately Held
Web: www.flawtech.com
SIC: 3548 Welding and cutting apparatus
and accessories, nec

(G-3365)
FLOWERS BKG CO JAMESTOWN LLC
2044 Kannapolis Hwy (28027-4147)
PHONE..............................704 305-0766
Mike Waites, Mgr
EMP: 4
SALES (corp-wide): 5.1B Publicly Held
SIC: 2051 Bread, cake, and related products
HQ: Flowers Baking Co. Of Jamestown, Llc
801 W Main St
Jamestown NC 27282
336 841-8840

(G-3366)
FORTILINE LLC (DH)
Also Called: Fortiline Waterworks
7025 Northwinds Dr Nw (28027)
P.O. Box 797507 (75379)
PHONE..............................704 788-9800
Tim Tysinger, Managing Member
Mike Swedick, *
▼ EMP: 35 EST: 1988

SALES (est): 90.92MM **Privately Held**
Web: www.fortiline.com
SIC: 3317 5085 Steel pipe and tubes; Valves and fittings
HQ: Fortiline, Inc.
7025 Northwinds Dr Nw
Concord NC 28027

(G-3367)
FUNCO INC
2583 Armentrout Dr (28025-5864)
PHONE.................................704 788-3003
Lewis Reid Junior, *Pr*
EMP: 5
SALES (corp-wide): 415.35MM **Privately Held**
Web: www.campechesportswear.com
SIC: 2321 Men's and boy's furnishings
HQ: Funco, Inc.
4735 Corp Dr Nw Ste 100
Concord NC 28027
704 788-3003

(G-3368)
GENIXUS CORP
Also Called: Genixus
4715 Corporate Dr Nw Ste 100
(28027-9104)
PHONE.................................877 436-4987
EMP: 5
SALES (corp-wide): 2.66MM **Privately Held**
Web: www.genixus.com
SIC: 2834 Pharmaceutical preparations
PA: Genixus, Corp.
150 N Research Campus Dr
Kannapolis NC 28081
877 436-4987

(G-3369)
GM DEFENSE LLC
4280 Defender Way Nw (28027-9174)
PHONE.................................800 462-8782
EMP: 64
SIC: 3711 3714 Motor vehicles and car bodies; Motor vehicle parts and accessories
HQ: Gm Defense Llc
300 Rnaissance Ctr Fl 24
Detroit MI 48243
313 462-8782

(G-3370)
GREY HOUSE PUBLISHING INC
Also Called: Grey House Publishing
624 Foxwood Dr Se (28025-2768)
PHONE.................................704 784-0051
EMP: 4
SALES (corp-wide): 5.54MM **Privately Held**
SIC: 2741 Miscellaneous publishing
PA: Grey House Publishing, Inc.
4919 Route 22
Amenia NY 12501
518 789-8700

(G-3371)
HARRIS SOLAR INC
356 Belvedere Dr Nw (28027-9604)
PHONE.................................704 490-8374
Rupert E Harris Junior, *Pr*
EMP: 5 **EST:** 2009
SALES (est): 292.05K **Privately Held**
SIC: 3674 Semiconductors and related devices

(G-3372)
HATLEYS SIGNS & SERVICE INC
4495 Motorsports Dr Sw Ste 110 # 1
(28027-8916)
PHONE.................................704 723-4027
Danny Hatley, *Owner*

EMP: 5 **EST:** 2008
SALES (est): 217.28K **Privately Held**
Web: hatleysignservice.weebly.com
SIC: 3993 Signs and advertising specialties

(G-3373)
HEIQ CHEMTEX INC (HQ)
2725 Armentrout Dr (28025-5878)
P.O. Box 5228 (28027-1503)
PHONE.................................704 795-9322
EMP: 5 **EST:** 2017
SALES (est): 19.07MM
SALES (corp-wide): 62.32MM **Privately Held**
Web: www.chemtexlaboratories.com
SIC: 5169 2869 2257 Chemicals and allied products, nec; Industrial organic chemicals, nec; Weft knit fabric mills
PA: Heiq Limited
18 Pall Mall
London SW1Y
207 389-5010

(G-3374)
HYDROMER INC (PA)
4715 Corporate Dr Nw Ste 200
(28027-9104)
PHONE.................................908 526-2828
Michael E Torti, *CEO*
Manfred F Dyck, *Ch Bd*
Robert Y Lee, *VP Fin*
Martin Von Dyck, *COO*
John Konar, *QA*
◆ **EMP:** 25 **EST:** 1980
SQ FT: 35,000
SALES (est): 5.56MM
SALES (corp-wide): 5.56MM **Publicly Held**
Web: www.hydromer.com
SIC: 8731 2261 Biotechnical research, commercial; Chemical coating or treating of cotton broadwoven fabrics

(G-3375)
ICS NORTH AMERICA CORP
Also Called: Reality Check Sports
323 Corban Ave Sw Ste 504 (28025-5176)
P.O. Box 1278 (28026-1278)
PHONE.................................704 794-6620
Terry Fahmey, *Pr*
▲ **EMP:** 20 **EST:** 2003
SALES (est): 4.82MM **Privately Held**
Web: www.ramcoapparel.com
SIC: 5136 5137 2329 2326 Men's and boys' sportswear and work clothing; Sportswear, women's and children's; Men's and boys' sportswear and athletic clothing; Medical and hospital uniforms, men's

(G-3376)
IMPACT TECHNOLOGIES LLC
4171 Deerfield Dr Nw (28027-4519)
PHONE.................................704 400-5364
EMP: 8 **EST:** 2014
SALES (est): 1.13MM **Privately Held**
Web: www.impactaudioandvideo.com
SIC: 2891 Sealants

(G-3377)
INGLE PROTECTIVE SYSTEMS INC
231 Pounds Ave Sw (28025-4700)
P.O. Box 586 (28026-0586)
PHONE.................................704 788-3327
Dean Andrews, *Pr*
Mark Andrews, *VP*
Christopher Andrews, *Treas*
Gregory Andrews, *Sec*
EMP: 6 **EST:** 1997
SQ FT: 10,000
SALES (est): 701.19K **Privately Held**
Web: www.worldfibers.net

SIC: 3842 Gloves, safety

(G-3378)
INTELLIGENT TOOL CORP
1151 Biscayne Dr (28027-8403)
PHONE.................................704 799-0449
Patrick Godwin, *Pr*
EMP: 15 **EST:** 1993
SALES (est): 690.2K **Privately Held**
Web: www.intelligenttoolcorp.com
SIC: 3599 7389 Machine shop, jobbing and repair; Grinding, precision: commercial or industrial

(G-3379)
INTERNATIONAL EMBROIDERY
2890 Highway 49 N (28025-6203)
PHONE.................................704 792-0641
Lori Jones, *Owner*
EMP: 4 **EST:** 1985
SQ FT: 11,000
SALES (est): 139.11K **Privately Held**
SIC: 2395 Embroidery products, except Schiffli machine

(G-3380)
INTERSTATE ALL BATTERIES CTR
8605 Concord Mills Blvd (28027-5400)
PHONE.................................704 979-3430
Mike Rushing, *Mgr*
Mike Rushing, *Prin*
EMP: 4 **EST:** 2001
SALES (est): 485.97K **Privately Held**
Web: www.interstatebatteries.com
SIC: 5063 3613 Storage batteries, industrial; Distribution boards, electric

(G-3381)
IPS
338 Webb Rd (28025-9018)
PHONE.................................704 788-3327
Dean Andrews, *Owner*
EMP: 5 **EST:** 2017
SALES (est): 46.43K **Privately Held**
Web: www.ips.us
SIC: 2791 Typesetting

(G-3382)
IRVAN-SMITH INC
1027 Central Dr Nw (28027-4201)
PHONE.................................704 788-2554
Vic Irvan, *Pr*
Kevin Smith, *VP*
Jo Irvan, *Sec*
Tracy Smith, *Treas*
▲ **EMP:** 10 **EST:** 1982
SQ FT: 10,000
SALES (est): 889.4K **Privately Held**
Web: www.irvansmith.com
SIC: 3465 5531 Body parts, automobile: stamped metal; Automotive parts

(G-3383)
ITEK GRAPHICS LLC
7075 Aviation Blvd Nw Ste B (28027-0080)
PHONE.................................704 357-6002
Rick Mitchell, *
Julli Goodwin, *
EMP: 40 **EST:** 2009
SQ FT: 90,000
SALES (est): 193.23K
SALES (corp-wide): 879.21K **Privately Held**
Web: www.itekrocks.com
SIC: 2752 2789 Offset printing; Bookbinding and related work
PA: Salem One, Inc.
5670 Shattalon Dr
Winston Salem NC 27105
336 744-9990

(G-3384)
JASPER PENSKE ENGINES
Also Called: Power Tech Engines
4361 Motorsports Dr Sw (28027-8977)
PHONE.................................704 788-8996
EMP: 16 **EST:** 1998
SALES (est): 1.09MM **Privately Held**
Web: www.teampenske.com
SIC: 3519 3711 Engines, diesel and semi-diesel or dual-fuel; Motor vehicles and car bodies

(G-3385)
JFL ENTERPRISES INC
Also Called: Failure Free Reading
82 Spring St Sw (28025-5003)
P.O. Box 386 (28026-0386)
PHONE.................................704 786-7838
Joseph F Lockavitch, *Pr*
Angela Lockavitch, *Sec*
EMP: 6 **EST:** 1988
SQ FT: 10,000
SALES (est): 493.1K **Privately Held**
Web: www.failurefree.com
SIC: 2731 7372 8299 Books, publishing only ; Publisher's computer software; Tutoring school

(G-3386)
JOHNSON CONCRETE COMPANY
Also Called: Johnson Concrete Products
106 Old Davidson Pl Nw (28027-4312)
PHONE.................................704 786-4204
EMP: 34
SALES (corp-wide): 24.88MM **Privately Held**
Web: www.johnsonproductsusa.com
SIC: 3271 Blocks, concrete or cinder: standard
PA: Johnson Concrete Company
217 Klumac Rd
Salisbury NC 28144
704 636-5231

(G-3387)
JOIE OF SEATING INC
4537 Orphanage Rd (28027-9633)
PHONE.................................704 795-7474
Randall Lajoie, *Pr*
Lisa Lajoie, *VP*
EMP: 6 **EST:** 1998
SALES (est): 764.83K **Privately Held**
Web: www.thejoieofseating.com
SIC: 2531 5947 Seats, automobile; Gift, novelty, and souvenir shop

(G-3388)
K&H ACQUISITION COMPANY LLC
Also Called: D A Moore
36 Oak Dr Sw (28027-7107)
P.O. Box 1150 (28026-1150)
PHONE.................................704 788-1128
EMP: 9 **EST:** 1973
SQ FT: 25,000
SALES (est): 1.44MM **Privately Held**
Web: www.damoorecorp.com
SIC: 3444 Sheet metalwork

(G-3389)
KANTHAL THERMAL PROCESS INC
180 International Dr Nw Ste A
(28027-9443)
PHONE.................................704 784-3001
Mark Samir, *Pr*
Frank Figoni, *
▲ **EMP:** 42 **EST:** 1981
SALES (est): 8.68MM
SALES (corp-wide): 12.03B **Privately Held**
SIC: 3559 Semiconductor manufacturing machinery
HQ: Sandvik, Inc.

1483 Dogwood Way
Mebane NC 27302
919 563-5008

(G-3390)
KETCHIE-HOUSTON INC
Also Called: Ketchie-Houston
201 Winecoff School Rd (28027-4143)
PHONE..............................704 786-5101
Robert Ketchie, *Pr*
Edgar Ketchie, *Ch Bd*
Ann Ketchie, *Sec*
Courtney Ketchie, *VP*
Bobby Ketchie, *Prin*
▲ EMP: 20 EST: 1947
SQ FT: 25,000
SALES (est): 7.7MM **Privately Held**
Web: www.ketchiemeansquality.com
SIC: 3462 3562 3568 3429 Gears, forged
steel; Ball bearings and parts; Power
transmission equipment, nec; Hardware,
nec

(G-3391)
LEGACY VULCAN LLC
Also Called: Mideast Division
7680 Poplar Tent Rd (28027-7593)
P.O. Box 3110 (28025)
PHONE..............................704 788-7833
David Holsinger, *Mgr*
EMP: 6
Web: www.vulcanmaterials.com
SIC: 3273 1423 Ready-mixed concrete;
Crushed and broken granite
HQ: Legacy Vulcan, Llc
1200 Urban Center Dr
Birmingham AL 35242
205 298-3000

(G-3392)
LEGENDS COUNTERTOPS LLC
138 Buffalo Ave Nw Unit 3 (28025-4622)
PHONE..............................980 230-4501
Jorge Guzman, *Managing Member*
EMP: 4
SALES (est): 236.57K **Privately Held**
SIC: 2499 Kitchen, bathroom, and
household ware: wood

(G-3393)
**LINDER INDUSTRIAL MACHINERY
CO**
5733 Davidson Hwy (28027-8482)
PHONE..............................980 777-8345
EMP: 14 EST: 2004
SALES (est): 2.99MM **Privately Held**
SIC: 3531 Construction machinery

(G-3394)
LIONEL LLC (PA)
6301 Performance Dr Sw (28027)
PHONE..............................704 454-4371
Howard Hitchcock, *CEO*
◆ EMP: 100 EST: 1986
SQ FT: 50,000
SALES (est): 21.66MM
SALES (corp-wide): 21.66MM **Privately
Held**
Web: www.lionelstore.com
SIC: 3944 Trains and equipment, toy:
electric and mechanical

(G-3395)
LOADING REPUBLIC INC
Also Called: Blackwater
191 Crowell Dr Nw (28025-4883)
PHONE..............................704 561-1077
Bradley Gresham, *CEO*
Caleb Clark, *COO*
EMP: 5 EST: 2014
SALES (est): 1.53MM **Privately Held**

Web: www.loadingrepublicammo.com
SIC: 3489 Ordnance and accessories, nec

(G-3396)
LOMAR SPECIALTY ADVG INC
Also Called: Lsa
7148 Weddington Rd Nw Ste 110
(28027-3663)
PHONE..............................704 788-4380
Marlo Lee, *Pr*
Lorraine Lee, *CEO*
▲ EMP: 10 EST: 2001
SALES (est): 982.45K **Privately Held**
Web: www.lomarspecialtyad.com
SIC: 7311 2393 2399 2392 Advertising
agencies; Textile bags; Sleeping bags;
Laundry, garment and storage bags

(G-3397)
LYNN ELECTRONICS CORPORATION
5409 Shoreview Dr (28025-9417)
PHONE..............................704 369-0093
John Stuart Lynn, *Pr*
Jean Griswold, *VP*
EMP: 5 EST: 1985
SQ FT: 15,000
SALES (est): 176.08K **Privately Held**
Web: www.specialmachines.com
SIC: 3625 3577 3541 Relays and industrial
controls; Encoders, computer peripheral
equipment; Machine tools, metal cutting
type

(G-3398)
MARTIN MARIETTA MATERIALS INC
Also Called: Martin Marietta Aggregates
7219 Weddington Rd Nw (28027-3468)
PHONE..............................704 786-8415
Ronald Borum, *Mgr*
EMP: 5
Web: www.martinmarietta.com
SIC: 1422 Crushed and broken limestone
PA: Martin Marietta Materials Inc
4123 Parklake Ave
Raleigh NC 27612

(G-3399)
MATEENBAR USA INC
2011 Highway 49 S (28027-8920)
PHONE..............................704 662-2005
Nick Crofts, *CEO*
EMP: 30 EST: 2020
SALES (est): 6.02MM **Privately Held**
Web: www.mateenbar.com
SIC: 3229 Glass fiber products

(G-3400)
MAX SOLUTIONS INC (PA)
Also Called: Max Solutions USA
700 Derita Rd Bldg B (28027)
PHONE..............................215 458-7050
Marc Shore, *CEO*
Richard Olear, *CEO*
Dennis Kaltman, *Pr*
Marc Shore, *Prin*
EMP: 22 EST: 2021
SALES (est): 66.9MM
SALES (corp-wide): 66.9MM **Privately
Held**
Web: www.biggerthanpackaging.com
SIC: 2657 Folding paperboard boxes

(G-3401)
MICHAEL SIMMONS
Also Called: Fluid Sealing Supply
6012 Bayfield Pkwy Ste 302 (28027-7597)
PHONE..............................704 298-1103
Michael Simmons, *Owner*
EMP: 4 EST: 2013
SALES (est): 221.72K **Privately Held**
Web: www.fluidsealingsupply.com

SIC: 3053 Gaskets, all materials

(G-3402)
MICHIGAN PACKAGING COMPANY
Also Called: Southeastern Packg Plant 2
2215 Mulberry Rd (28025-8951)
PHONE..............................704 455-4206
Todd Ross, *Mgr*
EMP: 25
SALES (corp-wide): 5.45B **Publicly Held**
SIC: 2653 Sheets, corrugated: made from
purchased materials
HQ: Michigan Packaging Company Inc
700 Eden Rd
Mason MI 48854
517 676-8700

(G-3403)
MINKA LIGHTING INC
Also Called: Madison Ave
435 Business Blvd Nw (28025-6556)
PHONE..............................704 785-9200
Dale Smith, *Mgr*
EMP: 79
SALES (corp-wide): 29.73B **Privately Held**
Web: www.minkagroup.net
SIC: 3634 5063 Ceiling fans; Electrical
apparatus and equipment
HQ: Minka Lighting, Llc
1151 Bradford Cir
Corona CA 92882
951 735-9220

(G-3404)
**MOORES CYLINDER HEADS LLC
(PA)**
Also Called: M C H
323 Corban Ave Sw Ste 515 (28025-5176)
P.O. Box 728 (28026-0728)
PHONE..............................704 786-8412
▲ EMP: 30 EST: 1995
SQ FT: 35,000
SALES (est): 3.18MM **Privately Held**
SIC: 3714 Cylinder heads, motor vehicle

(G-3405)
MOROIL CORP
Also Called: Moroil Technologies
6867 Belt Rd (28027-2966)
P.O. Box 127 (28036-0127)
PHONE..............................704 795-9595
Ronald M Powell, *Pr*
▼ EMP: 11 EST: 1949
SQ FT: 15,000
SALES (est): 4.97MM **Privately Held**
Web: www.moroil.com
SIC: 5172 2992 Lubricating oils and greases
; Brake fluid (hydraulic): made from
purchased materials

(G-3406)
**MUGO GRAVEL & GRADING INC
(PA)**
2600 Concord Pkwy S (28027-9045)
PHONE..............................704 782-3478
Karen Moore Christy, *Pr*
EMP: 40 EST: 2004
SALES (est): 4.03MM
SALES (corp-wide): 4.03MM **Privately
Held**
Web: www.mugogravelgrading.com
SIC: 1442 1794 Construction sand and
gravel; Excavation work

(G-3407)
MULCH SOLUTIONS LLC
900 Warren Coleman Blvd (28025-5888)
P.O. Box 2933 (28079-2933)
PHONE..............................704 956-2343
Mack O'neal Partee Junior, *Pr*

EMP: 15 EST: 2017
SALES (est): 908K **Privately Held**
Web: www.mulch-solutions.com
SIC: 2499 Mulch or sawdust products, wood

(G-3408)
MUSTANG REPRODUCTIONS INC
Also Called: Daniel Carpenter Mustang
4310 Concord Pkwy S (28027-4612)
PHONE..............................704 786-0990
Daniel Carpenter, *Pr*
▲ EMP: 10 EST: 1982
SQ FT: 38,000
SALES (est): 1.87MM **Privately Held**
Web: www.dcmustang.com
SIC: 3069 Weather strip, sponge rubber

(G-3409)
MYSTIC LIFESTYLE INC
Also Called: Ibd Outdoor Rooms
184 Academy Ave Nw (28025-4829)
P.O. Box 2074 (28026-2074)
PHONE..............................704 960-4530
Sheryl Isenhour, *Pr*
▲ EMP: 6 EST: 2002
SALES (est): 1.27MM **Privately Held**
Web: www.ibdodr.com
SIC: 3271 Blocks, concrete: chimney or
fireplace

(G-3410)
**OFFICE SUP SVCS INC CHARLOTTE
(PA)**
Also Called: Office Supply Services
4490 Artdale Rd Sw (28027-0438)
PHONE..............................704 786-4677
Linda Vreugdenhill, *Pr*
Garry G Vreugdenhil, *
Linda Vreugdenhil, *
EMP: 28 EST: 1985
SQ FT: 36,000
SALES (est): 929.08K
SALES (corp-wide): 929.08K **Privately
Held**
Web: www.ossone.com
SIC: 2752 5021 5199 5943 Commercial
printing, lithographic; Office furniture, nec;
Advertising specialties; Office forms and
supplies

(G-3411)
**OILES AMERICA CORPORATION
(HQ)**
4510 Enterprise Dr Nw (28027-6437)
PHONE..............................704 784-4500
Takahiko Uchida, *Pr*
Hiroshi Suda, *Sec*
Kazuhito Sato, *Sec*
Yasushi Honda, *Sec*
▲ EMP: 16 EST: 1998
SQ FT: 40,000
SALES (est): 42.91MM **Privately Held**
Web: www.oilesglobal.com
SIC: 3568 5085 Bearings, plain; Bearings
PA: Oiles Corporation
8, Kiriharacho
Fujisawa KNG 252-0

(G-3412)
OLDCASTLE INFRASTRUCTURE INC
4905 Stough Rd Sw (28027-8969)
PHONE..............................704 788-4050
David Shacklett, *Mgr*
EMP: 31
SALES (corp-wide): 34.95B **Privately Held**
Web: www.oldcastleinfrastructure.com
SIC: 3272 Pipe, concrete or lined with
concrete
HQ: Oldcastle Infrastructure, Inc.
7000 Central Pkwy Ste 800
Atlanta GA 30328
770 270-5000

▲ = Import ▼ = Export
◆ = Import/Export

(G-3413)
ON DEMAND SCREEN PRINTING LLC
2242 Roberta Rd (28025-5035)
PHONE.............................704 661-0788
Bobby Joe Sturdivant Junior, *Owner*
EMP: 4 EST: 2016
SALES (est): 92.3K **Privately Held**
Web: www.studioprintshop.com
SIC: 2752 Commercial printing, lithographic

(G-3414)
OWENS CORNING GLASS METAL SVCS
4535 Enterprise Dr Nw (28027-6437)
PHONE.............................704 721-2000
Jeff Smith, *Prin*
▲ EMP: 70 EST: 2003
SALES (est): 24.77MM **Publicly Held**
SIC: 3296 Fiberglass insulation
HQ: Owens Corning Sales, Llc
1 Owens Corning Pkwy
Toledo OH 43659
419 248-8000

(G-3415)
PASS & SEYMOUR INC
Also Called: Pass & Seymour Legrand
4515 Enterprise Dr Nw (28027-6437)
PHONE.............................315 468-6211
Jim Todd, *Brnch Mgr*
EMP: 550
SQ FT: 331,666
Web: www.legrand.us
SIC: 3694 3643 Engine electrical equipment;
Electric switches
HQ: Pass & Seymour, Inc.
50 Boyd Ave
Syracuse NY 13209
315 468-6211

(G-3416)
PATEL DEEPAL
Also Called: Power Clean Chem
4898 Aldridge Pl Nw (28027-3434)
PHONE.............................704 634-5141
EMP: 5 EST: 2019
SALES (est): 101.56K **Privately Held**
SIC: 2842 7349 Disinfectants, household or
industrial plant; Janitorial service, contract
basis

(G-3417)
PERDUE FARMS INC
Perdue Farms
862 Harris St Nw (28025-4308)
PHONE.............................704 789-2400
Karen Ray, *Mgr*
EMP: 895
SQ FT: 126,708
SALES (corp-wide): 1.24B **Privately Held**
Web: www.perdue.com
SIC: 2015 Chicken, processed: fresh
PA: Perdue Farms Incorporated
31149 Old Ocean City Rd
Salisbury MD 21804
800 473-7383

(G-3418)
PIEDMONT WELD & PIPE INC
172 Buffalo Ave Nw (28025-4662)
P.O. Box 1314 (28026-1314)
PHONE.............................704 782-7774
James Larry Templeton, *Pr*
EMP: 4 EST: 1983
SQ FT: 2,400
SALES (est): 456.52K **Privately Held**
SIC: 1799 7692 Welding on site; Welding
repair

(G-3419)
PILGRIMS PRIDE CORPORATION
Also Called: Pilgrims Pride Chkn Oprtons Di
2925 Armentrout Dr (28025-5841)
PHONE.............................704 721-3585
Douglas Jones, *Mgr*
EMP: 21
Web: www.pilgrims.com
SIC: 2015 Chicken, slaughtered and dressed
HQ: Pilgrim's Pride Corporation
1770 Promontory Cir
Greeley CO 80634
970 506-8000

(G-3420)
POWDER COATING BY 3 S X
4317 Triple Crown Dr Sw (28027-8978)
PHONE.............................704 784-3724
Steve Burrows, *Owner*
EMP: 4 EST: 2006
SALES (est): 121.95K **Privately Held**
Web: www.3sx.com
SIC: 3479 Coating of metals and formed
products

(G-3421)
PREGEL AMERICA INC (DH)
Also Called: Pregel America
4450 Fortune Ave Nw (28027-7901)
PHONE.............................704 707-0300
Marco Casol, *Pr*
Russell Chapman, *
◆ EMP: 115 EST: 1967
SQ FT: 140,000
SALES (est): 15.22MM
SALES (corp-wide): 184.98MM **Privately
Held**
Web: www.pregelamerica.com
SIC: 2099 Gelatin dessert preparations
HQ: Pre Gel Spa
Via Xi Settembre 2001 5/A
Scandiano RE 42019

(G-3422)
PREZIOSO VENTURES LLC
Also Called: A-Line
5410 Powerhouse Ct (28027-5339)
PHONE.............................704 793-1602
Charles Prezioso, *Pr*
Kristy Prezioso, *Sec*
EMP: 5 EST: 2015
SQ FT: 12,000
SALES (est): 2.32MM **Privately Held**
SIC: 3499 3999 Machine bases, metal;
Barber and beauty shop equipment

(G-3423)
PRIME BEVERAGE GROUP LLC
215 International Dr Nw Ste B
(28027-6890)
PHONE.............................704 385-5451
EMP: 156
SALES (corp-wide): 43.93MM **Privately
Held**
Web: www.primebev.com
SIC: 2087 Beverage bases
PA: Prime Beverage Group, Llc
12800 Jamesburg Dr
Huntersville NC 28078
704 385-5450

(G-3424)
PRO CAL PROF DECALS INC (PA)
4366 Triple Crown Dr Sw (28027)
P.O. Box 3321 (29732)
PHONE.............................704 795-6090
Robert L Hogue, *Pr*
Charlotte Hogue, *VP*
EMP: 19 EST: 1981
SALES (est): 2.79MM
SALES (corp-wide): 2.79MM **Privately
Held**

Web: www.procal1.com
SIC: 2759 2752 Decals: printing, nsk;
Commercial printing, lithographic

(G-3425)
PRO-FABRICATION INC
4328 Triple Crown Dr Sw (28027-8978)
PHONE.............................704 795-7563
Steve Sousley, *Pr*
Rhonda Wellmon, *Off Mgr*
EMP: 17 EST: 1995
SQ FT: 10,000
SALES (est): 4.98MM **Privately Held**
Web: www.profabrication.com
SIC: 3714 Mufflers (exhaust), motor vehicle

(G-3426)
PURPLE STAR GRAPHICS INC
32 Union St S (28025-5010)
PHONE.............................704 723-4020
Corrella S Moran, *Admn*
EMP: 5 EST: 2016
SALES (est): 216.72K **Privately Held**
Web: www.purplestargraphics.com
SIC: 3993 Signs and advertising specialties

(G-3427)
PURSER CENTL REWINDING CO INC (PA)
865 Concord Pkwy N (28027-6039)
P.O. Box 1217 (28026-1217)
PHONE.............................704 786-3131
Nicole Purser, *Pr*
Nancy H Purser, *Sec*
EMP: 10 EST: 1948
SQ FT: 6,000
SALES (est): 2.14MM
SALES (corp-wide): 2.14MM **Privately
Held**
Web: www.pursercentral.com
SIC: 7694 5085 Electric motor repair;
Industrial supplies

(G-3428)
QUEEN CITY ENGRG & DESIGN PLLC
51 Carpenter Ct Nw Ste A (28027-4639)
PHONE.............................704 918-5851
Rex Carriker, *Managing Member*
EMP: 6 EST: 2015
SALES (est): 1.5MM **Privately Held**
Web: www.queencityeng.com
SIC: 8711 3444 Building construction
consultant; Forming machine work, sheet
metal

(G-3429)
RACE TECHNOLOGIES CONCORD NC
7275 Westwinds Blvd Nw (28027-3310)
PHONE.............................704 799-0530
EMP: 7 EST: 2018
SALES (est): 102.2K **Privately Held**
Web: www.racetechnologies.com
SIC: 3714 Motor vehicle parts and
accessories

(G-3430)
RAMCO
323 Corban Ave Sw (28025-5173)
PHONE.............................704 794-6620
EMP: 4 EST: 2013
SALES (est): 831.83K **Privately Held**
Web: wholesale.ramcolifestyles.com
SIC: 2329 Men's and boys' sportswear and
athletic clothing

(G-3431)
RELIABLE WOODWORKS INC
Also Called: Reliable Hauling and Grading

2989 Old Salisbury Concord Rd
(28025-7827)
PHONE.............................704 785-9663
Josh W Airheart, *Pr*
Tamara Airheart, *VP*
EMP: 8 EST: 1991
SQ FT: 4,000
SALES (est): 5.88MM **Privately Held**
Web: www.reliablewoodworks.com
SIC: 2499 1611 Decorative wood and
woodwork; General contractor, highway
and street construction

(G-3432)
RICHARDSON RACING PRODUCTS INC
1028 Central Dr Nw Unit C (28027-4247)
PHONE.............................704 784-2602
Steven Richardson, *Pr*
EMP: 7 EST: 1987
SALES (est): 489.22K **Privately Held**
Web: www.rrpinc.com
SIC: 3714 Motor vehicle parts and
accessories

(G-3433)
ROBERT BLAKE
Also Called: Blake Enterprises
1522 La Forest Ln (28027-7508)
PHONE.............................704 720-9341
Robert Blake, *Owner*
EMP: 5 EST: 1968
SQ FT: 7,500
SALES (est): 332.26K **Privately Held**
SIC: 3592 5013 Carburetors; Automotive
supplies and parts

(G-3434)
ROMANOS PIZZA
Also Called: Romanos Pizza Italian Rest
349 Copperfield Blvd Ne Ste A
(28025-2408)
PHONE.............................704 782-5020
Salvatore Illiano, *Mgr*
EMP: 6 EST: 2000
SALES (est): 265.08K **Privately Held**
Web:
romanospizzainc.a-zcompanies.com
SIC: 2041 Pizza dough, prepared

(G-3435)
RP MOTOR SPORTS INC
Also Called: Roush's Racing
4202 Roush Pl Nw (28027-7112)
PHONE.............................704 720-4200
FAX: 704 720-4105
EMP: 32
SQ FT: 15,000
SALES (est): 1.87MM **Privately Held**
SIC: 7948 3714 3711 Auto race track
operation; Motor vehicle parts and
accessories; Motor vehicles and car bodies

(G-3436)
RQ INDUSTRIES INC
19 Franklin Ave Nw (28025-4703)
PHONE.............................704 701-1071
Robert Nixon, *Owner*
EMP: 5 EST: 2016
SALES (est): 121.5K **Privately Held**
SIC: 3999 Manufacturing industries, nec

(G-3437)
S & D COFFEE INC (HQ)
Also Called: S & D Coffee and Tea
300 Concord Pkwy S (28027)
P.O. Box 1628 (28026)
PHONE.............................704 782-3121
Scott T Ford, *CEO*
Christopher Pledger, *
William A Ford, *

Robert P Mckinney, *CLO*
Blake Schuhmacher, *CAO**
◆ **EMP:** 650 **EST:** 1927
SALES (est): 409.57MM **Publicly Held**
Web: www.westrockcoffee.com
SIC: 2095 5149 2086 Coffee roasting
(except by wholesale grocers); Coffee,
green or roasted; Tea, iced: packaged in
cans, bottles, etc.
PA: Westrock Coffee Company
4009 N Rdney Prham Rd # 4
Little Rock AR 72212

(G-3438)
SAFEWAZE LLC
225 Wilshire Ave Sw (28025-5631)
PHONE.............................704 262-7893
Brian Colton, *CEO*
▲ **EMP:** 100 **EST:** 2016
SALES (est): 10.7MM **Privately Held**
Web: www.safewaze.com
SIC: 3842 Personal safety equipment

(G-3439)
SES INTEGRATION
7575 Westwinds Blvd Nw Ste B
(28027-3328)
EMP: 5 **EST:** 2018
SALES (est): 877.92K **Privately Held**
Web: www.sesintegration.com
SIC: 3651 Household audio and video
equipment

(G-3440)
SIRIUS ENERGIES CORPORATION
(PA)
545 Hamberton Ct Nw (28027-6513)
PHONE.............................704 425-6272
Brooks Agnew, *Pr*
Robin H Lamb, *Sec*
▼ **EMP:** 5 **EST:** 2007
SALES (est): 327.92K **Privately Held**
SIC: 3621 Commutators, electric motor

(G-3441)
SNYDER PACKAGING INC
Also Called: Snyder Packaging
788 Harris St Nw (28025-4352)
PHONE.............................704 786-3111
EMP: 86 **EST:** 1925
SALES (est): 13.02MM **Privately Held**
Web: www.snyderpkg.com
SIC: 2675 2657 Paperboard die-cutting;
Folding paperboard boxes

(G-3442)
SONASPECTION INTERNATIONAL
6851 Belt Rd (28027-2966)
PHONE.............................704 262-3384
Roy Duce, *Opers Mgr*
EMP: 11 **EST:** 1997
SQ FT: 1,750
SALES (est): 4.75MM
SALES (corp-wide): 37.7MM **Privately
Held**
Web: www.sonaspection.com
SIC: 3699 Laser welding, drilling, and cutting
equipment
HQ: Sonaspection International Limited
10 Woodgate
Morecambe LANCS LA3 3
152434991

(G-3443)
SOUTHERN CONCRETE MATERIALS
2807 Armentrout Dr (28025-5866)
PHONE.............................704 641-9604
Aaron Barnes, *Prin*
EMP: 6 **EST:** 2017
SALES (est): 197.13K **Privately Held**
Web:

SIC: 3273 Ready-mixed concrete

(G-3444)
SPEED ENERGY DRINK LLC
7100 Weddington Rd Nw (28027-3412)
PHONE.............................704 949-1255
EMP: 5 **EST:** 2010
SALES (est): 483.59K **Privately Held**
Web: www.speedenergy.com
SIC: 2087 Concentrates, drink

(G-3445)
SPEED UTV LLC
Also Called: Speed Utv
7100 Weddington Rd Nw (28027-3412)
PHONE.............................704 949-1255
Robert W Gordon, *Managing Member*
EMP: 20 **EST:** 2019
SALES (est): 1.08MM **Privately Held**
Web: www.speedutv.com
SIC: 3799 5961 All terrain vehicles (ATV);
Electronic shopping

(G-3446)
STANLEY BLACK & DECKER INC
Also Called: Stanley Works The
1000 Stanley Dr (28027-7679)
PHONE.............................704 789-7000
Matt Gordon, *Brnch Mgr*
EMP: 220
SALES (corp-wide): 15.78B **Publicly Held**
Web: www.stanleyblackanddecker.com
SIC: 3699 3429 3546 3423 Security devices;
Builders' hardware; Power-driven handtools
; Hand and edge tools, nec
PA: Stanley Black & Decker, Inc.
1000 Stanley Dr
New Britain CT 06053
860 225-5111

(G-3447)
STANLEY CUSTOMER SUPPORT
DIVIS
1000 Stanley Dr (28027-7679)
PHONE.............................704 789-7000
Mike Gallagher, *Mgr*
EMP: 6 **EST:** 1996
SALES (est): 1.79MM **Privately Held**
SIC: 3546 Power-driven handtools

(G-3448)
STAR AMERICA INC (PA)
190 Cabarrus Ave W (28025-5151)
P.O. Box 1501 (28026-1501)
PHONE.............................704 788-4700
Harry D Hemphill Junior, *Pr*
Rebecca N Hemphill, ***
▲ **EMP:** 150 **EST:** 1987
SQ FT: 210,000
SALES (est): 3.13MM
SALES (corp-wide): 3.13MM **Privately
Held**
SIC: 2251 2252 Dyeing and finishing
women's full- and knee-length hosiery;
Tights, except women's

(G-3449)
STONEMASTER INC
2949 S Ridge Ave (28025-0827)
PHONE.............................704 333-0353
Zbigniew Habas, *Pr*
▼ **EMP:** 10 **EST:** 2006
SALES (est): 1.12MM **Privately Held**
Web: www.stonemasterhome.com
SIC: 1741 3281 Masonry and other
stonework; Stone, quarrying and
processing of own stone products

(G-3450)
SUNBELT ENTERPRISES INC
Also Called: Kennelpro
263 Litaker Ln (28025-8406)
PHONE.............................704 788-4749
John Franklin, *Pr*
EMP: 5 **EST:** 1998
SALES (est): 827.67K **Privately Held**
SIC: 3496 Fencing, made from purchased
wire

(G-3451)
TAMEKA BURROS
Also Called: Leanders
979 Ramsgate Dr Sw (28025-9222)
PHONE.............................330 338-8941
Tameka Burros, *Owner*
EMP: 6 **EST:** 2019
SALES (est): 15.5K **Privately Held**
SIC: 2599 Food wagons, restaurant

(G-3452)
TDC INTERNATIONAL LLC
Also Called: Technical Development
980 Derita Rd # B (28027-3680)
PHONE.............................704 875-1198
Keith Earhart, *Pr*
Kerry Earhart, *CFO*
▲ **EMP:** 7 **EST:** 1978
SALES (est): 8.85MM **Privately Held**
Web: www.technicaldevelopment.com
SIC: 3599 8711 Custom machinery;
Mechanical engineering

(G-3453)
TECHNICON INDUSTRIES INC
Also Called: Technicon Acoustics
4412 Republic Ct Nw (28027-7722)
PHONE.............................704 788-1131
Tyler Keeley, *Pr*
Joan Benner, ***
Mark Nye, ***
John Gagliardi, ***
EMP: 35 **EST:** 1980
SQ FT: 85,000
SALES (est): 11.97MM **Privately Held**
Web: www.techniconacoustics.com
SIC: 3086 Insulation or cushioning material,
foamed plastics

(G-3454)
TECHNIQUE CHASSIS LLC
4101 Roush Pl Nw (28027-8196)
PHONE.............................517 819-3579
Ronald W Johncox, *Managing Member*
EMP: 38 **EST:** 2020
SALES (est): 875.82K **Privately Held**
Web: www.techniquejobs.com
SIC: 7692 Automotive welding
PA: Technique, Inc.
1500 Technology Dr
Jackson MI 49201

(G-3455)
TEF INC
Also Called: Profection Embroidery
3650 Zion Church Rd (28025-7036)
PHONE.............................704 786-9577
Tony Freeze, *Owner*
EMP: 4 **EST:** 1995
SALES (est): 103.06K **Privately Held**
SIC: 2759 Screen printing

(G-3456)
TERRA TECH INC
965 Derita Rd (28027-3345)
P.O. Box 433 (49829-0433)
PHONE.............................906 399-0863
Gheorghe Oancea, *CEO*
Mihai Aurelian Oancea, *CFO*

EMP: 4 **EST:** 2012
SALES (est): 271.81K **Privately Held**
SIC: 1381 1623 Drilling oil and gas wells;
Water, sewer, and utility lines

(G-3457)
THERMAL CONTROL PRODUCTS
INC
6324 Performance Dr Sw (28027-3426)
PHONE.............................704 454-7605
Colleen Matte, *Pr*
Paul Matte, ***
EMP: 30 **EST:** 1996
SALES (est): 5.23MM **Privately Held**
Web: www.thermalcontrolproducts.com
SIC: 2261 Fire resistance finishing of cotton
broadwoven fabrics

(G-3458)
TICO POLISHING
2044 Wilshire Ct Sw (28025-6417)
PHONE.............................704 788-2466
Berto Barrida, *Owner*
EMP: 5 **EST:** 2005
SALES (est): 281.07K **Privately Held**
SIC: 3471 Polishing, metals or formed
products

(G-3459)
TRU-CONTOUR INC
Also Called: Tru-Contour Precast Division
165 Brumley Ave Ne (28025-3460)
PHONE.............................704 455-8700
Jim Srackangast, *Pr*
Elaine Srackangast, ***
EMP: 4 **EST:** 1982
SQ FT: 12,000
SALES (est): 492.7K **Privately Held**
Web: www.trucontourinc.com
SIC: 3087 3272 Custom compound
purchased resins; Concrete products, nec

(G-3460)
TUCKAWAY PINES INC
Also Called: Wild Brds Unlimited Concord NC
8609 Concord Mills Blvd (28027-5400)
PHONE.............................704 979-3443
Timothy Thornton, *Pr*
EMP: 5 **EST:** 2019
SALES (est): 74.35K **Privately Held**
Web: www.wbu.com
SIC: 2048 Bird food, prepared

(G-3461)
UNIQUE HOME THEATER INC
135 Scalybark Trl (28027-7550)
PHONE.............................704 787-3239
Viengkhone Saychay, *Pr*
EMP: 7 **EST:** 2019
SALES (est): 511.35K **Privately Held**
SIC: 3651 Home entertainment equipment,
electronic, nec

(G-3462)
UNITED HOUSE PUBLISHING
4671 Garrison Inn Ct Nw (28027-8063)
PHONE.............................248 605-3787
Amber Olafsson, *Prin*
EMP: 5 **EST:** 2018
SALES (est): 78.79K **Privately Held**
SIC: 2741 Miscellaneous publishing

(G-3463)
UTILITY PRECAST INC
1420 Ivey Cline Rd (28027-9529)
PHONE.............................704 721-0106
Travis Overcash, *Pr*
Isaac Harris Iii, *Pr*
William K Foster, ***
Larinda Buesch, ***

EMP: 35 EST: 1972
SQ FT: 80,000
SALES (est): 5.04MM **Privately Held**
Web: www.utilityprecastinc.com
SIC: 3272 Concrete products, precast, nec

(G-3464)
VH INDUSTRIES INC
Also Called: Safe Waze
4451 Raceway Dr Sw (28027-8979)
PHONE...............................704 743-2400
Gary Warren, *Pr*
Darrell W Hagler, *
▲ EMP: 9 EST: 1994
SQ FT: 5,000
SALES (est): 109.26K
SALES (corp-wide): 32.68B **Publicly Held**
Web: www.safewaze.com
SIC: 3199 5099 3842 Safety belts, leather;
Safety equipment and supplies; Surgical
appliances and supplies
HQ: Aearo Technologies Llc
7911 Zionsville Rd
Indianapolis IN 46268

(G-3465)
VISION MOTOR CARS INC (PA)
545 Hamberton Ct Nw (28027-6513)
PHONE...............................704 425-6271
Brooks Agnew, *CEO*
Tony Lanham, *Pr*
Robin Lamb, *Corporate Secretary*
EMP: 6 EST: 2009
SQ FT: 3,000
SALES (est): 165.51K
SALES (corp-wide): 165.51K **Privately
Held**
Web: www.visionmotorcars.com
SIC: 3711 Motor vehicles and car bodies

(G-3466)
WALLINGFORD COFFEE MILLS INC
(PA)
300 Concord Pkwy S (28027-6702)
PHONE...............................513 771-3131
Gary Weber Senior, *Pr*
▼ EMP: 80 EST: 1957
SALES (est): 2.24MM
SALES (corp-wide): 2.24MM **Privately
Held**
Web: www.westrockcoffee.com
SIC: 2095 2099 Coffee roasting (except by
wholesale grocers); Tea blending

(G-3467)
**WHATEVER YOU NEED SCREEN
PRINT**
531 Brightleaf Pl Nw (28027-4542)
PHONE...............................704 287-8603
Gary Patterson, *Owner*
EMP: 5 EST: 2003
SALES (est): 139.38K **Privately Held**
SIC: 2752 Commercial printing, lithographic

(G-3468)
WHITAKER S TIRE SERVICE INC
Also Called: Whitakers Tire & Wheel Service
530 Concord Pkwy N (28027-6739)
PHONE...............................704 786-6174
Donald Whitaker, *Pr*
EMP: 8 EST: 1965
SQ FT: 4,000
SALES (est): 954.89K **Privately Held**
Web: www.punchywhitaker.com
SIC: 5531 5014 5013 7539 Automotive tires;
Automobile tires and tubes; Wheels, motor
vehicle; Wheel alignment, automotive

(G-3469)
WORLD ELASTIC CORPORATION
(PA)
338 Webb Rd (28025-9018)
P.O. Box 463 (28026-0463)
PHONE...............................704 786-9508
Dean R Andrews, *Pr*
Chris Andrews, *VP*
Mark Andrews, *VP*
Greg Andrews, *Sec*
▲ EMP: 20 EST: 1973
SQ FT: 25,000
SALES (est): 7.08MM
SALES (corp-wide): 7.08MM **Privately
Held**
Web: www.worldfibers.net
SIC: 2281 2241 Yarn spinning mills; Yarns,
elastic: fabric covered

(G-3470)
WORLD FIBERS INC (PA)
338 Webb Rd (28025-9018)
P.O. Box 586 (28026-0586)
PHONE...............................704 786-9508
Dean R Andrews, *Prin*
▲ EMP: 5 EST: 2006
SALES (est): 947.97K **Privately Held**
Web: www.worldfibers.net
SIC: 2299 Fibers, textile: recovery from
textile mill waste and rags

(G-3471)
YEPZY INC
57 Union St S Pmb 1234 (28025-5009)
PHONE...............................855 461-2678
Christopher Dax Coan, *CEO*
EMP: 11 EST: 2021
SALES (est): 1.45MM **Privately Held**
SIC: 7372 Prepackaged software

(G-3472)
YUMMI FACTORY CORPORATION ✪
Also Called: Yummi Muffin
40 Concord Commons Pl Sw (28027-5025)
PHONE...............................980 248-1062
Eugenia Daniel, *Managing Member*
EMP: 50 EST: 2023
SALES (est): 844.38K **Privately Held**
SIC: 5461 2052 2051 Retail bakeries;
Cookies; Cakes, pies, and pastries

Connelly Springs
Burke County

(G-3473)
BAKER INTERIORS FURNITURE CO
(DH)
1 Baker Way (28612-7602)
PHONE...............................336 431-9115
Tsuan-chien Chang, *Pr*
Chen-kun Shih, *Sr VP*
Hau Ou-yang, *Sr VP*
◆ EMP: 97 EST: 1966
SALES (est): 23.93MM **Privately Held**
SIC: 2511 Wood household furniture
HQ: Samson Investment Holding Co.
2575 Penny Rd
High Point NC 27265

(G-3474)
CHAPMAN BROTHERS LOGGING
LLC
8849 Gus Peeler Rd (28612-8217)
PHONE...............................828 437-6498
Harold U Chapman, *Pt*
Garland W Chapman, *Pt*
EMP: 5 EST: 1966
SALES (est): 160.49K **Privately Held**

SIC: 2411 Logging camps and contractors

(G-3475)
CIRCA 1801
1 Jacquard Dr (28612-7851)
PHONE...............................828 397-7003
Mark Shelton, *Pr*
EMP: 6 EST: 1998
SQ FT: 167,000
SALES (est): 447.43K **Privately Held**
Web: www.valdeseweavers.com
SIC: 2211 2241 2231 Broadwoven fabric
mills, cotton; Narrow fabric mills;
Broadwoven fabric mills, wool

(G-3476)
ELK PRODUCTS INC
3266 Us Highway 70 (28612-7695)
P.O. Box 200 (28603-0208)
PHONE...............................828 397-4200
Kirk Phillips, *CEO*
▲ EMP: 26 EST: 1989
SQ FT: 56,000
SALES (est): 4.52MM **Privately Held**
Web: www.elkproducts.com
SIC: 3669 Burglar alarm apparatus, electric

(G-3477)
GRECON DIMTER INC
8658 Huffman Ave (28612-7689)
P.O. Box 3158 (28117-3158)
PHONE...............................828 397-5139
Jeff Davidson, *Pr*
Jeff Davidon, *
Skip Weber, *
Manfred Witte, *
▲ EMP: 6 EST: 1997
SALES (est): 439.89K **Privately Held**
SIC: 5084 3553 Woodworking machinery;
Woodworking machinery

(G-3478)
HIGH DEFINITION TOOL CORP
7600 Carolina Tool Dr (28612)
PHONE...............................828 397-2467
Gary Dyer, *CEO*
EMP: 46 EST: 1983
SQ FT: 21,000
SALES (est): 2.6MM **Privately Held**
Web: www.carolinatools.com
SIC: 3549 Metalworking machinery, nec

(G-3479)
JIMBUILT MACHINES INC
Also Called: Jimbuilt
2555 Israel Chapel Rd (28612-8002)
PHONE...............................828 874-3530
James A Southerland, *Pr*
Judy Southerland, *VP*
EMP: 6 EST: 1970
SQ FT: 5,500
SALES (est): 463.69K **Privately Held**
SIC: 3599 Machine shop, jobbing and repair

(G-3480)
MR BS FUN FOODS INC (PA)
2616 Israel Chapel Rd (28612-8003)
P.O. Box 218 (28690-0218)
PHONE...............................828 879-1901
Craig Pittman, *Pr*
Ann Benfield, *Sec*
EMP: 24 EST: 1933
SQ FT: 7,500
SALES (est): 2.86MM
SALES (corp-wide): 2.86MM **Privately
Held**
Web: www.mrbsfunfoods.com
SIC: 2064 2096 Candy and other
confectionery products; Popcorn, already
popped (except candy covered)

(G-3481)
PARKER INDUSTRIES INC
4867 Rhoney Rd (28612-8142)
PHONE...............................828 437-7779
Jeffrey Parker, *Pr*
EMP: 56 EST: 1959
SQ FT: 136,000
SALES (est): 17.14MM **Privately Held**
Web: www.parkerindustriesinc.com
SIC: 3469 3544 Stamping metal for the trade
; Die sets for metal stamping (presses)

(G-3482)
R EVANS HOSIERY LLC
Also Called: Evans Hosiery
8177 Grover Evans Sr Rd (28612-7798)
PHONE...............................828 397-3715
EMP: 22 EST: 1985
SQ FT: 8,000
SALES (est): 1.73MM **Privately Held**
SIC: 2252 Socks

(G-3483)
SPARTACRAFT INC
7690 Sparta Craft Dr (28612)
PHONE...............................828 397-4630
Jeff Smyre, *CFO*
Wade Moose, *
Krystal Tomlinson, *
Catherine Casali, *
▲ EMP: 45 EST: 1994
SQ FT: 80,000
SALES (est): 2.41MM **Privately Held**
Web: www.spartacraft.com
SIC: 2441 2541 2431 Nailed wood boxes
and shook; Display fixtures, wood; Millwork

(G-3484)
US OPTICS
100 Beiersdorf Dr (28612-7544)
PHONE...............................828 874-2242
EMP: 6 EST: 2019
SALES (est): 1.14MM **Privately Held**
Web: www.usoptics.com
SIC: 3827 Optical instruments and lenses

(G-3485)
W M CRAMER LUMBER CO (PA)
3486 Texs Fish Camp Rd (28612-7635)
P.O. Box 2888 (28603-2888)
PHONE...............................828 397-7481
Wendell M Cramer, *Pr*
Judith Cramer, *Stockholder**
Dave Peterson, *
Mark Vollinger, *
▲ EMP: 58 EST: 1969
SQ FT: 2,500
SALES (est): 7.45MM
SALES (corp-wide): 7.45MM **Privately
Held**
Web: www.cramerlumber.com
SIC: 5031 2426 2421 Lumber: rough,
dressed, and finished; Lumber, hardwood
dimension; Sawmills and planing mills,
general

Conover
Catawba County

(G-3486)
A OLIVER ARTHUR & SON INC
1904 Conover Blvd E (28613-9346)
P.O. Box 3075 (28603-3075)
PHONE...............................828 459-8000
Mike Oliver, *Brnch Mgr*
EMP: 10
SALES (corp-wide): 12.11MM **Privately
Held**
Web: www.aaoliver.com

GEOGRAPHIC

SIC: **5087** 2823 Upholsterers' equipment and supplies; Cellulosic manmade fibers
PA: A Oliver Arthur & Son Inc
2406 W English Rd
High Point NC
336 885-6191

(G-3487)
AB NEW BEGINNINGS INC
1211 Keisler Rd Se (28613-9336)
PHONE.............................828 465-6953
▲ **EMP:** 85
SIC: **2512** Upholstered household furniture

(G-3488)
ACACIA HOME & GARDEN INC
101 N Mclin Creek Rd (28613-8900)
P.O. Box 426 (28613-0426)
PHONE.............................828 465-1700
Alex U Te, *CEO*
Lorraine Te, *Dir*
▲ **EMP:** 10 **EST:** 1989
SQ FT: 87,000
SALES (est): 533.44K **Privately Held**
Web: www.acaciahomeandgarden.com
SIC: **5712** 2519 Outdoor and garden furniture
; Wicker and rattan furniture

(G-3489)
AMPHENOL ANTENNA SOLUTIONS INC
Also Called: Csa Wireless
1123 Industrial Dr Sw (28613-2754)
PHONE.............................828 324-6971
Jim Hartman, *Pr*
▲ **EMP:** 32 **EST:** 2002
SQ FT: 15,000
SALES (est): 2.93MM
SALES (corp-wide): 15.22B **Publicly Held**
Web: www.amphenol-antennas.com
SIC: **3663** Airborne radio communications equipment
HQ: Jaybeam Limited
Rutherford Drive
Wellingborough NORTHANTS NN8 6
193 340-8408

(G-3490)
AMPHENOL PROCOM INC
1123 Industrial Dr Sw (28613-2754)
PHONE.............................888 262-7542
Mette Brink, *Pr*
EMP: 99 **EST:** 2018
SALES (est): 4.77MM
SALES (corp-wide): 15.22B **Publicly Held**
Web: www.amphenolprocom.com
SIC: **3678** 3643 3661 Electronic connectors; Connectors and terminals for electrical devices; Fiber optics communications equipment
PA: Amphenol Corporation
358 Hall Ave
Wallingford CT 06492
203 265-8900

(G-3491)
ARMACELL LLC
1004 Keisler Rd Nw (28613)
PHONE.............................828 464-5880
David Cox, *Mgr*
EMP: 71
Web: www.armacell.com
SIC: **3086** Plastics foam products
HQ: Armacell, Llc
55 Vilcom Ctr Dr Ste 200
Chapel Hill NC 27514

(G-3492)
ASPEN CABINETRY INC
908 Industrial Dr Sw (28613-2762)
PHONE.............................828 466-0216

Chris Kunik, *Pr*
EMP: 6 **EST:** 1992
SQ FT: 3,500
SALES (est): 221.55K **Privately Held**
SIC: **2434** Wood kitchen cabinets

(G-3493)
AXJO AMERICA INC
221 S Mclin Creek Rd Ste A (28613)
PHONE.............................828 322-6046
Timothy Schultz, *Pr*
Robin Sigmon, *
▲ **EMP:** 62 **EST:** 2011
SALES (est): 12.31MM **Privately Held**
Web: www.axjo.com
SIC: **2655** 5113 Fiber spools, tubes, and cones; Fiber cans and drums
HQ: Axjo Europe Ab
Svarvargatan 6
Gislaved 332 3
371586730

(G-3494)
BLUE INC USA LLC
Also Called: Drnc
1808 Emmanuel Church Rd (28613-7328)
PHONE.............................828 346-8660
Cathy Nagel, *VP*
EMP: 45 **EST:** 2020
SALES (est): 8.91MM **Privately Held**
Web: www.blueincusa.com
SIC: **3541** Machine tools, metal cutting type

(G-3495)
BLUE RIDGE
121 Fairgrove Church Rd Se (28613-8173)
PHONE.............................828 325-4705
EMP: 9 **EST:** 2013
SALES (est): 838.52K **Privately Held**
Web: www.blueridgemolding.com
SIC: **3089** Injection molding of plastics

(G-3496)
BLUE RIDGE MOLDING LLC
Also Called: Blue Ridge Plastic Molding
121a Fairgrove Church Rd Se (28613-8173)
PHONE.............................828 485-2017
F Raymond Von Drehle Junior, *Managing Member*
Stephen P Von Drehle, *Managing Member*
EMP: 65 **EST:** 2012
SALES (est): 10.34MM
SALES (corp-wide): 467.3MM **Privately Held**
Web: www.blueridgemolding.com
SIC: **3089** Molding primary plastics
PA: Marcal Holdings Llc
1 Market St
Elmwood Park NJ 07407
201 796-4000

(G-3497)
C & S ANTENNAS INC
1123 Industrial Dr Sw (28613-2754)
PHONE.............................828 324-2454
Kirk Wentz, *Pr*
▲ **EMP:** 10 **EST:** 1985
SQ FT: 2,500
SALES (est): 1.47MM
SALES (corp-wide): 15.22B **Publicly Held**
Web: www.csantennas.com
SIC: **5731** 3669 Antennas; Emergency alarms
HQ: Amphenol Antenna Solutions, Inc.
1123 Industrial Dr Sw
Conover NC 28613

(G-3498)
CAMFIL USA INC
1008 1st St W (28613-9692)
PHONE.............................828 465-2880
EMP: 24
SALES (corp-wide): 95.11K **Privately Held**
Web: www.camfil.com
SIC: **3564** Blowers and fans
HQ: Camfil Usa, Inc.
1 N Corporate Dr
Riverdale NJ 07457
973 616-7300

(G-3499)
CAROLINA CHAIR INC
1822 Brian Dr Ne (28613-8852)
P.O. Box 11367 (28603-4867)
PHONE.............................828 459-1330
Hubert D Fry Iii, *Pr*
EMP: 14 **EST:** 2000
SQ FT: 15,000
SALES (est): 485.49K **Privately Held**
Web: www.carolinachair.com
SIC: **2512** 5712 Upholstered household furniture; Furniture stores

(G-3500)
CAROLINA GLOVE COMPANY (PA)
Also Called: Carolina Gloves & Safety Co
116 S Mclin Creek Rd (28613-9024)
P.O. Box 999 (28613-0999)
PHONE.............................828 464-1132
▲ **EMP:** 30 **EST:** 1946
SALES (est): 23.14MM
SALES (corp-wide): 23.14MM **Privately Held**
Web: www.carolinaglove.com
SIC: **2381** Gloves, work: woven or knit, made from purchased materials

(G-3501)
CARPENTER CO
2009 Keisler Dairy Rd (28613-9138)
P.O. Box 879 (28613-0879)
PHONE.............................828 464-9470
Gary Gilliam, *Mgr*
EMP: 54
SALES (corp-wide): 506.96MM **Privately Held**
Web: www.carpenter.com
SIC: **5999** 2821 Foam and foam products; Plastics materials and resins
PA: Carpenter Co.
5016 Monument Ave
Richmond VA 23230
804 359-0800

(G-3502)
CARROLL COMPANIES INC
Also Called: Carroll Leather
1226 Fedex Dr Sw (28613-7426)
PHONE.............................828 466-5489
Joe Franck, *Brnch Mgr*
EMP: 11
SQ FT: 27,621
SALES (corp-wide): 22.6MM **Privately Held**
Web: www.carrollleather.com
SIC: **5199** 3111 Leather, leather goods, and furs; Leather tanning and finishing
PA: Carroll Companies, Inc.
1640 Old 421 S
Boone NC 28607
828 264-2521

(G-3503)
CATAWBA VALLEY FABRICATION INC
1823 Brian Dr Ne (28613-8852)
P.O. Box 1257 (28610-1257)
PHONE.............................828 459-1191

William C Galliher, *Pr*
Darryl S Bost, *
Chad Stewart, *
EMP: 11 **EST:** 2003
SQ FT: 40,000
SALES (est): 1.96MM **Privately Held**
Web: www.lakemattress.biz
SIC: **3069** Foam rubber

(G-3504)
CLASSIC LEATHER INC (PA)
Also Called: St Timothy Chair Co Division
309 Simpson St Sw (28613-8208)
P.O. Box 2404 (28603-2404)
PHONE.............................828 328-2046
Thomas Shores Junior, *CEO*
Rachel Leclair, *
Guy Holbrook, *
▲ **EMP:** 400 **EST:** 1965
SQ FT: 750,000
SALES (est): 13.88MM
SALES (corp-wide): 13.88MM **Privately Held**
Web: www.centuryfurniture.com
SIC: **2512** 2521 2511 Upholstered household furniture; Wood office furniture; Wood household furniture

(G-3505)
COMMUNICATIONS & PWR INDS LLC
1700 Cable Dr Ne (28613-8991)
PHONE.............................650 846-2900
EMP: 33
Web: www.cpii.com
SIC: **3671** 3679 3699 Vacuum tubes; Microwave components; Electrical equipment and supplies, nec
HQ: Communications & Power Industries Llc
811 Hansen Way
Palo Alto CA 94304

(G-3506)
CONOVER LUMBER COMPANY INC
311 Conover Blvd E (28613-1926)
P.O. Box 484 (28613-0484)
PHONE.............................828 464-4591
O Kemit Lawing Junior, *Pr*
Tim Lawing, *VP*
Rodney Lawing, *Sec*
EMP: 18 **EST:** 1946
SQ FT: 30,000
SALES (est): 2.47MM **Privately Held**
Web: www.conoverlumber.net
SIC: **2421** 5031 Planing mills, nec; Lumber: rough, dressed, and finished

(G-3507)
CONOVER METAL PRODUCTS INC
315 S Mclin Creek Rd (28613-9026)
P.O. Box 1147 (28613-1147)
PHONE.............................828 464-9414
Victor S Scott, *Pr*
Phillip Anthony, *Ex VP*
Gary Matthews, *Treas*
B E Matthews, *Sec*
EMP: 13 **EST:** 1971
SQ FT: 41,024
SALES (est): 2.11MM **Privately Held**
Web: www.conovermetalproducts.com
SIC: **3441** Fabricated structural metal

(G-3508)
CPI SATCOM & ANTENNA TECH INC
Also Called: Etc Division
1700 Cable Dr Ne (28613-8991)
P.O. Box 850 (28658-0850)
PHONE.............................704 462-7330
Robert Featherstone, *Brnch Mgr*
EMP: 211
Web: www.cpii.com

SIC: 3444 3663 Sheet metalwork; Antennas, transmitting and communications
HQ: Cpi Satcom & Antenna Technologies Inc.
1700 Cable Dr Ne
Conover NC 28613
704 462-7330

(G-3509)
CPI SATCOM & ANTENNA TECH INC (DH)
1700 Cable Dr Ne (28613)
P.O. Box 850 (28658)
PHONE...............................704 462-7330
Christopher Marzilli, *Pr*
Mark Schalk, *
◆ **EMP: 24 EST:** 1994
SQ FT: 200,000
SALES (est): 444.87MM **Privately Held**
Web: www.cpii.com
SIC: 3663 Radio and t.v. communications equipment
HQ: Communications & Power Industries Llc
811 Hansen Way
Palo Alto CA 94304

(G-3510)
CREATIVE PROSTHETICS AND ORTHO
3305 16th Ave Se Ste 101 (28613-9213)
PHONE...............................828 994-4808
EMP: 4 EST: 2015
SALES (est): 1.3MM **Privately Held**
Web: www.creativep-o.com
SIC: 3842 Prosthetic appliances

(G-3511)
DAL LEATHER INC
2139 St Johns Church Rd Ne (28613-8975)
PHONE...............................828 302-1667
Dwight J Gryder, *Pr*
EMP: 4 EST: 2005
SALES (est): 232.58K **Privately Held**
SIC: 2512 Wood upholstered chairs and couches

(G-3512)
DALCO GF TECHNOLOGIES LLC
2050 Evergreen Dr Ne (28613-8166)
PHONE...............................828 459-2577
Joey Duncan, *CEO*
EMP: 79 EST: 2022
SALES (est): 607.91K **Privately Held**
SIC: 2297 Nonwoven fabrics

(G-3513)
DALCO GFT NONWOVENS LLC
2050 Evergreen Dr Ne (28613-8166)
P.O. Box 1479 (28613-1479)
PHONE...............................828 459-2577
Joey Duncan, *CEO*
Anita Litten, *
▲ **EMP: 79 EST:** 2003
SALES (est): 11.1MM **Privately Held**
Web: www.dalcononwovens.com
SIC: 2297 Nonwoven fabrics

(G-3514)
DEETAG USA INC (DH)
1232 Fedex Dr Sw (28613-7426)
PHONE...............................828 465-2644
Dean Gordon, *Pr*
Heather Nansy, *Sec*
▲ **EMP: 6 EST:** 2010
SQ FT: 4,000
SALES (est): 4.72MM
SALES (corp-wide): 437.91MM **Privately Held**
Web: www.deetag.com

SIC: 5084 3492 Hydraulic systems equipment and supplies; Hose and tube fittings and assemblies, hydraulic/pneumatic
HQ: Deetag Ltd
649 Third St
London ON N5V 2
519 659-4673

(G-3515)
DESIGN TOOL INC
1607 Norfolk Pl Sw (28613)
PHONE...............................828 328-6414
Victor Glenn, *CEO*
Kevin Church, *
▼ **EMP: 30 EST:** 1988
SQ FT: 16,000
SALES (est): 6.21MM **Privately Held**
Web: www.designtoolinc.com
SIC: 3549 3569 8742 3541 Screw driving machines; Robots, assembly line: industrial and commercial; Automation and robotics consultant; Screw machines, automatic

(G-3516)
DISTINCTION LEATHER COMPANY
210 Lap Rd Ne (28613-7618)
P.O. Box 397 (28613-0397)
EMP: 4 EST: 1982
SALES (est): 250.93K **Privately Held**
Web: www.fineleatherfurniture.com
SIC: 3111 Upholstery leather

(G-3517)
EDWARD HEIL SCREW PRODUCTS
1114 1st St W (28613-9620)
PHONE...............................828 345-6140
James G Heiligenthaler, *Pr*
EMP: 7 EST: 1938
SQ FT: 5,000
SALES (est): 893.39K **Privately Held**
Web: www.heilscrewproducts.com
SIC: 3451 Screw machine products

(G-3518)
ELITE COMFORT SOLUTIONS LLC
1115 Farrington St Sw Bldg 1 (28613-8251)
PHONE...............................828 328-2201
Daniel Williams, *Mgr*
EMP: 120
SALES (corp-wide): 5.15B **Publicly Held**
Web: www.elitecomfortsolutions.com
SIC: 3069 Foam rubber
HQ: Elite Comfort Solutions Llc
24 Herring Rd
Newnan GA 30265
770 502-8577

(G-3519)
ENGINEERED CONTROLS INTL LLC
911 Industrial Dr Sw (28613-2761)
PHONE...............................828 466-2153
Topper Andrade, *Mgr*
EMP: 193
SALES (corp-wide): 7.75B **Publicly Held**
Web: www.regoproducts.com
SIC: 3491 3494 3492 Regulators (steam fittings); Valves and pipe fittings, nec; Fluid power valves and hose fittings
HQ: Engineered Controls International, Llc
100 Rego Dr
Elon NC 27244

(G-3520)
EVERYTHING ATTACHMENTS
1506 Emmanuel Church Rd (28613-9017)
PHONE...............................828 464-0161
Theodore H Corriher, *Prin*
EMP: 11 EST: 2016
SALES (est): 4.05MM **Privately Held**
Web: www.everythingattachments.com

SIC: 3531 Construction machinery

(G-3521)
FIBRIX LLC (HQ)
Also Called: Cameo Fibers
1820 Evans St Ne (28613-9042)
P.O. Box 310 (28613-0310)
PHONE...............................828 459-7064
Keith White, *CEO*
Dean Cobb, *
Darren White, *
◆ **EMP: 50 EST:** 2007
SQ FT: 130,000
SALES (est): 46.63MM
SALES (corp-wide): 46.63MM **Privately Held**
Web: www.fibrix.com
SIC: 2824 Polyester fibers
PA: Polycor Holdings, Inc.
1820 Evans St Ne
Conover NC 28613
828 459-7064

(G-3522)
FORTRESS INTERNATIONAL CORP NC
Also Called: Fortress Forest International
1808 Emmanuel Church Rd (28613-7328)
PHONE...............................336 645-9365
Michael Menz, *Pr*
Matthew Carsaro, *VP*
EMP: 8 EST: 2014
SQ FT: 53,000
SALES (est): 2.33MM **Privately Held**
SIC: 3429 Furniture hardware

(G-3523)
FRAMEWRIGHT INC
1824 Brian Dr Ne (28613-8852)
P.O. Box 1390 (28613-1390)
PHONE...............................828 459-2284
Clifford Spencer, *Pr*
Stanley Lail, *VP*
George Spencer, *Treas*
EMP: 6 EST: 1976
SALES (est): 584.28K **Privately Held**
SIC: 2512 2426 Couches, sofas, and davenports: upholstered on wood frames; Hardwood dimension and flooring mills

(G-3524)
GKN SINTER METALS LLC
Also Called: GKN Sinter Metals - Conover
407 Thornburg Dr Se (28613-8845)
PHONE...............................828 464-0642
Rick Rice, *Brnch Mgr*
EMP: 142
SALES (corp-wide): 6.06B **Privately Held**
Web: www.gknpm.com
SIC: 3312 Sinter, iron
HQ: Gkn Sinter Metals, Llc
1670 Opdyke Ct
Auburn Hills MI 48326
248 883-4500

(G-3525)
HANES COMPANIES INC
Also Called: Hanes Inds A Div Hnes Cmpanies
500 N Mclin Creek Rd (28613-8856)
P.O. Box 457 (28613-0457)
PHONE...............................828 464-4673
Zach Cox, *Pr*
EMP: 312
SALES (corp-wide): 5.15B **Publicly Held**
Web: www.hanescompanies.com
SIC: 2221 Acetate broadwoven fabrics
HQ: Hanes Companies, Inc.
815 Buxton St
Winston Salem NC 27101
336 747-1600

(G-3526)
HANES COMPANIES - NJ LLC
Also Called: Hanes
500 N Mclin Creek Rd (28613)
PHONE...............................828 464-4673
Jim Curia, *Mgr*
▲ **EMP: 21 EST:** 1994
SALES (est): 1.1MM
SALES (corp-wide): 5.15B **Publicly Held**
Web: www.walmart.com
SIC: 2261 Dyeing cotton broadwoven fabrics
PA: Leggett & Platt, Incorporated
1 Leggett Rd
Carthage MO 64836
417 358-8131

(G-3527)
HAWORTH INC
Also Called: Haworth Conover Manufacturing
1610 Deborah Herman Rd Sw (28613-8218)
PHONE...............................828 328-5600
Vyanna Reddiar, *Brnch Mgr*
EMP: 40
SALES (corp-wide): 2.59B **Privately Held**
Web: www.haworth.com
SIC: 2522 2521 Office furniture, except wood; Wood office furniture
HQ: Haworth, Inc.
1 Haworth Ctr
Holland MI 49423
616 393-3000

(G-3528)
HAWORTH HEALTH ENVIRONMENTS LLC
1610 Deborah Herman Rd Sw (28613-8218)
P.O. Box 189 (28613-0189)
PHONE...............................828 328-5600
EMP: 40
SIC: 2521 Wood office chairs, benches and stools

(G-3529)
HICKORY PRINTING GROUP INC H
725 Reese Dr Sw (28613-2935)
P.O. Box 69 (28603-0069)
PHONE...............................828 465-3431
T Kol, *Prin*
EMP: 18 EST: 2011
SALES (est): 310.74K **Privately Held**
Web: www.rrd.com
SIC: 2752 Commercial printing, lithographic

(G-3530)
HICKORY PRINTING SOLUTIONS LLC
725 Reese Dr Sw (28613-2935)
PHONE...............................828 465-3431
EMP: 408 EST: 2010
SALES (est): 9.44MM
SALES (corp-wide): 15B **Privately Held**
Web: www.rrd.com
SIC: 2752 2759 2791 2789 Color lithography; Labels and seals: printing, nsk; Typesetting; Bookbinding and related work
HQ: Consolidated Graphics, Inc.
5858 Westheimer Rd # 200
Houston TX 77057

(G-3531)
HIGHLAND FOAM INC
1560 Deborah Herman Rd Sw (28613-8204)
P.O. Box 575 (28613-0575)
PHONE...............................828 327-0400
Gary L Fox, *Pr*
EMP: 8 EST: 1986
SALES (est): 1.02MM **Privately Held**
Web: www.highlandfoam.net
SIC: 3069 Foam rubber

(G-3532)
IDEAITLIA CNTMPORARY FURN CORP
1902 Emmanuel Church Rd (28613-7301)
P.O. Box 1298 (28613-1298)
PHONE...................................828 464-1000
Carlo Bargagli, *Pr*
▲ EMP: 140 EST: 2004
SQ FT: 300,000
SALES (est): 9.04MM Privately Held
Web: www.ideaitaliausa.com
SIC: 2426 5712 4226 Turnings, furniture: wood; Furniture stores; Household goods and furniture storage

(G-3533)
INNOVAKNITS LLC
350 5th Ave Se (28613-1941)
PHONE...................................828 536-9348
Jason Wilkins, *Admn*
EMP: 7 EST: 2015
SALES (est): 408.79K Privately Held
Web: www.innovaknits.com
SIC: 5949 2257 2258 2253 Knitting goods and supplies; Weft knit fabric mills; Warp and flat knit products; Cold weather knit outerwear including ski wear

(G-3534)
INTERSTATE FOAM & SUPPLY INC
306 Comfort Dr Ne (28613-9297)
P.O. Box 338 (28613-0338)
PHONE...................................828 459-9700
Mark A Webb, *Pr*
Lewis A Webb, *
▲ EMP: 215 EST: 1981
SQ FT: 240,000
SALES (est): 10.32MM Privately Held
Web: www.interstatefoamandsupply.com
SIC: 3069 Foam rubber

(G-3535)
J L FRAME SHOP INC
1310 Houston Mill Rd (28613-8503)
PHONE...................................828 256-6290
Jerry Hollar, *Pr*
Lynda Hollar, *Treas*
EMP: 5 EST: 1985
SALES (est): 328.71K Privately Held
SIC: 2426 Frames for upholstered furniture, wood

(G-3536)
LEATHERCRAFT INC
102 Section House Rd (28613)
PHONE...................................828 322-3305
Staley Keener, *CEO*
Herschel H Keener, *
John Jack Donahoe Junior, *Pr*
Kathy Stout, *
◆ EMP: 125 EST: 1967
SQ FT: 190,000
SALES (est): 2.32MM Privately Held
Web: www.leathercraft-furniture.com
SIC: 2512 2522 2521 2511 Upholstered household furniture; Office furniture, except wood; Wood office furniture; Wood household furniture

(G-3537)
LEE INDUSTRIES LLC (PA)
210 4th St Sw (28613-2628)
PHONE...................................828 464-8318
J Steve Shelor, *Prin*
Phyllis Starnes, *
J Steve Shelor, *Pr*
◆ EMP: 260 EST: 1969
SQ FT: 237,000
SALES (est): 33.33MM
SALES (corp-wide): 33.33MM Privately Held

Web: www.leeindustries.com
SIC: 2512 2599 Couches, sofas, and davenports: upholstered on wood frames; Hotel furniture

(G-3538)
LEGGETT & PLATT INCORPORATED
Also Called: L&P Dstribution Ctr Furn 8814
1401 Deborah Herman Rd Sw (28613-8247)
P.O. Box 609 (28613-0609)
PHONE...................................828 322-6855
Joe Dishman, *Brnch Mgr*
EMP: 48
SALES (corp-wide): 5.15B Publicly Held
Web: www.leggett.com
SIC: 2515 Mattresses and bedsprings
PA: Leggett & Platt, Incorporated
    1 Leggett Rd
    Carthage MO 64836
    417 358-8131

(G-3539)
MID-ATLANTIC DRAINAGE INC (PA)
105 Ge Plant Rd Sw (28613-8202)
P.O. Box 399 (28613-0399)
PHONE...................................828 324-0808
Howard Anderson, *Pr*
Laddie G Hiller, *Treas*
Ranny W Keys, *Sec*
EMP: 19 EST: 1984
SQ FT: 1,800
SALES (est): 5.06MM
SALES (corp-wide): 5.06MM Privately Held
Web: www.mid-atlanticdrainage.com
SIC: 5999 5074 3494 Plumbing and heating supplies; Plumbing and hydronic heating supplies; Plumbing and heating valves

(G-3540)
NC CUSTOM LEATHER INC
Also Called: Carolina Custom Leather
1118 1st St W (28613-9620)
P.O. Box 9 (28613-0009)
PHONE...................................828 404-2973
Todd Strud, *Pr*
EMP: 11 EST: 2008
SALES (est): 991.42K Privately Held
Web: www.ccleather.com
SIC: 2512 Upholstered household furniture

(G-3541)
NEPTUNE HLTH WLLNESS INNVTION
408 S Mclin Creek Rd (28613-9500)
PHONE...................................888 664-9166
Michael Cammarata, *Pr*
Pritpal Thind, *
EMP: 226 EST: 2020
SALES (est): 1.06MM Privately Held
SIC: 3999 2834 2077 5999
; Vitamin preparations; Marine fats, oils, and meals

(G-3542)
OYAMA CABINET INC
115 Ge Plant Rd Sw (28613-8202)
PHONE...................................828 327-2668
George C Ritchie, *Pr*
Donald R Lail, *VP*
Charlie M Ritchie, *Sec*
EMP: 7
SALES (est): 194.99K Privately Held
SIC: 2541 2431 2434 Store fixtures, wood; Millwork; Vanities, bathroom: wood

(G-3543)
PAN AMERICAN SCREW LLC (HQ)
630 Reese Dr Sw (28613-2932)
PHONE...................................828 466-0060
Phil Lail, *Pr*

◆ EMP: 69 EST: 1982
SQ FT: 40,000
SALES (est): 6.47MM
SALES (corp-wide): 424.23B Publicly Held
Web: www.panamericanscrew.com
SIC: 3452 Screws, metal
PA: Berkshire Hathaway Inc.
    3555 Farnam St Ste 1440
    Omaha NE 68131
    402 346-1400

(G-3544)
PIEDMONT TRUCK TIRES INC
1317 Emmanuel Church Rd (28613-9015)
P.O. Box 625 (28613-0625)
PHONE...................................828 202-5337
Dan Rice, *Prin*
EMP: 10
SALES (corp-wide): 636MM Privately Held
Web: www.piedmonttrucktires.com
SIC: 7534 5531 Tire retreading and repair shops; Automotive tires
HQ: Piedmont Truck Tires, Inc.
    312 S Regional Rd
    Greensboro NC 27409
    336 668-0091

(G-3545)
PLASTIC TECHNOLOGY INC
Also Called: P T I
1101 Farrington St Sw # 3 (28613-8251)
P.O. Box 819 (28603-0819)
PHONE...................................828 328-8570
EMP: 50
SALES (corp-wide): 898.03MM Privately Held
SIC: 3082 Unsupported plastics profile shapes
HQ: Plastic Technology, Inc.
    235 2nd Ave Nw
    Hickory NC 28601
    828 328-2201

(G-3546)
PLASTICS MLDING DSIGN PLUS LLC
Also Called: Conover Plastics
1803 Conover Blvd E (28613-9696)
P.O. Box 1268 (28613-1268)
PHONE...................................828 459-7853
EMP: 7 EST: 1974
SQ FT: 24,000
SALES (est): 1.63MM Privately Held
Web: www.conoverplastics.com
SIC: 3089 Injection molding of plastics

(G-3547)
POLYCOR HOLDINGS INC (PA)
1820 Evans St Ne (28613-9042)
PHONE...................................828 459-7064
Keith White, *Pr*
Darren White, *
Dean Cobb, *
▼ EMP: 52 EST: 2014
SQ FT: 130,000
SALES (est): 46.63MM
SALES (corp-wide): 46.63MM Privately Held
Web: www.fibrix.com
SIC: 2824 Polyester fibers

(G-3548)
PRECISION INDUSTRIES INC
305 N Mclin Creek Rd (28613-9093)
PHONE...................................828 465-3418
Conrad E Stewart, *Pr*
EMP: 12 EST: 1977
SQ FT: 25,000
SALES (est): 934.95K Privately Held

SIC: 3541 Screw machines, automatic

(G-3549)
PREGIS LLC
500 Thornburg Dr Se (28613-9096)
PHONE...................................828 465-9197
EMP: 22
SALES (corp-wide): 191.81K Privately Held
Web: www.pregis.com
SIC: 2891 Adhesives
HQ: Pregis Llc
    2345 Waukegan Rd Ste 120
    Bannockburn IL 60015

(G-3550)
PREMIUM CUSHION INC
1009 1st St W (28613-9692)
P.O. Box 1125 (28613-1125)
PHONE...................................828 464-4783
Ronnie Wike, *Pr*
Patty Brendle, *
EMP: 49 EST: 1999
SALES (est): 5.38MM Privately Held
SIC: 2392 Pillows, bed: made from purchased materials

(G-3551)
PREMIUM FABRICATORS LLC
419 4th St Sw (28613-2630)
P.O. Box 227 (28613-0227)
PHONE...................................828 464-3818
Ronnie A Wike, *Managing Member*
Christi Wike, *Managing Member*
EMP: 30 EST: 2011
SALES (est): 6.19MM Privately Held
SIC: 2396 Furniture trimmings, fabric

(G-3552)
PROFILE PRODUCTS LLC
219 Simpson St Sw (28613-8207)
PHONE...................................828 327-4165
Gary Bowers, *Brnch Mgr*
EMP: 96
SALES (corp-wide): 156.8MM Privately Held
Web: www.profileproducts.com
SIC: 2611 1459 2823 Pulp manufactured from waste or recycled paper; Fuller's earth mining; Cellulosic manmade fibers
PA: Profile Products Llc
    750 W Lk Cook Rd Ste 440
    Buffalo Grove IL 60089
    847 215-1144

(G-3553)
PSI-POLYMER SYSTEMS INC
1703 Pineview St Se (28613-9339)
PHONE...................................828 468-2600
Glenn Woodcock, *Pr*
Glen Woodcock, *Pr*
Carla Woodcock, *VP*
▲ EMP: 23 EST: 1994
SQ FT: 55,000
SALES (est): 8.86MM Privately Held
Web: www.psi-polymersystems.com
SIC: 3559 5084 Plastics working machinery; Industrial machinery and equipment

(G-3554)
RICHARD SHEW
Also Called: Elite Cushion Company
6202 N Nc 16 Hwy (28613-7411)
P.O. Box 1341 (28613-1341)
PHONE...................................828 781-3294
Richard Shew, *Owner*
EMP: 15 EST: 2017
SALES (est): 622.65K Privately Held
SIC: 2392 2512 Pillows, bed: made from purchased materials; Upholstered household furniture

(G-3555)
RMG LEATHER USA LLC
1226 Fedex Dr Sw (28613-7426)
PHONE..............................828 466-5489
EMP: 6 **EST:** 2021
SALES (est): 3.66MM
SALES (corp-wide): 500.31K **Privately Held**
Web: www.carrollleather.com
SIC: 2386 Garments, leather
HQ: Rino Mastrotto Group Spa
Via Dell'artigianato 100
Trissino VI 36070

(G-3556)
ROLLEASE ACMEDA INC
Also Called: Rollease Acmeda Dist Ctr
375 Workman St Sw (28613-8270)
PHONE..............................800 552-5100
EMP: 57
SALES (corp-wide): 1.49B **Privately Held**
Web: www.rolleaseacmeda.com
SIC: 2591 Window shade rollers and fittings
HQ: Rollease Acmeda, Inc.
750 E Main St Fl 7
Stamford CT 06902
800 552-5100

(G-3557)
RPM PLASTICS INC
Also Called: RPM Plastics
2041 S Mclin Creek Rd (28613-8399)
PHONE..............................704 871-0518
John R Hobson, *Pr*
EMP: 11 **EST:** 2008
SALES (est): 2.32MM **Privately Held**
SIC: 3089 Injection molding of plastics

(G-3558)
SCHENCK USA CORP
Also Called: Benz Tling A Bus Unit Schnck U
1232 Commerce St Sw (28613-8355)
PHONE..............................704 529-5300
Lars Kuenne, *Brnch Mgr*
EMP: 5
SALES (corp-wide): 5.03B **Privately Held**
Web: www.benztooling.com
SIC: 3541 Machine tools, metal cutting type
HQ: Schenck Usa Corp.
535 Acorn St
Deer Park NY 11729
631 242-4010

(G-3559)
SMART ELECTRIC NORTH AMER LLC
1550 Deborah Herman Rd Sw
(28613-8204)
P.O. Box 697 (28613-0697)
PHONE..............................828 323-1200
Jerry Yang, *Managing Member*
Kelvin Crisp, *Pr*
▲ **EMP:** 6 **EST:** 2012
SQ FT: 15,000
SALES (est): 689.41K **Privately Held**
Web: www.smartelectricoem.com
SIC: 3699 5063 Electrical equipment and supplies, nec; Electrical apparatus and equipment

(G-3560)
SOUTHLINE CONVERTING LLC
639 4th Street Pl Sw (28613-2646)
PHONE..............................828 781-6414
Russell D Woy, *Managing Member*
EMP: 5 **EST:** 2005
SQ FT: 120,000
SALES (est): 974.82K **Privately Held**
Web: www.southlineconverting.com

SIC: 2221 Textile mills, broadwoven: silk and manmade, also glass

(G-3561)
SOUTHWOOD DOORS LLC
1222 Emmanuel Church Rd Ste 6
(28613-9386)
PHONE..............................704 625-2578
Toni Dearstyne, *Managing Member*
EMP: 7 **EST:** 2017
SALES (est): 2.79MM **Privately Held**
Web: www.southwooddoors.com
SIC: 2431 Doors, wood

(G-3562)
STAR SNAX LLC
103b Somerset Dr Nw (28613-9217)
PHONE..............................828 261-0255
Michael Karp, *Managing Member*
Randall Wilson Ctrl, *Treas*
◆ **EMP:** 100 **EST:** 2002
SQ FT: 100,000
SALES (est): 24.94MM **Privately Held**
Web: www.starsnaxfoods.com
SIC: 2099 Food preparations, nec

(G-3563)
SUPREME ELASTIC CORPORATION
Also Called: U K I Supreme
325 Spencer Rd Ne (28613-8211)
P.O. Box 848 (28603-0848)
PHONE..............................828 302-3836
Terry M Taylor, *Prin*
Nathaniel Kolmes, *
Wes Christopher, *
Mathew Kolmes, *
◆ **EMP:** 50 **EST:** 1964
SQ FT: 52,000
SALES (est): 8.01MM **Privately Held**
Web: www.supremecorporation.com
SIC: 2241 2284 2281 Rubber thread and yarns, fabric covered; Thread mills; Yarn spinning mills

(G-3564)
TB ARHAUS LLC
1211 Keisler Rd Se (28613-9336)
P.O. Box 1628 (28613-3003)
PHONE..............................828 465-6953
Watkins Doug, *Genl Mgr*
Brenda Rodefeld Ctrl, *Prin*
EMP: 190 **EST:** 2015
SALES (est): 24.91MM
SALES (corp-wide): 1.27B **Publicly Held**
Web: www.arhaus.com
SIC: 2512 Upholstered household furniture
HQ: Arhaus, Llc
51 E Hines Hill Rd
Hudson OH 44236
440 439-7700

(G-3565)
TEXTILE-BASED DELIVERY INC
Also Called: Texdel
350 5th Ave Se (28613-1941)
PHONE..............................866 256-8420
Jordan Schindler, *CEO*
▲ **EMP:** 30 **EST:** 2013
SALES (est): 6.22MM **Privately Held**
Web: www.texdel.com
SIC: 2211 Dress fabrics, cotton

(G-3566)
TIMMERMAN MANUFACTURING INC
102 S Mclin Creek Rd (28613-9024)
P.O. Box 1148 (28613-1148)
PHONE..............................828 464-1778
Dan Timmerman, *Pr*
Paula Timmerman, *Sec*
EMP: 15 **EST:** 1968
SQ FT: 36,000

SALES (est): 2.24MM **Privately Held**
Web: www.timmermanmfg.com
SIC: 2514 3499 3446 Metal household furniture; Furniture parts, metal; Architectural metalwork

(G-3567)
TOP TIER PAPER PRODUCTS INC (PA)
409 Thornburg Dr Se (28613-8845)
PHONE..............................828 994-2222
Rajiv Kaushal, *Pr*
Tracy High, *Sec*
Rob Williams, *VP*
Minakshi Kaushal, *Ch Bd*
EMP: 5 **EST:** 2015
SALES (est): 1MM
SALES (corp-wide): 1MM **Privately Held**
Web: www.toptierpaper.com
SIC: 2676 Towels, napkins, and tissue paper products

(G-3568)
UNITAPE (USA) INC
620 Reese Dr Sw (28613-2932)
PHONE..............................828 464-5695
Kathy Weaber, *Acctnt*
▲ **EMP:** 9 **EST:** 2010
SALES (est): 974.15K **Privately Held**
Web: www.unitape.co.uk
SIC: 1731 3357 Fiber optic cable installation; Aircraft wire and cable, nonferrous

(G-3569)
UNITED MACHINE & METAL FAB INC
1220 Fedex Dr Sw (28613-7426)
P.O. Box 1234 (28613-1234)
PHONE..............................828 464-5167
Amir Rashidi, *Prin*
Tony Johnson, *VP*
EMP: 22 **EST:** 1991
SQ FT: 14,500
SALES (est): 4.76MM **Privately Held**
Web: www.ummf.com
SIC: 3441 3545 Fabricated structural metal; Machine tool accessories

(G-3570)
UNIVERSAL FURNITURE INTL INC
1099 2nd Avenue Pl Se (28613-2165)
PHONE..............................828 464-0311
Dale Smith, *Brnch Mgr*
EMP: 110
Web: www.universalfurniture.com
SIC: 2512 2511 Living room furniture: upholstered on wood frames; Tables, household: wood
HQ: Universal Furniture International Inc.
2575 Penny Rd
High Point NC 27265
336 822-8425

(G-3571)
VANGUARD FURNITURE CO INC (PA)
Also Called: Vanguard Furniture
109 Simpson St Sw (28613)
P.O. Box 2187 (28603)
PHONE..............................828 328-5601
John N Bray, *CEO*
Dixon Mitchell, *
Jay Andrew Bray, *
Lauren Hoover, *
Charles Snipes, *
◆ **EMP:** 325 **EST:** 1968
SQ FT: 400,000
SALES (est): 24.92MM
SALES (corp-wide): 24.92MM **Privately Held**
Web: www.vanguardfurniture.com

SIC: 2512 Couches, sofas, and davenports: upholstered on wood frames

(G-3572)
VPC FOAM USA INC (PA) ✪
1820 Evans St Ne (28613-9042)
PHONE..............................704 622-0552
Patricia Bohrer, *CFO*
EMP: 22 **EST:** 2023
SALES (est): 6.46MM
SALES (corp-wide): 6.46MM **Privately Held**
SIC: 3086 Plastics foam products

(G-3573)
WESLEY HALL INC
141 Fairgrove Church Rd Se (28613-8173)
P.O. Box Po Box9 (28603-0009)
PHONE..............................828 324-7466
Ron Deal, *Ch Bd*
Eddie Deal, *
William Whitener, *
Anne Deal Bradshaw, *
EMP: 180 **EST:** 1989
SQ FT: 120,000
SALES (est): 23.9MM **Privately Held**
Web: www.wesleyhall.com
SIC: 2512 2511 Upholstered household furniture; Wood household furniture

(G-3574)
WESTROCK RKT LLC
214 Conover Blvd E (28613-1925)
P.O. Box 669 (28613-0669)
PHONE..............................828 464-5560
Wayne A Noyes, *Mgr*
EMP: 245
Web: www.westrock.com
SIC: 2657 5113 Folding paperboard boxes; Bags, paper and disposable plastic
HQ: Westrock Rkt, Llc
1000 Abernathy Rd Ste 125
Atlanta GA 30328
770 448-2193

(G-3575)
WILLIS MANUFACTURING INC
Also Called: Willis Manufacturing
1924 Emmanuel Church Rd (28613-7301)
P.O. Box 335 (28613-0335)
PHONE..............................828 244-0435
Brenda Willis Cayll, *Pr*
EMP: 10 **EST:** 1972
SALES (est): 265.93K **Privately Held**
SIC: 3541 Screw machines, automatic

(G-3576)
WINDAK INC
1661 4th St Sw (28613-9633)
P.O. Box 517 (28613)
PHONE..............................828 322-2292
Dan Shelander, *Pr*
Urban Bollo, *VP*
Staffan Edstrom, *Treas*
◆ **EMP:** 15 **EST:** 1997
SQ FT: 6,500
SALES (est): 4.54MM
SALES (corp-wide): 734.75K **Privately Held**
Web: www.windakgroup.com
SIC: 3565 Packaging machinery
PA: Windak Holding Ab
Veddestavagen 13
JArfAlla 175 3
858038930

(G-3577)
WOOD TECHNOLOGY INC (PA)
1317 Emmanuel Church Rd (28613-9015)
PHONE..............................828 464-8049
Thomas Goff, *Pr*

Jeff Kaylor, *VP*
EMP: 20 **EST:** 1984
SQ FT: 14,000
SALES (est): 2.64MM **Privately Held**
Web: www.woodtechnology.com
SIC: 5021 2511 2517 2434 Racks; Stands, household, nec: wood; Wood television and radio cabinets; Wood kitchen cabinets

Conway
Northampton County

(G-3578)
NUTRIEN AG SOLUTIONS INC
Ampac Rd (27820)
PHONE..........................252 585-0282
James Hatcher, *Mgr*
EMP: 7
SALES (corp-wide): 29.06B **Privately Held**
Web: www.nutrienagsolutions.com
SIC: 2875 5191 Fertilizers, mixing only; Fertilizer and fertilizer materials
HQ: Nutrien Ag Solutions, Inc.
    3005 Rocky Mountain Ave
    Loveland CO 80538
    970 685-3300

Corapeake
Gates County

(G-3579)
G P KITTRELL & SON INC
1260 Nc Highway 32 N (27926-9748)
PHONE..........................252 465-8929
George P Kittrell Junior, *Pr*
John Kittrell, *VP*
George P Kittrell Iii, *Sec*
EMP: 6 **EST:** 1949
SQ FT: 500
SALES (est): 602.77K **Privately Held**
Web: gpkittrellandson.blogspot.com
SIC: 5191 3423 5261 Fertilizer and fertilizer materials; Garden and farm tools, including shovels; Retail nurseries and garden stores

Cordova
Richmond County

(G-3580)
ELEVATE TEXTILES INC
740 Old Cheraw Hwy (28330)
PHONE..........................910 997-5001
Joseph Gorga, *Prin*
EMP: 6
SALES (corp-wide): 1.98B **Privately Held**
Web: www.elevatetextiles.com
SIC: 2211 Broadwoven fabric mills, cotton
HQ: Elevate Textiles, Inc.
    121 W Trade St Ste 1700
    Charlotte NC 28202

(G-3581)
LAUREL HILL PAPER CO
126 1st St (28330)
P.O. Box 159 (28330-0159)
PHONE..........................910 997-4526
Kent Hogan, *Pr*
Phillip G Hogan, *
♦ **EMP:** 6 **EST:** 1974
SQ FT: 377,000
SALES (est): 397.78K **Privately Held**
SIC: 2621 Tissue paper

Cornelius
Mecklenburg County

(G-3582)
A M P LABORATORIES LTD
20905 Torrence Chapel Rd Ste 204 (28031-4300)
PHONE..........................704 894-9721
Dean Victoria, *Pr*
EMP: 4 **EST:** 2000
SALES (est): 149.43K **Privately Held**
SIC: 2844 5122 Cosmetic preparations; Cosmetics

(G-3583)
ADVANCED PHOTONIC CRYSTALS LLC
19825 North Cove Rd Ste 216 (28031-6446)
PHONE..........................803 547-0881
John J Egan, *Managing Member*
EMP: 7 **EST:** 2002
SALES (est): 204K **Privately Held**
SIC: 3827 Optical instruments and apparatus

(G-3584)
APPLIED TECHNOLOGIES GROUP
19701 Bethel Church Rd Ste 103 (28031-4072)
PHONE..........................618 977-9872
Tom Tragesser, *Owner*
EMP: 4 **EST:** 2014
SALES (est): 840.5K **Privately Held**
Web: marshunicorn.business.site
SIC: 3861 Photographic equipment and supplies

(G-3585)
AQUA BLUE INC
9624 Bailey Rd Ste 270 (28031-6120)
PHONE..........................704 896-9007
EMP: 4 **EST:** 2004
SALES (est): 153.03K **Privately Held**
SIC: 3999 5091 Preparation of slides and exhibits; Water slides (recreation park)

(G-3586)
ARTISAN DIRECT LLC
18335 Old Statesville Rd Ste L (28031-9013)
PHONE..........................704 655-9100
EMP: 7 **EST:** 2019
SALES (est): 228.13K **Privately Held**
Web: www.artisandirect.us
SIC: 3993 Signs and advertising specialties

(G-3587)
ARTISAN SIGNS AND GRAPHICS INC
Also Called: Artisan Graphics
18335 Old Statesville Rd Ste L (28031-9014)
PHONE..........................704 655-9100
Scott Crosbie, *Pr*
▲ **EMP:** 18 **EST:** 2004
SQ FT: 12,500
SALES (est): 4.98MM **Privately Held**
Web: www.artisansignsandgraphics.com
SIC: 3993 Signs, not made in custom sign painting shops

(G-3588)
BALANCED PHARMA INCORPORATED
18204 Mainsail Pointe Dr (28031-5198)
PHONE..........................704 278-7054
EMP: 5 **EST:** 2020
SALES (est): 285.53K **Privately Held**
Web: www.balancedpharma.com

SIC: 2834 Pharmaceutical preparations

(G-3589)
BLUE NANO INC
18946 Brigadoon Pl (28031-5500)
PHONE..........................888 508-6266
David Himebaugh, *Pr*
EMP: 10 **EST:** 2007
SALES (est): 243.29K **Privately Held**
Web: www.bluenanoinc.com
SIC: 2819 Industrial inorganic chemicals, nec

(G-3590)
BLUESTONE METALS & CHEM LLC
19720 Jetton Rd Ste 101 (28031-8263)
PHONE..........................704 662-8632
Wouter Vanloo, *Managing Member*
EMP: 4 **EST:** 2014
SQ FT: 80
SALES (est): 3.64MM **Privately Held**
Web: www.bluestonemc.com
SIC: 2819 Industrial inorganic chemicals, nec
HQ: Specialty Metals Resources
    Rue De Tenbosch 42a
    Bruxelles 1050

(G-3591)
BLUESTONE SPECIALTY CHEM LLC
19720 Jetton Rd Ste 101 (28031-8263)
PHONE..........................704 662-8632
Wouter Van Loo, *Managing Member*
EMP: 17 **EST:** 2010
SALES (est): 7.59MM **Privately Held**
SIC: 2819 Industrial inorganic chemicals, nec
PA: Specialty Metals Resources Holding Limited
    Rm 3602 36/F China Resources Bldg
    Wan Chai HK

(G-3592)
CAROLINA COPY SERVICES INC (PA)
21300 Blakely Shores Dr (28031-6610)
PHONE..........................704 375-9099
Perry Montgomery, *Pr*
EMP: 12 **EST:** 1998
SQ FT: 4,000
SALES (est): 1.32MM **Privately Held**
Web: www.carolinacopyservices.com
SIC: 7334 2752 Photocopying and duplicating services; Commercial printing, lithographic

(G-3593)
CAROLINA GYPS RECLAMATION LLC
19109 W Catawba Ave (28031-5611)
PHONE..........................704 895-4506
EMP: 8 **EST:** 2009
SALES (est): 479.55K **Privately Held**
SIC: 3999 Manufacturing industries, nec

(G-3594)
COASTAL CAROLINA WINERY
10301 Carriage Ct (28031-9249)
PHONE..........................843 443-9463
Gary Taylor, *Owner*
EMP: 7 **EST:** 2014
SALES (est): 205.08K **Privately Held**
Web: www.coastalcarolinawinery.com
SIC: 2084 Wines

(G-3595)
COOKE RENTALS MT AIRY NC INC
18518 Statesville Rd (28031-6748)
PHONE..........................336 789-5068
EMP: 6 **EST:** 2016
SALES (est): 207.61K **Privately Held**
Web: www.cookerentals.com
SIC: 3423 Tools or equipment for use with sporting arms

(G-3596)
COOLING TECHNOLOGY INC
7102 Windaliere Dr (28031-8728)
P.O. Box 560369 (28256-0369)
PHONE..........................704 596-4109
Pratap Oza, *Pr*
Meena Oza, *Sec*
▲ **EMP:** 8 **EST:** 1986
SALES (est): 990.17K **Privately Held**
Web: www.coolingtechnology.com
SIC: 3585 Refrigeration equipment, complete

(G-3597)
DEXIOS SERVICES LLC
10308 Bailey Rd Ste 430 (28031-9426)
PHONE..........................704 946-5101
EMP: 8
SALES (est): 1.23MM **Privately Held**
SIC: 2844 Perfumes, cosmetics and other toilet preparations

(G-3598)
E BY DESIGN LLC
20823 N Main St Ste 115 (28031-8206)
P.O. Box 2310 (28036-5310)
PHONE..........................980 231-5483
Heather Slosson Roberts, *CEO*
EMP: 4 **EST:** 2013
SQ FT: 1,000
SALES (est): 206.63K **Privately Held**
Web: www.ebydesign.net
SIC: 2299 Pillow fillings: curled hair, cotton waste, moss, hemp tow

(G-3599)
FAST PRO MEDIA LLC
Also Called: Speed Pro Imaging N Charlotte
10308 Bailey Rd Ste 422 (28031-9426)
PHONE..........................704 799-8040
EMP: 5 **EST:** 2017
SALES (est): 250K **Privately Held**
SIC: 2752 7389 7336 Commercial printing, lithographic; Printing broker; Graphic arts and related design

(G-3600)
FAST PRO MEDIA LLC
Also Called: Speed Pro Imaging N Charlotte
10308 Bailey Rd Ste 422 (28031-9426)
P.O. Box 1766 (28036-1766)
PHONE..........................704 799-8040
John Alan Casson, *Prin*
EMP: 4 **EST:** 2015
SALES (est): 22.34K **Privately Held**
SIC: 4899 2752 7389 7336 Communication services, nec; Commercial printing, lithographic; Business services, nec; Commercial art and graphic design

(G-3601)
FIRST RATE BLINDS
19701 Bethel Church Rd # 178 (28031-4072)
PHONE..........................800 655-1080
EMP: 5 **EST:** 2019
SALES (est): 72.97K **Privately Held**
Web: www.firstrateblinds.com
SIC: 2591 Window blinds

(G-3602)
GLAXOSMITHKLINE LLC
8625 Covedale Crossings Cir (28031-5698)
PHONE..........................704 962-5786
EMP: 5
SALES (corp-wide): 39.77B **Privately Held**
Web: us.gsk.com
SIC: 2834 Pharmaceutical preparations
HQ: Glaxosmithkline Llc
    2929 Walnut St Ste 1700
    Philadelphia PA 19112
    888 825-5249

▲ = Import ▼ = Export
♦ = Import/Export

(G-3603)
GO GREEN MIRACLE BALM
17810 Half Moon Ln Apt A (28031-8007)
PHONE..................................630 209-0226
Kristina Lewandowski, *Prin*
EMP: 4 **EST:** 2019
SALES (est): 147.76K **Privately Held**
SIC: 2844 Perfumes, cosmetics and other
toilet preparations

(G-3604)
GOURMET FOODS USA LLC
10415 Bailey Rd (28031-9442)
PHONE..................................704 248-1724
Calvin Glover, *Managing Member*
EMP: 5 **EST:** 2016
SALES (est): 241.38K **Privately Held**
SIC: 2099 5199 Popcorn, packaged: except
already popped; General merchandise, non-
durable

(G-3605)
HARRAH ENTERPRISE LTD
10308 Bailey Rd Ste 416 (28031-9426)
PHONE..................................336 253-3963
Mark E Harrah, *Prin*
EMP: 5 **EST:** 2017
SALES (est): 3.75MM **Privately Held**
Web: www.harrahenterprise.com
SIC: 3465 Body parts, automobile: stamped
metal

(G-3606)
HIAB USA INC
Also Called: Hiab
18627 Starcreek Dr (28031-9328)
PHONE..................................704 896-9089
Jim Hunsuck, *Mgr*
EMP: 10
Web: www.hiab.com
SIC: 5084 3724 Cranes, industrial; Engine
mount parts, aircraft
HQ: Hiab Usa Inc.
12233 Williams Rd
Perrysburg OH 43551
419 482-6000

(G-3607)
HOWELL & SONS CANVAS REPAIRS
29015 North Main St (28031)
P.O. Box 187 (28031-0187)
PHONE..................................704 892-7913
Nicholas Droffopoulous, *Pr*
EMP: 4 **EST:** 1972
SQ FT: 3,600
SALES (est): 167.29K **Privately Held**
Web: www.howellandsonscanvas.com
SIC: 2394 7219 Liners and covers, fabric:
made from purchased materials; Accessory
and non-garment cleaning and repair

(G-3608)
HUCK CYCLES CORPORATION
11020 Bailey Rd Ste D (28031-8102)
PHONE..................................704 275-1735
EMP: 5 **EST:** 2021
SALES (est): 655K **Privately Held**
Web: www.huckcycles.com
SIC: 3751 Bicycles and related parts

(G-3609)
HUNTER FAN COMPANY
20464 Chartwell Center Dr Ste H
(28031-9629)
PHONE..................................704 896-9250
Jeff Newman, *Prin*
EMP: 4 **EST:** 2007
SALES (est): 230.08K **Privately Held**
Web: www.hunterfan.com

SIC: 3564 5084 Blowers and fans; Fans,
industrial

(G-3610)
INNOVATIVE AWNGS & SCREENS
LLC
19825 North Cove Rd Ste B (28031-0149)
PHONE..................................833 337-4233
Andrew Hoyt, *Managing Member*
EMP: 11 **EST:** 2017
SALES (est): 1.56MM **Privately Held**
Web: www.innovativeawnings.com
SIC: 5999 5712 3448 Awnings; Outdoor and
garden furniture; Screen enclosures

(G-3611)
INSOURCE SFTWR SOLUTIONS INC
19421 Liverpool Pkwy Ste A (28031-6283)
PHONE..................................704 895-1052
Bill Migirditch, *Brnch Mgr*
EMP: 6
SALES (corp-wide): 12.67MM **Privately
Held**
Web: www.insource.solutions
SIC: 7372 Prepackaged software
PA: Insource Software Solutions, Inc.
10800 Midlothian Tpke # 2
North Chesterfield VA 23235
804 419-0674

(G-3612)
LAKE NORMAN EMB &
MONOGRAMMING
21228 Catawba Ave (28031-8428)
PHONE..................................704 892-8450
Sandra Carrigan, *Owner*
EMP: 5 **EST:** 1990
SALES (est): 174.81K **Privately Held**
Web: www.lknemb.com
SIC: 2395 2759 Emblems, embroidered;
Commercial printing, nec

(G-3613)
LAKESIDE CSTM TEES &
EMBROIDER
9216 Westmoreland Rd Ste B
(28031-5675)
PHONE..................................704 274-3730
Shelly Hawley, *Prin*
EMP: 4 **EST:** 2017
SALES (est): 135.24K **Privately Held**
Web:
www.lakenormangiftsandapparel.com
SIC: 2759 Screen printing

(G-3614)
LEBOS SHOE STORE INC
20605 Torrence Chapel Rd (28031-6878)
PHONE..................................704 987-6540
EMP: 11
SALES (corp-wide): 4.99MM **Privately
Held**
Web: www.lebos.com
SIC: 5661 2389 Shoes, orthopedic; Men's
miscellaneous accessories
PA: Lebo's Shoe Store, Inc.
2321 Crown Centre Dr
Charlotte NC 28227
704 321-5000

(G-3615)
OAKSTONE ASSOCIATES LLC
10308 Bailey Rd Ste 430 (28031-9426)
PHONE..................................704 946-5101
EMP: 10 **EST:** 2016
SALES (est): 2.02MM **Privately Held**
SIC: 2844 Depilatories (cosmetic)

(G-3616)
OLDCASTLE RETAIL INC
Also Called: Oldcastle Apg
18637 Northline Dr Ste S (28031-9322)
PHONE..................................704 799-8083
Randy Gottlieb, *Brnch Mgr*
EMP: 267
SALES (corp-wide): 34.95B **Privately Held**
SIC: 3273 3272 3271 3255 Ready-mixed
concrete; Concrete products used to
facilitate drainage; Concrete block and brick
; Clay refractories
HQ: Oldcastle Retail, Inc.
625 Griffith Rd Ste 100
Charlotte NC 28217
704 525-1621

(G-3617)
ORIGINAL NEW YORK SELTZER
LLC (HQ)
19109 W Catawba Ave Ste 200
(28031-5614)
PHONE..................................323 500-0757
EMP: 20 **EST:** 2015
SALES (est): 11.64MM
SALES (corp-wide): 15.47MM **Privately
Held**
Web: www.newyorkseltzer.com
SIC: 2086 Bottled and canned soft drinks
PA: Entertainment Arts Research, Inc.
19109 W Ctwba Ave Ste 200
Cornelius NC 28031
980 999-0270

(G-3618)
PINCO USA INC
10620 Bailey Rd Ste A (28031-9364)
PHONE..................................704 895-5766
S Paul Whitaker, *Pr*
David T Culp, *CEO*
Alistair H Deas, *VP Sls*
Frances W Smith, *Sec*
▲ **EMP:** 5 **EST:** 2005
SALES (est): 528.57K **Privately Held**
Web: www.allertex.com
SIC: 3552 Textile machinery
PA: Allertex Of America, Ltd.
10620 Bailey Rd Ste A
Cornelius NC 28031

(G-3619)
PREMIER TOOL LLC
20409 Zion Ave (28031-8549)
PHONE..................................704 895-8223
Diane Hoskins, *CEO*
EMP: 5 **EST:** 1987
SQ FT: 5,000
SALES (est): 479.02K **Privately Held**
Web: www.premiertoolcorp.com
SIC: 3545 Cutting tools for machine tools

(G-3620)
PRIMO INC
Also Called: Primo Print
19009 Peninsula Point Dr (28031-7601)
PHONE..................................888 822-5815
Marc Levack, *Pr*
▼ **EMP:** 8 **EST:** 2009
SALES (est): 1.97MM **Privately Held**
Web: www.primoprint.com
SIC: 2752 Offset printing

(G-3621)
PROMOTHREADS INC
19824 W Catawba Ave Ste C (28031-4046)
PHONE..................................704 248-0942
William V Brisbin, *Prin*
EMP: 8 **EST:** 2013
SALES (est): 212.51K **Privately Held**
Web: www.promothreadsonline.com
SIC: 2759 Screen printing

(G-3622)
RAWCO LLC
Also Called: Rawco Precision Manufacturing
18435 Train Station Dr (28031-8179)
P.O. Box 296 (07830-0296)
PHONE..................................908 832-7700
EMP: 8 **EST:** 2004
SALES (est): 206.58K **Privately Held**
Web: www.rawcoprecision.com
SIC: 3599 Machine shop, jobbing and repair

(G-3623)
RED 5 PRINTING LLC
18631 Northline Dr (28031-9357)
PHONE..................................704 996-3848
EMP: 4 **EST:** 2015
SALES (est): 265.18K **Privately Held**
Web: www.red5printing.com
SIC: 2752 Offset printing

(G-3624)
RPM INSTALLIONS INC
19843 Henderson Rd (28031-6879)
P.O. Box 1449 (28031-1449)
PHONE..................................704 907-0868
Christopher Mcauliffe, *CEO*
Edward Elacla, *Sec*
EMP: 4 **EST:** 1999
SALES (est): 77.09K **Privately Held**
SIC: 2541 Cabinets, lockers, and shelving

(G-3625)
RS INDUSTRIES INC
Also Called: Classic Molders
17776 Kings Point Dr (28031-6910)
P.O. Box 1051 (28111-1051)
PHONE..................................704 289-2734
Robert Snyder, *Pr*
Mary Snyder, *VP*
EMP: 8 **EST:** 1990
SQ FT: 15,000
SALES (est): 2.04MM **Privately Held**
Web: www.classicmolders.com
SIC: 3089 Injection molding of plastics

(G-3626)
SAFE HOME PRO INC
Also Called: Adams Line Striping
18635 Starcreek Dr Ste B (28031-9342)
P.O. Box 725 (28070-0725)
PHONE..................................704 662-2299
Nicole Lasarsky, *Pr*
Suzanne Roakes, *VP*
EMP: 16 **EST:** 2010
SQ FT: 4,000
SALES (est): 2.4MM **Privately Held**
Web: www.safehomepro.com
SIC: 1521 3842 Single-family housing
construction; Surgical appliances and
supplies

(G-3627)
TARHEEL PAVEMENT CLG SVCS INC
18636 Starcreek Dr Ste G (28031-9330)
PHONE..................................704 895-8015
Randy Humphry, *Pr*
EMP: 28 **EST:** 1996
SALES (est): 2.58MM **Privately Held**
SIC: 3991 Street sweeping brooms, hand or
machine

(G-3628)
TIER 1 GRAPHICS LLC
18525 Statesville Rd Ste D10 (28031-5722)
PHONE..................................704 625-6880
EMP: 5 **EST:** 2012
SALES (est): 520.21K **Privately Held**
Web: www.tieronegraphics.com
SIC: 3993 Signs, not made in custom sign
painting shops

(G-3629)
VORTEX USA INC
Also Called: Vortex Aquatic Structures USA
11024 Bailey Rd Ste C (28031-8107)
PHONE...............................972 410-3619
Kevin Spence, *Mgr*
Jim Spence, *Sls Mgr*
Erica Montgomery, *Sls Mgr*
EMP: 17 **EST:** 1995
SALES (est): 873.38K **Privately Held**
Web: www.vortex-intl.com
SIC: 3599 Amusement park equipment

(G-3630)
WHITE PICKET MEDIA INC
Also Called: Kitchens.com
21313 Island Forest Dr (28031-7131)
PHONE...............................773 769-8400
Steven Krengel, *Pr*
EMP: 6 **EST:** 2007
SALES (est): 273.45K **Privately Held**
Web: www.kitchens.com
SIC: 2741 Miscellaneous publishing

(G-3631)
YOURLOGOWEAR
18700 Statesville Rd (28031-6752)
PHONE...............................704 664-1290
Ken Brock, *Prin*
EMP: 4 **EST:** 2018
SALES (est): 173.08K **Privately Held**
Web: your-logo-wear.business.site
SIC: 2759 Screen printing

Cove City
Craven County

(G-3632)
WARMACK LUMBER CO INC
321 E Sunset Blvd (28523-9638)
P.O. Box 127 (28523-0127)
PHONE...............................252 638-1435
W Guy Warmack Iii, *Pr*
Alan Warmack, *VP*
▼ **EMP:** 5 **EST:** 1956
SQ FT: 420
SALES (est): 471.25K **Privately Held**
SIC: 2421 Lumber: rough, sawed, or planed

(G-3633)
WORLD WOOD COMPANY
12045 Old Us Highway 70 (28523-9539)
PHONE...............................252 523-0021
Henry Dessauer, *Pr*
EMP: 65 **EST:** 1960
SQ FT: 2,000
SALES (est): 3.59MM
SALES (corp-wide): 595.03MM **Privately Held**
SIC: 5031 2421 Lumber: rough, dressed, and finished; Kiln drying of lumber
PA: Baillie Lumber Co., L.P.
　　4002 Legion Dr
　　Hamburg NY 14075
　　800 950-2850

Cramerton
Gaston County

(G-3634)
BROOKLINE INC
112 Cramer Mountain Woods (28032-1624)
PHONE...............................704 824-1390
O'brien Brooks Junior, *Pr*
Debra Brooks, *VP*
EMP: 4 **EST:** 1981
SALES (est): 126.65K **Privately Held**

SIC: 2259 Convertors, knit goods

Creedmoor
Granville County

(G-3635)
AIRCRAFT BELTS INC (DH)
Also Called: A B I
1176 Telecom Dr (27522-8294)
PHONE...............................919 956-4395
Michael Donoho, *CEO*
Frank Mcknight, *Pr*
David Devine, *CEO*
▲ **EMP:** 20 **EST:** 1981
SQ FT: 7,500
SALES (est): 2.25MM
SALES (corp-wide): 480.55MM **Privately Held**
Web: www.aircraftbelts.com
SIC: 2399 7699 Seat belts, automobile and aircraft; Replating shop, except silverware
HQ: Firstmark Corp.
　　2742 Live Oak Ln
　　Midlothian VA 23113
　　724 759-2850

(G-3636)
AISIN NORTH CAROLINA CORP
1187 Telecom Dr (27522-8262)
PHONE...............................919 529-0951
EMP: 200
Web: www.aisinnc.com
SIC: 3714 Transmissions, motor vehicle
HQ: Aisin North Carolina Corporation
　　4112 Old Oxford Hwy
　　Durham NC 27712
　　919 479-6400

(G-3637)
ALTEC INDUSTRIES INC
1550 Aerial Ave (27522-8252)
PHONE...............................919 528-2535
Joe Gonenc, *Mgr*
EMP: 300
SALES (corp-wide): 1.21B **Privately Held**
Web: www.altec.com
SIC: 3531 3536 3713 3537 Derricks, except oil and gas field; Cranes, overhead traveling ; Truck bodies (motor vehicles); Industrial trucks and tractors
HQ: Altec Industries, Inc.
　　210 Inverness Center Drv
　　Birmingham AL 35242
　　205 991-7733

(G-3638)
ALTEC NORTHEAST LLC
1550 Aerial Ave (27522-8252)
PHONE...............................508 320-9041
▲ **EMP:** 50 **EST:** 2010
SALES (est): 4.54MM
SALES (corp-wide): 1.21B **Privately Held**
Web: www.altec.com
SIC: 3531 3536 3713 Derricks, except oil and gas field; Cranes, overhead traveling; Truck bodies (motor vehicles)
HQ: Altec Industries, Inc.
　　210 Inverness Center Drv
　　Birmingham AL 35242
　　205 991-7733

(G-3639)
APPLIED MEDICAL TECH INC (PA)
Also Called: Airclean Systems
2179 E Lyon Station Rd (27522)
PHONE...............................919 255-3220
Michael Kevin Mcgough, *Pr*
Stephen Mitchell Stott, *VP*
Susan F Dobbyn, *Treas*

William J Wickward Junior, *Corporate Secretary*
▲ **EMP:** 39 **EST:** 1992
SQ FT: 30,000
SALES (est): 13.9MM **Privately Held**
Web: aircleansystems.com
SIC: 3443 Hoods, industrial: metal plate

(G-3640)
BEACON COMPOSITES LLC
4007 Estate Dr Ste C (27522-9453)
PHONE...............................704 813-8408
Alexander Venegas, *Pr*
EMP: 5 **EST:** 2019
SALES (est): 376.03K **Privately Held**
Web: www.beaconcomposites.com
SIC: 1799 3089 Fiberglass work; Plastics processing

(G-3641)
BET-MAC WILSON STEEL INC
118 S Durham Ave (27522-8210)
P.O. Box 948 (27522-0948)
PHONE...............................919 528-1540
William A Mc Allister, *Pr*
EMP: 7 **EST:** 1982
SQ FT: 10,000
SALES (est): 462.69K **Privately Held**
Web: www.betmacwilson.com
SIC: 3441 Building components, structural steel

(G-3642)
BKC INDUSTRIES INC
2117 Will Suitt Rd (27522-8161)
P.O. Box 2446 (79105-2446)
PHONE...............................919 575-6699
Steve Aderholt, *Pr*
Helen Piehl, *Sec*
EMP: 9 **EST:** 1998
SALES (est): 1.97MM **Privately Held**
Web: www.western.group
SIC: 3715 Trailer bodies

(G-3643)
CAREFUSION 303 INC
Also Called: Cardinal Alaris Products
1515 Ivac Way (27522-8113)
PHONE...............................919 528-5253
Tom Parker, *Pr*
EMP: 9 **EST:** 1996
SALES (est): 3.96MM
SALES (corp-wide): 20.18B **Publicly Held**
SIC: 3841 Surgical and medical instruments
HQ: Carefusion 303, Inc.
　　10020 Pacific Mesa Blvd
　　San Diego CA 92121
　　858 617-2000

(G-3644)
CAROLINA SUNROCK LLC
3092 Rock Spring Church Rd (27522-8604)
PHONE...............................919 201-4201
Stuart Nanney, *Prin*
EMP: 4 **EST:** 2018
SALES (est): 51.16K **Privately Held**
Web: www.thesunrockgroup.com
SIC: 3273 Ready-mixed concrete

(G-3645)
CEDER CREEK GALLERY & POTTERY
Also Called: Cedar Creek Pot & Cft Gallery
1150 Fleming Rd (27522-9262)
PHONE...............................919 528-1041
Pat Oakley, *Pr*
EMP: 9 **EST:** 1969
SALES (est): 492.28K **Privately Held**
Web: www.cedarcreekgallery.com

SIC: 3269 5719 5947 Art and ornamental ware, pottery; Pottery; Artcraft and carvings

(G-3646)
CREEDMOOR FOREST PRODUCTS
2128 Hoerner Warldorf Rd (27522)
PHONE...............................919 529-1779
John Morgan, *Pr*
EMP: 32 **EST:** 2017
SALES (est): 2.18MM **Privately Held**
SIC: 2421 Building and structural materials, wood

(G-3647)
DANNIES LOGGING INC
2155 Tar River Rd (27522-8612)
PHONE...............................919 528-2370
Dannie Autrey, *Pr*
Brenda Autry, *Treas*
Brenda Autrey, *Sec*
EMP: 8 **EST:** 1998
SALES (est): 210.68K **Privately Held**
SIC: 2411 Logging camps and contractors

(G-3648)
FIRSTMARK AEROSPACE CORP
Also Called: Firstmark Controls
1176 Telecom Dr (27522-8294)
PHONE...............................919 956-4200
Bill Coogan, *CEO*
Teresa Triddle, *
EMP: 55 **EST:** 1998
SQ FT: 102
SALES (est): 15.7MM
SALES (corp-wide): 480.55MM **Privately Held**
Web: www.firstmarkaerospace.com
SIC: 3812 3825 3769 Space vehicle guidance systems and equipment; Instruments to measure electricity; Space vehicle equipment, nec
HQ: Firstmark Corp.
　　2742 Live Oak Ln
　　Midlothian VA 23113
　　724 759-2850

(G-3649)
GRANVILLE PUBLISHING CO INC
Also Called: Butner-Creedmoor News
418 N Main St (27522-8809)
P.O. Box 1919 (27588-1919)
PHONE...............................919 528-2393
Elizabeth Coleman, *Prin*
Harry R Coleman, *
Elizabeth Coleman, *Sec*
EMP: 4 **EST:** 1965
SALES (est): 206.53K **Privately Held**
SIC: 2711 Newspapers, publishing and printing

(G-3650)
J-M MANUFACTURING COMPANY INC
2602 W Lyon Station Rd (27522-7309)
PHONE...............................919 575-6515
James Song, *Mgr*
EMP: 79
SALES (corp-wide): 304.63MM **Privately Held**
Web: www.jmeagle.com
SIC: 2821 3084 Polyvinyl chloride resins, PVC; Plastics pipe
PA: J-M Manufacturing Company, Inc.
　　5200 W Century Blvd
　　Los Angeles CA 90045
　　310 693-8200

(G-3651)
JHD ENTERPRISE LLC
Also Called: Trendy Nails
1102 Lake Ridge Dr (27522-7140)

PHONE..............................919 612-1787
EMP: 4 EST: 2021
SALES (est): 814.61K Privately Held
SIC: 3999 Fingernails, artificial

(G-3652)
MABLES HEADSTONE & MONU CO LLP (PA)
206 West Wilton Ave (27522)
P.O. Box 341 (27522-0341)
PHONE..............................919 724-8705
Robert James Harris, Pt
EMP: 4 EST: 1978
SQ FT: 400
SALES (est): 74.99K
SALES (corp-wide): 74.99K Privately Held
SIC: 3281 5999 Granite, cut and shaped; Monuments, finished to custom order

(G-3653)
ONTIC ENGINEERING AND MFG INC
1176 Telecom Dr (27522-8294)
PHONE..............................919 395-3908
Gareth Hall, Prin
EMP: 311
SALES (corp-wide): 480.55MM Privately Held
Web: www.ontic.com
SIC: 5088 3728 Aircraft equipment and supplies, nec; Accumulators, aircraft propeller
PA: Ontic Engineering And Manufacturing, Inc.
20400 Plummer St
Chatsworth CA 91311
818 678-6555

(G-3654)
SOUTHERN STATES COOP INC
Also Called: West Jefferson Service
2089 Sam Moss Hayes Rd (27522-9331)
PHONE..............................336 246-3201
James D King, Mgr
EMP: 4
SALES (corp-wide): 1.71B Privately Held
Web: www.southernstates.com
SIC: 2048 2873 0181 2874 Prepared feeds, nec; Nitrogenous fertilizers; Bulbs and seeds; Phosphatic fertilizers
PA: Southern States Cooperative, Incorporated
6606 W Broad St Ste B
Richmond VA 23230
804 281-1000

(G-3655)
SOUTHERN STATES COOP INC
Also Called: S S C 7579 7
301 N Main St (27522)
PHONE..............................919 528-1516
Paul Kelly, Mgr
EMP: 39
SALES (corp-wide): 1.71B Privately Held
Web: www.southernstates.com
SIC: 2048 5999 Prepared feeds, nec; Farm equipment and supplies
PA: Southern States Cooperative, Incorporated
6606 W Broad St Ste B
Richmond VA 23230
804 281-1000

(G-3656)
STAY ONLINE LLC (PA)
1506 Ivac Way (27522-8112)
P.O. Box 52402 (27717)
PHONE..............................888 346-4688
Bellinda Higgins, Pr
James Higgins, *
Guido Guidotti, *
Sarah Smits Filippini, *

▲ EMP: 47 EST: 1993
SQ FT: 24,000
SALES (est): 9.08MM Privately Held
Web: www.stayonline.com
SIC: 3643 3625 Connectors and terminals for electrical devices; Industrial electrical relays and switches

(G-3657)
WALLS WELDING
212 Oak St (27522-8324)
P.O. Box 526 (27522-0526)
PHONE..............................919 201-7544
Norman Wall, Pr
Norman Wall, Owner
Derek Daigle, VP
EMP: 8 EST: 2011
SALES (est): 459.79K Privately Held
Web: www.wallswelding.net
SIC: 7692 Welding repair

Creston
Ashe County

(G-3658)
OSSIRIAND INC
Also Called: Potter's Lumber
106 Hidden Valley Rd (28615-9538)
P.O. Box 133 (28615-0133)
PHONE..............................336 385-1100
Jon Abrams, Pr
EMP: 26 EST: 2018
SALES (est): 4.24MM Privately Held
SIC: 2421 Sawmills and planing mills, general

Crouse
Lincoln County

(G-3659)
R-ANELL HOUSING GROUP LLC
235 Anthony Grove Rd (28033-8789)
P.O. Box 1143 (28021-1143)
PHONE..............................704 445-9610
Dennis Jones, Pr
Randy Cosby, *
Bill Mclucas, CFO
EMP: 51 EST: 2001
SQ FT: 237,000
SALES (est): 19.76MM
SALES (corp-wide): 1.79B Publicly Held
Web: www.r-anell.com
SIC: 2451 Mobile homes, except recreational
PA: Cavco Industries, Inc.
3636 N Centl Ave Ste 1200
Phoenix AZ 85012
602 256-6263

Crumpler
Ashe County

(G-3660)
CHANDLER CONCRETE INC
Also Called: Watauga Ready Mix
1992 Nc Highway 16 N (28617-9560)
PHONE..............................336 982-8760
Robbie Stevens, Brnch Mgr
EMP: 12
Web: www.chandlerconcrete.com
SIC: 3273 Ready-mixed concrete
PA: Chandler Concrete Co., Inc.
1006 S Church Street
Burlington NC 27215

(G-3661)
NORTH FORK ELECTRIC INC
1309 Willie Brown Rd (28617-9374)
PHONE..............................336 982-4020
Andrew D Feimster, Pr
Kathryn Feimster, Sec
▲ EMP: 4 EST: 1989
SQ FT: 288
SALES (est): 412.07K Privately Held
Web: www.nfei.com
SIC: 3629 Electronic generation equipment

(G-3662)
R L ROTEN WOODWORKING LLC
1312 Howard Colvard Rd (28617-9540)
PHONE..............................336 982-3830
Ronnie Roten, Owner
EMP: 5 EST: 2009
SALES (est): 202.2K Privately Held
Web: www.cabinetsbest.com
SIC: 2431 Millwork

Currituck
Currituck County

(G-3663)
CORRTRAC SYSTEMS CORPORATION
126 E Canvasback Dr (27929-9641)
P.O. Box 747 (27956-0747)
PHONE..............................252 232-3975
Beverly Belcher, Pr
Harvey Belcher Junior, VP
EMP: 4 EST: 1995
SALES (est): 478.91K Privately Held
SIC: 2819 Industrial inorganic chemicals, nec

Dallas
Gaston County

(G-3664)
ALERT METAL WORKS INC
105 Yates St (28034-9215)
P.O. Box 595 (28034-0595)
PHONE..............................704 922-3152
Fred Mcgee, Pr
Michael Mcgee, VP
EMP: 8 EST: 1951
SQ FT: 17,000
SALES (est): 1.48MM Privately Held
SIC: 3444 Sheet metalwork

(G-3665)
BOWEN MACHINE COMPANY INC
2006 Dallas Cherryville Hwy (28034-7707)
P.O. Box 76 (28034-0076)
PHONE..............................704 922-0423
Stuart J Bowen, Pr
Jonathan D Bowen, VP
EMP: 15 EST: 1978
SALES (est): 1.02MM Privately Held
Web: www.bowenmachine.com
SIC: 3599 Machine shop, jobbing and repair

(G-3666)
BROOKS OF DALLAS INC
Also Called: Productive Tool
203 E Lay St (28034)
P.O. Box 456 (28034)
PHONE..............................704 922-5219
Chris Brooks, Pr
Amy Brooks Prince, *
Ted H Brooks, *
EMP: 27 EST: 1963
SALES (est): 5.42MM Privately Held
Web: www.productive-tool.com

SIC: 3544 Special dies and tools

(G-3667)
C & J MACHINE COMPANY INC
3519 Philadelphia Church Rd (28034-7560)
PHONE..............................704 922-5913
Carolyn Hensley, Pr
Amy Hunt, Sec
Jerry Hensley, VP
EMP: 6 EST: 1976
SQ FT: 2,460
SALES (est): 448.12K Privately Held
Web: www.cjmachinecompany.com
SIC: 3541 3552 Machine tools, metal cutting type; Dyeing machinery, textile

(G-3668)
DIXON VALVE & COUPLING CO LLC
Also Called: Dixon Quick Coupling
2925 Chief Ct (28034-9562)
PHONE..............................704 334-9175
Bob Grace, Pr
▲ EMP: 10
SALES (corp-wide): 439.82MM Privately Held
Web: www.dixonvalve.com
SIC: 3492 5085 Fluid power valves and hose fittings; Hose, belting, and packing
HQ: Dixon Valve & Coupling Company, Llc
1 Dixon Sq
Chestertown MD 21620

(G-3669)
ELLERRE TECH INC
107 E Robinson St (28034-2233)
PHONE..............................704 524-9096
Rafaele Falciai, Pr
EMP: 9 EST: 2010
SALES (est): 2.42MM Privately Held
SIC: 3552 Textile machinery

(G-3670)
ERECTO MCH & FABRICATION INC
Also Called: Emf Industries
3653 Dallas Cherryville Hwy (28034-8763)
P.O. Box 556 (28034-0556)
PHONE..............................704 922-8621
J Lamar Whisnant, Pr
EMP: 7 EST: 1973
SALES (est): 192.74K Privately Held
SIC: 3599 Custom machinery

(G-3671)
FAB-TEC INC
3626 Dallas Hgh Shls Hwy (28034-7721)
PHONE..............................704 864-6872
David Bolding, Pr
Dana Bolding, *
EMP: 64 EST: 1997
SQ FT: 56,000
SALES (est): 8.89MM Privately Held
Web: www.fab-tec.com
SIC: 3599 Machine shop, jobbing and repair

(G-3672)
FREEMAN CONTAINER COMPANY INC
Also Called: Freeman Corrugated Containers
121 Freeman Franklin Rd (28034-7812)
PHONE..............................704 922-7972
John H Freeman Junior, Pr
John H Ffreeman Junior, Pr
Paula Freeman, Sec
EMP: 6 EST: 1986
SQ FT: 14,100
SALES (est): 178.15K Privately Held
Web: www.freemancontainer.com
SIC: 2653 5113 Boxes, corrugated: made from purchased materials; Corrugated and solid fiber boxes

(G-3673)
GNT USA LLC
One Exberry Dr (28034)
PHONE...............................914 524-0600
EMP: 40 EST: 2021
SALES (est): 1.5MM **Privately Held**
Web: www.exberry.com
SIC: 2087 Food colorings

(G-3674)
HANS KISSLE COMPANY LLC
5118 Apple Creek Pkwy (28034-6002)
PHONE...............................980 500-1630
Scott Moffitt, *Managing Member*
EMP: 150 EST: 2004
SALES (est): 6.61MM **Privately Held**
SIC: 5199 2099 Plant food; Salads, fresh or
refrigerated

(G-3675)
HEYCO WERK USA INC
5134 Apple Creek Pkwy (28034-6002)
PHONE...............................434 634-8810
Daniel Dittmar, *Mgr*
EMP: 25
SALES (corp-wide): 187.33MM **Privately**
Held
Web: www.heyco.de
SIC: 3089 Automotive parts, plastic
HQ: Heyco Werk Usa Inc.
220 N Main St Ste 500
Greenville SC 29601
434 634-8810

(G-3676)
ICONS AMERICA LLC ○
1055 Gastonia Technology Pkwy
(28034-6724)
PHONE...............................704 922-0041
Sue Nichols, *CEO*
EMP: 56 EST: 2023
SALES (est): 8.7MM **Privately Held**
SIC: 3081 Film base, cellulose acetate or
nitrocellulose plastics
PA: Icons Beauty Group Pte. Ltd.
51 Marsiling Road
Singapore 73911

(G-3677)
INDUSTRIAL MACHINE COMPANY
103 Nelda St (28034-9342)
P.O. Box 909 (28034-0909)
PHONE...............................704 922-9750
Harmon Rose, *Pr*
Jonathan Rose, *VP*
Melinda Rose, *Treas*
EMP: 10 EST: 1983
SQ FT: 2,750
SALES (est): 2.11MM **Privately Held**
Web: www.industrialmachineco.com
SIC: 3599 Machine shop, jobbing and repair

(G-3678)
LANXESS CORPORATION
1225 Gastonia Technology Pkwy
(28034-6720)
PHONE...............................704 923-0121
Flemming B Bjoernslev, *Pr*
EMP: 5
SALES (corp-wide): 7.3B **Privately Held**
Web: www.lanxess.com
SIC: 2821 Plastics materials and resins
HQ: Lanxess Corporation
111 Ridc Park W Dr
Pittsburgh PA 15275
412 809-1000

(G-3679)
MUNDY MACHINE CO INC
Also Called: Mundy Machine & Fabricating Co

3934 Puetts Chapel Rd (28034-8734)
PHONE...............................704 922-8663
Corwin Farris, *Pr*
Greg Farris, *VP*
Bryan Farris, *VP*
Gloria Farris, *Sec*
EMP: 11 EST: 1969
SQ FT: 9,000
SALES (est): 222.68K **Privately Held**
SIC: 1799 3441 3599 Welding on site;
Fabricated structural metal; Machine shop,
jobbing and repair

(G-3680)
NEW SOUTH FABRICATOR LLC
930 Ashebrook Park Rd (28034-9599)
PHONE...............................704 922-2072
Charles C Millsaps, *Admn*
EMP: 7 EST: 2016
SALES (est): 4.91MM **Privately Held**
Web: www.newsouthfabricators.com
SIC: 3441 Fabricated structural metal

(G-3681)
OWENS CRNING NN-WOVEN TECH
LLC
Also Called: Owens Corning Gastonia Plant
1230 Gastonia Technology Pkwy
(28034-6721)
PHONE...............................740 321-6131
Brad Lazorka, *Managing Member*
▲ **EMP: 8 EST:** 2012
SALES (est): 2.59MM **Publicly Held**
SIC: 1761 2282 Roofing contractor; Acetate
filament yarn: throwing, twisting, winding,
spooling
PA: Owens Corning
1 Owens Corning Pkwy
Toledo OH 43659

(G-3682)
PREMIX NORTH CAROLINA LLC
5119 Apple Creek Pkwy (28034-6002)
PHONE...............................704 412-7922
Jari-matti Mehto, *Managing Member*
EMP: 5 EST: 2022
SALES (est): 2.98MM
SALES (corp-wide): 38.53MM **Privately**
Held
Web: www.premixgroup.com
SIC: 3087 Custom compound purchased
resins
HQ: Premix, Inc.
5119 Apple Creek Pkwy
Dallas NC 28034
704 412-7922

(G-3683)
PRICE METAL SPINNING INC
3202 Puetts Chapel Rd (28034-8723)
P.O. Box 624 (28034-0624)
PHONE...............................704 922-3195
Helene Price, *Pr*
Tim Price, *VP*
EMP: 5 EST: 1984
SALES (est): 415.11K **Privately Held**
SIC: 3542 Spinning machines, metal

(G-3684)
R & R POWDER COATING INC
190 Gibson Ct (28034-8764)
P.O. Box 476 (28034-0476)
PHONE...............................704 853-0727
Ray Jenkins, *Pr*
Charlotte M Jenkins, *VP*
EMP: 17 EST: 2000
SQ FT: 20,000
SALES (est): 2.23MM **Privately Held**
Web: www.rrpowdercoating.com
SIC: 3479 Coating of metals and formed
products

(G-3685)
REPI LLC
2825 Repi Ct (28034-6722)
PHONE...............................704 648-0252
Michael Torti, *Managing Member*
Paolo Ferniani, *CFO*
▲ **EMP: 40 EST:** 2003
SALES (est): 16.69MM **Privately Held**
Web: www.repi.com
SIC: 5162 2865 2821 Plastics products, nec;
Acid dyes, synthetic; Acrylic resins

(G-3686)
ROECHLING INDUS GASTONIA LP
(DH)
Also Called: Rochling Engineering
903 Gastonia Technology Pkwy
(28034-7791)
PHONE...............................704 922-7814
Timothy Brown, *Pr*
◆ **EMP: 192 EST:** 1987
SQ FT: 167,000
SALES (est): 41.48MM
SALES (corp-wide): 2.96B **Privately Held**
Web: www.roechling.com
SIC: 3081 3082 Unsupported plastics film
and sheet; Unsupported plastics profile
shapes
HQ: Rochling Industrial Se & Co. Kg
Rochlingstr. 1
Haren (Ems) NI 49733
59347010

(G-3687)
ROMAC INDUSTRIES INC
114 Eason Rd (28034-9548)
PHONE...............................704 922-9595
EMP: 67
SALES (corp-wide): 99.54MM **Privately**
Held
Web: www.romac.com
SIC: 3491 Industrial valves
PA: Romac Industries, Inc.
21919 20th Ave Se Ste 100
Bothell WA 98021
425 951-6200

(G-3688)
ROMAC INDUSTRIES INC
Hays Fluid Control Division
400 E Fields St (28034-1723)
PHONE...............................704 915-3317
Steve Williams, *Brnch Mgr*
EMP: 60
SALES (corp-wide): 99.54MM **Privately**
Held
Web: www.romac.com
SIC: 3824 3494 3432 3492 Water meters;
Valves and pipe fittings, nec; Plumbers'
brass goods: drain cocks, faucets, spigots,
etc.; Fluid power valves and hose fittings
PA: Romac Industries, Inc.
21919 20th Ave Se Ste 100
Bothell WA 98021
425 951-6200

(G-3689)
SHERRILL CONTRACT MFG INC (PA)
110 Durkee Ln (28034-9793)
P.O. Box 478 (28034-0478)
PHONE...............................704 922-7871
Rick Hargis, *Pr*
EMP: 19 EST: 1956
SQ FT: 61,000
SALES (est): 6.31MM
SALES (corp-wide): 6.31MM **Privately**
Held
Web: www.sherrillcm.com
SIC: 3552 3535 5085 Looms, textile
machinery; Conveyors and conveying
equipment; Industrial supplies

(G-3690)
SLACK & PARR INTERNATIONAL
(HQ)
Hwy 321 (28034)
PHONE...............................704 527-2975
Ted Hallsworth, *Ch Bd*
Ted Hallsworth, *Ch Bd*
A G Kellar, *Ex VP*
Lith Wingsile, *Mgr*
EMP: 5 EST: 1976
SALES (est): 3.82MM
SALES (corp-wide): 18.45MM **Privately**
Held
SIC: 5084 3541 Pumps and pumping
equipment, nec; Machine tools, metal
cutting type
PA: Slack & Parr (Investments) Limited
Long Lane
Derby DE74
150 967-2306

(G-3691)
SYCAMORE CABINETRY INC
644 Dallas Bessemer City Hwy
(28034-9480)
PHONE...............................704 375-1617
Rodney Blackwell, *Prin*
Chuck Mcgee, *Pr*
EMP: 9 EST: 2000
SALES (est): 383.85K **Privately Held**
Web: www.sycamorecabinetry.com
SIC: 2434 Wood kitchen cabinets

(G-3692)
VENTURA SYSTEMS INC
160 Gibson Ct (28034-8764)
PHONE...............................704 712-8630
Sieto Ykema, *Prin*
EMP: 31 EST: 2017
SALES (est): 4.22MM **Privately Held**
Web: www.venturasystems.com
SIC: 2431 Doors, wood

(G-3693)
WW&S CONSTRUCTION INC
817 Dallas Spencer Mtn Rd (28034-7609)
PHONE...............................217 620-4042
Eric Shively, *Pr*
Steve Wilson, *VP*
Jason Woodhead, *Opers Mgr*
EMP: 6 EST: 2021
SALES (est): 553.54K **Privately Held**
SIC: 1389 7389 Construction, repair, and
dismantling services; Business Activities at
Non-Commercial Site

Dana
Henderson County

(G-3694)
BLUE RIDGE BLDG COMPONENTS
INC
208 Justice Hills Dr (28724)
P.O. Box 1038 (28724-1038)
PHONE...............................828 685-0452
Daniel J Hinkle Senior, *Pr*
Samuel Hinkle, *VP*
Rhonda Hinkle, *Sec*
EMP: 7 EST: 2002
SALES (est): 984.2K **Privately Held**
SIC: 2439 Trusses, wooden roof

GEOGRAPHIC

Danbury
Stokes County

(G-3695)
RAYMOND BROWN WELL COMPANY INC
1109 N Main St (27016-7413)
P.O. Box 337 (27016-0337)
PHONE..................................336 374-4999
Raymond Brown, *Owner*
Ardina Fulp, *Sec*
EMP: 6 **EST:** 1985
SALES (est): 642.33K **Privately Held**
Web: www.raymondbrownwellco.com
SIC: 1781 3561 Servicing, water wells;
Pumps and pumping equipment

Davidson
Mecklenburg County

(G-3696)
3A COMPOSITES HOLDING INC
721 Jetton St Ste 325 (28036-0359)
PHONE..................................704 658-3527
EMP: 67 **EST:** 2019
SALES (est): 4.17MM **Privately Held**
Web: www.3acompositesusa.com
SIC: 2821 Plastics materials and resins
PA: Schweiter Technologies Ag
Hinterbergstrasse 20
Steinhausen ZG 6312

(G-3697)
ACCUDYNE INDUSTRIES LLC
800 Beaty St Ste A (28036-6924)
PHONE..................................469 518-4777
Charles L Treadway, *CEO*
Kyle Lorentzen, *
EMP: 1540 **EST:** 2012
SALES (est): 2.06MM
SALES (corp-wide): 7.24B **Publicly Held**
SIC: 3463 Pump, compressor, turbine, and
engine forgings, except auto
PA: Ingersoll Rand Inc.
525 Harbor Pl Ste 600
Davidson NC 28036
704 896-4000

(G-3698)
CAIRN STUDIO LTD (PA)
121 N Main St (28036-9402)
P.O. Box 400 (28036)
PHONE..................................704 892-3581
Joe Poteat, *Pr*
▲ **EMP:** 4 **EST:** 1980
SALES (est): 658.38K
SALES (corp-wide): 658.38K **Privately Held**
Web: www.cairnstudio.com
SIC: 3299 Nonmetallic mineral statuary and
other decorative products

(G-3699)
CAROLINA HOUSING SOLUTIONS LLC
Also Called: Construction
437 Hudson Pl (28036-8657)
PHONE..................................704 995-7078
Shawn Newton, *CEO*
Shawn Newton, *Managing Member*
EMP: 8 **EST:** 2018
SALES (est): 445.37K **Privately Held**
SIC: 7371 1389 Computer software
development; Construction, repair, and
dismantling services

(G-3700)
CURTISS-WRIGHT CORPORATION (PA)
130 Harbour Place Dr Ste 300 (28036)
PHONE..................................704 869-4600
Lynn M Bamford, *Ch Bd*
Kevin M Rayment, *VP*
K Christopher Farkas, *VP*
Gary A Ogilby, *Corporate Vice President*
Robert F Freda, *VP*
EMP: 338 **EST:** 1929
SALES (est): 3.12B
SALES (corp-wide): 3.12B **Publicly Held**
Web: www.curtisswright.com
SIC: 3491 3621 3812 Industrial valves;
Motors and generators; Aircraft control
systems, electronic

(G-3701)
DAVIDSON HOUSE INC
Also Called: Contract Furniture Restoration
643 Portside Dr (28036-8927)
P.O. Box 2598 (28036-2598)
PHONE..................................704 791-0171
Shelia Kimball, *Pr*
Shelia Deal, *Pr*
EMP: 10 **EST:** 1995
SQ FT: 2,000
SALES (est): 449.81K **Privately Held**
Web: www.davidsonhouseinc.com
SIC: 7641 2522 Upholstery work; Office
furniture, except wood

(G-3702)
DAVIDSON WINE CO LLC
10930 Zac Hill Rd (28036-0420)
PHONE..................................614 738-0051
EMP: 10 **EST:** 2018
SALES (est): 4.08MM **Privately Held**
Web: www.davidsonwinecompany.com
SIC: 2084 Wines

(G-3703)
DIGITOME CORPORATION
210 Delburg St (28036-8655)
PHONE..................................860 651-5560
Donald Twyman, *Pr*
EMP: 6 **EST:** 2000
SALES (est): 176.91K **Privately Held**
Web: www.digitomesite.com
SIC: 3844 7372 X-ray apparatus and tubes;
Application computer software

(G-3704)
ELBORN HOLDINGS LLC
Also Called: Airdream.net
17408 Lynx Den Ct (28036-7834)
P.O. Box 354 (28166-0354)
PHONE..................................919 917-1419
Don E Owens Iii, *CFO*
EMP: 5 **EST:** 2005
SALES (est): 78.71K **Privately Held**
SIC: 2515 Mattresses, containing felt, foam
rubber, urethane, etc.

(G-3705)
G DENVER AND CO LLC (HQ)
800 Beaty St Ste A (28036-6924)
PHONE..................................704 896-4000
Vicente Reynal, *Ch*
Mark R Sweeney, *
Andrew Schiesl, *
Philip T Herndon, *
◆ **EMP:** 50 **EST:** 1993
SALES (est): 2.78B
SALES (corp-wide): 7.24B **Publicly Held**
Web: www.gardnerdenver.com
SIC: 3564 3561 3563 Blowers and fans;
Industrial pumps and parts; Air and gas
compressors including vacuum pumps
PA: Ingersoll Rand Inc.

525 Harbor Pl Dr Ste 600
Davidson NC 28036
704 896-4000

(G-3706)
HAMILTON
400 Avinger Ln (28036-8800)
PHONE..................................704 896-1427
Herman Hamilton, *Prin*
EMP: 5 **EST:** 2007
SALES (est): 143.89K **Privately Held**
SIC: 3826 Analytical instruments

(G-3707)
HEALTHLINE INFO SYSTEMS INC
705 Northeast Dr Ste 17 (28036-7431)
PHONE..................................704 655-0447
Russ Lane, *Pr*
Chuck Lane, *VP*
EMP: 10 **EST:** 2000
SQ FT: 3,000
SALES (est): 403.75K **Privately Held**
Web: www.healthlineis.com
SIC: 7372 Application computer software

(G-3708)
INDEPENDENCE LUMBER INC
18900 Riverwind Ln (28036-7849)
PHONE..................................276 773-3744
Eller Randall, *Pr*
Nelson D Weaver, *
Eller Damon Randell, *
Mike Bolling, *
Bolling Charles M, *
EMP: 100 **EST:** 1983
SALES (est): 3.26MM **Privately Held**
Web: www.independencelumberinc.com
SIC: 2421 Lumber: rough, sawed, or planed

(G-3709)
INGERSOLL RAND INC (PA)
525 Harbour Place Dr Ste 600 (28036)
PHONE..................................704 896-4000
Vicente Reynal, *Ch Bd*
Vikram Kini, *Sr VP*
Matt Emmerich, *CIO*
Kathleen M Keene, *Human Resources Officer*
Andrew Schiesl, *CCO*
EMP: 572 **EST:** 1859
SALES (est): 7.24B
SALES (corp-wide): 7.24B **Publicly Held**
Web: www.irco.com
SIC: 3561 3563 Pumps and pumping
equipment; Air and gas compressors
including vacuum pumps

(G-3710)
INGERSOLL-RAND INDUS US INC (HQ)
525 Harbour Place Dr Ste 600 (28036)
PHONE..................................704 896-4000
Vicente Reynal, *Ch*
Vikram Kini, *VP*
Mark Siler, *Sec*
Herbert Jameson, *Treas*
Francisco De Barros, *Asst Tr*
EMP: 54 **EST:** 2019
SALES (est): 82.26MM
SALES (corp-wide): 7.24B **Publicly Held**
Web: www.ingersollrand.com
SIC: 3561 3429 3546 3563 Pumps and
pumping equipment; Furniture, builders'
and other household hardware; Power-
driven handtools; Air and gas
compressors including vacuum pumps
PA: Ingersoll Rand Inc.
525 Harbor Pl Dr Ste 600
Davidson NC 28036
704 896-4000

(G-3711)
INGERSOLL-RAND INTL HOLDG
800 Beaty St (28036-9000)
PHONE..................................704 655-4000
Theodore Black, *Ch Bd*
James E Perrella, *
William G Mulligan, *
Thomas E Bennett, *
William J Armstrong, *
EMP: 300 **EST:** 1978
SALES (est): 5.93MM **Privately Held**
SIC: 3531 Construction machinery
HQ: Trane Technologies Company Llc
800-E Beaty St
Davidson NC 28036
704 655-4000

(G-3712)
INGERSOLL-RAND US HOLDCO INC (PA)
800 Beaty St Ste E (28036-6924)
PHONE..................................704 655-4000
EMP: 6
SALES (est): 477.58K
SALES (corp-wide): 477.58K **Privately Held**
SIC: 3569 General industrial machinery, nec

(G-3713)
MOTORSPORT INNOVATIONS INC
19220 Callaway Hills Ln (28036-7710)
PHONE..................................704 728-7837
David Holden, *Pr*
EMP: 8 **EST:** 1996
SQ FT: 1,200
SALES (est): 87.98K **Privately Held**
SIC: 8711 3714 Consulting engineer; Motor
vehicle parts and accessories

(G-3714)
NINE-AI INC
359 Armour St (28036-6901)
PHONE..................................781 825-3267
Joseph Zagrobelny, *CEO*
EMP: 10 **EST:** 2018
SALES (est): 227.73K **Privately Held**
Web: www.nine-ai.com
SIC: 3549 Assembly machines, including
robotic

(G-3715)
NUCLEUS RADIOPHARMA INC
130 Harbour Place Dr Ste 340
(28036-7442)
PHONE..................................980 483-1766
Charles Conroy, *CEO*
EMP: 27 **EST:** 2022
SALES (est): 1.36MM **Privately Held**
SIC: 7389 2834 Business Activities at Non-
Commercial Site; Pharmaceutical
preparations

(G-3716)
PRINTOLOGY SIGNS GRAPHICS LLC
10931 Zac Hill Rd (28036-0420)
PHONE..................................843 473-4984
Mark Russell, *Managing Member*
Wendi Russell, *Managing Member*
EMP: 4 **EST:** 2015
SALES (est): 184.27K **Privately Held**
SIC: 3993 2262 Signs and advertising
specialties; Printing, manmade fiber and
silk broadwoven fabrics

(G-3717)
PROCTORFREE INC
210 Delburg St (28036-8655)
PHONE..................................704 759-6569
Michael Murphy, *CEO*
Brad Davis, *CEO*

Velvet Nelson, *Prin*
Michael Murphy, *Prin*
EMP: 14 **EST:** 2014
SQ FT: 5,000
SALES (est): 942.72K **Privately Held**
Web: www.proctorfree.com
SIC: 7371 7372 Computer software development and applications; Educational computer software

(G-3718)
READY SOLUTIONS INC
112 Eden St (28036-8131)
P.O. Box 1333 (28031-1333)
PHONE.............................704 534-9221
Bob Confoy, *Pr*
Mike Geraghty, *Treas*
EMP: 6 **EST:** 2003
SALES (est): 483.46K **Privately Held**
Web: www.readysolutionsinc.com
SIC: 3081 Plastics film and sheet

(G-3719)
TELEPHYS INC
610 Jetton St Ste 120 (28036-9319)
PHONE.............................312 625-9128
Jan Pachon, *CEO*
EMP: 4 **EST:** 2018
SALES (est): 95.66K **Privately Held**
SIC: 7371 8011 3845 7299 Software programming applications; Radiologist; Magnetic resonance imaging device, nuclear; Information services, consumer

(G-3720)
THERMO KING CORPORATION
Also Called: Thermo King Svc
800 Beaty St (28036-9000)
PHONE.............................732 652-6774
EMP: 50
Web: www.thermoking.com
SIC: 3585 Refrigeration and heating equipment
HQ: Thermo King Llc
314 W 90th St
Bloomington MN 55420
952 887-2200

(G-3721)
TRANE TECHNOLOGIES COMPANY LLC (HQ)
800 Beaty St Ste E (28036-6924)
PHONE.............................704 655-4000
Dave Regnery, *CEO*
Chris Kuehn, *Ex VP*
Maria Green, *Sr VP*
Marcia J Avedon, *Senior Vice President Human Resources*
Paul Camuti, *Sr VP*
◆ **EMP:** 575 **EST:** 1871
SALES (est): 685.84MM **Privately Held**
Web: www.tranetechnologies.com
SIC: 3564 3585 Filters, air: furnaces, air conditioning equipment, etc.; Air conditioning equipment, complete
PA: Trane Technologies Public Limited Company
170/175 Lakeview Drive
Swords

(G-3722)
TRANE TECHNOLOGIES MFG LLC
800 Beaty St (28036-9000)
PHONE.............................704 655-4000
Dave Regnery, *CEO*
EMP: 6 **EST:** 2022
SALES (est): 832.89K **Privately Held**
Web: www.tranetechnologies.com
SIC: 3585 Air conditioning equipment, complete

PA: Trane Technologies Public Limited Company
170/175 Lakeview Drive
Swords

(G-3723)
TRANE US INC (DH)
Also Called: Trane
800 Beaty St Ste E (28036)
P.O. Box 6820 (08855)
PHONE.............................704 655-4000
Donald E Simmons, *Pr*
Chris Kuehn, *
◆ **EMP:** 638 **EST:** 1929
SALES (est): 2.11B **Privately Held**
Web: www.trane.com
SIC: 3564 3585 3822 3634 Ventilating fans: industrial or commercial; Air conditioning units, complete: domestic or industrial; Air conditioning and refrigeration controls; Dehumidifiers, electric: room
HQ: Trane Inc.
1 Centennial Ave Ste 101
Piscataway NJ 08854
732 652-7100

(G-3724)
UNITED VISIONS CORP
Also Called: Visions Interior Designs
428 S Main St Ste B Pmb 135 (28036-7012)
P.O. Box 518 (28036-0518)
PHONE.............................704 953-4555
Michael J Melicia, *Pr*
Susan A Melicia, *VP*
EMP: 6 **EST:** 1995
SALES (est): 910.87K **Privately Held**
SIC: 1522 1542 1389 2421 Residential construction, nec; Agricultural building contractors; Construction, repair, and dismantling services; Building and structural materials, wood

(G-3725)
VALSPAR CORPORATION
721 Jetton St (28036-7108)
PHONE.............................704 897-5700
EMP: 6 **EST:** 2015
SALES (est): 183.65K **Privately Held**
Web: www.valspar.com
SIC: 2851 Varnishes, nec

Davis
Carteret County

(G-3726)
HARVEY & SONS NET & TWINE
Also Called: Sound Trees
804 Hwy 70 Davis (28524-7038)
P.O. Box 84 (28579-0084)
PHONE.............................252 729-1731
Neal L Harvey, *Owner*
EMP: 6 **EST:** 1981
SQ FT: 3,000
SALES (est): 246.17K **Privately Held**
SIC: 2399 Fishing nets

Deep Gap
Watauga County

(G-3727)
APPALACHIAN CABINET INC
7373 Old 421 S (28618-8900)
PHONE.............................828 265-0830
Perry Clark, *Pr*
EMP: 4 **EST:** 1992
SQ FT: 3,800
SALES (est): 383.14K **Privately Held**

SIC: 2521 2541 2599 Cabinets, office: wood; Cabinets, lockers, and shelving; Factory furniture and fixtures

(G-3728)
NEW RIVER DISTILLING CO LLC
180 W Yuma Ln (28618-9811)
PHONE.............................732 673-4852
Danil Meehan, *Managing Member*
EMP: 6 **EST:** 2017
SALES (est): 486.97K **Privately Held**
Web: www.newriverdistilling.com
SIC: 2085 Distilled and blended liquors

(G-3729)
PEPSI BOTTLING VENTURES LLC
Also Called: Pepsi-Cola
7467 Old 421 S (28618-8928)
P.O. Box B (28618)
PHONE.............................828 264-7702
Stephen King, *Mgr*
EMP: 42
Web: www.pepsibottlingventures.com
SIC: 2086 Soft drinks: packaged in cans, bottles, etc.
HQ: Pepsi Bottling Ventures Llc
4141 Parklake Ave
Raleigh NC 27612
919 865-2300

(G-3730)
SMITH BROTHERS LOGGING
136 Clyde Ln (28618-9514)
PHONE.............................828 265-1506
Royce Smith, *Pt*
Richard Smith, *Pt*
Randy Smith, *Pt*
EMP: 4 **EST:** 1994
SALES (est): 214.52K **Privately Held**
SIC: 2411 Logging camps and contractors

(G-3731)
WANDA NICKEL
6764 Old 421 S (28618-8911)
PHONE.............................828 265-3246
Wanda Nickel, *Prin*
EMP: 6 **EST:** 2010
SALES (est): 230.25K **Privately Held**
SIC: 3356 Nickel

Deep Run
Lenoir County

(G-3732)
FUTRELL PRECASTING LLC
3430 Old Pink Hill Rd (28525-9446)
PHONE.............................252 568-3481
Odom M Futrell, *Pt*
EMP: 9 **EST:** 1962
SALES (est): 483.67K **Privately Held**
SIC: 3272 0213 Septic tanks, concrete; Hogs

(G-3733)
OUTLAW STEP CO
2491 Burncoat Rd (28525-9475)
PHONE.............................252 568-4384
Jimmie D Outlaw, *Owner*
EMP: 7 **EST:** 1980
SQ FT: 3,000
SALES (est): 67.32K **Privately Held**
SIC: 2452 5039 Prefabricated wood buildings ; Prefabricated structures

Delco
Columbus County

(G-3734)
BRACEY BROS LOGGING LLC
418 Lennon Rd (28436-9394)
PHONE.............................910 231-9543
EMP: 8 **EST:** 2017
SALES (est): 1.77MM **Privately Held**
SIC: 2411 Logging

(G-3735)
COLUMBUS PALLET COMPANY INC
813 Lennon Rd (28436-9591)
P.O. Box 70 (28436-0070)
PHONE.............................910 655-4513
Robert Lennon, *Pr*
Jeff Lennon, *Mgr*
Julia Blake, *VP*
Alisa Lennon, *Treas*
EMP: 8 **EST:** 1973
SQ FT: 5,000
SALES (est): 122.25K **Privately Held**
SIC: 2448 Pallets, wood

(G-3736)
J&J OUTDOOR ACCESSORIES
26955 Andrew Jackson Hwy E (28436-9819)
PHONE.............................910 742-1969
EMP: 4 **EST:** 2019
SALES (est): 129.95K **Privately Held**
Web: www.jandjoutdoorbuildings.com
SIC: 3448 Prefabricated metal buildings and components

(G-3737)
LR MANUFACTURING INC
60 Dream Ave (28436-8700)
PHONE.............................910 399-1410
Melissa Lester, *Prin*
EMP: 4 **EST:** 2017
SALES (est): 284.24K **Privately Held**
SIC: 3999 Manufacturing industries, nec

(G-3738)
OBRIEN LOGGING CO
988 Livingston Chapel Rd (28436-9298)
PHONE.............................910 655-3830
Richard O'brien, *Owner*
EMP: 4 **EST:** 1972
SALES (est): 243.25K **Privately Held**
SIC: 2411 Logging

(G-3739)
PREFERRED LOGGING
Also Called: Paul James O'Brian
969 Livingston Chapel Rd (28436-9299)
PHONE.............................910 471-4011
Paul James O'brian, *Owner*
EMP: 6 **EST:** 2005
SQ FT: 2,000
SALES (est): 224.6K **Privately Held**
SIC: 2411 Logging

Denton
Davidson County

(G-3740)
AUSTIN POWDER COMPANY
Also Called: Austin Powder South East
372 Ernest Smith Rd (27239-6933)
PHONE.............................828 645-4291
James Reese, *Mgr*
EMP: 27
SALES (corp-wide): 749.73MM **Privately Held**

▲ = Import ▼ = Export
◆ = Import/Export

Web: www.austinpowder.com
SIC: 2892 Explosives
HQ: Austin Powder Company
25800 Science Park Dr # 300
Cleveland OH 44122
216 464-2400

(G-3741)
CAGLE SAWMILL INC
7065 Charles Mountain Rd (27239-9003)
PHONE........................336 857-2274
Glen Cagle, *Pr*
Roger Cagle, *Sec*
EMP: 4 EST: 1976
SALES (est): 409.03K **Privately Held**
SIC: 2421 2426 Sawmills and planing mills,
general; Hardwood dimension and flooring
mills

(G-3742)
CENTURY HOSIERY INC (PA)
651 Garner Rd (27239-7542)
P.O. Box 1410 (27239-1410)
PHONE........................336 859-3806
Kathy Martin, *Pr*
Malcom Martin, *
EMP: 120 EST: 1990
SQ FT: 55,000
SALES (est): 4.69MM **Privately Held**
Web: www.centuryhosiery.com
SIC: 3143 3144 3149 Orthopedic shoes,
men's; Orthopedic shoes, women's;
Orthopedic shoes, children's

(G-3743)
CONSTRUCTION IMPTS DEPO INC
1248 N Main St (27239-7589)
P.O. Box 1230 (27239-1230)
PHONE........................336 859-2002
John Kevin Matney, *Pr*
Ira D Matney, *VP*
EMP: 20 EST: 2003
SQ FT: 22,300
SALES (est): 9.5MM **Privately Held**
Web: www.cidattachments.com
SIC: 3531 Construction machinery

(G-3744)
CONTEMPORARY FURNISHINGS CORP
Carter Furniture Company
6550 Scarlet Oak Dr (27239-9079)
PHONE........................336 857-2988
Claud Wolfe, *Mgr*
EMP: 5
SALES (corp-wide): 1.79MM **Privately Held**
SIC: 2426 Furniture dimension stock,
hardwood
PA: Contemporary Furnishings Corp
1000 N Long St
Salisbury NC 28144
704 633-8000

(G-3745)
COUNCILL COMPANY LLC
Also Called: Thomas & Gray
1156 N Main St (27239-7588)
P.O. Box 3444 (28603-3444)
PHONE........................336 859-2155
▲ EMP: 125
Web: www.kindelfurniture.com
SIC: 2512 2511 Upholstered household
furniture; Wood household furniture

(G-3746)
DENTON ORATOR
26 N Main St (27239-6594)
P.O. Box 1546 (27239-1546)
PHONE........................336 859-3131
Stan Bingham, *Owner*

EMP: 4 EST: 1995
SALES (est): 207.07K **Privately Held**
Web: www.dentonorator.com
SIC: 2711 Newspapers, publishing and
printing

(G-3747)
DIAMOND OUTDOOR ENTPS INC
9035 Nc Highway 49 S (27239-8368)
PHONE........................336 857-1450
Keith Chrismon, *Prin*
EMP: 6 EST: 2005
SQ FT: 1,744
SALES (est): 227.2K **Privately Held**
SIC: 3911 Medals, precious or semiprecious
metal

(G-3748)
DIMENSION MILLING CO INC
12885 Nc Highway 47 (27239-7437)
P.O. Box 1306 (27239-1306)
PHONE........................336 983-2820
Alan Myers, *Pr*
Henry Mcmullin, *VP*
Jeff Kings, *Mgr*
EMP: 9 EST: 1962
SALES (est): 455.95K **Privately Held**
SIC: 2426 Hardwood dimension and flooring
mills

(G-3749)
HARDISTER LOGGING
5571 Sandalwood Dr (27239-9043)
PHONE........................336 857-2397
Donny Hardister, *Owner*
EMP: 5 EST: 1973
SALES (est): 106.67K **Privately Held**
SIC: 2411 Logging

(G-3750)
HARRIS LOGGING LLC
7508 Brantley Gordon Rd (27239-9222)
PHONE........................336 859-2786
David Harris, *Prin*
EMP: 6 EST: 2003
SALES (est): 211.8K **Privately Held**
SIC: 2411 Logging camps and contractors

(G-3751)
JACOBS CREEK STONE COMPANY INC
2081 W Slate Mine Rd (27239)
P.O. Box 608 (27239-0608)
PHONE........................336 857-2602
Robert J Mckinney, *Pr*
EMP: 10 EST: 1948
SQ FT: 3,000
SALES (est): 973.99K **Privately Held**
Web: www.jacobscreekstone.com
SIC: 1411 3281 Flagstone mining;
Flagstones

(G-3752)
JOHNNY DANIEL
Also Called: Daniel, Johnny Logging
230 Bringle Ferry Rd (27239-9137)
PHONE........................336 859-2480
Johnny Daniel, *Owner*
EMP: 6 EST: 2001
SALES (est): 151.85K **Privately Held**
SIC: 2411 Logging camps and contractors

(G-3753)
LANIERS SCREEN PRINTING
6271 Bombay School Rd (27239-8332)
PHONE........................336 857-2699
Arnold Lanier, *Owner*
EMP: 4 EST: 1988
SALES (est): 168.76K **Privately Held**
SIC: 2759 Screen printing

(G-3754)
LATHAM INC
6509 Scarlet Oak Dr (27239-9079)
PHONE........................336 857-3702
Rayford Latham, *Pr*
Bunny Latham, *VP*
EMP: 5 EST: 1994
SQ FT: 7,000
SALES (est): 98.99K **Privately Held**
Web: www.lathamcenters.org
SIC: 2426 Furniture stock and parts,
hardwood

(G-3755)
LEONARD LOGGING CO
4057 Salem Church Rd (27239-9592)
PHONE........................336 857-2776
Ricky Leonard, *Prin*
EMP: 6 EST: 1999
SALES (est): 247.53K **Privately Held**
SIC: 2411 Logging camps and contractors

(G-3756)
LOFLIN FABRICATION LLC
Also Called: Loflin Fabrication
1379 Cranford Rd (27239-8952)
PHONE........................336 859-4333
Terry E Ferrell, *
▲ EMP: 35 EST: 1993
SQ FT: 69,000
SALES (est): 9.4MM **Privately Held**
Web: www.loflinfabrication.com
SIC: 3444 3531 Sheet metal specialties, not
stamped; Construction machinery

(G-3757)
M & M FRAME COMPANY INC
Also Called: M-M Components
18847 S Nc Highway 109 (27239-7716)
P.O. Box 1337 (27239-1337)
PHONE........................336 859-8166
Clark Rogers Junior, *Pr*
EMP: 9 EST: 1990
SALES (est): 441K **Privately Held**
SIC: 3499 2426 2512 Furniture parts, metal;
Frames for upholstered furniture, wood;
Upholstered household furniture

(G-3758)
NOLAN MANUFACTURING LLC
18868 S Nc Highway 109 (27239-7716)
PHONE........................336 490-0086
Christopher Biesecker, *Managing Member*
EMP: 4 EST: 2020
SALES (est): 2.48MM **Privately Held**
Web: www.nolanmanufacturing.com
SIC: 3537 Industrial trucks and tractors

(G-3759)
ROCKETPRINT SOFTWARE LLC
211 Hb Newsome Pl (27239-6982)
PHONE........................336 267-7272
Gil Newsom, *Mgr*
EMP: 6 EST: 2009
SALES (est): 611.09K **Privately Held**
Web: www.rocketprintsoftware.com
SIC: 7372 Prepackaged software

(G-3760)
SOUTHERN LOGGING INC
250 Piedmont School Rd (27239-8921)
P.O. Box 1379 (27239-1379)
PHONE........................336 859-5057
Timothy D Hardister, *Prin*
EMP: 6 EST: 2008
SALES (est): 446.05K **Privately Held**
SIC: 2411 Logging camps and contractors

(G-3761)
STONETREE SIGNS
5321 New Hope Rd (27239-9321)
PHONE........................336 625-0938
TOLL FREE: 866
Michele Bortree, *Owner*
EMP: 6 EST: 1996
SALES (est): 206.94K **Privately Held**
Web: www.stonetreesigns.com
SIC: 3993 Electric signs

(G-3762)
SURRATT HOSIERY MILL INC
22872 Nc Highway 8 (27239-8175)
PHONE........................336 859-4583
Irving A Surratt, *Pr*
Eric Surratt, *Sec*
EMP: 7 EST: 1965
SQ FT: 85,000
SALES (est): 470.76K **Privately Held**
Web: www.surratthosiery.com
SIC: 2251 2252 Women's hosiery, except
socks; Socks

(G-3763)
THERMO PRODUCTS LLC (HQ)
92 W Fourth St (27239-7287)
P.O. Box 217 (46366-0217)
PHONE........................800 348-5130
Allen A Kuehl, *Pr*
EMP: 47 EST: 1946
SQ FT: 70,000
SALES (est): 13.54MM
SALES (corp-wide): 240.55MM **Publicly
Held**
Web: www.thermopride.com
SIC: 3585 3433 Furnaces, warm air: electric;
Heating equipment, except electric
PA: Burnham Holdings, Inc.
1241 Harrisburg Pike
Lancaster PA 17604
717 390-7800

(G-3764)
TUCKER LOGGING
6957 Gravel Hill Rd (27239-8324)
PHONE........................336 857-2674
Jessie Tucker, *Owner*
EMP: 4 EST: 1990
SALES (est): 132.59K **Privately Held**
SIC: 2411 Logging camps and contractors

(G-3765)
ULTRA-MEK INC
487 Bombay Rd (27239-0130)
P.O. Box 518 (27239-0518)
PHONE........................336 859-4552
Steve Hoffman, *CEO*
Shane Hoffman, *
William S Bencini, *
◆ EMP: 100 EST: 1980
SQ FT: 75,000
SALES (est): 14.71MM **Privately Held**
Web: www.ultramek.com
SIC: 3429 Furniture hardware

(G-3766)
WST LOGGING LLC
7324 Checkmark Rd (27239-9025)
PHONE........................336 857-0147
William Stewart Tysinger, *Prin*
EMP: 6 EST: 2014
SALES (est): 125.37K **Privately Held**
SIC: 2411 Logging

Denver
Lincoln County

(G-3767)
ADMIRAL MARINE PDTS & SVCS INC
770 Crosspoint Dr (28037-7826)
PHONE.....................704 489-8771
Michael Digh, *Pr*
Waco S Digh, *VP*
EMP: 5 **EST:** 1981
SALES (est): 127.94K **Privately Held**
Web: www.admiralmarine.biz
SIC: 7699 5999 2221 Boat repair; Fiberglass materials, except insulation; Fiberglass fabrics

(G-3768)
ADVANCED MCH & FABRICATION INC
7842 Commerce Dr (28037-9101)
P.O. Box 749 (28037-0749)
PHONE.....................704 489-0096
Elizabeth Barr, *Pr*
Mike Barr, *VP*
EMP: 4 **EST:** 1999
SALES (est): 615.55K **Privately Held**
Web: www.advancemachinefab.com
SIC: 3599 Machine shop, jobbing and repair

(G-3769)
AMF-NC ENTERPRISE COMPANY LLC
3570 Denver Dr (28037-7217)
PHONE.....................704 489-2206
Jerry Soots, *Genl Mgr*
EMP: 13 **EST:** 2013
SQ FT: 6,000
SALES (est): 2.78MM **Privately Held**
Web: www.gray-mfg.com
SIC: 3465 3728 Body parts, automobile: stamped metal; Aircraft body assemblies and parts

(G-3770)
ANATECH LTD (PA)
771 Crosspoint Dr (28037-7826)
PHONE.....................704 489-1488
George Barr, *Pr*
Liliana Barr, *VP*
EMP: 19 **EST:** 2004
SQ FT: 5,000
SALES (est): 636.2K
SALES (corp-wide): 636.2K **Privately Held**
Web: www.industrialhardcarbon.com
SIC: 3479 2836 Coating of metals and formed products; Biological products, except diagnostic

(G-3771)
ANDY MAYLISH FABRICATION INC
5384 Stone Henge Dr (28037-8721)
PHONE.....................704 785-1491
Andrew Maylish, *Prin*
EMP: 4 **EST:** 2016
SALES (est): 56.31K **Privately Held**
SIC: 3999 Manufacturing industries, nec

(G-3772)
ARGOS USA LLC
Also Called: Redi-Mix Concrete
4451 N Nc 16 Business Hwy (28037-6777)
PHONE.....................704 483-4013
Tim Kinder, *Mgr*
EMP: 10
Web: www.argos-us.com
SIC: 3273 Ready-mixed concrete
HQ: Argos Usa Llc
3015 Windward Plz Ste 300
Alpharetta GA 30005
678 368-4300

(G-3773)
BILL PERFECT INC
4207 Burnwood Trl (28037-6212)
PHONE.....................954 889-6699
Michael Jlates Junior, *Pr*
EMP: 12 **EST:** 2015
SALES (est): 2.52MM **Privately Held**
Web: www.timelybill.com
SIC: 7372 Prepackaged software

(G-3774)
BILL PINK CARBURETORS LLC
6137 Denver Industrial Park Rd Ste A (28037-7838)
PHONE.....................704 575-1645
Bill Pink, *Prin*
EMP: 4 **EST:** 2017
SALES (est): 2.52MM **Privately Held**
Web: www.pinkcarburetors.com
SIC: 3592 Carburetors

(G-3775)
BIOMEDINNOVATIONS INC
Also Called: Bmi Organbank
771 Crosspoint Dr (28037-7826)
PHONE.....................704 489-1290
George Barr, *Ch Bd*
EMP: 5 **EST:** 2005
SQ FT: 5,000
SALES (est): 245.14K **Privately Held**
Web: www.bmi.llc
SIC: 8733 3841 Medical research; Surgical and medical instruments

(G-3776)
C A ZIMMER INC
Also Called: Cornell Zimmer Organ Builders
731 Crosspoint Dr (28037-7826)
P.O. Box 2309 (28037-2309)
PHONE.....................704 483-4560
Cornel A Zimmer, *Pr*
Ann Zimmer, *VP*
EMP: 8 **EST:** 1992
SQ FT: 9,000
SALES (est): 204.88K **Privately Held**
Web: www.zimmerorgans.com
SIC: 3931 Organs, all types: pipe, reed, hand, electronic, etc.

(G-3777)
CALICO TECHNOLOGIES INC (PA)
Also Called: Calico Coatings
5883 Balsom Ridge Rd (28037-9233)
P.O. Box 901 (28037-0901)
PHONE.....................704 483-2202
Tracy Trotter, *Pr*
EMP: 23 **EST:** 1997
SQ FT: 20,000
SALES (est): 7.25MM
SALES (corp-wide): 7.25MM **Privately Held**
Web: www.calicocoatings.com
SIC: 3479 Coating of metals and formed products

(G-3778)
CRAWFORD COMPOSITES LLC
Also Called: High Performance Adaptive
3501 Denver Dr (28037-7217)
PHONE.....................704 483-4175
Michael Joukowsky, *Managing Member*
Kathryn Becker, *Managing Member**
EMP: 47 **EST:** 2012
SALES (est): 10.35MM **Privately Held**
Web: www.crawfordcomposites.com
SIC: 3083 Thermoplastics laminates: rods, tubes, plates, and sheet

(G-3779)
CROWN DEFENSE LTD
2320 N Nc 16 Business Hwy (28037-8353)
PHONE.....................202 800-8848
EMP: 8
SALES (corp-wide): 932.19K **Privately Held**
Web: www.sosmil.org
SIC: 3799 3795 Off-road automobiles, except recreational vehicles; Amphibian tanks, military
PA: Crown Defense Ltd
160 Taylor St
Aberdeen NC 28315
202 800-8848

(G-3780)
DENVER WATERJET LLC
3865 N Nc 16 Business Hwy (28037-7906)
PHONE.....................980 222-7447
EMP: 4 **EST:** 2019
SALES (est): 1.12MM **Privately Held**
Web: www.denverwaterjet.com
SIC: 3599 Machine shop, jobbing and repair

(G-3781)
EARTH MATTERS INC
4943 Looking Glass Trl (28037-9032)
P.O. Box 1589 (21041-1589)
PHONE.....................410 747-4400
Michael P Wiley, *Pr*
Paul Van Doren, *VP*
EMP: 6 **EST:** 1998
SALES (est): 931.38K **Privately Held**
Web: www.earthmattersinc.com
SIC: 1381 Drilling oil and gas wells

(G-3782)
EP CUSTOM PRODUCTS INC
7823 Commerce Dr (28037-9101)
P.O. Box 1118 (28037-1118)
PHONE.....................704 483-8793
Michael Savigny, *Pr*
EMP: 8 **EST:** 2010
SALES (est): 2.92MM **Privately Held**
Web: www.epcustomproducts.com
SIC: 3444 Sheet metalwork

(G-3783)
FURNACE REBUILDERS INC
915 Dove Ct (28037-9211)
P.O. Box 1067 (28037-1067)
PHONE.....................704 483-4025
John Murphy, *Pr*
EMP: 12 **EST:** 1995
SQ FT: 10,000
SALES (est): 2.31MM **Privately Held**
Web: www.furnacerebuilders.com
SIC: 3398 Metal heat treating

(G-3784)
GARAGE SHOP LLC
4252 Burnwood Trl (28037-6212)
PHONE.....................980 500-0583
Aaron Brown, *CEO*
EMP: 15 **EST:** 2015
SALES (est): 2.26MM **Privately Held**
Web: www.thegarageshop200.com
SIC: 7389 7549 5531 7948 Personal service agents, brokers, and bureaus; Automotive maintenance services; Speed shops, including race car supplies; Race car owners

(G-3785)
GRAY MANUFACTURING TECH LLC
3570 Denver Dr (28037-7217)
PHONE.....................704 489-2206
Gary Holcomb, *CEO*
Paul Wilhelm, *VP*

Bill Canning, *VP*
EMP: 17 **EST:** 2020
SALES (est): 4.02MM **Privately Held**
Web: www.gray-mfg.com
SIC: 3465 3728 Body parts, automobile: stamped metal; Aircraft body assemblies and parts

(G-3786)
HEADBANDS OF HOPE LLC
7498 Waterside Peak Dr (28037-7899)
PHONE.....................919 323-4140
Jess Ekstrom, *CEO*
Lauren Athey, *Pr*
EMP: 5 **EST:** 2015
SALES (est): 465.88K **Privately Held**
Web: www.headbandsofhopewholesale.com
SIC: 2339 Scarves, hoods, headbands, etc.: women's

(G-3787)
HIGH CONCEPTS LLC
7806 Creek Park Dr (28037-9111)
PHONE.....................704 377-3467
EMP: 5 **EST:** 2018
SALES (est): 242.45K **Privately Held**
SIC: 2752 Commercial printing, lithographic

(G-3788)
HUBER TECHNOLOGY INC (DH)
1009 Airlie Pkwy (28037)
PHONE.....................704 949-1010
Henk-jan Van Ettekoven, *Pr*
Jennifer Covington, *
▲ **EMP:** 22 **EST:** 1999
SQ FT: 23,338
SALES (est): 45.79MM
SALES (corp-wide): 344.12MM **Privately Held**
Web: www.huber-technology.com
SIC: 5084 3491 Industrial machinery and equipment; Automatic regulating and control valves
HQ: Huber Se
Industriepark Erasbach A 1
Berching BY 92334
84622010

(G-3789)
HYDAC TECHNOLOGY CORP
Hydac International
1051 Airlie Pkwy (28037-7705)
PHONE.....................610 266-0100
Matthias Mueller, *Pr*
EMP: 85
SALES (corp-wide): 675.58MM **Privately Held**
Web: www.hydac-na.com
SIC: 3492 Fluid power valves and hose fittings
HQ: Hydac Technology Corp.
2260 City Line Rd
Bethlehem PA 18017
610 266-0100

(G-3790)
INDUSTRIAL HARD CARBON LLC
771 Crosspoint Dr (28037-7826)
PHONE.....................704 489-1488
George Barr, *Pr*
◆ **EMP:** 24 **EST:** 2010
SALES (est): 5.77MM **Privately Held**
Web: www.industrialhardcarbon.com
SIC: 3674 Thin film circuits

(G-3791)
JD2 COMPANY LLC
3527 Governors Island Dr (28037-8442)
PHONE.....................800 811-6441
Jeff Sisterhen, *Managing Member*

▲ = Import ▼ = Export
◆ = Import/Export

EMP: 4 EST: 2021
SALES (est): 639.64K Privately Held
SIC: 2671 Plastic film, coated or laminated for packaging

(G-3792)
LEONARD AUTOMATICS INC
Also Called: Leonard Frabrication & Design
5894 Balsom Ridge Rd (28037-9233)
P.O. Box 501 (28037-0501)
PHONE.............................704 483-9316
Jeffrey N Frushtick, *Pr*
Gwen B Frushtick, *Sec*
▼ **EMP: 22 EST: 1969**
SQ FT: 30,000
SALES (est): 8.04MM Privately Held
Web: www.leonardautomatics.com
SIC: 3582 Commercial laundry equipment

(G-3793)
MODACAM INCORPORATED
3762 Deer Run (28037-9157)
PHONE.............................704 489-8500
Bud Tschudin, *Pr*
Jonathan Elrod, *Prin*
EMP: 8 EST: 2001
SALES (est): 495.23K Privately Held
Web: www.modacam.com
SIC: 3321 Gray iron castings, nec

(G-3794)
MR TIRE INC
357 N Nc 16 Business Hwy (28037-8012)
PHONE.............................704 483-1500
Tim Mcgee, *Brnch Mgr*
EMP: 10
SALES (corp-wide): 1.28B Publicly Held
Web: locations.mrtire.com
SIC: 5941 5531 5014 5722 Bicycle and bicycle parts; Automotive tires; Tires and tubes; Household appliance stores
HQ: Mr. Tire Inc.
2078 New York Ave Unit 2
Huntington Station NY 11746
631 499-3700

(G-3795)
OLD HICKORY LOG HOMES INC
4279 Burnwood Trl (28037-6212)
P.O. Box 2069 (28037-2069)
PHONE.............................704 489-8989
Paul Norman, *Pr*
EMP: 8 EST: 2002
SALES (est): 300.85K Privately Held
Web: www.oldhickryloghomes.com
SIC: 1521 2452 New construction, single-family houses; Log cabins, prefabricated, wood

(G-3796)
OSTEC INDUSTRIES CORP
4103 Sinclair St (28037-6207)
PHONE.............................704 488-3841
Richard Coste, *Pr*
EMP: 6 EST: 2000
SQ FT: 6,500
SALES (est): 505.8K Privately Held
Web: www.ostecindustries.com
SIC: 3599 Machine shop, jobbing and repair

(G-3797)
PIEDMONT PIPE MFG LLC
7871 Commerce Dr (28037-9101)
PHONE.............................704 489-0911
EMP: 9 EST: 2013
SALES (est): 2.05MM Privately Held
Web: www.piedmontpipe.com
SIC: 3317 Steel pipe and tubes

(G-3798)
PIEDMONT STAIRWORKS LLC
8135 Mallard Rd (28037-8633)
PHONE.............................704 483-3721
Jack Watson, *Brnch Mgr*
EMP: 9
SALES (corp-wide): 2.23MM Privately Held
Web: www.piedmontstairworks.com
SIC: 2431 Millwork
PA: Piedmont Stairworks Llc
2246 Old Steele Creek Rd
Charlotte NC 28208
704 697-0259

(G-3799)
POTTER LOGGING
2037 Cameron Heights Cir (28037-7818)
PHONE.............................704 483-2738
Clifford Potter, *Owner*
EMP: 4 EST: 2000
SALES (est): 247.28K Privately Held
SIC: 2411 Logging camps and contractors

(G-3800)
PRECISION MCH COMPONENTS INC
8075 Pine Lake Rd (28037-8810)
PHONE.............................704 201-8482
Brian Holder, *Pr*
▲ **EMP: 8 EST: 2000**
SQ FT: 6,000
SALES (est): 330.12K Privately Held
Web: www.precision-machine.net
SIC: 3599 Machine shop, jobbing and repair

(G-3801)
R-ANELL CUSTOM HOMES INC
3549 N Nc 16 Business Hwy (28037-8267)
P.O. Box 428 (28037-0428)
PHONE.............................704 483-5511
Dennis L Jones, *Pr*
Rollan L Jones, *
Randy Cosby, *
Steve Purdy, *
EMP: 6 EST: 1972
SQ FT: 88,000
SALES (est): 253.57K Privately Held
Web: www.r-anell.com
SIC: 2452 2451 Prefabricated buildings, wood; Mobile homes, except recreational

(G-3802)
RED OAK SALES COMPANY (PA)
7912 Commerce Dr (28037-9112)
PHONE.............................704 483-8464
Alex Barnette, *Pr*
Lillian Barnette, *Sec*
EMP: 6 EST: 1989
SQ FT: 7,000
SALES (est): 1.1MM Privately Held
Web: www.redoaksales.com
SIC: 2399 8742 Emblems, badges, and insignia; Management consulting services

(G-3803)
S & L SAWMILL INC
3044 N Nc 16 Business Hwy (28037-8262)
P.O. Box 526 (28037-0526)
PHONE.............................704 483-3264
Randy Miller, *Owner*
Ralph D Sherrill, *Owner*
EMP: 13 EST: 1973
SQ FT: 3,000
SALES (est): 1.18MM Privately Held
SIC: 2421 Lumber: rough, sawed, or planed

(G-3804)
SEYMOUR ADVANCED TECH LLC
3593 Denver Dr Unit 964 (28037-7269)
PHONE.............................704 709-9070
Robert Seymour Junior, *Managing Member*
EMP: 5 EST: 2019
SALES (est): 3.34MM Privately Held
Web: www.seymouradvancedtechnologies.com
SIC: 3599 Industrial machinery, nec

(G-3805)
SIGN HERE OF LAKE NORMAN INC
Also Called: Sign Here
422 N Nc 16 Business Hwy (28037-8244)
P.O. Box 923 (28037-0923)
PHONE.............................704 483-6454
Jerry Allen Earnest, *Pr*
Jerry Earnest, *Pr*
June Earnest, *Sec*
EMP: 5 EST: 1994
SALES (est): 452.3K Privately Held
SIC: 3993 Electric signs

(G-3806)
SOUTHSTERN PRCESS EQP CNTRLS I
Also Called: Spec
7558 Townsend Dr (28037-8904)
P.O. Box 746 (28037-0746)
PHONE.............................704 483-1141
Marvin Mc Donald, *Pr*
Dickson Dorrier, *VP*
EMP: 12 EST: 1989
SQ FT: 12,000
SALES (est): 3.2MM Privately Held
Web: www.inkdispensingsystems.com
SIC: 3823 Industrial process measurement equipment

(G-3807)
STEELE RUBBER PRODUCTS INC
6180 Highway 150 E (28037-9650)
PHONE.............................704 483-9343
Joanna Shere, *Pr*
Walter D Vaughan Junior, *VP*
Eric J Saltrick, *
Debra Lail, *
◆ **EMP: 54 EST: 1956**
SQ FT: 36,100
SALES (est): 9.11MM Privately Held
Web: www.steelerubber.com
SIC: 3052 Automobile hose, rubber

(G-3808)
SUSPENSIONS LLC
Also Called: Just Suspension
4723 Mountain Creek Ave (28037-6790)
PHONE.............................704 809-1269
EMP: 16
SQ FT: 12,000
SALES (est): 3.5MM Privately Held
SIC: 3714 Ball joints, motor vehicle

(G-3809)
TABUR SERVICES
7845 Commerce Dr (28037-9109)
PHONE.............................704 483-1650
EMP: 5
SALES (est): 381.24K Privately Held
Web: www.taburservices.com
SIC: 3663 Radio and t.v. communications equipment

(G-3810)
TABUR SERVICES LLC
7845 Commerce Dr Unit D (28037-9110)
P.O. Box 1497 (28037-1497)
PHONE.............................704 483-1650
Theodore Burk, *Managing Member*
EMP: 4 EST: 2005
SQ FT: 1,800
SALES (est): 897.29K Privately Held
Web: www.taburservices.com

SIC: 3661 Telephone and telegraph apparatus

(G-3811)
TEXTILE SALES INTL INC
Also Called: Tsi
8172 Malibu Pointe Ln (28037-8580)
P.O. Box 5261 (28374)
PHONE.............................704 483-7966
Todd Phillips, *Prin*
R Todd Phillips, *VP S/s*
EMP: 5 EST: 1984
SQ FT: 20,000
SALES (est): 471.88K Privately Held
SIC: 3552 Bleaching machinery, textile

(G-3812)
THANET INC
3501 Denver Dr (28037-7217)
PHONE.............................704 483-4175
Maxwell C Crawford, *Pr*
Janice G Crawford, *
▼ **EMP: 9 EST: 1996**
SQ FT: 24,000
SALES (est): 2.11MM Privately Held
Web: www.crawfordcomposites.com
SIC: 3089 3624 2823 Automotive parts, plastic; Carbon and graphite products; Cellulosic manmade fibers

(G-3813)
TRI-STAR PLASTICS CORP
1387 N Nc 16 Business Hwy (28037-8637)
PHONE.............................704 598-2800
Dan Gettis, *Brnch Mgr*
EMP: 50
SALES (corp-wide): 21.54MM Privately Held
Web: www.tstar.com
SIC: 5162 3089 Plastics products, nec; Air mattresses, plastics
PA: Tri-Star Plastics Corp
906 Boston Tpke
Shrewsbury MA 01545
508 845-1111

(G-3814)
TRIPLE C COMPANIES LLC
7911 Commerce Dr (28037-9112)
PHONE.............................704 966-1999
Rachel Drake, *Managing Member*
EMP: 30 EST: 2020
SALES (est): 700K Privately Held
SIC: 2448 Wood pallets and skids

(G-3815)
UNIVERSAL RUBBER PRODUCTS INC
7780 Forest Oak Dr (28037-8830)
P.O. Box 546 (28037-0546)
PHONE.............................704 483-1249
Robert Davis, *Pr*
Emily Davis, *VP*
▲ **EMP: 7 EST: 1986**
SQ FT: 6,000
SALES (est): 702.36K Privately Held
Web: www.universalrubberproducts.com
SIC: 3053 Gaskets, all materials

(G-3816)
WHISPERING WILLOW SOAP CO LLC
Also Called: Whispering Willow
5851 Balsom Ridge Rd Ste B (28037-9220)
PHONE.............................828 455-0322
EMP: 4 EST: 2010
SALES (est): 455.39K Privately Held
Web: www.whisperingwillow.com
SIC: 2841 Soap and other detergents

(G-3817)
WIREWAY/HUSKY CORP (PA)
Also Called: Husky Rack and Wire
6146 Denver Industrial Park Rd (28037)
P.O. Box 645 (28037)
PHONE....................704 483-1135
Ron Young, *Pr*
Reginald Young, *
Greg Young, *
Susan Meyers, *
▼ **EMP:** 155 **EST:** 1980
SQ FT: 264,400
SALES (est): 23.8MM
SALES (corp-wide): 23.8MM **Privately Held**
Web: www.huskyrackandwire.com
SIC: 3496 2542 3315 Grilles and grillework, woven wire; Pallet racks: except wood; Welded steel wire fabric

(G-3818)
XELERA INC
137 Cross Center Rd (28037-5009)
PHONE....................540 915-6181
EMP: 5
SALES (est): 853.99K **Privately Held**
Web: www.xelera.us
SIC: 2899 Chemical preparations, nec

Dillsboro
Jackson County

(G-3819)
MOUNTAIN BEAR & CO INC
28 Church St (28725)
P.O. Box 391 (28725-0391)
PHONE....................828 631-0156
Tonya Williams, *Pr*
Robert Williams, *VP*
Tammy Sessoms, *Sec*
EMP: 8 **EST:** 1998
SQ FT: 1,000
SALES (est): 182K **Privately Held**
Web: www.dillsborochocolate.com
SIC: 2066 Chocolate and cocoa products

Dobson
Surry County

(G-3820)
CAROLINA CARPORTS INC (PA)
187 Cardinal Ridge Ln (27017-8652)
P.O. Box 1263 (27017-1263)
PHONE....................336 367-6400
Adela Herrera, *Pr*
◆ **EMP:** 77 **EST:** 1997
SQ FT: 12,900
SALES (est): 24.51MM
SALES (corp-wide): 24.51MM **Privately Held**
Web: www.carolinacarportsinc.com
SIC: 3448 Carports, prefabricated metal

(G-3821)
HODGES PRECISION MACHINE
116 Tobe Hudson Rd (27017-7636)
PHONE....................336 366-3024
David Hodges, *Owner*
EMP: 4 **EST:** 1989
SQ FT: 4,000
SALES (est): 505K **Privately Held**
SIC: 3599 Machine shop, jobbing and repair

(G-3822)
HUTTON VINEYARDS LLC
103 Buck Fork Rd (27017-7806)
PHONE....................336 374-2321
Malcolm Hutton, *Owner*
EMP: 6 **EST:** 2005
SALES (est): 84.13K **Privately Held**
Web: www.huttonwinery.com
SIC: 2084 Wines

(G-3823)
MILLENNIUM BUILDINGS INC
317 W Atkins St (27017-8711)
PHONE....................866 216-8499
EMP: 4 **EST:** 2020
SALES (est): 128.5K **Privately Held**
Web: www.millenniumbuildings.com
SIC: 3448 Prefabricated metal buildings and components

(G-3824)
RUGGED METAL DESIGNS INC
1004 Red Hill Creek Rd (27017-7735)
PHONE....................336 352-5150
Gary Wilmoth, *CEO*
Tony Stanley, *Pr*
Peggy Wilmoth, *Sec*
EMP: 9 **EST:** 2001
SQ FT: 30,000
SALES (est): 912.55K **Privately Held**
SIC: 3441 Fabricated structural metal

(G-3825)
SHELTON VINEYARDS INC
286 Cabernet Ln (27017-6322)
PHONE....................336 366-4818
Charles Shelton, *Pr*
R Edwin Shelton, *
EMP: 40 **EST:** 1998
SALES (est): 3.91MM **Privately Held**
Web: www.sheltonvineyards.com
SIC: 2084 0172 Wines; Grapes

(G-3826)
USA METAL STRUCTURE LLP
507 W Kapp St (27017-8829)
PHONE....................336 717-2884
Juan Lopez Cruz, *Pt*
Orlando Perez, *Pt*
EMP: 8 **EST:** 2021
SALES (est): 390.94K **Privately Held**
Web: www.usametalstructures.com
SIC: 3441 7371 Fabricated structural metal; Computer software development

(G-3827)
WAYNE FARMS LLC
Also Called: Wayne Farms
802 E Atkins St (27017-8707)
P.O. Box 383 (27017-0383)
PHONE....................336 386-8151
Paul Norton, *Mgr*
EMP: 481
SALES (corp-wide): 405K **Privately Held**
Web: www.waynesandersonfarms.com
SIC: 2015 Poultry slaughtering and processing
HQ: Wayne Farms Llc
4110 Continental Dr
Oakwood GA 30566

Dover
Craven County

(G-3828)
CAROLINA STONE LLC
10600 Nc Highway 55 W (28526-8932)
P.O. Box 186 (28586-0186)
PHONE....................252 208-1633
Andy Purifoy, *Genl Pt*
Allen Russell, *Genl Pt*
EMP: 10 **EST:** 2001
SALES (est): 1.01MM **Privately Held**
Web: www.captkerry.com
SIC: 1442 Construction sand and gravel

(G-3829)
TRACTOR COUNTRY INC
5763 Hwy 70 (28526-8871)
PHONE....................252 523-3007
Jonathan Care, *Prin*
EMP: 4 **EST:** 2016
SALES (est): 209.58K **Privately Held**
Web: www.tractorcountry.net
SIC: 5999 3523 7699 Farm equipment and supplies; Tractors, farm; Tractor repair

Drexel
Burke County

(G-3830)
POWELL WELDING INC
3156 Hwy 70 (28619)
P.O. Box 2655 (28619-2655)
PHONE....................828 433-0831
Donnie Powell, *Pr*
Rodney Powell, *Sec*
Scott Powell, *Treas*
EMP: 4 **EST:** 1958
SQ FT: 3,600
SALES (est): 231.37K **Privately Held**
SIC: 7692 Welding repair

Dublin
Bladen County

(G-3831)
DUBLIN WOODWORK SHOP
N S Hwy 87 E (28332)
P.O. Box 52 (28332-0052)
PHONE....................910 862-2289
David Hursey, *Owner*
EMP: 4 **EST:** 1945
SQ FT: 1,800
SALES (est): 211.9K **Privately Held**
SIC: 2434 Wood kitchen cabinets

(G-3832)
PEANUT PROCESSORS INC (PA)
Also Called: Peanut
7329 Albert St (28332-8901)
P.O. Box 160 (28332-0160)
PHONE....................910 862-2136
Houston N Brisson Junior, *Ch Bd*
David S Cox, *
EMP: 10 **EST:** 1961
SQ FT: 50,000
SALES (est): 6.48MM
SALES (corp-wide): 6.48MM **Privately Held**
SIC: 2099 Peanut butter

(G-3833)
PEANUT PROCESSORS SHERMAN INC
7329 Albert St (28332-8901)
P.O. Box 160 (28332-0160)
PHONE....................910 862-2136
Nile Brisson, *Pr*
David Cox, *VP*
EMP: 5 **EST:** 1992
SQ FT: 1,000
SALES (est): 128.66K **Privately Held**
SIC: 2099 Peanut butter

Dudley
Wayne County

(G-3834)
BEST MACHINE & FABRICATION INC
117 Sleepy Creek Rd (28333-6419)
P.O. Box 711 (28333-0711)
PHONE....................919 731-7101
Ray Best, *Pr*
Phyliss Lewis, *Off Mgr*
EMP: 5
SALES (est): 2.56MM **Privately Held**
SIC: 3089 Netting, plastics

(G-3835)
CASE FARMS LLC
330 Pecan Rd (28333-5369)
PHONE....................919 735-5010
EMP: 78
Web: www.casefarms.com
SIC: 2015 8731 Poultry slaughtering and processing; Commercial physical research
PA: Case Farms, L.L.C.
385 Pilch Rd
Troutman NC 28166

(G-3836)
GEORGIA-PACIFIC LLC
Also Called: Georgia-Pacific
139 Brewington Dr (28333-8197)
PHONE....................919 580-1078
Charles Mclendon, *Mgr*
EMP: 62
SALES (corp-wide): 64.44B **Privately Held**
Web: www.gp.com
SIC: 2493 2436 2435 Particleboard, plastic laminated; Softwood veneer and plywood; Hardwood veneer and plywood
HQ: Georgia-Pacific Llc
133 Peachtree St Ne
Atlanta GA 30303
404 652-4000

(G-3837)
GEORGIA-PACIFIC LLC
Also Called: Georgia-Pacific
2457b Old Mt Olive Hwy (28333-8131)
PHONE....................919 736-2722
William Collins, *Mgr*
EMP: 98
SALES (corp-wide): 64.44B **Privately Held**
Web: www.gp.com
SIC: 2621 Paper mills
HQ: Georgia-Pacific Llc
133 Peachtree St Ne
Atlanta GA 30303
404 652-4000

(G-3838)
NATIONAL SALVAGE & SVC CORP
430 Old Mt Olive Hwy (28333-5170)
PHONE....................919 739-5633
Hugh Bray, *Brnch Mgr*
EMP: 56
SALES (corp-wide): 54.54MM **Privately Held**
Web: www.nsscorp.com
SIC: 2499 Applicators, wood
PA: National Salvage & Service Corporation
6755 S Old State Road 37
Bloomington IN 47401
812 339-9000

▲ = Import ▼ = Export
◆ = Import/Export

Dunn
Harnett County

(G-3839)
48FORTY SOLUTIONS LLC
2 Dinan Rd (28334-6753)
PHONE..............................910 891-1534
EMP: 661
SALES (corp-wide): 462.5MM **Privately Held**
Web: www.48forty.com
SIC: 2448 Pallets, wood
PA: 48forty Solutions, Llc
11740 Katy Fwy
Houston TX 77079
678 722-3984

(G-3840)
A CLEANER TOMORROW DRY CLG LLC (PA)
Also Called: A Cleaner Tomorrow and Laundry
102 S Wilson Ave (28334-3200)
PHONE..............................919 639-6396
EMP: 8 EST: 2011
SALES (est): 1.63MM
SALES (corp-wide): 1.63MM **Privately Held**
Web: www.simplydivinenc.com
SIC: 3999 2842 7212 7216 Hosiery kits, sewing and mending; Laundry cleaning preparations; Retail agent, laundry and drycleaning; Drycleaning plants, except rugs

(G-3841)
ADA MARKETING INC
Also Called: Adams Handmade Soap
601 N Ashe Ave (28334-3611)
PHONE..............................910 221-2189
Anthony Adams, *Pr*
Maranatha Adams, *
Nathaniel Hinds, *
Kelby Mcclelland, *VP*
EMP: 40 EST: 2005
SALES (est): 3.57MM **Privately Held**
Web: www.naturalsoapwholesale.com
SIC: 2841 5169 Soap and other detergents; Detergents and soaps, except specialty cleaning

(G-3842)
ALLIED MOBILE SYSTEMS LLC
17665 Us 421 S (28334-6485)
PHONE..............................888 503-1501
James Godwin Junior, *Pr*
EMP: 5 EST: 2019
SALES (est): 2.74MM **Privately Held**
Web: www.alliedmobilesystems.com
SIC: 3593 Fluid power actuators, hydraulic or pneumatic

(G-3843)
ALPHIN BROTHERS INC
2302 Us 301 S (28334-6165)
P.O. Box 1310 (28335-1310)
PHONE..............................910 892-8751
Jesse C Alphin Junior, *Pr*
▲ EMP: 26 EST: 1947
SQ FT: 80,000
SALES (est): 3.11MM **Privately Held**
Web: www.alphinbrothers.com
SIC: 2037 2092 Frozen fruits and vegetables; Seafoods, frozen: prepared

(G-3844)
ARC3 GASES INC (PA)
1600 Us 301 S (28334-6791)
P.O. Box 1708 (28335-1708)
PHONE..............................910 892-4016
Emmett Aldredge Iii, *Pr*

Emmett Aldredge Junior, *Ch*
Christopher Aldredge, *
EMP: 24 EST: 2014
SQ FT: 9,600
SALES (est): 204.15MM
SALES (corp-wide): 204.15MM **Privately Held**
Web: www.arc3gases.com
SIC: 2813 5084 5169 7359 Industrial gases; Industrial machinery and equipment; Chemicals and allied products, nec; Equipment rental and leasing, nec

(G-3845)
ARGOS USA LLC
Also Called: Ready Mixed Concrete Co
401 N Fayetteville Ave (28334-3913)
P.O. Box 1067 (28335-1067)
PHONE..............................910 892-3188
Bob Batts, *Mgr*
EMP: 9
Web: www.argos-us.com
SIC: 3273 Ready-mixed concrete
HQ: Argos Usa Llc
3015 Windward Plz Ste 300
Alpharetta GA 30005
678 368-4300

(G-3846)
BEMCO SLEEP PRODUCTS INC
601 N Ashe Ave (28334-3611)
P.O. Box 697 (28335-0697)
PHONE..............................910 892-3107
Gene T Jernigan, *Pr*
Charlla M Jernigan, *
EMP: 25 EST: 1935
SQ FT: 36,000
SALES (est): 699.27K **Privately Held**
Web: www.bemco.com
SIC: 2515 Mattresses, containing felt, foam rubber, urethane, etc.

(G-3847)
CAROLINA FIRE PROTECTION INC
4055 Hodges Chapel Rd (28334-8655)
P.O. Box 250 (28335-0250)
PHONE..............................910 892-1700
Jeffrey R Dunn, *Pr*
Terry L Parrish, *
EMP: 36 EST: 2002
SQ FT: 5,700
SALES (est): 11.25MM **Privately Held**
Web: www.carolinafireprotection.com
SIC: 3569 1711 Sprinkler systems, fire: automatic; Plumbing, heating, air-conditioning

(G-3848)
CAROLINA PRECAST CONCRETE
452 Webb Rd (28334-8742)
PHONE..............................910 230-0028
Robert Hill, *Prin*
EMP: 8 EST: 2007
SALES (est): 418.99K **Privately Held**
Web: www.concretepandp.com
SIC: 3272 Concrete products, precast, nec

(G-3849)
CARR PRECAST CONCRETE INC
7519 Plain View Hwy (28334-6883)
P.O. Box 1283 (28335-1283)
PHONE..............................910 892-1151
Robert B Carr, *Pr*
Loray F Carr, *Sec*
EMP: 13 EST: 1976
SQ FT: 15,000
SALES (est): 2.47MM **Privately Held**
Web: www.carrprecast.com
SIC: 3272 Concrete products, precast, nec

(G-3850)
CCO HOLDINGS LLC
102 W Divine St (28334-5202)
PHONE..............................910 292-4083
EMP: 112
SALES (corp-wide): 55.09MM **Publicly Held**
SIC: 4841 3663 3651 Cable television services; Radio and t.v. communications equipment; Household audio and video equipment
HQ: Cco Holdings, Llc
400 Atlantic St
Stamford CT 06901
203 905-7801

(G-3851)
CONCRETE PIPE & PRECAST LLC
452 Webb Rd (28334-8742)
PHONE..............................910 892-6411
Howard Tindal, *Brnch Mgr*
EMP: 19
SALES (corp-wide): 23.07MM **Privately Held**
Web: www.concretepandp.com
SIC: 3272 Precast terrazzo or concrete products
PA: Concrete Pipe & Precast, Llc
11352 Virginia Precast Rd
Ashland VA 23005
804 798-6068

(G-3852)
CREATIVE CAPS INC
214 E Broad St (28334-4921)
P.O. Box 835 (27504-0835)
PHONE..............................919 701-1175
Eva Massengill, *Pr*
Brian Massengill, *VP*
EMP: 4 EST: 1990
SQ FT: 2,400
SALES (est): 512.57K **Privately Held**
Web: www.creativecaps.net
SIC: 2395 Embroidery products, except Schiffli machine

(G-3853)
DISCOUNT PALLET SERVICES LLC
319 Ira B Tart Rd (28334-6093)
PHONE..............................910 892-3760
Sherwood Glenn Barefoot, *Prin*
EMP: 4 EST: 2011
SALES (est): 481.86K **Privately Held**
Web: www.discountpalletservices.com
SIC: 5251 3537 Hardware stores; Platforms, stands, tables, pallets, and similar equipment

(G-3854)
DUNBAR FOODS CORPORATION
1000 S Fayetteville Ave (28334-6213)
P.O. Box 519 (28335-0519)
PHONE..............................910 892-3175
Stanley K Dunbar, *Pr*
Christina M Dunbar, *
EMP: 56 EST: 1984
SALES (est): 4.14MM
SALES (corp-wide): 63.59MM **Privately Held**
SIC: 2033 Vegetables: packaged in cans, jars, etc.
PA: Moody Dunbar, Inc.
2000 Waters Edge Dr # 21
Johnson City TN 37604
423 952-0100

(G-3855)
ENERGY CONVERSION SYSTE
10 Carlie Cs Dr (28334-3649)
PHONE..............................910 892-8081
N Farthing, *Admn*

EMP: 7 EST: 2014
SALES (est): 2.54MM **Privately Held**
Web: www.ecs-global.net
SIC: 3624 Carbon and graphite products

(G-3856)
ENVIROSERVE CHEMICALS INC
603 S Wilson Ave (28334-5832)
PHONE..............................910 892-1791
Gary Ballard, *Pr*
EMP: 13 EST: 1996
SQ FT: 55,000
SALES (est): 7.48MM **Privately Held**
Web: www.enviroservechemicals.com
SIC: 2899 Chemical preparations, nec

(G-3857)
FORTERRA PIPE & PRECAST LLC
452 Webb Rd (28334-8742)
PHONE..............................910 892-6411
Ray Rosser, *Brnch Mgr*
EMP: 7
Web: www.concretepandp.com
SIC: 3272 Precast terrazzo or concrete products
HQ: Forterra Pipe & Precast, Llc
511 E John Crptr Fwy Ste
Irving TX 75062
469 458-7973

(G-3858)
GODWIN MANUFACTURING CO INC (PA)
17666 Us 421 S (28334-6484)
P.O. Box 1147 (28335-1147)
PHONE..............................910 897-4995
James P Godwin Senior, *Pr*
James P Godwin Junior, *VP*
Pam Faircloth, *
Mark Fentress, *
◆ EMP: 179 EST: 1966
SQ FT: 25,000
SALES (est): 23.81MM
SALES (corp-wide): 23.81MM **Privately Held**
Web: www.godwinmfg.com
SIC: 3713 3714 Truck bodies (motor vehicles); Dump truck lifting mechanism

(G-3859)
GRAY METAL SOUTH INC (PA)
600 N Powell Ave (28334-4543)
P.O. Box 1126 (28335-1126)
PHONE..............................910 892-2119
Marguerite Gray, *Pr*
Joseph Gray, *
EMP: 100 EST: 1908
SQ FT: 135,000
SALES (est): 19.95MM **Privately Held**
Web: www.graymetalsouth.com
SIC: 3444 Sheet metal specialties, not stamped

(G-3860)
H & H PRODUCTS INCORPORATED (PA)
275 Carlie Cs Dr (28334-3651)
P.O. Box 366 (28335-0366)
PHONE..............................910 891-4276
Jerry Mel Hartman, *Pr*
Bob Holder, *VP*
EMP: 6 EST: 1982
SQ FT: 17,000
SALES (est): 9.37MM **Privately Held**
Web: www.hhprodinc.com
SIC: 2842 Specialty cleaning

(G-3861)
HERITAGE CONCRETE SERVICE CORP

1300 N Mckay Ave (28334-3128)
PHONE.....................910 892-4445
Mike Haire, *Mgr*
EMP: 8
SALES (corp-wide): 5.73MM **Privately Held**
Web: www.heritageconcreteservice.com
SIC: 3273 Ready-mixed concrete
PA: Heritage Concrete Service Corporation
    140 Deep River Rd
    Sanford NC 27330
    919 775-5014

(G-3862)
MORGAN ADVANCED MTLS TECH INC
MORGAN ADVANCED MATERIALS AND TECHNOLOGY, INC.
504 N Ashe Ave (28334-3610)
PHONE.....................910 892-9677
John Stang, *Brnch Mgr*
EMP: 141
SALES (corp-wide): 1.39B **Privately Held**
Web: www.morganadvancedmaterials.com
SIC: 3624 Carbon and graphite products
HQ: Pure Carbon Company, Inc.
    441 Hall Avenue
    Saint Marys PA 15857

(G-3863)
O-TASTE-N-C LLC
19 Gainey Rd (28334)
PHONE.....................919 696-9547
EMP: 5 EST: 2016
SALES (est): 56.51K **Privately Held**
SIC: 2099 Food preparations, nec

(G-3864)
PALLET WORLD
670 John Lee Rd (28334-8147)
PHONE.....................919 800-1113
Antwon Small, *Pr*
Shannon Lockamy, *CEO*
EMP: 5 EST: 2015
SALES (est): 83.44K **Privately Held**
SIC: 2448 Pallets, wood and wood with metal

(G-3865)
RAVEN ROCK MANUFACTURING INC
803 E Broad St (28334-5103)
PHONE.....................910 308-8430
Veronica Livinggood, *Pr*
EMP: 4 EST: 2006
SALES (est): 378.95K **Privately Held**
Web: www.ravenrockmfg.com
SIC: 2591 Blinds vertical

(G-3866)
RECORD PUBLISHING COMPANY
Also Called: Daily Record The
99 W Broad St (28334-6031)
P.O. Box 1448 (28335-1448)
PHONE.....................910 230-1948
Bart S Adams, *Pr*
Hoover Adams, *Emeritus**
Brenton D Adams, *
Mellicent Adams, *
EMP: 11 EST: 1950
SQ FT: 10,000
SALES (est): 750.19K **Privately Held**
Web: www.mydailyrecord.com
SIC: 2711 Newspapers, publishing and printing

(G-3867)
SALAZAR CUSTOM FRAMING LLC
111 Raynor Sands Dr (28334-8019)
PHONE.....................919 349-0830
Moises Salazar, *Prin*
EMP: 6 EST: 2016

SALES (est): 1.19MM **Privately Held**
SIC: 2499 Picture frame molding, finished

(G-3868)
SIGN & AWNING SYSTEMS INC
2785 Us 301 N (28334-8383)
PHONE.....................919 892-5900
Jason Honeycutt, *CEO*
Michael R Godwin, *
Mickey Hodges, *
EMP: 9 EST: 1978
SQ FT: 40,000
SALES (est): 987.6K **Privately Held**
Web: www.signandawning.com
SIC: 2394 3993 1799 Canvas awnings and canopies; Electric signs; Awning installation

(G-3869)
TRANS EAST INC
Also Called: Southeastern Transformer Co
405 E Edgerton St (28334-4223)
P.O. Box 127 (28335-0127)
PHONE.....................910 892-1081
L Avery Corning Iv, *Pr*
EMP: 51 EST: 2001
SQ FT: 5,500
SALES (est): 11MM **Privately Held**
Web: www.setransformer.com
SIC: 7629 3612 Electrical equipment repair, high voltage; Power transformers, electric

(G-3870)
TWYFORD PRINTING COMPANY INC
200 E Canary St (28334-5812)
P.O. Box 728 (28335-0728)
PHONE.....................910 892-3271
William V Stephens, *Pr*
Virginia Stephens, *VP*
EMP: 6 EST: 1945
SQ FT: 9,800
SALES (est): 235.58K **Privately Held**
Web: www.twyfordprinting.com
SIC: 2752 2759 Offset printing; Letterpress printing

(G-3871)
WARREN OIL COMPANY LLC (PA)
2340 Us 301 N (28334-8307)
P.O. Box 1507 (28335-1507)
PHONE.....................910 892-6456
William Irvin Warren, *Pr*
Larry Sanderson, *
▼ EMP: 86 EST: 1975
SQ FT: 125,000
SALES (est): 282.38MM
SALES (corp-wide): 282.38MM **Privately Held**
Web: www.warrenoil.com
SIC: 5171 3826 2911 5172 Petroleum bulk stations and terminals; Analytical instruments; Petroleum refining; Lubricating oils and greases

---

Durham
Durham County

(G-3872)
410 MEDICAL INC
68 Tw Alexander Dr (27709-0151)
P.O. Box 110085 (27709-5085)
PHONE.....................919 241-7900
Kyle Chenet, *CEO*
Mark Piehl, *CMO*
Galen Robertson, *COO*
Jamie Baker, *Contrlr*
EMP: 14 EST: 2013
SQ FT: 800
SALES (est): 100K **Privately Held**
Web: www.410medical.com

SIC: 3842 Surgical appliances and supplies

(G-3873)
510NANO INC
5441 Lumley Rd Ste 101 (27703-7726)
P.O. Box 110401 (27709-5401)
PHONE.....................919 521-5982
Reginald Parker, *CEO*
Craig Brubaker, *Dir*
Robin Parker, *Sec*
EMP: 10 EST: 2011
SALES (est): 1.58MM **Privately Held**
Web: www.510nano.com
SIC: 3674 5074 Solar cells; Heating equipment and panels, solar

(G-3874)
A & M PAPER AND PRINTING
4122 Bennett Memorial Rd Ste 108 (27705-1207)
PHONE.....................919 813-7852
EMP: 4 EST: 2017
SALES (est): 87.41K **Privately Held**
Web: ampaperprinting.espwebsite.com
SIC: 2752 Offset printing

(G-3875)
A BETTER IMAGE PRINTING INC
4310 Garrett Rd (27707-3432)
PHONE.....................919 967-0319
Michael Celeste, *Managing Member*
Diana Minta, *Pr*
Steve Minta, *VP*
EMP: 12 EST: 1985
SQ FT: 1,600
SALES (est): 3.68MM **Privately Held**
Web: www.abetterimageprinting.com
SIC: 2752 Offset printing

(G-3876)
A&B INTEGRATORS LLC
Also Called: Security 101 Raleigh
2800 Meridian Pkwy (27713-5252)
PHONE.....................919 371-0750
EMP: 14 EST: 2014
SALES (est): 5.86MM **Privately Held**
SIC: 5065 3699 5072 7382 Security control equipment and systems; Security control equipment and systems; Security devices, locks; Burglar alarm maintenance and monitoring

(G-3877)
ACADEMY ASSOCIATION INC
Also Called: Eli Research It Journals
2222 Sedwick Rd Ste 101 (27713-2658)
PHONE.....................919 544-0835
Leslie Norins, *Brnch Mgr*
EMP: 17
SALES (corp-wide): 2.66MM **Privately Held**
SIC: 8243 8742 2721 Software training, computer; Management consulting services ; Periodicals
PA: Academy Association, Inc.
    2222 Sedwick Rd
    Durham NC 27713
    919 544-0835

(G-3878)
ACERAGEN INC
15 Tw Alexander Dr 418 (27709-0152)
PHONE.....................919 271-1032
EMP: 10 EST: 2021
SALES (est): 27.98K **Publicly Held**
Web: www.aceragen.com
SIC: 2834 Pharmaceutical preparations
PA: Idera Pharmaceuticals, Inc.
    505 Eagleview Blvd # 212
    Exton PA 19341

(G-3879)
ACHELIOS THERAPEUTICS LLC
4364 S Alston Ave Ste 300 (27713-2565)
P.O. Box 13965 (27709-3965)
PHONE.....................919 354-6233
EMP: 5 EST: 2012
SALES (est): 249.26K **Privately Held**
Web: www.achelios.com
SIC: 2834 Pharmaceutical preparations

(G-3880)
AD SPICE MARKETING LLC
4310 Garrett Rd (27707-3432)
PHONE.....................919 286-7110
EMP: 5 EST: 2012
SQ FT: 2,000
SALES (est): 151.7K **Privately Held**
Web: www.adspicepromo.com
SIC: 7389 2752 Advertising, promotional, and trade show services; Promotional printing, lithographic

(G-3881)
ADVANCED DIGITAL SYSTEMS INC
Also Called: Mi-
4601 Creekstone Dr Ste 180 (27703-8496)
P.O. Box 991 (24063-0991)
PHONE.....................919 485-4819
Gregory J Clary, *Pr*
James Clary, *Ch*
Chris Dipierro, *Ofcr*
David Nakamura, *Ofcr*
Will Shook, *Ofcr*
EMP: 11 EST: 1999
SQ FT: 5,000
SALES (est): 2.28MM **Privately Held**
Web: www.ideagen.com
SIC: 7371 7372 Computer software development; Prepackaged software

(G-3882)
AERAMI THERAPEUTICS INC (PA)
600 Park Offices Dr (27709-1009)
PHONE.....................650 773-5926
John Patton, *CEO*
J Tyler Martin, *Pr*
Greg Santi, *CFO*
Barry Deutsch, *CFO*
Lisa Yanez, *COO*
EMP: 12 EST: 2009
SALES (est): 4.74MM **Privately Held**
Web: www.aerami.com
SIC: 2834 Pharmaceutical preparations

(G-3883)
AERIE PHARMACEUTICALS INC (HQ)
4301 Emperor Blvd Ste 400 (27703-7615)
PHONE.....................919 237-5300
Raj Kannan, *CEO*
Benjamin F Mcgraw Iii, *Interim Executive Chairman of the Board*
Peter Lang, *CFO*
Casey C Kopczynski, *CSO*
EMP: 8 EST: 2005
SQ FT: 61,000
SALES (est): 194.13MM **Privately Held**
Web: www.alcon.com
SIC: 2834 Pharmaceutical preparations
PA: Alcon Ag
    0
    Fribourg FR 1700

(G-3884)
AIRGAS USA LLC
Also Called: Airgas
2810 S Miami Blvd (27703-9247)
PHONE.....................919 544-1056
James Beasley, *Mgr*
EMP: 5
SALES (corp-wide): 114.13MM **Privately Held**

▲ = Import ▼ = Export
◆ = Import/Export

Web: www.airgas.com
SIC: 2813 5169 5999 Dry ice, carbon dioxide
(solid); Dry ice; Ice
HQ: Airgas Usa, Llc
259 N Rdnor Chster Rd Ste
Radnor PA 19087
216 642-6600

(G-3885)
AIRGAS USA LLC
630 United Dr (27713-1407)
PHONE..............................919 544-3773
Charlie Winston, *Brnch Mgr*
EMP: 5
SALES (corp-wide): 114.13MM **Privately
Held**
Web: www.airgas.com
SIC: 5169 5084 5085 2813 Industrial gases;
Welding machinery and equipment;
Welding supplies; Industrial gases
HQ: Airgas Usa, Llc
259 N Rdnor Chster Rd Ste
Radnor PA 19087
216 642-6600

(G-3886)
AISIN NORTH CAROLINA CORP (DH)
4112 Old Oxford Rd (27712-9428)
P.O. Box 15970 (27712)
PHONE..............................919 479-6400
Shuji Oda, *CEO*
Shigeo Tsuzuki, *
Mitsuru Fukumoto, *
Takashi Kurauchi, *
◆ EMP: 1800 EST: 1998
SQ FT: 316,000
SALES (est): 392.68MM **Privately Held**
Web: www.aisinnc.com
SIC: 3714 Transmissions, motor vehicle
HQ: Aisin Holdings Of America, Inc.
1665 E 4th St
Seymour IN 47274
812 524-8144

(G-3887)
ALCAMI CAROLINAS CORPORATION
Also Called: Alcami
4620 Creekstone Dr Ste 200 (27703-0108)
PHONE..............................919 957-5500
Stephan Kutzer, *Mgr*
EMP: 25
SALES (corp-wide): 418.48MM **Privately
Held**
Web: www.alcami.com
SIC: 2834 Pharmaceutical preparations
HQ: Alcami Carolinas Corporation
2320 Scientific Park Dr
Wilmington NC 28405

(G-3888)
ALDAGEN INC
2810 Meridian Pkwy Ste 148 (27713-2234)
PHONE..............................919 484-2571
Lyle A Hohnke, *CEO*
EMP: 10 EST: 2000
SQ FT: 4,000
SALES (est): 405.68K
SALES (corp-wide): 608.52K **Publicly
Held**
SIC: 3841 Surgical instruments and
apparatus
PA: Nuo Therapeutics, Inc.
8285 El Rio, Suite 150
Houston TX 77054
346 396-4770

(G-3889)
ALPHAMED COMPANY INC (PA)
Also Called: Alphamed Press
6100 Guess Rd (27712-9278)
P.O. Box 12723 (27709-2723)

PHONE..............................919 680-0011
Ann Murphy, *Pr*
EMP: 7 EST: 1996
SALES (est): 1.31MM **Privately Held**
Web: www.alphamedpress.com
SIC: 2741 Miscellaneous publishing

(G-3890)
**AMERICAN INST CRTIF PUB
ACCNTN (PA)**
Also Called: American Institute of Cpas
220 Leigh Farm Rd (27707-8110)
P.O. Box 52383 (27717-2383)
PHONE..............................919 402-0682
Barry C Melancon, *CPA*
Eric L Hansen, *
Tim Kristen, *
Gregory J Anton C.p.a., *Vice Chairman*
Richard Miller, *
▲ EMP: 450 EST: 1887
SQ FT: 105,000
SALES (est): 16.26MM
SALES (corp-wide): 16.26MM **Privately
Held**
Web: www.aicpa.org
SIC: 8299 8621 2721 Educational service,
nondegree granting: continuing educ.;
Professional organizations; Periodicals,
publishing only

(G-3891)
AMERICAN LABOR INC
1308 Broad St (27705-3533)
PHONE..............................919 286-0726
Michael Shiflett, *Owner*
EMP: 4
SALES (est): 383.18K **Privately Held**
SIC: 3841 Surgical and medical instruments

(G-3892)
AMKOR TECHNOLOGY INC
3021 Cornwallis Rd (27709-0146)
PHONE..............................919 248-1800
Wayne Machon, *Brnch Mgr*
EMP: 4
SALES (corp-wide): 6.32B **Publicly Held**
Web: www.amkor.com
SIC: 3674 Integrated circuits, semiconductor
networks, etc.
PA: Amkor Technology, Inc.
2045 E Innovation Cir
Tempe AZ 85284
480 821-5000

(G-3893)
AMO PHARMA SERVICES CORP
321 E Chapel Hill St 3rd Fl (27701-3351)
PHONE..............................215 826-7420
Michael Snape, *Pr*
EMP: 4 EST: 2015
SALES (est): 70.68K **Privately Held**
Web: www.amo-pharma.com
SIC: 2834 Pharmaceutical preparations

(G-3894)
AMPAC MACHINERY LLC
319 Us 70 Service Rd (27703-4525)
P.O. Box 21077 (27703-1077)
PHONE..............................919 596-5320
EMP: 10 EST: 2009
SALES (est): 4MM **Privately Held**
Web: www.ampacmachinery.com
SIC: 3531 Aggregate spreaders

(G-3895)
ANALOG DEVICES INC
4001 Nc Hwy 54 Ste 3100 (27709-0101)
PHONE..............................336 202-6503
EMP: 12
SALES (corp-wide): 9.43B **Publicly Held**
Web: www.analog.com

SIC: 3674 Integrated circuits, semiconductor
networks, etc.
PA: Analog Devices, Inc.
1 Analog Way
Wilmington MA 01887
781 935-5565

(G-3896)
APOLLONIAS CANDLES THINGS LLC
2112 Broad St Apt E8 (27705-3430)
PHONE..............................910 408-2508
Apollonia Fassett, *Owner*
EMP: 4 EST: 2016
SALES (est): 58.25K **Privately Held**
SIC: 3999 Candles

(G-3897)
ARC3 GASES INC
1001 Hill Dr (27703-7037)
PHONE..............................919 772-9500
Emmett C Aldredge Iii, *Brnch Mgr*
EMP: 9
SALES (corp-wide): 204.15MM **Privately
Held**
SIC: 2813 Industrial gases
PA: Arc3 Gases, Inc.
1600 Us-301 S
Dunn NC 28334
910 892-4016

(G-3898)
ARCHIVESOCIAL INC
Also Called: Archivesocial
212 W Main St Ste 500 (27701-3239)
P.O. Box 3330 (27702-3330)
PHONE..............................888 558-6032
Anil Chawla, *Pr*
EMP: 41 EST: 2011
SALES (est): 3.89MM **Privately Held**
Web: www.civicplus.com
SIC: 7372 Utility computer software

(G-3899)
ART SIGN CO
209 S Goley St (27701-4203)
P.O. Box 11116 (27703-0116)
PHONE..............................919 596-8681
Artis Plummer Senior, *Owner*
EMP: 5 EST: 1954
SALES (est): 246.72K **Privately Held**
Web: www.artsignco.com
SIC: 3993 Signs and advertising specialties

(G-3900)
ARTISTIC IRONWORKS LLC
700 E Club Blvd Ste B (27704-4506)
PHONE..............................919 908-6888
EMP: 9 EST: 2015
SALES (est): 435.49K **Privately Held**
SIC: 3499 3462 Metal household articles;
Iron and steel forgings

(G-3901)
**ASSOCTION INTL CRTIF PROF
ACCN (PA)**
220 Leigh Farm Rd (27707-8110)
PHONE..............................919 402-4500
Barry Melancon, *CEO*
Michael J Buddendeck, *
EMP: 550 EST: 2016
SQ FT: 125,000
SALES (est): 24.73MM
SALES (corp-wide): 24.73MM **Privately
Held**
Web: www.aicpa-cima.com
SIC: 8299 8621 2721 Educational service,
nondegree granting: continuing educ.;
Professional organizations; Periodicals,
publishing only

(G-3902)
**ASTRAZENECA
PHARMACEUTICALS LP**
4222 Emperor Blvd Ste 560 (27703-8466)
PHONE..............................919 647-4990
Charles J Bramlage, *Pr*
EMP: 104
SALES (corp-wide): 45.81B **Privately Held**
Web: www.astrazeneca.com
SIC: 2834 Pharmaceutical preparations
HQ: Astrazeneca Pharmaceuticals Lp
1800 Concord Pike
Wilmington DE 19850

(G-3903)
ATLANTIC PROSTHETICS ORTHTCS
6208 Fayetteville Rd Ste 101 (27713-6286)
PHONE..............................919 806-3260
Brandon Barham, *Pr*
EMP: 4 EST: 2017
SALES (est): 403.51K **Privately Held**
Web: www.atlanticpo.com
SIC: 3842 Prosthetic appliances

(G-3904)
ATLANTIS GRAPHICS INC (PA)
Also Called: Universal Printing & Pubg
2410 E Nc Highway 54 (27713-2254)
PHONE..............................919 361-5809
Robert Moura, *Pr*
Sandra Moura, *
EMP: 34 EST: 1979
SQ FT: 17,500
SALES (est): 2.49MM
SALES (corp-wide): 2.49MM **Privately
Held**
Web: www.universalprinting.com
SIC: 2791 2752 2789 Typesetting; Offset
printing; Bookbinding and related work

(G-3905)
ATLAS BOX AND CRATING CO INC
3829 S Miami Blvd Ste 100 (27703-5419)
PHONE..............................919 941-1023
EMP: 6
SIC: 2448 Pallets, wood
PA: Atlas Box And Crating Co., Inc.
223 Wrcster Prvdence Tpke
Sutton MA 01590

(G-3906)
ATSENA THERAPEUTICS INC
280 S Mangum St Ste 350 (27701-3681)
PHONE..............................352 273-9342
Patrick Ritschel, *CEO*
Kenji Fujita, *CMO*
Linda B Couto, *CSO*
EMP: 16 EST: 2019
SALES (est): 9.78MM **Privately Held**
Web: www.atsenatx.com
SIC: 2834 Pharmaceutical preparations

(G-3907)
AUROBINDO PHARMA USA INC
2929 Weck Dr (27703)
P.O. Box 12167 (27709-2167)
PHONE..............................732 839-9400
EMP: 22 EST: 2015
SALES (est): 9.67MM **Privately Held**
Web: www.aurobindousa.com
SIC: 2834 Pharmaceutical preparations
PA: Aurobindo Pharma Limited
Galaxy, Floor 22-24; Plot No 1,
Hyderabad TS 50003

(G-3908)
AUROLIFE PHARMA LLC
2929 Weck Dr (27709-0186)
PHONE..............................732 839-9408
Gangadhar Gorla, *VP Fin*

EMP: 40
Web: www.aurobindousa.com
SIC: 2834 Pharmaceutical preparations
HQ: Aurolife Pharma Llc
2400 Us Highway 130
Dayton NJ 08810

(G-3909)
AVIOQ INC (HQ)
76 Tw Alexander Dr (27709-0152)
P.O. Box 12808 (27709-2808)
PHONE..............................919 314-5535
Chamroen Chetty, *CEO*
X James Li, *Prin*
Zhiyuan Che, *Ch Bd*
Xingxiang Li, *Bd of Dir*
Samuel Chetty, *Fin Mgr*
▲ **EMP:** 16 **EST:** 2008
SQ FT: 80,000
SALES (est): 13.44MM Privately Held
Web: www.avioq.com
SIC: 3841 Diagnostic apparatus, medical
PA: Shandong Oriental Ocean Sci-Tech
Co.,Ltd.
No.18 Aokema St., Laishan Dist.
Yantai SD 26400

(G-3910)
AVISTA PHARMA SOLUTIONS INC
(HQ)
Also Called: Cambrex
3501 Tricenter Blvd Ste C (27713-1868)
PHONE..............................919 544-8600
Patrick Walsh, *CEO*
Eric Evans, *
Cathy Butler, *
Ken Domagalski, *
EMP: 50 **EST:** 2011
SQ FT: 200,000
SALES (est): 48.73MM
SALES (corp-wide): 523.07MM Privately
Held
Web: www.avistapharma.com
SIC: 8734 2834 Testing laboratories;
Pharmaceutical preparations
PA: Cambrex Corporation
1 Meadowlands Plz
East Rutherford NJ 07073
201 804-3000

(G-3911)
BAE SYSTEMS INFO ELCTRNIC
SYST
4721 Emperor Blvd Ste 330 (27703-8580)
PHONE..............................919 323-5800
James Baxter, *Il Technology Development*
EMP: 43
SALES (corp-wide): 28.77B Privately Held
Web: www.baesystems.com
SIC: 3663 7371 Global positioning systems
(GPS) equipment; Computer software
development and applications
HQ: Bae Systems Information And
Electronic Systems Integration Inc.
65 Spit Brook Rd
Nashua NH 03060
603 885-4321

(G-3912)
BAEBIES INC
25 Alexandria Way (27709)
P.O. Box 14403 (27709-4403)
PHONE..............................919 891-0432
Richard West, *CEO*
EMP: 85 **EST:** 2014
SQ FT: 30,000
SALES (est): 24.96MM Privately Held
Web: www.baebies.com
SIC: 2835 In vitro diagnostics

(G-3913)
BARRISTER AND BREWER LLC
Also Called: Mystic Farm & Distillery
1212 N Mineral Springs Rd (27703-2717)
PHONE..............................919 323-2777
Jonathan Blitz, *Managing Member*
EMP: 7 **EST:** 2013
SALES (est): 477.64K Privately Held
Web: www.whatismystic.com
SIC: 2085 Distilled and blended liquors

(G-3914)
BASF CORPORATION
2 Tw Alexander Dr (27709-0144)
P.O. Box 13911 (27709-3911)
PHONE..............................919 433-6773
EMP: 240
SALES (corp-wide): 74.89B Privately Held
Web: www.basf.com
SIC: 2869 Industrial organic chemicals, nec
HQ: Basf Corporation
100 Park Ave
Florham Park NJ 07932
800 962-7831

(G-3915)
BASF CORPORATION
26 Davis Dr (27709-0003)
P.O. Box 13528 (27709-3528)
PHONE..............................919 547-2000
John Rabby, *Brnch Mgr*
EMP: 1200
SALES (corp-wide): 74.89B Privately Held
Web: www.basf.com
SIC: 2869 Industrial organic chemicals, nec
HQ: Basf Corporation
100 Park Ave
Florham Park NJ 07932
800 962-7831

(G-3916)
BASF PLANT SCIENCE LP
26 Davis Dr (27709-0003)
P.O. Box 13528 (27709-3528)
PHONE..............................919 547-2000
Peter Eckes, *CEO*
EMP: 113 **EST:** 1999
SALES (est): 5.56MM
SALES (corp-wide): 74.89B Privately Held
Web: www.basf.com
SIC: 2869 Industrial organic chemicals, nec
PA: Basf Se
Carl-Bosch-Str. 38
Ludwigshafen Am Rhein RP 67056
621600

(G-3917)
BATTLE FERMENTABLES LLC (PA)
1604 Lathrop St (27703-2136)
PHONE..............................336 225-4585
EMP: 6 **EST:** 2022
SALES (est): 133.64K
SALES (corp-wide): 133.64K Privately
Held
SIC: 2084 Wines, brandy, and brandy spirits

(G-3918)
BAUSCH HEALTH AMERICAS INC
406 Blackwell St Ste 410 (27701-3985)
PHONE..............................949 461-6000
EMP: 11
SALES (corp-wide): 8.76B Privately Held
Web: www.valeant.com
SIC: 5912 2834 Drug stores and proprietary
stores; Pharmaceutical preparations
HQ: Bausch Health Americas, Inc.
400 Somerset Corp Blvd
Bridgewater NJ 08807
908 927-1400

(G-3919)
BAYER CORPORATION
Also Called: Bayer Agriculture
2 Tw Alexander Dr (27709-0144)
PHONE..............................800 242-5897
EMP: 43
SALES (corp-wide): 51.78B Privately Held
Web: cropscience.bayer.com
SIC: 2834 Pills, pharmaceutical
HQ: Bayer Corporation
100 Bayer Blvd
Whippany NJ 07981
412 777-2000

(G-3920)
BAYER CROPSCIENCE INC
2400 Ellis Rd (27703-5543)
P.O. Box 526 (63166-0526)
PHONE..............................412 777-2000
Phil Blake, *Pr*
◆ **EMP:** 33 **EST:** 2011
SALES (est): 11.21MM
SALES (corp-wide): 49.29B Privately Held
Web: cropscience.bayer.us
SIC: 2834 Pharmaceutical preparations
HQ: Bayer Corporation
100 Bayer Blvd
Whippany NJ 07981
412 777-2000

(G-3921)
BECKETT MEDIA LP
2222 Sedwick Rd Ste 102 (27713-2658)
PHONE..............................800 508-2582
Greg Lindberg, *Pt*
EMP: 9 **EST:** 2011
SALES (est): 1.21MM Privately Held
Web: www.beckett.com
SIC: 2741 Newsletter publishing

(G-3922)
BECTON DICKINSON AND
COMPANY
Also Called: Bd Medical Technology
21 Davis Dr (27709-0003)
PHONE..............................201 847-6800
EMP: 300
SALES (corp-wide): 20.18B Publicly Held
Web: www.bd.com
SIC: 3841 Hypodermic needles and syringes
PA: Becton, Dickinson And Company
1 Becton Dr
Franklin Lakes NJ 07417
201 847-6800

(G-3923)
BELL AND HOWELL LLC (PA)
3791 S Alston Ave (27713-1880)
PHONE..............................919 767-4401
Larry Blue, *Pr*
Arthur Bergens, *CFO*
▲ **EMP:** 1259 **EST:** 1907
SALES (est): 66.4MM Privately Held
Web: www.bellhowell.net
SIC: 3579 Envelope stuffing, sealing, and
addressing machines

(G-3924)
BELL AND HOWELL LLC
Also Called: Bh Holdings
3791 S Alston Ave (27713-1880)
PHONE..............................919 767-6400
EMP: 20 **EST:** 2010
SALES (est): 841.87K Privately Held
Web: www.bellhowell.net
SIC: 3579 Mailing machines

(G-3925)
BENNETT & ASSOCIATES INC
Also Called: Sir Speedy

3312 Guess Rd (27705-2106)
PHONE..............................919 477-7362
Terry M Bennett, *Pr*
EMP: 8 **EST:** 1982
SQ FT: 2,400
SALES (est): 381.8K Privately Held
Web: www.sirspeedy.com
SIC: 2752 2791 2789 Commercial printing,
lithographic; Typesetting; Bookbinding and
related work

(G-3926)
BILL S IRON SHOP INC
Also Called: Bill's Ornamental Iron Shop
2243 Glover Rd (27703-6032)
P.O. Box 11487 (27703-0487)
PHONE..............................919 596-8360
Bill Emory, *Pr*
Larry Emory, *VP*
EMP: 4 **EST:** 1964
SQ FT: 8,000
SALES (est): 561.08K Privately Held
Web: www.billironshopinc.com
SIC: 3441 Fabricated structural metal

(G-3927)
BILLSOFT INC
Also Called: Eztax
512 S Mangum St Ste 100 (27701-3973)
PHONE..............................913 859-9674
Timothy J Lopatofsky, *Pr*
Maria Hoofer, *
Amanda Meglemre, *
Vicki J Klein, *
Staci K Grew, *
EMP: 18 **EST:** 1997
SALES (est): 590.66K Privately Held
Web: www.avalara.com
SIC: 7373 7372 Systems software
development services; Prepackaged
software

(G-3928)
BIOCRYST PHARMACEUTICALS
INC (PA)
Also Called: Biocryst
4505 Emperor Blvd Ste 200 (27703)
PHONE..............................919 859-1302
Jon P Stonehouse, *Pr*
Nancy J Hutson, *Ch Bd*
Anthony J Doyle, *CFO*
Alane P Barnes, *CLO*
Helen M Thackray, *Research &
Development*
▲ **EMP:** 403 **EST:** 1986
SQ FT: 24,500
SALES (est): 450.71MM Publicly Held
Web: www.biocryst.com
SIC: 2834 Pharmaceutical preparations

(G-3929)
BIOGEN MA INC
5000 Davis Dr (27709-0200)
P.O. Box 14627 (27709-4627)
PHONE..............................919 941-1100
Hal Price, *Genl Mgr*
EMP: 126
SALES (corp-wide): 9.68B Publicly Held
Web: www.biogen.com
SIC: 2834 Pharmaceutical preparations
HQ: Biogen Ma Inc.
225 Binney St
Cambridge MA 02142
617 679-2000

(G-3930)
BIOMERIEUX INC (DH)
100 Rodolphe St (27712-9402)
PHONE..............................919 620-2000
Brian Armstrong, *Pr*
Gary Mills, *

▲ = Import ▼ = Export
◆ = Import/Export

▲ **EMP:** 500 **EST:** 1977
SALES (est): 511.52MM
SALES (corp-wide): 7.5MM **Privately Held**
Web: www.biomerieux-usa.com
SIC: 3845 8071 3841 3826 Automated blood
and body fluid analyzers, except lab;
Medical laboratories; Surgical and medical
instruments; Analytical instruments
HQ: Biomerieux Sa
376 Chemin De L'orme
Marcy-L'etoile ARA 69280
478872000

(G-3931)
BIOTECH PRSTHTICS ORTHTICS
DRH
314 Crutchfield St (27704-2725)
PHONE..............................919 471-4994
Michael Astilla, *Pr*
EMP: 8 **EST:** 2001
SALES (est): 2.97MM
SALES (corp-wide): 1.12B **Privately Held**
Web: www.biotechnc.com
SIC: 3842 Limbs, artificial
PA: Hanger, Inc.
10910 Domain Dr Ste 300
Austin TX 78758
512 777-3800

(G-3932)
BIOVENTUS INC (PA)
Also Called: BIOVENTUS
4721 Emperor Blvd Ste 100 (27703)
PHONE..............................919 474-6700
Kenneth M Reali, *CEO*
William A Hawkins, *Ch Bd*
John E Nosenzo, *CCO*
Gregory O Anglum, *Sr VP*
Katrina Church, *Chief Compliance Officer*
EMP: 94 **EST:** 2012
SALES (est): 573.28MM
SALES (corp-wide): 573.28MM **Publicly**
Held
Web: www.bioventus.com
SIC: 3841 3843 Surgical and medical
instruments; Orthodontic appliances

(G-3933)
BIOVENTUS LLC (HQ)
4721 Emperor Blvd Ste 100 (27703-7663)
PHONE..............................800 396-4325
Ken Reali, *CEO*
Greg Anglum, *
John Nosenzo, *
Anthony D'adamio, *Sr VP*
▲ **EMP:** 100 **EST:** 2012
SALES (est): 93.93MM
SALES (corp-wide): 573.28MM **Publicly**
Held
Web: www.bioventus.com
SIC: 3845 5122 Ultrasonic medical
equipment, except cleaning;
Pharmaceuticals
PA: Bioventus Inc.
4721 Emperor Blvd Ste 100
Durham NC 27703
919 474-6700

(G-3934)
BLACK TIRE SERVICE INC
1400 E Geer St (27704-5039)
PHONE..............................919 908-6347
Ricky Benton, *Pr*
▲ **EMP:** 5 **EST:** 2012
SALES (est): 543.08K **Privately Held**
Web: bts.tireweb.com
SIC: 3011 Tires and inner tubes

(G-3935)
BLUE BAY DISTRIBUTING INC
3720 Appling Way (27703-9227)
P.O. Box 31807 (27622-1807)
PHONE..............................919 957-1300
Sharon Cronauer, *Pr*
Robert Cronauer, *VP*
EMP: 7 **EST:** 1995
SQ FT: 2,300
SALES (est): 254.83K **Privately Held**
Web: www.bluebaydist.com
SIC: 2253 T-shirts and tops, knit

(G-3936)
BODY BILLBOARDS INC
4905 S Alston Ave (27713-4424)
PHONE..............................919 544-4540
William R Drago, *Pr*
EMP: 5 **EST:** 1982
SQ FT: 8,000
SALES (est): 400.52K **Privately Held**
Web: www.bodybillboards.com
SIC: 7336 2759 2396 2395 Silk screen
design; Screen printing; Automotive and
apparel trimmings; Pleating and stitching

(G-3937)
BOLTON INVESTORS INC
Also Called: Portable Outdoor Equipment
4914 N Roxboro St Ste 7 (27704-1464)
PHONE..............................919 471-1197
Melissa Bolton, *Pr*
EMP: 7 **EST:** 1990
SQ FT: 3,600
SALES (est): 684.04K **Privately Held**
Web:
portableoutdoorequipmentdurham.stihldealer.
net
SIC: 3546 5063 5251 Saws and sawing
equipment; Generators; Tools, power

(G-3938)
BOOKCASE SHOP (PA)
Also Called: Durham Bookcases
301 S Duke St (27701-2820)
PHONE..............................919 683-1922
Elaine S Fletcher, *Pr*
Phillip S Fletcher, *VP*
EMP: 6 **EST:** 1992
SQ FT: 26,000
SALES (est): 984.53K **Privately Held**
Web: www.bookcaseshop.com
SIC: 2511 5021 Wood household furniture;
Bookcases

(G-3939)
BOTTOM LINE TECHNOLOGIES INC
Also Called: Enviroclean Solutions
1000 Parliament Ct Ste 310 (27703-0088)
PHONE..............................919 472-0541
William Trent, *Pr*
Charles Blalock, *Stockholder*
Rodger Morrison, *Stockholder*
EMP: 10 **EST:** 2008
SALES (est): 99.8K **Privately Held**
SIC: 2841 Soap and other detergents

(G-3940)
BRIDGESTONE AMERICAS INC
101 W Chapel Hill St Ste 200 (27701-3255)
PHONE..............................984 888-0413
EMP: 101
Web: www.bridgestoneamericas.com
SIC: 3011 3493 2952 2822 Tires and inner
tubes; Steel springs, except wire; Asphalt
felts and coatings; Synthetic rubber
HQ: Bridgestone Americas, Inc.
200 4th Ave S Ste 100
Nashville TN 37201
615 937-1000

(G-3941)
BRIDGESTONE RET OPERATIONS
LLC
Also Called: Firestone
3809 N Duke St (27704-1727)
PHONE..............................919 471-4468
Colt Hunter, *Mgr*
EMP: 9
SQ FT: 5,176
Web: www.bridgestoneamericas.com
SIC: 5531 7534 Automotive tires; Rebuilding
and retreading tires
HQ: Bridgestone Retail Operations, Llc
200 4th Ave S Ste 100
Nashville TN 37201
615 937-1000

(G-3942)
BRIGHT VIEW TECHNOLOGIES
CORP
4022 Stirrup Creek Dr Ste 301
(27703-8971)
PHONE..............................919 228-4370
Jennifer Aspell, *CEO*
Emily Friedman, *CFO*
EMP: 23 **EST:** 2002
SQ FT: 37,000
SALES (est): 12.66MM **Privately Held**
Web: www.brightviewtechnologies.com
SIC: 3081 Plastics film and sheet

(G-3943)
BRII BIOSCIENCES INC
110 N Corcoran St Unit 5-130 (27701-5015)
PHONE..............................919 240-5605
Zhi Hong, *CEO*
EMP: 11 **EST:** 2020
SALES (est): 4.59MM **Privately Held**
Web: www.briibio.com
SIC: 2834 Pharmaceutical preparations

(G-3944)
BROADCOM CORPORATION
1030 Swabia Ct Ste 400 (27703-8070)
PHONE..............................919 865-2954
EMP: 51
SALES (corp-wide): 51.57B **Publicly Held**
Web: www.broadcom.com
SIC: 3674 Integrated circuits, semiconductor
networks, etc.
HQ: Broadcom Corporation
1320 Ridder Park Dr
San Jose CA 95131

(G-3945)
BROMMA INC
4400 Ben Franklin Blvd Ste 200
(27704-2386)
PHONE..............................919 620-8039
Terry E Howell, *Pr*
Johnny Alvarsson, *Ch Bd*
Robert H Clark, *VP*
◆ **EMP:** 36 **EST:** 1982
SQ FT: 65,000
SALES (est): 2.35MM **Privately Held**
Web: www.bromma.com
SIC: 3531 3537 Aggregate spreaders;
Industrial trucks and tractors

(G-3946)
BRONTO SOFTWARE LLC
324 Blackwell St Ste 410 (27701-3600)
PHONE..............................919 595-2500
Joe Colopy, *CEO*
Chaz Felix, *
EMP: 109 **EST:** 2002
SQ FT: 14,000
SALES (est): 18.25MM
SALES (corp-wide): 52.96B **Publicly Held**

SIC: 7372 Prepackaged software
HQ: Netsuite, Inc.
2955 Campus Dr Ste 100
San Mateo CA 94403
650 627-1000

(G-3947)
BUDD-PIPER ROOFING COMPANY
506 Ramseur St (27701-4891)
P.O. Box 708 (27702-0708)
PHONE..............................919 682-2121
Charles A Budd, *Pr*
Joseph E King, *VP*
EMP: 6 **EST:** 1905
SQ FT: 20,000
SALES (est): 436.01K **Privately Held**
Web: www.buddpiperdurhamroofing.com
SIC: 1761 3444 Roofing contractor; Sheet
metalwork

(G-3948)
BUFFALO CRUSHED STONE INC
Also Called: Carolina Sunrock
1503 Camden Ave (27704-4609)
PHONE..............................919 688-6881
Marty Frain, *Mgr*
EMP: 11
SALES (corp-wide): 1.15B **Privately Held**
Web: www.nesl.com
SIC: 1422 Crushed and broken limestone
HQ: Buffalo Crushed Stone, Inc.
500 Como Park Blvd
Buffalo NY 14227
716 826-7310

(G-3949)
BULL CITY DESIGNS LLC
Also Called: B C D
1111 Neville St (27701-2681)
PHONE..............................919 908-6252
EMP: 24 **EST:** 2011
SALES (est): 6.04MM **Privately Held**
Web: www.bullcitydesigns.com
SIC: 2521 2514 2519 7389 Wood office
furniture; Household furniture: upholstered
on metal frames; Household furniture,
except wood or metal: upholstered; Design,
commercial and industrial

(G-3950)
BULL CITY SHEET METAL LLC
4008 Comfort Ln (27705-6177)
PHONE..............................919 354-0993
EMP: 5 **EST:** 2019
SALES (est): 2.43MM **Privately Held**
Web: www.bullcitysheetmetal.com
SIC: 3444 Sheet metalwork

(G-3951)
BULL DURHAM BEER CO LLC
409 Blackwell St (27701-3972)
PHONE..............................919 744-3568
Michael Goodman, *Pr*
EMP: 6 **EST:** 2016
SALES (est): 238.33K **Privately Held**
Web: www.bulldurhambeer.com
SIC: 2082 Beer (alcoholic beverage)

(G-3952)
BULLDURHAMFABRICATIONS COM
5004 Mandel Rd (27712-2519)
PHONE..............................919 479-1919
Robert Pickard, *Mgr*
EMP: 4 **EST:** 2014
SALES (est): 162.43K **Privately Held**
Web: www.bulldurhamfabrications.com
SIC: 3441 Fabricated structural metal

(G-3953)
BURTS BEES INC (HQ)
210 W Pettigrew St (27701-3666)
P.O. Box 13489 (27709-3489)
PHONE................................919 998-5200
John Replogle, *CEO*
M Beth Springer, *
Daniel J Heinrich, *
Angela Hilt, *
Charles R Conradi, *
◆ **EMP: 130 EST:** 1991
SQ FT: 108,000
SALES (est): 46.64MM
SALES (corp-wide): 7.09B **Publicly Held**
Web: www.burtsbees.com
SIC: 2844 5122 5087 Cosmetic preparations
; Cosmetics, perfumes, and hair products;
Beauty parlor equipment and supplies
PA: The Clorox Company
1221 Broadway
Oakland CA 94612
510 271-7000

(G-3954)
BURTS BEES INC
701 Distribution Dr (27709)
PHONE................................919 998-5200
EMP: 400
SALES (corp-wide): 7.09B **Publicly Held**
Web: www.burtsbees.com
SIC: 2844 5122 Bath salts; Cosmetics,
perfumes, and hair products
HQ: Burt's Bees, Inc.
210 W Pettigrew St
Durham NC 27701

(G-3955)
CAMARGO PHRM SVCS LLC
800 Taylor St Ste 101 (27701-4893)
PHONE................................513 618-0325
Stuart Byham, *Prin*
EMP: 4
SALES (corp-wide): 25.54MM **Privately Held**
Web: www.premierconsulting.com
SIC: 2834 Proprietary drug products
HQ: Camargo Pharmaceutical Services, Llc
1 E 4th St Ste 1400
Cincinnati OH 45202

(G-3956)
CAMPUS SAFETY PRODUCTS LLC
2530 Meridian Pkwy Ste 300 (27713-5272)
PHONE................................919 321-1477
Ernest Johnson Iii, *CEO*
Surjeet Johnson, *Pr*
Lowell Oakley, *CFO*
EMP: 6 EST: 2014
SALES (est): 222.62K **Privately Held**
Web: www.campussafetyproducts.com
SIC: 7382 3699 Protective devices, security;
Security devices

(G-3957)
CANCER DIAGNOSTICS INC (PA)
Also Called: Anatech
116 Page Point Cir (27703-9120)
P.O. Box 1205 (48012-1205)
PHONE................................877 846-5393
Patrick O'neil, *Pr*
Michael Franskoviak, *
▲ **EMP: 31 EST:** 1998
SALES (est): 13.16MM
SALES (corp-wide): 13.16MM **Privately Held**
Web: www.cancerdiagnostics.com
SIC: 3841 Anesthesia apparatus

(G-3958)
**CARGOTEC PORT SECURITY LLC
(DH)**
4400 Ben Franklin Blvd Ste 200a
(27704-2385)
PHONE................................919 620-1763
Troy A Thompson, *Managing Member*
▲ **EMP: 6 EST:** 2008
SQ FT: 5,000
SALES (est): 1.46MM **Privately Held**
SIC: 3699 5065 Security control equipment
and systems; Security control equipment
and systems
HQ: Kalmar Solutions Llc
415 E Dundee St
Ottawa KS 66067
785 242-2200

(G-3959)
CAROLINA ACADEMIC PRESS LLC
700 Kent St (27701-3049)
PHONE................................919 489-7486
EMP: 55 EST: 1976
SQ FT: 4,300
SALES (est): 4.12MM **Privately Held**
Web: www.cap-press.com
SIC: 2741 Miscellaneous publishing

(G-3960)
**CAROLINA COMPONENTS GROUP
INC**
Also Called: Carolina Components Group
1001 Hill Dr (27703)
PHONE................................919 635-8438
John Cooling, *CEO*
Michael Walsh, *
EMP: 45 EST: 2020
SALES (est): 10.08MM **Privately Held**
Web: www.carolinaflow.com
SIC: 3492 3545 3053 Hose and tube fittings
and assemblies, hydraulic/pneumatic;
Gauges (machine tool accessories);
Gaskets, all materials

(G-3961)
**CAROLINA MECHANICAL SERVICES
INC**
5100 International Dr (27712-8947)
PHONE................................919 477-7100
EMP: 43 EST: 1994
SALES (est): 6.71MM **Privately Held**
Web: www.carolinamechanical.com
SIC: 3559 Pharmaceutical machinery

(G-3962)
**CAROLINA SGNS GRPHIC DSGNS
INC**
Also Called: Carolina Signs and Graphics,
3535 Hillsborough Rd (27705-2916)
PHONE................................919 383-3344
Christopher Cross, *Pr*
EMP: 4 EST: 1990
SQ FT: 2,000
SALES (est): 251.04K **Privately Held**
Web: www.carolinabanner.com
SIC: 3993 5999 2759 1799 Signs and
advertising specialties; Banners; Screen
printing; Sandblasting of building exteriors

(G-3963)
CAROLINA WREN PRESS INC
Also Called: BLAIR
811 9th St Ste 130-127 (27705-4149)
PHONE................................919 560-2738
Lynn York, *Pr*
Robin Miura, *VP*
EMP: 5 EST: 1999
SALES (est): 447.89K **Privately Held**
Web: www.carolinawrenpress.org

SIC: 2731 Books, publishing only

(G-3964)
CASEIRO INTERNATIONAL LLC
105 Hood St Ste 7 (27701-3794)
PHONE................................919 530-8333
Roquel Siqueira, *Ofcr*
EMP: 5 EST: 2001
SQ FT: 4,400
SALES (est): 117.77K **Privately Held**
SIC: 2037 Frozen fruits and vegetables

(G-3965)
CATALENT PHARMA SOLUTIONS INC
160 N Pharma Dr (27703)
PHONE................................919 465-8206
Charlotte Carroll, *Brnch Mgr*
EMP: 13
Web: www.catalent.com
SIC: 2834 Pharmaceutical preparations
HQ: Catalent Pharma Solutions, Inc.
14 Schoolhouse Rd
Somerset NJ 08873

(G-3966)
CELL MICROSYSTEMS INC
801 Capitola Dr Ste 10 (27713-4384)
P.O. Box 13169 (27709-3169)
PHONE................................919 608-2035
Gary Pace, *CEO*
EMP: 6 EST: 2010
SALES (est): 5.98MM **Privately Held**
Web: www.cellmicrosystems.com
SIC: 2834 Adrenal pharmaceutical
preparations

(G-3967)
**CENTER FOR ORTHTIC PRSTHTIC
CA (HQ)**
Also Called: Center For Orthtic Prsthtic Ca
4702 Creekstone Dr (27703-8410)
PHONE................................919 797-1230
Don Dixon, *Pr*
Keith Senn, *
David Sickles, *
Michael Mattingly, *
Timothy Nutgrass, *
EMP: 26 EST: 2011
SALES (est): 4.85MM
SALES (corp-wide): 1.12B **Privately Held**
Web: www.centeropcare.com
SIC: 3842 Limbs, artificial
PA: Hanger, Inc.
10910 Domain Dr Ste 300
Austin TX 78758
512 777-3800

(G-3968)
CENTROTHERM USA INC
Also Called: Centrtherm Phtvoltaics USA Inc
3333 Durham Chapel Hill Blvd Ste D200
(27707-6238)
PHONE................................360 626-4445
Robert M Hartung, *CEO*
Dirk Stenkamp, *COO*
Hans Michael Kraus, *Sec*
Oliver Albrecht, *CFO*
◆ **EMP: 4 EST:** 2008
SALES (est): 1.03MM
SALES (corp-wide): 355.83K **Privately
Held**
SIC: 8711 3674 Engineering services; Solar
cells
HQ: Centrotherm International Ag
Wurttemberger Str. 31
Blaubeuren BW 89143

(G-3969)
CHANDLER CONCRETE INC
Also Called: Ready Mix Concrete
2700 E Pettigrew St (27703-4410)

P.O. Box 131 (27016-0131)
PHONE................................919 598-1424
Bruce Oakley, *Mgr*
EMP: 12
SQ FT: 288
Web: www.chandlerconcrete.com
SIC: 3273 1611 Ready-mixed concrete;
Surfacing and paving
PA: Chandler Concrete Co., Inc.
1006 S Church Street
Burlington NC 27215

(G-3970)
CHATHAM STEEL CORPORATION
2702 Cheek Rd (27704-5263)
PHONE................................912 233-4182
Mike Young, *Owner*
EMP: 38
SALES (corp-wide): 13.84B **Publicly Held**
Web: www.chathamsteel.com
SIC: 5051 3462 Steel; Aircraft forgings,
ferrous
HQ: Chatham Steel Corporation
501 W Boundary St
Savannah GA 31401
912 233-4182

(G-3971)
**CHECKFREE SERVICES
CORPORATION**
Also Called: Checkfree Mobius
4819 Emperor Blvd Ste 300 (27703-5420)
PHONE................................919 941-2640
Randy Stalings, *Brnch Mgr*
EMP: 404
SALES (corp-wide): 20.46B **Publicly Held**
Web: www.checkfreecsp.com
SIC: 7374 7372 Data processing service;
Prepackaged software
HQ: Checkfree Services Corporation
2900 Westside Pkwy
Alpharetta GA 30004
678 375-3000

(G-3972)
**CHEMOGENICS BIOPHARMA LLC
(PA)**
3325 Durham Chapel Hill Blvd Ste 250
(27707-6235)
PHONE................................919 323-8133
EMP: 6 EST: 2009
SALES (est): 476.66K **Privately Held**
Web: www.chemogenicsbiopharma.com
SIC: 2834 Pharmaceutical preparations

(G-3973)
CHIMERIX INC (PA)
2505 Meridian Pkwy Ste 100 (27713)
PHONE................................919 806-1074
Michael T Andriole, *Pr*
Michael A Sherman, *
Michelle Laspaluto, *CFO*
Allen S Melemed, *CMO*
Thomas Riga, *Chief Operations*
EMP: 25 EST: 2000
SQ FT: 21,325
SALES (est): 324K
SALES (corp-wide): 324K **Publicly Held**
Web: www.chimerix.com
SIC: 2834 Pharmaceutical preparations

(G-3974)
CHINA FREE PRESS INC
4711 Hope Valley Rd # 122 (27707-5651)
PHONE................................919 308-9826
Watson Meng, *Ex Dir*
EMP: 4 EST: 2007
SALES (est): 131.58K **Privately Held**
SIC: 2741 Miscellaneous publishing

(G-3975)
CHUDY GROUP LLC
Also Called: Tcgrx
106 Roche Dr (27703-0359)
PHONE...................................262 279-5307
Neville Dowell, *
Matt Noffsinger, *
Mark Hoffmann, CIO*
▲ EMP: 65 EST: 2007
SQ FT: 20,000
SALES (est): 2.11MM
SALES (corp-wide): 20.18B Publicly Held
SIC: 3565 Packaging machinery
PA: Becton, Dickinson And Company
1 Becton Dr
Franklin Lakes NJ 07417
201 847-6800

(G-3976)
CLAIRVOYANT TECHNOLOGY INC
3622 Lyckan Pkwy Ste 2006 (27707-2565)
PHONE...................................919 491-5062
Thomas Frederick, Pr
EMP: 4 EST: 2010
SALES (est): 872.5K Privately Held
Web: www.clairvoyant-technology.com
SIC: 3825 5045 Radio frequency measuring
equipment; Computers, peripherals, and
software

(G-3977)
CLEAN GREEN INC
Also Called: Clean Green Environmental Svcs
928 Harvest Rd (27704-5216)
PHONE...................................919 596-3500
Charles T Wilkinson, Pr
Kathie Wilkinson, VP
EMP: 9 EST: 1997
SQ FT: 10,000
SALES (est): 668.64K Privately Held
Web: www.cleangreennc.com
SIC: 4953 3559 Recycling, waste materials;
Automotive related machinery

(G-3978)
CLOUD PHARMACEUTICALS INC
6 Davis Dr (27709-0003)
P.O. Box 110081 (27709-5081)
PHONE...................................919 558-1254
Edwin R Addison, CEO
Lyle Lohmeyer, CFO
Don Van Dyke, COO
EMP: 6 EST: 2009
SALES (est): 880.27K Privately Held
Web: www.cloudpharmaceuticals.com
SIC: 2834 Pharmaceutical preparations

(G-3979)
CLUTCH INC
Also Called: Carpe
120 W Parrish St (27701-3321)
PHONE...................................919 448-8654
David Spratte, CEO
EMP: 11 EST: 2014
SALES (est): 4.4MM Privately Held
Web: www.mycarpe.com
SIC: 2844 Face creams or lotions

(G-3980)
CODING INSTITUTE LLC
2222 Sedwick Rd Ste 1 (27713-2655)
PHONE...................................239 280-2300
Ajay Gupta, Managing Member
EMP: 40 EST: 2002
SALES (est): 480.85K Privately Held
Web: www.aapc.com
SIC: 2731 7389 Book publishing; Business
services, nec

(G-3981)
COLD WATER NO BLEACH LLC
914 Corona St (27707-4817)
PHONE...................................336 505-9584
Jamal Mcdonald, Pt
EMP: 4 EST: 2020
SALES (est): 95.66K Privately Held
Web: www.coldwaternobleach.com
SIC: 7336 2395 Commercial art and graphic
design; Embroidery products, except
Schiffli machine

(G-3982)
**COLLEGATE CLORS CHRISTN
COLORS**
Also Called: CC
4204 Destrier Dr (27703-3756)
PHONE...................................919 536-8179
Tonya J Mcmannen, Owner
EMP: 4 EST: 2008
SALES (est): 196.09K Privately Held
SIC: 2397 Schiffli machine embroideries

(G-3983)
COLOWRAP LLC
3333 Durham Chapel Hill Blvd Ste A200
(27707-6238)
PHONE...................................888 815-3376
EMP: 15 EST: 2012
SALES (est): 2.4MM Privately Held
Web: www.colowrap.com
SIC: 5047 3841 Medical and hospital
equipment; Surgical and medical
instruments

(G-3984)
COMAN PUBLISHING CO INC (PA)
324 Blackwell St Ste 560 (27701-3600)
P.O. Box 2331 (27702-2331)
PHONE...................................919 688-0218
J Stuart Coman Junior, Pr
J S Coman Junior, Pr
Helena Coman, VP
Linda P Autry, Sec
EMP: 14 EST: 1980
SQ FT: 2,138
SALES (est): 1.13MM
SALES (corp-wide): 1.13MM Privately
Held
Web: www.comanpub.com
SIC: 2711 2741 Newspapers: publishing
only, not printed on site; Miscellaneous
publishing

(G-3985)
COMFORT ENGINEERS INC (PA)
4008 Comfort Ln (27705-6177)
P.O. Box 2955 (27715-2955)
PHONE...................................919 383-0158
Alan Williams, Pr
Layne M Hessee, *
H Christopher Perry, *
Jerry W Overajer, *
Robert D Teer Junior, Stockholder
EMP: 40 EST: 1955
SQ FT: 20,000
SALES (est): 9.39MM
SALES (corp-wide): 9.39MM Privately
Held
Web: www.comfortengineers.com
SIC: 1711 3441 3444 Warm air heating and
air conditioning contractor; Fabricated
structural metal; Sheet metalwork

(G-3986)
COMTECH GROUP INC
Also Called: Geeks On Call
4819 Emperor Blvd Ste 400 (27703-5420)
P.O. Box 14443 (27709-4443)
PHONE...................................919 313-4800
Etner Hill, Pr

Etner Hill, Pr
Saron Hill, VP
EMP: 4 EST: 2003
SQ FT: 600
SALES (est): 493.4K Privately Held
Web: www.teamcomtech.com
SIC: 7379 3825 7378 Computer related
consulting services; Network analyzers;
Computer maintenance and repair

(G-3987)
**CONSOLDTED ELCTRNIC RSRCES
INC**
2933 S Miami Blvd Ste 124 (27703-9041)
PHONE...................................919 321-0004
Julio Cordoba, CEO
EMP: 5 EST: 1997
SALES (est): 1.51MM Privately Held
SIC: 3699 Electrical equipment and supplies,
nec

(G-3988)
CORNING INCORPORATED
Also Called: Corning
1 Becton Cir (27712-9483)
PHONE...................................919 620-6200
EMP: 237
SALES (corp-wide): 13.12B Publicly Held
Web: www.corning.com
SIC: 3821 3841 Pipettes, hemocytometer;
Surgical and medical instruments
PA: Corning Incorporated
1 Riverfront Plz
Corning NY 14831
607 974-9000

(G-3989)
CREELED INC
4001 E Hwy 54 Ste 2000 (27709)
PHONE...................................919 313-5330
Jack Pacheco, Pr
EMP: 270 EST: 2020
SALES (est): 7.24MM
SALES (corp-wide): 1.17B Publicly Held
Web: www.cree-led.com
SIC: 3674 Light emitting diodes
PA: Penguin Solutions, Inc.
1390 Mccarthy Blvd
Milpitas CA 95035
510 623-1231

(G-3990)
CRICKET FORGE LLC
2314 Operations Dr (27705-2336)
PHONE...................................919 680-3513
EMP: 5 EST: 2018
SALES (est): 2.2MM Privately Held
Web: www.cricketforge.com
SIC: 3441 Fabricated structural metal

(G-3991)
CRIZAF INC
Also Called: Crizaf Srl
2, 1534 Cher Dr, (27713)
PHONE...................................919 251-7661
EMP: 4 EST: 2015
SALES (est): 525.28K Privately Held
Web: www.crizaf.com
SIC: 5084 3639 4953 Food industry
machinery; Major kitchen appliances,
except refrigerators and stoves; Recycling,
waste materials
PA: Crizaf Srl
Via Edvar Hagerup Grieg 15
Saronno VA 21047

(G-3992)
CSC SHEET METAL INC
1310 E Cornwallis Rd (27713-1423)
PHONE...................................919 544-8887
▲ EMP: 12

Web: www.kmsheetmetal.com
SIC: 3444 Sheet metalwork

(G-3993)
CUPCAKE BAR
315 Monmouth Ave (27701-1816)
PHONE...................................919 816-2905
Anna Branly, Owner
EMP: 8 EST: 2011
SALES (est): 238.27K Privately Held
Web: www.cupcakebarbakery.com
SIC: 5812 2051 Family restaurants; Bakery,
for home service delivery

(G-3994)
CUSTOM LIGHT AND SOUND INC
Also Called: C L S
2506 Guess Rd (27705-3307)
PHONE...................................919 286-1122
Bob R Phelps, Pr
Stephen Brown, VP
EMP: 22 EST: 1977
SQ FT: 5,000
SALES (est): 3.81MM Privately Held
Web: www.customlightandsound.com
SIC: 1731 3699 5065 Voice, data, and video
wiring contractor; Electric sound equipment;
Paging and signaling equipment

(G-3995)
**CUSTOM SHEETMETAL SERVICES
INC**
5109 Neal Rd (27705-2364)
PHONE...................................919 282-1088
Joseph M Lee Iii, Pr
EMP: 4 EST: 2007
SALES (est): 1.52MM Privately Held
SIC: 3444 Sheet metalwork

(G-3996)
CUSTOM STEEL INCORPORATED
3161 Hillsborough Rd (27705-4336)
PHONE...................................919 383-9170
Wendy Walker, Owner
EMP: 5 EST: 2007
SALES (est): 965.18K Privately Held
Web: www.customsteel.org
SIC: 3441 Fabricated structural metal

(G-3997)
CYTONET LLC
801 Capitola Dr Ste 8 (27713-4384)
EMP: 12 EST: 2007
SQ FT: 8,000
SALES (est): 584.83K Privately Held
Web: www.cytonet.llc
SIC: 2836 Biological products, except
diagnostic

(G-3998)
DATA443 RISK MITIGATION INC
4000 Sancar Way Ste 400 (27709-1110)
PHONE...................................919 858-6542
Jason Remillard, Ch Bd
Greg Mccraw, CFO
EMP: 26 EST: 1998
SQ FT: 5,000
SALES (est): 5.58MM Privately Held
Web: www.data443.com
SIC: 7372 Prepackaged software

(G-3999)
DATABASE INCORPORATED
3342 Rose Of Sharon Rd (27712-3302)
P.O. Box 3054 (27715-3054)
PHONE...................................202 684-6252
W E Hammond Ii, Pr
Kay Hammond, VP
EMP: 7 EST: 1981
SQ FT: 1,500

SALES (est): 930.17K **Privately Held**
SIC: 7372 5045 Prepackaged software;
Computers, peripherals, and software

(G-4000)
DIGITAL TURBINE MEDIA INC (HQ)
410 Blackwell St (27701-3986)
PHONE..............................866 254-2453
Jud Bowman, *CEO*
Tim Oakley, *CFO*
Jamie Fellows, *Chief Product Officer*
EMP: 24 EST: 2008
SALES (est): 9.91MM **Publicly Held**
Web: www.digitalturbine.com
SIC: 7372 7371 Prepackaged software;
Custom computer programming services
PA: Digital Turbine, Inc.
110 San Antnio St Ste 160
Austin TX 78701

(G-4001)
DIGNIFY THERAPEUTICS LLC
2 Davis Dr (27709-0003)
P.O. Box 13169 (27709-3169)
PHONE..............................919 371-8138
EMP: 7 EST: 2013
SALES (est): 2.44MM **Privately Held**
Web: www.dignifytherapeutics.com
SIC: 2834 Pharmaceutical preparations

(G-4002)
DILISYM SERVICES INC
6 Davis Dr (27709-0003)
P.O. Box 12317 (27709-2317)
PHONE..............................919 558-1323
Brett Howell, *CEO*
EMP: 8 EST: 2014
SALES (est): 5.75MM **Publicly Held**
Web: www.simulations-plus.com
SIC: 7372 Prepackaged software
PA: Simulations Plus, Inc.
800 Park Offces Dr Ste 40
Research Triangle Pa NC 27709

(G-4003)
DOE & INGALLS INVESTORS INC (HQ)
4813 Emperor Blvd Ste 300 (27703-8467)
PHONE..............................919 598-1986
Thomas S Todd, *Pr*
EMP: 25 EST: 2005
SALES (est): 42.25MM
SALES (corp-wide): 42.86B **Publicly Held**
SIC: 3826 Analytical instruments
PA: Thermo Fisher Scientific Inc.
168 3rd Ave
Waltham MA 02451
781 622-1000

(G-4004)
DOE & INGALLS MANAGEMENT LLC (DH)
4813 Emperor Blvd Ste 300 (27703-8467)
PHONE..............................919 598-1986
Brian Parker, *
Genoffir Macleod, *
Lainie Herrington, *Prin*
Tammy Starr, *
EMP: 13 EST: 2005
SALES (est): 32.96MM
SALES (corp-wide): 42.86B **Publicly Held**
Web: www.thermofisher.com
SIC: 3826 Analytical instruments
HQ: Doe & Ingalls Investors, Inc.
4813 Emperor Blvd Ste 300
Durham NC 27703
919 598-1986

(G-4005)
DOE & INGLLS NRTH CRLINA OPRTI
4063 Stirrup Creek Dr (27703-9001)
PHONE..............................919 282-1792
John Hollenbach, *CEO*
Spencer Todd, *VP*
Henry Clark, *Dir*
Andrew Finn, *Dir*
Joe Frijia, *Dir*
▲ EMP: 21 EST: 2005
SALES (est): 21.19MM
SALES (corp-wide): 42.86B **Publicly Held**
SIC: 3826 Analytical instruments
HQ: Doe & Ingalls Management, Llc
4813 Emperor Blvd Ste 300
Durham NC 27703

(G-4006)
DRAXLOR INDUSTRIES INC
228 S Riverdale Dr (27712-2502)
PHONE..............................757 274-6771
Elliott Richter, *Prin*
EMP: 5 EST: 2016
SALES (est): 82.47K **Privately Held**
Web: www.draxlorindustries.com
SIC: 3999 Manufacturing industries, nec

(G-4007)
DRCH INC
Also Called: Dracor Water Systems
3518 Medford Rd (27705-2458)
P.O. Box 2993 (27715-2993)
PHONE..............................919 383-9421
TOLL FREE: 800
Richard M Hall, *Pr*
Susan B Hall, *Sec*
EMP: 8 EST: 1954
SQ FT: 6,500
SALES (est): 961.12K **Privately Held**
Web: www.dracorwatersystems.com
SIC: 5074 3589 Water purification equipment
; Water treatment equipment, industrial

(G-4008)
DRINK A BULL LLC
Also Called: Waldensian Style Wines
921 Holloway St Ste 103 (27701-3856)
PHONE..............................919 818-3321
Andrew Zimmerman, *Managing Member*
EMP: 5
SALES (corp-wide): 25K **Privately Held**
Web: www.drink-a-bull.com
SIC: 2084 5182 5921 Wines; Wine; Wine
and beer
PA: Drink A Bull Llc
3904 Sterling Ridge Ln
Durham NC 27707
984 219-1232

(G-4009)
DUKE HUMAN VACCINE INSTITUTE
2 Genome Ct (27710-3011)
PHONE..............................919 684-5384
EMP: 7 EST: 2015
SALES (est): 517.65K **Privately Held**
Web: dhvi.duke.edu
SIC: 8733 2836 Medical research; Agar
culture media

(G-4010)
DUKE STUDENT PUBLISHING CO INC
Also Called: THE CHRONICLE
101 Union Dr (27708-9980)
P.O. Box 90858 (27708-0858)
PHONE..............................919 684-3811
Jonathon Angier, *Genl Mgr*
Mary Weaver, *Opers Mgr*
EMP: 6 EST: 1993
SALES (est): 673.55K **Privately Held**
Web: www.dukechronicle.com

SIC: 2711 Commercial printing and
newspaper publishing combined

(G-4011)
DUKE UNIVERSITY
Also Called: Duke University Press
905 W Main St Ste 19 (27701-2076)
PHONE..............................919 687-3600
Steve Cohen, *Dir*
EMP: 52
SALES (corp-wide): 9.18MM **Privately Held**
Web: www.duke.edu
SIC: 2731 2721 Book publishing; Periodicals
PA: Duke University
324 Blckwell St Wash Bldg
Durham NC 27701
919 684-8111

(G-4012)
DUPONT ELECTRONIC POLYMERS L P (HQ)
14 Tw Alexander Dr (27709-0149)
PHONE..............................919 248-5135
EMP: 13 EST: 2003
SALES (est): 5.62MM
SALES (corp-wide): 12.39B **Publicly Held**
Web: www.dupont.com
SIC: 2822 Ethylene-propylene rubbers,
EPDM polymers
PA: Dupont De Nemours, Inc.
974 Centre Rd Bldg 730
Wilmington DE 19805
302 295-5783

(G-4013)
DUPONT SPECIALTY PDTS USA LLC
Also Called: Dupont
4020 Stirrup Creek Dr (27703-9410)
P.O. Box 13999 (27709-3999)
PHONE..............................919 248-5109
EMP: 50
SQ FT: 166,000
SALES (corp-wide): 12.39B **Publicly Held**
Web: www.dupont.com
SIC: 2819 5065 Industrial inorganic
chemicals, nec; Electronic parts and
equipment, nec
HQ: Dupont Specialty Products Usa, Llc
974 Centre Rd
Wilmington DE 19805
302 295-5783

(G-4014)
DURHAM COCA-COLA BOTTLING COMPANY (PA)
3214 Hillsborough Rd (27705-3005)
P.O. Box 31487 (28231-1487)
PHONE..............................919 383-1531
EMP: 150 EST: 1928
SALES (est): 30.49MM
SALES (corp-wide): 30.49MM **Privately Held**
Web: www.durhamcocacola.com
SIC: 2086 5962 Soft drinks: packaged in
cans, bottles, etc.; Sandwich and hot food
vending machines

(G-4015)
DURHAM DISTILLERY LLC
711 Washington St (27701-2147)
PHONE..............................919 937-2121
Melissa Katrincic, *Managing Member*
Lee Katrincic, *Managing Member*
EMP: 8 EST: 2013
SALES (est): 2.57MM
SALES (corp-wide): 9.96B **Publicly Held**
Web: www.durhamdistillery.com
SIC: 2085 Distilled and blended liquors
PA: Constellation Brands, Inc.
50 E Broad St

Rochester NY 14614
585 678-7100

(G-4016)
DYNAMAC CORPORATION
1910 Sedwick Rd Ste 300a (27713-4367)
PHONE..............................919 544-6428
Jay Early, *Brnch Mgr*
EMP: 38
SALES (corp-wide): 6.39MM **Privately Held**
Web: www.css-inc.com
SIC: 3822 7371 Environmental controls;
Computer software systems analysis and
design, custom
HQ: Dynamac Corporation
10301 Democracy Ln # 300
Fairfax VA 22030
703 691-4612

(G-4017)
ELI LILLY AND COMPANY
59 Moore Dr (27709-0009)
PHONE..............................317 296-1226
Graciela Romero, *Mgr*
EMP: 14
SALES (corp-wide): 45.04B **Publicly Held**
Web: www.lilly.com
SIC: 2834 Pharmaceutical preparations
PA: Eli Lilly And Company
1 Lilly Corporate Ctr
Indianapolis IN 46285
317 276-2000

(G-4018)
ELXR HEALTH INC
334 Blackwell St Ste B005 (27701-2395)
PHONE..............................919 917-8484
Paul Emanuel, *CEO*
Clinton Racine, *VP*
EMP: 5 EST: 2015
SALES (est): 230.65K **Privately Held**
Web: www.elxrhealth.com
SIC: 7372 7374 7375 Application computer
software; Service bureau, computer; On-
line data base information retrieval

(G-4019)
EMBREX LLC (HQ)
Also Called: Pfizer Poultry Health Embrex
1040 Swabia Ct (27703-8481)
P.O. Box P.O. Box 13989 (27709)
PHONE..............................919 941-5185
Clinton Lewis Junior, *Pr*
Don T Seaquist, *Corporate Secretary*
David M Baines, *Global Sales Vice President*
Joseph P Odowd, *Global Vice President*
Heidi Chen, *
▲ EMP: 114 EST: 1985
SQ FT: 60,000
SALES (est): 9.46MM
SALES (corp-wide): 8.54B **Publicly Held**
Web: www.poultryhealthtoday.com
SIC: 2836 3556 Vaccines and other
immunizing products; Poultry processing
machinery
PA: Zoetis Inc.
10 Sylvan Way
Parsippany NJ 07054
973 822-7000

(G-4020)
EMBROIDME
105 W Nc Highway 54 Ste 261
(27713-6646)
PHONE..............................919 316-1538
Mike Ganesan, *Owner*
EMP: 4 EST: 2014
SALES (est): 155.35K **Privately Held**
Web: www.fullypromoted.com

▲ = Import ▼ = Export
◆ = Import/Export

SIC: **5949** 3993 Sewing, needlework, and piece goods; Signs and advertising specialties

(G-4021)
EMC CORPORATION
4121 Surles Ct (27703-8055)
PHONE..............................919 767-0641
EMP: 12
Web: www.emc.com
SIC: 3572 Computer tape drives and components
HQ: Emc Corporation
176 S St
Hopkinton MA 01748
508 435-1000

(G-4022)
EMERGO THERAPEUTICS INC
6208 Fayetteville Rd Ste 104 (27713-6286)
PHONE..............................919 649-5544
Robin Hyde-deruyscher, *Pr*
EMP: 8 **EST:** 2016
SALES (est): 471.24K **Privately Held**
Web: www.emergotherapeutics.com
SIC: 2833 Medicinals and botanicals

(G-4023)
EMRISE CORPORATION
2530 Meridian Pkwy (27713-5272)
PHONE..............................408 200-3040
▲ **EMP:** 203
Web: www.emrise.com
SIC: 3679 3825 3661 3568 Electronic loads and power supplies; Instruments to measure electricity; Telephone and telegraph apparatus; Power transmission equipment, nec

(G-4024)
ENCUBE ETHICALS INC
200 Meredith Dr Ste 202 (27713)
PHONE..............................919 767-3292
EMP: 6 **EST:** 2019
SALES (est): 1.1MM **Privately Held**
Web: www.encubeusa.com
SIC: 2834 Pharmaceutical preparations

(G-4025)
ENDEAVOUR FBRICATION GROUP INC
Also Called: Endeavor Fabrication Group
1534 Cher Dr (27713-5423)
P.O. Box 733 (27510-0733)
PHONE..............................919 479-1453
Tom Schopler, *Pr*
Russell Shores, *VP*
EMP: 9 **EST:** 2005
SQ FT: 9,000
SALES (est): 893.73K **Privately Held**
SIC: 2541 Counter and sink tops

(G-4026)
ENTTEC AMERICAS LLC
3874 S Alston Ave Ste 103 (27713-1883)
P.O. Box 13965 (27709-3965)
PHONE..............................919 200-6468
EMP: 10 **EST:** 2016
SALES (est): 6.13MM **Privately Held**
Web: www.enttec.com
SIC: 3646 3648 Commercial lighting fixtures; Stage lighting equipment

(G-4027)
ENVIRONMENTAL SUPPLY CO INC
708 E Club Blvd (27704-4506)
PHONE..............................919 956-9688
David Hendricks, *Pr*
William D Ballard, *VP*
Carol Ballard, *VP*

Rachel Pleasants, *Sec*
Lewis Ballard, *Dir*
▲ **EMP:** 14 **EST:** 1995
SQ FT: 10,000
SALES (est): 4.86MM **Privately Held**
Web: www.environsupply.com
SIC: 3826 7389 8748 Analytical instruments; Air pollution measuring service; Business consulting, nec

(G-4028)
ENVISIA THERAPEUTICS INC
4301 Emperor Blvd Ste 200 (27703-7616)
P.O. Box 110065 (27709-5065)
PHONE..............................919 973-1440
Benjamin Yerxa, *Pr*
Shawn Glidden, *
Rhett M Schiffman, *CMO*
Tomas Navratil, *
Eric Linsley, *
EMP: 24 **EST:** 2013
SALES (est): 2.36MM **Privately Held**
Web: www.envisiatherapeutics.com
SIC: 2834 Pharmaceutical preparations

(G-4029)
EPI GROUP LLC (PA)
Also Called: Post & Courier, The
4020 Stirrup Creek Dr (27703-9410)
PHONE..............................843 577-7111
John P Barnwell, *CEO*
Pierre Manigault, *
Edward M Gilbreth, *
Daniel P Herres, *
Roger A Berardinis, *
▲ **EMP:** 350 **EST:** 1894
SALES (est): 93.4MM
SALES (corp-wide): 93.4MM **Privately Held**
Web: www.postandcourier.com
SIC: 2711 Newspapers, publishing and printing

(G-4030)
EPICYPHER INC
Also Called: Epicypher
6 Davis Dr (27709-0003)
P.O. Box 14453 (27709-4453)
PHONE..............................855 374-2461
James Bone, *Pr*
EMP: 11 **EST:** 2012
SALES (est): 7.8MM **Privately Held**
Web: www.epicypher.com
SIC: 8731 2836 Biotechnical research, commercial; Veterinary biological products

(G-4031)
EVOQUA WATER TECHNOLOGIES LLC
1301 S Briggs Ave Ste 116 (27703-5070)
PHONE..............................919 477-2161
Tom Bell, *Brnch Mgr*
EMP: 20
SQ FT: 2,400
Web: www.evoqua.com
SIC: 2834 5999 Chlorination tablets and kits (water purification); Water purification equipment
HQ: Evoqua Water Technologies Llc
210 6th Ave Ste 3300
Pittsburgh PA 15222
724 772-0044

(G-4032)
FIRST LEADS INC
Also Called: House Staffer
201 W Main St Ste 305 (27701-3228)
PHONE..............................919 672-5329
Michael Schneider, *CEO*
EMP: 6 **EST:** 2014
SALES (est): 2.81MM

SALES (corp-wide): 307.69MM **Publicly Held**
Web: www.first.io
SIC: 7372 Prepackaged software
PA: Re/Max Holdings, Inc.
5075 S Syracuse St
Denver CO 80237
303 770-5531

(G-4033)
FLEXGEN POWER SYSTEMS INC
2175 Presidential Dr Ste 100 (27703-0960)
PHONE..............................855 327-5674
EMP: 4
SALES (corp-wide): 50.38MM **Privately Held**
Web: www.flexgen.com
SIC: 4931 3674 Electric and other services combined; Semiconductors and related devices
PA: Flexgen Power Systems, Inc.
280 S Mangum St Ste 150
Durham NC 27701
855 327-5674

(G-4034)
FLEXGEN POWER SYSTEMS INC (PA)
280 S Mangum St Ste 150 (27701)
PHONE..............................855 327-5674
Kelcy Pegler, *CEO*
Diane Giacomozzi, *COO*
Gary Cristini, *CFO*
Aruna Chandra, *Ex VP*
EMP: 15 **EST:** 2015
SALES (est): 50.38MM
SALES (corp-wide): 50.38MM **Privately Held**
Web: www.flexgen.com
SIC: 4931 3674 Electric and other services combined; Semiconductors and related devices

(G-4035)
FORTREA HOLDINGS INC (PA)
Also Called: FORTREA
8 Moore Dr (27709)
PHONE..............................480 295-7600
Thomas Pike, *Ch Bd*
Jill Mcconnell, *CFO*
Mark Morais, *COO*
Robert A Parks, *CAO*
EMP: 43 **EST:** 1971
SALES (est): 2.7B
SALES (corp-wide): 2.7B **Publicly Held**
Web: www.fortrea.com
SIC: 2834 Pharmaceutical preparations

(G-4036)
FREUDENBERG NONWOVENS LIMITED PARTNERSHIP
3500 Industrial Dr (27704-9309)
P.O. Box 15910 (27704-0910)
PHONE..............................919 620-3900
▲ **EMP:** 691
SIC: 2297 5023 Nonwoven fabrics; Floor coverings

(G-4037)
FREUDENBERG PRFMCE MTLS LP (HQ)
Also Called: Freudenberg Nonwoven
3500 Industrial Dr (27704-9309)
P.O. Box 15910 (27704-0910)
PHONE..............................919 479-7443
Bruce Olson, *CEO*
Edward Cann, *VP*
Stephan Liozu, *VP*
◆ **EMP:** 36 **EST:** 2013
SALES (est): 96.31MM
SALES (corp-wide): 12.96B **Privately Held**

Web: www.freudenberg-pm.com
SIC: 2297 5131 Nonwoven fabrics; Piece goods and other fabrics
PA: Freudenberg & Co. Kg
Hohnerweg 2-4
Weinheim BW 69469
6201800

(G-4038)
FREUDENBERG PRFMCE MTLS LP
Also Called: FREUDENBERG PERFORMANCE MATERIALS L.P.
3440 Industrial Dr (27704-9429)
PHONE..............................919 620-3900
Heiner Heng, *Mgr*
EMP: 19
SALES (corp-wide): 12.96B **Privately Held**
Web: www.freudenberg-pm.com
SIC: 2821 Plastics materials and resins
HQ: Freudenberg Performance Materials L.P.
3500 Industrial Dr
Durham NC 27704
919 479-7443

(G-4039)
FS LLC
Also Called: Ram Jack Foundation Repair
4122 Bennett Memorial Rd Ste 304 (27705-1209)
PHONE..............................919 309-9727
Richard D Sykes, *Managing Member*
EMP: 40 **EST:** 1989
SQ FT: 25,000
SALES (est): 4.59MM **Privately Held**
Web: www.ramjack.com
SIC: 2295 Waterproofing fabrics, except rubberizing

(G-4040)
FUJIFILM DIOSYNTH BIOTECHNOLOG
6051 George Watts Hill Dr (27709-0218)
PHONE..............................919 337-4400
Michael Baldauff, *Brnch Mgr*
EMP: 8
SQ FT: 121,200
Web: www.fujifilmdiosynth.com
SIC: 2834 Pharmaceutical preparations
HQ: Fujifilm Diosynth Biotechnologies U.S.A., Inc.
101 J Mrris Cmmons Ln Ste
Morrisville NC 27560

(G-4041)
FUSION SPORT INC
122 E Parrish St (27701-3319)
PHONE..............................720 987-4403
Markus Deutsch, *CEO*
Leslie Milne, *
EMP: 35 **EST:** 2011
SALES (est): 467.94K **Privately Held**
Web: www.smartabase.com
SIC: 5941 7372 Sporting goods and bicycle shops; Publisher's computer software

(G-4042)
G1 THERAPEUTICS INC
Also Called: G1 Therapeutics
700 Park Offices Dr Ste 200 (27709)
P.O. Box 110341 (27709)
PHONE..............................919 213-9835
John E Bailey Junior, *Pr*
Garry A Nicholson, *
Terry L Murdock, *COO*
Jennifer K Moses, *CFO*
Rajesh K Malik, *CMO*
EMP: 122 **EST:** 2008
SQ FT: 60,000
SALES (est): 82.51MM
SALES (corp-wide): 62.41K **Privately Held**

Web: www.g1therapeutics.com
SIC: **2834** Pharmaceutical preparations
HQ: Pharmacosmos Therapeutics Inc.
120 Hdqrters Plz E Twr 6t
Morristown NJ

(G-4043)
GE AIRCRAFT ENGS HOLDINGS INC
Also Called: GE
3701 S Miami Blvd (27703-9131)
PHONE.....................919 361-4400
Tina Mitchum, *CFO*
▲ EMP: 525
SALES (corp-wide): 67.95B **Publicly Held**
Web: www.geaerospace.com
SIC: **3724 7699** Air scoops, aircraft; Aircraft
and heavy equipment repair services
HQ: Ge Aircraft Engines Holdings, Inc.
1 Aviation Way
Cincinnati OH 45215
888 999-5103

(G-4044)
GEA INTEC LLC
4319 S Alston Ave Ste 105 (27713-2488)
PHONE.....................919 433-0131
▲ EMP: 26
Web: www.intecvrt.com
SIC: **3556** Food products machinery

(G-4045)
GENESYS CLOUD SERVICES INC
Also Called: Interactive Intelligence
4307 Emperor Blvd Ste 300 (27703-8080)
PHONE.....................317 872-3000
EMP: 17
SALES (corp-wide): 241.26MM **Privately
Held**
Web: www.genesys.com
SIC: **7372** Business oriented computer
software
HQ: Genesys Cloud Services, Inc.
1302 El Cmino Real Ste 30
Menlo Park CA 94025

(G-4046)
GIGABEAM CORPORATION
4021 Stirrup Creek Dr Ste 400
(27703-9352)
P.O. Box 50266 (33074-0266)
PHONE.....................919 206-4426
Louis Slaughter, *Ch*
EMP: 6 EST: 2004
SALES (est): 786.8K **Privately Held**
SIC: **3663** Radio and t.v. communications
equipment

(G-4047)
GILERO LLC (PA)
Also Called: Eg-Gilero
4319 S Alston Ave Ste 100 (27713-2487)
PHONE.....................919 595-8220
Theodore Mosler, *CEO*
Todd Korogi, *
Kevin Miller, *
EMP: 394 EST: 2002
SALES (est): 24.91MM
SALES (corp-wide): 24.91MM **Privately
Held**
Web: www.gilero.com
SIC: **3841** Surgical and medical instruments

(G-4048)
GLASS JUG
5410 Nc Highway 55 Ste V (27713-7802)
PHONE.....................919 818-6907
Chris Creech, *Managing Member*
Kathryn Creech, *Managing Member*
EMP: 15 EST: 2014
SALES (est): 978.85K **Privately Held**
Web: www.glass-jug.com

SIC: **2082 5181 5921 5813** Beer (alcoholic
beverage); Beer and ale; Wine and beer;
Beer garden (drinking places)

(G-4049)
GLASS JUG LLC
5410 Nc Highway 55 Ste V (27713-7802)
PHONE.....................919 813-0135
Chris Creech, *Managing Member*
Kathryn Creech, *Managing Member*
EMP: 15 EST: 2014
SALES (est): 593.99K **Privately Held**
Web: www.glass-jug.com
SIC: **5921 2082 5181 5813** Wine and beer;
Beer (alcoholic beverage); Beer and ale;
Beer garden (drinking places)

(G-4050)
GLAXOSMITHKLINE LLC
5 3313 Gsk Co (27713)
PHONE.....................919 483-5302
EMP: 27
SQ FT: 8,556
SALES (corp-wide): 39.77B **Privately Held**
Web: us.gsk.com
SIC: **2834** Pharmaceutical preparations
HQ: Glaxosmithkline Llc
2929 Walnut St Ste 1700
Philadelphia PA 19112
888 825-5249

(G-4051)
GLAXOSMITHKLINE LLC
Also Called: Glaxosmithkline
410 Blackwell St (27701-3986)
P.O. Box 13398 (27709-3398)
PHONE.....................919 483-2100
EMP: 27
SALES (corp-wide): 39.77B **Privately Held**
Web: us.gsk.com
SIC: **2834** Pharmaceutical preparations
HQ: Glaxosmithkline Llc
2929 Walnut St Ste 1700
Philadelphia PA 19112
888 825-5249

(G-4052)
GLAXOSMITHKLINE LLC
406 Blackwell St (27701-3983)
PHONE.....................252 315-9774
EMP: 7
SALES (corp-wide): 39.77B **Privately Held**
Web: us.gsk.com
SIC: **2834 5122** Pharmaceutical preparations
; Pharmaceuticals
HQ: Glaxosmithkline Llc
2929 Walnut St Ste 1700
Philadelphia PA 19112
888 825-5249

(G-4053)
GLAXOSMITHKLINE LLC
2512 S Tricenter Blvd (27713-1852)
PHONE.....................919 483-2100
EMP: 10
SALES (corp-wide): 39.77B **Privately Held**
Web: us.gsk.com
SIC: **2834 5122** Pharmaceutical preparations
; Pharmaceuticals
HQ: Glaxosmithkline Llc
2929 Walnut St Ste 1700
Philadelphia PA 19112
888 825-5249

(G-4054)
GLAXOSMITHKLINE SERVICES INC
5 Moore Dr (27709-0143)
P.O. Box 13398 (27709-3398)
PHONE.....................919 483-2100
Ryan Harris, *Prin*
EMP: 453 EST: 1998

SALES (est): 41.01MM
SALES (corp-wide): 39.77B **Privately Held**
Web: www.gsk.com
SIC: **2834** Pharmaceutical preparations
PA: Gsk Plc
79 New Oxford Street
London WC1A
208 047-5000

(G-4055)
GRAEDON ENTERPRISES INC
Also Called: People's Pharmacy, The
5900 Beech Bluff Ln (27705-8114)
P.O. Box 52027 (27717-2027)
PHONE.....................919 493-0448
Joe Graedon, *Pr*
EMP: 8 EST: 1978
SALES (est): 521.96K **Privately Held**
Web: www.peoplespharmacy.com
SIC: **2731** Pamphlets: publishing only, not
printed on site

(G-4056)
GRAYBEARD DISTILLERY INC
4625 Industry Ln (27713-1497)
PHONE.....................919 361-9980
EMP: 10 EST: 2016
SALES (est): 1.91MM **Privately Held**
Web: www.bedlamvodka.com
SIC: **2085** Distilled and blended liquors

(G-4057)
GRIFOLS THERAPEUTICS LLC
85 Tw Alexander Dr (27709-0152)
PHONE.....................919 316-6214
Leslie Tremlett, *Mgr*
EMP: 10
Web: www.discovertheplasma.com
SIC: **2836** Blood derivatives
HQ: Grifols Therapeutics Llc
79 Tw Alexander Dr
Research Triangle Pa NC 27709

(G-4058)
HEIDELBERG MTLS US CEM LLC
1031 Drew St (27701-2630)
PHONE.....................919 682-5791
Buddy Howell, *Brnch Mgr*
EMP: 4
SQ FT: 816
SALES (corp-wide): 23.02B **Privately Held**
Web: www.heidelbergmaterials.us
SIC: **3273** Ready-mixed concrete
HQ: Heidelberg Materials Us Cement Llc
300 E John Crptr Fwy Ste
Irving TX 75062
877 534-4442

(G-4059)
HEMO BIOSCIENCE INC
4022 Stirrup Creek Dr Ste 311
(27703-8998)
PHONE.....................919 313-2888
Noel Brown, *Pr*
◆ EMP: 6 EST: 2003
SALES (est): 6.61MM **Privately Held**
Web: www.hemobioscience.com
SIC: **2819** Chemicals, reagent grade: refined
from technical grade

(G-4060)
HEMOSONICS LLC
4020 Stirrup Creek Dr Ste 105
(27703-8970)
PHONE.....................800 280-5589
Bob Roda, *Pr*
Steve Erwine, *CFO*
EMP: 18 EST: 2005
SALES (est): 4.72MM **Privately Held**
Web: www.hemosonics.com

SIC: **3845 3829** Ultrasonic scanning devices,
medical; Measuring and controlling devices,
nec

(G-4061)
HEMOSONICS LLC
4020 Stirrup Creek Dr (27703-9410)
PHONE.....................800 280-5589
EMP: 49
SALES (corp-wide): 8.49MM **Privately
Held**
Web: www.hemosonics.com
SIC: **3845 3829** Ultrasonic scanning devices,
medical; Measuring and controlling devices,
nec
PA: Hemosonics, Llc
400 Preston Ave Ste 250
Charlottesville VA 27703
800 280-5589

(G-4062)
HL JAMES LLC
1911 W Club Blvd (27705-3503)
PHONE.....................516 398-3311
EMP: 4 EST: 2014
SALES (est): 74.52K **Privately Held**
Web: www.hljames.com
SIC: **2323** Men's and boy's neckwear

(G-4063)
HONEYGIRL MEADERY LLC
1604 Lathrop St (27703-2136)
PHONE.....................919 399-3056
EMP: 6 EST: 2012
SALES (est): 248.91K **Privately Held**
Web: www.honeygirlmeadery.com
SIC: **2084** Wines

(G-4064)
HOODOO HONEY LLC
3600 N Duke St Ste 1 (27704-1769)
PHONE.....................252 548-0697
Ebone Hinnant, *Managing Member*
EMP: 8 EST: 2020
SALES (est): 270.82K **Privately Held**
SIC: **3999** Magic equipment, supplies, and
props

(G-4065)
HORTONWORKS INC
312 Blackwell St Ste 100 (27701-3669)
PHONE.....................855 846-7866
EMP: 4
SALES (corp-wide): 496.12MM **Privately
Held**
Web: www.cloudera.com
SIC: **7372** Prepackaged software
HQ: Hortonworks, Inc.
5470 Great America Pkwy
Santa Clara CA 95054

(G-4066)
**HYDRO SERVICE & SUPPLIES INC
(PA)**
513 United Dr (27713)
P.O. Box 12197 (27709)
PHONE.....................919 544-3744
Dave Currin, *Pr*
Charles S Atwater, *
Paul Rigsbee, *
Charles S Atwater Junior, *CFO*
Charles Riley, *
▲ EMP: 30 EST: 1967
SQ FT: 14,000
SALES (est): 11.19MM
SALES (corp-wide): 11.19MM **Privately
Held**
Web: www.hydroservice.com

SIC: **3589** 7699 Water treatment equipment, industrial; Industrial equipment services

(G-4067)
HYPERBRANCH MEDICAL TECH INC
800 Capitola Dr Ste 12 (27713-4385)
PHONE...................................919 433-3325
Jeffrey Clark, *CEO*
EMP: 13 **EST:** 2003
SALES (est): 5.81MM
SALES (corp-wide): 22.59B **Publicly Held**
Web: cmf.stryker.com
SIC: 3842 3841 Surgical appliances and supplies; Surgical and medical instruments
PA: Stryker Corporation
1941 Stryker Way
Portage MI 49002
269 385-2600

(G-4068)
ICAGEN LLC
1035 Swabia Ct Ste 110 (27703-0963)
PHONE...................................919 941-5206
Richard Cunningham, *CEO*
EMP: 84 **EST:** 2020
SALES (est): 2.5MM
SALES (corp-wide): 34.16MM **Publicly Held**
Web: www.icagen.com
SIC: 2834 Pharmaceutical preparations
PA: Omniab, Inc.
5980 Horton St Ste 600
Emeryville CA 94608
510 250-7800

(G-4069)
IDEABLOCK LLC
212 W Main St Ste 302 (27701-3239)
P.O. Box 29622 (27626-0622)
PHONE...................................919 551-5054
Eli M Sheets, *Pr*
EMP: 4 **EST:** 2018
SALES (est): 2.6MM **Privately Held**
Web: www.ideablock.io
SIC: 7372 Business oriented computer software

(G-4070)
IDEAL PRECAST INC
7020 Mount Hermon Church Rd (27705-8067)
P.O. Box 61219 (27715-1219)
PHONE...................................919 801-8287
Mary Beth Johen, *Prin*
EMP: 9 **EST:** 2008
SALES (est): 2.34MM **Privately Held**
Web: www.idealprecast.com
SIC: 3272 Concrete products, precast, nec

(G-4071)
IFTA USA INC
4819 Emperor Blvd Ste 400 (27703-5420)
PHONE...................................919 659-8393
EMP: 5 **EST:** 2015
SALES (est): 2.03MM **Privately Held**
Web: www.iftausa.com
SIC: 2048 Prepared feeds, nec
PA: Biovet Sa
Calle De Luxemburg 25
Constanti T 43120

(G-4072)
IMAGINEOPTIX CORPORATION
20 Tw Alexander Dr Ste 100 (27709-0148)
PHONE...................................919 757-4945
Erin Clark, *CEO*
Jason Kekas, *CFO*
Jon Warren, *Ex VP*
EMP: 18 **EST:** 2004
SALES (est): 4.5MM
SALES (corp-wide): 164.5B **Publicly Held**

SIC: **3827** Optical instruments and lenses
PA: Meta Platforms, Inc.
1 Meta Way
Menlo Park CA 94025
650 543-4800

(G-4073)
IMPLUS FOOTCARE LLC (DH)
Also Called: Apara
2001 Tw Alexander Dr (27709)
P.O. Box 13925 (27709)
PHONE...................................800 446-7587
Michael Polk, *Managing Member*
Seth Richards, *
Todd Vore, *
Rodney Bullock, *
◆ **EMP:** 300 **EST:** 1988
SQ FT: 315,000
SALES (est): 50.29MM
SALES (corp-wide): 300MM **Privately Held**
Web: www.implus.com
SIC: 5139 3949 7389 Footwear, athletic; Sporting and athletic goods, nec; Business Activities at Non-Commercial Site
HQ: Implus, Llc
2001 Tw Alexander Dr
Durham NC 27709
919 544-7900

(G-4074)
INDUSTRIAL MTAL FLAME SPRYERS
419 Salem St (27703-4255)
PHONE...................................919 596-9381
Dwight Crabtree, *Pr*
Mark Wilson, *VP*
EMP: 9 **EST:** 1961
SQ FT: 5,510
SALES (est): 461.94K **Privately Held**
SIC: 3544 3599 Extrusion dies; Machine shop, jobbing and repair

(G-4075)
INFERENSYS INC
112 Dare Pines Way (27703-8349)
PHONE...................................910 398-1200
Edwin Addison, *CEO*
Don Joder, *VP*
EMP: 4
SQ FT: 150
SALES (est): 98.37K **Privately Held**
Web: www.inferensys.net
SIC: 7372 Prepackaged software

(G-4076)
INFINITY COMMUNICATIONS LLC (PA)
5201 International Dr (27712-8950)
P.O. Box 91751 (27675)
PHONE...................................919 797-2334
Jeff Coffey, *Managing Member*
EMP: 23 **EST:** 2012
SALES (est): 10.37MM
SALES (corp-wide): 10.37MM **Privately Held**
Web: www.infinitycommgroup.net
SIC: 8748 8322 3825 4812 Telecommunications consultant; Disaster service; Network analyzers; Cellular telephone services

(G-4077)
INHALON BIOPHARMA INC
104 Tw Alexander Dr Rm 2021rtp (27709-0002)
PHONE...................................650 439-0110
Samuel Lai, *Pr*
EMP: 5 **EST:** 2018
SALES (est): 642.18K **Privately Held**
Web: www.inhalon.com

SIC: **2834** Pharmaceutical preparations

(G-4078)
INK WELL INC
Also Called: Ink Well
3112 N Roxboro St (27704-3252)
PHONE...................................919 682-8279
EMP: 5 **EST:** 2016
SALES (est): 171.27K **Privately Held**
Web: www.theinkwellusa.com
SIC: 2752 Offset printing

(G-4079)
INNAVASC MEDICAL INC
110 Swift Ave (27705-4880)
PHONE...................................813 902-2228
Joseph Knight, *CEO*
EMP: 10 **EST:** 2013
SALES (est): 2.01MM **Privately Held**
Web: www.innavasc.com
SIC: 3841 Surgical and medical instruments

(G-4080)
INTERNATIONAL BUS MCHS CORP
Also Called: IBM
3039 Cornwallis Rd (27709-0154)
P.O. Box 12195 (27709-2195)
PHONE...................................919 543-6919
Tina Wilson, *Brnch Mgr*
EMP: 464
SALES (corp-wide): 62.75B **Publicly Held**
Web: www.ibm.com
SIC: 7371 7373 3577 3571 Computer software systems analysis and design, custom; Computer systems analysis and design; Computer peripheral equipment, nec; Electronic computers
PA: International Business Machines Corporation
1 New Orchard Rd
Armonk NY 10504
914 499-1900

(G-4081)
INTUITIVE SURGICAL INC
Also Called: Biotechnology Center
1650 Tw Alexander Dr (27703-8584)
PHONE...................................408 523-2100
EMP: 6
Web: www.intuitivesurgical.com
SIC: 3841 Surgical and medical instruments
PA: Intuitive Surgical, Inc.
1020 Kifer Rd
Sunnyvale CA 94086

(G-4082)
IPAS
4711 Hope Valley Rd (27707-5651)
P.O. Box 9990 (27515-1990)
PHONE...................................919 967-7052
John Herrington, *Pr*
Terrence Cominski, *
Barbara Crane, *
EMP: 110 **EST:** 1973
SALES (est): 44.92MM **Privately Held**
Web: www.ipas.org
SIC: 8399 3842 Fund raising organization, non-fee basis; Gynecological supplies and appliances
PA: Ips
Addis Ababa

(G-4083)
IPS CORPORATION
Scigrip Americas
600 Ellis Rd (27703-6015)
P.O. Box 12729 (27709-2729)
PHONE...................................919 598-2400
Kevin Connolly, *Brnch Mgr*
EMP: 25
SQ FT: 32,934

Web: www.ipscorp.com
SIC: 5085 2891 Industrial supplies; Adhesives
HQ: Ips Corporation
455 W Victoria St
Compton CA 90220
310 898-3300

(G-4084)
IQVIA PHARMA INC (HQ)
Also Called: Quintiles Pharma, Inc.
4820 Emperor Blvd (27703-8426)
PHONE...................................919 998-2000
Pamela Long, *Ex Dir*
John Ratliff, *Pr*
R David Andrews, *Treas*
Kim L Rose, *Sec*
EMP: 55 **EST:** 2005
SALES (est): 22.32MM **Publicly Held**
SIC: 2834 Pharmaceutical preparations
PA: Iqvia Holdings Inc.
2400 Ellis Rd
Durham NC 27703

(G-4085)
ISA
67 Alexander Dr (27709-0185)
P.O. Box 12277 (27709-2277)
PHONE...................................919 549-8411
Jim Keabney, *Pr*
Tony Fragnito, *
EMP: 7 **EST:** 1985
SALES (est): 1.38MM
SALES (corp-wide): 16.48MM **Privately Held**
Web: www.isa.org
SIC: 2721 2731 Magazines: publishing only, not printed on site; Book publishing
PA: International Society Of Automation
67 T W Alexander Dr
Research Triangle Pa NC 27709
919 206-4176

(G-4086)
IXC DISCOVERY INC (PA)
4222 Emperor Blvd Ste 350 (27703-8030)
P.O. Box 14487 (27709-4487)
PHONE...................................919 941-5206
Richard Cunningham, *Pr*
Timothy C Tyson, *Non-Executive Chairman of the Board*
Mark Korb, *CFO*
Douglas Krafte, *CSO*
EMP: 27 **EST:** 2003
SALES (est): 9.19MM
SALES (corp-wide): 9.19MM **Privately Held**
SIC: 2834 Pharmaceutical preparations

(G-4087)
JAGGAER LLC (HQ)
Also Called: Jaggaer
700 Park Offices Dr (27713-2845)
P.O. Box 12768 (27709-2768)
PHONE...................................919 659-2100
Andy Hovancik, *CEO*
Jeff Laborde, *
Eva Skidmore, *CMO*
EMP: 89 **EST:** 1996
SQ FT: 78,500
SALES (est): 90.47MM
SALES (corp-wide): 93.22MM **Privately Held**
Web: www.jaggaer.com
SIC: 7372 Business oriented computer software
PA: Sciquest Parent, Llc
3020 Crrngton Mill Blvd S
Morrisville NC 27560
919 659-2100

(G-4088)
JASON CASE CORP
4809 Hillsborough Rd (27705-2237)
PHONE..............................212 786-2288
Jason Comparetto, *CEO*
EMP: 9 **EST:** 2015
SALES (est): 1.57MM **Privately Held**
Web: www.jasoncases.com
SIC: 3861 Photographic equipment and
supplies

(G-4089)
JOHNSON CONTROLS INC
Also Called: Johnson Controls
5 Moore Dr (27709-0143)
P.O. Box 13398 (27709-3398)
PHONE..............................919 905-5745
Seth Haywood, *Mgr*
EMP: 19
Web: www.johnsoncontrols.com
SIC: 2531 Seats, automobile
HQ: Johnson Controls, Inc.
5757 N Green Bay Ave
Milwaukee WI 53209
866 496-1999

(G-4090)
JUSTENOUGH SOFTWARE CORP INC
1009 Slater Rd Ste 420 (27703-8327)
PHONE..............................800 949-3432
Malcolm Edward Buxton, *Brnch Mgr*
EMP: 4
SALES (corp-wide): 48.98MM **Privately Held**
Web: www.justenoughsoftware.com
SIC: 7372 Business oriented computer software
HQ: Justenough Software Corporation, Inc.
15440 Laguna Canyon Rd # 100
Irvine CA 92618

(G-4091)
K&M SHEET METAL LLC
1310 E Cornwallis Rd (27713-1423)
PHONE..............................919 544-8887
EMP: 17 **EST:** 2019
SALES (est): 4.25MM **Privately Held**
Web: www.kmsheetmetal.com
SIC: 3444 Sheet metalwork

(G-4092)
KASHIF MAZHAR
68 Tw Alexander Dr (27709-0151)
PHONE..............................919 314-2891
Kashif Mazhar, *Prin*
EMP: 5
SALES (est): 625.02K **Privately Held**
SIC: 3841 Surgical and medical instruments

(G-4093)
KBI BIOPHARMA INC
2 Triangle Dr (27709-0005)
PHONE..............................919 479-9898
EMP: 6
Web: www.kbibiopharma.com
SIC: 2834 Pharmaceutical preparations
HQ: Kbi Biopharma, Inc.
1101 Hamlin Rd
Durham NC 27704
919 479-9898

(G-4094)
KBI BIOPHARMA INC (DH)
Also Called: K B I Biopharma
1101 Hamlin Rd (27704-9658)
P.O. Box 15579 (27704-0579)
PHONE..............................919 479-9898
J D Mowery, *CEO*
Timothy Kelly, *

Dan Povia, *
Dirk Lange, *
Marykay Marchigiani, *
EMP: 66 **EST:** 2001
SQ FT: 145,000
SALES (est): 430.83MM **Privately Held**
Web: www.kbibiopharma.com
SIC: 2834 8733 Pharmaceutical preparations
; Biotechnical research, noncommercial
HQ: Jsr Corporation
1-9-2, Higashishimbashi
Minato-Ku TKY 105-0

(G-4095)
KESTREL I ACQUISITION CORPORATION
1035 Swabia Ct (27703-8462)
P.O. Box 13582 (27709-3582)
PHONE..............................919 990-7500
EMP: 1567
SIC: 2822 2869 2899 2891 Butadiene-
acrylonitrile, nitrile rubbers, NBR; Vinyl
acetate; Rosin sizes; Adhesives

(G-4096)
KINETIC SYSTEMS INC
4900 Prospectus Dr Ste 500 (27713-4407)
PHONE..............................919 322-7200
James Wilber, *Opers Mgr*
EMP: 75
SALES (corp-wide): 242.12K **Privately Held**
Web: www.kinetics.net
SIC: 1711 3312 Mechanical contractor; Blast
furnaces and steel mills
HQ: Kinetic Systems, Inc.
4309 Hacienda Dr
Pleasanton CA 94588
510 683-6000

(G-4097)
KOLB BOYETTE & ASSOC INC
Also Called: Triangle Web Printing
514 United Dr Ste A (27713-1663)
P.O. Box 13345 (27709)
PHONE..............................919 544-7839
Al Thorn, *Pr*
Willis Roberson, *
Eric Kolb, *
EMP: 35 **EST:** 1992
SQ FT: 9,000
SALES (est): 5.31MM **Privately Held**
Web: www.triwebprinting.com
SIC: 2752 Offset printing

(G-4098)
KONAMI DIGITAL ENTRMT INC
1953 Tw Alexander Dr (27703-0397)
PHONE..............................310 220-8100
EMP: 42
SIC: 7372 Home entertainment computer
software
HQ: Konami Digital Entertainment, Inc.
1 Konami Way
Hawthorne CA 90250
310 220-8100

(G-4099)
KYMERA INTERNATIONAL LLC (PA)
2601 Weck Dr (27709)
PHONE..............................919 544-8090
Barton White, *CEO*
EMP: 25 **EST:** 2018
SALES (est): 76.78MM
SALES (corp-wide): 76.78MM **Privately Held**
SIC: 3399 3334 5169 Metal powders,
pastes, and flakes; Ingots (primary),
aluminum; Industrial chemicals

(G-4100)
L C INDUSTRIES INC (PA)
4500 Emperor Blvd (27703)
P.O. Box 13629 (27709)
PHONE..............................919 596-8277
Richard M Hudson, *Ch*
William L Hudson, *
Tom White, *
◆ **EMP:** 125 **EST:** 1938
SQ FT: 229,000
SALES (est): 7.49MM
SALES (corp-wide): 7.49MM **Privately Held**
Web: www.lcindustries.com
SIC: 5943 2675 2515 2253 Office forms and
supplies; Folders, filing, die-cut: made from
purchased materials; Mattresses and
foundations; Shirts(outerwear), knit

(G-4101)
LASER INK CORPORATION
Also Called: Laser Image Printing & Mktg
4018 Patriot Dr Ste 200 (27703-8083)
PHONE..............................919 361-5822
Richard Smith, *Pr*
Kelly Clark, *
▲ **EMP:** 30 **EST:** 1987
SALES (est): 4.06MM **Privately Held**
Web: www.laserimagenc.com
SIC: 2759 2741 7331 2752 Laser printing;
Miscellaneous publishing; Direct mail
advertising services; Commercial printing,
lithographic

(G-4102)
LEE MARKS (PA)
Also Called: Print Marks Screen Prtg & EMB
4304 Amesbury Ln (27707-5386)
PHONE..............................919 493-2208
Lee Marks, *Owner*
EMP: 5 **EST:** 1988
SALES (est): 200K **Privately Held**
Web: www.localprintnc.com
SIC: 2395 2396 Embroidery products,
except Schiffli machine; Screen printing on
fabric articles

(G-4103)
LEICA MICROSYSTEMS NC INC
4222 Emperor Blvd Ste 390 (27703-8030)
P.O. Box 13569 (27709-3569)
PHONE..............................919 428-9661
Eric L Buckland, *CEO*
Tom Livingston, *CFO*
Joseph E Vance, *VP*
George F Wildeman, *VP*
EMP: 10 **EST:** 2004
SQ FT: 2,000
SALES (est): 2.19MM **Privately Held**
Web: www.leica-microsystems.com
SIC: 3827 Optical instruments and apparatus

(G-4104)
LEXITAS PHARMA SERVICES INC (PA)
5425 Page Rd Ste 410 (27703-2059)
PHONE..............................919 205-0012
George Magrath, *CEO*
Jeanne Hecht, *
Chad Ice, *
EMP: 40 **EST:** 2011
SALES (est): 7.25MM
SALES (corp-wide): 7.25MM **Privately Held**
Web: www.lexitas.com
SIC: 8731 2834 Commercial physical
research; Pharmaceutical preparations

(G-4105)
LINDE GAS & EQUIPMENT INC
Also Called: Linde Gas North America
11 Triangle Dr (27709-0005)
P.O. Box 12338 (27709-2338)
PHONE..............................919 549-0633
Roger Wyett, *Mgr*
EMP: 58
Web: www.lindeus.com
SIC: 2813 8731 Oxygen, compressed or
liquefied; Commercial physical research
HQ: Linde Gas & Equipment Inc.
10 Riverview Dr
Danbury CT 06810
844 445-4633

(G-4106)
LIQUIDATING REICHHOLD INC
Also Called: Reichhold Liquidation, Inc.
1035 Swabia Ct (27703-8462)
P.O. Box 13582 (27709-3582)
PHONE..............................919 990-7500
◆ **EMP:** 550
SIC: 2821 2822 2869 2899 Plastics
materials and resins; Butadiene-
acrylonitrile, nitrile rubbers, NBR; Vinyl
acetate; Rosin sizes

(G-4107)
LMG HOLDINGS INC
4920 S Alston Ave (27713-4423)
PHONE..............................919 653-0910
Kathryn Claire Haertel, *Prin*
EMP: 11 **EST:** 1993
SALES (est): 4.06MM **Privately Held**
SIC: 3694 Ignition systems, high frequency

(G-4108)
LOGICBIT SOFTWARE LLC
Also Called: Houdiniesq
2530 Meridian Pkwy Ste 300 (27713-5272)
PHONE..............................888 366-2280
Francisco Rivera, *CEO*
Annie Zhang, *Sec*
Frank Rivera, *Managing Member*
EMP: 20 **EST:** 2008
SQ FT: 12,000
SALES (est): 451.59K **Privately Held**
Web: www.houdiniesq.com
SIC: 7371 7372 Computer software systems
analysis and design, custom; Prepackaged
software

(G-4109)
LOGO LABEL PRINTING COMPANY
4416 Bennett Memorial Rd Ste 101
(27705-2484)
PHONE..............................919 309-0007
Timothy Oats, *Pr*
Catherine Bacon, *VP*
EMP: 4 **EST:** 2006
SALES (est): 1.15MM **Privately Held**
Web: www.logolabelprinting.com
SIC: 2759 Screen printing

(G-4110)
LRW HOLDINGS INC
Also Called: Little Red Wagon Granola
2310 Sparger Rd Ste B (27705-1208)
PHONE..............................919 609-4172
Venmathy Mcmahan, *Pr*
EMP: 7 **EST:** 2019
SALES (est): 709.73K **Privately Held**
SIC: 5145 2043 Snack foods; Cereal
breakfast foods

(G-4111)
LULU PRESS INC
700 Park Offices Dr Ste 250 (27709)
P.O. Box 12018 (27709)

▲ = Import ▼ = Export
◆ = Import/Export

PHONE....................919 447-3290
Robert Young, *CEO*
Dale Pithers, *Finance*
Don Cvetko, *
EMP: 88 **EST:** 2003
SQ FT: 27,600
SALES (est): 10.32MM **Privately Held**
Web: www.lulu.com
SIC: 2731 Books, publishing and printing

(G-4112)
LUMEDICA INC
404 Hunt St Ste 520 (27701-2275)
PHONE....................919 886-1863
William Brown, *Pr*
EMP: 5 **EST:** 2014
SALES (est): 2.16MM **Privately Held**
Web: www.lumedicasystems.com
SIC: 3845 Retinoscopes, electromedical

(G-4113)
LUXOR HYDRATION LLC
3600 N Duke St (27704-1709)
PHONE....................919 568-5047
Maya Peacock, *Managing Member*
EMP: 11 **EST:** 2020
SALES (est): 300K **Privately Held**
SIC: 3841 7389 IV transfusion apparatus;
Business services, nec

(G-4114)
MACHINE CONSULTING SVCS INC
Also Called: MCS
1545 Cooper St (27703-5082)
PHONE....................919 596-3033
Mike Appel, *Pr*
EMP: 5 **EST:** 1998
SQ FT: 1,800
SALES (est): 2.06MM **Privately Held**
SIC: 3599 Machine shop, jobbing and repair

(G-4115)
MACOM TECHNOLOGY SOLUTIONS INC
3028 Cornwallis Rd Ste 200 (27709-0007)
PHONE....................919 407-4768
Stephen Daly, *Pr*
EMP: 55
Web: www.macom.com
SIC: 3663 Radio and t.v. communications
equipment
HQ: Macom Technology Solutions Inc.
100 Chelmsford St
Lowell MA 01851

(G-4116)
MAGIC FACTORY LLC
3818 Somerset Dr (27707-5017)
PHONE....................919 585-5644
Danielle Lemmon Zapotoczny, *
EMP: 25 **EST:** 2008
SALES (est): 870.78K **Privately Held**
Web: www.magicfactory.com
SIC: 2731 7812 Books, publishing only;
Motion picture production and distribution

(G-4117)
MANUFACTUR LLC
201 W Main St (27701-3228)
PHONE....................919 937-2090
EMP: 4 **EST:** 2018
SALES (est): 363.53K **Privately Held**
SIC: 3999 Manufacturing industries, nec

(G-4118)
MAPJOY LLC
4501 Marena Pl (27707-9220)
PHONE....................919 450-8360
Bryan Conner, *Prin*
EMP: 4 **EST:** 2014

SALES (est): 142.96K **Privately Held**
Web: www.mapjoync.com
SIC: 7372 Prepackaged software

(G-4119)
MAVERICK BIOFEULS
104 Tw Alexander Dr Bldg 4a (27709-0002)
P.O. Box 13108 (27709-3108)
PHONE....................919 749-8717
David Bradin, *Prin*
EMP: 5 **EST:** 2008
SALES (est): 436.89K **Privately Held**
Web: www.mavericksynfuels.com
SIC: 2869 Industrial organic chemicals, nec

(G-4120)
MAVERICK BIOFUELS
104 Tw Alexander Dr (27709-0002)
P.O. Box 13108 (27709-3108)
PHONE....................919 931-1434
Sam Yenne, *CEO*
EMP: 4 **EST:** 2011
SALES (est): 588.74K **Privately Held**
Web: www.mavericksynfuels.com
SIC: 1382 Oil and gas exploration services

(G-4121)
MCCORKLE SIGN COMPANY INC
1107 E Geer St (27704-5024)
P.O. Box 11384 (27703-0384)
PHONE....................919 687-7080
Tommy J Mccorkle, *Pr*
EMP: 21 **EST:** 1983
SQ FT: 12,000
SALES (est): 2.84MM **Privately Held**
Web:
www.signdesignandinstallation.com
SIC: 3993 1799 Electric signs; Sign
installation and maintenance

(G-4122)
MEASUREMENT INCORPORATED (PA)
Also Called: M I
423 Morris St (27701-2128)
PHONE....................919 683-2413
Henry H Scherich, *Pr*
Michael Bunch, *
Holly Baker, *
Kirk Ridge, *
Kendra Timberlake, *
EMP: 97 **EST:** 1980
SQ FT: 63,000
SALES (est): 90.64MM
SALES (corp-wide): 90.64MM **Privately Held**
Web: www.measurementinc.com
SIC: 2752 8748 2791 2789 Offset printing;
Testing service, educational or personnel;
Typesetting; Bookbinding and related work

(G-4123)
MED EXPRESS/MEDICAL SPC INC
3874 S Alston Ave Ste 103 (27713-1883)
P.O. Box 13816 (27709-3816)
PHONE....................919 572-2568
Curtis Beatty, *CEO*
Annette Beatty, *Sec*
EMP: 19 **EST:** 1996
SQ FT: 2,000
SALES (est): 2.39MM **Privately Held**
Web: www.specialtycma.com
SIC: 5047 3841 Medical equipment and
supplies; Surgical and medical instruments

(G-4124)
MEDKOO INC
Also Called: Medkoo Biosciences
2224 Sedwick Rd Ste 102 (27713-2656)
PHONE....................919 636-5577
Qingqi Chen, *Pr*

EMP: 6 **EST:** 2009
SQ FT: 1,900
SALES (est): 368.99K **Privately Held**
Web: www.medkoo.com
SIC: 2833 Medicinals and botanicals

(G-4125)
MEDLIO INC
Also Called: Medlio
3313 Old Chapel Hill Rd (27707-3611)
PHONE....................919 599-4870
David Brooks, *CEO*
EMP: 5 **EST:** 2013
SALES (est): 290.25K **Privately Held**
Web: www.medl.io
SIC: 7372 Application computer software

(G-4126)
MEMSCAP INC (HQ)
3021 E Cornwallis Rd Research Triangle Pk
(27709-0146)
P.O. Box 14486 (27709-4486)
PHONE....................919 248-4102
Jean Michel Karam, *CEO*
Ron Wages, *
Jan Hallenstvedt, *
Yann Cousinet, *
Nicolas Bertsch, *
EMP: 45 **EST:** 1999
SQ FT: 14,000
SALES (est): 5.67MM **Privately Held**
Web: www.memscap.com
SIC: 3674 Microcircuits, integrated
(semiconductor)
PA: Memscap
Parc Activillage
Crolles Cedex ARA 38926

(G-4127)
MEMSCAP INC
3026 Cornwallis Rd (27709-0007)
P.O. Box 13942 (27709-3942)
PHONE....................919 248-1441
James Carter, *Opers Mgr*
EMP: 110
SQ FT: 112,000
Web: www.memscap.com
SIC: 3699 Electrical equipment and supplies,
nec
HQ: Memscap, Inc.
3021 Cornwallis Rd
Durham NC 27709
919 248-4102

(G-4128)
MERCK SHARP & DOHME LLC
Also Called: Merck
5325 Old Oxford Rd (27712-8730)
PHONE....................919 425-4000
John Wagner, *Mgr*
EMP: 120
SALES (corp-wide): 64.17B **Publicly Held**
Web: www.merck.com
SIC: 2834 Pharmaceutical preparations
HQ: Merck Sharp & Dohme Llc
126 E Lincoln Ave
Rahway NJ 07065
908 740-4000

(G-4129)
MERCK TEKNIKA LLC
100 Rodolphe St Bldg 1300 (27712-9402)
PHONE....................919 620-7200
Rita Karachun, *Pr*
Caroline Litchfield, *
Jon Filderman, *
EMP: 35 **EST:** 2000
SALES (est): 10.93MM
SALES (corp-wide): 64.17B **Publicly Held**
SIC: 2834 Pharmaceutical preparations
PA: Merck & Co., Inc.

126 E Lincoln Ave
Rahway NJ 07065
908 740-4000

(G-4130)
MEREDITH MEDIA CO
Also Called: Fastsigns
4015 University Dr Ste 2d (27707-2548)
PHONE....................919 748-4808
EMP: 4 **EST:** 2020
SALES (est): 423.27K **Privately Held**
Web: www.fastsigns.com
SIC: 3993 Signs and advertising specialties

(G-4131)
METALCRAFT FABRICATING COMPANY
1316 Old Oxford Rd (27704-9500)
P.O. Box 15238 (27704-0238)
PHONE....................919 477-2117
James D Fletcher, *Pr*
EMP: 12 **EST:** 1956
SQ FT: 9,250
SALES (est): 1.01MM **Privately Held**
Web: www.metalfabricating.com
SIC: 3441 Fabricated structural metal

(G-4132)
MICELL TECHNOLOGIES INC
801 Capitola Dr Ste 1 (27713-4384)
PHONE....................919 313-2102
Arthur J Benvenuto, *CEO*
Jim Mcclain, *Sr VP*
James A Klein Junior, *CFO*
James B Mcclain, *Sr VP*
EMP: 47 **EST:** 1996
SQ FT: 12,000
SALES (est): 7.04MM **Privately Held**
Web: www.micell.com
SIC: 3841 Surgical and medical instruments

(G-4133)
MIKE DS BBQ LLC
455 S Driver St (27703-4201)
P.O. Box 11872 (27703-0872)
PHONE....................866 960-8652
Michael Delossantos, *Managing Member*
Michael De Los Santos, *Managing Member*
EMP: 5 **EST:** 2013
SALES (est): 206.73K **Privately Held**
Web: www.mikedsbbq.com
SIC: 5999 2033 5812 Miscellaneous retail
stores, nec; Barbecue sauce: packaged in
cans, jars, etc.; Restaurant, lunch counter

(G-4134)
MIKRON INDUSTRIES
2505 Meridian Pkwy # 250 (27713-1799)
PHONE....................253 398-1382
EMP: 8
SALES (est): 235.18K **Privately Held**
Web: www.mikron.com
SIC: 3999 Manufacturing industries, nec

(G-4135)
MILLENNIUM PACKAGING SVC LLC
1953 Tw Alexander Dr Ste A (27703-0397)
PHONE....................775 353-5127
EMP: 6
SALES (corp-wide): 5.02MM **Privately Held**
SIC: 2441 Nailed wood boxes and shook
PA: Millennium Packaging Service Llc
100 Enterprise
Carbondale PA 18407
570 282-2990

(G-4136)
MISONIX LLC (HQ)
Also Called: Misonix

4721 Emperor Blvd (27703-8579)
PHONE.............................631 694-9555
Stavros G Vizirgianakis, *CEO*
Joseph P Dwyer, *CFO*
Sharon W Klugewicz, *COO*
Jay Waggoner, *Executive Global Sales Vice President*
Robert S Ludecker, *S&M/VP*
EMP: 59 **EST:** 1967
SALES (est): 74.02MM
SALES (corp-wide): 573.28MM **Publicly Held**
Web: www.bioventussurgical.com
SIC: 3821 Laboratory apparatus and furniture
PA: Bioventus Inc.
　　4721 Emperor Blvd Ste 100
　　Durham NC 27703
　　919 474-6700

(G-4137)
MISONIX OPCO INC (DH)
4721 Emperor Blvd (27703-8579)
PHONE.............................631 694-9555
Stavros G Vizirgianakis, *CEO*
Stavros G Vizirgianakis, *Pr*
Joseph P Dwyer, *CFO*
Sharon Klugewicz, *COO*
Robert S Ludecker, *Senior Vice President Global Sales*
▲ **EMP:** 18 **EST:** 1959
SALES (est): 62.48MM
SALES (corp-wide): 573.28MM **Publicly Held**
Web: www.bioventussurgical.com
SIC: 3841 3845 3677 Surgical and medical instruments; Electromedical equipment; Electronic coils and transformers
HQ: Misonix, Llc
　　4721 Emperor Blvd
　　Durham NC 27703
　　631 694-9555

(G-4138)
MISS TORTILLAS INC
3801 Wake Forest Rd Ste 106
(27703-3637)
PHONE.............................919 598-8646
Marcelo Ocampo, *Pr*
▲ **EMP:** 6 **EST:** 2004
SALES (est): 212.67K **Privately Held**
SIC: 2099 Tortillas, fresh or refrigerated

(G-4139)
MITT S NITTS INC
1014 S Hoover Rd (27703-4338)
PHONE.............................919 596-6793
Dennis Russell, *Pr*
EMP: 45 **EST:** 1977
SQ FT: 25,000
SALES (est): 2.1MM **Privately Held**
Web: www.mittsnitts.com
SIC: 2253 2259 2297 2381 Sweaters and sweater coats, knit; Gloves, knit, except dress and semidress gloves; Nonwoven fabrics; Fabric dress and work gloves

(G-4140)
MURANO CORPORATION
68 Tw Alexander Dr Ste 207 (27709-0151)
PHONE.............................919 294-8233
Rajagopalan Sreekumar, *Prin*
EMP: 10 **EST:** 2010
SALES (est): 1.88MM **Privately Held**
Web: www.muranocorp.com
SIC: 7372 Prepackaged software

(G-4141)
NACHO INDUSTRIES INC
8 Heath Pl (27705-5713)
PHONE.............................919 937-9471
Jacob D Baldridge, *Pr*

EMP: 4 **EST:** 2012
SALES (est): 151.09K **Privately Held**
Web: www.nachoindustries.com
SIC: 3999 Manufacturing industries, nec

(G-4142)
NALA MEMBRANES INC
2 Davis Dr # 113 (27709-0003)
PHONE.............................540 230-5606
Beverly Mecham, *Pr*
EMP: 6 **EST:** 2018
SALES (est): 2.8MM **Privately Held**
Web: www.nalamembranes.com
SIC: 3589 Water treatment equipment, industrial

(G-4143)
NATURALLY ME BOUTIQUE INC
3231 Shannon Rd Apt 31c (27707-6306)
PHONE.............................919 519-0783
Chaudra Smith, *Pr*
EMP: 4 **EST:** 2012
SALES (est): 162.48K **Privately Held**
SIC: 2844 2841 Face creams or lotions; Soap and other detergents

(G-4144)
NDSL INC
1000 Parliament Ct (27703-8456)
PHONE.............................919 790-7877
Earl Philmon, *CEO*
Rob Willcock, *CFO*
▲ **EMP:** 37 **EST:** 1999
SALES (est): 8.3MM
SALES (corp-wide): 15.46MM **Privately Held**
Web: www.cellwatch.com
SIC: 3825 Electrical power measuring equipment
PA: Ndsl Group Limited
　　Gloucester House
　　Milton Keynes BUCKS MK9 2
　　190 830-3730

(G-4145)
NETAPP INC
7301 Kit Creek Rd (27709-0266)
PHONE.............................919 476-4571
EMP: 65
Web: www.rtp.org
SIC: 3572 Computer storage devices
PA: Netapp, Inc.
　　3060 Olsen Dr
　　San Jose CA 95128

(G-4146)
NETQEM LLC
1012 Park Glen Pl (27713-8998)
PHONE.............................919 544-4122
James Huan, *Dir Opers*
▲ **EMP:** 4 **EST:** 2005
SALES (est): 477.69K **Privately Held**
Web: www.netqem.us
SIC: 2819 Industrial inorganic chemicals, nec

(G-4147)
NEUROTRONIK INC
4021 Stirrup Creek Dr Ste 210
(27703-9352)
P.O. Box 98553 (27624-8553)
PHONE.............................919 883-4155
Shawn Peterson, *Pr*
EMP: 27 **EST:** 2013
SALES (est): 1.74MM **Privately Held**
SIC: 2834 Pharmaceutical preparations

(G-4148)
NEWS AND OBSERVER PUBG CO
Also Called: Herald-Sun, The
2530 Meridian Pkwy Ste 300 (27713-5272)

PHONE.............................919 419-6500
EMP: 43
SALES (corp-wide): 1.39B **Privately Held**
SIC: 2711 Newspapers, publishing and printing
HQ: The News And Observer Publishing Company
　　421 Fayetteville St # 104
　　Raleigh NC 27601
　　919 829-4500

(G-4149)
NOCTURNAL PRODUCT DEV LLC
8128 Renaissance Pkwy Ste 210
(27713-6695)
PHONE.............................919 321-1331
Kenneth Armstrong, *Prin*
EMP: 6 **EST:** 2010
SALES (est): 3.43MM **Privately Held**
Web: www.nocturnalpd.com
SIC: 3841 Surgical and medical instruments

(G-4150)
NOTEMEAL INC
122 E Parrish St (27701-3319)
PHONE.............................312 550-2049
James Coffos, *Pr*
EMP: 20 **EST:** 2019
SALES (est): 1.03MM **Privately Held**
Web: explore.teamworks.com
SIC: 7372 Prepackaged software

(G-4151)
NOVO NORDISK PHRM INDS LP
5235 International Dr (27712-8950)
PHONE.............................919 550-2200
Dale Pulczinski, *Pt*
EMP: 40
SALES (corp-wide): 39.23B **Privately Held**
Web: www.novonordisk-us.com
SIC: 2834 Pharmaceutical preparations
HQ: Novo Nordisk Pharmaceutical Industries, Lp
　　3612 Powhatan Rd
　　Clayton NC 27527

(G-4152)
NUVOTRONICS INC (DH)
2305 Presidential Dr (27703-8039)
PHONE.............................434 298-6940
Jean-marc Rollin, *Pr*
Scott Meller, *
Martin J Amen, *
EMP: 52 **EST:** 2008
SALES (est): 24.2MM
SALES (corp-wide): 1.48B **Privately Held**
Web: www.cubic.com
SIC: 8731 3679 Electronic research; Microwave components
HQ: Cubic Corporation
　　9233 Balboa Ave
　　San Diego CA 92123
　　858 277-6780

(G-4153)
NVIDIA CORPORATION
2600 Meridian Pkwy (27713-2203)
PHONE.............................408 486-2000
EMP: 11
Web: www.nvidia.com
SIC: 3674 Semiconductors and related devices
PA: Nvidia Corporation
　　2788 San Tomas Expy
　　Santa Clara CA 95051

(G-4154)
NVN LIQUIDATION INC (PA)
4020 Stirrup Creek Dr Ste 110
(27703-8970)
P.O. Box 64 (27312)

PHONE.............................212 765-9100
Paula Brown Stafford, *Ch Bd*
John A Donofrio, *Ex VP*
Brian M Johnson, *CCO*
EMP: 30 **EST:** 2006
SALES (est): 23.68MM **Privately Held**
Web: www.pelthos.com
SIC: 2834 Dermatologicals

(G-4155)
OLD CASTLE APG SOUTH INC
Also Called: Adams Products
106 S Lasalle St (27705-3017)
PHONE.............................919 383-2521
Hank Hox, *Mgr*
EMP: 4
SQ FT: 3,806
SALES (corp-wide): 34.95B **Privately Held**
Web: www.adamsproducts.com
SIC: 3271 5032 3272 Blocks, concrete or cinder: standard; Concrete building products ; Concrete products, precast, nec
HQ: Oldcastle Apg South, Inc.
　　333 N Greene St Ste 500
　　Greensboro NC 27401

(G-4156)
ONCOCEUTICS INC
2505 Meridian Pkwy Ste 100 (27713-2288)
PHONE.............................678 897-0563
Wolfgang Oster, *CEO*
Joshua Allen, *VP*
Lee Schalop, *CFO*
EMP: 12 **EST:** 2009
SALES (est): 285.07K
SALES (corp-wide): 324K **Publicly Held**
Web: www.chimerix.com
SIC: 2834 Pharmaceutical preparations
PA: Chimerix, Inc.
　　2505 Mridian Pkwy Ste 100
　　Durham NC 27713
　　919 806-1074

(G-4157)
ORGBOOK INC
4307 Emperor Blvd Ste 300 (27703-8080)
PHONE.............................615 483-5410
Glen Caplan, *Prin*
EMP: 5 **EST:** 2012
SALES (est): 231.44K **Privately Held**
SIC: 7372 Business oriented computer software

(G-4158)
ORGSPAN INC
4307 Emperor Blvd Ste 300 (27703-8080)
PHONE.............................855 674-7726
EMP: 5
SALES (est): 739.06K
SALES (corp-wide): 37.98MM **Privately Held**
SIC: 7372 Prepackaged software
HQ: Interactive Intelligence Group, Inc.
　　7601 Interactive Way
　　Indianapolis IN 46278
　　317 872-3000

(G-4159)
ORIEL THERAPEUTICS INC
630 Davis Dr Ste 120 (27713)
P.O. Box 14087 (27709-4087)
PHONE.............................919 313-1290
Richard Fuller, *CEO*
Paul J Atkins, *Pr*
EMP: 6 **EST:** 2001
SALES (est): 1.82MM **Privately Held**
SIC: 2834 Pharmaceutical preparations
HQ: Sandoz Inc.
　　100 College Rd W
　　Princeton NJ 08540
　　609 627-8500

▲ = Import ▼ = Export
◆ = Import/Export

(G-4160)

ORLANDOS CSTM DESIGN T-SHIRTS
2824 N Roxboro St (27704-3246)
PHONE...............................919 220-5515
Orlando Clark, *Owner*
EMP: 6 **EST:** 1995
SALES (est): 218.86K **Privately Held**
Web: www.orlandoscdp.com
SIC: 2759 7389 Screen printing; Embroidery advertising

(G-4161)

OVERSTREET SIGN CONTRS INC
2210 Page Rd Ste 101 (27703-5949)
PHONE...............................919 596-7300
Gregory L Overstreet, *Pr*
John E Couch Junior, *VP*
Martin J Horn, *Sec*
EMP: 7 **EST:** 1996
SQ FT: 3,750
SALES (est): 2.32MM **Privately Held**
Web: www.overstreetsigns.com
SIC: 3993 Displays and cutouts, window and lobby

(G-4162)

OYSTER MERGER SUB II LLC
4721 Emperor Blvd Ste 100 (27703-7663)
PHONE...............................919 474-6700
EMP: 109 **EST:** 2021
SALES (est): 880.23K
SALES (corp-wide): 573.28MM **Publicly Held**
SIC: 3841 Surgical and medical instruments
PA: Bioventus Inc.
4721 Emperor Blvd Ste 100
Durham NC 27703
919 474-6700

(G-4163)

PALLET ALLIANCE INC
318 Blackwell St Ste 260 (27701-2884)
PHONE...............................919 442-1400
Sandra Messinger, *Pr*
Paul Messinger, *Genl Mgr*
EMP: 13 **EST:** 1995
SALES (est): 7.4MM **Privately Held**
Web: www.tpai.com
SIC: 2448 Pallets, wood

(G-4164)

PANACEUTICS NUTRITION INC
6 Davis Dr (27709-0003)
PHONE...............................919 797-9623
Adam Monroe, *CEO*
EMP: 13
SALES (est): 519.64K **Privately Held**
Web: www.panaceutics.com
SIC: 2099 7389 Food preparations, nec; Business services, nec

(G-4165)

PARATA SYSTEMS LLC (HQ)
Also Called: Tcgrx
106 Roche Dr (27703-0359)
PHONE...............................888 727-2821
Rob Kill, *CEO*
Jason Buchwald, *General Vice President**
Mark Longley, *CCO**
Marcus Kennedy, *
Graham Schillmoller, *
EMP: 235 **EST:** 2001
SALES (est): 93.35MM
SALES (corp-wide): 20.18B **Publicly Held**
Web: www.parata.com
SIC: 3826 8733 Automatic chemical analyzers; Research institute
PA: Becton, Dickinson And Company
1 Becton Dr
Franklin Lakes NJ 07417
201 847-6800

(G-4166)

PARTY TABLES LAND CO LLC
2455 S Alston Ave (27713-1301)
P.O. Box 13447 (27709-3447)
PHONE...............................919 596-3521
EMP: 6 **EST:** 2019
SALES (est): 822.39K **Privately Held**
Web: www.partytables.com
SIC: 2392 Household furnishings, nec

(G-4167)

PATHEON INC
4815 Emperor Blvd Ste 100 (27703-8470)
PHONE...............................919 226-3200
EMP: 4
SALES (corp-wide): 42.86B **Publicly Held**
Web: www.patheon.com
SIC: 2834 Pharmaceutical preparations
HQ: Patheon Inc
2100 Syntex Crt
Mississauga ON L5N 7
905 821-4001

(G-4168)

PATHEON INC
4815 Emperor Blvd Ste 100 (27703-8470)
PHONE...............................919 226-3200
EMP: 1200
SIC: 2834 Pharmaceutical preparations

(G-4169)

PBM GRAPHICS INC
4102 S Miami Blvd (27703-9138)
P.O. Box 2665 (28221)
PHONE...............................919 544-6222
Daniel Pink, *Prin*
EMP: 114
SALES (corp-wide): 15B **Privately Held**
Web: www.rrd.com
SIC: 2752 Offset printing
HQ: Pbm Graphics, Inc.
3700 S Miami Blvd
Durham NC 27703
919 544-6222

(G-4170)

PBM GRAPHICS INC (DH)
Also Called: R. R. Donnelley & Sons
3700 S Miami Blvd (27703-9130)
P.O. Box 13603 (27709-3603)
PHONE...............................919 544-6222
Rick Jones, *CEO*
Adam Geerts, *
Dave Mattingly, *
Greg Simpson, *
Johnny Mendoza, *
◆ **EMP:** 230 **EST:** 1983
SQ FT: 130,000
SALES (est): 43.14MM
SALES (corp-wide): 15B **Privately Held**
Web: www.rrd.com
SIC: 2752 Offset printing
HQ: Consolidated Graphics, Inc.
5858 Westheimer Rd # 200
Houston TX 77057

(G-4171)

PEACE OF MIND PUBLICATIONS
1321 Shiley Dr (27704-1495)
PHONE...............................919 308-5137
Tonya Headen, *Prin*
EMP: 5 **EST:** 2013
SALES (est): 79.39K **Privately Held**
SIC: 2741 Miscellaneous publishing

(G-4172)

PEGASUS BUILDERS SUPPLY LLC
2228 Page Rd Ste 108 (27703-7933)
PHONE...............................919 244-1586
EMP: 6 **EST:** 2007

SALES (est): 487.3K **Privately Held**
Web: www.pegasusbuilderssupply.com
SIC: 2431 Doors, wood

(G-4173)

PERFORMANCE PRINT SERVICES LLC
1 Tw Alexander Dr Ste 130 (27709-0152)
PHONE...............................919 957-9995
EMP: 6 **EST:** 2017
SALES (est): 865K **Privately Held**
Web:
www.performanceprintservices.com
SIC: 2752 Offset printing

(G-4174)

PERSEUS INTERMEDIATE INC
4721 Emperor Blvd Ste 100 (27703-7663)
PHONE...............................919 474-6700
EMP: 34 **EST:** 2021
SALES (est): 1.43MM
SALES (corp-wide): 573.28MM **Publicly Held**
SIC: 3841 Surgical and medical instruments
HQ: Bioventus Llc
4721 Emperor Blvd Ste 100
Durham NC 27703
800 396-4325

(G-4175)

PETNET SOLUTIONS INC
2310 Presidential Dr Ste 108 (27703-8569)
PHONE...............................919 572-5544
Susan Gridgers, *Prin*
EMP: 4
SALES (corp-wide): 84.78B **Privately Held**
Web: www.siemens-healthineers.com
SIC: 2835 Radioactive diagnostic substances
HQ: Petnet Solutions, Inc.
810 Innovation Dr
Knoxville TN 37932
865 218-2000

(G-4176)

PFIZER INC
Also Called: Pfizer
1040 Swabia Ct (27703-8481)
PHONE...............................919 941-5185
Brian Hrudka, *Mgr*
EMP: 11
SALES (corp-wide): 63.63B **Publicly Held**
Web: www.pfizer.com
SIC: 2834 Pharmaceutical preparations
PA: Pfizer Inc.
66 Hudson Blvd E
New York NY 10001
212 733-2323

(G-4177)

PHITONEX INC
701 W Main St Ste 200 (27701-5012)
PHONE...............................855 874-4866
Mike Stadnisky, *CEO*
EMP: 7 **EST:** 2017
SALES (est): 2.24MM
SALES (corp-wide): 42.86B **Publicly Held**
Web: www.thermofisher.com
SIC: 3826 Analytical instruments
PA: Thermo Fisher Scientific Inc.
168 3rd Ave
Waltham MA 02451
781 622-1000

(G-4178)

PHONONIC INC (PA)
801 Capitola Dr (27713-4382)
PHONE...............................919 908-6300
Anthony Atti, *Pr*
Tom Werthan, *CFO*
Ron Tarter, *COO*
▲ **EMP:** 83 **EST:** 2008

SQ FT: 2,500
SALES (est): 26.04MM **Privately Held**
Web: www.phononic.com
SIC: 3674 7371 Semiconductors and related devices; Computer software development and applications

(G-4179)

PHOTONICARE INC
2800 Meridian Pkwy Ste 175 (27713-5257)
PHONE...............................866 411-3277
Ryan Shelton, *CEO*
Stephen Boppart, *CMO*
Ryan Nolan, *VP*
EMP: 23 **EST:** 2013
SALES (est): 4.16MM **Privately Held**
Web: www.photoni.care
SIC: 3841 Surgical and medical instruments

(G-4180)

PIE PUSHERS
625 Hugo St (27704-4554)
PHONE...............................919 901-0743
EMP: 6 **EST:** 2017
SALES (est): 341.38K **Privately Held**
Web: www.piepushers.com
SIC: 3545 Pushers

(G-4181)

PIECE OF PIE LLC
904 9th St (27705-4105)
PHONE...............................919 286-7421
EMP: 6 **EST:** 2006
SALES (est): 476.52K **Privately Held**
Web: www.regencycleaner.com
SIC: 2842 Laundry cleaning preparations

(G-4182)

PIEDMONT JOINERY INC
2322 Glendale Ave (27704-4168)
PHONE...............................919 632-3703
Tim Harrison, *Pr*
EMP: 4 **EST:** 2008
SALES (est): 137.41K **Privately Held**
Web: www.piedmontjoinery.com
SIC: 2431 Millwork

(G-4183)

PINE RES INSTRUMENTATION INC
2741 Campus Walk Ave Bldg 100
(27705-8878)
PHONE...............................919 782-8320
Joseph Hines, *Pr*
EMP: 16 **EST:** 2005
SQ FT: 5,000
SALES (est): 1.59MM **Privately Held**
Web: www.pineresearch.com
SIC: 3826 Protein analyzers, laboratory type

(G-4184)

PLANTATION HOUSE FOODS INC
3316 Stoneybrook Dr (27705-2423)
PHONE...............................919 381-5495
Doug Sharpe, *Pr*
EMP: 6 **EST:** 1991
SALES (est): 150.81K **Privately Held**
SIC: 2032 Mexican foods, nec: packaged in cans, jars, etc.

(G-4185)

PMG-DH COMPANY
1530 N Gregson St Ste 2a (27701-1164)
PHONE...............................919 419-6500
TOLL FREE: 888
David Paxton, *Pr*
EMP: 184 **EST:** 1896
SQ FT: 116,000
SALES (est): 950.15K
SALES (corp-wide): 147.64MM **Privately Held**

SIC: 2711 Newspapers, publishing and printing
PA: Paxton Media Group, Llc
100 Television Ln
Paducah KY 42003
270 575-8630

(G-4186)
POLAREAN INC
2500 Meridian Pkwy Ste 175 (27713-4214)
P.O. Box 14805 (27709-4805)
PHONE............................919 206-7900
Bastiaan Driehuys, *Pr*
Kenneth West, *Prin*
Charles Osborne Junior, *CFO*
EMP: 18 EST: 2011
SALES (est): 2.92MM **Privately Held**
Web: www.polarean.com
SIC: 3845 Respiratory analysis equipment, electromedical

(G-4187)
POMDEVICES LLC
178 Colvard Park Dr (27713-5815)
PHONE............................919 200-6538
Ajit Pendse, *Prin*
EMP: 10 EST: 2011
SALES (est): 516.12K **Privately Held**
SIC: 3669 Communications equipment, nec

(G-4188)
PONYSAURUS BREWING LLC
219 Hood St (27701-3715)
PHONE............................919 455-3737
Nick Johnson, *Pr*
EMP: 18 EST: 2015
SALES (est): 1.01MM **Privately Held**
Web: www.ponysaurusbrewing.com
SIC: 2082 Beer (alcoholic beverage)

(G-4189)
POSITIVE PRINTS PROF SVCS LLC
1821 Hillandale Rd Ste 1b Pmb 256
(27705-2659)
PHONE............................336 701-2330
Sharon Perkins, *Managing Member*
EMP: 5 EST: 2011
SALES (est): 111.29K **Privately Held**
SIC: 8742 2731 Marketing consulting services; Books, publishing only

(G-4190)
POSTAL LIQUIDATION INC
3791 S Alston Ave (27713-1803)
EMP: 132
SIC: 3579 Mailing, letter handling, and addressing machines

(G-4191)
POWERSECURE SOLAR LLC
Also Called: Powersecure Solar
4068 Stirrup Creek Dr (27703-9000)
PHONE............................919 213-0798
Marty Meadows, *
Eric Dupont, *
EMP: 122 EST: 2012
SALES (est): 4.54MM
SALES (corp-wide): 26.72B **Publicly Held**
Web: www.powersecure.com
SIC: 3674 Diodes, solid state (germanium, silicon, etc.)
HQ: Powersecure, Inc.
4068 Stirrup Creek Dr
Durham NC 27703
919 556-3056

(G-4192)
PPG INDUSTRIES INC
Also Called: PPG 4685
3161 Hillsborough Rd (27705-4336)

PHONE............................919 382-3100
Tommy Howard, *Mgr*
EMP: 4
SALES (corp-wide): 17.65B **Publicly Held**
Web: www.ppg.com
SIC: 2851 Paints and allied products
PA: Ppg Industries, Inc.
1 Ppg Pl
Pittsburgh PA 15272
412 434-3131

(G-4193)
PRAETEGO INC
68 Tw Alexander Dr (27709-0151)
P.O. Box 13628 (27709-3628)
PHONE............................919 237-7969
Pepper Landson, *CEO*
John Mazur, *Prin*
J Wesley Fox, *Prin*
EMP: 6 EST: 2017
SALES (est): 188.23K **Privately Held**
Web: www.praetego.com
SIC: 8731 2834 Biotechnical research, commercial; Pharmaceutical preparations

(G-4194)
PRECISION BIOSCIENCES INC (PA)
Also Called: Precision
302 E Pettigrew St Ste A100 (27701-2393)
PHONE............................919 314-5512
Michael Amoroso, *Pr*
Kevin J Buehler, *Ch Bd*
Alex Kelly, *CFO*
Jeff Smith, *CRO*
EMP: 47 EST: 2006
SQ FT: 71,305
SALES (est): 48.73MM **Publicly Held**
Web: www.precisionbiosciences.com
SIC: 2836 8731 Biological products, except diagnostic; Biotechnical research, commercial

(G-4195)
PRECISION FERMENTATIONS INC
2810 Meridian Pkwy (27713-5241)
PHONE............................919 717-3983
Jared Resnick, *CEO*
EMP: 31 EST: 2017
SALES (est): 7.97MM **Privately Held**
Web: www.precisionfermentation.com
SIC: 7372 Prepackaged software

(G-4196)
PREMEX INC
Also Called: Iluma Alliance
1307 Person St (27703)
PHONE............................561 962-4128
Alejandro Mesa, *CEO*
Carlos Valencia, *Treas*
◆ EMP: 15 EST: 2002
SALES (est): 3.58MM **Privately Held**
Web: www.premex.co
SIC: 2834 5122 8099 Vitamin preparations; Vitamins and minerals; Nutrition services
PA: Premex S A S
Carrera 50 2 Sur 251 Autopista Sur
Medellin ANT

(G-4197)
PRODUCT IDENTIFICATION INC
1725 Carpenter Fletcher Rd Ste 201
(27713-2271)
P.O. Box 13157 (27709-3157)
PHONE............................919 544-4136
Kingsley D Maynard, *Pr*
EMP: 20 EST: 1995
SQ FT: 8,900
SALES (est): 5.95MM **Privately Held**
Web: www.prod-id.com

SIC: 2759 3479 Labels and seals: printing, nsk; Name plates: engraved, etched, etc.

(G-4198)
PROFORMA PRINT SOURCE
3600 N Duke St (27704-1709)
P.O. Box 16592 (27516-6592)
PHONE............................919 383-2070
Vero Muzzillo, *CEO*
Michael Baucom, *Pr*
EMP: 6 EST: 2010
SALES (est): 206.67K **Privately Held**
SIC: 2752 Offset printing

(G-4199)
PROMETHERA BIOSCIENCES LLC
6 Davis Dr (27709-0003)
PHONE............................919 354-1930
EMP: 19
SALES (corp-wide): 1.57MM **Privately Held**
Web: www.cellaion.com
SIC: 2834 Pharmaceutical preparations
PA: Promethera Biosciences Llc
4700 Falls Of Neuse Rd # 400
Raleigh NC 27609
919 354-1933

(G-4200)
PSI PHARMA SUPPORT AMERICA INC
10 Laboratory Dr (27709-0161)
PHONE............................919 249-2660
EMP: 41
SIC: 2834 Pharmaceutical preparations
HQ: Psi Pharma Support America, Inc.
875 1st Ave
King Of Prussia PA 19406
267 464-2500

(G-4201)
PUMPS BLOWERS & ELC MTRS LLC
2712 Edmund St (27705-3909)
PHONE............................919 286-4975
EMP: 4 EST: 2005
SQ FT: 1,269
SALES (est): 739.22K **Privately Held**
Web: www.pumpsblowers.com
SIC: 7694 Electric motor repair

(G-4202)
QUALITY CLEANING SERVICES LLC
3639 Guess Rd (27705-6908)
PHONE............................919 638-4969
EMP: 12 EST: 2018
SALES (est): 1.4MM **Privately Held**
SIC: 3589 Commercial cleaning equipment

(G-4203)
QUALITY EQUIPMENT LLC
3821 Durham Chapel Hill Blvd
(27707-2523)
PHONE............................919 493-3545
Jason Jarrett, *Brnch Mgr*
EMP: 7
Web: www.qualityequip.com
SIC: 5261 5251 7699 5082 Lawnmowers and tractors; Chainsaws; Lawn mower repair shop; Contractor's materials
PA: Quality Equipment, Llc
2214 N Main St Ste 501
Fuquay Varina NC 27526

(G-4204)
QUEEN OF WINES LLC
122 Wright Hill Dr (27712-9093)
PHONE............................919 348-6630
Laure Levesque, *Pr*
EMP: 13 EST: 2014
SALES (est): 701.77K **Privately Held**

Web: www.queenofwines.com
SIC: 2084 Wines

(G-4205)
R R DONNELLEY & SONS COMPANY
Also Called: RR Donnelley
1 Litho Way (27703-8929)
PHONE............................919 596-8942
Michael Phelps, *Brnch Mgr*
EMP: 28
SALES (corp-wide): 15B **Privately Held**
Web: www.rrd.com
SIC: 2759 Commercial printing, nec
HQ: R. R. Donnelley & Sons Company
35 W Wacker Dr
Chicago IL 60601
312 326-8000

(G-4206)
R65 LABS INC
108.5 E Parrish St (27701)
PHONE............................919 219-1983
Mark Willams, *Pr*
Nancy Owens, *Treas*
EMP: 5 EST: 2013
SALES (est): 484.05K **Privately Held**
Web: www.r65labs.com
SIC: 7372 Application computer software

(G-4207)
RANDOM & KIND LLC
1348 Scholar Dr (27703-6565)
PHONE............................919 249-8809
EMP: 7
SALES (est): 268.21K **Privately Held**
SIC: 7389 3161 Business Activities at Non-Commercial Site; Clothing and apparel carrying cases

(G-4208)
RCWS INC (PA)
421 W Corporation St (27701-2164)
PHONE............................919 680-2655
Carlton Saul, *CEO*
Mona Saul, *Pr*
EMP: 17 EST: 1997
SQ FT: 50,000
SALES (est): 1.71MM **Privately Held**
SIC: 2521 Panel systems and partitions (free-standing), office: wood

(G-4209)
REALXPERIENCE LLC
5109 Sweet Clover Ct (27703-9108)
PHONE............................512 775-4386
EMP: 5 EST: 2010
SALES (est): 206.87K **Privately Held**
Web: www.realxperience.com
SIC: 3822 Air flow controllers, air conditioning and refrigeration

(G-4210)
REICHHOLD HOLDINGS US INC
1035 Swabia Ct (27703-0962)
P.O. Box 13582 (27709-3582)
PHONE............................919 990-7500
◆ EMP: 553
SIC: 2821 2822 2891 3089 Plastics materials and resins; Synthetic rubber; Adhesives and sealants; Bands, plastics

(G-4211)
RENAISSANCE INNOVATIONS LLC
Also Called: RENAISSANCE INNOVATIONS, LLC
2534 Whilden Dr (27713-1356)
PHONE............................774 901-4642
James Corwin, *Prin*
EMP: 4
SALES (corp-wide): 2.98MM **Privately Held**

▲ = Import ▼ = Export
◆ = Import/Export

Web: www.retique.com
SIC: 2851 Paints and allied products
PA: Corwin Collective, Llc
1322 Gloriosa St
Apex NC 27523
844 473-7246

(G-4212)
RENEW LIFE FORMULAS LLC (HQ)
Also Called: Renew Life Cleansing Co
210 W Pettigrew St (27701-3666)
PHONE..............................727 450-1061
Ron Fugate, CEO
Don Pollo, CFO
EMP: 49 EST: 1997
SQ FT: 30,000
SALES (est): 3.77MM
SALES (corp-wide): 7.09B Publicly Held
SIC: 2074 Cottonseed oil mills
PA: The Clorox Company
1221 Broadway
Oakland CA 94612
510 271-7000

(G-4213)
RESEARCH TRNGLE EDTRIAL SLTONS
9 Amador Pl (27712-1461)
PHONE..............................919 808-2719
Julie Vo, CEO
EMP: 5 EST: 2019
SALES (est): 68.29K Privately Held
SIC: 2741 Miscellaneous publishing

(G-4214)
RIBOMETRIX
701 W Main St Ste 200 (27701-5012)
P.O. Box 12878 (27709-2878)
PHONE..............................919 744-9634
Christina Davis, Prin
EMP: 4 EST: 2017
SALES (est): 971.82K Privately Held
Web: www.ribometrix.com
SIC: 3845 Electromedical equipment

(G-4215)
RIPSTOP BY ROLL LLC
1023 S Miami Blvd (27703)
PHONE..............................877 525-7210
Kyle Baker, CEO
EMP: 18 EST: 2014
SQ FT: 4,800
SALES (est): 3.71MM Privately Held
Web: www.ripstopbytheroll.com
SIC: 5131 2211 Piece goods and other
fabrics; Sheets, bedding and table cloths:
cotton

(G-4216)
RIVERBED TECHNOLOGY LLC
5425 Page Rd Ste 200 (27703-7009)
PHONE..............................415 247-8800
EMP: 35
SALES (corp-wide): 380MM Privately
Held
Web: www.riverbed.com
SIC: 3577 Computer peripheral equipment,
nec
HQ: Riverbed Technology Llc
275 Shoreline Dr
Redwood City CA 94065
415 247-8800

(G-4217)
ROCAS WELDING LLC
923 E Trinity Ave Ste F (27704-5076)
PHONE..............................252 290-2233
Roberto Lopez, Managing Member
EMP: 6
SALES (corp-wide): 2.26MM Privately
Held

Web: www.rocaswelding.com
SIC: 7692 Welding repair
PA: Roca's Welding Llc
5114 Cop Ridge Dr U 101
Durham NC 27707
919 362-1937

(G-4218)
ROI INDUSTRIES GROUP INC
Also Called: Roi Machinery & Automation
700a E Club Blvd (27704-4506)
P.O. Box 2884 (27715-2884)
PHONE..............................919 788-7728
Kevin Saylor, CEO
EMP: 5 EST: 2009
SQ FT: 10,000
SALES (est): 6.18MM Privately Held
Web: www.roiindustries.com
SIC: 5084 3556 3565 Industrial machinery
and equipment; Packing house machinery;
Packing and wrapping machinery

(G-4219)
S & D MACHINE & TOOL INC
1404 Old Oxford Rd (27704-9505)
PHONE..............................919 479-8433
Warren Daniels, Pr
Thomas Jones, VP
EMP: 21 EST: 1965
SQ FT: 30,000
SALES (est): 2.65MM Privately Held
Web: www.sdmachinetool.com
SIC: 3599 Machine shop, jobbing and repair

(G-4220)
SAPERE BIO INC
Also Called: Healthspan Dx
400 Park Offices Dr Ste 113 (27709-1015)
P.O. Box 13075 (27709-3075)
PHONE..............................919 260-2565
Claudia Black, Mgr
Natalia Mitin, Pr
EMP: 4 EST: 2013
SALES (est): 1.17MM Privately Held
Web: www.saperebio.com
SIC: 2835 Diagnostic substances

(G-4221)
SARDA TECHNOLOGIES INC
100 Capitola Dr Ste 308 (27713-4497)
PHONE..............................919 757-6825
Bob Conner, CEO
Larry Krauss, Prin
Brian Wong, Prin
John Cambier, Prin
Phil Anthony, Prin
EMP: 5 EST: 2011
SQ FT: 2,000
SALES (est): 881.81K Privately Held
Web: www.sardatech.com
SIC: 3674 Semiconductors and related
devices

(G-4222)
SATCO TRUCK EQUIPMENT INC
2007 Cheek Rd (27704-5115)
P.O. Box 3182 (27715-3182)
PHONE..............................919 383-5547
Michael Diruscio, Pr
EMP: 14 EST: 2010
SALES (est): 743.11K Privately Held
Web: www.satcotruck.com
SIC: 5046 1799 3713 3714 Commercial
equipment, nec; Hydraulic equipment,
installation and service; Utility truck bodies;
Dump truck lifting mechanism

(G-4223)
SATSUMA PHARMACEUTICALS INC
Also Called: Satsuma
4819 Emperor Blvd Ste 340 (27703-5420)

PHONE..............................650 410-3200
Shunji Haruta, Ex Dir
John Kollins, Pr
Heath Lukatch, Ch Bd
Tom O'neil, CFO
Detlef Albrecht, CMO
EMP: 14 EST: 2016
SQ FT: 4,148
Web: www.satsumarx.com
SIC: 2834 Pharmaceutical preparations

(G-4224)
SCALAWAG
318 Blackwell St (27701-2883)
PHONE..............................917 671-7240
EMP: 12 EST: 2019
SALES (est): 279.91K Privately Held
Web: www.scalawagmagazine.org
SIC: 2721 Periodicals

(G-4225)
SCIEPHARM LLC
Also Called: CRS Laboratories
5441 Lumley Rd Ste 103 (27703-7726)
PHONE..............................307 352-9559
Estela Molini, Managing Member
EMP: 13
SALES (corp-wide): 9.67MM Privately
Held
SIC: 2819 Industrial inorganic chemicals, nec
PA: Sciepharm Llc
2201 Candun Dr Ste 102
Apex NC 27523
307 352-9559

(G-4226)
SCIPHER MEDICINE CORPORATION
4134 S Alston Ave Ste 104 (27713-1870)
P.O. Box 110087 (27709-5087)
PHONE..............................781 755-2063
EMP: 5
SALES (est): 536.28K Privately Held
Web: www.sciphermedicine.com
SIC: 2834 Pharmaceutical preparations

(G-4227)
SCRIPTORIUM PUBG SVCS INC
4220 Apex Hwy Ste 340 (27713-5295)
P.O. Box 12761 (27709-2761)
PHONE..............................919 481-2701
Sarah O'keefe, Pr
Alan Pringle, Sec
EMP: 7 EST: 1993
SALES (est): 1.63MM Privately Held
Web: www.scriptorium.com
SIC: 2752 7371 Commercial printing,
lithographic; Custom computer
programming services

(G-4228)
SEAL SEASONS INC
4426 S Miami Blvd Ste 105 (27703-9144)
PHONE..............................919 245-3535
Patrick Mateer, CEO
Dawn Paffenroth Ctrl, Prin
EMP: 15 EST: 2014
SALES (est): 5.44MM Privately Held
Web: www.sealtheseasons.com
SIC: 2037 Frozen fruits and vegetables

(G-4229)
SECURITY SELF STORAGE
1945 E Cornwallis Rd (27713-1493)
PHONE..............................919 544-3969
Antoinette Caron, Mgr
EMP: 4 EST: 2005
SALES (est): 196.22K Privately Held
Web: www.selfstoragenc.com
SIC: 2741 7513 Miscellaneous publishing;
Truck rental and leasing, no drivers

(G-4230)
SENECA DEVICES INC
2 Davis Dr (27709-0003)
PHONE..............................301 412-3576
Samuel Fox, CEO
EMP: 10 EST: 2017
SALES (est): 687K Privately Held
Web: www.senecadevices.com
SIC: 3999 Manufacturing industries, nec

(G-4231)
SHIMADZU SCIENTIFIC INSTRS INC
4022 Stirrup Creek Dr Ste 312
(27703-9411)
PHONE..............................919 425-1010
Chris Gaylor, Mgr
EMP: 4
Web: www.shimadzu.com
SIC: 3826 Analytical instruments
HQ: Shimadzu Scientific Instruments
Incorporated
7102 Riverwood Dr
Columbia MD 21046
800 477-1227

(G-4232)
SHIPMAN TECHNOLOGIES INC
2933 S Miami Blvd Ste 122 (27703-9041)
PHONE..............................919 294-8405
Douglas Shipman, Pr
EMP: 6 EST: 1986
SQ FT: 20,000
SALES (est): 898.46K Privately Held
Web: www.shipmantech.com
SIC: 3699 Electrical equipment and supplies,
nec

(G-4233)
SHOPBOT TOOLS INC
3333b Industrial Dr (27704-9307)
PHONE..............................919 680-4800
Warren Hall, Pr
▲ EMP: 41 EST: 1996
SQ FT: 15,000
SALES (est): 6.25MM Privately Held
Web: www.shopbottools.com
SIC: 5251 3625 Tools; Actuators, industrial

(G-4234)
SIERRA NEVADA CORPORATION
Also Called: SIERRA NEVADA
CORPORATION
1030 Swabia Ct Ste 100 (27703-8070)
PHONE..............................919 595-8551
Jim Raines, Brnch Mgr
EMP: 22
SALES (corp-wide): 2.38B Privately Held
Web: www.sncorp.com
SIC: 3812 3728 Search and navigation
equipment; Aircraft parts and equipment,
nec
PA: Sierra Nevada Company, Llc
444 Salomon Cir
Sparks NV 89434
775 331-0222

(G-4235)
SIGMA XI SCNTFIC RES HNOR SOC
3200 Chapel Hill Nelson Hwy Ste 300
(27709-0013)
P.O. Box 13975 (27709-3975)
PHONE..............................919 549-4691
Jamie Vernon, Ex Dir
EMP: 26 EST: 1886
SQ FT: 52,000
SALES (est): 4.17MM Privately Held
Web: www.sigmaxi.org
SIC: 2721 8733 Magazines: publishing only,
not printed on site; Scientific research
agency

(G-4236)
SIGNS SEALED DELIVERED
6409 Fayetteville Rd (27613-6297)
PHONE..................................919 213-1280
K Shevon Skinner, *Owner*
EMP: 4 **EST:** 2017
SALES (est): 53.15K **Privately Held**
SIC: 3993 Signs and advertising specialties

(G-4237)
SIGNS UNLIMITED INC
6801 Mount Hermon Church Rd Unit C
(27705-8318)
PHONE..................................919 596-7612
Gaston Ballbe, *Pr*
EMP: 16 **EST:** 1997
SALES (est): 2.43MM **Privately Held**
Web: www.signsunlimitedusa.com
SIC: 3993 Electric signs

(G-4238)
SKYBIEN PRESS LLC ✪
1920 E Nc Highway 54 Ste 30
(27713-2293)
PHONE..................................919 544-1777
Seungkyoo B Lee, *Managing Member*
EMP: 4 **EST:** 2023
SALES (est): 533.14K **Privately Held**
SIC: 2741 2711 2621 Miscellaneous
   publishing; Commercial printing and
   newspaper publishing combined; Printing
   paper

(G-4239)
SMART WIRES INC (PA)
Also Called: S W G
1035 Swabia Ct Ste 130 (27703-0963)
P.O. Box 819 (27540)
PHONE..................................919 294-3999
Peter Wells, *Pr*
Thomas R Voss, *
EMP: 65 **EST:** 2010
SALES (est): 15.44MM **Privately Held**
Web: www.smartwires.com
SIC: 3677 Electronic coils and transformers

(G-4240)
SMG HEARTH AND HOME LLC
Also Called: Comfort Bilt
3871 S Alston Ave (27713)
PHONE..................................919 973-4079
▲ **EMP:** 26 **EST:** 2014
SALES (est): 1.06MM **Privately Held**
Web: www.comfortbilt.net
SIC: 3433 Gas infrared heating units

(G-4241)
SNP INC
1301 S Briggs Ave Ste 110 (27703-5070)
PHONE..................................919 598-0400
Joseph D Kehoe, *Pr*
◆ **EMP:** 10 **EST:** 1961
SALES (est): 4.67MM **Privately Held**
Web: www.snpinc.com
SIC: 2824 Acrylic fibers

(G-4242)
SOSTRAM CORPORATION
2525 Meridian Pkwy Ste 350 (27713-5243)
PHONE..................................919 226-1195
Lynn Brookhouser, *Pr*
Fred Hallemann, *Pr*
▲ **EMP:** 4 **EST:** 1999
SALES (est): 787.43K
SALES (corp-wide): 660.29MM **Privately
Held**
Web: www.sipcamagrousa.com
SIC: 2819 5169 7373 Industrial inorganic
   chemicals, nec; Industrial chemicals;
   Computer integrated systems design

HQ: Sipcam Agro Usa, Inc.
   2525 Mridian Pkwy Ste 100
   Durham NC 27713
   919 226-1195

(G-4243)
SOUTHERN ELECTRIC MOTOR CO
2121 Front St # 25 (27705-2518)
PHONE..................................919 688-7879
Martin E Rigsbee, *Pr*
Myra Rigsbee, *Sec*
EMP: 8 **EST:** 1961
SALES (est): 489.27K **Privately Held**
Web: www.southernelectricmotornc.com
SIC: 7694 5063 5999 Electric motor repair;
   Motors, electric; Motors, electric

(G-4244)
SPECTACULAR PUBLISHING INC
3333 Durham Chapel Hill Blvd Ste A101
(27707-6237)
PHONE..................................919 672-0289
Lawrence Davis Iii, *Prin*
EMP: 4 **EST:** 2017
SALES (est): 203.57K **Privately Held**
Web: www.spectacularmag.com
SIC: 2711 Newspapers, publishing and
   printing

(G-4245)
SPEE DEE QUE INSTANT PRTG INC
301 E Chapel Hill St (27701-3301)
P.O. Box 25243 (27702-5243)
PHONE..................................919 683-1307
H Thomas Driver, *Pr*
Gloria Driver, *Sec*
Mike Driver, *VP*
EMP: 6 **EST:** 1975
SQ FT: 2,000
SALES (est): 449.39K **Privately Held**
Web: www.speedeeque.com
SIC: 2752 Offset printing

(G-4246)
SPEEDPRO IMAGING DURHAM
1055 Stillwell Dr Unit 1141 (27707-6365)
PHONE..................................919 278-7964
EMP: 6 **EST:** 2018
SALES (est): 144.75K **Privately Held**
SIC: 3993 Signs and advertising specialties

(G-4247)
SPENCO MEDICAL CORPORATION
2001 Tw Alexander Dr (27709-0184)
PHONE..................................919 544-7900
Seth Richards, *CEO*
Todd Vore, *
Bill Alfano, *
Steve Head, *
▲ **EMP:** 23 **EST:** 1970
SQ FT: 160,000
SALES (est): 489.21K **Privately Held**
Web: www.spenco.com
SIC: 3842 Orthopedic appliances

(G-4248)
SPOONFLOWER INC (DH)
Also Called: Spoonflower
3871 S Alston Ave (27713-1805)
PHONE..................................919 886-7885
Gart Davis, *CEO*
Michael Jones, *
Stephen Fraser, *
Allison Polish, *
Donnie Steele, *
▲ **EMP:** 51 **EST:** 2008
SQ FT: 20,000
SALES (est): 26.18MM
SALES (corp-wide): 2.47B **Privately Held**
Web: www.spoonflower.com

SIC: 2262 Finishing plants, manmade
HQ: Shutterfly, Llc
   10 Almaden Blvd Ste 900
   San Jose CA 95113
   650 610-5200

(G-4249)
STEEL CITY SERVICES LLC
1129 E Geer St (27704-5024)
PHONE..................................919 698-2407
J D Mcqueen, *Pt*
EMP: 14 **EST:** 2010
SALES (est): 1.03MM **Privately Held**
Web: www.steelcityservices.com
SIC: 3312 1796 Rails, steel or iron; Installing
   building equipment

(G-4250)
STERLING CLEORA CORPORATION
3115 Buckingham Rd (27707-4505)
PHONE..................................919 563-5800
Chip Cappelletti, *Pr*
Rich Cappelletti, *
EMP: 12 **EST:** 1994
SALES (est): 4.22MM **Privately Held**
Web: www.csterling.com
SIC: 2541 8712 1542 Store fixtures, wood;
   Architectural services; Design and erection,
   combined: non-residential

(G-4251)
STIEFEL LABORATORIES INC
410 Blackwell St (27701-3986)
PHONE..................................888 784-3335
EMP: 110
SALES (corp-wide): 39.77B **Privately Held**
Web: www.stiefel.com
SIC: 5122 2834 Pharmaceuticals;
   Pharmaceutical preparations
HQ: Stiefel Laboratories, Inc.
   5 Moore Dr
   Research Triangle Pa NC 27709
   888 784-3335

(G-4252)
STRAWBRIDGE STUDIOS INC (PA)
3616 Hillsborough Rd Ste D (27705-2900)
P.O. Box 3005 (27715-3005)
PHONE..................................919 286-9512
EMP: 90 **EST:** 1923
SALES (est): 9.24MM
SALES (corp-wide): 9.24MM **Privately
Held**
Web: www.strawbridge.net
SIC: 7221 2741 School photographer;
   Directories, nec: publishing and printing

(G-4253)
STRYKER CORPORATION
Also Called: Hyperbranch
800 Capitola Dr Ste 12 (27713-4385)
PHONE..................................919 433-3325
EMP: 13
SALES (corp-wide): 22.59B **Publicly Held**
Web: www.stryker.com
SIC: 3842 3841 Surgical appliances and
   supplies; Surgical and medical instruments
PA: Stryker Corporation
   1941 Stryker Way
   Portage MI 49002
   269 385-2600

(G-4254)
SUMMIT AGRO USA LLC
240 Leigh Farm Rd Ste 415 (27707)
PHONE..................................984 260-0407
Bill Lewis, *Pr*
Ryan Mccue, *CFO*
▲ **EMP:** 7 **EST:** 2011
SALES (est): 4.65MM **Privately Held**
Web: www.summitagro-usa.com

SIC: 2879 Fungicides, herbicides
PA: Sumitomo Corporation
   2-3-2, Otemachi
   Chiyoda-Ku TKY 100-0

(G-4255)
SUNHS WAREHOUSE LLC
607 Ellis Rd Bldg 42a (27703-6014)
PHONE..................................919 908-1523
Arturo Leon, *Managing Member*
EMP: 4 **EST:** 2019
SALES (est): 264.88K **Privately Held**
Web: www.sunhswarehouse.com
SIC: 2434 Wood kitchen cabinets

(G-4256)
SWIR VISION SYSTEMS INC
3021 Cornwallis Rd (27709-0146)
P.O. Box 110373 (27709-5373)
PHONE..................................919 248-0032
George Wildeman, *CEO*
Ethan Klem, *VP*
Allan Hilton, *VP*
Chris Gregory, *VP*
EMP: 21 **EST:** 2018
SALES (est): 2.54MM **Privately Held**
Web: www.swirvisionsystems.com
SIC: 3663 Cameras, television

(G-4257)
SYNNOVATOR INC
104 Tw Alexander Dr # 1 (27709-0002)
PHONE..................................919 360-0518
Xin Wang, *Brnch Mgr*
EMP: 5
SALES (corp-wide): 101.75K **Privately
Held**
Web: www.thesynnovator.com
SIC: 2819 Chemicals, reagent grade: refined
   from technical grade
PA: Synnovator, Inc
   115 Centrewest Ct
   Cary NC 27513
   919 360-0518

(G-4258)
SYNTHON PHARMACEUTICALS INC
Also Called: Synthon
1007 Slater Rd Ste 150 (27703-8057)
P.O. Box 110487 (27709-5487)
PHONE..................................919 493-6006
Edwin De Rooij, *CEO*
Angelo Cornelissen, *
EMP: 42 **EST:** 1991
SQ FT: 1,429
SALES (est): 1.96MM **Privately Held**
Web: www.synthon.com
SIC: 2834 Pharmaceutical preparations
HQ: Synthon International Holding B.V.
   Microweg 22
   Nijmegen GE 6545
   243727700

(G-4259)
TAPPED TEES LLC
600 W Main St Apt 613 (27701-1796)
PHONE..................................919 943-9692
Benjamin Ingold, *Mgr*
EMP: 8 **EST:** 2017
SALES (est): 440K **Privately Held**
SIC: 2396 Screen printing on fabric articles

(G-4260)
TAVROS THERAPEUTICS INC
8 Davis Dr Ste 100 (27709-0003)
PHONE..................................919 602-2631
Eoin R Mcdonnell, *CEO*
Greg Mossinghoff, *Chief Business Officer*
EMP: 19 **EST:** 2019
SALES (est): 4.7MM **Privately Held**
Web: www.tavrostx.com

SIC: **2834** Druggists' preparations (pharmaceuticals)

(G-4261)
TELEFLEX INCORPORATED
Also Called: Teleflex
2917 Weck Dr Research Triangle Park (27709-0186)
PHONE...............................919 433-2575
EMP: 8
SALES (corp-wide): 3.05B **Publicly Held**
Web: www.teleflex.com
SIC: **3841** 3842 Surgical and medical instruments; Surgical appliances and supplies
PA: Teleflex Incorporated
550 E Swdsford Rd Ste 400
Wayne PA 19087
610 225-6800

(G-4262)
TELEFLEX INCORPORATED
Also Called: Teleflex
1805a Tw Alexander Dr (27703-8389)
PHONE...............................919 433-2575
EMP: 7
SALES (corp-wide): 3.05B **Publicly Held**
Web: www.teleflex.com
SIC: **3842** Surgical appliances and supplies
PA: Teleflex Incorporated
550 E Swdsford Rd Ste 400
Wayne PA 19087
610 225-6800

(G-4263)
TELEFLEX MEDICAL INCORPORATED
4024 Stirrup Creek Dr Ste 270 (27703-9464)
PHONE...............................919 544-8000
EMP: 5
SALES (corp-wide): 3.05B **Publicly Held**
Web: www.teleflex.com
SIC: **3841** Surgical and medical instruments
HQ: Teleflex Medical Incorporated
3015 Carrington Mill Blvd
Morrisville NC 27560
919 544-8000

(G-4264)
TELIT WIRELESS SOLUTIONS INC (PA)
5425 Page Rd Ste 120 (27703-7009)
PHONE...............................919 439-7977
Roger Dewey, *Pr*
Michael Ueland, *
Yariv Dafna, *
Teemu Vasankari, *
Inbal Barak-etzion, *Treas*
EMP: 69 EST: 2006
SQ FT: 4,100
SALES (est): 22.08MM **Privately Held**
Web: www.telit.com
SIC: **3674** 4813 Modules, solid state; Internet connectivity services

(G-4265)
TEMPEST ENVIRONMENTAL CORP
7 Al Acqua Dr (27707-9211)
PHONE...............................919 973-1609
Tom Sparks, *COO*
Roddy Tempest, *CEO*
Tim Pate, *CFO*
EMP: 9 EST: 1985
SQ FT: 4,576
SALES (est): 77.69K **Privately Held**
Web: www.tempestenvironmental.com

SIC: **8999** 4941 3589 8744 Scientific consulting; Water supply; Water treatment equipment, industrial; Environmental remediation

(G-4266)
TEMPEST ENVMTL SYSTEMS INC
Also Called: Tempest Environmental
7 Al Acqua Dr (27707-9211)
PHONE...............................919 973-1609
Roddy Tempest, *CEO*
Scott Jones, *Pr*
Connie Tempest, *VP*
Tom Sparks, *VP*
▼ EMP: 5 EST: 1985
SQ FT: 8,000
SALES (est): 835.12K **Privately Held**
Web: www.aquapura.com
SIC: **3589** Water purification equipment, household type

(G-4267)
TERARECON INC (PA)
4309 Emperor Blvd Ste 310 (27703-8069)
PHONE...............................650 372-1100
Dan Mcsweeney, *Pr*
Tiecheng Zhao, *Sr VP*
Dianne Oseto, *Corporate Secretary*
Martin Clanty, *CFO*
▲ EMP: 80 EST: 1997
SALES (est): 21.18MM
SALES (corp-wide): 21.18MM **Privately Held**
Web: www.terarecon.com
SIC: **3577** 5734 Computer peripheral equipment, nec; Computer peripheral equipment

(G-4268)
TERGUS PHARMA LLC (PA)
4018 Stirrup Creek Dr (27703-9000)
P.O. Box 12012 (27709-2012)
PHONE...............................919 549-9700
Michael Kane, *CEO*
Vijendra Nalamothu, *CSO**
Peter Geiger, *
EMP: 30 EST: 1995
SQ FT: 4,100
SALES (est): 21.29MM **Privately Held**
Web: www.terguspharma.com
SIC: **2834** 8734 Pharmaceutical preparations; Testing laboratories

(G-4269)
THERMO FISHER SCIENTIFIC INC
4063 Stirrup Creek Dr (27703-9001)
PHONE...............................800 955-6288
EMP: 14
SALES (corp-wide): 42.86B **Publicly Held**
Web: www.thermofisher.com
SIC: **3826** Analytical instruments
PA: Thermo Fisher Scientific Inc.
168 3rd Ave
Waltham MA 02451
781 622-1000

(G-4270)
THERMOCHEM RECOVERY INTL
5201 International Dr (27712-8950)
PHONE...............................919 606-3282
EMP: 5 EST: 2017
SALES (est): 1.76MM **Privately Held**
Web: www.tri-inc.net
SIC: **3312** Chemicals and other products derived from coking

(G-4271)
THIN LINE SADDLE PADS INC
2945 S Miami Blvd Ste 120-120 (27703-8024)
PHONE...............................919 680-6803

Elaine Lockhead, *Pr*
EMP: 7 EST: 2007
SALES (est): 84.34K **Privately Held**
Web: www.thinlineglobal.com
SIC: **3199** 2399 Leather goods, nec; Fabricated textile products, nec

(G-4272)
THOMAS WELDING SERVICE INC
1002 Communications Dr (27704)
PHONE...............................919 471-6852
Ronald E Thomas, *Pr*
Lydia Thomas, *Sec*
EMP: 5 EST: 1982
SALES (est): 476.95K **Privately Held**
Web: welding-services.cmac.ws
SIC: **7692** Welding repair

(G-4273)
THRIFTY TIRE
2903 N Roxboro St (27704-3247)
P.O. Box 1095 (27573-1095)
PHONE...............................919 220-7800
Rick Gamble, *Genl Mgr*
EMP: 6 EST: 2006
SALES (est): 506.78K **Privately Held**
Web: www.thriftytireonline.com
SIC: **5531** 7534 Automotive tires; Tire retreading and repair shops

(G-4274)
TIMMONS FABRICATIONS INC
2818 Pervis Rd (27704-5334)
PHONE...............................919 688-8998
David Timmons, *Pr*
Marianna Timmons, *Sec*
EMP: 10 EST: 1989
SQ FT: 15,000
SALES (est): 947.5K **Privately Held**
SIC: **3441** Fabricated structural metal

(G-4275)
TOSHIBA GLOBL CMMRCE SLTONS IN (DH)
Also Called: Toshiba
3901 S Miami Blvd (27703-9135)
PHONE...............................919 544-8427
Rance M Poehler, *Pr*
Sam Craig, *
John Gaydac, *
Kenneth Hammer, *CLO**
Willis Lumpkin, *
EMP: 43 EST: 2012
SALES (est): 506.36MM **Privately Held**
Web: commerce.toshiba.com
SIC: **3577** Input/output equipment, computer
HQ: Toshiba Global Commerce Solutions Holdings Corporation
2-17-2, Higashigotanda
Shinagawa-Ku TKY 141-0

(G-4276)
TRANSENTERIX SURGICAL INC
1 Tw Alexander Dr Ste 160 (27703-7035)
PHONE...............................919 765-8400
Todd M Pope, *Pr*
David N Gill, *
Richard M Mueller, *
▲ EMP: 65 EST: 2006
SALES (est): 2.67MM
SALES (corp-wide): 2.37B **Privately Held**
Web: www.asensus.com
SIC: **3841** Surgical and medical instruments
HQ: Asensus Surgical, Inc.
1 Tw Alexander Dr Ste 160
Durham NC 27703

(G-4277)
TRIANGLE BRICK COMPANY (PA)
6523 Nc Highway 55 (27713)
PHONE...............................919 544-1796

Scott D Mollenkopf, *Pr*
Wilhelm Roeben, *
Arch Lynch, *
▲ EMP: 25 EST: 1959
SQ FT: 10,000
SALES (est): 31.97MM
SALES (corp-wide): 31.97MM **Privately Held**
Web: www.trianglebrick.com
SIC: **3251** 5211 8741 Brick and structural clay tile; Brick; Management services

(G-4278)
TRIANGLE CONVERTING CORP
2021 S Briggs Ave (27703-6076)
P.O. Box 2244 (27702-2244)
PHONE...............................919 596-6656
James B Brame Junior, *Pr*
Anita W Brame, *
EMP: 30 EST: 1983
SQ FT: 20,000
SALES (est): 2.44MM **Privately Held**
Web: www.bramespecialty.com
SIC: **2679** 2675 2621 Paper products, converted, nec; Die-cut paper and board; Paper mills

(G-4279)
TRIANGLE GLASS SERVICE INC
1320 Old Oxford Rd Ste 12 (27704-2470)
P.O. Box 15429 (27704-0429)
PHONE...............................919 477-9508
John Beck, *Pr*
William James, *VP*
EMP: 5 EST: 1988
SQ FT: 2,400
SALES (est): 420.71K **Privately Held**
Web: www.triangleglassservice.com
SIC: **1793** 7699 5231 5084 Glass and glazing work; Door and window repair; Glass; Machine tools and accessories

(G-4280)
TRIANGLE PRCSION DGNOSTICS INC
2 Davis Dr Rm 203 (27709-0003)
PHONE...............................919 345-0110
Tong Zhou, *CEO*
Zhiyuan Hu, *VP*
Ping Zhang, *COO*
Jiechun Zhou, *CFO*
EMP: 4 EST: 2014
SALES (est): 235.8K **Privately Held**
SIC: **2835** 7389 In vivo diagnostics; Business Activities at Non-Commercial Site

(G-4281)
TRIANGLE SYSTEMS INC
4364 S Alston Ave (27713-2564)
PHONE...............................919 544-0090
Jim Ott, *Owner*
EMP: 8
SALES (corp-wide): 1.03MM **Privately Held**
Web: www.triangle-systems.com
SIC: **7372** Educational computer software
PA: Triangle Systems, Inc.
882 Pinehurst Dr
Chapel Hill NC 27517
919 544-0090

(G-4282)
TRIANGLE TRIBUNE
Also Called: Consuldated Media Group
115 Market St Ste 211 (27701-3241)
PHONE...............................704 376-0496
Gerald Johnson, *Pt*
EMP: 4 EST: 1998
SALES (est): 139.29K **Privately Held**
Web: www.triangletribune.com

SIC: 2711 Newspapers, publishing and printing

(G-4283)
TRUEFAB LLC
3401 Industrial Dr (27704-9430)
PHONE....................919 620-8158
Lloyd Johnson, *Prin*
EMP: 10 EST: 2016
SALES (est): 3.14MM **Privately Held**
SIC: 3441 3499 Fabricated structural metal; Fabricated metal products, nec

(G-4284)
TSENG INFORMATION SYSTEMS INC
813 Watts St (27701-1532)
PHONE....................919 682-9197
Larry Tseng, *Pr*
Charles Ellertson, *VP*
EMP: 7 EST: 1980
SALES (est): 116.99K **Privately Held**
SIC: 2791 Typesetting

(G-4285)
TWINVISION NORTH AMERICA INC
4018 Patriot Dr Ste 100 (27703-8083)
PHONE....................919 361-2155
Dave L Turney, *Pr*
Dave Turney, *
▲ EMP: 223 EST: 1996
SQ FT: 18,000
SALES (est): 470.04K
SALES (corp-wide): 70.71MM **Privately Held**
Web: www.twinvisionna.com
SIC: 3993 Signs and advertising specialties
HQ: Xdric, Inc.
13760 Noel Rd Ste 830
Dallas TX 75240
214 378-8992

(G-4286)
TYRATA INC
101 W Chapel Hill St Ste 200 (27701-3255)
PHONE....................919 210-8992
Jesko Windheim, *Pr*
Richard Scott, *VP*
Tracey Timothy, *Ch Bd*
EMP: 12 EST: 2017
SALES (est): 866.82K **Privately Held**
Web: www.tyrata.com
SIC: 3011 Retreading materials, tire

(G-4287)
UAI TECHNOLOGY INC
68 Tw Alexander Dr (27709-0056)
PHONE....................919 541-9339
Steven Maier, *Brnch Mgr*
EMP: 9
SALES (corp-wide): 4.85MM **Privately Held**
Web: www.phoenixhecht.com
SIC: 2741 Miscellaneous publishing
PA: Uai Technology, Inc.
68 Tw Alexander Dr
Durham NC 27709
919 541-9339

(G-4288)
UNIFIED2 GLOBL PACKG GROUP LLC
3829 S Miami Blvd Ste 300 (27703-5419)
PHONE....................774 696-3643
Arthur Mahassel, *Pr*
EMP: 200 EST: 2018
SALES (est): 9.31MM **Privately Held**
SIC: 5199 3086 Packaging materials; Cups and plates, foamed plastics

(G-4289)
UNITED THERAPEUTICS CORP
2 Maughan Dr (27709-1033)
PHONE....................919 246-9389
Martine Rothblatt, *CEO*
Michael Benkowitz, *Pr*
James Edgemond, *CFO*
Paul A Mahon, *Sec*
Matthew Kootman, *Asst Tr*
EMP: 41 EST: 1977
SALES (est): 5.21MM **Privately Held**
Web: www.unither.com
SIC: 2834 Pharmaceutical preparations

(G-4290)
UNIVERSITY DIRECTORIES LLC
Also Called: Around Campus Group, The
2520 Meridian Pkwy Ste 470 (27713-4202)
P.O. Box 364 (27302-0364)
PHONE....................800 743-5556
EMP: 59 EST: 1996
SALES (est): 770.14K **Privately Held**
Web: www.universitydirectories.com
SIC: 2741 Directories, telephone: publishing and printing

(G-4291)
UNSPECIFIED INC
65 Tw Alexander Dr Unit 110324 (27709-0943)
PHONE....................919 907-2726
EMP: 7 EST: 2018
SALES (est): 992.55K **Privately Held**
Web: www.unspecified.life
SIC: 7372 Prepackaged software

(G-4292)
UPPER DECK COMPANY
1750 Tw Alexander Dr (27703-9241)
PHONE....................760 496-9149
EMP: 6
SALES (est): 927.76K **Privately Held**
Web: www.upperdeck.com
SIC: 3131 Uppers

(G-4293)
UROVANT SCIENCES INC
324 Blackwell St Bay 11 (27701-3658)
PHONE....................919 323-8528
EMP: 10
SALES (corp-wide): 24.69MM **Privately Held**
Web: www.urovant.com
SIC: 2834 Pharmaceutical preparations
HQ: Urovant Sciences, Inc.
5281 California Ave # 100
Irvine CA
949 226-6029

(G-4294)
VALASSIS COMMUNICATIONS INC
Also Called: Valassis Durham Printing Div
4918 Prospectus Dr (27713-4407)
PHONE....................919 544-4511
Blaine G Gerber, *Brnch Mgr*
EMP: 69
SQ FT: 10,000
SALES (corp-wide): 15B **Privately Held**
Web: www.vericast.com
SIC: 2759 2752 Promotional printing; Commercial printing, lithographic
HQ: Valassis Communications, Inc.
19975 Victor Pkwy
Livonia MI 48152

(G-4295)
VALASSIS COMMUNICATIONS INC
Also Called: Valassis Wichita Printing
4918 Prospectus Dr (27713-4407)
PHONE....................919 361-7900

Michael A Wood, *Brnch Mgr*
EMP: 85
SALES (corp-wide): 15B **Privately Held**
Web: www.vericast.com
SIC: 2759 2752 Promotional printing; Commercial printing, lithographic
HQ: Valassis Communications, Inc.
19975 Victor Pkwy
Livonia MI 48152

(G-4296)
VESTARON CORPORATION (PA)
4025 Stirrup Creek Dr Ste 400 (27703-9398)
P.O. Box 12237 (27709-2237)
PHONE....................919 694-1022
Juan Estupinan, *Pr*
EMP: 6 EST: 2005
SALES (est): 8.02MM
SALES (corp-wide): 8.02MM **Privately Held**
Web: www.vestaron.com
SIC: 2879 Insecticides and pesticides

(G-4297)
VIASIC INC
5015 Southpark Dr Ste 240 (27713-7736)
PHONE....................336 774-2150
Lynn Hayden, *Pr*
Denise Hummell, *Sec*
EMP: 6 EST: 1999
SQ FT: 2,100
SALES (est): 219.34K **Privately Held**
Web: www.viasic.com
SIC: 7372 Application computer software

(G-4298)
VIIV HEALTHCARE COMPANY
Also Called: Viiv Healthcare US
410 Blackwell St (27701-3986)
PHONE....................919 483-2100
Deborah Waterhouse, *CEO*
Jill Anderson, *
EMP: 1100 EST: 2009
SALES (est): 70.12MM
SALES (corp-wide): 39.77B **Privately Held**
Web: www.viivhealthcare.com
SIC: 2834 7389 Pharmaceutical preparations; Business services, nec
HQ: Glaxosmithkline Llc
2929 Walnut St Ste 1700
Philadelphia PA 19112
888 825-5249

(G-4299)
VOGENX INC
3920 S Alston Ave (27713-1829)
PHONE....................919 659-5677
Steve Delmar, *CFO*
EMP: 5 EST: 2021
SALES (est): 272.77K **Privately Held**
Web: www.vogenx.com
SIC: 2834 Pharmaceutical preparations

(G-4300)
VOLUMETRICS MED SYSTEMS LLC
4711 Hope Valley Rd Ste 4f (27707-5651)
PHONE....................800 472-0900
Mark Foster, *Prin*
Olaf Von Ramm, *Prin*
Kent Moore, *Prin*
EMP: 4 EST: 2021
SALES (est): 514.21K **Privately Held**
SIC: 3845 Electromedical equipment

(G-4301)
WALKER DRAPERIES INC
Also Called: Walker's
2503 Broad St (27704-3007)
PHONE....................919 220-1424
W Barry Walker, *Pr*

Janet Walker, *Sec*
EMP: 10 EST: 1959
SQ FT: 8,500
SALES (est): 1.09MM **Privately Held**
Web: www.walkersdraperies.com
SIC: 2391 5714 Draperies, plastic and textile: from purchased materials; Draperies

(G-4302)
WATSON PARTY TABLES INC (PA)
2455 S Alston Ave (27713-1301)
P.O. Box 13447 (27709-3447)
PHONE....................919 294-9153
Shawn Watson, *Pr*
Ronnie Watson, *VP*
Vicky Watson, *Sec*
▲ EMP: 12 EST: 1986
SQ FT: 12,000
SALES (est): 946.03K **Privately Held**
Web: www.partytables.com
SIC: 2392 7359 Tablecloths: made from purchased materials; Dishes, silverware, tables, and banquet accessories rental

(G-4303)
WEST & ASSOCIATES OF NC
Also Called: Trims Unlimited
4502b Bennett Memorial Rd (27705-2310)
P.O. Box 72046 (27722-2046)
PHONE....................919 479-5680
Adrian West, *Pr*
Robin West, *VP*
▲ EMP: 9 EST: 1999
SQ FT: 2,000
SALES (est): 127.96K **Privately Held**
SIC: 5031 2241 Building materials, interior; Trimmings, textile

(G-4304)
WHIMSICAL PRINTS PAPER & GIFTS
5826 Fayetteville Rd Ste 105 (27713-8684)
PHONE....................919 544-8491
EMP: 5 EST: 2011
SALES (est): 201.18K **Privately Held**
Web: www.whimsicalprints.com
SIC: 2752 Commercial printing, lithographic

(G-4305)
WILLIAMS EASY HITCH INC
2310 Old Oxford Rd (27704-9583)
PHONE....................919 302-0062
EMP: 6 EST: 2010
SALES (est): 181.5K **Privately Held**
SIC: 3799 Transportation equipment, nec

(G-4306)
WINDLIFT INC
Also Called: WINDLIFT
2445 S Alston Ave (27713-1301)
P.O. Box 3324 Lassider St (27707)
PHONE....................919 490-8575
Robert Creighton, *CEO*
EMP: 5 EST: 2020
SALES (est): 3.71MM **Privately Held**
Web: www.windlift.com
SIC: 3511 3721 4911 Turbines and turbine generator sets; Research and development on aircraft by the manufacturer

(G-4307)
WOLFSPEED INC
Also Called: Lightcreed Labs
4601 Silicon Dr 3rd Fl (27703-8449)
PHONE....................919 407-5300
Billy Moon, *Mgr*
EMP: 6
SALES (corp-wide): 807.2MM **Publicly Held**
Web: www.wolfspeed.com
SIC: 3674 Semiconductors and related devices

PA: Wolfspeed, Inc.
4600 Silicon Dr
Durham NC 27703
919 407-5300

(G-4308)
WOLFSPEED INC (PA)
Also Called: Wolfspeed
4600 Silicon Dr (27703)
PHONE................................919 407-5300
Gregg A Lowe, *Pr*
Thomas Werner, *
Neill P Reynolds, *Ex VP*
▲ EMP: 175 EST: 1987
SQ FT: 1,054,000
SALES (est): 807.2MM
SALES (corp-wide): 807.2MM **Publicly Held**
Web: www.wolfspeed.com
SIC: 3674 3672 Integrated circuits, semiconductor networks, etc.; Printed circuit boards

(G-4309)
WOLFSPEED EMPLOYEE SERVICES CO
4600 Silicon Dr (27703-8475)
PHONE................................919 313-5300
Michael E Mcdevitt, *Pr*
EMP: 6 EST: 2014
SALES (est): 932.27K **Privately Held**
Web: www.wolfspeed.com
SIC: 3674 Semiconductors and related devices

(G-4310)
WRIGHT CHEMICALS LLC
4804 Page Creek Ln (27703-8582)
PHONE................................919 296-1771
EMP: 8
SALES (est): 518.12K **Privately Held**
SIC: 2869 Industrial organic chemicals, nec

(G-4311)
WRIT PRESS INC
1308 N Duke St (27701-1652)
PHONE................................815 988-7074
Adam Lewis, *Prin*
EMP: 5 EST: 2019
SALES (est): 65.16K **Privately Held**
Web: www.writpress.shop
SIC: 2741 Miscellaneous publishing

(G-4312)
WRITING PENN LLC
4400 Turnberry Cir (27712-9466)
PHONE................................301 529-5324
EMP: 5 EST: 2016
SALES (est): 103.91K **Privately Held**
SIC: 2741 Miscellaneous publishing

(G-4313)
WTVD TELEVISION LLC
Also Called: ABC 11
411 Liberty St (27701-3407)
PHONE................................919 683-1111
Ed O'connor, *Dir*
Caroline Welch, *Managing Member**
EMP: 150 EST: 2008
SQ FT: 40,000
SALES (est): 4.86MM
SALES (corp-wide): 91.36B **Publicly Held**
Web: www.abc11.com
SIC: 4833 4832 2711 Television broadcasting stations; News; Newspapers, publishing and printing
HQ: Abc, Inc.
77 W 66th St
New York NY 10023
212 456-7777

(G-4314)
X-CELEPRINT INC
2 Davis Dr (27709-0003)
P.O. Box 13169 (27709-3169)
PHONE................................919 248-0020
Kyle Benkendorfer, *CEO*
EMP: 10 EST: 2019
SALES (est): 2.24MM **Privately Held**
Web: www.x-celeprint.com
SIC: 3674 Hybrid integrated circuits

(G-4315)
XDRI INC
4018 Patriot Dr Ste 100 (27703-8083)
PHONE................................919 361-2155
David L Turney, *Pr*
David Turney, *Pr*
EMP: 8 EST: 1983
SALES (est): 326.74K **Privately Held**
SIC: 3652 Prerecorded records and tapes

(G-4316)
YEEKA LLC
11 Yarmouth Pl (27707-5537)
PHONE................................919 308-9826
Weican Meng, *Pt*
EMP: 5 EST: 2006
SALES (est): 92K **Privately Held**
Web: www.yeeka.com
SIC: 2741 Internet publishing and broadcasting

(G-4317)
YUKON MEDICAL LLC
4021 Stirrup Creek Dr Ste 200 (27703-9352)
PHONE................................919 595-8250
EMP: 6 EST: 2008
SALES (est): 2.05MM **Privately Held**
Web: www.yukonmedical.com
SIC: 3841 5047 Physiotherapy equipment, electrical; Medical equipment and supplies

(G-4318)
ZOETIS INC
1040 Swabia Ct (27703-8481)
PHONE................................919 941-5185
EMP: 220
SALES (corp-wide): 8.54B **Publicly Held**
Web: www.zoetis.com
SIC: 2834 Pharmaceutical preparations
PA: Zoetis Inc.
10 Sylvan Way
Parsippany NJ 07054
973 822-7000

Eagle Springs
Moore County

(G-4319)
T H BLUE INC
Also Called: T. H. Blue Mulch
226 Flowers Rd (27242-8172)
P.O. Box 97 (27242-0097)
PHONE................................910 673-3033
Tommy Blue, *CEO*
T Harold Blue Senior, *Pr*
Thomas H Blue Junior, *VP*
EMP: 32 EST: 1965
SQ FT: 7,000
SALES (est): 4.23MM **Privately Held**
Web: www.thbluemulch.com
SIC: 2875 4212 4213 2421 Potting soil, mixed; Local trucking, without storage; Trucking, except local; Sawmills and planing mills, general

(G-4320)
WAR SPORT LLC
13117 Nc Highway 24 27 (27242-8072)
PHONE................................910 948-2237
EMP: 5 EST: 2009
SALES (est): 2.43MM **Privately Held**
SIC: 3483 Ammunition components

(G-4321)
WHITNEY SCREEN PRINTING
2244 Nc Highway 211 (27242-7950)
PHONE................................910 673-0309
EMP: 4 EST: 2016
SALES (est): 71.57K **Privately Held**
SIC: 2752 Commercial printing, lithographic

East Bend
Yadkin County

(G-4322)
CROSS TECHNOLOGY INC (PA)
Also Called: Nu-Tech
101 Cross Tech Dr (27018)
PHONE................................336 725-4700
James F Inman, *Pr*
EMP: 37 EST: 2000
SALES (est): 9.09MM **Privately Held**
Web: www.crosstech.us
SIC: 3399 8711 3089 3545 Brads: aluminum, brass, or other nonferrous metal or wire; Engineering services; Injection molded finished plastics products, nec; Precision tools, machinists'

(G-4323)
DIVINE LLAMA VINEYARDS LLC
4126 Divine Llama Ln (27018-7498)
PHONE................................336 699-2525
Patrick West, *Brnch Mgr*
EMP: 5
SALES (corp-wide): 223.32K **Privately Held**
Web: www.divinellamavineyards.com
SIC: 2084 Wines
PA: Divine Llama Vineyards, Llc
3524 Yadkinville Rd
Winston Salem NC 27106
336 407-8413

(G-4324)
NU-TECH ENTERPRISES INC
340 E Nc 67 Highway Byp (27018-8865)
P.O. Box 340 (27018-0340)
PHONE................................336 725-1691
James Inman, *Pr*
EMP: 23 EST: 2001
SQ FT: 7,000
SALES (est): 497.76K **Privately Held**
Web: www.nu-tech.us
SIC: 3069 3599 Molded rubber products; Machine and other job shop work
PA: Cross Technology, Inc.
101 Cross Tech Dr
East Bend NC 27018

(G-4325)
REYNOLDA MFG SOLUTIONS INC
1200 Flint Hill Rd (27018-8502)
P.O. Box 455 (27023-0455)
PHONE................................336 699-4204
EMP: 6 EST: 2005
SALES (est): 517.1K **Privately Held**
Web: www.reynolda.com
SIC: 3599 Machine shop, jobbing and repair

(G-4326)
REYNOLDA MFG SOLUTIONS INC
1200 Flint Hill Rd (27018-8502)
P.O. Box 455 (27023-0455)

PHONE................................336 699-4204
Scott Riddles, *CEO*
Richard Sechrist, *
EMP: 30 EST: 1994
SALES (est): 5.13MM **Privately Held**
Web: www.reynolda.com
SIC: 3599 Machine shop, jobbing and repair

(G-4327)
TWIN CARPORTS LLC
1014 Melrose Ct (27018-7279)
PHONE................................336 790-8284
EMP: 4
SALES (corp-wide): 1.12MM **Privately Held**
Web: www.twincarports.com
SIC: 3448 Prefabricated metal buildings and components
PA: Twin Carports Llc
202 Hamlin Dr
Pilot Mountain NC 27041
866 486-3924

East Flat Rock
Henderson County

(G-4328)
AGILE VENTURES LLC
Also Called: Cosaint Arms
2107 Spartanburg Hwy (28726-2134)
PHONE................................202 716-7958
EMP: 5 EST: 2018
SALES (est): 2.23MM **Privately Held**
Web: www.cosaintarms.com
SIC: 3489 Guns or gun parts, over 30 mm.

(G-4329)
DEMMEL INC
100 Old World Cir (28726-0277)
PHONE................................828 585-6600
Cornel Broenner, *Ex Dir*
Cornel Broenner, *Genl Mgr*
Simone Diett, *
◆ EMP: 95 EST: 2016
SQ FT: 12,000
SALES (est): 10.36MM
SALES (corp-wide): 264.1MM **Privately Held**
Web: www.demmel-group.com
SIC: 3711 Automobile assembly, including specialty automobiles
PA: Demmel Ag
Gruntenweg 14
Scheidegg BY 88175
838191900

(G-4330)
ELKAMET INC
201 Mills St (28726-2116)
P.O. Box 265 (28726-0265)
PHONE................................828 233-4001
Eberhard Flammer, *Pr*
Michael Parsch, *
Carsten Erkel, *
Brent Coston, *
◆ EMP: 165 EST: 2006
SQ FT: 145,000
SALES (est): 31.14MM
SALES (corp-wide): 29.61MM **Privately Held**
Web: www.elkamet.com
SIC: 3089 Injection molding of plastics
PA: Elkamet Kunststofftechnik Gmbh
Georg-Kramer-Str. 3
Biedenkopf HE
64619300

GEOGRAPHIC

(G-4331)
GB INDUSTRIES
3005 Spartanburg Hwy (28726-2925)
PHONE..............................828 692-9163
Julia Staton, *Pr*
Alan Staton, *VP*
Mark Staton, *Sec*
EMP: 8 **EST:** 1995
SQ FT: 5,000
SALES (est): 426.18K **Privately Held**
SIC: 3441 Fabricated structural metal

(G-4332)
GREENLEAF CORPORATION
Technical Ceramics Div
761 Roper Rd (28726)
P.O. Box 756 (28726-0756)
PHONE..............................828 693-0461
Chuck Dziedzic, *Mgr*
EMP: 40
SALES (corp-wide): 36.32MM **Privately Held**
Web: www.greenleafcorporation.com
SIC: 3545 3264 Cutting tools for machine tools; Porcelain electrical supplies
PA: Greenleaf Corporation
18695 Greenleaf Dr
Saegertown PA 16433
814 763-2915

(G-4333)
MINUTE-MAN PRODUCTS INC
305 W King St (28726-2318)
PHONE..............................828 692-0256
Martha G Moreno, *Pr*
Thomas W Hackney, *
Pat Hudpheth, *Stockholder**
EMP: 35 **EST:** 1965
SQ FT: 45,000
SALES (est): 1.55MM **Privately Held**
Web: www.minutemanproducts.com
SIC: 3462 Anchors, forged

(G-4334)
MMA MANUFACTURING INC
Also Called: Minute Man Anchors
305 W King St (28726-2318)
PHONE..............................828 692-0256
Mark Vollan, *Pr*
William Hackney, *
EMP: 35 **EST:** 2019
SALES (est): 2.5MM **Privately Held**
Web: www.minutemanproducts.com
SIC: 3499 Fire- or burglary-resistive products

(G-4335)
VOCATNAL SLTONS HNDRSON CNTY I
Also Called: VOCATIONAL SOLUTONS
2110 Spartanburg Hwy (28726-2135)
PHONE..............................828 692-9626
Mike Horton, *Ex Dir*
EMP: 27 **EST:** 1967
SQ FT: 45,000
SALES (est): 1.42MM **Privately Held**
Web: www.vocsol.com
SIC: 8331 2396 2395 Vocational rehabilitation agency; Automotive and apparel trimmings; Pleating and stitching

(G-4336)
WRKCO INC
200 Tabor Rd (28726-2832)
PHONE..............................828 692-6254
EMP: 28
SIC: 2631 Paperboard mills
HQ: Wrkco Inc.
1000 Abrnthy Rd Ne Ste 12
Atlanta GA 30328
770 448-2193

Eastover
Cumberland County

(G-4337)
J & L BCKH/NVRNMENTAL SVCS INC
3043 Tom Geddie Rd (28312-8143)
PHONE..............................910 237-7351
Debra M Davis, *Pr*
Loyde L Davis, *VP*
Maxine J Mclaurin, *Vice Chairman*
Jack G Mclaurin, *Stockholder*
EMP: 4 **EST:** 1999
SQ FT: 900
SALES (est): 221.27K **Privately Held**
SIC: 1794 3443 1795 4213 Excavation work; Dumpsters, garbage; Demolition, buildings and other structures; Contract haulers

(G-4338)
TYSON FOODS INC
Also Called: Tyson
3281 Baywood Rd (28312-9033)
PHONE..............................910 483-3282
Mitchell Sessoms, *Mgr*
EMP: 13
SQ FT: 7,000
SALES (corp-wide): 53.31B **Publicly Held**
Web: www.tyson.com
SIC: 2015 Poultry slaughtering and processing
PA: Tyson Foods, Inc.
2200 W Don Tyson Pkwy
Springdale AR 72762
479 290-4000

Eden
Rockingham County

(G-4339)
A C FURNITURE COMPANY INC
724 Riverside Dr (27288-2634)
P.O. Box 40013 (24022-0013)
PHONE..............................336 623-3430
Lee Manick, *Brnch Mgr*
EMP: 325
SALES (corp-wide): 4.11MM **Privately Held**
Web: www.acfurniture.com
SIC: 2426 2531 2522 2521 Furniture stock and parts, hardwood; Public building and related furniture; Office furniture, except wood; Wood office furniture
PA: A. C. Furniture Company, Inc.
3872 Martin Dr
Axton VA 24054
276 650-3356

(G-4340)
ALADDIN MANUFACTURING CORP
712 Henry St (27288-6122)
P.O. Box 130 (27289-0130)
PHONE..............................336 623-6000
Phil C Raiford, *Brnch Mgr*
EMP: 1704
Web: www.mohawkind.com
SIC: 2273 Carpets: twisted paper, grass, reed, coir, sisal, jute, etc.
HQ: Aladdin Manufacturing Corporation
160 S Industrial Blvd
Calhoun GA 30701
706 629-7721

(G-4341)
ALLTECH INC
11761 Hwy 770 E (27288)
PHONE..............................336 635-5190
Jp Woodrum, *Brnch Mgr*
EMP: 20

SALES (corp-wide): 1.49B **Privately Held**
Web: www.alltech.com
SIC: 2869 Enzymes
PA: Alltech, Inc.
3031 Catnip Hill Rd
Nicholasville KY 40356
859 885-9613

(G-4342)
CANVAS MW LLC
Weil-Mclain Assembly Facility
523 S New St (27288-3623)
PHONE..............................336 627-6000
Ed Lodics, *Brnch Mgr*
EMP: 201
SALES (corp-wide): 1.83B **Privately Held**
Web: www.weil-mclain.com
SIC: 3433 Boilers, low-pressure heating: steam or hot water
HQ: Canvas Mw, Llc
500 Blaine St
Michigan City IN 46360
630 560-3703

(G-4343)
CHANDLER CONCRETE CO INC
234 Main St (27288)
PHONE..............................336 635-0975
Tommy M Edwards, *Mgr*
EMP: 4
Web: www.chandlerconcrete.com
SIC: 3273 Ready-mixed concrete
PA: Chandler Concrete Co., Inc.
1006 S Church Street
Burlington NC 27215

(G-4344)
CHANDLER CONCRETE INC
Also Called: CHANDLER CONCRETE INC
6354 Main St (27288)
PHONE..............................336 342-5771
Danny Manroind, *Dist Mgr*
EMP: 8
Web: www.chandlerconcrete.com
SIC: 3273 Ready-mixed concrete
PA: Chandler Concrete Co., Inc.
1006 S Church Street
Burlington NC 27215

(G-4345)
CLASSIC CARBURETOR REBUILDERS
1909 Stovall St (27288-4337)
PHONE..............................336 613-5715
EMP: 5 **EST:** 2016
SALES (est): 71.09K **Privately Held**
SIC: 3592 Carburetors

(G-4346)
FLOWERS BKG CO JAMESTOWN LLC
403 W Kings Hwy Ste C (27288-5075)
PHONE..............................704 305-0766
Mike Waites, *Mgr*
EMP: 27
SALES (corp-wide): 5.1B **Publicly Held**
SIC: 2051 Bread, cake, and related products
HQ: Flowers Baking Co. Of Jamestown, Llc
801 W Main St
Jamestown NC 27282
336 841-8840

(G-4347)
GILDAN ACTIVEWEAR (EDEN) INC
602 E Meadow Rd (27288-3426)
P.O. Box 1247 (27289)
PHONE..............................336 623-9555
Glenn Chamandry, *Pr*
Laurence G Sellyn, *
▼ **EMP:** 160 **EST:** 1985

SQ FT: 400,000
SALES (est): 19.66MM
SALES (corp-wide): 3.2B **Privately Held**
Web: www.gildancorp.com
SIC: 5136 5311 2258 Men's and boy's clothing; Department stores; Lace and warp knit fabric mills
PA: Les Vetements De Sport Gildan Inc
600 Boul De Maisonneuve O 33eme Etage
Montreal QC H3A 3
514 735-2023

(G-4348)
INNOFA USA LLC
716 Commerce Dr (27288-3681)
PHONE..............................336 635-2900
Roger Droge, *Managing Member*
◆ **EMP:** 34 **EST:** 2003
SQ FT: 84,000
SALES (est): 7.52MM **Privately Held**
Web: www.innofa.com
SIC: 2257 2824 Pile fabrics, circular knit; Organic fibers, noncellulosic
HQ: Innofa Beheer B.V.
Minosstraat 20
Tilburg NB 5048
134634205

(G-4349)
KARASTAN
335 Summit Rd (27288-2829)
PHONE..............................336 627-7200
Richard Scales, *Pr*
EMP: 5 **EST:** 2013
SALES (est): 91.99K **Privately Held**
Web: www.karastan.com
SIC: 2273 Finishers of tufted carpets and rugs

(G-4350)
KDH DEFENSE SYSTEMS INC
Also Called: Kdh Defense Systems
750a W Fieldcrest Rd (27288-3631)
PHONE..............................336 635-4158
David E Herbener, *CEO*
EMP: 140 **EST:** 2003
SQ FT: 250,000
SALES (est): 19.62MM
SALES (corp-wide): 8.99MM **Privately Held**
Web: www.armorexpress.com
SIC: 3812 Defense systems and equipment
PA: Praesidium Spa
Via Della Giustizia 10/A
Milano MI 20125
023030971

(G-4351)
KINGS CHANDELIER COMPANY
1023 Friendly Rd (27288-2805)
P.O. Box 667 (27289-0667)
PHONE..............................336 623-6188
Nancy Daniel, *Pr*
Tim Lillard, *VP*
EMP: 7 **EST:** 1934
SALES (est): 985.63K **Privately Held**
Web: www.chandelier.com
SIC: 3645 3646 Chandeliers, residential; Chandeliers, commercial

(G-4352)
LOPAREX LLC
816 W Fieldcrest Rd (27288-3633)
PHONE..............................336 635-0192
Chip Sheeran, *Brnch Mgr*
EMP: 160
Web: www.loparex.com
SIC: 2672 5199 Adhesive backed films, foams and foils; Packaging materials
HQ: Loparex Llc

▲ = Import ▼ = Export
◆ = Import/Export

1255 Crescent Green # 400
Cary NC 27518
919 678-7700

(G-4353)
NESTLE PURINA PETCARE COMPANY
863 E Meadow Rd (27288-3636)
PHONE..................314 982-1000
EMP: 116
Web: www.purina.com
SIC: 2047 Dog and cat food
HQ: Nestle Purina Petcare Company
800 Chouteau Ave
Saint Louis MO 63102
314 982-1000

(G-4354)
PIEDMONT SURFACES OF TRIAD LLC
615 Monroe St (27288-6110)
PHONE..................336 627-7790
EMP: 20 EST: 2011
SALES (est): 317.82K Privately Held
Web:
www.piedmonttriadflemingrealtors.com
SIC: 3272 Slabs, crossing: concrete

(G-4355)
RONNIE BOYDS LOGGING LLC
153 Nance St (27288-3084)
PHONE..................336 613-0229
Ronnie Boyd, Prin
EMP: 6 EST: 2010
SALES (est): 167.13K Privately Held
SIC: 2411 Logging camps and contractors

(G-4356)
SGRTEX LLC
335 Summit Rd (27288-2829)
PHONE..................336 635-9420
Ramkumar Varadarajan, Managing Member
EMP: 84 EST: 2013
SQ FT: 180,000
SALES (est): 1.76MM Privately Held
SIC: 2281 Yarn spinning mills
PA: Shri Govindaraja Mills Private Limited
258, Thiruchuli Road
Aruppukottai TN 62610

(G-4357)
SPX CORPORATION
Also Called: SPX CORPORATION
523 S New St (27288-3623)
PHONE..................336 627-6020
Dennis Chase, Mgr
EMP: 11
SALES (corp-wide): 1.83B Privately Held
Web: www.spx.com
SIC: 3443 Cooling towers, metal plate
HQ: Canvas Sx, Llc
6325 Ardrey Kell Rd Ste 4
Charlotte NC 28277
980 474-3700

Edenton
Chowan County

(G-4358)
A&W WELDING INC
1106 Haughton Rd 37 (27932-9462)
PHONE..................252 482-3233
Wade Nixon, Pr
EMP: 6 EST: 1988
SALES (est): 141.96K Privately Held
SIC: 7692 Welding repair

(G-4359)
ALB BOATS
140 Midway Dr (27932-8908)
PHONE..................252 482-7600
J Scott Harrell Junior, Prin
J Scott Harrell Junior, Prin
Burch Perry, *
Carol Ricketts, *
▼ EMP: 200 EST: 1978
SQ FT: 100,000
SALES (est): 874.07K Privately Held
Web: www.albemarleboats.com
SIC: 3732 Boats, fiberglass: building and repairing

(G-4360)
ALBEMARLE CORPORATION
140 Midway Dr (27932-8908)
PHONE..................252 482-7423
Carroll Bundy, COO
EMP: 5
Web: www.albemarleboats.com
SIC: 2821 Plastics materials and resins
PA: Albemarle Corporation
4250 Congress St Ste 900
Charlotte NC 28209

(G-4361)
ASHLEY WELDING & MACHINE CO
104 Tower Dr (27932-9762)
P.O. Box 383 (27932-0383)
PHONE..................252 482-3321
Mitchell Byrd, Pr
Mysi Fortenbery, Off Mgr
Steven Byrd, VP
EMP: 10 EST: 1947
SQ FT: 24,000
SALES (est): 1.13MM Privately Held
Web: www.ashleywelding.com
SIC: 3441 Fabricated structural metal

(G-4362)
BATEMAN LOGGING CO INC
1531 Virginia Rd (27932-9533)
PHONE..................252 482-8959
Cecil Ray Bateman, Pr
Teresa Bateman, *
EMP: 10 EST: 1978
SALES (est): 1.05MM Privately Held
SIC: 2411 Logging camps and contractors

(G-4363)
CC BOATS INC
140 Midway Dr (27932-8908)
P.O. Box 968 (27932-0968)
PHONE..................252 482-3699
Mac Privott, Pr
Joan R Privott, Sec
▼ EMP: 5 EST: 1992
SQ FT: 27,000
SALES (est): 220.08K Privately Held
Web: www.albemarleboats.com
SIC: 3732 Motorboats, inboard or outboard: building and repairing

(G-4364)
COX NRTH CRLINA PBLCATIONS INC
Also Called: Chowan Herald
421 S Broad St (27932-1935)
P.O. Box 207 (27932-0207)
PHONE..................252 482-4418
Robert S Piazza Iii, Prin
EMP: 9
SALES (corp-wide): 961.55MM Privately Held
Web: www.reflector.com
SIC: 2711 Newspapers, publishing and printing
HQ: Cox North Carolina Publications, Inc.
1150 Sugg Pkwy
Greenville NC 27834
252 329-9643

(G-4365)
DAEDALUS COMPOSITES LLC
Also Called: Daedalus Yachts
109 Anchors Way Dr (27932-9746)
P.O. Box 428 (27932-0428)
PHONE..................252 368-9000
Michael Reardon, Managing Member
◆ EMP: 15 EST: 2016
SALES (est): 3.64MM Privately Held
Web: www.daedalusyachts.com
SIC: 3732 Yachts, building and repairing

(G-4366)
EDENTON BOATWORKS LLC
Also Called: Albemarle Boats
140 Midway Dr (27932-8908)
PHONE..................252 482-7600
Burch Perry, Genl Mgr
EMP: 30 EST: 2015
SALES (est): 6.91MM Privately Held
Web: www.albemarleboats.com
SIC: 3731 Barges, building and repairing

(G-4367)
HERMES MARINE LLC (PA)
109 Anchors Way Dr (27932-9746)
PHONE..................252 368-9000
EMP: 29 EST: 2021
SALES (est): 1.1MM
SALES (corp-wide): 1.1MM Privately Held
SIC: 3732 Boat kits, not models

(G-4368)
LAYTONS CUSTOM BOATWORKS LLC
103 Anchors Way Dr (27932-9746)
P.O. Box 147 (27932-0147)
PHONE..................252 482-1504
Carlton Layton, Managing Member
Doug Layton, Managing Member
EMP: 9 EST: 1998
SALES (est): 992.45K Privately Held
Web: www.laytonscustomboatworks.com
SIC: 3732 Boatbuilding and repairing

(G-4369)
MORVEN PARTNERS LP
Also Called: Original Nuthouse Brand
185 Peanut Dr (27932-9604)
P.O. Box 465 (27932-0465)
PHONE..................252 482-2193
Paul Britton, Mgr
EMP: 38
SIC: 2099 Peanut butter
PA: Morven Partners, L.P.
11 Leigh Fisher Blvd
El Paso TX 79906

(G-4370)
NOBLE BROS CABINETS MLLWK LLC (PA)
107 Marine Dr (27932-9748)
PHONE..................252 482-9100
Scott Noble, Managing Member
EMP: 8 EST: 1985
SQ FT: 8,000
SALES (est): 966.79K
SALES (corp-wide): 966.79K Privately Held
Web: www.noblebroscabinets.com
SIC: 1521 2434 General remodeling, single-family houses; Wood kitchen cabinets

(G-4371)
REGULATOR MARINE INC
187 Peanut Dr (27932-9604)
P.O. Box 49 (27932-0049)
PHONE..................252 482-3837
▼ EMP: 65 EST: 1988
SALES (est): 15.94MM Privately Held
Web: www.regulatormarine.com
SIC: 3732 Fishing boats: lobster, crab, oyster, etc.: small

(G-4372)
UNIVERSAL BLANCHERS LLC
Also Called: Seabrook Ingredients
115 Peanut Dr (27932-9604)
P.O. Box 609 (27932-0609)
PHONE..................252 482-2112
Larry Hughs, Mgr
EMP: 75
SALES (corp-wide): 170.68MM Privately Held
SIC: 2099 2068 Peanut butter; Salted and roasted nuts and seeds
HQ: Universal Blanchers, L.L.C.
2077 Cnvntion Ctr Cncrse
Atlanta GA 30337
404 209-2600

(G-4373)
W E NIXONS WLDG & HDWR INC
3036 Rocky Hock Rd (27932-9556)
PHONE..................252 221-4348
William Thomas Nixon, Pr
Terry Nixon Britton, Credit Officer
Robin P Nixon, Sec
EMP: 7 EST: 1952
SQ FT: 30,000
SALES (est): 986.4K Privately Held
SIC: 7692 5251 5999 5661 Welding repair; Hardware stores; Farm equipment and supplies; Women's shoes

Efland
Orange County

(G-4374)
CHAPMAN WELDING LLC
Also Called: Cw Landscapes
4501 Gails Trl (27243-9237)
PHONE..................919 951-8131
EMP: 4 EST: 2019
SALES (est): 478.64K Privately Held
SIC: 7692 Welding repair

(G-4375)
CONVEYOR TECHNOLOGIES INC
1218 Blacksmith Rd (27243-9760)
PHONE..................919 732-8291
Bryan M Wood, Pr
EMP: 6 EST: 1994
SALES (est): 751.08K Privately Held
Web: www.conveyor-technologies.com
SIC: 3535 Belt conveyor systems, general industrial use

(G-4376)
USA DUTCH INC (PA)
3604 Southern Dr (27243-9704)
P.O. Box 1299 (27253-1299)
PHONE..................919 732-6956
Ronald Keizer, Pr
EMP: 25 EST: 1989
SQ FT: 13,500
SALES (est): 10MM Privately Held
Web: www.usadutchinc.com
SIC: 3444 Sheet metal specialties, not stamped

Elizabeth City
Pasquotank County

(G-4377)
ACUCAL INC
108 Enterprise Dr (27909-6340)
PHONE..................252 337-9975

Thomas N Efaw, *Brnch Mgr*
EMP: 9
Web: www.trescal.com
SIC: 3823 Industrial process control instruments
HQ: Acucal, Inc.
11090 Industrial Rd
Manassas VA 20109
703 369-3090

(G-4378)
ALBEMRLE ORTHOTICS PROSTHETICS
Also Called: East Crlina Orthtics Prsthtics
106 Medical Dr (27909-3361)
P.O. Box 1471 (27906-1471)
PHONE................................252 338-3002
Wesley Scott Truesdale, *Pr*
Jeanie Truesdale, *
EMP: 33 **EST:** 1994
SALES (est): 2.37MM **Privately Held**
Web: www.albemarleop.com
SIC: 3842 5047 Limbs, artificial; Medical and hospital equipment

(G-4379)
BERGMAN ENTERPRISES INC
786 Pitts Chapel Rd (27909-7864)
PHONE................................252 335-7294
Marcy Pritchard, *Pr*
Arthur Bergman, *
Marcy Bergman, *
Patti Bergman, *
EMP: 35 **EST:** 1970
SQ FT: 6,200
SALES (est): 7.23MM **Privately Held**
Web: www.motionsensors.com
SIC: 3823 Process control instruments

(G-4380)
C A PERRY & SON INC
683 Dry Ridge Rd (27909-7173)
PHONE................................252 330-2323
Daniel Birch, *Brnch Mgr*
EMP: 6
SALES (corp-wide): 11.26B **Publicly Held**
Web: www.caperryandson.com
SIC: 5159 5191 4221 5153 Peanuts (bulk), unroasted; Farm supplies; Farm product warehousing and storage; Grains
HQ: C. A. Perry & Son, Inc.
4033 Virginia Rd
Hobbsville NC 27946
252 221-4463

(G-4381)
CERAMAWIRE
786 Pitts Chapel Rd (27909-7864)
PHONE................................252 335-7411
Edward Hamilton, *Owner*
EMP: 4 **EST:** 2001
SALES (est): 211.89K **Privately Held**
Web: www.ceramawire.com
SIC: 3496 Woven wire products, nec

(G-4382)
COCA-COLA CONSOLIDATED INC
Also Called: Coca-Cola
1210 George Wood Dr (27909-9600)
PHONE................................252 334-1820
Ron Verstat, *Mgr*
EMP: 95
SALES (corp-wide): 6.9B **Publicly Held**
Web: www.coca-cola.com
SIC: 2086 5149 Bottled and canned soft drinks; Groceries and related products, nec
PA: Coca-Cola Consolidated, Inc.
4100 Coca-Cola Plz
Charlotte NC 28211
980 392-8298

(G-4383)
COMMERCIAL READY MIX PDTS INC
168 Knobbs Creek Dr (27909-7001)
PHONE................................252 335-9740
Steve Duncan, *Mgr*
EMP: 13
SALES (corp-wide): 48.13MM **Privately Held**
Web: www.crmpinc.com
SIC: 3273 Ready-mixed concrete
PA: Commercial Ready Mix Products, Inc.
115 Hwy 158 W
Winton NC 27986
252 358-5461

(G-4384)
COURTESY FORD INC
Also Called: Courtesy Ford Lincoln-Mercury
1310 N Road St (27909-3338)
PHONE................................252 338-4783
Frank Bernard, *Pr*
EMP: 6 **EST:** 1984
SQ FT: 25,000
SALES (est): 218.18K **Privately Held**
Web: www.lincoln.com
SIC: 5511 7538 7515 5531 Automobiles, new and used; General automotive repair shops; Passenger car leasing; Auto and home supply stores

(G-4385)
COX NRTH CRLINA PBLCATIONS INC
Daily Advance Newspaper
215 S Water St (27909-4844)
P.O. Box 588 (27907-0588)
PHONE................................252 335-0841
Tim Hobbs, *Publisher*
EMP: 110
SALES (corp-wide): 961.55MM **Privately Held**
Web: www.reflector.com
SIC: 2711 Newspapers, publishing and printing
HQ: Cox North Carolina Publications, Inc.
1150 Sugg Pkwy
Greenville NC 27834
252 329-9643

(G-4386)
DOUGLAS TEMPLE & SON INC
1273 Lynchs Corner Rd (27909-7515)
PHONE................................252 771-5676
Doug Temple, *Pr*
Linda Temple, *Sec*
EMP: 4 **EST:** 2001
SALES (est): 136.58K **Privately Held**
SIC: 2411 Logging

(G-4387)
ELECTRIC MOTOR REWINDING INC
407 N Poindexter St (27909-4039)
PHONE................................252 338-8856
Robert D Lunsford, *Pr*
EMP: 6 **EST:** 1956
SQ FT: 5,000
SALES (est): 913.91K **Privately Held**
SIC: 7694 Electric motor repair

(G-4388)
EVENT EXTRAVAGANZA LLC
407 S Griffin St Ste E (27909-4693)
PHONE................................252 679-7004
De'mondrae Harris, *Managing Member*
EMP: 15 **EST:** 2021
SALES (est): 190K **Privately Held**
Web: www.eventextravaganza.org
SIC: 2051 Bread, cake, and related products

(G-4389)
F & H PRINT SIGN DESIGN LLC
1725 City Center Blvd Ste C (27909-8962)
PHONE................................252 335-0181
EMP: 5 **EST:** 2017
SQ FT: 5,000
SALES (est): 480.96K **Privately Held**
Web: www.fhprintsign.com
SIC: 2396 Fabric printing and stamping

(G-4390)
HOCKMEYER EQUIPMENT CORP
Also Called: HOCKMEYER EQUIPMENT CORP.
6 Kitty Hawk Ln (27909-6726)
PHONE................................252 338-4705
Rick Vandesande, *Mgr*
EMP: 54
SQ FT: 37,500
SALES (corp-wide): 22.82MM **Privately Held**
Web: www.hockmeyer.com
SIC: 3559 3531 3443 3582 Anodizing equipment; Construction machinery; Fabricated plate work (boiler shop); Commercial laundry equipment
PA: Hockmeyer Equipment Corp
610 Supor Blvd
Harrison NJ 07029
973 482-0225

(G-4391)
HOFFER CALIBRATION SVCS LLC
1100 W Ehringhaus St Ste C (27909-6943)
P.O. Box 583 (27907-0583)
PHONE................................252 338-6379
Nixon R William, *Prin*
EMP: 4 **EST:** 2016
SALES (est): 1.09MM **Privately Held**
Web: www.hofferflow.com
SIC: 3823 Process control instruments

(G-4392)
HOFFER FLOW CONTROLS INC
107 Kitty Hawk Ln (27909-6756)
P.O. Box 2145 (27906-2145)
PHONE................................252 331-1997
Kenneth Hoffer, *CEO*
Bob Carrell, *
Sandee Kelly, *
▼ **EMP:** 80 **EST:** 1969
SQ FT: 32,000
SALES (est): 18.37MM **Privately Held**
Web: www.hofferflow.com
SIC: 3823 Flow instruments, industrial process type

(G-4393)
J W JONES LUMBER COMPANY INC (PA)
1443 Northside Rd (27909-8531)
PHONE................................252 771-2497
▼ **EMP:** 90 **EST:** 1939
SALES (est): 16.78MM
SALES (corp-wide): 16.78MM **Privately Held**
Web: www.jwjoneslumber.com
SIC: 2421 Lumber: rough, sawed, or planed

(G-4394)
KAYLA JONISE BERNHARDT CRUTCH
115 Carver St (27909-5833)
PHONE................................252 457-5367
K Jonise Bernhardt Crutch, *Owner*
EMP: 4 **EST:** 2020
SALES (est): 144.09K **Privately Held**
SIC: 2339 Women's and misses' athletic clothing and sportswear

(G-4395)
KWIK ELC MTR SLS & SVC INC (PA)
511 Witherspoon St (27909-5265)
P.O. Box 1602 (27906-1602)
PHONE................................252 335-2524
John T Cox, *Pr*
John Cox, *Pr*
Aubrey Snowden, *VP*
Elizabeth Snowden, *Sec*
EMP: 5 **EST:** 1973
SQ FT: 5,000
SALES (est): 681.98K
SALES (corp-wide): 681.98K **Privately Held**
SIC: 5999 3677 7694 Motors, electric; Coil windings, electronic; Rewinding services

(G-4396)
LEGACY VULCAN LLC
Also Called: Elizabeth City Yard
174 Knobbs Creek Dr (27909-7001)
PHONE................................252 338-2201
Rene Salamone, *Mgr*
EMP: 4
Web: www.vulcanmaterials.com
SIC: 3273 Ready-mixed concrete
HQ: Legacy Vulcan, Llc
1200 Urban Center Dr
Birmingham AL 35242
205 298-3000

(G-4397)
MARVIN BAILEY SCREEN PRINTING
Also Called: E Gads Screen Printing & EMB
1403 N Road St (27909-3241)
PHONE................................252 335-1554
Marvin Bailey, *Owner*
EMP: 5 **EST:** 1982
SQ FT: 3,600
SALES (est): 135.36K **Privately Held**
Web: www.egadsobx.com
SIC: 2261 2396 Finishing plants, cotton; Automotive and apparel trimmings

(G-4398)
MOTOR VHCLES LCENSE PLATE AGCY
1545 N Road St Ste E (27909-4268)
PHONE................................252 338-6965
Lynn Cartwright, *Pr*
EMP: 5 **EST:** 1994
SALES (est): 181.99K **Privately Held**
SIC: 2796 6411 Platemaking services; Insurance agents, brokers, and service

(G-4399)
NOBLE BROS CABINETS MLLWK LLC
505 E Church St Apt 2 (27909-4868)
PHONE................................252 335-1213
Scott Noble, *Brnch Mgr*
EMP: 8
SALES (corp-wide): 2.05MM **Privately Held**
Web: www.noblebroscabinets.com
SIC: 1521 2434 General remodeling, single-family houses; Wood kitchen cabinets
PA: Noble Brothers Cabinets & Millwork, Llc
107 Marine Dr
Edenton NC 27932
252 482-9100

(G-4400)
NORTHEASTERN READY MIX
183 Knobbs Creek Dr (27909-7002)
P.O. Box 1731 (27906-1731)
PHONE................................252 335-1931
James G Gaskins Junior, *Pr*
EMP: 7 **EST:** 1977
SALES (est): 1.04MM **Privately Held**

Web: www.crmpinc.com
SIC: 3273 3272 Ready-mixed concrete; Septic tanks, concrete

(G-4401)
PEPSI BOTTLING VENTURES LLC
109 Corporate Dr (27909-7028)
PHONE..............................252 335-4355
EMP: 41
Web: www.pepsibottlingventures.com
SIC: 2086 Carbonated soft drinks, bottled and canned
HQ: Pepsi Bottling Ventures Llc
4141 Parklake Ave
Raleigh NC 27612
919 865-2300

(G-4402)
PERDUE FARMS INC
Also Called: PERDUE FARMS INC.
1268 Us Highway 17 S (27909-7631)
PHONE..............................252 338-1543
EMP: 34
SALES (corp-wide): 1.24B Privately Held
Web: www.perdue.com
SIC: 2015 Poultry slaughtering and processing
PA: Perdue Farms Incorporated
31149 Old Ocean City Rd
Salisbury MD 21804
800 473-7383

(G-4403)
PITT ROAD LLC
Also Called: Pitt Road Ex Lube & Car Wash
711 N Hughes Blvd (27909-3532)
PHONE..............................252 331-5818
Jeanna Albertson, Prin
EMP: 5 EST: 1998
SALES (est): 589.78K Privately Held
SIC: 2911 Road oils

(G-4404)
PRECISION PRINTING
307 S Road St (27909-4759)
PHONE..............................252 338-2450
Jesse Carden, Owner
EMP: 4 EST: 1981
SQ FT: 5,000
SALES (est): 225.55K Privately Held
Web: www.precisionprint.com
SIC: 2752 Offset printing

(G-4405)
QUALITY FOODS FROM SEA INC
Also Called: Sea Food Express
173 Knobbs Creek Dr (27909-7002)
P.O. Box 1837 (27906-1837)
PHONE..............................252 338-5455
William E Barclift, Pr
William E Barclift Junior, Pr
Roy P Martin Iii, VP
Susan Martin, *
▲ **EMP:** 80 EST: 1986
SQ FT: 24,000
SALES (est): 4.75MM Privately Held
SIC: 2091 5146 Canned and cured fish and seafoods; Seafoods

(G-4406)
QUALITY SEAFOOD CO INC
177 Knobbs Creek Dr (27909-7002)
PHONE..............................252 338-2800
William E Barclift, Pr
Russell Barclift, *
EMP: 5 EST: 1983
SALES (est): 710.56K Privately Held
Web: www.qualityseafoodco.com
SIC: 5146 2092 2091 Seafoods; Fresh or frozen packaged fish; Canned and cured fish and seafoods

(G-4407)
R O GIVENS SIGNS INC
Also Called: Atlantic Screen Print
1145 Parsonage St (27909-3303)
P.O. Box 9 (27907-0009)
PHONE..............................252 338-6578
Robert O Givens Junior, Pr
Scott Givens, VP
Mary G Lane, Sec
EMP: 5 EST: 1947
SALES (est): 353.09K Privately Held
Web: www.rogivenssigns.com
SIC: 3993 7359 Signs and advertising specialties; Sign rental

(G-4408)
SANDERS COMPANY INC
410 N Poindexter St (27909-4040)
P.O. Box 324 (27907-0324)
PHONE..............................252 338-3995
H T Sanders, Pr
E Craig Sawyer, VP
Colleen Sanders, Stockholder
EMP: 15 EST: 1880
SQ FT: 12,000
SALES (est): 6.85MM Privately Held
Web: www.sandersco.com
SIC: 5085 3599 5051 Industrial supplies; Machine shop, jobbing and repair; Foundry products

(G-4409)
SAS INDUSTRIES INC
100 Corporate Dr (27909-7027)
P.O. Box 245 (11949-0245)
PHONE..............................631 727-1441
Steve Steckis, Pr
▲ **EMP:** 15 EST: 1973
SQ FT: 10,000
SALES (est): 1.88MM Privately Held
Web: www.sasindustries.com
SIC: 3053 5085 Gaskets, all materials; Industrial supplies

(G-4410)
STALLINGS CABINETS INC
508 N Hughes Blvd (27909-3529)
PHONE..............................252 338-6747
Don Stallings, Prin
EMP: 4 EST: 2010
SALES (est): 173.7K Privately Held
Web: www.stallingscabinets.com
SIC: 2434 Wood kitchen cabinets

(G-4411)
SUBSEA VIDEO SYSTEMS INC
611 Hull Dr (27909-6924)
P.O. Box 159 (27907-0159)
PHONE..............................252 338-1001
Fred Meyer, Pr
Walter Brunner, Sec
EMP: 8 EST: 1990
SQ FT: 10,000
SALES (est): 462.5K Privately Held
Web: subsea-video-systems-inc-in-elizabeth-city-nc.cityfos.com
SIC: 3861 8711 Cameras, still and motion picture (all types); Electrical or electronic engineering

(G-4412)
TCE MANUFACTURING LLC
1287 Salem Church Rd (27909-7415)
PHONE..............................252 330-9919
EMP: 4 EST: 1999
SQ FT: 11,000
SALES (est): 427.23K Privately Held
Web: www.tcemfg.com
SIC: 3441 Fabricated structural metal

(G-4413)
TCOM LIMITED PARTNERSHIP
Also Called: TCOM, LIMITED PARTNERSHIP
190 T Com Dr (27909-2942)
PHONE..............................252 330-5555
Charles Knauss, Brnch Mgr
EMP: 346
SQ FT: 10,000
SALES (corp-wide): 157.16MM Privately Held
Web: www.tcomlp.com
SIC: 3721 3829 3728 3537 Blimps; Measuring and controlling devices, nec; Aircraft parts and equipment, nec; Industrial trucks and tractors
HQ: Tcom, L.P.
7115 Thomas Edison Dr
Columbia MD 21046
410 312-2300

(G-4414)
TCOM GROUND SYSTEMS LP
Also Called: Tcom
190 T Com Dr (27909-2942)
PHONE..............................252 338-3200
Charlie Knauss, Owner
EMP: 10 EST: 1989
SALES (est): 3.6MM Privately Held
Web: www.tcomlp.com
SIC: 3531 Marine related equipment

(G-4415)
TELEPHONICS CORPORATION
1014 Consolidated Rd (27909-7835)
PHONE..............................631 755-7446
David M Simek, Brnch Mgr
EMP: 20
SALES (corp-wide): 2.44B Publicly Held
Web: www.telephonics.com
SIC: 3669 Intercommunication systems, electric
HQ: Telephonics Corporation
815 Broadhollow Rd
Farmingdale NY 11735
631 755-7000

(G-4416)
UNIVERSAL FOREST PRODUCTS INC
Also Called: Universal Forest Products
141 Knobbs Creek Dr (27909-7002)
PHONE..............................252 338-0319
Robert Clark, Genl Mgr
EMP: 13
SALES (corp-wide): 6.65B Publicly Held
Web: www.ufpi.com
SIC: 2491 2439 2426 2499 Wood preserving ; Structural wood members, nec; Dimension, hardwood; Fencing, docks, and other outdoor wood structural products
PA: Ufp Industries, Inc.
2801 E Beltline Ave Ne
Grand Rapids MI 49525
616 364-6161

Elizabethtown
Bladen County

(G-4417)
ANTHEM DISPLAYS LLC
518 Ben Green Industrial Park Rd (28337-1160)
PHONE..............................910 746-8988
EMP: 10 EST: 2014
SALES (est): 5.05MM
SALES (corp-wide): 496.73MM Privately Held
Web: www.anthemdisplays.com
SIC: 3993 Electric signs
PA: Circle Graphics, Inc.

120 9th Ave
Longmont CO 80501
303 532-2370

(G-4418)
ANTHEM DISPLAYS LLC
113 W Broad St (28337-9311)
P.O. Box 1945 (28337-1945)
PHONE..............................910 862-3550
Evan Brooks, Asst Sec
EMP: 6 EST: 2018
SALES (est): 961.67K Privately Held
Web: www.anthemdisplays.com
SIC: 3993 Electric signs

(G-4419)
BURNEY SWEETS & MORE INC (PA)
Also Called: Burneys Sweets & More
106-B Martin Luther King Dr (28337)
PHONE..............................910 862-2099
EMP: 8 EST: 2011
SALES (est): 6.29MM
SALES (corp-wide): 6.29MM Privately Held
SIC: 2051 2052 Bread, cake, and related products; Cookies and crackers

(G-4420)
CAPE FEAR CHEMICALS INC
Also Called: Tiger Products
4271 Us Highway 701 N (28337-6627)
P.O. Box 695 (28337-0695)
PHONE..............................910 862-3139
Henry James Brice Iii, Pr
Phyllis Brice, VP
Melody Lane Brice, Sec
Henry James Brice Junior, Stockholder
EMP: 8 EST: 1950
SQ FT: 35,750
SALES (est): 431.41K Privately Held
SIC: 2879 Insecticides, agricultural or household

(G-4421)
CAPE FEAR VINEYARD WINERY LLC
195 Vineyard Dr (28337-5748)
PHONE..............................844 846-3386
Homer Munroe, Prin
EMP: 13 EST: 2016
SALES (est): 701.85K Privately Held
Web: www.capefearwinery.com
SIC: 2084 Wines

(G-4422)
CAPE FEAR VINYRD & WINERY LLC
218 Aviation Pkwy Ste C (28337-8401)
PHONE..............................910 645-4292
EMP: 5 EST: 2014
SALES (est): 441.81K Privately Held
Web: www.capefearwinery.com
SIC: 2084 Wines

(G-4423)
CAROLINA SURFACES LLC
242 Woodlief Dr (28337-9737)
PHONE..............................910 874-1335
Doug Long, Brnch Mgr
EMP: 4
SALES (corp-wide): 498.94K Privately Held
SIC: 2434 Wood kitchen cabinets
PA: Carolina Surfaces Llc
414 Peanut Rd
Elizabethtown NC 28337
910 874-1335

(G-4424)
DANAHER INDUS SENSORS CONTRLS
2100 W Broad St (28337-8826)

PHONE...................910 862-5426
EMP: 6 **EST:** 2019
SALES (est): 2.23MM **Privately Held**
Web:
www.specialtyproducttechnologies.com
SIC: 3824 Fluid meters and counting devices

(G-4425)
DVINE FOODS
1585 Hwy 107 South (28337)
P.O. Box 490 (28337-0490)
PHONE...................910 862-2576
EMP: 6 **EST:** 2014
SALES (est): 687.26K **Privately Held**
Web: www.dvinefoods.com
SIC: 2033 Apple sauce: packaged in cans,
jars, etc.

(G-4426)
DYNAPAR CORPORATION (HQ)
2100 W Broad St (28337-8826)
PHONE...................800 873-8731
Joseph Alexander, *Pr*
Patrick K Murphy, *
Daniel B Kim, *
▲ **EMP:** 130 **EST:** 2016
SALES (est): 262.04MM
SALES (corp-wide): 6.23B **Publicly Held**
Web: www.dynapar.com
SIC: 3824 Controls, revolution and timing
instruments
PA: Fortive Corporation
6920 Seaway Blvd
Everett WA 98203
425 446-5000

(G-4427)
HOG SLAT INCORPORATED
2229 Us Highway 701 N (28337-6137)
PHONE...................910 862-7081
Pat Klemme, *Brnch Mgr*
EMP: 4
SALES (corp-wide): 451.86MM **Privately**
Held
Web: www.hogslat.com
SIC: 3523 Farm machinery and equipment
PA: Hog Slat, Incorporated
206 Fayetteville St
Newton Grove NC 28366
800 949-4647

(G-4428)
IMAGE DESIGN
113 W Broad St (28337-9311)
P.O. Box 835 (28337-0835)
PHONE...................910 862-8988
Hunt Cole, *Pr*
▲ **EMP:** 10 **EST:** 1993
SQ FT: 10,000
SALES (est): 579.55K **Privately Held**
Web: www.imagedesign.us
SIC: 3993 Signs and advertising specialties

(G-4429)
MCKOYS LOGGING COMPANY INC
3006 W Broad St (28337-7000)
P.O. Box 460 (28337-0460)
PHONE...................910 862-2706
Robert W Mccoy Junior, *Prin*
Mashonia Daniels, *Prin*
EMP: 5 **EST:** 2017
SALES (est): 193.82K **Privately Held**
SIC: 2411 Logging

(G-4430)
MERRITT LOGGING & CHIPPING CO
1109 W Swanzy St (28337-9069)
P.O. Box 1225 (28337-1225)
PHONE...................910 862-4905
Kenneth Merritt, *Pr*
Robert Merritt, *VP*

Sheila Merritt, *Sec*
EMP: 6 **EST:** 1969
SQ FT: 5,000
SALES (est): 380.21K **Privately Held**
SIC: 2411 Logging camps and contractors

(G-4431)
OCEANIA HARDWOODS LLC
474 Sweet Home Church Rd (28337-6122)
P.O. Box 310 (28337-0310)
PHONE...................910 862-4447
EMP: 6 **EST:** 2005
SALES (est): 204.3K **Privately Held**
SIC: 2426 Hardwood dimension and flooring
mills

(G-4432)
S & W READY MIX CON CO LLC
Also Called: S & W Ready Mix Concrete
1460 Mercer Mill Rd (28337-5620)
PHONE...................910 645-6868
David Cook, *Brnch Mgr*
EMP: 5
SALES (corp-wide): 8.01MM **Privately**
Held
Web: www.snwreadymix.com
SIC: 3273 Ready-mixed concrete
HQ: S & W Ready Mix Concrete Company
Llc
217 Lisbon St
Clinton NC 28329
910 592-1733

(G-4433)
SIGNLOGIC INC
174 S Poplar St (28337-9066)
P.O. Box 340 (28337-0340)
PHONE...................910 862-8965
Martha Walters, *Pr*
Scott Walters, *Pur Mgr*
Brant Allen, *VP*
EMP: 4 **EST:** 2004
SALES (est): 145.11K **Privately Held**
Web: www.signlogic.biz
SIC: 3993 Signs and advertising specialties

(G-4434)
TAYLOR MANUFACTURING INC
1585 Us Hwy 701 S (28337)
P.O. Box 518 (28337-0518)
PHONE...................910 862-2576
Ron Taylor, *Pr*
Denise Taylor Bridgers, *
Oren Taylor, *Stockholder*
Victoria Taylor, *Stockholder*
EMP: 50 **EST:** 1988
SQ FT: 22,400
SALES (est): 1.82MM **Privately Held**
Web: www.taylormfg.com
SIC: 3433 3732 3599 3523 Stoves, wood
and coal burning; Boatbuilding and repairing
; Machine shop, jobbing and repair; Cotton
pickers and strippers

(G-4435)
TAYLOR PRODUCTS INC
1585 Us Hwy 701 S (28337)
P.O. Box 490 (28337-0490)
PHONE...................910 862-2576
Denise T Bridgers, *Pr*
EMP: 5 **EST:** 1982
SALES (est): 431.51K **Privately Held**
SIC: 2097 Manufactured ice

(G-4436)
TURN BULL LUMBER COMPANY (PA)
474 Sweet Home Church Rd (28337-6122)
P.O. Box 310 (28337-0310)
PHONE...................910 862-4447
Pembroke N Jenkins, *Pr*
◆ **EMP:** 29 **EST:** 1993

SQ FT: 980
SALES (est): 5.44MM **Privately Held**
Web: www.turnbulllumber.com
SIC: 2426 2499 Lumber, hardwood
dimension; Mulch or sawdust products,
wood

(G-4437)
WESTWOOD MANUFACTURING INC
Also Called: Westwood Robotic Technology
370 Ben Green Industrial Park Rd
(28337-9756)
P.O. Box 1445 (28337-1445)
PHONE...................910 862-9992
Terry F Baxter, *Pr*
Rebecca Baxter, *Sec*
▲ **EMP:** 7 **EST:** 1985
SQ FT: 5,000
SALES (est): 2.52MM **Privately Held**
Web: www.wwcnc.com
SIC: 3535 Robotic conveyors

Elkin
Surry County

(G-4438)
ACC COATINGS LLC
620 E Main St (28621-3537)
PHONE...................336 701-0080
David Steele, *Managing Member*
EMP: 10 **EST:** 2005
SQ FT: 20,000
SALES (est): 6.73MM **Privately Held**
Web: www.acc-coatings.com
SIC: 2851 Coating, air curing

(G-4439)
BASALT SPECIALTY PRODUCTS INC
600 E Main St (28621-3537)
P.O. Box 457 (27018-0457)
PHONE...................336 835-5153
Anthony Fanale, *Pr*
EMP: 6 **EST:** 2004
SQ FT: 22,500
SALES (est): 340.61K **Privately Held**
Web: www.bspmat.com
SIC: 3644 Insulators and insulation
materials, electrical

(G-4440)
CAROLINA CANDLE
430 Gentry Rd (28621-9241)
PHONE...................336 835-6020
Charlie Leichtweis, *Prin*
EMP: 5 **EST:** 2008
SALES (est): 241.09K **Privately Held**
Web: www.carolinacandle.com
SIC: 3999 Candles

(G-4441)
CAVU PRINTING INC
339 Benham Church Rd (28621-8244)
PHONE...................336 818-9790
David Simms Senior, *CEO*
Deborah A Simms, *VP*
EMP: 6 **EST:** 2009
SALES (est): 319.17K **Privately Held**
Web: www.cavuprinting.com
SIC: 2752 Commercial printing, lithographic

(G-4442)
CROCKERS INC
1821 Joe Layne Mill Rd (28621-8411)
P.O. Box 500 (28621-0500)
PHONE...................336 366-2005
Patti Crocker, *Pr*
EMP: 10 **EST:** 1991
SQ FT: 4,000
SALES (est): 903.64K **Privately Held**

SIC: 3534 Elevators and equipment

(G-4443)
CROWN HERITAGE INC
296 Gentry Rd (28621-8511)
PHONE...................336 835-1424
Wayne Carter, *Mgr*
EMP: 34
Web: www.crownheritage.com
SIC: 2431 Millwork
PA: Crown Heritage, Inc.
1708 Industrial Dr
Wilkesboro NC 28697

(G-4444)
ECMD INC
Arndt & Herman Lumber Co
541 Gentry Rd (28621-9318)
P.O. Box 349 (28621-0349)
PHONE...................336 835-1182
Don Mclarry, *Mgr*
EMP: 133
SALES (corp-wide): 186.49MM **Privately**
Held
Web: www.ecmd.com
SIC: 2431 Millwork
PA: Ecmd, Inc.
2 Grandview St
North Wilkesboro NC 28659
336 667-5976

(G-4445)
ELKIN CREEK VINEYARD LLC
318 Elkin Creek Mill Rd (28621-8860)
PHONE...................336 526-5119
Mark Greene, *Prin*
EMP: 4 **EST:** 2004
SALES (est): 317.79K **Privately Held**
Web: www.elkincreekvineyard.com
SIC: 2084 Wines

(G-4446)
KATHIE S MC DANIEL
Also Called: Graphic Printing
765 Oakland Dr (28621)
PHONE...................336 835-1544
Kathie S Mcdaniel, *Pr*
EMP: 5 **EST:** 1989
SALES (est): 83.3K **Privately Held**
Web: www.graphicsprintingelkin.com
SIC: 2752 7334 7336 2791 Offset printing;
Photocopying and duplicating services;
Graphic arts and related design; Typesetting

(G-4447)
LEGACY VULCAN LLC
Mideast Division
12362 Nc 268 (28621-7332)
P.O. Box 71 (28621-0071)
PHONE...................336 835-1439
Tim Hendrix, *Mgr*
EMP: 6
Web: www.vulcanmaterials.com
SIC: 3273 Ready-mixed concrete
HQ: Legacy Vulcan, Llc
1200 Urban Center Dr
Birmingham AL 35242
205 298-3000

(G-4448)
MILLER BROTHERS LUMBER CO INC
Also Called: Miller Brothers Lumber Co
350 Elkin Wildlife Rd (28621-8728)
PHONE...................336 366-3400
Mike Miller, *Pr*
Ricky Miller, *
Brenda Miller, *
EMP: 30 **EST:** 1952
SQ FT: 10,000
SALES (est): 2.37MM **Privately Held**

SIC: 2421 Sawmills and planing mills, general

(G-4449)
MVP GROUP INTERNATIONAL INC (HQ)
Also Called: TLC
430 Gentry Rd (28621-9241)
PHONE...............................843 216-8380
Sean Peters, *CEO*
Gautham S Pai, *
Jayaraman Ramachandran, *
Karpe Laxminarayana Rao, *Dir*
Venkata Valiveti, *
◆ EMP: 40 EST: 1998
SALES (est): 98.8MM Privately Held
Web: www.mvpgroupint.com
SIC: 3999 5122 Candles; Perfumes
PA: Primacy Industries Private Limited
Udayavani Building, Press Corner
Udupi KA 57610

(G-4450)
PERDUE FARMS INC
Also Called: Perdue Farms
105 Greenwood Cir (28621-8391)
PHONE...............................336 366-2591
Spergie Blue, *Mgr*
EMP: 112
SALES (corp-wide): 1.24B Privately Held
Web: www.perdue.com
SIC: 2015 Chicken, processed: fresh
PA: Perdue Farms Incorporated
31149 Old Ocean City Rd
Salisbury MD 21804
800 473-7383

(G-4451)
PGW AUTO GLASS LLC
Also Called: Pgw
300 Pgw Dr (28621)
PHONE...............................336 258-4950
Ab Brown, *Brnch Mgr*
EMP: 300
SALES (corp-wide): 503.2MM Privately Held
Web: www.pgwglass.com
SIC: 3211 5013 5231 Flat glass; Automotive supplies and parts; Glass
PA: Pgw Auto Glass, Llc
51 Dutilh Rd Ste 310
Cranberry Township PA 16066
878 208-4001

(G-4452)
TAMPCO INC
316 Stainless Way (28621-3126)
PHONE...............................336 835-1895
Kenneth G Nicks Junior, *Pr*
Irving Miles, *
Ed Hagen, *
EMP: 70 EST: 1969
SQ FT: 32,000
SALES (est): 7.08MM Privately Held
Web: www.tampcoinc.com
SIC: 3446 Railings, banisters, guards, etc: made from metal pipe

(G-4453)
VAUGHAN-BASSETT FURN CO INC
Also Called: Elkin Furniture
4109 Poplar Springs Rd (28621-8461)
P.O. Box 230 (28621-0230)
PHONE...............................336 835-2670
Danny Arnold, *Mgr*
EMP: 503
SALES (corp-wide): 37.86MM Privately Held
Web: www.vaughanbassett.com

SIC: 2511 2515 2512 Wood household furniture; Mattresses and bedsprings; Upholstered household furniture
PA: Vaughan-Bassett Furniture Company, Incorporated
300 E Grayson St
Galax VA 24333
276 236-6161

(G-4454)
WAYNE FARMS LLC
Also Called: Wayne Farms
10949 Nc 268 (28621-8790)
PHONE...............................336 366-4413
Doug Hester, *Brnch Mgr*
EMP: 302
SALES (corp-wide): 405K Privately Held
Web: www.waynesandersonfarms.com
SIC: 2015 Chicken, processed, nsk
HQ: Wayne Farms Llc
4110 Continental Dr
Oakwood GA 30566

(G-4455)
WEYERHAEUSER COMPANY
Eastern Osb Business
184 Gentry Rd (28621-8489)
PHONE...............................336 835-5100
Ross Gardner, *Mgr*
EMP: 21
SALES (corp-wide): 7.12B Publicly Held
Web: www.weyerhaeuser.com
SIC: 2436 5031 2493 Softwood veneer and plywood; Plywood; Reconstituted wood products
PA: Weyerhaeuser Company
220 Occidental Ave S
Seattle WA 98104
206 539-3000

Ellenboro
Rutherford County

(G-4456)
CAMP S WELL AND PUMP CO INC
149 Ola Dr (28040-7690)
P.O. Box 429 (28040-0429)
PHONE...............................828 453-7322
David Camp, *Pr*
EMP: 6 EST: 1954
SALES (est): 775K Privately Held
Web: www.campswellandpumpco.com
SIC: 1781 3561 Servicing, water wells; Pumps, domestic: water or sump

(G-4457)
EDS PALLET WORLD INC
559 Race Path Church Rd (28040-8363)
P.O. Box 37 (28040-0037)
PHONE...............................828 453-8986
Ed Romney, *Pr*
Gurdy Angalin, *VP*
Aertia Angtail, *VP*
EMP: 15 EST: 1988
SQ FT: 2,600
SALES (est): 1.87MM Privately Held
Web: www.edspalletworld.com
SIC: 2448 Pallets, wood

(G-4458)
NEXT GENERATION PLASTICS INC
161 Bugger Hollow Rd (28040-9340)
PHONE...............................828 453-0221
John Lahrmer, *Pr*
EMP: 4 EST: 2008
SALES (est): 524.82K Privately Held
SIC: 1446 Molding sand mining

(G-4459)
PLASTIC SOLUTIONS INC
324 Tiney Rd (28040)
PHONE...............................678 353-2100
Bradley B Morgan, *CEO*
Richard R Hughes Junior, *Sec*
EMP: 18 EST: 2002
SALES (est): 6.8MM Privately Held
Web: www.plasticsolutions.net
SIC: 2821 Plastics materials and resins

(G-4460)
R & D WEAVING INC
376 Pinehurst Rd (28040-7600)
PHONE...............................828 248-1910
Robert Martin, *Pr*
EMP: 10 EST: 1988
SQ FT: 15,250
SALES (est): 816.48K Privately Held
Web: www.rdweaving.com
SIC: 2512 2392 Upholstered household furniture; Blankets, comforters and beddings

(G-4461)
THIEMAN MANUFACTURING TECH LLC
Also Called: Thieman Technology
531 Webb Rd (28040-8396)
P.O. Box 39 (28040-0039)
PHONE...............................828 453-1866
Keith Jackson, *CEO*
Todd Meldrum, *Prin*
EMP: 17 EST: 1998
SALES (est): 5.26MM Privately Held
Web: www.tmtfab.com
SIC: 3441 3444 3443 Fabricated structural metal; Sheet metalwork; Fabricated plate work (boiler shop)
PA: Maverick Corporate Partners, Llc
301 W Prospect St
Smithville OH 44677

Ellerbe
Richmond County

(G-4462)
RICHMOND SPECIALTY YARNS LLC
Also Called: Filspecusa
1748 N Us Highway 220 (28338-9336)
PHONE...............................910 652-5554
Ronald Audet, *Pr*
Nicolas Fournier, *
Kenneth Goodman, *Managing Member**
▲ EMP: 120 EST: 1976
SQ FT: 150,000
SALES (est): 601.26K
SALES (corp-wide): 330K Privately Held
Web: www.filspec.com
SIC: 2281 Yarn spinning mills
HQ: Filspec Inc
85 Rue De La Burlington
Sherbrooke QC J1L 1
819 573-8700

(G-4463)
ROCK INDUSTRIAL SERVICES INC
157 S Railroad St (28338)
P.O. Box 660 (28338-0660)
PHONE...............................910 652-6267
Carl Puckett, *Pr*
Carter Kelly, *VP*
EMP: 16 EST: 1983
SQ FT: 45,000
SALES (est): 2.09MM Privately Held
SIC: 3599 Machine shop, jobbing and repair

Elm City
Wilson County

(G-4464)
BOONE LOGGING COMPANY INC
1996 Vaughan Rd (27822-7921)
PHONE...............................252 443-7641
Vincent H Boone, *Pr*
EMP: 6 EST: 1991
SALES (est): 290.84K Privately Held
SIC: 2411 Logging camps and contractors

(G-4465)
EASTERN COMPOST LLC
8487 Battleboro-Leggett Rd (27822)
P.O. Box 460 (27809-0460)
PHONE...............................252 446-3636
Joel Boseman, *Prin*
EMP: 4 EST: 2005
SALES (est): 193.49K Privately Held
SIC: 2875 Compost

(G-4466)
QUALITY TRCK BODIES & REPR INC
5316 Rock Quarry Rd (27822-8728)
P.O. Box 1669 (27894-1669)
PHONE...............................252 245-5100
Michael D Gira, *Pr*
EMP: 30 EST: 1975
SQ FT: 54,000
SALES (est): 4.92MM Privately Held
SIC: 3713 7532 Truck bodies (motor vehicles); Body shop, trucks

(G-4467)
SENTRY VAULT SERVICE INC
6905 Shallingtons Mill Rd (27822-8903)
P.O. Box 904 (27822-0904)
PHONE...............................252 243-2241
John J Lee, *Pr*
Carrie Lee, *Sec*
EMP: 9 EST: 1966
SQ FT: 10,000
SALES (est): 394.72K Privately Held
SIC: 3272 Burial vaults, concrete or precast terrazzo

(G-4468)
WOODWRIGHT OF WILSON CO INC
Also Called: Woodwright Co
5753 Nc 58 (27822-9129)
PHONE...............................252 243-9663
Robert Clark, *Pr*
Barbara Clark, *Sec*
EMP: 4 EST: 1994
SQ FT: 3,500
SALES (est): 207.91K Privately Held
Web: www.thewoodwrightco.com
SIC: 5021 5712 2426 Household furniture; Furniture stores; Furniture stock and parts, hardwood

Elon
Alamance County

(G-4469)
ENGINEERED CONTROLS INTL LLC (HQ)
100 Rego Dr (27244)
P.O. Box 247 (27244)
PHONE...............................336 449-7707
Thomas Farrel, *Pr*
▲ EMP: 210 EST: 2010
SQ FT: 100,000
SALES (est): 95.65MM
SALES (corp-wide): 7.75B Publicly Held
Web: www.regoproducts.com

SIC: 3491 Pressure valves and regulators, industrial
PA: Dover Corporation
3005 Hghland Pkwy Ste 200
Downers Grove IL 60515
630 541-1540

(G-4470)
HEARSAY GUIDES LLC
5005 Windsor Ct (27244-9410)
PHONE....................................336 584-1440
EMP: 4 EST: 2022
SALES (est): 92.1K Privately Held
SIC: 2741 Internet publishing and broadcasting

(G-4471)
JENESIS SOFTWARE INC
Also Called: Agency Management Soluitons
307 Georgetowne Dr (27244-8316)
PHONE....................................828 245-1171
Eddie Price, Prin
Lisa Price, VP
EMP: 5 EST: 2000
SALES (est): 1.2MM Privately Held
Web: www.jenesissoftware.com
SIC: 7372 Prepackaged software

(G-4472)
TEAMWORK INC
1000 Georgetowne Dr (27244-8335)
PHONE....................................336 578-3456
Robert Weavil, Pr
EMP: 8 EST: 1985
SALES (est): 211.47K Privately Held
Web: www.teamwork.com
SIC: 2252 2251 Socks; Women's hosiery, except socks

Elon College
Alamance County

(G-4473)
CLAYTON ELECTRIC MTR REPR INC
1407 N Nc Highway 87 (27244-9712)
PHONE....................................336 584-3756
Jay Clayton, Pr
J Wayne Clayton, Pr
James W Clayton, VP
Nelda Cook, Sec
EMP: 11 EST: 1980
SQ FT: 2,000
SALES (est): 1.13MM Privately Held
Web:
www.claytonelectricmotorrepair.com
SIC: 7694 5063 Electric motor repair; Motors, electric

(G-4474)
MABRY INDUSTRIES INC
2903 Gibsonville Ossipee Rd (27244-9706)
P.O. Box 277 (27244-0277)
PHONE....................................336 584-1311
James B Mabry, Pr
James B Mabry Junior, VP
Linda D Mabry, *
▲ EMP: 28 EST: 1976
SQ FT: 25,000
SALES (est): 5.35MM Privately Held
Web: www.mabryind.com
SIC: 3599 Machine shop, jobbing and repair

(G-4475)
SONOCO PRODUCTS COMPANY
Also Called: Sonoco
212 Cook Rd (27244-9390)
P.O. Box 428 (27244-0428)
PHONE....................................336 449-7731
Chip Goodman, Mgr

EMP: 11
SALES (corp-wide): 5.31B Publicly Held
Web: www.sonoco.com
SIC: 2655 Fiber cans, drums, and similar products
PA: Sonoco Products Company
1 N 2nd St
Hartsville SC 29550
843 383-7000

(G-4476)
WILSON TIRE AND AUTOMOTIVE INC (PA)
Also Called: Tire Pros
1807 N Nc Highway 87 (27244)
PHONE....................................336 584-9638
Steven Moss, Pr
Susan Moss, VP
EMP: 7 EST: 1972
SQ FT: 3,300
SALES (est): 1.34MM
SALES (corp-wide): 1.34MM Privately Held
Web: www.wilsontireandautomotive.com
SIC: 5531 7534 Automotive tires; Tire repair shop

Emerald Isle
Carteret County

(G-4477)
AVERCAST LLC
8921 Crew Dr (28594-1927)
PHONE....................................208 538-5380
EMP: 18 EST: 2008
SALES (est): 806.42K Privately Held
Web: www.avercast.com
SIC: 7372 Prepackaged software

(G-4478)
NATIONAL MARBLE PRODUCTS INC
404 Channel Dr (28594)
P.O. Box 33 (28584)
PHONE....................................910 326-3005
Mat Matheson, Pr
EMP: 9 EST: 1986
SALES (est): 493.9K Privately Held
Web: www.nationalmarbleproducts.com
SIC: 3281 Marble, building: cut and shaped

(G-4479)
PROGRESSIVE ELC GREENVILLE LLC
8606 Canal Dr (28594-2503)
PHONE....................................252 413-6957
EMP: 5 EST: 2006
SQ FT: 12,000
SALES (est): 2.09MM Privately Held
SIC: 3559 Electronic component making machinery

(G-4480)
TEABAR PUBLISHING INC
201n James Dr (28594-3039)
PHONE....................................252 764-2453
Elaine Teachey, Prin
EMP: 4 EST: 2016
SALES (est): 40.43K Privately Held
SIC: 2741 Miscellaneous publishing

Enfield
Halifax County

(G-4481)
AMERICAP CO INC
276 Daniels Bridge Rd (27823-8897)
PHONE....................................252 445-2388

Carlton T Qualls Iii, Pr
Byron Ransdell, *
Carlton T Qualls Junior, VP
Craig Stephenson, *
Edwin Borden Junior, Dir
▲ EMP: 8 EST: 1989
SQ FT: 15,000
SALES (est): 587.04K Privately Held
Web: www.americap.com
SIC: 2353 Baseball caps

(G-4482)
ENFIELD TIRE SERVICE INC
301 N Mcdaniel St (27823-1241)
PHONE....................................252 445-5016
Lillian Cofield, Pr
Vivian Spence, Sec
Nathaniel Cofield, VP
EMP: 5 EST: 1971
SQ FT: 1,200
SALES (est): 694.22K Privately Held
SIC: 5531 7534 Automotive tires; Tire recapping

(G-4483)
HALIFAX EMC
12867 Nc Highway 481 (27823-8204)
PHONE....................................252 445-5111
EMP: 10 EST: 2014
SALES (est): 4.86MM Privately Held
Web: www.ncelectriccooperatives.com
SIC: 3572 Computer storage devices

(G-4484)
HEWLIN BROTHERS LUMBER CO
18555 Nc Highway 48 (27823-9244)
PHONE....................................252 586-6473
Rodward Hewlin, Pt
Tyrone Hewlin, Pt
EMP: 4 EST: 1965
SALES (est): 221.35K Privately Held
SIC: 2421 5211 Lumber: rough, sawed, or planed; Planing mill products and lumber

(G-4485)
NASH BRICK COMPANY
532 Nash Brick Rd (27823-9634)
P.O. Box 6579 (27628-6579)
PHONE....................................252 443-4965
Thomas G Fisher, Pr
Donald R Bowden, Sec
EMP: 13 EST: 1902
SQ FT: 1,500
SALES (est): 1.35MM Privately Held
Web: www.nashbrick.com
SIC: 3251 Brick clay: common face, glazed, vitrified, or hollow

(G-4486)
WILSON BROS LOGGING INC
72 Gennie Rd (27823-9666)
PHONE....................................252 445-5317
Daniel Wilson, Pr
EMP: 10 EST: 2002
SALES (est): 81.36K Privately Held
SIC: 2411 Logging camps and contractors

Enka
Buncombe County

(G-4487)
LEGACY VULCAN LLC
Mideast Division
Hwy 19 & 23 S (28728)
P.O. Box 549 (28728-0549)
PHONE....................................828 255-8561
Weldon Peek, Mgr
EMP: 5
Web: www.vulcanmaterials.com

SIC: 3273 1423 Ready-mixed concrete; Crushed and broken granite
HQ: Legacy Vulcan, Llc
1200 Urban Center Dr
Birmingham AL 35242
205 298-3000

(G-4488)
SOUTHEASTERN CONTAINER INC (PA)
1250 Sand Hill Rd (28728)
P.O. Box 909 (28728-0909)
PHONE....................................828 350-7200
Doug Wehrkamp, Pr
Mike Ramos, *
◆ EMP: 164 EST: 1982
SQ FT: 400,000
SALES (est): 319.93MM
SALES (corp-wide): 319.93MM Privately Held
Web: www.secontainer.com
SIC: 3085 Plastics bottles

Ennice
Alleghany County

(G-4489)
RONNIE L POOLE
14596 Nc Highway 18 N (28623-9409)
PHONE....................................336 657-3956
Ronnie L Poole, Prin
EMP: 6 EST: 2009
SALES (est): 419.7K Privately Held
SIC: 2411 Logging

Ernul
Craven County

(G-4490)
COASTAL CAROLINA LOGGIN
250 Aurora Rd (28527-9601)
PHONE....................................252 474-2165
Joseph Clydelockey Junior, Mgr
EMP: 4 EST: 2013
SALES (est): 480.9K Privately Held
SIC: 2411 Logging

Erwin
Harnett County

(G-4491)
MICHEAL LANGDON LOGGING INC
7249 Ross Rd (28339-8634)
PHONE....................................910 890-5295
Michael Langdon, Pr
EMP: 6 EST: 2000
SALES (est): 123.66K Privately Held
SIC: 2411 Logging camps and contractors

(G-4492)
SPECIALTY PRODUCTS INTL LTD
820 N 14th St (28339-2613)
PHONE....................................910 897-4706
Leigh Beadle, Prin
▲ EMP: 4 EST: 2010
SALES (est): 119.73K Privately Held
SIC: 2087 Extracts, flavoring

(G-4493)
VEGHERB LLC
Also Called: Scenery Solutions
200 N 13th St Ste 3b (28339-1746)
PHONE....................................800 914-9835
▲ EMP: 11 EST: 1997
SALES (est): 4.48MM Privately Held
Web: www.frameitall.com

SIC: **3524** 5261 Lawn and garden equipment ; Retail nurseries and garden stores

Ether
Montgomery County

(G-4494)
BLACKSTONE FURNITURE INDS INC
Also Called: Little River Furniture
624 Hogan Farm Rd (27247)
P.O. Box 212 (27247-0212)
PHONE.................................910 428-2833
Gary Mabe, *Pr*
Greg Mabe, *VP*
David Mcrae, *VP Fin*
Sandy Mcfarlane, *VP Opers*
EMP: 15 **EST:** 1992
SQ FT: 27,000
SALES (est): 2.01MM **Privately Held**
SIC: **2512** Upholstered household furniture

Etowah
Henderson County

(G-4495)
BOONDOCK S MANUFACTURING INC
Also Called: B C M Company
6085 Brevard Rd (28729-9758)
PHONE.................................828 891-4242
Mike Hodges, *Pr*
Ryan Hodges, *VP*
Greg Hodges, *Prin*
EMP: 6 **EST:** 1972
SQ FT: 8,643
SALES (est): 2.43MM **Privately Held**
SIC: **3792** 3448 5531 Campers, for mounting on trucks; Farm and utility buildings; Automotive accessories

(G-4496)
KILN DRYING SYSTEMS CMPNNTS IN
Also Called: K D S
234 Industrial Dr (28729)
PHONE.................................828 891-8115
Rob Girardi, *Prin*
Charles Moniotte, *VP*
Mary Girardi, *Sec*
▲ **EMP:** 21 **EST:** 1992
SQ FT: 22,000
SALES (est): 9.52MM **Privately Held**
Web: www.kdskilns.com
SIC: **3559** Kilns, lumber

Everetts
Martin County

(G-4497)
INTERTAPE POLYMER CORP
1622 Twin Bridges Rd (27825-8700)
PHONE.................................252 792-2083
EMP: 83
SALES (corp-wide): 571.43MM **Privately Held**
Web: www.itape.com
SIC: **2821** Plastics materials and resins
HQ: Intertape Polymer Corp.
100 Paramount Dr Ste 300
Sarasota FL 34232
888 898-7834

Evergreen
Columbus County

(G-4498)
EVERGREEN LOGGING LLC
686 Homer Nance Rd (28438-9516)
PHONE.................................910 654-1662
Lennon Hinson, *Prin*
EMP: 6 **EST:** 2014
SALES (est): 755.93K **Privately Held**
SIC: **2411** Logging camps and contractors

Fair Bluff
Columbus County

(G-4499)
PIPELINE PLASTICS LLC
15159 Andrew Jackson Hwy Sw (28439-9663)
PHONE.................................817 693-4100
Mike Leathers, *CEO*
EMP: 5
SALES (corp-wide): 17.54MM **Privately Held**
Web: www.pipe.us
SIC: **3089** 1623 Fittings for pipe, plastics; Pipeline construction, nsk
PA: Pipeline Plastics, Llc
1453 Fm 2264
Decatur TX 76234
940 627-9100

Fairmont
Robeson County

(G-4500)
APPAREL USA INC
102 Trinity St (28340-1636)
PHONE.................................212 869-5495
Sanjay Israni, *Brnch Mgr*
EMP: 25
SALES (corp-wide): 2MM **Privately Held**
Web: fashionbuyers.garmentbuyingagents.com
SIC: **5136** 5137 2389 2339 Men's and boy's clothing; Women's and children's clothing; Men's miscellaneous accessories; Women's and misses' accessories
PA: Apparel Usa Inc
57 W 38th St Fl 4
New York NY 10018
212 869-5495

(G-4501)
CLAYBOURN WALTERS LOG CO INC
16071 Nc Highway 130 E (28340-5571)
P.O. Box 26 (28375-0026)
PHONE.................................910 628-7075
Claybourn Walters, *Pr*
Michael Walters, *
EMP: 10 **EST:** 1978
SALES (est): 873.37K **Privately Held**
Web: www.claybournwalters.com
SIC: **2411** Logging camps and contractors

(G-4502)
J & D WOOD INC
4940 Centerville Church Rd (28340-8439)
P.O. Box 271 (28340-0271)
PHONE.................................910 628-9000
Johnie F Allen, *Pr*
Diane T Allen, *Treas*
EMP: 19 **EST:** 1987
SQ FT: 65,000
SALES (est): 4.23MM **Privately Held**
Web: www.qualitypinebedding.com

SIC: **2426** 2421 Dimension, hardwood; Sawdust, shavings, and wood chips

(G-4503)
MEATINTERNATIONAL LLC
266 Bethesda Church Rd (28340-9616)
PHONE.................................910 628-8267
EMP: 4 **EST:** 2014
SALES (est): 97.83K **Privately Held**
SIC: **2011** Pork products, from pork slaughtered on site

(G-4504)
ROGERS SCREENPRINTING EMB INC (PA)
10306 Nc Highway 41 S (28340-5934)
PHONE.................................910 628-1983
Missy Rogers, *Pr*
Keith Rogers, *VP*
Bonita Rogers, *Treas*
EMP: 9 **EST:** 1999
SQ FT: 12,000
SALES (est): 2.37MM
SALES (corp-wide): 2.37MM **Privately Held**
Web: www.rogersseinc.com
SIC: **2396** 2395 Screen printing on fabric articles; Embroidery and art needlework

Fairview
Buncombe County

(G-4505)
ARTEX GROUP INC
1004 Charlotte Hwy (28730-8795)
PHONE.................................866 845-1042
Richard Camuto, *Pr*
EMP: 7 **EST:** 2010
SALES (est): 301.57K **Privately Held**
Web: www.artexgroup.net
SIC: **2395** Embroidery products, except Schiffli machine

(G-4506)
BYRD DESIGNS INC
140 Lee Dotson Rd (28730-8642)
PHONE.................................828 628-0151
Jaime Byrd, *Pr*
EMP: 7 **EST:** 1992
SQ FT: 2,376
SALES (est): 166.33K **Privately Held**
Web: www.byrddesigns.com
SIC: **3911** 5944 3961 Jewelry, precious metal ; Jewelry stores; Costume jewelry

(G-4507)
HENSLEY CORPORATION
9 Madelyn Ln (28730-8524)
PHONE.................................828 230-9447
Jeff Hensley, *Admn*
EMP: 4 **EST:** 2016
SALES (est): 558.8K **Privately Held**
SIC: **3999** Manufacturing industries, nec

(G-4508)
INDUSTRY CHOICE SOLUTIONS LLC
98 Bishop Cove Rd (28730-9799)
PHONE.................................828 628-1991
Mark Puzerewski, *CEO*
EMP: 5 **EST:** 2005
SALES (est): 284.26K **Privately Held**
Web: www.icsolutions-hq.com
SIC: **3559** Semiconductor manufacturing machinery

(G-4509)
LAURA GASKIN
922 Garren Creek Rd (28730-8650)
PHONE.................................828 628-5891

Laura Gaskin, *Prin*
EMP: 4 **EST:** 2011
SALES (est): 77K **Privately Held**
Web: www.lauragaskin.com
SIC: **3999** Framed artwork

(G-4510)
ROOTS ORGANIC GOURMET LLC
Also Called: Roots Food
125 Winding Rdg (28730-8764)
PHONE.................................828 232-2828
EMP: 16 **EST:** 2007
SALES (est): 2.81MM **Privately Held**
SIC: **2099** 5072 5085 Food preparations, nec ; Hardware; Industrial supplies

(G-4511)
SMITHWAY INC
20 Smith Farm Rd (28730-9570)
PHONE.................................828 628-1756
Rocky Smith, *VP*
EMP: 8 **EST:** 2015
SALES (est): 1.89MM **Privately Held**
Web: www.smithwayinc.com
SIC: **3715** 3713 3537 Truck trailers; Truck and bus bodies; Industrial trucks and tractors

(G-4512)
SMITHWAY INC
Us Highway 74 A E (28730)
P.O. Box 188 (28730-0188)
PHONE.................................828 628-1756
G D Smith, *Pr*
Rocky Smith, *VP*
Scott Smith, *Sec*
▼ **EMP:** 21 **EST:** 1980
SQ FT: 17,280
SALES (est): 5.14MM **Privately Held**
Web: www.smithwayinc.com
SIC: **3715** 3713 3537 Truck trailers; Truck bodies (motor vehicles); Industrial trucks and tractors

(G-4513)
TE CONNECTIVITY CORPORATION
Also Called: Cii Technologies
1396 Charlotte Hwy (28730-1409)
PHONE.................................828 338-1000
Bill Foley, *Brnch Mgr*
EMP: 281
SALES (corp-wide): 9.17B **Privately Held**
Web: www.te.com
SIC: **3678** 3643 Electronic connectors; Current-carrying wiring services
HQ: Te Connectivity Corporation
1050 Westlakes Dr
Berwyn PA 19312
610 893-9800

(G-4514)
TE CONNECTIVITY CORPORATION
Also Called: Agastat
1396 Charlotte Hwy (28730-1409)
PHONE.................................828 338-1000
EMP: 15
SALES (corp-wide): 9.17B **Privately Held**
Web: www.te.com
SIC: **3625** Industrial electrical relays and switches
HQ: Te Connectivity Corporation
1050 Westlakes Dr
Berwyn PA 19312
610 893-9800

Faison
Duplin County

(G-4515)
BAY VALLEY FOODS LLC
354 N Faison Ave (28341-7608)
PHONE..............................910 267-4711
E Bailey, *Pr*
▲ **EMP:** 33 **EST:** 2011
SALES (est): 6.49MM
SALES (corp-wide): 3.35B **Publicly Held**
SIC: 2099 Vegetables, peeled for the trade
HQ: Bay Valley Foods, Llc
3200 Riverside Dr Ste A
Green Bay WI 54301
800 236-1119

(G-4516)
ENVIVA PELLETS SAMPSON LLC
5 Connector Rd (28341-6123)
PHONE..............................301 657-5560
EMP: 80 **EST:** 2013
SALES (est): 20MM
SALES (corp-wide): 1.18MM **Privately Held**
Web: www.envivabiomass.com
SIC: 2421 Wood chips, produced at mill
PA: Enviva, Llc
7500 Old Grgtown Rd Ste 1
Bethesda MD 20814
301 657-5560

(G-4517)
EUGENES TRUCKING INC
10422 Faison Hwy (28341-5878)
PHONE..............................910 267-0555
Eugene Pearsall, *Pr*
EMP: 5 **EST:** 2006
SALES (est): 2.36MM **Privately Held**
SIC: 3715 Truck trailers

(G-4518)
PICKLES MANUFACTURING LLC
354 N Faison Ave (28341-7608)
PHONE..............................910 267-4711
Steven Okland, *Managing Member*
EMP: 203 **EST:** 2022
SALES (est): 92.01MM
SALES (corp-wide): 3.35B **Publicly Held**
Web: www.mtolivepickles.com
SIC: 2099 Food preparations, nec
PA: Treehouse Foods, Inc.
2021 Spring Rd Ste 600
Oak Brook IL 60523
708 483-1300

(G-4519)
R D JONES PACKING CO INC
192 N Nc Hwy 50 (28341)
PHONE..............................910 267-2846
Taylor W Best, *Pr*
Joseph M Price, *Sec*
EMP: 8 **EST:** 1981
SQ FT: 1,782
SALES (est): 156.43K **Privately Held**
SIC: 2011 Beef products, from beef
slaughtered on site

Faith
Rowan County

(G-4520)
WOOD PRODUCTS PACKG INTL INC
3725 Faith Rd (28041)
PHONE..............................704 279-3011
Lloyd Pullen, *Pr*
EMP: 8 **EST:** 2003
SQ FT: 48,000

SALES (est): 533.23K **Privately Held**
SIC: 3086 Packaging and shipping
materials, foamed plastics

Falcon
Cumberland County

(G-4521)
REUBEN JAMES AUTO ELECTRIC
7386 N West St (28342)
P.O. Box 126 (28342-0126)
PHONE..............................910 980-1056
David James, *Owner*
EMP: 5 **EST:** 1981
SALES (est): 402.07K **Privately Held**
SIC: 3714 Motor vehicle parts and
accessories

Fallston
Cleveland County

(G-4522)
BOGGS FARM CENTER INC
807 E Stagecoach Trl (28042)
P.O. Box 660 (28042-0660)
PHONE..............................704 538-7176
A Max Boggs Junior, *Pr*
Mary Boggs, *VP*
EMP: 5 **EST:** 1930
SQ FT: 12,000
SALES (est): 468.16K **Privately Held**
SIC: 0724 5191 0191 0212 Cotton ginning;
Fertilizer and fertilizer materials; General
farms, primarily crop; Beef cattle, except
feedlots

(G-4523)
FURNLITE INC
Also Called: Furnlite
344 Wilson Rd (28042)
P.O. Box 159 (28042-0159)
PHONE..............................704 538-3193
Kieth Helms, *Genl Mgr*
▲ **EMP:** 23 **EST:** 1981
SQ FT: 4,400
SALES (est): 5.91MM
SALES (corp-wide): 4.79B **Publicly Held**
Web: www.furnlite.com
SIC: 3648 3645 Lighting equipment, nec;
Residential lighting fixtures
PA: Graham Holdings Company
1300 17th St N Ste 1700 F
Arlington VA 22209
703 345-6300

(G-4524)
SPECIALTY LIGHTING LLC
4203 Fallston Rd (28042)
P.O. Box 780 (28042-0780)
PHONE..............................704 538-6522
Gregg Carpenter, *Managing Member*
▲ **EMP:** 12 **EST:** 2009
SALES (est): 3.17MM **Privately Held**
Web: www.specialtylighting.com
SIC: 3646 Commercial lighting fixtures

Farmville
Pitt County

(G-4525)
CMP PHARMA INC
8026 East Marlboro Rd (27828-9656)
P.O. Box 147 (27828-0147)
PHONE..............................252 753-7111
Gerald D Sakowski, *CEO*
Henry Smith, *

Tracey Smith, *
Kelly F Whitley, *
Peter Jerome, *
EMP: 30 **EST:** 1975
SALES (est): 9.74MM **Privately Held**
Web: www.cmppharma.com
SIC: 2834 Pharmaceutical preparations

(G-4526)
D R BURTON HEALTHCARE LLC
3936 South Fields St (27828-8570)
P.O. Box 229 (27828-0229)
PHONE..............................252 228-7038
Dennis Cook, *Managing Member*
EMP: 10 **EST:** 2016
SALES (est): 5.88MM **Privately Held**
Web: www.drburtonhealthcare.com
SIC: 3841 Surgical and medical instruments

(G-4527)
DUCK-RABBIT CRAFT BREWERY INC
4519 West Pine St (27828-8526)
PHONE..............................252 753-7745
Paul Philippon, *Pr*
EMP: 8 **EST:** 2004
SQ FT: 10,000
SALES (est): 1MM **Privately Held**
Web: www.duckrabbitbrewery.com
SIC: 2082 Ale (alcoholic beverage)

(G-4528)
ESCO ELECTRONIC SERVICES INC
Also Called: Electronic Services
268 Hwy 121 And 264 Alternate (27828)
P.O. Box 732 (27828-0732)
PHONE..............................252 753-4433
Kenneth H Strickland, *Pr*
Pamela Jo Strickland, *VP*
▲ **EMP:** 10 **EST:** 1977
SQ FT: 15,000
SALES (est): 195.79K **Privately Held**
SIC: 7694 7629 Electric motor repair; Circuit
board repair

(G-4529)
GARRIS GRADING AND PAVING INC
5950 Gay Rd (27828-8901)
PHONE..............................252 749-1101
Angela Garris, *Pr*
EMP: 15 **EST:** 2003
SALES (est): 4.4MM **Privately Held**
Web:
www.asphaltgradingmillingpaving.com
SIC: 1611 1771 1794 2951 Surfacing and
paving; Parking lot construction; Excavation
and grading, building construction; Asphalt
and asphaltic paving mixtures (not from
refineries)

(G-4530)
HARVEY FERTILIZER AND GAS CO
Also Called: Morgan Fertilizer
4419 West Pine St (27828-4400)
P.O. Box 649 (27828-0649)
PHONE..............................252 753-2063
Glenn Shirley, *Genl Mgr*
EMP: 30
SALES (corp-wide): 80.5MM **Privately Held**
Web: www.harveyfertilizerandgas.com
SIC: 5191 2879 Fertilizer and fertilizer
materials; Agricultural chemicals, nec
PA: Harvey Fertilizer And Gas Co.
303 Bohannon Rd
Kinston NC 28501
252 526-4150

(G-4531)
HERMES MEDICAL SOLUTIONS INC
710 Cromwell Dr (27828)
PHONE..............................252 355-4373
Jan Bertling, *CEO*
Guy Asterius, *Sec*
EMP: 7 **EST:** 2001
SALES (est): 2.57MM
SALES (corp-wide): 15.7MM **Privately Held**
Web: www.hermesmedical.com
SIC: 3577 Computer peripheral equipment,
nec
HQ: Hermes Medical Solutions Limited
7-8 Henrietta Street
London
207 839-2513

(G-4532)
JACK A FARRIOR INC
Also Called: Farrior Steel Works
9585 Us Highway 264a (27828-9548)
P.O. Box 839 (27828-0839)
PHONE..............................252 753-2020
Mary Susan Farrior, *Pr*
David Baker, *
Edwin Mark Flanagan, *Prin*
EMP: 60 **EST:** 1962
SQ FT: 30,000
SALES (est): 11.03MM **Privately Held**
Web: www.farriorsteelworks.com
SIC: 3444 7692 3535 1796 Sheet metalwork
; Welding repair; Conveyors and conveying
equipment; Millwright

(G-4533)
JFL LLC
4353 West Perry St (27828-1970)
PHONE..............................919 440-3517
Johnel Jones, *Prin*
EMP: 5
SALES (est): 357.88K **Privately Held**
SIC: 7389 3161 Business Activities at Non-
Commercial Site; Trunks

(G-4534)
LIMITLESS WLDG FABRICATION LLC
3543 South Fields St (27828-1983)
P.O. Box 134 (27828)
PHONE..............................252 753-0660
Dustin Coffey, *CEO*
EMP: 5 **EST:** 2016
SALES (est): 420K **Privately Held**
Web: www.limitlesswelding.com
SIC: 7692 1799 3441 7699 Welding repair;
Hydraulic equipment, installation and
service; Fabricated structural metal;
Industrial machinery and equipment repair

(G-4535)
MESTEK INC
Sterling Heater Division
3576 South Fields St (27828)
P.O. Box 809 (27828)
PHONE..............................252 753-5323
James Burk, *Brnch Mgr*
EMP: 220
SQ FT: 70,000
SALES (corp-wide): 689.94MM **Privately Held**
Web: www.mestek.com
SIC: 3585 3634 3549 3433 Heating
equipment, complete; Heating units, electric
(radiant heat): baseboard or wall;
Metalworking machinery, nec; Heating
equipment, except electric
PA: Mestek, Inc.
260 N Elm St
Westfield MA 01085
413 568-9571

▲ = Import ▼ = Export
◆ = Import/Export

(G-4536)
MODLINS ANONIZED ALUMINUM WLDG
4551 Nc Highway 121 (27828-9363)
PHONE...................252 753-7274
Keith Modlin, *Owner*
EMP: 4 **EST:** 2003
SALES (est): 217.88K **Privately Held**
Web: www.modlinswelding.com
SIC: 7692 3548 Welding repair; Welding and cutting apparatus and accessories, nec

(G-4537)
PACKAGING CORPORATION AMERICA
Also Called: PCA
9156 West Marlboro Rd (27828-8504)
PHONE...................252 753-8450
Jason Tatum, *Brnch Mgr*
EMP: 5
SALES (corp-wide): 7.73B **Publicly Held**
Web: www.packagingcorp.com
SIC: 2653 Boxes, corrugated: made from purchased materials
PA: Packaging Corporation Of America
1 N Field Ct
Lake Forest IL 60045
847 482-3000

(G-4538)
PYXUS INTERNATIONAL INC
8958 West Marlboro Rd (27828-8571)
P.O. Box 166 (27828-0166)
PHONE...................252 753-8000
William Loyd, *Brnch Mgr*
EMP: 150
SALES (corp-wide): 2.03B **Privately Held**
Web: www.aointl.com
SIC: 2141 5159 Tobacco stemming and redrying; Tobacco, leaf
PA: Pyxus International, Inc.
6001 Hsptality Ct Ste 100
Morrisville NC 27560
919 379-4300

(G-4539)
SAG HARBOR INDUSTRIES INC
3595 Mandarin Dr (27828-8580)
P.O. Box 269 (27828-0269)
PHONE...................252 753-7175
Gene W Michelsen, *Manager*
EMP: 29
SALES (corp-wide): 24.73MM **Privately Held**
Web: www.sagharborind.com
SIC: 3621 Coils, for electric motors or generators
PA: Sag Harbor Industries, Inc.
1668 Bhmpton Sag Hbr Tpke
Sag Harbor NY 11963
631 725-0440

Fayetteville
Cumberland County

(G-4540)
21ST CENTURY TECH OF AMER
Also Called: 21st Century Technologies Amer
6316 Yadkin Rd (28303-2647)
PHONE...................910 826-3676
William Mathes Iii, *Pr*
EMP: 18 **EST:** 1997
SQ FT: 18,000
SALES (est): 400.3K **Privately Held**
SIC: 3545 Tools and accessories for machine tools

(G-4541)
822TEES INC
2598 Raeford Rd (28305-5118)
PHONE...................910 822-8337
Kurin S Keys, *Pr*
Sherin Keys, *Treas*
Ashley Brown, *Sec*
EMP: 7 **EST:** 2016
SQ FT: 2,500
SALES (est): 256.21K **Privately Held**
Web: www.822tees.com
SIC: 7311 8742 8743 2395 Advertising agencies; Marketing consulting services; Promotion service; Embroidery products, except Schiffli machine

(G-4542)
A2A INTEGRATED LOGISTICS INC
1830 Owen Dr Ste 102 (28304-3412)
PHONE...................800 493-3736
Anthony Bryant, *Pr*
▼ **EMP:** 4 **EST:** 2011
SALES (est): 3.88MM **Privately Held**
Web: www.a2a-logistics.com
SIC: 2834 Pharmaceutical preparations

(G-4543)
ADVANCED BRACE & LIMB INC
Also Called: Advanced Brace and Limb
4140 Ferncreek Dr Ste 803 (28314-2572)
PHONE...................910 483-5737
Christopher Eney, *VP*
EMP: 8 **EST:** 2010
SALES (est): 503.3K **Privately Held**
Web: www.advancedbraceandlimb.com
SIC: 3842 Limbs, artificial

(G-4544)
ADVANCED COMPUTER LRNG CO LLC
Also Called: Aclc
208 Hay St Ste 2c (28301-5534)
PHONE...................910 779-2254
Bradd Chi, *Managing Member*
EMP: 43 **EST:** 2003
SQ FT: 16,000
SALES (est): 1.96MM **Privately Held**
Web: www.goaclc.com
SIC: 7372 8299 7371 8711 Educational computer software; Educational services; Custom computer programming services; Engineering services

(G-4545)
ADVANTAGE NEWSPAPER
501 Executive Pl Ste B (28305-5391)
PHONE...................910 323-0349
Timothy O Dellinger, *Prin*
EMP: 31 **EST:** 2011
SALES (est): 2.47MM **Privately Held**
Web: www.newspaperconsultants.com
SIC: 2711 Newspapers, publishing and printing

(G-4546)
AEC CONSUMER PRODUCTS LLC
Also Called: AEC Consumer Products
3005 Bankhead Dr (28306-2683)
PHONE...................704 904-0578
Richard Guy, *CEO*
Tammy Claussen, *COO*
EMP: 10 **EST:** 2012
SALES (est): 261.29K **Privately Held**
Web: www.bac-d.com
SIC: 7822 2842 Motion picture and tape distribution; Sanitation preparations, disinfectants and deodorants

(G-4547)
AFA BILLING SERVICES
894 Elm St Ste D (28303-4384)
PHONE...................910 868-8324
Cornelius Williams, *Mgr*
EMP: 4 **EST:** 2017
SALES (est): 951.97K **Privately Held**
Web: www.afap.com
SIC: 3669 Communications equipment, nec

(G-4548)
ALASKA STRUCTURES INC
Also Called: ALASKA STRUCTURES, INC.
2545 Ravenhill Dr Ste 101 (28303-5460)
P.O. Box 64577 (28306-0577)
PHONE...................910 323-0562
Jimmy White, *Brnch Mgr*
EMP: 69
SALES (corp-wide): 75MM **Privately Held**
Web: www.alaskastructures.com
SIC: 3448 Buildings, portable: prefabricated metal
PA: Aks Industries, Inc.
6991 E Cmlback Rd Ste D21
Scottsdale AZ 85251
480 677-6088

(G-4549)
ALL SIGNS & GRAPHICS LLC
301 Hope Mills Rd (28304-3152)
PHONE...................910 323-3115
EMP: 7 **EST:** 2011
SALES (est): 498.69K **Privately Held**
Web: www.allsignsnc.com
SIC: 3944 3993 8721 Erector sets, toy; Electric signs; Accounting, auditing, and bookkeeping

(G-4550)
ALPEK POLYESTER USA LLC
Also Called: Dak Americas
3216 Cedar Creek Rd (28312-7955)
P.O. Box 1690 (28302-1690)
PHONE...................910 433-8200
Cindy Jergensen, *Brnch Mgr*
EMP: 115
Web: www.alpekpolyester.com
SIC: 2821 Polytetrafluoroethylene resins, teflon
HQ: Alpek Polyester Usa, Llc
7621 Little Ave Ste 500
Charlotte NC 28226
704 940-7500

(G-4551)
AMERICAN PHOENIX INC
318 Blount St (28301-5606)
PHONE...................910 484-4007
Tommy Stewart, *Brnch Mgr*
EMP: 127
Web: www.apimix.net
SIC: 3069 2899 Custom compounding of rubber materials; Chemical preparations, nec
PA: American Phoenix, Inc.
800 Wisconsin St Unit 11
Eau Claire WI 54703

(G-4552)
AMERICAN WOODWORKERY INC
802 Bladen Cir (28312-9268)
PHONE...................910 916-8098
EMP: 4 **EST:** 2015
SALES (est): 424.21K **Privately Held**
Web: www.uscustomwoodwork.com
SIC: 2431 Millwork

(G-4553)
**ARNOLDS WELDING SERVICE INC
(PA)**

Also Called: A W S
1405 Waterless St (28306-1611)
PHONE...................910 323-3822
Bill Arnold, *CEO*
EMP: 23 **EST:** 1970
SQ FT: 18,000
SALES (est): 6.19MM
SALES (corp-wide): 6.19MM **Privately Held**
SIC: 5084 3542 3949 Industrial machinery and equipment; Machine tools, metal forming type; Golf equipment

(G-4554)
AUTO MACHINE SHOP INC
309 Winslow St (28301-5553)
PHONE...................910 483-6016
Richard Butler Junior, *Pr*
EMP: 4 **EST:** 1949
SQ FT: 2,500
SALES (est): 236.59K **Privately Held**
Web: www.automachinefayetteville.com
SIC: 3599 5013 Machine shop, jobbing and repair; Automotive supplies and parts

(G-4555)
AUTO PARTS FAYETTEVILLE LLC
Also Called: Auto Parts USA
929 Bragg Blvd Ste 2 (28301-4509)
PHONE...................910 889-4026
EMP: 5 **EST:** 2019
SALES (est): 233.58K **Privately Held**
Web: www.carquest.com
SIC: 5015 3089 2851 7699 Automotive parts and supplies, used; Automotive parts, plastic; Paints and paint additives; Hydraulic equipment repair

(G-4556)
AVERY MACHINE & WELDING CO
1312 Longleaf Dr (28305-5207)
P.O. Box 339 (28657-0339)
PHONE...................828 733-4944
Todd Lecka, *Pr*
Steve Lecka, *VP*
EMP: 7 **EST:** 1984
SQ FT: 10,000
SALES (est): 499.99K **Privately Held**
SIC: 3599 7692 1799 Machine shop, jobbing and repair; Welding repair; Welding on site

(G-4557)
BARNHILL CONTRACTING COMPANY
1100 Robeson St (28305-5528)
P.O. Box 35376 (28303-0376)
PHONE...................910 488-1319
Kermit Moser, *Brnch Mgr*
EMP: 58
SQ FT: 2,000
SALES (corp-wide): 490.43MM **Privately Held**
Web: www.barnhillcontracting.com
SIC: 1611 1629 2951 1771 Grading; Drainage system construction; Asphalt paving mixtures and blocks; Concrete work
PA: Barnhill Contracting Company Inc
800 Tiffany Blvd Ste 200
Rocky Mount NC 27804
252 823-1021

(G-4558)
BLACKSAND METAL WORKS LLC
433 Delbert Dr (28306-8849)
P.O. Box 41627 (28309-1627)
PHONE...................703 489-8282
EMP: 10 **EST:** 2015
SQ FT: 21,780
SALES (est): 144.09K **Privately Held**

SIC: 7692 3317 3441 Welding repair; Welded pipe and tubes; Building components, structural steel

(G-4559)
BLASHFIELD SIGN COMPANY INC
303 Williams St (28301-5661)
PHONE................................910 485-7200
Matt Blashfield, *Pr*
Stacey Blashfield, *VP*
EMP: 9 EST: 1989
SALES (est): 932.53K Privately Held
Web: www.bcsignage.com
SIC: 3993 Electric signs

(G-4560)
BLINDS PLUS INC
5137 Raeford Rd (28304-3145)
P.O. Box 41035 (28309-1035)
PHONE................................910 487-5196
Letitia Libby, *Owner*
EMP: 5 EST: 2009
SALES (est): 85.53K Privately Held
SIC: 2431 5719 7699 Blinds (shutters), wood; Window furnishings; Venetian blind repair shop

(G-4561)
BRANDY THOMPSON
Also Called: Spa and Salon
6712 Bone Creek Dr Apt A (28314-2931)
P.O. Box 1704 (28302-1704)
PHONE................................321 252-2911
Brandy Thompson, *Prin*
Brandy Thompson, *Owner*
EMP: 10 EST: 2015
SALES (est): 60K Privately Held
SIC: 7231 3999 7299 Cosmetologist; Barber and beauty shop equipment; Personal appearance services

(G-4562)
BRIDGESTONE RET OPERATIONS LLC
Also Called: Firestone
660 Cross Creek Mall (28303-7266)
PHONE................................910 864-4106
Michael Diantonio, *Mgr*
EMP: 5
Web: www.bridgestoneamericas.com
SIC: 5531 7534 Automotive tires; Rebuilding and retreading tires
HQ: Bridgestone Retail Operations, Llc
200 4th Ave S Ste 100
Nashville TN 37201
615 937-1000

(G-4563)
BUVIC LLC
6798 Weeping Water Run (28314-5148)
PHONE................................910 302-7950
David Thompson, *Managing Member*
EMP: 6 EST: 2019
SALES (est): 484.31K Privately Held
SIC: 3578 Automatic teller machines (ATM)

(G-4564)
BUZZ SAW INC
Also Called: Sign-A-Rama
1015 Robeson St Ste 103 (28305-5635)
PHONE................................910 321-7446
Robert M Degroff, *Pr*
Crystal A Degroff, *VP*
EMP: 5 EST: 2012
SALES (est): 170.38K Privately Held
Web: www.signarama.com
SIC: 3993 Signs and advertising specialties

(G-4565)
CAPE FEAR CABINET CO INC
2908 Fort Bragg Rd (28303-4725)
P.O. Box 584 (28348-0584)
PHONE................................910 703-8760
William Konen, *Pr*
EMP: 6 EST: 2016
SALES (est): 468.07K Privately Held
Web: www.capefearcabinets.com
SIC: 2434 Wood kitchen cabinets

(G-4566)
CAPE FEAR ORTHTICS PRSTHTICS I
435 W Russell St (28301-5576)
P.O. Box 58611 (28305-8611)
PHONE................................910 483-0933
Demetri Sleem, *Prin*
EMP: 8 EST: 1999
SALES (est): 1.08MM Privately Held
Web: www.cfop.org
SIC: 5999 3842 8093 Orthopedic and prosthesis applications; Prosthetic appliances; Specialty outpatient clinics, nec

(G-4567)
CAPITOL BUMPER (PA)
126 Drake St (28301-4710)
PHONE................................919 772-7330
Curtis Rogers, *Mgr*
EMP: 8 EST: 2003
SALES (est): 241.55K
SALES (corp-wide): 241.55K Privately Held
SIC: 3471 Rechroming auto bumpers

(G-4568)
CAPITOL BUMPER
Also Called: Capital Bumper
126 Drake St (28301-4710)
PHONE................................919 772-7330
Curtis Rogers, *Mgr*
EMP: 7
SQ FT: 6,000
SALES (corp-wide): 241.55K Privately Held
SIC: 3471 5013 Rechroming auto bumpers; Motor vehicle supplies and new parts
PA: Capitol Bumper
126 Drake St
Fayetteville NC 28301
919 772-7330

(G-4569)
CARGILL INCORPORATED
Cargill
1754 River Rd (28312-7362)
PHONE................................800 227-4455
Walker Humpries, *Mgr*
EMP: 49
SQ FT: 17,778
SALES (corp-wide): 159.59B Privately Held
Web: www.cargill.com
SIC: 2075 2099 Soybean oil mills; Food preparations, nec
PA: Cargill, Incorporated
15407 Mcginty Rd W
Wayzata MN 55391
800 227-4455

(G-4570)
CAROLINA PWR SIGNALIZATION LLC
Also Called: Carolina Signals and Lightings
1416 Middle River Loop (28312-9182)
P.O. Box 53650 (28305-3650)
PHONE................................910 323-5589
Garrett L Fulcher, *Pr*
Brian L Fulcher, *VP*
EMP: 22 EST: 2008
SQ FT: 1,100

SALES (est): 1.77MM
SALES (corp-wide): 23.67B Publicly Held
Web: www.carolinapowerandsignalization.com
SIC: 3669 Traffic signals, electric
PA: Quanta Services, Inc.
2727 North Loop W
Houston TX 77008
713 629-7600

(G-4571)
CBA PRODUCTIONS INC
Also Called: Nomadic State of Mind
579 Baywood Rd (28312-8470)
PHONE................................703 568-4758
Chris Anderson, *Pr*
▲ EMP: 6 EST: 2007
SALES (est): 1.34MM Privately Held
Web: www.nomadicstateofmind.com
SIC: 3021 Sandals, rubber

(G-4572)
CCBCC OPERATIONS LLC
Also Called: Coca-Cola
800 Tom Starling Rd (28306-8100)
PHONE................................910 483-6158
Alan Clark, *Brnch Mgr*
EMP: 49
SQ FT: 45,333
SALES (corp-wide): 6.9B Publicly Held
Web: www.coca-cola.com
SIC: 2086 Bottled and canned soft drinks
HQ: Ccbcc Operations, Llc
4100 Coca-Cola Plz
Charlotte NC 28211
704 364-8728

(G-4573)
CHEMOURS COMPANY
22828 Nc Highway 87 W (28306-7332)
PHONE................................910 483-4681
EMP: 48
SALES (corp-wide): 6.03B Publicly Held
Web: www.chemours.com
SIC: 2879 Agricultural chemicals, nec
PA: The Chemours Company
1007 Market St
Wilmington DE 19898
302 773-1000

(G-4574)
CHEMOURS COMPANY FC LLC
22828 Nc Highway 87 W (28306-7332)
PHONE................................910 678-1314
EMP: 91
SALES (corp-wide): 6.03B Publicly Held
Web: www.chemours.com
SIC: 2879 Agricultural chemicals, nec
HQ: The Chemours Company Fc Llc
1007 Market St
Wilmington DE 19898
302 773-1000

(G-4575)
CITYVIEW PUBLISHING LLC
Also Called: Cityview Magazine
2533 Raeford Rd Ste A (28305-5094)
P.O. Box 53967 (28305-3967)
PHONE................................910 423-6500
Marshal Waren, *Pr*
EMP: 11 EST: 2008
SALES (est): 1.17MM Privately Held
Web: www.cityviewnc.com
SIC: 2721 Magazines: publishing only, not printed on site

(G-4576)
COLLIERS WELDING LLC
773 Mary Jordan Ln (28311-7076)
PHONE................................910 818-5728
Bert Bcollier, *Prin*

EMP: 5 EST: 2009
SALES (est): 130K Privately Held
SIC: 3441 Fabricated structural metal

(G-4577)
CONCRETE SERVICE CO INC (HQ)
130 Builders Blvd (28301-4703)
P.O. Box 1867 (28302-1867)
PHONE................................910 483-0396
Richard R Allen Senior, *Pr*
Jerry King, *
Richard R Allen Junior, *VP*
EMP: 40 EST: 1965
SQ FT: 4,500
SALES (est): 15.02MM
SALES (corp-wide): 47.32MM Privately Held
Web: www.concreteservice.com
SIC: 3273 5032 Ready-mixed concrete; Aggregate
PA: D.R. Allen & Son, Inc.
130 Builders Blvd
Fayetteville NC 28301
910 323-8509

(G-4578)
CONNECTED 2K LLC
Also Called: Sign Manufacturing
1015 Robeson St Ste 103 (28305-5635)
PHONE................................910 321-7446
Samanthia Cook, *CEO*
EMP: 4 EST: 2017
SALES (est): 476.47K Privately Held
Web: www.signarama.com
SIC: 3993 7336 5999 1799 Signs and advertising specialties; Graphic arts and related design; Banners, flags, decals, and posters; Sign installation and maintenance

(G-4579)
COUNCIL TRNSP & LOGISTICS LLC
6217 Rhemish Dr (28304-4751)
PHONE................................910 322-7588
EMP: 5
SALES (est): 272.08K Privately Held
SIC: 2519 7389 Household furniture, nec; Business Activities at Non-Commercial Site

(G-4580)
CREATIVE STONE FYETTEVILLE INC (PA)
Also Called: Creative Stone
918 Foxhunt Ln (28314-6077)
PHONE................................910 491-1225
Richard Johnson, *CEO*
EMP: 12 EST: 2014
SQ FT: 10,000
SALES (est): 3.35MM
SALES (corp-wide): 3.35MM Privately Held
Web: www.creativestonenc.com
SIC: 5722 1752 7299 3281 Kitchens, complete (sinks, cabinets, etc.); Wood floor installation and refinishing; Home improvement and renovation contractor agency; Granite, cut and shaped

(G-4581)
CROWDER TRUCKING LLC
6776 Saint Julian Way (28314-5816)
PHONE................................910 797-4163
Carlos D Crowder, *Pr*
EMP: 8 EST: 2005
SALES (est): 463.06K Privately Held
SIC: 4212 1611 1442 Local trucking, without storage; Highway and street construction; Construction sand and gravel

(G-4582)
CTS CLEANING SYSTEMS INC
2185 Angelia M St (28312-8398)
PHONE..............................910 483-5349
Fred R Adkins, *Pr*
Rodney Adkins, *Sec*
EMP: 6 EST: 1967
SALES (est): 2.39MM Privately Held
Web: www.ctsclean.com
SIC: 5087 5074 2841 Janitors' supplies;
Water purification equipment; Soap and
other detergents

(G-4583)
DARLING INGREDIENTS INC
Cape Fear Feed Products Div
1309 Industrial Dr (28301-6323)
P.O. Box 1659 (28302-1659)
PHONE..............................910 483-0473
Reed Park, *Brnch Mgr*
EMP: 25
SALES (corp-wide): 6.79B Publicly Held
Web: www.darpro-solutions.com
SIC: 2048 2077 Feed concentrates; Tallow
rendering, inedible
PA: Darling Ingredients Inc.
5601 N Macarthur Blvd
Irving TX 75038
972 717-0300

(G-4584)
**DAY 3 LWNCARE LDSCPG
PRFCTNIST**
1637 Woodfield Rd (28303-3844)
PHONE..............................910 574-8422
Kenneth Haywood, *Pt*
Charles Peele, *Pt*
EMP: 8 EST: 2014
SALES (est): 167.34K Privately Held
SIC: 0782 3524 7389 Mowing services, lawn
; Edgers, lawn; Business services, nec

(G-4585)
**DB NORTH CAROLINA HOLDINGS
INC (HQ)**
Also Called: Fayetteville Observer, The
458 Whitfield St (28306-1614)
P.O. Box 849 (28302-0849)
PHONE..............................910 323-4848
Robert Gruber, *Pr*
Jill Koonce, *VP*
EMP: 38 EST: 2015
SQ FT: 101,158
SALES (est): 96.3MM
SALES (corp-wide): 2.51B Publicly Held
Web: www.fayobserver.com
SIC: 2711 Newspapers, publishing and
printing
PA: Gannett Co., Inc.
175 Sully's Trl Ste 203
Pittsford NY 14534
703 854-6000

(G-4586)
DEFENSE LOGISTICS SERVICES LLC
231 Meed Ct Ste 104 (28303-2076)
PHONE..............................703 449-1620
Carey A Smith, *Prin*
EMP: 76 EST: 2011
SALES (est): 514.35K Publicly Held
SIC: 3812 Search and navigation equipment
HQ: Lockheed Martin Integrated Systems,
Llc
6801 Rockledge Dr
Bethesda MD 20817

(G-4587)
DELABY BRACE AND LIMB CO
405 Owen Dr (28304-3411)
P.O. Box 250 (28399-0250)

PHONE..............................910 484-2509
Joan Benner, *Pr*
Joan Benner, *Prin*
David Benner, *VP*
EMP: 5 EST: 2008
SALES (est): 250.08K Privately Held
SIC: 3842 Limbs, artificial

(G-4588)
DOMINOS PIZZA LLC
Also Called: Domino's
5133 Raeford Rd (28304-3145)
PHONE..............................910 424-4884
Joshua Long, *Brnch Mgr*
EMP: 10
SALES (corp-wide): 4.71MM Publicly
Held
Web: www.dominos.com
SIC: 5812 2045 Pizzeria, chain; Prepared
flour mixes and doughs
HQ: Domino's Pizza Llc
30 Frank Lloyd Wright Dr
Ann Arbor MI 48106
734 930-3030

(G-4589)
DUPONT TEIJIN FILMS
3216 Cedar Creek Rd (28312-7955)
PHONE..............................910 433-8200
Craig Leite, *Mgr*
EMP: 6 EST: 2018
SALES (est): 29.6K Privately Held
Web: www.mylar.com
SIC: 2821 Plastics materials and resins

(G-4590)
E-N-G MOBILE SYSTEMS LLC (HQ)
810 Tom Starling Rd (28306-8100)
PHONE..............................925 798-4060
EMP: 14 EST: 1977
SALES (est): 4.44MM
SALES (corp-wide): 9.42MM Privately
Held
Web: www.e-n-g.com
SIC: 3711 Automobile assembly, including
specialty automobiles
PA: Positiveid Corporation
1690 S Cngress Ave Ste 20
Delray Beach FL 33445
561 805-8000

(G-4591)
EAST COAST BIOLOGICS
311 Wagoner Dr (28303-4646)
PHONE..............................717 919-9980
Rachael Buzzelli, *Prin*
EMP: 4 EST: 2017
SALES (est): 48.34K Privately Held
Web: www.eastcoastbiologics.com
SIC: 2834 Pharmaceutical preparations

(G-4592)
EAST COAST DESIGNS LLC
781 Tobermory Rd (28306-9447)
PHONE..............................910 865-1070
James Baker, *Owner*
EMP: 9 EST: 2007
SALES (est): 433.77K Privately Held
Web: www.eastcoastdesigns.org
SIC: 2759 Screen printing

(G-4593)
EATON CORPORATION
2900 Doc Bennett Rd (28306-9219)
PHONE..............................910 677-5375
John Stanpfel, *Mgr*
EMP: 370
Web: www.dix-eaton.com
SIC: 3625 Electric controls and control
accessories, industrial
HQ: Eaton Corporation

1000 Eaton Blvd
Cleveland OH 44122
440 523-5000

(G-4594)
EDWIN REAVES
1630 Flintshire Rd (28304-4943)
PHONE..............................901 326-6382
Edwin Reaves, *Owner*
EMP: 8
SALES (est): 1.44MM Privately Held
SIC: 1389 Construction, repair, and
dismantling services

(G-4595)
EIDP INC
Also Called: Dupont
22828 Nc Highway 87 W (28306-7332)
PHONE..............................910 483-4681
Barry Hudson, *Brnch Mgr*
EMP: 107
SALES (corp-wide): 16.91B Publicly Held
Web: www.dupont.com
SIC: 2819 Industrial inorganic chemicals, nec
HQ: Eidp, Inc.
9330 Zionsville Rd
Indianapolis IN 46268
833 267-8382

(G-4596)
ELEVATE CLEANING SERVICE
2120 Fort Bragg Rd (28303-7030)
PHONE..............................347 928-4030
Misty Burch, *Owner*
EMP: 4 EST: 2021
SALES (est): 156.69K Privately Held
SIC: 2842 Cleaning or polishing
preparations, nec

(G-4597)
ENERGETICS INC
Also Called: Electrotek
455 Hillsboro St (28301-4861)
P.O. Box 1864 (28302-1864)
PHONE..............................910 483-2581
David Phillips Junior, *Pr*
Dave K Phillips, *Sec*
EMP: 9 EST: 1973
SQ FT: 13,500
SALES (est): 980.02K Privately Held
Web: www.electrotek.biz
SIC: 7694 Electric motor repair

(G-4598)
ENSYSTEX INC (PA)
202 Fairway Dr Ste A (28305-5575)
P.O. Box 87329 (28304-7329)
PHONE..............................888 398-3772
David R Nimocks Iii, *Pr*
C Keith Love, *
James B Haugh, *
Kenneth Kendall, *
Franklin Howard, *
◆ EMP: 25 EST: 1994
SALES (est): 10MM
SALES (corp-wide): 10MM Privately Held
Web: www.ensystex.com
SIC: 2879 Exterminating products, for
household or industrial use

(G-4599)
F B PUBLICATIONS INC
909 S Mcpherson Church Rd (28303-5350)
P.O. Box 53461 (28305-3461)
PHONE..............................910 484-6200
Bill Bowman, *Pr*
EMP: 10 EST: 2000
SALES (est): 109.76K Privately Held
SIC: 2711 Newspapers

(G-4600)
FAYBLOCK MATERIALS INC
130 Builders Blvd (28301-4703)
P.O. Box 1867 (28302-1867)
PHONE..............................910 323-9198
Richard R Allen Junior, *Pr*
Larry Little, *
Jerry T King, *
Keith T Mcfadyen, *Sec*
▼ EMP: 100 EST: 1991
SALES (est): 17.65MM
SALES (corp-wide): 47.32MM Privately
Held
Web: www.fayblock.com
SIC: 3272 4212 3271 Concrete products, nec
; Local trucking, without storage; Concrete
block and brick
PA: D.R. Allen & Son, Inc.
130 Builders Blvd
Fayetteville NC 28301
910 323-8509

(G-4601)
FAYETTEVILLE PUBLISHING CO (DH)
Also Called: Fayetteville Observer, The
302 Worth St (28301-5632)
P.O. Box 1181 (27239-1181)
PHONE..............................910 323-4848
Charles W Broadwell, *Pr*
Virginia L Yarborough, *
▲ EMP: 48 EST: 1923
SALES (est): 2.67MM
SALES (corp-wide): 2.51B Publicly Held
Web: www.fayobserver.com
SIC: 2711 2791 2759 2752 Commercial
printing and newspaper publishing
combined; Typesetting; Commercial
printing, nec; Commercial printing,
lithographic
HQ: Db North Carolina Holdings, Inc.
458 Whitfield St
Fayetteville NC 28306
910 323-4848

(G-4602)
FLAWLESS TOUCH DETAILING LLC
450 W Russell St Ste 102 (28301-5997)
PHONE..............................910 987-8093
Stanley Jacobs, *Prin*
EMP: 5 EST: 2019
SALES (est): 261.54K Privately Held
Web: www.flawlesstouchdetailingnc.com
SIC: 2396 Automotive and apparel trimmings

(G-4603)
FORTEM GENUS INC
427 Franklin St (28301-6143)
P.O. Box 9159 (28311-9081)
PHONE..............................910 574-5214
Don Feeney, *CEO*
Donald Feeney, *Pr*
EMP: 5 EST: 2016
SALES (est): 236.57K Privately Held
Web: www.fortemgenus.com
SIC: 3711 Military motor vehicle assembly

(G-4604)
FULCHER ELC FAYETTEVILLE INC
1744 Middle River Loop (28312-7366)
P.O. Box 2799 (28302-2799)
PHONE..............................910 483-7772
Frances Fulcher, *Pr*
EMP: 40 EST: 1993
SQ FT: 5,000
SALES (est): 4.65MM Privately Held
Web: www.fulcherelectric.com
SIC: 3669 Traffic signals, electric

(G-4605)
GOODYEAR TIRE & RUBBER COMPANY
Goodyear
6650 Ramsey St (28311-9318)
PHONE......................................910 488-9295
James R Konneker, *Manager*
EMP: 78
SALES (corp-wide): 18.88B **Publicly Held**
Web: www.goodyear.com
SIC: 3011 Agricultural inner tubes
PA: The Goodyear Tire & Rubber Company
200 Innovation Way
Akron OH 44316
330 796-2121

(G-4606)
GRAHAMS TRANSPORTATION LLC
Also Called: Trucking
6642 Keeler Dr (28303-2325)
PHONE......................................910 627-6880
Peter Graham, *CEO*
EMP: 4 EST: 2022
SALES (est): 159.56K **Privately Held**
SIC: 3711 7389 Truck tractors for highway
use, assembly of; Business services, nec

(G-4607)
H C PRODUCTION CO
218 Tolar St (28306-1534)
PHONE......................................910 483-5267
Judy Hart, *Owner*
EMP: 7 EST: 2001
SALES (est): 166.6K **Privately Held**
SIC: 3549 3629 Assembly machines,
including robotic; Electrical industrial
apparatus, nec

(G-4608)
HAWTHORNE SERVICES
1 Fort Bragg (28307-5000)
PHONE......................................910 436-9013
Dan Lawson, *Genl Mgr*
EMP: 4 EST: 2002
SALES (est): 312.64K **Privately Held**
SIC: 3721 Aircraft

(G-4609)
HECKLER BREWING COMPANY
5780 Ramsey St Ste 110 (28311-1414)
PHONE......................................910 748-0085
Daniel Miller, *Pr*
EMP: 6 EST: 2020
SALES (est): 268.63K **Privately Held**
Web: www.hecklerbeer.com
SIC: 2082 Malt beverages

(G-4610)
HEFTY CONCRETE INC
309 Ivan Dr (28306-3308)
PHONE......................................910 483-1598
Rafael Valdez, *Pr*
EMP: 4 EST: 2002
SALES (est): 126.7K **Privately Held**
SIC: 3271 Blocks, concrete or cinder:
standard

(G-4611)
HERCULES STEEL COMPANY INC (PA)
950 Country Club Dr (28301-2904)
P.O. Box 35208 (28303-0208)
PHONE......................................910 488-5110
Lewis Jourden, *Pr*
H C Bud Gore Junior, *VP*
Robert Petroski, *
EMP: 50 EST: 1954
SQ FT: 8,000
SALES (est): 2.89MM
SALES (corp-wide): 2.89MM **Privately
Held**

Web: www.herculessteelco.com
SIC: 3441 5051 Building components,
structural steel; Steel

(G-4612)
HEXION INC
Also Called: Borden
1411 Industrial Dr (28301-6325)
PHONE......................................910 483-1311
EMP: 28
SQ FT: 2,926
SALES (corp-wide): 1.26B **Privately Held**
Web: www.hexion.com
SIC: 2899 2869 2821 Chemical
preparations, nec; Industrial organic
chemicals, nec; Plastics materials and
resins
PA: Hexion Inc.
180 E Broad St
Columbus OH 43215
888 443-9466

(G-4613)
HIGHLAND PAVING CO LLC
1351 Wilmington Hwy (28306-3005)
P.O. Box 1843 (28302-1843)
PHONE......................................910 482-0080
EMP: 95 EST: 2003
SALES (est): 22.63MM **Privately Held**
Web: www.highlandpaving.com
SIC: 1611 2951 Highway and street paving
contractor; Asphalt and asphaltic paving
mixtures (not from refineries)

(G-4614)
ICAN CLOTHES COMPANY
1617 Owen Dr (28304-3425)
P.O. Box 25433 (28314-5007)
PHONE......................................910 670-1494
Shannon Battle, *CEO*
Kelsey Battle, *VP*
EMP: 12 EST: 2016
SQ FT: 5,000
SALES (est): 185.68K **Privately Held**
SIC: 2339 2329 2326 7218 Women's and
misses' athletic clothing and sportswear;
Athletic clothing, except uniforms: men's,
youths' and boys'; Men's and boy's work
clothing; Work clothing supply

(G-4615)
INDUSTRIAL POWER INC (PA)
703 Whitfield St (28306-1617)
PHONE......................................910 483-4230
William Merritt, *Pr*
Mike Hillenbrand, *VP*
▼ EMP: 7 EST: 1997
SQ FT: 1,250
SALES (est): 5.76MM **Privately Held**
Web: www.industrialpowerinc.com
SIC: 3052 Rubber hose

(G-4616)
INDUSTRIAL WELDING &
5936 Tabor Church Rd (28312-7377)
PHONE......................................910 309-8540
EMP: 4 EST: 2011
SALES (est): 46.38K **Privately Held**
SIC: 7692 Welding repair

(G-4617)
INKWELL
2823 Bragg Blvd (28303-4173)
PHONE......................................919 433-7539
James Vinson, *Prin*
EMP: 5 EST: 2018
SALES (est): 88.26K **Privately Held**
Web: www.theinkwellusa.com
SIC: 2752 Offset printing

(G-4618)
J & D MANAGEMENTS LLC
605 German St (28301-5496)
PHONE......................................910 321-7373
Maroof Jahangir, *Managing Member*
◆ EMP: 8 EST: 2002
SQ FT: 7,000
SALES (est): 2.08MM **Privately Held**
SIC: 3444 8741 8742 Sheet metalwork;
Management services; Business
management consultant

(G-4619)
J&R PRECISION HEATING AND AIR
1625 Cumberland Dr (28311-1283)
PHONE......................................910 480-8322
Richard Ford, *Pr*
EMP: 4 EST: 2017
SALES (est): 285.42K **Privately Held**
SIC: 3585 Heating and air conditioning
combination units

(G-4620)
JAMES KING
Also Called: Tactical Mobility Training
9998 Fayetteville Rd (28304-5969)
PHONE......................................910 308-8818
James King, *Prin*
James King, *Owner*
EMP: 6 EST: 2000
SQ FT: 10,000
SALES (est): 195.2K **Privately Held**
Web: www.tacticalmobilitytraining.com
SIC: 8748 9711 3751 Safety training service;
Military training schools; Frames,
motorcycle and bicycle

(G-4621)
JASIE BLANKS LLC
Also Called: Wholesale
3725 Ramsey St Ste 103c (28311-7669)
PHONE......................................910 485-0016
Sheri Fowler, *Pr*
▲ EMP: 16 EST: 2015
SALES (est): 1.92MM **Privately Held**
Web: www.jasieblanks.com
SIC: 7371 7389 3944 5111 Computer
software development and applications;
Business services, nec; Craft and hobby
kits and sets; Printing paper

(G-4622)
JB-ISECURITY LLC
505 Toxaway Ct (28314-0956)
PHONE......................................910 824-7601
Joseph Jenifer, *CEO*
EMP: 5 EST: 2021
SALES (est): 250K **Privately Held**
SIC: 3581 Automatic vending machines

(G-4623)
JFK CONFERENCES LLC
322 Ridgeway Ct (28311-0370)
PHONE......................................980 255-3336
EMP: 26 EST: 2020
SALES (est): 272.24K **Privately Held**
Web: www.jfkdallasconference.com
SIC: 7389 2731 Business services, nec;
Books, publishing only

(G-4624)
JO-NATTA TRANSPORTATION LLC
348 Foothill Ln (28311-6317)
PHONE......................................888 424-8789
EMP: 6 EST: 2011
SALES (est): 200K **Privately Held**
SIC: 3799 Transportation equipment, nec

(G-4625)
K & L RESOURCES
7809 Gallant Ridge Dr (28314-6219)
PHONE......................................910 494-3736
Keith Howard, *Owner*
EMP: 9 EST: 2003
SALES (est): 177.95K **Privately Held**
SIC: 7349 3676 Janitorial service, contract
basis; Resistor networks

(G-4626)
K FORMULA ENTERPRISES INC
829 Gillespie St Ste A (28306-1555)
PHONE......................................910 323-3315
Ronald L Formulak, *Pr*
EMP: 5 EST: 1979
SQ FT: 1,500
SALES (est): 90.35K **Privately Held**
Web: www.faynet.com
SIC: 2261 5699 Screen printing of cotton
broadwoven fabrics; T-shirts, custom printed

(G-4627)
KRAKEN-SKULLS
Also Called: Barber Shop AP Screen Prtg
822 Shannon Dr (28303-3950)
PHONE......................................910 500-9100
Chadwick Mckeown, *Owner*
Chadwick Mckeown, *Managing Member*
EMP: 12 EST: 2019
SALES (est): 96.81K **Privately Held**
Web: www.kraken-skulls.com
SIC: 7241 2395 7299 2759 Barber shops;
Embroidery and art needlework; Tattoo
parlor; Screen printing

(G-4628)
KUNTRYS SOUL-FOOD & BBQ LLC
418 Minnow Ct (28312-6549)
PHONE......................................910 797-0766
Monroe Junior, *Managing Member*
EMP: 6
SALES (est): 230.93K **Privately Held**
SIC: 2599 Food wagons, restaurant

(G-4629)
L C INDUSTRIES INC
4525 Campground Rd (28314-1435)
PHONE......................................919 596-8277
Tina Watson, *Mgr*
EMP: 200
SALES (corp-wide): 7.49MM **Privately
Held**
Web: www.lcindustries.com
SIC: 5943 2675 2515 Office forms and
supplies; Folders, filing, die-cut: made from
purchased materials; Mattresses and
foundations
PA: L C Industries Inc.
4500 Emperor Blvd
Durham NC 27703
919 596-8277

(G-4630)
LARRY S SAUSAGE COMPANY
1624 Middle River Loop (28312-7365)
P.O. Box 4 (28302-0004)
PHONE......................................910 483-5148
Larry Godwin, *CEO*
Sheila Abe, *
EMP: 35 EST: 1952
SQ FT: 32,000
SALES (est): 5.67MM **Privately Held**
Web: www.larryssausage.com
SIC: 2013 Sausages, from purchased meat

(G-4631)
LUXOTTICA OF AMERICA INC
Also Called: Lenscrafters
302 Cross Creek Mall (28303-7242)

▲ = Import ▼ = Export
◆ = Import/Export

PHONE.................910 867-0200
Steven Earwood, *Brnch Mgr*
EMP: 4
SALES (corp-wide): 7.66MM **Privately Held**
Web: www.luxottica.com
SIC: 5995 3851 Eyeglasses, prescription; Ophthalmic goods
HQ: Luxottica Of America Inc.
    4000 Luxottica Pl
    Mason OH 45040

(G-4632)
MANN+HMMEL PRLATOR FILTERS LLC (DH)
Also Called: Oe Filters
3200 Natal St Ste 64069 (28306-2845)
P.O. Box 64069 (28306)
PHONE.................910 425-4181
Kurk Wilks, *Pr*
Marion Grill, *
Matt Cloninger, *
Joel Ihrig, *
◆ **EMP:** 21 **EST:** 2006
SQ FT: 680,000
SALES (est): 312.75MM
SALES (corp-wide): 5.11B **Privately Held**
Web: www.purolatornow.com
SIC: 3714 Motor vehicle parts and accessories
HQ: Mann + Hummel Holding Gmbh
    Schwieberdinger Str. 126
    Ludwigsburg BW 71636
    7141980

(G-4633)
MANN+HMMEL PRLATOR FILTERS LLC
Facet Purolator
3200 Natal St (28306-2845)
P.O. Box 64069 (28306-0069)
PHONE.................910 425-4181
Rob Malone, *Mgr*
EMP: 121
SALES (corp-wide): 5.11B **Privately Held**
Web: www.purolatornow.com
SIC: 3714 Motor vehicle parts and accessories
HQ: Mann+Hummel Purolator Filters Llc
    3200 Natal St Ste 64069
    Fayetteville NC 28306

(G-4634)
MARK STODDARD
Also Called: Lava Cable
1935 Brawley Ave (28314-8491)
PHONE.................910 797-7214
Mark Stoddard, *Owner*
EMP: 5 **EST:** 2009
SALES (est): 419.03K **Privately Held**
SIC: 3355 7389 Aluminum wire and cable; Business services, nec

(G-4635)
MARTINS FMOUS PSTRY SHOPPE INC
2320 Southern Ave (28306-2260)
PHONE.................800 548-1200
EMP: 5
SALES (corp-wide): 149.7MM **Privately Held**
Web: www.potatorolls.com
SIC: 2051 Rolls, bread type: fresh or frozen
PA: Martin's Famous Pastry Shoppe, Inc.
    1000 Potato Roll Ln
    Chambersburg PA 17202
    800 548-1200

(G-4636)
MASS CONNECTION INC
Also Called: King Signs
2828 Enterprise Ave (28306-2005)
PHONE.................910 424-0940
Dean Holzinger, *Pr*
EMP: 9 **EST:** 2003
SALES (est): 763.14K **Privately Held**
Web: www.kingsignsnc.com
SIC: 3953 1611 2759 Stationery embossers, personal; Highway signs and guardrails; Promotional printing

(G-4637)
MASTER TOW INC
783 Slocomb Rd (28311-9367)
PHONE.................910 630-2000
John W Tart, *Pr*
Joi-anna Tart, *Sec*
▲ **EMP:** 30 **EST:** 1991
SQ FT: 14,000
SALES (est): 4.49MM **Privately Held**
Web: www.mastertow.com
SIC: 3715 3714 3537 Trailer bodies; Third axle attachments or six wheel units for motor vehicles; Industrial trucks and tractors

(G-4638)
MCCUNE TECHNOLOGY INC
Also Called: Fayetteville Steel
4801 Research Dr (28306-8149)
P.O. Box 53834 (28305-3834)
PHONE.................910 424-2978
David M Mccune Senior, *Pr*
David Mccune Junior, *VP*
EMP: 5 **EST:** 1976
SQ FT: 27,450
SALES (est): 1.25MM **Privately Held**
Web: www.mccune1.com
SIC: 3441 5051 3444 3443 Building components, structural steel; Steel; Sheet metalwork; Fabricated plate work (boiler shop)

(G-4639)
MCKINNON ENTERPRISE LLC
1449 Aultroy Dr (28306-3561)
PHONE.................919 408-6365
EMP: 4 **EST:** 2020
SALES (est): 828.51K **Privately Held**
SIC: 2721 Magazines: publishing only, not printed on site

(G-4640)
MERITOR INC
3200 Natal St (28306-2845)
PHONE.................910 425-4181
Richard Pitt, *Brnch Mgr*
EMP: 13
SALES (corp-wide): 34.1B **Publicly Held**
Web: www.meritor.com
SIC: 3714 Filters: oil, fuel, and air, motor vehicle
HQ: Meritor, Inc.
    2135 W Maple Rd
    Troy MI 48084

(G-4641)
MICHAELS CREAMERY INC
439 Westwood Shopping Ctr Ste 148 (28314-1532)
PHONE.................910 292-4172
Michael Sampson, *CEO*
EMP: 5 **EST:** 2011
SALES (est): 372.13K **Privately Held**
SIC: 2021 Creamery butter

(G-4642)
MOFFITT MACHINE COMPANY INC
232 Winslow St (28301-5594)

PHONE.................910 485-2159
John Marshall, *Pr*
Marie Marshall, *VP*
EMP: 5 **EST:** 1944
SQ FT: 5,700
SALES (est): 579.87K **Privately Held**
Web: www.moffittmachine.com
SIC: 3599 Machine shop, jobbing and repair

(G-4643)
MORE THAN JUST ART INC
6441 Yadkin Rd Ste E (28303-2166)
PHONE.................910 864-7797
Daniel Norman, *Prin*
Norma Norman, *Prin*
EMP: 4 **EST:** 1998
SALES (est): 227.85K **Privately Held**
Web: morethanjustart.squarespace.com
SIC: 5999 2759 Picture frames, ready made; Engraving, nec

(G-4644)
MURIEL HARRIS INVESTMENTS INC
Also Called: M H Investments
3900 Murchison Rd (28311)
PHONE.................800 932-3191
EMP: 10 **EST:** 2012
SALES (est): 760K **Privately Held**
SIC: 3334 1761 3312 3444 Primary aluminum; Architectural sheet metal work; Bars and bar shapes, steel, cold-finished: own hot-rolled; Pipe, sheet metal

(G-4645)
NEXT MAGAZINE
458 Whitfield St (28306-1614)
PHONE.................910 609-0638
Charles Broadwell, *Pr*
EMP: 6 **EST:** 2005
SALES (est): 77.75K **Privately Held**
Web: www.next-magazine.com
SIC: 2711 Newspapers, publishing and printing

(G-4646)
NORTH CRLINA LCENSE PLATE AGCY
815 Elm St (28303-4151)
PHONE.................910 485-1590
Marilyn Cullison, *Owner*
EMP: 5 **EST:** 2002
SALES (est): 305.81K **Privately Held**
SIC: 3469 Automobile license tags, stamped metal

(G-4647)
OHERNS WELDING INC
5379 Butler Nursery Rd (28306-7696)
PHONE.................910 484-2087
Michael Lewis O'hern, *Pr*
EMP: 7 **EST:** 2004
SALES (est): 1.26MM **Privately Held**
Web: www.ohernswelding.com
SIC: 7692 Welding repair

(G-4648)
OLDCASTLE INFRASTRUCTURE INC
3960 Cedar Creek Rd (28312-7965)
PHONE.................910 433-2931
EMP: 12
SALES (corp-wide): 34.95B **Privately Held**
Web: www.oldcastleinfrastructure.com
SIC: 3272 Concrete products, nec
HQ: Oldcastle Infrastructure, Inc.
    7000 Central Pkwy Ste 800
    Atlanta GA 30328
    770 270-5000

(G-4649)
OS PRESS LLC
Also Called: International Minute Press
1005 Arsenal Ave (28305-5329)
PHONE.................910 485-7955
EMP: 5 **EST:** 2009
SALES (est): 1.66MM **Privately Held**
Web: www.minutemangraphics.com
SIC: 2752 Commercial printing, lithographic

(G-4650)
PACKIQ LLC
Also Called: Packiq
800 Technology Dr Ste 110 (28306-9417)
PHONE.................910 964-4331
Mark Beck, *CEO*
EMP: 29
Web: www.packiq.com
SIC: 3441 Fabricated structural metal
PA: Packiq, Llc
    1 American Way
    Anderson SC 29621

(G-4651)
PAPA PARUSOS FOODS INC
3426 Clinton Rd (28312-6148)
P.O. Box 65029 (28306-1029)
PHONE.................910 484-8999
Charles G Manis, *Ch Bd*
Donna K Manis, *
EMP: 199 **EST:** 1989
SQ FT: 35,000
SALES (est): 15.32MM **Privately Held**
SIC: 2032 Italian foods, nec: packaged in cans, jars, etc.

(G-4652)
PARK SHIRT COMPANY
321 E Russell St (28301-5743)
PHONE.................931 879-5894
Rajan Shamdasani, *Prin*
▲ **EMP:** 5 **EST:** 2000
SQ FT: 20,000
SALES (est): 137.38K **Privately Held**
SIC: 2253 Knit outerwear mills

(G-4653)
PEACHES ENTERPRISES INC
Also Called: Painting By Bill
1014 Cain Rd (28303-4017)
P.O. Box 35636 (28303-0636)
PHONE.................910 868-5800
Kenneth Hardin, *Pr*
Catherine Wagner, *Sec*
EMP: 4 **EST:** 1977
SALES (est): 178.01K **Privately Held**
SIC: 1721 3993 Residential painting; Signs and advertising specialties

(G-4654)
PETER J HAMANN
Also Called: Arcright Welding Service
337 Mcmillan St (28301-5503)
PHONE.................910 484-7877
Peter J Hamann, *Owner*
EMP: 8 **EST:** 2000
SALES (est): 115.85K **Privately Held**
SIC: 3356 7692 3444 Welding rods; Welding repair; Sheet metalwork

(G-4655)
PPG ARCHITECTURAL FINISHES INC
Also Called: Glidden Professional Paint Ctr
894 Elm St Ste A (28303-4384)
PHONE.................910 484-5161
Tj Beasley, *Brnch Mgr*
EMP: 4
SALES (corp-wide): 17.65B **Publicly Held**
Web: www.ppgpmc.com

SIC: **2851** Paints and allied products
HQ: Ppg Architectural Finishes, Inc.
1 Ppg Pl
Pittsburgh PA 15272
412 434-3131

(G-4656)
PRECISION MACHINE TECH INC
Also Called: Pmt
230 S Eastern Blvd (28301-5950)
PHONE..............................910 678-8665
Wanda Hall, *Pr*
EMP: 10 **EST:** 1994
SQ FT: 7,000
SALES (est): 484.75K **Privately Held**
Web: www.spex1.com
SIC: **3599** Machine shop, jobbing and repair

(G-4657)
PRIMA ELEMENTS LLC
124 Anderson St (28301-5014)
PHONE..............................910 483-8406
Hilda Burgos, *Mgr*
EMP: 7 **EST:** 2012
SALES (est): 583.75K **Privately Held**
Web: www.primaelements.org
SIC: **3556** 7999 8299 Juice extractors, fruit
and vegetable: commercial type; Yoga
instruction; Meditation therapy

(G-4658)
PRINT USA INC
505 S Eastern Blvd (28301-6313)
P.O. Box 43352 (28309-3352)
PHONE..............................910 485-2254
Harriett Shooter, *Pr*
EMP: 5 **EST:** 2003
SQ FT: 20,000
SALES (est): 468.15K **Privately Held**
Web: www.printusa.com
SIC: **2752** Offset printing

(G-4659)
PRINT WORKS FAYETTEVILLE INC
Also Called: Allegra Print & Imaging
3724 Sycamore Dairy Rd Ste 100
(28303-3495)
PHONE..............................910 864-8100
Bruce S Sykes, *Pr*
Kathy Sykes, *VP*
EMP: 7 **EST:** 1986
SQ FT: 2,400
SALES (est): 654.66K **Privately Held**
Web: www.allegramarketingprint.com
SIC: **2752** Offset printing

(G-4660)
QUALITY CONCRETE CO INC
1587 Wilmington Hwy (28306-3103)
P.O. Box 53413 (28305-3413)
PHONE..............................910 483-7155
Marvin E Howell Junior, *Pr*
EMP: 16 **EST:** 1961
SQ FT: 1,200
SALES (est): 2.42MM **Privately Held**
Web: www.qualityconcretenc.net
SIC: **3273** Ready-mixed concrete

(G-4661)
R E MASON ENTERPRISES INC (PA)
Also Called: U-Teck
515 Person St (28301-5840)
P.O. Box 2484 (28302-2484)
PHONE..............................910 483-5016
EMP: 9 **EST:** 1984
SALES (est): 2.24MM
SALES (corp-wide): 2.24MM **Privately Held**
SIC: **3661** 5261 Telephone and telegraph
apparatus; Lawn and garden equipment

(G-4662)
RIVERSIDE MATTRESS CO INC
225 Dunn Rd (28312-5227)
PHONE..............................910 483-0461
William T Allen, *Pr*
Nancy Allen, *
EMP: 35 **EST:** 1932
SQ FT: 60,000
SALES (est): 1.28MM **Privately Held**
Web: www.riversidemattressinc.com
SIC: **2515** Mattresses, innerspring or box
spring

(G-4663)
RK ENTERPRISES LLC
Also Called: James Ricks
121 N Racepath St (28301-5258)
P.O. Box 428 (28391-0428)
PHONE..............................910 481-0777
Michael Sutton, *Prin*
Joshua Cain, *Prin*
James Ricks, *Prin*
▲ **EMP:** 4 **EST:** 2012
SALES (est): 134.24K **Privately Held**
SIC: **7699** 3827 3083 Fire control (military)
equipment repair; Optical instruments and
apparatus; Laminated plastics plate and
sheet

(G-4664)
ROBERT S CONCRETE SERVICE INC
508 Lamon St (28301-5158)
PHONE..............................910 391-3973
Robert Mace Junior, *Owner*
EMP: 4 **EST:** 1966
SALES (est): 89.94K **Privately Held**
SIC: **3273** Ready-mixed concrete

(G-4665)
S & W READY MIX CON CO LLC
1309 S Reilly Rd (28314-5513)
PHONE..............................910 864-0939
Earl Wells, *Brnch Mgr*
EMP: 19
SALES (corp-wide): 8.01MM **Privately
Held**
Web: www.snwreadymix.com
SIC: **3273** Ready-mixed concrete
HQ: S & W Ready Mix Concrete Company
Llc
217 Lisbon St
Clinton NC 28329
910 592-1733

(G-4666)
SCIENCE APPLICATIONS INTL CORP
4317 Ramsey St Ste 303 (28311-2161)
PHONE..............................910 822-2100
Karen Lounsberry, *Mgr*
EMP: 6
SALES (corp-wide): 7.44B **Publicly Held**
Web: www.saic.com
SIC: **7373** 7372 Systems integration services
; Prepackaged software
PA: Science Applications International
Corporation
12010 Sunset Hills Rd
Reston VA 20190
703 676-4300

(G-4667)
SELECT MOLD SERVICE INC
419 Glidden St (28301-5621)
PHONE..............................910 323-1287
Mary F Blaylock, *CEO*
Richard Fisher Senior, *Ch*
▲ **EMP:** 4 **EST:** 1973
SQ FT: 8,000
SALES (est): 451.58K **Privately Held**
SIC: **3544** Industrial molds

(G-4668)
SIERRA NEVADA CORPORATION
Also Called: SIERRA NEVADA
CORPORATION
3139 Doc Bennett Rd (28306-8669)
PHONE..............................910 307-0362
Paul Zeisman, *Brnch Mgr*
EMP: 12
SALES (corp-wide): 2.38B **Privately Held**
Web: www.sncorp.com
SIC: **3663** 3812 3699 Radio and t.v.
communications equipment; Search and
navigation equipment; Countermeasure
simulators, electric
PA: Sierra Nevada Company, Llc
444 Salomon Cir
Sparks NV 89434
775 331-0222

(G-4669)
SIGNIFY IT INC
Also Called: Fastsigns
700 Ramsey St (28301-4738)
PHONE..............................910 678-8111
Jim Pittman, *Sec*
Dellmarie Pittman, *CEO*
EMP: 10 **EST:** 1995
SALES (est): 338.99K **Privately Held**
Web: www.fastsigns.com
SIC: **3993** Signs and advertising specialties

(G-4670)
SILVER KNIGHT PCS LLC
1324 Bragg Blvd (28311)
PHONE..............................910 824-2054
Theodore Melkoumov, *CEO*
EMP: 5 **EST:** 2019
SALES (est): 937.13K **Privately Held**
Web: www.silverknightpcs.com
SIC: **5734** 3571 7378 7373 Computer and
software stores; Electronic computers;
Computer maintenance and repair;
Computer integrated systems design

(G-4671)
SINGER EQUIPMENT COMPANY INC
Also Called: Singer T&L
933 Robeson St (28305-5613)
PHONE..............................910 484-1128
Andrew O'quinn, *Pr*
EMP: 44
SQ FT: 20,000
SALES (corp-wide): 167.67MM **Privately
Held**
Web: www.singerequipment.com
SIC: **3469** 5046 Kitchen fixtures and
equipment: metal, except cast aluminum;
Restaurant equipment and supplies, nec
PA: Singer Equipment Company, Inc.
150 S Twin Valley Rd
Elverson PA 19520
610 387-6400

(G-4672)
SONARON LLC
7790 Cottonwood Ave (28314-6481)
PHONE..............................808 232-6168
Ronald Cogdell, *Pr*
Suniray Ballard, *CEO*
Anton Cogdell, *COO*
EMP: 8 **EST:** 2014
SALES (est): 447.3K **Privately Held**
SIC: **1541** 7622 8742 3442 Industrial
buildings and warehouses; Radio and
television receiver installation; Management
consulting services; Rolling doors for
industrial buildings or warehouses, metal

(G-4673)
SOUTHERN SOFTWARE INC
7231 Cayman Dr (28306-5609)
P.O. Box 877 (28327-0877)
PHONE..............................910 638-8700
Christy C Seawell, *Prin*
EMP: 4 **EST:** 2011
SALES (est): 610.9K **Privately Held**
Web: www.southernsoftware.com
SIC: **7372** Prepackaged software

(G-4674)
SPEEDIPRINT INC
164 Westwood Shopping Ctr (28314-1521)
PHONE..............................910 483-2553
John Lynch, *Pr*
Wanda Lynch, *VP*
EMP: 12 **EST:** 1972
SALES (est): 391.68K **Privately Held**
Web: www.fayettevilleprintshop.com
SIC: **2752** Offset printing

(G-4675)
STORK NEWS TM OF AMERICA (PA)
Also Called: Stork News
5075 Morganton Rd 12a (28314-1587)
PHONE..............................910 868-3065
Cheryl L Young, *Pr*
John M Young, *VP*
EMP: 11 **EST:** 1982
SQ FT: 1,600
SALES (est): 130.02K
SALES (corp-wide): 130.02K **Privately
Held**
SIC: **2741** 5641 Miscellaneous publishing;
Infants' wear

(G-4676)
**TACTICAL SUPPORT EQUIPMENT
INC**
Also Called: T S E
4039 Barefoot Rd (28306-8254)
PHONE..............................910 425-3360
Carl Beene, *Pr*
Wayne Dadetto, *CEO*
Richard Lovato, *VP*
EMP: 10 **EST:** 2002
SQ FT: 11,000
SALES (est): 2.03MM **Privately Held**
Web: www.tserecon.com
SIC: **3671** 5065 Electronic tube parts, except
glass blanks; Electronic parts and
equipment, nec

(G-4677)
**TALLADEGA MCHY & SUP CO NC
(PA)**
Also Called: Talledega Machinery & Supply
3510 Gillespie St (28306-9264)
PHONE..............................256 362-4124
Sam Yates, *Pr*
James W Heacock, *VP*
Gary M Heacock, *Sec*
EMP: 5 **EST:** 1986
SQ FT: 3,200
SALES (est): 2.45MM **Privately Held**
SIC: **5085** 5084 3492 Mill supplies; Hydraulic
systems equipment and supplies; Hose and
tube fittings and assemblies, hydraulic/
pneumatic

(G-4678)
**TAR HEEL GRND CMMNDERY
ORDER K**
1940 Caviness St (28314-8485)
PHONE..............................910 867-6764
Daniel L Dt Thompson, *Owner*
EMP: 4 **EST:** 2011
SALES (est): 105.64K **Privately Held**
SIC: **2865** Tar

▲ = Import ▼ = Export
◆ = Import/Export

(G-4679)
TEAM 21ST
6316 Yadkin Rd (28303-2647)
PHONE..............................910 826-3676
Bill Mathes, *CEO*
Vickie Mathes, *Pr*
EMP: 5 EST: 1995
SQ FT: 9,600
SALES (est): 196.72K **Privately Held**
Web: www.21sttactical.com
SIC: 3469 Machine parts, stamped or
pressed metal

(G-4680)
THOMPSON & LITTLE INC
933 Robeson St (28305-5613)
PHONE..............................910 484-1128
EMP: 20
Web: www.thompsonlittle.com
SIC: 3469 5046 Kitchen fixtures and
equipment: metal, except cast aluminum;
Restaurant equipment and supplies, nec

(G-4681)
TINT PLUS
2850 Owen Dr (28306-2937)
PHONE..............................910 229-5303
Charles Locklear, *Owner*
EMP: 6 EST: 2011
SALES (est): 441.62K **Privately Held**
SIC: 3211 1799 Window glass, clear and
colored; Glass tinting, architectural or
automotive

(G-4682)
**TIRE SLS SVC INC FYTTEVILLE NC
(PA)**
400 Person St (28301-5738)
P.O. Box 104 (28302-0104)
PHONE..............................910 485-1121
Jimmy Crumpler, *Pr*
Wendell Keith Phillips, *
EMP: 30 EST: 1972
SQ FT: 10,000
SALES (est): 1.27MM
SALES (corp-wide): 1.27MM **Privately
Held**
Web: www.tiresalesandserviceinc.com
SIC: 5531 7534 Automotive tires; Rebuilding
and retreading tires

(G-4683)
TROPHY HOUSE INC (PA)
3006 Bragg Blvd (28303-4098)
P.O. Box 35691 (28303-0691)
PHONE..............................910 323-1791
Jimmy Keefe, *Pr*
▲ EMP: 10 EST: 1967
SQ FT: 35,000
SALES (est): 2.38MM
SALES (corp-wide): 2.38MM **Privately
Held**
Web: www.thetrophyhouseinc.com
SIC: 5999 3953 5094 5961 Trophies and
plaques; Screens, textile printing; Trophies;
Catalog sales

(G-4684)
TURBOMED LLC
1830 Owen Dr Ste 9 (28304-1611)
PHONE..............................973 527-5299
Anthony Bryant, *CEO*
EMP: 10 EST: 2016
SALES (est): 222.68K **Privately Held**
SIC: 7699 3699 5049 2834 Life saving and
survival equipment, non-medical: repair;
Cleaning equipment, ultrasonic, except
medical and dental; Laboratory equipment,
except medical or dental; Barbituric acid
pharmaceutical preparations

(G-4685)
**UNION CORRUGATING COMPANY
(DH)**
Also Called: Orange Steel Roofing Products
701 S King St (28301)
PHONE..............................910 483-0479
Keith Medick, *CEO*
◆ EMP: 40 EST: 1934
SQ FT: 35,000
SALES (est): 45.89MM
SALES (corp-wide): 5.58B **Privately Held**
Web: www.unioncorrugating.com
SIC: 3444 5033 Metal roofing and roof
drainage equipment; Roofing and siding
materials
HQ: Cornerstone Building Brands, Inc.
5020 Weston Pkwy
Cary NC 27513
281 897-7788

(G-4686)
UNIQUE BODY BLENDS INC
1108 Strathdon Ave (28304-0349)
PHONE..............................910 302-5484
Regina Davis, *Pr*
EMP: 6 EST: 2012
SALES (est): 117.74K **Privately Held**
Web: www.uniquebodyblends.com
SIC: 2844 Perfumes, cosmetics and other
toilet preparations

(G-4687)
UNITED TL & STAMPING CO NC INC
2817 Enterprise Ave (28306-2004)
PHONE..............................910 323-8588
Bryant Van Vlaanderen, *Pr*
Marc Townsend, *
EMP: 72 EST: 1996
SQ FT: 90,000
SALES (est): 8.86MM **Privately Held**
Web: www.uts-nc.com
SIC: 3469 7692 3398 3479 Stamping metal
for the trade; Welding repair; Metal heat
treating; Painting, coating, and hot dipping

(G-4688)
UNIVERSAL MANIA INC
1031 Robeson St Ste A (28305-5727)
PHONE..............................866 903-0852
Kurt Krol, *Prin*
EMP: 4 EST: 2008
SALES (est): 321.89K **Privately Held**
SIC: 3663 Global positioning systems (GPS)
equipment

(G-4689)
UP & COMING MAGAZINE
Also Called: F B Publications
208 Rowan St (28301-4922)
P.O. Box 53461 (28305-3461)
PHONE..............................910 391-3859
William Bowman, *Pt*
EMP: 5 EST: 1996
SALES (est): 242.06K **Privately Held**
Web: www.upandcomingweekly.com
SIC: 2711 2721 Newspapers, publishing and
printing; Periodicals

(G-4690)
US LBM OPERATING CO 2009 LLC
Comtech
1001 S Reilly Rd Ste 639 (28314-5560)
PHONE..............................910 864-8787
EMP: 125
SALES (corp-wide): 141.88MM **Privately
Held**
SIC: 2439 Trusses, wooden roof
HQ: Us Lbm Operating Co. 2009, Llc
2150 E Lk Cook Rd Ste 101
Buffalo Grove IL 60089
706 266-8856

(G-4691)
US LOGOWORKS LLC
Also Called: US Logoworks
4200 Morganton Rd Ste 105 (28314-1564)
PHONE..............................910 307-0312
EMP: 10 EST: 2012
SALES (est): 489.95K **Privately Held**
Web: www.uslogoworks.com
SIC: 7389 3993 Embroidery advertising;
Signs and advertising specialties

(G-4692)
**USA TIRE SALES AND STORAGE
LLC**
3696 Gillespie St (28306-9266)
PHONE..............................910 424-5330
EMP: 4
SALES (est): 309.82K **Privately Held**
SIC: 7534 Tire retreading and repair shops

(G-4693)
USA WHOLESALE AND DISTRG INC
500 Blount St (28301-5610)
PHONE..............................888 484-6872
Ali Abdo, *Pr*
◆ EMP: 11 EST: 2012
SQ FT: 15,000
SALES (est): 2.39MM **Privately Held**
Web: www.usawdistributing.com
SIC: 5141 5947 3999 5812 Groceries,
general line; Novelties; Cigarette and cigar
products and accessories; Snack bar

(G-4694)
UTECK
159 Rock Hill Rd (28312-8276)
PHONE..............................910 483-5016
EMP: 13 EST: 2013
SALES (est): 2.41MM **Privately Held**
Web: www.uteck.com
SIC: 3661 Telephone and telegraph
apparatus

(G-4695)
VANGUARD CULINARY GROUP LTD
716 Whitfield St (28306-1618)
P.O. Box 65029 (28306-1029)
PHONE..............................910 484-8999
Charles Manis, *Pr*
Kenneth Reidy, *
EMP: 70 EST: 1998
SQ FT: 40,000
SALES (est): 22.67MM **Privately Held**
Web: www.vanguardculinary.com
SIC: 2099 Food preparations, nec

(G-4696)
WASTE CONTAINER REPAIR SVCS
2405 Wilmington Hwy (28306-3121)
PHONE..............................910 257-4474
Jesus Benitez, *Pr*
EMP: 7 EST: 2015
SQ FT: 2,000
SALES (est): 353.86K **Privately Held**
Web: www.dumpsterrepairshop.com
SIC: 7692 5084 3443 7699 Welding repair;
Waste compactors; Dumpsters, garbage;
Industrial equipment services

(G-4697)
WASTE CONTAINER SERVICES LLC
705 W Mountain Dr (28306-3230)
PHONE..............................910 257-4474
Jesus Benitez, *Mgr*
EMP: 6
SALES (corp-wide): 571.13K **Privately
Held**
Web: www.dumpsterrepairshop.com

SIC: 3411 3412 3444 Metal cans; Metal
barrels, drums, and pails; Sheet metalwork
PA: Waste Container Services, Llc
11 E Deer Ct
Midway GA 31320
912 980-5282

(G-4698)
WE PRINT T-SHIRTS INC
2598 Raeford Rd (28305-5118)
PHONE..............................910 822-8337
Kurin Keys, *Sec*
EMP: 4 EST: 2011
SALES (est): 186.81K **Privately Held**
Web: www.822tees.com
SIC: 2759 Screen printing

(G-4699)
WELBUILT HOMES INC
Also Called: Whi Sand & Gravel
2311 Clinton Rd (28312-6113)
P.O. Box 1382 (28302-1382)
PHONE..............................910 323-0098
Johnny Bullock, *VP*
Joyce Bullock, *Sec*
Greg Bullock, *Asst Tr*
EMP: 7 EST: 1973
SQ FT: 1,400
SALES (est): 842.06K **Privately Held**
Web: www.whisandandgravel.com
SIC: 1442 5032 Construction sand mining;
Sand, construction

(G-4700)
WIGAL WOOD WORKS
508 Anson Dr (28311-1530)
PHONE..............................580 890-9723
EMP: 4 EST: 2011
SALES (est): 66.22K **Privately Held**
SIC: 2431 Millwork

(G-4701)
WILLIAMS SKIN CO
1812 Sapona Rd (28312-6536)
PHONE..............................910 323-2628
Grace Hinton, *Pr*
Cybil Hinton, *Sec*
Michael Hinton, *Treas*
EMP: 4 EST: 1980
SQ FT: 4,000
SALES (est): 245.23K **Privately Held**
SIC: 2013 2099 Prepared pork products,
from purchased pork; Food preparations,
nec

(G-4702)
**YOUNGS WELDING & MACHINE
SVCS**
787 Mcarthur Rd (28311-1959)
PHONE..............................910 488-1190
Michael B Young, *Owner*
EMP: 4 EST: 2009
SALES (est): 193.41K **Privately Held**
SIC: 7692 3469 Welding repair; Machine
parts, stamped or pressed metal

Flat Rock
Henderson County

(G-4703)
AUTOMATED DESIGNS INC
105 Education Dr (28731-8572)
PHONE..............................828 696-9625
Larry T Orr, *Pr*
Denise Orr, *VP*
EMP: 10 EST: 1979
SQ FT: 5,400
SALES (est): 1.15MM **Privately Held**
Web: www.adinc.net

GEOGRAPHIC

SIC: **3531** 5085 8711　Construction machinery
; Industrial supplies; Industrial engineers

(G-4704)
BRUNNER & LAY INC
90 Reeds Way　(28731-0770)
PHONE..................................828 274-2770
Connie Byrd, *Brnch Mgr*
EMP: 5
SQ FT: 20,264
**SALES (corp-wide): 39.1MM Privately
Held**
Web: www.brunnerlay.com
SIC: 3532 Mining machinery
PA: Brunner & Lay, Inc.
　　1510 N Old Missouri Rd
　　Springdale AR 72764
　　479 756-0880

(G-4705)
CARROLL-BACCARI INC (PA)
Also Called: Mavidon
110 Commercial Blvd　(28731-7747)
PHONE..................................561 585-2227
Timothy Carroll, *Pr*
EMP: 7 **EST:** 1993
SQ FT: 17,000
SALES (est): 2.28MM Privately Held
Web: www.mavidon.com
SIC: 2891 Adhesives and sealants

(G-4706)
COASTAL AGROBUSINESS INC
814 Mcmurray Rd　(28731-5781)
P.O. Box 750　(28724-0750)
PHONE..................................828 697-2220
Chuck Francis, *Mgr*
EMP: 8
**SALES (corp-wide): 61.99MM Privately
Held**
Web: www.coastalagro.com
SIC: 5191 3523　Chemicals, agricultural;
　Sprayers and spraying machines,
　agricultural
PA: Coastal Agrobusiness, Inc.
　　112 Staton Rd
　　Greenville NC 27834
　　252 238-7391

(G-4707)
DURALINE IMAGING INC
580 Upward Rd Ste 1　(28731-9477)
P.O. Box 1763　(28731-1763)
PHONE..................................828 692-1301
William Wick, *Pr*
Thomas P Dunn, *Pr*
Derek Bryan, *VP*
EMP: 4 **EST:** 1970
SALES (est): 549.25K Privately Held
Web: www.duralineimaging.com
SIC: 3955 Ribbons, inked: typewriter, adding
　machine, register, etc.

(G-4708)
LEISURE CRAFT HOLDINGS LLC
940 Upward Rd　(28731-8799)
P.O. Box 1190　(28793-1190)
PHONE..................................828 693-8241
Richard Herman, *Pr*
EMP: 65 **EST:** 2021
SALES (est): 20.88MM Privately Held
Web: www.leisurecraftinc.com
SIC: 2514 2542 3411 2531　Metal household
　furniture; Partitions and fixtures, except
　wood; Metal cans; Public building and
　related furniture
PA: Palmer Hamilton Llc
　　143 S Jackson St Ste 1
　　Elkhorn WI 53121

(G-4709)
LEISURE CRAFT INC
Also Called: USA Display
940 Upward Rd　(28731-8799)
P.O. Box 1700　(28793-1700)
PHONE..................................828 693-8241
EMP: 132 **EST:** 1979
SALES (est): 17.66MM Privately Held
Web: www.leisurecraftinc.com
SIC: 2514 2542 3411 2531　Metal household
　furniture; Partitions and fixtures, except
　wood; Metal cans; Public building and
　related furniture

(G-4710)
MAP SUPPLY INC
132 Poplar Loop Dr　(28731-8583)
PHONE..................................336 731-3230
Al Cleveland, *Pr*
Tim Carpenter, *
Carol Cleveland, *
EMP: 4 **EST:** 1977
SQ FT: 9,000
SALES (est): 208.78K Privately Held
Web: www.mapservicescorp.com
SIC: 5199 2741　Maps and charts; Maps:
　publishing only, not printed on site

(G-4711)
**NATIONAL VOCTNL TECH HONOR
SOC**
Also Called: Nv-Ths
1011 Airport Rd　(28731-4725)
P.O. Box 1336　(28731-1336)
PHONE..................................828 698-8011
Allen Powell, *Ex Dir*
EMP: 6 **EST:** 1984
SQ FT: 1,932
SALES (est): 321.52K Privately Held
Web: www.nths.org
SIC: 3999 8748　Education aids, devices and
　supplies; Educational consultant

(G-4712)
R & D PLASTICS INC
526 Crest Rd　(28731-8796)
P.O. Box 219　(28704-0219)
PHONE..................................828 684-2692
R Dennis Weaver Senior, *Pr*
Shirley W Weaver, *
Gary M Branks, *
EMP: 35 **EST:** 1979
SALES (est): 6.52MM Privately Held
Web: www.rdplastics.net
SIC: 3089 Injection molding of plastics

(G-4713)
SALUDA MOUNTAIN PRODUCTS INC
561 S Allen Rd　(28731-9447)
PHONE..................................828 696-2296
Richard Canfield, *Pr*
EMP: 10 **EST:** 1992
SQ FT: 20,000
SALES (est): 176.99K Privately Held
Web: www.wncguide.com
SIC: 2541 2499　Store and office display
　cases and fixtures; Decorative wood and
　woodwork

(G-4714)
THREE GS ENTERPRISES INC
Also Called: Elite Auto Lights, Inc.
100 Tabor Road Ext　(28731-6744)
PHONE..................................828 696-2060
Dustin Gosnell, *Pr*
EMP: 17 **EST:** 2009
SALES (est): 2.88MM Privately Held
Web: www.bbbind.com
SIC: 3647 Automotive lighting fixtures, nec
HQ: Terrepower, Llc
　　29627 Renaissance Blvd

Daphne AL 36526
800 280-2737

Fleetwood
Ashe County

(G-4715)
CRANBERRY WOOD WORKS INC
Also Called: Carolina Leatherwork
13830 Us Highway 221 S　(28626-9827)
P.O. Box 31　(28618-0031)
PHONE..................................336 877-8771
Pete Yates, *Pr*
Edward J Greene, *VP*
EMP: 4 **EST:** 1990
SALES (est): 349.55K Privately Held
Web: www.cranberrywoodworks.com
SIC: 2499 2511　Decorative wood and
　woodwork; Wood lawn and garden furniture

Fletcher
Henderson County

(G-4716)
A 1 TIRE SERVICE INC
24 Cane Creek Rd　(28732-9707)
P.O. Box 1685　(28732-1685)
PHONE..................................828 684-1860
Earl Youngblood, *Pr*
Patrica Youngblood, *Sec*
Gene Youngblood, *Stockholder*
EMP: 4 **EST:** 1987
SQ FT: 3,450
SALES (est): 244.68K Privately Held
SIC: 7534 7539 5531　Tire repair shop; Brake
　services; Automotive tires

(G-4717)
ACCURATE TECHNOLOGY INC (PA)
270 Rutledge Rd　(28732-9398)
PHONE..................................828 654-7920
Ed Fiantaca, *Pr*
◆ **EMP:** 6 **EST:** 1989
SALES (est): 2.55MM Privately Held
Web: www.proscale.com
SIC: 3812 Distance measuring equipment

(G-4718)
ADVANCE CABINETRY INC
15 Design Ave Unit 201　(28732-7826)
PHONE..................................828 676-3550
EMP: 10 **EST:** 2019
SALES (est): 201.99K Privately Held
Web: www.advancecabinetry.com
SIC: 2434 Wood kitchen cabinets

(G-4719)
ALPHATECH INC
388 Cane Creek Rd　(28732-9471)
P.O. Box 519　(28732-0519)
PHONE..................................828 684-9709
Al Worley, *Pr*
EMP: 35 **EST:** 1999
SQ FT: 44,000
SALES (est): 4.42MM Privately Held
Web: www.atimfg.com
SIC: 3599 Machine shop, jobbing and repair

(G-4720)
ASHEVILLE QUICKPRINT
Also Called: Quick Print
8 Chanter Dr　(28732-8566)
PHONE..................................828 252-7667
Larry M Brady, *Owner*
EMP: 4 **EST:** 1981
SQ FT: 1,200
SALES (est): 176.59K Privately Held

SIC: **2752** 7334　Offset printing;
　Photocopying and duplicating services

(G-4721)
**ASHEVILLE THERMOFORM PLAS
INC**
200 Cane Creek Industrial Park Rd
(28732-9753)
PHONE..................................828 684-8440
William Trometer, *Pr*
EMP: 10 **EST:** 1998
SQ FT: 15,000
SALES (est): 2.01MM Privately Held
Web:
www.ashevillethermoformplastics.com
SIC: 3089 Injection molding of plastics

(G-4722)
AURALITES INC
9a National Ave　(28732-8655)
PHONE..................................828 687-7990
Martien Vloet, *Prin*
EMP: 8 **EST:** 2010
SALES (est): 439.55K Privately Held
Web: www.auralites.com
SIC: 3999 Candles

(G-4723)
BETECH INC
190 Continuum Dr　(28732-7459)
PHONE..................................828 687-9917
Ronald Brevard, *Pr*
Richard Brevard, *Sec*
Amy Rhinehart, *Prin*
EMP: 6 **EST:** 1991
SQ FT: 10,000
SALES (est): 2.16MM Privately Held
Web: www.betechinc.net
SIC: 3599 Custom machinery

(G-4724)
BLUE RIDGE BRACKET INC
66 Fletcher Commercial Dr　(28732-8628)
PHONE..................................828 808-3273
EMP: 4 **EST:** 2015
SALES (est): 224.53K Privately Held
Web: www.blueridgemetals.com
SIC: 3999 Manufacturing industries, nec

(G-4725)
**BLUE RIDGE METALS
CORPORATION**
180 Mills Gap Rd　(28732-8548)
P.O. Box 189　(28732-0189)
PHONE..................................828 687-2525
Kazumasa Yoshida, *Ch Bd*
Isao Yoshida, *
Shigero Goda, *
▲ **EMP:** 160 **EST:** 1988
SQ FT: 3,484,800
SALES (est): 15.87MM Privately Held
Web: www.blueridgemetals.com
SIC: 3399 3315　Aluminum atomized powder;
　Fencing made in wiredrawing plants
PA: Central Yoshida Corporation
　　1-4-1, Mori
　　Ama AIC 490-1

(G-4726)
BORG-WARNER AUTOMOTIVE INC
Cane Creek Ind Pk　(28732)
PHONE..................................828 684-3501
Jim Jones, *Prin*
EMP: 5 **EST:** 2011
SALES (est): 379.43K Privately Held
Web: www.borgwarner.com
SIC: 3714 Motor vehicle parts and
　accessories

(G-4727)
CANE CREEK CYCLING CMPNNTS INC
355 Cane Creek Rd (28732-7404)
P.O. Box 798 (28732-0798)
PHONE..................................828 684-3551
Brent Graves, *Pr*
▲ **EMP:** 35 **EST:** 1974
SQ FT: 28,035
SALES (est): 3.85MM **Privately Held**
Web: www.canecreek.com
SIC: 5941 3751 Bicycle and bicycle parts;
Motorcycles, bicycles and parts

(G-4728)
CERTIFICATION SERVICES INTERNATIONAL LLC
510 La White Dr Bldg 12 (28732-9118)
P.O. Box 813 (28758-0813)
PHONE..................................828 458-1573
EMP: 8
SIC: 3714 Motor vehicle parts and
accessories

(G-4729)
CLAYTON HOMES INC
Also Called: Oakwood Homes
5250 Hendersonville Rd (28732-6672)
PHONE..................................828 684-1550
Bryant Moss, *Brnch Mgr*
EMP: 6
SALES (corp-wide): 424.23B **Publicly Held**
Web: www.claytonhomes.com
SIC: 2451 Mobile homes
HQ: Clayton Homes, Inc.
5000 Clayton Rd.
Maryville TN 37802
865 380-3000

(G-4730)
COGENT DYNAMICS INC
33 Meadow Brook Dr (28732-9101)
PHONE..................................828 628-9025
Carl Tannenbum, *Pr*
EMP: 4 **EST:** 2005
SALES (est): 469.78K **Privately Held**
Web: www.motocd.com
SIC: 3555 0119 Printing trades machinery;
Barley farm

(G-4731)
CONTINENTAL AUTO SYSTEMS INC
1 Quality Way (28732-9303)
PHONE..................................828 654-2000
John D'haenens, *Prin*
EMP: 400
SQ FT: 254,000
SALES (corp-wide): 45.02B **Privately Held**
Web: www.continental-automotive.com
SIC: 3465 3714 Body parts, automobile:
stamped metal; Motor vehicle parts and
accessories
HQ: Continental Automotive Systems, Inc.
1 Continental Dr
Auburn Hills MI 48326
248 393-5300

(G-4732)
DAYSTAR MACHINING TECH INC
356 Cane Creek Rd (28732-7403)
P.O. Box 1377 (28732-1377)
PHONE..................................828 684-1316
James Lytle, *Pr*
Margaret Lytle, *
Anna Viands, *
James Lytle, *VP Opers*
◆ **EMP:** 40 **EST:** 1999
SQ FT: 25,000
SALES (est): 5.71MM **Privately Held**

Web: www.daystarmachining.com
SIC: 3599 Machine shop, jobbing and repair

(G-4733)
EMTELLE USA INC
101 Mills Gap Rd Unit A (28732)
PHONE..................................828 707-9970
Tony Rodgers, *CEO*
Debra Davenport, *
EMP: 35 **EST:** 2022
SALES (est): 22.97MM
SALES (corp-wide): 355.83K **Privately Held**
Web: www.emtelle.com
SIC: 3357 Fiber optic cable (insulated)
HQ: Emtelle Uk Limited
Haughhead
Hawick TD9 8
145 036-4000

(G-4734)
EQUILIBAR LLC
320 Rutledge Rd (28732-9328)
PHONE..................................828 650-6590
David Reed, *Pr*
Jeff Jennings, *
David Reed, *VP Opers*
EMP: 35 **EST:** 2007
SQ FT: 10,000
SALES (est): 8.69MM
SALES (corp-wide): 11.77MM **Privately Held**
Web: www.equilibar.com
SIC: 3491 Industrial valves
PA: Richards Industrials, Inc.
3170 Wasson Rd
Cincinnati OH 45209
513 533-5600

(G-4735)
EXCELSIOR SEWING LLC
125 Brickton Dr (28732-0358)
PHONE..................................828 398-8056
Judith D Gross, *Managing Member*
EMP: 10 **EST:** 2012
SALES (est): 380.83K **Privately Held**
Web: excelsiorsewing.business.site
SIC: 2326 Aprons, work, except rubberized
and plastic: men's

(G-4736)
FIELDCO MACHINING INC
5164 Old Haywood Rd (28732)
P.O. Box 1305 (28732-1305)
PHONE..................................828 891-4100
Steve Fields, *Pr*
Michael Fields, *VP*
Tammy Swayngim, *Sec*
EMP: 6 **EST:** 1989
SQ FT: 7,500
SALES (est): 1.11MM **Privately Held**
SIC: 3599 Machine shop, jobbing and repair

(G-4737)
FLETCHER LIMESTONE COMPANY INC
639 Fanning Bridge Rd (28732-8360)
P.O. Box 32626 (37930-2626)
PHONE..................................828 684-6701
Bob Stevens, *Pr*
John Brooks, *VP*
Barbara Stevens, *Sec*
Mark Stevens, *Asst VP*
EMP: 4 **EST:** 1948
SALES (est): 224.93K **Privately Held**
SIC: 3272 5032 Cast stone, concrete; Stone,
crushed or broken

(G-4738)
GASP INC
80 Emma Sharp Rd Ste 5 (28732)
PHONE..................................828 891-1628
Mark D Garrison, *Prin*
EMP: 5 **EST:** 2004
SALES (est): 881.88K **Privately Held**
Web: www.gaspinc.com
SIC: 3613 Power circuit breakers

(G-4739)
GREENS MACHINE & TOOL INC
8 Park Ridge Dr (28732-9339)
PHONE..................................828 654-0042
Donald C Green, *Pr*
Mary Green, *CEO*
Adam Green, *VP*
EMP: 7 **EST:** 1986
SQ FT: 1,344
SALES (est): 1.77MM **Privately Held**
Web: www.gmtcnc.com
SIC: 3599 Machine shop, jobbing and repair

(G-4740)
HASCO AMERICA INC
270 Rutledge Rd Unit B (28732-9399)
PHONE..................................828 650-2631
Marna Duckett, *Pr*
Sharon Chrisman, *Sec*
▲ **EMP:** 9 **EST:** 1999
SQ FT: 20,000
SALES (est): 2.55MM
SALES (corp-wide): 681.43MM **Privately Held**
Web: www.hasco.com
SIC: 3544 Industrial molds
HQ: Hasco Hasenclever Gmbh + Co Kg
Romerweg 4
Ludenscheid NW 58513
23519570

(G-4741)
HENSEL PHELPS ✪
171 Wright Brothers Way (28732-7808)
PHONE..................................828 585-4689
Richard G Tucker, *VP*
EMP: 7 **EST:** 2023
SALES (est): 2.51MM **Privately Held**
SIC: 1389 Construction, repair, and
dismantling services

(G-4742)
HORIBA INSTRUMENTS INC
270 Rutledge Rd Unit D (28732-9399)
PHONE..................................828 676-2801
Jai Hakhu, *Ch Bd*
EMP: 15
Web: www.horiba.com
SIC: 3826 Analytical instruments
HQ: Horiba Instruments Incorporated
9755 Research Dr
Irvine CA 92618
949 250-4811

(G-4743)
INTERNATIONAL TELA-COM INC
103 Underwood Rd Unit C (28732-8661)
PHONE..................................828 651-9801
Edmund C Horgan Iii, *Pr*
Dennis Deranek, *VP*
EMP: 8 **EST:** 1969
SQ FT: 2,000
SALES (est): 919.04K **Privately Held**
SIC: 1731 1542 3643 Electronic controls
installation; Commercial and office
buildings, renovation and repair; Current-
carrying wiring services

(G-4744)
KATTERMANN VENTURES INC
282 Cane Creek Rd (28732-7402)
P.O. Box 550 (28732-0550)
PHONE..................................828 651-8737
David W Kattermann Junior, *Pr*
Robert Kattermann, *
▲ **EMP:** 34 **EST:** 1974
SQ FT: 78,000
SALES (est): 1.71MM **Privately Held**
Web: www.bromleyplastics.com
SIC: 2821 Plastics materials and resins

(G-4745)
KYOCERA PRECISION TOOLS INC (DH)
1 Quality Way (28732-9303)
Rural Route 102 Indtrl Prk (28792)
PHONE..................................800 823-7284
Koichi Nosaka, *Pr*
Jim Good, *
▲ **EMP:** 7 **EST:** 2013
SALES (est): 9.94MM **Privately Held**
Web: www.kyoceraprecisiontools.com
SIC: 3545 3541 3845 3843 Machine tool
accessories; Machine tools, metal cutting
type; Endoscopic equipment,
electromedical, nec; Cutting instruments,
dental
HQ: Kyocera International, Inc.
8611 Balboa Ave
San Diego CA 92123
858 576-2600

(G-4746)
LEGACY PADDLESPORTS LLC
210 Old Airport Rd (28732-9273)
PHONE..................................828 684-1933
◆ **EMP:** 110
Web: www.legacypaddlesports.com
SIC: 3732 Kayaks, building and repairing

(G-4747)
LEVI INNOVATIONS INC
122 Continuum Dr (28732-7459)
PHONE..................................828 684-6640
Michael K Levi, *Pr*
EMP: 5 **EST:** 2008
SALES (est): 949.84K **Privately Held**
Web: www.levitool.com
SIC: 3599 Machine shop, jobbing and repair

(G-4748)
LINAMAR LIGHT METAL S-MR LLC
490 Ferncliff Park Dr (28732-8633)
PHONE..................................828 348-4010
Eric Showalter, *Managing Member*
EMP: 505 **EST:** 2016
SALES (est): 44.67MM
SALES (corp-wide): 7.09B **Privately Held**
SIC: 3363 Aluminum die-castings
PA: Linamar Corporation
287 Speedvale Ave W
Guelph ON N1H 1
519 836-7550

(G-4749)
LOW IMPACT TECH USA INC
269 Cane Creek Rd (28732-7401)
PHONE..................................828 428-6310
Nick Probert, *CEO*
Eddiebee Farrar, *Corporate Secretary*
Dale E Polk Junior, *Dir*
EMP: 7 **EST:** 2020
SALES (est): 2.37MM
SALES (corp-wide): 2.89MM **Privately Held**
Web: www.lowimpacts.com
SIC: 3433 Solar heaters and collectors
PA: D & D Manufacturing, Llc
2655 Cherrywood Ln

Titusville FL 32780
321 652-4509

(G-4750)
MAHLE MOTORSPORTS INC
270 Rutledge Rd Unit C (28732-9399)
PHONE.............................888 255-1942
Hans D Jehle, *Pr*
Lee Morse, *VP*
▲ **EMP:** 16 **EST:** 1999
SQ FT: 10,000
SALES (est): 4.05MM
SALES (corp-wide): 3.75MM **Privately Held**
Web: us.mahle.com
SIC: 3714 Motor vehicle parts and accessories
HQ: Mahle Engine Components Usa, Inc.
　　1 Mahle Dr
　　Morristown TN 37815
　　248 305-8200

(G-4751)
MAINETTI USA INC
101 Mills Gap Rd (28732)
PHONE.............................828 844-0105
EMP: 8
SALES (corp-wide): 8.01MM **Privately Held**
Web: www.mainetti.com
SIC: 3089 Clothes hangers, plastics
HQ: Mainetti Usa, Inc.
　　200 Connell Dr Ste 3100
　　Berkeley Heights NJ 07922
　　201 215-2900

(G-4752)
MDT BROMLEY LLC
Also Called: Bromley Plastics
282 Cane Creek Rd (28732-7402)
PHONE.............................828 651-8737
Terry Ingham, *Pr*
EMP: 34 **EST:** 2022
SALES (est): 9.72MM
SALES (corp-wide): 9.72MM **Privately Held**
Web:
www.materialdifferencetechnologies.com
SIC: 2821 5162 Plastics materials and resins ; Plastics materials and basic shapes
PA: Material Difference Technologies Llc
　　1401 Manatee Ave W #1015
　　Bradenton FL 34205
　　888 818-1283

(G-4753)
MEDI MALL INC
Also Called: Medmassager
189 Continuum Dr Ste A (28732-7459)
PHONE.............................877 501-6334
Michael Terblanche, *Pr*
◆ **EMP:** 6 **EST:** 2009
SALES (est): 1.06MM **Privately Held**
Web: www.medmassager.com
SIC: 5047 5999 3845 3841 Medical equipment and supplies; Medical apparatus and supplies; Electromedical equipment; Physiotherapy equipment, electrical

(G-4754)
MERITOR INC
1000 Rockwell Dr (28732-9494)
P.O. Box Ckwell Dr (28732)
PHONE.............................828 687-2000
Mark Kanapeel, *Brnch Mgr*
EMP: 19
SALES (corp-wide): 34.1B **Publicly Held**
Web: www.meritor.com
SIC: 3714 Axles, motor vehicle
HQ: Meritor, Inc.
　　2135 W Maple Rd

Troy MI 48084

(G-4755)
MERITOR INC
Also Called: Arvinmeritor Hvy Vhcl Systems
1000 Rockwell Dr (28732-9494)
P.O. Box Ckwell Dr (28732)
PHONE.............................828 687-2000
William Keith, *Mgr*
EMP: 157
SALES (corp-wide): 34.1B **Publicly Held**
Web: www.meritor.com
SIC: 3714 Axles, motor vehicle
HQ: Meritor, Inc.
　　2135 W Maple Rd
　　Troy MI 48084

(G-4756)
MICROTECH DEFENSE INDS INC
15a National Ave (28732-8655)
PHONE.............................828 684-4355
Anthony Marfione, *Pr*
Susan Marfione, *Prin*
EMP: 4 **EST:** 2013
SALES (est): 1.1MM **Privately Held**
Web: www.microtechdefense.com
SIC: 3484 Pistols or pistol parts, 30 mm. and below

(G-4757)
MOTO GROUP LLC
Also Called: Trojan Defense
40 Cane Creek Industrial Park Rd (28732-7754)
PHONE.............................828 350-7653
Joseph Taylor, *Prin*
EMP: 26 **EST:** 2010
SALES (est): 3.85MM **Privately Held**
SIC: 3751 Motorcycles and related parts

(G-4758)
MTI MEDICAL CABLES LLC
2133 Old Fanning Bridge Rd (28732)
PHONE.............................828 890-2888
EMP: 4 **EST:** 2015
SALES (est): 2.24MM
SALES (corp-wide): 40.67MM **Privately Held**
Web: www.lifesync.com
SIC: 3841 Medical instruments and equipment, blood and bone work
HQ: American Biosurgical, Llc
　　1850 Beaver Ridge Cir B
　　Norcross GA 30071

(G-4759)
NORTH AMERICAN TRADE LLC
Also Called: Nat
388 Cane Creek Rd Ste 22 (28732-9471)
PHONE.............................828 712-3004
Neil Myers, *CEO*
EMP: 5 **EST:** 2013
SQ FT: 3,000
SALES (est): 468.59K **Privately Held**
Web: www.natrade.net
SIC: 7389 3482 5091 3483 Business Activities at Non-Commercial Site; Small arms ammunition; Firearms, sporting; Ammunition components

(G-4760)
PEPSI COLA BOTTLING CO
200 Fanning Field (28732)
P.O. Box 1207 (28732-1207)
PHONE.............................828 650-7800
Lee Teeter, *VP*
EMP: 96 **EST:** 1937
SALES (est): 2.41MM
SALES (corp-wide): 28.58MM **Privately Held**
Web: www.pepsico.com

SIC: 2086 Carbonated soft drinks, bottled and canned
PA: Pepsi-Cola Bottling Company Of Hickory, N.C., Inc.
　　2401 14th Avenue Cir Nw
　　Hickory NC 28601
　　828 322-8090

(G-4761)
PROMATIC AUTOMATION INC
9a National Ave (28732-8655)
PHONE.............................828 684-1700
Jerry Mckeithan, *Pr*
Peter Fontaine, *VP*
Marilyn Mercer, *Sec*
EMP: 17 **EST:** 2000
SQ FT: 36,000
SALES (est): 4.8MM **Privately Held**
Web: www.promaticautomation.com
SIC: 3599 Machine shop, jobbing and repair

(G-4762)
PUTSCH & COMPANY INC (HQ)
Also Called: Putsch
352 Cane Creek Rd (28732-7403)
P.O. Box 5128 (28813-5128)
PHONE.............................828 684-0671
Carl Christian, *Pr*
Elisabeth Paumen Radinger, *VP*
Carol Eubank, *Sec*
Karl H Straus, *Sec*
▲ **EMP:** 23 **EST:** 1973
SQ FT: 16,000
SALES (est): 10.2MM
SALES (corp-wide): 9.23MM **Privately Held**
Web: www.putschusa.com
SIC: 3556 3541 3545 Sugar plant machinery ; Machine tools, metal cutting type; Machine tool accessories
PA: Putsch Gmbh & Co. Kg
　　Frankfurter Str. 5-21
　　Hagen NW 58095
　　23313990

(G-4763)
RESINART EAST INC
201 Old Airport Rd (28732-9273)
PHONE.............................828 687-0215
Thomas V Trombatore, *Pr*
EMP: 12 **EST:** 1992
SQ FT: 25,000
SALES (est): 3.65MM **Privately Held**
Web: www.resinart.com
SIC: 5031 3089 Molding, all materials; Injection molding of plastics

(G-4764)
RINEHART RACING INC
40 Cane Creek Industrial Park Rd (28732-7754)
PHONE.............................828 350-7653
Gerald Rinehart, *Pr*
Judd Hollifield, *CEO*
EMP: 24 **EST:** 1995
SALES (est): 2.66MM **Privately Held**
Web: www.rinehartracing.com
SIC: 3751 Bicycles and related parts

(G-4765)
SCITECK DIAGNOSTICS INC
317 Rutledge Rd (28732-9328)
P.O. Box 562 (28704-0562)
PHONE.............................828 650-0409
Kerstin Lanier, *CEO*
EMP: 4 **EST:** 1989
SQ FT: 15,000
SALES (est): 197.26K **Privately Held**
Web: www.sciteck.org

SIC: 2819 2835 3826 Industrial inorganic chemicals, nec; In vitro diagnostics; Automatic chemical analyzers

(G-4766)
SDV OFFICE SYSTEMS LLC
Also Called: Sdv Medical Services
34 Redmond Dr Apt C (28732-9315)
P.O. Box 2427 (28776-2427)
PHONE.............................844 968-9500
Tyler Whisnant, *Mgr*
Daniel Whisnant, *Pr*
Theresa Gilbert, *Treas*
Tyler Whisnant, *VP*
EMP: 18 **EST:** 2010
SALES (est): 78.56MM **Privately Held**
Web: www.sdvosystems.com
SIC: 2522 5112 2521 5047 Office cabinets and filing drawers, except wood; Office filing supplies; Wood office furniture; Medical equipment and supplies

(G-4767)
SHADOWTRACK 247 LLC
Also Called: Shadowtrack 24/7
45 Park Ridge Dr (28732-9339)
PHONE.............................828 398-0980
Jeffrey Stingel, *Pr*
EMP: 10 **EST:** 2018
SQ FT: 10,000
SALES (est): 3.95MM **Privately Held**
Web: www.shadowtrack247.com
SIC: 3663 Global positioning systems (GPS) equipment

(G-4768)
SILVER MOON NUTRACEUTICALS LLC
111 Fletcher Commercial Dr Ste B (28732-8635)
PHONE.............................828 698-5795
Dennis Putnam, *Managing Member*
EMP: 6 **EST:** 2016
SALES (est): 475.08K **Privately Held**
Web: www.silvermoonnutra.com
SIC: 2899 Oils and essential oils

(G-4769)
SKYLAND PRSTHTICS ORTHTICS INC
3845 Hendersonville Rd (28732-8241)
P.O. Box 428 (28776-0428)
PHONE.............................828 684-1644
Pippa Dolen, *Pr*
Shaun Dolen, *VP*
EMP: 20 **EST:** 1979
SQ FT: 1,500
SALES (est): 2.7MM **Privately Held**
Web: www.skylandprosthetics.net
SIC: 3842 Limbs, artificial

(G-4770)
SMARTRAC TECH FLETCHER INC
267 Cane Creek Rd (28732)
PHONE.............................828 651-6051
Christian Uhl, *CEO*
Mike Keen, *
◆ **EMP:** 217 **EST:** 2010
SQ FT: 50,000
SALES (est): 14.81MM
SALES (corp-wide): 8.76B **Publicly Held**
SIC: 3612 Transformers, except electric
PA: Avery Dennison Corporation
　　8080 Norton Pkwy
　　Mentor OH 44060
　　440 534-6000

(G-4771)
SOUTHERN CONCRETE MTLS INC
250 Old Hendersonville Rd (28732-9679)

PHONE..............828 681-5178
Billy Jackson, *Genl Mgr*
EMP: 9
SQ FT: 1,424
SALES (corp-wide): 238.17MM **Privately Held**
Web: www.scmusa.com
SIC: 3273 5039 Ready-mixed concrete; Septic tanks
HQ: Southern Concrete Materials, Inc.
35 Meadow Rd
Asheville NC 28803
828 253-6421

(G-4772)
T D M CORPORATION
333 White Pine Dr (28732-9717)
EMP: 23 **EST:** 1969
SALES (est): 898.56K **Privately Held**
Web:
tdm-corporation-in-fletcher-nc.cityfos.com
SIC: 3599 3544 Machine shop, jobbing and repair; Industrial molds

(G-4773)
TRANSYLVNIA VCATIONAL SVCS INC
1 Quality Way (28732-9303)
PHONE..............828 884-1548
John Safi, *Mgr*
EMP: 63
SALES (corp-wide): 27.47MM **Privately Held**
Web: www.tvsinc.org
SIC: 8093 8331 2652 Rehabilitation center, outpatient treatment; Job training and related services; Setup paperboard boxes
PA: Transylvania Vocational Services, Inc.
11 Mountain Industrial Dr
Brevard NC 28712
828 884-3195

(G-4774)
TWO TREES DISTILLING CO LLC
17 Continuum Dr (28732-7445)
PHONE..............803 767-1322
EMP: 8 **EST:** 2018
SALES (est): 571.67K **Privately Held**
Web: www.twotreesdistilling.com
SIC: 2085 Distilled and blended liquors

(G-4775)
UPM RAFLATAC INC
Also Called: Upm Raflatac At Fletcher Bus
535 Cane Creek Rd (28732-9703)
PHONE..............828 335-3289
EMP: 15
Web: www.upmraflatac.com
SIC: 2672 Paper; coated and laminated, nec
HQ: Upm Raflatac, Inc.
400 Broadpointe Dr
Mills River NC 28759
828 651-4800

(G-4776)
UPM RAFLATAC INC
Also Called: Smartrac Technology
267 Cane Creek Rd (28732-7401)
PHONE..............828 651-4800
Noel Mitchell, *Mgr*
EMP: 20
Web: www.upmraflatac.com
SIC: 2672 Paper; coated and laminated, nec
HQ: Upm Raflatac, Inc.
400 Broadpointe Dr
Mills River NC 28759
828 651-4800

(G-4777)
WC&R INTERESTS LLC
Also Called: Diamond Brand Canvas Products
145 Cane Creek Industrial Park Rd Ste 100 (28732-8306)
PHONE..............828 684-9848
▲ **EMP:** 150 **EST:** 1881
SALES (est): 3.62MM **Privately Held**
SIC: 2394 Canvas and related products

(G-4778)
WELDING SOLUTIONS LLC
Also Called: Metal Creations
3632 Butler Bridge Rd (28732)
PHONE..............828 665-4363
Gina Newnam, *Managing Member*
EMP: 21 **EST:** 1995
SQ FT: 15,000
SALES (est): 2.4MM **Privately Held**
Web: www.weldingunl.com
SIC: 3441 7692 Fabricated structural metal; Welding repair

(G-4779)
WILSONART LLC
145 Cane Creek Industrial Park Rd (28732-8306)
PHONE..............866 267-7360
EMP: 5
SALES (corp-wide): 982.77MM **Privately Held**
Web: www.wilsonart.com
SIC: 2541 Wood partitions and fixtures
HQ: Wilsonart Llc
2501 Wilsonart Dr
Temple TX 76504
254 207-7000

(G-4780)
WILSONART LLC
80 La White Dr (28732-9117)
PHONE..............828 684-2351
Tammy Alberg, *Mgr*
◆ **EMP:** 52
SALES (corp-wide): 982.77MM **Privately Held**
Web: www.wilsonart.com
SIC: 2821 Plastics materials and resins
HQ: Wilsonart Llc
2501 Wilsonart Dr
Temple TX 76504
254 207-7000

(G-4781)
WILSONART LLC
Wilson Art
300 Cane Creek Industrial Park Rd (28732-9754)
PHONE..............828 684-2351
Tim Gwennat, *Manager*
EMP: 27
SALES (corp-wide): 982.77MM **Privately Held**
Web: www.wilsonart.com
SIC: 3089 3083 Laminating of plastics; Laminated plastics plate and sheet
HQ: Wilsonart Llc
2501 Wilsonart Dr
Temple TX 76504
254 207-7000

(G-4782)
YANCEY STONE INC
5 Williams Rd (28732-9430)
PHONE..............828 684-5522
William Michael Mccrary, *Pr*
EMP: 7 **EST:** 1993
SALES (est): 588.12K **Privately Held**
SIC: 1429 Igneus rock, crushed and broken-quarrying

Forest City
Rutherford County

(G-4783)
AMERICAN WATER GRAPHICS INC
317 Vance St (28043-7747)
P.O. Box 86 (28043-0086)
PHONE..............828 247-0700
John Ruppe Junior, *Pr*
▲ **EMP:** 6 **EST:** 1988
SQ FT: 50,000
SALES (est): 741.72K **Privately Held**
Web: www.americanwatergraphics.com
SIC: 2893 Printing ink

(G-4784)
BIGANODES LLC
117 Westerly Hills Dr (28043-9690)
PHONE..............828 245-1115
Paul Skelton, *CEO*
EMP: 4 **EST:** 2015
SALES (est): 507.09K **Privately Held**
Web: www.biganodes.com
SIC: 5051 5085 3999 Metals service centers and offices; Industrial supplies; Atomizers, toiletry

(G-4785)
BOYD WELDING AND MFG INC
Also Called: Boyd's Welding and Fabrication
324 Pine St (28043-4505)
P.O. Box 414 (28043-0414)
PHONE..............828 247-0630
Marty Boyd, *Ex VP*
Marty Boyd, *VP*
▲ **EMP:** 12 **EST:** 1999
SQ FT: 16,000
SALES (est): 1.13MM **Privately Held**
Web: www.bwmcompany.com
SIC: 7692 Welding repair

(G-4786)
CMI ENTERPRISES
135 Pine St (28043-4590)
PHONE..............305 685-9651
EMP: 4 **EST:** 2017
SALES (est): 225.41K **Privately Held**
SIC: 2295 Coated fabrics, not rubberized

(G-4787)
DIVERSE CORPORATE TECH INC
Also Called: Plastic Oddities
289 Shiloh Rd (28043-6958)
P.O. Box 1528 (28139-1528)
PHONE..............828 245-3717
TOLL FREE: 800
Kent Covington, *Pr*
Martin Bryson, *
Russell Millwood, *
Diane Mckinny, *Prin*
Gregory Southerland, *
▲ **EMP:** 25 **EST:** 1996
SQ FT: 29,000
SALES (est): 4.74MM **Privately Held**
Web: www.plasticoddities.com
SIC: 3089 Injection molding of plastics

(G-4788)
EATON CORPORATION
240 Daniel Rd (28043-9186)
PHONE..............828 286-4157
Robert Williams, *Mgr*
EMP: 75
Web: www.dix-eaton.com
SIC: 3492 3052 Hose and tube fittings and assemblies, hydraulic/pneumatic; Rubber and plastics hose and beltings
HQ: Eaton Corporation
1000 Eaton Blvd

Cleveland OH 44122
440 523-5000

(G-4789)
EVEREST TEXTILE USA LLC
1331 W Main St (28043)
PHONE..............828 245-6755
Kao Shan Wu, *Pr*
Wen Kuei Winston Hsiang, *
EMP: 125 **EST:** 2016
SQ FT: 375,904
SALES (est): 24.9MM **Privately Held**
Web: www.everest.com.tw
SIC: 2221 2262 2257 Suiting fabrics, manmade fiber and silk; Printing, manmade fiber and silk broadwoven fabrics; Dyeing and finishing circular knit fabrics
PA: Everest Textile Co., Ltd.
No. 256, Minghe Vil.
Tainan City 74300

(G-4790)
FILER MICRO WELDING
251 Terry Filer Rd (28043-7016)
PHONE..............828 248-1813
Gary E Filer, *Owner*
Gary Filer, *Owner*
EMP: 5 **EST:** 1996
SALES (est): 237.16K **Privately Held**
Web: www.filermicrowelding.com
SIC: 7692 Welding repair

(G-4791)
HERITAGE CLASSIC WOVENS LLC
Also Called: Millstreet Design
155 Westerly Hills Dr (28043-9690)
PHONE..............828 247-6010
Jeff Carpenter, *Managing Member*
EMP: 4 **EST:** 2004
SALES (est): 478.3K **Privately Held**
Web: www.hcwllc.com
SIC: 2211 Upholstery fabrics, cotton

(G-4792)
KCH SERVICES INC
Also Called: Kch Engineered Systems
144 Industrial Dr (28043-9675)
P.O. Box 1287 (28043-1287)
PHONE..............828 245-9836
Ken Hankinson, *CEO*
Kyle Hankinson, *
Rick Hall, *
EMP: 40 **EST:** 1980
SQ FT: 35,000
SALES (est): 9.32MM **Privately Held**
Web: www.kchservices.com
SIC: 3564 Air purification equipment

(G-4793)
MAYSE MANUFACTURING CO INC (PA)
2201 Us Highway 221 S (28043-7058)
PHONE..............828 245-1891
Johnny L Mayse, *Pr*
Sandra Mayse, *VP*
EMP: 7 **EST:** 1972
SQ FT: 25,000
SALES (est): 948.85K
SALES (corp-wide): 948.85K **Privately Held**
Web: www.maysemfg.com
SIC: 3448 Buildings, portable: prefabricated metal

(G-4794)
MERITOR INC
160 Ash Dr (28043-7767)
PHONE..............828 247-0440
Lucille Gartman, *Mgr*
EMP: 106
SALES (corp-wide): 34.1B **Publicly Held**

GEOGRAPHIC

Web: www.meritor.com
SIC: **3714** Axles, motor vehicle
HQ: Meritor, Inc.
　　2135 W Maple Rd
　　Troy MI 48084

(G-4795)
PARKER-HANNIFIN CORPORATION
Also Called: Hydraulic Valve Division
203 Pine St (28043-4589)
PHONE..............................828 245-3233
Andy Ross, *Brnch Mgr*
EMP: 76
SALES (corp-wide): 19.93B **Publicly Held**
Web: www.parker.com
SIC: **5084 3491** Hydraulic systems
　　equipment and supplies; Automatic
　　regulating and control valves
PA: Parker-Hannifin Corporation
　　6035 Parkland Blvd
　　Cleveland OH 44124
　　216 896-3000

(G-4796)
**ROCKTENN IN-STORE SOLUTIONS
INC**
376 Pine St (28043-4505)
P.O. Box 4098 (30091-4098)
PHONE..............................828 245-9871
EMP: 400
SIC: **2653** Display items, corrugated: made
　　from purchased materials

(G-4797)
SONOCO PRODUCTS COMPANY
Also Called: Sonoco
323 Pine St (28043-4504)
P.O. Box 749 (28043-0749)
PHONE..............................828 245-0118
Steve Trummont, *Mgr*
EMP: 96
SALES (corp-wide): 5.31B **Publicly Held**
Web: www.sonoco.com
SIC: **3089** Plastics containers, except foam
PA: Sonoco Products Company
　　1 N 2nd St
　　Hartsville SC 29550
　　843 383-7000

(G-4798)
TRI CITY CONCRETE CO LLC
158 Withrow Rd (28043-9464)
P.O. Box 241 (28043-0241)
PHONE..............................828 245-2011
Steve Barnes, *Managing Member*
Bill Morris, *Managing Member*
EMP: 18 EST: 1949
SALES (est): 2.88MM **Privately Held**
SIC: **3273** Ready-mixed concrete

(G-4799)
**UNITED SOUTHERN INDUSTRIES
INC (DH)**
486 Vance St (28043-2958)
PHONE..............................866 273-1810
Joe Y Bennett, *CEO*
Todd Bennett, *
▲ EMP: 100 EST: 1983
SQ FT: 90,000
SALES (est): 2.82MM
SALES (corp-wide): 218.2MM **Privately
Held**
SIC: **3089 3524 3423** Injection molding of
　　plastics; Lawn and garden equipment;
　　Hand and edge tools, nec
HQ: Wilbert Plastic Services Acquisition Llc
　　1000 Oaks Pkwy
　　Belmont NC 28012

(G-4800)
**WELLS JNKINS WELLS MT PROC
INC**
145 Rollins Rd (28043-9324)
PHONE..............................828 245-5544
Grady H Wells, *Pr*
Jeffrey Wells, *VP*
William R Wells, *Sec*
EMP: 6 EST: 1972
SQ FT: 4,000
SALES (est): 455.77K **Privately Held**
SIC: **5421 2011** Meat markets, including
　　freezer provisioners; Beef products, from
　　beef slaughtered on site

(G-4801)
WESTROCK COMPANY
376 Pine Street Ext (28043-5800)
PHONE..............................828 248-4815
EMP: 12
Web: www.westrock.com
SIC: **2653** Boxes, corrugated: made from
　　purchased materials
HQ: Westrock Company
　　1000 Abernathy Rd Ne
　　Atlanta GA 30328
　　770 448-2193

(G-4802)
WESTROCK CONVERTING LLC
376 Pine St (28043-4505)
PHONE..............................828 245-9871
EMP: 400
Web: www.westrock.com
SIC: **2653** Boxes, corrugated: made from
　　purchased materials
HQ: Westrock Converting, Llc
　　1000 Abernathy Rd Ste 125
　　Atlanta GA 30328
　　770 448-2193

Fort Bragg
Cumberland County

(G-4803)
**GENERAL DYNMICS MSSION
SYSTEMS**
Also Called: General Dynamics Worldwide
6812 Butner Rd And Letterman St Bldg 8
(28310-0001)
P.O. Box 71158 (28307-1158)
PHONE..............................910 497-7900
Mike Divittorio, *Mgr*
EMP: 10
SALES (corp-wide): 47.72B **Publicly Held**
Web: www.gdmissionsystems.com
SIC: **3571** Electronic computers
HQ: General Dynamics Mission Systems,
　　Inc.
　　12450 Fair Lakes Cir
　　Fairfax VA 22033
　　877 449-0600

(G-4804)
HONEYWELL INTERNATIONAL INC
Also Called: Honeywell
1 Fort Bragg (28307-5000)
P.O. Box 73721 (28307-6721)
PHONE..............................910 436-5144
Mike Lovell, *Brnch Mgr*
EMP: 4
SALES (corp-wide): 38.5B **Publicly Held**
Web: www.honeywell.com
SIC: **3724** Aircraft engines and engine parts
PA: Honeywell International Inc.
　　855 S Mint St
　　Charlotte NC 28202
　　704 627-6200

(G-4805)
US PATRIOT LLC
Bldg Z 3252 - 1017 Canopy Lane (28307)
PHONE..............................803 787-9398
Phillips N Dee, *Brnch Mgr*
EMP: 10
SALES (corp-wide): 557.14MM **Privately
Held**
Web: www.uspatriottactical.com
SIC: **2311** Military uniforms, men's and
　　youths': purchased materials
HQ: Us Patriot, Llc
　　1340 Russell Cave Rd
　　Lexington KY 40505
　　800 805-5294

Fountain
Pitt County

(G-4806)
MARIETTA MARTIN MATERIALS INC
Also Called: Martin Marietta Aggregates
5368 Allen Gay Rd (27829-9506)
P.O. Box 187 (27829-0187)
PHONE..............................252 749-2641
Ed Judy, *Mgr*
EMP: 6
Web: www.martinmarietta.com
SIC: **1422** Crushed and broken limestone
PA: Martin Marietta Materials Inc
　　4123 Parklake Ave
　　Raleigh NC 27612

Four Oaks
Johnston County

(G-4807)
ALLEN & SON S CABINET SHOP INC
5942 Us Highway 301 S (27524-9328)
P.O. Box 370 (27524-0370)
PHONE..............................919 963-2196
Donald K Allen, *Pr*
EMP: 4 EST: 1972
SQ FT: 11,000
SALES (est): 237.86K **Privately Held**
Web: www.allenandsonscabinets.com
SIC: **2434** Vanities, bathroom: wood

(G-4808)
**BECTON DICKINSON AND
COMPANY**
130 Four Oaks Pkwy (27524-7228)
PHONE..............................919 963-1307
EMP: 33
SALES (corp-wide): 20.18B **Publicly Held**
Web: www.bd.com
SIC: **3841** Surgical and medical instruments
PA: Becton, Dickinson And Company
　　1 Becton Dr
　　Franklin Lakes NJ 07417
　　201 847-6800

(G-4809)
BOUNDLESS INC
102 S Main St (27524-8223)
P.O. Box 105 (27524-0105)
PHONE..............................919 622-9051
David Faircloth, *Pr*
EMP: 6 EST: 2020
SALES (est): 35K **Privately Held**
Web: www.boundlessnc.com
SIC: **7336 2752** Commercial art and graphic
　　design; Commercial printing, lithographic

(G-4810)
D & W LOGGING INC
1771 Stricklands Crossroads Rd
(27524-8710)

PHONE..............................919 820-0826
Daniel Knight, *Admn*
EMP: 4 EST: 2021
SALES (est): 701.27K **Privately Held**
SIC: **2411** Logging

(G-4811)
GENCO
130 Four Oaks Pkwy (27524-7228)
PHONE..............................919 963-4227
EMP: 5 EST: 2015
SALES (est): 95.88K **Privately Held**
SIC: **3841** Surgical and medical instruments

(G-4812)
GRADY & SON ATKINS LOGGING
1401 Devils Racetrack Rd (27524-9313)
PHONE..............................919 934-7785
Grady Atkins, *Pr*
Gary Atkins, *VP*
Patricia Atkins, *Sec*
EMP: 9 EST: 1989
SALES (est): 410.02K **Privately Held**
SIC: **2411** Logging camps and contractors

(G-4813)
HOUSE-AUTRY MILLS INC (PA)
7000 Us Highway 301 S (27524-7628)
P.O. Box 460 (27524-0460)
PHONE..............................919 963-6200
Roger F Mortenson, *Pr*
Robert T Depree, *
EMP: 46 EST: 1966
SQ FT: 50,000
SALES (est): 22.57MM
SALES (corp-wide): 22.57MM **Privately
Held**
Web: www.house-autry.com
SIC: **2041** Corn meal

(G-4814)
MAY-CRAFT FIBERGLASS PDTS INC
96 Hillsboro Rd (27524-8028)
P.O. Box 450 (27577-0450)
PHONE..............................919 934-3000
Kenneth L May, *Pr*
Dianne May, *Sec*
▼ EMP: 7 EST: 1992
SQ FT: 44,000
SALES (est): 879.81K **Privately Held**
Web: www.maycraftboats.com
SIC: **3732** Boats, fiberglass: building and
　　repairing

(G-4815)
ROY DUNN
Also Called: NAPA Auto Parts
101 Dunn St (27524-7105)
PHONE..............................919 963-3700
Roy Dunn, *Owner*
EMP: 4 EST: 1987
SALES (est): 110.99K **Privately Held**
Web: www.napaonline.com
SIC: **5531 3599** Automotive parts; Machine
　　shop, jobbing and repair

(G-4816)
SOUTHERN WOODS LUMBER INC
3872 Old School Rd (27524-8675)
PHONE..............................919 963-2233
EMP: 7 EST: 2017
SALES (est): 1.65MM **Privately Held**
SIC: **2421** Lumber: rough, sawed, or planed

(G-4817)
T E JOHNSON LUMBER CO INC
Also Called: T E Johnson Building and Rentl
3872 Old School Rd (27524-8675)
P.O. Box 341 (27504-0341)
PHONE..............................919 963-2233

▲ = Import ▼ = Export
◆ = Import/Export

Thom E Johnson, *Pr*
Lana Massengill, *VP*
Heather Cliston, *Sec*
Thom Johnson Iii, *Stockholder*
EMP: 4 **EST:** 1946
SQ FT: 10,000
SALES (est): 167.73K **Privately Held**
Web: www.tejohnsonlumber.com
SIC: 2421 5211 Lumber: rough, sawed, or planed; Lumber and other building materials

---

Franklin
Macon County

(G-4818)
BEASLEY FLOORING PRODUCTS INC
Also Called: Flooring Manufacturing
41 Hardwood Dr (28734-3012)
PHONE..............................828 349-7000
EMP: 35
SALES (corp-wide): 92.42MM **Privately Held**
Web: www.beasleyflooring.com
SIC: 2426 Hardwood dimension and flooring mills
HQ: Beasley Flooring Products, Inc.
770 Uvalda Hwy
Hazlehurst GA 31539

(G-4819)
BRYANT GRANT MUTUAL BURIAL ASN
105 W Main St (28734-2916)
PHONE..............................828 524-2411
Guy Grant, *Prin*
EMP: 6 **EST:** 2011
SALES (est): 160.68K **Privately Held**
Web: www.bryantgrantfuneralhome.com
SIC: 3272 Burial vaults, concrete or precast terrazzo

(G-4820)
CANVASMASTERS LLC
78 Cabe Cove Rd (28734-5979)
PHONE..............................828 369-0406
Gred Mcgaha, *Owner*
Greg Mcgaha, *Owner*
EMP: 4 **EST:** 1997
SALES (est): 188.7K **Privately Held**
Web: www.canvasmasterswnc.com
SIC: 2394 Canvas and related products

(G-4821)
COATES DESIGNERS & CRAFSTMEN
57 Mill St (28734-2710)
P.O. Box 1273 (28744-1273)
PHONE..............................828 349-9700
Alan F Coates, *Pr*
EMP: 8 **EST:** 1960
SQ FT: 8,000
SALES (est): 111K **Privately Held**
Web: www.coatesplaques.com
SIC: 3999 2821 3993 Plaques, picture, laminated; Polymethyl methacrylate resins, plexiglass; Signs and advertising specialties

(G-4822)
COMMUNITY NEWSPAPERS INC
Also Called: Cni Regional
690 Wayah St (28734-3390)
P.O. Box 530 (28744-0530)
PHONE..............................828 369-3430
Judy Waldrop, *Mgr*
EMP: 4
SALES (corp-wide): 40.95MM **Privately Held**
Web: www.cninewspapers.com

SIC: 2711 Newspapers, publishing and printing
PA: Community Newspapers, Inc.
2365 Prince Ave # A
Athens GA 30606
706 548-0010

(G-4823)
COWEE MOUNTAIN RUBY MINE
6771 Sylva Rd (28734-2243)
PHONE..............................828 369-5271
Sonja Eldridge, *Prin*
▲ **EMP:** 7 **EST:** 2002
SALES (est): 741.22K **Privately Held**
Web: www.coweemtnrubymine.com
SIC: 1241 Coal mining services

(G-4824)
DRAKE ENTERPRISES LTD
Also Called: Macon Printing
219 E Palmer St (28734-3049)
PHONE..............................828 524-7045
Billy Banhook, *Mgr*
EMP: 5
SALES (corp-wide): 43.29MM **Privately Held**
Web: www.maconprinting.com
SIC: 2752 Business form and card printing, lithographic
PA: Drake Enterprises, Ltd.
235 E Palmer St
Franklin NC 28734
828 524-2922

(G-4825)
DRAKE SOFTWARE LLC
235 E Palmer St (28734-3049)
PHONE..............................828 524-2922
Dominic Morea, *Pr*
Euan Menzies, *
Leslie Gibson, *
EMP: 339 **EST:** 2010
SALES (est): 24.65MM **Privately Held**
Web: www.drakesoftware.com
SIC: 7372 Business oriented computer software

(G-4826)
DUOTECH SERVICES LLC
245 Industrial Park Rd (28734-7920)
PHONE..............................828 369-5111
Daniel Bader, *CEO*
Brett Rogers, *Sec*
EMP: 45 **EST:** 1983
SQ FT: 35,000
SALES (est): 15MM
SALES (corp-wide): 26.27MM **Privately Held**
Web: www.duotechservices.com
SIC: 8711 3679 Engineering services; Electronic circuits
PA: Asg Operations, Llc
400 Convention St # 1010
Baton Rouge LA 70802
337 344-3088

(G-4827)
ELITE MOUNTAIN BUSINESS LLC
Also Called: Ridge Line Homes
21 Sanderstown Rd (28734-8622)
PHONE..............................828 349-0403
Carey Lannon, *Managing Member*
Cynthia Truesdale, *Managing Member*
EMP: 4 **EST:** 2015
SALES (est): 310.29K **Privately Held**
SIC: 2451 Mobile homes

(G-4828)
FRANKLIN MACHINE COMPANY LLC
231 Depot St (28734-3001)
P.O. Box 1149 (28744-1149)

PHONE..............................828 524-2313
Tommy Potts, *VP*
EMP: 6 **EST:** 1950
SALES (est): 1.52MM **Privately Held**
Web: www.franklinmachineandsteel.com
SIC: 3599 Machine shop, jobbing and repair

(G-4829)
FRANKLIN SHEET METAL SHOP INC
Also Called: Franklin Sheet Metal
791 Ulco Dr Ste A (28734-3365)
PHONE..............................828 524-2821
James T Mann Senior, *Pr*
Ed Cope, *Sec*
EMP: 9 **EST:** 1952
SALES (est): 452.08K **Privately Held**
SIC: 1711 3444 Warm air heating and air conditioning contractor; Sheet metalwork

(G-4830)
GOODER GRAFIX INC
522 E Main St (28734-2649)
PHONE..............................828 349-4097
Guy Gooder, *Pr*
Alicia Gooder, *VP*
EMP: 4 **EST:** 1982
SALES (est): 464.51K **Privately Held**
Web: www.goodergrafix.com
SIC: 3993 7261 Signs, not made in custom sign painting shops; Funeral service and crematories

(G-4831)
HARMONY HOUSE FOODS INC
277 Industrial Park Rd (28734-7920)
PHONE..............................800 696-1395
John Seaman, *Pr*
Linda Seaman, *VP*
EMP: 8 **EST:** 2005
SALES (est): 414.99K **Privately Held**
Web: www.harmonyhousefoods.com
SIC: 2099 Food preparations, nec

(G-4832)
K & M PRODUCTS OF NC INC
3248 Patton Rd (28734-7896)
PHONE..............................828 524-5905
Judy Kirkland, *Pr*
Ronald Lee Kirkland, *VP*
EMP: 5 **EST:** 1979
SALES (est): 1.02MM **Privately Held**
Web: www.kmproductsofnc.com
SIC: 3829 Surveying and drafting equipment

(G-4833)
LANDER TUBULAR PDTS USA INC
Also Called: Tricom Usa, Inc.
66 Van Raalte St (28734-2760)
PHONE..............................828 369-6682
Michael Welburn, *Pr*
David Leakey, *
Phillip Lee, *
▲ **EMP:** 110 **EST:** 2013
SQ FT: 60,000
SALES (est): 24.82MM **Privately Held**
Web: www.lander.co.uk
SIC: 3317 Steel pipe and tubes

(G-4834)
LIBASCI WOODWORKS INC
401 Dobson Mountain Rd R (28734-6157)
PHONE..............................828 524-7073
Gary Libasci, *Prin*
EMP: 4 **EST:** 2008
SALES (est): 107.31K **Privately Held**
SIC: 2431 Millwork

(G-4835)
LIBERTY WOOD PRODUCTS INC
874 Iotla Church Rd (28734-0329)

PHONE..............................828 524-7958
Tim Hubbs, *Pr*
Phil Drake, *Ch*
John Sapp, *Treas*
EMP: 14 **EST:** 1978
SQ FT: 5,000
SALES (est): 2.02MM **Privately Held**
Web: www.libertywoodproducts.net
SIC: 2431 Millwork

(G-4836)
MAJOR DISPLAY INC (PA)
131 Franklin Plaza Dr Ste 363 (28734-3249)
PHONE..............................800 260-1067
Glen Whittaker, *Pr*
EMP: 5 **EST:** 2015
SALES (est): 477.68K
SALES (corp-wide): 477.68K **Privately Held**
Web: www.majordisplay.com
SIC: 3993 Scoreboards, electric

(G-4837)
MOONSHINE PRESS
162 Riverwood Dr (28734-1375)
PHONE..............................828 371-8519
EMP: 4 **EST:** 2013
SALES (est): 60.52K **Privately Held**
SIC: 2741 Miscellaneous publishing

(G-4838)
PARRISH CONTRACTING LLC
3370 Bryson City Rd (28734-4315)
P.O. Box 1026 (28744-1026)
PHONE..............................828 524-9100
Matthew Holland, *Pr*
Jim Parrish, *Owner*
EMP: 8 **EST:** 2019
SALES (est): 3.03MM **Privately Held**
Web: www.desototrailrealty.com
SIC: 1721 1799 1442 Painting and paper hanging; Construction site cleanup; Construction sand and gravel

(G-4839)
SHAW INDUSTRIES INC
301 Depot St (28734-3060)
PHONE..............................828 369-1701
Tien Ellington, *Brnch Mgr*
EMP: 296
SALES (corp-wide): 424.23B **Publicly Held**
Web: www.shawinc.com
SIC: 2273 Carpets and rugs
HQ: Shaw Industries, Inc.
616 E Walnut Ave
Dalton GA 30722

(G-4840)
SOUTHERN CONCRETE MTLS INC
493 Wells Grove Rd (28734-7521)
PHONE..............................828 524-3555
Eddie Evans, *Manager*
EMP: 17
SALES (corp-wide): 238.17MM **Privately Held**
Web: www.scmusa.com
SIC: 3273 1771 Ready-mixed concrete; Driveway contractor
HQ: Southern Concrete Materials, Inc.
35 Meadow Rd
Asheville NC 28803
828 253-6421

(G-4841)
TEKTONE SOUND & SIGNAL MFG INC
324 Industrial Park Rd (28734-1006)
PHONE..............................828 524-9967
Carlos Mira, *Pr*

Manuel S Mira, *
Maria Mira, *
Teresa Knippel, *
◆ EMP: 90 EST: 1973
SQ FT: 32,800
SALES (est): 22.08MM Privately Held
Web: www.tektone.com
SIC: 7382 3669 Security systems services;
Burglar alarm apparatus, electric

(G-4842)
WATAUGA CREEK LLC
25 Setser Branch Rd (28734-9215)
PHONE..........................828 369-7881
Robert W Moyer, Owner
▲ EMP: 5 EST: 1982
SALES (est): 399.39K Privately Held
Web: www.wataugacreek.com
SIC: 5712 2512 5021 Mattresses;
Upholstered household furniture; Furniture

(G-4843)
WATERWHEEL FACTORY
320 Arbor Ln (28734-6116)
PHONE..........................828 369-5928
Robert Vitale, Owner
EMP: 4 EST: 1999
SALES (est): 264.19K Privately Held
Web: www.waterwheelfactory.com
SIC: 3511 Hydraulic turbine generator set
units, complete

(G-4844)
ZICKGRAF ENTERPRISES INC
Franklin Machine
231 Depot St (28734-3001)
P.O. Box 1149 (28744-1149)
PHONE..........................828 524-2313
Paul Thomas Potts, VP
EMP: 6
SQ FT: 2,000
SALES (corp-wide): 3.98MM Privately
Held
Web: www.nantahalaflooring.com
SIC: 7699 7692 7538 Industrial machinery
and equipment repair; Welding repair;
General automotive repair shops
PA: Zickgraf Enterprises, Inc.
301 Depot St
Franklin NC 28734
828 369-1200

(G-4845)
ZICKGRAF ENTERPRISES INC
301 Depot St (28734-3060)
PHONE..........................704 369-1200
Bodenheimer Fp, Prin
EMP: 4 EST: 2009
SALES (est): 151.05K Privately Held
SIC: 2426 Hardwood dimension and flooring
mills

Franklinton
Franklin County

(G-4846)
ARCHITECTURAL CRAFTSMAN LTD
Also Called: Craftsmanship Unlimited
315 Cedar Creek Rd (27525-9057)
PHONE..........................919 494-6911
Peter De Cuir, Pr
Suzy De Cuir, Dir
EMP: 35 EST: 1978
SALES (est): 300.68K Privately Held
SIC: 1799 2431 1751 Athletic and recreation
facilities construction; Millwork; Carpentry
work

(G-4847)
CONTAINER SYSTEMS INCORPORATED
6863 N Carolina 56 Hwy E (27525-7379)
P.O. Box 519 (27525-0519)
PHONE..........................919 496-6133
TOLL FREE: 800
EMP: 75
SIC: 2449 3565 2657 Shipping cases and
drums, wood: wirebound and plywood;
Packaging machinery; Folding paperboard
boxes

(G-4848)
FRANKLIN VENEERS INC
5735 Nc Hwy 56 E (27525)
P.O. Box 70 (27525-0070)
PHONE..........................919 494-2284
Richard H Morgan Junior, Pr
Richard H Morgan Iii, VP
Judy Morgan, *
EMP: 7 EST: 1937
SQ FT: 20,000
SALES (est): 969.58K Privately Held
SIC: 2435 2426 Veneer stock, hardwood;
Hardwood dimension and flooring mills

(G-4849)
KATESVILLE PALLET MILL INC
7119 Nc 56 Hwy (27525-7249)
PHONE..........................919 496-3162
David Kemp, Pr
EMP: 11 EST: 1971
SQ FT: 2,000
SALES (est): 2.61MM Privately Held
SIC: 2421 Sawmills and planing mills,
general

(G-4850)
LINDSAY PRECAST INC
Also Called: LINDSAY PRECAST, INC.
2675 Us 1 Hwy (27525-8499)
P.O. Box 580 (27525-0580)
PHONE..........................919 494-7600
Matt Blind, Genl Mgr
EMP: 50
SALES (corp-wide): 35.62MM Privately
Held
Web: www.lindsayprecast.com
SIC: 3272 Precast terrazzo or concrete
products
PA: Lindsay Precast, Llc
6845 Erie Ave Nw
Canal Fulton OH 44614
800 837-7788

(G-4851)
NOVOZYMES NORTH AMERICA INC (HQ)
Also Called: Novozymes
77 Perrys Chapel Church Rd (27525)
P.O. Box 610 (27525)
PHONE..........................919 494-2014
Adam Monroe, Ch Bd
Steen Riisgaard, *
Thomas Nagy, *
Per Falholt, *
Kristian Merser, *
◆ EMP: 62 EST: 1969
SALES (est): 522.07MM
SALES (corp-wide): 2.61B Privately Held
Web: www.novozymes.com
SIC: 2869 Enzymes
PA: Novozymes A/S
Krogshojvej 36
Bagsvard 2880
44460000

(G-4852)
PALLETS AND MORE
119 N Cheatham St (27525-1302)
PHONE..........................919 815-6134
Joshua Roberson, Prin
EMP: 5 EST: 2016
SALES (est): 129.42K Privately Held
SIC: 2448 Wood pallets and skids

(G-4853)
S T WOOTEN CORPORATION
Also Called: Franklinton Concrete Plant
255 Material Rd (27525)
PHONE..........................919 562-1851
Scott Wooten, Pr
EMP: 22
SALES (corp-wide): 319.83MM Privately
Held
Web: www.stwcorp.com
SIC: 3531 Concrete plants
PA: S. T. Wooten Corporation
3801 Black Creek Rd Se
Wilson NC 27894
252 291-5165

(G-4854)
STAY-RIGHT PRE-CAST CONCRETE INC
2675 Us1 Hwy (27525)
P.O. Box 580 (27525-0580)
PHONE..........................919 494-7600
EMP: 52
SIC: 3272 Concrete products, nec

Franklinville
Randolph County

(G-4855)
CAUSEKEEPERS INC
Also Called: 4 Your Cause
5068 Us Highway 64 E (27248-8656)
PHONE..........................336 824-2518
Donald Lafferty, Pr
Samuel Hicks, VP
◆ EMP: 20 EST: 2004
SQ FT: 120,000
SALES (est): 634.01K Privately Held
Web: www.causekeepers.com
SIC: 2759 2752 5199 7336 Screen printing;
Offset printing; Advertising specialties; Art
design services

(G-4856)
DEEP RIVER FABRICATORS INC
240 E Main St (27248-8603)
P.O. Box 100 (27248-0100)
PHONE..........................336 824-8881
Roy Luckenbach, Pr
Eric Luckenbach, Pr
EMP: 14 EST: 1993
SQ FT: 30,000
SALES (est): 4.08MM Privately Held
SIC: 3086 2392 Plastics foam products;
Household furnishings, nec

(G-4857)
KEN STALEY CO INC
4675 Us Highway 64 E Bldg 16
(27248-8611)
PHONE..........................336 685-4294
Ken Staley, Pr
Judi Mills, Sec
EMP: 7 EST: 1973
SALES (est): 97.93K Privately Held
Web: www.bleachers101.com
SIC: 2531 5941 1796 Stadium furniture;
Sporting goods and bicycle shops;
Installing building equipment

(G-4858)
UNIQUE TOOL AND MFG CO
2054 Bruce Pugh Rd (27248-8019)
P.O. Box 909 (27317-0909)
PHONE..........................336 498-2614
Jimmy Scott, Pr
Vincent Scott, *
Doris Scott, *
EMP: 46 EST: 1986
SQ FT: 30,000
SALES (est): 4.99MM Privately Held
Web: www.uniquetool.net
SIC: 3545 3724 3714 Precision tools,
machinists'; Aircraft engines and engine
parts; Motor vehicle transmissions, drive
assemblies, and parts

Fremont
Wayne County

(G-4859)
BIG SHOW FOODS INC
588 Turner Swamp Rd (27830-9300)
P.O. Box 3182 (27830-3182)
PHONE..........................919 242-7769
Tom Price, Pr
EMP: 5 EST: 1999
SQ FT: 75,000
SALES (est): 362.7K Privately Held
Web: www.bigshowfoods.com
SIC: 2099 Food preparations, nec

(G-4860)
SANCTUARY SYSTEMS LLC
701 S Wilson St (27830-8649)
P.O. Box 692 (27830-0692)
PHONE..........................305 989-0953
Jason Shockley, *
Andy Parker, *
EMP: 61 EST: 2016
SALES (est): 114.7K Privately Held
Web: www.sanctuarysystem.com
SIC: 2821 Plastics materials and resins

(G-4861)
VENTURA INC
7061 Pennwright Rd (27830-9565)
PHONE..........................252 291-7125
Reece Daniels, Pr
EMP: 7 EST: 1991
SQ FT: 5,000
SALES (est): 410.45K Privately Held
SIC: 3553 Cabinet makers' machinery

(G-4862)
VENTURE CABINETS
7061 Pennwright Rd (27830-9565)
PHONE..........................252 299-0051
EMP: 4 EST: 2019
SALES (est): 106.06K Privately Held
SIC: 3553 Woodworking machinery

Frisco
Dare County

(G-4863)
CASHMAN INC
Also Called: All Decked Out
53392 Hwy 12 (27936)
P.O. Box 363 (27943-0363)
PHONE..........................252 995-4319
Dale Cashman, Pr
Betty Swanson, VP
EMP: 5 EST: 1984
SQ FT: 1,500
SALES (est): 109.17K Privately Held

▲ = Import ▼ = Export
◆ = Import/Export

SIC: **2511** Wood lawn and garden furniture

Fuquay Varina
Wake County

(G-4864)
AMERICAN NETTING CORP
Also Called: Super-Net
3209 Air Park Rd (27526-8516)
PHONE.................................919 567-3737
Glenn Passner, *Pr*
▲ **EMP:** 10 **EST:** 1978
SQ FT: 3,900
SALES (est): 402.01K **Privately Held**
Web: www.supernetsusa.com
SIC: **3949** Baseball equipment and supplies, general

(G-4865)
APEX INSTRUMENTS
INCORPORATED
204 Technology Park Ln (27526-9310)
PHONE.................................919 557-7300
William H Howe, *Pr*
▲ **EMP:** 40 **EST:** 1988
SQ FT: 6,000
SALES (est): 10.33MM **Privately Held**
Web: www.apexinst.com
SIC: **8734** 3829 Pollution testing; Measuring and controlling devices, nec

(G-4866)
ARGOS USA LLC
Also Called: Ready Mixed Concrete Co Fuquay
1506 Holland Rd (27526-7895)
PHONE.................................919 552-2294
James Holmes, *Mgr*
EMP: 9
Web: www.argos-us.com
SIC: **3273** Ready-mixed concrete
HQ: Argos Usa Llc
3015 Windward Plz Ste 300
Alpharetta GA 30005
678 368-4300

(G-4867)
ART HOUSE
3325 Air Park Rd (27526-8518)
PHONE.................................919 552-7327
Newton Prince Junior, *Pr*
EMP: 4 **EST:** 1984
SQ FT: 4,200
SALES (est): 177.54K **Privately Held**
Web: www.arthouseinks.com
SIC: **2759** Screen printing

(G-4868)
ATLANTIC MOLD INC
1000 N Main St Ste 221 (27526-2056)
PHONE.................................919 832-8151
Danyelle Holland, *Pr*
EMP: 6 **EST:** 2008
SALES (est): 466.31K **Privately Held**
Web: www.atlanticmoldexperts.com
SIC: **3544** Industrial molds

(G-4869)
BECWILL CORP
3209 Air Park Rd (27526-8516)
P.O. Box 2294 (27529-2294)
PHONE.................................919 552-8266
Laura Passner, *Pr*
EMP: 6 **EST:** 2001
SQ FT: 5,000
SALES (est): 475.5K **Privately Held**
SIC: **3949** Baseball equipment and supplies, general

(G-4870)
BOB BARKER COMPANY INC (PA)
7925 Purfoy Rd (27526-8937)
P.O. Box 429 (27526-0429)
PHONE.................................800 334-9880
Robert J Barker Senior, *CEO*
Robert Barker Junior, *Pr*
Patricia M Barker, *
Mark Bacon, *CRO**
◆ **EMP:** 220 **EST:** 1972
SQ FT: 29,000
SALES (est): 69.72MM
SALES (corp-wide): 69.72MM **Privately Held**
Web: www.bobbarker.com
SIC: **5122** 5131 5136 2392 Toiletries; Linen piece goods, woven; Uniforms, men's and boys'; Household furnishings, nec

(G-4871)
BOEHRNGER INGLHEIM ANMAL HLTH
Also Called: Manufacturing
3225 Air Park Rd (27526-8516)
PHONE.................................919 577-9020
Brittni Hathcock, *Brnch Mgr*
EMP: 78
SALES (corp-wide): 25.08B **Privately Held**
Web: www.boehringer-ingelheim.com
SIC: **2836** Biological products, except diagnostic
HQ: Boehringer Ingelheim Animal Health Usa Inc.
3239 Satellite Blvd
Duluth GA 30096
800 325-9167

(G-4872)
CCL LABEL INC
7924 Purfoy Rd (27526-8936)
PHONE.................................919 713-0388
Geoff Martin, *CEO*
EMP: 62
SALES (corp-wide): 4.84B **Privately Held**
Web: www.cclind.com
SIC: **2759** Labels and seals: printing, nsk
HQ: Ccl Label, Inc.
161 Worcester Rd Ste 603
Framingham MA 01701
508 872-4511

(G-4873)
CLEAN AND VAC
2013 Sterling Hill Dr (27526-5368)
PHONE.................................919 753-7951
Joseph Mussanlevy, *Owner*
EMP: 6 **EST:** 2011
SALES (est): 312.44K **Privately Held**
SIC: **3635** Household vacuum cleaners

(G-4874)
COLUMN & POST INC
Also Called: Column & Post
8013 Purfoy Rd (27526-8939)
PHONE.................................919 255-1533
David Szilezy, *Pr*
Robert Koren, *VP*
Terry Slate, *Sec*
EMP: 6 **EST:** 2002
SALES (est): 989.25K **Privately Held**
Web: www.columnpost.com
SIC: **3272** Columns, concrete

(G-4875)
COMBAT SUPPORT PRODUCTS INC
3738 Rawls Church Rd (27526-8021)
PHONE.................................919 552-0205
James M Cottrell, *CEO*
Barbara Cottrell, *VP*
EMP: 4 **EST:** 2007
SQ FT: 1,800

SALES (est): 292.65K **Privately Held**
Web: www.combatsupportproducts.com
SIC: **3569** Firefighting and related equipment

(G-4876)
CROMPTON INSTRUMENTS
8000 Purfoy Rd (27526-8938)
PHONE.................................919 557-8698
Scarlett Sears, *Dir*
EMP: 4 **EST:** 2014
SALES (est): 565.23K **Privately Held**
Web: www.crompton-instruments.com
SIC: **3678** Electronic connectors

(G-4877)
DAVID BENNETT
80 H H Mckoy Ln (27526-5609)
PHONE.................................919 798-3424
Bennett David, *Prin*
EMP: 6 **EST:** 2012
SALES (est): 1.22MM **Privately Held**
SIC: **7692** Welding repair

(G-4878)
DEERE & COMPANY
Also Called: John Deere Turf Care
6501 S Nc 55 Hwy (27526-7834)
PHONE.................................919 567-6400
Greg Van Grinsvin, *Manager*
EMP: 400
SALES (corp-wide): 8.51B **Publicly Held**
Web: www.deere.com
SIC: **3523** 3524 Turf and grounds equipment; Lawn and garden equipment
PA: Deere & Company
1 John Deere Pl
Moline IL 61265
309 765-8000

(G-4879)
DIGGER SPECIALTIES INC
8013 Purfoy Rd (27526-8939)
PHONE.................................919 255-2533
EMP: 11
SALES (corp-wide): 22.11MM **Privately Held**
Web: www.diggerspecialties.com
SIC: **3089** Plastics hardware and building products
PA: Digger Specialties, Inc.
3446 Us Hwy 6
Bremen IN 46506
574 546-5999

(G-4880)
E & M CONCRETE INC
Also Called: M.C. Exteriors
7505 Troy Stone Dr (27526-7111)
PHONE.................................919 235-7221
Micke Douglas, *Pr*
EMP: 32 **EST:** 2013
SALES (est): 5.33MM **Privately Held**
Web: www.emconcretenc.com
SIC: **1771** 3273 Concrete work; Ready-mixed concrete

(G-4881)
EONCOAT LLC (PA)
3337 Air Park Rd Ste 6 (27526-7277)
PHONE.................................941 928-9401
Tony Collins, *CEO*
Merrick Albert, *Pr*
EMP: 7 **EST:** 2015
SALES (est): 4.97MM
SALES (corp-wide): 4.97MM **Privately Held**
Web: www.eoncoat.com
SIC: **2851** Lacquers, varnishes, enamels, and other coatings

(G-4882)
FUQUAY-VARINA BAKING CO INC
127 S Main St (27526-2220)
P.O. Box 665 (27526-0665)
PHONE.................................919 557-2237
Katie Dies, *Owner*
EMP: 5 **EST:** 2011
SALES (est): 267.43K **Privately Held**
Web: www.fuquay-varina.org
SIC: **2051** Bread, cake, and related products

(G-4883)
GRANDWELL INDUSTRIES INC
6109 S Nc 55 Hwy (27526-7920)
P.O. Box 5722 (27512-5722)
PHONE.................................919 557-1221
Charles Lai, *CEO*
Mei-chieng Lai, *VP*
Roger Lai, *VP*
▲ **EMP:** 20 **EST:** 1989
SQ FT: 8,000
SALES (est): 909.52K **Privately Held**
Web: www.grandwell.com
SIC: **3993** Electric signs

(G-4884)
INNOCRIN PHARMACEUTICALS INC
701 Wagstaff Rd (27526-8101)
PHONE.................................919 467-8539
Fred Eshelman, *CEO*
Andrew Von Eschenbach, *Prin*
James Rosen, *Prin*
Robert Schotzinger, *Prin*
Ed Torres, *Prin*
EMP: 6 **EST:** 2005
SALES (est): 931.39K **Privately Held**
Web: www.abcapotek.com
SIC: **2834** Pharmaceutical preparations

(G-4885)
INTERNATIONAL MINUTE PRESS
316 Angier Rd (27526-2209)
PHONE.................................919 762-0054
Dann Vander, *Mgr*
EMP: 4 **EST:** 2014
SALES (est): 234.44K **Privately Held**
Web: www.minuteman.com
SIC: **2752** Commercial printing, lithographic

(G-4886)
J&L MANUFACTURING INC
192 Jarco Dr (27526-5071)
PHONE.................................919 801-3219
Jim Thomas, *Pr*
Lee Revis, *VP*
EMP: 13 **EST:** 2021
SALES (est): 1.08MM **Privately Held**
SIC: **3625** Controls for adjustable speed drives

(G-4887)
MARSHALL MIDDLEBY INC
Southbend Division
1100 Old Honeycutt Rd (27526-9312)
PHONE.................................919 762-1000
John Peruccio, *Pr*
EMP: 75
SQ FT: 138,855
SALES (corp-wide): 3.88B **Publicly Held**
Web: www.middleby.com
SIC: **3589** 3631 3556 Cooking equipment, commercial; Household cooking equipment; Food products machinery
HQ: Middleby Marshall Inc.
1100 Old Honeycutt Rd
Fuquay Varina NC 27526
919 762-1000

(G-4888)
MARTIN MARIETTA MATERIALS INC
Also Called: Martin Marietta Aggregates
7400 Buckhorn Duncan Road (27526)
P.O. Box 1957 (27526-2957)
PHONE..................................919 557-7412
Les Goshorn, *Mgr*
EMP: 10
Web: www.martinmarietta.com
SIC: 3273 Ready-mixed concrete
PA: Martin Marietta Materials Inc
4123 Parklake Ave
Raleigh NC 27612

(G-4889)
MECO INC
501 Community Dr (27526-7108)
PHONE..................................919 557-7330
Don Batot, *Prin*
EMP: 4 **EST:** 2016
SALES (est): 279.85K **Privately Held**
Web: www.meco.com
SIC: 3589 Water treatment equipment,
industrial

(G-4890)
MERGE SCIENTIFIC SOLUTIONS LLC
208 Technology Park Ln Ste 108
(27526-5875)
PHONE..................................919 346-0999
EMP: 4 **EST:** 2022
SALES (est): 63.22K **Privately Held**
SIC: 3231 Aquariums and reflectors, glass

(G-4891)
MIDDLEBY MARSHALL INC (HQ)
Also Called: Southbend
1100 Old Honeycutt Rd (27526-9312)
PHONE..................................919 762-1000
John Perruccio, *Pr*
◆ **EMP:** 200 **EST:** 1888
SQ FT: 210,000
SALES (est): 482.34MM
SALES (corp-wide): 3.88B **Publicly Held**
Web: www.middleby.com
SIC: 3556 3585 3631 Ovens, bakery;
Refrigeration equipment, complete;
Household cooking equipment
PA: The Middleby Corporation
1400 Toastmaster Dr
Elgin IL 60120
847 741-3300

(G-4892)
NOLES CABINETS INC
2290 N Grassland Dr (27526-6893)
PHONE..................................919 552-4257
R Douglas Doug Noles, *Pr*
EMP: 6 **EST:** 1970
SQ FT: 10,000
SALES (est): 575.11K **Privately Held**
Web: www.nolescabinets.com
SIC: 2434 Wood kitchen cabinets

(G-4893)
NVENT THERMAL LLC
8000 Purfoy Rd (27526-8938)
PHONE..................................919 552-3811
EMP: 488
SALES (corp-wide): 69.83B **Privately Held**
Web: www.nvent.com
SIC: 3661 Telephone and telegraph
apparatus
HQ: Nvent Thermal Llc
15375 Memorial Dr
Houston TX 77079
650 216-1526

(G-4894)
OLDCASTLE INFRASTRUCTURE INC
1431 Products Rd (27526-8614)
P.O. Box 548 (27526-0548)
PHONE..................................919 552-2252
Gregory Levine, *Mgr*
EMP: 22
SQ FT: 5,500
SALES (corp-wide): 34.95B **Privately Held**
Web: locator.oldcastleinfrastructure.com
SIC: 3272 Manhole covers or frames,
concrete
HQ: Oldcastle Infrastructure, Inc.
7000 Central Pkwy Ste 800
Atlanta GA 30328
770 270-5000

(G-4895)
PRIORITY BACKGROUNDS LLC
118 N Johnson St (27526-1973)
P.O. Box 1589 (27526-1589)
PHONE..................................919 557-3247
EMP: 8 **EST:** 2005
SALES (est): 452.75K **Privately Held**
Web: www.prioritybackgrounds.com
SIC: 7372 Prepackaged software

(G-4896)
REVELS TURF AND TRACTOR LLC
(PA)
Also Called: John Deere
2217 N Main St (27526-8560)
PHONE..................................919 552-5697
▲ **EMP:** 35 **EST:** 1961
SALES (est): 12.41MM
SALES (corp-wide): 12.41MM **Privately Held**
Web: www.revelstractor.com
SIC: 3949 Golf equipment

(G-4897)
S T WOOTEN CORPORATION
Also Called: Banks Rd Concrete Plant
3625 Banks Rd (27526)
PHONE..................................919 772-7991
Scott Wooten, *Pr*
EMP: 22
SALES (corp-wide): 319.83MM **Privately Held**
Web: www.stwcorp.com
SIC: 3531 Concrete plants
PA: S. T. Wooten Corporation
3801 Black Creek Rd Se
Wilson NC 27894
252 291-5165

(G-4898)
TE CONNECTIVITY CORPORATION
8000 Purfoy Rd (27526-8938)
PHONE..................................919 552-3811
Barry Allen, *Prin*
EMP: 26
SALES (corp-wide): 9.17B **Privately Held**
Web: careers.te.com
SIC: 3678 Electronic connectors
HQ: Te Connectivity Corporation
1050 Westlakes Dr
Berwyn PA 19312
610 893-9800

(G-4899)
TE CONNECTIVITY CORPORATION
8009 Purfoy Rd (27526-8939)
PHONE..................................919 557-8425
Bob Fennel, *Brnch Mgr*
EMP: 7
SALES (corp-wide): 9.17B **Privately Held**
Web: careers.te.com
SIC: 3678 3643 Electronic connectors;
Current-carrying wiring services
HQ: Te Connectivity Corporation

1050 Westlakes Dr
Berwyn PA 19312
610 893-9800

(G-4900)
TE CONNECTIVITY CORPORATION
Tyco Electronics Energy Plant
8000 Purfoy Rd (27526-8938)
PHONE..................................919 552-3811
Jim Robert, *Mgr*
EMP: 15
SALES (corp-wide): 9.17B **Privately Held**
Web: careers.te.com
SIC: 3678 3643 Electronic connectors;
Current-carrying wiring services
HQ: Te Connectivity Corporation
1050 Westlakes Dr
Berwyn PA 19312
610 893-9800

(G-4901)
TEC GRAPHICS INC
101 Technology Park Ln (27526-9363)
PHONE..................................919 567-2077
Thomas Cherry, *Pr*
EMP: 10 **EST:** 1992
SQ FT: 10,000
SALES (est): 1.66MM **Privately Held**
Web: www.tecgraphics.com
SIC: 2759 3993 3643 2672 Screen printing;
Signs and advertising specialties; Current-
carrying wiring services; Paper; coated and
laminated, nec

(G-4902)
THOMAS CONCRETE CAROLINA INC
140 Pamela Ct (27526-5662)
PHONE..................................919 557-3144
John Holding, *VP*
EMP: 12
SALES (corp-wide): 1.15B **Privately Held**
Web: www.thomasconcrete.com
SIC: 3273 Ready-mixed concrete
HQ: Thomas Concrete Of Carolina, Inc.
1131 Nw Street
Raleigh NC 27603
919 832-0451

(G-4903)
TRIANGLE CUSTOM WOODWORKS LLC (PA)
526 Victoria Hills Dr S (27526-5680)
PHONE..................................919 637-8857
Melissa Myers, *Prin*
EMP: 7 **EST:** 2015
SALES (est): 245.51K
SALES (corp-wide): 245.51K **Privately Held**
Web:
www.trianglecustomwoodworks.com
SIC: 2431 Millwork

(G-4904)
VICTORY SIGNS LLC
2908 N Main St (27526-5497)
PHONE..................................919 642-3091
EMP: 4 **EST:** 2018
SALES (est): 88.2K **Privately Held**
SIC: 3993 Signs and advertising specialties

(G-4905)
WALKER STREET LLC
104 Birchland Dr (27526-6800)
PHONE..................................919 880-3959
Carl D Phelan, *Prin*
EMP: 4 **EST:** 2008
SALES (est): 345.77K **Privately Held**
SIC: 3842 Walkers

(G-4906)
WEATHERS MACHINE MFG INC
9535 Us 401 N (27526-8071)
PHONE..................................919 552-5945
Linda Weathers, *Pr*
Phillip Ray Weathers, *VP*
Gwen Weathers, *Sec*
EMP: 15 **EST:** 1973
SQ FT: 13,000
SALES (est): 4.24MM **Privately Held**
Web: www.weathersmfg.com
SIC: 5084 3599 Instruments and control
equipment; Machine shop, jobbing and
repair

(G-4907)
YOUR CHOICE PREGNANCY CLINIC
607 N Ennis St (27526-2014)
PHONE..................................919 577-9050
Tonya Nelson, *Brnch Mgr*
EMP: 4
SALES (corp-wide): 339.46K **Privately Held**
Web:
www.yourchoicepregnancyclinic.com
SIC: 2835 Pregnancy test kits
PA: Your Choice Pregnancy Clinic
1701 Jones Franklin Rd
Raleigh NC 27606
919 758-8444

Garland
Sampson County

(G-4908)
GARLAND APPAREL GROUP LLC
Also Called: Garland Heritage NC
120 S Church Ave (28441-1201)
P.O. Box 980368 (84098)
PHONE..................................646 647-2790
Kenneth Ragland, *Managing Member*
EMP: 40 **EST:** 2021
SALES (est): 2.54MM **Privately Held**
Web: www.garlandapparelgroup.com
SIC: 2326 Aprons, work, except rubberized
and plastic: men's

(G-4909)
GARLAND FARM SUPPLY INC (PA)
Also Called: Clinton Grains
250 N Belgrade Ave (28441-8100)
P.O. Box 741 (28441-0741)
PHONE..................................910 529-9731
Ernest Smith, *Pr*
Doris Smith, *VP*
Alfred Smith, *Sec*
Charles Smith, *Treas*
EMP: 15 **EST:** 1963
SQ FT: 15,000
SALES (est): 977.04K
SALES (corp-wide): 977.04K **Privately Held**
SIC: 0723 2048 Feed milling, custom
services; Prepared feeds, nec

(G-4910)
ROBERT L RICH TMBER HRVSTG INC
360 Rich Rd (28441-9718)
P.O. Box 272 (28441-0272)
PHONE..................................910 529-7321
Robert Rich, *Pr*
Daniel Rich, *VP*
Frances Rich, *Sec*
EMP: 8 **EST:** 1955
SALES (est): 242.78K **Privately Held**
SIC: 2411 2421 Logging camps and
contractors; Sawmills and planing mills,
general

▲ = Import ▼ = Export
◆ = Import/Export

Garner
Wake County

(G-4911)
A & G MACHINING LLC
333 Technical Ct Ste 33 (27529-2873)
PHONE..............................919 329-7207
Mark Paskovich, *Managing Member*
EMP: 5 EST: 2004
SALES (est): 918.69K Privately Held
Web: www.agmachinenc.com
SIC: 3599 Machine shop, jobbing and repair

(G-4912)
A BEAN COUNTER INC
176 Foxglove Dr (27529-7731)
PHONE..............................919 359-9586
Wilson L Feick, *Prin*
EMP: 4 EST: 2009
SALES (est): 196.67K Privately Held
SIC: 3131 Counters

(G-4913)
ALCAMI CAROLINAS CORPORATION
Also Called: Alcami
5100 Jones Sausage Rd Ste 110
(27529-3578)
PHONE..............................910 619-3952
EMP: 5
SALES (corp-wide): 418.48MM Privately
Held
Web: www.alcami.com
SIC: 2834 8734 8731 Drugs affecting
neoplasms and endrocrine systems;
Product testing laboratories; Biological
research
HQ: Alcami Carolinas Corporation
2320 Scientific Park Dr
Wilmington NC 28405

(G-4914)
**ALPHAGRAPHICS DOWNTOWN
RALEIGH**
Also Called: AlphaGraphics
3731 Centurion Dr (27529-8581)
PHONE..............................919 832-2828
EMP: 9 EST: 2019
SALES (est): 984.86K Privately Held
Web: www.alphagraphics.com
SIC: 2752 Commercial printing, lithographic

(G-4915)
AMERICAN LABEL TECH LLC
343 Technology Dr Ste 2106 (27529-6249)
PHONE..............................984 269-5078
Darrin Schmitt, *Pr*
Gustavo Garcia, *VP*
EMP: 11 EST: 2017
SQ FT: 12,000
SALES (est): 939.98K Privately Held
Web: www.americanlabeltech.com
SIC: 2759 Labels and seals: printing, nsk

(G-4916)
ARGOS USA LLC
Also Called: Redi-Mix Concrete
1915 W Garner Rd (27529-2819)
PHONE..............................919 772-4188
Kim Nielsen, *Mgr*
EMP: 37
SQ FT: 2,708
Web: www.argos-us.com
SIC: 3273 Ready-mixed concrete
HQ: Argos Usa Llc
3015 Windward Plz Ste 300
Alpharetta GA 30005
678 368-4300

(G-4917)
ASSEMBLY TECH COMPONENTS INC
Also Called: A T Components
467 Hein Dr (27529-7217)
P.O. Box 90697 (27675)
PHONE..............................919 773-0388
Mike Brown, *Pr*
EMP: 7 EST: 2000
SQ FT: 6,000
SALES (est): 2.02MM Privately Held
Web: www.atcomponents.com
SIC: 3625 Industrial controls: push button,
selector switches, pilot

(G-4918)
BUTTERBALL LLC (HQ)
Also Called: Gusto Packing Company
1 Butterball Ln (27529-5971)
P.O. Box 1547 (28086)
PHONE..............................919 255-7900
▼ EMP: 50 EST: 2006
SALES (est): 618.29MM
SALES (corp-wide): 9.1B Publicly Held
Web: www.butterballfoodservice.com
SIC: 2015 Turkey, processed, nsk
PA: Seaboard Corporation
9000 W 67th St
Merriam KS 66202
913 676-8928

(G-4919)
C E HICKS ENTERPRISES INC
Also Called: Auto Marine Boat Repairs
230 Us 70 Hwy E (27529-4050)
PHONE..............................919 772-5131
Ed Hicks, *Pr*
EMP: 10 EST: 1967
SALES (est): 490.68K Privately Held
SIC: 3732 Boatbuilding and repairing

(G-4920)
CARROLL CO
Also Called: East Carolina Trucks
5771 Nc Highway 42 W (27529-8445)
P.O. Box 18108 (27619-8108)
PHONE..............................919 779-1900
Robert Carroll, *Pr*
Robert Carrol, *Pr*
EMP: 10 EST: 1996
SALES (est): 1.93MM Privately Held
Web: www.carrollclean.com
SIC: 3713 3462 Truck bodies and parts; Iron
and steel forgings

(G-4921)
CBJ TRANSIT LLC
1220 Timber Dr E (27529-6917)
PHONE..............................252 417-9972
EMP: 56
SALES (est): 2.81MM Privately Held
SIC: 3537 Trucks: freight, baggage, etc.:
industrial, except mining

(G-4922)
COMMERCIAL PRINTING COMPANY
3731 Centurion Dr (27529-8581)
PHONE..............................919 832-2828
Ralph C Moore, *Pr*
Mory A Read, *VP*
Juliet B Moore, *Sec*
Linda Maxa, *Contrlr*
EMP: 20 EST: 1907
SALES (est): 4.73MM
SALES (corp-wide): 25.71MM Privately
Held
Web: www.comprintco.com
SIC: 2752 Offset printing
HQ: Alphagraphics, Inc.
143 Union Blvd Ste 650
Lakewood CO 80228
800 955-6246

(G-4923)
COMMSCOPE TECHNOLOGIES LLC
Also Called: Grayson Wireless
620 N Greenfield Pkwy (27529-6947)
PHONE..............................919 329-8700
Morgan Kurk, *Dir*
EMP: 9
SALES (corp-wide): 15.22B Publicly Held
Web: www.commscope.com
SIC: 3663 5065 Radio and t.v.
communications equipment; Electronic
parts and equipment, nec
HQ: Commscope Technologies Llc
3642 E Us Highway 70
Claremont NC 28610
828 324-2200

(G-4924)
COMPASS GROUP USA INC
Also Called: Canteen Raleigh/Durham
3300 Waterfield Dr (27529-6318)
PHONE..............................919 381-9577
EMP: 357
SALES (corp-wide): 42B Privately Held
Web: www.compass-usa.com
SIC: 5962 2099 Merchandising machine
operators; Food preparations, nec
HQ: Compass Group Usa, Inc.
2400 Yorkmont Rd
Charlotte NC 28217

(G-4925)
CONTEMPORARY PRODUCTS INC
275 Hein Dr (27529-7221)
PHONE..............................919 779-4228
Joan Squillini, *Pr*
EMP: 7 EST: 1979
SQ FT: 24,000
SALES (est): 189.68K Privately Held
Web:
www.ceocontemporaryproducts.com
SIC: 3499 3423 Trophies, metal, except
silver; Engravers' tools, hand

(G-4926)
CREEK LIFE LLC
Also Called: Merch Unlimited
471 Cleveland Crossing Dr Ste 101
(27529-7840)
PHONE..............................910 892-9337
Charles Royal, *Managing Member*
EMP: 7 EST: 2017
SALES (est): 79.67K Privately Held
SIC: 3999 Manufacturing industries, nec

(G-4927)
CROWN EQUIPMENT CORPORATION
Also Called: Crown Lift Trucks
1000 N Greenfield Pkwy Ste 1090
(27529-6955)
PHONE..............................919 773-4160
EMP: 42
SALES (corp-wide): 7.12B Privately Held
Web: www.crown.com
SIC: 3537 Lift trucks, industrial: fork,
platform, straddle, etc.
PA: Crown Equipment Corporation
44 S Washington St
New Bremen OH 45869
419 629-2311

(G-4928)
CUSTOM CANVAS WORKS INC
Also Called: Awnings Etc
540 Dynamic Dr (27529-2508)
PHONE..............................919 662-4800
Donald K Kelly, *Pr*
EMP: 9 EST: 1976
SQ FT: 6,000
SALES (est): 471.12K Privately Held
Web: www.customcanvasworks.com

SIC: 2394 Awnings, fabric: made from
purchased materials

(G-4929)
**GENERAL REFRIGERATION
COMPANY**
96 Shipwash Dr (27529-6861)
PHONE..............................919 661-4727
Jim Thompson, *Pr*
EMP: 8
SALES (corp-wide): 25.94MM Privately
Held
Web: www.generalrefrig.com
SIC: 1711 3494 7692 Refrigeration contractor
; Pipe fittings; Welding repair
PA: General Refrigeration Company
34971 Sussex Hwy
Delmar DE 19940
302 846-3073

(G-4930)
**HAMLIN SHEET METAL COMPANY
INCORPORATED (PA)**
1411 W Garner Rd (27529-3029)
P.O. Box 465 (27529-0465)
PHONE..............................919 772-8780
◆ EMP: 25 EST: 1954
SALES (est): 13.19MM
SALES (corp-wide): 13.19MM Privately
Held
Web: www.hamlincos.com
SIC: 3444 Ducts, sheet metal

(G-4931)
HIPRA SCIENTIFIC USA
3835 Generosity Ct Ste 108 (27529-6233)
PHONE..............................919 605-8256
EMP: 6 EST: 2019
SALES (est): 727.36K Privately Held
Web: www.hipra.com
SIC: 2834 Pharmaceutical preparations

(G-4932)
HOWARD BROTHERS MFG LLC
1321 Bobbitt Dr (27529-3039)
PHONE..............................919 772-4800
Matthew G Howard, *Managing Member*
EMP: 4 EST: 2012
SALES (est): 785.16K Privately Held
SIC: 2421 Building and structural materials,
wood

(G-4933)
HUDSON S HARDWARE INC (PA)
Also Called: Do It Best
305 Benson Rd (27529-3003)
PHONE..............................919 553-3030
Leigh S Hudson, *Pr*
Helen B Hudson, *Sec*
▲ EMP: 22 EST: 1958
SQ FT: 22,000
SALES (est): 3.89MM
SALES (corp-wide): 3.89MM Privately
Held
Web: www.hudsonshardware.com
SIC: 5251 3999 Hardware stores; Pet
supplies

(G-4934)
IMPROVED NATURE LLC
101 Vandora Springs Rd (27529-5336)
PHONE..............................919 588-2299
Richard Hawkins, *Pr*
EMP: 51 EST: 2015
SALES (est): 5.61MM Privately Held
Web: www.improvednature.com
SIC: 2099 Food preparations, nec

(G-4935)
KONICA MNLTA HLTHCARE AMRCAS I
2217 Us 70 Hwy E (27529-9424)
PHONE.................................919 792-6420
EMP: 38
Web: healthcare.konicaminolta.us
SIC: 8732 3825 Business research service; Digital test equipment, electronic and electrical circuits
HQ: Konica Minolta Healthcare Americas, Inc.
411 Newark Pompton Tpke
Wayne NJ 07470
973 633-1500

(G-4936)
LEGACY GRAPHICS INC
191 Technology Dr (27529-9289)
P.O. Box 5279 (27512-5279)
PHONE.................................919 741-6262
Peter A Reckert, Pr
Robert Price, VP
EMP: 10 EST: 2007
SQ FT: 7,500
SALES (est): 496.66K Privately Held
Web: www.resourcelabel.com
SIC: 2752 Offset printing

(G-4937)
MANNING BUILDING PRODUCTS LLC
108 Professional Ct Ste A (27529-7975)
PHONE.................................919 662-9894
David Manning, Managing Member
EMP: 6 EST: 2010
SQ FT: 4,200
SALES (est): 309.21K Privately Held
Web: www.permaboot.co
SIC: 2452 Prefabricated buildings, wood

(G-4938)
MARIETTA MARTIN MATERIALS INC
Also Called: Martin Marietta
1111 E Garner Rd (27529-8746)
P.O. Box 37 (27529-0037)
PHONE.................................919 772-3563
Ben Brown, Mgr
EMP: 9
SQ FT: 12,039
Web: www.martinmarietta.com
SIC: 1422 Crushed and broken limestone
PA: Martin Marietta Materials Inc
4123 Parklake Ave
Raleigh NC 27612

(G-4939)
MARTIN WELDING INC
816 Old Crowder Dr (27529-9768)
PHONE.................................919 436-8805
Martin Montes Maldonado, Pr
EMP: 6 EST: 2017
SALES (est): 500.4K Privately Held
SIC: 7692 Welding repair

(G-4940)
MDN CABINETS INC
Also Called: M D N Cabinets
3411 Integrity Dr Ste 100 (27529-6226)
PHONE.................................919 662-1090
Justin Hanlon, Pr
EMP: 7 EST: 1987
SALES (est): 4.19MM Privately Held
Web: www.mdncabinets.com
SIC: 2434 Wood kitchen cabinets

(G-4941)
MEDLIT SOLUTIONS
191 Technology Dr (27529-9289)
PHONE.................................919 878-6789

EMP: 6
SALES (est): 79.3K Privately Held
Web: www.medlitsolutions.com
SIC: 2752 Commercial printing, lithographic

(G-4942)
MEDLIT SOLUTIONS LLC (HQ)
191 Technology Dr (27529-9289)
PHONE.................................919 878-6789
Kevin Grogan, CEO
▲ EMP: 58 EST: 1987
SQ FT: 7,500
SALES (est): 14.81MM Privately Held
Web: www.resourcelabel.com
SIC: 2791 2752 2789 2759 Typesetting; Offset printing; Bookbinding and related work; Commercial printing, nec
PA: Resource Label Group, Llc
2550 Mridian Blvd Ste 370
Franklin TN 37067

(G-4943)
MODUSLINK CORPORATION
990 N Greenfield Pkwy (27529-6953)
PHONE.................................781 663-5000
Brenda Rice, Brnch Mgr
EMP: 24
SALES (corp-wide): 174.11MM Privately Held
Web: www.moduslink.com
SIC: 7372 Prepackaged software
HQ: Moduslink Corporation
2000 Midway Ln
Smyrna TN 37167
615 267-6100

(G-4944)
MOHAWK INDUSTRIES INC
Also Called: Mohawk Industries
2000 Pergo Pkwy (27529-8553)
PHONE.................................919 661-5590
EMP: 18
Web: www.mohawkind.com
SIC: 2273 Finishers of tufted carpets and rugs
PA: Mohawk Industries, Inc.
160 S Industrial Blvd
Calhoun GA 30701

(G-4945)
MOHAWK INDUSTRIES INC
800 N Greenfield Pkwy (27529-6951)
PHONE.................................919 609-4759
EMP: 8
Web: www.mohawkind.com
SIC: 5735 2273 Video discs and tapes, prerecorded; Carpets and rugs
PA: Mohawk Industries, Inc.
160 S Industrial Blvd
Calhoun GA 30701

(G-4946)
MONTYS WELDING & FABRICATION
157 Creek Commons Ave (27529-2881)
PHONE.................................919 337-7859
EMP: 5 EST: 2017
SALES (est): 50.04K Privately Held
Web: www.montyswelding.com
SIC: 7692 Welding repair

(G-4947)
MORRIS & ASSOCIATES INC
803 Morris Dr (27529-4037)
PHONE.................................919 582-9200
◆ EMP: 51 EST: 1949
SALES (est): 13.47MM Privately Held
Web: www.morristhermal.com
SIC: 3585 Refrigeration and heating equipment

(G-4948)
MUSIC & ARTS
2566 Timber Dr (27529-2589)
PHONE.................................919 329-6069
EMP: 4 EST: 1952
SALES (est): 43.98K Privately Held
Web: stores.musicarts.com
SIC: 8299 5736 3931 Schools and educational services, nec; Musical instrument stores; Musical instruments

(G-4949)
NEWS AND OBSERVER PUBG CO
Also Called: News & Observer Recycling Ctr
1402 Mechanical Blvd (27529-2539)
PHONE.................................919 829-8903
Danny Collins, Brnch Mgr
EMP: 43
SALES (corp-wide): 1.39B Privately Held
SIC: 2711 Newspapers, publishing and printing
HQ: The News And Observer Publishing Company
421 Fayetteville St # 104
Raleigh NC 27601
919 829-4500

(G-4950)
OLD SCHOOL CRUSHING CO INC
250 Old Mechanical Ct (27529-2596)
PHONE.................................919 661-0011
John Dillinger, Pr
EMP: 6 EST: 2012
SALES (est): 897.77K Privately Held
SIC: 2611 Pulp mills, mechanical and recycling processing

(G-4951)
PC SIGNS & GRAPHICS LLC
180 Hein Dr (27529-8546)
PHONE.................................919 661-5801
EMP: 7 EST: 1996
SALES (est): 747.62K Privately Held
Web: www.pcsigns.biz
SIC: 3993 7389 Signs and advertising specialties; Business Activities at Non-Commercial Site

(G-4952)
PEPSI BOTTLING VENTURES LLC
1900 Treygan Rd (27529-3592)
PHONE.................................919 865-2388
Derek Hill, CEO
EMP: 95
Web: www.pepsibottlingventures.com
SIC: 2086 Carbonated soft drinks, bottled and canned
HQ: Pepsi Bottling Ventures Llc
4141 Parklake Ave
Raleigh NC 27612
919 865-2300

(G-4953)
PEPSI BOTTLING VENTURES LLC
Also Called: Pepsi-Cola
1900 Pepsi Way Fl 1 (27529-7232)
PHONE.................................919 863-4000
Tom Wiza, Mgr
EMP: 234
Web: www.pepsibottlingventures.com
SIC: 2086 5149 Carbonated soft drinks, bottled and canned; Groceries and related products, nec
HQ: Pepsi Bottling Ventures Llc
4141 Parklake Ave
Raleigh NC 27612
919 865-2300

(G-4954)
POWERSOLVE CORPORATION LLC
117b Pierce Rd (27529-7909)
PHONE.................................919 662-8515
EMP: 11 EST: 2017
SALES (est): 4.96MM Privately Held
Web: www.powersolve.com
SIC: 7372 Prepackaged software

(G-4955)
PRECISION SIGNS INC
5455 Raynor Rd (27529-9452)
PHONE.................................919 615-0979
Laurie Peach, Pr
Daniel Peach, VP
EMP: 4 EST: 2013
SQ FT: 2,100
SALES (est): 360.24K Privately Held
Web: www.precisionsignsnc.com
SIC: 3993 Signs, not made in custom sign painting shops

(G-4956)
PROVEN PROF CNSTR SVCS LLC
Also Called: PPCS
463 Cleveland Crossing Dr Ste 101 (27529-7832)
PHONE.................................919 821-2696
Michael L Imes, Managing Member
EMP: 12 EST: 2011
SALES (est): 1.28MM Privately Held
Web: www.provenpcs.com
SIC: 1389 1711 Construction, repair, and dismantling services; Plumbing contractors

(G-4957)
R & H WELDING LLC
3020 Cornwallis Rd (27529-7617)
PHONE.................................919 763-7955
Ruben Hernandez-trejo, Prin
EMP: 4 EST: 2015
SALES (est): 831.86K Privately Held
Web: r-h-welding-llc.business.site
SIC: 7692 Welding repair

(G-4958)
RED ADEPT PUBLISHING LLC
104 Bugenfield Ct (27529-3790)
PHONE.................................919 798-7410
EMP: 4 EST: 2018
SALES (est): 109.38K Privately Held
Web: www.redadeptpublishing.com
SIC: 2741 Miscellaneous publishing

(G-4959)
ROOFING SUPPLY
3609 Jones Sausage Rd (27529-9495)
PHONE.................................919 779-6223
Joan Pitcer, Prin
EMP: 7 EST: 2016
SALES (est): 297.19K Privately Held
SIC: 3531 Construction machinery

(G-4960)
RVB SYSTEMS GROUP INC
5504 Quails Call Ct (27529-7421)
P.O. Box 966 (27512-0966)
PHONE.................................919 362-5211
Robert Brown, Pr
EMP: 5 EST: 1997
SALES (est): 763.67K Privately Held
Web: www.barcode-solutions.com
SIC: 5084 7372 7371 Industrial machinery and equipment; Business oriented computer software; Computer software development

(G-4961)
S T WOOTEN CORPORATION
Also Called: Newport/Morehead Cy Con Plant

12200 Cleveland Rd (27529-8181)
PHONE...................252 393-2206
Seth Wooten, *Pr*
EMP: 22
SALES (corp-wide): 319.83MM **Privately Held**
Web: www.stwcorp.com
SIC: 3531 Concrete plants
PA: S. T. Wooten Corporation
3801 Black Creek Rd Se
Wilson NC 27894
252 291-5165

(G-4962)
S T WOOTEN CORPORATION
Also Called: Garner Concrete Plant
925 E Garner Rd (27529-3328)
PHONE...................919 779-6089
Jeff Palmer, *Mgr*
EMP: 28
SALES (corp-wide): 319.83MM **Privately Held**
Web: www.stwcorp.com
SIC: 3531 Concrete plants
PA: S. T. Wooten Corporation
3801 Black Creek Rd Se
Wilson NC 27894
252 291-5165

(G-4963)
S T WOOTEN CORPORATION
Also Called: Garner Concrete Plant
12204 Cleveland Rd (27529-8181)
PHONE...................919 779-7589
Reed Dawson, *Mgr*
EMP: 40
SALES (corp-wide): 319.83MM **Privately Held**
Web: www.stwcorp.com
SIC: 3531 Concrete plants
PA: S. T. Wooten Corporation
3801 Black Creek Rd Se
Wilson NC 27894
252 291-5165

(G-4964)
SIGMA ENGINEERED SOLUTIONS PC (PA)
120 Sigma Dr (27529-8542)
PHONE...................919 773-0011
Viren Joshi, *Pr*
Niteen Inamdar, *
Neville Kharas, *
Umesh Joshi, *Executive Global Human Resources Vice-President**
Kirankumar Acharya, *Global Chief Financial Officer**
▲ EMP: 95 EST: 2008
SQ FT: 185,000
SALES (est): 97.51MM
SALES (corp-wide): 97.51MM **Privately Held**
Web:
www.sigmaengineeringsolutions.com
SIC: 5063 3644 Electrical fittings and construction materials; Noncurrent-carrying wiring devices

(G-4965)
SPECIALIZED RETAIL SVCS LLC
115 Callisto Way (27529-6181)
PHONE...................727 639-0804
David Rodriguez, *Managing Member*
EMP: 4 EST: 2006
SALES (est): 282.16K **Privately Held**
SIC: 2541 Store and office display cases and fixtures

(G-4966)
SPECTRUM SCREEN PRTG SVC INC
1232 Open Field Dr (27529)

PHONE...................919 481-9905
Harry Gould, *Pr*
Donna Gould, *Sec*
EMP: 10 EST: 1986
SALES (est): 386.94K **Privately Held**
Web: www.spectrumscreen.com
SIC: 2759 Screen printing

(G-4967)
T & R SIGNS
Also Called: T & R Signs & Screen Printing
110 E Main St (27529-3238)
PHONE...................919 779-1185
Stan Powell, *Owner*
EMP: 5 EST: 1983
SQ FT: 4,000
SALES (est): 106.71K **Privately Held**
SIC: 3993 2261 5199 2752 Signs, not made in custom sign painting shops; Screen printing of cotton broadwoven fabrics; Advertising specialties; Offset printing

(G-4968)
TRIANGLE STEEL SYSTEMS LLC
133 Us 70 Hwy W (27529-3942)
PHONE...................919 615-0282
Kyle Reece, *Pr*
EMP: 4 EST: 2014
SALES (est): 2.38MM **Privately Held**
Web: www.specifichouse.com
SIC: 3441 Fabricated structural metal

(G-4969)
UNIQUE CONCEPTS
310 Shipwash Dr Ste 101 (27529-6893)
P.O. Box 1471 (27528-1471)
PHONE...................919 366-2001
Lonnie Sawyer Junior, *Owner*
EMP: 4 EST: 2005
SALES (est): 466.44K **Privately Held**
Web: www.uniqueconcepts.com
SIC: 3599 Machine shop, jobbing and repair

(G-4970)
USA DREAMSTONE LLC
Also Called: Dreamstone Gran MBL & Quartz
128 Yeargan Rd Ste C (27529-5504)
PHONE...................919 615-4329
Rafael Preto, *Owner*
EMP: 4 EST: 2015
SALES (est): 1.25MM **Privately Held**
Web: www.usadreamstone.com
SIC: 3679 3281 Quartz crystals, for electronic application; Marble, building: cut and shaped

(G-4971)
VIZTEK LLC
2217 Us 70 Hwy E (27529-9424)
P.O. Box 122272 (75312-2272)
PHONE...................919 792-6420
EMP: 50
Web: healthcare.konicaminolta.us
SIC: 8732 3825 Business research service; Digital test equipment, electronic and electrical circuits

(G-4972)
WEBBS LOGISTICS LLC
111 Saint Marys St (27529-3129)
PHONE...................919 591-4308
EMP: 10 EST: 2020
SALES (est): 1.31MM **Privately Held**
SIC: 3537 Trucks, tractors, loaders, carriers, and similar equipment

(G-4973)
WELDING SPC & MECH SVCS INC
Also Called: Welding Specialties & Mech Svc
555 Dynamic Dr (27529-2509)

P.O. Box 818 (27529-0818)
PHONE...................919 662-7898
Victor Hocutt, *Pr*
Victor A Hocutt, *Pr*
Sandy S Council, *Pr*
Rose H Hocutt, *Sec*
EMP: 9 EST: 1994
SQ FT: 3,000
SALES (est): 838.75K **Privately Held**
Web: www.wsmsnc.com
SIC: 7692 Welding repair

(G-4974)
WILSONS PLANNING & CONSULTING
1402 Harth Dr (27529-4817)
PHONE...................919 592-0935
Wilson Latrice, *Prin*
EMP: 4 EST: 2017
SALES (est): 91.96K **Privately Held**
SIC: 2752 Commercial printing, lithographic

(G-4975)
WURTH REVCAR FASTENERS INC
Also Called: WURTH REVCAR FASTENERS, INC.
800 N Greenfield Pkwy Ste 810 (27529-6951)
PHONE...................919 772-9930
Ron Mcgaugh, *Brnch Mgr*
EMP: 28
SALES (corp-wide): 22.17B **Privately Held**
Web: www.wurthindustry.com
SIC: 3399 Metal fasteners
HQ: Wurth Industry Usa Inc.
1 Avery Row
Roanoke VA 24012
540 561-6565

(G-4976)
XYLEM INC
1328 Bobbitt Dr (27529-3040)
PHONE...................919 772-4126
Stefan Van Staveren, *Pr*
Jamie Smith, *VP*
EMP: 7 EST: 1995
SALES (est): 500K **Privately Held**
Web: www.xylemonline.com
SIC: 2434 2521 2511 Wood kitchen cabinets ; Wood office furniture; Wood household furniture

Garysburg
Northampton County

(G-4977)
PRIZE MANAGEMENT LLC
8287 Nc Highway 46 (27831-9616)
PHONE...................252 532-1939
EMP: 7 EST: 2018
SALES (est): 230.15K **Privately Held**
SIC: 1442 Sand mining

Gaston
Northampton County

(G-4978)
CLARY LUMBER COMPANY
204 Mitchell St (27832-9787)
PHONE...................252 537-2558
John C Lucy Junior, *Ch Bd*
John C Lucy Iii, *Pr*
EMP: 68 EST: 1969
SQ FT: 1,800
SALES (est): 1.69MM **Privately Held**
Web: www.clarylumber.com
SIC: 2421 2448 2426 Lumber: rough, sawed, or planed; Wood pallets and skids; Hardwood dimension and flooring mills

(G-4979)
MICHAEL H BRANCH INC
Also Called: Branch Welding Greensville Co
1621 Old Emporia Rd (27832-9570)
PHONE...................252 532-0930
Michael Branch, *Owner*
EMP: 8 EST: 2008
SALES (est): 768.74K **Privately Held**
Web: www.branchwelding.com
SIC: 3842 Welders' hoods

Gastonia
Gaston County

(G-4980)
277 METAL INC
201 Davis Heights Dr (28052-6392)
PHONE...................704 372-4513
Jeremy Yaekel, *Prin*
EMP: 6 EST: 2017
SALES (est): 482.84K **Privately Held**
Web: www.277metal.com
SIC: 7692 Welding repair

(G-4981)
310 SIGN COMPANY
5439 Candlewick Trl (28056-8935)
PHONE...................704 910-2242
Amy Nannini, *Prin*
EMP: 4 EST: 2010
SALES (est): 172.1K **Privately Held**
Web: www.310signs.com
SIC: 3993 Signs and advertising specialties

(G-4982)
A B CARTER INC (PA)
Also Called: Carter Traveler Division
4801 York Hwy (28052)
P.O. Box 518 (28053)
PHONE...................704 865-1201
J Bynum Carter, *CEO*
J Bynum Carter, *Ch Bd*
T Henderson Wise, *Pr*
Louis Mitchell, *VP Fin*
▲ EMP: 61 EST: 1922
SQ FT: 140,000
SALES (est): 24.75MM
SALES (corp-wide): 24.75MM **Privately Held**
Web: www.abcarter.com
SIC: 3315 3552 Welded steel wire fabric; Textile machinery

(G-4983)
ACME DIE & MACHINE CORPORATION
202 Trakas Blvd (28052-9221)
P.O. Box 12507 (28052-0021)
PHONE...................704 864-8426
Richard Littlejohn, *Pr*
Stephen Littlejohn, *VP*
Helen Littlejohn, *Treas*
Sandra Wilson, *Sec*
EMP: 10 EST: 1965
SQ FT: 12,000
SALES (est): 746.04K **Privately Held**
SIC: 3599 3544 Machine shop, jobbing and repair; Special dies, tools, jigs, and fixtures

(G-4984)
ADVANCE MACHINING CO GASTONIA
Also Called: Advanced Machining Co
3517 W Franklin Blvd (28052-9488)
P.O. Box 757 (28053-0757)
PHONE...................704 866-7411
Paul W Medford, *Pr*
Dwayne Medford, *VP*
Tina Medford, *Sec*

GEOGRAPHIC

EMP: 6 EST: 1980
SQ FT: 4,000
SALES (est): 204.56K **Privately Held**
SIC: 3544 3599 Special dies and tools;
　　Machine shop, jobbing and repair

(G-4985)
ALL AMERICAN BRAIDS INC
1613 Warren Ave (28054-7451)
P.O. Box 789 (28164-0789)
PHONE.........................704 852-4380
John L Larson Junior, *Pr*
Robyn Ann Larson, *
EMP: 30 EST: 1995
SALES (est): 1.08MM **Privately Held**
Web: www.allamericanbraids.com
SIC: 2241 2298 Braids, textile; Cordage and
　　twine

(G-4986)
ALLIANCE MCH & FABRICATION LLC
3421 Fairview Dr (28052-7162)
P.O. Box 76 (28034-0076)
PHONE.........................704 629-5677
Jeremy Burns, *Managing Member*
EMP: 7 EST: 2011
SALES (est): 3.21MM **Privately Held**
SIC: 3441 Fabricated structural metal

(G-4987)
ALTUS FINISHING LLC
1711 Sparta Ct (28052-9111)
P.O. Box 3736 (28054-0038)
PHONE.........................704 861-1536
Ron Sytz, *Pr*
Janet Sytz Ctrl, *Prin*
EMP: 25 EST: 2018
SALES (est): 1.61MM
SALES (corp-wide): 23.38MM **Privately
Held**
SIC: 2231 Bleaching, dying and specialty
　　treating: wool, mohair, etc.
PA: Beverly Knits, Inc.
　　1675 Garfield Dr
　　Gastonia NC 28052
　　704 861-1536

(G-4988)
AMBASSADOR SERVICES INC
Also Called: Beyond This Day
1520 S York Rd (28052-6138)
PHONE.........................800 576-8627
Robert M Gallagher, *CEO*
EMP: 185 EST: 1998
SALES (est): 1.14MM
SALES (corp-wide): 12.64MM **Privately
Held**
Web: www.milestonescompany.com
SIC: 2731 Books, publishing only
PA: Good Will Publishers, Inc.
　　1520 S York Rd
　　Gastonia NC 28052
　　704 853-3237

(G-4989)
AMERICAN & EFIRD LLC
401 Grover St (28054-3231)
P.O. Box 507 (28120-0507)
PHONE.........................704 867-3664
Brian Mull, *Brnch Mgr*
EMP: 19
SALES (corp-wide): 1.98B **Privately Held**
Web: www.amefird.com
SIC: 2284 Thread mills
HQ: American & Efird Llc
　　24 American St
　　Mount Holly NC 28120
　　704 827-4311

(G-4990)
AMERICAN & EFIRD LLC
Also Called: American & Efird 56
3200 York Hwy (28056)
PHONE.........................704 864-0977
Morris Dillenger, *Mgr*
EMP: 14
SALES (corp-wide): 1.98B **Privately Held**
Web: www.amefird.com
SIC: 2284 2281 Thread mills; Yarn spinning
　　mills
HQ: American & Efird Llc
　　24 American St
　　Mount Holly NC 28120
　　704 827-4311

(G-4991)
AMERICAN FORMS MFG INC (PA)
170 Tarheel Dr (28056-8719)
PHONE.........................704 866-9139
Calvin Price, *Ch*
David Price, *
Karen P Carpenter, *Stockholder**
Ann R Daniels, *Stockholder**
▲ **EMP: 26 EST:** 1990
SQ FT: 35,000
SALES (est): 2.31MM **Privately Held**
Web: www.americanformsmfg.com
SIC: 5943 2761 Office forms and supplies;
　　Manifold business forms

(G-4992)
AMERICAN LINC CORPORATION
159 Wolfpack Rd (28056-9776)
P.O. Box 518 (28053)
PHONE.........................704 861-9242
D Lynn Hoover, *Pr*
Danny Lockman, *
◆ **EMP: 30 EST:** 1985
SQ FT: 20,000
SALES (est): 2.74MM **Privately Held**
Web: www.americanlinc.com
SIC: 3599 5084 3552 Machine shop, jobbing
　　and repair; Industrial machinery and
　　equipment; Textile machinery

(G-4993)
**AMERICAN METAL FABRICATORS
INC**
2608 Lowell Rd (28054-1428)
PHONE.........................704 824-8585
EMP: 35 EST: 1988
SALES (est): 4.84MM **Privately Held**
Web: www.americanmetalfabinc.com
SIC: 3443 Fabricated plate work (boiler shop)

(G-4994)
AMPED EVENTS LLC
401 S Marietta St (28052-4651)
PHONE.........................888 683-4386
EMP: 12 EST: 2008
SQ FT: 4,000
SALES (est): 988.38K **Privately Held**
SIC: 2759 Screen printing

(G-4995)
ATKINSON INTERNATIONAL INC
3800 Little Mountain Rd (28056-6875)
P.O. Box 6303 (28056-6020)
PHONE.........................704 865-7750
Claire Atkinson, *Pr*
Darin Atkinson, *
Connie Atkinson, *
▲ **EMP: 23 EST:** 2004
SQ FT: 196,000
SALES (est): 4.94MM **Privately Held**
SIC: 3714 Air brakes, motor vehicle

(G-4996)
AZUSA INTERNATIONAL INC
2510 N Chester St (28052-1808)
P.O. Box 550336 (28055-0336)
PHONE.........................704 879-4464
Zeshan Lakhani, *Pr*
▲ **EMP: 5 EST:** 2011
SALES (est): 477.43K **Privately Held**
SIC: 2299 Fabrics: linen, jute, hemp, ramie

(G-4997)
BELT SHOP INC
1941 Chespark Dr (28052-9108)
PHONE.........................704 865-3636
Donna Badger, *Pr*
James Mull, *VP*
Gloria Mull, *CFO*
Mark Mull, *Sec*
EMP: 15 EST: 1988
SQ FT: 18,000
SALES (est): 4.08MM **Privately Held**
Web: www.industrialbeltshop.com
SIC: 3496 3052 2387 2386 Conveyor belts;
　　Transmission belting, rubber; Apparel belts;
　　Leather and sheep-lined clothing

(G-4998)
BETTER BUSINESS PRINTING INC
Also Called: International Minute Press
495 E Long Ave (28054-2526)
PHONE.........................704 867-3366
Pamela Joles, *Pr*
Bill Joles, *Pr*
EMP: 9 EST: 1991
SQ FT: 6,000
SALES (est): 1.7MM **Privately Held**
Web: www.impressnc.com
SIC: 2752 7334 Offset printing;
　　Photocopying and duplicating services

(G-4999)
BEVERLY KNITS INC
1640 Federal St (28052-0502)
PHONE.........................704 964-0835
Ronald M Sytz, *Pr*
EMP: 41
SALES (corp-wide): 23.38MM **Privately
Held**
Web: www.beverlyknits.com
SIC: 2211 Broadwoven fabric mills, cotton
PA: Beverly Knits, Inc.
　　1675 Garfield Dr
　　Gastonia NC 28052
　　704 861-1536

(G-5000)
BEVERLY KNITS INC (PA)
1675 Garfield Dr (28052-8403)
P.O. Box 3736 (28054-0038)
PHONE.........................704 861-1536
▲ **EMP: 49 EST:** 1980
SALES (est): 23.38MM
SALES (corp-wide): 23.38MM **Privately
Held**
Web: www.beverlyknits.com
SIC: 2211 Broadwoven fabric mills, cotton

(G-5001)
BLUE STEEL INC
4905 Sparrow Dairy Rd (28056-8940)
PHONE.........................704 864-2583
Jack Barbee, *Pr*
Dwain Barbee, *VP*
EMP: 4 EST: 1994
SALES (est): 662.59K **Privately Held**
SIC: 3599 Machine shop, jobbing and repair

(G-5002)
BOWEN MACHINE COMPANY INC
3421 Fairview Dr (28052-7162)

PHONE.........................704 629-9111
Stuart Bowen Junior, *Pr*
Jonathan Bowen, *
EMP: 5 EST: 1979
SQ FT: 20,000
SALES (est): 650.6K **Privately Held**
Web: www.bowenmachine.com
SIC: 3599 Machine shop, jobbing and repair

(G-5003)
BP ASSOCIATES INC (PA)
2408 Forbes Rd (28056-6267)
P.O. Box 12885 (28052-0043)
PHONE.........................704 864-3032
Roger Bingham, *Pr*
Pat Bingham, *
◆ **EMP: 139 EST:** 1994
SQ FT: 167,000
SALES (est): 37.26MM **Privately Held**
Web: www.ifabrication.com
SIC: 3441 Fabricated structural metal

(G-5004)
BP ASSOCIATES INC
105 Wolfpack Rd (28056-9776)
PHONE.........................704 833-1494
EMP: 411
Web: www.ifabrication.com
SIC: 3441 Fabricated structural metal
PA: Bp Associates Inc.
　　2408 Forbes Rd
　　Gastonia NC 28056

(G-5005)
**BRIDGESTONE RET OPERATIONS
LLC**
Also Called: Firestone
142 N New Hope Rd (28054-4755)
PHONE.........................704 861-8146
Davon Bryd, *Mgr*
EMP: 10
Web: www.bridgestoneamericas.com
SIC: 5531 7534 Automotive tires; Rebuilding
　　and retreading tires
HQ: Bridgestone Retail Operations, Llc
　　200 4th Ave S Ste 100
　　Nashville TN 37201
　　615 937-1000

(G-5006)
BULK SAK INTERNATIONAL INC
1302 Industrial Pike Rd (28052-8430)
PHONE.........................704 833-1361
EMP: 30
SALES (corp-wide): 104.52MM **Privately
Held**
Web: www.sonoco.com
SIC: 2673 Bags: plastic, laminated, and
　　coated
HQ: Bulk Sak International, Inc.
　　103 Industrial Dr
　　Malvern AR 72104

(G-5007)
**BURLAN MANUFACTURING LLC
(PA)**
Also Called: Carolina Strapping Buckles Co
2740 W Franklin Blvd (28052-9480)
PHONE.........................704 867-3548
William Lee Cornwell, *Pr*
Suzanne M Landis, *
Kevin Wassil, *
David Devane, *
David Hinson, *
◆ **EMP: 150 EST:** 1971
SQ FT: 200,000
SALES (est): 24.45MM
SALES (corp-wide): 24.45MM **Privately
Held**
Web: www.burlan.com

▲ = Import ▼ = Export
◆ = Import/Export

SIC: 2296 Fabric for reinforcing industrial belting

(G-5008)
BURNETT MACHINE COMPANY INC
924 Hanover St (28054-2452)
PHONE..............................704 867-7786
Robert D Burnett, *Pr*
Robert M Burnett, *Stockholder*
Tim Hickson, *VP*
EMP: 10 EST: 1976
SQ FT: 6,400
SALES (est): 916.38K Privately Held
Web: www.burnettmachine.com
SIC: 3552 3599 Textile machinery; Machine and other job shop work

(G-5009)
C & R HARD CHROME SERVICE INC
940 Hanover St (28054-2452)
PHONE..............................704 861-8831
William A Cottingham, *Pr*
Charles Martin Reynolds, *VP*
Dora Cottingham, *Sec*
Jerri Reynolds, *Treas*
EMP: 7 EST: 1967
SQ FT: 5,000
SALES (est): 720.62K Privately Held
Web: www.cr-plating.com
SIC: 3471 Chromium plating of metals or formed products

(G-5010)
C L RABB INC
103 Wolfpack Rd (28056-9776)
P.O. Box P.O. Box 6009 (28056-6000)
PHONE..............................704 865-0295
Bryan Rabb, *CEO*
Bryan E Rabb, *
Suzanne T Rabb, *
Chris Rabb, *
Beverly Mcdonald, *Sec*
EMP: 48 EST: 1986
SQ FT: 45,000
SALES (est): 24.56MM Privately Held
Web: www.clrabb.com
SIC: 5113 2655 2653 Industrial and personal service paper; Ammunition cans or tubes, board laminated with metal foil; Corrugated boxes, partitions, display items, sheets, and pad

(G-5011)
CAROLINA BRUSH COMPANY
3093 Northwest Blvd (28052-1166)
P.O. Box 2469 (28053-2469)
PHONE..............................704 867-0286
Fred P Spach, *Pr*
Barbara Glenn, *CEO*
Gerrii Spach, *Ch Bd*
▲ EMP: 46 EST: 1919
SQ FT: 27,000
SALES (est): 4.37MM
SALES (corp-wide): 4.37MM Privately Held
Web: www.carolinabrush.com
SIC: 5085 3991 Brushes, industrial; Brooms and brushes
PA: Carolina Brush Manufacturing Company Inc
3093 Northwest Blvd
Gastonia NC 28052
704 867-0286

(G-5012)
CAROLINA BRUSH MFG CO (PA)
3093 Northwest Blvd (28052-1166)
P.O. Box 2469 (28053-2469)
PHONE..............................704 867-0286
Fred Spach, *Pr*
Gerrii Spach, *Ch Bd*

Jonathan Hicks, *Treas*
▲ EMP: 43 EST: 1919
SQ FT: 27,000
SALES (est): 4.37MM
SALES (corp-wide): 4.37MM Privately Held
Web: www.carolinabrush.com
SIC: 3991 Brushes, household or industrial

(G-5013)
CAROLINA CUSTOM TANK LLC
924 Dr Martin Luther King Jr Way (28054-7301)
PHONE..............................980 406-3200
▲ EMP: 8 EST: 2012
SALES (est): 1.96MM Privately Held
Web: www.tricktank.com
SIC: 3795 Tanks and tank components

(G-5014)
CAROLINA WARP PRINTS INC
221 Meek Rd (28056-8122)
PHONE..............................704 866-4763
Vincent N Murphy, *Pr*
Vincent N Nat Murphy, *Pr*
Tessia Steele, *VP*
▲ EMP: 10 EST: 1988
SQ FT: 9,200
SALES (est): 238.81K Privately Held
SIC: 2752 Poster and decal printing, lithographic

(G-5015)
CENTURION INDUSTRIES INC
1990 Industrial Pike Rd (28052-8436)
PHONE..............................704 867-2304
EMP: 79
SALES (corp-wide): 242.37MM Privately Held
Web: www.centurionind.com
SIC: 3444 Canopies, sheet metal
PA: Centurion Industries, Inc.
1107 N Taylor Rd
Garrett IN 46738
260 357-6665

(G-5016)
CENTURY TEXTILE MFG INC
803 N Oakland St (28054-7300)
PHONE..............................704 869-6660
Alexander Gendelman, *Pr*
EMP: 14 EST: 2002
SQ FT: 100,000
SALES (est): 505.22K Privately Held
SIC: 2261 2257 Finishing plants, cotton; Dyeing and finishing circular knit fabrics

(G-5017)
CHAMPION ENTERPRISES LLC ✪
Also Called: Champion Powder Coating
1220 Industrial Ave (28054-4629)
P.O. Box 551179 (28055)
PHONE..............................704 866-8148
EMP: 22 EST: 2024
SALES (est): 1.1MM Privately Held
SIC: 3471 Finishing, metals or formed products

(G-5018)
CHAMPION THREAD COMPANY (PA)
Also Called: Ctc
165 Bluedevil Dr (28056-8610)
PHONE..............................704 867-6611
Robert Poovey Iii, *CEO*
Robert Poovey, *Ch*
William Poovey, *Pr*
Pj Mccord, *VP*
Jim Lee, *VP*
▲ EMP: 5 EST: 1979
SALES (est): 1.54MM
SALES (corp-wide): 1.54MM Privately Held

Web: www.championthread.com
SIC: 5131 2211 7389 Thread; Elastic fabrics, cotton; Business services, nec

(G-5019)
CHEM-TECH SOLUTIONS INC
1932 Jordache Ct (28052-5435)
PHONE..............................704 829-9202
Tony Phillips, *Pr*
EMP: 28 EST: 1999
SALES (est): 7.91MM Privately Held
Web: www.chemtechsolutions.com
SIC: 2842 2899 Polishes and sanitation goods; Acid resist for etching

(G-5020)
CHOICE USA BEVERAGE INC
809 E Franklin Blvd (28054-4254)
P.O. Box 40 (28098-0040)
PHONE..............................704 861-1029
Jim Mccune, *Mgr*
EMP: 40
SALES (corp-wide): 23.19MM Privately Held
Web: www.choiceusabeverage.com
SIC: 2086 Soft drinks: packaged in cans, bottles, etc.
PA: Choice U.S.A. Beverage, Inc.
603 Grove St
Lowell NC 28098
704 823-1651

(G-5021)
CHRONICLE MILL LAND LLC
3826 S New Hope Rd Ste 4 (28056-4401)
P.O. Box 810 (28012-0810)
PHONE..............................704 527-3227
John Church, *Prin*
EMP: 6 EST: 2012
SALES (est): 242.77K Privately Held
Web: www.thechroniclemill.com
SIC: 2711 Newspapers, publishing and printing

(G-5022)
CLOSED TIRE COMPANY INC
191 E Franklin Blvd (28052-4147)
P.O. Box 146 (28053-0146)
PHONE..............................704 864-5464
Kenneth H Parks Junior, *Pr*
Douglas H Parks, *VP*
EMP: 19 EST: 1939
SQ FT: 17,000
SALES (est): 2.13MM Privately Held
Web: www.roosevelttirepros.com
SIC: 5531 7534 Automotive tires; Tire retreading and repair shops

(G-5023)
CMC REBAR
2528 N Chester St (28052-1808)
P.O. Box 1928 (28053-1928)
PHONE..............................704 865-8571
▲ EMP: 8 EST: 2010
SALES (est): 1.01MM Privately Held
Web: www.cmc.com
SIC: 3441 Fabricated structural metal

(G-5024)
COLLINS FABRICATION & WLDG LLC
1204 N Chester St (28052-1855)
PHONE..............................704 861-9326
Mike Collins, *Prin*
EMP: 4 EST: 1985
SQ FT: 4,000
SALES (est): 362.09K Privately Held
SIC: 7692 1799 3444 3441 Welding repair; Welding on site; Sheet metalwork; Fabricated structural metal

(G-5025)
COMMERCIAL METALS COMPANY
Also Called: CMC Rebar
2528 N Chester St (28052-1808)
PHONE..............................919 833-9737
EMP: 6
SALES (corp-wide): 7.93B Publicly Held
Web: www.cmc.com
SIC: 3312 Blast furnaces and steel mills
PA: Commercial Metals Company
6565 N Mcrthur Blvd Ste 8
Irving TX 75039
214 689-4300

(G-5026)
CONCEPT STEEL INC
1801 Bradbury Ct (28052-9107)
PHONE..............................704 874-0414
Ryan Chapman, *Pr*
EMP: 25 EST: 1999
SQ FT: 2,000
SALES (est): 5.19MM Privately Held
Web: www.conceptsteel.com
SIC: 3449 3441 Miscellaneous metalwork; Fabricated structural metal

(G-5027)
CONFERENCE INC
259 W Main Ave (28052-4140)
PHONE..............................704 349-0203
Souheil Anthony Tony Azar, *Pr*
EMP: 6 EST: 2013
SALES (est): 141.08K Privately Held
Web: www.rxaap.com
SIC: 2819 Industrial inorganic chemicals, nec

(G-5028)
CONITEX SONOCO USA INC
1302 Industrial Pike Rd (28052-8430)
PHONE..............................704 864-5406
Joseph Artiga, *Pr*
David Monteith, *
Carl Smith, *
Michael Schmidlin, *
Joaquin Vinas, *
◆ EMP: 140 EST: 1982
SQ FT: 103,000
SALES (est): 13.25MM
SALES (corp-wide): 5.31B Publicly Held
Web: www.sonoco.com
SIC: 5199 2655 Packaging materials; Ammunition cans or tubes, board laminated with metal foil
PA: Sonoco Products Company
1 N 2nd St
Hartsville SC 29550
843 383-7000

(G-5029)
CONTEMPORARY CONCEPTS INC
2940 Audrey Dr (28054-7268)
P.O. Box 550910 (28055-0910)
PHONE..............................704 864-9572
Doug Cullen, *Pr*
EMP: 30 EST: 1982
SQ FT: 3,800
SALES (est): 916.13K Privately Held
Web: www.contemporaryconcepts.net
SIC: 2731 Books, publishing only

(G-5030)
CONTEMPORARY DESIGN CO LLC
Also Called: Carolina Custom Millwork
513 N Broad St (28054-2508)
PHONE..............................704 375-6030
EMP: 19 EST: 2019
SALES (est): 2.49MM Privately Held
SIC: 2599 2431 Cabinets, factory; Millwork

GEOGRAPHIC

(G-5031)
CREATIVE FABRIC SERVICES LLC
1675 Garfield Dr (28052-8403)
P.O. Box 3736 (28054-0038)
PHONE................................704 861-8383
Robert V Sytz, *Managing Member*
◆ **EMP: 5 EST:** 1997
SQ FT: 47,500
SALES (est): 5.49MM
SALES (corp-wide): 23.38MM **Privately Held**
Web: www.creativeticking.com
SIC: 2211 Broadwoven fabric mills, cotton
PA: Beverly Knits, Inc.
1675 Garfield Dr
Gastonia NC 28052
704 861-1536

(G-5032)
CRISP PRINTERS INC
2022 E Ozark Ave (28054-3361)
PHONE................................704 867-6663
Monty Teague, *Pr*
Melody Teague, *Sec*
EMP: 6 EST: 1961
SQ FT: 1,900
SALES (est): 525.65K **Privately Held**
Web: www.crispprinters.com
SIC: 2752 Offset printing

(G-5033)
CS ALLOYS
2888 Colony Woods Dr (28054-7779)
PHONE................................704 675-5810
Ray Cheek, *Owner*
EMP: 5 EST: 2009
SALES (est): 636.97K **Privately Held**
Web: www.csalloys.com
SIC: 3363 Aluminum die-castings

(G-5034)
CTC HOLDINGS LLC (PA)
165 Bluedevil Dr (28056-8610)
P.O. Box 150 (29703-0150)
PHONE................................704 867-6611
EMP: 9 EST: 2005
SALES (est): 2.38MM **Privately Held**
SIC: 2284 Sewing thread

(G-5035)
CURTISS-WRIGHT CONTROLS INC
3120 Northwest Blvd (28052-1167)
PHONE................................704 869-2320
EMP: 16
SALES (corp-wide): 3.12B **Publicly Held**
Web: www.curtisswright.com
SIC: 3728 Aircraft assemblies,
subassemblies, and parts, nec
HQ: Curtiss-Wright Controls, Inc.
15801 Brixham Hill Ave # 200
Charlotte NC 28277
704 869-4600

(G-5036)
CUSTOM MARKING & PRINTING INC
907 Bessemer City Rd (28052-1133)
P.O. Box 1772 (28053-1772)
PHONE................................704 866-8245
James G Silver, *Pr*
Laura A Silver, *Sec*
EMP: 6 EST: 1978
SQ FT: 5,000
SALES (est): 104.95K **Privately Held**
Web: www.petrolaenergy.com
SIC: 2752 3069 Offset printing; Stationer's
rubber sundries

(G-5037)
D BLOCK METALS LLC (PA)
1111 Jenkins Rd (28052-1158)

PHONE................................704 705-5895
Craig Hefner, *Pr*
Cheryl Hefner, *CFO*
▲ **EMP: 10 EST:** 2011
SQ FT: 37,000
SALES (est): 3.39MM
SALES (corp-wide): 3.39MM **Privately Held**
Web: www.dblockmetals.com
SIC: 3399 Powder, metal

(G-5038)
DAIMLER TRUCK NORTH AMER LLC
Also Called: Freightliner Parts Plant
1400 Tulip Dr (28052-1873)
PHONE................................704 868-5700
Bob Pacillas, *Brnch Mgr*
EMP: 1300
SALES (corp-wide): 60.75B **Privately Held**
Web: northamerica.daimlertruck.com
SIC: 3714 3713 Motor vehicle parts and
accessories; Truck and bus bodies
HQ: Daimler Truck North America Llc
4555 N Channel Ave
Portland OR 97217
503 745-8000

(G-5039)
DARLING INGREDIENTS INC
Carolina By Pdts Gastonia Div
5533 York Hwy (28052-8729)
PHONE................................704 864-9941
Paul Humphries, *Brnch Mgr*
EMP: 15
SALES (corp-wide): 6.79B **Publicly Held**
Web: www.darlingii.com
SIC: 2048 2077 Prepared feeds, nec; Tallow
rendering, inedible
PA: Darling Ingredients Inc.
5601 N Macarthur Blvd
Irving TX 75038
972 717-0300

(G-5040)
DAVIS MACHINE CO INC
158 Superior Stainless Rd (28052-8744)
P.O. Box 2183 (28053-2183)
PHONE................................704 865-2863
David B Davis, *Pr*
Robert M Davis, *Sr VP*
Sandra Davis, *VP*
D Allen Davis, *VP Mfg*
EMP: 6 EST: 1984
SQ FT: 7,700
SALES (est): 243.61K **Privately Held**
SIC: 3599 Machine shop, jobbing and repair

(G-5041)
DIABETIC SOCK CLUB
109 Crowders Creek Rd (28052-9787)
PHONE................................800 214-0218
Samantha Ledford, *Owner*
EMP: 5 EST: 2020
SALES (est): 265.53K **Privately Held**
Web: www.diabeticsockclub.com
SIC: 2252 Socks

(G-5042)
DIAMOND ORTHOPEDIC LLC
1669 Federal St (28052-0504)
P.O. Box 1470 (28012-1470)
PHONE................................704 585-8258
Roy Bivens, *CEO*
Jonathan Crumpler, *CFO*
Jd Williams, *VP Sls*
EMP: 5 EST: 2017
SQ FT: 2,000
SALES (est): 1.99MM **Privately Held**
Web: www.diamondortho.com
SIC: 3841 Surgical and medical instruments

(G-5043)
DRAMAR MACHINE DEVICES INC
108 Chickasaw Rd (28056-6235)
P.O. Box 635 (29703-0635)
PHONE................................704 866-0904
Howard Collmar, *Pr*
Danny Freeman, *VP*
EMP: 20 **EST:** 1994
SQ FT: 40,000
SALES (est): 2.11MM **Privately Held**
Web: www.dramarinc.com
SIC: 3599 Machine shop, jobbing and repair

(G-5044)
DYNAMIC STAMPINGS NC INC
1412 Castle Ct (28052-1198)
P.O. Box 307 (53089-0307)
PHONE................................704 509-2501
Linda Windsor, *Pr*
EMP: 6 EST: 2006
SALES (est): 2.26MM
SALES (corp-wide): 5.15MM **Privately Held**
Web: www.dynamicstampings.com
SIC: 3469 Stamping metal for the trade
PA: Dynamic Stampings, Inc.
W225 N6328 Village Dr
Sussex WI 53089
262 246-4433

(G-5045)
ELECTRICAL APPARATUS & MCH CO
5619 Gallagher Dr (28052-8702)
P.O. Box 37432 (28237-7432)
PHONE................................704 333-2987
Douglas G James, *Pr*
Bess Thompson, *Sec*
Alan K James, *VP*
Donald C James, *VP*
▲ **EMP: 10 EST:** 1975
SALES (est): 987.34K **Privately Held**
Web: www.electricalapparatus.net
SIC: 3599 Machine shop, jobbing and repair

(G-5046)
EQUIPMENT DSIGN FBRICATION INC
201 Davis Heights Dr (28052-6392)
PHONE................................704 372-4513
Terry D Miller, *Pr*
▲ **EMP: 9 EST:** 1964
SALES (est): 564.76K **Privately Held**
Web: www.equipmentdesignandfab.com
SIC: 3441 Fabricated structural metal

(G-5047)
FIDELITY ASSOCIATES INC
Also Called: Family Traditions
2936 Rousseau Ct (28054-2102)
P.O. Box 550968 (28055-0968)
PHONE................................704 864-3766
Chris Cherry, *FAMILY TRADITIONS*
EMP: 31 **EST:** 1982
SQ FT: 5,000
SALES (est): 2.11MM **Privately Held**
Web: www.fidelityassociates.com
SIC: 2731 8021 Book publishing; Offices and
clinics of dentists

(G-5048)
FILTER SHOP LLC
2403 Lowell Rd (28054-1427)
PHONE................................704 860-4822
EMP: 68 **EST:** 2013
SALES (est): 4.44MM **Privately Held**
Web: www.thefiltershopinc.com
SIC: 3564 5084 3999 Blowers and fans;
Sewing machines, industrial; Sewing kits,
novelty

(G-5049)
FRENCH APRON MANUFACTURING CO
1619 Madison St (28052-0846)
P.O. Box 2324 (28053-2324)
PHONE................................704 865-7666
Randy Beavers, *CEO*
Robert A Main Junior, *Pr*
William Main, *Ex VP*
Susan Main, *VP*
EMP: 9 EST: 1952
SQ FT: 10,000
SALES (est): 1.09MM
SALES (corp-wide): 20.05MM **Privately Held**
Web: www.french-apron.com
SIC: 3552 Textile machinery
PA: Main, Robert A & Sons Holding
Company Inc
20-21 Wagaraw Rd
Fair Lawn NJ 07410
201 447-3700

(G-5050)
GASTEX LLC
3051 Aberdeen Blvd (28054-0622)
P.O. Box 3806 (28054-0039)
PHONE................................704 824-9861
EMP: 5 EST: 1974
SQ FT: 32,000
SALES (est): 1.01MM **Privately Held**
SIC: 3552 7699 Textile machinery; Industrial
machinery and equipment repair

(G-5051)
GASTON GAZETTE LLP
1893 Remount Rd (28056)
P.O. Box 1538 (28053-1538)
PHONE................................704 869-1700
Marlene Smith, *Mgr*
EMP: 2552 **EST:** 1880
SQ FT: 89,000
SALES (est): 2.22MM
SALES (corp-wide): 2.51B **Publicly Held**
Web: www.gastongazette.com
SIC: 2711 Commercial printing and
newspaper publishing combined
HQ: Halifax Media Group, Llc
2339 Beville Rd
Daytona Beach FL 32119
386 265-6700

(G-5052)
GASTONIA
860 Summit Crossing Pl (28054-2216)
PHONE................................704 377-3687
EMP: 9 EST: 2019
SALES (est): 225.41K **Privately Held**
Web: www.gastongov.com
SIC: 2711 Newspapers, publishing and
printing

(G-5053)
GENTRY PLASTICS INC
Also Called: Gpi
1808 Bradbury Ct (28052-9107)
PHONE................................704 864-4300
Michael Stephens, *Pr*
▲ **EMP: 45 EST:** 2000
SQ FT: 6,000
SALES (est): 6.7MM **Privately Held**
Web: www.gentryplastics.com
SIC: 3089 Injection molded finished plastics
products, nec

(G-5054)
GOOD WILL PUBLISHERS INC (PA)
1520 S York Rd (28052-6138)
P.O. Box 269 (28053-0269)
PHONE................................704 853-3237
John Briody, *Pr*

▲ = Import ▼ = Export
◆ = Import/Export

Robert M Gallagher, *
Richard Hoefling, *
▲ EMP: 70 EST: 1949
SQ FT: 30,000
SALES (est): 12.64MM
SALES (corp-wide): 12.64MM Privately Held
Web: www.milestonescompany.com
SIC: 2731 5942 Books, publishing only; Book stores

(G-5055)
GRACEFULLY BROKEN LLC
2131 Autumn Cyprus Ave (28054-4071)
PHONE.................................980 474-0309
EMP: 5 EST: 2020
SALES (est): 102.36K Privately Held
SIC: 7389 2211 7929 Business Activities at Non-Commercial Site; Apparel and outerwear fabrics, cotton; Entertainment service

(G-5056)
GSM SERVICES INC
Also Called: GSM Services
1535 W May Ave (28052-1409)
P.O. Box 12216 (28052-0030)
PHONE.................................704 864-0344
Ronald J Long Junior, Pr
Steven D Long, *
Judy Long, Corporate Secretary*
EMP: 100 EST: 1925
SQ FT: 10,000
SALES (est): 28.99MM Privately Held
Web: www.gsmsince1927.com
SIC: 1761 1711 3444 Roofing contractor; Heating and air conditioning contractors; Sheet metalwork

(G-5057)
HALIFAX MEDIA GROUP
1893 Remount Rd (28054-7413)
PHONE.................................704 869-1700
EMP: 10 EST: 2014
SALES (est): 112.36K Privately Held
Web: www.gastongazette.com
SIC: 2711 Newspapers, publishing and printing

(G-5058)
HAM BROTHERS INC
205 Shamrock Rd (28056-7671)
P.O. Box 407 (28120-0407)
PHONE.................................704 827-1303
Tod Ham, Pr
Joseph F Ham, Pr
Todd Ham, Pr
EMP: 15 EST: 1976
SALES (est): 3.19MM Privately Held
Web: www.hambrothers.com
SIC: 3441 Fabricated structural metal

(G-5059)
HERMAN REEVES TEX SHTMTL INC
Also Called: Herman Reeves Sheet Metal
1617 E Ozark Ave (28054-3513)
P.O. Box 249 (28098-0249)
PHONE.................................704 865-2231
Michael W Clagg, Pr
Joshua Clagg, *
EMP: 42 EST: 1962
SQ FT: 7,000
SALES (est): 15.07MM Privately Held
Web: www.hermanreeves.com
SIC: 1761 3444 Sheet metal work, nec; Sheet metalwork

(G-5060)
HESTER ENTERPRISES INC
214 Superior Stainless Rd (28052-8747)
PHONE.................................704 865-4480

Janet Hester, Pr
Tom Hester, *
EMP: 35 EST: 1993
SQ FT: 37,000
SALES (est): 2.06MM Privately Held
Web: www.hesterenterprises.com
SIC: 2512 5084 Upholstered household furniture; Sewing machines, industrial

(G-5061)
IFAB CORP (HQ) ✪
2408 Forbes Rd (28056-6267)
PHONE.................................704 864-3032
Hugo L Ochoa, Pr
Olga C Ochoa, *
Darien Ledford, *
EMP: 16 EST: 2023
SALES (est): 1.06MM
SALES (corp-wide): 23.03MM Privately Held
Web: www.ifabrication.com
SIC: 3441 3449 Fabricated structural metal; Bars, concrete reinforcing: fabricated steel
PA: South American Parts Corp.
5301 Nw 74th Ave Ste 200
Miami FL 33166
305 594-2844

(G-5062)
IMAGEMARK BUSINESS SVCS INC (PA)
Also Called: Imagemark
3145 Northwest Blvd (28052)
PHONE.................................704 865-4912
Walter Payne, Pr
David Walsh, VP
Greg Sellers, CFO
Karen Kaufman, Ex VP
EMP: 9 EST: 1931
SQ FT: 11,000
SALES (est): 7.19MM
SALES (corp-wide): 7.19MM Privately Held
Web: www.imagemarkonline.com
SIC: 2752 2759 Offset printing; Letterpress printing

(G-5063)
INDUSTRIAL ELCPLTG CO INC
Also Called: Warehouse Facility
1401 Gaston Ave (28052-2027)
P.O. Box 1537 (28053-1537)
PHONE.................................704 867-4547
Walter Prescott, CEO
EMP: 4
SALES (corp-wide): 9.51MM Privately Held
Web: www.electroplate.biz
SIC: 3471 Electroplating of metals or formed products
PA: Industrial Electroplating Company, Inc.
307 Linwood Rd
Gastonia NC 28052
704 867-4547

(G-5064)
INDUSTRIAL ELCPLTG CO INC (PA)
307 Linwood Rd (28052-3720)
P.O. Box 1537 (28053-1537)
PHONE.................................704 867-4547
TOLL FREE: 800
Walter C Prescott, Owner
Terry Brooks, *
Kevin Prescott, *
Amelia Prescott, *
Anna S Clinton, *
EMP: 60 EST: 1971
SQ FT: 12,000
SALES (est): 9.51MM
SALES (corp-wide): 9.51MM Privately Held

Web: www.electroplate.biz
SIC: 3471 Plating of metals or formed products

(G-5065)
INDUSTRIAL GLASS TECH LLC
Also Called: Industrial Glass Technologies
112 Superior Stainless Rd (28052-8744)
PHONE.................................704 853-2429
Carroll Barger, Managing Member
▲ EMP: 15 EST: 2005
SALES (est): 2.39MM Privately Held
Web: www.industrialglasstech.com
SIC: 5231 3211 Glass; Antique glass

(G-5066)
INDUSTRIAL METAL CRAFT INC
901 Tulip Dr (28052-1825)
PHONE.................................704 864-3416
Max Clark Junior, Pr
Dan S Wise, VP
G Glen Adams, Sec
EMP: 16 EST: 1975
SQ FT: 23,000
SALES (est): 2.49MM
SALES (corp-wide): 6.31MM Privately Held
Web: www.imc.us
SIC: 3444 Sheet metalwork
PA: Sherrill Contract Manufacturing, Inc.
110 Durkee Ln
Dallas NC 28034
704 922-7871

(G-5067)
INSTANT IMPRINTS
2258 Helen Dr (28054-1936)
PHONE.................................704 864-1510
Gary Lutz, Owner
EMP: 4 EST: 2006
SALES (est): 228.71K Privately Held
Web: www.instantimprints.com
SIC: 2752 Commercial printing, lithographic

(G-5068)
INTRINSIC ADVANCED MTLS LLC
531 Cotton Blossom Cir (28054-5245)
PHONE.................................704 874-5000
Steve Staley, Managing Member
EMP: 8 EST: 2018
SALES (est): 718.03K Privately Held
SIC: 2821 Polymethyl methacrylate resins, plexiglass

(G-5069)
J & P ENTRPRSES OF CRLINAS INC
5640 Gallagher Dr (28052-8702)
PHONE.................................704 861-1867
C Lamar Greene, Pr
Jeffrey L Greene, VP
Paula Painter, Sec
▲ EMP: 20 EST: 1981
SQ FT: 25,000
SALES (est): 2.4MM Privately Held
SIC: 3552 5084 5199 Textile machinery; Industrial machinery and equipment; Fabrics, yarns, and knit goods

(G-5070)
J CHARLES SAUNDERS CO INC
Also Called: Saunders Thread Company
1004 E Long Ave (28054-3171)
P.O. Box 4016 (28054-0041)
PHONE.................................704 866-9156
Charles J Sanders, Pr
Sarah W Saunders, *
Dean Queen, *
◆ EMP: 40 EST: 1968
SQ FT: 55,000
SALES (est): 1.16MM Privately Held
Web: www.saunders-thread.com

SIC: 2282 2284 Throwing yarn; Sewing thread

(G-5071)
J F HEAT TREATING INC
409 Airport Rd (28056-8804)
PHONE.................................704 864-0998
TOLL FREE: 800
John Freeman Junior, Pr
Jimmy Freeman, VP
Emma Freeman, Sec
EMP: 7 EST: 1980
SQ FT: 10,000
SALES (est): 803.5K Privately Held
Web: www.jfheattreatinginc.com
SIC: 3398 Metal heat treating

(G-5072)
JIMMYS COATING UNLIMITED INC
420 N Morehead St (28054-2534)
PHONE.................................704 915-2420
Jimmy Collins, Prin
EMP: 4 EST: 2016
SALES (est): 98.02K Privately Held
Web: www.jimmyscoatingsunlimitedinc.com
SIC: 3479 Metal coating and allied services

(G-5073)
KINDRED ROLLING DOORS LLC
Also Called: The Rolling Door Company
3420 Country Club Dr (28056-6680)
PHONE.................................704 905-3806
EMP: 5 EST: 2016
SALES (est): 242.28K Privately Held
SIC: 3442 Baseboards, metal

(G-5074)
KRISPY KREME DOUGHNUT CORP
Also Called: Krispy Kreme
2990 E Franklin Sq (28052)
PHONE.................................919 669-6151
Chip Crump, Mgr
EMP: 31
SALES (corp-wide): 1.69B Publicly Held
Web: www.krispykreme.com
SIC: 5461 2051 Doughnuts; Doughnuts, except frozen
HQ: Krispy Kreme Doughnut Corp
2116 Hawkins St Ste 102
Charlotte NC 28203
980 270-7117

(G-5075)
L & R SPECIALTIES INC
2757 W Franklin Blvd (28052-9480)
P.O. Box 12805 (28052-0015)
PHONE.................................704 853-3296
Chit Jones, Pr
EMP: 10 EST: 1992
SQ FT: 12,000
SALES (est): 486.78K Privately Held
Web: www.landr-newbritain.com
SIC: 3541 Lathes

(G-5076)
L AND L MACHINE CO INC
158 Superior Stainless Rd (28052-8744)
P.O. Box 178 (29703-0178)
PHONE.................................704 864-5521
Robert Lamm, Pr
EMP: 11 EST: 1976
SQ FT: 7,500
SALES (est): 1.99MM Privately Held
SIC: 3599 Machine shop, jobbing and repair

(G-5077)
LANXESS CORPORATION
214 W Ruby Ave (28054-7507)
PHONE.................................704 868-7200

Richard Lissende, *Brnch Mgr*
EMP: 20
SALES (corp-wide): 7.3B **Privately Held**
Web: www.lanxess.com
SIC: 2899 2821 2822 2879 Chemical
supplies for foundries; Plastics materials
and resins; Synthetic rubber; Insecticides,
agricultural or household
HQ: Lanxess Corporation
111 Ridc Park W Dr
Pittsburgh PA 15275
412 809-1000

(G-5078)
LPM INC
2703 Ashbourne Dr (28056-7564)
PHONE.................................704 922-6137
Dana Bumgardner, *Pr*
Jeff Bumgardner, *VP*
EMP: 6 **EST:** 2000
SALES (est): 100.54K **Privately Held**
SIC: 2679 Labels, paper: made from
purchased material

(G-5079)
LSRWM CORP
Also Called: Rwm Casters
1225 Isley Rd (28052-8106)
P.O. Box 668 (28053-0668)
PHONE.................................704 866-8533
Peter D Comeau, *Pr*
◆ **EMP:** 49 **EST:** 1967
SQ FT: 87,000
SALES (est): 1.4MM **Privately Held**
SIC: 3562 Casters

(G-5080)
**LUBRIZOL GLOBAL MANAGEMENT
INC**
207 Telegraph Dr (28056-1306)
PHONE.................................704 865-7451
James Nelli, *Mgr*
EMP: 58
SALES (corp-wide): 424.23B **Publicly
Held**
Web: www.lubrizol.com
SIC: 2899 3087 2851 Chemical
preparations, nec; Custom compound
purchased resins; Paints and allied products
HQ: Lubrizol Global Management, Inc.
9911 Brecksville Rd
Cleveland OH 44141
216 447-5000

(G-5081)
M & M ELECTRIC SERVICE INC
Also Called: M & M Electric Service NC
1680 Garfield Dr (28052-8403)
P.O. Box 12847 (28052-0043)
PHONE.................................704 867-0221
Marvin R Foy, *Pr*
Jeffrey Foy, *
Sheryll Foy, *
EMP: 40 **EST:** 1973
SQ FT: 17,000
SALES (est): 12.18MM **Privately Held**
Web: www.mme.com
SIC: 1731 3643 General electrical contractor
; Bus bars (electrical conductors)

(G-5082)
**MANN+HMMEL FLTRTION TECH
GROUP (DH)**
1 Wix Way (28053)
PHONE.................................704 869-3300
Keith Wilson, *CEO*
Jorge Schertel, *Pr*
Steven Klueg S, *VP*
▲ **EMP:** 4 **EST:** 2004
SQ FT: 24,000
SALES (est): 811.77MM

SALES (corp-wide): 5.11B **Privately Held**
Web: fleetdirect.mann-hummel.com
SIC: 5013 3714 Automotive supplies and
parts; Motor vehicle brake systems and
parts
HQ: Mann+Hummel Filtration Technology
Intermediate Holdings Inc.
1 Wix Way
Gastonia NC 28054
704 869-3300

(G-5083)
**MANN+HMMEL FLTRTION TECH
INTRM (DH)**
1 Wix Way (28054-6142)
PHONE.................................704 869-3300
Keith A Wilson, *Pr*
Steven P Klueg, *Sr VP*
Karl J Westrick, *CIO*
Kay Teixeira, *Senior Vice President Human
Resources*
David E Sturgess, *Sr VP*
▼ **EMP:** 24 **EST:** 2004
SALES (est): 899MM
SALES (corp-wide): 5.11B **Privately Held**
Web: www.wixfilters.com
SIC: 3714 Filters: oil, fuel, and air, motor
vehicle
HQ: Mann + Hummel Usa, Inc.
6400 S Sprinkle Rd
Portage MI 49002
269 329-3900

(G-5084)
**MANN+HMMEL FLTRTION TECH US
LL**
Wix Filtration Products Div
1 Wix Way (28054-6142)
P.O. Box 1902 (28053-1902)
PHONE.................................704 869-3700
Keith Wilson, *Brnch Mgr*
EMP: 114
SQ FT: 36,000
SALES (corp-wide): 5.11B **Privately Held**
Web: www.wixfilters.com
SIC: 3714 Motor vehicle engines and parts
HQ: Mann+Hummel Filtration Technology
Us Llc
1 Wix Way
Gastonia NC 28054
704 869-3300

(G-5085)
**MANN+HMMEL FLTRTION TECH US
LL (DH)**
Also Called: Mannhmmel Fltration Tech Group
1 Wix Way (28054)
P.O. Box 1967 (28053)
PHONE.................................704 869-3300
Kurk Wilks, *CEO*
Keith Wilson, *
◆ **EMP:** 120 **EST:** 2004
SALES (est): 195.01MM
SALES (corp-wide): 5.11B **Privately Held**
Web: www.wixfilters.com
SIC: 3569 3677 3589 Filters, general line:
industrial; Filtration devices, electronic;
Sewage and water treatment equipment
HQ: Mann+Hummel Filtration Technology
Group Inc.
1 Wix Way
Gastonia NC 28053
704 869-3300

(G-5086)
**MANN+HMMEL PRLATOR FILTERS
LLC**
1 Wix Way (28054-6142)
PHONE.................................704 869-3441
EMP: 141
SALES (corp-wide): 5.11B **Privately Held**

Web: www.mann-hummel.com
SIC: 3714 Motor vehicle parts and
accessories
HQ: Mann+Hummel Purolator Filters Llc
3200 Natal St Ste 64069
Fayetteville NC 28306

(G-5087)
**MANN+HUMMEL FILTRATION
TECHNOL**
2900 Northwest Blvd (28052-1162)
PHONE.................................704 869-3500
David Palmer, *Brnch Mgr*
EMP: 96
SALES (corp-wide): 5.11B **Privately Held**
Web: www.mann-hummel.com
SIC: 3714 Motor vehicle parts and
accessories
HQ: Mann+Hummel Filtration Technology
Group Inc.
1 Wix Way
Gastonia NC 28053
704 869-3300

(G-5088)
**MANN+HUMMEL FILTRATION
TECHNOL**
Also Called: Wix Filtration Products
1551 Mount Olive Church Rd (28052-9412)
PHONE.................................704 869-3952
John Winters, *Brnch Mgr*
EMP: 7
SALES (corp-wide): 5.11B **Privately Held**
Web: www.wixfilters.com
SIC: 3714 3569 Filters: oil, fuel, and air,
motor vehicle; Filters
HQ: Mann+Hummel Filtration Technology
Us Llc
1 Wix Way
Gastonia NC 28054
704 869-3300

(G-5089)
**MANN+HUMMEL FILTRATION
TECHNOL**
Also Called: Wix Filters
2900 Northwest Blvd (28052-1162)
P.O. Box 1967 (28053-1967)
PHONE.................................704 869-3501
Steve Renfrow, *Brnch Mgr*
EMP: 114
SALES (corp-wide): 5.11B **Privately Held**
Web: www.wixfilters.com
SIC: 3569 3714 Filters, general line:
industrial; Motor vehicle parts and
accessories
HQ: Mann+Hummel Filtration Technology
Us Llc
1 Wix Way
Gastonia NC 28054
704 869-3300

(G-5090)
**MANN+HUMMEL FILTRATION
TECHNOLOGY HOLDINGS INC**
1 Wix Way (28054-6142)
PHONE.................................704 869-3300
◆ **EMP:** 5615
SIC: 3714 Filters: oil, fuel, and air, motor
vehicle

(G-5091)
MARC MACHINE WORKS INC
5042 York Hwy (28052-6818)
PHONE.................................704 865-3625
Frank Hubbard, *Pr*
Frances Hubbard, *VP*
EMP: 12 **EST:** 1984
SQ FT: 1,188
SALES (est): 958.61K **Privately Held**

Web: www.marcmachine.com
SIC: 3599 7692 Machine shop, jobbing and
repair; Welding repair

(G-5092)
MAYSTEEL PORTERS LLC
469 Hospital Dr Ste A (28054-4778)
PHONE.................................704 864-1313
Kevin Matkin, *CEO*
EMP: 300
SALES (corp-wide): 396.03MM **Privately
Held**
Web: www.maysteel.com
SIC: 3441 3317 Fabricated structural metal;
Steel pipe and tubes
HQ: Maysteel Porters, Llc
6199 County Rd W
Allenton WI 53002
262 251-1632

(G-5093)
MERIDIAN INDUSTRIES INC
Also Called: Meridian Dyed Yarn Group
40 Rex Ave (28054-3026)
PHONE.................................704 824-7880
Joel Goodrich, *Mgr*
EMP: 28
SALES (corp-wide): 331.16MM **Privately
Held**
Web: www.msyg.com
SIC: 2281 Acrylic yarn, spun: made from
purchased staple
PA: Meridian Industries, Inc.
735 N Water St Ste 630
Milwaukee WI 53202
414 224-0610

(G-5094)
**METAL IMPROVEMENT COMPANY
LLC**
Also Called: Mic Equip Rebuild
1931 Jordache Ct (28052-5435)
PHONE.................................414 536-1573
Steve Smtih, *Mgr*
EMP: 4
SALES (corp-wide): 3.12B **Publicly Held**
Web: www.imrtest.com
SIC: 3398 Shot peening (treating steel to
reduce fatigue)
HQ: Metal Improvement Company, Llc
80 Route 4 E Ste 310
Paramus NJ 07652
201 843-7800

(G-5095)
METRO FIRE LIFESAFETY LLC
2714 Forbes Rd (28056-6287)
PHONE.................................704 529-7348
Pierre Zenie, *Pr*
EMP: 6 **EST:** 2004
SALES (est): 2.85MM **Privately Held**
Web: www.metrolifesafety.com
SIC: 3569 Firefighting and related equipment

(G-5096)
METYX USA INC
2504 Lowell Rd (28054-3409)
PHONE.................................704 824-1030
Besim Ugur Ustunel, *Pr*
EMP: 70 **EST:** 2017
SALES (est): 9.39MM **Privately Held**
Web: www.metyx.com
SIC: 2221 Textile mills, broadwoven: silk and
manmade, also glass

(G-5097)
MIK ALL MACHINE CO INC (PA)
Also Called: Metal Treating Div
905 Hanover St (28054-2455)
PHONE.................................704 866-4302
Charles Allen, *Prin*

▲ = Import ▼ = Export
◆ = Import/Export

Ruby Fail, *VP*
EMP: 13 **EST:** 1976
SQ FT: 4,500
SALES (est): 781.93K
SALES (corp-wide): 781.93K **Privately Held**
Web: www.mikall.com
SIC: 3599 Machine shop, jobbing and repair

(G-5098)
MINGES PRINTING & ADVG CO
Also Called: Minges Printing Company
323 S Chestnut St (28054-4542)
PHONE..............................704 867-6791
Gene M Minges Senior, *Pr*
Gene M Minges Junior, *VP*
EMP: 6 **EST:** 1959
SQ FT: 2,700
SALES (est): 182.22K **Privately Held**
Web: www.mingesprinting.com
SIC: 2752 7389 Offset printing; Lettering and sign painting services

(G-5099)
MINUTEMAN PRESS OF GASTONIA ✪
Also Called: Minuteman Press
495 E Long Ave (28054-2526)
PHONE..............................704 867-3366
Toni Marder, *Owner*
EMP: 5 **EST:** 2023
SALES (est): 182.38K **Privately Held**
Web: www.minutemanpress.com
SIC: 2752 Commercial printing, lithographic

(G-5100)
MODENA SOUTHERN DYEING CORP
Also Called: Saunders Phrad
1010 E Ozark Ave (28054)
P.O. Box 4016 (28054-0041)
PHONE..............................704 866-9156
J Charles Saunders, *Pr*
David Saunders, *Sec*
Wallace Ammons, *VP Mfg*
Kathyrn V Saunders, *Stockholder*
Dorothy Z Saunders, *Stockholder*
EMP: 5 **EST:** 1983
SQ FT: 15,000
SALES (est): 99.42K **Privately Held**
SIC: 2211 Yarn-dyed fabrics, cotton

(G-5101)
MORNINGSTAR SIGNS AND BANNERS
307 E Franklin Blvd (28054-7134)
PHONE..............................704 861-0020
Robert Claiborne, *Owner*
EMP: 4 **EST:** 2003
SALES (est): 99.39K **Privately Held**
SIC: 5999 3993 Banners; Signs and advertising specialties

(G-5102)
MORRIS MACHINE COMPANY INC
Also Called: Morris Machine Sales
122 Stroupe Rd (28056-8499)
P.O. Box 550817 (28055-0817)
PHONE..............................704 824-4242
William Morris Junior, *Pr*
William Morris, *Pr*
EMP: 5 **EST:** 1986
SQ FT: 4,000
SALES (est): 424.92K **Privately Held**
Web: www.web-tite.com
SIC: 3599 5084 Machine shop, jobbing and repair; Industrial machinery and equipment

(G-5103)
MOTOR SHOP INC
5001 York Hwy (28052-6810)
P.O. Box 12885 (28052-0043)

PHONE..............................704 867-8488
Ken Gordon, *Pr*
Sarah Gordon, *Sec*
EMP: 8 **EST:** 1989
SQ FT: 60,000
SALES (est): 509.22K **Privately Held**
SIC: 5063 7694 7699 5999 Motors, electric; Electric motor repair; Pumps and pumping equipment repair; Motors, electric

(G-5104)
MOUNT OLIVE PICKLE COMPANY
1534 Union Rd Ste A (28054-2203)
PHONE..............................704 867-5585
EMP: 7
SALES (est): 76.29K **Privately Held**
Web: www.mtolivepickles.com
SIC: 2035 Pickles, vinegar

(G-5105)
MOUNT OLIVE PICKLE COMPANY INC
1534 Union Rd Ste A (28054-2203)
PHONE..............................704 867-5585
EMP: 33
SALES (corp-wide): 835.67K **Privately Held**
Web: www.mtolivepickles.com
SIC: 2035 Pickles, vinegar
PA: Mount Olive Pickle Company, Inc.
One Cucumber Blvd
Mount Olive NC 28365
919 658-2535

(G-5106)
NAPA FILTERS
1 Wix Way (28054-6142)
P.O. Box 1892 (28053-1892)
PHONE..............................704 864-6748
Keith Wilson, *Prin*
EMP: 4 **EST:** 2011
SALES (est): 306.21K **Privately Held**
Web: www.napaindustrialfilters.com
SIC: 3569 Filters

(G-5107)
NATIONAL ROLLER SUPPLY INC
811 Grover St (28054-3282)
P.O. Box 240321 (28224-0321)
PHONE..............................704 853-1174
Mike Harris, *Pr*
Dennis Crowley, *Pr*
Cathy P Stout, *Sec*
Mike Harris, *Mgr*
EMP: 5 **EST:** 1980
SQ FT: 18,000
SALES (est): 435.84K **Privately Held**
SIC: 3555 Printing trades machinery

(G-5108)
NEW CAN COMPANY INC
121 Crowders Creek Rd (28052-9787)
PHONE..............................704 853-3711
Rodney Huffstetler, *Mgr*
EMP: 4
SALES (corp-wide): 10.42MM **Privately Held**
Web: www.newcan.com
SIC: 3469 Metal stampings, nec
HQ: The New Can Company Inc
1 Mear Rd
Holbrook MA 02343
330 928-1191

(G-5109)
NEWCOMB SPRING CORP
Also Called: Newcomb Spring of Carolina
2633 Plastics Dr (28054-1419)
PHONE..............................704 588-2043
Keith Porter Junior, *Mgr*
EMP: 21

SALES (corp-wide): 42.63MM **Privately Held**
Web: www.newcombspring.com
SIC: 3495 Wire springs
PA: Newcomb Spring Corp.
3155 North Point Pkwy G220
Alpharetta GA 30005
770 981-2803

(G-5110)
NEWELL BRANDS DISTRIBUTION LLC
3211 Aberdeen Blvd (28054-0669)
PHONE..............................770 418-7000
Robert Westreich, *Pr*
EMP: 100
SALES (corp-wide): 7.58B **Publicly Held**
Web: newellbrands.dejobs.org
SIC: 3089 Plastics kitchenware, tableware, and houseware
HQ: Newell Brands Distribution Llc
6655 Pachtree Dunwoody Rd
Atlanta GA 30328
770 418-7000

(G-5111)
NOLEN MACHINE CO INC
119 Bob Nolen Rd (28056-9296)
P.O. Box 455 (28053-0455)
PHONE..............................704 867-7851
Bill Nolen, *Pr*
Herman E Nolen, *VP*
EMP: 4 **EST:** 1953
SQ FT: 4,000
SALES (est): 185.44K **Privately Held**
SIC: 3599 Machine shop, jobbing and repair

(G-5112)
NUSSBAUM AUTO SOLUTIONS LP (PA)
1932 Jorache Ct (28052-5435)
PHONE..............................704 864-2470
Kim Nivens, *Contrlr*
▲ **EMP:** 6 **EST:** 2012
SALES (est): 8.07MM
SALES (corp-wide): 8.07MM **Privately Held**
Web: www.nussbaum-usa.com
SIC: 3534 Automobile elevators

(G-5113)
OSTEEL BUILDINGS INC (PA)
1180 Old Redbud Dr (28056)
P.O. Box 3667 (29582-0667)
PHONE..............................704 824-6061
Beverly Lynn, *Pr*
Larry Lynn, *VP*
EMP: 15 **EST:** 1990
SQ FT: 5,000
SALES (est): 560.62K **Privately Held**
Web: www.osteel.com
SIC: 3448 Prefabricated metal buildings and components

(G-5114)
OVERWITH INC
Also Called: Xpress Powder Coat
1220 Industrial Ave (28054-4629)
PHONE..............................704 866-8148
EMP: 5 **EST:** 2002
SALES (est): 510.42K **Privately Held**
Web: www.championpowdercoat.com
SIC: 3479 Coating of metals and formed products

(G-5115)
PARK MANUFACTURING COMPANY (PA)
Also Called: Park Elevator Co
3112 Northwest Blvd (28052-1167)

P.O. Box 12866 (28052-0043)
PHONE..............................704 869-6128
Nilla Stevens, *Pr*
EMP: 19 **EST:** 1898
SQ FT: 10,000
SALES (est): 2.28MM
SALES (corp-wide): 2.28MM **Privately Held**
Web: www.parkelevators.com
SIC: 3534 1796 Elevators and equipment; Elevator installation and conversion

(G-5116)
PARKDALE INCORPORATED (PA)
531 Cotton Blossom Cir (28054)
P.O. Box 1787 (28053)
PHONE..............................704 874-5000
Charles Heilig, *Pr*
◆ **EMP:** 74 **EST:** 2013
SALES (est): 1.44B
SALES (corp-wide): 1.44B **Privately Held**
Web: www.parkdalemills.com
SIC: 2281 Polyester yarn, spun: made from purchased staple

(G-5117)
PARKDALE MILLS INCORPORATED (HQ)
531 Cotton Blossom Cir (28054)
P.O. Box 1787 (28053)
PHONE..............................704 874-5000
Anderson D Warlick, *CEO*
Charles Heilig, *
Chuck Hall, *Vice Chairman*
Cecelia Meade, *
◆ **EMP:** 100 **EST:** 1916
SQ FT: 20,000
SALES (est): 550.27MM
SALES (corp-wide): 1.44B **Privately Held**
Web: www.parkdalemills.com
SIC: 2281 2844 2241 Cotton yarn, spun; Perfumes, cosmetics and other toilet preparations; Cotton narrow fabrics
PA: Parkdale, Incorporated
531 Cotton Blossom Cir
Gastonia NC 28054
704 874-5000

(G-5118)
PAUL CHARLES ENGLERT
Also Called: Scrappy's Metal Recycling
1820 Spencer Mountain Rd (28054-9600)
PHONE..............................704 824-2102
Paul C Englert, *Owner*
Englert Paul, *Owner*
EMP: 4 **EST:** 2011
SALES (est): 289.62K **Privately Held**
SIC: 3449 Miscellaneous metalwork

(G-5119)
PETTY MACHINE COMPANY INC
2403 Forbes Rd (28056-6268)
P.O. Box 1888 (28053-1888)
PHONE..............................704 864-3254
Larry K Petty, *CEO*
Frank Hovis, *Pr*
Jane Griffin, *Sec*
EMP: 22 **EST:** 1936
SQ FT: 98,000
SALES (est): 6.16MM **Privately Held**
Web: www.pettymachinecompany.com
SIC: 3565 3559 3552 3621 Packaging machinery; Plastics working machinery; Card clothing, textile machinery; Motors, electric

(G-5120)
PIONEER MACHINE WORKS INC
1221 W 2nd Ave (28052-3749)
P.O. Box 12826 (28052-0017)
PHONE..............................704 864-5528

Hugh H Jones, *Pr*
Ray Jones, *VP*
EMP: 5 **EST:** 1970
SQ FT: 20,000
SALES (est): 1.17MM **Privately Held**
Web: www.pioneermachineworks.com
SIC: 3599 Machine shop, jobbing and repair

(G-5121)
PORTERS GROUP LLC
Also Called: Porter's Fabrications
469 Hospital Dr Ste A (28054-4778)
PHONE..............................704 864-1313
▲ **EMP:** 300
SIC: 3441 3317 Fabricated structural metal;
Steel pipe and tubes

(G-5122)
POWDER COATING SERVICES INC
Also Called: Pcsi
1260 Shannon Bradley Rd (28052-1076)
PHONE..............................704 349-4100
Daryn E Parnham, *Pr*
Robert Burford, *
Jose I Venegas, *
EMP: 38 **EST:** 1996
SQ FT: 50,000
SALES (est): 5.43MM **Privately Held**
Web: www.pcsi-nc.com
SIC: 3479 Coating of metals and formed
products

(G-5123)
PPG ARCHITECTURAL FINISHES INC
Also Called: Glidden Professional Paint Ctr
729 E Franklin Blvd (28054-7149)
PHONE..............................704 864-6783
Raymond Grahmn, *Brnch Mgr*
EMP: 5
SALES (corp-wide): 17.65B **Publicly Held**
Web: www.ppgpaints.com
SIC: 2851 Paints and allied products
HQ: Ppg Architectural Finishes, Inc.
1 Ppg Pl
Pittsburgh PA 15272
412 434-3131

(G-5124)
PRATT INDUSTRIES
975 Tulip Dr (28052-1825)
PHONE..............................704 864-4022
EMP: 5 **EST:** 2018
SALES (est): 231.17K **Privately Held**
Web: www.prattindustries.com
SIC: 2653 Boxes, corrugated: made from
purchased materials

(G-5125)
PRECISION COMB WORKS INC
2524 N Chester St (28052-1808)
P.O. Box 2167 (28053-2167)
PHONE..............................704 864-2761
Larry G Brown, *Pr*
Patricia Carter, *VP*
Joyce Swanson, *Mgr*
EMP: 6 **EST:** 1958
SQ FT: 3,500
SALES (est): 474.14K **Privately Held**
Web: www.precisioncombworks.com
SIC: 3552 Textile machinery

(G-5126)
PRECISION MACHINE PRODUCTS INC
2347 N Chester St (28052-1810)
P.O. Box 1576 (28053-1576)
PHONE..............................704 865-7490
Robert H Blalock Junior, *Pr*
Robert Blalock Iii, *VP*
Linda Bess, *
EMP: 70 **EST:** 1947

SQ FT: 40,000
SALES (est): 9.32MM **Privately Held**
Web: www.pmpgastonia.com
SIC: 3552 3444 Textile machinery; Sheet
metalwork

(G-5127)
PREMIER BODY ARMOR LLC
1552 Union Rd Ste E (28054-5523)
P.O. Box 335 (28086-0335)
PHONE..............................704 750-3118
Frank Stewart, *Managing Member*
EMP: 10 **EST:** 2013
SALES (est): 4.89MM **Privately Held**
Web: www.premierbodyarmor.com
SIC: 3842 Bulletproof vests

(G-5128)
PROTOTYPE TOOLING CO
1811 W Franklin Blvd (28052-1426)
PHONE..............................704 864-7777
William Hall, *Owner*
EMP: 4 **EST:** 1990
SQ FT: 5,600
SALES (est): 223.58K **Privately Held**
SIC: 3544 Special dies and tools

(G-5129)
QUIKNIT CRAFTING INC
1916 S York Rd (28052-6369)
PHONE..............................704 861-1030
Charles Quick, *Pr*
Loretta Trammell, *VP*
EMP: 6 **EST:** 1986
SQ FT: 165,000
SALES (est): 144.23K **Privately Held**
Web: www.quiknit.com
SIC: 2241 5199 Fringes, woven; Knit goods

(G-5130)
R A SERAFINI INC
111 Lagrande St (28056-6317)
P.O. Box 6100 (28056-6022)
PHONE..............................704 864-6763
Robert A Serafini, *Pr*
▼ **EMP:** 13 **EST:** 1965
SALES (est): 2.41MM **Privately Held**
Web: www.raserafini.com
SIC: 3544 Industrial molds

(G-5131)
R R DONNELLEY & SONS COMPANY
Also Called: R R Donnelley
1205 Isley Rd (28052-8106)
P.O. Box 1577 (28053-1577)
PHONE..............................704 864-5717
Ann Payne, *Mgr*
EMP: 5
SALES (corp-wide): 15B **Privately Held**
Web: www.rrd.com
SIC: 2761 2752 Manifold business forms;
Color lithography
HQ: R. R. Donnelley & Sons Company
35 W Wacker Dr
Chicago IL 60601
312 326-8000

(G-5132)
REDDY ICE LLC
2306 Lowell Rd (28054-3407)
PHONE..............................704 824-4611
Bob Joyner, *Mgr*
EMP: 4
SALES (corp-wide): 3.82B **Privately Held**
Web: www.reddyice.com
SIC: 2097 Manufactured ice
HQ: Reddy Ice Llc
5710 Lbj Fwy Ste 300
Dallas TX 75240
214 526-6740

(G-5133)
REEL-TEX INC
4905 Sparrow Dairy Rd (28056-8940)
PHONE..............................704 868-4419
Jack C Barbee, *Pr*
Joyce Barbee, *Sec*
Dwain Barbee, *VP*
EMP: 10 **EST:** 1979
SQ FT: 3,400
SALES (est): 389.44K **Privately Held**
Web: www.reeltex.com
SIC: 3599 Machine shop, jobbing and repair

(G-5134)
SANS TECHNICAL FIBERS LLC
Also Called: Sans
2020 Remount Rd (28054-7476)
PHONE..............................704 869-8311
John Nagle, *Managing Member*
◆ **EMP:** 10 **EST:** 2000
SALES (est): 2.44MM **Privately Held**
Web: www.sansfibers.com
SIC: 2284 Nylon thread
PA: Aeci Ltd
1st Floor Aeci Place, 24 The
Woodlands
Saxonwold GT 2196

(G-5135)
SCHWARTZ STEEL SERVICE INC
525 N Broad St (28054-2508)
P.O. Box 1055 (28053-1055)
PHONE..............................704 865-9576
EMP: 35
Web: www.pasteel.com
SIC: 5051 3444 Steel; Sheet metalwork

(G-5136)
SIGN CONNECTION INC
1660 Pacolet Dr (28052-9467)
PHONE..............................704 868-4500
Sidney W Chip Craig Junior, *Pr*
Sidney W Craig Senior, *Treas*
Brenda Craig, *Sec*
EMP: 18 **EST:** 1988
SQ FT: 8,500
SALES (est): 2.52MM **Privately Held**
Web: www.signcon.com
SIC: 1799 3993 Sign installation and
maintenance; Electric signs

(G-5137)
SIGNZ INC
Also Called: Signs Now
3608 S New Hope Rd (28056-8325)
P.O. Box 550399 (28055-0399)
PHONE..............................704 824-7446
Lanny J Henderson, *Pr*
Susan Henderson, *VP*
EMP: 7 **EST:** 1956
SQ FT: 4,000
SALES (est): 634.06K **Privately Held**
Web: www.signsnow.com
SIC: 3993 Signs and advertising specialties

(G-5138)
SIKA CORPORATION (DH)
1909 Kyle Ct (28052-8420)
PHONE..............................704 810-0500
Tim A Smith, *VP*
Thomas Adolf, *
◆ **EMP:** 20 **EST:** 1999
SQ FT: 90,000
SALES (est): 22.73MM **Privately Held**
Web: automotive.sika.com
SIC: 5531 1742 2891 Automotive parts;
Acoustical and insulation work; Adhesives
HQ: Sika Automotive Deutschland Gmbh
Flinschstr. 10-16
Frankfurt Am Main HE 60388
62413010

(G-5139)
SPECIALTY MACHINE CO INC
1669 Federal St (28052-0504)
P.O. Box 12634 (28052-0013)
PHONE..............................704 853-2102
James C Brooks, *Pr*
James Brooks, *Pr*
Bryan Brooks, *Treas*
EMP: 7 **EST:** 1977
SQ FT: 10,000
SALES (est): 628.85K **Privately Held**
SIC: 3544 Special dies and tools

(G-5140)
SPEEDWELL MACHINE WORKS INC
Also Called: Smw
1301 Crowders Creek Rd (28052-8148)
PHONE..............................704 866-7418
Amos R Benefield, *Pr*
Udora S Benefield, *
EMP: 25 **EST:** 1975
SQ FT: 14,000
SALES (est): 5.69MM **Privately Held**
Web: www.speedwellmachineworks.com
SIC: 3599 3545 Machine shop, jobbing and
repair; Machine tool accessories

(G-5141)
STABILUS INC (DH)
Also Called: Stabilus
1201 Tulip Dr (28052-1842)
PHONE..............................704 865-7444
Anthony Haba, *Pr*
Craig Pospiech, *
Tom Napoli, *
◆ **EMP:** 89 **EST:** 2001
SQ FT: 200,000
SALES (est): 61.75MM
SALES (corp-wide): 1.46B **Privately Held**
Web: www.stabilus.com
SIC: 3493 Steel springs, except wire
HQ: Stabilus Gmbh
Wallersheimer Weg 100
Koblenz RP 56070
26189000

(G-5142)
STABLE HOLDCO INC
1201 Tulip Dr (28052-1842)
PHONE..............................704 866-7140
Ansgar Kroetz, *Pr*
EMP: 401 **EST:** 2008
SALES (est): 3.42MM
SALES (corp-wide): 1.46B **Privately Held**
SIC: 3493 Steel springs, except wire
HQ: Stable Beteiligungs Gmbh
Wallersheimer Weg 100
Koblenz RP 56070
261 890-0226

(G-5143)
STAR WIPERS INC
2260 Raeford Ct (28052-8422)
PHONE..............................888 511-2656
EMP: 43
Web: www.starwipers.com
SIC: 2211 Scrub cloths
PA: Star Wipers, Inc.
1125 E Main St
Newark OH 43055

(G-5144)
STERLING RACK INC
176 Tarheel Dr (28056-8719)
PHONE..............................704 866-9131
Ron Dalrymple, *Pr*
EMP: 4 **EST:** 1981
SALES (est): 562.25K **Privately Held**
Web: www.sterlingrack.com

SIC: **2542** 3537 3471 Racks, merchandise display or storage: except wood; Industrial trucks and tractors; Plating and polishing

(G-5145)
SUBTLE IMPRESSIONS INC
1200 Industrial Ave (28054-4629)
P.O. Box 3688 (28054-0037)
EMP: 23 **EST:** 1987
SQ FT: 28,000
SALES (est): 4.77MM **Privately Held**
Web: www.subtleimpressions.com
SIC: 2759 2796 2789 2675 Embossing on paper; Platemaking services; Bookbinding and related work; Die-cut paper and board

(G-5146)
SUMMIT YARN LLC
531 Cotton Blossom Cir (28054-5245)
P.O. Box 1787 (28053-1787)
PHONE..............................704 874-5000
John K Nims, *Pr*
Daniel K Wilson, *CFO*
Charles Dickinson, *VP*
EMP: 7 **EST:** 1998
SALES (est): 618.65K
SALES (corp-wide): 1.44B **Privately Held**
SIC: 2281 Needle and handicraft yarns, spun
HQ: Parkdale Mills, Incorporated
531 Cotton Blossom Cir
Gastonia NC 28054
704 874-5000

(G-5147)
SUPERIOR PLASTICS INC
533 N Broad St (28054-2508)
P.O. Box 1812 (28053-1812)
PHONE..............................704 864-5472
Thurman E Looper, *Pr*
Charles Looper, *VP*
Glenda Looper, *Sec*
▲ **EMP:** 10 **EST:** 1969
SALES (est): 1MM **Privately Held**
Web: www.superiorplastics.com
SIC: 3089 Injection molding of plastics

(G-5148)
SUPERIOR POWDER COATING LLC
123 Shannon Bradley Rd (28052-9202)
P.O. Box 821 (28053-0821)
PHONE..............................704 869-0004
Antonia H Callahan, *Managing Member*
EMP: 8 **EST:** 2010
SQ FT: 16,000
SALES (est): 791.87K **Privately Held**
Web: www.superiorpowder.com
SIC: 3479 Coating of metals and formed products

(G-5149)
TCI MOBILITY INC
1720 Industrial Pike Rd (28052-8434)
P.O. Box 939 (28053-0939)
PHONE..............................704 867-8331
Hannes M Charen, *Pr*
▼ **EMP:** 16 **EST:** 1947
SQ FT: 18,000
SALES (est): 2.55MM **Privately Held**
Web: www.tcimobility.com
SIC: 5084 3552 3699 3537 Textile machinery and equipment; Textile machinery; Electrical equipment and supplies, nec; Industrial trucks and tractors

(G-5150)
TEXLON PLASTICS CORP
135 Wolfpack Rd (28053)
P.O. Box 1284 (28053-1284)
PHONE..............................704 866-8785
William Glover, *Pr*
Ellen Beam, *

EMP: 35 **EST:** 1976
SQ FT: 23,400
SALES (est): 3.32MM **Privately Held**
Web: www.texlonplastics.com
SIC: 3089 Injection molding of plastics

(G-5151)
TEXPACK USA INC
1302 Industrial Pike Rd (28052-8430)
PHONE..............................704 864-5406
Michael Schmidlin, *Pr*
EMP: 7 **EST:** 2000
SALES (est): 136.17K **Privately Held**
SIC: 2678 Stationery products

(G-5152)
TEXTILE PARTS AND MCH CO INC
Also Called: Stewart Gear Manufacturing
1502 W May Ave (28052-1410)
P.O. Box 12305 (28052-0020)
PHONE..............................704 865-5003
John G Stewart, *Pr*
David M Stewart Junior, *VP*
EMP: 5 **EST:** 1944
SQ FT: 25,000
SALES (est): 735.39K **Privately Held**
Web: www.stewartgear.com
SIC: 3569 Filters

(G-5153)
THE MCQUACKINS COMPANY LLC
2335 Jenkins Dairy Rd (28052-7157)
PHONE..............................980 254-2309
Eve Lowry, *Managing Member*
EMP: 4 **EST:** 2022
SALES (est): 182.43K **Privately Held**
SIC: 2389 7389 Apparel and accessories, nec; Business Activities at Non-Commercial Site

(G-5154)
THOMAS CONCRETE SC INC
Also Called: Thomas Concrete South Carolina
5614 Union Rd (28056-9578)
PHONE..............................704 868-4545
Earl Strickland, *Mgr*
EMP: 4
SALES (corp-wide): 1.15B **Privately Held**
Web: www.thomasconcrete.com
SIC: 5211 3273 Lumber and other building materials; Ready-mixed concrete
HQ: Thomas Concrete Of South Carolina, Inc.
2500 Cumberland Pkwy Se # 200
Atlanta GA 30339
919 832-0451

(G-5155)
TOMS KNIT FABRICS
699 Carlton Dr Apt A (28054-5265)
PHONE..............................704 867-4236
Tommy B Atkinson, *Owner*
EMP: 6 **EST:** 1962
SQ FT: 8,000
SALES (est): 340.08K **Privately Held**
SIC: 2257 Pile fabrics, circular knit

(G-5156)
TONY S ICE CREAM COMPANY INC (PA)
604 E Franklin Blvd (28054-7111)
PHONE..............................704 867-7085
Robert Coletta, *Pr*
▲ **EMP:** 18 **EST:** 1915
SQ FT: 4,500
SALES (est): 2.59MM
SALES (corp-wide): 2.59MM **Privately Held**
Web: www.tonysicecream.com

SIC: **2024** 5451 Ice cream and frozen deserts ; Ice cream (packaged)

(G-5157)
TONYS ICE CREAM CO INC
Also Called: TONY'S ICE CREAM CO INC
520 E Franklin Blvd (28054-7110)
PHONE..............................704 853-0018
Robert Coletta, *Pr*
EMP: 7
SALES (corp-wide): 2.59MM **Privately Held**
Web: www.tonysicecream.com
SIC: 5143 5812 2024 Ice cream and ices; Eating places; Ice cream and frozen deserts
PA: Tony S Ice Cream Company, Inc.
604 E Franklin Blvd
Gastonia NC 28054
704 867-7085

(G-5158)
TRAC PLASTICS INC
140 Superior Stainless Rd (28052-8744)
P.O. Box 12547 (28052-0035)
PHONE..............................704 864-9140
W D Turlington, *Pr*
Brenda Turlington, *Sec*
EMP: 10 **EST:** 1979
SQ FT: 20,000
SALES (est): 978.03K **Privately Held**
Web: www.tracplastics.com
SIC: 3089 Injection molding of plastics

(G-5159)
TRI STATE PLASTICS INC
507 E Davidson Ave (28054-2444)
PHONE..............................704 865-7431
Thomas A Hope Junior, *Pr*
Carol N Hope, *VP*
Cindy Lynn Hope, *Sec*
EMP: 5 **EST:** 1967
SQ FT: 15,000
SALES (est): 451.2K **Privately Held**
SIC: 3552 Textile machinery

(G-5160)
UNIVERSAL BLACK OXIDE INC
205 Oxford St (28054-5422)
P.O. Box 2041 (28053-2041)
PHONE..............................704 867-1772
Randy Lewallen, *Pr*
Kenneth Lewallen, *VP*
Daphene Lewallen, *Sec*
EMP: 5 **EST:** 1985
SQ FT: 3,600
SALES (est): 248.07K **Privately Held**
Web: www.universalblackoxide.com
SIC: 3479 3471 Coating of metals and formed products; Coloring and finishing of aluminum or formed products

(G-5161)
US COTTON LLC (DH)
531 Cotton Blossom Cir (28054-5245)
P.O. Box 1787 (28053-1787)
PHONE..............................216 676-6400
Anthony Thomas, *Ch Bd*
John B Nims, *
◆ **EMP:** 250 **EST:** 1983
SQ FT: 160,000
SALES (est): 92.29MM
SALES (corp-wide): 1.44B **Privately Held**
Web: www.uscotton.com
SIC: 2844 2241 Perfumes, cosmetics and other toilet preparations; Cotton narrow fabrics
HQ: Parkdale Mills, Incorporated
531 Cotton Blossom Cir
Gastonia NC 28054
704 874-5000

(G-5162)
VAL-U-KING GROUP INC
2312 Rufus Ratchford Rd (28056-8179)
PHONE..............................980 306-5342
Valdez Tilton, *CEO*
Valdez Hilton, *CEO*
EMP: 5 **EST:** 2019
SALES (est): 351.43K **Privately Held**
SIC: 5311 2519 Department stores, discount ; Furniture, household: glass, fiberglass, and plastic

(G-5163)
W D LEE & COMPANY
212 Trakas Blvd (28052-9221)
P.O. Box 12157 (28052-0011)
PHONE..............................704 864-0346
Dennis J Lee, *Pr*
Karen Rhyne, *Sec*
Selina Lee, *Treas*
EMP: 8 **EST:** 1954
SQ FT: 22,000
SALES (est): 1.36MM **Privately Held**
Web: www.wdlee.com
SIC: 3599 7692 3545 Machine shop, jobbing and repair; Welding repair; Machine tool accessories

(G-5164)
WANGS AND THANGS LLC
2309 Penny Park Dr Apt D (28052-6068)
PHONE..............................980 925-7010
EMP: 4
SALES (est): 234.87K **Privately Held**
SIC: 2599 Food wagons, restaurant

(G-5165)
WILDER TACTICAL LLC
120 Wolfpack Rd (28056-9776)
P.O. Box 335 (28086-0335)
PHONE..............................704 750-7141
EMP: 5 **EST:** 2017
SALES (est): 2.68MM **Privately Held**
Web: www.wildertactical.com
SIC: 3949 Ammunition belts, sporting type

(G-5166)
WOOD CREATIONS NC INC
2223 Plastics Dr (28054-1415)
PHONE..............................704 865-1822
Ronald Honeycutt, *Pr*
Ann Honeycutt, *
EMP: 6 **EST:** 1997
SQ FT: 48,000
SALES (est): 870.04K **Privately Held**
Web: www.woodcreations.com
SIC: 2431 Doors, wood

(G-5167)
WORK WELL HYDRTION SYSTEMS LLC
Also Called: Wwh Systems LLC
1680 Garfield Dr (28052-8403)
P.O. Box 551360 (28055-1360)
PHONE..............................704 853-7788
Scott Foy, *Managing Member*
Marvin Foy, *Managing Member*
EMP: 8 **EST:** 2012
SALES (est): 969.83K **Privately Held**
Web: www.workwellhs.com
SIC: 5074 3585 Water purification equipment ; Ice making machinery

(G-5168)
WV HOLDINGS INC
Also Called: Witten Vent Company
404 E Long Ave (28054-2527)
PHONE..............................704 853-8338
Erik H Witten, *Pr*
Alvin E Witten, *VP*

Susan Nichols, *Mgr*
EMP: 6 **EST:** 1969
SQ FT: 13,000
SALES (est): 493.03K **Privately Held**
Web: www.bestvents.com
SIC: 3564 3444 Blowers and fans; Metal ventilating equipment

Gatesville
Gates County

(G-5169)
ASHTON LEWIS LUMBER CO INC
96 Lewis Mill Rd (27938-8003)
P.O. Box 25 (27938-0025)
PHONE.............................252 357-0050
James Rane, *CEO*
Steven Good, *
EMP: 100 **EST:** 2017
SALES (est): 2.7MM **Privately Held**
Web: www.ashton-lewis.com
SIC: 2421 Sawmills and planing mills, general

(G-5170)
BUNDY LOGGING COMPANY INC
Also Called: Bundy Trucking
37 Main St (27938)
P.O. Box 597 (27938-0597)
PHONE.............................252 357-0191
Claude Bundy, *Pr*
Jackie Bundy, *VP*
EMP: 5 **EST:** 1966
SALES (est): 341K **Privately Held**
SIC: 2411 4214 4213 Logging camps and contractors; Local trucking with storage; Trucking, except local

(G-5171)
COXE-LEWIS CORPORATION
Also Called: Ashton Lewis Lumber
96 Lewis Mill Rd (27938-8003)
P.O. Box 25 (27938-0025)
PHONE.............................252 357-0050
Tom Coxe, *Pr*
Nan Coxe, *VP*
▼ **EMP:** 6 **EST:** 1953
SQ FT: 300,000
SALES (est): 661.72K **Privately Held**
Web: www.ashton-lewis.com
SIC: 2421 2435 2426 Lumber: rough, sawed, or planed; Hardwood veneer and plywood; Hardwood dimension and flooring mills

(G-5172)
GATES CUSTOM MILLING INC
681 Nc Highway 37 S (27938-9628)
P.O. Box 405 (27938-0405)
PHONE.............................252 357-0116
Mark Truck, *Pr*
Mark Tuck, *
Nancy Tuck, *
Caroline Martin, *Stockholder*
EMP: 40 **EST:** 1978
SQ FT: 24,900
SALES (est): 8.66MM **Privately Held**
Web: www.gatesmilling.com
SIC: 2426 2431 2435 2421 Hardwood dimension and flooring mills; Millwork; Hardwood veneer and plywood; Planing mills, nec

Germanton
Stokes County

(G-5173)
BOYLES SIGN SHOP INC
4050 Stafford Mill Rd (27019-9421)
PHONE.............................336 782-1189
Robbie Boyles, *Pr*
Joyce Boyles, *VP*
EMP: 6 **EST:** 1985
SALES (est): 68.44K **Privately Held**
SIC: 3993 Signs and advertising specialties

(G-5174)
BUFFALO CREEK FARM & CRMRY LLC
Also Called: Buffalo Creek Farm
3241 Buffalo Creek Farm Rd (27019-9596)
PHONE.............................336 969-5698
EMP: 4 **EST:** 1991
SALES (est): 218.91K **Privately Held**
Web: www.buffalocreekfarmandcreamery.com
SIC: 5451 0241 2022 Dairy products stores; Dairy farms; Cheese spreads, dips, pastes, and other cheese products

Gibson
Scotland County

(G-5175)
OIL MILL SALVAGE RECYCLERS INC
13840 Oil Mill Rd (28343-8273)
PHONE.............................910 268-2111
Daniel Junecampbell, *CEO*
EMP: 4 **EST:** 2015
SALES (est): 159.88K **Privately Held**
Web: oilmillsalvagerecyclers.business.site
SIC: 2074 Cottonseed oil mills

Gibsonville
Guilford County

(G-5176)
GRIFFIN TUBING COMPANY INC
906 Burlington Ave (27249-2952)
P.O. Box 228 (27249-0228)
PHONE.............................336 449-4822
Richard W Griffin, *Pr*
Adele L Griffin, *VP*
EMP: 7 **EST:** 1950
SQ FT: 5,000
SALES (est): 76.95K **Privately Held**
SIC: 2259 Bags and bagging, knit

(G-5177)
HARDWOOD STORE OF NC INC
106v E Railroad Ave (27249-2300)
P.O. Box 15 (27249-0015)
PHONE.............................336 449-9627
Hilton B Peel Junior, *Pr*
Hilton Peal Senior, *Treas*
▼ **EMP:** 12 **EST:** 1996
SQ FT: 43,000
SALES (est): 2.13MM **Privately Held**
Web: www.hardwoodstore.com
SIC: 2541 5211 Wood partitions and fixtures; Lumber products

(G-5178)
J C CUSTOM SEWING INC
106 E Railroad Ave (27249-2300)
P.O. Box 213 (27249-0213)
PHONE.............................336 449-4586
Josephine Feyrer, *Pr*

Christel Schappacher, *VP*
EMP: 9 **EST:** 1980
SQ FT: 16,000
SALES (est): 319.84K **Privately Held**
SIC: 2339 2392 2393 Aprons, except rubber or plastic: women's, misses', juniors'; Bags, laundry: made from purchased materials; Textile bags

(G-5179)
KECK LOGGING COMPANY
576 Browns Chapel Rd (27249-9522)
PHONE.............................336 538-6903
Charles Keck, *Owner*
EMP: 7 **EST:** 1972
SALES (est): 163.11K **Privately Held**
SIC: 2411 Logging camps and contractors

(G-5180)
LARRY D TROXLER
Also Called: L T Welding
6170 Nc Highway 87 N (27249-9323)
PHONE.............................336 585-1141
Larry D Troxler, *Owner*
EMP: 5 **EST:** 1996
SALES (est): 151.72K **Privately Held**
SIC: 7692 Welding repair

(G-5181)
LINDLEY LABORATORIES INC (PA)
106 E Railroad Ave (27249-2300)
P.O. Box 341 (27216-0341)
PHONE.............................336 449-7521
J Thomas Lindley Senior, *Ch Bd*
William Clarke Lindley, *Pr*
▼ **EMP:** 10 **EST:** 1977
SQ FT: 200,000
SALES (est): 671.85K
SALES (corp-wide): 671.85K **Privately Held**
Web: www.lindleylabs.com
SIC: 2843 6531 2869 Finishing agents; Real estate agents and managers; Industrial organic chemicals, nec

(G-5182)
MAGNOLIA LINEN INC
106 E Railroad Ave (27249-2300)
P.O. Box 65 (27249-0065)
PHONE.............................336 449-0447
Maria Price, *Pr*
EMP: 12 **EST:** 1997
SALES (est): 862.63K **Privately Held**
Web: www.magnolialineninc.com
SIC: 7213 2326 Linen supply, non-clothing; Work uniforms

(G-5183)
NEW GENERATION YARN CORP
1248 Springwood Church Rd (27249-2646)
PHONE.............................336 449-5607
Shartel Smith, *Pr*
EMP: 6 **EST:** 2006
SALES (est): 365.36K **Privately Held**
Web: www.newgenerationyarn.com
SIC: 2282 Nylon yarn: throwing, twisting, winding or spooling

(G-5184)
TEMPEST AERO GROUP
Also Called: Tempest Plus Marketing Group
1240 Springwood Church Rd (27249-2646)
PHONE.............................336 449-5054
Tim Henderson, *
Charles Henderson, *
EMP: 42 **EST:** 1984
SQ FT: 3,500
SALES (est): 12.38MM **Privately Held**
Web: www.aeroaccessories.com

SIC: 3728 3812 Aircraft parts and equipment, nec; Search and navigation equipment

(G-5185)
TOMMYS TUBING & STOCKENETTES
628 Wood St (27249-2557)
PHONE.............................336 449-6461
Thomas Tickle, *Pr*
Janice Tickle, *
EMP: 10 **EST:** 1969
SQ FT: 4,800
SALES (est): 217.09K **Privately Held**
SIC: 2259 2257 Meat bagging, knit; Weft knit fabric mills

Godwin
Sampson County

(G-5186)
ATS SERVICE COMPANY LLC
8442 Fayetteville Rd (28344-2400)
PHONE.............................512 905-9005
Joshua Murray, *CEO*
Joshua Murray, *Managing Member*
EMP: 4 **EST:** 2021
SALES (est): 175.82K **Privately Held**
SIC: 7389 3589 Financial services; Commercial cooking and foodwarming equipment

(G-5187)
BRITE SKY LLC
6461 Sherrill Baggett Rd (28344-8200)
PHONE.............................757 589-4676
Tracy Frith Carvalho, *Managing Member*
EMP: 6 **EST:** 2022
SALES (est): 227.41K **Privately Held**
SIC: 3999 7389 Manufacturing industries, nec; Business services, nec

(G-5188)
COASTAL PROTEIN PRODUCTS INC
Also Called: Martin Meats
1600 Martin Rd (28344-9068)
PHONE.............................910 567-6102
Carlton Martin, *Pr*
EMP: 4 **EST:** 1989
SQ FT: 40,000
SALES (est): 431.73K **Privately Held**
SIC: 2077 Animal and marine fats and oils

(G-5189)
KANSAS CITY SAUSAGE CO LLC
Also Called: Coastal Proteins
1600 Martin Rd (28344-9068)
PHONE.............................910 567-5604
EMP: 5
Web: www.pineridge.org
SIC: 2013 Sausages and other prepared meats
HQ: Kansas City Sausage Company, Llc
   8001 Nw 106th St
   Kansas City MO 64153

Gold Hill
Rowan County

(G-5190)
CAROLINA STALITE CO LTD PARTNR
16815 Old Beatty Ford Rd (28071)
PHONE.............................704 279-2166
EMP: 21
SALES (corp-wide): 7.41MM **Privately Held**
Web: www.stalite.com

SIC: 3281 0711 Slate products; Soil
chemical treatment services
PA: Carolina Stalite Company Limited
Partnership
205 Klumac Rd
Salisbury NC 28144
704 637-1515

(G-5191)
CAROLINA STALITE CO LTD PARTNR
17700 Old Beatty Ford Rd (28071-9655)
P.O. Box 1037 (28145-1037)
PHONE.............................704 279-2166
Jessie Penley, *Brnch Mgr*
EMP: 23
SALES (corp-wide): 7.41MM **Privately
Held**
Web: www.stalite.com
SIC: 3295 Clay for petroleum refining,
chemically processed
PA: Carolina Stalite Company Limited
Partnership
205 Klumac Rd
Salisbury NC 28144
704 637-1515

(G-5192)
H & M WOOD PRESERVING INC
Also Called: H&M Woodpreserving
280 Zion Church Rd (28071-8710)
PHONE.............................704 279-5188
John A Hammill, *Pr*
Rebbecca Barnard Hammill, *
John Allen Hammill Iii, *VP*
EMP: 40 EST: 1982
SQ FT: 1,700
SALES (est): 3.07MM **Privately Held**
Web: www.hmwoodpreserving.com
SIC: 4212 2491 Local trucking, without
storage; Wood preserving

(G-5193)
HAMMILL CONSTRUCTION CO INC
5051 St Stephens Church Rd (28071-9427)
PHONE.............................704 279-5309
Jerry Hammill, *Pr*
Jerry Hammill, *CEO*
Donna Hammill, *
Larry Hammill, *
EMP: 7 EST: 1957
SQ FT: 3,000
SALES (est): 3.93MM **Privately Held**
Web: www.puppylovedscspa.com
SIC: 1446 4212 Abrasive sand mining;
Dump truck haulage

(G-5194)
LEGACY VULCAN LLC
Mideast Division
16745 Old Beatty Ford Rd (28071-9710)
P.O. Box 188 (28071-0188)
PHONE.............................704 279-5566
Corey Viers, *Mgr*
EMP: 4
Web: www.vulcanmaterials.com
SIC: 3273 Ready-mixed concrete
HQ: Legacy Vulcan, Llc
1200 Urban Center Dr
Birmingham AL 35242
205 298-3000

(G-5195)
LYERLYS WLDG & FABRICATION INC
215 Woodson Rd (28071-9635)
PHONE.............................704 680-2317
Wesley Lyerly, *Pr*
EMP: 6 EST: 2014
SALES (est): 931.15K **Privately Held**
SIC: 7692 3441 Welding repair; Fabricated
structural metal

Goldsboro
Wayne County

(G-5196)
AIRGAS USA LLC
109 Hinnant Rd (27530-7618)
PHONE.............................919 735-5276
EMP: 5
SALES (corp-wide): 114.13MM **Privately
Held**
Web: www.airgas.com
SIC: 5169 5084 5085 2813 Industrial gases;
Welding machinery and equipment;
Welding supplies; Industrial gases
HQ: Airgas Usa, Llc
259 N Rdnor Chster Rd Ste
Radnor PA 19087
216 642-6600

(G-5197)
ALTA FOODS LLC
105 Industry Ct (27530-9124)
P.O. Box 1876 (27533-1876)
PHONE.............................919 734-0233
Donald Best Barnes Ii, *Managing Member*
EMP: 55 EST: 2007
SQ FT: 50,000
SALES (est): 8.96MM **Privately Held**
Web: www.altafoods.com
SIC: 5141 2099 Food brokers; Tortillas, fresh
or refrigerated

(G-5198)
ANCHOR COUPLING INC
106 Industry Ct (27530-9124)
PHONE.............................919 739-8000
EMP: 309
SALES (corp-wide): 64.81B **Publicly Held**
Web: www.anchorcoupling.com
SIC: 3492 Hose and tube couplings,
hydraulic/pneumatic
HQ: Anchor Coupling Inc.
5520 13th St
Menominee MI 49858
906 863-2672

(G-5199)
AP EMISSIONS TECHNOLOGIES LLC
Also Called: Airtek
300 Dixie Trl (27530)
PHONE.............................919 580-2000
Rich Biel, *Pr*
◆ EMP: 688 EST: 2013
SQ FT: 900,000
SALES (est): 44.54MM
SALES (corp-wide): 424.23B **Publicly
Held**
Web: www.apemissions.com
SIC: 3714 Mufflers (exhaust), motor vehicle
HQ: Marmon Holdings, Inc.
181 W Madison St Ste 3900
Chicago IL 60602
312 372-9500

(G-5200)
**ARNOLD-WILBERT CORPORATION
(PA)**
1401 W Grantham St (27530-1115)
PHONE.............................919 735-5008
John Williams, *Pr*
Ron Turner, *
Stephen L Velker, *General Vice President*
EMP: 70 EST: 1953
SQ FT: 12,000
SALES (est): 8.18MM
SALES (corp-wide): 8.18MM **Privately
Held**
Web: www.arnoldwilbert.com

SIC: 3272 Burial vaults, concrete or precast
terrazzo

(G-5201)
BOEING AROSPC OPERATIONS INC
Also Called: Boeing
1950 Jabara Ave Bldg 4517 (27531-2520)
PHONE.............................919 722-4351
James Clue, *Mgr*
EMP: 14
SALES (corp-wide): 66.52B **Publicly Held**
SIC: 3721 8711 Aircraft; Engineering services
HQ: Boeing Aerospace Operations, Inc.
6001 S A Depo Blvd Ste E
Oklahoma City OK 73150
405 622-6000

(G-5202)
**BRIDGESTONE RET OPERATIONS
LLC**
Also Called: Firestone
507 N Berkeley Blvd (27534-3442)
PHONE.............................919 778-0230
Terry Turnage Junior, *Mgr*
EMP: 8
Web: www.bridgestoneamericas.com
SIC: 5531 7534 Automotive tires; Rebuilding
and retreading tires
HQ: Bridgestone Retail Operations, Llc
200 4th Ave S Ste 100
Nashville TN 37201
615 937-1000

(G-5203)
BUTTERBALL LLC
938 Millers Chapel Rd (27534-7772)
PHONE.............................919 658-6743
EMP: 47
SALES (corp-wide): 9.1B **Publicly Held**
Web: www.butterball.com
SIC: 2015 Turkey, processed, nsk
HQ: Butterball, Llc
1 Butterball Ln
Garner NC 27529
919 255-7900

(G-5204)
CASE FARMS LLC
330 Westbrook Rd (27530-8476)
PHONE.............................919 658-2252
EMP: 50
Web: www.casefarms.com
SIC: 2015 8731 Poultry slaughtering and
processing; Commercial physical research
PA: Case Farms, L.L.C.
385 Pilch Rd
Troutman NC 28166

(G-5205)
CASE FOODS INC
Also Called: Case Farms
259 Sandhill Dr (27530-0901)
PHONE.............................919 736-4498
Gene Short, *Mgr*
EMP: 1200
SALES (corp-wide): 117.64MM **Privately
Held**
Web: www.casefarms.com
SIC: 2015 Poultry slaughtering and
processing
PA: Case Foods, Inc.
385 Pilch Rd
Troutman NC 28166
704 528-4501

(G-5206)
CLOTH BARN INC
Also Called: Home Fabrics
1701 E Ash St (27530-4042)
PHONE.............................919 735-3643
John M Bridgers, *Pr*

Elizabeth Bridgers, *VP*
Lillian O Bridgers, *Sec*
EMP: 15 EST: 1958
SQ FT: 16,000
SALES (est): 927.37K **Privately Held**
Web: www.theclothbarn.net
SIC: 5949 2211 5131 5714 Fabric stores
piece goods; Draperies and drapery fabrics,
cotton; Piece goods and other fabrics;
Upholstery materials

(G-5207)
COKER FEED MILL INC
1439 Hood Swamp Rd (27534-8563)
PHONE.............................919 778-3491
R Brantley Coker, *Pr*
Mabel S Coker, *VP*
Gaye Coker, *Sec*
EMP: 12 EST: 1949
SQ FT: 15,000
SALES (est): 5.36MM **Privately Held**
Web: www.cokerfeedmill.com
SIC: 2048 5411 Prepared feeds, nec;
Convenience stores

(G-5208)
CONETOE LAND & TIMBER LLC
3820 Stevens Mill Rd (27530-9705)
P.O. Box 160 (27819-0160)
PHONE.............................252 717-4648
G Forrest York, *Admn*
EMP: 7 EST: 2017
SALES (est): 780.96K **Privately Held**
SIC: 2411 Logging

(G-5209)
**COOPER-STANDARD AUTOMOTIVE
INC**
Also Called: Cooper
308 Fedelon Trl (27530-9001)
PHONE.............................919 735-5394
Renzo Bulgarelli, *Brnch Mgr*
EMP: 82
SALES (corp-wide): 2.73B **Publicly Held**
Web: www.cooperstandard.com
SIC: 3714 Motor vehicle parts and
accessories
HQ: Cooper-Standard Automotive Inc.
40300 Traditions Dr
Northville MI 48168
248 596-5900

(G-5210)
CORNELL & FERENCZ INC
301 S George St (27530)
PHONE.............................919 736-7373
June Hill, *Pr*
EMP: 5 EST: 1981
SQ FT: 4,225
SALES (est): 540.56K **Privately Held**
SIC: 5063 7694 Motors, electric; Electric
motor repair

(G-5211)
DAYSTAR MATERIALS INC
200 W Dewey St (27530-1304)
P.O. Box 10561 (27532-0561)
PHONE.............................919 734-0460
Larry Davis, *Mgr*
EMP: 20
SALES (corp-wide): 376.23K **Privately
Held**
SIC: 2891 5052 Epoxy adhesives; Coal and
other minerals and ores
PA: Daystar Materials, Inc
1712 Stablersville Rd
White Hall MD
410 357-4761

GEOGRAPHIC

(G-5212)
ELECTROPIN TECHNOLOGIES LLC
110 Centura Dr (27530-7745)
PHONE.............................919 288-1203
Keith Brenton, *Pr*
EMP: 6 **EST:** 2018
SALES (est): 2.56MM **Privately Held**
Web: www.electropintech.com
SIC: 3671 Cathode ray tubes, including
rebuilt

(G-5213)
EVERETTES INDUSTRIAL REPR SVC
117 Dobbs Pl (27534-7874)
PHONE.............................252 527-4269
Travis D Everette, *Owner*
EMP: 10 **EST:** 1989
SALES (est): 436.16K **Privately Held**
SIC: 3599 7692 3441 Machine shop, jobbing
and repair; Welding repair; Fabricated
structural metal

(G-5214)
FRANKLIN BAKING COMPANY LLC
(HQ)
Also Called: Flowers Bakery
500 W Grantham St (27530-1928)
P.O. Box 228 (27533-0228)
PHONE.............................919 735-0344
▲ **EMP:** 350 **EST:** 1939
SQ FT: 200,000
SALES (est): 19.11MM
SALES (corp-wide): 5.1B **Publicly Held**
Web: franklin-co4goldsboro.edan.io
SIC: 2051 Bread, all types (white, wheat,
rye, etc); fresh or frozen
PA: Flowers Foods, Inc.
1919 Flowers Cir
Thomasville GA 31757
229 226-9110

(G-5215)
GENERAL INDUSTRIES INC
3048 Thoroughfare Rd (27534-7728)
P.O. Box 1279 (27533-1279)
PHONE.............................919 751-1791
John T Wiggins, *Pr*
Teresa Finley, *Stockholder**
EMP: 45 **EST:** 1951
SQ FT: 50,000
SALES (est): 6.04MM **Privately Held**
Web: www.gitank.com
SIC: 3443 Tanks, standard or custom
fabricated: metal plate

(G-5216)
GOLDSBORO MILLING COMPANY
938 Millers Chapel Rd (27534-7772)
PHONE.............................919 778-3130
EMP: 194
Web: www.goldsboromilling.com
SIC: 2048 Poultry feeds

(G-5217)
GOLDSBORO NEON SIGN CO INC
712 N George St (27530-2428)
P.O. Box 1811 (27533-1811)
PHONE.............................919 735-2035
Donald Ray Westbrooke, *Pr*
Donald Ray Westbrook, *Pr*
Carolyn Weaks, *Treas*
James Westbrook, *Owner*
EMP: 4 **EST:** 1950
SQ FT: 5,000
SALES (est): 391.65K **Privately Held**
Web: www.goldsboroneonsignco.com
SIC: 3993 7389 Electric signs; Sign painting
and lettering shop

(G-5218)
GOLDSBORO STRTER ALTRNTOR
SVC
105 E Oak St (27530-2740)
PHONE.............................919 735-6745
Edward L Underwood, *Pr*
Richard Burgess, *VP*
Dianne Underwood, *Sec*
EMP: 5 **EST:** 1965
SQ FT: 5,000
SALES (est): 1.5MM **Privately Held**
SIC: 3694 3621 7539 Alternators, automotive
; Starters, for motors; Electrical services

(G-5219)
GRAPHIXX SCREEN PRINTING INC
601 N James St Ste B (27530-2700)
P.O. Box 1318 (27533-1318)
PHONE.............................919 736-3995
David Gibson, *Pr*
Jimmy Bryan, *VP*
Richard Narron, *Sec*
EMP: 6 **EST:** 1990
SALES (est): 101.54K **Privately Held**
SIC: 2759 Screen printing

(G-5220)
GRUMA CORPORATION
Also Called: Mission Foods
401 Gateway Dr (27534-7058)
PHONE.............................919 778-5553
EMP: 20
Web: www.gruma.com
SIC: 2096 Tortilla chips
HQ: Gruma Corporation
5601 Executive Dr Ste 800
Irving TX 75038
972 232-5000

(G-5221)
HAM WAYCO COMPANY
506 N William St (27530-2804)
P.O. Box 841 (27533-0841)
PHONE.............................919 735-3962
George A Worrell, *Pr*
Sallie B Worrell, *Sec*
EMP: 20 **EST:** 1947
SQ FT: 31,000
SALES (est): 1.99MM **Privately Held**
Web: www.waycohams.com
SIC: 2013 2011 Prepared pork products,
from purchased pork; Meat packing plants

(G-5222)
HARVEY FERTILIZER AND GAS CO
Patetown-Dixie Fert & Gas
2937 N William St (27530-8009)
P.O. Box 1454 (27533-1454)
PHONE.............................919 731-2474
Bobby Finch, *Mgr*
EMP: 18
SALES (corp-wide): 80.5MM **Privately**
Held
Web: www.harveyfertilizerandgas.com
SIC: 2873 2911 2875 Fertilizers: natural
(organic), except compost; Petroleum
refining; Fertilizers, mixing only
PA: Harvey Fertilizer And Gas Co.
303 Bohannon Rd
Kinston NC 28501
252 526-4150

(G-5223)
LEGACY BIOGAS LLC
Also Called: Legacy Biogas
107 Cassedale Dr (27534-9408)
PHONE.............................713 253-9013
Robert Hoffland, *Prin*
EMP: 5 **EST:** 2013
SALES (est): 83.61K **Privately Held**

SIC: 2813 Industrial gases

(G-5224)
LIGHTHOUSE OF WAYNE COUNTY
INC
405 E Walnut St (27530-4838)
P.O. Box 227 (27533-0227)
PHONE.............................919 736-1313
Cheryl Seronick, *Dir*
EMP: 4 **EST:** 1980
SALES (est): 228.08K **Privately Held**
Web: www.waynegov.com
SIC: 3731 8322 Lighthouse tenders, building
and repairing; Crisis intervention center

(G-5225)
LITTLE RIVER METALWORKS LLC
132 Blueberry Rd (27530-9502)
PHONE.............................919 920-0292
Casey Matthew Lee, *Asst Sec*
EMP: 5 **EST:** 2018
SALES (est): 97.16K **Privately Held**
Web: www.lrmetalworks.com
SIC: 3446 Architectural metalwork

(G-5226)
LUXOTTICA OF AMERICA INC
Also Called: Lenscrafters
611 N Berkeley Blvd Ste B (27534-3468)
PHONE.............................919 778-5692
Steven Earwood, *Brnch Mgr*
EMP: 4
SALES (corp-wide): 7.66MM **Privately**
Held
Web: www.luxottica.com
SIC: 5995 3851 Eyeglasses, prescription;
Ophthalmic goods
HQ: Luxottica Of America Inc.
4000 Luxottica Pl
Mason OH 45040

(G-5227)
MAJESTIC XPRESS HANDWASH INC
103 N John St Ste D (27530-3632)
PHONE.............................919 440-7611
Jomokenyatta Jones, *CEO*
EMP: 5 **EST:** 2019
SQ FT: 900
SALES (est): 324.5K **Privately Held**
SIC: 3589 Car washing machinery

(G-5228)
METAL CRAFTERS OF GOLDSBORO
NC
855 Nc 111 Hwy S (27534-6325)
P.O. Box 10008 (27532-0008)
PHONE.............................919 778-7200
C Brooks Marriner, *Pr*
Kenneth L Cox, *VP*
EMP: 6 **EST:** 1956
SQ FT: 7,200
SALES (est): 769.25K **Privately Held**
SIC: 2431 Staircases, stairs and railings

(G-5229)
METALCRAFT & MECH SVC INC
147 Aycock Dr (27530-9501)
PHONE.............................919 736-1029
Warren Woodard, *Pr*
Richard Woodard Senior, *Pr*
EMP: 6 **EST:** 1981
SQ FT: 2,500
SALES (est): 922.11K **Privately Held**
Web: www.alldriveshafts.com
SIC: 3714 Motor vehicle parts and
accessories

(G-5230)
MONK LEKEISHA
Also Called: Dukester Productions Entrmt Co

P.O. Box 405 (27533-0405)
PHONE.............................910 385-0361
Lekeisha Monk, *Owner*
EMP: 6 **EST:** 1999
SQ FT: 1,000
SALES (est): 367.5K **Privately Held**
SIC: 7389 2752 Decoration service for
special events; Commercial printing,
lithographic

(G-5231)
NORTH CAROLINA MFG INC
Also Called: NCM
100 Industry Ct (27530-9124)
PHONE.............................919 734-1115
Ray Mayo, *Pr*
Janice Mayo, *Sec*
EMP: 20 **EST:** 1990
SQ FT: 6,000
SALES (est): 5.02MM **Privately Held**
Web: www.ncmfginc.com
SIC: 3599 3545 Machine shop, jobbing and
repair; Machine tool accessories

(G-5232)
NRFP LOGGING LLC
206 Connie Cir (27530-9309)
PHONE.............................919 738-0989
Ason B Tew, *Prin*
EMP: 4 **EST:** 2018
SALES (est): 837.37K **Privately Held**
SIC: 2411 Logging camps and contractors

(G-5233)
OCCASIONS GROUP INC
Also Called: Taylor Prime Labels & Packg
305 N Spence Ave (27534-4346)
PHONE.............................919 751-2400
Kevin Coakley, *Mgr*
EMP: 4
SALES (corp-wide): 3.81B **Privately Held**
Web: www.theoccasionsgroup.com
SIC: 7334 2752 Blueprinting service;
Commercial printing, lithographic
HQ: The Occasions Group Inc
1750 Tower Blvd
North Mankato MN 56003

(G-5234)
PACKAGING CORPORATION
AMERICA
Also Called: PCA
801 N William St (27530-2469)
PHONE.............................336 434-0600
EMP: 5
SALES (corp-wide): 7.73B **Publicly Held**
Web: www.packagingcorp.com
SIC: 2653 Boxes, corrugated: made from
purchased materials
PA: Packaging Corporation Of America
1 N Field Ct
Lake Forest IL 60045
847 482-3000

(G-5235)
PCORE
Also Called: Reuel
200 W Dewey St (27530-1304)
PHONE.............................919 734-0460
EMP: 10 **EST:** 2017
SALES (est): 2.47MM **Privately Held**
Web: www.hubbell.com
SIC: 3644 Noncurrent-carrying wiring devices

(G-5236)
PEPSI BOTTLING VENTURES LLC
Also Called: Pepsi-Cola
2707 N Park Dr (27534-7483)
PHONE.............................919 778-8300
Rick Poillon, *Brnch Mgr*
EMP: 49

▲ = Import ▼ = Export
◆ = Import/Export

Web: www.pepsibottlingventures.com
SIC: 2086 Carbonated soft drinks, bottled and canned
HQ: Pepsi Bottling Ventures Llc
4141 Parklake Ave
Raleigh NC 27612
919 865-2300

(G-5237)
PETRA PRECISION MACHINING
3413 Central Heights Rd (27534-7713)
PHONE..............................919 751-3461
Ernest Richards, *Pr*
EMP: 4 **EST:** 2005
SALES (est): 402.66K **Privately Held**
SIC: 3599 Machine shop, jobbing and repair

(G-5238)
PROLEC-GE WAUKESHA INC
Also Called: Heavy Duty Electric
2701 Us Highway 117 S (27530-0915)
P.O. Box 268 (27533-0268)
PHONE..............................919 734-8900
Mark Krueger, *Mgr*
EMP: 280
Web: www.waukeshatransformers.com
SIC: 3677 Electronic coils and transformers
HQ: Prolec-Ge Waukesha, Inc.
400 S Prairie Ave
Waukesha WI 53186
262 547-0121

(G-5239)
REESE SIGN SERVICE INC
Also Called: Reese Sign Service
3271 Us Highway 117 N (27530-8837)
P.O. Box 10593 (27532-0593)
PHONE..............................919 580-0705
George Reese, *Pr*
Paul Reese, *VP*
Cathy Reese, *Sec*
EMP: 6 **EST:** 1990
SALES (est): 439.11K **Privately Held**
Web: www.reesesign.com
SIC: 3993 Electric signs

(G-5240)
REUEL INC
200 W Dewey St (27530-1304)
P.O. Box 10561 (27532-0561)
PHONE..............................919 734-0460
▲ **EMP:** 40
SIC: 3264 3699 3675 3674 Insulators, electrical: porcelain; Electrical equipment and supplies, nec; Electronic capacitors; Semiconductors and related devices

(G-5241)
ROSE MEDIA INC
200 N Cottonwood Dr (27530-9177)
PHONE..............................919 736-1154
Margaret Harrison, *Pr*
Ken Harrison, *Stockholder*
EMP: 10 **EST:** 1997
SQ FT: 1,800
SALES (est): 73.29K **Privately Held**
SIC: 2721 Magazines: publishing and printing

(G-5242)
RUSKIN LLC
166 Nc 581 Hwy S (27530-9404)
PHONE..............................919 583-5444
Melissa Watson, *Managing Member*
EMP: 5 **EST:** 2017
SALES (est): 948.46K **Privately Held**
Web: www.ruskin.com
SIC: 3822 Environmental controls

(G-5243)
S & W READY MIX CON CO LLC
624 Powell Rd (27534-7852)
PHONE..............................919 751-1796
Robbie Trice, *Mgr*
EMP: 19
SALES (corp-wide): 8.01MM **Privately Held**
Web: www.snwreadymix.com
SIC: 3273 Ready-mixed concrete
HQ: S & W Ready Mix Concrete Company Llc
217 Lisbon St
Clinton NC 28329
910 592-1733

(G-5244)
SLEEPY CREEK TURKEYS LLC
Also Called: Sleepy Creek Turkeys, Inc.
938 Millers Chapel Rd (27534-7772)
PHONE..............................919 778-3130
James L Maxwell Junior, *Pr*
H Gordon Maxwell Iii, *Sec*
EMP: 158 **EST:** 1979
SALES (est): 3.96MM
SALES (corp-wide): 9.18MM **Privately Held**
SIC: 0253 3523 Turkey farm; Feed grinders, crushers, and mixers
PA: Sleepy Creek Farms, Inc.
938 Millers Chapel Rd
Goldsboro NC 27534
919 778-3130

(G-5245)
SOUTHERN HLDINGS GOLDSBORO INC
501 Patetown Rd Ste 4 (27530-5570)
PHONE..............................919 920-6998
Stephanie Rhodes Myers, *Prin*
EMP: 6 **EST:** 2018
SALES (est): 944.47K **Privately Held**
SIC: 3273 Ready-mixed concrete

(G-5246)
SPX FLOW US LLC
Also Called: APV Heat Exchanger PDT Group
2719 Graves Dr Ste 10 (27534-4536)
P.O. Box 1718 (27533-1718)
PHONE..............................919 735-4570
Tim Taylor, *Brnch Mgr*
EMP: 200
SALES (corp-wide): 1.78B **Privately Held**
SIC: 3443 Fabricated plate work (boiler shop)
HQ: Spx Flow Us, Llc
135 Mt Read Blvd
Rochester NY 14611
585 436-5550

(G-5247)
STORMBERG FOODS LLC
1002b Sunburst Dr (27534-8667)
PHONE..............................919 947-6011
Gary William Moorcroft, *Managing Member*
EMP: 50 **EST:** 2016
SALES (est): 4.72MM **Privately Held**
Web: www.stormbergfoods.com
SIC: 5499 2096 Gourmet food stores; Cheese curls and puffs
PA: Stormberg Certified Organic Farms (Pty) Ltd
15 Buick St
Port Elizabeth EC 6000

(G-5248)
SUPER RETREAD CENTER INC (PA)
Also Called: Hill's Tire & Auto
1213 S George St (27530-6803)
PHONE..............................919 734-0073
Ila Hill, *Pr*
Janet Hill, *VP*

EMP: 19 **EST:** 1968
SQ FT: 20,000
SALES (est): 2.34MM
SALES (corp-wide): 2.34MM **Privately Held**
Web: www.hillstire.com
SIC: 5531 7534 Automotive tires; Tire recapping

(G-5249)
TELAIR US LLC
Also Called: Telair US Cargo Systems
500a Gateway Dr (27534-7071)
PHONE..............................919 705-2400
Christopher Spagnoletti, *Pr*
EMP: 150 **EST:** 2015
SALES (est): 49.63MM
SALES (corp-wide): 7.94B **Publicly Held**
Web: www.uscargosystems.com
SIC: 3728 Aircraft parts and equipment, nec
HQ: Transdigm, Inc.
1350 Euclid Ave
Cleveland OH 44115

(G-5250)
TURNER EQUIPMENT COMPANY INC
Also Called: Turner Greenhouses
1502 Us Highway 117 S (27530-8587)
P.O. Box 1260 (27533-1260)
PHONE..............................919 734-8328
Gary Smithwick, *Pr*
Nancy Lilly Sales, *Prin*
Ashley Fleming Sales, *Prin*
David Ellis Cad Shipping, *Prin*
Rhonda Stokes Bookkeeping, *Accounting*
EMP: 30 **EST:** 1939
SQ FT: 17,000
SALES (est): 6.05MM **Privately Held**
Web: www.turnertanks.com
SIC: 3443 3448 Fabricated plate work (boiler shop); Prefabricated metal buildings and components

(G-5251)
UCHIYAMA MFG AMER LLC (HQ)
494 Arrington Bridge Rd (27530-8538)
PHONE..............................919 731-2364
Taizo Uchiyama, *CEO*
Masatomo Sueki, *
Nick Gambella, *Managing Member**
Linda Jennings, *
▲ **EMP:** 13 **EST:** 1999
SQ FT: 89,000
SALES (est): 22.87MM **Privately Held**
Web: www.umc-net.co.jp
SIC: 5085 3714 Gaskets; Motor vehicle parts and accessories
PA: Uchiyama Manufacturing Corp.
338, Enami, Naka-Ku
Okayama OKA 702-8

(G-5252)
WAYNE PRINTING COMPANY INC
Also Called: Goldsboro News-Argus
310 N Berkeley Blvd (27534-4326)
P.O. Box 10629 (27532-0629)
PHONE..............................919 778-2211
Hal H Tanner Junior, *Pr*
Hal H Tanner Iii, *VP*
Barbara Sturm, *
▲ **EMP:** 10 **EST:** 1953
SQ FT: 21,000
SALES (est): 991.78K **Privately Held**
Web: www.newsargus.com
SIC: 2711 Newspapers, publishing and printing

(G-5253)
WESTLIFT LLC
Also Called: Westlift
186 Belfast Rd (27530-8160)

P.O. Box 100 (27863)
PHONE..............................919 242-4379
E West, *Mgr*
Heather Ferris, *CFO*
EMP: 17 **EST:** 2009
SQ FT: 2,700
SALES (est): 4.59MM **Privately Held**
Web: www.westliftllc.com
SIC: 3537 7699 Forklift trucks; Industrial equipment services

(G-5254)
WILSON GRADING LLC
132 Blue Bird Ln (27534-8104)
PHONE..............................919 778-1580
Regis Wilson, *Pt*
Dennis Wilson, *Pt*
EMP: 10 **EST:** 1965
SALES (est): 465.11K **Privately Held**
SIC: 1411 Gneiss, dimension-quarrying

Goldston
Chatham County

(G-5255)
ALOTECH INC
751 S Church St (27252-9551)
PHONE..............................919 774-1297
William H Murphy, *Pr*
◆ **EMP:** 50 **EST:** 1991
SQ FT: 15,000
SALES (est): 4.43MM **Privately Held**
Web: www.alotechinc.com
SIC: 3599 3484 3565 Machine shop, jobbing and repair; Small arms; Packaging machinery

(G-5256)
ALOTECH NORTH
751 S Church St (27252-9551)
PHONE..............................919 774-1297
EMP: 5 **EST:** 2012
SALES (est): 506.5K **Privately Held**
Web: www.alotechinc.com
SIC: 3599 Machine shop, jobbing and repair

(G-5257)
CONVEYOR TECH LLC
Also Called: Conveyor Technologies
751 S Church St (27252)
PHONE..............................919 776-7227
Gary Kabot, *CEO*
Thomas R Kirk Ii, *COO*
◆ **EMP:** 131 **EST:** 2017
SQ FT: 120,000
SALES (est): 21.64MM **Privately Held**
Web: www.conveyor-technologies.com
SIC: 3535 Conveyors and conveying equipment

(G-5258)
SANFORD STEEL CORPORATION
375 Claude Hash Rd (27252-9448)
PHONE..............................919 898-4799
Andy B Starling, *Pr*
B Andy Starling, *Pr*
Rhonda G Starling, *VP*
EMP: 10 **EST:** 1993
SQ FT: 26,000
SALES (est): 3MM **Privately Held**
Web: www.welcometosanford.com
SIC: 3441 Building components, structural steel

Graham
Alamance County

(G-5259)
ACUCOTE INC (DH)
Also Called: Acucote
910 E Elm St (27253-1908)
P.O. Box 538 (27253)
PHONE.....................336 578-1800
Eugene Lauffer, *Pr*
Kathryn Cummings, *
Scott Ellis, *
◆ EMP: 130 EST: 1987
SQ FT: 90,000
SALES (est): 82.08MM **Privately Held**
Web: www.acucote.com
SIC: 2672 2679 Adhesive backed films,
　foams and foils; Building paper, laminated:
　made from purchased material
HQ: Fedrigoni Spa
　　Via Enrico Fermi 13/F
　　Verona VR 37135

(G-5260)
ATLANTIC CUSTOM CONTAINER INC
327 E Elm St (27253-3023)
P.O. Box 1071 (27253-1071)
PHONE.....................336 437-9302
Edward O'brien, *Pr*
EMP: 7 EST: 2002
SQ FT: 30,000
SALES (est): 1.09MM **Privately Held**
Web:
www.atlanticcustomcontainers.com
SIC: 2655 Containers, laminated phenolic
　and vulcanized fiber

(G-5261)
BROOKS MANUFACTURING SOLUTIONS
1017 Davis Ln (27253-4618)
P.O. Box 846 (27216-0846)
PHONE.....................336 438-1280
Troy Brooks, *Pr*
EMP: 16 EST: 2008
SALES (est): 2.73MM **Privately Held**
Web: www.bmscontrolpanels.com
SIC: 3613 3999 Control panels, electric;
　Manufacturing industries, nec

(G-5262)
BURLINGTON MSCLLNEOUS MTLS LLC
3406 William Newlin Dr (27253-9821)
PHONE.....................336 376-1264
Michael Workman, *Prin*
EMP: 10 EST: 2014
SALES (est): 4.71MM **Privately Held**
Web: www.burlingtonmiscmetals.website
SIC: 3446 Stairs, staircases, stair treads:
　prefabricated metal

(G-5263)
CHANDLER CONCRETE INC
Also Called: Truck Shop
301 W River St (27253-1755)
PHONE.....................336 222-9716
Thomas E Chandler, *Owner*
EMP: 5
Web: www.chandlerconcrete.com
SIC: 3273 Ready-mixed concrete
PA: Chandler Concrete Co., Inc.
　　1006 S Church Street
　　Burlington NC 27215

(G-5264)
CITY OF GRAHAM
111 E Crescent Square Dr (27253-4013)
PHONE.....................336 570-6811

EMP: 11
Web: www.cityofgraham.com
SIC: 3469 Automobile license tags, stamped
　metal
PA: Graham, City Of (Inc)
　　201 S Main St
　　Graham NC 27253
　　336 570-6705

(G-5265)
CKS PACKAGING INC
943 Trollingwood Road (27253)
P.O. Box 478 (27253-0478)
PHONE.....................336 578-5800
Ken Pierce, *Brnch Mgr*
EMP: 91
SALES (corp-wide): 418.61MM **Privately Held**
Web: www.ckspackaging.com
SIC: 3089 3085 Plastics containers, except
　foam; Plastics bottles
PA: C.K.S. Packaging, Inc.
　　350 Great Sw Pkwy
　　Atlanta GA 30336
　　404 691-8900

(G-5266)
CSM MANUFACTURING INC
Also Called: CSM
913 Washington St (27253-1645)
PHONE.....................336 570-2282
Scott Cobb, *Pr*
Richard Shevlin, *VP*
EMP: 14 EST: 2001
SQ FT: 3,000
SALES (est): 809.68K **Privately Held**
Web: www.csm-mfg.com
SIC: 3599 Machine shop, jobbing and repair

(G-5267)
D & L CABINETS INC
1010 Rolling Oaks Dr (27253-9966)
PHONE.....................336 376-6009
Phil Demarco, *Pr*
EMP: 15 EST: 2003
SALES (est): 1.06MM **Privately Held**
Web: www.dandlcabinets.com
SIC: 2434 Wood kitchen cabinets

(G-5268)
FARM SERVICES INC
125 E Elm St (27253-3019)
P.O. Box 872 (27253-0872)
PHONE.....................336 226-7381
William Talley, *Pr*
Jennifer Talley, *VP*
EMP: 6 EST: 1955
SQ FT: 6,000
SALES (est): 600K **Privately Held**
Web: www.farmservicesgraham.com
SIC: 5261 5999 5083 3546 Fertilizer; Feed
　and farm supply; Mowers, power; Chain
　saws, portable

(G-5269)
GONZALEZ WELDING INC
817 E Parker St (27253-1957)
PHONE.....................336 270-8179
Gabriel Gonzalez, *CEO*
EMP: 5 EST: 2017
SALES (est): 509.81K **Privately Held**
Web: www.salemiindustries.com
SIC: 7692 Welding repair

(G-5270)
INDULOR AMERICA LP
932 E Elm St (27253-1908)
PHONE.....................336 578-6855
Sebastian Fengler, *Prin*
▲ EMP: 55 EST: 2008
SALES (est): 12.11MM **Privately Held**

Web: www.blankophor-oba.com
SIC: 2822 Ethylene-propylene rubbers,
　EPDM polymers

(G-5271)
IVARS SPORTSWEAR INC
408 W Interstate Service Rd (27253-3524)
P.O. Box 2449 (27216-2449)
PHONE.....................336 227-9683
Corbin Sapp, *Pr*
Corbin I Sapp, *Pr*
Adelaide Raye Sapp, *Sec*
Bennett Sapp, *VP*
EMP: 8 EST: 1976
SQ FT: 12,000
SALES (est): 1.45MM **Privately Held**
Web: www.ivars-sportswear.com
SIC: 2395 Embroidery products, except
　Schiffli machine

(G-5272)
JAMES FODS FRNCHISE CORP AMER
611 E Gilbreath St (27253-3747)
PHONE.....................336 437-0393
Charles Timothy James, *Pr*
EMP: 6 EST: 2014
SQ FT: 39,000
SALES (est): 179.41K **Privately Held**
SIC: 2038 5411 Frozen specialties, nec;
　Frozen food and freezer plans, except meat

(G-5273)
JAMES FOODS INC
611 E Gilbreath St (27253-3747)
PHONE.....................336 437-0393
Charles T James, *Pr*
Charles Timothy James, *Pr*
Wanda Metzger, *
EMP: 40 EST: 2004
SQ FT: 40,000
SALES (est): 4.82MM **Privately Held**
Web: www.jamesfoods.com
SIC: 2099 Food preparations, nec

(G-5274)
KAYSER-ROTH HOSIERY INC
714 W Interstate Service Rd (27253-3527)
PHONE.....................336 229-2269
Wayne Branch, *Pr*
▲ EMP: 17 EST: 1982
SALES (est): 4.63MM **Privately Held**
Web: www.kayser-roth.com
SIC: 2252 Socks
HQ: Kayser-Roth Corporation
　　102 Corporate Center Blvd
　　Greensboro NC 27408
　　336 852-2030

(G-5275)
LINDLEY MILLS INC
7763 Lindley Mill Rd (27253-8326)
PHONE.....................336 376-6190
Joe J Lindley Senior, *Treas*
Joe J Lindley, *Junior Principal*
EMP: 8 EST: 1976
SALES (est): 988.83K **Privately Held**
Web: www.lindleymills.com
SIC: 2041 Flour

(G-5276)
LOY & LOY INC
205 Travora St (27253-2339)
PHONE.....................919 942-6356
Michael W Loy, *Pr*
Joyce Loy, *Sec*
EMP: 4 EST: 1966
SALES (est): 247.96K **Privately Held**
SIC: 2899 Water treating compounds

(G-5277)
MARSH FURNITURE COMPANY
Also Called: Alamance Cabinets
605 W Harden St (27253-2106)
P.O. Box 1401 (27253-1401)
PHONE.....................336 229-5122
Jon Lawson, *Brnch Mgr*
EMP: 6
SALES (corp-wide): 43.69MM **Privately Held**
Web: www.marshfurniture.com
SIC: 2434 Wood kitchen cabinets
PA: Marsh Furniture Company
　　1001 S Centennial St
　　High Point NC 27260
　　336 884-7363

(G-5278)
METAL IMPACT EAST LLC
Also Called: Luxfer
235 Riverbend Rd (27253-2621)
PHONE.....................336 578-4515
Philip Kretekos, *Pr*
EMP: 110 EST: 2021
SALES (est): 17.67MM
SALES (corp-wide): 157.67MM **Privately Held**
SIC: 3354 Aluminum rod and bar
HQ: Metal Impact Llc
　　1501 Oakton St
　　Elk Grove Village IL 60007

(G-5279)
METAL IMPACT EAST LLC
Also Called: Thunderbird Metals East
1200 Jay Ln (27253-2614)
PHONE.....................743 205-1900
Csr Seraphina Senior, *Brnch Mgr*
EMP: 5
SALES (corp-wide): 1.94MM **Privately Held**
SIC: 3563 Air and gas compressors
PA: Metal Impact East Llc
　　900 Commerce Dr Ste 150
　　Oak Brook IL 60523
　　743 205-1900

(G-5280)
NEW SOUTH LUMBER COMPANY INC
4408 Mount Hermon Rock Crk Rd
(27253-8909)
PHONE.....................336 376-3130
Terry Bishop, *Mgr*
EMP: 135
SALES (corp-wide): 3.95B **Privately Held**
Web: www.canfor.com
SIC: 2421 5031 Lumber: rough, sawed, or
　planed; Lumber, plywood, and millwork
HQ: New South Lumber Company, Inc.
　　3700 Claypond Rd Ste 6
　　Myrtle Beach SC 29579
　　843 236-9399

(G-5281)
PIEDMONT TRUCK TIRES INC
Also Called: Bandag
704 Myrtle Dr (27253)
PHONE.....................336 223-9412
Mitch Glover, *Brnch Mgr*
EMP: 13
SALES (corp-wide): 636MM **Privately Held**
Web: www.piedmonttrucktires.com
SIC: 5014 5531 7534 Truck tires and tubes;
　Auto and home supply stores; Rebuilding
　and retreading tires
HQ: Piedmont Truck Tires, Inc.
　　312 S Regional Rd
　　Greensboro NC 27409
　　336 668-0091

▲ = Import ▼ = Export
◆ = Import/Export

(G-5282)
PRECISION BOAT MFG
808 Carraway Dr (27253-4457)
PHONE..............................336 395-8795
James Allen, *Prin*
EMP: 4 **EST:** 2017
SALES (est): 89.25K **Privately Held**
SIC: 3999 Manufacturing industries, nec

(G-5283)
PURE FLOW INC (PA)
Also Called: Pfi
1241 Jay Ln (27253-2615)
PHONE..............................336 532-0300
Daniel Johnson, *Pr*
Lucinda Johnson, *
Gary Allred, *
EMP: 83 **EST:** 1985
SQ FT: 65,847
SALES (est): 26.33MM
SALES (corp-wide): 26.33MM **Privately Held**
Web: www.pureflowinc.com
SIC: 3589 Water treatment equipment, industrial

(G-5284)
RED WOLFE INDUSTRIES LLC
Also Called: CSM Manufacturing
913 Washington St (27253-1645)
PHONE..............................336 570-2282
Grey Seymour, *Prin*
Julie Seymour, *Prin*
EMP: 15 **EST:** 2019
SALES (est): 3.41MM **Privately Held**
SIC: 3999 Manufacturing industries, nec

(G-5285)
SOLA PUBLISHING
1074 W Main St (27253-8546)
PHONE..............................336 226-8240
EMP: 8 **EST:** 2019
SALES (est): 143.28K **Privately Held**
Web: www.solapublishing.com
SIC: 2741 Miscellaneous publishing

(G-5286)
SOUTH ATLANTIC LLC
Also Called: South Atlantic Galvanizing
3025 Steelway Dr (27253)
P.O. Box 1380 (27253-1380)
PHONE..............................336 376-0410
David Monroe, *Brnch Mgr*
EMP: 16
SALES (corp-wide): 355.87MM **Privately Held**
Web: www.southatlanticllc.com
SIC: 3479 3547 Galvanizing of iron, steel, or end-formed products; Galvanizing lines (rolling mill equipment)
HQ: South Atlantic, Llc
1907 S 17th St Ste 2
Wilmington NC 28401
910 332-1900

(G-5287)
USA DUTCH INC
778 Woody Dr (27253-3813)
P.O. Box 1299 (27253-1299)
PHONE..............................336 227-8600
Ronald Keizer, *Pr*
EMP: 40
Web: www.usadutchinc.com
SIC: 3444 Sheet metalwork
PA: Usa Dutch, Inc.
3604 Southern Dr
Efland NC 27243

(G-5288)
VESUVIUS NC LLC
Also Called: Permatech, LLC
911 E Elm St (27253-1907)
PHONE..............................336 578-7728
Joseph D Trettel, *Pr*
John Schneider, *VP*
◆ **EMP:** 74 **EST:** 2003
SQ FT: 65,000
SALES (est): 10.56MM
SALES (corp-wide): 22.69MM **Privately Held**
Web: www.permatech.net
SIC: 3297 Alumina fused refractories
PA: Ccpi Inc.
838 Cherry St
Blanchester OH 45107
937 783-2476

(G-5289)
VINATORU ENTERPRISES INC
209 W Hanover Rd (27253-1723)
PHONE..............................336 227-4300
Mihai Vinatoru, *Pr*
EMP: 9 **EST:** 1980
SQ FT: 3,500
SALES (est): 1.27MM **Privately Held**
Web: www.vinatoru.com
SIC: 3829 Accelerometers

(G-5290)
ZIMMERMANN - DYNAYARN USA LLC
327 E Elm St (27253-3023)
P.O. Box 811 (27253-0811)
PHONE..............................336 222-8129
John A Holt, *Managing Member*
Tommy Crowson, *
◆ **EMP:** 32 **EST:** 1999
SQ FT: 100,000
SALES (est): 5.03MM **Privately Held**
Web: www.zimdyn.com
SIC: 2241 2251 2281 Rubber thread and yarns, fabric covered; Women's hosiery, except socks; Yarn spinning mills

Grandy
Currituck County

(G-5291)
WEEPING RADISH FARM BREWRY LLC
6810 Caratoke Hwy (27939-9635)
P.O. Box 1471 (27954-1471)
PHONE..............................252 491-5205
Uli Bennewitz, *Managing Member*
EMP: 4 **EST:** 2007
SALES (est): 477.53K **Privately Held**
Web: www.weepingradish.com
SIC: 2082 Beer (alcoholic beverage)

Granite Falls
Caldwell County

(G-5292)
80 ACRES URBAN AGRICULTURE INC
4141 Yorkview Ct (28630-8771)
PHONE..............................704 437-6115
Tracy Canipe, *Brnch Mgr*
EMP: 8
SALES (corp-wide): 37.82MM **Privately Held**
Web: www.80acresfarms.com
SIC: 3532 Mining machinery
PA: 80 Acres Urban Agriculture, Inc.
345 High St Fl 7

Hamilton OH 45011
513 218-4387

(G-5293)
A MCGEE WOOD PRODUCTS INC
171 N Main St (28630-1329)
P.O. Box 1009 (28630-1009)
PHONE..............................828 212-1700
T Andrew Mcgee, *CEO*
EMP: 10 **EST:** 2019
SALES (est): 280.14K **Privately Held**
SIC: 2441 Ammunition boxes, wood

(G-5294)
AMP SERVICES LLC
Also Called: Commercial Lighting Services
30 N Main St (28630-1402)
PHONE..............................828 313-1200
Austin Powell, *Managing Member*
EMP: 7 **EST:** 2013
SALES (est): 2.68MM **Privately Held**
Web: www.commerciallightingservices.com
SIC: 3699 Electrical equipment and supplies, nec

(G-5295)
ASSOCIATED HARDWOODS INC (PA)
650 N Main St (28630-8572)
P.O. Box 491 (28630-0491)
PHONE..............................828 396-3321
▲ **EMP:** 35 **EST:** 1978
SALES (est): 22.92MM
SALES (corp-wide): 22.92MM **Privately Held**
Web: www.associatedhardwoods.com
SIC: 2426 5031 Hardwood dimension and flooring mills; Lumber: rough, dressed, and finished

(G-5296)
AUTOMATED SOLUTIONS LLC (PA)
4101 Us Highway 321a (28630-9602)
PHONE..............................828 396-9900
◆ **EMP:** 11 **EST:** 1998
SQ FT: 75,000
SALES (est): 17.56MM
SALES (corp-wide): 17.56MM **Privately Held**
Web: www.automatedsolutionsllc.com
SIC: 2674 3496 2671 3111 Shipping bags or sacks, including multiwall and heavy duty; Conveyor belts; Plastic film, coated or laminated for packaging; Cutting of leather

(G-5297)
AUTUMN HOUSE INC
Also Called: Autumn Wood Products
1206 Premier Rd (28630-7400)
PHONE..............................828 728-1121
Howard L Pruitt, *CEO*
Howard L Pruitt, *Pr*
Ernest Rosenquist, *
▲ **EMP:** 65 **EST:** 1977
SQ FT: 90,000
SALES (est): 4.1MM **Privately Held**
Web: www.autumnhouse.com
SIC: 2435 Hardwood veneer and plywood

(G-5298)
CAROLINA PRCSION CMPONENTS INC
4181 Us Highway 321a (28630-9602)
PHONE..............................828 496-1045
Randy A Walker, *Pr*
Will Shuffler Qa, *Mgr*
Mike Smith, *
EMP: 38 **EST:** 1995
SQ FT: 52,000
SALES (est): 2.28MM **Privately Held**
Web: www.carpreco.com

SIC: 3599 Machine shop, jobbing and repair

(G-5299)
CASE BASKET CREATIONS
4975 J M Craig Rd (28630-9295)
PHONE..............................828 381-4908
EMP: 5 **EST:** 2018
SALES (est): 101.34K **Privately Held**
SIC: 3523 Farm machinery and equipment

(G-5300)
CHASE CORPORATION
Also Called: Granite Falls Plant
3908 Hickory Blvd (28630-8373)
P.O. Box 800 (28630-0800)
PHONE..............................828 396-2121
EMP: 4
Web: www.chasecorp.com
SIC: 3644 Insulators and insulation materials, electrical
HQ: Chase Corporation
375 University Ave
Westwood MA 02090
781 332-0700

(G-5301)
CUSTOM CABINET WORKS
180 N Main St (28630-1332)
PHONE..............................828 396-6348
William Fisher, *Owner*
EMP: 8 **EST:** 1997
SALES (est): 437.6K **Privately Held**
Web: www.customcabinetworks.net
SIC: 2434 Wood kitchen cabinets

(G-5302)
EVERGREEN PALLETS LLC
3815 N Main St (28630-8516)
PHONE..............................828 313-0050
EMP: 11 **EST:** 2005
SALES (est): 173.69K **Privately Held**
SIC: 2448 Pallets, wood and wood with metal

(G-5303)
FUELTEC SYSTEMS LLC
3821 N Main St (28630-8516)
P.O. Box 14889 (34979-4889)
PHONE..............................828 212-1141
Ronald Lenz, *Pt*
Ronald Lenz, *Managing Member*
EMP: 6 **EST:** 2008
SALES (est): 2.33MM **Privately Held**
Web: www.fueltecsystems.com
SIC: 3677 Filtration devices, electronic

(G-5304)
GRANITE FALLS FURNACES LLC
1230 Premier Rd (28630-7400)
PHONE..............................828 324-4394
David Duncan Junior, *Pr*
Matthew Duncan, *
EMP: 24 **EST:** 2002
SALES (est): 2.96MM **Privately Held**
Web: www.granitefallsfurnace.com
SIC: 3315 Steel wire and related products

(G-5305)
GRANITE TAPE CO
4 Cedar St (28630-1602)
P.O. Box 1012 (28630-1012)
PHONE..............................828 396-5614
Barton Potter, *Owner*
EMP: 6 **EST:** 1982
SQ FT: 18,000
SALES (est): 493.39K **Privately Held**
SIC: 2672 Tape, pressure sensitive: made from purchased materials

GEOGRAPHIC

(G-5306)
HOFFMAN MATERIALS LLC
230 Timberbrook Ln (28630-1976)
PHONE...................717 243-2011
Diana Rauchfuss, *CEO*
EMP: 16 **EST:** 2007
SALES (est): 2.4MM **Privately Held**
Web: www.hoffmanmaterials.com
SIC: 3674 Wafers (semiconductor devices)

(G-5307)
HOFFMAN MATERIALS INC
230 Timberbrook Ln (28630-1976)
PHONE...................717 243-2011
Diana Rauchfuss, *Ch Bd*
Marci E Staudte, *Ch Bd*
Tom Hardy, *CEO*
Mark S Rauchfuss, *Pr*
EMP: 9 **EST:** 1938
SALES (est): 2.24MM **Privately Held**
Web: www.hoffmanmaterials.com
SIC: 3679 Quartz crystals, for electronic
　application

(G-5308)
HUFFMAN FINISHING COMPANY INC
4919 Hickory Blvd (28630-8390)
P.O. Box 170 (28630)
PHONE...................828 396-1741
A W Huffman Junior, *Pr*
Adele H Mangan, *
Mildred Wike, *
Lee T Huffman, *
▲ **EMP:** 125 **EST:** 1945
SQ FT: 25,000
SALES (est): 7.36MM **Privately Held**
SIC: 2252 2251 2262 2261 Dyeing and
　finishing hosiery; Women's hosiery, except
　socks; Finishing plants, manmade;
　Finishing plants, cotton

(G-5309)
JORDAN-HOLMAN LUMBER CO INC
650 N Main St (28630-8572)
P.O. Box 436 (28630-0436)
PHONE...................828 396-3101
Rick Jordan, *Pr*
Jane T Jordan, *
EMP: 58 **EST:** 1981
SQ FT: 18,000
SALES (est): 2.78MM **Privately Held**
Web: www.associatedhardwoods.com
SIC: 2421 Kiln drying of lumber

(G-5310)
KNITWEAR AMERICA INC
5740 Rocky Mount Rd (28630-8308)
PHONE...................704 396-1193
Edna Dunne, *Pr*
EMP: 7 **EST:** 1995
SALES (est): 74.33K **Privately Held**
SIC: 2253 Warm weather knit outerwear,
　including beachwear

(G-5311)
LUBRIMETAL CORPORATION
Also Called: Lm
2889 Countryside Dr (28630-1996)
PHONE...................828 212-1083
Giorgio Corso, *Pr*
▲ **EMP:** 19 **EST:** 2012
SALES (est): 2.53MM **Privately Held**
Web: www.lubrimetal.com
SIC: 2992 Lubricating oils and greases

(G-5312)
MARX LLC
4276 Helena St (28630)
P.O. Box 826 (28630-0826)
PHONE...................828 396-6700

EMP: 90 **EST:** 2018
SALES (est): 8.47MM **Privately Held**
Web: www.marxllc.net
SIC: 3086 Plastics foam products

(G-5313)
MINDA NORTH AMERICA LLC
10 N Summit Ave (28630-1333)
P.O. Box 425 (28630-0425)
PHONE...................828 313-0092
Charles Martin, *CEO*
Todd Beal, *Managing Member**
EMP: 25 **EST:** 2012
SALES (est): 7.6MM **Privately Held**
Web: www.minda.com
SIC: 3441 Fabricated structural metal

(G-5314)
NEPTCO INCORPORATED
3908 Hickory Blvd (28630-8373)
P.O. Box 800 (28630-0800)
PHONE...................828 313-0149
Randy Dula, *Mgr*
EMP: 230
SQ FT: 8,460
Web: www.chasecorp.com
SIC: 2672 2823 Tape, pressure sensitive:
　made from purchased materials; Cellulosic
　manmade fibers
HQ: Neptco Incorporated
　295 University Ave
　Westwood MA 02090
　401 722-5500

(G-5315)
PACTIV LLC
3825 N Main St (28630-8516)
P.O. Box 750 (28630-0750)
PHONE...................828 396-2373
Darren Green, *Manager*
EMP: 11
SQ FT: 50,000
Web: www.pactivevergreen.com
SIC: 3086 4225 Insulation or cushioning
　material, foamed plastics; General
　warehousing and storage
HQ: Pactiv Llc
　1900 W Field Ct
　Lake Forest IL 60045
　847 482-2000

(G-5316)
PEPSI-COLA BTLG HICKRY NC INC
Also Called: Pepsi-Cola
47 Duke St (28630-1807)
PHONE...................828 322-8090
France Teeter, *Mgr*
EMP: 9
SALES (corp-wide): 28.58MM **Privately
Held**
Web: www.hickorync.gov
SIC: 5149 2086 Soft drinks; Bottled and
　canned soft drinks
PA: Pepsi-Cola Bottling Company Of
　Hickory, N.C., Inc.
　2401 14th Avenue Cir Nw
　Hickory NC 28601
　828 322-8090

(G-5317)
PLAT LLC
5740 Rocky Mount Rd (28630-8308)
P.O. Box 1303 (28603-1303)
PHONE...................828 358-4564
Pamela Jean Payne, *Mng Pt*
Jerry Strickland, *Mng Pt*
EMP: 10 **EST:** 2016
SQ FT: 5,000
SALES (est): 180.49K **Privately Held**
SIC: 2512 Upholstered household furniture

(G-5318)
**PREGIS INNOVATIVE PACKG LLC
(DH)**
3825 N Main St (28630-8516)
PHONE...................847 597-2200
Kevin Baudhuin, *Pr*
Keith Lavanway, *CFO*
EMP: 38 **EST:** 1997
SALES (est): 53.46MM
SALES (corp-wide): 191.81K **Privately
Held**
Web: www.pregis.com
SIC: 2671 5199 Paper; coated and
　laminated packaging; Packaging materials
HQ: Pregis Llc
　2345 Waukegan Rd Ste 120
　Bannockburn IL 60015

(G-5319)
PREGIS LLC
3825 N Main St (28630-8516)
PHONE...................828 396-2373
Tony Smith, *Mgr*
EMP: 48
SALES (corp-wide): 191.81K **Privately
Held**
Web: www.pregis.com
SIC: 5999 2621 Foam and foam products;
　Wrapping and packaging papers
HQ: Pregis Llc
　2345 Waukegan Rd Ste 120
　Bannockburn IL 60015

(G-5320)
RICHARDS WELDING AND REPR INC
3080 Dry Ponds Rd (28630-9653)
PHONE...................828 396-8705
Richard Miller, *Pr*
Kendra Miller, *Sec*
EMP: 6 **EST:** 1995
SALES (est): 919.89K **Privately Held**
Web:
www.richardsweldingandrepair.com
SIC: 7692 Automotive welding

(G-5321)
ROBLON US INC
3908 Hickory Blvd (28630-8373)
PHONE...................828 396-2121
Lars Stergaard, *Pr*
EMP: 60 **EST:** 2017
SALES (est): 20.99MM
SALES (corp-wide): 36.76MM **Privately
Held**
Web: www.roblon.com
SIC: 3229 Fiber optics strands
HQ: Roblon Aktieselskab
　Fabriksvej 7
　Frederikshavn 9900
　96203300

(G-5322)
ROYAL HOSIERY COMPANY INC (PA)
10 N Summit Ave (28630-1333)
P.O. Box 1053 (28630-1053)
PHONE...................828 496-2200
Zafar Shaheen, *Pr*
Ashraf Ali, *VP*
▲ **EMP:** 6 **EST:** 1988
SQ FT: 28,000
SALES (est): 307.8K **Privately Held**
Web: royalhosiery.blogspot.com
SIC: 2252 2251 Men's, boys', and girls'
　hosiery; Women's hosiery, except socks

(G-5323)
SHUFORD YARNS LLC
5100 Burns Rd (28630-8247)
PHONE...................828 396-2342
Mike Bradshaw, *Brnch Mgr*
EMP: 108

Web: www.shufordyarns.com
SIC: 2281 Manmade and synthetic fiber
　yarns, spun
PA: Shuford Yarns, Llc
　1985 Tate Blvd Se Ste 54
　Hickory NC 28602

(G-5324)
SPECTRUM ADHESIVES INC
3815 N Main St (28630-8516)
PHONE...................828 396-4200
Angela Clark, *Mgr*
EMP: 5
SALES (corp-wide): 8.06MM **Privately
Held**
Web: www.spectrumadhesives.com
SIC: 2891 Glue
PA: Spectrum Adhesives, Inc.
　5611 Universal Dr
　Memphis TN 38118
　901 795-1943

(G-5325)
W & S FRAME COMPANY INC
4833 J M Craig Rd (28630-9294)
PHONE...................828 728-6078
Mark Smith, *Pr*
Maxine Smith, *Treas*
Tracy Smith, *Sec*
EMP: 4 **EST:** 1976
SALES (est): 412.38K **Privately Held**
SIC: 2426 Frames for upholstered furniture,
　wood

Granite Quarry
Rowan County

(G-5326)
GRANITE KNITWEAR INC (PA)
Also Called: Cal-Cru
805 S Salisbury Ave (28072)
P.O. Box 498 (28072-0498)
PHONE...................704 279-5526
Michael R Jones, *Pr*
Billy Jones, *
▼ **EMP:** 38 **EST:** 1968
SQ FT: 31,200
SALES (est): 1.56MM
SALES (corp-wide): 1.56MM **Privately
Held**
Web: www.calcru.com
SIC: 2321 2339 2335 Polo shirts, men's and
　boys': made from purchased materials;
　Women's and misses' outerwear, nec;
　Women's, junior's, and misses' dresses

(G-5327)
ROWAN PRECISION MACHINING INC
707 N Salisbury Ave (28072)
P.O. Box 778 (28072-0778)
PHONE...................704 279-6092
Reginald J Hall Junior, *Pr*
Doris Hall, *Sec*
EMP: 8 **EST:** 1985
SALES (est): 1.35MM **Privately Held**
SIC: 3599 Machine shop, jobbing and repair

(G-5328)
**SOUTHERN ATL SPRING MFG SLS
LL**
127 Rowan St (28072)
P.O. Box 1165 (28072-1165)
PHONE...................704 279-1331
Tony Nielsen, *Manager*
EMP: 31 **EST:** 2007
SALES (est): 2.41MM **Privately Held**
SIC: 3493 Steel springs, except wire

▲ = Import ▼ = Export
◆ = Import/Export

GEOGRAPHIC

Grantsboro
Pamlico County

(G-5329)
BOBBY CAHOON CONSTRUCTION INC
Also Called: Bobby Choon Mar Cnstr Land Dev
6003 Neuse Rd (28529-9530)
PHONE......................252 249-1617
Teresa Cahoon, Pr
EMP: 25 **EST:** 1999
SALES (est): 4.78MM **Privately Held**
Web:
www.bobbycahoonconstruction.com
SIC: 1629 4212 1442 1794 Dams, waterways, docks, and other marine construction; Local trucking, without storage ; Construction sand and gravel; Excavation work

(G-5330)
C & C CHIPPING INC
Also Called: Cahoon, Bobby Logging
6003 Neuse Rd (28529-9530)
PHONE......................252 249-1617
Bobby Cahoon, Pr
EMP: 6 **EST:** 1990
SQ FT: 10,000
SALES (est): 430.49K **Privately Held**
Web:
www.bobbycahoonconstruction.com
SIC: 2421 2439 Chipper mill; Structural wood members, nec

(G-5331)
PAMLICO PACKING CO INC (PA)
66 Cross Rd S (28529-5805)
P.O. Box 336 (28529-0336)
PHONE......................252 745-3688
William Ed Cross, Pr
Douglas E Cross, VP
Don Cross, Sec
EMP: 10 **EST:** 1944
SQ FT: 1,400
SALES (est): 3.78MM
SALES (corp-wide): 3.78MM **Privately Held**
Web: www.bestseafood.com
SIC: 2092 2091 5146 Seafoods, fresh: prepared; Bouillon, clam: packaged in cans, jars, etc.; Fish and seafoods

Greensboro
Guilford County

(G-5332)
A M MOORE AND COMPANY INC (PA)
Also Called: McLean Lighting Works
1207 Park Ter (27403-1957)
P.O. Box 20345 (27420-0345)
PHONE......................336 294-6994
Alexander Moore, Pr
▲ **EMP:** 8 **EST:** 1977
SALES (est): 852.09K
SALES (corp-wide): 852.09K **Privately Held**
Web: www.mcleanlighting.com
SIC: 3645 2499 3646 Residential lighting fixtures; Decorative wood and woodwork; Commercial lighting fixtures

(G-5333)
A TASTE OF HEAVENLY SWEETNESS
4518 W Market St (27407-1542)
PHONE......................336 825-7321
Asheda Walker, Genl Pt

Tausha Moore, Pt
EMP: 7 **EST:** 2011
SQ FT: 1,000
SALES (est): 75.15K **Privately Held**
SIC: 2051 Cakes, bakery: except frozen

(G-5334)
A-1 SANDROCK INC (PA)
Also Called: A-1 Trucking
2606 Phoenix Dr Ste 518 (27406-6351)
PHONE......................336 855-8195
Ronald Eugene Petty, Pr
Betty Petty, VP
Ronald E Petty, VP
EMP: 24 **EST:** 1987
SQ FT: 3,000
SALES (est): 15.18MM
SALES (corp-wide): 15.18MM **Privately Held**
Web: www.a-1servicegroup.com
SIC: 1442 4953 1629 Sand mining; Recycling, waste materials; Waste disposal plant construction

(G-5335)
ABACON TELECOMMUNICATIONS LLC (PA)
4388 Federal Dr (27410-8172)
PHONE......................336 855-1179
EMP: 22 **EST:** 1985
SQ FT: 30,400
SALES (est): 446.69K
SALES (corp-wide): 446.69K **Privately Held**
SIC: 3661 5065 Telephone and telegraph apparatus; Telephone and telegraphic equipment

(G-5336)
ABB MOTORS AND MECHANICAL INC
Also Called: Baldor Motors & Drives
1220 Rotherwood Rd (27406-3826)
P.O. Box 16500 (27416-0500)
PHONE......................336 272-6104
David Cousins, Brnch Mgr
EMP: 7
Web: www.baldor.com
SIC: 3621 5063 Motors, electric; Motors, electric
HQ: Abb Motors And Mechanical Inc.
5711 R S Boreham Jr St
Fort Smith AR 72901
479 646-4711

(G-5337)
ABE ENTERCOM HOLDINGS LLC
Also Called: Lincoln Financial
100 N Greene St Ste M (27401-2530)
PHONE......................336 691-4337
Mendol Hoover, Mgr
EMP: 9
SALES (corp-wide): 1.17B **Publicly Held**
Web: www.audacyinc.com
SIC: 2759 Commercial printing, nec
HQ: Abe Entercom Holdings Llc
401 E City Ave Ste 809
Bala Cynwyd PA 19004
404 239-7211

(G-5338)
ABOLDER IMAGE
205 Aloe Rd (27409-2105)
P.O. Box 8565 (27419-0565)
PHONE......................336 856-1300
John Sturm, Prin
Ruth Sturm, Prin
EMP: 10 **EST:** 2016
SALES (est): 208.47K **Privately Held**
Web: www.abolderimage.net
SIC: 2752 Offset printing

(G-5339)
AC CORPORATION (HQ)
Also Called: AC Corporation North Carolina
301 Creek Ridge Rd (27406)
P.O. Box P.O. Box 16367 (27416)
PHONE......................336 273-4472
▲ **EMP:** 440 **EST:** 1935
SALES (est): 57.95MM
SALES (corp-wide): 112.11MM **Privately Held**
Web: www.accorporation.com
SIC: 1711 1731 3556 3823 Warm air heating and air conditioning contractor; Electrical work; Food products machinery; Industrial process control instruments
PA: Crete Mechanical Group, Inc.
2701 N Rcky Pt Dr Ste 660
Tampa FL 33607
833 273-8364

(G-5340)
ACTON CORPORATION
1451 S Elm Eugene St (27406-2200)
PHONE......................434 728-4491
Said Elfayar, CEO
EMP: 6 **EST:** 2013
SALES (est): 569.83K **Privately Held**
Web: www.accorporation.com
SIC: 2873 Fertilizers: natural (organic), except compost

(G-5341)
ADVANCE STORES COMPANY INC
Also Called: Advance Auto Parts
2514 Battleground Ave Ste A (27408-1939)
PHONE......................336 545-9091
West Gregory, Mgr
EMP: 10
SALES (corp-wide): 9.09B **Publicly Held**
Web: shop.advanceautoparts.com
SIC: 5531 7534 5063 Auto and truck equipment and parts; Tire retreading and repair shops; Storage batteries, industrial
HQ: Advance Stores Company Incorporated
4200 Six Forks Rd
Raleigh NC 27609
540 561-6900

(G-5342)
ADVANCED SUBSTRATE
7860 Thorndike Rd (27409-9690)
PHONE......................336 285-5955
Jerry Allen, Genl Mgr
EMP: 10 **EST:** 2009
SALES (est): 1.69MM **Privately Held**
Web: www.advancedsubstrate.com
SIC: 3679 Electronic circuits

(G-5343)
ADVANCED TECH SYSTEMS INC
2606 Phoenix Dr Ste 602 (27406-6355)
PHONE......................336 299-6695
Jeffery Bill, Pr
EMP: 15 **EST:** 2002
SALES (est): 2.56MM **Privately Held**
Web: www.atstriad.com
SIC: 3651 Household audio and video equipment

(G-5344)
ADVANCED TECHNOLOGY INC
Also Called: ATI Laminates
6106 W Market St (27409-2040)
PHONE......................336 668-0488
◆ **EMP:** 45 **EST:** 1979
SALES (est): 5.8MM **Privately Held**
Web: www.atilaminates.com
SIC: 3446 5162 Architectural metalwork; Plastics materials and basic shapes

(G-5345)
AKZO NOBEL COATINGS INC
Also Called: Car RE Finish
4500 Green Point Dr Ste 104 (27410-8125)
PHONE......................336 665-9897
Ross Alexander, Mgr
EMP: 8
SALES (corp-wide): 11.6B **Privately Held**
SIC: 5198 2851 Paints; Paints: oil or alkyd vehicle or water thinned
HQ: Akzo Nobel Coatings Inc.
535 Marriott Dr Ste 500
Nashville TN 37214
440 297-5100

(G-5346)
ALAMANCE IRON WORKS INC
3900 Patterson St (27407-3240)
PHONE......................336 852-5940
Kurt Lents, Pr
EMP: 8 **EST:** 1970
SQ FT: 900
SALES (est): 200.25K **Privately Held**
Web: www.alamanceironworks.com
SIC: 1799 1521 3446 Ornamental metal work ; General remodeling, single-family houses; Fences or posts, ornamental iron or steel

(G-5347)
ALAMEEN A HAQQ
4424 Gray Wolf Way (27406-8099)
PHONE......................336 965-8339
Alameen A Haqq, Prin
EMP: 6 **EST:** 2007
SALES (est): 105.35K **Privately Held**
SIC: 2711 Newspapers, publishing and printing

(G-5348)
ALBERDINGK BOLEY INC
6008 W Gate City Blvd (27407-7073)
PHONE......................336 454-5000
Thomas Baur, Pr
Frank Dreisoerner, *
Beth Foust, *
◆ **EMP:** 69 **EST:** 2000
SQ FT: 125,000
SALES (est): 43.49MM
SALES (corp-wide): 316.3MM **Privately Held**
Web: www.alberdingkusa.com
SIC: 2851 Coating, air curing
PA: Alberdingk Boley Gmbh
Dusseldorfer Str. 53
Krefeld NW 47829
21515280

(G-5349)
ALLEN INDUSTRIES INC (PA)
6434 Burnt Poplar Rd (27409-9712)
PHONE......................336 668-2791
Thomas L Allen, Pr
John Allen, General Vice President*
David W Allen, *
▼ **EMP:** 100 **EST:** 1931
SQ FT: 75,000
SALES (est): 51.31MM
SALES (corp-wide): 51.31MM **Privately Held**
Web: www.allenindustries.com
SIC: 3993 Electric signs

(G-5350)
ALLEN INDUSTRIES INC
4100 Sheraton Ct (27410-8120)
PHONE......................336 294-4777
Tom Allen, Brnch Mgr
EMP: 123
SQ FT: 69,650
SALES (corp-wide): 51.31MM **Privately Held**

Web: www.allenindustries.com
SIC: 3993 Electric signs
PA: Allen Industries, Inc.
   6434 Burnt Poplar Rd
   Greensboro NC 27409
   336 668-2791

(G-5351)
ALTERNATIVE INGREDIENTS INC
2826 S Elm Eugene St (27406-4410)
P.O. Box 16846 (27416-0846)
PHONE..........................336 378-5368
James A Murphy Junior, *Ch*
Robin W Conner, *VP*
Ashley Sutton, *Sec*
EMP: 4 EST: 2014
SALES (est): 370.77K Privately Held
SIC: 2087 Concentrates, flavoring (except drink)

(G-5352)
ALUMINUM SCREEN MANUFACTURING
4501 Green Point Dr Ste 104 (27410-8141)
PHONE..........................336 605-8080
Donny Rauschuber, *Pr*
EMP: 4 EST: 2006
SALES (est): 249.63K Privately Held
Web: www.nrmlaw.com
SIC: 3496 Screening, woven wire: made from purchased wire

(G-5353)
AMALFI SEMICONDUCTOR INC
7628 Thorndike Rd (27409-9421)
PHONE..........................336 664-1233
EMP: 6 EST: 2019
SALES (est): 2.5MM
SALES (corp-wide): 3.77B Publicly Held
Web: www.qorvo.com
SIC: 3674 Semiconductors and related devices
PA: Qorvo, Inc.
   7628 Thorndike Rd
   Greensboro NC 27409
   336 664-1233

(G-5354)
AMERICAN CITY BUS JOURNALS INC
Also Called: Triad Business Journal
101 S Elm St Ste 100 (27401-2649)
PHONE..........................336 271-6539
Douglas Copeland, *Publisher*
EMP: 55
SALES (corp-wide): 2.88B Privately Held
Web: www.acbj.com
SIC: 2711 Newspapers: publishing only, not printed on site
HQ: American City Business Journals, Inc.
   120 W Morehead St Ste 400
   Charlotte NC 28202
   704 973-1000

(G-5355)
AMERICAN CLTVTION EXTRCTION SV
245 E Friendly Ave Ste 100 (27401-2986)
PHONE..........................336 544-1072
EMP: 8 EST: 2019
SALES (est): 161.91K Privately Held
SIC: 2079 Edible fats and oils

(G-5356)
AMERICAN EXTRUDED PLASTICS INC
938 Reynolds Pl (27403-2212)
P.O. Box 7422 (27417-0422)
PHONE..........................336 274-1131
EMP: 30 EST: 1983

SALES (est): 4.77MM
SALES (corp-wide): 295.68MM Privately Held
Web: www.carolinaextrudedplast.com
SIC: 3082 Unsupported plastics profile shapes
PA: Pexco Llc
   3440 Preston Ridge Rd
   Alpharetta GA 30005
   678 990-1523

(G-5357)
AMERICAN INDIAN PRINTING INC
Also Called: Bulldog Printing
1310 Beaman Pl (27408-8704)
PHONE..........................336 230-1551
Robert Martin Bundy, *Pr*
EMP: 4 EST: 1994
SALES (est): 376.4K Privately Held
Web: www.ncbulldogprinting.com
SIC: 2752 Offset printing

(G-5358)
AMERICAN VALVE INC (PA)
Also Called: Accord Ventilation Products
4321 Piedmont Pkwy (27410-8114)
PHONE..........................336 668-0554
Seth Guterman, *Pr*
Seth Guterman, *CEO*
Jeff Shaver, *
Carolyn Hinterberger, *
Marcy Jane Crump, *
▲ EMP: 60 EST: 1994
SQ FT: 20,000
SALES (est): 8.78MM Privately Held
Web: www.americanvalve.com
SIC: 3494 5074 Plumbing and heating valves ; Plumbing fittings and supplies

(G-5359)
AMERITEK INC
122 S Walnut Cir Ste B (27401)
PHONE..........................336 292-1165
Bill Hicks, *Prin*
EMP: 16 EST: 2007
SALES (est): 5.09MM Privately Held
Web: www.ameritekinc.com
SIC: 3554 Paper industries machinery

(G-5360)
AMERITEK LASERCUT DIES INC
Also Called: Ameritek
122 S Walnut Cir Ste B (27409-2641)
PHONE..........................336 292-1165
Bill Hicks, *Pr*
EMP: 6 EST: 1960
SQ FT: 22,000
SALES (est): 786.95K Privately Held
Web: www.ameritekinc.com
SIC: 3544 Special dies and tools

(G-5361)
AMKOR TECHNOLOGY INC
7870 Thorndike Rd (27409-9690)
PHONE..........................336 605-8009
EMP: 5
SALES (corp-wide): 6.32B Publicly Held
Web: www.amkor.com
SIC: 3674 Semiconductors and related devices
PA: Amkor Technology, Inc.
   2045 E Innovation Cir
   Tempe AZ 85284
   480 821-5000

(G-5362)
AMPLIFIED ELCTRONIC DESIGN INC
Also Called: Amped
7617 Boeing Dr (27409-9046)
P.O. Box 747 (27310-0747)
PHONE..........................336 223-4811

Sidney L Flake Iii, *Pr*
Robin Flake, *Sec*
EMP: 13 EST: 2012
SALES (est): 929.78K Privately Held
Web: www.ampedco.com
SIC: 1731 3669 8748 7382 Voice, data, and video wiring contractor; Intercommunication systems, electric; Communications consulting; Protective devices, security

(G-5363)
ANALOG DEVICES INC
7910 Triad Center Dr (27409-9758)
PHONE..........................336 668-9511
Gary Selders, *Mgr*
EMP: 30
SQ FT: 6,000
SALES (corp-wide): 9.43B Publicly Held
Web: www.analog.com
SIC: 3674 Integrated circuits, semiconductor networks, etc.
PA: Analog Devices, Inc.
   1 Analog Way
   Wilmington MA 01887
   781 935-5565

(G-5364)
ANGUNIQUE
6190 Pine Cove Ct (27410-9570)
PHONE..........................336 392-5866
Kenneth Henderson, *Prin*
EMP: 5 EST: 2010
SALES (est): 113.77K Privately Held
Web: www.angunique.com
SIC: 2323 Men's and boy's neckwear

(G-5365)
APEX ANALYTIX LLC (HQ)
1501 Highwoods Blvd Ste 200 (27410)
PHONE..........................336 272-4669
Steve Yurko, *CEO*
John Roberts, *
EMP: 150 EST: 1988
SALES (est): 45.27MM
SALES (corp-wide): 45.27MM Privately Held
Web: www.apexanalytix.com
SIC: 8742 7389 7372 Management consulting services; Financial services; Prepackaged software
PA: Apex Analytix Holding Llc
   1501 Highwoods Blvd # 200
   Greensboro NC 27410
   336 272-4669

(G-5366)
APPLE ROCK ADVG & PROM INC (PA)
Also Called: Apple Rock Displays
7602 Business Park Dr (27409-9696)
PHONE..........................336 232-4800
Eric Burg, *Pr*
Eric Burg, *CEO*
Terri Burg, *
Diane Rowell, *
Heidi Sanfilippo, *
EMP: 45 EST: 1988
SQ FT: 110,000
SALES (est): 22.46MM Privately Held
Web: www.applerock.com
SIC: 7319 8743 3993 Display advertising service; Promotion service; Signs and advertising specialties

(G-5367)
ARC3 GASES INC
810 Post St (27405-7261)
PHONE..........................336 275-3333
Danny Hollifield, *Mgr*
EMP: 7
SALES (corp-wide): 204.15MM Privately Held

Web: www.arc3gases.com
SIC: 2813 5169 7359 7692 Industrial gases; Chemicals and allied products, nec; Equipment rental and leasing, nec; Welding repair
PA: Arc3 Gases, Inc.
   1600 Us-301 S
   Dunn NC 28334
   910 892-4016

(G-5368)
ARCHIE SUPPLY LLC (PA)
4762 Champion Ct (27410-6101)
PHONE..........................336 987-0895
Brent Archie, *CEO*
EMP: 5 EST: 2014
SALES (est): 729.27K
SALES (corp-wide): 729.27K Privately Held
Web: www.archiesupply.com
SIC: 0279 5712 5112 5111 Worm farms; Office furniture; Stationery and office supplies; Printing and writing paper

(G-5369)
ARK AVIATION INC
200 N Raleigh St (27401-4822)
PHONE..........................336 379-0900
Carl Rshew, *Pr*
EMP: 5 EST: 2021
SALES (est): 1.21MM Privately Held
Web: www.arkaviation.aero
SIC: 3728 Aircraft parts and equipment, nec

(G-5370)
ARROWHEAD GRAPHICS INC
508 Houston St (27401-2332)
PHONE..........................336 274-2419
Bill Revels, *Pr*
William Revels Junior, *Pr*
EMP: 4 EST: 1979
SQ FT: 3,100
SALES (est): 447.96K Privately Held
Web: www.arrowheadgraphics.com
SIC: 2752 2759 Offset printing; Letterpress printing

(G-5371)
ARTIST S NEEDLE INC
2611 Phoenix Dr (27406-6320)
PHONE..........................336 294-5884
Mike Warwick, *Pr*
EMP: 4 EST: 2002
SQ FT: 5,000
SALES (est): 195.3K Privately Held
Web: www.artistneedle.com
SIC: 5949 2395 Sewing supplies; Embroidery products, except Schiffli machine

(G-5372)
ASHDAN ENTERPRISES
608 Summit Ave Ste 201 (27405-7754)
P.O. Box 67 (27301-0067)
PHONE..........................336 375-9698
Melvin Good, *Owner*
EMP: 4 EST: 1970
SALES (est): 226.85K Privately Held
SIC: 5719 3469 Kitchenware; Household cooking and kitchen utensils, metal

(G-5373)
ASP DISTRIBUTION INC
100 Bonita Dr (27405-7602)
PHONE..........................336 375-5672
Michael Caviness, *Pr*
EMP: 10 EST: 2003
SALES (est): 258.53K Privately Held
SIC: 3281 Curbing, granite or stone

(G-5374)
ATLANTIC BANKCARD CENTER INC
Also Called: Cardservice of Carolinas
2920 Manufacturers Rd (27406-4606)
PHONE..................336 855-9250
David W Tesh, Pr
EMP: 4 EST: 1992
SQ FT: 1,500
SALES (est): 238.9K **Privately Held**
Web: www.posregister.com
SIC: 7389 3578 Credit card service; Cash
registers

(G-5375)
AURORIUM LLC
Also Called: Aurorium
2110 W Gate City Blvd (27403-2642)
PHONE..................336 292-1781
John Van Hulle, CEO
EMP: 100
SALES (corp-wide): 636.82MM **Privately
Held**
Web: www.aurorium.com
SIC: 2869 Industrial organic chemicals, nec
HQ: Aurorium Llc
201 N Ill St Ste 1800
Indianapolis IN 46204
317 247-8141

(G-5376)
AUTEL NEW ENERGY US INC
8420 Triad Dr (27409-9018)
PHONE..................336 810-7083
Deena Lepe, Prin
EMP: 11
SALES (est): 2.55MM **Privately Held**
SIC: 3714 Motor vehicle electrical equipment

(G-5377)
AUTUMN CREEK VINEYARDS INC
2105 Lafayette Ave (27408-6303)
PHONE..................336 548-9463
Timothy Quinton Haley, Prin
EMP: 7 EST: 2007
SALES (est): 228.54K **Privately Held**
Web: www.gioiadellamorecellars.com
SIC: 2084 Wines

(G-5378)
AVERY DENNISON CORPORATION
2100 Summit Ave (27405-5012)
PHONE..................336 621-2570
Simon Coulson, Genl Mgr
EMP: 75
SALES (corp-wide): 8.76B **Publicly Held**
Web: www.averydennison.com
SIC: 2672 Paper; coated and laminated, nec
PA: Avery Dennison Corporation
8080 Norton Pkwy
Mentor OH 44060
440 534-6000

(G-5379)
AVERY DENNISON CORPORATION
620 Green Valley Rd Ste 306 (27408-7729)
PHONE..................336 553-2436
Greg Knoll, VP
EMP: 5
SALES (corp-wide): 8.76B **Publicly Held**
Web: www.averydennison.com
SIC: 2672 Adhesive papers, labels, or tapes:
from purchased material
PA: Avery Dennison Corporation
8080 Norton Pkwy
Mentor OH 44060
440 534-6000

(G-5380)
AVERY DENNISON CORPORATION
1100 Revolution Mill Dr # 11 (27405-5067)

PHONE..................336 856-8235
Phil Wray, Brnch Mgr
EMP: 5
SALES (corp-wide): 8.76B **Publicly Held**
Web: www.averydennison.com
SIC: 2672 Adhesive backed films, foams and
foils
PA: Avery Dennison Corporation
8080 Norton Pkwy
Mentor OH 44060
440 534-6000

(G-5381)
AVERY DENNISON CORPORATION
Avery Dennison
1100 Revolution Mill Dr # 11 (27405-5067)
PHONE..................864 938-1400
Al Greene, Brnch Mgr
EMP: 5
SALES (corp-wide): 8.76B **Publicly Held**
Web: www.averydennison.com
SIC: 2672 Coated paper, except
photographic, carbon, or abrasive
PA: Avery Dennison Corporation
8080 Norton Pkwy
Mentor OH 44060
440 534-6000

(G-5382)
AVERY DENNISON CORPORATION
200 Citation Ct (27409-9026)
PHONE..................336 665-6481
David Bullard, Mgr
EMP: 11
SALES (corp-wide): 8.76B **Publicly Held**
Web: www.averydennison.com
SIC: 2672 Coated paper, except
photographic, carbon, or abrasive
PA: Avery Dennison Corporation
8080 Norton Pkwy
Mentor OH 44060
440 534-6000

(G-5383)
AVERY DENNISON RFID COMPANY
1100 Revolution Mill Dr # 11 (27405-5067)
PHONE..................626 304-2000
Starla Parrish, Dir
EMP: 6 EST: 2016
SALES (est): 129.39K **Privately Held**
SIC: 2672 Paper; coated and laminated, nec

(G-5384)
BAKEMARK USA LLC
720 Pegg Rd (27409-9888)
PHONE..................336 848-9790
EMP: 62
SALES (corp-wide): 194.2MM **Privately
Held**
SIC: 2051 Bakery: wholesale or wholesale/
retail combined
PA: Bakemark Usa Llc
7351 Crider Ave
Pico Rivera CA 90660
562 949-1054

(G-5385)
BARKER AND MARTIN INC
Also Called: Phil Barker's Refinishing
1316 Headquarters Dr (27405-7920)
PHONE..................336 275-5056
Phil Barker, Pr
EMP: 4 EST: 1976
SQ FT: 2,500
SALES (est): 232.56K **Privately Held**
Web: www.philbarkerantiques.com
SIC: 7641 2511 5932 Furniture refinishing;
Wood household furniture; Antiques

(G-5386)
BARRIER1 SYSTEMS INC
Also Called: Barrier1
8015 Thorndike Rd (27409-9412)
PHONE..................336 617-8478
Michael J Lamore, Pr
EMP: 12 EST: 2006
SALES (est): 3.87MM **Privately Held**
Web: www.barrier1.com
SIC: 3499 Barricades, metal

(G-5387)
BENNETT UNIFORM MFG INC (PA)
4377 Federal Dr (27410-8116)
PHONE..................336 232-5772
Ervon R Bennett, Pr
Beatrice R Bennett, Sec
◆ **EMP: 18 EST:** 1972
SQ FT: 36,000
SALES (est): 2.13MM
SALES (corp-wide): 2.13MM **Privately
Held**
Web: www.bennettuniform.com
SIC: 2337 2326 2339 Uniforms, except
athletic: women's, misses', and juniors';
Work uniforms; Women's and misses'
outerwear, nec

(G-5388)
BERCO OF AMERICA INC
615 Pegg Rd (27409-9414)
PHONE..................336 931-1415
Marco Malsatti, Brnch Mgr
EMP: 28
SALES (corp-wide): 39.13B **Privately Held**
Web: www.berco.com
SIC: 3531 5082 Construction machinery;
General construction machinery and
equipment
HQ: Berco Of America, Inc.
W229n1420 Westwood Dr
Waukesha WI 53186

(G-5389)
BIBEY MACHINE COMPANY INC
642 S Spring St (27406-1252)
PHONE..................336 275-9421
Ronald G Bibey, Pr
Ken Younger, *
Kathy Bibey, *
EMP: 30 EST: 1978
SQ FT: 25,000
SALES (est): 3.89MM **Privately Held**
Web: www.bibeymachine.com
SIC: 3599 Machine shop, jobbing and repair

(G-5390)
**BIO-TECH PRSTHTICS ORTHTICS IN
(HQ)**
Also Called: Hanger Clinic
2301 N Church St (27405-4309)
PHONE..................336 333-9081
Anthony Saia, Pr
Michael Neal, VP
EMP: 7 EST: 1995
SQ FT: 1,600
SALES (est): 5.81MM
SALES (corp-wide): 1.12B **Privately Held**
Web: www.hangerclinic.com
SIC: 3842 5999 5661 Prosthetic appliances;
Orthopedic and prosthesis applications;
Shoes, orthopedic
PA: Hanger, Inc.
10910 Domain Dr Ste 300
Austin TX 78758
512 777-3800

(G-5391)
BLACK & DECKER (US) INC
Also Called: Dewalt Industrial Tool
4621 W Gate City Blvd (27407-4239)

PHONE..................336 852-1300
Chris Dennis, Mgr
EMP: 5
SALES (corp-wide): 15.78B **Publicly Held**
Web: www.dewalt.com
SIC: 3546 Power-driven handtools
HQ: Black & Decker (U.S.) Inc.
1000 Stanley Dr
New Britain CT 06053
860 225-5111

(G-5392)
BLACKTIP SOLUTIONS
3125 Kathleen Ave Ste 221 (27408-7819)
PHONE..................336 303-1580
Kevin Walsh, Admn
EMP: 4 EST: 2019
SALES (est): 268.77K **Privately Held**
SIC: 7372 Application computer software

(G-5393)
BLUE SUN ENERGY INC
408 Gallimore Dairy Rd Ste C
(27409-9526)
PHONE..................336 218-6707
H Scott Brown, Pr
Phillip O'neal Ridge, VP
Glean Day, Sec
▲ **EMP: 4 EST:** 2009
SALES (est): 177.57K **Privately Held**
Web: www.bluesunenergy.com
SIC: 3648 5063 Lighting equipment, nec;
Light bulbs and related supplies

(G-5394)
**BLUESCOPE BUILDINGS N AMER
INC**
Also Called: Varco Pruden Buildings
7031 Albert Pick Rd Ste 200 (27409-9537)
PHONE..................336 996-4801
Tim Mcneely, Brnch Mgr
EMP: 134
Web: www.bluescopebuildings.com
SIC: 3448 Prefabricated metal buildings and
components
HQ: Bluescope Buildings North America,
Inc.
1540 Genessee St
Kansas City MO 64102

(G-5395)
BLUETICK INC
Also Called: Bluetick Services
1501 Highwoods Blvd Ste 104
(27410-2050)
PHONE..................336 294-4102
Michael Mills, Pr
EMP: 16 EST: 2009
SALES (est): 2.5MM **Privately Held**
Web: www.bluetickinc.com
SIC: 7379 4899 7375 7371 Online services
technology consultants; Data
communication services; On-line data base
information retrieval; Computer software
development and applications

(G-5396)
BLYTHE CONSTRUCTION INC
2606 Phoenix Dr (27406)
PHONE..................336 854-9003
David Melton, Mgr
EMP: 42
SALES (corp-wide): 21.74MM **Privately
Held**
Web: www.blytheconstruction.com
SIC: 1611 2951 Highway and street paving
contractor; Asphalt paving mixtures and
blocks
HQ: Blythe Construction, Inc.
2911 N Graham St
Charlotte NC 28206
704 375-8474

(G-5397)
BOX BOARD PRODUCTS INC
8313 Triad Dr (27409-9621)
P.O. Box 18863 (27419)
PHONE.................................336 668-3347
TOLL FREE: 800
▲ EMP: 220 EST: 1968
SALES (est): 22.28MM
SALES (corp-wide): 5.45B **Publicly Held**
Web: www.boxboardproducts.com
SIC: 5113 2671 Corrugated and solid fiber
　boxes; Paper; coated and laminated
　packaging
PA: Greif, Inc.
　　425 Winter Rd
　　Delaware OH 43015
　　740 549-6000

(G-5398)
BRICE MANUFACTURING CO INC
Also Called: Haeco Americas Cabin Solutions
8010 Piedmont Triad Pkwy (27409-9407)
PHONE.................................818 896-2938
Richard Kendall, *CEO*
Mark Peterman, *
Lee Fox, *
▲ EMP: 25 EST: 1968
SALES (est): 672.26K
SALES (corp-wide): 18.29B **Privately Held**
Web: www.timco.aero
SIC: 3728 7641 Aircraft parts and
　equipment, nec; Furniture repair and
　maintenance
HQ: Haeco Americas, Llc
　　623 Radar Rd
　　Greensboro NC 27410

(G-5399)
**BRIDGESTONE RET OPERATIONS
LLC**
Also Called: Firestone
3311 Battleground Ave (27410-2401)
PHONE.................................336 282-6646
Dylan Smith, *Mgr*
EMP: 8
Web: www.bridgestoneamericas.com
SIC: 5531 7534 Automotive tires; Rebuilding
　and retreading tires
HQ: Bridgestone Retail Operations, Llc
　　200 4th Ave S Ste 100
　　Nashville TN 37201
　　615 937-1000

(G-5400)
**BRIDGESTONE RET OPERATIONS
LLC**
Also Called: Firestone
3937 W Gate City Blvd (27407-4611)
PHONE.................................336 852-8524
Noel Cecil, *Mgr*
EMP: 10
SQ FT: 6,349
Web: www.bridgestoneamericas.com
SIC: 5531 7534 7539 Automotive tires;
　Rebuilding and retreading tires; Brake
　services
HQ: Bridgestone Retail Operations, Llc
　　200 4th Ave S Ste 100
　　Nashville TN 37201
　　615 937-1000

(G-5401)
**BRIDGESTONE RET OPERATIONS
LLC**
Also Called: Firestone
512 Pisgah Church Rd (27455-2524)
PHONE.................................336 282-4695
EMP: 6
Web: www.bridgestoneamericas.com

SIC: 5531 7538 7537 7534 Automotive tires;
　General automotive repair shops;
　Automotiv e transmission repair shops; Tire
　retreading and repair shops
HQ: Bridgestone Retail Operations, Llc
　　200 4th Ave S Ste 100
　　Nashville TN 37201
　　615 937-1000

(G-5402)
BRIDGETOWER MEDIA LLC (PA)
7025 Albert Pick Rd (27408)
PHONE.................................612 317-9420
Hal Cohen, *CEO*
Tom Callahan, *CFO*
EMP: 24 EST: 2015
SALES (est): 8.86MM
SALES (corp-wide): 8.86MM **Privately
Held**
Web: www.beddingconference.com
SIC: 2711 Newspapers: publishing only, not
　printed on site

(G-5403)
BRIGHTON WEAVING LLC
7736 Mccloud Rd Ste 300 (27409-9324)
PHONE.................................336 665-3000
EMP: 4 EST: 2003
SALES (est): 127.14K **Privately Held**
SIC: 2211 Broadwoven fabric mills, cotton

(G-5404)
BRILLIANT YOU LLC
1451 S Elm Eugene St Ste 1102
(27406-2200)
PHONE.................................336 343-5535
EMP: 4 EST: 2012
SALES (est): 493.65K **Privately Held**
Web: www.brilliantyoudenim.com
SIC: 2339 2325 Jeans: women's, misses',
　and juniors'; Men's and boys' jeans and
　dungarees

(G-5405)
BRISPA INVESTMENTS INC
4833 W Gate City Blvd (27407-5305)
P.O. Box 77634 (27417-7634)
PHONE.................................336 668-3636
Stephen K Bright, *Pr*
L Kirk Sparks, *
Joseph H Vest, *
Jo Anna Bright, *
▲ EMP: 105 EST: 1987
SQ FT: 115,000
SALES (est): 16.56MM **Privately Held**
Web: www.brightplastics.com
SIC: 3089 Injection molding of plastics

(G-5406)
BRISTOL-MYERS SQUIBB COMPANY
Bristol-Myers Squibb
211 American Ave (27409-1803)
PHONE.................................336 855-5500
Michael Hession, *Brnch Mgr*
EMP: 400
SALES (corp-wide): 48.3B **Publicly Held**
Web: www.bms.com
SIC: 2834 Pharmaceutical preparations
PA: Bristol-Myers Squibb Company
　　Route 206/Prvince Line Rd
　　Princeton NJ 08540
　　609 252-4621

(G-5407)
BRITTANY SMITH
Also Called: Glitzbybritt
2508 Glenhaven Dr (27406-4211)
PHONE.................................912 313-0588
Brittany Smith, *Owner*
EMP: 8 EST: 2021
SALES (est): 304.48K **Privately Held**

SIC: 3999 Hair and hair-based products

(G-5408)
BUCHANAN PRTG & GRAPHICS INC
1088 Boulder Rd (27409-9106)
PHONE.................................336 299-6868
David Buchanan, *Pr*
James Buchanan, *Ch Bd*
Nancy C Buchanan, *Sec*
EMP: 8 EST: 1990
SQ FT: 6,000
SALES (est): 268.4K **Privately Held**
Web: www.buchananprinting.com
SIC: 2752 Offset printing

(G-5409)
BUILDERS FIRSTSOURCE INC
7601 Boeing Dr (27409-9046)
PHONE.................................336 884-5454
Oza Humphrey, *Brnch Mgr*
EMP: 13
SALES (corp-wide): 16.4B **Publicly Held**
Web: www.bldr.com
SIC: 2421 5211 2431 Building and structural
　materials, wood; Lumber and other building
　materials; Doors and door parts and trim,
　wood
PA: Builders Firstsource, Inc.
　　6031 Cnnection Dr Ste 400
　　Irving TX 75039
　　214 880-3500

(G-5410)
BURLINGTON CHEMICAL CO LLC
8646 W Market St Ste 116 (27409-9447)
PHONE.................................336 584-0111
Bret Holmes, *Managing Member*
Michael Matzinger, *Prin*
◆ EMP: 7 EST: 1954
SQ FT: 23,000
SALES (est): 4.38MM **Privately Held**
Web: www.burco.com
SIC: 5169 2899 2865 Dyestuffs; Chemical
　preparations, nec; Cyclic crudes and
　intermediates

(G-5411)
BURLINGTON DISTRIBUTING CO
Also Called: Old Master Cabinets
2232 Westbrook St (27407-2524)
P.O. Box 5486 (27435-0486)
PHONE.................................336 292-1415
Joseph P Mitchell Senior, *Pr*
William S Mitchell, *VP*
Gerald R Mitchell, *VP*
EMP: 4 EST: 1958
SQ FT: 16,000
SALES (est): 247.01K **Privately Held**
SIC: 2434 Wood kitchen cabinets

(G-5412)
BURLINGTON HOUSE LLC
804 Green Valley Rd Ste 300 (27408-7013)
PHONE.................................336 379-6220
Joe Gorga, *CEO*
EMP: 11 EST: 2004
SALES (est): 1.11MM
SALES (corp-wide): 1.98B **Privately Held**
SIC: 2211 Sheets, bedding and table cloths:
　cotton
HQ: Elevate Textiles, Inc.
　　121 W Trade St Ste 1700
　　Charlotte NC 28202

(G-5413)
BURLINGTON INDUSTRIES III LLC
3330 W Friendly Ave (27410-4806)
P.O. Box 21207 (27420-1207)
PHONE.................................336 379-2000
EMP: 10 EST: 2001
SALES (est): 358.23K **Privately Held**

SIC: 2231 Worsted fabrics, broadwoven

(G-5414)
BURLINGTON INDUSTRIES LLC (DH)
804 Green Valley Rd Ste 300 (27408)
PHONE.................................336 379-6220
Joey Underwood, *Pr*
◆ EMP: 150 EST: 2003
SALES (est): 37.4MM
SALES (corp-wide): 1.98B **Privately Held**
Web: www.burlingtonfabrics.com
SIC: 2231 2211 2221 2273 Bleaching yarn
　and fabrics: wool or similar fibers; Denims;
　Polyester broadwoven fabrics; Carpets and
　rugs
HQ: Elevate Textiles, Inc.
　　121 W Trade St Ste 1700
　　Charlotte NC 28202

(G-5415)
C E SMITH CO INC
6396 Burnt Poplar Rd (27409-9710)
PHONE.................................336 273-0166
Kellie Barricks, *Mgr*
EMP: 23
SALES (corp-wide): 13.04MM **Privately
Held**
Web: www.cesmith.com
SIC: 3469 Metal stampings, nec
PA: C. E. Smith Co., Inc.
　　1001 Bitting St
　　Greensboro NC 27403
　　336 273-0166

(G-5416)
C E SMITH CO INC (PA)
1001 Bitting St (27403-2165)
P.O. Box 9948 (27429-0948)
PHONE.................................336 273-0166
Carl E Smith, *Pr*
Robert Barricks, *
▲ EMP: 50 EST: 1966
SQ FT: 60,000
SALES (est): 13.04MM
SALES (corp-wide): 13.04MM **Privately
Held**
Web: www.cesmith.com
SIC: 3469 3452 Metal stampings, nec;
　Screws, metal

(G-5417)
C P EAKES COMPANY
2012 Fairfax Rd (27407)
PHONE.................................336 574-1800
Patrick Eakes, *CEO*
Patrick Eakes, *Pr*
Kristen Eakes, *Sec*
EMP: 16 EST: 1996
SQ FT: 40,000
SALES (est): 2.89MM **Privately Held**
Web: www.cpeakes.com
SIC: 3444 3446 Sheet metalwork;
　Architectural metalwork

(G-5418)
CABINET TRANSITIONS INC
5310 Solar Pl (27406-9144)
PHONE.................................336 382-7154
EMP: 4 EST: 2019
SALES (est): 75.19K **Privately Held**
Web: www.cabinettransitions.com
SIC: 2434 Wood kitchen cabinets

(G-5419)
CAMCO MANUFACTURING LLC (PA)
121 Landmark Dr (27409-9626)
PHONE.................................336 668-7661
Demir Vangelov, *CEO*
Lisa Schoder, *CMO*
Danielle Conner, *COO*
◆ EMP: 160 EST: 1966

SQ FT: 302,000
SALES (est): 86.27MM
SALES (corp-wide): 86.27MM **Privately Held**
Web: www.camco.net
SIC: 2899 Chemical preparations, nec

(G-5420)
CANGILOSI SPCIALTY SAUSAGE INC
115 Landmark Dr (27409-9603)
PHONE..........................336 665-5775
Giacomo Cangialosi, *Pr*
EMP: 5 **EST:** 1991
SQ FT: 12,000
SALES (est): 965.95K **Privately Held**
Web: www.cangialosispecialtyinc.com
SIC: 2013 Sausages and other prepared
  meats

(G-5421)
CANPLAST USA INC
7104 Cessna Dr (27409-9793)
PHONE..........................336 668-9555
Charley Mays, *Manager*
EMP: 7 **EST:** 2009
SALES (est): 547.12K **Privately Held**
Web: www.surteco.com
SIC: 2821 Plastics materials and resins

(G-5422)
CARDINAL MILLWORK & SUPPLY INC
7620 W Market St (27409-1848)
PHONE..........................336 665-9811
Richie V Fahnestock, *CEO*
Chris Fahnestock, *
Dannie Fahnestock, *
Patti Byrd, *
EMP: 34 **EST:** 2003
SALES (est): 8.78MM **Privately Held**
Web: www.cardinalmillwork.com
SIC: 2431 Millwork

(G-5423)
CARLISLE FINISHING LLC
804 Green Valley Rd Ste 300 (27408-7039)
PHONE..........................864 466-4173
James Payne, *Pr*
EMP: 54
SALES (corp-wide): 1.98B **Privately Held**
SIC: 2231 Broadwoven fabric mills, wool
HQ: Carlisle Finishing Llc
     804 Green Valley Rd # 300
     Greensboro NC 27408
     336 379-6220

(G-5424)
CAROLINA BY-PRODUCTS CO
2410 Randolph Ave (27406-2910)
PHONE..........................336 333-3030
Mike Hooks, *Mgr*
EMP: 4 **EST:** 1985
SALES (est): 220.49K **Privately Held**
SIC: 8742 2077 2047 Management
  consulting services; Animal and marine fats
  and oils; Dog and cat food

(G-5425)
CAROLINA CSTM SIGNS & GRAPHICS
1023 Huffman St (27405-7209)
PHONE..........................336 681-4337
EMP: 4 **EST:** 2017
SALES (est): 163.04K **Privately Held**
Web: www.greensborosigncompany.com
SIC: 3993 Signs and advertising specialties

(G-5426)
CAROLINA EXTRUDED PLASTICS INC

728 Utility St (27405-7224)
P.O. Box 14728 (27415-4728)
PHONE..........................336 272-1191
◆ **EMP:** 24 **EST:** 1977
SALES (est): 2.7MM **Privately Held**
Web: www.carolinaextrudedplast.com
SIC: 3089 Extruded finished plastics
  products, nec

(G-5427)
CAROLINA LASER CUTTING INC
4400 S Holden Rd (27406-9508)
PHONE..........................336 292-1474
Bruce Cromes, *Pr*
Shirley Massingill, *Sec*
EMP: 20 **EST:** 1986
SQ FT: 12,000
SALES (est): 2.78MM **Privately Held**
Web: www.carolinalasercutting.com
SIC: 3599 Machine shop, jobbing and repair

(G-5428)
CAROLINA LOOM REED COMPANY INC
3503 Holts Chapel Rd (27401-4526)
P.O. Box 22111 (27420-2111)
PHONE..........................336 274-7631
Ernest J Mcfetters Junior, *Pr*
EMP: 4 **EST:** 1938
SQ FT: 30,000
SALES (est): 616.04K **Privately Held**
Web: www.loom.coffee
SIC: 3552 Textile machinery

(G-5429)
CAROLINA LQUID CHMISTRIES CORP (PA)
313 Gallimore Dairy Rd (27409-9724)
PHONE..........................336 722-8910
Phillip Shugart, *Pr*
Patricia Shugart, *COO*
◆ **EMP:** 49 **EST:** 1994
SALES (est): 9.85MM **Privately Held**
Web: www.carolinachemistries.com
SIC: 3841 Anesthesia apparatus

(G-5430)
CAROLINA MATERIAL HANDLING INC
Also Called: Caster House
2209 Patterson Ct (27407-2541)
PHONE..........................336 294-2346
TOLL FREE: 800
John Middleton, *CEO*
Mid Middleton, *Pr*
Jay Mitchell, *VP*
EMP: 18 **EST:** 1971
SQ FT: 4,000
SALES (est): 9.62MM **Privately Held**
Web: www.cmh-inc.com
SIC: 5084 3537 3496 Materials handling
  machinery; Cradles, drum; Cages, wire

(G-5431)
CAROLINA NEWSPAPERS INC
Also Called: Carolina Peacemaker
807 Summit Ave (27405-7833)
P.O. Box 20853 (27420-0853)
PHONE..........................336 274-7829
John Marshall Kilimanjaro, *Pr*
Vickie Kilimanjaro, *Prin*
Afrique Kilimanjaro, *Editor*
EMP: 6 **EST:** 1967
SQ FT: 1,000
SALES (est): 135.6K **Privately Held**
Web: www.peacemakeronline.com
SIC: 2711 2752 Newspapers: publishing
  only, not printed on site; Commercial
  printing, lithographic

(G-5432)
CARSON-DELLOSA PUBLISHING LLC
Also Called: Carson Dellosa Education
657 Brigham Rd Ste A (27409-9098)
PHONE..........................336 632-0084
Rich Lugo, *Brnch Mgr*
EMP: 45
SALES (corp-wide): 48.3MM **Privately Held**
Web: www.carsondellosa.com
SIC: 2741 Miscellaneous publishing
PA: Carson-Dellosa Publishing, Llc
     7027 Albert Pick Rd
     Greensboro NC 27409
     336 632-0084

(G-5433)
CARSON-DELLOSA PUBLISHING LLC (PA)
Also Called: Carson Dellosa Education
7027 Albert Pick Rd Ste 300 (27409-9828)
P.O. Box 35665 (27425)
PHONE..........................336 632-0084
Ira Hernowitz, *CEO*
Joshua Loew, *CMO*
◆ **EMP:** 100 **EST:** 2009
SALES (est): 21.94MM
SALES (corp-wide): 21.94MM **Privately Held**
Web: www.carsondellosa.com
SIC: 5943 2731 School supplies; Textbooks:
  publishing and printing

(G-5434)
CCBCC OPERATIONS LLC
Also Called: Coca-Cola
8200 Capital Dr 067 (27409-9038)
PHONE..........................336 664-1116
Mark Moore, *Brnch Mgr*
EMP: 56
SQ FT: 12,200
SALES (corp-wide): 6.9B **Publicly Held**
Web: www.coca-cola.com
SIC: 2086 Bottled and canned soft drinks
HQ: Ccbcc Operations, Llc
     4100 Coca-Cola Plz
     Charlotte NC 28211
     704 364-8728

(G-5435)
CED INCORPORATED
7910 Industrial Village Rd (27409-9691)
P.O. Box 2515 (28329-2515)
PHONE..........................336 378-0044
George Carver, *Prin*
Calvin Edward Davis, *Prin*
EMP: 10 **EST:** 2010
SALES (est): 2.21MM **Privately Held**
SIC: 3612 Distribution transformers, electric

(G-5436)
CENTER FOR CREATIVE LEADERSHIP (PA)
1 Leadership Pl (27410)
PHONE..........................336 288-7210
Martin Schneider, *Pr*
Bradley E Shumaker, *
EMP: 400 **EST:** 1970
SQ FT: 180,000
SALES (est): 123.52MM
SALES (corp-wide): 123.52MM **Privately Held**
Web: www.ccl.org
SIC: 8299 2731 Educational services; Book
  publishing

(G-5437)
CENTRAL CAROLINA CONCRETE LLC (HQ)

296 Edwardia Dr (27409-2604)
P.O. Box 8308 (27419-0308)
PHONE..........................704 372-2930
EMP: 15 **EST:** 2000
SALES (est): 28.58MM
SALES (corp-wide): 149.62MM **Privately Held**
Web: www.centralcarolinaconcrete.com
SIC: 3273 4212 Ready-mixed concrete;
  Local trucking, without storage
PA: Concrete Supply Holdings, Inc.
     3823 Raleigh St
     Charlotte NC 28206
     704 372-2930

(G-5438)
CENTRIC BRANDS LLC
620 S Elm St Ste 395 (27406-1399)
PHONE..........................646 582-6000
Jason Rabin, *CEO*
Anurup Pruthi, *CFO*
Joe Favuzza, *CSO*
EMP: 342 **EST:** 1987
SALES (est): 4.46MM **Privately Held**
Web: www.centricbrands.com
SIC: 2339 2311 2325 2387 Women's and
  misses' accessories; Men's and boy's suits
  and coats; Men's and boy's trousers and
  slacks; Apparel belts
PA: Centric Brands Llc
     350 5th Ave Fl 6
     New York NY 10118

(G-5439)
CGR PRODUCTS INC (PA)
4655 Us Highway 29 N (27405-9446)
PHONE..........................336 621-4568
Charles S Keeley Iii, *Pr*
Richard C Wilmoth, *
Thomas J Schultz, *
◆ **EMP:** 75 **EST:** 1963
SQ FT: 70,000
SALES (est): 20.76MM
SALES (corp-wide): 20.76MM **Privately Held**
Web: www.cgrproducts.com
SIC: 3053 Gaskets, all materials

(G-5440)
CHANDLER CONCRETE INC
Also Called: Chandler Concrete
300 S Swing Rd (27409-2010)
P.O. Box 9679 (27429-0679)
PHONE..........................336 297-1179
Tom Chandler, *Mgr*
EMP: 12
Web: www.chandlerconcrete.com
SIC: 3273 Ready-mixed concrete
PA: Chandler Concrete Co., Inc.
     1006 S Church Street
     Burlington NC 27215

(G-5441)
CHANDLER FOODS INC
2727 Immanuel Rd (27407-2515)
PHONE..........................336 299-1934
Jerry Hendrix, *Pr*
Doctor John E Chandler Iii, *VP*
Martha Chandler, *
EMP: 35 **EST:** 1955
SQ FT: 45,000
SALES (est): 16.65MM **Privately Held**
Web: www.chandlerfoodsinc.com
SIC: 2013 2032 2099 2038 Prepared pork
  products, from purchased pork; Chili, with
  or without meat: packaged in cans, jars, etc.
  ; Food preparations, nec; Frozen
  specialties, nec

(G-5442)
CHASE-LOGEMAN CORPORATION
303 Friendship Dr (27409-9332)
PHONE...........................336 665-0754
Douglas Logeman, *Pr*
Jean Logeman, *Sec*
EMP: 19 EST: 1939
SQ FT: 18,000
SALES (est): 7.13MM **Privately Held**
Web: www.chaselogeman.com
SIC: 5084 3565 Packaging machinery and
　equipment; Packaging machinery

(G-5443)
CHEMOL COMPANY INC
2300 Randolph Ave (27406-2908)
P.O. Box P.O Box 16286 (27416)
PHONE...........................336 333-3050
Scott Seydel, *SR*
Fred Wellons, *
Graham Marsh, *
Maria S White, *
EMP: 30 **EST:** 1969
SQ FT: 15,000
SALES (est): 15.35MM
SALES (corp-wide): 49.12MM **Privately
Held**
Web: www.seydel.com
SIC: 2869 2819 Industrial organic chemicals,
　nec; Industrial inorganic chemicals, nec
PA: The Seydel Companies
　　244 John B Brooks Rd
　　Pendergrass GA 30567
　　706 693-2266

(G-5444)
CINTAS CORPORATION NO 2
Also Called: Cintas
4345 Federal Dr (27410-8116)
PHONE...........................336 632-4412
Jeff Wilt, *Genl Mgr*
EMP: 44
SALES (corp-wide): 9.6B **Publicly Held**
Web: www.cintas.com
SIC: 5084 2395 Safety equipment;
　Embroidery products, except Schiffli
　machine
HQ: Cintas Corporation No. 2
　　6800 Cintas Blvd
　　Mason OH 45040

(G-5445)
CITI ENERGY LLC
2309 W Cone Blvd Ste 200 (27408-4047)
P.O. Box 39599 (27438-9599)
PHONE...........................336 379-0800
Derrick Mcdow, *Pr*
EMP: 6 **EST:** 2010
SALES (est): 1.33MM **Privately Held**
Web: www.citienergyllc.com
SIC: 1382 Oil and gas exploration services

(G-5446)
CITY OF GREENSBORO
Also Called: Mitchell Water/Filtering Plant
1041 Battleground Ave (27408-8322)
PHONE...........................336 373-5855
Steven Drew, *Mgr*
EMP: 55
SALES (corp-wide): 471.51MM **Privately
Held**
Web: www.greensboro-nc.gov
SIC: 3589 5541 Water filters and softeners,
　household type; Gasoline service stations
PA: City Of Greensboro
　　300 W Washington St
　　Greensboro NC 27401
　　336 373-2002

(G-5447)
CLAROLUX INC
2501 Greengate Dr (27406-5242)
P.O. Box 4554 (27404-4554)
PHONE...........................336 378-6800
Robert Groat, *Pr*
Brian Groat, *
▲ **EMP:** 25 **EST:** 2004
SALES (est): 7.1MM **Privately Held**
Web: www.clarolux.com
SIC: 5063 3645 Lighting fixtures; Boudoir
　lamps

(G-5448)
CLASSIC WOOD MANUFACTURING
1006 N Raleigh St (27405-7328)
PHONE...........................336 691-1344
Steve Cannon, *Owner*
EMP: 5 **EST:** 1985
SQ FT: 3,000
SALES (est): 484.65K **Privately Held**
Web: www.classicwoodproductsllc.com
SIC: 3714 Motor vehicle parts and
　accessories

(G-5449)
**CLEAN GREEN SUSTAINABLE LF
LLC**
610 N Elam Ave (27408-6810)
PHONE...........................855 946-8785
Vince Pinpin, *Managing Member*
EMP: 15
SALES (est): 199.05K **Privately Held**
SIC: 3999 Manufacturing industries, nec

(G-5450)
CLEAR DEFENSE LLC
2000 N Church St (27405-5634)
P.O. Box 41316 (27404-1316)
PHONE...........................336 370-1699
EMP: 9 **EST:** 2000
SQ FT: 1,200
SALES (est): 1.95MM **Privately Held**
SIC: 3081 3083 Unsupported plastics film
　and sheet; Laminated plastics plate and
　sheet

(G-5451)
CLINTON PRESS INC
2100 Tennyson Dr (27410-2234)
PHONE...........................336 275-8491
Walter C Jackson Iv, *Pr*
EMP: 10 **EST:** 1946
SALES (est): 857.58K **Privately Held**
Web: www.clintonpress.com
SIC: 2752 2741 Offset printing;
　Miscellaneous publishing

(G-5452)
**CLONDALKIN PHARMA &
HEALTHCARE**
1072 Boulder Rd (27409-9106)
PHONE...........................336 292-4555
Peter Hunt, *CEO*
EMP: 7 **EST:** 2019
SALES (est): 961.22K **Privately Held**
SIC: 2752 Commercial printing, lithographic

(G-5453)
COLONIAL TIN WORKS INC
7609 Canoe Rd (27409-9002)
P.O. Box 49909 (27419-1909)
PHONE...........................336 668-4126
Tom La Rose, *Pr*
Charlie Lederer, *
▲ **EMP:** 25 **EST:** 1980
SQ FT: 60,000
SALES (est): 933.9K **Privately Held**
Web: www.ctwhomecollection.com

SIC: 5947 3499 5023 Gift, novelty, and
　souvenir shop; Novelties and giftware,
　including trophies; Decorative home
　furnishings and supplies

(G-5454)
COLUMBIA FOREST PRODUCTS INC
Centruty Drive Ste 200 (27401)
PHONE...........................336 605-0429
Richard Parker, *Brnch Mgr*
EMP: 4
SALES (corp-wide): 494.11K **Privately
Held**
Web: www.columbiaforestproducts.com
SIC: 5031 2426 2273 Lumber: rough,
　dressed, and finished; Hardwood
　dimension and flooring mills; Carpets and
　rugs
PA: Columbia Forest Products, Inc.
　　7900 Mccloud Rd Ste 200
　　Greensboro NC 27409
　　336 605-0429

(G-5455)
**COLUMBIA FOREST PRODUCTS
INC (PA)**
7900 Mccloud Rd Ste 200 (27409)
PHONE...........................336 605-0429
Greg Pray, *Pr*
Ron Jordee, *
◆ **EMP:** 60 **EST:** 1976
SALES (est): 494.11K
SALES (corp-wide): 494.11K **Privately
Held**
Web: www.columbiaforestproducts.com
SIC: 5031 2435 Lumber: rough, dressed,
　and finished; Hardwood plywood,
　prefinished

(G-5456)
**COLUMBIA WEST VIRGINIA CORP
(HQ)**
7820 Thorndike Rd (27409-9690)
PHONE...........................336 605-0429
Harry L Demorest, *Pr*
Cliff Barry, *
▲ **EMP:** 38 **EST:** 1990
SALES (est): 56.92K
SALES (corp-wide): 494.11K **Privately
Held**
Web: www.columbiaforestproducts.com
SIC: 2411 Veneer logs
PA: Columbia Forest Products, Inc.
　　7900 Mccloud Rd Ste 200
　　Greensboro NC 27409
　　336 605-0429

(G-5457)
COMBILIFT USA LLC
303 Concord St (27406-3635)
PHONE...........................336 378-8884
▲ **EMP:** 14 **EST:** 2005
SALES (est): 10.58MM **Privately Held**
Web: www.combilift.com
SIC: 3537 Forklift trucks
PA: Combilift Unlimited Company
　　Annahagh
　　Monaghan

(G-5458)
COMEDYCD
400 Nottingham Rd (27408-7526)
PHONE...........................336 273-0077
Douglas Key, *Pt*
EMP: 5 **EST:** 2016
SALES (est): 73.28K **Privately Held**
SIC: 2759 Commercial printing, nec

(G-5459)
COMMERCIAL FLTER SVC OF TRIAD
107 Creek Ridge Rd Ste F (27406-4439)
PHONE...........................336 272-1443
Lacy Alton Cole Junior, *Pr*
Janice Cole, *VP*
EMP: 7 **EST:** 1989
SALES (est): 169.31K **Privately Held**
SIC: 1711 3564 Heating and air conditioning
　contractors; Filters, air: furnaces, air
　conditioning equipment, etc.

(G-5460)
COMMONWEALTH BRANDS INC
714 Green Valley Rd (27408-7018)
PHONE...........................336 634-4200
Ulrich Netels, *Brnch Mgr*
EMP: 230
Web: www.itgbrands.com
SIC: 2111 Cigarettes
HQ: Commonwealth Brands, Inc.
　　5900 N Andrews Ave Ste 11
　　Fort Lauderdale FL 33309

(G-5461)
COMMSCOPE TECHNOLOGIES LLC
Also Called: Te Connectivity
8420 Triad Dr (27409-9018)
PHONE...........................336 665-6000
Al Link, *Brnch Mgr*
EMP: 29
SALES (corp-wide): 15.22B **Publicly Held**
Web: www.commscope.com
SIC: 3663 Radio and t.v. communications
　equipment
HQ: Commscope Technologies Llc
　　3642 E Us Highway 70
　　Claremont NC 28610
　　828 324-2200

(G-5462)
CONE DENIM LLC (DH)
Also Called: Cone Denim Mills
804 Green Valley Rd Ste 300 (27408-7013)
PHONE...........................336 379-6165
Ken Kunberger, *CEO*
◆ **EMP:** 59 **EST:** 2004
SALES (est): 16MM
SALES (corp-wide): 1.98B **Privately Held**
Web: www.conedenim.com
SIC: 2211 Denims
HQ: Elevate Textiles, Inc.
　　121 W Trade St Ste 1700
　　Charlotte NC 28202

(G-5463)
CONSOLIDATED PIPE & SUP CO INC
Also Called: Store 72
2410 Binford St (27407-2502)
PHONE...........................336 294-8577
Jaret Ledermann, *Mgr*
EMP: 10
SALES (corp-wide): 385.83MM **Privately
Held**
Web: www.consolidatedpipe.com
SIC: 5051 5085 3462 3084 Pipe and tubing,
　steel; Valves and fittings; Nuclear power
　plant forgings, ferrous; Plastics pipe
PA: Consolidated Pipe & Supply Company,
　　Inc.
　　1205 Hilltop Pkwy
　　Birmingham AL 35204
　　205 323-7261

(G-5464)
CONVATEC INC
7815 National Service Rd Ste 600
　(27409-9403)
PHONE...........................336 297-3021
Sharon Tate, *Brnch Mgr*
EMP: 7

▲ = Import ▼ = Export
◆ = Import/Export

SALES (corp-wide): 2.14B **Privately Held**
Web: www.convatec.com
SIC: 3841 Surgical and medical instruments
HQ: Convatec Inc.
200 Crossing Blvd Ste 101
Bridgewater NJ 08807

(G-5465)
CONVATEC INC
7815 National Service Rd Ste 600
(27409-9403)
PHONE..................336 855-5500
Steven Forden, *Mgr*
EMP: 200
SALES (corp-wide): 2.14B **Privately Held**
Web: www.convatec.com
SIC: 3841 Surgical and medical instruments
HQ: Convatec Inc.
200 Crossing Blvd Ste 101
Bridgewater NJ 08807

(G-5466)
CONVERTING TECHNOLOGY INC
514 Teague St (27406-4314)
PHONE..................336 333-2386
Michael Keaton, *Pr*
John Norgard, *VP*
EMP: 6 EST: 2004
SALES (est): 492.69K **Privately Held**
Web: www.converting-technology.com
SIC: 3544 Special dies and tools

(G-5467)
COOPER INDUSTRIES LLC
3912 Battleground Ave (27410-8575)
PHONE..................304 545-1482
EMP: 4 EST: 2017
SALES (est): 335.55K **Privately Held**
SIC: 3999 Manufacturing industries, nec

(G-5468)
COPY KING INC (PA)
Also Called: Copy King Printing
611 W Gate City Blvd (27403-3034)
P.O. Box 1057 (27402-1057)
PHONE..................336 333-9900
Matthew N Hopman, *Pr*
Alana L Hopman, *Mgr*
Steven Hopman, *VP*
EMP: 8 EST: 1981
SQ FT: 2,400
SALES (est): 432.21K
SALES (corp-wide): 432.21K **Privately Held**
Web: www.copykinggso.com
SIC: 7334 2752 Blueprinting service; Offset printing

(G-5469)
CORE TECHNOLOGY MOLDING CORP (PA)
2911 E Gate City Blvd Ste 201 (27410)
PHONE..................336 294-2018
Geoff E Foster, *Pr*
Tonya O Foster, *VP*
EMP: 29 EST: 2006
SALES (est): 611.85K
SALES (corp-wide): 611.85K **Privately Held**
Web: www.coretechnologycorp.com
SIC: 8731 1799 3069 Commercial physical research; Fiberglass work; Floor coverings, rubber

(G-5470)
CORE TECHNOLOGY MOLDING CORP
5201 Hayward Dr (27406-8856)
PHONE..................336 294-2018
Geoff Foster, *CEO*

EMP: 31
SALES (corp-wide): 611.85K **Privately Held**
Web: www.coretechnologycorp.com
SIC: 3089 Injection molding of plastics
PA: Core Technology Molding Corp
2911 E Gate City Blvd
Greensboro NC 27410
336 294-2018

(G-5471)
CREST ELECTRONICS INC
3703 Alliance Dr Ste A (27407-2385)
P.O. Box 8073 (27419-0073)
PHONE..................336 855-6422
Dennis Castelli, *CEO*
▲ **EMP:** 5 EST: 1974
SQ FT: 12,514
SALES (est): 438.28K **Privately Held**
Web: www.crestelectronics.com
SIC: 3663 7382 3861 5731 Television closed circuit equipment; Protective devices, security; Cameras and related equipment; Video cameras and accessories

(G-5472)
CROSS TECHNOLOGIES INC (PA)
Also Called: Cross Precision Measurement
4400 Piedmont Pkwy (27410-8121)
P.O. Box 18508 (27419-8508)
PHONE..................800 327-7727
John King, *CEO*
Rock Able, *
Jerry Bohnsack, *
EMP: 50 EST: 1954
SQ FT: 67,000
SALES (est): 197.14MM
SALES (corp-wide): 197.14MM **Privately Held**
Web: www.crossco.com
SIC: 3492 5084 8734 3625 Hose and tube fittings and assemblies, hydraulic/pneumatic ; Industrial machine parts; Calibration and certification; Electric controls and control accessories, industrial

(G-5473)
CROSS TECHNOLOGIES INC
Also Called: Cross Hose and Fitting
3012 S Elm Eugene St Ste A (27406-4455)
PHONE..................336 370-4673
Wayne Scott, *Mgr*
EMP: 5
SALES (corp-wide): 197.14MM **Privately Held**
Web: www.crossco.com
SIC: 3492 5085 Hose and tube couplings, hydraulic/pneumatic; Hose, belting, and packing
PA: Cross Technologies, Inc.
4400 Piedmont Pkwy
Greensboro NC 27410
800 327-7727

(G-5474)
CROWN TROPHY INC
Also Called: National Reconition
201 Pomona Dr Ste C (27407-1635)
PHONE..................336 851-1011
Norb W Burske, *VP*
Lana Burske, *Pr*
EMP: 4 EST: 1999
SALES (est): 228.43K **Privately Held**
Web: www.crowntrophy.com
SIC: 5999 5199 3479 Trophies and plaques; Badges; Engraving jewelry, silverware, or metal

(G-5475)
CSC FAMILY HOLDINGS INC (PA)
Also Called: Hirschfeld Industries

101 Centreport Dr Ste 400 (27409-9422)
P.O. Box 20888 (27420-0888)
PHONE..................336 275-9711
W H Reeves, *Pr*
EMP: 41 EST: 1919
SQ FT: 65,000
SALES (est): 17.66MM
SALES (corp-wide): 17.66MM **Privately Held**
SIC: 3441 Fabricated structural metal

(G-5476)
CUMMINS INC
Also Called: Cummins
513 Preddy Blvd (27406-4314)
PHONE..................336 275-4531
Charlie Townsend, *Mgr*
EMP: 27
SALES (corp-wide): 34.1B **Publicly Held**
Web: www.cummins.com
SIC: 5084 5013 5531 3519 Engines and parts, diesel; Motor vehicle supplies and new parts; Auto and home supply stores; Internal combustion engines, nec
PA: Cummins Inc.
500 Jackson St
Columbus IN 47201
812 377-5000

(G-5477)
CURSED SOCIETY LLC
27 Covey Ln Apt G (27406-6828)
PHONE..................702 445-5601
Ahkim Evans, *Managing Member*
EMP: 5
SALES (est): 925.27K **Privately Held**
SIC: 3161 Clothing and apparel carrying cases

(G-5478)
CURTIS PACKING COMPANY (PA)
2416 Randolph Ave (27406-2910)
P.O. Box 1470 (27402-1470)
PHONE..................336 275-7684
Douglas B Curtis, *Pr*
John R Curtis, *
EMP: 100 EST: 1946
SQ FT: 40,000
SALES (est): 4.57MM
SALES (corp-wide): 4.57MM **Privately Held**
Web: www.curtispackingcompany.com
SIC: 2011 Frankfurters, from meat slaughtered on site

(G-5479)
CUSTOM ARMOR GROUP INC
4270 Piedmont Pkwy Ste 102 (27410-8160)
PHONE..................336 617-4667
Todd M Dix, *Pr*
EMP: 4 EST: 2011
SALES (est): 559.5K **Privately Held**
Web: www.customarmorgroup.com
SIC: 3483 Ammunition, except for small arms, nec

(G-5480)
CUSTOM CNVERTING SOLUTIONS INC
Also Called: C C S
1207 Boston Rd (27407-2107)
PHONE..................336 292-2616
Matthew O'connell, *Pr*
Laura O'connell, *VP*
▲ **EMP:** 40 EST: 2001
SQ FT: 44,000
SALES (est): 7.82MM **Privately Held**
Web:
www.customconvertingsolutions.com

SIC: 3711 3469 Automobile assembly, including specialty automobiles; Appliance parts, porcelain enameled

(G-5481)
CUSTOM INDUSTRIES INC (PA)
Also Called: Bio Air
215 Aloe Rd (27409-2105)
P.O. Box 18547 (27419-8547)
PHONE..................336 299-2885
James E Nagel, *Pr*
Wilbert Everett, *
▲ **EMP:** 30 EST: 1962
SQ FT: 85,000
SALES (est): 2.26MM
SALES (corp-wide): 2.26MM **Privately Held**
Web: www.customindustries.com
SIC: 3599 3444 5047 3429 Machine shop, jobbing and repair; Restaurant sheet metalwork; Medical equipment and supplies ; Marine hardware

(G-5482)
CYBER DEFENSE ADVISORS
3336 Wall Rd (27407-9726)
PHONE..................336 899-6072
Kevin Fiscus, *Prin*
EMP: 4 EST: 2017
SALES (est): 304.65K **Privately Held**
SIC: 3812 Defense systems and equipment

(G-5483)
CYGANY INC
2712 Denise Dr (27407-6648)
PHONE..................773 293-2999
Patricia L C Henderson, *Pr*
▲ **EMP:** 5 EST: 1996
SALES (est): 203.51K **Privately Held**
SIC: 3911 Jewelry apparel

(G-5484)
CYRCO INC
120 N Chimney Rock Rd (27409-1854)
P.O. Box 7292 (27417-0292)
PHONE..................336 668-0977
Peter Couture, *Pr*
Paul Couture, *
Paula C Mcgee, *Sec*
▲ **EMP:** 26 EST: 1980
SQ FT: 9,000
SALES (est): 8.65MM **Privately Held**
Web: www.cyrco.com
SIC: 3499 1796 Aerosol valves, metal; Installing building equipment

(G-5485)
D & D ENTPS GREENSBORO INC
Also Called: D & D Precision Tool
1337 Burnetts Chapel Rd (27406-8815)
PHONE..................336 495-3407
Ralph Davis, *Pr*
Harold Davis, *
EMP: 7 EST: 1976
SALES (est): 1.56MM **Privately Held**
Web: www.ddent-usa.com
SIC: 3599 Machine shop, jobbing and repair

(G-5486)
D C THOMAS GROUP INC (PA)
Also Called: Thomas Foods
6540 W Market St (27409-1836)
P.O. Box 8822 (27419-0822)
PHONE..................336 299-6263
Dwight C Thomas Senior, *Pr*
Dwight C Thomas Junior, *VP*
Becky Thomas, *Sec*
EMP: 6 EST: 1971
SALES (est): 2.12MM **Privately Held**
Web: www.thomasgourmetfoods.net

G
E
O
G
R
A
P
H
I
C

SIC: **2035** Pickles, sauces, and salad
dressings

(G-5487)
DAVID ORECK CANDLE
3500 N Ohenry Blvd (27405-3814)
PHONE..............................336 375-8411
James Mccain, *Prin*
EMP: 6 **EST:** 2012
SALES (est): 621.77K **Privately Held**
Web: www.davidoreckcandles.com
SIC: **3999** Candles

(G-5488)
DAVID R WEBB COMPANY INC
300 Standard Dr (27409-9641)
PHONE..............................336 605-3355
Gary Cox, *Mgr*
EMP: 4
SALES (corp-wide): 31.51MM **Privately**
Held
Web: www.danzer.com
SIC: **2435** 2436 Veneer stock, hardwood;
Veneer stock, softwood
HQ: David R. Webb Company, Inc.
206 S Holland St
Edinburgh IN 46124
812 526-2601

(G-5489)
DBT COATINGS LLC
3625 N Elm St Ste 100a (27455-2605)
P.O. Box 4121 (27404-4121)
PHONE..............................336 834-9700
Timothy Leeper, *CEO*
David Parker, *VP*
Daniel Sroka, *VP*
Thomas Mckenna, *COO*
David Leeper, *CFO*
EMP: 7 **EST:** 2011
SALES (est): 991.14K **Privately Held**
Web: www.polytexus.com
SIC: **2631** 2759 2891 Container, packaging,
and boxboard; Commercial printing, nec;
Adhesives and sealants

(G-5490)
DDP SPCLTY ELCTRNIC MTLS US 9
Also Called: CSS
2914 Patterson St (27407-3337)
PHONE..............................336 547-7112
Darren W Cammin, *Brnch Mgr*
EMP: 26
SALES (corp-wide): 12.39B **Publicly Held**
Web: www.dupont.com
SIC: **2821** 2869 2891 3569 Plastics
materials and resins; Industrial organic
chemicals, nec; Adhesives and sealants;
Filters
HQ: Ddp Specialty Electronic Materials Us
9, Llc
974 Centre Rd
Wilmington DE 19805
302 774-1000

(G-5491)
DEDON INC (DH)
657 Brigham Rd Ste C (27409-9153)
P.O. Box 2196 (27261)
PHONE..............................336 790-1070
Bobby Dekeyser, *Ch Bd*
David Kennedy, *
◆ **EMP:** 14 **EST:** 2009
SALES (est): 24.42MM
SALES (corp-wide): 355.83K **Privately**
Held
Web: www.dedon.de
SIC: **2511** 5712 Lawn furniture: wood;
Outdoor and garden furniture
HQ: Dedon Gmbh
Zeppelinstr. 22

Luneburg NI
413 122-4470

(G-5492)
DEEP RVER MLLS CTD FABRICS
INC (PA)
Also Called: Deep River Printing
1904 Lendew St (27408-7007)
P.O. Box 66 (27259-0066)
PHONE..............................910 464-3135
Larry Booth, *Pr*
Vicky Booth, *VP*
▲ **EMP:** 10 **EST:** 1979
SQ FT: 55,000
SALES (est): 2.45MM
SALES (corp-wide): 2.45MM **Privately**
Held
Web: www.deeprivermills.com
SIC: **2261** Chemical coating or treating of
cotton broadwoven fabrics

(G-5493)
DELTA PHOENIX INC
Also Called: Wysong Parts and Service
4820 Us Hwy 29 N (27405)
P.O. Box 21168 (27420-1168)
PHONE..............................336 621-3960
Russell F Hall Iii, *Pr*
Suzanne C Hall, *
William F Herr Ii, *VP*
Billy R Carter, *
EMP: 26 **EST:** 2011
SALES (est): 5.47MM **Privately Held**
Web: www.wysong.us
SIC: **3541** 3542 Machine tools, metal cutting
type; Brakes, metal forming

(G-5494)
DELUXE CORPORATION
3703 Farmington Dr (27407-5616)
PHONE..............................336 851-4600
Cheryl Anthony, *Brnch Mgr*
EMP: 19
SALES (corp-wide): 2.12B **Publicly Held**
Web: www.deluxe.com
SIC: **2782** Checkbooks
PA: Deluxe Corporation
801 Marquette Ave
Minneapolis MN 55402
651 483-7111

(G-5495)
DELVE INTERIORS LLC
7820 Thorndike Rd (27409-9690)
PHONE..............................336 274-4661
▲ **EMP:** 113
SIC: **2521** 5021 2426 1742 Wood office
furniture; Office and public building furniture
; Frames for upholstered furniture, wood;
Acoustical and insulation work

(G-5496)
DIGITAL PROGRESSIONS INC
5101 W Market St (27409-2613)
P.O. Box 16792 (27416-0792)
PHONE..............................336 676-6570
Thomas Wayman, *Pr*
Mark Woodall, *VP*
EMP: 5 **EST:** 1997
SQ FT: 3,000
SALES (est): 522.44K **Privately Held**
SIC: **3861** Printing equipment, photographic

(G-5497)
DIVISION EIGHT INC
2206 N Church St (27405-4308)
P.O. Box 14985 (27415)
PHONE..............................336 852-1275
Peter B Norton, *Pr*
EMP: 16 **EST:** 2004
SQ FT: 15,000

SALES (est): 2.74MM **Privately Held**
Web: www.divisioneightinc.com
SIC: **3429** 3261 Furniture hardware;
Bathroom accessories/fittings, vitreous
china or earthenware

(G-5498)
DOCUMENT COMM SOLUTIONS INC
Also Called: AlphaGraphics
205 Aloe Rd (27409-2105)
P.O. Box 8565 (27419-0565)
PHONE..............................336 856-1300
Ruth Sturm, *Pr*
John Sturm, *VP*
EMP: 4 **EST:** 1997
SQ FT: 2,700
SALES (est): 571.36K **Privately Held**
Web: www.alphagraphics.com
SIC: **2752** Commercial printing, lithographic

(G-5499)
DOGGIES R US
2940 E Market St (27405-7407)
PHONE..............................336 455-1113
William Goode, *Owner*
EMP: 4 **EST:** 2021
SALES (est): 154.77K **Privately Held**
SIC: **3199** Dog furnishings: collars, leashes,
muzzles, etc.: leather

(G-5500)
DOKJA INC (PA)
Also Called: Sir Speedy
602 S Edwardia Dr (27409-2806)
PHONE..............................336 852-5190
Ken Miller, *Pr*
Ken Miller, *CEO*
Paul Miller, *CEO*
EMP: 8 **EST:** 1993
SQ FT: 1,500
SALES (est): 982.08K **Privately Held**
Web: www.sirspeedy.com
SIC: **2752** 2791 2789 Commercial printing,
lithographic; Typesetting; Bookbinding and
related work

(G-5501)
DOUBLE HUNG LLC
2801 Patterson St (27407-2318)
PHONE..............................888 235-8956
David Hoggard, *Managing Member*
EMP: 47 **EST:** 2008
SALES (est): 5.16MM **Privately Held**
Web: www.double-hung.com
SIC: **2431** 5031 Door frames, wood;
Windows

(G-5502)
DOVE COMMUNICATIONS INC
7 Wendy Ct Ste B (27409-2248)
PHONE..............................336 855-5491
John Liner, *Pr*
E Gordon Liner, *Sec*
EMP: 8 **EST:** 1988
SQ FT: 6,800
SALES (est): 403.39K **Privately Held**
Web: www.dovecommunication.com
SIC: **2752** Offset printing

(G-5503)
DOW SILICONES CORPORATION
2914 Patterson St (27407-3337)
PHONE..............................336 547-7100
Jane Waldron, *Mgr*
EMP: 104
SALES (corp-wide): 42.96B **Publicly Held**
Web: www.dow.com
SIC: **2821** Plastics materials and resins
HQ: Dow Silicones Corporation
2200 W Salzburg Rd
Midland MI 48686
989 496-4000

(G-5504)
DP SOLUTIONS INC (HQ)
Also Called: Dpsi
1801 Stanley Rd Ste 301 (27407-2644)
P.O. Box 49003 (27419-1003)
PHONE..............................336 854-7700
Frederick M Riek, *Ch Bd*
Carol Owens, *Pr*
Eric Lynn Carriker, *Ex VP*
EMP: 12 **EST:** 1986
SQ FT: 13,464
SALES (est): 4.71MM
SALES (corp-wide): 16.68MM **Privately**
Held
Web: www.dpsi.com
SIC: **7372** Application computer software
PA: Valsoft Corporation Inc.
100-7405 Rte Transcanadienne
Montreal QC H4T 1
514 316-7647

(G-5505)
DS SMITH PACKAGING AND PAPER
4328 Federal Dr Ste 105 (27410-8115)
PHONE..............................336 668-0871
EMP: 7 **EST:** 2019
SALES (est): 2.86MM **Privately Held**
Web: www.dssmith.com
SIC: **2621** Packaging paper

(G-5506)
DTBTLA INC
4301 Waterleaf Ct (27410-8106)
PHONE..............................336 769-0000
Al Hutchison, *Pr*
Allie Hutchison Senior, *Ch Bd*
Douglas S Flynn, *
Terry Preston, *
Carrie Stankwytch, *
▼ **EMP:** 11 **EST:** 1931
SQ FT: 37,000
SALES (est): 916.34K **Privately Held**
SIC: **2752** 2759 Offset printing; Commercial
printing, nec

(G-5507)
DTP INC
1 Wendy Ct Ste E (27409-2247)
PHONE..............................336 272-5122
Steve Lacivita, *Pr*
EMP: 4 **EST:** 1987
SQ FT: 3,000
SALES (est): 123.44K **Privately Held**
SIC: **2796** 7338 7384 Color separations, for
printing; Proofreading service; Photofinish
laboratories

(G-5508)
DUCK HEAD LLC
816 S Elm St (27406-1332)
PHONE..............................855 457-1865
EMP: 4 **EST:** 2013
SALES (est): 104.04K **Privately Held**
Web: www.duckhead.com
SIC: **2389** Men's miscellaneous accessories

(G-5509)
EAGLE COMPRESSORS INC (PA)
Also Called: Eagle Compressors
3003 Thurston Ave (27406-4516)
PHONE..............................336 370-4159
Anthony M Gonzalez, *Prin*
▲ **EMP:** 24 **EST:** 1999
SQ FT: 30,000
SALES (est): 4.05MM **Privately Held**
Web: www.eaglecompressors.com
SIC: **3563** Air and gas compressors

(G-5510)
EASTH20 HOLDINGS LLC
Also Called: Miller Products Co
4224 Tudor Ln Ste 101 (27410-8145)
PHONE......................919 313-2100
John Westland, *Brnch Mgr*
EMP: 9
SALES (corp-wide): 7.45MM **Privately Held**
SIC: 3069 3061 3089 5085 Clothing, vulcanized rubber or rubberized fabric; Mechanical rubber goods; Blow molded finished plastics products, nec; Rubber goods, mechanical
PA: Easth20 Holdings, Llc.
15041 Bake Pkwy Ste F
Irvine CA 92618
714 533-2827

(G-5511)
EATUMUP LURE COMPANY INC
Also Called: Revi Technical Wear
116 S Walnut Cir (27409-2625)
PHONE......................336 218-0896
James Murray, *Pr*
EMP: 9 **EST:** 1982
SQ FT: 6,000
SALES (est): 361.64K **Privately Held**
Web: www.reviwear.com
SIC: 2329 2339 2759 Athletic clothing, except uniforms: men's, youths' and boys'; Athletic clothing: women's, misses', and juniors'; Commercial printing, nec

(G-5512)
ECOLAB INC
Also Called: Ecolab Kay Chemical Company
8300 Capital Dr (27409-9790)
PHONE......................336 931-2289
Steve Mosh, *Brnch Mgr*
EMP: 38
SALES (corp-wide): 15.32B **Publicly Held**
Web: www.ecolab.com
SIC: 2842 Specialty cleaning
PA: Ecolab Inc.
1 Ecolab Pl
Saint Paul MN 55102
800 232-6522

(G-5513)
EFA INC
Also Called: Elastic Fabrics of America
3112 Pleasant Garden Rd (27406-4608)
P.O. Box 21986 (27420-1986)
PHONE......................336 378-2603
James Robbins, *Pr*
Rick Bauer, *
Terry Murphy, *
▼ **EMP:** 230 **EST:** 2007
SALES (est): 4.72MM **Privately Held**
Web: www.elasticfabrics.com
SIC: 2221 Broadwoven fabric mills, manmade
HQ: Nueva Expresion Textil Sa.
Calle Isabel Colbrand 10
Madrid M

(G-5514)
EFA INC (DH)
Also Called: Elastic Fabric of America
3112 Pleasant Garden Rd (27406-4608)
P.O. Box 21986 (27420-1986)
PHONE......................336 275-9401
James Robbins, *Pr*
Sandra Jones, *
Terry Murphy, *
▼ **EMP:** 147 **EST:** 2007
SALES (est): 22.77MM **Privately Held**
Web: www.elasticfabrics.com

SIC: 2241 2221 Rubber and elastic yarns and fabrics; Elastic fabrics, manmade fiber and silk
HQ: Nueva Expresion Textil Sa.
Calle Isabel Colbrand 10
Madrid M

(G-5515)
ELANCO US INC
3200 Northline Ave Ste 300 (27408-7616)
PHONE......................812 230-2745
Neel Ambani, *CFO*
EMP: 14 **EST:** 1996
SALES (est): 624.97K **Privately Held**
Web: www.elanco.com
SIC: 2834 Pharmaceutical preparations

(G-5516)
ELECTRIC FSHING REEL SYSTEMS I
1700 Sullivan St (27405-7265)
P.O. Box 20411 (27420)
PHONE......................336 273-9101
Carl Huffman, *CEO*
▲ **EMP:** 5 **EST:** 1970
SQ FT: 15,000
SALES (est): 480.5K **Privately Held**
Web: www.elec-tra-mate.com
SIC: 5941 3949 Bait and tackle; Fishing equipment

(G-5517)
ELSAG NORTH AMERICA LLC (PA)
4221 Tudor Ln (27410-8105)
PHONE......................336 379-7135
Mark Windover, *Managing Member*
EMP: 36 **EST:** 2004
SALES (est): 10.21MM
SALES (corp-wide): 10.21MM **Privately Held**
Web: www.leonardocompany-us.com
SIC: 3829 Photogrammetrical instruments

(G-5518)
EM2 MACHINE CORPORATION
1030 Boulder Rd (27409-9106)
PHONE......................336 707-8409
Vince Simmons, *CEO*
EMP: 4 **EST:** 2006
SALES (est): 908.65K **Privately Held**
SIC: 3499 Friction material, made from powdered metal

(G-5519)
ENCERTEC INC
415 Pisgah Church Rd Ste 302 (27455-2590)
PHONE......................336 288-7226
Don Denison, *Pr*
▲ **EMP:** 4 **EST:** 1992
SQ FT: 1,200
SALES (est): 486.1K **Privately Held**
Web: www.encertec.com
SIC: 3559 5084 2621 Kilns; Industrial machinery and equipment; Absorbent paper

(G-5520)
ENDLESS PLASTICS LLC
3704 Alliance Dr Ste B (27407-2989)
PHONE......................336 346-1839
Robert Long, *Managing Member*
EMP: 10 **EST:** 2002
SQ FT: 12,000
SALES (est): 969.49K **Privately Held**
Web: www.endlessplastics.com
SIC: 5162 3993 2542 Plastics sheets and rods; Displays and cutouts, window and lobby; Stands, merchandise display: except wood

(G-5521)
ENGINEERED SOFTWARE
615 Guilford Ave (27401-1975)
PHONE......................336 299-4843
Bill L Stanley, *Pr*
Susan Stanley, *VP*
EMP: 6 **EST:** 2002
SALES (est): 318.2K **Privately Held**
Web: www.engsw.com
SIC: 7372 Prepackaged software

(G-5522)
ENNIS-FLINT INC (HQ)
Also Called: PPG Traffic Solutions
4161 Piedmont Pkwy Ste 370 (27410-8176)
PHONE......................800 331-8118
Edward Baiden, *Pr*
Laura Greer, *Sec*
Brice Hester, *VP*
John A Jankowski, *Treas*
◆ **EMP:** 14 **EST:** 1996
SALES (est): 110.85MM
SALES (corp-wide): 17.65B **Publicly Held**
Web: www.ppg.com
SIC: 2851 Paints and allied products
PA: Ppg Industries, Inc.
1 Ppg Pl
Pittsburgh PA 15272
412 434-3131

(G-5523)
ENTRUST SERVICES LLC
130 S Walnut Cir (27409-2625)
P.O. Box 35228 (27425)
PHONE......................336 274-5175
EMP: 18 **EST:** 2005
SALES (est): 4.72MM **Privately Held**
SIC: 2842 3463 Drain pipe solvents or cleaners; Plumbing fixture forgings, nonferrous

(G-5524)
EPSILON HOLDINGS LLC
Also Called: Box Drop Furniture Whl NC
2103 E Town Blvd Ste 105 (27455)
PHONE......................336 763-6147
Frank Park, *Mng Pt*
EMP: 4 **EST:** 2015
SQ FT: 4,000
SALES (est): 106.81K **Privately Held**
SIC: 2599 Bar furniture

(G-5525)
ETHERNGTON CNSERVATION CTR INC
1010 Arnold St (27405-7102)
PHONE......................336 665-1317
Donald G Etherington, *Pr*
EMP: 20 **EST:** 2001
SALES (est): 414.17K **Privately Held**
Web: www.hfgroup.com
SIC: 2789 5932 Bookbinding and related work; Used merchandise stores
PA: Hf Group, Llc
400 Arora Cmmons Cir Unit
Aurora OH 44202

(G-5526)
EVONIK CORPORATION
2401 Doyle St (27406-2911)
PHONE......................336 333-3565
Reinhold Brand, *Brnch Mgr*
EMP: 61
SALES (corp-wide): 16.03B **Privately Held**
Web: corporate.evonik.com
SIC: 2869 Industrial organic chemicals, nec
HQ: Evonik Corporation
2 Turner Pl
Piscataway NJ 08854
732 981-5060

(G-5527)
EXACT CUT INC
824 Winston St (27405-7236)
PHONE......................336 207-4022
John Bradley, *Pr*
EMP: 5 **EST:** 2007
SALES (est): 911.6K **Privately Held**
Web: www.exactcut.net
SIC: 3541 Machine tools, metal cutting type

(G-5528)
EXQUISITE GRANITE AND MBL INC
6207 Tri Port Ct (27409-2013)
PHONE......................336 851-8890
Jody Esque, *Owner*
EMP: 6 **EST:** 2013
SQ FT: 10,000
SALES (est): 376.12K **Privately Held**
Web: www.exquisitegranitestudio.com
SIC: 3281 Marble, building: cut and shaped

(G-5529)
FAINTING GOAT SPIRITS LLC
321 W Wendover Ave (27408-8401)
PHONE......................336 273-6221
Shelley A Johnson, *Prin*
EMP: 4 **EST:** 2015
SALES (est): 616.56K **Privately Held**
Web: www.faintinggoatspirits.com
SIC: 2085 Distilled and blended liquors

(G-5530)
FIBEX LLC
7109 Cessna Dr (27409-9793)
PHONE......................336 358-5014
Jeff Bruner, *Brnch Mgr*
EMP: 4
SALES (corp-wide): 419.89K **Privately Held**
SIC: 2822 Synthetic rubber
PA: Fibex Llc
5280 National Center Dr
Colfax NC 27235
336 605-9002

(G-5531)
FILTRATION TECHNOLOGY INC (PA)
110 Pomona Dr (27407-1616)
P.O. Box 18168 (27419-8168)
PHONE......................336 294-5655
Richard A Matthews, *Ch Bd*
Scott Matthews, *Pr*
▼ **EMP:** 8 **EST:** 1971
SQ FT: 12,500
SALES (est): 3.18MM
SALES (corp-wide): 3.18MM **Privately Held**
Web: www.filtrationtechnology.com
SIC: 1799 5075 3564 Decontamination services; Air conditioning and ventilation equipment and supplies; Purification and dust collection equipment

(G-5532)
FILTRATION TECHNOLOGY INC
Also Called: Filtration Technology
110 Pomona Dr (27407-1616)
P.O. Box 18168 (27419-8168)
PHONE......................336 509-9960
Scott Mathews, *Pr*
EMP: 7
SALES (corp-wide): 3.18MM **Privately Held**
Web: www.filtrationtechnology.com
SIC: 3564 Filters, air: furnaces, air conditioning equipment, etc.
PA: Filtration Technology, Inc.
110 Pomona Dr
Greensboro NC 27407
336 294-5655

GEOGRAPHIC

(G-5533)
FILTRONA FILTERS INC
303 Gallimore Dairy Rd (27409-9724)
PHONE..............................336 362-1333
Robert Pye, *CEO*
EMP: 93
SALES (corp-wide): 599.01MM **Privately Held**
Web: www.essentra.com
SIC: 3999 2621 Cigarette filters; Cigarette paper
HQ: Filtrona Filters Inc
    2 Westbrook Corp Ctr
    Westchester IL 60154

(G-5534)
FISKARS BRANDS INC
Ginger
322 Edwardia Dr Ste D (27409-2636)
PHONE..............................336 292-6237
Anca Vladu, *Brnch Mgr*
EMP: 23
SALES (corp-wide): 1.23B **Privately Held**
Web: www.fiskars.com
SIC: 3423 Hand and edge tools, nec
HQ: Fiskars Brands, Inc.
    7800 Discovery Dr
    Middleton WI 53562
    608 259-1649

(G-5535)
FLINT SPINNING LLC
7736 Mccloud Rd Ste 300 (27409-9324)
PHONE..............................336 665-3000
Authur C Wiener, *Ch Bd*
Authur C Wiener, *Pr*
EMP: 4 EST: 2001
SALES (est): 171.49K **Privately Held**
SIC: 2211 Broadwoven fabric mills, cotton

(G-5536)
FONTEM US LLC
Also Called: Blu Ecigs
628 Green Valley Rd Ste 500 (27408-7791)
PHONE..............................888 207-4588
Murray Kessler, *CEO*
Jim Raport, *Pr*
▲ EMP: 7 EST: 2012
SALES (est): 12.89MM **Privately Held**
Web: us.blu.com
SIC: 2111 5993 Cigarettes; Cigarette store
HQ: Itg Brands, Llc
    628 Green Valley Rd
    Greensboro NC 27408
    336 335-6669

(G-5537)
FORVESON CORP
322 Edwardia Dr Ste D (27409-2636)
PHONE..............................336 292-6237
Mauro Lizzoli, *Pr*
Angelo Lizzoli, *Sec*
Giacomo Lizzoli, *Treas*
▲ EMP: 4 EST: 2012
SALES (est): 853.87K **Privately Held**
Web: www.gingher.com
SIC: 3421 Scissors, shears, clippers, snips, and similar tools

(G-5538)
FRAGRANT PASSAGE CANDLE CO LP
3500 N Ohenry Blvd (27405-3814)
PHONE..............................336 375-8411
David Oreck, *Ch Bd*
Carol Ritchie, *Acctnt*
Kathy Lavanier, *Genl Mgr*
▲ EMP: 25 EST: 2004
SQ FT: 20,000
SALES (est): 377.8K **Privately Held**
Web: www.fpcandle.com

SIC: 3999 Candles

(G-5539)
FRED MARVIN AND ASSOCIATES INC
Also Called: Fred Marvin Associates
496 Gallimore Dairy Rd Ste D (27409-9202)
PHONE..............................330 784-9211
Jeff Mussay, *Pr*
▲ EMP: 6 EST: 1946
SALES (est): 434.43K **Privately Held**
Web: www.fredmarvin.com
SIC: 3421 Cutlery

(G-5540)
FREEDOM BEVERAGE COMPANY
4319 Waterleaf Ct Ste 101 (27410-8171)
PHONE..............................336 316-1260
Tim Booras, *Pr*
▲ EMP: 5 EST: 2013
SALES (est): 1.49MM **Privately Held**
Web: www.freedombev.com
SIC: 2087 Beverage bases, concentrates, syrups, powders and mixes

(G-5541)
FRONT LINE EXPRESS LLC
4086 Clovelly Dr (27406-8563)
PHONE..............................800 260-1357
EMP: 7 EST: 2019
SALES (est): 343.26K **Privately Held**
SIC: 3799 Transportation equipment, nec

(G-5542)
FT MEDIA HOLDINGS LLC (HQ)
Also Called: Progressive Business Media
7025 Albert Pick Rd Ste 200 (27409-9539)
PHONE..............................336 605-0121
Catherine Silver, *Pr*
EMP: 11 EST: 2013
SALES (est): 1.73MM
SALES (corp-wide): 8.86MM **Privately Held**
Web:
www.progressivebusinessmedia.com
SIC: 2741 2721 Business service newsletters: publishing and printing; Trade journals: publishing and printing
PA: Bridgetower Media, Llc
    7025 Albert Pick Rd
    Greensboro NC 27408
    612 317-9420

(G-5543)
FURNITURE TDAY MEDIA GROUP LLC
7025 Albert Pick Rd Ste 200 (27409-9539)
PHONE..............................336 605-0121
EMP: 64 EST: 2013
SALES (est): 587.41K
SALES (corp-wide): 8.86MM **Privately Held**
Web: www.furnituretoday.com
SIC: 2721 Magazines: publishing only, not printed on site
HQ: Ft Media Holdings Llc
    7025 Albert Pick Rd Ste 2
    Greensboro NC 27409
    336 605-0121

(G-5544)
G & G MANAGEMENT LLC
Also Called: AR Workshop Greensboro
1603 Battleground Ave Ste F (27408-8049)
PHONE..............................336 444-6271
Gabrielle W Gillett, *Pr*
Lawrence C Gillett, *VP*
EMP: 12 EST: 2020
SALES (est): 391.81K **Privately Held**
Web: www.arworkshop.com

SIC: 2499 5999 Decorative wood and woodwork; Miscellaneous retail stores, nec

(G-5545)
G & J MACHINE SHOP INC (PA)
7800 Boeing Dr (27409-9706)
P.O. Box 941 (27261-0941)
PHONE..............................336 668-0996
Michael Jones, *Pr*
EMP: 20 EST: 1950
SQ FT: 15,000
SALES (est): 5.35MM **Privately Held**
Web: www.gandjmachineshop.com
SIC: 3599 Machine shop, jobbing and repair

(G-5546)
GAME BOX LLC (PA)
Also Called: Game Box Builders
143 Industrial Ave (27406-4504)
PHONE..............................866 241-1882
Benjamin Haskin, *Managing Member*
EMP: 4 EST: 2016
SALES (est): 1.51MM
SALES (corp-wide): 1.51MM **Privately Held**
Web: www.gameboxbuilders.com
SIC: 3944 Video game machines, except coin-operated

(G-5547)
GAMMA JS INC
4101 Beechwood Dr (27410-8118)
P.O. Box 8608 (27419-0608)
PHONE..............................336 294-3838
EMP: 11
Web: www.hoffmanhydronics.com
SIC: 5074 5075 7692 5084 Plumbing and hydronic heating supplies; Air conditioning equipment, except room units, nec; Welding repair; Industrial machinery and equipment

(G-5548)
GASBOY INTERNATIONAL INC
7300 W Friendly Ave (27410-6232)
PHONE..............................336 547-5000
David Kaehler, *Prin*
EMP: 12 EST: 2016
SALES (est): 2.71MM **Privately Held**
Web: www.gasboy.com
SIC: 3586 Measuring and dispensing pumps

(G-5549)
GATE CITY KITCHENS LLC
201 Creek Ridge Rd Ste D (27406-4437)
PHONE..............................336 378-0870
▲ EMP: 4 EST: 2004
SQ FT: 8,302
SALES (est): 468.27K **Privately Held**
Web: www.gatecitykitchens.com
SIC: 2434 Wood kitchen cabinets

(G-5550)
GB BIOSCIENCES LLC (DH)
410 S Swing Rd (27409-2012)
PHONE..............................336 632-6000
Robert Woods, *CEO*
▲ EMP: 90 EST: 1986
SQ FT: 300,000
SALES (est): 17.93MM **Privately Held**
SIC: 2879 2834 2899 Pesticides, agricultural or household; Pharmaceutical preparations; Chemical preparations, nec
HQ: Syngenta Corporation
    3411 Silverside Rd Ste 100
    Wilmington DE 19810
    302 425-2000

(G-5551)
GEM ASSET ACQUISITION LLC
139 S Walnut Cir (27409-2624)
PHONE..............................336 854-8200
Renee Gilbert, *Brnch Mgr*
EMP: 5
SALES (corp-wide): 10.35MM **Privately Held**
Web: www.sealmaster.net
SIC: 2951 Asphalt paving mixtures and blocks
PA: Gem Asset Acquisition Llc
    1855 Lindbergh St Ste 500
    Charlotte NC 28208
    704 225-3321

(G-5552)
GEMS FRST STOP MED SLTIONS LLC
5807 W Gate City Blvd (27407-7004)
PHONE..............................336 965-9500
Benita Morgan, *Managing Member*
EMP: 6 EST: 2021
SALES (est): 270.63K **Privately Held**
Web: www.firststopmed.com
SIC: 8099 8621 8011 3821 Health screening service; Health association; Offices and clinics of medical doctors; Clinical laboratory instruments, except medical and dental

(G-5553)
GENERAL DYNMICS MSSION SYSTEMS
Also Called: Gdais
3801 Boren Dr (27407-2046)
PHONE..............................336 323-9752
Alex Eksir, *Mgr*
EMP: 243
SALES (corp-wide): 47.72B **Publicly Held**
Web: www.gdmissionsystems.com
SIC: 3663 Radio and t.v. communications equipment
HQ: General Dynamics Mission Systems, Inc.
    12450 Fair Lakes Cir
    Fairfax VA 22033
    877 449-0600

(G-5554)
GENERAL FERTILIZER EQP INC
Also Called: Speedy Spread
429 Edwardia Dr (27409-2607)
P.O. Box 19409 (27419-9409)
PHONE..............................336 299-4711
Ben Coston, *Pr*
Hunter Dalton Iii, *Treas*
Marshall Pike, *Sec*
EMP: 13 EST: 1985
SQ FT: 13,000
SALES (est): 5.45MM **Privately Held**
Web: www.speedyspread.com
SIC: 5083 3523 3531 Agricultural machinery and equipment; Fertilizing machinery, farm; Construction machinery

(G-5555)
GENERAL MOTOR REPAIR & SVC INC
2206 Westbrook St (27407-2592)
PHONE..............................336 292-1715
David Ross, *Pr*
Donna M Ross, *VP*
EMP: 8 EST: 1956
SALES (est): 1.01MM **Privately Held**
Web: www.generalmotorrepair.com
SIC: 5063 7694 Motors, electric; Electric motor repair

(G-5556)
GENEVA SOFTWARE COMPANY INC
445 Dolley Madison Rd Ste 402 (27410)
PHONE...................................336 275-8887
Thomas Vincent, *Pr*
EMP: 5 **EST:** 1990
SALES (est): 1.01MM **Privately Held**
Web: www.genevasoftware.com
SIC: 7372 Business oriented computer
software

(G-5557)
GEORGE W DAHL COMPANY INC
8439 Triad Dr (27409-9018)
PHONE...................................336 668-4444
Lawrence Nicolette, *Pr*
Anthony Simone, *VP*
▼ **EMP:** 20 **EST:** 1991
SQ FT: 87,000
SALES (est): 513.82K **Privately Held**
SIC: 3492 Fluid power valves and hose
fittings

(G-5558)
GERBINGS LLC
Also Called: Gerbing's Heated Clothing
816 S Elm St Ste D (27406-1332)
PHONE...................................800 646-5916
Steve Wuebker, *CEO*
▲ **EMP:** 69 **EST:** 2012
SALES (est): 770.25K
SALES (corp-wide): 1.2MM **Privately Held**
Web: www.gerbing.com
SIC: 2386 2253 Coats and jackets, leather
and sheep-lined; Blouses, shirts, pants, and
suits
PA: Prospect Brands, Llc
816 S Elm St
Greensboro NC 27406
336 790-0085

(G-5559)
**GIBBS MACHINE COMPANY
INCORPORATED**
2012 Fairfax Rd (27407-3065)
PHONE...................................336 856-1907
EMP: 22
Web: www.gibbsmachineco.com
SIC: 3599 7692 3444 Machine shop, jobbing
and repair; Welding repair; Sheet metalwork

(G-5560)
GILBARCO INC (HQ)
Also Called: Gilbarco Veeder-Root
7300 W Friendly Ave (27410-6200)
P.O. Box 22087 (27420-2087)
PHONE...................................336 547-5000
◆ **EMP:** 1500 **EST:** 1865
SALES (est): 545.88MM
SALES (corp-wide): 2.98B **Publicly Held**
Web: www.gilbarco.com
SIC: 3586 3578 2752 7372 Gasoline pumps,
measuring or dispensing; Cash registers;
Tag, ticket, and schedule printing:
lithographic; Business oriented computer
software
PA: Vontier Corporation
5438 Wade Pk Blvd Ste 600
Raleigh NC 27607
984 275-6000

(G-5561)
GLADIATOR ENTERPRISES INC
5505 Weslo Willow Dr (27409-1935)
PHONE...................................336 944-6932
Ivor Buffong, *CEO*
EMP: 4 **EST:** 2015
SALES (est): 304.27K **Privately Held**

SIC: 3559 8361 7991 3949 Semiconductor
manufacturing machinery; Rehabilitation
center, residential: health care incidental;
Physical fitness facilities; Protective
sporting equipment

(G-5562)
GLAXOSMITHKLINE LLC
3408 Old Barn Rd (27410-9606)
PHONE...................................336 392-3058
EMP: 5
SALES (corp-wide): 39.77B **Privately Held**
Web: us.gsk.com
SIC: 2834 Pharmaceutical preparations
HQ: Glaxosmithkline Llc
2929 Walnut St Ste 1700
Philadelphia PA 19112
888 825-5249

(G-5563)
GLOBAL PRODUCTS LLC
Also Called: Wiper Technologies
144 Industrial Ave (27406-4505)
P.O. Box 2883 (46515-2883)
PHONE...................................336 227-7327
Douglas Diaab, *Prin*
EMP: 5 **EST:** 2011
SALES (est): 2.64MM **Privately Held**
Web: www.globalproducts.llc
SIC: 3714 Motor vehicle parts and
accessories

(G-5564)
GLOBAL STONE IMPEX LLC
5088 Bartholomews Ln (27407-2722)
PHONE...................................336 609-1113
Neeraj Bhadouria, *Managing Member*
EMP: 6 **EST:** 2016
SALES (est): 1.02MM **Privately Held**
SIC: 3271 Blocks, concrete: landscape or
retaining wall

(G-5565)
GO GREEN SERVICES LLC
Also Called: Go Green Plumbing
300 Pomona Dr (27407-1620)
PHONE...................................336 252-2999
EMP: 67 **EST:** 2015
SALES (est): 7.34MM **Privately Held**
Web: www.gogreenplumb.com
SIC: 1711 3585 Plumbing contractors;
Heating and air conditioning combination
units

(G-5566)
GOAERO LLC
7680 Airline Rd Ste C (27409-1897)
PHONE...................................815 713-1190
Greg Denning, *CEO*
Neil Sparkman, *Pr*
EMP: 4 **EST:** 2013
SALES (est): 2.7MM **Privately Held**
Web: www.goaero.net
SIC: 3728 Aircraft parts and equipment, nec

(G-5567)
GOLD MEDAL NORTH CAROLINA II
410 Gallimore Dairy Rd Ste G
(27409-9780)
PHONE...................................336 665-4997
Rob Morgan, *Genl Mgr*
EMP: 4 **EST:** 2014
SALES (est): 343.76K **Privately Held**
Web: www.gmpopcorn.com
SIC: 3469 Utensils, household: metal,
except cast

(G-5568)
GOLD MEDAL PRODUCTS CO
Also Called: Gold Medal Products-Carolina

410 Gallimore Dairy Rd Ste G
(27409-9782)
PHONE...................................336 665-4997
Jeff Kellner, *Mgr*
EMP: 7
SALES (corp-wide): 78.04MM **Privately
Held**
Web: www.gmpopcorn.com
SIC: 5145 5113 5046 3589 Snack foods;
Industrial and personal service paper;
Commercial cooking and food service
equipment; Popcorn machines, commercial
PA: Gold Medal Products Co.
10700 Medallion Dr
Cincinnati OH 45241
513 769-7676

(G-5569)
GOOD GRIEF MARKETING LLC
2609 E Market St (27401-4839)
PHONE...................................336 989-1984
Kishon Francis, *CEO*
EMP: 5 **EST:** 2017
SALES (est): 193.87K **Privately Held**
SIC: 7319 5943 3537 Advertising, nec;
Notary and corporate seals; Trucks,
tractors, loaders, carriers, and similar
equipment

(G-5570)
GPX INTELLIGENCE INC
Also Called: Logistimatics
620a S Elm St (27406-1328)
PHONE...................................888 260-0706
Gabriel Weeks, *CEO*
Matthew Oliver Hannam, *CIO**
Brendan Christopher Younger, *
EMP: 28 **EST:** 2021
SALES (est): 4.52MM **Privately Held**
Web: www.logistimatics.com
SIC: 4899 3663 Data communication
services; Global positioning systems (GPS)
equipment

(G-5571)
GRAHAM CRACKER LLC
514 Pisgah Church Rd (27455-2524)
PHONE...................................336 288-4440
Grant Chilton, *Prin*
EMP: 8 **EST:** 2006
SALES (est): 1.37MM **Privately Held**
SIC: 2052 Graham crackers

(G-5572)
GRAPHIC COMPONENTS LLC
2800 Patterson St (27407-2319)
PHONE...................................336 542-2128
Vince Cvijanovic, *Prin*
EMP: 22 **EST:** 2012
SALES (est): 3.25MM **Privately Held**
Web: www.graphiccomponents.com
SIC: 7336 3993 Graphic arts and related
design; Advertising artwork

(G-5573)
GRAPHIC FINSHG SOLUTIONS LLC
1207 Boston Rd (27407-2107)
PHONE...................................336 255-7857
EMP: 5 **EST:** 2003
SQ FT: 6,000
SALES (est): 460.09K **Privately Held**
SIC: 2679 2752 Tags and labels, paper; Tag,
ticket, and schedule printing: lithographic

(G-5574)
GRAPHIC SYSTEMS INTL INC
Also Called: G S I
7 Lockheed Ct (27409-9060)
P.O. Box 18345 (27419-8345)
PHONE...................................336 662-8686
Robert Kisstoth, *Pr*

Lisa Elkins, *
Brian Cagle, *
Jason Carrol, *
▼ **EMP:** 25 **EST:** 1978
SQ FT: 17,000
SALES (est): 3.47MM **Privately Held**
Web: www.gsi-signage.com
SIC: 3993 Signs, not made in custom sign
painting shops

(G-5575)
GREENHECK FAN CO
3816 Patterson St (27407-3238)
PHONE...................................336 852-5788
Patrice Pergolski, *COO*
EMP: 7 **EST:** 2005
SALES (est): 191.95K **Privately Held**
Web: www.greenheck.com
SIC: 3564 Blowing fans: industrial or
commercial

(G-5576)
GREENSBORO DISTILLING LLC
321 W Wendover Ave (27408-8401)
PHONE...................................336 273-6221
Shelley A Johnson, *Admn*
EMP: 6 **EST:** 2016
SALES (est): 617.25K **Privately Held**
Web: www.faintinggoatspirits.com
SIC: 2085 Distilled and blended liquors

(G-5577)
**GREENSBORO NEWS & RECORD
LLC**
3001 S Elm Eugene St (27406-4448)
PHONE...................................336 373-7000
Robin Saul, *Pr*
EMP: 600
SALES (est): 8.81MM
SALES (corp-wide): 611.38MM **Publicly
Held**
Web: www.greensboro.com
SIC: 2711 2791 2796 2752 Newspapers,
publishing and printing; Typesetting;
Platemaking services; Commercial printing,
lithographic
HQ: Bh Media Group, Inc.
1314 Douglas St Ste 1500
Omaha NE 68102
402 444-1154

(G-5578)
**GREENSBORO TIRE & AUTO
SERVICE**
Also Called: Greensboro Tire 3
4615 W Market St Ste A (27407-2973)
PHONE...................................336 294-9495
Dustin Allred, *Mgr*
EMP: 6
SALES (corp-wide): 1.65MM **Privately
Held**
Web: www.greensborotireandauto.com
SIC: 7534 7538 5531 Tire recapping;
General automotive repair shops;
Automotive tires
PA: Greensboro Tire & Auto Service
Center, Inc.
1901 E Bessemer Ave
Greensboro NC
336 273-6748

(G-5579)
GREENSBORO VOICE
407 E Washington St (27401-2930)
PHONE...................................336 255-1006
Susan Thomas, *Prin*
EMP: 10 **EST:** 2015
SALES (est): 60.02K **Privately Held**
Web: www.greensboro.com
SIC: 2711 Newspapers, publishing and
printing

(G-5580)
GRIFFIN MARKETING GROUP
4608 Knightbridge Rd (27455-1916)
PHONE..................................336 558-5802
EMP: 6 EST: 2018
SALES (est): 118.86K Privately Held
Web: www.griffinreps.com
SIC: 3556 Food products machinery

(G-5581)
GSO PRINTING
317 S Westgate Dr Ste A (27407-1633)
PHONE..................................336 292-1601
Mike Ealley, Mng Pt
Mary Ealley, Pt
EMP: 5 EST: 2008
SALES (est): 117.42K Privately Held
SIC: 2752 Offset printing

(G-5582)
GSO PRINTING INC
2 Hill Valley Ct (27410-9628)
PHONE..................................336 288-5778
Darrell Ealley, Pr
EMP: 4 EST: 2003
SQ FT: 2,100
SALES (est): 233.76K Privately Held
SIC: 2752 Commercial printing, lithographic

(G-5583)
GUERRILLA RF INC
2000 Pisgah Church Rd (27455-3308)
PHONE..................................336 510-7840
Ryan Pratt, CEO
Jeff Broxson, *
Alan Ake, *
Mark Mason, *
Steven Smith, *
EMP: 68 EST: 2013
SQ FT: 10,000
SALES (est): 15.08MM Privately Held
Web: www.guerrilla-rf.com
SIC: 3674 Monolithic integrated circuits
(solid state)

(G-5584)
GUILFORD ORTHTIC PROTHETIC INC
405 Parkway St Ste G (27401-1693)
PHONE..................................336 676-5394
Randy Johnson, Owner
EMP: 5 EST: 2014
SALES (est): 51.81K Privately Held
SIC: 3842 Limbs, artificial

(G-5585)
HAECO AMERICAS LLC (DH)
Also Called: Haeco Americas
623 Radar Rd (27410-6221)
PHONE..................................336 668-4410
Richard Kendall, Managing Member
Doug Rasmussen, Managing Member*
Bruce Patterson, Managing Member*
Lee Fox, Managing Member*
◆ EMP: 1000 EST: 1989
SQ FT: 190,000
SALES (est): 463.61MM
SALES (corp-wide): 18.29B Privately Held
Web: www.haeco.aero
SIC: 5088 4581 2396 Transportation
equipment and supplies; Aircraft servicing
and repairing; Automotive trimmings, fabric
HQ: Haeco Usa Holdings, Llc
623 Radar Rd
Greensboro NC 27410
336 668-4410

(G-5586)
HALL TIRE AND BATTERY CO INC
2222 Martin Luther King Jr Dr (27406-3710)

PHONE..................................336 275-3812
Frank I Hall, Pr
Mary Hall, VP
Gregory F Hall, Sec
EMP: 10 EST: 1960
SQ FT: 4,000
SALES (est): 2.28MM Privately Held
Web: www.halltire.com
SIC: 5531 7539 7534 Automotive tires;
Wheel alignment, automotive; Tire repair
shop

(G-5587)
HARTLEY READY MIX CON MFG INC
1040 Boulder Rd (27409-9106)
P.O. Box 1719 (27374-1719)
PHONE..................................336 294-5995
Scott Ball, Brnch Mgr
EMP: 7
SALES (corp-wide): 6.36MM Privately
Held
Web: www.hartleyreadymix.com
SIC: 3273 Ready-mixed concrete
PA: Hartley Ready Mix Concrete
Manufacturing, Inc.
3510 Rothrock St
Winston Salem NC 27107
336 788-3928

(G-5588)
HATRACK RIVER ENTERPRISES INC
401 Willoughby Blvd (27408-3135)
P.O. Box 18184 (27419-8184)
PHONE..................................336 282-9848
Orson Scott Card, Pr
EMP: 7 EST: 1997
SALES (est): 115.41K Privately Held
Web: www.hatrack.com
SIC: 2731 Books, publishing only

(G-5589)
HB FULLER COMPANY
2302 W Meadowview Rd (27407-3721)
PHONE..................................336 294-5939
Jamie Mittel, Brnch Mgr
EMP: 4
SALES (corp-wide): 3.57B Publicly Held
Web: www.hbfuller.com
SIC: 2891 Adhesives
PA: H.B. Fuller Company
1200 Willow Lake Blvd
Saint Paul MN 55110
651 236-5900

(G-5590)
HDB INC
3901 Riverdale Dr (27406-7599)
PHONE..................................800 403-2247
EMP: 4 EST: 1984
SALES (est): 81.13K Privately Held
SIC: 2393 Bags and containers, except
sleeping bags: textile

(G-5591)
HEALING SPRINGS FARMACY
812 Stoney Hill Cir (27406-9187)
PHONE..................................336 549-6159
Laylah Cooper Holman, Pr
Tinece Holman, Ex Dir
EMP: 4 EST: 2015
SALES (est): 466.29K Privately Held
Web: www.viyc.org
SIC: 2833 Medicinals and botanicals
PA: Volunteer In Your Community Inc.
805 Stoney Hill Cir
Greensboro NC 27406

(G-5592)
HEARTH & HOME TECHNOLOGIES LLC
Also Called: HEARTH & HOME
TECHNOLOGIES, LLC

215 Industrial Ave Ste A (27406-4546)
PHONE..................................336 274-1663
Jessica Schrader, Mgr
EMP: 149
SALES (corp-wide): 2.53B Publicly Held
Web: www.fireside.com
SIC: 3259 3433 3429 Flue lining, clay;
Heating equipment, except electric;
Fireplace equipment, hardware: andirons,
grates, screens
HQ: Hearth & Home Technologies, Llc
7571 215th St W
Lakeville MN 55044

(G-5593)
HEMISPHERES MAGAZINE
1301 Carolina St (27401-1032)
PHONE..................................336 255-0195
David Brown, Prin
EMP: 16 EST: 2008
SALES (est): 241.85K Privately Held
Web: www.paceco.com
SIC: 2721 Magazines: publishing only, not
printed on site

(G-5594)
HERSHEY GROUP LLC
2010 New Garden Rd Ste A (27410-2528)
PHONE..................................336 855-3888
Erik Hershey, Managing Member
EMP: 5 EST: 2018
SALES (est): 231.15K Privately Held
Web: www.thehersheygroup.com
SIC: 3999 4783 Handbag and luggage
frames and handles; Packing goods for
shipping

(G-5595)
HF GROUP LLC
Also Called: Mid Atlantic Book Bindery
1010 Arnold St (27405-7102)
PHONE..................................336 931-0800
Keith Roberts, Brnch Mgr
EMP: 48
Web: www.hfgroup.com
SIC: 2732 Books, printing and binding
PA: Hf Group, Llc
400 Arora Cmmons Cir Unit
Aurora OH 44202

(G-5596)
HIGHLAND COMPOSITES
416 Gallimore Dairy Rd Ste N
(27409-9535)
PHONE..................................704 924-3090
EMP: 6 EST: 2017
SALES (est): 397.19K Privately Held
SIC: 2211 Broadwoven fabric mills, cotton

(G-5597)
HIGHLAND INDUSTRIES INC
629 Green Valley Rd Ste 300 (27408-7726)
PHONE..................................336 547-1600
EMP: 40
SALES (corp-wide): 7.79B Privately Held
Web: www.highlandindustries.com
SIC: 2221 Automotive fabrics, manmade fiber
HQ: Highland Industries, Inc.
650 Chesterfield Hwy
Cheraw SC 29520
336 992-7500

(G-5598)
HIGHLAND INDUSTRIES INC
10 Northline Pl (27410-4842)
PHONE..................................336 855-0625
Frank Roe, Prin
EMP: 45
SALES (corp-wide): 7.79B Privately Held
Web: www.highlandindustries.com

SIC: 2221 Automotive fabrics, manmade fiber
HQ: Highland Industries, Inc.
650 Chesterfield Hwy
Cheraw SC 29520
336 992-7500

(G-5599)
HIGHLAND TANK NC INC
2700 Patterson St (27407-2317)
PHONE..................................336 218-0801
Michael Vanlenten, CEO
John Jacob, *
Charles A Frey, *
EMP: 140 EST: 1994
SQ FT: 43,000
SALES (est): 9.44MM Privately Held
Web: www.highlandtank.com
SIC: 3443 Tanks, standard or custom
fabricated: metal plate

(G-5600)
HIRSCHFELD INDUSTRIES BRDG LLC
Also Called: Hirschfeld Industries-Bridge
101 Centreport Dr Ste 400 (27409-9422)
P.O. Box 20888 (27420-0888)
PHONE..................................336 271-8252
John O'quinn, Ex VP
Rodney L Goodwill, *
EMP: 717 EST: 1994
SQ FT: 885,000
SALES (est): 1.91MM Privately Held
Web: www.wwafcosteel.com
SIC: 3441 Fabricated structural metal
PA: Hirschfeld Holdings Lp
112 W 29th St
San Angelo TX 76903

(G-5601)
HOFFMAN BUILDING TECH INC (PA)
Also Called: Thermatec
3816 Patterson St (27407-3238)
PHONE..................................336 292-8777
William M Easterday, Pr
Louis Hoffman, *
EMP: 194 EST: 2016
SQ FT: 20,000
SALES (est): 17.81MM
SALES (corp-wide): 17.81MM Privately
Held
Web: www.hbtech.com
SIC: 3822 Temperature controls, automatic

(G-5602)
HOFFMAN HYDRONICS LLC
Hoffman Hydronics Div
4321 Piedmont Pkwy (27410-8114)
PHONE..................................800 842-3328
EMP: 51
SALES (corp-wide): 166.15MM Privately
Held
Web: www.hoffmanhydronics.com
SIC: 3433 Heating equipment, except electric
HQ: Hoffman Hydronics, Llc
321 Piedmont Pkwy
Greensboro NC 27410
336 294-3838

(G-5603)
HOFFMAN HYDRONICS LLC (HQ)
Also Called: Heat Transfer Sales, LLC
321 Piedmont Pkwy (27410)
P.O. Box 8608 (27419-0608)
PHONE..................................336 294-3838
Joseph Britt, Pr
Casey Gardner Ctrl, Prin
EMP: 11 EST: 2019
SALES (est): 17.15MM
SALES (corp-wide): 166.15MM Privately
Held
Web: www.hoffmanhydronics.com

▲ = Import ▼ = Export
◆ = Import/Export

SIC: **3433** 3585 Heating equipment, except electric; Refrigeration and heating equipment
PA: Hoffman & Hoffman, Inc.
3816 Patterson St
Greensboro NC 27407
336 292-8777

(G-5604)
HONDA AIRCRAFT COMPANY LLC
Also Called: Honda Aircraft Co Service Ctr
6420 Ballinger Rd Bldg 400 (27410-9063)
PHONE..............................336 662-0246
David Sunda, *Mgr*
EMP: 20
Web: www.hondajet.com
SIC: **3721** Aircraft
HQ: Honda Aircraft Company, Llc
6430 Ballinger Rd
Greensboro NC 27410

(G-5605)
HONDA AIRCRAFT COMPANY LLC
404 S Chimney Rock Rd (27409-9260)
PHONE..............................336 662-0246
Timothy Peters, *Prin*
EMP: 20
Web: www.hondajet.com
SIC: **3721** Aircraft
HQ: Honda Aircraft Company, Llc
6430 Ballinger Rd
Greensboro NC 27410

(G-5606)
HONDA AIRCRAFT COMPANY LLC (HQ)
6430 Ballinger Rd (27410)
PHONE..............................336 662-0246
Michimasa Fujino, *Managing Member*
Tetsuo Iwamura, *
Hiroshi Soda, *
◆ **EMP:** 390 **EST:** 2011
SQ FT: 256,000
SALES (est): 257.52MM **Privately Held**
Web: www.hondajet.com
SIC: **3721** Aircraft
PA: Honda Motor Co., Ltd.
2-1-1, Minamiaoyama
Minato-Ku TKY 107-0

(G-5607)
HORIZON TOOL INC
Also Called: Cal-Van
7918 Industrial Village Rd (27409-9691)
PHONE..............................336 299-4182
Sean Kenny, *Pr*
▲ **EMP:** 111 **EST:** 1989
SQ FT: 35,000
SALES (est): 12.27MM **Privately Held**
Web: www.cal-vantools.com
SIC: **3423** Hand and edge tools, nec

(G-5608)
HUBERGROUP USA INC
651 Brigham Rd Ste C (27409-9078)
PHONE..............................336 292-5501
EMP: 17
SALES (corp-wide): 242.12K **Privately Held**
Web: www.hubergroup.com
SIC: **2893** Printing ink
HQ: Hubergroup Usa Inc.
4500 Western Ave
Lisle IL 60532
815 929-9293

(G-5609)
HUDSON OVERALL COMPANY INC
Also Called: Hudson's Hill
527 S Elm St (27406-1325)
PHONE..............................336 314-5024

William Clayton, *Pr*
Harold Clayton, *Sec*
Evan Morrison, *Prin*
EMP: 4 **EST:** 2014
SALES (est): 141.23K **Privately Held**
SIC: **5611** 2329 Men's and boys' clothing stores; Athletic clothing, except uniforms: men's, youths' and boys'

(G-5610)
HUGHES METAL WORKS LLC
Also Called: Hughes Metal Works
1914 Fairfax Rd (27407-4145)
P.O. Box 7363 (27417-0363)
PHONE..............................336 297-0808
EMP: 23 **EST:** 1994
SQ FT: 11,000
SALES (est): 2.19MM **Privately Held**
Web: www.hughesmetalworks.com
SIC: **3441** Fabricated structural metal

(G-5611)
I & I SLING INC
3824 Patterson St (27407-3238)
PHONE..............................336 323-1532
Dennis St Germain Junior, *Mgr*
EMP: 9
SALES (corp-wide): 19.76MM **Privately Held**
Web: www.iandisling.com
SIC: **3496** Miscellaneous fabricated wire products
PA: I & I Sling, Inc.
205 Bridgewater Rd
Aston PA 19014
610 485-8500

(G-5612)
ICON BOILER INC
2025 16th St (27405-5119)
PHONE..............................844 562-4266
Jim Brady, *Pr*
EMP: 23 **EST:** 2020
SALES (est): 2.54MM **Privately Held**
Web: www.iconboiler.com
SIC: **3443** Boiler and boiler shop work

(G-5613)
IDEACODE INC
11010 W Northwood St (27408)
PHONE..............................919 341-5170
Charles Bettini, *Pr*
John Acre, *VP*
EMP: 5 **EST:** 2000
SALES (est): 83.22K **Privately Held**
Web: www.ideacode.com
SIC: **7371** 8243 5734 7372 Computer software development; Software training, computer; Software, computer games; Application computer software

(G-5614)
IDEXX PHARMACEUTICALS INC
7009 Albert Pick Rd (27409-9654)
PHONE..............................336 834-6500
Doug Hepler, *Ex VP*
Steve Capps, *VP Fin*
EMP: 5 **EST:** 1996
SALES (est): 801.94M
SALES (corp-wide): 3.9B **Publicly Held**
Web: www.idexx.com
SIC: **2834** Pharmaceutical preparations
PA: Idexx Laboratories, Inc.
1 Idexx Dr
Westbrook ME 04092
207 556-0300

(G-5615)
IN GREENSBORO
2722 N Church St Ste P (27405-3661)
PHONE..............................336 621-0279

James E Avent Junior, *Prin*
EMP: 7 **EST:** 2017
SALES (est): 52.76K **Privately Held**
Web: www.greensboro.com
SIC: **2711** Newspapers, publishing and printing

(G-5616)
INDUSTRIAL AIR INC ✪
428 Edwardia Dr (27409-2608)
P.O. Box 8769 (27419-0769)
PHONE..............................336 292-1030
EMP: 125 **EST:** 2023
SALES (est): 46.32MM
SALES (corp-wide): 518.78MM **Publicly Held**
Web: www.industrialairinc.com
SIC: **1711** 3443 Warm air heating and air conditioning contractor; Tanks, standard or custom fabricated: metal plate
PA: Limbach Holdings, Inc.
1251 Wterfront Pl Ste 201
Pittsburgh PA 15222
412 359-2100

(G-5617)
INDUSTRIES OF BLIND INC (PA)
920 W Gate City Blvd (27403-2803)
PHONE..............................336 274-1591
David Thompson, *Prin*
David Thompson, *Prin*
EMP: 194 **EST:** 1932
SQ FT: 100,000
SALES (est): 5.28MM
SALES (corp-wide): 5.28MM **Privately Held**
Web: www.industriesoftheblind.com
SIC: **3951** Fountain pens and fountain pen desk sets

(G-5618)
INNOBIOACTIVES LLC
7325 W Friendly Ave Ste H (27410-6211)
PHONE..............................336 235-0838
Chen Chen, *Managing Member*
▲ **EMP:** 8 **EST:** 2007
SALES (est): 325.35K **Privately Held**
SIC: **2834** Pharmaceutical preparations

(G-5619)
INNOVATIVE KITCHENS BATHS INC
2912 Manufacturers Rd (27406-4606)
PHONE..............................336 279-1188
Patrick Bunn, *Pr*
EMP: 7 **EST:** 2004
SQ FT: 9,200
SALES (est): 835.53K **Privately Held**
Web: www.ikbgreensboro.com
SIC: **2434** Wood kitchen cabinets

(G-5620)
INSECT SHIELD LLC (PA)
814 W Market St (27401-1813)
P.O. Box 10129 (27404-0129)
PHONE..............................336 272-4157
Haynes G Griffin, *Managing Member*
Richard Lane, *
▲ **EMP:** 38 **EST:** 2002
SALES (est): 9.74MM
SALES (corp-wide): 9.74MM **Privately Held**
Web: www.insectshield.com
SIC: **2269** Finishing plants, nec

(G-5621)
INTERTECH CORPORATION
Also Called: Funball
3240 N Ohenry Blvd (27405-3808)
P.O. Box 14690 (27415-4690)
PHONE..............................336 621-1891
TOLL FREE: 800

EMP: 65 **EST:** 1968
SALES (est): 5.54MM
SALES (corp-wide): 868.81MM **Privately Held**
SIC: **3089** 3085 Blow molded finished plastics products, nec; Plastics bottles
PA: Pretium Packaging, L.L.C.
1555 Page Industrial Blvd
Saint Louis MO 63132
314 727-8200

(G-5622)
IQE INC
Also Called: Iqe PA
494 Gallimore Dairy Rd Ste A (27409-9240)
PHONE..............................610 861-6930
Andrew Nelson, *Pr*
Stephen Gergar, *
▲ **EMP:** 100 **EST:** 1988
SALES (est): 23.84MM
SALES (corp-wide): 143.65MM **Privately Held**
Web: www.iqep.com
SIC: **3674** Wafers (semiconductor devices)
PA: Iqe Plc
Pascal Close
Cardiff S GLAM CF3 0
292 083-9400

(G-5623)
IQE NORTH CAROLINA LLC
494 Gallimore Dairy Rd (27409-9514)
PHONE..............................336 609-6270
William Chin, *CPO*
EMP: 11 **EST:** 2012
SALES (est): 1.64MM **Privately Held**
Web: www.iqep.com
SIC: **5045** 7371 3674 Computer software; Computer software systems analysis and design, custom; Computer logic modules

(G-5624)
IQE RF LLC
494 Gallimore Dairy Rd Ste A (27409-9240)
PHONE..............................732 271-5990
Alex Ceruzzi, *Managing Member*
◆ **EMP:** 71 **EST:** 2006
SALES (est): 1.95MM
SALES (corp-wide): 143.65MM **Privately Held**
Web: www.iqep.com
SIC: **3679** Electronic circuits
PA: Iqe Plc
Pascal Close
Cardiff S GLAM CF3 0
292 083-9400

(G-5625)
IQE USA INC
494 Gallimore Dairy Rd (27409-9514)
PHONE..............................610 861-6930
Steven Kreider, *Prin*
Andrew Nelson, *Prin*
EMP: 5 **EST:** 2015
SALES (est): 1.85MM **Privately Held**
SIC: **3679** Electronic circuits

(G-5626)
ITG BRANDS
420 N English St (27405-7310)
PHONE..............................336 335-6600
Martin Orlowsky, *Mgr*
EMP: 89
Web: www.itgbrands.com
SIC: **2111** Cigarettes
HQ: Itg Brands
714 Green Valley Rd
Greensboro NC 27408
336 335-7000

(G-5627)
ITG BRANDS LLC (HQ)
628 Green Valley Rd Ste 500 (27408-7791)
P.O. Box 10529 (27404-0529)
PHONE..................................336 335-6669
EMP: 44 **EST:** 2012
SALES (est): 477MM **Privately Held**
Web: www.itgbrands.com
SIC: 2111 Cigarettes
PA: Imperial Brands Plc
121 Winterstoke Road
Bristol BS3 2

(G-5628)
ITG HOLDINGS INC
Also Called: I T G
804 Green Valley Rd Ste 300 (27408-7039)
PHONE..................................336 379-6220
◆ **EMP:** 4000
SIC: 2211 2231 2221 2273 Denims; Worsted
fabrics, broadwoven; Polyester broadwoven
fabrics; Carpets and rugs

(G-5629)
ITG HOLDINGS USA INC
714 Green Valley Rd (27408-7018)
PHONE..................................954 772-9000
Kevin Freudenchal, *Pr*
EMP: 19 **EST:** 2007
SALES (est): 689K **Privately Held**
Web: www.itgbrands.com
SIC: 2131 Chewing and smoking tobacco
PA: Imperial Brands Plc
121 Winterstoke Road
Bristol BS3 2

(G-5630)
ITM LTD SOUTH
1903 Brassfield Rd (27410-2155)
PHONE..................................336 883-2400
Scott Vanderlinder, *Pr*
◆ **EMP:** 6 **EST:** 1959
SALES (est): 388.73K **Privately Held**
Web: www.itmsouth.com
SIC: 3552 Textile machinery

(G-5631)
IVEY LN INC
Also Called: Ivey Lane
103 Ward Rd (27405-9651)
P.O. Box 29185 (27429-9185)
PHONE..................................336 230-0062
Peter Lane, *Pr*
Leslie Lane, *VP*
EMP: 10 **EST:** 1992
SALES (est): 919.67K **Privately Held**
Web: www.iveylane.com
SIC: 5211 1799 3281 Counter tops; Counter
top installation; Cut stone and stone
products

(G-5632)
J MORGAN SIGNS INC
4421 S Elm Eugene St (27406-8931)
PHONE..................................336 274-6509
Jeff Morgan, *Pr*
EMP: 10 **EST:** 1972
SALES (est): 633.52K **Privately Held**
Web: jmorgansigns.wordpress.com
SIC: 3993 Signs and advertising specialties

(G-5633)
JAMES M PLEASANTS COMPANY INC (PA)
Also Called: Jpm
603 Diamond Hill Ct (27406)
P.O. Box 16706 (27416)
PHONE..................................800 365-9010
TOLL FREE: 800
J Chris Edmonson, *Pr*

Jamie Edmondson, *
G David Pleasants, *
EMP: 50 **EST:** 1963
SQ FT: 26,000
SALES (est): 48.99MM
SALES (corp-wide): 48.99MM **Privately
Held**
Web: www.jmpco.com
SIC: 5075 3585 3561 3494 Warm air heating
and air conditioning; Refrigeration and
heating equipment; Pumps and pumping
equipment; Valves and pipe fittings, nec

(G-5634)
JAMES M PLEASANTS COMPANY INC
Hyfab
206 E Seneca Rd (27406-4533)
PHONE..................................888 902-8324
EMP: 11
SALES (corp-wide): 48.99MM **Privately
Held**
Web: www.hyfabco.com
SIC: 3494 Valves and pipe fittings, nec
PA: James M Pleasants Company
Incorporated
603 Diamond Hill Ct
Greensboro NC 27406
800 365-9010

(G-5635)
JBT AEROTECH SERVICES
6035 Old Oak Ridge Rd (27410-9240)
PHONE..................................336 740-3737
EMP: 4 **EST:** 2010
SALES (est): 482.09K **Privately Held**
Web: www.jbtc.com
SIC: 3556 Food products machinery

(G-5636)
JEWERS DOORS US INC
3714 Alliance Dr Ste 305 (27407-2060)
P.O. Box 16639 (27416-0639)
PHONE..................................888 510-5331
Michael Peters, *CEO*
Michael L Peters, *
April H Peters, *
EMP: 50 **EST:** 2020
SALES (est): 1.55MM **Privately Held**
SIC: 3442 1751 Metal doors, sash, and trim;
Window and door installation and erection

(G-5637)
JMS REBAR INC
1211 Rotherwood Rd (27406-3825)
PHONE..................................336 273-9084
Michael Ward, *Pr*
EMP: 8 **EST:** 2014
SALES (est): 4.46MM **Privately Held**
Web: www.jmsrebar.com
SIC: 3499 Fire- or burglary-resistive products

(G-5638)
JOCHUM INDUSTRIES
710 Freemasons Dr (27407-1862)
PHONE..................................336 288-7975
Jim Jochum, *Prin*
EMP: 4 **EST:** 2008
SALES (est): 102.72K **Privately Held**
SIC: 3999 Manufacturing industries, nec

(G-5639)
JONES FABRICARE INC (PA)
Also Called: Jones Furs
502 E Cornwallis Dr (27405-5680)
PHONE..................................336 272-7261
Hugh N Jones, *Pr*
EMP: 7 **EST:** 1906
SQ FT: 20,000
SALES (est): 252.9K
SALES (corp-wide): 252.9K **Privately Held**

SIC: 7219 2371 5632 Fur garment cleaning,
repairing, and storage; Fur coats and other
fur apparel; Fur apparel

(G-5640)
JORLINK USA INC
Also Called: Jorlink.com
3714 Alliance Dr Ste 100 (27407-2060)
PHONE..................................336 288-1613
Mackenzie J Quiros, *CEO*
EMP: 10 **EST:** 1988
SQ FT: 5,000
SALES (est): 3.54MM **Privately Held**
Web: www.jorlink.com
SIC: 5087 3564 Engraving equipment and
supplies; Dust or fume collecting
equipment, industrial

(G-5641)
K & C MACHINE CO INC
601 Industrial Ave (27406-4696)
PHONE..................................336 373-0745
Barry Collins, *Ch Bd*
Jeff Collins, *Pr*
Anita Jones, *Sec*
EMP: 6 **EST:** 1975
SQ FT: 10,000
SALES (est): 1.17MM **Privately Held**
Web: www.kcmachine.com
SIC: 3599 Machine shop, jobbing and repair

(G-5642)
KAY CHEMICAL COMPANY
Also Called: Ecolab
8300 Capital Dr (27409-9790)
PHONE..................................336 668-7290
◆ **EMP:** 620
SIC: 2842 Specialty cleaning

(G-5643)
KAYSER-ROTH CORPORATION (DH)
Also Called: No Nonsense
102 Corporate Center Blvd (27408)
P.O. Box 26530 (27408)
PHONE..................................336 852-2030
Nicola Galloti, *Ch Bd*
Kevin Toomey, *
◆ **EMP:** 120 **EST:** 1985
SALES (est): 348.67MM **Privately Held**
Web: www.kayser-roth.com
SIC: 5961 2251 3842 8741 Women's
apparel, mail order; Women's hosiery,
except socks; Surgical appliances and
supplies; Management services
HQ: Golden Lady Company Spa
Via Giacomo Leopardi 3/5
Castiglione Delle Stiviere MN 46043
037 694-1211

(G-5644)
KAYSER-ROTH HOSIERY INC
102 Corporate Center Blvd (27408-3172)
P.O. Box 26530 (27415-6530)
PHONE..................................336 852-2030
EMP: 37 **EST:** 1955
SALES (est): 7.39MM **Privately Held**
Web: www.kayser-roth.com
SIC: 2389 2252 Men's miscellaneous
accessories; Socks

(G-5645)
KCS IMPRV & CNSTR CO INC
Also Called: General Contractor
510 N Church St Ste C (27401-6097)
PHONE..................................336 288-3865
R Crabtree, *Pr*
Keith Crabtree, *Pr*
EMP: 5 **EST:** 1982
SQ FT: 3,500
SALES (est): 2.05MM **Privately Held**
Web: www.kcsimprovement.com

SIC: 1521 1389 General remodeling, single-
family houses; Construction, repair, and
dismantling services

(G-5646)
KELLER CRES U TO BE PHRMGRAPHI
1072 Boulder Rd (27409-9106)
PHONE..................................336 851-1150
Bill Wentz, *CFO*
EMP: 26 **EST:** 2019
SALES (est): 898.26K **Privately Held**
SIC: 2752 Commercial printing, lithographic

(G-5647)
KIMBEES INC
317 Martin Luthe (27406)
PHONE..................................336 323-8773
EMP: 4
SALES (est): 314.34K **Privately Held**
SIC: 2099 Tea blending

(G-5648)
KINDERMUSIK INTERNATIONAL INC
Also Called: Kindermusik
237 Burgess Rd Ste C (27409-9787)
PHONE..................................800 628-5687
Scott Kinsey, *CEO*
Judy L Harris, *
▲ **EMP:** 40 **EST:** 1980
SALES (est): 4.2MM **Privately Held**
Web: www.kindermusik.com
SIC: 8299 2741 Music school; Music, book:
publishing and printing

(G-5649)
KIRK & BLUM MANUFACTURING CO
8735 W Market St (27409-9653)
P.O. Box 35423 (27425)
PHONE..................................801 728-6533
Paul Gillespie, *Mgr*
EMP: 78
Web: www.cecoenviro.com
SIC: 3444 5075 3564 3443 Sheet metal
specialties, not stamped; Dust collecting
equipment; Blowers and fans; Fabricated
plate work (boiler shop)
HQ: The Kirk & Blum Manufacturing
Company
4625 Red Bank Rd Ste 200
Cincinnati OH 45227
513 458-2600

(G-5650)
KLB ENTERPRISES INCORPORATED
Also Called: Carolina Fine Snacks
209 Citation Ct (27409-9026)
PHONE..................................336 605-0773
Phillip Kosak, *Pr*
Jim Buck, *VP*
▲ **EMP:** 10 **EST:** 1982
SQ FT: 30,000
SALES (est): 3.56MM **Privately Held**
SIC: 2096 2064 Corn chips and other corn-
based snacks; Nuts, candy covered

(G-5651)
KLOUD HEMP CO
2701 S Elm Eugene St Ste E (27406-3634)
PHONE..................................336 740-2528
Katrina Travis, *Pr*
EMP: 4 **EST:** 2019
SALES (est): 177.63K **Privately Held**
SIC: 2299 2099 5999 Hemp yarn, thread,
roving, and textiles; Tea blending;
Miscellaneous retail stores, nec

(G-5652)
KONTOOR BRANDS INC
Also Called: Vf

400 N Elm St (27401-2143)
P.O. Box 21407 (27420-1407)
PHONE...............................336 332-3586
EMP: 87
SALES (corp-wide): 2.61B Publicly Held
Web: www.kontoorbrands.com
SIC: 2325 2331 Men's and boy's trousers
and slacks; Shirts, women's and juniors':
made from purchased materials
PA: Kontoor Brands, Inc.
400 N Elm St
Greensboro NC 27401
336 332-3400

(G-5653)
KONTOOR BRANDS INC (PA)
Also Called: Kontoor
400 N Elm St (27401)
PHONE...............................336 332-3400
Scott H Baxter, Ch Bd
Thomas E Waldron, Ex VP
Joseph A Alkire, Ex VP
Thomas L Doerr Junior, Ex VP
Jennifer H Broyles, Ex VP
EMP: 900 EST: 2018
SQ FT: 140,000
SALES (est): 2.61B
SALES (corp-wide): 2.61B Publicly Held
Web: www.kontoorbrands.com
SIC: 2326 2339 5699 Work apparel, except
uniforms; Service apparel, washable:
women's; Work clothing

(G-5654)
KONTOOR BRANDS INC
1421 S Elm Eugene St (27406-2237)
PHONE...............................336 332-3577
EMP: 49
SALES (corp-wide): 2.61B Publicly Held
Web: www.kontoorbrands.com
SIC: 2221 Acetate broadwoven fabrics
PA: Kontoor Brands, Inc.
400 N Elm St
Greensboro NC 27401
336 332-3400

(G-5655)
KRISPY KREME DOUGHNUT CORP
Also Called: Krispy Kreme
3704 W Gate City Blvd (27407-4628)
PHONE...............................336 854-8275
Clifford Janes, Brnch Mgr
EMP: 26
SALES (corp-wide): 1.69B Publicly Held
Web: www.krispykreme.com
SIC: 5461 2051 Doughnuts; Doughnuts,
except frozen
HQ: Krispy Kreme Doughnut Corp
2116 Hawkins St Ste 102
Charlotte NC 28203
980 270-7117

(G-5656)
L & R INSTALLATIONS INC
2303 Adams Farm Pkwy (27407-5406)
PHONE...............................336 547-8998
Lamar Coward Junior, Pr
Bobbiejo Coward, Sec
EMP: 4 EST: 1989
SALES (est): 210K Privately Held
SIC: 2531 Pews, church

(G-5657)
LAKE SHORE RADIATOR INC
211c Creek Ridge Rd (27406-4419)
PHONE...............................336 271-2626
TOLL FREE: 800
Mark Dean, Mgr
EMP: 10
SALES (corp-wide): 2.07MM Privately
Held

Web: lake-doctors-lake.edan.io
SIC: 5013 3714 Automotive supplies and
parts; Radiators and radiator shells and
cores, motor vehicle
PA: Lake Shore Radiator, Inc.
5355 Ramona Blvd
Jacksonville FL 32205
904 786-0954

(G-5658)
LEE APPAREL COMPANY INC (DH)
Also Called: Lee
400 N Elm St (27401-2143)
PHONE...............................336 332-3400
Scott Baxter, Pr
L R Pugh, Dir
G G Johnson, Dir
Mackey J Mcdonald, Dir
Frank C Pickard Iii, Dir
EMP: 450 EST: 1889
SQ FT: 147,000
SALES (est): 5.2MM
SALES (corp-wide): 2.61B Publicly Held
Web: www.lee.com
SIC: 2325 2339 Jeans: men's, youths', and
boys'; Jeans: women's, misses', and juniors'
HQ: Kontoor Us, Llc
400 N Elm St
Greensboro NC 27401

(G-5659)
LEE SPRING COMPANY LLC
104 Industrial Ave (27406-4505)
PHONE...............................336 275-3631
Jorge Cortes, Brnch Mgr
EMP: 20
SQ FT: 12,544
SALES (corp-wide): 46.66MM Privately
Held
Web: www.leespring.com
SIC: 3495 3493 5085 3315 Mechanical
springs, precision; Steel springs, except
wire; Springs; Wire and fabricated wire
products
PA: Lee Spring Company Llc
140 58th St Ste 3c
Brooklyn NY 11220
888 777-4647

(G-5660)
LEGGETT & PLATT INCORPORATED
Matrex
911 Northridge St (27403-2112)
P.O. Box 444 (27402-0444)
PHONE...............................336 379-7777
Roger Tornero, Prin
EMP: 125
SALES (corp-wide): 5.15B Publicly Held
Web: www.matrex-seating.com
SIC: 2515 Mattresses and bedsprings
PA: Leggett & Platt, Incorporated
1 Leggett Rd
Carthage MO 64836
417 358-8131

(G-5661)
**LEONARDO US CYBER SEC
SLTONS L (PA)**
Also Called: Leonardo
4221 Tudor Ln (27410-8105)
PHONE...............................336 379-7135
Bill Nieuwkerk, Pr
▼ EMP: 75 EST: 2001
SALES (est): 39.21MM
SALES (corp-wide): 39.21MM Privately
Held
Web: www.leonardocompany-us.com
SIC: 3993 3663 3699 Signs and advertising
specialties; Radio and t.v. communications
equipment; Security devices

(G-5662)
LEVEL 4 DESIGNS CORP
7027 Albert Pick Rd Ste 103 (27409-9828)
PHONE...............................336 235-3450
Robert Price, Pr
▲ EMP: 4 EST: 2012
SALES (est): 7.56MM Privately Held
Web: www.level4designs.com
SIC: 2512 Upholstered household furniture

(G-5663)
LOGIKSAVVY SOLUTIONS LLC
2204 Flora Vista Ct (27406-8557)
P.O. Box 1572 (27402-1572)
PHONE...............................336 392-6149
EMP: 6 EST: 2013
SALES (est): 935.01K Privately Held
Web: www.logiksavvysolutions.com
SIC: 3841 7371 7379 8742 Surgical and
medical instruments; Custom computer
programming services; Online services
technology consultants; New business start-
up consultant

(G-5664)
LONGWOOD INDUSTRIES INC (DH)
706 Green Valley Rd Ste 212 (27408-7023)
PHONE...............................336 272-3710
Kimberly L Rice, Sr VP
Joseph E Mihalick, Sr VP
James J Mcdonnell, Ex VP
Michael R Groves, Dir
▲ EMP: 10 EST: 1991
SALES (est): 43.49MM Publicly Held
SIC: 3069 3081 Molded rubber products;
Unsupported plastics film and sheet
HQ: Wabtec Components Llc
30 Isabella St
Pittsburgh PA 15212
412 825-1000

(G-5665)
**LORILLARD TOBACCO COMPANY
LLC**
714 Green Valley Rd (27408-7018)
P.O. Box 10529 (27404-0529)
PHONE...............................336 335-6600
◆ EMP: 2700
SIC: 2111 Cigarettes

(G-5666)
LOVE KNOT CANDLES
4603 Barn Owl Ct (27406-8065)
PHONE...............................336 456-1619
Sharon Bennett, Prin
EMP: 5 EST: 2016
SALES (est): 46.82K Privately Held
SIC: 3999 Candles

(G-5667)
LOVEJOY CORPORATION INC
Also Called: Hip Labels
2207 Granville Rd (27408)
PHONE...............................336 472-0674
Robert L Lovejoy, CEO
EMP: 11 EST: 2001
SALES (est): 704.07K Privately Held
Web: www.lovejoy-inc.com
SIC: 3568 Power transmission equipment,
nec

(G-5668)
M G NEWELL CORPORATION (PA)
301 Citation Ct (27409-9027)
P.O. Box 18765 (27419-8765)
PHONE...............................336 393-0100
J Michael Sherrill, Pr
Grey Sherill, *
EMP: 60 EST: 1885
SQ FT: 32,000

SALES (est): 24.08MM
SALES (corp-wide): 24.08MM Privately
Held
Web: www.mgnewell.com
SIC: 3556 Bakery machinery

(G-5669)
M&J OLDCO INC
Also Called: Mail Box Book Company, The
3515 W Market St Ste 200 (27403-4442)
P.O. Box 9753 (27429-0753)
PHONE...............................336 854-0309
▲ EMP: 70
SIC: 2721 Magazines: publishing and printing

(G-5670)
MACK TRUCKS INC (HQ)
7900 National Service Rd (27409-9416)
P.O. Box 26259 (27402)
PHONE...............................336 291-9001
Terry Mack, CEO
Stephen Roy, *
Gregory T Higgins, *
◆ EMP: 800 EST: 1974
SALES (est): 1.32B
SALES (corp-wide): 52.58B Privately Held
Web: www.macktrucks.com
SIC: 3711 3714 5012 6141 Motor trucks,
except off-highway, assembly of; Motor
vehicle parts and accessories; Truck
tractors; Financing: automobiles, furniture,
etc., not a deposit bank
PA: Ab Volvo
Amazonvagen 8
Goteborg 418 7
31660000

(G-5671)
**MAGNUSSEN HOME FURNISHINGS
INC (HQ)**
Also Called: Magnussen
4523 Green Point Dr Ste 109 (27410-8167)
PHONE...............................336 841-4424
Nathan Cressman, Pr
Kent Macfarlane, CFO
EMP: 7 EST: 1931
SALES (est): 4.85MM
SALES (corp-wide): 57.54MM Privately
Held
Web: www.magnussen.com
SIC: 2511 5021 Wood household furniture;
Household furniture
PA: Magnussen Home Furnishings Ltd
2-94 Bridgeport Rd E
Waterloo ON N2J 2
519 662-3040

(G-5672)
MANN MEDIA INC
Also Called: Our State Magazine
800 Green Valley Rd Ste 106 (27408-7027)
P.O. Box 4552 (27404-4552)
PHONE...............................336 286-0600
Bernard Mann, Pr
Lynn Tutterow, *
Roberta Mann, *
EMP: 33 EST: 1978
SQ FT: 7,000
SALES (est): 2.31MM Privately Held
Web: www.ourstate.com
SIC: 2721 Magazines: publishing only, not
printed on site

(G-5673)
MARIETTA MARTIN MATERIALS INC
Also Called: Martin Marietta Aggregates
413 S Chimney Rock Rd (27409-9260)
P.O. Box 30013 (27622-0013)
PHONE...............................336 668-3253
Dean Hardy, Genl Mgr
EMP: 9

Web: www.martinmarietta.com
SIC: 1422 Crushed and broken limestone
PA: Martin Marietta Materials Inc
  4123 Parklake Ave
  Raleigh NC 27612

(G-5674)
MARK/TRECE INC
Also Called: Mark Trece
902 Norwalk St (27407-2027)
PHONE....................973 884-1005
EMP: 19
SALES (corp-wide): 24.32MM **Privately Held**
Web: www.marktrece.com
SIC: 3555 Printing trades machinery
PA: Mark/Trece, Inc.
  2001 Stockton Rd
  Joppa MD 21085
  410 879-0060

(G-5675)
MARKET DEPOT USA NC INC ✪
4501 Green Point Dr Ste 500 (27410-8141)
PHONE....................888 417-8685
Mirtala A Castillo, *Pr*
EMP: 10 **EST:** 2023
SALES (est): 528.31K **Privately Held**
SIC: 2032 Spanish foods: packaged in cans, jars, etc.

(G-5676)
MARSH FURNITURE COMPANY
Also Called: Kitchen Art
2503 Greengate Dr (27406-5242)
PHONE....................336 273-8196
David Gainey, *Brnch Mgr*
EMP: 18
SALES (corp-wide): 43.69MM **Privately Held**
Web: www.marshkb.com
SIC: 2434 5211 1799 1751 Wood kitchen cabinets; Cabinets, kitchen; Counter top installation; Cabinet and finish carpentry
PA: Marsh Furniture Company
  1001 S Centennial St
  High Point NC 27260
  336 884-7363

(G-5677)
MARSHALL USA LLC
7130 Bentley Rd (27409)
PHONE....................301 481-1241
EMP: 4 **EST:** 2021
SALES (est): 2.9MM
SALES (corp-wide): 400.48MM **Privately Held**
SIC: 3721 Airplanes, fixed or rotary wing
PA: Marshall Of Cambridge (Holdings) Limited
  Control Building
  Cambridge CAMBS CB5 8
  122 337-3427

(G-5678)
MARTIN MARIETTA MATERIALS INC
Also Called: Martin Marietta Aggregates
5800 Eckerson Rd (27405-9466)
PHONE....................336 375-7584
Terry Small, *Brnch Mgr*
EMP: 8
Web: www.martinmarietta.com
SIC: 1422 Crushed and broken limestone
PA: Martin Marietta Materials Inc
  4123 Parklake Ave
  Raleigh NC 27612

(G-5679)
MARTIN MARIETTA MATERIALS INC
Also Called: Martin Marietta Aggregates
3957 Liberty Rd (27406-6109)

P.O. Box 16867 (27416-0867)
PHONE....................336 674-0836
David Thorn, *Brnch Mgr*
EMP: 6
Web: www.martinmarietta.com
SIC: 1422 5032 Crushed and broken limestone; Stone, crushed or broken
PA: Martin Marietta Materials Inc
  4123 Parklake Ave
  Raleigh NC 27612

(G-5680)
MARTIN MATERIALS INC
4801 Burlington Rd (27405-8615)
PHONE....................336 697-1800
Roger D Martin, *Pr*
Amanda Hopkins, *VP*
EMP: 4 **EST:** 2009
SALES (est): 827.69K **Privately Held**
Web: www.martinmaterialsinc.com
SIC: 2611 Pulp mills, mechanical and recycling processing

(G-5681)
MATTHEWS MOBILE MEDIA LLC
6343 Burnt Poplar Rd (27409-9711)
PHONE....................336 303-4982
Bradley J Matthews, *Managing Member*
EMP: 6 **EST:** 2019
SALES (est): 568.06K **Privately Held**
Web: www.matthewsmobile.com
SIC: 3993 Signs and advertising specialties

(G-5682)
MATTHEWS SPCIALTY VEHICLES INC
211 American Ave (27409-1803)
PHONE....................336 297-9600
Bradley Mathews, *Pr*
Glenn Matthews, *
Kathy Drapeau, *
EMP: 55 **EST:** 1994
SALES (est): 14.74MM **Privately Held**
Web: www.msvehicles.com
SIC: 3711 3713 3716 Ambulances (motor vehicles), assembly of; Truck and bus bodies; Recreational van conversion (self-propelled), factory basis

(G-5683)
MAXSON & ASSOCIATES
Also Called: Maxson and Assoc Greensboro
2618 Battleground Ave (27408-1924)
PHONE....................336 632-0524
William Maxson, *Owner*
EMP: 4 **EST:** 1976
SALES (est): 400.68K **Privately Held**
Web: www.maxsonassociates.com
SIC: 3537 7699 5211 5084 Loading docks: portable, adjustable, and hydraulic; Door and window repair; Door and window products; Materials handling machinery

(G-5684)
MAYNARD S FABRICATORS INC
2227 W Lee St Ste A (27403-2503)
PHONE....................336 230-1048
John Maynard, *Pr*
Adrienne K Maynard, *Sec*
Ann Maynards, *Treas*
EMP: 4 **EST:** 1989
SALES (est): 206.69K **Privately Held**
Web: www.waterfordatgoldmarkapts.com
SIC: 7692 1799 Welding repair; Welding on site

(G-5685)
MB-F INC (PA)
620 Industrial Ave (27406-4619)
P.O. Box 22107 (27420-2107)
PHONE....................336 379-9352

Bobby Christiansen, *Pr*
Fred Lyman, *
Dorie Crowe, *
EMP: 75 **EST:** 1967
SQ FT: 40,000
SALES (est): 4.47MM
SALES (corp-wide): 4.47MM **Privately Held**
Web: www.infodog.com
SIC: 7331 2721 7999 2759 Direct mail advertising services; Periodicals; Animal shows in circuses, fairs, and carnivals; Commercial printing, nec

(G-5686)
MCAD INC
Also Called: Carolina Custom Surfaces
100 Landmark Dr (27409-9602)
PHONE....................336 299-3030
Joe Duszka, *Pr*
EMP: 50 **EST:** 1995
SQ FT: 2,500
SALES (est): 3.4MM **Privately Held**
SIC: 3281 2541 Bathroom fixtures, cut stone ; Table or counter tops, plastic laminated

(G-5687)
MCLEAN SBSRFACE UTLITY ENGRG L
Also Called: Engineering Consulting Svcs
3015 E Bessemer Ave (27405-7503)
PHONE....................336 340-0024
Stacey Slaw, *CEO*
Stacey E Slaw, *Prin*
EMP: 10 **EST:** 2015
SALES (est): 413.96K **Privately Held**
SIC: 1389 8713 8711 1623 Testing, measuring, surveying, and analysis services ; Surveying services; Engineering services; Underground utilities contractor

(G-5688)
MECHANICAL SPECIALTY INC
1901 E Wendover Ave (27405-6899)
PHONE....................336 272-5606
David Smith, *Pr*
EMP: 6 **EST:** 1948
SQ FT: 20,000
SALES (est): 2.67MM **Privately Held**
Web: www.mechspecialty.com
SIC: 3599 Machine shop, jobbing and repair

(G-5689)
MEMIOS LLC
7609 Business Park Dr # B (27409-9696)
PHONE....................336 664-5256
EMP: 80 **EST:** 2003
SALES (est): 6.65MM **Privately Held**
Web: www.memios.com
SIC: 3535 Conveyors and conveying equipment

(G-5690)
MERCH CONNECT STUDIOS INC
1724 Holbrook St (27403-2713)
PHONE....................336 501-6722
EMP: 4 **EST:** 2021
SALES (est): 84.45K **Privately Held**
Web: www.merchconnect.com
SIC: 2759 Screen printing

(G-5691)
MERCHANT 1 MARKETING LLC
2900 Pacific Ave (27406-4513)
PHONE....................888 853-9992
William B Turner Junior, *Managing Member*
EMP: 4 **EST:** 2009
SALES (est): 91.38K **Privately Held**
Web: www.m1mequipment.com

SIC: 5013 3559 Automotive supplies and parts; Automotive maintenance equipment

(G-5692)
MIDSOUTH POWER EQP CO INC
518 Corliss St (27406-5216)
P.O. Box 16025 (27416-0025)
PHONE....................336 389-0515
Roger Johnson, *Pr*
Cathy Johnson, *VP*
EMP: 12 **EST:** 1999
SQ FT: 15,000
SALES (est): 1.54MM **Privately Held**
Web: www.clyde-industries.com
SIC: 3589 Commercial cleaning equipment

(G-5693)
MILLENIUM PRINT GROUP (PA)
4301 Waterleaf Ct (27410-8106)
PHONE....................919 818-1229
Tina Barham, *Prin*
EMP: 4 **EST:** 2022
SALES (est): 6.24MM
SALES (corp-wide): 6.24MM **Privately Held**
SIC: 2759 Commercial printing, nec

(G-5694)
MISCHIEF MAKERS LOCAL 816 LLC
Also Called: Home State Apparel
1504 Rainbow Dr (27403-3158)
PHONE....................336 763-2003
EMP: 25 **EST:** 2009
SALES (est): 818.02K **Privately Held**
SIC: 2389 Men's miscellaneous accessories

(G-5695)
MODERN RECREATIONAL TECH INC
Valvtect Petroleum Products
7625 Thorndike Rd (27409-9421)
PHONE....................847 272-2278
Gerald H Nessenson, *Prin*
EMP: 54
SALES (corp-wide): 7.34B **Publicly Held**
Web: www.kop-coat.com
SIC: 2851 Paints and allied products
HQ: Kop-Coat, Inc.
  3040 William Pitt Way
  Pittsburgh PA 15238
  412 227-2426

(G-5696)
MODERN RECREATIONAL TECH INC
Kop-Coat Marine Group
7625 Thorndike Rd (27409-9421)
PHONE....................800 221-4466
Linda Smith, *Brnch Mgr*
EMP: 50
SALES (corp-wide): 7.34B **Publicly Held**
Web: www.pettitpaint.com
SIC: 2851 2891 5198 Paints and paint additives; Adhesives and sealants; Paints
HQ: Kop-Coat, Inc.
  3040 William Pitt Way
  Pittsburgh PA 15238
  412 227-2426

(G-5697)
MOTHER MURPHYS LABS INC
300 Dougherty St (27406-4306)
PHONE....................336 273-1737
Robert B Murphy, *Ch*
EMP: 41
SALES (corp-wide): 105.82MM **Privately Held**
Web: www.mothermurphys.com
SIC: 2087 Extracts, flavoring
PA: Mother Murphy's Laboratories, Inc.
  2826 S Elm Eugene St
  Greensboro NC 27406
  336 273-1737

(G-5698)
MOTHER MURPHYS LABS INC (PA)
2826 S Elm Eugene St (27406-4435)
P.O. Box 16846 (27416-0846)
PHONE......................336 273-1737
Robert B Murphy, *Ch*
David Murphy, *
James A Murphy, *
Timothy Hansen, *
Janet Murphy, *
EMP: 79 **EST:** 1946
SQ FT: 39,000
SALES (est): 105.82MM
SALES (corp-wide): 105.82MM **Privately Held**
Web: www.mothermurphys.com
SIC: 2087 Extracts, flavoring

(G-5699)
MULTI PACKAGING SOLUTIONS
Also Called: MPS Greensboro
7915 Industrial Village Rd (27409-9691)
PHONE......................336 855-7142
EMP: 967 **EST:** 1987
SQ FT: 57,000
SALES (est): 7.09MM **Privately Held**
SIC: 2752 2759 7336 2671 Commercial printing, lithographic; Labels and seals: printing, nsk; Commercial art and graphic design; Paper; coated and laminated packaging
HQ: Lansing Mps Inc
5800 W Grand River Ave
Lansing MI 48906
517 323-9000

(G-5700)
MULTIGEN DIAGNOSTICS LLC
1100 Revolution Mill Dr Ste 1 (27405-5067)
PHONE......................336 510-1120
Thuraiayah Moorthy, *Managing Member*
EMP: 6 **EST:** 2015
SALES (est): 500.88K **Privately Held**
SIC: 3841 2835 Diagnostic apparatus, medical; Cytology and histology diagnostic agents

(G-5701)
MUNIBILLING
3300 Battleground Ave Ste 402 (27410-2465)
PHONE......................800 259-7020
John A Vergey, *Prin*
EMP: 26 **EST:** 2017
SALES (est): 3.81MM **Privately Held**
Web: www.munibilling.com
SIC: 7372 Business oriented computer software

(G-5702)
MUSIC MATTERS INC
Also Called: Music Garden
507 Arlington St (27406-1407)
PHONE......................336 272-5303
Lorna Heyge, *Pr*
Jeff Stickard, *VP*
▲ **EMP:** 7 **EST:** 1994
SALES (est): 214.08K **Privately Held**
Web: www.musikgarten.org
SIC: 2741 5736 Music, book: publishing and printing; Sheet music

(G-5703)
MYLAN PHARMACEUTICALS INC
Also Called: Lpmylan Specialty
2898 Manufacturers Rd (27406-4600)
PHONE......................336 271-6571
Larry Salmon, *Mgr*
EMP: 40
SQ FT: 160,642
SALES (corp-wide): 2.39MM **Publicly Held**
Web: www.viatris.com
SIC: 2834 Druggists' preparations (pharmaceuticals)
HQ: Mylan Pharmaceuticals Inc.
3711 Collins Ferry Road
Morgantown WV 26505
304 599-2595

(G-5704)
NATIVE NATURALZ INC
805 Stoney Hill Cir (27406-8135)
PHONE......................336 334-2984
Tinece Holman, *Pr*
EMP: 10 **EST:** 2013
SALES (est): 135.03K **Privately Held**
SIC: 8999 8748 5211 2911 Earth science services; Urban planning and consulting services; Insulation and energy conservation products; Mineral oils, natural

(G-5705)
NB CORPORATION
Also Called: Greensboro Industrial Platers
123 S Edwardia Dr (27409-2601)
P.O. Box 4466 (27404-4466)
PHONE......................336 852-8786
Allison Davis, *Mgr*
EMP: 10
SALES (corp-wide): 2.44MM **Privately Held**
Web: www.gboroplaters.com
SIC: 3471 Electroplating of metals or formed products
PA: Nb Corporation
725 Kenilworth St
Greensboro NC 27403
336 274-7654

(G-5706)
NB CORPORATION (PA)
Also Called: Greensboro Industrial Platers
725 Kenilworth St (27403-2417)
P.O. Box 4466 (27404)
PHONE......................336 274-7654
Harold O'tuel, *Pr*
Allison Davis, *Pr*
EMP: 20 **EST:** 1933
SQ FT: 28,000
SALES (est): 2.44MM
SALES (corp-wide): 2.44MM **Privately Held**
Web: www.gboroplaters.com
SIC: 3471 Electroplating of metals or formed products

(G-5707)
NEW GROWTH PRESS LLC
1301 Carolina St Ste 124 (27401-1090)
P.O. Box 4485 (27404-4485)
PHONE......................336 378-7775
Mark Teears, *CEO*
EMP: 5 **EST:** 2004
SALES (est): 679.82K **Privately Held**
Web: www.newgrowthpress.com
SIC: 2731 Books, publishing only

(G-5708)
NEWS & RECORD COMMERCIAL PRTG
200 E Market St (27401-2910)
PHONE......................336 373-7300
Jeff Newman, *Mgr*
EMP: 17 **EST:** 1965
SALES (est): 478.15K **Privately Held**
Web: www.greensboro.com
SIC: 2759 2711 Commercial printing, nec; Newspapers

(G-5709)
NICHOLS SPDMTR & INSTR CO INC
Also Called: Nichols Speedometer & Instr Co
1336 Oakland Ave (27403-2748)
P.O. Box 4281 (27404-4281)
PHONE......................336 273-2881
Charles Nichols, *Pr*
Renee Nichols, *Sec*
EMP: 8 **EST:** 1962
SQ FT: 1,900
SALES (est): 270.15K **Privately Held**
Web: www.nsifleet.com
SIC: 7539 5013 3824 Automotive repair shops, nec; Motor vehicle supplies and new parts; Speedometers

(G-5710)
NOMADIC DISPLAY LLC
7602 Business Park Dr (27409-9696)
PHONE......................800 336-5019
Franklin Gaskins, *Prin*
EMP: 4 **EST:** 2016
SALES (est): 147.57K **Privately Held**
Web: www.nomadicdisplay.com
SIC: 3993 Signs and advertising specialties

(G-5711)
NOMADIC NORTH AMERICA LLC (HQ)
Also Called: Nomadic Display
7602 Business Park Dr (27409-9696)
PHONE......................703 866-9200
▲ **EMP:** 44 **EST:** 1975
SALES (est): 957.54K **Privately Held**
Web: www.nomadicdisplay.com
SIC: 3993 Displays and cutouts, window and lobby
PA: Apple Rock Advertising & Promotion, Inc.
7602 Business Park Dr
Greensboro NC 27409

(G-5712)
NORCOR TECHNOLOGIES CORP
4291 Harbor Ridge Dr (27406-8576)
PHONE......................704 309-4101
Mark Clayton, *Pr*
Marquis Bey, *Sec*
Robert Warner, *VP*
EMP: 5 **EST:** 1989
SALES (est): 103.65K **Privately Held**
Web: www.norcortechnologies.com
SIC: 1711 5052 1311 2911 Solar energy contractor; Coal and other minerals and ores; Crude petroleum and natural gas; Petroleum refining

(G-5713)
NOREGON SYSTEMS INC
7823 National Service Rd Ste 100 (27409-9464)
PHONE......................336 615-8555
William Hathaway, *CEO*
EMP: 220 **EST:** 1993
SALES (est): 46.08MM **Privately Held**
Web: www.noregon.com
SIC: 7371 3578 Computer software development; Automatic teller machines (ATM)

(G-5714)
NOUVEAU VERRE HOLDINGS INC (DH)
3802 Robert Porcher Way (27410-2190)
PHONE......................336 545-0011
Phillipe Porcher, *CEO*
James R Henderson, *Ofcr*
Philippe R Dorier, *CFO*
EMP: 15 **EST:** 2004
SALES (est): 275.37MM
SALES (corp-wide): 2.67MM **Privately Held**
SIC: 2221 3624 2241 2295 Glass broadwoven fabrics; Fibers, carbon and graphite; Glass narrow fabrics; Mats, varnished glass
HQ: Porcher Industries
2440 Rd 1085
Eclose-Badinieres ARA 38300
474431010

(G-5715)
NOVALENT LTD
2319 Joe Brown Dr (27405-3960)
P.O. Box 10610 (28461)
PHONE......................336 375-7555
Joseph E Mason, *Pr*
Babu Patel, *VP*
▼ **EMP:** 15 **EST:** 1981
SQ FT: 30,000
SALES (est): 8.92MM **Privately Held**
Web: www.novalent.com
SIC: 2819 2842 2899 Industrial inorganic chemicals, nec; Polishes and sanitation goods; Chemical preparations, nec

(G-5716)
NUVASIVE INC
1250 Revolution Mill Dr (27405-5191)
PHONE......................336 430-3169
EMP: 7 **EST:** 1998
SALES (est): 414.67K **Privately Held**
Web: www.nuvasive.com
SIC: 3841 Surgical and medical instruments

(G-5717)
NVH INC (DH)
3802 Robert Porcher Way (27410-2190)
PHONE......................336 545-0011
Philippe Porcher, *CEO*
Philippe R Dorier, *CFO*
EMP: 7 **EST:** 2004
SALES (est): 247.83MM
SALES (corp-wide): 2.67MM **Privately Held**
SIC: 2221 3624 2241 2295 Glass broadwoven fabrics; Fibers, carbon and graphite; Glass narrow fabrics; Mats, varnished glass
HQ: Nouveau Verre Holdings, Inc.
3802 Robert Porcher Way
Greensboro NC 27410

(G-5718)
OAKHURST TEXTILES INC
Also Called: Logan Text Fabrics
203 Citation Ct (27409-9026)
P.O. Box 18744 (27419-8744)
PHONE......................336 668-0733
Richard L Stark Junior, *CEO*
Richard Wotring, *
Matthew Brennan, *OK Vice President*
▲ **EMP:** 27 **EST:** 1975
SQ FT: 84,000
SALES (est): 1.55MM **Privately Held**
SIC: 5131 2299 Piece goods and notions; Fabrics: linen, jute, hemp, ramie

(G-5719)
OLDCASTLE APG SOUTH INC
139 S Walnut Cir (27409-2624)
PHONE......................336 854-8200
Robert Carter, *Brnch Mgr*
EMP: 5
SALES (corp-wide): 34.95B **Privately Held**
Web: www.adamsproducts.com
SIC: 3272 Concrete products, nec
HQ: Oldcastle Apg South, Inc.
333 N Greene St Ste 500
Greensboro NC 27401

GEOGRAPHIC

(G-5720)

OLYMPIC PRODUCTS LLC (PA)
4100 Pleasant Garden Rd (27406-7699)
PHONE..............................336 378-9620
Mike Cooke, *Pr*
Joe Cladey, *Managing Member**
EMP: 71 EST: 2006
SALES (est): 17.68MM **Privately Held**
Web: www.olympic-products.com
SIC: 2821 Plastics materials and resins

(G-5721)

OLYMPIC PRODUCTS LLC
Also Called: Vita Foam
4100 Pleasant Garden Rd (27406-7699)
PHONE..............................336 378-9620
Britt Keaton, *Genl Mgr*
EMP: 76
Web: www.olympic-products.com
SIC: 2821 5199 Plastics materials and resins
; Foams and rubber
PA: Olympic Products Llc
4100 Pleasant Garden Rd
Greensboro NC 27406

(G-5722)

ONE FURNITURE GROUP CORP
6520 Airport Center Dr Ste 204
(27409-9072)
PHONE..............................336 235-0221
Robert L Price, *Pr*
EMP: 4 EST: 2010
SALES (est): 34.01K **Privately Held**
SIC: 2511 Wood household furniture

(G-5723)

**ONE SOURCE DOCUMENT
SOLUTIONS**
311 Pomona Dr Ste D (27407-1694)
PHONE..............................336 482-2360
John Kinney, *Owner*
EMP: 4 EST: 2018
SALES (est): 103.9K **Privately Held**
SIC: 2759 Commercial printing, nec

(G-5724)

**ONE SRCE DCUMENT SOLUTIONS
INC**
4355 Federal Dr Ste 140 (27410-8143)
P.O. Box 8227 (27419-0227)
PHONE..............................800 401-9544
Kevin Smith, *Pr*
EMP: 35 EST: 1994
SALES (est): 2.43MM **Privately Held**
Web: www.osdsinc.com
SIC: 7372 8742 Prepackaged software;
Management consulting services

(G-5725)

OPTICAL PLACE INC (PA)
Also Called: Optical Wholesale
2633 Randleman Rd (27406-5107)
P.O. Box 16087 (27416-0087)
PHONE..............................336 274-1300
William R Fonner, *Pr*
Jerry Burleson, ***
Maurice P Johnson, ***
EMP: 25 EST: 1976
SALES (est): 1.21MM
SALES (corp-wide): 1.21MM **Privately
Held**
Web: www.opticalplacenc.com
SIC: 5995 5049 3851 Opticians; Optical
goods; Ophthalmic goods

(G-5726)

OPTICS INC
Also Called: Layton Optics
1607 Westover Ter Ste B (27408-1997)
PHONE..............................336 288-9504

Bernie Dehoog, *Owner*
EMP: 5
SALES (corp-wide): 672.45K **Privately
Held**
Web: www.optics-eyewear.com
SIC: 8042 3827 5995 Offices and clinics of
optometrists; Optical instruments and lenses
; Opticians
PA: Optics Inc
1105 N Lindsay St Side
High Point NC 27262
336 884-5677

(G-5727)

ORPAK USA INC
7300 W Friendly Ave (27410-6232)
PHONE..............................201 441-9820
Shlomo Slotwiner, *Pr*
Vito Cantatore, *Contrlr*
EMP: 11 EST: 1991
SQ FT: 4,000
SALES (est): 593.82K **Privately Held**
Web: www.gilbarco.com
SIC: 7549 3829 Fuel system conversion,
automotive; Measuring and controlling
devices, nec
PA: Orpak Systems Ltd
Green Work Building E
Yakum 60972

(G-5728)

P R SPARKS ENTERPRISES INC
Also Called: Perfection Products Co
1333 Headquarters Dr (27405-7919)
P.O. Box 14571 (27415-4571)
PHONE..............................336 272-7200
Paul Sparks, *Pr*
Patricia L Sparks, *Sec*
EMP: 5 EST: 1980
SQ FT: 11,000
SALES (est): 114.93K **Privately Held**
SIC: 2434 2511 2431 Wood kitchen cabinets
; Whatnot shelves: wood; Doors, wood

(G-5729)

PACE COMMUNICATIONS INC (PA)
1301 Carolina St Ste 200 (27401-1022)
PHONE..............................336 378-6065
Bonnie Mcelveen-hunter, *CEO*
Leigh Ann Klee, ***
Grodon Locke, ***
Patricia M Mc Connell, ***
▲ EMP: 225 EST: 1983
SQ FT: 22,000
SALES (est): 24.86MM
SALES (corp-wide): 24.86MM **Privately
Held**
Web: www.paceco.com
SIC: 8742 2721 Marketing consulting
services; Magazines: publishing only, not
printed on site

(G-5730)

PACTIV LLC
520 Radar Rd (27410-6212)
PHONE..............................336 292-2796
Ernie Calahan, *Brnch Mgr*
EMP: 62
Web: www.pactivevergreen.com
SIC: 2679 5113 Book covers, paper;
Containers, paper and disposable plastic
HQ: Pactiv Llc
1900 W Field Ct
Lake Forest IL 60045
847 482-2000

(G-5731)

PALMETTO AND ASSOCIATE LLC
223 S Elm St (27401-2602)
PHONE..............................336 382-7432
Carlos Brown, *CEO*

EMP: 8 EST: 2010
SALES (est): 499.73K **Privately Held**
SIC: 2099 Food preparations, nec

(G-5732)

PARK COMMUNICATIONS LLC
Also Called: Millennium Print Group
4301 Waterleaf Ct (27410-8106)
PHONE..............................336 292-4000
EMP: 67
Web: www.mprintgroup.com
SIC: 2752 2791 2789 2759 Commercial
printing, lithographic; Typesetting;
Bookbinding and related work; Commercial
printing, nec
HQ: Park Communications, Llc
10900 World Trade Blvd
Raleigh NC 27617
919 852-1117

(G-5733)

**PARKER METAL FINISHING
COMPANY**
719 W Gate City Blvd Ste D (27403-3065)
P.O. Box 16084 (27406)
PHONE..............................336 275-9657
Jack R Parker, *Pr*
Tracy Dickerson, *Sec*
Yvonne Parker, *VP*
EMP: 7 EST: 1981
SQ FT: 3,000
SALES (est): 655.61K **Privately Held**
Web: www.parkermetalfinishing.com
SIC: 3471 Electroplating of metals or formed
products

(G-5734)

PARKER-HANNIFIN CORPORATION
Also Called: Hose Products Division
125 E Meadowview Rd (27406-4518)
PHONE..............................336 373-1761
Lonnie Gallup, *Brnch Mgr*
EMP: 68
SALES (corp-wide): 19.93B **Publicly Held**
Web: www.parker.com
SIC: 2241 5085 Hose fabric, tubular;
Industrial supplies
PA: Parker-Hannifin Corporation
6035 Parkland Blvd
Cleveland OH 44124
216 896-3000

(G-5735)

PARRISH TIRE COMPANY
2809 Thurston Ave (27406-4514)
PHONE..............................336 334-9979
Tony George, *Brnch Mgr*
EMP: 38
SALES (corp-wide): 378.88MM **Privately
Held**
Web: www.parrishtire.com
SIC: 7539 7537 7534 5531 Frame and front
end repair services; Automotiv e
transmission repair shops; Tire retreading
and repair shops; Automotive tires
PA: Parrish Tire Company
5130 Indiana Ave
Winston Salem NC 27106
800 849-8473

(G-5736)

PATHEON SOFTGELS INC
Also Called: Federal Ridge
7902 Indlea Point Ste 112 (27409)
PHONE..............................336 812-8700
Michelle Stinson, *Mgr*
EMP: 10
SALES (corp-wide): 42.86B **Publicly Held**
Web: www.patheon.com
SIC: 2834 4225 Vitamin preparations;
General warehousing and storage

HQ: Patheon Softgels Inc.
4125 Premier Dr
High Point NC 27265
336 812-8700

(G-5737)

PBM GRAPHICS INC
Also Called: Rrd Packaging Solutions
415 Westcliff Rd (27409-9786)
PHONE..............................336 664-5800
Steve Welch, *Mgr*
EMP: 114
SQ FT: 115,400
SALES (corp-wide): 15B **Privately Held**
Web: www.rrd.com
SIC: 2752 Offset printing
HQ: Pbm Graphics, Inc.
3700 S Miami Blvd
Durham NC 27703
919 544-6222

(G-5738)

**PERFORMANCE ENTPS & PARTS
INC**
4104 Burlington Rd (27405-8629)
PHONE..............................336 621-6572
Alfred Williams, *Pr*
EMP: 5 EST: 1964
SALES (est): 184.88K **Privately Held**
Web: www.performance-enterprises.com
SIC: 7539 3465 Machine shop, automotive;
Body parts, automobile: stamped metal

(G-5739)

PHARMACEUTICAL DIMENSIONS
7353 W Friendly Ave # A (27410-6233)
PHONE..............................336 297-4851
Michael P Deason, *Pr*
▲ EMP: 7 EST: 2004
SALES (est): 484.37K **Privately Held**
Web: www.phdreturns.com
SIC: 2834 Pharmaceutical preparations

(G-5740)

PIEDMONT ANIMAL HEALTH INC
Also Called: Triad Specialty Products
204 Muirs Chapel Rd Ste 200 (27410-6173)
PHONE..............................336 544-0320
Roland Johnson, *CEO*
Michael F Kelly, *CFO*
EMP: 20 EST: 2019
SALES (est): 1.24MM **Privately Held**
Web: www.animalhealthjobs.com
SIC: 2834 Pharmaceutical preparations

(G-5741)

**PIEDMONT AVI CMPONENT SVCS
LLC**
Also Called: Tat Piedmont
7102 Cessna Dr (27409-9793)
PHONE..............................336 423-5100
Dean Hall, ***
Todd Schwarz, ***
EMP: 108 EST: 1954
SQ FT: 65,000
SALES (est): 42.94MM **Privately Held**
Web: piedmont.tat-technologies.com
SIC: 4581 3721 Aircraft maintenance and
repair services; Aircraft
HQ: Limco Airepair Inc.
5304 S Lawton Ave
Tulsa OK 74107
918 445-4300

(G-5742)

PIEDMONT GRAPHICS INC
6903 International Dr (27409-9028)
P.O. Box 4509 (27404-4509)
PHONE..............................336 230-0040
John Rutledge, *Pr*

▲ = Import ▼ = Export
◆ = Import/Export

Cindy Rutledge, *
▲ **EMP:** 26 **EST:** 1993
SQ FT: 24,000
SALES (est): 4.35MM **Privately Held**
Web: www.source4greensboro.com
SIC: 2752 Offset printing

(G-5743)
PIEDMONT LMINATING COATING INC
1812 Sullivan St (27405-7216)
PHONE..............................336 272-1600
Tom Snyder, *Pr*
Guy Pawson, *Genl Mgr*
EMP: 10 **EST:** 1991
SALES (est): 253.69K **Privately Held**
Web: www.piedmontlaminating.com
SIC: 3479 Coating of metals and formed
products

(G-5744)
PIEDMONT PAPER STOCK LLC
Also Called: Record Stor Depot-Shred Depo
3909 Riverdale Dr (27406-7505)
P.O. Box 20146 (27420-0146)
PHONE..............................336 285-8592
EMP: 16
SALES (corp-wide): 943.59K **Privately
Held**
Web: www.piedmontpaperstock.com
SIC: 5093 3589 Waste paper; Shredders,
industrial and commercial
PA: Piedmont Paper Stock, Llc
2235 Cesnna Dr
Burlington NC 27215
336 437-8500

(G-5745)
PIEDMONT PLATING CORPORATION
3005 Holts Chapel Rd (27401-4454)
PHONE..............................336 272-2311
Matthew T Marsh, *Pr*
Mitchell T Marsh, *VP*
David A Willox, *Treas*
EMP: 49 **EST:** 2007
SALES (est): 1.03MM
SALES (corp-wide): 24.79MM **Privately
Held**
Web: www.piedmontplating.com
SIC: 3471 Electroplating of metals or formed
products
PA: Marsh Plating Corporation
103 N Grove St
Ypsilanti MI 48198
734 483-5767

(G-5746)
PIEDMONT TRUCK TIRES INC (HQ)
312 S Regional Rd (27409-9674)
P.O. Box 18228 (27419-8228)
PHONE..............................336 668-0091
Dan Rice, *Pr*
Mitch Glover, *
Greg Herring, *
EMP: 30 **EST:** 1978
SQ FT: 24,000
SALES (est): 41.24MM
SALES (corp-wide): 636MM **Privately
Held**
Web: www.piedmonttrucktires.com
SIC: 5014 5531 7534 Truck tires and tubes;
Auto and home supply stores; Rebuilding
and retreading tires
PA: Mccarthy Tire Service Company Inc
340 Kidder St
Wilkes Barre PA 18702
570 822-3151

(G-5747)
PIG POUNDER LLC
Also Called: Pig Pounder Brewery
1107 Grecade St (27408-8709)

PHONE..............................336 255-1306
William Kotis, *Prin*
EMP: 9 **EST:** 2016
SALES (est): 517.23K **Privately Held**
Web: www.pigpounder.com
SIC: 2084 Wines

(G-5748)
PIKE ELECTRIC LLC
Also Called: Pike Electric
3511 W Market St (27403-4443)
PHONE..............................336 316-7068
EMP: 246
SALES (corp-wide): 1.08B **Privately Held**
Web: www.pike.com
SIC: 4911 3699 1731 Electric services;
Electrical equipment and supplies, nec;
Electrical work
HQ: Pike Electric, Llc
100 Pike Way
Mount Airy NC 27030
336 789-2171

(G-5749)
PIRANHA NAIL AND STAPLE INC
Also Called: Piranha
901 Norwalk St Ste E (27407-2039)
PHONE..............................336 852-8358
Mike Mitchell, *Pr*
EMP: 5 **EST:** 1999
SQ FT: 3,000
SALES (est): 2.19MM **Privately Held**
Web: www.piranhanail.com
SIC: 3399 5049 Metal fasteners; Precision
tools

(G-5750)
PITNEY BOWES INC
Also Called: Pitney Bowes
4161 Piedmont Pkwy (27410-8175)
PHONE..............................336 805-3320
EMP: 13
SALES (corp-wide): 2.03B **Publicly Held**
Web: www.pitneybowes.com
SIC: 3579 Postage meters
PA: Pitney Bowes Inc.
3001 Summer St
Stamford CT 06926
203 356-5000

(G-5751)
PLATESETTERSCOM
114 Industrial Ave (27406-4505)
PHONE..............................888 380-7483
EMP: 7 **EST:** 2016
SALES (est): 742.09K **Privately Held**
Web: www.platesetters.com
SIC: 2752 Commercial printing, lithographic

(G-5752)
POWER INTEGRITY CORP
2109 Patterson St (27407-2531)
P.O. Box 9682 (27429-0682)
PHONE..............................336 379-9773
James T Fesmire, *Pr*
Debbie Wilson, *VP*
EMP: 20 **EST:** 1980
SALES (est): 2.52MM **Privately Held**
Web: www.powerintegritycorp.com
SIC: 3629 3612 1731 Electronic generation
equipment; Transformers, except electric;
Electric power systems contractors

(G-5753)
POWERTAC USA INC
3702 Alliance Dr Ste C (27407-2052)
PHONE..............................919 239-4470
James Rath, *Prin*
Bamrung Carroll, *Prin*
Jian Li, *Prin*
EMP: 7 **EST:** 2017

SALES (est): 878.17K **Privately Held**
Web: www.powertac.com
SIC: 3648 Lighting equipment, nec

(G-5754)
PPG ARCHITECTURAL FINISHES INC
Also Called: Glidden Professional Paint Ctr
5103 W Market St (27409-2644)
PHONE..............................336 273-9761
Jim Fausett, *Genl Mgr*
EMP: 4
SALES (corp-wide): 17.65B **Publicly Held**
Web: www.ppgpaints.com
SIC: 2851 Paints and allied products
HQ: Ppg Architectural Finishes, Inc.
1 Ppg Pl
Pittsburgh PA 15272
412 434-3131

(G-5755)
PPG INDUSTRIES INC
4347 Baylor St (27455-2563)
PHONE..............................919 772-3093
EMP: 4
SALES (corp-wide): 17.65B **Publicly Held**
Web: www.ppg.com
SIC: 2851 3211 3231 3229 Paints and allied
products; Flat glass; Strengthened or
reinforced glass; Glass fiber products
PA: Ppg Industries, Inc.
1 Ppg Pl
Pittsburgh PA 15272
412 434-3131

(G-5756)
PPG INDUSTRIES INC
Also Called: Industrial Coatings
109 P P G Rd (27409-1801)
PHONE..............................336 856-9280
Scott Mcmillen, *Mgr*
EMP: 201
SALES (corp-wide): 17.65B **Publicly Held**
Web: www.ppg.com
SIC: 2851 Coating, air curing
PA: Ppg Industries, Inc.
1 Ppg Pl
Pittsburgh PA 15272
412 434-3131

(G-5757)
**PRECISION FABRICS GROUP INC
(PA)**
333 N Greene St Ste 100 (27401-2142)
PHONE..............................336 281-3049
Lanty Smith, *Ch*
Pat Burns, *
Walter Jones, *CEO*
◆ **EMP:** 49 **EST:** 1988
SALES (est): 198.9MM
SALES (corp-wide): 198.9MM **Privately
Held**
Web: www.precisionfabrics.com
SIC: 2262 2221 Decorative finishing of
manmade broadwoven fabrics; Manmade
and synthetic broadwoven fabrics

(G-5758)
PRECISION PRINTING
2832 Randleman Rd Ste D (27406-5158)
PHONE..............................336 273-5794
Wayne Willard, *Owner*
EMP: 4 **EST:** 1988
SALES (est): 241.58K **Privately Held**
SIC: 2752 Offset printing

(G-5759)
PRECISION WALLS INC
7215 Cessna Dr (27409-9685)
PHONE..............................336 852-7710
Bruce Wolfe, *Brnch Mgr*
EMP: 8

SALES (corp-wide): 131.34MM **Privately
Held**
Web: www.precisionwalls.com
SIC: 1743 5046 3275 2631 Tile installation,
ceramic; Partitions; Gypsum products;
Paperboard mills
PA: Precision Walls, Inc.
1230 N E Maynard Rd
Cary NC 27513
919 832-0380

(G-5760)
PRECOR INCORPORATED
1818 Youngs Mill Rd (27406-9060)
PHONE..............................336 603-1000
Chris Torgtler, *Brnch Mgr*
EMP: 233
SALES (corp-wide): 2.7B **Publicly Held**
Web: www.precor.com
SIC: 3949 Ammunition belts, sporting type
HQ: Precor Incorporated
24309 Snhmish Wdnville Rd
Woodinville WA 98072
425 486-9292

(G-5761)
PREMEDIA GROUP LLC
7605 Business Park Dr Ste F (27409-9460)
PHONE..............................336 274-2421
EMP: 13 **EST:** 2005
SQ FT: 20,000
SALES (est): 2.42MM **Privately Held**
Web: www.premediagroup.com
SIC: 2782 Account books

(G-5762)
PRETIUM PACKAGING LLC
Also Called: Pretium Packaging
3240 N Ohenry Blvd (27405-3808)
PHONE..............................336 621-1891
Jim Sitton, *Pr*
EMP: 50
SALES (corp-wide): 868.81MM **Privately
Held**
Web: www.pretiumpkg.com
SIC: 5199 3089 Packaging materials; Air
mattresses, plastics
PA: Pretium Packaging, L.L.C.
1555 Page Industrial Blvd
Saint Louis MO 63132
314 727-8200

(G-5763)
PREVOST CAR (US) INC (DH)
Also Called: Novabus
7817 National Service Rd (27409)
PHONE..............................908 222-7211
Gaetan Bolduc, *Pr*
▲ **EMP:** 35 **EST:** 1993
SALES (est): 97.88MM
SALES (corp-wide): 52.58B **Privately Held**
Web: www.prevostcar.com
SIC: 3711 5013 7539 3713 Buses, all types,
assembly of; Motor vehicle supplies and
new parts; Automotive repair shops, nec;
Truck and bus bodies
HQ: Volvo Trucks North America, Inc.
7900 National Service Rd
Greensboro NC 27409
336 393-2000

(G-5764)
PRINTERY
2100 Fairfax Rd Ste 101a (27407-3010)
PHONE..............................336 852-9774
Galen Hill, *Owner*
EMP: 10 **EST:** 1985
SQ FT: 4,500
SALES (est): 1.25MM **Privately Held**
Web: www.printeryweb.com

SIC: 2752 2791 Offset printing; Typesetting

(G-5765)
PRINTING SVCS GREENSBORO INC
Also Called: P S G
2206 N Church St (27405-4308)
PHONE.................................336 274-7663
Eddie Franklin Brame, Pr
Russ Brame, Treas
EMP: 4 EST: 1969
SQ FT: 29,000
SALES (est): 251.33K Privately Held
Web: www.phase3communications.com
SIC: 2752 7334 2791 2789 Offset printing;
Photocopying and duplicating services;
Typesetting; Bookbinding and related work

(G-5766)
PRO-FACE AMERICA LLC (HQ)
Also Called: Proface America
235 Burgess Rd Ste D (27409-9778)
PHONE.................................734 477-0600
Jeff Roberts, Off Mgr
▲ EMP: 48 EST: 1968
SALES (est): 2.33MM
SALES (corp-wide): 1.09K Privately Held
Web: www.profaceamerica.com
SIC: 3571 3575 3577 Minicomputers;
Computer terminals; Computer peripheral
equipment, nec
PA: Schneider Electric Se
35 Rue Joseph Monier
Rueil-Malmaison IDF
146046982

(G-5767)
PROCTER & GAMBLE MFG CO
Also Called: Procter & Gamble
100 S Swing Rd (27409-2006)
P.O. Box 18647 (27419-8647)
PHONE.................................336 954-0000
Mary Jane Harris, Brnch Mgr
EMP: 91
SALES (corp-wide): 84.04B Publicly Held
Web: us.pg.com
SIC: 2844 2676 3421 2842 Deodorants,
personal; Towels, napkins, and tissue paper
products; Razor blades and razors;
Specialty cleaning
HQ: The Procter & Gamble Manufacturing
Company
1 Procter And Gamble Plz
Cincinnati OH 45202
513 983-1100

(G-5768)
PROGRESSIVE TOOL & MFG INC
245 Standard Dr (27409-9600)
PHONE.................................336 664-1130
Daniel Thompson, Pr
Richard Thompson, VP
EMP: 18 EST: 1984
SQ FT: 15,000
SALES (est): 2.55MM Privately Held
Web: www.progtool.net
SIC: 3544 Special dies and tools

(G-5769)
PROXIMITY FOODS CORPORATION
Also Called: Proximity Bakery
1117 W Cornwallis Dr (27408-6331)
PHONE.................................336 691-1700
Natalie Hyde, Pr
EMP: 4 EST: 2003
SALES (est): 60.39K Privately Held
SIC: 2041 Bread and bread-type roll mixes

(G-5770)
PUBLIC HEALTH CORPS INC
Also Called: Sanicap
3300 Battleground Ave Ste 270
(27410-2465)

P.O. Box 39253 (27438-9253)
PHONE.................................336 545-2999
Bryan D Hill, Pr
Mari Solano, VP
EMP: 5 EST: 1993
SALES (est): 528.36K Privately Held
Web: www.sanicap.com
SIC: 2842 Industrial plant disinfectants or
deodorants

(G-5771)
PUROLATOR FACET INC (HQ)
Also Called: Purolator Advanced Filtration
8439 Triad Dr (27409-9018)
PHONE.................................336 668-4444
Russell D Stellfox, Pr
Richard Wolfson, *
David Fallon, *
▲ EMP: 40 EST: 1999
SQ FT: 90,000
SALES (est): 22.6MM
SALES (corp-wide): 19.93B Publicly Held
Web: www.purolator-afg.com
SIC: 3677 5085 3728 3564 Filtration
devices, electronic; Filters, industrial;
Aircraft parts and equipment, nec; Blowers
and fans
PA: Parker-Hannifin Corporation
6035 Parkland Blvd
Cleveland OH 44124
216 896-3000

(G-5772)
QORVO INC
7908 Piedmont Triad Pkwy Bldg D
(27409-9417)
PHONE.................................336 664-1233
Robert Bruggeworth, CEO
EMP: 147
SALES (corp-wide): 3.77B Publicly Held
Web: www.qorvo.com
SIC: 3674 Semiconductors and related
devices
PA: Qorvo, Inc.
7628 Thorndike Rd
Greensboro NC 27409
336 664-1233

(G-5773)
QORVO INC (PA)
Also Called: QORVO
7628 Thorndike Rd (27409-9421)
PHONE.................................336 664-1233
Robert A Bruggeworth, Pr
Walden C Rhines, *
Grant A Brown, Sr VP
Paul J Fego, Senior Vice President Global
Operations
Gina B Harrison, Corporate Vice President
EMP: 900 EST: 1957
SALES (est): 3.77B
SALES (corp-wide): 3.77B Publicly Held
Web: www.qorvo.com
SIC: 3674 3825 Semiconductors and related
devices; Oscillators, audio and radio
frequency (instrument types)

(G-5774)
**QORVO INTERNATIONAL HOLDG
INC (DH)**
7628 Thorndike Rd (27409-9421)
PHONE.................................336 664-1233
Robert A Bruggeworth, Pr
EMP: 10 EST: 2000
SALES (est): 715.36K
SALES (corp-wide): 3.77B Publicly Held
Web: www.qorvo.com
SIC: 3674 Semiconductors and related
devices
HQ: Qorvo Us, Inc.
2300 Ne Brookwood Pkwy

Hillsboro OR 97124
503 615-9000

(G-5775)
QORVO INTERNATIONAL SVCS INC
7628 Thorndike Rd (27409-9421)
PHONE.................................336 664-1233
Robert Bruggeworth, CEO
EMP: 7 EST: 2016
SALES (est): 914.17K
SALES (corp-wide): 3.77B Publicly Held
Web: www.qorvo.com
SIC: 3674 Semiconductors and related
devices
HQ: Qorvo Us, Inc.
2300 Ne Brookwood Pkwy
Hillsboro OR 97124
503 615-9000

(G-5776)
QORVO US INC
7907 Piedmont Triad Pkwy (27409-9457)
PHONE.................................336 662-1150
Vic Steel, Mgr
EMP: 7
SQ FT: 147,705
SALES (corp-wide): 3.77B Publicly Held
Web: www.qorvo.com
SIC: 3674 Semiconductors and related
devices
HQ: Qorvo Us, Inc.
2300 Ne Brookwood Pkwy
Hillsboro OR 97124
503 615-9000

(G-5777)
QORVO US INC
7914 Piedmont Triad Pkwy (27409-9417)
PHONE.................................336 931-8298
EMP: 42
SALES (corp-wide): 3.77B Publicly Held
Web: www.qorvo.com
SIC: 3674 Integrated circuits, semiconductor
networks, etc.
HQ: Qorvo Us, Inc.
2300 Ne Brookwood Pkwy
Hillsboro OR 97124
503 615-9000

(G-5778)
QUALITY HOUSING CORPORATION
Also Called: Insul Kor
1400 Battleground Ave Ste 205
(27408-8042)
PHONE.................................336 274-2622
S Sanders Junior, Pr
Major S Sanders Junior, Pr
Kenneth Lenz, Treas
Chris Samuels, Prin
EMP: 11 EST: 2000
SALES (est): 130.32K Privately Held
Web: www.gha-nc.org
SIC: 2452 Prefabricated wood buildings

(G-5779)
QUALITY PRTG CARTRIDGE FCTRY
Also Called: M C B Displays
6700 W Market St (27409-1890)
PHONE.................................336 852-2505
Bonnie Ferguson, Pr
Mary Beisner, VP
EMP: 6 EST: 1978
SQ FT: 5,800
SALES (est): 318.38K Privately Held
Web: www.qualityprinting.info
SIC: 2752 2791 2789 Offset printing;
Typesetting; Bookbinding and related work

(G-5780)
RALPH LAUREN CORPORATION
4100 Beechwood Dr (27425)
P.O. Box 35868 (27425)
PHONE.................................336 632-5000
EMP: 6
SALES (corp-wide): 6.63B Publicly Held
Web: www.ralphlauren.com
SIC: 2325 Men's and boy's trousers and
slacks
PA: Ralph Lauren Corporation
650 Madison Ave
New York NY 10022
212 318-7000

(G-5781)
RANDALL PRINTING INC
1029 Huffman St (27405-7209)
PHONE.................................336 272-3333
Charles Younts, Pr
Patricia Younts, VP
EMP: 8 EST: 1991
SQ FT: 4,598
SALES (est): 408.22K Privately Held
Web: www.randallprinting.com
SIC: 2752 7389 Offset printing; Printing
broker

(G-5782)
RESCO PRODUCTS INC
3600 W Wendover Ave (27407-1508)
PHONE.................................336 299-1441
EMP: 22 EST: 2019
SALES (est): 3.7MM Privately Held
Web: www.rescoproducts.com
SIC: 3255 Clay refractories

(G-5783)
RESCO PRODUCTS INC
North State Prophyllite Div
3600 W Wendover Ave (27407-1508)
P.O. Box 7247 (27417-0247)
PHONE.................................336 299-1441
R B Arthur Junior, VP
EMP: 10
SQ FT: 5,000
SALES (corp-wide): 178.92MM Privately
Held
Web: www.rescoproducts.com
SIC: 3255 3297 Ladle brick, clay; Cement:
high temperature, refractory (nonclay)
PA: Resco Products, Inc.
1 Robinson Plz Ste 300
Pittsburgh PA 15205
412 494-4491

(G-5784)
RESIDEO LLC
Also Called: ADI Global Distribution
4500 Green Point Dr Ste 103 (27409)
PHONE.................................336 668-3644
Anna Ferguson, Brnch Mgr
EMP: 6
SALES (corp-wide): 6.76B Publicly Held
Web: www.adiglobaldistribution.us
SIC: 5063 3669 Electrical apparatus and
equipment; Emergency alarms
HQ: Resideo Llc
275 Bradhollow Rd Ste 400
Melville NY 11747
631 692-1000

(G-5785)
RF MICRO DEVICES INC
Also Called: Rfmd
7628 Thorndike Rd (27409-9421)
PHONE.................................336 664-1233
▲ EMP: 3482
Web: www.qorvo.com
SIC: 3674 Semiconductors and related
devices

(G-5786)
RFMD LLC
7628 Thorndike Rd (27409-9421)
PHONE..................................336 664-1233
EMP: 143 **EST:** 2019
SALES (est): 6.31MM
SALES (corp-wide): 3.77B **Publicly Held**
Web: www.qorvo.com
SIC: 3674 Semiconductors and related
devices
PA: Qorvo, Inc.
7628 Thorndike Rd
Greensboro NC 27409
336 664-1233

(G-5787)
RHINOCEROS TIMES
Also Called: Hammer Publications
216 W Market St (27401-2504)
P.O. Box 9023 (27429-0023)
PHONE..................................336 763-4170
William Hammer, *Pt*
John Hammer, *Pt*
EMP: 5 **EST:** 1993
SQ FT: 4,500
SALES (est): 156.74K **Privately Held**
Web: www.rhinotimes.com
SIC: 2711 Newspapers, publishing and
printing

(G-5788)
RIDGEWOOD MANAGEMENT LLC
Also Called: Stonefield Homes
808 James Doak Pkwy (27455-8305)
PHONE..................................336 644-0006
Michelle James, *Mgr*
EMP: 4
SALES (est): 361.43K **Privately Held**
Web: www.ridgewoodswimtennis.net
SIC: 2451 Mobile homes

(G-5789)
RLM/UNIVERSAL PACKAGING INC
Also Called: Universal Packaging
8607 Cedar Hollow Rd (27455-8253)
PHONE..................................336 644-6161
Celeste C Manning, *Pr*
Rocky Manning, *VP*
EMP: 15 **EST:** 1996
SQ FT: 70,000
SALES (est): 709.29K **Privately Held**
SIC: 2653 5113 7319 5199 Corrugated and
solid fiber boxes; Corrugated and solid fiber
boxes; Display advertising service;
Packaging materials

(G-5790)
ROBERT D STARR
Also Called: Starr's Party Ice
1211 Youngs Mill Rd (27405-9650)
PHONE..................................336 697-0286
Robert Starr, *Owner*
EMP: 5 **EST:** 1963
SALES (est): 265.95K **Privately Held**
SIC: 2097 Manufactured ice

(G-5791)
ROBIX AMERICA INC
7104 Cessna Dr (27409-9793)
PHONE..................................336 668-9555
▲ **EMP:** 210
SQ FT: 65,000
SALES (est): 15.7MM **Privately Held**
Web: www.canplast.com
SIC: 2891 2821 Adhesives; Polyvinyl
chloride resins, PVC

(G-5792)
ROCK-WELD INDUSTRIES INC
3515 Associate Dr (27405-3879)

PHONE..................................336 375-6862
Chris Salter, *Pr*
Mike Salter, *VP*
EMP: 9 **EST:** 1946
SQ FT: 17,000
SALES (est): 1.37MM **Privately Held**
Web: www.rockweld.com
SIC: 3545 5084 Diamond cutting tools for
turning, boring, burnishing, etc.; Drilling bits

(G-5793)
ROEHRIG ENGINEERING INC
Also Called: MTS Systems Roehrig
603 Woodland Dr (27408-7416)
P.O. Box 728 (27299-0728)
PHONE..................................336 956-3800
Kurt Roehrig, *Pr*
Scott Treichler, *VP*
Carmella Roehrig, *Treas*
Kimberly Elliot, *Sec*
EMP: 4 **EST:** 1977
SQ FT: 2,500
SALES (est): 2.24MM
SALES (corp-wide): 16.11B **Publicly Held**
Web: www.roehrigengineering.com
SIC: 3829 8711 Physical property testing
equipment; Consulting engineer
HQ: Mts Systems Corporation
14000 Technology Dr
Eden Prairie MN 55344
952 937-4000

(G-5794)
ROOBRIK INC
301 S Elm St Ste 421 (27401)
PHONE..................................919 667-7750
Nate O'keefe, *CEO*
EMP: 5 **EST:** 2015
SALES (est): 3.33MM **Privately Held**
Web: www.roobrik.com
SIC: 7372 Business oriented computer
software

(G-5795)
ROUTH SIGN SERVICE
318 Creek Ridge Rd Ste B (27406-4459)
PHONE..................................336 272-0895
John Humble, *Owner*
EMP: 6 **EST:** 1984
SQ FT: 2,200
SALES (est): 426.9K **Privately Held**
Web: www.routhsigns.com
SIC: 3993 Signs and advertising specialties

(G-5796)
ROYAL CAROLINA CORPORATION
7305 Old Friendly Rd (27410-6236)
PHONE..................................336 292-8845
Felix A Euforbia, *Ch Bd*
Alice E Parker, *
▼ **EMP:** 32 **EST:** 1971
SQ FT: 71,500
SALES (est): 5.01MM **Privately Held**
Web: www.royalcarolina.com
SIC: 3229 Fiber optics strands

(G-5797)
**RUSSELL STANDARD
CORPORATION**
1124 S Holden Rd (27407-2914)
PHONE..................................336 292-6875
EMP: 15
SALES (corp-wide): 97.54MM **Privately
Held**
Web: www.russellstandard.com
SIC: 1611 2951 Highway and street paving
contractor; Asphalt paving mixtures and
blocks
PA: Russell Standard Corporation
285 Kappa Dr Ste 300
Pittsburgh PA 15238

412 449-0700

(G-5798)
RUSSELL STANDARD NC LLC
Also Called: Russell Standard
1124 S Holden Rd (27407-2914)
PHONE..................................336 292-6875
Matthew Wjohnson, *Mgr*
EMP: 74 **EST:** 2008
SALES (est): 3.75MM
SALES (corp-wide): 97.54MM **Privately
Held**
SIC: 2951 Asphalt paving mixtures and
blocks
PA: Russell Standard Corporation
285 Kappa Dr Ste 300
Pittsburgh PA 15238
412 449-0700

(G-5799)
RUSSELL-FSHION FOOT HSY MLLS I
3804 Buncombe Dr (27407-7326)
P.O. Box 732 (27371-0732)
PHONE..................................336 299-0741
William J Sullivan, *Pr*
EMP: 5 **EST:** 1988
SALES (est): 171.84K **Privately Held**
Web: www.russellsocks.com
SIC: 2252 Socks

(G-5800)
SAFETY & SECURITY INTL INC
4270 Piedmont Pkwy Ste 102 (27410-8161)
PHONE..................................336 285-8673
Michael Dix, *Pr*
Brittany Grady, *Dir Opers*
EMP: 8 **EST:** 2009
SQ FT: 1,500
SALES (est): 5.15MM **Privately Held**
Web: www.safesecint.com
SIC: 3728 2311 Military aircraft equipment
and armament; Military uniforms, men's
and youths': purchased materials

(G-5801)
SAGE MULE
608 Battleground Ave (27401-2015)
PHONE..................................336 209-9183
EMP: 4 **EST:** 2019
SALES (est): 373.6K **Privately Held**
Web: www.thesagemule.com
SIC: 2099 Food preparations, nec

(G-5802)
SARAHS SALSA INC
622 Myers Ln (27408-7522)
PHONE..................................336 508-3033
Sarah Ward, *Pr*
Susan Kennedy, *VP*
Katherine Meadows, *VP*
Wes Ward, *Sec*
Mike Kennedy, *CFO*
EMP: 5 **EST:** 2005
SALES (est): 159.65K **Privately Held**
SIC: 2099 Salads, fresh or refrigerated

(G-5803)
SC JOHNSON PROF USA INC
2408 Doyle St (27406-2912)
PHONE..................................704 263-4240
EMP: 51
Web: www.scjp.com
SIC: 2841 Textile soap
HQ: Sc Johnson Professional Usa, Inc.
2815 Clseum Cntre Dr Ste
Charlotte NC 28217

(G-5804)
SECOND EARTH INC
3716 Alliance Dr Ste C (27407-2387)

PHONE..................................336 740-9333
Robert Haskin, *CEO*
Gary Slack, *CFO*
EMP: 5 **EST:** 2010
SALES (est): 377.93K **Privately Held**
SIC: 2899 5999 Water treating compounds;
Water purification equipment

(G-5805)
SEE CLEARLY INC
Also Called: Sippin Snax Cft Beer Wine Snck
207 S Westgate Dr Ste B (27407-1655)
PHONE..................................929 464-6887
Melissa Wallace, *CEO*
EMP: 4 **EST:** 2010
SALES (est): 150K **Privately Held**
SIC: 2068 Nuts: dried, dehydrated, salted or
roasted

(G-5806)
SELPRO LLC
408 Gallimore Dairy Rd Ste C (27409)
PHONE..................................336 513-0550
Kerry Martin, *Prin*
▲ **EMP:** 8 **EST:** 2010
SALES (est): 1.12MM **Privately Held**
Web: www.norbridgecabinets.com
SIC: 2434 Wood kitchen cabinets

(G-5807)
**SENNETT SECURITY PRODUCTS
LLC (PA)**
21 Beech Ridge Ct (27455-1278)
PHONE..................................336 404-3284
Michelle Finn, *Pr*
Sandra Lane, *Managing Member*
James Tolbert, *Dir*
▲ **EMP:** 7 **EST:** 1987
SQ FT: 2,500
SALES (est): 9.9MM
SALES (corp-wide): 9.9MM **Privately Held**
Web: www.sspsecure.com
SIC: 2752 Commercial printing, lithographic

(G-5808)
SENSORY ANALYTICS LLC
405b Pomona Dr (27407-1431)
PHONE..................................336 315-6090
Greg Frisby, *CEO*
EMP: 49 **EST:** 2004
SALES (est): 12.93MM **Privately Held**
Web: www.specmetrix.com
SIC: 3826 Analytical optical instruments

(G-5809)
SHAMROCK CORPORATION (PA)
Also Called: Innisbrook Wraps
422 N Chimney Rock Rd (27410-6249)
P.O. Box 19448 (27419-9448)
PHONE..................................336 574-4200
Alexander W Worth, *Pr*
David M Worth, *
Robert P Worth, *
◆ **EMP:** 125 **EST:** 1957
SQ FT: 253,000
SALES (est): 20.79MM
SALES (corp-wide): 20.79MM **Privately
Held**
Web: www.shamrockwraps.com
SIC: 2754 Rotogravure printing

(G-5810)
SHERWIN-WILLIAMS COMPANY
Also Called: Sherwin-Williams
113 Stage Coach Trl (27409-1859)
PHONE..................................336 292-3000
Mark Hamilton, *Mgr*
EMP: 43
SQ FT: 20,048
SALES (corp-wide): 23.1B **Publicly Held**
Web: www.sherwin-williams.com

SIC: 5231 5198 2851 Paint; Paints; Coating, air curing
PA: The Sherwin-Williams Company
101 W Prospect Ave
Cleveland OH 44115
216 566-2000

(G-5811)
SID JENKINS INC
Also Called: Tiffany Marble Company
3004 Harnett Dr (27407-6102)
PHONE..........................336 632-0707
Sid Jenkins, *Pr*
Jano Jenkins, *Sec*
▲ EMP: 5 EST: 1975
SQ FT: 5,000
SALES (est): 102.76K **Privately Held**
SIC: 5032 1793 3496 3281 Brick, stone, and related material; Glass and glazing work; Miscellaneous fabricated wire products; Cut stone and stone products

(G-5812)
SIERRA SOFTWARE LLC
Also Called: Acetrace
143 Industrial Ave (27406-4504)
PHONE..........................877 285-2867
Bradley Snyder, *Prin*
EMP: 7 EST: 2013
SALES (est): 2.57MM **Privately Held**
Web: www.sierrasoftwarellc.com
SIC: 7372 Prepackaged software

(G-5813)
SIMONTIC COMPOSITE INC
2901 E Gate City Blvd Ste 2500 (27401-4898)
PHONE..........................336 897-9885
Simon Senibi, *CEO*
EMP: 20 EST: 2010
SALES (est): 478.08K **Privately Held**
Web: simonticcomposite.comcastbiz.net
SIC: 3999 Advertising curtains

(G-5814)
SINGLEY SPECIALTY CO INC
1025 Willowbrook Dr (27403-2059)
PHONE..........................336 852-8581
Charles P Kennedy, *Pr*
S B Kennedy, *Sec*
EMP: 6 EST: 1952
SQ FT: 2,000
SALES (est): 385.47K **Privately Held**
SIC: 3553 Sanding machines, except portable floor sanders: woodworking

(G-5815)
SKINNER COMPANY
414 E Montcastle Dr (27406-5387)
PHONE..........................336 580-4716
EMP: 4 EST: 2017
SALES (est): 54.38K **Privately Held**
Web: www.skinnerco.com
SIC: 3429 Hardware, nec

(G-5816)
SKYWORKS SOLUTIONS INC
406 Gallimore Dairy Rd (27409-9725)
PHONE..........................336 291-4200
EMP: 21
SALES (corp-wide): 4.18B **Publicly Held**
Web: www.skyworksinc.com
SIC: 3674 Semiconductors and related devices
PA: Skyworks Solutions, Inc.
5260 California Ave
Irvine CA 92617
949 231-3000

(G-5817)
SMART MACHINE TECHNOLOGIES INC
Also Called: Fmt Food and Beverage Systems
2105 Mimosa Dr (27403)
P.O. Box 4828 (24115)
PHONE..........................276 632-9853
Richard Gibb, *Ch*
Mark Gibb, *
Kim Wehrenberg, *
Duane Doerle, *
▲ EMP: 65 EST: 1976
SALES (est): 8.4MM **Privately Held**
Web: www.smartmachine.com
SIC: 3556 3552 5084 3469 Food products machinery; Textile machinery; Food product manufacturing machinery; Metal stampings, nec

(G-5818)
SMITH ARCHITECTURAL METALS LLC
4536 S Holden Rd (27406-9510)
P.O. Box 16303 (27416-0303)
PHONE..........................336 273-1970
EMP: 30 EST: 1997
SQ FT: 30,000
SALES (est): 5.43MM **Privately Held**
Web: www.smithmetals.net
SIC: 3441 Fabricated structural metal

(G-5819)
SNAP PUBLICATIONS LLC
Also Called: Rhino Times
216 W Market St Ste A (27401-2504)
P.O. Box 9846 (27429-0846)
PHONE..........................336 274-8531
Roy Carroll, *Managing Member*
EMP: 4 EST: 2013
SALES (est): 215.22K **Privately Held**
Web: www.rhinotimes.com
SIC: 2711 Newspapers, publishing and printing

(G-5820)
SNIDER TIRE INC
330 E Lindsay St (27401-2924)
PHONE..........................336 691-5480
Marty Snider, *Mgr*
EMP: 17
SALES (corp-wide): 501.16MM **Privately Held**
Web: www.sniderfleet.com
SIC: 5531 7534 7538 Automotive tires; Tire recapping; General automotive repair shops
PA: Snider Tire, Inc.
1081 Red Ventures Dr
Fort Mill SC 29707
800 528-2840

(G-5821)
SOLVEKTA LLC
2110 Rockglen Ln (27410-2481)
PHONE..........................336 944-4677
EMP: 4 EST: 2012
SALES (est): 174.2K **Privately Held**
Web: www.solvekta.com
SIC: 2834 Pharmaceutical preparations

(G-5822)
SOUTH / WIN LLC (DH)
112 Maxfield Rd (27405-8643)
P.O. Box 20461 (27420-0461)
PHONE..........................336 398-5650
William H Dubose, *Pr*
EMP: 57 EST: 1987
SALES (est): 21.39MM
SALES (corp-wide): 741.18MM **Privately Held**
Web: www.highlinewarren.com

SIC: 2841 5169 Detergents, synthetic organic or inorganic alkaline; Detergents
HQ: Highline Warren Llc
8700 W Trail Lk Dr Ste 30
Memphis TN 38125
800 986-2211

(G-5823)
SOUTHEASTER PLASTIC INC
Also Called: Southeastern Plastics
605 Diamond Hill Ct (27406-4617)
P.O. Box 36256 (27416-6256)
PHONE..........................336 275-6616
Al Faust, *Prin*
Al Faust, *Pr*
David Faust, *VP*
EMP: 10 EST: 1980
SQ FT: 4,500
SALES (est): 1.09MM **Privately Held**
Web: www.seplastics.com
SIC: 3089 Injection molding of plastics

(G-5824)
SOUTHEASTERN DIE OF NC
510 Corliss St (27406-5272)
PHONE..........................336 275-5212
Bert Ficquette, *Genl Mgr*
EMP: 4 EST: 2010
SALES (est): 299.13K **Privately Held**
SIC: 3544 Special dies and tools

(G-5825)
SOUTHERN DIGITAL WATCH REPAIR
4009 Groometown Rd (27407-7915)
PHONE..........................336 299-6718
Betty Matthews, *Owner*
EMP: 5 EST: 1978
SALES (est): 429.79K **Privately Held**
SIC: 3873 7631 Clocks, except timeclocks; Watch repair

(G-5826)
SOUTHERN HOME SPA AND WTR PDTS
Also Called: Southern Home Spa & Water Pdts
105 Edwardia Dr (27409-2601)
PHONE..........................336 286-3564
TOLL FREE: 800
John J Mathews, *Pr*
EMP: 4 EST: 1981
SQ FT: 4,700
SALES (est): 184.61K **Privately Held**
Web: www.southernhomespas.com
SIC: 3999 7991 Hot tubs; Spas

(G-5827)
SOUTHERN RUBBER COMPANY INC
2209 Patterson St (27407-2533)
PHONE..........................336 299-2456
H Edward Bowman, *Pr*
David J Delman, *
Carol S Bowman, *
EMP: 29 EST: 1925
SQ FT: 30,000
SALES (est): 7.42MM **Privately Held**
Web: www.southernrubber.com
SIC: 3053 5085 Gaskets, all materials; Rubber goods, mechanical

(G-5828)
SOUTHERN TRADE PUBLICATIONS CO (PA)
6520 Airport Center Dr Ste 204 (27409-9072)
P.O. Box 7344 (27417-0344)
PHONE..........................336 454-3516
Emmet D Atkins Iii, *Pr*
EMP: 5 EST: 1957
SALES (est): 113.92K

SALES (corp-wide): 113.92K **Privately Held**
Web: www.southernphc.com
SIC: 2721 Trade journals: publishing only, not printed on site

(G-5829)
SPECIALIZED PACKAGING RADISSON LLC
Also Called: Specialized Packaging Flexo
600 Industrial Ave (27406-4604)
PHONE..........................336 574-1513
EMP: 75
SIC: 2657 Folding paperboard boxes

(G-5830)
SPORTSEDGE INC
3425 Derby Pl (27405-3601)
P.O. Box 837 (28166-0837)
PHONE..........................704 528-0188
Russell Petty, *Prin*
EMP: 19 EST: 1997
SALES (est): 224.36K **Privately Held**
Web: www.sportsedge.com
SIC: 3949 Sporting and athletic goods, nec

(G-5831)
SPRING AIR MATTRESS CORP
401 N Raleigh St (27401-4842)
P.O. Box 20028 (27420-0028)
PHONE..........................336 272-1141
John R Grove Senior, *CEO*
Frank Grove Iii, *Ch Bd*
Mathew Grove, *
John R Grove Senior, *Pr*
EMP: 85 EST: 1926
SQ FT: 80,000
SALES (est): 8.21MM **Privately Held**
Web: www.mattressgrove.com
SIC: 2515 Mattresses, innerspring or box spring

(G-5832)
SPRING REPAIR SERVICE INC
Also Called: Olens B Enterprises
5800 W Gate City Blvd (27407-7097)
PHONE..........................336 299-5660
Harry Owensby, *Pr*
Larry J Owensby, *Sec*
EMP: 6 EST: 1954
SQ FT: 5,000
SALES (est): 473.07K **Privately Held**
Web: www.angelakenbokphotography.com
SIC: 7699 7538 3715 7519 Welding equipment repair; General automotive repair shops; Truck trailers; Trailer rental

(G-5833)
ST JOHNS PACKAGING USA LLC
Also Called: North State Flexibles
2619 Phoenix Dr (27406-6320)
P.O. Box 5466 (27435)
PHONE..........................336 292-9911
T W Mages, *
Bill M Wentz, *
W Battle Wall, *
Tim Mages, *
▲ EMP: 190 EST: 1997
SQ FT: 122,000
SALES (est): 26.36MM **Privately Held**
Web: www.sjpack.com
SIC: 2671 7336 2759 Paper; coated and laminated packaging; Package design; Commercial printing, nec

(G-5834)
STAGE DECORATION AND SUPS INC
Also Called: Stage Dec
3519 Associate Dr (27405-3879)
PHONE..........................336 621-5454

▲ = Import ▼ = Export
◆ = Import/Export

Robert J Thurston, *Pr*
Eric Lowell, *Sec*
Melanie Baynes, *VP*
Beth Cole, *Treas*
▲ **EMP:** 6 **EST:** 1923
SQ FT: 13,500
SALES (est): 624.72K **Privately Held**
Web: www.stagedec.com
SIC: 3999 7922 2391 Stage hardware and
equipment, except lighting; Equipment
rental, theatrical; Curtains and draperies

(G-5835)
**STAMPING & SCRAPBOOKING RM
INC**
2806 Randleman Rd (27406-5265)
PHONE...............................336 389-9538
Eric Sarachik, *VP*
EMP: 4 **EST:** 2005
SALES (est): 65.17K **Privately Held**
SIC: 8299 2782 Arts and crafts schools;
Scrapbooks, albums, and diaries

(G-5836)
STANDARD TOOLS AND EQP CO
Also Called: Tools USA
4810 Clover Rd (27405-9607)
PHONE...............................336 697-7177
Kat Mendenhall, *CEO*
Robert G Shepley, *
◆ **EMP:** 28 **EST:** 1996
SQ FT: 67,000
SALES (est): 6MM **Privately Held**
Web: www.paint-booths.com
SIC: 3444 Booths, spray: prefabricated
sheet metal

(G-5837)
STATE ELECTRIC SUPPLY COMPANY
2709 Patterson St (27407-2316)
PHONE...............................336 855-8200
Rick Sheets, *Mgr*
EMP: 11
SALES (corp-wide): 303.01MM **Privately
Held**
Web: www.stateelectric.com
SIC: 5063 3625 Electrical supplies, nec;
Motor control accessories, including
overload relays
HQ: State Electric Supply Company
2010 2nd Ave
Huntington WV 25703
304 523-7491

(G-5838)
STAUNTON CAPITAL INC (PA)
Also Called: Rwm Casters
3406 W Wendover Ave Ste E (27407-1527)
P.O. Box 668 (28053-0668)
PHONE...............................704 866-8533
Peter D Comeau, *Pr*
EMP: 49 **EST:** 1948
SQ FT: 87,000
SALES (est): 12.28MM **Privately Held**
Web: www.rwmcasters.com
SIC: 3562 Casters

(G-5839)
**STERLING PRODUCTS
CORPORATION**
Also Called: Sterling Sign
3924 S Holden Rd (27406-8962)
P.O. Box 7069 (27417-0069)
PHONE...............................646 423-3175
Robert P Hilemn, *Pr*
EMP: 4 **EST:** 1986
SALES (est): 86.17K **Privately Held**
SIC: 3993 Signs and advertising specialties

(G-5840)
STEVENS PACKING INC
Also Called: Triad Meats
3023 Randleman Rd (27406-6610)
PHONE...............................336 274-6033
Darren Keith Stevens, *Pr*
EMP: 6 **EST:** 2004
SALES (est): 519.39K **Privately Held**
Web: www.triadmeat.com
SIC: 5421 5411 5147 2013 Meat markets,
including freezer provisioners; Grocery
stores; Meats and meat products;
Sausages and other prepared meats

(G-5841)
STITCHMASTER LLC
Also Called: Stitchmaster
309 S Regional Rd (27409-9674)
PHONE...............................336 852-6448
EMP: 11 **EST:** 1984
SQ FT: 1,000
SALES (est): 242.31K **Privately Held**
Web: www.stitchmaster.com
SIC: 7374 2395 3999 Computer graphics
service; Embroidery and art needlework;
Embroidery kits

(G-5842)
**STOCKHAUSEN SUPERABSORBER
LLC (DH)**
2401 Doyle St (27406)
PHONE...............................336 333-7540
Frank Canepa, *Managing Member*
Michael Terhart, *Genl Mgr*
EMP: 20 **EST:** 2021
SQ FT: 50
SALES (est): 126.33MM
SALES (corp-wide): 16.03B **Privately Held**
Web: www.stockhausen.com
SIC: 2821 Acrylic resins
HQ: Evonik Corporation
2 Turner Pl
Piscataway NJ 08854
732 981-5060

(G-5843)
STRANDBERG ENGRG LABS INC
1302 N Ohenry Blvd (27405-6768)
PHONE...............................336 274-3775
John A Strandberg, *Pr*
EMP: 10 **EST:** 1949
SQ FT: 31,000
SALES (est): 979.79K **Privately Held**
Web: www.strandberg.com
SIC: 3823 3822 3625 Industrial process
control instruments; Environmental controls
; Relays and industrial controls

(G-5844)
SUMMIT AVIATION INC
243 Burgess Rd Ste A (27409-9314)
PHONE...............................302 834-5400
Ralph Kunz, *Pr*
EMP: 16
SALES (corp-wide): 441.54MM **Publicly
Held**
Web: www.summitaviationmfg.com
SIC: 3721 4581 Aircraft; Airports, flying
fields, and services
HQ: Summit Aviation, Inc.
4200 Summit Bridge Rd
Middletown DE 19709
302 834-5400

(G-5845)
SUPERSKINSYSTEMS INC
3329 N Rockingham Rd (27407-7270)
PHONE...............................336 601-6005
Stuart Smith, *Prin*
EMP: 4 **EST:** 2010
SALES (est): 149.91K **Privately Held**

SIC: 2821 Plastics materials and resins

(G-5846)
SURTECO USA INC
Also Called: Surteco SE
7104 Cessna Dr (27409-9793)
PHONE...............................336 668-9555
Friedhelm Pafgen, *Ch*
Tim Valters, *Pr*
Kenneth Seeto, *Sec*
▲ **EMP:** 50 **EST:** 2008
SQ FT: 65,000
SALES (est): 16.14MM
SALES (corp-wide): 292.57MM **Privately
Held**
Web: www.surteco.com
SIC: 3089 Bands, plastics
HQ: Surteco Group Se
Johan-Viktor-Bausch-Str. 2
Buttenwiesen BY 86647
827499880

(G-5847)
SWK TECHNOLOGIES INC
2309 W Cone Blvd Ste 220 (27408-4047)
PHONE...............................336 230-0200
Christopher Oates, *Brnch Mgr*
EMP: 10
SALES (corp-wide): 85.32MM **Publicly
Held**
Web: www.swktech.com
SIC: 7372 Business oriented computer
software
HQ: Swk Technologies, Inc.
120 Eagle Rock Ave # 330
East Hanover NJ 07936

(G-5848)
SYD INC
Also Called: American Sign
5223c W Market St Ste C (27409-2629)
PHONE...............................336 294-8807
Mike Linville, *CEO*
EMP: 7 **EST:** 1990
SQ FT: 1,300
SALES (est): 282.65K **Privately Held**
Web: www.theamericansignshop.com
SIC: 3993 Signs and advertising specialties

(G-5849)
SYSTEL BUSINESS EQP CO INC
Also Called: Systel Office Automation
3517 W Wendover Ave (27407-1505)
PHONE...............................336 808-8000
Jeff Dalto, *Mgr*
EMP: 42
SALES (corp-wide): 50.23MM **Privately
Held**
Web: www.systeloa.com
SIC: 5044 2752 Copying equipment;
Publication printing, lithographic
PA: Systel Business Equipment Co., Inc.
2604 Fort Bragg Rd
Fayetteville NC 28303
910 483-7114

(G-5850)
**TALLEY MACHINERY
CORPORATION (HQ)**
7009 Cessna Dr (27409-9792)
PHONE...............................336 664-0012
Randy Vansparrentak, *VP*
◆ **EMP:** 5 **EST:** 1902
SQ FT: 14,750
SALES (est): 4.52MM
SALES (corp-wide): 36.56MM **Privately
Held**
Web: www.tingue.com
SIC: 3582 5087 Commercial laundry
equipment; Laundry equipment and supplies
PA: Tingue, Brown & Co.

535 N Midland Ave
Saddle Brook NJ 07663
201 796-4490

(G-5851)
TAPESTRIES LTD
Also Called: Debbing Inspirations
6 Westmount Ct (27410-2183)
PHONE...............................336 883-9864
Nancy Herman, *Pr*
Andrew Kane, *Sec*
▲ **EMP:** 6 **EST:** 1973
SQ FT: 2,300
SALES (est): 211.01K **Privately Held**
Web: www.heirloomtapestries.com
SIC: 5023 2221 Decorative home furnishings
and supplies; Upholstery, tapestry, and wall
covering fabrics

(G-5852)
TAR HEEL CREDIT COUNCILING
2223 N Church St (27405-4307)
PHONE...............................336 254-0348
Latonya Swift, *Pt*
EMP: 6 **EST:** 2011
SALES (est): 283.06K **Privately Held**
SIC: 2865 Tar

(G-5853)
TAXATION STATION LLC
800 W Smith St Ste 209 (27401-1960)
PHONE...............................336 209-3933
Jessica Smith, *CEO*
EMP: 5 **EST:** 2021
SALES (est): 267.67K **Privately Held**
SIC: 3999 Massage machines, electric:
barber and beauty shops

(G-5854)
TBC RETAIL GROUP INC
Also Called: Ntb
2514 Battleground Ave Ste B (27408-1938)
PHONE...............................336 540-8066
William Miller, *Brnch Mgr*
EMP: 8
SQ FT: 12,099
SALES (corp-wide): 2.41B **Privately Held**
Web: jobs.tbccorp.com
SIC: 7534 7539 Tire repair shop; Brake
services
HQ: Tbc Retail Group, Inc.
4280 Prof Ctr Dr Ste 400
Palm Beach Gardens FL 33410
561 383-3000

(G-5855)
TE CONNECTIVITY CORPORATION
8300 Triad Dr (27409-9621)
PHONE...............................336 428-7200
EMP: 12
SALES (corp-wide): 9.17B **Privately Held**
Web: www.te.com
SIC: 3678 Electronic connectors
HQ: Te Connectivity Corporation
1050 Westlakes Dr
Berwyn PA 19312
610 893-9800

(G-5856)
TE CONNECTIVITY CORPORATION
Also Called: Tyco Electronics
8000 Piedmont Triad Pkwy (27409-9407)
PHONE...............................336 664-7000
Randy Krull, *Brnch Mgr*
EMP: 104
SALES (corp-wide): 9.17B **Privately Held**
Web: www.te.com
SIC: 3678 Electronic connectors
HQ: Te Connectivity Corporation
1050 Westlakes Dr
Berwyn PA 19312
610 893-9800

(G-5857)

TE CONNECTIVITY CORPORATION
719 Pegg Rd Bldg 253 (27409-9672)
PHONE....................................336 665-4400
John Cramfort, *Brnch Mgr*
EMP: 237
SALES (corp-wide): 9.17B **Privately Held**
Web: careers.te.com
SIC: 3678 3471 Electronic connectors;
Plating and polishing
HQ: Te Connectivity Corporation
1050 Westlakes Dr
Berwyn PA 19312
610 893-9800

(G-5858)

TENCARVA MACHINERY COMPANY LLC
Essco
1800 Sullivan St (27405-7216)
PHONE....................................336 665-1435
Stan Shelton, *Brnch Mgr*
EMP: 8
SALES (corp-wide): 235.69MM **Privately Held**
Web: www.tencarva.com
SIC: 5063 3613 7694 Motors, electric;
Control panels, electric; Electric motor repair
HQ: Tencarva Machinery Company, Llc
1115 Pleasant Ridge Rd
Greensboro NC 27409
336 665-1435

(G-5859)

TEVA PHARMACEUTICALS USA INC
100 S Swing Rd (27409-2006)
PHONE....................................336 316-4132
Bob Cowan, *Finance*
EMP: 52
Web: www.tevausa.com
SIC: 2834 Pharmaceutical preparations
HQ: Teva Pharmaceuticals Usa, Inc.
400 Interpace Pkwy Bldg A
Parsippany NJ 07054
215 591-3000

(G-5860)

TEXINNOVATE INC
7109 Cessna Dr (27409-9793)
PHONE....................................336 279-7800
Jeffrey W Bruner, *Pr*
Robert Benko, *
Elaine Miller, *
EMP: 39 EST: 2017
SALES (est): 1.61MM **Privately Held**
Web: www.hempblack.com
SIC: 2221 Broadwoven fabric mills, manmade

(G-5861)

TEXTRON AVIATION INC
Also Called: Cessna Grnsboro Cttion Svc Ctr
615 Service Center Rd (27410-6250)
PHONE....................................336 605-7000
Jack Blondeau, *Genl Mgr*
EMP: 145
SALES (corp-wide): 13.7B **Publicly Held**
Web: www.txtav.com
SIC: 3721 4581 Airplanes, fixed or rotary
wing; Aircraft servicing and repairing
HQ: Textron Aviation Inc.
1 Cessna Blvd
Wichita KS 67215
316 517-6000

(G-5862)

THEM INTERNATIONAL INC
1005 N Eugene St (27401-1612)
PHONE....................................336 855-7880
Mike Stokes, *Pr*
Robert Darby, *VP*

▼ EMP: 6 EST: 1985
SALES (est): 271.64K **Privately Held**
Web: www.them-int.com
SIC: 3089 Plastics containers, except foam

(G-5863)

THOMCO INC
2005 Boulevard St Ste F (27407-4557)
P.O. Box 130 (27868-0130)
PHONE....................................336 292-3300
Stephen R Thompson, *Pr*
Jim Gibbons, *VP*
EMP: 5 EST: 1980
SQ FT: 2,200
SALES (est): 890.02K **Privately Held**
Web: www.thomcoincorporated.com
SIC: 3577 2759 5113 2657 Bar code
(magnetic ink) printers; Labels and seals:
printing, nsk; Containers, paper and
disposable plastic; Folding paperboard
boxes

(G-5864)

THOMPSON TRADERS INC
2024 E Market St (27401-3345)
P.O. Box 7404 (27417-0404)
PHONE....................................336 272-3003
Cliff Thompson, *Pr*
Alexandria Thompson, *VP*
◆ EMP: 15 EST: 1995
SQ FT: 28,000
SALES (est): 4.72MM **Privately Held**
Web: www.thompsontraders.com
SIC: 3431 Sinks: enameled iron, cast iron, or
pressed metal

(G-5865)

THUNDRBIRD MLDING GRNSBORO LLC
Also Called: Bright Plastic
7205 Cessna Dr (27409-9685)
PHONE....................................336 668-3636
EMP: 16
SALES (corp-wide): 157.67MM **Privately Held**
Web: www.brightplastics.com
SIC: 3089 Injection molding of plastics
HQ: Thunderbird Molding Greensboro Llc
4833 W Gate City Blvd
Greensboro NC 27407
336 668-3636

(G-5866)

THUNDRBIRD MLDING GRNSBORO LLC (DH)
4833 W Gate City Blvd (27407-5305)
PHONE....................................336 668-3636
Kirk Sparks, *Pr*
Mackenzie Bone Ctrl, *Prin*
EMP: 48 EST: 2022
SALES: 16.69MM
SALES (corp-wide): 157.67MM **Privately Held**
Web: www.brightplastics.com
SIC: 3089 Injection molding of plastics
HQ: Thunderbird Parent Plastics Llc
900 Commerce Dr Ste 105
Oak Brook IL

(G-5867)

TK ELEVATOR CORPORATION
22 Oak Branch Dr Ste C (27407-2448)
PHONE....................................336 272-4563
Brian James, *Brnch Mgr*
EMP: 83
SALES (corp-wide): 2.67MM **Privately Held**
Web: www.thyssenkrupp.com
SIC: 5084 7699 3999 Elevators; Elevators:
inspection, service, and repair; Wheelchair
lifts

HQ: Tk Elevator Corporation
788 Crcle 75 Pkwy Se Ste
Atlanta GA 30339
678 319-3240

(G-5868)

TRANE US INC
Also Called: Trane
3101 S Elm Eugene St # 100 (27406-5201)
PHONE....................................336 273-6353
John White, *Mgr*
EMP: 8
Web: www.trane.com
SIC: 3585 Refrigeration and heating
equipment
HQ: Trane U.S. Inc.
800-E Beaty St
Davidson NC 28036
704 655-4000

(G-5869)

TRANE US INC
Also Called: Trane
1915 N Church St (27405-5631)
P.O. Box 13587 (27415-3587)
PHONE....................................336 378-0670
Don Brady, *Brnch Mgr*
EMP: 10
Web: www.trane.com
SIC: 3585 Refrigeration and heating
equipment
HQ: Trane U.S. Inc.
800-E Beaty St
Davidson NC 28036
704 655-4000

(G-5870)

TRANE US INC
Also Called: Trane
8408 Triad Dr (27409-9018)
PHONE....................................336 387-1735
Baron Qualls, *Brnch Mgr*
EMP: 8
Web: www.bradyservices.com
SIC: 3585 Heating equipment, complete
HQ: Trane U.S. Inc.
800-E Beaty St
Davidson NC 28036
704 655-4000

(G-5871)

TREEFORMS INC
Also Called: Treeforms Lockers
4242 Regency Dr (27410-8100)
PHONE....................................336 292-8998
William B Richardson, *Pr*
Carol Bauer, *
Ellen Richardson, *
▼ EMP: 35 EST: 1973
SQ FT: 70,000
SALES (est): 5.7MM **Privately Held**
Web: www.treeforms.com
SIC: 2541 2511 2499 2542 Lockers, except
refrigerated: wood; Wood household
furniture; Decorative wood and woodwork;
Partitions and fixtures, except wood

(G-5872)

TRI-CITY MECHANICAL CONTRS INC
706 Utility St (27405-7224)
P.O. Box 21546 (27420-1546)
PHONE....................................336 272-9495
Richard G Nester, *Pr*
Claude E Holder, *
Dick Nester, *
Gene Holder, *
Claude Smith, *
EMP: 85 EST: 1983
SQ FT: 10,000
SALES (est): 9.45MM **Privately Held**
Web: www.tricitymech.com

SIC: 1711 3441 3643 5013 Mechanical
contractor; Fabricated structural metal;
Current-carrying wiring services; Exhaust
systems (mufflers, tail pipes, etc.)

(G-5873)

TRIAC CORPORATION
611 Norwalk St (27407-1409)
PHONE....................................336 297-1130
Leonard Antonelli, *Pr*
Andrea Antonelli, *Sec*
Fred Antonelli, *Dir*
Kabbie Morrone, *Operations Officer*
EMP: 10 EST: 1995
SQ FT: 3,500
SALES (est): 3.1MM
SALES (corp-wide): 23.59MM **Privately Held**
Web: www.triaccorporation.com
SIC: 3625 Relays and industrial controls
PA: Portwest Corporation
30 Larsen Way
North Attleboro MA 02763
508 809-5112

(G-5874)

TRIAD ANODIZING & PLATING INC
3502 Spring Garden St (27407-1830)
P.O. Box 154 (27235-0154)
PHONE....................................336 292-7028
Patricia T Proco, *Pr*
Steve M Proco, *VP*
EMP: 5 EST: 1972
SQ FT: 1,500
SALES (est): 154.59K **Privately Held**
SIC: 3471 Electroplating of metals or formed
products

(G-5875)

TRIAD BUSINESS CARD ASSOC
3201 Summit Ave (27405-3741)
PHONE....................................336 706-2729
Donald Harnage, *Ofcr*
EMP: 6 EST: 2009
SALES (est): 229.69K **Privately Held**
Web: www.triadbusinessbank.com
SIC: 2752 Business form and card printing,
lithographic

(G-5876)

TRIAD POWER & CONTROLS INC
215 Industrial Ave Ste G (27406-4546)
PHONE....................................336 375-9780
Billy Parrish, *Pr*
Shayn Hayes, *Prin*
EMP: 9 EST: 2005
SALES (est): 4.59MM **Privately Held**
Web: www.triadpowerandcontrols.com
SIC: 3643 Power line cable

(G-5877)

TRIAD PREFINISH & LBR SLS INC
3514 Associate Dr (27405-3878)
P.O. Box 13496 (27415-3496)
PHONE....................................336 375-4849
Ronald Cottelli, *Pr*
Donna Cottelli, *Sec*
EMP: 6 EST: 1989
SQ FT: 10,000
SALES (est): 1.06MM **Privately Held**
Web: www.triadprefinish.com
SIC: 5211 5031 2431 Millwork and lumber;
Lumber: rough, dressed, and finished;
Exterior and ornamental woodwork and trim

(G-5878)

TRIAD PRINTING NC INC
Also Called: Triad Printing NC
1306 E Wendover Ave (27405-6717)
PHONE....................................336 422-8752
Alan E Martinez, *Admn*

▲ = Import ▼ = Export
◆ = Import/Export

EMP: 4 **EST:** 2015
SALES (est): 207.85K **Privately Held**
Web: www.triadprintingnc.com
SIC: 2759 Commercial printing, nec

(G-5879)
TRIAD SHEET METAL & MECH INC
300 Lowdermilk St (27401-4437)
PHONE..............................336 379-9891
Harold Amick Junior, *Pr*
Dwayne Bingman, *VP*
EMP: 10 **EST:** 1990
SQ FT: 2,200
SALES (est): 3.82MM **Privately Held**
Web: www.triadsheetmetalhvac.com
SIC: 3444 5051 1711 Sheet metalwork;
    Copper products; Mechanical contractor

(G-5880)
TRIDENT FIBERS INC
7109 Cessna Dr (27409-9793)
PHONE..............................336 605-9002
Jeffrey W Bruner, *Prin*
EMP: 5 **EST:** 2015
SALES (est): 400.07K **Privately Held**
SIC: 2655 Fiber cans, drums, and similar
    products

(G-5881)
TRU-CAST INC
1208 Rail St (27407-2199)
P.O. Box 18167 (27419-8167)
PHONE..............................336 294-2370
S Wayne Gibbs, *Prin*
Paula Tuggle, *
EMP: 35 **EST:** 1978
SQ FT: 24,000
SALES (est): 4.74MM **Privately Held**
Web: www.trucastnc.com
SIC: 3369 3599 Nonferrous foundries, nec;
    Machine shop, jobbing and repair

(G-5882)
TRUFLO PUMPS INC
7105 Cessna Dr (27409-9793)
PHONE..............................336 664-9225
Fred Wilson, *Pr*
◆ **EMP:** 10 **EST:** 2000
SALES (est): 3.89MM **Privately Held**
Web: www.truflo.com
SIC: 5084 3561 Pumps and pumping
    equipment, nec; Pumps and pumping
    equipment

(G-5883)
TURN BULL LUMBER COMPANY
1027 Arnold St (27405-7101)
PHONE..............................336 272-5200
Edward Cosby, *Prin*
EMP: 14
SIC: 2411 Timber, cut at logging camp
PA: Turn Bull Lumber Company
    474 Sweet Home Church Rd
    Elizabethtown NC 28337

(G-5884)
TWISTED PAPER PRODUCTS INC
7100 Cessna Dr (27409-9793)
PHONE..............................336 393-0273
Massimo Fantechi, *Pr*
▲ **EMP:** 45 **EST:** 1976
SQ FT: 60,000
SALES (est): 6.59MM **Privately Held**
Web: www.twistedpaperproducts.com
SIC: 2621 Paper mills

(G-5885)
UKG KRONOS SYSTEMS LLC
Also Called: Kronos Carolinas
101 Centreport Dr Ste 340 (27409-9446)

PHONE..............................800 225-1561
Jim Beacham, *Mgr*
EMP: 8
SALES (corp-wide): 1.85B **Privately Held**
Web: www.ukg.com
SIC: 7372 Business oriented computer
    software
HQ: Ukg Kronos Systems, Llc
    900 Chelmsford St
    Lowell MA 01851
    978 250-9800

(G-5886)
ULTIMIX RECORDS
Also Called: Carolina Custom Pressing
3404 W Wendover Ave Ste E (27407-1524)
P.O. Box 16062 (27261)
PHONE..............................336 288-7566
John Deets, *Pr*
EMP: 5 **EST:** 1986
SQ FT: 17,000
SALES (est): 180.01K **Privately Held**
Web: www.ultimix.com
SIC: 5735 3652 Records, audio discs, and
    tapes; Phonograph record blanks

(G-5887)
UNIFI INC (PA)
Also Called: Unifi
7201 W Friendly Ave (27410)
P.O. Box 19109 (27419)
PHONE..............................336 294-4410
Edmund M Ingle, *CEO*
Albert P Carey, *
Hongjun Ning, *Ex VP*
Gregory K Sigmon, *Corporate Secretary*
Aj Eaker, *Ex VP*
◆ **EMP:** 100 **EST:** 1969
SQ FT: 121,000
SALES (est): 582.21MM
SALES (corp-wide): 582.21MM **Publicly
Held**
Web: www.unifi.com
SIC: 2281 2282 2221 Nylon yarn, spinning of
    staple; Polyester filament yarn: throwing,
    twisting, winding, etc.; Spandex
    broadwoven fabrics

(G-5888)
UNIFI MANUFACTURING INC (HQ)
7201 W Friendly Ave (27410-6237)
P.O. Box 19109 (27419-9109)
PHONE..............................336 294-4410
William L Jasper, *CEO*
Brian D Moore, *Pr*
Sean D Goodman, *CFO*
Thomas H Caudle Junior, *VP*
W Randy Eaddy, *Sec*
◆ **EMP:** 119 **EST:** 1996
SALES (est): 42.64MM
SALES (corp-wide): 582.21MM **Publicly
Held**
Web: www.unifi.com
SIC: 2281 Nylon yarn, spinning of staple
PA: Unifi, Inc.
    7201 W Friendly Ave
    Greensboro NC 27410
    336 294-4410

(G-5889)
UNIQUE COLLATING & BINDERY SVC
Also Called: Carson Dellosa Publishing
237 Burgess Rd Ste A (27409-9787)
P.O. Box 35665 (27425-5665)
PHONE..............................336 664-0960
Ronnie Kennedy, *Pr*
Ronnie Kennedy, *Pr*
▲ **EMP:** 20 **EST:** 1987
SALES (est): 942.86K
SALES (corp-wide): 942.86K **Privately
Held**

Web: www.carsondellosa.com
SIC: 2789 Binding only: books, pamphlets,
    magazines, etc.
PA: Cookie Jar Education Inc.
    7027 Albert Pick Rd Fl 3
    Greensboro NC 27409
    336 362-0084

(G-5890)
UNIQUE OFFICE SOLUTIONS INC
408 Gallimore Dairy Rd Ste E (27409-9541)
PHONE..............................336 854-0900
Amy Lane, *Pr*
William Lane, *VP*
EMP: 16 **EST:** 1996
SQ FT: 12,000
SALES (est): 3.46MM **Privately Held**
Web: www.uosinc.com
SIC: 1799 5712 2522 5021 Office furniture
    installation; Office furniture; Office furniture,
    except wood; Office furniture, nec

(G-5891)
**UNITED MTAL FNSHG INC
GRNSBORO**
Also Called: United Metal Finishing
133 Blue Bell Rd (27406-5301)
P.O. Box 16623 (27416)
PHONE..............................336 272-8107
Claude Church, *Pr*
EMP: 9 **EST:** 1985
SQ FT: 1,000
SALES (est): 2.19MM **Privately Held**
Web: www.unitedmetalfinishing.us
SIC: 3471 Electroplating of metals or formed
    products

(G-5892)
UNITEX CHEMICAL CORP
520 Broome Rd (27406-3799)
P.O. Box 16344 (27416-0344)
PHONE..............................336 378-0965
◆ **EMP:** 35
Web: www.unitexchemical.com
SIC: 2899 Chemical preparations, nec

(G-5893)
US CUSTOM SOCKS CO LLC
2522 Brandt Forest Ct (27455-1983)
PHONE..............................336 549-1088
Dennis J Finnegan, *Prin*
EMP: 5 **EST:** 2012
SALES (est): 84.86K **Privately Held**
Web: www.uscustomsocks.com
SIC: 2252 Socks

(G-5894)
US LABEL CORPORATION
2118 Enterprise Rd (27408-7004)
PHONE..............................336 332-7000
John M Andrew, *Pr*
H Allen Andrew, *Ch Bd*
Clyde M Andrew, *
James N Grant, *
Edward Tidaback, *
EMP: 7 **EST:** 1960
SQ FT: 92,000
SALES (est): 145.66K **Privately Held**
SIC: 2241 2269 Fabric tapes; Labels, cotton:
    printed

(G-5895)
VALLEY PROTEINS (DE) INC
Also Called: Carolina By-Products
2410 Randolph Ave (27406-2910)
PHONE..............................336 333-3030
David Rosenstein, *Brnch Mgr*
EMP: 375
SALES (corp-wide): 6.79B **Publicly Held**
Web: www.darpro-solutions.com

SIC: 2048 7699 2077 Prepared feeds, nec;
    Waste cleaning services; Animal and
    marine fats and oils
HQ: Valley Proteins (De), Llc
    151 Randall Stuewe Dr
    Winchester VA 22603
    540 877-2533

(G-5896)
VAN BLAKE DIXON
378 Air Harbor Rd (27455-9280)
PHONE..............................336 282-1861
Van Blake Dixon, *Owner*
EMP: 10 **EST:** 2011
SALES (est): 504.75K **Privately Held**
SIC: 3315 Welded steel wire fabric

(G-5897)
VECOPLAN LLC
Also Called: Vecoplan
501 Gallimore Dairy Rd (27409-9728)
P.O. Box 7224 (27264-7224)
PHONE..............................336 861-6070
Werner Berens, *CEO*
Jeff Queen, *
Len Buesse, *
◆ **EMP:** 49 **EST:** 1969
SALES (est): 19.7MM
SALES (corp-wide): 445.87MM **Privately
Held**
Web: www.vecoplanllc.com
SIC: 3999 Grinding and pulverizing of
    materials, nec
HQ: Vecoplan Ag
    Vor Der Bitz 10
    Bad Marienberg (Westerwald) RP
    56470
    266162670

(G-5898)
VERITIV OPERATING COMPANY
International Paper
3 Centerview Dr Ste 100 (27407-3727)
PHONE..............................336 834-3488
Harrison Stewart, *Mgr*
EMP: 5
SALES (corp-wide): 7.15B **Privately Held**
Web: www.veritiv.com
SIC: 2679 5113 Paper products, converted,
    nec; Industrial and personal service paper
HQ: Veritiv Operating Company
    1000 Abrnthy Rd Ste 1700
    Atlanta GA 30328
    770 391-8200

(G-5899)
VF CORPORATION
105 Corporate Center Blvd (27408-3194)
PHONE..............................336 424-6000
Steve Rendle, *Pr*
Scott A Roe, *Ex VP*
EMP: 4 **EST:** 1998
SALES (est): 176.53K **Privately Held**
Web: www.vfc.com
SIC: 5139 2211 Footwear; Apparel and
    outerwear fabrics, cotton

(G-5900)
VF CORPORATION
105 Corp Ctr Blvd (27408-3194)
PHONE..............................336 424-6000
EMP: 10
SALES (est): 73.4K **Privately Held**
Web: www.vfc.com
SIC: 2211 5139 Apparel and outerwear
    fabrics, cotton; Footwear

(G-5901)
VF JEANSWEAR INC (PA)
105 Corporate Center Blvd (27408-3194)
P.O. Box 21647 (27420-1647)

PHONE..................336 332-3400
EMP: 17 **EST:** 1986
SALES (est): 3.67MM
SALES (corp-wide): 3.67MM **Privately
Held**
Web: www.vfc.com
SIC: 2323 Men's and boys' neckties and bow
ties

(G-5902)
VF RECEIVABLES LP
105 Corporate Center Blvd (27408-3194)
PHONE..................336 424-6000
EMP: 8 **EST:** 2014
SALES (est): 2.77MM
SALES (corp-wide): 10.45B **Publicly Held**
Web: www.vfc.com
SIC: 2325 Jeans: men's, youths', and boys'
PA: V.F. Corporation
1551 Wewatta St
Denver CO 80202
720 778-4000

(G-5903)
VIC INC
Also Called: Sign-A-Rama
3410 W Wendover Ave Ste C (27407-1585)
PHONE..................336 545-1124
Vince V Cvijanovic, *Pr*
Mathew S Cvijanovic, *
Ivy J Cvijanovic, *
EMP: 14 **EST:** 2004
SQ FT: 23,500
SALES (est): 1.02MM **Privately Held**
Web: www.signarama.com
SIC: 3993 Signs and advertising specialties

(G-5904)
VIVET INC (PA)
Also Called: Vivet Home Brands
1150 Pleasant Ridge Rd Ste A (27409)
PHONE..................909 390-1039
Mark L Feng, *CEO*
Jing Chen, *CFO*
Hao Howard Pan, *Sec*
EMP: 27 **EST:** 2017
SALES (est): 85.93MM
SALES (corp-wide): 85.93MM **Privately
Held**
SIC: 2426 1771 Flooring, hardwood;
Flooring contractor

(G-5905)
VNA HOLDING INC (HQ)
7825 National Service Rd (27409)
PHONE..................336 393-4890
Ava Persson, *CEO*
Eva Pesson, *
Donald W Shumaker, *
Therence Pickett, *
◆ **EMP:** 3700 **EST:** 1996
SALES (est): 3.74B
SALES (corp-wide): 52.58B **Privately Held**
SIC: 6159 3713 5012 5013 Equipment and
vehicle finance leasing companies;
Specialty motor vehicle bodies; Commercial
vehicles; Motor vehicle supplies and new
parts
PA: Ab Volvo
Amazonvagen 8
Goteborg 418 7
31660000

(G-5906)
**VOLVO GROUP NORTH AMERICA
LLC (DH)**
Also Called: Volvo Trucks North America
7900 National Service Rd (27409)
P.O. Box 26115 (27402)
PHONE..................336 393-2000
Per Carlsson, *CEO*

Stephen Roy, *
Lars Thoren, *
Therence Pickett, *
Gregory Higgins, *
◆ **EMP:** 600 **EST:** 1998
SQ FT: 60,000
SALES (est): 1.77B
SALES (corp-wide): 52.58B **Privately Held**
Web: www.volvogroup.com
SIC: 3713 5012 5013 Specialty motor
vehicle bodies; Commercial vehicles; Motor
vehicle supplies and new parts
HQ: Vna Holding Inc.
7825 National Service Rd
Greensboro NC 27409
336 393-4890

(G-5907)
**VOLVO GROUP NORTH AMERICA
LLC**
Also Called: Volvo Trucks Uptime Center
8003 Piedmont Triad Pkwy (27409-9407)
PHONE..................336 393-2000
EMP: 3763
SALES (corp-wide): 52.58B **Privately Held**
Web: www.volvocars.com
SIC: 3713 5012 5013 Specialty motor
vehicle bodies; Commercial vehicles; Motor
vehicle supplies and new parts
HQ: Volvo Group North America, Llc
7900 National Service Rd
Greensboro NC 27409

(G-5908)
**VOLVO GROUP NORTH AMERICA
LLC**
8203 Piedmont Triad Pkwy (27409-9454)
PHONE..................336 393-2000
EMP: 5013
SALES (corp-wide): 52.58B **Privately Held**
Web: www.volvocars.com
SIC: 3713 5012 5013 Specialty motor
vehicle bodies; Commercial vehicles; Motor
vehicle supplies and new parts
HQ: Volvo Group North America, Llc
7900 National Service Rd
Greensboro NC 27409

(G-5909)
**VOLVO GROUP NORTH AMERICA
LLC**
7821 National Service Rd 1 (27409-9667)
PHONE..................731 968-0151
Therence Pickett, *Owner*
EMP: 5049
SALES (corp-wide): 52.58B **Privately Held**
Web: www.volvogroup.com
SIC: 3429 Motor vehicle hardware
HQ: Volvo Group North America, Llc
7900 National Service Rd
Greensboro NC 27409

(G-5910)
**VOLVO LOGISTICS NORTH
AMERICA INC**
7900 National Service Rd (27409-9416)
PHONE..................336 393-4746
◆ **EMP:** 163
Web: www.volvotrucks.us
SIC: 3713 8741 Truck and bus bodies;
Management services

(G-5911)
**VOLVO TRUCKS NORTH AMERICA
INC (DH)**
7900 National Service Rd (27409)
P.O. Box 26115 (27402)
PHONE..................336 393-2000
Peter Karlsten Pickett, *Pr*
Gary Mccartney, *Sr VP*

◆ **EMP:** 600 **EST:** 1986
SQ FT: 60,000
SALES (est): 353.69MM
SALES (corp-wide): 52.58B **Privately Held**
Web: www.volvotrucks.us
SIC: 5511 5012 5013 3713 Automobiles,
new and used; Commercial vehicles; Motor
vehicle supplies and new parts; Truck
bodies and parts
HQ: Vna Holding Inc.
7825 National Service Rd
Greensboro NC 27409
336 393-4890

(G-5912)
VPM LIQUIDATING INC
2110 W Gate City Blvd (27403-2642)
PHONE..................336 292-1781
◆ **EMP:** 10
SIC: 2869 2879 Plasticizers, organic: cyclic
and acyclic; Agricultural chemicals, nec

(G-5913)
W&W-AFCO STEEL LLC
101 Centreport Dr Ste 400 (27409-9422)
PHONE..................336 275-9711
Jenny Carter, *Brnch Mgr*
EMP: 50
SALES (corp-wide): 424.23B **Publicly
Held**
Web: www.wwafcosteel.com
SIC: 3441 Fabricated structural metal
HQ: W&W-Afco Steel Llc
1730 W Reno Ave
Oklahoma City OK 73106
405 235-3621

(G-5914)
WEB 4 HALF LLC
Also Called: Direct Promotional
1301 Carolina St Ste 125a (27401-1090)
PHONE..................855 762-4638
Blesson George, *CEO*
EMP: 50 **EST:** 2010
SQ FT: 15,000
SALES (est): 6.76MM **Privately Held**
Web: www.directpromotionals.com
SIC: 7371 3999 3993 Computer software
development; Advertising display products;
Signs and advertising specialties

(G-5915)
**WELSH CSTM SLTTING RWNDING
LLC**
200 Citation Ct (27409-9026)
PHONE..................336 665-6481
▲ **EMP:** 31 **EST:** 2011
SQ FT: 105,000
SALES (est): 13.23MM **Privately Held**
Web: www.welshslitting.com
SIC: 2679 Paper products, converted, nec

(G-5916)
**WESTERN ROTO ENGRAVERS
INCORPORATED (PA)**
Also Called: Wre/Colortech
533 Banner Ave (27401-4397)
PHONE..................336 275-9821
EMP: 36 **EST:** 1951
SALES (est): 12.93MM
SALES (corp-wide): 12.93MM **Privately
Held**
Web: www.wrecolor.com
SIC: 2759 Engraving, nec

(G-5917)
WHEEL PROS LLC
2606 Phoenix Dr Ste 804 (27406-6357)
PHONE..................336 851-6705
Corey Kiesel, *Mgr*

EMP: 6
SALES (corp-wide): 731.01MM **Privately
Held**
Web: www.wheelpros.com
SIC: 3312 Wheels
HQ: Wheel Pros, Llc
5347 S Vlntia Way Ste 200
Greenwood Village CO 80111

(G-5918)
WIKOFF COLOR CORPORATION
7212 Cessna Dr (27409-9685)
PHONE..................336 668-3423
David Hall, *Mgr*
EMP: 27
SQ FT: 7,872
SALES (corp-wide): 156.45MM **Privately
Held**
Web: www.wikoff.com
SIC: 2893 Printing ink
PA: Wikoff Color Corporation
1886 Merritt Rd
Fort Mill SC 29715
803 548-2210

(G-5919)
WILBERT FUNERAL SERVICES INC
Also Called: Greensboro Wilbert
108 Buchanan Church Rd (27405-8631)
PHONE..................800 828-5879
Tom Shank, *Mgr*
EMP: 30
SALES (corp-wide): 424.23B **Publicly
Held**
Web: www.greensborowilbert.com
SIC: 3272 Burial vaults, concrete or precast
terrazzo
HQ: Wilbert Funeral Services, Inc.
10965 Granada Ln Ste 300
Overland Park KS 66211
913 345-2120

(G-5920)
**WINDSORS CBNETRY FOR KIT
BATHS**
1816 Pembroke Rd Ste 2 (27408-7910)
PHONE..................336 275-0190
Dale Windsor, *Prin*
EMP: 4 **EST:** 2011
SALES (est): 98.34K **Privately Held**
Web: www.windsorscabinetry.com
SIC: 2434 Wood kitchen cabinets

(G-5921)
**WITH PURPOSE PRESSURE WSHG
LLC**
2702 Renee Dr (27407-5946)
PHONE..................336 965-9473
EMP: 8 **EST:** 2019
SALES (est): 319.01K **Privately Held**
Web: www.martinspressurewashing.com
SIC: 1521 1389 1799 Patio and deck
construction and repair; Construction,
repair, and dismantling services; Cleaning
building exteriors, nec

(G-5922)
WLC LLC
5509b W Friendly Ave Ste 201
(27410-4270)
PHONE..................336 852-6422
EMP: 5 **EST:** 1997
SALES (est): 140.89K **Privately Held**
SIC: 2731 Books, publishing only

(G-5923)
WOMACK NEWSPAPER INC
Also Called: Yes Weekly
5500 Adams Farm Ln Ste 204
(27407-7063)

PHONE..............................336 316-1231
Charles Womack, *Brnch Mgr*
EMP: 4
SALES (corp-wide): 2.2MM Privately Held
Web: www.yesweekly.com
SIC: 2711 Newspapers, publishing and printing
PA: Womack Newspaper, Inc.
30 N Main St
Chatham VA 24531
434 432-1654

(G-5924)
WORKWEAR OUTFITTERS LLC
Also Called: Vf
No Physical Location (27420)
P.O. Box 21647 (27420-1647)
PHONE..............................877 824-0613
EMP: 33
SALES (corp-wide): 2.07B Privately Held
Web: www.redkap.com
SIC: 2326 Men's and boy's work clothing
HQ: Workwear Outfitters, Llc
545 Marriott Dr
Nashville TN 37214
800 733-5271

(G-5925)
WRANGLER APPAREL CORP
Also Called: Wrangler
400 N Elm St (27401-2143)
PHONE..............................336 332-3400
Scott Baxter, *Pr*
EMP: 500 EST: 1993
SALES (est): 2.45MM
SALES (corp-wide): 2.61B Publicly Held
Web: www.kontoorbrands.com
SIC: 2325 2321 2329 2339 Men's and boy's trousers and slacks; Sport shirts, men's and boys': from purchased materials; Jackets (suede, leatherette, etc.), sport: men's and boys'; Jeans: women's, misses', and juniors'
PA: Kontoor Brands, Inc.
400 N Elm St
Greensboro NC 27401
336 332-3400

(G-5926)
WRIGHT ROLLER COMPANY
1800 Fairfax Rd Ste K (27407-4124)
P.O. Box 7753 (27417-0753)
PHONE..............................336 852-8393
Toni Wright, *Pr*
Rodney Dabbs, *VP*
Carrie Moyel, *Off Mgr*
EMP: 8 EST: 1988
SQ FT: 14,000
SALES (est): 503.34K Privately Held
Web: www.wrightroller.com
SIC: 3069 Roll coverings, rubber

(G-5927)
WUKO INC
3505 Associate Dr (27405-3879)
PHONE..............................980 938-0512
Lucia Hakala, *Pr*
EMP: 5 EST: 2014
SALES (est): 599.49K Privately Held
Web: www.wuko.at
SIC: 3542 Machine tools, metal forming type

(G-5928)
WYSONG AND MILES COMPANY
Also Called: Wysong Parts & Service
4820 Us 29 N (27405)
PHONE..............................336 621-3960
Russell F Hall Iii, *Pr*
Thomas Adkisson, *VP Opers*
Suzanne Hall, *Dir*
Patricia Herr, *Dir*
Franz Herr, *Dir*

EMP: 20 EST: 1903
SQ FT: 104,000
SALES (est): 4.97MM Privately Held
Web: www.wysong.us
SIC: 3542 Machine tools, metal forming type

(G-5929)
YELLOW DOG DESIGN INC
112 Oconnor St (27406-2206)
PHONE..............................336 553-2172
Donald Brian Dempsey, *Pr*
▲ EMP: 15 EST: 2000
SQ FT: 15,000
SALES (est): 2.05MM Privately Held
Web: www.yellowdog-design.com
SIC: 2399 Pet collars, leashes, etc.: non-leather

(G-5930)
YKK AP AMERICA INC
4524 Green Point Dr Ste 106 (27410-8123)
PHONE..............................336 665-1963
Kim Law, *Mgr*
EMP: 15
Web: www.ykkap.com
SIC: 3442 Sash, door or window: metal
HQ: Ykk Ap America Inc.
101 Mretta St Nw Ste 2100
Atlanta GA 30303

(G-5931)
ZIEHL-ABEGG INC (DH)
719 N Regional Rd (27419)
P.O. Box 19971 (27419)
PHONE..............................336 834-9339
▲ EMP: 24 EST: 2003
SQ FT: 240,000
SALES (est): 157MM
SALES (corp-wide): 688.71MM Privately Held
Web: www.ziehl-abegg.com
SIC: 3694 3443 3564 Engine electrical equipment; Fabricated plate work (boiler shop); Blowers and fans
HQ: Ziehl - Abegg Elektrizitats-Gmbh
Heinz-Ziehl-Str.
Kunzelsau BW 74653

(G-5932)
ZIM ARCRAFT CBIN SOLUTIONS LLC (DH)
Also Called: Haeco Americas Cabin Solutions
8010 Piedmont Triad Pkwy (27409-9407)
PHONE..............................336 862-1418
Richard Kendall, *CEO*
Mark Peterman, *
Lee Fox, *
EMP: 10 EST: 2006
SALES (est): 27.8MM Privately Held
Web: www.timco.aero
SIC: 4581 2531 Aircraft maintenance and repair services; Seats, aircraft
HQ: Zim Aircraft Seating Gmbh
Graf-Von-Soden-Str. 1
Immenstaad Am Bodensee BW 88090
754495720

(G-5933)
ZOETIS PRODUCTS LLC
620 S Elm St Ste 363 (27406-1398)
PHONE..............................336 333-9356
April Willis, *Brnch Mgr*
EMP: 9
SALES (corp-wide): 8.54B Publicly Held
Web: www.zoetis.com
SIC: 2834 Pharmaceutical preparations
HQ: Zoetis Products Llc
100 Campus Dr Ste 3
Florham Park NJ 07932
973 660-5000

Greenville
Pitt County

(G-5934)
ACCULINK
1055 Greenville Blvd Sw (27834-7021)
PHONE..............................252 321-5805
EMP: 19
SALES (est): 5.49MM Privately Held
SIC: 2759 Promotional printing

(G-5935)
AMERICAN MATERIALS COMPANY LLC
2703 Nc Highway 222 (27834-7483)
PHONE..............................252 752-2124
Harry Shaw, *Brnch Mgr*
EMP: 6
Web: www.americanmaterialsco.com
SIC: 1442 Construction sand mining
HQ: American Materials Company, Llc
1410 Commwl Dr Ste 201
Wilmington NC 28403
910 799-1411

(G-5936)
ANGSTROM MEDICA INC
Also Called: Pioneer Srgical Orthobiologics
1800 N Greene St Ste A (27834-9013)
PHONE..............................781 933-6121
Paul Mraz, *CEO*
Edward Ahn, *Pr*
EMP: 10 EST: 2001
SQ FT: 6,500
SALES (est): 753.9K
SALES (corp-wide): 81.98MM Publicly Held
SIC: 3841 Surgical and medical instruments
HQ: Pioneer Surgical Technology, Inc.
7 Switchbud Pl Ste 192-18
The Woodlands TX 77380

(G-5937)
APG/EAST LLC
1150 Sugg Pkwy (27834-9077)
P.O. Box 1967 (27835-1967)
PHONE..............................252 329-9500
EMP: 198 EST: 2016
SALES (est): 4.39MM
SALES (corp-wide): 333.51MM Privately Held
Web: www.reflector.com
SIC: 2711 Newspapers, publishing and printing
PA: Adams Publishing Group, Llc
4095 Coon Rapids Blvd Nw
Minneapolis MN 55433
218 348-3391

(G-5938)
ARCHIE S STEEL SERVICE INC
4575 Us Highway 13 S (27834-0044)
PHONE..............................252 355-5007
Archie Oakley, *Pr*
Janie Oakley, *VP*
Archie Oakley Junior, *Pr*
EMP: 6 EST: 1985
SALES (est): 135.7K Privately Held
SIC: 7692 Welding repair

(G-5939)
ASMO GREENVILLE OF NORTH CAROLINA INC
Also Called: Asamo Co
1125 Sugg Pkwy (27834-9009)
PHONE..............................252 754-1000
▲ EMP: 463
Web: www.greenvilleconventioncenter.com

SIC: 3594 Fluid power motors

(G-5940)
ASSOCIATED HYGIENIC PDTS LLC (PA)
Also Called: Associated Hygienic Products
1029 Old Creek Rd (27834-8178)
P.O. Box 1749 (30096-0031)
PHONE..............................770 497-9800
Brandon Wang, *
▲ EMP: 70 EST: 2000
SALES (est): 55.64MM
SALES (corp-wide): 55.64MM Privately Held
Web: www.attindas.com
SIC: 2676 Diapers, paper (disposable): made from purchased paper

(G-5941)
ATTENDS HEALTHCARE PDTS INC
1029 Old Creek Rd (27834-8178)
PHONE..............................252 752-1100
EMP: 7
SALES (corp-wide): 90.15MM Privately Held
Web: www.attends.com
SIC: 2676 Sanitary paper products
PA: Attends Healthcare Products Inc.
8020 Arco Corp Dr Ste 200
Raleigh NC 27617
800 428-8363

(G-5942)
ATTINDAS HYGIENE PARTNERS INC
350 Industrial Blvd (27834-9014)
PHONE..............................252 752-1100
EMP: 159
SALES (corp-wide): 18.86MM Privately Held
Web: www.attindas.com
SIC: 2621 Paper mills
PA: Attindas Hygiene Partners Inc.
8020 Arco Corp Dr Ste 200
Raleigh NC 27617
919 237-4000

(G-5943)
AVIENT PROTECTIVE MTLS LLC (HQ)
Also Called: DSM Hpf
5750 Martin Luther King Jr Hwy (27834)
PHONE..............................252 707-2547
Scott Mcintyre, *Pr*
Avery Johnson, *
Robert K James, *
◆ EMP: 64 EST: 2001
SALES (est): 25.66MM Publicly Held
SIC: 2821 Plastics materials and resins
PA: Avient Corporation
33587 Walker Rd
Avon Lake OH 44012

(G-5944)
BAILEYS SAUCES INC
3765 Mills Rd (27858-8269)
PHONE..............................252 756-7179
Dale Bailey, *Pr*
Nikki Bailey, *VP*
EMP: 4 EST: 2002
SALES (est): 89.45K Privately Held
SIC: 2033 Barbecue sauce: packaged in cans, jars, etc.

(G-5945)
BANILLA GAMES INC
3506 Greenville Blvd Ne (27834-8980)
PHONE..............................252 329-7977
Garrett Blackwelder, *Pr*
EMP: 8 EST: 2014
SALES (est): 1.78MM Privately Held
Web: www.banillagames.com

GEOGRAPHIC

SIC: **3944** Board games, children's and adults'

(G-5946)
BARNHILL CONTRACTING COMPANY
Also Called: APAC
562 Barrus Construction Rd (27834-7365)
P.O. Box 1467 (27835-1467)
PHONE..............................252 752-7608
Eddie Briley, *Pr*
EMP: 30
SALES (corp-wide): 490.43MM **Privately Held**
Web: www.barnhillcontracting.com
SIC: 1611 2951 Highway and street paving contractor; Asphalt paving mixtures and blocks
PA: Barnhill Contracting Company Inc
800 Tiffany Blvd Ste 200
Rocky Mount NC 27804
252 823-1021

(G-5947)
BELVOIR MANUFACTURING CORP (PA)
4081 Nc Highway 33 W (27834-7349)
PHONE..............................252 746-1274
Robert Danzger, *Pr*
Joshua Danzger, *
Joanne Palmer, *
▲ **EMP:** 55 **EST:** 1981
SQ FT: 60,000
SALES (est): 2.13MM
SALES (corp-wide): 2.13MM **Privately Held**
SIC: 2389 2339 2326 Hospital gowns; Women's and misses' outerwear, nec; Men's and boy's work clothing

(G-5948)
BOSTIK INC
130 Commerce St (27858-5025)
PHONE..............................864 535-3759
EMP: 18
SALES (corp-wide): 134.78MM **Privately Held**
SIC: 2891 Adhesives and sealants
HQ: Bostik, Inc.
11320 W Wtertown Plank Rd
Wauwatosa WI 53226
414 774-2250

(G-5949)
CARGILL INCORPORATED
Also Called: Cargill
6 Miles East Farmville (27834)
P.O. Box 31a (27835-0031)
PHONE..............................252 752-1879
Michael Foster, *Brnch Mgr*
EMP: 25
SALES (corp-wide): 159.59B **Privately Held**
Web: www.cargill.com
SIC: 2048 Prepared feeds, nec
PA: Cargill, Incorporated
15407 Mcginty Rd W
Wayzata MN 55391
800 227-4455

(G-5950)
CARLINA SHOTWELL LLC
Also Called: ASAP Marketing
204 E Arlington Blvd Ste C-103 (27858-5022)
PHONE..............................252 417-8688
Carlina Shotwell, *CEO*
Carlina Whiting, *CEO*
EMP: 4 **EST:** 2016
SALES (est): 240.43K **Privately Held**

SIC: **2731** Book publishing

(G-5951)
CAROLINA WINDOWS AND DOORS INC
3203 S Memorial Dr (27834-6718)
PHONE..............................252 756-2585
Blake Bailey, *Pr*
Jeff Bailey, *Pr*
Wayne Bailey, *Sec*
Wanda Kennedy, *Acctnt*
EMP: 18 **EST:** 1984
SQ FT: 14,000
SALES (est): 9.36MM **Privately Held**
Web: www.cwdnc.com
SIC: 3999 5211 1751 3448 Barber and beauty shop equipment; Siding; Window and door (prefabricated) installation; Sunrooms, prefabricated metal

(G-5952)
CATALENT GREENVILLE INC
1240 Sugg Pkwy (27834)
PHONE..............................252 752-3800
Alessandro Masseli, *Pr*
EMP: 100 **EST:** 2022
SALES (est): 36.58MM **Privately Held**
Web: www.catalent.com
SIC: 2834 Solutions, pharmaceutical
HQ: Catalent Pharma Solutions, Inc.
14 Schoolhouse Rd
Somerset NJ 08873

(G-5953)
CCBCC OPERATIONS LLC
Also Called: Coca-Cola
1051 Staton Rd (27834-9052)
PHONE..............................252 752-2446
Chuck Jenkins, *Mgr*
EMP: 37
SALES (corp-wide): 6.9B **Publicly Held**
Web: www.coca-cola.com
SIC: 2086 Bottled and canned soft drinks
HQ: Ccbcc Operations, Llc
4100 Coca-Cola Plz
Charlotte NC 28211
704 364-8728

(G-5954)
CLASSY SASSY 5 JEWELS BOUTIQUE ✪
P.O. Box 3743 (27836-1743)
PHONE..............................252 481-8144
Kimiko Moore, *Owner*
EMP: 4 **EST:** 2024
SALES (est): 1.1MM **Privately Held**
SIC: 3911 7389 Jewelry, precious metal; Business Activities at Non-Commercial Site

(G-5955)
COASTAL AGROBUSINESS INC (PA)
112 Staton Rd (27834)
P.O. Box 856 (27835)
PHONE..............................252 238-7391
James C Whitehurst Iii, *Pr*
James C Whitehurst Junior, *Ch Bd*
Mike Seymour, *VP*
Ann H Whitehurst, *Sec*
◆ **EMP:** 55 **EST:** 1953
SQ FT: 50,000
SALES (est): 61.99MM
SALES (corp-wide): 61.99MM **Privately Held**
Web: www.coastalagro.com
SIC: 5191 3523 Chemicals, agricultural; Sprayers and spraying machines, agricultural

(G-5956)
COLLINS BANKS INVESTMENTS INC
Also Called: Super Shred
311 Staton Rd (27834-9038)
P.O. Box 2725 (27836-0725)
PHONE..............................252 439-1200
Ruth Collins, *Pr*
EMP: 9 **EST:** 1999
SALES (est): 492.99K **Privately Held**
SIC: 2611 Pulp manufactured from waste or recycled paper

(G-5957)
CONWAY DEVELOPMENT INC (PA)
Also Called: Greenville Marble & Gran Works
2218 Dickinson Ave (27834-5104)
P.O. Box 103 (27835-0103)
PHONE..............................252 756-2168
John A Conway Iii, *Pr*
Pat Conway, *VP*
EMP: 15 **EST:** 1933
SALES (est): 2.67MM
SALES (corp-wide): 2.67MM **Privately Held**
Web: www.go2gmg.com
SIC: 5099 5999 3281 Monuments and grave markers; Monuments and tombstones; Cut stone and stone products

(G-5958)
COOKE COMMUNICATIONS NC LLC
1150 Sugg Pkwy (27834-9077)
P.O. Box 1967 (27835-1967)
PHONE..............................252 329-9500
EMP: 11 **EST:** 2012
SALES (est): 2.33MM **Privately Held**
Web: www.reflector.com
SIC: 2711 Commercial printing and newspaper publishing combined

(G-5959)
COPYMATIC UNITED CEREBRAL
Also Called: Copymatic of Greenville
200 W 4th St (27858-1816)
PHONE..............................252 695-6155
Mark Carter, *Ex Dir*
EMP: 10 **EST:** 2004
SALES (est): 93.3K **Privately Held**
Web: www.copymatic.ai
SIC: 2752 Cards, lithographed

(G-5960)
COTTON BELT INC
Also Called: Sleepworthy
310 Staton Rd (27834-9037)
P.O. Box 108 (27864-0108)
PHONE..............................252 689-6847
EMP: 100 **EST:** 1932
SALES (est): 13.39MM **Privately Held**
Web: www.edgecombe.com
SIC: 2515 2512 Box springs, assembled; Living room furniture: upholstered on wood frames

(G-5961)
COX NRTH CRLINA PBLCATIONS INC (DH)
Also Called: Daily Reflector , The
1150 Sugg Pkwy (27834-9077)
P.O. Box 1967 (27835-1967)
PHONE..............................252 329-9643
Jay Smith, *Pr*
Brian G Cooper, *
Andrew Merdek, *
EMP: 200 **EST:** 1882
SQ FT: 90,000
SALES (est): 4.94MM
SALES (corp-wide): 961.55MM **Privately Held**
Web: www.reflector.com

SIC: **2711** Newspapers, publishing and printing
HQ: Cox Newspapers, Inc.
6205 Pchtree Dnwody Rd N
Atlanta GA 30328

(G-5962)
CYPRESS MOUNTAIN COMPANY (HQ)
107 Staton Ct (27834-9016)
PHONE..............................252 758-2179
M Michael Richardson, *Pr*
Michael Richardson, *Pr*
Harry H Esbenshade Iii, *Sec*
Michael D Cain, *Treas*
Barry T Sugg, *VP*
EMP: 5 **EST:** 2000
SALES (est): 24.89MM
SALES (corp-wide): 94.28MM **Privately Held**
SIC: 3444 1761 Sheet metalwork; Roofing, siding, and sheetmetal work
PA: The Mountain Company
166 60th St
Parkersburg WV 26105
304 295-0036

(G-5963)
DENSO MANUFACTURING NC INC
Also Called: Dmnc Greenville Plant
1125 Sugg Pkwy (27834-9078)
PHONE..............................252 754-1000
EMP: 463
Web: www.denso.com
SIC: 3594 Fluid power motors
HQ: Denso Manufacturing North Carolina, Inc.
470 Crawford Rd
Statesville NC 28625

(G-5964)
DEXTERITY LLC
104 Azalea Dr (27858-5401)
PHONE..............................919 524-7732
EMP: 10 **EST:** 2012
SQ FT: 2,000
SALES (est): 637.03K **Privately Held**
Web: www.4dpick.com
SIC: 3089 3663 Cases, plastics; Mobile communication equipment

(G-5965)
DIGITAL PRINT & IMAGING INC
115 Red Banks Rd Ste A (27858-5703)
PHONE..............................910 341-3005
Brian Carter, *Pr*
Matt Carter, *VP*
EMP: 7 **EST:** 2002
SALES (est): 281.23K **Privately Held**
SIC: 2759 5112 5044 Screen printing; Stationery and office supplies; Office equipment

(G-5966)
DOMTAR PAPER COMPANY LLC
1029 Old Creek Rd (27834-8178)
PHONE..............................252 752-1100
EMP: 69
Web: www.domtar.com
SIC: 5099 2621 Pulpwood; Paper mills
HQ: Domtar Paper Company, Llc
234 Kingsley Park Dr
Fort Mill SC 29715

(G-5967)
DPI NEWCO LLC
Also Called: Newco
5900 Martin Luther King Jr Hwy (27834-8628)
PHONE..............................252 758-3436
Jim Mullen, *CEO*

EMP: 1200 **EST:** 2014
SALES (est): 5.46MM
SALES (corp-wide): 42.86B **Publicly Held**
SIC: 2834 Pharmaceutical preparations
HQ: Patheon Holdings I B.V.
De Posthoornstraat 7
Tilburg NB

(G-5968)
DSM
202 Crestline Blvd (27834-6816)
PHONE..............................408 582-2610
EMP: 14 **EST:** 2017
SALES (est): 151.2K **Privately Held**
Web: www.dsm.com
SIC: 2834 Pharmaceutical preparations

(G-5969)
DSM PHARMACEUTICALS INC
5900 Martin Luther King Jr Hwy
(27834-8628)
P.O. Box 127 (27889-0127)
PHONE..............................252 758-3436
▲ **EMP:** 53 **EST:** 2011
SALES (est): 2.02MM **Privately Held**
Web: www.dsm.com
SIC: 2834 Pharmaceutical preparations

(G-5970)
DSM PHARMACEUTICALS INC
Also Called: Dpi
5900 Martin Luther King Jr Hwy
(27834-8628)
P.O. Box 2451 (30903-2451)
PHONE..............................252 758-3436
▲ **EMP:** 1200
SIC: 2834 Pharmaceutical preparations

(G-5971)
E C U UNIV PRTG & GRAPHICS
Also Called: Ecu Print Shop
2612 E 10th St (27858-3122)
PHONE..............................252 737-1301
Anne Weingartz, Dir
EMP: 16 **EST:** 1980
SALES (est): 170.12K **Privately Held**
Web: www.ecu.edu
SIC: 2752 Commercial printing, lithographic

(G-5972)
EASTERN CRLINA VCTONAL CTR INC (PA)
Also Called: Ecvc
2100 N Greene St (27834-9024)
P.O. Box 1686 (27835-1686)
PHONE..............................252 758-4188
Jason Thomas, CEO
Beth Davis, *
EMP: 77 **EST:** 1965
SQ FT: 145,000
SALES (est): 13.64MM
SALES (corp-wide): 13.64MM **Privately Held**
Web: www.ecvcinc.com
SIC: 8331 4953 3069 Vocational training agency; Refuse systems; Battery boxes, jars, or parts, hard rubber

(G-5973)
ELECTRIC MTR SLS SVC PITT CNTY
202 Hooker Rd (27834-5121)
P.O. Box 7044 (27835)
PHONE..............................252 752-3170
Bobby Bowen, Pr
Marshall Bowen, VP
EMP: 7 **EST:** 1977
SQ FT: 10,000
SALES (est): 2.01MM **Privately Held**
Web:
www.electricmotorsalesgreenville.com

SIC: 5063 7694 Motors, electric; Electric motor repair

(G-5974)
ENERGY SVERS WINDOWS DOORS INC
Also Called: Home Security Bars
1806 Dickinson Ave (27834-3804)
PHONE..............................252 758-8700
Charles H Hagan Junior, Pr
EMP: 4 **EST:** 1986
SALES (est): 146.1K **Privately Held**
SIC: 5211 3442 Windows, storm: wood or metal; Storm doors or windows, metal

(G-5975)
FERVENT PHARMACEUTICALS LLC
740 Greenville Blvd Ste 400-151
(27834-6715)
PHONE..............................252 558-9700
George E Royster Junior, CEO
EMP: 4 **EST:** 2011
SALES (est): 233.78K **Privately Held**
Web: www.ferventpharma.com
SIC: 2834 Pharmaceutical preparations

(G-5976)
FIXED-NC LLC
1830a Old Fire Tower Rd (27858-7985)
PHONE..............................252 751-1911
EMP: 9 **EST:** 2018
SQ FT: 1,500
SALES (est): 349.52K **Privately Held**
Web: www.fixednc.com
SIC: 1389 1521 7299 8322 Construction, repair, and dismantling services; Repai ing fire damage, single-family houses; Home improvement and renovation contractor agency; Disaster service

(G-5977)
FORWARD DSPTCHING LGISTICS LLC
3033 Clubway Dr Apt 124 (27834-8978)
PHONE..............................252 907-9797
EMP: 4
SALES (est): 286.06K **Privately Held**
SIC: 3537 7389 Trucks: freight, baggage, etc.: industrial, except mining; Business services, nec

(G-5978)
FRANKLIN BAKING COMPANY LLC
1107 Myrtle St (27834-3141)
PHONE..............................252 752-4600
Billy Killian, Brnch Mgr
EMP: 14
SALES (corp-wide): 5.1B **Publicly Held**
Web: franklin-co4goldsboro.edan.io
SIC: 2051 Bread, cake, and related products
HQ: Franklin Baking Company, Llc
500 W Grantham St
Goldsboro NC 27530
919 735-0344

(G-5979)
FRANKLIN BAKING COMPANY LLC
3350 Frog Level Rd (27834-8086)
PHONE..............................252 752-4600
Paul Frankum, Mgr
EMP: 10
SALES (corp-wide): 5.1B **Publicly Held**
Web: franklin-co4goldsboro.edan.io
SIC: 2051 Bread, all types (white, wheat, rye, etc); fresh or frozen
HQ: Franklin Baking Company, Llc
500 W Grantham St
Goldsboro NC 27530
919 735-0344

(G-5980)
FUJI SILYSIA CHEMICAL LTD
1215 Sugg Pkwy (27834-9008)
PHONE..............................919 484-4158
Brian Baymiller, Brnch Mgr
EMP: 10
Web: www.fujisilysia.com
SIC: 8732 2819 Market analysis or research; Silica compounds
PA: Fuji Silysia Chemical Ltd.
2-1846, Kozojicho
Kasugai AIC 487-0

(G-5981)
FUJI SILYSIA CHEMICAL USA LTD
1215 Sugg Pkwy (27834-9008)
PHONE..............................252 413-0003
Seiji Takahashi, Pr
Brian R Baymiller, *
Yasuo Ezaki, *
▲ **EMP:** 31 **EST:** 1998
SQ FT: 60,000
SALES (est): 18.11MM **Privately Held**
Web: www.fuji-silysia.co.jp
SIC: 2819 Industrial inorganic chemicals, nec
PA: Fuji Silysia Chemical Ltd.
2-1846, Kozojicho
Kasugai AIC 487-0

(G-5982)
GOOD VIBRATIONZ LLC ✪
1020 Red Banks Rd Ste 150 (27858-5466)
P.O. Box 7203 (27835-7203)
PHONE..............................919 820-3084
EMP: 7 **EST:** 2024
SALES (est): 344.75K **Privately Held**
SIC: 2024 Ice cream, packaged: molded, on sticks, etc.

(G-5983)
GRADY-WHITE BOATS INC
5121 Martin Luther King Jr Hwy (27834)
P.O. Box 1527 (27835)
PHONE..............................252 752-2111
▼ **EMP:** 200 **EST:** 1968
SALES (est): 24.86MM **Privately Held**
Web: www.gradywhite.com
SIC: 3732 Boats, fiberglass: building and repairing

(G-5984)
GREGORY POOLE EQUIPMENT CO
Also Called: Yale Material Handling
5200 Martin Luther King Jr Hwy
(27834-8614)
PHONE..............................252 931-5100
Paul Dougherty, Brnch Mgr
EMP: 7
SALES (corp-wide): 592.57MM **Privately Held**
Web: www.gregorypoolelift.com
SIC: 5084 3537 Materials handling machinery; Industrial trucks and tractors
HQ: Gregory Poole Equipment Company
4807 Beryl Rd
Raleigh NC 27606
919 828-0641

(G-5985)
GROVER GAMING INC (PA)
Also Called: New Market
3506 Greenville Blvd Ne (27834)
PHONE..............................252 329-7900
Garrett Blackwelder, Pr
EMP: 51 **EST:** 2013
SALES (est): 11.52MM
SALES (corp-wide): 11.52MM **Privately Held**
Web: www.grovergaming.com

SIC: 7993 5734 3823 Game machines; Software, computer games; Absorption analyzers: infrared, x-ray, etc.: industrial

(G-5986)
H&A SCIENTIFIC INC
105 Regency Blvd Ste A (27834-4699)
P.O. Box 8133 (27835-8133)
PHONE..............................252 752-4315
Craig Hamilton, Pr
▲ **EMP:** 8 **EST:** 1992
SALES (est): 427.55K **Privately Held**
Web: www.hascientific.com
SIC: 7371 3577 Custom computer programming services; Computer peripheral equipment, nec

(G-5987)
HATTERAS HAMMOCKS INC
Also Called: Hatteras Canvas Products
305 Industrial Blvd (27834-9015)
P.O. Box 1602 (27835-1602)
PHONE..............................252 758-0641
◆ **EMP:** 125 **EST:** 1973
SALES (est): 21.88MM **Privately Held**
Web: www.hatterashammocks.com
SIC: 2399 2298 2394 Hammocks, fabric: made from purchased materials; Rope, except asbestos and wire; Canvas and related products

(G-5988)
HYSTER-YALE GROUP INC
Yale Materials Handling
1400 Sullivan Dr (27834-9007)
PHONE..............................252 931-5100
Chuck Pascarelli, Pr
EMP: 40
Web: www.hyster-yale.com
SIC: 3537 Aircraft engine cradles
HQ: Hyster-Yale Materials Handling, Inc.
1400 Sullivan Dr
Greenville NC 27834
252 931-5100

(G-5989)
HYSTER-YALE GROUP INC
Also Called: HYSTER-YALE GROUP, INC.
5200 Martin Luther King Jr Hwy
(27834-8614)
P.O. Box 12010 (27835-2010)
PHONE..............................252 931-5100
Christopher Goodwin, Engr
EMP: 10
Web: www.hyster-yale.com
SIC: 3537 Forklift trucks
HQ: Hyster-Yale Materials Handling, Inc.
1400 Sullivan Dr
Greenville NC 27834
252 931-5100

(G-5990)
HYSTER-YALE MATERIALS HDLG INC (HQ)
Also Called: Yale Materials Handling
1400 Sullivan Dr (27834-9007)
P.O. Box 12010 (27835-2010)
PHONE..............................252 931-5100
Anthony J Salgado, CEO
Rajiv K Prasad, Pr
Charles A Bittenbender, Senior Vice President Law*
Gregory J Breier, Tax Vice President*
Brian K Frentzko, *
◆ **EMP:** 67 **EST:** 1993
SQ FT: 25,000
SALES (est): 1.41B **Publicly Held**
Web: www.hyster-yale.com
SIC: 3537 Forklift trucks
PA: Hyster-Yale, Inc.
5875 Lndrbrook Dr Ste 300

Cleveland OH 44124

(G-5991)
INSTITUTE FOR RESCH BIOTECNOLY
2905 S Memorial Dr (27834-6222)
PHONE................................252 689-2205
Farid Ahmed, *Dir*
EMP: 6
SALES (est): 178.6K **Privately Held**
SIC: 3826 Analytical instruments

(G-5992)
IOTO USA LLC
1997 N Greene St (27834-9021)
P.O. Box 1811 (27835-1811)
PHONE................................252 413-7343
▲ **EMP:** 10 **EST:** 2006
SALES (est): 1MM **Privately Held**
Web: www.iotointernational.com
SIC: 2131 2834 Chewing and smoking tobacco; Pharmaceutical preparations

(G-5993)
J & P MACHINE WORKS INC
4291 Us Highway 264 E (27834-0707)
PHONE................................252 758-1719
John Mccoy, *Pr*
Barbara Mccoy, *VP*
EMP: 6 **EST:** 1989
SALES (est): 410.18K **Privately Held**
SIC: 3599 Machine shop, jobbing and repair

(G-5994)
JANUS DEVELOPMENT GROUP INC
218 E Arlington Blvd (27858-5058)
PHONE................................252 551-9042
Alan Newton, *Pr*
EMP: 6 **EST:** 2000
SALES (est): 751.52K **Privately Held**
Web: www.janusdevelopment.com
SIC: 3841 5047 Surgical and medical instruments; Medical and hospital equipment

(G-5995)
JEFFERSON GROUP INC
Transeast
225 Martin St (27834-1479)
P.O. Box 39 (27835-0039)
PHONE................................252 752-6195
Edward Glenn, *Sec*
EMP: 25
SQ FT: 60,000
SALES (corp-wide): 2.11MM **Privately Held**
Web: www.newgrowthdesigns.com
SIC: 5193 3999 Artificial flowers; Chairs, hydraulic, barber and beauty shop
PA: Jefferson Group, Inc.
310 W 9th St
Greenville NC 27834
252 355-5600

(G-5996)
JKL INC (PA)
Also Called: Jenni K Jewelry
727 Red Banks Rd (27858-5832)
PHONE................................252 355-6714
Jenni Kolczynski Landis, *Pr*
Gerald Landis Junior, *Sec*
Gerald Landis Senior, *VP*
Christine Kolczynski, *Treas*
EMP: 19 **EST:** 1987
SQ FT: 8,700
SALES (est): 631.1K
SALES (corp-wide): 631.1K **Privately Held**
Web: www.jennik.com

SIC: 3911 5944 7631 5921 Jewelry, precious metal; Jewelry stores; Watch, clock, and jewelry repair; Wine

(G-5997)
JOHNNYS TIRE SALES AND SVC INC
2400 S Memorial Dr Ste 3a (27834-5031)
PHONE................................252 353-8473
John Edmison, *Pr*
Johnny Joyner, *VP*
EMP: 11 **EST:** 2010
SQ FT: 10,000
SALES (est): 980.65K **Privately Held**
Web: www.johnnystire.com
SIC: 5014 5531 7534 Automobile tires and tubes; Automotive tires; Tire repair shop

(G-5998)
KERDEA TECHNOLOGIES INC
1800 N Greene St (27834-9013)
PHONE................................971 900-1113
Douglas Carnes, *CEO*
Douglas Carnes Md Ph.d., *CEO*
Lloyd A Pearson, *CFO*
EMP: 12 **EST:** 2012
SALES (est): 431.66K **Privately Held**
SIC: 5531 3999 Automotive parts; Atomizers, toiletry

(G-5999)
LBA GROUP INC (PA)
3400 Tupper Dr (27834-0781)
P.O. Box 8026 (27835-8026)
PHONE................................252 329-9243
Lawrence Behr, *Ch*
Wayne Hildebrandt, *CFO*
Jerry Brown, *COO*
EMP: 22 **EST:** 1985
SQ FT: 12,000
SALES (est): 6.35MM **Privately Held**
Web: www.lbagroup.com
SIC: 3663 3661 8711 Antennas, transmitting and communications; Telephones and telephone apparatus; Consulting engineer

(G-6000)
LBA TECHNOLOGY INC
3400 Tupper Dr (27834-0781)
P.O. Box 8026 (27835-8026)
PHONE................................252 757-0279
Lawrence V Behr, *CEO*
Wayne A Hildebrandt, *
Jerry Brown, *
◆ **EMP:** 25 **EST:** 1975
SQ FT: 10,000
SALES (est): 2.26MM **Privately Held**
Web: www.lbagroup.com
SIC: 3663 3661 Antennas, transmitting and communications; Telephones and telephone apparatus
PA: Lba Group, Inc.
3400 Tupper Dr
Greenville NC 27834

(G-6001)
LDR DESIGNS
3113 Cleere Ct (27858-5570)
PHONE................................252 375-4484
Lakisha Randolph, *CEO*
Lakisha Randolph, *Owner*
EMP: 6 **EST:** 2008
SALES (est): 390.98K **Privately Held**
Web: www.ldr-designs.com
SIC: 2759 7389 7336 7379 Letterpress and screen printing; Apparel designers, commercial; Art design services; Online services technology consultants

(G-6002)
MAOLA MILK AND ICE CREAM CO
Also Called: MAOLA MILK AND ICE CREAM COMPANY
107 Hungate Dr (27858-8046)
PHONE................................252 756-3160
Harold Suber, *Brnch Mgr*
EMP: 45
SALES (corp-wide): 177.64MM **Privately Held**
Web: www.maolamilk.com
SIC: 2026 2024 Fluid milk; Ice cream, bulk
HQ: Maola Milk And Ice Cream Company, Llc
5500 Chestnut Ave
Newport News VA 23605
252 638-1131

(G-6003)
METALLIX REFINING INC
251 Industrial Blvd (27834-9004)
PHONE................................252 413-0346
John Santos, *Brnch Mgr*
EMP: 34
SALES (corp-wide): 23.19MM **Privately Held**
Web: www.metallix.com
SIC: 3356 2819 3339 Solder: wire, bar, acid core, and rosin core; Industrial inorganic chemicals, nec; Precious metals
PA: Metallix Refining Inc.
59 Ave At The Cmmons Ste
Shrewsbury NJ 07702
732 945-4132

(G-6004)
METROHOSE INCORPORATED
2009 N Greene St (27834-9023)
PHONE................................252 329-9891
Mark Jozwicki, *Brnch Mgr*
EMP: 4
SIC: 3492 4225 Hose and tube fittings and assemblies, hydraulic/pneumatic; General warehousing and storage
PA: Metrohose, Incorporated
2211 W 3rd St
Farmville VA 23901

(G-6005)
MODERN LIGHTNING PROTECTION CO
Also Called: Ftp Co
302 Queen Annes Rd (27858-6303)
PHONE................................252 756-3006
Ben Gibbs, *Pr*
EMP: 11 **EST:** 1944
SALES (est): 1.02MM **Privately Held**
Web: www.modernlightning.com
SIC: 7382 3643 Burglar alarm maintenance and monitoring; Current-carrying wiring services

(G-6006)
MOJO SPORTSWEAR INC
Also Called: Mojo Sportwear
1016 Myrtle St (27834-3140)
PHONE................................252 758-4176
EMP: 6 **EST:** 1985
SQ FT: 3,000
SALES (est): 490.49K **Privately Held**
Web: www.mojosportswear.com
SIC: 2261 2395 Screen printing of cotton broadwoven fabrics; Emblems, embroidered

(G-6007)
NEW EAST CARTRIDGE INC
1809 Dickinson Ave (27834-3803)
PHONE................................252 329-0837
Mack Taha, *CEO*
EMP: 6 **EST:** 2002
SALES (est): 472.63K **Privately Held**

SIC: 3955 Print cartridges for laser and other computer printers

(G-6008)
NORTH STATE STEEL INC (PA)
1010 W Gum Rd (27834-1191)
P.O. Box 5003 (27835-5003)
PHONE................................252 830-8884
EMP: 30 **EST:** 1984
SALES (est): 11.76MM
SALES (corp-wide): 11.76MM **Privately Held**
Web: www.northstatesteel.com
SIC: 3441 Fabricated structural metal

(G-6009)
OCCASIONS GROUP INC
Also Called: Taylor Prime Labels & Packg
1055 Greenville Blvd Sw (27834-7021)
PHONE................................252 321-5805
Tom Obrien, *Brnch Mgr*
EMP: 20
SALES (corp-wide): 3.81B **Privately Held**
Web: www.theoccasionsgroup.com
SIC: 2752 7334 2789 7389 Photo-offset printing; Photocopying and duplicating services; Bookbinding and related work; Labeling bottles, cans, cartons, etc.
HQ: The Occasions Group Inc
1750 Tower Blvd
North Mankato MN 56003

(G-6010)
PATHEON MANUFACTURING SVCS LLC
Also Called: Patheon
5900 Martin Luther King Jr Hwy (27834-8628)
PHONE................................252 758-3436
Claudia Harrington, *Managing Member*
▲ **EMP:** 99 **EST:** 2014
SALES (est): 75.95MM
SALES (corp-wide): 42.86B **Publicly Held**
Web: www.patheon.com
SIC: 2834 Druggists' preparations (pharmaceuticals)
PA: Thermo Fisher Scientific Inc.
168 3rd Ave
Waltham MA 02451
781 622-1000

(G-6011)
PEA CREEK MINE LLC
4747 Us Highway 264 E (27834-0716)
PHONE................................252 814-1388
EMP: 4 **EST:** 2007
SALES (est): 633.67K **Privately Held**
Web: www.peacreeksandmine.com
SIC: 3273 Ready-mixed concrete

(G-6012)
PENCO PRODUCTS INC (DH)
1820 Stonehenge Dr (27858-5965)
PHONE................................252 917-5287
TOLL FREE: 800
Greg Grogan, *Pr*
Charlie Mcbride, *VP*
Alan Kolody, *
Thomas Kulikawski, *
◆ **EMP:** 50 **EST:** 1979
SQ FT: 50,000
SALES (est): 48.99MM
SALES (corp-wide): 459.42MM **Privately Held**
Web: www.pencoproducts.com
SIC: 2599 2542 Factory furniture and fixtures ; Lockers (not refrigerated): except wood
HQ: Industrial Manufacturing Company Llc
8223 Brcksvlle Rd Ste 100
Brecksville OH 44141
440 838-4700

▲ = Import ▼ = Export
◆ = Import/Export

(G-6013)
PERDUE FARMS INC
Also Called: Perdue Farms Warehouse
1623 N Greene St (27834-1285)
PHONE..................................252 758-2141
EMP: 6
SALES (corp-wide): 1.24B Privately Held
Web: www.perdue.com
SIC: 2015 Poultry slaughtering and
processing
PA: Perdue Farms Incorporated
31149 Old Ocean City Rd
Salisbury MD 21804
800 473-7383

(G-6014)
PERFUSIO CORP
102a Hungate Dr (27858-8045)
P.O. Box 2611 (27602-2611)
PHONE..................................252 656-0404
Monte B Tucker, CEO
Jeffrey Basham, Prin
Phillip Hodges, Prin
Cheng Chen, Prin
Peter Geiger, Prin
EMP: 9 EST: 2014
SQ FT: 400
SALES (est): 3.04MM Privately Held
Web: www.perfusio.com
SIC: 3841 Diagnostic apparatus, medical

(G-6015)
PIONEER SRGCAL ORTHBLOGICS INC (DH)
1800 N Greene St Ste A (27834-9013)
PHONE..................................252 355-4405
Anton Lewis Usala, Ch Bd
Mark Metzger, Ex VP
EMP: 14 EST: 1991
SALES (est): 3.49MM
SALES (corp-wide): 81.98MM Publicly
Held
Web: www.rtix.com
SIC: 3841 Surgical and medical instruments
HQ: Pioneer Surgical Technology, Inc.
7 Switchbud Pl Ste 192-18
The Woodlands TX 77380

(G-6016)
PURILUM LLC
967 Woodridge Park Rd (27834-0055)
P.O. Box 1673 (27835-1673)
PHONE..................................252 931-8020
Bianca Iodice, Pr
EMP: 23 EST: 2013
SALES (est): 4.75MM Privately Held
Web: www.purilum.com
SIC: 3999 Cigarette and cigar products and
accessories

(G-6017)
RANDOM RUES BOTANICAL LLC
1290 E Arlington Blvd (27858-7854)
PHONE..................................252 214-2759
Christmas Smith, Pr
EMP: 8 EST: 2016
SALES (est): 166.59K Privately Held
SIC: 5499 3842 5963 5122 Spices and herbs
; Cosmetic restorations; Cosmetic sales,
house-to-house; Cosmetics, perfumes, and
hair products

(G-6018)
RENASCENCE INC
Also Called: PIP Printing
3185 Moseley Dr (27858-4245)
PHONE..................................252 355-1636
Donald Stocks, Pr
EMP: 8 EST: 1990
SQ FT: 5,000
SALES (est): 2.87MM Privately Held

Web: www.pip.com
SIC: 2752 Offset printing

(G-6019)
ROBERT BOSCH TOOL CORPORATION
Also Called: Greenville Division
310 Staton Rd (27834-9037)
PHONE..................................252 551-7512
Gary W Utz, Mgr
EMP: 11
SALES (corp-wide): 391.51MM Privately
Held
Web: www.boschtools.com
SIC: 3545 3423 Drills (machine tool
accessories); Hand and edge tools, nec
HQ: Robert Bosch Tool Corporation
1800 W Central Rd
Mount Prospect IL 60056

(G-6020)
SALT WOOD PRODUCTS INC (PA)
Also Called: Salt Wood Products 2
3016 Jones Park Rd (27834-8361)
PHONE..................................252 830-8875
Gary Salt, Pr
Teresa Salt, Sec
Alger Salt, Stockholder
EMP: 6 EST: 1957
SQ FT: 12,000
SALES (est): 1.75MM
SALES (corp-wide): 1.75MM Privately
Held
Web: www.saltwoodproducts.com
SIC: 2452 5031 5211 Prefabricated
buildings, wood; Lumber, plywood, and
millwork; Lumber and other building
materials

(G-6021)
SERVICE ROOFING AND SHTMTL CO
107 Staton Ct (27834-9016)
P.O. Box 1864 (27835-1864)
PHONE..................................252 758-2179
M Michael Richardson, Pr
Harry H Esbenshade Iii, Ch Bd
Max Michael Richardson, Pr
Barry Sugg, VP
Paul E Tyndall, VP
EMP: 86 EST: 1960
SQ FT: 6,000
SALES (est): 3.62MM
SALES (corp-wide): 94.28MM Privately
Held
Web: www.tri-stateservicegroup.com
SIC: 3444 1761 Sheet metalwork; Roofing,
siding, and sheetmetal work
HQ: The Cypress Mountain Company
107 Staton Ct
Greenville NC 27834
252 758-2179

(G-6022)
SIGNS NOW 103 LLC
Also Called: Signs Now
118b Greenville Blvd Se (27858-5706)
PHONE..................................252 355-0768
EMP: 6 EST: 1989
SQ FT: 2,000
SALES (est): 204.15K Privately Held
Web: www.signsnow.com
SIC: 3993 Signs and advertising specialties

(G-6023)
SIGNSMITH CUSTOM SIGNS & AWNIN
1709 Evans St (27834-5772)
PHONE..................................252 752-4321
Leighton Blount, Owner
EMP: 11 EST: 2007
SALES (est): 968.72K Privately Held

Web: www.signsmithinc.com
SIC: 3993 Signs, not made in custom sign
painting shops

(G-6024)
SIMPLY BTIFUL EVENTS DECOR LLC
1263 Windsong Dr (27858-9750)
PHONE..................................252 375-3839
EMP: 5 EST: 2021
SALES (est): 150K Privately Held
Web: www.simplybeautifuldecor.ca
SIC: 2621 Printing paper

(G-6025)
SPHENODON TOOL CO INC
Also Called: STC Precision Cutting Tools
3530 Tupper Dr (27834-0755)
PHONE..................................252 757-3460
Jeffery A Dill, Pr
Amy Dill, VP
EMP: 6 EST: 1981
SQ FT: 6,500
SALES (est): 1.82MM Privately Held
Web: www.sphenodontool.com
SIC: 3599 Machine shop, jobbing and repair

(G-6026)
TEAM GSG LLC
Also Called: Greenville Seamless Gutters
851 Black Jack Simpson Rd (27858-8728)
PHONE..................................252 830-1032
EMP: 5 EST: 2010
SALES (est): 369.53K Privately Held
Web: www.greenvillegutters.com
SIC: 3089 Gutters (glass fiber reinforced),
fiberglass or plastics

(G-6027)
THURMAN TOLER
Also Called: Toler Welding & Repair
1229 Sheppard Mill Rd (27834-8271)
PHONE..................................252 758-4082
Thurman Toler, Owner
EMP: 6 EST: 1988
SALES (est): 174.83K Privately Held
Web: www.tolerswelding.com
SIC: 7692 Welding repair

(G-6028)
TIMOTHY L GRIFFIN ✪
Also Called: T.L.g Atelier
477 Huntingridge Rd Apt B (27834-5906)
PHONE..................................336 317-8314
Timothy Lee Griffin, Owner
EMP: 8 EST: 2023
SALES (est): 1.22MM Privately Held
SIC: 3299 7699 7336 7335 Architectural
sculptures: gypsum, clay, papier mache, etc.
; Welding equipment repair; Graphic arts
and related design; Photographic studio,
commercial

(G-6029)
UNITED MACHINE WORKS INC
1716 Nc Highway 903 N (27834-6009)
PHONE..................................252 752-7434
Herbert Brown, Pr
C Russell Brown, *
EMP: 34 EST: 1964
SQ FT: 23,750
SALES (est): 4.21MM Privately Held
Web: www.unitedmachineworksnc.com
SIC: 3599 Machine shop, jobbing and repair

(G-6030)
UNX-CHRISTEYNS LLC (PA)
707 E Arlington Blvd (27858)
P.O. Box 7206 (27858)
PHONE..................................252 756-8616
Joshua Clark, Pr

EMP: 22 EST: 2019
SALES (est): 22.34MM
SALES (corp-wide): 22.34MM Privately
Held
Web: www.unxchristeyns.com
SIC: 2841 Soap and other detergents

(G-6031)
UNX-CHRISTEYNS LLC
1704 E Arlington Blvd Ste A (27858-7828)
PHONE..................................252 355-8433
Joe Daxtor, Supervisor
EMP: 6
SALES (corp-wide): 22.34MM Privately
Held
Web: www.unxchristeyns.com
SIC: 2842 2841 Automobile polish;
Detergents, synthetic organic or inorganic
alkaline
PA: Unx-Christeyns, Llc
707 E Arlington Blvd
Greenville NC 27858
252 756-8616

(G-6032)
UNX-CHRISTEYNS LLC
201 W 9th St (27835)
PHONE..................................252 756-8616
Ben Wilson, Brnch Mgr
EMP: 54
SALES (corp-wide): 22.34MM Privately
Held
Web: www.unxchristeyns.com
SIC: 2842 Bleaches, household: dry or liquid
PA: Unx-Christeyns, Llc
707 E Arlington Blvd
Greenville NC 27858
252 756-8616

(G-6033)
WATSON ELECTRICAL CNSTR CO LLC
3121 Bismarck St (27834-6807)
P.O. Box 1250 (27835-1250)
PHONE..................................252 756-4550
Greg Philligin, Mgr
EMP: 54
SALES (corp-wide): 278.97MM Privately
Held
Web: www.watsonelec.com
SIC: 1731 7694 General electrical contractor
; Electric motor repair
HQ: Watson Electrical Construction Co Llc
1500 Charleston St Se
Wilson NC 27893
252 237-7511

Grifton
Pitt County

(G-6034)
COVATION BIOMATERIALS LLC
Also Called: Kinston Plant
4693 Highway 11 N (28530-0017)
PHONE..................................252 643-7000
EMP: 115
Web: www.covationbio.com
SIC: 2824 Organic fibers, noncellulosic
HQ: Covation Biomaterials Llc
800 Prdes Crssing Ste 201
Newark DE 19713
865 279-1414

(G-6035)
EIDP INC
Also Called: Dupont
4693 Highway 11 N (28530-0017)
P.O. Box 800 (28502-0800)
PHONE..................................252 522-6111

G
E
O
G
R
A
P
H
I
C

Harold Thomas, *Mgr*
EMP: 60
SALES (corp-wide): 16.91B **Publicly Held**
Web: www.dupont.com
SIC: 2819 Industrial inorganic chemicals, nec
HQ: Eidp, Inc.
  9330 Zionsville Rd
  Indianapolis IN 46268
  833 267-8382

(G-6036)
ENGLISHS ALL WOOD HOMES INC
Also Called: Carolina Vinyl Products
608 Queen St (28530-7347)
P.O. Box 1137 (28530-1137)
PHONE..............................252 524-5000
Patsy English, *Pr*
Jerry English, *VP*
EMP: 18 **EST:** 1995
SQ FT: 12,000
SALES (est): 2.28MM **Privately Held**
Web: www.carolinavp.com
SIC: 1799 3089 Fence construction; Air
  mattresses, plastics

(G-6037)
MAGNUM ENTERPRIZE INC
Also Called: Magnum Telemetry
525 Country Acres Rd (28530-8909)
P.O. Box 1060 (28530-1060)
PHONE..............................252 524-5391
Gary Tripp, *Pr*
Tracy Tripp, *Sec*
▲ **EMP:** 7 **EST:** 1997
SQ FT: 6,000
SALES (est): 481.63K **Privately Held**
Web: www.magnumtelemetry.com
SIC: 3699 Sound signaling devices, electrical

(G-6038)
ROADMSTER TRCK CONVERSIONS INC
Also Called: Roadmaster Truck Company
6482 N Highland Blvd (28530-8101)
PHONE..............................252 412-3980
Ronald Lassiter, *Pr*
EMP: 5 **EST:** 2011
SQ FT: 800
SALES (est): 659.33K **Privately Held**
Web: www.roadmastertruck.com
SIC: 2515 Sleep furniture

(G-6039)
WEYERHAEUSER COMPANY
371 E Hanrahan Rd (28530-8717)
P.O. Box 280 (28513-0280)
PHONE..............................252 746-7200
Alaen Sherrington, *Mgr*
EMP: 12
SALES (corp-wide): 7.12B **Publicly Held**
Web: www.weyerhaeuser.com
SIC: 4226 2426 2421 Lumber terminal
  (storage for hire); Hardwood dimension and
  flooring mills; Sawmills and planing mills,
  general
PA: Weyerhaeuser Company
  220 Occidental Ave S
  Seattle WA 98104
  206 539-3000

Grimesland
Pitt County

(G-6040)
BEC-FAYE LLC
3393 Mobleys Bridge Rd (27837-8857)
PHONE..............................252 714-8700
Overton V Parker, *Prin*
EMP: 6 **EST:** 2005

SALES (est): 163.62K **Privately Held**
SIC: 3721 Aircraft

Grover
Cleveland County

(G-6041)
A B C SCREENPRINTING AND EMB
106 Sprouse Ln (28073-9600)
P.O. Box 324 (28073-0324)
PHONE..............................704 937-3452
Angie Richardson, *VP*
Angie Richardson, *Cnslt*
Donna Mabry, *Treas*
EMP: 6 **EST:** 1999
SALES (est): 59.02K **Privately Held**
SIC: 2759 Screen printing

(G-6042)
CELANESE INTL CORP
Also Called: Celanese
2523 Blacksburg Rd (28073-9641)
PHONE..............................704 480-5798
EMP: 9 **EST:** 2016
SALES (est): 1.54MM **Privately Held**
SIC: 2821 Plastics materials and resins

(G-6043)
GENERAL SHALE BRICK INC
1622 Longbranch Rd (28073-8501)
PHONE..............................704 937-7431
Dale Russell, *Mgr*
EMP: 12
SALES (corp-wide): 4.59B **Privately Held**
Web: www.generalshale.com
SIC: 3251 5211 Structural brick and blocks;
  Brick
HQ: General Shale Brick, Inc.
  3015 Bristol Hwy
  Johnson City TN 37601
  423 282-4661

(G-6044)
GROVER INDUSTRIES INC (PA)
219 Laurel Ave (28073-1207)
PHONE..............................828 859-9125
James A Harry, *Pr*
O John Harry, *VP*
Ronald W Hewett, *VP Sls*
Gregory D Blalock, *Sec*
▲ **EMP:** 10 **EST:** 1962
SQ FT: 200,000
SALES (est): 2.27MM
SALES (corp-wide): 2.27MM **Privately Held**
SIC: 2269 Bleaching: raw stock, yarn, and
  narrow fabrics

(G-6045)
UNIQUETEX LLC
700 S Battleground Ave (28073-9541)
PHONE..............................704 457-3003
Fang Wang, *Managing Member*
EMP: 50 **EST:** 2015
SALES (est): 9.13MM **Privately Held**
Web: www.uniquetex.com
SIC: 2221 Textile mills, broadwoven: silk and
  manmade, also glass
PA: Guangdong Beautiful Health Co., Ltd.
  Shatou Shijiang Industrial Zone,
  Nanhai District
  Foshan GD 52820

Halifax
Halifax County

(G-6046)
CCBCC OPERATIONS LLC
Also Called: Coca-Cola
80 Industrial Dr (27839-9276)
PHONE..............................252 536-3611
Dan Treadway, *Brnch Mgr*
EMP: 39
SALES (corp-wide): 6.9B **Publicly Held**
Web: www.cokeconsolidated.com
SIC: 2086 Bottled and canned soft drinks
HQ: Ccbcc Operations, Llc
  4100 Coca-Cola Plz
  Charlotte NC 28211
  704 364-8728

(G-6047)
PERDUE FARMS INC
Also Called: Perdue Farms
1201 State Rd (27839)
P.O. Box 508 (27839-0508)
PHONE..............................252 583-5731
Darrell Bryant, *Mgr*
EMP: 78
SALES (corp-wide): 1.24B **Privately Held**
Web: www.perdue.com
SIC: 2015 Poultry slaughtering and
  processing
PA: Perdue Farms Incorporated
  31149 Old Ocean City Rd
  Salisbury MD 21804
  800 473-7383

Hamilton
Martin County

(G-6048)
COASTAL AGROBUSINESS INC
12011 Nc 125 (27840-9705)
PHONE..............................252 798-3481
Andy Tuer, *Mgr*
EMP: 9
SALES (corp-wide): 61.99MM **Privately Held**
Web: www.coastalagro.com
SIC: 5191 3523 Chemicals, agricultural;
  Sprayers and spraying machines,
  agricultural
PA: Coastal Agrobusiness, Inc.
  112 Staton Rd
  Greenville NC 27834
  252 238-7391

(G-6049)
PENCO PRODUCTS INC
1301 Penco Dr Hwy 125 (27840)
P.O. Box 400 (27840-0400)
PHONE..............................252 798-4000
Bruce Woodword, *Brnch Mgr*
EMP: 200
SALES (corp-wide): 459.42MM **Privately Held**
Web: www.pencoproducts.com
SIC: 3499 2599 5021 3444 Tablets, bronze
  or other metal; Factory furniture and fixtures
  ; Lockers; Sheet metalwork
HQ: Penco Products, Inc.
  1820 Stonehenge Dr
  Greenville NC 27858

Hamlet
Richmond County

(G-6050)
ASSOCIATED DISTRIBUTORS INC
120 Doe Loop (28345-9305)
PHONE..............................910 895-5800
Sheila Locklear, *Pr*
Wyatt Pegram, *Sec*
Mitchell Spivey, *VP*
EMP: 9 **EST:** 1992
SQ FT: 5,000
SALES (est): 201.76K **Privately Held**
Web: www.associateddistributors.ne
SIC: 2253 5136 Shirts(outerwear), knit;
  Shirts, men's and boys'

(G-6051)
BOX COMPANY OF AMERICA LLC
12 Ev Hogan Dr (28345-8822)
PHONE..............................910 582-0100
EMP: 50 **EST:** 2022
SALES (est): 3.89MM **Privately Held**
Web: www.boxcompanyofamerica.com
SIC: 2631 2679 5113 2675 Chip board;
  Corrugated paper: made from purchased
  material; Corrugated and solid fiber boxes;
  Die-cut paper and board

(G-6052)
CAVCO INDUSTRIES INC
Also Called: Cavco of North Carolina
106 Innovative Way (28345-4440)
PHONE..............................910 410-5050
EMP: 55
SALES (corp-wide): 1.79B **Publicly Held**
Web: www.cavco.com
SIC: 2452 Modular homes, prefabricated,
  wood
PA: Cavco Industries, Inc.
  3636 N Centl Ave Ste 1200
  Phoenix AZ 85012
  602 256-6263

(G-6053)
CCBCC OPERATIONS LLC
Also Called: Coca-Cola
1662 E Us 74 Hwy (28345-8102)
P.O. Box 711 (28345-0711)
PHONE..............................910 582-3543
Wayne Andrews, *Brnch Mgr*
EMP: 33
SALES (corp-wide): 6.9B **Publicly Held**
Web: www.coca-cola.com
SIC: 2086 Bottled and canned soft drinks
HQ: Ccbcc Operations, Llc
  4100 Coca-Cola Plz
  Charlotte NC 28211
  704 364-8728

(G-6054)
DR LOGGING LLC
506 Bauersfeld St (28345-2103)
PHONE..............................910 417-9643
EMP: 4 **EST:** 2011
SALES (est): 485.9K **Privately Held**
SIC: 2411 Logging camps and contractors

(G-6055)
FERROFAB INC
1416 Hylan Ave (28345-4743)
PHONE..............................910 557-5624
Willy Hauer, *Pr*
▲ **EMP:** 27 **EST:** 2012
SALES (est): 5.71MM **Privately Held**
Web: www.ferro-fab.com
SIC: 3441 Fabricated structural metal

(G-6056)
GLOBAL PACKAGING INC
106 Marks Creek Ln (28345-7273)
PHONE..................610 666-1608
EMP: 82
SALES (corp-wide): 78.16MM **Privately Held**
Web: www.glopkg.com
SIC: 5199 3089 Packaging materials; Air mattresses, plastics
PA: Global Packaging, Inc.
209 Brower Ave
Oaks PA 19456
610 666-1608

(G-6057)
HOOD PACKAGING CORPORATION
Also Called: Hamlet Paper Packaging
740 Cheraw Rd (28345-7157)
PHONE..................910 582-1842
Jimmy Dawkins, *Brnch Mgr*
EMP: 200
Web: www.hoodpkg.com
SIC: 2674 2673 Shipping bags or sacks, including multiwall and heavy duty; Bags: plastic, laminated, and coated
HQ: Hood Packaging Corporation
25 Woodgreen Pl
Madison MS 39110
601 853-7260

(G-6058)
IMPACT PLASTICS INC
1057 County Home Rd (28345-4390)
PHONE..................910 205-1493
John Sousa, *Prin*
EMP: 6 **EST:** 2005
SALES (est): 1.92MM **Privately Held**
Web: www.impactplastics.co
SIC: 3089 Injection molding of plastics

(G-6059)
LATICRETE INTERNATIONAL INC
299 Industry Dr (28345-7324)
PHONE..................910 582-2252
Ron Nunnerlyn, *Brnch Mgr*
EMP: 19
SALES (corp-wide): 135.71MM **Privately Held**
Web: www.laticrete.com
SIC: 2891 2899 Epoxy adhesives; Chemical preparations, nec
PA: Laticrete International, Inc.
91 Amity Rd
Bethany CT 06524
203 393-0010

(G-6060)
P & P DISTRIBUTING COMPANY
Also Called: Page Plantation Shuttering Co
307 Industry Dr (28345-7323)
PHONE..................910 582-1968
Willard Page, *Pr*
Judy Page, *Sec*
EMP: 5 **EST:** 1990
SQ FT: 21,000
SALES (est): 222.75K **Privately Held**
Web: www.pageplantationshutter.com
SIC: 2431 5031 Louver doors: wood; Lumber, plywood, and millwork

(G-6061)
R R MICKEY LOGGING INC
1014 Boyd Lake Rd (28345-8146)
PHONE..................910 205-0525
Richard R Mickey, *Pr*
Donna Reishel, *Sec*
EMP: 9 **EST:** 1980
SALES (est): 178.53K **Privately Held**
SIC: 2411 Logging camps and contractors

(G-6062)
RICHMOND COUNTY GMRS INC
109 George Dawkins Dr (28345-4368)
PHONE..................910 461-0260
Andy Baucom, *CEO*
EMP: 4
SALES (est): 334.19K **Privately Held**
SIC: 7389 3663 Business Activities at Non-Commercial Site; Radio broadcasting and communications equipment

(G-6063)
THUASNE LLC
167 Marks Creek Ln (28345)
P.O. Box 495 (28338)
PHONE..................910 557-5378
Mark W L Smith, *Pr*
EMP: 140
SALES (corp-wide): 1.25MM **Privately Held**
Web: www.knitrite.com
SIC: 3842 Orthopedic appliances
HQ: Thuasne Llc
120 Osage Ave
Kansas City KS 66105
913 279-6310

(G-6064)
TRINITY MANUFACTURING INC
11 Ev Hogan Dr (28345-8821)
P.O. Box 1519 (28345)
PHONE..................910 582-5650
Dean Storkan, *Pr*
◆ **EMP:** 68 **EST:** 1989
SQ FT: 7,000
SALES (est): 23.12MM **Privately Held**
Web: www.trinitymfg.com
SIC: 2879 2869 Agricultural chemicals, nec; Industrial organic chemicals, nec

(G-6065)
VISTA PRODUCTS INC
10 Ev Hogan Dr (28345-8822)
PHONE..................910 582-0130
Alen Courtwright, *Mgr*
EMP: 75
Web: www.vistaproducts.com
SIC: 2591 5072 Blinds vertical; Hardware
HQ: Vista Products, Inc.
8801 Corporate Square Ct
Jacksonville FL 32216
904 725-2242

Hampstead
Pender County

(G-6066)
ALLFUEL HST INC ✪
109 W High Bluff Dr (28443-7133)
PHONE..................919 868-9410
Joe Cochran, *CEO*
EMP: 10 **EST:** 2024
SALES (est): 1.03MM **Privately Held**
SIC: 3259 7389 Chimney pipe and tops, clay ; Business Activities at Non-Commercial Site

(G-6067)
ALLIED MARINE CONTRACTORS LLC
92 Harold Ct (28443-8247)
PHONE..................910 367-2159
EMP: 9 **EST:** 2007
SALES (est): 1.11MM **Privately Held**
Web: www.alliedmarinecontractors.com
SIC: 3531 Marine related equipment

(G-6068)
ATLANTIC TOOL & DIE CO INC
2363 Nc Highway 210 W (28443-3455)
PHONE..................910 270-2888
Hugh Hawthorne, *Pr*
Andy Hawkins, *VP*
EMP: 9 **EST:** 1987
SQ FT: 6,000
SALES (est): 278.85K **Privately Held**
Web: www.atlantictoolanddie.com
SIC: 3544 3469 Special dies and tools; Metal stampings, nec

(G-6069)
BABINE LAKE CORPORATION (PA)
Also Called: Whisper Soft Mills
113 Dogwood Cir (28443-2596)
PHONE..................910 285-7955
Nicholas Sokol, *Pr*
Richard F Tunner Junior, *Ex VP*
◆ **EMP:** 25 **EST:** 1973
SQ FT: 100,000
SALES (est): 1.52MM
SALES (corp-wide): 1.52MM **Privately Held**
SIC: 2392 Sheets, fabric: made from purchased materials

(G-6070)
CAISON YACHTS INC
405 Lewis Rd (28443-8605)
P.O. Box 991 (28443-0991)
PHONE..................910 270-6394
Don Caison, *CEO*
EMP: 6 **EST:** 2007
SALES (est): 844.29K **Privately Held**
Web: www.caisonyachts.com
SIC: 3732 Yachts, building and repairing

(G-6071)
ELAND INDUSTRIES INC
353 Washington Acres Rd (28443-3737)
PHONE..................910 304-5353
Tim Ennis, *Pr*
Kevin Ennis, *
EMP: 24 **EST:** 2017
SALES (est): 1.57MM **Privately Held**
SIC: 3449 Miscellaneous metalwork

(G-6072)
FOXSTER OPCO LLC
118 Circle Dr (28443-2108)
PHONE..................910 297-6996
Adam Fox, *Managing Member*
EMP: 22 **EST:** 2016
SALES (est): 552.94K **Privately Held**
SIC: 5088 7372 Transportation equipment and supplies; Business oriented computer software

(G-6073)
GREG PRICE
Also Called: Wood and Anvil
107 Patton Ln (28443-7600)
PHONE..................847 778-4426
Greg Price, *Owner*
EMP: 9 **EST:** 2021
SALES (est): 561.18K **Privately Held**
SIC: 3479 2514 Coating of metals and formed products; Kitchen cabinets: metal

(G-6074)
ONSLOW BAY BOATWORKS & MARINE
175 Sloop Point Loop Rd (28443-2616)
PHONE..................910 270-3703
EMP: 6
SALES (est): 1.05MM **Privately Held**
SIC: 3732 Boatbuilding and repairing

(G-6075)
RAYS CLASSIC VINYL REPAIR INC
440 Crooked Creek Rd (28443-7977)
PHONE..................910 520-1626
EMP: 5 **EST:** 2003
SALES (est): 233.82K **Privately Held**
Web: www.nbccbakersfield.com
SIC: 3081 Vinyl film and sheet

(G-6076)
TECH-TOOL INC
2561 Country Club Dr (28443-2528)
PHONE..................919 906-6229
Richard Tilley, *Pr*
EMP: 8 **EST:** 1993
SQ FT: 10,000
SALES (est): 217.07K **Privately Held**
SIC: 3599 Machine shop, jobbing and repair

(G-6077)
TOPSAIL SPORTSWEAR INC
15530 Us Highway 17 (28443-3084)
P.O. Box 995 (28443-0995)
PHONE..................910 270-4903
Bill Lanier, *Pr*
Mitch Lanier, *VP*
EMP: 4 **EST:** 1986
SALES (est): 242.99K **Privately Held**
Web: www.topsailsportswear.com
SIC: 2395 Embroidery products, except Schiffli machine

(G-6078)
TOPSAIL VOICE LLC
Also Called: Hampstead Publishing
14886 Us Highway 17 (28443-3217)
P.O. Box 880 (28443-0880)
PHONE..................910 270-2944
Lockwood Phillips, *Pr*
EMP: 9 **EST:** 1991
SALES (est): 58.37K **Privately Held**
Web: www.topsailvoice.com
SIC: 2711 Newspapers, publishing and printing

(G-6079)
UTILITY METERING SOLUTIONS INC
Also Called: Carolina Meter and Supply
231 Sloop Point Loop Rd (28443-2618)
P.O. Box 12448 (28405-0119)
PHONE..................910 270-2885
Barry Hales, *CEO*
Nancy S Jones, *CFO*
EMP: 4 **EST:** 1999
SALES (est): 405.21K **Privately Held**
SIC: 3824 Water meters

(G-6080)
WATERS CORPORATION
15430 Us Highway 17 (28443-3549)
P.O. Box 998 (28443-0998)
PHONE..................910 270-3137
Lee Piver, *Brnch Mgr*
EMP: 4
Web: www.waters.com
SIC: 3826 Chromatographic equipment, laboratory type
PA: Waters Corporation
34 Maple St
Milford MA 01757

Hamptonville
Yadkin County

(G-6081)
AMERICAN IMAGE PRESS
5043 Highland Grove Pl (27020-8190)
P.O. Box 42 (27020-0042)
PHONE..................336 468-2796

Vonda Blackburn, *Prin*
EMP: 4 **EST:** 2010
SALES (est): 165.02K **Privately Held**
Web: www.ifpo.net
SIC: 2741 Miscellaneous publishing

(G-6082)
BESANA-LOVATI INC (PA)
4112 W Old Us 421 Hwy (27020-8413)
PHONE..............................336 768-6064
Angelo Lovati, *Pr*
Annibale Besana, *VP*
Stewart Walmsley, *Sec*
Lorendana Lovati, *Treas*
Darrell Green, *Sec*
▲ **EMP:** 11 **EST:** 1990
SALES (est): 1.05MM **Privately Held**
Web: www.besana-usa.com
SIC: 3559 Glass making machinery: blowing,
molding, forming, etc.

(G-6083)
DUTCH KETTLE LLC
Also Called: Dutch Kettle, The
5016 Hunting Creek Church Rd
(27020-7750)
PHONE..............................336 468-8422
Paul Peachey, *Managing Member*
▲ **EMP:** 5 **EST:** 1986
SALES (est): 1.96MM **Privately Held**
Web: www.dutchkettle.net
SIC: 2033 Jams, jellies, and preserves,
packaged in cans, jars, etc.

(G-6084)
GOLD CREEK INC
3441 Lone Hickory Rd (27020-7201)
PHONE..............................336 468-4495
Dale Wooten, *Pr*
EMP: 4 **EST:** 1982
SALES (est): 92.99K **Privately Held**
SIC: 2411 Logging camps and contractors

(G-6085)
IFPO - IFMO/AMERICAN IMAGE INC
Also Called: Today's Photographer Magazine
5043 Highland Grove Pl (27020-8190)
P.O. Box 42 (27020-0042)
PHONE..............................336 945-9867
Vonda Blackburn, *Pr*
Jack Gallimore, *Sec*
EMP: 4 **EST:** 1984
SQ FT: 4,500
SALES (est): 89.34K **Privately Held**
Web: www.ifpo.net
SIC: 2721 7311 Magazines: publishing only,
not printed on site; Advertising agencies

(G-6086)
LAUREL GRAY VINEYARDS INC
5726 W Old Us 421 Hwy (27020-8225)
PHONE..............................336 468-9463
Kim Myers, *Pr*
EMP: 7 **EST:** 2004
SALES (est): 245.18K **Privately Held**
Web: www.laurelgray.com
SIC: 2084 Wines

(G-6087)
LYDALL INC
1241 Buck Shoals Rd (27020)
PHONE..............................336 468-8522
Joe Abbruzzi, *Brnch Mgr*
EMP: 4
Web: www.lydall.com
SIC: 2297 Nonwoven fabrics
HQ: Lydall, Inc.
180 Glstnbury Blvd Ste 12
Glastonbury CT 06033
860 646-1233

(G-6088)
**LYDECH THERMAL ACOUSTICAL
INC (HQ)**
Also Called: Thermal Acoustical Group
1245 Buck Shoals Rd (27020)
P.O. Box 109 (27020)
PHONE..............................248 277-4900
Collin Malcolm, *CEO*
Mary Brandon, *
▲ **EMP:** 68 **EST:** 1977
SQ FT: 60,000
SALES (est): 98.01MM
SALES (corp-wide): 921.67MM **Privately
Held**
Web: www.lydech.com
SIC: 3441 Fabricated structural metal
PA: Regent, Lp
9720 Wilshire Blvd Fl 6
Beverly Hills CA 90212
310 299-4100

(G-6089)
LYDECH THERMAL ACOUSTICAL INC
Fibers
1241 Buck Shoals Rd (27020-7624)
PHONE..............................336 468-8522
William Hume, *Mgr*
EMP: 527
SALES (corp-wide): 921.67MM **Privately
Held**
Web: www.lydallautomotive.com
SIC: 3441 Fabricated structural metal
HQ: Lydech Thermal Acoustical, Inc.
1245 Buck Shoals Rd
Hamptonville NC 27020
248 277-4900

(G-6090)
MAST WOODWORKS
5328 Saint Paul Church Rd (27020-7839)
PHONE..............................336 468-1194
Alvin Dale Mast, *Owner*
EMP: 10 **EST:** 2000
SALES (est): 750K **Privately Held**
Web:
www.affordablebuildingsonline.com
SIC: 3448 2452 Prefabricated metal
buildings and components; Log cabins,
prefabricated, wood

(G-6091)
ROLLFORMING LLC
4708 Hunting Creek Church Rd
(27020-7747)
PHONE..............................336 468-4317
Gabriel Schlabach, *Managing Member*
EMP: 5 **EST:** 2020
SALES (est): 297.64K **Privately Held**
SIC: 3542 Machine tools, metal forming type

(G-6092)
STEELMAN LUMBER & PALLET LLC
4744 Us 21 Hwy (27020-7322)
PHONE..............................336 468-2757
Spencer Steelman, *Managing Member*
EMP: 12 **EST:** 2015
SALES (est): 1.21MM **Privately Held**
Web: www.steelmanlumber.com
SIC: 4953 2448 5031 Recycling, waste
materials; Wood pallets and skids; Pallets,
wood

(G-6093)
TARHEEL SAND & STONE INC
1108 Tuckda Way (27020-8398)
PHONE..............................336 468-4003
Keith Adams, *Pr*
Terry Jester, *VP*
EMP: 4 **EST:** 1989
SALES (est): 916.2K **Privately Held**

SIC: 1411 1442 Dimension stone;
Construction sand and gravel

(G-6094)
VINYL STRUCTURES LLC
Also Called: Trupoint Backyards
4708 Hunting Creek Church Rd
(27020-7747)
PHONE..............................336 468-4311
Mark Schlabach, *Managing Member*
EMP: 5 **EST:** 1997
SQ FT: 12,000
SALES (est): 2.36MM **Privately Held**
SIC: 3448 Buildings, portable: prefabricated
metal

Harbinger
Currituck County

(G-6095)
GRAPHIC ATTACK INC
Harbinger Commercial Park Ste 34 (27941)
P.O. Box 38 (27941)
PHONE..............................252 491-2174
Guy R Grazetti, *Pr*
▼ **EMP:** 4 **EST:** 1987
SQ FT: 6,000
SALES (est): 142.18K **Privately Held**
Web: www.graphicattack.com
SIC: 2261 Screen printing of cotton
broadwoven fabrics

(G-6096)
TRI-H MOLDING CO
135 W Side Ln (27941)
P.O. Box 159 (27941-0159)
PHONE..............................252 491-8530
Stanley Hopkins, *Pr*
David S Hopkins, *Stockholder*
EMP: 4 **EST:** 1985
SQ FT: 7,500
SALES (est): 150.39K **Privately Held**
SIC: 2491 Structural lumber and timber,
treated wood

Harmony
Iredell County

(G-6097)
ASSOCIATED METAL WORKS INC
137 E Memorial Hwy (28634-9131)
P.O. Box 449 (28634-0449)
PHONE..............................704 546-7002
Ernest White, *Pr*
EMP: 36 **EST:** 1997
SQ FT: 30,000
SALES (est): 5.82MM **Privately Held**
Web: www.associatedmetalworks.com
SIC: 3564 Air purification equipment

(G-6098)
G & G LUMBER COMPANY INC
179 Lumber Dr (28634-9200)
PHONE..............................704 539-5110
Cecil S Gregory, *Pr*
EMP: 6 **EST:** 1973
SQ FT: 4,000
SALES (est): 474.72K **Privately Held**
Web: www.gandglumber.com
SIC: 2435 2421 Hardwood plywood,
prefinished; Sawmills and planing mills,
general

(G-6099)
SOMERS LUMBER AND MFG INC
126 Oakleaf Rd (28634-9222)
P.O. Box 87 (28689-0087)
PHONE..............................704 539-4751

Keith Somers, *Pr*
Aaron Somers, *Sec*
EMP: 11 **EST:** 1964
SQ FT: 21,000
SALES (est): 2MM **Privately Held**
Web: www.somerslumber.com
SIC: 5031 2448 2421 Lumber: rough,
dressed, and finished; Wood pallets and
skids; Sawmills and planing mills, general

Harrells
Sampson County

(G-6100)
DNL SERVICES LLC
64 Blue Heron Dr (28444-8889)
PHONE..............................910 689-8759
EMP: 8 **EST:** 2016
SALES (est): 211.49K **Privately Held**
SIC: 3271 Blocks, concrete: landscape or
retaining wall

(G-6101)
**LAKE CREEK LOGGING & TRCKG
INC**
3744 Nc Highway 210 E (28444-8919)
PHONE..............................910 532-2041
Mark Long, *Pr*
Jill Long, *Sec*
EMP: 10 **EST:** 1991
SALES (est): 971.08K **Privately Held**
SIC: 2411 Logging camps and contractors

(G-6102)
NORTH CAPE FEAR LOGGING LLC
125 Charlie Smith Dr (28444-8043)
PHONE..............................910 876-3197
EMP: 5 **EST:** 2014
SALES (est): 135.92K **Privately Held**
SIC: 2411 Logging

(G-6103)
THOMAS TIMBER INC
3344 Nc Highway 210 E (28444-8924)
PHONE..............................910 532-4542
G Dean Thomas, *Pr*
Winnie Lewis, *Sec*
EMP: 5 **EST:** 1946
SALES (est): 234K **Privately Held**
SIC: 2411 2421 Logging camps and
contractors; Chipper mill

Harrellsville
Hertford County

(G-6104)
**SANDY LAND PEANUT COMPANY
INC**
229 Swains Mill Rd (27942-9779)
P.O. Box 38 (27924-0038)
PHONE..............................252 356-2679
Greg Dyer, *Managing Member*
James Beasley, *Pr*
Horace P Beasley, *VP*
EMP: 19 **EST:** 2007
SALES (est): 1.78MM **Privately Held**
Web: www.sandylandpeanut.com
SIC: 0723 2068 Crop preparation services
for market; Nuts: dried, dehydrated, salted
or roasted

Harrisburg
Cabarrus County

(G-6105)
CARBON-LESS INDUSTRIES INC
12059 University City Blvd (28075-8466)
PHONE......................704 361-1231
John Meeks, *Prin*
EMP: 5 EST: 2016
SALES (est): 76.45K **Privately Held**
SIC: 3999 Manufacturing industries, nec

(G-6106)
CEMEX MATERIALS LLC
Also Called: Cemex
5601 Pharr Mill Rd (28075-0390)
PHONE......................704 455-1100
Rick Santiago, *Mgr*
EMP: 112
SIC: 3273 Ready-mixed concrete
HQ: Cemex Materials Llc
1720 Cntrpark Dr E Ste 10
West Palm Beach FL 33401
561 833-5555

(G-6107)
DOT BLUE READI-MIX LLC
7406 Millbrook Rd (28075-7410)
PHONE......................704 247-2778
Ken Hall, *Manager*
EMP: 27
SALES (corp-wide): 23.52MM **Privately Held**
Web: www.bluedotreadimix.com
PA: Blue Dot Readi-Mix, Llc
11330 Bain School Rd
Mint Hill NC 28227
704 971-7676

(G-6108)
GALVAN INDUSTRIES INC
7315 Galvan Way (28075-4300)
P.O. Box 369 (28075-0369)
PHONE......................704 455-5102
Laurens Willard, *Pr*
Elizabeth Willard, *
Brad Wittensoldner, *
◆ EMP: 150 EST: 1960
SQ FT: 100,000
SALES (est): 18.83MM **Privately Held**
Web: www.galvan-ize.com
SIC: 3479 Coating of metals and formed products

(G-6109)
GARICK LLC
Also Called: Tar Heel Bark
8829 Rocky River Rd (28075-7636)
PHONE......................704 455-6418
Shane Baucom, *Brnch Mgr*
EMP: 8
SALES (corp-wide): 22.06B **Publicly Held**
Web: www.garick.com
SIC: 2499 Mulch, wood and bark
HQ: Garick, Llc
8400 Sweet Vly Dr Ste 408
Cleveland OH 44125
216 581-0100

(G-6110)
J F FABRICATORS LLC (PA)
7315 Millbrook Rd (28075-7489)
PHONE......................704 454-7224
EMP: 5 EST: 2008
SQ FT: 20,000
SALES (est): 1.54MM **Privately Held**
SIC: 3449 Fabricated bar joists and concrete reinforcing bars

(G-6111)
KCI LLC
Also Called: Kci
5924 Caldwell Park Dr (28075-7402)
PHONE......................843 675-2626
Kevin Carpenter, *Owner*
EMP: 34 EST: 2016
SALES (est): 263.07K **Privately Held**
Web: www.kcitelecom.com
SIC: 2599 Hospital beds

(G-6112)
MALLARD CREEK POLYMERS LLC
2388 Speedrail Dr (28075-0378)
PHONE......................704 547-0622
EMP: 8
Web: www.mcpolymers.com
SIC: 2821 Plastics materials and resins
PA: Mallard Creek Polymers, Llc
8901 Research Dr
Charlotte NC 28262

(G-6113)
MARCON INTERNATIONAL INC
Also Called: Keyper Systems
5679 Harrisburg Ind Pk Dr (28075-7412)
P.O. Box 1540 (28075-1540)
PHONE......................704 455-9400
Ric Stone, *CEO*
Walt Leaver, *
▲ EMP: 30 EST: 1993
SQ FT: 20,000
SALES (est): 8.37MM
SALES (corp-wide): 17.42MM **Privately Held**
Web: www.marcon.com
SIC: 7382 3429 Protective devices, security; Keys and key blanks
PA: Ucc-Kp Investment, Llc
485 W Putnam Ave
Greenwich CT 06830
203 580-5740

(G-6114)
MAUSER USA LLC
Also Called: Berenfield Containers
12180 University Cy Blvd (28075-7406)
PHONE......................704 455-2111
EMP: 60
SIC: 3412 Drums, shipping: metal
HQ: Mauser Usa, Llc
2 Tower Center Blvd
East Brunswick NJ 60523

(G-6115)
PEPSI BOTTLING VENTURES LLC
Also Called: Pepsi-Cola
22 Pepsi Way (28075-8416)
PHONE......................704 455-0800
David Brown Michael Mills, *Brnch Mgr*
EMP: 250
Web: www.pepsibottlingventures.com
SIC: 2086 Carbonated soft drinks, bottled and canned
HQ: Pepsi Bottling Ventures Llc
4141 Parklake Ave
Raleigh NC 27612
919 865-2300

(G-6116)
RINKER MATERIALS
2268 Speedrail Dr (28075-0390)
PHONE......................704 455-1100
EMP: 15 EST: 2018
SALES (est): 3.84MM **Privately Held**
SIC: 3273 Ready-mixed concrete

(G-6117)
S FOIL INCORPORATED
2283 Nc Highway 49 S (28075-7549)
P.O. Box 296 (28075-0296)
PHONE......................704 455-5134
Ralph M Torrence, *Pr*
EMP: 16 EST: 1947
SQ FT: 10,000
SALES (est): 2.45MM **Privately Held**
Web: www.foilsinc.com
SIC: 5093 3341 Metal scrap and waste materials; Secondary nonferrous metals

(G-6118)
THREE WISHES MONOGRAMMING
8200 Blackjack Oak Ct (28075-7612)
PHONE......................980 298-2981
EMP: 4 EST: 2017
SALES (est): 47.02K **Privately Held**
SIC: 2395 Embroidery and art needlework

(G-6119)
US LEGEND CARS INTL INC
Also Called: 600 Racing Service
5245 Nc Highway 49 S (28075-8476)
PHONE......................704 455-3896
Bill Brooks, *Sec*
◆ EMP: 40 EST: 1992
SQ FT: 93,000
SALES (est): 4.48MM
SALES (corp-wide): 125.61MM **Privately Held**
Web: www.uslegendcars.com
SIC: 3944 5091 3714 3711 Go-carts, children's; Go-carts; Motor vehicle parts and accessories; Motor vehicles and car bodies
HQ: Speedway Motorsports, Llc
5555 Concord Pkwy S
Concord NC 28027

(G-6120)
VENATOR CHEMICALS LLC
Also Called: Mineral Research & Development
5910 Pharr Mill Rd (28075-8625)
P.O. Box 640 (28075-0640)
PHONE......................704 454-4811
Jona Stein, *Brnch Mgr*
EMP: 100
SQ FT: 93,472
SALES (corp-wide): 2.17B **Privately Held**
Web: www.mrdc.com
SIC: 2819 8731 2899 Industrial inorganic chemicals, nec; Commercial physical research; Chemical preparations, nec
HQ: Venator Chemicals Llc
10001 Wdloch Frest Dr 600
The Woodlands TX 77380
704 455-4135

(G-6121)
WILBERT PLSTIC SVCS ACQSTION L
7301 Caldwell Rd (28075-7413)
PHONE......................704 455-5191
Tony Colson, *Brnch Mgr*
▲ EMP: 21
SALES (corp-wide): 218.2MM **Privately Held**
Web: www.wilbertplastics.com
SIC: 5162 3089 Plastics products, nec; Thermoformed finished plastics products, nec
HQ: Wilbert Plastic Services Acquisition Llc
1000 Oaks Pkwy
Belmont NC 28012

Havelock
Craven County

(G-6122)
ABC SIGNS AND GRAPHICS LLC
160 Us Highway 70 W (28532-9506)
PHONE......................252 652-6620
Dennis Baker, *Dir Opers*
EMP: 4 EST: 2015
SALES (est): 890.31K **Privately Held**
Web: www.abcsignsnc.com
SIC: 3993 Electric signs

(G-6123)
MERCHANTS INC
Also Called: Merchants
174 Us Highway 70 W (28532-9506)
PHONE......................252 447-2121
Orland Wolford, *Pr*
EMP: 9 EST: 1963
SQ FT: 16,000
SALES (est): 216.23K **Privately Held**
SIC: 5531 7534 Automotive tires; Tire recapping

(G-6124)
NORTHROP GRMMAN TCHNCAL SVCS I
4280 6th Ave Cherry Point Air Station (28532)
P.O. Box 2070 (28532-4070)
PHONE......................252 447-7575
Armand Escobio, *Prin*
EMP: 42
SIC: 3812 Search and navigation equipment
HQ: Northrop Grumman Technical Services, Inc.
7575 Colshire Dr
Mc Lean VA 22102
703 556-1144

(G-6125)
PARKER-HANNIFIN CORPORATION
245 Belltown Rd (28532-2705)
PHONE......................252 652-6592
Donald E Washkewicz, *Brnch Mgr*
EMP: 8
SALES (corp-wide): 19.93B **Publicly Held**
Web: www.parker.com
SIC: 3594 Fluid power pumps and motors
PA: Parker-Hannifin Corporation
6035 Parkland Blvd
Cleveland OH 44124
216 896-3000

(G-6126)
RED BULL DISTRIBUTION CO INC
95 Outer Banks Dr (28532-1603)
PHONE......................910 500-1566
Jay Hutzler, *Brnch Mgr*
EMP: 15
SALES (corp-wide): 11.47B **Privately Held**
Web: www.redbulldistributioncompany.com
SIC: 2086 Carbonated soft drinks, bottled and canned
HQ: Red Bull Distribution Company, Inc.
1740 Stewart St
Santa Monica CA 90404

(G-6127)
SMYRNA READY MIX CONCRETE LLC
417 Miller Blvd (28532-2643)
PHONE......................252 447-5356
Van Valkenburg, *Manager*
EMP: 8
SALES (corp-wide): 471.79MM **Privately Held**

(PA)=Parent Co (HQ)=Headquarters
✪ = New Business established in last 2 years

Web: www.argos-us.com
SIC: 3273 Ready-mixed concrete
PA: Smyrna Ready Mix Concrete, Llc
1000 Hollingshead Cir
Murfreesboro TN 37129
615 355-1028

(G-6128)
TANDEMLOC INC
824 Nc Highway 101 Fontana Blvd (28532)
PHONE..............................252 447-7155
EMP: 56 EST: 1984
SALES (est): 10.34MM **Privately Held**
Web: www.tandemloc.com
SIC: 3531 Construction machinery

Haw River
Alamance County

(G-6129)
ANDERSEN ENERGY INC
3151 Caroline Dr (27258-9575)
PHONE..............................336 376-0107
H W Anderson, *Prin*
H W Andersen, *Pr*
EMP: 4 EST: 1980
SALES (est): 426.42K **Privately Held**
Web: www.sterility.com
SIC: 3841 Surgical and medical instruments

(G-6130)
ANDERSEN PRODUCTS INC
3202 Caroline Dr (27258-9564)
PHONE..............................336 376-3000
Harold W Andersen, *Pr*
Shirley Andersen, *
▼ EMP: 50 EST: 1958
SQ FT: 24,000
SALES (est): 8.37MM **Privately Held**
Web: www.anpro.com
SIC: 8731 3841 3842 Commercial research
laboratory; Surgical and medical
instruments; Surgical appliances and
supplies

(G-6131)
ANDERSEN STERILIZERS INC
Also Called: Andersen Products
3202 Caroline Dr (27258-9564)
PHONE..............................336 376-8622
William K Andersen, *Pr*
C E Andersen, *
Bruce Fenn, *
Shirley Andersen, *
Harold Andersen, *
EMP: 45 EST: 1995
SALES (est): 9.82MM **Privately Held**
Web: www.anpro.com
SIC: 3841 3842 Surgical and medical
instruments; Surgical appliances and
supplies

(G-6132)
INTERSTATE NARROW FABRICS INC
1101 Porter Ave (27258-9547)
P.O. Box 28 (27253-0028)
PHONE..............................336 578-1037
Tony Vailati, *Pr*
Marie Vailati, *
Anthony H Vailati, *
▲ EMP: 90 EST: 1985
SALES (est): 2.64MM **Privately Held**
Web: www.interstatenarrowfabrics.com
SIC: 2241 Elastic narrow fabrics, woven or
braided

(G-6133)
JOCEPHUS ORIGINALS INC
1003 W Main St Ste A4 (27258-8930)

PHONE..............................336 229-9600
Joe Wade, *Pr*
Joe Wade, *Owner*
EMP: 10 EST: 1998
SALES (est): 379.93K **Privately Held**
Web: www.jocephusoriginals.com
SIC: 2384 Bathrobes, men's and women's:
made from purchased materials

(G-6134)
NOVAFLEX HOSE INC
449 Trollingwood Rd (27258-8750)
PHONE..............................336 578-2161
Melinda Donnelly, *Pr*
Claire Howard, *
▲ EMP: 85 EST: 1986
SQ FT: 8,500
SALES (est): 17.94MM
SALES (corp-wide): 49.34MM **Privately
Held**
Web: www.novaflex.com
SIC: 5085 3061 Hose, belting, and packing;
Mechanical rubber goods
HQ: Z-Flex Realty, Inc.
20 Commerce Park North # 107
Bedford NH 03110

(G-6135)
SUE-LYNN TEXTILES INC (PA)
Also Called: 21st Century Hosiery
302 Roxboro St (27258-9673)
P.O. Box 939 (27258-0939)
PHONE..............................336 578-0871
Thurman B Oakley, *Pr*
Mary L Oakley, *
Randy Ector, *
Diane Ector, *
EMP: 32 EST: 1971
SQ FT: 70,000
SALES (est): 2.15MM
SALES (corp-wide): 2.15MM **Privately
Held**
SIC: 2251 5137 Panty hose; Hosiery:
women's, children's, and infants'

(G-6136)
UNICHEM IV LTD (PA)
916 W Main St (27258-9661)
P.O. Box 612 (27258)
PHONE..............................336 578-5476
◆ EMP: 15 EST: 1981
SALES (est): 9.76MM
SALES (corp-wide): 9.76MM **Privately
Held**
Web: www.unichem.com
SIC: 2819 Industrial inorganic chemicals, nec

Hayesville
Clay County

(G-6137)
**ADVANCED DIGITAL CABLE INC
(PA)**
Also Called: ADC
94 Eagle Fork Rd (28904-5255)
P.O. Box 305 (30546-0305)
PHONE..............................828 389-1652
Steve Payne, *Pr*
Adam C Payne, *VP*
Mary Payne, *
▲ EMP: 49 EST: 1997
SQ FT: 105,000
SALES (est): 26.52MM
SALES (corp-wide): 26.52MM **Privately
Held**
Web: www.adcable.com
SIC: 3671 Cathode ray tubes, including
rebuilt

(G-6138)
CLAY COUNTY FOOD PANTRY INC
2278 Hinton Center Rd (28904-4884)
P.O. Box 853 (28904-0853)
PHONE..............................828 389-1657
Bert Wiley, *Pr*
EMP: 9 EST: 2005
SALES (est): 197.73K **Privately Held**
Web: www.claycountyfoodpantry.org
SIC: 8322 2099 5149 Meal delivery program;
Ready-to-eat meals, salads, and
sandwiches; Dried or canned foods

(G-6139)
COLEMAN CABLE LLC
Intercomp Wire & Cable
788 Tusquittee Rd (28904-7889)
P.O. Box 206 (28904-0206)
PHONE..............................828 389-8013
Lee Ferguson, *Mgr*
EMP: 57
SALES (corp-wide): 602.03MM **Privately
Held**
Web: www.colemancable.com
SIC: 3496 3678 3643 3357 Cable,
uninsulated wire: made from purchased wire
; Electronic connectors; Current-carrying
wiring services; Nonferrous wiredrawing
and insulating
HQ: Coleman Cable, Llc
1 Overlook Pt
Lincolnshire IL 60069
847 672-2300

(G-6140)
COMMUNITY NEWSPAPERS INC
Also Called: Clay County Progress
43 Main St (28904-5808)
P.O. Box 483 (28904-0483)
PHONE..............................828 389-8431
Becky Long, *Prin*
EMP: 9
SALES (corp-wide): 40.95MM **Privately
Held**
Web: www.cninewspapers.com
SIC: 2711 Newspapers, publishing and
printing
PA: Community Newspapers, Inc.
2365 Prince Ave # A
Athens GA 30606
706 548-0010

(G-6141)
**GOLDEN RCTANGLE ENTEPRISES
INC**
2966 Nc 69 (28904-7256)
P.O. Box 34 (28904-0034)
PHONE..............................828 389-3336
Cathy Jones, *Genl Mgr*
EMP: 4 EST: 2005
SALES (est): 166.93K **Privately Held**
SIC: 2512 Upholstered household furniture

(G-6142)
LIDSEEN NORTH CAROLINA INC
6382 Old Hwy 64 W (28904)
PHONE..............................828 389-8082
Melvin Swanson, *Pr*
Edwin James, *Treas*
Mitchell Swanson, *VP*
Merinda Woody, *Sec*
EMP: 5 EST: 1901
SQ FT: 24,000
SALES (est): 709.65K **Privately Held**
Web: www.chicagopipebender.com
SIC: 3423 3469 Hand and edge tools, nec;
Metal stampings, nec

(G-6143)
**POWER SUPPORT ENGINEERING
INC**
653 Barlow Fields Dr (28904-8054)
PHONE..............................813 909-1199
G Brian Blatt, *Pr*
Kelly Blatt, *Ex VP*
EMP: 4 EST: 1995
SALES (est): 395.54K **Privately Held**
Web: www.powersupporteng.com
SIC: 1731 3612 1796 Computer power
conditioning; Transformers, except electric;
Power generating equipment installation

(G-6144)
SENTINEL NEWSPAPERS (PA)
Also Called: Union Sentinal
23 Riverwalk Cir (28904-7949)
PHONE..............................828 389-8338
Frank Bradley, *Owner*
EMP: 16 EST: 1987
SQ FT: 3,000
SALES (est): 157.06K **Privately Held**
SIC: 2711 Newspapers: publishing only, not
printed on site

Hays
Wilkes County

(G-6145)
C & L MANUFACTURING
1519 Oak Ridge Church Rd (28635)
P.O. Box 250 (28635-0250)
PHONE..............................336 957-8359
Charles Farrington, *Owner*
EMP: 5 EST: 1976
SQ FT: 3,568
SALES (est): 231.78K **Privately Held**
SIC: 2253 Collar and cuff sets, knit

Henderson
Vance County

(G-6146)
A R PERRY CORPORATION
Also Called: Perry Glass Co
220 Old Epsom Rd (27536-5342)
P.O. Box 206 (27536-0206)
PHONE..............................252 492-6181
Richard A Davis Iii, *Pr*
Richard A Davis Iv, *VP*
EMP: 5 EST: 1920
SQ FT: 25,000
SALES (est): 457.29K **Privately Held**
Web: www.arperryglass.com
SIC: 1793 7536 5085 3442 Glass and
glazing work; Automotive glass
replacement shops; Welding supplies;
Metal doors, sash, and trim

(G-6147)
AIR CONTROL INC
237 Raleigh Rd (27536-4977)
P.O. Box 1738 (27536-1738)
PHONE..............................252 492-2300
EMP: 25 EST: 1961
SALES (est): 5MM **Privately Held**
Web: www.aircontrol-inc.com
SIC: 3564 3821 3674 3561 Air purification
equipment; Laboratory apparatus and
furniture; Semiconductors and related
devices; Pumps and pumping equipment

(G-6148)
CAROLINA COPACKING LLC
860 Commerce Dr (27537-7450)
PHONE..............................252 433-0130

▲ = Import ▼ = Export
◆ = Import/Export

Sherri Matthews, *Off Mgr*
EMP: 22 **EST:** 2017
SQ FT: 80,000
SALES (est): 9.51MM **Privately Held**
Web: www.carolinacopacking.com
SIC: 3221 Bottles for packing, bottling, and canning: glass

(G-6149)
CAROLINA GIANT TIRES INC
389 Americal Rd (27537-3381)
P.O. Box 872 (27522-0872)
PHONE..............................919 609-9077
Shawn Reaves, *Pr*
EMP: 13 **EST:** 2014
SQ FT: 6,400
SALES (est): 1.11MM **Privately Held**
Web: www.carolinagianttirellc.com
SIC: 7534 3011 Tire retreading and repair shops; Tires and inner tubes

(G-6150)
CAROLINA WOODWORKS TRIM OF NC
625 Parham Rd (27536-2624)
PHONE..............................252 492-9259
Bill Atkinson, *Owner*
EMP: 4 **EST:** 2006
SALES (est): 203.79K **Privately Held**
SIC: 2431 Millwork

(G-6151)
COMMERCIAL SEAMING CO INC
501 Walnut St (27536)
P.O. Box 39 (27536-0039)
PHONE..............................252 492-6178
Doug Capps, *Pr*
Faye Capps, *
◆ **EMP:** 5 **EST:** 1979
SQ FT: 43,000
SALES (est): 452.65K **Privately Held**
Web: www.commercialseaming.com
SIC: 2262 Finishing plants, manmade

(G-6152)
COUNTRY SNACKS MFG INC
513 Commerce Dr (27537-9551)
PHONE..............................252 433-4644
Dwight M Frazier, *Pr*
EMP: 25 **EST:** 2000
SQ FT: 10,000
SALES (est): 4.66MM **Privately Held**
Web: www.ccsnacks.com
SIC: 2013 Prepared pork products, from purchased pork

(G-6153)
D C THOMAS GROUP INC
Also Called: Carolina Co Packaging LLC
860 Commerce Dr (27537-7450)
PHONE..............................252 433-0132
Dwight C Thomas Senior, *Pr*
EMP: 30
Web: www.thomasgourmetfoods.net
SIC: 2035 Pickles, sauces, and salad dressings
PA: D. C. Thomas Group, Inc.
6540 W Market St
Greensboro NC 27409

(G-6154)
EDWARDS UNLIMITED INC
Also Called: Metal Fabrication
3355 Raleigh Rd (27537-7461)
PHONE..............................252 226-4583
Boyd C Edwards Iv, *Pr*
EMP: 9 **EST:** 2005
SALES (est): 1.18MM **Privately Held**
Web: www.edwardsunlimitednc.com

SIC: 3441 3599 Fabricated structural metal; Machine and other job shop work

(G-6155)
FLORIDA MARINE TANKS INC (HQ)
Also Called: Fmt
120 Peter Gill Rd (27537-4297)
PHONE..............................305 620-9030
Rose Marie Fiori, *Pr*
Vince G Di Rosa, *VP*
Jennie Di Rosa, *VP*
James A Pearson, *Prin*
Steven A Lurus, *Prin*
◆ **EMP:** 12 **EST:** 1974
SQ FT: 54,000
SALES (est): 13.82MM
SALES (corp-wide): 3.72B **Publicly Held**
Web: www.floridamarinetanks.com
SIC: 3443 3231 Tanks, standard or custom fabricated: metal plate; Windshields, glass: made from purchased glass
PA: Patrick Industries, Inc.
107 W Franklin St
Elkhart IN 46516
574 294-7511

(G-6156)
FLOWERS BKG CO JAMESTOWN LLC
875 S Beckford Dr (27536-5910)
PHONE..............................252 492-1519
Johnny Moodiham, *Mgr*
EMP: 6
SALES (corp-wide): 5.1B **Publicly Held**
Web: www.flowersfoods.com
SIC: 2051 Bread, cake, and related products
HQ: Flowers Baking Co. Of Jamestown, Llc
801 W Main St
Jamestown NC 27282
336 841-8840

(G-6157)
GREYSTONE CONCRETE PDTS INC
2100 Us 1/158 Hwy (27537-8265)
P.O. Box 680 (27536-0680)
PHONE..............................252 438-5144
John F Cannady Iii, *Pr*
Samuel Cannady, *
Ernestine C Cannady, *
John F Cannady Iv, *Ex VP*
Susan Martin, *Stockholder*
EMP: 27 **EST:** 1946
SQ FT: 3,000
SALES (est): 5.95MM **Privately Held**
Web:
www.greystoneconcreteproducts.com
SIC: 3271 3273 3272 Blocks, concrete or cinder: standard; Ready-mixed concrete; Building materials, except block or brick: concrete

(G-6158)
HENDERSON NEWSPAPERS INC
Also Called: Daily Dispatch
420 S Garnett St (27536-4540)
PHONE..............................252 436-2700
J Edward Publisher, *Prin*
Rick Bean, *Pr*
James Edwards, *Publisher*
EMP: 11 **EST:** 1994
SALES (est): 2.26MM
SALES (corp-wide): 147.64MM **Privately Held**
Web: www.hendersondispatch.com
SIC: 2711 Newspapers, publishing and printing
PA: Paxton Media Group, Llc
100 Television Ln
Paducah KY 42003
270 575-8630

(G-6159)
HIGH AND HIGH INC
268 Country Club Dr (27536-4711)
P.O. Box 201 (27586-0201)
PHONE..............................252 257-2390
Robert High, *Pr*
EMP: 18
SALES (corp-wide): 2.3MM **Privately Held**
SIC: 2421 Sawmills and planing mills, general
PA: High And High Inc
2843 Triplet Rd
Lawrenceville VA
434 577-2372

(G-6160)
HOLLAND SUPPLY COMPANY
Also Called: Holland Industrial
518 W Montgomery St (27536-3318)
P.O. Box 987 (27536-0987)
PHONE..............................252 492-7541
EMP: 35 **EST:** 1946
SALES (est): 18.45MM **Privately Held**
Web: www.hollandindustrial.com
SIC: 5085 5063 7694 Industrial supplies; Motors, electric; Rebuilding motors, except automotive

(G-6161)
IDAHO TIMBER NC LLC (HQ)
1431 Nicholas St (27536-5330)
P.O. Box 847 (27536-0847)
PHONE..............................252 430-0030
EMP: 22 **EST:** 1998
SALES (est): 13.8MM
SALES (corp-wide): 308.2MM **Privately Held**
Web: www.idahotimber.com
SIC: 2421 5031 2439 Lumber: rough, sawed, or planed; Lumber: rough, dressed, and finished; Structural wood members, nec
PA: Hampton Investment Company
9600 Sw Barnes Rd 200
Portland OR 97225
503 297-7691

(G-6162)
J & J LOGGING INC
255 J P Taylor Rd (27537-4290)
P.O. Box 785 (27536-0785)
PHONE..............................252 430-1110
Joe Ross, *Pr*
EMP: 24 **EST:** 1976
SQ FT: 800
SALES (est): 2.25MM **Privately Held**
SIC: 2411 Logging camps and contractors

(G-6163)
KENNAMETAL INC
139 Warehouse Rd (27537-4214)
P.O. Box 159 (27536-0159)
PHONE..............................252 492-4163
John V Lazar, *Mgr*
EMP: 76
SALES (corp-wide): 2.05B **Publicly Held**
Web: www.kennametal.com
SIC: 3545 Machine tool accessories
PA: Kennametal Inc.
525 Wlliam Penn Pl Ste 33
Pittsburgh PA 15219
412 248-8000

(G-6164)
LEGACY VULCAN LLC
Mideast Division
696 Greystone Rd (27537-5513)
P.O. Box 470 (27536-0470)
PHONE..............................252 438-3161
Billy Stevenson, *Mgr*
EMP: 4
Web: www.vulcanmaterials.com

SIC: 3273 Ready-mixed concrete
HQ: Legacy Vulcan, Llc
1200 Urban Center Dr
Birmingham AL 35242
205 298-3000

(G-6165)
LUMENFOCUS LLC
Also Called: Lumenfocus
880 Facet Rd (27537-5412)
PHONE..............................252 430-6970
EMP: 10 **EST:** 2016
SQ FT: 90,000
SALES (est): 4.96MM **Privately Held**
Web: www.lumenfocus.com
SIC: 3646 Commercial lighting fixtures

(G-6166)
MARS PETCARE US INC
Also Called: IAMS
845 Commerce Dr (27537-7450)
PHONE..............................252 438-1600
Pickson Pratt, *Mgr*
EMP: 62
SALES (corp-wide): 42.84B **Privately Held**
Web: www.marspetcare.com
SIC: 2047 Dog food
HQ: Mars Petcare Us, Inc.
2013 Ovation Pkwy
Franklin TN 37067
615 807-4626

(G-6167)
NUNNERY-FREEMAN INC
Also Called: Nunnery-Freeman Mfg Co
2117 Coleman Pl (27536-3839)
P.O. Box 332 (27536-0332)
PHONE..............................252 438-3149
Gary Freeman, *Pr*
Ann Freeman, *Sec*
EMP: 6 **EST:** 1949
SQ FT: 6,000
SALES (est): 650.59K **Privately Held**
SIC: 3589 5812 Cooking equipment, commercial; Barbecue restaurant

(G-6168)
OPTIMUM LIGHTING LLC
Also Called: Optimum Lighting
880 Facet Rd (27537-5412)
PHONE..............................508 646-3324
EMP: 40
Web: www.signify.com
SIC: 3646 Fluorescent lighting fixtures, commercial

(G-6169)
PACIFIC COAST FEATHER LLC
Also Called: Southern Quilters
100 Comfort Dr (27537-5933)
PHONE..............................252 492-0051
Richard Aldrich, *Brnch Mgr*
EMP: 4
SALES (corp-wide): 46.93MM **Privately Held**
Web: www.pacificcoast.com
SIC: 2392 2395 Bedspreads and bed sets: made from purchased materials; Pleating and stitching
PA: Pacific Coast Feather, Llc
901 W Yamato Rd Ste 250
Boca Raton FL 33431
206 624-1057

(G-6170)
PROFILFORM US INC
101 Eastern Minerals Rd (27537-4288)
PHONE..............................252 430-0392
Thilo Hessler, *Pr*
Friedrizh Hessler, *
▲ **EMP:** 40 **EST:** 1998

SQ FT: 24,000
SALES (est): 4.84MM **Privately Held**
Web: www.versatrim.com
SIC: 2431 Moldings, wood: unfinished and prefinished

(G-6171)
QUALITY INSULATION COMPANY
132 Carey Chapel Rd (27537-8473)
P.O. Box 866 (27536-0866)
PHONE.....................................252 438-3711
Judith S Riley, *Owner*
EMP: 4 EST: 1983
SALES (est): 105.29K **Privately Held**
SIC: 2493 Insulation board, cellular fiber

(G-6172)
QUALITY INVESTMENTS INC
Also Called: V I P
1902 N Garnett St (27536-2723)
P.O. Box 1528 (27536-1528)
PHONE.....................................252 492-8777
Phillip White, *Pr*
EMP: 50 EST: 1972
SQ FT: 1,380
SALES (est): 2.83MM **Privately Held**
SIC: 5531 7534 7538 5521 Automotive tires; Tire repair shop; General automotive repair shops; Automobiles, used cars only

(G-6173)
QUICK PRINT HENDERSON INC
416 Dabney Dr (27536-3944)
PHONE.....................................252 492-8905
Warren Nelms, *Pr*
EMP: 7 EST: 2000
SALES (est): 254.36K **Privately Held**
Web: www.quickprint.biz
SIC: 2752 Offset printing

(G-6174)
RALEIGH ROAD BOX CORPORATION
Rr 9 Box 403 (27536)
PHONE.....................................252 438-7401
Charlie M Smith, *Pr*
Mary Smith, *Sec*
Ronnie Smith, *VP*
EMP: 6 EST: 1975
SALES (est): 124.2K **Privately Held**
SIC: 4212 2449 Lumber (log) trucking, local; Casks, wood: coopered

(G-6175)
ROBCO MANUFACTURING INC
Also Called: Alumadock Marine Structure
651 Bearpond Rd (27536)
P.O. Box 2600 (27536-6600)
PHONE.....................................252 438-7399
M Thomas Roberson, *Pr*
Annette C Roberson, *
Michael T Roberson Junior, *VP Sls*
▲ EMP: 30 EST: 1983
SQ FT: 35,000
SALES (est): 4.65MM **Privately Held**
Web: www.alumadock.com
SIC: 3448 Docks, prefabricated metal

(G-6176)
ROY BRIDGMOHAN
596 Industry Dr (27537-8795)
PHONE.....................................804 426-9652
Roy Bridgmohan, *Owner*
EMP: 4 EST: 2001
SALES (est): 268.32K **Privately Held**
SIC: 3812 Search and navigation equipment

(G-6177)
SANFORD S ATV REPAIR LLC
887 Weldon Rd (27537-9152)
PHONE.....................................252 438-2730

Freddy Sanford, *Owner*
EMP: 4 EST: 1995
SALES (est): 673.49K **Privately Held**
SIC: 3799 All terrain vehicles (ATV)

(G-6178)
SCREEN MASTER
904 Buckhorn St (27536-3004)
PHONE.....................................252 492-8407
Eugene Watkins, *Pt*
Lorraine Watkins, *Pt*
EMP: 6 EST: 1976
SALES (est): 148.2K **Privately Held**
Web:
www.screenmasterofhenderson.com
SIC: 5941 5699 2261 5999 Sporting goods and bicycle shops; T-shirts, custom printed; Screen printing of cotton broadwoven fabrics; Trophies and plaques

(G-6179)
SOUTHEASTERN MINERALS INC
Also Called: SOUTHEASTERN MINERALS, INC.
170 Eastern Minerals Rd (27537-4288)
P.O. Box 226 (27536-0226)
PHONE.....................................252 492-0831
Charles Gordon, *Mgr*
EMP: 22
SALES (corp-wide): 13.03MM **Privately Held**
Web: www.seminerals.com
SIC: 2048 3295 2879 Prepared feeds, nec; Minerals, ground or treated; Agricultural chemicals, nec
PA: Eastern Minerals, Inc.
1100 Dothan Rd
Bainbridge GA 39817
229 246-3396

(G-6180)
TARHEEL WOODCRAFTERS INC
1570 Hicksboro Rd (27537-7762)
PHONE.....................................252 432-3035
John D Edwards, *Pr*
EMP: 5 EST: 1998
SALES (est): 177.22K **Privately Held**
SIC: 2434 Wood kitchen cabinets

(G-6181)
TIMBERLINE ACQUISITION LLC
Also Called: Timberline
235 Warehouse Rd (27537-4229)
P.O. Box 1457 (27536-1457)
PHONE.....................................252 492-6144
EMP: 25 EST: 1973
SQ FT: 90,000
SALES (est): 4.46MM **Privately Held**
Web: www.timberlinellc.com
SIC: 2448 2441 Pallets, wood; Nailed wood boxes and shook

(G-6182)
VESCOM AMERICA INC
2289 Ross Mill Rd (27537-5966)
P.O. Box 1698 (27536-1698)
PHONE.....................................252 431-6200
Joe Berasi, *Pr*
▲ EMP: 20 EST: 1969
SQ FT: 50,000
SALES (est): 9.58MM **Privately Held**
Web: www.vescom.com
SIC: 2295 Coated fabrics, not rubberized

Hendersonville
Henderson County

(G-6183)
ACME MACHINE LLC
95 Commercial Hill Dr (28792-4563)
PHONE.....................................828 483-6440
EMP: 13 EST: 2018
SALES (est): 3.54MM **Privately Held**
Web: www.acmemachinenc.com
SIC: 3599 Machine shop, jobbing and repair

(G-6184)
AMERICAN PRIDE INC
135 Sugarloaf Rd (28792-9326)
PHONE.....................................828 697-8847
Joe Bright, *Genl Mgr*
Joe Bright, *Genl Mgr*
▲ EMP: 22 EST: 1984
SQ FT: 17,500
SALES (est): 1.67MM
SALES (corp-wide): 6.08MM **Privately Held**
Web: www.apcabinets.com
SIC: 2393 Textile bags
HQ: Zwd Products Corporation
400 Lukens Dr
Historic New Castle DE 19720
302 326-8200

(G-6185)
BARRY CALLEBAUT USA LLC
Also Called: Mona Lisa Foods
51 Saint Pauls Rd (28792-1625)
PHONE.....................................828 685-2443
Peter Thom, *Mgr*
EMP: 87
Web: www.barry-callebaut.com
SIC: 2066 Chocolate
HQ: Barry Callebaut U.S.A. Llc
600 W Chicago Ave Ste 860
Chicago IL 60654

(G-6186)
BAY BREEZE SEAFOOD REST INC
Also Called: Bay Breeze Seafood
1830 Asheville Hwy (28791-2310)
PHONE.....................................828 697-7106
Bill Katsadouros, *CEO*
Jimmy Katsadouros, *Prin*
EMP: 12 EST: 2010
SALES (est): 2.36MM **Privately Held**
Web: www.baybreezeseafood.com
SIC: 5146 2091 Fish and seafoods; Canned and cured fish and seafoods

(G-6187)
BLUE RIDGE JAMS
75 Lytle Rd (28792-6475)
P.O. Box 6 (28724-0006)
PHONE.....................................828 685-1783
Steve Pridmore, *Owner*
EMP: 5 EST: 1961
SALES (est): 246.66K **Privately Held**
Web: www.blueridgejam.com
SIC: 5499 2033 Gourmet food stores; Canned fruits and specialties

(G-6188)
BLUE RIDGE PLATING COMPANY
127 Foxwood Dr (28791-8504)
PHONE.....................................828 274-1795
Carolyn Benfield, *Pr*
Ken Schmidt, *Genl Mgr*
EMP: 4 EST: 1967
SQ FT: 10,000
SALES (est): 241.1K **Privately Held**
SIC: 3471 Electroplating of metals or formed products

(G-6189)
BOLD LIFE PUBLICATION
105 S Main St Ste A (28792-5028)
PHONE.....................................828 692-3230
Mary Diorio, *Owner*
EMP: 7 EST: 2008
SALES (est): 67.86K **Privately Held**
Web: www.boldlife.com
SIC: 2741 Miscellaneous publishing

(G-6190)
BON WORTH INC (PA)
Also Called: Bon Worth Factory Outlets
219 Commercial Hill Dr (28792-7089)
P.O. Box 2890 (28793-2890)
PHONE.....................................800 355-5131
Gurusankar Gurumoorthy, *COO*
Nick Dmytryszyn, *Prin*
▲ EMP: 25 EST: 1971
SALES (est): 21.71MM
SALES (corp-wide): 21.71MM **Privately Held**
Web: www.bonworth.com
SIC: 2339 2335 2337 5621 Slacks: women's, misses', and juniors'; Dresses,paper, cut and sewn; Skirts, separate: women's, misses', and juniors'; Ready-to-wear apparel, women's

(G-6191)
BURNTSHIRT VINEYARDS LLC
3737 Howard Gap Rd (28792-3174)
PHONE.....................................828 685-2402
Oates Lemuel, *Prin*
EMP: 16 EST: 2013
SALES (est): 467.45K **Privately Held**
Web: www.burntshirtvineyards.com
SIC: 2084 Wines

(G-6192)
BYERS PRCISION FABRICATORS INC
675 Dana Rd (28792-3005)
P.O. Box 5127 (28793-5127)
PHONE.....................................828 693-4088
Roger Byers, *CEO*
Shirley Byers, *
Charlene Case, *
▲ EMP: 28 EST: 1943
SQ FT: 60,000
SALES (est): 1.04MM **Privately Held**
Web: www.byersprecision.com
SIC: 3444 Sheet metal specialties, not stamped

(G-6193)
CARBO-CUT INC
3937 Chimney Rock Rd (28792-9385)
P.O. Box 674 (28793-0674)
PHONE.....................................828 685-7890
Ludwik Bochynek, *Pr*
William Synder, *VP*
EMP: 6 EST: 1992
SQ FT: 2,500
SALES (est): 242.54K **Privately Held**
SIC: 3545 Machine tool accessories

(G-6194)
CAROLINA BLIND OUTLET INC (PA)
225 Duncan Hill Rd (28792-2714)
PHONE.....................................828 697-8525
Joel Wayne Patterson Ii, *Pr*
Tony Edward Goodwin, *VP*
EMP: 4 EST: 1992
SQ FT: 1,870
SALES (est): 873.83K **Privately Held**
Web: www.carolinablinds.com
SIC: 5719 2591 Window furnishings; Blinds vertical

▲ = Import ▼ = Export
◆ = Import/Export

(G-6195)
CAROLINA HOME GARDEN
Also Called: Verve
105 S Main St (28792-5022)
PHONE..............................828 692-3230
Mary Diorio, *Pt*
Mary Diorio, *Prin*
EMP: 5 **EST:** 2010
SALES (est): 135.46K **Privately Held**
Web: www.carolinahomegarden.com
SIC: 2721 Magazines: publishing only, not
printed on site

(G-6196)
CJT MACHINE INC
Also Called: Cjt Machine
1172 Terrys Gap Rd (28792-0236)
PHONE..............................828 376-3693
Christopher Hare, *Pr*
EMP: 5 **EST:** 2013
SALES (est): 1.44MM **Privately Held**
Web: www.cjtmachine.com
SIC: 3599 Machine shop, jobbing and repair

(G-6197)
CLEMENT PAPPAS NC LLC
125 Industrial Park Rd (28792-9012)
PHONE..............................856 455-1000
Mark Mcneil, *Pr*
Caroline Lemoine, *Sec*
Glenn Mckellar, *Treas*
EMP: 4
SALES (est): 123.72K **Privately Held**
SIC: 2033 Fruit juices: packaged in cans,
jars, etc.

(G-6198)
CONTINENTAL TOOL WORKS INC
690 Shepherd St (28792-6470)
PHONE..............................828 692-2578
Douglas L Marshall, *Pr*
EMP: 8 **EST:** 1992
SQ FT: 10,000
SALES (est): 868.04K **Privately Held**
Web: www.flatrocktoolandmold.com
SIC: 3544 Special dies and tools

(G-6199)
COPY WORKS
348 7th Ave E (28792-3706)
PHONE..............................828 698-7622
Don Bowman, *Ex Dir*
EMP: 4 **EST:** 2008
SALES (est): 238.99K **Privately Held**
Web: www.allegrawnc.com
SIC: 2752 Offset printing

(G-6200)
DAMPP-CHASER ELECTRONICS CORP
Also Called: Dampp-Chaser
1410 Spartanburg Hwy (28792-6445)
P.O. Box 1610 (28793-1610)
PHONE..............................828 692-8271
Gayle Mair, *Pr*
Roger Wheelock, *
▲ **EMP:** 25 **EST:** 1947
SQ FT: 6,000
SALES (est): 4.46MM **Privately Held**
Web: www.pianolifesaver.com
SIC: 3634 3822 Dehumidifiers, electric: room
; Humidistats: wall, duct, and skeleton

(G-6201)
DANA FANCY FOODS
101 Lytle Rd (28792-6476)
P.O. Box 192 (28724-0192)
PHONE..............................828 685-2937
Robert Morris, *Owner*
EMP: 6 **EST:** 2012

SALES (est): 170K **Privately Held**
SIC: 2035 Pickles, vinegar

(G-6202)
DIGITAL AUDIO CORPORATION
Also Called: Salient Sciences
116 Brightwater Heights Dr (28791-9705)
PHONE..............................919 572-6767
Donald Tunstall, *Pr*
Donald E Tunstall, *Pr*
Jason Williams, *VP*
Kelly K Smith, *Sec*
Peter Salas, *Ex Dir*
EMP: 10 **EST:** 1979
SALES (est): 2.49MM **Privately Held**
Web: www.salientsciences.com
SIC: 3571 7372 Electronic computers;
Prepackaged software
PA: Dolphin Equity Partners, Lp
4924 Frst Cast Hwy Ste 12
Fernandina Beach FL 32034

(G-6203)
DOWNTOWN TIRE CENTER INC
Also Called: Downtown Tire
108 S King St (28792)
PHONE..............................828 693-1676
Robert R Roland, *Pr*
EMP: 7 **EST:** 1999
SQ FT: 6,000
SALES (est): 234.82K **Privately Held**
Web: www.downtowntirecenter.com
SIC: 7539 7534 Brake repair, automotive;
Tire retreading and repair shops

(G-6204)
EDDIE S MOUNTAIN MACHINE INC
Also Called: Mountain Machine
2011 Pilot Mountain Rd (28792-8806)
P.O. Box 331 (28727-0331)
PHONE..............................828 685-0733
Eddie Merrell, *Pr*
Brian Merrell, *VP*
EMP: 4 **EST:** 1985
SALES (est): 305.96K **Privately Held**
SIC: 3599 Machine shop, jobbing and repair

(G-6205)
FIMIA INC
201 Arbutus Ln (28739-3903)
PHONE..............................828 697-8447
John Brookshire, *Pr*
Betty Kay Brookshire, *VP*
EMP: 4 **EST:** 1990
SALES (est): 90.81K **Privately Held**
SIC: 2299 Broadwoven fabrics: linen, jute,
hemp, and ramie

(G-6206)
FLAME-TEC LLC
136 Hillview Blvd (28792-5333)
PHONE..............................844 352-6383
EMP: 12 **EST:** 2016
SALES (est): 1.19MM **Privately Held**
Web: www.flame-tec.com
SIC: 3822 Air flow controllers, air
conditioning and refrigeration

(G-6207)
FLANAGAN PRINTING COMPANY INC
127 3rd Ave W (28792-4313)
P.O. Box 1613 (28793-1613)
PHONE..............................828 693-7380
Dennis Brooks, *Pr*
EMP: 4 **EST:** 1931
SQ FT: 3,750
SALES (est): 119.75K **Privately Held**
Web: www.flanaganprinting.com
SIC: 2752 Offset printing

(G-6208)
FLAT ROCK TOOL & MOLD INC
690 Shepherd St (28792-6470)
PHONE..............................828 692-2578
Lewis Kuykendall, *Pr*
Anthony R Corn, *Sec*
EMP: 8 **EST:** 2010
SALES (est): 933.6K **Privately Held**
Web: www.flatrocktoolandmold.com
SIC: 3544 Special dies and tools

(G-6209)
FOGLE COMPUTING CORPORATION
131 Camellia Way (28739-9306)
P.O. Box 1045 (28793-1045)
PHONE..............................828 697-9080
John B Fogle, *CEO*
Carolyn Fogle, *VP*
EMP: 7 **EST:** 1981
SALES (est): 211.28K **Privately Held**
Web: www.foglecomputing.com
SIC: 7372 Application computer software

(G-6210)
GOLDSMITH BY RUDI LTD
434 N Main St (28792-4901)
PHONE..............................828 693-1030
Rudolf H Haug, *Pr*
Yvonne Hill, *Adm/Dir*
EMP: 8 **EST:** 1975
SALES (est): 483.36K **Privately Held**
Web: www.thegoldsmithbyrudi.com
SIC: 3911 Jewelry, precious metal

(G-6211)
HALIFAX MEDIA HOLDINGS LLC
1717 Four Seasons Blvd (28792-2859)
PHONE..............................828 692-5763
Jon Brooks, *Brnch Mgr*
EMP: 4
SALES (corp-wide): 34.82MM **Privately
Held**
Web: www.news-journalonline.com
SIC: 2711 Commercial printing and
newspaper publishing combined
PA: Halifax Media Holdings, Llc
901 6 St
Daytona Beach FL 32117
386 681-2404

(G-6212)
HAYNES INTERNATIONAL INC
Also Called: Haynes Wire Company
158 N Egerton Rd (28792-1130)
PHONE..............................765 456-6000
EMP: 26
SALES (corp-wide): 589.96MM **Privately
Held**
Web: www.haynesintl.com
SIC: 3356 Nickel
PA: Haynes International, Inc.
1020 W Park Ave
Kokomo IN 46904
765 456-6000

(G-6213)
HEARTWOOD REFUGE
389 Courtland Blvd (28791-8545)
PHONE..............................828 513-5016
EMP: 8 **EST:** 2016
SALES (est): 233.35K **Privately Held**
Web: www.heartwoodrefuge.org
SIC: 2499 Wood products, nec

(G-6214)
HELENA AGRI-ENTERPRISES LLC
3642 Chimney Rock Rd (28792-9382)
PHONE..............................828 685-1182
Travis Nix, *Mgr*
EMP: 5

Web: www.helenaagri.com
SIC: 5191 2879 Chemicals, agricultural;
Pesticides, agricultural or household
HQ: Helena Agri-Enterprises, Llc
225 Schilling Blvd
Collierville TN 38017
901 761-0050

(G-6215)
HENDERSNVLLE AFFRDBL HSING COR
203 N Justice St (28739-4943)
P.O. Box 1106 (28793-1106)
PHONE..............................828 692-6175
Diana Brow, *Prin*
Ronnie Pepper, *Prin*
Garry Sherill, *Prin*
Dan Williams, *Prin*
Mike Wagner, *Prin*
EMP: 13 **EST:** 2018
SALES (est): 3.37MM **Privately Held**
Web: www.hendersonvillelightning.com
SIC: 2711 Newspapers, publishing and
printing

(G-6216)
HIVIZ LED LIGHTING LLC
149 Twin Springs Rd (28792-9262)
P.O. Box 1553 (27546-1553)
PHONE..............................703 662-3458
Sam Massa, *Managing Member*
EMP: 10 **EST:** 2011
SALES (est): 1.48MM **Privately Held**
Web: www.hivizleds.com
SIC: 3674 Light emitting diodes

(G-6217)
HIVIZ LIGHTING INC
Also Called: Firetech
149 Twin Springs Rd (28792-9262)
P.O. Box 565 (28760-0565)
PHONE..............................703 382-5675
Sam Massa, *Prin*
EMP: 6 **EST:** 2019
SALES (est): 4.16MM **Privately Held**
Web: www.hivizleds.com
SIC: 3641 Electric lamps

(G-6218)
KIMBERLY-CLARK CORPORATION
Kimberly-Clark
32 Smyth Ave (28792-8503)
PHONE..............................828 698-5230
Stephen King, *Mgr*
EMP: 250
SALES (corp-wide): 20.06B **Publicly Held**
Web: www.kimberly-clark.com
SIC: 2621 2676 Sanitary tissue paper;
Sanitary paper products
PA: Kimberly-Clark Corporation
351 Phelps Dr
Irving TX 75038
972 281-1200

(G-6219)
L & B JANDREW ENTERPRISES
Also Called: Animal Supply House
1927 Spartanburg Hwy (28792-6528)
PHONE..............................828 687-8927
Larry Jandrew, *Pr*
Barbara Jandrew, *VP*
EMP: 7 **EST:** 1999
SALES (est): 308.65K **Privately Held**
SIC: 3999 5999 Pet supplies; Pets

(G-6220)
LANTERN OF HENDERSONVILLE LLC
755 N Main St (28792-5079)
PHONE..............................828 513-5033

John Bell, *VP*
EMP: 6 **EST:** 2015
SALES (est): 86.04K **Privately Held**
Web: www.thecharleston.net
SIC: 2711 Newspapers

(G-6221)
LEGACY VULCAN LLC
Mideast Division
2960 Clear Creek Rd (28792-8515)
P.O. Box 905 (28793-0905)
PHONE..............................828 692-0254
Sammy Peak, *Mgr*
EMP: 7
Web: www.vulcanmaterials.com
SIC: 3273 Ready-mixed concrete
HQ: Legacy Vulcan, Llc
    1200 Urban Center Dr
    Birmingham AL 35242
    205 298-3000

(G-6222)
M T INDUSTRIES INC
1584 Airport Rd (28792-9155)
PHONE..............................828 697-2864
Gary D Salvaggio, *Pr*
Bart Salvaggio, *VP*
Dale Bradshaw, *VP*
EMP: 10 **EST:** 1985
SQ FT: 15,000
SALES (est): 975.82K **Privately Held**
SIC: 3861 Photographic equipment and
    supplies

(G-6223)
MANNA CORP NORTH CAROLINA
(PA)
Also Called: Manna Designs
508 N Main St (28792-5070)
PHONE..............................828 696-3642
Charles Paskus, *Pr*
Kathleen Paskus, *VP*
EMP: 4 **EST:** 1993
SALES (est): 455.95K **Privately Held**
SIC: 2396 2395 5699 . Screen printing on
    fabric articles; Embroidery and art
    needlework; Customized clothing and
    apparel

(G-6224)
MANUAL WOODWORKERS
WEAVERS INC (PA)
Also Called: Mww On Demand
3737 Howard Gap Rd (28792-3174)
PHONE..............................828 692-7333
Travis L Oates, *CEO*
Molly Oates Sherrill, *
James Clarke, *
Lemuel Oates, *Adviser*
Sandra T Oates, *
◆ **EMP:** 201 **EST:** 1932
SQ FT: 500,000
SALES (est): 19.59MM
SALES (corp-wide): 19.59MM **Privately
Held**
Web: www.manualww.com
SIC: 2392 Household furnishings, nec

(G-6225)
MCF OPERATING LLC
352 Jet St (28792-8004)
PHONE..............................828 685-8821
John Webber, *Mgr*
EMP: 42
Web: www.mrsclarks.com
SIC: 2033 2099 Fruit juices: fresh; Food
    preparations, nec
PA: Mcf Operating, Llc
    740 Se Dalbey Dr
    Ankeny IA 50021

(G-6226)
MESA QUALITY FENESTRATION INC
Also Called: Mesa Quality
968 Crab Creek Rd (28739-8437)
P.O. Box 494 (28793-0494)
PHONE..............................828 393-0132
Warren Morris, *Pr*
EMP: 5 **EST:** 2016
SALES (est): 1.21MM **Privately Held**
Web: www.mesaquality.com
SIC: 2431 5031 Millwork; Millwork

(G-6227)
MICHELSON ENTERPRISES INC
Also Called: Oriole Mill, The
701 Oriole Dr (28792-2642)
PHONE..............................828 693-5500
Stephan Michelson, *Pr*
EMP: 8 **EST:** 2010
SALES (est): 177.27K **Privately Held**
Web: www.theoriolemill.com
SIC: 2231 Weaving mill, broadwoven fabrics:
    wool or similar fabric

(G-6228)
MOUNTAIN SHOWCASE GROUP INC
Also Called: Mountain Showcase
211 Sugarloaf Rd (28792-9386)
PHONE..............................828 692-9494
Dan Casto, *Pr*
David Manning, *VP*
EMP: 23 **EST:** 1997
SQ FT: 10,000
SALES (est): 5.72MM **Privately Held**
Web: www.mountainshowcase.com
SIC: 1751 5211 2517 2434 Cabinet building
    and installation; Cabinets, kitchen; Wood
    television and radio cabinets; Wood kitchen
    cabinets

(G-6229)
MURPHY S CUSTOM CABINETRY INC
351 Hidden Woods Ln (28791-5500)
PHONE..............................828 891-3050
Paul Defoy Murphy, *Pr*
Jewell Irene Murphy, *Sec*
EMP: 4 **EST:** 1976
SQ FT: 4,000
SALES (est): 177.85K **Privately Held**
Web:
www.murphyscustomcabinetry.com
SIC: 5712 2434 5031 Cabinet work, custom;
    Wood kitchen cabinets; Kitchen cabinets

(G-6230)
NC PRINTING LLC
1524 Haywood Rd (28791-2338)
PHONE..............................828 393-4615
EMP: 4 **EST:** 2010
SALES (est): 251.81K **Privately Held**
Web: www.ncprinting.com
SIC: 2752 Offset printing

(G-6231)
NORMAC INCORPORATED (PA)
Also Called: Normac
93 Industrial Dr (28739-7895)
P.O. Box 69 (28704-0069)
PHONE..............................828 209-9000
Raymond Bodie, *Pr*
Mark Kushigian, *
Patricia Hunnicutt, *
Emmanuel Gauzer, *
◆ **EMP:** 40 **EST:** 1967
SQ FT: 27,000
SALES (est): 9.87MM
SALES (corp-wide): 9.87MM **Privately
Held**
Web: www.normac.com
SIC: 3541 Grinding machines, metalworking

(G-6232)
OHLINS USA INC
703 S Grove St (28792-5794)
PHONE..............................828 692-4525
Scott Macdonald, *Ex Dir*
▲ **EMP:** 36 **EST:** 1997
SALES (est): 25MM
SALES (corp-wide): 18.04B **Privately Held**
Web: www.ohlinsusa.com
SIC: 3714 Shock absorbers, motor vehicle
HQ: Ohlins Racing Ab
    Instrumentvagen 8-10
    Upplands VAsby 194 5
    859002500

(G-6233)
OKLAWAHA BREWING COMPANY
LLC
147 1st Ave E (28792-5191)
PHONE..............................828 595-9956
Joseph Dinan, *Prin*
Josep Dinan, *Owner*
EMP: 10 **EST:** 2015
SALES (est): 170.74K **Privately Held**
Web: www.oklawahabrewing.com
SIC: 5813 2084 Bars and lounges; Wine
    cellars, bonded: engaged in blending wines

(G-6234)
PAMELA TAYLOR
Also Called: Carolina Press
101 1st Ave W (28792-5009)
PHONE..............................828 692-8599
Pamela Taylor, *Owner*
EMP: 5 **EST:** 1985
SQ FT: 9,000
SALES (est): 93.08K **Privately Held**
SIC: 2752 Offset printing

(G-6235)
PATTY CAKES
5 Star Ln (28791-9058)
PHONE..............................828 696-8240
Patricia Lowes, *Pr*
Charles Moore, *VP*
EMP: 4 **EST:** 1999
SALES (est): 175.26K **Privately Held**
SIC: 2051 Cakes, pies, and pastries

(G-6236)
PLANE DEFENSE LTD
175 N Mason Way (28792-1159)
P.O. Box 193 (28726-0193)
PHONE..............................828 254-6061
Stephen J Wilde, *Pr*
EMP: 5 **EST:** 2005
SALES (est): 301.81K **Privately Held**
SIC: 3812 Defense systems and equipment

(G-6237)
PRINTPACK INC
3510 Asheville Hwy (28791-0739)
PHONE..............................828 693-1723
Timothy Garrity, *Brnch Mgr*
EMP: 164
SALES (corp-wide): 684.49MM **Privately
Held**
Web: www.printpack.com
SIC: 2673 Bags: plastic, laminated, and
    coated
HQ: Printpack, Inc.
    2800 Overlook Pkwy Ne
    Atlanta GA 30339
    404 460-7000

(G-6238)
QRMC LTD
11 S Egerton Rd (28792-1129)
P.O. Box 709 (28793-0709)
PHONE..............................828 696-2000

L A Lorenzo, *Ch Bd*
Bernard J Garcarz, *VP*
T J Hoyland, *VP*
Brian Lavell, *Sec*
▲ **EMP:** 7 **EST:** 1939
SQ FT: 72,000
SALES (est): 785.64K **Privately Held**
Web: www.qualityrubber.com
SIC: 3544 3069 Extrusion dies; Molded
    rubber products

(G-6239)
SAINT PAUL MOUNTAIN VINEYARDS
588 Chestnut Gap Rd (28792-3256)
PHONE..............................828 685-4002
Alan Ward, *Owner*
EMP: 14 **EST:** 2013
SALES (est): 578.87K **Privately Held**
Web: www.saintpaulfarms.com
SIC: 2084 Wines

(G-6240)
SELEE CORPORATION (DH)
700 Shepherd St (28792-6400)
PHONE..............................828 697-2411
Mark Morse, *Pr*
Tim Kriegel, *
Watt Jackson, *
Daren Rogers, *
◆ **EMP:** 170 **EST:** 1992
SQ FT: 135,000
SALES (est): 50.37MM
SALES (corp-wide): 213.47MM **Privately
Held**
Web: www.selee.com
SIC: 3269 Filtering media, pottery
HQ: Porvair Corporation
    700 Shepherd St
    Hendersonville NC 28792

(G-6241)
SOFWARE LLC (PA)
Also Called: Sofware
217 Covington Cove Ln (28739-5844)
PHONE..............................828 820-2810
EMP: 7 **EST:** 2011
SALES (est): 1.28MM **Privately Held**
Web: www.sofwarellc.com
SIC: 7372 Application computer software

(G-6242)
SOUTHERN AG INSECTICIDES INC
511 Maple St (28792-3752)
P.O. Box 429 (28793-0429)
PHONE..............................828 692-2233
Richard Baxter, *Mgr*
EMP: 25
SALES (corp-wide): 22.18MM **Privately
Held**
Web: www.southernag.com
SIC: 5191 2879 2875 Insecticides;
    Agricultural chemicals, nec; Fertilizers,
    mixing only
PA: Southern Agricultural Insecticides Inc.
    7500 Bayshore Rd
    Palmetto FL 34221
    941 722-3285

(G-6243)
SOUTHERN CONCRETE MTLS INC
715 Shepherd St (28792-6473)
PHONE..............................828 692-6517
John Holt, *Mgr*
EMP: 20
SQ FT: 6,311
SALES (corp-wide): 238.17MM **Privately
Held**
Web: www.scmusa.com
SIC: 3273 5039 Ready-mixed concrete;
    Septic tanks
HQ: Southern Concrete Materials, Inc.

▲ = Import ▼ = Export
◆ = Import/Export

35 Meadow Rd
Asheville NC 28803
828 253-6421

(G-6244)
STANDARD TYTAPE COMPANY INC
1495 N Main St (28792-2568)
P.O. Box 2270 (28793-2270)
PHONE.....................828 693-6594
Robert Herrmann, *Pr*
EMP: 7 **EST:** 1935
SQ FT: 35,000
SALES (est): 974.25K **Privately Held**
Web: www.tytape.com
SIC: 2396 2241 2298 Automotive and
apparel trimmings; Braids, textile; Cordage
and twine

(G-6245)
TODDS RV & MARINE INC
130 Lyndale Rd (28739-6119)
PHONE.....................828 651-0007
Daniel Todd, *Pr*
Edwina Garrison, *VP*
Alineen Todd, *Sec*
EMP: 5 **EST:** 1956
SQ FT: 62,000
SALES (est): 202.5K **Privately Held**
Web: www.toddsrvandmarine.com
SIC: 5561 5551 7699 3732 Motor homes;
Motor boat dealers; Recreational vehicle
repair services; Motorized boat, building
and repairing

(G-6246)
UNDERGROUND BAKING CO LLC
304 Yon Hill Rd (28792-2460)
PHONE.....................828 674-7494
Matthew N Hickman, *Prin*
EMP: 8 **EST:** 2010
SALES (est): 149.59K **Privately Held**
Web: www.undergroundbaking.com
SIC: 2051 Bakery: wholesale or wholesale/
retail combined

(G-6247)
VILLAGE CERAMICS INC
320 Q P Ln (28792-5600)
PHONE.....................828 685-9491
Q P Anderson, *Pr*
Elaine Anderson, *Sec*
EMP: 4 **EST:** 1970
SALES (est): 490.74K **Privately Held**
SIC: 3843 3842 8072 Denture materials;
Prosthetic appliances; Dental laboratories

(G-6248)
VULCAN MATERIALS COMPANY
2284 Clear Creek Rd (28792-9078)
PHONE.....................828 692-0039
EMP: 4
Web: www.vulcanmaterials.com
SIC: 3273 Ready-mixed concrete
PA: Vulcan Materials Company
1200 Urban Center Dr
Birmingham AL 35242

(G-6249)
WARM PRODUCTS INC
Also Called: Warm Industrial Nonwovens
581 Old Sunset Hill Rd (28792-8362)
PHONE.....................425 248-2424
Robert Whaley, *Brnch Mgr*
EMP: 18
SALES (corp-wide): 9.92MM **Privately
Held**
Web: www.warmindustrial.com
SIC: 5131 2297 Piece goods and notions;
Nonwoven fabrics
PA: Warm Products, Inc.
5529 186th Pl Sw

Lynnwood WA 98037
425 248-2424

(G-6250)
WIRTZ WIRE EDM LLC
65a Commercial Hill Dr (28792-4563)
PHONE.....................828 696-0830
W Wirtz, *Managing Member*
Patrick Wirtz, *Pr*
EMP: 14 **EST:** 1993
SQ FT: 4,500
SALES (est): 974.8K **Privately Held**
Web: www.wirtzwireedm.com
SIC: 3544 Special dies and tools

Hertford
Perquimans County

(G-6251)
BILLY HARRELL LOGGING INC
108 Iiilda Dr (27944-9559)
PHONE.....................252 426-1362
Billy Harrell, *Prin*
EMP: 5 **EST:** 2016
SALES (est): 961.73K **Privately Held**
SIC: 2411 Logging camps and contractors

(G-6252)
CROSSROADS FUEL SERVICE INC
395 Ocean Hwy N (27944-8956)
P.O. Box 67 (27944-0067)
PHONE.....................252 426-5216
Billy Lewis, *Brnch Mgr*
EMP: 26
SALES (corp-wide): 52.91MM **Privately
Held**
Web: www.crossroadsfuel.com
SIC: 5172 2893 Fuel oil; Printing ink
PA: Crossroads Fuel Service, Inc.
1441 Fentress Rd
Chesapeake VA 23322
757 482-2179

(G-6253)
EAST COAST STL FABRICATION INC
116 N Granby St (27944)
PHONE.....................757 351-2601
Cynthia Overman, *Prin*
Mark Overman, *
Mary Miller, *
▲ **EMP:** 37 **EST:** 2006
SALES (est): 5.32MM **Privately Held**
Web: www.ecsfi.com
SIC: 3441 3317 Fabricated structural metal;
Boiler tubes (wrought)

(G-6254)
HERTFORD ABC BOARD
803 S Church St (27944-1210)
P.O. Box 23 (27944-0023)
PHONE.....................252 426-5290
Don Keaton, *Mgr*
EMP: 6 **EST:** 2010
SALES (est): 219.77K **Privately Held**
Web: www.townofhertfordnc.com
SIC: 2084 Wines, brandy, and brandy spirits

(G-6255)
**JOHNIE GREGORY TRCK BODIES
INC**
337 Old Us Highway 17 (27944-9111)
PHONE.....................252 264-2626
Johnie M Gregory, *Pr*
William J Gregory, *VP*
Ashley Gregory, *Sec*
Tim Gregory, *Stockholder*
EMP: 6 **EST:** 1898
SQ FT: 6,000
SALES (est): 1.94MM **Privately Held**

Web:
www.johniegregorytruckbodies.com
SIC: 3713 Truck bodies (motor vehicles)

(G-6256)
R & S LOGGING INC
771 Lake Rd (27944-8752)
PHONE.....................252 426-5880
Janis Rhodes, *Pr*
James Rhodes, *Prin*
EMP: 7 **EST:** 1998
SALES (est): 2.1MM **Privately Held**
Web: www.insiteshred.com
SIC: 2411 Logging camps and contractors

(G-6257)
WHITEHAT SEED FARMS INC
102 Whitehat Rd (27944-9008)
PHONE.....................252 264-2427
Burt Eure, *Pr*
Karl M Eure, *Stockholder*
Betty Eure, *Treas*
Paige Eure, *Sec*
EMP: 7 **EST:** 1956
SQ FT: 55,000
SALES (est): 396.12K **Privately Held**
Web: www.whitehat.com.au
SIC: 2041 2083 2075 Oat flour; Barley malt;
Soybean oil, cake or meal

Hickory
Catawba County

(G-6258)
057 TECHNOLOGY LLC
728 11th Street Pl Nw (28601-3441)
P.O. Box 2127 (28603-2127)
PHONE.....................855 557-7057
Jason Hughes, *Pr*
Jason David Hughes, *Managing Member*
EMP: 4 **EST:** 2018
SQ FT: 31,000
SALES (est): 1.69MM **Privately Held**
Web: www.057tech.com
SIC: 3621 7373 Motors, electric; Computer
integrated systems design

(G-6259)
A PLUS SERVICE INC
2233a Highland Ave Ne (28601-8162)
P.O. Box 1390 (28603-1390)
PHONE.....................828 324-4397
Bill Hasty, *Pr*
EMP: 8 **EST:** 2005
SQ FT: 60,000
SALES (est): 736.55K **Privately Held**
Web: www.aplusserviceinc.com
SIC: 3086 Plastics foam products

(G-6260)
ABB INSTALLATION PRODUCTS INC
415 19th Street Dr Se (28602-4446)
PHONE.....................828 322-1855
EMP: 41
Web: elis-secure.abb.com
SIC: 3643 3312 3567 Electric connectors;
Structural shapes and pilings, steel;
Heating units and devices, industrial:
electric
HQ: Abb Installation Products Inc.
860 Rdg Lake Blvd
Memphis TN 38120
901 252-5000

(G-6261)
AIKEN-BLACK TIRE SERVICE INC
823 1st Ave Nw (28601-6064)
P.O. Box 1605 (28603-1605)
PHONE.....................828 322-3736

David Black, *Pr*
John Black, *
EMP: 40 **EST:** 1960
SQ FT: 20,500
SALES (est): 10.7MM **Privately Held**
Web: www.aikenblacktire.com
SIC: 5531 7534 7538 Automotive tires; Tire
recapping; General automotive repair shops

(G-6262)
ALL GLASS INC
1125 S Center St (28602-3446)
P.O. Box 11002 (28603-4502)
PHONE.....................828 324-8609
Bob Inman, *Owner*
Ray Prewitt, *Pr*
Beth Prewitt, *VP*
EMP: 9 **EST:** 1993
SALES (est): 899.81K **Privately Held**
Web: www.allglasscompany.com
SIC: 5211 5999 3231 Screens, door and
window; Alarm signal systems; Aquariums
and reflectors, glass

(G-6263)
AMERICAN SPEEDY PRINTING CTRS
Also Called: American Speedy Printing
337 Maln Ave Ne (28601-5121)
PHONE.....................828 322-3981
Marcus Woodie, *Pr*
EMP: 6 **EST:** 2018
SALES (est): 99.15K **Privately Held**
Web: www.americanspeedy.com
SIC: 2752 Offset printing

(G-6264)
ANEW LOOK HOMES LLC
1717 Highland Ave Ne Ste 102
(28601-5305)
PHONE.....................800 796-5152
Melissa Hall, *Managing Member*
EMP: 12 **EST:** 2016
SALES (est): 591.88K **Privately Held**
Web: www.anewlookhomes.com
SIC: 8742 6531 1389 6798 Management
consulting services; Real estate leasing
and rentals; Construction, repair, and
dismantling services; Real estate
investment trusts

(G-6265)
APPLIED COMPONENTS MFG LLC
101 33rd Street Dr Se (28602-8375)
PHONE.....................828 323-8915
Hans Peterson, *Prin*
EMP: 6 **EST:** 2009
SALES (est): 808.67K **Privately Held**
Web: www.appliedcompmfg.com
SIC: 3999 Manufacturing industries, nec

(G-6266)
AQUA PLASTICS INC
1474 17th St Ne (28601-2824)
PHONE.....................828 324-6284
Miguel Crouch, *Pr*
Ana Crouch, *VP*
◆ **EMP:** 15 **EST:** 2006
SALES (est): 1.41MM **Privately Held**
Web: www.aquaplasticsusa.com
SIC: 2821 3089 3081 Thermoplastic
materials; Molding primary plastics;
Unsupported plastics film and sheet

(G-6267)
ARGOS USA LLC
Also Called: Redi-Mix Concrete
2001 Main Ave Se (28602-1404)
P.O. Box 1847 (28603-1847)
PHONE.....................828 322-9325
Chet Miller, *Brnch Mgr*
EMP: 59

Web: www.argos-us.com
SIC: 3273 Ready-mixed concrete
HQ: Argos Usa Llc
3015 Windward Plz Ste 300
Alpharetta GA 30005
678 368-4300

(G-6268)
B & M ELECTRIC MOTOR SERVICE
20 17th Street Pl Nw (28601-5819)
P.O. Box 2676 (28603-2676)
PHONE..............................828 267-0829
Shannon Mcdonald, *Pr*
Dee Dee Brittin, *Sec*
▲ **EMP:** 7 **EST:** 2001
SQ FT: 11,000
SALES (est): 1.11MM **Privately Held**
Web: www.clearelectricinc.net
SIC: 7694 Electric motor repair

(G-6269)
B&P ENTERPRISE NC INC
4128 Icard Ridge Rd (28601-7656)
PHONE..............................727 669-6877
James Jackson, *Pr*
EMP: 9 **EST:** 1998
SALES (est): 608.64K **Privately Held**
SIC: 3993 7311 Electric signs; Advertising
consultant

(G-6270)
BETHLEHEM MANUFACTURING CO
(PA)
Also Called: Molds of Bethlehem
36 Bethlehem Manufacturing Ln
(28601-7831)
PHONE..............................828 495-7731
Latt Moretz, *Pr*
Ashley Moretz, *VP*
EMP: 13 **EST:** 1963
SQ FT: 2,400
SALES (est): 1.36MM
SALES (corp-wide): 1.36MM **Privately Held**
Web: www.moldsofbethlehem.com
SIC: 3544 3537 Industrial molds; Trucks,
tractors, loaders, carriers, and similar
equipment

(G-6271)
BLL INNOVATIONS INC
77 Pine Ridge Dr (28602)
PHONE..............................888 501-0678
Donald Warmbold, *Prin*
EMP: 5
SALES (est): 312.7K **Privately Held**
SIC: 2421 Sawmills and planing mills,
general

(G-6272)
BLOSSMAN PROPANE GAS & APPL
2315 Catawba Valley Blvd Se (28602-4162)
PHONE..............................828 396-0144
Jimmy Daley, *Genl Mgr*
EMP: 12 **EST:** 1951
SALES (est): 338.07K **Privately Held**
Web: www.blossmangas.com
SIC: 5984 3634 Propane gas, bottled;
Heating units, for electric appliances

(G-6273)
BLUE LAGOON INC
Also Called: TEC-Ops
1011 10th Street Blvd Nw (28601-3459)
P.O. Box 1890 (28603-1890)
PHONE..............................828 324-2333
Peter Menzies, *Pr*
EMP: 4 **EST:** 2008
SALES (est): 1.07MM **Privately Held**
Web: www.covertthreads.com

SIC: 2253 Knit outerwear mills

(G-6274)
BLUE RIDGE PRODUCTS CO INC
3050 Main Ave Nw (28601-5663)
P.O. Box 2028 (28603-2028)
PHONE..............................828 322-7990
Charles Ingle, *Pr*
EMP: 4 **EST:** 1950
SQ FT: 125,000
SALES (est): 172.56K **Privately Held**
Web: www.blueridgeproducts.com
SIC: 2515 2426 2392 Spring cushions;
Hardwood dimension and flooring mills;
Household furnishings, nec

(G-6275)
BRADINGTON-YOUNG LLC (HQ)
4040 10th Avenue Dr Sw (28602-4535)
PHONE..............................704 435-5881
C Scott Young, *Managing Member*
▲ **EMP:** 200 **EST:** 1978
SALES (est): 7.41MM
SALES (corp-wide): 433.23MM **Publicly Held**
Web: www.bradington-young.com
SIC: 2512 Chairs: upholstered on wood
frames
PA: Hooker Furnishings Corporation
440 Commonwealth Blvd E
Martinsville VA 24112
276 632-2133

(G-6276)
BURRIS MACHINE COMPANY INC
1631 Main Avenue Dr Nw (28601-5834)
PHONE..............................828 322-6914
Jerry Sellers, *Brnch Mgr*
EMP: 6
SALES (corp-wide): 1.61MM **Privately Held**
Web: www.burrismachineco.com
SIC: 3599 Machine shop, jobbing and repair
PA: Burris Machine Company Inc
3155 Highland Ave Ne
Hickory NC 28601
828 322-6914

(G-6277)
BURRIS MACHINE COMPANY INC
(PA)
3155 Highland Ave Ne (28601-8106)
P.O. Box 2858 (28603-2858)
PHONE..............................828 322-6914
Jerry Sellers, *Pr*
EMP: 9 **EST:** 1976
SQ FT: 28,100
SALES (est): 1.61MM
SALES (corp-wide): 1.61MM **Privately Held**
Web: www.burrismachineco.com
SIC: 5084 3469 3599 Industrial machinery
and equipment; Metal stampings, nec;
Machine and other job shop work

(G-6278)
C R LAINE FURNITURE CO INC
2829 Us Highway 70 Se (28602-8692)
P.O. Box 2128 (28603-2128)
PHONE..............................828 328-1831
C E Roseman Junior, *Pr*
Warren L Frye, *
Lori Whisnant, *
▲ **EMP:** 155 **EST:** 1958
SQ FT: 130,000
SALES (est): 9.85MM **Privately Held**
Web: www.crlaine.com
SIC: 2512 Chairs: upholstered on wood
frames

(G-6279)
CABINET DOOR WORLD LLC
1711 11th Ave Sw (28602-4909)
PHONE..............................877 929-2750
Richard Healey, *Prin*
EMP: 10 **EST:** 2012
SALES (est): 829.3K **Privately Held**
Web: www.cabinetdoorworld.com
SIC: 2434 Wood kitchen cabinets

(G-6280)
CABINET SOLUTIONS USA INC
2001 Startown Rd (28602-8788)
PHONE..............................828 358-2349
James Christopher Robinson, *Pr*
EMP: 33 **EST:** 2017
SALES (est): 2.91MM **Privately Held**
Web: www.usacabinetsolutions.com
SIC: 2434 3429 1751 1799 Wood kitchen
cabinets; Cabinet hardware; Cabinet and
finish carpentry; Kitchen cabinet installation

(G-6281)
CABLE DEVICES INCORPORATED
(HQ)
Also Called: Cable Exchange
3642 Us Highway 70 Sw (28602)
PHONE..............................714 554-4370
Charles L Treadway, *CEO*
Kyle D Lorentzen, *
Frank B Wyatt, *
▲ **EMP:** 150 **EST:** 1979
SALES (est): 37.85MM **Publicly Held**
Web: www.commscope.com
SIC: 3577 Computer peripheral equipment,
nec
PA: Commscope Holding Company, Inc.
3642 E Us Hwy 70
Claremont NC 28610

(G-6282)
CANIPE & LYNN ELC MTR REPR INC
1909 1st Ave Sw (28602-2224)
P.O. Box 1422 (28603-1422)
PHONE..............................828 322-9052
Sherry Lynn, *Pr*
Dock Lynn, *VP*
Ramona Lynn, *Sec*
EMP: 9 **EST:** 1959
SALES (est): 244.45K **Privately Held**
SIC: 5999 7694 Motors, electric; Electric
motor repair

(G-6283)
CAROLINA CLTCH BRAKE RBLDRS
IN
430 Us Highway 70 Se (28602-5122)
PHONE..............................828 327-9358
EMP: 6 **EST:** 2019
SALES (est): 137.63K **Privately Held**
Web: www.carolinaclutch.com
SIC: 3714 Motor vehicle parts and
accessories

(G-6284)
CAROLINA CONTAINER LLC
Also Called: Digital High Point
61 30th St Nw (28601-5630)
P.O. Box 2166 (27261-2166)
PHONE..............................828 322-3380
Jack Pressley, *Mgr*
EMP: 27
SALES (corp-wide): 644.8MM **Privately Held**
Web: www.carolinacontainer.com
SIC: 2653 Boxes, corrugated: made from
purchased materials
HQ: Carolina Container Company
909 Prospect St
High Point NC 27260
336 883-7146

(G-6285)
CAROLINA PAVING HICKORY INC
Also Called: Carolina Asphalt
445 9th St Se (28602-4041)
PHONE..............................828 328-3909
Jim Taylor, *Mgr*
EMP: 4
SALES (corp-wide): 5.62MM **Privately Held**
Web: www.carolinapaving.com
SIC: 1611 3531 Grading; Asphalt plant,
including gravel-mix type
PA: Carolina Paving Of Hickory, Inc.
3203 Highland Ave Ne
Hickory NC 28601
828 322-1706

(G-6286)
CAROLINA PAVING HICKORY INC
(PA)
3203 Highland Ave Ne (28601-9375)
PHONE..............................828 322-1706
Marie H Huffman, *Pr*
E Dane Huffman, *VP*
EMP: 17 **EST:** 1964
SQ FT: 2,000
SALES (est): 5.62MM
SALES (corp-wide): 5.62MM **Privately Held**
Web: www.carolinapaving.com
SIC: 1611 3531 Grading; Asphalt plant,
including gravel-mix type

(G-6287)
CAROLINA SOLVENTS INC
Also Called: C S I
2274 1st St Se (28602-5338)
P.O. Box 9206 (28603-9206)
PHONE..............................828 322-1920
EMP: 24 **EST:** 1969
SALES (est): 7.53MM **Privately Held**
Web: www.carolinasolventsinc.com
SIC: 2952 2891 Asphalt felts and coatings;
Sealants

(G-6288)
CAROLINA SWATCHING INC
725 14th Street Dr Sw (28602-3128)
P.O. Box 9255 (28603-9255)
PHONE..............................828 327-9499
David Robinson, *Pr*
Katherine Robinson, *Sec*
EMP: 12 **EST:** 1993
SQ FT: 10,000
SALES (est): 1.21MM **Privately Held**
Web: www.carolinaswatching.com
SIC: 2789 2782 Swatches and samples;
Blankbooks and looseleaf binders

(G-6289)
CAROLINA TAPE & SUPPLY CORP
502 19th Street Pl Se (28602-4403)
P.O. Box 2488 (28603-2488)
PHONE..............................828 322-3991
TOLL FREE: 800
K Shawn Dagenhardt, *Pr*
D W Dagenhardt, *
Marcus B Dagenhardt, *
James Dagenhardt, *
◆ **EMP:** 29 **EST:** 1966
SQ FT: 30,000
SALES (est): 11.14MM **Privately Held**
Web: www.carolinatape.com
SIC: 5113 2512 2672 Pressure sensitive tape
; Upholstered household furniture; Tape,
pressure sensitive: made from purchased
materials

▲ = Import ▼ = Export
◆ = Import/Export

(G-6290)
CARPENTER CO
30 29th St Nw (28601-5650)
PHONE.....................828 322-6545
Randy Hefner, *Mgr*
EMP: 26
SALES (corp-wide): 506.96MM **Privately Held**
Web: www.carpenter.com
SIC: 3086 2821 Insulation or cushioning material, foamed plastics; Plastics materials and resins
PA: Carpenter Co.
5016 Monument Ave
Richmond VA 23230
804 359-0800

(G-6291)
CATAWBA VLY YOUTH SOCCER ASSOC
3404 6th Street Dr Nw (28601-9092)
P.O. Box 2246 (28603-2246)
PHONE.....................828 234-7082
James Knuckles, *Prin*
EMP: 6 **EST:** 2016
SALES (est): 298.35K **Privately Held**
Web: www.cvysa.org
SIC: 2711 Newspapers, publishing and printing

(G-6292)
CCBCC OPERATIONS LLC
Also Called: Coca-Cola
820 1st Ave Nw (28601-6063)
PHONE.....................828 322-5097
Phillip Davidson, *Mgr*
EMP: 47
SALES (corp-wide): 6.9B **Publicly Held**
Web: www.coca-cola.com
SIC: 2086 Bottled and canned soft drinks
HQ: Ccbcc Operations, Llc
4100 Coca-Cola Plz
Charlotte NC 28211
704 364-8728

(G-6293)
CCO HOLDINGS LLC
483 Us Highway 70 Sw (28602-5019)
PHONE.....................828 270-7016
EMP: 280
SALES (corp-wide): 55.09MM **Publicly Held**
SIC: 4841 3663 3651 Cable television services; Radio and t.v. communications equipment; Household audio and video equipment
HQ: Cco Holdings, Llc
400 Atlantic St
Stamford CT 06901
203 905-7801

(G-6294)
CENTRAL TOOL & MFG CO INC
1021 17th St Sw (28602-4925)
P.O. Box 2325 (28603-2325)
PHONE.....................828 328-2383
Charles Threewitt, *Pr*
June Threewitt, *Sec*
EMP: 6 **EST:** 1967
SQ FT: 15,000
SALES (est): 472.87K **Privately Held**
SIC: 7699 3545 3541 Precision instrument repair; Machine tool attachments and accessories; Machine tools, metal cutting type

(G-6295)
CENTURY FURNITURE LLC
Also Called: Century Furniture Uphl Plant
535 27th St Nw (28601-4551)
PHONE.....................828 326-8410

Terry Jennings, *Mgr*
EMP: 53
SALES (corp-wide): 87.25MM **Privately Held**
Web: www.centuryfurniture.com
SIC: 2511 Wood household furniture
HQ: Century Furniture, Llc
401 11th St Nw
Hickory NC 28601
828 267-8739

(G-6296)
CENTURY FURNITURE LLC
Also Called: Century Case Goods Division
420 12th Street Dr Nw (28601-4741)
P.O. Box 608 (28603-0608)
PHONE.....................828 326-8201
Wade Yount, *Div Mgr*
EMP: 124
SALES (corp-wide): 87.25MM **Privately Held**
Web: www.centuryfurniture.com
SIC: 2511 2512 Wood household furniture; Upholstered household furniture
HQ: Century Furniture, Llc
401 11th St Nw
Hickory NC 28601
828 267-8739

(G-6297)
CENTURY FURNITURE LLC
Also Called: Technical Center
25 18th St Nw (28601-5822)
PHONE.....................828 326-8535
Jim Conley, *Mgr*
EMP: 53
SALES (corp-wide): 87.25MM **Privately Held**
Web: www.centuryfurniture.com
SIC: 2511 8711 Wood household furniture; Engineering services
HQ: Century Furniture, Llc
401 11th St Nw
Hickory NC 28601
828 267-8739

(G-6298)
CENTURY FURNITURE LLC
Chair
3086 Main Ave Nw (28601-5663)
P.O. Box 608 (28603-0608)
PHONE.....................828 326-8458
Kevin Boyle, *Mgr*
EMP: 98
SQ FT: 390,000
SALES (corp-wide): 87.25MM **Privately Held**
Web: www.centuryfurniture.com
SIC: 2511 2512 Chairs, household, except upholstered: wood; Chairs: upholstered on wood frames
HQ: Century Furniture, Llc
401 11th St Nw
Hickory NC 28601
828 267-8739

(G-6299)
CENTURY FURNITURE LLC
420 27th St Nw (28601-4550)
P.O. Box 608 (28603-0608)
PHONE.....................828 326-8410
Terry Jennings, *Mgr*
EMP: 53
SALES (corp-wide): 87.25MM **Privately Held**
Web: www.centuryfurniture.com
SIC: 2512 Upholstered household furniture
HQ: Century Furniture, Llc
401 11th St Nw
Hickory NC 28601
828 267-8739

(G-6300)
CENTURY FURNITURE LLC
820 21st St Nw (28601-3354)
P.O. Box 608 (28603-0608)
PHONE.....................828 326-8650
Norman Carson, *Brnch Mgr*
EMP: 53
SALES (corp-wide): 87.25MM **Privately Held**
Web: www.centuryfurniture.com
SIC: 2512 Upholstered household furniture
HQ: Century Furniture, Llc
401 11th St Nw
Hickory NC 28601
828 267-8739

(G-6301)
CENTURY FURNITURE LLC
126 33rd St Nw (28601-5676)
PHONE.....................828 326-8495
EMP: 10
SALES (corp-wide): 87.25MM **Privately Held**
Web: www.centuryfurniture.com
SIC: 2512 Chairs: upholstered on wood frames
HQ: Century Furniture, Llc
401 11th St Nw
Hickory NC 28601
828 267-8739

(G-6302)
CENTURY FURNITURE LLC (HQ)
Also Called: Highland House
401 11th St Nw (28601-4750)
P.O. Box 608 (28603-0608)
PHONE.....................828 267-8739
◆ **EMP:** 160 **EST:** 1946
SALES (est): 49.18MM
SALES (corp-wide): 87.25MM **Privately Held**
Web: www.centuryfurniture.com
SIC: 2512 5021 Living room furniture: upholstered on wood frames; Household furniture
PA: Rhf Investments, Inc.
401 11th St Nw
Hickory NC 28601
828 326-8350

(G-6303)
CHASE CORPORATION
1954 Main Ave Se (28602-1401)
PHONE.....................828 855-9316
EMP: 6
Web: www.chasecorp.com
SIC: 2821 Plastics materials and resins
HQ: Chase Corporation
375 University Ave
Westwood MA 02090
781 332-0700

(G-6304)
CODE LLC
Also Called: Coaxle Optical Device and Eqp
2013 1st St Se (28602-5353)
PHONE.....................828 328-6004
Daryl Finger, *VP*
EMP: 20 **EST:** 2002
SALES (est): 1.88MM **Privately Held**
Web: www.codecorp.com
SIC: 3661 5063 8748 Telephone station equipment and parts, wire; Electrical apparatus and equipment; Telecommunications consultant

(G-6305)
COMFORT BAY HOME FASHIONS INC
Also Called: Dromma Bed
2200 Main Ave Se (28602-1407)

PHONE.....................843 442-7477
EMP: 4
SIC: 2515 Bedsprings, assembled
PA: Comfort Bay Home Fashions, Inc.
428 Hudson River Rd
Waterford NY 12188

(G-6306)
COMMSCOPE INC NORTH CAROLINA
2908 2nd Ave Nw (28601-5648)
PHONE.....................828 324-2200
Jeff Wossord, *Mgr*
EMP: 10
Web: www.commscope.com
SIC: 3663 Radio and t.v. communications equipment
HQ: Commscope, Inc. Of North Carolina
3642 E Us Highway 70
Claremont NC 28610
828 324-2200

(G-6307)
COMMSCOPE CNNCTVITY SLTONS LLC
1100 Commscope Pl Se (28602-3619)
P.O. Box 1729 (28603-1729)
PHONE.....................828 324-2200
EMP: 10
SALES (est): 1.1MM **Privately Held**
Web: www.commscope.com
SIC: 3663 Microwave communication equipment

(G-6308)
COMMSCOPE TECHNOLOGIES LLC
1100 Commscope Pl Se (28602-3619)
PHONE.....................828 324-2200
EMP: 26
SALES (corp-wide): 15.22B **Publicly Held**
Web: www.commscope.com
SIC: 3643 Power line cable
HQ: Commscope Technologies Llc
3642 E Us Highway 70
Claremont NC 28610
828 324-2200

(G-6309)
CONOVER MACHINE AND DESIGN INC
231 33rd Street Dr Se (28602-8399)
P.O. Box 977 (28613-0977)
PHONE.....................828 328-6737
Herman T Christenbury, *Pr*
Hal E Lail, *Sec*
EMP: 6 **EST:** 1985
SQ FT: 14,000
SALES (est): 554.99K **Privately Held**
SIC: 3599 Machine shop, jobbing and repair

(G-6310)
CONTRACT SEATING INC
796 20th St Ne 4 (28601-4316)
P.O. Box 3485 (28603-3485)
PHONE.....................828 322-6662
Randy Stillwell, *Pr*
Ron Woody, *COO*
EMP: 4 **EST:** 1986
SQ FT: 22,000
SALES (est): 154.11K **Privately Held**
Web: www.montagegalleries.com
SIC: 2512 Upholstered household furniture

(G-6311)
COPYMASTERS PRINTING SVCS INC
818 1st Ave Sw (28602-2614)
P.O. Box 3738 (28603-3738)
PHONE.....................828 324-0532
Sandy Mangum, *Pr*
Jimmy Mangum, *VP*

EMP: 4 **EST:** 1987
SQ FT: 2,000
SALES (est): 246.38K **Privately Held**
Web: www.copymastersprinting.com
SIC: 2752 Offset printing

(G-6312)
CORNING OPTCAL CMMNCATIONS LLC
Also Called: Corning
1164 23rd St Se (28602-7320)
PHONE..............................828 327-5290
Steve Thomas, *Mgr*
EMP: 1680
SALES (corp-wide): 13.12B **Publicly Held**
Web: www.corning.com
SIC: 3357 Communication wire
HQ: Corning Optical Communications Llc
    4200 Corning Pl
    Charlotte NC 28216
    828 901-5000

(G-6313)
COX MANUFACTURING COMPANY INC
220 10th St Sw (28602-2518)
PHONE..............................828 397-4123
Mark R Romeo, *Pr*
▲ **EMP:** 25 **EST:** 1932
SALES (est): 3.77MM **Privately Held**
Web: www.coxmfg.com
SIC: 2512 Upholstered household furniture

(G-6314)
CRAYMER MCELWEE HOLDINGS INC
6429 Hildebran Shelby Rd (28602-8748)
P.O. Box 1028 (28603-1028)
PHONE..............................828 326-6100
Carrie B Cramer, *Pr*
Nathan Mcelwee Junior, *VP*
EMP: 6 **EST:** 2000
SQ FT: 74,000
SALES (est): 827.2K **Privately Held**
Web: www.ourhousedesigns.com
SIC: 2512 Upholstered household furniture

(G-6315)
CUSHION MANUFACTURING INC
1343 9th Ave Ne (28601-4101)
PHONE..............................828 324-9555
Sonny Lackey, *Pr*
EMP: 4 **EST:** 1988
SALES (est): 230.59K **Privately Held**
SIC: 2393 Cushions, except spring and carpet: purchased materials

(G-6316)
CV INDUSTRIES INC (PA)
Also Called: Century Furniture Industries
401 11th St Nw (28601-4750)
P.O. Box 608 (28603-0608)
PHONE..............................828 328-1851
A Alex Shuford Ii, *Pr*
Harley F Shuford Junior, *Ch Bd*
Nancy S Dowdy, *VP*
Brandon Hucks, *CFO*
Richard L Reese, *Sec*
◆ **EMP:** 6 **EST:** 1973
SQ FT: 700,000
SALES (est): 22.83MM **Privately Held**
Web: www.centuryfurniture.com
SIC: 2511 2512 2211 Wood household furniture; Upholstered household furniture; Upholstery fabrics, cotton

(G-6317)
DAVIS BROTHERS ROOFING
2404 N Center St Unit B (28601-1335)
PHONE..............................828 578-8561

Joshua Bellew, *Prin*
EMP: 4 **EST:** 2018
SALES (est): 958.35K **Privately Held**
Web: www.davisbrosroofing.com
SIC: 3499 Fabricated metal products, nec

(G-6318)
DB POWER SPORTS
2830 Springs Rd Ne (28601-9106)
PHONE..............................828 324-1500
Damon Bowman, *Owner*
EMP: 4 **EST:** 2009
SALES (est): 128.73K **Privately Held**
SIC: 3949 Sporting and athletic goods, nec

(G-6319)
DEERHUNTER TREE STANDS INC
5944 Leil Rd (28602-7199)
PHONE..............................704 462-1116
Kenneth Benfield, *Pr*
Bradley Scott Benfield, *VP*
Jody Vance Benfield, *Sec*
EMP: 4 **EST:** 1977
SALES (est): 120.75K **Privately Held**
SIC: 3949 Hunting equipment

(G-6320)
DEL-MARK INC
1225 Main Ave Sw (28602-2438)
P.O. Box 1988 (28603-1988)
PHONE..............................828 322-6180
J Wells Walker, *Pr*
Davis Walker, *VP*
Wells Walker, *Pr*
EMP: 10 **EST:** 1947
SQ FT: 30,000
SALES (est): 748.03K **Privately Held**
Web: www.delmarktransfers.com
SIC: 2752 Transfers, decalcomania or dry: lithographed

(G-6321)
DELUXE PRINTING CO INC
Also Called: Deluxe Printing Group
10 9th St Nw (28601-6025)
P.O. Box 9467 (28603-9467)
PHONE..............................828 322-1329
Tom K East Junior, *Pr*
Jeremy East, *Genl Mgr*
Chad East, *Sls Mgr*
EMP: 23 **EST:** 1974
SQ FT: 25,000
SALES (est): 2.28MM **Privately Held**
Web: www.deluxeprintinggroup.com
SIC: 2752 Offset printing

(G-6322)
DESIGNMASTER FURNITURE INC
1283 23rd St Se (28602-7333)
PHONE..............................828 324-7992
▲ **EMP:** 20 **EST:** 1989
SALES (est): 2.56MM **Privately Held**
Web: www.designmasterfurniture.com
SIC: 2511 5021 Dining room furniture: wood; Dining room furniture

(G-6323)
DIAMOND ENTERPRISES
Also Called: Diamond Research and Dev
5171 Icard Ridge Rd (28601-8968)
PHONE..............................828 495-4448
Darryl Diamond, *Pr*
Georgia Diamond, *Sec*
EMP: 5 **EST:** 1986
SQ FT: 20,000
SALES (est): 250K **Privately Held**
SIC: 3599 Machine shop, jobbing and repair

(G-6324)
DR PEPPER/SEVEN-UP BOTTLING
2401 14th Avenue Cir Nw (28601-7336)
P.O. Box 550 (28603-0550)
PHONE..............................828 322-8090
Lee Teeter, *Prin*
EMP: 4 **EST:** 1984
SALES (est): 201.75K **Privately Held**
Web: www.drpepper.com
SIC: 2086 Soft drinks: packaged in cans, bottles, etc.

(G-6325)
DYNISCO INSTRUMENTS LLC
Also Called: Dynisco Bearing
1291 19th Street Ln Nw (28601-4677)
PHONE..............................828 326-9888
Randy Pierson, *Mgr*
EMP: 31
SALES (corp-wide): 476.13MM **Privately Held**
Web: www.dynisco.com
SIC: 3829 8734 3561 Aircraft and motor vehicle measurement equipment; Testing laboratories; Pumps and pumping equipment
HQ: Dynisco Instruments Llc
    38 Forge Pkwy
    Franklin MA 02038
    508 541-9400

(G-6326)
EAGLE SUPERABRASIVES INC
141 33rd Street Dr Se (28602-8375)
P.O. Box 3856 (28603-3856)
PHONE..............................828 261-7281
Robert Comer, *Pr*
EMP: 9 **EST:** 2009
SALES (est): 952.26K **Privately Held**
Web: www.eaglesuperabrasives.com
SIC: 3291 Abrasive products

(G-6327)
EARLY BIRD HOSIERY MILLS INC
1011 10th Street Blvd Nw (28601-3459)
P.O. Box 1890 (28603-1890)
PHONE..............................828 324-6745
Eljoe Mullins, *Pr*
Martha Mullins, *Sec*
EMP: 6 **EST:** 1948
SQ FT: 10,000
SALES (est): 307.01K **Privately Held**
SIC: 2257 Weft knit fabric mills

(G-6328)
EARTH EDGE LLC
940 23rd St Sw (28602-4861)
P.O. Box 849 (28603-0849)
PHONE..............................828 624-0252
EMP: 11 **EST:** 2010
SALES (est): 1.58MM **Privately Held**
Web: www.earthedgeproducts.com
SIC: 3069 Latex, foamed

(G-6329)
ENECO EAST INC
P.O. Box 2531 (28603-2531)
PHONE..............................828 322-6008
David Snyder, *CEO*
EMP: 4 **EST:** 1975
SALES (est): 217.05K **Privately Held**
Web: www.ruthrauffsauer.com
SIC: 3585 Air conditioning equipment, complete

(G-6330)
EVERSHARP SAW & TOOL INC
1241 13th St Ne (28601-4135)
PHONE..............................828 345-1200
Art Chaffee, *Pr*

Diane Chaffee, *VP*
Christina Chaffee, *Sec*
EMP: 4 **EST:** 1992
SQ FT: 4,500
SALES (est): 355.78K **Privately Held**
Web: www.eversharpsawandtool.com
SIC: 7629 3545 Tool repair, electric; Machine tool attachments and accessories

(G-6331)
FAIRGROVE FURNITURE CO INC
1350 21st Street Dr Se (28602-8386)
PHONE..............................828 322-8570
Melvin M Jones, *Pt*
Steve Jones, *Pt*
Adrian Jones, *Pt*
EMP: 7 **EST:** 1963
SQ FT: 15,000
SALES (est): 205.18K **Privately Held**
SIC: 2426 Frames for upholstered furniture, wood

(G-6332)
FASTRACK PUBLISHING CO INC
1602 Corral Dr (28602-9786)
P.O. Box 1590 (28603-1590)
PHONE..............................828 294-0544
EMP: 5 **EST:** 2011
SALES (est): 57.74K **Privately Held**
SIC: 2741 Miscellaneous publishing

(G-6333)
FIBER-LINE LLC
280 Performance Dr Se (28602-4045)
PHONE..............................828 326-8700
Robert Stulpin, *Brnch Mgr*
EMP: 75
Web: www.fiber-line.com
SIC: 2295 2281 Coated fabrics, not rubberized; Manmade and synthetic fiber yarns, spun
HQ: Fiber-Line, Llc
    3050 Campus Dr
    Hatfield PA 19440
    215 997-9181

(G-6334)
FILL PAC LLC
1140 Tate Blvd Se (28602-4025)
PHONE..............................828 322-1916
William F Hadley, *Managing Member*
▲ **EMP:** 10 **EST:** 2006
SALES (est): 823K **Privately Held**
Web: www.fill-pac.com
SIC: 3999 Pet supplies

(G-6335)
FREUDNBERG RSDNTIAL FLTRTION T (DH)
Also Called: Protect Plus Air
420 3rd Ave Nw (28601)
PHONE..............................828 328-1142
Jeri Lemke, *Pr*
Kevin Ruff, *CFO*
Brian Craven, *Treas*
Monica Navarro, *Sec*
EMP: 20 **EST:** 2017
SALES (est): 30.25MM
SALES (corp-wide): 12.96B **Privately Held**
SIC: 3585 5075 Heating and air conditioning combination units; Warm air heating and air conditioning
HQ: Freudenberg Filtration Technologies Gmbh & Co. Kg
    Hohnerweg 2-4
    Weinheim BW 69469
    6201800

(G-6336)
FURNITURE CONCEPTS
909 10th St Ne (28601-4035)
PHONE...............................828 323-1590
Herman Fox, *Owner*
EMP: 15 **EST:** 1984
SALES (est): 237.52K **Privately Held**
Web: www.furnitureconcepts.com
SIC: 2512 2511 Chairs: upholstered on wood
frames; Chairs, household, except
upholstered: wood

(G-6337)
GAINES MOTOR LINES INC (PA)
2349 13th Ave Sw (28602-4740)
P.O. Box 1549 (28603-1549)
PHONE...............................828 322-2000
Forest M Gaines, *CEO*
Timothy Gaines, *Prin*
Corey Gaines, *Prin*
Sara Gaines, *Prin*
EMP: 110 **EST:** 1940
SQ FT: 76,000
SALES (est): 9.05MM
SALES (corp-wide): 9.05MM **Privately
Held**
Web: www.gainesml.com
SIC: 3715 4731 Truck trailers; Freight
transportation arrangement

(G-6338)
GIFTED HANDS STYLING SALON
1316 Us Highway 70 Sw (28602-3133)
PHONE...............................828 781-2781
Gwendolyn Roseboro, *Owner*
EMP: 9 **EST:** 2014
SALES (est): 43.84K **Privately Held**
SIC: 7231 3999 Beauty shops; Hair and hair-
based products

(G-6339)
GLASS WORKS OF HICKORY INC
1040 Old Lenoir Rd Ste B (28601-3473)
PHONE...............................828 322-2122
David L Fowler, *Pr*
Steve Fowler, *VP*
EMP: 4 **EST:** 1995
SQ FT: 3,000
SALES (est): 273.32K **Privately Held**
Web: www.glassworksofhickory.com
SIC: 3231 5719 Mirrored glass; Mirrors

(G-6340)
GRASCHE USA INC
Also Called: Grasche
240 Performance Dr Se (28602-4045)
P.O. Box 1348 (28603-1348)
PHONE...............................828 322-1226
Guenter Grass, *Pr*
Klaus Jensen, *
Guenter Grass, *Stockholder*
Astrid Grass, *Stockholder*
Michael Downing, *
▲ **EMP:** 26 **EST:** 1979
SQ FT: 30,000
SALES (est): 4.43MM **Privately Held**
Web: www.grasche.com
SIC: 3425 5085 Saws, hand: metalworking
or woodworking; Knives, industrial

(G-6341)
H W S COMPANY INC (HQ)
Also Called: Hickory White Company
856 7th Ave Se (28602-3938)
P.O. Box 189 (28603-0189)
PHONE...............................828 322-8624
Harold W Sherrill, *Pr*
Michael E Powers, *
Thom Woller, *
Robert L Choppa Junior, *VP*
▲ **EMP:** 300 **EST:** 1997

SQ FT: 479,200
SALES (est): 6.74MM
SALES (corp-wide): 49.81MM **Privately
Held**
Web: www.sandhpools.com
SIC: 2512 Couches, sofas, and davenports:
upholstered on wood frames
PA: Sherrill Furniture Company Inc
2405 Highland Ave Ne
Hickory NC 28601
828 322-2640

(G-6342)
**HARGENRADER CSTM
WOODCRAFT LLC**
2481 23rd St Ne (28601-9193)
PHONE...............................828 896-7182
Luke Hargenrader, *Prin*
EMP: 4 **EST:** 2014
SALES (est): 335.52K **Privately Held**
Web:
www.hargenradercustomwoodcraft.com
SIC: 2434 Wood kitchen cabinets

(G-6343)
HDM FURNITURE INDUSTRIES INC
Also Called: Pearson Company
37 9th Street Pl Se (28602-1215)
PHONE...............................336 882-8135
EMP: 165
SALES (corp-wide): 384.13MM **Privately
Held**
SIC: 2511 Wood household furniture
PA: Hdm Furniture Industries Inc
1925 Eastchester Dr
High Point NC 27265
336 888-4800

(G-6344)
HDM FURNITURE INDUSTRIES INC
Hickory Chair Company
37 9th Street Pl Se (28602-1215)
P.O. Box 2147 (28603-2147)
PHONE...............................800 349-4579
EMP: 1770
SALES (corp-wide): 384.13MM **Privately
Held**
SIC: 2512 2511 Chairs: upholstered on wood
frames; Wood household furniture
PA: Hdm Furniture Industries Inc
1925 Eastchester Dr
High Point NC 27265
336 888-4800

(G-6345)
HEICO FASTENERS INC (HQ)
2377 8th Ave Nw (28601-4511)
P.O. Box 2905 (28601)
PHONE...............................828 261-0184
Stefan Waltermann, *Pr*
Michael Zeller, *Sec*
◆ **EMP:** 23 **EST:** 1996
SQ FT: 75,000
SALES (est): 5.57MM
SALES (corp-wide): 77.27MM **Privately
Held**
Web: www.heicofasteners.com
SIC: 3965 Fasteners
PA: Theo Heimann Holding Gmbh & Co. Kg
Osterweg 21
Ense NW 59469
29388050

(G-6346)
HICKORY ADCHEM INC
123 23rd St Sw (28602-2154)
P.O. Box 1451 (28603-1451)
PHONE...............................828 327-0936
Robert G Hadley, *Pr*
Elaine Hadley, *VP*
EMP: 7 **EST:** 1968

SQ FT: 42,000
SALES (est): 84.07K **Privately Held**
SIC: 2891 Adhesives

(G-6347)
HICKORY BRANDS INC
429 27th St Nw (28601-4549)
PHONE...............................828 322-2600
Nisson Joseph, *Pr*
Julie Huffman, *
Catherine Pitts, *
◆ **EMP:** 91 **EST:** 1987
SQ FT: 80,000
SALES (est): 7.2MM **Privately Held**
Web: www.hickorybrands.com
SIC: 2241 2842 Shoe laces, except leather;
Shoe polish or cleaner

(G-6348)
**HICKORY BUSINESS FURNITURE
LLC (HQ)**
Also Called: Hbf Textiles
900 12th Street Dr Nw (28601-4763)
P.O. Box 8 (28603-0008)
PHONE...............................828 328-2064
Stan A Askren, *Ch*
Steven M Bradford, *VP*
Kurt A Tjaden, *CFO*
Don Mead, *Ex VP*
▲ **EMP:** 325 **EST:** 1979
SQ FT: 200,000
SALES (est): 45.17MM
SALES (corp-wide): 2.53B **Publicly Held**
Web: www.hbf.com
SIC: 2521 2299 Wood office furniture;
Batting, wadding, padding and fillings
PA: Hni Corporation
600 E 2nd St
Muscatine IA 52761
563 272-7400

(G-6349)
HICKORY CHAIR COMPANY
Also Called: Hickory Chair
37 9th Street Pl Se (28602-1215)
P.O. Box 2147 (28603-2147)
PHONE...............................800 225-0265
◆ **EMP:** 58
SIC: 2511 Wood household furniture

(G-6350)
HICKORY DYG & WINDING CO INC
Also Called: Hickory Yarns
1025 10th St Ne (28601-4037)
P.O. Box 1975 (28603-1975)
PHONE...............................828 322-1550
Robert Miller Junior, *Pr*
▲ **EMP:** 13 **EST:** 1938
SQ FT: 70,000
SALES (est): 1.54MM **Privately Held**
Web: www.hickoryyarns.com
SIC: 2282 2281 Throwing and winding mills;
Yarn spinning mills

(G-6351)
**HICKORY HERITAGE OF FALLING
CREEK INC**
3211b Falling Creek Rd (28601-9606)
EMP: 22 **EST:** 2010
SALES (est): 1.83MM **Privately Held**
SIC: 2221 Upholstery fabrics, manmade
fiber and silk

(G-6352)
HICKORY PUBLISHING CO INC
Also Called: Hickory Daily Record
1100 Park Place 11th Ave Se (28601)
PHONE...............................828 322-4510
Suzanne G Millholland, *Pr*
Kenneth Millholland, *

John G Millholland, *
David K Millholland, *
EMP: 27 **EST:** 1915
SQ FT: 40,000
SALES (est): 777.55K **Privately Held**
Web: www.hickoryrecord.com
SIC: 2711 Newspapers, publishing and
printing

(G-6353)
HICKORY SAW & TOOL INC
406 9th St Se (28602-4040)
PHONE...............................828 324-5585
Mike L Pannell, *Pr*
J Robert Busbee, *
Barry Whisnant, *
Larry C Pannell, *
Don Jones, *Stockholder*
▲ **EMP:** 24 **EST:** 1983
SQ FT: 10,000
SALES (est): 5.35MM **Privately Held**
Web: www.hickorysawandtool.com
SIC: 3545 7699 Cutting tools for machine
tools; Knife, saw and tool sharpening and
repair

(G-6354)
HICKORY SPRINGS CALIFORNIA LLC
235 2nd Ave Nw (28601-4950)
P.O. Box 128 (28603-0128)
PHONE...............................828 328-2201
David Underdown, *Ch*
Parks C Underdown Junior, *Ch Bd*
J Donald Coleman, *
Lee Lunsford, *
▲ **EMP:** 607 **EST:** 1985
SQ FT: 30,000
SALES (est): 52.07K
SALES (corp-wide): 430.3MM **Privately
Held**
Web: www.hickorysprings.com
SIC: 3429 3086 Furniture hardware; Plastics
foam products
PA: Hickory Springs Manufacturing
Company
235 2nd Ave Nw
Hickory NC 28601
828 328-2201

(G-6355)
**HICKORY SPRINGS
MANUFACTURING COMPANY (PA)**
Also Called: Hsm Solutions
235 2nd Ave Nw (28601-4950)
P.O. Box 128 (28603-0128)
PHONE...............................828 328-2201
◆ **EMP:** 100 **EST:** 1944
SALES (est): 430.3MM
SALES (corp-wide): 430.3MM **Privately
Held**
Web: www.hickorysprings.com
SIC: 3069 3495 2514 5072 Foam rubber;
Furniture springs, unassembled; Frames for
box springs or bedsprings: metal; Furniture
hardware, nec

(G-6356)
HICKORY SPRINGS MFG CO
871 Highland Ave Ne (28601-4053)
PHONE...............................828 322-7994
Robert L Campbell Junior, *Brnch Mgr*
EMP: 7
SALES (corp-wide): 430.3MM **Privately
Held**
Web: www.hsmsolutions.com
SIC: 3069 Foam rubber
PA: Hickory Springs Manufacturing
Company
235 2nd Ave Nw
Hickory NC 28601
828 328-2201

(G-6357)
HICKORY SPRINGS MFG CO
2230 Main Ave Se (28602-1407)
P.O. Box 128 (28603-0128)
PHONE..................................828 328-2201
Jim Tate, *Mgr*
EMP: 62
SALES (corp-wide): 430.3MM **Privately Held**
Web: www.hsmsolutions.com
SIC: 3429 Furniture hardware
PA: Hickory Springs Manufacturing
Company
235 2nd Ave Nw
Hickory NC 28601
828 328-2201

(G-6358)
HICKORY SPRINGS MFG CO
Also Called: Hickory Springs - Metal Plant
140 Mcdonald Pkwy (28603)
PHONE..................................828 325-4757
EMP: 8
SALES (corp-wide): 430.3MM **Privately Held**
SIC: 2514 Metal household furniture
PA: Hickory Springs Manufacturing
Company
235 2nd Ave Nw
Hickory NC 28601
828 328-2201

(G-6359)
HICKORY THROWING COMPANY
520 20th St Se (28602-4400)
PHONE..................................828 322-1158
William H Taylor Senior, *Ch Bd*
William H Taylor Junior, *Pr*
Nancy Pittman, *
◆ **EMP:** 45 **EST:** 1958
SQ FT: 48,500
SALES (est): 2.16MM **Privately Held**
Web: www.hickorythrowing.com
SIC: 2281 2282 Yarn spinning mills; Twisting yarn

(G-6360)
HICKORY WIRE INC
1711 11th Ave Sw (28602-4909)
P.O. Box 1229 (29585-1229)
PHONE..................................828 322-9473
Robert Moser, *Pr*
Sharon Moser, *Sec*
EMP: 10 **EST:** 1990
SQ FT: 66,000
SALES (est): 1.72MM **Privately Held**
Web: www.fenceprohickory.com
SIC: 3351 Wire, copper and copper alloy

(G-6361)
HM LIQUIDATION INC
Also Called: Cabot Wrenn
166 Hancock & Moore Ln (28601)
PHONE..................................828 495-8235
Jack Glasheen, *CEO*
Timothy Rogers, *Pr*
Jimmy Moore, *VP*
EMP: 4 **EST:** 1981
SQ FT: 150,000
SALES (est): 1.29MM **Privately Held**
Web: www.hancockandmoore.com
SIC: 2512 2522 Couches, sofas, and davenports: upholstered on wood frames; Chairs, office: padded or plain: except wood

(G-6362)
HOME IMPRESSIONS INC
420 3rd Ave Nw (28601-4983)
P.O. Box 9181 (28603-9181)
PHONE..................................828 328-1142
Cliff Tucker, *Pr*

▲ **EMP:** 458 **EST:** 1994
SQ FT: 10,000
SALES (est): 2.29MM
SALES (corp-wide): 1.31B **Publicly Held**
Web: www.homeimpressions.com
SIC: 5099 3469 Containers: glass, metal or plastic; Metal stampings, nec
HQ: Solar Group, Inc.
107 Fellowship Rd
Taylorsville MS 39168
601 785-4711

(G-6363)
HUNTINGTON HOUSE INC (PA)
661 Rink Dam Rd (28601)
P.O. Box 6231 (28603-6231)
PHONE..................................828 495-4400
▲ **EMP:** 101 **EST:** 1985
SALES (est): 19.15MM
SALES (corp-wide): 19.15MM **Privately Held**
Web: www.huntingtonhouse.com
SIC: 2512 Upholstered household furniture

(G-6364)
IMAGINE ONE LLC
420 3rd Ave Nw (28601-4983)
P.O. Box 9349 (28603-9349)
PHONE..................................828 324-6454
EMP: 4 **EST:** 2001
SALES (est): 2.65MM **Privately Held**
Web: www.imagine-one.com
SIC: 3589 Water filters and softeners, household type

(G-6365)
IMAGINE ONE RESOURCES LLC
420 3rd Ave Nw (28601-4983)
P.O. Box 9181 (28603-9181)
PHONE..................................828 328-1142
Robert W Lackey, *Managing Member*
Robert W Lackey Junior, *Managing Member*
EMP: 8 **EST:** 2011
SALES (est): 4.6MM
SALES (corp-wide): 14.44MM **Privately Held**
Web: www.imagine-one.com
SIC: 3589 Water treatment equipment, industrial
PA: Protect Plus Llc
420 3rd Ave Nw
Hickory NC 28601
828 328-1142

(G-6366)
IMMUNOTEK BIO CENTERS LLC
1040 2nd St Ne (28601-3844)
PHONE..................................828 569-6264
Matthew Lindstaedt, *Mgr*
EMP: 36
SALES (corp-wide): 27MM **Privately Held**
Web: www.immunotek.com
SIC: 2836 Blood derivatives
PA: Immunotek Bio Centers, L.L.C.
1430 E Sthlake Blvd Ste 2
Southlake TX 76092
337 500-1175

(G-6367)
IMPLUS LLC
Balega
1279 19th Street Ln Nw (28601-4677)
PHONE..................................828 485-3318
EMP: 16
SALES (corp-wide): 300MM **Privately Held**
Web: www.implus.com
SIC: 2252 Socks
HQ: Implus, Llc
2001 Tw Alexander Dr
Durham NC 27709
919 544-7900

(G-6368)
INFORM INC
Also Called: Fogleman and Partners
415 1st Ave Nw (28601-6170)
PHONE..................................828 322-7766
Paul F Fogleman, *Pr*
Martha Fogleman, *Sec*
EMP: 15 **EST:** 1968
SQ FT: 8,000
SALES (est): 410.91K **Privately Held**
SIC: 7311 8743 2711 Advertising consultant; Public relations and publicity; Newspapers, publishing and printing

(G-6369)
ING SOURCE LLC
1340 14th Avenue Ct Sw (28602)
PHONE..................................828 855-0481
David Higgins, *CEO*
David B Higgins, *CEO*
▲ **EMP:** 19 **EST:** 2008
SALES (est): 2.63MM **Privately Held**
Web: www.ingsource.com
SIC: 3842 Orthopedic appliances

(G-6370)
INOTEC AMD INC
1350 4th St Nw (28601-2444)
PHONE..................................888 354-9772
Jenifer Walter, *CEO*
EMP: 6 **EST:** 2018
SALES (est): 1.86MM **Privately Held**
Web: www.natroxwoundcare.com
SIC: 3829 Thermometers, including digital: clinical

(G-6371)
INTERNTONAL SPECIALTY PDTS INC
1720 Tate Blvd Se (28602-4246)
P.O. Box 3826 (28603-3826)
PHONE..................................828 326-9053
Heather Gragg, *VP*
▲ **EMP:** 7 **EST:** 1993
SALES (est): 467.93K **Privately Held**
SIC: 3312 Wire products, steel or iron

(G-6372)
INVICTUS LIGHTING LLC
1401 Main Ave Sw (28602-2440)
P.O. Box 2708 (28603-2708)
PHONE..................................828 855-9324
Eric Mcmillan, *Managing Member*
Peter Lohr, *Mng Pt*
Erik Mcmillan, *Managing Member*
EMP: 9 **EST:** 2015
SQ FT: 2,250
SALES (est): 1.77MM **Privately Held**
Web: www.invictuslighting.com
SIC: 3646 3641 Commercial lighting fixtures; Electric lamps and parts for generalized applications

(G-6373)
JACOB HOLTZ COMPANY LLC
747 22nd Street Pl Se (28602-7316)
PHONE..................................828 328-1003
Buddy Burchan, *Mgr*
EMP: 22
SALES (corp-wide): 2.28MM **Privately Held**
Web: www.jacobholtz.com
SIC: 3429 3469 Furniture hardware; Metal stampings, nec
PA: Jacob Holtz Company, Llc
10 Industrial Hwy Ste Ms6
Philadelphia PA 19113
215 423-2800

(G-6374)
JAMES OXYGEN AND SUPPLY CO (PA)
Also Called: James O 2
30 Us Highway 321 Nw (28601-6801)
P.O. Box 159 (28603-0159)
PHONE..................................704 322-5438
Vance T James Junior, *Pr*
Andrew C James, *
Margaret James, *
EMP: 31 **EST:** 1956
SQ FT: 14,000
SALES (est): 8.36MM
SALES (corp-wide): 8.36MM **Privately Held**
Web: www.jameso2.com
SIC: 5169 5084 2813 Gases, compressed and liquefied; Welding machinery and equipment; Industrial gases

(G-6375)
JBS USA LLC
1207 25th Street Pl Se (28602-9658)
PHONE..................................828 855-9571
EMP: 10 **EST:** 2018
SALES (est): 1.01MM **Privately Held**
Web: www.jbsfoodsgroup.com
SIC: 2011 Meat packing plants

(G-6376)
KELLY HOSIERY MILL INC
6450 Applehill Dr (28602-8744)
PHONE..................................828 324-6456
Joe J Watts, *Pr*
Orlee Watts, *VP*
EMP: 6 **EST:** 1965
SALES (est): 482.77K **Privately Held**
Web: www.kellyhosiery.com
SIC: 2252 Socks

(G-6377)
KERRS HICKRY READY-MIXED CON (PA)
Also Called: Kerr's H R M Concrete
1126 1st Ave Sw (28602-2606)
P.O. Box 1924 (28603-1924)
PHONE..................................828 322-3157
Helen Kerr, *Pr*
James Kerr Junior, *VP*
Roger S Kerr, *
Donna Kerr, *
EMP: 45 **EST:** 1920
SQ FT: 3,000
SALES (est): 9.85MM
SALES (corp-wide): 9.85MM **Privately Held**
Web: www.kerrsconcrete.com
SIC: 3273 Ready-mixed concrete

(G-6378)
KING HICKORY FURNITURE COMPANY
728 Highland Ave Ne (28601-4028)
PHONE..................................828 324-0472
EMP: 7
SALES (corp-wide): 9.7MM **Privately Held**
Web: www.kinghickory.com
SIC: 2512 Couches, sofas, and davenports: upholstered on wood frames
PA: King Hickory Furniture Company
1820 Main Ave Se
Hickory NC 28602
828 322-6025

(G-6379)
KING HICKORY FURNITURE COMPANY (PA)
1820 Main Ave Se (28602-1340)
P.O. Box 1179 (28603-1179)
PHONE..................................828 322-6025

▲ = Import ▼ = Export
◆ = Import/Export

Robert E Palmer, *Ch*
▲ **EMP:** 180 **EST:** 1958
SQ FT: 30,000
SALES (est): 9.7MM
SALES (corp-wide): 9.7MM **Privately Held**
Web: www.kinghickory.com
SIC: 2512 Couches, sofas, and davenports: upholstered on wood frames

(G-6380)
KLINGSPOR ABRASIVES INC (HQ)
Also Called: Klingspor
2555 Tate Blvd Se (28602)
P.O. Box 2367 (28603)
PHONE..............................828 322-3030
Christoph Klingspor, *Pr*
Berthold Spatz, *
◆ **EMP:** 209 **EST:** 1979
SQ FT: 150,000
SALES (est): 49.87MM
SALES (corp-wide): 336.57MM **Privately Held**
Web: www.klingspor.com
SIC: 3291 Coated abrasive products
PA: Klingspor Ag
Huttenstr. 36
Haiger HE 35708
27739220

(G-6381)
KOHNLE CABINETRY
250 Rocky Acres Rd (28601-8354)
PHONE..............................828 640-2498
EMP: 4 **EST:** 2014
SALES (est): 137.49K **Privately Held**
SIC: 2434 Wood kitchen cabinets

(G-6382)
KONTANE LOGISTICS INC (PA)
3876 Martin Fish Pond St (28603)
P.O. Box 1702 (28601)
PHONE..............................828 397-5501
▲ **EMP:** 4 **EST:** 1975
SALES (est): 11.2MM
SALES (corp-wide): 11.2MM **Privately Held**
Web: www.kontanelogistics.com
SIC: 2441 2449 Shipping cases, wood: nailed or lock corner; Wood containers, nec

(G-6383)
L & R KNITTING INC
6350 Claude Brittain Rd (28602-9571)
PHONE..............................828 874-2960
Ronnie Brittain, *Pr*
Loretta Brittain, *Sec*
EMP: 6 **EST:** 1972
SQ FT: 14,000
SALES (est): 243.05K **Privately Held**
SIC: 2252 Men's, boys', and girls' hosiery

(G-6384)
LARLIN CUSHION COMPANY
1950 Fairgrove Church Rd (28602)
PHONE..............................828 465-5599
Lawrence Swaney, *Owner*
EMP: 10 **EST:** 1975
SQ FT: 15,000
SALES (est): 116.98K **Privately Held**
Web: www.larlincushion.com
SIC: 2515 Spring cushions

(G-6385)
LCF ENTERPRISE (PA)
719 6th Ave Nw (28601-3509)
PHONE..............................208 415-4300
Lorna Finman, *Owner*
EMP: 9 **EST:** 1986
SALES (est): 863.14K
SALES (corp-wide): 863.14K **Privately Held**

SIC: 3663 Amplifiers, RF power and IF

(G-6386)
LEATHER MIRACLES LLC
3350 20th Ave Se (28602)
P.O. Box 2171 (28603-2171)
PHONE..............................828 464-7448
David Mathison, *Managing Member*
Timothy Scopes, *Managing Member**
Michael R Cobb, *
◆ **EMP:** 40 **EST:** 2000
SQ FT: 50,000
SALES (est): 5.73MM **Privately Held**
Web: www.leathermiracles.com
SIC: 5199 3111 Leather and cut stock; Leather tanning and finishing

(G-6387)
LITTLE RIVER YACHTS LLC
1100 Commscope Pl Se (28602-3619)
P.O. Box 9212 (28603-9212)
PHONE..............................828 323-4955
Sandra O Walters, *Managing Member*
EMP: 4 **EST:** 2009
SALES (est): 119.05K **Privately Held**
Web: www.commscope.com
SIC: 3663 Radio and t.v. communications equipment

(G-6388)
LOVEKIN & YOUNG PC
110 N Center St (28601-6294)
P.O. Box 585 (10536-0585)
PHONE..............................828 322-5435
Gary F Young, *Prin*
EMP: 4 **EST:** 2014
SALES (est): 65.76K **Privately Held**
Web: www.lovekinandyoung.com
SIC: 2741 Miscellaneous publishing

(G-6389)
LTLB HOLDING COMPANY (PA)
Also Called: American Roller Bearing Co
1350 4th Street Dr Nw (28601-2524)
PHONE..............................828 624-1460
Benjamin S Succop, *Pr*
Larry Succop, *CEO*
Marshall Kim Harkins, *CFO*
Lawrence N Succop, *Ch Bd*
Tim Hopkins, *CFO*
▲ **EMP:** 18 **EST:** 2007
SQ FT: 21,000
SALES (est): 45.63MM
SALES (corp-wide): 45.63MM **Privately Held**
Web: www.amroll.com
SIC: 3562 Ball and roller bearings

(G-6390)
MAA UMIYA INC
Also Called: Raceway 6739
1141 Lenoir Rhyne Blvd Se (28602-5128)
PHONE..............................410 818-6811
Catrina Serrano, *Prin*
EMP: 5 **EST:** 2007
SALES (est): 491.3K **Privately Held**
SIC: 3644 Raceways

(G-6391)
MARCAL PAPER MILLS LLC
612 3rd Ave Ne (28601-5164)
PHONE..............................828 322-1805
EMP: 500
SALES (corp-wide): 467.3MM **Privately Held**
Web: www.marcalpaper.com
SIC: 2676 Towels, napkins, and tissue paper products
HQ: Marcal Paper Mills, Llc
1 Market St
Elmwood Park NJ 07407
828 322-1805

(G-6392)
MARIETTA MARTIN MATERIALS INC
Also Called: Martin Marietta Aggregates
1989 11th Ave Se (28602-4325)
PHONE..............................828 322-8386
Justin Nelson, *Brnch Mgr*
EMP: 6
Web: www.martinmarietta.com
SIC: 1422 Crushed and broken limestone
PA: Martin Marietta Materials Inc
4123 Parklake Ave
Raleigh NC 27612

(G-6393)
MAXIMIZER SYSTEMS INC
1010 21st Street Dr Se (28602-8320)
PHONE..............................828 345-6036
Richard Neville-dove, *Prin*
EMP: 8 **EST:** 2018
SALES (est): 3.7MM **Privately Held**
Web: www.maximizersystems.com
SIC: 3999 Manufacturing industries, nec

(G-6394)
MCCRORIE GROUP LLC (PA)
Also Called: McCrorie Wood Products
330 19th St Se (28602-4229)
P.O. Box 9007 (28603-9007)
PHONE..............................828 328-4538
EMP: 21 **EST:** 1969
SQ FT: 100,000
SALES (est): 2.4MM
SALES (corp-wide): 2.4MM **Privately Held**
Web: www.mccroriewoodproducts.com
SIC: 2499 Carved and turned wood

(G-6395)
MILLENIA USA LLC
3211c Falling Creek Rd (28601-9606)
▲ **EMP:** 16 **EST:** 2006
SALES (est): 413.05K **Privately Held**
Web: www.millenia-furniture.com
SIC: 2519 Lawn and garden furniture, except wood and metal

(G-6396)
MINELLI USA LLC
1245 26th St Se (28602-7317)
PHONE..............................828 578-6734
Alberto Tansi, *Prin*
EMP: 6 **EST:** 2017
SALES (est): 1.01MM **Privately Held**
Web: www.minelligroup.com
SIC: 2499 Wood products, nec

(G-6397)
MORETZ & SIPE INC
3261 Highland Ave Ne (28601-9375)
PHONE..............................828 327-8661
Pauline Moretz, *Pr*
EMP: 6 **EST:** 1951
SALES (est): 550K **Privately Held**
Web: www.toddstapley.com
SIC: 1611 3272 Highway and street paving contractor; Septic tanks, concrete

(G-6398)
MR TIRE INC
2105 N Center St (28601-1317)
PHONE..............................828 322-8130
Baron Bobgarner, *Brnch Mgr*
EMP: 10
SALES (corp-wide): 1.28B **Publicly Held**
Web: locations.mrtire.com
SIC: 3714 5531 7538 7534 Automotive wiring harness sets; Automotive tires; General automotive repair shops; Tire recapping
HQ: Mr. Tire Inc.
2078 New York Ave Unit 2

Huntington Station NY 11746
631 499-3700

(G-6399)
NELSON HOLDINGS NC INC
Also Called: Nelson Oil Company
5 20th St Sw (28602-2216)
P.O. Box 1472 (28603-1472)
PHONE..............................828 322-9226
Andrew N Hines, *Pr*
Leslie Hines Iii, *VP*
EMP: 10 **EST:** 1925
SALES (est): 4.38MM **Privately Held**
Web: www.nelsonlubricants.com
SIC: 5172 3586 Petroleum products, nec; Measuring and dispensing pumps

(G-6400)
NETWORK INTEGRITY SYSTEMS INC
Also Called: Network Integrity Systems
1937 Tate Blvd Se (28602-1430)
PHONE..............................828 322-2181
David Vokey, *Pr*
Joe Giovannini, *VP*
EMP: 5 **EST:** 2003
SQ FT: 5,767
SALES (est): 2.46MM **Privately Held**
Web: www.networkintegritysystems.com
SIC: 3825 Network analyzers

(G-6401)
NEW CARBON COMPANY LLC
Also Called: Ncd Hickory
1040 Old Lenoir Rd Unit 1040 (28601-3472)
PHONE..............................574 247-2270
Beth Morganti, *Mgr*
EMP: 4
SALES (corp-wide): 263.3MM **Privately Held**
Web: www.goldenwaffles.com
SIC: 2041 Flour and other grain mill products
HQ: New Carbon Company, Llc
50 Applied Bank Blvd
Glen Mills PA 19342
224 246-1347

(G-6402)
NORDSON CORPORATION
Also Called: Nordson Xaloy
1291 19th Street Ln Nw (28601-4677)
PHONE..............................724 656-5600
EMP: 11
SALES (corp-wide): 2.69B **Publicly Held**
Web: www.nordson.com
SIC: 3563 Air and gas compressors
PA: Nordson Corporation
28601 Clemens Rd
Westlake OH 44145
440 892-1580

(G-6403)
NORTH CAROLINA SOCK INC
Also Called: N C Sock
5521 Suttlemyre Ln (28601-9426)
PHONE..............................828 327-4664
Dennis E Martin, *Pr*
EMP: 5 **EST:** 1994
SQ FT: 25,000
SALES (est): 100.92K **Privately Held**
SIC: 2252 2251 Socks; Women's hosiery, except socks

(G-6404)
NOT JUST ARCHERY
2201 Moss Farm Rd (28602-8313)
PHONE..............................828 294-7727
Ty Drum, *Owner*
EMP: 4 **EST:** 1993
SQ FT: 2,400
SALES (est): 182.94K **Privately Held**

SIC: **3949** 7699 Sporting and athletic goods, nec; Gun services

(G-6405)
OMNI GROUP LLC
1140 Tate Blvd Se (28602-4025)
PHONE................................828 404-3104
Janet Anderson, *Prin*
EMP: 4 EST: 2008
SALES (est): 250.13K **Privately Held**
SIC: **3532** Screeners, stationary

(G-6406)
ONEH2 INC
620 23rd St Nw (28601-4526)
PHONE................................844 996-6342
Paul Dawson, *CEO*
EMP: 42 EST: 2015
SALES (est): 30.55MM **Privately Held**
Web: www.oneh2.com
SIC: **2819** Industrial inorganic chemicals, nec

(G-6407)
ORTHOPEDIC APPLIANCE COMPANY
910 Tate Blvd Se (28602-4030)
PHONE................................828 348-1960
EMP: 5 EST: 2018
SALES (est): 445.57K **Privately Held**
Web: www.orthopedicapplianceco.com
SIC: **3842** Orthopedic appliances

(G-6408)
OVERNIGHT SOFA CORPORATION
3043 1st Ave Sw (28602-1821)
P.O. Box 2608 (28603-2608)
PHONE................................828 324-2271
Amy Johnson, *Pr*
Mark Madnick, *
Jeremy Johnson, *
◆ **EMP: 40 EST:** 1989
SQ FT: 34,000
SALES (est): 8.72MM **Privately Held**
Web: www.overnightsofa.net
SIC: **2512** Living room furniture: upholstered on wood frames

(G-6409)
PEPSI-COLA BTLG HICKRY NC INC
Also Called: Pepsi-Cola
2640 Main Ave Nw (28601-5655)
PHONE................................828 322-8090
Frans Katherine, *Ex VP*
EMP: 64
SALES (corp-wide): 28.58MM **Privately Held**
Web: www.hickorync.gov
SIC: **5149** 2086 Soft drinks; Soft drinks: packaged in cans, bottles, etc.
PA: Pepsi-Cola Bottling Company Of Hickory, N.C., Inc.
2401 14th Avenue Cir Nw
Hickory NC 28601
828 322-8090

(G-6410)
PEPSI-COLA BTLG HICKRY NC INC (PA)
Also Called: Pepsi-Cola
2401 14th Avenue Cir Nw (28601-7336)
P.O. Box 550 (28603-0550)
PHONE................................828 322-8090
James Lee Teeter, *Pr*
Katherine Frans, *
Margaret Brady, *
Mary Teeter, *
John Teeter, *
EMP: 115 EST: 1926
SQ FT: 53,000
SALES (est): 28.58MM

SALES (corp-wide): 28.58MM **Privately Held**
Web: www.hickorync.gov
SIC: **2086** 5149 Carbonated soft drinks, bottled and canned; Soft drinks

(G-6411)
PERFECTION FABRICS INC
841a F Avenue Dr Se (28602-1123)
P.O. Box 2946 (28603-2946)
PHONE................................828 328-3322
George Lane, *Pr*
EMP: 8 EST: 1993
SQ FT: 12,500
SALES (est): 493.54K **Privately Held**
SIC: **3582** Washing machines, laundry: commercial, incl. coin-operated

(G-6412)
PIEDMONT PRECISION PRODUCTS
347 Highland Ave Se (28602-3033)
P.O. Box 3171 (28603-3171)
PHONE................................828 304-0791
David Ridgeway, *Pr*
Eric Harwell, *VP*
EMP: 7 EST: 1997
SQ FT: 5,000
SALES (est): 728.66K **Privately Held**
Web: www.piedmontprecision.com
SIC: **3599** Machine shop, jobbing and repair

(G-6413)
PIEDMONT SPRINGS COMPANY INC
118 11th Street Pl Sw (28602-2608)
P.O. Box 335 (28603-0335)
PHONE................................828 322-5347
Robert A Gaston, *Pr*
Ed Henry, *Mgr*
Jo Henry, *VP*
EMP: 4 EST: 1956
SQ FT: 2,975
SALES (est): 497.9K **Privately Held**
SIC: **3495** Furniture springs, unassembled

(G-6414)
PLASTIC TECHNOLOGY INC (HQ)
Also Called: Pti
235 2nd Ave Nw (28601-4950)
P.O. Box 128 (28603-0128)
PHONE................................828 328-2201
J Donald Coleman, *Pr*
Parks C Underdown Junior, *Ch Bd*
Stephen W Ellif, *CFO*
C Hampton Queen, *Asst Tr*
David F Underdown, *Sec*
EMP: 15 EST: 1983
SQ FT: 44,000
SALES (est): 9.44MM
SALES (corp-wide): 430.3MM **Privately Held**
Web: www.ptifoam.com
SIC: **3082** Unsupported plastics profile shapes
PA: Hickory Springs Manufacturing Company
235 2nd Ave Nw
Hickory NC 28601
828 328-2201

(G-6415)
POPPE INC
Also Called: Resource Recovery Company
313 Main Ave Ne (28601-5121)
PHONE................................828 345-6036
Dean Poppe, *Pr*
Denise Johnson, *Off Mgr*
EMP: 10 EST: 2001
SQ FT: 6,500
SALES (est): 458.46K **Privately Held**
SIC: **3443** Heat exchangers, condensers, and components

(G-6416)
PRIME COATINGS LLC
442 Highland Ave Se (28602-1148)
P.O. Box 3874 (28603-3874)
PHONE................................828 855-1136
EMP: 4 EST: 2007
SALES (est): 326.74K **Privately Held**
Web: www.ecustomcoatings.com
SIC: **3479** Metal coating and allied services

(G-6417)
PRINT PATH LLC
1215 15th Street Dr Ne (28601-4269)
PHONE................................828 855-9966
David Filmore Wooten Iii, *Prin*
EMP: 29 EST: 2010
SALES (est): 9.33MM **Privately Held**
Web: www.printpathllc.com
SIC: **2752** Commercial printing, lithographic

(G-6418)
PRINTMARKETING LLC
320 19th St Se (28602-4229)
PHONE................................828 261-0063
Gerald Wayne Miller, *Prin*
EMP: 6 EST: 2011
SALES (est): 979.7K **Privately Held**
Web: www.printmarketingnc.com
SIC: **2752** Offset printing

(G-6419)
PROTECT PLUS PRO LLC
420 3rd Ave Nw Ste A (28601-4984)
PHONE................................828 328-1142
EMP: 10 EST: 2017
SALES (est): 2.37MM **Privately Held**
Web: www.protectplus.com
SIC: **3589** Water treatment equipment, industrial

(G-6420)
PROTECTION PRODUCTS INC
1010 3rd Ave Nw (28601-4851)
PHONE................................828 324-2173
Jeff Hale, *Pr*
▲ **EMP: 25 EST:** 2010
SALES (est): 1.99MM **Privately Held**
Web: www.p-p-i.com
SIC: **3842** 5047 Personal safety equipment; Medical equipment and supplies

(G-6421)
PRYSMIAN CBLES SYSTEMS USA LLC
1711 11th Ave Sw (28602-4909)
PHONE................................828 322-9473
Scott Bachman, *Mgr*
EMP: 25
Web: na.prysmian.com
SIC: **3496** Miscellaneous fabricated wire products
HQ: Prysmian Cables And Systems Usa, Llc
4 Tesseneer Dr
Highland Heights KY 41076
859 572-8000

(G-6422)
PURTHERMAL LLC
Also Called: Manufacturer
1720 Tate Blvd Se (28602-4246)
PHONE................................828 855-0108
Todd Duckwitz, *CEO*
EMP: 5 EST: 2020
SALES (est): 2.39MM **Privately Held**
Web: www.purthermal.com
SIC: **3443** 3479 3498 Heat exchangers, condensers, and components; Painting, coating, and hot dipping; Tube fabricating (contract bending and shaping)

(G-6423)
QUANTUM SOLUTIONS
365 Main Ave Sw (28602-2928)
P.O. Box 141 (28613-0141)
PHONE................................828 615-7500
Michael Mcneely, *Prin*
EMP: 6 EST: 2012
SALES (est): 1.63MM **Privately Held**
SIC: **3572** Computer storage devices

(G-6424)
QUIKTRON INC
925 Old Lenoir Rd (28601-3446)
PHONE................................828 327-6009
Steve Rockwell, *Pr*
▲ **EMP: 7 EST:** 2004
SALES (est): 831K **Privately Held**
Web: www.quiktron.com
SIC: **3643** Current-carrying wiring services

(G-6425)
R H BOLICK & COMPANY INC
1210 9th Ave Ne (28601-4108)
PHONE................................828 322-7847
Richard H Bolick, *Pr*
Judy Bolick, *VP*
▲ **EMP: 8 EST:** 1970
SQ FT: 6,000
SALES (est): 1.96MM **Privately Held**
Web: www.rhbolick.com
SIC: **3599** Machine shop, jobbing and repair

(G-6426)
R&D PLASTICS OF HICKORY LTD
345 26th Street Dr Se (28602-1459)
PHONE................................828 431-4660
David Duncan, *Pr*
Robert Canterbury, *
▲ **EMP: 27 EST:** 1999
SQ FT: 40,000
SALES (est): 2.91MM **Privately Held**
Web: www.randdplastics.com
SIC: **3089** Injection molding of plastics

(G-6427)
REDI-FRAME INC
207 20th St Se (28602-1414)
PHONE................................828 322-4227
Joseph Parris, *Pr*
EMP: 6 EST: 2001
SALES (est): 733.56K **Privately Held**
SIC: **2426** Frames for upholstered furniture, wood

(G-6428)
RHF INVESTMENTS INC (PA)
401 11th St Nw (28601-4750)
P.O. Box 608 (28603-0608)
PHONE................................828 326-8350
Brandon M Hucks, *CEO*
A Alex Shuford Iii, *Pr*
A Shuford, *Pr*
EMP: 5 EST: 2013
SALES (est): 87.25MM
SALES (corp-wide): 87.25MM **Privately Held**
Web: www.centuryfurniture.com
SIC: **6799** 5023 2512 Investors, nec; Decorative home furnishings and supplies; Upholstered household furniture

(G-6429)
RILEY DEFENSE INC
25 18th St Nw (28601-5822)
PHONE................................704 507-9224
EMP: 5 EST: 2015
SALES (est): 1.99MM **Privately Held**
Web: www.rileydefense.com
SIC: **3482** 3484 Small arms ammunition; Small arms

▲ = Import ▼ = Export
◆ = Import/Export

(G-6430)
ROBERT ABBEY INC (PA)
3166 Main Ave Se (28602-8374)
PHONE...............................828 322-3480
Jerry Rose, *Pr*
Joseph Rose Junior, *VP*
Ken Wilkinson, *
◆ **EMP:** 249 **EST:** 1946
SQ FT: 350,000
SALES (est): 20.72MM
SALES (corp-wide): 20.72MM **Privately Held**
Web: www.robertabbey.biz
SIC: 3645 3641 Residential lighting fixtures; Electric lamps

(G-6431)
ROL-MOL INC
2205 Us Highway 70 Sw (28602-4827)
P.O. Box 1686 (28603-1686)
PHONE...............................828 328-1210
Steve Whisnant, *Pr*
Rush Whisnant, *Asst VP*
Connie Whisnant, *Sec*
EMP: 6 **EST:** 1966
SQ FT: 16,000
SALES (est): 482.15K **Privately Held**
Web: www.rolmol.com
SIC: 3531 Rollers, road: steam or other power

(G-6432)
ROLL-TECH MOLDING PRODUCTS LLC
Also Called: Roll-Tech
243 Performance Dr Se (28602-4046)
PHONE...............................828 431-4515
Patrice Bertrand, *Managing Member*
◆ **EMP:** 26 **EST:** 1995
SQ FT: 26,000
SALES (est): 4.95MM
SALES (corp-wide): 2.5MM **Privately Held**
Web: www.roll-tech.net
SIC: 3011 Tires and inner tubes
HQ: Roll-Gom
Zone Industrielle Est
Tilloy Les Mofflaines HDF 62217
321249495

(G-6433)
RPM INDSTRIAL CTINGS GROUP INC (HQ)
Also Called: Finishworks
2220 Us Highway 70 Se Ste 100 (28602-5192)
PHONE...............................828 261-0325
Johnny Green Junior, *Pr*
Ronnie G Holman, *
Glenn R Hasman, *
Wesley Harris, *
Edward Winslow Moore, *
▲ **EMP:** 338 **EST:** 1977
SALES (est): 205.9MM
SALES (corp-wide): 7.34B **Publicly Held**
Web: www.ccicoatings.com
SIC: 2851 Lacquers, varnishes, enamels, and other coatings
PA: Rpm International Inc.
2628 Pearl Rd
Medina OH 44258
330 273-5090

(G-6434)
RPM INDSTRIAL CTINGS GROUP INC
C C I Division
22 S Center St (28602-3028)
PHONE...............................828 261-0325
Philip Kyriacou, *Brnch Mgr*
EMP: 101
SALES (corp-wide): 7.34B **Publicly Held**
Web: www.mohawk-finishing.com

SIC: 2851 2893 3479 Lacquers, varnishes, enamels, and other coatings; Printing ink; Coating of metals and formed products
HQ: Rpm Industrial Coatings Group, Inc.
2220 Us Hwy 70 Se Ste 100
Hickory NC 28602
828 261-0325

(G-6435)
RPM INDSTRIAL CTINGS GROUP INC
Mohawk Finishing Products Div
22 S Center St (28602-3028)
PHONE...............................828 261-0325
Robert Clusker, *VP*
EMP: 101
SALES (corp-wide): 7.34B **Publicly Held**
Web: www.rpmwfg.com
SIC: 2851 5072 Stains: varnish, oil, or wax; Furniture hardware, nec
HQ: Rpm Industrial Coatings Group, Inc.
2220 Us Hwy 70 Se Ste 100
Hickory NC 28602
828 261-0325

(G-6436)
RUSKIN INC
1189 27th Street Dr Se (28602-8394)
P.O. Box 9350 (28603-9350)
PHONE...............................828 324-6500
Jay Rubino, *Pr*
Pedie King, *VP*
EMP: 5 **EST:** 1999
SQ FT: 21,500
SALES (est): 178.07K **Privately Held**
SIC: 2426 2511 Furniture stock and parts, hardwood; Wood household furniture

(G-6437)
RUST911 INC
1206 8th Ave Sw (28602-3117)
PHONE...............................607 425-2882
Howard Philips Junior, *Pr*
EMP: 4 **EST:** 2015
SALES (est): 232.21K **Privately Held**
Web: www.rust911.com
SIC: 2899 Chemical preparations, nec

(G-6438)
S E LAB GROUP INC
5565 Icard Ridge Rd (28601-8972)
PHONE...............................707 253-8852
Jerry Orr, *Pr*
Lyn Codron, *VP*
▲ **EMP:** 8 **EST:** 1984
SALES (est): 2.2MM **Privately Held**
Web: www.selabgroup.net
SIC: 3821 Laboratory apparatus and furniture

(G-6439)
SHERRILL FURNITURE COMPANY
Also Called: Hickory Mfg Division
856 7th Ave Se (28602-3938)
P.O. Box 998 (28603-0998)
PHONE...............................828 322-8624
Chuck Auten, *Prin*
EMP: 14
SALES (corp-wide): 49.81MM **Privately Held**
Web: www.sherrillfurniture.com
SIC: 2512 Upholstered household furniture
PA: Sherrill Furniture Company Inc
2405 Highland Ave Ne
Hickory NC 28601
828 322-2640

(G-6440)
SHERRILL FURNITURE COMPANY
Also Called: Cth-Shrrill Occsional Furn Div
2425 Highland Ave Ne (28601-8164)
PHONE...............................828 328-5241
Chuck Auten, *Brnch Mgr*

EMP: 18
SQ FT: 184,000
SALES (corp-wide): 49.81MM **Privately Held**
Web: www.sherrillfurniture.com
SIC: 2512 Upholstered household furniture
PA: Sherrill Furniture Company Inc
2405 Highland Ave Ne
Hickory NC 28601
828 322-2640

(G-6441)
SHERRILL FURNITURE COMPANY (PA)
Also Called: Sherrill Furniture
2405 Highland Ave Ne (28601-8164)
P.O. Box 189 (28603-0189)
PHONE...............................828 322-2640
Harold W Sherrill, *Pr*
Michael E Powers, *Admn Execs*
Steve Cartee, *VP*
William Smith, *VP Engg*
Walter Bost, *VP*
◆ **EMP:** 460 **EST:** 1943
SQ FT: 265,000
SALES (est): 49.81MM
SALES (corp-wide): 49.81MM **Privately Held**
Web: www.sherrillfurniture.com
SIC: 2512 2511 Couches, sofas, and davenports: upholstered on wood frames; Wood household furniture

(G-6442)
SHUFORD MILLS LLC (HQ)
Also Called: Shuford Yarns
1985 Tate Blvd Se Ste 54 (28602-1433)
P.O. Box 1530 (28603-1530)
PHONE...............................828 324-4265
Stephen Shuford, *Pr*
C Hunt Shuford Junior, *Sec*
Amy Hawn, *Contrlr*
Marvin Smith, *VP*
◆ **EMP:** 5 **EST:** 1926
SQ FT: 25,000
SALES (est): 9.33MM
SALES (corp-wide): 787.56MM **Privately Held**
Web: www.shufordyarns.com
SIC: 2221 Broadwoven fabric mills, manmade
PA: Stm Industries, Inc.
1712 8th Street Dr Se
Hickory NC 28602
828 322-2700

(G-6443)
SHUFORD YARNS LLC (PA)
1985 Tate Blvd Se Ste 54 (28602-1433)
PHONE...............................828 324-4265
Marvin Smith, *CEO*
Khalid Majeed, *COO*
▲ **EMP:** 92 **EST:** 2006
SQ FT: 560,000
SALES (est): 24.01MM **Privately Held**
Web: www.shufordyarns.com
SIC: 2281 Yarn spinning mills

(G-6444)
SHUFORD YARNS MANAGEMENT INC
1985 Tate Blvd Se Ste 54 (28602-1433)
PHONE...............................828 324-4265
EMP: 5 **EST:** 2018
SALES (est): 46.58K **Privately Held**
Web: www.shufordyarns.com
SIC: 2281 Yarn spinning mills

(G-6445)
SHURTAPE TECHNOLOGIES LLC
1985 Tate Blvd Se (28603)
PHONE...............................828 304-8302
Steve Byrd, *Brnch Mgr*
EMP: 5
SALES (corp-wide): 787.56MM **Privately Held**
Web: www.shurtape.com
SIC: 2672 Tape, pressure sensitive: made from purchased materials
HQ: Shurtape Technologies, Llc
1712 8th St Dr Se
Hickory NC 28602

(G-6446)
SIGN SYSTEMS INC
315 9th St Se (28602-4039)
P.O. Box 3767 (28603-3767)
PHONE...............................828 322-5622
Charles Hines, *CEO*
EMP: 12 **EST:** 1954
SQ FT: 9,000
SALES (est): 2.87MM **Privately Held**
Web: www.signsystemsnc.com
SIC: 1799 3993 Sign installation and maintenance; Signs, not made in custom sign painting shops

(G-6447)
SIGNATURE SEATING INC
1718 9th Ave Nw (28601-3328)
PHONE...............................828 325-0174
Don Mcmullin, *Pr*
Jean Mcmullin, *Treas*
Leigh Ann Huffman, *
Michael J Huffman, *
EMP: 50 **EST:** 2001
SQ FT: 15,000
SALES (est): 5.5MM **Privately Held**
Web: corporate.lippert.com
SIC: 2392 Cushions and pillows

(G-6448)
SIMMONS HOSIERY MILL INC (PA)
3715 9th Street Cir Ne (28601-9630)
PHONE...............................828 327-4890
Marion Roseman, *Pr*
EMP: 8 **EST:** 1981
SQ FT: 100,000
SALES (est): 245.03K
SALES (corp-wide): 245.03K **Privately Held**
SIC: 5136 5137 2252 2251 Hosiery, men's and boys'; Hosiery: women's, children's, and infants'; Hosiery, nec; Women's hosiery, except socks

(G-6449)
SIPES CARVING SHOP INC
1450 10th Ave Sw (28602-4902)
PHONE...............................828 327-3077
Darrell Wilson, *Pr*
Teddy Wilson, *VP*
Christine Wilson, *Sec*
EMP: 8 **EST:** 1946
SALES (est): 946.94K **Privately Held**
SIC: 2426 Carvings, furniture: wood

(G-6450)
SNIDER TIRE INC
1226 21st Street Dr Se (28602-8350)
PHONE...............................828 324-9955
David Benfield, *Opers Mgr*
EMP: 5
SALES (corp-wide): 501.16MM **Privately Held**
Web: www.sniderfleet.com
SIC: 5531 7534 Automotive tires; Tire recapping
PA: Snider Tire, Inc.

GEOGRAPHIC

1081 Red Ventures Dr
Fort Mill SC 29707
800 528-2840

(G-6451)
SOCK FACTORY INC
1371 13th St Sw (28602-4918)
P.O. Box 40 (28637-0040)
PHONE...............................828 328-5207
Michael Banks Senior, *Pr*
Michael Banks Junior, *VP*
EMP: 30 **EST:** 1991
SQ FT: 22,000
SALES (est): 8.27MM **Privately Held**
Web: www.thesockfactory.com
SIC: 2252 Socks

(G-6452)
SOLOMON ENGINEERING INC
Also Called: SEI Technologies
340 9th St Se (28602-4038)
PHONE...............................828 855-1652
Constantin Solomon, *Pr*
EMP: 20 **EST:** 1997
SQ FT: 6,000
SALES (est): 3.1MM **Privately Held**
Web: www.seitechnologies.com
SIC: 3599 Machine shop, jobbing and repair

(G-6453)
SONOCO HICKORY INC (HQ)
1246 Main Ave Se (28602-1238)
P.O. Box 2029 (28603-2029)
PHONE...............................828 328-2466
Rodger D Fuller, *Pr*
Julie C Albrecht, *
R Howard Coker, *
Russell Grissett, *
Harold G Cummings Iii, *Treas*
◆ **EMP:** 89 **EST:** 1921
SQ FT: 185,000
SALES (est): 14.83MM
SALES (corp-wide): 5.31B **Publicly Held**
SIC: 5199 3089 Packaging materials;
Injection molded finished plastics products,
nec
PA: Sonoco Products Company
1 N 2nd St
Hartsville SC 29550
843 383-7000

(G-6454)
SONOCO PRODUCTS COMPANY
1214 Highland Ave Ne (28601-4146)
PHONE...............................828 322-8844
David Tumey, *Brnch Mgr*
EMP: 18
SALES (corp-wide): 5.31B **Publicly Held**
Web: www.sonoco.com
SIC: 2655 Fiber cans, drums, and similar
products
PA: Sonoco Products Company
1 N 2nd St
Hartsville SC 29550
843 383-7000

(G-6455)
SOVEREIGN TECHNOLOGIES LLC
3908 Pinecrest Dr Ne (28601-8748)
PHONE...............................828 358-5355
EMP: 9 **EST:** 2012
SALES (est): 2.22MM **Privately Held**
Web: www.sovereigntechinc.com
SIC: 2869 Industrial organic chemicals, nec

(G-6456)
SQUAREHEAD TECHNOLOGY LLC
200 1st Ave Nw (28601-6113)
PHONE...............................571 299-4849
Stig Nyvold, *CEO*
EMP: 5 **EST:** 2015

SALES (est): 397.77K **Privately Held**
Web: www.sqhead.com
SIC: 5049 3669 8731 Law enforcement
equipment and supplies; Emergency alarms
; Commercial physical research

(G-6457)
**STEWART SUPERABSORBENTS
LLC**
1954 Main Ave Se (28602-1401)
PHONE...............................828 855-9316
Kip Clyburn, *Managing Member*
▲ **EMP:** 6 **EST:** 1999
SQ FT: 22,000
SALES (est): 3.1MM **Publicly Held**
Web: www.chasecorp.com
SIC: 2869 Industrial organic chemicals, nec
HQ: Chase Corporation
375 University Ave
Westwood MA 02090
781 332-0700

(G-6458)
STITCHCRAFTERS INCORPORATED
7923 Houston Ave (28602-8616)
PHONE...............................828 397-7656
Tommy Fraley, *Pr*
EMP: 7 **EST:** 1992
SQ FT: 7,700
SALES (est): 236.75K **Privately Held**
Web: www.stitchcraftersinc.com
SIC: 2395 2396 Embroidery products,
except Schiffli machine; Automotive and
apparel trimmings

(G-6459)
STM INDUSTRIES INC (PA)
Also Called: Shurtech Brands
1712 8th Street Dr Se (28602-9656)
P.O. Box 1530 (28603-1530)
PHONE...............................828 322-2700
Stephen Sufford, *CEO*
James B Shuford, *
Don Pomeroy, *
Matt Raymer, *
◆ **EMP:** 50 **EST:** 1996
SQ FT: 25,000
SALES (est): 787.56MM
SALES (corp-wide): 787.56MM **Privately
Held**
Web: www.shurtapetech.com
SIC: 2672 Tape, pressure sensitive: made
from purchased materials

(G-6460)
STYLE UPHOLSTERING INC
33 23rd Ave Ne (28601-1499)
P.O. Box 1368 (28603-1368)
PHONE...............................828 322-4882
Ralph F Bowman, *Pr*
Nathan Bowman, *
Sylvia Bowman, *
EMP: 4 **EST:** 1948
SQ FT: 35,000
SALES (est): 455.71K **Privately Held**
Web: www.styleupholstering.com
SIC: 2512 2511 2221 Chairs: upholstered on
wood frames; Wood household furniture;
Broadwoven fabric mills, manmade

(G-6461)
SURE WOOD PRODUCTS INC
980 3rd Ave Se (28602-4009)
P.O. Box 1507 (28658-4507)
PHONE...............................828 261-0004
J L Murtagh, *Pr*
Gary Truesdale, *Sec*
EMP: 5 **EST:** 1988
SQ FT: 45,000
SALES (est): 462.34K **Privately Held**

SIC: 2426 Furniture stock and parts,
hardwood

(G-6462)
**TAILORED CHEMICAL PRODUCTS
INC (PA)**
Also Called: Tailored Chemical
700 12th Street Dr Nw Ste B (28601)
P.O. Box P.O. Box 4186 (28603)
PHONE...............................828 322-6512
E J Temple Iii, *Pr*
E J Temple Junior, *Pr*
E J Temple Iii, *VP*
Mark Huckabee, *
William Pope, *
◆ **EMP:** 96 **EST:** 1977
SQ FT: 120,000
SALES (est): 36.41MM
SALES (corp-wide): 36.41MM **Privately
Held**
Web: www.tailoredchemical.com
SIC: 2899 2891 2672 2821 Insulating
compounds; Adhesives and sealants;
Adhesive papers, labels, or tapes: from
purchased material; Polyurethane resins

(G-6463)
TCS DESIGNS INC
1851 9th Ave Ne (28601-4209)
PHONE...............................828 324-9944
Jobie Redmond, *Pr*
Susie Redmond, *Sec*
EMP: 11 **EST:** 1994
SQ FT: 30,000
SALES (est): 1.7MM **Privately Held**
Web: www.tcsdesignsfurniture.com
SIC: 2512 Upholstered household furniture

(G-6464)
TECHMET CARBIDES INC
Also Called: Techmet
730 21st Street Dr Se (28602-4443)
P.O. Box 1658 (28613-3003)
PHONE...............................828 624-0222
James E Kuykendall, *CEO*
▲ **EMP:** 71 **EST:** 1998
SALES (est): 9.24MM **Privately Held**
Web: www.techmet-carbide.com
SIC: 3549 2819 Cutting and slitting
machinery; Carbides

(G-6465)
**THE SOUTHWOOD FURNITURE
CORPORATION**
2860 Nathan St (28601)
P.O. Box 1054 (27282-1054)
PHONE...............................828 465-1776
▲ **EMP:** 5
Web: www.southwoodfurn.com
SIC: 2512 2511 2426 Couches, sofas, and
davenports: upholstered on wood frames;
Wood household furniture; Frames for
upholstered furniture, wood

(G-6466)
THE WHEELCHAIR PLACE LLC
920 Tate Blvd Se Ste 104 (28602-4032)
PHONE...............................828 855-9099
EMP: 5 **EST:** 2007
SALES (est): 3.08MM **Privately Held**
Web: www.thewheelchairplace.com
SIC: 3842 Wheelchairs

(G-6467)
THOMASVILLE UPHOLSTERY INC
890 F Avenue Dr Se (28602-1122)
P.O. Box 500 (28603-0500)
PHONE...............................828 345-6225
EMP: 120

SIC: 2512 2521 Couches, sofas, and
davenports: upholstered on wood frames;
Chairs, office: padded, upholstered, or
plain: wood

(G-6468)
TIGRA USA INC
1106 8th Street Ct Se (28602-3403)
P.O. Box 9197 (28603-9197)
PHONE...............................828 324-8227
Bernd Motzer, *CEO*
▲ **EMP:** 9 **EST:** 2000
SQ FT: 24,000
SALES (est): 3.37MM
SALES (corp-wide): 1.07MM **Privately
Held**
Web: www.tigra.com
SIC: 3541 Machine tools, metal cutting type
PA: Tigra Gmbh
Gewerbering 2
Oberndorf A. Lech BY 86698
909 096-8001

(G-6469)
TILEWARE GLOBAL LLC
Also Called: Tileware
1021 16th St Ne (28601-4236)
P.O. Box 793 (28603-0793)
PHONE...............................828 322-9273
David Scalise, *Managing Member*
▲ **EMP:** 4 **EST:** 2010
SQ FT: 6,000
SALES (est): 337.28K **Privately Held**
Web: www.tilewareproducts.com
SIC: 3261 Bathroom accessories/fittings,
vitreous china or earthenware

(G-6470)
TRUE CABINET LLC
2401 Us Highway 70 Sw (28602-4751)
PHONE...............................828 855-9200
EMP: 6 **EST:** 2015
SALES (est): 786.58K **Privately Held**
Web: www.truecabinet.com
SIC: 2434 Wood kitchen cabinets

(G-6471)
TSG FINISHING LLC
Also Called: Synthetics Finishing
2246 Us Highway 70 Se (28602-4827)
PHONE...............................828 328-5522
EMP: 5
SALES (corp-wide): 27.54MM **Privately
Held**
Web: www.tsgfinishing.com
SIC: 3552 Textile machinery
PA: Tsg Finishing, Llc
7 N Waterloo Rd
Devon PA 19333
215 628-2000

(G-6472)
TSG FINISHING LLC
Long View Machinary Co
515 23rd St Sw (28602-2106)
PHONE...............................828 328-5541
Darr Grater, *VP*
EMP: 47
SALES (corp-wide): 27.54MM **Privately
Held**
Web: www.tsgfinishing.com
SIC: 3552 Textile machinery
PA: Tsg Finishing, Llc
7 N Waterloo Rd
Devon PA 19333
215 628-2000

(G-6473)
TSG FINISHING LLC
Also Called: Synthetic Finishing
515 23rd St Sw (28602-2106)

▲ = Import ▼ = Export
◆ = Import/Export

P.O. Box 2141 (28603-2141)
PHONE..............................828 328-5522
Rich Grecki, *Brnch Mgr*
EMP: 28
SQ FT: 31,001
SALES (corp-wide): 27.54MM **Privately Held**
Web: www.tsgfinishing.com
SIC: 3552 2261 Textile machinery; Finishing plants, cotton
  PA: Tsg Finishing, Llc
     7 N Waterloo Rd
     Devon PA 19333
     215 628-2000

(G-6474)
TSG FINISHING LLC
Also Called: Synthetic Finishing Co
1006 19th St Ne (28601-4314)
P.O. Box 2141 (28603-2141)
PHONE..............................828 328-5535
David Poody, *Brnch Mgr*
EMP: 65
SALES (corp-wide): 27.54MM **Privately Held**
Web: www.tsgfinishing.com
SIC: 2269 2261 Dyeing: raw stock, yarn, and narrow fabrics; Finishing plants, cotton
  PA: Tsg Finishing, Llc
     7 N Waterloo Rd
     Devon PA 19333
     215 628-2000

(G-6475)
TUCKER PRODUCTION INCORPORATED
Also Called: Focus Newspaper
264 1st Ave Nw (28601-6103)
P.O. Box 1721 (28603)
PHONE..............................828 322-1036
Tammy Panther, *Pr*
Lynn Jenkins, *Sec*
Tammy Panther, *VP*
John Tucker, *Pr*
EMP: 4 **EST:** 1977
SQ FT: 3,400
SALES (est): 68.67K **Privately Held**
Web: www.focusnewspaper.com
SIC: 2711 Newspapers, publishing and printing

(G-6476)
TURBOCOATING CORP
Also Called: Lincotek Surface Solutions
1928 Main Ave Se (28602-1401)
PHONE..............................828 328-8726
Rudi Bakker, *CEO*
▲ **EMP:** 33 **EST:** 2010
SALES (est): 9.9MM
SALES (corp-wide): 283.47MM **Privately Held**
Web: www.lincoteksurfacesolutions.com
SIC: 3479 Coating of metals and formed products
  HQ: Lincotek Rubbiano Spa
     Via Mistrali 7
     Solignano PR 43046
     052 530-5808

(G-6477)
UNIFOUR FINISHERS INC (PA)
Also Called: Division One
120 21st St Nw (28601-4678)
P.O. Box 1965 (28603-1965)
PHONE..............................828 322-9435
Harold D Setzer, *CEO*
Richard Setzer, *
EMP: 32 **EST:** 1979
SQ FT: 23,000
SALES (est): 6.83MM
SALES (corp-wide): 6.83MM **Privately Held**

Web: www.unifourfinishers.com
SIC: 2257 2261 Dyeing and finishing circular knit fabrics; Finishing plants, cotton

(G-6478)
UNIFOUR FINISHERS INC
Also Called: Division II
54 29th St Nw (28601-5650)
P.O. Box 1965 (28603-1965)
PHONE..............................828 322-9435
Rick Setzer, *Mgr*
EMP: 34
SALES (corp-wide): 6.83MM **Privately Held**
Web: www.unifourfinishers.com
SIC: 2257 2261 Dyeing and finishing circular knit fabrics; Finishing plants, cotton
  PA: Unifour Finishers, Inc.
     120 21st St Nw
     Hickory NC 28601
     828 322-9435

(G-6479)
UNIGEL INC
1027 19th St Sw (28602-4812)
PHONE..............................828 228-2095
Jiry Robinson, *Pr*
◆ **EMP:** 4 **EST:** 2010
SQ FT: 35,000
SALES (est): 2.02MM **Privately Held**
Web: www.unigel.co.uk
SIC: 2511 Wood household furniture

(G-6480)
UPHOLSTERY DESIGNS HICKORY INC
Also Called: Upholstery Design
1251 19th St Ne (28601-2833)
P.O. Box 2561 (28603-2561)
PHONE..............................828 324-2002
Henry Lail, *Pr*
Bob E Watts, *
Piero Caglies, *
EMP: 6 **EST:** 1984
SQ FT: 80,000
SALES (est): 927.14K
SALES (corp-wide): 97.46MM **Privately Held**
Web: www.hickoryfurniture.com
SIC: 2512 2521 Upholstered household furniture; Wood office furniture
  PA: Chateau D'ax Spa
     Via Nazionale 159
     Lentate Sul Seveso MB 20823
     036 256-9068

(G-6481)
US CONEC LTD
830 21st Street Dr Se (28602-8376)
PHONE..............................828 323-8883
EMP: 5
SALES (corp-wide): 13.12B **Publicly Held**
Web: www.usconec.com
SIC: 3357 Fiber optic cable (insulated)
  HQ: Us Conec Ltd.
     1138 25th St Se
     Hickory NC 28602

(G-6482)
US CONEC LTD (HQ)
1138 25th St Se (28602-7313)
P.O. Box 2306 (28603)
PHONE..............................828 323-8883
Joe Graham, *Pr*
Russell Granger, *
David Kiel, *
Shannon Fichter, *
EMP: 92 **EST:** 1992
SQ FT: 6,200
SALES (est): 30.01MM
SALES (corp-wide): 13.12B **Publicly Held**

Web: www.usconec.com
SIC: 3357 3678 Fiber optic cable (insulated); Electronic connectors
  PA: Corning Incorporated
     1 Riverfront Plz
     Corning NY 14831
     607 974-9000

(G-6483)
US DRAINAGE SYSTEMS LLC
26 5th St Se (28602-1112)
PHONE..............................828 855-1906
Travis Obermeyer, *Managing Member*
EMP: 6 **EST:** 2011
SQ FT: 60,000
SALES (est): 1.47MM **Privately Held**
Web: www.usdrainage.co
SIC: 3089 Thermoformed finished plastics products, nec

(G-6484)
UTILITY SOLUTIONS INC
101 33rd S Dr Se (28602)
PHONE..............................828 323-8914
Hans Peterson, *CEO*
Bryan Lackey, *CFO*
Matt Nolte, *COO*
◆ **EMP:** 4 **EST:** 1990
SQ FT: 10,250
SALES (est): 5.1MM
SALES (corp-wide): 13.2MM **Privately Held**
Web: www.utilitysolutionsinc.com
SIC: 3679 3699 Electronic loads and power supplies; Electrical equipment and supplies, nec
  PA: Evolution Sustainability Group Llc
     1 E Uwchlan Ave Ste 312
     Exton PA 19341
     877 280-4655

(G-6485)
VACUUM HANDLING NORTH AMER LLC
Also Called: Joulin
2551 Us Highway 70 Sw (28602-4744)
PHONE..............................828 327-2290
Francois Joulin, *Managing Member*
▲ **EMP:** 47 **EST:** 2007
SALES (est): 6.42MM **Privately Held**
Web: www.joulin.com
SIC: 3635 Household vacuum cleaners

(G-6486)
VOLEX INC
915 Tate Blvd Se Ste 144 (28602-4042)
PHONE..............................828 485-4500
Martin May, *CEO*
EMP: 24
SQ FT: 8,000
SALES (corp-wide): 912.8MM **Privately Held**
Web: www.volex.com
SIC: 3089 Injection molded finished plastics products, nec
  HQ: Volex Inc.
     511 E San Ysdro Blvd Ste
     San Ysdro CA 92173
     669 444-1740

(G-6487)
VOLEX INC
915 Tate Blvd Se (28602-4042)
PHONE..............................828 485-4500
EMP: 38
SALES (corp-wide): 912.8MM **Privately Held**
Web: www.volex.com
SIC: 3089 Injection molded finished plastics products, nec
  HQ: Volex Inc.

511 E San Ysdro Blvd Ste
     San Ysdro CA 92173
     669 444-1740

(G-6488)
WB FRAMES INC
3771 Sandy Ford Rd (28602-8938)
PHONE..............................828 459-2147
Wayne Bollinger, *Pr*
Janie Bollinger, *VP*
Gary Bollinger, *Treas*
EMP: 4 **EST:** 2000
SALES (est): 227.75K **Privately Held**
SIC: 2426 Hardwood dimension and flooring mills

(G-6489)
WEN BRAY HEATING & AC
6034 Norcross Ln (28601-9007)
PHONE..............................828 267-0635
Joseph W Icard, *Pr*
Carol A Icard, *VP*
EMP: 4 **EST:** 1980
SALES (est): 250.51K **Privately Held**
SIC: 1711 5722 7841 3585 Warm air heating and air conditioning contractor; Electric household appliances; Video disk/tape rental to the general public; Refrigeration and heating equipment

(G-6490)
WOOTEN JOHN
3763 1st Ave Sw (28602-1605)
P.O. Box 4095 (28603-4095)
PHONE..............................828 322-4031
John Wooten, *Owner*
EMP: 5 **EST:** 2000
SALES (est): 347.61K **Privately Held**
SIC: 7538 3599 General automotive repair shops; Machine shop, jobbing and repair

(G-6491)
WRIGHT BUSINESS CONCEPTS INC
Also Called: A Sign Co
1320 Fairgrove Church Rd (28603)
P.O. Box 1709 (28603-1709)
PHONE..............................828 466-1044
Donna Wright, *Pr*
Rudy Wright, *VP*
EMP: 5 **EST:** 1995
SQ FT: 1,400
SALES (est): 401.34K **Privately Held**
Web: www.asigncohickory.com
SIC: 3993 Signs, not made in custom sign painting shops

(G-6492)
XALOY EXTRUSION LLC
Also Called: Nordson Xaloy
1291 19th Street Ln Nw (28601-4677)
PHONE..............................828 326-9888
Randy Pearson, *Pr*
◆ **EMP:** 48 **EST:** 2000
SQ FT: 40,000
SALES (est): 4.69MM **Privately Held**
Web: www.xaloy.com
SIC: 5084 3561 Plastic products machinery; Pumps and pumping equipment

---

Hiddenite
Alexander County

(G-6493)
AMERICAN ROLLER BEARING INC
1095 Mcclain Rd (28636-6202)
PHONE..............................828 624-1460
Michael J Connors, *Pr*
EMP: 200
SALES (corp-wide): 4.57B **Publicly Held**

Web: www.amroll.com
SIC: 3562 Roller bearings and parts
HQ: American Roller Bearing Inc.
    307 Burke Dr
    Morganton NC 28655
    828 624-1460

(G-6494)
CRAFTMASTER FURNITURE INC
(DH)
221 Craftmaster Rd (28636-9309)
P.O. Box 759 (28681)
PHONE.................................828 632-9786
Alex Reeves, Pr
Anderson Shih, *
◆ EMP: 350 EST: 2006
SQ FT: 175,000
SALES (est): 34.98MM Privately Held
Web: www.cmfurniture.com
SIC: 2512 Couches, sofas, and davenports:
    upholstered on wood frames
HQ: Samson Investment Holding Co.
    2575 Penny Rd
    High Point NC 27265

(G-6495)
CRAFTMASTER FURNITURE INC
750 Sharpe Ln (28636-8389)
P.O. Box 759 (28681-0759)
PHONE.................................828 632-8127
Harold Bentley, Mgr
EMP: 693
Web: www.cmfurniture.com
SIC: 2512 2511 Couches, sofas, and
    davenports: upholstered on wood frames;
    Wood household furniture
HQ: Craftmaster Furniture, Inc.
    221 Craftmaster Rd
    Hiddenite NC 28636
    828 632-9786

(G-6496)
FORTNER LUMBER INC
991 Liberty Church Rd (28636-9336)
P.O. Box 39 (28636-0039)
PHONE.................................704 585-2383
Ronald L Fortner, Pr
Justin Fortner, VP
Josh Fortner, Sec
EMP: 4 EST: 1961
SQ FT: 800
SALES (est): 187.34K Privately Held
SIC: 2426 Lumber, hardwood dimension

(G-6497)
HICKORY SPRINGS MFG CO
Sharpe Rd (28636)
P.O. Box 116 (28636-0116)
PHONE.................................828 632-9733
Candy Duffey, Mgr
EMP: 40
SALES (corp-wide): 430.3MM Privately
Held
Web: www.hickorysprings.com
SIC: 3086 Insulation or cushioning material,
    foamed plastics
PA: Hickory Springs Manufacturing
    Company
    235 2nd Ave Nw
    Hickory NC 28601
    828 328-2201

(G-6498)
HIDDENITE CONFERENCE CTR LLC
Also Called: Parchment Press
471 Sulphur Springs Rd (28636-5141)
P.O. Box 100 (28636-0100)
PHONE.................................828 352-9200
David Burleigh, Managing Member
EMP: 5 EST: 2011
SALES (est): 235.84K Privately Held

Web: www.hiddenitearts.org
SIC: 2741 Miscellaneous publishing

(G-6499)
HIDDENITE GEMS INC
Also Called: Emerald Hollow Gems
484 Emerald Hollow Mine Dr (28636-7393)
PHONE.................................828 632-3394
Dorothy Watkins, Pr
EMP: 4 EST: 1986
SALES (est): 462.41K Privately Held
Web: www.emeraldhollowmine.com
SIC: 1499 Gem stones (natural) mining, nec

(G-6500)
INDUSTRIAL TIMBER LLC
330 White Plains Rd (28636-8767)
PHONE.................................704 919-1215
EMP: 82
SALES (corp-wide): 37.25MM Privately
Held
Web: www.thesmartplay.com
SIC: 2493 5031 Reconstituted wood products
    ; Lumber, plywood, and millwork
PA: Industrial Timber, Llc
    6441 Hendry Rd Ste B
    Charlotte NC 28269
    704 919-1215

(G-6501)
KDS FABRICATING AND MCH SP LLC
4838 Nc Highway 90 E (28636-9396)
P.O. Box 2868 (42002-2868)
PHONE.................................828 632-5091
Robert Petter Junior, Mgr
Olivia Petter, Prin
Meredith Petter, Prin
Bruce Wilcox, Mgr
EMP: 10 EST: 2017
SALES (est): 1.15MM Privately Held
SIC: 3498 3549 Tube fabricating (contract
    bending and shaping); Wiredrawing and
    fabricating machinery and equipment, ex.
    die

(G-6502)
LTLB HOLDING COMPANY
1095 Mcclain Rd (28636-6202)
P.O. Box 117 (28636-0117)
PHONE.................................704 585-2908
Frank Dickson, Pr
EMP: 91
SALES (corp-wide): 45.63MM Privately
Held
Web: www.amroll.com
SIC: 3562 Ball and roller bearings
PA: Ltlb Holding Company
    1350 4th Street Dr Nw
    Hickory NC 28601
    828 624-1460

(G-6503)
ON TIME METAL LLC
31 Wayfound Church Rd (28636-7333)
PHONE.................................828 635-1001
EMP: 7 EST: 2016
SALES (est): 1.15MM Privately Held
Web: www.ontimemetal.com
SIC: 1761 3444 Roofing contractor; Metal
    roofing and roof drainage equipment

(G-6504)
PALADIN INDUSTRIES INC
Also Called: Paladin Furniture
5270 Nc Highway 90 E (28636-8300)
P.O. Box 218 (28636-0218)
PHONE.................................828 635-0448
Timothy R Bolick, Pr
Elaine Bolick, *
◆ EMP: 100 EST: 2002
SQ FT: 120,000

SALES (est): 10.02MM Privately Held
Web: www.paladinfurniture.com
SIC: 2512 Upholstered household furniture

(G-6505)
STATESVILLE PALLET COMPANY
INC
351 Old Mountain Rd (28636-8306)
P.O. Box 36 (28636-0036)
PHONE.................................828 632-0268
Eric Sloop, Pr
Regina Pierce, Sec
EMP: 6 EST: 1988
SQ FT: 35,000
SALES (est): 562.36K Privately Held
SIC: 2448 Pallets, wood

High Point
Guilford County

(G-6506)
615 ALTON PLACE LLC
615 Alton Pl (27263-2272)
PHONE.................................336 431-4487
Herbert R Bolick Junior, Prin
EMP: 6 EST: 2012
SALES (est): 634.78K Privately Held
Web: www.nimbusinc.com
SIC: 3672 Printed circuit boards

(G-6507)
A LAND OF FURNITURE INC
430 S Main St Ste 431 (27260-6635)
PHONE.................................336 882-3866
Phillip Shaw, Pr
Dottie Shaw, Sec
▲ EMP: 4 EST: 1990
SQ FT: 6,000
SALES (est): 177.17K Privately Held
SIC: 2299 Upholstery filling, textile

(G-6508)
ACME SAMPLE BOOKS INC
Also Called: Asb Graphics
603 Fraley Rd (27263-1762)
PHONE.................................336 883-4336
Steve Lambert, VP
EMP: 20
SQ FT: 17,765
SALES (corp-wide): 3.85MM Privately
Held
Web: www.asbgraphics.com
SIC: 2752 Offset printing
PA: Acme Sample Books, Inc.
    2410 Schirra Pl
    High Point NC
    336 883-4187

(G-6509)
ADAMS WOOD TURNING INC
Also Called: Sedgefield By Adams
216 Woodbine St (27260-8340)
P.O. Box 1113 (32778-1113)
PHONE.................................336 882-0196
Walter Blackburn, Pr
Terri Thomas, Sec
Sherri Mickey, VP
▲ EMP: 4 EST: 1958
SQ FT: 50,000
SALES (est): 504.45K Privately Held
Web: www.adamswoodturning.com
SIC: 2426 3645 3641 Turnings, furniture:
    wood; Table lamps; Electric lamps

(G-6510)
ADWOOD CORPORATION
260 Durand Ave (27263-9761)
P.O. Box 1195 (27261-1195)
PHONE.................................336 884-1846

Rudolf Stockinger, Pr
▲ EMP: 21 EST: 1981
SQ FT: 20,000
SALES (est): 11.11MM
SALES (corp-wide): 440.85MM Privately
Held
Web: www.adwood.com
SIC: 5084 2435 Woodworking machinery;
    Hardwood veneer and plywood
PA: Jowat Se
    Ernst-Hilker-Str. 10-14
    Detmold NW 32758
    52317490

(G-6511)
AGM CAROLINA INC
1031 E Springfield Rd (27263-2157)
PHONE.................................336 431-4100
Carman Parrente, Pr
Chad William, VP
▲ EMP: 8 EST: 2012
SQ FT: 2,000
SALES (est): 1.97MM Privately Held
Web: www.agmcarolina.com
SIC: 5072 5251 3334 Hardware; Hardware
    stores; Aluminum ingots and slabs

(G-6512)
AKZO NOBEL COATINGS INC
Also Called: Akzo Nobel Coatings
1431 Progress Ave (27260-8322)
PHONE.................................336 841-5111
James Burray, Brnch Mgr
EMP: 30
SALES (corp-wide): 11.6B Privately Held
SIC: 2851 Paints and allied products
HQ: Akzo Nobel Coatings Inc.
    535 Marriott Dr Ste 500
    Nashville TN 37214
    440 297-5100

(G-6513)
ALAMANCE STEEL FABRICATORS
5926 Prospect St (27263-3970)
PHONE.................................336 887-3015
Scott Troxler, Pr
EMP: 6 EST: 1974
SQ FT: 7,000
SALES (est): 701.32K Privately Held
Web: www.alamancesteel.com
SIC: 3446 3441 Railings, prefabricated metal
    ; Fabricated structural metal

(G-6514)
ALEXANDER PRESS INC
701 Greensboro Rd (27260-2651)
PHONE.................................336 884-8063
Mary Fay Bodenheimer, Owner
Mary Fay Bodenheimer, Prin
EMP: 6 EST: 2010
SALES (est): 69.47K Privately Held
SIC: 2752 Commercial printing, lithographic

(G-6515)
ALI GROUP NORTH AMERICA CORP
Also Called: Carpigiani Corporation America
738 Gallimore Dairy Rd Ste 113
(27265-9721)
PHONE.................................800 648-4389
EMP: 26
SALES (corp-wide): 4.67B Privately Held
Web: www.aligroup.com
SIC: 3589 Cooking equipment, commercial
HQ: Ali Group North America Corporation
    101 Corporate Woods Pkwy
    Vernon Hills IL 60061
    847 215-6565

(G-6516)
ALL BAKED OUT COMPANY
629 Mcway Dr (27263-2059)
PHONE..............................336 861-1212
Marlene Felisberto, *Pr*
Rodney Hensley, *VP*
EMP: 15 **EST:** 2010
SALES (est): 2.59MM **Privately Held**
Web: www.bigbossbaking.com
SIC: 2051 Bakery: wholesale or wholesale/
retail combined

(G-6517)
ALLRED METAL STAMPING WORKS INC
1305 Old Thomasville Rd (27260-8459)
P.O. Box 2566 (27261-2566)
PHONE..............................336 886-5221
EMP: 35 **EST:** 1964
SALES (est): 6.55MM **Privately Held**
Web: www.allredmetal.com
SIC: 3469 Stamping metal for the trade

(G-6518)
AMADA AMERICA INC
109 Penny Rd (27260-2500)
PHONE..............................877 262-3287
EMP: 6
Web: www.amada.com
SIC: 5084 3541 Metalworking machinery;
Machine tools, metal cutting type
HQ: Amada America, Inc.
7025 Firestone Blvd
Buena Park CA 90621
714 739-2111

(G-6519)
AMCASE INC
2214 Shore St (27263-2512)
PHONE..............................336 784-5992
Lindy Mulford, *CEO*
Mike Mulford, *
EMP: 34 **EST:** 1984
SALES (est): 8.22MM **Privately Held**
Web: www.amcase.com
SIC: 2521 2542 2541 2531 Wood office
furniture; Office and store showcases and
display fixtures; Wood partitions and fixtures
; Public building and related furniture

(G-6520)
AMERICAN METALLURGY INC
Also Called: American Metal Treating
505 Garrison St (27260-7042)
P.O. Box 4912 (27263-4912)
PHONE..............................336 889-3277
Michael Ram, *Pr*
EMP: 5 **EST:** 1990
SALES (est): 206.11K **Privately Held**
Web:
www.americanmetaltreatinginc.com
SIC: 3398 Metal heat treating

(G-6521)
AMERICAN OF HIGH POINT INC
2224 Shore St (27263-2512)
P.O. Box 7103 (27264)
PHONE..............................336 431-1513
David Richardson, *Pr*
Bobbie Richardson, *
EMP: 16 **EST:** 1959
SQ FT: 83,000
SALES (est): 2.05MM **Privately Held**
Web: www.american-woodcrafters.com
SIC: 2511 Wood household furniture

(G-6522)
AMERICAN SILK MILLS LLC (PA)
329 S Wrenn St Ste 101 (27260-6684)
PHONE..............................570 822-7147

Cynthia Dluthit, *Pr*
◆ **EMP:** 14 **EST:** 1930
SQ FT: 3,700
SALES (est): 3.36MM
SALES (corp-wide): 3.36MM **Privately Held**
Web: www.americansilk.com
SIC: 2211 2221 Cotton broad woven goods;
Broadwoven fabric mills, manmade

(G-6523)
AMERIFAB INTERNATIONAL INC
203 Feld Ave (27263-1929)
PHONE..............................336 882-9010
Raj Mehta, *CEO*
Kajal Bhat, *
▲ **EMP:** 48 **EST:** 1994
SALES (est): 5.55MM **Privately Held**
Web: www.amerifabintl.com
SIC: 2211 Draperies and drapery fabrics,
cotton

(G-6524)
APOLLO DESIGNS LLC (PA)
Also Called: Apollo Designs
2147 Brevard Rd (27263-1703)
PHONE..............................336 886-0260
Nihar Upadhyaya, *CEO*
Janki Upadhyaya, *Pr*
▲ **EMP:** 25 **EST:** 2015
SALES (est): 4.28MM
SALES (corp-wide): 4.28MM **Privately Held**
Web: www.apollodesigns.net
SIC: 5021 3272 2511 2499 Furniture; Stone,
cast concrete; Vanity dressers: wood;
Kitchen, bathroom, and household ware:
wood

(G-6525)
ARCHDALE PRINTING COMPANY INC
1316 Trinity Ave (27260-8358)
P.O. Box 433 (27370-0433)
PHONE..............................336 884-5312
Ed Smith, *Pr*
EMP: 4 **EST:** 2006
SALES (est): 248.59K **Privately Held**
SIC: 2752 Offset printing

(G-6526)
ARE MANAGEMENT LLC
1420 Lorraine Ave (27263-2040)
PHONE..............................336 855-7800
▲ **EMP:** 25 **EST:** 1993
SALES (est): 7.45MM **Privately Held**
Web: www.ancoeaglin.com
SIC: 3556 Food products machinery

(G-6527)
ARGOS USA LLC
406 Tomlinson St (27260-6639)
PHONE..............................336 841-3379
Howard Hepler, *Brnch Mgr*
EMP: 31
Web: www.argos-us.com
SIC: 3273 Ready-mixed concrete
HQ: Argos Usa Llc
3015 Windward Plz Ste 300
Alpharetta GA 30005
678 368-4300

(G-6528)
ARISTON HOSPITALITY INC
Also Called: Motivo Furniture
1581 Prospect St (27260-8457)
PHONE..............................626 458-8668
Tony Tsai, *CEO*
Tony Tsai, *Prin*
▲ **EMP:** 30 **EST:** 2006
SALES (est): 1.62MM **Privately Held**
Web: www.aristonhospitality.com

SIC: 2599 2426 Furniture and fixtures, nec;
Furniture stock and parts, hardwood

(G-6529)
ARPER USA (PA)
660 Southwest St (27260-8107)
PHONE..............................336 434-2376
Danielle Incati, *Genl Mgr*
▲ **EMP:** 6 **EST:** 2015
SALES (est): 639.29K
SALES (corp-wide): 639.29K **Privately Held**
SIC: 2599 Furniture and fixtures, nec

(G-6530)
ARTISANS GUILD INCORPORATED
639 Mcway Dr Ste 101 (27263-2492)
PHONE..............................336 841-4140
Bruce Thomas, *Pr*
Cindy Thomas, *VP*
EMP: 5 **EST:** 1970
SQ FT: 5,000
SALES (est): 95.43K **Privately Held**
Web: www.artisansguild.biz
SIC: 2511 2392 5023 2531 Novelty furniture:
wood; Household furnishings, nec; Floor
cushion and padding; School furniture

(G-6531)
AXALTA COATING SYSTEMS LTD
1717 W English Rd (27262-7205)
PHONE..............................336 802-5701
EMP: 13
SALES (corp-wide): 5.28B **Publicly Held**
Web: www.axalta.com
SIC: 2851 Paints and allied products
PA: Axalta Coating Systems Ltd.
1050 Constitution Ave
Philadelphia PA 19112
855 547-1461

(G-6532)
AXALTA COATING SYSTEMS LTD
2137 Brevard Rd (27263-1703)
PHONE..............................336 802-4392
Charlie Jacobs, *Mgr*
EMP: 25
SALES (corp-wide): 5.28B **Publicly Held**
Web: www.axalta.com
SIC: 2851 Paints and paint additives
PA: Axalta Coating Systems Ltd.
1050 Constitution Ave
Philadelphia PA 19112
855 547-1461

(G-6533)
AXALTA COATING SYSTEMS USA LLC
1717 W English Rd (27262-7205)
PHONE..............................336 802-5701
EMP: 10 **EST:** 2017
SALES (est): 8.86MM
SALES (corp-wide): 5.28B **Publicly Held**
Web: www.axalta.com
SIC: 2952 Asphalt felts and coatings
HQ: Axalta Coating Systems, Llc
50 Applied Bnk Blvd Ste 3
Glen Mills PA 19342
855 547-1461

(G-6534)
B&H MILLWORK AND FIXTURES INC
1130 Bedford St (27263-1604)
PHONE..............................336 431-0068
EMP: 32
Web: www.bandhmillwork.com
SIC: 2542 2431 2521 Partitions and fixtures,
except wood; Millwork; Cabinets, office:
wood

(G-6535)
B/E AEROSPACE INC
2376 Hickswood Rd Ste 106 (27265-7918)
PHONE..............................336 841-7698
John Gonzalez, *Brnch Mgr*
EMP: 6
SALES (corp-wide): 80.74B **Publicly Held**
Web: www.collinsaerospace.com
SIC: 3728 Aircraft parts and equipment, nec
HQ: B/E Aerospace, Inc.
2730 West Tyvola Rd
Charlotte NC 28217
704 423-7000

(G-6536)
BAKEBOXX COMPANY ✪
Also Called: Big Boss Baking Company
629 Mcway Dr (27263-2059)
PHONE..............................336 861-1212
Melissa Shenker, *Pr*
Edward Shenker, *VP*
EMP: 10 **EST:** 2023
SALES (est): 508.51K **Privately Held**
SIC: 5461 2064 2043 5149 Retail bakeries;
Granola and muesli, bars and clusters;
Cereal breakfast foods; Breakfast cereals

(G-6537)
BAKER INTERIORS FURNITURE CO
Also Called: Baker Furniture
2219 Shore St (27263-2511)
PHONE..............................336 431-9115
William Simmons, *Mgr*
EMP: 8
SIC: 2511 2512 Wood household furniture;
Upholstered household furniture
HQ: Baker Interiors Furniture Company
1 Baker Way
Connelly Springs NC 28612
336 431-9115

(G-6538)
BANNER LIFE SCIENCES LLC
3980 Premier Dr Ste 110 (27265-8409)
PHONE..............................336 812-8700
Michael Lytton, *Pr*
Aqeel Fatmi, *
EMP: 50 **EST:** 2014
SALES (est): 3.76MM **Privately Held**
Web: www.bannerls.com
SIC: 2834 Vitamin preparations

(G-6539)
BARSINA PUBLISHING
3510 Pine Valley Rd (27265-2015)
PHONE..............................336 869-2849
Cherl T Harrison, *Owner*
EMP: 4 **EST:** 2014
SALES (est): 41.35K **Privately Held**
SIC: 2741 Miscellaneous publishing

(G-6540)
BARUDAN AMERICA INC
9826 Us Highway 311 Ste 4 (27263-8844)
PHONE..............................800 627-4776
Dave Davidson, *Brnch Mgr*
EMP: 7
Web: www.barudanamerica.com
SIC: 3552 Embroidery machines
HQ: Barudan America, Inc.
30901 Carter St Frnt A
Solon OH 44139
440 248-8770

(G-6541)
BEAMER TIRE & AUTO REPAIR INC
245 E Parris Ave (27262-7710)
PHONE..............................336 882-7043
Douglas F Beamer, *Pr*
EMP: 17 **EST:** 2009

SALES (est): 939.75K **Privately Held**
Web: www.beamertire.com
SIC: **5531** 7538 7534 7539 Automotive tires;
General automotive repair shops; Tire
retreading and repair shops; Automotive
repair shops, nec

(G-6542)
BEAST CHAINS
733 Spinning Wheel Pt (27265-3452)
PHONE..............................336 346-9081
EMP: 4 EST: 2017
SALES (est): 96.61K **Privately Held**
Web: www.beastchains.com
SIC: **3999** Manufacturing industries, nec

(G-6543)
BEAUFURN LLC
Also Called: Beaufurn
1005 W Fairfield Rd (27263-1609)
P.O. Box 1795 (27012-1795)
PHONE..............................336 768-2544
Bill Bongaerts, *Managing Member*
Moniquie Bongaerts, *
◆ EMP: 24 EST: 1996
SALES (est): 4.91MM **Privately Held**
Web: www.beaufurn.com
SIC: **2599** 2531 5021 Bar, restaurant and
cafeteria furniture; Assembly hall furniture;
Office and public building furniture

(G-6544)
BEDEX LLC
210 Swathmore Ave (27263-1932)
PHONE..............................336 617-6755
EMP: 40 EST: 2012
SALES (est): 1.46MM **Privately Held**
Web: www.gobedex.com
SIC: **7641** 2515 Reupholstery and furniture
repair; Spring cushions

(G-6545)
BELWITH PRODUCTS LLC
1006 N Main St (27262-3166)
PHONE..............................336 841-3899
Mark Smith, *Brnch Mgr*
EMP: 4
SQ FT: 3,666
Web: www.belwith-keeler.com
SIC: **3469** 3465 3429 5072 Metal stampings,
nec; Automotive stampings; Furniture
hardware; Hardware
PA: Belwith Products, Llc
3100 Broadway Ave Sw
Grandville MI 49418

(G-6546)
BERKELEY HOME FURNITURE LLC
2228 Shore St (27263-2512)
P.O. Box 5023 (27262-5023)
PHONE..............................336 882-0012
EMP: 8 EST: 2017
SQ FT: 60,000
SALES (est): 604.93K **Privately Held**
SIC: **2512** Living room furniture: upholstered
on wood frames

(G-6547)
BERRY GLOBAL INC
314 Mandustry St (27262-8139)
PHONE..............................336 841-1723
EMP: 5
Web: www.berryglobal.com
SIC: **3089** 3081 Bottle caps, molded plastics;
Unsupported plastics film and sheet
HQ: Berry Global, Inc.
101 Oakley St
Evansville IN 47710

(G-6548)
BLUE RIDGE TOOL INC
2546 Willard Dairy Rd (27265-8117)
PHONE..............................336 993-8111
Ronald Lamy, *Pr*
EMP: 5 EST: 1993
SQ FT: 3,000
SALES (est): 430.03K **Privately Held**
Web: www.blueridgetool.net
SIC: **3599** Machine shop, jobbing and repair

(G-6549)
BOOK LOVER SEARCH
P.O. Box 694 (27261-0694)
PHONE..............................336 889-6127
Denise Jones, *Owner*
EMP: 5 EST: 2002
SALES (est): 78.82K **Privately Held**
SIC: **5192** 2789 Books; Binding and repair of
books, magazines, and pamphlets

(G-6550)
BOSS DESIGN US INC
2014 Chestnut Street Ext (27262-4408)
PHONE..............................844 353-7834
Richard K Schell, *Prin*
EMP: 5 EST: 2014
SALES (est): 527.29K **Privately Held**
Web: www.bossdesign.com
SIC: **2521** Wood office furniture

(G-6551)
BRYAN AUSTIN
Also Called: UPS
1589 Skeet Club Rd Ste 102 (27265-8817)
PHONE..............................336 841-6573
Bryan Austin, *Owner*
EMP: 4 EST: 2007
SALES (est): 553.41K **Privately Held**
Web: www.uscellphonedetective.com
SIC: **7389** 2759 5044 Mailbox rental and
related service; Commercial printing, nec;
Office equipment

(G-6552)
BUILDING AUTOMATION SVCS LLC
1515 Bethel Dr (27260-8348)
PHONE..............................336 884-4026
Robert Koonts, *Pr*
EMP: 10 EST: 2017
SALES (est): 5.03MM **Privately Held**
Web: www.basllco.com
SIC: **3822** Environmental controls

(G-6553)
CAMBREX HIGH POINT INC
4180 Mendenhall Oaks Pkwy (27265)
PHONE..............................336 841-5250
Steven Klosk, *Pr*
EMP: 62 EST: 1999
SQ FT: 35,000
SALES (est): 37.5MM
SALES (corp-wide): 523.07MM **Privately
Held**
Web: www.cambrex.com
SIC: **2834** Pharmaceutical preparations
PA: Cambrex Corporation
1 Meadowlands Plz
East Rutherford NJ 07073
201 804-3000

(G-6554)
CARBIDE SAWS INCORPORATED
701 Garrison St (27260-7098)
PHONE..............................336 882-6835
Rogene Mc Guinn, *Pr*
Jane Goodman Burnette, *VP*
EMP: 7 EST: 1954
SQ FT: 1,600
SALES (est): 457.14K **Privately Held**

Web: www.carbidesawsinc.com
SIC: **7699** 3553 Knife, saw and tool
sharpening and repair; Woodworking
machinery

(G-6555)
CARGILL & PENDLETON INC
Also Called: Cargill
330 N Hamilton St (27260-5034)
PHONE..............................336 882-5510
Sumner Finch, *Mgr*
EMP: 24
SIC: **2512** Upholstered household furniture
HQ: Cargill & Pendleton, Inc.
411 Tomlinson St
High Point NC 27260
336 472-7540

(G-6556)
CAROLINA BUSINESS FURN INC
535 Archdale Blvd (27263-8590)
P.O. Box 4398 (27263)
PHONE..............................336 431-9400
Hank Menke, *Pr*
Ryan Menke, *General Vice President**
Robert H Menke Junior, *Pr*
Jeff Eckert, *
Michael Wagner, *
▲ EMP: 1815 EST: 1999
SQ FT: 65,000
SALES (est): 3MM
SALES (corp-wide): 13.85MM **Privately
Held**
Web:
www.carolinabusinessfurniture.com
SIC: **2511** 2599 Wood household furniture;
Hospital furniture, except beds
PA: Ofs Brands Inc.
1204 E 6th St
Huntingburg IN 47542
800 521-5381

(G-6557)
CAROLINA CASTING INC
1416 Progress Ave (27260-8319)
P.O. Box 7091 (27264-7091)
PHONE..............................336 884-7311
Michael D Goldman, *Pr*
Bill Hurd, *
EMP: 50 EST: 1997
SQ FT: 52,000
SALES (est): 2.3MM **Privately Held**
Web: www.carolinacasting.com
SIC: **2519** Fiberglass and plastic furniture

(G-6558)
**CAROLINA CONTAINER COMPANY
(HQ)**
Also Called: Digital High Point
909 Prospect St (27260-8273)
P.O. Box 2166 (27261-2166)
PHONE..............................336 883-7146
Nicholas Smith, *CEO*
Ronald T Sessions, *
Randall L Black, *
◆ EMP: 100 EST: 1928
SQ FT: 9,200
SALES (est): 101.35MM
SALES (corp-wide): 644.8MM **Privately
Held**
Web: www.carolinacontainer.com
SIC: **2653** 2679 Boxes, corrugated: made
from purchased materials; Corrugated
paper: made from purchased material
PA: New-Indy Jv Corp.
3500 Porsche Way Ste 150
Ontario CA 91764
909 296-3400

(G-6559)
**CAROLINA CUSTOM BOOTH CO
LLC**
Also Called: Carolina Custom Booth
901 W Market Center Dr (27260-8238)
P.O. Box 150 (27261-0150)
PHONE..............................336 886-3127
Renee Surratt, *
Stephanie Roberts, *
Amy Blum Grady, *
◆ EMP: 26 EST: 2010
SALES (est): 4.94MM **Privately Held**
Web: www.carolinacustombooth.com
SIC: **3444** Booths, spray: prefabricated
sheet metal

(G-6560)
CARPENTER CO
1021 E Springfield Rd Ste 101
(27263-2157)
PHONE..............................336 861-5730
Randy Wisner, *Genl Mgr*
EMP: 58
SQ FT: 127,616
SALES (corp-wide): 506.96MM **Privately
Held**
Web: www.carpenter.com
SIC: **3086** 2821 Insulation or cushioning
material, foamed plastics; Plastics materials
and resins
PA: Carpenter Co.
5016 Monument Ave
Richmond VA 23230
804 359-0800

(G-6561)
CARR MILL SUPPLIES INC
1015 Manley St (27260-7062)
P.O. Box 2766 (27261-2766)
PHONE..............................336 883-0135
Sara W Carr, *Pr*
Guy E Carr Junior, *VP*
Doctor Jennifer Savitz, *Sec*
EMP: 9 EST: 1952
SQ FT: 9,600
SALES (est): 381.38K **Privately Held**
SIC: **3599** 5085 Machine shop, jobbing and
repair; Industrial supplies

(G-6562)
CARTRIDGE WORLD
Also Called: Earnmoore
2640 Willard Dairy Rd Ste 114
(27265-8708)
PHONE..............................336 885-0989
James Steven Moore, *Owner*
Robert Wessman, *Prin*
EMP: 4 EST: 2004
SALES (est): 137.84K **Privately Held**
Web: www.cartridgeworld.com
SIC: **5112** 3955 Office filing supplies; Print
cartridges for laser and other computer
printers

(G-6563)
CASCADE DIE CASTING GROUP INC
Also Called: Atlantic Division
501 Old Thomasville Rd (27260-8430)
PHONE..............................336 882-0186
Kent Nifong, *Prin*
EMP: 38
SALES (corp-wide): 97.08MM **Privately
Held**
Web: www.cascade-cdc.com
SIC: **3544** Special dies and tools
PA: Cascade Die Casting Group Inc
7441 S Division Ave
Grand Rapids MI 49548
616 281-1660

(G-6564)
CASCADE DIE CASTING GROUP INC
Also Called: Cascade Die Casting
1800 Albertson Rd (27260-8206)
P.O. Box 8045 (27264-8045)
PHONE..............................336 882-0186
Phil Torchio, *Brnch Mgr*
EMP: 230
SQ FT: 40,000
SALES (corp-wide): 97.08MM **Privately Held**
Web: www.cascade-cdc.com
SIC: 3364 3365 3363 Zinc and zinc-base alloy die-castings; Aluminum foundries; Aluminum die-castings
PA: Cascade Die Casting Group Inc
7441 S Division Ave
Grand Rapids MI 49548
616 281-1660

(G-6565)
CECIL-JOHNSON MFG INC
1445 Jackson Lake Rd (27263-9764)
PHONE..............................336 431-5233
Richard Pokrivka, *Pr*
Katherine Johnson, *Treas*
Evon Pokrivka, *Sec*
EMP: 27 **EST:** 1979
SQ FT: 20,000
SALES (est): 3.02MM **Privately Held**
SIC: 2426 Frames for upholstered furniture, wood

(G-6566)
CENTURY FURNITURE LLC
Also Called: Highpoint Century Showroom
200 Steele St (27260-5153)
PHONE..............................336 889-8286
Sandra Royals, *Mgr*
EMP: 5
SALES (corp-wide): 87.25MM **Privately Held**
Web: www.centuryfurniture.com
SIC: 2511 Wood household furniture
HQ: Century Furniture, Llc
401 11th St Nw
Hickory NC 28601
828 267-8739

(G-6567)
CHATEAU DAX USA LTD
1838 Eastchester Dr Ste 106 (27265-1494)
PHONE..............................336 885-9777
Giulio Rainoldi, *CEO*
Walter Colombo, *Pr*
Amir Kalipour, *Sec*
Giolio Rainoldi, *CEO*
◆ **EMP:** 7 **EST:** 1985
SQ FT: 2,500
SALES (est): 2.28MM
SALES (corp-wide): 97.46MM **Privately Held**
SIC: 2512 5021 Upholstered household furniture; Chairs
PA: Chateau D'ax Spa
Via Nazionale 159
Lentate Sul Seveso MB 20823
036 256-9068

(G-6568)
CHILDERS CONCRETE COMPANY
200 Wise Ave (27260-7646)
P.O. Box 777 (27261-0777)
PHONE..............................336 841-3111
Mitchel L Childers Junior, *Pr*
Kelly Vickers, *Sec*
EMP: 12 **EST:** 1946
SQ FT: 1,200
SALES (est): 3.31MM **Privately Held**
Web: www.childersconcrete.com

SIC: 3273 Ready-mixed concrete

(G-6569)
CLARIOS LLC
Also Called: Johnson Controls
211 S Hamilton St (27260-5232)
PHONE..............................336 884-5832
EMP: 32
SALES (corp-wide): 69.83B **Privately Held**
Web: www.clarios.com
SIC: 2531 Seats, automobile
HQ: Clarios, Llc
5757 N Green Bay Ave Flor
Glendale WI 53209

(G-6570)
CLARKE HARLAND CORP
4475 Premier Dr (27265-8336)
PHONE..............................210 697-8888
Julie Kellman, *Prin*
EMP: 8
Web: www.harlandclarke.com
SIC: 2782 Bank checkbooks and passbooks
HQ: Harland Clarke Corp.
15955 La Cantera Pkwy
San Antonio TX 78256
830 609-5500

(G-6571)
COAST TO COAST LEA & VINYL INC
Also Called: Southeast Leather
1022 Porter St (27263-1638)
PHONE..............................336 886-5050
Cicki Reez, *Mgr*
EMP: 4
SALES (corp-wide): 2.09MM **Privately Held**
Web: www.coast2coastleather.com
SIC: 3111 3199 Mechanical leather; Leather garments
PA: Coast To Coast Leather & Vinyl, Inc.
1 Crossman Rd S
Sayreville NJ 08872
732 525-8877

(G-6572)
COLONIAL LLC (PA)
536 Townsend Ave (27263)
P.O. Box 148 (27261)
PHONE..............................336 434-5600
Mark Hobson, *Managing Member*
James R Keever, *Managing Member*
Jim Keever Senior, *Pr*
Wes Keever, *VP*
Jimmy Keever, *VP*
▲ **EMP:** 40 **EST:** 1982
SQ FT: 22,000
SALES (est): 6.93MM
SALES (corp-wide): 6.93MM **Privately Held**
Web: www.colonialllc.com
SIC: 2395 Embroidery and art needlework

(G-6573)
COLUMBIA PANEL MFG CO INC
100 Giles St (27263-2108)
P.O. Box 7447 (27264-7447)
PHONE..............................336 861-4100
Todd Rush, *Pr*
Brenda Rush, *
EMP: 70 **EST:** 1920
SQ FT: 46,000
SALES (est): 13.33MM **Privately Held**
Web: www.columbiapanel.com
SIC: 2435 Hardwood veneer and plywood

(G-6574)
COMPETITION TOOLING INC
219 Dublin Ave (27260-8352)
P.O. Box 7203 (27264)
PHONE..............................336 887-4414

Carl L Warrell, *Pr*
Johnnie Cox, *Sec*
EMP: 8 **EST:** 1968
SQ FT: 9,000
SALES (est): 1.05MM **Privately Held**
Web: www.competitionengineering.net
SIC: 3599 Machine shop, jobbing and repair

(G-6575)
COMPUTERWAY FOOD SYSTEMS INC
2700 Westchester Dr (27262-8037)
PHONE..............................336 841-7289
Jeff Jackson, *CEO*
EMP: 28 **EST:** 2017
SALES (est): 4.17MM **Privately Held**
Web: www.mycfs.com
SIC: 7373 3596 Computer integrated systems design; Scales and balances, except laboratory

(G-6576)
CONCEPT PLASTICS INC (PA)
Also Called: Craft-Tex
1210 Hickory Chapel Rd (27260-7187)
P.O. Box 847 (27261-0847)
PHONE..............................336 889-2001
Paul Saperstein, *Pr*
Sara L Saperstein, *
EMP: 144 **EST:** 1970
SALES (est): 4.08MM
SALES (corp-wide): 4.08MM **Privately Held**
Web: www.cpico.com
SIC: 3089 Injection molding of plastics

(G-6577)
CRAFTWOOD VENEERS INC
822 Herman Ct (27263-2166)
PHONE..............................336 434-2158
Victor Furr, *Pr*
EMP: 4 **EST:** 2015
SALES (est): 668.37K **Privately Held**
Web: www.craftwoodproducts.com
SIC: 2449 Containers, plywood and veneer wood

(G-6578)
CRAVEN SIGN SERVICES INC
508 Old Thomasville Rd (27260-8431)
PHONE..............................336 883-7306
TOLL FREE: 800
Tony Craven, *Pr*
EMP: 4 **EST:** 1965
SQ FT: 1,200
SALES (est): 830.98K **Privately Held**
Web: www.cravensigns.com
SIC: 3993 Signs, not made in custom sign painting shops

(G-6579)
CRAWFORD INDUSTRIES INC
Also Called: Artistic Quilting
108 Lane Ave (27260-8719)
P.O. Box 5171 (27262-5171)
PHONE..............................336 884-8822
Kent Crawford, *Pr*
Lynn Crawford, *VP*
▼ **EMP:** 5 **EST:** 1985
SQ FT: 11,000
SALES (est): 400.98K **Privately Held**
Web: www.artisticquiltinginc.com
SIC: 2395 Quilting and quilting supplies

(G-6580)
CREATIVE SERVICES USA INC
1231 Montlieu Ave (27262-3560)
P.O. Box 2344 (27282-2344)
PHONE..............................336 887-1958
Michael West, *Pr*
EMP: 6 **EST:** 1970

SQ FT: 30,000
SALES (est): 540.96K **Privately Held**
Web: www.creativeservicesusa.com
SIC: 2789 Swatches and samples

(G-6581)
CROWN FOAM PRODUCTS INC
921 Baker Rd Ste 3 (27263-2127)
P.O. Box 1224 (27261-1224)
PHONE..............................336 434-4024
Steve Roach, *Pr*
Betty Roach, *Sec*
EMP: 12 **EST:** 1973
SQ FT: 20,000
SALES (est): 963.62K **Privately Held**
SIC: 3086 Plastics foam products

(G-6582)
CULP INC (PA)
1823 Eastchester Dr (27265)
P.O. Box 2686 (27265)
PHONE..............................336 889-5161
Robert G Culp Iv, *Pr*
Franklin N Saxon, *
Kenneth R Bowling, *Ex VP*
Ashley C Durbin, *Corporate Secretary*
Teresa Huffman, *Chief Human Resource Officer*
EMP: 102 **EST:** 1972
SQ FT: 36,643
SALES (est): 225.33MM
SALES (corp-wide): 225.33MM **Publicly Held**
Web: www.culp.com
SIC: 2221 Upholstery fabrics, manmade fiber and silk

(G-6583)
CUSTOM AIR TRAYS INC (PA)
2112 S Elm St (27260-8811)
P.O. Box 7026 (27264-7026)
PHONE..............................336 889-8729
Jim Hardy, *Genl Mgr*
▼ **EMP:** 10 **EST:** 1992
SALES (est): 2.41MM **Privately Held**
Web: www.customairtrays.com
SIC: 2449 7261 Shipping cases and drums, wood: wirebound and plywood; Funeral service and crematories

(G-6584)
CUSTOM FINISHERS INC (PA)
Also Called: Eagle Laser
2213 Shore St (27263-2511)
P.O. Box 7008 (27264-7008)
PHONE..............................336 431-7141
Christopher Wayne Wilkins, *Pr*
Sylvia Hicks, *
EMP: 39 **EST:** 1972
SQ FT: 45,000
SALES (est): 8.38MM
SALES (corp-wide): 8.38MM **Privately Held**
Web: www.customfinishers.com
SIC: 2493 7389 Hardboard; Metal cutting services

(G-6585)
D & B CONCEPTS INC
613 Prospect St (27260-1522)
PHONE..............................336 885-8292
William Slate, *Pr*
Thomas Waterhouse, *VP*
EMP: 6 **EST:** 2004
SALES (est): 736.6K **Privately Held**
Web: www.dandbconcepts.com
SIC: 5031 2541 Lumber, plywood, and millwork; Bar fixtures, wood

GEOGRAPHIC

(G-6586)
D3 SOFTWARE INC
277 Creekside Dr (27265-9254)
PHONE..................336 870-9138
EMP: 5 EST: 2016
SALES (est): 96.07K Privately Held
SIC: 7372 Prepackaged software

(G-6587)
DANI LEATHER USA INC
635 Southwest St Ste A (27260-8223)
PHONE..................973 598-0890
Silvano Fumei, Prin
▲ EMP: 6 EST: 2005
SALES (est): 804.1K
SALES (corp-wide): 161.52MM Privately Held
Web: www.gruppodani.com
SIC: 3111 Leather tanning and finishing
HQ: Dani Spa
Via Concia 186
Arzignano VI 36071
044 445-4111

(G-6588)
DARRAN FURNITURE INDS INC
Also Called: Darran Furniture
2402 Shore St (27263)
P.O. Box 7614 (27264)
PHONE..................336 861-2400
Jennifer H Cushion, Pr
EMP: 135 EST: 1977
SQ FT: 225,000
SALES (est): 20.67MM Privately Held
Web: www.darran.com
SIC: 2521 Wood office furniture

(G-6589)
DAVIS FURNITURE INDUSTRIES INC
(PA)
2401 College Dr (27260-8816)
P.O. Box 2065 (27261-2065)
PHONE..................336 889-2009
Danny Davis, Pr
◆ EMP: 165 EST: 1942
SQ FT: 350,000
SALES (est): 23.13MM
SALES (corp-wide): 23.13MM Privately Held
Web: www.davisfurniture.com
SIC: 2521 2531 2522 2511 Chairs, office: padded, upholstered, or plain: wood; Public building and related furniture; Office furniture, except wood; Wood household furniture

(G-6590)
DESIGN CONCEPTS INCORPORATED
341 South Rd (27262-8198)
PHONE..................336 887-1932
Hal A Kennerly Junior, Pr
Kay Miller, *
EMP: 13 EST: 1968
SQ FT: 36,000
SALES (est): 1.15MM Privately Held
Web: www.designconceptslv.com
SIC: 2782 2221 Sample books; Broadwoven fabric mills, manmade

(G-6591)
DESIGN THEORY LLC
1020 Surrett Dr (27260-8821)
PHONE..................336 912-0155
Scott Kim, Managing Member
EMP: 11 EST: 2014
SALES (est): 2.66MM Privately Held
Web: www.designtheoryhp.com
SIC: 2512 Upholstered household furniture

(G-6592)
DFP INC (PA)
Also Called: Edward Ferrell Lewis Mittman
685 Southwest St (27260-8108)
PHONE..................336 841-3028
Ira Glazer, Pr
▲ EMP: 100 EST: 1972
SALES (est): 8.58MM
SALES (corp-wide): 8.58MM Privately Held
Web: www.ferrellmittman.com
SIC: 2512 2531 Upholstered household furniture; Public building and related furniture

(G-6593)
DIGITAL HIGHPOINT LLC
401 Model Farm Rd Ste 101 (27263-1827)
P.O. Box 2166 (27261-2166)
PHONE..................336 883-7146
Ronald T Sessions, CEO
EMP: 110 EST: 2004
SALES (est): 1.21MM
SALES (corp-wide): 644.8MM Privately Held
Web: www.carolinacontainer.com
SIC: 3555 3955 5084 Printing plates; Print cartridges for laser and other computer printers; Printing trades machinery, equipment, and supplies
HQ: Carolina Container Company
909 Prospect St
High Point NC 27260
336 883-7146

(G-6594)
DISTINCTION HOSPITALITY INC
4100 Mendenhall Oaks Pkwy Ste 200 (27265-8075)
PHONE..................336 875-3043
Stanley Sapp, Pr
Tamera Sapp, Sec
EMP: 10 EST: 2014
SALES (est): 2.37MM Privately Held
Web: www.distinctionhospitality.com
SIC: 2599 Hotel furniture

(G-6595)
DIX ENTERPRISES INC
2436 Lake Oak (27265-9256)
PHONE..................336 558-9512
Michael Dix, Pr
EMP: 10 EST: 1992
SALES (est): 75.73K Privately Held
Web: www.dixgroupinc.com
SIC: 3949 7389 Sporting and athletic goods, nec; Fund raising organizations

(G-6596)
DOMENICKS FURNITURE MFR LLC
1107 Tate St (27260-7846)
PHONE..................336 442-3348
EMP: 20 EST: 2017
SALES (est): 2.41MM Privately Held
Web: www.domenicksfurniture.com
SIC: 2512 Upholstered household furniture

(G-6597)
DRAKE S FRESH PASTA COMPANY
636 Southwest St (27260-8107)
P.O. Box 5072 (27262-5072)
PHONE..................336 861-5454
Richard Drake, Ch
Simone Drake, *
▲ EMP: 50 EST: 1985
SALES (est): 10.71MM Privately Held
Web: www.drakesfreshpasta.com
SIC: 2099 Food preparations, nec

(G-6598)
DREXEL HERITAGE HOME FURNSNGS
741 W Ward Ave (27260-1645)
PHONE..................336 812-4430
Bryon Milleson, CFO
EMP: 5 EST: 2016
SALES (est): 57.78K Privately Held
SIC: 2599 Furniture and fixtures, nec

(G-6599)
DRUM FILTER MEDIA INC
901 W Fairfield Rd (27263-1607)
PHONE..................336 434-4195
John C Hollinger Iii, Pr
EMP: 4 EST: 1992
SALES (est): 531.18K Privately Held
Web: www.dfmiusa.com
SIC: 3569 5084 Filters, general line: industrial; Industrial machinery and equipment

(G-6600)
E FEIBUSCH COMPANY INC
Also Called: Swatchcraft
516 Townsend Ave (27263-2046)
PHONE..................336 434-5095
Gerald Feibusch, Pr
▲ EMP: 48 EST: 1934
SALES (est): 3.87MM Privately Held
Web: www.swatchcraft.com
SIC: 2782 2789 Blankbooks and looseleaf binders; Swatches and samples

(G-6601)
EAGLE PRODUCTS INC
1200 Surrett Dr (27260-8823)
P.O. Box 7387 (27264-7387)
PHONE..................336 886-5688
EMP: 4 EST: 1981
SALES (est): 231.52K Privately Held
SIC: 2674 Bags: uncoated paper and multiwall

(G-6602)
EAGLESTONE TECHNOLOGY INC
1401 Kensington Dr (27262-7319)
PHONE..................336 476-0244
Robert M Barnard, Pr
EMP: 10 EST: 1993
SALES (est): 1.61MM Privately Held
SIC: 3599 Machine shop, jobbing and repair

(G-6603)
ECOLAB INC
1101 Gallimore Dairy Rd (27265-9742)
PHONE..................336 931-3423
EMP: 11
SALES (corp-wide): 15.32B Publicly Held
Web: www.ecolab.com
SIC: 2841 Soap and other detergents
PA: Ecolab Inc.
1 Ecolab Pl
Saint Paul MN 55102
800 232-6522

(G-6604)
ED KEMP ASSOCIATES INC
Also Called: Ed Kemp Associates
3001 N Main St (27265-1938)
PHONE..................336 869-2155
Jon Kemp, CEO
Tony Faucette, VP
EMP: 8 EST: 1961
SQ FT: 1,500
SALES (est): 243.55K Privately Held
Web: www.edkemp.com
SIC: 7311 2752 8743 Advertising consultant; Commercial printing, lithographic; Public relations and publicity

(G-6605)
ELECTRICAL PANEL & CONTRLS INC
645 Mcway Dr (27263-2398)
PHONE..................336 434-4445
Martin Goodpasture, Pr
Paul Jones, VP
EMP: 5 EST: 2000
SQ FT: 15,000
SALES (est): 189.37K Privately Held
SIC: 3823 Process control instruments

(G-6606)
ELITE FURNITURE MFG INC
928 Millis St (27260-7237)
PHONE..................336 882-0406
Tim Miller, Pr
Todd Miller, VP
Terry Miller, Sec
EMP: 9 EST: 1997
SQ FT: 158,000
SALES (est): 152.84K Privately Held
SIC: 2512 5021 Upholstered household furniture; Household furniture

(G-6607)
ELITE GRAPHICS INC
Also Called: Fastsigns
1305 N Main St (27262-3128)
PHONE..................336 887-2923
Angela Riddle, Pr
EMP: 6 EST: 1996
SQ FT: 2,100
SALES (est): 437.22K Privately Held
Web: www.fastsigns.com
SIC: 3993 Signs and advertising specialties

(G-6608)
ELITE TEXTILES FABRICATION INC
1124 Roberts Ln Ste 101 (27260-7211)
PHONE..................888 337-0977
Ryan West, CEO
EMP: 12 EST: 2018
SALES (est): 939.21K Privately Held
Web: www.draperyfabrication.com
SIC: 2591 Window blinds

(G-6609)
EMB INC
4180 Mendenhall Oaks Pkwy Ste 100 (27265-8017)
PHONE..................336 945-0759
EMP: 4 EST: 2010
SALES (est): 46.38K Privately Held
SIC: 2395 Embroidery products, except Schiffli machine

(G-6610)
ENDURA PRODUCTS LLC
210 E Commerce Ave (27260-6686)
PHONE..................336 991-8818
EMP: 21
Web: www.enduraproducts.com
SIC: 3429 Hardware, nec
HQ: Endura Products, Llc
8817 W Market St
Colfax NC 27235
336 668-2472

(G-6611)
ENGCON NORTH AMERICA INC
2827 Earlham Pl (27263-1948)
PHONE..................203 691-5920
Krister Blomgren, Prin
EMP: 16 EST: 2017
SALES (est): 971.48K Privately Held
SIC: 3531 Construction machinery

▲ = Import ▼ = Export
◆ = Import/Export

(G-6612)
ENGLAND INC
222 S Main St (27260-5208)
PHONE..............................336 861-5266
Otis Sawyer, *Prin*
EMP: 56
SALES (corp-wide): 2.05B **Publicly Held**
Web: www.englandfurniture.com
SIC: 2512 Upholstered household furniture
HQ: England, Inc.
    145 England Dr
    New Tazewell TN 37825
    423 626-5211

(G-6613)
ENNIS-FLINT INC
4189 Eagle Hill Dr Ste 110 (27265-8316)
PHONE..............................800 331-8118
EMP: 4
SALES (corp-wide): 17.65B **Publicly Held**
Web: www.ennisflint.com
SIC: 2851 Paints and allied products
HQ: Ennis-Flint, Inc.
    4161 Pedmont Pkwy Ste 370
    Greensboro NC 27410
    800 331-8118

(G-6614)
ESTATE MENTORS INC ✪
3980 Premier Dr Ste 110 (27265)
PHONE..............................877 378-7567
EMP: 4 **EST:** 2024
SALES (est): 1.33MM **Privately Held**
SIC: 7372 Prepackaged software

(G-6615)
ETHNICRAFT USA LLC
101 Prospect St (27260-7259)
PHONE..............................336 885-2055
Jack G Hendrix, *Admn*
EMP: 18 **EST:** 2016
SALES (est): 5.4MM **Privately Held**
SIC: 2022 Processed cheese

(G-6616)
EUROHANSA INC
1213 Dorris Ave (27260-1575)
P.O. Box 6416 (27262-6416)
PHONE..............................336 885-1010
Hans Zoellinger, *Pr*
Frank H Zoellinger, *VP*
▲ **EMP:** 9 **EST:** 1988
SQ FT: 15,000
SALES (est): 375.19K **Privately Held**
Web: www.eurohansa.com
SIC: 3553 Woodworking machinery

(G-6617)
F C C LLC
Also Called: Furniture City Color
4045 Premier Dr Ste 200 (27265-9431)
P.O. Box 35304 (27425)
PHONE..............................336 883-7314
Tim Frye, *Managing Member*
Bill Franklin, *Managing Member*
EMP: 4 **EST:** 1969
SQ FT: 7,000
SALES (est): 210.52K **Privately Held**
Web: www.lastnamefirst.com
SIC: 2796 2759 2791 Lithographic plates,
    positives or negatives; Commercial printing,
    nec; Typesetting

(G-6618)
FACES SOUTH INC
1330 Lincoln Dr (27260-1515)
P.O. Box 1837 (27261-1837)
PHONE..............................336 883-0647
John Michael Ritch, *Pr*
Donna Ritch, *VP*

EMP: 5 **EST:** 1995
SALES (est): 976.65K **Privately Held**
Web: www.ritchfaceveneer.com
SIC: 2436 Softwood veneer and plywood

(G-6619)
FFNC INC
Also Called: Future Foam
1300 Prospect St (27260-8329)
P.O. Box 1017 (68101-1017)
PHONE..............................336 885-4121
◆ **EMP:** 83
SIC: 3086 Plastics foam products

(G-6620)
FIBER CUSHIONING INC
113 Motsinger St (27260-8836)
P.O. Box 4877 (27263-4877)
PHONE..............................336 887-4782
Dob Mc Gee, *Brnch Mgr*
EMP: 14
SALES (corp-wide): 3.1MM **Privately Held**
Web: www.fibercushioning.com
SIC: 2392 Household furnishings, nec
PA: Fiber Cushioning, Inc.
    4454 Us Highway 220 Bus S
    Asheboro NC 27205
    336 629-8442

(G-6621)
FORTRESS WOOD PRODUCTS INC
3874 Bethel Drive Ext (27260-8465)
P.O. Box 4991 (24115-4991)
PHONE..............................336 854-5121
Brandt A Mitchell, *Pr*
N Dillard Jones, *VP*
Janet M Decker, *Sec*
EMP: 12 **EST:** 1986
SQ FT: 1,500
SALES (est): 16.47MM
SALES (corp-wide): 44.45MM **Privately
Held**
Web: www.fortresswood.com
SIC: 2491 Wood preserving
PA: The Lester Group Inc
    101 E Commonwealth Blvd
    Martinsville VA 24112
    276 638-8834

(G-6622)
FRENCH HERITAGE INC (PA)
1638 W English Rd (27262-7204)
P.O. Box 2054 (27285)
PHONE..............................336 882-3565
Jacques Wayser, *Pr*
Hennessy Wayser, *VP*
▲ **EMP:** 16 **EST:** 1994
SALES (est): 904.36K
SALES (corp-wide): 904.36K **Privately
Held**
Web: www.frenchheritage.com
SIC: 2519 5021 Household furniture, except
    wood or metal: upholstered; Household
    furniture

(G-6623)
FRESH AS A DAISY INC
Also Called: Fresh As A Daisy
3601 Huntingridge Dr (27265-1258)
PHONE..............................336 869-3002
Edythe Golden, *Pr*
James Golden, *
EMP: 4 **EST:** 1999
SALES (est): 363.12K **Privately Held**
Web: www.faadinc.com
SIC: 2842 Cleaning or polishing
    preparations, nec

(G-6624)
FREUD AMERICA INC
Also Called: Freud
218 Feld Ave (27263-1930)
P.O. Box 7187 (27264-7187)
PHONE..............................800 334-4107
Russell Kohl, *Pr*
David Lewis, *
Russell Kohl, *Chief Executive Officer Freud
US*
Jim Brewer, *
Gregory Thiess, *
◆ **EMP:** 120 **EST:** 1991
SQ FT: 50,000
SALES (est): 46.84MM
SALES (corp-wide): 391.51MM **Privately
Held**
SIC: 5072 3546 3545 Cutlery; Power-driven
    handtools; Machine tool accessories
HQ: Bosch Rexroth Ag
    Zum EisengieBer 1
    Lohr A. Main BY 97816
    9352180

(G-6625)
FUTURE FOAM INC
Also Called: Ffnc
1300 Prospect St (27260-8329)
P.O. Box 7185 (27264-7185)
PHONE..............................336 885-4121
Tim Akins, *Brnch Mgr*
EMP: 98
SALES (corp-wide): 495.02MM **Privately
Held**
Web: www.futurefoam.com
SIC: 2821 3086 Plastics materials and resins
    ; Insulation or cushioning material, foamed
    plastics
PA: Future Foam, Inc.
    1610 Ave N
    Council Bluffs IA 51501
    712 323-9122

(G-6626)
FXI INC
2222 Surrett Dr (27263-8508)
PHONE..............................336 431-1171
EMP: 90
Web: www.fxi.com
SIC: 3086 Carpet and rug cushions, foamed
    plastics
HQ: Fxi, Inc.
    100 Mtsnford Rd 5 Rdnor C
    Radnor PA 19087

(G-6627)
GBF INC
Also Called: Guilford Business Forms
2427 Penny Rd (27265-8120)
P.O. Box 16128 (27261-6128)
PHONE..............................336 665-0205
Danny Bowman, *CEO*
Jason Bowman, *
Coy Shields, *
EMP: 72 **EST:** 1964
SQ FT: 240,000
SALES (est): 22.14MM **Privately Held**
Web: www.gbf-inc.com
SIC: 2835 2899 5112 Diagnostic substances
    ; Drug testing kits, blood and urine;
    Business forms

(G-6628)
**GERSAN INDUSTRIES
INCORPORATED**
607 Blake Ave (27260-8371)
P.O. Box 7043 (27264-7043)
PHONE..............................336 886-5455
Gerald Swanson, *Owner*
EMP: 4 **EST:** 1972
SQ FT: 8,000

SALES (est): 487.45K **Privately Held**
Web: www.gersanindustries.com
SIC: 2821 Plastics materials and resins

(G-6629)
GLASS UNLIMITED HIGH POINT INC
Also Called: Glass Unlimited
2149 Brevard Rd (27263-1703)
P.O. Box 528 (27261-0528)
PHONE..............................336 889-4551
Keith Eichhorn, *Pr*
Clint Field, *
▲ **EMP:** 55 **EST:** 1977
SQ FT: 75,000
SALES (est): 9.31MM **Privately Held**
Web: www.glass-unlimited.com
SIC: 3231 Products of purchased glass

(G-6630)
GLOBAL BIOPROTECT LLC
2714 Uwharrie Rd (27263-1680)
PHONE..............................336 861-0162
EMP: 10 **EST:** 2016
SALES (est): 2.49MM **Privately Held**
Web: www.globalbioprotect.com
SIC: 2899 Chemical preparations, nec

(G-6631)
GLOBAL VENEER SALES INC
112 Hodgin St (27262-7909)
P.O. Box 5829 (27262-5829)
PHONE..............................336 885-5061
Elwood S Cain Junior, *Pr*
Sandra Cain, *Sec*
David Hiatt, *VP*
▲ **EMP:** 6 **EST:** 1985
SQ FT: 20,000
SALES (est): 393.17K **Privately Held**
Web: www.globalveneer.com
SIC: 5031 7534 Veneer; Vulcanizing tires
    and tubes

(G-6632)
GOLD REFINERY
3954 Huttons Lake Ct (27265-1873)
PHONE..............................336 471-4817
Angela Tripp, *Prin*
EMP: 8 **EST:** 2010
SALES (est): 78.37K **Privately Held**
SIC: 3559 Refinery, chemical processing,
    and similar machinery

(G-6633)
GP FOAM FABRICATORS INC
220 Swathmore Ave (27263-1932)
P.O. Box 7483 (27264-7483)
PHONE..............................336 434-3600
Bob Pace, *Pr*
Elsie Pace, *
EMP: 14 **EST:** 1987
SQ FT: 20,000
SALES (est): 2.74MM **Privately Held**
SIC: 3069 Foam rubber

(G-6634)
GRAPHIK DIMENSIONS LIMITED
Also Called: Pictureframes.com
2103 Brentwood St (27263-1807)
PHONE..............................800 332-8884
Lauri Feinsod, *Pr*
Joan Feinsod, *
Dave Shelton, *
Mike Keyes, *
◆ **EMP:** 100 **EST:** 1966
SQ FT: 108,000
SALES (est): 18.44MM
SALES (corp-wide): 496.73MM **Privately
Held**
Web: www.pictureframes.com

GEOGRAPHIC

SIC: **3499** 2499 7379 Picture frames, metal;
Picture and mirror frames, wood; Computer
related consulting services
PA: Circle Graphics, Inc.
120 9th Ave
Longmont CO 80501
303 532-2370

(G-6635)
GUILFORD FABRICATORS INC
5261 Glenola Industrial Dr (27263-8152)
P.O. Box 7245 (27264-7245)
PHONE................................336 434-3163
Don Payne, *Pr*
Randy Rains, *VP*
Trudy Payne, *Sec*
▲ **EMP: 13 EST:** 1977
SQ FT: 28,000
SALES (est): 597.98K **Privately Held**
SIC: **5999** 3086 Foam and foam products;
Plastics foam products

(G-6636)
GUM DROP CASES LLC
1515 W Green Dr (27260-1657)
PHONE................................206 805-0818
EMP: 6 **EST:** 2018
SALES (est): 532.93K **Privately Held**
Web: www.gumdropcases.com
SIC: **3523** Farm machinery and equipment

(G-6637)
H & H WOODWORKING INC
530 Gatewood Ave (27262-4720)
PHONE................................336 884-5848
H Michael Hedrick, *Pr*
Susan Hedrick, *VP*
EMP: 8 **EST:** 1976
SQ FT: 13,000
SALES (est): 730K **Privately Held**
SIC: **1751** 2431 Cabinet building and
installation; Millwork

(G-6638)
HARRISS & COVINGTON HSY MILLS
1232 Hickory Chapel Rd (27260-7187)
PHONE................................336 882-6811
EMP: 5 **EST:** 1920
SALES (est): 71.04K **Privately Held**
Web: www.harrissandcov.com
SIC: **2252** Socks

(G-6639)
HARRISS CVINGTON HSY MILLS INC
Also Called: Harriss & Covington Hosiery
1250 Hickory Chapel Rd (27260-7187)
P.O. Box 1909 (27261-1909)
PHONE................................336 882-6811
Edward H Covington, *Pr*
Darrell Frye, *
Danny Mcnair, *VP*
Edward Covington, *Prin*
◆ **EMP:** 240 **EST:** 1920
SQ FT: 130,000
SALES (est): 24.66MM **Privately Held**
Web: www.harrissandcov.com
SIC: **2252** Socks

(G-6640)
HAWORTH INC
1673 W English Rd (27262-7203)
P.O. Box 189 (28613-0189)
PHONE................................336 885-4021
Steve Snyder, *Mgr*
EMP: 7
SALES (corp-wide): 2.59B **Privately Held**
Web: www.haworth.com
SIC: **2521** 2531 Wood office chairs, benches
and stools; Public building and related
furniture
HQ: Haworth, Inc.

1 Haworth Ctr
Holland MI 49423
616 393-3000

(G-6641)
HDM FURNITURE INDUSTRIES INC
741 W Ward Ave Plant37 (27260-1645)
PHONE................................336 812-4434
EMP: 38
SALES (corp-wide): 384.13MM **Privately
Held**
SIC: **2512** Upholstered household furniture
PA: Hdm Furniture Industries Inc
1925 Eastchester Dr
High Point NC 27265
336 888-4800

(G-6642)
HEALING CRAFTER
4435 Garden Club St (27265-1196)
PHONE................................336 567-1620
Brandi Oliver, *Owner*
EMP: 4
SALES (est): 125.39K **Privately Held**
SIC: **2389** Apparel and accessories, nec

(G-6643)
HEDGECOCK RACING ENTPS INC
1520 Horneytown Rd (27265-9255)
PHONE................................336 887-4221
Jay Hedgecock Junior, *Pr*
EMP: 10 **EST:** 1982
SQ FT: 16,700
SALES (est): 2.09MM **Privately Held**
Web: www.hedgecockracing.com
SIC: **3711** Automobile assembly, including
specialty automobiles

(G-6644)
HENDRIX BATTING COMPANY
2310 Surrett Dr (27263-8509)
P.O. Box 7408 (27264-7408)
PHONE................................336 431-1181
Kenneth Hendrix Junior, *Pr*
Lesley Theirault, *
Angela Hendrix Bennett, *
▲ **EMP:** 150 **EST:** 1960
SQ FT: 125,000
SALES (est): 4.66MM **Privately Held**
Web: www.hendrixbatting.com
SIC: **2299** 2297 Batting, wadding, padding
and fillings; Nonwoven fabrics

(G-6645)
HENRY WILLIAMS JR (PA)
Also Called: Henry The Great
455 S Main St (27260-6634)
PHONE................................336 897-8714
Henry Williams Junior, *Owner*
EMP: 6 **EST:** 2022
SALES (est): 285.97K
SALES (corp-wide): 285.97K **Privately
Held**
SIC: **3999** Hair clippers for human use, hand
and electric

(G-6646)
HEXION INC
Also Called: Borden
1717 W Ward Ave (27260-1537)
PHONE................................336 884-8918
EMP: 5
SALES (corp-wide): 1.26B **Privately Held**
Web: www.hexion.com
SIC: **2891** 2821 Adhesives; Plastics
materials and resins
PA: Hexion Inc.
180 E Broad St
Columbus OH 43215
888 443-9466

(G-6647)
HICKORY SPRINGS MFG CO
Triad-Fabco Industries
1325 Baker Rd (27263-2031)
PHONE................................336 861-4195
Donald Leonard, *VP Opers*
EMP: 68
SALES (corp-wide): 430.3MM **Privately
Held**
Web: www.hsmsolutions.com
SIC: **3086** 2392 Insulation or cushioning
material, foamed plastics; Cushions and
pillows
PA: Hickory Springs Manufacturing
Company
235 2nd Ave Nw
Hickory NC 28601
828 328-2201

(G-6648)
HICKORY SPRINGS MFG CO
Also Called: Ultra Flex
1905 Alleghany St (27263-2027)
P.O. Box 4549 (27263-4549)
PHONE................................336 491-4131
Faye Glevins, *Brnch Mgr*
EMP: 19
SALES (corp-wide): 430.3MM **Privately
Held**
Web: www.hsmsolutions.com
SIC: **2241** 3714 Webbing, woven; Motor
vehicle parts and accessories
PA: Hickory Springs Manufacturing
Company
235 2nd Ave Nw
Hickory NC 28601
828 328-2201

(G-6649)
HIGH POINT ENTERPRISE INC
Also Called: Archdale Trinity News
213 Woodbine St (27260-8339)
PHONE................................336 434-2716
Kathy Stuart, *Brnch Mgr*
EMP: 5
SALES (corp-wide): 147.64MM **Privately
Held**
Web: www.hpenews.com
SIC: **2711** Newspapers, publishing and
printing
HQ: The High Point Enterprise Llc
213 Woodbine St
High Point NC 27260
336 888-3500

(G-6650)
HIGH POINT ENTERPRISE INC
Also Called: Region 3 Tasc Services
712 W Lexington Ave (27262-2583)
PHONE................................336 883-2839
EMP: 13
SALES (corp-wide): 147.64MM **Privately
Held**
Web: www.hpenews.com
SIC: **2711** Newspapers, publishing and
printing
HQ: The High Point Enterprise Llc
213 Woodbine St
High Point NC 27260
336 888-3500

(G-6651)
HIGH POINT ENTERPRISE LLC (HQ)
Also Called: High Point Enterprise, Inc.
213 Woodbine St (27260-8339)
P.O. Box 1009 (27261-1009)
PHONE................................336 888-3500
Fred Paxton, *Pr*
David Paxton, *
Nick Maheras, *
John Mcclure, *Dir*

Nancy Baker, *
EMP: 160 **EST:** 1884
SALES (est): 4.78MM
SALES (corp-wide): 147.64MM **Privately
Held**
Web: www.hpenews.com
SIC: **2711** Commercial printing and
newspaper publishing combined
PA: Paxton Media Group, Llc
100 Television Ln
Paducah KY 42003
270 575-8630

(G-6652)
HIGH POINT FIBERS INC
601 Old Thomasville Rd (27260-8432)
PHONE................................336 887-8771
John Hailey, *Pr*
Ronny Odell, *
Robert Hampton, *
▼ **EMP:** 30 **EST:** 1998
SQ FT: 31,496
SALES (est): 3.47MM **Privately Held**
Web: www.highpointfibers.com
SIC: **2299** Padding and wadding, textile

(G-6653)
HIGH POINT FURNITURE INDS INC
(PA)
Also Called: Hpfi
1104 Bedford St (27263-1604)
P.O. Box 2063 (27261-2063)
PHONE................................336 431-7101
Spencer O'meara, *CEO*
Harry Samet, *
Jerry Samet, *
Joan Samet, *
Jon Goskolka, *
▲ **EMP:** 92 **EST:** 1958
SQ FT: 180,000
SALES (est): 7.61MM
SALES (corp-wide): 7.61MM **Privately
Held**
Web: www.hpfi.com
SIC: **2521** Chairs, office: padded,
upholstered, or plain: wood

(G-6654)
HIGH POINT PHARMACEUTICALS
LLC
4170 Mendenhall Oaks Pkwy (27265-8345)
PHONE................................336 841-0300
Stephen L Holcombe, *Pr*
EMP: 12 **EST:** 2009
SALES (est): 200.75K **Privately Held**
Web: www.highpointctc.com
SIC: **2834** Pharmaceutical preparations

(G-6655)
HIGH POINT QUILTING INC
1601 Blandwood Dr (27260-8302)
P.O. Box 311 (27370-0311)
PHONE................................336 861-4180
Gary Weavil, *CEO*
Jerrine Mathis, *Sec*
▼ **EMP:** 14 **EST:** 1986
SQ FT: 125,000
SALES (est): 1.06MM **Privately Held**
Web: www.highpointquilting.com
SIC: **2395** Quilted fabrics or cloth

(G-6656)
HIGHTOWER GROUP LLC
211 Fraley Rd (27263-1711)
PHONE................................816 286-1051
Marty Peterson, *Managing Member*
Kristin Goodman, *Prin*
Casandra Sheyman, *Prin*
▲ **EMP:** 11 **EST:** 2006
SALES (est): 3.82MM **Privately Held**
Web: www.hightower.design

▲ = Import ▼ = Export
◆ = Import/Export

SIC: 2599 Factory furniture and fixtures

(G-6657)
HILL-PAK INC
5453 Lilly Flower Rd (27263-8002)
PHONE...............................336 431-3833
Walter J Hill, *Pr*
EMP: 7
SALES (corp-wide): 3.14MM **Privately Held**
SIC: 2679 Paper products, converted, nec
PA: Hill-Pak, Inc.
5825 Edgar Rd
High Point NC 27263
336 431-3833

(G-6658)
HOFFMAN PLASTI-FORM COMPANY
Also Called: Hoffman Plasti
5432 Edgar Rd (27263-8102)
PHONE...............................336 431-2934
Nancy Hoffman, *Pr*
EMP: 5 EST: 1972
SQ FT: 6,000
SALES (est): 550.4K **Privately Held**
SIC: 3089 Molding primary plastics

(G-6659)
HOLT GROUP INC (PA)
Also Called: Holt Group
4198 Eagle Hill Dr Ste 105 (27265-8330)
PHONE...............................336 668-2770
Mike Cirsculoo, *Pr*
EMP: 13 EST: 1975
SQ FT: 7,500
SALES (est): 5.29MM
SALES (corp-wide): 5.29MM **Privately Held**
Web: www.holtxp.com
SIC: 2541 Bar fixtures, wood

(G-6660)
HOME MERIDIAN GROUP LLC (HQ)
Also Called: Hmi USA
2485 Penny Rd (27265-8375)
PHONE...............................336 819-7200
EMP: 66 EST: 2016
SQ FT: 40,000
SALES (est): 9.75MM
SALES (corp-wide): 433.23MM **Publicly Held**
SIC: 2511 Wood household furniture
PA: Hooker Furnishings Corporation
440 Commonwealth Blvd E
Martinsville VA 24112
276 632-2133

(G-6661)
HOME MERIDIAN HOLDINGS INC
Also Called: Pulaski Furniture
2485 Penny Rd (27265-8375)
PHONE...............................336 887-1985
▲ EMP: 200
SIC: 2511 Wood household furniture

(G-6662)
HOOKER FURNISHINGS CORPORATION
Home Meridian International
2485 Penny Rd Fl 2 (27265-8375)
PHONE...............................336 819-7200
Lee Boone, *Pr*
EMP: 130
SALES (corp-wide): 433.23MM **Publicly Held**
Web: www.hookerfurnishings.com
SIC: 2511 Wood bedroom furniture
PA: Hooker Furnishings Corporation
440 Commonwealth Blvd E
Martinsville VA 24112
276 632-2133

(G-6663)
HOPE TREE PUBLISHING LLC
916 Big Creek Ct (27265-3173)
PHONE...............................336 858-5301
Paige Lyerly, *Prin*
EMP: 5 EST: 2016
SALES (est): 92.98K **Privately Held**
SIC: 2741 Miscellaneous publishing

(G-6664)
HUNTER FARMS
Also Called: Hunter Farms
1900 N Main St (27262-2132)
PHONE...............................336 822-2300
Dwight Moore, *VP*
Chester Marsh, *
EMP: 130 EST: 1917
SALES (est): 9.6MM
SALES (corp-wide): 150.04B **Publicly Held**
SIC: 2024 Dairy based frozen desserts
HQ: Harris Teeter, Llc
701 Crestdale Rd
Matthews NC 28105
704 844-3100

(G-6665)
I2E GROUP LLC
Also Called: NTI Systems
2108 S Elm St (27260-8811)
PHONE...............................336 884-2014
EMP: 6 EST: 2013
SALES (est): 1.35MM **Privately Held**
Web: www.innov2exec.com
SIC: 3571 3599 Computers, digital, analog or hybrid; Custom machinery

(G-6666)
IDENTITY CUSTOM SIGNAGE INC
324 Burton Ave (27262-8070)
PHONE...............................336 882-7446
Matt Craven, *Pr*
EMP: 7 EST: 2007
SALES (est): 742.51K **Privately Held**
Web: www.identitycustomsignage.com
SIC: 3993 Signs and advertising specialties

(G-6667)
IMAGE INNOVATION GROUP INC
Also Called: Image Innovation Group
3301 N Main St (27265-1918)
P.O. Box 6265 (27262-6265)
PHONE...............................336 883-6010
Ermon R Rush, *Pr*
EMP: 7 EST: 2005
SALES (est): 489.1K **Privately Held**
Web: www.imageinnovationgroup.com
SIC: 3993 Signs, not made in custom sign painting shops

(G-6668)
IMMUNOTEK BIO CENTERS LLC
1628 S Main St Ste 105 (27260-4498)
PHONE...............................336 781-4901
Frank Perrotto, *Mgr*
EMP: 30
SALES (corp-wide): 27MM **Privately Held**
Web: www.immunotek.com
SIC: 2836 Blood derivatives
PA: Immunotek Bio Centers, L.L.C.
1430 E Sthlake Blvd Ste 2
Southlake TX 76092
337 500-1175

(G-6669)
INDIANA MILLS & MANUFACTURING
Also Called: Immi Safeguard
200 Swathmore Ave (27263-1932)
PHONE...............................336 862-7519
Chad Blankenship, *Brnch Mgr*

EMP: 209
SALES (corp-wide): 241.71MM **Privately Held**
Web: www.imminet.com
SIC: 2531 Seats, automobile
PA: Indiana Mills & Manufacturing Inc
18881 Immi Way
Westfield IN 46074
317 896-9531

(G-6670)
INDUSTRIAL CONTAINER CORP
Also Called: ICC
107 Motsinger St (27260-8836)
PHONE...............................336 886-7031
Daniel Ross, *Pr*
Bernard Rosinsky, *Pr*
Daniel Ross, *VP*
Randy Chambers, *Genl Mgr*
EMP: 19 EST: 1965
SQ FT: 34,000
SALES (est): 2.36MM **Privately Held**
Web: www.iccpkg.com
SIC: 2653 Boxes, corrugated: made from purchased materials

(G-6671)
INDUSTRIAL CONTAINER INC
107 Motsinger St (27260-8836)
PHONE...............................336 882-1310
Bernie Rosinski, *Pr*
Ron Horny, *Genl Mgr*
Dan Roth, *VP*
EMP: 4 EST: 1970
SQ FT: 85,000
SALES (est): 352.62K **Privately Held**
SIC: 6512 2653 Commercial and industrial building operation; Corrugated and solid fiber boxes

(G-6672)
INNOSPEC ACTIVE CHEMICALS LLC (HQ)
Also Called: Innospec
510 W Grimes Ave (27260)
PHONE...............................336 882-3308
Patrick Williams, *Managing Member*
Ian Clemison, *
David E Williams, *
▲ EMP: 83 EST: 2001
SQ FT: 86,000
SALES (est): 102.92MM
SALES (corp-wide): 1.85B **Publicly Held**
SIC: 2869 Industrial organic chemicals, nec
PA: Innospec Inc.
8310 S Valley Hwy Ste 350
Englewood CO 80112
303 792-5554

(G-6673)
INTENSA INC
1810 S Elm St (27260-8703)
P.O. Box 5981 (27262-5981)
PHONE...............................336 884-4096
Marty Cagle, *Pr*
Dwan Richardson, *VP*
William Gurney, *Sec*
EMP: 20 EST: 2002
SQ FT: 40,000
SALES (est): 762.64K
SALES (corp-wide): 42.78MM **Privately Held**
Web: www.intensa.net
SIC: 3821 Laboratory apparatus and furniture
PA: Gf Health Products, Inc.
1 Graham Field Way
Atlanta GA 30340
770 368-4700

(G-6674)
INTENSA INC
1810 S Elm St (27260-8703)
P.O. Box 5981 (27262-5981)
PHONE...............................336 884-4003
Dwan Richardson, *Pr*
▲ EMP: 6 EST: 1998
SQ FT: 40,000
SALES (est): 244.24K **Privately Held**
Web: www.intensa.net
SIC: 2512 2522 Upholstered household furniture; Office furniture, except wood

(G-6675)
INTERIOR WOOD SPECIALTIES INC
Also Called: I W S
1130 Bedford St (27263-1604)
PHONE...............................336 431-0068
Huig Zuiderent, *Pr*
EMP: 35 EST: 1984
SQ FT: 40,000
SALES (est): 6.04MM **Privately Held**
Web: www.interiorwoodspecialties.com
SIC: 2531 School furniture

(G-6676)
JACK CARTWRIGHT INCORPORATED
2014 Chestnut Street Ext (27262-7160)
P.O. Box 2798 (27261-2798)
PHONE...............................336 889-9400
Brian Murray, *Pr*
Steve Bannister, *
▲ EMP: 50 EST: 1963
SQ FT: 100,000
SALES (est): 4.05MM
SALES (corp-wide): 57.7MM **Privately Held**
Web: www.jackcartwright.com
SIC: 2512 Chairs: upholstered on wood frames
HQ: Boss Design Limited
Boss Drive
Dudley W MIDLANDS DY2 8
138 445-5570

(G-6677)
JAMES G GOUGE
Also Called: International Minute Press
1001 Phillips Ave (27262-7252)
P.O. Box 18424 (27419-8424)
PHONE...............................336 854-1551
Jim Gouge, *Owner*
EMP: 6 EST: 2002
SALES (est): 403.97K **Privately Held**
Web: www.greensboroimp.com
SIC: 2752 Offset printing

(G-6678)
JESSICA CHARLES LLC
535 Townsend Ave (27263-2047)
P.O. Box 3444 (28603-3444)
PHONE...............................336 434-2124
▲ EMP: 80
Web: www.jessicacharles.com
SIC: 2512 Chairs: upholstered on wood frames

(G-6679)
JONES FRAME INC
5456 Uwharrie Rd (27263-4165)
P.O. Box 153 (27370-0153)
PHONE...............................336 434-2531
Molly Jones, *CEO*
Rick Hartley, *
Carolee Hartley, *
EMP: 30 EST: 1978
SQ FT: 60,000
SALES (est): 2.26MM **Privately Held**

G E O G R A P H I C

SIC: **2511** 2426 2515 Bed frames, except water bed frames: wood; Hardwood dimension and flooring mills; Mattresses and bedsprings

(G-6680)
K & S TOOL & MANUFACTURING CO
1247 Elon Pl (27263-9745)
P.O. Box 2037 (27282-2037)
PHONE..............................336 410-7260
Kenneth Hughes, *Pr*
EMP: 19
SALES (corp-wide): 14.46MM **Privately Held**
Web: www.ks-tool.com
SIC: **3599** Machine shop, jobbing and repair
PA: K & S Tool & Manufacturing Company
614 Hendrix St
High Point NC 27260
336 410-7260

(G-6681)
K & S TOOL & MANUFACTURING CO (PA)
614 Hendrix St (27260-4306)
P.O. Box 2037 (27282-2037)
PHONE..............................336 410-7260
Kenneth Hughes, *Pr*
Joe Hughes, *
Sally Hughes, *
◆ **EMP:** 50 **EST:** 1974
SQ FT: 80,000
SALES (est): 14.46MM
SALES (corp-wide): 14.46MM **Privately Held**
Web: www.ks-tool.com
SIC: **3469** 3441 Stamping metal for the trade ; Fabricated structural metal

(G-6682)
KAMP USA INC
Also Called: Keya USA
2321 E Martin Luther King Jr Dr (27260-6287)
PHONE..............................336 668-1169
Abdul Khaleque Pathan, *Prin*
Bill Van Dolan, *VP Mktg*
Greg Brown, *Sr VP*
Chris Douglass, *Dir Fin*
Rose Timmons, *Contrlr*
◆ **EMP:** 10 **EST:** 2009
SQ FT: 60,000
SALES (est): 302.67K **Privately Held**
Web: www.keyagroupbd.com
SIC: **2253** T-shirts and tops, knit

(G-6683)
KAO SPECIALTIES AMERICAS LLC (HQ)
Also Called: KSA
243 Woodbine St (27260-8339)
P.O. Box 2316 (27261-2316)
PHONE..............................336 884-2214
Yasuo Monoe, *Pr*
Terry Singleton, *
Gerald Sykes, *
Hisanori Hagi, *
Shinichiro Suda, *
◆ **EMP:** 160 **EST:** 1999
SQ FT: 3,049,200
SALES (est): 104.24MM **Privately Held**
Web: chemical.kao.com
SIC: **2869** Industrial organic chemicals, nec
PA: Kao Corporation
1-14-10, Nihombashikayabacho
Chuo-Ku TKY 103-0

(G-6684)
KENMAR INC
2531 Willard Dairy Rd (27265-8117)
PHONE..............................336 884-8722

Jimmy Clegg, *Pr*
Marion Shoemaker, *VP*
EMP: 15 **EST:** 1963
SQ FT: 1,100
SALES (est): 2.35MM **Privately Held**
Web: www.kenmarprecision.com
SIC: **3569** 3545 Firefighting apparatus; Precision tools, machinists'

(G-6685)
KING HICKORY FURNITURE COMPANY
Also Called: Showroom
2016 W Green Dr (27260-8709)
P.O. Box 1179 (28603-1179)
PHONE..............................336 841-6140
Bob Palmer, *Brnch Mgr*
EMP: 8
SALES (corp-wide): 9.7MM **Privately Held**
Web: www.kinghickory.com
SIC: **2512** Upholstered household furniture
PA: King Hickory Furniture Company
1820 Main Ave Se
Hickory NC 28602
828 322-6025

(G-6686)
KREBER
Also Called: Kreber Enterprises
221 Swathmore Ave (27263-1931)
PHONE..............................336 861-2700
EMP: 61 **EST:** 1967
SQ FT: 249,600
SALES (est): 2.77MM
SALES (corp-wide): 19.37MM **Privately Held**
Web: www.kreber.com
SIC: **7336** 2752 2789 7335 Graphic arts and related design; Color lithography; Swatches and samples; Color separation, photographic and movie film
PA: Kreber Graphics, Inc.
2580 Westbelt Dr
Columbus OH 43228
614 529-5701

(G-6687)
KRUEGER INTERNATIONAL INC
217 Feld Ave (27263-1929)
PHONE..............................336 434-5011
Kenneth Neves, *Brnch Mgr*
EMP: 15
SALES (corp-wide): 484.48MM **Privately Held**
Web: www.ki.com
SIC: **2531** School furniture
PA: Krueger International, Inc.
1330 Bellevue St
Green Bay WI 54302
920 468-8100

(G-6688)
LA BARGE INC
1925 Eastchester Dr (27265-1404)
PHONE..............................336 812-2400
EMP: 6 **EST:** 2018
SALES (est): 464.61K **Privately Held**
Web: www.labargeinc.com
SIC: **2426** Frames for upholstered furniture, wood

(G-6689)
LACQUER CRAFT HOSPITALITY INC (DH)
Also Called: Samson Marketing
2575 Penny Rd (27265-8334)
PHONE..............................336 822-8086
Noel Chitwood, *CEO*
Bennie Corbett, *Sec*
◆ **EMP:** 105 **EST:** 2010
SALES (est): 13.63MM **Privately Held**

Web: lacquercraft.great-site.net
SIC: **2511** Wood household furniture
HQ: Samson Investment Holding Co.
2575 Penny Rd
High Point NC 27265

(G-6690)
LEGGETT & PLATT INCORPORATED
Also Called: High Point Spring 1506
1629 Blandwood Dr (27260-8302)
P.O. Box 7327 (27264-7327)
PHONE..............................336 884-4306
Gerald Rigney, *Brnch Mgr*
EMP: 68
SALES (corp-wide): 5.15B **Publicly Held**
Web: www.leggett.com
SIC: **2515** Mattresses and bedsprings
PA: Leggett & Platt, Incorporated
1 Leggett Rd
Carthage MO 64836
417 358-8131

(G-6691)
LEGGETT & PLATT INCORPORATED
Also Called: High Point Furniture 0n64
1430 Sherman Ct (27260-8200)
P.O. Box 7107 (27264-7107)
PHONE..............................336 889-2600
Murray Catton, *Brnch Mgr*
EMP: 115
SQ FT: 213,652
SALES (corp-wide): 5.15B **Publicly Held**
Web: www.leggett.com
SIC: **2515** Mattresses and bedsprings
PA: Leggett & Platt, Incorporated
1 Leggett Rd
Carthage MO 64836
417 358-8131

(G-6692)
LEGGETT & PLATT INCORPORATED
Leggett & Platt 0n64
1430 Sherman Ct (27260-8200)
PHONE..............................336 889-2600
Murray Catton, *Mgr*
EMP: 57
SALES (corp-wide): 5.15B **Publicly Held**
Web: www.leggett.com
SIC: **3495** 3496 Furniture springs, unassembled; Miscellaneous fabricated wire products
PA: Leggett & Platt, Incorporated
1 Leggett Rd
Carthage MO 64836
417 358-8131

(G-6693)
LLOYDS CHATHAM LTD PARTNERSHIP
511 Dorado Dr (27265-8670)
PHONE..............................919 742-4692
James Lloyd, *Genl Pt*
▲ **EMP:** 28 **EST:** 1996
SALES (est): 1.23MM **Privately Held**
SIC: **2512** Upholstered household furniture

(G-6694)
MAC PANEL COMPANY LLC (PA)
Also Called: Mac Panel
551 W Fairfield Rd (27263-1741)
P.O. Box 7728 (27264-7728)
PHONE..............................336 861-3100
Joseph L Craycroft Junior, *Ch*
Tom Craycroft, *
Anthony Sedberry, *
▲ **EMP:** 44 **EST:** 1987
SQ FT: 60,000
SALES (est): 10.57MM
SALES (corp-wide): 10.57MM **Privately Held**
Web: www.macpanel.com

SIC: **3823** 3672 Computer interface equipment, for industrial process control; Circuit boards, television and radio printed

(G-6695)
MACHINEX
716 Gallimore Dairy Rd (27265-9176)
PHONE..............................336 665-5030
Pierre Stare, *Pr*
EMP: 6 **EST:** 2012
SALES (est): 601.24K **Privately Held**
Web: www.machinexrecycling.com
SIC: **3599** 5084 Machine shop, jobbing and repair; Industrial machinery and equipment

(G-6696)
MACHINEX TECHNOLOGIES INC
716 Gallimore Dairy Rd (27265-9176)
PHONE..............................773 867-8801
Nicolas Belanger, *Pr*
Pierre Pare, *VP*
Paul Fortier, *VP*
EMP: 10 **EST:** 1996
SALES (est): 3.27MM **Privately Held**
Web: www.machinexrecycling.com
SIC: **5084** 3535 Conveyor systems; Conveyors and conveying equipment

(G-6697)
MANNINGTON MILLS INC
Mannington Wood Floors Company
210 N Pendleton St (27260-5800)
PHONE..............................336 884-5600
Douglas Brown, *VP*
EMP: 26
SALES (corp-wide): 686.34MM **Privately Held**
Web: www.mannington.com
SIC: **2426** 2435 Flooring, hardwood; Veneer stock, hardwood
PA: Mannington Mills Inc.
75 Mannington Mills Rd
Salem NJ 08079
800 356-6787

(G-6698)
MARINE TOOLING TECHNOLOGY INC
2100 E Martin Luther King Jr Dr Ste 106 (27260-5834)
P.O. Box 2564 (27261-2564)
PHONE..............................336 887-9577
William D Burris, *Pr*
Regina Burris, *Sec*
EMP: 4 **EST:** 1999
SALES (est): 675.31K **Privately Held**
Web: www.marinetooling.com
SIC: **3429** 3732 Marine hardware; Boats, fiberglass: building and repairing

(G-6699)
MARLOWE-VAN LOAN CORPORATION
Also Called: Marlowe Loans Sales
1224 W Ward Ave (27260-1534)
P.O. Box 1851 (27261-1851)
PHONE..............................336 886-7126
Paul Tharp, *Pr*
EMP: 8 **EST:** 1933
SQ FT: 55,000
SALES (est): 1.42MM **Privately Held**
Web: marlowevanloan.lookchem.com
SIC: **2869** 2865 2819 Industrial organic chemicals, nec; Cyclic crudes and intermediates; Industrial inorganic chemicals, nec

(G-6700)
MARLOWE-VAN LOAN SALES CO
Also Called: Hickory Color & Chemical Co

1224 W Ward Ave (27260-1534)
P.O. Box 1851 (27261-1851)
PHONE..................................336 882-3351
Donald W Van Loan, *Pt*
Kathleen Poag Minchak, *Pt*
EMP: 4 **EST:** 1933
SQ FT: 15,000
SALES (est): 146.38K **Privately Held**
Web: www.marlowevanloan.lookchem.com
SIC: 5169 2899 Chemicals, industrial and heavy; Chemical preparations, nec

(G-6701)
MARQUIS CONTRACT CORPORATION (PA)
Also Called: Marquis Seating
231 South Rd (27262-8152)
P.O. Box 2208 (27261-2208)
PHONE..................................336 884-8200
Gary M Lindenberg, *Pr*
Jana M Lindenberg, *Sec*
▲ **EMP:** 38 **EST:** 1992
SALES (est): 9.99MM **Privately Held**
Web: www.marquisseating.com
SIC: 2512 Upholstered household furniture

(G-6702)
MARSH FURNITURE COMPANY
Also Called: Marsh Kitchens of High Point
1015 S Centennial St (27260-7850)
P.O. Box 870 (27261-0870)
PHONE..................................336 884-7393
Steve Schadt, *Brnch Mgr*
EMP: 10
SALES (corp-wide): 43.69MM **Privately Held**
Web: www.marshfurniture.com
SIC: 2434 Wood kitchen cabinets
PA: Marsh Furniture Company
1001 S Centennial St
High Point NC 27260
336 884-7363

(G-6703)
MARSH FURNITURE COMPANY (PA)
Also Called: Marsh Kitchens
1001 S Centennial St (27260-8126)
P.O. Box 870 (27261-0870)
PHONE..................................336 884-7363
▲ **EMP:** 484 **EST:** 1906
SALES (est): 43.69MM
SALES (corp-wide): 43.69MM **Privately Held**
Web: www.marshfurniture.com
SIC: 2434 5712 2421 Wood kitchen cabinets ; Cabinets, except custom made: kitchen; Lumber: rough, sawed, or planed

(G-6704)
MARSH-ARMFIELD INCORPORATED
1237 Hickory Chapel Rd (27260-7189)
P.O. Box 1407 (27261-1407)
PHONE..................................336 882-4175
Ben Armfield, *Pr*
Sharee Mcarthur, *Sec*
Bonnie Black, *Off Mgr*
EMP: 15 **EST:** 1945
SQ FT: 75,000
SALES (est): 1.14MM **Privately Held**
Web: www.marsharmfield.com
SIC: 2672 Adhesive backed films, foams and foils

(G-6705)
MARTIES MINIATURES
392 Northbridge Dr (27265-3061)
PHONE..................................336 869-5952
Martha Tyler, *Prin*
EMP: 5 **EST:** 2010
SALES (est): 73K **Privately Held**
SIC: 3999 Miniatures

(G-6706)
MASTER DISPLAYS INC
Also Called: Design Master Displays
5657 Prospect St (27263-3967)
PHONE..................................336 884-5575
◆ **EMP:** 90 **EST:** 1984
SALES (est): 8.72MM **Privately Held**
Web: www.masterdisplays.com
SIC: 2542 Office and store showcases and display fixtures

(G-6707)
MATCHEM INC
1115 Clinton Ave (27260-1581)
P.O. Box 808 (27261-0808)
PHONE..................................336 886-5000
Thomas Mattocks, *Pr*
Rebecca Mattocks, *VP*
EMP: 4 **EST:** 1983
SQ FT: 2,500
SALES (est): 67.76K **Privately Held**
SIC: 2899 Water treating compounds

(G-6708)
MAXIM LABEL PACKG HIGH PT INC (PA)
506 Townsend Ave (27263-2046)
PHONE..................................336 861-1666
Roy J Johnston, *Pr*
Sam Chororos, *VP*
▲ **EMP:** 19 **EST:** 1985
SQ FT: 31,000
SALES (est): 9.55MM
SALES (corp-wide): 9.55MM **Privately Held**
Web: www.jcmfg.com
SIC: 2672 2759 2752 Labels (unprinted), gummed: made from purchased materials; Commercial printing, nec; Commercial printing, lithographic

(G-6709)
METAL WORKS HIGH POINT INC
918 W Kivett Dr (27262-6814)
P.O. Box 2002 (27261-2002)
PHONE..................................336 886-4612
J Campbell Hall Iii, *Pr*
Margaret Ann Hall, *
EMP: 56 **EST:** 1969
SQ FT: 39,000
SALES (est): 12.28MM **Privately Held**
Web: www.metalworkshp.com
SIC: 3499 3469 Aerosol valves, metal; Metal stampings, nec

(G-6710)
MICKEY TRUCK BODIES INC
1425 Bethel Dr (27260-8307)
PHONE..................................336 882-6806
EMP: 4
SALES (corp-wide): 488.43K **Privately Held**
Web: www.mickeybody.com
SIC: 3713 Truck and bus bodies
PA: Mickey Truck Bodies Inc.
1305 Trinity Ave
High Point NC 27261
336 882-6806

(G-6711)
MICKEY TRUCK BODIES INC (PA)
1305 Trinity Ave (27261)
P.O. Box 2044 (27261)
PHONE..................................336 882-6806
Matt Sink, *CEO*
Tom Arland, *
Carl F Mickey Junior, *Ex VP*
Kent Lapp, *
Carolyn Sink, *
▼ **EMP:** 275 **EST:** 1904
SQ FT: 108,000

SALES (est): 488.43K
SALES (corp-wide): 488.43K **Privately Held**
Web: www.mickeybody.com
SIC: 3713 7532 3711 3715 Beverage truck bodies; Body shop, trucks; Motor vehicles and car bodies; Truck trailers

(G-6712)
MICROTRONIC US LLC
401 Dorado Dr (27265-8669)
PHONE..................................336 869-0429
EMP: 8 **EST:** 2010
SALES (est): 181.72K **Privately Held**
Web: www.microtronicus.com
SIC: 5932 3581 Used merchandise stores; Automatic vending machines

(G-6713)
MLG TRNSCNDENT TRCKG TRNSP SVC
3495 Hickswood Forest Dr (27265-7925)
PHONE..................................336 905-1192
Melvin Green Li, *CEO*
EMP: 6 **EST:** 2019
SALES (est): 692.35K **Privately Held**
SIC: 3537 Trucks: freight, baggage, etc.: industrial, except mining

(G-6714)
MORBERN LLC
401 Fraley Rd (27263-1715)
PHONE..................................336 883-4332
EMP: 16 **EST:** 2019
SALES (est): 2.54MM **Privately Held**
Web: www.morbern.com
SIC: 2824 Vinyl fibers

(G-6715)
MORBERN USA INC (HQ)
401 Fraley Rd (27263-1715)
P.O. Box 7404 (27264-7404)
PHONE..................................336 883-4332
David Bloomfield, *CEO*
Mark Bloomfield, *
Tom Mccuddy, *VP*
Richard Fox, *
Mike Leap, *
▲ **EMP:** 25 **EST:** 1995
SQ FT: 42,000
SALES (est): 11.18MM
SALES (corp-wide): 94.6MM **Privately Held**
Web: www.morbern.com
SIC: 2295 5131 Buckram: varnished, waxed, and impregnated; Coated fabrics
PA: Morbern Inc
80 Boundary Rd
Cornwall ON
613 932-8811

(G-6716)
MOTORSPORTS DESIGNS INC
300 Old Thomasville Rd (27260-8189)
PHONE..................................336 454-1181
John Mc Kenzie, *CEO*
Mark Sexton, *
EMP: 10 **EST:** 1982
SQ FT: 13,172
SALES (est): 838.67K **Privately Held**
SIC: 2759 3993 2752 2396 Screen printing; Signs and advertising specialties; Commercial printing, lithographic; Automotive and apparel trimmings

(G-6717)
NEIL ALLEN INDUSTRIES INC
2101 E Martin Luther King Jr Dr (27260-5819)
PHONE..................................336 887-6500
Neil Aberman, *Pr*

Debbi Aberman, *Sec*
EMP: 8 **EST:** 1986
SQ FT: 30,000
SALES (est): 985.39K **Privately Held**
Web: www.neilallenindustries.com
SIC: 2599 5712 Hotel furniture; Furniture stores

(G-6718)
NEWELL BRANDS INC
4110 Premier Dr (27265-8343)
PHONE..................................336 812-8181
Jeff Heoler, *Brnch Mgr*
EMP: 18
SALES (corp-wide): 7.58B **Publicly Held**
Web: www.newellbrands.com
SIC: 2591 Window blinds
PA: Newell Brands Inc
6655 Pachtree Dunwoody Rd
Atlanta GA 30328
770 418-7000

(G-6719)
OAKHURST COMPANY INC (PA)
Also Called: Clayton & Co
2016 Van Buren St # 101 (27260-1564)
P.O. Box 433 (27261-0433)
PHONE..................................336 474-4600
Walter J Haarsgaard, *Pr*
Margaret Haarsgaard, *Sec*
▲ **EMP:** 9 **EST:** 1991
SALES (est): 1.12MM **Privately Held**
Web: www.claytoncolamps.com
SIC: 3645 Residential lighting fixtures

(G-6720)
OBX BOATWORKS LLC
2100 E Martin Luther King Jr Dr Ste 121 (27260-5834)
P.O. Box 5181 (27262-5181)
PHONE..................................336 878-9490
EMP: 6 **EST:** 2009
SALES (est): 744.72K **Privately Held**
Web: www.obx-boatworks.com
SIC: 3732 Boatbuilding and repairing

(G-6721)
OPTICS INC (PA)
1105 N Lindsay St Side Side (27262-3935)
PHONE..................................336 884-5677
Harry Allen, *Pr*
EMP: 5 **EST:** 1947
SQ FT: 2,120
SALES (est): 672.45K
SALES (corp-wide): 672.45K **Privately Held**
Web: www.optics-eyewear.com
SIC: 3827 8042 Optical instruments and lenses; Offices and clinics of optometrists

(G-6722)
OTTO AND MOORE INC
Also Called: Otto & Moore Furn Designers
701 Eastchester Dr (27262-7637)
P.O. Box 5627 (27262-5627)
PHONE..................................336 887-0017
William Dudley Moore, *CEO*
William Dudley Moore Junior, *Pr*
EMP: 12 **EST:** 1960
SQ FT: 2,700
SALES (est): 1.3MM **Privately Held**
Web: www.furniturelibrary.com
SIC: 2519 7641 Lawn and garden furniture, except wood and metal; Furniture repair and maintenance

(G-6723)
PACKAGE CRAFTERS INCORPORATED
1040 E Springfield Rd (27263-2158)
P.O. Box 2563 (27261-2563)

PHONE....................336 431-9700
Gary Brewer, *Pr*
Wayne Brewer, *
EMP: 51 EST: 2003
SQ FT: 72,500
SALES (est): 11.99MM **Privately Held**
Web: www.packagecrafters.com
SIC: 2653 Boxes, corrugated: made from
purchased materials

(G-6724)
PAG ASB LLC
Also Called: Acme Sample Books
2410 Schirra Pl (27263-1730)
PHONE....................336 883-4187
EMP: 6 EST: 2019
SALES (est): 2.74MM **Privately Held**
SIC: 3999 Manufacturing industries, nec

(G-6725)
PARAGON GLOBAL LLC
2415 W English Rd (27262-8057)
PHONE....................336 899-8525
Kellena Daigle, *Pr*
EMP: 7 EST: 2007
SALES (est): 331.16K **Privately Held**
Web: www.paragonglobaltextiles.com
SIC: 2211 Chenilles, tufted textile

(G-6726)
PARAGON ID HIGH POINT US INC
Also Called: EDM Technology Inc.
210 Old Thomasville Rd (27260)
PHONE....................336 882-8115
John Rogers, *CEO*
EMP: 23 EST: 2021
SALES (est): 8.56MM
SALES (corp-wide): 308.16K **Privately Held**
Web: www.paragon-id.com
SIC: 2752 2759 Business form and card
printing, lithographic; Tickets: printing, nsk
HQ: Paragon Id
Les Aubepins
Argent-Sur-Sauldre CVL 18410

(G-6727)
PATHEON PHARMACEUTICALS INC
4125 Premier Dr (27265-8144)
PHONE....................866 728-4366
Michelle Stinson, *Brnch Mgr*
EMP: 1930
SALES (corp-wide): 42.86B **Publicly Held**
Web: www.patheon.jp
SIC: 2834 Pharmaceutical preparations
HQ: Patheon Pharmaceuticals Inc.
3900 Paramount Pkwy
Morrisville NC 27560
919 226-3200

(G-6728)
PATHEON SOFTGELS INC (DH)
4125 Premier Dr (27265-8144)
PHONE....................336 812-8700
Michelle Stinson, *Genl Mgr*
◆ EMP: 47 EST: 1971
SQ FT: 21,920
SALES (est): 19.7MM
SALES (corp-wide): 42.86B **Publicly Held**
Web: www.patheon.com
SIC: 2834 Vitamin preparations
HQ: Patheon U.S. Holdings Inc.
4815 Emperor Blvd Ste 110
Durham NC 27703

(G-6729)
PAULS WATER TREATMENT LLC
1224 W Ward Ave (27260-1534)
P.O. Box 567 (27261-0567)
PHONE....................336 886-5600
Paul Thaurp, *Owner*

▲ EMP: 8 EST: 2003
SALES (est): 1.75MM **Privately Held**
SIC: 3589 Water treatment equipment,
industrial

(G-6730)
PHOENIX HOME FURNISHINGS INC
2485 Penny Rd (27265-8375)
◆ EMP: 113
Web: www.hookerfurnishings.com
SIC: 2511 Wood household furniture

(G-6731)
PIEDMONT CHEMICAL INDS I LLC
331 Burton Ave (27261)
P.O. Box 2728 (27261)
PHONE....................336 885-5131
Fred Wilson Junior, *Managing Member*
Ray Soyars, *
▼ EMP: 68 EST: 1996
SALES (est): 3.41MM
SALES (corp-wide): 92.45MM **Privately Held**
Web: www.piedmontchemical.com
SIC: 2869 Industrial organic chemicals, nec
PA: Syntha Group, Inc.
331 Burton Ave
High Point NC 27262
336 885-5131

(G-6732)
PIEDMONT PACKAGING INC (PA)
1141 Foust Ave (27260-8706)
P.O. Box 7025 (27264-7025)
PHONE....................336 886-5043
Edward L Lee, *Pr*
EMP: 16 EST: 1973
SQ FT: 50,000
SALES (est): 4.68MM
SALES (corp-wide): 4.68MM **Privately Held**
Web: www.ppihp.com
SIC: 2653 Boxes, corrugated: made from
purchased materials

(G-6733)
PILOT VIEW WOOD WORKS INC
Also Called: Pilot View Wood Works
412 Berkley St (27260-8458)
PHONE....................336 883-2511
Rickie Garner, *Pr*
Nolan S Garner, *
Norma Smith, *
Brent Garner, *
Pauline B Garner, *
EMP: 4 EST: 1960
SQ FT: 6,800
SALES (est): 370.22K **Privately Held**
SIC: 2426 Furniture stock and parts,
hardwood

(G-6734)
PIONEER SQUARE BRANDS INC (PA)
Also Called: Brenthaven
1515 W Green Dr (27260-1657)
PHONE....................360 733-5608
Michael Ferren, *CEO*
EMP: 5 EST: 2017
SALES (est): 4.96MM
SALES (corp-wide): 4.96MM **Privately Held**
SIC: 3172 Card cases

(G-6735)
PLAN NINE PUBLISHING INC
1237 Elon Pl (27263-9745)
PHONE....................336 454-7766
David Allen, *Pr*
EMP: 5 EST: 1996
SALES (est): 60.14K **Privately Held**

Web: www.plan9publishing.com
SIC: 2731 Books, publishing only

(G-6736)
PLATAINE INC
319 Ardmore Cir (27262-3001)
PHONE....................336 883-7657
Norman Bolick, *Brnch Mgr*
EMP: 5
Web: www.plataine.com
SIC: 7372 Application computer software
PA: Plataine, Inc.
168 Main St
Goshen NY 10924

(G-6737)
PLUSH COMFORTS
508 Ashe St (27262-4628)
PHONE....................336 882-9185
Jonathan Connor, *Prin*
EMP: 4 EST: 2006
SALES (est): 122.69K **Privately Held**
SIC: 2221 Plushes, manmade fiber and silk

(G-6738)
PNB MANUFACTURING
2315 E Martin Luther King Jr Dr Ste A
(27260-6292)
PHONE....................336 883-0021
Tonya C Stratton, *Pr*
EMP: 6 EST: 2014
SALES (est): 210.71K **Privately Held**
SIC: 3999 Manufacturing industries, nec

(G-6739)
POLY PACKAGING SYSTEMS INC
2150 Brevard Rd (27263-1704)
P.O. Box 4506 (27263-4506)
PHONE....................336 889-8334
▼ EMP: 80
SIC: 2621 2671 3086 5199 Towels, tissues
and napkins; paper and stock; Paper;
coated and laminated packaging; Plastics
foam products; Packaging materials

(G-6740)
PRECISION DESIGN MACHINERY
Also Called: ADI/PDM Trade Group
1509 Bethel Dr (27260-8348)
PHONE....................336 889-8157
Chad Butler, *Pr*
Joseph White, *VP*
EMP: 7 EST: 1998
SALES (est): 2.41MM **Privately Held**
Web: www.arcdoyle.com
SIC: 3599 Machine shop, jobbing and repair

(G-6741)
PRECISION FABRICATION INC
2000 Nuggett Rd (27263-2009)
PHONE....................336 885-6091
Allen Henkel, *Pr*
Leann Henkel, *VP*
EMP: 11 EST: 1993
SQ FT: 15,720
SALES (est): 2.05MM **Privately Held**
Web: www.precisionfabricationinc.com
SIC: 3441 Fabricated structural metal

(G-6742)
PRECISION TEXTILES LLC
Also Called: Precision Textiles
5522 Uwharrie Rd (27263-4166)
PHONE....................336 861-0168
EMP: 105
SALES (corp-wide): 48.14MM **Privately Held**
Web: www.precisiontextiles-usa.com
SIC: 2295 Coated fabrics, not rubberized
PA: Precision Textiles Llc

90 New Dutch Ln
Fairfield NJ 07004
973 890-3873

(G-6743)
PREFERRED DATA CORPORATION
1208 Eastchester Dr (27265-3170)
P.O. Box 16102 (27261-6103)
PHONE....................336 886-3282
Wade Wellborn, *Pr*
EMP: 5 EST: 1987
SALES (est): 799.63K **Privately Held**
Web: www.pdcsoftware.com
SIC: 5734 7371 7372 Computer peripheral
equipment; Custom computer programming
services; Prepackaged software

(G-6744)
PREVOST CAR (US) INC
1951 Eastchester Dr Unit E (27265-2477)
PHONE....................336 812-3504
Dann Wiltgen, *Brnch Mgr*
EMP: 15
SALES (corp-wide): 52.58B **Privately Held**
Web: www.prevostcar.com
SIC: 3711 Motor vehicles and car bodies
HQ: Prevost Car (Us) Inc.
7817 National Service Rd
Greensboro NC 27409
908 222-7211

(G-6745)
PRICELY INC
7210 Suits Rd (27263-4019)
P.O. Box 7626 (27264-7626)
PHONE....................336 431-2055
Fredrick Price, *Pr*
Rebecca Ly, *
EMP: 30 EST: 1993
SQ FT: 30,000
SALES (est): 2.46MM **Privately Held**
Web: www.uwharriechair.com
SIC: 2511 Wood lawn and garden furniture

(G-6746)
PRIME MILL LLC
Also Called: Sparta Plastics
1946 W Green Dr (27260-1666)
PHONE....................336 819-4300
EMP: 15 EST: 2007
SQ FT: 3,000
SALES (est): 509.2K **Privately Held**
Web: www.primemill.com
SIC: 3089 5021 Thermoformed finished
plastics products, nec; Furniture

(G-6747)
PRODUCTION SYSTEMS INC
1500 Trinity Ave (27260-8362)
P.O. Box 5373 (27262-5373)
PHONE....................336 886-7161
William A Ball, *Pr*
Brian T Ball, *
Alice F Ball, *
William A Ball Junior, *Stockholder*
Alyssa Ball, *Stockholder**
▲ EMP: 37 EST: 1973
SQ FT: 25,000
SALES (est): 6.34MM **Privately Held**
Web: www.productionsystems-usa.com
SIC: 3444 3563 3567 3535 Booths, spray:
prefabricated sheet metal; Spraying and
dusting equipment; Paint baking and drying
ovens; Conveyors and conveying equipment

(G-6748)
PROFESSINAL SALES ASSOCIATES
2783 Nc Highway 68 S Ste 116
(27265-8324)
PHONE....................336 210-2756
Greg Phillips, *Pr*

EMP: 4 EST: 2007
SALES (est): 83.01K Privately Held
SIC: 2521 5021 Wood office furniture; Office furniture, nec

(G-6749)
PROFORMA HANSON BRANDING
4257 Wallburg High Point Rd (27265-7619)
PHONE..............................210 437-3061
Sonya L Hanson, *Prin*
EMP: 4 EST: 2008
SALES (est): 241.04K Privately Held
Web:
proformahansonbranding.proforma.com
SIC: 2759 Commercial printing, nec

(G-6750)
QUALITY PACKAGING CORP (PA)
255 Swathmore Ave (27263-1931)
PHONE..............................336 881-5300
Jerry Hill, *CEO*
Dewey Hill, *Pr*
Joey Hill, *VP*
Tommy Hill, *Sec*
EMP: 7 EST: 1977
SALES (est): 27.17MM
SALES (corp-wide): 27.17MM Privately Held
Web: www.qualitypackagingcorp.com
SIC: 2679 2671 Corrugated paper: made from purchased material; Paper; coated and laminated packaging

(G-6751)
QUALITY SAW SHOP INC
1208 Elon Pl (27263-9745)
PHONE..............................336 882-1722
Tony Taylor, *Pr*
Jeremy Taylor, *Sec*
EMP: 5 EST: 1955
SQ FT: 2,500
SALES (est): 126.28K Privately Held
Web: www.qualitysawandtool.com
SIC: 3425 Saw blades and handsaws

(G-6752)
RALPH LAUREN CORPORATION
4190 Eagle Hill Dr (27265-8237)
P.O. Box 35868 (27425-5868)
PHONE..............................336 632-5000
George Cloppin, *VP*
EMP: 4
SALES (corp-wide): 6.63B Publicly Held
Web: www.ralphlauren.com
SIC: 5651 2329 Family clothing stores; Athletic clothing, except uniforms: men's, youths' and boys'
PA: Ralph Lauren Corporation
650 Madison Ave
New York NY 10022
212 318-7000

(G-6753)
RALPH S FRAME WORKS INC
2231 Shore St (27263-2511)
P.O. Box 7192 (27264-7192)
PHONE..............................336 431-2168
Ralph Thomas Rice Junior, *Pr*
Lennis Ashe, *
EMP: 100 EST: 1950
SQ FT: 60,000
SALES (est): 3.79MM Privately Held
Web: www.ralphsframe.com
SIC: 2511 Wood household furniture

(G-6754)
RBC INC
Also Called: Ashley Interiors
310 S Elm St (27260-6617)
PHONE..............................336 889-7573
Bob Holt, *Mgr*

EMP: 5
SALES (corp-wide): 23.83MM Privately Held
SIC: 2512 Upholstered household furniture
PA: Rbc, Inc.
7310 Us Highway 311
Sophia NC 27350
336 861-5800

(G-6755)
RELENTLESS WLDG & FABRICATION
903 Londonderry Dr (27265-2792)
PHONE..............................336 402-3749
EMP: 4 EST: 2018
SALES (est): 48.86K Privately Held
Web: www.mandmweldingnc.com
SIC: 7692 Welding repair

(G-6756)
RELIABLE QUILTING COMPANY
414 South Rd (27262-8155)
PHONE..............................336 886-7036
Robert Parris, *Pr*
EMP: 7 EST: 2016
SALES (est): 92.33K Privately Held
SIC: 2515 Mattresses and bedsprings

(G-6757)
RIFLED AIR CONDITIONING INC
2810 Earlham Pl (27263-1949)
PHONE..............................800 627-1707
Bradley J Matthews, *Pr*
Glenn J Matthews, *
EMP: 35 EST: 1997
SQ FT: 55,000
SALES (est): 4.58MM Privately Held
Web: www.rifledair.com
SIC: 3585 Air conditioning units, complete: domestic or industrial

(G-6758)
RITCH FACE VENEER COMPANY
1330 Lincoln Dr (27260-1515)
P.O. Box 1837 (27261-1837)
PHONE..............................336 883-4184
John Michael Ritch, *Pr*
Donna Ritch, *
EMP: 8 EST: 1941
SQ FT: 45,000
SALES (est): 2.13MM Privately Held
Web: www.ritchfaceveneer.com
SIC: 2435 2426 Veneer stock, hardwood; Hardwood dimension and flooring mills

(G-6759)
ROADSAFE TRAFFIC SYSTEMS INC
913 Finch Ave (27263-1623)
PHONE..............................919 772-9401
Rick Dean, *Brnch Mgr*
EMP: 5
Web: www.roadsafetraffic.com
SIC: 3531 Construction machinery
PA: Roadsafe Traffic Systems, Inc.
8750 W Bryn Mawr Ave Ste
Chicago IL 60631

(G-6760)
ROUTER BIT SERVICE COMPANY INC
7018 Tomball Rd (27263-9754)
PHONE..............................336 431-5535
Buren Scott Andrews, *Pr*
EMP: 11 EST: 1972
SQ FT: 2,000
SALES (est): 1.91MM Privately Held
Web: www.routerbitservice.com
SIC: 3553 7699 Saws, power: bench and table, except portable: woodworking; Knife, saw and tool sharpening and repair

(G-6761)
ROWLAND WOODWORKING INC
111 E Market Center Dr (27260-7865)
P.O. Box 1510 (27261-1510)
PHONE..............................336 887-0700
Jeffrey S Cox, *Pr*
Marion Rowland Junior, *VP*
Kristine M Cox, *
EMP: 25 EST: 1992
SQ FT: 20,000
SALES (est): 9.68MM Privately Held
Web: www.rowlandwoodworking.com
SIC: 2541 2431 Cabinets, except refrigerated: show, display, etc.: wood; Millwork

(G-6762)
ROYALL DEVELOPMENT CO INC
325 Kettering Rd (27263-1719)
P.O. Box 519 (38879-0519)
PHONE..............................336 889-2569
Mickey James, *Pr*
Joseph Lanham, *
EMP: 215 EST: 1990
SALES (est): 9.51MM Privately Held
SIC: 3443 Metal parts

(G-6763)
SAMPLETECH INC
2101 W Green Dr (27260-8710)
PHONE..............................336 882-1717
Eric Doss, *Pr*
▲ EMP: 10 EST: 1997
SALES (est): 279.17K Privately Held
SIC: 2789 Swatches and samples

(G-6764)
SEALED AIR CORPORATION
Also Called: Jiffy Division
2150 Brevard Rd (27263-1704)
P.O. Box 2083 (27261-2083)
PHONE..............................336 883-9184
Roger Jackson, *Brnch Mgr*
EMP: 55
SQ FT: 2,500
SALES (corp-wide): 5.39B Publicly Held
Web: www.sealedair.com
SIC: 3086 Packaging and shipping materials, foamed plastics
PA: Sealed Air Corporation
2415 Cascade Pointe Blvd
Charlotte NC 28208
980 221-3235

(G-6765)
SEAM-CRAFT INC
702 Prospect St (27260-8230)
P.O. Box 7045 (27264-7045)
PHONE..............................336 861-4156
Greg Parlier, *Pr*
EMP: 7 EST: 1972
SALES (est): 581.21K Privately Held
SIC: 2512 Upholstered household furniture

(G-6766)
SEAM-CRAFT INC
1501 Potts Ave (27260-1558)
PHONE..............................336 861-4156
Giles H Parlier, *Pr*
Greg G Parlier, *VP*
▲ EMP: 12 EST: 1972
SQ FT: 54,000
SALES (est): 289.87K Privately Held
Web: www.carolinacushion.com
SIC: 2512 Upholstered household furniture

(G-6767)
SELECT FURNITURE COMPANY INC
408 South Rd (27262-8155)
P.O. Box 817 (27261-0817)

PHONE..............................336 886-3572
Lloyd Graves, *Pr*
EMP: 17 EST: 1981
SQ FT: 20,000
SALES (est): 733.32K Privately Held
Web: www.selectfurniturecompany.com
SIC: 2512 Living room furniture: upholstered on wood frames

(G-6768)
SHERRILL FURNITURE COMPANY
Also Called: Precedent Furniture
301 Steele St Ste 4 (27260-5100)
P.O. Box 189 (28603-0189)
PHONE..............................336 884-0974
Buddy Sherrill, *Mgr*
EMP: 14
SALES (corp-wide): 49.81MM Privately Held
Web: www.sherrillfurniture.com
SIC: 2512 Upholstered household furniture
PA: Sherrill Furniture Company Inc
2405 Highland Ave Ne
Hickory NC 28601
828 322-2640

(G-6769)
SIDES FURNITURE INC
Also Called: Sides Custom Furniture
1812 Homeytown Rd (27265-9279)
PHONE..............................336 869-5509
Judy Sides, *Pr*
EMP: 7 EST: 1981
SQ FT: 796
SALES (est): 80.49K Privately Held
SIC: 2512 5712 Upholstered household furniture; Furniture stores

(G-6770)
SIGMA PLASTICS GROUP
Also Called: Southern Film Extruders
2319 W English Rd (27262-8055)
PHONE..............................336 885-8091
EMP: 32 EST: 2014
SALES (est): 6.5MM Privately Held
Web: www.sigmaplasticsgroup.com
SIC: 3089 Injection molding of plastics

(G-6771)
SIGN MINE INC
2211 Eastchester Dr (27265-1456)
PHONE..............................336 884-5780
Michael Hague, *Pr*
Mary Hague, *VP*
EMP: 4 EST: 2004
SALES (est): 200.64K Privately Held
Web: www.signmineinc.com
SIC: 3993 Signs, not made in custom sign painting shops

(G-6772)
SIGN TECHNOLOGY INC
311 Berkley St (27260-8103)
P.O. Box 866 (30549-0866)
PHONE..............................336 887-3211
Lonnie Poole, *Pr*
Debra Poole, *VP*
EMP: 5 EST: 1989
SQ FT: 5,000
SALES (est): 410.63K Privately Held
SIC: 3993 Signs and advertising specialties

(G-6773)
SIGNATURE SIGNS INC
211 Berkley St (27260-8101)
PHONE..............................336 431-2072
Jeffrey A Curtis, *Pr*
Julie A Curtis, *Sec*
Matt Craven, *VP*
EMP: 7 EST: 1988
SQ FT: 15,000

GEOGRAPHIC

SALES (est): 977.44K **Privately Held**
Web: www.signaturesignage.com
SIC: 3993 5046 5099 Electric signs; Neon
signs; Signs, except electric

(G-6774)
SILICONES INC
211 Woodbine St (27260)
P.O. Box 363 (27261)
PHONE..........................336 886-5018
Gerald Swanson, *Pr*
Richie Ashburn, *VP*
▲ **EMP:** 17 **EST:** 1974
SQ FT: 72,000
SALES (est): 5.85MM **Privately Held**
Web: www.silicones-inc.com
SIC: 2869 Industrial organic chemicals, nec

(G-6775)
SIMPLICITY SOFAS INC
414 Grayson St (27260-7302)
PHONE..........................800 813-2889
Jeff Frank, *Pr*
Ann Sankevitsch, *VP*
EMP: 4 **EST:** 2018
SALES (est): 191.49K **Privately Held**
Web: www.simplicitysofas.com
SIC: 2512 5021 5714 Upholstered
household furniture; Furniture; Drapery and
upholstery stores

(G-6776)
**SIMPSON STRONG-TIE COMPANY
INC**
4485 Premier Dr Ste 101 (27265-8389)
PHONE..........................336 841-1338
EMP: 8
SALES (corp-wide): 2.23B **Publicly Held**
Web: www.strongtie.com
SIC: 3449 Joists, fabricated bar
HQ: Simpson Strong-Tie Company Inc.
5956 W Las Positos Blvd
Pleasanton CA 94588
925 560-9000

(G-6777)
SINGSA
2401 Penny Rd (27265-8162)
PHONE..........................336 882-9160
Singha Srikumfun, *Owner*
EMP: 4 **EST:** 2010
SALES (est): 178.22K **Privately Held**
SIC: 3421 Table and food cutlery, including
butchers'

(G-6778)
SKEEN DECORATIVE FABRICS INC
1220 W Market Center Dr (27260-8236)
P.O. Box 329 (27370-0329)
PHONE..........................336 884-4044
Brian M Skeen, *Pr*
Karmen Skeen, *Dir*
EMP: 7 **EST:** 2015
SALES (est): 1.2MM **Privately Held**
SIC: 2211 Broadwoven fabric mills, cotton

(G-6779)
SKEEN TEXTILES INC
1900 S Elm St (27260-8807)
P.O. Box 2283 (27261-2283)
PHONE..........................336 884-4044
◆ **EMP:** 11
Web: www.skeentextiles.com
SIC: 2299 Fabrics: linen, jute, hemp, ramie

(G-6780)
SKEEN TXTILES AUTO FABRICS INC
1900 S Elm St (27260-8807)
PHONE..........................336 884-4044
Stephen Skeen, *Prin*

EMP: 7 **EST:** 2015
SALES (est): 777.04K **Privately Held**
SIC: 2299 Fabrics: linen, jute, hemp, ramie

(G-6781)
SLANE HOSIERY MILLS INC
313 S Centennial St (27260-6753)
P.O. Box 2486 (27261-2486)
PHONE..........................336 883-4136
Jim Cobb, *CEO*
Gloria White, *
◆ **EMP:** 219 **EST:** 1915
SQ FT: 180,000
SALES (est): 10.86MM **Privately Held**
Web: www.slanehosiery.com
SIC: 2251 2252 Women's hosiery, except
socks; Men's, boys', and girls' hosiery

(G-6782)
SNYDER PAPER CORPORATION
Also Called: Chushion Division
1104 W Ward Ave (27260-1533)
PHONE..........................336 884-1172
Robert Dutnell, *Mgr*
EMP: 30
SALES (corp-wide): 41.68MM **Privately
Held**
Web: www.snydersolutions.com
SIC: 2392 Cushions and pillows
PA: Snyder Paper Corporation
250 26th Street Dr Se
Hickory NC 28602
828 328-2501

(G-6783)
SOLACE HEALTHCARE FURN LLC
815 W Ward Ave (27260-1526)
PHONE..........................336 884-0046
Geovanny Brown, *Managing Member*
EMP: 12 **EST:** 2018
SALES (est): 1.07MM **Privately Held**
Web: www.hcfbysolace.com
SIC: 2599 Furniture and fixtures, nec

(G-6784)
SOLID FRAMES INC
Also Called: Hale's Sample Shop
501 Garrison St (27260-7042)
PHONE..........................336 882-5082
Jerry Walker, *Pr*
EMP: 7 **EST:** 1988
SQ FT: 12,000
SALES (est): 232.42K **Privately Held**
SIC: 2426 Frames for upholstered furniture,
wood

(G-6785)
SONY MUSIC HOLDINGS INC
921 Eastchester Dr (27262-7646)
PHONE..........................336 886-1807
John Cannon, *Pr*
EMP: 8
Web: www.sonymusic.com
SIC: 3652 5099 Prerecorded records and
tapes; Phonograph records
HQ: Sony Music Holdings Inc.
25 Madison Ave Fl 26
New York NY 10010
212 833-8000

(G-6786)
SOUTHANDENGLISH LLC
1314 Starr Dr (27260-8204)
PHONE..........................336 888-8333
David Ebbetts, *CEO*
David Ebbetts, *Managing Member*
Palmer Smith, *Managing Member*
Kathy Wilson, *Opers Mgr*
EMP: 4 **EST:** 2019
SALES (est): 126.46K **Privately Held**
Web: www.southandenglish.com

SIC: 2512 5021 Upholstered household
furniture; Household furniture

(G-6787)
SOUTHERN ENGRAVING COMPANY
3008 Windchase Ct (27265-3015)
PHONE..........................336 656-0084
G Jordan Clapp Junior, *Pr*
Carole W Clapp, *Sec*
Charles K Williams, *VP*
EMP: 5 **EST:** 1921
SALES (est): 79.33K **Privately Held**
Web: www.southernengraving.com
SIC: 2759 Invitation and stationery printing
and engraving

(G-6788)
SOUTHERN FILM EXTRUDERS INC
2319 W English Rd (27262-8055)
P.O. Box 2104 (27261-2104)
PHONE..........................336 885-8091
EMP: 145
SIC: 3081 Polyethylene film

(G-6789)
SOUTHFIELD LTD
Also Called: Southfield Upholstered Furn
2224 Shore St (27260-2512)
P.O. Box 2064 (27261-2064)
PHONE..........................336 434-6220
Mike Gulledge, *Pr*
EMP: 12 **EST:** 1997
SQ FT: 100,000
SALES (est): 5.35MM **Privately Held**
Web: www.southfieldfurniture.net
SIC: 2512 Wood upholstered chairs and
couches

(G-6790)
SPECIALTY NAILS COMPANY
5050 Prospect St (27263-3961)
P.O. Box 1213 (27261-1213)
PHONE..........................336 883-0135
Guy E Carr Junior, *Owner*
EMP: 6 **EST:** 1981
SQ FT: 22,000
SALES (est): 490.58K **Privately Held**
SIC: 3315 Nails, steel: wire or cut

(G-6791)
**STANLEY FURNITURE COMPANY
LLC**
200 N Hamilton St No 200 (27260-5032)
PHONE..........................336 884-7700
Richard Ledger, *CEO*
EMP: 101 **EST:** 2017
SALES (est): 2.99MM **Privately Held**
SIC: 2511 Wood household furniture

(G-6792)
STEPHEN J MCCUSKER
1705 Heathgate Pt (27262-7462)
PHONE..........................336 884-1916
Stephen Mccusker, *Owner*
EMP: 7 **EST:** 1979
SALES (est): 62.74K **Privately Held**
SIC: 2741 Technical manual and paper
publishing

(G-6793)
STERI-AIR LLC
2109 Brevard Rd (27263-1703)
PHONE..........................336 434-1166
EMP: 4
SALES (est): 118.6K **Privately Held**
SIC: 3999 Manufacturing industries, nec

(G-6794)
STONE RESOURCE INC
2101 E Martin Luther King Jr Dr
(27260-5819)
PHONE..........................336 889-7800
Neil Aberman, *Pr*
◆ **EMP:** 30 **EST:** 1989
SQ FT: 30,000
SALES (est): 3.94MM **Privately Held**
Web: www.thestoneresource.com
SIC: 3281 Furniture, cut stone

(G-6795)
SUN FABRICATORS INC
701 W Ward Ave (27260-1645)
P.O. Box 2898 (27361-2898)
PHONE..........................336 885-0095
Betty Easley, *Pr*
EMP: 40 **EST:** 1997
SQ FT: 57,000
SALES (est): 2.21MM **Privately Held**
Web: www.sunfabricators.com
SIC: 3069 Latex, foamed

(G-6796)
SUNBELT ABRASIVES INC
1507 Bethel Dr (27260-8348)
PHONE..........................336 882-6837
Betty Goodman, *VP*
EMP: 6 **EST:** 1984
SQ FT: 10,000
SALES (est): 313.42K **Privately Held**
Web: www.sunbeltabrasives.com
SIC: 3291 Abrasive products

(G-6797)
SWAIM INC (PA)
Also Called: Classics
1801 S University Pkwy (27260-7854)
P.O. Box 4189 (27263-4189)
PHONE..........................336 885-6131
Richard A Swaim, *Pr*
Glenn E Swaim Junior, *Ch Bd*
Andy Swaim, *
Rhonda S Warren, *
Zachary A Swaim, *
◆ **EMP:** 185 **EST:** 1945
SQ FT: 178,587
SALES (est): 10.03MM
SALES (corp-wide): 10.03MM **Privately
Held**
Web: www.swaim-inc.com
SIC: 2514 2512 Tables, household: metal;
Living room furniture: upholstered on wood
frames

(G-6798)
SWATCHCRAFT LLC
516 Townsend Ave (27263)
PHONE..........................336 434-5095
Lynda Forken, *CFO*
EMP: 6 **EST:** 2022
SALES (est): 552.05K **Privately Held**
Web: www.swatchcraft.com
SIC: 2752 Commercial printing, lithographic

(G-6799)
SWEET ROOM LLC
4435 Garden Club St (27265-1196)
PHONE..........................336 567-1620
EMP: 4 **EST:** 2015
SALES (est): 249.5K **Privately Held**
SIC: 5813 2051 5812 5632 Bars and lounges
; Cakes, bakery: except frozen; Caterers;
Apparel accessories

(G-6800)
SYNTEC INC
200 Swathmore Ave (27263-1932)
PHONE..........................336 861-9023

▲ = Import ▼ = Export
◆ = Import/Export

◆ **EMP:** 78
SIC: 2531 8742 Seats, miscellaneous public conveyances; Marketing consulting services

(G-6801)
SYNTHA GROUP INC (PA)
331 Burton Ave (27262-8071)
P.O. Box 2728 (27261-2728)
PHONE................................336 885-5131
Fred Wilson Junior, *Pr*
Fred Wilson Iii, *VP*
Bill Goodman, *
Lloyd Roghelia, *
Ray Soyars, *
◆ **EMP:** 100 **EST:** 1958
SQ FT: 500,000
SALES (est): 92.45MM
SALES (corp-wide): 92.45MM **Privately Held**
Web: www.piedmontchemical.com
SIC: 2841 2843 Textile soap; Surface active agents

(G-6802)
TASMAN INDUSTRIES INC
1011 Porter St Ste 103 (27263-1637)
PHONE................................502 587-0701
EMP: 19
SALES (corp-wide): 22.97MM **Privately Held**
Web: www.tasmanusa.com
SIC: 3111 Accessory products, leather
PA: Tasman Industries, Inc.
930 Geiger St
Louisville KY 40206
502 785-7477

(G-6803)
TAYLOR COMMUNICATIONS INC
4189 Eagle Hill Dr Ste 101 (27265-8315)
PHONE................................336 841-7700
Eric Brown, *Mgr*
EMP: 13
SALES (corp-wide): 3.81B **Privately Held**
Web: www.taylor.com
SIC: 2761 Manifold business forms
HQ: Taylor Communications, Inc.
1725 Roe Crest Dr
North Mankato MN 56003
866 541-0937

(G-6804)
TEMPO PRODUCTS LLC
2130 Brevard Rd (27263-1704)
P.O. Box 2005 (27261-2005)
PHONE................................336 434-8649
Martha Kennedy Romer, *Managing Member*
▲ **EMP:** 22 **EST:** 2004
SQ FT: 20,000
SALES (est): 2.44MM **Privately Held**
Web: www.tempohomeproducts.com
SIC: 2392 Pillows, bed: made from purchased materials

(G-6805)
THAYER COGGIN INC
Also Called: Thayer Coggin
230 South Rd (27262-8153)
PHONE................................336 841-6000
Royale Wiggin, *COO*
Doris Coggin, *
Clarence Coggin, *
◆ **EMP:** 55 **EST:** 1956
SQ FT: 200,000
SALES (est): 7.96MM **Privately Held**
Web: www.thayercoggin.com
SIC: 2511 Wood household furniture

(G-6806)
THERMO FISHER SCIENTIFIC INC
4125 Premier Dr (27265-8144)
PHONE................................800 955-6288
EMP: 4
SALES (corp-wide): 42.86B **Publicly Held**
Web: www.thermofisher.com
SIC: 3826 Analytical instruments
PA: Thermo Fisher Scientific Inc.
168 3rd Ave
Waltham MA 02451
781 622-1000

(G-6807)
THOMAS BUILT BUSES INC (DH)
Also Called: Thomas Buses
1408 Courtesy Rd (27260-7248)
P.O. Box 2450 (27261-2450)
PHONE................................336 889-4871
EMP: 1749 **EST:** 1916
SALES (est): 68.04MM
SALES (corp-wide): 60.75B **Privately Held**
Web: www.thomasbuiltbuses.com
SIC: 3713 3711 Bus bodies (motor vehicles); Chassis, motor vehicle
HQ: Daimler Truck North America Llc
4555 N Channel Ave
Portland OR 97217
503 745-8000

(G-6808)
THOMASVILLE-DEXEL INCORPORATED
Also Called: Td Fiber
420 Fraley Rd (27263-1716)
P.O. Box 2278 (27261-2278)
PHONE................................336 819-5550
Blair L Whitworth, *Pr*
Doris P Deal, *
EMP: 50 **EST:** 1925
SALES (est): 13.78MM **Privately Held**
Web: www.tdfiber.com
SIC: 2824 Organic fibers, noncellulosic

(G-6809)
TRANSARCTIC NORTH CAROLINA INC
Also Called: Transarctic
5270 Glenola Industrial Dr (27263-8152)
P.O. Box 98 (27361-0098)
PHONE................................336 861-6116
Michael Marlin, *Pr*
Dale Mason, *
James Stewart, *
EMP: 25 **EST:** 2002
SQ FT: 1,000
SALES (est): 2.3MM **Privately Held**
Web: www.transarctic.com
SIC: 3585 Air conditioning equipment, complete

(G-6810)
TRANSTECH PHARMA LLC (PA)
Also Called: Vtv Therapeutics
3980 Premier Dr Ste 310 (27265-8409)
PHONE................................336 841-0300
Stephen Holcombe, *Pr*
Stephen L Holcombe, *Pr*
EMP: 119 **EST:** 1999
SALES (est): 9.1MM
SALES (corp-wide): 9.1MM **Privately Held**
Web: www.ttpharma.com
SIC: 2834 Pharmaceutical preparations

(G-6811)
TRIANGLE CABINET COMPANY
809 Aberdeen Rd (27265-1306)
PHONE................................336 869-6401
Daniel Adams, *Owner*
EMP: 6 **EST:** 1980

SALES (est): 129.4K **Privately Held**
SIC: 2434 Wood kitchen cabinets

(G-6812)
TRIUNE BUSINESS FURNITURE INC
1101 Roberts Ln (27260-7196)
P.O. Box 1270 (27261-1270)
PHONE................................336 884-8341
Charles Baker, *Pr*
Charley Stephens, *VP*
EMP: 8 **EST:** 1993
SQ FT: 10,000
SALES (est): 444.13K **Privately Held**
Web: www.triuneseating.com
SIC: 2521 Wood office furniture

(G-6813)
TRUE PORTION INC
Also Called: Millennium Landscaping
5220 High Point Rd (27265-1146)
PHONE................................336 362-6326
Richard V Knowles, *Pr*
Brenda S Knowles, *Treas*
EMP: 14 **EST:** 1992
SQ FT: 5,500
SALES (est): 733.45K **Privately Held**
SIC: 3596 5046 Weighing machines and apparatus; Scales, except laboratory

(G-6814)
TUBS-USA LLC
322 Fraley Rd (27263-1714)
PHONE................................336 884-5737
Hp Mccoy, *Managing Member*
EMP: 12 **EST:** 2022
SALES (est): 2.34MM **Privately Held**
SIC: 3431 Shower stalls, metal

(G-6815)
TWE NONWOVENS US INC (HQ)
Also Called: Vita Nonwovens
2215 Shore St (27263-2511)
PHONE................................336 431-7187
Kevin Womble, *Pr*
Dave Kame, *
Jason Johnson, *
◆ **EMP:** 25 **EST:** 2012
SQ FT: 339,000
SALES (est): 93.97MM
SALES (corp-wide): 395.26MM **Privately Held**
Web: www.twenonwovensus.com
SIC: 2297 Nonwoven fabrics
PA: Twe Group Gmbh
Hollefeldstr. 46
Emsdetten NW 48282
25722050

(G-6816)
ULLMANIQUE INC
323 Old Thomasville Rd (27260-8190)
P.O. Box 1636 (27261-1636)
PHONE................................336 885-5111
Thomas L Ullman, *Pr*
William L Ullman, *VP*
Carol M Young, *Sec*
EMP: 8 **EST:** 1992
SQ FT: 7,000
SALES (est): 446.09K **Privately Held**
SIC: 2521 Tables, office: wood

(G-6817)
ULTRA COATINGS INCORPORATED
3509 Jamac Rd (27260-7179)
P.O. Box 57 (27261-0057)
PHONE................................336 883-8853
Floyd Zeno Moore, *Pr*
Michael Moore, *
Bonnie Moore, *
EMP: 12 **EST:** 1964
SQ FT: 40,000

SALES (est): 2.45MM **Privately Held**
Web: www.ultracoatings.com
SIC: 3479 2816 Painting of metal products; Inorganic pigments

(G-6818)
UNITED FINISHERS INTL INC
1950 W Green Dr (27260-1666)
P.O. Box 5462 (27262-5462)
PHONE................................336 883-3901
Juan C Hernandez, *Pr*
Carlos Hernandez, *VP*
Robert D Gross, *Treas*
▲ **EMP:** 8 **EST:** 1993
SALES (est): 2.4MM **Privately Held**
Web: www.unitedfinishers.com
SIC: 5031 2431 2426 Kitchen cabinets; Millwork; Hardwood dimension and flooring mills

(G-6819)
UNIVERSAL FURNITURE LIMITED (PA)
Also Called: Universal Bedroom Furniture
2575 Penny Rd (27265-8334)
PHONE................................336 822-8888
Ronald J Hoffman, *Pr*
Larry Lilan, *Sr VP*
Tom Lyons, *CTRL*
Catherine T Mcgee, *VP*
Peggy R Cook, *Sec*
◆ **EMP:** 70 **EST:** 1973
SQ FT: 150,000
SALES (est): 13.07MM
SALES (corp-wide): 13.07MM **Privately Held**
Web: www.universalfurniture.com
SIC: 2511 2512 Dining room furniture: wood; Couches, sofas, and davenports: upholstered on wood frames

(G-6820)
UWHARRIE CHAIR COMPANY LLC
5873 Parker St (27263-8502)
PHONE................................336 431-2055
Erica Lloyd, *Managing Member*
EMP: 6 **EST:** 2015
SALES (est): 798.98K **Privately Held**
Web: www.uwharriechair.com
SIC: 2511 Wood household furniture

(G-6821)
V AND E COMPONENTS INC (PA)
720 W Fairfield Rd (27263-1746)
P.O. Box 7352 (27264-7352)
PHONE................................336 884-0088
Bill Vest, *Pr*
Woody Vest, *Sec*
Karen Hamilton, *VP*
▲ **EMP:** 17 **EST:** 1976
SQ FT: 50,000
SALES (est): 3.03MM
SALES (corp-wide): 3.03MM **Privately Held**
SIC: 3089 Injection molding of plastics

(G-6822)
VAUGHAN-BASSETT FURN CO INC
210 E Commerce Ave (27260-6686)
PHONE................................336 889-9111
Candace Hicks, *Mgr*
EMP: 504
SALES (corp-wide): 37.86MM **Privately Held**
Web: www.vaughanbassett.com
SIC: 2511 Wood household furniture
PA: Vaughan-Bassett Furniture Company, Incorporated
300 E Grayson St
Galax VA 24333
276 236-6161

(G-6823)
VAULT LLC
Also Called: Vault Enclosures
1515 W Green Dr (27260-1657)
PHONE..............................336 698-3796
EMP: 13 EST: 2013
SQ FT: 40,000
SALES (est): 4.96MM
SALES (corp-wide): 4.96MM **Privately Held**
Web: www.byvault.com
SIC: 3089 Plastics containers, except foam
PA: Pioneer Square Brands, Inc.
1515 W Green Dr
High Point NC 27260
360 733-5608

(G-6824)
VERELLEN INC
5297 Prospect St (27263-3963)
P.O. Box 1018 (27261-1018)
PHONE..............................336 889-7379
Tom Verellen, *Prin*
◆ EMP: 49 EST: 2007
SALES (est): 9.29MM **Privately Held**
Web: www.verellen.biz
SIC: 5712 2512 Furniture stores; Chairs: upholstered on wood frames

(G-6825)
VERENA DESIGNS INC (PA)
812 W Green Dr (27260-7336)
P.O. Box 869 (27261-0869)
PHONE..............................336 869-8235
Verena Houghtaling, *Pr*
EMP: 25 EST: 1990
SQ FT: 11,000
SALES (est): 821.69K
SALES (corp-wide): 821.69K **Privately Held**
Web: www.verenadesigns.com
SIC: 2254 2341 Shorts, shirts, slips, and panties (underwear): knit; Women's and children's underwear

(G-6826)
VIOLINO USA LTD
123 S Hamilton St (27260-5230)
PHONE..............................336 889-6623
EMP: 20 EST: 2015
SALES (est): 987.21K **Privately Held**
Web: www.violino.us
SIC: 2512 Living room furniture: upholstered on wood frames

(G-6827)
VISION CONTRACT MFG LLC
1327 Lincoln Dr (27260-1514)
PHONE..............................336 405-8784
Chris Morris, *Prin*
Woon Lee, *
EMP: 30 EST: 2021
SALES (est): 4.77MM **Privately Held**
Web: www.visioncontractmfg.com
SIC: 3999 Manufacturing industries, nec

(G-6828)
VISUAL PRODUCTS INC
1019 Porter St (27263-1637)
PHONE..............................336 883-0156
TOLL FREE: 800
Gail Wright, *Pr*
Sylvia J Breed, *Sec*
Marsha Talton, *VP*
Angela Osborne, *VP*
EMP: 12 EST: 1967
SQ FT: 20,000
SALES (est): 851.46K **Privately Held**
Web: www.visualproductsinc.com
SIC: 2782 Blankbooks and looseleaf binders

(G-6829)
VRUSH INDUSTRIES INC
Also Called: Rushfurniture.com
118 N Wrenn St (27260-5020)
PHONE..............................336 886-7700
Vicky L Rush, *Pr*
Mike Rush, *Ex VP*
◆ EMP: 5 EST: 2009
SALES (est): 344K **Privately Held**
Web: www.vrushinc.com
SIC: 5045 5021 7379 3469 Computer peripheral equipment; Furniture; Computer related consulting services; Furniture components, porcelain enameled

(G-6830)
VTV THERAPEUTICS LLC
3980 Premier Dr Ste 310 (27265-8409)
PHONE..............................336 841-0300
EMP: 7 EST: 2015
SALES (est): 384.77K **Publicly Held**
Web: www.vtvtherapeutics.com
SIC: 2834 Pharmaceutical preparations
PA: Vtv Therapeutics Inc.
3980 Premier Dr Ste 310
High Point NC 27265
336 841-0300

(G-6831)
W V DOYLE ENTERPRISES INC
Also Called: Doyle Enterprises
1816 Belmar St (27260-8401)
PHONE..............................336 885-2035
Randy Doyle, *Pr*
Roger Doyle, *VP*
Walter Doyle Junior, *Treas*
Carolyn Doyle Cobler, *Sec*
EMP: 8 EST: 1981
SQ FT: 56,000
SALES (est): 237.43K **Privately Held**
SIC: 3554 Box making machines, paper

(G-6832)
WARRIOR BOATS
2100 E Martin Luther King Jr Dr (27260-5834)
PHONE..............................336 885-2628
Brian Kilgariff, *Owner*
EMP: 4 EST: 1992
SALES (est): 111.99K **Privately Held**
Web: www.thewarriorboat.com
SIC: 3732 Boatbuilding and repairing

(G-6833)
WEBER AND WEBER INC
Also Called: Sir Speedy
117 W Lexington Ave (27262-2531)
PHONE..............................336 889-6322
Dwight Shaw, *Genl Mgr*
EMP: 8
SALES (corp-wide): 4.56MM **Privately Held**
Web: www.sirspeedy.com
SIC: 2752 Offset printing
PA: Weber And Weber, Inc.
1011 Burke St
Winston Salem NC 27101
336 722-4109

(G-6834)
WHITEWOOD CONTRACTS LLC
Also Called: Sedgewick Industries
667 W Ward Ave (27260-1644)
PHONE..............................336 885-9300
Kim Crossman, *Brnch Mgr*
EMP: 44
SALES (corp-wide): 20.02MM **Privately Held**
Web: www.customcontract.com
SIC: 2512 2389 Chairs: upholstered on wood frames; Hospital gowns

HQ: Whitewood Contracts, Llc
100 Liberty Dr
Thomasville NC 27360
336 882-8565

(G-6835)
WILLOW CREEK FURNITURE INC
1949 W Green Dr (27260-1686)
PHONE..............................336 889-0076
Steve Shumate, *Pr*
EMP: 5 EST: 1989
SQ FT: 12,000
SALES (est): 143.19K **Privately Held**
Web: www.willowcreekfurniture.com
SIC: 2511 Wood household furniture

(G-6836)
WINTER BELL COMPANY (PA)
2018 Brevard Rd (27261-1702)
P.O. Box 48 (27261-0048)
PHONE..............................336 887-2651
Richard Lewis, *Pr*
Gurney L Stroud Ii, *VP*
Glenda Kemp, *Sec*
▼ EMP: 5 EST: 1960
SQ FT: 70,000
SALES (est): 4.82MM
SALES (corp-wide): 4.82MM **Privately Held**
Web: www.winterbell.com
SIC: 2679 Paper products, converted, nec

(G-6837)
WISE LIVING INC (PA)
216 Woodbine St (27260-8340)
PHONE..............................323 541-0410
Jose A Pinedo, *CEO*
EMP: 16 EST: 2009
SALES (est): 4.54MM
SALES (corp-wide): 4.54MM **Privately Held**
Web: www.wiselivinginc.com
SIC: 2519 Household furniture, except wood or metal: upholstered

(G-6838)
WISE LIVING INC
Also Called: Living Wise
216 Woodbine St (27260-8340)
PHONE..............................336 991-5346
EMP: 19
SALES (corp-wide): 4.54MM **Privately Held**
Web: www.wiselivinginc.com
SIC: 2512 2511 Wood upholstered chairs and couches; Wood household furniture
PA: Wise Living, Inc.
216 Woodbine St
High Point NC 27260
323 541-0410

(G-6839)
WOODMARK ORIGINALS INC
1920 Jarrell St (27260-8812)
PHONE..............................336 841-6409
Dan Masters, *Prin*
▲ EMP: 105 EST: 1964
SQ FT: 90,000
SALES (est): 254.45K
SALES (corp-wide): 1.21MM **Privately Held**
SIC: 2512 Upholstered household furniture
PA: Howard Miller Company
860 E Main Ave
Zeeland MI 49464
616 772-9131

(G-6840)
WOOLFOAM CORPORATION
Also Called: Wool Novelty
107 Whittier Ave (27262-8042)

PHONE..............................336 886-4964
Bernard Lodzyski, *Brnch Mgr*
EMP: 6
SQ FT: 25,000
SALES (corp-wide): 4.61MM **Privately Held**
SIC: 3552 Loopers, textile machinery
HQ: The Woolfoam Corporation
3000 Hmpstead Tpk Ste 302
Levittown NY
516 731-5380

(G-6841)
YORKSHIRE HOUSE INC
1904 Alleghany St (27263-2028)
P.O. Box 5872 (27262-5872)
PHONE..............................336 869-9714
Michael Beaver, *Pr*
Thomas J Beaver, *CEO*
▲ EMP: 5 EST: 1990
SQ FT: 1,100
SALES (est): 255.93K **Privately Held**
Web: www.modernhistoryhome.com
SIC: 2511 Wood household furniture

Highlands
Macon County

(G-6842)
ALLAN DRTH SONS GNRTOR SLS SVC
Also Called: Allan Dearth and Sons
11259 Buck Creek Rd (28741-8918)
P.O. Box 2768 (28741-2768)
PHONE..............................828 526-9325
Allan Dearth, *Pr*
Margaret Dearth, *VP*
Bryan Dearth, *Sec*
EMP: 4 EST: 2007
SALES (est): 2.47MM **Privately Held**
Web: www.adsemergencypower.com
SIC: 3621 7629 Motors and generators; Generator repair

(G-6843)
BLACK ROCK GRANITE & CABINETRY
2543 Cashiers Rd (28741-0089)
PHONE..............................828 787-1100
Kevin J Bradle, *Prin*
EMP: 6 EST: 2010
SALES (est): 552.66K **Privately Held**
Web: www.blackrockgraniteandcabinetry.com
SIC: 2434 Wood kitchen cabinets

(G-6844)
CASHIERS PRINTING INC
Also Called: Cashiers Printing & Graphics
68 Highlands Walk (28741-8375)
P.O. Box 39 (28741-0039)
PHONE..............................828 787-1324
Russel Majors, *Pr*
EMP: 5 EST: 1983
SQ FT: 3,000
SALES (est): 470.24K **Privately Held**
Web: www.cashiersareachamber.com
SIC: 2752 Offset printing

(G-6845)
DIVINE SOUTH BAKING CO LLC
2254 Dillard Rd (28741-6679)
PHONE..............................828 421-2042
Krysti Henderson, *Managing Member*
EMP: 6 EST: 2022
SALES (est): 500K **Privately Held**
Web: www.lovechocolateheaven.com
SIC: 2052 Bakery products, dry

(G-6846)
TIGER MOUNTAIN WOODWORKS INC
Also Called: The Summer House
2089 Dillard Rd (28741-6677)
P.O. Box 1088 (28741-1088)
PHONE...............................828 526-5577
Paula Jones, *Pr*
Barry Jones, *
▲ **EMP:** 11 **EST:** 1988
SQ FT: 3,000
SALES (est): 1.09MM **Privately Held**
Web: www.summerhousehighlands.com
SIC: 5712 2511 2431 Customized furniture
and cabinets; Wood household furniture;
Millwork

Hildebran
Burke County

(G-6847)
CONTOUR ENTERPRISES LLC
3345 Clarence Towery Cir (28637-8231)
P.O. Box 945 (28637-0945)
PHONE...............................828 328-1550
David L Baird, *Mgr*
EMP: 75 **EST:** 2003
SALES (est): 5.49MM **Privately Held**
SIC: 3069 Rubberized fabrics

(G-6848)
DE FEET INTERNATIONAL INC
Also Called: De Feet
371 I40 Access Rd (28637-8041)
PHONE...............................828 397-7025
Shane Cooper, *Pr*
EMP: 8 **EST:** 1993
SQ FT: 30,000
SALES (est): 744.2K **Privately Held**
Web: www.defeet.com
SIC: 2251 2252 Women's hosiery, except
socks; Socks

(G-6849)
FABRIC SERVICES HICKORY INC
130 Kline Industrial Park 3rd St Ne (28637)
P.O. Box 2102 (28603-2102)
PHONE...............................828 397-7331
Stanley Knox, *Pr*
▲ **EMP:** 4 **EST:** 1969
SQ FT: 2,000
SALES (est): 220.01K **Privately Held**
Web: www.allenrussellchase.com
SIC: 2395 Quilted fabrics or cloth

(G-6850)
GEIGER INTERNATIONAL INC
218 Cline Park Dr (28637-8115)
P.O. Box 22 (53551-0022)
PHONE...............................828 324-6500
Michael Glassford, *Mgr*
EMP: 16
SALES (corp-wide): 3.63B **Publicly Held**
Web: www.geigerfurniture.com
SIC: 2521 2512 Wood office furniture;
Upholstered household furniture
HQ: Geiger International, Inc.
6095 Fulton Indus Blvd Sw
Atlanta GA 30336
404 344-1100

(G-6851)
HUITT MILLS INC (PA)
115 10th St Ne (28637-8102)
P.O. Box 640 (28637-0640)
PHONE...............................828 322-8628
Kevin Huitt, *Pr*
Susan Huitt, *
Kenneth Huitt, *

Norine Huitt, *
EMP: 26 **EST:** 1946
SQ FT: 20,000
SALES (est): 2.01MM
SALES (corp-wide): 2.01MM **Privately
Held**
Web: www.huitt.com
SIC: 2252 Socks

(G-6852)
**INDUSTRIAL MECHANICAL
SERVICES**
2354 Us Hwy 70 (28637)
P.O. Box 580 (28637-0580)
PHONE...............................828 397-3231
Johnny R Williams, *Pr*
Pat Honeycutt, *
EMP: 4 **EST:** 1971
SALES (est): 208.18K **Privately Held**
SIC: 3441 1711 Fabricated structural metal;
Mechanical contractor

(G-6853)
LYON ROOFING INC
Also Called: Lyon Metal & Supply
323 S Center St (28637-8306)
PHONE...............................828 397-2301
Brett Lyon, *Brnch Mgr*
EMP: 10
Web: www.lyonmetalroofing.com
SIC: 3444 Sheet metalwork
PA: Lyon Roofing, Inc.
485 Industrial Park Rd
Piney Flats TN 37686

(G-6854)
MARVES INDUSTRIES INC
205 Cline Park Dr (28637-8114)
P.O. Box 946 (28637-0946)
PHONE...............................828 397-4400
Elias Gomez, *Pr*
EMP: 68 **EST:** 2009
SALES (est): 8.78MM **Privately Held**
Web: www.marvesindustries.com
SIC: 3086 Insulation or cushioning material,
foamed plastics

(G-6855)
TAB STEEL & FABRICATING INC
3345 Clarence Towery Cir (28637-8231)
P.O. Box 9516 (28603-9516)
PHONE...............................828 323-8300
Tripp Burns, *Pr*
Jamie Burns, *Sec*
EMP: 6 **EST:** 2000
SQ FT: 8,000
SALES (est): 864.86K **Privately Held**
SIC: 3441 Fabricated structural metal

(G-6856)
ZION INDUSTRIES INC
9480 Neuville Ave (28637-8374)
PHONE...............................828 397-2701
Mark Shoemaker, *Brnch Mgr*
EMP: 22
SALES (corp-wide): 10.21MM **Privately
Held**
Web: www.zioninduction.com
SIC: 3398 Brazing (hardening) of metal
PA: Zion Industries, Inc.
6229 Grafton Rd
Valley City OH 44280
330 483-4650

Hillsborough
Orange County

(G-6857)
ACCIDENTAL BAKER
115 Boone Square St (27278-2561)
PHONE...............................919 732-6777
Jennie Mccray, *Owner*
EMP: 5 **EST:** 2011
SALES (est): 144.74K **Privately Held**
Web: www.theaccidentalbakernc.com
SIC: 2051 Bread, cake, and related products

(G-6858)
ARGOS USA LLC
Also Called: Union Concrete
411 Valley Forge Rd (27278-8544)
PHONE...............................919 732-7509
Marcus William, *Brnch Mgr*
EMP: 4
Web: www.argos-us.com
SIC: 3273 Ready-mixed concrete
HQ: Argos Usa Llc
3015 Windward Plz Ste 300
Alpharetta GA 30005
678 368-4300

(G-6859)
ATHOL ARBOR CORPORATION
Also Called: Hardwood Designs
511 Valley Forge Rd (27278-9502)
PHONE...............................919 643-1100
EMP: 17
SIC: 2431 1751 Millwork; Carpentry work

(G-6860)
BIG SPOON ROASTERS LLC
500 Meadowlands Dr (27278-8504)
PHONE...............................919 309-9100
Mark Overbay, *Prin*
▼ **EMP:** 10 **EST:** 2011
SALES (est): 1.79MM **Privately Held**
Web: www.bigspoonroasters.com
SIC: 2068 Salted and roasted nuts and seeds

(G-6861)
BRIAN MCGREGOR ENTERPRISE
2207 Leah Dr (27278-9010)
PHONE...............................919 732-2317
Brian Mcgregor, *Owner*
EMP: 8 **EST:** 2005
SALES (est): 481.05K **Privately Held**
Web: www.videogaming.com
SIC: 3999 Coin-operated amusement
machines

(G-6862)
CAROLINA GYM SUPPLY CORP
575 Dimmocks Mill Rd (27278-2352)
PHONE...............................919 732-6999
Benjamin S Edkins, *Pr*
▲ **EMP:** 6 **EST:** 1978
SALES (est): 1.33MM **Privately Held**
Web: www.carolinagym.com
SIC: 5941 3949 Gymnasium equipment, nec
; Gymnasium equipment

(G-6863)
CHANDLER CONCRETE INC
Also Called: CHANDLER CONCRETE INC
1501 Old North Carolina Hwy 10
(27278-9510)
P.O. Box 131 (27216-0131)
PHONE...............................919 644-1058
Marvin Thrasher, *Mgr*
EMP: 33
Web: www.chandlerconcrete.com
SIC: 3273 Ready-mixed concrete
PA: Chandler Concrete Co., Inc.

1006 S Church Street
Burlington NC 27215

(G-6864)
CMA SIGNS LLC
610 Meadowlands Dr (27278-8561)
PHONE...............................919 245-8339
Smyrna Robinson, *Managing Member*
EMP: 12 **EST:** 2020
SALES (est): 1.87MM **Privately Held**
Web: www.cmasigns.com
SIC: 3993 Signs and advertising specialties

(G-6865)
ENO SCIENTIFIC LLC
1606 Faucette Mill Rd (27278-7556)
P.O. Box 1586 (27278-1586)
PHONE...............................910 778-2660
Stephen Judd, *Pt*
Stephen Judd, *Managing Member*
▲ **EMP:** 5 **EST:** 2009
SQ FT: 2,000
SALES (est): 940.14K **Privately Held**
Web: www.enoscientific.com
SIC: 3823 Pressure measurement
instruments, industrial

(G-6866)
HARTFORD PRODUCTS INC
6224 Acorn Ridge Trl (27278-8890)
PHONE...............................919 471-5937
Robert B Hartford, *Pr*
EMP: 4 **EST:** 1997
SALES (est): 208.41K **Privately Held**
SIC: 3944 Trains and equipment, toy:
electric and mechanical

(G-6867)
HOMETOWN SPORTS INC
Also Called: Hometown Sports Embroidery
3301 St Marys Rd (27278-9726)
PHONE...............................919 732-7090
Robert R Castona Junior, *Pr*
Linda Castona, *Sec*
Susan Billat, *International Marketing
Director*
Bill Berard, *Dir*
George Horton, *Dir*
EMP: 5 **EST:** 1994
SALES (est): 171.33K **Privately Held**
SIC: 2395 5961 Embroidery products,
except Schiffli machine; Novelty
merchandise, mail order

(G-6868)
INNEROPTIC TECHNOLOGY INC
3421 Carriage Trl (27278-9512)
PHONE...............................919 732-2090
Kurtis Keller, *Ex Dir*
EMP: 6 **EST:** 2002
SALES (est): 1.04MM **Privately Held**
Web: www.inneroptic.com
SIC: 2833 7371 3845 Endocrine products;
Software programming applications;
Ultrasonic medical equipment, except
cleaning

(G-6869)
KAYE PRODUCTS INC
535 Dimmocks Mill Rd (27278-2352)
PHONE...............................919 732-6444
◆ **EMP:** 35 **EST:** 1976
SALES (est): 5.39MM **Privately Held**
Web: www.kayeproducts.com
SIC: 3842 Orthopedic appliances

(G-6870)
KOTEK HOLDINGS INC
Also Called: HARDWOOD DESIGNS
511 Valley Forge Rd (27278-9502)

PHONE..............................919 643-1100
Michael Kaisersatt, *CEO*
EMP: 25 **EST:** 2016
SALES (est): 4.66MM **Privately Held**
Web: www.hardwooddesigns.com
SIC: 2431 Door sashes, wood

(G-6871)
LUTHIERS WORKSHOP LLC
Also Called: Pre - War Guitars Co.
2207 Leah Dr Ste 102 (27278-9010)
PHONE..............................919 241-4578
EMP: 8 **EST:** 2015
SALES (est): 835.08K **Privately Held**
SIC: 3931 Musical instruments

(G-6872)
MAPLE VIEW ICE CREAM
6900 Rocky Ridge Rd (27278-7952)
PHONE..............................919 960-5535
Muffin Brosig, *Owner*
EMP: 10 **EST:** 2001
SALES (est): 878.5K **Privately Held**
Web: www.mapleviewfarm.com
SIC: 2024 Ice cream and frozen deserts

(G-6873)
MDM MFG LLC
206 Stockbridge Pl (27278-9773)
PHONE..............................919 908-6574
EMP: 4 **EST:** 2019
SALES (est): 543.15K **Privately Held**
Web: www.mdm-mfg.com
SIC: 3599 Machine shop, jobbing and repair

(G-6874)
NORTHSIDE MILLWORK INC
301 Millstone Dr (27278-8777)
PHONE..............................919 732-6100
Peter Singer, *Pr*
Debra Singer, *
EMP: 35 **EST:** 1982
SQ FT: 25,000
SALES (est): 5.55MM **Privately Held**
Web: www.northsidemillwork.com
SIC: 2431 Millwork

(G-6875)
PICASSOMOESLLC ✪
513 Patriots Pointe Dr (27278-9030)
PHONE..............................216 703-4547
Maurice Morrison, *CEO*
EMP: 5 **EST:** 2023
SALES (est): 97.55K **Privately Held**
SIC: 3161 5999 2051 5046 Clothing and apparel carrying cases; Miscellaneous retail stores, nec; Bakery: wholesale or wholesale/retail combined; Store equipment

(G-6876)
REDUX BEVERAGES LLC
2318 Oakhurst Trl (27278-6639)
PHONE..............................951 304-1144
James Kirby, *Managing Member*
EMP: 5 **EST:** 2006
SALES (est): 161.95K **Privately Held**
Web: www.reduxdirect.com
SIC: 2086 Soft drinks: packaged in cans, bottles, etc.

(G-6877)
SHEET METAL DUCT SUPPLIERS LLC
214 Millstone Dr (27278-8776)
PHONE..............................919 732-4362
Larry F Warren, *Prin*
EMP: 4 **EST:** 2009
SALES (est): 235.14K **Privately Held**
Web: www.sheetmetalductsuppliers.com
SIC: 3444 Sheet metalwork

(G-6878)
SOMMERVILLE ENTERPRISES LLC
Also Called: Open South Imports
202 Holiday Park Rd (27278-8603)
PHONE..............................919 924-1594
Steve Sommerville, *Pr*
EMP: 11 **EST:** 2018
SALES (est): 338.91K **Privately Held**
SIC: 2084 Wines

(G-6879)
TOUCHAMERICA INC
437 Dimmocks Mill Rd (27278-2300)
P.O. Box 1304 (27278-1304)
PHONE..............................919 732-6968
Stewart Griffith, *Pr*
◆ **EMP:** 5 **EST:** 1985
SALES (est): 467.93K **Privately Held**
Web: www.touchamerica.com
SIC: 3841 Surgical and medical instruments

(G-6880)
TRACKX TECHNOLOGY LLC
437 Dimmocks Mill Rd Ste 28 (27278-2379)
PHONE..............................888 787-2259
Robert Isaacs, *CEO*
EMP: 15 **EST:** 2016
SALES (est): 3.3MM **Privately Held**
Web: www.trackx.tech
SIC: 3845 Ultrasonic scanning devices, medical

(G-6881)
WILMORE ELECTRONICS COMPANY INC (PA)
Also Called: Wilmore Electronics
607 Us Highway 70a E (27278-8526)
P.O. Box 1329 (27278-1329)
PHONE..............................919 732-9351
EMP: 55 **EST:** 1963
SALES (est): 13.2MM
SALES (corp-wide): 13.2MM **Privately Held**
Web: www.wilmoreelectronics.com
SIC: 3699 Electrical equipment and supplies, nec

(G-6882)
WOMACK PUBLISHING CO INC
Also Called: News of Orange County
109 E King St (27278-2570)
P.O. Box 580 (27278-0580)
PHONE..............................919 732-2171
Keith Coleman, *Genl Mgr*
EMP: 4
SALES (corp-wide): 4.28MM **Privately Held**
Web: www.womackpublishing.com
SIC: 2711 Newspapers: publishing only, not printed on site
PA: Womack Publishing Company, Inc.
28 N Main St
Chatham VA 24531
434 432-2791

Hobbsville
Gates County

(G-6883)
C A PERRY & SON INC (DH)
4033 Virginia Rd (27946)
PHONE..............................252 221-4463
Sidney L Perry, *Owner*
Sydney Kopland, *
EMP: 33 **EST:** 1950
SQ FT: 100,000
SALES (est): 26.01MM
SALES (corp-wide): 11.26B **Publicly Held**
Web: www.caperryandson.com

SIC: 5159 5191 4221 5153 Peanuts (bulk), unroasted; Farm supplies; Farm product warehousing and storage; Grains
HQ: Lansing Trade Group, Llc
11350 Switzer Rd
Overland Park KS 66210
913 748-3000

(G-6884)
MURPHY-BROWN LLC
Also Called: Smithfield Grain
4033 Virginia Rd (27946)
PHONE..............................252 221-4463
Marcus Hawkins, *Brnch Mgr*
EMP: 8
SIC: 2041 5153 Flour and other grain mill products; Grain elevators
HQ: Murphy-Brown Llc
2822 W Nc 24 Hwy
Warsaw NC 28398
910 293-3434

Hoffman
Richmond County

(G-6885)
SOUTHERN PRODUCTS COMPANY INC
4303 Us Hwy 1 N (28347)
P.O. Box 189 (28347-0189)
PHONE..............................910 281-3189
TOLL FREE: 800
Marshall B Gilchrist, *Pr*
Peter Gilchrist Iii, *Sec*
EMP: 25 **EST:** 1970
SQ FT: 12,000
SALES (est): 2.31MM **Privately Held**
Web: www.sandandgravel.net
SIC: 3295 3569 Minerals, ground or treated; Filters

Holly Ridge
Onslow County

(G-6886)
ABOVE TOPSAIL LLC
301 Us Highway 17 S (28445-8788)
PHONE..............................910 803-1759
Jeffery Wenzel, *Managing Member*
EMP: 4 **EST:** 2017
SALES (est): 809.04K **Privately Held**
Web: www.abovetopsail.com
SIC: 7335 3861 Commercial photography; Printing frames, photographic

(G-6887)
BULK TRANSPORT SERVICE INC
169 Preston Wells Rd (28445-8543)
PHONE..............................910 329-0555
Kendall R Moore, *Pr*
EMP: 7 **EST:** 1994
SQ FT: 500
SALES (est): 384.75K **Privately Held**
SIC: 1442 Common sand mining

(G-6888)
GULFSTREAM STEEL & SUPPLY INC
Also Called: Gulfstream Steel & Supply
301 Us Highway 17 S Ste 1 (28445-8785)
P.O. Box 38 (28445-0038)
PHONE..............................910 329-5100
Thomas C Rollins, *Pr*
Bernie A Rollins, *
EMP: 45 **EST:** 1988
SQ FT: 24,000
SALES (est): 1.18MM **Privately Held**
Web: www.gulfstreamsteel.com

SIC: 3291 3312 3449 5051 Abrasive metal and steel products; Stainless steel; Bars, concrete reinforcing: fabricated steel; Metals service centers and offices

(G-6889)
JAXONSIGNS
874 E Ocean Hwy (28445-8714)
PHONE..............................910 467-3409
Cathy Jackson, *Mgr*
EMP: 4 **EST:** 2015
SALES (est): 162.25K **Privately Held**
Web: www.jaxonsigns.com
SIC: 3993 Signs and advertising specialties

(G-6890)
JOHNNY SLICKS INC
624 Us Highway 17 S Unit 1 (28445-8660)
PHONE..............................910 803-2159
Johnny Raushi, *Prin*
EMP: 7 **EST:** 2019
SALES (est): 511.51K **Privately Held**
Web: www.johnnyslicks.com
SIC: 5999 5087 3999 2844 Miscellaneous retail stores, nec; Beauty parlor equipment and supplies; Hair and hair-based products; Lotions, shaving

(G-6891)
S & W READY MIX CON CO LLC
Also Called: S & W Ready Mix Concrete
307 W Ocean Rd (28445-7871)
PHONE..............................910 329-1201
Chuck Jewett, *Brnch Mgr*
EMP: 19
SALES (corp-wide): 8.01MM **Privately Held**
Web: www.snwreadymix.com
SIC: 3273 Ready-mixed concrete
HQ: S & W Ready Mix Concrete Company Llc
217 Lisbon St
Clinton NC 28329
910 592-1733

Holly Springs
Wake County

(G-6892)
ASI SIGNAGE NORTH CAROLINA
600 Irving Pkwy (27540-8445)
P.O. Box 819 (27540-0819)
PHONE..............................919 362-9669
EMP: 21 **EST:** 2019
SALES (est): 1.01MM **Privately Held**
Web: www.asisignage.net
SIC: 3993 Signs and advertising specialties

(G-6893)
AVIATOR BREWING COMPANY INC
5504 Caleb Knolls Dr (27540-7611)
PHONE..............................919 601-5497
Mark D Doble, *Pr*
EMP: 9 **EST:** 2008
SQ FT: 2,500
SALES (est): 602.76K **Privately Held**
Web: www.aviatorbrew.com
SIC: 2082 5182 5921 Beer (alcoholic beverage); Wine and distilled beverages; Beer (packaged)

(G-6894)
BEAZER EAST INC
7000 Cass Holt Rd (27540-9781)
PHONE..............................919 567-9512
Jim Hilton, *Mgr*
EMP: 10
SQ FT: 4,672
SALES (corp-wide): 23.02B **Privately Held**

SIC: 3241 1442 Natural cement;
Construction sand and gravel
HQ: Beazer East, Inc.
600 River Ave Ste 200
Pittsburgh PA 15212
412 428-9407

(G-6895)
BOMBSHELL BEER COMPANY LLC
120 Quantum St (27540-8861)
PHONE..................919 823-1933
Ellen Joyner, Pr
EMP: 11 EST: 2012
SALES (est): 1.97MM Privately Held
Web: www.bombshellbeer.com
SIC: 2082 5813 Beer (alcoholic beverage);
Drinking places

(G-6896)
C & J WELDING INC
136 Acorn Ridge Ln (27540-7337)
P.O. Box 1299 (27526-1299)
PHONE..................919 552-0275
Chuck Wombles, Prin
EMP: 6 EST: 2003
SALES (est): 388.57K Privately Held
SIC: 7692 Welding repair

(G-6897)
CHENTECH CORP
524 Texanna Way (27540-7352)
PHONE..................919 749-8765
Richard Chen, Admn
EMP: 4 EST: 2015
SALES (est): 247.27K Privately Held
SIC: 3851 Contact lenses

(G-6898)
DS SMITH PLC
301 Thomas Mill Rd (27540-8447)
PHONE..................919 557-3148
EMP: 25
SALES (corp-wide): 8.62B Privately Held
Web: www.dssmith.com
SIC: 2653 2542 2671 Boxes, corrugated:
made from purchased materials; Partitions
and fixtures, except wood; Paper; coated
and laminated packaging
PA: Ds Smith Limited
Level 3
London W2 1D
754 542-9001

(G-6899)
DYNAGRAPHICS SCREENPRINTNG
125 Quantum St (27540-8862)
PHONE..................919 212-2898
Steve Knight, Pr
Shelley L Knight, VP
EMP: 5 EST: 1997
SQ FT: 2,500
SALES (est): 503.26K Privately Held
Web: www.tshirtsraleigh.com
SIC: 2759 Screen printing

(G-6900)
EW JACKSON TRANSPORTATION LLC
113 Gingerlilly Ct (27540-7868)
PHONE..................919 586-2514
Vinson Jackson, Prin
EMP: 7 EST: 2016
SALES (est): 895.04K Privately Held
SIC: 3547 Primary rolling mill equipment

(G-6901)
FIVE STAR COFFEE ROASTERS LLC
108 Thomas Mill Rd Ste 101 (27540-9253)
PHONE..................919 671-0645
Nelson Amador, Pr

EMP: 8 EST: 2016
SALES (est): 199.09K Privately Held
Web: www.5starcoffeeroasters.com
SIC: 2095 Coffee roasting (except by
wholesale grocers)

(G-6902)
FRESH POINT LLC
237 Kenmont Dr (27540-7404)
PHONE..................919 895-0790
EMP: 6
SALES (est): 710.81K Privately Held
SIC: 7389 2082 Business Activities at Non-
Commercial Site; Ale (alcoholic beverage)

(G-6903)
GOODYEAR TIRE & RUBBER COMPANY
Also Called: Goodyear
932 N Main St (27540-8782)
PHONE..................919 552-9340
Mike Correll, Mgr
EMP: 5
SALES (corp-wide): 18.88B Publicly Held
Web: www.goodyear.com
SIC: 5531 3714 3011 Automotive tires;
Motor vehicle wheels and parts; Tires and
inner tubes
PA: The Goodyear Tire & Rubber Company
200 Innovation Way
Akron OH 44316
330 796-2121

(G-6904)
JEBCO INC
121 Thomas Mill Rd (27540-9320)
PHONE..................919 557-2001
EMP: 37
SALES (corp-wide): 17.29MM Privately Held
SIC: 3631 5812 8741 Barbecues, grills, and
braziers (outdoor cooking); Eating places;
Management services
PA: Jebco, Inc.
7798 Ga Highway 88 E
Keysville GA 30816
706 465-3378

(G-6905)
LAFAUCI
5001 Sunset Forest Cir (27540-7817)
PHONE..................919 244-5912
EMP: 4 EST: 2018
SALES (est): 73.16K Privately Held
SIC: 2721 Periodicals

(G-6906)
LOVEGRASS KITCHEN INC
300 S Main St Ste 108 (27540-4201)
PHONE..................919 205-8426
Meron Kassa, CEO
Samson Kassa, Ex Dir
Meron Afework, Owner
EMP: 15 EST: 2017
SALES (est): 640.7K Privately Held
Web: www.lovegrasskitchen.com
SIC: 2064 2045 5812 Granola and muesli,
bars and clusters; Pancake mixes,
prepared: from purchased flour; Cafe

(G-6907)
MAKE AN IMPRESSION INC
202 Premier Dr (27540-8413)
PHONE..................919 557-7400
Dawn Joseph, Pr
Joann Randall, VP
James R Randall, Treas
James L Joseph, Sec
EMP: 7 EST: 2001
SQ FT: 3,012
SALES (est): 636.41K Privately Held

Web: www.makeanimpressioninc.com
SIC: 2759 7334 Screen printing;
Photocopying and duplicating services

(G-6908)
NOVARTIS VCCNES DAGNOSTICS INC (HQ)
475 Green Oaks Pkwy (27540-7976)
PHONE..................617 871-7000
Joerg Reinhardt, CEO
▲ EMP: 500 EST: 1986
SQ FT: 119,600
SALES (est): 56.11MM
SALES (corp-wide): 39.77B Privately Held
SIC: 2835 2836 2834 Diagnostic substances
; Vaccines and other immunizing products;
Drugs affecting parasitic and infective
diseases
PA: Gsk Plc
79 New Oxford Street
London WC1A
208 047-5000

(G-6909)
OFM LLC
Also Called: Office Furniture Marketing
161 Tradition Trl (27540-7045)
PHONE..................919 303-6389
Steven M Bradford, Managing Member
Barbara Zalcberg, *
▲ EMP: 91 EST: 1995
SQ FT: 124,000
SALES (est): 19.62MM
SALES (corp-wide): 2.53B Publicly Held
Web: www.ofminc.com
SIC: 2521 Wood office furniture
PA: Hni Corporation
600 E 2nd St
Muscatine IA 52761
563 272-7400

(G-6910)
PEAK TRUSS BUILDERS LLC
1220 N Main St (27540-9396)
P.O. Box 639 (27540-0639)
PHONE..................919 552-5933
Le Greene, Managing Member
EMP: 9 EST: 2011
SQ FT: 8,000
SALES (est): 1MM Privately Held
Web: www.peaktruss.com
SIC: 2439 Trusses, wooden roof

(G-6911)
RODNEY S CSTM CUT SIGN CO INC
Also Called: Rodney's Sign Company
600 Irving Pkwy (27540-8445)
P.O. Box 819 (27540-0819)
PHONE..................919 362-9669
Tayler Dalpe, Pr
John Dalpe Junior, COO
EMP: 27 EST: 1983
SQ FT: 45,000
SALES (est): 5.95MM Privately Held
Web: www.asisignage.net
SIC: 3993 2499 Signs, not made in custom
sign painting shops; Handles, poles, dowels
and stakes: wood
PA: Asi Sign Systems, Inc.
8181 Jetstar Dr Ste 100
Irving TX 75063

(G-6912)
ROMEO SIX LLC
260 Premier Dr (27540-5303)
PHONE..................919 589-7150
David Mannheim, Admn
W David Mannheim, Prin
EMP: 10 EST: 2015
SALES (est): 3.18MM Privately Held
Web: www.romeosix.com

SIC: 7373 7379 3669 Local area network
(LAN) systems integrator; Computer related
consulting services; Emergency alarms

(G-6913)
S&F PRODUCTS
6112 N Deer Ridge Dr (27540-7809)
PHONE..................714 412-1298
Fred Brown, Owner
◆ EMP: 4 EST: 2002
SALES (est): 209.53K Privately Held
SIC: 2851 Paints and allied products

(G-6914)
SEQIRUS INC (DH)
475 Green Oaks Pkwy (27540-7976)
PHONE..................919 577-5000
Dave Sehgal, Pr
EMP: 18 EST: 2015
SALES (est): 62.5MM Privately Held
Web: www.csl.com
SIC: 2836 Vaccines and other immunizing
products
HQ: Seqirus Uk Limited
Point
Maidenhead BERKS SL6 8
162 864-1500

(G-6915)
SOFTWARE GOLDSMITH INC
5305 Lake Edge Dr (27540-9340)
PHONE..................919 346-0403
Swapna Gangopadhyay, Pr
EMP: 18 EST: 2001
SALES (est): 377.75K Privately Held
Web: www.softsmithinc.com
SIC: 7372 Prepackaged software

(G-6916)
SPLENDIDCRM SOFTWARE INC
705 Laurel Bay Ln (27540-8741)
PHONE..................919 604-1258
Paul Rony, Prin
EMP: 5 EST: 2005
SALES (est): 665.42K Privately Held
Web: www.splendidcrm.com
SIC: 7372 7371 Prepackaged software;
Software programming applications

(G-6917)
SWORD CONSERVATORY INC
112 Tonks Trl (27540-8280)
PHONE..................919 557-4465
Stephenson Lindbeck, Prin
EMP: 5 EST: 2016
SALES (est): 132.49K Privately Held
SIC: 3421 Cutlery

(G-6918)
VERTICAL SOLUTIONS OF NC INC
5040 Kinderston Dr (27540-9165)
P.O. Box 451 (27540-0451)
PHONE..................919 285-2251
Michael L Lassiter, Prin
EMP: 4 EST: 2010
SALES (est): 232.65K Privately Held
SIC: 2591 Blinds vertical

(G-6919)
W G OF SOUTHWEST RALEIGH INC
413 Redhill Rd (27540-6272)
P.O. Box 1151 (27540-1151)
PHONE..................919 629-7327
Micheal Boone, Pr
EMP: 4 EST: 2012
SALES (est): 270.18K Privately Held
SIC: 7349 2842 Window cleaning; Specialty
cleaning

(G-6920)
WARP TECHNOLOGIES INC
601 Irving Pkwy (27540-8446)
P.O. Box 500 (27540-0500)
PHONE...............................919 552-2311
Shartel Smith, *Pr*
EMP: 130 EST: 1988
SQ FT: 150,000
SALES (est): 2.36MM **Privately Held**
SIC: 2824 2258 Polyester fibers; Lace and warp knit fabric mills

---

Hookerton
Greene County

(G-6921)
AMERICAN MADE PRODUCTS INC
606 5th St (28538)
P.O. Box 176 (62626-0176)
PHONE...............................252 747-2010
Pherick Moore, *Mgr*
EMP: 10
SALES (corp-wide): 877.31K **Privately Held**
SIC: 2381 Gloves, work: woven or knit, made from purchased materials
PA: American Made Products Inc.
   1155 Morgan St
   Carlinville IL
   217 854-4496

Hope Mills
Cumberland County

(G-6922)
AEC IMAGING & GRAPHICS LLC (PA)
5755 Dove Dr (28348-1707)
PHONE...............................910 693-1034
EMP: 4 EST: 1998
SALES (est): 497.09K
SALES (corp-wide): 497.09K **Privately Held**
Web: www.aecimaging.com
SIC: 7334 5049 2752 Blueprinting service; Drafting supplies; Commercial printing, lithographic

(G-6923)
C & F CUSTOM CABINETS INC
140 Sanders St (28348-8985)
PHONE...............................910 424-7475
Frank Carter, *Pr*
Steve Ford, *VP*
EMP: 20 EST: 1987
SQ FT: 16,000
SALES (est): 2.37MM **Privately Held**
Web: www.cfcustomcabinets.com
SIC: 2434 Wood kitchen cabinets

(G-6924)
CAROLINA MCH FAYETTEVILLE INC
3465 Black And Decker Rd (28348-9332)
P.O. Box 632 (28348-0632)
PHONE...............................910 425-9115
James Dietzen, *Pr*
Elek Torok, *VP*
Cnythia Torok, *Prin*
EMP: 4 EST: 1973
SQ FT: 7,000
SALES (est): 469.93K **Privately Held**
SIC: 3599 Machine shop, jobbing and repair

(G-6925)
CCI HAIR BOUTIQUE LLC
3059 N Main St (28348-2798)
PHONE...............................407 216-9213
EMP: 15 EST: 2018
SALES (est): 240.28K **Privately Held**

SIC: 3999 Hair and hair-based products

(G-6926)
COMSET MANAGEMENT GROUP
3926 Gaithersburg Ln (28348-2092)
PHONE...............................910 574-6007
Darrell Williams, *Owner*
EMP: 5 EST: 2000
SALES (est): 234.21K **Privately Held**
SIC: 1499 Gemstone and industrial diamond mining

(G-6927)
FRANKLIN BAKING COMPANY LLC
Also Called: Branch 0457
217 Woodington Rd (28348-8551)
PHONE...............................910 425-5090
Joseph Mulligan, *Brnch Mgr*
EMP: 10
SALES (corp-wide): 5.1B **Publicly Held**
Web: franklin-co4goldsboro.edan.io
SIC: 2051 Bread, cake, and related products
HQ: Franklin Baking Company, Llc
   500 W Grantham St
   Goldsboro NC 27530
   919 735-0344

(G-6928)
WILLIAM GEORGE PRINTING LLC
Also Called: Relyus
3469 Black And Decker Rd (28348-9332)
PHONE...............................910 221-2700
Marshall Waren, *Pr*
▲ **EMP: 46 EST:** 2004
SQ FT: 95,000
SALES (est): 11.78MM **Privately Held**
Web: www.relyus.com
SIC: 2752 7331 Offset printing; Direct mail advertising services

---

Horse Shoe
Henderson County

(G-6929)
LIBERTY HSE UTILITY BUILDINGS
65 Dalton Rd (28742-9759)
PHONE...............................828 209-3390
Phillip C Whitaker, *Pr*
Rhonda Whitaker, *Sec*
EMP: 4 EST: 2004
SALES (est): 483.36K **Privately Held**
SIC: 2511 Storage chests, household: wood

(G-6930)
MICHAELIAN & KOHLBERG INC (PA)
5216 Brevard Rd (28742-9664)
P.O. Box 398 (28742-0398)
PHONE...............................828 891-8511
William T Sumner, *Ch Bd*
Sandra Lemke, *VP*
▲ **EMP: 5 EST:** 1920
SQ FT: 2,600
SALES (est): 1.27MM
SALES (corp-wide): 1.27MM **Privately Held**
Web: www.michaelian.com
SIC: 5023 2273 Rugs; Carpets and rugs

(G-6931)
ZUMCO INC
199 Forest Knolls Pl (28742-4767)
PHONE...............................828 891-3300
Daniel Zumstein, *Pr*
Virginia Zumstein, *VP*
EMP: 5 EST: 1974
SQ FT: 15,000
SALES (est): 790.27K **Privately Held**
SIC: 3599 Machine shop, jobbing and repair

Hot Springs
Madison County

(G-6932)
BLUFF MOUNTAIN OUTFITTERS INC
152 Bridge St (28743-9231)
P.O. Box 114 (28743-0114)
PHONE...............................828 622-7162
Wayne Crosby, *Pr*
Daniel Gallagher, *VP*
EMP: 7 EST: 1997
SQ FT: 4,800
SALES (est): 437.86K **Privately Held**
SIC: 3949 5945 5411 Sporting and athletic goods, nec; Hobby, toy, and game shops; Grocery stores, independent

(G-6933)
MADISON MANUFACTURING COMPANY
Also Called: Peerless Blowers
172 S Andrews Ave (28743-9213)
P.O. Box 187 (28743-0187)
PHONE...............................828 622-7500
Craig Neuhardt, *Pr*
Margaret Mcinnis, *Sec*
▲ **EMP: 91 EST:** 1991
SALES (est): 13.57MM **Privately Held**
Web: www.peerlessblowers.com
SIC: 3634 Electric housewares and fans

(G-6934)
RONNY D PHELPS
12 E Lawson Rd (28743-7780)
PHONE...............................828 206-6339
Ronny D Phelps, *Prin*
EMP: 6 EST: 2005
SALES (est): 157.39K **Privately Held**
SIC: 3531 Backhoes

Hubert
Onslow County

(G-6935)
MEDALS TO HONOR INC
176 Oyster Ln (28539-3759)
P.O. Box 96 (28539-0096)
PHONE...............................910 326-4275
Michelle Holmquist, *Pr*
Karen Golden, *Sec*
EMP: 4 EST: 1999
SALES (est): 893.51K **Privately Held**
Web: www.medalstohonor.com
SIC: 2541 Store and office display cases and fixtures

(G-6936)
QUEENS CREEK SEAFOOD
105 Huffman Ln (28539)
PHONE...............................910 326-4801
Randy Tallman, *Owner*
Kenny Callan, *Owner*
EMP: 5 EST: 2010
SALES (est): 179.31K **Privately Held**
SIC: 2091 Clams: packaged in cans, jars, etc.

(G-6937)
WATERLINE SYSTEMS INC
270 Hogans Rd (28539-4508)
PHONE...............................910 708-1000
Randall Borges, *Pr*
Tracy Gable, *Prin*
Nicholas Vann, *Prin*
EMP: 8 EST: 2019
SALES (est): 868.92K **Privately Held**
Web: www.waterlinesystems.com

SIC: 3731 Shipbuilding and repairing

(G-6938)
WILLIAM STONE & TILE INC
1525 Freedom Way (28539-3641)
PHONE...............................910 353-0914
William S Cucksee, *CEO*
▲ **EMP: 4 EST:** 2005
SQ FT: 22,500
SALES (est): 582.45K **Privately Held**
Web: www.williamstoneandtile.com
SIC: 2541 5211 Counter and sink tops; Counter tops

(G-6939)
WINTER CUSTOM YACHTS INC
270 Hogans Rd (28539-4508)
P.O. Box 40 (28539-0040)
PHONE...............................910 325-7583
Katelyn Miller, *CEO*
EMP: 10 EST: 2018
SALES (est): 1.16MM **Privately Held**
Web: www.wintercustomyachts.com
SIC: 3732 Boat kits, not models

Hudson
Caldwell County

(G-6940)
ADHEZION BIOMEDICAL LLC
506 Pine Mountain Rd (28638-8793)
PHONE...............................828 728-6116
Caridad Rahim, *Brnch Mgr*
EMP: 5
SALES (corp-wide): 3.57B **Publicly Held**
Web: www.adhezion.com
SIC: 3841 Surgical and medical instruments
HQ: Adhezion Biomedical, Llc
   1 Meridian Blvd Ste 1b02
   Wyomissing PA 19610

(G-6941)
ARCONA LEATHER COMPANY LLC (PA)
Also Called: JP Leather Arcona Division
2615 Mission Rd (28638-9043)
P.O. Box 399 (28638-0399)
PHONE...............................828 396-7728
Robert Hollar, *Pr*
▲ **EMP: 9 EST:** 1979
SALES (est): 912.48K
SALES (corp-wide): 912.48K **Privately Held**
Web: www.arconaleather.com
SIC: 5199 3111 Leather, leather goods, and furs; Leather tanning and finishing

(G-6942)
BEOCARE INC
1905 International Blvd (28638-2734)
PHONE...............................828 728-7300
James Berberg, *Pr*
▲ **EMP: 105 EST:** 2010
SQ FT: 85,000
SALES (est): 20.35MM
SALES (corp-wide): 12.8MM **Privately Held**
Web: www.beocare.net
SIC: 3842 Surgical appliances and supplies
PA: Fra Production Spa
   Via Delle Poste 16
   Dusino San Michele AT 14010
   014 197-9911

(G-6943)
BEOCARE GROUP INC (PA)
1905 International Blvd (28638-2734)
PHONE...............................828 728-7300
Peter Vanderbruggen, *CEO*

▲ = Import ▼ = Export
◆ = Import/Export

Matt Valego, *
Peter Vanderbruggen, *Pr*
Steve De Backer, *
James Verberg, *
◆ **EMP:** 104 **EST:** 2009
SQ FT: 85,000
SALES (est): 3.44MM
SALES (corp-wide): 3.44MM **Privately Held**
Web: www.beocare.net
SIC: 2399 Hand woven apparel

(G-6944)
CAJAH CORPORATION
Also Called: Cajah Mountain Hosiery Mills
1905 International Blvd (28638-2734)
P.O. Box 369 (28638-0369)
PHONE..............................828 728-7300
Jim Verberg, *Mgr*
▲ **EMP:** 110 **EST:** 1993
SQ FT: 1,000
SALES (est): 2.11MM **Privately Held**
Web: www.mountzionhudson.org
SIC: 2251 Women's hosiery, except socks

(G-6945)
CALDWELL CABINETS NC LLC
Also Called: Caseworx
3441 Hickory Blvd (28638-9025)
P.O. Box 547 (28638-0547)
PHONE..............................828 212-0000
Dianne Green, *
EMP: 28 **EST:** 2016
SQ FT: 20,000
SALES (est): 6.51MM **Privately Held**
Web: www.caseworxnc.com
SIC: 2434 Wood kitchen cabinets

(G-6946)
CAROLINA BASE - PAC CORP
3157 Freezer Locker Rd (28638-8759)
P.O. Box 783 (28638-0783)
PHONE..............................828 728-7304
Weidner Abernathy, *Pr*
EMP: 50 **EST:** 1982
SQ FT: 25,000
SALES (est): 4.41MM **Privately Held**
Web: www.carolinabasepac.com
SIC: 2448 3089 Pallets, wood; Plastics processing

(G-6947)
CAROLINA LEG SUPPLY LLC
111 Davis St (28638-2524)
P.O. Box 2154 (28645-2154)
PHONE..............................828 446-6838
Charles Roy Munday, *Managing Member*
William Hunter Munday, *Managing Member*
EMP: 5 **EST:** 2015
SALES (est): 592.83K **Privately Held**
Web: www.carolinalegco.com
SIC: 2426 Furniture stock and parts, hardwood

(G-6948)
CEDAR ROCK HOME FURNISHINGS
3483 Hickory Blvd (28638-9025)
P.O. Box 515 (28638-0515)
PHONE..............................828 396-2361
Leonard G Widner, *Pr*
Jimmie Kaye Widner, *Sec*
EMP: 4 **EST:** 1986
SQ FT: 12,000
SALES (est): 305.24K **Privately Held**
Web: www.cedarrockfurniture.com
SIC: 5712 2512 Mattresses; Living room furniture: upholstered on wood frames

(G-6949)
CEDAR VALLEY HOSIERY MILL INC
3074 Deal Mill Rd (28638-9216)
PHONE..............................828 396-1804
Monti Hall, *VP*
Carroll Hall, *Pr*
Dorothy Hall, *Sec*
Karen Roberts, *Treas*
EMP: 7 **EST:** 1979
SQ FT: 2,000
SALES (est): 70.12K **Privately Held**
SIC: 2252 Socks

(G-6950)
J & M WOODWORKING INC
432 Pine Mountain Rd (28638-2638)
P.O. Box 145 (28638-0145)
PHONE..............................828 728-3253
Todd Bumgarner, *Pr*
Jerry A Bumgarner, *Sec*
▲ **EMP:** 10 **EST:** 1963
SQ FT: 11,250
SALES (est): 827.34K **Privately Held**
Web: www.jandmwoodworking.org
SIC: 2431 Millwork

(G-6951)
JP LEATHER COMPANY INC
2615 Mission Rd (28638-9043)
P.O. Box 11066 (28603-4566)
PHONE..............................828 396-7728
Robert D Haller, *Pr*
▲ **EMP:** 6 **EST:** 1995
SQ FT: 20,000
SALES (est): 136.86K **Privately Held**
SIC: 2386 Leather and sheep-lined clothing

(G-6952)
KELLEYS SPORTS AND AWARDS INC
2636 Hickory Blvd (28638-9100)
P.O. Box 2579 (28645-2579)
PHONE..............................828 728-4600
Robert Peircy, *Pr*
Robert Piercy, *Pr*
Todd Rayle, *VP*
EMP: 9 **EST:** 1983
SQ FT: 10,000
SALES (est): 247.56K **Privately Held**
Web: www.kelleyssports.net
SIC: 2759 2395 5941 5999 Screen printing; Embroidery and art needlework; Sporting goods and bicycle shops; Trophies and plaques

(G-6953)
KINCAID FURNITURE COMPANY INC (HQ)
240 Pleasant Hill Rd (28638-2244)
P.O. Box 605 (28638-0605)
PHONE..............................828 728-3261
Steven M Kincaid, *Pr*
Bob Lemons, *VP Sls*
Reggie Probst, *VP Opers*
Gary Lake, *Contrlr*
▲ **EMP:** 70 **EST:** 1946
SALES (est): 23.68MM
SALES (corp-wide): 2.05B **Publicly Held**
Web: www.kincaidfurniture.com
SIC: 2511 2512 Wood household furniture; Upholstered household furniture
PA: La-Z-Boy Incorporated
1 Lazboy Dr
Monroe MI 48162
734 242-1444

(G-6954)
LEA INDUSTRIES INC
240 Pleasant Hill Rd (28638-2244)
PHONE..............................336 294-5233

Jack Richardson, *Pr*
▲ **EMP:** 250 **EST:** 1973
SALES (est): 1.96MM
SALES (corp-wide): 2.05B **Publicly Held**
SIC: 2511 Wood bedroom furniture
PA: La-Z-Boy Incorporated
1 Lazboy Dr
Monroe MI 48162
734 242-1444

(G-6955)
MARX INDUSTRIES INCORPORATED
Also Called: Marx Industries
4276 Helena St (28638-9023)
P.O. Box 826 (28630-0826)
PHONE..............................828 396-6700
EMP: 50
SIC: 3069 3086 Foam rubber; Plastics foam products

(G-6956)
POPES SIGNATURE GALLERY
Also Called: Signature Gallery
3965 Us Highway 321a (28638-9505)
P.O. Box 1013 (28638-1013)
PHONE..............................828 396-9494
Lonnie Pope, *Owner*
EMP: 5 **EST:** 1988
SQ FT: 7,500
SALES (est): 82.11K **Privately Held**
Web: signaturegallery.tripod.com
SIC: 2512 Upholstered household furniture

(G-6957)
RPM INDSTRIAL CTINGS GROUP INC
C C I Division
3190 Hickory Blvd (28638-2661)
PHONE..............................828 728-8266
Sam Hinson, *Mgr*
EMP: 101
SALES (corp-wide): 7.34B **Publicly Held**
Web: www.mohawk-finishing.com
SIC: 2851 2893 3479 Lacquers, varnishes, enamels, and other coatings; Printing ink; Coating of metals and formed products
HQ: Rpm Industrial Coatings Group, Inc.
2220 Us Hwy 70 Se Ste 100
Hickory NC 28602
828 261-0325

(G-6958)
SATTLER CORP
Also Called: Outdura
447 Main St (28638-2329)
PHONE..............................828 759-2100
Manfred Heissenberg, *Pr*
Andreas Freiler, *
Jonathan Murphy, *
Charlie Church, *
◆ **EMP:** 80 **EST:** 2010
SQ FT: 175,000
SALES (est): 11.56MM
SALES (corp-wide): 148.5MM **Privately Held**
Web: usa.sattler.com
SIC: 2211 Broadwoven fabric mills, cotton
PA: Sattler Ag
SattlerstraBe 45
Gossendorf 8077
31641040

(G-6959)
SEALED AIR CORPORATION
Polyethylene Foam Div
2001 International Blvd (28638-2731)
PHONE..............................828 728-6610
Ed Frost, *Mgr*
EMP: 100
SALES (corp-wide): 5.39B **Publicly Held**
Web: www.sealedair.com

SIC: 3087 3086 3089 2676 Custom compound purchased resins; Plastics foam products; Plastics containers, except foam; Sanitary paper products
PA: Sealed Air Corporation
2415 Cascade Pointe Blvd
Charlotte NC 28208
980 221-3235

(G-6960)
SUPERIOR DRY KILNS INC
Also Called: Boldesigns
2601 Withers Dr (28638-9062)
P.O. Box 1586 (28645-1586)
PHONE..............................828 754-7001
Brett Bollinger, *Pr*
EMP: 20 **EST:** 1984
SALES (est): 4.85MM **Privately Held**
Web: www.boldesigninc.com
SIC: 3559 3531 3541 3537 Kilns, lumber; Construction machinery; Machine tools, metal cutting type; Industrial trucks and tractors

(G-6961)
TIMBER WOLF FOREST PRODUCTS
3189 Freezer Locker Rd (28638-8759)
P.O. Box 608 (28638-0608)
PHONE..............................828 728-7500
Randy Roper, *Pr*
Rita Roper, *VP*
EMP: 13 **EST:** 1998
SQ FT: 13,000
SALES (est): 3.93MM **Privately Held**
Web: www.timberwolfforest.com
SIC: 2431 Millwork

Huntersville
Mecklenburg County

(G-6962)
760 CRAFT WORKS LLC
100 Gilead Rd (28078-7825)
PHONE..............................704 274-5216
Knox Ramsey, *Managing Member*
EMP: 15 **EST:** 2019
SALES (est): 367.03K **Privately Held**
Web: www.760craftworks.com
SIC: 2082 5813 7389 Malt beverages; Drinking places; Business Activities at Non-Commercial Site

(G-6963)
AKOUSTIS TECHNOLOGIES INC (PA)
Also Called: Akoustis
9805 Northcross Center Ct Ste A (28078)
PHONE..............................704 997-5735
Mark D Podgainy Fto, *Prin*
Kamran Cheema, *CPO*
Kenneth E Boller, *CFO*
EMP: 4 **EST:** 2013
SQ FT: 22,400
SALES (est): 27.38MM
SALES (corp-wide): 27.38MM **Publicly Held**
Web: www.akoustis.com
SIC: 3663 Amplifiers, RF power and IF

(G-6964)
AMERICAN WOODMARK CORPORATION
Also Called: Timberlake Cabinet Company
9825 Northcross Center Ct Ste N (28078-7338)
P.O. Box 65524 (28216)
PHONE..............................704 947-3280
Tim Argall, *Mgr*
EMP: 48
SALES (corp-wide): 1.85B **Publicly Held**

Web: www.americanwoodmark.com
SIC: 2431 Millwork
PA: American Woodmark Corporation
    561 Shady Elm Rd
    Winchester VA 22602
    540 665-9100

(G-6965)
AMEROCK LLC (DH)
Also Called: Piedmont Hardware Brands
10115 Kincey Ave Ste 210 (28078-6483)
PHONE..............................800 435-6959
Ian T Graham, *
▲ EMP: 18 EST: 1928
SALES (est): 1.86MM
SALES (corp-wide): 29.73B Privately Held
SIC: 3429 Cabinet hardware
HQ: Ferguson Enterprises, Llc
    751 Lakefront Cmns
    Newport News VA 23606
    757 874-7795

(G-6966)
APEX TOOL GROUP LLC
13620 Reese Blvrd Pkwy E Ste 410
(28078)
PHONE..............................410 773-7800
EMP: 65
SQ FT: 180,000
SALES (corp-wide): 2.81B Privately Held
Web: www.apextoolgroup.com
SIC: 3423 Hand and edge tools, nec
HQ: Apex Tool Group, Llc
    910 Ridgebrook Rd Ste 200
    Sparks Glencoe MD 21152

(G-6967)
AREVA
11515 Vanstory Dr Ste 140 (28078-6388)
PHONE..............................704 805-2935
EMP: 7 EST: 2018
SALES (est): 126.37K Privately Held
SIC: 3823 Process control instruments

(G-6968)
ASHLAND PRODUCTS INC
Also Called: Ashland Hardware Systems
8936 N Exec Dr S 250 (28078)
PHONE..............................815 266-0250
▲ EMP: 200
SIC: 3089 Plastics hardware and building
    products

(G-6969)
ATOM POWER INC
Also Called: Atom Power
13245 Reese Blvd W Ste 130 (28078-6349)
PHONE..............................844 704-2866
Bharat Vats, CEO
Eric Dana, *
EMP: 98 EST: 2014
SALES (est): 22.57MM Privately Held
Web: www.atompower.com
SIC: 3699 Electrical equipment and supplies,
    nec

(G-6970)
AUTOMATED CONTROLS LLC
13416 S Old Statesville Rd (28078-7261)
P.O. Box 1952 (28070-1952)
PHONE..............................704 724-7625
Joshua J Penn, Prin
EMP: 8 EST: 2008
SQ FT: 1,500
SALES (est): 978.83K Privately Held
Web: www.automatedcontrolsnc.com
SIC: 1799 7382 1731 3446 Fence
    construction; Fire alarm maintenance and
    monitoring; Access control systems
    specialization; Gates, ornamental metal

(G-6971)
AUTOMEDX LLC
13359 Reese Blvd E (28078-6591)
PHONE..............................888 617-2904
James Evans, Prin
EMP: 5 EST: 2004
SALES (est): 1.69MM Privately Held
Web: www.automedx.com
SIC: 3845 Electromedical equipment

(G-6972)
BELEV EN U WATER MFG CO
Also Called: Bottle Water Manufacture
13620 Reese Blvd E Ste 120 (28078-6453)
P.O. Box 240351 (28224-0351)
PHONE..............................704 458-9950
Norman Mundy Junior, CEO
Norman Mundy, CEO
EMP: 5 EST: 2021
SALES (est): 710.71K Privately Held
SIC: 3999 Manufacturing industries, nec

(G-6973)
BELTSERVICE CORPORATION
9540 Julian Clark Ave (28078-3346)
PHONE..............................704 947-2264
Jim Mcnery, Mgr
EMP: 26
SALES (corp-wide): 135.54MM Privately
Held
Web: www.beltservice.com
SIC: 3052 3535 Rubber belting; Conveyors
    and conveying equipment
PA: Beltservice Corporation
    4143 Rider Trail N
    Earth City MO 63045
    314 344-8500

(G-6974)
BURKERT USA CORPORATION
Also Called: Burkert Fluid Control Systems
11425 Mount Holly Hntrsvlle Rd
(28078-7763)
PHONE..............................800 325-1405
Andreas Ruzic, Pr
Heribert Peter Rohrbeck, *
Dietrich Glas, *
Marco Ivan Steinemann, *
EMP: 138 EST: 1984
SQ FT: 198,000
SALES (est): 39.34MM
SALES (corp-wide): 144.19K Privately
Held
Web: www.burkert.com
SIC: 3491 Industrial valves
HQ: Burkert International Ag
    Bosch 71
    Hunenberg ZG 6331

(G-6975)
CELESTIAL PRODUCTS INC
9632 Skybluff Cir (28078-2412)
PHONE..............................540 338-4040
Larry Bohlayer, Pr
Barbara C Bohlayer, VP
EMP: 4 EST: 1980
SALES (est): 123.17K Privately Held
SIC: 2752 Calendars, lithographed

(G-6976)
CITIZEN MEDIA INC
403 N Old Statesville Rd (28078-7203)
PHONE..............................704 363-6062
EMP: 4 EST: 2017
SALES (est): 62.99K Privately Held
SIC: 2711 Newspapers

(G-6977)
COMBAT MEDICAL SYSTEMS LLC
Also Called: Safeguard America

13359 Reese Blvd E (28078-6591)
PHONE..............................704 705-1222
Greg Keyes, Dir
Kim Salvi, *
EMP: 25 EST: 2008
SALES (est): 11.03MM
SALES (corp-wide): 13.86MM Privately
Held
Web: www.combatmedical.com
SIC: 3845 5047 Arc lamp units,
    electrotherapeutic (except IR and UV);
    Medical equipment and supplies
PA: Safeguard Us Operating, Llc
    5555 Harrisburg Ind Pk Dr
    Harrisburg NC 28075
    855 428-6074

(G-6978)
COMMON PART GROUPINGS LLC
Also Called: Cpg
11601 Hambright Rd (28078-7666)
P.O. Box 2368 (28070-2368)
PHONE..............................704 948-0097
James Lang, Managing Member
▲ EMP: 10 EST: 2006
SQ FT: 48,000
SALES (est): 3.43MM Privately Held
Web: www.commonpartgroupings.com
SIC: 3441 Fabricated structural metal

(G-6979)
CORSAN LLC
13201 Reese Blvd W Ste 100 (28078-7945)
PHONE..............................704 765-9979
Rusty Broome, Managing Member
Brad Edwards, COO
EMP: 15 EST: 2013
SALES (est): 10.94MM Privately Held
Web: www.corsan.com
SIC: 5051 3999 Miscellaneous nonferrous
    products; Barber and beauty shop
    equipment

(G-6980)
COVIA HOLDINGS CORPORATION
Also Called: COVIA HOLDINGS
CORPORATION
9930 Kincey Ave # 200 (28078-6541)
PHONE..............................980 495-2092
Reid Carlson, Mgr
EMP: 5
SALES (corp-wide): 1.47B Privately Held
Web: www.coviacorp.com
SIC: 1446 Industrial sand
PA: Covia Holdings Llc
    3 Summit Park Dr Ste 700
    Independence OH 44131
    800 243-9004

(G-6981)
CRC PRINTING CO INC
15700 Old Statesville Rd (28078-7238)
PHONE..............................704 875-1804
Robin Holder, Pr
EMP: 4 EST: 1984
SQ FT: 2,660
SALES (est): 171.3K Privately Held
Web: www.crc123.net
SIC: 2752 Offset printing

(G-6982)
DOOR WORKS HUNTERSVILLE LLC
11701 Mccord Rd Bldg 11 (28078-7293)
P.O. Box 430 (28164-0430)
PHONE..............................704 947-1900
EMP: 32 EST: 2003
SALES (est): 4.74MM Privately Held
Web: www.doorworkscompany.com
SIC: 2431 Louver doors: wood

(G-6983)
DURAFIBER TECHNOLOGIES
13620 Reese Blvd E # 400 (28078-6417)
PHONE..............................704 912-3700
EMP: 1500
SALES (est): 103.96K
SALES (corp-wide): 17.78B Privately Held
SIC: 2824 Organic fibers, noncellulosic
HQ: Sun Performance Fibers, Llc
    5200 Town Center Cir # 470
    Boca Raton FL

(G-6984)
DURAFIBER TECHNOLOGIES (DFT)
INC
13620 Reese Blvd E Ste 400 (28078-6417)
PHONE..............................704 912-3700
▲ EMP: 1200
SIC: 2824 Organic fibers, noncellulosic

(G-6985)
DURAFIBER TECHNOLOGIES (DFT)
OPERATIONS LLC
13620 Reese Blvd E Ste 400 (28078-6417)
PHONE..............................704 912-3770
◆ EMP: 650
SIC: 2824 Organic fibers, noncellulosic

(G-6986)
EAGLE MACHINING USA INC
13728 Statesville Rd (28078-9038)
PHONE..............................717 235-9383
Anthony Lazarek, Pr
Dave Rietschy, *
Marc Childs, *
EMP: 18 EST: 1998
SALES (est): 700.01K Privately Held
SIC: 3599 Machine shop, jobbing and repair

(G-6987)
ESHER LLC
9911 Rose Commons Dr (28078-0323)
PHONE..............................704 975-1463
Joslyn Fyffe, Prin
EMP: 6 EST: 2015
SALES (est): 1.07MM Privately Held
SIC: 3446 Ornamental metalwork

(G-6988)
FANUC AMERICA CORPORATION
Also Called: Fanuc Robotics
13245 Reese Blvd W Ste 140 (28078-6307)
PHONE..............................704 596-5121
Jim Kosmala, Brnch Mgr
EMP: 61
Web: www.fanucamerica.com
SIC: 3559 3548 3569 Metal finishing
    equipment for plating, etc.; Electric welding
    equipment; Robots, assembly line:
    industrial and commercial
HQ: Fanuc America Corporation
    3900 W Hamlin Rd
    Rochester Hills MI 48309
    248 377-7000

(G-6989)
FIDELITY PHARMACEUTICALS LLC
11957 Ramah Church Rd (28078-7271)
PHONE..............................704 274-3192
Joseph Pfeiffer, CEO
Matthew Damato, CEO
EMP: 5 EST: 2021
SALES (est): 488.3K Privately Held
Web: www.fidelitypharmaceuticals.com
SIC: 2834 5122 5047 Pharmaceutical
    preparations; Drugs, proprietaries, and
    sundries; Medical and hospital equipment

▲ = Import ▼ = Export
◆ = Import/Export

(G-6990)
FINNORD NORTH AMERICA CORP
14514 Sunset Walk Ln (28078-0602)
PHONE.................................704 723-4913
Delln Murphy, *Genl Mgr*
▲ EMP: 15 EST: 2011
SALES (est): 2.25MM **Privately Held**
Web: www.finnord.it
SIC: 8711 3679 Engineering services;
Electronic circuits
HQ: Meccanica Finnord Spa
Via Dante Alighieri 51
Jerago Con Orago VA 21040

(G-6991)
FIRELINE SHIELDS LLC
15336 Old Statesville Rd (28078-7234)
PHONE.................................704 948-3680
Gregory Braham, *Prin*
EMP: 6 EST: 2011
SALES (est): 193.3K **Privately Held**
Web: www.firelineshields.com
SIC: 3559 Special industry machinery, nec

(G-6992)
FORBO BELTING
12201 Vanstory Dr (28078-8395)
PHONE.................................704 948-0800
Natlie Deal, *Mgr*
EMP: 23 EST: 2007
SALES (est): 2.56MM **Privately Held**
Web: www.forbo.com
SIC: 3052 Rubber belting

(G-6993)
FORBO SIEGLING LLC
13245 Reese Blvd W (28078-6307)
PHONE.................................704 948-0800
EMP: 13
Web: www.forbo.com
SIC: 3052 Rubber and plastics hose and
beltings
HQ: Forbo Siegling, Llc
12201 Vanstory Dr
Huntersville NC 28078
704 948-0800

(G-6994)
FORBO SIEGLING LLC
12120 Herbert Wayne Ct (28078-6326)
PHONE.................................704 948-0800
EMP: 13
Web: www.forbo.com
SIC: 3052 Rubber belting
HQ: Forbo Siegling, Llc
12201 Vanstory Dr
Huntersville NC 28078
704 948-0800

(G-6995)
FORBO SIEGLING LLC (HQ)
12201 Vanstory Dr (28078)
P.O. Box 60943 (28260)
PHONE.................................704 948-0800
Wayne E Hoffman, *Pr*
Chris Flannigan, *
John Casali, *
Norm Nelson, *
This E Schneider, *
▲ EMP: 274 EST: 1956
SQ FT: 100,000
SALES (est): 47.97MM **Privately Held**
Web: www.forbo.com
SIC: 3052 3535 Rubber belting; Conveyors
and conveying equipment
PA: Forbo Holding Ag
Lindenstrasse 8
Baar ZG 6340

(G-6996)
GREAT STAR INDUSTRIAL USA LLC (DH)
9836 Northcross Center Ct Ste A
(28078-7345)
PHONE.................................704 892-4965
▲ EMP: 4 EST: 2012
SQ FT: 5,000
SALES (est): 13.41MM **Privately Held**
SIC: 3423 Carpenters' hand tools, except
saws: levels, chisels, etc.
HQ: Great Star Tools Usa, Inc.
271 Mayhill St
Saddle Brook NJ 07663
201 562-1232

(G-6997)
HERALD HUNTERSVILLE
Also Called: Mechlanburg Newspaper Group
200 S Old Statesville Rd (28078-3924)
PHONE.................................704 766-2100
Tucker Mitchell, *Owner*
EMP: 4 EST: 2002
SALES (est): 204.16K **Privately Held**
Web: www.lakenormanpublications.com
SIC: 2711 Newspapers, publishing and
printing

(G-6998)
HERTZ KOMPRESSOREN USA INC
11910 Mount Holly Hntrsvlle Rd
(28078-6592)
Rural Route 3320 Service St (28206)
PHONE.................................704 579-5900
EMP: 9 EST: 2016
SALES (est): 4.25MM **Privately Held**
Web: www.hertz-kompressoren.com
SIC: 3563 Air and gas compressors

(G-6999)
HIRSCH SOLUTIONS LLC
11515 Vanstory Dr Ste 145 (28078-6387)
P.O. Box 18004 (11788-8804)
PHONE.................................631 701-2112
Brian Rees, *Mgr*
EMP: 5 EST: 2018
SALES (est): 488.23K **Privately Held**
Web: www.hsi.us
SIC: 2323 Men's and boy's neckwear

(G-7000)
IDEA PEOPLE INC
14311 Reese Blvd W (28078-7954)
PHONE.................................704 398-4437
Jay Joyce, *Pr*
Bill Mccown, *VP*
EMP: 6 EST: 1994
SQ FT: 7,000
SALES (est): 778.13K **Privately Held**
Web: www.theideapeople.com
SIC: 7372 7311 5942 8748 Application
computer software; Advertising agencies;
Children's books; Publishing consultant

(G-7001)
INNOVASOURCE LLC
11515 Vanstory Dr Ste 110 (28078-6388)
PHONE.................................704 584-0072
▲ EMP: 10 EST: 2009
SQ FT: 12,000
SALES (est): 2.45MM
SALES (corp-wide): 2.89B **Publicly Held**
Web: www.innovasource.com
SIC: 2841 Soap and other detergents
PA: Energizer Holdings, Inc.
8235 Forsyth Blvd Ste 100
Saint Louis MO 63105
314 985-2000

(G-7002)
INTERACTIVE SAFETY PDTS INC
9825 Northcross Center Ct Ste A
(28078-7338)
P.O. Box 315 (18407-0315)
PHONE.................................704 664-7377
Jan Korny, *CFO*
▲ EMP: 7 EST: 1996
SQ FT: 15,000
SALES (est): 1.39MM
SALES (corp-wide): 103.27MM **Privately Held**
Web: www.gentexcorp.com
SIC: 3469 Helmets, steel
HQ: Helmet Integrated Systems Limited
Unit 3 Focus
Letchworth Garden City HERTS SG6 2
146 247-8000

(G-7003)
IRWIN
8936 N Pointe Executive P (28078-4810)
PHONE.................................704 987-4339
EMP: 6 EST: 2014
SALES (est): 93.46K **Privately Held**
Web: www.irwin.com
SIC: 3423 Hand and edge tools, nec

(G-7004)
IRWIN INDUSTRIAL TOOL COMPANY (HQ)
Also Called: Irwin Construction Accessories
8935 N Pointe Executive Park Dr
(28078-4857)
PHONE.................................704 987-4555
Michael B Polk, *CEO*
Neil R Eibeler, *
◆ EMP: 200 EST: 1985
SALES (est): 27.31MM
SALES (corp-wide): 15.78B **Publicly Held**
Web: www.irwintools.com
SIC: 3423 3545 3421 Screw drivers, pliers,
chisels, etc. (hand tools); Drill bits,
metalworking; Snips, tinners'
PA: Stanley Black & Decker, Inc.
1000 Stanley Dr
New Britain CT 06053
860 225-5111

(G-7005)
JAG INDUSTRIES LLC
10408 Remembrance Trl (28078-5914)
PHONE.................................704 655-2507
Joseph Grouse, *Prin*
EMP: 4 EST: 2018
SALES (est): 77.07K **Privately Held**
Web: www.jagconstructioncorp.com
SIC: 3999 Manufacturing industries, nec

(G-7006)
KELLANOVA
Also Called: Kellog
13801 Reese Blvd W (28078-6308)
PHONE.................................704 370-1658
Michelle Piegaro, *Mgr*
EMP: 4
SALES (corp-wide): 13.12B **Publicly Held**
Web: www.kellanova.com
SIC: 2043 Cereal breakfast foods
PA: Kellanova
412 N Wells St
Chicago IL 60654
269 961-2000

(G-7007)
KELLER TECHNOLOGY CORPORATION
11905 Vanstory Dr (28078-8121)
PHONE.................................704 875-1605
Robert Paschka, *Brnch Mgr*

EMP: 40
SALES (corp-wide): 150MM **Privately Held**
Web: www.kellertechnology.com
SIC: 8711 3569 Engineering services;
Robots, assembly line: industrial and
commercial
PA: Keller Technology Corporation
2320 Military Rd
Tonawanda NY 14150
716 693-3840

(G-7008)
KURZ TRANSFER PRODUCTS LP (HQ)
11836 Patterson Rd (28078-9732)
P.O. Box 63182 (28283)
PHONE.................................704 927-3700
Walter Kurz, *Pt*
Kurz Charlotte, *
Peter Kurz, *
Konrad Kurz, *
▲ EMP: 100 EST: 1992
SALES (est): 101.89MM
SALES (corp-wide): 1B **Privately Held**
Web: www.kurzusa.com
SIC: 3497 Metal foil and leaf
PA: Leonhard Kurz Stiftung & Co. Kg
Schwabacher Str. 482
Furth BY 90763
91171410

(G-7009)
LANART INTERNATIONAL INC
10325 Hambright Rd (28078-7655)
PHONE.................................704 875-1972
Angelo Ponce, *Pr*
EMP: 4 EST: 1979
SQ FT: 3,458
SALES (est): 363.26K **Privately Held**
Web: www.lanartalpaca.com
SIC: 2211 Alpacas, cotton

(G-7010)
LEHR LLC
12703 Commerce Station Dr (28078-6825)
PHONE.................................704 827-9368
Patrick Mccullagh, *CEO*
EMP: 18 EST: 2014
SALES (est): 2.3MM **Privately Held**
Web: www.golehr.com
SIC: 3519 Marine engines

(G-7011)
LIECHTI AMERICA
13245 Reese Blvd W Ste 100 (28078-6307)
PHONE.................................704 948-1277
Philip Ward, *COO*
▲ EMP: 6 EST: 2012
SALES (est): 418.27K **Privately Held**
SIC: 3462 Pump, compressor, and turbine
forgings

(G-7012)
MAX DAETWYLER CORP (DH)
Also Called: Daetwyler Cstm Fbrction McHnin
13420 Reese Blvd W (28078-7925)
PHONE.................................704 875-1200
Ralph Daetwyler, *Pr*
Walter Siegenthaler, *
Kurt Oegerli, *
◆ EMP: 21 EST: 1975
SQ FT: 72,000
SALES (est): 14.61MM **Privately Held**
Web: www.daetwyler-usa.com
SIC: 3599 Electrical discharge machining
(EDM)
HQ: Mdc Max Daetwyler Ag
Flugplatz
Bleienbach BE 3368

(G-7013)
MICROBAN PRODUCTS COMPANY (DH)
Also Called: Microban
11400 Vanstory Dr (28078-8147)
PHONE...............704 766-4267
David Mayers, *Pr*
Richard Chapman, *VP*
Tom Bowlds, *CFO*
▲ **EMP:** 40 **EST:** 1987
SQ FT: 50,000
SALES (est): 22.96MM
SALES (corp-wide): 390.28MM **Privately Held**
Web: www.microban.com
SIC: 2842 2819 2821 2899 Specialty cleaning; Industrial inorganic chemicals, nec ; Thermoplastic materials; Chemical preparations, nec
HQ: Microban International, Ltd.
11400 Vanstory Dr
Huntersville NC 28078

(G-7014)
MIRACLE RECREATION EQP CO
11515 Vanstory Dr Ste 100 (28078-6300)
PHONE...............704 875-6550
Erin Hampton, *Prin*
EMP: 137
Web: www.softplay.com
SIC: 3949 Playground equipment
HQ: Miracle Recreation Equipment Company
878 E Us Highway 60
Monett MO 65708
888 458-2752

(G-7015)
MK PRO LOGISTICS LLC
7001 Sweetfield Dr (28078-7750)
PHONE...............980 420-8156
EMP: 6
SALES (est): 341.83K **Privately Held**
SIC: 7389 3799 Business Activities at Non-Commercial Site; Transportation equipment, nec

(G-7016)
MLB SCREEN PRINTING
12008 Regal Lily Ln (28078-2396)
PHONE...............704 363-6124
Michelle L Backstrom, *Prin*
EMP: 5 **EST:** 2013
SALES (est): 143.5K **Privately Held**
SIC: 2752 Commercial printing, lithographic

(G-7017)
MOMENTIVE PERFORMANCE MTLS INC
Also Called: Momentive Performance Mtls USA
13620 Reese Blvd E Ste 310 (28078-6418)
PHONE...............704 805-6200
Sara Gherman, *Brnch Mgr*
EMP: 50
Web: www.momentive.com
SIC: 2869 Silicones
HQ: Momentive Performance Materials Inc.
2750 Balltown Rd
Niskayuna NY 12309

(G-7018)
MOUNTAINEER YELLOWPAGES
16126 Glen Miro Dr (28078-2259)
PHONE...............866 758-0123
David C Wolding, *Pr*
David Wolding, *Pr*
EMP: 4 **EST:** 2008
SALES (est): 165.84K **Privately Held**
Web: www.mountaineeryellowpages.com

SIC: 2741 Telephone and other directory publishing

(G-7019)
NEWELL BRANDS INC
Also Called: Testing Facility
9815 Northcross Center Ct Ste 8 (28078-7340)
PHONE...............704 987-4760
Gary Decarr, *Mgr*
EMP: 30
SALES (corp-wide): 7.58B **Publicly Held**
Web: www.newellbrands.com
SIC: 3089 Plastics kitchenware, tableware, and houseware
PA: Newell Brands Inc.
6655 Pachtree Dunwoody Rd
Atlanta GA 30328
770 418-7000

(G-7020)
NEWELL BRANDS INC
Rubbermaid
8935 N Pointe Executive Park Dr (28078-4857)
PHONE...............704 895-8082
EMP: 48
SALES (corp-wide): 7.58B **Publicly Held**
Web: www.rubbermaidcommercial.com
SIC: 3089 Plastics kitchenware, tableware, and houseware
PA: Newell Brands Inc.
6655 Pachtree Dunwoody Rd
Atlanta GA 30328
770 418-7000

(G-7021)
NINOS WLDG & CNSTR SVCS LLC
11901 Everett Keith Rd (28078-3661)
PHONE...............980 214-5804
Joaquin Guevara Nino, *Prin*
EMP: 4 **EST:** 2016
SALES (est): 350.77K **Privately Held**
SIC: 7692 Welding repair

(G-7022)
NORMAN LAKE GRAPHICS INC
9735 Northcross Center Ct Ste L (28078-7326)
P.O. Box 2280 (28031-2280)
PHONE...............704 896-8444
Robert C Carter, *Pr*
Jean Carter, *Sec*
EMP: 5 **EST:** 1991
SALES (est): 244.8K **Privately Held**
Web: www.lakenormanchamber.org
SIC: 2752 Commercial printing, lithographic

(G-7023)
NOVA WILDCAT DRAPERY HDWR LLC
Also Called: Drapery Hardware
10115 Kincey Ave Ste 210 (28078-6483)
PHONE...............704 696-5110
EMP: 50 **EST:** 2013
SALES (est): 2.15MM **Privately Held**
SIC: 2591 Drapery hardware and window blinds and shades

(G-7024)
NSI INDUSTRIES
9730 Northcross Center Ct (28078-7301)
PHONE...............800 321-5847
EMP: 100
SALES (corp-wide): 9.22MM **Privately Held**
SIC: 3625 Relays and industrial controls
PA: Nsi Industries
9730 Northcross Center Ct
Huntersville NC
914 664-3542

(G-7025)
NUTEC INC
11830 Mount Holly Hntrsvlle Rd (28078-7628)
PHONE...............877 318-2430
Gilberto Wells, *CEO*
EMP: 30 **EST:** 2015
SALES (est): 19.23MM **Privately Held**
Web: www.nutec.com
SIC: 3567 Heating units and devices, industrial; electric
PA: Grupo Nutec, S.A. De C.V.
Jardin De San Jeronimo No. 225
Monterrey NLE 64640

(G-7026)
OCUFII INC ✪
11211 James Coy Rd (28078-5131)
PHONE...............804 874-4036
William Sandoval, *Pr*
EMP: 4 **EST:** 2023
SALES (est): 363.37K **Privately Held**
SIC: 7372 7389 Prepackaged software; Business Activities at Non-Commercial Site

(G-7027)
OERLIKON AM US INC
12012 Vanstory Dr (28078-8324)
PHONE...............980 260-2827
Roland Fischer, *CEO*
EMP: 50 **EST:** 2017
SALES (est): 16.97MM **Privately Held**
SIC: 5084 2851 Industrial machinery and equipment; Coating, air curing
PA: Oc Oerlikon Corporation Ag, Pfaffikon
Churerstrasse 120
PfAffikon SZ 8808

(G-7028)
OERLIKON METCO (US) INC
12012 Vanstory Dr (28078-8324)
PHONE...............713 715-6300
EMP: 11
Web: www.oerlikon.com
SIC: 3399 5084 3479 Powder, metal; Industrial machinery and equipment; Coating of metals and formed products
HQ: Oerlikon Metco (Us) Inc.
1101 Prospect Ave
Westbury NY 11590
516 334-1300

(G-7029)
ORANGE BAKERY INC
13400 Reese Blvd W (28078-7925)
PHONE...............704 875-3003
Yoshiaki Okacaki, *Dir*
EMP: 30
SQ FT: 45,063
Web: www.orangebakery.com
SIC: 2038 2053 2051 Frozen specialties, nec ; Frozen bakery products, except bread; Bread, cake, and related products
HQ: Orange Bakery, Inc.
17751 Cowan
Irvine CA 92614
949 863-1377

(G-7030)
PCS COLLECTIBLES LLC (PA)
Also Called: Culture Shock Toys
9825 Northcross Center Ct (28078-7338)
PHONE...............805 306-1140
Anthony Adams, *Managing Member*
EMP: 9 **EST:** 2017
SALES (est): 8.28MM
SALES (corp-wide): 8.28MM **Privately Held**
Web: www.collectpcs.com
SIC: 3942 Dolls and stuffed toys

(G-7031)
PEAK CLEAN ENERGY LLC
11330 Vanstory Dr (28078)
PHONE...............303 588-2789
EMP: 5 **EST:** 2016
SALES (est): 679.3K **Privately Held**
Web: www.peakcleanenergy.com
SIC: 3621 8711 Windmills, electric generating ; Energy conservation engineering

(G-7032)
PERFORMANCE FIBERS
12721 Longstock Ct (28078-5718)
PHONE...............704 947-7193
Gareth Jones, *Prin*
EMP: 15 **EST:** 2010
SALES (est): 317.52K **Privately Held**
SIC: 2221 Polyester broadwoven fabrics

(G-7033)
PLAYPOWER INC (DH)
11515 Vanstory Dr Ste 100 (28078)
PHONE...............704 949-1600
Bryan Yeazel, *CEO*
Michael Pruss, *
Lynn Vandever, *
Brenda Mcclelland, *Contrlr*
◆ **EMP:** 24 **EST:** 1993
SQ FT: 124,260
SALES (est): 167.16MM **Privately Held**
Web: www.playpower.com
SIC: 3949 Playground equipment
HQ: Playpower Holdings Inc.
11515 Vanstory Dr Ste 100
Huntersville NC 28078

(G-7034)
POLY-TECH INDUSTRIAL INC
11330 Vanstory Dr (28078-8143)
PHONE...............704 992-8100
Daniel Cedrone, *Prin*
EMP: 5 **EST:** 2015
SALES (est): 784.29K **Privately Held**
Web: www.ensinger-pc.com
SIC: 3089 Injection molding of plastics

(G-7035)
POLY-TECH INDUSTRIAL INC
13728 Statesville Rd (28078-9038)
PHONE...............704 948-8055
EMP: 35 **EST:** 2001
SALES (est): 6.03MM
SALES (corp-wide): 652MM **Privately Held**
Web: www.ensinger-pc.com
SIC: 5162 3089 Plastics materials and basic shapes; Molding primary plastics
HQ: Ensinger Polytech, Inc.
13728 Statesville Rd
Huntersville NC 28078
704 992-8100

(G-7036)
PRATT MLLER ENGRG FBRCTION LLC
9801 Kincey Ave Ste 175 (28078-3104)
PHONE...............704 977-0642
Christopher Gilligan, *Brnch Mgr*
EMP: 175
SALES (corp-wide): 10.73B **Publicly Held**
Web: www.prattmiller.com
SIC: 3711 8711 Automobile assembly, including specialty automobiles; Engineering services
HQ: Pratt & Miller Engineering & Fabrication, Llc
29600 Wk Smith Dr
New Hudson MI 48165

▲ = Import ▼ = Export
◆ = Import/Export

(G-7037)
PRECISION CONCEPTS INTL LLC (PA)
16810 Kenton Dr (28078-4831)
PHONE.....................704 360-8923
Ray Grupinski, *CEO*
Dave Bell, *CFO*
EMP: 7 EST: 2011
SALES (est): 93.83MM
SALES (corp-wide): 93.83MM **Privately Held**
Web: www.pcinternational.com
SIC: 3085 3221 7336 Plastics bottles; Glass containers; Package design

(G-7038)
PRIME BEVERAGE GROUP LLC (PA)
12800 Jamesburg Dr (28078)
PHONE.....................704 385-5450
Brian Hughs, *Managing Member*
EMP: 94 EST: 2019
SALES (est): 43.93MM
SALES (corp-wide): 43.93MM **Privately Held**
Web: www.primebev.com
SIC: 2087 Beverage bases

(G-7039)
PRINT SOCIAL
403 Gilead Rd Ste A (28078-6814)
PHONE.....................980 430-4483
EMP: 4 EST: 2016
SALES (est): 86.67K **Privately Held**
Web: www.primoprint.com
SIC: 2752 Offset printing

(G-7040)
PROJECT BEAN LLC
Also Called: Water-Jel Technologies
13359 Reese Blvd E (28078-6591)
PHONE.....................201 438-1598
James Hartnett, *Pr*
Mark Lait, *
▲ EMP: 70 EST: 1999
SALES (est): 3.87MM
SALES (corp-wide): 16.02MM **Privately Held**
Web: www.safeguardmedical.com
SIC: 3842 5199 First aid, snake bite, and burn kits; First aid supplies
PA: Safeguard Medical Alarms, Inc.
 13359 Reese Blvd E
 Huntersville NC 28078
 312 506-2900

(G-7041)
REACREDENCE IT SOLUTIONS INC
8936 N Pointe Executive Park Dr Ste 240
(28078-4810)
PHONE.....................980 399-4071
Danielle Renee Marlowe, *Brnch Mgr*
EMP: 4
SALES (corp-wide): 62.28K **Privately Held**
Web: www.reacredence.com
SIC: 7372 Application computer software
PA: Reacredence It Solutions Inc.
 13526 Winterhaven Dr
 Dallas TX

(G-7042)
REYNOLDS CONSUMER PRODUCTS INC
Also Called: Reynolds Consumer Products
14201 Meacham Farm Dr (28078-8000)
PHONE.....................704 371-5550
Andy Bass, *Mgr*
EMP: 527
Web: www.reynoldsbrands.com

SIC: 2673 3497 3089 2621 Food storage and trash bags (plastic); Metal foil and leaf; Plastics containers, except foam; Pressed and molded pulp and fiber products
HQ: Reynolds Consumer Products Inc.
 1900 W Field Ct
 Lake Forest IL 60045
 800 879-5067

(G-7043)
RICURA CORPORATION
11515 Vanstory Dr Ste 110 (28078-6388)
PHONE.....................704 875-0366
Glen Cueman, *Pr*
Barnwell Ramsey, *VP*
▲ EMP: 10 EST: 1996
SQ FT: 12,000
SALES (est): 586.02K **Privately Held**
Web: www.ricura.com
SIC: 3564 5075 Filters, air: furnaces, air conditioning equipment, etc.; Air pollution control equipment and supplies

(G-7044)
ROYAL FAIRES INC (PA)
16445 Poplar Tent Rd (28078-4620)
PHONE.....................704 896-5555
Jeffrey Siegel, *Prin*
Robert Levine C F O, *Prin*
EMP: 12 EST: 1993
SALES (est): 2.46MM **Privately Held**
SIC: 7922 2731 Theatrical producers and services; Book publishing

(G-7045)
RUBBERMAID COMMERCIAL PDTS LLC (DH)
Also Called: Rubbermaid
8900 N Pointe Executive Park Dr
(28078-4857)
PHONE.....................540 667-8700
Mike Mcdermott, *CEO*
◆ EMP: 1000 EST: 1968
SQ FT: 750,000
SALES (est): 49.18MM
SALES (corp-wide): 7.58B **Publicly Held**
Web: www.rubbermaidcommercial.com
SIC: 3089 2673 Plastics containers, except foam; Bags: plastic, laminated, and coated
HQ: Rubbermaid Incorporated
 6655 Pachtree Dunwoody Rd
 Atlanta GA 30328
 888 895-2110

(G-7046)
RUBBERMAID INCORPORATED
Also Called: Rubbermaid
8936 N Pointe Executive Park Dr
(28078-4809)
PHONE.....................704 987-4339
Steve Taylor, *Brnch Mgr*
EMP: 1102
SALES (corp-wide): 7.58B **Publicly Held**
Web: www.rubbermaidcommercial.com
SIC: 3089 Buckets, plastics
HQ: Rubbermaid Incorporated
 6655 Pachtree Dunwoody Rd
 Atlanta GA 30328
 888 895-2110

(G-7047)
RUBBERMAID INCORPORATED
Also Called: Rubbermaid
16905 Northcross Dr Ste 120 (28078-5097)
PHONE.....................888 859-8294
David Walsh, *Brnch Mgr*
EMP: 1632
SALES (corp-wide): 7.58B **Publicly Held**
Web: www.newellbrands.com
SIC: 3089 Buckets, plastics
HQ: Rubbermaid Incorporated

6655 Pachtree Dunwoody Rd
Atlanta GA 30328
888 895-2110

(G-7048)
SAERTEX MULTICOM LP (DH)
12200 Mount Holly Hntrsvlle Rd
(28078-7632)
PHONE.....................704 946-9229
Frank Mersamann, *Pt*
▲ EMP: 10 EST: 2013
SQ FT: 100,000
SALES (est): 21.49MM
SALES (corp-wide): 324.24MM **Privately Held**
Web: www.saertex-multicom.de
SIC: 3312 Pipes and tubes
HQ: Saertex Holding Gmbh & Co.Kg
 Brochterbecker Damm 52
 Saerbeck NW 48369
 25749020

(G-7049)
SAERTEX MULTICOM LP
12200 Mount Holly Hntrsvlle Rd Ste A
(28078-7632)
PHONE.....................704 946-9229
Frank Mersamann, *Pt*
EMP: 20
SALES (corp-wide): 324.24MM **Privately Held**
Web: www.saertex-multicom.de
SIC: 3312 Pipes and tubes
HQ: Saertex Multicom Lp
 12200 Mt Hly Hntrsvle Rd A
 Huntersville NC 28078
 704 946-9229

(G-7050)
SAERTEX USA LLC
12200 Mount Holly Hntrsvlle Rd
(28078-7631)
PHONE.....................704 464-5998
Ulrich Tombuelt, *COO*
◆ EMP: 200 EST: 2000
SQ FT: 22,000
SALES (est): 44.41MM
SALES (corp-wide): 324.24MM **Privately Held**
Web: www.saertex.com
SIC: 2297 Nonwoven fabrics
HQ: Saertex Beteiligungsges. Mbh
 Brochterbecker Damm 52
 Saerbeck NW 48369
 25749020

(G-7051)
SAFEGUARD MEDICAL
13359 Reese Blvd E (28078-6591)
PHONE.....................855 428-6074
EMP: 91
SALES (est): 6.78MM **Privately Held**
Web: www.safeguardmedical.com
SIC: 3841 Surgical and medical instruments

(G-7052)
SAFEGUARD MEDICAL ALARMS INC (PA)
13359 Reese Blvd E (28078-6591)
PHONE.....................312 506-2900
Adam Johnson, *CEO*
EMP: 11 EST: 2003
SALES (est): 16.02MM
SALES (corp-wide): 16.02MM **Privately Held**
Web: www.safeguardmedical.com
SIC: 3669 5999 Emergency alarms; Medical apparatus and supplies

6655 Pachtree Dunwoody Rd
Atlanta GA 30328
888 895-2110

(G-7053)
SAINT-GOBAIN VETROTEX AMER INC
8936 N Pointe Executive Park Dr Ste 165
(28078-0806)
PHONE.....................704 895-5906
Miguel Furray, *Mgr*
EMP: 152
SALES (corp-wide): 402.18MM **Privately Held**
Web:
www.saint-gobain-northamerica.com
SIC: 3089 Spouting, plastics and glass fiber reinforced
HQ: Saint-Gobain Vetrotex America, Inc.
 20 Moores Rd
 Valley Forge PA 19482

(G-7054)
SEG SYSTEMS LLC
10701 Hambright Rd (28078-7659)
PHONE.....................704 579-5800
Reid Johnson, *Pr*
EMP: 13 EST: 2014
SALES (est): 1.54MM
SALES (corp-wide): 48.12MM **Privately Held**
Web: www.segsystems.com
SIC: 3354 Aluminum extruded products
PA: Orbus, Llc
 9033 Murphy Rd
 Woodridge IL 60517
 630 226-1155

(G-7055)
SMC CORPORATION OF AMERICA
9801 Kincey Ave Ste 150 (28078-3106)
PHONE.....................704 947-7556
Lisa Shue, *Mgr*
EMP: 11
Web: www.smcusa.com
SIC: 3652 Prerecorded records and tapes
HQ: Smc Corporation Of America
 10100 Smc Blvd
 Noblesville IN 46060
 317 899-4440

(G-7056)
SOUTHWIRE COMPANY LLC
Also Called: Southwire
12331 Commerce Station Dr (28078-6823)
PHONE.....................704 379-9600
EMP: 28
SALES (corp-wide): 602.03MM **Privately Held**
Web: www.southwire.com
SIC: 3355 Aluminum rolling and drawing, nec
PA: Southwire Company, Llc
 One Southwire Dr
 Carrollton GA 30119
 770 832-4242

(G-7057)
STANLEY BLACK & DECKER
9829 Northcross Center Ct (28078-7302)
PHONE.....................704 987-2271
EMP: 11 EST: 2018
SALES (est): 726.51K **Privately Held**
Web: www.stanleyblackanddecker.com
SIC: 3546 Power-driven handtools

(G-7058)
STANLEY BLACK & DECKER INC
9930 Kincey Ave (28078-6541)
PHONE.....................704 293-9392
EMP: 5
SALES (corp-wide): 15.78B **Publicly Held**
Web: www.stanleyblackanddecker.com
SIC: 3545 Machine tool accessories
PA: Stanley Black & Decker, Inc.
 1000 Stanley Dr

New Britain CT 06053
860 225-5111

(G-7059)
SUNCAST CORPORATION
9801 Kincey Ave (28078-3110)
PHONE..............................704 274-5394
Jennifer Fensley, *Owner*
EMP: 24
SALES (corp-wide): 104.7MM **Privately Held**
Web: www.suncast.com
SIC: 2519 Lawn furniture, except wood, metal, stone, or concrete
PA: Suncast Corporation
701 N Kirk Rd
Batavia IL 60510
630 879-2050

(G-7060)
TRUNORTH WRRNTY PLANS N AMER L
16740 Birkdale Commons Pkwy (28078-4460)
PHONE..............................800 903-7489
EMP: 34 **EST:** 2015
SALES (est): 2.42MM **Privately Held**
Web: www.trunorthwarranty.com
SIC: 3537 Trucks, tractors, loaders, carriers, and similar equipment

(G-7061)
TUDG MULTIMEDIA FIRM
Also Called: Grapgic Design
12523 Surreykirt Ln (28078-4306)
PHONE..............................704 916-9819
Corey Newton, *Prin*
EMP: 7 **EST:** 2011
SALES (est): 191.31K **Privately Held**
SIC: 2741 Miscellaneous publishing

(G-7062)
WIRENET INC
16740 Birkdale Commons Pkwy Ste 306 (28078-4463)
PHONE..............................513 774-7759
Kenneth Cowan, *Pr*
EMP: 11 **EST:** 2000
SQ FT: 5,000
SALES (est): 855.12K **Privately Held**
SIC: 1623 8742 3663 3441 Transmitting tower (telecommunication) construction; Management consulting services; Radio and t.v. communications equipment; Fabricated structural metal

(G-7063)
YAT USA INC
10506 Bryton Corporate Center Dr (28078-0142)
PHONE..............................480 584-4096
Todd Murphy, *Pr*
EMP: 8 **EST:** 2017
SALES (est): 2.25MM **Privately Held**
SIC: 3545 5072 5251 Tools and accessories for machine tools; Power tools and accessories; Tools, power

Icard
Burke County

(G-7064)
ARTCRAFT PRESS INC
7814 Old Hwy 10 (28666)
P.O. Box 130 (28666-0130)
PHONE..............................828 397-8612
Mike Wallace, *Pr*
EMP: 6 **EST:** 1947
SQ FT: 6,200

SALES (est): 460.96K **Privately Held**
Web: www.artcraftpress.org
SIC: 2752 2759 Offset printing; Letterpress printing

Indian Trail
Union County

(G-7065)
3 STAR ENTERPRISES LLC
Also Called: Bce South
108 Business Park Dr (28079-9432)
P.O. Box 829 (28079-0829)
PHONE..............................704 821-7503
EMP: 20 **EST:** 1989
SQ FT: 5,600
SALES (est): 2.35MM **Privately Held**
Web: www.bcesouth.com
SIC: 2752 Visiting cards, lithographed

(G-7066)
ADD-ON TECHNOLOGIES INC
7000 Stinson Hartis Rd Ste D (28079-8807)
PHONE..............................704 882-2227
Ray Van Vynckt, *Pr*
EMP: 10 **EST:** 1994
SALES (est): 1.52MM **Privately Held**
Web: www.addontechnologies.com
SIC: 7371 3578 Computer software development; Billing machines

(G-7067)
ANDARK GRAPHICS INC
7204 Stinson Hartis Rd Ste A (28079-8835)
PHONE..............................704 882-1400
Rob Sellers, *Prin*
EMP: 6 **EST:** 2007
SALES (est): 470.65K **Privately Held**
Web: www.andarkgraphics.com
SIC: 3993 Signs and advertising specialties

(G-7068)
ANDRONICS CONSTRUCTION INC
Also Called: Andronx
110 Business Park Dr (28079-9432)
PHONE..............................704 400-9562
Yelena Andronic, *Pr*
Ivan Andronic, *
EMP: 30 **EST:** 2005
SQ FT: 13,000
SALES (est): 2.09MM **Privately Held**
Web: www.andronx.com
SIC: 2431 1751 Staircases and stairs, wood; Cabinet building and installation

(G-7069)
AUDIO VDEO CONCEPTS DESIGN INC
Also Called: Co-Da
1409 Babbage Ln Ste B (28079-3458)
PHONE..............................704 821-2823
Chris Wissa, *Pr*
Robert Burns, *VP*
EMP: 5 **EST:** 2011
SALES (est): 2.32MM **Privately Held**
Web: www.co-da.com
SIC: 3699 1731 Security control equipment and systems; Electronic controls installation

(G-7070)
AUSTIN BUSINESS FORMS INC
Also Called: Austin Print Solutions
241 Post Office Dr Ste A5 (28079-7676)
P.O. Box 1905 (28106-1905)
PHONE..............................704 821-6165
Robert L Austin, *Pr*
Terry S Austin, *VP*
Bart Austin, *VP*
EMP: 10 **EST:** 1991

SALES (est): 950.33K **Privately Held**
Web: austin.untapd.us
SIC: 5112 2759 Business forms; Commercial printing, nec

(G-7071)
B & B INDUSTRIES INC
4824 Unionville Indian Trail Rd W Ste A (28079-9567)
PHONE..............................704 882-4688
Gary Beck, *Pr*
Sandra Beck, *Sec*
EMP: 6 **EST:** 1992
SQ FT: 7,000
SALES (est): 888.93K **Privately Held**
Web: www.coloradogolflinks.com
SIC: 3599 Machine shop, jobbing and repair

(G-7072)
BRANCH OFFICE SOLUTIONS INC
4391 Indian Trail Fairview Rd Ste A (28079-9656)
PHONE..............................800 743-1047
Jeffrey Pitney, *Pr*
Jeffery Pitney, *Pr*
Chris Heffner, *VP*
EMP: 6 **EST:** 2008
SQ FT: 4,000
SALES (est): 140.73K **Privately Held**
Web: www.branchscan.com
SIC: 5044 3955 3577 7334 Office equipment ; Print cartridges for laser and other computer printers; Printers, computer; Photocopying and duplicating services

(G-7073)
CALL PRINTING & COPYING
311 Indian Trail Rd S (28079-9101)
P.O. Box 31 (28079-0031)
PHONE..............................704 821-6554
Greg Rogers, *Owner*
EMP: 6 **EST:** 1981
SQ FT: 3,200
SALES (est): 236.83K **Privately Held**
Web: www.callprinting.com
SIC: 2752 Offset printing

(G-7074)
COATINGS TECHNOLOGIES INC
Also Called: C T I
214 Plyler Rd (28079-7589)
P.O. Box 2400 (28079-2400)
PHONE..............................704 821-8231
David C Mccallister, *Pr*
David C Mc Callister Junior, *Pr*
Nancy Mc Callister, *Sec*
EMP: 7 **EST:** 1988
SQ FT: 3,200
SALES (est): 820.18K **Privately Held**
Web: www.coatingstechnologies.com
SIC: 3479 Coating of metals and formed products

(G-7075)
CPS RESOURCES INC
2000 Innovation Dr (28079-5504)
PHONE..............................704 628-7678
Craig Smith, *Pr*
Paul Smith, *
▲ **EMP:** 26 **EST:** 1987
SALES (est): 2.51MM **Privately Held**
Web: www.cpsresources.com
SIC: 3089 5084 2791 2752 Injection molding of plastics; Plastic products machinery; Typesetting; Commercial printing, lithographic

(G-7076)
CRYSTAL IMPRESSIONS LTD
14200 E Independence Blvd (28079-7833)
P.O. Box 280 (28079-0280)

PHONE..............................704 821-7678
Clive Berman, *Pr*
EMP: 10 **EST:** 1985
SALES (est): 242.2K **Privately Held**
Web: www.thecrystalshoppe.com
SIC: 2759 2396 Screen printing; Automotive and apparel trimmings

(G-7077)
DRYDOG BARRIERS LLC
2034 Van Buren Ave Ste C (28079-5596)
P.O. Box 743 (28106-0743)
PHONE..............................704 334-8222
▲ **EMP:** 5
Web: www.drydogbarriers.com
SIC: 1799 2385 Waterproofing; Aprons, waterproof: made from purchased materials

(G-7078)
ELIZABETH LOGISTIC LLC
1000 Loudoun Rd (28079-8478)
PHONE..............................803 920-3931
Melody Williams, *Managing Member*
EMP: 65 **EST:** 2017
SALES (est): 2.5MM **Privately Held**
SIC: 4731 4214 7372 Freight forwarding; Local trucking with storage; Application computer software

(G-7079)
ETK INTERNATIONAL INC
1005 Andrea Pl (28079-5529)
P.O. Box 2394 (28079-2394)
PHONE..............................704 819-1541
Douglas Todd, *Pr*
Dunja Todd, *Treas*
▲ **EMP:** 4 **EST:** 2003
SALES (est): 419.72K **Privately Held**
Web: www.etkinternational.com
SIC: 3553 Woodworking machinery

(G-7080)
EXHIBIT WORLD INC
13701 E Independence Blvd (28079-7600)
PHONE..............................704 882-2272
Dennis J Rogers, *Pr*
Phyllis Rogers, *VP*
EMP: 6 **EST:** 1974
SQ FT: 35,000
SALES (est): 248.31K **Privately Held**
Web: www.exhibit-world.com
SIC: 7389 3993 Exhibit construction by industrial contractors; Signs and advertising specialties

(G-7081)
FERGUSON HIGHWAY PRODUCTS INC
212 Old Dutch Rd W (28079-8771)
PHONE..............................704 320-3087
Helen Ferguson, *Pr*
Patrick Ferguson, *VP*
EMP: 5 **EST:** 2004
SALES (est): 517.01K **Privately Held**
Web: www.fergusonhp.com
SIC: 3531 Construction machinery

(G-7082)
GENERAL ELECTRIC COMPANY
Also Called: GE
171 Associate Ln (28079-7840)
PHONE..............................704 821-8260
Cheerie Shelton, *Brnch Mgr*
EMP: 10
SALES (corp-wide): 38.7B **Publicly Held**
Web: www.ge.com
SIC: 3829 Measuring and controlling devices, nec
PA: General Electric Company
1 Aviation Way
Cincinnati OH 45215

▲ = Import ▼ = Export
◆ = Import/Export

617 443-3000

(G-7083)
HITECH CIRCUITS INC
Also Called: Circuits
7711 Idlewild Rd (28079-7628)
P.O. Box 1796 (28079-1796)
PHONE.................................336 838-3420
Jerambhai Patel, *Pr*
Ramesh M Sanghani, *VP*
Kiran Patel, *Prin*
Ramnik Sanghani, *Sec*
Mahesh Patel, *Treas*
EMP: 7 **EST:** 1987
SQ FT: 22,000
SALES (est): 667.29K **Privately Held**
SIC: 3672 Printed circuit boards

(G-7084)
INDUSTRIAL ALLOYS INC
3013 Eaton Ave (28079-8830)
P.O. Box 1210 (28079-1210)
PHONE.................................704 882-2887
Chris Cauthen, *VP*
Chris Cauthen, *Pr*
Joye Cauthen, *Treas*
Kim Cauthen, *VP*
EMP: 18 **EST:** 1983
SQ FT: 20,000
SALES (est): 24.83MM **Privately Held**
Web: www.iaifab.com
SIC: 5051 3312 Iron or steel semifinished
  products; Primary finished or semifinished
  shapes

(G-7085)
KC STONE ENTERPRISE INC
3006 Sardis Dr (28079-3625)
PHONE.................................704 907-1361
Esselito Solano, *Pr*
EMP: 4 **EST:** 2015
SALES (est): 147.24K **Privately Held**
SIC: 2434 Wood kitchen cabinets

(G-7086)
KNIGHT COMMUNICATIONS INC
Also Called: Carolina Fire Journal
6301 Creft Cir (28079-9544)
PHONE.................................704 568-7804
Randall Baxter Knight, *Pr*
EMP: 12 **EST:** 1974
SALES (est): 1.79MM **Privately Held**
Web: www.baxterknight.com
SIC: 2721 7389 Magazines: publishing and
  printing; Advertising, promotional, and trade
  show services

(G-7087)
LARU INDUSTRIES INC
Also Called: Bce South
115 Business Park Dr (28079-9432)
P.O. Box 829 (28079-0829)
PHONE.................................704 821-7503
Larry Kunar, *Pr*
Ruth Kunar, *Sec*
EMP: 4 **EST:** 1989
SQ FT: 5,500
SALES (est): 183.21K **Privately Held**
Web: www.bcesouth.com
SIC: 2759 Thermography

(G-7088)
LIQUID PROCESS SYSTEMS INC
1025 Technology Dr Ste A (28079-5514)
PHONE.................................704 821-1115
Judy Shums, *Pr*
▼ **EMP:** 5 **EST:** 1992
SQ FT: 5,600
SALES (est): 960.51K **Privately Held**
Web: www.lps-filtration.com

SIC: 3677 3569 Filtration devices, electronic;
  Filters

(G-7089)
LOGIC MANUFACTURING INC
4009 Fawnbrooke Dr (28079-3704)
PHONE.................................704 821-0535
Teresa Wilkie-hoefl, *Ch*
Robert Hoefl Ii, *Pr*
EMP: 27 **EST:** 1997
SQ FT: 10,000
SALES (est): 4.36MM **Privately Held**
Web: www.logicmfginc.com
SIC: 3599 Machine shop, jobbing and repair

(G-7090)
M & M TECHNOLOGY INC
7711 Idlewild Rd (28079-7628)
P.O. Box 1796 (28079-1796)
PHONE.................................704 882-9432
Majid Babaie, *CEO*
Jerambhai Patel, ***
Ramnik Sanghani, ***
▲ **EMP:** 26 **EST:** 1996
SQ FT: 24,000
SALES (est): 6.15MM **Privately Held**
Web: www.mandm-tech.com
SIC: 3672 Printed circuit boards

(G-7091)
MICRO LENS TECHNOLOGY INC
2001 Van Buren Ave (28079-5573)
PHONE.................................704 893-2109
Mary Ellen Conley, *Mgr*
EMP: 7
SQ FT: 2,250
SALES (corp-wide): 735.49K **Privately
Held**
Web: www.microlens.com
SIC: 3089 Injection molding of plastics
PA: Micro Lens Technology, Inc
  3308 Mikelynn Dr
  Matthews NC 28105
  704 847-9234

(G-7092)
NORTHERN STAR TECHNOLOGIES INC
1712 Price Rd (28079-7512)
PHONE.................................516 353-3333
Chris Zbodula, *Pr*
EMP: 6 **EST:** 2002
SALES (est): 423.95K **Privately Held**
SIC: 3444 7389 Metal ventilating equipment;
  Business Activities at Non-Commercial Site

(G-7093)
OPTO ALIGNMENT TECHNOLOGY INC
1034 Van Buren Ave Ste A (28079-5632)
PHONE.................................704 893-0399
Guy Pearlman, *Pr*
Sahsha Pearlman, *Pr*
Guy Pearlman, *Prin*
▲ **EMP:** 20 **EST:** 1992
SALES (est): 6.05MM **Privately Held**
Web: www.optoalignment.com
SIC: 3827 Optical instruments and lenses

(G-7094)
ORYX SYSTEMS INC
3056 Eaton Ave (28079)
PHONE.................................704 519-8803
David K Lacey, *Pr*
EMP: 5 **EST:** 1999
SALES (est): 3.45MM **Privately Held**
Web: www.oryxsystems.com
SIC: 3823 Process control instruments

(G-7095)
PIERCE FARRIER SUPPLY INC
9705 Pierce Rd (28079-7710)
PHONE.................................704 753-4358
Ben Pierce, *Owner*
EMP: 4 **EST:** 1988
SALES (est): 202.39K **Privately Held**
Web: www.piercefarriersupply.com
SIC: 3462 Horseshoes

(G-7096)
PREVENTIVE TECHNOLOGIES INC
Also Called: Preventech
4330 Matthews Indian Trail Rd
(28079-3779)
PHONE.................................704 684-1211
Fred Alton King, *Pr*
EMP: 5 **EST:** 1995
SQ FT: 7,500
SALES (est): 2.41MM **Privately Held**
Web: www.preventech.com
SIC: 3843 8021 Dental equipment; Offices
  and clinics of dentists

(G-7097)
RADIATOR SPECIALTY COMPANY (PA)
Also Called: Gunk
600 Radiator Rd (28079-5225)
P.O. Box 1890 (28079-1890)
PHONE.................................704 688-2302
Mike Guggenheimer, *CEO*
Alan Blumenthal, *Ch*
Ronald Weiner, *VP*
◆ **EMP:** 55 **EST:** 1923
SQ FT: 351,000
SALES (est): 19.29MM
SALES (corp-wide): 19.29MM **Privately
Held**
Web: www.rscbrands.com
SIC: 2899 Chemical preparations, nec

(G-7098)
RSC CHEMICAL SOLUTIONS LLC
600 Radiator Rd (28079-5225)
P.O. Box 159 (28079)
PHONE.................................704 821-7643
C Michale Guggenheimer, *Mgr*
EMP: 16 **EST:** 2010
SALES (est): 1.64MM **Privately Held**
Web: www.rscbio.com
SIC: 2899 Chemical preparations, nec

(G-7099)
SOUTHERN ELECTRICAL EQP CO INC
Also Called: Seeco
1015 Van Buren Ave (28079-5541)
PHONE.................................704 392-1396
Kathleen Panto, *Mgr*
EMP: 7
SALES (corp-wide): 10.18MM **Privately
Held**
Web: www.seecoswitch.com
SIC: 3625 3613 Relays and industrial
  controls; Switchgear and switchgear
  accessories, nec
PA: Southern Electrical Equipment
  Company, Inc.
  4045 Hargrove Ave
  Charlotte NC 28208
  704 392-1396

(G-7100)
STAFFORD CUTTING DIES INC
131 Business Park Dr (28079-9432)
P.O. Box 566 (28079-0566)
PHONE.................................704 821-6330
EMP: 97 **EST:** 1991
SALES (est): 7.84MM **Privately Held**

Web: www.gostafford.com
SIC: 3544 Special dies and tools

(G-7101)
SUNSEEKER NORTH AMERICA INC ✪
Also Called: Manufacturer
4330 Matthews Indian Trail Rd Ste A
(28079-3780)
PHONE.................................704 684-5709
Miaowu Ma, *Pr*
Lin Xin, *Treas*
Justin Novosel, *Sec*
EMP: 15 **EST:** 2024
SALES (est): 1.37MM **Privately Held**
SIC: 3524 Lawn and garden equipment

(G-7102)
SUNSEEKER US INC
4330 Matthews Indian Trail Rd
(28079-3779)
PHONE.................................443 253-1546
Terry Ma, *Pr*
Ned Cox, *General Vice President*
Justin Novosel, *Ex VP*
EMP: 6 **EST:** 2016
SALES (est): 2.11MM **Privately Held**
Web: www.shopsunseekertech.com
SIC: 3524 Blowers and vacuums, lawn

(G-7103)
TEXTILE RUBBER AND CHEM CO INC
1020 Forsyth Ave Ste 100 (28079-0019)
PHONE.................................704 376-3582
Chip Howalt, *Brnch Mgr*
EMP: 8
SALES (corp-wide): 94.1MM **Privately
Held**
Web: www.tiarcochem.com
SIC: 5169 2891 Chemicals and allied
  products, nec; Adhesives
PA: Textile Rubber And Chemical
  Company, Inc.
  1400 Tiarco Dr Sw
  Dalton GA 30721
  706 277-1300

(G-7104)
WINDCO LLC
1505 Turring Dr Ste B (28079-8475)
PHONE.................................704 846-6029
EMP: 4 **EST:** 2017
SALES (est): 443.8K **Privately Held**
SIC: 3541 Machine tools, metal cutting type

(G-7105)
WMF AMERICAS INC
Also Called: Wmf USA
3521 Faith Church Rd (28079-9321)
PHONE.................................704 882-3898
◆ **EMP:** 50
Web: www.wmfamericas.com
SIC: 3589 Coffee brewing equipment

Iron Station
Lincoln County

(G-7106)
PRINTING PRO
1310 L R Schronce Ln (28080-6731)
PHONE.................................704 748-9396
Jonathan Lester, *Prin*
EMP: 4 **EST:** 2006
SQ FT: 1,809
SALES (est): 124.47K **Privately Held**
SIC: 2752 Commercial printing, lithographic

(G-7107)
R & R LOGGING INC
1040 N Ingleside Farm Rd (28080-9242)
PHONE..............................704 483-5733
Mark A Reel, *Pr*
Ronald Reel, *Sec*
EMP: 7 EST: 1953
SALES (est): 352.71K **Privately Held**
SIC: 2411 Logging camps and contractors

(G-7108)
TIMKEN COMPANY
1000 Timken Pl (28080-8771)
PHONE..............................704 736-2700
Todd Lautzenheiser, *Genl Mgr*
EMP: 248
SQ FT: 1,248
SALES (corp-wide): 4.57B **Publicly Held**
Web: www.timken.com
SIC: 3562 Ball and roller bearings
PA: The Timken Company
4500 Mount Pleasant St Nw
North Canton OH 44720
234 262-3000

Ivanhoe
Sampson County

(G-7109)
AMERICAN MATERIALS COMPANY LLC
3596 Dr Kerr Rd (28447-9611)
PHONE..............................910 532-6070
Tim Bizzal, *Mgr*
EMP: 50
Web: www.americanmaterialsco.com
SIC: 1442 Construction sand mining
HQ: American Materials Company, Llc
1410 Commwl Dr Ste 201
Wilmington NC 28403
910 799-1411

(G-7110)
BLACK RIVER LOGGING INC
20289 North Carolina Hwy 210 E
(28447-9552)
PHONE..............................910 669-2850
Mike Squires, *Pr*
EMP: 7 EST: 1978
SALES (est): 121.84K **Privately Held**
SIC: 2411 Logging

(G-7111)
JOHNSON LUMBER PRODUCTS INC
911 Eddie L Jones Rd (28447-3601)
P.O. Box 37 (28447-0037)
PHONE..............................910 532-4201
Earnest C Johnson, *Pr*
Mickey Johnson, *Admn*
EMP: 6 EST: 1975
SALES (est): 109.23K **Privately Held**
SIC: 2499 Surveyors' stakes, wood

Jacksonville
Onslow County

(G-7112)
910 SIGN CO LLC
614 Richlands Hwy (28540-3655)
PHONE..............................910 353-2298
Lisa Marshburn, *Managing Member*
Michael Marshburn, *Managing Member*
EMP: 4 EST: 2014
SALES (est): 284.37K **Privately Held**
Web: www.910signco.com
SIC: 3993 Signs and advertising specialties

(G-7113)
ALCRETE PELL CITY LLC
Also Called: Alcrete Industries
620 Mildred Thomas Ct (28540-8905)
PHONE..............................910 455-7040
Justin Norman, *CEO*
EMP: 11
SALES (corp-wide): 1.55MM **Privately Held**
Web: www.alcrete.com
SIC: 3272 Concrete products, precast, nec
PA: Alcrete Pell City Llc
1 Alcrete Way
Pell City AL 35125
205 675-0845

(G-7114)
ALEXANDERS
165 Blue Creek School Rd (28540-3305)
PHONE..............................910 938-0013
Kimberly Reust, *Genl Mgr*
EMP: 4 EST: 2006
SALES (est): 158.33K **Privately Held**
Web: www.alexandersofjacksonville.com
SIC: 2599 Bar, restaurant and cafeteria furniture

(G-7115)
ALLEN R GOODSON LOGGING CO
Also Called: Allen Goodson Logging Co
1417 Kellum Loop Rd (28546-3311)
PHONE..............................910 455-4177
Allen R Goodson, *Pr*
Margaret Goodson, *Sec*
EMP: 6 EST: 1963
SALES (est): 335.91K **Privately Held**
SIC: 2411 Logging camps and contractors

(G-7116)
BARNES DMND GLLERY JWLY MFRS I
120 College Plz (28546-6820)
PHONE..............................910 347-4300
Carol T Barnes, *Pr*
Jimmy Barnes, *VP*
EMP: 6 EST: 1991
SQ FT: 2,100
SALES (est): 254.43K **Privately Held**
Web: www.barnesdiamondgallery.com
SIC: 5944 3911 Jewelry, precious stones and precious metals; Jewelry, precious metal

(G-7117)
BPC PLASMA INC
113 Yopp Rd (28540-3509)
PHONE..............................910 463-2603
EMP: 18
SQ FT: 15,000
Web: www.grifolsplasma.com
SIC: 2834 Pharmaceutical preparations
HQ: Bpc Plasma, Inc.
901 W Yamato Rd Ste 101
Boca Raton FL 33431

(G-7118)
BUTLER TRIEU INC
1183 Kellum Loop Rd (28546-3305)
P.O. Box 343 (28541-0343)
PHONE..............................910 346-4929
Tim Butler, *Pr*
Vy Trieu, *

EMP: 5 EST: 2011
SQ FT: 5,000
SALES (est): 812.7K **Privately Held**
Web: www.butlertrieu.com
SIC: 4959 3589 0781 0782 Sweeping service: road, airport, parking lot, etc.; High pressure cleaning equipment; Landscape services; Landscape contractors

(G-7119)
CAMP LEJEUNE GLOBE
149 Rea St (28546-5773)
PHONE..............................910 939-0705
EMP: 12 EST: 2017
SALES (est): 261.49K **Privately Held**
Web: www.jdnews.com
SIC: 2711 Newspapers, publishing and printing

(G-7120)
CAROLINA COASTAL COATINGS
400 White St (28546-6732)
PHONE..............................910 346-9607
Jeffrey Bailey, *Sec*
EMP: 10 EST: 2018
SALES (est): 655.23K **Privately Held**
SIC: 3479 Painting, coating, and hot dipping

(G-7121)
CHRONICLES
121 Mendover Dr (28546-9207)
PHONE..............................252 617-1774
EMP: 4 EST: 2018
SALES (est): 102.72K **Privately Held**
Web: www.highlandsnews.com
SIC: 2711 Newspapers, publishing and printing

(G-7122)
DBF INC
Also Called: Patriot Blinds & More
100 Fall Creek Dr Ste A (28540-8495)
PHONE..............................910 548-6725
Stephen James, *Pr*
EMP: 5 EST: 2015
SQ FT: 1,500
SALES (est): 617.29K **Privately Held**
Web: www.patriotblinds.com
SIC: 5719 2591 1799 Venetian blinds; Window blinds; Glass tinting, architectural or automotive

(G-7123)
FOUR POINTS RECYCLING LLC
309 King Rd (28540-8438)
P.O. Box 87 (28541-0087)
PHONE..............................910 333-5961
EMP: 12 EST: 2000
SALES (est): 1.23MM **Privately Held**
Web: www.fourpointsrecycling.com
SIC: 3531 1799 Graders, road (construction machinery); Construction site cleanup

(G-7124)
FURNITURE FAIR INC
418 White St (28546-6732)
PHONE..............................910 455-4044
EMP: 38
SALES (corp-wide): 20.72MM **Privately Held**
Web: www.furniture-fair.net
SIC: 5712 2273 Furniture stores; Carpets and rugs
PA: Furniture Fair, Inc.
507 Bell Fork Rd
Jacksonville NC 28540
910 455-9595

(G-7125)
GOODSON S ALL TERRAIN LOG INC
173 Goodson Trl (28546-4127)
PHONE..............................910 347-7919
Bobby Goodson, *Pr*
Lori Goodson, *Sec*
EMP: 6 EST: 1992
SALES (est): 490.71K **Privately Held**
SIC: 2411 Logging camps and contractors

(G-7126)
HOME TEAM ATHLETICS INC
242 Wilmington Hwy 17 (28540-3506)
PHONE..............................910 938-0862
Dennis Jones, *CEO*
EMP: 5 EST: 1993
SQ FT: 955
SALES (est): 169.29K **Privately Held**
Web: home-team-athletics.ueniweb.com
SIC: 5941 2395 2759 Team sports equipment ; Embroidery products, except Schiffli machine; Screen printing

(G-7127)
ICEE COMPANY
13 E Doris Ave Ste H (28540-5149)
PHONE..............................910 346-3937
EMP: 4
SALES (corp-wide): 1.57B **Publicly Held**
Web: www.icee.com
SIC: 2038 Frozen specialties, nec
HQ: The Icee Company
265 Mason Rd
La Vergne TN 37086
800 426-4233

(G-7128)
JACKSONVILLE METAL MFG INC
181 Piney Green Rd (28546-8125)
PHONE..............................910 938-7635
William T Humphrey, *Pr*
EMP: 5 EST: 1989
SALES (est): 1.05MM
SALES (corp-wide): 18.42MM **Privately Held**
SIC: 3444 Ducts, sheet metal
PA: W. T. Humphrey, Inc.
2423 N Marine Blvd
Jacksonville NC 28546
910 455-3555

(G-7129)
LACEYS TREE SERVICE
221 Jenkins Rd (28540-8434)
PHONE..............................910 330-2868
Jeremy Lacey, *Owner*
Jeremy Lacey, *Prin*
EMP: 4 EST: 2007
SALES (est): 240.14K **Privately Held**
SIC: 2411 Logging

(G-7130)
LUXURIOUSLY NATURAL SOAPS LLC
Also Called: Natural Bath and Body Products
3620 Wilmington Hwy (28540-8320)
PHONE..............................910 378-9064
Sonya Black, *CEO*
EMP: 5 EST: 2012
SALES (est): 163.03K **Privately Held**
Web: www.lnsoaps.com
SIC: 5999 3999 2841 Toiletries, cosmetics, and perfumes; Candles; Soap and other detergents

(G-7131)
MICHAEL L GOODSON LOGGING INC
171 Goodson Trl (28546-4127)
PHONE..............................910 346-8399
Michael L Goodson, *Pr*
Cathy Goodson, *Sec*
EMP: 9 EST: 1991
SALES (est): 5.29MM **Privately Held**
SIC: 2411 Logging camps and contractors

(G-7132)
MINUTEMAN QUICK COPY SVC INC
207 W Bayshore Blvd (28540-5339)
PHONE..............................910 455-5353
Debbie Phillips, *Pr*

Dwain Phillips, *Sec*
EMP: 5 **EST:** 1977
SQ FT: 800
SALES (est): 144.52K **Privately Held**
SIC: 2752 Offset printing

(G-7133)
MSA SAFETY SALES LLC
352 White St (28546-6730)
PHONE...............................910 353-1540
J Ryan, *BD*
EMP: 80
SALES (corp-wide): 1.81B **Publicly Held**
Web: ru.msasafety.com
SIC: 3842 Personal safety equipment
HQ: Msa Safety Sales, Llc
   1000 Cranberry Woods Dr
   Cranberry Township PA 16066
   800 672-2222

(G-7134)
NC LICENSE PLATE AGENCY
521 Yopp Rd (28540-3595)
PHONE...............................910 347-1000
Cecil Hargett, *Prin*
EMP: 9 **EST:** 1993
SALES (est): 479.24K **Privately Held**
SIC: 3469 Automobile license tags, stamped metal

(G-7135)
NEALS CARPENTRY & CNSTR
153 White Oak Blvd (28546-4538)
PHONE...............................910 346-6154
Robert Neal, *Pr*
EMP: 4 **EST:** 1992
SALES (est): 236.57K **Privately Held**
SIC: 1751 3448 1521 Cabinet and finish carpentry; Prefabricated metal buildings and components; Single-family home remodeling, additions, and repairs

(G-7136)
NEWTON SIGN CO INC
310 Preston Rd (28540-5655)
PHONE...............................910 347-1661
Richard S Newton, *Pr*
EMP: 5 **EST:** 1974
SALES (est): 413.99K **Privately Held**
SIC: 3993 Signs and advertising specialties

(G-7137)
PETTEWAY BODY SHOP INC
Also Called: Petteway Rentals
1362 Old Maplehurst Rd (28540-3215)
PHONE...............................910 455-3272
Joel C Petteway, *Pr*
Wayne Petteway, *VP*
EMP: 4 **EST:** 1972
SQ FT: 3,336
SALES (est): 340.96K **Privately Held**
SIC: 3599 Grinding castings for the trade

(G-7138)
PRINT EXPRESS INC
Also Called: Express Printing
117 N Marine Blvd (28540-6508)
PHONE...............................910 455-4554
Carol Cross, *VP*
EMP: 10 **EST:** 1984
SQ FT: 1,500
SALES (est): 207.78K **Privately Held**
Web: www.expressprintingjacksonville.com
SIC: 2752 7334 2759 Offset printing; Photocopying and duplicating services; Commercial printing, nec

(G-7139)
PROFESSNAL ALTERATIONS EMB INC
Also Called: Shirleys Prof Alterations EMB
2113 Lejeune Blvd (28546-8251)
PHONE...............................910 577-8484
Shirley Stanley, *Pr*
EMP: 4 **EST:** 1991
SALES (est): 114.22K **Privately Held**
SIC: 2395 7219 7389 Embroidery products, except Schiffli machine; Garment alteration and repair shop; Personal service agents, brokers, and bureaus

(G-7140)
PROGRESSIVE SERVICE DIE CO
226 White St (28546-6318)
PHONE...............................910 353-4836
Brian France, *Pr*
George France, *VP*
EMP: 19 **EST:** 1913
SQ FT: 30,000
SALES (est): 947.32K **Privately Held**
Web: www.psdcdies.com
SIC: 3544 Special dies and tools

(G-7141)
RANDOLPH GOODSON LOGGING INC
170 Jenkins Rd (28540-8466)
PHONE...............................910 347-5117
Randolph D Goodson, *Pr*
Judy Carroll Goodson, *Sec*
EMP: 9 **EST:** 1987
SALES (est): 70.68K **Privately Held**
SIC: 2411 Logging camps and contractors

(G-7142)
RUSH MASONRY MANAGEMENT LLC
234 Clayton James Rd (28540-9549)
PHONE...............................910 787-9100
Kendra Blackmon, *Pr*
Travis Plymell, *VP*
EMP: 6 **EST:** 2011
SALES (est): 1.5MM **Privately Held**
Web: www.rushconstruction.org
SIC: 3423 Masons' hand tools

(G-7143)
SEMPER FI WATER LLC
508 Cozy Crow Trl (28540-4818)
PHONE...............................910 381-3569
Norine Rosetti, *Managing Member*
EMP: 4 **EST:** 2022
SALES (est): 927.88K **Privately Held**
Web: www.semperfihomeinspectionsllc.com
SIC: 3589 Water treatment equipment, industrial

(G-7144)
SILKSCREEN SPECIALISTS
2239 Lejeune Blvd (28546-8253)
PHONE...............................910 353-8859
Jerry Copeland, *Owner*
EMP: 5 **EST:** 1991
SALES (est): 109.64K **Privately Held**
Web: www.silkscreenspecialists.com
SIC: 2759 Screen printing

(G-7145)
SL LIQUIDATION LLC
408 White St (28546-6732)
PHONE...............................910 353-3666
Paul Peterson, *Brnch Mgr*
EMP: 100
SALES (corp-wide): 325.81MM **Privately Held**
Web: www.stanadyne.com

SIC: 3714 Motor vehicle parts and accessories
HQ: Sl Liquidation Llc
   405 White St
   Jacksonville NC 28546
   860 525-0821

(G-7146)
SL LIQUIDATION LLC (DH)
405 White St (28546-6731)
PHONE...............................860 525-0821
John A Pinson, *CEO*
Costas Loukellis, *
◆ **EMP:** 21 **EST:** 1988
SALES (est): 25.24MM
SALES (corp-wide): 325.81MM **Privately Held**
Web: www.stanadyne.com
SIC: 3714 Fuel pumps, motor vehicle
HQ: Stanadyne Intermediate Holdings, Llc
   405 White St
   Jacksonville NC 28546

(G-7147)
SL LIQUIDATION LLC
Also Called: Stanadyne Diesel Systems
405 White St (28546-6731)
PHONE...............................910 353-3666
Rich Pasqualune, *Brnch Mgr*
EMP: 360
SALES (corp-wide): 325.81MM **Privately Held**
Web: www.stanadyne.com
SIC: 3714 3561 3432 Fuel systems and parts, motor vehicle; Pumps and pumping equipment; Plumbing fixture fittings and trim
HQ: Sl Liquidation Llc
   405 White St
   Jacksonville NC 28546
   860 525-0821

(G-7148)
SONOCO PRODUCTS COMPANY
Also Called: Sonoco Recycling
417 Meadowview Rd (28540-7313)
PHONE...............................910 455-6903
Jim Foster, *Brnch Mgr*
EMP: 4
SALES (corp-wide): 5.31B **Publicly Held**
Web: www.sonoco.com
SIC: 2631 3085 Cardboard; Plastics bottles
PA: Sonoco Products Company
   1 N 2nd St
   Hartsville SC 29550
   843 383-7000

(G-7149)
SOUNDSIDE ORTHTICS PRSTHTICS L
1715 Country Club Rd Ste B (28546-6009)
PHONE...............................910 238-2026
Stephen Truesdale, *Bd of Dir*
EMP: 4 **EST:** 2004
SALES (est): 360.97K **Privately Held**
SIC: 3842 Surgical appliances and supplies

(G-7150)
SOUTHEASTERN STEEL CNSTR INC
225 Ellis Blvd (28540-6332)
P.O. Box 190 (28541-0190)
PHONE...............................910 346-4462
Valerie Dail, *Pr*
EMP: 10 **EST:** 2003
SQ FT: 5,000
SALES (est): 500.01K **Privately Held**
Web: www.southeasternsteel.com
SIC: 3441 Building components, structural steel

(G-7151)
SOUTHERN LEISURE BUILDERS INC
2444 Commerce Rd (28546-7560)
PHONE...............................910 381-0426
Shannon Kellum, *Mgr*
EMP: 4
SALES (corp-wide): 907.52K **Privately Held**
Web: www.southernleisurebuilders.com
SIC: 3448 Sunrooms, prefabricated metal
PA: Southern Leisure Builders Inc
   172 Willis Pkwy Ste A
   Jacksonville NC 28546
   910 219-0438

(G-7152)
STANADYNE INTRMDATE HLDNGS LLC (HQ)
405 White St (28546-6790)
PHONE...............................860 525-0821
David P Galuska, *CEO*
John A Pinson, *
Steve Rodgers, *
Stephen S Langin, *
▲ **EMP:** 250 **EST:** 1997
SALES (est): 325.81MM
SALES (corp-wide): 325.81MM **Privately Held**
Web: www.stanadyne.com
SIC: 3714 3492 Fuel systems and parts, motor vehicle; Control valves, fluid power: hydraulic and pneumatic
PA: Htpps Liquidation, Inc.
   405 White St
   Jacksonville NC 28546
   860 525-0821

(G-7153)
STANADYNE JACKSONVILLE LLC ✪
405 White St (28546-6790)
PHONE...............................860 683-4553
Rob Mallory, *CEO*
EMP: 190 **EST:** 2023
SALES (est): 4.91MM
SALES (corp-wide): 38.46MM **Privately Held**
Web: www.stanadyne.com
SIC: 3714 Motor vehicle engines and parts
HQ: Stanadyne Operating Company Llc
   405 White St
   Jacksonville NC 28546
   910 353-3666

(G-7154)
STANADYNE OPERATING CO LLC (DH) ✪
405 White St (28546-6790)
PHONE...............................910 353-3666
Rob Mallory, *Managing Member*
EMP: 24 **EST:** 2023
SALES (est): 38.46MM
SALES (corp-wide): 38.46MM **Privately Held**
Web: www.stanadyne.com
SIC: 3714 Motor vehicle parts and accessories
HQ: Stanadyne Ppt Holdings, Inc.
   405 White Street
   Jacksonville NC

(G-7155)
STONE CLLINS MTR REWINDING INC
Also Called: Sams Motor Rewinding
111 Ramsey Rd (28546-9366)
PHONE...............................910 347-2775
Kevin Collins, *Pr*
Vernancia Collins, *VP*
EMP: 5 **EST:** 1970
SQ FT: 8,000
SALES (est): 1.33MM **Privately Held**

SIC: **7694** 5063 Electric motor repair;
Motors, electric

(G-7156)
TIMBER HARVESTER INC (PA)
3862 Richlands Hwy (28540-7123)
P.O. Box 164 (28541-0164)
PHONE...............................910 346-9754
Charles Rawls, *Pr*
Anthony Rawls, *VP*
Myrtie Rawls, *Sec*
EMP: 6 **EST:** 1984
SALES (est): 138.27K
SALES (corp-wide): 138.27K **Privately Held**
SIC: **2411** Logging camps and contractors

(G-7157)
VEXEA MX LLC
205 America Ct (28540-5060)
PHONE...............................910 787-9391
Adam Baldwin, *Prin*
EMP: 5 **EST:** 2015
SALES (est): 58.8K **Privately Held**
SIC: **3751** Gears, motorcycle and bicycle

(G-7158)
W T HUMPHREY INC (PA)
2423 N Marine Blvd (28546-6906)
P.O. Box 1268 (28541-1268)
PHONE...............................910 455-3555
Steven Wangerin, *CEO*
William Troy Humphrey, *
Wanda Flud, *
Frances Humphrey, *
EMP: 42 **EST:** 1967
SQ FT: 7,500
SALES (est): 18.42MM
SALES (corp-wide): 18.42MM **Privately Held**
Web: www.wthumphrey.com
SIC: **8741** 1711 1542 3444 Management
services; Plumbing, heating, air-conditioning
; Commercial and office building, new
construction; Ducts, sheet metal

(G-7159)
WALTONS DISTILLERY INC
261 Ben Williams Rd (28540-9213)
PHONE...............................910 347-7770
Donald Walton, *Pr*
EMP: 7 **EST:** 2015
SALES (est): 1.15MM **Privately Held**
Web: www.waltonsdistillery.com
SIC: **2085** Distilled and blended liquors

(G-7160)
**WORLD ART GALLERY
INCORPORATED**
Also Called: Carriage House Furniture Co
1116 Gum Branch Rd (28540-5743)
PHONE...............................910 989-0203
Dora Smith, *Pr*
Richard Smith, *Sec*
EMP: 8 **EST:** 1971
SQ FT: 8,000
SALES (est): 850.38K **Privately Held**
Web:
www.carriagehousefurnitureco.com
SIC: **5712** 2499 5999 Furniture stores;
Picture and mirror frames, wood; Art dealers

Jamestown
Guilford County

(G-7161)
**FLOWERS BKG CO JAMESTOWN
LLC (HQ)**
Also Called: Flowers Bakery

801 W Main St (27282-9562)
P.O. Box 819 (27282-0819)
PHONE...............................336 841-8840
Roger Tooley, *Pr*
Paul Houser, *
EMP: 56 **EST:** 2000
SQ FT: 110,000
SALES (est): 15.82MM
SALES (corp-wide): 5.1B **Publicly Held**
SIC: **2051** Bread, all types (white, wheat,
rye, etc); fresh or frozen
PA: Flowers Foods, Inc.
1919 Flowers Cir
Thomasville GA 31757
229 226-9110

(G-7162)
GEO-LIN INC
Also Called: Budget Printing
107 Hillstone Dr (27282-8924)
PHONE...............................336 884-0648
Jason Spangler, *Pr*
EMP: 4 **EST:** 1986
SQ FT: 1,700
SALES (est): 101.97K **Privately Held**
SIC: **2752** Offset printing

(G-7163)
GOCAISSONCOM
3210 Dillon Rd (27282-9129)
PHONE...............................336 454-4610
EMP: 5 **EST:** 2016
SALES (est): 90.04K **Privately Held**
Web: www.gocaisson.com
SIC: **3679** Electronic components, nec

(G-7164)
HEMCO WIRE PRODUCTS INC
Also Called: Greensboro Metal Parts
301 Scientific St (27282-9537)
P.O. Box 1648 (27282-1648)
PHONE...............................336 454-7280
Mark Myers, *Pr*
EMP: 6 **EST:** 1943
SQ FT: 48,000
SALES (est): 487.44K **Privately Held**
SIC: **3496** 3479 3694 2542 Miscellaneous
fabricated wire products; Painting, coating,
and hot dipping; Engine electrical equipment
; Partitions and fixtures, except wood

(G-7165)
HIGHLAND CONTAINERS INC (DH)
100 Ragsdale Rd (27282-9874)
PHONE...............................336 887-5400
Doug Johnston, *Pr*
▲ **EMP:** 200 **EST:** 1992
SQ FT: 179,000
SALES (est): 9.79MM **Privately Held**
SIC: **2653** Boxes, corrugated: made from
purchased materials
HQ: Stronghaven, Incorporated
2727 Paces Ferry Rd Se
Atlanta GA 30336
678 235-2713

(G-7166)
HIGHLAND CONTAINERS INC
3520 Dillon Rd (27282-9802)
PHONE...............................336 887-5400
Travis Wright, *Brnch Mgr*
EMP: 250
Web: www.hoodcontainer.com
SIC: **2653** Boxes, corrugated: made from
purchased materials
HQ: Highland Containers, Inc.
100 Ragsdale Rd
Jamestown NC 27282

(G-7167)
HOOD CONTAINER CORPORATION
3520 Dillon Rd (27282-9802)
PHONE...............................336 887-5400
EMP: 20
Web: www.hoodcontainer.com
SIC: **2653** Boxes, corrugated: made from
purchased materials
HQ: Hood Container Corporation
2100 Rvredge Pkwy Ste 650
Atlanta GA 30328
855 605-6317

(G-7168)
IMAGE WORKS INC
120 Wade St Ste A (27282-9846)
PHONE...............................336 668-3338
Arnold Riewe, *Pr*
Linda Riewe, *Sec*
▲ **EMP:** 5 **EST:** 1994
SQ FT: 11,000
SALES (est): 69.13K **Privately Held**
SIC: **2752** Offset printing

(G-7169)
INSPIRATION LEATHER DESIGN INC
4713 Barrington Place Ct (27282-7976)
PHONE...............................336 420-2265
Vicki Ann Reed, *Pr*
Kenneth Reed, *Sec*
EMP: 6 **EST:** 2012
SALES (est): 80.03K **Privately Held**
SIC: **2386** 3111 7389 Garments, leather;
Upholstery leather; Business services, nec

(G-7170)
JAMESTOWN NEWS
Also Called: Womack Newspapers
206 E Main St Ste 1a (27282-8005)
P.O. Box 307 (27282-0307)
PHONE...............................336 841-4933
Charles Womack, *Pr*
Carolyn Lewis, *Off Mgr*
EMP: 5 **EST:** 1990
SALES (est): 228.74K **Privately Held**
Web: www.yesweekly.com
SIC: **2711** Newspapers, publishing and
printing

(G-7171)
MARIETTA MARTIN MATERIALS INC
Martin Marietta Aggregates
5725 Riverdale Dr (27282-9172)
P.O. Box 937 (27282-0937)
PHONE...............................336 886-5015
Steve Carter, *Genl Mgr*
EMP: 5
Web: www.martinmarietta.com
SIC: **1422** Crushed and broken limestone
PA: Martin Marietta Materials Inc
4123 Parklake Ave
Raleigh NC 27612

(G-7172)
NAVELITE LLC
3220 Peninsula Dr (27282-8700)
PHONE...............................336 509-9924
John Price, *Prin*
EMP: 4 **EST:** 2015
SALES (est): 286.23K **Privately Held**
Web: www.navelite.com
SIC: **3812** Search and navigation equipment

(G-7173)
NC SIGN AND LIGHTING SVC LLC
213 Hillstone Pl (27282-2000)
PHONE...............................586 764-0563
EMP: 11 **EST:** 2015
SALES (est): 2.12MM **Privately Held**
Web: www.yesco.com

SIC: **3993** Signs and advertising specialties

(G-7174)
OAKDALE COTTON MILLS
710 Oakdale Rd (27282)
PHONE...............................336 454-1144
William Ragsdale, *Pr*
William G Ragsdale Iii, *Pr*
Norma Knight, *
EMP: 5 **EST:** 1865
SQ FT: 50,000
SALES (est): 133.96K **Privately Held**
SIC: **2281** 2298 Yarn spinning mills; Twine,
nec

(G-7175)
**PERFORMANCE PLASTICS PDTS
INC**
126 Wade St Ste D (27282-9848)
PHONE...............................336 454-0350
James Mchon, *Brnch Mgr*
EMP: 80
SALES (corp-wide): 15.99MM **Privately
Held**
Web: www.3pcorporate.com
SIC: **3089** 3498 3312 3084 Plastics
hardware and building products; Fabricated
pipe and fittings; Blast furnaces and steel
mills; Plastics pipe
HQ: Performance Plastics Products, Inc.
11718 Mcgallion Rd
Houston TX

(G-7176)
QORVO US INC
4113 Devondale Ct (27282-7793)
PHONE...............................503 615-9000
Andrew Labaziewicz, *Brnch Mgr*
EMP: 9
SALES (corp-wide): 3.77B **Publicly Held**
Web: www.qorvo.com
SIC: **3674** Semiconductors and related
devices
HQ: Qorvo Us, Inc.
2300 Ne Brookwood Pkwy
Hillsboro OR 97124
503 615-9000

(G-7177)
R & D LABEL LLC
117 Wade St (27282-9567)
P.O. Box 6 (27282-0006)
PHONE...............................336 889-2900
EMP: 7 **EST:** 2006
SALES (est): 753.93K **Privately Held**
Web: ns1.hxmi.com
SIC: **2752** Commercial printing, lithographic

(G-7178)
R D TILLSON & ASSOCIATES INC
Also Called: Tillson Engineering Laboratory
105 Cottonwood Dr (27282-9468)
PHONE...............................336 454-1410
David K Tillson, *Pr*
EMP: 4 **EST:** 1953
SALES (est): 83.24K **Privately Held**
SIC: **8711** 3621 Consulting engineer; Motors
and generators

(G-7179)
SBS DIVERSIFIED TECH INC
Also Called: Diversified Technologies
125 Wade St (27282-9567)
P.O. Box 2039 (27282-2039)
PHONE...............................336 884-5564
EMP: 15 **EST:** 1979
SQ FT: 21,000
SALES (est): 391.13K **Privately Held**
SIC: **3672** Printed circuit boards

▲ = Import ▼ = Export
◆ = Import/Export

(G-7180)
TEKNOR APEX COMPANY
3518 Dillon Rd (27282-9802)
PHONE..............................401 642-3598
EMP: 54
SALES (corp-wide): 731.88MM **Privately Held**
Web: www.teknorapexcareers.com
SIC: 3087 3084 Custom compound purchased resins; Plastics pipe
PA: Teknor Apex Company
505 Central Ave
Pawtucket RI 02861
401 725-8000

(G-7181)
UNIVERSAL PLASTIC PRODUCTS INC
3220 Peninsula Dr (27282-8700)
PHONE..............................336 856-0882
John K Price, Prin
EMP: 4 EST: 1996
SALES (est): 256.97K **Privately Held**
SIC: 3089 Injection molding of plastics

Jamesville
Martin County

(G-7182)
ARRANTS LOGGING INC
3600 Jerden Thicket Rd (27846-9151)
P.O. Box 30 (27846-0030)
PHONE..............................252 792-1889
Frankie Arrants, Pr
Danette Arrants, Sec
EMP: 18 EST: 1978
SQ FT: 3,600
SALES (est): 2.41MM **Privately Held**
SIC: 2411 Logging camps and contractors

(G-7183)
EVANS LOGGING INC
1047 Fleming Cir (27846-9148)
P.O. Box 156 (27846-0156)
PHONE..............................252 792-3865
Gary Evans, Pr
Larry Evans, VP
EMP: 10 EST: 1925
SALES (est): 972.39K **Privately Held**
SIC: 2411 Logging camps and contractors

(G-7184)
PRICE LOGGING INC
1901 Mill Rd (27846-9237)
PHONE..............................252 792-5687
Alfred Price Senior, Pr
Alfred Price Junior, VP
EMP: 12 EST: 1983
SQ FT: 4,200
SALES (est): 1.01MM **Privately Held**
SIC: 2411 2426 2421 Logging camps and contractors; Hardwood dimension and flooring mills; Sawmills and planing mills, general

Jarvisburg
Currituck County

(G-7185)
CAROLINA CSUAL OTDOOR FURN INC
Also Called: Salt Marsh Home
7359 Caratoke Hwy (27947-9705)
PHONE..............................252 491-5171
Michael Mcclanahan, Pr
Susan Mcclanahan, VP
EMP: 15 EST: 2016

SALES (est): 1.56MM **Privately Held**
Web: www.carolinacasual.com
SIC: 2511 5021 Porch furniture and swings: wood; Household furniture

(G-7186)
SOUNDSIDE RECYCLING & MTLS INC
7565 Caratoke Hwy (27947-9709)
PHONE..............................252 491-8666
Kimberly Newbern, CEO
Kimberly Newbern, Pr
Horatio D Newbern Iv, VP
EMP: 8 EST: 1999
SQ FT: 1,000
SALES (est): 2.71MM **Privately Held**
Web: www.soundsiderecycling.com
SIC: 1442 1795 4953 1629 Construction sand and gravel; Concrete breaking for streets and highways; Recycling, waste materials; Waste disposal plant construction

Jefferson
Ashe County

(G-7187)
CARDINAL STONE COMPANY INC
1608 Us Highway 221 N (28640-9808)
P.O. Box 635 (28640-0635)
PHONE..............................336 846-7191
James M Vannoy, Pr
EMP: 8 EST: 1986
SALES (est): 808.58K **Privately Held**
Web: www.jrvannoy.com
SIC: 1429 3531 Igneus rock, crushed and broken-quarrying; Asphalt plant, including gravel-mix type

(G-7188)
HALCORE GROUP INC
American Emergency Vehicles
101 Gates Ln (28640-9704)
PHONE..............................336 982-9824
Mark Van Arnam, Mgr
EMP: 36
Web: www.hortonambulance.com
SIC: 3711 Ambulances (motor vehicles), assembly
HQ: Halcore Group, Inc.
3800 Mcdowell Rd
Grove City OH 43123
614 539-8181

(G-7189)
HALCORE GROUP INC
Also Called: American Emergency Vehicles
101 Gates Ln (28640-9704)
PHONE..............................336 846-8010
Mark Van Arnam, Pr
Mark Van Arnam, Prin
Randy Hanson, General Vice President*
Dino Cusumano, *
Chris Eppel, *
◆ EMP: 366 EST: 1997
SALES (est): 24.26MM **Publicly Held**
Web: www.aev.com
SIC: 3711 Ambulances (motor vehicles), assembly of
PA: Rev Group, Inc.
245 S Exec Dr Ste 100
Brookfield WI 53005

(G-7190)
LOG HOMES OF AMERICA INC
Also Called: Log Home Cooperative America
2999 Us Highway 221 N (28640-9408)
PHONE..............................336 982-8989
Charles A Maney, Pr
Betty P Maney, Sec

EMP: 6 EST: 1989
SQ FT: 400
SALES (est): 2.35MM **Privately Held**
Web: www.loghomesofamerica.com
SIC: 2452 Log cabins, prefabricated, wood

(G-7191)
MC FARLAND & COMPANY INC
960 Nc Highway 88 W (28640-8813)
P.O. Box 611 (28640-0611)
PHONE..............................336 246-4460
Robert Franklin, Pr
Rhonda Herman, *
Michael Strand, *
EMP: 48 EST: 1979
SQ FT: 6,500
SALES (est): 3.42MM **Privately Held**
Web: www.mcfarlandbooks.com
SIC: 2731 Books, publishing only

(G-7192)
NEXT SAFETY INC
676 S Main St (28640-9571)
P.O. Box 547 (28640-0547)
PHONE..............................336 246-7700
C Eric Hunter, Ch
Ron Criss, Pr
Lyndell Devall, Sec
EMP: 19 EST: 2002
SQ FT: 25,000
SALES (est): 774.24K **Privately Held**
Web: www.nextsafety.net
SIC: 3841 Surgical and medical instruments

(G-7193)
VANNOY CONSTRUCTION ARCFT LLC
1608 Us Highway 221 N (28640-9808)
PHONE..............................336 846-7191
James B Maloney, Prin
EMP: 5 EST: 2008
SALES (est): 2.14MM **Privately Held**
Web: www.jrvannoy.com
SIC: 3728 Aircraft parts and equipment, nec

Jonesville
Yadkin County

(G-7194)
CHATEAU JOURDAIN LLC
2406 Swan Creek Rd (28642-9436)
PHONE..............................786 273-2869
Joseph Jourdain, Prin
Glennis Rodriguez, Prin
EMP: 4 EST: 2019
SALES (est): 245.03K **Privately Held**
Web: www.chateaujourdain.com
SIC: 2084 Wines

(G-7195)
FOOTHILLS SUG CURED CNTRY HAMS
522 S Main St (28642-2726)
PHONE..............................336 835-2411
Greg Purdue, Pt
Stephen Edwards, Pt
EMP: 11 EST: 1997
SQ FT: 2,000
SALES (est): 4.18MM **Privately Held**
SIC: 2011 Meat packing plants

(G-7196)
GENERATIONS L LLC
220 Winston Rd (28642-2209)
PHONE..............................336 835-3095
Doug Longworth, Prin
EMP: 4 EST: 2008
SALES (est): 741.92K **Privately Held**

SIC: 3421 Table and food cutlery, including butchers'

(G-7197)
GRANDEUR MANUFACTURING INC
Also Called: Salt Water Lite
2200 Nc Highway 67 (28642-9251)
P.O. Box 216 (28642-0216)
PHONE..............................336 526-2468
Mike Phillips, Pr
Tricia Phillips, Sec
Jennie Wilkins, Adm/Asst
EMP: 22 EST: 1989
SQ FT: 12,500
SALES (est): 2.47MM **Privately Held**
Web: stonykns.wixsite.com
SIC: 3599 Custom machinery

(G-7198)
PARRISH TIRE COMPANY
547 Winston Rd (28642-2217)
PHONE..............................704 872-6565
Tim Chaffin, Mgr
EMP: 43
SALES (corp-wide): 378.88MM **Privately Held**
Web: www.parrishtire.com
SIC: 5531 5014 7534 Automotive tires; Tires and tubes; Tire recapping
PA: Parrish Tire Company
5130 Indiana Ave
Winston Salem NC 27106
800 849-8473

(G-7199)
TOWN OF JONESVILLE
Also Called: Jonesville Water Plant
399 Shaw St (28642-2155)
PHONE..............................336 835-2250
Scott Buffkin, Mgr
EMP: 5
Web: www.jonesvillenc.gov
SIC: 3589 Water treatment equipment, industrial
PA: Town Of Jonesville
1503 Nc Highway 67
Jonesville NC 28642
336 835-3426

Julian
Guilford County

(G-7200)
BATTLGRUND STRTER GNERATOR INC
4497 Folger Rd (27283-8009)
PHONE..............................336 685-4511
Jerry Brown, VP
Sylvia C Brown, Sec
EMP: 4 EST: 1978
SQ FT: 2,400
SALES (est): 368.6K **Privately Held**
SIC: 3621 Starters, for motors

(G-7201)
HOMELAND CREAMERY LLC
6506 Bowman Dairy Rd (27283-9122)
PHONE..............................336 685-6455
Bowman Theresa, Prin
EMP: 4 EST: 2003
SQ FT: 2,069
SALES (est): 992.12K **Privately Held**
Web: www.homelandcreamery.com
SIC: 2024 Ice cream, bulk

Kannapolis
Cabarrus County

(G-7202)
ARTISTIC FRAME CORP
401 N Little Texas Rd (28083-6355)
PHONE..............................212 289-2100
EMP: 495
SIC: 2426 5021 Frames for upholstered
furniture, wood; Office furniture, nec
PA: Artistic Frame Corp.
981 3rd Ave
New York NY 10022

(G-7203)
BOMMERANG IMPRINTS
2305 Beaver Pond Rd (28083-6504)
PHONE..............................704 933-9075
Donna Haywood, *Prin*
EMP: 5 EST: 2007
SALES (est): 73.63K **Privately Held**
SIC: 3949 Boomerangs

(G-7204)
BRIGHT PATH LABORATORIES INC
150 N Research Campus Dr (28081-3384)
PHONE..............................858 281-8121
Tony Quinones, *Prin*
Phil Lichtenberger, *Prin*
John Lalonde, *Prin*
Matt Demarey, *Prin*
Todd Smith, *Prin*
EMP: 8 EST: 2017
SALES (est): 4.7MM **Privately Held**
Web: www.brightpathlabs.com
SIC: 2834 Pharmaceutical preparations

(G-7205)
BROWN CABINET CO
1510 N Ridge Ave (28083-1703)
P.O. Box 122 (28082-0122)
PHONE..............................704 933-2731
Doug Brown, *Owner*
EMP: 4 EST: 1935
SQ FT: 5,000
SALES (est): 226.57K **Privately Held**
Web: www.browncabinetcompany.com
SIC: 2511 2434 Wood household furniture;
Wood kitchen cabinets

(G-7206)
DALE RAY FABRICS LLC
1121 N Main St (28081-2256)
PHONE..............................704 932-6411
Dale Ray Cathcart, *Owner*
EMP: 7 EST: 1978
SQ FT: 10,000
SALES (est): 246.65K **Privately Held**
Web: www.dalerayfabrics.com
SIC: 2392 5719 5714 Cushions and pillows;
Wicker, rattan, or reed home furnishings;
Upholstery materials

(G-7207)
DIAGNOSTIC SHOP INC
Also Called: Diagnostic Shop and Repair
723 Fairview St (28083-5201)
PHONE..............................704 933-3435
Joshua Rachels, *Pr*
EMP: 5 EST: 2014
SQ FT: 4,500
SALES (est): 913.09K **Privately Held**
Web: www.diagnosticshop.guru
SIC: 3011 7549 7539 5531 Automobile tires,
pneumatic; Emissions testing without
repairs, automotive; Brake repair,
automotive; Automotive tires

(G-7208)
ENVIRNMNTAL CMFORT SLTIONS INC
1400 S Main St (28081-5918)
PHONE..............................980 272-7327
Michelle Setzekorn, *CEO*
Jonathan Setzekorn, *
EMP: 26 EST: 2005
SQ FT: 5,000
SALES (est): 2.11MM **Privately Held**
Web:
www.environmentalcomfortsolutions.com
SIC: 5063 5075 3625 8748 Electrical
apparatus and equipment; Warm air
heating and air conditioning; Relays and
industrial controls; Energy conservation
consultant

(G-7209)
GENIXUS CORP (PA)
Also Called: Genixus
150 N Research Campus Dr (28081-3384)
PHONE..............................877 436-4987
Kendall Foster, *CEO*
EMP: 10 EST: 2020
SALES (est): 2.66MM
SALES (corp-wide): 2.66MM **Privately Held**
Web: www.genixus.com
SIC: 2834 Pharmaceutical preparations

(G-7210)
HANGING C FARMS
709 China Grove Rd (28083-8800)
PHONE..............................704 239-6691
Elizabeth Cox, *Owner*
EMP: 12 EST: 2011
SALES (est): 753.06K **Privately Held**
SIC: 3537 Industrial trucks and tractors

(G-7211)
HYGEIA MARKETING CORPORATION
729 S Main St (28081-4915)
PHONE..............................704 933-5190
John A Bishop, *Pr*
Malcom Bishop, *VP*
EMP: 4 EST: 1986
SALES (est): 296.4K **Privately Held**
SIC: 3069 Birth control devices, rubber

(G-7212)
INNOVATIVE CUSTOM CABINETS INC
1018 Robinhood Ln (28081-5744)
PHONE..............................813 748-0655
Angel L Ortiz, *Prin*
EMP: 4 EST: 2011
SALES (est): 199.35K **Privately Held**
SIC: 2434 Wood kitchen cabinets

(G-7213)
KANNAPOLIS AWARDS AND GRAPHICS
1103 Central Dr (28083-3736)
PHONE..............................704 224-3695
Derik Wieland, *Mgr*
EMP: 4 EST: 2017
SALES (est): 93.95K **Privately Held**
SIC: 2759 Screen printing

(G-7214)
KONTEK INDUSTRIES INC
805 Mccombs Ave (28083-3680)
P.O. Box 69 (63801-0069)
PHONE..............................704 273-5040
Charles Merrill, *CEO*
Kris Knoe, *Treas*
EMP: 10 EST: 1990
SQ FT: 5,000
SALES (est): 10.92MM **Privately Held**
Web: www.kontekindustries.com

SIC: 3449 Bars, concrete reinforcing:
fabricated steel

(G-7215)
LOLLIPOP CENRAL
3111 Mocking Bird Ln (28083-9225)
PHONE..............................704 934-0015
EMP: 5 EST: 2016
SALES (est): 64.26K **Privately Held**
SIC: 2064 Lollipops and other hard candy

(G-7216)
MRA SERVICES INC
2500 S Cannon Blvd (28083-6912)
PHONE..............................704 933-4300
James J Miller, *Pr*
EMP: 12 EST: 1986
SALES (est): 388.25K **Privately Held**
Web: www.mraservices.net
SIC: 2741 8711 Technical manual and paper
publishing; Consulting engineer

(G-7217)
O GRAYSON COMPANY
6509 Grayson Ln (28081-9608)
PHONE..............................704 932-6195
Van D Stamey, *Pr*
G O'dell Stamey, *Sec*
▲ EMP: 50 EST: 1973
SQ FT: 52,000
SALES (est): 7.96MM **Privately Held**
SIC: 2844 Hair preparations, including
shampoos

(G-7218)
PASB INC
303 N Cannon Blvd (28083-3822)
PHONE..............................704 490-2556
Lee N Forrest, *Pr*
EMP: 5 EST: 2003
SALES (est): 703.66K **Privately Held**
SIC: 2273 Art squares, textile fiber

(G-7219)
SALUBRENT PHRMA SOLUTIONS CORP
150 N Research Campus Dr Ste 3700
(28081-3384)
PHONE..............................301 980-7224
Terry Novak, *CEO*
EMP: 5 EST: 2020
SALES (est): 942.77K **Privately Held**
Web: www.salubrent.com
SIC: 2834 Pharmaceutical preparations

(G-7220)
SMITHFIELD FOODS INC
2975 Dale Earnhardt Blvd (28083-1404)
PHONE..............................704 298-0936
EMP: 11
Web: www.smithfieldfoods.com
SIC: 2011 Meat packing plants
HQ: Smithfield Foods, Inc.
200 Commerce St
Smithfield VA 23430
757 365-3000

(G-7221)
SUNDROP PRINTING
700 N Cannon Blvd (28083-3798)
PHONE..............................704 960-1592
EMP: 5 EST: 2016
SALES (est): 83.91K **Privately Held**
Web: www.sundropgraphics.com
SIC: 2752 Commercial printing, lithographic

(G-7222)
TOWEL CITY TIRE & WHEEL LLC
1601 N Ridge Ave (28083-2788)
PHONE..............................704 933-2143

Herbert O Cauble Iii, *Pr*
Herbert O Cauble Junior, *Treas*
Danny R Cauble, *VP*
EMP: 8 EST: 1935
SQ FT: 5,000
SALES (est): 422.63K **Privately Held**
Web: www.towelcityracingtires.com
SIC: 7534 5531 5014 Tire recapping;
Automotive tires; Automobile tires and tubes

Kelly
Bladen County

(G-7223)
TOPLINK PUBLISHING
2227 Natmore Rd (28448-8677)
PHONE..............................888 375-9818
EMP: 4 EST: 2017
SALES (est): 66.03K **Privately Held**
SIC: 2741 Miscellaneous publishing

Kenansville
Duplin County

(G-7224)
AG PROVISION LLC (PA)
277 Faison W Mcgowan Rd (28349-8948)
PHONE..............................910 296-0302
▲ EMP: 30 EST: 1990
SQ FT: 182,000
SALES (est): 24.78MM **Privately Held**
Web: www.agprovisionllc.com
SIC: 5191 2841 Chemicals, agricultural;
Detergents, synthetic organic or inorganic
alkaline

(G-7225)
COX NRTH CRLINA PBLCATIONS INC
Also Called: Duplin Times
102 Front St (28349)
P.O. Box 69 (28349-0069)
PHONE..............................910 296-0239
Gary Scott, *Mgr*
EMP: 4
SALES (corp-wide): 961.55MM **Privately Held**
Web: www.reflector.com
SIC: 2711 Newspapers: publishing only, not
printed on site
HQ: Cox North Carolina Publications, Inc.
1150 Sugg Pkwy
Greenville NC 27834
252 329-9643

(G-7226)
LEAR CORPORATION
1754 N Nc 11 903 Hwy (28349-8738)
P.O. Box 509 (28349-0509)
PHONE..............................910 296-8671
John Emmett, *Pr*
EMP: 50
SALES (corp-wide): 23.31B **Publicly Held**
Web: www.lear.com
SIC: 2258 2282 Cloth, warp knit; Acetate
filament yarn: throwing, twisting, winding,
spooling
PA: Lear Corporation
21557 Telegraph Rd
Southfield MI 48033
248 447-1500

(G-7227)
QUO VADEMUS LLC
277 Faison W Mcgowan Rd (28349-8948)
PHONE..............................910 296-1632
Gabriela Greilinger, *Managing Member*
EMP: 9 EST: 2008
SALES (est): 147.05K **Privately Held**

▲ = Import ▼ = Export
◆ = Import/Export

SIC: 2836 Veterinary biological products

Kenly
Johnston County

(G-7228)
CCO HOLDINGS LLC
607 W 2nd St (27542-7723)
PHONE..............................919 502-4007
EMP: 168
SALES (corp-wide): 55.09MM **Publicly Held**
SIC: 4841 3663 3651 Cable television services; Radio and t.v. communications equipment; Household audio and video equipment
HQ: Cco Holdings, Llc
400 Atlantic St
Stamford CT 06901
203 905-7801

(G-7229)
CONESTOGA WOOD SPC CORP
621 Johnston Pkwy (27542-7516)
PHONE..............................919 284-2258
Roger Anderson, *Brnch Mgr*
EMP: 100
SALES (corp-wide): 44.21MM **Privately Held**
Web: www.conestogawood.com
SIC: 2514 2434 Kitchen cabinets: metal; Wood kitchen cabinets
PA: Conestoga Wood Specialties Corporation
245 Reading Rd
East Earl PA 17519
717 445-6701

(G-7230)
CUMMINS INC
Also Called: Cummins
350 Cummins Dr (27542-7545)
PHONE..............................919 284-9111
Michael Stanford, *Mgr*
EMP: 5
SALES (corp-wide): 34.1B **Publicly Held**
Web: www.cummins.com
SIC: 5084 3519 Engines and parts, diesel; Internal combustion engines, nec
PA: Cummins Inc.
500 Jackson St
Columbus IN 47201
812 377-5000

(G-7231)
CUMMINS INC
350 Cummins Dr (27542-7545)
PHONE..............................919 284-9111
Michael Stanford, *Brnch Mgr*
EMP: 6
SALES (corp-wide): 34.1B **Publicly Held**
Web: www.cummins.com
SIC: 3714 Motor vehicle parts and accessories
PA: Cummins Inc.
500 Jackson St
Columbus IN 47201
812 377-5000

(G-7232)
DAUGHTERS & RYAN INC
207 Johnston Pkwy (27542-7503)
PHONE..............................919 284-0153
EMP: 9
SALES (est): 142.68K **Privately Held**
SIC: 3069 Pipestems or bits, tobacco: hard rubber

(G-7233)
HERSHEY COMPANY
Also Called: Hershey
104 Hershey Dr (27542-7536)
PHONE..............................919 284-0272
Ronald Wishall, *Mgr*
EMP: 10
SALES (corp-wide): 11.16B **Publicly Held**
Web: www.thehersheycompany.com
SIC: 2064 5143 Candy and other confectionery products; Dairy products, except dried or canned
PA: Hershey Company
19 E Chocolate Ave
Hershey PA 17033
717 534-4200

(G-7234)
PERDUE FARMS INC
Also Called: Perdue Farms
9266 Revell Rd (27542-9204)
PHONE..............................919 284-2033
Darryl Bryant, *Brnch Mgr*
EMP: 123
SALES (corp-wide): 1.24B **Privately Held**
Web: www.perdue.com
SIC: 2015 Poultry slaughtering and processing
PA: Perdue Farms Incorporated
31149 Old Ocean City Rd
Salisbury MD 21804
800 473-7383

(G-7235)
PETROLEUM TANK CORPORATION
Also Called: Petco
600 N Gardner Ave (27542)
P.O. Box 429 (27542-0429)
PHONE..............................919 284-2418
Greg Narron, *Pr*
Lois Narron, *Sec*
EMP: 16 EST: 1954
SQ FT: 1,000
SALES (est): 1.81MM **Privately Held**
Web: www.pettank.com
SIC: 3713 7699 5084 Tank truck bodies; Tank repair and cleaning services; Textile and leather machinery

(G-7236)
RICHARD D STEWART
Also Called: Kenly News
201 W 2nd St (27542-5001)
P.O. Box 39 (27542-0039)
PHONE..............................919 284-2295
Richard D Stewart, *Owner*
EMP: 7 EST: 1973
SQ FT: 6,000
SALES (est): 113.13K **Privately Held**
Web: www.kenlynews.com
SIC: 2711 2791 Newspapers, publishing and printing; Typesetting

(G-7237)
RPP ACQUISITION LLC
Also Called: Quantum Plastics Raleigh
131 Johnston Pkwy (27542-7504)
PHONE..............................919 248-9001
Ron Embree, *CEO*
Lisa Fiorenza, *
EMP: 25 EST: 2018
SQ FT: 45,000
SALES (est): 9.99MM **Privately Held**
SIC: 3089 Injection molded finished plastics products, nec
HQ: Qp Holdings, Llc
3730 Wheeler Ave
Fort Smith AR 72901
479 646-3473

Kernersville
Forsyth County

(G-7238)
A & S TOOL & DIE CO INC
1510 Brookford Industrial Dr (27284-9412)
P.O. Box 890 (27285-0890)
PHONE..............................336 993-3440
Jack Hale, *Pr*
Ken Hale, *VP*
EMP: 6 EST: 1958
SQ FT: 7,000
SALES (est): 679.96K **Privately Held**
SIC: 3599 Machine shop, jobbing and repair

(G-7239)
ADVANTAGE FITNESS PRODUCTS INC
115 Gralin St (27284-3998)
P.O. Box 710 (29566-0710)
PHONE..............................336 643-8810
Brent Johnson, *Pr*
EMP: 6 EST: 2005
SALES (est): 431.51K **Privately Held**
Web: www.afpnorthamerica.com
SIC: 3949 Exercise equipment

(G-7240)
ALLIED TOOL AND MACHINE CO (PA)
115 Corum St (27284-2927)
P.O. Box 706 (27285-0706)
PHONE..............................336 993-2131
Nan Kollar, *Pr*
Joe Kollar, *VP*
Mildred Ballard, *Sec*
EMP: 7 EST: 1945
SQ FT: 40,000
SALES (est): 6.63MM
SALES (corp-wide): 6.63MM **Privately Held**
SIC: 3469 3444 Appliance parts, porcelain enameled; Sheet metalwork

(G-7241)
ALTERNATIVE CARE GROUP LLC
931 S Main St Ste A (27284-7459)
PHONE..............................336 499-5644
James Guarino, *Pr*
EMP: 4 EST: 2009
SALES (est): 421.6K **Privately Held**
Web: www.alternativecaregroup.com
SIC: 3842 Prosthetic appliances

(G-7242)
AMANZI MARBLE & GRANITE LLC
703 Park Lawn Ct (27284-8967)
PHONE..............................336 993-9998
EMP: 6 EST: 2004
SALES (est): 4.06MM **Privately Held**
Web: www.amanzigranite.com
SIC: 3281 Granite, cut and shaped

(G-7243)
AMERICAN CYLINDER PRODUCTS INC
115 Furlong Industrial Dr (27284-3242)
P.O. Box 408 (27285-0408)
PHONE..............................336 993-7722
Phillip E Fuller Junior, *Pr*
Tony W Seaford, *VP*
Darlene S Fuller, *Treas*
EMP: 5 EST: 2010
SALES (est): 935.54K **Privately Held**
Web: www.americancylinderproducts.com
SIC: 3599 Machine shop, jobbing and repair

(G-7244)
AMERICAN WOOD REFACE OF TRIAD
5339 Valleydale Rd (27284-7874)
PHONE..............................336 345-2837
EMP: 4 EST: 2017
SALES (est): 64.21K **Privately Held**
Web: www.woodreface.com
SIC: 2434 Wood kitchen cabinets

(G-7245)
ARTWEAR EMBROIDERY INC (PA)
621 Indeneer Dr (27284-3581)
PHONE..............................336 992-2166
Cindy Cox-wilson, *Pr*
Jerry Davis, *VP*
EMP: 24 EST: 1993
SALES (est): 3.87MM **Privately Held**
Web: www.artwearinc.com
SIC: 2395 Embroidery products, except Schiffli machine

(G-7246)
ATLANTIC MANUFACTURING LLC
1322 S Park Dr (27284-3151)
PHONE..............................336 497-5500
EMP: 5 EST: 2017
SALES (est): 91.1K **Privately Held**
SIC: 3999 Manufacturing industries, nec

(G-7247)
BEESON SIGN CO INC
213 Berry Garden Rd (27284-9449)
PHONE..............................336 993-5617
Chris Beeson, *Pr*
Allan Lamper, *Mgr*
EMP: 6 EST: 1972
SALES (est): 536.78K **Privately Held**
Web: www.beesonsignco.com
SIC: 3993 Electric signs

(G-7248)
BRIDGPORT RESTORATION SVCS INC
742 Park Lawn Ct (27284-8967)
P.O. Box 1051 (27285-1051)
PHONE..............................336 996-1212
Carol Horton, *Pr*
EMP: 4 EST: 1987
SQ FT: 1,500
SALES (est): 432.19K **Privately Held**
Web: www.bridgeportrestoration.com
SIC: 7217 1799 2269 7342 Carpet and upholstery cleaning; Post disaster renovations; Finishing plants, nec; Disinfecting and deodorizing

(G-7249)
CARAUSTAR INDUS CNSMR PDTS GRO
Also Called: Kernersville Adhesives Plant
1485 Plaza South Dr (27284-3515)
PHONE..............................336 564-2163
EMP: 8
SALES (corp-wide): 5.45B **Publicly Held**
SIC: 2655 Fiber cans, drums, and similar products
HQ: Caraustar Industrial And Consumer Products Group Inc
5000 Austell Powder Ste
Austell GA 30106
803 548-5100

(G-7250)
CARAUSTAR INDUS CNSMR PDTS GRO
Also Called: Kernsville Tube Plant
1045 Industrial Park Dr (27284-9481)
PHONE..............................336 996-4165
David Partin, *Mgr*

EMP: 43
SALES (corp-wide): 5.45B **Publicly Held**
SIC: 2655 Fiber cans, drums, and similar products
HQ: Caraustar Industrial And Consumer Products Group Inc
5000 Austell Powder Ste
Austell GA 30106
803 548-5100

(G-7251)
CARAUSTAR INDUSTRIES INC
1496 Plaza South Dr (27284-3514)
PHONE.............................336 992-1053
Charlie Burton, *Manager*
EMP: 22
SALES (corp-wide): 5.45B **Publicly Held**
Web: www.greif.com
SIC: 2655 Tubes, fiber or paper: made from purchased material
HQ: Caraustar Industries, Inc.
5000 Astell Pwdr Sprng Rd
Austell GA 30106
770 948-3101

(G-7252)
CAROLINA NORTH MFG INC
1161 S Park Dr (27284-3114)
P.O. Box 339 (27358-0339)
PHONE.............................336 992-0082
Kent Southard, *Pr*
Linda Southard, *Sec*
▲ **EMP:** 6 **EST:** 1991
SQ FT: 9,000
SALES (est): 851.66K **Privately Held**
Web: www.roperatchet.com
SIC: 3429 Marine hardware

(G-7253)
CARTER PUBLISHING COMPANY INC
Also Called: Kernersville News
300 E Mountain St (27284-2943)
P.O. Box 337 (27285-0337)
PHONE.............................336 993-2161
Meredith Harrell, *Pr*
EMP: 10 **EST:** 1938
SQ FT: 20,000
SALES (est): 2.4MM
SALES (corp-wide): 147.64MM **Privately Held**
Web: www.kernersvillenews.com
SIC: 2711 5943 2759 Commercial printing and newspaper publishing combined; Office forms and supplies; Letterpress printing
PA: Paxton Media Group, Llc
100 Television Ln
Paducah KY 42003
270 575-8630

(G-7254)
CASTLE SHIRT COMPANY LLC
621 Indeneer Dr Ste 1 (27284-3570)
P.O. Box 8666 (27419-0666)
PHONE.............................336 992-7727
Jenny Zmuda, *Managing Member*
Jinny Zmuda, *Managing Member*
▲ **EMP:** 4 **EST:** 1999
SALES (est): 247.68K **Privately Held**
SIC: 2759 Screen printing

(G-7255)
CGMI ACQUISITION COMPANY LLC
Also Called: Clearlight Glass and Mirror
1318 Shields Rd (27284-3532)
PHONE.............................919 533-6123
EMP: 17 **EST:** 2017
SALES (est): 5.14MM **Privately Held**
Web: www.clearlightglass.com
SIC: 3231 Mirrored glass

(G-7256)
CHICHIBONE INC (PA)
Also Called: McNamara & Company
1310 Grindelwald Dr (27284-8673)
P.O. Box 667 (27284)
PHONE.............................919 785-0090
Pat Mcnamara, *Pr*
Phil Mcnamara, *Sr VP*
Dick Polenm, *CFO*
EMP: 15 **EST:** 1999
SALES (est): 23.23MM
SALES (corp-wide): 23.23MM **Privately Held**
Web: www.trs-sesco.com
SIC: 3585 7623 3561 Heating and air conditioning combination units; Refrigeration service and repair; Pumps and pumping equipment

(G-7257)
CLARIOS LLC
Also Called: Johnson Controls
2701 Johnson Controls Dr (27284-5200)
P.O. Box 1667 (27285-1667)
PHONE.............................336 761-1550
Dick Tryor, *Mgr*
EMP: 199
SQ FT: 250,000
SALES (corp-wide): 69.83B **Privately Held**
Web: www.clarios.com
SIC: 2531 3692 3691 Seats, automobile; Primary batteries, dry and wet; Storage batteries
HQ: Clarios, Llc
5757 N Green Bay Ave Flor
Glendale WI 53209

(G-7258)
COLUMBIANA HI TECH LLC
1621 Old Greensboro Rd (27284-6855)
PHONE.............................336 497-3600
EMP: 6
SIC: 3443 Nuclear shielding, metal plate

(G-7259)
CORILAM FABRICATING CO
5211 Macy Grove Rd (27284-0204)
P.O. Box 361 (27285-0361)
PHONE.............................336 993-2371
Bradley Robins, *Pr*
Brad Robins, *
Miles West, *
Andrew J Robins, *
Charles Gray, *
▲ **EMP:** 45 **EST:** 1975
SQ FT: 84,000
SALES (est): 7.65MM **Privately Held**
Web: www.corilam.com
SIC: 2541 2531 2521 2434 Wood partitions and fixtures; Public building and related furniture; Wood office furniture; Wood kitchen cabinets

(G-7260)
COVINGTON BARCODING INC
1800 Watmead Rd (27284-8761)
PHONE.............................336 996-5759
Mark Covington, *Prin*
EMP: 4 **EST:** 2015
SALES (est): 791.75K **Privately Held**
Web: www.covingtonbarcoding.com
SIC: 3577 7389 Bar code (magnetic ink) printers; Business Activities at Non-Commercial Site

(G-7261)
CUSTOM MACHINING INC
121 Majestic Way Ct Ste D (27284-3259)
P.O. Box 1605 (27285-1605)
PHONE.............................336 996-0855
Alan Mellott, *Pr*

EMP: 6 **EST:** 1991
SQ FT: 2,000
SALES (est): 994.28K **Privately Held**
SIC: 3599 Machine shop, jobbing and repair

(G-7262)
CUSTOM PRINTING SOLUTIONS INC
1355 S Park Dr (27284-3150)
P.O. Box 450 (27285-0450)
PHONE.............................336 992-1161
Devin Lineberry, *Pr*
Jodi Lineberry, *VP*
EMP: 8 **EST:** 2004
SALES (est): 738.05K **Privately Held**
SIC: 2752 Offset printing

(G-7263)
DANBY BARCODING LLC
1800 Watmead Rd (27284-8761)
PHONE.............................770 416-9845
EMP: 5
SALES (est): 920.38K **Privately Held**
Web: www.covingtonbarcoding.com
SIC: 3565 7389 Labeling machines, industrial ; Business services, nec

(G-7264)
DANISSON USA TRADING LTD LLC
Also Called: Danisson Trading
210 Serenity Pointe Dr (27284-9822)
PHONE.............................704 965-8317
Efstratios Ferentinos, *Pr*
Nick Delis, *VP*
EMP: 4 **EST:** 2010
SALES (est): 297K **Privately Held**
SIC: 1389 5172 Cementing oil and gas well casings; Petroleum brokers

(G-7265)
DEERE & COMPANY
Also Called: Deere-Hitachi Cnstr McHy
1000 John Deere Rd (27284-2275)
PHONE.............................336 996-8100
EMP: 4
SALES (corp-wide): 8.51B **Publicly Held**
Web: www.deere.com
SIC: 3523 Farm machinery and equipment
PA: Deere & Company
1 John Deere Pl
Moline IL 61265
309 765-8000

(G-7266)
DIXON CUSTOM CABINETRY LLC
129 Furlong Industrial Dr (27284-3242)
PHONE.............................336 992-3306
EMP: 10 **EST:** 2006
SALES (est): 1.8MM **Privately Held**
Web: www.dixoncabinetry.com
SIC: 3553 5031 Cabinet makers' machinery; Kitchen cabinets

(G-7267)
DJ POWDERCOATING IRONWORK LLC
Also Called: Dj Powder Coating
232 Industrial Way Dr Ste A (27284-3260)
PHONE.............................336 310-4725
Marvin Young, *Managing Member*
Denny Young, *Managing Member*
EMP: 5 **EST:** 2008
SALES (est): 916.98K **Privately Held**
Web: www.djpowdercoating.com
SIC: 3479 Coating of metals and formed products

(G-7268)
DONE-GONE ADIOS INC
1318 Shields Rd (27284-3532)
PHONE.............................336 993-7300

Robert Johnson, *Pr*
EMP: 12 **EST:** 1994
SQ FT: 75,000
SALES (est): 2.11MM **Privately Held**
Web: www.clearlightglass.com
SIC: 5231 3231 Glass; Aquariums and reflectors, glass

(G-7269)
DREAM KREAMS LLC
549 Arbor Hill Rd Apt 5a (27284-3333)
PHONE.............................919 491-1984
Kendra Sharlese Vanhook, *CEO*
EMP: 4 **EST:** 2019
SALES (est): 238.98K **Privately Held**
SIC: 2024 Ice cream and frozen deserts

(G-7270)
EDC INC (PA)
950 Old Winston Rd (27284-8193)
PHONE.............................336 993-0468
EMP: 65 **EST:** 1981
SALES (est): 9.94MM
SALES (corp-wide): 9.94MM **Privately Held**
Web: www.edcinc.com
SIC: 3679 Electronic circuits

(G-7271)
EMERALD TOOL AND MOLD INC
106 Furlong Industrial Dr (27284-3241)
P.O. Box 2462 (27285-2462)
PHONE.............................336 996-6445
Joe Russell, *Pr*
Michael T Young, *VP*
▲ **EMP:** 13 **EST:** 1992
SQ FT: 4,800
SALES (est): 2.46MM **Privately Held**
Web: www.emeraldtoolandmold.com
SIC: 3544 Dies, plastics forming

(G-7272)
EUROGOLD ART
251 N Main St (27284-2879)
P.O. Box 2215 (27285-2215)
PHONE.............................336 989-6205
Mariam Martinca, *Prin*
EMP: 6 **EST:** 2005
SALES (est): 96.48K **Privately Held**
SIC: 3911 Jewelry, precious metal

(G-7273)
EXOTICS POWER COAT
745 Cinema Ct (27284-2494)
PHONE.............................336 831-3865
George Debidart Iii, *Prin*
EMP: 4 **EST:** 2014
SALES (est): 149.77K **Privately Held**
SIC: 3479 Coating of metals and formed products

(G-7274)
FELICE HOSIERY CO INC
118 Burke St (27284-2687)
P.O. Box 1116 (27285-1116)
PHONE.............................336 996-2371
Daniel Hayworth, *Mgr*
EMP: 42
SALES (corp-wide): 676.48K **Privately Held**
Web: www.iwsocks.com
SIC: 2252 2251 Socks; Women's hosiery, except socks
PA: Felice Hosiery Co, Inc
632 W Roosevelt Rd
Chicago IL 60607
312 922-3710

(G-7275)
GET CUSTOM PRINT
504 Edgewood St (27284-3137)
PHONE..............................336 682-3891
Elmer Ramos, *Prin*
EMP: 4 EST: 2018
SALES (est): 178.92K Privately Held
SIC: 2752 Commercial printing, lithographic

(G-7276)
GHX INDUSTRIAL LLC
1295 S Park Dr (27284-3198)
PHONE..............................336 996-7271
Daniel Ahuero, *CEO*
EMP: 8
SALES (corp-wide): 884.09MM Privately Held
Web: www.ghxinc.com
SIC: 5085 3052 3053 Packing, industrial; Air line or air brake hose, rubber or rubberized fabric; Gaskets; packing and sealing devices
HQ: Ghx Industrial, Llc
13311 Lockwood Rd
Houston TX 77044
713 341-3407

(G-7277)
GRASS AMERICA INC
1202 Nc Highway 66 S (27284-3537)
PHONE..............................336 996-4041
Tom Kipp, *Pr*
Scott Bjork, *
Matthias Bulla, *
◆ EMP: 201 EST: 1977
SQ FT: 190,000
SALES (est): 30.11MM
SALES (corp-wide): 22.17B Privately Held
Web: www.grassusa.com
SIC: 5072 3429 Hardware; Furniture, builders' and other household hardware
HQ: Wurth Group Of North America Inc.
93 Grant St
Ramsey NJ 07446

(G-7278)
HEDRICK CONSTRUCTION
838 Crosscreek Rd (27284-8442)
PHONE..............................336 362-3443
Jeff Hedrick, *Owner*
EMP: 5 EST: 1995
SALES (est): 126.28K Privately Held
Web: www.hedrickconstructionco.com
SIC: 2431 Interior and ornamental woodwork and trim

(G-7279)
IDEAL PRINTING SERVICES INC
4240 Kernersville Rd Ste D (27284-8101)
P.O. Box 161 (27051-0161)
PHONE..............................336 784-0074
Bobby Wolfington, *Pr*
Mark Wolfington, *Sec*
EMP: 5 EST: 1964
SQ FT: 3,000
SALES (est): 125.26K Privately Held
SIC: 2752 Offset printing

(G-7280)
ILLINOIS TOOL WORKS INC
Texwipe
1210 S Park Dr (27284-3104)
PHONE..............................336 996-7046
Les Josey, *Genl Mgr*
EMP: 200
SALES (corp-wide): 16.11B Publicly Held
Web: www.itw.com
SIC: 2842 Specialty cleaning
PA: Illinois Tool Works Inc.
155 Harlem Ave
Glenview IL 60025

224 661-8870

(G-7281)
JOHN DEERE KERNERSVILLE LLC
1000 John Deere Rd (27284-2275)
P.O. Box 1187 (27285)
PHONE..............................336 996-8100
John C May, *CEO*
▲ EMP: 691 EST: 1988
SALES (est): 49.54MM
SALES (corp-wide): 8.51B Publicly Held
Web: www.dhkernersville.com
SIC: 3531 Bituminous, cement and concrete related products and equip.
PA: Deere & Company
1 John Deere Pl
Moline IL 61265
309 765-8000

(G-7282)
LOFLIN CONCRETE CO INC
2105 Pisgah Church Rd (27284-8063)
PHONE..............................336 904-2788
Richard G Loflin, *Pr*
Denise Loflin, *Sec*
EMP: 35 EST: 1925
SQ FT: 23,000
SALES (est): 5.12MM Privately Held
Web: www.loflinconcrete.com
SIC: 3273 4214 Ready-mixed concrete; Local trucking with storage

(G-7283)
M & S SYSTEMS INC
Also Called: M & S Systems
951 Nc Highway 66 S Ste 6b (27284-3101)
P.O. Box 610 (27235-0610)
PHONE..............................336 996-7118
Marvin R Keel, *Pr*
EMP: 4 EST: 1987
SQ FT: 600
SALES (est): 149.64K Privately Held
Web: www.stenclabl.net
SIC: 2752 5999 Commercial printing, lithographic; Packaging materials: boxes, padding, etc.

(G-7284)
MARIETTA MARTIN MATERIALS INC
Also Called: Salem Stone Quarry
4572 High Point Rd (27284-9158)
PHONE..............................336 769-3803
David Thorne, *Bookkpr*
EMP: 5
Web: www.martinmarietta.com
SIC: 1422 5032 Crushed and broken limestone; Granite building stone
PA: Martin Marietta Materials Inc
4123 Parklake Ave
Raleigh NC 27612

(G-7285)
MARTINS FMOUS PSTRY SHOPPE INC
1031 E Mountain St Bldg 314 (27284-7998)
PHONE..............................800 548-1200
EMP: 5
SALES (corp-wide): 149.7MM Privately Held
Web: www.potatorolls.com
SIC: 2051 Rolls, bread type: fresh or frozen
PA: Martin's Famous Pastry Shoppe, Inc.
1000 Potato Roll Ln
Chambersburg PA 17202
800 548-1200

(G-7286)
MEPLA-ALFIT INCORPORATED
1202 Nc Highway 66 S (27284-3537)
PHONE..............................336 289-2300
▼ EMP: 45 EST: 1977

SQ FT: 100,000
SALES (est): 5.51MM
SALES (corp-wide): 12.52B Privately Held
SIC: 3429 Furniture hardware
HQ: Wurth Group Of North America Inc.
93 Grant St
Ramsey NJ 07446
201 818-8877

(G-7287)
MOCHA MEMOIR PRESS
931 S Main St (27284-7493)
PHONE..............................336 404-7445
EMP: 5 EST: 2013
SALES (est): 118.33K Privately Held
Web: www.mochamemoirspress.com
SIC: 2741 Miscellaneous publishing

(G-7288)
MORE THAN BILLBOARDS INC
Also Called: Associated Posters
2737 W Mountain St (27284-9332)
PHONE..............................336 723-1018
Robert Arnold, *Pr*
Nina Hill, *VP*
EMP: 36 EST: 2017
SALES (est): 4.81MM Privately Held
Web: www.associatedposters.com
SIC: 2752 Commercial printing, lithographic

(G-7289)
OLD CASTLE SERVICE INC
920 Old Winston Rd (27284-8119)
PHONE..............................336 992-1601
Bob Jackson, *Genl Mgr*
EMP: 5 EST: 2012
SALES (est): 80.11K Privately Held
SIC: 2541 Counter and sink tops

(G-7290)
OLIVE EURO OIL LLC
1369 S Park Dr (27284-3150)
PHONE..............................336 310-4624
Francesco Caccamo, *Managing Member*
EMP: 8 EST: 2018
SALES (est): 191.44K Privately Held
SIC: 2079 Olive oil

(G-7291)
PALADIN CUSTOM WORKS
230 Perry Rd (27284-2148)
PHONE..............................336 996-2796
Jason Oswalt, *Prin*
EMP: 5 EST: 2016
SALES (est): 947.52K Privately Held
Web: www.paladinattachments.com
SIC: 3531 Construction machinery

(G-7292)
PAM TRADING CORPORATION
1135 Snow Bridge Ln (27284-8429)
P.O. Box 819 (27235-0819)
PHONE..............................336 668-0901
▲ EMP: 38 EST: 1983
SALES (est): 12.89MM Privately Held
Web: www.paminjectionmolding.com
SIC: 5084 3089 Textile machinery and equipment; Injection molding of plastics

(G-7293)
PRINTING PARTNERS INC
365 W Bodenhamer St (27284-2528)
P.O. Box 837 (27235)
PHONE..............................336 996-2268
Barbara A Hannon, *Pr*
EMP: 8 EST: 2002
SQ FT: 7,500
SALES (est): 293.35K Privately Held
SIC: 2752 2791 Offset printing; Typesetting

(G-7294)
PROCOATERS INC
216 Industrial Way Dr (27284-3200)
P.O. Box 426 (27285-0426)
PHONE..............................336 992-0012
Berrick Swaim, *CEO*
John Ogle, *Pr*
Norman Bennett, *VP*
Connie Trainer, *Sec*
EMP: 10 EST: 1995
SQ FT: 12,000
SALES (est): 1.77MM Privately Held
Web: www.procoatersinc.com
SIC: 3479 Painting of metal products

(G-7295)
QMF MTAL ELCTRNIC SLUTIONS INC
324 Berry Garden Rd (27284-9450)
PHONE..............................336 992-8002
Tina H Rierson, *Pr*
Clarence Rierson, *
▲ EMP: 85 EST: 2002
SQ FT: 75,000
SALES (est): 8.45MM Privately Held
Web: www.qmf-usa.com
SIC: 3444 3679 Sheet metal specialties, not stamped; Antennas, receiving

(G-7296)
QUALITY MACHINE & TOOL
1793 Union Cross Rd (27284-7582)
PHONE..............................336 769-9131
George Yountz, *Pr*
Zachary Yountz, *VP*
Juanita Yountz, *Sec*
EMP: 8 EST: 1978
SQ FT: 8,640
SALES (est): 597.85K Privately Held
SIC: 3599 Machine shop, jobbing and repair

(G-7297)
RUGBY ACQUISITION LLC
637 Graves St (27284-3205)
PHONE..............................336 993-8686
Doug Forstrom, *Genl Mgr*
EMP: 62
SALES (corp-wide): 2.58B Privately Held
Web: www.rugbyabp.com
SIC: 5031 2821 2541 2434 Lumber: rough, dressed, and finished; Plastics materials and resins; Wood partitions and fixtures; Wood kitchen cabinets
HQ: Rugby Acquisition Llc
1 Pillsbury St Ste 302
Concord NH 03301
603 369-4710

(G-7298)
SAF-HOLLAND INC
952 Kensal Green Dr (27284-7668)
PHONE..............................336 310-4595
EMP: 5 EST: 2017
SALES (est): 481.27K Privately Held
Web: www.safholland.com
SIC: 3714 Motor vehicle parts and accessories

(G-7299)
SALEM ONE INC
Also Called: Postmark
1155 Distribution Ct (27284-0039)
PHONE..............................336 722-2886
John Bowman, *Brnch Mgr*
EMP: 15
SALES (corp-wide): 879.21K Privately Held
Web: www.postmark.ws
SIC: 7331 8742 2752 Mailing service; Marketing consulting services; Commercial printing, lithographic
PA: Salem One, Inc.

G
E
O
G
R
A
P
H
I
C

5670 Shattalon Dr
Winston Salem NC 27105
336 744-9990

(G-7300)
SIGN RESOURCES OF NC
673 Gralin St Ste B (27284-3457)
PHONE..................................336 310-4611
James Braun, *Prin*
EMP: 4 **EST:** 2009
SALES (est): 136.62K **Privately Held**
Web: www.signresourcesnc.com
SIC: 3993 Signs and advertising specialties

(G-7301)
SOUTH-EAST LUMBER COMPANY
1896 W Mountain St (27284-2140)
P.O. Box 745 (27285-0745)
PHONE..................................336 996-5322
Steve Brackett, *Pr*
Thad Brackett, *
Teresa Brackett, *
EMP: 28 **EST:** 1960
SQ FT: 2,400
SALES (est): 8.91MM **Privately Held**
Web: www.south-eastlumber.com
SIC: 5031 2452 Lumber: rough, dressed,
and finished; Log cabins, prefabricated,
wood

(G-7302)
SPARTAN MANUFACTURING CORP
(PA)
Also Called: Pressure Power Systems
1536 Brookford Industrial Dr (27284-9412)
P.O. Box 917 (27285-0917)
PHONE..................................336 996-5585
Ronald W Robarge, *Pr*
Marilyn C Robarge, *Stockholder**
EMP: 25 **EST:** 1974
SQ FT: 12,500
SALES (est): 2.42MM
SALES (corp-wide): 2.42MM **Privately
Held**
Web: www.smcwashers.com
SIC: 3699 Cleaning equipment, ultrasonic,
except medical and dental

(G-7303)
SPECIALTY NATIONAL INC
119 Furlong Industrial Dr Ste E
(27284-3274)
P.O. Box 488 (27285-0488)
PHONE..................................336 996-8783
Tom Corns, *Pr*
Ronald L Styers, *
EMP: 7 **EST:** 1989
SQ FT: 112,000
SALES (est): 1.44MM **Privately Held**
Web: www.specialtynational.com
SIC: 2841 Soap and other detergents

(G-7304)
TECGRACHEM INC
1957 Nc Highway 66 S (27284-3903)
P.O. Box 2120 (27285-2120)
PHONE..................................336 993-6785
John R Peters, *Pr*
EMP: 5 **EST:** 1979
SQ FT: 542
SALES (est): 227.69K **Privately Held**
SIC: 2819 Industrial inorganic chemicals, nec

(G-7305)
TEX-TECH COATINGS LLC
215 Drummond St (27284-2849)
PHONE..................................336 992-7500
EMP: 80
Web: www.textechindustries.com

SIC: 2296 Tire cord and fabrics
HQ: Tex-Tech Coatings, Llc
1350 Bridgeport Dr Ste 1
Kernersville NC 27284
336 992-7500

(G-7306)
TEX-TECH COATINGS LLC (HQ)
1350 Bridgeport Dr Ste 1 (27284-3794)
PHONE..................................336 992-7500
Ciaran Lynch, *CEO*
Peter Manos, *Pr*
John Stankiewicz, *Treas*
Stephen Judge, *Ex VP*
Erica Son, *Asst VP*
EMP: 15 **EST:** 2019
SALES (est): 39.63MM **Privately Held**
Web: www.textechindustries.com
SIC: 2296 2261 Tire cord and fabrics;
Finishing plants, cotton
PA: Tex-Tech Industries, Inc.
1350 Bridgeport Dr Ste 1
Kernersville NC 27284

(G-7307)
TEX-TECH INDUSTRIES INC (PA)
Also Called: Tex Tech Industries
1350 Bridgeport Dr Ste 1 (27284-3794)
PHONE..................................207 756-8606
Scott Burkhart, *Pr*
John Stankiewicz, *
Stephen Judge, *
▲ **EMP:** 185 **EST:** 1983
SQ FT: 3,000
SALES (est): 117.25MM **Privately Held**
Web: www.textechindustries.com
SIC: 2299 Batting, wadding, padding and
fillings

(G-7308)
TORTILLERIA DUVY LLC
1261 Nc Highway 66 S (27284-3550)
PHONE..................................336 497-1510
EMP: 4 **EST:** 2022
SALES (est): 82.04K **Privately Held**
SIC: 2032 Tortillas: packaged in cans, jars,
etc.

(G-7309)
TRIAD FABRICATION AND MCH INC
1080 Industrial Park Dr (27284-9410)
P.O. Box 1053 (27285-1053)
PHONE..................................336 993-6042
John Ogle, *Pr*
Norman Bennett, *VP*
Avalon Potts, *Treas*
EMP: 9 **EST:** 1988
SQ FT: 20,000
SALES (est): 2.28MM **Privately Held**
SIC: 3599 3444 Machine and other job shop
work; Sheet metalwork

(G-7310)
TRS-SESCO LLC
721 Park Centre Dr Ste A (27284-3895)
PHONE..................................336 996-2220
Burton Hong, *
Ed Dunlap, *
Colleen Catalano, *
Ray Badua, *
EMP: 95 **EST:** 2020
SALES (est): 962.18K
SALES (corp-wide): 3.88B **Publicly Held**
Web: www.trs-sesco.com
SIC: 3585 7623 3561 Heating and air
conditioning combination units;
Refrigeration service and repair; Pumps
and pumping equipment
HQ: Coolsys Commercial & Industrial
Solutions, Inc.
145 S State College Blvd

Brea CA 92821

(G-7311)
US INDUSTRIAL PIPING INC
105 Woodland Trl (27284-2159)
P.O. Box 889 (27285-0889)
PHONE..................................336 993-9505
John C Dixon, *Pr*
Cassius Dixon, *
EMP: 56 **EST:** 1992
SALES (est): 7.8MM **Privately Held**
Web: www.usindustrialpiping.com
SIC: 3498 Fabricated pipe and fittings

(G-7312)
VESTAL BUICK GMC INC
Also Called: Vestal Pontiac Buick GMC Truck
900 Hwy 66 South (27284)
PHONE..................................336 310-0261
Timothy Vestal, *Pr*
EMP: 63 **EST:** 1966
SQ FT: 5,500
SALES (est): 4.27MM **Privately Held**
Web:
www.parksbuickgmckernersville.com
SIC: 5511 7534 Automobiles, new and used;
Tire repair shop

(G-7313)
VULCAN MATERIALS COMPANY
2874 Nc Highway 66 S (27284-9175)
PHONE..................................336 869-2148
D Gray Kimel Junior, *Prin*
EMP: 5
Web: www.vulcanmaterials.com
SIC: 3273 Ready-mixed concrete
PA: Vulcan Materials Company
1200 Urban Center Dr
Birmingham AL 35242

Kill Devil Hills
Dare County

(G-7314)
ATLANTIC COASTAL SHUTTERS
LLC
2701 N Croatan Hwy (27948-9062)
P.O. Box 1243 (27948-1243)
PHONE..................................252 441-4358
EMP: 6 **EST:** 2000
SALES (est): 495.97K **Privately Held**
Web:
www.atlanticcoastalshuttersobx.com
SIC: 3442 Shutters, door or window: metal

(G-7315)
COUNTY OF DARE
Dare County Water
600 S Mustian St (27948-8459)
P.O. Box 1000 (27954-1000)
PHONE..................................252 475-5990
Bob Oreskovich, *Mgr*
EMP: 114
Web: www.darenc.gov
SIC: 3589 Sewage and water treatment
equipment
PA: County Of Dare
954 Marshall C Collins Dr
Manteo NC 27954
252 475-5000

(G-7316)
EPIC KITES LLC
508 Schooner Ct (27948-9600)
PHONE..................................203 209-6831
Dimitri Maramedides, *Prin*
▲ **EMP:** 4 **EST:** 2009
SALES (est): 310K **Privately Held**
SIC: 3944 Kites

(G-7317)
GMG GROUP LLC
Also Called: Good Measure Graphics
115 W Saint Clair St (27948-6955)
P.O. Box 7804 (27948-5804)
PHONE..................................252 441-8374
EMP: 5 **EST:** 2012
SALES (est): 188.82K **Privately Held**
Web: www.goodmeasuregraphics.com
SIC: 2759 3993 7336 5941 Commercial
printing, nec; Signs and advertising
specialties; Commercial art and graphic
design; Sporting goods and bicycle shops

(G-7318)
OUTER BANKS INTERNET INC
3116 N Croatan Hwy Ste 104 (27948-6200)
P.O. Box 2560 (27948-2560)
PHONE..................................252 441-6698
Chris Hess, *Pr*
Tricia Honeycutt, *Corporate Secretary*
EMP: 4 **EST:** 1996
SALES (est): 212.41K **Privately Held**
Web: www.outerbanksinternet.com
SIC: 7374 2741 Computer graphics service;
Internet publishing and broadcasting

(G-7319)
PPG INDUSTRIES INC
Also Called: PPG 4655
2800 N Croatan Hwy (27948-9267)
PHONE..................................252 480-1970
Ryan Smithson, *Mgr*
EMP: 6
SALES (corp-wide): 17.65B **Publicly Held**
Web: www.ppg.com
SIC: 2851 Paints and allied products
PA: Ppg Industries, Inc.
1 Ppg Pl
Pittsburgh PA 15272
412 434-3131

(G-7320)
TIMES PRINTING COMPANY INC
1500 S Croatan Hwy (27948-8714)
PHONE..................................252 441-2223
EMP: 6
SALES (corp-wide): 1.5MM **Privately Held**
SIC: 2759 5943 2711 Commercial printing,
nec; Office forms and supplies; Newspapers
PA: Times Printing Company Inc
501 Budleigh St
Manteo NC 27954
252 473-2105

King
Stokes County

(G-7321)
BLUE LIGHT IMAGES COMPANY INC
(PA)
Also Called: Camel City Posters
428 Newsome Rd (27021-8508)
P.O. Box 2409 (27021-2409)
PHONE..................................336 983-4986
Danny Hoots, *Pr*
John Keats, *VP*
EMP: 17 **EST:** 1988
SALES (est): 5.45MM
SALES (corp-wide): 5.45MM **Privately
Held**
Web: www.camelcityposters.com
SIC: 3993 Signs and advertising specialties

(G-7322)
BUCK RACING ENGINES INC
205 Old Newsome Rd (27021-8532)
PHONE..................................336 983-6562
Charlie Buck, *Pr*

▲ = Import ▼ = Export
◆ = Import/Export

EMP: 6 EST: 1993
SALES (est): 504.26K **Privately Held**
Web: www.buckracingengines.com
SIC: 3537 Engine stands and racks, metal

(G-7323)
CAROLINA SIGNS & LIGHTING INC
928 Spainhour Rd (27021-9395)
P.O. Box 1037 (27045)
PHONE..................................336 399-1400
Chris Smith, *Pr*
EMP: 4 EST: 2000
SALES (est): 480.33K **Privately Held**
Web: www.carolinasignsandlighting.com
SIC: 3993 Signs and advertising specialties

(G-7324)
CARROLL SIGNS & ADVERTISING
151 Jefferson Church Rd Ste B
(27021-8605)
P.O. Box 809 (27021-0809)
PHONE..................................336 983-3415
Lewis N Carroll, *Owner*
EMP: 4 EST: 1966
SQ FT: 8,000
SALES (est): 218.3K **Privately Held**
Web: www.carrollsigns.com
SIC: 5199 2752 Advertising specialties;
Commercial printing, lithographic

(G-7325)
CRES TOBACCO COMPANY LLC
Also Called: Alliance One International
3000 Big Oaks Rd (27021)
P.O. Box 2559 (27021-2559)
PHONE..................................336 983-7727
Pete Harrison, *Pr*
Ed Dilda, *
Mark W Kehaya, *
▲ EMP: 25 EST: 1994
SQ FT: 130,000
SALES (est): 2.44MM
SALES (corp-wide): 2.03B **Privately Held**
SIC: 2131 Chewing and smoking tobacco
PA: Pyxus International, Inc.
6001 Hsptality Ct Ste 100
Morrisville NC 27560
919 379-4300

(G-7326)
DYNAMIC MACHINING X MFG LLC
157 Industrial Dr (27021-8221)
P.O. Box 429 (27021-0429)
PHONE..................................336 362-3425
Joseph H Landry, *Managing Member*
Leonard Speaks, *VP*
EMP: 23 EST: 2004
SALES (est): 4.41MM **Privately Held**
Web: www.dmxm.com
SIC: 3599 Machine shop, jobbing and repair

(G-7327)
HIM INC
P.O. Box 851 (27021-0851)
PHONE..................................336 409-7795
Richard Hammon, *CEO*
Shannon Bowles, *Ofcr*
EMP: 12 EST: 2017
SALES (est): 496.11K **Privately Held**
SIC: 3442 Metal doors

(G-7328)
IMPERIAL VAULT COMPANY
1 Sun Dr (27021)
P.O. Box 950 (27021-0950)
PHONE..................................336 983-6343
Nancy Carter-griffin, *Pr*
Todd Carter, *
Terry Carter, *
Timothy Carter, *
EMP: 11 EST: 1935

SQ FT: 26,000
SALES (est): 2.09MM **Privately Held**
Web: www.imperialvaultcompany.com
SIC: 3272 5087 Burial vaults, concrete or
precast terrazzo; Concrete burial vaults and
boxes

(G-7329)
**KING INTERNATIONAL
CORPORATION**
275 S Main St (27021-9012)
P.O. Box 1009 (27021-1009)
PHONE..................................336 983-5171
Shelby Smith, *Ch Bd*
George C Smith Senior, *Pr*
▲ EMP: 28 EST: 1964
SQ FT: 20,000
SALES (est): 3.59MM **Privately Held**
Web: www.ki-corp.com
SIC: 2752 2396 Decals, lithographed;
Automotive and apparel trimmings

(G-7330)
MAGNET AMERICA INTL INC
Also Called: Magnet America
512 Newsome Rd (27021-8510)
PHONE..................................336 985-0320
Leigh Anne Parker, *CEO*
Paul Parker, *COO*
Chris Weeks, *VP Opers*
EMP: 20 EST: 2012
SQ FT: 10,000
SALES (est): 2.21MM **Privately Held**
Web: www.magnetamerica.com
SIC: 2759 Decals: printing, nsk

(G-7331)
MERFIN SYSTEMS LLC
105 Industrial Dr (27021-8221)
PHONE..................................800 874-6373
◆ EMP: 60
SQ FT: 92,000
SALES (est): 11.69MM
SALES (corp-wide): 40.63B **Privately Held**
Web: www.merfin.com
SIC: 2676 Towels, napkins, and tissue paper
products
HQ: Buckeye Technologies Inc.
1001 Tillman St
Memphis TN 38112

(G-7332)
MILPAK GRAPHICS INC
2880 Big Oaks Dr (27021)
P.O. Box 490 (27021-0490)
PHONE..................................336 347-8772
Roby B Kilby, *Pr*
Bill G Kilby, *
Jean M Kilby, *
EMP: 36 EST: 1967
SALES (est): 2.47MM **Privately Held**
Web: www.milpak.com
SIC: 2679 Labels, paper: made from
purchased material

(G-7333)
N C COIL INC
529b S Main St (27021-9015)
PHONE..................................336 983-4440
Danny Isaacs, *Prin*
EMP: 6 EST: 2008
SALES (est): 89.08K **Privately Held**
Web: www.nccoil.com
SIC: 3495 Wire springs

(G-7334)
NVIZION INC
129 Charles Rd (27021-8247)
P.O. Box 2424 (27021-2424)
PHONE..................................336 985-3862
Frank Lawson, *Pr*

EMP: 6 EST: 2008
SALES (est): 447.56K **Privately Held**
Web: www.nvizioninc.com
SIC: 2759 Screen printing

(G-7335)
**PERFORMANCE MACHINE & FAB
INC**
1050 Denny Rd (27021-8312)
PHONE..................................336 983-0414
Joshua Pruitt, *Prin*
EMP: 6 EST: 2015
SALES (est): 2.81MM **Privately Held**
Web: www.performancemfnc.com
SIC: 3599 Machine shop, jobbing and repair

(G-7336)
SCORPION PRODUCTS INC
741 Spainhour Rd (27021-9393)
P.O. Box 834 (27045-0834)
PHONE..................................336 813-3241
Joseph Sabo, *Prin*
▲ EMP: 11 EST: 2014
SALES (est): 478.59K **Privately Held**
SIC: 3714 Motor vehicle parts and
accessories

(G-7337)
SIGNATURE CUSTOM WDWKG INC
1050 Denny Rd (27021-8312)
P.O. Box 345 (27021-0345)
PHONE..................................336 983-9905
Randy Bennett, *Pr*
EMP: 8 EST: 2004
SQ FT: 22,000
SALES (est): 984.81K **Privately Held**
Web: www.signaturecw.com
SIC: 2431 Millwork

(G-7338)
USA ATTACHMENTS INC
105 Industrial Dr (27021-8221)
PHONE..................................336 983-0763
Jeff Hamilton, *Pr*
▼ EMP: 25 EST: 2003
SQ FT: 10,000
SALES (est): 3.91MM **Privately Held**
Web: www.excavatorthumb.com
SIC: 3531 Construction machinery
attachments

(G-7339)
**WEST STKES WLDCAT GRDRON
CLB I**
321 Logan Ct (27021-9463)
PHONE..................................336 985-6152
Tonya Smith, *Prin*
EMP: 5 EST: 2016
SALES (est): 64.02K **Privately Held**
SIC: 2711 Newspapers, publishing and
printing

(G-7340)
WINSTON TOOL COMPANY INC
1025 Gause Dr (27021-8096)
PHONE..................................336 983-3722
Herman Denny, *Pr*
Dennis Gause, *VP*
Ashley Bennett, *Sec*
EMP: 4 EST: 1975
SALES (est): 473.27K **Privately Held**
Web: www.winstontool.com
SIC: 3599 Machine shop, jobbing and repair

(G-7341)
**WOODMASTERS WOODWORKING
INC**
Also Called: Woodmaster Woodworking
402 Newsome Rd (27021-8509)
PHONE..................................336 985-4000

Donnald L Dunnagan Junior, *Owner*
EMP: 4 EST: 1989
SALES (est): 63.5K **Privately Held**
SIC: 2434 Wood kitchen cabinets

Kings Mountain
Cleveland County

(G-7342)
**ABB MOTORS AND MECHANICAL
INC**
101 Reliance Rd (28086-8512)
PHONE..................................704 734-2500
Brain Brehmer, *Brnch Mgr*
EMP: 300
Web: www.baldor.com
SIC: 3621 Electric motor and generator
auxiliary parts
HQ: Abb Motors And Mechanical Inc.
5711 R S Boreham Jr St
Fort Smith AR 72901
479 646-4711

(G-7343)
ACTEGA NORTH AMERICA INC
Also Called: Actega Wit
101 Reliance Rd (28086-8512)
PHONE..................................704 736-9389
EMP: 4
SALES (corp-wide): 4.44B **Privately Held**
Web: www.actega.com
SIC: 2851 2952 Paints and allied products;
Coating compounds, tar
HQ: Actega North America, Inc.
1450 Taylors Ln
Cinnaminson NJ 08077
856 829-6300

(G-7344)
ADVANCE CONVEYING TECH LLC
171 Kings Rd (28086-2089)
P.O. Box 189 (28086-0189)
PHONE..................................704 710-4001
EMP: 20 EST: 2011
SQ FT: 26,500
SALES (est): 4.91MM **Privately Held**
Web: act.us.com
SIC: 3535 Conveyors and conveying
equipment

(G-7345)
ALBEMARLE CORPORATION
348 Holiday Inn Dr (28086-3615)
PHONE..................................704 739-2501
EMP: 105
Web: www.albemarle.com
SIC: 2819 Industrial inorganic chemicals, nec
PA: Albemarle Corporation
4250 Congress St Ste 900
Charlotte NC 28209

(G-7346)
ALBEMARLE US INC (DH)
348 Holiday Inn Dr (28086)
PHONE..................................704 739-2501
Steffen Haber, *Ch*
Thomas J Riordan, *
Robert J Zatta, *
Michael W Valente, *
Marcus Brune, *
◆ EMP: 112 EST: 1876
SQ FT: 6,500
SALES (est): 116.25MM **Publicly Held**
Web: www.albemarle.com
SIC: 2819 Lithium compounds, inorganic
HQ: Rockwood Specialties Group, Inc.
100 Overlook Cntr
Princeton NJ 08540
609 514-0300

(G-7347)

ALCO METAL FABRICATORS INC
307 S Cansler St (28086-3501)
P.O. Box 1158 (28086-1158)
PHONE................................704 739-1168
Charles D Cody, *Pr*
Jeffrey Cody, *VP*
Kevin Cody, *Sec*
EMP: 16 **EST:** 1999
SQ FT: 24,000
SALES (est): 2.43MM **Privately Held**
Web: www.alcometalfabricatorsinc.com
SIC: 3441 Fabricated structural metal

(G-7348)

B & D ENTERPRISES INC
Also Called: Tom's Coin Laundry
736 Stony Point Rd (28086-8567)
PHONE................................704 739-2958
Thomas G Brooks, *Pr*
James Brooks, *VP*
Rose E Brooks, *Sec*
EMP: 6 **EST:** 1963
SQ FT: 2,000
SALES (est): 453.87K **Privately Held**
SIC: 5411 7692 7542 7033 Convenience
stores, independent; Welding repair;
Carwash, automatic; Trailer park

(G-7349)

BAY VALLEY FOODS LLC
120 Woodlake Pkwy (28086-9225)
PHONE................................704 476-7141
EMP: 45
SALES (corp-wide): 3.35B **Publicly Held**
Web: www.bayvalleyfoods.com
SIC: 2099 Food preparations, nec
HQ: Bay Valley Foods, Llc
3200 Riverside Dr Ste A
Green Bay WI 54301
800 236-1119

(G-7350)

**BLACHFORD RBR ACQUISITION
CORP**
Also Called: Blachford Rp Corporation
707 Broadview Dr (28086-3176)
PHONE................................704 730-1005
John Blachford, *Pr*
Bill Hayes, *
▲ **EMP:** 26 **EST:** 2001
SALES (est): 5.05MM
SALES (corp-wide): 17.57MM **Privately
Held**
Web: www.blachford.com
SIC: 3069 Mats or matting, rubber, nec
HQ: Blachford Enterprises, Inc.
1400 Nuclear Dr
West Chicago IL 60185

(G-7351)

**BUCKEYE FIRE EQUIPMENT
COMPANY (PA)**
110 Kings Rd (28086-2090)
P.O. Box 428 (28086-0428)
PHONE................................704 739-7415
Kevin Bower, *Pr*
Thomas J Bower, *
William Cowley, *
◆ **EMP:** 45 **EST:** 1968
SQ FT: 265,000
SALES (est): 49.71MM
SALES (corp-wide): 49.71MM **Privately
Held**
Web: www.buckeyef.com
SIC: 3569 Firefighting apparatus

(G-7352)

C & C PRECISION MACHINE INC
418 Canterbury Rd (28086-8627)

PHONE................................704 739-0505
Joe Cunningham, *CEO*
Joseph S Cunningham, *Pr*
Jeff Cunningham, *VP*
EMP: 20 **EST:** 1990
SQ FT: 22,000
SALES (est): 6.06MM **Privately Held**
Web: www.e-ccpm.com
SIC: 3599 3545 Machine shop, jobbing and
repair; Precision tools, machinists'

(G-7353)

CA FOY MACHINE CO
265 Kings Rd (28086-2093)
P.O. Box 706 (28086-0706)
PHONE................................704 734-4833
Chip Foy, *Pr*
Charles A Foy, *
Aixa Foy, *
EMP: 30 **EST:** 1983
SQ FT: 29,000
SALES (est): 5.99MM **Privately Held**
Web: www.cafoy.com
SIC: 3599 Machine shop, jobbing and repair

(G-7354)

CARDINAL PLASTICS INC
4910 Barrett Rd (28086-8547)
PHONE................................704 739-9420
John F Hess, *VP*
Linda Hess, *Pr*
EMP: 5 **EST:** 1991
SQ FT: 6,000
SALES (est): 930.08K **Privately Held**
Web: www.cardinalplastics.com
SIC: 5162 3081 Plastics materials and basic
shapes; Unsupported plastics film and sheet

(G-7355)

CAROLINA FINSHG & COATING INC
441 Countryside Rd (28086-8914)
PHONE................................704 730-8233
Gorham J Samuel Iii, *Prin*
EMP: 10 **EST:** 2008
SALES (est): 2.3MM **Privately Held**
Web: www.cfcanodizing.com
SIC: 3471 Electroplating of metals or formed
products

(G-7356)

CAROLINA PIPING SERVICES INC
307 S Cansler St (28086-3501)
P.O. Box 186 (28086-0186)
PHONE................................704 405-0297
Harold K Green, *Pr*
Michele Green, *VP*
EMP: 9 **EST:** 2006
SALES (est): 3.22MM **Privately Held**
Web: www.carolinapiping.com
SIC: 3443 Fabricated plate work (boiler shop)

(G-7357)

CAROLINA TEX SLS GASTONIA INC
Also Called: Carolina Textile Sls Gastonia
521 N Sims St (28086-3261)
P.O. Box 637 (28086-0637)
PHONE................................704 739-1646
Pam Grimsley, *CEO*
Greg Mccomas, *VP*
EMP: 5 **EST:** 1977
SQ FT: 8,000
SALES (est): 940.61K **Privately Held**
SIC: 3599 3552 3699 Machine and other job
shop work; Textile machinery; Electrical
equipment and supplies, nec

(G-7358)

CHAPMAN MACHINE
109 Joanne Dr (28086-7735)
PHONE................................704 739-1834
Tim L Chapman, *Owner*

EMP: 4 **EST:** 1989
SALES (est): 967.73K **Privately Held**
SIC: 3599 Machine shop, jobbing and repair

(G-7359)

DIRECT WHOLESALE SIGNS LLC
711 York Rd (28086-3662)
PHONE................................704 750-2842
Teresa Gardner Caldwell, *Admn*
EMP: 6 **EST:** 2016
SALES (est): 1.51MM **Privately Held**
Web: www.directwholesalesigns.co
SIC: 3993 Signs and advertising specialties

(G-7360)

DIVERSIFIED TEXTILE MCHY CORP
Also Called: D T M
133 Kings Rd (28086-2089)
P.O. Box 809 (28086-0809)
PHONE................................704 739-2121
Ronald Goble, *Pr*
Janice Goble, *VP*
Flay Washburn, *VP*
EMP: 8 **EST:** 1986
SQ FT: 30,000
SALES (est): 1.88MM **Privately Held**
Web: www.diversifiedtextilemach.com
SIC: 3552 Creels, textile machinery

(G-7361)

EAS INCORPORATED
420 Canterbury Rd (28086-8627)
P.O. Box 2029 (28086-6029)
PHONE................................704 734-4945
Jeff Fish, *Pr*
EMP: 8 **EST:** 1987
SALES (est): 2.43MM **Privately Held**
Web: www.eassheetmetal.com
SIC: 3564 Air cleaning systems

(G-7362)

EATON CORPORATION
Eaton Transmission Div
744 S Battleground Ave (28086-3610)
P.O. Box 1728 (28086-1728)
PHONE................................704 937-7411
Jon Sczesny, *Brnch Mgr*
EMP: 121
Web: www.dix-eaton.com
SIC: 3714 Transmissions, motor vehicle
HQ: Eaton Corporation
1000 Eaton Blvd
Cleveland OH 44122
440 523-5000

(G-7363)

EDDIE HSR S PRCSION MCHNING IN
Also Called: Precision McHning Eddie Husers
613 Slater St (28086-3148)
P.O. Box 887 (28086-0887)
PHONE................................704 750-4244
Eddie Houser, *Pr*
Joyce Houser, *Clerk*
EMP: 6 **EST:** 1989
SALES (est): 472.15K **Privately Held**
SIC: 3599 Machine shop, jobbing and repair

(G-7364)

FIRESTONE FIBERS TEXTILES LLC
100 Firestone Ln (28086-7706)
P.O. Box 1369 (28086-1369)
PHONE................................704 734-2110
James Pridgen, *Pr*
◆ **EMP:** 520 **EST:** 2007
SQ FT: 400,000
SALES (est): 48.3MM **Privately Held**
Web: commercial.firestone.com
SIC: 2299 Textile mill waste and remnant
processing
HQ: Bridgestone Americas, Inc.
200 4th Ave S Ste 100

Nashville TN 37201
615 937-1000

(G-7365)

IMERYS MICA KINGS MOUNTAIN INC
1469 S Battleground Ave (28086-3906)
PHONE................................704 739-3616
Damien Caby, *VP*
◆ **EMP:** 10 **EST:** 2007
SALES (est): 2.47MM
SALES (corp-wide): 5.36MM **Privately
Held**
SIC: 3295 Minerals, ground or treated
HQ: Imerys Usa, Inc.
100 Mansell Ct E Ste 300
Roswell GA 30076
770 645-3300

(G-7366)

J E HERNDON COMPANY (HQ)
1020 Je Herndon Access Rd (28086-2000)
P.O. Box 1608 (28086-1608)
PHONE................................704 739-4711
Patrick Mullen, *Pr*
▼ **EMP:** 20 **EST:** 1928
SQ FT: 60,000
SALES (est): 3.03MM
SALES (corp-wide): 63.42MM **Privately
Held**
Web: www.steinfibers.com
SIC: 2299 Fibers, textile: recovery from
textile mill waste and rags
PA: Stein Fibers, Llc
4 Computer Dr W
Albany NY 12205
518 489-5700

(G-7367)

KEYSTONE POWDERED METAL CO
779 Sunnyside Shady Rest Rd
(28086-8404)
PHONE................................704 730-8805
Monty Rhea, *Owner*
EMP: 54
Web: www.keystonepm.com
SIC: 2899 Fluxes: brazing, soldering,
galvanizing, and welding
HQ: Keystone Powdered Metal Co
251 State St
Saint Marys PA 15857
814 781-1591

(G-7368)

KINGDOM WOODWORKS INC
405 Margrace Rd (28086-3873)
PHONE................................704 678-8134
Bryan Morrow, *Prin*
EMP: 4 **EST:** 2009
SALES (est): 87.06K **Privately Held**
SIC: 2431 Millwork

(G-7369)

KINGS MOUNTAIN INTL INC
1755 S Battleground Ave (28086-9237)
PHONE................................704 739-4227
Steve Wagenknight, *Pr*
John Spencer, *
◆ **EMP:** 65 **EST:** 2004
SQ FT: 140,000
SALES (est): 8.87MM **Privately Held**
Web: www.kmiinc.net
SIC: 3471 Electroplating of metals or formed
products

(G-7370)

KINGS PLUSH INC
Also Called: STI
515 Marie St (28086-3147)
P.O. Box 398 (28086-0398)
PHONE................................704 739-9931
John Kay, *Pr*

Sean D Gibbons, *
Mark Hovis, *
◆ **EMP:** 200 **EST:** 1964
SQ FT: 150,000
SALES (est): 24.08MM **Privately Held**
Web: www.stifabrics.com
SIC: 2221 Nylon broadwoven fabrics
PA: Specialty Textiles Inc
515 Marie St
Kings Mountain NC 28086

(G-7371)
LNS TURBO INC (DH)
203 Turbo Dr (28086-7641)
PHONE..............................704 739-7111
▲ **EMP:** 100 **EST:** 1977
SALES (est): 27.72MM
SALES (corp-wide): 15.41MM **Privately Held**
Web: www.lns-northamerica.com
SIC: 3535 Conveyors and conveying equipment
HQ: Lns Holding Sa
C/O Coworking Neuchatel Sarl
NeuchAtel NE 2000

(G-7372)
MARIETTA MARTIN MATERIALS INC
Also Called: Martin Marietta Aggregates
181 Quarry Rd (28086-3896)
P.O. Box 747 (28086-0747)
PHONE..............................704 739-4761
Donald Champion, *Brnch Mgr*
EMP: 6
Web: www.martinmarietta.com
SIC: 1422 Crushed and broken limestone
PA: Martin Marietta Materials Inc
4123 Parklake Ave
Raleigh NC 27612

(G-7373)
MR TIRE INC
407 S Battleground Ave (28086-3603)
PHONE..............................704 739-6456
Stephen Honbaier, *Brnch Mgr*
EMP: 6
SALES (corp-wide): 1.28B **Publicly Held**
Web: locations.mrtire.com
SIC: 5722 5014 7538 7534 Household appliance stores; Tires and tubes; General automotive repair shops; Tire recapping
HQ: Mr. Tire Inc.
2078 New York Ave Unit 2
Huntington Station NY 11746
631 499-3700

(G-7374)
NVR INC
Also Called: NVR Building Products
132 Riverside Ct (28086-8901)
PHONE..............................704 484-7170
Jim Kepple, *Mgr*
EMP: 100
Web: www.nvrinc.com
SIC: 1521 2439 New construction, single-family houses; Structural wood members, nec
PA: Nvr, Inc.
11700 Plz Amer Dr Ste 500
Reston VA 20190

(G-7375)
PARKDALE MILLS INCORPORATED
Also Called: Parkdale Plant 5
500 S Railroad Ave (28086-3351)
PHONE..............................704 739-7411
Jeff Johnson, *Brnch Mgr*
EMP: 24
SALES (corp-wide): 1.44B **Privately Held**
Web: www.parkdalemills.com

SIC: 2281 Yarn spinning mills
HQ: Parkdale Mills, Incorporated
531 Cotton Blossom Cir
Gastonia NC 28054
704 874-5000

(G-7376)
PARKER-HANNIFIN CORPORATION
Also Called: Parker Hydraulics
101 Canterbury Rd (28086-9433)
P.O. Box 219 (28086-0219)
PHONE..............................704 739-9781
Bob Mcbride, *Brnch Mgr*
EMP: 350
SALES (corp-wide): 19.93B **Publicly Held**
Web: www.parker.com
SIC: 3594 Fluid power pumps and motors
PA: Parker-Hannifin Corporation
6035 Parkland Blvd
Cleveland OH 44124
216 896-3000

(G-7377)
PATRICK YARN MILL INC
Also Called: Patrick Yarns
501 York Rd (28086-3158)
P.O. Box 1847 (28086-1847)
PHONE..............................704 739-4119
Gilbert H Patrick, *Pr*
Janice Patrick, *VP*
Thomas Koval, *Treas*
▲ **EMP:** 190 **EST:** 1963
SQ FT: 200,000
SALES (est): 48.77MM
SALES (corp-wide): 1.39B **Privately Held**
Web: www.patrickyarns.com
SIC: 2281 Yarn spinning mills
PA: Coats Group Plc
4th Floor
London EC2V
208 210-5010

(G-7378)
PLASTIC PRODUCTS INC
1051 York Rd (28086-9713)
PHONE..............................704 739-7463
Jay E Raxter, *Brnch Mgr*
EMP: 16
SALES (corp-wide): 10.26MM **Privately Held**
Web: www.plastic-products.com
SIC: 3089 Injection molding of plastics
PA: Plastic Products, Inc.
1413 Bessemer City
Bessemer City NC 28016
704 739-7463

(G-7379)
PRETTY PAID LLC
608 York Rd (28086)
PHONE..............................980 443-3876
EMP: 5 **EST:** 2017
SALES (est): 167.76K **Privately Held**
Web: prettypaidboutique.com
SIC: 5621 3949 5651 2752 Boutiques; Sporting and athletic goods, nec; Family clothing stores; Commercial printing, lithographic

(G-7380)
QUALTECH INDUSTRIES INC
311 Industrial Dr (28086-3888)
PHONE..............................704 734-0345
Jeffrey P Latchaw, *Prin*
EMP: 8 **EST:** 2009
SALES (est): 616.04K **Privately Held**
Web: www.qualtechindustries.com
SIC: 3999 Manufacturing industries, nec

(G-7381)
R AND L COLLISION CENTER INC
Also Called: R & L
1207 S Battleground Ave (28086-3901)
PHONE..............................704 739-2500
Richard Smith, *Prin*
Lara Smtih, *Prin*
EMP: 10 **EST:** 1995
SALES (est): 334.28K **Privately Held**
SIC: 7532 3993 Truck painting and lettering; Signs and advertising specialties

(G-7382)
RIDDLEY RETAIL FIXTURES INC
119 Bess Rd (28086-8106)
PHONE..............................704 435-8829
Terry Riddley, *Prin*
Terry A Riddley, *
Alan Riddley, *
Lorie Riddley, *
EMP: 50 **EST:** 1990
SQ FT: 5,000
SALES (est): 10.29MM **Privately Held**
Web: www.riddleyinc.com
SIC: 1751 5046 2541 Cabinet and finish carpentry; Store fixtures and display equipment; Cabinets, lockers, and shelving

(G-7383)
ROCKWOOD LITHIUM
348 Holiday Inn Dr (28086-3615)
PHONE..............................704 739-2501
EMP: 48 **EST:** 2019
SALES (est): 3.49MM **Privately Held**
Web: www.albemarle.com
SIC: 2819 Industrial inorganic chemicals, nec

(G-7384)
SCIVOLUTIONS INC
811 Floyd St (28086-3130)
P.O. Box 234 (28637-0234)
PHONE..............................704 853-0100
Fritz Schulte, *CEO*
▲ **EMP:** 6 **EST:** 1986
SQ FT: 28,000
SALES (est): 838.11K **Privately Held**
SIC: 3842 Bandages and dressings

(G-7385)
SOUTHEASTERN CONTAINER INC
293 Industrial Dr (28086-3949)
PHONE..............................704 710-4200
Sam Schember, *Mgr*
EMP: 42
SALES (corp-wide): 319.93MM **Privately Held**
Web: www.secontainer.com
SIC: 3085 Plastics bottles
PA: Southeastern Container, Inc.
1250 Sand Hill Rd
Enka NC 28728
828 350-7200

(G-7386)
SPECIALTY TEXTILES INC
Also Called: STI
822 Floyd St (28086-3131)
PHONE..............................704 710-8657
EMP: 7
Web: www.stifabrics.com
SIC: 2299 Fibers, textile: recovery from textile mill waste and rags
PA: Specialty Textiles Inc
515 Marie St
Kings Mountain NC 28086

(G-7387)
SPECIALTY TEXTILES INC (PA)
Also Called: King Splash
515 Marie St (28086-3147)

P.O. Box 398 (27263)
PHONE..............................704 739-4503
John Kay, *Pr*
EMP: 150 **EST:** 2007
SQ FT: 250,000
SALES (est): 25.07MM **Privately Held**
Web: yuri-greene.squarespace.com
SIC: 2299 Fibers, textile: recovery from textile mill waste and rags

(G-7388)
STOUT BEVERAGES LLC (PA)
518 N Sims St (28086-3262)
PHONE..............................704 293-7640
Cody Sommer, *Managing Member*
▲ **EMP:** 20 **EST:** 2011
SALES (est): 651.77K
SALES (corp-wide): 651.77K **Privately Held**
SIC: 2082 Beer (alcoholic beverage)

(G-7389)
STOUT BRANDS LLC
518 N Sims St (28086-3262)
PHONE..............................704 293-7640
Cody Sommer, *Managing Member*
David Scott, *Bd of Dir*
▲ **EMP:** 29 **EST:** 2012
SQ FT: 21,000
SALES (est): 606.45K
SALES (corp-wide): 651.77K **Privately Held**
SIC: 2082 Stout (alcoholic beverage)
PA: Stout Beverages, Llc
518 N Sims St
Kings Mountain NC 28086
704 293-7640

(G-7390)
WEDE CORPORATION
133 Industrial Dr (28086-3889)
PHONE..............................704 864-1313
Hans Wede, *Pr*
EMP: 5 **EST:** 1969
SQ FT: 20,000
SALES (est): 305.59K **Privately Held**
SIC: 3441 3444 Fabricated structural metal; Sheet metalwork

Kinston
Lenoir County

(G-7391)
ADAMSON GLOBAL TECHNOLOGY CORP (PA)
2018 W Vernon Ave (28504-0001)
P.O. Box 6246 (28501-0246)
PHONE..............................252 523-5200
J Ward Mcconnell Junior, *Pr*
Marc Mcconnel, *VP*
EMP: 5 **EST:** 1995
SQ FT: 10,000
SALES (est): 940.86K **Privately Held**
Web: www.adamsontank.com
SIC: 3443 Tanks, standard or custom fabricated: metal plate

(G-7392)
ADVANTAGE PRINTING & DESIGN
2425 N Herritage St (28501-1613)
PHONE..............................252 523-8133
Gordon Vermillione, *Pr*
EMP: 7 **EST:** 1988
SQ FT: 7,000
SALES (est): 88.76K **Privately Held**
SIC: 2752 Offset printing

GEOGRAPHIC

(G-7393)
ALSIDE WINDOW CO
3800 Window Way (28504-8038)
PHONE.............................407 293-9010
EMP: 9 EST: 2019
SALES (est): 2.72MM Privately Held
Web: www.alside.com
SIC: 3442 Metal doors, sash, and trim

(G-7394)
ARGOS USA LLC
3350 Nc Highway 11 N (28501-7344)
PHONE.............................252 527-8008
Ricky Gray, Brnch Mgr
EMP: 30
Web: www.argos-us.com
SIC: 3273 Ready-mixed concrete
HQ: Argos Usa Llc
3015 Windward Plz Ste 300
Alpharetta GA 30005
678 368-4300

(G-7395)
**BARNHILL CONTRACTING
COMPANY**
604 E New Bern Rd (28504-6742)
PHONE.............................252 527-8021
William F Davis, Mgr
EMP: 20
SALES (corp-wide): 490.43MM Privately
Held
Web: www.barnhillcontracting.com
SIC: 1611 1771 3531 5032 Highway and
street paving contractor; Parking lot
construction; Asphalt plant, including gravel-
mix type; Sand, construction
PA: Barnhill Contracting Company Inc
800 Tiffany Blvd Ste 200
Rocky Mount NC 27804
252 823-1021

(G-7396)
BLUE MOUNTAIN ENTERPRISES INC
Also Called: Blue Mountain Flavors
4000 Commerce Dr (28504-7906)
PHONE.............................252 522-1544
▼ EMP: 37 EST: 1988
SALES (est): 7.21MM Privately Held
Web: www.bluemountainflavors.com
SIC: 2087 Extracts, flavoring

(G-7397)
**BRIDGESTONE RET OPERATIONS
LLC**
Also Called: Firestone
1901 W Vernon Ave (28504-3327)
PHONE.............................252 522-5126
Ricky Morris, Mgr
EMP: 7
Web: www.bridgestoneamericas.com
SIC: 5531 7534 Automotive tires; Rebuilding
and retreading tires
HQ: Bridgestone Retail Operations, Llc
200 4th Ave S Ste 100
Nashville TN 37201
615 937-1000

(G-7398)
**CAROLINA GREENHOUSE PLANTS
INC**
1504 Cunningham Rd (28501-1838)
P.O. Box 1140 (28503-1140)
PHONE.............................252 523-9300
Dwight Howard, Pr
EMP: 9 EST: 1982
SQ FT: 6,000
SALES (est): 1.47MM Privately Held
Web: www.carolinagreenhouses.com

SIC: 3448 5191 Greenhouses, prefabricated
metal; Greenhouse equipment and supplies

(G-7399)
CAROLINA ICE INC
2466 Old Poole Rd (28504-9234)
PHONE.............................252 527-3178
TOLL FREE: 800
Thomas L Edwards, Pr
Merle Edwards, *
EMP: 30 EST: 1983
SALES (est): 4.14MM Privately Held
Web: www.carolinaice.com
SIC: 2097 Manufactured ice

(G-7400)
CAROLINA WELDING & CNSTR
1806 N Herritage St (28501-2216)
PHONE.............................252 814-8740
Meldon Dail, CEO
EMP: 5 EST: 2012
SALES (est): 194.15K Privately Held
Web: www.carolinawelding.us
SIC: 7692 Welding repair

(G-7401)
CAULEY CONSTRUCTION COMPANY
2385 Westdowns Ter (28504-7545)
PHONE.............................252 522-1078
William B Cauley, Pr
C B Cauley, VP
Kattie L Cauley, Sec
EMP: 7 EST: 1962
SALES (est): 65.47K Privately Held
SIC: 2411 0191 0212 Logging camps and
contractors; General farms, primarily crop;
Beef cattle, except feedlots

(G-7402)
COCA-COLA CONSOLIDATED INC
Also Called: Coca-Cola
4194 W Vernon Ave (28504-9673)
P.O. Box 337 (28502-0337)
PHONE.............................704 551-4500
Stene Walton, Mgr
EMP: 48
SALES (corp-wide): 6.9B Publicly Held
Web: www.cokeconsolidated.com
SIC: 2086 Bottled and canned soft drinks
PA: Coca-Cola Consolidated, Inc.
4100 Coca-Cola Plz
Charlotte NC 28211
980 392-8298

(G-7403)
CROWN EQUIPMENT CORPORATION
Also Called: Crown Lift Trucks
2000 Dobbs Farm Rd (28504-8907)
PHONE.............................252 522-3088
EMP: 325
SALES (corp-wide): 7.12B Privately Held
Web: us-careers.crown.com
SIC: 3537 Forklift trucks
PA: Crown Equipment Corporation
44 S Washington St
New Bremen OH 45869
419 629-2311

(G-7404)
DAILS PALLET & PRODUCE INC
2884 Neuse Rd (28501-9119)
PHONE.............................252 717-1338
Gail Dail, Prin
EMP: 5 EST: 2009
SALES (est): 393.99K Privately Held
SIC: 2448 Pallets, wood

(G-7405)
DISCOVERY INSURANCE COMPANY
604 N Queen St (28501-4340)

P.O. Box 200 (28502-0200)
PHONE.............................800 876-1492
Stephen B Hill, CEO
Michael J Minor, Pr
Glenn Scott Gannett, Treas
Robert O Hill Senior, VP
Robert O Hill Junior, VP
EMP: 47 EST: 1993
SQ FT: 20,000
SALES (est): 10.2MM Privately Held
Web: www.discoveryinsurance.com
SIC: 6331 7372 Property damage insurance;
Application computer software

(G-7406)
**DOMESTIC FABRICS BLANKETS
CORP**
2002 W Vernon Ave (28504-3330)
PHONE.............................252 523-7948
Donna Wilfong, Ch
David E Wilfong, *
Jonathan Wilfong, *
EMP: 46 EST: 2009
SQ FT: 70,000
SALES (est): 4.39MM Privately Held
Web: www.domesticfabrics.com
SIC: 5131 2396 Piece goods and notions;
Apparel and other linings, except millinery

(G-7407)
EFFIKAL LLC
2630 Airport Rd (28504-7319)
PHONE.............................252 522-3031
Patrick Holleran, Pr
▲ EMP: 10 EST: 1977
SQ FT: 30,000
SALES (est): 886.1K Privately Held
Web: www.fieldcontrols.com
SIC: 3822 3444 Damper operators:
pneumatic, thermostatic, electric; Sheet
metalwork
HQ: Field Controls, L.L.C.
2630 Airport Rd
Kinston NC 28504
252 208-7300

(G-7408)
EIDP INC
Also Called: Dupont
2204 Pink Hill Rd (28504)
PHONE.............................252 522-6896
Tommy Burns, Brnch Mgr
EMP: 6
SALES (corp-wide): 16.91B Publicly Held
Web: www.dupont.com
SIC: 2819 Industrial inorganic chemicals, nec
HQ: Eidp, Inc.
9330 Zionsville Rd
Indianapolis IN 46268
833 267-8382

(G-7409)
EIDP INC
Also Called: Dupont
4693 Hwy 11 N (28502)
PHONE.............................252 522-6286
Harold Thomas, Manager
EMP: 6
SALES (corp-wide): 16.91B Publicly Held
Web: www.dupont.com
SIC: 2821 Plastics materials and resins
HQ: Eidp, Inc.
9330 Zionsville Rd
Indianapolis IN 46268
833 267-8382

(G-7410)
**ELECTROLUX HOME PRODUCTS
INC**
ELECTROLUX HOME PRODUCTS, INC.
4850 W Vernon Ave (28504-7544)

PHONE.............................252 527-5100
Bill Hilling, Mgr
EMP: 400
SALES (corp-wide): 3.83B Privately Held
Web: www.electroluxprofessional.com
SIC: 5722 3631 Household appliance stores;
Household cooking equipment
HQ: Electrolux Home Products, Llc
10200 David Taylor Dr
Charlotte NC 28262

(G-7411)
FARVAL LUBRICATION SYSTEMS
2685 Airport Rd (28504-7335)
PHONE.............................252 527-6001
John Short, Manager
EMP: 44
SALES (corp-wide): 459.42MM Privately
Held
Web: www.farval.com
SIC: 3569 Lubricating equipment
HQ: Farval Lubrication Systems, Inc
808 Aviation Pkwy
Kinston NC 28504

(G-7412)
**FARVAL LUBRICATION SYSTEMS
(DH)**
808 Aviation Parkway (28504)
PHONE.............................252 527-6001
Thomas W Arndt, Pr
Roger M Yamamoto, VP Fin
John V Curci, Sec
▲ EMP: 50 EST: 1993
SQ FT: 46,000
SALES (est): 3.33MM
SALES (corp-wide): 459.42MM Privately
Held
Web: www.farval.com
SIC: 3569 Lubricating equipment
HQ: Industrial Manufacturing Company Llc
8223 Brcksvlle Rd Ste 100
Brecksville OH 44141
440 838-4700

(G-7413)
FIELD CONTROLS LLC (DH)
2630 Airport Rd (28504)
PHONE.............................252 208-7300
Patrick T Holleran, Pr
Michael Afarian, *
Tony Schrank, *
Bobby Nelson, *
▲ EMP: 84 EST: 1927
SQ FT: 100,000
SALES (est): 16.27MM Privately Held
Web: www.fieldcontrols.com
SIC: 3829 3564 3444 Measuring and
controlling devices, nec; Blowers and fans;
Sheet metalwork
HQ: Pettibone L.L.C.
27501 Bella Vista Pkwy
Warrenville IL 60555
630 353-5000

(G-7414)
HARVEY FERTILIZER AND GAS CO
1291 Hwy 258 N (28504-7209)
PHONE.............................252 523-9090
Frakie Hill, CFO
EMP: 12
SALES (corp-wide): 80.5MM Privately
Held
Web: www.harveyfertilizerandgas.com
SIC: 5191 2873 2875 Fertilizer and fertilizer
materials; Nitrogenous fertilizers;
Fertilizers, mixing only
PA: Harvey Fertilizer And Gas Co.
303 Bohannon Rd
Kinston NC 28501
252 526-4150

▲ = Import ▼ = Export
◆ = Import/Export

(G-7415)
HARVEY FERTILIZER AND GAS CO (PA)
Also Called: Harvey Gin & Cotton
303 Bohannon Rd (28501-7434)
P.O. Box 189 (28502)
PHONE............................252 526-4150
Herbert Rouse, Pr
Llyod E Cooper, *
Frankie Hill, *
▲ EMP: 42 EST: 1871
SQ FT: 25,000
SALES (est): 80.5MM
SALES (corp-wide): 80.5MM Privately Held
Web: www.harveyfertilizerandgas.com
SIC: 2875 2873 5191 Fertilizers, mixing only; Nitrogenous fertilizers; Chemicals, agricultural

(G-7416)
JARED SASNETT LOGGING CO INC
1976 Neuse Rd (28501-9188)
PHONE............................252 939-6289
Jared Sasnett, Owner
EMP: 6 EST: 2008
SALES (est): 458.23K Privately Held
SIC: 2411 Logging camps and contractors

(G-7417)
KINSTON FREE PRESS COMPANY
Also Called: Free Press, The
2103 N Queen St (28501-1622)
P.O. Box 129 (28502-0129)
PHONE............................252 527-3191
Patrick Holmes, Associate Publisher
Lee Raynor, Managing Editor*
EMP: 35 EST: 1882
SQ FT: 16,000
SALES (est): 930.04K
SALES (corp-wide): 2.51B Publicly Held
Web: www.kinston.com
SIC: 2711 Newspapers, publishing and printing
HQ: Gatehouse Media, Llc
175 Sllys Trf Fl 3 Corp C
Pittsford NY 14534
585 598-0030

(G-7418)
KINSTON NEUSE CORPORATION
2000 Dobbs Farm Rd (28504-8907)
PHONE............................252 522-3088
◆ EMP: 250
Web: www.visitkinston.com
SIC: 3537 Pallet loaders and unloaders

(G-7419)
KINSTON OFFICE SUPPLY CO INC (PA)
Also Called: Corporate Resources
704 Plaza Blvd Ste B (28501-1554)
P.O. Box 696 (28502-0696)
PHONE............................252 523-7654
Scott H Bowen, Pr
Craig Bowen, *
Barbara Bowen, *
EMP: 26 EST: 1951
SQ FT: 30,000
SALES (est): 1.83MM
SALES (corp-wide): 1.83MM Privately Held
Web: ci.kinston.nc.us
SIC: 5712 5942 2752 Office furniture; Books, religious; Offset printing

(G-7420)
LYNN JONES RACE CARS
1168 Woodington Rd (28504-7057)
PHONE............................252 522-0705

Lynn Jones, Owner
EMP: 4 EST: 1999
SALES (est): 78.68K Privately Held
SIC: 3711 Cars, electric, assembly of

(G-7421)
MAGIC MILE MEDIA INC
Also Called: Davidson Daily
105 W Blount St (28501-4807)
PHONE............................252 572-1330
Bj Murphy, CEO
Aleatha Thrower, VP
EMP: 12 EST: 2016
SALES (est): 523.59K Privately Held
Web: www.magicmilemedia.com
SIC: 2711 7379 Newspapers: publishing only, not printed on site; Online services technology consultants

(G-7422)
MASTERBRAND CABINETS LLC
651 Collier Loftin Rd (28504-6847)
P.O. Box 3567 (28502-3567)
PHONE............................252 523-4131
Steve Woolard, Mgr
EMP: 61
SALES (corp-wide): 2.7B Publicly Held
Web: www.masterbrand.com
SIC: 2434 Wood kitchen cabinets
HQ: Masterbrand Cabinets Llc
3300 Entp Pkwy Ste 300
Beachwood OH 44122
812 482-2527

(G-7423)
MOTHER EARTH BREWING LLC
311 N Herritage St (28501-4823)
PHONE............................252 208-2437
Trent E Mooring, Managing Member
▲ EMP: 6 EST: 2008
SALES (est): 2.42MM Privately Held
Web: www.motherearthbrewing.com
SIC: 2082 Beer (alcoholic beverage)

(G-7424)
NORTH CRLINA DEPT CRIME CTRL P
Also Called: Highway Patrol
2214 W Vernon Ave (28504-3334)
PHONE............................252 522-1511
Charles L Johnston, Chief
EMP: 6
SALES (corp-wide): 74.26B Privately Held
Web: www.ncdps.gov
SIC: 3711 9229 Patrol wagons (motor vehicles), assembly of; Public order and safety, State government
HQ: North Carolina Department Of Crime Control And Public Safety
512 N Salisbury St
Raleigh NC 27604

(G-7425)
PACTIV LLC
1447 Enterprise Blvd (28504-7598)
PHONE............................252 527-6300
Mike Tutowski, Mgr
EMP: 107
Web: www.pactivevergreen.com
SIC: 2657 2671 2631 Food containers, folding: made from purchased material; Paper; coated and laminated packaging; Paperboard mills
HQ: Pactiv Llc
1900 W Field Ct
Lake Forest IL 60045
847 482-2000

(G-7426)
S & W READY MIX CON CO LLC
604 E New Bern Rd (28504-6742)
PHONE............................252 527-1881

Johnny Jarman, Brnch Mgr
EMP: 16
SALES (corp-wide): 8.01MM Privately Held
Web: www.snwreadymix.com
SIC: 3273 Ready-mixed concrete
HQ: S & W Ready Mix Concrete Company Llc
217 Lisbon St
Clinton NC 28329
910 592-1733

(G-7427)
SANDERSON FARMS INC
Also Called: Production Division
1536 Smithfield Way (28504-9272)
PHONE............................252 208-0036
Wes Hall, Mgr
EMP: 14
SALES (corp-wide): 4.8B Privately Held
Web: www.sandersonfarms.com
SIC: 2015 Poultry slaughtering and processing
HQ: Sanderson Farms, Llc
127 Flynt Rd
Laurel MS 39443
601 649-4030

(G-7428)
SMITHFIELD FOODS INC
1780 Smithfield Way (28504-9244)
PHONE............................252 208-4700
Gerry Koster, Manager
EMP: 98
Web: www.smithfieldfoods.com
SIC: 2013 2011 Sausages and other prepared meats; Boxed beef, from meat slaughtered on site
HQ: Smithfield Foods, Inc.
200 Commerce St
Smithfield VA 23430
757 365-3000

(G-7429)
SOUTHERN VINYL MFG INC
2010 Smithfield Way (28504-6200)
PHONE............................252 523-2520
Wes Seegars, CEO
Dean Ervin, Pr
EMP: 12 EST: 1997
SALES (est): 1.9MM Privately Held
Web: www.svmnc.com
SIC: 3089 Fences, gates, and accessories: plastics

(G-7430)
SPIRIT AEROSYSTEMS NC INC
2600 Aerosystems Blvd (28504-7356)
PHONE............................252 208-4645
Jeff Turner, CEO
◆ EMP: 10 EST: 2006
SALES (est): 5.88MM Publicly Held
Web: www.spiritaero.com
SIC: 3728 Aircraft parts and equipment, nec
PA: Spirit Aerosystems Holdings, Inc.
3801 S Oliver St
Wichita KS 67210

(G-7431)
THREE STACKS DISTILLING CO LLC
Also Called: Three Stacks Distilling Co.
906 Atlantic Ave (28501-4109)
PHONE............................252 468-0779
EMP: 8 EST: 2017
SALES (est): 578.9K Privately Held
SIC: 2085 Distilled and blended liquors

(G-7432)
UNIFI KINSTON LLC
4693 Hwy 11 (28504)
PHONE............................252 522-6518

Bill Lowe, CEO
▲ EMP: 5 EST: 2004
SALES (est): 962.86K
SALES (corp-wide): 582.21MM Publicly Held
SIC: 2821 Polyesters
PA: Unifi, Inc.
7201 W Friendly Ave
Greensboro NC 27410
336 294-4410

(G-7433)
URBAN TACTICAL AND CSTM ARMORY
643 Tyree Rd (28504-6343)
PHONE............................252 686-0122
EMP: 5 EST: 2015
SALES (est): 170.86K Privately Held
SIC: 3484 Small arms

(G-7434)
VILLABONA IRON WORKS INC
1415 W New Bern Rd (28504-4717)
P.O. Box 6549 (28501-0549)
PHONE............................252 522-4005
John Villabona, Owner
EMP: 10 EST: 1994
SQ FT: 60,000
SALES (est): 537.31K Privately Held
SIC: 7692 Welding repair

(G-7435)
WALL-LENK CORPORATION
Also Called: Craftmark
1950 Dr Martin Luther King Jr Blvd (28501-2462)
P.O. Box 3349 (28502-3349)
PHONE............................252 527-4186
▲ EMP: 26 EST: 1864
SALES (est): 5.3MM Privately Held
Web: www.wlenk.com
SIC: 3423 3821 5112 3546 Soldering tools; Laboratory heating apparatus; Marking devices; Power-driven handtools

(G-7436)
WEST PHARMACEUTICAL SVCS INC
1028 Innovation Way (28504-7616)
PHONE............................252 522-8956
Thomas Clagoen, Mgr
EMP: 4
SALES (corp-wide): 2.89B Publicly Held
Web: www.westpharma.com
SIC: 2834 Pharmaceutical preparations
PA: West Pharmaceutical Services, Inc.
530 Herman O West Dr
Exton PA 19341
610 594-2900

(G-7437)
WILLIAM BARNET & SON LLC
Kinston Division
1411 Hwy 258 S (28504-5379)
P.O. Box 3449 (28502-3449)
PHONE............................252 522-2418
Thomas Parker, Brnch Mgr
EMP: 200
SALES (corp-wide): 67.95MM Privately Held
Web: www.barnet.com
SIC: 2299 Textile mill waste and remnant processing
PA: William Barnet & Son, Llc
1300 Hayne St
Spartanburg SC 29301
864 576-7154

Kittrell
Vance County

(G-7438)
BOBBITT SIGNS INC
2232 Rocky Ford Rd (27544-9576)
PHONE..........................252 492-7326
Bryant Bobbitt, *Pr*
Lisa Cottrell, *Sec*
EMP: 4 **EST:** 1974
SALES (est): 126.31K **Privately Held**
Web: www.bobbittsigns.com
SIC: 3993 Signs, not made in custom sign
painting shops

(G-7439)
BUFFALOE MILLING COMPANY INC
196 Buffalo Mill Rd (27544-9048)
P.O. Box 145 (27544-0145)
PHONE..........................252 438-8637
John D Spencer, *Pr*
James K Spencer Junior, *VP*
Marilove Spencer, *Treas*
Christina Spencer, *Sec*
EMP: 10 **EST:** 1855
SQ FT: 13,000
SALES (est): 2.46MM **Privately Held**
Web: www.buffaloemilling.com
SIC: 2041 Corn flour

(G-7440)
CAROLINA SUNROCK LLC
214 Sunrock Rd (27544-8012)
PHONE..........................252 433-4617
EMP: 33
SALES (corp-wide): 51.02MM **Privately
Held**
Web: www.thesunrockgroup.com
SIC: 3273 Ready-mixed concrete
HQ: Carolina Sunrock Llc
　　1001 W B St
　　Butner NC 27509
　　919 575-4502

(G-7441)
GES INDUSTRIES (PA)
78 Walter Grissom Rd (27544-9129)
PHONE..........................252 430-8851
▲ **EMP:** 35
SALES (est): 3MM **Privately Held**
SIC: 2499 Laundry products, wood

(G-7442)
NC GRAPHIC PROS LLC
2232 Rocky Ford Rd (27544-9576)
PHONE..........................252 492-7326
Jennifer Stanley, *Prin*
EMP: 4 **EST:** 2016
SALES (est): 207.54K **Privately Held**
Web: www.ncgraphicpros.com
SIC: 3993 7336 5131 5999 Letters for signs,
metal; Commercial art and graphic design;
Flags and banners; Trophies and plaques

Kitty Hawk
Dare County

(G-7443)
ALPHA-ADVANTAGE INC
891 Emeline Ln (27949-4271)
PHONE..........................252 441-3766
Robert Walde Junior, *Pr*
EMP: 5 **EST:** 1999
SALES (est): 879.58K **Privately Held**
Web: www.alpha-advantage.com
SIC: 3589 Water treatment equipment,
industrial

(G-7444)
DUSTY RHOADS HVAC INC
Also Called: Honeywell Authorized Dealer
3822 Elijah Baum Dr (27949-4253)
P.O. Box 444 (27949-0444)
PHONE..........................252 261-5892
Dusty Rhoads, *Pr*
Bonnie Rhoads, *Sec*
EMP: 7 **EST:** 1987
SALES (est): 371.52K **Privately Held**
Web: www.honeywell.com
SIC: 1711 3444 Warm air heating and air
conditioning contractor; Sheet metalwork

(G-7445)
IDENTIFY YOURSELF LLC
6146 N Croatan Hwy Unit C (27949-3866)
P.O. Box 432 (27949-0432)
PHONE..........................252 202-1452
Alex Lefevre, *Prin*
Emily Ausband, *Prin*
EMP: 12 **EST:** 2004
SALES (est): 4.12MM **Privately Held**
Web: www.idyourself.com
SIC: 5199 2759 Advertising specialties;
Promotional printing

(G-7446)
OBBC INC
Also Called: Outer Banks Press
75 E Dogwood Trl (27949-3322)
PHONE..........................252 261-0612
Linda L Lauby, *Pr*
▲ **EMP:** 6 **EST:** 1997
SALES (est): 61.11K **Privately Held**
Web: www.outerbankspress.com
SIC: 2721 5812 Magazines: publishing and
printing; Eating places

(G-7447)
TNT SERVICES INC
3908 Poor Ridge Rd (27949-4332)
P.O. Box 296 (27966-0296)
PHONE..........................252 261-3073
Roy Lee Etheridge, *Pr*
Karen Etheridge, *VP*
EMP: 6 **EST:** 1981
SQ FT: 5,000
SALES (est): 418K **Privately Held**
SIC: 1771 1711 3272 1629 Driveway
contractor; Septic system construction;
Septic tanks, concrete; Land clearing
contractor

Knightdale
Wake County

(G-7448)
AMETEK ELECTRONICS SYSTEMS
8001 Knightdale Blvd Ste 121
(27545-9023)
PHONE..........................800 645-9721
EMP: 12 **EST:** 2017
SALES (est): 7.08MM **Privately Held**
Web: www.ametekesp.com
SIC: 3629 Electronic generation equipment

(G-7449)
BULLDOG INDUSTRIES INC
205 Forest Dr (27545-9604)
PHONE..........................919 217-6170
Walker Knox, *Pr*
EMP: 20 **EST:** 2015
SALES (est): 2.43MM **Privately Held**
Web: www.mid-atlanticfab.com
SIC: 3444 Sheet metalwork

(G-7450)
CARTER PRINTING
1105 Great Falls Ct Ste A (27545-5800)
P.O. Box 385 (27545-0385)
PHONE..........................919 373-0531
Herb Steward, *Owner*
EMP: 4 **EST:** 2015
SALES (est): 77.41K **Privately Held**
SIC: 2752 Offset printing

(G-7451)
CARTER PRINTING & GRAPHICS INC
1001 Steeple Square Ct (27545-8072)
P.O. Box 385 (27545-0385)
PHONE..........................919 266-5280
Gene Carter, *Pr*
Joyce Carter, *
EMP: 10 **EST:** 1985
SQ FT: 33,000
SALES (est): 233.35K **Privately Held**
Web: www.carterprintingnc.com
SIC: 2752 Offset printing

(G-7452)
LEN CORPORATION
Also Called: Royce Company
525 Hinton Oaks Blvd (27545-5834)
PHONE..........................919 876-2964
Len Johnson, *Pr*
Scott Shulz, *VP*
EMP: 18 **EST:** 1982
SALES (est): 2.74MM
SALES (corp-wide): 170.37MM **Privately
Held**
Web: www.roycecompany.com
SIC: 3444 Sheet metal specialties, not
stamped
PA: Handy Distribution Llc
　　65 10th St
　　Lynchburg VA 24504
　　434 847-4495

(G-7453)
MYRICKS CABINET SHOP INC
2329 Hodge Rd (27545-8601)
PHONE..........................919 266-3720
Steve Myrick, *Prin*
EMP: 5 **EST:** 2007
SALES (est): 692.04K **Privately Held**
Web: www.myrickscabinetshop.com
SIC: 2434 Wood kitchen cabinets

(G-7454)
OLD RM CO LLC
512 Three Sisters Rd (27545)
P.O. Box 1697 (27312)
PHONE..........................919 217-0222
James Lochren, *Managing Member*
Jeff Bowes, *Prin*
EMP: 57 **EST:** 2008
SALES (est): 9.86MM **Privately Held**
Web: www.capitalreadymixconcrete.com
SIC: 3273 Ready-mixed concrete

(G-7455)
PCX HOLDING LLC
370 Spectrum Dr (27545-5144)
PHONE..........................919 550-2800
EMP: 74
SALES (corp-wide): 5.63B **Publicly Held**
Web: www.pcxcorp.com
SIC: 3699 Electrical equipment and supplies,
nec
HQ: Pcx Holding Llc
　　33 Pony Farm Rd
　　Clayton NC 27520
　　919 550-2800

(G-7456)
PROGRESSIVE INTL ELEC INC
1106 Great Falls Ct (27545-5801)
PHONE..........................919 266-4442
Ted Warn, *Pr*
EMP: 8 **EST:** 1978
SQ FT: 5,000
SALES (est): 502.26K **Privately Held**
Web: www.pie-corp.com
SIC: 3823 Process control instruments

(G-7457)
PROTRONICS INC
Also Called: Pro Tronics
861 Old Knight Rd Ste 102 (27545-6056)
PHONE..........................919 217-0007
Jan Alford, *Pr*
Teresa Alford, *VP*
EMP: 15 **EST:** 1993
SQ FT: 5,300
SALES (est): 3.83MM **Privately Held**
Web: www.protronics-inc.com
SIC: 3672 7629 Circuit boards, television
and radio printed; Circuit board repair

(G-7458)
SCHNEIDER ELECTRIC USA INC
Also Called: Schneider Electric
Hwy 64 East (27545)
PHONE..........................919 266-3671
Harry Hyatt, *Brnch Mgr*
EMP: 282
SALES (corp-wide): 1.09K **Privately Held**
Web: www.se.com
SIC: 3613 3625 Switchgear and switchboard
apparatus; Relays and industrial controls
HQ: Schneider Electric Usa, Inc.
　　1 Boston Pl Ste 2700
　　Boston MA 02108
　　617 904-9422

(G-7459)
THREE SISTERS READY MIX LLC
512 Three Sisters Rd (27545-8202)
PHONE..........................919 217-0222
EMP: 6 **EST:** 2009
SALES (est): 194.61K **Privately Held**
Web: www.capitalreadymixconcrete.com
SIC: 3273 Ready-mixed concrete

(G-7460)
TRADE VENTURE STONES LLC
Also Called: Tvs
365 Spectrum Dr Ste 100 (27545-5144)
PHONE..........................919 803-3923
David Kim, *Pr*
▲ **EMP:** 6 **EST:** 2015
SALES (est): 10.12MM **Privately Held**
Web: www.tvs-usa.com
SIC: 3281 5032 Table tops, marble; Granite
building stone

(G-7461)
TRESMC LLC
2509 Ferdinand Dr (27545-7460)
PHONE..........................919 900-0868
Angela Clemmons, *Pr*
EMP: 5 **EST:** 2006
SALES (est): 208.95K **Privately Held**
SIC: 5699 5137 2311 Uniforms; Uniforms,
women's and children's; Men's and boys'
uniforms

(G-7462)
WAKE STONE CORPORATION (PA)
6821 Knightdale Blvd (27545-9651)
P.O. Box 190 (27545-0190)
PHONE..........................919 266-1100
Samuel T Bratton, *Pr*
John R Bratton, *

Theodore D Bratton, *
Thomas B Oxholm, *
M Holt Browning, *
EMP: 48 **EST:** 1970
SQ FT: 8,500
SALES (est): 23.51MM
SALES (corp-wide): 23.51MM **Privately Held**
Web: www.wakestonecorp.com
SIC: 3281 Cut stone and stone products

Kure Beach
New Hanover County

(G-7463)
ANDREWS VIOLINIST
546 Anchor Way (28449-4802)
PHONE.................................910 458-1226
EMP: 4 **EST:** 2012
SALES (est): 81.56K **Privately Held**
SIC: 3931 Violins and parts

(G-7464)
DNA SERVICES INC
Also Called: Fireplace Guy, The
770 Settlers Ln (28449-4907)
PHONE.................................910 279-2775
EMP: 6 **EST:** 2014
SALES (est): 73.45K **Privately Held**
Web: www.fireplaceguy.net
SIC: 3433 1799 Logs, gas fireplace;
Prefabricated fireplace installation

La Grange
Lenoir County

(G-7465)
COOPER BUSSMANN LLC
Cooper Bussmann-Automotive
4758 Washington St (28551-8173)
PHONE.................................252 566-0278
Steve Tate, *Genl Mgr*
EMP: 189
SIC: 3613 3545 Fuses, electric; Machine tool
accessories
HQ: Cooper Bussmann, Llc
114 Old State Rd
Ellisville MO 63021
636 394-2877

(G-7466)
COOPER CROUSE-HINDS LLC
4758 Washington St (28551-8173)
PHONE.................................252 566-3014
Alexander M Cutler, *CEO*
EMP: 63
Web: www.coopercrouse-hinds.com
SIC: 3069 3679 Hard rubber and molded
rubber products; Electronic circuits
HQ: Cooper Crouse-Hinds, Llc
1201 Wolf St
Syracuse NY 13208
315 477-7000

(G-7467)
DUDLEYS FENCE COMPANY
4126 Fields Station Rd (28551-7933)
PHONE.................................252 566-5759
Sherman Dudley, *Pr*
EMP: 5 **EST:** 1997
SALES (est): 629.9K **Privately Held**
Web: dudleysfence.webs.com
SIC: 3446 5084 Fences, gates, posts, and
flagpoles; Cleaning equipment, high
pressure, sand or steam

(G-7468)
FOSS INDUSTRIAL RECYCLING LLC
7037 Us Highway 70 W (28551-8932)
PHONE.................................336 342-4812
Jimmie C Foss Junior, *Pr*
EMP: 21 **EST:** 2015
SALES (est): 7.41MM **Privately Held**
Web: www.fossrecycling.com
SIC: 3569 Baling machines, for scrap metal,
paper, or similar material

(G-7469)
M M M INC (PA)
501 W Railroad St (28551-1641)
P.O. Box 188 (28551-0188)
PHONE.................................252 527-0229
J Ward Mc Connell, *Ch Bd*
EMP: 6 **EST:** 1818
SQ FT: 48,000
SALES (est): 683.3K
SALES (corp-wide): 683.3K **Privately Held**
Web: www.mmmpots.com
SIC: 3443 Tanks, lined: metal plate

(G-7470)
P & D ARCHTECTURAL PRECAST INC
323 E Railroad St (28551-1844)
P.O. Box 477 (28551-0477)
PHONE.................................252 566-9811
Mark Fairman, *Pr*
EMP: 15 **EST:** 1980
SQ FT: 17,000
SALES (est): 4.31MM **Privately Held**
Web: www.pdarchprecast.com
SIC: 3272 Concrete products, precast, nec

Lake Waccamaw
Columbus County

(G-7471)
COUNCIL TOOL COMPANY INC (PA)
345 Pecan Ln (28450-2325)
PHONE.................................910 646-3011
John M Council Iii, *Pr*
Virginia P Council, *VP*
▲ **EMP:** 50 **EST:** 1886
SQ FT: 2,500
SALES (est): 7.71MM
SALES (corp-wide): 7.71MM **Privately Held**
Web: www.counciltool.com
SIC: 3423 Carpenters' hand tools, except
saws: levels, chisels, etc.

(G-7472)
TOP TOBACCO LP
204 Top Tobacco Rd (28450-2220)
PHONE.................................910 646-3014
Claus Platt, *Pr*
EMP: 106
SALES (corp-wide): 24.73MM **Privately Held**
Web: www.republicbrands.com
SIC: 2131 2141 0132 Smoking tobacco;
Tobacco stemming and redrying; Tobacco
PA: Top Tobacco L.P.
2301 Ravine Way
Glenview IL 60025
847 832-9700

Landis
Rowan County

(G-7473)
CECO FRICTION PRODUCTS INC
2525 N Hwy 29 (28088)

P.O. Box 150 (28088-0150)
PHONE.................................704 857-1156
Phillip Coan, *Pr*
Thomas Young, *VP*
Paul B Coan, *Treas*
EMP: 14 **EST:** 1973
SQ FT: 18,000
SALES (est): 1.39MM **Privately Held**
Web: www.cecofriction.com
SIC: 3714 Motor vehicle brake systems and
parts

(G-7474)
MARTIN MARIETTA MATERIALS INC
Also Called: Martin Marietta Aggregates
P.O. Box 8108 (28088-8108)
PHONE.................................704 932-4379
Ronnie Borum, *Brnch Mgr*
EMP: 10
Web: www.martinmarietta.com
SIC: 3273 Ready-mixed concrete
PA: Martin Marietta Materials Inc
4123 Parklake Ave
Raleigh NC 27612

(G-7475)
PARKDALE MILLS INCORPORATED
Also Called: Parkdale Plant 23
100 S Main St (28088-1310)
P.O. Box 1787 (28053-1787)
PHONE.................................704 855-3164
Brett Lowder, *Brnch Mgr*
EMP: 46
SALES (corp-wide): 1.44B **Privately Held**
Web: www.parkdalemills.com
SIC: 2281 Yarn spinning mills
HQ: Parkdale Mills, Incorporated
531 Cotton Blossom Cir
Gastonia NC 28054
704 874-5000

(G-7476)
PARKDALE MILLS INC
Also Called: Parkdale Plant 24
414 N Meriah St (28088-1039)
PHONE.................................704 857-3456
Brett Lowder, *Brnch Mgr*
EMP: 24
SALES (corp-wide): 1.44B **Privately Held**
Web: www.parkdalemills.com
SIC: 2281 Cotton yarn, spun
HQ: Parkdale Mills, Incorporated
531 Cotton Blossom Cir
Gastonia NC 28054
704 874-5000

Lansing
Ashe County

(G-7477)
JERRY BLEVINS
Also Called: High Country Chair Weaving
1162 Deep Ford Rd (28643-9240)
PHONE.................................336 384-3726
Jerry Blevins, *Owner*
EMP: 6 **EST:** 1996
SQ FT: 2,400
SALES (est): 191.79K **Privately Held**
SIC: 5021 2426 Chairs; Chair seats,
hardwood

(G-7478)
MOLLEY CHOMPER LLC
1124 Jerd Branch Rd (28643-9186)
PHONE.................................404 769-1439
Kathleen Arscott-mills, *Admn*
EMP: 4 **EST:** 2015
SALES (est): 309.85K **Privately Held**
Web: www.molleychomper.com

SIC: 2084 Wines

(G-7479)
UNITED CHEMI-CON INC
185 Mcneil Rd (28643-8308)
PHONE.................................336 384-6903
Noburu Tokushige, *Mgr*
EMP: 300
Web: www.chemi-con.com
SIC: 3675 5065 Electronic capacitors;
Capacitors, electronic
HQ: United Chemi-Con, Inc.
1701 Golf Rd Ste 1-1200
Rolling Meadows IL 60008
847 696-2000

Lattimore
Cleveland County

(G-7480)
KLEAROPTICS INC
150 N Reasearch Campus Dr Ste 3505
(28089)
PHONE.................................760 224-6770
Ali Dahi, *Pr*
Ramazan Benrashid, *VP*
EMP: 5 **EST:** 2017
SALES (est): 60.56K **Privately Held**
SIC: 7389 3827 Business Activities at Non-
Commercial Site; Optical instruments and
apparatus

(G-7481)
MARTINS WOODWORKING LLC
Also Called: Martins Woodworking
100 Martin St (28089)
P.O. Box 256 (28089-0256)
PHONE.................................704 473-7617
Jackson Martin, *Managing Member*
EMP: 10 **EST:** 2011
SALES (est): 551.19K **Privately Held**
Web: www.martinswoodworking.com
SIC: 2431 Millwork

Laurel Hill
Scotland County

(G-7482)
EAST COAST UMBRELLA INC
6321 Andrew Jackson Hwy (28351-8561)
PHONE.................................910 462-2500
Darrell L Day, *Pr*
Dewayne Day, *
Christine Oxendine, *
▲ **EMP:** 45 **EST:** 1987
SQ FT: 68,000
SALES (est): 1.65MM **Privately Held**
Web: www.eastcoastumbrella.com
SIC: 3999 2393 5712 Umbrellas, garden or
wagon; Cushions, except spring and
carpet: purchased materials; Outdoor and
garden furniture

(G-7483)
HANESBRANDS INC
Also Called: Champion Products
18400 Fieldcrest Rd (28351-8351)
P.O. Box 70 (28351-0070)
PHONE.................................910 462-2001
Stodd Mcewan, *Brnch Mgr*
EMP: 4
SQ FT: 165,000
Web: www.hanes.com
SIC: 5621 2253 Women's sportswear; Knit
outerwear mills
PA: Hanesbrands Inc.
1000 E Hanes Mill Rd
Winston Salem NC 27105

(G-7484)
HYGIENE SYSTEMS INC
Also Called: Omni Systems
10442 Old Wire Rd (28351-9386)
PHONE..............................910 462-2661
EMP: 30 EST: 1996
SALES (est): 760.91K **Privately Held**
SIC: 2676 Sanitary paper products

(G-7485)
KORDSA INC
17780 Armstrong Rd (28351-9394)
PHONE..............................910 462-2051
Daniel Pelton V Press, *Brnch Mgr*
EMP: 135
Web: careers.indokordsa.com
SIC: 2281 Nylon yarn, spinning of staple
HQ: Kordsa, Inc.
    4501 N Access Rd
    Chattanooga TN 37415
    423 643-8300

(G-7486)
KRODSA USA INC
17780 Armstrong Rd (28351-9394)
PHONE..............................910 462-2041
Thomas Harmen, *Ofcr*
EMP: 5 EST: 2014
SALES (est): 64.07K **Privately Held**
SIC: 2281 Yarn spinning mills

(G-7487)
LAWRENCE WILLIAMS
Also Called: Williams Machine & Tool
10200 Andrew Jackson Hwy (28351-9579)
PHONE..............................910 462-2332
Lawrence Williams, *Owner*
EMP: 6 EST: 1995
SQ FT: 3,000
SALES (est): 1.8MM **Privately Held**
Web: www.williamsmachineandtool.com
SIC: 3599 Machine shop, jobbing and repair

(G-7488)
TONY D HILDRETH
Also Called: Hildreth Mechanical & Maint
22945 Broadwell Rd (28351-9704)
PHONE..............................910 276-1803
Tony D Hildreth, *Owner*
EMP: 10 EST: 1990
SQ FT: 6,000
SALES (est): 213.28K **Privately Held**
SIC: 1711 7389 3599 1799 Mechanical
    contractor; Crane and aerial lift service;
    Machine shop, jobbing and repair; Welding
    on site

Laurel Springs
Alleghany County

(G-7489)
L F DELP LUMBER CO INC
2601 Nc Highway 113 (28644-9149)
PHONE..............................336 359-8202
Larry Delp, *Pr*
Linda Delp, *
EMP: 4 EST: 1979
SALES (est): 215.53K **Privately Held**
SIC: 2421 2426 Sawmills and planing mills,
    general; Hardwood dimension and flooring
    mills

(G-7490)
THISTLE MEADOW WINERY INC
102 Thistle Mdw (28644-8333)
PHONE..............................800 233-1505
Thomas Burgess, *Pr*
EMP: 9 EST: 2003
SALES (est): 138.19K **Privately Held**

Web: www.thistlemeadowwinery.com
SIC: 2084 Wines

(G-7491)
TOM BURGISS
Also Called: Burgiss Farm Bed & Breakfast
294 Elk Knob Rd (28644-8374)
PHONE..............................336 359-2995
Thomas Burgiss, *Owner*
EMP: 5 EST: 1987
SALES (est): 210K **Privately Held**
Web: www.thistlemeadowwinery.com
SIC: 2084 7011 Wines; Bed and breakfast
    inn

Laurinburg
Scotland County

(G-7492)
AVERITT ENTERPRISES INC
Also Called: Averitt Electric Motor Repair
14121 Highland Rd (28352-4045)
P.O. Box 1793 (28353-1793)
PHONE..............................910 276-1294
Ronnie Averitt, *Pr*
Levinia Averitt, *Sec*
EMP: 10 EST: 1964
SQ FT: 10,500
SALES (est): 595.55K **Privately Held**
Web: www.averittcontainer.com
SIC: 7694 Electric motor repair

(G-7493)
BUIE MANUFACTURING COMPANY
Also Called: Buie and Company
105 Sterling Ln (28352-5526)
PHONE..............................910 610-3504
Clifton Poole Buie, *Pr*
EMP: 25 EST: 2020
SALES (est): 1.49MM **Privately Held**
SIC: 3429 Furniture hardware

(G-7494)
CAROLINA CONTAINER LLC
Also Called: Carocon
16100 Joy St (28352)
P.O. Box 2166 (27261-2166)
PHONE..............................910 277-0400
Susan Medlis, *Brnch Mgr*
EMP: 27
SALES (corp-wide): 644.8MM **Privately
Held**
Web: www.carolinacontainer.com
SIC: 2653 Boxes, corrugated: made from
    purchased materials
HQ: Carolina Container Company
    909 Prospect St
    High Point NC 27260
    336 883-7146

(G-7495)
CAROLINA CRATING INC
430 Hillside Ave (28352-3046)
PHONE..............................910 276-7170
Linda Pate, *Pr*
Catherine Boone, *
Archibald Mclean Junior, *VP*
EMP: 45 EST: 1971
SQ FT: 75,000
SALES (est): 2.19MM **Privately Held**
Web: www.carolinacratinginc.com
SIC: 2441 2448 Shipping cases, wood:
    nailed or lock corner; Pallets, wood

(G-7496)
CHAMPION MEDIA LLC
Also Called: Laurinburg Exchange
915 S Main St Ste H (28352-4700)
PHONE..............................910 506-3021

EMP: 218
SALES (corp-wide): 12.2MM **Privately
Held**
Web: www.championcarolinas.com
SIC: 2711 Newspapers, publishing and
    printing
PA: Champion Media Llc
    116 Morlake Dr Ste 203
    Mooresville NC 28117
    704 746-3955

(G-7497)
CHARLES CRAFT INC (PA)
Also Called: Burch Industries
21381 Charles Craft Ln (28352)
P.O. Box 1049 (28353-1049)
PHONE..............................910 844-3521
▲ **EMP:** 7 EST: 1966
SALES (est): 4.94MM
SALES (corp-wide): 4.94MM **Privately
Held**
Web: www.charlescraftinc.com
SIC: 2281 2015 Manmade and synthetic
    fiber yarns, spun; Egg albumen

(G-7498)
ED S TIRE LAURINBURG INC
300 Biggs St (28352-3806)
PHONE..............................910 277-0565
Alan Smith, *Pr*
Deneane Smith, *Sec*
EMP: 6 EST: 1982
SALES (est): 556.89K **Privately Held**
SIC: 5531 7534 5014 Automotive tires; Tire
    repair shop; Automobile tires and tubes

(G-7499)
EDWARDS WOOD PRODUCTS INC
19500 Old Lumberton Rd (28352-6632)
P.O. Box 1527 (28353-1527)
PHONE..............................910 276-6870
Carroll Edwards, *Ch*
Jeff Edwards, *
EMP: 65 EST: 1989
SQ FT: 2,500
SALES (est): 5.72MM **Privately Held**
Web: www.ewpi.com
SIC: 2421 Sawmills and planing mills,
    general

(G-7500)
ELECTRICAL EQUIPMENT COMPANY
226 N Wilkinson Dr (28352-2927)
PHONE..............................910 276-2141
Bill Litton, *Mgr*
EMP: 28
SALES (corp-wide): 231.46MM **Privately
Held**
Web: www.eecoonline.com
SIC: 5063 7629 7694 Electrical supplies, nec
    ; Electrical equipment repair services;
    Armature rewinding shops
PA: Electrical Equipment Company Inc
    1440 Diggs Dr
    Raleigh NC 27603
    919 828-5411

(G-7501)
FCC (NORTH CAROLINA) LLC
Also Called: FCC
18000 Fieldcrest Rd (28352-6798)
PHONE..............................910 462-4465
▲ **EMP:** 185 EST: 2001
SQ FT: 75,000
SALES (est): 24.8MM **Privately Held**
Web: www.fcc-na.com
SIC: 3714 Clutches, motor vehicle
PA: F.C.C.Co., Ltd.
    7000-36, Hosoechonakagawa,
    Hamana-Ku
    Hamamatsu SZO 431-1

(G-7502)
**FEEDER INNOVATIONS
CORPORATION**
9781 Mccoll Rd (28352-8901)
P.O. Box 816 (28031-0816)
PHONE..............................910 276-3511
Douglas Bowen, *Pr*
Lawrence Bowen, *Sec*
EMP: 4 EST: 1985
SALES (est): 243.85K **Privately Held**
Web: www.feederinnovations.com
SIC: 3549 Metalworking machinery, nec

(G-7503)
HANEYS TIRE RECAPPING SVC LLC
Also Called: Haney's Tire
1663 S Main St (28352-5412)
PHONE..............................910 276-2636
Mike Coughenour, *Managing Member*
EMP: 7 EST: 1961
SQ FT: 10,000
SALES (est): 951.67K **Privately Held**
Web: www.haneystire.com
SIC: 5531 7534 7538 5014 Automotive tires;
    Tire recapping; General automotive repair
    shops; Automobile tires and tubes

(G-7504)
KING BUSINESS SERVICE INC
Also Called: UPS Stores 2922, The
1680 S Main St (28352-5413)
PHONE..............................910 610-1030
Greg King, *Pr*
EMP: 8 EST: 1996
SQ FT: 1,750
SALES (est): 632.08K **Privately Held**
Web: locations.theupsstore.com
SIC: 7389 7331 5943 5087 Mailbox rental
    and related service; Mailing service; Office
    forms and supplies; Moving equipment and
    supplies

(G-7505)
LAURINBURG MACHINE COMPANY
715 Park Cir (28352-4417)
PHONE..............................910 276-0360
William D Lytch Junior, *Pr*
James A Lytch, *VP*
EMP: 6 EST: 1909
SQ FT: 35,000
SALES (est): 765.33K **Privately Held**
SIC: 3713 3599 5085 Truck and bus bodies;
    Machine shop, jobbing and repair; Mill
    supplies

(G-7506)
M C C OF LAURINBURG INC
Also Called: Evans, Bill Co
200 Johns Rd (28352-4735)
P.O. Box 669 (28353-0669)
PHONE..............................910 276-0519
M C Cathcart, *Pr*
EMP: 7 EST: 1937
SQ FT: 10,000
SALES (est): 324.49K **Privately Held**
Web: www.laurinburg.org
SIC: 2752 5712 5943 Offset printing; Office
    furniture; Office forms and supplies

(G-7507)
MARMON ENGINE CONTROLS LLC
Also Called: Marmonpowertrain
2519 Dana Dr (28352-4000)
PHONE..............................843 701-5145
Jeff Mccurley, *Pr*
Patrick Fennell, *
EMP: 42 EST: 2017
SALES (est): 4.92MM **Privately Held**
SIC: 3714 Motor vehicle parts and
    accessories

(G-7508)
MARMON HOLDINGS INC
Also Called: Rostra Powertrain Controls
2519 Dana Dr (28352-4000)
PHONE..................910 291-2571
Justin Tatum, *Mgr*
EMP: 6
SALES (corp-wide): 424.23B **Publicly Held**
Web: www.rostrapowertrain.com
SIC: 3714 3679 Acceleration equipment, motor vehicle; Solenoids for electronic applications
HQ: Marmon Holdings, Inc.
181 W Madison St Ste 3900
Chicago IL 60602
312 372-9500

(G-7509)
MCKENZIE SUPPLY COMPANY
1600 Us Highway 401 Byp S (28352-5401)
P.O. Box 1068 (28353-1068)
PHONE..................910 276-1691
Fred Johnson, *Mgr*
EMP: 7
SALES (corp-wide): 11.53MM **Privately Held**
Web: www.mckenziesupplyco.com
SIC: 5074 5063 5064 3625 Plumbing fittings and supplies; Electrical supplies, nec; Water heaters, electric; Motor control accessories, including overload relays
PA: Mckenzie Supply Company
726 E 16th St
Lumberton NC 28358
910 738-4801

(G-7510)
MURPHY-BROWN LLC
Also Called: Laurinburg Feed Mill
19600 Andrew Jackson Hwy (28352-4067)
PHONE..................910 277-8999
Cesar Menendez Feedmill, *Mgr*
EMP: 59
Web: www.smithfieldfoods.com
SIC: 2048 Prepared feeds, nec
HQ: Murphy-Brown Llc
2822 W Nc 24 Hwy
Warsaw NC 28398
910 293-3434

(G-7511)
PILKINGTON NORTH AMERICA INC
13121 S Rocky Ford Rd (28352-6216)
PHONE..................910 276-5630
David Robinson, *Brnch Mgr*
EMP: 27
Web: www.pilkington.com
SIC: 3211 Flat glass
HQ: Pilkington North America, Inc.
811 Madison Ave
Toledo OH 43604
419 247-3731

(G-7512)
QUALPAK LLC
16000 Joy St (28352-0402)
P.O. Box 2277 (44309-2277)
PHONE..................910 610-1213
Dick Palin, *Managing Member*
Joseph S Kanfer, *Managing Member*
▲ EMP: 9 EST: 2003
SQ FT: 200,000
SALES (est): 1.8MM
SALES (corp-wide): 802.21MM **Privately Held**
SIC: 2841 Soap: granulated, liquid, cake, flaked, or chip
PA: Gojo Industries, Inc.
1 Gojo Plz Ste 500
Akron OH 44311

330 255-6000

(G-7513)
SAM M BUTLER INC
Also Called: Service Thread Manufacturing
504 S King St (28352-3735)
PHONE..................910 276-2360
Jim Myers, *Brnch Mgr*
EMP: 45
SQ FT: 115,000
SALES (corp-wide): 12.55MM **Privately Held**
Web: www.servicethread.com
SIC: 2282 Throwing and winding mills
PA: Sam M. Butler, Inc.
17900 Dana Dr
Laurinburg NC 28352
910 277-7456

(G-7514)
SAM M BUTLER INC (PA)
Also Called: Service Thread Manufacturing
17900 Dana Dr (28352-4031)
P.O. Box 673 (28353)
PHONE..................910 277-7456
◆ EMP: 20 EST: 1949
SALES (est): 12.55MM
SALES (corp-wide): 12.55MM **Privately Held**
Web: www.servicethread.com
SIC: 2284 2295 3552 Thread mills; Yarns, plastic coated: made from purchased yarns; Textile machinery

(G-7515)
SMC HOLDCO INC
22261 Skyway Church Rd (28353)
P.O. Box 1067 (28353-1067)
PHONE..................910 844-3956
Wayne Cain, *Prin*
EMP: 105 EST: 1991
SQ FT: 50,000
SALES (est): 20.69MM
SALES (corp-wide): 56.63MM **Privately Held**
Web: www.scotlandmanufacturing.com
SIC: 3469 Stamping metal for the trade
PA: Spartanburg Steel Products, Inc.
1290 New Cut Rd
Spartanburg SC 29303
864 585-5211

(G-7516)
THOMAS LCKLARS CBNETS LRNBURG
21720 Wagram Rd (28352-6770)
PHONE..................910 369-2094
Thomas Locklear, *Pr*
Joann Locklear, *VP*
EMP: 8 EST: 1977
SALES (est): 386.87K **Privately Held**
SIC: 2434 1799 Wood kitchen cabinets; Kitchen cabinet installation

Lawndale
Cleveland County

(G-7517)
JA SMITH INC
Also Called: Smith Electric Co
305 Plainsview Church Rd (28090-7405)
P.O. Box 550 (28042-0550)
PHONE..................704 860-4910
Joe A Smith, *Pr*
EMP: 4 EST: 1984
SALES (est): 235.21K **Privately Held**
Web: www.jasmithinc.com

SIC: 1731 8711 5063 3625 General electrical contractor; Engineering services; Electrical apparatus and equipment; Relays and industrial controls

(G-7518)
MCNEILLYS INC
Also Called: McNeilly Champion Furniture
229 Carpenters Grove Church Rd (28090-9256)
PHONE..................704 300-1712
Leonard J Mcneilly, *Pr*
EMP: 35 EST: 2000
SALES (est): 948.11K **Privately Held**
Web: www.mcneillychampionfurniture.com
SIC: 2512 5712 Chairs: upholstered on wood frames; Furniture stores

Lawsonville
Stokes County

(G-7519)
HIGH-TECH FABRICATIONS INC
3045 Nc 704 Hwy E (27022-7851)
PHONE..................336 871-2990
Jerry Lawrence, *Pr*
Jerry William Lawrence, *Pr*
Avalon Potts, *Sec*
Jerry W Lawrence, *Owner*
EMP: 10 EST: 1999
SQ FT: 14,500
SALES (est): 878.78K **Privately Held**
Web: www.high-techfab.com
SIC: 3441 Fabricated structural metal

(G-7520)
SPRINGMILL PRODUCTS INC
1147 Walter Mabe Rd (27022-8256)
P.O. Box 291 (27016-0291)
PHONE..................336 406-9050
William F Fels, *Pr*
Thomas Sparacio, *VP*
Rhonda C Fels, *Sec*
▼ EMP: 5 EST: 2002
SQ FT: 75,000
SALES (est): 67.66K **Privately Held**
SIC: 2048 Dry pet food (except dog and cat)

Leicester
Buncombe County

(G-7521)
ALTOM FUEL CELLS LLC
117 Jones Rd (28748-5128)
PHONE..................828 231-6889
EMP: 4 EST: 2008
SALES (est): 240.34K **Privately Held**
SIC: 3621 Motors and generators

(G-7522)
CREATIVE WOODCRAFTERS INC
42 West Rd (28748-7739)
PHONE..................828 252-9663
Michael Keleher, *Pr*
Jennifer P Keleher, *VP*
EMP: 4 EST: 1976
SQ FT: 12,000
SALES (est): 132.12K **Privately Held**
SIC: 2434 Wood kitchen cabinets

(G-7523)
DYNAMIC SYSTEMS INC
104 Morrow Branch Rd (28748-9635)
PHONE..................828 683-3523
Robin Yost, *Pr*
▲ EMP: 24 EST: 1967
SQ FT: 16,000

SALES (est): 3.82MM **Privately Held**
Web: www.sunmatecushions.com
SIC: 3086 Insulation or cushioning material, foamed plastics

(G-7524)
FLAT IRON MILL WORKS LLC
22 Pear Tree Ln (28748-5500)
PHONE..................828 768-7770
Rachel R Brown, *Owner*
EMP: 4 EST: 2017
SALES (est): 827.33K **Privately Held**
SIC: 2431 Millwork

(G-7525)
GREEN LINE DEFENSE LLC
36 Renaissance Pl (28748-8438)
PHONE..................828 707-5236
Shawn Patrick Martin, *Owner*
EMP: 5 EST: 2017
SALES (est): 83.36K **Privately Held**
SIC: 3812 Defense systems and equipment

(G-7526)
INDUSTRIAL TLING SVCS ASHVLLE
1259 Alexander Rd (28748-6338)
P.O. Box 877 (28748-0877)
PHONE..................828 683-4168
Cliff Johnson, *Pr*
EMP: 8 EST: 1973
SQ FT: 5,000
SALES (est): 501.54K **Privately Held**
SIC: 3599 Machine shop, jobbing and repair

(G-7527)
MELT YOUR HEART LLC
Also Called: Melt Your Heart
162 Brookshire Rd (28748-5140)
PHONE..................828 989-6749
Steven Paulson, *Prin*
EMP: 5 EST: 2016
SALES (est): 108.22K **Privately Held**
SIC: 2599 Food wagons, restaurant

(G-7528)
NEWFOUND TIRE & QUICK LUBE INC
642 Newfound Rd (28748-9769)
PHONE..................828 683-3232
Stacy Gossett, *Pr*
EMP: 4 EST: 2006
SQ FT: 4,000
SALES (est): 482.83K **Privately Held**
Web: www.newfoundtireandquicklube.com
SIC: 7549 7534 Lubrication service, automotive; Tire retreading and repair shops

(G-7529)
SOUTHERN SIGNWORKS
45 Single Tree Gap Rd (28748-4505)
PHONE..................828 683-8726
Doc Welty, *Prin*
EMP: 5 EST: 2005
SALES (est): 128.27K **Privately Held**
SIC: 3993 Signs and advertising specialties

Leland
Brunswick County

(G-7530)
33RD STRIKE GROUP LLC
9101 Lackey Rd Ne Ste 4 (28451-3308)
PHONE..................910 371-9688
Christopher Chen, *Pr*
▲ EMP: 4 EST: 2014
SQ FT: 106,000
SALES (est): 189.62K **Privately Held**
SIC: 3732 Boatbuilding and repairing

(G-7531)
ADAMS BEVERAGES NC LLC
Also Called: Adams Beverages Leland
2265 Mercantile Dr (28451-4058)
PHONE...............................910 763-6216
Casey Cranor, *Mgr*
EMP: 75
SALES (corp-wide): 8.55MM **Privately Held**
Web: www.wilmingtonchamber.org
SIC: 2084 Wine coolers (beverages)
PA: Adams Beverages Of North Carolina, Llc
7505 Statesville Rd
Charlotte NC 28269
704 509-3000

(G-7532)
BOAT LIFT US INC
2216 Mercantile Dr (28451-4091)
PHONE...............................239 283-9040
Terry J Hamilton, *Prin*
▲ EMP: 6 EST: 2006
SALES (est): 1.87MM **Privately Held**
Web: www.boatliftus.com
SIC: 3536 Boat lifts

(G-7533)
BOLIVIA LUMBER COMPANY LLC (PA)
405 Old Mill Rd Ne (28451-7594)
P.O. Box 1387 (28402-1387)
PHONE...............................910 371-2515
Thomas Garner, *Pr*
EMP: 15 EST: 1960
SQ FT: 75,000
SALES (est): 4.75MM
SALES (corp-wide): 4.75MM **Privately Held**
Web: www.bolivialumber.com
SIC: 2448 5031 Pallets, wood; Lumber: rough, dressed, and finished

(G-7534)
BOONE ENTERPRISES LLC
Also Called: Infinity Custom Cabinets
497 Olde Waterford Way Ste 103
(28451-4183)
PHONE...............................910 859-8299
Brian Boone, *Managing Member*
EMP: 6 EST: 2009
SALES (est): 117.58K **Privately Held**
SIC: 2521 Cabinets, office: wood

(G-7535)
BRADFORD PRODUCTS LLC (PA)
Also Called: Bradford Products
2101 Enterprise Dr Ne (28451-8807)
PHONE...............................910 791-2202
Dale Brodeur Junior, *Pr*
Dale Brodeur Senior, *Managing Member*
Mike Brodeur, *
Mark Miller, *
◆ EMP: 89 EST: 1997
SQ FT: 50,000
SALES (est): 36.54MM
SALES (corp-wide): 36.54MM **Privately Held**
Web: www.bradfordproducts.com
SIC: 3999 1799 Hot tubs; Spa or hot tub installation or construction

(G-7536)
C&V POWDER COATING
1068 Ashland Way (28451-9112)
PHONE...............................910 228-1173
Nijel Richburg, *Prin*
EMP: 5 EST: 2018
SALES (est): 84.6K **Privately Held**

SIC: 3479 Coating of metals and formed products

(G-7537)
CDB CORPORATION
2304 Mercantile Dr Ne (28451-4066)
PHONE...............................910 383-6464
Markus Hirsch, *CEO*
H W Heipl, *
Eric Moschik, *
Hermann Hirsch, *
▲ EMP: 50 EST: 1989
SQ FT: 10,900
SALES (est): 4.22MM **Privately Held**
Web: www.cdbcorp.net
SIC: 3843 8072 Orthodontic appliances; Dental laboratories

(G-7538)
COASTAL TRIMWORKS INC
1114 Maplechase Dr Se (28451-9569)
PHONE...............................910 231-8532
EMP: 6 EST: 2006
SALES (est): 144.74K **Privately Held**
SIC: 3732 Boatbuilding and repairing

(G-7539)
COCA-COLA CONSOLIDATED INC
Also Called: Coca-Cola
2210 Mercantile Dr (28451-4091)
PHONE...............................919 763-3172
Paul Summerlin, *Brnch Mgr*
EMP: 4
SALES (corp-wide): 6.9B **Publicly Held**
Web: www.cokeconsolidated.com
SIC: 2086 Bottled and canned soft drinks
PA: Coca-Cola Consolidated, Inc.
4100 Coca-Cola Plz
Charlotte NC 28211
980 392-8298

(G-7540)
EIDP INC
Also Called: Dupont
3500 Daniels Rd Ne (28451-4174)
PHONE...............................910 371-4000
Tom Harris, *Mgr*
EMP: 4
SALES (corp-wide): 16.91B **Publicly Held**
Web: www.dupont.com
SIC: 2819 Industrial inorganic chemicals, nec
HQ: Eidp, Inc.
9330 Zionsville Rd
Indianapolis IN 46268
833 267-8382

(G-7541)
FELLER LLC (DH)
9100 Industrial Blvd Ne (28451-9037)
PHONE...............................910 383-6920
Doug Fox, *
Rod Linville, *
◆ EMP: 25 EST: 1984
SQ FT: 30,000
SALES (est): 6.58MM
SALES (corp-wide): 242.12K **Privately Held**
Web: www.feller-us.com
SIC: 3699 Accelerating waveguide structures
HQ: Feller U.S. Corp.
9100 Industrial Blvd Ne
Leland NC 28451
910 383-6920

(G-7542)
FLOW SCIENCES INC
2025 Mercantile Dr (28451-4054)
PHONE...............................910 763-1717
Raymond F Ryan, *Pr*
Ruth Gensinger, *
◆ EMP: 38 EST: 1987

SQ FT: 37,000
SALES (est): 8.8MM **Privately Held**
Web: www.flowsciences.com
SIC: 3821 Laboratory equipment: fume hoods, distillation racks, etc.

(G-7543)
FLOWSERVE CORPORATION
Flowserve
2216 Mercantile Dr (28451-4091)
PHONE...............................910 371-9011
Sue Russell, *Mgr*
EMP: 7
SALES (corp-wide): 4.56B **Publicly Held**
Web: www.flowserve.com
SIC: 3561 Pumps and pumping equipment
PA: Flowserve Corporation
5215 N Ocnnor Blvd Ste 70
Irving TX 75039
972 443-6500

(G-7544)
GALE GLOBAL RESEARCH INC
Also Called: Ggr
7007 Robert Ruark Dr (28451)
PHONE...............................910 795-8595
William Gale, *Pr*
Joe Hatem, *VP*
EMP: 6 EST: 2013
SALES (est): 66.82K **Privately Held**
Web: www.galeglobalresearch.com
SIC: 2834 8731 Druggists' preparations (pharmaceuticals); Medical research, commercial

(G-7545)
GENERAL WOOD PRESERVING CO INC
1901 Wood Treatment Rd Ne (28451-9655)
P.O. Box 370 (28451-0370)
PHONE...............................910 371-3131
Karl Boatright, *CEO*
EMP: 4 EST: 1979
SQ FT: 2,000
SALES (est): 184.48K **Privately Held**
SIC: 2491 2411 Poles and pole crossarms, treated wood; Logging

(G-7546)
GLYCOTECH INC
2271 Andrew Jackson Hwy Ne (28451-9627)
P.O. Box 1956 (28451-1956)
PHONE...............................910 371-2234
Margaret Heitman Collins, *Pr*
Eddie Collins, *
EMP: 4 EST: 2008
SALES (est): 353.4K **Privately Held**
SIC: 2611 Pulp mills, chemical and semichemical processing

(G-7547)
INX INTERNATIONAL INK CO
1901 Popular St (28451-8181)
PHONE...............................910 371-3184
EMP: 4
SIC: 2893 Printing ink
HQ: Inx International Ink Co.
150 N Mrtngale Rd Ste 700
Schaumburg IL 60173
630 382-1800

(G-7548)
INX INTRNTNAL CTINGS ADHESIVES ✪
1901 Popular St (28451-8181)
PHONE...............................910 371-3184
Pryce Kristo, *CEO*
EMP: 146 EST: 2024
SALES (est): 2.42MM **Privately Held**
SIC: 2891 Adhesives

HQ: The Inx Group Ltd
150 N Martingale Rd # 700
Schaumburg IL 60173
630 382-1800

(G-7549)
LANDSDOWN MINING CORPORATION
3949 Blue Banks Loop Rd Ne
(28451-4077)
PHONE...............................704 753-5400
Vincenzo La Barbera, *Pr*
EMP: 11 EST: 2018
SALES (est): 2.56MM **Privately Held**
SIC: 1442 Sand mining

(G-7550)
LELAND MACHINE SHOP INC
767 Village Rd Ne (28451-8469)
PHONE...............................910 371-0360
Glenn Johnson, *Pr*
EMP: 4 EST: 1990
SALES (est): 289.59K **Privately Held**
SIC: 3599 Machine shop, jobbing and repair

(G-7551)
LIBRA LIFE GROUP LLC
Also Called: Libra Logistics/Escort
9371 Cassadine Ct (28451-1860)
PHONE...............................910 550-8664
Lwanda Green, *CEO*
EMP: 8 EST: 2020
SALES (est): 190.05K **Privately Held**
SIC: 3799 Transportation equipment, nec

(G-7552)
LUCID INNOVATIVE TECH LLC
9244 Industrial Blvd Ne (28451-7517)
P.O. Box 2107 (28451-2107)
PHONE...............................910 233-5214
Hanson O Peterson Iii, *Pr*
EMP: 5 EST: 2019
SALES (est): 206.45K **Privately Held**
SIC: 3599 Machine shop, jobbing and repair

(G-7553)
MANUFACTURING METHODS LLC
9244 Industrial Blvd Ne (28451-7517)
P.O. Box 2105 (28451)
PHONE...............................910 371-1700
Hanson Peterson, *Managing Member*
David Ott, *CFO*
EMP: 25 EST: 2007
SQ FT: 40,000
SALES (est): 4.63MM **Privately Held**
Web: www.manufacturingmethods.com
SIC: 3441 3549 Fabricated structural metal; Metalworking machinery, nec

(G-7554)
MARTIN MARIETTA MATERIALS INC
Also Called: Martin Marietta Aggregates
1635 Malmo Loop Rd Ne (28451-7866)
PHONE...............................910 371-3848
Tommy Shepard, *Brnch Mgr*
EMP: 5
Web: www.martinmarietta.com
SIC: 1422 Crushed and broken limestone
PA: Martin Marietta Materials Inc
4123 Parklake Ave
Raleigh NC 27612

(G-7555)
MICROSOLV TECHNOLOGY CORP
9158 Industrial Blvd Ne (28451-9037)
PHONE...............................720 949-1302
EMP: 11 EST: 2018
SALES (est): 2.92MM **Privately Held**
Web: www.mtc-usa.com

SIC: 3826 Analytical instruments

(G-7556)
PACON MANUFACTURING CO LLC
Also Called: Baumgartner Associates
100 Quality Dr (28451)
PHONE...............................910 239-3001
Dorothy H Shannon, *Ch Bd*
Paul Guth, *
Lawrence H Shannon, *
A Vernon Shannon Iii, *Treas*
Micheal Shannon, *
▲ EMP: 125 EST: 1946
SQ FT: 168,000
SALES (est): 23.48MM Privately Held
Web: www.paconmfg.com
SIC: 2676 3821 3842 Sanitary paper
products; Incubators, laboratory; Surgical
appliances and supplies

(G-7557)
QUAD CITY HIGH PRFMCE COATINGS
1427 Green Hill Rd Ne (28451-8619)
PHONE...............................937 623-2282
Zachary Rgambrell, *Pr*
EMP: 6 EST: 2014
SALES (est): 975.71K Privately Held
SIC: 3479 Metal coating and allied services

(G-7558)
RAMCO MACHINE & PUMP SVC INC
1054 Thistle Downs St Se (28451-9550)
PHONE...............................910 371-3388
Jimmy U Ramsey, *Pr*
J Scott Ramsey, *VP*
Phyllis Ramsey, *Sec*
Alecia Williams, *Treas*
EMP: 5 EST: 1993
SALES (est): 393.42K Privately Held
SIC: 3599 Machine shop, jobbing and repair

(G-7559)
TECHNICAL COATING INTL INC
150 Backhoe Rd Ne (28451)
PHONE...............................910 371-0860
Burt E Moody, *CEO*
Sean E Moody, *Pr*
David Stanbury, *VP*
◆ EMP: 44 EST: 1992
SQ FT: 65,000
SALES (est): 14.82MM Privately Held
Web: www.tciinc.com
SIC: 2672 2679 3089 Paper; coated and
laminated, nec; Building, insulating, and
packaging paper; Plastics containers,
except foam

(G-7560)
THUNDER ALLEY ENTERPRISES
1224 Magnolia Village Way (28451-9464)
PHONE...............................910 371-0119
Kevin Groves, *Mgr*
EMP: 6 EST: 2009
SALES (est): 137.3K Privately Held
Web: www.thunderalleybowling.com
SIC: 3949 Bowling balls

(G-7561)
TRI-TECH FORENSICS INC (PA)
Also Called: Tri Tech Forensics National La
3811 International Blvd Ne Ste 100
(28451-4299)
PHONE...............................910 457-6600
Jim Seidel, *CEO*
James Cesar, *VP*
Eric Barton, *VP*
Phil Corey, *RESCUE ESSEN*
Sara Jensen, *RESCUE ESSEN*
EMP: 61 EST: 1983
SALES (est): 26.7MM

SALES (corp-wide): 26.7MM Privately Held
Web: www.tritechforensics.com
SIC: 3999 5049 Fingerprint equipment; Law
enforcement equipment and supplies

(G-7562)
USW-MENARD INC
3600 Andrew Jackson Hwy Ne
(28451-7988)
PHONE...............................910 371-1899
Mark Palmatier, *Pr*
◆ EMP: 4 EST: 1994
SQ FT: 100,000
SALES (est): 716.6K Privately Held
Web: www.menardusa.com
SIC: 3499 Drain plugs, magnetic

(G-7563)
VICTAULIC COMPANY
Also Called: Victaulic Leland Facility
2010 Enterprise Dr Ne (28451-8804)
PHONE...............................910 371-5588
Ron Hower, *Mgr*
EMP: 33
SALES (corp-wide): 574.15MM Privately
Held
Web: www.victaulic.com
SIC: 3494 3498 3432 3053 Couplings,
except pressure and soil pipe; Fabricated
pipe and fittings; Plumbing fixture fittings
and trim; Gaskets; packing and sealing
devices
PA: Victaulic Company
4901 Kesslersville Rd
Easton PA 18040
610 559-3300

(G-7564)
WALEX PRODUCTS COMPANY INC (PA)
1949 Popular St (28451-8181)
P.O. Box P.O. Box 3785 (28406-0785)
PHONE...............................910 371-2242
Bill Williams Walex, *Pr*
Bill Williams, *
William A Williams, *
Robert A Williams, *
◆ EMP: 15 EST: 1986
SQ FT: 60,000
SALES (est): 10.45MM
SALES (corp-wide): 10.45MM Privately
Held
Web: www.walex.com
SIC: 2842 2844 Polishes and sanitation
goods; Perfumes, cosmetics and other
toilet preparations

Lenoir
Caldwell County

(G-7565)
A FORBES COMPANY
Also Called: Forbes Printing
1035 Harper Ave Sw (28645-5092)
EMP: 19 EST: 1984
SALES (est): 2.25MM Privately Held
Web: www.aforbescompany.com
SIC: 2752 Offset printing

(G-7566)
ACTION SIGN COMPANY LENOIR INC
Also Called: Actionsign Group
511 Creekway Dr Nw (28645-4958)
PHONE...............................828 754-4116
Steve Harvey, *Pr*
Benny Hamby, *CEO*
EMP: 6 EST: 1978
SQ FT: 6,500

SALES (est): 217.69K Privately Held
Web: www.actionsign.com
SIC: 7312 3993 Billboard advertising;
Electric signs

(G-7567)
AIKEN DEVELOPMENT LLC
Also Called: Aikencontrols
1028 West Ave Nw (28645-5127)
PHONE...............................828 572-4040
Christopher E Aiken, *Pr*
EMP: 9 EST: 2006
SALES (est): 2.5MM Privately Held
Web: www.aikencontrols.com
SIC: 3625 7371 Control circuit relays,
industrial; Computer software development
and applications

(G-7568)
AIR SYSTEMS MFG OF LENOIR INC
2621 Hogan Dr (28645-9424)
P.O. Box 1736 (28645-1736)
PHONE...............................828 757-3500
EMP: 30 EST: 1988
SALES (est): 4.71MM Privately Held
Web: www.airsystemsmfglenoir.com
SIC: 3564 Dust or fume collecting
equipment, industrial

(G-7569)
ALAN WALSH LOGGING LLC
Also Called: Alan Walsh Logging
2687 Nc Highway 268 (28645-6544)
PHONE...............................828 234-7500
EMP: 6 EST: 1980
SALES (est): 233.64K Privately Held
SIC: 2411 Logging camps and contractors

(G-7570)
ALBION MEDICAL HOLDINGS INC (DH)
Also Called: Stallergenes Greer
639 Nuway Cir (28645)
P.O. Box 800 (28645)
PHONE...............................800 378-3906
EMP: 10 EST: 1999
SALES (est): 30.69MM Privately Held
Web: www.stallergenesgreer.com
SIC: 2836 8734 2834 Vaccines; Testing
laboratories; Pharmaceutical preparations
HQ: Stallergenes Greer Ltd
30 Old Bailey
London EC4M
203 910-7600

(G-7571)
AMERICAN & EFIRD LLC
619 Connelly Springs Rd Sw (28645-6331)
PHONE...............................828 754-9066
Morris Dellinger, *Mgr*
EMP: 17
SALES (corp-wide): 1.98B Privately Held
Web: www.amefird.com
SIC: 2281 2284 Yarn spinning mills; Thread
mills
HQ: American & Efird Llc
24 American St
Mount Holly NC 28120
704 827-4311

(G-7572)
ANNAS MACHINE SHOP INC
1751 Main St Nw (28645-3955)
PHONE...............................828 754-4184
Mark Annas, *Pr*
EMP: 5 EST: 1961
SQ FT: 500
SALES (est): 232.22K Privately Held
SIC: 3599 Machine shop, jobbing and repair

(G-7573)
ARIA DESIGNS LLC
800 Hickory Blvd Sw (28645-5858)
PHONE...............................828 572-4303
Jeffrey Arditti, *CEO*
▲ EMP: 14 EST: 2011
SALES (est): 882K Privately Held
Web: www.ariadesigns.us
SIC: 7389 5712 2512 Design services;
Furniture stores; Chairs: upholstered on
wood frames

(G-7574)
AUTOMATED LUMBER HANDLING INC
723 Virginia St Sw (28645-6172)
P.O. Box 796 (28645-0796)
PHONE...............................828 754-4662
William Dugger, *Pr*
Teresa Dugger, *VP*
Tracy Richardson, *Engg Mgr*
Wayne Parton, *Mfg Mgr*
Rose Younce, *Sec*
EMP: 5 EST: 1988
SALES (est): 1.81MM Privately Held
SIC: 3553 3535 Woodworking machinery;
Conveyors and conveying equipment

(G-7575)
B & E WOODTURNING INC
2395 Howard Arnett Rd (28645-7012)
P.O. Box 469 (28645-0469)
PHONE...............................828 758-2843
James Greer, *Pr*
Sandra Poarch, *VP*
Lewis F Bentley, *Sec*
EMP: 4 EST: 1969
SQ FT: 23,200
SALES (est): 329.54K Privately Held
Web: www.bandewoodturning.com
SIC: 2426 Turnings, furniture: wood

(G-7576)
BAREWOODWORKING INC
4400 Fox Rd (28645-7557)
PHONE...............................828 758-0694
Ron Bare, *Pr*
EMP: 13 EST: 2011
SALES (est): 411.97K Privately Held
Web: www.barewoodworking.com
SIC: 2431 Millwork

(G-7577)
BEARD HOSIERY CO
652 Nuway Cir (28645-3646)
P.O. Box 2369 (28645-2369)
PHONE...............................828 758-1942
David W Beard, *Pr*
Joyce Beard, *
EMP: 52 EST: 1954
SQ FT: 10,000
SALES (est): 636.71K Privately Held
SIC: 2252 Socks

(G-7578)
BEMIS MANUFACTURING COMPANY
Bemis Contract Group
201 Industrial Ct (28645-8174)
PHONE...............................828 754-1086
Jim Chapman, *Mgr*
EMP: 200
SALES (corp-wide): 636.83K Privately
Held
Web: www.bemismfg.com
SIC: 0782 3083 Landscape contractors;
Laminated plastics plate and sheet
PA: Bemis Manufacturing Company Inc
300 Mill St
Sheboygan Falls WI 53085
920 467-4621

(G-7579)
BERNHARDT FURNITURE COMPANY
Also Called: Bernhardt Design Plant 3
1502 Morganton Blvd Sw (28645-5561)
P.O. Box 740 (28645-0740)
PHONE..............................828 759-6245
Enno Roellgen, *Manager*
EMP: 56
SALES (corp-wide): 252.62MM **Privately Held**
Web: www.bernhardtdesign.com
SIC: 2521 2522 Wood office furniture; Office furniture, except wood
HQ: Bernhardt Furniture Company
1839 Morganton Blvd Sw
Lenoir NC 28645
828 758-9811

(G-7580)
BERNHARDT FURNITURE COMPANY
Also Called: Bfc Plant 2
1828 Morganton Blvd Sw (28645-5337)
P.O. Box 740 (28645-0740)
PHONE..............................828 759-6652
Chris Tanner, *Manager*
EMP: 56
SALES (corp-wide): 252.62MM **Privately Held**
Web: www.bernhardt.com
SIC: 2511 2512 Wood household furniture; Upholstered household furniture
HQ: Bernhardt Furniture Company
1839 Morganton Blvd Sw
Lenoir NC 28645
828 758-9811

(G-7581)
BERNHARDT FURNITURE COMPANY
Also Called: Plant 6
1840 Morganton Blvd Sw (28645-5337)
P.O. Box 740 (28645-0740)
PHONE..............................828 758-9811
Gary Shuffler, *Manager*
EMP: 56
SALES (corp-wide): 252.62MM **Privately Held**
Web: www.bernhardt.com
SIC: 2511 2521 2512 Wood household furniture; Wood office furniture; Upholstered household furniture
HQ: Bernhardt Furniture Company
1839 Morganton Blvd Sw
Lenoir NC 28645
828 758-9811

(G-7582)
BERNHARDT FURNITURE COMPANY (HQ)
1839 Morganton Blvd Sw (28645)
P.O. Box 740 (28645)
PHONE..............................828 758-9811
Alex Bernhardt Junior, *Pr*
Rountree Collett, *COO*
John E Cahill, *CFO*
William Burton Collett, *COO*
◆ EMP: 200 EST: 1889
SQ FT: 55,000
SALES (est): 252.62MM
SALES (corp-wide): 252.62MM **Privately Held**
Web: www.bernhardt.com
SIC: 2511 2512 2521 2522 Dining room furniture: wood; Couches, sofas, and davenports: upholstered on wood frames; Desks, office: wood; Chairs, office: padded or plain: except wood
PA: Bernhardt Industries, Inc.
1839 Morganton Blvd Sw
Lenoir NC 28645
828 758-9811

(G-7583)
BERNHARDT FURNITURE COMPANY
Also Called: Bfc Plant 5a
1814 Morganton Blvd Sw (28645-5337)
PHONE..............................828 572-4664
Debbie Robbins, *Brnch Mgr*
EMP: 56
SALES (corp-wide): 252.62MM **Privately Held**
Web: www.bernhardt.com
SIC: 2512 Upholstered household furniture
HQ: Bernhardt Furniture Company
1839 Morganton Blvd Sw
Lenoir NC 28645
828 758-9811

(G-7584)
BERNHARDT FURNITURE COMPANY
Also Called: Bernhardt Design Plant 7
1402 Morganton Blvd Sw (28645-5508)
P.O. Box 740 (28645-0740)
PHONE..............................828 759-6205
G Alex Bernhardt Junior, *CEO*
EMP: 37
SALES (corp-wide): 252.62MM **Privately Held**
Web: www.bernhardt.com
SIC: 5712 2511 2521 2512 Furniture stores; Wood household furniture; Wood office furniture; Upholstered household furniture
HQ: Bernhardt Furniture Company
1839 Morganton Blvd Sw
Lenoir NC 28645
828 758-9811

(G-7585)
BERNHARDT INDUSTRIES INC (PA)
Also Called: Bernhardt Furniture Company
1839 Morganton Blvd Sw (28645-5338)
P.O. Box 740 (28645-0740)
PHONE..............................828 758-9811
Alex Bernhardt Junior, *Pr*
William B Collett, *
Harland Dick, *
J Rountree Collett Junior, *COO*
Peter W Craymer, *
◆ EMP: 146 EST: 1927
SALES (est): 252.62MM
SALES (corp-wide): 252.62MM **Privately Held**
Web: www.bernhardtdesign.com
SIC: 2511 2521 2512 2522 Wood household furniture; Wood office furniture; Upholstered household furniture; Office furniture, except wood

(G-7586)
BIOGENIV INC
640 Nuway Cir (28645-3646)
PHONE..............................828 850-1007
EMP: 8 EST: 2018
SALES (est): 323.16K **Privately Held**
SIC: 3841 Surgical and medical instruments

(G-7587)
BIONUTRA LIFE SCIENCES LLC
2464 Norwood St Sw (28645-8924)
PHONE..............................828 572-2838
Meena Tummuru, *Pr*
Ranga Namburi, *Techl Dir*
EMP: 4 EST: 2022
SALES (est): 227.69K **Privately Held**
SIC: 2023 Dietary supplements, dairy and non-dairy based

(G-7588)
BLUE RDGE ELC MMBERS FNDTION I
Also Called: BLUE RIDGE ELECTRIC MEMBERS FOUNDATION, INC.
219 Nuway Cir (28645-3644)

PHONE..............................828 754-9071
Kenneth Greene, *Brnch Mgr*
EMP: 93
SALES (corp-wide): 161.96MM **Privately Held**
Web: www.blueridgeenergy.com
SIC: 3272 Fireplaces, concrete
PA: Blue Ridge Energy Members Foundation
1216 Blowing Rock Blvd Ne
Lenoir NC 28645
828 758-2383

(G-7589)
BRUEX INC
312 Lutz St Sw (28645-5328)
P.O. Box 1623 (28645-1623)
PHONE..............................828 754-1186
Keith Johnston, *Pr*
Bruce Johnston Junior, *Pr*
EMP: 22 EST: 1993
SQ FT: 12,500
SALES (est): 2.39MM **Privately Held**
Web: www.bruexinc.net
SIC: 2426 Furniture stock and parts, hardwood

(G-7590)
CAROLINA PRIME PET INC
Also Called: Carolina Prime
2040 Morganton Blvd Sw (28645-4971)
P.O. Box P.O. Box 635 (28906-0635)
PHONE..............................888 370-2360
Van H Brown, *Pr*
▲ EMP: 45 EST: 1997
SQ FT: 260,000
SALES (est): 14.97MM **Privately Held**
Web: www.carolinaprimepet.com
SIC: 2047 Dog food

(G-7591)
CAROLINA YOGURT INC
Also Called: TCBY
208 Morganton Blvd Sw (28645-5219)
PHONE..............................828 754-9685
Melanie Cromer, *Mgr*
EMP: 7
SALES (corp-wide): 397.84K **Privately Held**
Web: www.tcby.com
SIC: 5812 2026 Frozen yogurt stand; Fluid milk
PA: Carolina Yogurt Inc
2170 E 116th St
Carmel IN
317 844-2885

(G-7592)
CCO HOLDINGS LLC
1048 Harper Ave Nw (28645-5085)
PHONE..............................828 394-0635
EMP: 168
SALES (corp-wide): 55.09MM **Publicly Held**
SIC: 4841 3663 3651 Cable television services; Radio and t.v. communications equipment; Household audio and video equipment
HQ: Cco Holdings, Llc
400 Atlantic St
Stamford CT 06901
203 905-7801

(G-7593)
CHASE CORPORATION
2012 Hickory Blvd Sw (28645-6406)
PHONE..............................828 726-6023
EMP: 11
Web: www.chasecorp.com
SIC: 3644 Insulators and insulation materials, electrical

HQ: Chase Corporation
375 University Ave
Westwood MA 02090
781 332-0700

(G-7594)
CITY MACHINE COMPANY INC
723 Virginia St Sw (28645-6172)
P.O. Box 723 (28645-0723)
PHONE..............................828 754-9661
Larry Setzer Senior, *Pr*
Mitchell Setzer Senior, *VP*
EMP: 25 EST: 1958
SQ FT: 40,000
SALES (est): 2.19MM **Privately Held**
Web: www.machtechsol.com
SIC: 3599 3441 Machine shop, jobbing and repair; Fabricated structural metal

(G-7595)
COMPAGNIE PARENTO INC
340 Industrial Ct (28645-8100)
PHONE..............................828 758-2525
Roger T Kiley, *Pr*
Joyce Kiley, *VP*
EMP: 5 EST: 1920
SALES (est): 151.02K **Privately Held**
Web: www.compagnieparento.com
SIC: 2869 Perfume materials, synthetic

(G-7596)
CONSTRUCTION ATTACHMENTS INC
Also Called: Construction Attachments
1160 Cal Ct (28645)
PHONE..............................828 758-2674
Charles Corriher Junior, *Pr*
Michelle Clark, *
▲ EMP: 75 EST: 1976
SQ FT: 47,000
SALES (est): 7.69MM **Privately Held**
Web: www.constructionattachmentsinc.com
SIC: 3531 Construction machinery

(G-7597)
CUSTOM VENEERS INC
1790 Cedar Dr (28645-9144)
P.O. Box 986 (28645)
PHONE..............................828 758-7001
David S Martin, *Prin*
Mac Martin, *Pr*
David Martin, *VP*
EMP: 4 EST: 1964
SALES (est): 240.9K **Privately Held**
Web: www.customveneers.us
SIC: 2435 Veneer stock, hardwood

(G-7598)
CUT ABOVE CONSTRUCTION
3815 Charles White Ln (28645-7535)
PHONE..............................828 758-8557
Charles White, *Owner*
EMP: 4 EST: 1994
SALES (est): 170K **Privately Held**
SIC: 2434 Wood kitchen cabinets

(G-7599)
D R KINCAID CHAIR CO INC
3122 Sheely Rd (28645-9778)
P.O. Box 925 (28645-0925)
PHONE..............................828 754-0255
▲ EMP: 45 EST: 1983
SALES (est): 3.61MM **Privately Held**
Web: www.drkincaidchair.com
SIC: 2512 Chairs: upholstered on wood frames

▲ = Import ▼ = Export
◆ = Import/Export

(G-7600)
DISTINCTIVE FURNITURE INC (PA)
1750 Taylorsville Rd Se (28645-8330)
PHONE.............................828 754-3947
Edward Andrews, *Pr*
Phyllis Andrews, *Sec*
EMP: 5 **EST:** 1995
SALES (est): 110.97K **Privately Held**
SIC: 2512 5712 7389 5949 Upholstered
household furniture; Furniture stores;
Design, commercial and industrial; Fabric
stores piece goods

(G-7601)
DREXEL HERITAGE FURNISHINGS
825 Visionary St (28645-8365)
PHONE.............................828 391-6400
Robert Curby, *Maint Supr*
EMP: 5 **EST:** 2018
SALES (est): 96.09K **Privately Held**
SIC: 2511 Wood household furniture

(G-7602)
EONCOAT LLC
1333 Virginia St Sw (28645-8177)
PHONE.............................941 928-9401
Tony Collins, *CEO*
EMP: 5
SALES (corp-wide): 4.97MM **Privately Held**
Web: www.eoncoat.com
SIC: 2899 Chemical preparations, nec
PA: Eoncoat, Llc
3337 Air Park Rd Ste 6
Fuquay Varina NC 27526
941 928-9401

(G-7603)
EXELA DRUG SUBSTANCE LLC
1245 Blowing Rock Blvd (28645-3618)
PHONE.............................828 758-5474
Phanesh Koneru, *Admn*
EMP: 7 **EST:** 2016
SALES (est): 288.34K **Privately Held**
Web: www.exelapharma.com
SIC: 2834 Pharmaceutical preparations

(G-7604)
EXELA PHARMA SCIENCES LLC (PA)
1245 Blowing Rock Blvd (28645-3618)
P.O. Box 818 (28645-0818)
PHONE.............................828 758-5474
Phanesh Koneru, *CEO*
Jonathon Sterling, *Prin*
EMP: 21 **EST:** 2008
SALES (est): 49.8MM **Privately Held**
Web: www.exelapharma.com
SIC: 2834 Pharmaceutical preparations

(G-7605)
FAIRFIELD CHAIR COMPANY
606 Kincaid Cir (28645-9429)
PHONE.............................828 785-5571
EMP: 40
SALES (corp-wide): 16.38MM **Privately Held**
Web: www.fairfieldchair.com
SIC: 2512 2511 Chairs: upholstered on wood
frames; Wood household furniture
PA: Fairfield Chair Company
1331 Harper Ave Sw
Lenoir NC 28645
828 758-5571

(G-7606)
FAIRFIELD CHAIR COMPANY (PA)
1331 Harper Ave Sw (28645-5098)
P.O. Box 1710 (28645-1710)
PHONE.............................828 758-5571

J Harper Beall, *Ch*
J Harper Beall Iii, *CEO*
Dick Posey, *
Larry E Hollar, *
Alvin W Daughtridge, *TRAFFIC Customer
Service*
◆ **EMP:** 129 **EST:** 1921
SQ FT: 500,000
SALES (est): 16.38MM
SALES (corp-wide): 16.38MM **Privately Held**
Web: www.fairfieldchair.com
SIC: 2512 2511 Chairs: upholstered on wood
frames; Wood household furniture

(G-7607)
FLEETGENIUS OF NC INC
1808 Norwood St Sw (28645-6431)
PHONE.............................828 726-3001
Andreas Y Gruson, *Pr*
▼ **EMP:** 131 **EST:** 1981
SQ FT: 55,000
SALES (est): 27.43MM
SALES (corp-wide): 95.38MM **Privately Held**
Web: www.fleetgenius.com
SIC: 3443 3411 Dumpsters, garbage; Metal
cans
PA: Fleetgenius, Llc
2525 Tarpon Rd
Naples FL 34102
714 912-8353

(G-7608)
GRAND MANOR FURNITURE INC
929 Harrisburg Dr Sw (28645-6126)
P.O. Box 1286 (28645)
PHONE.............................828 758-5521
William R Johnson, *CEO*
EMP: 100 **EST:** 1963
SQ FT: 70,000
SALES (est): 8.34MM **Privately Held**
Web: www.grandmanorfurniture.com
SIC: 2512 Chairs: upholstered on wood
frames
HQ: Lacquer Craft Hospitality, Inc.
2575 Penny Rd
High Point NC 27265

(G-7609)
GREER LABORATORIES INC
Hwy 90 (28645)
P.O. Box 800 (28645-0800)
PHONE.............................828 758-2388
EMP: 28
Web: www.stagrallergy.com
SIC: 2836 8731 8734 Vaccines; Commercial
physical research; Testing laboratories
HQ: Greer Laboratories, Inc.
639 Nuway Circle Ne
Lenoir NC 28645
828 754-5327

(G-7610)
GREER LABORATORIES INC (DH)
Also Called: Stallergenes Greer
639 Nuway Cir (28645)
P.O. Box 800 (28645)
PHONE.............................828 754-5327
Rick Russell, *Pr*
Robert E Esch, *
Anthony Palombo, *
William White Junior, *Dir*
Terrance C Coyne, *Chief Medical Officer*
▲ **EMP:** 186 **EST:** 1946
SQ FT: 150,000
SALES (est): 29.91MM **Privately Held**
Web: www.stagrallergy.com
SIC: 2836 8734 2834 Vaccines; Testing
laboratories; Pharmaceutical preparations
HQ: Albion Medical Holdings Inc

639 Nuway Cir Ne
Lenoir NC 28645
800 378-3906

(G-7611)
H PARSONS INCORPORATED
100 Parsons Park Dr (28645-8844)
PHONE.............................828 757-9191
Harold V Parsons, *Pr*
EMP: 15 **EST:** 1986
SQ FT: 90,000
SALES (est): 4.9MM **Privately Held**
SIC: 2421 2448 Sawmills and planing mills,
general; Pallets, wood

(G-7612)
H&H METAL FAB
3050 Mcmillan Pl (28645-7615)
PHONE.............................828 757-3747
Shawn Haigler, *Owner*
EMP: 4 **EST:** 1997
SALES (est): 347.76K **Privately Held**
SIC: 3999 Parasols and frames: handles,
parts, and trimmings

(G-7613)
HAMBY BROTHERS CONCRETE INC
2051 Morganton Blvd Sw (28645-4970)
P.O. Box 844 (28645-0844)
PHONE.............................828 754-2176
Randall Hamby, *Pr*
EMP: 19 **EST:** 1979
SQ FT: 1,000
SALES (est): 2.09MM **Privately Held**
SIC: 3273 Ready-mixed concrete

(G-7614)
HICKORY SPRINGS MFG CO
Also Called: Hickory Springs Mfg Rubbr
2145 Norwood St Sw (28645-8921)
PHONE.............................828 728-9274
John Paul Eisenhower, *Mgr*
EMP: 61
SALES (corp-wide): 430.3MM **Privately Held**
Web: www.hsmsolutions.com
SIC: 3069 Foam rubber
PA: Hickory Springs Manufacturing
Company
235 2nd Ave Nw
Hickory NC 28601
828 328-2201

(G-7615)
HOLDERS RESTAURANT FURNITURE
2310 Morganton Blvd Sw (28645-4972)
P.O. Box 1198 (28638-1198)
PHONE.............................828 754-8383
Robert Holder, *Pr*
EMP: 6 **EST:** 1990
SQ FT: 500
SALES (est): 498.22K **Privately Held**
Web:
www.holdersrestaurantfurniture.com
SIC: 2599 Carts, restaurant equipment

(G-7616)
I G P
1477 Connelly Springs Rd (28645-7824)
PHONE.............................828 728-5338
Craig Osborne, *Owner*
EMP: 6 **EST:** 1982
SQ FT: 12,500
SALES (est): 472.45K **Privately Held**
Web: www.igptools.com
SIC: 3545 Diamond cutting tools for turning,
boring, burnishing, etc.

(G-7617)
JBS USA LLC
Also Called: Jbs Case Ready
1450 Homegrown Ct (28645-8175)
PHONE.............................828 725-7000
▲ **EMP:** 35 **EST:** 2020
SALES (est): 17.51MM **Privately Held**
Web: www.jbsfoodsgroup.com
SIC: 2011 Meat packing plants

(G-7618)
LEGACY VULCAN LLC
2008 Wilkesboro Blvd (28645-4646)
P.O. Box 1796 (28645-1796)
PHONE.............................828 754-5348
John Peck, *Brnch Mgr*
EMP: 4
Web: www.vulcanmaterials.com
SIC: 3273 Ready-mixed concrete
HQ: Legacy Vulcan, Llc
1200 Urban Center Dr
Birmingham AL 35242
205 298-3000

(G-7619)
LENOIR CONCRETE CNSTR CO
562 Abington Rd (28645-3993)
PHONE.............................828 759-0449
Marie Sanders, *Owner*
EMP: 8 **EST:** 1961
SALES (est): 122.77K **Privately Held**
Web: www.kerrsconcrete.com
SIC: 3273 Ready-mixed concrete

(G-7620)
LENOIR MIRROR COMPANY
401 Kincaid St (28645-9476)
P.O. Box 1650 (28645-1650)
PHONE.............................828 728-3271
A G Jonas Junior, *Ch Bd*
Drew Mayberry, *
Myron L Moore Junior, *Treas*
Linda T Jonas, *
Joyce Bumgarner, *
▲ **EMP:** 155 **EST:** 1929
SQ FT: 260,000
SALES (est): 23.24MM **Privately Held**
Web: www.lenoirmirror.com
SIC: 3231 Mirrored glass

(G-7621)
LENOIR PRINTING INC
Also Called: Lenoir Printing Solutions
401 Harper Ave Sw (28645-5068)
P.O. Box 739 (28645-0739)
PHONE.............................828 758-7260
Robert P Booth Junior, *Pr*
Glenda Booth, *VP*
Jean Booth, *Prin*
EMP: 5 **EST:** 1987
SQ FT: 4,000
SALES (est): 355.33K **Privately Held**
Web: www.printdirtcheap.com
SIC: 2752 Offset printing

(G-7622)
M & S WAREHOUSE INC (PA)
Also Called: M & S Manufacturing
1712 Hickory Blvd Sw (28645-6446)
P.O. Box 929 (28638-0929)
PHONE.............................828 728-3733
David Miller, *Pr*
Jane Miller, *VP*
Angie Coffey, *Sec*
◆ **EMP:** 20 **EST:** 1992
SQ FT: 5,000
SALES (est): 2.39MM **Privately Held**
SIC: 2426 7389 5712 Furniture stock and
parts, hardwood; Furniture finishing;
Furniture stores

GEOGRAPHIC

(G-7623)
MARLIN COMPANY INC
1211 Underdown Ave Sw (28645-5552)
PHONE.....................828 758-9999
Marty Waters, *Brnch Mgr*
EMP: 5
Web: www.marlinchemical.net
SIC: 2891 2841 Glue; Soap and other
　detergents
HQ: Marlin Company, Inc.
　1333 Virginia St Sw
　Lenoir NC 28645

(G-7624)
MARLIN COMPANY INC (HQ)
1333 Virginia St Sw (28645-8177)
P.O. Box 639 (28645-0639)
PHONE.....................828 754-0980
Marty Waters, *Pr*
◆ EMP: 23 EST: 1992
SALES (est): 9.1MM Privately Held
Web: www.marlinchemical.net
SIC: 2891 2841 Glue; Soap and other
　detergents
PA: Brenntag Se
　Messeallee 11
　Essen NW 45131

(G-7625)
MARTIN MARIETTA MATERIALS INC
Also Called: Martin Marietta Aggregates
1325 Bradford Mountain Rd (28645-8117)
PHONE.....................828 754-3077
Linwood Hanrick, *Mgr*
EMP: 10
Web: www.martinmarietta.com
SIC: 1422 Crushed and broken limestone
PA: Martin Marietta Materials Inc
　4123 Parklake Ave
　Raleigh NC 27612

(G-7626)
MC GEES CRATING INC
1640 Wilkesboro Blvd (28645-8283)
P.O. Box 1588 (28645-1588)
PHONE.....................828 758-4660
Tommy L Mc Gee, *Pr*
Diane Davis, *
EMP: 30 EST: 1969
SQ FT: 32,000
SALES (est): 2.28MM Privately Held
SIC: 2441 2426 2448 Shipping cases, wood:
　nailed or lock corner; Furniture stock and
　parts, hardwood; Pallets, wood

(G-7627)
MR TIRE INC
1306 Morganton Blvd Sw (28645-5506)
PHONE.....................828 758-0047
Clayton Brant, *Brnch Mgr*
EMP: 5
SQ FT: 4,028
SALES (corp-wide): 1.28B Publicly Held
Web: locations.mrtire.com
SIC: 7549 7534 5014 7538 Automotive
　maintenance services; Tire recapping; Tires
　and tubes; General automotive repair shops
HQ: Mr. Tire Inc.
　2078 New York Ave Unit 2
　Huntington Station NY 11746
　631 499-3700

(G-7628)
MURPHY USA INC
Also Called: Murphy USA
915 Blowing Rock Blvd (28645-3711)
PHONE.....................828 758-7055
EMP: 30
Web: www.murphyusa.com
SIC: 5541 2911 Filling stations, gasoline;
　Petroleum refining

PA: Murphy Usa Inc.
　200 Peach St
　El Dorado AR 71730

(G-7629)
NEPTCO INCORPORATED
Also Called: Neptco
2012 Hickory Blvd Sw (28645-6406)
P.O. Box 1766 (28645-1766)
PHONE.....................828 728-5951
Mark Kenroberts, *Mgr*
EMP: 243
Web: www.chasecorp.com
SIC: 2672 3357 Tape, pressure sensitive:
　made from purchased materials;
　Nonferrous wiredrawing and insulating
HQ: Neptco Incorporated
　295 University Ave
　Westwood MA 02090
　401 722-5500

(G-7630)
NPS HOLDINGS LLC
Blue Ridge Tissue
1427 Yadkin River Rd (28645-9041)
PHONE.....................828 757-7501
Jim Brown, *Pr*
EMP: 40
SALES (corp-wide): 22.35MM Privately
Held
Web: www.npsholdings.com
SIC: 2679 Paper products, converted, nec
PA: Nps Holdings Llc
　3303 Spirit Way
　Green Bay WI 54304
　920 983-9223

(G-7631)
NUTEX CONCEPTS NC CORP
2424 Norwood St Sw (28645-8924)
P.O. Box 3359 (28645-3359)
PHONE.....................828 726-8801
Arnold D Moore Iii, *Pr*
◆ EMP: 25 EST: 2001
SQ FT: 35,000
SALES (est): 9.43MM Privately Held
Web: www.nutexconcepts.com
SIC: 2297 Nonwoven fabrics

(G-7632)
PACTIV LLC
303 Advantage Ct (28645-8379)
PHONE.....................828 758-7580
Mike Crump, *Brnch Mgr*
EMP: 12
Web: www.pactivevergreen.com
SIC: 3086 5113 Packaging and shipping
　materials, foamed plastics; Industrial and
　personal service paper
HQ: Pactiv Llc
　1900 W Field Ct
　Lake Forest IL 60045
　847 482-2000

(G-7633)
PARSONS METAL FABRICATORS INC
265 Wildwood Rd (28645-8280)
P.O. Box 310 (28645-0310)
PHONE.....................828 758-7521
Kevin Parsons, *Pr*
Douglas Parsons, *VP*
Mark Parsons, *Asst VP*
Jill Parsons, *Sec*
EMP: 10 EST: 1981
SQ FT: 6,000
SALES (est): 303.45K Privately Held
SIC: 3441 Fabricated structural metal

(G-7634)
PMG ACQUISITION CORP
Also Called: PMG Acquisitions Group Div
123 Pennton Ave Nw (28645-4313)
P.O. Box 1110 (28645-1110)
PHONE.....................828 758-7381
Deborah Murray, *Brnch Mgr*
EMP: 74
SALES (corp-wide): 147.64MM Privately
Held
Web: www.newstopicnews.com
SIC: 2711 2752 Newspapers: publishing
　only, not printed on site; Commercial
　printing, lithographic
HQ: Pmg Acquisition Corp.
　201 S 4th St
　Paducah KY 42003

(G-7635)
POLYCHEM ALLOY INC
Also Called: PCA
240 Polychem Ct (28645-8688)
PHONE.....................828 754-7570
Chakra V Gupta, *CEO*
Heather Justice, *
▲ EMP: 35 EST: 1989
SQ FT: 5,000
SALES (est): 3.85MM Privately Held
Web: www.polychemalloy.com
SIC: 2821 Plastics materials and resins

(G-7636)
PRE FLIGHT INC
1035 Harper Ave Sw (28645-5092)
P.O. Box 2430 (28645-2430)
PHONE.....................828 758-1138
Esley S Forbes, *Pr*
EMP: 5 EST: 1994
SALES (est): 69.83K Privately Held
SIC: 2796 2759 Platemaking services;
　Ready prints

(G-7637)
ROLLING UMBRELLAS INC
1932 Valway Rd (28645-3988)
PHONE.....................828 754-4200
EMP: 6 EST: 2015
SALES (est): 267.82K Privately Held
Web: www.rollingumbrellas.com
SIC: 3999 Manufacturing industries, nec

(G-7638)
**SANDERS ELECTRIC MOTOR SVC
INC**
Also Called: Sanders Electric Motor Svc
285 Wildwood Rd (28645-8280)
PHONE.....................828 754-0513
Roger Sanders, *Pr*
Mike Sanders, *
Fred M Sanders, *
EMP: 26 EST: 1985
SQ FT: 13,000
SALES (est): 15.19MM Privately Held
Web: www.sanderselectricmotors.com
SIC: 5063 5999 7694 Motors, electric;
　Motors, electric; Electric motor repair

(G-7639)
SEALED AIR CORPORATION
2075 Valway Rd (28645-3969)
P.O. Box 1018 (28645-1018)
PHONE.....................828 726-2100
Roger Jackson, *Mgr*
EMP: 100
SALES (corp-wide): 5.39B Publicly Held
Web: www.sealedair.com
SIC: 3086 Packaging and shipping
　materials, foamed plastics
PA: Sealed Air Corporation
　2415 Cascade Pointe Blvd
　Charlotte NC 28208

980 221-3235

(G-7640)
STRUCTURAL MATERIALS INC
802 Old North Rd Nw (28645-3916)
P.O. Box 598 (28645-0598)
PHONE.....................828 754-6413
E J Temple Junior, *Pr*
EMP: 6 EST: 1991
SQ FT: 8,000
SALES (est): 2.46MM Privately Held
Web: www.structuralmaterialsinc.com
SIC: 5085 3312 Industrial supplies;
　Structural shapes and pilings, steel

(G-7641)
TEIJIN AUTOMOTIVE TECH INC
2424 Norwood St Sw Unit 300
(28645-8924)
PHONE.....................828 757-8313
David Stearman, *Opers Mgr*
EMP: 5
SQ FT: 90,000
Web: www.teijinautomotive.com
SIC: 3089 Injection molding of plastics
HQ: Teijin Automotive Technologies, Inc.
　255 Rex Blvd
　Auburn Hills MI 48326
　248 237-7800

(G-7642)
TEIJIN AUTOMOTIVE TECH INC
601 Hibriten Dr Sw (28645-6389)
P.O. Box 820 (28645-0820)
PHONE.....................828 754-8441
John Eller, *Mgr*
EMP: 107
Web: www.teijinautomotive.com
SIC: 3714 Motor vehicle parts and
　accessories
HQ: Teijin Automotive Technologies, Inc.
　255 Rex Blvd
　Auburn Hills MI 48326
　248 237-7800

(G-7643)
VERDANTE BIOENERGY SVCS LLC
Also Called: Verdante
628 Harper Ave Nw # D (28645-5056)
PHONE.....................828 394-1246
G David Waechter, *CEO*
EMP: 5 EST: 2014
SALES (est): 209.12K Privately Held
Web: www.grainit.net
SIC: 7379 7372 8731 Computer related
　consulting services; Business oriented
　computer software; Natural resource
　research

(G-7644)
W G CANNON PAINT CO INC (PA)
Also Called: Cannon Paint and Abbraisives
1015 Zacks Fork Rd (28645-8306)
P.O. Box 1976 (28645-1976)
PHONE.....................828 754-5376
Greg Pilkenton, *Pr*
Stephen Pilkenton, *Pr*
Charlie Pilkenton, *VP*
Jeff Pilkenton, *VP*
Pamela Pilkenton, *Sec*
EMP: 5 EST: 1946
SQ FT: 12,000
SALES (est): 683.91K
SALES (corp-wide): 683.91K Privately
Held
Web: www.cannonpaint.com
SIC: 5231 3291 Paint and painting supplies;
　Abrasive buffs, bricks, cloth, paper, stones,
　etc.

▲ = Import ▼ = Export
◆ = Import/Export

(G-7645)
WATSON CONCRETE PIPE COMPANY
2532 Morganton Blvd Sw (28645-9692)
PHONE.....................828 754-6476
Thomas Ray Hoover, *Pr*
Elizabeth Davis, *Sec*
Monica T Hoover, *VP*
EMP: 6 EST: 1949
SQ FT: 4,700
SALES (est): 348.18K **Privately Held**
Web: www.watsonconcrete.com
SIC: 3272 Pipe, concrete or lined with
concrete

(G-7646)
WOODSMITHS COMPANY
Also Called: Woodsmiths
418 Prospect St Nw (28645-5017)
P.O. Box 1318 (28645-1318)
PHONE.....................406 626-3102
Michael Munoz, *Pr*
EMP: 8 EST: 1977
SQ FT: 350,000
SALES (est): 561.29K **Privately Held**
Web: www.woodsmiths.com
SIC: 2599 2521 3281 2511 Cabinets, factory
; Cabinets, office: wood; Table tops, marble;
Wood household furniture

Lewiston Woodville
Bertie County

(G-7647)
PERDUE FARMS INC
Also Called: PERDUE FARMS INC.
3539 Governors Rd (27849-9241)
P.O. Box 460 (27849-0460)
PHONE.....................252 348-4200
Ron Flagg, *Prin*
EMP: 515
SALES (corp-wide): 1.24B **Privately Held**
Web: www.perdue.com
SIC: 2015 Chicken, processed, nsk
PA: Perdue Farms Incorporated
31149 Old Ocean City Rd
Salisbury MD 21804
800 473-7383

(G-7648)
VALLEY PROTEINS
3539 Governors Rd (27849-9241)
P.O. Box 10 (27849-0010)
PHONE.....................252 348-4200
EMP: 10 EST: 2012
SALES (est): 938.25K **Privately Held**
Web: www.darpro-solutions.com
SIC: 2077 Animal and marine fats and oils

Lewisville
Forsyth County

(G-7649)
AD RUNNER MBL OUTDOOR ADVG INC
2555 Williams Rd (27023-8298)
PHONE.....................336 945-1190
Zebulon Williams, *Owner*
EMP: 8 EST: 2005
SALES (est): 310.16K **Privately Held**
Web: www.adrunnertrucks.com
SIC: 3993 Signs and advertising specialties

(G-7650)
FIBER COMPANY
8863 Belhaven Ct (27023-7740)
PHONE.....................336 725-5277

EMP: 6 EST: 1985
SALES (est): 352.85K **Privately Held**
Web: fibercompany.blogspot.com
SIC: 2221 7336 Specialty broadwoven
fabrics, including twisted weaves; Art
design services

(G-7651)
GRYPHON HOUSE INC
Also Called: Robins Lane Press
1310 Lewisville Clemmons Rd
(27023-9635)
P.O. Box 10 (27023-0010)
PHONE.....................800 638-0928
Matthew Marceron, *Pr*
▲ **EMP: 12 EST:** 1969
SQ FT: 43,000
SALES (est): 440.93K **Privately Held**
Web: www.gryphonhouse.com
SIC: 2731 5192 Textbooks: publishing only,
not printed on site; Books

(G-7652)
MEDALONI CELLARS LLC
470 Yadkin Valley Trl (27023-8733)
P.O. Box 4486 (27404)
PHONE.....................305 509-2004
Joey Medaloni, *Owner*
EMP: 6 EST: 2019
SALES (est): 534.98K **Privately Held**
Web: www.medalonicellars.com
SIC: 2084 Wines

(G-7653)
SIGN A RAMA INC
Also Called: Sign-A-Rama
5054 Styers Ferry Rd (27023-9634)
PHONE.....................336 893-8042
John Barnes, *Genl Mgr*
EMP: 4
Web: www.signarama.com
SIC: 3993 Signs and advertising specialties
HQ: Sign A Rama Inc.
2121 Vista Pkwy
West Palm Beach FL 33411
561 640-5570

Lexington
Davidson County

(G-7654)
A-1 FACE INC
480 Dixon St Ste C (27292-7594)
PHONE.....................336 248-5555
Loyd Leonard, *Pr*
Leonard Loyd, *Pr*
EMP: 4 EST: 1988
SQ FT: 50,000
SALES (est): 473.09K **Privately Held**
SIC: 2435 2436 2499 Veneer stock,
hardwood; Veneer stock, softwood; Veneer
work, inlaid

(G-7655)
AMERICAN ATTACHMENTS INC
702 N Silver St (27292-6192)
PHONE.....................336 859-2002
EMP: 6 EST: 2018
SALES (est): 202.13K **Privately Held**
Web: www.americanattachments.com
SIC: 3531 Construction machinery

(G-7656)
ARNEG LLC
Also Called: Arneg USA
750 Old Hargrave Rd (27295-7514)
PHONE.....................336 956-5300
Louis Moschetta, *Managing Member*
◆ **EMP: 70 EST:** 1988

SQ FT: 66,000
SALES (est): 14MM **Privately Held**
Web: www.arnegusa.com
SIC: 3585 Refrigeration equipment, complete
HQ: Arneg Spa
Via Venezia 58
Campo San Martino PD 35010
049 969-9333

(G-7657)
ASCO POWER TECHNOLOGIES LP
325 Welcome Center Blvd (27295-9018)
PHONE.....................336 731-5000
Bob Kinross, *Brnch Mgr*
EMP: 11
SALES (corp-wide): 1.09K **Privately Held**
Web: www.ascopower.com
SIC: 3699 Electrical equipment and supplies,
nec
HQ: Asco Power Technologies, L.P.
160 Park Ave
Florham Park NJ 07932

(G-7658)
BARNHARTS TECH TIRE REPAIR INC
278 Rocky Trail Rd (27292-8200)
PHONE.....................336 337-1569
Kathlyn Pletcher, *Prin*
EMP: 4 EST: 2008
SALES (est): 213.49K **Privately Held**
SIC: 5531 7538 7534 7539 Automotive tires;
General automotive repair shops; Tire
retreading and repair shops; Automotive
repair shops, nec

(G-7659)
BLACK CONCRETE INC
705 Cotton Grove Rd (27292-3823)
P.O. Box 664 (27293-0664)
PHONE.....................336 243-1388
TOLL FREE: 800
Jerry B Black, *Prin*
EMP: 9 EST: 1973
SQ FT: 2,500
SALES (est): 834.82K **Privately Held**
Web: www.blackconcreteinc.com
SIC: 3273 Ready-mixed concrete

(G-7660)
BORDER CONCEPTS INC
115 Lexington Pkwy (27295-8524)
PHONE.....................336 248-2419
Neal Miller, *Pr*
EMP: 4
Web: www.borderconcepts.com
SIC: 3317 3469 3441 Steel pipe and tubes;
Metal stampings, nec; Fabricated structural
metal
PA: Border Concepts, Inc.
15720 Brixham Hill Ave
Charlotte NC 28277

(G-7661)
CARTER MILLWORK INC
Also Called: Flex Tram
117 Cedar Lane Dr (27292-5709)
P.O. Box 189 (27299-0189)
PHONE.....................800 861-0734
Greg Carter, *Pr*
Alan Carter, *
Lisa Carter, *
EMP: 60 EST: 1996
SQ FT: 28,000
SALES (est): 9.76MM **Privately Held**
Web: www.carterflex.com
SIC: 2431 Moldings, wood: unfinished and
prefinished

(G-7662)
CEPRINT SOLUTIONS INC
Also Called: Carolina Envelope
564 Dixon St (27292-7516)
P.O. Box 1229 (27293-1229)
PHONE.....................336 956-6327
Tony S Townsend, *CEO*
Tony S Townsend Junior, *CEO*
Carolyn Townsend, *
Michelle T O'bryant, *Ex VP*
Jill Koontz, *
EMP: 28 EST: 1979
SQ FT: 60,000
SALES (est): 1.83MM **Privately Held**
Web: www.ceprint.com
SIC: 2752 Offset printing

(G-7663)
CHILDRESS VINEYARDS LLC
1000 Childress Vinyard Rd (27295-2061)
P.O. Box 847 (27293-0847)
PHONE.....................336 236-9463
▲ **EMP: 20 EST:** 2002
SALES (est): 3.36MM **Privately Held**
Web: www.childressvineyards.com
SIC: 2084 Wines

(G-7664)
CHILDRESS WINERY LLC
9160 Hampton Rd (27295-9785)
P.O. Box 847 (27293-0847)
PHONE.....................336 775-0522
▲ **EMP: 7 EST:** 2002
SALES (est): 519.14K **Privately Held**
Web: www.childressvineyards.com
SIC: 2084 Wines

(G-7665)
CIDER BROS LLC
Also Called: Bull City Ciderworks
599 S Railroad St (27292-3318)
PHONE.....................919 943-9692
John Clowney, *Mgr*
EMP: 13 EST: 2015
SQ FT: 2,000
SALES (est): 2.77MM **Privately Held**
Web: www.bullcityciderworks.com
SIC: 2084 Wines, brandy, and brandy spirits

(G-7666)
CITY OF LEXINGTON
Also Called: Lexington Gas Dept, City of
425 Carolina Ave (27292-4325)
PHONE.....................336 248-3945
John Everhart, *Mgr*
EMP: 20
Web: www.lexingtonnc.gov
SIC: 1311 Natural gas production
PA: City Of Lexington
28 W Center St
Lexington NC 27292
336 243-2489

(G-7667)
COL-EVE METAL PRODUCTS CO
702 Bryant Rd (27292-8117)
P.O. Box 2067 (27361-2067)
PHONE.....................336 472-7039
Tammy Carrick, *Pr*
EMP: 5 EST: 1963
SQ FT: 8,000
SALES (est): 897.52K **Privately Held**
Web: www.coleve.com
SIC: 3469 Stamping metal for the trade

(G-7668)
COMER SANITARY SERVICE INC
Also Called: Comer Trucking
3039 Greensboro Street Ext (27295-4806)
P.O. Box 1083 (27293-1083)

GEOGRAPHIC

PHONE.................................336 629-8311
Charlie Comer, *Prin*
EMP: 4 **EST:** 1968
SQ FT: 1,092
SALES (est): 268.05K **Privately Held**
Web: www.comersanitary.com
SIC: 7359 4214 3431 4212 Portable toilet rental; Local trucking with storage; Metal sanitary ware; Dump truck haulage

(G-7669)
CPM ACQUISITION CORP
Also Called: TSA Griddle System
121 Proctor Ln (27292-7630)
PHONE.................................972 243-8070
Ted Waitman, *Pr*
EMP: 10
SALES (corp-wide): 227.38MM **Privately Held**
Web: www.cpmroskamp.com
SIC: 3634 Griddles or grills, electric: household
HQ: Cpm Acquisition Corp.
2975 Airline Circle
Waterloo IA 50703
319 232-8444

(G-7670)
CPM WOLVERINE PROCTOR LLC
121 Proctor Ln (27292-7630)
PHONE.................................336 479-2983
David Scrauss, *Mgr*
EMP: 10
SALES (corp-wide): 227.38MM **Privately Held**
Web: www.wolverineproctor.com
SIC: 3542 Mechanical (pneumatic or hydraulic) metal forming machines
HQ: Cpm Wolverine Proctor, Llc
251 Gibraltar Rd
Horsham PA 19044

(G-7671)
CPM WOLVERINE PROCTOR LLC
Also Called: Wolverine Proctor
121 Proctor Ln (27292-7630)
PHONE.................................336 248-5181
Ryan Dietzenbach, *Mgr*
EMP: 100
SALES (corp-wide): 227.38MM **Privately Held**
Web: www.wolverineproctor.com
SIC: 3542 Mechanical (pneumatic or hydraulic) metal forming machines
HQ: Cpm Wolverine Proctor, Llc
251 Gibraltar Rd
Horsham PA 19044

(G-7672)
CSI ARMORING INC
425 Industrial Dr (27295-7542)
PHONE.................................336 313-8561
Usman Bashir, *Pr*
▼ **EMP:** 8 **EST:** 2004
SQ FT: 20,000
SALES (est): 1.26MM **Privately Held**
Web: www.csiarmoring.com
SIC: 3711 Automobile bodies, passenger car, not including engine, etc.

(G-7673)
CUNNINGHAM BRICK COMPANY
Also Called: Scenic Scape
701 N Main St (27292-2692)
P.O. Box 2063 (27293-2063)
PHONE.................................336 248-8541
TOLL FREE: 800
EMP: 134
Web: cunninghambrik.openfos.com
SIC: 3251 Brick and structural clay tile

(G-7674)
CURVED PLYWOOD INC
111 E 7th Ave (27292-3861)
P.O. Box 1092 (27293-1092)
PHONE.................................336 249-6901
Thomas S Payne, *Pr*
EMP: 4 **EST:** 1978
SALES (est): 74.8K **Privately Held**
SIC: 2426 Furniture stock and parts, hardwood

(G-7675)
DAVIDSON PRINTING INC
Also Called: Davidsonspeed Printing
223 S Main St Ste D (27292-3352)
P.O. Box 1534 (27293-1534)
PHONE.................................336 357-0555
Ron Hutcheson, *Pr*
EMP: 5 **EST:** 1974
SALES (est): 442.53K **Privately Held**
Web: www.davidsonspeed.com
SIC: 2752 Offset printing

(G-7676)
DELIVERIGHT LOGISTICS INC
176 L F I Complex Ln (27295)
P.O. Box 20763 (10023-1488)
PHONE.................................862 279-7332
Doug Ladden, *CEO*
Ori Anavim, *
EMP: 120 **EST:** 2015
SALES (est): 14.98MM **Privately Held**
Web: www.deliveright.com
SIC: 4731 7372 Truck transportation brokers ; Application computer software

(G-7677)
DIAMONDBACK INDUSTRIES LLC
4683 Old Salisbury Rd (27295-7826)
PHONE.................................336 956-8871
EMP: 30 **EST:** 2018
SALES (est): 5.33MM **Privately Held**
Web: diamondback-industries-llc.business.site
SIC: 3441 Fabricated structural metal

(G-7678)
DIAMONDBACK PRODUCTS INC
40 W 12th Ave (27292-3126)
P.O. Box 2235 (27374-2235)
PHONE.................................336 236-9800
Eric Surratt, *CEO*
▲ **EMP:** 7 **EST:** 1998
SALES (est): 2.82MM **Privately Held**
Web: www.diamondbackproducts.com
SIC: 3714 Dump truck lifting mechanism

(G-7679)
DIRECT WOOD PRODUCTS
Also Called: DIRECT WOOD PRODUCTS
808 Grimes Blvd (27292-7640)
P.O. Box 856 (23181-0856)
PHONE.................................336 238-2516
Chris Davis, *Mgr*
EMP: 5
SALES (corp-wide): 5.34MM **Privately Held**
Web: www.dwp-inc.com
SIC: 2448 Pallets, wood
PA: Direct Wood Products, Incorporated
18501 Eltham Rd
West Point VA 23181
804 843-4642

(G-7680)
DRAFT DOT INTERNATIONAL LLC
Also Called: DOT Master
5450 N Nc Highway 150 (27295-9754)
P.O. Box 2164 (27374-2164)
PHONE.................................336 775-0525

Richard Everhart, *Pr*
Omaey Everhart, *VP*
EMP: 6 **EST:** 1972
SALES (est): 129.85K **Privately Held**
SIC: 2759 2672 Labels and seals: printing, nsk; Tape, pressure sensitive: made from purchased materials

(G-7681)
EBERT SIGN COMPANY INC
7815 N Nc Highway 150 (27295-9387)
P.O. Box 24274 (27114-4274)
PHONE.................................336 768-2867
Roger Ebert, *Pr*
EMP: 5 **EST:** 1985
SALES (est): 595.94K **Privately Held**
Web: www.ebertsigns.com
SIC: 3993 1799 Electric signs; Sign installation and maintenance

(G-7682)
ELECTRIC GLASS FIBER AMER LLC
473 New Jersey Church Rd (27292-6726)
P.O. Box 949 (27293-0949)
PHONE.................................336 357-8151
Todd Douthit, *Brnch Mgr*
EMP: 213
Web: www.neg.co.jp
SIC: 2851 Paint removers
HQ: Electric Glass Fiber America, Llc
940 Washburn Switch Rd
Shelby NC 28150
704 434-2261

(G-7683)
ELEMENT WEST LLC
266 Haywood Rd (27295-9610)
PHONE.................................336 853-6118
Erik A Ullring, *Prin*
EMP: 4 **EST:** 2015
SALES (est): 260.25K **Privately Held**
SIC: 2819 Industrial inorganic chemicals, nec

(G-7684)
ELIZABETH CARBIDE NC INC
Also Called: Elizabeth Carbide Die Co
5801 E Us Highway 64 (27292-6607)
PHONE.................................336 472-5555
Robert Miller, *Genl Mgr*
EMP: 6 **EST:** 1979
SALES (est): 2.72MM
SALES (corp-wide): 40.63MM **Privately Held**
Web: www.eliz.com
SIC: 3544 Special dies and tools
PA: Linden St. Holdings, Inc
601 Linden St
Mckeesport PA 15132
412 751-3000

(G-7685)
ESC BRANDS LLC (PA)
664 Old Hargrave Rd (27295-7504)
PHONE.................................888 331-8332
EMP: 6 **EST:** 2017
SQ FT: 25,000
SALES (est): 1.7MM
SALES (corp-wide): 1.7MM **Privately Held**
Web: www.escbrands.com
SIC: 2834 Antiseptics, medicinal

(G-7686)
EXEMPLAR LABORATORIES LLC ✪
405 E Center St (27292-4109)
PHONE.................................336 817-6794
Maegan Chriscoe, *Pr*
EMP: 5 **EST:** 2024
SALES (est): 298.68K **Privately Held**
SIC: 2834 Pharmaceutical preparations

(G-7687)
FLETCHER MACHINE INDS INC
4305 E Us Highway 64 (27292-8041)
P.O. Box 2096 (27293-2096)
PHONE.................................336 249-6101
Ray Fletcher, *Pr*
Bryan Eunlip, *General Vice President**
Carolyn Smith, *
EMP: 52 **EST:** 2014
SQ FT: 104,000
SALES (est): 4.43MM **Privately Held**
Web: www.fletcher-machine.com
SIC: 3553 Woodworking machinery

(G-7688)
FOSTER TIRE SALES INC
1609 S Main St (27292-2843)
P.O. Box 823 (27293-0823)
PHONE.................................336 248-6726
Joe A Foster Junior, *Pr*
EMP: 4 **EST:** 1961
SQ FT: 6,000
SALES (est): 424.91K **Privately Held**
SIC: 7534 5531 Tire recapping; Automotive tires

(G-7689)
FRANKS MILLWRIGHT SERVICES
1207 Ashland Dr (27295-2631)
PHONE.................................336 248-6692
Joe Frank, *Owner*
EMP: 4 **EST:** 1965
SALES (est): 134.9K **Privately Held**
SIC: 7692 7389 Welding repair; Business Activities at Non-Commercial Site

(G-7690)
FRENZELIT INC
4165 Old Salisbury Rd (27295-6870)
P.O. Box 1853 (27293-1853)
PHONE.................................336 814-4317
Phil Howell, *Pr*
Wolfgang Wagner Ph.d., *Ch Bd*
Thorsten Sowa, *OF TEXTILES**
Torsten Aeugle, *OF GASKETS**
Richard Hammer, *OF EXPANSION JOINTS**
EMP: 49 **EST:** 2017
SALES (est): 11.05MM
SALES (corp-wide): 109.35MM **Privately Held**
Web: www.frenzelit.com
SIC: 3069 3357 Expansion joints, rubber; Nonferrous wiredrawing and insulating
PA: Frenzelit Gmbh
Frankenhammer 7
Bad Berneck I. Fichtelgebirge BY
95460
9273720

(G-7691)
GAINSBOROUGH BATHS LLC
Also Called: Gainsbrough Specialist Bathing
41 Rogers Rd (27292-5802)
PHONE.................................336 357-0797
Gordon T Farmiloe, *Managing Member*
Daniel Mills, *General Vice President**
Cynthia Byrd, *
▲ **EMP:** 10 **EST:** 2011
SQ FT: 45,000
SALES (est): 2.58MM **Privately Held**
SIC: 3088 1799 Tubs (bath, shower, and laundry), plastics; Fiberglass work

(G-7692)
GB LABS LLC
794 American Way (27295-1156)
PHONE.................................919 606-7253
Dave Obrien, *Managing Member*
Robert Lewis, *Managing Member*
EMP: 4 **EST:** 2019

SALES (est): 316.16K **Privately Held**
Web: www.gblabs.com
SIC: 3565 Bottling machinery: filling,
  capping, labeling

(G-7693)
**GOOSE AND MONKEY BREWHOUSE
LLC**
Also Called: Goose and The Monkey
Brewhouse
401 S Railroad St (27292-3337)
PHONE................................336 239-0206
Ashlee Moore, *CEO*
Ashlee Moore, *Pr*
Brent Moore, *Pr*
EMP: 17 **EST:** 2019
SALES (est): 1.19MM **Privately Held**
Web:
www.gooseandthemonkeybrewhouse.com
SIC: 2082 Ale (alcoholic beverage)

(G-7694)
H & V PROCESSING INC
251 Primrose Drive Ext (27292-0607)
P.O. Box 1172 (27293-1172)
PHONE................................336 224-2985
James Harris, *Pr*
Bernice Volpe, *VP*
Hildur Harris, *Sec*
▲ **EMP:** 5 **EST:** 1997
SQ FT: 20,900
SALES (est): 372.37K **Privately Held**
Web: www.hvprocessing.com
SIC: 2621 Paper mills

(G-7695)
H HORSESHOE
194 Sandy Creek Ln (27295-0358)
PHONE................................336 853-5913
Albert Bruce Hinson, *Admn*
EMP: 7 **EST:** 2010
SALES (est): 53.37K **Privately Held**
SIC: 3462 Horseshoes

(G-7696)
**HARVEST HOMES AND HANDI
HOUSES (PA)**
2100 S Main St (27292-3624)
PHONE................................336 243-2382
Elizabeth Bunce, *Pr*
Dearl L Bunce Ii, *VP*
EMP: 8 **EST:** 1986
SQ FT: 960
SALES (est): 2.27MM
SALES (corp-wide): 2.27MM **Privately
Held**
Web: www.buncebuildings.com
SIC: 3448 Buildings, portable: prefabricated
  metal

(G-7697)
**HEDRICK BROTHERS LUMBER CO
INC**
6736 Nc Highway 47 (27292-7764)
PHONE................................336 746-5885
Terry Hedrick, *Pr*
Charles Ricky Hedrick, *Sec*
Danny Lee Hedrick, *VP*
William D Hedrick, *Stockholder*
EMP: 17 **EST:** 1920
SQ FT: 4,000
SALES (est): 552.57K **Privately Held**
SIC: 2421 Sawmills and planing mills,
  general

(G-7698)
HIGH POINT PRECAST PDTS INC
4130 W Us Highway 64 (27295-7763)
PHONE................................336 434-1815
James Shoaf, *Pr*

Carlton Shoaf, *VP*
EMP: 6 **EST:** 1997
SALES (est): 2.39MM **Privately Held**
Web: www.hpprecast.com
SIC: 3272 5074 Precast terrazzo or concrete
  products; Plumbing fittings and supplies

(G-7699)
HITCH CRAFTERS LLC
853 Cid Rd (27292-6184)
PHONE................................336 859-3257
Jason Hughes, *Managing Member*
EMP: 7 **EST:** 2005
SALES (est): 1.27MM **Privately Held**
Web: www.hitchcrafter.com
SIC: 3714 Acceleration equipment, motor
  vehicle

(G-7700)
J E JONES LUMBER COMPANY
Also Called: Carolina Dry Kiln
7255 E Us Highway 64 (27292-7603)
PHONE................................336 472-3478
Jim Leonard, *Brnch Mgr*
EMP: 25
SQ FT: 95,262
SALES (corp-wide): 1.72MM **Privately
Held**
SIC: 5031 2421 Lumber, plywood, and
  millwork; Sawmills and planing mills,
  general
PA: J. E. Jones Lumber Company
  1301 Kimberly Rd
  New Bern NC 28562
  252 638-5717

(G-7701)
JEWEL MASTERS INC (PA)
Also Called: Ellis Jewelers
221 W Us Highway 64 (27295-2567)
PHONE................................336 243-2711
Leonard M Defelice, *Pr*
▲ **EMP:** 17 **EST:** 1951
SQ FT: 4,500
SALES (est): 2.32MM
SALES (corp-wide): 2.32MM **Privately
Held**
Web: www.ellisjewelers.com
SIC: 5944 3915 Jewelry, precious stones
  and precious metals; Jewelers' materials
  and lapidary work

(G-7702)
JOHNSON CONCRETE COMPANY
Also Called: Piedmont Block
514 Burgin Dr (27292-2740)
PHONE................................336 248-2918
David Bates, *Mgr*
EMP: 33
SALES (corp-wide): 24.88MM **Privately
Held**
Web: www.johnsonproductsusa.com
SIC: 3271 Blocks, concrete or cinder:
  standard
PA: Johnson Concrete Company
  217 Klumac Rd
  Salisbury NC 28144
  704 636-5231

(G-7703)
K12 COMPUTERS
1203 Winston Rd (27295-1754)
PHONE................................336 754-6111
Coty Burke, *Managing Member*
EMP: 9 **EST:** 2022
SALES (est): 1.42MM **Privately Held**
Web: www.k12computers.us
SIC: 3571 Electronic computers

(G-7704)
KAUFMAN TRAILERS INC
702 N Silver St (27292-6192)
PHONE................................336 790-6800
Robb Kaufman, *Pr*
Tim Carter, *
▼ **EMP:** 30 **EST:** 1986
SALES (est): 5.34MM **Privately Held**
Web: www.kaufmantrailers.com
SIC: 5599 5084 3799 3537 Utility trailers;
  Trailers, industrial; Trailers and trailer
  equipment; Industrial trucks and tractors

(G-7705)
KEPLEY-FRANK HARDWOOD CO INC
Also Called: Kfh
975 Conrad Hill Mine Rd (27292-7090)
PHONE................................336 746-5419
Jim Kepley, *Pr*
J Herbert Frank Junior, *VP*
EMP: 50 **EST:** 1959
SQ FT: 10,000
SALES (est): 9.58MM **Privately Held**
Web: www.kepleyfrank.us
SIC: 2421 Sawmills and planing mills,
  general

(G-7706)
KURZ TRANSFER PRODUCTS LP
4939 N Nc Highway 150 (27295-9749)
PHONE................................336 764-4128
Richard Tilley, *Mgr*
EMP: 80
SQ FT: 37,118
SALES (corp-wide): 1B **Privately Held**
Web: www.kurzusa.com
SIC: 3497 Metal foil and leaf
HQ: Kurz Transfer Products, Lp
  11836 Patterson Rd
  Huntersville NC 28078
  704 927-3700

(G-7707)
LACY J MILLER MACHINE
7987 Old Us Highway 52 (27295-7333)
PHONE................................336 764-0518
Lacy Miller, *Prin*
EMP: 5 **EST:** 2005
SALES (est): 497.04K **Privately Held**
SIC: 3599 Machine shop, jobbing and repair

(G-7708)
LAKE CITY ELECTRIC MOTOR REPR
Also Called: Lexington Electric Motor Repr
915 S Talbert Blvd (27292-3937)
PHONE................................336 248-2377
Joe Frye, *Pr*
EMP: 4 **EST:** 2010
SALES (est): 370.74K **Privately Held**
Web: www.lexingtonelectric.net
SIC: 7694 Electric motor repair

(G-7709)
LEGGETT & PLATT INCORPORATED
161 Proctor Ln (27292-7630)
P.O. Box 668 (27293-0668)
PHONE................................855 853-3539
EMP: 4
SALES (corp-wide): 5.15B **Publicly Held**
Web: www.leggett.com
SIC: 2515 Mattresses and bedsprings
PA: Leggett & Platt, Incorporated
  1 Leggett Rd
  Carthage MO 64836
  417 358-8131

(G-7710)
LIBERTY SIGN AND LIGHTING LLC
375 Ridge Rd (27295-9184)
P.O. Box 2152 (27293-2152)

PHONE................................336 703-7465
Zach Wishon, *Prin*
EMP: 4 **EST:** 2018
SALES (est): 731.21K **Privately Held**
Web: www.libertysignllc.com
SIC: 3993 Signs and advertising specialties

(G-7711)
LINDEN ST HOLDINGS INC
Elizabeth Carbide NC
5801 E Us Highway 64 (27292-6607)
PHONE................................336 472-5555
Robert B Miller, *Brnch Mgr*
EMP: 12
SALES (corp-wide): 40.63MM **Privately
Held**
Web: www.eliz.com
SIC: 3544 Special dies, tools, jigs, and
  fixtures
PA: Linden St. Holdings, Inc
  601 Linden St
  Mckeesport PA 15132
  412 751-3000

(G-7712)
LINWOOD INC
3979 Old Linwood Rd (27292-7528)
P.O. Box 5129 (27113-5129)
PHONE................................336 300-8307
Jimmy Kepley, *Pr*
▼ **EMP:** 6 **EST:** 2005
SQ FT: 47,611
SALES (est): 179.58K **Privately Held**
Web: www.linwoodbc.com
SIC: 2511 Wood household furniture

(G-7713)
LJM MACHINE CO INC
7987 Old Us Highway 52 (27295-7333)
PHONE................................336 764-0518
James T Donley, *Owner*
Craig Donley, *
Nancy Donley, *
Jeff Lookabill, *
EMP: 4 **EST:** 1967
SQ FT: 51,000
SALES (est): 476.58K **Privately Held**
Web: www.ljmmachineco.com
SIC: 3599 Machine shop, jobbing and repair

(G-7714)
M AND M DOCKS LLC
10235 Nc Highway 8 (27292-6495)
PHONE................................336 537-0092
EMP: 10 **EST:** 2021
SALES (est): 432.31K **Privately Held**
Web: www.mandmdocks.com
SIC: 1389 Construction, repair, and
  dismantling services

(G-7715)
MASTERBRAND CABINETS INC
632 Dixon St (27292-7558)
PHONE................................765 491-2385
EMP: 30 **EST:** 2015
SALES (est): 5.53MM **Privately Held**
Web: www.masterbrand.com
SIC: 2434 Wood kitchen cabinets

(G-7716)
MASTERWRAP INC
969 American Way (27295)
P.O. Box 1219 (27374-1219)
PHONE................................336 243-4515
Richard Goff, *Pr*
▲ **EMP:** 50 **EST:** 1994
SQ FT: 63,000
SALES (est): 2.5MM **Privately Held**
Web: www.masterwrap.com
SIC: 2431 Millwork

(G-7717)
MATCOR MTAL FBRCTION WLCOME IN
835 Salem Rd (27295-1086)
PHONE..................................336 731-5700
Arthur Artuso, *Pr*
Frank Lucus, *
Rod Harrison, *
Manfred Kretschmer, *
Galliano Tiberini, *
▲ **EMP:** 140 **EST:** 2009
SALES (est): 24.37MM **Privately Held**
Web: www.matcormetalfab.com
SIC: 3541 Machine tools, metal cutting type

(G-7718)
MEDCOR INC
550 Scout Rd (27292-5215)
PHONE..................................888 579-1050
Mike Adkins, *Pr*
EMP: 7 **EST:** 1996
SALES (est): 482.08K **Privately Held**
SIC: 5047 3841 Hospital equipment and
supplies, nec; Surgical and medical
instruments

(G-7719)
MYERS TOOL AND MACHINE CO INC
156 Dixon St (27292-7565)
P.O. Box 219 (27299-0219)
PHONE..................................336 956-1324
H Donald Myers, *Pr*
Eric Myers, *
Judy Myers, *
EMP: 70 **EST:** 1982
SQ FT: 66,000
SALES (est): 5.26MM **Privately Held**
Web: www.myerstoolandmachine.com
SIC: 3599 Machine shop, jobbing and repair

(G-7720)
NC IMPRINTS INC
3199 E Holly Grove Rd (27292-9631)
PHONE..................................336 790-4546
EMP: 5 **EST:** 2016
SALES (est): 116.28K **Privately Held**
SIC: 2752 Commercial printing, lithographic

(G-7721)
NC MOULDING ACQUISITION LLC
Also Called: North Carolina Moulding Co
808 Martin Luther King Jr Blvd
(27292-3793)
PHONE..................................336 249-7309
Kevin Mallory, *Managing Member*
EMP: 11 **EST:** 2018
SALES (est): 2.04MM **Privately Held**
SIC: 2499 Picture frame molding, finished

(G-7722)
NIPPON ELECTRIC GLASS CO LTD
Also Called: Lexington Plant Nippon Elc GL
473 New Jersey Church Rd (27292-6726)
PHONE..................................336 357-8151
Motoharu Matsumoto, *Pr*
EMP: 6
Web: www.neg-us.com
SIC: 3229 Glassware, industrial
PA: Nippon Electric Glass Co., Ltd.
2-7-1, Seiran
Otsu SGA 520-0

(G-7723)
NORTH AMERICAN IMPLEMENTS
12608 E Old Us Highway 64 (27292-7324)
P.O. Box 2840 (27361-2840)
PHONE..................................336 476-2904
Eric Garner, *Pr*
EMP: 45 **EST:** 2014
SALES (est): 2.39MM **Privately Held**

Web:
www.northamericanimplements.com
SIC: 3537 Trucks, tractors, loaders, carriers,
and similar equipment

(G-7724)
NORTH STATE MACHINE INC
1775 Tyro Rd (27295-7804)
PHONE..................................336 956-1441
David Wayne Smith, *Pr*
Kim Smith, *Sec*
EMP: 12 **EST:** 1985
SALES (est): 1.87MM **Privately Held**
Web: www.northstatemachine.com
SIC: 3599 Machine shop, jobbing and repair

(G-7725)
NUCOR CORPORATION
Also Called: Nucor Steel Lexington
6776 E Us Highway 64 (27292-7600)
PHONE..................................336 481-7924
Mike Hess, *Genl Mgr*
EMP: 101
SALES (corp-wide): 30.73B **Publicly Held**
Web: www.nucor.com
SIC: 3312 3441 3448 Blast furnaces and
steel mills; Fabricated structural metal;
Prefabricated metal buildings and
components
PA: Nucor Corporation
1915 Rexford Rd
Charlotte NC 28211
704 366-7000

(G-7726)
NUTRA-PHARMA MFG CORP NC
130 Lexington Pkwy (27295-8524)
PHONE..................................631 846-2500
Oscar Ramjeet, *Pr*
Joseph Kramer, *CFO*
EMP: 60 **EST:** 2014
SALES (est): 4.52MM **Privately Held**
SIC: 2834 Pharmaceutical preparations

(G-7727)
NUTRACEUTICAL LF SCIENCES INC
Also Called: Nls
130 Lexington Pkwy (27295-8524)
PHONE..................................336 956-0800
EMP: 109 **EST:** 2007
SALES (est): 840.55K
SALES (corp-wide): 150.04B **Publicly Held**
SIC: 2834 Tablets, pharmaceutical
HQ: Vitacost.Com Inc.
4700 Exchange Ct Ste 200
Boca Raton FL 33431

(G-7728)
PALLET RESOURCE OF NC INC
4572 N Nc Highway 150 (27295-9745)
PHONE..................................336 731-8338
TOLL FREE: 800
Forrest M Grimes, *Pr*
Laura Grimes, *
EMP: 95 **EST:** 1970
SQ FT: 45,000
SALES (est): 4.42MM **Privately Held**
Web: www.prnc.com
SIC: 2448 Pallets, wood

(G-7729)
PARKDALE MILLS INCORPORATED
Also Called: Parkdale Plants 3 & 4
100 Mill St (27295-1624)
PHONE..................................336 243-2141
Dan Thompson, *Brnch Mgr*
EMP: 50
SALES (corp-wide): 1.44B **Privately Held**
Web: www.parkdalemills.com

SIC: 2281 Polyester yarn, spun: made from
purchased staple
HQ: Parkdale Mills, Incorporated
531 Cotton Blossom Cir
Gastonia NC 28054
704 874-5000

(G-7730)
PHASE II CREATIONS INC
109 E 7th Ave (27292-3861)
PHONE..................................336 249-0673
John Adkins, *Prin*
EMP: 6 **EST:** 1987
SALES (est): 330.97K **Privately Held**
SIC: 2821 Acrylic resins

(G-7731)
PIEDMONT CANDY COMPANY
305 E Us Highway 64 (27292-4274)
PHONE..................................336 248-2477
EMP: 18
SALES (corp-wide): 10.27MM **Privately
Held**
Web: www.redbirdcandies.com
SIC: 2064 Candy and other confectionery
products
PA: Piedmont Candy Company
404 Market St
Lexington NC 27292
336 248-2477

(G-7732)
PIEDMONT CANDY COMPANY (PA)
404 Market St (27292-1293)
P.O. Box 1722 (27293-1722)
PHONE..................................336 248-2477
Mark Stephens, *CEO*
Chris Reid, *Pr*
J Douglas Reid, *Pr*
Heath Cagle, *VP*
Mary Cox, *VP*
▲ **EMP:** 58 **EST:** 1890
SQ FT: 38,000
SALES (est): 10.27MM
SALES (corp-wide): 10.27MM **Privately
Held**
Web: www.redbirdcandies.com
SIC: 2064 Lollipops and other hard candy

(G-7733)
PMB INDUSTRIES INC
632 Dixon St (27292-7558)
PHONE..................................336 453-3121
Diane Mcbride, *CFO*
EMP: 5 **EST:** 2013
SALES (est): 404.29K **Privately Held**
SIC: 3999 Barber and beauty shop
equipment

(G-7734)
PRINTCRAFT COMPANY INC
259 City Lake Rd (27295-8437)
P.O. Box 1558 (28151-1558)
PHONE..................................336 248-2544
Boyce J Hanna, *Pr*
EMP: 60 **EST:** 1953
SALES (est): 9.59MM **Privately Held**
Web: www.printcraftcompany.com
SIC: 2759 Tags: printing, nsk

(G-7735)
RIVERWOOD INC
Also Called: Riverwood Casual
632 Dixon St (27292-7558)
PHONE..................................336 956-3034
EMP: 20
SIC: 2519 Garden furniture, except wood,
metal, stone, or concrete

(G-7736)
RP FLETCHER MACHINE CO INC
4305 E Us Highway 64 (27292-8041)
PHONE..................................336 249-6101
Richard Piselli, *Pr*
▲ **EMP:** 85 **EST:** 1962
SQ FT: 125,000
SALES (est): 2.3MM **Privately Held**
Web: www.fletcher-machine.com
SIC: 3553 3545 3069 3544 Woodworking
machinery; Diamond cutting tools for
turning, boring, burnishing, etc.; Molded
rubber products; Special dies, tools, jigs,
and fixtures

(G-7737)
SAUERS & COMPANY INC
Also Called: Sauers & Co Processed Veneers
363 Dixon St (27292-7574)
PHONE..................................336 956-1200
Laurence C Sauers, *Pr*
Laurence C Sauers Junior, *VP*
Jeffrey A Sauers, *VP*
▲ **EMP:** 10 **EST:** 1999
SQ FT: 15,000
SALES (est): 2.59MM **Privately Held**
Web: www.sveneers.com
SIC: 5031 2435 Veneer; Veneer stock,
hardwood

(G-7738)
SCHUTZ CONTAINER SYSTEMS INC
138 Walser Rd (27295-1338)
PHONE..................................336 249-6816
Ian Miller, *Brnch Mgr*
EMP: 52
SALES (corp-wide): 3.08B **Privately Held**
Web: www.schuetz-packaging.net
SIC: 2653 5199 Corrugated and solid fiber
boxes; Packaging materials
HQ: Schutz Container Systems, Inc.
200 Aspen Hill Rd
Branchburg NJ 08876

(G-7739)
SCOOTATRAILERTM
1370 Payne Rd (27295-9027)
PHONE..................................336 671-0444
Gregory W Tesh, *Prin*
EMP: 4 **EST:** 2008
SALES (est): 980.63K **Privately Held**
Web: www.scootatrailer.com
SIC: 3537 Forklift trucks

(G-7740)
SHOAF PRECAST SEPTIC TANK INC
Also Called: Shoaf Precasting
4130 W Us Highway 64 (27295-7763)
PHONE..................................336 787-5826
Jimmy Shoaf, *Pr*
James Shoaf, *Pr*
Dennis Shoaf, *VP*
EMP: 9 **EST:** 1966
SQ FT: 20,000
SALES (est): 2.81MM **Privately Held**
Web: www.shoafprecast.com
SIC: 3272 Concrete products, precast, nec

(G-7741)
SIGNWORKS NORTH CAROLINA INC
373 Marco Blvd (27295-7563)
P.O. Box 1090 (27299-1090)
PHONE..................................336 956-7446
Jeff Cooper, *Pr*
Janet Cooper, *Sec*
Corey Cooper, *VP*
EMP: 7 **EST:** 1991
SQ FT: 5,200
SALES (est): 960.05K **Privately Held**
Web: www.signworksofnc.com

▲ = Import ▼ = Export
◆ = Import/Export

SIC: 3993 Letters for signs, metal

(G-7742)
SMITH COMPANIES LEXINGTON INC (PA)
720 W Center St (27292-2718)
P.O. Box 594 (27293)
PHONE...................................336 249-4941
Jerry F Smith, *Pr*
M Steve Smith, *VP*
R B Smith, *Treas*
EMP: 5 **EST:** 1978
SALES (est): 11.03MM
SALES (corp-wide): 11.03MM **Privately Held**
Web: www.gwsmithlumber.com
SIC: 5211 2431 1531 Lumber and other building materials; Millwork; Speculative builder, single-family houses

(G-7743)
SMITH MILLWORK INC
920 Robbins Cir (27292-3138)
P.O. Box T (27293-9394)
PHONE...................................800 222-8498
Keith Smith, *Pr*
Jerry F Smith, *
M Steve Smith, *
R B Smith, *Stockholder*
▲ **EMP:** 30 **EST:** 1921
SQ FT: 99,000
SALES (est): 5.33MM
SALES (corp-wide): 11.03MM **Privately Held**
Web: www.smithmillwork.com
SIC: 5031 2431 Doors and windows; Windows and window parts and trim, wood
PA: Smith Companies Of Lexington, Inc.
720 W Center St
Lexington NC 27292
336 249-4941

(G-7744)
SOUTHEASTERN INSTALLATION INC (PA)
Also Called: Sii Dry Kilns
207 Cedar Lane Dr (27292-5711)
P.O. Box I (27293-9383)
PHONE...................................704 352-7146
Dan R Mathews, *Pr*
Paula Turlington, *
EMP: 48 **EST:** 1969
SQ FT: 65,000
SALES (est): 19.07MM
SALES (corp-wide): 19.07MM **Privately Held**
Web: www.siidrykilns.com
SIC: 3559 3567 Kilns, lumber; Industrial furnaces and ovens

(G-7745)
SPECIAL FAB & MACHINE INC
Also Called: S F M
4133 Old Salisbury Rd (27295-6870)
P.O. Box 808 (27299-0808)
PHONE...................................336 956-2121
W Avalon Potts, *Pr*
Avalon Potts, *
EMP: 50 **EST:** 1993
SQ FT: 70,000
SALES (est): 10.42MM **Privately Held**
Web: www.specialfabinc.com
SIC: 3599 Machine shop, jobbing and repair

(G-7746)
STITCHERY INC
134 Elk St (27292-4028)
P.O. Box 1693 (27293-1693)
PHONE...................................336 248-5604
Todd A Klass, *Pr*
Amy S Klass, *Sec*

EMP: 5 **EST:** 1989
SQ FT: 8,500
SALES (est): 87.44K **Privately Held**
Web: www.stitcherync.com
SIC: 2395 Emblems, embroidered

(G-7747)
SUPERIOR FINISHING SYSTEMS LLC
2132 Beckner Rd (27292-8884)
PHONE...................................336 956-2000
EMP: 9 **EST:** 1995
SALES (est): 659.88K **Privately Held**
Web:
www.superiorfinishingsystems.com
SIC: 3569 3567 3444 3563 Gas producers, generators, and other gas related equipment; Paint baking and drying ovens; Booths, spray: prefabricated sheet metal; Spraying and dusting equipment

(G-7748)
TARHEEL PLASTICS LLC
2018 E Us Highway 64 (27292-8083)
EMP: 20
Web: www.tarheelplastics.com
SIC: 3089 Injection molded finished plastics products, nec

(G-7749)
THERMAL PANE INC
200 S Main St (27292-3324)
PHONE...................................336 722-9977
EMP: 5 **EST:** 2011
SALES (est): 106.64K **Privately Held**
SIC: 3724 Aircraft engines and engine parts

(G-7750)
THOMASVLLE MTAL FBRICATORS INC (PA)
200 Prospect Dr (27292-3751)
PHONE...................................336 248-4992
Scott Ten Eyck, *Pr*
EMP: 25 **EST:** 1995
SQ FT: 40,000
SALES (est): 1.71MM **Privately Held**
Web: www.tier1isp.com
SIC: 3441 3444 2542 Fabricated structural metal; Sheet metalwork; Partitions and fixtures, except wood

(G-7751)
THOMSON PLASTICS INC
2018 E Us Highway 64 (27292-8083)
PHONE...................................336 843-4255
Genu Revattaro, *Genl Mgr*
EMP: 91
Web: www.thomsonplastics.com
SIC: 3949 3089 Sporting and athletic goods, nec; Plastics containers, except foam
PA: Thomson Plastics, Inc.
130 Quality Dr Nw
Thomson GA 30824

(G-7752)
TIMELESS BEDDING INC
306 Beech Retreat Dr (27292-9195)
P.O. Box 336 (27350-0336)
PHONE...................................336 472-6603
Robert Allen, *Pr*
Betty Allen, *
Sharon Gainey, *
▼ **EMP:** 4 **EST:** 1983
SQ FT: 55,000
SALES (est): 126.93K **Privately Held**
SIC: 2515 Mattresses and bedsprings

(G-7753)
TODCO INC
1123 Roy Lopp Rd (27292-9613)
PHONE...................................336 248-2001

Todd Warfford, *Pr*
Cherie Warfford, *Sec*
EMP: 10 **EST:** 1992
SALES (est): 2.42MM **Privately Held**
Web: www.todcoinc.com
SIC: 4953 2611 Sanitary landfill operation; Pulp manufactured from waste or recycled paper

(G-7754)
TUBULAR TEXTILE MACHINERY
85 Hargrave Rd (27293)
P.O. Box 2097 (27293-2097)
PHONE...................................336 956-6444
William Milligan, *Pr*
▲ **EMP:** 4 **EST:** 1965
SALES (est): 1.01MM **Privately Held**
Web: www.hkwinc.com
SIC: 3552 Textile machinery

(G-7755)
TYSINGER HOSIERY MILL INC
1294 Old Nc Highway 109 (27292-9411)
PHONE...................................336 472-2148
Bradley Tysinger, *Pr*
E Vernon Tysinger, *VP*
Shirley Tysinger, *Sec*
EMP: 10 **EST:** 1974
SQ FT: 8,800
SALES (est): 340.71K **Privately Held**
SIC: 2252 Socks

(G-7756)
VALENDRAWERS INC
Also Called: Valendrawers
555 Dixon St Sapona Business Park (27293)
P.O. Box 1169 (27293-1169)
PHONE...................................336 956-2118
Amedeo D Valentina, *Ch Bd*
Piero Della Valentina, *
Carla Della Valentina, *
Diane Mcbride, *Sec*
Michele Cassin, *
▲ **EMP:** 50 **EST:** 1984
SQ FT: 75,000
SALES (est): 9.3MM **Privately Held**
Web: www.valenusa.com
SIC: 2426 Furniture stock and parts, hardwood

(G-7757)
WEATHERVANE WINERY INC
1452 Welcome Arcadia Rd (27295-5475)
PHONE...................................336 793-3366
Sid Proctor, *Prin*
EMP: 5 **EST:** 2010
SALES (est): 178.57K **Privately Held**
Web: www.weathervanewinery.com
SIC: 2084 Wines

(G-7758)
WRKCO INC
Also Called: Westrock
101 Lexington Pkwy (27295-8524)
PHONE...................................336 956-6000
EMP: 25
SIC: 2653 Boxes, corrugated: made from purchased materials
HQ: Wrkco Inc.
1000 Abrnthy Rd Ne Ste 12
Atlanta GA 30328
770 448-2193

Liberty
Randolph County

(G-7759)
AERO PRECISION MACHINE INC
6024 Smithwood Rd (27298-9125)
P.O. Box 216 (27283-0216)
PHONE...................................336 685-0016
Michael P Langlois, *Pr*
Mabel Langlois, *VP*
Joseph Langlois, *Rgnl Mgr*
EMP: 10 **EST:** 1992
SALES (est): 1.65MM **Privately Held**
Web: www.aeroprecisionmachine.com
SIC: 3599 Machine shop, jobbing and repair

(G-7760)
AMOR FURNITURE AND BEDDING LLC
Also Called: Amor Furniture
143 S Asheboro St (27298-7517)
P.O. Box 63 (27298-0063)
PHONE...................................336 795-0044
Spiro Laousis, *Banking Manager*
EMP: 10 **EST:** 2010
SQ FT: 10,000
SALES (est): 253.34K **Privately Held**
Web: www.amorfurniture.com
SIC: 2512 5021 Upholstered household furniture; Beds and bedding

(G-7761)
AMT/BCU INC
Also Called: American Modular Technologies
6306 Old 421 Rd (27298-8285)
P.O. Box 1069 (27298-1069)
PHONE...................................336 622-6200
EMP: 37
Web:
www.americanmodulartechnologies.com
SIC: 3441 3448 Fabricated structural metal; Prefabricated metal buildings and components

(G-7762)
CUMINS MACHINERY CORP
312 W Luther Ave (27298-8634)
PHONE...................................336 622-1000
Edward W Cumins, *Pr*
EMP: 6 **EST:** 1967
SQ FT: 12,000
SALES (est): 327.6K **Privately Held**
Web: www.cumins.com
SIC: 5084 2281 Textile machinery and equipment; Yarn spinning mills

(G-7763)
DANIELS LUMBER SALES INC
3224 Staley Store Rd (27298-9500)
PHONE...................................336 622-5486
Gene Aldridge, *Pr*
Nancy Aldridge, *VP*
EMP: 4 **EST:** 1980
SQ FT: 5,600
SALES (est): 267.61K **Privately Held**
Web: www.danielslumbersales.com
SIC: 2421 Planing mills, nec

(G-7764)
EDWARDS WOOD PRODUCTS INC
9979 Old Liberty Rd (27298-8628)
PHONE...................................704 624-5098
EMP: 62
SALES (corp-wide): 29.48MM **Privately Held**
Web: www.ewpi.com
SIC: 2421 Sawmills and planing mills, general
PA: Edwards Wood Products, Inc.

2215 Old Lawyers Rd
Marshville NC 28103
704 624-3624

(G-7765)
EDWARDS WOOD PRODUCTS INC
3231 Staley Store Rd (27298-9500)
PHONE....................336 622-7537
Don Blair, *Brnch Mgr*
EMP: 63
SQ FT: 34,116
SALES (corp-wide): 29.48MM **Privately Held**
Web: www.ewpi.com
SIC: 2421 Sawmills and planing mills, general
PA: Edwards Wood Products, Inc.
    2215 Old Lawyers Rd
    Marshville NC 28103
    704 624-3624

(G-7766)
EULISS OIL COMPANY INC
122 S Foster St (27298-9661)
P.O. Box 789 (27298-0789)
PHONE....................336 622-3055
John K Stanley Junior, *Pr*
EMP: 8 EST: 1954
SQ FT: 3,500
SALES (est): 776.78K **Privately Held**
Web: www.eulisspropane.com
SIC: 1321 5983 5172 5984 Propane (natural) production; Fuel oil dealers; Gasoline; Liquefied petroleum gas, delivered to customers' premises

(G-7767)
HOLDER BACKHOE & HAULING INC
4660 Randolph Church Rd (27298-8108)
PHONE....................336 622-7388
Christopher R Holder, *Pr*
EMP: 5 EST: 2014
SALES (est): 914.95K **Privately Held**
SIC: 3531 Backhoes

(G-7768)
INDIANA CHAIR FRAME COMPANY
Also Called: Indiana Chair Frame 3200
330 N Greensboro St (27298-2605)
PHONE....................574 825-9355
Terry Gabhart, *Pr*
David Haffner, *
▲ EMP: 5 EST: 1985
SALES (est): 534.24K
SALES (corp-wide): 5.15B **Publicly Held**
Web: www.lpworkfurniture.com
SIC: 2512 Upholstered household furniture
PA: Leggett & Platt, Incorporated
    1 Leggett Rd
    Carthage MO 64836
    417 358-8131

(G-7769)
KENNY ROBINSON S WLDG SVC INC
8975 Moody Rd (27298-8923)
PHONE....................760 213-6454
Kenny G Robinson, *Pr*
EMP: 4 EST: 1991
SALES (est): 102.64K **Privately Held**
Web: www.robinsonsinc.net
SIC: 7692 Welding repair

(G-7770)
LEGGETT & PLATT INCORPORATED
Also Called: Cincro
330 N Greensboro St (27298-2605)
PHONE....................336 622-0121
Terry Gabhart, *Brnch Mgr*
EMP: 16
SALES (corp-wide): 5.15B **Publicly Held**
Web: www.lpworkfurniture.com

SIC: 2515 Mattresses and bedsprings
PA: Leggett & Platt, Incorporated
    1 Leggett Rd
    Carthage MO 64836
    417 358-8131

(G-7771)
LIBERTY DRY KILN CORP
3246 Staley Store Rd (27298-9500)
PHONE....................336 622-5490
Doug Younts, *Pr*
Joe Younts, *Prin*
EMP: 4 EST: 1996
SALES (est): 213.35K **Privately Held**
SIC: 2421 Sawmills and planing mills, general

(G-7772)
LIBERTY LUMBER COMPANY
9979 Old Liberty Rd (27298-8628)
P.O. Box 271 (27248-0271)
PHONE....................336 622-4901
Paul James Skiver Ii, *Pr*
EMP: 16 EST: 1974
SQ FT: 62,000
SALES (est): 1.49MM **Privately Held**
Web: www.ewpi.com
SIC: 5031 2421 Lumber: rough, dressed, and finished; Sawmills and planing mills, general

(G-7773)
LIBERTY TRAILERS LLC
5806 York Martin Rd (27298-8479)
PHONE....................219 866-7141
EMP: 5 EST: 2014
SALES (est): 2.14MM **Privately Held**
Web: www.libertytrailers.com
SIC: 3715 Bus trailers, tractor type

(G-7774)
NORCRAFT COMPANIES LP
Also Called: Ultra Craft Companies
6163 Old 421 Rd (27298-8283)
PHONE....................336 622-4281
David Andrew, *Mgr*
EMP: 250
SQ FT: 217,457
SALES (corp-wide): 2.7B **Publicly Held**
Web: www.ultracraft.com
SIC: 2434 Wood kitchen cabinets
HQ: Norcraft Companies, L.P.
    1 Masterbrand Cabinets Dr
    Jasper IN 47546
    812 482-2527

(G-7775)
PALLET EXPRESS INC
6306 Old 421 Rd (27298-8285)
P.O. Box 1998 (27298-1998)
PHONE....................336 621-2266
TOLL FREE: 800
Michael Briggs, *Pr*
Lynn Bell, *
EMP: 115 EST: 1993
SQ FT: 10,000
SALES (est): 19.8MM **Privately Held**
Web: www.palletexpress.com
SIC: 2448 Pallets, wood

(G-7776)
PMA PRODUCTS INC
6120 Smithwood Rd (27298-9126)
PHONE....................800 762-0844
Charles G Causey, *Pr*
EMP: 7 EST: 2005
SALES (est): 499.82K **Privately Held**
Web: www.pmaproducts.com
SIC: 3728 Aircraft parts and equipment, nec

(G-7777)
ROBINSONS WELDING SERVICE
3465 Staley Store Rd (27298-9527)
PHONE....................336 622-3150
Kenny Robinson, *Pr*
Ronda W Robinson, *Sec*
EMP: 8 EST: 1989
SALES (est): 1.12MM **Privately Held**
Web: www.robinsonsinc.net
SIC: 7692 1542 Welding repair; Commercial and office buildings, prefabricated erection

(G-7778)
RUBBER MILL INC
Also Called: Rubber Mill
9897 Old Liberty Rd (27298-8627)
P.O. Box 1329 (27298-1329)
PHONE....................336 622-1680
▲ EMP: 20 EST: 1986
SALES (est): 6.35MM **Privately Held**
Web: www.rubbermill.com
SIC: 3069 5085 3569 3053 Molded rubber products; Rubber goods, mechanical; Filters ; Gaskets; packing and sealing devices

(G-7779)
SFP RESEARCH INC
Also Called: Gen Trak
121 W Swannanoa Ave (27298-3215)
P.O. Box 1290 (27298-1290)
PHONE....................336 622-5266
Steve Repp, *Pr*
EMP: 8 EST: 1991
SQ FT: 10,000
SALES (est): 866.86K **Privately Held**
Web: www.gentrakinc.com
SIC: 3841 Medical instruments and equipment, blood and bone work

(G-7780)
SUMMIT PEAK PENS AND WD WORKS
412 E Starmount Ave (27298-3008)
PHONE....................336 404-8312
EMP: 5 EST: 2010
SALES (est): 63.7K **Privately Held**
SIC: 2431 Millwork

(G-7781)
SUPERTEX INC
Also Called: Earthknit
312 W Luther Ave (27298-8634)
PHONE....................336 622-1000
Edward Cumins, *Pr*
Howard Cumins, *
Cheryl Severson, *
▲ EMP: 35 EST: 1982
SQ FT: 350,000
SALES (est): 2.02MM **Privately Held**
Web: www.supertex-inc.com
SIC: 2258 Lace and warp knit fabric mills

(G-7782)
TOYOTA BATTERY MFG INC
5938 Julian Airport Rd (27298)
PHONE....................469 292-6094
Sean Suggs, *Pr*
EMP: 33 EST: 2021
SALES (est): 1.11MM **Privately Held**
Web: www.toyota.com
SIC: 5531 3691 Batteries, automotive and truck; Storage batteries

(G-7783)
VISION METALS INC
Also Called: Ferree Trailer
5806 York Martin Rd (27298-8479)
P.O. Box 1169 (27298-1169)
PHONE....................336 622-7300
EMP: 5 EST: 1992

SALES (est): 415.43K **Privately Held**
SIC: 3715 3596 Truck trailers; Weighing machines and apparatus

Lilesville
Anson County

(G-7784)
COUNTY OF ANSON
Also Called: Anson County Water Treatment
567 Filtration Rd (28091-6086)
PHONE....................704 848-4849
John Turner, *Genl Mgr*
EMP: 9
Web: co.anson.nc.us
SIC: 3589 4941 Water treatment equipment, industrial; Water supply
PA: County Of Anson
    101 S Green St
    Wadesboro NC 28170
    704 994-3200

(G-7785)
HEDRICK B V GRAVEL & SAND CO
403 Gravel Plant Rd (28091)
P.O. Box 418 (28091-0418)
PHONE....................704 848-4165
Judith Johnson, *Pt*
EMP: 9 EST: 1925
SQ FT: 4,000
SALES (est): 2.37MM **Privately Held**
Web: www.hedrickind.com
SIC: 1442 Construction sand mining

(G-7786)
HORNWOOD INC (PA)
766 Haileys Ferry Rd (28091-6051)
PHONE....................704 848-4121
Charles D Horne, *Pr*
Larry W Adams, *
Kenneth W Horne Junior, *Ex VP*
Paula Tice, *
◆ EMP: 320 EST: 1945
SQ FT: 230,000
SALES (est): 46.97MM
SALES (corp-wide): 46.97MM **Privately Held**
Web: www.hornwoodinc.com
SIC: 2258 Cloth, warp knit

(G-7787)
KING CHARLES INDUSTRIES LLC
766 Haileys Ferry Rd (28091-6051)
PHONE....................704 848-4121
Charles Horne, *Prin*
EMP: 5 EST: 2016
SALES (est): 1.07MM **Privately Held**
SIC: 3999 Manufacturing industries, nec

Lillington
Harnett County

(G-7788)
ARMTEC ESTERLINE CORP
608 E Mcneill St (27546-9189)
PHONE....................910 814-3029
Lena Olving, *COO*
EMP: 18 EST: 2006
SALES (est): 5.32MM
SALES (corp-wide): 7.94B **Publicly Held**
Web: www.armtecdefense.com
SIC: 3823 Process control instruments
HQ: Esterline Technologies Corp
    1350 Euclid Ave Ste 1600
    Cleveland OH 44114
    216 706-2960

(G-7789)
BARLIN RANCH & PETS INC
390 D R Harvell Ln (27546-5512)
PHONE..................................910 814-1930
EMP: 4
SALES (est): 293.93K **Privately Held**
SIC: 3131 Quarters

(G-7790)
BRIGHT LIGHT TECHNOLOGIES LLC
2217 Keith Hills Rd (27546-7692)
PHONE..................................910 212-6869
Jessica Wynns, Pr
EMP: 5 EST: 2020
SALES (est): 151.22K **Privately Held**
Web: www.brightlighttech.net
SIC: 3648 5999 5065 Ultraviolet lamp fixtures
; Air purification equipment; Security control
equipment and systems

(G-7791)
CAPITAL MARBLE CREATIONS INC
309 W Duncan St (27546-9462)
P.O. Box 1417 (27546-1417)
PHONE..................................910 893-2462
Thomas E Wood, Pr
Bruce W Morris, Sec
EMP: 7 EST: 1972
SQ FT: 29,540
SALES (est): 999.21K **Privately Held**
Web: www.capitalmarblecreations.com
SIC: 3281 3431 Household articles, except
furniture: cut stone; Metal sanitary ware

(G-7792)
CFI READY MIX LLC
304 E Mcneill St (27546-8408)
P.O. Box 970 (27546-0970)
PHONE..................................910 814-4238
Wayne Underwood, Managing Member
EMP: 5 EST: 2007
SALES (est): 246.76K **Privately Held**
SIC: 3273 Ready-mixed concrete

(G-7793)
CHAMPION HOME BUILDERS INC
Also Called: Champion
4055 Us 401 S (27546-6829)
PHONE..................................910 893-5713
Gary Wilkinson, Mgr
EMP: 279
SALES (corp-wide): 2.02B **Publicly Held**
Web: www.championhomes.com
SIC: 1521 2451 New construction, single-
family houses; Mobile homes, except
recreational
HQ: Champion Home Builders, Inc.
755 W Big Bevr Rd Ste 100
Troy MI 48084
248 614-8200

(G-7794)
CHEMTECH NORTH CAROLINA LLC
1030 S Main St (27546-5633)
P.O. Box 58 (27546-0058)
PHONE..................................910 514-9575
EMP: 26 EST: 2008
SALES (est): 2.04MM **Privately Held**
Web: www.chemtechglobal.com
SIC: 2899 Chemical preparations, nec

(G-7795)
DONALD R YOUNG LOGGING INC
165 Buie Farm Ln (27546-6180)
PHONE..................................910 934-6769
Donald R Young, Prin
EMP: 6 EST: 2010
SALES (est): 266.45K **Privately Held**
SIC: 2411 Logging camps and contractors

(G-7796)
ESTERLINE TECHNOLOGIES CORP
Also Called: Esterline Defense Technologies
608 E Mcneill St (27546-9189)
P.O. Box 1179 (27546-1179)
PHONE..................................910 814-1222
Robert W Cremin, CEO
R Brad Lawrence, CEO
Jerry D Leitman, Ch
EMP: 5 EST: 2009
SALES (est): 1.58MM
SALES (corp-wide): 7.94B **Publicly Held**
Web: www.armtecdefense.com
SIC: 3728 Aircraft parts and equipment, nec
PA: Transdigm Group Incorporated
1350 Euclid Ave Ste 1600
Cleveland OH 44115
216 706-2960

(G-7797)
**HEIDELBERG MTLS STHAST AGG
LLC**
Sr 2016 (27546)
PHONE..................................910 893-2111
James Godwin, Mgr
EMP: 16
SALES (corp-wide): 23.02B **Privately Held**
Web: www.hansonbiz.com
SIC: 1423 Crushed and broken granite
HQ: Heidelberg Materials Southeast Agg Llc
3237 Satellite Blvd # 30
Duluth GA 30096
770 491-2756

(G-7798)
KELKEN ENTERPRISES LLC
12 Caco Dr (27546-7974)
PHONE..................................910 890-7211
Kelley Peregoy, Prin
EMP: 4 EST: 2017
SALES (est): 251.8K **Privately Held**
Web: www.kelkengolf.com
SIC: 3949 Sporting and athletic goods, nec

(G-7799)
KRIGEN PHARMACEUTICALS LLC
800 Edwards Dr (27546)
PHONE..................................919 523-7530
Dhruvkumar Patel, Prin
EMP: 6 EST: 2018
SALES (est): 426.3K **Privately Held**
Web: www.krigenpharmaceuticals.com
SIC: 2834 Pharmaceutical preparations

(G-7800)
MARLINWOODWORKS LLC
50 Otto Rd (27546-6276)
PHONE..................................919 343-2605
Doug Courtright, Prin
EMP: 4 EST: 2016
SALES (est): 480.04K **Privately Held**
SIC: 2499 Wood products, nec

(G-7801)
POINT BLANK ENTERPRISES INC
Also Called: Gould & Goodrich
709 E Mcneill St (27546-9188)
PHONE..................................910 893-2071
Scott Nelson, Brnch Mgr
EMP: 67
Web: www.gouldusa.com
SIC: 3199 2387 3172 2221 Holsters, leather;
Apparel belts; Personal leather goods, nec;
Broadwoven fabric mills, manmade
HQ: Point Blank Enterprises, Inc.
2102 Sw 2nd St
Pompano Beach FL 33069
954 630-0900

(G-7802)
SAAB BARRACUDA LLC
608 E Mcneill St (27546-9189)
PHONE..................................910 814-3088
▲ EMP: 27 EST: 2002
SQ FT: 156,000
SALES (est): 3.59MM
SALES (corp-wide): 2.78B **Privately Held**
SIC: 5511 1711 2399 Automobiles, new and
used; Heating systems repair and
maintenance; Parachutes
HQ: Saab, Inc.
20700 Loudoun County Pkwy # 100
Ashburn VA 20147
703 406-7200

(G-7803)
SORRELLS CABINET CO INC
490 Chesterfield Lake Rd (27546-8138)
PHONE..................................919 639-4320
Corbin Sorrell, Pr
Dann Sorrell, VP
Kathy Sorrell, Sec
EMP: 4 EST: 1977
SALES (est): 464.87K **Privately Held**
Web: www.sorrellscabinets.com
SIC: 2434 5211 Wood kitchen cabinets;
Lumber and other building materials

(G-7804)
TIN CANS LLC
906 S 8th St (27546-5947)
P.O. Box 208 (27546-0208)
PHONE..................................910 322-2626
Mark L Centrella, Prin
EMP: 6 EST: 2014
SALES (est): 2.27MM **Privately Held**
Web: www.calltincans.com
SIC: 3411 Tin cans

(G-7805)
ZOEYS BTQ STYLE SPCLTY TRATS
896 Shawtown Rd (27546-9080)
P.O. Box 721 (27546-0721)
PHONE..................................910 808-1778
EMP: 4 EST: 2021
SALES (est): 23K **Privately Held**
SIC: 2389 Apparel and accessories, nec

Lincolnton
Lincoln County

(G-7806)
A & D PRECAST INC
1032 N Flint St (28092-3026)
P.O. Box 1198 (28093-1198)
PHONE..................................704 735-3337
David C Gilbert, Pr
EMP: 5 EST: 2011
SALES (est): 590.5K **Privately Held**
Web: www.adprecast.com
SIC: 3272 Concrete products, precast, nec

(G-7807)
A R BYRD COMPANY INC
Also Called: A R Byrd Company
171 Joshua Ct (28092-7508)
PHONE..................................704 732-5675
Alan R Byrd, Pr
EMP: 5 EST: 1987
SALES (est): 235.79K **Privately Held**
Web: www.arbyrdcompany.com
SIC: 5712 1542 2522 1541 Cabinet work,
custom; Nonresidential construction, nec;
Cabinets, office: except wood; Renovation,
remodeling and repairs: industrial buildings

(G-7808)
ACTEGA WIT INC
125 Technolgy Dr (28092-4290)
P.O. Box 10 (28093-0010)
PHONE..................................704 735-8282
▲ EMP: 150
Web: www.inkmiser2.com
SIC: 2893 Printing ink

(G-7809)
ACTIVE CONCEPTS LLC
110 Technolgy Dr (28092-4288)
PHONE..................................704 276-7372
EMP: 9
SALES (corp-wide): 9.44MM **Privately
Held**
Web: www.activeconceptsllc.com
SIC: 2844 Cosmetic preparations
PA: Active Concepts, Llc
107 Technolgy Dr
Lincolnton NC 28092
704 276-7100

(G-7810)
ACTIVE CONCEPTS LLC (PA)
107 Technolgy Dr (28092-4290)
PHONE..................................704 276-7100
Durant Scholz, Managing Member
▲ EMP: 24 EST: 2021
SQ FT: 7,000
SALES (est): 9.44MM
SALES (corp-wide): 9.44MM **Privately
Held**
Web: www.activeconceptsllc.com
SIC: 2844 Cosmetic preparations

(G-7811)
AIRBORN INDUSTRIES INC
115 Industrial Park Rd (28092-8359)
PHONE..................................704 483-5000
Donald J Barry, Pr
EMP: 25 EST: 2002
SALES (est): 4.66MM **Privately Held**
Web: www.airbornusa.com
SIC: 3523 3639 Balers, farm: hay, straw,
cotton, etc.; Trash compactors, household

(G-7812)
**AMERICAN CONVERTING CO LTD
LLC**
Also Called: Amerikrate
1161 Burris Blvd (28092-6014)
PHONE..................................704 479-5025
Tom Eubanks, Managing Member
EMP: 25 EST: 2003
SQ FT: 210,000
SALES (est): 8.59MM **Privately Held**
Web: www.americanconverting.com
SIC: 2679 Paper products, converted, nec

(G-7813)
**AMERICAN WOODMARK
CORPORATION**
838 Lincoln County Pkwy (28092-6126)
PHONE..................................828 428-6300
EMP: 53
SALES (corp-wide): 1.85B **Publicly Held**
Web: www.americanwoodmark.com
SIC: 2434 Wood kitchen cabinets
PA: American Woodmark Corporation
561 Shady Elm Rd
Winchester VA 22602
540 665-9100

(G-7814)
**ANNIHILARE MEDICAL SYSTEMS
INC**
311 Motz Ave # E (28092-2532)
PHONE..................................855 545-5677
Parker Sipes, Pr

Steve Cobb, *CFO*
Marty Paris, *CEO*
Bill Bath, *Dir*
Diana Seifert, *Dir*
EMP: 10 **EST:** 2015
SALES (est): 1.73MM **Privately Held**
Web: www.annihilare.com
SIC: 8099 2842 Medical services
organization; Polishes and sanitation goods

(G-7815)
APTARGROUP INC
3300 Finger Mill Rd (28092-6129)
PHONE.....................828 970-6300
Tim Decrow, *Brnch Mgr*
EMP: 150
Web: www.aptar.com
SIC: 3586 Measuring and dispensing pumps
PA: Aptargroup, Inc.
265 Exchange Dr Ste 301
Crystal Lake IL 60014

(G-7816)
ARBOR ORGANIC TECHNOLOGIES LLC
107 Technolgy Dr (28092-4290)
PHONE.....................704 276-7100
Durant Scholz, *Managing Member*
EMP: 25 **EST:** 2011
SALES (est): 626.6K **Privately Held**
SIC: 2834 Extracts of botanicals: powdered,
pilular, solid, or fluid

(G-7817)
BR LEE INDUSTRIES INC
500 Lincoln County Parkway Ext
(28092-6132)
PHONE.....................704 966-3317
Calvin Majeskie, *Prin*
EMP: 6 **EST:** 2010
SALES (est): 198.38K **Privately Held**
SIC: 3999 Manufacturing industries, nec

(G-7818)
CAMPBELL & SONS MACHINING CO
230 W Congress St (28092-2507)
PHONE.....................704 394-0291
Leroy Campbell, *Pr*
Ronnie Campbell, *VP*
Steven Campbell, *Sec*
EMP: 5 **EST:** 1979
SQ FT: 128
SALES (est): 635.88K **Privately Held**
Web: www.lincolneda.org
SIC: 3599 7699 Machine shop, jobbing and
repair; Industrial machinery and equipment
repair

(G-7819)
CATALER NORTH AMERICA CORP (DH)
2002 Cataler Dr (28092-6138)
PHONE.....................828 970-0026
Hiroaki Sunakawa, *Pr*
Rikizo Yoshikawa, *
Albert Alvarez, *
Hironao Kawai, *
▲ **EMP:** 197 **EST:** 2001
SQ FT: 200,000
SALES (est): 23.98MM **Privately Held**
Web: www.cataler.co.jp
SIC: 3714 Exhaust systems and parts, motor
vehicle
HQ: Cataler Corporation
7800, Chihama
Kakegawa SZO 437-1

(G-7820)
CCO HOLDINGS LLC
644 Center Dr (28092-3712)

PHONE.....................704 308-3361
EMP: 112
SALES (corp-wide): 55.09MM **Publicly Held**
SIC: 4841 3663 3651 Cable television
services; Radio and t.v. communications
equipment; Household audio and video
equipment
HQ: Cco Holdings, Llc
400 Atlantic St
Stamford CT 06901
203 905-7801

(G-7821)
CHARLOTTE METAL FINISHING INC
Also Called: CMF
2708 E Main St (28092-4281)
PHONE.....................704 732-7570
Michael Wise, *Mgr*
Thomas L Finger, *Pr*
Kay C Finger, *Sec*
EMP: 10 **EST:** 1983
SQ FT: 10,000
SALES (est): 1.05MM
SALES (corp-wide): 13.14MM **Privately Held**
Web: www.t-fab.com
SIC: 3471 Electroplating of metals or formed
products
PA: T L F Inc
280 Cane Creek Rd.
Fletcher NC 28732
828 681-5343

(G-7822)
COMMERCIAL PRTG LINCOLNTON NC
Also Called: Commercial Printing
523 N Aspen St (28092-2105)
P.O. Box 675 (28093-0675)
PHONE.....................704 735-6831
Russell Cornwell Ii, *Pr*
Dorothy Cornwell, *Sec*
Debra Cornwell, *VP*
◆ **EMP:** 4 **EST:** 1958
SQ FT: 4,600
SALES (est): 166.44K **Privately Held**
SIC: 2752 Offset printing

(G-7823)
COSETTE PHARMACEUTICALS INC
1877 Kawai Rd (28092-5905)
PHONE.....................704 735-5700
Greg Sherwood, *Mgr*
EMP: 180
SALES (corp-wide): 91.68MM **Privately Held**
Web: www.cosettepharma.com
SIC: 2834 Pharmaceutical preparations
PA: Cosette Pharmaceuticals, Inc.
101 Coolidge St
South Plainfield NJ 07080
800 922-1038

(G-7824)
COSETTE PHRMCTCALS NC LABS LLC
1877 Kawai Rd (28092-5905)
PHONE.....................908 753-2000
▲ **EMP:** 150 **EST:** 2014
SALES (est): 8.75MM
SALES (corp-wide): 91.68MM **Privately Held**
SIC: 2834 Pharmaceutical preparations
PA: Cosette Pharmaceuticals, Inc.
101 Coolidge St
South Plainfield NJ 07080
800 922-1038

(G-7825)
CREATIVE PRINTING STANLEY INC
4147 Stoney Creek Dr (28092-6107)
PHONE.....................704 732-6398
Gary Wooten, *Prin*
EMP: 5 **EST:** 2010
SALES (est): 98.3K **Privately Held**
SIC: 2752 Offset printing

(G-7826)
CSC BEARING NORTH AMERICA INC
Also Called: Zwz Bearing USA
1574 Startown Rd (28092)
PHONE.....................734 456-6206
Robert Waters, *Sls Mgr*
EMP: 22
SALES (corp-wide): 4.63MM **Privately Held**
Web: www.zwzbearingusa.com
SIC: 3366 Bushings and bearings
PA: Csc Bearing North America, Inc.
535 Brea Canyon Rd
City Of Industry CA 91789
909 598-6238

(G-7827)
CUSTOM GEARS INC
3565 Hwy 155 S (28092)
P.O. Box 1736 (28093-1736)
PHONE.....................704 735-6883
George Bundy, *Pr*
Brenda Bundy, *Sec*
EMP: 4 **EST:** 1990
SQ FT: 3,500
SALES (est): 168.13K **Privately Held**
SIC: 2299 Fibers, textile: recovery from
textile mill waste and rags

(G-7828)
D BLOCK METALS LLC
1808 Indian Creek Rd (28092-6916)
PHONE.....................980 238-2600
EMP: 4
SALES (corp-wide): 3.39MM **Privately Held**
Web: www.dblockmetals.com
SIC: 3399 Powder, metal
PA: D Block Metals, Llc
1111 Jenkins Rd
Gastonia NC 28052
704 705-5895

(G-7829)
DUSTIN ELLIS LOGGING
1186 Confederate Rd (28092-9091)
PHONE.....................704 732-6027
Dustin Ellis, *Owner*
Wendy Ellis, *Owner*
EMP: 5 **EST:** 1985
SALES (est): 253.76K **Privately Held**
Web: rambo.sites.c21.homes
SIC: 2411 Logging

(G-7830)
EXCEL INC
509 Lee Ave (28092-2522)
P.O. Box 459 (28093-0459)
PHONE.....................704 735-6535
Charles Eurey, *Pr*
Paul Eurey, *Sec*
▼ **EMP:** 5 **EST:** 1945
SQ FT: 40,000
SALES (est): 447.94K **Privately Held**
Web: www.excelhandling.com
SIC: 3552 Textile machinery

(G-7831)
FMS ENTERPRISES USA INC
2001 Kawai Rd (28092-6976)
PHONE.....................704 735-4249

Daniel Blum, *Pr*
Avi Blum, *VP*
◆ **EMP:** 55 **EST:** 2005
SQ FT: 65,000
SALES (est): 6.98MM **Privately Held**
SIC: 2396 Linings, apparel: made from
purchased materials

(G-7832)
HUGGER INC
1443 E Gaston St (28092-4401)
P.O. Box 489 (28093-0489)
PHONE.....................704 735-7422
Carol Grove, *Pr*
Thomas D Grove, *
Harris Jones, *VP Fin*
Sonnie G Herbert, *
EMP: 150 **EST:** 1977
SQ FT: 100,000
SALES (est): 881.21K **Privately Held**
SIC: 2253 2335 T-shirts and tops, knit;
Women's, junior's, and misses' dresses

(G-7833)
J WISE INC
Also Called: Vapor Honing Technologies
313a Motz Ave (28092-2532)
PHONE.....................828 202-5563
Johnathan Wise, *Pr*
EMP: 25 **EST:** 2013
SQ FT: 4,000
SALES (est): 1.89MM **Privately Held**
Web:
www.vaporhoningtechnologies.com
SIC: 5993 3549 Tobacco stores and stands;
Assembly machines, including robotic

(G-7834)
JAX BROTHERS INC
Also Called: Gametime Imagewear
536 N Generals Blvd (28092-3561)
PHONE.....................704 732-3351
Michael Hopkins, *Pr*
EMP: 5 **EST:** 2008
SALES (est): 243.1K **Privately Held**
Web: www.gametimeimagewear.com
SIC: 2759 Screen printing

(G-7835)
LAWING MARBLE CO INC
2523 E Highway 150 (28092-4188)
PHONE.....................704 732-0360
Candace Heavner, *Pr*
Candance Heavner, *Pr*
EMP: 5 **EST:** 1989
SQ FT: 3,000
SALES (est): 95.46K **Privately Held**
Web: www.lawingmarble.com
SIC: 3281 5719 Marble, building: cut and
shaped; Bath accessories

(G-7836)
LEDFORD UPHOLSTERY
Also Called: Ledford Upholstery & Fabrics
202 W Pine St (28092-2159)
PHONE.....................704 732-0233
Bill Ledford, *Owner*
EMP: 5 **EST:** 1978
SALES (est): 109.25K **Privately Held**
Web: ledfordupholstery.theinfocity.com
SIC: 2221 7641 5949 Upholstery fabrics,
manmade fiber and silk; Upholstery work;
Fabric stores piece goods

(G-7837)
LINCOLN COUNTY FABRICATORS INC
513 Jason Rd (28092-6451)
PHONE.....................704 735-1398
Jason Carpenter, *CEO*
Kenneth Carpenter, *

▲ = Import ▼ = Export
◆ = Import/Export

David Carpenter, *
▼ **EMP:** 30 **EST:** 1972
SALES (est): 12.94MM **Privately Held**
Web: www.lincolncountyfabricators.com
SIC: 3441 Fabricated structural metal

(G-7838)
LINCOLN HERALD LLC
611 N Laurel St (28092-2917)
PHONE.................................704 735-3620
Jacob Dellinger, *Prin*
EMP: 9 **EST:** 2012
SALES (est): 76.33K **Privately Held**
Web: www.lincolnherald.com
SIC: 2711 Newspapers, publishing and
   printing

(G-7839)
LITTLE BEEKEEPER LLC
3978 Stoney Creek Dr (28092-6105)
PHONE.................................704 215-9690
Johnnie Hunt, *CEO*
EMP: 5 **EST:** 2018
SALES (est): 125K **Privately Held**
Web: www.thelittlebeekeeper.com
SIC: 2087 Syrups, drink

(G-7840)
LUCKY COUNTRY USA LLC
3333 Finger Mill Rd (28092-6129)
PHONE.................................828 428-8313
▲ **EMP:** 30 **EST:** 2000
SALES (est): 2.15MM **Privately Held**
SIC: 2064 Licorice candy
HQ: Darrell Lea Confectionery Co Pty Ltd
   3 Brooks Rd
   Ingleburn NSW 2565

(G-7841)
MAIN FILTER LLC
1443 E Gaston St (28092)
PHONE.................................704 735-0009
Andrew Perkel, *Pr*
Todd Crawford, *CFO*
EMP: 27 **EST:** 2021
SALES (est): 5.15MM
SALES (corp-wide): 5.15MM **Privately
Held**
Web: mainfilter.com
SIC: 3569 Filter elements, fluid, hydraulic line
PA: Hengst Filtration Usa, Llc
   1443 East Gaston St
   Lincolnton NC
   704 735-0009

(G-7842)
MARILYN COOK
Also Called: Gerald's Yarns
2628 Buffalo Forest Rd (28092-7271)
PHONE.................................704 735-4414
Marilyn Cook, *Owner*
EMP: 4 **EST:** 1980
SQ FT: 5,000
SALES (est): 240.22K **Privately Held**
SIC: 2282 2281 Rewinding of yarn; Yarn
   spinning mills

(G-7843)
MCMURRAY FABRICS INC
1140 N Flint St (28092-5238)
P.O. Box 893 (28093-0893)
PHONE.................................704 732-9613
Johnathan Yoder, *Mgr*
EMP: 54
SALES (corp-wide): 48.46MM **Privately
Held**
Web: www.mcmurrayfabrics.com
SIC: 2262 2261 5949 Finishing plants,
   manmade; Finishing plants, cotton; Fabric
   stores piece goods
PA: Mcmurray Fabrics, Inc.

105 Vann Pl
Aberdeen NC 28315
910 944-2128

(G-7844)
MOHICAN MILLS INC
1419 E Gaston St (28092-4425)
P.O. Box 190 (28093-0190)
PHONE.................................704 735-3343
▼ **EMP:** 307
Web: www.mohicanmills.com
SIC: 2258 Cloth, warp knit

(G-7845)
**MOORES UPHOLSTERING
INTERIORS**
Also Called: AMF Custom Upholstery
308 S Poplar St (28092-3324)
PHONE.................................704 240-8393
Alex F Moore, *Pr*
Karen Moore, *VP*
EMP: 5 **EST:** 1985
SQ FT: 1,100
SALES (est): 246.93K **Privately Held**
SIC: 7641 2512 Reupholstery; Upholstered
   household furniture

(G-7846)
MR TIRE INC
609 E Main St (28092-3411)
PHONE.................................704 735-8024
Thomas Hand, *Brnch Mgr*
EMP: 9
SALES (corp-wide): 1.28B **Publicly Held**
Web: locations.mrtire.com
SIC: 5941 5014 7538 5531 Bicycle and
   bicycle parts; Tires and tubes; General
   automotive repair shops; Automotive tires
HQ: Mr. Tire Inc.
   2078 New York Ave Unit 2
   Huntington Station NY 11746
   631 499-3700

(G-7847)
NORTH CRLINA SPNNING MILLS INC
104 Industrial Park Rd (28092-8358)
P.O. Box 818 (28093-0818)
PHONE.................................704 732-1171
William Kaplan, *Pr*
Robert Lehrer, *
Sharon Hovis, *
▲ **EMP:** 32 **EST:** 1964
SQ FT: 150,000
SALES (est): 1.22MM **Privately Held**
SIC: 2281 Yarn spinning mills

(G-7848)
**NORTH CROLINA TORTILLA MFG
LLC** ✿
Also Called: Our Home - Lincolnton
3181 Progress Dr (28092-5203)
PHONE.................................270 861-5956
Michael Karp, *Managing Member*
EMP: 60 **EST:** 2024
SALES (est): 3.31MM **Privately Held**
SIC: 2052 2096 Pretzels; Potato chips and
   similar snacks

(G-7849)
PUNKER LLC
1112 Lincoln County Pkwy (28092-6135)
PHONE.................................828 322-1951
Ryan Kilkelly, *Managing Member*
▲ **EMP:** 18 **EST:** 2011
SALES (est): 6.21MM
SALES (corp-wide): 86.01MM **Privately
Held**
Web: www.punker-usa.com
SIC: 3564 Blowers and fans
HQ: Punker Gmbh

Niewark 1
Eckernforde SH 24340
43514720

(G-7850)
R W GARCIA CO INC
3181 Progress Dr (28092-5203)
PHONE.................................828 428-0115
Greg Taylor, *Managing Member*
EMP: 20
SALES (corp-wide): 20.33MM **Privately
Held**
Web: www.rwgarcia.com
SIC: 2096 Tortilla chips
PA: R. W. Garcia Co., Inc.
   900 High St
   Hanover PA 17331
   408 287-4616

(G-7851)
**ROBERT BOSCH TOOL
CORPORATION**
Vermont American Tool Company
1980 Indian Creek Rd (28092-6939)
PHONE.................................704 735-7464
Shane Jones, *Genl Mgr*
EMP: 27
SALES (corp-wide): 391.51MM **Privately
Held**
Web: www.boschtools.com
SIC: 3425 5085 Saw blades and handsaws;
   Tools, nec
HQ: Robert Bosch Tool Corporation
   1800 W Central Rd
   Mount Prospect IL 60056

(G-7852)
RSI HOME PRODUCTS INC
General Marble
838 Lincoln County Pkwy (28092-6126)
PHONE.................................828 428-6300
Karen Eakins, *Prin*
EMP: 132
SALES (corp-wide): 1.85B **Publicly Held**
Web: www.americanwoodmark.com
SIC: 3281 5031 Cut stone and stone
   products; Lumber, plywood, and millwork
HQ: Rsi Home Products Llc
   400 E Orangethorpe Ave
   Anaheim CA 92801
   714 449-2200

(G-7853)
SIA ABRASIVES INC USA
Also Called: Abrasives Industries AG
1980 Indian Creek Rd (28092-6939)
PHONE.................................704 587-7355
Julia Chayun, *Dir*
Katina Xouria, *
Ute Lepple, *
Tom Williams, *
David Machnyk, *
▲ **EMP:** 100 **EST:** 1995
SQ FT: 70,000
SALES (est): 10.55MM
SALES (corp-wide): 391.51MM **Privately
Held**
Web: www.siaabrasives.com
SIC: 3291 Abrasive products
HQ: Sia Abrasives Industries Ag
   Muhlewiesenstrasse 20
   Frauenfeld TG 8501

(G-7854)
SOUTHERN FIBER INC (PA)
1041 S Grove Extension (28093)
PHONE.................................704 736-0011
Robert Ruberti, *Pr*
▼ **EMP:** 20 **EST:** 1996
SQ FT: 65,000
SALES (est): 8.5MM

SALES (corp-wide): 8.5MM **Privately Held**
Web: www.southernfiberinc.com
SIC: 2824 Polyester fibers

(G-7855)
SPANTEK EXPANDED METAL INC
352 N Generals Blvd (28092-3557)
PHONE.................................704 479-6210
Mike Gilboy, *Pr*
EMP: 26 **EST:** 1970
SQ FT: 60,000
SALES (est): 7.97MM
SALES (corp-wide): 57.58MM **Privately
Held**
Web: www.spantek.com
SIC: 3312 Blast furnaces and steel mills
PA: Umi Company, Inc.
   1520 5th St S
   Hopkins MN 55343
   952 935-8431

(G-7856)
ST ENGINEERING LEEBOY INC
Also Called: Leeboy
500 Lincoln County Parkway Ext
(28092-6132)
PHONE.................................704 966-3300
Shannon Seymour, *Pr*
Christina Strange, *
Jay Horn, *
EMP: 460 **EST:** 2019
SALES (est): 4.78MM **Privately Held**
Web: www.leeboy.com
SIC: 3531 Railway track equipment
HQ: St Engineering North America, Inc.
   99 Canal Ctr Plz Ste 220
   Alexandria VA 22314
   703 739-2610

(G-7857)
STEPHANIE BAXTER
1089 Peach Tree St (28092-8699)
PHONE.................................803 203-8467
Stephanie Baxter, *Owner*
EMP: 7
SALES (est): 226.85K **Privately Held**
SIC: 2519 7389 Household furniture, nec;
   Business Activities at Non-Commercial Site

(G-7858)
SVCM
Also Called: Svcm International
536 N Generals Blvd (28092-3561)
PHONE.................................305 767-3595
Stanley Clark-munoz, *Owner*
EMP: 5 **EST:** 2017
SALES (est): 181.37K **Privately Held**
SIC: 2299 4226 5131 2221 Textile goods,
   nec; Textile warehousing; Textiles, woven,
   nec; Textile mills, broadwoven: silk and
   manmade, also glass

(G-7859)
TAIJI MEDICAL SUPPLIES INC
3211 Progress Dr (28092-5204)
PHONE.................................888 667-6658
EMP: 9 **EST:** 2020
SALES (est): 793.21K **Privately Held**
Web: www.taijimedical.com
SIC: 5047 3842 Medical equipment and
   supplies; Personal safety equipment

(G-7860)
TENOWO INC (DH)
1968 Kawai Rd (28092-5916)
PHONE.................................704 732-3525
◆ **EMP:** 14 **EST:** 1991
SALES (est): 27.59MM
SALES (corp-wide): 679.88MM **Privately
Held**
Web: www.tenowo.com

SIC: **2297** Nonwoven fabrics
HQ: Tenowo Gmbh
Fabrikzeile 21
Hof BY 95028
9281490

(G-7861)
TENOWO INC
1582 Startown Rd (28092-8040)
PHONE..............................704 732-3525
EMP: 1486
SALES (corp-wide): 679.88MM **Privately
Held**
Web: www.tenowo.com
SIC: 3714 Motor vehicle parts and
accessories
HQ: Tenowo Inc.
1968 Kawai Rd
Lincolnton NC 28092

(G-7862)
TEXTILE PIECE DYEING CO INC
319 N Generals Blvd (28092-3558)
P.O. Box 370 (28093-0370)
PHONE..............................704 732-4200
Dan Doherr, *Pr*
Thomas A Rosse, *
EMP: 114 **EST:** 1986
SQ FT: 200,000
SALES (est): 766.51K **Privately Held**
SIC: 2253 Dyeing and finishing knit
outerwear, excl. hosiery and glove
PA: Dartmouth Textile International Inc
185 Devonshire St Fl 9
Boston MA 02110

(G-7863)
TEXTURE PLUS INC
1477 Roseland Dr (28092-7007)
PHONE..............................631 218-9200
EMP: 40 **EST:** 1980
SQ FT: 16,000
SALES (est): 3.19MM **Privately Held**
Web: www.textureplus.com
SIC: 2952 Siding materials

(G-7864)
**THORNBURG MACHINE & SUP CO
INC**
1699 Smith Farm Rd (28092-0902)
P.O. Box 981 (28093-0981)
PHONE..............................704 735-5421
B C Lineberger, *Pr*
Mike Nale, *
EMP: 28 **EST:** 1926
SQ FT: 31,000
SALES (est): 2.68MM **Privately Held**
Web: www.thornburgmachine.com
SIC: 7692 3599 Welding repair; Machine
shop, jobbing and repair

(G-7865)
TWO PERCENT LLC
204 N Laurel St (28092-3408)
P.O. Box 15 (28093-0015)
PHONE..............................301 401-2750
Allison Levitt, *Prin*
EMP: 4 **EST:** 2015
SALES (est): 257.77K **Privately Held**
Web: www.barebites.com
SIC: 2048 Canned pet food (except dog and
cat)

(G-7866)
UCS INC
Also Called: U C S
511 Hoffman Rd (28092-8230)
P.O. Box 657 (28093-0657)
PHONE..............................704 732-9922
Jeffrey Schwartz, *Pr*
Lawrence H Schwartz, *

◆ **EMP:** 70 **EST:** 2005
SALES (est): 7.28MM **Privately Held**
Web: www.ucsspirit.com
SIC: 3949 Track and field athletic equipment

(G-7867)
UMI COMPANY INC
Also Called: Cemco
352 N Generals Blvd (28092-3557)
PHONE..............................704 479-6210
Vince Hendrickson, *Mgr*
EMP: 8
SALES (corp-wide): 57.58MM **Privately
Held**
Web: www.spantek.com
SIC: 3469 3449 Cash and stamp boxes,
stamped metal; Miscellaneous metalwork
PA: Umi Company, Inc.
1520 5th St S
Hopkins MN 55343
952 935-8431

(G-7868)
UNITED CANVAS & SLING INC
Also Called: U C S
511 Hoffman Rd (28092-8230)
P.O. Box 657 (28093-0657)
PHONE..............................704 732-9922
Jeffrey Schwartz, *Pr*
Lawrence Schwartz, *
Jason Schwartz, *
◆ **EMP:** 50 **EST:** 1967
SQ FT: 130,000
SALES (est): 4.73MM **Privately Held**
Web: www.ucsspirit.com
SIC: 3949 Track and field athletic equipment

(G-7869)
VT LEEBOY INC
Also Called: Leeboy
500 Lincoln County Parkway Ext
(28092-6132)
P.O. Box 370 (28092)
PHONE..............................704 966-3300
Shannon Seymour, *CEO*
Jay Horn, *
Anthony Fadel, *
◆ **EMP:** 460 **EST:** 1978
SQ FT: 150,000
SALES (est): 45.43MM **Privately Held**
Web: www.leeboy.com
SIC: 3531 Drags, road (construction and
road maintenance equipment)
HQ: St Engineering North America, Inc.
99 Canal Ctr Plz Ste 220
Alexandria VA 22314
703 739-2610

(G-7870)
WALTER REYNOLDS (PA)
Also Called: T&J Sales
216 Old Lincolnton Crouse Rd
(28092-7040)
P.O. Box 1858 (28093-1858)
PHONE..............................704 735-6050
Walter Reynolds, *Owner*
EMP: 6 **EST:** 1994
SALES (est): 429.17K **Privately Held**
SIC: 2329 2339 5137 5136 Men's and boys'
sportswear and athletic clothing; Women's
and misses' athletic clothing and sportswear
; Women's and children's clothing; Men's
and boy's clothing

(G-7871)
WEST DYNAMICS US INC
1443 E Gaston St (28092-4401)
PHONE..............................704 735-0009
Steve Turmaine, *Pr*
EMP: 30 **EST:** 2011
SALES (est): 6.25MM **Privately Held**

Web: www.mainfilter.com
SIC: 5084 3569 Industrial machinery and
equipment; Assembly machines, non-
metalworking

Linden
Cumberland County

(G-7872)
A HOUSE OF HEMP LLC
235 Shepard Dr (28356-9589)
PHONE..............................910 984-1441
Sheila Hill, *CEO*
EMP: 5 **EST:** 2019
SALES (est): 468.19K **Privately Held**
Web: www.ahouseofhemp.com
SIC: 2833 5999 5169 Botanical products,
medicinal: ground, graded, or milled;
Essential oils

(G-7873)
DAVID RAYNOR LOGGING INC
4718 Long St (28356-8008)
P.O. Box 70 (28356-0070)
PHONE..............................910 980-0129
David Raynor, *Pr*
Sue Raynor, *Sec*
EMP: 22 **EST:** 1973
SALES (est): 940.27K **Privately Held**
SIC: 2411 2426 2421 Logging camps and
contractors; Hardwood dimension and
flooring mills; Sawmills and planing mills,
general

(G-7874)
DELTA CONTRACTORS INC
6309 Castlebrooke Ln (28356-8046)
P.O. Box 68 (28356-0068)
PHONE..............................817 410-9481
Maria Madriz, *CEO*
EMP: 10 **EST:** 2009
SALES (est): 104.49K **Privately Held**
SIC: 2851 7363 Removers and cleaners;
Temporary help service

(G-7875)
PAGES HYDRO DIPPING COATINGS
7455 Lane Rd (28356-9125)
PHONE..............................910 322-2077
Stephen Page, *Prin*
EMP: 5 **EST:** 2017
SALES (est): 87.31K **Privately Held**
SIC: 3479 Metal coating and allied services

Linwood
Davidson County

(G-7876)
EGGER WOOD PRODUCTS LLC
Also Called: Egger
300 Egger Pkwy (27299-9030)
PHONE..............................336 843-7000
Gerald Jobst, *Managing Member*
Michael Egger, *
Fritz Egger, *
EMP: 284 **EST:** 2016
SALES (est): 97.6MM
SALES (corp-wide): 355.83K **Privately
Held**
Web: www.egger.com
SIC: 2493 Particleboard, plastic laminated
PA: Egger Gmbh
Dollach 23
Liezen
361 282-6300

(G-7877)
EVERETTES COMPANY INC
4805 Old Linwood Rd (27299-9614)
P.O. Box 640 (27299-0640)
PHONE..............................336 956-2097
Ronald M Everette, *Pr*
Geraldine Everette, *Pr*
EMP: 4 **EST:** 1978
SALES (est): 448.38K **Privately Held**
SIC: 3599 Machine shop, jobbing and repair

(G-7878)
FERGUSON COMPANIES
Also Called: Ferguson Fibers
1638 Clyde Fitzgerald Rd (27299-9264)
▲ **EMP:** 8 **EST:** 1972
SQ FT: 78,000
SALES (est): 905.92K **Privately Held**
SIC: 3552 3589 Textile machinery; Car
washing machinery

(G-7879)
LIVENGOOD INNOVATIONS LLC
12068 S Nc Highway 150 (27299-9677)
PHONE..............................336 925-7604
EMP: 4
SALES (est): 264.29K **Privately Held**
SIC: 1389 7389 Construction, repair, and
dismantling services; Business Activities at
Non-Commercial Site

(G-7880)
OLDE LEXINGTON PRODUCTS INC
480 Cedarwood Dr (27299)
P.O. Box 673 (27293-0673)
PHONE..............................336 956-2355
Barry Sink, *Pr*
Renee Sink, *Sec*
EMP: 5 **EST:** 1990
SALES (est): 197.73K **Privately Held**
Web: www.oldelexington.com
SIC: 2431 5712 Moldings, wood: unfinished
and prefinished; Furniture stores

(G-7881)
STROBELS SUPPLY INC
1638 Clyde Fitzgerald Rd (27299-9264)
PHONE..............................607 324-1721
Mike Fortuna, *Pr*
EMP: 14
SIC: 5085 3479 2851 Industrial supplies;
Painting of metal products; Lacquers,
varnishes, enamels, and other coatings
PA: Strobels Supply Inc.
40 Shawmut Industrial Pk
Hornell NY 14843

Little Switzerland
Mcdowell County

(G-7882)
EMERALD VILLAGE INC
387 Mckinney Mine Rd (28749)
P.O. Box 98 (28749-0098)
PHONE..............................828 765-6463
Robert Schabilion, *Pr*
Allan Schabilion, *Pr*
EMP: 5 **EST:** 1980
SQ FT: 40,000
SALES (est): 242.61K **Privately Held**
Web: www.emeraldvillage.com
SIC: 8412 1499 Museum; Gem stones
(natural) mining, nec

▲ = Import ▼ = Export
◆ = Import/Export

Littleton
Halifax County

(G-7883)
AIRBOSS HEATING AND COOLG INC
Also Called: Honeywell Authorized Dealer
127 W South Main St (27850-0046)
P.O. Box 25 (27850-0025)
PHONE.............................252 586-0500
Joanne Lynch, *Prin*
EMP: 5 EST: 2004
SALES (est): 482.17K Privately Held
Web:
www.airbossheatingandcooling.com
SIC: 3585 1711 Air conditioning units,
complete: domestic or industrial; Plumbing,
heating, air-conditioning

(G-7884)
BOAT LIFT STORE INC
1557 Nc Highway 903 (27850-8374)
P.O. Box 850 (27850-0850)
PHONE.............................252 586-5437
Lewis Fields, *Pr*
Marie Fields, *VP*
EMP: 9 EST: 1985
SQ FT: 7,500
SALES (est): 878.94K Privately Held
Web: www.dooziboatlifts.com
SIC: 3536 Boat lifts

(G-7885)
ENTERPRISE LOGGERS COMPANY
INC
681 Enterprise Rd (27850-8179)
PHONE.............................252 586-4805
Burnice Hilliard, *Pr*
Teresa W Hilliard, *Sec*
Ronnie West, *VP*
Lynne West, *Treas*
EMP: 10 EST: 1987
SALES (est): 239.86K Privately Held
SIC: 2411 Logging camps and contractors

(G-7886)
GLOVERS WELDING LLC
638 Oak Grove Church Rd (27850)
P.O. Box 1109 (27850-1109)
PHONE.............................252 586-7692
EMP: 10 EST: 2006
SQ FT: 8,000
SALES (est): 968.12K Privately Held
Web: www.gloverswelding.com
SIC: 7692 3441 Welding repair; Fabricated
structural metal for ships

(G-7887)
STONE HOUSE CREEK LOGGING
615 Fleming Dairy Rd (27850-7722)
PHONE.............................252 586-4477
Tim Capp, *Owner*
Karoao Capp, *Sec*
EMP: 7 EST: 1997
SQ FT: 800
SALES (est): 238.28K Privately Held
SIC: 2411 Logging camps and contractors

(G-7888)
WOMACK PUBLISHING CO INC
Also Called: Lake Gaston Gazette
378 Lizard Creek Rd (27850-8390)
P.O. Box 1166 (27850-1166)
PHONE.............................252 586-2700
Francis Dunn, *Mgr*
EMP: 5
SALES (corp-wide): 4.28MM Privately
Held
Web: www.womackpublishing.com

SIC: 2711 Newspapers: publishing only, not
printed on site
PA: Womack Publishing Company, Inc.
28 N Main St
Chatham VA 24531
434 432-2791

Locust
Stanly County

(G-7889)
CARNES-MILLER GEAR COMPANY
INC
362 Browns Hill Rd (28097-6614)
P.O. Box 268 (28097-0268)
PHONE.............................704 888-4448
Daniel M Tweed Junior, *Pr*
EMP: 17 EST: 1974
SQ FT: 20,000
SALES (est): 1.9MM Privately Held
Web: www.cmgear.us
SIC: 3599 Machine shop, jobbing and repair

(G-7890)
CHICAGO TUBE AND IRON
COMPANY
Also Called: Chicago Tube and Iron
421 Browns Hill Rd (28097-6615)
P.O. Box 548 (28129-0548)
PHONE.............................704 781-2060
Jerry Osborne, *Brnch Mgr*
EMP: 65
SALES (corp-wide): 1.94B Publicly Held
Web: www.chicagotube.com
SIC: 5051 7699 3498 3443 Steel; Boiler
repair shop; Fabricated pipe and fittings;
Fabricated plate work (boiler shop)
HQ: Chicago Tube And Iron Company
1 Chicago Tube Dr
Romeoville IL 60446
815 834-2500

(G-7891)
DIARKIS LLC
142 Cara Ct (28097-9740)
PHONE.............................704 888-5244
EMP: 4 EST: 2007
SQ FT: 500
SALES (est): 237.46K Privately Held
Web: www.upt-usa.com
SIC: 2843 Surface active agents

(G-7892)
ENZYME CUSTOMS
515 Redah Ave (28097-8708)
PHONE.............................704 888-8278
Mason Mcnaught, *Prin*
EMP: 5 EST: 2013
SALES (est): 98.04K Privately Held
SIC: 2869 Enzymes

(G-7893)
FLEXTROL CORPORATION
192 Browns Hill Rd (28097-6609)
PHONE.............................704 888-1120
Richard B Patterson, *Pr*
William R Patterson, *Stockholder*
EMP: 15 EST: 1982
SQ FT: 8,000
SALES (est): 2.74MM Privately Held
Web: www.flextrol.com
SIC: 3052 3568 Rubber hose; Joints and
couplings

(G-7894)
KENZIE LAYNE COMPANY
506 Running Creek Church Rd
(28097-6213)
PHONE.............................704 485-2282

Darryl Page, *Pr*
James Page, *VP*
EMP: 6 EST: 1993
SQ FT: 4,050
SALES (est): 98.21K Privately Held
SIC: 2511 Wood household furniture

(G-7895)
LOCUST MONUMENT LLC
713 Main St W (28097-9715)
P.O. Box 221 (28097-0221)
PHONE.............................704 888-5600
Stan Dry, *Owner*
EMP: 5 EST: 1960
SALES (est): 207.77K Privately Held
Web: www.locustnc.com
SIC: 3281 Monuments, cut stone (not
finishing or lettering only)

(G-7896)
NORMAC KITCHENS INC
607 N Central Ave (28097-7131)
PHONE.............................704 485-1911
Robin Zaretsky, *Brnch Mgr*
EMP: 52
SALES (corp-wide): 29.62MM Privately
Held
Web: www.normackitchens.com
SIC: 3553 Cabinet makers' machinery
HQ: Normac Kitchens, Inc.
226 S Main St
Oakboro NC 28129

(G-7897)
PSI LIQUIDATING INC
605 N Central Ave Ste A (28097-7312)
PHONE.............................704 888-9930
Christopher Meurett, *Pr*
EMP: 7 EST: 2006
SALES (est): 2.46MM Privately Held
Web: www.powerstreamindustries.com
SIC: 3599 Machine shop, jobbing and repair

(G-7898)
QUICK-DECK INC
137 Pine Forest Rd (28097-9404)
P.O. Box 537 (94514-0537)
PHONE.............................704 888-0327
Fred A Wagner Iii, *Pr*
Graham L Scott, *VP*
John Wintz, *CEO*
Lauren Wintz, *VP*
EMP: 22 EST: 1983
SQ FT: 2,500
SALES (est): 1.9MM Privately Held
Web: www.quick-deck.com
SIC: 3448 3537 7352 Ramps, prefabricated
metal; Platforms, cargo; Medical equipment
rental

(G-7899)
READY MIX OF CAROLINAS INC
364 Browns Hill Rd (28097-6614)
P.O. Box 325 (28097-0325)
PHONE.............................704 888-3027
EMP: 31 EST: 2015
SALES (est): 4.52MM Privately Held
Web:
ready-mix-of-the-carolinas-inc.business.site
SIC: 3273 Ready-mixed concrete

(G-7900)
REDY MIX OF CAROLINAS INC
364 Browns Hill Rd (28097-6614)
P.O. Box 325 (28097-0325)
PHONE.............................704 888-2224
Rick Alexander, *Pr*
EMP: 7 EST: 2015
SALES (est): 808.97K Privately Held
Web:
ready-mix-of-the-carolinas-inc.business.site

SIC: 3273 Ready-mixed concrete

(G-7901)
SERVICE ELECTRIC AND CONTROL
703 Redah Ave (28097-8712)
P.O. Box 969 (28097-0969)
PHONE.............................704 888-5100
Ronald Wolfarth, *Pr*
EMP: 7 EST: 2012
SALES (est): 3.58MM Privately Held
Web: www.seac-inc.com
SIC: 3699 1731 Electrical equipment and
supplies, nec; Electrical work

(G-7902)
SOUTHERN ESTATES METAL
ROOFING
614 Maple St (28097-9447)
PHONE.............................704 245-2023
Zack Criscoe, *Pr*
EMP: 4 EST: 1996
SALES (est): 187.29K Privately Held
SIC: 1389 1761 Construction, repair, and
dismantling services; Roofing contractor

(G-7903)
STEEL CONSTRUCT SYSTEMS LLC
118 Pine Forest Rd (28097-9404)
PHONE.............................704 781-5575
EMP: 20 EST: 2011
SALES (est): 2.27MM Privately Held
Web: www.lgscs.com
SIC: 3441 Fabricated structural metal

(G-7904)
STREETS AUTO SALES & FOUR WD
814 Main St W (28097-9716)
PHONE.............................704 888-8686
EMP: 4 EST: 2011
SALES (est): 94.06K Privately Held
SIC: 5511 5012 3711 New and used car
dealers; Busses; Buses, all types,
assembly of

(G-7905)
T W HATHCOCK LOGGING INC
25341 Millingport Rd (28097-8327)
PHONE.............................704 485-9457
Todd Hathcock, *Prin*
EMP: 4 EST: 2010
SALES (est): 244.84K Privately Held
SIC: 2411 Logging

(G-7906)
UFP SITE BUILT LLC
Also Called: Ufp Mid-Atlantic
147 Locust Level Dr (28097-8715)
PHONE.............................704 781-2520
Corie Misenheimer, *Brnch Mgr*
EMP: 42
SALES (corp-wide): 6.65B Publicly Held
Web: www.ufpi.com
SIC: 2439 Trusses, except roof: laminated
lumber
HQ: Ufp Site Built, Llc
2801 E Beltline Ave Ne
Grand Rapids MI 49525
616 634-6161

(G-7907)
UNITED PROTECTIVE TECH LLC
142 Cara Ct (28097-9740)
P.O. Box 1149 (28097-1149)
PHONE.............................704 888-2470
EMP: 20 EST: 2002
SQ FT: 20,000
SALES (est): 6.81MM Privately Held
Web: www.upt-usa.com
SIC: 3842 Clothing, fire resistant and
protective

Louisburg
Franklin County

(G-7908)
ADVANTAGE MARKETING
129 Bartholomew Rd (27549-8267)
PHONE..................................919 872-8610
John A Parrish, *Owner*
EMP: 4 **EST:** 1984
SALES (est): 171.72K **Privately Held**
SIC: 2759 Screen printing

(G-7909)
ALBERT E MANN
106 Clifton Ridge Ct (27549-9030)
PHONE..................................919 497-0815
Albert Mann, *Ch*
EMP: 4 **EST:** 2016
SALES (est): 67K **Privately Held**
SIC: 3571 Electronic computers

(G-7910)
BRODIE-JONES PRINTING CO INC
Also Called: Finch's Print Shop
253 Ronald Tharrington Rd (27549-7418)
PHONE..................................252 438-7992
Thomas Finch, *Pr*
EMP: 5 **EST:** 1972
SALES (est): 481.39K **Privately Held**
SIC: 2752 Offset printing

(G-7911)
CAROLINA DESIGN & MFG INC
Also Called: CDM Wireless
239 Wiggins Rd (27549-9161)
P.O. Box 865 (27596-0865)
PHONE..................................919 554-1823
Thomas G Albright, *CEO*
EMP: 5 **EST:** 2006
SALES (est): 391.42K **Privately Held**
Web: www.cdmwireless.com
SIC: 3663 Radio and t.v. communications
equipment

(G-7912)
CHEMTECH INDUSTRIAL INC
61 T Kemp Rd (27549-6707)
PHONE..................................919 400-5743
Nereida Berdeicia, *CEO*
Linda E Rivera, *Sec*
Leslie Gard, *Treas*
EMP: 9 **EST:** 2010
SQ FT: 37,000
SALES (est): 1.02MM **Privately Held**
SIC: 2869 Industrial organic chemicals, nec

(G-7913)
DANA INDUSTRIES
Timberlake Rd (27549)
PHONE..................................919 496-3262
Dana Lewis, *Prin*
EMP: 6 **EST:** 1996
SALES (est): 185.7K **Privately Held**
Web: www.danaindustries.com
SIC: 3823 Industrial flow and liquid
measuring instruments

(G-7914)
EN FLEUR CORPORATION
Also Called: Paramason
124 Fairview Rd (27549-9792)
PHONE..................................919 556-1623
Brenda D Lewis, *Pr*
EMP: 5 **EST:** 1984
SALES (est): 339.61K **Privately Held**
SIC: 7372 Prepackaged software

(G-7915)
FRANKLIN COUNTY NEWSPAPERS INC
Also Called: Franklin Times
109 S Bickett Blvd (27549-2468)
P.O. Box 119 (27549-0119)
PHONE..................................919 496-6503
Gary R Cunard, *Pr*
EMP: 4 **EST:** 1952
SALES (est): 300.48K **Privately Held**
Web: www.thefranklintimes.com
SIC: 2711 Newspapers, publishing and
printing

(G-7916)
FRED R HARRRIS LOGGING INC
527 Schloss Rd (27549-8037)
PHONE..................................919 853-2266
Fred R Harris, *Pr*
Rachel Harris, *Sec*
EMP: 6 **EST:** 1975
SALES (est): 118.48K **Privately Held**
SIC: 2411 Logging camps and contractors

(G-7917)
H&M WOODWORKS INC
504 S Bickett Blvd (27549-2804)
PHONE..................................919 496-5993
John Daniel, *Pr*
EMP: 10 **EST:** 2020
SALES (est): 1.32MM **Privately Held**
Web: www.hmwoodworksnc.com
SIC: 2431 Millwork

(G-7918)
HUNT LOGGING CO
2233 Person Rd (27549-8030)
PHONE..................................919 853-2850
James T Hunt, *Pt*
Lonnie Hunt, *Pt*
EMP: 4 **EST:** 1984
SALES (est): 68.7K **Privately Held**
SIC: 2411 Logging

(G-7919)
JIMMY D NELMS LOGGING INC
Also Called: Jimmie Nelms Trucking
4021 Nc 561 Hwy (27549-9677)
PHONE..................................919 853-2597
Jimmie D Nelms, *Pr*
EMP: 6 **EST:** 1968
SALES (est): 411.9K **Privately Held**
SIC: 2411 Logging camps and contractors

(G-7920)
NORTH STATE STEEL INC
Also Called: North State Steel At Louisburg
1801 Nc 98 Hwy W (27549-7612)
PHONE..................................919 496-2506
Rick Fleming, *Genl Mgr*
EMP: 16
SALES (corp-wide): 8.94MM **Privately Held**
Web: www.northstatesteel.com
SIC: 3441 Building components, structural
steel
PA: North State Steel, Inc.
1010 W Gum Rd
Greenville NC 27834
252 830-8884

(G-7921)
PACKO BOTTLING INC
Also Called: Bobbees Bottling
42 Golden Leaf Dr (27549-2853)
PHONE..................................919 496-4286
Jack Pyritz, *Pr*
Patty Pyritz, *VP*
◆ **EMP:** 20 **EST:** 1982
SQ FT: 89,000

SALES (est): 5.07MM **Privately Held**
Web: www.bobbeesbottling.com
SIC: 2086 Bottled and canned soft drinks

(G-7922)
PALZIV NORTH AMERICA INC
Also Called: Palziv North America
7966 Nc 56 Hwy (27549-8633)
PHONE..................................919 497-0010
Paul Robertson, *COO*
Rick Merkley, *
▲ **EMP:** 190 **EST:** 2008
SQ FT: 200,000
SALES (est): 24.4MM **Privately Held**
Web: www.palzivna.com
SIC: 3086 Packaging and shipping
materials, foamed plastics
PA: Palziv Ein Hanaziv Agricultural Coop
Society Ltd.
Kibbutz
Ein Hanatziv 10805

(G-7923)
PUETT TRUCKING & LOGGING
1796 Person Rd (27549-7936)
PHONE..................................919 853-2071
Gene Puett, *Owner*
EMP: 5 **EST:** 1988
SALES (est): 62.7K **Privately Held**
SIC: 2411 Logging camps and contractors

(G-7924)
QUALITY PRECAST INC
100 Gayline Dr (27549-8612)
PHONE..................................919 497-0660
Roland Lindsay, *Pr*
Timothy Gessaman, *VP*
Linda Lindsay, *Treas*
EMP: 5 **EST:** 2003
SALES (est): 225.75K
SALES (corp-wide): 35.62MM **Privately
Held**
Web: www.qualityprecast.com
SIC: 3272 Precast terrazzo or concrete
products
PA: Lindsay Precast, Llc
6845 Erie Ave Nw
Canal Fulton OH 44614
800 837-7788

(G-7925)
REGIMENTAL FLAG & T SHIRTS
29 Secession Ln (27549-7065)
PHONE..................................919 496-2888
Jane Langley, *Owner*
EMP: 5 **EST:** 2002
SALES (est): 248.97K **Privately Held**
Web: www.kudzutshirts.com
SIC: 2396 Screen printing on fabric articles

(G-7926)
RICHARD C JONES
Also Called: B J Logging
7823 Nc 561 Hwy (27549-8862)
PHONE..................................919 853-2096
Richard Jones, *Owner*
EMP: 8 **EST:** 1997
SQ FT: 1,620
SALES (est): 87.7K **Privately Held**
SIC: 2411 Logging camps and contractors

(G-7927)
TAR RIVER THINNING INC
176 Paul Sledge Rd (27549-7040)
PHONE..................................919 497-1647
David Jones, *Pr*
Rebecca Jones, *
EMP: 6 **EST:** 2001
SALES (est): 461.15K **Privately Held**
SIC: 2411 Logging camps and contractors

(G-7928)
TONEY LUMBER COMPANY INC
309 Bunn Rd (27549-2707)
P.O. Box 447 (27549-0447)
PHONE..................................919 496-5711
Roger Melvin, *Pr*
Elizabeth Toney Melvin, *
Susan Toney, *
Conrad Sturges, *
EMP: 68 **EST:** 1948
SQ FT: 2,600
SALES (est): 9.28MM **Privately Held**
Web: www.toneyhardware.com
SIC: 5031 2421 Lumber: rough, dressed,
and finished; Sawmills and planing mills,
general

(G-7929)
WOOD BARN INC (PA)
206 Clifton Ridge Ct (27549-9031)
P.O. Box 819 (27549-0819)
PHONE..................................919 496-6714
Jerry Faulkner, *Pr*
EMP: 20 **EST:** 1992
SQ FT: 150,000
SALES (est): 322.79K **Privately Held**
Web: www.woodbarn.com
SIC: 2431 Staircases and stairs, wood

Lowell
Gaston County

(G-7930)
CHOICE USA BEVERAGE INC (PA)
Also Called: Sun-Drop Bottling Co
603 Groves St (28098-1702)
PHONE..................................704 823-1651
James P Falls Senior, *Ch Bd*
Linda Medley, *
Sam L Robinson, *
J Falls Junior, *Owner*
EMP: 75 **EST:** 1933
SQ FT: 18,000
SALES (est): 23.19MM
SALES (corp-wide): 23.19MM **Privately
Held**
Web: www.choiceusabeverage.com
SIC: 2086 2087 Carbonated beverages,
nonalcoholic: pkged. in cans, bottles;
Syrups, drink

(G-7931)
FRYEDAY COFFEE ROASTERS LLC
106 E 1st St Unit B (28098-1573)
PHONE..................................704 879-9083
Alisa Frye, *Managing Member*
EMP: 4 **EST:** 2017
SALES (est): 343.72K **Privately Held**
Web: www.fryedaycoffeeroasters.com
SIC: 2095 Coffee roasting (except by
wholesale grocers)

(G-7932)
IMPERIAL PRINTING PDTS CO INC
141 Robins St (28098-1940)
P.O. Box 240905 (28224-0905)
PHONE..................................704 554-1188
Stuart Cojac, *Pr*
EMP: 6 **EST:** 1936
SQ FT: 25,000
SALES (est): 203.72K **Privately Held**
SIC: 2752 Offset printing

(G-7933)
INDIAN MOTORCYCLE COMPANY
Also Called: Indian Motorcycle Charlotte
110 Indian Walk (28098-2030)
PHONE..................................704 879-4560
Mark Moses, *Brnch Mgr*

▲ = Import ▼ = Export
◆ = Import/Export

EMP: 7
SALES (corp-wide): 7.18B Publicly Held
Web:
www.indianmotorcyclecharlotte.com
SIC: 3751 7699 Motorcycles and related
parts; Motorcycle repair service
HQ: Indian Motorcycle Company
2100 Hwy 55
Hamel MN 55340
763 542-0500

(G-7934)
S & L CREATIONS INC
120 E 1st St (28098-1573)
P.O. Box 334 (28098-0334)
PHONE.....................704 824-1930
James F Smith, Pr
Pamela Smith, Sec
EMP: 5 EST: 1984
SQ FT: 2,700
SALES (est): 81.72K Privately Held
SIC: 2261 5999 Screen printing of cotton
broadwoven fabrics; Trophies and plaques

(G-7935)
U S ALLOY CO
Also Called: Washington Alloy
825 Groves St (28098-1706)
PHONE.....................888 522-8296
Joe Dearborn, Mgr
EMP: 16
SALES (corp-wide): 1.99MM Privately
Held
Web: www.washingtonalloy.com
SIC: 3548 Welding wire, bare and coated
PA: U. S. Alloy Co.
8885 White Oak Ave Ste 10
Rancho Cucamonga CA 91730
800 830-9033

Lowland
Pamlico County

(G-7936)
TRAWLER INCORPORATED
569 Kelly Watson Rd (28552-9653)
PHONE.....................252 745-3751
Carol Potter, Prin
EMP: 4 EST: 2002
SALES (est): 174.49K Privately Held
SIC: 3732 Fishing boats: lobster, crab,
oyster, etc.: small

Lucama
Wilson County

(G-7937)
JOHNSON INDUSTRIAL MCHY SVCS
7160 Us Highway 117 (27851-8805)
P.O. Box 3877 (27895-3877)
PHONE.....................252 239-1944
Jimmy R Johnson, Pr
Lynda Johnson, *
Angela Fulghum, *
EMP: 20 EST: 1972
SQ FT: 7,500
SALES (est): 3.26MM Privately Held
Web: www.jimsinc.net
SIC: 1796 3523 3599 Machinery installation;
Farm machinery and equipment; Machine
shop, jobbing and repair

(G-7938)
R & J ROAD SERVICE INC
5014 Saint Marys Church Rd (27851-9699)
PHONE.....................252 239-1404
Rufus Gallyn, Pr
EMP: 4 EST: 2005

SALES (est): 1.83MM Privately Held
Web: www.rjroadservice.com
SIC: 3669 Emergency alarms

Lumber Bridge
Robeson County

(G-7939)
MOUNTAIRE FARMS LLC
Also Called: Piedmont Poultry
17269 Nc 71 Hwy N (28357)
P.O. Box 129 (28357-0129)
PHONE.....................910 843-3332
EMP: 134
SALES (corp-wide): 2.07B Privately Held
Web: www.mountaire.com
SIC: 2015 Poultry slaughtering and
processing
HQ: Mountaire Farms Inc.
1901 Napa Valley Dr
Little Rock AR 72212
501 372-6524

(G-7940)
MOUNTAIRE FARMS LLC
Also Called: Mountaire Farms, L.L.C.
17269 N Carolina Hwy 71 (28357-8089)
PHONE.....................910 843-5942
EMP: 273
SALES (corp-wide): 2.07B Privately Held
Web: www.mountaire.com
SIC: 2015 Poultry slaughtering and
processing
HQ: Mountaire Farms Inc.
1901 Napa Valley Dr
Little Rock AR 72212
501 372-6524

(G-7941)
MOUNTAIRE FARMS INC
17269 Hwy 71 (28357)
P.O. Box 339 (28357-0339)
PHONE.....................910 843-5942
John Wise, Brnch Mgr
EMP: 825
SALES (corp-wide): 2.07B Privately Held
Web: www.mountaire.com
SIC: 2015 Poultry slaughtering and
processing
HQ: Mountaire Farms Inc.
1901 Napa Valley Dr
Little Rock AR 72212
501 372-6524

Lumberton
Robeson County

(G-7942)
ADAMS BEVERAGES NC LLC
Also Called: Adams Beverages Lumberton
797 Caton Rd (28360-0457)
PHONE.....................910 738-8165
Casey Cranor, Mgr
EMP: 75
SALES (corp-wide): 8.55MM Privately
Held
Web: www.adamsbeverages.net
SIC: 2084 Wine coolers (beverages)
PA: Adams Beverages Of North Carolina,
Llc
7505 Statesville Rd
Charlotte NC 28269
704 509-3000

(G-7943)
ALAMAC AMERICAN KNITS LLC
1885 Alamac Rd (28358-8859)
P.O. Box 1347 (28359-1347)

PHONE.....................910 618-2248
◆ EMP: 240
Web: www.alamacknits.com
SIC: 2211 Broadwoven fabric mills, cotton

(G-7944)
ALLENS GUTTER SERVICE
209 T P Rd (28358-7897)
PHONE.....................910 738-9509
Jerry C Allen, Owner
EMP: 5 EST: 1978
SQ FT: 5,000
SALES (est): 230.34K Privately Held
SIC: 1761 5051 3444 Gutter and downspout
contractor; Metals service centers and
offices; Sheet metalwork

(G-7945)
ASBURY GRAPHITE MILLS
191 Magna Blvd (28360-4807)
PHONE.....................910 671-4141
EMP: 8 EST: 2019
SALES (est): 1.96MM Privately Held
Web: www.asbury.com
SIC: 3624 Carbon and graphite products

(G-7946)
BFT LUMBERTON OPS CORP
Also Called: Bft Lumberton
1000 Noir St (28358-6660)
PHONE.....................910 737-3200
James Posa, CEO
▲ EMP: 30 EST: 1968
SQ FT: 150,000
SALES (est): 5.32MM Privately Held
SIC: 2611 Pulp produced from non-wood
fiber base, nec
HQ: Bast Fibre Technologies Usa Inc.
148 River St Ste 202
Greenville SC 29601
778 433-2278

(G-7947)
CANAL WOOD LLC
1866 Hestertown Rd (28358-8284)
PHONE.....................910 733-7436
Boyd Mclaurin, Prin
Boyd Mclaurin, VP
Tim Foley, Mgr
EMP: 5 EST: 2000
SALES (est): 86.97K Privately Held
Web: www.canalwood.com
SIC: 2421 Sawmills and planing mills,
general

(G-7948)
CONTEMPORA FABRICS INC
351 Contempora Dr (28358-0445)
PHONE.....................910 345-0150
Ronald Roach, Pr
Carey M Read, *
Gerald Cauthen, PROD*
EMP: 145 EST: 1972
SQ FT: 150,000
SALES (est): 23.02MM Privately Held
Web: www.contemporafabrics.com
SIC: 2253 5949 2257 Dresses and skirts;
Sewing, needlework, and piece goods;
Weft knit fabric mills

(G-7949)
**DUE PROCESS STABLE TRDG CO
LLC**
4111 W 5th St (28358-0411)
PHONE.....................910 608-0284
David Grasse, Managing Member
▲ EMP: 25 EST: 2004
SALES (est): 585.56K Privately Held
SIC: 2273 1771 Carpets and rugs; Flooring
contractor

(G-7950)
ELKAY OHIO PLUMBING PDTS CO
880 Caton Rd (28360-0458)
PHONE.....................910 739-8181
EMP: 3454
Web: www.zurnelkay.com
SIC: 3431 Sinks: enameled iron, cast iron, or
pressed metal
HQ: Elkay Ohio Plumbing Products
Company
7634 New West Rd
Toledo OH 43617
419 841-1820

(G-7951)
ELKAY PLUMBING PRODUCTS CO
880 Caton Rd (28360-0458)
PHONE.....................910 739-8181
EMP: 5
SALES (corp-wide): 2.69MM Privately
Held
Web: www.elkay.com
SIC: 3431 Metal sanitary ware
PA: Elkay Plumbing Products Company
855 Caton Rd
Lumberton NC 28360
910 737-3057

(G-7952)
EXPRESSIVE SCREEN PRINTING
504 Peterson Dr (28358-2600)
PHONE.....................910 739-3221
Victor A Dorais, Owner
EMP: 4 EST: 1983
SQ FT: 3,000
SALES (est): 205.97K Privately Held
SIC: 2759 2396 Screen printing; Automotive
and apparel trimmings

(G-7953)
FAITH COMPUTER REPAIRS
3404 Nc Highway 211 W (28360-3571)
PHONE.....................910 730-1731
Daniel Jacobs, Owner
EMP: 6 EST: 2011
SQ FT: 2,000
SALES (est): 250.82K Privately Held
SIC: 3577 Computer peripheral equipment,
nec

(G-7954)
FEX STRAW MANUFACTURING INC
191 Magna Blvd (28360-4807)
PHONE.....................910 671-4141
Jim Mcalpine, Pr
▲ EMP: 4 EST: 2003
SALES (est): 245.39K Privately Held
SIC: 2399 Horse and pet accessories, textile

(G-7955)
FLO-TITE INC VALVES & CONTRLS
4815 W 5th St (28358-0425)
P.O. Box 1293 (28359-1293)
PHONE.....................910 738-8904
Martin Gibbons, CEO
▲ EMP: 47 EST: 2004
SALES (est): 18MM Privately Held
Web: www.flotite.com
SIC: 3492 5085 Control valves, aircraft:
hydraulic and pneumatic; Valves and fittings

(G-7956)
GUNMAR MACHINE CORPORATION
310 Hines St (28358-6624)
PHONE.....................910 738-6295
Dennis Martin, Pr
Joanne Martin, Sec
EMP: 10 EST: 1972
SQ FT: 7,900
SALES (est): 1.49MM Privately Held

SIC: **3599** 7692 Machine shop, jobbing and repair; Welding repair

(G-7957)
HIGH VACUUM ELECTRONICS INC
2200 Cox Rd (28358)
P.O. Box 1044 (28359-1044)
PHONE................................910 738-1219
Alexander Stanton, *Pr*
Bruce Job, *Sec*
EMP: 7 EST: 1985
SALES (est): 170.63K **Privately Held**
SIC: **3679** Electronic switches

(G-7958)
INTERNATIONAL PAPER COMPANY
International Paper
820 Caton Rd (28360-0458)
PHONE................................910 738-6214
Mark Witt, *Genl Mgr*
EMP: 87
SALES (corp-wide): 18.62B **Publicly Held**
Web: www.internationalpaper.com
SIC: **2653** Boxes, corrugated: made from purchased materials
PA: International Paper Company
6400 Poplar Ave
Memphis TN 38197
901 419-7000

(G-7959)
INTERNATIONAL PAPER COMPANY
Also Called: International Paper
2060 W 5th St (28358-5453)
PHONE................................910 738-8930
EMP: 5
SALES (corp-wide): 18.62B **Publicly Held**
Web: www.internationalpaper.com
SIC: **2621** Paper mills
PA: International Paper Company
6400 Poplar Ave
Memphis TN 38197
901 419-7000

(G-7960)
KR PUBLICATIONS
4100 Nelson Way (28360-9102)
PHONE................................910 852-1525
Kadan Thompson, *Owner*
EMP: 4 EST: 2018
SALES (est): 99.81K **Privately Held**
SIC: **2731** Books, publishing only

(G-7961)
LUMBERTON OVERHEAD DOORS INC
1519 Carthage Rd Ste C (28358-3488)
P.O. Box 3837 (28359-3837)
PHONE................................910 739-6426
Stanford L Wiggins, *CEO*
EMP: 9 EST: 2019
SALES (est): 1.38MM **Privately Held**
SIC: **2431** Garage doors, overhead, wood

(G-7962)
MILITARY WRAPS INC
Also Called: Mw Defense Systems
3400a David St (28358-6900)
PHONE................................910 671-0008
Trevor Kracker, *Pr*
EMP: 4 EST: 2007
SALES (est): 291.08K **Privately Held**
Web: www.militarywraps.com
SIC: **2824** Vinyl fibers

(G-7963)
NUCOR REBAR FABRICATION NC INC
2790 Kenny Biggs Rd (28358-3771)
PHONE................................910 739-9747

EMP: 117
SALES (corp-wide): 40.2MM **Privately Held**
Web: www.harrisrebar.com
SIC: **3441** Fabricated structural metal
HQ: Nucor Rebar Fabrication North Carolina Inc.
803 S Market St
Benson NC 27504
919 894-3900

(G-7964)
NYP CORP FRMRLY NEW YRKR-PTERS
Ampack
299 Osterneck Robetex Dr (28358-0804)
PHONE................................910 739-4403
Chris Labelle, *Brnch Mgr*
EMP: 12
SALES (corp-wide): 21.65MM **Privately Held**
Web: www.nyp-corp.com
SIC: **2393** Textile bags
PA: Nyp Corp. (Formerly New Yorker-Peters Corporation)
1640 Vauxhall Rd
Union NJ 07083
908 351-6550

(G-7965)
PERDUE FARMS INC
Also Called: PERDUE FARMS INC.
1801 Godwin Ave (28358-3193)
PHONE................................910 738-8581
W Parker, *Pr*
EMP: 34
SALES (corp-wide): 1.24B **Privately Held**
Web: www.perdue.com
SIC: **2015** Poultry slaughtering and processing
PA: Perdue Farms Incorporated
31149 Old Ocean City Rd
Salisbury MD 21804
800 473-7383

(G-7966)
QUICKIE MANUFACTURING CORP
2880 Kenny Biggs Rd (28358-6332)
PHONE................................910 737-6500
Bob Carson, *VP*
EMP: 147
SALES (corp-wide): 7.58B **Publicly Held**
Web: www.quickie.com
SIC: **3991** 2392 Brooms and brushes; Mops, floor and dust
HQ: Quickie Manufacturing Corp
3124 Valley Ave
Winchester VA 22601
856 829-7900

(G-7967)
QUIK PRINT INC
232 E 4th St (28358-5525)
P.O. Box 805 (28359-0805)
PHONE................................910 738-6775
Betty M Evans, *Pr*
EMP: 6 EST: 1985
SQ FT: 4,500
SALES (est): 390.56K **Privately Held**
SIC: **2752** 2759 Offset printing; Commercial printing, nec

(G-7968)
REDDY ICE LLC
903 E Elizabethtown Rd (28358-4163)
PHONE................................910 738-9930
Steve Musslewhite, *Mgr*
EMP: 8
SALES (corp-wide): 3.82B **Privately Held**
Web: www.reddyice.com

SIC: **2097** Manufactured ice
HQ: Reddy Ice Llc
5710 Lbj Fwy Ste 300
Dallas TX 75240
214 526-6740

(G-7969)
REMPAC LLC
2005 Starlite Dr (28358-6951)
PHONE................................910 737-6557
Mike Vanepen, *Dir Opers*
EMP: 33
SALES (corp-wide): 16.29MM **Privately Held**
Web: www.rempac.com
SIC: **3069** 3053 Sponge rubber and sponge rubber products; Gaskets; packing and sealing devices
PA: Rempac Llc
370 W Passaic St Ste A
Rochelle Park NJ 07662
201 843-4585

(G-7970)
ROBETEX INC (PA)
2504 Fayetteville Rd (28358-3114)
P.O. Box 1489 (30740-1489)
PHONE................................910 671-8787
David G Talbot, *Ch Bd*
Cary Talbot, *Pr*
John Moravec, *Sec*
Kerry Talbot, *Prin*
▲ EMP: 19 EST: 1994
SALES (est): 2.07MM **Privately Held**
Web: www.robetexinc.com
SIC: **3089** 3083 3082 Reinforcing mesh, plastics; Laminated plastics plate and sheet ; Unsupported plastics profile shapes

(G-7971)
ROGERS SCREENPRINTING EMB INC
1988 N Roberts Ave (28358-3120)
PHONE................................910 738-6208
Keith Rogers, *Brnch Mgr*
EMP: 5
SALES (corp-wide): 2.37MM **Privately Held**
Web: www.rogersseinc.com
SIC: **2759** Screen printing
PA: Rogers Screenprinting & Embroidery, Inc.
10306 Nc Highway 41 S
Fairmont NC 28340
910 628-1983

(G-7972)
SANDERSON FARMS LLC
Also Called: St. Pauls Hatchery
6762 Nc Highway 41 N (28358-2583)
PHONE................................910 887-2284
EMP: 5
SALES (corp-wide): 4.8B **Privately Held**
Web: www.sandersonfarms.com
SIC: **2015** Poultry slaughtering and processing
HQ: Sanderson Farms, Llc
127 Flynt Rd
Laurel MS 39443
601 649-4030

(G-7973)
SUMMIT LOGGING LLC
1485 Beulah Church Rd (28358-8115)
PHONE................................910 734-8787
Thomas L Odum, *Prin*
EMP: 4 EST: 2014
SALES (est): 218.71K **Privately Held**
SIC: **2411** Logging

(G-7974)
TAYLCO INC
Also Called: Green State Landscape & Nrsry
2643 W Carthage Rd (28360-8859)
PHONE................................910 739-0405
Myra Norton, *Pr*
G Keith Taylor, *
Myra T Norton, *
EMP: 30 EST: 1985
SQ FT: 4,000
SALES (est): 4.33MM **Privately Held**
SIC: **3271** 0181 0782 1711 Blocks, concrete: landscape or retaining wall; Flowers: grown under cover (e.g., greenhouse production); Landscape contractors; Irrigation sprinkler system installation

(G-7975)
TITAN FLOW CONTROL INC (PA)
290 Corporate Dr (28358-1110)
P.O. Box 7408 (28359)
PHONE................................910 735-0000
Martin Gibbons, *Pr*
◆ EMP: 20 EST: 2000
SQ FT: 10,000
SALES (est): 14.46MM
SALES (corp-wide): 14.46MM **Privately Held**
Web: www.titanfci.com
SIC: **3494** Valves and pipe fittings, nec

(G-7976)
WILBERT BURIAL VAULT COMPANY
1015 S Roberts Ave (28358-7975)
P.O. Box 934 (28359-0934)
PHONE................................910 739-7276
Wanda Ouzts, *Pr*
EMP: 6 EST: 1959
SQ FT: 8,000
SALES (est): 757.24K **Privately Held**
Web: www.wilbert.com
SIC: **3272** Burial vaults, concrete or precast terrazzo

(G-7977)
XAVIER POWER SYSTEMS
885 Shawn Rd (28358-8953)
P.O. Box 234 (28384-0234)
PHONE................................910 734-7813
EMP: 10
SALES (est): 142.73K **Privately Held**
Web: www.xavier.edu
SIC: **3621** Motors, electric

(G-7978)
ZURN ELKAY WTR SOLUTIONS CORP
102 Elkay Way (28358-2476)
PHONE................................910 501-1853
Todd A Adams, *Ch Bd*
EMP: 7
Web: www.zurnelkay.com
SIC: **3491** Industrial valves
PA: Zurn Elkay Water Solutions Corporation
511 W Freshwater Way
Milwaukee WI 53204

Macclesfield
Edgecombe County

(G-7979)
CALHOUN WELDING INC
7367 Tory Pl (27852-9512)
PHONE................................252 281-1455
Joe Calhoun, *Prin*
EMP: 5 EST: 2012
SALES (est): 448.67K **Privately Held**
SIC: **7692** Welding repair

▲ = Import ▼ = Export
◆ = Import/Export

(G-7980)
HALES WELDING AND FABRICATION
900 Carr Farm Rd (27852-9040)
PHONE..............................252 907-5508
Charles Hales, *Owner*
Stephanie Spencer C.p.a., *Prin*
EMP: 5 **EST:** 2012
SALES (est): 117.08K **Privately Held**
SIC: 7692 Welding repair

(G-7981)
WIZARDS WOOD WERKS
7114 Shallingtons Mill Rd (27852-9803)
PHONE..............................252 813-3929
Walt Williams, *Prin*
EMP: 5 **EST:** 2016
SALES (est): 54.13K **Privately Held**
SIC: 2431 Millwork

Macon
Warren County

(G-7982)
ARCOLA LOGGING CO INC
134 Chip Capps Rd (27551-8929)
PHONE..............................252 257-3205
Weldon C Capps Junior, *Pr*
Sarah P Capps, *Sec*
EMP: 9 **EST:** 1986
SQ FT: 3,000
SALES (est): 946.36K **Privately Held**
SIC: 2411 Logging camps and contractors

Madison
Rockingham County

(G-7983)
ACE INDUSTRIES INC
213 Carlton Rd (27025)
P.O. Box 891 (27025-0891)
PHONE..............................336 427-5316
Jim L Allred Senior, *Pr*
EMP: 4 **EST:** 1977
SQ FT: 5,000
SALES (est): 357.05K **Privately Held**
Web: www.aceindustries.com
SIC: 5087 2842 Service establishment equipment; Cleaning or polishing preparations, nec

(G-7984)
COMPTON TAPE & LABEL INC
Also Called: Compton Tape and Converting
3520 Us Highway 220 (27025-8310)
P.O. Box 370 (27025-0370)
PHONE..............................336 548-4400
Thomas A Compton, *Pr*
William C Compton, *VP*
EMP: 12 **EST:** 1996
SQ FT: 8,800
SALES (est): 480.38K **Privately Held**
SIC: 2259 Convertors, knit goods

(G-7985)
CUSTOM SCREENS INC
Also Called: Cs Ink
2216 Us Highway 311 (27025-8456)
P.O. Box 368 (27025-0368)
PHONE..............................336 427-0265
John Pleas Mcmichael, *CEO*
Chris Mcmichael, *VP*
EMP: 6 **EST:** 1961
SQ FT: 41,000
SALES (est): 441.98K **Privately Held**
Web: www.csink.net

SIC: 2262 2396 Screen printing: manmade fiber and silk broadwoven fabrics; Automotive and apparel trimmings

(G-7986)
DEEP SOUTH HOLDING COMPANY INC
Also Called: Csi
2216 Us Highway 311 (27025-8456)
P.O. Box 250 (27025-0250)
PHONE..............................336 427-0265
William Hemrck, *Pr*
▲ **EMP:** 100 **EST:** 2009
SQ FT: 40,000
SALES (est): 4.56MM **Privately Held**
SIC: 2759 Screen printing

(G-7987)
DICKS STORE
547 Mccollum Rd (27025-7808)
PHONE..............................336 548-9358
Richard R Cartwright, *Owner*
EMP: 5 **EST:** 1962
SALES (est): 248.65K **Privately Held**
SIC: 2396 5199 Screen printing on fabric articles; Advertising specialties

(G-7988)
JOB SHOP FABRICATORS INC
3522 Us Highway 220 (27025-8310)
P.O. Box 1003 (27025-1003)
PHONE..............................336 427-7300
Jerry Hilliard, *Ch Bd*
Gerald Hudson, *Pr*
Elaine Hudson, *Treas*
Judy Hilliard, *Sec*
EMP: 8 **EST:** 1989
SQ FT: 10,000
SALES (est): 943.6K **Privately Held**
SIC: 3443 Fabricated plate work (boiler shop)

(G-7989)
KREBS CORPORATION
Also Called: Seal Master
703 W Decatur St (27025-1817)
P.O. Box 826 (27025-0826)
PHONE..............................336 548-3250
Robert Krebs, *Pr*
EMP: 9 **EST:** 2004
SALES (est): 5.25MM **Privately Held**
Web: www.sealmaster.net
SIC: 2951 Asphalt paving mixtures and blocks

(G-7990)
LIBERTY EMBROIDERY INC
301 K Fork Rd (27025-7532)
P.O. Box 707 (27025-0707)
PHONE..............................336 548-1802
EMP: 600 **EST:** 1980
SQ FT: 87,000
SALES (est): 18.34MM **Privately Held**
SIC: 2395 Embroidery products, except Schiffli machine

(G-7991)
LICHTENBERG INC
Also Called: Hell On Horsecreek Brewing
107 E Murphy St (27025-1919)
PHONE..............................336 949-9438
David Peters, *Pr*
EMP: 4 **EST:** 2018
SALES (est): 76.29K **Privately Held**
SIC: 2391 Curtains and draperies

(G-7992)
MADISON COMPANY INC (PA)
Also Called: Gem-Dandy
200 W Academy St (27025-2002)
P.O. Box 657 (27025-0657)

PHONE..............................336 548-9624
Fred Burke, *Pr*
George R Penn, *VP*
Donald Wilson, *VP*
▲ **EMP:** 20 **EST:** 1921
SQ FT: 107,000
SALES (est): 5.7MM
SALES (corp-wide): 5.7MM **Privately Held**
Web: www.gem-dandy.com
SIC: 2387 2389 5136 2386 Apparel belts; Suspenders; Men's and boy's clothing; Leather and sheep-lined clothing

(G-7993)
MARTIN WOOD PRODUCTS INC
Also Called: McW Custom Doors
680 Bald Hill Loop (27025-7613)
PHONE..............................336 548-3470
Eddie Martin, *Owner*
EMP: 5 **EST:** 1994
SQ FT: 4,050
SALES (est): 340.4K **Privately Held**
Web: www.mcwcustomdoors.com
SIC: 2431 Woodwork, interior and ornamental, nec

(G-7994)
NATURESRULES INC
2094 Ellisboro Rd (27025-8063)
PHONE..............................336 427-2526
EMP: 6 **EST:** 2019
SALES (est): 225.78K **Privately Held**
Web: www.naturesrules.com
SIC: 2034 Dried and dehydrated fruits, vegetables and soup mixes

(G-7995)
PIEDMONT DISTILLERS INC
3960 Us Highway 220 (27025-8314)
P.O. Box 472 (27025-0472)
PHONE..............................336 445-0055
Joseph Michalek, *Pr*
Katherine Michalek, *
Candy W Bowlin, *
EMP: 82 **EST:** 1997
SALES (est): 8.98MM **Privately Held**
Web: www.piedmontdistillers.com
SIC: 2085 Distiller's dried grains and solubles, and alcohol

(G-7996)
PINE HALL BRICK CO INC
634 Lindsey Bridge Rd (27025-9477)
P.O. Box 836 (27025-0836)
PHONE..............................336 721-7500
W Steele, *Brnch Mgr*
EMP: 14
SALES (corp-wide): 44.87MM **Privately Held**
Web: www.pinehallbrick.com
SIC: 3259 5211 Adobe brick; Brick
PA: Pine Hall Brick Co., Inc.
2701 Shorefair Dr
Winston Salem NC 27105
336 721-7500

(G-7997)
PMG SM HOLDINGS LLC
Also Called: Seal Master
703 W Decatur St (27025-1817)
PHONE..............................336 548-3250
EMP: 5 **EST:** 2020
SALES (est): 2.19MM **Privately Held**
Web: www.sealmaster.net
SIC: 2851 Wood fillers or sealers

(G-7998)
REMINGTON ARMS COMPANY LLC
H&R 1871
870 Remington Dr (27025-8331)
P.O. Box 1849 (45071-1849)

PHONE..............................800 544-8892
Rebecca Wood, *Brnch Mgr*
EMP: 211
SALES (corp-wide): 97.62MM **Privately Held**
Web: www.remington.com
SIC: 3484 Guns (firearms) or gun parts, 30 mm. and below
PA: Remington Arms Company, Llc
2592 Arkansas Hwy 15n
Lonoke AR 72086
336 548-8700

(G-7999)
REMINGTON ARMS COMPANY LLC
Marlin Firearms Company
870 Remington Dr (27025-8331)
P.O. Box 1849 (45071-1849)
PHONE..............................800 544-8892
Robert Behn, *Brnch Mgr*
EMP: 104
SALES (corp-wide): 97.62MM **Privately Held**
Web: www.remington.com
SIC: 3484 Rifles or rifle parts, 30 mm. and below
PA: Remington Arms Company, Llc
2592 Arkansas Hwy 15n
Lonoke AR 72086
336 548-8700

(G-8000)
SOUTHERN STEEL AND WIRE INC
100 Minich Rd (27025-8474)
PHONE..............................336 548-9611
David Kendrick, *VP*
EMP: 95
SQ FT: 37,520
SIC: 3544 3315 Wire drawing and straightening dies; Steel wire and related products
HQ: Southern Steel And Wire, Incorporated
1111 6th St
Highland IL 62249
618 654-2161

(G-8001)
THE MADISON COMPANY INC
Also Called: Gem-Dandy
200 W Academy St (27025-2002)
PHONE..............................336 548-9624
Tom Robinson, *Brnch Mgr*
EMP: 25
SALES (corp-wide): 5.7MM **Privately Held**
Web: www.gem-dandy.com
SIC: 2387 2341 2389 Apparel belts; Women's and children's undergarments; Suspenders
PA: The Madison Company Inc
200 W Academy St
Madison NC 27025
336 548-9624

(G-8002)
UNIFI INC
Also Called: Unifi Plant 3
805 Island Dr (27025)
P.O. Box 737 (27025)
PHONE..............................336 427-1890
Carol Sparks, *Mgr*
EMP: 201
SALES (corp-wide): 582.21MM **Publicly Held**
Web: www.unifi.com
SIC: 2281 Manmade and synthetic fiber yarns, spun
PA: Unifi, Inc.
7201 W Friendly Ave
Greensboro NC 27410
336 294-4410

(G-8003)
WENTWORTH CORPORATION
301 K Fork Rd (27025-7532)
PHONE..................................336 548-1802
Phillip Ray Junior, *Pr*
Betty S Harter, *Sec*
John B Sealy Junior, *Prin*
Steve Hassenfelt, *Prin*
Donald Orr, *Prin*
▲ EMP: 6 EST: 1971
SQ FT: 24,000
SALES (est): 250.77K **Privately Held**
Web: www.wentworthcorp.com
SIC: 2387 Apparel belts

(G-8004)
WRIGHT PRINTING SERVICE INC
1510 W Academy St (27025-9320)
P.O. Box 483 (27025-0483)
PHONE..................................336 427-4768
Daniel F Wright, *Pr*
EMP: 6 EST: 1986
SQ FT: 4,800
SALES (est): 485.19K **Privately Held**
Web: www.wrightprinting.net
SIC: 2752 5943 Offset printing; Office forms
and supplies

Maggie Valley
Haywood County

(G-8005)
CAROLINA ASPHALT MAINTENANCE
Also Called: Asphalt
5490 Soco Rd (28751-9522)
PHONE..................................828 944-0425
Tracy Price, *Pr*
EMP: 4 EST: 2019
SALES (est): 247.54K **Privately Held**
Web: www.camasphalt.com
SIC: 2951 Asphalt and asphaltic paving
mixtures (not from refineries)

(G-8006)
TOWN OF MAGGIE VALLEY INC
Also Called: Maggie Valley Sanitary Dst
45 Water Plant Rd (28751)
P.O. Box 1029 (28751-1029)
PHONE..................................828 926-0145
Niel Carpenter, *Mgr*
EMP: 10
Web: maggiewater.myruralwater.com
SIC: 3589 6531 Water treatment equipment,
industrial; Real estate agents and managers
PA: Town Of Maggie Valley Inc
3987 Soco Rd
Maggie Valley NC 28751
828 926-0866

Maiden
Catawba County

(G-8007)
BEN PUSHPA INC
2896 E Maiden Rd (28650-9605)
PHONE..................................828 428-8590
Nayana Patel, *Prin*
EMP: 8 EST: 2005
SALES (est): 1.42MM **Privately Held**
SIC: 3873 Watches, clocks, watchcases,
and parts

(G-8008)
C O JELLIFF CORPORATION
Also Called: L G M
4292 Providence Mill Rd (28650-8593)
P.O. Box 456 (28650-0456)
PHONE..................................828 428-3672

Mark Beals, *Brnch Mgr*
EMP: 8
SALES (corp-wide): 3.41MM **Privately
Held**
Web: www.jelliff.com
SIC: 3357 3825 Automotive wire and cable,
except ignition sets: nonferrous; Ignition
testing instruments
PA: C. O. Jelliff Corporation
354 Pequot Ave Ste 300
Southport CT 06890
203 259-1615

(G-8009)
**CALDWELLS MT PROCESS
ABATTOIRS**
3726 Goodson Rd (28650-8216)
PHONE..................................828 428-8833
Kevin Caldwell, *Owner*
EMP: 4 EST: 1971
SALES (est): 163.29K **Privately Held**
SIC: 2011 Meat packing plants

(G-8010)
**CAROLINA MILLS INCORPORATED
(PA)**
618 N Carolina Ave (28650-1170)
P.O. Box 157 (28650-0157)
PHONE..................................828 428-9911
Bryan E Beal, *Pr*
George A Moretz, *Sec*
◆ EMP: 96 EST: 1928
SQ FT: 100,000
SALES (est): 6.52MM
SALES (corp-wide): 6.52MM **Privately
Held**
Web: www.carolinamills.com
SIC: 2281 2211 2221 2257 Knitting yarn,
spun; Upholstery fabrics, cotton; Upholstery
fabrics, manmade fiber and silk; Dyeing
and finishing circular knit fabrics

(G-8011)
CAROLINA NONWOVENS LLC
Also Called: Cnc
1106 Jw Abernathy Plant Rd (28650-9697)
PHONE..................................704 735-5600
Frederick Fink, *Pr*
S Paul Whitaker, *Ex VP*
▲ EMP: 15 EST: 2006
SQ FT: 75,000
SALES (est): 2.68MM
SALES (corp-wide): 40.55MM **Privately
Held**
Web: www.carolinanonwovens.com
SIC: 2297 Nonwoven fabrics
PA: National Spinning Co., Inc.
1481 W 2nd St
Washington NC 27889
252 975-7111

(G-8012)
ETHAN ALLEN RETAIL INC
Also Called: Ethan Allen Maiden Division
700 S Main Ave (28650-8211)
PHONE..................................828 428-9361
Wade Spears, *Mgr*
EMP: 38
Web: www.ethanallen.com
SIC: 5712 2511 2426 Furniture stores; Wood
household furniture; Hardwood dimension
and flooring mills
HQ: Ethan Allen Retail, Inc.
25 Lake Avenue Ext
Danbury CT 06811
203 743-8000

(G-8013)
FAIRVIEW WOODCARVING INC
2092 Anaconda Ln (28650-9361)
PHONE..................................828 428-9491

Samuel Dellinger, *Pr*
Sherry Dellinger, *Sec*
EMP: 6 EST: 1989
SALES (est): 402.93K **Privately Held**
SIC: 2499 Carved and turned wood

(G-8014)
GREGORY HILL FRAME
108 W Cemetery St (28650-1172)
PHONE..................................828 428-0007
Gregg Campbell, *Owner*
EMP: 10 EST: 1994
SALES (est): 173.03K **Privately Held**
SIC: 2426 Frames for upholstered furniture,
wood

(G-8015)
KEENER WOOD PRODUCTS INC
4274 Providence Mill Rd (28650-8593)
P.O. Box 566 (28650-0566)
PHONE..................................828 428-1562
Ronnie Keener, *VP*
Chad Dale Keener, *Pr*
EMP: 4 EST: 1997
SALES (est): 220.09K **Privately Held**
Web: www.keenerwoodproducts.com
SIC: 2421 2499 Wood chips, produced at mill
; Carved and turned wood

(G-8016)
PARKER SOUTHERN INC
15 W Holly St (28650-8596)
P.O. Box 568 (28650-0568)
PHONE..................................828 428-3506
Tony Parker, *Pr*
Gary Parker, *VP*
EMP: 10 EST: 1991
SQ FT: 60,000
SALES (est): 1.41MM
SALES (corp-wide): 11.23MM **Privately
Held**
Web: www.parkersouthern.com
SIC: 2512 2521 Upholstered household
furniture; Wood office furniture
PA: Temple, Inc.
102 S 7th Avenue Ext
Maiden NC 28650
828 428-8031

(G-8017)
SOUTH FORK INDUSTRIES INC
100 W Pine St (28650-1261)
P.O. Box 742 (28650-0742)
PHONE..................................828 428-9921
EMP: 75 EST: 1988
SALES (est): 4.25MM **Privately Held**
Web: www.southforkind.com
SIC: 2257 2269 2261 Dyeing and finishing
circular knit fabrics; Finishing plants, nec;
Finishing plants, cotton

(G-8018)
TEMPLE INC (PA)
Also Called: Temple Furniture
102 S 7th Avenue Ext (28650-1451)
P.O. Box 185 (28650-0185)
PHONE..................................828 428-8031
Tony A Parker, *Pr*
Gary Parker, *
Adrian Parker, *
EMP: 85 EST: 1977
SQ FT: 67,500
SALES (est): 11.23MM
SALES (corp-wide): 11.23MM **Privately
Held**
Web: www.templefurniture.com
SIC: 2512 Couches, sofas, and davenports:
upholstered on wood frames

(G-8019)
TOUCH UP SOLUTIONS INC
4372 Providence Mill Rd (28650-8594)
P.O. Box 368 (28650-0368)
PHONE..................................828 428-9094
Troy W Pait, *Pr*
William T Brown, *VP*
EMP: 22 EST: 2006
SQ FT: 44,760
SALES (est): 1.36MM **Privately Held**
Web: www.touchupsolutions.com
SIC: 2599 7641 Factory furniture and fixtures
; Furniture repair and maintenance

Manns Harbor
Dare County

(G-8020)
MANN CUSTOM BOATS INC
6300 Us Highway 64 # 264 (27953-9574)
P.O. Box 239 (27953-0239)
PHONE..................................252 473-1716
Paul Mann, *Pr*
Robin Mann, *VP*
EMP: 20 EST: 1987
SQ FT: 8,000
SALES (est): 2.06MM **Privately Held**
Web: www.paulmanncustomboats.com
SIC: 3732 5551 Boats, fiberglass: building
and repairing; Boat dealers

(G-8021)
SPENCER YACHTS INC
5698 Us Highway 64 # 264 (27953-9517)
P.O. Box 210 (27953-0210)
PHONE..................................252 473-2660
Paul Spencer, *Pr*
Shelly Spencer, *
EMP: 25 EST: 1997
SQ FT: 8,000
SALES (est): 437.11K **Privately Held**
Web: www.spenceryachtsinc.com
SIC: 3732 Fishing boats: lobster, crab,
oyster, etc.: small

Manson
Vance County

(G-8022)
INTERNATIONAL PAPER COMPANY
Also Called: International Paper
967 Us Highway 1 S (27553-9085)
P.O. Box 338 (27553-0338)
PHONE..................................252 456-3111
Bob Breneman, *VP*
EMP: 5
SALES (corp-wide): 18.62B **Publicly Held**
Web: www.internationalpaper.com
SIC: 2653 Boxes, corrugated: made from
purchased materials
PA: International Paper Company
6400 Poplar Ave
Memphis TN 38197
901 419-7000

Manteo
Dare County

(G-8023)
ARTHUR DEMAREST
Also Called: Art Press
419 Skyco Rd (27954-9394)
P.O. Box 580 (27981-0580)
PHONE..................................252 473-1449
Arthur Demarest, *Owner*
EMP: 5 EST: 1923

SQ FT: 20,000
SALES (est): 198.07K **Privately Held**
Web: www.artpressprinters.com
SIC: 2752 Offset printing

(G-8024)
TIMES PRINTING COMPANY (PA)
Also Called: Coastland Times
501 Budleigh St (27954)
P.O. Box 400 (27954-0400)
PHONE.........................252 473-2105
Francis W Meekins, *Pr*
Susan M Simpson, *
EMP: 40 **EST:** 1935
SQ FT: 10,000
SALES (est): 986.99K
SALES (corp-wide): 986.99K **Privately Held**
Web: www.thecoastlandtimes.com
SIC: 2711 5943 Commercial printing and newspaper publishing combined; Office forms and supplies

Maple Hill
Pender County

(G-8025)
CAROLINA COASTAL COATINGS INC
375 Padgett Rd (28454-8576)
PHONE.........................910 346-9607
Jenaca Wasicki, *Prin*
Jeffrey D Bailey, *Prin*
EMP: 10 **EST:** 2018
SALES (est): 106.92K **Privately Held**
SIC: 3479 7389 Painting, coating, and hot dipping; Business services, nec

(G-8026)
SEASHORE BUILDERS INC
5930 Nc Hwy 50 (28454-8175)
PHONE.........................910 259-3404
Elizabeth Raynor, *Pr*
Elizabeth G Raynor, *
Stephen L Raynor, *
EMP: 27 **EST:** 2001
SALES (est): 1.61MM **Privately Held**
Web: www.seashorebuilders.net
SIC: 1522 1541 1542 1751 Residential construction, nec; Industrial buildings and warehouses; Commercial and office buildings, renovation and repair; Framing contractor

Marble
Cherokee County

(G-8027)
PAMELA STOEPPELWERTH
Also Called: Mountain Manner Exotic Jellies
929 Coalville Rd (28905-8519)
PHONE.........................828 837-7293
Pamela Stoeppelwerth, *Owner*
EMP: 4 **EST:** 1997
SALES (est): 165.59K **Privately Held**
Web: www.mountainmanna.net
SIC: 2033 Jams, jellies, and preserves, packaged in cans, jars, etc.

(G-8028)
VALWOOD CORPORATION
35 Coalville Rd (28905-8888)
PHONE.........................828 321-4717
Chris Logan, *Pr*
Tom Buchanon, *VP*
EMP: 7 **EST:** 1972
SALES (est): 1.82MM **Privately Held**
SIC: 2421 Wood chips, produced at mill

Marion
Mcdowell County

(G-8029)
ABB MOTORS AND MECHANICAL INC
Also Called: Marian Manufacturing Plant
510 Rockwell Dr (28752-8821)
PHONE.........................479 646-4711
Ronald E Tucker, *CEO*
EMP: 8
Web: www.baldor.com
SIC: 3621 Electric motor and generator parts
HQ: Abb Motors And Mechanical Inc.
5711 R S Boreham Jr St
Fort Smith AR 72901
479 646-4711

(G-8030)
AJS DEZIGNS INC
Also Called: Allied Industrial
Ashworth Rd (28752)
P.O. Box 1360 (28762-1360)
PHONE.........................828 652-6304
Len Warren, *Pr*
Anita F Warren, *Treas*
EMP: 8 **EST:** 1987
SQ FT: 8,400
SALES (est): 362.73K **Privately Held**
Web: www.alliedindustrial.net
SIC: 2541 2431 Cabinets, except refrigerated: show, display, etc.: wood; Millwork

(G-8031)
AMERICAN PLASTIC INC
136 W Marion Business Park (28752-5574)
P.O. Box 1269 (28752-1269)
PHONE.........................828 652-3511
Jim Hall, *Pr*
EMP: 9 **EST:** 1997
SQ FT: 5,000
SALES (est): 420.83K **Privately Held**
Web: www.americanplastics.com
SIC: 3089 Injection molding of plastics

(G-8032)
B V HEDRICK GRAVEL & SAND CO
Also Called: Cumberland Gravel
1182 Old Glenwood Rd (28752-7785)
PHONE.........................828 738-0332
John Brown, *Mgr*
EMP: 9
SALES (corp-wide): 238.17MM **Privately Held**
Web: www.hedrickind.com
SIC: 1442 Construction sand and gravel
PA: B. V. Hedrick Gravel & Sand Company
120 1/2 Church St
Salisbury NC 28144
704 633-5982

(G-8033)
BALDOR DODGE RELIANCE
510 Rockwell Dr (28752-8821)
PHONE.........................828 652-0074
Terry Fulmer, *Prin*
▲ **EMP:** 22 **EST:** 2008
SALES (est): 6.45MM **Privately Held**
SIC: 3562 Ball bearings and parts

(G-8034)
BAXTER HEALTHCARE CORPORATION
65 Pitts Station Rd (28752-7925)
PHONE.........................828 756-6623
Keely Elkins, *Mgr*
EMP: 10
SALES (corp-wide): 10.64B **Publicly Held**

Web: www.baxter.com
SIC: 2834 Pharmaceutical preparations
HQ: Baxter Healthcare Corporation
1 Baxter Pkwy
Deerfield IL 60015
224 948-2000

(G-8035)
BAXTER HEALTHCARE CORPORATION
Also Called: Baxter US
65 Pitts Station Rd (28752-7925)
P.O. Box 1390 (28752-1390)
PHONE.........................828 756-6600
Tony Johnson, *Mgr*
EMP: 329
SALES (corp-wide): 10.64B **Publicly Held**
Web: www.baxter.com
SIC: 2834 Pharmaceutical preparations
HQ: Baxter Healthcare Corporation
1 Baxter Pkwy
Deerfield IL 60015
224 948-2000

(G-8036)
BOYD STONE & QUARRIES
2207 Cannon Rd (28752-2944)
P.O. Box 579 (28752-0579)
PHONE.........................828 659-6862
Mark Boyd, *Pt*
EMP: 5 **EST:** 1987
SALES (est): 509.44K **Privately Held**
SIC: 1422 Crushed and broken limestone

(G-8037)
BUECHEL STONE CORP
7274 Us 221 N (28752-6103)
PHONE.........................800 236-4474
EMP: 70
SALES (corp-wide): 15.32MM **Privately Held**
Web: www.buechelstone.com
SIC: 3281 Cut stone and stone products
PA: Buechel Stone Corp.
W3639 County Road H
Chilton WI 53014
920 922-4790

(G-8038)
CAROLINA CHOCOLATIERS INC
20 N Main St (28752-3936)
PHONE.........................828 652-4496
Kelly Lewis, *Pr*
EMP: 5 **EST:** 1981
SALES (est): 153.93K **Privately Held**
SIC: 2064 Chocolate candy, except solid chocolate

(G-8039)
CAROLINA PALLET RECYCLING INC
2855 Nc 226 I 40 (28752-7775)
P.O. Box 1233 (28752-1233)
PHONE.........................828 652-6818
Randall O Crowder, *Pr*
Janet Crowder, *VP*
EMP: 6 **EST:** 1992
SQ FT: 30,000
SALES (est): 588.12K **Privately Held**
SIC: 2448 Pallets, wood

(G-8040)
CHATTER FREE TLING SLTIONS INC
1877 Rutherford Rd (28752-4764)
PHONE.........................828 659-7379
Joel Hardin, *Prin*
EMP: 4 **EST:** 2011
SALES (est): 98.38K **Privately Held**
SIC: 3999 Manufacturing industries, nec

(G-8041)
EDWARDS WOOD PDTS INC/ WOODLAWN
8482 Us 221 N (28752-7564)
P.O. Box 219 (28103-0219)
PHONE.........................828 756-4758
Jeffrey G Edwards, *CEO*
EMP: 6 **EST:** 2010
SALES (est): 138.94K **Privately Held**
Web: www.ewpi.com
SIC: 2421 Sawmills and planing mills, general

(G-8042)
HALDEX INC
5334 Us Hwy 221 N (28752-6100)
P.O. Box 1129 (28752-1129)
PHONE.........................828 652-9308
EMP: 115
SALES (corp-wide): 472.17MM **Privately Held**
SIC: 3714 3568 3561 Motor vehicle brake systems and parts; Power transmission equipment, nec; Pumps and pumping equipment
HQ: Haldex, Inc.
10930 N Pomona Ave
Kansas City MO 64153
816 891-2470

(G-8043)
HUNTER LIVER MUSH INC
98 Poteat Rd (28752-9014)
PHONE.........................828 652-7902
Jerry Hunter, *Pr*
Carolyn Hunter, *VP*
Phyllis Harmon, *Sec*
Louise Rumfelt, *Treas*
EMP: 9 **EST:** 1959
SQ FT: 5,000
SALES (est): 310.44K **Privately Held**
SIC: 2013 Sausages and other prepared meats

(G-8044)
ITL CORP
203 College Dr (28752-7723)
PHONE.........................828 659-9663
EMP: 16
Web: www.itlcorp.com
SIC: 2421 Sawmills and planing mills, general
HQ: Itl Corp.
23925 Commerce Park
Cleveland OH 44122
216 831-3140

(G-8045)
JELD-WEN INC
Also Called: Fiber N C Div
100 Henry Mccall Rd (28752-7412)
PHONE.........................828 724-9511
Jim English, *Mgr*
EMP: 60
Web: www.jeld-wen.ca
SIC: 2431 Doors, wood
HQ: Jeld-Wen, Inc.
2645 Silver Crescent Dr
Charlotte NC 28273
800 535-3936

(G-8046)
JOHNSON PAVING COMPANY INC
3101 Us 221 North (28752)
P.O. Box 1066 (28752-1066)
PHONE.........................828 652-4911
Gregory Johnson, *Pr*
Virginia Johnson, *Sec*
EMP: 12 **EST:** 1968
SQ FT: 150
SALES (est): 1.65MM **Privately Held**

Web: www.johnsonpavingcompany.com
SIC: **1499** 1611 2951 Asphalt mining and bituminous stone quarrying; Highway and street paving contractor; Asphalt paving mixtures and blocks

(G-8047)
JOSEPH SOTANSKI
Also Called: Forever Outdoors
632 College Dr (28752-8729)
PHONE.................................407 324-6187
Joseph Sotanski, *Owner*
EMP: 30
SALES (corp-wide): 429.28K **Privately Held**
SIC: **2519** 3999 Garden furniture, except wood, metal, stone, or concrete; Lawn ornaments
PA: Joseph Sotanski
2260 Old Lake Mary Rd
Sanford FL 32771
407 324-6187

(G-8048)
KEY GAS COMPONENTS INC (PA)
160 Clay St (28752-3570)
PHONE.................................828 655-1700
Roy Kuhn, *CEO*
Jim Kuhn, *
Mary Ann Kuhn, *Stockholder**
Henderson Cathcart, *
Michelle Cline, *
▲ EMP: 34 EST: 1986
SQ FT: 50,000
SALES (est): 12.19MM
SALES (corp-wide): 12.19MM **Privately Held**
Web: www.keygas.com
SIC: **3498** 3491 3494 3432 Manifolds, pipe: fabricated from purchased pipe; Gas valves and parts, industrial; Valves and pipe fittings, nec; Plumbing fixture fittings and trim

(G-8049)
MARION CULTURED MARBLE INC
Also Called: Wilson Marble
4805 Us 70 W (28752-7448)
P.O. Box 2562 (28752-2562)
PHONE.................................828 724-4782
Randy Wilson, *Pr*
Kenny Wilson, *VP*
Bernice Wilson, *Treas*
EMP: 5 EST: 1972
SQ FT: 26,250
SALES (est): 248.84K **Privately Held**
SIC: **3281** 3088 Marble, building: cut and shaped; Plastics plumbing fixtures

(G-8050)
MARION MACHINE LLC
169 Machine Shop Rd (28752-2812)
PHONE.................................800 627-1639
Howard Mcneil, *Brnch Mgr*
EMP: 40
SALES (corp-wide): 71.76MM **Privately Held**
Web: www.marionmachinellc.com
SIC: **3599** Machine shop, jobbing and repair
HQ: Marion Machine Llc
14937 Warfordsburg Rd
Hancock MD 21750
301 678-2000

(G-8051)
MASTERS HAND PRINT WORKS INC
5 Old Greenlee Rd W (28752-6226)
P.O. Box 190 (28752-0190)
PHONE.................................828 652-5833
Brian K Johnston, *Pr*
Linda Johnston, *Stockholder*

EMP: 4 EST: 2006
SALES (est): 169.42K **Privately Held**
Web: www.mastershandprint.com
SIC: **2752** 2759 Offset printing; Commercial printing, nec

(G-8052)
MCC HOLDINGS INC
Also Called: Crane Resistoflex
1 Quality Way (28752-9410)
PHONE.................................828 724-4000
EMP: 170
SALES (corp-wide): 2.13B **Publicly Held**
Web: www.cranecpe.com
SIC: **3492** Control valves, fluid power: hydraulic and pneumatic
HQ: Mcc Holdings, Inc.
4526 Res Frest Dr Ste 400
The Woodlands TX 77381
936 271-6500

(G-8053)
MCDOWELL CEMENT PRODUCTS CO (HQ)
S Garden St (28752)
PHONE.................................828 652-5721
Robert H Boone, *Pr*
John Boone, *VP*
Susan B Gardin, *Sec*
EMP: 11 EST: 1947
SALES (est): 2.29MM
SALES (corp-wide): 5.15MM **Privately Held**
Web: www.mcdowellnews.com
SIC: **3273** Ready-mixed concrete
PA: Explosives Supply Company
167 Roan Rd
Spruce Pine NC 28777
828 765-2762

(G-8054)
MCDOWELL COUNTY MILLWORK LLC
4 Old West Henderson St (28752-7889)
P.O. Box 726 (28714-0726)
PHONE.................................828 682-6215
Deanna French, *Mgr*
EMP: 6 EST: 2006
SALES (est): 553.81K **Privately Held**
Web: www.mcdowellchamber.com
SIC: **2434** Wood kitchen cabinets

(G-8055)
MCDOWELL LFAC
Also Called: Farmers of The Foothills
263 Barnes Rd Ste J (28752-6989)
PHONE.................................828 289-5553
Molly Sandfoss, *Pr*
EMP: 15 EST: 2018
SALES (est): 453.77K **Privately Held**
Web: www.foothillsfoodhub.org
SIC: **2711** Newspapers, publishing and printing

(G-8056)
MPV MORGANTON PRESSU
1 Alfredo Baglioni Dr (28752-5104)
PHONE.................................828 652-3704
EMP: 11
SALES (est): 3.71MM **Privately Held**
Web: www.morgantonpv.com
SIC: **1382** Oil and gas exploration services

(G-8057)
MPV MRGNTON PRSSURE VSSELS NC
Also Called: Morganton Pressure Vessels LLC
1 Alfredo Baglioni Dr (28752-5104)
PHONE.................................828 652-3704
Franco Tartaglino, *Managing Member*

▲ EMP: 118 EST: 2006
SQ FT: 110,000
SALES (est): 26.74MM **Privately Held**
Web: www.morgantonpv.com
SIC: **3491** Pressure valves and regulators, industrial
HQ: Baglioni Spa
Strada Biandrate 24
Novara NO 28100

(G-8058)
NEW WORLD TECHNOLOGIES INC
Also Called: Midnight Machining
78 W Marion Business Park (28752-5041)
PHONE.................................828 652-8662
Alex Lee Hawkins, *Treas*
Misty Callahan, *Sec*
Greg Ward, *Pr*
EMP: 4 EST: 1997
SQ FT: 8,200
SALES (est): 178.14K **Privately Held**
SIC: **3599** Machine shop, jobbing and repair

(G-8059)
ORA INC
315 Baldwin Ave (28752-6656)
PHONE.................................540 903-7177
Steven Parks, *Pr*
EMP: 7 EST: 2016
SQ FT: 20,000
SALES (est): 548.24K **Privately Held**
SIC: **3542** 3569 3599 3442 High energy rate metal forming machines; Testing chambers for altitude, temperature, ordnance, power; Custom machinery; Metal doors

(G-8060)
PEPSICO INC
Also Called: Pepsico
8337 Us 221 N (28752-9647)
P.O. Box 550 (28603-0550)
PHONE.................................828 756-4662
Dan Revis, *Brnch Mgr*
EMP: 6
SALES (corp-wide): 91.47B **Publicly Held**
Web: www.pepsico.com
SIC: **2086** Carbonated soft drinks, bottled and canned
PA: Pepsico, Inc.
700 Anderson Hill Rd
Purchase NY 10577
914 253-2000

(G-8061)
PLEASANT GARDENS MACHINE INC
2708 Us 70 W (28752-8815)
PHONE.................................828 724-4173
Michael L Queen, *Pr*
Lawrence Queen, *Treas*
EMP: 11 EST: 1965
SQ FT: 43,000
SALES (est): 2.34MM **Privately Held**
Web: www.pgmachine.com
SIC: **3599** Machine shop, jobbing and repair

(G-8062)
RATOON AGROPROCESSING LLC
5290 Nc 226 S (28752-8733)
PHONE.................................828 273-9114
EMP: 6 EST: 2019
SALES (est): 631.73K **Privately Held**
Web: www.ratoonagroprocessing.com
SIC: **3999** Manufacturing industries, nec

(G-8063)
ROCKWELL AUTOMATION INC
510 Rockwell Dr (28752-8821)
PHONE.................................828 652-0074
Mark Early, *Mgr*
EMP: 12
Web: www.rockwellautomation.com

SIC: **3625** Electric controls and control accessories, industrial
PA: Rockwell Automation, Inc.
1201 S 2nd St
Milwaukee WI 53204

(G-8064)
ROSS SKID PRODUCTS INC
7 Landis Rd (28752-7711)
P.O. Box 1455 (28752-1455)
PHONE.................................828 652-7450
Perry Jack Ross, *Pr*
EMP: 20 EST: 1972
SQ FT: 6,000
SALES (est): 937.24K **Privately Held**
SIC: **2448** Pallets, wood

(G-8065)
SMITHS CUSTOM KITCHEN INC
58 Butterfly Dr (28752-7848)
PHONE.................................828 652-9033
Darryl K Smith, *Pr*
Brenda Smith, *VP*
EMP: 5 EST: 1982
SALES (est): 163.13K **Privately Held**
SIC: **2434** Wood kitchen cabinets

(G-8066)
SPEER OPERATIONAL TECH LLC
315 Baldwin Ave (28752-6656)
PHONE.................................864 631-2512
Amanda Westmoreland, *Pr*
Ted Westmorland, *Genl Mgr*
EMP: 4 EST: 2007
SALES (est): 165.21K **Privately Held**
SIC: **5099** 3999 5999 5047 Safety equipment and supplies; Fire extinguishers, portable; Alarm and safety equipment stores; Instruments, surgical and medical

(G-8067)
SSS LOGGING INC
29 Liberty Dr (28752-5159)
P.O. Box 281 (28752-0281)
PHONE.................................828 467-1155
Doyle Shuford, *Pr*
EMP: 7 EST: 2002
SALES (est): 549.07K **Privately Held**
SIC: **2411** Logging

(G-8068)
SUPERIOR MACHINE CO SC INC
Also Called: Marion Machine Div
169 Machine Shop Rd (28752-2812)
PHONE.................................828 652-6141
E L Cunningham, *Brnch Mgr*
EMP: 35
SALES (corp-wide): 47.88MM **Privately Held**
Web: www.smco.net
SIC: **3599** 7629 3444 Machine shop, jobbing and repair; Electrical repair shops; Sheet metalwork
HQ: Superior Machine Co. Of South Carolina, Inc.
692 N Cashua Dr
Florence SC 29501
843 468-9200

(G-8069)
TILSON MACHINE INC (PA)
632 College Dr (28752-8729)
PHONE.................................828 668-4416
EMP: 81 EST: 1988
SALES (est): 9.51MM
SALES (corp-wide): 9.51MM **Privately Held**
Web: www.tilsonmachine.com
SIC: **3599** Machine and other job shop work

(G-8070)
TOOLCRAFT INC NORTH CAROLINA (PA)
1877 Rutherford Rd (28752-4764)
PHONE................828 659-7379
Darvy Hensley, *Pr*
EMP: 15 EST: 1978
SQ FT: 40,000
SALES (est): 4.58MM
SALES (corp-wide): 4.58MM **Privately Held**
Web: www.toolcraftinc.com
SIC: 3545 3469 Tools and accessories for machine tools; Machine parts, stamped or pressed metal

(G-8071)
UNIVERSAL MACHINE AND TOOL INC
1114 W Marion Business Park (28752)
P.O. Box 756 (28762-0756)
PHONE................828 659-2002
David Lytle, *Pr*
EMP: 7 EST: 1995
SQ FT: 5,000
SALES (est): 1.65MM **Privately Held**
SIC: 3599 Machine shop, jobbing and repair

(G-8072)
WESTROCK RKT LLC
468 Carolina Ave (28752-2846)
PHONE................828 655-1303
Pat Warner, *Brnch Mgr*
EMP: 32
Web: www.westrock.com
SIC: 2653 Boxes, corrugated: made from purchased materials
HQ: Westrock Rkt, Llc
1000 Abernathy Rd Ste 125
Atlanta GA 30328
770 448-2193

(G-8073)
WESTROCK RKT LLC
1659 E Court St (28752-4565)
PHONE................770 448-2193
Steve Arrell, *Mgr*
EMP: 258
Web: www.westrock.com
SIC: 2657 2752 Folding paperboard boxes; Commercial printing, lithographic
HQ: Westrock Rkt, Llc
1000 Abernathy Rd Ste 125
Atlanta GA 30328
770 448-2193

(G-8074)
WNC DRY KILN INC (PA)
65 Jacktown Rd (28752-9206)
P.O. Box 777 (28752-0777)
PHONE................828 652-0050
Joe Lyle, *Pr*
Tom Thrash, *VP*
Tommy Orr, *Sec*
EMP: 10 EST: 2003
SQ FT: 10,000
SALES (est): 1.22MM
SALES (corp-wide): 1.22MM **Privately Held**
Web: www.wncpallet.com
SIC: 5093 2421 Lumber scrap; Lumber: rough, sawed, or planed

(G-8075)
WOODLAWN TIRE AND ALGNMT INC
Also Called: Woodlawn Tire & Alignment
8021 Us 221 N (28752-7565)
PHONE................828 756-4212
Andrew Winters, *CEO*
EMP: 6 EST: 2006

SALES (est): 189.15K **Privately Held**
SIC: 7534 Tire repair shop

Mars Hill
Madison County

(G-8076)
ADVANCED SUPERABRASIVES INC
1270 N Main St (28754-7500)
P.O. Box 1390 (28754-1390)
PHONE................828 689-3200
Jonathan Szucs, *Pr*
Attila Szucs, *
EMP: 28 EST: 1993
SQ FT: 34,000
SALES (est): 5.18MM **Privately Held**
Web: www.asiwheels.com
SIC: 3545 3291 Diamond cutting tools for turning, boring, burnishing, etc.; Abrasive products

(G-8077)
FFR ELECTRICS LLC
Also Called: Outrider USA
400 Hickory Dr Unit 2 (28754-0479)
PHONE................828 654-7555
Jesse Lee, *Prin*
EMP: 10 EST: 2013
SALES (est): 448.7K **Privately Held**
Web: www.outriderusa.com
SIC: 5941 3751 Sporting goods and bicycle shops; Motorcycles, bicycles and parts

(G-8078)
TREE CRAFT LOG HOMES INC
43 Back Hollow Rd (28754-6702)
PHONE................828 689-2240
Don Fosson, *Pr*
Edward A Fosson, *VP*
Nancy A Fosson, *Sec*
EMP: 5 EST: 1978
SQ FT: 6,400
SALES (est): 61.15K **Privately Held**
Web: www.treecraft.net
SIC: 2452 Log cabins, prefabricated, wood

Marshall
Madison County

(G-8079)
DERINGER-NEY INC
155 Deringer Dr (28753)
P.O. Box 159 (28753-0159)
PHONE................828 649-3232
Richard Rzeszotarski, *Brnch Mgr*
EMP: 42
SALES (corp-wide): 96.37MM **Privately Held**
Web: www.deringerney.com
SIC: 3643 Contacts, electrical
PA: Deringer-Ney Inc.
353 Woodland Ave
Bloomfield CT 06002
860 242-2281

(G-8080)
GANNETT MEDIA CORP
News Record & Sentinal
58 Back St (28753)
P.O. Box 999 (28754)
PHONE................828 649-1075
Christina Rice, *Brnch Mgr*
EMP: 6
SALES (corp-wide): 2.51B **Publicly Held**
Web: www.gannett.com
SIC: 2711 Newspapers, publishing and printing
HQ: Gannett Media Corp.

7950 Jones Branch Dr
Mclean VA 22102
703 854-6000

(G-8081)
MEDICAL MISSIONARY PRESS
491 Blue Hill Rd (28753-5366)
PHONE................828 649-3976
Bob Jorgensen, *Dir*
EMP: 4 EST: 1985
SQ FT: 4,500
SALES (est): 51.96K **Privately Held**
Web: www.mmpress.info
SIC: 2741 Miscellaneous publishing

(G-8082)
PRINTPACK INC
Also Called: Printpack Medical Store
100 Kenpak Ln (28753-0770)
PHONE................828 649-3800
Cha Taoshwan, *Brnch Mgr*
EMP: 188
SALES (corp-wide): 684.49MM **Privately Held**
Web: www.printpack.com
SIC: 3081 Film base, cellulose acetate or nitrocellulose plastics
HQ: Printpack, Inc.
2800 Overlook Pkwy Ne
Atlanta GA 30339
404 460-7000

(G-8083)
RED SHED WOODWORKS INC
200 Carl Bowman Rd (28753-4409)
P.O. Box 53 (28753-0053).
PHONE................828 768-3854
Matt Yeakley, *Pr*
Morgan Yeakley, *VP*
EMP: 8 EST: 2004
SALES (est): 1.24MM **Privately Held**
Web: www.redshedwoodworks.com
SIC: 2431 Millwork

Marshallberg
Carteret County

(G-8084)
BUDSIN WOOD CRAFT
142 Moore Ln (28553-9713)
PHONE................252 729-1540
Tom Hesselink, *Owner*
EMP: 4 EST: 1987
SALES (est): 149.89K **Privately Held**
Web: www.budsin.com
SIC: 3732 Boats, fiberglass: building and repairing

Marshville
Union County

(G-8085)
ALLYN INTERNATIONAL TRDG CORP (PA)
412 College St (28103-1343)
P.O. Box 1682 (28111-1682)
PHONE................877 858-2482
Ernest Allen, *Pr*
EMP: 8 EST: 2016
SQ FT: 28,000
SALES (est): 952.77K
SALES (corp-wide): 952.77K **Privately Held**
Web: www.aitc-steel.com
SIC: 8741 5085 2297 3842 Management services; Industrial supplies; Nonwoven fabrics; Surgical appliances and supplies

(G-8086)
CAROLINA WD PDTS MRSHVILLE INC
1112 Doctor Blair Rd (28103-9704)
P.O. Box 523 (28103-0523)
PHONE................704 624-2119
Robert Horne Junior, *CEO*
Ronald Horne, *
Randy Horne, *
Frances Horne, *
EMP: 65 EST: 1969
SQ FT: 70,220
SALES (est): 4.86MM **Privately Held**
Web: www.carolinawood.net
SIC: 2448 2449 2441 Pallets, wood; Wood containers, nec; Nailed wood boxes and shook

(G-8087)
EDWARDS TIMBER COMPANY INC (PA)
2215 Old Lawyers Rd (28103-8002)
P.O. Box 219 (28103-0219)
PHONE................704 624-5098
Carroll Edwards, *CEO*
EMP: 6 EST: 1969
SALES (est): 2.29MM
SALES (corp-wide): 2.29MM **Privately Held**
Web: www.ewpi.com
SIC: 2421 Sawmills and planing mills, general

(G-8088)
EDWARDS WOOD PRODUCTS INC (PA)
Also Called: Edwards Transportation
2215 Old Lawyers Rd (28103-8002)
P.O. Box 219 (28103-0219)
PHONE................704 624-3624
Jeffrey G Edwards, *Pr*
Tina Edwards, *
Elona Edwards, *
Michelle Medlin, *
Lisa E Ammons, *
◆ EMP: 250 EST: 1969
SQ FT: 48,000
SALES (est): 29.48MM
SALES (corp-wide): 29.48MM **Privately Held**
Web: www.ewpi.com
SIC: 2448 2421 2631 2426 Pallets, wood; Sawmills and planing mills, general; Chip board; Hardwood dimension and flooring mills

(G-8089)
GRIFFIN INDUSTRIES LLC
Also Called: Bakery Feeds
5805 Highway 74 E (28103-7035)
PHONE................704 624-9140
John Lerch, *Mgr*
EMP: 52
SALES (corp-wide): 6.79B **Publicly Held**
Web: www.griffinind.com
SIC: 5083 2048 Agricultural machinery and equipment; Prepared feeds, nec
HQ: Griffin Industries Llc
4221 Alexandria Pike
Cold Spring KY 41076
859 781-2010

(G-8090)
HIGHS WELDING SHOP
1027 Unarco Rd (28103-9328)
P.O. Box 312 (28103-0312)
PHONE................704 624-5707
Thomas High, *Owner*
Douglas High Junior, *Prin*
EMP: 6 EST: 1973
SQ FT: 11,500

G E O G R A P H I C

(PA)=Parent Co (HQ)=Headquarters
✪ = New Business established in last 2 years

SALES (est): 294.37K **Privately Held**
SIC: **7692** Welding repair

(G-8091)
PAUL HOGE CREATIONS INC
Also Called: Www.candlevision.com
7105 E Marshville Blvd (28103-1237)
P.O. Box 540 (28103-0540)
PHONE..............................704 624-6860
Paul Hoge, *Pr*
◆ **EMP:** 15 **EST:** 1976
SQ FT: 15,000
SALES (est): 3.58MM **Privately Held**
Web: www.paulhogecreations.com
SIC: **3999** Candles

(G-8092)
PILGRIMS PRIDE CORPORATION
5901 Hwy 74 E (28103)
PHONE..............................704 624-2171
EMP: 293
Web: www.pilgrims.com
SIC: **2015** 0254 0252 2048 Chicken,
slaughtered and dressed; Chicken hatchery
; Chicken eggs; Poultry feeds
HQ: Pilgrim's Pride Corporation
1770 Promontory Cir
Greeley CO 80634
970 506-8000

(G-8093)
POLY PLASTIC PRODUCTS NC INC
1206 Traywick Rd (28103-9502)
PHONE..............................704 624-2555
Steve Redlich, *Pr*
▼ **EMP:** 78 **EST:** 2003
SALES (est): 11.41MM **Privately Held**
Web: www.sigmaplasticsgroup.com
SIC: **2673** Plastic bags: made from
purchased materials
PA: Alpha Industries Management, Inc.
2919 Center Port Cir
Pompano Beach FL 33064

(G-8094)
SEAFARER LLC (PA)
Also Called: Seagoing Uniform
220 E Main St (28103-1149)
PHONE..............................704 624-3200
Hugh M Efird, *Pr*
Aaron H Efird, *VP*
Debbie Gibson, *Off Mgr*
EMP: 4 **EST:** 1938
SQ FT: 14,000
SALES (est): 1.15MM
SALES (corp-wide): 1.15MM **Privately
Held**
SIC: **2326** 2339 5136 5137 Work shirts:
men's, youths', and boys'; Women's and
misses' outerwear, nec; Men's and boy's
clothing; Women's and children's clothing

(G-8095)
STONY KNOLL FORGE
1309 Hamiltons Cross Rd (28103-9513)
P.O. Box 3352 (28111-3352)
PHONE..............................704 507-0179
William Kiker, *Prin*
EMP: 4 **EST:** 2018
SALES (est): 122.56K **Privately Held**
Web: www.stonyknollforge.com
SIC: **3446** Architectural metalwork

(G-8096)
UNION PLASTICS COMPANY
132 E Union St (28103-1141)
P.O. Box 512 (28103-0512)
PHONE..............................704 624-2112
Carroll H Osborn, *Pr*
Sandra Osborn, *Sec*
EMP: 8 **EST:** 1967

SQ FT: 7,500
SALES (est): 392.13K **Privately Held**
SIC: **3432** Plastic plumbing fixture fittings,
assembly

(G-8097)
WALCO INTERNATIONAL
531 E Main St Ste B (28103-1503)
PHONE..............................704 624-2473
Dale Zaimey, *Prin*
EMP: 5 **EST:** 2009
SALES (est): 151.91K **Privately Held**
SIC: **3999** Pet supplies

Matthews
Mecklenburg County

(G-8098)
AARONS QUALITY SIGNS
524 E Charles St (28105-4788)
P.O. Box 1303 (28106)
PHONE..............................704 841-7733
Catherine Lewis, *Owner*
Catherine Lewis, *Prin*
EMP: 5 **EST:** 1986
SALES (est): 232.57K **Privately Held**
Web: www.aqsigns.com
SIC: **3993** Signs, not made in custom sign
painting shops

(G-8099)
BODY ENGINEERING INC
701 Matthews Mint Hill Rd (28105-1706)
PHONE..............................704 650-3434
Kathy Feldman, *CEO*
Ross Leveque, *Pr*
EMP: 6 **EST:** 2003
SALES (est): 499.46K **Privately Held**
SIC: **2023** Dietary supplements, dairy and
non-dairy based

(G-8100)
BORNEMANN PUMPS INC
901a Matthews Mint Hill Rd (28105-1704)
P.O. Box 1769 (28106-1769)
PHONE..............................704 849-8636
Tim Mabes, *Prin*
EMP: 5 **EST:** 2013
SALES (est): 981.41K **Privately Held**
SIC: **3561** Pumps and pumping equipment

(G-8101)
CAROLINA BG
624 Matthews Mint Hill Rd Ste B
(28105-1761)
PHONE..............................704 847-8840
Thomas Scott, *Mgr*
EMP: 5 **EST:** 2008
SALES (est): 477.02K **Privately Held**
Web:
www.carolinabenefitconsultants.com
SIC: **5169** 2911 Oil additives; Fuel additives

(G-8102)
CAROLINA CONCRETE INC (PA)
1316 Waxhaw Rd (28105)
PHONE..............................704 821-7645
James R Mc Clain, *Pr*
C Louise Mc Clain, *
EMP: 30 **EST:** 1972
SQ FT: 3,000
SALES (est): 1.79MM
SALES (corp-wide): 1.79MM **Privately
Held**
SIC: **3273** Ready-mixed concrete

(G-8103)
CAROTEK INC (HQ)
Also Called: Carotek

700 Sam Newell Rd (28105-4515)
P.O. Box 1395 (28106-1395)
PHONE..............................704 844-1100
James Addison Bell, *CEO*
Deryl L Bell, *
Tara D Snyder, *
▲ **EMP:** 80 **EST:** 1965
SALES (est): 27.72MM
SALES (corp-wide): 664.84MM **Privately
Held**
Web: www.carotek.com
SIC: **7692** 5084 Welding repair; Industrial
machinery and equipment
PA: Sts Operating, Inc.
2301 Windsor Ct
Addison IL 60101
630 317-2700

(G-8104)
CHANNELTIVITY LLC
301 E John St (28106-4201)
P.O. Box 3449 (28106-3449)
PHONE..............................704 408-3560
EMP: 10 **EST:** 2007
SALES (est): 1.53MM **Privately Held**
Web: www.channeltivity.com
SIC: **7372** Business oriented computer
software

(G-8105)
CHARLOTTE OBSERVER PUBG CO
Also Called: Charlotte Observer
10810 Independence Pointe Pkwy Ste H
(28105-1754)
PHONE..............................704 358-6020
Glenn Hargett, *Brnch Mgr*
EMP: 47
SALES (corp-wide): 1.39B **Privately Held**
Web: www.carpet-cleaning-charlotte.com
SIC: **2711** 2741 Newspapers, publishing and
printing; Miscellaneous publishing
HQ: The Charlotte Observer Publishing
Company
550 S Caldwell St Fl 10
Charlotte NC 28202
704 358-5000

(G-8106)
CITY PRINTS LLC
5008 Helena Park Ln (28105-7718)
PHONE..............................404 273-5741
Anthony N Rodono, *Prin*
EMP: 5 **EST:** 2013
SALES (est): 269.25K **Privately Held**
Web: www.cityprintsmapart.com
SIC: **2752** Commercial printing, lithographic
PA: Vertitex Spa
Via Pietro Ferloni 42
Bulgarograsso CO 22070

(G-8107)
COC USA INC
624 Matthews Mint Hill Rd Ste C
(28105-1761)
PHONE..............................888 706-0059
Eiichi Kobayashi, *CEO*
Devin Ware, *Pr*
EMP: 5 **EST:** 2022
SALES (est): 966.18K **Privately Held**
SIC: **3562** Ball and roller bearings

(G-8108)
COCOA BOTANICS CORPORATION
✪
2217 Matthews Township Pkwy Ste D-113
(28105-4815)
PHONE..............................980 565-7739
Ahmed Banya, *CEO*
EMP: 10 **EST:** 2025
SALES (est): 401.73K **Privately Held**

SIC: **2844** Toilet preparations

(G-8109)
**COG GLBAL MEDIA/CONSULTING
LLC**
738 Ablow Dr (28105-8905)
PHONE..............................980 239-8042
EMP: 20 **EST:** 2014
SALES (est): 301.86K **Privately Held**
SIC: **7812** 4841 2741 Audio-visual program
production; Subscription television services;
Miscellaneous publishing

(G-8110)
DELCOR POLYMERS INC
2536 Winterbrooke Dr (28105-8859)
PHONE..............................704 847-0640
John Buhlinger, *Pr*
Jenevieve Buhlinger, *VP*
EMP: 5 **EST:** 1999
SQ FT: 1,500
SALES (est): 859.01K **Privately Held**
Web: www.delcorpolymers.com
SIC: **2821** Plastics materials and resins

(G-8111)
EVERGLOW NA INC
1122 Industrial Dr Ste 112 (28105-5419)
P.O. Box 830 (28106-0830)
PHONE..............................704 841-2580
Markus Thrun, *Pr*
Charles Barlow, *VP*
EMP: 20 **EST:** 2004
SALES (est): 983.65K
SALES (corp-wide): 7.39MM **Privately
Held**
Web: www.everglow.us
SIC: **3993** 1799 Signs, not made in custom
sign painting shops; Sign installation and
maintenance
HQ: Everglow Gmbh
Draisstr. 19a-B
Muggensturm BW 76461

(G-8112)
EVERGREEN SILKS NC INC
Also Called: Evergreen Silks
901 Sam Newell Rd Ste I (28105-9400)
P.O. Box 1138 (28106-1138)
PHONE..............................704 845-5577
Mary Fehl, *Pr*
Jim Fehl, *VP*
EMP: 11 **EST:** 1992
SQ FT: 12,000
SALES (est): 922.26K **Privately Held**
Web: www.anysizeart.com
SIC: **3999** Artificial trees and flowers

(G-8113)
GALAXY GRAPHICS INC
1028 Brenham Ln (28105-8815)
P.O. Box 2191 (28106-2191)
PHONE..............................704 724-9057
Roger Walton, *Owner*
EMP: 5 **EST:** 1991
SALES (est): 93.46K **Privately Held**
Web: www.galaxygraphicsprinting.com
SIC: **2752** Offset printing

(G-8114)
H2H BLINDS
13137 Bleinheim Ln (28105-5092)
PHONE..............................704 628-5084
EMP: 5 **EST:** 2019
SALES (est): 321.7K **Privately Held**
Web: www.h2hinstall.com
SIC: **2591** Window blinds

(G-8115)
HARRIS TEETER LLC
Also Called: Harris Teeter 157
1811 Matthews Township Pkwy
(28105-4659)
PHONE..........................704 846-7117
Christi Larson, *Mgr*
EMP: 93
SALES (corp-wide): 150.04B **Publicly Held**
Web: www.harristeeter.com
SIC: 5411 5992 5912 2051 Supermarkets, chain; Florists; Drug stores and proprietary stores; Bread, cake, and related products
HQ: Harris Teeter, Llc
701 Crestdale Rd
Matthews NC 28105
704 844-3100

(G-8116)
HIGH MOBILITY SOLUTIONS INC
Also Called: Hsm
648 Matthews Mint Hill Rd Ste D
(28105-1767)
P.O. Box 1299 (28106-1299)
PHONE..........................704 849-8242
Ernest Aschermann, *Pr*
Brooks Bloxom, *VP*
EMP: 8 **EST:** 1976
SALES (est): 413.09K **Privately Held**
SIC: 3695 Computer software tape and disks: blank, rigid, and floppy

(G-8117)
HOLLINGSWORTH & VOSE COMPANY
143 Sardis Pointe Rd (28105-5326)
PHONE..........................704 708-5913
John Fry, *Genl Mgr*
EMP: 5
SALES (corp-wide): 584.59MM **Privately Held**
Web: www.hollingsworth-vose.com
SIC: 2621 Paper mills
PA: Hollingsworth & Vose Company
112 Washington St
East Walpole MA 02032
508 850-2000

(G-8118)
HYPE WORLD INC
2817 Summergrove Ct (28105-6455)
PHONE..........................336 588-8666
Tyre Shoffner, *CEO*
EMP: 8 **EST:** 2022
SALES (est): 292.16K **Privately Held**
SIC: 7372 Prepackaged software

(G-8119)
JODY STOWE
Also Called: Charlottes Crown
2848 Lakeview Cir (28105-7562)
PHONE..........................704 519-6560
Jody Stowe, *Owner*
EMP: 5 **EST:** 1997
SALES (est): 224.57K **Privately Held**
SIC: 2431 Interior and ornamental woodwork and trim

(G-8120)
KALEIDA SYSTEMS INC
2530 Plantation Center Dr Ste A
(28105-5298)
PHONE..........................704 814-4429
David Glenn, *Pr*
Russell Roux, *Prin*
EMP: 8 **EST:** 2001
SALES (est): 1.24MM **Privately Held**
Web: www.kaleidasystems.com

SIC: 7372 Business oriented computer software

(G-8121)
KARL OGDEN ENTERPRISES INC
Also Called: Ogden Enterprises
1320 Industrial Dr (28105-5307)
PHONE..........................704 845-2785
Karl Ogden, *Pr*
Brenley Ogden, *Sec*
◆ **EMP:** 9 **EST:** 1983
SQ FT: 20,000
SALES (est): 947.48K **Privately Held**
Web: www.ogden-group.com
SIC: 3553 Woodworking machinery

(G-8122)
KERN-LIEBERS USA TEXTILE INC
Also Called: Kern-Liebers
921 Matthews Mint Hill Rd Ste C-D (28105)
P.O. Box 519 (28106)
PHONE..........................704 329-7153
Tasslo Baeuerle, *Pr*
Larry Ausley, *Contrlr*
▲ **EMP:** 21 **EST:** 2004
SQ FT: 9,600
SALES (est): 1.33MM
SALES (corp-wide): 844.66MM **Privately Held**
Web: www.kern-liebers-textile.com
SIC: 3552 Textile machinery
PA: Kern Liebers Gmbh & Co. Kg
Dr.-Kurt-Steim-Str. 35
Schramberg BW 78713
74225110

(G-8123)
KITCHEN TUNE-UP
10810 Independence Pointe Pkwy Ste H (28105)
PHONE..........................833 259-1838
EMP: 4 **EST:** 1986
SALES (est): 213.37K **Privately Held**
Web: www.kitchentuneup.com
SIC: 2434 1799 1522 1521 Wood kitchen cabinets; Special trade contractors, nec; Residential construction, nec; Single-family housing construction

(G-8124)
KME CONSOLIDATED INC
Also Called: Ballabox
529 Crestdale Rd (28105)
P.O. Box 851 (28106-0851)
PHONE..........................704 847-9888
Kate B Young, *Pr*
Jim Kutcher, *
EMP: 30 **EST:** 1957
SQ FT: 51,300
SALES (est): 3.93MM **Privately Held**
Web: www.ballabox.com
SIC: 2657 2631 Folding paperboard boxes; Folding boxboard

(G-8125)
KRAL USA INC
901a Matthews Mint Hill Rd (28105-1704)
P.O. Box 2990 (28106-2990)
PHONE..........................704 814-6164
Otmar E Krautler, *Pr*
Richard Meighan, *Sec*
▲ **EMP:** 9 **EST:** 2001
SALES (est): 1.02MM **Privately Held**
Web: www.kral-usa.com
SIC: 3561 Industrial pumps and parts

(G-8126)
LAUNDRY SVC TECH LTD LBLTY CO
Also Called: Pro Laundry Equipment
2217 Matthews Township Pkwy Ste D (28105-4815)

PHONE..........................908 327-1997
EMP: 4 **EST:** 2008
SALES (est): 801.05K **Privately Held**
Web: www.mylaundrycare.com
SIC: 3582 5087 Commercial laundry equipment; Laundry equipment and supplies

(G-8127)
LIZZYS LOGOS INC
3118 Savannah Hills Dr (28105-6732)
PHONE..........................704 321-2588
Elizabeth Thomas, *Prin*
EMP: 4 **EST:** 2010
SALES (est): 120.72K **Privately Held**
Web: www.lizzyslogosembroidery.com
SIC: 2323 Men's and boy's neckwear

(G-8128)
MACHINE CONTROL COMPANY INC
1030 Industrial Dr (28105-5371)
P.O. Box 703 (28106-0703)
PHONE..........................704 708-5782
Chris Trapp, *Pr*
EMP: 4 **EST:** 1995
SALES (est): 1.93MM **Privately Held**
Web: www.machinecontrolco.com
SIC: 3699 Electrical equipment and supplies, nec

(G-8129)
MANA NUTRITIVE AID PDTS INC (PA)
Also Called: Mana Nutrition
130 Library Ln Ste A (28105-5345)
P.O. Box 763 (28106-0763)
PHONE..........................855 438-6262
Mark Moore, *CEO*
Amy Robbins, *Ch*
David Todd Harmon, *Dir Opers*
▼ **EMP:** 6 **EST:** 2009
SQ FT: 3,000
SALES (est): 29.22MM **Privately Held**
Web: www.mananutrition.org
SIC: 2099 Food preparations, nec

(G-8130)
MATTHEWS BUILDING SUPPLY CO
325 W Matthews St (28105-5320)
P.O. Box 607 (28106-0607)
PHONE..........................704 847-2106
Eric Hulsey, *Pr*
EMP: 50 **EST:** 1946
SQ FT: 30,000
SALES (est): 3.31MM **Privately Held**
Web: www.matthewsbuildingsupply.com
SIC: 5211 5251 2431 Lumber products; Hardware stores; Millwork

(G-8131)
MCGEE CORPORATION
Also Called: North Carolina McGee
12100 Stallings Commerce Dr (28105-5098)
P.O. Box 1375 (28106-1375)
PHONE..........................704 882-1500
Richard M Mc Gee, *Pr*
John C Oakes, *
Arthur K Cates, *
Tommy L Broome, *
▼ **EMP:** 80 **EST:** 1948
SQ FT: 175,000
SALES (est): 20.24MM **Privately Held**
Web: www.mcgeecorp.com
SIC: 3448 3441 3444 Prefabricated metal buildings and components; Fabricated structural metal; Sheet metalwork

(G-8132)
METALFAB OF NORTH CAROLINA LLC
Also Called: Select Stainless
11145 Monroe Rd (28105-6564)

PHONE..........................704 841-1090
EMP: 160
SIC: 3431 3469 5078 2431 Metal sanitary ware; Kitchen fixtures and equipment: metal, except cast aluminum; Refrigerators, commercial (reach-in and walk-in); Millwork

(G-8133)
MICRO LENS TECHNOLOGY INC (PA)
3308 Mikelynn Dr (28105-3885)
P.O. Box 656 (28691-0656)
PHONE..........................704 847-9234
Kenneth Conley, *Pr*
Mary Ellen Conley, *VP Fin*
▲ **EMP:** 8 **EST:** 1997
SQ FT: 2,000
SALES (est): 735.49K
SALES (corp-wide): 735.49K **Privately Held**
Web: www.microlens.com
SIC: 3089 Engraving of plastics

(G-8134)
MID CAROLINA CABINETS INC
Also Called: Kitchen Distributors of South
1418 Industrial Dr (28105-5414)
PHONE..........................704 358-9950
Andrew H Estes, *Pr*
EMP: 6 **EST:** 2004
SALES (est): 313.9K **Privately Held**
Web: www.jwcabinets.com
SIC: 2434 Wood kitchen cabinets

(G-8135)
NATIONWIDE ANALGESICS LLC
3116 Weddington Rd Ste 900 (28105-9406)
PHONE..........................704 651-5551
Marcy Huey, *Prin*
EMP: 4 **EST:** 2010
SALES (est): 165.76K **Privately Held**
SIC: 2834 Analgesics

(G-8136)
NONTOXIC PTHGEN ERDCTION CONS
1258 Mann Dr Ste 200 (28105-5548)
PHONE..........................800 308-1094
Charles Cole, *Managing Member*
Neal Speight, *Managing Member*
EMP: 8 **EST:** 2020
SALES (est): 121.3K **Privately Held**
SIC: 2834 Pharmaceutical preparations

(G-8137)
OGDEN SALES GROUP LLC
Also Called: Ogden Group
1320 Industrial Dr (28105-5307)
PHONE..........................704 845-2785
Karl Ogden, *Owner*
▲ **EMP:** 7 **EST:** 2009
SQ FT: 18,000
SALES (est): 2.74MM **Privately Held**
Web: www.ogden-group.com
SIC: 3553 Woodworking machinery

(G-8138)
OMNIA INDUSTRIES LLC
1430 Industrial Dr Ste A (28105-5300)
PHONE..........................704 707-6062
Denise Skinner, *Managing Member*
David Klinko, *Managing Member*
EMP: 4 **EST:** 2019
SALES (est): 745.78K **Privately Held**
SIC: 3429 Keys, locks, and related hardware

(G-8139)
ORACLE SYSTEMS CORPORATION
Also Called: Oracle
1608 Nightshade Pl (28105-0308)
PHONE..........................704 423-1426

GEOGRAPHIC

Emily Kao, *Brnch Mgr*
EMP: 5
SALES (corp-wide): 52.96B **Publicly Held**
SIC: 7372 Prepackaged software
HQ: Oracle Systems Corporation
500 Oracle Pkwy
Redwood City CA 94065

(G-8140)
PACELINE INC (PA)
Also Called: Rx Textiles
10737 Independence Pointe Pkwy Ste 103
(28105-2885)
PHONE.............................704 290-5007
Joseph Davant, *Pr*
Anne S Davant, *
Herman Pfisterer, *
▲ **EMP:** 51 **EST:** 1985
SQ FT: 15,000
SALES (est): 9.57MM
SALES (corp-wide): 9.57MM **Privately Held**
Web: www.paceline.com
SIC: 3842 2259 Prosthetic appliances;
Stockinettes, knit

(G-8141)
PPG ARCHITECTURAL FINISHES INC
Also Called: Glidden Professional Paint Ctr
1600 Matthews Mint Hill Rd Ste B
(28105-1848)
PHONE.............................704 847-7251
Doug Ernhart, *Brnch Mgr*
EMP: 4
SALES (corp-wide): 17.65B **Publicly Held**
Web: www.ppgpaints.com
SIC: 2851 Paints and allied products
HQ: Ppg Architectural Finishes, Inc.
1 Ppg Pl
Pittsburgh PA 15272
412 434-3131

(G-8142)
PUBLISHING GROUP INC
Also Called: Publishing Group, The
211 W Matthews St Ste 105 (28105-1310)
P.O. Box 79320 (28271-7063)
PHONE.............................704 847-7150
Eddis Fulghum, *Pr*
EMP: 6 **EST:** 1988
SQ FT: 1,323
SALES (est): 145.97K **Privately Held**
Web:
www.thevolunteerfiremanonline.com
SIC: 2741 Miscellaneous publishing

(G-8143)
R82 INC
13137 Bleinheim Ln (28105-5092)
P.O. Box 1739 (28106-1739)
PHONE.............................704 882-0668
Ryan Williams, *Pr*
Ro Octave, *
▲ **EMP:** 25 **EST:** 1987
SQ FT: 25,000
SALES (est): 4.95MM
SALES (corp-wide): 6.85MM **Privately Held**
Web: www.etac.com
SIC: 3842 Orthopedic appliances
HQ: Etac Ab
Farogatan 33
Kista 164 4
86334700

(G-8144)
REHAB SOLUTIONS INC
3029 Senna Dr (28105-6727)
PHONE.............................800 273-3418
EMP: 6 **EST:** 2019
SALES (est): 198.37K **Privately Held**

SIC: 2741 Miscellaneous publishing

(G-8145)
RFSPROTECH LLC
1320 Industrial Dr (28105-5307)
PHONE.............................704 845-2785
Russell Hass, *
▼ **EMP:** 25 **EST:** 2006
SQ FT: 20,000
SALES (est): 5.54MM **Privately Held**
Web: www.ogden-group.com
SIC: 3553 Woodworking machinery

(G-8146)
RSA SECURITY LLC
250 N Trade St (28105-9449)
PHONE.............................704 847-4725
Jim Fisher, *Brnch Mgr*
EMP: 22
SALES (corp-wide): 1.44B **Privately Held**
Web: www.rsa.com
SIC: 3577 Computer peripheral equipment,
nec
PA: Rsa Security Llc
2 Burlington Wods Dr Ste 2
Burlington MA 01803
800 995-5095

(G-8147)
SECOND MAIN PHASE SLUTIONS LLC
407 Clairview Ln (28105-0208)
PHONE.............................704 303-0090
Jason Lu, *Prin*
EMP: 4 **EST:** 2019
SALES (est): 987.68K **Privately Held**
SIC: 7372 Prepackaged software

(G-8148)
SHUTTERCRAFT INC
Also Called: Blind Factory of Charlotte
921 Matthews Mint Hill Rd Ste D
(28105-2406)
PHONE.............................704 708-9079
Aaron Stephens, *Pr*
Luanne Stephens, *Sec*
EMP: 16 **EST:** 1999
SQ FT: 7,200
SALES (est): 200.49K **Privately Held**
SIC: 2591 5719 Blinds vertical; Vertical blinds

(G-8149)
SOUTHERN CABINET CO INC
1418 Industrial Dr (28105-5414)
PHONE.............................704 373-2299
James F Freeze Junior, *Pr*
Brian Freeze, *
Steve Foster, *
EMP: 6 **EST:** 1989
SQ FT: 40,000
SALES (est): 249.72K **Privately Held**
Web: www.lathamremodel.com
SIC: 2434 Wood kitchen cabinets

(G-8150)
SPEEDWAY LINK INC
3727 Weddington Ridge Ln (28105-7700)
PHONE.............................704 338-2028
Mykoala Nagornyy, *Pr*
EMP: 6 **EST:** 2005
SQ FT: 8,000
SALES (est): 615.41K **Privately Held**
Web: www.speedway.com
SIC: 3715 4789 Truck trailers; Pipeline
terminal facilities, independently operated

(G-8151)
STRONGHAVEN INCORPORATED
11135 Monroe Rd (28105-6564)
P.O. Box 1300 (28106-1300)

PHONE.............................770 739-6080
Rodney Benson, *Genl Mgr*
EMP: 100
Web: www.hoodcontainer.com
SIC: 2653 Boxes, corrugated: made from
purchased materials
HQ: Stronghaven, Incorporated
2727 Paces Ferry Rd Se
Atlanta GA 30336
678 235-2713

(G-8152)
TOTAL CONTROLS INC
4420 Friendship Dr Ste A (28105-5902)
P.O. Box 629 (28106-0629)
PHONE.............................704 821-6341
Wayne K Seale, *Pr*
Gary Rawls, *VP*
EMP: 8 **EST:** 1995
SQ FT: 4,000
SALES (est): 988.2K **Privately Held**
Web: www.totalcontrols.com
SIC: 3625 1731 Relays and industrial
controls; Electronic controls installation

(G-8153)
TRANSCONTINENTAL AC US LLC (HQ)
700 Crestdale Rd (28105-4700)
PHONE.............................704 847-9171
Francois Olivier, *Managing Member*
▲ **EMP:** 19 **EST:** 2007
SALES (est): 34.66MM
SALES (corp-wide): 2.09B **Privately Held**
Web:
www.transcontinentaladvancedcoatings.com
SIC: 2631 2621 Container, packaging, and
boxboard; Wrapping and packaging papers
PA: Transcontinental Inc
1 Place Ville-Marie Bureau 3240
Montreal QC H3B 0
514 954-4000

(G-8154)
TRANSCONTINENTAL AC US LLC
Also Called: Intellicoat Technologies
700 Crestdale Rd (28105-4700)
P.O. Box 368 (28106-0368)
PHONE.............................704 847-9171
Harry Barto, *Mgr*
EMP: 18
SALES (corp-wide): 2.09B **Privately Held**
Web:
www.transcontinentaladvancedcoatings.com
SIC: 2671 8731 3083 2851 Paper; coated
and laminated packaging; Commercial
physical research; Laminated plastics plate
and sheet; Paints and allied products
HQ: Transcontinental Ac Us Llc
700 Crestdale Rd
Matthews NC 28105

(G-8155)
TVL INTERNATIONAL LLC
165 S Trade St (28105-5771)
P.O. Box 2278 (28106-2278)
PHONE.............................704 814-0930
▲ **EMP:** 4 **EST:** 2004
SALES (est): 486.29K **Privately Held**
Web: www.gaswatch.com
SIC: 3491 Process control regulator valves

(G-8156)
VRG COMPONENTS INC
2020 Independence Commerce Dr Ste G
(28105-4202)
PHONE.............................980 244-3862
Sarah Warren, *CEO*
Ruben Gutierrez, *CEO*
Sarah Warren, *Prin*
EMP: 6 **EST:** 2014

SALES (est): 12.58MM **Privately Held**
Web: www.vrgcomponents.com
SIC: 5065 3674 5084 Connectors, electronic
; Integrated circuits, semiconductor
networks, etc.; Industrial machinery and
equipment

(G-8157)
WATKINS CABINETS LLC
1418 Industrial Dr (28105-5414)
PHONE.............................704 634-1724
John Watkins Estes, *Prin*
EMP: 5 **EST:** 2013
SALES (est): 239.32K **Privately Held**
SIC: 2434 Wood kitchen cabinets

Matthews
Union County

(G-8158)
ASSOCIATED BATTERY COMPANY
3469 Gribble Rd (28104-8114)
P.O. Box 1590 (28079-1590)
PHONE.............................704 821-8311
Dwight Hobbs, *Pr*
EMP: 5 **EST:** 1980
SALES (est): 667.96K **Privately Held**
Web: www.associatedbattery.com
SIC: 3691 Storage batteries

(G-8159)
B P PRINTING AND COPYING INC
3756 Pleasant Plains Rd (28104-5960)
PHONE.............................704 821-8219
Boyce Paysoyce, *Pr*
EMP: 4 **EST:** 1998
SALES (est): 100.26K **Privately Held**
SIC: 2752 Offset printing

(G-8160)
BERRY GLOBAL FILMS LLC
303 Seaboard Dr (28104-8155)
PHONE.............................704 821-2316
Donald L Brafford, *Mgr*
EMP: 233
Web: www.berryglobal.com
SIC: 3081 2673 Polyethylene film; Bags:
plastic, laminated, and coated
HQ: Berry Global Films, Llc
95 Chestnut Ridge Rd
Montvale NJ 07645
201 641-6600

(G-8161)
BULLDOG MACHINE INC
3330 Smith Farm Rd (28104-5040)
PHONE.............................704 200-7838
James Rublee, *Pr*
EMP: 4 **EST:** 2017
SALES (est): 123.87K **Privately Held**
SIC: 3599 Machine shop, jobbing and repair

(G-8162)
CEM CORPORATION (HQ)
Also Called: Innovtors In McRwave Technolgy
3100 Smith Farm Rd (28104-5044)
P.O. Box 200 (28106)
PHONE.............................704 821-7015
Michael J Collins, *Pr*
Richard N Decker, *
◆ **EMP:** 180 **EST:** 1971
SQ FT: 70,000
SALES (est): 43.68MM **Privately Held**
Web: www.cem.com
SIC: 3826 3679 Moisture analyzers;
Microwave components
PA: Cem Holdings Corporation
3100 Smith Farm Rd
Matthews NC 28104

(G-8163)
CEM HOLDINGS CORPORATION (PA)
3100 Smith Farm Rd (28104-5044)
P.O. Box 200 (28104)
PHONE...........................704 821-7015
Michael J Collins, *CEO*
EMP: 27 **EST:** 1971
SALES (est): 52.82MM **Privately Held**
Web: www.cem.com
SIC: 3826 Moisture analyzers

(G-8164)
CHOICE AWARDS & SIGNS
4036 Matthews Indian Trail Rd
(28104-3920)
PHONE...........................704 844-0860
Deforest Kenemer, *Owner*
EMP: 6 **EST:** 1994
SQ FT: 5,000
SALES (est): 419.42K **Privately Held**
Web: choice-awards-signs.hub.biz
SIC: 3993 Signs, not made in custom sign
painting shops

(G-8165)
DAVIS STEEL AND IRON CO INC
1035 Commercial Dr (28104-5001)
P.O. Box 3450 (28106-3450)
PHONE...........................704 821-7676
EMP: 9 **EST:** 1967
SALES (est): 2.01MM **Privately Held**
Web: www.davissteel.com
SIC: 3441 3449 3446 Fabricated structural
metal; Miscellaneous metalwork;
Ornamental metalwork

(G-8166)
ELEKTRIKREDD LLC
2123 Stevens Mill Rd (28104-4248)
PHONE...........................704 805-0110
EMP: 5 **EST:** 2020
SALES (est): 1.16MM **Privately Held**
SIC: 3537 Trucks: freight, baggage, etc.:
industrial, except mining

(G-8167)
EZ CUSTOM SCREEN PRINTING
600 Union West Blvd Ste B (28104-8841)
PHONE...........................704 821-8488
Ed Jones, *Owner*
EMP: 23 **EST:** 2014
SALES (est): 969.52K **Privately Held**
Web: www.ezcustomscreenprinting.com
SIC: 2759 Screen printing

(G-8168)
**EZ CUSTOM SCRNPRINTING EMB
INC**
200 Foxton Rd (28104-7307)
PHONE...........................704 821-9641
Ez Jones, *Owner*
EMP: 7 **EST:** 2006
SALES (est): 56.16K **Privately Held**
Web: www.ezcustomscreenprinting.com
SIC: 2759 Screen printing

(G-8169)
FIRE RETARDANT CHEM TECH LLC
Also Called: Frct
3465 Gribble Rd (28104-8114)
PHONE...........................980 253-8880
Futong Cui, *Pr*
EMP: 5 **EST:** 2014
SQ FT: 2,000
SALES (est): 2.07MM
SALES (corp-wide): 6.65B **Publicly Held**
SIC: 2899 8733 Fire retardant chemicals;
Research institute
HQ: Prowood, Llc
2801 E Beltline Ave Ne

Grand Rapids MI

(G-8170)
FISHER TEXTILES INC
4211 Matthews Indian Trail Rd
(28104-5005)
P.O. Box 307 (28079-0307)
PHONE...........................800 554-8886
Larry Fisher, *CEO*
Scott Fisher, *
◆ **EMP:** 34 **EST:** 1988
SQ FT: 43,000
SALES (est): 28.17MM **Privately Held**
Web: www.fishertextiles.com
SIC: 2259 2211 Convertors, knit goods;
Broadwoven fabric mills, cotton

(G-8171)
FRESH AIR TECHNOLOGIES LLC
2246 Stevens Mill Rd Ste B (28104-4210)
PHONE...........................704 622-7877
Fred Lanzy, *Pr*
Alan Shorts, *Manager*
EMP: 17 **EST:** 2010
SALES (est): 2.93MM **Privately Held**
Web: www.thefreshaircompanies.com
SIC: 3563 Air and gas compressors

(G-8172)
GLOBAL SYNERGY GROUP INC
13663 Providence Rd Ste 370
(28104-9373)
PHONE...........................704 254-9886
Larayne Whitehead, *CEO*
EMP: 5 **EST:** 2009
SALES (est): 106.76K **Privately Held**
SIC: 3482 Small arms ammunition

(G-8173)
HMF INC
3479 Gribble Rd (28104-8114)
PHONE...........................704 821-6765
Robert T Hucks, *Pr*
Kathy T Hucks, *Sec*
EMP: 8 **EST:** 1985
SQ FT: 9,500
SALES (est): 2.53MM **Privately Held**
Web: www.hmf.com
SIC: 3599 Machine shop, jobbing and repair

(G-8174)
HUNTER MILLWORK INC
422 Seaboard Dr (28104-5073)
P.O. Box 2483 (28106-2483)
PHONE...........................704 821-0144
Glenn Ronald Hunter, *Pr*
EMP: 14 **EST:** 1997
SALES (est): 848.5K **Privately Held**
Web: www.huntermillwork.com
SIC: 5211 2431 Door and window products;
Awnings, blinds and shutters: wood

(G-8175)
**INTERNATIONAL CNSTR EQP INC
(PA)**
Also Called: Ice
301 Warehouse Dr (28104-8100)
PHONE...........................704 821-8200
T Richard Morris, *Pr*
Thomas P Cunningham, *VP*
Kurt W Seufort, *CFO*
Brock Hemmingsen, *Genl Mgr*
Dick Morris, *Prin*
◆ **EMP:** 25 **EST:** 1974
SQ FT: 50,000
SALES (est): 21.6MM
SALES (corp-wide): 21.6MM **Privately
Held**
Web: www.iceusa.com

SIC: 7353 3531 Heavy construction
equipment rental; Vibrators for concrete
construction

(G-8176)
ITC MILLWORK LLC (PA)
Also Called: Interior Trim Creations
3619 Gribble Rd (28104-8112)
P.O. Box 1618 (28079-1618)
PHONE...........................704 821-1470
EMP: 85 **EST:** 1999
SQ FT: 49,000
SALES (est): 8.97MM
SALES (corp-wide): 8.97MM **Privately
Held**
Web: www.itcmillwork.com
SIC: 2431 Moldings and baseboards,
ornamental and trim

(G-8177)
J J JENKINS INCORPORATED
3380 Smith Farm Rd (28104-5040)
P.O. Box 1949 (28106-1949)
PHONE...........................704 821-6648
EMP: 27 **EST:** 1984
SALES (est): 7.5MM **Privately Held**
Web: www.jjjenkinsinc.com
SIC: 8711 5084 3552 Designing: ship, boat,
machine, and product; Textile machinery
and equipment; Textile machinery

(G-8178)
JOHN W FOSTER SALES INC
3491 Gribble Rd (28104-8114)
P.O. Box 2883 (28106-2883)
PHONE...........................704 821-3822
Debi Long, *Pr*
John W Foster, *Pr*
Debbie Long, *VP*
EMP: 6 **EST:** 1973
SALES (est): 1MM **Privately Held**
SIC: 3569 Filters, general line: industrial

(G-8179)
LIQUID ICE CORPORATION
500 Union West Blvd Ste C (28104-8802)
PHONE...........................704 882-3505
Henry Rabinovich, *Pr*
EMP: 10 **EST:** 2002
SALES (est): 954.45K **Privately Held**
Web: www.liquidicecoolant.com
SIC: 2899 Chemical preparations, nec

(G-8180)
M3 PRODUCTS COM
Also Called: Scienscope Products
1537 Golden Rain Dr (28104-6215)
P.O. Box 1657 (28106-1657)
PHONE...........................631 938-1245
Susan Vincenti, *Pt*
EMP: 5 **EST:** 2008
SALES (est): 263.12K **Privately Held**
Web: www.scienscopeproducts.com
SIC: 3827 Optical instruments and lenses

(G-8181)
MANG SYSTEMS INC
500 Union West Blvd Ste B (28104-8802)
PHONE...........................704 292-1041
Hienz Roth, *Pr*
EMP: 5 **EST:** 1988
SQ FT: 16,000
SALES (est): 164.29K **Privately Held**
Web: www.pdm-at.com
SIC: 5084 3599 Industrial machinery and
equipment; Machine shop, jobbing and
repair

(G-8182)
MASTER FORM INC
500 Union West Blvd Ste B (28104-8802)
PHONE...........................704 292-1041
Heinz Roth, *Pr*
▲ **EMP:** 8 **EST:** 1993
SQ FT: 16,000
SALES (est): 425.02K **Privately Held**
SIC: 3471 3444 3441 Finishing, metals or
formed products; Sheet metalwork;
Fabricated structural metal

(G-8183)
MASTER KRAFT INC
3350 Smith Farm Rd (28104-5040)
PHONE...........................704 234-2673
Michael Kovalev, *Prin*
EMP: 30 **EST:** 2006
SALES (est): 2.79MM **Privately Held**
Web: www.masterkraftinc.com
SIC: 2431 Millwork

(G-8184)
MCNEELY MOTORSPORTS INC
340 Seaboard Dr (28104-8119)
PHONE...........................704 426-7430
Myra Holt Mcneely, *Prin*
EMP: 4 **EST:** 2011
SALES (est): 162.78K **Privately Held**
SIC: 3949 Sporting and athletic goods, nec

(G-8185)
**MELLTRONICS INDUSTRIAL INC
(PA)**
3479 Gribble Rd (28104-8114)
P.O. Box 2368 (28079-2368)
PHONE...........................704 821-6651
Frederick Mellon, *Pr*
Gregory Barker, *Sec*
Scott W Mellon, *VP*
EMP: 5 **EST:** 1993
SQ FT: 2,000
SALES (est): 3.88MM **Privately Held**
Web: www.melltronics.com
SIC: 3625 Motor controls and accessories

(G-8186)
MMDI INC
Also Called: Steelpoint
200 Beltway Blvd (28104-8807)
PHONE...........................704 882-4550
Michael J Edwards, *Pr*
Deborah L Edwards, *
EMP: 55 **EST:** 2010
SQ FT: 60,000
SALES (est): 9.45MM **Privately Held**
Web: www.mmdicorp.com
SIC: 3441 Fabricated structural metal

(G-8187)
**NORTHEAST TOOL AND MFG
COMPANY**
15200 Idlewild Rd (28104-1418)
P.O. Box 55 (28079-0055)
PHONE...........................704 882-1187
EMP: 45 **EST:** 1964
SALES (est): 6MM **Privately Held**
Web: www.northeasttool.us
SIC: 3444 3495 3544 3541 Sheet metalwork
; Mechanical springs, precision; Special
dies and tools; Grinding machines,
metalworking

(G-8188)
OPTOMILL SOLUTIONS LLC
1223 Clover Ln (28104-6119)
PHONE...........................704 560-4037
Colleen A Davies, *Managing Member*
EMP: 4 **EST:** 2017
SALES (est): 153.54K **Privately Held**

SIC: 3999 Manufacturing industries, nec

(G-8189)
ORNAMENTAL SPECIALTIES INC
3488 Gribble Rd (28104-8105)
P.O. Box 1980 (28079-1980)
PHONE..............................704 821-9154
Darlene Novak, *Pr*
EMP: 12 **EST:** 1994
SALES (est): 2.01MM **Privately Held**
Web: www.ornamentalspecialties.com
SIC: 3446 Ornamental metalwork

(G-8190)
PRECISION MACHINE TOOLS CORP
500 Union West Blvd Ste A (28104-8802)
PHONE..............................704 882-3700
Henry S Rabinovich, *Pr*
Susan Rabinovich, *Sec*
EMP: 6 **EST:** 1988
SQ FT: 8,000
SALES (est): 487.69K **Privately Held**
Web: www.pmtcorporation.com
SIC: 3599 Machine shop, jobbing and repair

(G-8191)
RIVET SOLUTIONS INC ✪
308 Wheatberry Hill Dr (28104-6133)
PHONE..............................888 487-3849
Christopher Hart, *Prin*
EMP: 7 **EST:** 2023
SALES (est): 1.15MM **Privately Held**
SIC: 7372 Business oriented computer software

(G-8192)
SCR CONTROLS INC
Also Called: SCR/ Melltronics
3479 Gribble Rd (28104-8114)
P.O. Box 2368 (28079-2368)
PHONE..............................704 821-6651
Fred Mellon, *Pr*
Scott Mellon, *VP*
Pamela Holly, *Sec*
EMP: 12 **EST:** 1981
SQ FT: 6,000
SALES (est): 3.88MM **Privately Held**
Web: www.scrcontrols.com
SIC: 3621 7629 8711 Electric motor and generator parts; Electronic equipment repair ; Electrical or electronic engineering
PA: Melltronics Industrial, Inc.
3479 Gribble Rd
Matthews NC 28104

(G-8193)
SORBE LTD
111 Cupped Oak Dr Ste A (28104-8823)
P.O. Box 457 (28106-0457)
PHONE..............................704 562-2991
Neal Kronovet, *Pr*
David Kronovet, *VP*
▲ **EMP:** 5 **EST:** 1995
SQ FT: 17,000
SALES (est): 437.05K **Privately Held**
SIC: 2339 5137 Sportswear, women's; Women's and children's clothing

(G-8194)
STEELCO INC
1020 Commercial Dr (28104-5004)
PHONE..............................704 896-1207
Brooks Davis, *Pr*
Jean Davis, *Sec*
EMP: 10 **EST:** 1993
SQ FT: 14,000
SALES (est): 344.15K **Privately Held**
Web: www.steelco.co
SIC: 3441 Fabricated structural metal

(G-8195)
STS SCREEN PRINTING INC
107 Industrial Dr (28104-5147)
PHONE..............................704 821-8488
Devonne Smith, *Pr*
EMP: 6 **EST:** 1994
SQ FT: 5,000
SALES (est): 83.74K **Privately Held**
SIC: 2759 2395 Screen printing; Embroidery and art needlework

(G-8196)
TECHSOUTH INC
601 Union West Blvd (28104-8820)
P.O. Box 1799 (28106-1799)
PHONE..............................704 334-1100
Joe Kloiber, *Pr*
▲ **EMP:** 9 **EST:** 1983
SQ FT: 15,000
SALES (est): 1.99MM **Privately Held**
Web: www.techsouthinc.com
SIC: 3545 7699 Cutting tools for machine tools; Welding equipment repair

(G-8197)
WATSON STEEL & IRON WORKS LLC
3624 Gribble Rd (28104-8107)
PHONE..............................704 821-7140
Douglas B Watson, *Managing Member*
Mary Evelyn Watson, *
EMP: 23 **EST:** 1975
SQ FT: 2,400
SALES (est): 3.54MM **Privately Held**
Web: www.watsonsteelandiron.com
SIC: 1791 3446 7389 Iron work, structural; Architectural metalwork; Crane and aerial lift service

(G-8198)
WILDCAT PETROLEUM SERVICE INC
326 Hawksnest Ct (28104-4261)
P.O. Box 690816 (28227-7014)
PHONE..............................704 379-0132
EMP: 7 **EST:** 1999
SALES (est): 3.58MM **Privately Held**
Web: www.wildcatpetroleuminc.com
SIC: 3728 Refueling equipment for use in flight, airplane

Maxton
Robeson County

(G-8199)
ADVANCED CUTTING TECH INC
Also Called: Adcut
12760 Airport Rd (28364-9429)
PHONE..............................910 944-3028
Mike Dixon, *Pr*
Chris Dixon, *Sec*
EMP: 8 **EST:** 1995
SQ FT: 6,750
SALES (est): 1.17MM **Privately Held**
Web: www.adcut.net
SIC: 3599 Machine shop, jobbing and repair

(G-8200)
EMBREX POULTRY HEALTH LLC
22300 Skyway Church Rd (28364-6412)
P.O. Box 190 (28364-0190)
PHONE..............................910 844-5566
EMP: 4 **EST:** 2003
SALES (est): 495.6K
SALES (corp-wide): 8.54B **Publicly Held**
SIC: 2834 Pharmaceutical preparations
PA: Zoetis Inc.
10 Sylvan Way
Parsippany NJ 07054
973 822-7000

(G-8201)
HUVEPHARMA INC
22300 Skyway Church Rd (28364-6412)
PHONE..............................910 506-4649
Glen Wilkinson, *Pr*
EMP: 10 **EST:** 2016
SALES (est): 1.87MM **Privately Held**
Web: www.huvepharma.com
SIC: 2834 Veterinary pharmaceutical preparations

(G-8202)
MERITOR INC
Also Called: Arvinmeritor Automotive
22021 Skyway Church Rd Ste B (28364-6946)
PHONE..............................910 844-9401
Rick Martello, *Mgr*
EMP: 17
SALES (corp-wide): 34.1B **Publicly Held**
Web: www.meritor.com
SIC: 3714 Motor vehicle parts and accessories
HQ: Meritor, Inc.
2135 W Maple Rd
Troy MI 48084

(G-8203)
MERITOR INC
Also Called: Transmission Div
22021 Skyway Church Rd Ste A (28364-6946)
PHONE..............................910 844-9401
David Coleman, *Manager*
EMP: 100
SALES (corp-wide): 34.1B **Publicly Held**
Web: www.meritor.com
SIC: 3714 3568 Motor vehicle parts and accessories; Power transmission equipment, nec
HQ: Meritor, Inc.
2135 W Maple Rd
Troy MI 48084

(G-8204)
MOUNTAIRE FARMS INC
10800 Pell Dr (28364-5641)
PHONE..............................910 844-3126
Gary Scott, *Brnch Mgr*
EMP: 58
SALES (corp-wide): 2.07B **Privately Held**
Web: www.mountaire.com
SIC: 2048 5191 Prepared feeds, nec; Animal feeds
HQ: Mountaire Farms Inc.
1901 Napa Valley Dr
Little Rock AR 72212
501 372-6524

(G-8205)
RAILROAD FRICTION PDTS CORP
13601 Airport Rd (28364-6819)
P.O. Box 1349 (28353-1349)
PHONE..............................910 844-9709
Rafael Santana, *CEO*
Matthew Jurinski, *
◆ **EMP:** 150 **EST:** 1954
SQ FT: 800
SALES (est): 26.18MM **Publicly Held**
Web: www.wabteccorp.com
SIC: 3743 Railroad equipment, except locomotives
PA: Westinghouse Air Brake Technologies Corporation
30 Isabella St
Pittsburgh PA 15212

Mayodan
Rockingham County

(G-8206)
BMS INVESTMENT HOLDINGS LLC
225 Commerce Ln (27027-8597)
P.O. Box 37 (27027-0037)
PHONE..............................336 949-4107
Scott Mcneil, *Genl Mgr*
Sara Brust, *
▼ **EMP:** 45 **EST:** 2009
SQ FT: 2,500
SALES (est): 8.81MM **Privately Held**
Web: www.blowmoldedsolutions.com
SIC: 3089 Injection molding of plastics

(G-8207)
MCMICHAEL MILLS INC (PA)
130 Shakey Rd (27027-8587)
P.O. Box 507 (27025-0507)
PHONE..............................336 548-4242
Dalton L Mcmichael Junior, *Pr*
Martha Ford, *
Brac Brigman, *
◆ **EMP:** 200 **EST:** 1993
SQ FT: 87,000
SALES (est): 18.34MM **Privately Held**
Web: www.mcmichaelmills.com
SIC: 2241 Rubber and elastic yarns and fabrics

(G-8208)
MILLIKEN & COMPANY
Also Called: Two Rivers Plant
109 Turner Rd (27027-8251)
PHONE..............................336 548-5680
Mark Rice, *Brnch Mgr*
EMP: 19
SALES (corp-wide): 1.69B **Privately Held**
Web: www.milliken.com
SIC: 2281 Yarn spinning mills
PA: Milliken & Company
920 Milliken Rd
Spartanburg SC 29303
864 503-2020

(G-8209)
STURM RUGER & COMPANY INC
700 S Ayersville Rd (27027-2827)
PHONE..............................336 427-0286
EMP: 302
SALES (corp-wide): 535.64MM **Publicly Held**
Web: www.ruger.com
SIC: 5941 3489 Firearms; Artillery or artillery parts, over 30 mm.
PA: Sturm, Ruger & Company, Inc.
1 Lacey Pl
Southport CT 06890
203 259-7843

Maysville
Jones County

(G-8210)
BRADLEY TODD BAUGUS
6444 White Oak River Rd (28555-7081)
PHONE..............................252 665-4901
Bradley Todd Baugus, *Prin*
EMP: 7 **EST:** 2016
SALES (est): 149.59K **Privately Held**
SIC: 2411 Logging

(G-8211)
MARIETTA MARTIN MATERIALS INC
Also Called: Martin Marietta Aggregates
2998 Belgrade Swansboro Rd (28555-9427)

P.O. Box 99 (28555-0099)
PHONE..............................910 743-6471
Jerry Fraizer, *Mgr*
EMP: 5
Web: www.martinmarietta.com
SIC: 1422 Cement rock, crushed and broken-
quarrying
PA: Martin Marietta Materials Inc
4123 Parklake Ave
Raleigh NC 27612

(G-8212)
STEVE & RAY BANKS LOGGING INC
Also Called: Banks, Steve and Ray Logging
7625 New Bern Hwy (28555-9322)
P.O. Box 448 (28555-0448)
PHONE..............................910 743-3051
Steven Banks, *Pr*
Ray Bank, *VP*
Ruth Banks, *Sec*
EMP: 4 **EST:** 1953
SALES (est): 197.78K **Privately Held**
SIC: 2411 Pulpwood contractors engaged in
cutting

Mc Adenville
Gaston County

(G-8213)
COATS HP INC
Also Called: Pharr Ph/Crescent Plant
300 Dickson Rd (28101)
PHONE..............................704 824-9904
▲ **EMP:** 323
SQ FT: 2,268
SALES (corp-wide): 1.39B **Privately Held**
SIC: 2281 2282 2824 Manmade and
synthetic fiber yarns, spun; Manmade and
synthetic fiber yarns, twisting, winding, etc.;
Acrylic fibers
HQ: Coats Hp Inc.
14120 Bllntyne Corp Pl St
Charlotte NC 28277
704 329-5800

(G-8214)
MANNINGTON MILLS INC
Also Called: Pharr Fibers and Yarns
200 Saxony Dr (28101)
PHONE..............................704 824-3551
EMP: 64
SALES (corp-wide): 686.34MM **Privately
Held**
Web: www.mannington.com
SIC: 2281 2824 Manmade and synthetic
fiber yarns, spun; Acrylic fibers
PA: Mannington Mills Inc.
75 Mannington Mills Rd
Salem NJ 08079
800 356-6787

(G-8215)
**PHARR MCADENVILLE
CORPORATION (PA)**
100 Main St (28101-9705)
P.O. Box 1939 (28101-1939)
PHONE..............................704 824-3551
William J P Carstarphen, *Pr*
EMP: 72 **EST:** 2003
SALES (est): 39.79MM
SALES (corp-wide): 39.79MM **Privately
Held**
Web: www.pharrcorp.com
SIC: 6719 2281 2282 2824 Investment
holding companies, except banks;
Manmade and synthetic fiber yarns, spun;
Manmade and synthetic fiber yarns,
twisting, winding, etc.; Acrylic fibers

Mc Farlan
Anson County

(G-8216)
**HOW GREAT THOU ART
PUBLICATION**
Hwy 52 Sr 1003 Ste 357 (28102)
P.O. Box 48 (28102-0048)
PHONE..............................704 851-3117
Barry Stebbing, *Owner*
EMP: 4 **EST:** 1991
SQ FT: 700
SALES (est): 226.23K **Privately Held**
Web: www.howgreatthouart.com
SIC: 2731 Book publishing

Mc Grady
Wilkes County

(G-8217)
WILKES WELDING AND MCH CO INC
1018 Mulberry Rd (28649-9618)
P.O. Box 1067 (28659-1067)
PHONE..............................336 670-2742
Jeral Sebastian, *Pr*
Doris Sebastian, *Treas*
EMP: 5 **EST:** 1955
SQ FT: 6,500
SALES (est): 218.45K **Privately Held**
SIC: 3599 7692 Machine shop, jobbing and
repair; Welding repair

Mc Leansville
Guilford County

(G-8218)
BIG TIRE OUTFITTERS
5210 Cragganmore Dr (27301-9524)
PHONE..............................919 568-9605
Brian Roberts, *Owner*
EMP: 8 **EST:** 2015
SALES (est): 216.78K **Privately Held**
SIC: 7534 Rebuilding and retreading tires

(G-8219)
BLUEWATER PALLET SOLUTIONS
5517 Burlington Rd (27301-9622)
PHONE..............................336 697-9109
Marc Scudder, *Owner*
EMP: 4 **EST:** 2009
SALES (est): 172.53K **Privately Held**
SIC: 2448 Pallets, wood

(G-8220)
CONTINENTAL MANUFACTURING CO
814c Knox Rd Ste E (27301-9227)
PHONE..............................336 697-2591
Briz Walia, *Owner*
EMP: 4 **EST:** 2004
SALES (est): 241.01K **Privately Held**
SIC: 2899 3999 Concrete curing and
hardening compounds; Manufacturing
industries, nec

(G-8221)
DECAL SOURCE INC
804 Knox Rd (27301-9227)
PHONE..............................336 574-3141
Anthony Johnson, *Pr*
Jeffrey L Fischer, *Stockholder**
Brian T Fleming, *Stockholder**
Vass A Barbour, *Stockholder**
Charlie L Christopher, *Stockholder**
▲ **EMP:** 24 **EST:** 1998
SQ FT: 1,500
SALES (est): 4.22MM **Privately Held**

Web: www.thedecalsource.com
SIC: 2752 Decals, lithographed

(G-8222)
**GENERAL DYNAMICS
CORPORATION**
5440 Millstream Rd Ste W300
(27301-9282)
PHONE..............................336 698-8571
Earl Mc Bride, *Brnch Mgr*
EMP: 25
SALES (corp-wide): 47.72B **Publicly Held**
Web: www.gdmissionsystems.com
SIC: 7372 Prepackaged software
PA: General Dynamics Corporation
11011 Sunset Hills Rd
Reston VA 20190
703 876-3000

(G-8223)
**GENERAL DYNMICS MSSION
SYSTEMS**
5440 Millstream Rd Ste W300
(27301-9274)
PHONE..............................336 698-8000
Harry Grant, *Prin*
EMP: 234
SALES (corp-wide): 47.72B **Publicly Held**
Web: www.gdmissionsystems.com
SIC: 3669 3812 7373 8711 Emergency
alarms; Search and navigation equipment;
Computer integrated systems design;
Engineering services
HQ: General Dynamics Mission Systems,
Inc.
12450 Fair Lakes Cir
Fairfax VA 22033
877 449-0600

(G-8224)
IRSI AUTOMATION INC
3703 Hines Chapel Rd (27301-9113)
PHONE..............................336 303-5320
Kenneth Moore, *Pr*
Gary Floyd, *Treas*
EMP: 5 **EST:** 2015
SALES (est): 334.51K **Privately Held**
SIC: 3569 7699 8711 8742 Liquid
automation machinery and equipment;
Industrial machinery and equipment repair;
Machine tool design; Automation and
robotics consultant

(G-8225)
MMS LOGISTICS INCORPORATED
1509 Guinness Dr (27301-9512)
PHONE..............................336 214-3552
Ranaldo Harden, *CEO*
EMP: 5 **EST:** 2016
SALES (est): 847.53K **Privately Held**
SIC: 4789 3537 Transportation services, nec
; Trucks: freight, baggage, etc.: industrial,
except mining

(G-8226)
QUICK COLOR SOLUTIONS
829 Knox Rd (27301-9227)
PHONE..............................336 698-0951
Mary Benton, *Prin*
EMP: 6 **EST:** 2009
SALES (est): 701.54K **Privately Held**
Web: www.quickcolorsolutions.com
SIC: 2752 Offset printing

Mebane
Alamance County

(G-8227)
AIRSPEED LLC
1413 S Third Street Ext (27302-8186)
PHONE..............................919 644-1222
C Scott Clendinin, *Managing Member*
Toby Nichols, *
▲ **EMP:** 31 **EST:** 1996
SALES (est): 6.01MM **Privately Held**
Web: www.airspeedllc.com
SIC: 3399 5051 3442 8711 Nails: aluminum,
brass, or other nonferrous metal or wire;
Castings, rough: iron or steel; Moldings and
trim, except automobile: metal; Mechanical
engineering

(G-8228)
AKG NORTH AMERICA INC
7315 Oakwood Street Ext (27302-9211)
P.O. Box 365 (27302-0365)
PHONE..............................919 563-4286
Ralf Hutter, *VP*
Richard White, *
Peter Feuerle, *
Ron Prichard, *
Alexander Gress, *VP*
◆ **EMP:** 28 **EST:** 1981
SALES (est): 9.58MM **Privately Held**
Web: www.akg-america.com
SIC: 3443 Fabricated plate work (boiler shop)

(G-8229)
**AKG NRTH AMERCN OPERATIONS
INC (DH)**
7315 Oakwood Street Ext (27302-9211)
PHONE..............................919 563-4286
Wolfgang Dahlman, *Pr*
◆ **EMP:** 10 **EST:** 2010
SALES (est): 33.88MM
SALES (corp-wide): 1.2MM **Privately Held**
Web: www.akg-america.com
SIC: 3443 Cooling towers, metal plate
HQ: Autokuhler Gmbh & Co. Kg
Am Hohlen Weg 31
Hofgeismar HE 34369
56718830

(G-8230)
AKG OF AMERICA INC (DH)
7315 Oakwood Street Ext (27302-9211)
P.O. Box 370 (27302-0370)
PHONE..............................919 563-4286
G Richard White, *Pr*
◆ **EMP:** 36 **EST:** 1981
SQ FT: 100,000
SALES (est): 28.62MM
SALES (corp-wide): 1.2MM **Privately Held**
Web: www.akg-america.com
SIC: 3443 Heat exchangers, condensers,
and components
HQ: Autokuhler Gmbh & Co. Kg
Am Hohlen Weg 31
Hofgeismar HE 34369
56718830

(G-8231)
ARMACELL US HOLDINGS LLC
7600 Oakwood Street Ext (27302-9577)
PHONE..............................919 304-3846
Ulrich Weimer, *Pr*
James F Mars Junior, *VP*
EMP: 200 **EST:** 2000
SALES (est): 3.08MM **Privately Held**
Web: www.armacell.com
SIC: 3086 Plastics foam products
PA: Insulation United States Holdings, Llc
7600 Oakwood St

Mebane NC 27302

(G-8232)
BIOMERICS LLC ✪
1413 S Third Street Ext (27302-8186)
PHONE..................................336 810-7178
EMP: 5 EST: 2023
SALES (est): 2.08MM Privately Held
SIC: 3089 Plastics products, nec

(G-8233)
BROADSIGHT SYSTEMS INC
1023 Corporate Park Dr (27302-8368)
PHONE..................................336 837-1272
Takeshi Fujita, Pr
▲ EMP: 5 EST: 2011
SALES (est): 898.3K Privately Held
Web: www.broadsightsystems.com
SIC: 7539 3599 Machine shop, automotive;
Machine and other job shop work
HQ: Cbc America Holding Corp
1023 Corporate Park Dr
Mebane NC 27302
919 230-8700

(G-8234)
CAMBBRO MANUFACTURING COMPANY
1268 W Holt St (27302-8174)
PHONE..................................919 568-8506
EMP: 16 EST: 2016
SALES (est): 3.09MM Privately Held
SIC: 3999 Atomizers, toiletry

(G-8235)
CAMBRO (PA)
1268 Holt St (27302-9148)
PHONE..................................919 563-0761
Jon Skiffington, Pr
EMP: 5 EST: 2015
SALES (est): 2.19MM
SALES (corp-wide): 2.19MM Privately Held
Web: www.cambro.com
SIC: 3999 Manufacturing industries, nec

(G-8236)
COMFORTLAND INTERNATIONAL LLC
709 A O Smith Rd (27302-2752)
PHONE..................................866 277-3135
Lois Tsui, Pr
◆ EMP: 12 EST: 2010
SQ FT: 10,000
SALES (est): 2.58MM Privately Held
Web: www.comfortlandmed.com
SIC: 3842 Orthopedic appliances

(G-8237)
D & S INTERNATIONAL INC
700 Trollingwood Hawflds Rd (27302-8169)
P.O. Box 40 (27302-0040)
PHONE..................................336 578-3800
Frank Strohlein, Pr
Emy Strohlein, VP
Bonnie Philips, VP
◆ EMP: 14 EST: 1982
SQ FT: 102,000
SALES (est): 777.59K Privately Held
Web: www.dandsinternational.com
SIC: 3552 Textile machinery

(G-8238)
DORMER PRAMET LLC
1483 Dogwood Way (27302-9115)
PHONE..................................800 877-3745
◆ EMP: 232 EST: 2010
SALES (est): 2.55MM
SALES (corp-wide): 12.03B Privately Held
Web: www.dormerpramet.com

SIC: 3545 Drills (machine tool accessories)
HQ: Sandvik, Inc.
1483 Dogwood Way
Mebane NC 27302
919 563-5008

(G-8239)
EAST COAST DIGITAL INC
100 E Ruffin St (27302-2441)
P.O. Box 483 (27302-0483)
PHONE..................................919 304-1142
John Cornett, Pr
Glenn Cornett, VP
Christie Aaron, Sec
EMP: 10 EST: 2004
SALES (est): 270.87K Privately Held
Web: www.eastcoastdigital.com
SIC: 3651 Household audio equipment

(G-8240)
FORMA-FAB METALS INC
5816 Us 70 W (27302-8807)
P.O. Box 710 (27302-0710)
PHONE..................................919 563-5630
Richie Richmond, Pr
John Medlin, *
EMP: 35 EST: 1995
SQ FT: 50,000
SALES (est): 4.67MM Privately Held
Web: www.formafab.com
SIC: 3441 Fabricated structural metal

(G-8241)
GENERAL ELECTRIC COMPANY
Also Called: GE
I-85 Buckhorn Rd (27302)
PHONE..................................919 563-7445
Rodger Gasaway, Brnch Mgr
EMP: 15
SALES (corp-wide): 38.7B Publicly Held
Web: www.ge.com
SIC: 3625 3537 Control circuit relays,
industrial; Industrial trucks and tractors
PA: General Electric Company
1 Aviation Way
Cincinnati OH 45215
617 443-3000

(G-8242)
GENERAL ELECTRIC COMPANY
GE
6801 Industrial Dr (27302-8603)
PHONE..................................919 563-5561
Eric Tate, Mgr
EMP: 460
SQ FT: 9,514
SALES (corp-wide): 38.7B Publicly Held
Web: www.ge.com
SIC: 3625 3537 3613 Control circuit relays,
industrial; Industrial trucks and tractors;
Switchgear and switchboard apparatus
PA: General Electric Company
1 Aviation Way
Cincinnati OH 45215
617 443-3000

(G-8243)
GKN DNA INC
Also Called: Alamance Facility
1067 Trollingwood Hawflds Rd
(27302-9740)
PHONE..................................919 304-7378
Arnaud Lesschaev, Pr
EMP: 8 EST: 2010
SALES (est): 707.89K Privately Held
SIC: 3714 Universal joints, motor vehicle

(G-8244)
GKN DRIVELINE NORTH AMER INC
Also Called: GKN Automotive Grinding Whee
1067 Trollingwood Hawflds Rd
(27302-9740)

PHONE..................................919 304-7200
Bob Carvel, Brnch Mgr
EMP: 600
SALES (corp-wide): 6.06B Privately Held
SIC: 3694 3714 Automotive electrical
equipment, nec; Motor vehicle parts and
accessories
HQ: Gkn Driveline North America, Inc.
2200 N Opdyke Rd
Auburn Hills MI 48326
248 296-7000

(G-8245)
GOODYEAR TIRE & RUBBER COMPANY
Also Called: Goodyear
1352 Trollingwood Hawflds Rd
(27302-9743)
PHONE..................................984 983-0161
Rich Mccallum, Brnch Mgr
EMP: 5
SALES (corp-wide): 18.88B Publicly Held
Web: www.goodyear.com
SIC: 7534 5511 5531 Tire retreading and
repair shops; Trucks, tractors, and trailers:
new and used; Automotive tires
PA: The Goodyear Tire & Rubber Company
200 Innovation Way
Akron OH 44316
330 796-2121

(G-8246)
HONEYWELL SEC AMERICAS LLC
1027 Corporate Park Dr (27302-8368)
PHONE..................................919 563-5911
Scott Little, Brnch Mgr
EMP: 42
SALES (corp-wide): 38.5B Publicly Held
Web: corporate.carrier.com
SIC: 3669 Burglar alarm apparatus, electric
HQ: Honeywell Security Americas, Llc
855 S Mint St
Charlotte NC 28202

(G-8247)
KINGSDOWN INCORPORATED (HQ)
110 S Fourth St (27302-2640)
P.O. Box 388 (27302-0388)
PHONE..................................919 563-3531
Frank Hood, Pr
Timothy Price, *
◆ EMP: 25 EST: 1904
SALES (est): 35.01MM
SALES (corp-wide): 84.16MM Privately Held
Web: www.kingsdown.com
SIC: 2515 5712 5023 Mattresses,
innerspring or box spring; Mattresses;
Homefurnishings
PA: Kingsdown Holdings Inc.
110 S Fourth St
Mebane NC 27302
919 563-3531

(G-8248)
KINGSDOWN ACQUISITION CORP
126 W Holt St (27302-2622)
PHONE..................................919 563-3531
Eric Hinshaw, Prin
EMP: 8 EST: 1995
SALES (est): 125.24K Privately Held
Web: www.kingsdown.com
SIC: 2515 5023 Mattresses, innerspring or
box spring; Homefurnishings

(G-8249)
LIGGETT GROUP LLC (DH)
100 Maple Ln (27302-8160)
PHONE..................................919 304-7700
James A Taylor, *
Steven H Erikson, *

Jerry R Loftin, *
John R Long, *
▲ EMP: 372 EST: 1911
SQ FT: 300,000
SALES (est): 30.75MM Privately Held
Web: www.liggettvectorbrands.com
SIC: 2111 Cigarettes
HQ: Vgr Holding Llc
4400 Biscayne Blvd Fl 10
Miami FL 33131

(G-8250)
LOTUS BAKERIES US LLC
2010 Park Center Dr (27302-9817)
PHONE..................................415 956-8956
Jan Boone, CEO
Ignace Heyman, COO
EMP: 5 EST: 2017
SALES (est): 6.22MM
SALES (corp-wide): 92.63MM Privately
Held
SIC: 5963 5145 5149 2052 Food services,
direct sales; Snack foods; Health foods;
Bakery products, dry
HQ: Lotus Bakeries North America, Inc.
1000 Sansome St Ste 350
San Francisco CA 94111

(G-8251)
MAJORPOWER CORPORATION
7011 Industrial Dr (27302-8605)
PHONE..................................919 563-6610
Oren Nutik, Pr
Samuel Norman, *
▲ EMP: 25 EST: 1990
SQ FT: 20,000
SALES (est): 2.63MM Privately Held
Web: www.majorpower.com
SIC: 5065 3629 Communication equipment;
Inverters, nonrotating: electrical

(G-8252)
MORINAGA AMERICA FOODS INC
Also Called: Morinaga America
4391 Wilson Rd (27302-9823)
PHONE..................................919 643-2439
Toshiaki Fukunaga, CEO
Masao Hoshino, Pr
Teruhiro Kawabe, COO
Tomohiko Nakatogawa, CFO
▲ EMP: 26 EST: 2013
SALES (est): 7.52MM Privately Held
Web: www.morinaga-america-foods.com
SIC: 2064 Chewing candy, not chewing gum

(G-8253)
NYPRO INC
Also Called: Nypro Mebane
1018 Corporate Park Dr (27302-8368)
PHONE..................................919 304-1400
Gordon Lankton, Brnch Mgr
EMP: 5209
SALES (corp-wide): 28.88B Publicly Held
Web: www.nypromold.com
SIC: 3089 Injection molding of plastics
HQ: Nypro Inc.
101 Union St
Clinton MA 01510
978 365-9721

(G-8254)
PAK-LITE INC
6508 E Washington Street Ext
(27302-7222)
PHONE..................................919 563-1097
Jimmy Reily, Brnch Mgr
EMP: 37
SALES (corp-wide): 40.78MM Privately
Held
Web: www.pliusa.com

▲ = Import ▼ = Export
◆ = Import/Export

SIC: 3086 Packaging and shipping
materials, foamed plastics
PA: Pak-Lite, Inc.
550 Old Peachtree Rd Nw
Suwanee GA 30024
770 447-5123

(G-8255)
PARK COURT PROPERTIES RE INC
1404 Dogwood Way Unit C (27302-9586)
PHONE..............................919 304-3110
Doug Mahar, *Mgr*
EMP: 10
SALES (corp-wide): 1.93MM **Privately**
Held
SIC: 3823 Water quality monitoring and
control systems
PA: Park Court Properties Real Estate, Inc.
207a Park Ct
Ridgeland MS 39157
601 605-3000

(G-8256)
PIEDMONT METALWORKS LLC
5902 Us 70 W (27302-8808)
PHONE..............................919 598-6500
Ron Hamilton, *Pr*
Ron Hamilton, *Pr*
EMP: 5 EST: 2007
SALES (est): 2.89MM **Privately Held**
Web: www.piedmontmetalworks.com
SIC: 3441 Fabricated structural metal

(G-8257)
PRECISION CONCEPTS MEBANE
LLC (DH)
1403a S Third Street Ext (27302)
PHONE..............................919 563-9292
James M Piermarini, *Pr*
▲ EMP: 76 EST: 1984
SQ FT: 50,000
SALES (est): 24.69MM **Privately Held**
Web: www.pcinternational.com
SIC: 3089 Injection molding of plastics
HQ: Biomerics, Llc
6030 W Harold Gatty Dr
Salt Lake City UT 84116

(G-8258)
SANDVIK INC (HQ)
Also Called: Sandvik Coromant
1483 Dogwood Way (27302)
P.O. Box 428 (07410)
PHONE..............................919 563-5008
Rick Askin, *Pr*
◆ EMP: 250 EST: 1963
SALES (est): 911.74MM
SALES (corp-wide): 12.03B **Privately Held**
Web: www.home.sandvik
SIC: 3316 3317 3356 3315 Strip, steel, cold-
rolled, nec: from purchased hot-rolled,;
Tubes, seamless steel; Zirconium and
zirconium alloy: rolling, drawing,or extruding
; Wire products, ferrous/iron: made in
wiredrawing plants
PA: Sandvik Ab
Spangvagen 10
Sandviken 811 3
26260000

(G-8259)
SANDVIK MCHNING SLTONS USA
LLC
295 Maple Ln (27302-0748)
PHONE..............................919 563-5008
EMP: 14
SALES (corp-wide): 12.03B **Privately Held**
SIC: 3545 Machine tool accessories
HQ: Sandvik Machining Solutions Usa Llc
2424 Sandifer Blvd
Westminster SC 29693
800 726-3845

(G-8260)
SANDVIK TOOLING
1483 Dogwood Way (27302-9115)
PHONE..............................919 563-5008
Jogendra Saxena, *Mgr*
EMP: 4 EST: 2010
SALES (est): 554.08K **Privately Held**
SIC: 3541 Drilling machine tools (metal
cutting)

(G-8261)
TECH MEDICAL PLASTICS INC
1403 Dogwood Way (27302-9115)
PHONE..............................919 563-9272
James Piermarini, *Pr*
Alberto Rossato, *VP Opers*
Pamela Ward, *CFO*
EMP: 6 EST: 1989
SQ FT: 15,000
SALES (est): 375.07K **Privately Held**
SIC: 3089 3083 Injection molded finished
plastics products, nec; Laminated plastics
plate and sheet

(G-8262)
UNIVERSAL PRESERVACHEM INC
Also Called: Upi Chem Distribution Center
2390 Park Center Dr (27302-9848)
PHONE..............................732 568-1266
Daniel Ravitz, *Pr*
Herbert Ravitz, *
Michael Ravitz, *
Jim Sardi, *
◆ EMP: 81 EST: 1969
SALES (est): 3.65MM **Privately Held**
Web: www.upichem.com
SIC: 5169 2844 2834 Chemicals and allied
products, nec; Perfumes, cosmetics and
other toilet preparations; Pharmaceutical
preparations

(G-8263)
WALTER KIDDE PORTABLE EQP INC
(HQ)
Also Called: Kidde Safety
1016 Corporate Park Dr (27302-8368)
PHONE..............................919 563-5911
Isis Wu, *Pr*
Kenneth Cammarato, *
Jack Parow, *
Chris Rovenstine, *
◆ EMP: 269 EST: 1987
SQ FT: 100,000
SALES (est): 94.17MM
SALES (corp-wide): 22.49B **Publicly Held**
Web: www.kidde.com
SIC: 3669 5099 Smoke detectors; Fire
extinguishers
PA: Carrier Global Corporation
13995 Pasteur Blvd
Palm Beach Gardens FL 33418
561 365-2000

(G-8264)
WALTON LUMBER CO
302 Circle Dr (27302-2726)
P.O. Box 218 (27302-0218)
PHONE..............................919 563-6565
Sam L White, *Pt*
Ellen White Turner, *Pt*
EMP: 7 EST: 1950
SALES (est): 125.58K **Privately Held**
SIC: 2426 5211 Lumber, hardwood
dimension; Planing mill products and lumber

(G-8265)
WOMACK PUBLISHING CO INC
Also Called: Mebane Enterprise
106 N Fourth St (27302-2428)
PHONE..............................919 563-3555
Jackie Brown, *Mgr*

EMP: 5
SQ FT: 1,850
SALES (corp-wide): 4.28MM **Privately**
Held
Web: www.womackpublishing.com
SIC: 2711 Newspapers: publishing only, not
printed on site
PA: Womack Publishing Company, Inc.
28 N Main St
Chatham VA 24531
434 432-2791

(G-8266)
WRKCO INC
7411 Oakwood Street Ext (27302-9212)
PHONE..............................919 304-0300
Joe Royal, *Owner*
EMP: 28
SIC: 2631 Paperboard mills
HQ: Wrkco Inc.
1000 Abrnthy Rd Ne Ste 12
Atlanta GA 30328
770 448-2193

Merritt
Pamlico County

(G-8267)
CUSTOM STEEL BOATS INC
102 Yacht Dr (28556-9433)
P.O. Box 148 (28556-0148)
PHONE..............................252 745-7447
Rodney Flowers, *Pr*
Teresa Flowers, *VP*
EMP: 15 EST: 1981
SQ FT: 16,000
SALES (est): 1.65MM **Privately Held**
Web: www.customsteelboats.com
SIC: 3732 1799 1721 Boats, fiberglass:
building and repairing; Sandblasting of
building exteriors; Commercial painting

Merry Hill
Bertie County

(G-8268)
AVOCA LLC (DH)
841 Avoca Rd (27957)
P.O. Box 129 (27957-0129)
PHONE..............................252 482-2133
Augustinus Gerritsen, *Pr*
Robin E Lampkin, *
Donald E Meyer, *
Matthew K Spence, *
William C Whitaker, *
▲ EMP: 100 EST: 1962
SQ FT: 172,000
SALES (est): 23.83MM
SALES (corp-wide): 2.11B **Publicly Held**
Web: www.avocainc.com
SIC: 2099 Food preparations, nec
HQ: Ashland Chemco Inc.
1979 Atlas St
Columbus OH 43228
859 815-3333

(G-8269)
TATE & LYLE SOLUTIONS USA LLC
841 Avoca Farm Rd Ste 2 (27957)
PHONE..............................252 482-0402
Michele Mcguire, *Quality*
EMP: 50
SALES (corp-wide): 1.16B **Privately Held**
Web: www.tateandlyle.com
SIC: 2099 Food preparations, nec
HQ: Tate & Lyle Solutions Usa Llc
5450 Prairie Stone Pkwy
Hoffman Estates IL 60192
217 423-4411

Micaville
Yancey County

(G-8270)
BOONE-WOODY MINING COMPANY
INC
Also Called: B & W Stone Company
4456 E Us Hwy 19 E (28755)
P.O. Box 209 (28755-0209)
PHONE..............................828 675-5188
Tim Boone, *Pr*
Paul Boone, *Sec*
Chris Boone, *VP*
EMP: 6 EST: 1961
SQ FT: 560
SALES (est): 561.73K **Privately Held**
SIC: 3281 Stone, quarrying and processing
of own stone products

Middleburg
Vance County

(G-8271)
GEORGIA-PACIFIC LLC
Also Called: Georgia-Pacific
Hwy 158 And Interstate 85 (27556)
P.O. Box 99 (27556-0099)
PHONE..............................252 438-2238
Mark Tucker, *Mgr*
EMP: 5
SALES (corp-wide): 64.44B **Privately Held**
Web: www.gp.com
SIC: 2621 Paper mills
HQ: Georgia-Pacific Llc
133 Peachtree St Ne
Atlanta GA 30303
404 652-4000

Middlesex
Nash County

(G-8272)
CONCEPT FUSION LLC
Also Called: Concept Fusion
8200 Planer Mill Rd (27557-7439)
PHONE..............................252 406-7052
Nathan Brindle, *Pr*
EMP: 6 EST: 2015
SALES (est): 1.82MM **Privately Held**
Web:
www.conceptfusionmanufacturing.com
SIC: 3446 Architectural metalwork

(G-8273)
EAGLE SPORTSWEAR LLC
10447 S Nash St (27557-7825)
P.O. Box 430 (27557-0430)
PHONE..............................252 235-4082
William Lucas, *Prin*
EMP: 4 EST: 2014
SALES (est): 645.32K **Privately Held**
SIC: 2339 Women's and misses' outerwear,
nec

(G-8274)
EASTCOAST PACKAGING INC
Also Called: E C P
10235 E Finch Ave (27557-7400)
P.O. Box 279 (27557-0279)
PHONE..............................919 562-6060
Kevin Carden, *Pr*
Jimmy Royall, *
Crystal Nines, *
▲ EMP: 35 EST: 1995
SQ FT: 70,000
SALES (est): 1.75MM **Privately Held**

Web: www.ecpkg.com
SIC: **2675** 2671 2652 5113 Paperboard die-
cutting; Paper; coated and laminated
packaging; Setup paperboard boxes;
Folding paperboard boxes

(G-8275)
FREDERICK AND FREDERICK ENTP
Also Called: Shutter Works, The
8520 Hilliard Rd (27557-9350)
PHONE.....................252 235-4849
Judith Frederick, *Pr*
Walter Frederick, *VP*
EMP: 10 **EST:** 1993
SQ FT: 15,000
SALES (est): 223.54K **Privately Held**
Web: www.shutterworksandblinds.com
SIC: **2431** Millwork

(G-8276)
GERSON & GERSON INC
10601 E Finch Ave (27557-9223)
P.O. Box 97 (27557-0097)
PHONE.....................252 235-2441
Barbara Bowen, *Mgr*
EMP: 50
SALES (corp-wide): 22.9MM **Privately
Held**
Web: www.gersonandgerson.com
SIC: **5137** 2335 Women's and children's
clothing; Women's, junior's, and misses'
dresses
PA: Gerson & Gerson, Inc.
499 7th Ave Fl 5
New York NY 10018
212 244-6775

(G-8277)
MIDDLESEX PLANT
8171 Planer Mill Rd (27557-7407)
PHONE.....................252 235-2121
Greg Eatmon, *Prin*
EMP: 6 **EST:** 2010
SALES (est): 285.74K **Privately Held**
SIC: **3625** Relays and industrial controls

(G-8278)
NORTH CAROLINA MULCH INC
3277 Prong Creek Rd (27557-7969)
PHONE.....................252 478-4609
Kurk Stickland, *Pr*
EMP: 4 **EST:** 1997
SALES (est): 288.52K **Privately Held**
Web: www.northcarolinamulch.com
SIC: **2499** Mulch, wood and bark

(G-8279)
PENCCO INC
10143 Us 264a (27557-9257)
PHONE.....................252 235-5300
Jerry Murphy, *Brnch Mgr*
EMP: 10
SALES (corp-wide): 28.16MM **Privately
Held**
Web: www.pencco.com
SIC: **2899** 5169 2819 Water treating
compounds; Chemicals and allied products,
nec; Industrial inorganic chemicals, nec
PA: Pencco, Inc.
831 Bartlett Rd
Sealy TX 77474
979 885-0005

(G-8280)
PHYNIX PC INC
51 Abba Cir (27557-7301)
PHONE.....................503 890-1444
Angel Klett, *Pr*
EMP: 14 **EST:** 2022
SALES (est): 999.48K **Privately Held**

SIC: **3575** 7389 Computer terminals,
monitors and components; Business
Activities at Non-Commercial Site

Midland
Cabarrus County

(G-8281)
BOOMERANG WATER LLC
13570 Broadway Ave (28107-9733)
PHONE.....................833 266-6420
EMP: 15 **EST:** 2017
SALES (est): 2.96MM **Privately Held**
Web: www.boomerangwater.com
SIC: **5093** 3949 Bottles, waste; Ammunition
belts, sporting type

(G-8282)
CARRIFF CORPORATION INC (PA)
Also Called: Carriff Engineered Fabrics
3500 Fieldstone Trce (28107-9534)
PHONE.....................704 888-3330
◆ **EMP:** 7 **EST:** 1993
SALES (est): 5.66MM **Privately Held**
Web: www.carriff.com
SIC: **2221** Polyester broadwoven fabrics

(G-8283)
CF STEEL LLC
12322 Old Camden Rd (28107-7463)
P.O. Box 148 (28129-0148)
PHONE.....................704 516-1750
Tim Liescheidt, *Managing Member*
EMP: 6 **EST:** 2011
SALES (est): 2.48MM **Privately Held**
Web: www.flattruss.com
SIC: **3448** Prefabricated metal buildings and
components

(G-8284)
CORNING INCORPORATED
Also Called: Corning
14556 S Us Hwy 601 (28107-9245)
P.O. Box 1700 (28026-1700)
PHONE.....................704 569-6000
Tom Nettleman, *Brnch Mgr*
EMP: 99
SALES (corp-wide): 13.12B **Publicly Held**
Web: www.corning.com
SIC: **3211** 3357 Flat glass; Nonferrous
wiredrawing and insulating
PA: Corning Incorporated
1 Riverfront Plz
Corning NY 14831
607 974-9000

(G-8285)
CROSSROADS TIRE STORE INC
4430 Albemarle Rd (28107-9722)
P.O. Box 13 (28107-0013)
PHONE.....................704 888-2064
Dennis Hathcock, *Pr*
Claudia Hathcock, *Treas*
EMP: 5 **EST:** 1962
SQ FT: 6,000
SALES (est): 92.9K **Privately Held**
SIC: **5531** 7534 Automotive tires; Tire
recapping

(G-8286)
E T SALES INC
Also Called: Carolina Counters
13570 Broadway Ave (28107-9733)
P.O. Box 39 (28107-0039)
PHONE.....................704 888-4010
Nell M Eudy, *Pr*
Henry Eudy, *
Mark Eudy, *
EMP: 18 **EST:** 1982

SQ FT: 30,000
SALES (est): 622.21K **Privately Held**
Web: www.carolinacounters.com
SIC: **3281** 2541 Cut stone and stone
products; Wood partitions and fixtures

(G-8287)
H & R MULLIS MACHINE INC
151 Highway 24 27 E (28107-6420)
P.O. Box 229 (28107-0229)
PHONE.....................704 791-4149
Ronald L Mullis, *Pr*
Harold C Mullis, *Stockholder**
EMP: 4 **EST:** 1978
SQ FT: 10,000
SALES (est): 420.55K **Privately Held**
Web: www.hrmullis.com
SIC: **3599** Machine shop, jobbing and repair

(G-8288)
INTERTAPE POLYMER CORP
Also Called: Intertape Polymer Group
13722 Bill Mcgee Rd (28107-9539)
PHONE.....................980 907-4871
Jason Brauch, *Opers Mgr*
EMP: 55
SALES (corp-wide): 571.43MM **Privately
Held**
Web: www.itape.com
SIC: **2672** Paper; coated and laminated, nec
HQ: Intertape Polymer Corp.
100 Paramount Dr Ste 300
Sarasota FL 34232
888 898-7834

(G-8289)
**KNAPHEIDE TRCK EQP CO
MIDSOUTH**
Also Called: Knapheide Truck Equipment Ctrs
3572 Fieldstone Trce (28107-9534)
P.O. Box 318 (28107-0318)
PHONE.....................910 484-0558
Harold W Knapheide, *Pr*
Hardy Harris, *
EMP: 25 **EST:** 2004
SALES (est): 3.93MM
SALES (corp-wide): 47.7MM **Privately
Held**
Web: www.knapheide.com
SIC: **3713** Truck bodies (motor vehicles)
PA: The Knapheide Manufacturing
Company
1848 Westphalia Strasse
Quincy IL 62305
217 222-7131

(G-8290)
MESSER LLC
375 Nc Hwy 24 (28107)
PHONE.....................908 464-8100
EMP: 23
SALES (corp-wide): 2.29B **Privately Held**
Web: www.messeramericas.com
SIC: **2813** Industrial gases
HQ: Messer Llc
200 Smrset Corp Blvd Ste
Bridgewater NJ 08807
800 755-9277

(G-8291)
PEPSI BOTTLING GROUP INC
Also Called: Pepsico
5047 Highway 24 27 E (28107-5762)
PHONE.....................704 507-4031
EMP: 7
SIC: **2086** Carbonated soft drinks, bottled
and canned

(G-8292)
POEHLER ENTERPRISES INC
10515 Jim Sossoman Rd (28107-7707)
PHONE.....................704 239-1166
Sylvia Poehler, *Pr*
David F Poehler Junior, *VP*
EMP: 5 **EST:** 1997
SALES (est): 476.81K **Privately Held**
Web: www.poentinc.com
SIC: **3446** 1796 3534 Architectural metalwork
; Installing building equipment; Elevators
and moving stairways

(G-8293)
PREMIER MFG CO
3520 Fieldstone Trce (28107-9534)
PHONE.....................704 781-4001
EMP: 50 **EST:** 2019
SQ FT: 36,000
SALES (est): 9.13MM **Privately Held**
Web: pm.drtholdingsllc.com
SIC: **3599** Machine shop, jobbing and repair
HQ: Drt Precision Mfg., Llc
1985 Campbell Rd
Sidney OH 45365
937 507-4308

(G-8294)
QUARRY & KILN LLC
1334 Nc-24 W (28107)
P.O. Box 23027 (28227-0272)
PHONE.....................704 888-0775
EMP: 4 **EST:** 2016
SALES (est): 2.59MM **Privately Held**
Web: www.quarryandkiln.com
SIC: **3559** Kilns

(G-8295)
ROCKY RIVER VINEYARDS LLC
11685 Reed Mine Rd (28107-8617)
PHONE.....................704 781-5035
David Elliott, *Managing Member*
EMP: 7 **EST:** 2005
SALES (est): 167.67K **Privately Held**
Web: www.rockyrivervineyards.com
SIC: **2084** Wines

(G-8296)
SOTA VISION INC
1325 Aj Tucker Loop (28107-0030)
PHONE.....................800 807-7187
Daniel Ilnitskiy, *CEO*
EMP: 38 **EST:** 2018
SALES (est): 2.38MM **Privately Held**
Web: www.sotavision.com
SIC: **3823** Process control instruments

(G-8297)
SQUEEGEE TEES & MORE INC
12410 Grey Commercial Rd (28107-9400)
P.O. Box 159 (28107-0159)
PHONE.....................704 888-0336
Laurie Levinsky, *Pr*
Diane Levinsky, *Sec*
EMP: 6 **EST:** 1990
SQ FT: 6,000
SALES (est): 127.69K **Privately Held**
SIC: **2759** Screen printing

(G-8298)
WHITLEY HOLDING COMPANY (PA)
Also Called: Whitley Manufacturing
3827 Whitley Rd (28107-7242)
P.O. Box 112 (28107-0112)
PHONE.....................704 888-2625
Arlene Whitley, *Pr*
▲ **EMP:** 30 **EST:** 1960
SALES (est): 4.53MM **Privately Held**
Web: www.whitleyhandle.com
SIC: **2499** Handles, wood

(G-8299)
WHITLEY/MONAHAN HANDLE LLC
3827 Whitley Rd (28107-7242)
P.O. Box 112 (28107-0112)
PHONE..................................704 888-2625
Patrick Peeples, *
◆ **EMP: 40 EST:** 2007
SALES (est): 2.31MM Privately Held
Web: www.whitleyhandle.com
SIC: 2499 Handles, wood

Mill Spring
Polk County

(G-8300)
C & M INDUSTRIAL SUPPLY CO
748 N Hwy 16 (28756)
P.O. Box 911 (28037-0911)
PHONE..................................704 483-4001
Susan Donaldson, Pr
EMP: 4 EST: 2008
SALES (est): 244.12K Privately Held
SIC: 5251 5211 3069 Hardware stores;
Home centers; Tubing, rubber

(G-8301)
HTC LOGGING INC
1055 Cooper Gap Rd (28756-9670)
PHONE..................................828 625-1601
Hoyle Jackson, Pr
EMP: 5 EST: 1988
SALES (est): 113.65K Privately Held
SIC: 2411 Logging camps and contractors

(G-8302)
PACK BROTHERS LOGGING
Also Called: Pack Brothers Log & Grading
1559 Highway 9 S (28756-4716)
PHONE..................................828 894-2191
Kevin Pack, Pt
Kyle Pack, Pt
Bryan Pack, Pt
EMP: 5 EST: 1999
SALES (est): 373.01K Privately Held
SIC: 2411 Logging

(G-8303)
SUNNY VIEW PALLET COMPANY
3057 Big Level Rd (28756-6714)
PHONE..................................828 625-9907
James V Searcy, Owner
EMP: 4 EST: 1978
SALES (est): 231.25K Privately Held
SIC: 2448 Pallets, wood

Millers Creek
Wilkes County

(G-8304)
CHURCH & CHURCH LUMBER LLC
Also Called: Select Hardwoods Div
185 Hensley Eller Rd (28651-9132)
P.O. Box 619 (28651-0619)
PHONE..................................336 838-1256
EMP: 12
SALES (corp-wide): 15.41MM Privately Held
Web: www.churchandchurchlumber.com
SIC: 2426 2421 Hardwood dimension and
flooring mills; Sawmills and planing mills,
general
PA: Church & Church Lumber, Llc
863 New Browns Ford Rd
Wilkesboro NC 28697
336 973-5700

(G-8305)
KEITH CALL LOGGING LLC
P.O. Box 1407 (28651-1407)
PHONE..................................336 262-3681
Keith Call, Prin
EMP: 4 EST: 2001
SALES (est): 487.27K Privately Held
SIC: 2411 Logging camps and contractors

(G-8306)
OPENFIRE SYSTEMS
5450 Boone Trl (28651-9197)
PHONE..................................336 251-3991
Daniel Pereira, Pr
EMP: 8 EST: 2013
SALES (est): 92.08K Privately Held
Web: www.openfiresystems.com
SIC: 3949 7371 Target shooting equipment;
Computer software systems analysis and
design, custom

(G-8307)
RETAIL INSTALLATION SVCS LLC
142 Lexi Dr (28651-9241)
PHONE..................................336 818-1333
Jonathan Gorich, Owner
Steven Kilbey, Dir Opers
EMP: 4 EST: 2010
SALES (est): 193.88K Privately Held
SIC: 3993 1799 1542 Signs and advertising
specialties; Office furniture installation;
Commercial and office building, new
construction

(G-8308)
WILLIAM SHAWN STALEY
Also Called: Staley Logging & Grading
838 Green Acres Mill Rd (28651-8756)
P.O. Box 800 (28651-0800)
PHONE..................................336 838-9193
William S Staley, Owner
EMP: 4 EST: 2000
SALES (est): 239.92K Privately Held
SIC: 2411 Logging

Mills River
Henderson County

(G-8309)
A & M TOOL INC
125 School House Rd (28759-9742)
P.O. Box 309 (28742-0309)
PHONE..................................828 891-9990
James Awald, Pr
Anna Awald, VP
EMP: 19 EST: 1980
SQ FT: 9,000
SALES (est): 2.31MM Privately Held
Web: www.amtoolusa.com
SIC: 3544 Forms (molds), for foundry and
plastics working machinery

(G-8310)
ALAN KIMZEY
Also Called: National Wood Products
42 Sawmill Rd (28759-9730)
PHONE..................................828 891-8720
Billy Kimzey, Owner
EMP: 6 EST: 1979
SALES (est): 201.02K Privately Held
SIC: 2421 2448 Sawmills and planing mills,
general; Wood pallets and skids

(G-8311)
BLUE RIDGE CAB CONNECTION LLC
7 Brandy Branch Rd (28759-8715)
PHONE..................................828 891-2281
EMP: 4 EST: 2018
SALES (est): 614.04K Privately Held
Web:
www.blueridgecabinetconnection.com
SIC: 2434 Wood kitchen cabinets

(G-8312)
BOLD ROCK PARTNERS LP
Also Called: Bold Rock Hard Cider
72 School House Rd (28759-9712)
PHONE..................................828 595-9940
Brian Shanks, Pt
▲ **EMP: 15 EST:** 2011
SALES (est): 2.35MM
**SALES (corp-wide): 10.75MM Privately
Held**
Web: www.boldrock.com
SIC: 5813 2085 Bars and lounges; Applejack
(alcoholic beverage)
PA: Craft Revolution, Llc
4001 Yancey Rd Ste A
Charlotte NC 28217
347 924-7540

(G-8313)
DOVER FOODS INC
Also Called: American Quality Foods
353 Banner Farm Rd (28759-8707)
P.O. Box 519 (28704-0519)
PHONE..................................800 348-7416
Kathy S Milner, Pr
Joseph Mckay, VP
EMP: 32 EST: 1994
SQ FT: 17,000
SALES (est): 5.2MM Privately Held
Web: www.americanqualityfoods.com
SIC: 2099 Food preparations, nec

(G-8314)
HIGHLAND TOOL AND GAUGE INC
Also Called: Highland Tool
5500 Old Haywood Rd (28759-2008)
PHONE..................................828 891-8557
Bill Lafever, Pr
Lillie Lafever, Sec
EMP: 8 EST: 1985
SQ FT: 9,500
SALES (est): 1.67MM Privately Held
SIC: 3599 Machine shop, jobbing and repair

(G-8315)
HILLS MACHINERY COMPANY LLC
5481 Old Haywood Rd (28759-2007)
PHONE..................................828 820-5265
EMP: 4
**SALES (corp-wide): 37.47MM Privately
Held**
Web: www.hillsmachinery.com
SIC: 3531 Construction machinery
PA: Hills Machinery Company, Llc
1014 Atlas Way
Columbia SC 29209
803 658-0200

(G-8316)
JABIL INC
724 Broadpointe Dr (28759-0018)
PHONE..................................828 209-4202
Drew Friedman, Mgr
EMP: 5
SALES (corp-wide): 28.88B Publicly Held
Web: www.jabil.com
SIC: 3672 Printed circuit boards
PA: Jabil Inc.
10800 Roosevelt Blvd N
Saint Petersburg FL 33716
727 577-9749

(G-8317)
MEDICAL CABLE SPECIALISTS INC
Also Called: M T I
2133 Old Fanning Bridge Rd (28759-3418)
PHONE..................................828 890-2888
EMP: 20
Web: www.lifesync.com
SIC: 3089 Injection molded finished plastics
products, nec

(G-8318)
MICROTECH KNIVES INC (PA)
Also Called: Microtech
321 Fanning Fields Rd (28759-4610)
PHONE..................................828 684-4355
Anthony L Marfione, Pr
Susan A Marfione, VP
EMP: 57 EST: 2005
SALES (est): 12.27MM
**SALES (corp-wide): 12.27MM Privately
Held**
Web: www.microtechknives.com
SIC: 3423 Hand and edge tools, nec

(G-8319)
PRINCE GROUP LLC
Also Called: Prince Mfg - Greenville
209 Broadpointe Dr (28759-4995)
PHONE..................................828 681-8860
Bill White, Prin
EMP: 51
**SALES (corp-wide): 133.52MM Privately
Held**
Web: www.princemanufacturing.com
SIC: 3479 3471 Coating of metals and
formed products; Plating and polishing
HQ: Prince Group, Llc
3227 Sunset Blvd Ste E101
West Columbia SC 29169
803 708-4789

(G-8320)
PRINCE MANUFACTURING CORP
Also Called: Prince Mfg - Asheville
209 Broadpointe Dr (28759-4995)
PHONE..................................828 681-8860
Steven Floyd, Mgr
EMP: 150
**SALES (corp-wide): 133.52MM Privately
Held**
Web: www.princemanufacturing.com
SIC: 2759 3479 Commercial printing, nec;
Coating of metals and formed products
HQ: Prince Manufacturing Corporation
203 W Main St Ste A3
Lexington SC 29072
803 708-4789

(G-8321)
SKYLINE PLASTIC SYSTEMS INC
2220 Jeffress Rd (28759-4192)
PHONE..................................828 891-2515
Dean Smithson, Pr
Deborah P Smithson, Sec
Wayne Parrish, Dir
Doctor S A Burnette, Dir
EMP: 14 EST: 1990
SQ FT: 3,000
SALES (est): 5.86MM Privately Held
Web: www.skylineplastics.com
SIC: 3089 Injection molding of plastics

(G-8322)
UPM RAFLATAC INC (HQ)
400 Broadpointe Dr (28759-4652)
P.O. Box 13457 (19101-3457)
PHONE..................................828 651-4800
Jussi Vanhanen, Pr
Mark Pollard, *
Greg Owen, Business*
◆ **EMP: 315 EST:** 1985
SQ FT: 235,000
SALES (est): 223.96MM Privately Held
Web: www.upmraflatac.com

GEOGRAPHIC

SIC: 2672 3083 Labels (unprinted),
gummed: made from purchased materials;
Laminated plastics plate and sheet
PA: Upm-Kymmene Oyj
Alvar Aallon Katu 1
Helsinki 00100

(G-8323)
VAN WINGERDEN GRNHSE CO INC
Also Called: Vwgc
4078 Haywood Rd (28759-9762)
PHONE.................................828 891-7389
Richard Van Wingerden, *Pr*
James Gapinski, *
◆ **EMP:** 25 **EST:** 1972
SQ FT: 83,000
SALES (est): 4.57MM **Privately Held**
Web: www.van-wingerden.com
SIC: 3448 3231 Greenhouses, prefabricated
metal; Products of purchased glass

(G-8324)
**WESTERN CRLINA TL MOLD CORP
IN**
Also Called: Repair Services
3 Brandy Branch Rd (28759-8708)
PHONE.................................828 890-4448
Woody Scott, *Pr*
Alan W Scott Junior, *Pr*
Danny Grant, *VP*
David Holland, *VP*
Aubrey Laubter, *VP*
EMP: 14 **EST:** 1997
SQ FT: 7,000
SALES (est): 976.6K **Privately Held**
Web: www.wescartool.com
SIC: 7699 3544 Miscellaneous building item
repair services; Special dies, tools, jigs, and
fixtures

(G-8325)
WOODPECKER SAWMILL
Also Called: National Wood Product
52 Sawmill Rd (28759-9730)
P.O. Box 127 (28742-0127)
PHONE.................................828 891-8720
Allen Kimzey, *Pt*
Billy Kimzey, *Pt*
EMP: 6 **EST:** 1980
SALES (est): 131.25K **Privately Held**
Web: www.nationalwoodproducts.com
SIC: 2421 Sawmills and planing mills,
general

Milton
Caswell County

(G-8326)
RFH TACTICAL MOBILITY INC
748 Dotmond Rd (27305-9660)
PHONE.................................910 916-0284
EMP: 15 **EST:** 2008
SALES (est): 888.78K **Privately Held**
Web: www.rhtacticalmobility.com
SIC: 3711 8299 Ambulances (motor
vehicles), assembly of; Vehicle driving
school

Mineral Springs
Union County

(G-8327)
MINERAL SPRINGS FERTILIZER INC
5901 Eubanks (28108)
P.O. Box 8 (28108-0008)
PHONE.................................704 843-2683
Burt Fincher, *Pr*
Crystal F Hinson, *VP*

EMP: 6 **EST:** 1957
SQ FT: 15,000
SALES (est): 1.01MM **Privately Held**
Web: www.mineralspringsfertilizer.com
SIC: 2873 0723 5261 Nitrogenous fertilizers;
Grain milling; custom services; Nursery
stock, seeds and bulbs

(G-8328)
PARKDALE MILLS INCORPORATED
Also Called: Plant 21
Hwy 75 (28108)
PHONE.................................704 292-1255
Pam Haywood, *Mgr*
EMP: 28
SALES (corp-wide): 1.44B **Privately Held**
Web: www.parkdalemills.com
SIC: 2281 Yarn spinning mills
HQ: Parkdale Mills, Incorporated
531 Cotton Blossom Cir
Gastonia NC 28054
704 874-5000

Mint Hill
Mecklenburg County

(G-8329)
AFL NETWORK SERVICES INC
11211 Allen Station Dr (28227-7202)
P.O. Box 2580 (28111-2580)
PHONE.................................704 289-5522
Dick Phillips, *Brnch Mgr*
EMP: 35
Web: www.aflglobal.com
SIC: 3357 Nonferrous wiredrawing and
insulating
HQ: Afl Network Services, Inc.
170 Ridgeview Ctr Dr
Duncan SC 29334
864 433-0333

(G-8330)
ATLANTIC TUBE & FITTING LLC
4475 Morris Park Dr Ste L (28227-8260)
P.O. Box 690366 (28227-7007)
PHONE.................................704 545-6166
EMP: 5 **EST:** 2011
SALES (est): 1.56MM **Privately Held**
Web: www.atlantictubeandfitting.com
SIC: 3494 Pipe fittings

(G-8331)
BIG FISH DPI
9740 Lawyers Rd (28227-5134)
PHONE.................................704 545-8112
Jeff Love, *Pt*
EMP: 6 **EST:** 2012
SALES (est): 180.88K **Privately Held**
Web: www.bigfishdpi.com
SIC: 2754 7336 7374 Commercial printing,
gravure; Commercial art and graphic design
; Computer graphics service

(G-8332)
BLUE DOT READI-MIX LLC (PA)
11330 Bain School Rd (28227)
P.O. Box 23029 (28227)
PHONE.................................704 971-7676
Jj Dixon, *Managing Member*
EMP: 15 **EST:** 2004
SALES (est): 23.52MM
SALES (corp-wide): 23.52MM **Privately
Held**
Web: www.bluedotreadimix.com
SIC: 3273 Ready-mixed concrete

(G-8333)
C & M ENTERPRISE INC
Also Called: C & M Tag

6808 Wilgrove Mint Hill Rd (28227-3428)
P.O. Box 23226 (28227-0275)
PHONE.................................704 545-1180
Charles S Jones, *Pr*
Marlene Jones, *VP*
EMP: 8 **EST:** 1982
SQ FT: 2,000
SALES (est): 730.01K **Privately Held**
Web: www.cmenterprise.net
SIC: 5199 7519 2759 Advertising specialties;
Trailer rental; Tags: printing, nsk

(G-8334)
CARDINAL GRAPHICS INC
4475 Morris Park Dr Ste H (28227-8260)
P.O. Box 23367 (28227-0276)
PHONE.................................704 545-4144
Kelly Moore, *Ch Bd*
Ray Dulin, *Pr*
EMP: 5 **EST:** 1983
SQ FT: 4,000
SALES (est): 237.47K **Privately Held**
SIC: 2752 Offset printing

(G-8335)
**CAROLINA STAKE AND WD PDTS
INC**
11223 Blair Rd Ste 4 (28227-6870)
PHONE.................................704 545-7774
L Nelson Welch Junior, *Pr*
EMP: 5 **EST:** 1993
SALES (est): 490.14K **Privately Held**
Web: www.carolinawoodstakes.com
SIC: 2499 Surveyors' stakes, wood

(G-8336)
DATASCOPE NORTH AMERICA INC
4427 Wilgrove Mint Hill Rd (28227-3468)
PHONE.................................980 819-5244
Anton Jurgens, *Pr*
EMP: 27 **EST:** 2016
SALES (est): 3.15MM **Privately Held**
Web: www.datascopewms.com
SIC: 7372 Prepackaged software

(G-8337)
FAT MAN FABRICATIONS INC
8621c Fairview Rd (28227-7619)
PHONE.................................704 545-0369
Brent K Vandervort, *Pr*
Deborah Vandervort, *
EMP: 29 **EST:** 1985
SQ FT: 13,000
SALES (est): 4.81MM **Privately Held**
Web: www.fatmanfab.com
SIC: 3714 Frames, motor vehicle

(G-8338)
LUMENLUX LLC
8037 Fairview Rd Ste J-3 (28227-8953)
PHONE.................................704 222-7787
EMP: 5 **EST:** 2017
SALES (est): 452.08K **Privately Held**
Web: www.lumenluxllc.com
SIC: 3674 Light emitting diodes

(G-8339)
MAIN STREET RAG PUBLISHING CO
4614 Wilgrove Mint Hill Rd Ste G3
(28227-0130)
P.O. Box 690100 (28227-7001)
PHONE.................................704 573-2516
M Scott Douglass, *Pt*
EMP: 6 **EST:** 1996
SALES (est): 212.89K **Privately Held**
Web: www.mainstreetrag.com
SIC: 2741 Miscellaneous publishing

(G-8340)
MEUSBURGER US INC
4600 Lebanon Rd Ste A-1 (28227-8252)
PHONE.................................704 526-0330
Reinhard Von Hennigs, *Prin*
Michael Winship, *Prin*
▲ **EMP:** 21 **EST:** 2011
SALES (est): 2MM **Privately Held**
Web: www.meusburger.com
SIC: 3544 Diamond dies, metalworking

(G-8341)
MINT HILL INDUSTRIES
7313 Old Oak Ln (28227-5122)
PHONE.................................704 545-8852
Raymond Filz, *Prin*
EMP: 4 **EST:** 2008
SALES (est): 75.01K **Privately Held**
Web: www.minthill.com
SIC: 3999 Manufacturing industries, nec

(G-8342)
MOSACK GROUP LLC
Also Called: Apollo By Mosack Group
11210 Allen Station Dr (28227-7105)
P.O. Box 247 (28106-0247)
PHONE.................................888 229-2874
Glenn Mosack, *CEO*
Taylor Nelson, *
EMP: 75 **EST:** 2018
SALES (est): 8.8MM **Privately Held**
Web: www.apolloflow.com
SIC: 3494 Valves and pipe fittings, nec

(G-8343)
S Y SHOP INC
4475 Morris Park Dr Ste G (28227-8285)
PHONE.................................704 545-7710
Sam Yue, *Pr*
EMP: 6 **EST:** 1991
SQ FT: 2,500
SALES (est): 69.7K **Privately Held**
Web: www.syshopinc.com
SIC: 3999 Models, general, except toy

(G-8344)
UTD TECHNOLOGY CORP
4455 Morris Park Dr Ste J (28227-8264)
PHONE.................................704 612-0121
Johan Marte, *Prin*
EMP: 6 **EST:** 2010
SALES (est): 527.23K **Privately Held**
Web: www.utdtechnology.com
SIC: 3571 5999 7372 7373 Electronic
computers; Audio-visual equipment and
supplies; Home entertainment computer
software; Computer integrated systems
design

Mocksville
Davie County

(G-8345)
22ND CENTURY GROUP INC (PA)
321 Farmington Rd (27028-7638)
PHONE.................................716 270-1523
Lawrence D Firestone, *CEO*
Daniel Otto, *CFO*
EMP: 11 **EST:** 1998
SALES (est): 32.2MM
SALES (corp-wide): 32.2MM **Publicly
Held**
Web: www.xxiicentury.com
SIC: 8731 2111 6794 Biotechnical research,
commercial; Cigarettes; Franchises, selling
or licensing

▲ = Import ▼ = Export
◆ = Import/Export

(G-8346)
ABLE GRAPHICS COMPANY LLC
126 Horn St (27028-2449)
PHONE..................336 753-1812
William R Freeman, *Prin*
EMP: 6 **EST:** 2010
SALES (est): 148.83K **Privately Held**
Web: www.ablegraphicsprinting.com
SIC: 2752 Offset printing

(G-8347)
AMARR COMPANY
275 Enterprise Way (27028-4417)
PHONE..................336 936-0010
Tony East, *Brnch Mgr*
EMP: 6
Web: www.amarr.com
SIC: 1751 3442 2431 5031 Garage door, installation or erection; Baseboards, metal; Doors and door parts and trim, wood; Lumber, plywood, and millwork
HQ: Amarr Company
165 Carriage Ct
Winston Salem NC 27105
336 744-5100

(G-8348)
ATEC COATINGS LLC
111 Bailey St (27028-2408)
PHONE..................336 753-8888
EMP: 7 **EST:** 2009
SALES (est): 553.89K **Privately Held**
Web: www.ateccoatings.com
SIC: 2851 Coating, air curing

(G-8349)
ATEC WIND ENERGY PRODUCTS LLC
Also Called: Atec
111 Bailey St (27028-2408)
PHONE..................336 753-8888
EMP: 6 **EST:** 2009
SALES (est): 283.78K **Privately Held**
Web: www.ateccoatings.com
SIC: 2851 Undercoatings, paint

(G-8350)
AVGOL AMERICA INC
Also Called: Avgol Nonwovens
178 Avgol Dr (27028-2558)
PHONE..................336 936-2500
Shlomo Liran, *CEO*
Nir Peleg, *
Kazann Joyner, *
Shachar Rachim, *
◆ **EMP:** 140 **EST:** 2001
SALES (est): 42.84MM **Privately Held**
Web: www.avgol.com
SIC: 2297 Nonwoven fabrics
HQ: Avgol Industries 1953 Ltd
9 Shimshon
Petah Tikva 49527

(G-8351)
BEAR CREEK LOG TMBER HOMES LLC
371 Valley Rd (27028-2080)
PHONE..................336 751-6180
Kevin Nunn, *Owner*
EMP: 5 **EST:** 2005
SALES (est): 3.92MM **Privately Held**
Web: www.loghomesofnc.com
SIC: 2452 Log cabins, prefabricated, wood

(G-8352)
BUS SAFETY INC
Also Called: Bus Safety Solutions
133 Avgol Dr (27028-2559)
PHONE..................336 671-0838
Scott Geyer, *Pr*

Robert Geyer, *Pr*
Scott Geyer, *VP*
EMP: 6 **EST:** 2017
SALES (est): 975.13K **Privately Held**
Web: www.bussafetysolutions.com
SIC: 3711 Buses, all types, assembly of

(G-8353)
CAROLINA PRCSION MACHINING INC
1500 N Main St (27028-2719)
PHONE..................336 751-7788
Steven B Vick, *Pr*
Jansen Vick, *Mgr*
EMP: 29 **EST:** 1994
SQ FT: 15,000
SALES (est): 4.9MM **Privately Held**
Web: www.cpmmachining.com
SIC: 3599 Machine shop, jobbing and repair

(G-8354)
CAROLINA PRECISION MACHINING
130 Funder Dr (27028-2884)
PHONE..................336 751-7788
Steve Vick, *Pr*
EMP: 5 **EST:** 2016
SALES (est): 903.38K **Privately Held**
Web: www.cpmmachining.com
SIC: 3599 Machine shop, jobbing and repair

(G-8355)
CAROLINA PRECISION PLAS LLC
Also Called: Cpp Global
111 Cpp Global Dr (27028-5979)
PHONE..................336 283-4700
Tim Stafford, *Mgr*
EMP: 100
SALES (corp-wide): 500.49MM **Privately Held**
Web: www.cppglobal.com
SIC: 3089 Injection molding of plastics
HQ: Carolina Precision Plastics, L.L.C.
405 Commerce Pl
Asheboro NC 27203
336 498-2654

(G-8356)
CAROLINA SQUARE INC
Also Called: Diamond Apparel
1164 Cherry Hill Rd (27028-6629)
PHONE..................336 793-3222
Dan Cagle, *Pr*
Janet J Cagle, *VP*
EMP: 5 **EST:** 1993
SALES (est): 175.4K **Privately Held**
Web: www.diamondgolfshirts.com
SIC: 2491 Structural lumber and timber, treated wood

(G-8357)
DAVIE COUNTY PUBLISHING CO (HQ)
Also Called: Clemmons Courier
171 S Main St (27028-2424)
P.O. Box 99 (27028-0099)
PHONE..................336 751-2120
Dwight Sparks, *VP*
EMP: 13 **EST:** 1920
SALES (est): 1.67MM
SALES (corp-wide): 93.4MM **Privately Held**
Web: www.ourdavie.com
SIC: 2711 5735 Newspapers: publishing only, not printed on site; Records
PA: Epi Group, Llc.
4020 Stirrup Creek Dr
Durham NC 27703
843 577-7111

(G-8358)
DFA US INC
300 Bethel Church Rd (27028-2872)
PHONE..................336 756-0590
Ralf Dopheide, *Pr*
Reinhard Hecht, *
Denise Harrism, *
EMP: 35 **EST:** 2015
SQ FT: 100
SALES (est): 8.39MM **Privately Held**
Web: www.dfa-us.com
SIC: 5531 3296 Auto and home supply stores ; Mineral wool insulation products

(G-8359)
DUNLOP AIRCRAFT TYRES INC
205 Enterprise Way (27028-4417)
PHONE..................336 283-0979
John Seawell, *Mgr*
◆ **EMP:** 30 **EST:** 2015
SQ FT: 110,000
SALES (est): 5.63MM
SALES (corp-wide): 88.96MM **Privately Held**
Web: www.dunlopaircrafttyres.co.uk
SIC: 7534 5014 Rebuilding and retreading tires; Tires and tubes
HQ: Dunlop Aircraft Tyres Limited
40 Fort Parkway
Birmingham W MIDLANDS B24 9

(G-8360)
DWIGGINS METAL MASTERS INC
122 Wilkesboro St (27028-2322)
PHONE..................336 751-2379
Mike Dwiggins, *Pr*
David Dwiggins, *VP*
Peggy Dwiggins, *Sec*
EMP: 7 **EST:** 1922
SQ FT: 3,200
SALES (est): 545.54K **Privately Held**
SIC: 3446 3449 3444 3441 Stairs, staircases, stair treads: prefabricated metal; Miscellaneous metalwork; Sheet metalwork ; Fabricated structural metal

(G-8361)
EEKKOHART FLOORS & LBR CO INC
1133 N Main St (27028-2215)
PHONE..................336 409-2672
Daniel Ehrlich, *Ch Bd*
EMP: 4 **EST:** 2010
SALES (est): 243.41K **Privately Held**
SIC: 2426 Hardwood dimension and flooring mills

(G-8362)
FILET OF CHICKEN
251 Eaton Rd (27028-8653)
PHONE..................336 751-4752
Marty Gautreau, *Owner*
EMP: 10 **EST:** 2015
SALES (est): 760.43K **Privately Held**
Web: www.houseofraeford.com
SIC: 2015 Chicken, processed: cooked

(G-8363)
FULLER WLDG & FABRICATORS INC
980 Salisbury Rd (27028-9301)
PHONE..................336 751-3712
Phillip E Fuller Junior, *Pr*
Darlene Fuller, *Sec*
EMP: 21 **EST:** 1972
SQ FT: 30,000
SALES (est): 4.07MM **Privately Held**
Web: www.fullerwelding.com
SIC: 3441 Fabricated structural metal

(G-8364)
FUNDER AMERICA INC
Ilbau America
200 Funder Dr (27028-2886)
PHONE..................336 751-3501
Peter Funder, *Brnch Mgr*
EMP: 18
SALES (corp-wide): 89.73MM **Privately Held**
Web: www.funderamerica.com
SIC: 5021 2431 Furniture; Panel work, wood
HQ: Funder America, Inc.
200 Funder Dr
Mocksville NC 27028
336 751-3501

(G-8365)
FUNDER AMERICA INC (HQ)
200 Funder Dr (27028-2886)
P.O. Box 729 (27028)
PHONE..................336 751-3501
Peter Funder, *Pr*
Lisl Funder, *
Erhard Grossnigg, *
◆ **EMP:** 110 **EST:** 1972
SQ FT: 120,000
SALES (est): 16.43MM
SALES (corp-wide): 89.73MM **Privately Held**
Web: www.funderamerica.com
SIC: 2431 Millwork
PA: Genesis Products, Llc
1853 Eisenhower Dr S
Goshen IN 46526
877 266-8292

(G-8366)
GENTLE MACHINE AND TOOL INC
2716 Us Highway 601 N (27028-5952)
PHONE..................336 492-5055
Jimmy Gentle, *Pr*
Melinda Gentle, *VP*
EMP: 4 **EST:** 1970
SQ FT: 4,000
SALES (est): 869.5K **Privately Held**
SIC: 3599 Machine shop, jobbing and repair

(G-8367)
GESIPA FASTENERS USA INC
Also Called: Tooling Division
126 Quality Dr (27028-4415)
PHONE..................336 751-1555
Milo Edwards, *Brnch Mgr*
EMP: 21
SALES (corp-wide): 6.37MM **Privately Held**
Web: www.gesipausa.com
SIC: 3599 3542 3965 3452 Machine shop, jobbing and repair; Riveting machines; Fasteners; Rivets, metal
PA: Gesipa Fasteners Usa, Inc.
126 Quality Dr
Mocksville NC 27028
609 208-1740

(G-8368)
GESIPA FASTENERS USA INC (PA)
126 Quality Dr (27028-4415)
PHONE..................609 208-1740
Guy C Krone, *Pr*
Erik Olshall, *General Vice President*
Bill Schuler, *VP*
◆ **EMP:** 12 **EST:** 1975
SALES (est): 6.37MM
SALES (corp-wide): 6.37MM **Privately Held**
Web: www.gesipausa.com
SIC: 5251 3542 3965 3599 Builders' hardware; Riveting machines; Fasteners; Machine shop, jobbing and repair

(G-8369)

HOUSE OF RAEFORD FARMS LA LLC
251 Eaton Rd (27028-8653)
PHONE..............................336 751-4752
EMP: 173
SALES (corp-wide): 1.79B Privately Held
Web: www.houseofraeford.com
SIC: 2015 Poultry slaughtering and processing
HQ: House Of Raeford Farms Of Louisiana, L.L.C.
3867 2nd St
Arcadia LA 71001
318 263-9004

(G-8370)

HUNCKLER FABRICATION LLC
123 S Park Pl (27028-9305)
PHONE..............................336 753-0905
Roger Hunckler, Managing Member
EMP: 14 EST: 2009
SALES (est): 1.44MM Privately Held
Web: www.magneshade.com
SIC: 3716 5719 Motor homes; Window shades, nec

(G-8371)

INGERSOLL RAND INC
501 Sanford Ave (27028-2919)
PHONE..............................828 375-8240
EMP: 8
SALES (corp-wide): 7.24B Publicly Held
Web: www.irco.com
SIC: 3561 Pumps and pumping equipment
PA: Ingersoll Rand Inc.
525 Harbor Pl Dr Ste 600
Davidson NC 28036
704 896-4000

(G-8372)

JONES DOORS & WINDOWS INC
533 Joe Rd (27028-7253)
PHONE..............................336 998-8624
David Tkach, Pr
Albert Tkach, VP
EMP: 12 EST: 1996
SQ FT: 15,000
SALES (est): 4.75MM Privately Held
Web: www.jonesdoors.net
SIC: 2431 Millwork

(G-8373)

LANDMARK COATINGS LLC
Also Called: Landmark Coatings
933 Danner Rd (27028-5731)
P.O. Box 1602 (27028-1602)
PHONE..............................336 492-2492
EMP: 5 EST: 1997
SQ FT: 10,000
SALES (est): 485.11K Privately Held
Web: www.landmarkcoatings.com
SIC: 3479 Coating of metals and formed products

(G-8374)

LEWTAK PIPE ORGAN BUILDERS INC
211 Parsley Ln (27028-6771)
PHONE..............................336 554-2251
Tomasz Lewtak, Pr
▲ EMP: 4 EST: 2008
SALES (est): 154.83K Privately Held
Web: www.lewtak.com
SIC: 1521 3931 New construction, single-family houses; Musical instruments

(G-8375)

MCDANIEL DELMAR (PA)
Also Called: Uniform Express
144 Whetstone Dr (27028-6932)
PHONE..............................336 284-6377
Delmar Mc Daniel, Owner
EMP: 24 EST: 1984
SQ FT: 35,000
SALES (est): 920.23K
SALES (corp-wide): 920.23K Privately Held
Web: www.duckscrubs.com
SIC: 2311 2339 2326 5699 Men's and boys' uniforms; Women's and misses' outerwear, nec; Men's and boy's work clothing; Uniforms and work clothing

(G-8376)

MEGA MACHINE SHOP INC
130 Macy Langston Ln (27028-6227)
P.O. Box 1252 (27028-1252)
PHONE..............................336 492-2728
Kimberly Howard, Pr
Todd Howard, VP
EMP: 8 EST: 1993
SQ FT: 5,500
SALES (est): 530.56K Privately Held
Web: www.megamachineinc.com
SIC: 3599 Machine shop, jobbing and repair

(G-8377)

METAL SALES MANUFACTURING CORP
188 Quality Dr (27028-4415)
PHONE..............................704 859-0550
Jerry Ace, Mgr
EMP: 25
SALES (corp-wide): 443.57MM Privately Held
Web: metalsales.us.com
SIC: 3444 Roof deck, sheet metal
HQ: Metal Sales Manufacturing Corporation
545 S 3rd St Ste 200
Louisville KY 40202
502 855-4300

(G-8378)

MILLER SHEET METAL CO INC
2038 Us Highway 601 S (27028-6904)
P.O. Box 158 (27028-0158)
PHONE..............................336 751-2304
Cletus R Miller, Pr
Mildred M Miller, Sec
Ed Miller, VP
EMP: 4 EST: 1969
SQ FT: 1,025
SALES (est): 240.32K Privately Held
SIC: 1711 7692 Warm air heating and air conditioning contractor; Welding repair

(G-8379)

MOCK TIRE & AUTOMOTIVE INC
Also Called: Beroth Tire of Mocksville
132 Interstate Dr (27028-4195)
PHONE..............................336 753-8473
EMP: 36
SALES (corp-wide): 6.96MM Privately Held
Web: www.mockberothtire.com
SIC: 5531 7539 7534 Automotive tires; Auto front end repair; Tire repair shop
PA: Mock Tire & Automotive Inc
4752 Country Club Rd
Winston Salem NC 27104
336 768-1010

(G-8380)

MOUNTAINTOP CHEESECAKES LLC
209 Sunburst Ln (27028-5378)
PHONE..............................336 391-9127
Dustin Horner, Owner
EMP: 6 EST: 2017
SALES (est): 120.67K Privately Held
SIC: 2591 Window blinds

(G-8381)

NEWRIVERWELDING
271 Merrells Lake Rd (27028-7321)
PHONE..............................336 413-3040
EMP: 5 EST: 2014
SALES (est): 493.33K Privately Held
SIC: 7692 Welding repair

(G-8382)

NPC CORPORATION
140 Theodore Dr (27028)
P.O. Box 2011 (27006-2011)
PHONE..............................336 998-2386
Jerry Smith, CEO
Brock Agee, Pr
Eddie Scott, Contrlr
Kathy Woodrum, Dir
Ashley Seamon, Dir
EMP: 6 EST: 2006
SALES (est): 433.44K Privately Held
Web: www.mightymuscadine.com
SIC: 2023 Dietary supplements, dairy and non-dairy based

(G-8383)

OLON INDUSTRIES INC (US)
Also Called: Eurodrawer
279 Bethel Church Rd (27028-2871)
P.O. Box 669 (47501-0669)
PHONE..............................630 232-4705
Dagmar Deich, Mgr
EMP: 11
SALES (corp-wide): 38.47MM Privately Held
Web: www.olon.ca
SIC: 2493 3081 Particleboard products; Unsupported plastics film and sheet
HQ: Olon Industries Inc. (Us)
411 Union St
Geneva IL 60134
630 232-4705

(G-8384)

PALLETONE NORTH CAROLINA INC
Pallet One
165 Turkey Foot Rd (27028-5930)
PHONE..............................336 492-5565
Brian Dyson, Brnch Mgr
EMP: 98
SALES (corp-wide): 6.65B Publicly Held
Web: www.palletone.com
SIC: 2448 Pallets, wood
HQ: Palletone Of North Carolina, Inc.
2340 Ike Brooks Rd
Siler City NC 27344
704 462-1882

(G-8385)

PRO REFRIGERATION INC
319 Farmington Rd (27028-7638)
PHONE..............................336 283-7281
James L Vander Giessen Senior, Pr
EMP: 25
Web: www.prochiller.com
SIC: 3585 Refrigeration equipment, complete
PA: Pro Refrigeration Inc.
326 8th St Sw
Auburn WA 98001

(G-8386)

QST INDUSTRIES INC
Quick Service Textiles
140 Lionheart Dr (27028-9440)
PHONE..............................336 751-1000
Nathan Varner, Mgr
EMP: 15
SALES (corp-wide): 43.51MM Privately Held
Web: www.qst.com
SIC: 2396 Waistbands, trouser
PA: Qst Industries, Inc.

1755 Park St
Naperville IL 60563
312 930-9400

(G-8387)

REEB MILLWORK CORPORATION
346 Bethel Church Rd (27028-2872)
PHONE..............................336 751-4650
EMP: 15
SALES (corp-wide): 766.45MM Privately Held
Web: www.reeb.com
SIC: 2431 Millwork
HQ: Reeb Millwork Corporation
1000 Maloney Cir
Bethlehem PA 18015
610 867-6160

(G-8388)

SCOTT BADER INC
212 Quality Dr (27028-4430)
PHONE..............................330 920-4410
Kevin Matthews, Pr
EMP: 21 EST: 2008
SALES (est): 8.52MM Privately Held
SIC: 2891 Adhesives and sealants

(G-8389)

SIGNLITE SERVICES INC
151 Industrial Blvd (27028-2773)
P.O. Box 1207 (27028-1207)
PHONE..............................336 751-9543
Daniel Des Noyers, Pr
EMP: 4 EST: 1987
SQ FT: 3,000
SALES (est): 150.22K Privately Held
Web: www.signliteonline.com
SIC: 7312 3993 Outdoor advertising services; Signs, not made in custom sign painting shops

(G-8390)

SOISA INC
111 Dalton Business Ct Ste 101 (27028-5195)
PHONE..............................336 940-4006
Van Fulp, Prin
Roberto Romero, CEO
Jacobo Mesta, VP
Jesus Mesta, Prin
Javier Mesta, Prin
EMP: 5 EST: 2019
SALES (est): 104.33K Privately Held
SIC: 2396 3728 Automotive trimmings, fabric; Aircraft parts and equipment, nec

(G-8391)

SPORTSFIELD SPECIALTIES INC
Also Called: Sportsfield Specialties
155 Boyce Dr (27028-4187)
P.O. Box 2489 (28145-2489)
PHONE..............................704 637-2140
EMP: 22
Web: www.sportsfield.com
SIC: 3949 Sporting and athletic goods, nec
PA: Sportsfield Specialties, Inc.
41155 State Hwy 10
Delhi NY 13753

(G-8392)

STEPHENS MECHANICAL
714 Cherry Hill Rd (27028-6625)
PHONE..............................336 998-2141
Vickie Stephens, Owner
EMP: 4 EST: 1986
SQ FT: 15,000
SALES (est): 1.47MM Privately Held
Web: www.stephensmechanical.com
SIC: 3441 Fabricated structural metal

(G-8393)
TAR HEEL LANDWORKS LLC
6858 Nc Highway 801 S (27028-6733)
PHONE..............................336 941-3009
Brian R Williams, *Owner*
EMP: 6 **EST:** 2018
SALES (est): 1.72MM **Privately Held**
SIC: 2865 Cyclic crudes and intermediates

(G-8394)
TRANE TECHNOLOGIES COMPANY LLC
Ingersoll-Rand
501 Sanford Ave (27028-2919)
P.O. Box 868 (27028-0868)
PHONE..............................336 751-3561
Carl Nascar, *Brnch Mgr*
EMP: 450
Web: www.tranetechnologies.com
SIC: 3621 3563 3441 Motors and generators
; Air and gas compressors; Fabricated
structural metal
HQ: Trane Technologies Company Llc
800-E Beaty St
Davidson NC 28036
704 655-4000

(G-8395)
TRIM INC
351 Bethel Church Rd (27028-2873)
P.O. Box 905 (27028-0905)
PHONE..............................336 751-3591
Paul Hauser, *Pr*
Neil Hauser, *Sec*
EMP: 7 **EST:** 1970
SQ FT: 45,000
SALES (est): 1.07MM **Privately Held**
SIC: 2431 3442 Moldings and baseboards,
ornamental and trim; Metal doors, sash,
and trim

(G-8396)
WNYH LLC
155 Boyce Dr (27028-4187)
PHONE..............................716 853-1800
▲ **EMP:** 250
SIC: 3841 Medical instruments and
equipment, blood and bone work

Moncure
Chatham County

(G-8397)
3M COMPANY
3M
4191 Hwy 87 S (27559)
PHONE..............................919 642-0006
John Lowery, *Mgr*
EMP: 100
SALES (corp-wide): 32.68B **Publicly Held**
Web: www.3m.com
SIC: 3295 Roofing granules
PA: 3m Company
3m Center
Saint Paul MN 55144
651 733-1110

(G-8398)
ACONCAGUA TIMBER CORP
Also Called: Franklin Partleboard
985 Corinth Rd (27559-9740)
PHONE..............................919 542-2128
◆ **EMP:** 500
SIC: 2493 Particleboard products

(G-8399)
ARAUCO NORTH AMERICA INC
985 Corinth Rd (27559-9740)
PHONE..............................919 542-2128

EMP: 76
Web: www.arauco.com
SIC: 2493 Reconstituted wood products
HQ: Arauco North America, Inc.
400 Prmter Ctr Terr Ste 7
Atlanta GA 30346

(G-8400)
ARCLIN USA LLC
Also Called: Dynea
790 Corinth Rd (27559-9345)
PHONE..............................919 542-2526
Larry Sanders, *Brnch Mgr*
EMP: 7
SALES (corp-wide): 146.06MM **Privately Held**
Web: www.arclin.com
SIC: 2821 2891 Plastics materials and resins
; Adhesives and sealants
HQ: Arclin Usa Llc
1150 Sanctuary Pkwy
Alpharetta GA 30009
678 999-2100

(G-8401)
CABINET CREATIONS INC
585 Carl Foushee Rd (27559-9220)
PHONE..............................919 542-3722
Wayne Foushee, *Pr*
Kathie Foushee, *VP*
EMP: 8 **EST:** 1980
SALES (est): 534.2K **Privately Held**
Web: www.cabinetcreationsnc.com
SIC: 2434 Wood kitchen cabinets

(G-8402)
CAPITAL RDYMX PITTSBORO LLC
270 Moncure Pittsboro Rd (27559-9721)
PHONE..............................919 217-0222
EMP: 20 **EST:** 2017
SALES (est): 4.22MM **Privately Held**
Web: www.capitalreadymixconcrete.com
SIC: 3273 Ready-mixed concrete

(G-8403)
EAST COAST FIREWOOD LLC
840 Moncure Pittsboro Rd (27559-9222)
PHONE..............................919 542-0792
J Perry Hunt, *Managing Member*
EMP: 10 **EST:** 2016
SALES (est): 520.1K **Privately Held**
Web: www.ecfirewood.com
SIC: 2421 Lumber: rough, sawed, or planed

(G-8404)
ELKINS SAWMILL INC
670 King Rd (27559-9653)
PHONE..............................919 362-1235
Billy H Elkins, *Prin*
EMP: 28
SALES (corp-wide): 5.39MM **Privately Held**
Web: www.elkinssawmill.com
SIC: 2421 Sawmills and planing mills,
general
PA: Elkins Sawmill, Inc.
6855 Pittsboro Rd
Goldston NC 27252
919 898-4689

(G-8405)
GENERAL SHALE BRICK INC
300 Brick Plant Rd (27559-9519)
PHONE..............................919 775-2121
Jerry Whitfield, *Mgr*
EMP: 30
SALES (corp-wide): 4.59B **Privately Held**
Web: www.generalshale.com
SIC: 3251 3271 Brick clay: common face,
glazed, vitrified, or hollow; Concrete block
and brick

HQ: General Shale Brick, Inc.
3015 Bristol Hwy
Johnson City TN 37601
423 282-4661

(G-8406)
HEARTWOOD PINE FLOORS INC
2722 Nc 87 S (27559-9780)
PHONE..............................919 542-4394
Larry Green Junior, *Prin*
▼ **EMP:** 8 **EST:** 2004
SALES (est): 357.95K **Privately Held**
Web: www.heartwoodpine.com
SIC: 5713 2499 Floor covering stores;
Applicators, wood

(G-8407)
KINDLED PROVISIONS LLC ✪
840 Moncure Pittsboro Rd (27559)
P.O. Box 877 (27312)
PHONE..............................919 542-0792
J Perry Hunt, *Managing Member*
EMP: 10 **EST:** 2024
SALES (est): 401.73K **Privately Held**
SIC: 2499 7389 Wood products, nec;
Business Activities at Non-Commercial Site

(G-8408)
LUCK STONE CORPORATION
Also Called: Luck Stone - Pittsboro
4189 Nc Highway 87 S (27559)
P.O. Box 59 (27312-0059)
PHONE..............................919 545-0027
Steve Demeyer, *Prin*
EMP: 65
SALES (corp-wide): 366.46MM **Privately Held**
Web: www.luckstone.com
SIC: 1429 Grits mining (crushed stone)
PA: Luck Stone Corporation
515 Stone Mill Dr
Manakin Sabot VA 23103
804 784-6300

(G-8409)
SOUTHERN VNEER SPCLTY PDTS LLC
306 Corinth Rd (27559-9295)
PHONE..............................919 642-7004
EMP: 13 **EST:** 2019
SALES (est): 9.25MM **Privately Held**
SIC: 2435 5031 Hardwood plywood,
prefinished; Veneer

(G-8410)
TRIANGLE BRICK COMPANY
Also Called: Triangle Brick Merryoaks Plant
294 King Rd (27559-9580)
PHONE..............................919 387-9257
Ricky Marit, *Genl Mgr*
EMP: 77
SALES (est): 49.63MM **Privately Held**
Web: www.trianglebrick.com
SIC: 3251 Brick and structural clay tile
PA: Triangle Brick Company
6523 Nc Highway 55
Durham NC 27713
919 544-1796

(G-8411)
UNIBOARD USA LLC
985 Corinth Rd (27559-9740)
PHONE..............................919 542-2128
◆ **EMP:** 250
SIC: 2493 Reconstituted wood products

(G-8412)
WAKE STONE CORPORATION
9725 Stone Quarry Rd (27559)

P.O. Box 158 (27559-0158)
PHONE..............................919 775-7349
Floyd Drake, *Brnch Mgr*
EMP: 26
SALES (corp-wide): 23.51MM **Privately Held**
Web: www.wakestonecorp.com
SIC: 1423 5032 Crushed and broken granite;
Stone, crushed or broken
PA: Wake Stone Corporation
6821 Knightdale Blvd
Knightdale NC 27545
919 266-1100

(G-8413)
WILLIAMS LOGGING INC
2371 Charlie Brooks Rd (27559-9325)
PHONE..............................919 542-2740
Richard Williams, *Pr*
EMP: 5 **EST:** 1989
SALES (est): 485.81K **Privately Held**
SIC: 2411 Logging camps and contractors

Monroe
Union County

(G-8414)
A C S ENTERPRISES NC INC
Also Called: Whitecaps
307 N Secrest Ave (28110-3801)
PHONE..............................704 226-9898
Jeffrey W White, *Pr*
EMP: 8 **EST:** 1989
SALES (est): 697.8K **Privately Held**
SIC: 3444 Sheet metalwork

(G-8415)
ACHEM INDUSTRY AMERICA INC
2910 Stitt St (28110-3914)
PHONE..............................704 283-6144
Kenny Liu, *Brnch Mgr*
EMP: 8
SALES (corp-wide): 24.61MM **Privately Held**
Web: www.achem.com.tw
SIC: 2672 Tape, pressure sensitive: made
from purchased materials
PA: Achem Industry America, Inc.
4250 N Harbor Blvd
Fullerton CA 92835
562 802-0998

(G-8416)
ACME NAMEPLATE & MFG INC
300 Acme Dr (Off Hwy 74 E) (28112-4199)
PHONE..............................704 283-8175
Bromley B Schuett, *Ch Bd*
Peter C Collias, *
Stephen L Ebbers, *
Jack L Sharrett, *
EMP: 5 **EST:** 1937
SQ FT: 60,000
SALES (est): 183.43K **Privately Held**
Web: www.boydcorp.com
SIC: 3479 3089 Name plates: engraved,
etched, etc.; Engraving of plastics

(G-8417)
ADVANCED DIGITAL TEXTILES LLC
600 Broome St (28110-3947)
PHONE..............................704 226-9600
▲ **EMP:** 20 **EST:** 2006
SQ FT: 34,000
SALES (est): 7.62MM **Privately Held**
Web: www.advdigitaltextiles.com
SIC: 2269 2261 2262 Linen fabrics: dyeing,
finishing, and printing; Printing of cotton
broadwoven fabrics; Printing, manmade
fiber and silk broadwoven fabrics

(G-8418)
ADVANCED PLATING TECHNOLOGIES
2600 Stitt St (28110-3836)
PHONE.................................704 291-9325
Robert Parker, *Pr*
EMP: 8 **EST:** 1996
SQ FT: 10,000
SALES (est): 331.54K **Privately Held**
Web: www.advplating.com
SIC: 3356 3471 Nickel and nickel alloy pipe, plates, sheets, etc.; Plating and polishing

(G-8419)
ADVPLATING LLC
2600 Stitt St (28110-3836)
PHONE.................................704 291-9325
Kyle Caniglia, *Managing Member*
EMP: 9 **EST:** 2015
SQ FT: 17,000
SALES (est): 1.9MM **Privately Held**
Web: www.advplating.com
SIC: 3471 Electroplating of metals or formed products

(G-8420)
AIR-WE-GO LLC
Also Called: Aie We Go
4507 W Highway 74 (28110-0430)
PHONE.................................704 289-6565
Andrew A Adams, *Managing Member*
Margret England, *Mgr*
EMP: 39
SALES (est): 2.22MM **Privately Held**
SIC: 3728 Aircraft parts and equipment, nec

(G-8421)
ALLIED PRESSROOM PRODUCTS INC (PA)
4814 Persimmon Ct (28110-9313)
PHONE.................................954 920-0909
Richard H Sures, *Pr*
Jeffrey H Rose, *
▼ **EMP:** 20 **EST:** 1952
SQ FT: 1,530
SALES (est): 4.14MM
SALES (corp-wide): 4.14MM **Privately Held**
Web: www.croftgateusa.com
SIC: 2893 2851 Printing ink; Paints: oil or alkyd vehicle or water thinned

(G-8422)
AMERICAN REWINDING NC INC
Also Called: American Rewinding Co
1825 N Rocky River Rd (28110-7961)
P.O. Box 890377 (28289-0377)
PHONE.................................704 289-4177
Paula Huber, *CEO*
Michael Huber, *
Lewis Stegall, *
Danny Plyler, *
EMP: 40 **EST:** 1972
SQ FT: 15,000
SALES (est): 12.08MM **Privately Held**
Web: www.americanmts.com
SIC: 7694 3599 Rewinding services; Machine shop, jobbing and repair

(G-8423)
AMERICAN REWINDING OF NC INC
1825 N Rocky River Rd (28110-7961)
PHONE.................................704 589-1020
EMP: 20 **EST:** 2002
SALES (est): 1.03MM **Privately Held**
Web: www.americanmts.com
SIC: 7694 Electric motor repair

(G-8424)
AMERICAN WICK DRAIN CORP
1209 Airport Rd (28110-7389)
PHONE.................................704 296-5801
T Richard Morris, *Pr*
Thomas P Cunningham, *
▼ **EMP:** 35 **EST:** 1974
SQ FT: 105,000
SALES (est): 5.6MM **Privately Held**
Web: www.awd-usa.com
SIC: 3444 3089 Sheet metalwork; Thermoformed finished plastics products, nec

(G-8425)
AMSTED INDUSTRIES INCORPORATED
4515 Corporate Dr (28110)
PHONE.................................704 226-5243
EMP: 4
SALES (corp-wide): 3.96B **Privately Held**
Web: www.conmet.com
SIC: 3714 Motor vehicle parts and accessories
PA: Amsted Industries Incorporated
111 S Wacker Dr Ste 4400
Chicago IL 60606
312 645-1700

(G-8426)
ANCIENT MARINER INC
1402 Walkup Ave (28110-3524)
P.O. Box 1277 (28111-1277)
PHONE.................................704 635-7911
Jessica Cann, *Pr*
EMP: 15 **EST:** 2016
SALES (est): 357.83K **Privately Held**
Web: www.ancientmarinersigns.com
SIC: 3993 Signs and advertising specialties

(G-8427)
AP&T NORTH AMERICA INC
4817 Persimmon Ct (28110-9314)
PHONE.................................704 292-2900
Adam Allansson, *Pr*
◆ **EMP:** 15 **EST:** 1990
SQ FT: 5,800
SALES (est): 4.8MM
SALES (corp-wide): 884.44K **Privately Held**
Web: www.aptgroup.com
SIC: 3499 5084 Aerosol valves, metal; Hydraulic systems equipment and supplies
HQ: Automation, Press And Tooling, A.P.& T. Ab
Ronnasgatan 3a
Ulricehamn 523 3

(G-8428)
AQUA LOGIC INC
2806 Gray Fox Rd (28110-8422)
PHONE.................................858 292-4773
Douglas Russell, *Pr*
▼ **EMP:** 20 **EST:** 1989
SQ FT: 20,000
SALES (est): 4.73MM **Privately Held**
Web: www.aqualogicinc.com
SIC: 3585 Refrigeration and heating equipment

(G-8429)
ARC3 GASES INC
2411 Nelda Dr (28110-8583)
PHONE.................................704 220-1029
Matthew Wright, *Mgr*
EMP: 9
SALES (corp-wide): 204.15MM **Privately Held**
Web: www.arc3gases.com

SIC: 2813 5084 5169 7359 Industrial gases; Industrial machinery and equipment; Chemicals and allied products, nec; Equipment rental and leasing, nec
PA: Arc3 Gases, Inc.
1600 Us-301 S
Dunn NC 28334
910 892-4016

(G-8430)
AS INC
Also Called: St.clair Coatings
1920 Tower Industrial Dr (28110-8513)
PHONE.................................704 225-1700
Arthur St Clair, *Pr*
EMP: 5 **EST:** 2010
SALES (est): 464.93K **Privately Held**
Web: www.stclaircoatings.com
SIC: 3479 Coating of metals and formed products

(G-8431)
ASSA ABLOY AB
1902 Airport Rd (28110-7396)
PHONE.................................704 283-2101
▲ **EMP:** 44 **EST:** 2010
SALES (est): 2.16MM **Privately Held**
SIC: 3695 Magnetic and optical recording media

(G-8432)
ASSA ABLOY ACC DOOR CNTRLS GRO (DH)
Also Called: Assa Abloy
1902 Airport Rd (28110-7396)
PHONE.................................877 974-2255
Lucas Boselli, *Pr*
Page Heslin, *
Joseph Hurley, *
◆ **EMP:** 200 **EST:** 1864
SQ FT: 130,000
SALES (est): 208.04MM **Privately Held**
SIC: 3429 3466 Locks or lock sets; Crowns and closures
HQ: Assa Abloy Inc.
110 Sargent Dr
New Haven CT 06511

(G-8433)
ASSA ABLOY ACCESSORIES AND
Also Called: Norton Door Controls Yale SEC
3000 E Highway 74 (28112-9152)
PHONE.................................704 233-4011
Doug Millikan, *Mgr*
EMP: 276
SIC: 3429 3812 3699 Door locks, bolts, and checks; Search and navigation equipment; Electrical equipment and supplies, nec
HQ: Assa Abloy Accessories And Door Controls Group, Inc.
1902 Airport Rd
Monroe NC 28110
877 974-2255

(G-8434)
ASSA ABLOY ENTRNCE SYSTEMS US (DH)
Also Called: Besam Entrance Solution
1900 Airport Rd (28110)
PHONE.................................866 237-2687
Michael Mccaslin, *Pr*
Michael Fisher, *
Michael W Griffin, *
Michael Drury, *
◆ **EMP:** 120 **EST:** 1975
SALES (est): 450.22MM **Privately Held**
Web: www.assaabloyentrance.com
SIC: 3699 1796 3442 Door opening and closing devices, electrical; Installing building equipment; Metal doors
HQ: Assa Abloy Entrance Systems Ab

Lodjursgatan 10
Landskrona 261 4
104747000

(G-8435)
ASSA ABLOY INC
Rixson Specialty Door Controls
3000 E Highway 74 (28112-9152)
PHONE.................................704 776-8773
EMP: 12
Web: www.assaabloydss.com
SIC: 3568 Pivots, power transmission
HQ: Assa Abloy Inc.
110 Sargent Dr
New Haven CT 06511

(G-8436)
ATI ALLVAC
6400 Alloy Way (28110-8329)
PHONE.................................541 967-9000
EMP: 10 **EST:** 2020
SALES (est): 489.76K **Privately Held**
Web: www.allvaccu.com
SIC: 3356 Battery metal

(G-8437)
AUSTIN PRINTING COMPANY INC
1823 Morgan Mill Rd (28110-3644)
PHONE.................................704 289-1445
Jeff Austin, *Pr*
Debbie Austin, *VP*
Donna Austin Whitley, *Pt*
EMP: 4 **EST:** 1976
SQ FT: 2,400
SALES (est): 252.95K **Privately Held**
Web: www.austinprinting.com
SIC: 2752 2791 Offset printing; Typesetting

(G-8438)
B+E MANUFACTURING CO INC
Also Called: Stainless Valve Co
4811 Persimmon Ct (28110-9314)
PHONE.................................704 236-8439
EMP: 22 **EST:** 1993
SALES (est): 2.33MM
SALES (corp-wide): 4.98MM **Privately Held**
Web: www.bemfg.com
SIC: 3599 Machine and other job shop work
PA: Dal Investment Inc.
4811 Persimmon Ct
Monroe NC 28110
704 847-1423

(G-8439)
BERRY GLOBAL INC
3414 Wesley Chapel Stouts Rd (28110-7945)
PHONE.................................704 289-1526
Jeff Godsey, *Brnch Mgr*
EMP: 121
Web: www.berryglobal.com
SIC: 3089 3081 Bottle caps, molded plastics; Unsupported plastics film and sheet
HQ: Berry Global, Inc.
101 Oakley St
Evansville IN 47710

(G-8440)
BMC SOFTWARE INC
Also Called: BMC Software
2980 Mason St (28110-3942)
PHONE.................................704 283-8179
Randy Rogers, *Brnch Mgr*
EMP: 7
SALES (corp-wide): 1.5B **Privately Held**
Web: www.bmc.com
SIC: 7372 Prepackaged software
PA: Bmc Software, Inc.
2103 Citywest Blvd
Houston TX 77042

▲ = Import ▼ = Export
◆ = Import/Export

713 918-8800

(G-8441)
BOGGS MATERIALS INC (PA)
Also Called: Boggs Materials Plant 1
1613 W Roosevelt Blvd (28110-2754)
P.O. Box 689 (28111)
PHONE..................704 289-8482
Drew Boggs, *Pr*
Chris Boggs, *
EMP: 6 **EST:** 1997
SALES (est): 24.81MM
SALES (corp-wide): 24.81MM **Privately Held**
Web: www.truerockholdings.com
SIC: 2951 Asphalt and asphaltic paving mixtures (not from refineries)

(G-8442)
BOGGS TRANSPORT INC
Also Called: Boggs Group
2318 Concord Hwy (28110-8768)
PHONE..................704 289-8482
Carl A Boggs Junior, *Pr*
David Boggs, *VP*
EMP: 7 **EST:** 1997
SALES (est): 1.13MM **Privately Held**
Web: www.truerockholdings.com
SIC: 2951 Asphalt and asphaltic paving mixtures (not from refineries)

(G-8443)
BONA USA
4275 Corporate Center Dr (28110-1314)
PHONE..................704 220-6943
EMP: 11 **EST:** 2018
SALES (est): 3.3MM **Privately Held**
Web: www.bona.com
SIC: 2426 Flooring, hardwood

(G-8444)
BONAKEMI USA INCORPORATED
Also Called: Bona US
4275 Corporate Center Dr (28110-1314)
PHONE..................704 218-3917
Paul England, *VP Opers*
EMP: 72
SALES (corp-wide): 365.42MM **Privately Held**
SIC: 5198 2431 Stain; Awnings, blinds and shutters: wood
HQ: Bonakemi Usa, Incorporated
24 Inverness Pl E Ste 100
Englewood CO 80112
303 371-1411

(G-8445)
BONAKEMI USA INCORPORATED
Also Called: Bona US Dc2
4110 Propel Way (28110-8398)
PHONE..................704 220-6943
EMP: 54
SALES (corp-wide): 365.42MM **Privately Held**
SIC: 5198 5169 5023 2851 Stain; Waxes, except petroleum; Floor coverings; Paints and allied products
HQ: Bonakemi Usa, Incorporated
24 Inverness Pl E Ste 100
Englewood CO 80112
303 371-1411

(G-8446)
BOYD GMN INC
Also Called: GM Nameplate NC Division
300 Acme Dr (28112-4199)
PHONE..................206 284-2200
Jack Sharratt, *Mgr*
EMP: 165
SQ FT: 58,408
Web: www.boydcorp.com

SIC: 3479 3089 3993 Name plates: engraved, etched, etc.; Engraving of plastics ; Signs and advertising specialties
HQ: Boyd Gmn, Inc.
2040 15th Ave W
Seattle WA 98119
206 284-2200

(G-8447)
BROOKS TOOL INC
524 Marshall St (28112-4676)
P.O. Box 1695 (28111-1695)
PHONE..................704 283-0112
Randy Brooks, *Pr*
Mandy Brooks, *Sec*
EMP: 5 **EST:** 1985
SQ FT: 5,000
SALES (est): 464.75K **Privately Held**
Web: www.kutcheyfamilyfarm.com
SIC: 3544 Industrial molds

(G-8448)
BROWN EQUIPMENT AND CAPITL INC
650 Broome St (28110-3947)
P.O. Box 32214 (28232-2214)
PHONE..................704 921-4644
Neil N Brown, *Pr*
Patrick N Brown, *VP*
EMP: 17 **EST:** 1946
SQ FT: 33,000
SALES (est): 3.61MM **Privately Held**
Web: www.brownequipment.com
SIC: 3541 Machine tools, metal cutting type

(G-8449)
C & C TOOL AND MACHINE INC
903 Icemorlee St (28110-2631)
P.O. Box 845 (28111-0845)
PHONE..................704 226-1363
Jerry Collins, *Pr*
Barbara Collins, *Treas*
Greg Collins, *VP*
Randy Clountz, *VP*
EMP: 9 **EST:** 1980
SQ FT: 11,000
SALES (est): 755.37K **Privately Held**
Web: www.c-ctool.com
SIC: 3599 Machine shop, jobbing and repair

(G-8450)
CARDINAL BAG & ENVELOPE CO INC
2861 Gray Fox Rd (28110-6405)
PHONE..................704 225-9636
David T Van Blarcom, *Pr*
▲ **EMP:** 25 **EST:** 1957
SQ FT: 34,000
SALES (est): 5.61MM **Privately Held**
Web: www.cardinalbag.com
SIC: 2674 Paper bags: made from purchased materials

(G-8451)
CAROLINA BOTTLE MFR LLC
2630 Nelda Dr Ste B (28110-8485)
PHONE..................704 635-8759
EMP: 5 **EST:** 2017
SALES (est): 395.21K **Privately Held**
Web: www.carolinabottle.com
SIC: 2899 Distilled water

(G-8452)
CAROLINA CLASSIFIEDSCOM LLC (PA)
Also Called: Carolina Money Saver
1609 Airport Rd (28110-7393)
PHONE..................704 246-0900
Scott Patterson, *Managing Member*
EMP: 68 **EST:** 2006

SALES (est): 1.29MM **Privately Held**
Web: www.carolinamoneysaver.com
SIC: 2759 Advertising literature: printing, nsk

(G-8453)
CAROLINA ELECTRIC MTR REPR LLC
1812 Skyway Dr (28110-2715)
PHONE..................704 289-3732
EMP: 4 **EST:** 2016
SALES (est): 542.36K **Privately Held**
SIC: 7699 3699 Repair services, nec; Electrical equipment and supplies, nec

(G-8454)
CAROLINA READY-MIX LLC
1901 Valley Pkwy Ste 100 (28110-6515)
PHONE..................704 225-1112
Eric W Mccomb, *Prin*
EMP: 5 **EST:** 2008
SALES (est): 2.35MM **Privately Held**
Web: www.carolinareadymix.com
SIC: 3273 Ready-mixed concrete

(G-8455)
CCBCC OPERATIONS LLC
Also Called: Coca-Cola
4268 Capital Dr (28110-7681)
PHONE..................704 225-1973
Devin Dunway, *Brnch Mgr*
EMP: 49
SALES (corp-wide): 6.9B **Publicly Held**
Web: www.coca-cola.com
SIC: 2086 Bottled and canned soft drinks
HQ: Ccbcc Operations, Llc
4100 Coca-Cola Plz
Charlotte NC 28211
704 364-8728

(G-8456)
CEDAR VALLEY FINISHING CO INC
603 Broome St (28110-3946)
PHONE..................704 289-9546
Richard Quick, *Pr*
EMP: 10 **EST:** 1982
SQ FT: 20,000
SALES (est): 650K **Privately Held**
Web: www.wcfcourier.com
SIC: 2262 Finishing plants, manmade

(G-8457)
CHARLOTTE PIPE AND FOUNDRY CO
Also Called: Charlotte Plastics
4210 Old Charlotte Hwy (28110-7333)
P.O. Box 1339 (28111-1339)
PHONE..................704 372-3650
Charles E Cobb, *VP*
EMP: 550
SALES (corp-wide): 841.88MM **Privately Held**
Web: www.charlottepipe.com
SIC: 3084 Plastics pipe
PA: Charlotte Pipe And Foundry Company
2109 Randolph Rd
Charlotte NC 28207
800 438-6091

(G-8458)
CIRCOR PRECISION METERING LLC (DH)
1710 Airport Rd (28110-7394)
P.O. Box 5020 (28111-5020)
PHONE..................704 289-6511
Darryl Mayhorn, *CEO*
▲ **EMP:** 63 **EST:** 2000
SALES (est): 7.17MM **Publicly Held**
Web: www.zenithpumps.com
SIC: 3561 Pumps and pumping equipment
HQ: Circor International, Inc.

30 Corporate Dr Ste 200
Burlington MA 01803
781 270-1200

(G-8459)
CIRCOR PUMPS NORTH AMERICA LLC (DH)
1710 Airport Rd (28110-7394)
PHONE..................704 289-6511
EMP: 58 **EST:** 2017
SALES (est): 34.32MM **Publicly Held**
Web: pumps.circor.com
SIC: 3561 3829 Pumps and pumping equipment; Aircraft and motor vehicle measurement equipment
HQ: Circor International, Inc.
30 Corporate Dr Ste 200
Burlington MA 01803
781 270-1200

(G-8460)
CIRCOR PUMPS NORTH AMERICA LLC
Also Called: Circor Pumping Technologies
1710 Airport Rd (28110-7394)
PHONE..................877 853-7867
EMP: 211
Web: pumps.circor.com
SIC: 3491 Industrial valves
HQ: Circor Pumps North America, Llc
1710 Airport Rd
Monroe NC 28110
704 289-6511

(G-8461)
CLASSIC SIGN SERVICES LLC
Also Called: Fastsigns
2242 W Roosevelt Blvd Ste F (28110-3070)
PHONE..................704 401-1466
Judith Stuebs, *Prin*
EMP: 6 **EST:** 2018
SALES (est): 560.47K **Privately Held**
Web: www.fastsigns.com
SIC: 3993 Signs and advertising specialties

(G-8462)
COCHRANE STEEL INDUSTRIES INC
Also Called: Cochrane Steel
5529 Cannon Dr (28110-7982)
PHONE..................704 291-9330
John Turnblom, *Pr*
EMP: 17 **EST:** 1974
SQ FT: 13,500
SALES (est): 1.75MM **Privately Held**
Web: www.cochranesteelusa.com
SIC: 3441 Fabricated structural metal

(G-8463)
COLFAX PUMP GROUP
Also Called: IMO Pump
1710 Airport Rd (28110-7394)
PHONE..................704 289-6511
▲ **EMP:** 200
SIC: 3561 Industrial pumps and parts

(G-8464)
COLONY GUMS LLC
2626 Executive Point Dr (28110-8523)
PHONE..................704 226-9666
Robert Muhlsteff, *Pr*
Christopher Muhlsteff, *VP*
◆ **EMP:** 29 **EST:** 1938
SQ FT: 20,000
SALES (est): 10.89MM **Privately Held**
Web: www.colonygums.com
SIC: 2041 Sorghum grain flour
PA: Brenntag Se
Messeallee 11
Essen NW 45131

(G-8465)

CONN-SELMER INC

Also Called: Ludwig Industries

2806 Mason St (28110-3826)

PHONE............................704 289-6459

Jim Kinsey, *Mgr*

EMP: 74

SALES (corp-wide): 478.63MM **Privately Held**

Web: www.connselmer.com

SIC: 3161 3931 Musical instrument cases; Musical instruments

HQ: Conn-Selmer, Inc.

600 Industrial Pkwy

Elkhart IN 46516

574 522-1675

(G-8466)

CONSOLIDATED METCO INC

780 Patton Ave (28110-2438)

PHONE............................704 289-6492

Wayne Duncan, *Genl Mgr*

EMP: 11

SQ FT: 6,000

SALES (corp-wide): 3.96B **Privately Held**

Web: www.conmet.com

SIC: 3365 Aluminum and aluminum-based alloy castings

HQ: Consolidated Metco, Inc.

5701 Se Columbia Way

Vancouver WA 98661

360 828-2599

(G-8467)

CONSOLIDATED METCO INC

1700 N Charlotte Ave (28110-8481)

PHONE............................704 289-6491

EMP: 39

SALES (corp-wide): 3.96B **Privately Held**

Web: www.conmet.com

SIC: 3365 Aluminum and aluminum-based alloy castings

HQ: Consolidated Metco, Inc.

5701 Se Columbia Way

Vancouver WA 98661

360 828-2599

(G-8468)

CONSOLIDATED METCO INC

Also Called: Conmet

4220 Propel Way (28110-8399)

PHONE............................704 226-5246

Thomas White, *Mgr*

EMP: 42

SALES (corp-wide): 3.96B **Privately Held**

Web: www.conmet.com

SIC: 3714 Motor vehicle parts and accessories

HQ: Consolidated Metco, Inc.

5701 Se Columbia Way

Vancouver WA 98661

360 828-2599

(G-8469)

COOLANT & CLEANING TECH INC

7421 Morgan Mill Rd (28110-7546)

PHONE............................704 753-1333

C A Williams, *Pr*

Eric D Williams, *VP*

Betty Williams, *Sec*

EMP: 4 **EST:** 1998

SQ FT: 22,500

SALES (est): 208.17K **Privately Held**

SIC: 3714 Cleaners, air, motor vehicle

(G-8470)

COX MACHINE CO INC

2336 Concord Hwy (28110-8768)

P.O. Box 1979 (28079-1979)

PHONE............................704 296-0118

Douglas L Cox, *Pr*

Sue Cox, *Sec*

EMP: 4 **EST:** 1987

SQ FT: 1,500

SALES (est): 989.04K **Privately Held**

SIC: 3559 3714 3444 Degreasing machines, automotive and industrial; Motor vehicle parts and accessories; Sheet metalwork

(G-8471)

CRH AMERICAS INC

1139 N Charlotte Ave (28110-2512)

PHONE............................704 282-8443

Randy Lake, *CEO*

EMP: 218

SALES (corp-wide): 34.95B **Privately Held**

Web: www.crhamericas.com

SIC: 3273 Ready-mixed concrete

HQ: Crh Americas, Inc.

900 Ashwood Pkwy Ste 600

Atlanta GA 30338

770 804-3363

(G-8472)

CUSTOM AUTOMATED MACHINES INC

509 E Windsor St (28112-4831)

PHONE............................704 289-7038

Tom Land, *Pr*

EMP: 4 **EST:** 1993

SQ FT: 6,000

SALES (est): 2.8MM **Privately Held**

Web: www.customautomatedmachines.com

SIC: 3599 Machine shop, jobbing and repair

(G-8473)

CYRIL BATH COMPANY (PA)

1610 Airport Rd (28110-7393)

PHONE............................704 289-8531

Patrick Braun, *Prin*

◆ **EMP:** 18 **EST:** 1999

SQ FT: 65,000

SALES (est): 8.49MM

SALES (corp-wide): 8.49MM **Privately Held**

Web: www.cyrilbath.com

SIC: 3542 Machine tools, metal forming type

(G-8474)

DARNEL INC

1809 Airport Rd (28110)

PHONE............................704 625-9869

Charles Odle, *Dir Opers*

Albert Tverus, *Pr*

◆ **EMP:** 5 **EST:** 2006

SALES (est): 9.33MM **Privately Held**

Web: www.darnelgroup.com

SIC: 2821 Plastics materials and resins

(G-8475)

DECORE-ATIVE SPC NC LLC

701 Industrial Dr (28110-8155)

PHONE............................704 291-9669

Todd Shapiro, *Mgr*

EMP: 111

SALES (corp-wide): 95.6MM **Privately Held**

Web: www.decore.com

SIC: 2431 Doors, wood

PA: Decore-Ative Specialties Nc Llc

2772 Peck Rd

Monrovia CA 91016

626 254-9191

(G-8476)

DENTONICS INC

Also Called: Microbrush International

2833 Top Hill Rd (28110-9310)

PHONE............................704 238-0245

Randall Leander, *Pr*

Elaine Leander, *Sec*

▲ **EMP:** 16 **EST:** 1988

SALES (est): 997.54K **Privately Held**

Web: www.dentonics.com

SIC: 5047 3843 Dentists' professional supplies; Dental equipment and supplies

(G-8477)

DOT BLUE READI-MIX LLC

1703 Morgan Mill Rd (28110-3642)

PHONE............................704 247-2777

Monny Taylor, *Manager*

EMP: 27

SALES (corp-wide): 23.52MM **Privately Held**

Web: www.bluedotreadimix.com

SIC: 3273 Ready-mixed concrete

PA: Blue Dot Readi-Mix, Llc

11330 Bain School Rd

Mint Hill NC 28227

704 971-7676

(G-8478)

DUCO-SCI INC

6004 Stitt St (28110-8186)

PHONE............................704 289-9502

Joanne South, *Prin*

EMP: 19 **EST:** 2007

SALES (est): 846.36K

SALES (corp-wide): 24.67MM **Privately Held**

SIC: 3264 Insulators, electrical: porcelain

PA: Du-Co Ceramics Company

155 S Rebecca St

Saxonburg PA 16056

724 352-1511

(G-8479)

DUNN MANUFACTURING CORP (PA)

Also Called: Mutual Dropcloth

1400 Goldmine Rd (28110-2664)

P.O. Box 810 (28111-0810)

PHONE............................704 283-2147

◆ **EMP:** 210 **EST:** 1905

SALES (est): 9.77MM

SALES (corp-wide): 9.77MM **Privately Held**

Web: www.dunnmfg.com

SIC: 2241 2394 2299 Cotton narrow fabrics; Canvas and related products; Flags, fabric

(G-8480)

DYNA-TECH MANUFACTURING INC

5639 Cannon Dr (28110-9139)

PHONE............................704 839-0203

Ronald Elliott Eodom, *Pr*

EMP: 13 **EST:** 2013

SALES (est): 2.12MM **Privately Held**

Web: www.dyna-techmfg.com

SIC: 3599 Machine shop, jobbing and repair

(G-8481)

EDUCATRX INC

504 Kintyre Dr (28112-4111)

PHONE............................980 328-0013

Tony Burrus, *VP*

EMP: 4 **EST:** 2015

SALES (est): 155.97K **Privately Held**

SIC: 8742 7389 7372 Management consulting services; Business Activities at Non-Commercial Site; Educational computer software

(G-8482)

EMINESS TECHNOLOGIES INC

1412 Airport Rd (28110-7391)

PHONE............................704 283-2600

Boyd Brown, *Mgr*

EMP: 24

SALES (corp-wide): 4.67MM **Privately Held**

Web: www.pureon.com

SIC: 2842 5169 Cleaning or polishing preparations, nec; Polishes, nec

PA: Eminess Technologies, Inc.

7272 E Indian School Rd # 350

Scottsdale AZ 85251

480 505-3409

(G-8483)

ENGINEERING MFG SVCS CO

5634 Cannon Dr (28110-9139)

P.O. Box 1771 (28079-1771)

PHONE............................704 821-7325

Gale Orem, *Pr*

EMP: 18 **EST:** 1985

SQ FT: 12,400

SALES (est): 2.35MM **Privately Held**

Web: www.emsco-nc.com

SIC: 3491 Industrial valves

(G-8484)

ENOVIS CORPORATION

Colfax Fluid Handling

1710 Airport Rd (28110-7394)

PHONE............................704 289-6511

Barry Butler, *Prin*

EMP: 16

SALES (corp-wide): 2.11B **Publicly Held**

Web: www.enovis.com

SIC: 3561 Pump jacks and other pumping equipment

PA: Enovis Corporation

2711 Cntrville Rd Ste 400

Wilmington DE 19808

301 252-9160

(G-8485)

EQUIPMENT & SUPPLY INC

4507 W Highway 74 (28110-0430)

PHONE............................704 289-6565

Andrew A Adams, *Pr*

Geroge Griffith, *

L Jester, *

EMP: 41 **EST:** 1972

SQ FT: 140,000

SALES (est): 12.44MM **Privately Held**

Web: www.equipsy.com

SIC: 3728 3423 Aircraft parts and equipment, nec; Hand and edge tools, nec

(G-8486)

EUCLID CHEMICAL COMPANY

914 N Johnson St (28110-4676)

PHONE............................704 283-2544

EMP: 5

SALES (corp-wide): 7.34B **Publicly Held**

Web: www.euclidchemical.com

SIC: 2899 Chemical preparations, nec

HQ: The Euclid Chemical Company

19215 Redwood Rd

Cleveland OH 44110

800 321-7628

(G-8487)

FAIZON GLOBAL INC

Also Called: Kraze Custom Prints

2115 W Roosevelt Blvd # 70 (28110-2712)

PHONE............................704 774-1141

EMP: 5

SIC: 2211 Print cloths, cotton

(G-8488)

FERNCREST FASHIONS INC

4813 Starcrest Dr (28110-8496)

PHONE............................704 283-6422

Steve Seaborn, *Pr*

Daniel Seaborn, *

John Seaborn, *Stockholder**

▲ **EMP:** 60 **EST:** 1978

SQ FT: 30,000

SALES (est): 1.66MM **Privately Held**

▲ = Import ▼ = Export

◆ = Import/Export

SIC: 2211 2391 Draperies and drapery fabrics, cotton; Curtains and draperies

(G-8489)
FLOWERS BKG CO JAMESTOWN LLC
5524 W Highway 74 (28110-8461)
PHONE.............................704 296-1000
Jim Fergerson, *Mgr*
EMP: 7
SALES (corp-wide): 5.1B **Publicly Held**
SIC: 2051 Bread, cake, and related products
HQ: Flowers Baking Co. Of Jamestown, Llc
801 W Main St
Jamestown NC 27282
336 841-8840

(G-8490)
FORWARD DESIGN & PRINT CO INC
1903 Tom Williams Rd (28112-9610)
PHONE.............................704 776-9304
David W Nowlan, *Pr*
Angela R Ammons, *VP*
EMP: 4 EST: 2010
SALES (est): 196.18K **Privately Held**
SIC: 2752 Offset printing

(G-8491)
GARY FORTE WOODWORKING INC
1424 Forest Ln (28112-7716)
PHONE.............................704 780-0095
Gary Forte, *Prin*
EMP: 4 EST: 2009
SALES (est): 121.75K **Privately Held**
Web: www.garyfortewoodworking.com
SIC: 2431 Millwork

(G-8492)
GLENMARK PHRMCEUTICALS INC USA
Glenmark Generics
4147 Goldmine Rd (28110-7759)
PHONE.............................704 218-2600
EMP: 60
Web: www.glenmarkpharma-us.com
SIC: 5122 2834 Pharmaceuticals; Adrenal pharmaceutical preparations
HQ: Glenmark Pharmaceuticals Inc., Usa
750 Corporate Dr
Mahwah NJ 07430
201 684-8000

(G-8493)
GOODRICH CORPORATION
Also Called: Customer Service Spare
4115 Corporate Center Dr (28110-1313)
PHONE.............................704 282-2500
Christa Mcmanus, *Admn*
EMP: 5
SALES (corp-wide): 80.74B **Publicly Held**
Web: www.collinsaerospace.com
SIC: 3728 Aircraft parts and equipment, nec
HQ: Goodrich Corporation
2730 W Tyvola Rd
Charlotte NC 28217
704 423-7000

(G-8494)
GOODRICH CORPORATION
Also Called: Customer Service Center Repair
4115 Corporate Center Dr (28110-1313)
PHONE.............................704 282-2500
Robert Butz, *Genl Mgr*
EMP: 160
SALES (corp-wide): 80.74B **Publicly Held**
Web: www.collinsaerospace.com
SIC: 3728 Aircraft parts and equipment, nec
HQ: Goodrich Corporation
2730 W Tyvola Rd
Charlotte NC 28217
704 423-7000

(G-8495)
GOULSTON TECHNOLOGIES INC (HQ)
700 N Johnson St (28110)
PHONE.............................704 289-6464
Frederick Edwards, *Pr*
Hisao Yamamoto, *
Andrew Starzecki, *
Srinivasan Ranganathan, *
Alan Gold, *
◆ EMP: 43 EST: 1956
SQ FT: 300,000
SALES (est): 41.57MM **Privately Held**
Web: www.goulston.com
SIC: 2671 2899 2822 Plastic film, coated or laminated for packaging; Laundry sours; Ethylene-propylene rubbers, EPDM polymers
PA: Takemoto Oil & Fat Co., Ltd.
2-5, Minatomachi
Gamagori AIC 443-0

(G-8496)
GREINER BIO-ONE NORTH AMER INC (DH)
Also Called: Greiner-Bio-One
4238 Capital Dr (28110)
PHONE.............................704 261-7800
A C Marchionne, *Ch Bd*
Eric J Mcinnis, *VP Fin*
Roland Keller, *Operations**
◆ EMP: 260 EST: 1997
SQ FT: 180,000
SALES (est): 88.96MM
SALES (corp-wide): 2.18B **Privately Held**
Web: www.gbo.com
SIC: 5047 3841 Medical laboratory equipment; Surgical and medical instruments
HQ: Greiner Bio-One Gmbh
Bad HallerstraBe 32
Kremsmunster 4550
758367910

(G-8497)
H & H FARM MACHINE CO INC
7916 Unionville Brief Rd (28110-9025)
PHONE.............................704 753-1555
Brian Nance, *Pr*
EMP: 15 EST: 1981
SQ FT: 4,500
SALES (est): 2.41MM **Privately Held**
Web: www.hhspray.com
SIC: 3523 3524 Sprayers and spraying machines, agricultural; Lawn and garden equipment

(G-8498)
HELMS MACHINE COMPANY
216 N Bivens Rd (28110-8110)
P.O. Box 1355 (28111-1355)
PHONE.............................704 289-5571
Walter C Helms, *Pr*
Jane Helms, *Sec*
EMP: 9 EST: 1972
SQ FT: 10,500
SALES (est): 1.36MM **Privately Held**
SIC: 3599 Machine shop, jobbing and repair

(G-8499)
HILTON VINEYARDS LLC
3310 Crow Rd (28112-7558)
PHONE.............................704 776-9656
EMP: 4 EST: 2015
SALES (est): 99.95K **Privately Held**
Web: www.hiltonvineyardatthevine.com
SIC: 2084 Wines

(G-8500)
HOSER INC
1132 Curtis St (28112-5058)
PHONE.............................704 989-7151
Joseph Paul Dugick, *Pr*
EMP: 6 EST: 2020
SALES (est): 3.15MM **Privately Held**
Web: www.hoserinc.com
SIC: 3599 Hose, flexible metallic

(G-8501)
HUNEYWOOD INC
Also Called: Huneywood Frames
7123 Sugar And Wine Rd (28110-1072)
PHONE.............................704 385-9785
Wayne Huneycutt, *Pr*
EMP: 6 EST: 1984
SALES (est): 197.05K **Privately Held**
Web: huneywood-inc.hub.biz
SIC: 2499 Picture frame molding, finished

(G-8502)
IDENTIGRAPH SIGNS & AWNINGS
1132 Curtis St (28112-5058)
PHONE.............................704 635-7911
Bill Petroff, *CEO*
EMP: 6 EST: 2011
SQ FT: 1,000
SALES (est): 504.51K **Privately Held**
Web: www.identigraphsigns.com
SIC: 3089 Awnings, fiberglass and plastics combination

(G-8503)
IMO INDUSTRIES INC (HQ)
Also Called: Zenith Pumps
420 National Business Pkwy Fl 5 (28110)
P.O. Box 5020 (28111-5020)
PHONE.............................301 323-9000
Darryl Mayhorn, *CEO*
▲ EMP: 61 EST: 1931
SALES (est): 23.46MM
SALES (corp-wide): 2.11B **Publicly Held**
Web: www.imo-pump.com
SIC: 3561 3829 Pumps and pumping equipment; Aircraft and motor vehicle measurement equipment
PA: Enovis Corporation
2711 Cntrville Rd Ste 400
Wilmington DE 19808
301 252-9160

(G-8504)
IMO INDUSTRIES INC
IMO Pump Division
1710 Airport Rd (28110-7394)
P.O. Box 5020 (28111-5020)
PHONE.............................704 289-6511
Christian Sahlman, *Prin*
EMP: 188
SQ FT: 268,488
SALES (corp-wide): 2.11B **Publicly Held**
Web: www.imo-pump.com
SIC: 5084 3561 Pumps and pumping equipment, nec; Cylinders, pump
HQ: Imo Industries Inc.
420 Ntional Bus Pkwy Fl 5
Monroe NC 28110
301 323-9000

(G-8505)
INTEGRITY ENVMTL SOLUTIONS LLC (PA)
Also Called: Carlson Envmtl Cons Prof Corp
1127 Curtis St Ste 110 (28112)
PHONE.............................704 283-9765
Seth Nunes, *Pr*
Kristofer L Carlson, *
Seth Nunes, *
Jeff Mcnabb, *VP*
EMP: 73 EST: 2004

SQ FT: 5,000
SALES (est): 45.28MM
SALES (corp-wide): 45.28MM **Privately Held**
Web: www.cecenv.com
SIC: 8711 4959 1381 1623 Consulting engineer; Sanitary services, nec; Drilling oil and gas wells; Oil and gas pipeline construction

(G-8506)
IVEY FIXTURE & DESIGN INC
2814 N Rocky River Rd (28110-9266)
PHONE.............................704 283-4398
Tim Ivey, *Pr*
J B Ivey, *Pr*
Barbara Ivey, *Sec*
Tim Ivey, *VP*
Marty Barbee, *VP*
EMP: 4 EST: 1977
SQ FT: 7,000
SALES (est): 226.41K **Privately Held**
SIC: 2541 Store fixtures, wood

(G-8507)
J L ANDERSON CO INC
Also Called: Palmetto Brick-Florence
4812 W Highway 74 (28110-8454)
PHONE.............................704 289-9599
Ricky Taylor, *Brnch Mgr*
EMP: 7
SALES (corp-wide): 32.63MM **Privately Held**
Web: www.palmettobrick.com
SIC: 3251 Brick clay: common face, glazed, vitrified, or hollow
PA: J. L. Anderson Co., Inc.
3501 Brickyard Rd
Wallace SC 29596
843 537-7861

(G-8508)
JAMES IRON & STEEL INC
2819 Top Hill Rd (28110-9310)
PHONE.............................704 283-2299
Eric James, *Pr*
Robert James, *Contrlr*
Robert Darren, *VP*
EMP: 8 EST: 1952
SQ FT: 8,500
SALES (est): 703.02K **Privately Held**
Web: www.jamesironandsteel.com
SIC: 1799 3446 Ornamental metal work; Stairs, staircases, stair treads: prefabricated metal

(G-8509)
JAMES RIVER EQUIPMENT
Also Called: John Deere Authorized Dealer
2112 Morgan Mill Rd (28110-8845)
PHONE.............................704 821-7399
James D Black, *Pr*
EMP: 12 EST: 1988
SALES (est): 1.19MM **Privately Held**
Web: www.jamesriverequipment.com
SIC: 3523 5082 Tractors, farm; Construction and mining machinery

(G-8510)
JD APPAREL INC
Also Called: Pine Island Sportswear
1680 Williams Rd (28110-8563)
PHONE.............................704 289-5600
Jaime Winter, *Pr*
◆ EMP: 20 EST: 2006
SQ FT: 15,000
SALES (est): 978.09K **Privately Held**
SIC: 2321 Polo shirts, men's and boys': made from purchased materials

(G-8511)
JESKRI ASSOCIATES INC
1821 N Rocky River Rd (28110-7961)
PHONE....................................704 291-9991
Josef Pennigar, *Pr*
EMP: 9 EST: 2004
SALES (est): 97.72K **Privately Held**
SIC: 2899 Drug testing kits, blood and urine

(G-8512)
KELLER COSMETICS INC
Also Called: Hazel Keller Cosmetics
2620 Stitt St (28110-3836)
P.O. Box 77064 (28271-7000)
PHONE....................................704 399-2226
Amy Kramer Kennedy, *Pr*
EMP: 4 EST: 1956
SALES (est): 230.47K **Privately Held**
Web: www.kellercosmetics.com
SIC: 5122 2844 Cosmetics; Cosmetic
preparations

(G-8513)
KROOPS BRANDS LLC
2913 Chamber Dr (28110-8474)
PHONE....................................704 635-7963
Andrew B Tremblay, *Mgr*
EMP: 5 EST: 2008
SALES (est): 589.68K **Privately Held**
Web: www.kroops.com
SIC: 5999 3851 Sunglasses; Goggles: sun,
safety, industrial, underwater, etc.

(G-8514)
LD DAVIS INDUSTRIES INC
Also Called: L D Davis
2031 E Roosevelt Blvd (28112-4133)
PHONE....................................704 289-4551
Barry Barto, *Mgr*
EMP: 43
SALES (corp-wide): 15.72MM **Privately
Held**
Web: www.lddavis.com
SIC: 2891 Adhesives
PA: L.D. Davis Industries, Inc.
1725 The Fairway
Jenkintown PA 19046
800 883-6199

(G-8515)
LEATHER MAGIC INC
1104 Leewood Dr (28112-5175)
PHONE....................................704 283-5078
Danny Yunker, *Pr*
Susan Yunker, *VP*
EMP: 8 EST: 1991
SQ FT: 12,500
SALES (est): 194.16K **Privately Held**
Web: www.leathermagic.com
SIC: 3111 Leather processing

(G-8516)
LEGACY MECHANICAL
2715 Gray Fox Rd (28110-8421)
PHONE....................................704 225-8558
Melvin Thomas, *Prin*
Melvin Thomas Senior, *VP*
▲ **EMP: 10 EST:** 1987
SQ FT: 7,000
SALES (est): 730.85K **Privately Held**
SIC: 3542 Robots for metal forming:
pressing, extruding, etc.

(G-8517)
LIMESTONE PRODUCTS INC (PA)
3302 W Highway 74 B (28110-8439)
P.O. Box 1309 (28111-1309)
PHONE....................................704 283-9492
Larry Rogers, *Pr*
Thomas L Broome, *VP*

Arthur K Cates, *VP*
Jerry Sutton, *Sec*
EMP: 6 EST: 1985
SALES (est): 8.77MM
SALES (corp-wide): 8.77MM **Privately
Held**
Web: www.limestoneproductsinc.com
SIC: 1422 Lime rock, ground

(G-8518)
**LLEWELLYN MTAL FABRICATORS
INC**
4816 Persimmon Ct (28110-9313)
PHONE....................................704 283-4816
Joe Llewellyn, *Pr*
Brenda Llewellyn, *VP*
EMP: 5 EST: 1986
SALES (est): 435.67K **Privately Held**
Web: www.lmetalfabrication.com
SIC: 3441 Fabricated structural metal

(G-8519)
LOGO DOGZ
4808 Persimmon Ct (28110-9313)
PHONE....................................888 827-8866
Traci Mcdonald, *Owner*
EMP: 5 EST: 2018
SALES (est): 132.16K **Privately Held**
Web: www.logodogz.com
SIC: 2759 Screen printing

(G-8520)
LONGHORN ROOFING INC
1302 Walkup Ave (28110-3522)
PHONE....................................704 774-1080
Luis Perez, *Pr*
EMP: 10 EST: 2017
SALES (est): 1.01MM **Privately Held**
Web: www.longhornroofinginc.com
SIC: 5033 1761 3069 2952 Roofing, asphalt
and sheet metal; Roofing and gutter work;
Roofing, membrane rubber; Roofing felts,
cements, or coatings, nec

(G-8521)
M & J STUCCO LLC
P.O. Box 513 (29714-0513)
PHONE....................................704 634-2249
Jennifer Lloyd, *Managing Member*
Mark Lloyd, *Managing Member*
EMP: 4 EST: 2011
SALES (est): 148.45K **Privately Held**
Web: www.mandjstucco.com
SIC: 3299 Stucco

(G-8522)
**MACHINING TECHNOLOGY
SERVICES**
1817 N Rocky River Rd (28110-7961)
PHONE....................................704 282-1071
Sherrill Connell, *Pr*
Lindy Williams, *VP*
Terry Thompson, *Sec*
EMP: 6 EST: 1988
SQ FT: 4,000
SALES (est): 1.44MM **Privately Held**
Web:
www.machiningtechnologyservices.com
SIC: 3433 Stokers, mechanical: domestic or
industrial

(G-8523)
**MANUFACTURING SYSTEMS EQP
INC**
2812 Chamber Dr (28110-8473)
PHONE....................................704 283-2086
Charles Earhart, *CEO*
Keith Earhart, *Pr*
Ruth Earhart, *Sec*
Kerry Earhart, *VP Fin*

Kim Earhart, *VP Mktg*
▲ **EMP: 18 EST:** 1987
SQ FT: 33,300
SALES (est): 2.31MM **Privately Held**
SIC: 5063 3612 3694 Transformers and
transmission equipment; Power
transformers, electric; Engine electrical
equipment

(G-8524)
MARIETTA MARTIN MATERIALS INC
Also Called: Martin Marietta Aggregates
2111 N Rocky River Rd (28110-7964)
P.O. Box 458 (28111-0458)
PHONE....................................704 283-4915
Larry Thomas, *Mgr*
EMP: 7
Web: www.martinmarietta.com
SIC: 1422 Crushed and broken limestone
PA: Martin Marietta Materials Inc
4123 Parklake Ave
Raleigh NC 27612

(G-8525)
MASTER SCREENS SOUTH LLC
600 Broome St (28110-3947)
PHONE....................................704 226-9600
▲ **EMP: 4 EST:** 1997
SQ FT: 30,000
SALES (est): 220.58K **Privately Held**
SIC: 2754 Rotogravure printing

(G-8526)
MATTHEWS MILLWORK INC
1105 Jim Cir (28110-5101)
PHONE....................................704 821-4499
Roger I Leslie, *Pr*
EMP: 7 EST: 1987
SQ FT: 7,000
SALES (est): 816.21K **Privately Held**
Web: www.matthewsmillwork.com
SIC: 2431 Millwork

(G-8527)
MAVERICK ENTERPRISES INTL INC
Also Called: Maverick Enterprises
818 Circle Trace Rd (28110-7677)
PHONE....................................704 291-9474
Margaret L Harty, *Pr*
Leslie Harty, *Pr*
Edward Harty, *Prin*
EMP: 6 EST: 2006
SALES (est): 182.66K **Privately Held**
Web: www.maverickent.net
SIC: 2673 Garment and wardrobe bags,
(plastic film)

(G-8528)
MBP ACQUISITION LLC
Also Called: Hamilton Drywall Products
6090 Willis Way (28110-8365)
PHONE....................................704 349-5055
Mark Hamilton, *Managing Member*
EMP: 23 EST: 2017
SALES (est): 1.11MM **Privately Held**
Web: www.hamiltondrywallproducts.com
SIC: 3275 Acoustical plaster, gypsum

(G-8529)
MCCOTTER INDUSTRIES INC
Also Called: Sports To You
108 S Hayne St (28112-5500)
PHONE....................................704 282-2102
Cindy Mccotter, *Pr*
EMP: 10 EST: 1999
SQ FT: 2,500
SALES (est): 401.94K **Privately Held**
Web: sportstoyou.com
SIC: 2759 2395 Screen printing; Embroidery
and art needlework

(G-8530)
MCDONALD SERVICES INC (PA)
7427 Price Tucker Rd (28110-8297)
P.O. Box 1192 (28070-1192)
PHONE....................................704 753-9669
Jim Mcdonald, *Pr*
Margaret Mcdonald, *VP*
EMP: 4 EST: 1983
SQ FT: 30,000
SALES (est): 4.54MM
SALES (corp-wide): 4.54MM **Privately
Held**
Web: www.msibalers.com
SIC: 5084 3559 Industrial machinery and
equipment; Recycling machinery

(G-8531)
MINT HILL CABINET SHOP INC
Also Called: Mint Hill Cabinet Shop
5519 Cannon Dr (28110-7982)
P.O. Box 2069 (28079-2069)
PHONE....................................704 821-9373
John Carriker, *Pr*
Richard Carriker, *
EMP: 30 EST: 1961
SQ FT: 25,000
SALES (est): 2.75MM **Privately Held**
Web: www.minthillcabinets.com
SIC: 2434 5031 5211 Wood kitchen cabinets
; Kitchen cabinets; Cabinets, kitchen

(G-8532)
MITCHELL MEDLIN MACHINE SHOP
1394 Walkup Ave Ste C (28110-3565)
PHONE....................................704 289-2840
Louceil Medlin, *Pr*
EMP: 6 EST: 1979
SQ FT: 3,500
SALES (est): 461.58K **Privately Held**
SIC: 3599 Machine shop, jobbing and repair

(G-8533)
MONARCH KNITTING MCHY CORP
Also Called: Vanguard Supreme Div
601 Mcarthur Cir (28110-3622)
PHONE....................................704 283-8171
William Moody, *Brnch Mgr*
EMP: 22
SALES (corp-wide): 12.43MM **Privately
Held**
Web: www.monarchknitting.org
SIC: 3552 Knitting machines
PA: Monarch Knitting Machinery Corp.
115 N Secrest Ave
Monroe NC 28110
704 291-3300

(G-8534)
**MONARCH KNITTING MCHY CORP
(PA)**
Also Called: Monarch Manufacturing
115 N Secrest Ave (28110-6807)
P.O. Box 5009 (28111-5009)
PHONE....................................704 291-3300
David Pernick, *Ch Bd*
Bruce Pernick, *Pr*
Jose Rodriguez, *CFO*
Stewart Bader, *Sec*
◆ **EMP: 15 EST:** 1964
SQ FT: 6,000
SALES (est): 12.43MM
SALES (corp-wide): 12.43MM **Privately
Held**
Web: www.monarchknitting.org
SIC: 3552 5084 Knitting machines; Textile
machinery and equipment

(G-8535)
MONARCH MANUFACTURING CORP
Also Called: Vanguard Supreme
115 N Secrest Ave (28110-6807)

▲ = Import ▼ = Export
◆ = Import/Export

P.O. Box 9 (28111-0009)
PHONE..................................704 283-8171
David Pernick, *Pr*
◆ **EMP**: 10 **EST**: 1986
SALES (est): 2.5MM
SALES (corp-wide): 12.43MM **Privately Held**
Web: www.monarchknitting.org
SIC: 3552 Knitting machines
PA: Monarch Knitting Machinery Corp.
    115 N Secrest Ave
    Monroe NC 28110
    704 291-3300

(G-8536)
MONROE METAL MANUFACTURING INC
Also Called: Monroe Metal Manufacturing
6025 Stitt St (28110-8187)
PHONE..................................800 366-1391
Bobby F Pope, *Pr*
Janice Pope, *
▼ **EMP**: 55 **EST**: 1968
SQ FT: 180,000
SALES (est): 2.79MM **Privately Held**
SIC: 3444 Ducts, sheet metal

(G-8537)
NORTHSTAR COMPUTER TECH INC
5014 Hampton Meadows Rd (28110-9351)
PHONE..................................980 272-1969
Daniel Beltz, *CEO*
EMP: 4 **EST**: 2008
SALES (est): 105.8K **Privately Held**
Web: www.northstarcomp.com
SIC: 5734 3812 3674 Computer and software stores; Defense systems and equipment; Microcircuits, integrated (semiconductor)

(G-8538)
NORTON DOOR CONTROLS
3000 E Highway 74 (28112-9152)
PHONE..................................704 233-4011
Cavanna Steve, *Prin*
◆ **EMP**: 17 **EST**: 1957
SALES (est): 4.19MM **Privately Held**
Web: www.nortonrixson.com
SIC: 3429 5099 Locks or lock sets; Locks and lock sets

(G-8539)
ORO MANUFACTURING COMPANY
5000 Stitt St (28110-4000)
PHONE..................................704 283-2186
Robert Engel, *Pr*
Patricia Engel, *
Robert Engel, *VP*
Nancy Engel, *
Susan Hagarty, *
EMP: 41 **EST**: 1945
SQ FT: 80,000
SALES (est): 5.17MM **Privately Held**
Web: www.oromfg.com
SIC: 2542 3499 3728 3444 Fixtures, office: except wood; Wheels: wheelbarrow, stroller, etc.: disc, stamped metal; Aircraft assemblies, subassemblies, and parts, nec; Sheet metalwork

(G-8540)
PAXTON MEDIA GROUP
Also Called: Inquire Journal, The
1508 Skyway Dr (28110-3008)
PHONE..................................704 289-1541
Marvin Enderle, *Publisher*
EMP: 8 **EST**: 1997
SALES (est): 203.46K **Privately Held**
Web: www.paducahsun.com
SIC: 2711 Newspapers, publishing and printing

(G-8541)
PEARL RIVER GROUP LLC
Also Called: Altior Industries
6027 Stitt St (28110-8370)
PHONE..................................704 283-4667
◆ **EMP**: 6 **EST**: 1996
SQ FT: 16,000
SALES (est): 950.96K **Privately Held**
SIC: 2389 Disposable garments and accessories

(G-8542)
PEELLE COMPANY
115 N Secrest Ave (28110-6807)
PHONE..................................631 231-6000
C J Wagenhauser, *Prin*
EMP: 8
SALES (corp-wide): 4.02MM **Privately Held**
Web: www.peelledoor.com
SIC: 3442 Metal doors
PA: The Peelle Company
    34 E Main St Ste 372
    Smithtown NY 11787
    631 231-6000

(G-8543)
POPLIN & SONS MACHINE CO INC
2118 Stafford Street Ext (28110-9650)
PHONE..................................704 289-2079
Ronny Poplin, *Pr*
Gary Poplin, *Treas*
Kathy Presson, *Sec*
EMP: 11 **EST**: 1975
SQ FT: 12,300
SALES (est): 1.06MM **Privately Held**
SIC: 3599 Machine shop, jobbing and repair

(G-8544)
PRIVETTE ENTERPRISES INC
2751 Old Charlotte Hwy (28110-9107)
P.O. Box 1189 (28110)
PHONE..................................704 634-3291
David Privette, *Pr*
EMP: 22 **EST**: 2001
SALES (est): 4.16MM **Privately Held**
Web: www.peigrading.com
SIC: 5211 2499 2879 4212 Sand and gravel; Mulch, wood and bark; Soil conditioners; Dump truck haulage

(G-8545)
PUREON INC
1412 Airport Rd (28110-7391)
PHONE..................................480 505-3409
Daniel Spring, *CEO*
Martin Spring, *
Karen Miles, *
Jeanie Coudright Ctrl, *Prin*
EMP: 52 **EST**: 2007
SALES (est): 9.37MM **Privately Held**
Web: www.pureon.com
SIC: 2842 Polishes and sanitation goods

(G-8546)
QSPAC INDUSTRIES INC
506 Miller St (28110-3180)
PHONE..................................704 635-7815
EMP: 28
Web: www.qspac.com
SIC: 3999 Atomizers, toiletry
PA: Qspac Industries, Inc.
    15020 Marquardt Ave
    Santa Fe Springs CA 90670

(G-8547)
RABUNS TRLR REPR TIRE SVC INC
4519 Old Pageland Monroe Rd (28112-8182)
PHONE..................................704 764-7841

Bobby Rabun, *Prin*
EMP: 5 **EST**: 2003
SALES (est): 749.85K **Privately Held**
SIC: 5531 7538 7534 7539 Automotive tires; General automotive repair shops; Tire retreading and repair shops; Automotive repair shops, nec

(G-8548)
RANDALL SUPPLY INC (PA)
2409 Walkup Ave (28110-3841)
PHONE..................................704 289-6479
Kenneth R Randall Junior, *Pr*
Eleanor Randall, *
EMP: 24 **EST**: 1954
SQ FT: 19,000
SALES (est): 2.55MM
SALES (corp-wide): 2.55MM **Privately Held**
Web: www.randallsupply.com
SIC: 7694 5063 Electric motor repair; Motors, electric

(G-8549)
RECORD USA INC (PA)
4324 Phil Hargett Ct (28110-7671)
P.O. Box 3099 (28111-3099)
PHONE..................................704 289-9212
Marty Licciardello, *Pr*
▲ **EMP**: 50 **EST**: 1995
SQ FT: 35,000
SALES (est): 48.14MM **Privately Held**
Web: www.recorddoors.com
SIC: 3699 Electrical equipment and supplies, nec

(G-8550)
RELIABLE CONSTRUCTION CO INC
100 N Sutherland Ave Ste A (28110-3992)
P.O. Box 688 (28111-0688)
PHONE..................................704 289-1501
Douglas S Moore, *Pr*
Galard C Moore Junior, *VP*
Phyllis Garrison, *Sec*
EMP: 7 **EST**: 1965
SQ FT: 3,000
SALES (est): 949.61K **Privately Held**
SIC: 1542 2541 2431 Bank building construction; Wood partitions and fixtures; Millwork

(G-8551)
RELIANCE MANAGEMENT GROUP INC
Also Called: Logodogz
4910 Starcrest Dr (28110-8497)
PHONE..................................704 282-2255
Rodney Mcdonald, *Pr*
Anthony Mizzi, *VP*
George Bohle, *VP*
EMP: 12 **EST**: 2000
SALES (est): 3.59MM **Privately Held**
SIC: 2759 Screen printing

(G-8552)
ROBERT HAMMS LLC
Also Called: Custom Wood Products
3028 Proverbs Ct (28110-7896)
PHONE..................................704 605-8057
Robert Hamm, *Managing Member*
EMP: 7 **EST**: 2016
SALES (est): 215.17K **Privately Held**
SIC: 2499 7699 Applicators, wood; Customizing services

(G-8553)
ROVERTYM
3308 Westwood Industrial Dr Ste E (28110-5234)
PHONE..................................704 635-7305
Larry Harrell, *Pr*

EMP: 4 **EST**: 2011
SALES (est): 203.01K **Privately Held**
SIC: 3441 Fabricated structural metal

(G-8554)
SAFE FIRE DETECTION INC
Also Called: Westek
5915 Stockbridge Dr (28110-8106)
PHONE..................................704 821-7920
Ronald Robertson, *Pr*
▲ **EMP**: 18 **EST**: 1995
SALES (est): 4.33MM **Privately Held**
Web: www.safefiredetection.com
SIC: 3669 Fire alarm apparatus, electric

(G-8555)
SCOTT TECHNOLOGIES INC (HQ)
Also Called: Scott Safety
4320 Goldmine Rd (28110-7355)
P.O. Box 569 (28111-0569)
PHONE..................................704 291-8300
Andrew Chrostowski, *Pr*
◆ **EMP**: 44 **EST**: 1983
SQ FT: 10,000
SALES (est): 120.68MM
SALES (corp-wide): 32.68B **Publicly Held**
Web: scottu.3m.com
SIC: 3569 Firefighting and related equipment
PA: 3m Company
    3m Center
    Saint Paul MN 55144
    651 733-1110

(G-8556)
SDFC LLC
Also Called: Mocaro Dyeing & Finishing
3511 Essex Pointe Dr (28110-7733)
PHONE..................................704 878-6645
Abid Ali, *Managing Member*
EMP: 14 **EST**: 2016
SALES (est): 2.42MM **Privately Held**
Web: www.mocaro.com
SIC: 2257 Dyeing and finishing circular knit fabrics

(G-8557)
SELECT AIR SYSTEMS USA INC
Also Called: Select Air Systems
2716 Chamber Dr (28110-8472)
PHONE..................................704 289-1122
Gary D Smith, *Pr*
Trecia Thomas, *Pr*
Jody Reynolds, *VP*
EMP: 20 **EST**: 2001
SQ FT: 150,000
SALES (est): 4.17MM **Privately Held**
Web: www.selectairsystemsinc.com
SIC: 3564 Ventilating fans: industrial or commercial

(G-8558)
SIGNATURE CUSTOM CABINETS LLC
2106 E Highway 218 (28110-7031)
PHONE..................................704 753-4874
Charles Medlin Junior, *Prin*
EMP: 4 **EST**: 2011
SALES (est): 228.44K **Privately Held**
SIC: 2434 Wood kitchen cabinets

(G-8559)
SMALL BROTHERS TIRE CO INC
Also Called: Small Tire Company
1725 Concord Ave (28110-2917)
P.O. Box 852 (28111-0852)
PHONE..................................704 289-3531
Alan L Small, *Pr*
Sadie H Small, *Sec*
EMP: 6 **EST**: 1945
SQ FT: 8,000
SALES (est): 921.08K **Privately Held**

Web: www.monroetiresnc.com
SIC: **5531** 7534 Automotive tires; Tire recapping

(G-8560)
SOUTHERN RANGE BREWING LLC
151 S Stewart St (28112-5548)
PHONE.............................704 289-4049
Dustin Gatliff, *Managing Member*
EMP: 8 EST: 2016
SALES (est): 971.01K **Privately Held**
Web: www.southernrangebrewing.com
SIC: **2082** 2084 Beer (alcoholic beverage); Wines

(G-8561)
SPT TECHNOLOGY INC
3107 Chamber Dr (28110-0439)
PHONE.............................612 332-1880
Daryl Sandberg, *Pr*
Mary Van Horne, *Ex VP*
▲ EMP: 14 EST: 1996
SQ FT: 6,280
SALES (est): 487.46K
SALES (corp-wide): 9.57MM **Privately Held**
Web: www.paceline.com
SIC: **2821** 3229 2241 2299 Polyesters; Yarn, fiberglass; Tie tapes, woven or braided; Scouring and carbonizing of textile fibers
PA: Paceline, Inc.
10737 Indpndnce Pnte Pkwy
Matthews NC 28105
704 290-5007

(G-8562)
SPT TECHNOLOGY INC
Also Called: Paceline
4808 Persimmon Ct (28110-9313)
PHONE.............................704 290-5007
Anthony Mizzi, *Prin*
EMP: 5 EST: 2012
SALES (est): 248.24K **Privately Held**
Web: www.paceline.com
SIC: **2821** Plastics materials and resins

(G-8563)
STAINLESS SUPPLY INC
Also Called: JW Metal Products
307 N Secrest Ave (28110-3801)
PHONE.............................704 635-2064
Jeffrey White, *Prin*
EMP: 19 EST: 2012
SALES (est): 4.59MM **Privately Held**
Web: www.stainlesssupply.com
SIC: **3444** Sheet metalwork

(G-8564)
STEGALL PETROLEUM INC
Also Called: SPI Express
1907 Old Charlotte Hwy (28110-9146)
P.O. Box 766 (28111-0766)
PHONE.............................704 283-5058
Danny Seagall, *Owner*
EMP: 5 EST: 2005
SALES (est): 155.46K **Privately Held**
Web: www.marathonoil.com
SIC: **2741** Miscellaneous publishing

(G-8565)
SUN VALLEY STL FABRICATION INC
1810 Tower Industrial Dr (28110-8575)
PHONE.............................704 289-5830
Timothy Curtis Meggs, *Pr*
Debbie Meggs, *Sec*
EMP: 10 EST: 1989
SALES (est): 2.11MM **Privately Held**
SIC: **5051** 3599 Steel; Machine shop, jobbing and repair

(G-8566)
SWANSON SHEETMETAL INC
320 Broome St (28110-3908)
PHONE.............................704 283-3955
Karen Swanson, *Pr*
EMP: 11 EST: 1991
SQ FT: 30,000
SALES (est): 2.33MM **Privately Held**
Web: www.swansonsheetmetal.com
SIC: **3444** Sheet metal specialties, not stamped

(G-8567)
SYNTHOMER INC
Also Called: Printworld
2011 N Rocky River Rd (28110-7963)
PHONE.............................704 225-1872
Rick Creedmore, *Dir*
EMP: 52
SQ FT: 78,502
SALES (corp-wide): 2.46B **Privately Held**
Web: www.omnova.com
SIC: **2621** 2754 Paper mills; Commercial printing, gravure
HQ: Synthomer Inc.
25435 Harvard Rd
Beachwood OH 44122
216 682-7000

(G-8568)
TAYLOR COMMUNICATIONS INC
1803 N Rocky River Rd (28110-7961)
P.O. Box 989 (28111-0989)
PHONE.............................704 282-0989
Dan Buchholtz, *Mgr*
EMP: 32
SALES (corp-wide): 3.81B **Privately Held**
Web: www.taylor.com
SIC: **2761** Manifold business forms
HQ: Taylor Communications, Inc.
1725 Roe Crest Dr
North Mankato MN 56003
866 541-0937

(G-8569)
TEXTROL LABORATORIES INC
111 W Sandy Ridge Rd (28112-9541)
PHONE.............................704 764-3400
E F White, *Pr*
Francis H White, *
B E Wallace, *
▲ EMP: 30 EST: 1971
SQ FT: 22,000
SALES (est): 2.4MM **Privately Held**
Web: www.textrollabs.com
SIC: **3625** 8711 3552 Electric controls and control accessories, industrial; Consulting engineer; Textile machinery

(G-8570)
TRIMWORKS INC
Also Called: Haigler Electric & Cnstr
4705 Carriker Rd (28110-7491)
PHONE.............................704 753-4149
Michelle Haiger, *Pr*
Ronnie Haiger, *VP*
Michelle Haigler, *Pr*
EMP: 4 EST: 1993
SQ FT: 2,000
SALES (est): 149.29K **Privately Held**
SIC: **2431** Moldings and baseboards, ornamental and trim

(G-8571)
TS WOODWORKS & RAD DESIGN INC
3213 Westwood Industrial Dr (28110-5228)
PHONE.............................704 238-1015
Toral Jagani, *Pr*
Kamlesh Jagani, *VP*
EMP: 12 EST: 2015

SQ FT: 18,000
SALES (est): 6.29MM **Privately Held**
Web: www.tswoodworks.com
SIC: **2431** 2541 2434 Millwork; Table or counter tops, plastic laminated; Vanities, bathroom: wood

(G-8572)
TYSON FOODS INC
Also Called: Tyson
2023 Hasty St (28112-5997)
PHONE.............................704 283-7571
EMP: 20
SALES (corp-wide): 53.31B **Publicly Held**
Web: www.tyson.com
SIC: **2015** Poultry slaughtering and processing
PA: Tyson Foods, Inc.
2200 W Don Tyson Pkwy
Springdale AR 72762
479 290-4000

(G-8573)
TYSON FOODS INC
2715 Cureton St (28112-4128)
PHONE.............................704 201-8654
EMP: 5
SALES (corp-wide): 53.31B **Publicly Held**
Web: www.tyson.com
SIC: **2015** 2032 Chicken slaughtering and processing; Ethnic foods, canned, jarred, etc.
PA: Tyson Foods, Inc.
2200 W Don Tyson Pkwy
Springdale AR 72762
479 290-4000

(G-8574)
US SPECIALTY COLOR CORP
5624 Cannon Dr (28110-9139)
P.O. Box 2669 (28079-2669)
PHONE.............................704 292-1476
James Seiferheld, *Pr*
Mark Huff, *Mgr*
▲ EMP: 6 EST: 1985
SQ FT: 7,800
SALES (est): 427.02K **Privately Held**
Web: www.usspecialty.com
SIC: **2865** 2819 Dyes and pigments; Inorganic metal compounds or salts, nec

(G-8575)
VANGUARD PAI LUNG LLC
Also Called: Vanguard Pailung
601 Mcarthur Cir (28110-3622)
P.O. Box 9 (28111-0009)
PHONE.............................704 283-8171
Christopher Skinner, *Pr*
Chien Chang James Wang, *Ch*
◆ EMP: 9 EST: 2009
SALES (est): 17.29MM **Privately Held**
Web: www.vanguardpailung.com
SIC: **5084** 3552 Textile machinery and equipment; Knitting machines

(G-8576)
VANN S WLDG & ORNA WORKS INC
709 Sikes Mill Rd (28110-9759)
PHONE.............................704 289-6056
Vann Mcmanus, *Pr*
Judy Mc Manus, *Sec*
EMP: 17 EST: 1983
SQ FT: 10,000
SALES (est): 3.74MM **Privately Held**
Web: www.vannsweldingnc.com
SIC: **3446** 3441 Ornamental metalwork; Fabricated structural metal

(G-8577)
W F HARRIS LIGHTING INC
4015 Airport Extension Rd (28110-7398)
P.O. Box 5023 (28111-5023)
PHONE.............................704 283-7477
▲ EMP: 18 EST: 1971
SALES (est): 2.81MM **Privately Held**
Web: www.wfharris.com
SIC: **3646** 3645 3648 Fluorescent lighting fixtures, commercial; Fluorescent lighting fixtures, residential; Lighting equipment, nec

(G-8578)
WDM INC
Also Called: Wood Designs
608 Broome St (28110-3947)
P.O. Box 1308 (28111-1308)
PHONE.............................704 283-7508
Dennis Gosney, *Pr*
Deborah Gosney, *
◆ EMP: 50 EST: 1981
SQ FT: 70,000
SALES (est): 9.96MM **Privately Held**
Web: www.wooddesigns.com
SIC: **2511** Children's wood furniture

(G-8579)
WEISS USA LLC
2213 Stafford Street Ext (28110-9651)
P.O. Box 509 (28111-0509)
PHONE.............................704 282-4496
T W Kirkpatrick, *Pr*
▲ EMP: 4 EST: 2009
SALES (est): 482.05K **Privately Held**
Web: www.usa-weiss.com
SIC: **2891** Adhesives

(G-8580)
WILLIAM GOODYEAR CO (PA)
2802 Gray Fox Rd (28110-8422)
PHONE.............................704 283-7824
Edward W Goodyear Junior, *Pr*
Sylvia Goodyear, *Sec*
▲ EMP: 19 EST: 1986
SQ FT: 16,400
SALES (est): 4.74MM
SALES (corp-wide): 4.74MM **Privately Held**
Web: www.wmgoodyear.com
SIC: **3069** Hard rubber and molded rubber products

(G-8581)
WILLIAMS READY MIX PDTS INC
2465 Old Charlotte Hwy (28110-7366)
PHONE.............................704 283-1137
Mitchell C Crook, *Pr*
Paula W Crook, *Sec*
EMP: 17 EST: 1987
SQ FT: 500
SALES (est): 3.16MM **Privately Held**
Web: ivj.sgz.mybluehost.me
SIC: **3273** Ready-mixed concrete

(G-8582)
WINDSOR WINDOW COMPANY
1400 N Sutherland Ave (28110-4013)
PHONE.............................704 283-7459
EMP: 63
SALES (corp-wide): 160.53MM **Privately Held**
Web: www.woodgrain.com
SIC: **2431** Millwork
HQ: Windsor Window Company
300 Nw 16th St
Fruitland ID 83619
800 452-3801

▲ = Import ▼ = Export
◆ = Import/Export

Mooresboro
Cleveland County

(G-8583)
CLIFFSIDE TECHNOLOGIES INC
4734 Us 221a Hwy (28114-6611)
P.O. Box 249 (29702-0249)
PHONE..................................828 657-4477
Kyle Bullock, *Pr*
EMP: 7 **EST:** 1991
SQ FT: 12,000
SALES (est): 2.19MM **Privately Held**
Web: www.crosslinkgroup.com
SIC: 2843 Textile finishing agents

(G-8584)
FULTON TECHNOLOGY CORPORATION
337 S Pea Ridge Rd (28114-7681)
P.O. Box 159 (28019-0159)
PHONE..................................828 657-1611
Jane Fulton, *Pr*
Nathan Fulton, *VP*
EMP: 5 **EST:** 1999
SQ FT: 10,000
SALES (est): 3.46MM **Privately Held**
Web: www.fultontechnology.com
SIC: 3599 Machine shop, jobbing and repair

(G-8585)
ROGERS GROUP INC
1385 Ferry Rd (28114-8649)
PHONE..................................828 657-9331
EMP: 9
SALES (corp-wide): 1.05B **Privately Held**
Web: www.rogersgroupincint.com
SIC: 1442 Construction sand and gravel
PA: Rogers Group, Inc.
421 Great Cir Rd
Nashville TN 37228
615 242-0585

(G-8586)
SUNRISE DEVELOPMENT LLC
Also Called: Sunrise Development USA
650 Nc 120 Hwy (28114-6713)
P.O. Box 35 (28040-0035)
PHONE..................................828 453-0590
Quinxin Zhu, *Pr*
▲ **EMP:** 12 **EST:** 2009
SQ FT: 50,000
SALES (est): 1.36MM **Privately Held**
Web: www.sunrise-usa.com
SIC: 2299 2221 2392 5137 Batting, wadding, padding and fillings; Bedding, manmade or silk fabric; Pillows, bed: made from purchased materials; Baby goods

(G-8587)
THOMPSON PRINTING & PACKG INC
2457 Mccraw Rd (28114-7721)
PHONE..................................704 313-7323
Robert Thompson, *CEO*
EMP: 5 **EST:** 2022
SALES (est): 233.84K **Privately Held**
Web: www.tpphome.com
SIC: 7389 3086 5199 2752 Packaging and labeling services; Packaging and shipping materials, foamed plastics; Packaging materials; Commercial printing, lithographic

Mooresville
Iredell County

(G-8588)
1ST CHOICE ACTIVEWEAR II LLC
Also Called: ARIA APPAREL

118 Overhill Dr Ste 101 (28117-8021)
PHONE..................................704 528-7814
Richard Johnson, *Pr*
EMP: 22 **EST:** 2012
SALES (est): 1.22MM **Privately Held**
Web: www.1stchoiceactivewear.com
SIC: 2759 Screen printing

(G-8589)
27 SOFTWARE US INC
Also Called: Dxterity Solutions
153 Farm Knoll Way (28117-0010)
PHONE..................................704 968-2879
Darrel Woodruff, *CEO*
EMP: 10 **EST:** 2018
SALES (est): 765.25K **Privately Held**
Web: www.dxteritysolutions.com
SIC: 7371 7372 Computer software systems analysis and design, custom; Prepackaged software

(G-8590)
ACCESS TECHNOLOGIES LLC
163 Cooley Rd (28117-9253)
PHONE..................................574 286-1255
Stefan Savastano, *Managing Member*
EMP: 5 **EST:** 2005
SALES (est): 491.14K **Privately Held**
SIC: 2819 5169 Industrial inorganic chemicals, nec; Industrial chemicals

(G-8591)
ADVANCED DETECTION TECH LLC
215 Overhill Dr 1 (28117-7036)
PHONE..................................704 663-1949
Jan Zickerman, *Managing Member*
EMP: 20 **EST:** 2006
SQ FT: 4,000
SALES (est): 4.83MM **Privately Held**
Web:
www.advanced-detection-technology.com
SIC: 7382 3812 Security systems services; Search and detection systems and instruments

(G-8592)
ALCON COMPONENTS USA INC
Also Called: Alcon Components
121 Oakpark Dr (28115-7811)
PHONE..................................704 799-2723
EMP: 5 **EST:** 2018
SALES (est): 711.76K **Privately Held**
Web: www.alcon.co.uk
SIC: 3625 Electromagnetic clutches or brakes

(G-8593)
ALEXANDERS HAM COMPANY INC
5920 Highway 152 W (28115-7330)
P.O. Box 57 (28088-0057)
PHONE..................................704 857-9222
Carl W Alexander Junior, *Pr*
Kathy Teague, *Sec*
Ricky Lipe, *VP*
Harry K Smith, *VP*
EMP: 10 **EST:** 1952
SQ FT: 6,300
SALES (est): 323.37K **Privately Held**
Web: www.alexanderham.com
SIC: 5147 2013 2011 Meats, cured or smoked; Sausages and other prepared meats; Meat packing plants

(G-8594)
ALTERNATIVE HEALTH DIST LLC
106 N Commercial Dr Ste A (28115)
PHONE..................................336 465-6618
Lee Vantine Iii, *CEO*
Yasser Abdelhalim, *CFO*
Nicholas Groat, *COO*
EMP: 13 **EST:** 2016

SALES (est): 1.1MM **Privately Held**
Web: www.ahdist.com
SIC: 2833 Drugs and herbs: grading, grinding, and milling

(G-8595)
AMERICAN DURAFILM CO INC
117 Infield Ct (28117-8026)
PHONE..................................704 895-7701
Jeff Allegrti, *Pr*
EMP: 6 **EST:** 2017
SALES (est): 1.03MM **Privately Held**
Web: www.americandurafilm.com
SIC: 2821 Plastics materials and resins

(G-8596)
AMERITECH DIE & MOLD INC
107 Knob Hill Rd (28117)
PHONE..................................704 664-0801
Steven Rotman, *Prin*
Mark Rotman, *Prin*
EMP: 20 **EST:** 1985
SALES (est): 3.95MM **Privately Held**
Web: www.amdiemold.com
SIC: 3544 Industrial molds

(G-8597)
AMERITECH DIE & MOLD SOUTH INC (PA)
107 Knob Hill Rd (28117-6847)
PHONE..................................704 664-0801
Steven J Rotman, *Pr*
Wayne E Rotman, *VP*
EMP: 10 **EST:** 1985
SQ FT: 26,000
SALES (est): 3.84MM
SALES (corp-wide): 3.84MM **Privately Held**
Web: www.amdiemold.com
SIC: 3544 Industrial molds

(G-8598)
AMIAD FILTRATION SYSTEMS LTD (PA)
Also Called: Amiad Water Systems
120 Talbert Rd Ste J (28117-7119)
PHONE..................................805 377-0288
Michael Poth, *Pr*
Matthew Miles, *
◆ **EMP:** 24 **EST:** 2012
SALES (est): 6.97MM
SALES (corp-wide): 6.97MM **Privately Held**
Web: www.amiad.com
SIC: 3677 3589 Filtration devices, electronic; Water treatment equipment, industrial

(G-8599)
AMIAD USA INC (DH)
120 Talbert Rd Ste J (28117-7119)
PHONE..................................704 662-3133
Tom Akehurst, *Pr*
▲ **EMP:** 17 **EST:** 2011
SALES (est): 11.09MM **Privately Held**
Web: us.amiad.com
SIC: 3589 Water treatment equipment, industrial
HQ: Amiad Filtration Solutions (2004) Ltd
Kibbutz
Amiad 12335

(G-8600)
ARGOS USA LLC
Also Called: Redi-Mix Concrete
Hwy 150 E (28115)
PHONE..................................704 872-9566
John Wood, *Brnch Mgr*
EMP: 5
Web: www.argos-us.com

SIC: 3273 Ready-mixed concrete
HQ: Argos Usa Llc
3015 Windward Plz Ste 300
Alpharetta GA 30005
678 368-4300

(G-8601)
ATTIC TENT INC
Also Called: Insulsure
164 Mill Pond Ln (28115-7777)
PHONE..................................704 892-5399
Steve Williams, *Pr*
Tammy Williams, *Sec*
David Williams, *VP*
▲ **EMP:** 5 **EST:** 1996
SQ FT: 1,200
SALES (est): 238.41K **Privately Held**
Web: www.attictent.com
SIC: 2493 1711 1742 Insulation and roofing material, reconstituted wood; Plumbing, heating, air-conditioning; Insulation, buildings

(G-8602)
AUTOMAIL LLC
2987 Charlotte Hwy (28117-8052)
PHONE..................................704 677-0152
Kent Hovey, *Prin*
EMP: 4 **EST:** 2012
SALES (est): 250.66K **Privately Held**
Web: www.automail1.com
SIC: 2711 Commercial printing and newspaper publishing combined

(G-8603)
AVANT PUBLICATIONS LLC
116 Morlake Dr Ste 203 (28117-9211)
PHONE..................................704 897-6048
Scott Champion, *CEO*
Corey Champion, *CFO*
EMP: 7 **EST:** 2019
SALES (est): 938.39K **Privately Held**
SIC: 2759 Publication printing

(G-8604)
AVINTIV SPECIALTY MTLS INC
111 Excellance Ln (28115-9305)
PHONE..................................704 660-6242
Fernando Apolinario, *Bd of Dir*
EMP: 104
Web: www.berryglobal.com
SIC: 2297 Nonwoven fabrics
HQ: Avintiv Specialty Materials Inc.
9335 Hrris Crners Pkwy St
Charlotte NC 28269

(G-8605)
B & B FABRICATION INC
Also Called: Billy Boat Performance Exhaust
125 Infield Ct (28117-8026)
PHONE..................................623 581-7600
William Boat, *Pr*
Andrea Boat, *VP*
▲ **EMP:** 10 **EST:** 1986
SALES (est): 2.42MM **Privately Held**
Web: www.bbexhaust.com
SIC: 3714 Exhaust systems and parts, motor vehicle

(G-8606)
BAY STATE MILLING COMPANY
448 N Main St (28115-2456)
P.O. Box 358 (28115-0358)
PHONE..................................704 664-4873
Leslie A Lovett, *Mgr*
EMP: 27
SALES (corp-wide): 131.82MM **Privately Held**
Web: www.baystatemilling.com
SIC: 2041 2048 Flour: blended, prepared, or self-rising; Prepared feeds, nec

GEOGRAPHIC

PA: Bay State Milling Company
100 Congress St
Quincy MA 02169
617 328-4400

(G-8607)
BEN HUFFMAN ENTERPRISES LLC
516 River Hwy Ste D (28117-6830)
PHONE.............................704 724-4705
EMP: 6 **EST:** 2018
SALES (est): 1.6MM **Privately Held**
SIC: 3714 Motor vehicle parts and
accessories

(G-8608)
BERRY GLOBAL INC
Also Called: Berry Plastics
111 Excellance Ln (28115-9305)
PHONE.............................704 664-3733
Steve Ford, *Prin*
EMP: 101
Web: www.berryglobal.com
SIC: 3089 Plastics containers, except foam
HQ: Berry Global, Inc.
101 Oakley St
Evansville IN 47710

(G-8609)
BESTCO HOLDINGS INC
288 Mazeppa Rd (28115-7928)
P.O. Box 329 (28115-0329)
PHONE.............................704 664-4300
Richard Zulman, *CEO*
Tim Condron, *Pr*
Mark Knight, *Ex VP*
Steve Berkowitz, *Ex VP*
Scott Wattenberg, *CFO*
◆ **EMP:** 424 **EST:** 1990
SQ FT: 140,000
SALES (est): 23.17MM **Privately Held**
Web: www.bestco.com
SIC: 2064 Candy and other confectionery
products

(G-8610)
BESTCO LLC
Also Called: Accounting Office
137 Bestco Ln (28115)
PHONE.............................704 664-4300
Richard Zulman, *Brnch Mgr*
EMP: 39
SALES (corp-wide): 299.17MM **Privately
Held**
Web: www.bestco.com
SIC: 2023 Dietary supplements, dairy and
non-dairy based
PA: Bestco Llc
288 Mazeppa Rd
Mooresville NC 28115
704 664-4300

(G-8611)
BESTCO LLC
119 E Super Sport Dr (28117-6311)
PHONE.............................704 664-4300
EMP: 35
SALES (corp-wide): 299.17MM **Privately
Held**
Web: www.bestco.com
SIC: 2834 Pharmaceutical preparations
PA: Bestco Llc
288 Mazeppa Rd
Mooresville NC 28115
704 664-4300

(G-8612)
BESTCO LLC
139 Camp Ln (28115)
P.O. Box 329 (28115-0329)
PHONE.............................704 664-4300
Tim Condron, *Brnch Mgr*

EMP: 150
SALES (corp-wide): 299.17MM **Privately
Held**
Web: www.bestco.com
SIC: 2834 Pharmaceutical preparations
PA: Bestco Llc
288 Mazeppa Rd
Mooresville NC 28115
704 664-4300

(G-8613)
BESTCO LLC
208 Manufacturers Blvd (28115-6001)
PHONE.............................704 664-4300
Tim Condron, *CEO*
EMP: 250
SALES (corp-wide): 299.17MM **Privately
Held**
Web: www.bestco.com
SIC: 2834 Pharmaceutical preparations
PA: Bestco Llc
288 Mazeppa Rd
Mooresville NC 28115
704 664-4300

(G-8614)
BESTCO LLC (PA)
288 Mazeppa Rd (28115)
P.O. Box 329 (28115)
PHONE.............................704 664-4300
Tim Condron, *Pr*
John Dahldorf, *
Mark Knight, *
Andrew B Hochman, *
Amy Rockwell, *
◆ **EMP:** 133 **EST:** 2013
SQ FT: 334,000
SALES (est): 299.17MM
SALES (corp-wide): 299.17MM **Privately
Held**
Web: www.bestco.com
SIC: 2834 Lozenges, pharmaceutical

(G-8615)
BIZ TECHNOLOGY SOLUTIONS LLC
353 Oates Rd (28117-6824)
PHONE.............................704 658-1707
Mahmoud Chouffani, *Pr*
Reda Chouffani, *OK Vice President**
EMP: 40 **EST:** 2001
SQ FT: 8,000
SALES (est): 5.41MM **Privately Held**
Web: www.biztechnologysolutions.com
SIC: 7378 7372 Computer maintenance and
repair; Prepackaged software

(G-8616)
BLACK & DECKER CORPORATION
Also Called: Black & Decker
134 Talbert Pointe Dr (28117-4377)
PHONE.............................704 799-3929
EMP: 5
SALES (corp-wide): 15.78B **Publicly Held**
Web: www.blackanddecker.com
SIC: 3546 Power-driven handtools
HQ: The Black & Decker Corporation
701 E Joppa Rd
Towson MD 21286
410 716-3900

(G-8617)
BOARDS AND BOWLS LLC
141 Brookleaf Ln (28115-6788)
PHONE.............................704 293-2004
David Paventi, *Prin*
EMP: 5 **EST:** 2019
SALES (est): 95.41K **Privately Held**
Web: www.spencerpeterman.com
SIC: 2499 Wood products, nec

(G-8618)
BODYCOTE THERMAL PROC INC
Also Called: Bodycote Thermal Processing
128 Speedway Ln (28117-6879)
PHONE.............................704 664-1808
EMP: 11
SALES (corp-wide): 1B **Privately Held**
Web: www.bodycote.com
SIC: 3398 Metal heat treating
HQ: Bodycote Thermal Processing, Inc.
12750 Merit Dr Ste 1400
Dallas TX 75251
214 904-2420

(G-8619)
BRANDSPEED
915 River Hwy (28117-9245)
PHONE.............................410 204-1032
EMP: 6 **EST:** 2018
SALES (est): 131.66K **Privately Held**
Web: www.brandspeed.us
SIC: 2299 Textile goods, nec

(G-8620)
BRANFORD FILTRATION LLC (PA)
Also Called: Fibrix Filtration
119 Poplar Pointe Dr Ste C (28117-9428)
PHONE.............................704 394-2111
Keith White, *CEO*
Michael Rush, *CFO*
Jr Baccus, *Pr*
EMP: 60 **EST:** 2020
SALES (est): 72.75MM
SALES (corp-wide): 72.75MM **Privately
Held**
SIC: 3677 Filtration devices, electronic

(G-8621)
BRAVO TEAM LLC
603 N Church St (28115-2303)
PHONE.............................704 309-1918
EMP: 39 **EST:** 2018
SALES (est): 5.93MM **Privately Held**
Web: www.bravoteam.tech
SIC: 3451 7371 Screw machine products;
Computer software development and
applications

(G-8622)
BRUMLEY/SOUTH INC
Also Called: Brumley-South
422 N Broad St (28115-3040)
P.O. Box 1237 (28115-1237)
PHONE.............................704 664-9251
Thomas Norment, *Pr*
Cindy Norment, *Treas*
▲ **EMP:** 7 **EST:** 1992
SQ FT: 25,000
SALES (est): 2.09MM **Privately Held**
Web: www.brumleysouth.com
SIC: 3674 Wafers (semiconductor devices)

(G-8623)
BSCI INC (PA)
170 Barley Park Ln (28115-7912)
P.O. Box 1203 (28115-1203)
PHONE.............................704 664-3005
Karen B Ray, *Pr*
Luke Ray, *VP*
▲ **EMP:** 7 **EST:** 1990
SQ FT: 6,000
SALES (est): 2.48MM
SALES (corp-wide): 2.48MM **Privately
Held**
Web: www.rollbarpadding.com
SIC: 3069 Foam rubber

(G-8624)
BUCHER MUNICIPAL N AMER INC
Also Called: Jna

105 Motorsports Rd (28115-8258)
P.O. Box 388 (28115)
PHONE.............................704 658-1333
Todd Parsons, *Pr*
Todd W Parsons, *
Bob Ohara, *
Colin Madden, *
◆ **EMP:** 33 **EST:** 2011
SQ FT: 12,000
SALES (est): 7.46MM **Privately Held**
Web: www.buchermunicipal.com
SIC: 3711 Motor vehicles and car bodies
HQ: Bucher Municipal Limited
Gate 3
Dorking RH4 1
130 688-4722

(G-8625)
C TEK LEAN SOLUTIONS INC
460 E Plaza Dr Ste A (28115-8020)
PHONE.............................704 895-0090
Daniel Sanderson, *Ch*
Chris Dawson, *Pr*
◆ **EMP:** 20 **EST:** 2017
SALES (est): 4.86MM **Privately Held**
Web: www.ctekleansolutions.com
SIC: 3441 8711 Building components,
structural steel; Consulting engineer

(G-8626)
C&K PLASTICS NC LLC
Also Called: C&K Plastics North Carolina
164 Mckenzie Rd (28115-9302)
PHONE.............................833 232-4848
EMP: 7 **EST:** 2021
SALES (est): 5.29MM **Privately Held**
SIC: 3089 Plastics containers, except foam

(G-8627)
CAIRN STUDIO LTD
200 Mckenzie Rd (28115-7975)
P.O. Box 400 (28036-0400)
PHONE.............................704 664-7128
Clarence Atwell, *Mgr*
EMP: 28
SALES (corp-wide): 658.38K **Privately
Held**
Web: www.cairnstudio.com
SIC: 3269 3544 4226 Figures: pottery, china,
earthenware, and stoneware; Special dies,
tools, jigs, and fixtures; Special
warehousing and storage, nec
PA: Cairn Studio, Ltd.
121 N Main St
Davidson NC 28036
704 892-3581

(G-8628)
CARDINAL GLASS INDUSTRIES INC
Also Called: Cardinal Fg
342 Mooresville Blvd (28115-7909)
PHONE.............................704 660-0900
Jim Stevens, *Manager*
EMP: 250
SALES (corp-wide): 1B **Privately Held**
Web: www.cardinalcorp.com
SIC: 3211 Float glass
PA: Cardinal Glass Industries Inc
775 Pririe Ctr Dr Ste 200
Eden Prairie MN 55344
952 229-2600

(G-8629)
CAROLINA BEVERAGE GROUP LLC
313 Mooresville Blvd (28115-7909)
PHONE.............................704 799-3627
EMP: 32
SALES (corp-wide): 167.48MM **Privately
Held**
Web: www.carolinabeveragegroup.com

SIC: **2082** Beer (alcoholic beverage)
HQ: Carolina Beverage Group, Llc
110 Barley Park Ln
Mooresville NC 28115
704 799-2337

(G-8630)
CAROLINA BEVERAGE GROUP LLC (HQ)
Also Called: Carolina Beer Company
110 Barley Park Ln (28115)
P.O. Box 1183 (28115)
PHONE..............................704 799-2337
Brian Demos, *CEO*
Brian Demos, *Pr*
J Michael Smith, *Managing Member*
John Stritch, *
Eric Pearce, *
▲ EMP: 38 EST: 1997
SQ FT: 30,000
SALES (est): 105.25MM
SALES (corp-wide): 167.48MM **Privately Held**
Web: www.carolinabeveragegroup.com
SIC: **2086** Soft drinks: packaged in cans, bottles, etc.
PA: Cold Spring Brewing Company
219 Red River Ave N
Cold Spring MN 56320
651 637-3360

(G-8631)
CAROLINA BUILDING SERVICES INC (PA)
Also Called: CBS Windows & Doors
207 Timber Rd (28115-7868)
P.O. Box 414 (28123-0414)
PHONE..............................704 664-7110
John S Alden, *Pr*
Garry Dunne, *VP*
EMP: 15 EST: 1992
SQ FT: 5,000
SALES (est): 2.22MM **Privately Held**
Web: www.carolinabuildingservices.com
SIC: **2431** Windows and window parts and trim, wood

(G-8632)
CAROLINA PRECISION MFG LLC
1138 Gateway Dr (28115-8208)
PHONE..............................704 662-3480
EMP: 20 EST: 1998
SQ FT: 12,000
SALES (est): 4.92MM **Privately Held**
Web: www.carolinaprecision.com
SIC: **7539 3599** Automotive repair shops, nec; Machine shop, jobbing and repair

(G-8633)
CAROLINA PRECISION TECH LLC
1055 Gateway Dr Ste A (28115-8342)
PHONE..............................215 675-4590
Kevin Burke, *Managing Member*
EMP: 50 EST: 1998
SALES (est): 4.69MM **Privately Held**
Web: www.carolinaprecision.com
SIC: **3841 3724** Surgical and medical instruments; Aircraft engines and engine parts

(G-8634)
CASETEC PRECISION MACHINE LLC
Also Called: Casetec
178 Attleboro Pl (28117-7106)
PHONE..............................704 663-6043
Jon R Carlson, *Managing Member*
▲ EMP: 8 EST: 2006
SQ FT: 2,500
SALES (est): 474.6K **Privately Held**

SIC: **3599 3541** Machine shop, jobbing and repair; Numerically controlled metal cutting machine tools

(G-8635)
CAVOTEC USA INC (DH)
500 S Main St # 1 (28115-3549)
PHONE..............................704 873-3009
Stefan Widegren, *CEO*
Erik Wilhelmsen, *Pr*
Risto Toukola, *VP*
Art Avlon, *VP*
◆ EMP: 24 EST: 1990
SALES (est): 20.66MM **Privately Held**
Web: www.cavotec.com
SIC: **5082 3568** Cranes, construction; Pulleys, power transmission
HQ: Cavotec Group Holdings N.V.
Meent 106 Minervahuis 1
Rotterdam ZH 3011
348460160

(G-8636)
CBT SUPPLY
Also Called: Smart Desks
109 Farmers Folly Dr (28117-8572)
P.O. Box 64 (28117)
PHONE..............................803 617-8230
Roger Lampkin, *Pr*
Jeffery Korber, *Pr*
EMP: 7 EST: 1998
SALES (est): 2.45MM **Privately Held**
Web: www.smartdesks.com
SIC: **2521** Wood office furniture

(G-8637)
CHAMPION MEDIA LLC (PA)
Also Called: Robesonion
116 Morlake Dr Ste 203 (28117-9211)
PHONE..............................704 746-3955
Scott Champion, *Managing Member*
EMP: 23 EST: 2017
SALES (est): 12.2MM
SALES (corp-wide): 12.2MM **Privately Held**
Web: www.championcarolinas.com
SIC: **7379 7371 2711** Computer related maintenance services; Computer software development and applications; Newspapers

(G-8638)
CKS PACKAGING
289 Rolling Hill Rd (28117-6845)
PHONE..............................704 663-6510
Marshall Henderson, *Pr*
EMP: 10 EST: 1983
SQ FT: 40,000
SALES (est): 4.36MM **Privately Held**
Web: www.ckspackaging.com
SIC: **3089** Plastics containers, except foam

(G-8639)
CKS PACKAGING INC
289 Rolling Hill Rd (28117-6845)
PHONE..............................704 663-6510
Marshall Henderson, *Prin*
EMP: 48
SALES (corp-wide): 418.61MM **Privately Held**
Web: www.ckspackaging.com
SIC: **3089 2656** Plastics containers, except foam; Sanitary food containers
PA: C.K.S. Packaging, Inc.
350 Great Sw Pkwy
Atlanta GA 30336
404 691-8900

(G-8640)
CLARIANT CORPORATION
337 Timber Rd (28115-7855)
PHONE..............................704 235-5700

Raymond Sloan, *Brnch Mgr*
EMP: 23
Web: www.clariant.com
SIC: **2869** Industrial organic chemicals, nec
HQ: Clariant Corporation
500 E Morehead St Ste 400
Charlotte NC 28202
704 331-7000

(G-8641)
COCONUT PARADISE INC
803 Performance Rd (28115-9597)
PHONE..............................704 662-3443
George Brunnhoelzl, *Pr*
Robin Hansen, *Sec*
EMP: 8 EST: 1993
SQ FT: 18,000
SALES (est): 834.87K **Privately Held**
Web: www.brunnhoelzl.com
SIC: **3423 3714** Jacks: lifting, screw, or ratchet (hand tools); Motor vehicle parts and accessories

(G-8642)
COMPOSITE FACTORY LLC
255 Raceway Dr (28117-6510)
PHONE..............................484 264-3306
EMP: 10 EST: 2019
SALES (est): 1.78MM **Privately Held**
Web: www.fibreworkscomposites.com
SIC: **3449** Bars, concrete reinforcing: fabricated steel

(G-8643)
COREGRP LLC
Also Called: Coregroup Displays
631 Brawley School Rd (28117-6204)
P.O. Box 210 (12534)
PHONE..............................845 876-5109
Daniel Riso, *Pr*
◆ EMP: 15 EST: 2003
SALES (est): 2.35MM **Privately Held**
Web: www.coregroupdisplays.com
SIC: **2542** Partitions and fixtures, except wood

(G-8644)
CRC
Also Called: CRC Powder Coating
2425 Statesville Hwy (28115-7968)
PHONE..............................704 664-1242
Paul Daigrepont, *Prin*
EMP: 5 EST: 2015
SALES (est): 921.85K **Privately Held**
Web: www.crcpowdercoating.com
SIC: **3479** Coating of metals and formed products

(G-8645)
CRP USA LLC
127 Goodwin Cir (28115-7971)
P.O. Box 728 (28115-0728)
PHONE..............................704 660-0258
Chris Brewster, *CEO*
EMP: 12 EST: 2009
SALES (est): 1.38MM **Privately Held**
Web: www.crp-usa.net
SIC: **3087** Custom compound purchased resins

(G-8646)
CURTIS L MACLEAN L C
227 Manufacturers Blvd (28115-6001)
PHONE..............................704 940-5531
Paul R Hojnacki, *Pr*
EMP: 110
SQ FT: 55,000
SALES (corp-wide): 1.15B **Privately Held**
Web: www.macleanfoggcs.com

SIC: **3451 3714** Screw machine products; Motor vehicle parts and accessories
HQ: Curtis L Maclean L C
50 Thielman Dr
Buffalo NY 14206
716 898-7800

(G-8647)
CUSTOM PRODUCTS INC
1618 Landis Hwy (28115-6906)
P.O. Box 1141 (28115-1141)
PHONE..............................704 663-4159
▲ EMP: 99
SIC: **2531** Seats, aircraft

(G-8648)
CUTTING EDGE STONEWORKS INC
Also Called: Cutting Edge Stoneworks
161 Mckenzie Rd (28115-7976)
P.O. Box 4931 (28117-4931)
PHONE..............................704 799-1227
Michael Giordano, *Pr*
EMP: 5 EST: 2008
SALES (est): 3.52MM **Privately Held**
Web: www.cuttingedgestoneworks.com
SIC: **2541** Counter and sink tops

(G-8649)
CYCLE PRO LLC
261 Rolling Hill Rd Ste 1a (28117-6505)
PHONE..............................704 662-6682
▲ EMP: 5 EST: 2000
SALES (est): 499.1K **Privately Held**
Web: www.cycleprollc.com
SIC: **8748 3714** Business consulting, nec; Motor vehicle parts and accessories

(G-8650)
DANBARTEX LLC
120 Commercial Dr Ste A (28115-8039)
P.O. Box 681748 (28216-0033)
PHONE..............................704 323-8728
Danny L Barrett, *Managing Member*
▲ EMP: 6 EST: 2007
SALES (est): 494.86K **Privately Held**
Web: www.danbartex.com
SIC: **5999 2426** Business machines and equipment; Hardwood dimension and flooring mills

(G-8651)
DAP PRODUCTS INC
125 Infield Ct (28117-8026)
PHONE..............................704 799-9640
Michael Morris, *Prin*
EMP: 16
SALES (corp-wide): 7.34B **Publicly Held**
Web: www.dap.com
SIC: **2891** Caulking compounds
HQ: Dap Products Inc.
2400 Boston St Ste 200
Baltimore MD 21224
800 543-3840

(G-8652)
DCE INC
138 Cayuga Dr Ste C (28117-8260)
PHONE..............................704 230-4649
David Cunliffe, *Pr*
Sandra Cunliffe, *VP*
◆ EMP: 8 EST: 2012
SQ FT: 2,500
SALES (est): 3.47MM
SALES (corp-wide): 1.05MM **Privately Held**
Web: us.dcemotorsport.com
SIC: **3714** Automotive wiring harness sets
PA: D.C. Electronics Motorsport Specialist Limited
Unit 1
Maldon CM9 5

(G-8653)

DEBOTECH INC
130 Infield Ct (28117-8026)
PHONE..............................704 664-1361
Hans Debot, *CEO*
Hans Debot, *Pr*
Jamye Debot, *
▼ **EMP:** 150 **EST:** 1998
SQ FT: 25,000
SALES (est): 7.74MM **Privately Held**
Web: www.debotech.com
SIC: 3089 3624 Automotive parts, plastic;
Carbon and graphite products

(G-8654)

DEHN INC (HQ)
500 S Main St Ste 115 (28115-3550)
PHONE..............................772 460-9315
Helmet Pusch, *Pr*
Thomas Dehn, *
EMP: 11 **EST:** 2003
SALES (est): 11.47MM
SALES (corp-wide): 459.7MM **Privately
Held**
Web: www.dehn-usa.com
SIC: 3643 5063 Lightning protection
equipment; Circuit breakers
PA: Hans Dehn Holding Se + Co Kg
Hans-Dehn-Str. 1
Neumarkt I.D.Opf. BY 92318
91819060

(G-8655)

DEJ HOLDINGS LLC (PA)
349 Cayuga Dr (28117-8216)
P.O. Box 330 (28115-0330)
PHONE..............................704 799-4800
Dale Earnhardt Junior, *Managing Member*
EMP: 25 **EST:** 1999
SALES (est): 2.8MM **Privately Held**
Web: www.thedalejrfoundation.org
SIC: 3711 Motor vehicles and car bodies

(G-8656)

DYNAMIC MOUNTING
120b Pitt Rd (28115-6782)
PHONE..............................704 978-8723
EMP: 4 **EST:** 2019
SALES (est): 39.69K **Privately Held**
Web: www.mantelmount.com
SIC: 3999 Manufacturing industries, nec

(G-8657)

E G A PRODUCTS INC
Also Called: Ega Southeast
208 Mckenzie Rd (28115-7975)
PHONE..............................704 664-1221
Gary Green, *Prin*
EMP: 10
SALES (corp-wide): 6.57MM **Privately
Held**
Web: www.egaproducts.com
SIC: 3542 2542 Machine tools, metal
forming type; Partitions and fixtures, except
wood
PA: E G A Products, Inc.
4275 N 127th St
Brookfield WI 53005
262 781-7899

(G-8658)

E-LIQUID BRANDS LLC
120 Commercial Dr (28115-8036)
PHONE..............................828 385-5090
EMP: 30 **EST:** 2014
SALES (est): 638.45K **Privately Held**
Web: www.eliquidbrandsllc.com
SIC: 3999 Cigarette and cigar products and
accessories

(G-8659)

EARTH-KIND INC
Also Called: Crane Creek Garden
346 E Plaza Dr Ste D (28115-8050)
PHONE..............................701 751-4456
Kari Warberg, *Pr*
John Warberg, *Sec*
EMP: 5 **EST:** 1993
SALES (est): 4.47MM **Privately Held**
Web: www.earthkind.com
SIC: 3999 Artificial trees and flowers

(G-8660)

ECLIPSE COMPOSITE ENGRG INC
Also Called: Eclipse Composites Engineering
138 Cedar Pointe Dr (28117)
PHONE..............................801 601-8559
Chad Dailey, *CEO*
EMP: 20 **EST:** 2018
SALES (est): 2.82MM **Privately Held**
Web: www.eclipsecomposites.com
SIC: 3679 Antennas, receiving

(G-8661)

EXECUTIVE PROMOTIONS INC
Also Called: Mailing Solutions Plus
2987 Charlotte Hwy 21 (28117-8052)
PHONE..............................704 663-4000
Kent Hovey, *Pr*
Kirsten Hovey, *VP*
EMP: 12 **EST:** 1990
SQ FT: 4,000
SALES (est): 458.33K **Privately Held**
SIC: 2754 7311 Commercial printing, gravure
; Advertising agencies

(G-8662)

FABRINEERING LLC
8955 W Nc 152 Hwy (28115-4240)
PHONE..............................704 999-9906
EMP: 6 **EST:** 2015
SALES (est): 3.25MM **Privately Held**
Web: www.fabrineering.co
SIC: 3441 Fabricated structural metal

(G-8663)

FIBREWORKS COMPOSITES LLC
143 Thunder Rd (28115-6000)
PHONE..............................704 696-1084
Gunther Steiner, *CEO*
Joseph G Hofmann, *
EMP: 36 **EST:** 2008
SALES (est): 9.84MM **Privately Held**
Web: www.fibreworkscomposites.com
SIC: 3089 7948 Composition stone, plastics;
Stock car racing

(G-8664)

FIRERESQ INCORPORATED
Also Called: Fire Hose Direct
115 Corporate Center Dr Ste J
(28117-0080)
P.O. Box 3455 (28117-3455)
PHONE..............................888 975-0858
Barry Mcconaghey, *Pr*
Daniel Weber, *VP*
▼ **EMP:** 10 **EST:** 2011
SQ FT: 12,000
SALES (est): 3.1MM **Privately Held**
Web: www.fireresq.com
SIC: 3429 3569 5999 5087 Nozzles, fire
fighting; Firefighting and related equipment;
Alarm and safety equipment stores;
Firefighting equipment

(G-8665)

FITT USA INC
136 Corporate Park Dr Ste I (28117-6960)
PHONE..............................866 348-8872
Federico Cuman, *Pr*

Andrea Budano, *Sec*
EMP: 11 **EST:** 2018
SALES (est): 9.67MM **Privately Held**
Web: usa.fitt.com
SIC: 3084 Plastics pipe
HQ: Fitt Group Spa
Viale Del Mercato Nuovo 44/G
Vicenza VI 36100

(G-8666)

FLYNN BURNER CORPORATION
225 Mooresville Blvd (28115-7965)
PHONE..............................704 660-1500
Dom Medina, *Pr*
Edward Flynn, *
Julian Modzeleski, *
◆ **EMP:** 50 **EST:** 1946
SQ FT: 25,000
SALES (est): 4.47MM **Privately Held**
Web: www.flynnburner.com
SIC: 3433 Gas burners, industrial

(G-8667)

**FOUR CORNERS FRMNG GALLERY
INC**
148 N Main St (28115-2526)
PHONE..............................704 662-7154
Kim Saragoni, *Owner*
EMP: 5 **EST:** 2006
SALES (est): 169.19K **Privately Held**
Web: www.fcfgframing.com
SIC: 5999 5023 3499 2499 Picture frames,
ready made; Frames and framing, picture
and mirror; Picture frames, metal; Picture
and mirror frames, wood

(G-8668)

FUNNY BONE EMB & SCREENING
829 Plaza Ln (28115-9555)
PHONE..............................704 663-4711
Daniel Dougherty, *Owner*
EMP: 6 **EST:** 2003
SALES (est): 470.6K **Privately Held**
Web: www.funnybonenc.com
SIC: 2395 5699 2759 Embroidery products,
except Schiffli machine; Miscellaneous
apparel and accessory stores; Screen
printing

(G-8669)

G-LOC BRAKES LLC
Also Called: Gee-Lock
503 Performance Rd (28115-9594)
PHONE..............................704 765-0213
James Rogerson, *Managing Member*
EMP: 6 **EST:** 2016
SALES (est): 649.17K **Privately Held**
Web: www.g-locbrakes.com
SIC: 3714 Air brakes, motor vehicle

(G-8670)

GA COMMUNICATIONS INC
136 Fairview Rd Ste 220 (28117-8547)
PHONE..............................704 360-1860
Mike Hynson, *Mgr*
EMP: 36
Web: www.purered.net
SIC: 2796 Color separations, for printing
PA: Ga Communications, Inc.
2196 W Park Ct
Stone Mountain GA 30087

(G-8671)

GARRETTCOM INC (HQ)
Also Called: Califrnia Grrett Cmmnctons Inc
1113 N Main St (28115-2359)
PHONE..............................510 438-9071
EMP: 62 **EST:** 1989
SALES (est): 2.8MM
SALES (corp-wide): 2.46B **Publicly Held**
Web: www.belden.com

SIC: 3577 Input/output equipment, computer
PA: Belden Inc.
1 N Brentwood Blvd Fl 15
Saint Louis MO 63105
314 854-8000

(G-8672)

GEOSURFACES SOUTHEAST INC
Also Called: Medallion Athletic Products
150 River Park Rd (28117-8929)
PHONE..............................704 660-3000
Charles Dawson, *CEO*
EMP: 20 **EST:** 2018
SALES (est): 2.96MM
SALES (corp-wide): 19.54MM **Privately
Held**
Web: www.geosurfaces.com
SIC: 3949 Sporting and athletic goods, nec
PA: Geosurfaces, Inc.
7080 St Gabriel Ave Ste A
Saint Gabriel LA 70776
877 663-5968

(G-8673)

GLACIER FORESTRY INC
135 Jocelyn Ln Apt 108 (28117-5270)
PHONE..............................704 902-2594
Jaime L Hutton, *Pr*
EMP: 7 **EST:** 2015
SALES (est): 71.17K **Privately Held**
SIC: 2411 Logging camps and contractors

(G-8674)

GO GREEN RACING
409 Performance Rd (28115-9593)
PHONE..............................916 295-2621
Tim Barile, *CEO*
EMP: 8 **EST:** 2015
SALES (est): 711.72K **Privately Held**
Web: www.gofasracing.com
SIC: 3711 Automobile assembly, including
specialty automobiles

(G-8675)

GRACIE & LUCAS LLC
Also Called: Transmission Unlimited
224 Wiredell Ave (28115)
PHONE..............................704 707-3207
EMP: 4 **EST:** 2017
SALES (est): 1.51MM **Privately Held**
SIC: 3714 Wheels, motor vehicle

(G-8676)

GRAY OX INC
155 Quiet Cove Rd (28117-8892)
PHONE..............................704 662-8247
Roger M Oxidine, *Pr*
Troy C Graham, *Sec*
EMP: 10 **EST:** 2001
SALES (est): 200.3K **Privately Held**
Web: www.grayox.com
SIC: 3253 Ceramic wall and floor tile

(G-8677)

**GREENWORKS NORTH AMERICA
LLC (PA)**
Also Called: Greenworks Tools
500 S Main St Ste 450 (28115-3550)
PHONE..............................888 909-6757
Klaus Hahn, *Managing Member*
◆ **EMP:** 100 **EST:** 2006
SQ FT: 2,000
SALES (est): 33.33MM **Privately Held**
SIC: 5072 3423 Power tools and accessories
; Garden and farm tools, including shovels

(G-8678)

H M ELLIOTT INC
387 Pitt Rd (28115-6777)
PHONE..............................704 663-8226

Brenda Elliott, *Pr*
▲ **EMP:** 4 **EST:** 1990
SQ FT: 12,000
SALES (est): 421.05K **Privately Held**
Web: www.hmelliottcoatings.com
SIC: 3479 Coating of metals and formed
products

(G-8679)
H&S AUTOSHOT LLC
302 Rolling Hill Rd (28117-6846)
PHONE................................847 662-8500
EMP: 20 **EST:** 2016
SALES (est): 2.43MM **Privately Held**
Web: www.hsautoshot.com
SIC: 3444 Studs and joists, sheet metal

(G-8680)
HEALTH SUPPLY US LLC
205 Raceway Dr Ste 3 (28117-6524)
PHONE................................888 408-1694
Christopher Garcia, *Owner*
Christopher Garcia, *CEO*
EMP: 12 **EST:** 2020
SALES (est): 4.61MM **Privately Held**
Web: www.healthsupplyus.com
SIC: 5047 3841 3842 2389 Medical
equipment and supplies; Surgical and
medical instruments; Personal safety
equipment; Hospital gowns

(G-8681)
HENKEL US OPERATIONS CORP
150 Fairview Rd Ste 225 (28117-9515)
PHONE................................704 799-0385
Kevin Kruger, *Mgr*
EMP: 5
SALES (corp-wide): 22.83B **Privately Held**
Web: www.henkel.com
SIC: 2891 Adhesives
HQ: Henkel Us Operations Corporation
1 Henkel Way
Rocky Hill CT 06067
860 571-5100

(G-8682)
HI & DRI BOAT LIFT SYSTEMS INC
1277 River Hwy (28117-9088)
P.O. Box 3744 (28117-3744)
PHONE................................704 663-5438
John Louttit, *Pr*
EMP: 4 **EST:** 1988
SALES (est): 317.67K **Privately Held**
Web:
hi-dri-boat-lift-systems.business.site
SIC: 3536 Boat lifts

(G-8683)
HI-TECH SCREENS INC
188 Blossom Ridge Dr (28117-5834)
PHONE................................828 452-5151
Chris Hartley, *Pr*
Wallace Foutch Ii, *CEO*
EMP: 4 **EST:** 2000
SALES (est): 345.24K **Privately Held**
Web: www.hitechscreens.com
SIC: 2396 Screen printing on fabric articles

(G-8684)
HIGHLINE PERFORMANCE GROUP
Also Called: Fitzbradshaw Racing
114 Meadow Hill Cir (28117-8089)
PHONE................................704 799-3500
Armando Fitz, *Pr*
EMP: 50 **EST:** 2000
SQ FT: 20,000
SALES (est): 803.09K **Privately Held**
Web: www.fitzbradshawracing.com
SIC: 3711 Automobile assembly, including
specialty automobiles

(G-8685)
HOGANS RACING MANIFOLDS INC
115 Thunder Rd (28115-6000)
PHONE................................704 799-3424
Tim M Hogan, *Pr*
EMP: 4 **EST:** 2013
SALES (est): 1.51MM **Privately Held**
Web: www.hogansracingmanifolds.com
SIC: 3714 Manifolds, motor vehicle

(G-8686)
HOLZ-HER US INC (DH)
124 Crosslake Park Dr (28117-8016)
P.O. Box 3158 (28117-3158)
PHONE................................704 587-3400
Wulf W Reich, *Ch*
Stephen Carey, *
Richard Hannigan, *
◆ **EMP:** 17 **EST:** 1984
SQ FT: 83,000
SALES (est): 4.45MM **Privately Held**
Web: www.holzherusa.com
SIC: 3553 Furniture makers machinery,
woodworking
HQ: Weinig Holz-Her Usa, Inc.
124 Crosslake Park Dr
Mooresville NC 28117
704 799-0100

(G-8687)
HOTCHKIS BRYDE INCORPORATED
118 Infield Ct Ste A (28117-8212)
PHONE................................704 660-3060
Kevin Bryde, *Prin*
EMP: 4 **EST:** 2013
SALES (est): 845.84K **Privately Held**
Web: www.hotchkis.net
SIC: 3714 Motor vehicle parts and
accessories

(G-8688)
HOTCHKIS PERFORMANCE MFG INC
118 Infield Ct Ste A (28117-8212)
PHONE................................704 660-3060
John Hotchkis, *Pr*
EMP: 8 **EST:** 2013
SALES (est): 2.61MM **Privately Held**
Web: www.hotchkis.net
SIC: 3446 Acoustical suspension systems,
metal

(G-8689)
HYDROHOIST OF NORTH CAROLINA
Also Called: Hydrohoist of The Carolinas
1258 River Hwy (28117-9088)
PHONE................................704 799-1910
Mike Lineberger, *Owner*
EMP: 5 **EST:** 2004
SQ FT: 600
SALES (est): 376.58K **Privately Held**
Web: www.hydrohoistofthecarolinas.com
SIC: 3536 Boat lifts

(G-8690)
ICKLER MANUFACTURING LLC
229 Pitt Rd (28115-6783)
PHONE................................704 658-1195
Brian Ickler, *Managing Member*
EMP: 5 **EST:** 2014
SQ FT: 13,000
SALES (est): 3.74MM **Privately Held**
Web: www.icklermfg.com
SIC: 3841 3812 Diagnostic apparatus,
medical; Search and navigation equipment

(G-8691)
ILMOR MARINE LLC
186 Penske Way (28115-8094)
PHONE................................704 360-1901
Paul Ray, *Pr*

Ronald Brown, *
Julie Bernard, *
John Fraas, *
Edwin Baumgartner, *
▲ **EMP:** 25 **EST:** 2008
SQ FT: 50,000
SALES (est): 8.85MM **Privately Held**
Web: www.ilmor.com
SIC: 3519 Marine engines
PA: Ilmor Engineering Inc.
43939 Plymouth Oaks Blvd
Plymouth MI 48170

(G-8692)
INFRASTRCTURE SLTONS GROUP INC
505 E Plaza Dr (28115-8071)
PHONE................................704 833-8048
Eric Rocchiccioli, *Pr*
Ben Jones, *VP*
EMP: 19 **EST:** 1999
SALES (est): 1.09MM **Privately Held**
SIC: 3531 Construction machinery

(G-8693)
INNOVATIVE TECHNOLOGY MFG LLC
136 Lugnut Ln Ste C (28117-9398)
PHONE................................980 248-3731
Matthew Blankenship, *Prin*
EMP: 6 **EST:** 2019
SALES (est): 2.53MM **Privately Held**
SIC: 3999 Manufacturing industries, nec

(G-8694)
INTERNTNAL AGRCLTURE GROUP LLC
106 Langtree Village Dr Ste 301
(28117-7593)
PHONE................................908 323-3246
Maurice Moragne, *Managing Member*
David Skea, *Managing Member*
Humberto Wedderburn, *Managing Member*
Julio Vasquez, *Managing Member*
EMP: 10 **EST:** 2017
SALES (est): 169.54K **Privately Held**
Web: www.iagnubana.com
SIC: 2833 5149 5122 2034 Vitamins, natural
or synthetic: bulk, uncompounded; Flour;
Vitamins and minerals; Fruit flour, meal,
and powder

(G-8695)
IOMAX USA LLC ✪
133 River Park Rd (28117-8929)
PHONE................................704 662-1840
Kelly C Howard, *CEO*
Matthew G Kiser, *CFO*
James H Flatley Iv, *COO*
Nicholas J Bishop, *VP Engg*
Kevin A Oakes, *Senior Program Manager*
EMP: 27 **EST:** 2024
SALES (est): 3.25MM **Privately Held**
SIC: 3721 8711 Aircraft; Engineering services

(G-8696)
IQMETRIX USA INC
184 Longboat Rd (28117-8202)
PHONE................................704 987-9903
Erick Stachowski, *Pr*
EMP: 65 **EST:** 2010
SALES (est): 6.7MM
SALES (corp-wide): 17.2MM **Privately Held**
Web: www.iqmetrix.com
SIC: 7372 Business oriented computer
software
PA: Iqmetrix Software Development Corp
1333 Johnston St Unit 200
Vancouver BC V6H 3
866 476-3874

(G-8697)
ISLAND MACHINING LLC
Also Called: Machine Shop
265 Pitt Rd (28115-6783)
PHONE................................704 278-3553
Melissa Fleming, *Owner*
Melissa Fleming, *Prin*
EMP: 4 **EST:** 2007
SALES (est): 984.35K **Privately Held**
Web: www.islandmachiningllc.com
SIC: 3599 Machine shop, jobbing and repair

(G-8698)
JASPER ENGINE EXCHANGE INC
Also Called: Jasper Motor Sports
200 Penske Way (28115-8022)
PHONE................................704 664-2300
Mark Harraah, *Brnch Mgr*
EMP: 40
SALES (corp-wide): 418.4MM **Privately
Held**
Web: www.jasperengines.com
SIC: 3714 3711 Rebuilding engines and
transmissions, factory basis; Motor vehicles
and car bodies
PA: Jasper Engine Exchange, Inc.
815 Wernsing Rd
Jasper IN 47546
812 482-1041

(G-8699)
JRI DEVELOPMENT GROUP LLC
136 Knob Hill Rd (28117-6847)
PHONE................................704 660-8346
Dan Kungl, *Managing Member*
▲ **EMP:** 12 **EST:** 2007
SQ FT: 2,500
SALES (est): 857.21K **Privately Held**
Web: www.jrishocks.com
SIC: 3714 Motor vehicle parts and
accessories

(G-8700)
JRI SHOCKS LLC
116 Infield Ct (28117-8026)
PHONE................................704 660-8346
Det Cullum, *Prin*
EMP: 19 **EST:** 2018
SALES (est): 5.42MM **Privately Held**
Web: www.jrishocks.com
SIC: 3714 Motor vehicle parts and
accessories

(G-8701)
JUSTICE BEARING LLC
Also Called: Justice Bearings
243 Overhill Dr Ste D (28117-7019)
PHONE................................800 355-2500
Shawn Barnett Sabatino, *CEO*
John E Miller Iii, *Pr*
EMP: 4 **EST:** 2015
SALES (est): 3.69MM **Privately Held**
Web: www.justicebearing.com
SIC: 3562 5085 7389 Ball and roller bearings
; Industrial supplies; Business Activities at
Non-Commercial Site

(G-8702)
KEMMLER PRODUCTS INC
250 Canvasback Rd (28117-8109)
PHONE................................704 663-5678
Bruce Kemmler, *Pr*
Tom Pearce, *Ex VP*
EMP: 5 **EST:** 2001
SALES (est): 258.04K **Privately Held**
Web: www.shocktec.com
SIC: 2299 Padding and wadding, textile

(G-8703)
KENNYS COMPONENTS INC
112 Loma Hill Dr Ste 101 (28117-8210)
P.O. Box 330 (28166-0330)
PHONE..................................704 662-0777
Kenny Koldsbaek, *Pr*
EMP: 10 **EST:** 2001
SQ FT: 3,750
SALES (est): 1.64MM **Privately Held**
Web: www.kennyscomponents.com
SIC: 3442 3089 3599 Moldings and trim,
except automobile: metal; Injection molded
finished plastics products, nec; Machine
shop, jobbing and repair

(G-8704)
KGT ENTERPRISES INC
Also Called: Dse
185 Mckenzie Rd (28115)
PHONE..................................704 662-3272
Kyle G Tucker, *Pr*
Stacy Tucker, *
EMP: 49 **EST:** 2006
SQ FT: 30,000
SALES (est): 9.3MM **Privately Held**
Web: www.detroitspeed.com
SIC: 3714 5531 Motor vehicle parts and
accessories; Automotive parts
PA: Qa1 Precision Products, Inc.
9574 217th St W
Lakeville MN 55044

(G-8705)
KIDSVIDZ PRODUCTIONS
694 Big Indian Loop (28117-9047)
PHONE..................................704 663-4487
EMP: 4 **EST:** 2016
SALES (est): 107.32K **Privately Held**
Web: www.jcrproductions.com
SIC: 3674 Semiconductors and related
devices

(G-8706)
L B PLASTICS LLC
482 E Plaza Dr (28115-8021)
P.O. Box 907 (28115-0907)
PHONE..................................704 663-1543
Matt Cobb, *Pr*
▲ **EMP:** 60 **EST:** 1977
SQ FT: 279,000
SALES (est): 11.03MM
SALES (corp-wide): 1.44B **Publicly Held**
Web: www.lbplastics.com
SIC: 3089 2522 3069 Plastics hardware and
building products; Office cabinets and filing
drawers, except wood; Mats or matting,
rubber, nec
PA: The Azek Company Inc
1330 W Fulton St Ste 350
Chicago IL 60607
877 275-2935

(G-8707)
L G SOURCING INC (HQ)
Also Called: Lowes Global Sourcing
1000 Lowes Blvd (28117-8520)
P.O. Box 1111 (28656)
PHONE..................................704 758-1000
Robert F Posthauer, *Pr*
David R Green, *VP*
Amber Lason, *Sec*
Benjamin S Adams Junior, *Treas*
◆ **EMP:** 34 **EST:** 1997
SALES (est): 34.89MM
SALES (corp-wide): 86.38B **Publicly Held**
Web: www.loweslink.com
SIC: 5031 2499 5023 Building materials,
exterior; Picture and mirror frames, wood;
Decorative home furnishings and supplies
PA: Lowe's Companies, Inc.
1000 Lowes Blvd

Mooresville NC 28117
704 758-1000

(G-8708)
LASER DYNAMICS INC
104 Performance Rd (28115-9590)
PHONE..................................704 658-9769
Patrick Folmar, *Owner*
EMP: 7 **EST:** 2004
SALES (est): 1.6MM **Privately Held**
Web: www.laserdynamicsinc.com
SIC: 3599 Machine shop, jobbing and repair

(G-8709)
LELANTOS GROUP INC
132 Joe Knox Ave Ste 100 (28117-9203)
PHONE..................................704 780-4127
Michael Strohl, *CEO*
Derek Strohl, *Sr VP*
John Barb, *COO*
Monique Nicolai, *Admn*
EMP: 95 **EST:** 2013
SALES (est): 2.32MM **Privately Held**
Web: www.lelantosgroup.com
SIC: 7382 3312 2311 3711 Protective
devices, security; Armor plate; Military
uniforms, men's and youths': purchased
materials; Universal carriers, military,
assembly of

(G-8710)
LI-ION MOTORS CORP
158 Rolling Hill Rd (28117-8804)
PHONE..................................704 662-0827
Stacey Fling, *Pr*
Benjamin Roseberry, *
EMP: 6 **EST:** 2006
SQ FT: 40,000
SALES (est): 310.36K **Privately Held**
SIC: 3621 Motors and generators

(G-8711)
LIBURDI DIMETRICS CORPORATION
Also Called: Liburdi
2599 Charlotte Hwy (28117-9463)
PHONE..................................704 230-2510
Joe Liburdi, *Pr*
▲ **EMP:** 35 **EST:** 1997
SQ FT: 15,000
SALES (est): 9.86MM
SALES (corp-wide): 25.02MM **Privately
Held**
Web: www.liburdigapco.com
SIC: 3612 3548 Transformers, except electric
; Welding and cutting apparatus and
accessories, nec
PA: Liburdi Engineering Limited
400 Hwy 6 N
Dundas ON L9H 7
905 689-0734

(G-8712)
LIBURDI TURBINE SERVICES LLC
2599 Charlotte Hwy (28117-9463)
PHONE..................................704 230-2510
Joe Liburdi, *Prin*
▲ **EMP:** 15 **EST:** 2008
SALES (est): 5.05MM **Privately Held**
Web: www.liburditurbine.com
SIC: 3823 Turbine flow meters, industrial
process type

(G-8713)
LITEX INDUSTRIES INC
120 N Commercial Dr (28115-7801)
PHONE..................................704 799-3758
Greg Tronti, *VP*
EMP: 5 **EST:** 2001
SALES (est): 106.68K **Privately Held**
SIC: 2844 Cosmetic preparations

(G-8714)
LOGONATION INC
128 Overhill Dr Ste 102 (28117-8025)
P.O. Box 3847 (28117-3847)
PHONE..................................704 799-0612
Denny Watson, *Pr*
Jennifer Watson, *
EMP: 26 **EST:** 1998
SQ FT: 4,000
SALES (est): 947.5K **Privately Held**
Web: www.logonation.com
SIC: 2759 Screen printing

(G-8715)
M & A EQUIPMENT INC (PA)
Also Called: Quantum Machinery Group
156 Exmore Rd Ste 100 (28117)
PHONE..................................704 703-9400
Michael Bucciero, *Pr*
Alberto Solano, *VP*
▲ **EMP:** 4 **EST:** 2002
SALES (est): 724.39K
SALES (corp-wide): 724.39K **Privately
Held**
Web: www.quantummachinerygroup.com
SIC: 3542 Presses: hydraulic and
pneumatic, mechanical and manual

(G-8716)
M 5 SCENTIFIC GLASSBLOWING INC
Also Called: Edge Welding Supply
706c Performance Rd (28115-9596)
PHONE..................................704 663-0101
Eric Mueller, *Pr*
Stacia Mueller, *VP*
EMP: 5 **EST:** 2012
SQ FT: 2,500
SALES (est): 870.39K **Privately Held**
Web: www.edgeweldingsupply.com
SIC: 3231 3229 Scientific and technical
glassware: from purchased glass; Scientific
glassware

(G-8717)
M I CONNECTION
435 S Broad St (28115-3208)
P.O. Box 90 (28115-0090)
PHONE..................................704 662-3255
John N Venzon, *Ch*
EMP: 17 **EST:** 2009
SALES (est): 490.01K **Privately Held**
Web: www.ourtds.com
SIC: 7389 7372 4841 4813 Telephone
services; Prepackaged software; Cable and
other pay television services; Online
service providers

(G-8718)
**MAMMOTH MACHINE AND DESIGN
LLC**
197 Pitt Rd (28115-6782)
PHONE..................................704 727-3330
Ali Bahar, *CEO*
Eric Winkler, *Genl Mgr*
EMP: 7 **EST:** 2016
SALES (est): 2.67MM **Privately Held**
Web: www.mammothmachine.com
SIC: 3599 3999 Machine shop, jobbing and
repair; Barber and beauty shop equipment

(G-8719)
MASCO CORPORATION
Also Called: Masco
344 E Plaza Dr (28115-8041)
PHONE..................................704 658-9646
EMP: 5
SALES (corp-wide): 7.83B **Publicly Held**
Web: www.masco.com
SIC: 3432 Faucets and spigots, metal and
plastic
PA: Masco Corporation

17450 College Pkwy
Livonia MI 48152
313 274-7400

(G-8720)
**MATT BIENEMAN ENTERPRISES
LLC**
1375 Deal Rd (28115-6721)
PHONE..................................704 856-0200
EMP: 4 **EST:** 2002
SQ FT: 3,000
SALES (est): 669.65K **Privately Held**
Web: www.mbellc.com
SIC: 3469 Machine parts, stamped or
pressed metal

(G-8721)
MAXAM NORTH AMERICA INC (PA)
106 Langtree Village Dr Ste 301 (28117)
P.O. Box 140906 (75014)
PHONE..................................214 736-8100
German Morales, *CEO*
James Bryan, *CAO*
Rocio Summers, *CFO*
Stanton Johnso, *Pr*
John Watson, *VP*
◆ **EMP:** 17 **EST:** 2000
SQ FT: 3,000
SALES (est): 35.93MM
SALES (corp-wide): 35.93MM **Privately
Held**
SIC: 2892 5169 Explosives; Explosives

(G-8722)
MEMORIES OF ORANGEBURG INC
Also Called: Memories
126 Foxfield Park Dr (28115-7885)
PHONE..................................803 533-0035
Jay C Pearson, *Pr*
James Avinger, *Sec*
Robert F Fulmur, *VP*
EMP: 8 **EST:** 1972
SQ FT: 3,800
SALES (est): 117.16K **Privately Held**
SIC: 2759 5199 5099 Screen printing;
Advertising specialties; Novelties, durable

(G-8723)
METAL STRUCTURES PLUS LLC
561 Oak Tree Rd (28117-5919)
PHONE..................................704 896-7155
EMP: 4 **EST:** 2013
SALES (est): 732.83K **Privately Held**
SIC: 3399 3444 Primary metal products;
Sheet metalwork

(G-8724)
MITSUBISHI MATERIALS USA CORP
105 Corporate Center Dr Ste A
(28117-0078)
PHONE..................................980 312-3100
EMP: 9 **EST:** 2019
SALES (est): 965.42K **Privately Held**
Web: www.mmc-carbide.com
SIC: 3545 Angle rings

(G-8725)
**MOORESVILLE ICE CREAM
COMPANY LLC**
Also Called: Front Porch Ice Cream
172 N Brd St (28115)
P.O. Box 118 (28115-0118)
PHONE..................................704 664-5456
▲ **EMP:** 20 **EST:** 2009
SALES (est): 2.34MM **Privately Held**
Web: www.visitmooresville.com
SIC: 2024 5451 Ice cream and ice milk; Ice
cream (packaged)

(G-8726)
MOORESVILLE NC
174 Mandarin Dr (28117-8156)
PHONE.............................704 909-6459
EMP: 5 **EST:** 2018
SALES (est): 257.2K **Privately Held**
Web: www.mooresvillenc.org
SIC: 2711 Newspapers, publishing and printing

(G-8727)
MOORESVLLE PUB WRKS SNTTION DE
2523 Charlotte Hwy (28117-9463)
P.O. Box 878 (28115-0878)
PHONE.............................704 664-4278
Ryan Rafe, *Dir*
John Yvars Sanitation, *Superintnt*
EMP: 4 **EST:** 2002
SQ FT: 1,210
SALES (est): 257.04K **Privately Held**
Web: www.mooresvillenc.gov
SIC: 2842 Sanitation preparations

(G-8728)
MOTORING INC
139 Golden Pond Ln (28117-8875)
PHONE.............................704 809-1265
Jayme H Freitas, *Pr*
EMP: 7 **EST:** 2016
SALES (est): 173.62K **Privately Held**
SIC: 3714 Motor vehicle parts and accessories

(G-8729)
MOULDING SOURCE INCORPORATED
184 Azalea Rd (28115-7252)
PHONE.............................704 658-1111
Rick Dinardo, *Pr*
EMP: 4 **EST:** 1996
SALES (est): 236.05K **Privately Held**
Web: www.themouldingsource.com
SIC: 2431 5031 Moldings, wood: unfinished and prefinished; Lumber, plywood, and millwork

(G-8730)
MSI DEFENSE SOLUTIONS LLC
Also Called: MSI
136 Knob Hill Rd (28117-6847)
P.O. Box 5506 (28117-0506)
PHONE.............................704 660-8348
David Holden, *Pr*
David J Holden, *
Eric Dana, *
EMP: 64 **EST:** 2007
SQ FT: 69,000
SALES (est): 30.42MM **Privately Held**
Web: www.msidefense.com
SIC: 8711 3714 Engineering services; Motor vehicle parts and accessories

(G-8731)
NATIONAL PRINT SERVICES INC
678 Big Indian Loop (28117-9047)
P.O. Box 2055 (28031-2055)
PHONE.............................704 892-9209
Daniel Preiss, *Prin*
▲ **EMP:** 6 **EST:** 2009
SALES (est): 505.96K **Privately Held**
SIC: 2752 Color lithography

(G-8732)
NC SOFTBALL SALES
117 E Statesville Ave (28115-2321)
PHONE.............................704 663-2134
Matt Haines, *Owner*
EMP: 4 **EST:** 2007
SALES (est): 160.23K **Privately Held**

Web: www.ncsoftballsales.com
SIC: 3949 Sporting and athletic goods, nec

(G-8733)
NGK CERAMICS USA INC (HQ)
119 Mazeppa Rd (28115-7927)
PHONE.............................704 664-7000
◆ **EMP:** 6 **EST:** 1988
SALES (est): 200MM **Privately Held**
Web: www.ngkceramics.com
SIC: 3559 Automotive related machinery
PA: Ngk Insulators, Ltd.
2-56, Sudacho, Mizuho-Ku
Nagoya AIC 467-0

(G-8734)
NIAGARA BOTTLING LLC
178 Mooresville Blvd (28115-7433)
PHONE.............................909 815-6310
EMP: 6
SALES (corp-wide): 45.74MM **Privately Held**
Web: www.niagarawater.com
SIC: 2086 Water, natural: packaged in cans, bottles, etc.
PA: Niagara Bottling, Llc
1440 Bridgegate Dr
Diamond Bar CA 91765
909 230-5000

(G-8735)
NISSENS COOLING SOLUTIONS INC
110 Oakpark Dr Ste 105 (28115-0137)
PHONE.............................704 696-8575
Alan Steighner, *Pr*
Hans Erik Obling, *Pr*
Christian Gunnar Retboell, *Treas*
Edward J Wright Junior, *Sec*
EMP: 13 **EST:** 2013
SALES (est): 221.02K
SALES (corp-wide): 2.41MM **Privately Held**
SIC: 3585 Parts for heating, cooling, and refrigerating equipment
HQ: Kk Wind Solutions Holding A/S
Bogildvej 3
Ikast 7430

(G-8736)
NITRO MANUFACTURING INC
510 Performance Rd (28115-9594)
PHONE.............................704 663-3155
Danny Timmons, *Pr*
Valerie Timmons, *Sec*
EMP: 10 **EST:** 1998
SQ FT: 12,000
SALES (est): 2.28MM **Privately Held**
Web: www.nitromfg.com
SIC: 3444 Sheet metalwork

(G-8737)
NORTHEAST TEXTILES
105 Oakpark Dr Ste A (28115-8029)
P.O. Box 2147 (29342-2147)
PHONE.............................704 799-2235
Denise Evans, *Owner*
EMP: 4 **EST:** 2015
SALES (est): 103.75K **Privately Held**
SIC: 2299 Textile goods, nec

(G-8738)
OLEKSYNPRANNYK LLC
Also Called: Olpr.leather goods Co.
149 Cayuga Dr Ste A3 (28117-8343)
PHONE.............................704 450-0182
Pavlo Prannyk, *CEO*
EMP: 12 **EST:** 2015
SALES (est): 266.17K **Privately Held**
Web: www.olpr.com

SIC: 3199 2399 5947 3999 Leather goods, nec; Fabricated textile products, nec; Gift shop; Manufacturing industries, nec

(G-8739)
ONE SOURCE SEC & SOUND INC
122 Summerville Dr Ste 101 (28115-8037)
PHONE.............................281 850-9487
Jason Smith, *Pr*
EMP: 7
SALES (corp-wide): 4.64MM **Privately Held**
Web: www.os2s.com
SIC: 7382 3578 7539 Security systems services; Calculating and accounting equipment; Automotive repair shops, nec
PA: One Source Security & Sound, Inc.
2925 Fm 1960 Rd E
Humble TX 77338
888 848-6727

(G-8740)
P4RTS LLC
Also Called: A V E Parts & Accesories
106 Langtree Village Dr Ste 301 (28117-7594)
PHONE.............................561 717-7580
Steve Sparks, *Managing Member*
EMP: 44 **EST:** 2014
SALES (est): 17MM **Privately Held**
Web: www.autopartswholesalellc.com
SIC: 3714 Motor vehicle parts and accessories

(G-8741)
PACKAGING CORPORATION AMERICA
Also Called: Pca/Regional Design Center
307 Oates Rd Ste B (28117-6985)
PHONE.............................704 664-5010
Carmine Buclo, *Brnch Mgr*
EMP: 9
SALES (corp-wide): 7.73B **Publicly Held**
Web: www.packagingcorp.com
SIC: 2653 5113 Boxes, corrugated: made from purchased materials; Corrugated and solid fiber boxes
PA: Packaging Corporation Of America
1 N Field Ct
Lake Forest IL 60045
847 482-3000

(G-8742)
PARKER-HANNIFIN CORPORATION
Also Called: Parker Service Center
2559 Charlotte Hwy (28117-9463)
PHONE.............................704 664-1922
Tom Boyer, *Brnch Mgr*
EMP: 25
SQ FT: 48,602
SALES (corp-wide): 19.93B **Publicly Held**
Web: www.parker.com
SIC: 3429 5012 Clamps and couplings, hose ; Automobiles and other motor vehicles
PA: Parker-Hannifin Corporation
6035 Parkland Blvd
Cleveland OH 44124
216 896-3000

(G-8743)
PATRIOT CLEAN FUEL LLC
214 Mazeppa Rd (28115-7928)
PHONE.............................704 896-3600
EMP: 14 **EST:** 2006
SALES (est): 5MM **Privately Held**
Web: www.patriotcleanfuel.com
SIC: 2899 Fuel tank or engine cleaning chemicals

(G-8744)
PEGGS RECREATION INC
408 N Main St (28115-2456)
P.O. Box 917 (28115-0917)
PHONE.............................704 660-0007
Eric Lowder, *Prin*
EMP: 4 **EST:** 2011
SALES (est): 493.96K **Privately Held**
Web: www.peggsrecreation.com
SIC: 3949 Playground equipment

(G-8745)
PENROCK LLC
Also Called: Leviosa Motor Shades
251 Knoxview Ln (28117-9689)
PHONE.............................704 800-6722
David Biedermann, *Dir*
Caroline Biedermann, *Dir*
EMP: 27 **EST:** 2016
SQ FT: 3,000
SALES (est): 788.9K **Privately Held**
Web: www.leviosashades.com
SIC: 2591 Window shades

(G-8746)
PENSKE RACING SOUTH INC (DH)
Also Called: Team Penske
200 Penske Way (28115-8022)
P.O. Box 500 (28115)
PHONE.............................704 664-2300
Roger S Penske, *Ch Bd*
Timothy J Cindric, *
David N Hoffert, *
Michael Nelson Junior, *VP*
Lawrence N Bluth, *
▲ **EMP:** 200 **EST:** 1990
SQ FT: 427,000
SALES (est): 23.16MM
SALES (corp-wide): 32.13B **Publicly Held**
Web: www.teampenske.com
SIC: 3711 8711 8731 7948 Motor vehicles and car bodies; Engineering services; Commercial physical research; Motor vehicle racing and drivers
HQ: Penske Company Llc
2555 Telegraph Rd
Bloomfield Hills MI 48302
248 648-2000

(G-8747)
PEP FILTERS INC
Also Called: Pep Filters
120 Talbert Rd Ste J (28117-7119)
PHONE.............................704 662-3133
Michael Poth, *Pr*
▲ **EMP:** 22 **EST:** 1975
SQ FT: 20,000
SALES (est): 5.12MM **Privately Held**
Web: www.pepfilters.com
SIC: 3589 Water treatment equipment, industrial

(G-8748)
PERFORMANCE PARTS INTL LLC
Also Called: Ppi
104 Blue Ridge Trl (28117-8477)
PHONE.............................704 660-1084
John Vitale, *Pr*
EMP: 11 **EST:** 2020
SALES (est): 1.3MM **Privately Held**
Web: www.thepropad.com
SIC: 3751 7389 Motorcycles and related parts; Business Activities at Non-Commercial Site

(G-8749)
PERFORMANCE RACING WHSE INC
Also Called: Performance Center
145 Blossom Ridge Dr (28117-5834)
PHONE.............................704 838-1400
Roger Johnson Iii, *Pr*

GEOGRAPHIC

Kim Kurzejewski, *VP*
EMP: 6 **EST:** 2010
SALES (est): 251.76K **Privately Held**
Web: www.performcenter.com
SIC: 3711 Cars, electric, assembly of

(G-8750)
POLYTEC INC (PA)
191 Barley Park Ln (28115-7912)
P.O. Box 659 (28115-0659)
PHONE..............................704 277-3960
Jack Harmon, *Pr*
▲ **EMP:** 23 **EST:** 1994
SQ FT: 33,000
SALES (est): 25.74MM **Privately Held**
Web: www.polytecinc.net
SIC: 5169 2899 Industrial chemicals;
Chemical preparations, nec

(G-8751)
PPG ARCHITECTURAL FINISHES INC
Also Called: Glidden Professional Paint Ctr
142 S Cardigan Way (28117-8536)
PHONE..............................704 658-9250
Charles Bunch, *Brnch Mgr*
EMP: 6
SALES (corp-wide): 17.65B **Publicly Held**
Web: www.ppgpmc.com
SIC: 2851 Paints and allied products
HQ: Ppg Architectural Finishes, Inc.
1 Ppg Pl
Pittsburgh PA 15272
412 434-3131

(G-8752)
PPG INDUSTRIES INC
128 Overhill Dr Ste 104 (28117-8025)
PHONE..............................704 658-9250
Kevin Braun, *Mgr*
EMP: 7
SALES (corp-wide): 17.65B **Publicly Held**
Web: www.ppg.com
SIC: 2851 Paints and allied products
PA: Ppg Industries, Inc.
1 Ppg Pl
Pittsburgh PA 15272
412 434-3131

(G-8753)
PRATT & WHITNEY ENG SVCS INC
Also Called: Pratt & Whitney
169 Stumpy Creek Rd (28117-8492)
PHONE..............................704 660-9999
Greg Miller, *Mgr*
EMP: 325
SALES (corp-wide): 80.74B **Publicly Held**
Web: www.prattwhitney.com
SIC: 3724 Aircraft engines and engine parts
HQ: Pratt & Whitney Engine Services, Inc.
1525 Midway Park Rd
Bridgeport WV 26330
304 842-5421

(G-8754)
PRECISION METAL FINISHING INC
962 N Main St (28115-2356)
PHONE..............................704 799-0250
Eric Wilkinson, *Owner*
EMP: 5 **EST:** 2007
SALES (est): 323.39K **Privately Held**
SIC: 3471 Finishing, metals or formed
products

(G-8755)
PRO-MOTOR ENGINES INC
Also Called: PME
102 S Iredell Industrial Park Rd
(28115-7128)
PHONE..............................704 664-6800
Peter F Guild, *Pr*
Ann Guild, *Sec*

EMP: 7 **EST:** 1992
SQ FT: 15,000
SALES (est): 1.83MM **Privately Held**
Web: www.pmeengines.com
SIC: 5013 8732 7699 7549 Automotive
supplies and parts; Research services,
except laboratory; Marine engine repair;
High performance auto repair and service

(G-8756)
PRO-SYSTEM INC
121 Oakpark Dr (28115-7811)
P.O. Box 685 (28115-0685)
PHONE..............................704 799-8100
Ashley Page, *Pr*
Chris Norburn, *VP*
Helen Miller, *Sec*
EMP: 10 **EST:** 1994
SQ FT: 8,400
SALES (est): 1.03MM **Privately Held**
Web: www.prosystembrakes.com
SIC: 2396 5012 Automotive and apparel
trimmings; Automobiles and other motor
vehicles

(G-8757)
QUEEN CITY PASTRY LLC
137 Speedway Ln (28117-6879)
PHONE..............................704 660-5706
EMP: 45 **EST:** 1996
SQ FT: 6,500
SALES (est): 9.91MM **Privately Held**
Web: www.queencitypastry.com
SIC: 2051 5143 Bakery: wholesale or
wholesale/retail combined; Frozen dairy
desserts

(G-8758)
REVOLUTION OIL INC
291 Cayuga Dr (28117-8179)
PHONE..............................704 577-2546
Edward Conz, *Prin*
EMP: 4 **EST:** 2011
SALES (est): 144.97K **Privately Held**
SIC: 2992 Lubricating oils and greases

(G-8759)
RILEY TECHNOLOGIES LLC
170 Overhill Dr (28117-8006)
P.O. Box 4447 (28117)
PHONE..............................704 663-6319
Bob Riley, *Pr*
Bill Riley, *VP*
▲ **EMP:** 35 **EST:** 1990
SQ FT: 57,000
SALES (est): 8.15MM **Privately Held**
Web: www.rileytech.com
SIC: 3711 7389 Automobile assembly,
including specialty automobiles; Design
services

(G-8760)
RITCHIE FOAM COMPANY INC
214 E Waterlynn Rd (28117-8075)
PHONE..............................704 663-2533
Ted W Ritchie, *Pr*
Wayne Ritchie, *VP*
EMP: 4 **EST:** 1980
SALES (est): 542.19K **Privately Held**
Web: www.ritchiefoam.com
SIC: 3086 Plastics foam products

(G-8761)
ROOSTERFISH MEDIA LLC
Also Called: Real Producers
129 Ashford Hollow Ln (28115-7695)
PHONE..............................980 722-7454
Tom Bramhall, *Owner*
EMP: 4 **EST:** 2018
SALES (est): 216.67K **Privately Held**
Web: www.roosterfish.media

SIC: 2741 Miscellaneous publishing

(G-8762)
ROUSH & YATES RACING ENGS LLC
Also Called: Roush Yates Mfg Solutions
112 Byers Creek Rd (28117-4376)
PHONE..............................704 799-6216
EMP: 55
SALES (corp-wide): 43.73MM **Privately
Held**
Web: www.roushyates.com
SIC: 3462 Automotive forgings, ferrous:
crankshaft, engine, axle, etc.
PA: Roush & Yates Racing Engines Llc
297 Rolling Hill Rd
Mooresville NC 28117
704 799-6216

(G-8763)
ROUSH & YATES RACING ENGS LLC
(PA)
297 Rolling Hill Rd (28117)
P.O. Box 3788 (28117)
PHONE..............................704 799-6216
Jack Roush, *
Robert Yates, *
▲ **EMP:** 110 **EST:** 2003
SQ FT: 12,000
SALES (est): 43.73MM
SALES (corp-wide): 43.73MM **Privately
Held**
Web: www.roushyates.com
SIC: 3462 Automotive forgings, ferrous:
crankshaft, engine, axle, etc.

(G-8764)
ROWDY MANUFACTURING LLC
Also Called: Rowdy Manufacturing
161 Byers Creek Rd (28117-4440)
PHONE..............................704 662-0000
Kyle Busch, *Managing Member*
EMP: 4 **EST:** 2010
SALES (est): 1.11MM **Privately Held**
Web: www.rowdymfg.com
SIC: 3711 3599 Automobile assembly,
including specialty automobiles; Machine
and other job shop work

(G-8765)
RUST-OLEUM CORPORATION
Also Called: Rust-Oleum
157 Cedar Pointe Dr Ste A (28117-6975)
PHONE..............................704 662-7730
Norm Bowman, *Brnch Mgr*
EMP: 4
SALES (corp-wide): 7.34B **Publicly Held**
Web: www.rustoleum.com
SIC: 2851 Paints and allied products
HQ: Rust-Oleum Corporation
11 Hawthorn Pkwy
Vernon Hills IL 60061
847 367-7700

(G-8766)
SAUDER WOODWORKING CO
119 Magnolia Park Dr (28117-8928)
PHONE..............................704 799-6782
EMP: 6 **EST:** 2019
SALES (est): 54.13K **Privately Held**
Web: www.sauder.com
SIC: 2431 Millwork

(G-8767)
SCOTTS COMPANY LLC
319 Oates Rd Ste A (28117-7041)
PHONE..............................704 663-6088
Pete Carpentier, *Mgr*
EMP: 9
SALES (corp-wide): 3.55B **Publicly Held**
Web: www.scotts.com

SIC: 2873 2874 2879 Fertilizers: natural
(organic), except compost; Phosphates;
Fungicides, herbicides
HQ: The Scotts Company Llc
14111 Scottslawn Rd
Marysville OH 43040
937 644-0011

(G-8768)
SHEETS LAUNDRY CLUB INC
211 Mckenzie Rd (28115-7975)
PHONE..............................704 662-8696
Chris Videau, *Prin*
EMP: 8 **EST:** 2019
SALES (est): 2.37MM **Privately Held**
Web: www.sheetslaundryclub.com
SIC: 2841 Soap and other detergents

(G-8769)
SHUR LINE INC
116 Exmore Rd (28117-9422)
PHONE..............................317 442-8850
EMP: 39 **EST:** 2017
SALES (est): 989.08K **Privately Held**
Web: www.shurline.com
SIC: 3991 Brooms and brushes

(G-8770)
SHURTECH BRANDS LLC
150 Fairview Rd (28117-9504)
PHONE..............................704 799-0779
EMP: 5
SALES (corp-wide): 787.56MM **Privately
Held**
Web: www.shurtapetech.com
SIC: 2671 Plastic film, coated or laminated
for packaging
HQ: Shurtech Brands, Llc
32150 Just Imagine Dr
Avon OH 44011

(G-8771)
SIR SPEEDY PRINTING
Also Called: Sir Speedy
124 E Plaza Dr Ste C (28115-8103)
PHONE..............................704 664-1911
EMP: 5 **EST:** 2017
SALES (est): 181.87K **Privately Held**
Web: www.sirspeedy.com
SIC: 2752 Commercial printing, lithographic

(G-8772)
SMITH FABRICATION INC
2136 Coddle Creek Hwy (28115-8250)
PHONE..............................704 660-5170
Jeffery Brian Smith, *Pr*
EMP: 5 **EST:** 1996
SALES (est): 222.62K **Privately Held**
SIC: 3599 3711 3444 Machine and other job
shop work; Motor vehicles and car bodies;
Sheet metalwork

(G-8773)
SPECTRUM BRANDS INC
307 Oates Rd Ste F (28117-6985)
PHONE..............................704 658-2060
Jeff Johnson, *Brnch Mgr*
EMP: 5
SALES (corp-wide): 2.96B **Publicly Held**
Web: www.spectrumbrands.com
SIC: 3691 Alkaline cell storage batteries
HQ: Spectrum Brands, Inc.
3001 Deming Way
Middleton WI 53562
608 275-3340

(G-8774)
SRI PERFORMANCE LLC
122 Knob Hill Rd (28117-6847)
P.O. Box 5478 (28117-0478)

PHONE.............................704 662-6982
EMP: 43 EST: 2016
SALES (est): 6.64MM Privately Held
Web: www.sriperformance.com
SIC: 3714 Motor vehicle parts and
accessories

(G-8775)
SS HANDCRAFTED ART LLC
107 Glade Valley Ave (28117-8705)
PHONE.............................704 664-2544
Jose Conde, Brnch Mgr
◆ EMP: 6
SALES (corp-wide): 242.88K Privately
Held
Web: www.sshandart.com
SIC: 2395 Embroidery and art needlework
PA: Ss Handcrafted Art Llc
195 E Waterlynn Rd
Mooresville NC 28117
866 352-9377

(G-8776)
**STARHGEN AROSPC COMPONENTS
LLC**
333 Oates Rd (28117-6824)
PHONE.............................704 660-1001
◆ EMP: 13 EST: 2012
SALES (est): 4.13MM Privately Held
SIC: 3728 Aircraft parts and equipment, nec

(G-8777)
STITCH 98 INC
154 Talbert Pointe Dr Ste 101 (28117-4314)
PHONE.............................704 235-5783
Marci Athey, Pr
EMP: 18 EST: 2007
SALES (est): 975.63K Privately Held
Web: www.stitch98.com
SIC: 2395 Embroidery products, except
Schiffli machine

(G-8778)
STONERY LLC
1077 Mecklenburg Hwy (28115-7853)
PHONE.............................704 662-8702
EMP: 7 EST: 2006
SALES (est): 164.08K Privately Held
Web: www.thestonery.com
SIC: 2541 Counter and sink tops

(G-8779)
STORAGEMOTION INC
216 Overhill Dr Ste 104 (28117-7000)
PHONE.............................704 746-3700
Kurtis Krohn, Pr
Tina Krohn, Sec
▲ EMP: 6 EST: 2005
SALES (est): 472.16K Privately Held
Web: www.storagemotion.com
SIC: 2511 China closets

(G-8780)
STRUCTURE MEDICAL LLC
123 Cayuga Dr (28117-8239)
PHONE.............................704 799-3450
Robert Boody, Mgr
EMP: 90
Web: www.structuremedical.com
SIC: 3842 Orthopedic appliances
HQ: Structure Medical, Llc
9935 Business Cir
Naples FL 34112
239 262-5551

(G-8781)
STRUCTURE MEDICAL LLC
123 Cayuga Dr (28117-8239)
PHONE.............................256 461-0900
EMP: 90

Web: www.structuremedical.com
SIC: 3842 Orthopedic appliances
HQ: Structure Medical, Llc
9935 Business Cir
Naples FL 34112
239 262-5551

(G-8782)
SUGAR POPS
248 N Main St (28115-2528)
PHONE.............................704 799-0959
EMP: 5 EST: 2012
SALES (est): 246.09K Privately Held
SIC: 3421 7299 5441 Table and food cutlery,
including butchers'; Party planning service;
Candy

(G-8783)
SYSMETRIC USA
107 Infield Ct (28117-8026)
PHONE.............................704 522-8778
Itzhak Livni, Pr
EMP: 6 EST: 2016
SALES (est): 2.84MM Privately Held
Web: sysmetric-usa.business.site
SIC: 3089 Plastics containers, except foam

(G-8784)
TEXTILE DESIGNED MACHINE CO
1320 Shearers Rd (28115-7778)
PHONE.............................704 664-1374
Dan Newton, Pr
Richard Newton, Pr
EMP: 10 EST: 1961
SQ FT: 12,000
SALES (est): 1.03MM Privately Held
Web: www.tdmc-rolls.com
SIC: 3599 Machine shop, jobbing and repair

(G-8785)
THOMAS MENDOLIA MD
Also Called: Tri County Gastroenterology
146 Reids Cove Dr (28117-8307)
PHONE.............................336 835-5688
Thomas Mendolia Md, Owner
EMP: 6 EST: 1991
SALES (est): 167.89K Privately Held
SIC: 8011 3845 Gastronomist;
Colonascopes, electromedical

(G-8786)
**THYSSENKRUPP BILSTEIN AMER
INC**
Also Called: Shock Absorber Division
293 Timber Rd (28115-7868)
PHONE.............................704 663-7563
Scott Mcdonald, Brnch Mgr
EMP: 10
SALES (corp-wide): 39.13B Privately Held
Web: www.bilstein.com
SIC: 3714 Motor vehicle parts and
accessories
HQ: Thyssenkrupp Bilstein Of America, Inc.
8685 Bilstein Blvd
Hamilton OH 45015
513 881-7600

(G-8787)
TREADZ LLC
2118 Charlotte Hwy (28117-9468)
PHONE.............................704 664-0995
James Hubschmitt, Pr
James Hubschmitt, Managing Member
EMP: 4 EST: 2017
SALES (est): 639.07K Privately Held
Web: www.treadznc.com
SIC: 5531 7539 7534 Automotive
accessories; Automotive repair shops, nec;
Tire repair shop

(G-8788)
TRIBODYN TECHNOLOGIES INC
124 Tulip Dr (28117-6060)
PHONE.............................859 750-6299
Mark Wheatley, Pr
EMP: 6 EST: 2012
SALES (est): 1.95MM Privately Held
Web: www.tribodyn.com
SIC: 2899 Chemical preparations, nec

(G-8789)
UTSEY DUSKIE & ASSOCIATES
243 Overhill Dr Ste B (28117-7016)
PHONE.............................704 663-0036
Libby Duskie, Prin
EMP: 8
SALES (corp-wide): 415.11K Privately
Held
SIC: 3556 Food products machinery
PA: Utsey Duskie & Associates
386 Williamson Rd
Mooresville NC 28117
704 663-0036

(G-8790)
VERTICALFX INC ✪
107 Mcneil Ln (28117-5995)
PHONE.............................704 594-5000
Blair Fuller, CEO
EMP: 5 EST: 2024
SALES (est): 261.15K Privately Held
SIC: 2752 Commercial printing, lithographic

(G-8791)
VICTORY 1 PERFORMANCE INC
159 Lugnut Ln (28117-9300)
PHONE.............................704 799-1955
Derek Dahl, Pr
Conner Dahl, Prin
EMP: 15 EST: 1980
SQ FT: 18,000
SALES (est): 4.85MM
SALES (corp-wide): 195.05MM Privately
Held
Web: www.titaniumvalve.com
SIC: 3462 Automotive and internal
combustion engine forgings
PA: Race Winning Brands, Inc.
7201 Industrial Park Blvd
Mentor OH 44060
440 951-6600

(G-8792)
VICTORY PRESS LLC
114 Eastbend Ct Ste 4 (28117-4310)
PHONE.............................704 660-0348
EMP: 9 EST: 2006
SALES (est): 804.12K Privately Held
Web: www.victorypress.biz
SIC: 2752 Offset printing

(G-8793)
VINE & BRANCH WOODWORKS LLC
388 E Plaza Dr (28115-8047)
PHONE.............................704 663-0077
Shawn A Copeland, Admn
EMP: 6 EST: 2016
SALES (est): 383.06K Privately Held
Web:
www.vineandbranchwoodworks.com
SIC: 2434 Wood kitchen cabinets

(G-8794)
WATER TECH SOLUTIONS INC
178 Cayuga Dr (28117-8239)
PHONE.............................704 408-8391
Greg Sanders, Pr
EMP: 5 EST: 2004
SALES (est): 761.11K Privately Held
Web: www.ozonesalesandservice.com

SIC: 3823 Process control instruments

(G-8795)
**WEBER SCREWDRIVING SYSTEMS
INC**
149 Knob Hill Rd (28117-6847)
PHONE.............................704 360-5820
EMP: 35 EST: 1979
SALES (est): 15.85MM
SALES (corp-wide): 105.31MM Privately
Held
Web: www.weberusa.com
SIC: 3546 Power-driven handtools
PA: Weber Schraubautomaten
Gesellschaft Mit Beschrankter Haftung
Hans-Urmiller-Ring 56
Wolfratshausen BY 82515
81714060

(G-8796)
WEBER STEPHEN PRODUCTS LLC
200 Overhill Dr (28117-7033)
PHONE.............................704 662-0335
EMP: 12 EST: 2015
SALES (est): 747.33K Privately Held
SIC: 3631 Household cooking equipment

(G-8797)
WESTROCK - SOUTHERN CONT LLC
279 Mooresville Blvd (28115-7965)
P.O. Box 1009 (28115-1009)
PHONE.............................704 662-8496
David Easom, Brnch Mgr
EMP: 50
Web: www.smurfitwestrock.com
SIC: 2653 Boxes, corrugated: made from
purchased materials
HQ: Westrock - Southern Container, Llc
1000 Abernathy Rd Ne
Atlanta GA 30328
770 448-2193

(G-8798)
WESTROCK RKT LLC
279 Mooresville Blvd (28115-7965)
P.O. Box 1009 (28115-1009)
PHONE.............................704 662-8494
Don Kasun, Brnch Mgr
EMP: 97
Web: www.westrock.com
SIC: 2653 2652 2631 Boxes, corrugated:
made from purchased materials; Setup
paperboard boxes; Paperboard mills
HQ: Westrock Rkt, Llc
1000 Abernathy Rd Ste 125
Atlanta GA 30328
770 448-2193

(G-8799)
WHITE STONE LABS INC
178 Cayuga Dr (28117-8239)
PHONE.............................704 775-5274
Gregory Sanders, Pr
EMP: 4
SALES (est): 243.09K Privately Held
SIC: 2833 Medicinals and botanicals

(G-8800)
**WOMACK PUBLISHING COMPANY
INC**
Also Called: Lake Norman Times
548 Williamson Rd Ste 3 (28117-9111)
PHONE.............................704 660-5520
Chris Montgomery, Dir
EMP: 10
SALES (corp-wide): 4.28MM Privately
Held
Web: www.womackpublishing.com
SIC: 2711 Newspapers: publishing only, not
printed on site

PA: Womack Publishing Company, Inc.
28 N Main St
Chatham VA 24531
434 432-2791

(G-8801)
XXXTREME MOTORSPORT
292 Rolling Hill Rd (28117-6845)
PHONE.............................704 663-1500
John Cohen, *Owner*
EMP: 7 EST: 2012
SALES (est): 207.92K **Privately Held**
SIC: 3799 Recreational vehicles

(G-8802)
YATES PRECISION MACHINING LLC
133 Byers Creek Rd Unit D (28117-4376)
P.O. Box 5450 (28117-0450)
PHONE.............................704 662-7165
EMP: 6 EST: 2008
SALES (est): 1.01MM **Privately Held**
Web: www.roushyates.com
SIC: 3462 Iron and steel forgings

(G-8803)
YUKON PACKAGING LLC (PA)
122 Backstretch Ln (28117-8071)
PHONE.............................704 214-0579
Chris Poore, *Managing Member*
EMP: 5 EST: 2022
SALES (est): 7.74MM
SALES (corp-wide): 7.74MM **Privately Held**
SIC: 2656 Frozen food containers: made from purchased material

(G-8804)
YUMMY TUMMY GA LLC
Also Called: Planet Smoothie
2105 Brawley School Rd (28117-7081)
PHONE.............................704 658-0445
Bill Renton, *Pr*
Mo Rafiq, *VP*
EMP: 9 EST: 2007
SALES (est): 357.96K **Privately Held**
Web: www.planetsmoothie.com
SIC: 5812 2024 Soft drink stand; Ice cream and frozen deserts

(G-8805)
ZEKELMAN INDUSTRIES INC
Wheatland Tube A Div Zklman In
111 Pin Oak Ln (28117-7501)
PHONE.............................704 560-6768
EMP: 10
Web: www.zekelman.com
SIC: 3317 Pipes, seamless steel
PA: Zekelman Industries, Inc.
227 W Monroe St Ste 2600
Chicago IL 60606

(G-8806)
ZIBRA LLC (PA)
172 Broad Sound Pl (28117-6050)
PHONE.............................704 271-4503
▲ EMP: 4 EST: 2004
SALES (est): 1.75MM **Privately Held**
Web: www.enjoyzibra.com
SIC: 3991 3699 Brushes, household or industrial; Household electrical equipment

Moravian Falls
Wilkes County

(G-8807)
AMERICAN ALCOHOLLERY LLC
385 Hose Rd (28654-9671)
PHONE.............................704 960-7243
Amanda Holman, *Prin*

EMP: 5 EST: 2015
SALES (est): 80.68K **Privately Held**
SIC: 2084 Wines

(G-8808)
BROCK AND TRIPLETT MACHINE SP
Also Called: Brock & Triplett Machine
285 E Meadows Rd (28654-9600)
PHONE.............................336 667-6951
Donnie A Brock, *Pr*
Warren E Triplett, *VP*
EMP: 4 EST: 1961
SALES (est): 154.36K **Privately Held**
Web: www.discoverymobilehomes.com
SIC: 3599 Custom machinery

(G-8809)
CHARLES FERGUSON LOGGING
245 Jack Russell Rd (28654-9641)
P.O. Box 235 (28606-0235)
PHONE.............................336 921-3126
Charles E Ferguson, *Owner*
EMP: 4 EST: 1984
SALES (est): 155.14K **Privately Held**
SIC: 2411 Logging camps and contractors

(G-8810)
NI4L ANTENNAS AND ELEC LLC
Also Called: Unadilla Antenna Mfg Co
3861 Mount Olive Church Rd (28654-9576)
PHONE.............................828 738-6445
EMP: 5 EST: 2013
SALES (est): 776.76K **Privately Held**
Web: www.ni4l.com
SIC: 3663 5063 5731 7389 Antennas, transmitting and communications; Antennas, receiving, satellite dishes; Antennas; Business Activities at Non-Commercial Site

Morehead City
Carteret County

(G-8811)
ACE MARINE RIGGING & SUPPLY INC (PA)
600 Arendell St (28557-4233)
PHONE.............................252 726-6620
◆ EMP: 12 EST: 1990
SALES (est): 2.7MM **Privately Held**
Web: www.acemarinerigging.com
SIC: 5031 5251 5551 2298 Building materials, exterior; Hardware stores; Marine supplies, nec; Slings, rope

(G-8812)
ACTION SURFBOARDS
Also Called: Action Surf Shop
4130 Arendell St (28557-2801)
P.O. Box 276 (28570-0276)
PHONE.............................252 240-1818
Bob Webb, *Owner*
EMP: 6 EST: 1981
SQ FT: 5,800
SALES (est): 124.69K **Privately Held**
Web: www.actionsurf.com
SIC: 5941 3949 Surfing equipment and supplies; Surfboards

(G-8813)
AQUA 10 CORPORATION
Also Called: Bio D
5112 Midyette Ave (28557-2694)
PHONE.............................252 726-5421
William E Campell Iii, *Pr*
EMP: 8 EST: 1972
SQ FT: 12,000
SALES (est): 101.57K **Privately Held**

SIC: 2879 Agricultural chemicals, nec

(G-8814)
ASPHALT EMULSION INDS LLC
107 Arendell St (28557-4248)
PHONE.............................252 726-0653
Carter Dabney, *Managing Member*
EMP: 4 EST: 2011
SALES (est): 253.4K **Privately Held**
Web: www.asphalt-emulsion.com
SIC: 5032 3531 Paving materials; Aggregate spreaders

(G-8815)
BALLY REFRIGERATED BOXES INC (PA)
135 Little Nine Rd (28557-8483)
PHONE.............................252 240-2829
Michael Coyle, *Pr*
John Reilly, *
Nicholas Hope, *
Carmen Carosella, *
◆ EMP: 175 EST: 1995
SQ FT: 200,000
SALES (est): 45.77MM **Privately Held**
Web: www.ballyrefboxes.com
SIC: 5078 3585 Refrigeration equipment and supplies; Air conditioning condensers and condensing units

(G-8816)
BIG ROCK INDUSTRIES INC
Also Called: Big Rock Propellers
111 Turners Dairy Rd Ste A (28557-4530)
PHONE.............................252 222-3618
Adam Pierce, *Pr*
Thomas Healey, *Sec*
EMP: 4 EST: 2014
SALES (est): 223.39K **Privately Held**
Web: www.bigrockpropellers.com
SIC: 8711 3731 Marine engineering; Fishing vessels, large: building and repairing

(G-8817)
BIRCHER INCORPORATED
Also Called: Beaufort Naval Armorers
119 Industrial Dr (28557-8481)
PHONE.............................252 726-5470
James T Bircher, *Pr*
EMP: 5 EST: 1984
SQ FT: 7,200
SALES (est): 431.7K **Privately Held**
Web: www.bircherinc.com
SIC: 3599 Machine shop, jobbing and repair

(G-8818)
BLACKBEARDS BOATWORKS
4531 Arendell St (28557-2707)
PHONE.............................252 726-6161
Joy Edmundson, *Prin*
EMP: 4 EST: 2016
SALES (est): 82.41K **Privately Held**
Web: www.shearlineboatworks.com
SIC: 3732 Boatbuilding and repairing

(G-8819)
BOARDWALK INC
4911 Bridges St Ext # A (28557-8978)
PHONE.............................252 240-1095
Garry Mckeel, *Pr*
EMP: 5 EST: 1994
SALES (est): 86.75K **Privately Held**
Web: www.boardwalkscreenprinting.com
SIC: 2396 5999 Screen printing on fabric articles; Trophies and plaques

(G-8820)
CABINET SHOP INC
4915 Arendell St Ste 309 (28557-2659)
PHONE.............................252 726-6965

Paul Pagliughi, *Pr*
EMP: 6 EST: 1983
SQ FT: 24,090
SALES (est): 180.22K **Privately Held**
Web: www.cabinet-shop.com
SIC: 2434 Wood kitchen cabinets

(G-8821)
CAPE LOOKOUT CANVAS & CUSTOMS
4444 Arendell St Ste D (28557-2701)
PHONE.............................252 726-3751
William Hoke Page Junior, *Owner*
EMP: 4 EST: 2003
SALES (est): 181.31K **Privately Held**
SIC: 2394 Canvas and related products

(G-8822)
CAROLINA ATL SEAFOOD ENTPS
Also Called: Ottis' Fish Market
711 Shepard St (28557-4206)
P.O. Box 3576 (28557)
PHONE.............................252 728-2552
Doug Brady, *Pr*
EMP: 6 EST: 1982
SQ FT: 30,000
SALES (est): 139.6K **Privately Held**
SIC: 5146 5421 2092 2091 Seafoods; Fish markets; Fresh or frozen packaged fish; Canned and cured fish and seafoods

(G-8823)
CARTERET PUBLISHING COMPANY (PA)
Also Called: This Week Magazine
5039 Executive Dr Ste 300 (28557-2579)
P.O. Box 1679 (28557-1679)
PHONE.............................252 726-7081
Bonnie Pollock, *Managing Editor*
Walter D Phillips, *
Lockwood B Phillips, *
EMP: 100 EST: 1944
SALES (est): 2.17MM
SALES (corp-wide): 2.17MM **Privately Held**
Web: www.carolinacoastonline.com
SIC: 2711 Newspapers, publishing and printing

(G-8824)
CASE-CLOSED INVESTIGATIONS
5032 Hwy 70 W (28557-4502)
P.O. Box 218 (28557-0218)
PHONE.............................336 794-2274
Jamesc Stevens, *Mgr*
EMP: 4 EST: 2013
SALES (est): 241.04K **Privately Held**
Web: www.case-closed.com
SIC: 3523 Farm machinery and equipment

(G-8825)
CHRISTIAN FOCUS MAGAZINE
Also Called: Creative Clout Agency
706 Wagon Cir (28557-3172)
P.O. Box 102 (28557-0102)
PHONE.............................252 240-1656
Janet Landenburger, *Owner*
EMP: 5 EST: 2004
SALES (est): 116.1K **Privately Held**
SIC: 2721 Magazines: publishing only, not printed on site

(G-8826)
COASTAL AWNINGS INC
Also Called: Coastal Awngs Hrrcane Shutters
5300 High St Unit 0 (28557-4520)
PHONE.............................252 222-0707
Bobby Berckman, *Pr*
Judy Berckman, *Sec*
EMP: 13 EST: 1999

SALES (est): 1.11MM **Privately Held**
Web: www.crystalcoastawnings.com
SIC: **2394** 3442 Awnings, fabric: made from
purchased materials; Louvers, shutters,
jalousies, and similar items

(G-8827)
COASTAL PRESS INC
Also Called: Down East Printing
1706 Arendell St (28557-4040)
PHONE..............................252 726-1549
Tiffany Dawn Brock, *Pr*
Chris Brock, *VP*
EMP: 4 EST: 1948
SQ FT: 2,600
SALES (est): 317.05K **Privately Held**
Web: www.coastalpressinc.com
SIC: **2791** 2789 2752 7336 Typesetting;
Bookbinding and related work; Commercial
printing, lithographic; Commercial art and
graphic design

(G-8828)
CONSUMER CONCEPTS
Also Called: ASAP Embroideries
1506 Bridges St (28557-3649)
PHONE..............................252 247-7000
Sara West, *Pr*
Nancy Carrier, *Prin*
EMP: 10 EST: 1976
SQ FT: 2,000
SALES (est): 2.4MM **Privately Held**
Web: www.ncpromotionalproducts.com
SIC: **5199** 2759 3993 2396 Advertising
specialties; Commercial printing, nec; Signs
and advertising specialties; Automotive and
apparel trimmings

(G-8829)
DIVINE CREATIONS
216 Glenn Abby Dr (28557-2578)
PHONE..............................704 364-5844
Donna Snipes, *Owner*
EMP: 8 EST: 1988
SALES (est): 142.61K **Privately Held**
Web: www.divinecreationsusa.com
SIC: **2339** Women's and misses' outerwear,
nec

(G-8830)
DUOCRAFT CABINETS & DIST CO
(PA)
1306 Bridges St (28557-3757)
PHONE..............................252 240-1476
Alan Tate, *Prin*
EMP: 5 EST: 2006
SALES (est): 612.96K **Privately Held**
Web: www.duocraft.com
SIC: **2434** Wood kitchen cabinets

(G-8831)
EAST CAROLINA BRACE LIMB INC
209 N 35th St Ste 1 (28557-3179)
PHONE..............................252 726-8068
Cynthia T Monroe, *Brnch Mgr*
EMP: 9
SALES (corp-wide): 2.61MM **Privately
Held**
Web: www.ecblnc.com
SIC: **3842** Limbs, artificial
PA: East Carolina Brace & Limb Co., Inc.
4110 M L King Jr Blvd C
New Bern NC 28562
252 638-1312

(G-8832)
ESKIMO 7 LIMITED
Also Called: Windows & More
5317 Hwy 70 W (28557-4509)
PHONE..............................252 726-8181
Sharon Yeomans, *Owner*

EMP: 7 EST: 2006
SALES (est): 199.06K **Privately Held**
Web: www.windows-and-more.com
SIC: **2426** Flooring, hardwood

(G-8833)
GOVERNMENT SALES LLC
4644 Arendell St Ste A (28557-2759)
PHONE..............................252 726-6315
Charles Robinson, *Managing Member*
EMP: 6 EST: 1993
SQ FT: 800
SALES (est): 2.01MM **Privately Held**
Web: www.governmentsalesllc.com
SIC: **5046** 5193 5023 2599 Restaurant
equipment and supplies, nec; Artificial
flowers; Homefurnishings; Factory furniture
and fixtures

(G-8834)
HEIDELBERG MTLS STHAST AGG
LLC
5101 Business Dr (28557-6313)
PHONE..............................252 222-0812
Joseph Martin, *Brnch Mgr*
EMP: 6
SALES (corp-wide): 23.02B **Privately Held**
Web: www.hansonbiz.com
SIC: **1423** Crushed and broken granite
HQ: Heidelberg Materials Southeast Agg Llc
3237 Satellite Blvd # 30
Duluth GA 30096
770 491-2756

(G-8835)
HERALD PRINTING INC
201 N 17th St (28557-3627)
PHONE..............................252 726-3534
Pete Wenk, *Pr*
EMP: 5 EST: 1983
SQ FT: 1,000
SALES (est): 176.3K **Privately Held**
SIC: **2752** 2759 Offset printing; Commercial
printing, nec

(G-8836)
IVP FOREST PRODUCTS LLC
125 Horton Dr (28557-4528)
PHONE..............................252 241-8126
Ingrid Pfaff-niebauer, *CEO*
Carl Heinz Pfaff, *CSO*
◆ EMP: 15 EST: 2012
SALES (est): 1.85MM **Privately Held**
Web: www.ivplogs.com
SIC: **2411** 0831 Wooden logs; Gathering of
forest products

(G-8837)
JONES BROTHERS MARINE MFG
INC
Also Called: Jbm Manufacturing
100 Bateau Blvd (28557-6314)
PHONE..............................252 240-1995
Mary Raines Jones, *VP*
Donnie H Jones Iii, *Pr*
EMP: 5 EST: 1993
SQ FT: 46,520
SALES (est): 809.45K **Privately Held**
Web: www.jonesbrothersmarine.com
SIC: **3732** Motorized boat, building and
repairing

(G-8838)
LAMCO MACHINE TOOL INC
135 Industrial Dr (28557-8481)
P.O. Box 2357 (28557-2357)
PHONE..............................252 247-4360
Lois Fowler, *Pr*
EMP: 15 EST: 1990
SQ FT: 40,000

SALES (est): 592.51K **Privately Held**
Web: www.lamcomachine.com
SIC: **3089** Injection molding of plastics

(G-8839)
NCOAST COMMUNICATIONS (PA)
Also Called: Coaster Magazine Carteret Cnty
201 N 17th St (28557-3627)
PHONE..............................252 247-7442
Jennifer Star, *Pr*
EMP: 19 EST: 1984
SALES (est): 269.93K **Privately Held**
SIC: **2721** Magazines: publishing only, not
printed on site

(G-8840)
QUILLEN WELDING SERVICES LLC
110 Bonner Ave (28557-3212)
PHONE..............................252 269-4908
Jared Quillen, *Pr*
EMP: 4 EST: 2017
SALES (est): 175K **Privately Held**
Web: www.quillenwelding.com
SIC: **7692** Welding repair

(G-8841)
QWS LLC
110 Bonner Ave (28557-3212)
PHONE..............................252 723-2106
Jared Quillen, *Managing Member*
EMP: 25 EST: 2017
SALES (est): 1.22MM **Privately Held**
Web: www.quillenwelding.com
SIC: **3548** Electric welding equipment

(G-8842)
S & W READY MIX CON CO LLC
5161 Business Dr (28557-6313)
PHONE..............................252 726-2566
EMP: 16
SALES (corp-wide): 8.01MM **Privately
Held**
Web: www.snwreadymix.com
SIC: **3273** Ready-mixed concrete
HQ: S & W Ready Mix Concrete Company
Llc
217 Lisbon St
Clinton NC 28329
910 592-1733

(G-8843)
SEA STRIKER INC
158 Little Nine Rd (28557-8482)
P.O. Box 459 (28557-0459)
PHONE..............................252 247-4113
Phyllis Henry, *Pr*
Troy D Henry Junior, *VP*
Troy D Henry Iii, *Stockholder*
Phillip Henry, *Stockholder*
◆ EMP: 5 EST: 1992
SQ FT: 8,000
SALES (est): 453.47K **Privately Held**
Web: www.calcuttaoutdoors.com
SIC: **3949** Fishing tackle, general

(G-8844)
SHEARLINE BOATWORKS LLC
127 Hestron Dr (28557-6303)
P.O. Box 579 (28557-0579)
PHONE..............................252 726-6916
EMP: 8 EST: 2000
SALES (est): 230.55K **Privately Held**
Web: www.shearlineboatworks.com
SIC: **3732** Boats, fiberglass: building and
repairing

(G-8845)
SOUTHEASTERN ELEVATOR LLC
143 Industrial Dr (28557-8481)
P.O. Box 2148 (28557-2148)

PHONE..............................252 726-9983
EMP: 6 EST: 2013
SALES (est): 695.7K **Privately Held**
Web: www.southeasternelevatorllc.com
SIC: **1796** 3534 Elevator installation and
conversion; Elevators and equipment

(G-8846)
SURGICAL CENTER OF MOREHEA
3714 Guardian Ave Ste W (28557-2975)
PHONE..............................252 247-0314
Thomas Bates, *Pr*
EMP: 15 EST: 2011
SALES (est): 2.56MM **Privately Held**
Web: www.surgicalcenterofmhc.com
SIC: **3842** 8011 Trusses, orthopedic and
surgical; Plastic surgeon

(G-8847)
TAYLOR BOAT WORKS
200 Pensacola Ave (28557-2730)
P.O. Box 1346 (28557-1346)
PHONE..............................252 726-6374
John Mc Callum, *Owner*
EMP: 6 EST: 1965
SALES (est): 202.78K **Privately Held**
SIC: **3732** Boatbuilding and repairing

(G-8848)
V M TRUCKING INC
4915 Arendell St (28557-2659)
PHONE..............................984 239-4853
Franco Hill, *Pr*
EMP: 4 EST: 2017
SALES (est): 670.41K **Privately Held**
SIC: **4212** 3537 7513 Dump truck haulage;
Trucks: freight, baggage, etc.: industrial,
except mining; Truck leasing, without drivers

Morganton
Burke County

(G-8849)
ALL 4 U HOME MEDICAL LLC
617 S Green St Ste 100 (28655-3517)
P.O. Box 1393 (28680-1393)
PHONE..............................828 437-0684
Jerrol Smith, *Managing Member*
Wesley Smith, *Opers Mgr*
Laura Clark, *Treas*
EMP: 8 EST: 2010
SQ FT: 2,800
SALES (est): 2.61MM **Privately Held**
Web: www.all4uhomemedical.com
SIC: **5999** 3842 Medical apparatus and
supplies; Wheelchairs

(G-8850)
AMERICAN ROLLER BEARING INC
(HQ)
307 Burke Dr (28655-5334)
PHONE..............................828 624-1460
Michael J Connors, *Pr*
Hansal N Patel, *Sec*
Teresa L Wilson, *Treas*
EMP: 13 EST: 2022
SALES (est): 11.11MM
SALES (corp-wide): 4.57B **Publicly Held**
Web: www.amroll.com
SIC: **3562** Roller bearings and parts
PA: The Timken Company
4500 Mount Pleasant St Nw
North Canton OH 44720
234 262-3000

(G-8851)
ARPRO M-TEC LLC
Also Called: Whole Sale Printing Inks
212 E Fleming Dr (28655-3676)

PHONE..................................828 433-0699
EMP: 15 EST: 2011
SALES (est): 3.95MM **Privately Held**
Web: www.arproinks.com
SIC: 2893 Printing ink

(G-8852)
BAREFOOT CNC INC
Also Called: H D Technologies
1004 Carbon City Rd (28655)
PHONE..................................828 438-5038
James Wakeford, *Pr*
EMP: 7 EST: 1997
SALES (est): 933.85K **Privately Held**
Web: www.barefootcnc.com
SIC: 5734 3451 Software, business and non-game; Screw machine products

(G-8853)
BORDEN CHEMICAL
Also Called: Borden
114 Industrial Blvd (28655-8285)
PHONE..................................828 584-3800
Rooney Borden, *Prin*
EMP: 6 EST: 2014
SALES (est): 276.76K **Privately Held**
SIC: 2819 Industrial inorganic chemicals, nec

(G-8854)
BURKE VENEERS INC
2170 Fr Coffey Rd (28655-9399)
PHONE..................................828 437-8510
Wendell Powell, *Pr*
Carolyn Powell, *
EMP: 6 EST: 1980
SQ FT: 10,500
SALES (est): 474.64K **Privately Held**
SIC: 2435 Hardwood veneer and plywood

(G-8855)
CHELTEC INC
647 Hopewell Rd Ste C (28655)
PHONE..................................941 355-1045
Denise Delancy, *Pr*
Tom O'neill, *VP*
EMP: 7 EST: 1996
SALES (est): 952.84K **Privately Held**
Web: www.cheltec.com
SIC: 2819 Chemicals, high purity: refined from technical grade

(G-8856)
CHESTERFIELD WOOD PRODUCTS INC
1810 Us 64 (28655-8868)
P.O. Box 1792 (28680-1792)
PHONE..................................828 433-0042
Wendell Powell, *Pr*
Robin Powell, *Sec*
EMP: 13 EST: 1991
SQ FT: 20,000
SALES (est): 1.08MM **Privately Held**
SIC: 2499 2435 Furniture inlays (veneers); Hardwood veneer and plywood

(G-8857)
CITY OF MORGANTON
100 Coulter St (28655-4114)
PHONE..................................828 584-1460
EMP: 10
Web: ci.morganton.nc.us
SIC: 3569 Filters
PA: City Of Morganton
305 E Union St Ste A100
Morganton NC 28655
828 438-5376

(G-8858)
CONSOLIDATED ELEC DISTRS INC
Also Called: Ced

208 W Fleming Dr Ste D (28655-3969)
PHONE..................................828 433-4689
EMP: 6
SALES (corp-wide): 1.5B **Privately Held**
Web: www.cedcareers.com
SIC: 5099 3699 Firearms and ammunition, except sporting; High-energy particle physics equipment
PA: Consolidated Electrical Distributors, Inc.
1920 Westridge Dr
Irving TX 75038
972 582-5300

(G-8859)
CONTINENTAL AUTO SYSTEMS INC
Also Called: Continental Teves
1103 Jamestown Rd (28655-9285)
PHONE..................................828 584-4500
David Jones, *Brnch Mgr*
EMP: 252
SALES (corp-wide): 45.02B **Privately Held**
Web: www.continental-automotive.com
SIC: 3714 Motor vehicle brake systems and parts
HQ: Continental Automotive Systems, Inc.
1 Continental Dr
Auburn Hills MI 48326
248 393-5300

(G-8860)
DIRECT DIAGNOSTIC SERVICES LLC
Also Called: Direct Diagnostic Services
125 Wamsutta Mill Rd Ste A (28655-5522)
PHONE..................................843 708-3891
EMP: 10 EST: 2013
SALES (est): 1.06MM **Privately Held**
Web: www.directdiagnosticservices.com
SIC: 3829 Medical diagnostic systems, nuclear

(G-8861)
E J VICTOR INC (PA)
Also Called: E J Victor Furniture
110 Wamsutta Mill Rd (28655-5551)
P.O. Box 309 (28680-0309)
PHONE..................................828 437-1991
John Victor Jokinen, *Pr*
Edward W Phifer Iii, *Sr VP*
Daniel C Breeden, *
William G Morrison Junior, *VP*
◆ **EMP: 160 EST:** 1989
SQ FT: 232,000
SALES (est): 24.34MM **Privately Held**
Web: www.ejvictor.com
SIC: 2512 2511 Couches, sofas, and davenports: upholstered on wood frames; Dining room furniture: wood

(G-8862)
EMERY CORPORATION
1523 N Green St (28655-6744)
P.O. Box 1104 (28680-1104)
PHONE..................................828 433-1536
Beverly Emery, *CEO*
Mark Emery, *
Meryl Taulbee, *
Ronald Emery, *
Sheryl Emery Burdick, *
◆ **EMP: 75 EST:** 1955
SQ FT: 80,000
SALES (est): 2.11MM **Privately Held**
Web: www.emerycorp.com
SIC: 3542 3545 3544 Machine tools, metal forming type; Gauges (machine tool accessories); Jigs: inspection, gauging, and checking

(G-8863)
ENVIRONMENTAL INKS AND COATINGS CANADA LTD

1 Quality Products Rd (28655-4759)
PHONE..................................828 433-1922
▲ **EMP:** 200
Web: www.siegwerk.com
SIC: 2893 Printing ink

(G-8864)
FENCE QUARTER LLC
318 Burke Dr (28655-5395)
PHONE..................................800 205-0128
Christopher Price, *Managing Member*
EMP: 4 EST: 2017
SALES (est): 167.84K **Privately Held**
Web: www.fencequarter.com
SIC: 1799 2499 Fence construction; Applicators, wood

(G-8865)
FERGUSON CABINET WORKS
4188 Nc 181 (28655-7597)
P.O. Box 925 (28680-0925)
PHONE..................................828 433-8710
James Ferguson, *Owner*
EMP: 4 EST: 1987
SQ FT: 7,000
SALES (est): 193.63K **Privately Held**
Web: www.fergusoncabinetworks.com
SIC: 2434 Wood kitchen cabinets

(G-8866)
FREAKIN PEKIN
D114 Morganton Heights Blvd (28655-5214)
PHONE..................................828 705-3313
Caroline Holt, *Managing Member*
EMP: 5 EST: 2018
SALES (est): 260.06K **Privately Held**
Web: www.thefreakinpekin.com
SIC: 2841 Soap and other detergents

(G-8867)
G & G MOULDING INC
Also Called: G and G Art and Frame
801 N Green St (28655-5611)
P.O. Box 830 (28680-0830)
PHONE..................................828 438-1112
▲ **EMP:** 37
Web: www.internationalmoulding.com
SIC: 5023 2499 5719 Decorative home furnishings and supplies; Picture and mirror frames, wood; Lighting, lamps, and accessories

(G-8868)
GERRESHEIMER GLASS INC
114 Wamsutta Mill Rd (28655-5551)
PHONE..................................828 433-5000
Jim Baldwin, *Mgr*
EMP: 17
SALES (corp-wide): 2.2B **Privately Held**
Web: www.gerresheimer.com
SIC: 3221 3231 Glass containers; Products of purchased glass
HQ: Gerresheimer Glass Inc.
537 Crystal Ave
Vineland NJ 08360

(G-8869)
GUY CHADDOCK AND COMPANY LLC
Also Called: Chaddock Home
100 Reep Dr (28655-8441)
PHONE..................................828 584-0664
Andrew Crone, *Pr*
EMP: 200 EST: 2004
SALES (est): 3.08MM **Privately Held**
SIC: 2511 Wood household furniture

(G-8870)
HAIRFIELD WILBERT BURIAL VLT
3098 Morganton Furniture Rd (28655)
P.O. Box 146 (28680-0146)
PHONE..................................828 437-4319
Joseph B Hairfield, *Pr*
Steven Hairfield, *VP*
EMP: 8 EST: 1952
SQ FT: 7,500
SALES (est): 847.62K **Privately Held**
SIC: 3272 Burial vaults, concrete or precast terrazzo

(G-8871)
HEXION INC
114 Industrial Blvd (28655-8285)
PHONE..................................828 584-3800
EMP: 40
SQ FT: 1,872
SALES (corp-wide): 1.26B **Privately Held**
Web: www.hexion.com
SIC: 2821 Plastics materials and resins
PA: Hexion Inc.
180 E Broad St
Columbus OH 43215
888 443-9466

(G-8872)
HFI WIND DOWN INC
109 E Fleming Dr 7 (28655-3675)
PHONE..................................828 438-5767
EMP: 180
SQ FT: 1,707
SALES (corp-wide): 511.79MM **Privately Held**
SIC: 5712 2512 2426 Furniture stores; Upholstered household furniture; Hardwood dimension and flooring mills
PA: Hfi Wind Down, Inc.
1925 Eastchester Dr
High Point NC 27265
336 888-4800

(G-8873)
HFI WIND DOWN INC
410 Hogan St (28655-3616)
PHONE..................................828 430-3355
EMP: 133
SALES (corp-wide): 511.79MM **Privately Held**
SIC: 2511 Wood household furniture
PA: Hfi Wind Down, Inc.
1925 Eastchester Dr
High Point NC 27265
336 888-4800

(G-8874)
ICE RIVER SPRINGS USA INC (HQ)
Also Called: Ice River Springs Water
601 E Union St (28655-3457)
PHONE..................................519 925-2929
EMP: 11 EST: 2005
SALES (est): 4.88MM
SALES (corp-wide): 143.34MM **Privately Held**
SIC: 2086 Water, natural: packaged in cans, bottles, etc.
PA: Ice River Springs Water Co. Inc
485387 Sideroad 30 Dufferin County Rd 11
Shelburne ON
844 764-7336

(G-8875)
JAMES TOOL MACHINE & ENGRG INC (PA)
Also Called: JAMES TOOL COMPANY
130 Reep Dr (28655-8441)
P.O. Box 1665 (28680-1665)
PHONE..................................828 584-8722
Jeff Toner, *Pr*

Elizabeth Burleson, *
Kevin Moses, *
Tim King, *
▲ **EMP:** 115 **EST:** 1987
SALES (est): 23.23MM
SALES (corp-wide): 23.23MM **Privately Held**
Web: www.jamestool.com
SIC: 3599 3724 3728 3764 Machine and other job shop work; Aircraft engines and engine parts; Aircraft parts and equipment, nec; Space propulsion units and parts

(G-8876)
JARRETT BROTHERS
200 Carbondale Ln (28655-4381)
PHONE..................828 433-8036
Kirby Jarrett, *Pt*
Michael Jarrett, *Pt*
▼ **EMP:** 5 **EST:** 1979
SQ FT: 8,000
SALES (est): 162.16K **Privately Held**
SIC: 2512 Upholstered household furniture

(G-8877)
LEGACY VULCAN LLC
Mideast Division
Causby Quarry Rd (28655)
P.O. Box 69 (28680-0069)
PHONE..................828 437-2616
Brad Allison, *Mgr*
EMP: 5
Web: www.vulcanmaterials.com
SIC: 3273 Ready-mixed concrete
HQ: Legacy Vulcan, Llc
1200 Urban Center Dr
Birmingham AL 35242
205 298-3000

(G-8878)
LEVITON MANUFACTURING CO INC
113 Industrial Blvd (28655-8285)
PHONE..................828 584-1611
Leonard Causby, *Brnch Mgr*
EMP: 30
SALES (corp-wide): 1.46B **Privately Held**
Web: www.leviton.com
SIC: 3643 3357 Current-carrying wiring services; Nonferrous wiredrawing and insulating
PA: Leviton Manufacturing Co., Inc.
201 N Service Rd
Melville NY 11747
800 323-8920

(G-8879)
LLC FERGUSON COPELAND (HQ)
Also Called: Chaddock
100 Reep Dr (28655-8441)
P.O. Box 10 (28680-0010)
PHONE..................828 584-0664
Andrew Crone, *Managing Member*
◆ **EMP:** 120 **EST:** 1996
SQ FT: 110,000
SALES (est): 24.96MM
SALES (corp-wide): 25.47MM **Privately Held**
Web: www.fergusoncopeland.com
SIC: 2512 Chairs: upholstered on wood frames
PA: Eighteen Seventy Corporation
1700 E Putnam Ave Ste 202
Old Greenwich CT 06870
203 769-1873

(G-8880)
MATERIAL RETURN LLC
Also Called: Chrysalis
647 Hopewell Rd (28655-8267)
P.O. Box 71 (28680-0071)
PHONE..................828 234-5368

EMP: 4 **EST:** 2018
SALES (est): 283.38K **Privately Held**
Web: www.thematerialreturn.com
SIC: 2282 Acetate filament yarn: throwing, twisting, winding, spooling

(G-8881)
MERITOR INC
105 Wamsutta Mill Rd (28655-5552)
PHONE..................828 433-4600
Brad Kendall, *Manager*
EMP: 250
SQ FT: 5,970
SALES (corp-wide): 34.1B **Publicly Held**
Web: www.meritor.com
SIC: 3312 3714 3713 Axles, rolled or forged: made in steel mills; Motor vehicle parts and accessories; Truck and bus bodies
HQ: Meritor, Inc.
2135 W Maple Rd
Troy MI 48084

(G-8882)
MOLDED FIBR GL CMPNY/NRTH CRLI
Also Called: Molded Fiber Glass
213 Reep Dr (28655-8253)
PHONE..................828 584-4974
Richard S Morrison, *Pr*
Joseph A Cotman, *
Stuart W Cordell, *
EMP: 215 **EST:** 1994
SQ FT: 110,000
SALES (est): 19.22MM
SALES (corp-wide): 360.86MM **Privately Held**
Web: www.moldedfiberglass.com
SIC: 3089 Air mattresses, plastics
PA: Molded Fiber Glass Companies
2925 Mfg Pl
Ashtabula OH 44004
440 997-5851

(G-8883)
MULLS CON & SEPTIC TANKS INC
Also Called: Mull's Concrete & Septic Tanks
2416 Mount Home Church Rd (28655-6405)
PHONE..................828 437-0959
Richard Mulls, *Pr*
Susan Mulls, *VP*
EMP: 8 **EST:** 1969
SALES (est): 243.65K **Privately Held**
SIC: 7699 3273 Septic tank cleaning service; Ready-mixed concrete

(G-8884)
NELSON RODRIGUEZ
341 E Parker Rd (28655-5112)
PHONE..................828 433-1223
Nelson Rodriguez, *Prin*
EMP: 4 **EST:** 2010
SALES (est): 347.42K **Privately Held**
SIC: 3843 Enamels, dentists'

(G-8885)
NORELL INC
1001 Innovation Dr (28655-6955)
P.O. Box 1707 (28680-1707)
PHONE..................828 584-2600
Gregory Norell, *Ch*
Theresa Norell, *VP*
EMP: 8 **EST:** 1967
SALES (est): 1.16MM **Privately Held**
Web: shop.nmrtubes.com
SIC: 3231 2821 Laboratory glassware; Polytetrafluoroethylene resins, teflon

(G-8886)
OPTICONCEPTS INC
911 W Union St (28655-4253)
P.O. Box 1170 (28690-1170)
PHONE..................828 320-0138
Chris J Pons, *Pr*
EMP: 5 **EST:** 2000
SQ FT: 3,000
SALES (est): 909.98K **Privately Held**
Web: www.opticoncepts.com
SIC: 3357 Fiber optic cable (insulated)

(G-8887)
PACKAGING CORPORATION AMERICA
Also Called: Pca/Morganton 354
114 Dixie Blvd (28655-8244)
PHONE..................828 584-1511
Rich De Augustinis, *Brnch Mgr*
EMP: 50
SALES (corp-wide): 7.73B **Publicly Held**
Web: www.packagingcorp.com
SIC: 2653 Boxes, corrugated: made from purchased materials
PA: Packaging Corporation Of America
1 N Field Ct
Lake Forest IL 60045
847 482-3000

(G-8888)
PPG ARCHITECTURAL FINISHES INC
Also Called: Glidden Professional Paint Ctr
511 Burkemont Ave (28655-4409)
PHONE..................828 438-9210
Richard Sharp, *Mgr*
EMP: 5
SALES (corp-wide): 17.65B **Publicly Held**
Web: www.ppgpaints.com
SIC: 2851 Paints and allied products
HQ: Ppg Architectural Finishes, Inc.
1 Ppg Pl
Pittsburgh PA 15272
412 434-3131

(G-8889)
PRO ULTRASONICS INC
3076 Hwy 18 N / Us 64 (28655-8350)
P.O. Box 999 (28761-0961)
PHONE..................828 584-1005
Danny Kentch, *Pr*
Joanna Kentch, *VP*
▲ **EMP:** 8 **EST:** 2001
SQ FT: 4,000
SALES (est): 1.03MM **Privately Held**
Web: www.proultrasonics.com
SIC: 3699 Generators, ultrasonic

(G-8890)
R & R IRONWORKS INC
Also Called: R&R Iron Works
501 Salem Rd (28655-4718)
PHONE..................828 448-0524
Roy Moseley, *Pr*
EMP: 5 **EST:** 2014
SALES (est): 1.78MM **Privately Held**
Web: www.rrironworks.com
SIC: 3441 Expansion joints (structural shapes), iron or steel

(G-8891)
R S SKILLEN
2080 Us 70 E (28655-8952)
PHONE..................828 433-5353
Kwang Chung, *Prin*
EMP: 4 **EST:** 2007
SALES (est): 310.98K **Privately Held**
SIC: 3728 Aircraft parts and equipment, nec

(G-8892)
ROBERT BERGELIN COMPANY (PA)
120 S Sterling St (28655-3441)
PHONE..................828 437-6409
Christopher A Bergelin, *Pr*
Marilyn Bergelin, *
Thad Bergelin, *
EMP: 25 **EST:** 1995
SQ FT: 48,000
SALES (est): 1.16MM **Privately Held**
Web: www.rbcfurn.com
SIC: 2511 Wood household furniture

(G-8893)
SACK-UPS CORPORATION
Also Called: Sandviper
1611 Jamestown Rd (28655-9289)
P.O. Box 3051 (28680-3051)
PHONE..................828 584-4579
Warren Norman, *VP*
EMP: 10 **EST:** 2014
SQ FT: 20,000
SALES (est): 817.93K **Privately Held**
Web: www.sackups.com
SIC: 2282 Knitting yarn: twisting, winding, or spooling

(G-8894)
SEIREN NORTH AMERICA LLC (HQ)
1500 E Union St (28655-5325)
P.O. Box 130 (28680-0130)
PHONE..................828 430-3456
Jeff Kale, *
▲ **EMP:** 19 **EST:** 2001
SQ FT: 437,000
SALES (est): 48.49MM **Privately Held**
Web: www.seiren-na.com
SIC: 2221 Automotive fabrics, manmade fiber
PA: Seiren Co.,Ltd.
1-10-1, Keya
Fukui FKI 918-8

(G-8895)
SGL CARBON LLC
Also Called: S G L Carbon
307 Jamestown Rd (28655-9948)
PHONE..................828 437-3221
Andy Stinson, *Genl Mgr*
EMP: 4
SALES (corp-wide): 1.18B **Privately Held**
Web: www.sglcarbon.com
SIC: 3624 3823 Carbon and graphite products; Process control instruments
HQ: Sgl Carbon, Llc
10715 Dvid Tylor Dr Ste 4
Charlotte NC 28262
704 593-5100

(G-8896)
SHERRILL FURNITURE COMPANY
Also Called: Motioncraft By Sherrill Div
516 Drexel Rd (28655-8949)
P.O. Box 9145 (28603-9145)
PHONE..................828 437-2256
Johnny Suddreth, *Brnch Mgr*
EMP: 14
SQ FT: 52,000
SALES (corp-wide): 49.81MM **Privately Held**
Web: www.sherrillfurniture.com
SIC: 2512 Upholstered household furniture
PA: Sherrill Furniture Company Inc
2405 Highland Ave Ne
Hickory NC 28601
828 322-2640

(G-8897)
SIEGWERK EIC LLC (DH)
Also Called: Environmental Inks
1 Quality Products Rd (28655-4759)
PHONE..................800 368-4657

Herbert Forkner, *CEO*
▲ **EMP:** 11 **EST:** 2010
SALES (est): 11.18MM
SALES (corp-wide): 2.67MM **Privately Held**
Web: www.siegwerk.com
SIC: 2893 Printing ink
HQ: Siegwerk Usa Inc.
   3535 Sw 56th St
   Des Moines IA 50321
   515 471-2100

(G-8898)
SKELLY INC
628 E Meeting St (28655-3435)
P.O. Box 3853 (28680-3853)
PHONE.....................828 433-7070
Robert Skelly, *Pr*
EMP: 11 **EST:** 2003
SALES (est): 1.01MM **Privately Held**
Web: www.skellyinc.net
SIC: 3069 Foam rubber

(G-8899)
SOUTH MOUNTAIN CRAFTS
Also Called: Craft Village
300 Enola Rd (28655-4608)
PHONE.....................828 433-2607
June Hollingsworth, *Mgr*
EMP: 4 **EST:** 2001
SALES (est): 248.96K **Privately Held**
SIC: 2511 3944 5999 Wood household
   furniture; Craft and hobby kits and sets;
   Miscellaneous retail stores, nec

(G-8900)
SOUTHERN DEVICES INC
113 Industrial Blvd (28655-8285)
PHONE.....................828 584-1611
Grady Redis, *Prin*
EMP: 6 **EST:** 2014
SALES (est): 1.88MM **Privately Held**
SIC: 3643 Current-carrying wiring services

(G-8901)
STONE & LEIGH LLC
1020 N Green St (28655-9029)
PHONE.....................919 971-2096
EMP: 6 **EST:** 2018
SALES (est): 2.2MM **Privately Held**
Web: www.stoneandleigh.com
SIC: 5032 2512 Stone, crushed or broken;
   Chairs: upholstered on wood frames

(G-8902)
SUSTAINABLE CORRUGATED LLC
1000 Chain Dr (28655-7239)
PHONE.....................828 608-0990
Bobby Hunter, *Brnch Mgr*
EMP: 80
SQ FT: 160,000
Web: www.sustainablecorrugated.com
SIC: 2653 Boxes, corrugated: made from
   purchased materials
HQ: Sustainable Corrugated, Llc
   2852 Five Springs Rd
   Dalton GA 30720
   706 529-8101

(G-8903)
T DISTRIBUTION NC INC
Also Called: International Moulding NC
801 N Green St (28655-5611)
PHONE.....................828 438-1112
Jason Whisnant, *Pr*
EMP: 28 **EST:** 2014
SQ FT: 82,000
SALES (est): 4.51MM
SALES (corp-wide): 4.51MM **Privately Held**

SIC: 5023 2499 Frames and framing, picture
   and mirror; Picture frame molding, finished
PA: International Mouldings, Inc.
   33 Omega St S
   Birmingham AL 35205
   205 324-5783

(G-8904)
TABLE ROCK PRINTERS LLC
205 N Sterling St (28655-3344)
PHONE.....................828 433-1377
Ronald Perry, *Owner*
EMP: 5 **EST:** 1986
SALES (est): 246.05K **Privately Held**
Web: www.tablerockprinters.com
SIC: 2752 Offset printing

(G-8905)
TONER MACHINING TECH INC
1523 N Green St (28655-6744)
P.O. Box 2876 (28680)
PHONE.....................828 432-8007
James C Toner Junior, *Pr*
EMP: 80 **EST:** 2001
SQ FT: 25,000
SALES (est): 15MM **Privately Held**
Web: www.tonermachining.com
SIC: 3469 3544 3545 Machine parts,
   stamped or pressed metal; Special dies,
   tools, jigs, and fixtures; Machine tool
   accessories

(G-8906)
TONER MACHINING TECHNOLOGIES
212 E Fleming Dr (28655-3676)
P.O. Box 2876 (28680-2876)
PHONE.....................828 432-8007
EMP: 10
SALES (est): 254.85K **Privately Held**
Web: www.tonermachining.com
SIC: 3599 Machine shop, jobbing and repair

(G-8907)
UNIX PACKAGING LLC
100 Ceramic Tile Dr (28655-6772)
PHONE.....................310 877-7979
Bobby Melameds, *CEO*
EMP: 144
SALES (corp-wide): 88.94MM **Privately Held**
Web: www.unixpackaging.com
SIC: 2086 Mineral water, carbonated:
   packaged in cans, bottles, etc.
PA: Unix Packaging, Llc
   9 Minson Way
   Montebello CA 90640
   213 627-5050

(G-8908)
VEKA EAST INC
90 Ceramic Tile Dr (28655-6734)
PHONE.....................800 654-5589
EMP: 496 **EST:** 2017
SALES (est): 5.45MM
SALES (corp-wide): 1.8B **Privately Held**
Web: www.veka.com
SIC: 3089 Injection molding of plastics
HQ: Veka Inc.
   100 Veka Dr
   Fombell PA 16123
   800 654-5589

(G-8909)
VLR LLC
Also Called: Stone & Leigh Furniture
1020 N Green St (28655-9029)
PHONE.....................252 355-4610
Brad Garner, *Managing Member*
EMP: 31 **EST:** 2018
SQ FT: 25,000
SALES (est): 8MM **Privately Held**

SIC: 2211 Upholstery fabrics, cotton

(G-8910)
VX AEROSPACE CORPORATION
2080 Us 70 E (28655-8952)
PHONE.....................828 433-5353
Raymond Jones, *Pr*
Robert Skillen, *CEO*
EMP: 14 **EST:** 2006
SALES (est): 2.03MM **Privately Held**
Web: www.vxaerospace.com
SIC: 3721 3728 Research and development
   on aircraft by the manufacturer; Aircraft
   parts and equipment, nec

(G-8911)
VX AEROSPACE HOLDINGS INC
2080 Us 70 E (28655-8952)
PHONE.....................828 433-5353
Robert Skillen, *CEO*
EMP: 10 **EST:** 2016
SALES (est): 261.69K **Privately Held**
Web: www.vxaerospace.com
SIC: 3721 Helicopters

(G-8912)
WB EMBROIDERY INC
Also Called: Wendy Bs Cstm EMB Screen
Prtg
3076 Nc 18 S (28655-7476)
PHONE.....................828 432-0076
Wendy Bradshaw, *Pr*
Linda Norville, *Sec*
EMP: 5 **EST:** 2004
SQ FT: 4,300
SALES (est): 574.83K **Privately Held**
Web: www.wbembinc.com
SIC: 2395 Embroidery products, except
   Schiffli machine

Morrisville
Wake County

(G-8913)
623 MEDICAL LLC
Also Called: 623 Medical
635 Davis Dr Ste 100 (27560-7183)
PHONE.....................877 455-0112
Ty Schandler, *CEO*
EMP: 10 **EST:** 2020
SALES (est): 678.59K **Privately Held**
Web: www.623medical.com
SIC: 3841 Anesthesia apparatus

(G-8914)
6TH SENSE ANALYTICS
1 Copley Pkwy Ste 560 (27560-7424)
PHONE.....................919 439-4740
Gregory Burnell, *CEO*
EMP: 4 **EST:** 2019
SALES (est): 305.87K **Privately Held**
SIC: 7372 Prepackaged software

(G-8915)
AAA MOBILE SIGNS LLC
Also Called: Signs Now
10404 Chapel Hill Rd Ste 110 (27560-0218)
PHONE.....................919 463-9768
Lisa Dyrd, *Mgr*
EMP: 5
SALES (corp-wide): 2.4MM **Privately Held**
Web: www.signsnow.com
SIC: 3993 Signs and advertising specialties
PA: Aaa Mobile Signs, L.C.
   1570 Lakeview Dr Ste 108
   Sebring FL 33870
   863 471-1800

(G-8916)
AAE NORTH AMERICA LLC
Also Called: Solara Automation
155 Kitty Hawk Dr (27560)
PHONE.....................919 534-1500
Manon Pijnenburg, *Ex Dir*
EMP: 14 **EST:** 2004
SQ FT: 10,000
SALES (est): 4.97MM **Privately Held**
Web: www.solaraautomation.com
SIC: 3569 Assembly machines, non-
   metalworking

(G-8917)
ACCULABS TECHNOLOGIES INC
1018 Morrisville Pkwy Ste E (27560-0308)
P.O. Box 1579 (27312-1579)
PHONE.....................919 468-8780
Tom Wilkie, *Pr*
Cameron Stephens, *Treas*
EMP: 5 **EST:** 1997
SALES (est): 117.49K **Privately Held**
Web: www.acculabstech.com
SIC: 3564 Air cleaning systems

(G-8918)
ACTERNA LLC
1100 Perimeter Park Dr Ste 101
(27560-9119)
PHONE.....................919 388-5100
John Govert, *Brnch Mgr*
EMP: 19
SALES (corp-wide): 1B **Publicly Held**
SIC: 3669 7379 3825 5065
   Intercommunication systems, electric;
   Computer related consulting services;
   Instruments to measure electricity;
   Electronic parts and equipment, nec
HQ: Acterna Llc
   20250 Cntury Blvd Ste 100
   Germantown MD 20874
   301 353-1550

(G-8919)
ADAMS PRODUCTS COMPANY
5701 Mccrimmon Pkwy Ste 201
(27560-8340)
P.O. Box 189 (27560-0189)
PHONE.....................919 467-2218
Joseph Mc Cullough, *V Ch Bd*
Michael Lynch, *Sec*
▲ **EMP:** 180 **EST:** 1946
SQ FT: 11,000
SALES (est): 8.77MM
SALES (corp-wide): 34.95B **Privately Held**
Web: www.adamsproducts.com
SIC: 3271 5032 3272 Blocks, concrete or
   cinder: standard; Concrete building products
   ; Concrete products, nec
HQ: Crh Americas, Inc.
   900 Ashwood Pkwy Ste 600
   Atlanta GA 30338
   770 804-3363

(G-8920)
ADR HYDRO-CUT INC
125 International Dr Ste E (27560-7390)
PHONE.....................919 388-2251
David Brooks, *Pr*
Al Ely, *VP*
Ron Harris, *VP*
EMP: 5 **EST:** 1998
SQ FT: 10,000
SALES (est): 979.16K **Privately Held**
Web: www.adrhydrocut.com
SIC: 3589 Water treatment equipment,
   industrial

(G-8921)
ADVANCED MICRO DEVICES INC
3000 Rdu Center Dr Ste 230 (27560-7671)
PHONE..............................919 840-8080
Ted Donnelly, *Mgr*
EMP: 4
SALES (corp-wide): 25.79B **Publicly Held**
Web: www.amd.com
SIC: 3674 Integrated circuits, semiconductor
networks, etc.
PA: Advanced Micro Devices, Inc.
2485 Augustine Dr
Santa Clara CA 95054
408 749-4000

(G-8922)
ALCAMI CAROLINAS CORPORATION
627 Davis Dr Ste 100 (27560-7101)
PHONE..............................910 254-7000
EMP: 10
SALES (corp-wide): 418.48MM **Privately
Held**
Web: www.alcami.com
SIC: 2834 Pharmaceutical preparations
HQ: Alcami Carolinas Corporation
2320 Scientific Park Dr
Wilmington NC 28405

(G-8923)
ALCAMI CAROLINAS CORPORATION
419 Davis Dr Ste 300 (27560-7552)
PHONE..............................910 254-7000
EMP: 4
SALES (corp-wide): 418.48MM **Privately
Held**
Web: www.alcami.com
SIC: 2834 Drugs affecting neoplasms and
endrocrine systems
HQ: Alcami Carolinas Corporation
2320 Scientific Park Dr
Wilmington NC 28405

(G-8924)
ALCAMI CAROLINAS CORPORATION
200 Innovation Ave Ste 150 (27560-8562)
PHONE..............................910 254-7000
EMP: 4
SALES (corp-wide): 418.48MM **Privately
Held**
Web: www.alcami.com
SIC: 2834 8731 Drugs affecting neoplasms
and endrocrine systems; Biological research
HQ: Alcami Carolinas Corporation
2320 Scientific Park Dr
Wilmington NC 28405

(G-8925)
ALTERNATIVE PWR SLS & RENT LLP
1000 Northgate Ct (27560-6295)
PHONE..............................919 467-8001
Don Bitting Mg, *Pt*
Don Bitting, *Mng Pt*
EMP: 6 **EST:** 2004
SALES (est): 678.81K **Privately Held**
Web: www.alternativepower.com
SIC: 3621 Motors and generators

(G-8926)
AMG CASEWORK LLC
10315 Chapel Hill Rd (27560-8707)
P.O. Box 1338 (27560-1338)
PHONE..............................919 462-9203
Anita Mcleod, *Managing Member*
EMP: 10 **EST:** 2019
SALES (est): 928.34K **Privately Held**
Web: www.amgcasework.com
SIC: 2599 Cabinets, factory

(G-8927)
ANUTRA MEDICAL INC
1000 Perimeter Park Dr Ste E
(27560-9658)
PHONE..............................919 648-1215
Derek Lorati, *Admn*
EMP: 22 **EST:** 2013
SALES (est): 4.8MM **Privately Held**
Web: www.anutramedical.com
SIC: 3843 Dental equipment

(G-8928)
ANUVA SERVICES INC
Also Called: Anuva
140 Southcenter Ct Ste 600 (27560-8538)
PHONE..............................919 468-6441
▲ **EMP:** 14
Web: www.anuva.com
SIC: 3679 7629 Electronic circuits;
Electronic equipment repair

(G-8929)
APEX MARBLE AND GRANITE INC
10315b Chapel Hill Rd (27560-8707)
P.O. Box 1338 (27560-1338)
PHONE..............................919 462-9202
Nathan Mcleod, *Pr*
Anital Mcleod, *Sec*
EMP: 24 **EST:** 1999
SQ FT: 100
SALES (est): 986.03K **Privately Held**
Web: www.apexmarbleandgranite.com
SIC: 3281 1743 Granite, cut and shaped;
Marble installation, interior

(G-8930)
APJET INC (PA)
523 Davis Dr Ste 100 (27560-6554)
PHONE..............................919 595-5538
John A Emrich, *CEO*
EMP: 6 **EST:** 2014
SALES (est): 1.27MM
SALES (corp-wide): 1.27MM **Privately
Held**
Web: www.apjet.com
SIC: 3599 Industrial machinery, nec

(G-8931)
ARRAY BIOPHARMA INC
3005 Carrington Mill Blvd (27560-8885)
PHONE..............................303 381-6600
Tricia Haugeto, *Off Mgr*
EMP: 99
SALES (corp-wide): 63.63B **Publicly Held**
Web: www.pfizer.com
SIC: 2834 Pharmaceutical preparations
HQ: Array Biopharma Inc.
3200 Walnut St
Boulder CO 80301
303 381-6600

(G-8932)
ARRIVO MANAGEMENT LLC
3000 Rdu Center Dr (27560-7643)
PHONE..............................919 460-9500
Michael Ackermann, *Mgr*
EMP: 8 **EST:** 2015
SALES (est): 560.74K **Privately Held**
Web: www.arrivobio.com
SIC: 2834 Proprietary drug products

(G-8933)
ASCOM (US) INC
300 Perimeter Park Dr Ste D (27560-9703)
PHONE..............................877 712-7266
Tim Whelehan, *Pr*
Tom Mckearney, *VP*
Robert Goldman, *
Nancy Duffy, *
EMP: 150 **EST:** 2000

SQ FT: 10,000
SALES (est): 29.73MM **Privately Held**
Web: www.ascom.com
SIC: 3663 Radio broadcasting and
communications equipment
HQ: Ascom Solutions Ag
Gewerbepark
MAgenwil AG 5506

(G-8934)
ASTEELFLASH USA CORP
6833 Mount Herman Rd (27560-9261)
PHONE..............................919 882-5400
Pat Mcnally, *Mgr*
EMP: 138
Web: www.asteelflash.com
SIC: 3672 Printed circuit boards
HQ: Asteelflash Usa Corp.
1940 Milmont Dr
Milpitas CA 95035
510 440-2840

(G-8935)
ATC PANELS INC
2000 Aerial Center Pkwy Ste 113
(27560-9294)
PHONE..............................919 653-6053
Rony Obach, *Pr*
Jim Skinner, *VP*
◆ **EMP:** 4 **EST:** 2005
SALES (est): 181.57K **Privately Held**
SIC: 2493 Reconstituted wood products

(G-8936)
**AUTOMATED MACHINE
TECHNOLOGIES**
10404 Chapel Hill Rd Ste 100
(27560-6900)
P.O. Box 1186 (27560-1186)
PHONE..............................919 361-0121
Ted Kemnitz, *Pr*
EMP: 6 **EST:** 1994
SQ FT: 2,000
SALES (est): 1.82MM **Privately Held**
Web: www.amtliquidfilling.com
SIC: 3565 5084 3599 Packaging machinery;
Packaging machinery and equipment;
Custom machinery

(G-8937)
BASF CORPORATION
3500 Paramount Pkwy (27560-7218)
PHONE..............................919 461-6500
EMP: 46
SALES (corp-wide): 74.89B **Privately Held**
Web: www.basf.com
SIC: 2869 Industrial organic chemicals, nec
HQ: Basf Corporation
100 Park Ave
Florham Park NJ 07932
800 962-7831

(G-8938)
BAYER HEALTHCARE LLC
Also Called: Bayer Technology and Services
3500 Paramount Pkwy (27560-7218)
PHONE..............................919 461-6525
Neil Cleveland, *Brnch Mgr*
EMP: 10
SALES (corp-wide): 49.29B **Privately Held**
Web: www.bayercare.com
SIC: 2834 Pharmaceutical preparations
HQ: Bayer Healthcare Llc
100 Bayer Blvd
Whippany NJ 07981
862 404-3000

(G-8939)
BEAZER EAST INC
3131 Rdu Center Dr Ste 220 (27560-7687)
PHONE..............................919 380-2610

Jim Sprinkle, *Mgr*
EMP: 8
SQ FT: 1,836
SALES (corp-wide): 23.02B **Privately Held**
SIC: 3272 Concrete products, nec
HQ: Beazer East, Inc.
600 River Ave Ste 200
Pittsburgh PA 15212
412 428-9407

(G-8940)
BESPAK LABORATORIES INC
511 Davis Dr Ste 100 (27560-6804)
P.O. Box 14748 (27709-4748)
PHONE..............................919 884-2064
Kevin Clancy, *Ex Dir*
Francois Billard, *
Roger Francis, *
Anne Flodin, *
EMP: 50 **EST:** 1997
SQ FT: 29,811
SALES (est): 19.62MM **Privately Held**
Web: www.bespak.com
SIC: 2834 Pharmaceutical preparations
PA: Kemwell Biopharma Private Limited
Kemell House No.11,
Bengaluru KA 56002

(G-8941)
BIOSUPPLYNET INC
Also Called: Sciquest
3020 Carrington Mill Blvd Ste 100
(27560-5432)
PHONE..............................919 659-2121
Stephen J Wiehe, *CEO*
EMP: 10 **EST:** 1996
SALES (est): 9.92MM
SALES (corp-wide): 93.22MM **Privately
Held**
Web: www.blaze.ae
SIC: 5049 2721 Scientific and engineering
equipment and supplies; Periodicals,
publishing only
HQ: Jaggaer, Llc
700 Park Offices Dr
Durham NC 27713
919 659-2100

(G-8942)
BLUE FORCE TECHNOLOGIES LLC
627 Distribution Dr Ste D (27560-7100)
PHONE..............................919 443-1660
Babak Siavoshy, *Managing Member*
Joseph Murray, *
EMP: 90 **EST:** 2011
SALES (est): 19.52MM
SALES (corp-wide): 457.43MM **Privately
Held**
Web: www.blueforcetech.com
SIC: 3728 Fuselage assembly, aircraft
PA: Anduril Industries, Inc.
1400 Anduril
Costa Mesa CA 92626
949 891-1607

(G-8943)
BRAVOSOLUTION US INC (DH)
3020 Carrington Mill Blvd Ste 100
(27560-5432)
PHONE..............................312 373-3100
Marc Bergeron, *General*
Chandler Hall, *
Kristian O'meara, *VP*
Richard Long, *
Chris Horacek, *
▲ **EMP:** 25 **EST:** 1995
SALES (est): 9.57MM
SALES (corp-wide): 93.22MM **Privately
Held**
SIC: 7372 Prepackaged software
HQ: Jaggaer, Llc

700 Park Offices Dr
Durham NC 27713
919 659-2100

(G-8944)
BROWN BUILDING CORPORATION
1111 Copeland Oaks Dr (27560-6611)
P.O. Box 91206 (27675-1206)
PHONE...............................919 782-1800
Peter D Brown, *Pr*
Jan Brown, *Sec*
EMP: 10 EST: 1993
SALES (est): 273.46K **Privately Held**
SIC: 1521 1389 1611 Single-family housing
construction; Construction, repair, and
dismantling services; General contractor,
highway and street construction

(G-8945)
BUEHLER MOTOR INC (HQ)
1100 Perimeter Park Dr Ste 118
(27560-9119)
PHONE...............................919 380-3333
Peter Muhr, *CEO*
Ray Welterlin, *
Stephanie Denkowicz, *
Karl Wagner, *
◆ EMP: 25 EST: 2004
SALES (est): 46.3MM
SALES (corp-wide): 311.47MM **Privately
Held**
Web: www.buehlermotor.com
SIC: 3621 Motors, electric
PA: Buhler Motor Gmbh
Anne-Frank-Str. 33-35
Nurnberg BY 90459
91145040

(G-8946)
BURTS BEES INC
900 Aviation Pkwy Ste 400 (27560-9218)
PHONE...............................919 238-6450
Brian Buchanan, *Dir*
EMP: 243
SALES (corp-wide): 7.09B **Publicly Held**
Web: www.burtsbees.com
SIC: 2844 5122 Perfumes, cosmetics and
other toilet preparations; Drugs,
proprietaries, and sundries
HQ: Burt's Bees, Inc.
210 W Pettigrew St
Durham NC 27701

(G-8947)
BUSIAPP CORPORATION
Also Called: Lightjunction
400 Innovation Ave Ste 150 (27560-8557)
PHONE...............................877 558-2518
Yi Zhou, *Pr*
▲ EMP: 6 EST: 2013
SALES (est): 2.49MM **Privately Held**
Web: www.busiappcorp.com
SIC: 3648 Lighting equipment, nec

(G-8948)
CARRIER CORPORATION
200 Perimeter Park Dr Ste A (27560-9714)
PHONE...............................704 494-2600
Ronald Reitler, *Brnch Mgr*
EMP: 4
SALES (corp-wide): 22.49B **Publicly Held**
Web: www.carrier.com
SIC: 3585 Refrigeration and heating
equipment
HQ: Carrier Corporation
13995 Pasteur Blvd
Palm Beach Gardens FL 33418
561 365-2000

(G-8949)
**CATALENT PHARMA SOLUTIONS
LLC**
140 Southcenter Ct (27560-8538)
PHONE...............................919 481-4855
EMP: 7
Web: www.catalent.com
SIC: 2834 Pharmaceutical preparations
HQ: Catalent Pharma Solutions, Llc
14 Schoolhouse Rd
Somerset NJ 08873

(G-8950)
**CATALENT PHARMA SOLUTIONS
LLC**
Also Called: Catalent Biologics
120 Southcenter Ct Ste 900 (27560-8460)
PHONE...............................919 465-8101
EMP: 8
Web: www.catalent.com
SIC: 2834 Pharmaceutical preparations
HQ: Catalent Pharma Solutions, Llc
14 Schoolhouse Rd
Somerset NJ 08873

(G-8951)
CATALENT PHARMA SOLUTIONS INC
120 Southcenter Ct Ste 100 (27560-6664)
PHONE...............................919 481-2614
Russ Winstead, *Brnch Mgr*
EMP: 9
Web: www.catalent.com
SIC: 2834 Pharmaceutical preparations
HQ: Catalent Pharma Solutions, Inc.
14 Schoolhouse Rd
Somerset NJ 08873

(G-8952)
**CATALENT PHARMA SOLUTIONS
LLC**
160s N Pharma Dr (27560-9570)
PHONE...............................919 481-4855
Ramon Ceron, *Govt*
EMP: 11
SALES (est): 4.9MM **Privately Held**
SIC: 2834 8734 Pharmaceutical preparations
; Product testing laboratories

(G-8953)
CDV LLC (PA)
Also Called: Trimaco
2300 Gateway Centre Blvd Ste 200
(27560-9669)
PHONE...............................919 674-3460
◆ EMP: 18 EST: 2002
SQ FT: 22,000
SALES (est): 46.04MM
SALES (corp-wide): 46.04MM **Privately
Held**
SIC: 2851 2621 2672 2679 Paints and allied
products; Poster and art papers; Masking
tape: made from purchased materials;
Building paper, laminated: made from
purchased material

(G-8954)
CHARLES & COLVARD LTD (PA)
Also Called: Charles & Colvard
170 Southport Dr (27560)
PHONE...............................919 468-0399
Don O'connell, *Pr*
Neal I Goldman, *Ch Bd*
▲ EMP: 18 EST: 1995
SQ FT: 36,350
SALES (est): 29.95MM
SALES (corp-wide): 29.95MM **Publicly
Held**
Web: www.charlesandcolvard.com
SIC: 3911 Jewelry, precious metal

(G-8955)
CHARLES & COLVARD DIRECT LLC
300 Perimeter Park Dr Ste A (27560-9703)
PHONE...............................919 468-0399
Randall N Mccullough, *CEO*
EMP: 14 EST: 2011
SALES (est): 326.84K
SALES (corp-wide): 29.95MM **Publicly
Held**
SIC: 3915 Jewelers' materials and lapidary
work
PA: Charles & Colvard, Ltd.
170 Southport Dr
Morrisville NC 27560
919 468-0399

(G-8956)
CHARLESANDCOLVARDCOM LLC
Also Called: Moissanite.com, LLC
170 Southport Dr (27560-7327)
PHONE...............................877 202-5467
EMP: 21 EST: 2011
SALES (est): 910.19K
SALES (corp-wide): 29.95MM **Publicly
Held**
Web: www.charlesandcolvard.com
SIC: 3915 Jewelers' materials and lapidary
work
PA: Charles & Colvard, Ltd.
170 Southport Dr
Morrisville NC 27560
919 468-0399

(G-8957)
CHICHIBONE INC
600 Airport Blvd Ste 1400 (27560-9138)
PHONE...............................919 785-0090
Pat Mcnamara, *Pr*
EMP: 7
SALES (corp-wide): 23.23MM **Privately
Held**
Web: www.trs-sesco.com
SIC: 3561 1711 Pumps and pumping
equipment; Heating and air conditioning
contractors
PA: Chichibone, Inc.
1310 Grindelwald Pond Cir
Kernersville NC 27284
919 785-0090

(G-8958)
CISCO SYSTEMS INC
Also Called: Cisco Systems
7100 Kit Creek Rd (27560-8663)
PHONE...............................919 392-2000
John Chambers, *CEO*
EMP: 27
SALES (corp-wide): 53.8B **Publicly Held**
Web: www.cisco.com
SIC: 3577 3578 Data conversion equipment,
media-to-media: computer; Automatic teller
machines (ATM)
PA: Cisco Systems, Inc.
170 W Tasman Dr
San Jose CA 95134
408 526-2000

(G-8959)
CISCO SYSTEMS INC
Also Called: Cisco Systems
7025 Kit Creek Rd (27560-9741)
P.O. Box 14987 (27709-4987)
PHONE...............................919 392-2000
EMP: 2500
SALES (corp-wide): 53.8B **Publicly Held**
Web: www.cisco.com
SIC: 3577 8731 Data conversion equipment,
media-to-media: computer; Commercial
physical research
PA: Cisco Systems, Inc.
170 W Tasman Dr

San Jose CA 95134
408 526-4000

(G-8960)
CORTINA SYSTEMS
523 Davis Dr Ste 300 (27560-7165)
PHONE...............................919 226-1800
George Kaldani, *Prin*
EMP: 4 EST: 2007
SALES (est): 474.33K **Privately Held**
SIC: 3674 Semiconductors and related
devices

(G-8961)
CURRENT ENTERPRISES INC
125 International Dr Ste J (27560-7390)
PHONE...............................919 469-1227
Eugene Creech, *Pr*
George Welch, *Sec*
EMP: 6 EST: 1977
SQ FT: 10,130
SALES (est): 833.57K **Privately Held**
SIC: 3599 Machine shop, jobbing and repair

(G-8962)
DATAR CANCER GENETICS INC
500 Perimeter Park Dr Unit A (27560-9637)
PHONE...............................919 377-2119
Dadasaheb Akolkar, *Prin*
EMP: 14 EST: 2021
SALES (est): 1.16MM **Privately Held**
Web: www.datarpgx.com
SIC: 2835 In vitro diagnostics

(G-8963)
DCS USA CORPORATION
3000 Bear Cat Way Ste 118 (27560-7353)
P.O. Box 1233 (27560)
PHONE...............................919 535-8000
Annesophie Dorey, *Pr*
EMP: 5 EST: 2014
SALES (est): 283.85K **Privately Held**
Web: www.converting-systems.com
SIC: 3549 3423 3621 Cutting and slitting
machinery; Cutting dies, except metal
cutting; Rotary converters (electrical
equipment)

(G-8964)
DIGITAL RECORDERS INC
598 Airport Blvd Ste 300 (27560-7214)
PHONE...............................919 361-2155
Francis X Coleman Iii, *Prin*
Francis X Coleman Iii, *Pr*
Francis J Ingrassia, *
Andrew Stanton, *
EMP: 208 EST: 2012
SALES (est): 472.23K
SALES (corp-wide): 54.82MM **Privately
Held**
SIC: 3652 Prerecorded records and tapes
PA: Clever Devices Ltd.
300 Crossways Prk Dr
Woodbury NY 11797
516 433-6100

(G-8965)
DISCO HI-TEC AMERICA INC
3000 Aerial Center Pkwy Ste 140
(27560-9132)
PHONE...............................919 468-6003
Joel Sigmund, *Mgr*
EMP: 7
Web: www.dicing-grinding.com
SIC: 5065 3674 Semiconductor devices;
Semiconductors and related devices
HQ: Disco Hi-Tec America, Inc.
5921 Optical Ct
San Jose CA 95138
408 987-3776

▲ = Import ▼ = Export
◆ = Import/Export

(G-8966)
DOBLE ENGINEERING COMPANY
2200 Gateway Centre Blvd Ste 207
(27560-9122)
PHONE..................919 380-7461
Lawrence H Nordt, *Brnch Mgr*
EMP: 6
Web: www.doble.com
SIC: 8711 1389 Electrical or electronic
engineering; Pipe testing, oil field service
HQ: Doble Engineering Company
123 Felton St
Marlborough MA 01752
617 926-4900

(G-8967)
DOCU SOURCE OF NC
951 Aviation Pkwy Ste 600 (27560-6636)
PHONE..................919 459-5900
Derek Dorroh, *Prin*
EMP: 17 EST: 2013
SALES (est): 1.29MM **Privately Held**
Web: www.docusourceofnc.com
SIC: 2752 Offset printing

(G-8968)
DOCUSOURCE NORTH CAROLINA LLC
2800 Slater Rd (27560-8436)
PHONE..................919 459-5900
EMP: 35 EST: 2001
SQ FT: 26,500
SALES (est): 4.28MM **Privately Held**
Web: www.docusourceofnc.com
SIC: 2759 2789 2796 Publication printing;
Bookbinding and related work; Platemaking
services

(G-8969)
DOVA PHARMACEUTICALS INC (HQ)
Also Called: Dova Pharmaceuticals
3015 Carrington Mill Blvd (27560-5437)
PHONE..................919 748-5975
Duane Barnes, *Pr*
Guled Adam, *Sec*
Christine Belin, *Treas*
Mark W Hahn, *CFO*
Lee F Allen, *CMO*
EMP: 31 EST: 2016
SALES (est): 7.02MM
SALES (corp-wide): 1.32B **Privately Held**
Web: www.sobi-northamerica.com
SIC: 2834 Pharmaceutical preparations
PA: Swedish Orphan Biovitrum Ab (Publ)
Norra Stationsgatan 93a
Stockholm 113 6
86972000

(G-8970)
ELMARCO INC
1101 Aviation Pkwy Ste E (27560-7389)
PHONE..................919 334-6495
Kenneth L Donahue, *Pr*
EMP: 6 EST: 2009
SALES (est): 1.43MM **Privately Held**
Web: www.elmarco.com
SIC: 3552 Textile machinery

(G-8971)
EMITBIO INC
615 Davis Dr (27560-6845)
PHONE..................919 321-1726
Neal Hunter, *Ofcr*
David Emerson, *CEO*
John C Oakley, *CFO*
EMP: 6 EST: 2020
SALES (est): 2.9MM
SALES (corp-wide): 5.86MM **Privately Held**
Web: www.emitbio.com

SIC: 3841 Surgical and medical instruments
PA: Know Bio, Llc
615 Davis Dr Ste 800
Morrisville NC 27560
919 321-1726

(G-8972)
ENDAXI COMPANY INC
Also Called: Business Card Express Raleigh
137 Trans Air Dr (27560-7211)
P.O. Box 565 (27560-0565)
PHONE..................919 467-8895
Marshall Bates, *Pr*
Lyle Blue, *
Marilyn S Bates, *
EMP: 32 EST: 1989
SQ FT: 10,000
SALES (est): 794.01K **Privately Held**
Web: www.bcesouth.com
SIC: 2759 Thermography

(G-8973)
EXTREME NETWORKS INC (PA)
Also Called: Extreme
2121 Rdu Center Dr Ste 300 (27560)
PHONE..................408 579-2800
Edward B Meyercord Iii, *Pr*
John C Shoemaker, *
Kevin Rhodes, *Ex VP*
◆ EMP: 423 EST: 1996
SQ FT: 54,530
SALES (est): 1.12B **Publicly Held**
Web: www.extremenetworks.com
SIC: 3661 7373 7372 Telephone and
telegraph apparatus; Computer integrated
systems design; Prepackaged software

(G-8974)
FINELINE PROTOTYPING INC
3700 Pleasant Grove Church Rd
(27560-8942)
PHONE..................919 781-7702
Robert I Connelly, *Pr*
EMP: 53 EST: 2000
SQ FT: 11,000
SALES (est): 2.45MM
SALES (corp-wide): 500.89MM **Publicly Held**
Web: www.protolabs.com
SIC: 3089 Injection molding of plastics
PA: Proto Labs, Inc.
5540 Pioneer Creek Dr
Maple Plain MN 55359
763 479-3680

(G-8975)
FLEXTRONICS INTL USA INC
1000 Innovation Ave (27560)
PHONE..................919 998-4000
Debrie Johnson, *Brnch Mgr*
EMP: 218
Web: www.flex.com
SIC: 3672 8711 Printed circuit boards;
Engineering services
HQ: Flextronics International Usa, Inc.
12455 Research Blvd
Austin TX 78759

(G-8976)
FLOLOGIC INC
1015 Aviation Pkwy Ste 900 (27560-8556)
PHONE..................919 878-1808
Charles Desmet, *Pr*
▼ EMP: 5 EST: 1997
SQ FT: 4,200
SALES (est): 1.18MM **Privately Held**
Web: www.flologic.com
SIC: 5999 3432 5074 Plumbing and heating
supplies; Plumbing fixture fittings and trim;
Plumbing fittings and supplies

(G-8977)
FUJIFILM DSYNTH BTCHNLGIES USA (DH)
101 J Morris Commons Ln Ste 300
(27560-0287)
PHONE..................919 337-4400
Steve Spearman, *Managing Member*
Steve Spearman, *Managing Member*
EMP: 99 EST: 2011
SQ FT: 137,000
SALES (est): 152.61MM **Privately Held**
Web: www.fujifilmdiosynth.com
SIC: 2834 Pharmaceutical preparations
HQ: Fujifilm Holdings America Corporation
200 Summit Lake Dr
Valhalla NY 10595

(G-8978)
FURIEX PHARMACEUTICALS LLC
3900 Paramount Pkwy Ste 150
(27560-5401)
PHONE..................919 456-7800
A Robert D Bailey, *Pr*
Rita Weinberger, *Treas*
Kira Schwartz, *Sec*
EMP: 10 EST: 2009
SQ FT: 4,650
SALES (est): 1.1MM
SALES (corp-wide): 56.33B **Publicly Held**
Web: news.abbvie.com
SIC: 2834 Pharmaceutical preparations
HQ: Allergan Sales, Llc
2525 Dupont Dr
Irvine CA 92612

(G-8979)
GAINSPAN CORPORATION
3131 Rdu Center Dr Ste 135 (27560-7687)
PHONE..................408 627-6500
Yosi Fait, *CEO*
Yariv Dafna, *CDO*
Alon Segal, *
Michael Galai, *CLO*
Eran Edri, *
EMP: 58 EST: 2006
SALES (est): 4.74MM **Privately Held**
Web: www.telit.com
SIC: 3674 Semiconductors and related
devices

(G-8980)
GAMMA TECHNOLOGIES INC (PA)
125 International Dr Ste B (27560-7390)
P.O. Box 350 (27560-0350)
PHONE..................919 319-5272
Marc Verhoeven, *Pr*
EMP: 8 EST: 1983
SQ FT: 15,000
SALES (est): 1.07MM **Privately Held**
Web:
gammatechnologies.wordpress.com
SIC: 3451 3599 Screw machine products;
Machine shop, jobbing and repair

(G-8981)
GANNETT MEDIA CORP
U S A Today
107b Quail Fields Ct (27560-8798)
PHONE..................919 467-1402
Paul Cimino Circulation, *Mgr*
EMP: 10
SALES (corp-wide): 2.51B **Publicly Held**
Web: www.gannett.com
SIC: 2711 Newspapers, publishing and
printing
HQ: Gannett Media Corp.
7950 Jones Branch Dr
Mclean VA 22102
703 854-6000

(G-8982)
GILMORE GLOBL LGSTICS SVCS INC
101 Southcenter Ct Ste 100-E
(27560-8539)
PHONE..................919 277-2700
Bob Gilmore, *CEO*
Brian Wright, *
Dennis Quon, *
Robert E Gilmore, *Prin*
EMP: 100 EST: 1999
SQ FT: 50,000
SALES (est): 10.67MM
SALES (corp-wide): 96.89MM **Privately Held**
Web: www.gilmoreglobal.com
SIC: 7389 2752 2759 Printing broker;
Commercial printing, lithographic;
Commercial printing, nec
PA: Gilmore, R. E. Investments Corp
120 Herzberg Rd
Kanata ON K2K 3
613 592-2944

(G-8983)
GLAXOSMITHKLINE LLC
7030 Kit Creek Rd (27560-9761)
PHONE..................919 628-3630
EMP: 5
SALES (corp-wide): 39.77B **Privately Held**
Web: us.gsk.com
SIC: 2834 Pharmaceutical preparations
HQ: Glaxosmithkline Llc
2929 Walnut St Ste 1700
Philadelphia PA 19112
888 825-5249

(G-8984)
GLOBAL RESOURCE CORPORATION
Also Called: (A Development Stage Company)
9400 Globe Center Dr Ste 101
(27560-6213)
PHONE..................919 972-7803
Peter A Worthington, *CEO*
Peter A Worthington, *Interim Chairman of the Board*
Jeffrey J Andrews, *CFO*
Ken Kinsella, *Pr*
▲ EMP: 5 EST: 2000
SQ FT: 5,124
SALES (est): 403.12K **Privately Held**
SIC: 3559 Automotive related machinery

(G-8985)
HATTERAS NETWORKS INC
637 Davis Dr (27560-6835)
PHONE..................919 991-5440
Mike Aquino, *Pr*
Kevin Sheehan, *CEO*
Jeff White, *Pr*
Vincent Zumbo, *CFO*
▲ EMP: 17 EST: 1999
SQ FT: 16,275
SALES (est): 2.92MM **Privately Held**
Web: www.hatterasnetworks.com
SIC: 3661 Telephone and telegraph
apparatus

(G-8986)
HB FULLER ADHESIVES LLC
523 Davis Dr Ste 400 (27560-7165)
PHONE..................415 878-7202
EMP: 35
SALES (corp-wide): 3.57B **Publicly Held**
Web: www.hbfuller.com
SIC: 2891 Adhesives
HQ: H.B. Fuller Adhesives, Llc
1200 Willow Lake Blvd
Saint Paul MN 55110
651 236-5823

(G-8987)
HERITAGE DESIGN & SUPPLY LLC
Also Called: Cabinetry Div
6833 Mount Herman Rd (27560-9261)
PHONE..................................919 453-1622
Adam R Nix, *Managing Member*
Matthew Wallace, *Managing Member*
EMP: 23 EST: 2022
SALES (est): 1.74MM **Privately Held**
Web: www.heritagedesignandsupply.com
SIC: 2434 1771 Wood kitchen cabinets;
Flooring contractor

(G-8988)
HEXATECH INC
991 Aviation Pkwy Ste 800 (27560-8458)
PHONE..................................919 481-4412
John Goehrke, *CEO*
Zlatko Sitar, *Pr*
Raoul Schleffer, *VP*
Kathy Morris, *CFO*
▲ EMP: 13 EST: 2001
SALES (est): 8.94MM **Privately Held**
Web: www.hexatechinc.com
SIC: 3674 Semiconductors and related
devices

(G-8989)
HZO INC (PA)
Also Called: Hzo
5151 Mccrimmon Pkwy Ste 208
(27560-8425)
PHONE..................................919 439-0505
Richard Holder, *CEO*
Glen Marder, *
EMP: 48 EST: 2009
SALES (est): 19.78MM
SALES (corp-wide): 19.78MM **Privately
Held**
Web: www.hzo.com
SIC: 2899 Waterproofing compounds

(G-8990)
ICONTACT LLC
Also Called: Broadwick
2450 Perimeter Park Dr Ste 105
(27560-8443)
PHONE..................................919 957-6150
Nate Simmons, *Pr*
EMP: 67 EST: 2003
SALES (est): 4.7MM
SALES (corp-wide): 21.6MM **Privately
Held**
Web: www.icontact.com
SIC: 7372 Business oriented computer
software
HQ: Cision Us Inc.
300 S Riverside Plz
Chicago IL 60606
877 297-8912

(G-8991)
IFS INDUSTRIES INC
Also Called: Ifs Industries
100 Southcenter Ct Ste 300 (27560-9125)
PHONE..................................919 234-1397
EMP: 22
SALES (corp-wide): 76.91MM **Privately
Held**
Web: www.ifscos.com
SIC: 2899 Chemical preparations, nec
PA: Ifs Industries, Inc.
400 Orton Ave
Reading PA 19603
610 378-1381

(G-8992)
IMBRIUM THERAPEUTICS LP
400 Park Offices Dr Ste Ll 102 (27560)
PHONE..................................984 439-1075
David Igo, *Brnch Mgr*

EMP: 11
SALES (corp-wide): 458.51MM **Privately
Held**
Web: www.purduepharma.com
SIC: 2834 Pharmaceutical preparations
HQ: Imbrium Therapeutics L.P.
201 Tresser Blvd
Stamford CT 06901
888 827-0622

(G-8993)
INI POWER SYSTEMS INC
Also Called: I N I
137 Trans Air Dr (27560-7211)
PHONE..................................919 677-7112
EMP: 12
Web: www.inipower.com
SIC: 3621 Motors and generators

(G-8994)
**INTERPACE PHARMA SOLUTIONS
INC**
133 Southcenter Ct Ste 400 (27560-8537)
PHONE..................................919 678-7024
EMP: 4 EST: 2019
SALES (est): 426.75K **Privately Held**
Web: www.interpace.com
SIC: 2834 Pharmaceutical preparations

(G-8995)
JOHNSON CONTROLS INC
2700 Perimeter Park Dr (27560-8448)
PHONE..................................866 285-8345
George Oliver, *CEO*
Joanne Birtwistle, *VP*
Tomas Brannemo, *VP*
EMP: 4 EST: 1926
SALES (est): 121.27K **Privately Held**
SIC: 1389 7372 4911 Grading oil and gas
well foundations; Prepackaged software;
Transmission, electric power

(G-8996)
KDY AUTOMATION SOLUTIONS INC
150 Dominion Dr Ste E (27560-9205)
PHONE..................................888 219-0049
Allan Salant, *Pr*
Douglas Mecvey, *VP*
EMP: 6 EST: 2006
SALES (est): 4.2MM **Privately Held**
Web: www.kdyautomation.com
SIC: 7371 8711 3429 3823 Computer
software development; Engineering services
; Hardware, nec; Industrial process control
instruments

(G-8997)
KEEL LABS INC
1015 Aviation Pkwy Ste 400 (27560-8540)
PHONE..................................917 848-9066
Aaron Nesser, *CEO*
Aleksandra Gosiewski, *Dir*
Wayne Cheng, *Prin*
EMP: 5 EST: 2019
SALES (est): 2.22MM **Privately Held**
Web: www.keellabs.com
SIC: 7389 2282 Design services; Acetate
filament yarn: throwing, twisting, winding,
spooling

(G-8998)
KODAK
1100 Perimeter Park Dr Ste 108
(27560-9119)
PHONE..................................919 559-7232
Chuck Bowen, *Mgr*
EMP: 6 EST: 2011
SALES (est): 484.03K **Privately Held**
Web: www.kodakalaris.com

SIC: 3861 Photographic equipment and
supplies

(G-8999)
KORBER PHARMA INC
Also Called: Korber Medipak Systems N Amer
1001 Aviation Pkwy Ste 200 (27560-6607)
PHONE..................................727 538-4644
Kerry Fillmore, *Pr*
EMP: 37
SALES (corp-wide): 54.57MM **Privately
Held**
Web: www.koerber-pharma.com
SIC: 3565 Packaging machinery
HQ: Korber Pharma, Inc.
2243 Energy Dr
Apex NC 27502
727 538-4644

(G-9000)
KOWA RESEARCH INSTITUTE INC
430 Davis Dr Ste 200 (27560-6802)
PHONE..................................919 433-1600
Gary Gordon, *Pr*
EMP: 21 EST: 2003
SALES (est): 8.43MM **Privately Held**
Web: www.kowaus.com
SIC: 2834 Pharmaceutical preparations
HQ: Kowa Holdings America, Inc.
55 E 59th St Fl 19a
New York NY 10022

(G-9001)
KSEP SYSTEMS LLC
598 Airport Blvd Ste 600 (27560-7205)
PHONE..................................919 339-1850
Sunil Mehta, *Pr*
Tod Herman, *Dir*
EMP: 4 EST: 2011
SALES (est): 245.25K **Privately Held**
SIC: 2834 Pharmaceutical preparations

(G-9002)
LAIRD THERMAL SYSTEMS INC
629 Davis Dr Ste 200 (27560-7890)
PHONE..................................919 597-7300
Karine Brand, *CEO*
Robert Baxter, *Sec*
◆ EMP: 23 EST: 2019
SQ FT: 14,150
SALES (est): 10.58MM
SALES (corp-wide): 12.39B **Publicly Held**
Web: www.lairdthermal.com
SIC: 3629 Electronic generation equipment
HQ: Laird Technologies, Inc.
16401 Swngley Rdge Rd Ste
Chesterfield MO 63017
636 898-6000

(G-9003)
LAMBDA TECHNOLOGIES INC
2200 Gateway Centre Blvd (27560-6217)
PHONE..................................919 462-1919
Richard Garard, *Pr*
▲ EMP: 20 EST: 1994
SALES (est): 5.01MM **Privately Held**
Web: www.microcure.com
SIC: 3567 Heating units and devices,
industrial: electric

(G-9004)
LENOVO (UNITED STATES) INC
5241 Paramount Pkwy (27560-8496)
PHONE..................................919 486-9627
Julia Deigh, *Brnch Mgr*
EMP: 5
Web: www.lenovo.com
SIC: 3571 Electronic computers
HQ: Lenovo (United States) Inc.
8001 Development Dr
Morrisville NC 27560
855 253-6686

(G-9005)
LENOVO (UNITED STATES) INC
7001 Development Dr Bldg 7 (27560-8105)
PHONE..................................919 237-8389
EMP: 135
Web: www.lenovo.com
SIC: 3571 Electronic computers
HQ: Lenovo (United States) Inc.
8001 Development Dr
Morrisville NC 27560
855 253-6686

(G-9006)
LENOVO (UNITED STATES) INC (HQ)
Also Called: Lenovo International
8001 Development Dr (27560-7416)
PHONE..................................855 253-6686
Yang Yuanqing, *CEO*
Gianfranco Lanci, *
Liu Chuanzhi, *
Wong W Ming, *
David Roman, *
▲ EMP: 1518 EST: 2005
SALES (est): 653.89MM **Privately Held**
Web: www.lenovo.com
SIC: 3571 7371 Electronic computers;
Computer software development and
applications
PA: Lenovo Group Limited
23/F Taikoo Place Lincoln Hse
Quarry Bay HK

(G-9007)
LENOVO GLOBAL TECH US INC (HQ)
8001 Development Dr (27560-7416)
PHONE..................................855 253-6686
Yang Yuanqing Wins, *CEO*
Gianfranco Lanci, *COO*
Wong Wai Ming, *VP*
EMP: 592 EST: 2016
SALES (est): 3.9B **Privately Held**
Web: www.lenovo.com
SIC: 3571 Electronic computers
PA: Lenovo Group Limited
23/F Taikoo Place Lincoln Hse
Quarry Bay HK

(G-9008)
**LENOVO HOLDING COMPANY INC
(HQ)**
8001 Development Dr (27560-7416)
PHONE..................................855 253-6686
Kurt Cranor, *Pr*
EMP: 14 EST: 2007
SALES (est): 48.16MM **Privately Held**
Web: www.lenovocareers.com
SIC: 3571 Personal computers
(microcomputers)
PA: Lenovo Group Limited
23/F Taikoo Place Lincoln Hse
Quarry Bay HK

(G-9009)
LENOVO US FULFILLMENT CTR LLC
1009 Think Pl (27560-9002)
P.O. Box 1009 (27560-1009)
PHONE..................................855 253-6686
Yang Yuanqing, *CEO*
John Pershke, *Managing Member**
▲ EMP: 11 EST: 2007
SALES (est): 24.9MM **Privately Held**
Web: www.lenovo.com
SIC: 3571 Electronic computers
HQ: Lenovo Holding Company, Inc.
8001 Development Dr
Morrisville NC 27560
855 253-6686

2025 Harris North Carolina
Manufacturers Directory

▲ = Import ▼ = Export
◆ = Import/Export

(G-9010)
LIBERTY INVESTMENT & MGT CORP
Also Called: Metaltek
455 Kitty Hawk Dr (27560-8515)
P.O. Box 30399 (27622-0399)
PHONE....................................919 544-0344
Alfred F Yarur, *Pr*
Nickolas J Yarur, *VP*
▲ **EMP:** 15 **EST:** 1973
SQ FT: 10,000
SALES (est): 3.09MM **Privately Held**
Web: www.playmatetennis.com
SIC: 3949 Tennis equipment and supplies

(G-9011)
LIGHTJUNCTION
400 Innovation Ave # 150 (27560-8557)
PHONE....................................919 607-9717
EMP: 5 **EST:** 2014
SALES (est): 205.1K **Privately Held**
Web: www.lightjunction.com
SIC: 3648 Lighting equipment, nec

(G-9012)
LIPOSCIENCE INC
Also Called: Liposcience
100 Perimeter Park Dr Ste C (27560-9715)
PHONE....................................919 212-1999
Howard B Doran, *Pr*
William C Cromwell, *Chief Medical Officer**
Lucy G Martindale, *
James D Otvos, *
EMP: 239 **EST:** 2000
SQ FT: 83,000
SALES (est): 9.09MM
SALES (corp-wide): 13.01B **Publicly Held**
Web: www.liposcience.com
SIC: 8071 2835 Testing laboratories;
Diagnostic substances
HQ: Laboratory Corporation Of America
531 S Spring St
Burlington NC 27215
336 229-1127

(G-9013)
LONZA RTP
523 Davis Dr Ste 400 (27560-7165)
PHONE....................................800 748-8979
EMP: 6
SALES (est): 260.38K **Privately Held**
Web: www.lonza.com
SIC: 2834 Pharmaceutical preparations

(G-9014)
LQ3 PHARMACEUTICALS INC
Also Called: Lq3 Pharmaceuticals
419 Davis Dr Ste 100 (27560-7551)
PHONE....................................919 794-7391
Kyle Chenet, *CEO*
Kevin Herlihy, *Dir*
Drew Folk, *Dir*
Enrique Alvarez, *Prin*
EMP: 4 **EST:** 2013
SALES (est): 430.8K **Privately Held**
Web: www.lq3pharma.com
SIC: 2834 Pharmaceutical preparations

(G-9015)
LULU TECHNOLOGY CIRCUS INC
Also Called: Lulu.com
860 Aviation Pkwy Ste 300 (27560-7396)
PHONE....................................919 459-5858
Robert Young, *CEO*
Gart Davis, *
Tim Albury, *
Bryce Boothby Junior, *COO*
EMP: 20 **EST:** 2002
SQ FT: 13,800
SALES (est): 906.93K **Privately Held**
SIC: 8299 2731 Educational services;
Books, publishing and printing

(G-9016)
MACOM TECHNOLOGY SOLUTIONS INC
523 Davis Dr Ste 500 (27560-7165)
PHONE....................................919 807-9100
EMP: 72
Web: www.macom.com
SIC: 3674 Semiconductors and related
devices
HQ: Macom Technology Solutions Inc.
100 Chelmsford St
Lowell MA 01851

(G-9017)
MARVELL SEMICONDUCTOR INC
3015 Carrington Mill Blvd (27560-5437)
PHONE....................................408 222-2500
EMP: 90
SALES (corp-wide): 5.51B **Publicly Held**
Web: www.marvell.com
SIC: 3674 Semiconductors and related
devices
HQ: Marvell Semiconductor, Inc.
5488 Marvell Ln
Santa Clara CA 95054

(G-9018)
**MATERIAL HANDLING
TECHNOLOGIES INC (PA)**
Also Called: Material Handling Tech - NC
113 International Dr (27560-8792)
PHONE....................................919 388-0050
EMP: 60 **EST:** 1992
SALES (est): 20.51MM **Privately Held**
Web: www.materialhandlingtech.com
SIC: 5084 3535 Materials handling
machinery; Conveyors and conveying
equipment

(G-9019)
MAXIMUM ASP
9221 Globe Center Dr Ste 120
(27560-6205)
PHONE....................................919 544-7900
D Foster C, *Technology Officer*
EMP: 5 **EST:** 2015
SALES (est): 712.85K **Privately Held**
SIC: 3841 Surgical and medical instruments

(G-9020)
MICROPORE TECHNOLOGIES INC
2121 Tw Alexander Dr Ste 124-8
(27560-6815)
PHONE....................................984 344-7499
Dai Hayward, *CEO*
EMP: 16 **EST:** 2019
SALES (est): 903.94K **Privately Held**
Web: www.microporetech.com
SIC: 3559 Pharmaceutical machinery

(G-9021)
MOTOROLA MOBILITY LLC
7001 Development Dr (27560-8105)
PHONE....................................919 294-1289
EMP: 31
Web: www.motorola.com
SIC: 3663 Mobile communication equipment
HQ: Motorola Mobility Llc
222 W Mdse Mart Plz Ste 1
Chicago IL 60654

(G-9022)
NCONTACT SURGICAL LLC
Also Called: Atricure
1001 Aviation Pkwy Ste 400 (27560-9135)
EMP: 19 **EST:** 2004
SQ FT: 3,500
SALES (est): 1.83MM **Privately Held**
Web: www.ncontactinc.com

SIC: 3841 Surgical and medical instruments

(G-9023)
NEOMONDE BAKING COMPANY (PA)
Also Called: Neomonde Bakery
220 Dominion Dr Ste A (27560-7307)
PHONE....................................919 469-8009
Sam Saleh, *Pr*
Joseph Saleh, *
Mounir Saleh, *
EMP: 50 **EST:** 1977
SALES (est): 10.69MM
SALES (corp-wide): 10.69MM **Privately
Held**
Web: www.neomonde.com
SIC: 2051 5812 Bakery: wholesale or
wholesale/retail combined; Delicatessen
(eating places)

(G-9024)
NEURONEX INC
9001 Aerial Center Pkwy Ste 110
(27560-9731)
PHONE....................................919 460-9500
Moise A Khayrallah Ph.d., *CEO*
EMP: 5 **EST:** 2010
SALES (est): 468.25K **Publicly Held**
SIC: 2834 Pharmaceutical preparations
PA: Acorda Therapeutics, Inc.
2 Blue Hill Plz Fl 3
Pearl River NY 10965

(G-9025)
NHANCED SEMICONDUCTORS INC
800 Perimeter Park Dr Ste B (27560-7271)
PHONE....................................630 561-6813
Robert Patti, *Pr*
EMP: 20
SALES (corp-wide): 2.08MM **Privately
Held**
Web: www.nhanced-semi.com
SIC: 3674 Semiconductors and related
devices
PA: Nhanced Semiconductors, Inc.
1201 N Raddant Rd
Batavia IL 60510
331 701-7070

(G-9026)
NITRONEX LLC
523 Davis Dr Ste 500 (27560-7165)
PHONE....................................919 807-9100
Greg Baker, *Pr*
EMP: 30 **EST:** 1999
SQ FT: 12,000
SALES (est): 2.76MM **Publicly Held**
Web: www.macom.com
SIC: 3674 Semiconductors and related
devices
HQ: Macom Technology Solutions Inc.
100 Chelmsford St
Lowell MA 01851

(G-9027)
NITTA GELATIN HOLDINGS INC (HQ)
598 Airport Blvd Ste 900 (27560-7205)
PHONE....................................919 238-3300
Raymond Merz, *Pr*
EMP: 26 **EST:** 1996
SQ FT: 24,000
SALES (est): 7.62MM **Privately Held**
Web: www.nitta-gelatin.com
SIC: 2899 Gelatin
PA: Nitta Gelatin Inc.
2-22, Futamata
Yao OSK 581-0

(G-9028)
NITTA GELATIN USA INC
598 Airport Blvd (27560-7214)
PHONE....................................910 484-0457

Raymond Merz, *Pr*
Tsuneo Sasaki, *
Hiroshi Takase, *
▲ **EMP:** 25 **EST:** 2004
SALES (est): 7.13MM **Privately Held**
Web: www.nitta-gelatin.com
SIC: 2899 Gelatin
HQ: Nitta Gelatin Holdings, Inc.
598 Airport Blvd Ste 900
Morrisville NC 27560

(G-9029)
**NORTHROP GRUMMAN SYSTEMS
CORP**
Also Called: Northrop Grumman Info Systems
3005 Carrington Mill Blvd (27560-8885)
PHONE....................................919 465-5020
Cindy Hicks, *Brnch Mgr*
EMP: 120
Web: www.northropgrumman.com
SIC: 3812 Search and navigation equipment
HQ: Northrop Grumman Systems
Corporation
2980 Fairview Park Dr
Falls Church VA 22042
703 280-2900

(G-9030)
NOVOZYMES NORTH AMERICA INC
9000 Development Dr (27560-7427)
PHONE....................................919 494-3220
EMP: 42
SALES (corp-wide): 2.61B **Privately Held**
Web: www.novozymes.com
SIC: 2869 Industrial organic chemicals, nec
HQ: Novozymes North America, Inc.
77 Perry Chapel Church Rd
Franklinton NC 27525
919 494-2014

(G-9031)
NOXON AUTOMATION USA LLC
150 Dominion Dr Ste B (27560-9205)
PHONE....................................919 390-1560
Marcel Zachmann, *Managing Member*
EMP: 5 **EST:** 2015
SALES (est): 677.26K **Privately Held**
Web: www.noxon-automation.com
SIC: 3599 Custom machinery

(G-9032)
ONION PEEL SOFTWARE INC
1 Copley Pkwy Ste 480 (27560-7423)
PHONE....................................919 460-1789
Douglas R Austin, *Pr*
EMP: 4 **EST:** 1994
SQ FT: 15,000
SALES (est): 293.59K **Privately Held**
SIC: 7372 7379 7371 Business oriented
computer software; Computer related
consulting services; Custom computer
programming services

(G-9033)
ORACLE CORPORATION
Also Called: Oracle
5200 Paramount Pkwy Ste 100
(27560-5470)
PHONE....................................919 595-2500
EMP: 65
SALES (corp-wide): 52.96B **Publicly Held**
Web: www.oracle.com
SIC: 7372 Prepackaged software
PA: Oracle Corporation
2300 Oracle Way
Austin TX 78741
737 867-1000

(G-9034)
PATHEON CALCULUS MERGER LLC
3900 Paramount Pkwy (27560-7200)
PHONE.....................................919 226-3200
EMP: 4 EST: 2018
SALES (est): 457.95K
SALES (corp-wide): 42.86B **Publicly Held**
SIC: 2834 Pharmaceutical preparations
PA: Thermo Fisher Scientific Inc.
 168 3rd Ave
 Waltham MA 02451
 781 622-1000

(G-9035)
**PATHEON PHARMACEUTICALS INC
(DH)**
Also Called: Patheon
3900 Paramount Pkwy (27560-7200)
PHONE.....................................919 226-3200
James C Mullen, *CEO*
Frank Mccune, *Sec*
Bradley Mitchell, *Treas*
Michael Lehmann, *Pr*
Stuart Grant, *Ex VP*
◆ **EMP: 58 EST:** 2002
SALES (est): 89.15MM
SALES (corp-wide): 42.86B **Publicly Held**
SIC: 2834 Pharmaceutical preparations
HQ: Patheon U.S. Holdings Inc.
 4815 Emperor Blvd Ste 110
 Durham NC 27703

(G-9036)
**PATHEON PHRMCEUTICALS SVCS
INC (DH)**
Also Called: Patheon
3900 Paramount Pkwy (27560-7200)
PHONE.....................................919 226-3200
James Mullen, *CEO*
EMP: 48 EST: 2009
SALES (est): 24.68MM
SALES (corp-wide): 42.86B **Publicly Held**
Web: www.patheon.com
SIC: 2834 Pharmaceutical preparations
HQ: Patheon U.S. Holdings Inc.
 4815 Emperor Blvd Ste 110
 Durham NC 27703

(G-9037)
PATHOLDCO INC (HQ)
108 Nova Dr (27560-8244)
P.O. Box 46449 (27620-6449)
PHONE.....................................919 212-1300
Scott R Ahrens, *Pr*
Lynn M Heatherly, *VP*
Todd M Ahrens, *Treas*
EMP: 8 EST: 1994
SALES (est): 4.3MM
SALES (corp-wide): 15.19MM **Privately
Held**
Web: www.precisionairtechnology.com
SIC: 3564 Filters, air: furnaces, air
 conditioning equipment, etc.
PA: Technical Safety Services, Llc
 4225 Executive Sq Ste 370
 La Jolla CA 92037
 510 845-5591

(G-9038)
PRACTICHEM LLC
Also Called: Practichem
10404 Chapel Hill Rd Ste 112 (27560-6900)
PHONE.....................................919 714-8430
Nicholas Demarco, *Prin*
EMP: 7 EST: 2010
SALES (est): 1.22MM **Privately Held**
Web: www.practichem.com
SIC: 3826 Chromatographic equipment,
 laboratory type

(G-9039)
PROGRESS SOFTWARE CORP
3005 Carrington Mill Blvd (27560-8885)
PHONE.....................................919 461-4200
EMP: 14 EST: 2014
SALES (est): 2.91MM **Privately Held**
Web: www.progress.com
SIC: 7372 Business oriented computer
 software

(G-9040)
PROTO LABS INC
3700 Pleasant Grove Church Rd
(27560-8942)
PHONE.....................................833 245-8827
Craig Goss, *of Strat*
EMP: 86
SALES (corp-wide): 500.89MM **Publicly
Held**
Web: www.protolabs.com
SIC: 3089 Plastics containers, except foam
PA: Proto Labs, Inc.
 5540 Pioneer Creek Dr
 Maple Plain MN 55359
 763 479-3680

(G-9041)
QUATROBIO LLC
3000 Rdu Center Dr (27560-7643)
PHONE.....................................919 460-9500
EMP: 6 EST: 2016
SALES (est): 252.46K **Privately Held**
Web: www.arrivobio.com
SIC: 2834 Pharmaceutical preparations

(G-9042)
QUEST SOFTWARE INC
Also Called: QUEST SOFTWARE, INC.
133 Southcenter Ct (27560-8537)
PHONE.....................................919 337-4719
Mike Sharrett, *Brnch Mgr*
EMP: 4
SALES (corp-wide): 647.68MM **Privately
Held**
Web: www.quest.com
SIC: 7372 Prepackaged software
PA: Quest Software Inc.
 20 Enterprise Ste 100
 Aliso Viejo CA 92656
 949 754-8000

(G-9043)
RFHIC US CORPORATION
920 Morrisville Pkwy (27560-8799)
PHONE.....................................919 677-8780
Stella Bae, *Pr*
EMP: 8 EST: 2012
SALES (est): 2.79MM **Privately Held**
Web: www.rfhic.com
SIC: 3674 Integrated circuits, semiconductor
 networks, etc.
PA: Rfhic Corporation
 110 Gwacheon-Daero 12-Gil
 Gwacheon 13824

(G-9044)
SCHELLING AMERICA INC
301 Kitty Hawk Dr (27560-8581)
P.O. Box 80367 (27623-0367)
PHONE.....................................919 544-0430
▲ **EMP: 30 EST:** 1986
SALES (est): 19.67MM
SALES (corp-wide): 419.4MM **Privately
Held**
Web: www.imaschelling.us
SIC: 5084 3541 Woodworking machinery;
 Machine tools, metal cutting type
HQ: Ima Schelling Austria Gmbh
 Gebhard Schwarzler-StraBe 34
 Schwarzach 6858
 55723960

(G-9045)
SCHNEIDER ELECTRIC USA INC
Also Called: Schneider Electric
1101 Shiloh Glenn Dr # 100 (27560-5419)
PHONE.....................................888 778-2733
Charlie Denny, *Brnch Mgr*
EMP: 152
SALES (corp-wide): 1.09K **Privately Held**
Web: www.se.com
SIC: 3613 Switchgear and switchboard
 apparatus
HQ: Schneider Electric Usa, Inc.
 1 Boston Pl Ste 2700
 Boston MA 02108
 617 904-9422

(G-9046)
SCHUNK INTEC INC
Also Called: Schunk
211 Kitty Hawk Dr (27560-8548)
P.O. Box 91023 (27675-1023)
PHONE.....................................919 572-2705
Milton Guerry, *Pr*
Heinz D Schunk, *
Henrik Schunk, *
◆ **EMP: 80 EST:** 1992
SQ FT: 37,000
SALES (est): 22.81MM
SALES (corp-wide): 47.12MM **Privately
Held**
Web: www.schunk.com
SIC: 3542 5084 3594 3544 Machine tools,
 metal forming type; Machine tools and
 metalworking machinery; Fluid power
 pumps and motors; Special dies, tools, jigs,
 and fixtures
PA: Schunk Se & Co. Kg Spanntechnik
 Greiftechnik Automatisierungstechnik
 Bahnhofstr. 106-134
 Lauffen Am Neckar BW 74348
 71331030

(G-9047)
SCIQUEST HOLDINGS INC
5151 Mccrimmon Pkwy Ste 216
(27560-8425)
PHONE.....................................919 659-2100
Stephen J Wiehe, *CEO*
EMP: 89 EST: 2004
SALES (est): 873.7K **Privately Held**
SIC: 7372 Educational computer software

(G-9048)
SCIQUEST PARENT LLC (PA)
3020 Carrington Mill Blvd Ste 100
(27560-5433)
PHONE.....................................919 659-2100
EMP: 11 EST: 2016
SALES (est): 93.22MM
SALES (corp-wide): 93.22MM **Privately
Held**
Web: www.jaggaer.com
SIC: 7372 Business oriented computer
 software

(G-9049)
SCORPIUS HOLDINGS INC (PA)
Also Called: Scorpius
627 Davis Dr Ste 400 (27560)
PHONE.....................................919 240-7133
Jeffrey Wolf, *Ch Bd*
William L Ostrander, *CFO*
EMP: 24 EST: 2008
SQ FT: 15,996
SALES (est): 6.99MM **Publicly Held**
Web: www.nighthawkbio.com
SIC: 2834 Pharmaceutical preparations

(G-9050)
SENSUS USA INC
639 Davis Dr (27560-6835)
PHONE.....................................919 879-3200
Darrin Sutherland, *Brnch Mgr*
EMP: 246
Web: www.sensus.com
SIC: 3824 Gasmeters, domestic and large
 capacity: industrial
HQ: Sensus Usa Inc.
 637 Davis Dr
 Morrisville NC 27560

(G-9051)
SENSUS USA INC (HQ)
Also Called: Sensus
637 Davis Dr (27560-6835)
P.O. Box 30160 (77842-3160)
PHONE.....................................919 845-4000
◆ **EMP: 24 EST:** 1989
SALES (est): 529.31MM **Publicly Held**
Web: www.sensus.com
SIC: 3824 3363 2891 3491 Gasmeters,
 domestic and large capacity: industrial;
 Aluminum die-castings; Sealants; Industrial
 valves
PA: Xylem Inc.
 301 Water St Se Ste 200
 Washington DC 20003

(G-9052)
SENSUS USA INC
Also Called: Sensus Metering Systems
400 Perimeter Park Dr Ste K (27560-9744)
Rural Route 639 Davis Dr (27560)
PHONE.....................................919 576-6185
EMP: 200
Web: www.sensus.com
SIC: 3824 3363 3491 2891 Gasmeters,
 domestic and large capacity: industrial;
 Aluminum die-castings; Industrial valves;
 Sealants
HQ: Sensus Usa Inc.
 637 Davis Dr
 Morrisville NC 27560

(G-9053)
SHIFTWIZARD INC
909 Aviation Pkwy Ste 700 (27560-6632)
PHONE.....................................866 828-3318
Christain Pardue, *Pr*
David Moes, *VP*
Shane Pearker, *VP*
EMP: 10 EST: 2005
SQ FT: 1,000
SALES (est): 4.47MM **Publicly Held**
Web: www.shiftwizard.com
SIC: 3571 Electronic computers
PA: Healthstream, Inc.
 500 11th Ave N Ste 1000
 Nashville TN 37203

(G-9054)
SICEL TECHNOLOGIES INC
3800 Gateway Centre Blvd (27560-6220)
PHONE.....................................919 465-2236
Charles Scarantino, *Ch Bd*
Michael D Riddle, *
Jennifer Pierce, *
EMP: 48 EST: 1994
SQ FT: 17,625
SALES (est): 2.38MM **Privately Held**
SIC: 3841 Diagnostic apparatus, medical

(G-9055)
SIGNATURE FLIGHT AIR INC
Also Called: TAC Air
1725 E International Dr (27560-7690)
P.O. Box 90995 (27675-0995)
PHONE.....................................919 840-4400
Greg Arnold, *CEO*

▲ = Import ▼ = Export
◆ = Import/Export

EMP: 30
SALES (corp-wide): 703.02MM **Privately Held**
Web: www.tacenergy.com
SIC: **3721** Aircraft
PA: Signature Flight Air Inc.
100 Crescent Ct Ste 1600
Dallas TX 75201
903 794-3835

(G-9056)
SOBI INC
3015 Carrington Mill Blvd Ste 410
(27560-5437)
PHONE...........................844 506-3682
Mian M Ashraf, *Prin*
EMP: 4
SALES (corp-wide): 1.32B **Privately Held**
Web: www.sobi.com
SIC: **2834** Pharmaceutical preparations
HQ: Sobi, Inc
77 4th Ave Fl 3
Waltham MA 02451
781 786-7370

(G-9057)
SOUTHPORT GRAPHICS LLC
9400 Globe Center Dr Ste 101
(27560-6213)
P.O. Box 91709 (27675-1709)
PHONE...........................919 650-3822
EMP: 6 EST: 2010
SQ FT: 5,600
SALES (est): 2.54MM **Privately Held**
Web: www.southportgraphics.com
SIC: **2752** Offset printing

(G-9058)
SPENCER HEALTH SOLUTIONS INC
2501 Aerial Center Pkwy Ste 100 (27560)
PHONE...........................866 971-8564
Thomas Rhoads, *CEO*
Nancy Thomason, *
EMP: 25 EST: 2015
SALES (est): 8.72MM **Privately Held**
SIC: **3829 8082** Measuring and controlling
devices, nec; Home health care services

(G-9059)
STOP N GO LLC
2916 Homebrook Ln (27560-7174)
PHONE...........................919 523-7355
EMP: 7
SALES (corp-wide): 4.14MM **Privately Held**
Web: www.kwiktrip.com
SIC: **2911** Petroleum refining
PA: Stop N Go Llc
2028 Mill Gate Ln
Cary NC

(G-9060)
SUNTECH MEDICAL INC
5827 S Miami Blvd Ste 100 (27560-8394)
PHONE...........................919 654-2300
▼ EMP: 80 EST: 1983
SALES (est): 24.5MM
SALES (corp-wide): 2.58B **Privately Held**
Web: www.suntechmed.com
SIC: **5047 3841** Medical equipment and
supplies; Anesthesia apparatus
HQ: Halma Holdings Inc.
535 Sprngfeld Ave Ste 110
Summit NJ 07901
513 772-5501

(G-9061)
SYNEOS HEALTH CONSULTING INC
1030 Sync St (27560-5468)
PHONE...........................919 876-9300
Colin Shannon, *CEO*

Michael Brooks, *COO*
Michael Bonello, *CFO*
EMP: 27 EST: 1997
SALES (est): 2.18MM
SALES (corp-wide): 5.39B **Privately Held**
Web: www.syneoshealth.com
SIC: **2834** Pharmaceutical preparations
PA: Syneos Health, Inc.
1030 Sync St
Morrisville NC 27560
919 876-9300

(G-9062)
SYNOPSYS INC
710 Slater Rd (27560-6438)
PHONE...........................919 941-6600
Jonathan White, *Brnch Mgr*
EMP: 9
SALES (corp-wide): 6.13B **Publicly Held**
Web: www.synopsys.com
SIC: **7372 7371 5065** Application computer
software; Custom computer programming
services; Semiconductor devices
PA: Synopsys, Inc.
675 Almanor Ave
Sunnyvale CA 94085
650 584-5000

(G-9063)
TARHEEL WOOD TREATING COMPANY
10309 Chapel Hill Rd (27560-5413)
P.O. Box 480 (27560-0480)
PHONE...........................919 467-9176
James S Gallup, *Pr*
Vickie Gallup, *Sec*
EMP: 10 EST: 1956
SQ FT: 3,000
SALES (est): 2.37MM **Privately Held**
Web: www.tarheelwoodtreating.com
SIC: **2491** Structural lumber and timber,
treated wood

(G-9064)
TEARSCIENCE INC
5151 Mccrimmon Pkwy Ste 250
(27560-0177)
PHONE...........................919 459-4880
Steve Grenon, *VP*
Brian Regan, *
Doug Pinotti, *
Donald Korb, *
Joe Boorady, *
▲ EMP: 90 EST: 2005
SALES (est): 8.03MM
SALES (corp-wide): 88.82B **Publicly Held**
Web: www.jnjvisionpro.com
SIC: **3845** Electromedical equipment
PA: Johnson & Johnson
1 Johnson And Johnson Plz
New Brunswick NJ 08933
732 524-0400

(G-9065)
TEKELEC INC
5200 Paramount Pkwy (27560-5469)
▲ EMP: 211 EST: 2012
SALES (est): 9.4MM
SALES (corp-wide): 52.96B **Publicly Held**
SIC: **3661 3825 7371** Telephone and
telegraph apparatus; Test equipment for
electronic and electrical circuits; Computer
software development and applications
PA: Oracle Corporation
2300 Oracle Way
Austin TX 78741
737 867-1000

(G-9066)
TEKELEC GLOBAL INC
Also Called: Tekelec
5200 Paramount Pkwy (27560-5469)
PHONE...........................919 460-5500
EMP: 1291
SIC: **3661 3825 7371** Telephone and
telegraph apparatus; Test equipment for
electronic and electrical circuits; Computer
software development and applications

(G-9067)
TELEFLEX INCORPORATED
Also Called: Teleflex
3015 Carrington Mill Blvd (27560-5437)
PHONE...........................919 544-8000
EMP: 21
SALES (corp-wide): 3.05B **Publicly Held**
Web: www.teleflex.com
SIC: **3841** Catheters
PA: Teleflex Incorporated
550 E Swdsford Rd Ste 400
Wayne PA 19087
610 225-6800

(G-9068)
TELEFLEX MEDICAL INCORPORATED (HQ)
3015 Carrington Mill Blvd (27560-5437)
P.O. Box 12600 (27709-2600)
PHONE...........................919 544-8000
Liam Kelly, *CEO*
George Babich Junior, *CEO*
Gregg W Winter, *
Cynthia Sharo, *
C Jeffrey Jacobs, *
◆ EMP: 79 EST: 1955
SALES (est): 412.29MM
SALES (corp-wide): 3.05B **Publicly Held**
Web: www.teleflex.com
SIC: **3841** Surgical and medical instruments
PA: Teleflex Incorporated
550 E Swdsford Rd Ste 400
Wayne PA 19087
610 225-6800

(G-9069)
TG THERAPEUTICS INC (PA)
Also Called: Tg Therapeutics
3020 Carrington Mill Blvd Ste 475 (27560)
PHONE...........................877 575-8489
Michael S Weiss, *Ch Bd*
Sean A Power, *Corporate Secretary*
EMP: 57 EST: 1993
SALES (est): 329MM **Publicly Held**
Web: www.tgtherapeutics.com
SIC: **2834** Pharmaceutical preparations

(G-9070)
THERMO FISHER SCIENTIFIC INC
Also Called: Ppd Clinical Research
3900 Paramount Pkwy (27560-7200)
PHONE...........................919 380-2000
Jessica Stevenson, *Proj Mgr*
EMP: 4
SALES (corp-wide): 42.86B **Publicly Held**
Web: www.thermofisher.com
SIC: **3826** Analytical instruments
PA: Thermo Fisher Scientific Inc.
168 3rd Ave
Waltham MA 02451
781 622-1000

(G-9071)
THOMAS CONCRETE CAROLINA INC
220 International Dr (27560-8708)
PHONE...........................919 460-5317
Justin Hartley, *Mgr*
EMP: 11

SQ FT: 9,595
SALES (corp-wide): 1.15B **Privately Held**
Web: www.thomasconcrete.com
SIC: **3273** Ready-mixed concrete
HQ: Thomas Concrete Of Carolina, Inc.
1131 Nw Street
Raleigh NC 27603
919 832-0451

(G-9072)
TICKETS PLUS INC (PA)
Also Called: Star Tickets Plus
909 Aviation Pkwy Ste 900 (27560-9000)
PHONE...........................616 222-4000
Jack Krasula, *Pr*
Henry Mast, *
Robert Struyk, *
Larry D Fredericks, *
Kevin Einfeld, *
EMP: 35 EST: 1994
SALES (est): 3.68MM **Privately Held**
SIC: **2759 7999** Tickets: printing, nsk; Ticket
sales office for sporting events, contract

(G-9073)
TOMORROWMED PHARMA LLC ✪
1101 Shiloh Glenn Dr Unit 1108
(27560-5419)
PHONE...........................832 615-2880
Welton Wayne Wilson, *Managing Member*
EMP: 25 EST: 2024
SALES (est): 1.38MM **Privately Held**
SIC: **2834** Pharmaceutical preparations

(G-9074)
TRANE US INC
Also Called: Trane
401 Kitty Hawk Dr (27560-8271)
PHONE...........................919 781-0458
Randy Zatz, *Mgr*
EMP: 6
Web: www.bradyservices.com
SIC: **3585** Refrigeration and heating
equipment
HQ: Trane U.S. Inc.
800-E Beaty St
Davidson NC 28036
704 655-4000

(G-9075)
TRIANGLE COATINGS INC
6721 Mount Herman Rd (27560-9223)
PHONE...........................919 781-6108
Terry Overton, *Pr*
Deborah Overton, *Sec*
EMP: 9 EST: 1978
SQ FT: 10,000
SALES (est): 757.44K **Privately Held**
Web: www.trianglepowdercoating.com
SIC: **3479** Coating of metals and formed
products

(G-9076)
TRIANGLE INNER VISION COMPANY
Also Called: Speedpro of Northwest Raleigh
100 Dominion Dr Ste 110 (27560)
PHONE...........................919 460-6013
Jerry Parise, *Pr*
Kim Parise, *VP*
EMP: 4 EST: 2009
SQ FT: 3,000
SALES (est): 332.31K **Privately Held**
Web: www.speedpro.com
SIC: **2752** Commercial printing, lithographic

(G-9077)
TRIANGLE READY MIX LLC
241 International Dr (27560-8411)
PHONE...........................919 859-4190
Nelson Loureiro, *Managing Member*
EMP: 20 EST: 2018

(PA)=Parent Co (HQ)=Headquarters
✪ = New Business established in last 2 years

GEOGRAPHIC

SALES (est): 2.52MM **Privately Held**
SIC: 3273 Ready-mixed concrete

(G-9078)
TRIMACO INC (PA)
2300 Gateway Centre Blvd Ste 200
(27560-9669)
PHONE....................919 674-3460
Drew Cook, *Sec*
EMP: 6 **EST:** 2018
SALES (est): 7.58MM
SALES (corp-wide): 7.58MM **Privately Held**
Web: www.trimaco.com
SIC: 2394 Canvas covers and drop cloths

(G-9079)
TRIO LABS INC
133 Southcenter Ct Ste 900 (27560-6604)
P.O. Box 13169 (27709-3169)
PHONE....................919 818-9646
Adam Steege, *CEO*
Ken Purchase, *COO*
Scott Schiller, *CCO*
EMP: 15 **EST:** 2015
SALES (est): 2.89MM **Privately Held**
Web: www.triolabs.com
SIC: 3555 Printing trades machinery

(G-9080)
TRIPHARM SERVICES INC
627 Davis Dr Ste 100 (27560-7101)
PHONE....................984 243-0800
Patrick Walsh, *CEO*
EMP: 10 **EST:** 2019
SALES (est): 2.08MM
SALES (corp-wide): 418.48MM **Privately Held**
Web: www.alcami.com
SIC: 2834 Solutions, pharmaceutical
PA: Alcami Corporation
2320 Scientific Park Dr
Wilmington NC 28405
910 254-7000

(G-9081)
TUFF SHED INC
409 Airport Blvd (27560-8426)
PHONE....................919 413-2494
EMP: 6
SALES (corp-wide): 347.42MM **Privately Held**
Web: www.tuffshed.com
SIC: 2452 Prefabricated wood buildings
PA: Tuff Shed, Inc.
1777 S Harrison St # 600
Denver CO 80210
303 753-8833

(G-9082)
TYRATECH INC
5151 Mccrimmon Pkwy Ste 275
(27560-5425)
PHONE....................919 415-4275
Bruno Jactel, *CEO*
Alan Reid, *
Peter K Jerome, *
Vincent T Morgus, *
EMP: 35 **EST:** 2007
SALES (est): 12.23MM
SALES (corp-wide): 579.37MM **Publicly Held**
Web: www.tyratech.com
SIC: 2879 Insecticides, agricultural or household
PA: American Vanguard Corporation
4695 Macarthur Ct
Newport Beach CA 92660
949 260-1200

(G-9083)
UNLIMTED POTENTIAL SANFORD INC
Also Called: Millennium Print Group
9301 Globe Center Dr Ste 120
(27560-6203)
PHONE....................919 852-1117
Darren Spivey, *Pr*
David Lane, *VP*
EMP: 21 **EST:** 1989
SALES (est): 7.29MM **Privately Held**
SIC: 7334 2752 Photocopying and duplicating services; Offset printing

(G-9084)
VASONOVA INC
3015 Carrington Mill Blvd 3 (27560-5437)
PHONE....................650 327-1412
▲ **EMP:** 17
SIC: 3841 Surgical and medical instruments

(G-9085)
VAST THERAPEUTICS INC
Also Called: Novoclem
615 Davis Dr Ste 800 (27560-6845)
PHONE....................919 321-1403
Neal Hunter, *CEO*
John Oakley, *CFO*
Paul Bruinenberg, *Chief Medical Officer*
EMP: 6 **EST:** 2017
SALES (est): 10.69MM **Privately Held**
Web: www.vasttherapeutics.com
SIC: 2834 Drugs acting on the respiratory system

(G-9086)
VIAVI SOLUTIONS INC
1100 Perimeter Park Dr Ste 101
(27560-9119)
PHONE....................919 388-5100
EMP: 4
SALES (corp-wide): 1B **Publicly Held**
Web: www.viavisolutions.com
SIC: 3674 Semiconductors and related devices
PA: Viavi Solutions Inc.
1445 S Spctrum Blvd Ste 1
Chandler AZ 85286
408 404-3600

(G-9087)
VYSE GELATIN LLC
598 Airport Blvd Ste 900 (27560-7205)
PHONE....................919 238-3300
Seiichi Nishikawa, *CEO*
Ikuo Okamura, *Sec*
Shunsuke Otani, *Treas*
EMP: 8 **EST:** 2016
SALES (est): 55.71MM **Privately Held**
Web: www.nitta-gelatin.com
SIC: 2899 Chemical preparations, nec

(G-9088)
WE PHARMA INC
Also Called: Wep Clinical
951 Aviation Pkwy Ste 200 (27560-6637)
PHONE....................919 389-1478
Jaswinder Khera, *CEO*
Jaswinder Singh, *Managing Member**
EMP: 60 **EST:** 2011
SQ FT: 400
SALES (est): 7.88MM **Privately Held**
Web: www.wepclinical.com
SIC: 2834 Pharmaceutical preparations

(G-9089)
WEBSTER FINE ART LIMITED (PA)
2800 Perimeter Park Dr Ste A
(27560-0176)
PHONE....................919 349-8455

Brandin Myers, *Pr*
Tim Myers, *VP*
◆ **EMP:** 4 **EST:** 1987
SALES (est): 242.71K **Privately Held**
Web: www.websterspages.com
SIC: 2741 Art copy: publishing only, not printed on site

(G-9090)
WESTROCK PAPER AND PACKG LLC
Also Called: Kapstone Paper Packaging
5150 Mccrimmon Pkwy (27560-0179)
PHONE....................919 463-3100
EMP: 480
Web: www.westrock.com
SIC: 2653 Boxes, corrugated: made from purchased materials
HQ: Westrock Paper And Packaging, Llc
1000 Abernathy Rd Ne
Atlanta GA 30328

(G-9091)
XSCHEM INC (PA)
Also Called: Nterline
1500 Perimeter Park Dr Ste 300
(27560-0195)
PHONE....................919 379-3500
Fulton Breen, *CEO*
Bill Barton, *
EMP: 22 **EST:** 1998
SALES (est): 2.32MM
SALES (corp-wide): 2.32MM **Privately Held**
SIC: 7372 Business oriented computer software

(G-9092)
YOUR CABINET CONNECTION INC
10315 Chapel Hill Rd (27560-8707)
P.O. Box 1507 (27502-3507)
PHONE....................919 641-2877
Marvin Eugene Allen Iii, *Pr*
EMP: 4 **EST:** 2017
SALES (est): 231.46K **Privately Held**
Web:
www.yourcabinetconnectionnc.com
SIC: 2434 Wood kitchen cabinets

(G-9093)
ZEBRA COMMUNICATIONS INC (PA)
Also Called: Zebra Print Solutions
9401 Globe Center Dr Ste 130
(27560-6211)
PHONE....................919 314-3700
Charlotte Dileonardo, *CEO*
Patrick Dileonardo, *Pr*
EMP: 21 **EST:** 1991
SQ FT: 10,000
SALES (est): 2.64MM
SALES (corp-wide): 2.64MM **Privately Held**
Web: www.zebraprintsolutions.com
SIC: 7334 2752 7336 Photocopying and duplicating services; Offset printing; Graphic arts and related design

(G-9094)
ZIPTRONIX INC
800 Perimeter Park Dr Ste B (27560-7271)
PHONE....................919 459-2400
Dan Donabedian, *CEO*
EMP: 16 **EST:** 2003
SQ FT: 1,200
SALES (est): 953.64K
SALES (corp-wide): 376.02MM **Publicly Held**
Web: www.ziptronix.com
SIC: 3674 Semiconductors and related devices
HQ: Tessera Technologies, Inc.
3025 Orchard Pkwy

San Jose CA 95134
408 321-6000

Mount Airy
Surry County

(G-9095)
ACME STONE COMPANY INC
1700 Fancy Gap Rd (27030-1800)
P.O. Box 925 (27030-0925)
PHONE....................336 786-6978
Mark Stevens, *Pr*
Cathy Stevens, *Off Mgr*
▲ **EMP:** 11 **EST:** 1957
SQ FT: 2,250
SALES (est): 1.17MM **Privately Held**
Web: www.acmestonenc.com
SIC: 3281 5999 1799 Monument or burial stone, cut and shaped; Monuments and tombstones; Counter top installation

(G-9096)
ADVANCED ELECTRONIC SVCS INC (PA)
Also Called: Ces
101 Technology Ln (27030-6683)
PHONE....................336 789-0792
Steve Cooke, *Pr*
Leslie M Cooke, *CEO*
▲ **EMP:** 46 **EST:** 1992
SQ FT: 2,800
SALES (est): 24.77MM **Privately Held**
Web: www.aesintl.com
SIC: 7629 3699 Electronic equipment repair; Accelerating waveguide structures

(G-9097)
ALTEC INDUSTRIES INC
Also Called: Altec Inds Mt Airy Operations
200 Altec Way (27030-9934)
PHONE....................336 786-3623
EMP: 28
SALES (corp-wide): 1.21B **Privately Held**
Web: www.altec.com
SIC: 3531 Derricks, except oil and gas field
HQ: Altec Industries, Inc.
210 Inverness Center Drv
Birmingham AL 35242
205 991-7733

(G-9098)
AMERICAN CARPORTS STRUCTURES
152 Eastwind Ct (27030-7818)
PHONE....................336 710-1091
EMP: 4 **EST:** 2018
SALES (est): 99.72K **Privately Held**
Web: www.carportcentral.com
SIC: 3448 Prefabricated metal buildings and components

(G-9099)
AWESOME PRODUCTS INC
1625 Sheep Farm Rd (27030-6379)
PHONE....................336 374-5900
Loksarang D Hardas, *Admn*
EMP: 5 **EST:** 2013
SALES (est): 850.17K **Privately Held**
Web: www.lastotallyawesome.com
SIC: 2842 Cleaning or polishing preparations, nec

(G-9100)
B & M WHOLESALE INC
Also Called: B & M Wholesale
1800 Sparger Rd (27030-7565)
PHONE....................336 789-3916
Michael B Waddell, *Pr*
Blanche Waddell, *Sec*

▲ = Import ▼ = Export
◆ = Import/Export

Buernie Waddell, *VP*
EMP: 6 **EST:** 1949
SALES (est): 733.44K **Privately Held**
Web: b-m-wholesale.edan.io
SIC: 5099 5085 2252 Novelties, durable; Industrial tools; Socks

(G-9101)
BARNHARDT MANUFACTURING CO
Also Called: Ncfi Polyurethanes
1515 Carter St (27030-5721)
P.O. Box 1528 (27030-1528)
PHONE..............................336 789-9161
Steve Riddle, *Brnch Mgr*
EMP: 170
SALES (corp-wide): 268.75MM **Privately Held**
Web: www.barnhardt.net
SIC: 3086 Plastics foam products
PA: Barnhardt Manufacturing Company
1100 Hawthorne Ln
Charlotte NC 28205
800 277-0377

(G-9102)
BED IN A BOX
199 Woltz St (27030-7832)
PHONE..............................800 588-5720
EMP: 22 **EST:** 2020
SALES (est): 40.95K **Privately Held**
Web: www.bedinabox.com
SIC: 2392 Mattress pads

(G-9103)
BGI RECOVERY LLC
127 Belvue Dr (27030-5190)
PHONE..............................336 429-6976
Tonya Ferguson, *Prin*
EMP: 5 **EST:** 2010
SALES (est): 133.89K **Privately Held**
SIC: 3531 Automobile wrecker hoists

(G-9104)
BOTTOMLEY ENTERPRISES INC
452 Oak Grove Church Rd (27030-8769)
P.O. Box 70 (28623-0070)
PHONE..............................336 657-6400
Mitchell Bottomley, *CEO*
Deanna Bottomley, *
Michelle Voss, *
EMP: 84 **EST:** 2004
SALES (est): 13.42MM **Privately Held**
Web: www.bottomleyenterprises.com
SIC: 3537 Trucks: freight, baggage, etc.: industrial, except mining

(G-9105)
BRAY S RECAPPING SERVICE INC (PA)
1120 W Lebanon St (27030-2226)
P.O. Box 804 (27030-0804)
PHONE..............................336 786-6182
E Dean Bray Iii, *Pr*
E Dean Bray Junior, *VP*
Rebecca Bray, *VP*
Shannon Bray, *VP*
EMP: 22 **EST:** 1930
SALES (est): 423.31K
SALES (corp-wide): 423.31K **Privately Held**
SIC: 7534 5531 Tire recapping; Automotive tires

(G-9106)
CARDINAL CT COMPANY
630 Derby St (27030-4400)
PHONE..............................336 719-6857
EMP: 40
SALES (corp-wide): 1B **Privately Held**
Web: www.cardinalcorp.com
SIC: 3211 Tempered glass

HQ: Cardinal Ct Company
775 Pririe Ctr Dr Ste 200
Eden Prairie MN 55344

(G-9107)
CAROLINA CONNECTIONS INC
Also Called: Unique Background Solutions
805 Merita St (27030-2763)
P.O. Box 1604 (27030-1604)
PHONE..............................336 786-7030
Norwood A Barnes Junior, *Pr*
Michael Barnes, *VP*
EMP: 9 **EST:** 2002
SALES (est): 950.88K **Privately Held**
Web: www.uniquebackground.com
SIC: 7389 2899 7375 Personal service agents, brokers, and bureaus; Drug testing kits, blood and urine; Information retrieval services

(G-9108)
CAROLINA EXPEDITERS LLC
1415 Fancy Gap Rd (27030-1821)
P.O. Box 207 (27030-0207)
PHONE..............................888 537-5330
Jason Lee Ring, *Mgr*
EMP: 4 **EST:** 2008
SALES (est): 950.29K **Privately Held**
Web: www.freightemergency.com
SIC: 3537 4789 Containers (metal), air cargo ; Cargo loading and unloading services

(G-9109)
CAROLINA NORTH GRANITE CORP
151 Granite Quarry Trl (27030-3970)
PHONE..............................336 719-2600
C Richard Vaughn, *Ch Bd*
Donald R Shelton, *
Joan H Gammons, *
D Sam Brintle, *
◆ **EMP:** 90 **EST:** 1889
SQ FT: 25,000
SALES (est): 13.96MM
SALES (corp-wide): 2.1MM **Privately Held**
Web: www.polycor.com
SIC: 3281 Building stone products
HQ: Polycor Inc
100-76 Rue Saint-Paul
Quebec QC G1K 3
418 692-4695

(G-9110)
CARPENTER CO
220 Woltz St (27030-9973)
PHONE..............................336 789-9161
Travis Gnida, *Brnch Mgr*
EMP: 150
SALES (corp-wide): 506.96MM **Privately Held**
Web: www.carpenter.com
SIC: 3086 Plastics foam products
PA: Carpenter Co.
5016 Monument Ave
Richmond VA 23230
804 359-0800

(G-9111)
CARPORT CENTRAL INC (PA)
1372 Boggs Dr (27030)
P.O. Box 1308 (27030)
PHONE..............................336 673-6020
Alvaro Lara, *Pr*
EMP: 25 **EST:** 2014
SALES (est): 7.76MM
SALES (corp-wide): 7.76MM **Privately Held**
Web: www.carportcentral.com
SIC: 5211 3448 Doors, wood or metal, except storm; Prefabricated metal buildings and components

(G-9112)
CCBCC OPERATIONS LLC
Also Called: Coca-Cola
2516 W Pine St (27030-8544)
PHONE..............................336 789-7111
Sid Harris, *Brnch Mgr*
EMP: 46
SALES (corp-wide): 6.9B **Publicly Held**
Web: www.coca-cola.com
SIC: 2086 Bottled and canned soft drinks
HQ: Ccbcc Operations, Llc
4100 Coca-Cola Plz
Charlotte NC 28211
704 364-8728

(G-9113)
CENTRAL STATES MFG INC
751 Piedmont Triad West Dr (27030-9851)
PHONE..............................336 719-3280
Charlie Cox, *Brnch Mgr*
EMP: 146
SALES (corp-wide): 148.14MM **Privately Held**
Web: www.centralstatesco.com
SIC: 3353 3448 Aluminum sheet, plate, and foil; Prefabricated metal buildings and components
PA: Central States Manufacturing, Inc.
171 Naples St
Tontitown AR 72762
800 356-2733

(G-9114)
CENTRAL STEEL BUILDINGS INC
181 Woltz St (27030-7832)
PHONE..............................336 789-7896
Hai Yong Chen, *Pr*
Zack Mcmillian, *Genl Mgr*
Jody Casstevens, *Genl Mgr*
Eric Aparicio, *Genl Mgr*
Rick York, *Prin*
▲ **EMP:** 10 **EST:** 2015
SALES (est): 1.36MM **Privately Held**
Web: www.centralsteelbuildings.com
SIC: 3448 1541 Carports, prefabricated metal ; Steel building construction

(G-9115)
COAST TO COAST CARPORTS INC
Also Called: COAST TO COAST CARPORTS INC.
170 Holly Springs Rd (27030-6688)
P.O. Box 100 (72845-0100)
PHONE..............................336 783-3015
Primo Castillo, *Prin*
EMP: 27
SALES (corp-wide): 3.42MM **Privately Held**
Web: www.coast-to-coastcarports.com
SIC: 3448 Carports, prefabricated metal
PA: Coast To Coast Carports, Inc.
22525 I-40 Knoxville
Knoxville AR 72845
479 885-1258

(G-9116)
CREATIVE LIQUID COATINGS INC
710 Piedmont Triad West Dr (27030-9851)
PHONE..............................336 415-6214
Josh Ault, *Brnch Mgr*
EMP: 73
Web: www.creativeliquidcoatings.com
SIC: 3089 Injection molding of plastics
PA: Creative Liquid Coatings, Inc.
2620 Marion Dr
Kendallville IN 46755

(G-9117)
EAGLE CARPORTS INC (PA)
210 Airport Rd (27030)
PHONE..............................800 579-8589

Gabriel Torrez, *Pr*
EMP: 25 **EST:** 1997
SQ FT: 1,800
SALES (est): 23.31MM
SALES (corp-wide): 23.31MM **Privately Held**
Web: www.eaglecarports.com
SIC: 1541 3448 Steel building construction; Buildings, portable: prefabricated metal

(G-9118)
EASYGLASS INC
Also Called: Andrew Pearson Design
1 Andrew Pearson Dr (27030-2124)
PHONE..............................336 786-1800
Harold Brownfield, *Pr*
Susanne Brownfield Ph.d., *Ex VP*
▲ **EMP:** 7 **EST:** 1990
SQ FT: 70,000
SALES (est): 1.13MM **Privately Held**
SIC: 3229 2511 3231 Pressed and blown glass, nec; Wood household furniture; Furniture tops, glass: cut, beveled, or polished

(G-9119)
ESTES MACHINE CO
256 Snowhill Dr (27030-4392)
PHONE..............................336 786-7680
Don Estes, *Pt*
Benny East, *Pt*
EMP: 14 **EST:** 1990
SQ FT: 10,000
SALES (est): 218.76K **Privately Held**
SIC: 3599 7692 Machine shop, jobbing and repair; Welding repair

(G-9120)
EVERVIEW
201 Technology Ln (27030-6684)
PHONE..............................800 549-4722
Eric W Ek, *CEO*
EMP: 4 **EST:** 2018
SALES (est): 349.88K **Privately Held**
SIC: 7372 Prepackaged software

(G-9121)
FIBRECRETE PPRSRVTION TECH INC
Also Called: Fpt Infrastructure
131 Saint James Way (27030-6068)
PHONE..............................336 789-7259
Jonathan Simmons, *Pr*
Mark O'neal, *VP*
Rick Marion, *Contrlr*
Mark E Mcgonigle, *Treas*
Edward W Moore, *Sec*
EMP: 9 **EST:** 2016
SALES (est): 5.54MM
SALES (corp-wide): 7.34B **Publicly Held**
Web: www.fptinfrastructure.com
SIC: 2951 Road materials, bituminous (not from refineries)
HQ: Rpm Performance Coatings Group, Inc.
280 West Ave
Long Branch NJ 07740
888 788-4323

(G-9122)
GENESYS TECHNOLOGY INC
506 Bennett St (27030-5873)
PHONE..............................336 789-0763
Mark E Coleman, *Owner*
EMP: 6 **EST:** 2003
SALES (est): 314.14K **Privately Held**
Web: www.genesys.com
SIC: 7372 Business oriented computer software

(G-9123)
GEORGIA-CAROLINA QUARRIES INC (PA)
1700 Fancy Gap Rd (27030-1800)
P.O. Box 925 (27030-0925)
PHONE..................................336 786-6978
Bob Stevens, *Pr*
Mary Laura Stevens, *Sec*
Mark Steven, *VP*
EMP: 20 **EST:** 1979
SQ FT: 50
SALES (est): 677.72K
SALES (corp-wide): 677.72K **Privately Held**
SIC: 1423 3281 Crushed and broken granite; Curbing, granite or stone

(G-9124)
GRANITE MEMORIALS INC
636 S Main St (27030-4722)
P.O. Box 790 (27041-0790)
PHONE..................................336 786-6596
EMP: 8
SALES (est): 400K **Privately Held**
SIC: 3281 5999 Cut stone and stone products; Monuments and tombstones

(G-9125)
GRANITE TACTICAL VEHICLES INC
915 Newsome St (27030-5421)
PHONE..................................336 789-5555
Christopher Berman, *Pr*
Tammy Geldenhuys, *VP*
EMP: 12 **EST:** 2006
SALES (est): 400.67K **Privately Held**
Web: www.granitetacticalvehicles.com
SIC: 3711 Cars, armored, assembly of

(G-9126)
HANESBRANDS INC
Also Called: L'Eggs - Hanes - Bali
645 W Pine St (27030-4439)
PHONE..................................336 789-6118
Doug St Louis, *Mgr*
EMP: 5
Web: www.hanes.com
SIC: 2251 2252 Women's hosiery, except socks; Hosiery, nec
PA: Hanesbrands Inc.
1000 E Hanes Mill Rd
Winston Salem NC 27105

(G-9127)
HAO WEI LAI INC
2021 Rockford St (27030-5203)
PHONE..................................336 789-9969
Wu Lin, *Prin*
EMP: 7 **EST:** 2012
SALES (est): 85.58K **Privately Held**
SIC: 3421 Table and food cutlery, including butchers'

(G-9128)
HARVEST TIME BREAD COMPANY
501 Piedmont Triad West Dr (27030-9850)
EMP: 100
SIC: 2051 Breads, rolls, and buns

(G-9129)
HICKS WTERSTOVES SOLAR SYSTEMS
Also Called: Hicks Mechanical
2649 S Main St (27030-7219)
PHONE..................................336 789-4977
Mark Hicks, *Pr*
Mark Hicks, *Pr*
Carol Hicks, *VP*
EMP: 11 **EST:** 1981
SQ FT: 13,000
SALES (est): 1.97MM **Privately Held**

Web: www.hickswaterstoves.com
SIC: 1711 3433 3441 Process piping contractor; Heating equipment, except electric; Fabricated structural metal

(G-9130)
HULL BROTHERS LUMBER CO INC
579 Maple Hollow Rd (27030-9731)
PHONE..................................336 789-5252
Howard W Hull, *Pr*
Chad W Hull, *Sec*
Brent Hull, *VP*
Howard Hull Junior, *Asst VP*
EMP: 6 **EST:** 1943
SQ FT: 900
SALES (est): 436.88K **Privately Held**
SIC: 2421 2426 Sawmills and planing mills, general; Hardwood dimension and flooring mills

(G-9131)
INSTEEL INDUSTRIES INC (PA)
Also Called: Insteel
1373 Boggs Dr (27030)
PHONE..................................336 786-2141
H O Woltz Iii, *Pr*
Richard T Wagner, *Sr VP*
James R York, *Sr VP*
Scot R Jafroodi, *VP*
Elizabeth C Southern, *CLO*
◆ **EMP:** 169 **EST:** 1953
SALES (est): 529.2MM
SALES (corp-wide): 529.2MM **Publicly Held**
Web: www.insteel.com
SIC: 3441 Fabricated structural metal

(G-9132)
INSTEEL WIRE PRODUCTS COMPANY (HQ)
1373 Boggs Dr (27030-2145)
PHONE..................................336 719-9000
H O Woltz Iii, *Pr*
James F Petelle, *
Richard Wagner, *General Vice President*
Michael C Gazmarian, *
Lyle Bullington, *Vice-President Information Systems*
◆ **EMP:** 38 **EST:** 1981
SQ FT: 43,000
SALES (est): 480.78MM
SALES (corp-wide): 529.2MM **Publicly Held**
Web: www.insteel.com
SIC: 3315 Welded steel wire fabric
PA: Insteel Industries Inc.
1373 Boggs Dr
Mount Airy NC 27030
336 786-2141

(G-9133)
INTERCONTINENTAL METALS CORP
1373 Boggs Dr (27030-2145)
PHONE..................................336 786-2141
Howard Woltz Iii, *Pr*
Gary Kniskern, *
EMP: 75 **EST:** 1955
SALES (est): 1.16MM
SALES (corp-wide): 529.2MM **Publicly Held**
SIC: 3496 Concrete reinforcing mesh and wire
PA: Insteel Industries Inc.
1373 Boggs Dr
Mount Airy NC 27030
336 786-2141

(G-9134)
INTERLAM CORPORATION
391 Hickory St (27030-2264)
PHONE..................................336 786-6254

Alvin Eckenrod, *Pr*
◆ **EMP:** 20 **EST:** 1987
SQ FT: 70,000
SALES (est): 7.12MM **Privately Held**
Web: www.interlam-design.com
SIC: 2541 5162 Bar fixtures, wood; Plastics materials and basic shapes

(G-9135)
INTERSTATE SIGN COMPANY INC
1990 Rockford St (27030-5202)
PHONE..................................336 789-3069
Ricky Shelton, *Pr*
Steve Barnard, *Sec*
EMP: 23 **EST:** 1991
SQ FT: 6,000
SALES (est): 3.8MM **Privately Held**
Web: www.interstatesign.com
SIC: 1799 3993 Sign installation and maintenance; Electric signs

(G-9136)
JANTEC SIGN GROUP LLC
196 Sexton Rd (27030-8784)
PHONE..................................336 429-5010
Jan Day Legere, *Mgr*
EMP: 34 **EST:** 2017
SALES (est): 2.6MM **Privately Held**
Web: www.jantecneon.com
SIC: 3993 Signs and advertising specialties

(G-9137)
K & D SIGNS LLC
1078 S Main St (27030-4730)
P.O. Box 1546 (27030-1546)
PHONE..................................336 786-1111
Tony Kirby, *Admn*
EMP: 10 **EST:** 2014
SALES (est): 1.8MM **Privately Held**
Web: www.kdsignsllc.com
SIC: 3993 Signs and advertising specialties

(G-9138)
KAT DESIGNS INC
Also Called: T W Signs & Graphics
280 Hickory St (27030-2212)
PHONE..................................336 789-7288
Kim Jones, *Pr*
EMP: 6 **EST:** 1996
SALES (est): 231.84K **Privately Held**
Web: www.twsigns.net
SIC: 3993 Signs, not made in custom sign painting shops

(G-9139)
KB SOCKS INC
661 Linville Rd (27030-3101)
P.O. Box 908 (27030-0908)
PHONE..................................336 719-8000
Karen Bell, *CEO*
EMP: 5 **EST:** 2011
SALES (est): 1.51MM
SALES (corp-wide): 3.26B **Privately Held**
Web: www.kbellsocks.com
SIC: 2252 Socks
HQ: Renfro Llc
661 Linville Rd
Mount Airy NC 27030
336 719-8000

(G-9140)
KEN HORTON LOGGING LLC
120 W Elm St (27030-3502)
PHONE..................................336 789-2849
Ken Horton, *Owner*
EMP: 4 **EST:** 1985
SALES (est): 228.32K **Privately Held**
Web: www.getfitwithida.com
SIC: 2411 Logging camps and contractors

(G-9141)
KIEFFER STARLITE COMPANY
609 Junction St (27030-3719)
PHONE..................................800 659-2493
EMP: 4 **EST:** 2019
SALES (est): 171.21K **Privately Held**
SIC: 2752 Commercial printing, lithographic

(G-9142)
KINGS PRTBLE WLDG FBRCTION LLC
832 W Lebanon St (27030-2220)
PHONE..................................336 789-2372
Jack King, *Owner*
EMP: 4 **EST:** 1971
SQ FT: 4,500
SALES (est): 420.1K **Privately Held**
Web: kings-portable-welding-fabrication-llc.business.site
SIC: 7692 3443 Welding repair; Fabricated plate work (boiler shop)

(G-9143)
KUSTOM KRAFT WDWRKS MT AIRY IN
Also Called: Surry Collection
3096 Westfield Rd (27030-9553)
PHONE..................................336 786-2831
Claybern Taylor, *Pr*
Peggy Taylor, *VP*
EMP: 4 **EST:** 1976
SQ FT: 8,500
SALES (est): 95.45K **Privately Held**
SIC: 2511 Wood household furniture

(G-9144)
LAB DESIGNS LLC (PA)
Also Called: Lab Dsgns Archtctural Laminate
391 Hickory St (27030-2264)
PHONE..................................336 429-4114
Joseph Ervin, *Managing Member*
▲ **EMP:** 7 **EST:** 2010
SQ FT: 10,000
SALES (est): 1.56MM
SALES (corp-wide): 1.56MM **Privately Held**
Web: www.labdesignlaminate.com
SIC: 3299 Mica, laminated

(G-9145)
LAZEREDGE LLC
244 Brunswick Ln (27030-3765)
P.O. Box 15 (27030-0015)
PHONE..................................336 480-7934
William Pfitzner, *Prin*
EMP: 10 **EST:** 2015
SALES (est): 2.44MM **Privately Held**
Web: www.lazeredge.com
SIC: 3555 Blocks, wood: engravers'

(G-9146)
LEONARD ALUM UTLITY BLDNGS INC (PA)
Also Called: Leonard Building & Trck Covers
630 W Independence Blvd Ste 3 (27030-3568)
P.O. Box 1728 (27030-1728)
PHONE..................................336 789-5018
Sandra P Leonard, *Pr*
David Oneal, *
Michael J Leonard, *
Bruce Strohl, *
EMP: 75 **EST:** 1967
SQ FT: 100,000
SALES (est): 98.91MM
SALES (corp-wide): 98.91MM **Privately Held**
Web: www.leonardusa.com

SIC: 5531 3448 Truck equipment and parts; Prefabricated metal buildings

(G-9147)
LL CULTURED MARBLE INC
1184 Maple Grove Church Rd (27030-7552)
PHONE...............................336 789-3908
Doris Holder, *Pr*
EMP: 4 EST: 1976
SALES (est): 291.93K **Privately Held**
Web: www.llmarble.com
SIC: 2493 3088 Marbleboard (stone face hard board); Plastics plumbing fixtures

(G-9148)
LS STARRETT COMPANY
1372 Boggs Dr (27030-2144)
PHONE...............................336 789-5141
EMP: 52
SALES (corp-wide): 256.18MM **Privately Held**
Web: www.starrett.com
SIC: 3545 Machine tool accessories
PA: The L S Starrett Company
121 Crescent St
Athol MA 01331
978 249-3551

(G-9149)
LUCK STONE CORPORATION
525 Quarry Rd (27030-9959)
PHONE...............................336 786-4693
Charles S Luck Iii, *Ch Bd*
EMP: 28
SALES (corp-wide): 366.46MM **Privately Held**
Web: www.luckstone.com
SIC: 1423 Crushed and broken granite
PA: Luck Stone Corporation
515 Stone Mill Dr
Manakin Sabot VA 23103
804 784-6300

(G-9150)
LYONS HOSIERY INC
719 S South St (27030-4425)
P.O. Box 1833 (27030-6833)
PHONE...............................336 789-2651
Clancy Lyons, *Pr*
Trent Lyons, *Stockholder*
Sandy Lyons, *Sec*
Susan Simmons, *Stockholder*
▲ EMP: 6 EST: 1980
SQ FT: 40,000
SALES (est): 287.94K **Privately Held**
Web: www.bargain-bulk-sock-sales.com
SIC: 2252 Socks

(G-9151)
M & M SIGNS AND AWNINGS INC
1465 Ladonia Church Rd (27030-9080)
PHONE...............................336 352-4300
TOLL FREE: 800
Dale Golding, *Pr*
Melissa Golding, *Sec*
EMP: 10 EST: 1970
SQ FT: 2,500
SALES (est): 975.01K **Privately Held**
Web:
SIC: 3993 2394 Signs, not made in custom sign painting shops; Canvas and related products

(G-9152)
MAYBERRY DISTILLERY
461 N South St (27030-3533)
PHONE...............................336 719-6860
James Mayberry, *Prin*
Vann Mccoy, *Managing Member*
EMP: 4 EST: 2013

SALES (est): 243.25K **Privately Held**
Web: www.mayberryspirits.com
SIC: 2085 Distilled and blended liquors

(G-9153)
MICHAEL TATE
Also Called: Mike's Hosiery
1455 Simpson Mill Rd (27030-8573)
PHONE...............................336 374-4695
Michael Tate, *Owner*
EMP: 4 EST: 1981
SALES (est): 163.18K **Privately Held**
SIC: 2252 Hosiery, nec

(G-9154)
MOUNT AIRY SIGNS & LETTERS INC
1543 Fancy Gap Rd (27030-1823)
PHONE...............................336 786-5777
Bobby Bodenhamer, *Pr*
EMP: 16 EST: 1990
SQ FT: 8,000
SALES (est): 839.46K **Privately Held**
SIC: 3993 Signs, not made in custom sign painting shops

(G-9155)
MT AIRY MEAT CENTER INC
133 Old Buck Shoals Rd (27030-7597)
PHONE...............................336 786-2023
Gray Gwyn, *Pr*
Wade Johnson, *Sec*
EMP: 5 EST: 1977
SQ FT: 6,000
SALES (est): 976.3K **Privately Held**
Web: www.mtairyncchamber.org
SIC: 2011 5421 Meat packing plants; Meat markets, including freezer provisioners

(G-9156)
MVP GROUP INTERNATIONAL INC
830 Fowler Rd (27030-2750)
PHONE...............................336 527-2238
EMP: 22
Web: www.mvpgroupint.com
SIC: 3999 Candles
HQ: Mvp Group International, Inc.
430 Gentry Rd
Elkin NC 28621
843 216-8380

(G-9157)
NC QUALITY SALES LLC
136 Greyhound Rd (27030-4885)
PHONE...............................336 786-7211
EMP: 10 EST: 2010
SQ FT: 20,000
SALES (est): 779.14K **Privately Held**
Web: www.ncqualitysales.net
SIC: 2252 Socks

(G-9158)
NCFI POLYURETHANES
Also Called: Ncfi
1515 Carter St (27030)
P.O. Box 1528 (27030)
PHONE...............................336 789-9161
Chip Holton, *CEO*
◆ EMP: 200 EST: 1964
SQ FT: 3,000
SALES (est): 24.85MM
SALES (corp-wide): 268.75MM **Privately Held**
Web: www.ncfi.com
SIC: 3086 Insulation or cushioning material, foamed plastics
PA: Barnhardt Manufacturing Company
1100 Hawthorne Ln
Charlotte NC 28205
800 277-0377

(G-9159)
NESTER HOSIERY INC
Also Called: NESTER HOSIERY, INC.
1400 Carter St (27030-5711)
PHONE...............................336 789-0026
Martin W Nester, *Brnch Mgr*
EMP: 70
Web: www.nesterhosiery.com
SIC: 2252 Socks
PA: Nester Hosiery, Llc
1546 Carter St
Mount Airy NC 27030

(G-9160)
NESTER HOSIERY LLC (PA)
Also Called: Nester Hosiery
1546 Carter St (27030)
P.O. Box 1343 (27030)
PHONE...............................336 789-0026
Kelly Nester, *CEO*
Dusty Wade Nester, *Sec*
Keith Nester, *CFO*
Donna Anderson, *VP*
▲ EMP: 30 EST: 1993
SQ FT: 50,000
SALES (est): 20.91MM **Privately Held**
Web: www.nesterhosiery.com
SIC: 2252 Socks

(G-9161)
OLD NORTH STATE WINERY INC
Also Called: Fish Hippie
308 N Main St (27030-3812)
P.O. Box 631 (27030)
PHONE...............................336 789-9463
Ben Webb, *Pr*
EMP: 11 EST: 2006
SALES (est): 703.22K **Privately Held**
Web: www.oldnorthstatewinery.com
SIC: 2084 Wines

(G-9162)
OTTENWELLER CO INC
401 Technology Ln (27030-5039)
PHONE...............................336 783-6959
Carl Brodhun, *Brnch Mgr*
EMP: 43
SALES (corp-wide): 18.18MM **Privately Held**
Web: www.ottenweller.com
SIC: 3441 Fabricated structural metal
PA: Ottenweller Co., Inc.
3011 Congressional Pkwy
Fort Wayne IN 46808
260 484-3166

(G-9163)
OUTPUT SERVICES GROUP INC
201 Technology Ln (27030-6684)
PHONE...............................336 783-5948
EMP: 30
SALES (corp-wide): 460.53MM **Privately Held**
Web: www.osgconnect.com
SIC: 7372 Prepackaged software
HQ: Output Services Group, Inc.
75905 Kennedy Blvd
North Bergen NJ 07047

(G-9164)
PINE STATE CORPORATE AP LLC
Also Called: Pine State Corporative Apparel
219 Frederick St (27030-5603)
PHONE...............................336 789-9437
EMP: 10 EST: 2003
SALES (est): 129.93K **Privately Held**
Web: www.pinestatemarketing.com
SIC: 2395 5621 Embroidery and art needlework; Women's clothing stores

(G-9165)
PIONEER PRINTING COMPANY INC
203 N South St (27030-3560)
P.O. Box 407 (27030-0407)
PHONE...............................336 789-4011
Robin Owens, *Pr*
Anita Nichols, *Treas*
Vicky Fields, *Sec*
Douglas Nichols, *VP*
EMP: 6 EST: 1971
SQ FT: 5,000
SALES (est): 487.86K **Privately Held**
Web: www.pioneerprintingco.com
SIC: 2752 Offset printing

(G-9166)
POP DESIGNS MKTG SOLUTIONS LLC
1153 Holly Springs Rd (27030-9539)
PHONE...............................336 444-4033
Rick G Hunter, *CEO*
Teresa Martin, *COO*
EMP: 7 EST: 2014
SALES (est): 108.86K **Privately Held**
SIC: 2759 Screen printing

(G-9167)
PSM ENTERPRISES INC
219 Frederick St (27030-5603)
PHONE...............................336 789-8888
EMP: 10 EST: 2006
SALES (est): 952.03K **Privately Held**
Web: www.pinestatemarketing.com
SIC: 2396 5199 Fabric printing and stamping ; Advertising specialties

(G-9168)
RENFRO LLC
Also Called: Willow Street Plant
304 Willow St (27030-3550)
PHONE...............................336 786-3000
EMP: 10
SALES (corp-wide): 3.26B **Privately Held**
Web: www.renfro.com
SIC: 2252 Hosiery, nec
HQ: Renfro Llc
661 Linville Rd
Mount Airy NC 27030
336 719-8000

(G-9169)
RENFRO LLC
801 W Lebanon St (27030-2219)
PHONE...............................336 719-8290
Norman Smith, *Mgr*
EMP: 75
SALES (corp-wide): 3.26B **Privately Held**
Web: www.renfro.com
SIC: 2252 Socks
HQ: Renfro Llc
661 Linville Rd
Mount Airy NC 27030
336 719-8000

(G-9170)
RENFRO LLC (HQ)
Also Called: Renfro Brands
661 Linville Rd (27030-3101)
P.O. Box 908 (27030)
PHONE...............................336 719-8000
Stanley Jewell, *CEO*
Susan Bevard, *
Kieth Venable, *
◆ EMP: 168 EST: 1921
SQ FT: 180,000
SALES (est): 476.65MM
SALES (corp-wide): 3.26B **Privately Held**
Web: www.renfro.com
SIC: 2252 Socks
PA: The Renco Group Inc
1 Rockefeller Plz Fl 29

New York NY 10020
212 541-6000

(G-9171)
RENFRO MEXICO HOLDINGS LLC
661 Linville Rd (27030-3101)
PHONE..............................336 786-3501
EMP: 6 EST: 2002
SALES (est): 196.64K Privately Held
Web: www.renfro.com
SIC: 2252 Socks

(G-9172)
ROGERS KNITTING INC
181 Beasley Rd (27030-9212)
PHONE..............................336 789-4155
Roger Delnorman, Pr
Tina Marshall, Sec
EMP: 5 EST: 1988
SQ FT: 2,400
SALES (est): 319.63K Privately Held
SIC: 2251 7389 Women's hosiery, except
socks; Textile and apparel services

(G-9173)
ROUND PEAK VINEYARDS LLC
765 Round Peak Church Rd (27030-8421)
PHONE..............................336 352-5595
George Little, Managing Member
Susan Little, Managing Member
Ken Gulaian, Managing Member
Kari Heerdt, Managing Member
EMP: 6 EST: 2004
SALES (est): 237.03K Privately Held
Web: www.roundpeak.com
SIC: 2084 Wines

(G-9174)
SARA LEE SOCKS
100 Woltz St (27030-7832)
PHONE..............................336 789-6118
EMP: 4
SALES (est): 285.72K Privately Held
SIC: 2252 Socks

(G-9175)
SAWYERS SIGN SERVICE INC
608 Allred Mill Rd (27030-2204)
EMP: 19 EST: 1996
SQ FT: 30,000
SALES (est): 528.81K Privately Held
SIC: 1799 2394 3993 Sign installation and
maintenance; Canvas and related products;
Signs and advertising specialties

(G-9176)
SIGN MEDIC INC
1410 Boggs Dr (27030-2146)
PHONE..............................336 789-5972
Scott Simmons, Pr
▼ EMP: 8 EST: 2000
SQ FT: 30,000
SALES (est): 555.75K Privately Held
Web: www.signmedicinc.com
SIC: 3993 Electric signs

(G-9177)
SOUTHEASTERN SIGN WORKS INC
609 Junction St (27030-3719)
P.O. Box 1206 (27030-1206)
PHONE..............................336 789-5516
Teresa Martin, Pr
Bob Gravley, VP
Rick Vaughn, Treas
EMP: 7 EST: 1999
SALES (est): 489.71K Privately Held
SIC: 3993 5046 Electric signs; Signs,
electrical

(G-9178)
SOUTHERN STATES COOP INC
Also Called: S S C 7793-7
202 Snowhill Dr (27030-4392)
PHONE..............................336 786-7545
Mike Midkiff, Mgr
EMP: 35
SALES (corp-wide): 1.71B Privately Held
Web: www.southernstates.com
SIC: 2048 2873 0181 2874 Prepared feeds,
nec; Nitrogenous fertilizers; Bulbs and
seeds; Phosphatic fertilizers
PA: Southern States Cooperative,
Incorporated
6606 W Broad St Ste B
Richmond VA 23230
804 281-1000

(G-9179)
SPECIFIED METALS INC
391 Hickory St (27030-2264)
PHONE..............................336 786-6254
Alvin Eckenrod, Pr
Catherine Eckenrod, VP
EMP: 6 EST: 2015
SALES (est): 317.1K Privately Held
Web: www.specifiedmetals.com
SIC: 3444 Sheet metalwork

(G-9180)
SUITS USA INC
Also Called: Suits US
1219a W Lebanon St (27030-2227)
PHONE..............................336 786-8808
Linda Dollyhigh, Pr
Stephanie Combs, Sec
EMP: 5 EST: 1995
SALES (est): 1.79MM Privately Held
Web: www.suitsusainc.com
SIC: 3842 Suits, firefighting (asbestos)

(G-9181)
**SURRY CHEMICALS
INCORPORATED**
241 Hickory St (27030-2211)
P.O. Box 1447 (27030-1447)
PHONE..............................336 786-4607
Sherman H Shepherd, Pr
Vicki Shepherd, *
William Shepherd, *
◆ EMP: 28 EST: 1977
SQ FT: 50,000
SALES (est): 6.66MM Privately Held
Web: www.surrychemicals.co
SIC: 2843 2841 2899 Textile finishing agents
; Soap and other detergents; Chemical
preparations, nec

(G-9182)
SYNERGEM TECHNOLOGIES INC
371 Windrush Ln (27030-7930)
PHONE..............................866 859-0911
EMP: 29 EST: 2019
SALES (est): 4.79MM Privately Held
Web: www.synergemtech.com
SIC: 7379 7372 Computer related consulting
services; Business oriented computer
software

(G-9183)
T P SUPPLY CO INC
Also Called: Material Handling
483 Belvue Dr (27030-5196)
P.O. Box 1543 (27030-1543)
PHONE..............................336 789-2337
Troy Payne Junior, Pr
EMP: 22 EST: 1979
SQ FT: 4,500
SALES (est): 4.81MM Privately Held
Web: www.tpsupplyco.com

SIC: 2448 5084 5085 Pallets, wood and
metal combination; Materials handling
machinery; Mill supplies

(G-9184)
T-N-T CARPORTS INC
1050 Worth St (27030-4453)
PHONE..............................336 789-3818
EMP: 8
SALES (corp-wide): 3.67MM Privately
Held
Web: www.tntcarports.com
SIC: 3448 Prefabricated metal buildings and
components
PA: T-N-T Carports, Inc.
170 Holly Springs Rd
Mount Airy NC 27030
336 789-3818

(G-9185)
T-N-T CARPORTS INC (PA)
170 Holly Springs Rd (27030-6688)
PHONE..............................336 789-3818
Venancio Torres, CEO
▼ EMP: 26 EST: 1995
SQ FT: 12,000
SALES (est): 3.67MM
SALES (corp-wide): 3.67MM Privately
Held
Web: www.tntcarports.com
SIC: 3448 Carports, prefabricated metal

(G-9186)
TIGER STEEL INC
998 W Pine St (27030-3439)
PHONE..............................336 624-4481
Arturo Lopez, Pr
EMP: 5 EST: 2020
SALES (est): 1.08MM Privately Held
SIC: 3291 Abrasive metal and steel products

(G-9187)
TRAVIS L BUNKER
Also Called: L C B of Mount Airy
6198 W Pine St (27030-6185)
PHONE..............................336 352-3289
Travis L Bunker, Owner
EMP: 4 EST: 1983
SALES (est): 147.31K Privately Held
SIC: 2261 Finishing plants, cotton

(G-9188)
TRI-STATE CARPORTS INC (PA)
304 Franklin St (27030-4588)
PHONE..............................276 755-2081
Torres Gabriel, Pr
Florencio Torres, VP
Hilario Torres, Sec
EMP: 7 EST: 2000
SALES (est): 774.79K
SALES (corp-wide): 774.79K Privately
Held
Web: www.tristatecarports.com
SIC: 3448 Carports, prefabricated metal

(G-9189)
TRIPLETTE FENCING SUPPLY INC
Also Called: Triplette Competition Arms
786 W Lebanon St (27030)
PHONE..............................336 835-1205
Walter Triplette, Pr
▲ EMP: 5 EST: 1977
SALES (est): 410.5K Privately Held
Web: www.triplette.com
SIC: 3949 5091 5941 Sporting and athletic
goods, nec; Sporting and recreation goods;
Sporting goods and bicycle shops

(G-9190)
TRITON INDUSTRIES LLC
830 Fowler Rd (27030-2750)
PHONE..............................336 816-3794
EMP: 10 EST: 2022
SALES (est): 1.06MM Privately Held
SIC: 3448 Prefabricated metal buildings and
components

(G-9191)
TRUESTEEL STRUCTURES LLC ✪
Also Called: Carports.com
1050 Worth St (27030-4453)
PHONE..............................336 789-3818
Jason Torres, Managing Member
EMP: 20 EST: 2023
SALES (est): 1.04MM Privately Held
SIC: 3448 Carports, prefabricated metal

(G-9192)
UNITED PLASTICS CORPORATION
511 Hay St (27030-5629)
P.O. Box 807 (27030-0807)
PHONE..............................336 786-2127
Monty K Venable, Ch Bd
Nick Antonnechia, *
Johnny Collins, *
▲ EMP: 105 EST: 1947
SQ FT: 143,000
SALES (est): 10.14MM Privately Held
Web: www.unitedplastics.com
SIC: 3082 5162 Unsupported plastics profile
shapes; Plastics sheets and rods

(G-9193)
WHATZ COOKIN LLC
123 Old Brintle St (27030-5970)
PHONE..............................336 353-0227
Bernetta Simmons, Managing Member
EMP: 4 EST: 2022
SALES (est): 182.43K Privately Held
SIC: 2599 7389 Food wagons, restaurant;
Business Activities at Non-Commercial Site

(G-9194)
WHOLESALE MONUMENT COMPANY
3539 W Pine St (27030-9004)
P.O. Box 68 (27030-0068)
PHONE..............................336 789-2031
Delma Beck, Pr
Ginger Beck, Sec
Darell Beck, VP
EMP: 9 EST: 1976
SQ FT: 4,396
SALES (est): 499.56K Privately Held
Web: www.wholesalemonument.com
SIC: 3281 Marble, building: cut and shaped

(G-9195)
WILLOW TEX LLC
Also Called: Izitleather
501 Piedmont Triad West Dr (27030)
PHONE..............................336 789-1009
Dew Claybough, *
▲ EMP: 24 EST: 1964
SQ FT: 18,000
SALES (est): 4.56MM Privately Held
Web: www.izitleather.com
SIC: 3111 Upholstery leather

(G-9196)
WISE STORAGE SOLUTIONS LLC
1372 Boggs Dr (27030-2144)
P.O. Box 804 (27030-0804)
PHONE..............................336 789-5141
Neil Willard, Brnch Mgr
EMP: 45
SALES (corp-wide): 1.67MM Privately
Held

SIC: **3545** Machine tool accessories
PA: Wise Storage Solutions, Llc
1219 N South St
Mount Airy NC 27030
336 786-6182

(G-9197)
YADKIN VALLEY CABINET CO INC
135 Red Laurel Ln (27030-7920)
P.O. Box 6048 (27030-6048)
PHONE..................................336 786-9860
Thelma Hill, *Pr*
EMP: 8 EST: 2006
SALES (est): 669.44K **Privately Held**
Web: www.yvccinc.com
SIC: **2434** Wood kitchen cabinets

Mount Gilead
Montgomery County

(G-9198)
CAPITOL FUNDS INC
Also Called: Piedmont Components
409 N Main St (27306-9038)
P.O. Box 1253 (27306-1253)
PHONE..................................910 439-5275
Jimmy Eudy, *Mgr*
EMP: 16
SALES (corp-wide): 6.94MM **Privately Held**
Web: www.capitolfundsinc.com
SIC: **6552 5231 5251 2439** Land subdividers and developers, commercial; Paint; Hardware stores; Structural wood members, nec
PA: Capitol Funds, Inc.
720 S Lafayette St
Shelby NC 28150
704 487-8547

(G-9199)
J R B AND J KNITTING INC
4543 Nc Highway 109 S (27306-9496)
P.O. Box 833 (27306-0833)
PHONE..................................910 439-4242
Jessie R Bowles Junior, *Pr*
Joyce T Sedberry, *VP*
Marty B Richardson, *Sec*
Jessie Bowles Junior, *Pr*
EMP: 4 EST: 1981
SQ FT: 2,400
SALES (est): 71.52K **Privately Held**
SIC: **2252** Socks

(G-9200)
JORDAN LUMBER & SUPPLY INC
Also Called: Cotton Creek Chip Co
1939 Nc Highway 109 S (27306-8455)
P.O. Box 98 (27306-0098)
PHONE..................................910 439-6121
Bob Jordan, *Brnch Mgr*
EMP: 106
SALES (corp-wide): 26.93MM **Privately Held**
Web: www.jordanlumber.com
SIC: **2421** Lumber: rough, sawed, or planed
PA: Jordan Lumber & Supply, Inc.
1939 Nc Hwy 109 S
Mount Gilead NC 27306
910 439-6121

(G-9201)
JORDAN LUMBER & SUPPLY INC (PA)
1939 Nc Highway 109 S (27306-8455)
P.O. Box 98 (27306-0098)
PHONE..................................910 439-6121
Bob Jordan, *Pr*
Jack P Jordan, *

Robert B Jordan Iv, *VP*
EMP: 250 EST: 1939
SQ FT: 6,000
SALES (est): 26.93MM
SALES (corp-wide): 26.93MM **Privately Held**
Web: www.jordanlumber.com
SIC: **2421** Lumber: rough, sawed, or planed

(G-9202)
MCLENDON LOGGING INCORPORATED
671 Nc Highway 731 W (27306-8608)
PHONE..................................910 439-6223
Tommy Mclendon, *Pr*
EMP: 4 EST: 1980
SALES (est): 158.08K **Privately Held**
SIC: **2411** Logging camps and contractors

(G-9203)
MCRAE INDUSTRIES INC
Mc Rae Footwear
125 Wadeville Fire Station Rd (27306-6004)
P.O. Box 1239 (27306-1239)
PHONE..................................910 439-6149
Kelly Hamilton, *CFO*
EMP: 180
SALES (corp-wide): 24.66MM **Publicly Held**
Web: www.mcraeindustries.com
SIC: **5139 6153 3021** Boots; Short-term business credit institutions, except agricultural; Arctics, rubber or rubber soled fabric
PA: Mcrae Industries, Inc.
400 N Main St
Mount Gilead NC 27306
910 439-6147

(G-9204)
MCRAE INDUSTRIES INC (PA)
400 N Main St (27306-9038)
P.O. Box 1239 (27306)
PHONE..................................910 439-6147
D Gary Mc Rae, *Ch Bd*
Victor A Karam, *FOOTWEAR* *
Harold W Smith, *
James W Mc Rae, *
▲ **EMP: 40 EST:** 1959
SQ FT: 71,000
SALES (est): 24.66MM
SALES (corp-wide): 24.66MM **Publicly Held**
Web: www.mcraeindustries.com
SIC: **3143 3144** Boots, dress or casual: men's; Women's footwear, except athletic

(G-9205)
MEGAWOOD INC
670 W Allenton St (27306-9238)
P.O. Box 464 (27371-0464)
PHONE..................................910 572-3796
Billy Hamilton, *Pr*
Sue Hamilton, *VP*
EMP: 6 EST: 1985
SQ FT: 7,200
SALES (est): 367.28K **Privately Held**
SIC: **2421** Cants, resawed (lumber)

(G-9206)
MEGAWOOD HOLDINGS INC
610 W Allenton St (27306-9238)
P.O. Box 1227 (27306-1227)
PHONE..................................910 439-2124
EMP: 4 EST: 2015
SALES (est): 439.03K **Privately Held**
SIC: **2499** Wood products, nec

(G-9207)
MOHAWK INDUSTRIES INC
Unilin US Mdf
149 Homanit Usa Rd (27306-8649)
P.O. Box 69 (27306-0069)
PHONE..................................910 439-6959
Gunter Heyen, *Pr*
EMP: 197
Web: www.mohawkind.com
SIC: **2493** Insulation board, cellular fiber
PA: Mohawk Industries, Inc.
160 S Industrial Blvd
Calhoun GA 30701

(G-9208)
MT GILEAD CUT & SEW INC
112 N Main St (27306-9276)
PHONE..................................910 439-9909
Geraldine Craven, *Pr*
EMP: 10 EST: 2019
SALES (est): 425.93K **Privately Held**
SIC: **3639** Sewing equipment

(G-9209)
PAPERWORKS INDUSTRIES INC
5465 Nc Highway 73 W (27306-9316)
PHONE..................................910 439-6137
EMP: 227
Web: www.onepaperworks.com
SIC: **2653** Boxes, corrugated: made from purchased materials
PA: Paperworks Industries, Inc.
1300 Virginia Dr Ste 220
Fort Washington PA 19034

(G-9210)
TIMBER STAND IMPROVEMENTS INC
1939 Nc Highway 109 S (27306-8455)
P.O. Box 98 (27306-0098)
PHONE..................................910 439-6121
Bruce Evans, *Pr*
Jack P Jordan, *Sec*
EMP: 8 EST: 1988
SQ FT: 6,000
SALES (est): 555.46K **Privately Held**
Web: www.jordanlumber.com
SIC: **2411** Logging camps and contractors

(G-9211)
TOBE MANUFACTURING INC
603 W Allenton St (27306-9238)
P.O. Box 447 (27306-0447)
PHONE..................................910 439-6203
Gary Haywood, *Pr*
Brenda Haywood, *CFO*
EMP: 15 EST: 1983
SQ FT: 30,000
SALES (est): 1.88MM **Privately Held**
Web: www.tobemfg.com
SIC: **3599** Machine shop, jobbing and repair

(G-9212)
WOODLAND HOSIERY INC
118 Hudson Ln (27306-8972)
PHONE..................................910 439-4843
Jimmy Bowles, *Pr*
EMP: 4 EST: 1997
SALES (est): 402.31K **Privately Held**
Web: www.woodlandhosiery.com
SIC: **2252** Socks

Mount Holly
Gaston County

(G-9213)
AMERICAN & EFIRD GLOBAL LLC (DH)
22 American St (28120-2150)
P.O. Box 507 (28120-0507)

PHONE..................................704 827-4311
Mary Ann Sigler, *
EMP: 28 EST: 1968
SALES (est): 1.81MM
SALES (corp-wide): 1.98B **Privately Held**
Web: www.amefird.com
SIC: **2284** Thread mills
HQ: Elevate Textiles, Inc.
121 W Trade St Ste 1700
Charlotte NC 28202

(G-9214)
AMERICAN & EFIRD LLC
Regal Thread & Notions
22 American St (28120-2150)
PHONE..................................704 827-4311
Jerome Golden, *Mgr*
EMP: 12
SALES (corp-wide): 1.98B **Privately Held**
Web: www.amefird.com
SIC: **2284** Thread from natural fibers
HQ: American & Efird Llc
24 American St
Mount Holly NC 28120
704 827-4311

(G-9215)
AMERICAN & EFIRD LLC (DH)
24 American St (28120-2150)
P.O. Box 507 (28120-0507)
PHONE..................................704 827-4311
Les Miller, *CEO*
Lindell Stoker, *
L Richard Heavener, *Credit Vice President* *
Ronnie Ensley, *
Al Irvine, *
◆ **EMP: 200 EST:** 1891
SQ FT: 20,000
SALES (est): 238.44MM
SALES (corp-wide): 1.98B **Privately Held**
Web: www.amefird.com
SIC: **2284** Thread from natural fibers
HQ: Elevate Textiles, Inc.
121 W Trade St Ste 1700
Charlotte NC 28202

(G-9216)
AMERICAN & EFIRD LLC
101 Mill St (28120-1534)
PHONE..................................704 823-2501
Eddie Eaker, *Mgr*
EMP: 16
SALES (corp-wide): 1.98B **Privately Held**
Web: www.amefird.com
SIC: **2284** Sewing thread
HQ: American & Efird Llc
24 American St
Mount Holly NC 28120
704 827-4311

(G-9217)
ARROCHEM INC
201 Westland Farm Rd (28120-9533)
P.O. Box 5 (28120-0005)
PHONE..................................704 827-0216
David A Hostetler, *Pr*
Patty M Hostetler, *VP*
EMP: 15 EST: 1979
SQ FT: 18,000
SALES (est): 6.68MM **Privately Held**
Web: www.arrochem.com
SIC: **2843** Emulsifiers, except food and pharmaceutical

(G-9218)
BELMONT TEXTILE MACHINERY CO
1212 W Catawba Ave (28120-1111)
P.O. Box 568 (28120-0568)
PHONE..................................704 827-5836
Walter P Rhyne, *CEO*
Jeff T Rhyne, *

▲ **EMP:** 48 **EST:** 1955
SQ FT: 59,000
SALES (est): 4.59MM **Privately Held**
Web: www.btmc.com
SIC: 3552 Winders, textile machinery

(G-9219)
BOXMAN STUDIOS LLC
1310 Charles Raper Jonas Hwy Ste B
(28120-1234)
PHONE................................704 333-3733
David Campbell, *Managing Member*
EMP: 6 **EST:** 2009
SALES (est): 23.29MM **Privately Held**
Web: www.boxmanstudios.com
SIC: 5085 3448 Commercial containers;
Buildings, portable: prefabricated metal

(G-9220)
BUCKEYE TECHNOLOGIES INC
Also Called: BUCKEYE TECHNOLOGIES
INC.
100 Buckeye Dr (28120-1278)
PHONE................................704 822-6400
John Crows, *Prin*
EMP: 176
SALES (corp-wide): 64.44B **Privately Held**
Web: www.bkitech.com
SIC: 2611 2621 Pulp mills; Paper mills
HQ: Georgia-Pacific Nonwovens Llc
1001 Tillman
Memphis TN 38112

(G-9221)
CAROLINA FAB INC
2129 Charles Raper Jonas Hwy
(28120-1276)
P.O. Box 672 (28120-0672)
PHONE................................704 820-8694
Deborah Evans, *Pr*
William Evans, *VP*
Christian Evans, *VP*
EMP: 17 **EST:** 1998
SALES (est): 3.52MM **Privately Held**
Web: www.carolinafabinc.com
SIC: 3441 Fabricated structural metal

(G-9222)
CEKAL SPECIALTIES INC
101 Brickyard Rd (28120-8800)
P.O. Box 788 (28120-0788)
PHONE................................704 822-6206
Dallas Crotts, *Pr*
Jimmy Lawing, *Stockholder*
Jeff Lawing, *VP*
◆ **EMP:** 20 **EST:** 1992
SQ FT: 10,000
SALES (est): 4.57MM **Privately Held**
Web: www.cekalspecialties.com
SIC: 2393 Textile bags

(G-9223)
CHARAH LLC
175 Steam Plant Rd (28120-9740)
PHONE................................502 873-6993
EMP: 138
SALES (corp-wide): 293.17MM **Publicly Held**
Web: www.charah.com
SIC: 1081 Metal mining exploration and
development services
HQ: Charah, Llc
12601 Plantside Dr
Louisville KY 40299

(G-9224)
CLARIANT CORPORATION
Also Called: Mount Holly West Plant
625 E Catawba Ave (28120-2270)
PHONE................................704 822-2100
Ken Golder, *Pr*

EMP: 40
Web: www.clariant.com
SIC: 2869 Industrial organic chemicals, nec
HQ: Clariant Corporation
500 E Morehead St Ste 400
Charlotte NC 28202
704 331-7000

(G-9225)
CLIFT INDUSTRIES INC
201 Westland Farm Rd (28120-9533)
PHONE................................704 752-0031
Layne Finchur, *Pr*
EMP: 5
SALES (corp-wide): 3.08MM **Privately Held**
Web: www.cliftindustries.com
SIC: 2819 Industrial inorganic chemicals, nec
PA: Clift Industries, Inc.
3033 Eaton Ave
Indian Trail NC 28079
704 752-0031

(G-9226)
CRAZIE TEES
177 Brookstone Dr (28120-2811)
PHONE................................704 898-2272
Theresa Wilson, *Prin*
EMP: 4 **EST:** 2018
SALES (est): 90.31K **Privately Held**
SIC: 2759 Screen printing

(G-9227)
**DAVID VIZARD MOTORTEC
FEATURES**
109 Mistywood Dr (28120-9267)
PHONE................................865 850-0666
EMP: 4 **EST:** 2017
SALES (est): 148.96K **Privately Held**
SIC: 3714 Motor vehicle parts and
accessories

(G-9228)
DIVERSFIED HOLDINGS DALLAS INC
124 W Catawba Ave (28120-1602)
P.O. Box 515 (28034-0515)
PHONE................................704 922-5293
David W Hoyle Junior, *Pr*
EMP: 7 **EST:** 2009
SALES (est): 2.03MM **Privately Held**
SIC: 3499 Fabricated metal products, nec

(G-9229)
**ENVIRNMNTAL PRCESS SYSTEMS
INC**
227 Lamplighter Ln (28120-9243)
PHONE................................704 827-0740
Ben Taylor, *Pr*
Elaine Taylor, *Sec*
EMP: 6 **EST:** 1996
SQ FT: 4,000
SALES (est): 558.26K **Privately Held**
Web: www.epsiusa.com
SIC: 3589 Water treatment equipment,
industrial

(G-9230)
EPSIUSA
1124 W Charlotte Ave (28120-1212)
PHONE................................704 827-0740
Ben Taylor, *Prin*
EMP: 4 **EST:** 2010
SALES (est): 346.76K **Privately Held**
SIC: 3589 Service industry machinery, nec

(G-9231)
**GASTON COUNTY DYEING
MACHINE COMPANY**
Also Called: Gaston Fabrication
1310 Charles Raper Jonas Hwy
(28120-1234)

PHONE................................704 822-5000
▼ **EMP:** 100 **EST:** 1921
SALES (est): 9.74MM **Privately Held**
Web: www.gaston-county.com
SIC: 3443 3552 Tanks, standard or custom
fabricated: metal plate; Dyeing machinery,
textile

(G-9232)
GASTONIA ORNAMENTAL WLDG INC
Also Called: Gastonia Iron Works
624 Legion Rd (28120-1424)
P.O. Box 748 (28120-0748)
PHONE................................704 827-1146
Katherine C Pace, *Pr*
Jerry N Pace Senior, *VP*
EMP: 15 **EST:** 1940
SQ FT: 2,400
SALES (est): 1.05MM **Privately Held**
SIC: 3449 1799 Bars, concrete reinforcing:
fabricated steel; Ornamental metal work

(G-9233)
GLATFELTER MT HOLLY LLC
100 Buckeye Dr (28120-1278)
PHONE................................704 812-2299
◆ **EMP:** 98 **EST:** 1999
SQ FT: 15,563
SALES (est): 23.44MM
SALES (corp-wide): 1.39B **Publicly Held**
Web: www.mtholly.us
SIC: 2611 Pulp produced from non-wood
fiber base, nec
PA: Magnera Corporation
9335 Hrris Crners Pkwy St
Charlotte NC 28269
866 744-7380

(G-9234)
J & B TOOL MAKING INC
14522 Lucia Riverbend Hwy (28120-9703)
PHONE................................704 827-4805
EMP: 6 **EST:** 1985
SQ FT: 7,000
SALES (est): 597.22K **Privately Held**
SIC: 3541 Drilling machine tools (metal
cutting)

(G-9235)
**LEONINE PROTECTION SYSTEMS
LLC**
309 Dutchmans Meadow Dr (28120-3015)
PHONE................................704 296-2675
EMP: 6 **EST:** 2003
SALES (est): 310.05K **Privately Held**
SIC: 3699 Security control equipment and
systems

(G-9236)
MAC/FAB COMPANY INC
913 W Catawba Ave (28120-1411)
P.O. Box 452 (28120-0452)
PHONE................................704 822-1103
R G Pfaff, *Pr*
Jeffery Pfaff, *VP*
EMP: 20 **EST:** 1982
SQ FT: 10,000
SALES (est): 4.66MM **Privately Held**
Web: www.macfab.net
SIC: 3444 3469 3599 Sheet metalwork;
Metal stampings, nec; Machine and other
job shop work

(G-9237)
METRO PRINT INC
800 W Central Ave (28120-1675)
P.O. Box 374 (28120-0374)
PHONE................................704 827-3796
Frank Kemp, *Pr*
Angela Kemp, *Sec*
EMP: 10 **EST:** 2011

SQ FT: 10,000
SALES (est): 1.37MM **Privately Held**
Web: www.signsbymetroprint.com
SIC: 3993 Signs and advertising specialties

(G-9238)
MODERN MOLD & TOOL COMPANY
Also Called: Machine Shop of Charlotte, The
1050 Ironwood Dr (28299-5313)
P.O. Box 5313 (28299-5313)
PHONE................................704 377-2300
Robin Hood, *Pr*
Dora A Hood, *VP*
Elizabeth Patton, *Sec*
EMP: 6 **EST:** 1968
SALES (est): 779.27K **Privately Held**
Web: www.tonerplastics.com
SIC: 3544 Special dies and tools

(G-9239)
MUDDY RIVER DISTILLERY LLC
250 N Main St (28120-1770)
PHONE................................336 516-4190
Robert Jeffrey Delaney, *Prin*
EMP: 4 **EST:** 2011
SALES (est): 265.05K **Privately Held**
Web: www.muddyriverdistillery.com
SIC: 2085 Distilled and blended liquors

(G-9240)
NATIONAL COLOR GRAPHICS INC
98 Rutledge Rd (28120-9407)
PHONE................................704 263-3187
Hugh Taylor, *Pr*
EMP: 4 **EST:** 1980
SALES (est): 159.37K **Privately Held**
SIC: 3555 Plates, offset

(G-9241)
PARKDALE MILLS INCORPORATED
Also Called: Parkdale Plant 68
101 Mill St (28120-1534)
PHONE................................704 822-0778
EMP: 24
SALES (corp-wide): 1.44B **Privately Held**
Web: www.parkdalemills.com
SIC: 2281 Cotton yarn, spun
HQ: Parkdale Mills, Incorporated
531 Cotton Blossom Cir
Gastonia NC 28054
704 874-5000

(G-9242)
PROCESS ELECTRONICS CORP
100 Brickyard Rd (28120-8800)
P.O. Box 505 (28120-0505)
PHONE................................704 827-9019
Carolyn Berry, *Ch Bd*
EMP: 19 **EST:** 1984
SQ FT: 16,000
SALES (est): 2.25MM **Privately Held**
Web: www.pecrectifier.com
SIC: 3699 Accelerating waveguide structures

(G-9243)
**PROFORM FINISHING PRODUCTS
LLC**
1725 Wester Rd (28120-9483)
PHONE................................704 398-3900
Thomas Nelson, *Prin*
EMP: 23
SALES (corp-wide): 795.88MM **Privately Held**
Web: www.nationalgypsum.com
SIC: 3275 Gypsum products
HQ: Proform Finishing Products, Llc
2001 Rexford Rd
Charlotte NC 28211

(G-9244)
RINKER MATERIALS
1725 Drywall Dr (28120-8453)
PHONE.................704 827-8175
Earl Wood, *Prin*
EMP: 7 **EST:** 2010
SALES (est): 98.49K **Privately Held**
SIC: 3273 Ready-mixed concrete

(G-9245)
WARREN PLASTICS INC
511 Rankin Ave (28120-1565)
PHONE.................704 827-9887
Mark V Warren, *Pr*
Betty Warren, *VP*
EMP: 5 **EST:** 1981
SQ FT: 5,500
SALES (est): 476.06K **Privately Held**
Web: www.warrenplasticsinc.com
SIC: 3089 Injection molding of plastics

Mount Olive
Wayne County

(G-9246)
AFL NETWORK SERVICES INC
Also Called: Impulse NC
100 Impulse Way (28365-8691)
P.O. Box 889 (28365-0889)
PHONE.................919 658-2311
EMP: 25
Web: www.aflglobal.com
SIC: 3357 Nonferrous wiredrawing and
insulating
HQ: Afl Network Services, Inc.
170 Ridgeview Ctr Dr
Duncan SC 29334
864 433-0333

(G-9247)
BENMOT PUBLISHING COMPANY INC
Also Called: Mount Olive Tribune
214 N Center St (28365-1702)
PHONE.................919 658-9456
Larry Mcphail, *Genl Mgr*
EMP: 4 **EST:** 2012
SALES (est): 210.1K **Privately Held**
SIC: 2711 Newspapers, publishing and
printing

(G-9248)
BIO-ADHESIVE ALLIANCE INC
225 Daniel Chestnutt Rd (28365-5258)
PHONE.................336 285-3676
Mahour Mellat-parast, *Pr*
EMP: 4 **EST:** 2013
SALES (est): 241.52K **Privately Held**
Web: www.baa-usa.com
SIC: 2891 Adhesives and sealants

(G-9249)
BOBBY A HERRING LOGGING
324 Alum Springs Rd (28365-9270)
PHONE.................919 658-9768
Bobby Herring, *Owner*
EMP: 7 **EST:** 1982
SALES (est): 419.73K **Privately Held**
SIC: 2411 Logging camps and contractors

(G-9250)
BUTTERBALL LLC
Also Called: Carolina Turkeys
1628 Garner Chapel Rd (28365-6167)
P.O. Box 599 (28365-0599)
PHONE.................919 658-6743
EMP: 99
SALES (corp-wide): 9.1B **Publicly Held**
Web: www.butterballfoodservice.com

SIC: 2015 Turkey, processed, nsk
HQ: Butterball, Llc
1 Butterball Ln
Garner NC 27529
919 255-7900

(G-9251)
CAROLINA NUT INC
Also Called: Golden Grove USA
1180 Stanley Chapel Church Rd
(28365-8614)
PHONE.................910 293-4209
Nicholas Swinson, *Pr*
EMP: 10 **EST:** 2017
SALES (est): 1.04MM **Privately Held**
Web: www.carolinanutcracker.com
SIC: 2068 Nuts: dried, dehydrated, salted or
roasted

(G-9252)
CASE FARMS LLC
Also Called: Calypso Feed Mill
188 Broadhurst Rd (28365-9541)
PHONE.................919 635-2390
Johnny Milkovits, *Mgr*
EMP: 83
Web: www.casefarms.com
SIC: 2015 Poultry slaughtering and
processing
PA: Case Farms, L.L.C.
385 Pilch Rd
Troutman NC 28166

(G-9253)
CONSOLIDATED INSPECTIONS INC
526 Norwood Ezzell Rd (28365-5361)
P.O. Box 450 (28365-0450)
PHONE.................919 658-5800
Sam Wilson, *Pr*
Susan Wilson, *Sec*
EMP: 5 **EST:** 1991
SALES (est): 341.18K **Privately Held**
Web: www.conspect.com
SIC: 3599 Machine shop, jobbing and repair

(G-9254)
GOSHEN ENGINEERING INC
439 Nc Highway 55 E (28365-8001)
P.O. Box 1170 (28365-3170)
PHONE.................919 429-9798
Jason Stevens, *Dir*
EMP: 4 **EST:** 2006
SALES (est): 2.74MM **Privately Held**
Web: www.goshenengineering.com
SIC: 8711 8742 3599 Electrical or electronic
engineering; Automation and robotics
consultant; Custom machinery

(G-9255)
IMPULSE NC LLC
100 Impulse Way (28365-8691)
PHONE.................919 658-2311
▲ **EMP:** 25
SIC: 3612 Transformers, except electric

(G-9256)
JACKSON LOGGING
2936 Summerlins Crossroad Rd
(28365-6416)
PHONE.................919 658-2757
Ricki Jackson, *Owner*
EMP: 4 **EST:** 1980
SALES (est): 246.02K **Privately Held**
SIC: 2411 Logging camps and contractors

(G-9257)
MOUNT OLIVE PICKLE COMPANY INC (PA)
Also Called: That's Picklicious
1 Cucumber Blvd (28365)

P.O. Box 609 (28365)
PHONE.................919 658-2535
William H Bryan, *Ch*
Robert D Frye Junior, *Pr*
A Douglas Brock, *
Richard D Bowen, *
◆ **EMP:** 203 **EST:** 1926
SQ FT: 400,000
SALES (est): 835.67K
SALES (corp-wide): 835.67K **Privately Held**
Web: www.mtolivepickles.com
SIC: 2035 Pickles, vinegar

(G-9258)
SOUTHERN MACHINE SERVICES
300 Waller Rd (28365-7570)
PHONE.................919 658-9300
Carl Graves, *Owner*
EMP: 4 **EST:** 1996
SQ FT: 2,500
SALES (est): 235.09K **Privately Held**
SIC: 3599 3569 Machine shop, jobbing and
repair; Robots, assembly line: industrial and
commercial

(G-9259)
SOUTHERN STATES COOP INC
Also Called: S S C 7795-7
301 N Chestnut St (28365-1615)
P.O. Box 419 (28365-0419)
PHONE.................919 658-5061
Sammy Fields, *Mgr*
EMP: 35
SALES (corp-wide): 1.71B **Privately Held**
Web: www.southernstates.com
SIC: 2048 2873 0181 2874 Prepared feeds,
nec; Nitrogenous fertilizers; Bulbs and
seeds; Phosphatic fertilizers
PA: Southern States Cooperative,
Incorporated
6606 W Broad St Ste B
Richmond VA 23230
804 281-1000

(G-9260)
SWELL HOME SOLUTIONS INC
109 Barfield St (28365-2624)
PHONE.................919 440-4692
EMP: 4 **EST:** 2017
SALES (est): 200.39K **Privately Held**
SIC: 3524 Lawn and garden equipment

Mount Pleasant
Cabarrus County

(G-9261)
CREATIONS BY TAYLOR
2892 Long Run Farm Rd (28124-8830)
PHONE.................410 269-6430
Barry Taylor, *Owner*
EMP: 8 **EST:** 1986
SALES (est): 157.48K **Privately Held**
Web: www.creationsbytaylor.com
SIC: 2512 Upholstered household furniture

(G-9262)
IVEY ICENHOUR DBA
5690 Barrier Georgeville Rd (28124-9158)
PHONE.................704 786-0676
Ivey Icenhour, *Prin*
EMP: 6 **EST:** 2010
SALES (est): 111.29K **Privately Held**
SIC: 2411 Logging

(G-9263)
PASTURE MANAGEMENT SYSTEMS INC
10325 Nc Highway 49 N (28124-9666)

P.O. Box 1120 (28124-1120)
PHONE.................704 436-6401
David A Hill, *Pr*
W C Cannon Junior, *Sec*
▲ **EMP:** 17 **EST:** 1991
SQ FT: 23,500
SALES (est): 4.19MM **Privately Held**
Web: www.pasturemgmt.com
SIC: 3523 Farm machinery and equipment

(G-9264)
PIEDMONT HARDWOOD LBR CO INC
9000 Nc Highway 49 N (28124-9656)
P.O. Box 535 (28124-0535)
PHONE.................704 436-9311
L Joe Stirewalt, *Pr*
Curtis L Stirewalt, *VP*
Randy Bingham, *Off Mgr*
EMP: 10 **EST:** 1960
SQ FT: 1,200
SALES (est): 4.35MM **Privately Held**
SIC: 2421 2426 Lumber: rough, sawed, or
planed; Hardwood dimension and flooring
mills

(G-9265)
TOMMY W SMITH INC
Also Called: Cabinet Creations
9825 Bowman Barrier Rd (28124-8713)
P.O. Box 267 (28124-0267)
PHONE.................704 436-6616
Tommy W Smith, *Owner*
Tommy W Smith, *Pr*
Debbie Smith, *VP*
EMP: 5 **EST:** 1988
SQ FT: 5,000
SALES (est): 141.03K **Privately Held**
SIC: 2434 Wood kitchen cabinets

(G-9266)
TUSCARORA YARNS INC
8760 Franklin St E (28124-8788)
P.O. Box 218 (28124-0218)
PHONE.................704 436-6527
◆ **EMP:** 305
Web: www.tuscarorayarns.com
SIC: 2281 Knitting yarn, spun

Mount Ulla
Rowan County

(G-9267)
CAROLINA STAIRS INC
255 Belk Rd (28125-9769)
P.O. Box 572 (28125-0572)
PHONE.................704 664-5032
Charles Johnson, *Pr*
EMP: 17 **EST:** 1981
SQ FT: 16,000
SALES (est): 2.31MM **Privately Held**
Web: www.bigframer.com
SIC: 2431 Staircases and stairs, wood

(G-9268)
CWC FABRICATING
2530 Graham Rd (28125-9652)
PHONE.................704 360-8264
EMP: 4 **EST:** 2017
SALES (est): 225.7K **Privately Held**
SIC: 3441 Fabricated structural metal

(G-9269)
HODGE FARMS LLC
11235 Nc Highway 801 (28125-8640)
PHONE.................704 278-2684
Robie Hodge, *Owner*
EMP: 4 **EST:** 1962
SALES (est): 236.59K **Privately Held**

GEOGRAPHIC

SIC: 2048 Rolled oats, prepared as animal feed

(G-9270)
PIEDMONT WELL COVERS INC
1135 Mazeppa Rd (28125-9703)
PHONE...................................704 664-8488
William Wainscott, *Pr*
Pam Wainscott, *VP*
EMP: 10 **EST:** 1994
SALES (est): 894.17K **Privately Held**
Web: www.piedmontwellcovers.com
SIC: 3432 1799 3443 3229 Plumbing fixture fittings and trim; Fiberglass work; Heat exchangers, condensers, and components; Glass fiber products

(G-9271)
PROTECH FABRICATION INC
575 Edmiston Rd (28125-8746)
PHONE...................................704 663-1721
Harold G Moore, *Pr*
Christy Moore, *Sec*
EMP: 13 **EST:** 1992
SQ FT: 7,500
SALES (est): 2.13MM **Privately Held**
Web: www.protechnc.net
SIC: 3498 3441 Fabricated pipe and fittings; Fabricated structural metal

(G-9272)
WAGGONER MANUFACTURING CO
1065 Hall Rd (28125-9668)
PHONE...................................704 278-2000
Luther W Waggoner, *Owner*
Luther W Waggoner, *Pr*
Peggy Waggoner, *Sec*
EMP: 20 **EST:** 1964
SQ FT: 1,350
SALES (est): 4.45MM **Privately Held**
Web: www.waggonermanufacturing.com
SIC: 3498 7699 Fabricated pipe and fittings; Industrial machinery and equipment repair

(G-9273)
WILLIAMS PERFORMANCE INC
3140 Corriher Grange Rd (28125-7820)
PHONE...................................704 603-4431
Nicholas Williams, *Pr*
▲ **EMP:** 6 **EST:** 2005
SQ FT: 9,000
SALES (est): 4.14MM **Privately Held**
Web: www.williamsperformance.net
SIC: 3559 Automotive related machinery

Mountain Home
Henderson County

(G-9274)
HAYNES WIRE COMPANY
Also Called: Haynes International
158 N Edgerton Rd (28758)
P.O. Box 677 (28758-0677)
PHONE...................................828 692-5791
TOLL FREE: 800
▲ **EMP:** 52
SIC: 3315 Wire and fabricated wire products

Moyock
Currituck County

(G-9275)
ANDREA L GRIZZLE
Also Called: Unified Logistics NC
101 Trinity Ln Box 751 (27958-5900)
PHONE...................................252 202-3278
Andrea Grizzle, *Owner*
Lorie Grizzle, *Prin*

Mary Dorsey, *Prin*
Andre Grizzle, *Prin*
EMP: 4 **EST:** 2010
SALES (est): 330.71K **Privately Held**
Web: www.unifiedlogisticsnc.com
SIC: 3661 2621 Telephone central office equipment, dial or manual; Cleansing paper

(G-9276)
BAY PAINTING CONTRACTORS
128 Bayside Dr (27958-9056)
PHONE...................................252 435-5374
Brad Forehand, *Owner*
EMP: 4 **EST:** 2008
SALES (est): 172.53K **Privately Held**
SIC: 2851 Paints and allied products

(G-9277)
BUILT TO LAST NC LLC
417h Caratoke Hwy (27958-8608)
PHONE...................................252 232-0055
Daniel W Aston, *Managing Member*
EMP: 17 **EST:** 2019
SALES (est): 1.05MM **Privately Held**
SIC: 2519 Fiberglass and plastic furniture

(G-9278)
COMMERCIAL READY MIX PDTS INC
115 Windchaser Way (27958-8794)
PHONE...................................252 232-1250
EMP: 9
SALES (corp-wide): 48.13MM **Privately Held**
Web: www.crmpinc.com
SIC: 3273 Ready-mixed concrete
PA: Commercial Ready Mix Products, Inc.
115 Hwy 158 W
Winton NC 27986
252 358-5461

(G-9279)
MIDWEST MODULAR SERVICES LTD
216 Tarheel Dr (27958-8027)
PHONE...................................847 417-0010
Matthew Brennan, *Pr*
EMP: 12 **EST:** 2019
SALES (est): 3.18MM **Privately Held**
SIC: 1389 Construction, repair, and dismantling services

(G-9280)
QUALITY MCH & FABRICATION INC
444 Guinea Mill Rd (27958-9293)
P.O. Box 460 (27958-0460)
PHONE...................................252 435-6041
Deborah Brackett, *Pr*
EMP: 5 **EST:** 1990
SALES (est): 352.99K **Privately Held**
Web: www.qualitymachineandfabrication.com
SIC: 3599 Machine shop, jobbing and repair

Murfreesboro
Hertford County

(G-9281)
BORNEO INC
10 Commerce St (27855)
PHONE...................................252 398-3100
Jacques Y Gamard, *Pr*
Peter Martone, *
EMP: 5 **EST:** 1987
SQ FT: 85,000
SALES (est): 629.26K **Privately Held**
SIC: 3089 Plastics kitchenware, tableware, and houseware

(G-9282)
JIF LOGGING INC
411 E Woodrow School Rd (27855-9417)
PHONE...................................252 398-2249
John Futrell, *Pr*
Debra H Futrell, *Sec*
EMP: 7 **EST:** 1993
SALES (est): 118.07K **Privately Held**
SIC: 2411 Logging camps and contractors

(G-9283)
METAL TECH MURFREESBORO INC (PA)
Also Called: Metal Tech of Murfreesboro
314 W Broad St (27855-1442)
PHONE...................................252 398-4041
Ray Felton, *Pr*
Edward Drock, *
Judy H Felton, *
Brock Felton, *
▲ **EMP:** 45 **EST:** 1971
SQ FT: 21,500
SALES (est): 27.61MM
SALES (corp-wide): 27.61MM **Privately Held**
Web: www.metaltechnc.com
SIC: 3441 Fabricated structural metal

(G-9284)
PERDUE FARMS INC
Also Called: Perdue Farms
Hwy 158 W (27855)
P.O. Box 532 (27855-0532)
PHONE...................................252 398-5112
Dale Evans, *Mgr*
EMP: 112
SALES (corp-wide): 1.24B **Privately Held**
Web: www.perdue.com
SIC: 2015 Poultry slaughtering and processing
PA: Perdue Farms Incorporated
31149 Old Ocean City Rd
Salisbury MD 21804
800 473-7383

(G-9285)
PRODUCERS GIN MURFREESBORO LLC
336 Benthall Bridge Rd (27855-9672)
PHONE...................................252 398-3762
EMP: 6 **EST:** 2010
SALES (est): 256.28K **Privately Held**
SIC: 3999 Manufacturing industries, nec

Murphy
Cherokee County

(G-9286)
ACORN WOODWORKS NC LLC
1221 Warren Dr (28906-3102)
PHONE...................................828 361-9953
John Lachance, *Prin*
EMP: 4 **EST:** 2019
SALES (est): 65.49K **Privately Held**
SIC: 2431 Millwork

(G-9287)
AEGIS POWER SYSTEMS INC
805 Greenlawn Cemetery Rd (28906-9137)
P.O. Box 429 (28906-0429)
PHONE...................................828 837-4029
Arlissa Vaughn, *Pr*
Jeffrey Martin, *
Arlissa Vaughn, *Ch*
Zoe Scroggs, *
EMP: 25 **EST:** 1995
SQ FT: 10,000
SALES (est): 8.41MM **Privately Held**
Web: www.aegispower.com

SIC: 3699 Electrical equipment and supplies, nec

(G-9288)
BEAR PAGES
99 Smoke Rise Cir (28906-9005)
PHONE...................................828 837-0785
Weldon Beach, *Owner*
EMP: 6 **EST:** 2007
SALES (est): 159.65K **Privately Held**
Web: www.bearpagespaperarts.com
SIC: 3069 3953 5084 5945 Rubber tape; Embossing seals and hand stamps; Industrial machinery and equipment; Hobbies, nec

(G-9289)
CHI RESOURCES
Also Called: Indian Health Spring Water
1115 Horton Rd (28906-3580)
P.O. Box 860 (28906-0860)
PHONE...................................828 835-7878
David Lawrence, *Pr*
EMP: 4 **EST:** 1997
SALES (est): 238.23K **Privately Held**
SIC: 3221 Water bottles, glass

(G-9290)
INDIAN HEAD INDUSTRIES INC
Also Called: MGM Brakes
229 Park Ave (28906-2745)
P.O. Box 70 (28906-0070)
PHONE...................................704 547-7411
Robin Jenkins, *Mgr*
EMP: 88
SALES (corp-wide): 30.92MM **Privately Held**
Web: www.mgmbrakes.com
SIC: 3714 Motor vehicle brake systems and parts
PA: Indian Head Industries, Inc.
6200 Hars Tech Blvd
Charlotte NC 28269
704 547-7411

(G-9291)
LEDFORD LOGGING CO INC
1737 Sunny Point Rd (28906-7393)
PHONE...................................828 644-5410
Robert Ledford, *Pr*
Robert Buddy Ledford, *Pr*
Linda Ledford, *Mgr*
Linda Ledford, *Sec*
EMP: 4 **EST:** 1967
SALES (est): 129.79K **Privately Held**
SIC: 2411 Logging camps and contractors

(G-9292)
MCLOUD MEDIA
Also Called: Late Model Digest
1192 Andrews Rd Ste H (28906-2809)
P.O. Box 340 (28906-0340)
PHONE...................................828 837-9539
Carolyn Mcloud, *Owner*
EMP: 5 **EST:** 1989
SALES (est): 258.39K **Privately Held**
SIC: 2711 Newspapers: publishing only, not printed on site

(G-9293)
MOOG INC
Also Called: Moog Components Group
1995 Nc Highway 141 (28906-6864)
P.O. Box 160 (28906-0160)
PHONE...................................828 837-5115
Terry Martin, *Brnch Mgr*
EMP: 400
SQ FT: 130,000
SALES (corp-wide): 3.32B **Publicly Held**
Web: www.moog.com

Al Bannister Junior, *Pr*
EMP: 7 **EST:** 1983
SALES (est): 1.5MM **Privately Held**
SIC: 3599 Machine shop, jobbing and repair

(G-9340)
BENDER APPAREL & SIGNS INC
1841 Old Airport Rd (28562-9453)
PHONE.................................252 636-8337
John Berry Bender, *Pr*
Wade Bender, *VP*
EMP: 8 **EST:** 1996
SQ FT: 2,400
SALES (est): 968.69K **Privately Held**
Web: www.bendershirts.com
SIC: 2759 Screen printing

(G-9341)
BROADWAY LOGGING CO INC
Also Called: Broadway Chipping Co.
1525 Saints Delight Church Rd
(28560-7305)
PHONE.................................252 633-2693
B F Broadway, *Pr*
Gail Broadway, *
EMP: 50 **EST:** 1978
SALES (est): 534.92K **Privately Held**
SIC: 2411 Logging camps and contractors

(G-9342)
BSH HOME APPLIANCES CORP
120 Bosch Blvd (28562-6924)
PHONE.................................252 636-4454
Clemence Schaller, *Brnch Mgr*
EMP: 34
SALES (corp-wide): 391.51MM **Privately Held**
Web: www.bosch-home.com
SIC: 3631 Convection ovens, including portable; household
HQ: Bsh Home Appliances Corporation
1901 Main St Ste 600
Irvine CA 92614

(G-9343)
BSH HOME APPLIANCES CORP
Also Called: Bsh International Trade
100 Bosch Blvd (28562-6924)
PHONE.................................252 672-9155
Clemens Schaller, *Brnch Mgr*
EMP: 400
SALES (corp-wide): 391.51MM **Privately Held**
Web: www.bosch-home.com
SIC: 7629 3632 Electrical household appliance repair; Household refrigerators and freezers
HQ: Bsh Home Appliances Corporation
1901 Main St Ste 600
Irvine CA 92614

(G-9344)
BSH HOME APPLS A LTD PARTNR
100 Bosch Blvd (28562-6924)
PHONE.................................252 636-4200
Fred Hohage, *Pt*
EMP: 270 **EST:** 1996
SQ FT: 160,000
SALES (est): 22.95MM
SALES (corp-wide): 391.51MM **Privately Held**
SIC: 3639 Dishwashing machines, household
HQ: Bsh Hausgerate Gmbh
Carl-Wery-Str. 34
Munchen BY 81739
89459001

(G-9345)
BURKETT WELDING SERVICES INC
1401 B St (28560-9300)
P.O. Box 314 (28586-0314)

PHONE.................................252 635-2814
Kevin L Burkett, *Pr*
EMP: 10 **EST:** 2008
SALES (est): 1.15MM **Privately Held**
Web: www.burkettindustrial.com
SIC: 1799 3441 Welding on site; Fabricated structural metal

(G-9346)
C & S REPAIR CENTER INC
2081 Royal Pines Dr (28560-1807)
PHONE.................................610 524-9724
Shirley Lynn, *VP*
Carl Ressler, *Pr*
EMP: 6 **EST:** 1992
SALES (est): 262.78K **Privately Held**
Web: www.candsrepaircenter.com
SIC: 7694 5999 Rebuilding motors, except automotive; Engine and motor equipment and supplies

(G-9347)
CARAWAY LOGGING INC
1939 Olympia Rd (28560-5110)
PHONE.................................252 633-1230
John Dee Caraway, *Pr*
John Dee Caraway Iii, *VP*
EMP: 9 **EST:** 1990
SALES (est): 494.23K **Privately Held**
SIC: 2411 Logging camps and contractors

(G-9348)
CAROLINA EAST TIMBER INC
2145 Saints Delight Church Rd
(28560-7317)
PHONE.................................252 638-1914
John P Ipock Iii, *Pr*
Mary W Ipock, *Sec*
EMP: 5 **EST:** 1992
SALES (est): 300.63K **Privately Held**
Web: www.carolinaeasthealth.com
SIC: 2411 Logging camps and contractors

(G-9349)
CAROLINA GROUND SVC EQP INC (PA)
Also Called: Carolina GSE
430 Executive Pkwy (28562-9794)
PHONE.................................252 565-0288
John Werner, *Pr*
EMP: 11 **EST:** 2002
SALES (est): 3.77MM
SALES (corp-wide): 3.77MM **Privately Held**
Web: www.carolinagse.com
SIC: 3728 5088 Aircraft parts and equipment, nec; Aircraft and parts, nec

(G-9350)
CAROLINA HOME EXTERIORS LLC
252 Kale Rd (28562-7055)
PHONE.................................252 637-6599
David Thereault, *Managing Member*
EMP: 10 **EST:** 1980
SQ FT: 23,000
SALES (est): 2.31MM **Privately Held**
Web: www.carolinahomeexteriorsenc.com
SIC: 1521 3089 5033 Patio and deck construction and repair; Window screening, plastics; Siding, except wood

(G-9351)
CAT LOGISTICS INC
Also Called: Caterpillar
7970 Hwy 70 E (28560-8487)
PHONE.................................252 447-2490
Daniel Shannon, *Mgr*
EMP: 10
SALES (corp-wide): 64.81B **Publicly Held**

SIC: 3365 Aerospace castings, aluminum
HQ: C.A.T. Logistics Inc.
500 N Morton Ave
Morton IL 61550
309 675-1000

(G-9352)
CCBCC OPERATIONS LLC
Also Called: Coca-Cola
3710 Dr M L King Jr Blvd (28562)
PHONE.................................252 637-3157
George Walker, *Mgr*
EMP: 43
SALES (corp-wide): 6.9B **Publicly Held**
Web: www.coca-cola.com
SIC: 2086 Bottled and canned soft drinks
HQ: Ccbcc Operations, Llc
4100 Coca-Cola Plz
Charlotte NC 28211
704 364-8728

(G-9353)
CCBCC OPERATIONS LLC
3710 Dr M L King Jr Blvd (28562)
PHONE.................................252 671-4515
J Frank Harrison Iii, *Mgr*
EMP: 72
SALES (corp-wide): 6.9B **Publicly Held**
SIC: 2086 Bottled and canned soft drinks
HQ: Ccbcc Operations, Llc
4100 Coca-Cola Plz
Charlotte NC 28211
704 364-8728

(G-9354)
CHATSWORTH PRODUCTS INC
Also Called: CPI
701 Industrial Dr (28562-5447)
PHONE.................................252 514-2779
David Parker, *Genl Mgr*
EMP: 110
Web: www.chatsworth.com
SIC: 3499 3496 3444 3441 Machine bases, metal; Miscellaneous fabricated wire products; Sheet metalwork; Fabricated structural metal
PA: Chatsworth Products, Inc.
4175 Guardian St
Simi Valley CA 93063

(G-9355)
COASTAL CUSTOM WOOD WORKS LLC
111 Premier Dr (28562-9591)
PHONE.................................252 675-8732
Eric Williams Massey, *VP*
EMP: 4 **EST:** 2013
SALES (est): 128.51K **Privately Held**
SIC: 2431 Millwork

(G-9356)
COUNTER EFFECT
115 Justin Dr (28562-9143)
PHONE.................................252 636-0080
Chuck Arcomdak, *Dir*
EMP: 5 **EST:** 2011
SALES (est): 263.2K **Privately Held**
Web: www.countereffect.net
SIC: 3131 Counters

(G-9357)
CRAVEN TIRE INC
318 1st St (28560-5506)
PHONE.................................252 633-0200
Robert R Northington, *Pr*
Tim Tart, *VP*
EMP: 6 **EST:** 1975
SQ FT: 4,820
SALES (est): 875.98K **Privately Held**
Web: www.craventireandautomotive.com

SIC: 5999 3272 Concrete products, pre-cast; Concrete products, nec

(G-9358)
CREEKRAFT CULTURED MARBLE INC
3205 Old Cherry Point Rd (28560-6967)
P.O. Box 3413 (28564-3413)
PHONE.................................252 636-5488
Guy Hopewell, *Pr*
EMP: 4 **EST:** 1990
SQ FT: 10,000
SALES (est): 447.31K **Privately Held**
Web: www.creekraftmarble.com
SIC: 3088 Hot tubs, plastics or fiberglass

(G-9359)
CRYSTAL COAST MACHINE LLC
190 Aeronautical Way (28562-0015)
PHONE.................................252 876-3859
Donald Dimattia, *Pr*
Donald Dimattia Junior, *Pr*
EMP: 9 **EST:** 2015
SALES (est): 824K **Privately Held**
Web: www.crystalcoastmachine.com
SIC: 3599 Machine shop, jobbing and repair

(G-9360)
CUSTOM MARINE FABRICATION INC
2401 Us Highway 70 E (28560-6795)
PHONE.................................252 638-5422
Donald A Willis Senior, *Pr*
Donald Willis Junior, *VP*
EMP: 8 **EST:** 1986
SQ FT: 12,500
SALES (est): 670.94K **Privately Held**
Web: www.nccustommarine.com
SIC: 5091 3732 5941 Boat accessories and parts; Boatbuilding and repairing; Fishing equipment

(G-9361)
CUSTOM SURFACES CORPORATION
115 Justin Dr (28562-9143)
P.O. Box 12849 (28561-2849)
PHONE.................................252 638-3800
Denny Murdock, *Pr*
Charles Murdock, *VP*
Amy Upton, *Off Mgr*
EMP: 8 **EST:** 2015
SQ FT: 3,600
SALES (est): 423.21K **Privately Held**
SIC: 2434 2541 Wood kitchen cabinets; Table or counter tops, plastic laminated

(G-9362)
D2 GOVERNMENT SOLUTIONS LLC (PA)
820 Aviation Dr Ste 1 (28562-8117)
PHONE.................................662 655-4554
Dave Ricker, *CEO*
Darryl Centanni, *Pr*
EMP: 35 **EST:** 2015
SALES (est): 23.69MM **Privately Held**
Web: www.d2-gs.com
SIC: 3728 4512 4522 4581 Aircraft parts and equipment, nec; Air transportation, scheduled; Air transportation, nonscheduled; Aircraft maintenance and repair services

(G-9363)
DAMCO INC
1103 Us Highway 17 N (28560-5061)
P.O. Box 1656 (28563-1656)
PHONE.................................252 633-1404
Asa Dail, *Pr*
Beverly Dail, *Sec*
EMP: 15 **EST:** 1975
SQ FT: 20,000
SALES (est): 3.7MM **Privately Held**

Web: www.damcoinc.net
SIC: 3599 Machine shop, jobbing and repair

(G-9364)
DERROW ENTERPRISES INC
Also Called: Trailer Plus
7001 Us Highway 70 E (28562-8716)
PHONE..............................252 635-3375
Scott Derrow, *Pr*
EMP: 7 EST: 2013
SALES (est): 224.14K Privately Held
SIC: 3011 3792 5014 5561 Tires and inner
tubes; Travel trailers and campers; Tires
and tubes; Recreational vehicle parts and
accessories

(G-9365)
DIVISION SIX INCORPORATED
115 Justin Dr (28562-9143)
PHONE..............................910 420-3305
Chuck Murdock, *Pr*
EMP: 5 EST: 2019
SALES (est): 476.97K Privately Held
SIC: 2431 Millwork

(G-9366)
DRADURA USA CORP
197 Bosch Blvd (28562-6924)
PHONE..............................252 637-9660
Wolfgang Stein, *Pr*
▲ EMP: 90 EST: 2007
SALES (est): 9.29MM
SALES (corp-wide): 711.66K Privately
Held
Web: www.dradura.com
SIC: 3496 Miscellaneous fabricated wire
products
HQ: Dradura Holding Gmbh & Co. Kg
Talstr. 2
Altleiningen RP 67317
63569660

(G-9367)
ELLIS PUBLISHING COMPANY INC
Also Called: The Havelock News
3200 Wellons Blvd (28562-5234)
P.O. Box 777 (28532-0777)
PHONE..............................252 444-1999
Gene Mace, *Pr*
Lea Stifflemire, *Sec*
EMP: 4 EST: 1985
SALES (est): 171.28K Privately Held
Web: www.havenews.com
SIC: 2711 Newspapers, publishing and
printing

(G-9368)
FRANKIE YORK LOGGING CO
2250 Us Highway 17 N (28560-9660)
PHONE..............................252 633-4825
Frankie York, *Owner*
EMP: 4 EST: 1971
SALES (est): 243.34K Privately Held
SIC: 2411 Logging camps and contractors

(G-9369)
G & H BROADWAY LOGGING INC
145 Territorial Rd (28560-8894)
PHONE..............................252 229-4594
Gregory A Broadway, *Pr*
EMP: 4 EST: 2016
SALES (est): 464.82K Privately Held
SIC: 2411 Logging camps and contractors

(G-9370)
HATTERAS YACHTS INC
110 N Glenburnie Rd (28560-2703)
PHONE..............................252 633-3101
◆ EMP: 1320

SIC: 3732 Yachts, building and repairing

(G-9371)
**INNOVATIVE LAMINATIONS
COMPANY**
51a Halls Creek Rd (28560-5766)
PHONE..............................252 745-8133
Andreas Penz, *Pr*
Peter Hofmann, *Sec*
EMP: 18 EST: 2000
SQ FT: 21,000
SALES (est): 7.11MM
SALES (corp-wide): 329.03MM Privately
Held
Web: www.innovative-laminations.com
SIC: 3083 Laminated plastics sheets
HQ: Trodat Gmbh
Linzer StraBe 156
Wels 4600
72422390

(G-9372)
INTERNATIONAL PAPER COMPANY
Also Called: International Paper
1785 Weyerhaeuser Rd (28563)
PHONE..............................252 633-7407
EMP: 5
SALES (corp-wide): 18.62B Publicly Held
Web: www.internationalpaper.com
SIC: 2653 Boxes, corrugated: made from
purchased materials
PA: International Paper Company
6400 Poplar Ave
Memphis TN 38197
901 419-7000

(G-9373)
JOESIGNS INC
2617 Trent Rd (28562-2025)
PHONE..............................252 638-1622
Joey Pontiff, *Pr*
Paige Pontiff, *Sec*
EMP: 4 EST: 1992
SALES (est): 249.61K Privately Held
Web: www.joesigns.com
SIC: 3993 Signs, not made in custom sign
painting shops

(G-9374)
JOHNSON MACHINE CO INC
8 Batts Hill Rd (28562-7364)
PHONE..............................252 638-2620
Junius P Johnson Junior, *Pr*
Paul Johnson, *Pr*
EMP: 6 EST: 1944
SQ FT: 2,500
SALES (est): 97.5K Privately Held
SIC: 7538 5013 3599 Engine rebuilding:
automotive; Automotive supplies and parts;
Machine shop, jobbing and repair

(G-9375)
LIFTAVATOR INC
4430 Us Highway 70 E (28560-7513)
PHONE..............................252 634-1717
Roger Grear, *Pr*
Kelly Grear, *
EMP: 24 EST: 1985
SQ FT: 15,000
SALES (est): 3.9MM Privately Held
Web: www.liftavator.com
SIC: 3534 Elevators and moving stairways

(G-9376)
M & K LOGGING LLC
310 Parker Rd (28562-9215)
PHONE..............................252 349-8975
Miguel Bryant, *Prin*
EMP: 6 EST: 2016
SALES (est): 960.24K Privately Held

SIC: 2411 Logging camps and contractors

(G-9377)
MAOLA MILK AND ICE CREAM CO
307 N First Ave (28560-2850)
PHONE..............................844 287-1970
Dwayne Myers, *Prin*
EMP: 11 EST: 1945
SALES (est): 731.85K Privately Held
Web: www.maolamilk.com
SIC: 2026 Acidophilus milk

(G-9378)
MARCO PRODUCTS INC
Also Called: Marco Pproducts
214 Kale Rd (28562-7055)
P.O. Box 826 (28571-0826)
PHONE..............................215 956-0313
Arden Martenz, *Pr*
Cameon Funk, *VP*
EMP: 10 EST: 1983
SALES (est): 147.41K Privately Held
Web: www.youthlight.com
SIC: 2731 Books, publishing only

(G-9379)
MARSHALL GROUP OF NC INC
2400 Trent Rd (28562-2020)
PHONE..............................252 638-8585
Jason Voyce, *Prin*
EMP: 5 EST: 1991
SQ FT: 2,000
SALES (est): 111.58K Privately Held
Web: www.themarshallgroup.net
SIC: 2531 Public building and related
furniture

(G-9380)
MARTIN MARIETTA MATERIALS INC
Also Called: Martin Marietta Aggregates
1315 Old Us 70 W (28560)
P.O. Box 12326 (28561-2326)
PHONE..............................252 633-5308
Larry Windsor, *Brnch Mgr*
EMP: 6
Web: www.martinmarietta.com
SIC: 1422 Crushed and broken limestone
PA: Martin Marietta Materials Inc
4123 Parklake Ave
Raleigh NC 27612

(G-9381)
MASS ENTERPRISES LLC
Also Called: Pocket Yacht Company
4310 Us Highway 70 E (28560-7913)
PHONE..............................443 585-0732
Mark Schulstad, *Managing Member*
EMP: 19 EST: 2011
SALES (est): 261.37K Privately Held
SIC: 3732 Yachts, building and repairing

(G-9382)
MILLER SAWS & SUPPLIES INC
115 Ridgewood Trl (28560-9462)
PHONE..............................252 636-3347
EMP: 5
SALES (est): 631.62K Privately Held
SIC: 3524 Lawn and garden equipment

(G-9383)
MINGES BOTTLING GROUP
256 Middle St (28560-2142)
PHONE..............................252 636-5898
Larry Cook, *Prin*
EMP: 14 EST: 2011
SALES (est): 242.05K Privately Held
Web: www.pepsistore.com
SIC: 2086 Soft drinks: packaged in cans,
bottles, etc.

(G-9384)
MOEN INCORPORATED
Also Called: Moen
101 Industrial Dr (28562-9607)
PHONE..............................252 638-3300
Brian Donato, *Brnch Mgr*
EMP: 77
SQ FT: 60,000
SALES (corp-wide): 4.61B Publicly Held
Web: www.moen.com
SIC: 3088 Shower stalls, fiberglass and
plastics
HQ: Moen Incorporated
25300 Al Moen Dr
North Olmsted OH 44070
800 289-6636

(G-9385)
MONTE ENTERPRISES INC
Also Called: Monte Printing Co
3204 Neuse Blvd (28560-4113)
P.O. Box 12391 (28561-2391)
PHONE..............................252 637-5803
Peter T Monte, *Pr*
EMP: 5 EST: 1952
SALES (est): 133.8K Privately Held
Web: www.monteprinting.com
SIC: 2752 Offset printing

(G-9386)
NOMAD HOUSEBOATS INC
208 Outrigger Rd (28562-8844)
PHONE..............................252 288-5670
Warren Lloyd, *Pr*
Judy Lloyd, *Sec*
EMP: 5 EST: 2000
SQ FT: 5,000
SALES (est): 126.66K Privately Held
Web: www.nomadhouseboats.com
SIC: 5551 3732 Motor boat dealers;
Boatbuilding and repairing

(G-9387)
OWEN G DUNN CO INC (PA)
3731 Trent Rd (28562-2221)
P.O. Box 13216 (28561-3216)
PHONE..............................252 633-3197
Owen D Andrews, *Pr*
Donald R Andrews Junior, *VP*
Debra C Andrews, *Sec*
EMP: 8 EST: 1902
SQ FT: 18,000
SALES (est): 5.02MM
SALES (corp-wide): 5.02MM Privately
Held
Web: www.printelect.com
SIC: 2752 5943 2791 2789 Commercial
printing, lithographic; Office forms and
supplies; Typesetting; Bookbinding and
related work

(G-9388)
PHILLIP DUNN LOGGING CO INC
508 Madam Moores Ln (28562-6440)
PHONE..............................252 633-4577
Phillip Dunn, *Pr*
EMP: 7 EST: 1970
SALES (est): 244.62K Privately Held
SIC: 2411 Logging camps and contractors

(G-9389)
PUCUDA INC
Also Called: Leading Edge Safety Systems
3100 Oaks Rd (28560-2841)
P.O. Box 471 (06443-0471)
PHONE..............................860 526-8004
John Rexroad, *Pr*
◆ EMP: 15 EST: 1992
SQ FT: 12,500
SALES (est): 2.39MM Privately Held
Web: www.netting.com

SIC: 3089 Netting, plastics

(G-9390)
R E BENGEL SHEET METAL CO
1311 N Craven St (28560-3249)
PHONE..............................252 637-3404
Steve Bengel, *Pr*
Ella Bengel, *Sec*
Sabrina Bengel, *Treas*
EMP: 7 EST: 1912
SQ FT: 3,000
SALES (est): 691.28K **Privately Held**
Web: www.rebengel.com
SIC: 1761 3444 Sheet metal work, nec;
Sheet metalwork

(G-9391)
ROBERT LASKOWSKI
232 Stony Branch Rd (28562-9329)
PHONE..............................203 732-0846
Robert Laskowski, *Prin*
EMP: 6 EST: 2012
SALES (est): 104.71K **Privately Held**
SIC: 2711 Newspapers, publishing and
printing

(G-9392)
S & W READY MIX CON CO LLC
1300 Us Highway 17 N (28560-5013)
PHONE..............................252 633-2115
Daniel Bordeaux, *Mgr*
EMP: 16
SALES (corp-wide): 8.01MM **Privately
Held**
Web: www.snwreadymix.com
SIC: 3273 Ready-mixed concrete
HQ: S & W Ready Mix Concrete Company
Llc
217 Lisbon St
Clinton NC 28329
910 592-1733

(G-9393)
S T WOOTEN CORPORATION
Also Called: New Bern Asphalt Plant
245 Parker Rd (28562-9214)
PHONE..............................252 636-2568
Scott Wooten, *Pr*
EMP: 22
SALES (corp-wide): 319.83MM **Privately
Held**
Web: www.stwcorp.com
SIC: 3531 Asphalt plant, including gravel-mix
type
PA: S. T. Wooten Corporation
3801 Black Creek Rd Se
Wilson NC 27894
252 291-5165

(G-9394)
S ZAYTOUN CUSTOM CABINETS INC
1206 Pollock St (28560-5538)
PHONE..............................252 638-8390
John E Zaytoun Junior, *Pr*
Michael F Zaytoun, *VP*
Michael Zaytoun Junior, *Treas*
EMP: 9 EST: 1972
SQ FT: 25,000
SALES (est): 1.96MM **Privately Held**
Web: www.zaytouncustomcabinets.com
SIC: 2541 2434 Cabinets, lockers, and
shelving; Wood kitchen cabinets

(G-9395)
SCHLAADT USA LIMITED
Also Called: Schlaadt Plastics Limited
198 Bosch Blvd (28562-6924)
P.O. Box 15409 (28561-5409)
PHONE..............................252 634-9494
Stefan Schlaadt, *Pr*
▲ EMP: 15 EST: 2005

SALES (est): 6.91MM
SALES (corp-wide): 355.83K **Privately
Held**
Web: www.schlaadt.de
SIC: 2821 Plastics materials and resins
HQ: Schlaadt Gmbh
Schwalbacher Str. 123
Lorch HE 65391
67268030

(G-9396)
SHOPPER
Also Called: Shopper The
3200 Wellons Blvd (28562-5234)
P.O. Box 12367 (28561-2367)
PHONE..............................252 633-1153
Judy Avery, *Pr*
EMP: 4 EST: 1968
SQ FT: 3,600
SALES (est): 237.03K **Privately Held**
Web: login-validation.imedidata.net
SIC: 2711 Newspapers, publishing and
printing

(G-9397)
**SMYRNA READY MIX CONCRETE
LLC**
Also Called: Ready Mixed Concrete
1715 Race Track Rd (28562-4117)
P.O. Box 877 (27835-0877)
PHONE..............................252 637-4155
Carl Norris, *Manager*
EMP: 12
SALES (corp-wide): 471.79MM **Privately
Held**
Web: www.argos-us.com
SIC: 3273 Ready-mixed concrete
PA: Smyrna Ready Mix Concrete, Llc
1000 Hollingshead Cir
Murfreesboro TN 37129
615 355-1028

(G-9398)
SUN-JOURNAL INCORPORATED
4901 Us Highway 17 S (28562-8880)
PHONE..............................252 638-8101
Mike Distelhorst, *Prin*
David Threshie, *Ch*
Richard A Wallace, *
Albert W Bassett, *
EMP: 30 EST: 1929
SALES (est): 1.01MM
SALES (corp-wide): 2.51B **Publicly Held**
Web: www.newbernsj.com
SIC: 2711 Commercial printing and
newspaper publishing combined
HQ: Gatehouse Media, Llc
175 Sllys Trl Fl 3 Corp C
Pittsford NY 14534
585 598-0030

(G-9399)
TEST ME OUT INC
Also Called: Second Nature
3262 Wellons Blvd (28562-5234)
PHONE..............................252 635-6770
Janis T Gaskill, *Pr*
Anna Hardison, *VP*
EMP: 5 EST: 2009
SALES (est): 1.93MM **Privately Held**
Web: www.secondnaturedme.com
SIC: 3842 5047 Surgical appliances and
supplies; Medical equipment and supplies

(G-9400)
THERMIK CORPORATION
3498a Martin Dr (28562-5145)
P.O. Box 12786 (28561-2786)
PHONE..............................252 636-5720
Fred Goeckerman, *Pr*
Terry Dixon, *Sec*

EMP: 20 EST: 1987
SQ FT: 5,000
SALES (est): 5.27MM
SALES (corp-wide): 55.3MM **Privately
Held**
Web: www.thermik.de
SIC: 3822 Air conditioning and refrigeration
controls
HQ: Thermik Geratebau Gmbh
Salzstr. 11
Sondershausen TH 99706
363254120

(G-9401)
TRIAD MARINE CENTER INC
Also Called: Boats Unlimited
4316 Us Highway 70 E (28560-7913)
PHONE..............................252 634-1880
Jerry Bryant, *Prin*
EMP: 6
SALES (corp-wide): 5.18MM **Privately
Held**
SIC: 5551 3732 Motor boat dealers;
Boatbuilding and repairing
PA: Triad Marine Center, Inc.
2102 N Elm St Ste E
Greensboro NC 27408
336 379-7000

(G-9402)
TRYHARD INFINITY LLC
3019 Brunswick Ave (28562-4126)
PHONE..............................252 269-0985
EMP: 4 EST: 2022
SALES (est): 294.56K **Privately Held**
SIC: 7372 7389 Prepackaged software;
Business Activities at Non-Commercial Site

(G-9403)
URETHANE INNOVATORS INC
403 Industrial Dr (28562-5437)
PHONE..............................252 637-7110
▲ EMP: 40 EST: 1983
SALES (est): 9.83MM **Privately Held**
Web: www.urethaneusa.com
SIC: 3562 Roller bearings and parts

(G-9404)
US ARMS & AMMUNITION LLC
119 Mellen Rd (28562-8766)
PHONE..............................252 652-7400
EMP: 8 EST: 2019
SALES (est): 498.66K **Privately Held**
Web: www.usarmsandammo.com
SIC: 3484 Small arms

(G-9405)
WHEATSTONE CORPORATION (PA)
600 Indl Dr (28562)
PHONE..............................252 638-7000
Gary C Snow, *Pr*
Kathleen Snow, *
Denny Murdock, *
▲ EMP: 97 EST: 1974
SQ FT: 51,000
SALES (est): 13.04MM
SALES (corp-wide): 13.04MM **Privately
Held**
Web: www.wheatstone.com
SIC: 3663 3651 2522 Radio and t.v.
communications equipment; Household
audio and video equipment; Office furniture,
except wood

(G-9406)
WHITE RIVER MARINE GROUP LLC
Also Called: Hatteras Yachts
110 N Glenburnie Rd (28560-2703)
PHONE..............................252 633-3101
Don Farlow, *Mgr*
EMP: 159

Web: www.trackermarine.com
SIC: 3519 3732 Outboard motors; Yachts,
building and repairing
HQ: White River Marine Group, Llc
2500 E Kearney St
Springfield MO 65898
417 873-5900

(G-9407)
WHITES TIRE SVC NEW BERN INC
2813 Neuse Blvd (28562-2838)
PHONE..............................252 633-1170
Samuel E White, *Pr*
Victoria White, *Sec*
EMP: 4 EST: 1961
SQ FT: 10,000
SALES (est): 374.66K **Privately Held**
Web: www.whitestireserviceinc.com
SIC: 5531 7534 5014 Automotive tires; Tire
recapping; Automobile tires and tubes

(G-9408)
WIRTHWEIN NEW BERN CORP
901 Industrial Dr (28562-5403)
PHONE..............................252 634-2871
Udo Wirthwein, *Pr*
Marh Hansen Om, *Prin*
◆ EMP: 150 EST: 2002
SQ FT: 101,000
SALES (est): 16.83MM
SALES (corp-wide): 377.18MM **Privately
Held**
Web: www.wirthwein.de
SIC: 3089 Injection molding of plastics
PA: Wirthwein Se
Walter-Wirthwein-Str. 2-10
Creglingen BW 97993
79337020

New Hill
Wake County

(G-9409)
DAS OIL WERKS LLC
198 Hidden Field Ln (27562-8847)
PHONE..............................919 267-5781
William M White, *Prin*
▲ EMP: 4 EST: 2012
SALES (est): 1.43MM **Privately Held**
SIC: 1382 Oil and gas exploration services

(G-9410)
MCGILL ENVIRONMENTAL GP LLC
634 Christian Chapel Church Rd
(27562-8867)
PHONE..............................919 362-1161
EMP: 10 EST: 2022
SALES (est): 2.21MM **Privately Held**
SIC: 2875 Compost

(G-9411)
MUDDY DOG LLC
Also Called: Muddy Dog Roasting Co
5196 Beaver Creek Rd (27562-9053)
PHONE..............................919 371-2818
EMP: 5 EST: 2006
SALES (est): 150.6K **Privately Held**
Web: www.coffeedans.com
SIC: 2095 Coffee extracts

(G-9412)
PLAN B ENTERPRISES LLC
3217 Hinsley Rd (27562-8978)
PHONE..............................919 387-4856
Michael P Klatt, *Ch*
EMP: 5 EST: 2000
SALES (est): 370.39K **Privately Held**
Web: www.planbenterprises.com

SIC: **3699** 8711 Security control equipment
and systems; Consulting engineer

New London
Stanly County

(G-9413)
ARTECH GRAPHICS INC
176 Yadkin Falls Rd (28127-9135)
PHONE.............................704 545-9804
David Carpenter, *Pr*
EMP: 9 **EST:** 1969
SQ FT: 4,200
SALES (est): 160.46K **Privately Held**
Web: www.artechgraphicsinc.com
SIC: 2752 Offset printing

(G-9414)
CAPITAL WOOD PRODUCTS INC
38081 Saw Mill Rd (28127-9569)
PHONE.............................704 982-2417
Ronnie Carter, *Pr*
Allen Herlocker, *VP*
EMP: 6 **EST:** 1980
SQ FT: 30,000
SALES (est): 362.58K **Privately Held**
SIC: 2421 Sawmills and planing mills,
general

(G-9415)
FIBER COMPOSITES LLC (HQ)
Also Called: Fiberon
181 Random Dr (28127-8735)
PHONE.............................704 463-7120
◆ **EMP:** 290 **EST:** 1997
SQ FT: 300,000
SALES (est): 184.13MM
SALES (corp-wide): 4.61B **Publicly Held**
Web: www.fiberondecking.com
SIC: 2899 Plastic wood
PA: Fortune Brands Innovations, Inc.
520 Lake Cook Rd
Deerfield IL 60015
847 484-4400

(G-9416)
FIBER COMPOSITES LLC
Also Called: Fiberon Recycling
44017 Us 52 Hwy N (28127-9726)
PHONE.............................704 463-7118
Susan Saunders, *Mgr*
EMP: 62
SALES (corp-wide): 4.61B **Publicly Held**
Web: www.fiberondecking.com
SIC: 3089 4953 Air mattresses, plastics;
Recycling, waste materials
HQ: Fiber Composites, Llc
181 Random Dr
New London NC 28127
704 463-7120

(G-9417)
H W CULP LUMBER COMPANY
491 Us Hwy 52 N (28127)
PHONE.............................704 463-7311
H W Culp Junior, *Pr*
H W Culp Iii, *VP*
Amy Shelton, *
Jewel Culp, *
EMP: 92 **EST:** 1924
SQ FT: 5,000
SALES (est): 20.51MM **Privately Held**
Web: www.culplumber.com
SIC: 2421 Sawmills and planing mills,
general

(G-9418)
HARRIS WOOD PRODUCTS INC
40425 Tower Rd (28127-8527)

PHONE.............................704 550-5494
James Harris, *Pr*
Susan Harris, *VP*
EMP: 4 **EST:** 1985
SALES (est): 183.29K **Privately Held**
SIC: 5031 2541 Millwork; Cabinets, except
refrigerated: show, display, etc.: wood

(G-9419)
MAGNUM MANUFACTURING LLC
40867 Airport Rd (28127-9597)
PHONE.............................704 983-1340
James Murphy, *Pr*
EMP: 10 **EST:** 2001
SQ FT: 600
SALES (est): 766.06K **Privately Held**
Web: www.magnumbolts.com
SIC: 3965 3452 Fasteners; Bolts, nuts,
rivets, and washers

(G-9420)
POTTS LOGGING INC
39342 Holly Ridge Rd (28127-8517)
PHONE.............................704 463-7549
James L Potts, *Pr*
Linda Potts, *VP*
Randy Potts, *Mgr*
EMP: 9 **EST:** 1975
SALES (est): 98.6K **Privately Held**
SIC: 2411 Logging camps and contractors

(G-9421)
PREFORMED LINE PRODUCTS CO
Also Called: Preformed Line Products Co
446 Glenbrook Spg (28127-9140)
PHONE.............................336 461-3513
EMP: 4
SALES (corp-wide): 593.71MM **Publicly
Held**
Web: www.plp.com
SIC: 3644 Noncurrent-carrying wiring devices
PA: Preformed Line Products Company
660 Beta Dr
Mayfield Village OH 44143
440 461-5200

(G-9422)
SOUTHERN PIPE INC (PA)
135 Random Dr (28127-8735)
P.O. Box 606 (28127-0606)
PHONE.............................704 463-5202
Bryan Mitchell, *Pr*
Kevin Mitchell, *
Patricia Mitchell, *
◆ **EMP:** 39 **EST:** 2005
SQ FT: 55,475
SALES (est): 14.87MM
SALES (corp-wide): 14.87MM **Privately
Held**
Web: www.southern-pipe.com
SIC: 3084 Plastics pipe

(G-9423)
UFP NEW LONDON LLC
Also Called: U F P
174 Random Dr (28127-8735)
PHONE.............................704 463-1400
John Devitto, *Mgr*
EMP: 18 **EST:** 2011
SALES (est): 2.87MM
SALES (corp-wide): 6.65B **Publicly Held**
SIC: 2452 2436 2435 2439 Prefabricated
wood buildings; Softwood veneer and
plywood; Hardwood veneer and plywood;
Trusses, except roof: laminated lumber
HQ: Ufp Factory Built, Llc
2801 E Beltline Ave Ne
Grand Rapids MI 49525
616 364-6161

Newland
Avery County

(G-9424)
AVERY COUNTY RECAPPING CO INC
Also Called: Avery County Tire
405 Linville St (28657)
P.O. Box 505 (28657)
PHONE.............................828 733-0161
John Phillips, *Pr*
James Phillips, *
EMP: 8 **EST:** 1964
SQ FT: 12,000
SALES (est): 2.44MM **Privately Held**
Web: www.averytirepros.com
SIC: 5531 7539 7534 Automotive tires;
Automotive repair shops, nec; Tire
recapping

(G-9425)
BLUMER & STANTON ENTPS INC
275 Bridge Ln (28657-9195)
P.O. Box 967 (28777-0967)
PHONE.............................828 765-2800
Roger Stanton, *Brnch Mgr*
EMP: 4
SALES (corp-wide): 4.91MM **Privately
Held**
Web: www.blumerandstanton.com
SIC: 2431 Woodwork, interior and
ornamental, nec
PA: Blumer & Stanton Enterprises, Inc.
5112 Georgia Ave
West Palm Beach FL 33405
561 585-2525

(G-9426)
BRASWELL REALTY
320 Linville St (28657-8037)
P.O. Box 1208 (28657-1208)
PHONE.............................828 733-5800
Pamela Braswell, *Pr*
EMP: 7 **EST:** 1992
SALES (est): 521.18K **Privately Held**
Web: www.braswellrealty.com
SIC: 6531 2452 Real estate agent,
commercial; Log cabins, prefabricated,
wood

(G-9427)
CCO HOLDINGS LLC
520 Pineola St (28657-7604)
PHONE.............................828 528-4004
EMP: 112
SALES (corp-wide): 55.09MM **Publicly
Held**
SIC: 4841 3663 3651 Cable television
services; Radio and t.v. communications
equipment; Household audio and video
equipment
HQ: Cco Holdings, Llc
400 Atlantic St
Stamford CT 06901
203 905-7801

(G-9428)
DICKIE JONES
Also Called: Bowman Distribution
883 Whitaker Branch Rd (28657-9170)
PHONE.............................828 733-5084
Dickie Jones, *Owner*
EMP: 5 **EST:** 1996
SALES (est): 80.32K **Privately Held**
SIC: 3492 Hose and tube fittings and
assemblies, hydraulic/pneumatic

(G-9429)
GARDEN METALWORK
3640 Rd (28657)

P.O. Box 41 (28662-0041)
PHONE.............................828 733-1077
Bruce Yak, *Owner*
EMP: 5 **EST:** 2008
SALES (est): 230.18K **Privately Held**
Web: www.gardenmetalwork.com
SIC: 1791 3442 Iron work, structural; Sash,
door or window: metal

(G-9430)
HIGH COUNTRY MEDIA LLC
Also Called: Avery Journal Times
428 Pineola St (28657-7603)
PHONE.............................828 733-2448
Sam Calhoun, *Editor*
EMP: 4 **EST:** 1959
SALES (est): 89.58K **Privately Held**
Web: www.averyjournal.com
SIC: 2711 Newspapers, publishing and
printing

(G-9431)
LINVILLE FALLS WINERY
9557 Linville Falls Hwy (28657-8920)
P.O. Box 517 (28657-0517)
PHONE.............................828 733-9021
EMP: 6 **EST:** 2014
SALES (est): 106.97K **Privately Held**
Web: www.linvillefallswinery.com
SIC: 2084 Wines

(G-9432)
**MOUNTAIN RCRTION LOG CBINS
LLC**
8007 Linville Falls Hwy (28657-8293)
PHONE.............................828 387-6688
Shane Ollis, *Prin*
EMP: 5 **EST:** 2011
SALES (est): 120K **Privately Held**
Web:
www.mountainrecreationlogcabins.com
SIC: 2452 Log cabins, prefabricated, wood

(G-9433)
NORTH CAROLINA DEPT TRNSP
Also Called: Equipment Shop
North Carolina Hwy 181 (28657-7818)
P.O. Box 631 (28657-0631)
PHONE.............................828 733-9002
Nathan Clark, *Mgr*
EMP: 4
SALES (corp-wide): 74.26B **Privately Held**
Web: www.ncdot.gov
SIC: 3799 9621 Trailers and trailer
equipment; Regulation, administration of
transportation
HQ: North Carolina Department Of
Transportation
1 S Wilmington St
Raleigh NC 27610

(G-9434)
**S BANNER CABINETS
INCORPORATED**
299 Watauga St (28657-7100)
P.O. Box 1390 (28657-1390)
PHONE.............................828 733-2031
Joseph E Banner Senior, *Pr*
Joseph E Banner Junior, *VP*
Debbie Banner, *
EMP: 38 **EST:** 1942
SQ FT: 55,000
SALES (est): 2.34MM **Privately Held**
Web: www.bannerscabinets.com
SIC: 5712 2431 2434 Cabinet work, custom;
Millwork; Wood kitchen cabinets

(G-9435)
**SUGAR MOUNTAIN WOODWORKS
INC**

▲ = Import ▼ = Export
◆ = Import/Export

3030 Sugar Mountain 2 Rd (28657-8397)
PHONE..................423 292-6245
EMP: 4 **EST:** 2020
SALES (est): 236.16K **Privately Held**
SIC: 2431 Millwork

Newport
Carteret County

(G-9436)
ABC SIGNS
214 Roberts Rd (28570-7932)
PHONE..................252 223-5900
Joyce Tferrell, *Prin*
EMP: 4 **EST:** 2011
SALES (est): 56.78K **Privately Held**
Web: www.abcsigns.biz
SIC: 3993 Signs and advertising specialties

(G-9437)
ARGOS USA LLC
Also Called: Readymixed
247 Carl Garner Rd (28570-7956)
PHONE..................252 223-4348
Duncan Kimbro, *Genl Mgr*
EMP: 8
Web: www.argos-us.com
SIC: 3273 Ready-mixed concrete
HQ: Argos Usa Llc
3015 Windward Plz Ste 300
Alpharetta GA 30005
678 368-4300

(G-9438)
BOGUE SOUND DISTILLERY INC
108 Bogue Commercial Dr (28570-8224)
PHONE..................252 241-1606
Richard Chapmin, *CEO*
EMP: 10 **EST:** 2013
SALES (est): 682.62K **Privately Held**
Web: www.boguesounddistillery.com
SIC: 2085 Distilled and blended liquors

(G-9439)
CAROLINA TAILORS INC (PA)
Also Called: Promotional Products Plus
2896 Highway 24 Ste D (28570-5088)
PHONE..................252 247-6469
George Gardner, *Pr*
EMP: 6 **EST:** 1979
SALES (est): 183.25K **Privately Held**
Web: www.ctailors.com
SIC: 5136 2759 Uniforms, men's and boys';
Screen printing

(G-9440)
DL HOPPER & ASSOCIATES INC
402 Sea Gate Dr (28570-6270)
PHONE..................252 838-1062
David Hopper, *Ch*
Elizabeth Hopper, *CFO*
B D Hall, *VP*
EMP: 4 **EST:** 1994
SQ FT: 3,500
SALES (est): 336.6K **Privately Held**
SIC: 7372 Prepackaged software

(G-9441)
OFFSHORE MARINE ELEC LLC
1381 Old Winberry Rd (28570-6163)
PHONE..................252 504-2624
EMP: 7 **EST:** 2007
SALES (est): 1.1MM **Privately Held**
SIC: 3699 Electrical equipment and supplies,
nec

(G-9442)
PRISCLLAS CRYSTAL CAST WNES IN
187 Hibbs Road Ext (28570-9172)
PHONE..................252 422-8336
Priscilla Livingston, *Pr*
EMP: 4 **EST:** 2007
SALES (est): 190.2K **Privately Held**
SIC: 2084 Wines, brandy, and brandy spirits

(G-9443)
RIGEM RIGHT
173 Hankison Dr (28570-9170)
PHONE..................252 726-9508
Matthew Cagle, *Managing Member*
▲ **EMP:** 8 **EST:** 2011
SALES (est): 551.29K **Privately Held**
Web: www.rigemright.com
SIC: 3949 Hunting equipment

(G-9444)
SHORTWAY BREWING COMPANY LLC (PA)
228 Chatham St (28570-8515)
PHONE..................252 777-3065
Matt Shortway, *Prin*
EMP: 5 **EST:** 2017
SALES (est): 494.6K
SALES (corp-wide): 494.6K **Privately Held**
Web: www.shortwaybrewing.com
SIC: 5813 2082 Bars and lounges; Malt
beverages

(G-9445)
TRF MANUFACTURING NC INC
Also Called: Frank Door Company
413 Howard Blvd (28570-9530)
P.O. Box 1720 (28570-1720)
PHONE..................252 223-1112
Terry Frank, *Pr*
Maryanne Frank, *
▲ **EMP:** 30 **EST:** 1996
SQ FT: 50,000
SALES (est): 8.6MM **Privately Held**
Web: www.frankdoor.com
SIC: 3822 5078 5211 Refrigeration/air-
conditioning defrost controls; Commercial
refrigeration equipment; Door and window
products

(G-9446)
VENEER TECHNOLOGIES INC (PA)
Also Called: Cloverdale Co Inc Roanoke Co
611 Verdun St (28570-8088)
P.O. Box 1145 (28570-1145)
PHONE..................252 223-5600
Christian Weygoldt, *Pr*
Michael Kraszeksi, *
Ilse Moehring, *
▲ **EMP:** 135 **EST:** 1992
SQ FT: 100,000
SALES (est): 22.77MM **Privately Held**
Web: www.veneertech.com
SIC: 2435 2426 2421 Veneer stock,
hardwood; Hardwood dimension and
flooring mills; Sawmills and planing mills,
general

Newton
Catawba County

(G-9447)
ABZORBIT INC
2628 Northwest Blvd (28658-3729)
P.O. Box 1538 (28613)
PHONE..................828 464-9944
Stephanie Setzer, *Pr*
Ron Setzer, *Sec*
EMP: 10 **EST:** 1994

SQ FT: 15,000
SALES (est): 465.6K **Privately Held**
Web: www.abzorbit.com
SIC: 2621 2842 Absorbent paper; Polishes
and sanitation goods

(G-9448)
ADVANCED GRADING & EXCVTG LLC
4360 Caldwell Rd (28658-8104)
PHONE..................828 320-7465
Jonathan Setzer, *Prin*
EMP: 4 **EST:** 2013
SALES (est): 694.79K **Privately Held**
SIC: 3531 Plows: construction, excavating,
and grading

(G-9449)
ASHFAR ENTERPRISES INC
Also Called: Catawba Valley Mills
3772 Plateau Rd (28658-8812)
P.O. Box 10233 (28603)
PHONE..................704 462-4672
Anis Satar, *Mgr*
EMP: 10
SALES (corp-wide): 9.61MM **Privately
Held**
Web: www.ashfar.com
SIC: 2221 Broadwoven fabric mills,
manmade
PA: Ashfar Enterprises Inc.
200 Metroplex Dr Ste 275
Edison NJ 08817
848 202-1581

(G-9450)
BA ROBBINS COMPANY LLC
110 E 15th St (28658-2957)
P.O. Box 645 (28658-0645)
PHONE..................828 466-3900
Adam Robbins, *Owner*
EMP: 4 **EST:** 2002
SALES (est): 181.05K **Privately Held**
Web: www.windingnc.com
SIC: 2282 Winding yarn

(G-9451)
BASSETT FURNITURE INDS NC LLC
Also Called: Bassett Upholstery Division
1111 E 20th St (28658-1955)
P.O. Box 47 (28658-0047)
PHONE..................828 465-7700
Mark Jordan, *Brnch Mgr*
EMP: 1219
SALES (corp-wide): 329.92MM **Publicly
Held**
Web: www.bassettfurniture.com
SIC: 2512 5712 Upholstered household
furniture; Furniture stores
HQ: Bassett Furniture Industries Of North
Carolina Llc
3525 Fairystone Park Hwy
Bassett VA 24055
276 629-6000

(G-9452)
CATAWBA FARMS ENTERPRISES LLC
1670 Southwest Blvd (28658-7439)
PHONE..................828 464-5780
Michael Waltuch, *Pt*
Twyla Mcdermott, *Pt*
James D Baucom, *Pt*
EMP: 10 **EST:** 2015
SQ FT: 1,481,040
SALES (est): 415.88K **Privately Held**
Web: www.catawbafarms.com
SIC: 5153 7011 2084 0191 Field beans;
Vacation lodges; Wines, brandy, and
brandy spirits; General farms, primarily crop
PA: Second Nature Technology Inc.

19 N College Ave
Newton NC 28658

(G-9453)
CATAWBA VALLEY FINISHING LLC (PA)
1609 Northwest Blvd (28658-3759)
P.O. Box 410 (28658-0410)
PHONE..................828 464-2252
Renee Woody, *CEO*
EMP: 45 **EST:** 1941
SQ FT: 68,000
SALES (est): 3.46MM
SALES (corp-wide): 3.46MM **Privately
Held**
SIC: 2252 2251 Men's, boys', and girls'
hosiery; Women's hosiery, except socks

(G-9454)
CLEVELAND-CLIFFS PLATE LLC
Also Called: Cleveland-Cliffs Piedmont
2027 S Mclin Creek Rd (28658-1957)
PHONE..................828 464-9214
Debbie Mccurry, *Brnch Mgr*
EMP: 979
SALES (corp-wide): 19.18B **Publicly Held**
SIC: 3312 Plate, steel
HQ: Cleveland-Cliffs Plate Llc
139 Modena Rd
Coatesville PA 19320
610 383-2000

(G-9455)
COCA-COLA CONSOLIDATED INC
Also Called: Coca-Cola
820 E 1st St (28658-1803)
PHONE..................828 322-5096
Frank Wood, *Brnch Mgr*
EMP: 47
SALES (corp-wide): 6.9B **Publicly Held**
Web: www.cokeconsolidated.com
SIC: 2086 Bottled and canned soft drinks
PA: Coca-Cola Consolidated, Inc.
4100 Coca-Cola Plz
Charlotte NC 28211
980 392-8298

(G-9456)
COMMERCIAL FABRICATORS INC
2045 Industrial Dr (28658-7703)
P.O. Box 165 (28658-0165)
PHONE..................828 465-1010
Richard J Tucker, *Pr*
Richard J Tucker, *VP*
Diann B Icenhour, *
EMP: 30 **EST:** 1962
SQ FT: 34,600
SALES (est): 5.26MM **Privately Held**
Web: www.commfab.com
SIC: 3441 3446 Fabricated structural metal;
Architectural metalwork

(G-9457)
COMMSCOPE INC NORTH CAROLINA
Also Called: Comm Scope Network Cable Div
1545 Saint James Church Rd (28658-8938)
PHONE..................828 466-8600
Randy Crenshaw, *Brnch Mgr*
EMP: 14
Web: www.commscope.com
SIC: 3663 Radio and t.v. communications
equipment
HQ: Commscope, Inc. Of North Carolina
3642 E Us Highway 70
Claremont NC 28610
828 324-2200

(G-9458)

COMMUNITY BREWING VENTURES LLC (PA)
Also Called: Bevana
116 W A St (28658-3342)
PHONE...........................800 579-6539
Andrew Durstewitz, CEO
EMP: 5 EST: 2019
SALES (est): 4.27MM
SALES (corp-wide): 4.27MM **Privately Held**
Web: www.bevana.com
SIC: **5084** 3556 Brewery products manufacturing machinery, commercial; Beverage machinery

(G-9459)

CONCEPT FRAMES INC
2015 Industrial Dr (28658-7703)
P.O. Box 248 (28658-0248)
PHONE...........................828 465-2015
C John Wiley, Pr
Diann B Icenhour, *
Daniel L Gibbs, *
Cindy L Payne, *
EMP: 60 EST: 1984
SQ FT: 35,000
SALES (est): 4.97MM **Privately Held**
Web: www.conceptframes.com
SIC: **3441** Fabricated structural metal

(G-9460)

CORNING INCORPORATED
Also Called: Corning
1500 Prodelin Dr (28658-7819)
PHONE...........................828 465-0016
EMP: 11
SALES (corp-wide): 13.12B **Publicly Held**
Web: www.corning.com
SIC: **3229** Glass fiber products
PA: Corning Incorporated
1 Riverfront Plz
Corning NY 14831
607 974-9000

(G-9461)

COUNTRY AT HOME FURNITURE INC
2010 Log Barn Rd (28658-8889)
P.O. Box 39 (28637-0039)
PHONE...........................828 464-7498
William Coulter, Pr
Robert Davis, VP
EMP: 10 EST: 2003
SALES (est): 784.21K **Privately Held**
SIC: **2512** Upholstered household furniture

(G-9462)

CRAFT DOORS USA LLC
1516 Mount Olive Church Rd (28658-1706)
PHONE...........................828 469-7029
EMP: 10 EST: 2020
SALES (est): 1.51MM **Privately Held**
Web: www.craftdoorsusa.com
SIC: **2431** Garage doors, overhead, wood

(G-9463)

CUSTOM SOCKS INK INC
Also Called: Csi
2011 N Main Ave (28658-2825)
P.O. Box 14 (28658-0014)
PHONE...........................828 695-9869
Alton Rockett, Pr
Ranae Woody, *
EMP: 29 EST: 2014
SALES (est): 1.98MM
SALES (corp-wide): 3.46MM **Privately Held**
Web: www.customsocksink.com
SIC: **2252** Socks
PA: Catawba Valley Finishing, Llc
1609 Northwest Blvd

Newton NC 28658
828 464-2252

(G-9464)

ERIC ARNOLD KLEIN
Also Called: Pioneer Diversities
504a W 25th St (28658-3701)
PHONE...........................828 464-0001
Eric A Klein, Owner
EMP: 10 EST: 1990
SQ FT: 10,000
SALES (est): 482.75K **Privately Held**
SIC: **3479** Painting, coating, and hot dipping

(G-9465)

FLAGSHIP BRANDS LLC (PA)
Also Called: Feetures Company
2084 Fairgrove Church Rd (28658-8598)
PHONE...........................888 801-7227
John Gaither, Managing Member
▲ EMP: 31 EST: 2002
SALES (est): 10.46MM
SALES (corp-wide): 10.46MM **Privately Held**
Web: www.feetures.com
SIC: **5136** 2257 Men's and boys' sportswear and work clothing; Weft knit fabric mills

(G-9466)

GKN DRIVELINE NEWTON LLC (HQ)
Also Called: GKN Automotive
1848 Gkn Way (28658)
PHONE...........................828 428-3711
Markus Bannert, CEO
Sean Bannon, *
Thierry Minel, CPO*
Mark Gabriel, CCO*
◆ EMP: 551 EST: 1980
SQ FT: 250,000
SALES (est): 85.21MM
SALES (corp-wide): 6.06B **Privately Held**
Web: www.gknautomotive.com
SIC: **3462** 3714 Iron and steel forgings; Gears, motor vehicle
PA: Dowlais Group Plc
2nd Floor
London SW1E

(G-9467)

GKN DRIVELINE NEWTON LLC
Also Called: GKN Automotive
2900 S Us 321 Hwy (28658-8154)
PHONE...........................828 428-5292
EMP: 39
SALES (corp-wide): 6.06B **Privately Held**
Web: www.gknautomotive.com
SIC: **3714** Motor vehicle parts and accessories
HQ: Gkn Driveline Newton, Llc
1848 Gkn Way
Newton NC 28658
828 428-3711

(G-9468)

GLENN MAUSER COMPANY INC
3240 20th Ave Se (28658-8572)
PHONE...........................828 464-8996
H Glenn Mauser, Pr
EMP: 10 EST: 1983
SQ FT: 25,000
SALES (est): 385.25K **Privately Held**
Web: www.glennmauserplastics.com
SIC: **3089** Injection molding of plastics

(G-9469)

GOLD TOE STORES INC (DH)
514 W 21st St (28658-3763)
PHONE...........................828 464-0751
John M Moretz, CEO
◆ EMP: 8 EST: 1982
SQ FT: 42,600

SALES (est): 4.56MM
SALES (corp-wide): 3.2B **Privately Held**
SIC: **2252** 5136 Hosiery, nec; Men's and boy's clothing
HQ: Gold Toe Moretz Holdings Corp.
2121 Heilig Rd
Salisbury NC 28146
828 464-0751

(G-9470)

GOLDTOEMORETZ LLC
514 W 21st St (28658-3763)
P.O. Box 580 (28658-0580)
PHONE...........................828 464-0751
◆ EMP: 500
SIC: **2251** 2252 Women's hosiery, except socks; Socks

(G-9471)

HANES INDUSTRIES-NEWTON
2042 Fairgrove Church Rd (28658-8598)
P.O. Box 457 (28613-0457)
PHONE...........................828 469-2000
Tyler Newton, Prin
▲ EMP: 8 EST: 2004
SALES (est): 253.27K **Privately Held**
Web: www.hanescompanies.com
SIC: **3999** Barber and beauty shop equipment

(G-9472)

HM FRAME COMPANY INC
1903 Gkn Way (28658-9073)
PHONE...........................828 428-3354
Kevin Hefner, Pr
Daren Hefner, *
Jan S Hefner, *
EMP: 30 EST: 1984
SQ FT: 55,000
SALES (est): 1.61MM **Privately Held**
Web: www.hmwoodworkinginc.com
SIC: **2512** 2511 2435 2426 Upholstered household furniture; Wood household furniture; Hardwood veneer and plywood; Hardwood dimension and flooring mills

(G-9473)

HORIZON PUBLICATIONS INC
Also Called: Observer News Enterprise
309 N College Ave (28658-3255)
P.O. Box 48 (28658-0048)
PHONE...........................828 464-0221
Seth Mabry, Mgr
EMP: 12
SALES (corp-wide): 47.1MM **Privately Held**
Web: www.observernewsonline.com
SIC: **2711** Newspapers, publishing and printing
PA: Horizon Publications, Inc.
1120 N Carbon St Ste 100
Marion IL 62959
618 993-1711

(G-9474)

IMAGE INDUSTRIES NC INC
1848 Saint Pauls Church Rd (28658-9521)
PHONE...........................828 464-8882
Jerry Mallonee Junior, CEO
Tony Trado, Pr
▲ EMP: 19 EST: 1997
SQ FT: 15,000
SALES (est): 2.18MM **Privately Held**
Web: www.iionc.com
SIC: **3955** Ribbons, inked: typewriter, adding machine, register, etc.

(G-9475)

INDUSTRIAL RECYCLING SERVICES
Also Called: A Palletone Company
2815 Woodtech Dr (28658-8967)

PHONE...........................704 462-1882
EMP: 7 EST: 2015
SALES (est): 116.13K **Privately Held**
SIC: **2448** Pallets, wood

(G-9476)

INK TEC INC
1838 Saint Pauls Church Rd (28658-9521)
P.O. Box 909 (28671-0909)
PHONE...........................828 465-6411
Ivan Livas, CEO
Renato Livas, Pr
Myrna Livas, VP
▲ EMP: 15 EST: 1995
SQ FT: 14,000
SALES (est): 1.66MM **Privately Held**
Web: www.inktecinc.com
SIC: **2893** Printing ink

(G-9477)

INTER-CONTINENTAL CORPORATION
2575 N Ashe Ave (28658-2766)
P.O. Box 1119 (28613-1119)
PHONE...........................828 464-8250
David B Radke, Ch Bd
Mark Radke, *
Steve Radke, *
▲ EMP: 70 EST: 1969
SQ FT: 70,000
SALES (est): 16.31MM **Privately Held**
Web: www.iccboxes.com
SIC: **2653** 3412 Boxes, corrugated: made from purchased materials; Metal barrels, drums, and pails

(G-9478)

INTERNATIONAL PAPER COMPANY
International Paper
1525 Mount Olive Church Rd (28658-1740)
PHONE...........................828 464-3841
Larry Wise, Mgr
EMP: 56
SALES (corp-wide): 18.62B **Publicly Held**
Web: www.internationalpaper.com
SIC: **2621** Paper mills
PA: International Paper Company
6400 Poplar Ave
Memphis TN 38197
901 419-7000

(G-9479)

LEE INDUSTRIES LLC
402 W 25th St (28658-3755)
PHONE...........................828 464-8318
EMP: 219
SALES (corp-wide): 33.33MM **Privately Held**
Web: www.leeindustries.com
SIC: **2512** Chairs: upholstered on wood frames
PA: Lee Industries, Llc
210 4th St Sw
Conover NC 28613
828 464-8318

(G-9480)

LEE INDUSTRIES LLC
1620 Fisher Ct (28658-7821)
PHONE...........................828 464-8318
EMP: 219
SALES (corp-wide): 33.33MM **Privately Held**
Web: www.leeindustries.com
SIC: **2512** Couches, sofas, and davenports: upholstered on wood frames
PA: Lee Industries, Llc
210 4th St Sw
Conover NC 28613
828 464-8318

(G-9481)
MCCREARY MODERN INC (PA)
2564 S Us 321 Hwy (28658-9349)
P.O. Box 130 (28658-0130)
PHONE..............................828 464-6465
Robert Mccreary, *CEO*
Bob Mccreary, *Ch Bd*
Rick Coffey, *
Michele Mccreary, *Sec*
Doug Yoder, *
◆ **EMP:** 425 **EST:** 1985
SQ FT: 160,000
SALES (est): 24.29MM
SALES (corp-wide): 24.29MM **Privately Held**
Web: www.mccrearymodern.com
SIC: 2512 2421 Living room furniture: upholstered on wood frames; Kiln drying of lumber

(G-9482)
MIDSTATE MILLS INC
Also Called: Tenda Bake
11 N Brady Ave (28658-3245)
P.O. Box 350 (28658-0350)
PHONE..............................828 464-1611
Steven Arndt, *Pr*
Cindy Gabriel, *
Dianne Fulbright, *
Cynthia Drum, *
EMP: 120 **EST:** 1935
SQ FT: 10,000
SALES (est): 1.85MM **Privately Held**
Web: www.midstatemills.com
SIC: 2041 2048 Wheat flour; Prepared feeds, nec

(G-9483)
OBSERVER NEWS ENTERPRISE INC
Also Called: County Nws-Ntrprs-Maiden Times
309 N College Ave (28658-3255)
P.O. Box 48 (28658-0048)
PHONE..............................828 464-0221
Steve Garland, *Publisher*
EMP: 4 **EST:** 1879
SQ FT: 10,000
SALES (est): 704.2K
SALES (corp-wide): 12.26MM **Privately Held**
Web: www.observernewsonline.com
SIC: 2711 2752 Newspapers, publishing and printing; Commercial printing, lithographic
PA: Horizon Publications, Inc.
1120 N Carbon St Ste 100
Marion IL 62959
618 993-1711

(G-9484)
OLD HICKORY TANNERY INC (PA)
970 Locust St (28658-9235)
PHONE..............................828 465-6599
Willard G Black, *Pr*
Clint Black, *
Sharee Huffman, *
▲ **EMP:** 38 **EST:** 1962
SQ FT: 80,000
SALES (est): 7.59MM
SALES (corp-wide): 7.59MM **Privately Held**
Web: www.ohtfurniture.com
SIC: 2522 2512 Office furniture, except wood ; Upholstered household furniture

(G-9485)
OWENS QUILTING INC
101 E 11th St Ste 13 (28658-2274)
PHONE..............................828 695-1495
William Douglas Owens, *Pr*
Diane Owens, *VP*
EMP: 4 **EST:** 2001

SQ FT: 4,000
SALES (est): 229.33K **Privately Held**
Web: www.losego.net
SIC: 2392 7299 Slip covers and pads; Quilting for individuals

(G-9486)
P1 CATAWBA DEVELOPMENT CO LLC
2815 Woodtech Dr (28658-8967)
PHONE..............................704 462-1882
Howe Wallace, *Pr*
EMP: 9 **EST:** 2010
SALES (est): 378.2K
SALES (corp-wide): 6.65B **Publicly Held**
SIC: 2448 Pallets, wood
HQ: Palletone, Inc.
6001 Foxtrot Ave
Bartow FL 33830
866 336-6032

(G-9487)
PERRYS FRAME INC
3785 Thompson St (28658-9528)
PHONE..............................828 327-4681
Ricky Travis, *Pr*
Christine Travis, *VP*
EMP: 13 **EST:** 1965
SALES (est): 589.75K **Privately Held**
SIC: 2426 Frames for upholstered furniture, wood

(G-9488)
PIEDMONT BUSINESS FORMS INC
Also Called: Piedmont Office Products
703 W C St (28658-4304)
P.O. Box 281 (28658-0281)
PHONE..............................828 464-0010
Ken Ferguson, *Pr*
Gary Wagner, *VP*
EMP: 4 **EST:** 1955
SQ FT: 13,000
SALES (est): 182.47K **Privately Held**
SIC: 2752 2789 2759 Offset printing; Bookbinding and related work; Commercial printing, nec

(G-9489)
POWDER RIVER TECHNOLOGIES INC
1987 Industrial Dr (28658-7702)
PHONE..............................828 465-2894
Mark Sigmon, *Pr*
Myron Yount, *VP*
EMP: 8 **EST:** 1980
SALES (est): 493.74K **Privately Held**
Web: www.powderriverinc.com
SIC: 2514 Chairs, household: metal

(G-9490)
RENWOOD MILLS LLC
Also Called: Renwood Mills
11 N Brady Ave (28658-3245)
P.O. Box 350 (28658-0350)
PHONE..............................828 465-0302
Tommy Lynn, *CEO*
Robin Sigmon, *
EMP: 94 **EST:** 2013
SALES (est): 8.59MM
SALES (corp-wide): 211.12MM **Privately Held**
Web: www.homegrownfamilyfood.com
SIC: 0723 2041 Flour milling, custom services; Cake flour
PA: The Mennel Milling Company
319 S Vine St
Fostoria OH 44830
419 435-8151

(G-9491)
RMC ADVANCED TECHNOLOGIES INC
1400 Burris Rd (28658-1753)
PHONE..............................704 325-7100
Soroush Nazarpour, *Pr*
Aly Karnib, *VP Opers*
EMP: 52 **EST:** 2019
SALES (est): 8.76MM
SALES (corp-wide): 90.32MM **Privately Held**
SIC: 3448 Prefabricated metal components
PA: Nanoxplore Inc
4500 Boul Thimens
Montreal QC H4R 2
514 935-1377

(G-9492)
RUDISILL FRAME SHOP INC
780 Buchanan Pl (28658-8595)
PHONE..............................828 464-7020
Gary Rudisill, *Pr*
Dawn Rudisill, *Sec*
EMP: 23 **EST:** 1982
SALES (est): 1.66MM **Privately Held**
Web: www.yardstickinteriors.com
SIC: 2426 Furniture stock and parts; hardwood

(G-9493)
SARSTEDT INC (PA)
1025 Saint James Church Rd (28658-8937)
P.O. Box 468 (28658-0468)
PHONE..............................828 465-4000
Walter Sarstedt, *Pr*
▲ **EMP:** 198 **EST:** 1973
SALES (est): 49.38MM
SALES (corp-wide): 49.38MM **Privately Held**
Web: www.sarstedt.com
SIC: 5047 3821 Medical laboratory equipment; Laboratory apparatus and furniture

(G-9494)
SHERRILL FURNITURE COMPANY
Also Called: Precedent Furniture
1425 Smyre Farm Rd (28658-9361)
P.O. Box 189 (28603-0189)
PHONE..............................828 465-0844
Woody Williams, *Brnch Mgr*
EMP: 77
SQ FT: 103,000
SALES (corp-wide): 49.81MM **Privately Held**
Web: www.sherrillfurniture.com
SIC: 2512 Upholstered household furniture
PA: Sherrill Furniture Company Inc
2405 Highland Ave Ne
Hickory NC 28601
828 322-2640

(G-9495)
SMITH WOODTURNING INC
2427 Claremont Rd (28658-9615)
PHONE..............................828 464-2230
Linda Smith, *Prin*
EMP: 4 **EST:** 2005
SALES (est): 488.35K **Privately Held**
SIC: 3553 Woodworking machinery

(G-9496)
SNYDER PAPER CORPORATION
Also Called: Snyder Paper
1813 Mount Olive Church Rd (28658-1642)
PHONE..............................828 464-1189
Bill Schultz, *Brnch Mgr*
EMP: 20
SALES (corp-wide): 41.68MM **Privately Held**
Web: www.snydersolutions.com

SIC: 5199 2392 Foams and rubber; Household furnishings, nec
PA: Snyder Paper Corporation
250 26th Street Dr Se
Hickory NC 28602
828 328-2501

(G-9497)
SOUTHERN GLOVE INC
749 Ac Little Dr (28658-3769)
PHONE..............................828 464-4884
Brent A Fidler, *Pr*
Jeff Carter, *VP*
Doug Dickson, *CFO*
◆ **EMP:** 300 **EST:** 1945
SQ FT: 34,440
SALES (est): 3.15MM
SALES (corp-wide): 80.12MM **Privately Held**
Web: www.twusa.com
SIC: 2381 Gloves, work: woven or knit, made from purchased materials
PA: Techniweld Usa, Inc.
6205 Boat Rock Blvd Sw
Atlanta GA 30336
404 699-9900

(G-9498)
SPECIALTY TRNSP SYSTEMS INC
Also Called: Specialty Transportation
2720 N Main Ave (28658-2732)
P.O. Box 334 (28658-0334)
PHONE..............................828 464-9738
Dexter Warren, *Pr*
Carry Warren, *VP*
EMP: 4 **EST:** 1992
SALES (est): 506.69K **Privately Held**
SIC: 7549 5047 3999 Automotive customizing services, nonfactory basis; Medical equipment and supplies; Wheelchair lifts

(G-9499)
SPECIALTY WELDING & MCH INC
505 E 16th St (28658-2102)
PHONE..............................828 464-1104
Dennis Hefner, *Pr*
Gail Hefner, *Sec*
EMP: 8 **EST:** 1993
SQ FT: 16,000
SALES (est): 1.05MM **Privately Held**
Web: www.specweld.biz
SIC: 3441 1799 Fabricated structural metal; Welding on site

(G-9500)
SUN CLEANERS & LAUNDRY INC
Also Called: Frsteam By Sun Cleaners
2306 N Main Ave (28658-2724)
PHONE..............................704 325-3722
Nick Babamov, *Pr*
Ashley Babamov, *Sec*
EMP: 4 **EST:** 2001
SALES (est): 359.5K **Privately Held**
SIC: 2842 Polishes and sanitation goods

(G-9501)
SUNQEST INC (PA)
1555 N Rankin Ave (28658-2028)
PHONE..............................828 325-4910
Greg Baer, *Pr*
Delores Baer, *VP*
EMP: 8 **EST:** 1988
SQ FT: 12,000
SALES (est): 1MM
SALES (corp-wide): 1MM **Privately Held**
Web: www.sunqest.com
SIC: 3433 5074 8711 1799 Solar heaters and collectors; Heating equipment (hydronic); Engineering services; Home/office interiors finishing, furnishing and remodeling

(G-9502)
TECHNIBILT LTD (DH)
Also Called: Wanzl North America
700 Technibilt Dr (28658-8991)
P.O. Box 310 (28658-0310)
PHONE..............................828 464-7388
Ben Hinnen, *Pr*
Lynda Farrell, *
◆ **EMP:** 47 **EST:** 1946
SQ FT: 300,000
SALES (est): 43.95MM
SALES (corp-wide): 912.17MM **Privately Held**
Web: www.technibilt.com
SIC: 3799 2542 5046 3496 Pushcarts; Partitions and fixtures, except wood; Shelving, commercial and industrial; Grocery carts, made from purchased wire
HQ: Wanzl Gmbh & Co. Kgaa
   Rudolf-Wanzl-Str. 4
   Leipheim BY 89340
   82217290

(G-9503)
TEIJIN AUTOMOTIVE TECH INC
1400 Burris Rd (28658-1753)
PHONE..............................828 466-7000
Rick Spaulding, *Mgr*
EMP: 101
Web: www.teijinautomotive.com
SIC: 3714 Motor vehicle parts and accessories
HQ: Teijin Automotive Technologies, Inc.
   255 Rex Blvd
   Auburn Hills MI 48326
   248 237-7800

(G-9504)
TEMPRANO TECHVESTORS INC
2105 Northwest Blvd (28658-3723)
P.O. Box 492 (28673)
PHONE..............................877 545-1509
Luke Walling, *Pr*
EMP: 18 **EST:** 2005
SQ FT: 8,000
SALES (est): 3.16MM **Privately Held**
Web: www.temprano.com
SIC: 7372 Business oriented computer software

(G-9505)
TREE BRAND PACKAGING INC (PA)
2800 Woodtech Dr (28658-8967)
PHONE..............................704 483-0719
Al Helms, *CEO*
Michael Helms, *
Chris Helms, *
EMP: 53 **EST:** 1991
SALES (est): 3.21MM **Privately Held**
Web: www.treebrand.com
SIC: 2448 Pallets, wood

(G-9506)
TREE MASTERS INC
101 E 11th St Ste 1 (28658-2275)
P.O. Box 1095 (28658-1095)
PHONE..............................828 464-9443
Robert Baker Junior, *Pr*
Edsel Shusort, *
Cecelia Baker, *
◆ **EMP:** 45 **EST:** 1997
SQ FT: 75,000
SALES (est): 2.49MM **Privately Held**
Web: www.treemastersinc.com
SIC: 3999 Artificial trees and flowers

(G-9507)
UNIFOUR TECH INC
2845 Robinson Rd (28658-8547)
P.O. Box 1235 (28613-1235)
PHONE..............................828 256-4962

Spencer Fredell, *Pr*
EMP: 6 **EST:** 1996
SQ FT: 5,000
SALES (est): 804.89K **Privately Held**
SIC: 3625 Relays and industrial controls

(G-9508)
UNITED GLOVE INC
2017 N Stewart Ave (28658-2800)
P.O. Box 7 (28658-0007)
PHONE..............................828 464-2510
Dan Long, *Pr*
Michael C Long, *
◆ **EMP:** 50 **EST:** 1984
SQ FT: 33,000
SALES (est): 2.2MM **Privately Held**
Web: www.unitedglove.com
SIC: 2259 2381 Gloves and mittens, knit; Gloves, work: woven or knit, made from purchased materials

(G-9509)
WALLACE PRINTING INC
2032 Fairgrove Church Rd (28658-8598)
P.O. Box 1238 (28658-1238)
PHONE..............................828 466-3300
Kim Wallace, *Pr*
Danny Wallace, *VP*
EMP: 11 **EST:** 1989
SQ FT: 5,000
SALES (est): 901.28K **Privately Held**
Web: www.wallaceprinting.com
SIC: 2752 Offset printing

(G-9510)
WAREHOUSE DISTILLERY LLC
2628 Northwest Blvd (28658-3729)
PHONE..............................828 464-5183
EMP: 4 **EST:** 2015
SALES (est): 217.92K **Privately Held**
Web: www.warehousedistillery.com
SIC: 4225 2085 Miniwarehouse, warehousing ; Applejack (alcoholic beverage)

(G-9511)
WAYNE FARMS LLC
332 E A St (28658-2304)
P.O. Box 383 (27017-0383)
PHONE..............................770 538-2120
Andrea Stewart, *Acctnt*
EMP: 11 **EST:** 2000
SALES (est): 4.55MM **Privately Held**
Web: www.waynesandersonfarms.com
SIC: 2015 Poultry slaughtering and processing

(G-9512)
WEYERHAEUSER CO
1525 Mount Olive Church Rd (28658-1740)
P.O. Box 408 (28658-0408)
PHONE..............................828 464-3841
Jerry Thomas, *Genl Mgr*
EMP: 7 **EST:** 2009
SALES (est): 149.18K **Privately Held**
Web: www.weyerhaeuser.com
SIC: 2653 Corrugated and solid fiber boxes

(G-9513)
ZF CHASSIS COMPONENTS LLC
Also Called: ZF Lemforder
1570 E P Street Ext (28658-7803)
PHONE..............................828 468-3711
Mike Curtis, *Manager*
EMP: 128
SQ FT: 188,250
SALES (corp-wide): 144.19K **Privately Held**
Web: www.zf.com
SIC: 3714 Steering mechanisms, motor vehicle
HQ: Zf Chassis Components, Llc

3300 John Conley Dr
Lapeer MI 48446
810 245-2000

Newton Grove
Sampson County

(G-9514)
HOG SLAT INCORPORATED (PA)
Also Called: Georgia Poultry Equipment Co
206 Fayetteville St (28366-9071)
P.O. Box 300 (28366-0300)
PHONE..............................800 949-4647
William Herring Senior, *Ch Bd*
William Herring Ii, *Pr*
Mark Herring, *
David Herring, *
◆ **EMP:** 360 **EST:** 1970
SQ FT: 16,000
SALES (est): 451.86MM
SALES (corp-wide): 451.86MM **Privately Held**
Web: www.hogslat.com
SIC: 1542 3272 3523 0213 Farm building construction; Floor slabs and tiles, precast concrete; Hog feeding, handling, and watering equipment; Hogs

(G-9515)
HOG SLAT INCORPORATED
117 W Weeksdale Dr (28366-7762)
PHONE..............................800 949-4647
EMP: 12
SALES (corp-wide): 451.86MM **Privately Held**
Web: www.hogslat.com
SIC: 3523 Balers, farm: hay, straw, cotton, etc.
PA: Hog Slat, Incorporated
   206 Fayetteville St
   Newton Grove NC 28366
   800 949-4647

(G-9516)
MACS FARMS SAUSAGE CO INC
209 Raleigh St (28366-7613)
P.O. Box 190 (28366-0190)
PHONE..............................910 594-0095
Scott Mclamb, *Pr*
Shelton Mclamb, *Mgr*
Terry Mclamb, *VP*
EMP: 6 **EST:** 1994
SALES (est): 223.58K **Privately Held**
SIC: 2013 Sausages and other prepared meats

(G-9517)
SAMPSON GIN COMPANY INC
Also Called: Cotton Gin and Warehouse
5625 Newton Grove Hwy (28366-6255)
P.O. Box 526 (28366-0526)
PHONE..............................910 567-5111
Henry F Chancy, *Prin*
Henry F Chancy, *Pr*
Arthur T Lee, *
R Gerald Warren, *
EMP: 5 **EST:** 1990
SQ FT: 71,800
SALES (est): 480.73K **Privately Held**
SIC: 0724 2211 Cotton ginning; Broadwoven fabric mills, cotton

(G-9518)
STICKY LIFE
321 Goldsboro St (28366-7705)
P.O. Box 10 (28366-0010)
PHONE..............................910 817-4531
EMP: 4 **EST:** 2013
SALES (est): 112.19K **Privately Held**

Web: www.stickylife.com
SIC: 3993 Signs and advertising specialties

(G-9519)
TRANSFORMER SALES & SERVICE
1392 Massey Rd (28366-8542)
P.O. Box 808 (27577-0808)
PHONE..............................910 594-1495
Roger C Mayo, *Pr*
Daryl Mayo, *Treas*
William F Outlaw, *VP Opers*
EMP: 6 **EST:** 1979
SALES (est): 155.97K **Privately Held**
Web: www.transmaint.com
SIC: 7629 3612 Electrical equipment repair, high voltage; Power transformers, electric

Norlina
Warren County

(G-9520)
CLAYPRO LLC
Also Called: Orca Tactical
343 Warren Plains Norlina Rd (27563)
P.O. Box 1024 (27563-1024)
PHONE..............................828 301-6309
EMP: 6
SALES (est): 246.6K **Privately Held**
SIC: 3949 Sporting and athletic goods, nec

North Wilkesboro
Wilkes County

(G-9521)
ANCHOR COFFEE CO INC
Also Called: Anchor Coffee Co.
313b 9th St Ste 1 (28659-4168)
PHONE..............................336 265-7458
Nathaniel Griffin, *Pr*
Greg Brady, *VP*
Barry Mitchell, *Sec*
EMP: 5 **EST:** 2014
SQ FT: 6,000
SALES (est): 343.77K **Privately Held**
Web: shop.anchorcoffeeco.com
SIC: 5812 2095 Coffee shop; Roasted coffee

(G-9522)
B & C CONCRETE PRODUCTS INC
228 New Brickyard Rd (28659-8961)
P.O. Box 1014 (28659-1014)
PHONE..............................336 838-4201
Keith Blackburn, *Pr*
Joyce Blackburn, *VP*
EMP: 5 **EST:** 1977
SQ FT: 6,000
SALES (est): 946.6K **Privately Held**
Web: www.bc-concrete.com
SIC: 3272 Concrete products, precast, nec

(G-9523)
BLISSFULL MEMORIES
101 6th St (28659-4238)
PHONE..............................336 903-1835
Ronald Ording, *Owner*
EMP: 4 **EST:** 2007
SALES (est): 177.99K **Privately Held**
Web: www.blissfulmemories.com
SIC: 2782 Scrapbooks

(G-9524)
CERTAINTEED LLC
1149 Abtco Rd (28659-9633)
PHONE..............................336 696-2007
Don Veronie, *Mgr*
EMP: 11
SALES (corp-wide): 402.18MM **Privately Held**

▲ = Import ▼ = Export
◆ = Import/Export

Web: www.certainteed.com
SIC: 3292 Asbestos building materials, except asbestos paper
HQ: Certainteed Llc
20 Moores Rd
Malvern PA 19355
610 893-5000

(G-9525)
COMMERCIAL PROPERTY LLC
Also Called: Carolina Heritage Cabinetry
209 Elkin Hwy (28659-3478)
PHONE.....................336 818-1078
Scott Nase, *Pt*
Jeff Sigmon, *
EMP: 23 EST: 2002
SALES (est): 2.66MM Privately Held
Web: www.chcabinetry.com
SIC: 2434 Wood kitchen cabinets

(G-9526)
COPPER BARREL DISTILLERY LLC
532 Main St (28659-4406)
PHONE.....................336 262-6500
George L Smith, *CEO*
EMP: 9 EST: 2015
SALES (est): 487.59K Privately Held
Web: www.copperbarrel.com
SIC: 2085 Distilled and blended liquors

(G-9527)
CUB CREEK KITCHENS & BATHS INC
309 Wilkesboro Ave (28659-4227)
PHONE.....................336 651-8983
William M Walker, *Pr*
Debbie Walker, *Sec*
EMP: 8 EST: 1999
SALES (est): 1.29MM Privately Held
Web:
www.cubcreekkitchensandbaths.com
SIC: 2542 2541 Partitions and fixtures, except wood; Wood partitions and fixtures

(G-9528)
D & D DISPLAYS INC
126 Shaver St (28659-3403)
P.O. Box 1809 (28659-1809)
PHONE.....................336 667-8765
Glenn Harrs, *Pr*
J D Brown, *
◆ EMP: 30 EST: 2000
SQ FT: 100,000
SALES (est): 1.01MM Privately Held
SIC: 2541 Display fixtures, wood

(G-9529)
ECMD INC (PA)
Also Called: East Coast Mouldings
2 Grandview St (28659-3109)
P.O. Box 278 (28659)
PHONE.....................336 667-5976
▲ EMP: 100 EST: 1981
SALES (est): 186.49MM
SALES (corp-wide): 186.49MM Privately Held
Web: www.ecmd.com
SIC: 2431 5031 Moldings, wood: unfinished and prefinished; Millwork

(G-9530)
GARDNER GLASS PRODUCTS INC
Carolina Mirror Division
201 Elkin Hwy (28659-3463)
PHONE.....................336 838-2151
Mike Jordan, *Mgr*
EMP: 12
SALES (corp-wide): 22.87MM Privately Held
Web: www.dreamwalls.com
SIC: 3231 Mirrored glass
PA: Gardner Glass Products, Inc.

301 Elkin Hwy
North Wilkesboro NC 28659
336 651-9300

(G-9531)
GARDNER GLASS PRODUCTS INC (PA)
Also Called: Gardner Glass Products
301 Elkin Hwy (28659-3444)
P.O. Box 1570 (28659-1570)
PHONE.....................336 651-9300
Randy Brooks, *CEO*
Melissa Lackey, *
Tommy Huskey, *
Edd Gardner, *
◆ EMP: 175 EST: 1961
SQ FT: 70,000
SALES (est): 22.87MM
SALES (corp-wide): 22.87MM Privately Held
Web: www.dreamwalls.com
SIC: 3231 Mirrored glass

(G-9532)
GREENE MOUNTAIN OUTDOORS LLC
2321 Yellow Banks Rd (28659-8700)
PHONE.....................336 670-2186
EMP: 14 EST: 2008
SALES (est): 1.29MM Privately Held
Web: www.greenemountain.net
SIC: 2311 3111 3199 3792 Coats, overcoats and vests; Die-cutting of leather; Holsters, leather; Pickup covers, canopies or caps

(G-9533)
HAMBY BROTHER S INCORPORATED
Us Hwy 421 (28659)
P.O. Box 973 (28659-0973)
PHONE.....................336 667-1154
Joe D Hamby, *Pr*
Gail Hamby, *Sec*
EMP: 10 EST: 1963
SQ FT: 500
SALES (est): 717.9K Privately Held
SIC: 3273 Ready-mixed concrete

(G-9534)
HIGH COUNTRY ELECTRIC MTRS LLC
1268 Suncrest Orchard Rd (28659-9461)
P.O. Box 1262 (28659-1262)
PHONE.....................336 838-4808
EMP: 6 EST: 2005
SALES (est): 606.86K Privately Held
SIC: 7694 5999 Electric motor repair; Motors, electric

(G-9535)
HOBES COUNTRY HAMS INC (PA)
389 Elledge Mill Rd (28659-9241)
P.O. Box 350 (28697-0350)
PHONE.....................336 670-3401
Hobert D Gambill, *Pr*
David Gambill, *
Carolyn Wagoner, *
EMP: 35 EST: 1977
SALES (est): 4.9MM
SALES (corp-wide): 4.9MM Privately Held
Web: www.hobescountryham.com
SIC: 2011 5421 Meat packing plants; Meat markets, including freezer provisioners

(G-9536)
JELD-WEN INC
Also Called: Jeld-Wen Composite
205 Lanes Dr (28659-8376)
P.O. Box 1329 (97601-0268)
PHONE.....................336 838-0292

Arnie Hoyle, *Brnch Mgr*
EMP: 125
Web: www.jeld-wen.ca
SIC: 2421 3442 3089 2448 Sawmills and planing mills, general; Metal doors, sash, and trim; Windows, plastics; Pallets, wood
HQ: Jeld-Wen, Inc.
2645 Silver Crescent Dr
Charlotte NC 28273
800 535-3936

(G-9537)
JENKINS PROPERTIES INC
Also Called: Jenkins Interiors
102 Chestnut St Ste 101 (28659-4450)
P.O. Box 1509 (28659-1509)
PHONE.....................336 667-4282
Lewis Jenkins Senior, *Pr*
Ira D Morris, *
Lewis H Jenkins Junior, *VP*
EMP: 25 EST: 1950
SQ FT: 50,000
SALES (est): 518.65K Privately Held
SIC: 6512 5199 7532 3714 Commercial and industrial building operation; Leather, leather goods, and furs; Antique and classic automobile restoration; Motor vehicle body components and frame

(G-9538)
JOHNSTON CASUALS FURNITURE INC
121 Shaver St (28659-3445)
P.O. Box 668 (28659-0668)
PHONE.....................336 838-5178
Joe Johnston, *Pr*
Gary Cogdill, *
▼ EMP: 100 EST: 1955
SQ FT: 100,000
SALES (est): 5.33MM Privately Held
Web: www.johnstoncasuals.com
SIC: 2511 Wood household furniture

(G-9539)
JORDAN PIPING INC
300 8th St (28659-0100)
PHONE.....................336 818-9252
James Jordan, *Prin*
EMP: 8 EST: 2018
SALES (est): 2.26MM Privately Held
Web: www.jpiping.com
SIC: 1389 Oil field services, nec

(G-9540)
LEGACY VULCAN LLC
Mideast Division
776 Quarry Rd # 115 (28659-7806)
PHONE.....................336 838-8072
Bob Church, *Mgr*
EMP: 4
Web: www.vulcanmaterials.com
SIC: 3273 Ready-mixed concrete
HQ: Legacy Vulcan, Llc
1200 Urban Center Dr
Birmingham AL 35242
205 298-3000

(G-9541)
LIFESPAN INCORPORATED
Ls Solutions
2070 River Rd Liberty Grove Rd (28659-7314)
PHONE.....................336 838-2614
Scott Mauney, *Genl Mgr*
EMP: 95
SALES (corp-wide): 19.26MM Privately Held
Web: www.lifespanservices.org
SIC: 8211 3842 School for retarded, nec; Surgical appliances and supplies
PA: Lifespan Incorporated

1511 Shopton Rd Ste A
Charlotte NC 28217
704 944-5100

(G-9542)
LIFT BODIES INC
1675 Elkin Hwy 268 (28659-8827)
P.O. Box 1321 (28659-1321)
PHONE.....................336 667-2588
Danny Wagoner, *Pr*
Phyllis Wagoner, *Sec*
EMP: 6 EST: 1982
SQ FT: 21,000
SALES (est): 1.58MM Privately Held
Web: www.liftbodies.com
SIC: 3713 Dump truck bodies

(G-9543)
LOUISIANA-PACIFIC CORPORATION
Also Called: L P
1068 Abtco Rd (28659-9632)
P.O. Box 98 (28669-0098)
PHONE.....................336 696-2751
Mike Blosser, *Mgr*
EMP: 194
SALES (corp-wide): 2.94B Publicly Held
Web: www.lpcorp.com
SIC: 2493 Hardboard
PA: Louisiana-Pacific Corporation
1610 West End Ave Ste 200
Nashville TN 37203
615 986-5600

(G-9544)
LURAY TEXTILES INC
Also Called: Luray Textiles & Knitting
300 Luray Rd (28659-9709)
PHONE.....................336 670-3725
Raymond Church, *Pr*
Diane Royall, *
EMP: 15 EST: 1986
SQ FT: 18,000
SALES (est): 2.15MM Privately Held
Web: www.luraytextiles.com
SIC: 2257 2211 Jersey cloth; Terry woven fabrics, cotton

(G-9545)
MATHIS QUARRIES INC
873 Cove Creek Dr (28659-7829)
PHONE.....................336 984-4010
Bart C Mathis, *Pr*
EMP: 4 EST: 2010
SALES (est): 428.7K Privately Held
SIC: 3295 Minerals, ground or treated

(G-9546)
MEADOWS MILLS INC
1352 W D St (28659-3506)
P.O. Box 1288 (28659-1288)
PHONE.....................336 838-2282
Robert Hege Iii, *Pr*
Bob Hege, *
June Hege, *
Brian Hege, *
Corey Sheets, *
▼ EMP: 37 EST: 1902
SQ FT: 52,000
SALES (est): 4.48MM Privately Held
Web: www.meadowsmills.com
SIC: 3531 3553 3556 3599 Hammer mills (rock and ore crushing machines), portable; Sawmill machines; Food products machinery; Machine shop, jobbing and repair

(G-9547)
MICHAEL S NORTH WILKESBORO INC
Also Called: Michaels Jewelry
900 Main St (28659-4216)

PHONE..............336 838-5964
Michael Parsons, *Pr*
Vickie Parsons, *Sec*
EMP: 5 **EST:** 1985
SQ FT: 1,250
SALES (est): 182.11K **Privately Held**
Web: www.michaelsjewelry.com
SIC: 5944 3911 5947 Jewelry, precious
  stones and precious metals; Jewelry,
  precious metal; Gift shop

(G-9548)
MILLER BEE SUPPLY INC
496 Yellow Banks Rd (28659-8773)
PHONE..............336 670-2249
Presley Miller, *Pr*
EMP: 12 **EST:** 2003
SALES (est): 852.67K **Privately Held**
Web: www.millerbeesupply.com
SIC: 2499 3999 Beekeeping supplies, wood;
  Beekeepers' supplies

(G-9549)
PLYCEM USA LLC
Allura Fiber Cement
1149 Abtco Rd (28659-9633)
PHONE..............336 696-2007
Jerry Shermer, *Mgr*
EMP: 101
Web: www.alluransa.com
SIC: 2952 3292 5032 Roof cement: asphalt,
  fibrous, or plastic; Siding, asbestos cement;
  Cement
HQ: Plycem Usa Llc
  396 W Green Rd Ste 300
  Houston TX 77067
  844 525-5872

(G-9550)
RAGG CO INC
627 Elkin Hwy (28659-3405)
PHONE..............336 838-4895
Tim R Clonch, *Pr*
EMP: 4 **EST:** 1987
SALES (est): 217.22K **Privately Held**
Web: www.theraggcompany.com
SIC: 2759 Screen printing

(G-9551)
**THOMAS BROTHERS SLAUGHTER
HSE**
Also Called: Thomas Brothers Meat Proc
347 Thomas St (28659-3168)
PHONE..............336 667-1346
Buddy Joe Thomas, *Pt*
Charlie P Thomas, *Pt*
EMP: 5 **EST:** 1971
SQ FT: 4,000
SALES (est): 293.56K **Privately Held**
SIC: 0751 2011 Slaughtering: custom
  livestock services; Meat packing plants

(G-9552)
WESLACOVA CORP
2070 River Rd Liberty Grove Rd
(28659-7314)
PHONE..............336 838-2614
Scott Mauney, *Pr*
EMP: 7 **EST:** 2020
SALES (est): 1.12MM **Privately Held**
Web: www.weslacova.com
SIC: 3841 Surgical and medical instruments

Norwood
Stanly County

(G-9553)
AQUADALE QUERY
12423 Old Aquadale Rd (28128-7548)

P.O. Box 987 (28002-0987)
PHONE..............704 474-3165
Jeffrey Goodman, *Owner*
EMP: 6 **EST:** 2008
SALES (est): 1.16MM **Privately Held**
Web: www.hedrickind.com
SIC: 1442 Construction sand and gravel

(G-9554)
CAROLINA STALITE CO LTD PARTNR
12423 Old Aquadale Rd (28128-7548)
PHONE..............704 474-3165
Mike Farrington, *Brnch Mgr*
EMP: 16
SALES (corp-wide): 7.41MM **Privately
Held**
Web: www.stalite.com
SIC: 3281 Slate products
PA: Carolina Stalite Company Limited
  Partnership
  205 Klumac Rd
  Salisbury NC 28144
  704 637-1515

(G-9555)
CUMBERLAND SAND AND GRAVEL
12423 Old Aquadale Rd (28128-7548)
PHONE..............704 474-3165
EMP: 6 **EST:** 2010
SALES (est): 1.43MM **Privately Held**
Web: www.hedrickind.com
SIC: 1442 Construction sand and gravel

(G-9556)
M & R RETREADING & OIL CO INC
337 W Whitley St (28128-8712)
PHONE..............704 474-4101
Reggie Barfield, *Pr*
Mitchell Barfield, *Pr*
Reggie Barfield, *Dir*
Wesley Smith, *Dir*
EMP: 8 **EST:** 1971
SQ FT: 15,000
SALES (est): 936.68K **Privately Held**
Web: mr-retreading.business.site
SIC: 5014 5531 7534 5983 Automobile tires
  and tubes; Automotive tires; Tire recapping;
  Fuel oil dealers

(G-9557)
NEW FINISH INC
8353 Us 52 Hwy S (28128-6592)
PHONE..............704 474-4116
Steve Bradley, *Pr*
Brenda Bradley, *
EMP: 47 **EST:** 2001
SALES (est): 9.85MM **Privately Held**
Web: www.newfinishinc.com
SIC: 2851 4212 Epoxy coatings; Local
  trucking, without storage

(G-9558)
NORWOOD MANUFACTURING INC
680 Lanier Rd (28128-8448)
PHONE..............704 474-0505
Allen Kuehl, *Pr*
EMP: 47 **EST:** 2004
SQ FT: 77,920
SALES (est): 3.87MM
SALES (corp-wide): 240.55MM **Publicly
Held**
SIC: 3448 Prefabricated metal components
PA: Burnham Holdings, Inc.
  1241 Harrisburg Pike
  Lancaster PA 17604
  717 390-7800

(G-9559)
RUSCO FIXTURE COMPANY INC
Also Called: Rusco Fixture
11635 Nc 138 Hwy (28128-7509)

P.O. Box 598 (28129-0598)
PHONE..............704 474-3184
EMP: 37 **EST:** 1976
SALES (est): 3.96MM **Privately Held**
SIC: 2541 Store fixtures, wood

(G-9560)
STANLY FIXS ACQUISITION LLC
Also Called: Stanly Fixtures
11635 Nc 138 Hwy (28128-7509)
P.O. Box 616 (28128-0616)
PHONE..............704 474-3184
Kinny Bowers, *
Boyce Thompson, *
EMP: 8 **EST:** 1959
SQ FT: 128,000
SALES (est): 824.98K **Privately Held**
Web: www.stanlyfixtures.com
SIC: 2541 Store fixtures, wood

(G-9561)
STANLY FIXTURES COMPANY INC
11635 Nc 138 Hwy (28128-7509)
P.O. Box 616 (28128-0616)
PHONE..............704 474-3184
Todd Curlee, *Pr*
EMP: 7 **EST:** 2006
SALES (est): 823.95K **Privately Held**
SIC: 2542 Partitions and fixtures, except
  wood

(G-9562)
TILLERY ACCESSORIES INC
7041 Riverview Rd (28128-9623)
PHONE..............704 474-3013
Yvonne Pinion, *Pr*
Roger Pinion, *VP*
EMP: 7 **EST:** 1993
SQ FT: 3,000
SALES (est): 119.35K **Privately Held**
SIC: 2326 Work uniforms

(G-9563)
UWHARRIE KNITS INC
957 N Main St (28128-6526)
P.O. Box 890 (28128-0890)
PHONE..............704 474-4123
Doug Forman, *Pr*
▲ **EMP:** 12 **EST:** 1999
SALES (est): 481.27K **Privately Held**
SIC: 5949 2258 Knitting goods and supplies;
  Lace and warp knit fabric mills

Oak Island
Brunswick County

(G-9564)
BURLINGTON OUTLET (PA)
5817 E Oak Island Dr (28465-5040)
PHONE..............910 278-3442
James R Taylor, *Owner*
EMP: 7 **EST:** 1983
SQ FT: 8,000
SALES (est): 160.4K
SALES (corp-wide): 160.4K **Privately Held**
Web: www.burlingtonoutlet.com
SIC: 2339 5945 5947 Beachwear: women's,
  misses', and juniors'; Toys and games; Gift
  shop

(G-9565)
ELITE WOOD CLASSICS INC
4392 Long Beach Rd Se (28461-8617)
PHONE..............910 454-8745
Merrideth Herr, *Prin*
EMP: 6 **EST:** 2005
SALES (est): 459.74K **Privately Held**
SIC: 2431 Millwork

(G-9566)
LAKEBROOK CORPORATION
Also Called: Leonard Products
3506 E Yacht Dr (28465-5721)
PHONE..............207 947-4051
Elizabeth A R Long, *Pr*
EMP: 4 **EST:** 1997
SALES (est): 111.08K **Privately Held**
SIC: 2672 2675 Tape, pressure sensitive:
  made from purchased materials; Die-cut
  paper and board

(G-9567)
PARKWOOD CORPORATION
3506 E Yacht Dr (28465-5721)
PHONE..............910 815-4300
Robert L Long, *Pr*
EMP: 5 **EST:** 2003
SALES (est): 100.08K **Privately Held**
SIC: 2631 Paperboard mills

(G-9568)
RC BOLDT PUBLISHING LLC (PA)
804 Ocean Dr (28465-8217)
PHONE..............904 624-0033
EMP: 6 **EST:** 2016
SALES (est): 72.02K **Privately Held**
SALES (corp-wide): 72.02K **Privately Held**
SIC: 2741 Miscellaneous publishing

Oak Ridge
Guilford County

(G-9569)
B & B WELDING INC
Also Called: Spencer Bowman Customs
2900 Oak Ridge Rd (27310-8705)
PHONE..............336 643-5702
Spencer G Bowman, *Pr*
Spencer E Bowman, *VP*
Wanda Bowman, *Sec*
EMP: 7 **EST:** 1971
SQ FT: 5,000
SALES (est): 566.56K **Privately Held**
SIC: 3751 7538 Motorcycles and related
  parts; General automotive repair shops

(G-9570)
BLUM INC
594 Carson Ridge Dr (27310-9693)
PHONE..............919 345-6214
Ben Houston, *Prin*
EMP: 6 **EST:** 2010
SALES (est): 116.77K **Privately Held**
Web: www.blum.com
SIC: 3429 Hardware, nec

(G-9571)
EDUCATION CENTER LLC
Also Called: Mailbox, The
8886 Rymack Dr (27310-8804)
PHONE..............336 854-0309
EMP: 49 **EST:** 2012
SALES (est): 1.55MM **Privately Held**
Web: www.themailbox.com
SIC: 2721 Periodicals

(G-9572)
NUCLAMP SYSTEM LLC
Also Called: Nuclamp
8585 Benbow Merrill Rd (27310-9509)
PHONE..............336 643-1766
EMP: 5 **EST:** 2011
SALES (est): 250.92K **Privately Held**
Web: www.nuclamp.com
SIC: 3429 Clamps, metal

(G-9573)
OAKBROOK SOLUTIONS INC
Also Called: Cornerstone Software
5930 Tarleton Dr (27310-9632)
PHONE..............................336 714-0321
Craig Cook, *Brnch Mgr*
EMP: 38
SALES (corp-wide): 2.58MM **Privately Held**
Web: www.f2strategy.com
SIC: 7372 Prepackaged software
HQ: Caco Holdings Inc.
301 N Main St Ste 2424
Winston Salem NC 27101
336 714-0321

(G-9574)
PIEDMONT MARBLE INC
5014 Robdot Dr (27310-9208)
P.O. Box 1047 (27402-1047)
PHONE..............................336 274-1800
Tony Parrish, *Pr*
Rene Parrish, *VP*
Louise Hobbs, *Off Mgr*
EMP: 8 EST: 1985
SALES (est): 264.27K **Privately Held**
SIC: 3281 Household articles, except furniture: cut stone

Oakboro
Stanly County

(G-9575)
CHARLOTTE PIPE AND FOUNDRY CO
10145 Lighthouse Rd (28129-8988)
P.O. Box 35430 (28235-5430)
PHONE..............................704 887-8015
Mike Hall, *Manager*
EMP: 510
SALES (corp-wide): 841.88MM **Privately Held**
Web: www.charlottepipe.com
SIC: 3084 Plastics pipe
PA: Charlotte Pipe And Foundry Company
2109 Randolph Rd
Charlotte NC 28207
800 438-6091

(G-9576)
CONCRETE PIPE & PRECAST LLC
20047 Silver Rd (28129-8986)
PHONE..............................704 485-4614
James B Kennedy, *Pr*
EMP: 19
SALES (corp-wide): 23.07MM **Privately Held**
Web: www.concretepandp.com
SIC: 3272 Precast terrazzo or concrete products
PA: Concrete Pipe & Precast, Llc
11352 Virginia Precast Rd
Ashland VA 23005
804 798-6068

(G-9577)
CT COMMERCIAL PAPER LLC
349 S Main St (28129)
PHONE..............................704 485-3212
EMP: 42 EST: 2014
SALES (corp-wide): 1.71B **Privately Held**
Web: www.ctcpaper.com
SIC: 3089 2621 Tissue dispensers, plastics; Towels, tissues and napkins; paper and stock
PA: Pmc Global, Inc.
12243 Branford St
Sun Valley CA 91352

818 896-1101

(G-9578)
ENTERPRISE RENDERING COMPANY
28821 Bethlehem Church Rd (28129-8758)
PHONE..............................704 485-3018
Carroll Braun Senior, *Pr*
EMP: 9 EST: 1964
SQ FT: 8,000
SALES (est): 1.23MM **Privately Held**
Web: www.enterpriserendering.com
SIC: 2077 Bone meal, except as animal feed

(G-9579)
FAB-CON MACHINERY DEV CORP (PA)
Also Called: Fab-Con
201 E 10th St (28129-9621)
P.O. Box 591 (11050)
PHONE..............................704 486-7120
Frank Catallo, *Pr*
James Catallo, *
◆ EMP: 70 EST: 1966
SQ FT: 20,000
SALES (est): 9.46MM
SALES (corp-wide): 9.46MM **Privately Held**
Web: www.fab-con.com
SIC: 5084 3552 Textile machinery and equipment; Knitting machines

(G-9580)
LITTLE LOGGING INC
1513 N Main St (28129-9012)
P.O. Box 801 (28129-0801)
PHONE..............................704 201-8185
Michael D Little Ii, *Pr*
Ashlee N Little, *VP*
EMP: 10 EST: 2007
SALES (est): 1MM **Privately Held**
SIC: 2411 Logging camps and contractors

(G-9581)
MORGANS CABINETS INC
8056 Rocky River Rd (28129-8879)
P.O. Box 269 (28129-0269)
PHONE..............................704 485-8693
Claude Morgan, *Prin*
EMP: 10 EST: 1995
SALES (est): 414.82K **Privately Held**
SIC: 2434 Wood kitchen cabinets

(G-9582)
NORMAC KITCHENS INC (HQ)
226 S Main St (28129-7718)
P.O. Box 479 (28129-0479)
PHONE..............................704 485-1911
Hans Marcus, *Pr*
EMP: 10 EST: 1993
SQ FT: 5,000
SALES (est): 8.81MM
SALES (corp-wide): 29.62MM **Privately Held**
Web: www.normackitchens.com
SIC: 2434 2541 2431 Wood kitchen cabinets; Wood partitions and fixtures; Millwork
PA: Normac Kitchens Limited
59 Glen Cameron Rd
Thornhill ON L3T 5
905 889-1342

(G-9583)
SWB LOGGING LLC
213 Glenwood Dr (28129-9406)
PHONE..............................704 485-3411
Scott Broadaway, *Pr*
EMP: 5 EST: 2001
SALES (est): 564.92K **Privately Held**
SIC: 2411 Logging camps and contractors

(G-9584)
VALLEY PROTEINS (DE) INC
Also Called: Valley Proteins (de), Inc.
28844 Bethlehem Church Rd (28129-8758)
PHONE..............................540 877-2533
EMP: 154
SALES (corp-wide): 6.79B **Publicly Held**
Web: www.darpro-solutions.com
SIC: 2077 Animal and marine fats and oils
HQ: Valley Proteins (De), Llc
151 Randall Stuewe Dr
Winchester VA 22603
540 877-2533

(G-9585)
WEST STANLY FABRICATION INC
16431 Sr 24/27 (28129)
PHONE..............................704 254-2967
Christopher West, *Pr*
EMP: 5 EST: 2007
SALES (est): 129.68K **Privately Held**
SIC: 7692 Welding repair

Ocean Isle Beach
Brunswick County

(G-9586)
BRUNSWICK SCREEN PRTG & EMB
570 Meadow Summit Dr (28469-6185)
PHONE..............................910 579-1234
Paul Saah, *Prin*
EMP: 6 EST: 2016
SALES (est): 601.97K **Privately Held**
SIC: 2759 Commercial printing, nec

(G-9587)
CENTRAL SITE GROUP LLC
15 Scotland St (28469-7629)
PHONE..............................336 380-4121
Travis E Sharpe, *Managing Member*
EMP: 6 EST: 2016
SALES (est): 1.26MM **Privately Held**
SIC: 1389 Construction, repair, and dismantling services

(G-9588)
OCEAN WOODWORKING INC
6863 Beach Dr Sw (28469-5747)
PHONE..............................910 579-2233
Laurence Moore, *Pr*
Rita Moore, *VP*
EMP: 4 EST: 1999
SQ FT: 8,000
SALES (est): 496.44K **Privately Held**
Web: www.oceanwoodworking.com
SIC: 2521 2517 Cabinets, office: wood; Home entertainment unit cabinets, wood

Old Fort
Mcdowell County

(G-9589)
AURIA OLD FORT LLC (DH)
1506 E Main St (28762-0168)
PHONE..............................828 668-7601
Brian Pour, *Pr*
▲ EMP: 206 EST: 2007
SALES (est): 3.62MM
SALES (corp-wide): 19K **Privately Held**
Web: www.blueridgetraveler.com
SIC: 3714 Motor vehicle parts and accessories
HQ: Auria Solutions Usa Inc.
26999 Cntl Pk Blvd Ste 30
Southfield MI 48076
248 728-8000

(G-9590)
AURIA OLD FORT II LLC
1542 E Main St (28762-0168)
PHONE..............................828 668-3277
Brian Pour, *Pr*
▲ EMP: 71 EST: 2007
SALES (est): 22.2MM
SALES (corp-wide): 19K **Privately Held**
SIC: 3714 Motor vehicle parts and accessories
HQ: Auria Solutions Usa Inc.
26999 Cntl Pk Blvd Ste 30
Southfield MI 48076
248 728-8000

(G-9591)
COLUMBIA FOREST PRODUCTS INC
369 Columbia Carolina Rd (28762-8629)
P.O. Box 1148 (28762-1148)
PHONE..............................828 724-9495
Jeff Wakefield, *Mgr*
EMP: 209
SALES (corp-wide): 494.11K **Privately Held**
Web: www.columbiaforestproducts.com
SIC: 5031 2435 Lumber, plywood, and millwork; Hardwood plywood, prefinished
PA: Columbia Forest Products, Inc.
7900 Mccloud Rd Ste 200
Greensboro NC 27409
336 605-0429

(G-9592)
COLUMBIA PLYWOOD CORPORATION
Also Called: Columbia Carolina Division
369 Columbia Carolina Rd (28762-8629)
P.O. Box 1148 (28762-1148)
PHONE..............................828 724-4191
Jeff Tuckey, *Mgr*
EMP: 447
SALES (corp-wide): 494.11K **Privately Held**
Web: www.columbiaforestproducts.com
SIC: 2435 2426 Plywood, hardwood or hardwood faced; Hardwood dimension and flooring mills
HQ: Columbia Plywood Corporation
222 Sw Columbia Ste 1575
Portland OR 97201
503 224-5300

(G-9593)
HI-TEC MACHINE CORP
2082 Silvers Welch Rd (28762-8728)
PHONE..............................828 652-1060
Russell D Wysong Iii, *Pr*
Todd Mustin, *
Richard T Mustin, *
EMP: 26 EST: 1998
SQ FT: 5,000
SALES (est): 4.76MM **Privately Held**
Web: www.hitechmachines.com
SIC: 3599 Machine shop, jobbing and repair

(G-9594)
JANESVILLE LLC
157 Lackey Town Rd (28762-7758)
P.O. Box 1209 (28762)
PHONE..............................828 668-9251
John Berghammer, *Brnch Mgr*
EMP: 180
SIC: 3086 Insulation or cushioning material, foamed plastics
HQ: Janesville, Llc
88 East 48th St
Holland MI 49423
248 948-1811

(G-9595)
LEWIS MACHINE COMPANY INC
712 Catawba River Rd (28762-7642)
PHONE......................828 668-7752
Gary Lewis, *Pr*
EMP: 8 **EST:** 1985
SQ FT: 2,500
SALES (est): 496.8K **Privately Held**
SIC: 3599 Machine shop, jobbing and repair

(G-9596)
PARKER HOSIERY COMPANY INC
Also Called: Parker Legwear
78 Catawba Ave (28762-8920)
P.O. Box 1799 (28762-1799)
PHONE......................828 668-7628
Jeffrey W Parker, *Pr*
Amy L Parker, *
◆ **EMP:** 30 **EST:** 1946
SQ FT: 100,000
SALES (est): 2.52MM **Privately Held**
Web: www.parkerlegwear.com
SIC: 5137 2252 Gloves, women's and children's; Hosiery, nec

(G-9597)
POPPY HANDCRAFTED POPCORN INC
78 Catawba Ave Ste A (28762-8920)
PHONE......................828 552-3149
Carmen Cabrera, *Mgr*
EMP: 10
SALES (corp-wide): 6.62MM **Privately Held**
Web:
www.poppyhandcraftedpopcorn.com
SIC: 2099 Food preparations, nec
PA: Poppy Handcrafted Popcorn Inc.
12 Gerber Rd
Asheville NC 28803
828 552-3149

Olin
Iredell County

(G-9598)
WOODWORKING UNLIMITED INC
675 Bussell Rd (28660-9450)
PHONE......................704 903-8080
David Haynes, *Prin*
EMP: 6 **EST:** 2007
SALES (est): 141.56K **Privately Held**
SIC: 2431 Millwork

Oriental
Pamlico County

(G-9599)
COLLIN MFG INC
99 Pelican Cir (28571-9808)
PHONE......................919 917-6264
Steve Price, *Prin*
EMP: 5 **EST:** 2005
SALES (est): 109.59K **Privately Held**
SIC: 3999 Manufacturing industries, nec

(G-9600)
J C LAWRENCE CO
Also Called: Medlin Office Supply
9526 Connie Cove Rd (28571-9493)
PHONE......................919 553-3044
Jennifer Lawrence, *Pr*
Charels Chuck Lawrence, *VP*
EMP: 5 **EST:** 1985
SALES (est): 100.4K **Privately Held**
SIC: 5932 2759 Used merchandise stores; Commercial printing, nec

(G-9601)
M & J MARINE LLC
Also Called: Sailcraft Service
1218 Lupton Dr (28571-9629)
PHONE......................252 249-0522
Jennifer Pawlikowski, *Managing Member*
EMP: 10 **EST:** 2018
SALES (est): 499.86K **Privately Held**
SIC: 5551 3731 7699 3732 Boat dealers; Shipbuilding and repairing; Recreational sporting equipment repair services; Motorized boat, building and repairing

(G-9602)
RUSSO MIKE DBA LRGER THAN LF I
Also Called: Larger Than Life Inflatables
1109 Yardarm Dr (28571-9142)
P.O. Box 492 (92007-0492)
PHONE......................760 942-0289
Michael Russo, *Owner*
Mike Russo, *Owner*
EMP: 6 **EST:** 1993
SALES (est): 462.28K **Privately Held**
Web: www.inflatables.net
SIC: 3069 Balloons, advertising and toy: rubber

(G-9603)
VILLAGE GRAPHICS
204 Freemason St (28571-9202)
P.O. Box 61 (28509-0061)
PHONE......................252 745-4600
Greg Winfrey, *Owner*
EMP: 4 **EST:** 1986
SALES (est): 157,76K **Privately Held**
SIC: 7336 2752 Graphic arts and related design; Commercial printing, lithographic

Orrum
Robeson County

(G-9604)
PRO-KAY SUPPLY INC
5032 Atkinson Rd (28369-9057)
P.O. Box 93 (28369-0093)
PHONE......................910 628-0882
Wilton P Caulder, *Pr*
Sabrina Caulder, *Sec*
EMP: 16 **EST:** 1984
SALES (est): 2.42MM **Privately Held**
Web: www.prokaysupply.com
SIC: 2431 Millwork

(G-9605)
RICHARD LEWIS VON
1928 Indian Swamp Rd (28369-9650)
PHONE......................910 628-9292
Richard Lewis, *Owner*
EMP: 7 **EST:** 2007
SALES (est): 208.88K **Privately Held**
SIC: 2411 Logging

Otto
Macon County

(G-9606)
J CULPEPPER & CO
Also Called: Infinity Stingray Products
8285 Georgia Rd (28763-8339)
P.O. Box 690 (28763-0690)
PHONE......................828 524-6842
Joe Culpepper, *Pr*
Kristi Culpepper, *VP*
▲ **EMP:** 5 **EST:** 1995
SALES (est): 340.79K **Privately Held**
Web: www.knifehandles.com
SIC: 3421 Cutlery

Oxford
Granville County

(G-9607)
CERTAINTEED LLC
200 Certainteed Dr (27565-3597)
PHONE......................919 603-1971
Mark Hielman, *Mgr*
EMP: 250
SALES (corp-wide): 402.18MM **Privately Held**
Web: www.certainteed.com
SIC: 2952 Roofing felts, cements, or coatings, nec
HQ: Certainteed Llc
20 Moores Rd
Malvern PA 19355
610 893-5000

(G-9608)
COBLE PRINTING CO INC
120 Hillsboro St (27565-3212)
P.O. Box 667 (27565-0667)
PHONE......................919 693-4622
Kevin King, *Pr*
Laurie Stephens, *Sec*
Claudia King, *VP*
EMP: 4 **EST:** 1928
SQ FT: 3,000
SALES (est): 177.97K **Privately Held**
Web: www.cobleprinting.com
SIC: 2752 Offset printing

(G-9609)
CREATIVE TEXTILES INC
615 Hillsboro St (27565-3102)
P.O. Box 587 (27565-0587)
PHONE......................919 693-4427
Michael Newton, *Pr*
Thomas D Newton Junior, *VP*
EMP: 7 **EST:** 1984
SQ FT: 16,000
SALES (est): 244.25K **Privately Held**
Web: www.notiremarks.com
SIC: 2299 2392 Quilt fillings: curled hair, cotton waste, moss, hemp tow; Pillows, bed: made from purchased materials

(G-9610)
CROSCILL HOME LLC
200 Ne Outer Loop (27565-5014)
PHONE......................919 735-7111
EMP: 160
SALES (corp-wide): 1.17K **Privately Held**
Web: www.croscill.com
SIC: 3431 Bathroom fixtures, including sinks
HQ: Croscill Home Llc
1333 Broadway Fl 8
New York NY 10018

(G-9611)
CURVEMAKERS INC
115 Corporation Dr (27565-4000)
PHONE......................919 690-1121
EMP: 9
SALES (corp-wide): 1.25MM **Privately Held**
Web: www.curvemakers.com
SIC: 2431 Millwork
PA: Curvemakers, Inc.
703 W Johnson St
Raleigh NC 27603
919 821-5792

(G-9612)
DAN MORTON LOGGING
1671 Sunset Rd (27565-8213)
PHONE......................919 693-1898
Martha Morton, *Prin*

EMP: 5 **EST:** 2017
SALES (est): 66.84K **Privately Held**
SIC: 2411 Logging

(G-9613)
DILL AIR CONTROLS PRODUCTS LLC (PA)
1145 Se Industry Dr (27565)
P.O. Box 159 (27565)
PHONE......................919 692-2300
Charles Zhang, *
Holly Chen, *
▲ **EMP:** 160 **EST:** 2005
SALES (est): 27.91MM
SALES (corp-wide): 27.91MM **Privately Held**
Web: www.dillvalves.com
SIC: 3714 Tire valve cores

(G-9614)
GATE PRECAST COMPANY
3800 Oxford Loop (27565)
P.O. Box 1604 (27565-1604)
PHONE......................919 603-1633
Laurie Nusso, *Mgr*
EMP: 120
SALES (corp-wide): 172.28MM **Privately Held**
Web: www.gateprecast.com
SIC: 3272 Concrete products, nec
HQ: Gate Precast Company
9540 San Jose Blvd
Jacksonville FL 32257
904 732-7668

(G-9615)
GRANVILLE EQUIPMENT LLC
4602a Watkins Rd (27565-7995)
PHONE......................919 693-1425
Don Watkins, *Prin*
▲ **EMP:** 10 **EST:** 2005
SALES (est): 1.84MM **Privately Held**
Web: www.granvilleequipment.com
SIC: 3523 Farm machinery and equipment

(G-9616)
GRANVILLE PALLET CO INC
3566 Us Highway 15 (27565-8519)
PHONE......................919 528-2347
J Glen Watkins, *Pr*
Angela Watkins, *
EMP: 68 **EST:** 1979
SQ FT: 25,000
SALES (est): 5.27MM **Privately Held**
Web: www.granvillepallet.com
SIC: 2448 Pallets, wood

(G-9617)
IDAHO WOOD INC
114 Southgate Dr (27565-3280)
PHONE......................208 263-9521
J T Vaughn, *Pr*
EMP: 10 **EST:** 2021
SALES (est): 1.02MM **Privately Held**
SIC: 2431 3646 Woodwork, interior and ornamental, nec; Commercial lighting fixtures

(G-9618)
IDEAL FASTENER CORPORATION (PA)
Also Called: Ideal Accessories
603 W Industry Dr (27565-3593)
P.O. Box 548 (27565-0548)
PHONE......................919 693-3115
TOLL FREE: 800
Ralph Gut, *Pr*
Carol Critcher, *
◆ **EMP:** 150 **EST:** 1936
SQ FT: 105,000

▲ = Import ▼ = Export
◆ = Import/Export

SALES (est): 26.35MM
SALES (corp-wide): 26.35MM **Privately Held**
Web: www.idealfastener.com
SIC: 3965 5085 Buckles and buckle parts; Fasteners, industrial: nuts, bolts, screws, etc.

(G-9619)
LEDGER PUBLISHING COMPANY
Also Called: Oxford Public Ledger
200 W Spring St (27565-3247)
P.O. Box 643 (27565-0643)
PHONE.................................919 693-2646
Ronnie Critcher, *Pr*
Charles Critcher, *VP*
EMP: 4 **EST:** 1932
SQ FT: 6,400
SALES (est): 286.32K **Privately Held**
Web: www.oxfordledger.com
SIC: 2711 Newspapers, publishing and printing

(G-9620)
NELSON LOGGING COMPANY INC
9557 Nc Highway 96 (27565-7647)
PHONE.................................919 849-2547
James Ray Nelson, *Pr*
Connie Nelson, *Treas*
EMP: 10 **EST:** 2004
SALES (est): 2.35MM **Privately Held**
SIC: 2421 Sawmills and planing mills, general

(G-9621)
OMNIA LLC
Also Called: Omnia Products
115 Certainteed Dr (27565-3587)
PHONE.................................919 696-2193
EMP: 5 **EST:** 1994
SQ FT: 6,000
SALES (est): 271.29K **Privately Held**
Web: www.omnia-products.com
SIC: 5131 2295 Piece goods and other fabrics; Coated fabrics, not rubberized

(G-9622)
OMNIA PRODUCTS LLC
115 Certainteed Dr (27565-3587)
PHONE.................................919 514-3977
John Dispennette, *Pr*
EMP: 4 **EST:** 2011
SQ FT: 6,000
SALES (est): 524.55K **Privately Held**
Web: www.omnia-products.com
SIC: 2824 Organic fibers, noncellulosic

(G-9623)
PERRY BROTHERS TIRE SVC INC
Also Called: Goodyear
606 Lewis St (27565-3524)
P.O. Box 869 (27565-0869)
PHONE.................................919 693-2128
Harry Wilkins, *Mgr*
EMP: 10
SALES (corp-wide): 3.29MM **Privately Held**
Web: www.blackstire.com
SIC: 5531 7534 5731 5014 Automotive tires; Tire recapping; Television sets; Automobile tires and tubes
PA: Perry Brothers Tire Service, Inc.
610 Wicker St
Sanford NC 27330
919 775-7225

(G-9624)
PLANTD INC
3220 Knotts Grove Rd (27565-7421)
PHONE.................................434 906-3445
Nathan Silvernail, *CEO*

Huade Tan, *
EMP: 57 **EST:** 2021
SALES (est): 5.22MM **Privately Held**
SIC: 3999 Grasses, artificial and preserved

(G-9625)
PLASTIC INGENUITY INC
113 Certainteed Dr (27565-3587)
PHONE.................................919 693-2009
Charles Polichnowski, *Mgr*
EMP: 83
SALES (corp-wide): 49.11MM **Privately Held**
Web: www.plasticingenuity.com
SIC: 3089 3081 Plastics containers, except foam; Packing materials, plastics sheet
PA: Plastic Ingenuity, Inc.
1017 Park St
Cross Plains WI 53528
608 798-3071

(G-9626)
PREMIER QUILTING CORPORATION
720 W Industry Dr (27565-3599)
PHONE.................................919 693-1151
Louis Lobraico, *Pr*
Louis J Lobraico, *
EMP: 7 **EST:** 1965
SQ FT: 52,000
SALES (est): 460.23K **Privately Held**
Web: www.premierquiltingcorp.com
SIC: 2221 Comforters and quilts, manmade fiber and silk

(G-9627)
PROMETALS INC
510 1/2 Hillsboro St (27565-3218)
P.O. Box 532 (27565-0532)
PHONE.................................919 693-8884
Tim Sobolak, *Pr*
Jean Sobolak, *Treas*
EMP: 7 **EST:** 1962
SALES (est): 456.06K **Privately Held**
Web: www.prometals.com
SIC: 3599 Machine shop, jobbing and repair

(G-9628)
REVLON INC
Also Called: Revlon Accounts Payable
1501 Williamsboro St (27565-3461)
P.O. Box 6114 (27565-2114)
PHONE.................................919 603-2782
EMP: 153
Web: www.revlon.com
SIC: 2844 Cosmetic preparations
HQ: Revlon, Inc.
55 Water St
New York NY 10041

(G-9629)
REVLON INC
1501 Williamsboro St (27565-3461)
P.O. Box 6111 (27565-6111)
PHONE.................................919 603-2000
William Conover, *Brnch Mgr*
EMP: 50
Web: www.revloncorp.com
SIC: 2844 5122 Cosmetic preparations; Drugs, proprietaries, and sundries
HQ: Revlon, Inc.
55 Water St
New York NY 10041

(G-9630)
REVLON CONSUMER PRODUCTS CORP
Also Called: Cnd
1501 Williamsboro St (27565-3461)
P.O. Box 6112 (27565-2112)
PHONE.................................919 603-2000
Art Curtis, *Brnch Mgr*

EMP: 100
Web: www.revlon.com
SIC: 2844 Cosmetic preparations
HQ: Revlon Consumer Products Llc
55 Water St
New York NY 10004

(G-9631)
RFR METAL FABRICATION INC
Also Called: Rfr
3204 Knotts Grove Rd (27565-7421)
P.O. Box 1627 (27565-1627)
PHONE.................................919 693-1354
Randall Williams, *Pr*
EMP: 58 **EST:** 1999
SQ FT: 20,000
SALES (est): 18.86MM **Privately Held**
Web: www.rfr-metalfab.com
SIC: 3444 3331 3469 Sheet metal specialties, not stamped; Bars (primary), copper; Electronic enclosures, stamped or pressed metal

(G-9632)
SANTA FE NATURAL TOB CO INC
104 Enterprise Ct (27565-6179)
P.O. Box 3000 (27102-3000)
PHONE.................................919 690-1905
Michael R Ball, *Pr*
Alden H Smith, *Sec*
John R Whitener, *Treas*
EMP: 5 **EST:** 2016
SALES (est): 3.52MM **Privately Held**
Web: www.sfntc.com
SIC: 2121 Cigars
HQ: Santa Fe Natural Tobacco Company Foundation
401 N Main St
Winston Salem NC 27101
800 332-5595

(G-9633)
SANTA FE NTURAL TOB FOUNDATION
3220 Knotts Grove Rd (27565-7421)
P.O. Box 129 (27565-0129)
PHONE.................................919 690-0880
Mike Little, *Sr VP*
EMP: 140
Web: www.americanspirit.com
SIC: 2111 Cigarettes
HQ: Santa Fe Natural Tobacco Company Foundation
401 N Main St
Winston Salem NC 27101
800 332-5595

(G-9634)
SHALAG US INC
Also Called: Shalag Nonwovens
917 Se Industry Dr (27565)
P.O. Box 225 (27565-0225)
▲ **EMP:** 95 **EST:** 2009
SQ FT: 12,000
SALES (est): 27.73MM **Privately Held**
Web: www.shalag.com
SIC: 2297 Nonwoven fabrics
HQ: Shalag Industries Ltd
Kibbutz
Shamir 12135

(G-9635)
SOUTHERN DATA SYSTEMS INC
7758 Nc Highway 96 (27565-8841)
P.O. Box 65 (23962-0065)
PHONE.................................919 781-7603
Robert Drew, *Pr*
Michelle Sparrow, *VP*
EMP: 10 **EST:** 1979
SQ FT: 5,500
SALES (est): 185.03K **Privately Held**

SIC: 7379 3577 Computer related consulting services; Computer peripheral equipment, nec

(G-9636)
SOUTHERN STATES COOP INC
Also Called: S S C Oxford Svc
607 Hillsboro St (27565-3102)
PHONE.................................919 693-6136
Steve Timberlake, *Mgr*
EMP: 39
SALES (corp-wide): 1.71B **Privately Held**
Web: www.southernstates.com
SIC: 2048 5999 Prepared feeds, nec; Farm equipment and supplies
PA: Southern States Cooperative, Incorporated
6606 W Broad St Ste B
Richmond VA 23230
804 281-1000

(G-9637)
SOUTHERN WOODCRAFT DESIGN LLC
114 Southgate Dr (27565-3280)
PHONE.................................919 693-8995
EMP: 7 **EST:** 2005
SALES (est): 1.55MM **Privately Held**
Web: www.southernwoodcraft.net
SIC: 2431 Millwork

(G-9638)
TED WHEELER
Also Called: Ted's Service Company
2651 Hwy 158 (27565-8478)
P.O. Box 1457 (27302-1457)
PHONE.................................252 438-0820
Ted Wheeler, *Owner*
EMP: 4 **EST:** 2005
SALES (est): 201.41K **Privately Held**
SIC: 2099 Food preparations, nec

(G-9639)
TRUE MACHINE LLC
6575 Huntsboro Rd (27565-7548)
P.O. Box 1607 (27565-1607)
PHONE.................................919 270-2552
Sylvester Moltisanti, *Admn*
EMP: 4 **EST:** 2015
SALES (est): 368.44K **Privately Held**
Web: www.truemachineautomation.com
SIC: 3599 Machine shop, jobbing and repair

(G-9640)
WINSTONS WOODWORKS
600 Sunset Ave (27565-2842)
PHONE.................................919 693-4120
Winston Brooks, *Owner*
EMP: 5 **EST:** 1985
SALES (est): 247.43K **Privately Held**
Web: www.winstonswoodworks.com
SIC: 2434 Wood kitchen cabinets

Pantego
Beaufort County

(G-9641)
CAHOON BROTHERS LOGGING LLC
26606 Us Highway 264 E (27860-9388)
PHONE.................................252 943-9901
Ronnie Cahoon, *Managing Member*
Ronnie W Cahoon, *Managing Member*
EMP: 10 **EST:** 2003
SALES (est): 1.63MM **Privately Held**
SIC: 2411 Logging camps and contractors

(G-9642)
COASTAL CAROLINA GIN LLC
Also Called: Coastal Carolina Gin
4851 Terra Ceia Rd (27860-9315)
PHONE..................................252 943-6990
EMP: 11 EST: 1996
SQ FT: 4,000
SALES (est): 1.77MM **Privately Held**
Web: www.coastalcarolinagin.com
SIC: 0724 3559 Cotton ginning; Cotton
    ginning machinery

(G-9643)
**EAST CRLINA OLSEED PRCSSORS
LL**
Also Called: Perdue Ecop Crushing
2015 Nc Highway 45 N (27860-9110)
PHONE..................................252 935-5553
Darrel Dun, *Manager*
EMP: 63 EST: 2011
SALES (est): 492.31K
SALES (corp-wide): 1.24B **Privately Held**
SIC: 5159 3556 Oil nuts, kernels, seeds;
    Oilseed crushing and extracting machinery
HQ: Perdue Agribusiness Llc
    31149 Old Ocean City Rd
    Salisbury MD 21804

(G-9644)
IBX LUMBER LLC
405 Mainstem Rd (27860-9214)
PHONE..................................252 935-4050
Leland Hershey, *Managing Member*
EMP: 8 EST: 2016
SALES (est): 757.27K **Privately Held**
SIC: 2421 Sawmills and planing mills,
    general

(G-9645)
**J&R COHOON LOGGING &
TIDEWATER**
25912 Us Highway 264 E (27860-9404)
P.O. Box 429 (27860-0429)
PHONE..................................252 943-6300
Barbara Cahoon, *Owner*
EMP: 5 EST: 2005
SALES (est): 282.75K **Privately Held**
SIC: 2411 Logging camps and contractors

(G-9646)
MARTIN LUMBER & MULCH LLC
301 Mainstem Rd (27860-9212)
PHONE..................................252 935-5294
Malvrin Martin, *Managing Member*
EMP: 14 EST: 1996
SALES (est): 1.36MM **Privately Held**
Web: www.martinlumberllc.com
SIC: 5031 2499 Lumber: rough, dressed,
    and finished; Mulch or sawdust products,
    wood

(G-9647)
NATHAN BEILER
Also Called: Pungo River Timber Company
2685 Nc Highway 45 N (27860-9108)
PHONE..................................252 935-5141
Nathan Beiler, *Pt*
Tom Beiler, *Pt*
Brenda Beiler, *Sec*
EMP: 6 EST: 1992
SALES (est): 84.89K **Privately Held**
SIC: 2411 Logging

(G-9648)
PRECISION PALLET LLC
405 Mainstem Rd (27860-9214)
PHONE..................................252 935-5355
EMP: 11 EST: 2005
SALES (est): 3.07MM **Privately Held**
Web: www.palletnc.com

SIC: 2448 Pallets, wood

Paw Creek
Mecklenburg County

(G-9649)
LETS TALK SOME SHIT
7400 Old Mount Holly Rd (28130-2001)
PHONE..................................704 264-6212
Orlando Parker, *CEO*
EMP: 4 EST: 2020
SALES (est): 261.67K **Privately Held**
SIC: 3663 Television broadcasting and
    communications equipment

Peachland
Anson County

(G-9650)
ANSON METALS LLC
2905 Hopewell Church Rd (28133-9168)
P.O. Box 74 (28133-0074)
PHONE..................................704 272-7878
EMP: 11 EST: 2002
SALES (est): 1.15MM **Privately Held**
Web: www.ansonmachine.com
SIC: 3599 Machine shop, jobbing and repair

(G-9651)
DAVIS MECHANICAL INC
4368 Nc 218 (28133-9179)
P.O. Box 488 (28103-0488)
PHONE..................................704 272-9366
Robert Delane Davis, *Pr*
Robert Delane Davis Ii, *VP*
EMP: 17 EST: 2002
SALES (est): 5.18MM **Privately Held**
SIC: 1623 2431 Water, sewer, and utility lines
    ; Millwork

(G-9652)
**PEACHLAND DSIGN FBRICATION
LLC**
3129 Deep Springs Church Rd
(28133-9056)
PHONE..................................704 272-9296
Dona F Black, *CEO*
Tom Black, *VP*
EMP: 13 EST: 2016
SALES (est): 2.44MM **Privately Held**
Web:
www.peachlanddesignandfabrication.com
SIC: 3441 Fabricated structural metal

(G-9653)
QUIKRETE COMPANIES LLC
Also Called: Quikrete Peachland
13471 Us Highway 74 W (28133-9524)
P.O. Box 99 (28133-0099)
PHONE..................................704 272-7677
Maury Goodloe, *Mgr*
EMP: 37
Web: www.quikrete.com
SIC: 3272 3273 Concrete products, nec;
    Ready-mixed concrete
HQ: The Quikrete Companies Llc
    5 Concourse Pkwy Ste 1900
    Atlanta GA 30328
    404 634-9100

(G-9654)
**SOUTHERN PDMONT PPING
FBRCTION**
2798 Lower White Store Rd (28133-8227)
P.O. Box 100 (28133-0100)
PHONE..................................704 272-7936
Katrenia M Davis, *Pr*

Kristina Forbes, *VP*
EMP: 13 EST: 1983
SQ FT: 3,500
SALES (est): 2.51MM **Privately Held**
Web: www.southernpiedmontpiping.com
SIC: 1711 3444 Process piping contractor;
    Sheet metalwork

Pelham
Caswell County

(G-9655)
NORAG TECHNOLOGY LLC (PA)
1214 Nc Highway 700 (27311-8913)
PHONE..................................336 316-0417
Floyd Guidry, *CEO*
Eresterine Guidiy, *CFO*
▼ EMP: 5 EST: 2007
SQ FT: 700
SALES (est): 1.16MM **Privately Held**
Web: www.noragtech.com
SIC: 2869 Industrial organic chemicals, nec

Pembroke
Robeson County

(G-9656)
**ARROW EDUCATIONAL PRODUCTS
INC**
208 Union Chapel Rd # 101 (28372-7419)
P.O. Box 1287 (28372-1287)
PHONE..................................910 521-0840
Riginald Oxendine, *Pr*
Reginald Oxendine Junior, *CEO*
EMP: 5 EST: 1988
SQ FT: 1,000
SALES (est): 168.53K **Privately Held**
SIC: 7372 Prepackaged software

(G-9657)
COLLEGE SUN DO
701 W 3rd St (28372-7979)
P.O. Box 1575 (28372-1575)
PHONE..................................910 521-9189
Edsel Lowry, *Owner*
Kelby Lowry, *Owner*
EMP: 4 EST: 1981
SQ FT: 2,000
SALES (est): 475.79K **Privately Held**
SIC: 5541 7534 Filling stations, gasoline;
    Tire retreading and repair shops

(G-9658)
DESIGNER WOODWORK
1616 Hiawatha Rd (28372)
P.O. Box 2663 (28372-2663)
PHONE..................................910 521-1252
Elwood Deese, *Owner*
EMP: 6 EST: 1982
SQ FT: 5,000
SALES (est): 143.64K **Privately Held**
SIC: 2434 Vanities, bathroom: wood

(G-9659)
SIMMIE BULLARD
Also Called: Simmie Bullard Construction
787 Goins Rd (28372-8341)
PHONE..................................910 600-3191
Simmie Bullard, *Owner*
EMP: 7 EST: 2020
SALES (est): 269.92K **Privately Held**
SIC: 1389 Construction, repair, and
    dismantling services

(G-9660)
STEVEN-ROBERT ORIGINALS LLC
Also Called: Steven-Robert Original Dessert

701 S Jones St (28372-9696)
PHONE..................................910 521-0199
Steven Fabos, *CEO*
EMP: 150
SALES (corp-wide): 350.86MM **Privately
Held**
Web: www.originaldesserts.com
SIC: 2052 Cookies and crackers
HQ: Steven-Robert Originals, Llc
    2780 Tower Rd
    Aurora CO 80011

Pendleton
Northampton County

(G-9661)
COMMERCIAL READY MIX PDTS INC
1231 Vougemills Rd (27862)
P.O. Box 189 (27986-0189)
PHONE..................................252 585-1777
Laverne Howell, *Brnch Mgr*
EMP: 13
SALES (corp-wide): 48.13MM **Privately
Held**
Web: www.crmpinc.com
SIC: 3273 Ready-mixed concrete
PA: Commercial Ready Mix Products, Inc.
    115 Hwy 158 W
    Winton NC 27986
    252 358-5461

Penrose
Transylvania County

(G-9662)
MERRILL RESOURCES INC
99 Cascade Lake Rd (28766-8716)
PHONE..................................828 877-4450
Dustin Merrill, *Pr*
EMP: 9 EST: 1946
SQ FT: 2,000
SALES (est): 894.36K **Privately Held**
Web: www.merrillresources.com
SIC: 5251 1781 3561 1623 Pumps and
    pumping equipment; Water well drilling;
    Pumps and pumping equipment; Pumping
    station construction

Pfafftown
Forsyth County

(G-9663)
CLASSIC PACKAGING COMPANY
5570 Bethania Rd (27040-9596)
P.O. Box 310 (27010)
PHONE..................................336 922-4224
Geraldine Pilla, *CEO*
Joseph Pilla, *
▲ EMP: 80 EST: 1990
SQ FT: 41,000
SALES (est): 4.41MM **Privately Held**
Web: www.classicpackaging.com
SIC: 2673 3086 Bags: plastic, laminated,
    and coated; Packaging and shipping
    materials, foamed plastics

(G-9664)
**NORTHWEST COATINGS SYSTEMS
INC**
5640 Clinedale Ct (27040-9308)
PHONE..................................336 924-1459
William Miller, *Pr*
EMP: 5 EST: 1980
SALES (est): 68.09K **Privately Held**
SIC: 2851 Paints and allied products

(G-9665)
SPEVCO INC
8118 Reynolda Rd (27040)
P.O. Box 11845 (27116)
PHONE...........................336 924-8100
Frank M Tharpe Junior, *CEO*
Fran Weller, *
Frank M Tharpe Iii, *Pr*
EMP: 65 **EST:** 1979
SQ FT: 40,000
SALES (est): 9.99MM **Privately Held**
Web: www.spevco.com
SIC: 3711 Trucks, pickup, assembly of

Pikeville
Wayne County

(G-9666)
BASF
703 Nor Am Rd (27863-8420)
PHONE...........................919 731-1700
EMP: 4 **EST:** 2019
SALES (est): 249.09K **Privately Held**
SIC: 2869 Industrial organic chemicals, nec

(G-9667)
BENTON & SONS FABRICATION INC
1921 N Nc 581 Hwy (27863-8756)
PHONE...........................919 734-1700
Binford Benton, *Pr*
Binford Benton Junior, *VP*
Cheryl Benton, *
Bruce Benton, *
Donna Myers, *
EMP: 38 **EST:** 1981
SQ FT: 70,000
SALES (est): 7.43MM **Privately Held**
Web: www.bentonsfabrication.com
SIC: 3599 3444 Machine shop, jobbing and
repair; Sheet metalwork

(G-9668)
STEEL SMART INCORPORATED
1042 Airport Rd Ne (27863-9130)
PHONE...........................919 736-0681
Brandon Hall, *Pr*
April Hall, *Sec*
Gerald Hall, *VP*
Linda Hall, *Treas*
EMP: 20 **EST:** 1962
SQ FT: 5,000
SALES (est): 2.56MM **Privately Held**
Web: www.steelsmartinc.com
SIC: 3446 3449 Architectural metalwork;
Miscellaneous metalwork

(G-9669)
WHEELER INDUSTRIES INC
Also Called: Wheeler Industries
4573 Us Highway 117 N (27863-9016)
P.O. Box 1521 (27533-1521)
PHONE...........................919 736-4256
Horace Gillett, *Pr*
EMP: 6 **EST:** 1992
SQ FT: 17,000
SALES (est): 1.15MM **Privately Held**
Web: www.wheeler-industries.com
SIC: 2448 4214 Pallets, wood; Local trucking
with storage

Pilot Mountain
Surry County

(G-9670)
BROWN & CHURCH NECK WEAR CO
118 Mary Moore Ln (27041-8692)
PHONE...........................336 368-5502
Larry Marshall, *COO*

▲ **EMP:** 45 **EST:** 1980
SQ FT: 7,500
SALES (est): 2.28MM
SALES (corp-wide): 665.91MM **Privately
Held**
Web: www.brownandchurch.com
SIC: 2323 Men's and boy's neckwear
PA: Tom James Company
263 Seaboard Ln
Franklin TN 37067
615 771-1122

(G-9671)
JOLO WINERY & VINEYARDS LLC
219 Jolo Winery Ln (27041-8717)
PHONE...........................954 816-5649
Kristen Ray, *Prin*
EMP: 24 **EST:** 2012
SALES (est): 3.63MM **Privately Held**
Web: www.jolovineyards.com
SIC: 2084 Wines

(G-9672)
PROTECHNOLOGIES INC
Also Called: Pti
331 Shellybrook Dr (27041-7572)
P.O. Box 950 (27041-0950)
PHONE...........................336 368-1375
Ian Edmonds, *CEO*
Raymond H Roc, *Pr*
Iris Stonestreet, *
Julie Sanson Rees, *
▲ **EMP:** 31 **EST:** 1985
SQ FT: 20,000
SALES (est): 11.37MM
SALES (corp-wide): 101MM **Privately
Held**
Web: www.protechnologies.com
SIC: 3679 Harness assemblies, for
electronic use: wire or cable
PA: Universal Power Group, Inc.
120 Dividend Dr Ste 100
Coppell TX 75019
469 892-1122

(G-9673)
RACK WORKS INC
207 Premier Ln (27041-9108)
PHONE...........................336 368-1302
Michael Francis, *Pr*
Sandra Francis, *
EMP: 35 **EST:** 1990
SQ FT: 3,500
SALES (est): 6.23MM **Privately Held**
Web: www.rackworksinc.com
SIC: 3496 3315 5021 3443 Miscellaneous
fabricated wire products; Baskets, steel wire
; Racks; Fabricated plate work (boiler shop)

(G-9674)
SPORTS SOLUTIONS INC
Also Called: No Sweat Specialties
614 E Main St (27041-8517)
P.O. Box 596 (27041-0596)
PHONE...........................336 368-1100
Charles Badgett, *Pr*
EMP: 18 **EST:** 2001
SALES (est): 2.33MM **Privately Held**
Web: www.noswetspecialties.com
SIC: 2252 Socks

(G-9675)
**VEGA CONSTRUCTION COMPANY
INC**
137 W Main St Unit 8 (27041-9304)
P.O. Box 1901 (27030-6901)
PHONE...........................336 756-3477
Carlos Vega, *CEO*
Socorro Vega, *
EMP: 28 **EST:** 2018
SALES (est): 4.82MM **Privately Held**

SIC: 3241 1741 Masonry cement; Masonry
and other stonework

(G-9676)
WOUND-ABOUT INC
309 Nelson St (27041-8618)
P.O. Box 201 (27053-0201)
PHONE...........................336 368-5001
Kyle Wallace, *Pr*
EMP: 7 **EST:** 2001
SALES (est): 923.78K **Privately Held**
Web: www.woundabout.com
SIC: 2298 Rope, except asbestos and wire

Pine Hall
Stokes County

(G-9677)
WIELAND COPPER PRODUCTS LLC
3990 Us 311 Hwy N (27042-8166)
P.O. Box 160 (27042)
PHONE...........................336 445-4500
▲ **EMP:** 470 **EST:** 1988
SQ FT: 560,000
SALES (est): 40.83MM **Privately Held**
Web: www.wieland.com
SIC: 3351 Bands, copper and copper alloy
HQ: Wieland-Werke Ag
Graf-Arco-Str. 36
Ulm BW 89079
7319440

Pine Level
Johnston County

(G-9678)
CUSTOM ASSEMBLIES INC
330 E Main St (27568-9210)
P.O. Box 177 (27568-0177)
PHONE...........................919 202-4533
Jack Peacock, *Pr*
Gayle Peacock, *
EMP: 43 **EST:** 1996
SQ FT: 18,500
SALES (est): 7.22MM **Privately Held**
Web: www.customassemblies.com
SIC: 3069 3841 Medical and laboratory
rubber sundries and related products;
Surgical and medical instruments

(G-9679)
CUSTOM MEDICAL SPECIALTIES INC
330 E Main St (27568-9210)
P.O. Box 177 (27568-0177)
PHONE...........................919 202-8462
Jack Peacock, *CEO*
Jim Perkins, *Pr*
▼ **EMP:** 4 **EST:** 1999
SALES (est): 428.86K **Privately Held**
Web:
www.custommedicalspecialties.com
SIC: 3842 Surgical appliances and supplies

(G-9680)
GENERAL METALS INC
Also Called: G M I
328 E Main St (27568-9210)
P.O. Box Po Box99 (27568-0099)
PHONE...........................919 202-0100
Eric Welak, *Pr*
Leslie Liles, *
Kenneth Lee, *
EMP: 25 **EST:** 1994
SQ FT: 25,000
SALES (est): 6.38MM **Privately Held**
Web: www.generalmetalsllc.com
SIC: 3444 Sheet metalwork

(G-9681)
HINNANT FARMS VINEYARD LLC
826 Pine Level Micro Road (27568)
P.O. Box 189 (27568-0189)
PHONE...........................919 965-3350
EMP: 18 **EST:** 1990
SALES (est): 767.38K **Privately Held**
Web: www.hinnantvineyards.com
SIC: 0172 2084 Grapes; Brandy

(G-9682)
JABB OF CAROLINAS INC
302 E Brown St (27568-9062)
P.O. Box 310 (27568-0310)
PHONE...........................919 965-9007
James J Arends, *Pr*
William Black, *VP*
EMP: 6 **EST:** 1994
SQ FT: 6,000
SALES (est): 471.4K **Privately Held**
Web: www.jabbthecarolinas.com
SIC: 2879 Insecticides, agricultural or
household

(G-9683)
NEW INNOVATIVE PRODUCTS INC
Also Called: Starlight Cases
2180 Hyw 70 E (27568)
PHONE...........................919 631-6759
Steve L Ramos Senior, *Pr*
Betty Ramos, *Pr*
Steve L Ramos, *VP*
▲ **EMP:** 8 **EST:** 1994
SQ FT: 10,000
SALES (est): 375.32K **Privately Held**
Web:
new-innovative-products-inc-in-pine-level-
nc.cityfos.com
SIC: 3669 3089 Emergency alarms; Plastics
containers, except foam

Pinebluff
Moore County

(G-9684)
ATEX TECHNOLOGIES INC
120 W Monroe Ave (28373-8333)
PHONE...........................910 255-2839
Brian L Mc Murray, *Pr*
Martin Monestere, *
Konni A Mc Murray, *
▲ **EMP:** 125 **EST:** 2001
SQ FT: 60,000
SALES (est): 23.63MM **Privately Held**
Web: www.atextechnologies.com
SIC: 2299 Fabrics: linen, jute, hemp, ramie

(G-9685)
**BALLISTIC RECOVERY SYSTEMS
INC (PA)**
Also Called: Brs Aerospace
41383 Us 1 Hwy (28373-8330)
PHONE...........................651 457-7491
Fernando De Caralt, *CEO*
Robert L Nelson, *Sec*
▲ **EMP:** 30 **EST:** 1980
SALES (est): 24.79MM
SALES (corp-wide): 24.79MM **Publicly
Held**
Web: www.brsaerospace.com
SIC: 3728 2399 Aircraft parts and
equipment, nec; Parachutes

(G-9686)
BLUE MAIDEN DEFENSE
165 Laurel Oak Ln (28373-8020)
PHONE...........................678 292-8342
Christy Wentzell, *Prin*
EMP: 4 **EST:** 2018

SALES (est): 220.96K **Privately Held**
SIC: 3812 Defense systems and equipment

(G-9687)
MANNING FABRICS INC
42028 Us 1 Hwy (28373-8014)
PHONE..................910 295-1970
Ned Manning, *Mgr*
EMP: 33
SALES (corp-wide): 6.04MM **Privately Held**
Web: www.manningcorporation.com
SIC: 2211 Broadwoven fabric mills, cotton
PA: Manning Fabrics, Inc.
650a Page St
Pinehurst NC 28374
910 295-1970

Pinehurst
Moore County

(G-9688)
CAROLINA PERFUMER INC (PA)
102 Berwick Ct (28374-8142)
PHONE..................910 295-5600
Janet Coffman, *Pr*
Ronald L Coffman, *Sec*
EMP: 9 EST: 1981
SQ FT: 6,000
SALES (est): 255.45K
SALES (corp-wide): 255.45K **Privately Held**
SIC: 3999 2844 5947 Potpourri; Perfumes and colognes; Gift shop

(G-9689)
CAROLINA VINYL PRINTING
14 Troon Dr (28374-6710)
PHONE..................910 603-3036
Yolanda Mccarty, *Prin*
EMP: 4 EST: 2018
SALES (est): 128.24K **Privately Held**
SIC: 2752 Commercial printing, lithographic

(G-9690)
CUSTOM MARBLE CORPORATION (PA)
150 Safford Dr (28374-8221)
PHONE..................910 215-0679
Anthony J Leo Junior, *Pr*
Christine Leo, *Sec*
EMP: 9 EST: 1974
SQ FT: 25,000
SALES (est): 262.13K
SALES (corp-wide): 262.13K **Privately Held**
SIC: 3261 5031 3431 3281 Bathroom accessories/fittings, vitreous china or earthenware; Lumber, plywood, and millwork; Metal sanitary ware; Cut stone and stone products

(G-9691)
EATON CORPORATION
Also Called: Golf Pride
15 Centennial Blvd (28374-0400)
P.O. Box 58 (28388-0058)
PHONE..................910 695-2900
James Ledford, *Mgr*
EMP: 99
Web: www.golfpride.com
SIC: 3069 3568 Grips or handles, rubber; Power transmission equipment, nec
HQ: Eaton Corporation
1000 Eaton Blvd
Cleveland OH 44122
440 523-5000

(G-9692)
GILLEY PRINTERS INC
Also Called: Village Printers
22 Rattlesnake Trl (28374-7612)
P.O. Box 2139 (28370-2139)
PHONE..................910 295-6317
Kim Gilley, *Pr*
Tony Gilley, *VP*
EMP: 5 EST: 1951
SALES (est): 201.54K **Privately Held**
Web: www.villageprinters.com
SIC: 2752 Offset printing

(G-9693)
GOLFSTAR TECHNOLOGY LLC
75 Lakewood Dr (28374-8292)
PHONE..................910 420-3122
Graham Ballingall, *CEO*
EMP: 6 EST: 2010
SALES (est): 191.26K **Privately Held**
SIC: 5091 3663 Golf equipment; Global positioning systems (GPS) equipment

(G-9694)
KS PRECIOUS METALS LLC
P.O. Box 3686 (28374-3686)
PHONE..................910 687-0244
EMP: 4 EST: 2008
SALES (est): 167.83K **Privately Held**
Web: www.pinehurstcoins.com
SIC: 3339 Precious metals

(G-9695)
M & P POLYMERS INC
135 Applecross Rd (28374-8521)
P.O. Box 2229 (28388-2229)
PHONE..................910 246-6585
Maurice V Smith, *Pr*
◆ EMP: 6 EST: 2008
SALES (est): 253.11K **Privately Held**
SIC: 2822 Ethylene-propylene rubbers, EPDM polymers

(G-9696)
MANNING FABRICS INC (PA)
Also Called: Manning and Co.
650a Page St (28374)
P.O. Box 6300 (28374-6300)
PHONE..................910 295-1970
Edward N Manning Senior, *Ch Bd*
Edward N Manning Junior, *Pr*
EMP: 7 EST: 1967
SQ FT: 3,000
SALES (est): 6.04MM
SALES (corp-wide): 6.04MM **Privately Held**
Web: www.manningcorporation.com
SIC: 2211 3083 3089 2891 Broadwoven fabric mills, cotton; Laminated plastics plate and sheet; Extruded finished plastics products, nec; Adhesives and sealants

(G-9697)
MCDONALDS
260 Ivey Ln (28374-9818)
PHONE..................910 295-1112
EMP: 10 EST: 2020
SALES (est): 57.19K **Privately Held**
Web: www.mcdonalds.com
SIC: 5813 5812 5499 2038 Drinking places; Eating places; Miscellaneous food stores; Frozen specialties, nec

(G-9698)
PAPER PERFECTOR LLC
125 Brookfield Dr (28374-8783)
PHONE..................910 695-1092
EMP: 5 EST: 2018
SALES (est): 82.48K **Privately Held**
SIC: 2621 Paper mills

(G-9699)
PERFORMANCE ADDITIVES LLC
222 Central Park Ave (28374-8803)
PHONE..................215 321-4388
Arthur Van Nostrand, *Pr*
▲ EMP: 15 EST: 2005
SALES (est): 12.67MM **Privately Held**
Web: www.performanceadditives.us
SIC: 2821 7389 Plastics materials and resins; Business services, nec

(G-9700)
PRINT PROFESSIONALS
280 Oakmont Cir (28374-8343)
PHONE..................607 279-3335
Edward Emnett, *Pr*
EMP: 5 EST: 2010
SALES (est): 175.15K **Privately Held**
SIC: 2752 Offset printing

(G-9701)
PROTECH METALS LLC
3619 Murdocksville Rd (28374)
P.O. Box 1925 (28370-1925)
PHONE..................910 295-6905
Wiliiam Hall, *Mng Pt*
EMP: 13 EST: 2011
SALES (est): 2.29MM **Privately Held**
Web: www.protechmetals.net
SIC: 3599 3479 3449 3446 Machine and other job shop work; Metal coating and allied services; Miscellaneous metalwork; Architectural metalwork

(G-9702)
ROOT SPRING SCRAPER CO
1 York Pl (28374-8512)
PHONE..................269 382-2025
Frederick Root Junior, *Pr*
Rodney Root, *
William Root, *
▼ EMP: 6 EST: 1891
SALES (est): 248.41K **Privately Held**
Web: www.rootsnowplows.com
SIC: 3531 3524 Snow plow attachments; Lawn and garden equipment

(G-9703)
SHUTTERBUG GRAFIX & SIGNS
300 Kelly Rd Ste B3 (28374-8276)
PHONE..................910 315-1556
EMP: 4 EST: 2014
SALES (est): 83.04K **Privately Held**
Web: www.shutterbuggrafixnc.com
SIC: 3993 Signs and advertising specialties

(G-9704)
TERIDA LLC
40 Augusta National Dr (28374-7140)
P.O. Box 5897 (28374-5897)
PHONE..................910 693-1633
Teri Prince, *Pr*
EMP: 10 EST: 2003
SALES (est): 237.49K **Privately Held**
Web: www.terida.com
SIC: 7379 7371 7372 Online services technology consultants; Computer software systems analysis and design, custom; Application computer software

Pinetops
Edgecombe County

(G-9705)
ABB INC
Also Called: A B B Power Technolgies
3022 Nc 43 N (27864-9575)
P.O. Box 22114 (27420)
PHONE..................252 827-2121
Tobias Lynch, *Mgr*
EMP: 101
Web: www.abb.com
SIC: 5063 3613 Motor controls, starters and relays: electric; Switchgear and switchboard apparatus
HQ: Abb Inc.
305 Gregson Dr
Cary NC 27511

(G-9706)
HARRIS-ROBINETTE INC
412 Harris Acre Ln (27864-7026)
P.O. Box 158 (27864-0158)
PHONE..................252 813-5794
Harris Robinette, *Pr*
EMP: 7 EST: 2012
SALES (est): 165.2K **Privately Held**
Web: www.harrisrobinette.com
SIC: 2013 Prepared beef products, from purchased beef

Pinetown
Beaufort County

(G-9707)
ACRE STATION MEAT FARM INC
Also Called: Meat Farm
17076 Nc Highway 32 N (27865-9502)
PHONE..................252 927-3700
Ronald Huettmann, *Pr*
Richard Huettmann, *VP*
Nancy Huettmann, *Treas*
EMP: 12 EST: 1977
SQ FT: 2,000
SALES (est): 1.48MM **Privately Held**
Web: www.acrestationmeatfarm.com
SIC: 5421 2011 Meat markets, including freezer provisioners; Meat packing plants

(G-9708)
CAHOON LOGGING COMPANY INC
Also Called: Cahoon Logging
6848 Free Union Church Rd (27865-9539)
P.O. Box 579 (27860-0579)
PHONE..................252 943-6805
Christine Cahoon, *Pr*
EMP: 9 EST: 1994
SALES (est): 1.03MM **Privately Held**
SIC: 2411 Logging camps and contractors

(G-9709)
R W BRITT LOGGING INC
7281 Long Ridge Rd (27865)
P.O. Box 833 (27962)
PHONE..................252 799-7682
Robert W Britt, *Prin*
EMP: 5 EST: 1990
SALES (est): 447.6K **Privately Held**
SIC: 2411 Logging camps and contractors

(G-9710)
TERRY LEGGETT LOGGING CO INC
4403 Long Ridge Rd (27865-9618)
PHONE..................252 927-4671
Terry W Leggett, *Pr*
Gretta Leggett, *VP*
EMP: 37 EST: 1984
SQ FT: 6,400
SALES (est): 5.27MM **Privately Held**
SIC: 2411 Logging camps and contractors

(G-9711)
WADE BIGGS LOGGING INC
2173 Biggs Rd (27865-9471)
PHONE..................252 927-4470
Wade T Biggs, *Pr*
Caroline Biggs, *Sec*
EMP: 9 EST: 1985

SALES (est): 799.61K **Privately Held**
SIC: **2411** Logging camps and contractors

Pineville
Mecklenburg County

(G-9712)
AMERICAN MOISTENING CO INC
Also Called: Amoco
10402 Rodney St (28134-8832)
P.O. Box 1066 (28134-1066)
PHONE......................704 889-7281
James O Alexander, *CEO*
Mario Giammattei, *Pr*
EMP: 15 EST: 1983
SQ FT: 50,000
SALES (est): 2.57MM **Privately Held**
Web: www.amco.com
SIC: **3585** 3613 Humidifiers and dehumidifiers; Control panels, electric

(G-9713)
AMERICAN SPRINKLE CO INC
11240 Rivers Edge Rd (28134-7385)
PHONE......................800 408-6708
William Brockmann, *Pr*
Kenneth Brockmann, *Prin*
Robert Brockman, *Prin*
Douglas Brockmann, *Prin*
EMP: 35 EST: 2001
SQ FT: 60,000
SALES (est): 11.52MM **Privately Held**
Web: www.americansprinkle.com
SIC: **2064** Candy and other confectionery products

(G-9714)
B G V INC
12245 Nations Ford Rd Ste 503 (28134-8444)
P.O. Box 7725 (28241-7725)
PHONE......................704 588-3047
John H Hopkins, *Pr*
Ida Mae Hopkins, *Sec*
EMP: 5 EST: 1969
SQ FT: 3,000
SALES (est): 975.14K **Privately Held**
Web: sell.sawbrokers.com
SIC: **3823** Process control instruments

(G-9715)
BLACK BOX CORPORATION
10817 Southern Loop Blvd (28134-7384)
PHONE......................704 248-6430
EMP: 6
Web: www.blackbox.com
SIC: **3577** Computer peripheral equipment, nec
HQ: Black Box Corporation
2701 N Dllas Pkwy Ste 510
Plano TX 75093
724 746-5500

(G-9716)
BLP PRODUCTS AND SERVICES INC
Also Called: Embroidery 2
605 N Polk St Ste D (28134-7435)
PHONE......................704 899-5505
Nick Vona, *CEO*
EMP: 4 EST: 2010
SALES (est): 178.53K **Privately Held**
Web: www.embroidery2.com
SIC: **2759** Screen printing

(G-9717)
BUILDING CENTER INC (PA)
10201 Industrial Dr (28134-6520)
P.O. Box 357 (28134)
PHONE......................704 889-8182

Edgar L Norris Senior, *Ch Bd*
Edgar L Norris Junior, *Pr*
Judith Norris, *
Grant Phillip, *
Amanda N Arnett, *
EMP: 96 EST: 1977
SQ FT: 52,000
SALES (est): 73.96MM
SALES (corp-wide): 73.96MM **Privately Held**
Web: www.thebuildingcenterinc.com
SIC: **5031** 2431 Lumber, plywood, and millwork; Millwork

(G-9718)
CABLE DEVICES INCORPORATED
Also Called: Cable Exchange
10540 Southern Loop Blvd (28134)
PHONE......................704 588-0859
EMP: 10
Web: www.commscope.com
SIC: **3663** Radio and t.v. communications equipment
HQ: Cable Devices Incorporated
3642 E Us Highway 70
Hickory NC 28602
714 554-4370

(G-9719)
CAROLINA FOODS LLC
12031 Carolina Logistics Dr (28134-1400)
PHONE......................704 333-9812
Dan Myers, *Brnch Mgr*
EMP: 400
SALES (corp-wide): 85.24MM **Privately Held**
Web: www.carolinafoodsinc.com
SIC: **2051** Breads, rolls, and buns
PA: Carolina Foods, Llc
1807 S Tryon St
Charlotte NC 28203
704 333-9812

(G-9720)
CONTAINER GRAPHICS CORP
Also Called: Cgc
10430 Southern Loop Blvd (28134-8468)
PHONE......................704 588-7230
Bill Farber, *Mgr*
EMP: 47
SQ FT: 3,168
SALES (corp-wide): 3.99MM **Privately Held**
Web: www.containergraphics.com
SIC: **5084** 3544 2796 Machine tools and accessories; Special dies, tools, jigs, and fixtures; Platemaking services
PA: Container Graphics Corp.
114 Ednbrgh S Drv Ste 104
Cary NC 27511
919 481-4200

(G-9721)
CONTROLS SOUTHEAST INC
Also Called: Csi
12201 Nations Ford Rd (28134)
P.O. Box 7500 (28241)
PHONE......................704 644-5000
Fred H Stubblefield Iii, *Pr*
Fred Stubblefield Junior, *Sec*
Michael D Cockram, *Design Vice President*
Jackson Roper, *
Brian Walsh, *
◆ EMP: 220 EST: 1962
SQ FT: 150,000
SALES (est): 42.07MM
SALES (corp-wide): 6.94B **Publicly Held**
Web: www.csiheat.com

SIC: **3498** 3494 3312 Piping systems for pulp, paper, and chemical industries; Valves and pipe fittings, nec; Blast furnaces and steel mills
PA: Ametek, Inc.
1100 Cassatt Rd
Berwyn PA 19312
610 647-2121

(G-9722)
CREATIVE TOOLING SOLUTIONS INC
10809 Southern Loop Blvd (28134-7425)
PHONE......................704 504-5415
Catherine Micalizzi, *Pr*
▲ EMP: 6 EST: 2010
SALES (est): 216.17K **Privately Held**
Web: www.creativetoolingsolutions.net
SIC: **3545** Tools and accessories for machine tools

(G-9723)
CUMMINS INC
11101 Nations Ford Rd (28134-9437)
PHONE......................704 588-1240
Russell Dallas, *Brnch Mgr*
EMP: 4
SALES (corp-wide): 34.1B **Publicly Held**
Web: www.cummins.com
SIC: **3519** 3714 3694 3621 Internal combustion engines, nec; Motor vehicle parts and accessories; Engine electrical equipment; Generator sets: gasoline, diesel, or dual-fuel
PA: Cummins Inc.
500 Jackson St
Columbus IN 47201
812 377-5000

(G-9724)
DIENES APPARATUS INC
9220 Rodney St (28134-9200)
P.O. Box 549 (28134-0549)
PHONE......................704 525-3770
Dan Miller, *Pr*
▲ EMP: 6 EST: 1981
SQ FT: 12,000
SALES (est): 340.66K
SALES (corp-wide): 1.64MM **Privately Held**
Web: www.dienes.net
SIC: **3585** Refrigeration and heating equipment
PA: Dienes Apparatebau Gesellschaft Mit Beschrankter Haftung
Philipp-Reis-Str. 16
Muhlheim Am Main HE 63165
61087070

(G-9725)
DIVERSIFIED WELDING AND STEEL
10801 Nations Ford Rd (28134-9440)
PHONE......................704 504-1111
EMP: 4 EST: 2016
SALES (est): 151.79K **Privately Held**
Web: www.diversifiedweldingllc.com
SIC: **7692** Welding repair

(G-9726)
ELNIK SYSTEMS LLC
12004 Carolina Logistics Dr Ste A (28134-1400)
PHONE......................973 239-6066
EMP: 20 EST: 2002
SALES (est): 1.08MM **Privately Held**
SIC: **3621** Motors and generators

(G-9727)
FERGUSON WATERWORKS
10039 Industrial Dr (28134-8384)
P.O. Box 1147 (28134-1147)
PHONE......................704 540-7225

Trae Farthing, *Mgr*
EMP: 4 EST: 2018
SALES (est): 755.58K **Privately Held**
SIC: **3589** Service industry machinery, nec

(G-9728)
FORKLIFT PRO INC
Also Called: Bellatony
9801 Industrial Dr (28134-6515)
P.O. Box 99 (28134-0099)
PHONE......................704 716-3636
Bill Zemak, *Pr*
Jaclyn Smith Ctrl, *Prin*
◆ EMP: 18 EST: 1999
SQ FT: 21,200
SALES (est): 3.89MM **Privately Held**
Web: www.theforkliftpro.com
SIC: **3537** Forklift trucks

(G-9729)
GALAXY PRESSURE WASHING INC
10810 Southern Loop Blvd Ste 12 (28134-8365)
P.O. Box 832 (28106-0832)
PHONE......................888 299-3129
Saqer Hejji, *Pr*
EMP: 5 EST: 2011
SALES (est): 383.03K **Privately Held**
Web: www.galaxypressurewashing.com
SIC: **7389** 7699 7349 3589 Business Activities at Non-Commercial Site; Cleaning services; Building cleaning service; Commercial cleaning equipment

(G-9730)
GRAPHIC PACKAGING INTL LLC
8800 Crump Rd (28134-8607)
P.O. Box 411288 (28241-1288)
PHONE......................704 588-1750
Jim Seel, *Brnch Mgr*
EMP: 217
Web: www.graphicpkg.com
SIC: **2657** 2631 2671 Folding paperboard boxes; Paperboard mills; Paper; coated and laminated packaging
HQ: Graphic Packaging International, Llc
1500 Rvredge Pkwy Ste 100
Atlanta GA 30328

(G-9731)
GRIFFITHS CORPORATION
Wrico Stamping Co NC
10134 Industrial Dr (28134-6516)
PHONE......................704 552-6793
Ed Schleicher, *Mgr*
EMP: 100
SALES (corp-wide): 147.92MM **Privately Held**
Web: www.griffithscorp.com
SIC: **3469** Stamping metal for the trade
HQ: Griffiths Corporation
2717 Niagara Ln N
Minneapolis MN 55447
763 557-8935

(G-9732)
GRIFFITHS CORPORATION
Also Called: K-Tek Crlina Prcsion Spclty Mf
10240 Industrial Dr (28134-6517)
PHONE......................704 554-5657
John Kirkpatrick, *Mgr*
EMP: 65
SALES (corp-wide): 147.92MM **Privately Held**
Web: www.ktek-net.com
SIC: **3469** 3544 3444 3451 Stamping metal for the trade; Special dies, tools, jigs, and fixtures; Sheet metal specialties, not stamped; Screw machine products
HQ: Griffiths Corporation
2717 Niagara Ln N

Minneapolis MN 55447
763 557-8935

(G-9733)
HLMF LOGISTICS INC
11516 Downs Rd (28134-8416)
PHONE.....................704 782-0356
Amy Bush, *Pr*
EMP: 4 **EST:** 2003
SALES (est): 758.84K **Privately Held**
SIC: 3621 7699 Electric motor and generator
parts; Filter cleaning

(G-9734)
HYPER NETWORKS LLC
12249 Nations Ford Rd (28134)
PHONE.....................704 837-8411
Ryan Draayer, *Managing Member*
EMP: 46 **EST:** 2022
SALES (est): 3.19MM **Privately Held**
Web: www.hypernetworksinc.com
SIC: 1623 3531 Pipeline wrapping; Cranes,
nec

(G-9735)
IPEX USA LLC (DH)
10100 Rodney St (28134)
P.O. Box 240696 (28224)
PHONE.....................704 889-2431
Thomas E Torokvei, *CEO*
Katherine Serafino, *
◆ **EMP:** 130 **EST:** 2000
SALES (est): 294.62MM
SALES (corp-wide): 8.01MM **Privately
Held**
Web: www.ipexna.com
SIC: 3084 Plastics pipe
HQ: Ipex Inc
1425 North Service Rd E Suite 3
Oakville ON L6H 1
289 881-0120

(G-9736)
IPEX USA LLC
Eslon Thermo Plastics
10100 Rodney St (28134-7538)
P.O. Box 240696 (28224-0696)
PHONE.....................704 889-2431
Wayne Peterson, *Mgr*
EMP: 13
SALES (corp-wide): 8.01MM **Privately
Held**
Web: www.ipexna.com
SIC: 3084 3498 Plastics pipe; Fabricated
pipe and fittings
HQ: Ipex Usa Llc
10100 Rodney Blvd
Pineville NC 28134

(G-9737)
JGI INC (PA)
Also Called: Signs Etc
10108 Industrial Dr (28134-6516)
PHONE.....................704 522-8860
Spencer Brower, *Pr*
Sherry Brower, *Sec*
EMP: 20 **EST:** 1980
SALES (est): 2.42MM
SALES (corp-wide): 2.42MM **Privately
Held**
SIC: 3993 Signs, not made in custom sign
painting shops

(G-9738)
KRANKEN SIGNS VEHICLE WRAPS
310 N Polk St (28134-8133)
P.O. Box 1025 (28134-1025)
PHONE.....................704 339-0059
Clifford Smith, *Owner*
EMP: 4 **EST:** 2013
SALES (est): 407.33K **Privately Held**

Web: www.krankensigns.com
SIC: 3993 Signs and advertising specialties

(G-9739)
LEKE LLC
Also Called: A S I
10800 Nations Ford Rd (28134)
PHONE.....................704 523-1452
Lawrence Eichorn, *Pr*
Kevin Eichorn, *
EMP: 6 **EST:** 1929
SQ FT: 20,000
SALES (est): 1.58MM **Privately Held**
SIC: 2819 2869 5169 Industrial inorganic
chemicals, nec; Industrial organic
chemicals, nec; Industrial chemicals
HQ: Colonial Chemical Solutions, Inc.
916 W Lathrop Ave
Savannah GA 31415
912 236-7891

(G-9740)
LOCK DRIVES INC
11198 Downs Rd (28134-8445)
P.O. Box 501 (28134-0501)
PHONE.....................704 588-1844
John Walters, *Pr*
▲ **EMP:** 4 **EST:** 2008
SALES (est): 1.13MM **Privately Held**
Web: www.lockdrives.com
SIC: 3523 1542 3448 5084 Barn, silo,
poultry, dairy, and livestock machinery;
Commercial and office buildings, renovation
and repair; Greenhouses, prefabricated
metal; Industrial machinery and equipment

(G-9741)
LSC COMMUNICATIONS INC
10519 Industrial Dr (28134-6527)
PHONE.....................704 889-5800
EMP: 11
SALES (corp-wide): 8.23B **Privately Held**
Web: www.lsccom.com
SIC: 2732 Book printing
HQ: Lsc Communications, Inc.
4101 Winfield Rd
Warrenville IL 60555
844 572-5720

(G-9742)
**MEXICHEM SPCALTY COMPOUNDS
INC**
9635 Industrial Dr (28134-8835)
P.O. Box 490 (28134-0490)
PHONE.....................704 889-7821
Robert N Gingue, *Brnch Mgr*
EMP: 80
SQ FT: 60,000
Web: www.alphagary.com
SIC: 2821 Plastics materials and resins
HQ: Mexichem Specialty Compounds, Inc.
170 Pioneer Dr
Leominster MA 01453
978 537-8071

(G-9743)
MPE USA INC
10424 Rodney St (28134-8832)
P.O. Box 713 (28134-0713)
PHONE.....................704 340-4910
Barbara Duncan, *Off Mgr*
▲ **EMP:** 21 **EST:** 2003
SQ FT: 70,000
SALES (est): 2.98MM
SALES (corp-wide): 74.75MM **Privately
Held**
Web: www.mpeplastics.com
SIC: 5162 3089 Plastics materials and basic
shapes; Injection molding of plastics
PA: M.P.E. Srl
Via Dell'industria 15

Villanova Canavese TO 10070

(G-9744)
NCSMJ INC
Also Called: Skatells Mfg Jewelers
9433 Pineville Matthews Rd (28134-6588)
PHONE.....................704 544-1118
Anthony Skatell, *Pr*
EMP: 10 **EST:** 1994
SQ FT: 14,638
SALES (est): 104.76K **Privately Held**
Web: www.skatellsnc.com
SIC: 3911 5094 5944 5045 Jewelry, precious
metal; Jewelry and precious stones;
Jewelry stores; Computers, peripherals,
and software

(G-9745)
OMEGA STUDIOS INC
10519 Industrial Dr (28134-6527)
PHONE.....................704 889-5800
Tom Palmer, *Pr*
EMP: 6 **EST:** 2017
SALES (est): 83.91K **Privately Held**
SIC: 2752 Commercial printing, lithographic

(G-9746)
ORAMENTAL POST
10108 Industrial Dr (28134-6516)
PHONE.....................704 376-8111
John Iyoob, *Pr*
▲ **EMP:** 6 **EST:** 1984
SQ FT: 10,000
SALES (est): 627.18K **Privately Held**
Web: www.ornamentalpost.com
SIC: 3993 Signs and advertising specialties

(G-9747)
**PINNACLE CONVERTING EQP &
SVCS**
11325 Nations Ford Rd Ste A (28134-8319)
PHONE.....................704 376-3855
Thomas Kepper, *Prin*
EMP: 20 **EST:** 2014
SALES (est): 1.18MM **Privately Held**
Web: www.pinnacleconverting.com
SIC: 3599 Machine and other job shop work

(G-9748)
**PINNACLE CONVERTING EQP INC
(PA)**
11325 Nations Ford Rd Ste A (28134-8319)
PHONE.....................704 376-3855
Bob Hillebrand, *Pr*
Kathy Hillebrand, *Sec*
Robert D Hillebrand, *Pr*
EMP: 23 **EST:** 1983
SALES (est): 4.36MM **Privately Held**
Web: www.pinnacleconverting.com
SIC: 3599 3621 Machine and other job shop
work; Motors and generators

(G-9749)
R S INTEGRATORS INC
11172 Downs Rd (28134-8445)
PHONE.....................704 588-8288
Ronald Sigmon, *Pr*
EMP: 6 **EST:** 1995
SQ FT: 4,000
SALES (est): 872.09K
SALES (corp-wide): 29.3MM **Privately
Held**
Web: www.rsintegrators.com
SIC: 3613 7539 Control panels, electric;
Electrical services
PA: Advanced Industrial Devices Company
Llc
4323 S Elwood Ave
Tulsa OK 74107
918 445-1254

(G-9750)
ROYAL WELDING LLC
413 N Polk St Unit H (28134-7457)
PHONE.....................704 750-9353
Gilman Derosier, *Managing Member*
Elisa Maria Derosier, *Member Finance*
EMP: 8 **EST:** 2009
SQ FT: 2,400
SALES (est): 754.82K **Privately Held**
Web:
www.royalweldingandsteelfabricationofcharlott
e.com
SIC: 7692 Welding repair

(G-9751)
RUSSELL FINEX INC
625 Eagleton Downs Dr (28134-7424)
P.O. Box 69 (28134-0069)
PHONE.....................704 588-9808
Rob Ward, *Pr*
John Edwards, *Pr*
Ernest W Reigel, *Sec*
◆ **EMP:** 16 **EST:** 1970
SQ FT: 25,000
SALES (est): 9.47MM
SALES (corp-wide): 62.09MM **Privately
Held**
Web: www.russellfinex.com
SIC: 5084 3569 Industrial machinery and
equipment; Assembly machines, non-
metalworking
PA: Russell Finex Limited
Russell House
Feltham MIDDX TW13
208 818-2000

(G-9752)
RUTLAND GROUP INC (HQ)
10021 Rodney St (28134-8574)
PHONE.....................704 553-0046
Jeff Leone, *CEO*
Hortensia Ladr, *
◆ **EMP:** 110 **EST:** 1986
SQ FT: 75,000
SALES (est): 16.09MM **Publicly Held**
SIC: 3087 2821 Custom compound
purchased resins; Plastics materials and
resins
PA: Avient Corporation
33587 Walker Rd
Avon Lake OH 44012

(G-9753)
RUTLAND HOLDINGS LLC (PA)
Also Called: Rutland Plastic Technologies
10021 Rodney St (28134-8574)
P.O. Box 339 (28134-0339)
PHONE.....................704 553-0046
◆ **EMP:** 33 **EST:** 2004
SALES (est): 7.49MM **Privately Held**
Web: www.avientspecialtyinks.com
SIC: 3087 2821 Custom compound
purchased resins; Plastics materials and
resins

(G-9754)
**SAPPHIRE TCHNCAL SOLUTIONS
LLC**
10230 Rodney St (28134-7539)
PHONE.....................704 561-3100
Michael Piscitelli, *Managing Member*
EMP: 9 **EST:** 2005
SQ FT: 21,000
SALES (est): 3.71MM **Privately Held**
Web: www.sapphirests.com
SIC: 8734 3829 3823 3826 Testing
laboratories; Measuring and controlling
devices, nec; Industrial process
measurement equipment; Analytical
instruments

(G-9755)
SCI SHARP CONTROLS INC
11331 Downs Rd (28134-8441)
PHONE...............................704 394-1395
Chrinstine Lopez-blossfled, *CEO*
EMP: 6 **EST:** 2007
SALES (est): 994.12K **Privately Held**
Web: www.sharpcontrols.com
SIC: 3494 3492 3594 Valves and pipe
  fittings, nec; Fluid power valves and hose
  fittings; Fluid power pumps and motors

(G-9756)
SCRIBBLES SOFTWARE LLC
10617 Southern Loop Blvd (28134-7381)
PHONE...............................704 390-5690
EMP: 22 **EST:** 2016
SALES (est): 6.89MM **Privately Held**
Web: www.scribsoft.com
SIC: 7372 Prepackaged software

(G-9757)
SIGNS NOW CHARLOTTE
Also Called: Signs Now
600 Towne Centre Blvd Ste 404
(28134-8476)
PHONE...............................704 844-0552
Michael Lutz, *Pr*
Janet Lutz, *Sec*
EMP: 4 **EST:** 1996
SALES (est): 486.9K **Privately Held**
Web: www.signsnow.com
SIC: 3993 Signs and advertising specialties

(G-9758)
SIQNARAMA PINEVILLW
10615 Industrial Dr Ste 200 (28134-6526)
PHONE...............................704 835-1123
EMP: 4 **EST:** 2018
SALES (est): 46.08K **Privately Held**
SIC: 3993 Signs and advertising specialties

(G-9759)
**STRONG MEDICAL PARTNERS LLC
(PA)**
Also Called: Strong Manufacturers
11519 Nations Ford Rd Ste 200
(28134-9447)
PHONE...............................716 626-9400
Alan Bagliore, *CEO*
EMP: 27 **EST:** 2016
SALES (est): 9.23MM
SALES (corp-wide): 9.23MM **Privately
Held**
Web: www.strongmanufacturers.com
SIC: 3841 Surgical and medical instruments

(G-9760)
STRONG MEDICAL PARTNERS LLC
Also Called: Strong Manufacturers
11515 Nations Ford Rd (28134-9540)
PHONE...............................716 507-4476
EMP: 93
SALES (corp-wide): 9.23MM **Privately
Held**
Web: www.strongmanufacturers.com
SIC: 3841 Surgical and medical instruments
PA: Strong Medical Partners Llc
  11519 Nations Ford Rd # 2
  Pineville NC 28134
  716 626-9400

(G-9761)
STUDIO DISPLAYS INC
11150 Rivers Edge Rd (28134-8478)
PHONE...............................704 588-6590
EMP: 13
SALES (corp-wide): 6.44MM **Privately
Held**
Web: www.studiodisplays.com

SIC: 3993 7336 Signs and advertising
  specialties; Graphic arts and related design
PA: Studio Displays, Inc.
  9081 Northfield Dr
  Indian Land SC 29707
  704 588-6590

(G-9762)
SUPERIOR FIRE HOSE CORP
10000 Industrial Dr Ste B (28134-8624)
P.O. Box 3527 (91744-0527)
PHONE...............................704 643-5888
Paul Sposato, *CEO*
Richard Bergeron, *
▲ **EMP:** 27 **EST:** 1996
SQ FT: 56,000
SALES (est): 922.82K **Privately Held**
Web: www.superiorfirehose.com
SIC: 3052 Fire hose, rubber

(G-9763)
URBAN INDUSTRIES CORP
12245 Nations Ford Rd Ste 505
(28134-7456)
PHONE...............................980 209-9471
Mark Urban, *Prin*
EMP: 7 **EST:** 2017
SALES (est): 1.15MM **Privately Held**
Web: www.urbanind.com
SIC: 3999 Manufacturing industries, nec

Pink Hill
Lenoir County

(G-9764)
BACKWOODS LOGGING LLC
1066 Sumner Rd (28572-7918)
PHONE...............................910 298-3786
EMP: 6 **EST:** 2012
SALES (est): 769.71K **Privately Held**
SIC: 2411 Logging camps and contractors

(G-9765)
CORDSET DESIGNS INC
100 W New St (28572-8569)
P.O. Box 528 (31007-0528)
PHONE...............................252 568-4001
Steven Peltz, *Pr*
Gary Payne, *Pr*
Ben Byrnside, *Sec*
▲ **EMP:** 7 **EST:** 1991
SQ FT: 43,000
SALES (est): 2.48MM **Privately Held**
Web: www.cordsetdesigns.com
SIC: 3357 3699 Appliance fixture wire,
  nonferrous; Electrical equipment and
  supplies, nec

(G-9766)
PINK HILL WELLNESS EDU CENTER
301 S Pine St (28572-8097)
PHONE...............................252 568-2425
Jennifer Scott, *Dir*
EMP: 8 **EST:** 2012
SALES (est): 246.42K **Privately Held**
Web:
pinkhillwellnessandeducation.yolasite.com
SIC: 8099 3674 Health and allied services,
  nec; Computer logic modules

Pinnacle
Stokes County

(G-9767)
B & B HOSIERY MILL
3608 Volunteer Rd (27043-8525)
PHONE...............................336 368-4849
Bernie Young, *Owner*

EMP: 5 **EST:** 1981
SALES (est): 198.73K **Privately Held**
SIC: 2252 Socks

(G-9768)
FELTS LUMBER CO INC
1377 Perch Rd (27043-8314)
P.O. Box 8 (27043-0008)
PHONE...............................336 368-5667
Brent Felts, *Pr*
Debra Felts, *Sec*
EMP: 7 **EST:** 1972
SALES (est): 133.75K **Privately Held**
SIC: 2421 Lumber: rough, sawed, or planed

Pisgah Forest
Transylvania County

(G-9769)
GLATFELTER CORPORATION
Also Called: Glatfelter Composite Fibers NA
2795 King Rd (28768-7880)
PHONE...............................828 877-2110
Jim Turra, *Genl Mgr*
EMP: 6
SALES (corp-wide): 1.39B **Publicly Held**
Web: www.glatfelter.com
SIC: 2621 Specialty papers
PA: Magnera Corporation
  9335 Hrris Crners Pkwy St
  Charlotte NC 28269
  866 744-7380

(G-9770)
KEOWEE PUBLISHING CO INC
96 Merle Farm Ln (28768-9960)
PHONE...............................828 877-4742
Gerald Harris, *Prin*
EMP: 9 **EST:** 2002
SALES (est): 73.98K **Privately Held**
SIC: 2741 Miscellaneous publishing

(G-9771)
MCJAST INC
Also Called: American Carolina Lighting
6497 Old Hendersonville Hwy
(28768-8851)
P.O. Box 1079 (28729-1079)
PHONE...............................828 884-4809
Janet Mcnabb, *Pr*
Steve Mcnabb, *CEO*
EMP: 10 **EST:** 1987
SQ FT: 8,000
SALES (est): 810.59K **Privately Held**
Web: www.americancarolinalighting.net
SIC: 3496 3599 3469 3452 Miscellaneous
  fabricated wire products; Grinding castings
  for the trade; Metal stampings, nec; Bolts,
  nuts, rivets, and washers

(G-9772)
PISGAH LABORATORIES INC
3222 Old Hendersonville Hwy
(28768-9213)
PHONE...............................828 884-2789
David W Bristol, *Pr*
Cliff King, *VP*
Belinda Novick, *Sec*
▲ **EMP:** 20 **EST:** 1979
SQ FT: 30,000
SALES (est): 5.35MM **Privately Held**
Web: www.pisgahlabs.com
SIC: 2833 2869 Medicinals and botanicals;
  Industrial organic chemicals, nec
PA: Ipca Laboratories Limited
  125, Kandivli Industrial Estate, Kandivli
  (West),
  Mumbai MH 40006

(G-9773)
TNW VENTURES INC
60 Bishop Ln (28768-7602)
P.O. Box 152 (28768-0152)
PHONE...............................828 216-4089
EMP: 6 **EST:** 2004
SALES (est): 69.94K **Privately Held**
SIC: 2064 Breakfast bars

(G-9774)
TREND PERFORMANCE PRODUCTS
114 Lime Kiln Ln (28768-8914)
PHONE...............................828 862-8290
Robert Fox, *Brnch Mgr*
EMP: 5
SALES (corp-wide): 1.34MM **Privately
Held**
Web: www.trendperform.com
SIC: 3714 Motor vehicle parts and
  accessories
PA: Trend Performance Products Inc
  23444 Schoenherr Rd
  Warren MI 48089
  586 447-0400

(G-9775)
WINS SMOKEHOUSE SERVICES LTD
45 S Ridge Rd (28768-8506)
PHONE...............................828 884-7476
Pete Wiencek, *Pr*
Holly Wiencek, *Sec*
EMP: 6 **EST:** 1996
SALES (est): 1.16MM **Privately Held**
Web: www.winssmokehouse.com
SIC: 3556 Smokers, food processing
  equipment

Pittsboro
Chatham County

(G-9776)
BIOLEX THERAPEUTICS INC
158 Credle St (27312-4130)
PHONE...............................919 542-9901
Jan Turek, *Pr*
Dale A Sander, *
David Spencer Ph.d., *COO*
Glen Williams, *
Bipin Dalmia Ph.d., *Sr VP*
EMP: 46 **EST:** 1998
SALES (est): 4.88MM **Privately Held**
Web: www.biolex.com
SIC: 2834 Digitalis pharmaceutical
  preparations

(G-9777)
BUDDY CUT INC
760 Redgate Rd (27312-7936)
P.O. Box 160 (27312-0160)
PHONE...............................888 608-4701
Joshua Esnard, *CEO*
EMP: 5 **EST:** 2017
SALES (est): 734.01K **Privately Held**
Web: www.thecutbuddy.com
SIC: 5961 3999 Electronic shopping; Barber
  and beauty shop equipment

(G-9778)
CARR AMPLIFIERS INC
433 W Salisbury St (27312-9451)
PHONE...............................919 545-0747
Steve Carr, *Pr*
EMP: 10 **EST:** 1998
SQ FT: 2,800
SALES (est): 597.8K **Privately Held**
Web: www.carramps.com
SIC: 3651 Amplifiers: radio, public address,
  or musical instrument

GEOGRAPHIC

(G-9779)
CHANDLER CONCRETE INC
Also Called: Chandler Concrete Company
246 Chatham Forest Dr (27312-5729)
PHONE................................919 542-4242
Ronnie Mannes, *Mgr*
EMP: 7
Web: www.chandlerconcrete.com
SIC: 3273 Ready-mixed concrete
PA: Chandler Concrete Co., Inc.
   1006 S Church Street
   Burlington NC 27215

(G-9780)
COUNTRY CORNER
2193 Us 64 Business E (27312-7672)
PHONE................................919 444-9663
Alicia Womble, *Owner*
EMP: 6 EST: 2004
SALES (est): 207.85K Privately Held
SIC: 3581 Automatic vending machines

(G-9781)
DEVMIR LEGWEAR INC
136 Fayetteville St (27312-0750)
PHONE................................919 545-5500
Altug Sipal, *Pr*
▲ EMP: 4 EST: 2010
SALES (est): 417.74K Privately Held
Web: www.devmir.com
SIC: 2252 Anklets (hosiery)

(G-9782)
DLSS MANUFACTURING LLC
697 Hillsboro St (27312-5979)
P.O. Box 1549 (27312-1549)
PHONE................................919 619-7594
Erik Berg, *Managing Member*
EMP: 4 EST: 2010
SALES (est): 555.22K Privately Held
Web: www.dlssmfg.com
SIC: 3446 Architectural metalwork

(G-9783)
FAIR GAME BEVERAGE COMPANY
220 Lorax Ln Unit 15 (27312-8898)
PHONE................................919 245-5434
Lyle Estill, *Pr*
Chris Jude, *COO*
▲ EMP: 4 EST: 2015
SALES (est): 251.2K Privately Held
Web: www.fairgamebeverage.com
SIC: 2085 2084 Distilled and blended liquors
; Wines, brandy, and brandy spirits

(G-9784)
HOMESERVE NC LLC
2225 Castle Rock Farm Rd (27312-9648)
PHONE................................740 552-8497
EMP: 4 EST: 2022
SALES (est): 261.94K Privately Held
SIC: 1389 Construction, repair, and
dismantling services

(G-9785)
HOMS LLC
Also Called: Homs
193 Lorax Ln (27312-5763)
P.O. Box 1887 (27312-1887)
PHONE................................919 533-4752
▲ EMP: 8 EST: 1998
SQ FT: 15,000
SALES (est): 997.19K Privately Held
Web: www.homs.com
SIC: 2879 Pesticides, agricultural or
household

(G-9786)
PROPELLA THERAPEUTICS INC
120 Mosaic Blvd Ste 120-3 (27312-4966)

PHONE................................703 631-7523
William Moore, *Pr*
EMP: 6 EST: 2020
SALES (est): 497.86K Privately Held
Web: www.propellatx.com
SIC: 2834 Pharmaceutical preparations
PA: Astellas Pharma Inc.
   2-5-1, Nihombashihoncho
   Chuo-Ku TKY 103-0

(G-9787)
RANCHO PARK PUBLISHING INC
8 Matchwood (27312-8601)
PHONE................................919 942-9493
Stan Cheren, *Pr*
EMP: 5 EST: 1992
SALES (est): 55.17K Privately Held
Web: www.ranchopark.com
SIC: 2741 Miscellaneous publishing

(G-9788)
REVOLUTION PD LLC
379 White Smith Rd (27312-6028)
PHONE................................919 949-0241
EMP: 4 EST: 2011
SALES (est): 1.57MM Privately Held
Web: www.revolutionpd.com
SIC: 3089 3465 Molding primary plastics;
Moldings or trim, automobile: stamped metal

(G-9789)
ROLLS ENTERPRISES INC
2277 Otis Johnson Rd (27312-6275)
PHONE................................919 545-9401
Rollo T Varkey, *Pr*
▲ EMP: 4 EST: 2000
SALES (est): 385.86K Privately Held
Web: www.keralacurry.com
SIC: 2099 Ready-to-eat meals, salads, and
sandwiches

(G-9790)
TYNDALL MACHINE TOOL INC
Also Called: Tyndall Machine Technologies
154 Dogwood Ln (27312-4119)
PHONE................................919 542-4014
Dwight Tyndall, *Pr*
EMP: 6 EST: 1983
SALES (est): 175.9K Privately Held
SIC: 3599 Machine shop, jobbing and repair

(G-9791)
US MICROWAVE INC
164 Fearrington Post (27312-8553)
PHONE................................520 891-2444
Ana C Brownstein, *Pr*
Dennis Brownstein, *VP*
EMP: 6 EST: 1984
SALES (est): 408.31K Privately Held
SIC: 3679 5065 Microwave components;
Communication equipment

Pleasant Garden
Guilford County

(G-9792)
MEDLEY S GARAGE WELDING
5879 Cherokee Trl (27313-9600)
PHONE................................336 674-0422
Garland Medley, *Prin*
EMP: 4 EST: 2008
SALES (est): 347.62K Privately Held
SIC: 7692 Welding repair

(G-9793)
PLEASANT GARDEN DRY KILN
1221 Briarcrest Dr (27313-9234)
P.O. Box 457 (27313-0457)
PHONE................................336 674-2863

Derrick Milliken, *Pt*
EMP: 9 EST: 1969
SQ FT: 200
SALES (est): 120.7K Privately Held
SIC: 2421 Kiln drying of lumber

(G-9794)
SMITH FAMILY SCREEN PRINTING
5311 Appomattox Rd (27313-8255)
PHONE................................336 317-4849
EMP: 4 EST: 2017
SALES (est): 83.91K Privately Held
SIC: 2752 Commercial printing, lithographic

(G-9795)
TARHEEL SOLUTIONS LLC
6463 Walter Wright Rd (27313-9715)
PHONE................................336 420-9265
Marcus B Talcott, *Pr*
EMP: 4 EST: 2014
SALES (est): 92.36K Privately Held
SIC: 2834 Pharmaceutical preparations

(G-9796)
WYRICK MACHINE AND TOOL CO
1215 Kearns Hackett Rd (27313-8217)
P.O. Box 573 (27313-0573)
PHONE................................336 841-8261
Chet Wyrick, *Pr*
Ann Wyrick, *Treas*
EMP: 6 EST: 1987
SQ FT: 2,000
SALES (est): 1.1MM Privately Held
SIC: 3599 Machine shop, jobbing and repair

Pleasant Hill
Northampton County

(G-9797)
GLOVER MATERIALS INC (PA)
4493 Us Highway 301 (27866-9687)
P.O. Box 40 (27866-0040)
PHONE................................252 536-2660
John M Glover, *Pr*
Matthew B Glover, *VP*
Jewel G Glover, *Sec*
EMP: 5 EST: 1987
SALES (est): 2.43MM Privately Held
Web: www.gloverconstruction.com
SIC: 5211 1442 Masonry materials and
supplies; Construction sand mining

Plymouth
Washington County

(G-9798)
BARNES LOGGING CO INC
308 Golf Rd (27962-1114)
P.O. Box 665 (27962-0665)
PHONE................................252 799-6016
Jack O Barnes Junior, *Pr*
Jack O Barnes Senior, *VP*
Connie Barnes, *Treas*
Christine Barnes, *Sec*
EMP: 14 EST: 1984
SQ FT: 1,100
SALES (est): 1.53MM Privately Held
SIC: 2411 Logging camps and contractors

(G-9799)
BASTROP SKID COMPANY (PA)
111 W Water St (27962-1305)
PHONE................................252 793-6600
Thomas Harrison, *Pr*
Rexanne Harrison, *VP*
Trudy C Respess, *Sec*
EMP: 9 EST: 1982
SQ FT: 1,000

SALES (est): 2.69MM
SALES (corp-wide): 2.69MM Privately
Held
SIC: 2448 5031 Pallets, wood; Lumber:
rough, dressed, and finished

(G-9800)
CAROLINA MAT INCORPORATED
193 Hwy 149 N (27962-9309)
P.O. Box 339 (27962-0339)
PHONE................................252 793-1111
Susan Harrison, *Pr*
Margaret Harrison, *Pr*
Susan Harrison, *VP*
EMP: 15 EST: 1985
SQ FT: 6,000
SALES (est): 712.84K Privately Held
Web: www.carolinamat.com
SIC: 2448 Pallets, wood

(G-9801)
DIVERSIFIED WOOD PRODUCTS INC
Also Called: Dwp
111 W Water St Ste 1 (27962-1347)
P.O. Box 706 (27962-0706)
PHONE................................252 793-6600
Thomas Harrison, *Pr*
Thomas J Harrison, *Pr*
Roxanne Harrison, *VP*
Trudy Respess, *Sec*
EMP: 15 EST: 1995
SQ FT: 10,000
SALES (est): 4.14MM Privately Held
Web: www.dwpworks.com
SIC: 2448 Pallets, wood

(G-9802)
DOMTAR PAPER COMPANY LLC
Also Called: Plymouth Mill
1375 Nc Hwy 149 N (27962)
P.O. Box 747 (27962-0747)
PHONE................................252 793-8111
Jack Bray, *Brnch Mgr*
EMP: 375
Web: www.domtar.com
SIC: 2621 2631 2421 Paper mills;
Paperboard mills; Sawmills and planing
mills, general
HQ: Domtar Paper Company, Llc
   234 Kingsley Park Dr
   Fort Mill SC 29715

(G-9803)
EDSEL G BARNES JR INC
1458 Morrattock Rd (27962-8401)
PHONE................................252 793-4170
Edsel G Barnes Junior, *Pr*
EMP: 13 EST: 2013
SALES (est): 1.08MM Privately Held
SIC: 2411 Logging

(G-9804)
GEO SPECIALTY CHEMICALS INC
Main St Extension (27962)
P.O. Box 68 (27962-0068)
PHONE................................252 793-2121
Herb Myers, *Mgr*
EMP: 4
SALES (corp-wide): 214.44MM Privately
Held
Web: www.geosc.com
SIC: 2819 Industrial inorganic chemicals, nec
HQ: Geo Specialty Chemicals, Inc.
   105 N Axtel St
   Milford IL 60953

(G-9805)
H & L LOGGING INC
1166 Long Ridge Rd (27962-8707)
PHONE................................252 793-2778
Louis E White, *Pr*

2025 Harris North Carolina
Manufacturers Directory
▲ = Import ▼ = Export
◆ = Import/Export

Vanessa White, *VP*
EMP: 17 EST: 1999
SALES (est): 1.09MM **Privately Held**
Web: www.renttoownlewistonme.com
SIC: 2411 Logging camps and contractors

(G-9806)
M M & D HARVESTING INC
385 Roxie Reese Rd (27962-9084)
PHONE..................................252 793-4074
Robert Holcomb, *Pr*
Debbie Holcomb, *Sec*
EMP: 5 EST: 1994
SALES (est): 517.83K **Privately Held**
SIC: 2411 Logging

(G-9807)
RICHARD WEST CO INC
1174 Us Highway 64 W (27962-8846)
P.O. Box 868 (27962-0868)
PHONE..................................252 793-4440
Harvey West, *Pr*
Richard G West, *VP*
Ethel West, *Sec*
EMP: 8 EST: 1937
SQ FT: 22,000
SALES (est): 350.96K **Privately Held**
Web: www.richardwestcompany.com
SIC: 2448 Pallets, wood

(G-9808)
WEYERHAEUSER COMPANY
1000 Nc Highway 149 N (27962-9544)
P.O. Box 787 (27962-0787)
PHONE..................................252 791-3200
Kenneth Mcride, *Mgr*
EMP: 11
SALES (corp-wide): 7.12B **Publicly Held**
Web: www.weyerhaeuser.com
SIC: 5031 2421 Lumber: rough, dressed,
and finished; Lumber: rough, sawed, or
planed
PA: Weyerhaeuser Company
220 Occidental Ave S
Seattle WA 98104
206 539-3000

Point Harbor
Currituck County

(G-9809)
BUFFALO CITY DISTILLERY LLC
8821 Caratoke Hwy (27964-9602)
PHONE..................................252 256-1477
Clifford C Byrum Junior, *Managing Member*
EMP: 5 EST: 2018
SALES (est): 370.91K **Privately Held**
Web: www.buffalocitydistillery.com
SIC: 2085 Distilled and blended liquors

Polkton
Anson County

(G-9810)
A B METALS OF POLKTON LLC
6245 Us Highway 74 W (28135-8432)
PHONE..................................704 694-6635
EMP: 6 EST: 2020
SALES (est): 364.61K **Privately Held**
Web: www.abmetalsllc.com
SIC: 3444 Metal roofing and roof drainage
equipment

(G-9811)
**AMERICAN BUILDERS ANSON INC
(PA)**
8564 Hwy 74 W (28135-8446)

P.O. Box 8 (28135-0008)
PHONE..................................704 272-7655
W Bruce Thomas, *Pr*
Walter G Thomas Junior, *VP*
Ralph E Thomas, *VP*
Patricia M Thomas, *Sec*
EMP: 20 EST: 1972
SQ FT: 2,400
SALES (est): 955.57K
SALES (corp-wide): 955.57K **Privately
Held**
SIC: 1542 3325 Farm building construction;
Rolling mill rolls, cast steel

(G-9812)
AMP AGENCY
Also Called: Residential/Commercial Cnstr
7550 Us Highway 74 W (28135-8436)
PHONE..................................704 430-2313
Akeiamarie Saunders, *CEO*
EMP: 5 EST: 2022
SALES (est): 541.77K **Privately Held**
Web: www.ampagency.com
SIC: 1389 7389 Construction, repair, and
dismantling services; Design, commercial
and industrial

(G-9813)
ANSON MACHINE WORKS INC
100 Efird Cir (28135-2100)
P.O. Box 269 (28133-0269)
PHONE..................................704 272-7657
Steve Garris, *Pr*
Lynn Godwin, *VP*
Randy Smith, *Sec*
Joel L Godwin, *Treas*
EMP: 22 EST: 1988
SQ FT: 17,500
SALES (est): 4.08MM **Privately Held**
Web: www.ansonmachine.com
SIC: 3599 Machine shop, jobbing and repair

(G-9814)
D & T SOY CANDLES
152 Hawk Rd (28135-7223)
PHONE..................................704 320-2804
Teresa Mercer, *Prin*
EMP: 4 EST: 2015
SALES (est): 70.95K **Privately Held**
SIC: 3999 Candles

(G-9815)
SOUTHERN FABRICATORS INC
8188 Us Highway 74 W (28135-8442)
P.O. Box 97 (28135-0097)
PHONE..................................704 272-7615
Ken Carpenter Senior, *Pr*
Hugh Efird, *Stockholder**
Ken Carpenter Junior, *Prin*
▲ **EMP: 80 EST:** 1968
SQ FT: 100,000
SALES (est): 22.22MM **Privately Held**
Web: www.southernfabricators.net
SIC: 3444 Sheet metalwork

Pollocksville
Jones County

(G-9816)
**ADVANCED PLASTIC EXTRUSION
LLC**
Also Called: Apex
213 Sermon Rd (28573-9218)
PHONE..................................252 224-1444
Ronald Buck, *Managing Member*
EMP: 7 EST: 2014
SALES (est): 2.68MM **Privately Held**
Web: www.apex-extrusion.com

SIC: 3089 Injection molding of plastics

(G-9817)
MARINE & INDUSTRIAL PLASTICS
Hwy 17 Sermon Lane (28573)
PHONE..................................252 224-1000
C Hunter Williams, *Pr*
Susan T Williams, *Sec*
EMP: 8 EST: 1991
SALES (est): 117.37K **Privately Held**
SIC: 3089 3081 Plastics boats and other
marine equipment; Unsupported plastics
film and sheet

(G-9818)
MIKE S CUSTOM CABINETS INC
587 Island Creek Rd (28573-9451)
PHONE..................................252 224-5351
Michael Meadows, *Pr*
Kimberly A Meadows, *Sec*
EMP: 8 EST: 1991
SALES (est): 392.45K **Privately Held**
Web: www.mikescustomcabinetsinc.com
SIC: 2434 Wood kitchen cabinets

Potecasi
Northampton County

(G-9819)
BRANT & LASSITER SEPTIC TANK
Hwy 35 (27867)
P.O. Box 157 (27867-0157)
PHONE..................................252 587-4321
David Cooper, *Pr*
Felisia Cooper, *VP*
EMP: 6 EST: 1968
SQ FT: 3,000
SALES (est): 497.31K **Privately Held**
Web: www.bryantandlassiter.com
SIC: 3272 7699 Septic tanks, concrete;
Aircraft and heavy equipment repair
services

Powells Point
Currituck County

(G-9820)
CAROLINA CUSTOM CABINETS INC
Also Called: Carolina Cstm Cabinets & Furn
102 Park Dr (27966-9616)
P.O. Box 252 (27949-0252)
PHONE..................................252 491-5475
Rex Filion, *Pr*
Arlene Filion, *Sec*
EMP: 8 EST: 1989
SQ FT: 5,000
SALES (est): 330.24K **Privately Held**
Web: www.carolinacustomcabinet.com
SIC: 2434 Wood kitchen cabinets

(G-9821)
HARCO AIR LLC
116 Ballast Rock Rd Unit L (27966-9614)
PHONE..................................252 491-5220
Phillip Rose, *Managing Member*
Robert Harwood Junior, *Managing Member*
EMP: 8 EST: 2017
SALES (est): 284.55K **Privately Held**
SIC: 1711 3444 Heating and air conditioning
contractors; Ducts, sheet metal

(G-9822)
JAMES LAMMERS
Also Called: Lammers Glass & Design
7715 Caratoke Hwy (27966-9738)
P.O. Box 428 (27966-0428)
PHONE..................................252 491-2303
James Lammers, *Owner*

Theresa G Lammers, *Genl Mgr*
EMP: 4 EST: 1972
SALES (est): 245.52K **Privately Held**
Web: www.lammersglass.com
SIC: 5947 3231 Gift shop; Stained glass:
made from purchased glass

Princeton
Johnston County

(G-9823)
CAROLINA PRINTING CO
640 Quarterhorse Rd (27569-8645)
PHONE..................................919 834-0433
Steve Yancey, *Owner*
EMP: 4 EST: 1982
SALES (est): 245.94K **Privately Held**
Web: www.carolinaprintingcompany.com
SIC: 2752 2759 Offset printing; Letterpress
printing

(G-9824)
**HEIDELBERG MTLS STHAST AGG
LLC**
476 Edwards Rd (27569-7041)
P.O. Box 180 (27569-0180)
PHONE..................................919 936-4221
Jesse Bizzell, *Mgr*
EMP: 24
SALES (corp-wide): 23.02B **Privately Held**
Web: www.hansonbiz.com
SIC: 1422 1521 Crushed and broken
limestone; Single-family housing
construction
HQ: Heidelberg Materials Southeast Agg Llc
3237 Satellite Blvd # 30
Duluth GA 30096
770 491-2706

(G-9825)
POWERSECURE INC
Also Called: Southern Flow Companies
6137 Princeton Kenly Rd (27569-7955)
PHONE..................................919 818-8700
Christ Edge, *Brnch Mgr*
EMP: 9
SALES (corp-wide): 26.72B **Publicly Held**
Web: www.powersecure.com
SIC: 3621 Power generators
HQ: Powersecure, Inc.
4068 Stirrup Creek Dr
Durham NC 27703
919 556-3056

(G-9826)
S T WOOTEN CORPORATION
Princeton Commercial Cnstr Off
6401 Us Highway 70 E (27569-7828)
PHONE..................................919 965-9880
Reade Dawson, *Mgr*
EMP: 22
SALES (corp-wide): 319.83MM **Privately
Held**
Web: www.stwcorp.com
SIC: 2951 1611 1794 Asphalt paving
mixtures and blocks; Highway and street
construction; Excavation work
PA: S. T. Wooten Corporation
3801 Black Creek Rd Se
Wilson NC 27894
252 291-5165

(G-9827)
S T WOOTEN CORPORATION
Also Called: Princeton Asphalt Plant
6401 Us Highway 70 E (27569-7828)
PHONE..................................919 965-7176
David Fountain, *Mgr*
EMP: 22

SALES (corp-wide): 319.83MM **Privately Held**
Web: www.stwcorp.com
SIC: 3531 Asphalt plant, including gravel-mix type
PA: S. T. Wooten Corporation
3801 Black Creek Rd Se
Wilson NC 27894
252 291-5165

Princeville
Edgecombe County

(G-9828)
SOUTHERN STATES COOP INC
Also Called: Tarboro Serv
142 Commercial Rd (27886-9728)
P.O. Box 1214 (27886-1214)
PHONE.............................252 823-2520
Joe Dupree, *Mgr*
EMP: 7
SALES (corp-wide): 1.71B **Privately Held**
Web: www.southernstates.com
SIC: 2048 5999 Prepared feeds, nec; Farm equipment and supplies
PA: Southern States Cooperative, Incorporated
6606 W Broad St Ste B
Richmond VA 23230
804 281-1000

Prospect Hill
Caswell County

(G-9829)
ROYAL PARK UNIFORMS INC
14139 Nc Highway 86 S (27314-9488)
P.O. Box 24 (27314-0024)
PHONE.............................336 562-3345
William K Royal, *Pr*
Geraldine Royal, *
Steven R Royal, *
Gregory W Royal, *
◆ **EMP:** 7 **EST:** 1973
SQ FT: 175,000
SALES (est): 309.6K **Privately Held**
Web: www.royal-park.com
SIC: 2389 Uniforms and vestments

(G-9830)
W T MANDER & SON INC
1587 Egypt Rd (27314-9525)
PHONE.............................336 562-5755
Tom Mander, *Pr*
Joy Mander, *VP*
Jacob Mander, *Treas*
EMP: 5 **EST:** 1998
SALES (est): 216.1K **Privately Held**
SIC: 3545 Machine tool accessories

Purlear
Wilkes County

(G-9831)
GREENE LOGGING
9145 Boone Trl (28665-9191)
PHONE.............................336 667-6960
Scott Greene, *Owner*
EMP: 5 **EST:** 2000
SALES (est): 150.15K **Privately Held**
Web: www.greenelogging.com
SIC: 2411 Logging camps and contractors

Raeford
Hoke County

(G-9832)
BENNETT ELEC MAINT & CNSTR LLC
Also Called: Electrical
586 Allegiance St (28376-8656)
PHONE.............................910 231-0300
Jimmy Bennett, *CEO*
EMP: 5 **EST:** 2001
SALES (est): 79.27K **Privately Held**
Web: www.fayetteville-nc-electrician.com
SIC: 1521 1389 1731 Single-family housing construction; Construction, repair, and dismantling services; Electrical work

(G-9833)
BUTTERBALL LLC
1140 E Central Ave (28376-3000)
PHONE.............................910 875-8711
EMP: 275
SALES (corp-wide): 9.1B **Publicly Held**
Web: www.butterballfoodservice.com
SIC: 2015 Turkey, processed, nsk
HQ: Butterball, Llc
1 Butterball Ln
Garner NC 27529
919 255-7900

(G-9834)
CONOPCO INC
Also Called: Unilever
100 Faberge Blvd (28376-3406)
PHONE.............................910 875-4121
Kevin Beck, *Genl Mgr*
EMP: 290
SALES (corp-wide): 64.79B **Privately Held**
Web: www.conopco.com
SIC: 2844 Perfumes, cosmetics and other toilet preparations
HQ: Conopco, Inc.
700 Sylvan Ave
Englewood Cliffs NJ 07632
201 894-7760

(G-9835)
COPIA LABS INC
2501 Hwy 401 Bus (28376-5776)
P.O. Box 447 (28376-0447)
PHONE.............................910 904-1000
J Todd Sumner, *Pr*
Frances Sumner, *Sec*
EMP: 5 **EST:** 1994
SQ FT: 6,700
SALES (est): 238.07K **Privately Held**
Web: www.copialabs.net
SIC: 2899 Chemical preparations, nec

(G-9836)
CURRIE MOTORSPORTS INC
Also Called: CMS Printing Services
611 College Dr (28376-2403)
P.O. Box 972 (28376-0972)
PHONE.............................910 580-1765
Robie W Currie, *CEO*
Linda Cadlett, *Sec*
EMP: 4 **EST:** 2007
SALES (est): 183.36K **Privately Held**
SIC: 2752 Commercial printing, lithographic

(G-9837)
FARM CHEMICALS INC (PA)
Also Called: Fci-An Agricultural Service Co
2274 Saint Pauls Dr (28376-5616)
P.O. Box 667 (28376-0667)
PHONE.............................910 875-4277
Alfred K Leach Junior, *Pr*
Earl Hendrix, *Sec*

▲ **EMP:** 12 **EST:** 1964
SQ FT: 2,500
SALES (est): 13.75MM
SALES (corp-wide): 13.75MM **Privately Held**
Web: www.fciag.com
SIC: 5153 2873 Grains; Nitrogen solutions (fertilizer)

(G-9838)
GARNERS SEPTIC TANK INC
8574 Turnpike Rd (28376-6327)
PHONE.............................919 718-5181
Eddie Garner, *Pr*
EMP: 9 **EST:** 2017
SALES (est): 1.19MM **Privately Held**
Web: www.garnersseptictank.com
SIC: 3272 Septic tanks, concrete

(G-9839)
GINAS PROCESSING & PRTG CTR
114 Harris Ln (28376-9647)
PHONE.............................910 476-0037
EMP: 4 **EST:** 2014
SALES (est): 83.91K **Privately Held**
SIC: 2752 Commercial printing, lithographic

(G-9840)
HOUSE OF RAEFORD FARMS INC
1000 E Central Ave (28376-3039)
P.O. Box 3628 (29070-1628)
PHONE.............................910 289-3191
Donald Taber, *Ch*
EMP: 734
SALES (corp-wide): 1.79B **Privately Held**
Web: www.houseofraeford.com
SIC: 2015 Poultry slaughtering and processing
HQ: House Of Raeford Farms, Inc.
3333 S Us Highway 117
Rose Hill NC 28458
912 222-4090

(G-9841)
I T G RAEFORD
1001 Turnpike Rd (28376-8566)
PHONE.............................910 875-3736
Barry Tapp, *Prin*
EMP: 4 **EST:** 2010
SALES (est): 267.74K **Privately Held**
SIC: 2231 Broadwoven fabric mills, wool

(G-9842)
MOES HNDY SVCS FNCE INSTL MNO
185 Desert Orchid Cir (28376-1546)
PHONE.............................910 712-1402
Jamie Mclaurin, *CEO*
EMP: 5 **EST:** 2022
SALES (est): 75.42K **Privately Held**
SIC: 7699 3312 Repair services, nec; Fence posts, iron and steel

(G-9843)
NATURES CUP LLC
1930 Club Pond Rd (28376-8691)
PHONE.............................910 795-2700
Aundrea Dinkins, *Managing Member*
EMP: 6 **EST:** 2021
SALES (est): 150K **Privately Held**
SIC: 2099 Tea blending

(G-9844)
PARACLETE XP SKY VENTURE LLC
190 Paraclete Dr (28376-6844)
PHONE.............................910 848-2600
EMP: 12 **EST:** 2009
SALES (est): 267.46K **Privately Held**
Web: www.paracletexp.com
SIC: 7999 2759 Instruction schools, camps, and services; Screen printing

(G-9845)
PARACLETE XP SKYVENTURE LLC
925 Doc Brown Rd (28376-8081)
PHONE.............................910 904-0027
Timothy D'annunzio, *Managing Member*
EMP: 35 **EST:** 2007
SALES (est): 1.29MM **Privately Held**
Web: www.paracletexp.com
SIC: 7999 2759 Instruction schools, camps, and services; Screen printing

(G-9846)
PARISH SIGN & SERVICE INC
627 Laurinburg Rd (28376-2526)
P.O. Box 766 (28376-0766)
PHONE.............................910 875-6121
William R Parish, *Pr*
Linda Parish, *Sec*
EMP: 20 **EST:** 1982
SQ FT: 7,000
SALES (est): 2.43MM **Privately Held**
Web: www.parishsigns.com
SIC: 3993 1799 Electric signs; Sign installation and maintenance

(G-9847)
PENNSYLVANIA TRANS TECH INC
Also Called: Pennsylvania Transformer Co
201 Carolina Dr (28376-9272)
PHONE.............................910 875-7600
Ravi Rahangdera, *Pr*
EMP: 65
SALES (corp-wide): 23.67B **Publicly Held**
Web: www.patransformer.com
SIC: 3612 Distribution transformers, electric
HQ: Pennsylvania Transformer Technology, Llc
30 Curry Ave Ste 2
Canonsburg PA 15317
724 873-2100

(G-9848)
PRECISE SHEET METAL MECH LLC
124 Winterfield Dr (28376-5408)
P.O. Box 1740 (28376-1740)
PHONE.............................336 693-3246
Adela Garcia, *Prin*
EMP: 5 **EST:** 2019
SALES (est): 2.16MM **Privately Held**
SIC: 3444 Sheet metalwork

(G-9849)
RAINEY AND WILSON LOGISTICS
1308 Checker Dr (28376-5041)
PHONE.............................910 736-8540
Lawerence Rainey, *Prin*
EMP: 4 **EST:** 2020
SALES (est): 275.7K **Privately Held**
SIC: 3537 Trucks, tractors, loaders, carriers, and similar equipment

(G-9850)
REBECCA TRICKEY
Also Called: Rebecca Kaye International
389 Gibson Dr (28376-5569)
PHONE.............................910 584-5549
EMP: 6 **EST:** 2012
SALES (est): 361.67K **Privately Held**
SIC: 2844 7389 Hair preparations, including shampoos; Business Activities at Non-Commercial Site

(G-9851)
ROCKFISH CREEK WINERY LLC
1709 Arabia Rd (28376-7062)
PHONE.............................910 729-0648
Imberly Rulli, *Prin*
EMP: 6 **EST:** 2018
SALES (est): 524.31K **Privately Held**
Web: www.rockfishcreekwinery.com

▲ = Import ▼ = Export
◆ = Import/Export

SIC: 2084 Wines

(G-9852)
SPC-USA INC
Also Called: Sun Path Contracting
404 W Edinborough Ave (28376-2832)
PHONE..............................910 875-9002
Patricia Thomas, *Pr*
EMP: 5 **EST:** 2005
SALES (est): 225.14K **Privately Held**
Web: www.sunpath.com
SIC: 2399 Fabricated textile products, nec

(G-9853)
SUN PATH PRODUCTS INC
404 W Edinborough Ave (28376-2832)
PHONE..............................910 875-9002
Patricia Thomas, *Pr*
EMP: 90 **EST:** 1986
SQ FT: 28,000
SALES (est): 9.87MM **Privately Held**
Web: www.sunpath.com
SIC: 3429 Parachute hardware

(G-9854)
TYTON NC BIOFUELS LLC
800 Pate Rd (28376-9189)
PHONE..............................910 878-7820
Benjamin Steves, *
EMP: 45 **EST:** 2014
SQ FT: 4,000
SALES (est): 2.55MM **Privately Held**
Web: www.tytonbiofuels.com
SIC: 2869 Ethyl alcohol, ethanol

(G-9855)
UNILEVER
4152 Turnpike Rd (28376-7343)
PHONE..............................910 988-1054
Lauren Garner, *Prin*
EMP: 14 **EST:** 2019
SALES (est): 140.7K **Privately Held**
Web: www.unilever.com
SIC: 2844 Perfumes, cosmetics and other
   toilet preparations

(G-9856)
WILLIAM BRANTLEY
Also Called: Professnal Prprty Prservations
637 Dunrobin Dr (28376-9149)
PHONE..............................910 627-7286
William Brantley, *Owner*
EMP: 4 **EST:** 2020
SALES (est): 83K **Privately Held**
SIC: 1389 Construction, repair, and
   dismantling services

Raleigh
Wake County

(G-9857)
2391 EATONS FERRY RD ASSOC LLC
7610 Six Forks Rd Ste 200 (27615-5049)
PHONE..............................919 844-0565
Rabon Robert Gary, *Prin*
EMP: 4 **EST:** 2014
SALES (est): 830.22K **Privately Held**
SIC: 3625 Motor controls and accessories

(G-9858)
4 OVER LLC
Also Called: ASAP Printing
5609 Departure Dr (27616-1842)
PHONE..............................919 875-3187
Ed Dignam, *Brnch Mgr*
EMP: 15
SALES (corp-wide): 172.36MM **Privately
Held**
Web: www.4over.com

SIC: 2752 Offset printing
HQ: 4 Over, Llc
   1225 Loa Angeles St
   Glendale CA 91204
   818 246-1170

(G-9859)
A & B CHEM-DRY
4208 Bertram Dr (27604-2658)
PHONE..............................919 878-02ᴿ8
EMP: 16 **EST:** 1999
SALES (est): 213.93K **Privately Held**
Web: www.abchemdry.com
SIC: 7349 2842 Building maintenance
   services, nec; Polishes and sanitation goods

(G-9860)
A1GUMBALLS
Also Called: A1 Vending
316 W Millbrook Rd Ste 113 (27609-4482)
PHONE..............................919 494-1322
Scott Tidball, *Owner*
EMP: 5 **EST:** 2000
SALES (est): 1.01MM **Privately Held**
Web: www.frugalburger.com
SIC: 3556 Chewing gum machinery

(G-9861)
AARDVARK SCREEN PRINTING
1600 Automotive Way (27604-2050)
PHONE..............................919 829-9058
Greg A Clayton, *Pt*
EMP: 5 **EST:** 1999
SALES (est): 88.94K **Privately Held**
Web: www.aardvarkscreenprinting.net
SIC: 2759 Screen printing

(G-9862)
ABB ENTERPRISE SOFTWARE INC
Also Called: Power Technologies
1021 Main Campus Dr (27606-5238)
P.O. Box 90999 (27675-0999)
PHONE..............................919 582-3283
Jamie Travino, *Dir*
EMP: 150
Web: new.abb.com
SIC: 3612 8711 3613 3625 Transformers,
   except electric; Engineering services;
   Switchgear and switchboard apparatus;
   Relays and industrial controls
HQ: Abb Inc.
   305 Gregson Dr
   Cary NC 27511

(G-9863)
ABB INC
901 Main Campus Dr Ste 300
(27606-5293)
PHONE..............................919 856-3920
EMP: 7
Web: www.abb.com
SIC: 3612 Transformers, except electric
HQ: Abb Inc.
   305 Gregson Dr
   Cary NC 27511

(G-9864)
ABB INC
Also Called: ABB Power Systems
1021 Main Campus Dr (27606-5239)
P.O. Box 91209 (27675-1209)
PHONE..............................919 856-2360
Greg Scheu, *Brnch Mgr*
EMP: 76
Web: new.abb.com
SIC: 3613 3675 3612 Switchgear and
   switchboard apparatus; Electronic
   capacitors; Power and distribution
   transformers
HQ: Abb Inc.
   305 Gregson Dr

Cary NC 27511

(G-9865)
ABB POWER SYSTEMS INC
901 Main Campus Dr Ste 300
(27606-5293)
PHONE..............................919 856-2389
EMP: 4 **EST:** 2016
SALES (est): 563.76K **Privately Held**
Web: www.abb.com
SIC: 3612 Transformers, except electric
PA: Abb Ltd
   Affolternstrasse 44
   Zurich ZH 8050

(G-9866)
ABB POWER T & D COMPANY INC
1021 Main Campus Dr (27606-5238)
P.O. Box 91471 (27675-1471)
PHONE..............................919 856-3806
Enrique Santacana, *Pr*
▼ **EMP:** 1300 **EST:** 1988
SALES (est): 20.17MM **Privately Held**
SIC: 3612 Distribution transformers, electric
HQ: Abb Inc.
   305 Gregson Dr
   Cary NC 27511

(G-9867)
ABC FITNESS PRODUCTS LLC (PA)
8541 Glenwood Ave (27612-7358)
PHONE..............................704 649-0000
▲ **EMP:** 6 **EST:** 2011
SALES (est): 1.09MM
SALES (corp-wide): 1.09MM **Privately
Held**
Web: www.abcfitnessproducts.com
SIC: 3949 Exercise equipment

(G-9868)
ABLE SOFTSYSTEMS CORP
1017 Main Campus Dr Ste 1501
(27606-5204)
PHONE..............................919 241-7907
John Kahsai, *Pr*
Ruth Kahsai, *Prin*
EMP: 5 **EST:** 2002
SALES (est): 342.81K **Privately Held**
SIC: 7372 7371 Prepackaged software;
   Software programming applications

(G-9869)
ABS SOUTHEAST LLC (PA)
5902 Fayetteville Rd (27603-4530)
PHONE..............................919 329-0014
Wayne Sullivan, *Managing Member*
EMP: 10 **EST:** 2012
SALES (est): 3.91MM
SALES (corp-wide): 3.91MM **Privately
Held**
Web: www.truteam.com
SIC: 3089 1742 Gutters (glass fiber
   reinforced), fiberglass or plastics;
   Insulation, buildings

(G-9870)
ABSOLENT INC
6541 Meridien Dr Ste 125 (27616-3211)
P.O. Box 1279 (27596-1279)
PHONE..............................919 570-2862
Joshua Hannah, *Pr*
Edwin Sithes, *Pr*
Charles Sithes, *VP*
Brittany Long, *Mgr*
▲ **EMP:** 17 **EST:** 2006
SALES (est): 4.95MM **Privately Held**
Web: www.avanienvironmental.com
SIC: 3564 Air purification equipment

(G-9871)
ACC SPORTS JOURNAL
3012 Highwoods Blvd Ste 200
(27604-1037)
PHONE..............................919 846-7502
David Glenn, *Editor*
EMP: 4 **EST:** 2010
SALES (est): 101.35K **Privately Held**
Web: www.accsports.com
SIC: 2711 Newspapers, publishing and
   printing

(G-9872)
ACCESS NEWSWIRE INC (PA)
Also Called: Issuer Direct
1 Glenwood Ave Ste 1001 (27603)
PHONE..............................919 481-4000
Brian R Balbirnie, *Pr*
Timothy Pitoniak, *CFO*
Steven Knerr, *CFO*
EMP: 104 **EST:** 1988
SQ FT: 9,766
SALES (est): 33.38MM **Publicly Held**
Web: www.issuerdirect.com
SIC: 7372 8742 Application computer
   software; Management consulting services

(G-9873)
ACCORD HEALTHCARE INC (HQ)
8041 Arco Corporate Dr Ste 200
(27617-2091)
PHONE..............................919 941-7878
Gerald Price, *Pr*
Burt Sullivan, *
▼ **EMP:** 35 **EST:** 2005
SQ FT: 6,160
SALES (est): 14.75MM **Privately Held**
Web: www.accordhealthcare.us
SIC: 2834 8011 Pharmaceutical preparations
   ; Oncologist
PA: Intas Pharmaceuticals Limited
   Corporate House, Plot No. 255,
   Magnet Corporate Park,
   Ahmedabad GJ 38005

(G-9874)
ACCUMED CORP (HQ)
160 Mine Lake Ct Ste 200 (27615-6417)
PHONE..............................800 278-6796
Jason Cardew, *CEO*
EMP: 100 **EST:** 2014
SALES (est): 32.16MM
SALES (corp-wide): 23.31B **Publicly Held**
Web: www.accumedtech.com
SIC: 3841 Medical instruments and
   equipment, blood and bone work
PA: Lear Corporation
   21557 Telegraph Rd
   Southfield MI 48033
   248 447-1500

(G-9875)
ACCURATE MACHINE & TOOL LLC
5124 Trademark Dr (27610-3024)
PHONE..............................919 212-0266
EMP: 14 **EST:** 2003
SQ FT: 20,300
SALES (est): 1.39MM **Privately Held**
Web: www.accuratemachining.com
SIC: 3599 Machine shop, jobbing and repair

(G-9876)
**ACROPLIS CNTRLS ENGINEERS
PLLC**
313 S Blount St Ste 200d (27601-1861)
PHONE..............................919 275-3884
Terence Morrison, *Pr*
EMP: 15 **EST:** 2014
SALES (est): 1.31MM **Privately Held**
Web: www.acropolisepc.com

SIC: 8711 7373 3613 Electrical or electronic engineering; Turnkey vendors, computer systems; Control panels, electric

(G-9877)
ACW TECHNOLOGY INC
3725 Althorp Dr (27616-8457)
▲ EMP: 530
SIC: 3699 3841 Electrical equipment and supplies, nec; Medical instruments and equipment, blood and bone work

(G-9878)
ADAPTIVE TECHNOLOGIES LLC
Also Called: Beacon Prosthetics & Orthotics
3224 Lake Woodard Dr Ste 100 (27604-3659)
PHONE.................................919 231-6890
Eddie White, *Brnch Mgr*
EMP: 6
SALES (corp-wide): 38.46MM Privately Held
Web: www.beaconpo.com
SIC: 3842 Prosthetic appliances
HQ: Adaptive Technologies, Llc
3224 Lake Woodard Dr # 100
Raleigh NC 27604
919 231-6890

(G-9879)
ADS PRINTING CO INC
733 W Hargett St (27603-1601)
P.O. Box 25667 (27611-5667)
PHONE.................................919 834-0579
W Bruce Cash, *Pr*
Sylvia M Cash, *VP*
EMP: 9 EST: 1958
SQ FT: 7,500
SALES (est): 476.86K Privately Held
SIC: 2752 Lithographing on metal

(G-9880)
ADVANCED NON-LETHAL TECH INC
8311 Brier Creek Pkwy Ste 106-88 (27617-7328)
PHONE.................................847 812-6450
David Chlystek, *Managing Member*
Felix Batts, *CEO*
Deloris E Jordan, *COO*
Dave Chlystek, *VP*
EMP: 6 EST: 2019
SALES (est): 167.69K Privately Held
SIC: 8731 7389 3489 Engineering laboratory, except testing; Design services; Smoke generators (ordnance)

(G-9881)
ADVANTAGE CONVEYOR INC
Also Called: Advantage Manufacturing
8816 Gulf Ct Ste C (27617-4629)
P.O. Box 91686 (27675-1686)
PHONE.................................919 781-0055
Vann C Webb, *Pr*
EMP: 10 EST: 1991
SQ FT: 6,250
SALES (est): 2.72MM Privately Held
Web: www.advantageconveyor.com
SIC: 3535 Conveyors and conveying equipment

(G-9882)
ADVOCACY TO ALLVATE HMLESSNESS
4000 Wake Forest Rd Ste 102 (27609-6859)
PHONE.................................919 810-3431
Janet Hocutt-hairston, *CEO*
Dwight Jones, *Treas*
Nina Heath, *Asst Tr*
EMP: 4 EST: 2016
SALES (est): 130.66K Privately Held

Web: www.aah-inc.org
SIC: 2221 2522 Upholstery, tapestry, and wall covering fabrics; Office furniture, except wood

(G-9883)
AER THERAPEUTICS INC
400 W North St Ste 112 (27603-1570)
PHONE.................................919 345-4256
EMP: 7 EST: 2014
SALES (est): 381.9K Privately Held
Web: www.aertherapeutics.com
SIC: 2834 Pharmaceutical preparations

(G-9884)
AEROFABB LLC
3312 Marcony Way (27610-4076)
PHONE.................................919 793-8487
EMP: 4 EST: 2018
SALES (est): 231.8K Privately Held
SIC: 3714 Motor vehicle parts and accessories

(G-9885)
AFI CAPITAL INC
801 Beacon Lake Dr (27610-1377)
PHONE.................................919 212-6400
Gregory W Page, *Pr*
Craven B Page, *
Greg Newey, *
▼ EMP: 120 EST: 1972
SQ FT: 82,000
SALES (est): 22.15MM Privately Held
Web: www.accufabnc.com
SIC: 3444 Sheet metal specialties, not stamped

(G-9886)
AIR PURIFICATION INC (PA)
8121 Ebenezer Church Rd (27612-7307)
PHONE.................................919 783-6161
TOLL FREE: 800
Ron Stumpo, *Pr*
Duane Dorsay, *VP*
EMP: 16 EST: 1986
SQ FT: 10,000
SALES (est): 4.33MM
SALES (corp-wide): 4.33MM Privately Held
Web: www.airpurificationinc.com
SIC: 3564 Blowers and fans

(G-9887)
AJINOMOTO HLTH NTRTN N AMER IN
Also Called: Ajinomoto
4020 Ajinomoto Dr (27610-2911)
PHONE.................................919 231-0100
Brad Bigger, *Brnch Mgr*
EMP: 140
Web: www.ajihealthandnutrition.com
SIC: 2099 Food preparations, nec
HQ: Ajinomoto Health & Nutrition North America, Inc.
250 East Devon Ave
Itasca IL 60143
630 931-6800

(G-9888)
ALAMO NORTH TEXAS RAILROAD CO
2710 Wycliff Rd (27607-3033)
PHONE.................................919 787-9504
EMP: 8 EST: 2009
SALES (est): 2.45MM Publicly Held
SIC: 1423 Crushed and broken granite
PA: Martin Marietta Materials Inc
4123 Parklake Ave
Raleigh NC 27612

(G-9889)
ALCON
6425 Belle Crest Dr (27612-2871)
PHONE.................................919 624-5868
Julie Johnson, *Prin*
EMP: 7 EST: 2010
SALES (est): 600.38K Privately Held
Web: www.alcon.com
SIC: 3841 Surgical and medical instruments

(G-9890)
ALERT PROTECTION SYSTEMS INC
1401 Monkwood Pl (27603-3952)
PHONE.................................919 467-4357
Larry Beaton, *Pr*
Brian Beaton, *Cnslt*
EMP: 9 EST: 1985
SALES (est): 470.7K Privately Held
SIC: 3699 5065 Security devices; Security control equipment and systems

(G-9891)
ALK INVESTMENTS LLC
Also Called: Batteries Plus
6812 Glenwood Ave Ste 100 (27612-7133)
PHONE.................................984 233-5353
Mark Doggett, *Pr*
EMP: 9 EST: 2011
SALES (est): 1.37MM Privately Held
Web: www.batteriesplus.com
SIC: 3612 5063 3641 5531 Ballasts for lighting fixtures; Flashlights; Electric light bulbs, complete; Batteries, automotive and truck

(G-9892)
ALLEN KELLY & CO INC
Also Called: Honeywell Authorized Dealer
220 Tryon Rd Ste A (27603-3587)
PHONE.................................919 779-4197
Allen Kelly, *Pr*
Joan Kelly, *
Jc Moeller, *CFO*
EMP: 77 EST: 1986
SQ FT: 5,000
SALES (est): 9.03MM Privately Held
Web: www.allenkelly.com
SIC: 1711 3444 1731 Warm air heating and air conditioning contractor; Sheet metalwork; Electrical work

(G-9893)
ALTERA CORPORATION
5540 Centerview Dr Ste 318 (27606-3388)
PHONE.................................919 852-1004
Jeff Wills, *Mgr*
EMP: 6
SALES (corp-wide): 54.23B Publicly Held
Web: www.intel.com
SIC: 3674 7372 3577 Metal oxide silicon (MOS) devices; Application computer software; Data conversion equipment, media-to-media: computer
HQ: Altera Corporation
101 Innovation Dr
San Jose CA 95134
408 544-7000

(G-9894)
ALYWILLOW
5301 Hillsborough St Ste 100 (27606-6343)
PHONE.................................919 454-4826
Angela Suggs, *Owner*
EMP: 6 EST: 2017
SALES (est): 177.69K Privately Held
Web: www.alywillow.com
SIC: 2844 Perfumes, cosmetics and other toilet preparations

(G-9895)
AMBER ALERT INTERNATIONAL TM (PA)
6537 English Oaks Dr (27615-6306)
PHONE.................................919 641-8773
James M Thrasher, *Pr*
EMP: 4 EST: 2006
SALES (est): 401.6K Privately Held
SIC: 2754 Business form and card printing, gravure

(G-9896)
AMBER BROOKS PUBLISHING LLC
7233 Mine Shaft Rd (27615-6019)
PHONE.................................704 582-1035
Amber Brooks, *Prin*
EMP: 4 EST: 2017
SALES (est): 64.05K Privately Held
SIC: 2741 Miscellaneous publishing

(G-9897)
AMERICAN SOIL AND MULCH INC
1109 Athens Dr (27606-2420)
PHONE.................................919 460-1349
Russell W Tarlton, *Pr*
EMP: 7 EST: 1966
SALES (est): 1.01MM Privately Held
Web: www.americansoilandmulch.com
SIC: 2499 5261 Mulch, wood and bark; Top soil

(G-9898)
AMERICAN SOLUTIONS FOR BU
9201 Leesville Rd Ste 120 (27613-7540)
PHONE.................................919 848-2442
Michael P Arata, *Prin*
EMP: 5 EST: 2006
SALES (est): 100K Privately Held
SIC: 2759 Commercial printing, nec

(G-9899)
AMERICAN WELDING & GAS INC (PA)
Also Called: Compressed Gas Solutions
4900 Falls Of Neuse Rd Ste 150 (27609-5490)
PHONE.................................984 222-2600
EMP: 6 EST: 1983
SALES (est): 166.62MM
SALES (corp-wide): 166.62MM Privately Held
Web: www.awggases.com
SIC: 3548 Gas welding equipment

(G-9900)
AMS USA INC
Also Called: AMS
353 E Six Forks Rd Ste 250 (27609-7881)
P.O. Box 97414 (27624-7414)
PHONE.................................919 755-2889
Ravi Jhota, *Prin*
EMP: 8 EST: 2007
SALES (est): 788.4K Privately Held
SIC: 3674 Infrared sensors, solid state

(G-9901)
AMTAI MEDICAL EQUIPMENT INC
5605 Primavera Ct (27616-1840)
PHONE.................................919 872-1803
Alan Sou Cheng Lee, *VP*
▲ EMP: 14 EST: 2008
SALES (est): 2.34MM Privately Held
Web: www.amtai.com
SIC: 5047 3842 Medical equipment and supplies; Surgical appliances and supplies

(G-9902)
ANALOG DEVICES INC
223 S West St Ste 1400 (27603-4094)
PHONE.................................919 831-2790

▲ = Import ▼ = Export
◆ = Import/Export

Tony Montalvo, *Mgr*
EMP: 10
SALES (corp-wide): 9.43B **Publicly Held**
Web: www.analog.com
SIC: 3674 Integrated circuits, semiconductor
networks, etc.
PA: Analog Devices, Inc.
1 Analog Way
Wilmington MA 01887
781 935-5565

(G-9903)
ANDRITZ FABRICS AND ROLLS INC
8521 Six Forks Rd (27615-5278)
PHONE..............................919 556-7235
Thomas Gutierrez, *Brnch Mgr*
EMP: 14
SALES (corp-wide): 1.13B **Privately Held**
Web: www.andritz.com
SIC: 3069 Printers' rolls and blankets: rubber
or rubberized fabric
HQ: Andritz Fabrics And Rolls Inc.
8521 Six Forks Rd
Raleigh NC 27615
919 526-1400

(G-9904)
**ANDRITZ FABRICS AND ROLLS INC
(HQ)**
Also Called: Xerium
8521 Six Forks Rd Ste 300 (27615-5294)
PHONE..............................919 526-1400
Mark Staton, *Pr*
Clifford E Pietrafitta, *
William S Butterfield, *
Phillip B Kennedy, *
EMP: 74 **EST:** 2002
SALES (est): 497.23MM
SALES (corp-wide): 1.13B **Privately Held**
Web: www.andritz.com
SIC: 2221 3069 Broadwoven fabric mills,
manmade; Printers' rolls and blankets:
rubber or rubberized fabric
PA: Andritz Ag
Stattegger StraBe 18
Graz 8045
31669020

(G-9905)
ANTKAR LLC
Also Called: Flavors Ice Cream
2831 Jones Franklin Rd (27606-4007)
PHONE..............................919 322-4100
Elisa Mclean, *Managing Member*
EMP: 6 **EST:** 2020
SALES (est): 135.43K **Privately Held**
Web: www.flavorsicecream.net
SIC: 2024 Dairy based frozen desserts

(G-9906)
ANUMA AEROSPACE LLC
720 Pebblebrook Dr (27609-5345)
PHONE..............................919 600-0142
Diana Little, *CEO*
EMP: 4 **EST:** 2021
SALES (est): 627.4K **Privately Held**
Web: www.anumaaerospace.com
SIC: 3721 Aircraft

(G-9907)
APAC-ATLANTIC INC (DH)
Also Called: APAC
2626 Glenwood Ave Ste 550 (27608-1370)
P.O. Box 399 (28502-0399)
PHONE..............................336 412-6800
David L Schwartz, *Pr*
David H Kilpatrick, *VP*
Thomas G Kindred, *VP*
E S Arthur Junior, *VP*
Barry L Johnson, *VP*
EMP: 100 **EST:** 1945

SQ FT: 5,000
SALES (est): 7.32MM
SALES (corp-wide): 34.95B **Privately Held**
Web: www.thompsonarthur.com
SIC: 1611 1771 3531 5032 Highway and
street paving contractor; Parking lot
construction; Asphalt plant, including gravel-
mix type; Sand, construction
HQ: Crh Americas Materials, Inc.
900 Ashwood Pkwy Ste 600
Atlanta GA 30338

(G-9908)
APEX STEEL CORP
301 Petfinder Ln (27603-2874)
PHONE..............................919 362-6611
Bridgette Burks, *Pr*
Ronald E Clemmons, *
Teresa L Clemmons, *
EMP: 45 **EST:** 1985
SQ FT: 20,000
SALES (est): 10.65MM **Privately Held**
Web: www.apexsteelcorp.com
SIC: 1791 3446 1799 Iron work, structural;
Ornamental metalwork; Welding on site

(G-9909)
AQUARIUS DESIGNS & LOGO WEAR
4429 Beryl Rd (27606-1457)
PHONE..............................919 821-4646
Michel Kelkalezic, *Owner*
EMP: 5 **EST:** 1983
SALES (est): 126.38K **Privately Held**
SIC: 2759 Screen printing

(G-9910)
ARBOR PHARMACEUTICALS INC
5511 Capital Center Dr Ste 224
(27606-3380)
PHONE..............................919 792-1700
Ed Schutter, *CEO*
EMP: 5 **EST:** 2018
SALES (est): 287.3K **Privately Held**
Web: www.arborpharma.com
SIC: 2834 Pharmaceutical preparations

(G-9911)
ARCHANGEL ARMS LLC
3405 Banks Rd (27603-8998)
PHONE..............................984 235-2536
Jeremy Jones, *Managing Member*
EMP: 7 **EST:** 2011
SALES (est): 113.13K **Privately Held**
Web: www.archangelarms.com
SIC: 3949 Sporting and athletic goods, nec

(G-9912)
**ARGOS READY MIX (CAROLINAS)
CORP**
Also Called: Ready Mixed Concrete Company
3610 Bush St (27609-7511)
P.O. Box 27326 (27611-7326)
PHONE..............................919 790-1520
EMP: 475
SIC: 3273 Ready-mixed concrete

(G-9913)
ARGOS USA LLC
Also Called: Ready Mixed Concrete Co
3200 Spring Forest Rd Ste 210
(27616-2812)
PHONE..............................919 828-3695
George Turner, *Pr*
EMP: 10
Web: www.argos-us.com
SIC: 3273 Ready-mixed concrete
HQ: Argos Usa Llc
3015 Windward Plz Ste 300
Alpharetta GA 30005
678 368-4300

(G-9914)
ARGOS USA LLC
Also Called: Ready Mix Concrete of Sanford
3200 Spring Forest Rd Ste 210
(27616-2811)
PHONE..............................919 775-5441
Mike Sakzer, *Mgr*
EMP: 10
Web: www.argos-us.com
SIC: 3273 Ready-mixed concrete
HQ: Argos Usa Llc
3015 Windward Plz Ste 300
Alpharetta GA 30005
678 368-4300

(G-9915)
ARGOS USA LLC
Also Called: Argos Ready Mix
3200 Spring Forest Rd Ste 210
(27616-2811)
PHONE..............................919 790-1520
EMP: 44
Web: www.argos-us.com
SIC: 3273 Ready-mixed concrete
HQ: Argos Usa Llc
3015 Windward Plz Ste 300
Alpharetta GA 30005
678 368-4300

(G-9916)
ARMAC INC
4027 Atlantic Ave (27604-1732)
P.O. Box 1985 (27526-2985)
PHONE..............................919 878-9836
Rusty Young, *CEO*
Sue Parker, *
Dorothy Young, *Stockholder**
EMP: 13 **EST:** 1983
SQ FT: 21,000
SALES (est): 2.14MM **Privately Held**
Web: www.tecgraphics.com
SIC: 2759 Screen printing

(G-9917)
ASC ENGINEERED SOLUTIONS LLC
920 Friar Tuck Rd (27610-3635)
PHONE..............................919 395-5222
EMP: 18
SALES (corp-wide): 836.12MM **Privately
Held**
Web: www.asc-es.com
SIC: 3498 Fabricated pipe and fittings
PA: Asc Engineered Solutions, Llc
2001 Spring Rd Ste 300
Oak Brook IL 60523
800 301-2701

(G-9918)
ASCEPI MEDICAL GROUP LLC
3344 Hillsborough St Ste 100 (27607-5469)
PHONE..............................919 336-4246
EMP: 7 **EST:** 2020
SALES (est): 420.98K **Privately Held**
Web: www.ascepimed.com
SIC: 3841 Medical instruments and
equipment, blood and bone work

(G-9919)
ASEPTIA INC
723 W Johnson St Ste 100 (27603-1244)
PHONE..............................678 373-6751
David Clark, *Pr*
Michael Drozd, *
Mac Mcaulay, *CFO*
John Winnie, *
Lindsey Lacy, *
EMP: 125 **EST:** 2006
SALES (est): 3.07MM **Privately Held**
Web: www.wrightfoods.com

SIC: 3356 5199 5148 Battery metal;
Packaging materials; Fresh fruits and
vegetables

(G-9920)
ATLANTIC GROUP USA INC (PA)
3401 Gresham Lake Rd Ste 118
(27615-4243)
PHONE..............................919 623-7824
Brett Block, *CEO*
EMP: 10 **EST:** 1990
SQ FT: 1,000
SALES (est): 13.7MM **Privately Held**
Web: www.agunc.com
SIC: 6411 8748 1522 3999 Insurance
adjusters; Business consulting, nec;
Residential construction, nec; Atomizers,
toiletry

(G-9921)
**ATTENDS HEALTHCARE PRODUCTS
INC (PA)**
8020 Arco Corporate Dr Ste 200 (27617)
PHONE..............................800 428-8363
◆ **EMP:** 280 **EST:** 2002
SALES (est): 90.15MM
SALES (corp-wide): 90.15MM **Privately
Held**
Web: www.attends.com
SIC: 2676 Sanitary paper products

(G-9922)
**ATTINDAS HYGIENE PARTNERS INC
(PA)**
8020 Arco Corporate Dr Ste 200 (27617)
PHONE..............................919 237-4000
Esther Berrozpe, *Pr*
Brad Goodwin, *OF GLOBAL
COMMERCIAL MARKETS*
Avia Graves Senior, *Vice-President Global
Human Resources*
David Struhs, *OF GLOBAL Corporate
Services*
Crichton Waddell, *Senior Vice President
Global Operations*
EMP: 15 **EST:** 2013
SALES (est): 18.86MM
SALES (corp-wide): 18.86MM **Privately
Held**
Web: www.attends.com
SIC: 2621 Paper mills

(G-9923)
AUDIO ADVICE LLC
8621 Glenwood Ave Ste 117 (27617)
PHONE..............................919 881-2005
EMP: 92 **EST:** 1978
SALES (est): 10.2MM **Privately Held**
Web: www.audioadvice.com
SIC: 3663 Studio equipment, radio and
television broadcasting

(G-9924)
AXIAL EXCHANGE INC
1111 Haynes St Ste 113 (27604-1454)
P.O. Box 6486 (27628-6486)
PHONE..............................919 576-9988
Joanne Rohde, *Pr*
John Casey, *VP*
EMP: 5 **EST:** 2012
SALES (est): 397.76K **Privately Held**
Web: www.axialexchange.com
SIC: 7372 Business oriented computer
software

(G-9925)
AXITARE CORPORATION
1717 Brassfield Rd (27614-9448)
PHONE..............................919 256-8196
Jim Passe, *Pr*

(PA)=Parent Co (HQ)=Headquarters
✪ = New Business established in last 2 years

EMP: 4 **EST:** 2005
SALES (est): 350K **Privately Held**
SIC: 2834 Pharmaceutical preparations

(G-9926)
AXON LLC
Also Called: Axon Styrotech
3080 Business Park Dr Ste 103
(27610-3094)
PHONE....................919 772-8383
▲ **EMP:** 44 **EST:** 1991
SALES (est): 9.51MM **Privately Held**
Web: www.axoncorp.com
SIC: 3565 Packaging machinery
HQ: Pro Mach, Inc.
     50 E Rvrcnter Blvd Ste 18
     Covington KY 41011
     513 831-8778

(G-9927)
B&B CAP LINERS LLC
3208 Spottswood St Ste 115 (27615-8130)
PHONE....................585 598-1828
EMP: 4 **EST:** 2011
SALES (est): 1.05MM **Privately Held**
Web: www.bbcapliners.com
SIC: 3443 Liners, industrial: metal plate

(G-9928)
B&C XTERIOR CLEANING SVC INC
Also Called: Xterior Sales & Service
142 Annaron Ct (27603-3640)
PHONE....................919 779-7905
C Mike Baker, *Pr*
Mary Baker, *VP*
EMP: 8 **EST:** 1977
SQ FT: 3,000
SALES (est): 655.84K **Privately Held**
Web: www.landanc.com
SIC: 3589 5251 7699 7542 High pressure
cleaning equipment; Hardware stores;
Cleaning services; Carwashes

(G-9929)
B6USA INC
Also Called: Bay Six
414 Dupont Cir (27603-2076)
PHONE....................919 833-3851
Katherine Hite, *Pr*
EMP: 8 **EST:** 2005
SALES (est): 575.55K **Privately Held**
SIC: 2395 Embroidery products, except
Schiffli machine

(G-9930)
BANDWIDTH INC (PA)
Also Called: Bandwidth
2230 Bandmate Way (27607)
PHONE....................800 808-5150
David A Morken, *Ch Bd*
Rebecca G Bottorff, *CPO**
Daryl E Raiford, *CFO*
Kade Ross, *CIO*
EMP: 305 **EST:** 2000
SQ FT: 534,000
SALES (est): 601.12MM
SALES (corp-wide): 601.12MM **Publicly
Held**
Web: www.bandwidth.com
SIC: 7372 Prepackaged software

(G-9931)
BAR SQUARED INC
Also Called: Caromed
5605 Spring Ct (27616-2920)
P.O. Box 4360 (18043-4360)
PHONE....................919 878-0578
Thomas Barnett, *Pr*
Barbara Beck, *VP*
EMP: 18 **EST:** 1992
SALES (est): 162.04K **Privately Held**

Web: www.caromed.us
SIC: 3842 Bandages and dressings

(G-9932)
BAR-S FOODS CO
2101 Westinghouse Blvd Ste 109
(27604-2477)
PHONE....................847 652-3238
EMP: 40
Web: www.bar-sfoods.com
SIC: 2013 Sausages and other prepared
meats
HQ: Bar-S Foods Co.
     18700 N Hayden Rd Ste 545
     Scottsdale AZ 85255
     602 264-7272

(G-9933)
BAREFOOT PRESS INC
731 Pershing Rd (27608-2711)
PHONE....................919 283-6396
Richard Kilby, *Pr*
EMP: 5 **EST:** 1987
SQ FT: 6,500
SALES (est): 526.78K **Privately Held**
Web: www.barefootpress.com
SIC: 2752 Offset printing

(G-9934)
**BAYER HLTHCARE
PHARMACEUTICALS**
1820 Liatris Ln (27613-6583)
PHONE....................602 469-6846
Vilushis Byrd, *Sls Mgr*
EMP: 5 **EST:** 2017
SALES (est): 319.19K **Privately Held**
SIC: 2834 Pharmaceutical preparations

(G-9935)
BAYSIX USA
414 Dupont Cir (27603-2076)
PHONE....................919 833-3851
Katherine Hite, *Prin*
▲ **EMP:** 16 **EST:** 2010
SALES (est): 489.04K **Privately Held**
Web: www.wearebaysix.com
SIC: 2395 Embroidery products, except
Schiffli machine

(G-9936)
BEAKER INC
700 Spring Forest Rd Ste 121
(27609-9124)
PHONE....................919 803-7422
Jeffrey Clark, *CEO*
EMP: 17 **EST:** 2013
SALES (est): 957.54K **Privately Held**
Web: www.beaker.com
SIC: 2834 Pharmaceutical preparations

(G-9937)
**BEAUTIMAR MANUFACTURED MBL
INC**
1221 Home Ct (27603-4541)
PHONE....................919 779-1181
Howard B Mills, *Pr*
Gail Mills, *Sec*
EMP: 4 **EST:** 1969
SQ FT: 9,000
SALES (est): 378.81K **Privately Held**
Web: www.beautimar.com
SIC: 3281 Marble, building: cut and shaped

(G-9938)
BEECH STREET VENTURES LLC
Also Called: Videri Chocolate Factory
327 W Davie St Ste 100 (27601-1703)
PHONE....................919 755-5053
Sam Ratto, *Managing Member*
EMP: 22 **EST:** 2018

SALES (est): 1.02MM **Privately Held**
Web: www.viderichocolatefactory.com
SIC: 5441 2066 Candy; Cacao bean
processing

(G-9939)
BELKOZ INC
4900 Thornton Rd (27616-5878)
PHONE....................919 703-0694
Zoltan Laszlovszky, *Prin*
EMP: 4 **EST:** 2012
SALES (est): 862.29K **Privately Held**
Web: www.belkoz.com
SIC: 3541 3423 8711 Milling machines;
Soldering tools; Engineering services

(G-9940)
BEYOND ELECTRONICS CORP
Also Called: BEC
12405 Cilcain Ct (27614-8959)
PHONE....................919 231-8000
Richard Goodell, *Pr*
EMP: 5 **EST:** 2005
SALES (est): 864.05K **Privately Held**
Web: www.beyondelectronics.us
SIC: 3812 Acceleration indicators and
systems components, aerospace

(G-9941)
BFS ASSET HOLDINGS LLC (HQ)
Also Called: Builders Firstsource
4800 Falls Of Neuse Rd Ste 400
(27609-8142)
PHONE....................303 784-4288
David Flitman, *Managing Member*
Peter Jackson, *
Timothy Johnson, *
▲ **EMP:** 286 **EST:** 1987
SALES (est): 540.04MM
SALES (corp-wide): 16.4B **Publicly Held**
SIC: 5211 2431 2439 5031 Lumber and
other building materials; Millwork; Trusses,
wooden roof; Lumber, plywood, and
millwork
PA: Builders Firstsource, Inc.
     6031 Cnnection Dr Ste 400
     Irving TX 75039
     214 880-3500

(G-9942)
BFS OPERATIONS LLC (HQ)
4800 Falls Of Neuse Rd (27609)
PHONE....................919 431-1000
David Keltner, *Pr*
James F Major Junior, *Ex VP*
Lisa Hamblet, *
Mike Mtgaugh, *
Donna Thagard, *
▲ **EMP:** 1500 **EST:** 1922
SALES (est): 1B
SALES (corp-wide): 16.4B **Publicly Held**
SIC: 5211 2431 5031 5713 Millwork and
lumber; Millwork; Lumber: rough, dressed,
and finished; Floor covering stores
PA: Builders Firstsource, Inc.
     6031 Cnnection Dr Ste 400
     Irving TX 75039
     214 880-3500

(G-9943)
BIG DELICIOUS BRAND INC
1632 Lorraine Rd (27607-6626)
P.O. Box 12606 (27605-2606)
PHONE....................919 270-7324
James Marion Milican Junior, *Pr*
EMP: 10 **EST:** 2017
SALES (est): 106.55K **Privately Held**
Web: www.bigdelish.com
SIC: 2022 Cheese spreads, dips, pastes,
and other cheese products

(G-9944)
BIJUR DELIMON INTL INC (DH)
5909 Falls Of Neuse Rd Ste 201
(27609-4000)
PHONE....................919 465-4448
Roger M Yamamoto, *Pr*
Roger M Yamamoto, *CFO*
John V Curci, *
Karen Johnson, *
Nancy S Lenhart, *
▲ **EMP:** 40 **EST:** 1965
SALES (est): 21.52MM
SALES (corp-wide): 459.42MM **Privately
Held**
Web: www.farval.com
SIC: 3569 Lubricating equipment
HQ: Industrial Manufacturing Company Llc
     8223 Brcksvlle Rd Ste 100
     Brecksville OH 44141
     440 838-4700

(G-9945)
BIOLOGICS INC
625 Oberlin Rd (27605-1126)
PHONE....................919 546-9810
EMP: 4 **EST:** 2019
SALES (est): 108.7K **Privately Held**
Web: biologics.mckesson.com
SIC: 2514 Metal household furniture

(G-9946)
BIOMERIEUX INC
3300 Tarheel Dr (27609-7538)
PHONE....................800 682-2666
Donna Pickett, *Brnch Mgr*
EMP: 5
SALES (corp-wide): 7.5MM **Privately Held**
Web: www.biomerieux-usa.com
SIC: 3829 Ion chambers
HQ: Biomerieux, Inc.
     100 Rodolphe St
     Durham NC 27712
     919 620-2000

(G-9947)
BIZNET SOFTWARE INC
8529 Six Forks Rd Ste 400 (27615-4972)
PHONE....................919 872-7800
George Mcmann, *Pr*
Paula Anthony Mcmann, *Sec*
Lori Shwenn, *CFO*
EMP: 12 **EST:** 1996
SALES (est): 3.51MM
SALES (corp-wide): 109.78MM **Privately
Held**
Web: www.insightsoftware.com
SIC: 7372 Business oriented computer
software
PA: Insightsoftware, Llc
     8529 Six Forks Rd
     Raleigh NC 27615
     919 872-7800

(G-9948)
BLACK & DECKER CORPORATION
Also Called: Black & Decker
2930 Capital Blvd (27604-3235)
PHONE....................919 878-0357
Benjamin G Beeker, *Mgr*
EMP: 5
SALES (corp-wide): 15.78B **Publicly Held**
Web: www.blackanddecker.com
SIC: 3546 Power-driven handtools
HQ: The Black & Decker Corporation
     701 E Joppa Rd
     Towson MD 21286
     410 716-3900

(G-9949)
BLUE WOLF TECHNOLOGIES LLP
9650 Strickland Rd Ste 103 (27615-1902)
PHONE...................................919 810-1508
Ernest Johnson, *Pt*
Joseph E Freed, *Pt*
EMP: 6 **EST:** 2012
SALES (est): 538.84K **Privately Held**
SIC: 7372 7373 7379 Business oriented
computer software; Local area network
(LAN) systems integrator; Online services
technology consultants

(G-9950)
BLUEBIRD CUPCAKES
2524 Beech Gap Ct (27603-5876)
PHONE...................................919 616-7347
Cynthia Mcgee, *Prin*
EMP: 5 **EST:** 2011
SALES (est): 190.21K **Privately Held**
SIC: 2051 Bread, cake, and related products

(G-9951)
BMI WOOD PRODUCTS INC
2506 Yonkers Rd (27604-2241)
PHONE...................................919 829-9505
Sandy Mullin, *Pr*
Courtney Mullin, *CEO*
EMP: 4 **EST:** 1975
SALES (est): 419.26K **Privately Held**
Web: www.barrmullin.com
SIC: 3553 Sawmill machines

(G-9952)
BOLTON CONSTRUCTION & SVC LLC
Also Called: Bolton
1623 Old Louisburg Rd (27604-1589)
PHONE...................................919 861-1500
William E Bolton Iv, *Managing Member*
EMP: 55 **EST:** 2002
SQ FT: 14,000
SALES (est): 5.05MM **Privately Held**
Web: www.boltonservice.com
SIC: 3444 1623 4924 1711 Sheet metalwork;
Water, sewer, and utility lines; Natural gas
distribution; Plumbing, heating, air-
conditioning

(G-9953)
BONAVENTURE GROUP INC
Also Called: Afex
6031 Oak Forest Dr (27616-1903)
PHONE...................................919 781-6610
EMP: 14 **EST:** 1986
SALES (est): 4.04MM **Privately Held**
Web: www.afexsystems.com
SIC: 3999 Fire extinguishers, portable

(G-9954)
BOND TECHNOLOGIES
909 Walkertown Dr (27614-7177)
PHONE...................................919 866-0075
Brian Scarboro, *Prin*
EMP: 6 **EST:** 2010
SALES (est): 68.16K **Privately Held**
Web: www.bondtechnologies.net
SIC: 3599 Machine shop, jobbing and repair

(G-9955)
BOON EDAM INC (DH)
421 Northj Harrington St (27603)
PHONE...................................910 814-3800
Mark G Borto, *Ch Bd*
Thomas Devine, *
Valerie Anderson, *
Daniel Camp, *
◆ **EMP:** 37 **EST:** 1981
SQ FT: 50,000
SALES (est): 46.21MM

SALES (corp-wide): 194.28MM **Privately Held**
Web: www.boonedam.com
SIC: 3829 Turnstiles, equipped with counting
mechanisms
HQ: Boon Edam B.V.
Ambachtstraat 4
Edam NH 1135
299380808

(G-9956)
BOSS KEY PRODUCTIONS INC
230 Fayetteville St Ste 300 (27601-1587)
P.O. Box 90126 (27675-0126)
PHONE...................................919 659-5704
Cliff Bleszinski, *CEO*
Arjan Brussee, *
EMP: 57 **EST:** 2014
SQ FT: 5,000
SALES (est): 1.37MM **Privately Held**
Web: www.bosskey.com
SIC: 7372 Home entertainment computer
software

(G-9957)
BRANDILLY OF NC INC
Also Called: Brandilly Marketing Creative
1053 E Whitaker Mill Rd Ste 115
(27604-5311)
PHONE...................................919 278-7896
Kemah Washington, *Pr*
EMP: 4 **EST:** 2015
SALES (est): 315.5K **Privately Held**
Web: www.bcgnc.com
SIC: 7336 2752 Graphic arts and related
design; Commercial printing, lithographic

(G-9958)
BRIDGESTONE RET OPERATIONS LLC
Also Called: Firestone
5058 N New Hope Rd (27604-4400)
PHONE...................................919 872-6402
Nathan Barbour, *Mgr*
EMP: 6
Web: www.bridgestoneamericas.com
SIC: 5531 7534 Automotive tires; Rebuilding
and retreading tires
HQ: Bridgestone Retail Operations, Llc
200 4th Ave S Ste 100
Nashville TN 37201
615 937-1000

(G-9959)
BRIDGESTONE RET OPERATIONS LLC
Also Called: Firestone
4305 Wake Forest Rd (27609-6276)
PHONE...................................919 872-6566
Paul Morton, *Brnch Mgr*
EMP: 8
SQ FT: 7,744
Web: www.bridgestoneamericas.com
SIC: 5531 7534 Automotive tires; Rebuilding
and retreading tires
HQ: Bridgestone Retail Operations, Llc
200 4th Ave S Ste 100
Nashville TN 37201
615 937-1000

(G-9960)
BRIGHT HOLDINGS USA INC
8900 Capital Blvd (27616-3117)
PHONE...................................919 327-5500
David Vogt, *Dir*
EMP: 249
Web: www.sagentpharma.com
SIC: 2834 Pharmaceutical preparations
HQ: Bright Holdings Usa, Inc.
1901 N Roselle Rd Ste 450
Schaumburg IL 60195

(G-9961)
BROOKHURST ASSOCIATES
Also Called: Fundamental Playgrounds
2400 Saint Pauls Sq (27614-7424)
PHONE...................................919 792-0987
G Mark Hockenyos, *Owner*
EMP: 4 **EST:** 1995
SALES (est): 159.19K **Privately Held**
SIC: 3949 6531 Playground equipment; Real
estate agents and managers

(G-9962)
BUSINESS MOGUL LLC
2120 Breezeway Dr Unit 112 (27614-7461)
PHONE...................................919 605-2165
Sheria Rowe, *Pr*
EMP: 6 **EST:** 2018
SALES (est): 173.96K **Privately Held**
Web: www.thebusinessmogul.com
SIC: 2759 2836 Publication printing; Culture
media

(G-9963)
BUSINESS TO BUSINESS INC (PA)
Also Called: Business Leader
3801 Wake Forest Rd Ste 102
(27609-6864)
PHONE...................................919 872-7077
Chris Verk, *Prin*
Daniel Davies, *Prin*
Martin Feligson, *VP*
EMP: 7 **EST:** 1989
SQ FT: 18,000
SALES (est): 912.09K **Privately Held**
Web: www.businessleader.com
SIC: 2721 Magazines: publishing only, not
printed on site

(G-9964)
CABINETWORKS GROUP MICH LLC
6221 Westgate Rd Ste 100 (27617-4722)
PHONE...................................919 868-8174
Keith Allen, *Brnch Mgr*
EMP: 29
SALES (corp-wide): 501.27MM **Privately Held**
Web: www.cabinetworksgroup.com
SIC: 2434 Wood kitchen cabinets
PA: Cabinetworks Group Michigan, Llc
20000 Victor Pkwy
Livonia MI 48152
734 205-4600

(G-9965)
CANALTA ENTERPRISES LLC
Also Called: Phillips Iron Works
4809 Auburn Knightdale Rd (27610-8230)
PHONE...................................919 615-1570
Maryanne Mah-throndson, *CEO*
Ronald Throndson, *Pr*
EMP: 25 **EST:** 2013
SALES (est): 5.33MM **Privately Held**
Web: www.phillipsiw.com
SIC: 3449 1791 Miscellaneous metalwork;
Structural steel erection

(G-9966)
CAPITAL CITY CUISINE LLC
4808 Wallingford Dr (27616-7032)
PHONE...................................919 432-2126
EMP: 4 **EST:** 2021
SALES (est): 234.75K **Privately Held**
SIC: 2599 7389 Food wagons, restaurant;
Business services, nec

(G-9967)
CAPITAL CITY SEALANTS LLC
3101 Stony Brook Dr Ste 166 (27604-3786)
P.O. Box 41014 (27629-1014)
PHONE...................................919 427-4077

EMP: 8 **EST:** 2010
SALES (est): 481.91K **Privately Held**
SIC: 2891 Sealants

(G-9968)
CAPITAL LGHTNING PRTECTION INC
Also Called: Quality Lightning Protection
743 Pershing Rd (27608-2711)
P.O. Box 162 (27602-0162)
PHONE...................................919 832-5574
Thomas J Cottle Junior, *Pr*
Charles Stephenson, *VP*
EMP: 6 **EST:** 1944
SQ FT: 5,000
SALES (est): 858.74K
SALES (corp-wide): 3.57MM **Privately Held**
SIC: 3643 Lightning protection equipment
PA: Quality Lightning Protection, Inc.
743 Pershing Rd
Raleigh NC 27608
919 832-9399

(G-9969)
CAPITAL SIGN SOLUTIONS LLC
5800 Mchines Pl Ste 110 (27616-1952)
PHONE...................................919 789-1452
EMP: 28 **EST:** 2011
SALES (est): 4.15MM **Privately Held**
Web: www.capitalsignsolutions.com
SIC: 3993 Signs and advertising specialties

(G-9970)
CAPITOL CITY LUMBER COMPANY
Also Called: Do It Best
4216 Beryl Rd (27606-1449)
P.O. Box 33065 (27636-3065)
PHONE...................................919 832-6492
TOLL FREE: 800
Cheyney A Nicholson, *Pr*
Edward A Nicholson, *VP*
Rachel Nicholson, *Sec*
Alice Nicksa, *Stockholder*
Sara J Inglis, *Stockholder*
EMP: 15 **EST:** 1947
SQ FT: 18,000
SALES (est): 2.82MM **Privately Held**
Web: www.capitolcitylumber.com
SIC: 5211 2421 Lumber and other building
materials; Lumber: rough, sawed, or planed

(G-9971)
CAPPER MCCALL CO
9650 Strickland Rd Ste 103420
(27615-1902)
PHONE...................................919 270-8813
EMP: 9 **EST:** 2019
SALES (est): 2.33MM **Privately Held**
Web: www.cappermccall.com
SIC: 3599 Industrial machinery, nec

(G-9972)
CAPTIVE-AIRE SYSTEMS INC (PA)
Also Called: Aqua-Matic
4641 Paragon Park Rd Ste 104
(27616-3407)
PHONE...................................919 882-2410
Robert L Luddy, *Pr*
William H Francis Junior, *VP Fin*
◆ **EMP:** 130 **EST:** 1978
SQ FT: 90,000
SALES (est): 485.13MM
SALES (corp-wide): 485.13MM **Privately Held**
Web: www.captiveaire.com
SIC: 3444 Restaurant sheet metalwork

(G-9973)
CARDINAL CABINETWORKS INC
4900 Craftsman Dr Ste A (27609-5665)
PHONE...................................919 829-3634

L Hardin Sigmon, *Pr*
EMP: 9 **EST:** 1994
SALES (est): 989.7K **Privately Held**
Web: www.cardinalcabinetworks.com
SIC: 2434 Wood kitchen cabinets

(G-9974)
CAROLINA COUNTERTOPS OF GARNER
3800 Tryon Rd Ste F (27606-4247)
PHONE......................919 832-3335
Robert Lilly, *Pr*
Hal Lilly, *VP*
A Lilly, *Sec*
EMP: 15 **EST:** 1985
SQ FT: 9,000
SALES (est): 441.19K **Privately Held**
SIC: 2541 Counters or counter display cases, wood

(G-9975)
CAROLINA FABRICATORS LLC
Also Called: Carolina Fabricators
6016 Triangle Dr (27617-4743)
PHONE......................919 510-8410
Scott Kisner, *Managing Member*
EMP: 18 **EST:** 1998
SQ FT: 16,000
SALES (est): 4.87MM
SALES (corp-wide): 4.87MM **Privately Held**
Web: www.carolinametalfabricators.com
SIC: 3441 Fabricated structural metal
PA: Directus Holdings, Llc
　　6016 Triangle Dr
　　Raleigh NC 27617
　　919 510-8410

(G-9976)
CAROLINA FUR DRESSING COMPANY
900 Freedom Dr (27610-1424)
PHONE......................919 231-0086
Rick Morgan, *Pr*
▲ **EMP:** 28 **EST:** 1980
SQ FT: 30,000
SALES (est): 890.86K **Privately Held**
Web: www.carolinafurdressing.com
SIC: 3111 Leather tanning and finishing

(G-9977)
CAROLINA LASERS
Also Called: Clausen Carolina Lasers
5508 Old Wake Forest Rd (27609-5279)
PHONE......................919 872-8001
Wayne Clausen, *Prin*
EMP: 5 **EST:** 2009
SALES (est): 515.93K **Privately Held**
Web: www.carolinalasers.com
SIC: 3829 Measuring and controlling devices, nec

(G-9978)
CAROLINA PACKAGING & SUP INC (PA)
5609 Departure Dr (27616-1842)
P.O. Box 98599 (27624-8599)
PHONE......................919 201-5592
Ralph J Sigler Junior, *Pr*
Ralph Jeremy Sigler Iii, *VP*
EMP: 61 **EST:** 1994
SALES (est): 4.69MM **Privately Held**
Web: www.carolinapackaging.com
SIC: 2653 Boxes, corrugated: made from purchased materials

(G-9979)
CAROLINA SUNROCK LLC
8620 Barefoot Industrial Rd (27617-4703)
PHONE......................919 861-1860

Bryan Postol, *Owner*
EMP: 33
SALES (corp-wide): 51.02MM **Privately Held**
Web: www.thesunrockgroup.com
SIC: 3273 Ready-mixed concrete
HQ: Carolina Sunrock Llc
　　1001 W B St
　　Butner NC 27509
　　919 575-4502

(G-9980)
CAROLINIAN PUBG GROUP LLC
1504 New Bern Ave (27610-2536)
P.O. Box 25308 (27611-5308)
PHONE......................919 834-5558
Adria Jervay, *Pr*
EMP: 7 **EST:** 1940
SALES (est): 125.56K **Privately Held**
Web: www.caro.news
SIC: 2711 Newspapers, publishing and printing

(G-9981)
CAROMED INTERNATIONAL INC
Also Called: Polli Garment
5605 Spring Ct (27616-2920)
P.O. Box 4360 (18043-4360)
PHONE......................919 878-0578
Barbara Beck, *Pr*
Thomas A Barnett, *
Brian Madigan, *
EMP: 5 **EST:** 1983
SQ FT: 15,000
SALES (est): 485.84K **Privately Held**
Web: www.caromed.us
SIC: 3842 Bandages and dressings

(G-9982)
CARROLL RUSSELL MFG INC
2009 Carr Pur Dr (27603-8885)
PHONE......................919 779-2273
John Kissock, *Ch*
Russell K Carroll Junior, *Pr*
Donna Watkins, *
Connie Carroll, *
EMP: 45 **EST:** 1976
SQ FT: 52,000
SALES (est): 9.77MM **Privately Held**
Web: www.russwood.com
SIC: 2511 Wood household furniture

(G-9983)
CARY AUDIO DESIGN LLC
6301 Chapel Hill Rd (27607-5115)
PHONE......................919 355-0010
William W Wright Junior, *Managing Member*
▲ **EMP:** 24 **EST:** 1989
SQ FT: 10,000
SALES (est): 1.7MM **Privately Held**
Web: www.caryaudio.com
SIC: 3651 Household audio equipment

(G-9984)
CARY PRINTING
1528 Crickett Rd (27610-9300)
PHONE......................919 266-9005
Larry Whitaker, *Prin*
EMP: 5 **EST:** 2010
SALES (est): 159.76K **Privately Held**
SIC: 2752 Commercial printing, lithographic

(G-9985)
CASCADAS NYE CORPORATION
Also Called: Sir Speedy
2109 Avent Ferry Rd Ste 103 (27606-2198)
PHONE......................919 834-8128
Phillip Nye, *Pr*
Margaret Nye, *Stockholder*
Edith Nye, *Stockholder*
EMP: 10 **EST:** 1989

SALES (est): 402.67K **Privately Held**
Web: www.sirspeedy.com
SIC: 2752 Commercial printing, lithographic

(G-9986)
CASE SPECIALISTS
2033 Longwood Dr (27612-2814)
PHONE......................919 818-4476
Wayne Evans, *Owner*
EMP: 5 **EST:** 2003
SALES (est): 74.86K **Privately Held**
Web: www.casespecialists.com
SIC: 2449 Shipping cases and drums, wood: wirebound and plywood

(G-9987)
CAST IRON ELEGANCE INC
Also Called: Elite Custom Coatings
831 Purser Dr Ste 103 (27603-4181)
PHONE......................919 662-8777
Matt Vaughn, *CEO*
EMP: 15 **EST:** 2005
SALES (est): 1.93MM **Privately Held**
Web: www.castironelegance.com
SIC: 3446 2851 Architectural metalwork; Coating, air curing

(G-9988)
CCL LABEL
308 S Rogers Ln (27610-2925)
PHONE......................919 713-0388
▲ **EMP:** 10 **EST:** 2011
SALES (est): 1.2MM **Privately Held**
Web: www.ccllabel.com
SIC: 2759 Labels and seals: printing, nsk

(G-9989)
CELTIC CERAMICS
4140 Mardella Dr (27613-1529)
PHONE......................919 510-6817
Edward Gallagher, *Prin*
EMP: 5 **EST:** 2010
SALES (est): 245.5K **Privately Held**
SIC: 3269 Pottery products, nec

(G-9990)
CENGAGE LEARNING INC
Also Called: Webassign
1791 Varsity Dr Ste 200 (27606-5242)
P.O. Box 37665 (27627-7665)
PHONE......................919 829-8181
Michael Hansen, *Brnch Mgr*
EMP: 25
Web: www.webassign.com
SIC: 4813 7372 Internet connectivity services ; Educational computer software
HQ: Cengage Learning, Inc.
　　5191 Natorp Blvd
　　Mason OH 45040

(G-9991)
CENTICE CORPORATION
7283 Nc Highway 42 Ste 102 (27603-7529)
PHONE......................919 653-0424
John Goehrke, *CEO*
Rob Mclaughlin, *Sec*
Prasant Potuluri, *
EMP: 18 **EST:** 2003
SQ FT: 14,000
SALES (est): 1.74MM **Privately Held**
Web: www.centice.com
SIC: 3823 3826 5049 Process control instruments; Spectroscopic and other optical properties measuring equip.; Precision tools

(G-9992)
CHEF MARTINI LLC
1908 Falls Of Neuse Rd Ste 215 (27615)
P.O. Box 99806 (27624-9806)

PHONE......................919 327-3183
EMP: 1129 **EST:** 1989
SQ FT: 2,500
SALES (est): 1.62MM **Privately Held**
Web: www.chefmartini.us
SIC: 5149 5046 2035 2023 Natural and organic foods; Commercial cooking and food service equipment; Seasonings, meat sauces (except tomato and dry); Canned milk, whole

(G-9993)
CHESNICK CORPORATION
3236 Lake Woodard Dr (27604-3659)
PHONE......................919 231-2899
Mark A Chesnick, *Pr*
Charlie Lingenfelser, *VP*
Susan Latta, *Sec*
EMP: 15 **EST:** 1996
SQ FT: 20,000
SALES (est): 1.01MM **Privately Held**
Web: www.chesnick.com
SIC: 2431 2434 Moldings and baseboards, ornamental and trim; Wood kitchen cabinets

(G-9994)
CHOICE PRINTING LLC
4100 Wingate Dr (27609-6053)
PHONE......................919 790-0680
EMP: 5 **EST:** 2001
SALES (est): 115.3K **Privately Held**
SIC: 2752 Offset printing

(G-9995)
CIRCLE GRAPHICS INC
10700 World Trade Blvd (27617-4220)
PHONE......................919 864-4518
Hank Ridless, *Pr*
EMP: 250
SALES (corp-wide): 496.73MM **Privately Held**
Web: www.circlegraphicsonline.com
SIC: 2759 Commercial printing, nec
PA: Circle Graphics, Inc.
　　120 9th Ave
　　Longmont CO 80501
　　303 532-2370

(G-9996)
CIVES CORP
1621 Morning Mountain Rd (27614-9388)
PHONE......................919 518-2140
Howard Lachlar, *Owner*
EMP: 4 **EST:** 2002
SALES (est): 215.43K **Privately Held**
Web: www.cives.com
SIC: 3441 Fabricated structural metal

(G-9997)
CLARK ART SHOP INC
12705 Scenic Dr (27614-9183)
PHONE......................919 832-8319
Owen Walker Iii, *Pr*
Doris C Walker, *Sec*
EMP: 8 **EST:** 1923
SQ FT: 4,000
SALES (est): 245.89K **Privately Held**
Web: www.clarknow.org
SIC: 7999 2394 1799 Art gallery, commercial ; Awnings, fabric: made from purchased materials; Window treatment installation

(G-9998)
CLASSIC CLEANING LLC
Also Called: Commercial Cnstr Jantr Svcs
8601 Six Forks Rd Ste 400 (27615-2965)
PHONE......................800 220-7101
Patricia Mathis, *Pr*
Marcus Brinson, *
EMP: 30 **EST:** 2016
SALES (est): 1.41MM **Privately Held**

SIC: **7699** 0782 3315 7349 Cleaning services ; Lawn care services; Chain link fencing; Janitorial service, contract basis

(G-9999)
CLICK ELECTRONICS LLC
4030 Wake Forest Rd Ste 349
(27609-0010)
PHONE..............................704 840-6855
Jovan Ortiz, *Mgr*
EMP: 12
SALES (est): 1.39MM **Privately Held**
Web: www.clickic.net
SIC: **3679** Electronic components, nec

(G-10000)
CLINETIC INC
520 Guilford Cir (27608-1698)
PHONE..............................513 295-1332
Thomas Kaminski, *CEO*
EMP: 10 EST: 2017
SALES (est): 500K **Privately Held**
Web: www.clinetic.com
SIC: **7372** Business oriented computer software

(G-10001)
CLOSURE MEDICAL CORPORATION
5250 Greens Dairy Rd (27616-4612)
PHONE..............................919 876-7800
Daniel A Pelak, *Pr*
EMP: 123 EST: 1987
SQ FT: 69,000
SALES (est): 3.35MM
SALES (corp-wide): 88.82B **Publicly Held**
SIC: **2834** Pharmaceutical preparations
HQ: Ethicon Inc.
1000 Route 202
Raritan NJ 08869
800 384-4266

(G-10002)
CLOUD SFTWR GROUP HOLDINGS INC
Also Called: Citrix Sharefile
120 S West St (27603-1834)
PHONE..............................919 839-6139
EMP: 600
SALES (corp-wide): 4.38B **Privately Held**
Web: www.sharefile.com
SIC: **7372** Business oriented computer software
HQ: Cloud Software Group Holdings, Inc.
851 W Cypress Creek Rd
Fort Lauderdale FL 33309
954 267-3000

(G-10003)
COLD OFF PRESS LLC
416 W South St Ste 100 (27601-2242)
PHONE..............................984 444-9006
EMP: 4 EST: 2013
SALES (est): 195.29K **Privately Held**
Web: www.coldoffthepress.com
SIC: **5499** 2033 Juices, fruit or vegetable; Fruit juices: fresh

(G-10004)
COMPETITIVE SOLUTIONS INC (PA)
8340 Bandford Way Ste 103 (27615-2755)
PHONE..............................919 851-0058
John Pyecha, *CEO*
Anna Versteeg, *
John Pyecha, *Treas*
Shane Yount, *
EMP: 25 EST: 1991
SALES (est): 3.81MM **Privately Held**
Web: www.csipbl.com

SIC: **8742** 7372 8741 8748 Business management consultant; Business oriented computer software; Business management; Business consulting, nec

(G-10005)
COMPLETE COMP ST OF RALGH INC
Also Called: Digitz
3016 Hillsborough St Ste 100 (27607-0149)
P.O. Box 847 (27522-0847)
PHONE..............................919 828-5227
Joseph K Alukal, *Pr*
Maria J Alukal, *VP*
EMP: 20 EST: 1984
SQ FT: 7,700
SALES (est): 731.73K **Privately Held**
SIC: **5734** 7378 3955 Personal computers; Computer and data processing equipment repair/maintenance; Print cartridges for laser and other computer printers

(G-10006)
COMPUTER TASK GROUP INC
8801 Fast Park Dr Ste 101 (27617-4853)
PHONE..............................919 677-1313
Tom Stephenson, *Owner*
EMP: 26
SALES (corp-wide): 30.1MM **Privately Held**
Web: www.ctg.com
SIC: **7371** 7379 7374 7372 Custom computer programming services; Computer related consulting services; Data processing and preparation; Prepackaged software
HQ: Computer Task Group, Incorporated
300 Corp Pkwy Ste 214n
Amherst NY 14226
716 882-8000

(G-10007)
CONNECTMEDIA VENTURES LLC
425 N Boylan Ave (27603-1200)
PHONE..............................773 551-7446
EMP: 6 EST: 2009
SQ FT: 1,500
SALES (est): 455.66K **Privately Held**
Web: www.cmvmobile.com
SIC: **7372** Prepackaged software

(G-10008)
CONSOLIDATED MFG INTL LLC (PA)
Also Called: C M I
5816 Triangle Dr (27617-4705)
PHONE..............................919 781-3411
◆ EMP: 6 EST: 2002
SQ FT: 12,600
SALES (est): 2.62MM
SALES (corp-wide): 2.62MM **Privately Held**
Web: www.cmiwebsite.com
SIC: **3699** Electrical equipment and supplies, nec

(G-10009)
CONSOLIDATED SCIENCES INC
Also Called: Micro Technology Unlimited
8390 Six Forks Rd Ste 101 (27615-3060)
P.O. Box 80124 (27623-0124)
PHONE..............................919 870-0344
David B Cox, *Pr*
Bryan Cox, *
Benjamin Bryan Cox, *VP*
EMP: 5 EST: 1977
SQ FT: 1,500
SALES (est): 419.1K **Privately Held**
SIC: **3695** Computer software tape and disks: blank, rigid, and floppy

(G-10010)
CONTECH ENGNERED SOLUTIONS LLC
4917 Waters Edge Dr Ste 271
(27606-5416)
PHONE..............................919 858-7820
Brent Brewbaker, *Mgr*
EMP: 6
Web: www.conteches.com
SIC: **3443** Fabricated plate work (boiler shop)
HQ: Contech Engineered Solutions Llc
9025 Centre Pointe Dr # 400
West Chester OH 45069
513 645-7000

(G-10011)
CONTECH ENGNERED SOLUTIONS LLC
6115 Chapel Hill Rd (27607-5111)
PHONE..............................919 851-2880
Greg Demerjian, *Mgr*
EMP: 9
Web: www.conteches.com
SIC: **3443** Fabricated plate work (boiler shop)
HQ: Contech Engineered Solutions Llc
9025 Centre Pointe Dr # 400
West Chester OH 45069
513 645-7000

(G-10012)
CONTEGO MEDICAL INC
3801 Lake Boone Trl Ste 100 (27607-2994)
PHONE..............................919 606-3917
Ravish Sachar, *CEO*
Jay Yadav, *CEO*
Nathalie Greene, *VP*
EMP: 29 EST: 2010
SALES (est): 2.7MM **Privately Held**
Web: www.contegomedical.com
SIC: **3841** Surgical and medical instruments

(G-10013)
CONTEMPORARY PUBLISHING CO
1460 Diggs Dr Ste C (27603-2771)
P.O. Box 767 (27502-0767)
PHONE..............................919 834-4432
Ronald B Rose, *Pr*
Ellen Rose, *VP*
EMP: 5 EST: 1975
SALES (est): 53.99K **Privately Held**
SIC: **2731** Textbooks: publishing only, not printed on site

(G-10014)
CONTRACT PRINTING & GRAPHICS
2417 Bertie Dr (27610-1730)
PHONE..............................919 832-7178
Charles L Ethridge, *Owner*
EMP: 5 EST: 1975
SALES (est): 174.07K **Privately Held**
SIC: **7336** 2759 Commercial art and graphic design; Commercial printing, nec

(G-10015)
COOL RUNNINGS JAMAICAN LLC (PA)
Also Called: Millys Jamaican Jerk Seasoning
2700 Hidden Glen Ln (27606-8307)
PHONE..............................919 818-9220
Stephen Millington, *Managing Member*
EMP: 8 EST: 2019
SALES (est): 54.38K
SALES (corp-wide): 54.38K **Privately Held**
SIC: **2099** Seasonings and spices

(G-10016)
CORE SOUND IMAGING INC
5510 Six Forks Rd Ste 200 (27609-8620)
PHONE..............................919 277-0636
Mark Smith, *Pr*

Laurie Smith, *VP*
EMP: 39 EST: 2007
SALES (est): 2.76MM **Privately Held**
Web: app.corestudycast.com
SIC: **3841** Surgical and medical instruments

(G-10017)
CORNERSTONE KITCHENS INC
6300 Westgate Rd Ste C (27617-4754)
PHONE..............................919 510-4200
Scott Baltz, *Pr*
EMP: 4 EST: 1983
SALES (est): 94.45K **Privately Held**
Web: www.cornerstonekitchensnc.com
SIC: **2434** Wood kitchen cabinets

(G-10018)
COVIDIEN HOLDING INC
8800 Durant Rd (27616-3104)
PHONE..............................919 878-2930
Bob Hassebrock, *Brnch Mgr*
EMP: 177
SQ FT: 121,800
Web: www.medtronic.com
SIC: **3841** Surgical and medical instruments
HQ: Covidien Holding Inc.
710 Medtronic Pkwy
Minneapolis MN 55432

(G-10019)
CREATIONS CABINETRY DESIGN LLC
3825 Junction Blvd (27603-5264)
PHONE..............................919 865-5979
EMP: 6 EST: 2013
SALES (est): 1.4MM **Privately Held**
Web: www.creationscabinetry.com
SIC: **2434** Wood kitchen cabinets

(G-10020)
CREATIVE T-SHIRTS IMAGING LLC
2526 Hillsborough St Ste 101 (27607-7275)
PHONE..............................919 828-0204
Geraldine Jones, *Owner*
EMP: 4 EST: 2016
SALES (est): 149.91K **Privately Held**
Web: www.creativeteesraleigh.com
SIC: **2759** Screen printing

(G-10021)
CRMNEXT INC
702 Oberlin Rd Ofc Ofc (27605-1321)
PHONE..............................415 424-4644
Joseph Salesky, *Prin*
EMP: 34 EST: 2016
SALES (est): 7.88MM **Privately Held**
Web: www.businessnext.com
SIC: **7372** Business oriented computer software
PA: Acidaes Solutions Private Limited
Unitech Infospace, Block B, Plot No.2,
Tower 1
Noida UP 20130

(G-10022)
CRUDE LLC
501 E Davie St (27601-1917)
PHONE..............................919 391-8185
Craig Rudewicz, *Managing Member*
EMP: 5 EST: 2015
SALES (est): 261.23K **Privately Held**
Web: www.crudebitters.com
SIC: **2087** Flavoring extracts and syrups, nec

(G-10023)
CRUMBLE CUPS LLC
2161 S Wilmington St (27603-2539)
P.O. Box 2331 (27612)
PHONE..............................919 520-7414
Najia Ch, *Managing Member*

GEOGRAPHIC

EMP: 4 EST: 2022
SALES (est): 457.17K **Privately Held**
SIC: 2053 Cakes, bakery: frozen

(G-10024)
CRYOGEN LLC
Also Called: Glia Beauty
2626 Glenwood Ave Ste 140 (27608-1367)
PHONE.................................919 649-7027
Criollo Vinueza, *Managing Member*
Valeria Margarita, *Managing Member*
EMP: 15 EST: 2021
SQ FT: 1,174
SALES (est): 338.27K **Privately Held**
SIC: 2844 Perfumes, cosmetics and other
toilet preparations

(G-10025)
CTI PROPERTY SERVICES INC
Also Called: C T I Pressure Washing
5450 Old Wake Forest Rd (27609-5012)
P.O. Box 58635 (27658-8635)
PHONE.................................919 787-3789
Tim Felton, *Pr*
EMP: 37 EST: 1995
SALES (est): 2.56MM **Privately Held**
Web: www.ctipropertyservices.com
SIC: 0783 3271 1721 Removal services,
bush and tree; Blocks, concrete: insulating;
Painting and paper hanging

(G-10026)
CUPCAKE STOP SHOP LLC
6902 Cameron Crest Cir Apt 118
(27613-7348)
PHONE.................................919 457-7900
Stephanie Jones, *CEO*
EMP: 4 EST: 2022
SALES (est): 182.43K **Privately Held**
SIC: 2051 7389 Cakes, bakery: except frozen
; Business services, nec

(G-10027)
CURVEMAKERS INC (PA)
703 W Johnson St (27603-1295)
P.O. Box 33706 (27636-3706)
PHONE.................................919 821-5792
John Thomas, *Pr*
EMP: 9 EST: 1996
SQ FT: 20,000
SALES (est): 1.25MM
SALES (corp-wide): 1.25MM **Privately
Held**
Web: www.curvemakers.com
SIC: 2431 Doors, wood

(G-10028)
CUSTOM BRICK COMPANY INC
Also Called: Custom Brick and Supplied Co.
1833 Capital Blvd (27604-2144)
P.O. Box 6245 (27628-6245)
PHONE.................................919 832-2804
TOLL FREE: 800
Tom G Fisher, *Pr*
Steve Frazier, *VP*
Grant Fisher, *Treas*
EMP: 22 EST: 1961
SQ FT: 6,000
SALES (est): 8.81MM **Privately Held**
Web: www.custombrick.com
SIC: 5032 3271 2951 3272 Brick, stone, and
related material; Concrete block and brick;
Paving blocks; Cast stone, concrete

(G-10029)
**CUSTOM CONTROLS UNLIMITED
LLC**
2600 Garner Station Blvd (27603-4187)
PHONE.................................919 812-6553
Melissa Carroll, *Pr*
Devin Carrol, *VP*

EMP: 18 EST: 2000
SQ FT: 16,000
SALES (est): 2.66MM **Privately Held**
Web: www.ccuinc.com
SIC: 7373 1731 3625 8711 Systems
engineering, computer related; Electronic
controls installation; Electric controls and
control accessories, industrial; Engineering
services

(G-10030)
CUSTOM PATCH HATS LLC
1505 Capital Blvd Ste 14b (27603-1199)
PHONE.................................919 424-7723
Scott Alexander, *Managing Member*
EMP: 31 EST: 2018
SALES (est): 3.41MM **Privately Held**
Web: www.custompatchhats.com
SIC: 2353 2389 Hats, caps, and millinery;
Apparel and accessories, nec

(G-10031)
CYBER IMAGING SYSTEMS INC
8300 Falls Of Neuse Rd (27615-3449)
PHONE.................................919 872-5179
Hal E Wilson, *Pr*
James Welch, *Sec*
EMP: 10 EST: 1996
SQ FT: 2,000
SALES (est): 961.41K **Privately Held**
Web: www.eyeweb.com
SIC: 7372 Prepackaged software

(G-10032)
D & B PRINTING CO
3000 Trawick Rd (27604-3753)
PHONE.................................919 876-3530
Shirley Blake, *Owner*
EMP: 6 EST: 1975
SQ FT: 3,000
SALES (est): 369.23K **Privately Held**
SIC: 2752 Offset printing

(G-10033)
DAIRY SERVICES
100 Cordova Ct (27606)
PHONE.................................919 303-2442
Tyrone Tazewell, *Owner*
EMP: 4 EST: 1989
SALES (est): 197.33K **Privately Held**
SIC: 3523 Dairy equipment (farm), nec

(G-10034)
DALES WELDING SERVICE
7352 Berkshire Downs Dr (27616-5636)
PHONE.................................919 872-6969
Dale Kraynak, *Owner*
EMP: 5 EST: 1986
SALES (est): 239.28K **Privately Held**
Web: www.daleswelding.com
SIC: 7692 Welding repair

(G-10035)
DALLAS TRANS LLC
4030 Wake Forest Rd Ste 349
(27609-0010)
PHONE.................................704 965-6057
EMP: 8 EST: 2018
SALES (est): 1.75MM **Privately Held**
Web: www.dallastranstrucking.com
SIC: 3799 Transportation equipment, nec

(G-10036)
DATASPECTRUM
4700 Falls Of Neuse Rd (27609-6200)
PHONE.................................919 341-3300
David E Williams, *Prin*
EMP: 5 EST: 2004
SALES (est): 166.79K **Privately Held**

SIC: 2834 Pharmaceutical preparations

(G-10037)
DAUNTLESS DISCOVERY LLC
4141 Parklake Ave Ste 130 (27612-2333)
PHONE.................................610 909-7383
EMP: 132 EST: 2017
SALES (est): 2.16MM **Privately Held**
Web: www.dauntlessdiscovery.com
SIC: 7372 Prepackaged software

(G-10038)
DAVCOM ENTERPRISES INC
Also Called: Fastsigns
2621 Spring Forest Rd Ste 105
(27616-1830)
PHONE.................................919 872-9522
Tonya Davis, *Pr*
EMP: 8 EST: 1989
SQ FT: 2,800
SALES (est): 444.18K **Privately Held**
Web: www.fastsigns.com
SIC: 3993 Signs and advertising specialties

(G-10039)
DAVID ALLEN COMPANY INC (PA)
150 Rush St (27603-3594)
P.O. Box 27705 (27611-7705)
PHONE.................................919 821-7100
Robert C Roberson, *Ch*
Donald R Scott, *
David Roberson, *
Philip Halcomb, *
Martin Howard, *
▲ EMP: 150 EST: 1920
SQ FT: 25,000
SALES (est): 40.81MM
SALES (corp-wide): 40.81MM **Privately
Held**
Web: www.davidallen.com
SIC: 1743 3272 Tile installation, ceramic;
Areaways, basement window: concrete

(G-10040)
DDI PRINT
Also Called: Ddi
5210 Western Blvd (27606-1642)
PHONE.................................919 829-8810
EMP: 10 EST: 2010
SALES (est): 98.5K **Privately Held**
Web: www.documentsdirectinc.com
SIC: 2752 Offset printing

(G-10041)
DESCHER LLC
Also Called: Descher Automation
1613 Old Louisburg Rd (27604-1300)
PHONE.................................919 828-7708
EMP: 5 EST: 2008
SQ FT: 4,500
SALES (est): 777.39K **Privately Held**
Web: www.descher-automation.com
SIC: 3569 8711 7373 Assembly machines,
non-metalworking; Machine tool design;
Computer-aided design (CAD) systems
service

(G-10042)
DESIGN SPECIALTIES INC
Also Called: Presicion Wall
3640 Banks Rd (27603-8918)
PHONE.................................919 772-6955
Loy C Allen, *Pr*
Loy C Allen Junior, *VP*
Gary Roth, *Sec*
Jim Womble, *Sec*
EMP: 5 EST: 1985
SQ FT: 2,000
SALES (est): 181.4K **Privately Held**

SIC: 5032 5039 3355 Brick, stone, and
related material; Architectural metalwork;
Aluminum rolling and drawing, nec

(G-10043)
DESIGN SURFACES INC
Also Called: Design Surfaces of Raleigh
1212 Front St (27609-7527)
PHONE.................................919 781-0310
▲ EMP: 5 EST: 1989
SALES (est): 237.53K **Privately Held**
SIC: 5031 2499 5211 Structural assemblies,
prefabricated: wood; Decorative wood and
woodwork; Counter tops

(G-10044)
DESIGNELEMENT
972 Trinity Rd (27607-4940)
PHONE.................................919 383-5561
EMP: 14 EST: 2019
SALES (est): 408.1K **Privately Held**
Web: www.designelement-us.com
SIC: 3993 Signs and advertising specialties

(G-10045)
DEXTER INC (PA)
Also Called: Dexter Furniture
8411 Glenwood Ave Ste 101 (27612-7312)
PHONE.................................919 510-5050
Thomas Collins, *Pr*
EMP: 4 EST: 1985
SALES (est): 960.65K
SALES (corp-wide): 960.65K **Privately
Held**
Web: www.dexterfurniture.com
SIC: 5712 2512 Mattresses; Upholstered
household furniture

(G-10046)
DIMILL ENTERPRISES LLC
Also Called: Prism Specialties NC
531 Pylon Dr (27606-1414)
PHONE.................................919 629-2011
EMP: 5 EST: 2012
SALES (est): 331.71K **Privately Held**
Web: www.prismspecialties.com
SIC: 7699 3571 8999 5045 Antique repair
and restoration, except furniture, autos;
Electronic computers; Art restoration;
Computers and accessories, personal and
home entertainment

(G-10047)
DIRECT LEGAL MAIL LLC
8800 Westgate Park Dr Ste 110
(27617-4833)
PHONE.................................919 353-9158
Steve Darren Immelman, *Managing
Member*
EMP: 4 EST: 2019
SALES (est): 280.65K **Privately Held**
Web: www.directlegalmail.com
SIC: 2741 Miscellaneous publishing

(G-10048)
DIRECTUS HOLDINGS LLC (PA)
Also Called: Carolina Metal Fabricators
6016 Triangle Dr (27617-4743)
PHONE.................................919 510-8410
Jeffrey Matuszak, *Managing Member*
EMP: 5 EST: 1998
SALES (est): 4.87MM
SALES (corp-wide): 4.87MM **Privately
Held**
SIC: 3441 Fabricated structural metal

(G-10049)
DISCOVER NIGHT LLC
Also Called: Night
4030 Wake Forest Rd Ste 349
(27609-0010)

▲ = Import ▼ = Export
◆ = Import/Export

PHONE..................888 825-6282
Kalle Simpson, *Managing Member*
EMP: 12 **EST:** 2021
SALES (est): 1.31MM **Privately Held**
Web: www.discovernight.com
SIC: 2392 Pillows, bed: made from
purchased materials

(G-10050)
DIVERSE SECURITY SYSTEMS INC
8831 Westgate Park Dr Ste 100
(27617-4815)
PHONE.....................919 848-9599
Alan Brain, *Pr*
EMP: 4 **EST:** 1999
SALES (est): 917.82K **Privately Held**
Web:
www.diversesecuritysystemsinc.com
SIC: 3699 Security control equipment and
systems

(G-10051)
DNA GROUP INC (PA)
2841 Plaza Pl Ste 200 (27612-6746)
PHONE.....................919 881-0889
Eric Vaughn, *CEO*
W Michael Owens, *
Bill Romick, *Prin*
▲ **EMP:** 46 **EST:** 1987
SQ FT: 25,000
SALES (est): 6.71MM **Privately Held**
Web: www.dnagroup.com
SIC: 5063 3822 3643 3621 Electrical
apparatus and equipment; Environmental
controls; Current-carrying wiring services;
Motors and generators

(G-10052)
DOCMAGNET INC
6220 Angus Dr Ste 100 (27617-4752)
PHONE.....................919 788-7999
▲ **EMP:** 4
Web: www.docmagnet.com
SIC: 3499 Magnets, permanent: metallic

(G-10053)
DOCUMENT DIRECTS INC
5210 Western Blvd (27606-1642)
PHONE.....................919 829-8810
Quinn Wesson, *Pr*
EMP: 6 **EST:** 2005
SALES (est): 105.07K **Privately Held**
Web: www.documentsdirectinc.com
SIC: 2759 Commercial printing, nec

(G-10054)
DOCUMENT IMAGING SYSTEMS INC
Also Called: Engineering Reprographics
8709 Stage Ford Rd (27615-1826)
PHONE.....................919 460-9440
Laura Evans-sharp, *Pr*
Laura Evans, *Pr*
EMP: 4 **EST:** 1993
SALES (est): 346.6K **Privately Held**
Web:
www.documentimagingsystems.com
SIC: 7334 2741 Blueprinting service; Art
copy: publishing and printing

(G-10055)
DOLAN LLC
Also Called: North Carolina Lawyers Weekly
107 Fayetteville St 3rd Fl (27601-1398)
PHONE.....................919 829-9333
Liz Irwin, *Brnch Mgr*
EMP: 10
SALES (corp-wide): 83.73MM **Privately
Held**
Web: www.dolanmedia.com
SIC: 2711 Newspapers, publishing and
printing

HQ: Dolan Llc
222 S 9th St Ste 2300
Minneapolis MN 55402

(G-10056)
DOOR STORE OF AMERICA INC
Also Called: DSA Master Crafted Doors
10681 World Trade Blvd (27617-4304)
PHONE.....................919 781-3200
Eric Burkam, *Pr*
Eddie Wang, *VP*
▲ **EMP:** 19 **EST:** 2001
SQ FT: 25,000
SALES (est): 6.99MM **Privately Held**
Web: www.dsadoors.com
SIC: 2431 Doors, wood

(G-10057)
DOWNTOWN RALEIGH
402 Glenwood Ave (27603-1220)
PHONE.....................919 821-7897
EMP: 6 **EST:** 2014
SALES (est): 160.51K **Privately Held**
Web: www.welovedowntown.com
SIC: 2752 Commercial printing, lithographic

(G-10058)
DREAMSHIP INC
Also Called: Dreamshipper
12212 Kyle Abbey Ln (27613-6271)
PHONE.....................908 601-8152
William G Bricker Iii, *CEO*
EMP: 4 **EST:** 2018
SALES (est): 479.02K **Privately Held**
Web: www.dreamship.com
SIC: 7372 7389 Prepackaged software;
Business services, nec

(G-10059)
DRIVER DISTRIBUTION INC
Also Called: Eastern Bikes
9413 Owls Nest Dr (27613-7526)
PHONE.....................984 204-2929
Jon Byers, *CEO*
EMP: 6
SALES (corp-wide): 935.42K **Privately
Held**
Web: www.easternbikes.com
SIC: 3751 Motorcycles and related parts
PA: Driver Distribution, Inc.
624 N Carolina Ave Bldg 4
Maiden NC 28650
984 204-2929

(G-10060)
DRS TRANSPORTATION INC
Also Called: Drs Consulting
10820 Oliver Rd Apt 101 (27614-7341)
PHONE.....................919 215-2770
Lenny Gibson, *Prin*
EMP: 4 **EST:** 2013
SALES (est): 344.12K **Privately Held**
SIC: 3537 7389 Trucks: freight, baggage,
etc.: industrial, except mining; Business
Activities at Non-Commercial Site

(G-10061)
DSM INC
266 W Millbrook Rd (27609-4684)
PHONE.....................919 876-2802
Ralph Mullins, *Prin*
EMP: 8 **EST:** 2009
SALES (est): 137.89K **Privately Held**
Web: www.dsmbuildersinc.com
SIC: 2834 Pharmaceutical preparations

(G-10062)
DUCDUC LLC
Also Called: Ducduc Nyc
3200 Wake Forest Rd Ste 204
(27609-7451)

PHONE.....................212 226-1868
Philip Eidles, *Managing Member*
EMP: 8
Web: www.ducducnyc.com
SIC: 2511 Children's wood furniture
PA: Ducduc Llc
200 Lexington Ave Rm 715
New York NY 10016

(G-10063)
DUKE ENERGY CENTER
2 E South St (27601-2337)
PHONE.....................919 464-0960
EMP: 10 **EST:** 2019
SALES (est): 2.36MM **Privately Held**
Web: www.martinmariettacenter.com
SIC: 1389 Oil field services, nec

(G-10064)
DUNCAN DESIGN LTD
2308 Wake Forest Rd Ste E (27608-1756)
PHONE.....................919 834-7713
Todd Duncan, *Pr*
Susan Duncan, *VP*
EMP: 4 **EST:** 1986
SQ FT: 1,600
SALES (est): 219.29K **Privately Held**
SIC: 3911 5094 5944 Jewelry, precious metal
; Jewelry; Jewelry stores

(G-10065)
DUPONT
5816 Raddington St (27613-5719)
PHONE.....................919 414-0089
EMP: 6 **EST:** 2017
SALES (est): 398.01K **Privately Held**
Web: www.dupont.com
SIC: 2879 Agricultural chemicals, nec

(G-10066)
DURHAM COCA-COLA BOTTLING CO
Also Called: Coca-Cola
1 Floretta Pl (27613)
PHONE.....................919 510-0574
Tommy Dorsett, *Mgr*
EMP: 4
SALES (corp-wide): 30.49MM **Privately
Held**
Web: www.durhamcocacola.com
SIC: 2086 Bottled and canned soft drinks
PA: Durham Coca-Cola Bottling Company
3214 Hillsborough Rd
Durham NC 27705
919 383-1531

(G-10067)
EAGLE ROCK CONCRETE LLC (PA)
8310 Bandford Way (27615-2752)
PHONE.....................919 781-3744
Jay Loftin, *Pr*
Henry Willeym, *
Adam Loftin, *
Lyman Austin, *
Dexter Tart, *
EMP: 24 **EST:** 2011
SALES (est): 22.7MM
SALES (corp-wide): 22.7MM **Privately
Held**
Web: www.eaglerockconcrete.com
SIC: 3273 Ready-mixed concrete

(G-10068)
EAGLE ROCK CONCRETE LLC
Also Called: Raleigh Plant
8311 Bandford Way Ste 7 (27615-2761)
PHONE.....................919 281-0120
Jay Loftin, *Pr*
EMP: 44
SALES (corp-wide): 22.7MM **Privately
Held**
Web: www.eaglerockconcrete.com

SIC: 3273 Ready-mixed concrete
PA: Eagle Rock Concrete Llc
8310 Bandford Way
Raleigh NC 27615
919 781-3744

(G-10069)
**EAST CRLINA METAL TREATING INC
(PA)**
Also Called: Virginia Mtal Trting Lynchburg
1117 Capital Blvd (27603-1113)
PHONE.....................919 834-2100
Roscoe L Strickland Iii, *Pr*
Don Bryant, *
James D Ramm, *
EMP: 33 **EST:** 1976
SQ FT: 45,000
SALES (est): 6.13MM
SALES (corp-wide): 6.13MM **Privately
Held**
Web: www.ecmtinc.com
SIC: 3398 Metal heat treating

(G-10070)
EASTER SEALS UCP NC & VA INC
Also Called: Copymatic Document Solutions
2533 Atlantic Ave (27604-1567)
PHONE.....................919 856-0250
Greg Card, *Mgr*
EMP: 51
SALES (corp-wide): 91.81MM **Privately
Held**
Web: www.eastersealsucp.com
SIC: 8322 2759 Individual and family
services; Commercial printing, nec
PA: Easter Seals Ucp North Carolina &
Virginia, Inc.
5171 Glenwood Ave Ste 211
Raleigh NC 27612
919 832-3787

(G-10071)
EASTERN ELEVATOR INC
176 Mine Lake Ct (27615-6417)
PHONE.....................877 840-2638
Rob Rauch, *VP*
EMP: 4 **EST:** 2015
SALES (est): 570.25K **Privately Held**
SIC: 3534 Stair elevators, motor powered

(G-10072)
EATON CORPORATION
8609 Six Forks Rd (27615-2966)
PHONE.....................919 870-3000
EMP: 227
Web: www.dix-eaton.com
SIC: 3625 Motor controls and accessories
HQ: Eaton Corporation
1000 Eaton Blvd
Cleveland OH 44122
440 523-5000

(G-10073)
EATON CORPORATION
Also Called: Eaton US Raleigh
8380 Capital Blvd (27616-3146)
PHONE.....................864 433-1603
Steve Laughinghouse, *Mgr*
EMP: 74
Web: poweradvantage.eaton.com
SIC: 3629 7629 Power conversion units, a.c.
to d.c.: static-electric; Electrical equipment
repair services
HQ: Eaton Corporation
1000 Eaton Blvd
Cleveland OH 44122
440 523-5000

GEOGRAPHIC

(G-10074)
EATON CORPORATION
3301 Spring Forest Rd (27616-2922)
PHONE..............................919 872-3020
Mark Ascolese, *Pr*
EMP: 110
Web: poweradvantage.eaton.com
SIC: 3629 7629 3699 Power conversion
　units, a.c. to d.c.: static-electric; Electrical
　equipment repair services; Electrical
　equipment and supplies, nec
HQ: Eaton Corporation
　　1000 Eaton Blvd
　　Cleveland OH 44122
　　440 523-5000

(G-10075)
EATON POWER QUALITY CORP
8609 Six Forks Rd (27615-2966)
P.O. Box 58189 (27658-8189)
PHONE..............................919 872-3020
A M Cutler, *Pr*
Thomas Gutierrez, *Power Systems Division President*
Richard Nicholas, *Controller Power Systems Division*
R W Carson, *VP*
R H Fearon, *VP*
EMP: 11 **EST:** 1962
SQ FT: 93,000
SALES (est): 4.49MM **Privately Held**
Web: poweradvantage.eaton.com
SIC: 3629 7629 Power conversion units, a.c.
　to d.c.: static-electric; Electrical equipment
　repair services
HQ: Eaton Corporation
　　1000 Eaton Blvd
　　Cleveland OH 44122
　　440 523-5000

(G-10076)
EATON POWER QUALITY GROUP INC (DH)
8609 Six Forks Rd (27615-2966)
PHONE..............................919 872-3020
A M Cutler, *Pr*
David P Johnson, *VP*
Earl R Franklin, *VP*
Herve Tardy, *VP*
Loraine Leavell, *Prin*
▲ **EMP:** 4 **EST:** 2004
SALES (est): 1.8MM **Privately Held**
Web: poweradvantage.eaton.com
SIC: 3629 7629 Power conversion units, a.c.
　to d.c.: static-electric; Electrical equipment
　repair services
HQ: Eaton Corporation
　　1000 Eaton Blvd
　　Cleveland OH 44122
　　440 523-5000

(G-10077)
ECO-KIDS LLC
6316 J Richard Dr Ste C (27617-4614)
PHONE..............................207 899-2752
Cammie Weeks, *CEO*
Edward Weeks, *Pr*
EMP: 12 **EST:** 2008
SALES (est): 561.33K **Privately Held**
Web: www.ecokidsusa.com
SIC: 3952 Crayons: chalk, gypsum,
　charcoal, fusains, pastel, wax, etc.

(G-10078)
EDTECH SYSTEMS LLC
6115 Corporate Ridge Rd (27607-5473)
PHONE..............................919 341-0613
EMP: 5 **EST:** 2007
SALES (est): 460.1K **Privately Held**
SIC: 2676 Sanitary paper products

(G-10079)
EISAI INC
4130 Parklake Ave Ste 500 (27612-4462)
PHONE..............................919 941-6920
Dan Povia, *Mgr*
EMP: 13
Web: www.eisai.com
SIC: 2834 Pharmaceutical preparations
HQ: Eisai Inc.
　　200 Metro Blvd
　　Nutley NJ 07110
　　201 692-1100

(G-10080)
EIZI GROUP LLC
9008 Riverview Park Dr (27613-5392)
PHONE..............................919 397-3638
Gaurav Sharma, *Mng Pt*
EMP: 5 **EST:** 2016
SALES (est): 517.28K **Privately Held**
SIC: 3589 5063 3491 3312 Water treatment
　equipment, industrial; Electrical fittings and
　construction materials; Pressure valves and
　regulators, industrial; Galvanized pipes,
　plates, sheets, etc.: iron and steel

(G-10081)
ELECTRO SWITCH CORP
Also Called: Electroswitch
2010 Yonkers Rd (27604-2258)
P.O. Box 41129 (27629-1129)
PHONE..............................919 833-0707
Kyle Martin, *Brnch Mgr*
EMP: 105
SALES (corp-wide): 39.86MM **Privately Held**
Web: www.electroswitch.com
SIC: 3613 Switches, electric power except
　snap, push button, etc.
HQ: Electro Switch Corp.
　　775 Pleasant St Ste 1
　　Weymouth MA 02189
　　781 335-1195

(G-10082)
ELLEDGE FAMILY INC
Also Called: A Place To Copy
2900 Spring Forest Rd Ste 101
(27616-1896)
P.O. Box 58040 (27658)
PHONE..............................919 876-2300
Keith Ford, *Admn Mgr*
Susan Ford, *Sec*
Christoper Ford, *Dir*
EMP: 10 **EST:** 1990
SQ FT: 8,000
SALES (est): 839.45K **Privately Held**
Web: www.aplacetocopy.com
SIC: 2752 Offset printing

(G-10083)
ELSTER SOLUTIONS LLC
Also Called: Elster Electricity
201 S Rogers Ln (27610-4336)
PHONE..............................919 212-4819
Ray Schmitt, *Brnch Mgr*
EMP: 300
SALES (corp-wide): 38.5B **Publicly Held**
Web: portal.elstersolutions.com
SIC: 3825 Meters: electric, pocket, portable,
　panelboard, etc.
HQ: Elster Solutions, Llc
　　208 S Rogers Ln
　　Raleigh NC 27610
　　919 212-4800

(G-10084)
ELSTER SOLUTIONS LLC (DH)
Also Called: Electric Meter Division
208 S Rogers Ln (27610)
PHONE..............................919 212-4800

Mark Munday, *Pr*
Mark Fronmuller, *
Patrick Corrigan, *
◆ **EMP:** 415 **EST:** 2002
SQ FT: 115,500
SALES (est): 90.06MM
SALES (corp-wide): 38.5B **Publicly Held**
Web: www.elster-instromet.com
SIC: 3825 Meters: electric, pocket, portable,
　panelboard, etc.
HQ: Elster Gmbh
　　Steinern Str. 19-21
　　Mainz-Kastel HE 55252
　　61346050

(G-10085)
EMC CORPORATION
701 Corporate Center Dr Ste 425
(27607-5245)
PHONE..............................919 851-3241
Randall Gresset, *Mgr*
EMP: 9
Web: www.emc.com
SIC: 3572 Computer storage devices
HQ: Emc Corporation
　　176 S St
　　Hopkinton MA 01748
　　508 435-1000

(G-10086)
ENEPAY CORPORATION
7226 Summit Waters Ln (27613-7479)
PHONE..............................919 788-1454
Gary Stewart, *Prin*
EMP: 5 **EST:** 2008
SALES (est): 240.24K **Privately Held**
Web: www.enepay.com
SIC: 3999 Manufacturing industries, nec

(G-10087)
ENERGY SOLUTIONS (US) LLC
Also Called: Energy Solutions (US) LLC
9650 Strickland Rd Ste 103 (27615-1903)
PHONE..............................919 786-4555
Glewn Simon, *Brnch Mgr*
EMP: 144
SALES (corp-wide): 8.01MM **Privately Held**
Web: www.solvay.com
SIC: 2819 Industrial inorganic chemicals, nec
HQ: Solvay Usa Llc
　　504 Carnegie Ctr
　　Princeton NJ 08540
　　609 860-4000

(G-10088)
ENVIRONMENTAL SPECIALTIES LLC (DH)
4412 Tryon Rd (27606-4246)
PHONE..............................919 829-9300
Tim Whitener, *CEO*
Steve Draper, *
Chris Berrier, *
John Walters, *
EMP: 100 **EST:** 1973
SQ FT: 20,000
SALES (est): 20.23MM
SALES (corp-wide): 14.57B **Publicly Held**
Web: www.eschambers.com
SIC: 3826 7623 3564 Environmental testing
　equipment; Refrigeration service and repair
　; Blowers and fans
HQ: Bahnson, Inc.
　　4731 Commercial Park Ct
　　Clemmons NC 27012

(G-10089)
ENVISION INC
625 Hutton St Ste 102 (27606-6321)
PHONE..............................919 832-8962
James Friedrich, *Pr*

EMP: 6
Web: www.envisionllc.com
SIC: 3669 Intercommunication systems,
　electric
PA: Envision Inc
　　1025 Old Monrovia Rd Nw
　　Huntsville AL 35806

(G-10090)
EQUAGEN ENGINEERS PLLC
Also Called: Equagen Engineers
8045 Arco Corporate Dr Ste 220
(27617-2093)
PHONE..............................919 444-5442
Moti Kc, *CEO*
Moti Kc, *Prin*
EMP: 44 **EST:** 2018
SALES (est): 7.72MM **Privately Held**
Web: www.equagen.com
SIC: 8711 3999 3629 8741 Engineering
　services; Barber and beauty shop
　equipment; Electronic generation equipment
　; Construction management

(G-10091)
ESCAZU ARTISAN CHOCOLATE LLC
936 N Blount St (27604-1128)
PHONE..............................919 832-3433
EMP: 10 **EST:** 2007
SQ FT: 1,650
SALES (est): 281.15K **Privately Held**
Web: www.escazuchocolates.com
SIC: 5149 2066 Chocolate; Chocolate

(G-10092)
ESCO GROUP LLC
3221 Durham Dr Ste 118 (27603-3507)
PHONE..............................919 900-8226
Dean Heaney, *Mgr*
EMP: 8
SALES (corp-wide): 3.29B **Privately Held**
Web: www.escocorp.com
SIC: 3535 Conveyors and conveying
　equipment
HQ: Esco Group Llc
　　1631 Nw Thurman St
　　Portland OR 97209
　　503 228-2141

(G-10093)
EVANS AND MCCLAIN LLC
555 Fayetteville St Ste 201 (27601-3030)
PHONE..............................919 374-5578
EMP: 4 **EST:** 2021
SALES (est): 200K **Privately Held**
SIC: 2326 Men's and boy's work clothing

(G-10094)
EVENT 1 SOFTWARE INC
8529 Six Forks Rd Ste 400 (27615-4972)
PHONE..............................360 567-3752
Michael Newland, *Pr*
EMP: 9 **EST:** 2006
SALES (est): 1.31MM
SALES (corp-wide): 109.78MM **Privately Held**
Web: www.insightsoftware.com
SIC: 7372 Business oriented computer
　software
PA: Insightsoftware, Llc
　　8529 Six Forks Rd
　　Raleigh NC 27615
　　919 872-7800

(G-10095)
EVERGREEN PACKAGING LLC
Also Called: Raleigh Facility
2215 S Wilmington St (27603-2541)
PHONE..............................919 828-9134
Tom David, *Brnch Mgr*
EMP: 267

▲ = Import ▼ = Export
◆ = Import/Export

Web: www.pactivevergreen.com
SIC: 2621 Paper mills
HQ: Evergreen Packaging Llc
1900 W Field Ct
Lake Forest IL 60045

(G-10096)
EVIEW TECHNOLOGY INC
4909 Green Rd Ste 133 (27616-3419)
PHONE...................................919 878-5199
Sharon Gregory, *Pr*
Trent Gregory, *Dir*
▼ EMP: 6 EST: 1999
SQ FT: 5,000
SALES (est): 601.87K Privately Held
Web: www.precisely.com
SIC: 7372 Prepackaged software

(G-10097)
EVOLUTION TECHNOLOGIES INC
1121 Situs Ct Ste 130 (27606-4164)
PHONE...................................919 544-3777
Bradley Deifer, *Pr*
Donald Deifer, *VP*
▼ EMP: 6 EST: 2000
SQ FT: 3,100
SALES (est): 116.93K Privately Held
SIC: 3651 Household audio and video
equipment

(G-10098)
EXECUTIVE GROOMING LLC
5910 Duraleigh Rd Ste 133 (27612-2581)
PHONE...................................919 706-5382
EMP: 5 EST: 2017
SALES (est): 76.05K Privately Held
Web:
executive-grooming-services.business.site
SIC: 7241 7372 Hair stylist, men; Application
computer software

(G-10099)
EXPOSURE SOFTWARE LLC
1111 Haynes St Ste 107 (27604-1454)
PHONE...................................919 832-4124
EMP: 16 EST: 1993
SALES (est): 1.59MM Privately Held
Web: www.exposure.software
SIC: 7372 Application computer software

(G-10100)
EXTRON ELECTRONICS
2500 N Raleigh Blvd (27604-2478)
PHONE...................................919 850-1000
Robert Barra, *Prin*
EMP: 6 EST: 2019
SALES (est): 10.5MM Privately Held
SIC: 5065 3578 Sound equipment, electronic
; Automatic teller machines (ATM)

(G-10101)
FAIRWAY OUTDOOR ADVG LLC
FAIRWAY OUTDOOR ADVERTISING LLC
508 Capital Blvd (27603-1318)
PHONE...................................919 755-1900
Paul Hitman, *Mgr*
EMP: 5
SQ FT: 2,200
SIC: 7312 3993 Billboard advertising; Signs
and advertising specialties
HQ: Fairway Outdoor Advertising Llc
420 The Pkwy Bldg H
Greer SC 29650

(G-10102)
FAIRWAY PRINTING INC
821 Purser Dr Ste A (27603-4185)
P.O. Box 37429 (27627-7429)
PHONE...................................919 779-4797
Don Beasley, *Pr*

James Nichols, *Sec*
Neal Champion, *VP*
Jeanette Burlock, *VP*
EMP: 9 EST: 1988
SQ FT: 6,500
SALES (est): 237.54K Privately Held
Web: www.fairwayprintingofnc.com
SIC: 2752 Offset printing

(G-10103)
**FALLS OF NEUSE MANAGEMENT
LLC**
Also Called: National Coatings & Supplies
4900 Falls Of Neuse Rd Ste 150
(27609-5490)
PHONE...................................919 573-2900
Temple O Sloan Junior, *Managing Member*
EMP: 3599 EST: 2012
SALES (est): 35.62MM Privately Held
Web: www.fnmllc.com
SIC: 3559 Automotive maintenance
equipment

(G-10104)
FAMILY INDUSTRIES INC
Also Called: Woodplay
631 Macon Pl (27609-5649)
P.O. Box 97995 (27624-7995)
PHONE...................................919 875-4499
James Sally, *Pr*
John Sally Junior, *Stockholder*
James W Sally, *
Thomas Marenyi, *Stockholder**
EMP: 7 EST: 1976
SQ FT: 70,000
SALES (est): 326.13K Privately Held
SIC: 3949 7336 Playground equipment;
Commercial art and graphic design

(G-10105)
FEEDTRAIL INCORPORATED
811 Handsworth Ln Apt 108 (27607-5260)
PHONE...................................757 618-7760
Paul Jaglowski, *Pr*
EMP: 14 EST: 2017
SALES (est): 2.45MM Privately Held
Web: www.feedtrail.com
SIC: 7372 Operating systems computer
software

(G-10106)
FIELDX INC
7504 Deer Track Dr (27613-3508)
PHONE...................................919 926-7001
EMP: 4 EST: 2015
SALES (est): 245.03K Privately Held
Web: www.fieldx.com
SIC: 7372 Prepackaged software

(G-10107)
FIESTIC INC
555 Fayetteville St Ste 201 (27601-3030)
PHONE...................................888 935-3999
Jacob Ongwiseth, *CEO*
Nipith Ongwiseth, *CEO*
Jacob Ongwiseth, *Pr*
EMP: 15 EST: 2014
SQ FT: 1,200
SALES (est): 1.03MM Privately Held
Web: www.fiestic.com
SIC: 7372 7336 7371 Business oriented
computer software; Commercial art and
graphic design; Software programming
applications

(G-10108)
FIL-CHEM INC
3808 Evander Way (27613-5370)
P.O. Box 90833 (27675-0833)
PHONE...................................919 878-1270
Jerome Bogus, *Pr*

Felice Bogus, *VP*
EMP: 6 EST: 1966
SQ FT: 7,500
SALES (est): 114.24K Privately Held
Web: www.fil-chem.com
SIC: 2819 5169 3559 3812 Industrial
inorganic chemicals, nec; Chemical
additives; Metal finishing equipment for
plating, etc.; Search and navigation
equipment

(G-10109)
FINTRONX LLC
5995 Chapel Hill Rd Ste 119 (27607-0118)
PHONE...................................919 324-3960
Brenda Yatef, *CFO*
Pat Forbis, *Ch Bd*
▲ EMP: 10 EST: 2002
SQ FT: 7,000
SALES (est): 9MM Privately Held
Web: www.fintronx.com
SIC: 3641 5719 5063 Electric light bulbs,
complete; Lighting, lamps, and accessories;
Light bulbs and related supplies

(G-10110)
FIT1MEDIA LLC
8601 Six Forks Rd Ste 400 (27615-2965)
PHONE...................................919 925-2200
EMP: 4 EST: 2018
SALES (est): 870.41K Privately Held
Web: www.fit1media.com
SIC: 2741 7311 Internet publishing and
broadcasting; Advertising agencies

(G-10111)
FLAMEOFF COATINGS INC (PA)
3915 Beryl Rd Ste 130 (27607-5609)
PHONE...................................888 816-7468
Jim Turner, *Pr*
EMP: 8 EST: 2014
SALES (est): 1.39MM
SALES (corp-wide): 1.39MM Privately
Held
Web: www.flameoffcoatings.com
SIC: 3569 7371 Firefighting and related
equipment; Computer software
development and applications

(G-10112)
FLORES WELDING INC
961 Palace Garden Way (27603-2892)
PHONE...................................919 838-1060
Julio Flores, *Pr*
Marielle Flores, *VP*
Marielle Belhassen, *VP*
EMP: 7 EST: 1996
SQ FT: 4,000
SALES (est): 466.01K Privately Held
Web: www.floresweldinginc.com
SIC: 7692 Welding repair

(G-10113)
**FLORIDA PROGRESS
CORPORATION (DH)**
Also Called: Progress Energy Florida
410 S Wilmington St (27601-1849)
PHONE...................................704 382-3853
Richard D Keller, *CEO*
William D Johnson, *
Peter M Scott Iii, *Ex VP*
Robert B Mcgehee, *Ex VP*
EMP: 242 EST: 1982
SQ FT: 35,000
SALES (est): 6.59B
SALES (corp-wide): 30.36B Publicly Held
Web: www.duke-energy.com

SIC: 1221 4911 4011 4449 Bituminous coal
and lignite-surface mining; Generation,
electric power; Railroads, line-haul
operating; River transportation, except on
the St. Lawrence Seaway
HQ: Progress Energy, Inc.
410 S Wilmington St
Raleigh NC 27601
704 382-3853

(G-10114)
FLOWSERVE US INC
Also Called: Flowserve US Inc.
1900 S Saunders St (27603-2318)
P.O. Box 1961 (27602-1961)
PHONE...................................972 443-6500
EMP: 11
SALES (corp-wide): 4.56B Publicly Held
Web: www.flowserve.com
SIC: 3561 Pump jacks and other pumping
equipment
HQ: Flowserve Us Company
5215 N Ocnnor Blvd Ste 70
Irving TX 75039
972 443-6500

(G-10115)
FOCUSALES INC
6113 Chowning Ct (27612-6704)
PHONE...................................919 614-3076
Terry J Carlton, *Pr*
EMP: 6 EST: 2004
SALES (est): 432.36K Privately Held
Web: www.focusalesinc.com
SIC: 2782 Account books

(G-10116)
FOOTHOLD PUBLICATIONS INC
2656 Garden Knoll Ln (27614-8970)
PHONE...................................770 891-3423
Phillip A Lombardi, *CEO*
EMP: 5 EST: 2015
SALES (est): 48.89K Privately Held
SIC: 2741 Miscellaneous publishing

(G-10117)
FORTOVIA THERAPEUTICS INC (PA)
8540 Colonnade Center Dr Ste 101
(27615-3052)
PHONE...................................919 872-5578
Peter Melnyk, *CEO*
Craig Cook, *CMO*
Tim Sparey, *Chief Business Officer*
Dan Palmer, *CSO*
Ernest De Paolantonio, *CFO*
EMP: 8 EST: 1993
SQ FT: 7,520
SALES (est): 2.45MM Privately Held
Web: www.mcdbolatopone.com
SIC: 2834 Pharmaceutical preparations

(G-10118)
FRANKLIN BAKING COMPANY LLC
1404 S Bloodworth St (27610-3902)
PHONE...................................919 832-7942
Robert Reegs, *Mgr*
EMP: 6
SQ FT: 12,768
SALES (corp-wide): 5.1B Publicly Held
Web: franklin-co4goldsboro.edan.io
SIC: 2051 Bread, cake, and related products
HQ: Franklin Baking Company, Llc
500 W Grantham St
Goldsboro NC 27530
919 735-0344

(G-10119)
FREEMAN CUSTOM WELDING INC
2108 Langdon Rd (27604-3616)
PHONE...................................919 210-6267
Sie Freeman, *Pt*

EMP: 4 EST: 2006
SALES (est): 210.8K **Privately Held**
SIC: 7692 Welding repair

(G-10120)
FROEHLING & ROBERTSON INC
310 Hubert St (27603-2302)
PHONE..............................804 264-2701
Daniel Schaefer, *Mgr*
EMP: 44
SQ FT: 13,570
SALES (corp-wide): 42.68MM **Privately Held**
Web: www.fandr.com
SIC: 7389 8711 3829 8734 Inspection and testing services; Engineering services; Measuring and controlling devices, nec; Testing laboratories
PA: Froehling & Robertson Inc
    3015 Dumbarton Rd
    Richmond VA 23228
    804 264-2701

(G-10121)
FSC HOLDINGS INC
Also Called: Asphalt Plant 1
6001 Westgate Rd (27617-5222)
PHONE..............................919 782-1247
Donald Schell, *Mgr*
EMP: 5
SALES (corp-wide): 8.99MM **Privately Held**
Web: www.fredsmithcompany.net
SIC: 2951 Asphalt paving mixtures and blocks
PA: Fsc Holdings, Inc.
    6105 Chapel Hill Rd
    Raleigh NC 27607
    919 783-5700

(G-10122)
FSC II LLC (HQ)
Also Called: Fred Smith Company
701 Corporate Center Dr Ste 101 (27607-5084)
PHONE..............................919 783-5700
Fred Smith Iii, *Pr*
Jule Smith, *Pr*
EMP: 15 EST: 1998
SALES (est): 77.19MM
SALES (corp-wide): 1.82B **Publicly Held**
Web: www.fredsmithcompany.net
SIC: 5032 1499 Asphalt mixture; Asphalt (native) mining
PA: Construction Partners, Inc.
    290 Healthwest Dr Ste 2
    Dothan AL 36303
    334 673-9763

(G-10123)
FUN PUBLICATIONS INC
12513 Birchfalls Dr (27614-9675)
PHONE..............................919 847-5263
Brian Savage, *Pr*
Becky Savage, *VP*
EMP: 5 EST: 1992
SALES (est): 52.95K **Privately Held**
SIC: 2711 Newspapers: publishing only, not printed on site

(G-10124)
GATEWAY CAMPUS
1306 Hillsborough St (27605-1827)
PHONE..............................919 833-0096
Wendy Banister, *Prin*
EMP: 4 EST: 2007
SALES (est): 249.37K **Privately Held**
Web: www.gatewaywomens.care
SIC: 2835 Pregnancy test kits

(G-10125)
GEAMI LTD
3401 Gresham Lake Rd Ste 110 (27615-4243)
P.O. Box 8004 (44077-8004)
PHONE..............................919 654-7700
EMP: 25
Web: www.ranpak.com
SIC: 2621 5199 Packaging paper; Packaging materials

(G-10126)
GELDER & ASSOCIATES INC
3901 Gelder Dr (27603-5699)
PHONE..............................919 772-6895
EMP: 109 EST: 1953
SALES (est): 2.54MM
SALES (corp-wide): 1.82B **Publicly Held**
Web: www.gelderandassociates.com
SIC: 2951 1611 Asphalt paving mixtures and blocks; Surfacing and paving
PA: Construction Partners, Inc.
    290 Healthwest Dr Ste 2
    Dothan AL 36303
    334 673-9763

(G-10127)
GENERAL SHALE BRICK INC
7101 Creedmoor Rd (27613-1682)
PHONE..............................919 775-2121
Bill Brown, *Principal B*
EMP: 27
SALES (corp-wide): 4.59B **Privately Held**
Web: www.generalshale.com
SIC: 3251 5032 Brick and structural clay tile; Brick, stone, and related material
HQ: General Shale Brick, Inc.
    3015 Bristol Hwy
    Johnson City TN 37601
    423 282-4661

(G-10128)
GEORGE CLINICAL INC
120 Penmarc Dr (27603-2574)
PHONE..............................919 789-2022
EMP: 5 EST: 2017
SALES (est): 193.75K **Privately Held**
Web: www.georgeclinical.com
SIC: 2834 Pharmaceutical preparations

(G-10129)
GEORGIA PRATT BOX INC
5620 Departure Dr (27616-1841)
PHONE..............................919 872-3007
EMP: 103
Web: www.prattindustries.com
SIC: 2653 Boxes, corrugated: made from purchased materials
HQ: Georgia Pratt Box Inc
    1800 Sarasot Bus Pkwy Ne
    Conyers GA 30013
    864 963-0992

(G-10130)
GEOSONICS INC
5874 Faringdon Pl Ste 100 (27609-3932)
PHONE..............................919 790-9500
William Powell, *Genl Mgr*
EMP: 5
SALES (corp-wide): 9.71MM **Privately Held**
Web: www.geosonicsvibratech.com
SIC: 8999 3829 Geological consultant; Seismographs
PA: Geosonics, Inc.
    359 Northgate Dr Ste 200
    Warrendale PA 15086
    724 934-2900

(G-10131)
GERDAU AMERISTEEL US INC
Ameristeel Rligh Fab Rnfrcing
2126 Garner Rd (27610-4608)
PHONE..............................919 833-9737
Ron Long, *Brnch Mgr*
EMP: 27
SQ FT: 36,484
SALES (corp-wide): 1.56B **Privately Held**
Web: gerdau.com
SIC: 3449 3441 Miscellaneous metalwork; Fabricated structural metal
HQ: Gerdau Ameristeel Us Inc.
    4221 W Boy Scout Blvd Ste
    Tampa FL 33607
    813 286-8383

(G-10132)
GETBRIDGE LLC
Also Called: Bridge
434 Fayetteville St Fl 9 (27601-1891)
PHONE..............................919 645-2800
Peter Brussard, *Pr*
Jocelyn Karney, *CFO*
Eric Fairbanks, *CMO*
EMP: 155 EST: 2020
SALES (est): 13.35MM
SALES (corp-wide): 700.88MM **Privately Held**
Web: www.getbridge.com
SIC: 7372 Educational computer software
HQ: Learning Technologies Group Inc.
    300 5th Ave
    Waltham MA 02451
    781 530-2000

(G-10133)
GIK INC
Also Called: Sir Speedy
1801 Saint Albans Dr Ste B (27609-6286)
PHONE..............................919 872-9498
Lloyd Newton, *Pr*
Colleen Newton, *Sec*
Frank Shepphard Stkldr, *Prin*
EMP: 12 EST: 1981
SQ FT: 6,000
SALES (est): 2.34MM **Privately Held**
Web: www.sirspeedy.com
SIC: 2752 7334 2791 2789 Commercial printing, lithographic; Photocopying and duplicating services; Typesetting; Bookbinding and related work

(G-10134)
GILEAD SCIENCES INC
305 Church At North Hills St (27609-2666)
PHONE..............................650 574-3000
EMP: 4
SALES (corp-wide): 28.75B **Publicly Held**
Web: www.gilead.com
SIC: 2834 Pharmaceutical preparations
PA: Gilead Sciences, Inc.
    333 Lakeside Dr
    Foster City CA 94404
    650 574-3000

(G-10135)
GK SOFTWARE USA INC
Also Called: GK Software USA
9121 Anson Way Ste 150 (27615-5858)
PHONE..............................984 255-7995
Michael Jaszczyk, *Pr*
EMP: 45 EST: 2013
SALES (est): 14.62MM
SALES (corp-wide): 187.5MM **Privately Held**
Web: www.gk-software.com
SIC: 7372 Business oriented computer software
PA: Gk Software Se
    Waldstr. 7

Schoneck/Vogtl. SN 08261
37464840

(G-10136)
GLASER DESIGNS INC
2825 Seclusion Ct Apt A (27612-6632)
PHONE..............................415 552-3188
Myron Glaser, *Pr*
Kari Glaser, *VP*
EMP: 10 EST: 1975
SALES (est): 306.28K **Privately Held**
Web: www.shapingsoundco.com
SIC: 3171 3172 3161 Handbags, women's; Personal leather goods, nec; Clothing and apparel carrying cases

(G-10137)
GLOBAL FILTER SOURCE LLC
6212 Westgate Rd Ste A (27617-4847)
P.O. Box 99215 (27624-9215)
PHONE..............................919 571-4945
Paul Bryant, *Owner*
EMP: 4 EST: 2005
SALES (est): 662.41K **Privately Held**
Web: www.globalfiltersource.com
SIC: 3569 Filters

(G-10138)
GLOBAL SOFTWARE LLC
Also Called: GLOBAL SOFTWARE, LLC
3200 Atlantic Ave Ste 200 (27604-1668)
PHONE..............................919 872-7800
Zack Michael Schuch, *Owner*
EMP: 8
SALES (corp-wide): 109.78MM **Privately Held**
Web: www.insightsoftware.com
SIC: 7372 Prepackaged software
PA: Insightsoftware, Llc
    8529 Six Forks Rd
    Raleigh NC 27615
    919 872-7800

(G-10139)
GLOVER CORPORATION INC
Also Called: Glover Printing Company
2401 Atlantic Ave (27604-1409)
PHONE..............................919 821-5535
Louis M Goldberg, *Pr*
Brian Goldberg, *Sec*
EMP: 38 EST: 1963
SALES (est): 1.67MM **Privately Held**
Web: www.gloverconstruction.com
SIC: 5045 5084 2752 Printers, computer; Packaging machinery and equipment; Offset and photolithographic printing

(G-10140)
GOUNMANNED LLC
533 Pylon Dr (27606-1414)
PHONE..............................919 835-2140
Maria Kolar, *Prin*
EMP: 4 EST: 2017
SALES (est): 1.02MM **Privately Held**
Web: www.gounmanned.com
SIC: 3728 Aircraft parts and equipment, nec

(G-10141)
GP TECHNOLOGY LLC
Also Called: Sitech Precision
4807 Beryl Rd (27606-1406)
PHONE..............................919 876-3666
EMP: 14 EST: 2020
SALES (est): 715.87K **Privately Held**
SIC: 1389 Construction, repair, and dismantling services

(G-10142)
GRACEFULLY GIFTED HANDS LLC
8480 Honeycutt Rd Ste 200 (27615-2261)

PHONE..............845 248-8743
Crystal Hines, *Managing Member*
EMP: 5 **EST:** 2019
SALES (est): 205.73K **Privately Held**
SIC: 3944 Craft and hobby kits and sets

(G-10143)
GREENE IMAGING & DESIGN INC
Also Called: Image 360, Raleigh-Rtp
6320 Angus Dr Ste E (27617-4756)
PHONE..............919 787-3737
Robert N Greene, *Pr*
EMP: 5 **EST:** 2007
SQ FT: 1,800
SALES (est): 235.68K **Privately Held**
SIC: 3993 Signs and advertising specialties

(G-10144)
GREENOLOGY PRODUCTS LLC
7020 Cynrow Blvd (27615-5739)
PHONE..............877 473-3650
Adam Mccarthy, *CEO*
Adam Mccarthy, *Pr*
Shanna Redkey, *Marketing**
Frank Lemanski, ***
▼ **EMP:** 25 **EST:** 2008
SQ FT: 3,000
SALES (est): 4.63MM **Privately Held**
Web: www.greenshieldorganic.com
SIC: 5169 2841 Detergents; Soap and other detergents

(G-10145)
GREENWICH BAY TRADING CO INC
5809 Triangle Dr Ste C (27617-4809)
P.O. Box 90787 (27675-0787)
PHONE..............919 781-5008
Richard Huntwork, *Mgr*
EMP: 23
SALES (corp-wide): 4.12MM **Privately Held**
Web: www.gbsoaps.com
SIC: 2844 2841 Perfumes, cosmetics and other toilet preparations; Soap and other detergents
PA: Greenwich Bay Trading Co Inc
216 Spencer Ave
East Greenwich RI 02818
401 885-0144

(G-10146)
GREGORY POOLE EQUIPMENT CO
2620 Discovery Dr (27616-1817)
PHONE..............919 872-2691
EMP: 10
SALES (corp-wide): 592.57MM **Privately Held**
Web: www.gregorypoolelift.com
SIC: 7359 5084 5082 3569 Garage facility and tool rental; Industrial machinery and equipment; Construction and mining machinery; Assembly machines, non-metalworking
HQ: Gregory Poole Equipment Company
4807 Beryl Rd
Raleigh NC 27606
919 828-0641

(G-10147)
GRIFFIN PRINTING INC
500 Uwharrie Ct Ste A (27606-1469)
P.O. Box 10812 (27605-0812)
PHONE..............919 832-6931
Jack Griffin, *Pr*
▲ **EMP:** 4 **EST:** 1976
SALES (est): 106.43K **Privately Held**
Web: www.griffinprint.com
SIC: 2752 Offset printing

(G-10148)
GRIFOLS THERAPEUTICS LLC
1017 Main Campus Dr Ste 2580 (27606-5204)
PHONE..............919 316-6612
Greg Rich, *Brnch Mgr*
EMP: 4199
Web: www.discovertheplasma.com
SIC: 2836 Blood derivatives
HQ: Grifols Therapeutics Llc
79 Tw Alexander Dr
Research Triangle Pa NC 27709

(G-10149)
GRIP POD SYSTEMS INTL LLC
6321 Swallow Cove Ln (27614-7161)
PHONE..............239 233-3694
Joseph Gaddini, *Managing Member*
EMP: 5 **EST:** 2012
SALES (est): 761.65K **Privately Held**
Web: www.grippod.com
SIC: 3484 Guns (firearms) or gun parts, 30 mm. and below

(G-10150)
GRT ELECTRONICS LLC
Also Called: G R T Electronics
3805 Beryl Rd (27607-5244)
PHONE..............919 821-1996
▲ **EMP:** 19 **EST:** 2001
SQ FT: 6,000
SALES (est): 3.62MM **Privately Held**
Web: www.grtelectronics.com
SIC: 3672 Circuit boards, television and radio printed

(G-10151)
GT RHYNO CONSTRUCTION LLC
7061 Fox Meadow Ln Apt 911 (27616-7649)
PHONE..............919 737-3620
EMP: 6
SALES (est): 264.29K **Privately Held**
SIC: 1389 7389 Construction, repair, and dismantling services; Business services, nec

(G-10152)
GUERBET LLC
Also Called: Guerbet
8800 Durant Rd Ste 800 (27616-3104)
PHONE..............919 878-2930
Justin Cappelmann, *Brnch Mgr*
EMP: 19
SALES (corp-wide): 532.38MM **Privately Held**
Web: www.guerbet.com
SIC: 2833 5122 Medicinals and botanicals; Drugs, proprietaries, and sundries
HQ: Guerbet Llc
214 Carnegie Ctr Ste 300
Princeton NJ 08540
812 333-0059

(G-10153)
HAIRCUTTERS OF RALEIGH INC
4024 Barrett Dr Ste 102 (27609-6625)
PHONE..............919 781-3465
Renee Tilley, *Owner*
EMP: 4 **EST:** 1985
SQ FT: 1,000
SALES (est): 175.74K **Privately Held**
Web: www.heir-raleigh.com
SIC: 7231 2844 Hairdressers; Manicure preparations

(G-10154)
HAMILTON MACHINE WORKS LLC
908 Withers Rd (27603-6095)
P.O. Box 37516 (27627-7516)
PHONE..............919 779-6892
Robert Hamilton Junior, *Pt*
Linwood Hamilton, *Pt*
EMP: 8 **EST:** 1967
SQ FT: 4,400
SALES (est): 1.02MM **Privately Held**
Web: www.hamiltonmachineworks.com
SIC: 3599 Machine shop, jobbing and repair

(G-10155)
HARGROVE COUNTERTOPS & ACC INC
Also Called: Atlantic Counter Top & ACC
5250 Old Wake Forest Rd Ste 100 (27609-5275)
PHONE..............919 981-0163
Michael Orlikoff, *Pr*
EMP: 20 **EST:** 1994
SQ FT: 12,000
SALES (est): 2.13MM **Privately Held**
Web: www.atlanticcountertops.com
SIC: 2541 5211 5084 Counter and sink tops; Counter tops; Countersinks

(G-10156)
HARRIS TEETER LLC
Also Called: Harris Teeter 038
5563 Western Blvd Ste 38 (27606-1595)
PHONE..............919 859-0110
Doug Benton, *Mgr*
EMP: 58
SALES (corp-wide): 150.04B **Publicly Held**
Web: www.harristeeter.com
SIC: 5411 2051 Supermarkets, chain; Bread, cake, and related products
HQ: Harris Teeter, Llc
701 Crestdale Rd
Matthews NC 28105
704 844-3100

(G-10157)
HAYDON & COMPANY
1803 Oberlin Rd (27608-2043)
PHONE..............919 781-1293
Kenneth W Haydon, *Pr*
EMP: 8 **EST:** 1976
SQ FT: 4,200
SALES (est): 905.12K **Privately Held**
Web: www.haydonco.com
SIC: 5944 3911 Jewelry, precious stones and precious metals; Jewelry, precious metal

(G-10158)
HEALTHLINK EUROPE
611 Creekside Dr (27609-7807)
PHONE..............919 368-2187
EMP: 10 **EST:** 2015
SALES (est): 740.73K **Privately Held**
Web: www.healthlinkeurope.com
SIC: 3841 Surgical and medical instruments

(G-10159)
HEALTHLINK EUROPE
3737 Glenwood Ave Ste 100 (27612-5515)
PHONE..............919 783-4142
Richard Hughes, *Pr*
Rick Hughes, *Pr*
EMP: 17 **EST:** 2010
SALES (est): 678.56K **Privately Held**
Web: www.healthlinkeurope.com
SIC: 3841 Medical instruments and equipment, blood and bone work

(G-10160)
HEALTHLINK INTERNATIONAL INC
Also Called: Healthlink Europe & Intl
2235 Gateway Access Pt (27607-3070)
PHONE..............877 324-2837
EMP: 9 **EST:** 2013

SALES (est): 4.15MM **Privately Held**
Web: www.healthlinkeurope.com
SIC: 3841 Muscle exercise apparatus, ophthalmic
HQ: Healthlink Europe B.V.
Pettelaarpark 114
's-Hertogenbosch NB 5216
135479300

(G-10161)
HEIDELBERG MTLS STHAST AGG LLC
5001 Duraleigh Rd (27612-7627)
P.O. Box 52039 (27612-0039)
PHONE..............919 787-0613
Kenneth W Kennedy, *Mgr*
EMP: 36
SALES (corp-wide): 23.02B **Privately Held**
Web: www.hansonbiz.com
SIC: 1429 Igneus rock, crushed and broken-quarrying
HQ: Heidelberg Materials Southeast Agg Llc
3237 Satellite Blvd # 30
Duluth GA 30096
770 491-2756

(G-10162)
HELIUM AGENCY LLC
2207 Alexander Rd (27608-1644)
PHONE..............919 833-1358
Wilbur Garner Lingo Iii, *Owner*
EMP: 5 **EST:** 2018
SALES (est): 131.44K **Privately Held**
Web: www.helium-agency.com
SIC: 2813 Helium

(G-10163)
HEXATECH INC
8311 Brier Creek Pkwy (27617-7328)
PHONE..............919 633-0583
Raoul Schlesser, *Prin*
EMP: 4 **EST:** 2010
SALES (est): 648.18K **Privately Held**
Web: www.hexatechinc.com
SIC: 3674 Semiconductors and related devices

(G-10164)
HEYEL CUSTOM METAL
1224 Home Ct (27603-4541)
PHONE..............919 957-8442
EMP: 7
SALES (est): 123.72K **Privately Held**
Web: www.heyelcustommetal.com
SIC: 3441 Fabricated structural metal

(G-10165)
HEYEL CUSTOM METAL INC
1224 Home Ct (27603-4541)
P.O. Box 13527 (27709-3527)
PHONE..............919 957-8442
Stuart Heyel, *Pr*
David Quate, *VP*
Marshall Quate, *Sec*
EMP: 10 **EST:** 1995
SQ FT: 7,000
SALES (est): 1.15MM **Privately Held**
Web: www.heyelcustommetal.com
SIC: 3441 Fabricated structural metal

(G-10166)
HI-TECH FABRICATION INC
222 Glenwood Ave Apt 503 (27603-1496)
P.O. Box 80668 (27623-0668)
PHONE..............919 781-6150
▲ **EMP:** 145
Web: www.htfi.com

SIC: **3469** 3444 3479 3471 Stamping metal for the trade; Sheet metalwork; Painting of metal products; Chromium plating of metals or formed products

(G-10167)
HIGH PERFORMANCE MARKETING INC
158 Wind Chime Ct (27615-6433)
PHONE...................................919 870-9915
Jay Langley, *CEO*
EMP: 7 EST: 1991
SQ FT: 2,000
SALES (est): 446.01K **Privately Held**
Web: www.hpmmail.com
SIC: **7336** 2759 Commercial art and graphic design; Commercial printing, nec

(G-10168)
HITACHI ENERGY USA INC
Also Called: Hitachi ABB Power Grids
901 Main Campus Dr (27606-5293)
PHONE...................................919 649-7022
Yoann Barbosa, *CFO*
EMP: 17
SIC: **7372** Prepackaged software
HQ: Hitachi Energy Usa Inc
901 Main Campus Dr
Raleigh NC 27606
919 856-2360

(G-10169)
HITACHI ENERGY USA INC
1345 Express Dr (27603-4156)
PHONE...................................919 324-5403
EMP: 13
SIC: **3675** Electronic capacitors
HQ: Hitachi Energy Usa Inc
901 Main Campus Dr
Raleigh NC 27606
919 856-2360

(G-10170)
HITACHI ENERGY USA INC (HQ)
901 Main Campus Dr (27606-5293)
P.O. Box 90774 (27675)
PHONE...................................919 856-2360
Yoann Barbosa, *CEO*
Anthony Allard, ***
EMP: 200 EST: 1997
SQ FT: 10,000
SALES (est): 503.54MM **Privately Held**
SIC: **3675** 3699 3621 Electronic capacitors; Electrical equipment and supplies, nec; Motors and generators
PA: Hitachi, Ltd.
1-6-6, Marunouchi
Chiyoda-Ku TKY 100-0

(G-10171)
HOLLEY SELINDA
Also Called: Helpmehelpu
700 Peterson St (27610-0053)
PHONE...................................919 351-9466
Selinda Holley, *Owner*
Selinda Holley, *Mgr*
EMP: 5 EST: 2015
SALES (est): 134.31K **Privately Held**
SIC: **2761** Manifold business forms

(G-10172)
HOLLISTER INCORPORATED
5959 Triangle Town Blvd Ste 1085 (27616-3270)
PHONE...................................919 792-2095
Caroline Knorr, *Brnch Mgr*
EMP: 6
SALES (corp-wide): 709.48MM **Privately Held**
Web: www.hollisterco.com

SIC: **3842** Surgical appliances and supplies
PA: Hollister Incorporated
2000 Hollister Dr
Libertyville IL 60048
847 680-1000

(G-10173)
HONEYWELL INTERNATIONAL INC
Also Called: Honeywell
201 S Rogers Ln (27610-4336)
PHONE...................................919 662-7539
Vince Iamunno, *Brnch Mgr*
EMP: 657
SALES (corp-wide): 38.5B **Publicly Held**
Web: www.honeywell.com
SIC: **3724** Aircraft engines and engine parts
PA: Honeywell International Inc.
855 S Mint St
Charlotte NC 28202
704 627-6200

(G-10174)
HORBALLS INC
1009 Lila Ln (27614-9118)
PHONE...................................919 925-0483
EMP: 5 EST: 2017
SALES (est): 230.21K **Privately Held**
Web: www.horballs.com
SIC: **2099** Food preparations, nec

(G-10175)
HORIZON FREST PDTS WLMNGTON LP
Also Called: Horizon Forest Products
4115 Commodity Pkwy (27610-2973)
P.O. Box 46809 (27620-6809)
PHONE...................................919 424-8265
Jeff Myer, *Pr*
David Wiilliams, *VP*
EMP: 100 EST: 1992
SQ FT: 10,000
SALES (est): 1.64MM **Privately Held**
Web: www.horizonforest.com
SIC: **2426** Flooring, hardwood

(G-10176)
HORSEWARE TRIPLE CROWN BLANKET
1030 N Rogers Ln (27610-6083)
P.O. Box 6328 (28501-0328)
PHONE...................................252 208-0080
▲ **EMP: 13 EST:** 1996
SALES (est): 1MM **Privately Held**
Web: www.horseware.com
SIC: **2399** Horse blankets

(G-10177)
HOUSE OF HOPS
6909 Glenwood Ave (27612-7100)
PHONE...................................919 819-0704
EMP: 4 EST: 2015
SALES (est): 236.32K **Privately Held**
Web: www.houseofhopsnc.com
SIC: **2082** Malt beverages

(G-10178)
HRTMS INCORPORATED
801 Corporate Center Dr Ste 130 (27607-5243)
PHONE...................................919 741-5099
Andrew Ellerhorst, *Pr*
EMP: 9 EST: 2005
SALES (est): 5.35MM **Privately Held**
Web: www.jdxpert.com
SIC: **7372** 7389 Prepackaged software; Business services, nec

(G-10179)
HUBER USA INC
1101 Nowell Rd # 110 (27607-5242)

PHONE...................................919 674-4266
Georg Kiefer, *CEO*
EMP: 19 EST: 2014
SALES (est): 5.6MM
SALES (corp-wide): 166.62K **Privately Held**
Web: www.huber-usa.com
SIC: **3822** Environmental controls
PA: Huber Kg
Werner-Von-Siemens-Str. 1
Offenburg BW
781 960-3244

(G-10180)
HUMBOLDT MFG CO INC
2525 Atlantic Ave (27604-1411)
PHONE...................................919 832-6509
Mahir Alnadaf, *VP*
EMP: 8 EST: 2015
SALES (est): 820.91K **Privately Held**
Web: www.humboldtmfg.com
SIC: **3999** Manufacturing industries, nec

(G-10181)
HUNTER INNOVATIONS LTD
1201 Corporation Pkwy (27610-1349)
P.O. Box 17105 (27619-7105)
PHONE...................................919 848-8814
Al Hunter, *Pr*
Nancy Hunter, *VP*
EMP: 7 EST: 1986
SQ FT: 17,000
SALES (est): 937.51K **Privately Held**
Web: www.oakcitycolumns.com
SIC: **2431** 5031 Millwork; Millwork

(G-10182)
I MUST GARDEN LLC
1500 Garner Rd Ste D (27610-6669)
PHONE...................................919 929-2299
▲ **EMP: 5 EST:** 2004
SALES (est): 1.23MM **Privately Held**
Web: www.imustgarden.com
SIC: **5261** 5941 2879 Lawn and garden equipment; Golf goods and equipment; Agricultural disinfectants

(G-10183)
ICARE USA INC
Also Called: Icare Tonomoter
809 Faulkner Pl (27609-5943)
PHONE...................................919 877-9607
EMP: 4
SALES (corp-wide): 100.72MM **Privately Held**
Web: www.icare-world.com
SIC: **3822** Hydronic pressure or temperature controls
HQ: Icare Finland Oy
Ayritie 22
Vantaa 01510

(G-10184)
IDEA SOFTWARE INC
10814 Greater Hills St (27614-8653)
PHONE...................................407 453-3883
David E Terry, *Prin*
EMP: 5 EST: 2009
SALES (est): 123.95K **Privately Held**
SIC: **7372** Prepackaged software

(G-10185)
IDEAL PRECISION METER INC
5816 Creedmoor Rd Ste 103 (27612-2310)
PHONE...................................919 571-2000
Mohamed El-refai, *Pr*
EMP: 7 EST: 1972
SQ FT: 25,000
SALES (est): 453.71K **Privately Held**
Web: www.idealmeter.com

SIC: **3825** Indicating instruments, electric

(G-10186)
ILUKA RESOURCES INC
4208 Six Forks Rd Ste 1000 (27609-5733)
PHONE...................................904 284-9832
Matthew Blackwell, *Pr*
◆ **EMP: 4 EST:** 1984
SALES (est): 3.42MM **Privately Held**
Web: www.iluka.com
SIC: **1499** Peat mining and processing
HQ: Iluka Resources Inc
4701 Owens Way Ste 500
Prince George VA 23875

(G-10187)
INDIVIOR MANUFACTURING LLC ✪
8900 Capital Blvd (27616-3117)
PHONE...................................804 594-0974
Mark Erossley, *Managing Member*
EMP: 65 EST: 2023
SALES (est): 1.84MM
SALES (corp-wide): 1.09B **Privately Held**
SIC: **2834** Pharmaceutical preparations
HQ: Indivior Inc.
10710 Mdlthian Tpke Ste 1
North Chesterfield VA 23235

(G-10188)
INDUCTION FOOD SYSTEMS INC
2609 Discovery Dr Ste 115 (27616-1905)
PHONE...................................919 907-0179
Francesco Aimone, *CEO*
George Sadler, *Pr*
EMP: 5 EST: 2017
SALES (est): 1.4MM **Privately Held**
Web: www.inductionfoodsystems.com
SIC: **3556** 5499 Food products machinery; Gourmet food stores

(G-10189)
INDUSTRIAL AUTOMATION COMPANY
544 Pylon Dr (27606-1415)
PHONE...................................877 727-8757
Will Jacobson, *Owner*
EMP: 12 EST: 2019
SALES (est): 11.17MM **Privately Held**
Web: www.industrialautomationco.com
SIC: **3569** Liquid automation machinery and equipment

(G-10190)
INDUSTRIAL HEAT LLC
1017 Main Campus Dr Ste 3800 (27606-5505)
PHONE...................................919 743-5727
Thomas Francis Darden, *Pr*
J T Vaughn, *VP*
EMP: 8 EST: 2012
SALES (est): 3.07MM **Privately Held**
SIC: **3822** Environmental controls

(G-10191)
INDUSTRIAL MCH SOLUTIONS INC
3734 Overlook Rd (27616-3039)
P.O. Box 40026 (27629-0026)
PHONE...................................919 872-0016
Bill Hayes, *Pr*
EMP: 8 EST: 2001
SQ FT: 23,500
SALES (est): 988.9K **Privately Held**
Web: www.industrialmachine.net
SIC: **3541** 3599 7692 Machine tools, metal cutting type; Machine shop, jobbing and repair; Welding repair

(G-10192)
INDY WEEK
709 W Jones St (27603-1426)

▲ = Import ▼ = Export
◆ = Import/Export

PHONE....................919 832-8774
Pete Weber, *Pr*
EMP: 7 **EST:** 2015
SALES (est): 112.14K **Privately Held**
Web: www.indyweek.com
SIC: 2711 Newspapers, publishing and printing

(G-10193)
INEOS AUTOMOTIVE AMERICAS LLC
2020 Progress Ct Ste 100-112 (27608-2767)
PHONE....................404 513-8577
George Ratcliffe, *Pr*
Darryl Cohen, *Finance Treasurer*
Lynn Calder, *Mgr*
EMP: 8 **EST:** 2021
SALES (est): 1.73MM **Privately Held**
SIC: 3694 Distributors, motor vehicle engine

(G-10194)
INFINITE BLUE INC
8913 Brandon Station Rd Ste A (27613-1305)
PHONE....................919 744-7704
EMP: 4 **EST:** 2013
SALES (est): 210.26K **Privately Held**
SIC: 3699 3691 3643 3357 Electrical equipment and supplies, nec; Storage batteries; Current-carrying wiring services; Communication wire

(G-10195)
INFORMATION TECH WORKS LLC (HQ)
4809 Little Falls Dr (27609-5983)
PHONE....................919 232-5332
Jim Wrenn, *Pr*
EMP: 7 **EST:** 2001
SALES (est): 1.07MM
SALES (corp-wide): 13.58MM **Privately Held**
SIC: 7372 7371 5734 Prepackaged software; Software programming applications; Computer software and accessories
PA: Cayuse, Llc
1050 Sw 6th Ave
Portland OR 97204
503 297-2108

(G-10196)
INNOVATIVE FABRICATION INC
1730 Round Rock Dr (27615-5740)
PHONE....................919 544-0254
Michael Yarur, *Pr*
EMP: 5 **EST:** 2005
SALES (est): 3.85MM **Privately Held**
Web: www.innovativefabrication.com
SIC: 2392 Sheets, fabric: made from purchased materials

(G-10197)
INNOWERA LTD LIABILITY COMPANY
8529 Six Forks Rd Ste 400 (27615-4972)
PHONE....................214 295-9508
Mickey Shah, *SAP SOLUTIONS ARC*
EMP: 6 **EST:** 2007
SALES (est): 2.32MM
SALES (corp-wide): 109.78MM **Privately Held**
Web: www.insightsoftware.com
SIC: 7372 Application computer software
HQ: Magnitude Software, Inc.
8904 Westminster Glen Ave
Austin TX 78730
866 466-3849

(G-10198)
INOVAETION INC
8601 Six Forks Rd Ste 400 (27615-2965)
PHONE....................919 651-1628
Kimthanh Do Le, *Pr*
EMP: 11 **EST:** 2015
SALES (est): 1.12MM **Privately Held**
Web: www.pteverywhere.com
SIC: 7372 Application computer software

(G-10199)
INPRIMO SOLUTIONS INC
7925 Vandemere Ct (27615-4601)
PHONE....................919 390-7776
Vann R James, *Prin*
EMP: 4 **EST:** 2013
SALES (est): 284.23K **Privately Held**
Web: www.inprimosolutions.com
SIC: 2752 Offset printing

(G-10200)
INSIGHTSOFTWARE LLC (PA)
Also Called: Insightsoftware
8529 Six Forks Rd Ste 300 (27615-4972)
PHONE....................919 872-7800
Michael Sullivan, *CEO*
Matthew Kupferman, *
Spencer Kupferman, *
EMP: 50 **EST:** 1981
SALES (est): 109.78MM
SALES (corp-wide): 109.78MM **Privately Held**
Web: www.insightsoftware.com
SIC: 7371 7372 Computer software development; Application computer software

(G-10201)
INSPECTIONXPERT CORPORATION
1 Glenwood Ave Ste 500 (27603-2580)
P.O. Box 991 (24063-0991)
PHONE....................919 249-6442
EMP: 14 **EST:** 2004
SALES (est): 3.17MM
SALES (corp-wide): 355.83K **Privately Held**
Web: www.inspectionxpert.com
SIC: 7372 7371 Prepackaged software; Computer software development
HQ: Ideagen Limited
Mere Way Ruddington Fields Business Park
Nottingham NOTTS NG11
162 969-9100

(G-10202)
INSTANTIATIONS INC
4917 Waters Edge Dr Ste 268 (27606-2459)
PHONE....................855 476-2558
Seth Berman, *Pr*
EMP: 10 **EST:** 2010
SALES (est): 1MM **Privately Held**
Web: www.instantiations.com
SIC: 7372 Prepackaged software

(G-10203)
INSURANCE SYSTEMS GROUP INC
Also Called: I S G
827 N Bloodworth St (27604-1231)
PHONE....................919 834-4907
Charles Kerr, *CEO*
Duncan Kerr, *VP*
EMP: 10 **EST:** 1984
SALES (est): 243.77K **Privately Held**
Web: www.isg-online.com
SIC: 7372 Business oriented computer software

(G-10204)
INTAS PHARMACEUTICALS LIMITED
8041 Arco Corporate Dr Ste 200 (27617-2091)
PHONE....................919 941-7878
Samir Mehta, *Pr*
EMP: 39 **EST:** 2006
SALES (est): 741.26K **Privately Held**
Web: www.intaspharma.com
SIC: 2834 Pharmaceutical preparations
PA: Intas Pharmaceuticals Limited
Corporate House, Plot No. 255,
Magnet Corporate Park,
Ahmedabad GJ 38005

(G-10205)
INTELLIGENT APPS LLC
12113 Oakwood View Dr Apt 202 (27614-6878)
PHONE....................919 628-6256
Ruba Abughazaleh, *VP*
EMP: 4 **EST:** 2014
SALES (est): 226.04K **Privately Held**
Web: www.intelligentappsinc.com
SIC: 7371 7372 8742 7389 Computer software systems analysis and design, custom; Application computer software; Management consulting services; Business Activities at Non-Commercial Site

(G-10206)
INTERECO USA BELT FILTER PRESS
7474 Creedmoor Rd (27613-1663)
PHONE....................919 349-6041
Stephanie Richardson, *Prin*
▲ **EMP:** 4 **EST:** 2008
SALES (est): 94.15K **Privately Held**
SIC: 2741 Miscellaneous publishing

(G-10207)
INTERNATIONAL PAPER COMPANY
Also Called: International Paper
5 W Hargett St Rm 914 (27601-2936)
PHONE....................919 831-4764
Deano Orr, *Brnch Mgr*
EMP: 5
SALES (corp-wide): 18.62B **Publicly Held**
Web: www.internationalpaper.com
SIC: 2621 Paper mills
PA: International Paper Company
6400 Poplar Ave
Memphis TN 38197
901 419-7000

(G-10208)
INTERNTNAL CHLDBRTH EDCATN ASS
Also Called: I C E A
1500 Sunday Dr Ste 102 (27607-5151)
PHONE....................919 863-9487
Cheryl Coleman, *Pr*
EMP: 7 **EST:** 1960
SQ FT: 4,200
SALES (est): 183.63K **Privately Held**
Web: www.icea.org
SIC: 8641 2741 Civic associations; Technical manuals: publishing only, not printed on site

(G-10209)
IRON BOX LLC
Also Called: Iron Box
1349 Express Dr (27603-4156)
P.O. Box 19422 (27619)
PHONE....................919 890-0025
Elizabeth Knout, *Pt*
Christopher Knout, *VP*
Brittany Dedafoe, *Genl Mgr*
Elizabeth Knout, *Pr*
▲ **EMP:** 21 **EST:** 2021
SALES (est): 15.43MM **Privately Held**
Web: www.customavrack.com

SIC: 5051 5063 3679 Metals service centers and offices; Wire and cable; Harness assemblies, for electronic use: wire or cable

(G-10210)
ITG BRANDS
900 E Six Forks Rd Unit 210 (27604-1822)
PHONE....................919 366-0220
Steven Brooks, *Brnch Mgr*
EMP: 89
Web: www.itgbrands.com
SIC: 2111 Cigarettes
HQ: Itg Brands
714 Green Valley Rd
Greensboro NC 27408
336 335-7000

(G-10211)
ITRON INC
8529 Six Forks Rd Ste 100 (27615-4972)
PHONE....................919 876-2600
Dave Godwin, *Dir*
EMP: 85
SALES (corp-wide): 2.44B **Publicly Held**
Web: na.itron.com
SIC: 3663 3571 Radio and t.v. communications equipment; Electronic computers
PA: Itron, Inc.
2111 N Molter Rd
Liberty Lake WA 99019
509 924-9900

(G-10212)
J A KING
7239 Acc Blvd Ste 101 (27617-4882)
PHONE....................800 327-7727
EMP: 8 **EST:** 2018
SALES (est): 187.18K **Privately Held**
Web: www.crossco.com
SIC: 7692 Welding repair

(G-10213)
JARRETT BAY OFFSHORE
4209 Lassiter Mill Rd Ste 126 (27609-5794)
PHONE....................919 803-1990
EMP: 4 **EST:** 2017
SALES (est): 49.42K **Privately Held**
Web: shop.jarrettbay.com
SIC: 3732 Boatbuilding and repairing

(G-10214)
JEFFREY SHEFFER
Also Called: Atc Conversions
3901 Commerce Park Dr (27610-2776)
PHONE....................919 861-9126
Jeffrey Sheffer, *Owner*
EMP: 7 **EST:** 2014
SQ FT: 1,600
SALES (est): 424.61K **Privately Held**
SIC: 3499 Automobile seat frames, metal

(G-10215)
JEREMY WEITZEL
Also Called: Allkindsa Signs
1228 United Dr (27603-2241)
P.O. Box 883 (27526-0883)
PHONE....................919 878-4474
Jeremy Weitzel, *Pr*
EMP: 5 **EST:** 1985
SALES (est): 245.88K **Privately Held**
Web: www.allkindsa.com
SIC: 3993 Signs and advertising specialties

(G-10216)
JESTER-CROWN INC
Also Called: Sign-A-Rama
4721 Atlantic Ave Ste 119 (27604-8106)
PHONE....................919 872-1070
Randy Warren, *Owner*

EMP: 4 **EST:** 1990
SQ FT: 1,050
SALES (est): 311.03K **Privately Held**
Web: www.signarama.com
SIC: 3993 Signs and advertising specialties

(G-10217)
JOHN LINDENBERGER
6429 Grassy Knoll Ln (27616-8875)
PHONE.............................919 337-6741
John Lindenberger, *Prin*
EMP: 5 **EST:** 2017
SALES (est): 76.15K **Privately Held**
SIC: 2431 Millwork

(G-10218)
JOHN WEST AUTO SERVICE INC
3216 Lake Woodard Dr (27604-3659)
PHONE.............................919 250-0825
John West, *Pr*
EMP: 7 **EST:** 1976
SQ FT: 10,000
SALES (est): 482.86K **Privately Held**
Web:
www.johnwestautorepairservice.com
SIC: 3599 7538 Machine shop, jobbing and
repair; General automotive repair shops

(G-10219)
JOHNSON CONTROLS INC
Also Called: Johnson Controls
633 Hutton St Ste 104 (27606-6319)
PHONE.............................919 743-3500
Roland Robustelli, *Brnch Mgr*
EMP: 90
Web: www.johnsoncontrols.com
SIC: 2531 7623 Seats, automobile; Air
conditioning repair
HQ: Johnson Controls, Inc.
5757 N Green Bay Ave
Milwaukee WI 53209
866 496-1999

(G-10220)
JOHNSON HARN VNGAR GEE GL PLLC
434 Fayetteville St Ste 2200 (27601-1701)
PHONE.............................919 213-6163
Samuel H Johnson, *Prin*
EMP: 10 **EST:** 2017
SALES (est): 411.9K **Privately Held**
Web: www.jhvgglaw.com
SIC: 2099 Vinegar

(G-10221)
JOSEPH C WOODARD PRTG CO INC
2815 S Saunders St (27603-3519)
PHONE.............................919 829-0634
Joyce W Woodard, *Pr*
Kimberly W Hall, *VP*
Joseph C Woodard Junior, *VP*
Ryan S Woodard, *VP*
Jason H Woodard, *VP*
EMP: 19 **EST:** 1967
SQ FT: 11,000
SALES (est): 2.49MM **Privately Held**
Web: www.josephcwoodard.com
SIC: 2752 2791 2789 Offset printing;
Typesetting; Bookbinding and related work

(G-10222)
JPS COMMUNICATIONS INC
5800 Departure Dr (27616-1857)
PHONE.............................919 534-1168
Carl S Kist, *Pr*
Rochelle Graham, *
EMP: 60 **EST:** 1988
SQ FT: 16,000
SALES (est): 969.74K
SALES (corp-wide): 80.74B **Publicly Held**
Web: www.jps.com

SIC: 8748 3577 3663 3661 Communications
consulting; Computer peripheral equipment,
nec; Radio and t.v. communications
equipment; Telephone and telegraph
apparatus
HQ: Raytheon Company
870 Winter St
Waltham MA 02451
781 522-3000

(G-10223)
JPS INTRPRBILITY SOLUTIONS INC
5800 Departure Dr (27616-1857)
PHONE.............................919 332-5009
Donald Scott, *CEO*
Arthur Powers, *
EMP: 26 **EST:** 2016
SALES (est): 3.57MM **Privately Held**
Web: www.jps.com
SIC: 3663 Receivers, radio communications

(G-10224)
JS PRINTING LLC
Also Called: International Minute Press
1824 Garner Station Blvd (27603-3643)
PHONE.............................919 773-1103
EMP: 6 **EST:** 1999
SQ FT: 2,000
SALES (est): 532.27K **Privately Held**
Web: www.minuteman.com
SIC: 2752 Offset printing

(G-10225)
JT INTERNATIONAL USA INC ✪
4000 Center At North Hills St (27609)
PHONE.............................201 871-1210
Eddy Pirard, *Pr*
Vasillis Vovos, *Ex VP*
EMP: 21 **EST:** 2023
SALES (est): 2.75MM **Privately Held**
SIC: 3559 Tobacco products machinery

(G-10226)
JULIAS SOUTHERN FOODS LLC
Also Called: Julia's Pantry
5608 Primavera Ct Ste G (27616-1848)
PHONE.............................919 609-6745
Reta Washington, *Managing Member*
EMP: 6 **EST:** 2011
SALES (est): 244.2K **Privately Held**
Web: www.juliaspantry.com
SIC: 2096 2099 2045 Pork rinds;
Seasonings: dry mixes; Pancake mixes,
prepared: from purchased flour

(G-10227)
JUNIPER NETWORKS INC
1730 Varsity Dr Ste 10 (27606-2188)
PHONE.............................888 586-4737
EMP: 13
Web: www.juniper.net
SIC: 7373 7372 Computer integrated
systems design; Prepackaged software
PA: Juniper Networks, Inc.
1133 Innovation Way
Sunnyvale CA 94089

(G-10228)
KALEIDO INC
16 W Martin St Fl 7 (27601-1341)
PHONE.............................984 205-9436
Steve Cerveny, *CEO*
Sophia Lopez, *Prin*
Joseph Lubin, *Prin*
EMP: 19 **EST:** 2020
SALES (est): 4.3MM **Privately Held**
Web: www.kaleido.io
SIC: 7372 Prepackaged software

(G-10229)
KAOTIC PARTS LLC
4114 Pearl Rd (27610-6110)
PHONE.............................919 766-6040
Omaine Avery, *CEO*
Omaine Avery, *Managing Member*
EMP: 5 **EST:** 2017
SALES (est): 329.57K **Privately Held**
Web: kaotic-parts.square.site
SIC: 7389 3357 7549 7539 Business
Activities at Non-Commercial Site;
Automotive wire and cable, except ignition
sets: nonferrous; Inspection and diagnostic
service, automotive; Brake services

(G-10230)
KARAMEDICA INC
509 W North St (27603-1414)
PHONE.............................919 302-1325
Andrew Crofton, *CEO*
Wolff Kirsch, *CEO*
Taub Swartz, *CFO*
Andrew Crofton, *COO*
Sam Hudson, *Ofcr*
EMP: 7 **EST:** 2016
SALES (est): 1.28MM **Privately Held**
Web: www.karamedica.com
SIC: 3841 5122 Surgical and medical
instruments; Biotherapeutics

(G-10231)
KARL RL MANUFACTURING
11937 Appaloosa Run E (27613-7111)
PHONE.............................919 846-3801
Randy Karl, *Prin*
EMP: 5 **EST:** 2010
SALES (est): 63.74K **Privately Held**
SIC: 3999 Manufacturing industries, nec

(G-10232)
KEGLERS WOODWORKS LLC
330 Dupont Cir (27603-1928)
PHONE.............................919 608-7220
Allen Keglers, *Prin*
EMP: 4 **EST:** 2009
SALES (est): 163.5K **Privately Held**
SIC: 2431 Millwork

(G-10233)
KENN M LLC
6046 Inona Pl (27606-1198)
PHONE.............................678 755-6607
Kenneth C Mathara, *CEO*
EMP: 5 **EST:** 2019
SALES (est): 228.14K **Privately Held**
SIC: 7389 4731 3799 Business Activities at
Non-Commercial Site; Freight
transportation arrangement; Transportation
equipment, nec

(G-10234)
KI AGENCY LLC
Also Called: Capital Wraps
5812 Triangle Dr (27617-4705)
P.O. Box 80371 (27623-0371)
PHONE.............................919 977-7075
Keoni Denison, *Managing Member*
Keoni Denison Mng Mr, *Prin*
EMP: 8 **EST:** 2010
SALES (est): 1.39MM **Privately Held**
Web: www.capitalwraps.com
SIC: 3993 Signs and advertising specialties

(G-10235)
KING TUTT GRAPHICS LLC
1113 Transport Dr (27603-4146)
PHONE.............................877 546-4888
EMP: 21 **EST:** 2018
SALES (est): 3.5MM **Privately Held**
Web: www.kingtuttgraphics.com

SIC: 3993 Signs and advertising specialties

(G-10236)
KISNER CORPORATION
Also Called: Carolina Fabricators
6016 Triangle Dr (27617-4743)
PHONE.............................919 510-8410
Scott Kisner, *Pr*
EMP: 10 **EST:** 2007
SALES (est): 208.88K **Privately Held**
Web: www.carolinametalfabricators.com
SIC: 3441 Fabricated structural metal

(G-10237)
KITCHEN BATH GLLRIES N HLLS LL
Also Called: K&B Galleries
4209 Lassiter Mill Rd Ste 130 (27609-5794)
PHONE.............................919 600-6200
Rachel Roberts, *Owner*
EMP: 6 **EST:** 2008
SALES (est): 2.1MM **Privately Held**
Web: www.kandbgalleries.com
SIC: 3429 Cabinet hardware

(G-10238)
KITCHEN CABINET DESIGNERS LLC
Also Called: Kitchen Cabinet Distributors
431 Milburnie Lake Dr (27610-8058)
PHONE.............................919 833-6532
Randy Goldstein, *CEO*
Roberto Rivera, *
Patrick Dickinson, *
Michael Weiner, *
Pauline Gambill, *
▲ **EMP:** 119 **EST:** 2014
SALES (est): 17MM **Privately Held**
Web: www.kcdus.com
SIC: 2434 5712 Vanities, bathroom: wood;
Customized furniture and cabinets

(G-10239)
KNOWLEDGE MANAGEMENT ASSOC LLC
Also Called: Metal Graphic
8529 Six Forks Rd Ste 400 (27615-4972)
PHONE.............................781 250-2001
David Goldstein, *Managing Member*
Jorge Rodriguez, *Sec*
▼ **EMP:** 9 **EST:** 1995
SALES (est): 347.14K **Privately Held**
Web: www.mekkographics.com
SIC: 7372 Prepackaged software

(G-10240)
KOL INCORPORATED
Also Called: Ward's Grocery
5700 Buffaloe Rd (27616-6036)
PHONE.............................919 872-2340
Byung Kim, *Pr*
EMP: 6 **EST:** 1953
SALES (est): 91.92K **Privately Held**
SIC: 3949 5411 Hunting equipment; Grocery
stores

(G-10241)
KUENZ AMERICA INC
9321 Focal Pt Ste 8 (27617-8770)
PHONE.............................984 255-1018
Clemens Horacek, *Pr*
Reinhard Hennings, *Sec*
▲ **EMP:** 19 **EST:** 1997
SQ FT: 6,000
SALES (est): 2.89MM **Privately Held**
Web: www.kuenz.com
SIC: 3536 3589 Cranes, industrial plant;
Commercial cooking and foodwarming
equipment

▲ = Import ▼ = Export
◆ = Import/Export

(G-10242)
KYMA TECHNOLOGIES INC
Also Called: Carolina Sputter Solutions
8829 Midway West Rd (27617-4606)
PHONE..................919 789-8880
Keith R Evans, *Pr*
Mark Williams, *COO*
Karen Nield, *Dir Fin*
Edward Preble, *VP*
▼ EMP: 13 EST: 1998
SQ FT: 7,000
SALES (est): 4.64MM **Privately Held**
Web: www.kymatech.com
SIC: 3674 Integrated circuits, semiconductor
networks, etc.

(G-10243)
LABEL & PRINTING SOLUTIONS INC
201 Buncombe St (27609-6369)
P.O. Box 18647 (27619-8647)
PHONE..................919 782-1242
Michael Tollison, *CEO*
EMP: 5 EST: 1996
SALES (est): 460.21K **Privately Held**
Web: www.labelandprinting.com
SIC: 2679 2759 7389 2752 Tags and labels,
paper; Decals: printing, nsk; Packaging and
labeling services; Commercial printing,
lithographic

(G-10244)
LAND AND LOFT LLC
Also Called: Lie Loft
701 Georgetown Rd (27608-2703)
PHONE..................315 560-7060
Luke Davis, *CEO*
EMP: 5 EST: 2015
SALES (est): 213.07K **Privately Held**
SIC: 2741 5941 Art copy: publishing and
printing; Golf goods and equipment

(G-10245)
LANDMARK PRINTING INC
901 W Hodges St (27608-1704)
PHONE..................919 833-5151
Teresa Davis, *Prin*
Jerry Davis, *Prin*
EMP: 6 EST: 1989
SALES (est): 103.06K **Privately Held**
Web: www.landmarkprintingink.com
SIC: 2752 Offset printing

(G-10246)
LANDMARK PRINTING CO INC
901 W Hodges St (27608-1704)
PHONE..................919 833-5151
Teresa Davis, *Pr*
Tim Davis, *Pr*
Jerry Davis, *VP*
EMP: 6 EST: 1982
SQ FT: 3,500
SALES (est): 262.07K **Privately Held**
Web:
landmarkprintingink.secureprintorder.com
SIC: 2752 Offset printing

(G-10247)
LANE CONSTRUCTION CORPORATION
3010 Gresham Lake Rd (27615-4221)
PHONE..................919 876-4550
Eddie Spencer, *Mgr*
EMP: 246
SALES (corp-wide): 10.16B **Privately Held**
Web: www.laneconstruct.com
SIC: 1611 2951 Highway and street paving
contractor; Asphalt paving mixtures and
blocks
HQ: The Lane Construction Corporation
90 Fieldstone Ct
Cheshire CT 06410
203 235-3351

(G-10248)
LARRYS BEANS INC
1507 Gavin St (27608-2613)
PHONE..................919 828-1234
Larry Larson, *Pr*
Kevin Bobal, *VP*
▲ EMP: 9 EST: 1993
SQ FT: 8,700
SALES (est): 1.72MM **Privately Held**
Web: www.larryscoffee.com
SIC: 5149 2095 2087 Coffee, green or
roasted; Roasted coffee; Flavoring extracts
and syrups, nec

(G-10249)
LATINO COMMUNICATIONS INC
150 Fayetteville St Ste 110 (27601-2919)
PHONE..................919 645-1680
Federico Van Gelderen, *Brnch Mgr*
EMP: 18
SALES (corp-wide): 1.2MM **Privately Held**
Web: www.quepasamedia.com
SIC: 2711 7313 4832 Newspapers:
publishing only, not printed on site;
Newspaper advertising representative;
Radio broadcasting stations
PA: Latino Communications, Inc.
3067 Waughtown St
Winston Salem NC 27107
336 714-2823

(G-10250)
LC FOODS LLC
3809 Frazier Dr Ste 101 (27610-1358)
PHONE..................919 510-6688
Glen A Frederich, *Prin*
EMP: 6 EST: 2010
SALES (est): 520.67K **Privately Held**
Web: www.lowcarbfoods.com
SIC: 5499 2051 2099 2046 Health foods;
Bread, cake, and related products; Pasta,
uncooked: packaged with other ingredients;
Wheat gluten

(G-10251)
LEASEACCELERATOR INC (PA)
Also Called: Leaseaccelerator
8529 Six Forks Rd (27615-4971)
PHONE..................866 446-0980
Michael J Keeler, *CEO*
Keith Haas, *CFO*
David Mitchell, *CRO*
EMP: 12 EST: 2000
SALES (est): 5MM
SALES (corp-wide): 5MM **Privately Held**
Web: explore.leaseaccelerator.com
SIC: 7372 Business oriented computer
software

(G-10252)
LEGALIS DMS LLC
1315 Oakwood Ave (27610-2247)
PHONE..................919 741-8260
Craig Mcgannon, *CEO*
Robert Almoney, *Pr*
Brandie Beebe, *COO*
EMP: 11 EST: 2014
SQ FT: 27,000
SALES (est): 1.09MM **Privately Held**
Web: www.legalis.com
SIC: 7334 4226 7389 7374 Photocopying
and duplicating services; Document and
office records storage; Document storage
service; Optical scanning data service

(G-10253)
LEOFORCE LLC
500 W Peace St (27603-1102)
PHONE..................919 539-5434
Madhusudan Modugu, *Managing Member*
Amit Singh, *

EMP: 28 EST: 2013
SALES (est): 4.33MM **Privately Held**
Web: www.leoforce.com
SIC: 7372 Application computer software

(G-10254)
LEONARD ALUM UTLITY BLDNGS INC
Also Called: Leonard Building & Truck ACC
4239 Capital Blvd (27604-4310)
PHONE..................919 872-4442
Thomas Brown, *Mgr*
EMP: 7
SALES (corp-wide): 98.91MM **Privately Held**
Web: www.leonardusa.com
SIC: 3448 3713 3089 3714 Prefabricated
metal buildings; Truck tops; Molding
primary plastics; Motor vehicle parts and
accessories
PA: Leonard Aluminum Utility Buildings,
Inc.
630 W Indpndnce Blvd
Mount Airy NC 27030
336 789-5018

(G-10255)
LIEBEL-FLARSHEIM COMPANY LLC
8800 Durant Rd (27616-3104)
PHONE..................919 878-2930
Chris Guerdan, *Mgr*
EMP: 137
SALES (corp-wide): 532.38MM **Privately Held**
SIC: 3841 2835 Diagnostic apparatus,
medical; Diagnostic substances
HQ: Liebel-Flarsheim Company Llc
1034 S Brntwood Blvd Ste
Saint Louis MO 63117
314 376-4768

(G-10256)
LIGHTNING PRTCTION SYSTEMS LLC
Also Called: VFC Lightning Protection
5901 Triangle Dr (27617-4742)
PHONE..................252 213-9900
Kirk John Partridge, *Brnch Mgr*
EMP: 76
Web: www.vfclp.com
SIC: 3643 Lightning protection equipment
PA: Lightning Protection Systems, Llc
90 Cutler Dr
North Salt Lake UT 84054

(G-10257)
LITHO PRITING INC
Also Called: Lithography Design
1501 S Blount St (27603-2507)
P.O. Box 26344 (27611-6344)
PHONE..................919 755-9542
Carl Dereth, *Pr*
Elizabeth Dereth, *VP*
EMP: 5 EST: 1990
SQ FT: 19,000
SALES (est): 215.68K **Privately Held**
SIC: 2752 Offset printing

(G-10258)
LLS INVESTMENTS INC (PA)
Also Called: Craters and Freighters Raleigh
3400 Lake Woodard Dr (27604-3854)
P.O. Box 98895 (27624-8895)
PHONE..................919 662-7283
Evan Lennon, *Pr*
John Lennon, *Treas*
EMP: 10 EST: 2011
SALES (est): 3.42MM
SALES (corp-wide): 3.42MM **Privately Held**

Web:
www.cratersandfreightersraleigh.com
SIC: 4783 2653 5113 4731 Packing and
crating; Corrugated and solid fiber boxes;
Shipping supplies; Freight transportation
arrangement

(G-10259)
LM SHEA LLC
8201 Candelaria Dr (27616-5860)
PHONE..................919 608-1901
EMP: 4 EST: 2020
SALES (est): 111.01K **Privately Held**
SIC: 2339 6799 Women's and misses'
accessories; Real estate investors, except
property operators

(G-10260)
LOBBYGUARD SOLUTIONS LLC
4700 Six Forks Rd Ste 300 (27609)
P.O. Box 4458 (77210)
PHONE..................919 785-3301
Kevin Allen, *Pr*
EMP: 15 EST: 2005
SALES (est): 2.29MM
SALES (corp-wide): 11.35MM **Privately Held**
Web: www.lobbyguard.com
SIC: 7372 Business oriented computer
software
PA: Raptor Technologies, Llc
2900 North Loop W Ste 900
Houston TX 77092
713 880-8902

(G-10261)
LUMEOVA INC
3801 Lake Boone Trl Ste 260 (27607-0044)
PHONE..................908 229-4651
Mohammad Khatibzadeh, *CEO*
EMP: 5 EST: 2014
SALES (est): 1.83MM **Privately Held**
Web: www.lumeova.com
SIC: 3674 Monolithic integrated circuits
(solid state)

(G-10262)
LUXEMARK COMPANY
6909 Glenwood Ave Ste 106 (27612-7101)
PHONE..................919 863-0101
Michael Armstrong, *Pr*
EMP: 4 EST: 2008
SALES (est): 897.06K **Privately Held**
Web: www.luxemarkcompany.com
SIC: 2434 Wood kitchen cabinets

(G-10263)
LXD RESEARCH & DISPLAY LLC
7516 Precision Dr Ste 100 (27617-8748)
PHONE..................919 600-6440
Todd Bolanz, *Pr*
Timothy Harrison, *Sec*
▲ EMP: 15 EST: 2010
SALES (est): 3.96MM **Privately Held**
Web: www.lxdinc.com
SIC: 3679 Liquid crystal displays (LCD)

(G-10264)
M2 OPTICS INC
5621 Departure Dr Ste 117 (27616-1911)
PHONE..................919 342-5619
Kevin Miller, *CEO*
EMP: 4
SALES (corp-wide): 978.23K **Privately Held**
Web: www.m2optics.com
SIC: 1731 3699 3675 3082 Electrical work;
Electrical equipment and supplies, nec;
Electronic capacitors; Unsupported plastics
profile shapes
PA: M2 Optics, Inc.

GEOGRAPHIC

100 Parksouth Ln
Holly Springs NC 27540
919 342-5619

(G-10265)
MADIX
2326 Hales Rd (27608-1446)
PHONE....................804 456-3007
Clayton Allen, *Prin*
EMP: 4 **EST:** 2010
SALES (est): 75.77K **Privately Held**
Web: www.madixinc.com
SIC: 2542 Partitions and fixtures, except
wood

(G-10266)
MAGAZINE NAKIA LASHAWN
Also Called: Hair Collection, The
2833 Roundleaf Ct (27604-5474)
PHONE....................919 875-1156
Nakia L Magazine, *Owner*
EMP: 7 **EST:** 2007
SALES (est): 200.87K **Privately Held**
SIC: 2721 Magazines: publishing and printing

(G-10267)
**MAKHTESHIM AGAN NORTH AMER
INC (DH)**
Also Called: Adama US
8601 Six Forks Rd Ste 300 (27615-2965)
PHONE....................919 256-9300
Jake Brodsgaard, *CEO*
Joseph Mark Hough, *
Craig Lupton-smith, *CFO*
◆ **EMP:** 50 **EST:** 1991
SQ FT: 12,000
SALES (est): 85.32MM **Privately Held**
Web: www.manainc.com
SIC: 2879 Agricultural chemicals, nec
HQ: Adama Ltd.
93 Beijing East Road
Jingzhou HB 43400

(G-10268)
MALLINCKRODT LLC
8801 Capital Blvd (27616-3116)
PHONE....................919 878-2800
Keitha Buckingham, *Brnch Mgr*
EMP: 63
Web: www.mallinckrodt.com
SIC: 2834 Pharmaceutical preparations
HQ: Mallinckrodt Llc
675 Mcdonnell Blvd
Hazelwood MO 63042
314 654-2000

(G-10269)
MALLINCKRODT LLC
8800 Durant Rd (27616-3104)
PHONE....................919 878-2900
Michael Collins, *Brnch Mgr*
EMP: 6
Web: www.mallinckrodt.com
SIC: 2834 3829 3841 2833 Pharmaceutical
preparations; Medical diagnostic systems,
nuclear; Catheters; Codeine and derivatives
HQ: Mallinckrodt Llc
675 Mcdonnell Blvd
Hazelwood MO 63042
314 654-2000

(G-10270)
MARIETTA MARTIN MATERIALS INC
Also Called: Martin Marietta Aggregates
6028 Triangle Dr (27617-4743)
PHONE....................919 788-4392
Todd Tucker, *Mgr*
EMP: 10
Web: www.martinmarietta.com

SIC: 1422 Crushed and broken limestone
PA: Martin Marietta Materials Inc
4123 Parklake Ave
Raleigh NC 27612

(G-10271)
MARIUS PHARMACEUTICALS LLC
2301 Sugar Bush Rd Ste 510 (27612-3382)
PHONE....................919 374-1913
Om Dhingra, *CEO*
Shalin Y Shah, *CFO*
EMP: 6 **EST:** 2016
SALES (est): 2.78MM **Privately Held**
Web: www.mariuspharma.com
SIC: 2834 Pharmaceutical preparations

(G-10272)
MARKET OF RALEIGH LLC
4111 New Bern Ave (27610-1372)
PHONE....................919 212-2100
EMP: 4 **EST:** 2019
SALES (est): 83.3K **Privately Held**
Web: www.seortp.com
SIC: 2519 Furniture, household: glass,
fiberglass, and plastic

(G-10273)
**MARTIN MARIETTA MAGNESIA
SPECIALTIES LLC (HQ)**
Also Called: Martin Marietta
4123 Parklake Ave (27612-2309)
P.O. Box 30013 (27622-0013)
PHONE....................800 648-7400
▲ **EMP:** 73 **EST:** 1888
SALES (est): 49.38MM **Publicly Held**
Web: www.magnesiaspecialties.com
SIC: 3295 Magnesite, crude: ground,
calcined, or dead-burned
PA: Martin Marietta Materials Inc
4123 Parklake Ave
Raleigh NC 27612

(G-10274)
MARTIN MARIETTA MATERIALS INC
2235 Gateway Access Pt Ste 400
(27607-3076)
PHONE....................919 664-1700
Ron Kopplin, *Div Pres*
EMP: 6
Web: www.martinmarietta.com
SIC: 3273 Ready-mixed concrete
PA: Martin Marietta Materials Inc
4123 Parklake Ave
Raleigh NC 27612

(G-10275)
MARTIN MARIETTA MATERIALS INC
Also Called: Aggregates Div
4123 Parklake Ave (27612-2309)
P.O. Box 30013 (27622-0013)
PHONE....................360 424-3441
Rosa Naprstek, *CFO*
EMP: 11
Web: www.martinmarietta.com
SIC: 1422 1442 Cement rock, crushed and
broken-quarrying; Construction sand and
gravel
PA: Martin Marietta Materials Inc
4123 Parklake Ave
Raleigh NC 27612

(G-10276)
MARTIN MARIETTA MATERIALS INC
Also Called: Martin Marietta Aggregates
2501 Blue Ridge Rd (27607-0159)
PHONE....................919 863-4305
EMP: 6
Web: www.martinmarietta.com
SIC: 1423 Crushed and broken granite
PA: Martin Marietta Materials Inc
4123 Parklake Ave

Raleigh NC 27612

(G-10277)
**MARTIN MARIETTA MATERIALS INC
(PA)**
Also Called: Martin Marietta
4123 Parklake Ave (27612)
P.O. Box 30013 (27612)
PHONE....................919 781-4550
C Howard Nye, *Ch Bd*
James A J Nickolas, *Ex VP*
Roselyn R Bar, *Ex VP*
Donald A Mccunniff, *Chief Human
Resource Officer*
Robert J Cardin, *CAO*
◆ **EMP:** 150 **EST:** 1993
SALES (est): 6.54B **Publicly Held**
Web: www.martinmarietta.com
SIC: 1423 1422 1442 3295 Crushed and
broken granite; Crushed and broken
limestone; Construction sand and gravel;
Magnesite, crude: ground, calcined, or
dead-burned

(G-10278)
**MARTINEZ WLDG FABRICATION
CORP**
2901 Carpenter Pond Rd (27613-8165)
PHONE....................919 957-8904
EMP: 10 **EST:** 2020
SALES (est): 3.26MM **Privately Held**
SIC: 3441 Fabricated structural metal

(G-10279)
**MASTER MARKETING GROUP LLC
(PA)**
4801 Glenwood Ave Ste 310 (27612-3857)
PHONE....................870 932-4491
Eran Salu, *Managing Member*
EMP: 5 **EST:** 2014
SALES (est): 1.42MM
SALES (corp-wide): 1.42MM **Privately
Held**
SIC: 2752 Offset printing

(G-10280)
MASTERS MOVING SERVICES INC
4220 Gallatree Ln (27616-0728)
PHONE....................919 523-9836
William Porter, *Pr*
EMP: 6 **EST:** 2008
SALES (est): 274.84K **Privately Held**
SIC: 2519 Household furniture, nec

(G-10281)
MAYNE PHARMA COMMERCIAL LLC
Also Called: Mayne Pharma
3301 Benson Dr Ste 401 (27609-7380)
PHONE....................984 242-1400
Shawn Patrick O'brien, *CEO*
Wes Edwards, *
EMP: 350 **EST:** 1994
SQ FT: 44,000
SALES (est): 42.47MM **Publicly Held**
Web: www.maynepharma.com
SIC: 2834 Pharmaceutical preparations
PA: Mayne Pharma Group Limited
1538 Main North Road
Salisbury South SA 5106

(G-10282)
MAYNE PHARMA LLC
3301 Benson Dr Ste 401 (27609-7380)
PHONE....................252 752-3800
Shawn Patrick O'brien, *CEO*
EMP: 145 **EST:** 2014
SALES (est): 10.53MM **Publicly Held**
Web: www.maynepharma.com
SIC: 2834 Pharmaceutical preparations
PA: Mayne Pharma Group Limited

1538 Main North Road
Salisbury South SA 5106

(G-10283)
MAYNE PHARMA VENTURES LLC
3301 Benson Dr Ste 401 (27609-7380)
PHONE....................252 752-3800
Shawn O'brien, *CEO*
Stefan Cross, *Pr*
John Ross, *VP*
Nick Freeman, *CFO*
EMP: 5 **EST:** 2014
SALES (est): 821.9K **Publicly Held**
Web: www.maynepharma.com
SIC: 2834 Pharmaceutical preparations
PA: Mayne Pharma Group Limited
1538 Main North Road
Salisbury South SA 5106

(G-10284)
MC CLATCHY INTERACTIVE USA
1101 Haynes St (27604-1455)
PHONE....................919 861-1200
Christian A Hendrick, *Prin*
EMP: 9 **EST:** 2013
SALES (est): 331.45K **Privately Held**
Web: www.mcclatchy.com
SIC: 2711 Newspapers, publishing and
printing

(G-10285)
MCKNIGHT15 INC
Also Called: Fastsigns 111701
3912 Bluffwind Dr (27603)
PHONE....................919 326-6488
Douglas J Mcknight, *Owner*
EMP: 6 **EST:** 2018
SALES (est): 1.06MM **Privately Held**
Web: www.fastsigns.com
SIC: 3993 Signs and advertising specialties

(G-10286)
MECHA INC
6204 Daimler Way Ste 107 (27607-5479)
PHONE....................919 858-0372
Bobby Boyd, *Pr*
EMP: 13 **EST:** 2008
SQ FT: 6,000
SALES (est): 1.3MM **Privately Held**
Web: www.mechainc.com
SIC: 3599 3499 Custom machinery; Metal
household articles

(G-10287)
MECHANICAL SPC CONTRS INC
Also Called: Bahnson Mechanical Specialties
4412 Tryon Rd (27606-4218)
PHONE....................919 829-9300
Anthony Triano, *Pr*
Chris Berrier, *
Steve Draper, *
Lisa Cunningham, *
EMP: 70 **EST:** 1996
SQ FT: 12,000
SALES (est): 8.77MM
SALES (corp-wide): 14.57B **Publicly Held**
Web: www.mscpiping.com
SIC: 1711 3312 3449 Process piping
contractor; Pipes, iron and steel; Bars,
concrete reinforcing: fabricated steel
HQ: Bahnson, Inc.
4731 Commercial Park Ct
Clemmons NC 27012

(G-10288)
MEDAPTUS INC
4917 Waters Edge Dr Ste 135
(27606-2380)
PHONE....................617 896-4000
Dennis Mitchelle, *Brnch Mgr*
EMP: 11

▲ = Import ▼ = Export
◆ = Import/Export

SALES (corp-wide): 8.41B Privately Held
Web: www.medaptus.com
SIC: 7372 Business oriented computer software
HQ: Medaptus, Inc.
101 Arch St Fl 4
Boston MA 02110
617 896-4000

(G-10289)
MEDVERTICAL LLC
Also Called: Beewell
3725 National Dr Ste 160 (27612-4832)
PHONE..................................919 867-4268
Alden Parsons, Managing Member
EMP: 6 EST: 2015
SALES (est): 714.98K Privately Held
SIC: 7372 Application computer software

(G-10290)
MERCHANTS METALS LLC
Also Called: Merchants Metals
6512 Mount Herman Rd (27617-9401)
PHONE..................................919 598-8471
Greg Morton, Mgr
EMP: 7
SALES (corp-wide): 1.06B Privately Held
Web: www.merchantsmetals.com
SIC: 3496 Miscellaneous fabricated wire products
HQ: Merchants Metals Llc
3 Ravinia Dr Ste 1750
Atlanta GA 30346
770 741-0300

(G-10291)
MERGE LLC
1410 Hillsborough St (27605-1829)
PHONE..................................919 832-3924
EMP: 9 EST: 2003
SQ FT: 2,000
SALES (est): 443.1K Privately Held
Web: www.mergellc.com
SIC: 7336 3993 Commercial art and graphic design; Advertising artwork

(G-10292)
MERIDIAN GRANITE COMPANY
2710 Wycliff Rd (27607-3033)
PHONE..................................919 781-4550
EMP: 5 EST: 1997
SALES (est): 1.7MM Publicly Held
SIC: 1423 3281 Crushed and broken granite; Cut stone and stone products
PA: Martin Marietta Materials Inc
4123 Parklake Ave
Raleigh NC 27612

(G-10293)
MERZ INCORPORATED
Also Called: Merz
6501 Six Forks Rd (27615-6515)
P.O. Box 18806 (27419-8806)
PHONE..................................919 582-8196
Bill Humphries, CEO
John Delaney, *
Doctor J Huckmann, Ch Bd
R G Boulton, *
James M Iseman Junior, Sec
▲ EMP: 135 EST: 1986
SQ FT: 60,000
SALES (est): 43.02MM
SALES (corp-wide): 1.81B Privately Held
Web: www.merzaesthetics.com
SIC: 2834 Pharmaceutical preparations
HQ: Merz Pharma Gmbh & Co. Kgaa
Eckenheimer Landstr. 100
Frankfurt Am Main HE 60318
6915030

(G-10294)
MERZ NORTH AMERICA INC (DH)
Also Called: Neocutis
6501 Six Forks Rd (27615-6515)
PHONE..................................919 582-8000
Bob Rhatigan, CEO
Patrick Urban, Pr
Alana Sine, VP
Matt Anderson, Technology Operations Vice President
Joseph Barry, CCO
EMP: 16 EST: 1999
SQ FT: 20,000
SALES (est): 149.66MM
SALES (corp-wide): 1.81B Privately Held
Web: www.merzusa.com
SIC: 2834 Pharmaceutical preparations
HQ: Merz Pharma Gmbh & Co. Kgaa
Eckenheimer Landstr. 100
Frankfurt Am Main HE 60318
6915030

(G-10295)
MERZ PHARMACEUTICALS LLC
6601 Six Forks Rd (27615-6589)
PHONE..................................919 582-8000
Kevin O Brien, Pr
Chad Duncan, *
Alana Sine, *
Bill Edwards, *
Michal Yarborough, *
▲ EMP: 110 EST: 1951
SALES (est): 37.53MM
SALES (corp-wide): 1.81B Privately Held
Web: www.merz.it
SIC: 2834 Pharmaceutical preparations
HQ: Merz Pharmaceuticals Gmbh
Eckenheimer Landstr. 100
Frankfurt Am Main HE 60318
6915031

(G-10296)
METRO PRODUCTIONS INC
6005 Chapel Hill Rd (27607-5109)
PHONE..................................919 851-6420
Charles Underwood Senior, Pr
Charles Underwood Junior, VP
Clara Underwood, Sec
EMP: 12 EST: 1988
SQ FT: 6,500
SALES (est): 848.39K Privately Held
Web: www.metroproductions.com
SIC: 2752 7336 7812 7331 Offset printing; Commercial art and graphic design; Video production; Mailing service

(G-10297)
METTECH INC (PA)
105 S Wilmington St (27601-1431)
P.O. Box 25609 (27611-5609)
PHONE..................................919 833-9460
Michael Mettrey, Pr
Iris Mettrey, VP
▲ EMP: 9 EST: 1970
SQ FT: 9,000
SALES (est): 413.67K
SALES (corp-wide): 413.67K Privately Held
Web: www.met-techbilliards.com
SIC: 5941 5091 3949 Pool and billiard tables ; Billiard equipment and supplies; Billiard and pool equipment and supplies, general

(G-10298)
MICHAEL PARKER CABINETRY
Also Called: Eidolon Designs
414 Dupont Cir Ste 4 (27603-2083)
PHONE..................................919 833-5117
Micheal Parker, Pr
Anne Cowperthwaite, VP
EMP: 5 EST: 1984

SALES (est): 198.6K Privately Held
Web: www.eidolondesigns.com
SIC: 2511 2521 2541 Wood household furniture; Wood office furniture; Wood partitions and fixtures

(G-10299)
MICRO EPSILON AMER LTD PARTNR (PA)
Also Called: Micro Epsilon America
8120 Brownleigh Dr (27617-7410)
PHONE..................................919 787-9707
Richard Auxer, Genl Pt
Karl Wisspeintner, Pt
▲ EMP: 5 EST: 1998
SQ FT: 1,000
SALES (est): 3.73MM
SALES (corp-wide): 3.73MM Privately Held
Web: www.micro-epsilon.com
SIC: 3829 Measuring and controlling devices, nec

(G-10300)
MICRO SCRIBE PUBLISHING INC
732 Lanham Pl (27615-1536)
P.O. Box 14142 (27709-4142)
PHONE..................................919 848-0388
James Edwards, Pr
EMP: 6 EST: 1999
SALES (est): 126.09K Privately Held
Web: www.microscribepub.com
SIC: 2741 Micropublishing

(G-10301)
MICRO-OHM CORPORATION
14460 Falls Of Neuse Rd Ste 149-273 (27614-8227)
P.O. Box 99748 (27624-9748)
PHONE..................................800 845-5167
EMP: 4 EST: 2010
SALES (est): 1.63MM
SALES (corp-wide): 7.08B Publicly Held
Web: www.microohm.com
SIC: 3674 Solar cells
PA: On Semiconductor Corporation
5701 N Pima Rd
Scottsdale AZ 85250
602 244-6600

(G-10302)
MICROCHIP TECHNOLOGY INC
7901 Strickland Rd Ste 101 (27615-3189)
PHONE..................................919 844-7510
Jim Hallman, Brnch Mgr
EMP: 10
SALES (corp-wide): 7.63B Publicly Held
Web: www.microchip.com
SIC: 3674 Microcircuits, integrated (semiconductor)
PA: Microchip Technology Inc
2355 W Chandler Blvd
Chandler AZ 85224
480 792-7200

(G-10303)
MICROTHERMICS INC
3216 Wellington Ct Ste 102 (27615-4122)
PHONE..................................919 878-8045
John J Miles, Pr
David M Miles, VP
▲ EMP: 12 EST: 1989
SQ FT: 7,200
SALES (est): 4.02MM Privately Held
Web: www.microthermics.com
SIC: 3556 8742 Beverage machinery; Food and beverage consultant

(G-10304)
MID-ATLANTIC CRANE AND EQP CO
3224 Northside Dr (27615-4125)
PHONE..................................919 790-3535
Mitchell E Filip, Pr
▲ EMP: 25 EST: 1980
SQ FT: 10,000
SALES (est): 30.15MM Privately Held
Web: www.midatlanticcrane.com
SIC: 5084 3531 Materials handling machinery; Aerial work platforms: hydraulic/ elec. truck/carrier mounted

(G-10305)
MID-ATLANTIC SPECIALTIES INC
5200 Trademark Dr Ste 102 (27610-3087)
P.O. Box 98749 (27624-8749)
PHONE..................................919 212-1939
Thomas Harward, Prin
EMP: 4 EST: 2007
SALES (est): 951.27K Privately Held
Web: www.midatlanticspecialties.com
SIC: 5033 3296 Insulation materials; Acoustical board and tile, mineral wool

(G-10306)
MIDLAND BOTTLING LLC
4141 Parklake Ave Ste 600 (27612-2380)
PHONE..................................919 865-2300
David Obryant, Admn
EMP: 4 EST: 2013
SALES (est): 162.08K Privately Held
Web: www.pepsibottlingventures.com
SIC: 2086 Carbonated soft drinks, bottled and canned

(G-10307)
MILL ART WOOD
1500 Capital Blvd (27603-1122)
PHONE..................................919 828-7376
Rob Christian, Pr
EMP: 5 EST: 2011
SALES (est): 963.34K Privately Held
Web: www.millwoodart.com
SIC: 3553 Woodworking machinery

(G-10308)
MINCAR GROUP INC
215 Tryon Rd (27603-3527)
PHONE..................................919 772-7170
Josephine D Jones, Pr
Ronnie Jones, VP
Dwight Jones, Sec
EMP: 9 EST: 1995
SQ FT: 7,500
SALES (est): 158.96K Privately Held
Web: www.morethanamailbox.com
SIC: 3444 Mail (post office) collection or storage boxes, sheet metal

(G-10309)
MIRCHANDANI INC
3904 Peppertree Pl (27604-3443)
PHONE..................................919 872-8871
Mike Mirchandani, Prin
EMP: 4 EST: 2002
SALES (est): 61.45K Privately Held
SIC: 2893 Printing ink

(G-10310)
MISSION SRGCAL INNOVATIONS LLC
7424 Acc Blvd Ste 104 (27617)
PHONE..................................678 699-6057
EMP: 4 EST: 2019
SALES (est): 638.9K Privately Held
Web: www.safeviewsurgery.com
SIC: 3841 Surgical and medical instruments

(G-10311)
MLF COMPANY LLC
3248 Lake Woodard Dr (27604-3659)
PHONE......................919 231-9401
Michael Ficalora, *Pr*
EMP: 14 EST: 2000
SQ FT: 8,000
SALES (est): 2MM Privately Held
Web: www.ficaloramfg.com
SIC: 2514 3446 Household furniture:
upholstered on metal frames; Architectural
metalwork

(G-10312)
MON MACARON LLC
111 Seaboard Ave Ste 118 (27604-1152)
PHONE......................984 200-1387
Autumn C Butler, *Managing Member*
EMP: 8 EST: 2019
SALES (est): 1.95MM Privately Held
Web: www.monmacaron.us
SIC: 2051 Bakery: wholesale or wholesale/
retail combined

(G-10313)
MONTH9 BOOKS LLC (PA)
4208 Six Forks Rd Ste 1000 (27609-5733)
PHONE......................919 645-5786
EMP: 5 EST: 2014
SALES (est): 321.79K
SALES (corp-wide): 321.79K Privately
Held
Web: www.month9books.com
SIC: 2741 Miscellaneous publishing

(G-10314)
MOORE PRINTING & GRAPHICS INC
Also Called: Lewis Moore Prtg & Graphics
5320 Departure Dr (27616-1836)
PHONE......................919 821-3293
Sharry Layton, *Pr*
Barbara Moore, *Sec*
EMP: 10 EST: 1977
SQ FT: 4,500
SALES (est): 968.23K Privately Held
Web:
www.mooreprintingandgraphics.com
SIC: 7334 2752 Photocopying and
duplicating services; Offset printing

(G-10315)
MOTOR RITE INC
1001 Corporation Pkwy Ste 100
(27610-1859)
PHONE......................919 625-3653
David Brooks, *Prin*
EMP: 8 EST: 2002
SALES (est): 1.69MM Privately Held
Web: www.motorrite.com
SIC: 3621 Electric motor and generator parts

(G-10316)
MR TOBACCO
4011 Capital Blvd Ste 125 (27604-3486)
PHONE......................919 747-9052
EMP: 4 EST: 2012
SALES (est): 190.63K Privately Held
SIC: 5194 2111 Smoking tobacco; Cigarettes

(G-10317)
MRR SOUTHERN LLC
5842 Faringdon Pl Ste 1 (27609-3930)
PHONE......................919 436-3571
Francis Hector, *Prin*
EMP: 8 EST: 2015
SALES (est): 4.99MM Privately Held
SIC: 3443 Dumpsters, garbage

(G-10318)
MULCH MASTERS OF NC INC
Also Called: Mulch Masters
10200 Durant Rd (27614-9783)
PHONE......................919 676-0031
Randolph Keith Caruthers, *Pr*
Catherine Caruthers, *VP*
EMP: 7 EST: 1993
SALES (est): 623.05K Privately Held
Web: www.themulchmasters.com
SIC: 2499 Mulch, wood and bark

(G-10319)
MY ALABASTER BOX LLC
5412 Cahaba Way (27616-3192)
PHONE......................919 873-1442
Barbara Lennon, *Owner*
EMP: 5 EST: 2017
SALES (est): 76.33K Privately Held
Web: www.myalabasterboxllc.com
SIC: 2741 Miscellaneous publishing

(G-10320)
MYFUTURENC INC
311 New Bern Ave Unit 26246
(27611-0179)
PHONE......................919 649-7834
Cecilia Holden, *Pr*
EMP: 18 EST: 2019
SALES (est): 3.87MM Privately Held
Web: www.myfuturenc.org
SIC: 3999 Education aids, devices and
supplies

(G-10321)
N2 FRANCHISING INC
Also Called: Belocal
160 Mine Lake Ct Ste 200 (27615)
PHONE......................844 353-5378
Duane Hixon, *CEO*
EMP: 13 EST: 2006
SQ FT: 1,000
SALES (est): 77.45MM Privately Held
Web: www.strollmag.com
SIC: 2741 Miscellaneous publishing

(G-10322)
NATIONAL AIR FILTERS INC
1109 N New Hope Rd (27610-1415)
PHONE......................919 231-8596
James R Grubbs Iii, *Pr*
EMP: 13 EST: 2010
SALES (est): 2.78MM Privately Held
Web: www.filtersonline.com
SIC: 3564 Filters, air: furnaces, air
conditioning equipment, etc.

(G-10323)
NATIONAL CTR FOR SOCIAL IMPACT
1053 E Whitaker Mill Rd Ste 115
(27604-5311)
PHONE......................984 212-2285
Daniel Demaionewton, *Ex Dir*
EMP: 6 EST: 2016
SALES (est): 175.26K Privately Held
SIC: 8742 4832 8299 3999 Human resource
consulting services; Educational;
Educational services; Education aids,
devices and supplies

(G-10324)
NATIONAL MASTERCRAFT INDS INC
Also Called: Mastercraft
14 Glenwood Ave Ste 22 (27603-1700)
P.O. Box 27643 (27611-7643)
PHONE......................919 896-8858
Barry W Carter, *Pr*
Sherry O Stegall, *Sec*
EMP: 6 EST: 1936
SQ FT: 12,000

SALES (est): 173.59K Privately Held
SIC: 2391 Curtains, window: made from
purchased materials

(G-10325)
NATRX INC
6220 Angus Dr Ste 101 (27617-4752)
PHONE......................919 263-0667
Tad Schwendler, *Admn*
Matthew Campbell, *CEO*
Leonard Nelson, *VP*
William Theodore Schwendler Iii, *Prin*
EMP: 20 EST: 2018
SALES (est): 3.53MM Privately Held
Web: www.natrx.io
SIC: 7371 3999 Software programming
applications; Barber and beauty shop
equipment

(G-10326)
NATURAL GRANITE & MARBLE INC
3100 Stony Brook Dr Ste N1 (27604-3768)
PHONE......................919 872-1508
Issam Hachicho, *Pr*
Sam Coelho, *Genl Mgr*
▲ EMP: 7 EST: 2008
SQ FT: 3,000
SALES (est): 700K Privately Held
Web: www.naturalgranitemarble.com
SIC: 3281 Marble, building: cut and shaped

(G-10327)
NC SOLAR NOW INC
Also Called: NC Solar
2517 Atlantic Ave (27604-1411)
PHONE......................919 833-9096
Stephen Nicolas, *Pr*
EMP: 15 EST: 2010
SALES (est): 4.89MM Privately Held
Web: www.ncsolarnow.com
SIC: 1711 3699 Solar energy contractor;
Electrical equipment and supplies, nec

(G-10328)
NCI GROUP INC
Also Called: Metal Depots
5115 New Bern Ave (27610)
PHONE......................919 926-4800
Ed Collier, *Mgr*
EMP: 9
SALES (corp-wide): 5.58B Privately Held
Web: www.metaldepots.com
SIC: 3448 3446 Prefabricated metal buildings
; Architectural metalwork
HQ: Nci Group, Inc.
5020 Weston Pkwy
Cary NC 27513
281 897-7788

(G-10329)
NEIGHBORHOOD SMOOTHIE LLC
10115 Second Star Ct (27613-4157)
PHONE......................919 845-5513
John Agori, *Prin*
EMP: 4 EST: 2014
SALES (est): 359.99K Privately Held
SIC: 2037 Frozen fruits and vegetables

(G-10330)
NEW PHOENIX AEROSPACE INC
6008 Triangle Dr Ste 101 (27617-4784)
PHONE......................919 380-8500
Cynthia Ezami, *Pr*
EMP: 15 EST: 2004
SALES (est): 831.07K Privately Held
Web: www.npaero.com
SIC: 3812 Acceleration indicators and
systems components, aerospace

(G-10331)
NEWS AND OBSERVER PUBG CO
(DH)
Also Called: Gold Leaf Publishers
421 Fayetteville St Ste 104 (27601-3010)
PHONE......................919 829-4500
Orage Quarles Iii, *Pr*
George Mccanless, *VP*
▲ EMP: 700 EST: 1894
SQ FT: 20,000
SALES (est): 24.76MM
SALES (corp-wide): 1.39B Privately Held
SIC: 2711 2741 2721 2752 Newspapers,
publishing and printing; Shopping news:
publishing and printing; Magazines:
publishing and printing; Commercial
printing, lithographic
HQ: Mcclatchy Newspapers, Inc.
1601 Alhambra Blvd # 100
Sacramento CA 95816
916 321-1855

(G-10332)
NINE THIRTEEN LLC
Also Called: Instant Imprints
5300 Atlantic Ave Ste 105 (27609-1123)
PHONE......................919 876-8070
Sharon Sawyer, *Owner*
Tyron Freeman, *Store Mgr*
EMP: 4 EST: 2006
SALES (est): 1.2MM Privately Held
Web: www.instantimprints.com
SIC: 2752 Commercial printing, lithographic

(G-10333)
NOKIA OF AMERICA CORPORATION
Also Called: Alcatel-Lucent USA
2301 Sugar Bush Rd Ste 300 (27601)
PHONE......................919 850-6000
EMP: 7
SALES (corp-wide): 24.19B Privately Held
Web: www.nokia.com
SIC: 3674 Integrated circuits, semiconductor
networks, etc.
HQ: Nokia Of America Corporation
600 Mountain Ave Ste 700
Murray Hill NJ 07974

(G-10334)
NORCA ENGINEERED PRODUCTS
LLC
7201 Creedmoor Rd Ste 150 (27613-1688)
PHONE......................919 846-2010
Jim Pollan, *Pr*
EMP: 28 EST: 1988
SALES (est): 4.07MM Privately Held
Web: www.norcaeng.com
SIC: 3325 Alloy steel castings, except
investment

(G-10335)
NORTH CAROLINA DEPT LABOR
Also Called: Elevator & Amusement DVC Bur
1101 Mail Service Ctr (27699-1100)
PHONE......................919 807-2770
Jonathan Brooks, *Pr*
EMP: 16
SALES (corp-wide): 74.26B Privately Held
Web: labor.nc.gov
SIC: 9311 3599 Finance, taxation, and
monetary policy, State government;
Amusement park equipment
HQ: North Carolina Department Of Labor
4 W Edenton St
Raleigh NC 27601

(G-10336)
NORTH CAROLINA STATE UNIV
Also Called: North Carolina State Dar Plant
Food Science Bldg Rm 12 (27695-0001)

P.O. Box 7624 (27695-0001)
PHONE..................919 515-2760
Gary Cartwright, *Mgr*
EMP: 9
SALES (corp-wide): 5.82MM **Privately Held**
Web: www.ncsu.edu
SIC: 2024 8221 Ice cream and frozen deserts
; University
HQ: North Carolina State University
2601 Wolf Village Way
Raleigh NC 27607
919 515-2011

(G-10337)
NORTH CRLINA DEPT ADULT CRRCTO
Also Called: Enterprise Metal Tag Plant
1150 Martin Luther King Jr Blvd (27601)
PHONE..................919 733-0867
Yonny Mclamb, *Mgr*
EMP: 7
SQ FT: 706,810
SALES (corp-wide): 74.26B **Privately Held**
Web: www.ncdps.gov
SIC: 3555 9223 Plates, metal: engravers';
Correctional institutions
HQ: North Carolina Department Of Adult
Corrections
214 W Jones St
Raleigh NC 27603

(G-10338)
NORTH CRLINA RNWABLE PRPTS LLC
176 Mine Lake Ct Ste 100 (27615-6417)
PHONE..................407 536-5346
EMP: 5 **EST:** 2011
SALES (est): 1.52MM
SALES (corp-wide): 30.36B **Publicly Held**
Web: www.energync.org
SIC: 3674 Semiconductors and related
devices
PA: Duke Energy Corporation
525 S Tryon St
Charlotte NC 28202
704 382-3853

(G-10339)
NORTH STATE SIGNS INC
553 Pylon Dr Ste D (27606-1466)
PHONE..................919 977-7053
Cyrus Gill, *Owner*
EMP: 5 **EST:** 2016
SALES (est): 233.25K **Privately Held**
Web: www.northstatesigns.com
SIC: 3993 Signs and advertising specialties

(G-10340)
NORTRIA INC
8801 Fast Park Dr Ste 301 (27617-4853)
PHONE..................919 440-3253
Bobby Butler, *CEO*
EMP: 12 **EST:** 2019
SALES (est): 926.9K **Privately Held**
SIC: 2834 Pharmaceutical preparations

(G-10341)
NOVISYSTEMS INC
1315 Ileagnes Rd (27603-3432)
PHONE..................919 205-5005
John Bass, *Ex Dir*
John Bass, *Prin*
Michael Kowolenko, *CEO*
EMP: 4 **EST:** 2018
SALES (est): 364.49K **Privately Held**
Web: www.novisurvey.net
SIC: 7371 7372 Computer software
development; Business oriented computer
software

(G-10342)
NSI LAB SOLUTIONS INC
7212 Acc Blvd (27617-8736)
PHONE..................919 789-3000
Mark Hammersla, *Pr*
Deborah Hammersla, *Sec*
EMP: 15 **EST:** 1991
SQ FT: 10,000
SALES (est): 8.52MM **Privately Held**
Web: www.nsilabsolutions.com
SIC: 2899 Chemical preparations, nec

(G-10343)
OBJECTIVE SECURITY CORPORATION
555 Fayetteville St Ste 201 (27601-3034)
PHONE..................415 997-9967
Grace Nordin, *CEO*
Thomas Nordin, *Pr*
EMP: 15 **EST:** 2003
SALES (est): 441.07K **Privately Held**
Web: www.objectivefs.com
SIC: 7372 Application computer software

(G-10344)
OLDCASTLE INFRASTRUCTURE INC
Also Called: NC Products
920 Withers Rd (27603-6095)
P.O. Box 27077 (27611-7077)
PHONE..................919 772-6269
Bill Hobson, *Mgr*
EMP: 26
SALES (corp-wide): 34.95B **Privately Held**
Web: locator.oldcastleinfrastructure.com
SIC: 1791 3272 5013 Precast concrete
structural framing or panels, placing of;
Concrete products, nec; Automobile glass
HQ: Oldcastle Infrastructure, Inc.
7000 Central Pkwy Ste 800
Atlanta GA 30328
770 270-5000

(G-10345)
OLIVENTURES INC (PA)
6325 Falls Of Neuse Rd Ste 35-122
(27615-6877)
PHONE..................800 231-2619
EMP: 4 **EST:** 2009
SALES (est): 228.35K
SALES (corp-wide): 228.35K **Privately Held**
SIC: 2079 Olive oil

(G-10346)
ONTARGET LABS INC (PA)
8605 Bell Grove Way (27615-3168)
PHONE..................919 846-3877
Steven Dmiszewicki, *Prin*
EMP: 5 **EST:** 2010
SALES (est): 233.8K **Privately Held**
SIC: 2834 Pharmaceutical preparations

(G-10347)
OPTOPOL USA INC
3915 Beryl Rd Ste 130 (27607-5609)
PHONE..................833 678-6765
Robert Padula, *Pr*
EMP: 4 **EST:** 2020
SALES (est): 1.23MM **Privately Held**
Web: www.optopolusa.com
SIC: 3841 Ophthalmic instruments and
apparatus

(G-10348)
OPULENCE OF SOUTHERN PINE
400 Daniels St (27605-1315)
PHONE..................919 467-1781
EMP: 7 **EST:** 2013
SALES (est): 126.88K **Privately Held**

Web:
www.opulenceofsouthernpines.com
SIC: 2299 Linen fabrics

(G-10349)
ORACLE OF GOD MINISTRIES NC
Also Called: Oracle
5731 New Bern Ave (27610-9305)
PHONE..................919 522-2113
EMP: 6 **EST:** 2015
SALES (est): 735.18K **Privately Held**
SIC: 7372 Prepackaged software

(G-10350)
ORACLE SYSTEMS CORPORATION
Also Called: Oracle
8081 Arco Corporate Dr Ste 270
(27617-2042)
PHONE..................919 257-2300
Frank Myers, *Brnch Mgr*
EMP: 10
SALES (corp-wide): 52.96B **Publicly Held**
SIC: 7372 Prepackaged software
HQ: Oracle Systems Corporation
500 Oracle Pkwy
Redwood City CA 94065

(G-10351)
OSLO PRESS INC
2316 Foxtrot Rd (27610-5048)
PHONE..................919 606-2028
EMP: 4 **EST:** 2008
SALES (est): 127.4K **Privately Held**
SIC: 2741 Miscellaneous publishing

(G-10352)
PACKAGING SERVICES
4112 Willow Oak Rd (27604-4729)
PHONE..................919 630-4145
EMP: 5 **EST:** 2010
SALES (est): 102.41K **Privately Held**
SIC: 2631 Container, packaging, and
boxboard

(G-10353)
PALACE GREEN LLC
Also Called: Palace Green
4701 Violet Fields Way (27612-5661)
P.O. Box 308 (27512-0308)
PHONE..................919 827-7950
EMP: 4 **EST:** 2013
SALES (est): 215.78K **Privately Held**
SIC: 2033 Jams, jellies, and preserves,
packaged in cans, jars, etc.

(G-10354)
PALETRIA LA MNRCA MCHACANA LLC
3901 Capital Blvd Ste 155 (27604-6072)
PHONE..................919 803-0636
Azucena Morales, *Managing Member*
EMP: 4 **EST:** 2016
SALES (est): 274.2K **Privately Held**
SIC: 5451 2024 Ice cream (packaged); Ice
cream and frozen deserts

(G-10355)
PAMELA A ADAMS
Also Called: Insty-Prints
3812 Tarheel Dr Ste D (27609-7535)
PHONE..................919 876-5949
Pamela J Atkins Adams, *Owner*
EMP: 4 **EST:** 1983
SQ FT: 1,575
SALES (est): 199.66K **Privately Held**
Web: www.instyprints.com
SIC: 2752 2791 2789 Commercial printing,
lithographic; Typesetting; Bookbinding and
related work

(G-10356)
PAMOR FINE PRINT
5924 Crepe Myrtle Ct (27609-4245)
PHONE..................919 559-2846
Bill Griggs, *Owner*
EMP: 6 **EST:** 2010
SALES (est): 106.73K **Privately Held**
Web: www.pamorfineprint.com
SIC: 2752 Offset printing

(G-10357)
PAPER SPECIALTIES INC
2708 Discovery Dr Ste J (27616-1961)
PHONE..................919 431-0028
Henry K Tingley, *Pr*
Charles Tingley, *VP*
EMP: 5 **EST:** 1981
SQ FT: 6,000
SALES (est): 153.16K **Privately Held**
SIC: 2675 Paper die-cutting

(G-10358)
PARK COMMUNICATIONS LLC (HQ)
Also Called: Millenium Print Group
10900 World Trade Blvd (27617-4202)
PHONE..................919 852-1117
Terry Pegram, *Managing Member*
EMP: 9 **EST:** 2013
SALES (est): 136.13MM **Privately Held**
Web: www.mprintgroup.com
SIC: 2759 Commercial printing, nec
PA: Pokemon Company, The
6-10-1, Roppongi
Minato-Ku TKY 106-0

(G-10359)
PASCHAL ASSOCIATES LTD
324 S Wilmington St (27601-1847)
PHONE..................336 625-2535
EMP: 10 **EST:** 2016
SALES (est): 1.02MM **Privately Held**
Web: www.paschalassociates.com
SIC: 3532 Mining machinery

(G-10360)
PATHOLDCO INC
5217 Blue Stem Ct (27606-9373)
PHONE..................919 369-0345
Scott Ahrens, *Pr*
EMP: 9
SALES (corp-wide): 38.72MM **Privately Held**
Web: www.precisionairtechnology.com
SIC: 3564 Filters, air: furnaces, air
conditioning equipment, etc.
HQ: Patholdco., Inc.
108 Nova Dr
Morrisville NC 27560

(G-10361)
PATHWAY TECHNOLOGIES INC (PA)
8400 Six Forks Rd Ste 202 (27615-3068)
PHONE..................919 847-2680
Donald Frazier, *CEO*
Donald Frazier, *Pr*
EMP: 40 **EST:** 2008
SQ FT: 1,000
SALES (est): 24.42MM
SALES (corp-wide): 24.42MM **Privately Held**
Web: www.pathwaytech.com
SIC: 3699 Security control equipment and
systems

(G-10362)
PATTY KNIO
Also Called: Tube-Tech Solar
3008 Campbell Rd (27606-4422)
PHONE..................919 995-2670
Patty Knio, *Owner*

EMP: 8 **EST:** 2010
SALES (est): 99.66K **Privately Held**
SIC: 5013 3533 Pumps, oil and gas; Oil and gas field machinery

(G-10363)
PB & J INDUSTRIES INC
8805 Running Oak Dr (27617-4621)
PHONE..................................919 661-2738
Jonathan Pulverhouse, *CEO*
EMP: 18 **EST:** 2006
SALES (est): 2.46MM **Privately Held**
Web: www.pbandjindustries.com
SIC: 2434 Wood kitchen cabinets

(G-10364)
PDM LIGHTING LLC
3737 Glenwood Ave Ste 100 (27612-5515)
P.O. Box 61151 (27661-1151)
PHONE..................................919 771-3230
Ponce D Moody, *Owner*
Ponce D Moody, *Prin*
EMP: 6 **EST:** 2015
SALES (est): 1.61MM **Privately Held**
Web: www.poncemoody.com
SIC: 3648 Lighting equipment, nec

(G-10365)
PELICAN VENTURES LLC
5924 Wild Orchid Trl (27613-8550)
PHONE..................................919 518-8203
Jim Tarleton, *Mgr*
EMP: 7 **EST:** 2010
SALES (est): 58.35K **Privately Held**
Web: www.pelican.com
SIC: 3648 Lighting equipment, nec

(G-10366)
PEPSI BOTTLING VENTURES LLC (DH)
Also Called: Pepsi-Cola
4141 Parklake Ave (27612)
PHONE..................................919 865-2300
Derek Hill, *Pr*
Matthew Bucherati, *
Mark Johnson, *
Claire Niver, *
▲ **EMP:** 60 **EST:** 1999
SQ FT: 3,000
SALES (est): 521.69MM **Privately Held**
Web: www.pepsibottlingventures.com
SIC: 2086 Carbonated soft drinks, bottled and canned
HQ: Suntory International
　4141 Park Lk Ave Ste 600
　Raleigh NC 27612
　917 756-2747

(G-10367)
PHOTOLYNX INC
2020 Progress Ct (27608-2767)
PHONE..................................760 787-1177
Chris Burton, *Prin*
EMP: 6 **EST:** 2008
SALES (est): 2.71MM **Privately Held**
Web: www.photolynx.com
SIC: 7372 Prepackaged software

(G-10368)
PIPE BRIDGE PRODUCTS INC
5208 Rembert Dr (27612-6244)
P.O. Box 10544 (27605-0544)
PHONE..................................919 786-4499
David Clemmer, *Pr*
EMP: 5 **EST:** 1999
SALES (est): 84.62K **Privately Held**
Web: www.daveclemmer.com
SIC: 3272 Sewer pipe, concrete

(G-10369)
PITNEY BOWES INC
Also Called: Pitney Bowes
3150 Spring Forest Rd Ste 122 (27616-2880)
P.O. Box 27407 (27611-7407)
PHONE..................................919 785-3480
Elisabeth Crut, *Brnch Mgr*
EMP: 4
SALES (corp-wide): 2.03B **Publicly Held**
Web: www.pitneybowes.com
SIC: 3579 Postage meters
PA: Pitney Bowes Inc.
　3001 Summer St
　Stamford CT 06926
　203 356-5000

(G-10370)
PLASMA GAMES
208 Bracken Ct (27615-6101)
PHONE..................................252 721-3294
Hunter Moore, *Prin*
EMP: 4 **EST:** 2018
SALES (est): 74.42K **Privately Held**
Web: www.plasma.games
SIC: 2836 Plasmas

(G-10371)
PLASMA GAMES INC
112 Wind Chime Ct (27615-6433)
PHONE..................................919 627-1252
Hunter Moore, *Prin*
EMP: 33 **EST:** 2019
SALES (est): 855.06K **Privately Held**
Web: www.plasma.games
SIC: 2836 Plasmas

(G-10372)
PLASTIC ART DESIGN INC
5811 Mchines Pl (27616-1914)
PHONE..................................919 878-1672
Ricky Chua, *Pr*
EMP: 4 **EST:** 1986
SQ FT: 4,000
SALES (est): 354.11K **Privately Held**
Web: www.plasticartdesign.com
SIC: 3993 5712 Displays and cutouts, window and lobby; Customized furniture and cabinets

(G-10373)
PLEXUS CORP
5511 Capital Center Dr Ste 600 (27606-3365)
PHONE..................................919 807-8000
Randy Hrnick, *Mgr*
EMP: 55
SALES (corp-wide): 3.96B **Publicly Held**
Web: www.plexus.com
SIC: 3841 3672 Surgical and medical instruments; Printed circuit boards
PA: Plexus Corp.
　1 Plexus Way
　Neenah WI 54957
　920 969-6000

(G-10374)
PLUSHH LLC
3633 Top Of The Pines Ct (27604-5053)
PHONE..................................919 647-7911
Bianca Williams, *Managing Member*
EMP: 7 **EST:** 2015
SALES (est): 100K **Privately Held**
SIC: 5699 3999 Costumes and wigs; Wigs, including doll wigs, toupees, or wiglets

(G-10375)
POGO SOFTWARE INC
Also Called: Pogo
8212 Oak Leaf Ct (27615-5116)

PHONE..................................407 267-4864
Joseph Farrell, *Pr*
EMP: 6 **EST:** 2010
SALES (est): 454.36K **Privately Held**
Web: www.pogocorporation.com
SIC: 7372 7371 Prepackaged software; Computer software development

(G-10376)
POGOMAXY INC
3737 Benson Dr (27609-7324)
P.O. Box 2477 (27602-2477)
PHONE..................................919 623-0118
Murali Bashyam, *CEO*
EMP: 4 **EST:** 2015
SQ FT: 2,800
SALES (est): 334.29K **Privately Held**
SIC: 7372 Application computer software

(G-10377)
POOLE PRINTING COMPANY INC
1400 Mapleside Ct (27609-4075)
P.O. Box 58487 (27658-8487)
PHONE..................................919 876-5260
A Richard Poole, *Pr*
Henry W Poole Junior, *Sec*
EMP: 7 **EST:** 1947
SQ FT: 8,500
SALES (est): 934.1K **Privately Held**
Web: www.pooleprinting.com
SIC: 2752 2759 Offset printing; Letterpress printing

(G-10378)
POWDER COAT USA
4200 Atlantic Ave Ste 130 (27604-1752)
PHONE..................................919 954-7170
Debbie Ainolhayat, *Prin*
EMP: 7 **EST:** 2008
SALES (est): 242.1K **Privately Held**
Web: www.powdercoatusa.com
SIC: 3479 Coating of metals and formed products

(G-10379)
POWERAMERICA INSTITUTE
930 Main Campus Dr Ste 20 (27606-5560)
PHONE..................................919 515-6013
Victor Veliadis, *Ex Dir*
EMP: 14 **EST:** 2017
SALES (est): 867.82K **Privately Held**
Web: www.poweramericainstitute.com
SIC: 3674 Semiconductors and related devices

(G-10380)
POWERHOUSE RESOURCES INTL LLC
2710 Wycliff Rd Ste 105 (27607-3033)
PHONE..................................919 291-1783
Wes Pierce, *Pr*
Roger Pierce, *
Linda Mandel, *
Trish Stover, *
David West Pierce, *
EMP: 59 **EST:** 2010
SQ FT: 16,000
SALES (est): 1.85MM
SALES (corp-wide): 2.37MM **Privately Held**
Web: www.powerhrllc.com
SIC: 4581 3559 Aircraft maintenance and repair services; Automotive maintenance equipment
PA: Vetpride Services, Inc
　2710 Wycliff Rd Ste 105
　Raleigh NC 27607
　910 920-2220

(G-10381)
POWERLYTE PAINTBALL GAME PDTS
5811 Mchines Pl Ste 105 (27616-1914)
PHONE..................................919 713-4317
Paul Fernandez, *Pr*
Carson Fernandez, *VP*
▲ **EMP:** 4 **EST:** 1999
SALES (est): 311.13K **Privately Held**
SIC: 3398 7389 Tempering of metal; Design services

(G-10382)
POZEN INC
8310 Bandford Way (27615-2752)
PHONE..................................919 913-1030
EMP: 12
SIC: 2834 Pharmaceutical preparations

(G-10383)
PPG ARCHITECTURAL FINISHES INC
Also Called: Glidden Professional Paint Ctr
2205 Westinghouse Blvd 11 (27604-2495)
PHONE..................................919 872-6500
Pom Joens, *Mgr*
EMP: 5
SALES (corp-wide): 17.65B **Publicly Held**
Web: www.ppgpaints.com
SIC: 2851 Paints and allied products
HQ: Ppg Architectural Finishes, Inc.
　1 Ppg Pl
　Pittsburgh PA 15272
　412 434-3131

(G-10384)
PPG ARCHITECTURAL FINISHES INC
Also Called: Glidden Professional Paint Ctr
1458 Garner Station Blvd (27603-3600)
PHONE..................................919 779-5400
Bill Stevenson, *Mgr*
EMP: 6
SALES (corp-wide): 17.65B **Publicly Held**
Web: www.ppgpaints.com
SIC: 2851 Paints and allied products
HQ: Ppg Architectural Finishes, Inc.
　1 Ppg Pl
　Pittsburgh PA 15272
　412 434-3131

(G-10385)
PPG INDUSTRIES INC
Also Called: PPG 4669
5500 Atlantic Springs Rd (27616-1856)
PHONE..................................919 981-0600
David Brady, *Brnch Mgr*
EMP: 4
SALES (corp-wide): 17.65B **Publicly Held**
Web: www.ppgpaints.com
SIC: 2851 Paints and allied products
PA: Ppg Industries, Inc.
　1 Ppg Pl
　Pittsburgh PA 15272
　412 434-3131

(G-10386)
PRACTICE FUSION INC (DH)
Also Called: Ringadoc
305 Church At North Hills St Ste 100 (27609-2667)
PHONE..................................415 346-7700
Tom Langan, *CEO*
Jonathan Malek, *
▲ **EMP:** 101 **EST:** 2005
SALES (est): 2.91MM
SALES (corp-wide): 1.5B **Publicly Held**
Web: www.practicefusion.com
SIC: 7372 Prepackaged software
HQ: Veradigm Llc
　305 Church At North Hills
　Raleigh NC 27609
　919 847-8102

(G-10387)
PRATT INDUSTRIES INC
Also Called: Converting Division
5620 Departure Dr (27616-1841)
PHONE..................919 334-7400
Mike Keepers, *Brnch Mgr*
EMP: 52
Web: www.prattindustries.com
SIC: 2653 5113 Boxes, corrugated: made
from purchased materials; Corrugated and
solid fiber boxes
PA: Pratt Industries, Inc.
4004 Smmit Blvd Ne Ste 10
Atlanta GA 30319

(G-10388)
PRECAST TERRAZZO ENTPS INC
1107 N New Hope Rd (27610-1415)
PHONE..................919 231-6200
Keith Oliver, *Pr*
EMP: 25 EST: 1996
SQ FT: 15,000
SALES (est): 4.7MM **Privately Held**
Web: www.precastterrazzo.com
SIC: 3272 3253 2511 Concrete products, nec
; Ceramic wall and floor tile; Wood
household furniture

(G-10389)
PRECISION ALLOYS INC
1040 Corporation Pkwy Ste T (27610-0129)
P.O. Box 41143 (27629-1143)
PHONE..................919 231-6329
William L Russell Junior, *Pr*
Richard W Zendzian, *VP*
EMP: 4 EST: 1988
SQ FT: 4,500
SALES (est): 210.33K **Privately Held**
SIC: 3471 Finishing, metals or formed
products

(G-10390)
PRECISION MCH FABRICATION INC
1100 N New Hope Rd (27610-1416)
PHONE..................919 231-8648
Gene Richardson, *Pr*
Don Turner, *
Richard Wheeler, *
▲ EMP: 65 EST: 1978
SQ FT: 100,000
SALES (est): 9.88MM **Privately Held**
Web: www.pmfweb.com
SIC: 3599 3613 3444 Machine shop, jobbing
and repair; Switchgear and switchboard
apparatus; Sheet metalwork

(G-10391)
PREDATAR INC
4208 Six Forks Rd Ste 1000 (27609-5733)
PHONE..................919 827-4516
Brandon S Neuman, *Prin*
EMP: 4 EST: 2021
SALES (est): 419.04K **Privately Held**
Web: www.predatar.com
SIC: 7371 7372 Custom computer
programming services; Application
computer software

(G-10392)
PREMIER CAKES LLC
Also Called: Premier Cakes
6617 Falls Of Neuse Rd Ste 105
(27615-6879)
PHONE..................919 274-8511
Bobby Outlaw, *Pr*
EMP: 5 EST: 2008
SQ FT: 1,700
SALES (est): 561.5K **Privately Held**
Web: www.premier-cakes.com
SIC: 2051 Cakes, bakery: except frozen

(G-10393)
PRESTIGE FARMS INC
2414 Crabtree Blvd (27604-2233)
PHONE..................919 861-8867
Chandler Thompson, *Mgr*
EMP: 34
SALES (corp-wide): 22.15MM **Privately Held**
Web: www.prestigefarms.com
SIC: 2015 Poultry slaughtering and
processing
PA: Prestige Farms, Inc.
7120 Orr Rd
Charlotte NC 28213
704 596-2824

(G-10394)
PRIME WATER SERVICES INC
9400 Ransdell Rd Ste 9 (27603-8980)
PHONE..................919 504-1020
Phillip Minor, *Pr*
EMP: 8 EST: 2015
SQ FT: 2,000
SALES (est): 121.13K **Privately Held**
Web: www.primewaterservices.com
SIC: 1711 3639 4941 Plumbing contractors;
Hot water heaters, household; Water supply

(G-10395)
PRIMEVIGILANCE INC
5430 Wade Park Blvd Ste 208
(27607-4191)
PHONE..................781 703-5540
Aleksandra Seisert, *Off Mgr*
EMP: 6 EST: 2016
SALES (est): 1.38MM **Privately Held**
Web: www.primevigilance.com
SIC: 3821 Clinical laboratory instruments,
except medical and dental

(G-10396)
PRINTSURGE INCORPORATED
2308 Beaver Oaks Ct (27606-9287)
PHONE..................919 854-4376
Greg Card, *Prin*
EMP: 6 EST: 2007
SALES (est): 59.03K **Privately Held**
SIC: 2752 Offset printing

(G-10397)
PRISM RESEARCH GLASS INC
6004 Triangle Dr Ste B (27617-4743)
P.O. Box 14187 (27709-4187)
PHONE..................919 571-0078
John Foscato, *Pr*
Steve Foscato, *VP*
▲ EMP: 15 EST: 1990
SQ FT: 17,000
SALES (est): 3.66MM **Privately Held**
Web: www.prismresearchglass.com
SIC: 3231 Laboratory glassware

(G-10398)
PRO CHOICE CONTRACTORS CORP
2405 Churchill Rd (27608-1927)
PHONE..................919 696-7383
Frank Marina, *Pr*
EMP: 6 EST: 2007
SALES (est): 549.62K **Privately Held**
SIC: 1521 1542 1799 2449 General
remodeling, single-family houses;
Commercial and office building contractors;
Post disaster renovations; Shipping cases
and drums, wood: wirebound and plywood

(G-10399)
PROBLEM SOLVER INC
1053 E Whitaker Mill Rd Ste 115 (27604)
PHONE..................919 596-5555
Robert A Wiener, *Pr*

▼ EMP: 10 EST: 2009
SALES (est): 931.94K **Privately Held**
Web: www.businessfurnitureshop.com
SIC: 3562 3499 Casters; Furniture parts,
metal

(G-10400)
PRODUCTION MEDIA INC
Also Called: Church Production Magazine
2501 Blue Ridge Rd Ste 250 (27607-6346)
PHONE..................919 325-0120
Brian Blackmore, *Pr*
Terri L South, *VP*
EMP: 10 EST: 1998
SQ FT: 1,500
SALES (est): 460.55K **Privately Held**
Web: www.churchproduction.com
SIC: 2741 7389 Miscellaneous publishing;
Decoration service for special events

(G-10401)
PROGRESS SOLAR SOLUTIONS LLC
Also Called: Manufacturing
1108 N New Hope Rd (27610)
P.O. Box 19540 (27619)
PHONE..................919 363-3738
◆ EMP: 18 EST: 2008
SQ FT: 25,000
SALES (est): 3.16MM **Privately Held**
Web: www.progresssolarsolutions.com
SIC: 3645 3621 3648 1711 Residential
lighting fixtures; Generator sets: gasoline,
diesel, or dual-fuel; Lighting equipment, nec
; Solar energy contractor

(G-10402)
PROGRESSIVE GRAPHICS INC
Also Called: Tristitch
3707 Hillsborough St (27607-5410)
PHONE..................919 821-3223
Richard Puckett, *Sec*
Norwood Mcdowell, *Pr*
EMP: 10 EST: 1989
SQ FT: 5,000
SALES (est): 1.73MM **Privately Held**
Web: www.progressivegraphics.net
SIC: 2759 Screen printing

(G-10403)
PROMETHERA BIOSCIENCES LLC (PA)
4700 Falls Of Neuse Rd Ste 400
(27609-6200)
PHONE..................919 354-1933
Mark B Johnston, *Pr*
EMP: 5 EST: 2016
SALES (est): 1.57MM
SALES (corp-wide): 1.57MM **Privately Held**
Web: www.cellaion.com
SIC: 2834 Pharmaceutical preparations

(G-10404)
PROMETHEUS GROUP HOLDINGS LLC
4601 Six Forks Rd Ste 220 (27609-5210)
PHONE..................919 835-0810
Eric Huang, *CEO*
EMP: 85 EST: 2015
SALES (est): 4.48MM **Privately Held**
SIC: 7372 Business oriented computer
software

(G-10405)
PROPHARMA GROUP LLC (HQ)
Also Called: Acadeus
107 W Hargett St (27601-1700)
P.O. Box 12090 (66282)
PHONE..................888 242-0559

Dawn Sherman, *CEO*
Jeff Hargroves, *
Brian Tuttle, *
Joe Biehl, *
Steve Swantek, *
EMP: 60 EST: 2001
SALES (est): 35.93MM
SALES (corp-wide): 91.99MM **Privately Held**
Web: www.propharmagroup.com
SIC: 8742 8731 7372 Quality assurance
consultant; Commercial physical research;
Prepackaged software
PA: Linden, Llc
111 S Wacker Dr Ste 3350
Chicago IL 60606
312 506-5657

(G-10406)
PROSAPIENT INC
Also Called: Prosapient
555 Fayetteville St Ste 700 (27601-3030)
PHONE..................984 282-2823
Jordan Shlosberg, *Pr*
EMP: 6 EST: 2019
SALES (est): 4.52MM
SALES (corp-wide): 35.26MM **Privately Held**
SIC: 7372 Prepackaged software
PA: Prosapient Limited
5 Floor
London EC1N
208 505-0500

(G-10407)
PROXIMAL DESIGN LABS LLC
1421 Carolina Pines Ave (27603-2739)
PHONE..................919 599-5742
EMP: 4 EST: 2020
SALES (est): 376.15K **Privately Held**
SIC: 7372 Educational computer software

(G-10408)
PT MARKETING INCORPORATED
Also Called: Tech Marketing
8360 Six Forks Rd Ste 204 (27615-5087)
PHONE..................412 471-8995
Patrick Teen, *Pr*
Aileen Bryant, *Admn*
EMP: 9 EST: 1994
SALES (est): 879.17K **Privately Held**
Web: www.techmarketing.biz
SIC: 3679 Electronic circuits

(G-10409)
PUNY HUMAN LLC
6278 Glenwood Ave (27612-2723)
PHONE..................919 420-4538
Michael Sanders, *Prin*
EMP: 8 EST: 2011
SALES (est): 462.5K **Privately Held**
Web: www.punyhuman.com
SIC: 3652 Prerecorded records and tapes

(G-10410)
QPLOT CORPORATION
3245 Lewis Farm Rd (27607-6761)
PHONE..................949 302-7928
Zhengzheng Hu, *CEO*
EMP: 5 EST: 2011
SALES (est): 246.65K **Privately Held**
Web: www.qplot.com
SIC: 7373 7371 8748 7372 Systems
engineering, computer related; Custom
computer programming services; Systems
engineering consultant, ex. computer or
professional; Application computer software

(G-10411)
QUADRON HOLDINGS INC
4105 Glen Laurel Dr (27612-3716)
PHONE..............................919 523-5376
Daniel Pratl, *CEO*
EMP: 5
SALES (est): 341.83K **Privately Held**
SIC: 7389 7372 Business Activities at Non-
Commercial Site; Business oriented
computer software

(G-10412)
QUALCOMM DATACENTER TECH
INC
8045 Arco Corporate Dr (27617-2025)
PHONE..............................858 567-1121
EMP: 58
SALES (corp-wide): 38.96B **Publicly Held**
SIC: 3674 Integrated circuits, semiconductor
networks, etc.
HQ: Qualcomm Datacenter Technologies,
Inc.
5775 Morehouse Dr
San Diego CA 92121
858 567-1121

(G-10413)
QUALIA NETWORKS INC
Also Called: Qni
3732 Westbury Lake Dr (27603-5187)
PHONE..............................805 637-2083
George Wayne, *Pr*
Edward Carney, *Bd of Dir*
Byron Shaw, *Bd of Dir*
Michael Wayne, *VP*
EMP: 6 EST: 2013
SALES (est): 335.76K **Privately Held**
SIC: 3674 3663 3812 3822 Integrated
circuits, semiconductor networks, etc.;
Antennas, transmitting and communications
; Aircraft control systems, electronic;
Environmental controls

(G-10414)
QUALITY CONTEMPORARY
FURNITURE
2517 Floyd Dr # B (27610-5529)
PHONE..............................919 758-7277
Milton Simpkins, *Pr*
EMP: 5 EST: 2009
SALES (est): 155.9K **Privately Held**
SIC: 2511 Wood household furniture

(G-10415)
QUALITY LGHTNING PRTECTION
INC (PA)
Also Called: Capital Lightng Protection
743 Pershing Rd (27608-2711)
P.O. Box 162 (27602-0162)
PHONE..............................919 832-9399
TOLL FREE: 800
Thomas J Cottle Junior, *Pr*
Charles Stephenson, *VP*
Marsha S Caviness, *Treas*
EMP: 12 EST: 1976
SQ FT: 8,000
SALES (est): 3.57MM
SALES (corp-wide): 3.57MM **Privately**
Held
Web: www.qualitylighting.com
SIC: 3643 Current-carrying wiring services

(G-10416)
QUANTUM NEWSWIRE
150 Fayetteville St 2800d108 (27601-1395)
PHONE..............................919 439-8800
EMP: 4 EST: 2019
SALES (est): 118.96K **Privately Held**
Web: www.quantumnewswire.app

SIC: 3572 Computer storage devices

(G-10417)
R JACOBS FINE PLBG & HDWR INC
8613 Glenwood Ave Ste 103 (27617-7553)
PHONE..............................919 720-4202
Nikole B Mariencheck, *Prin*
EMP: 7 EST: 2012
SALES (est): 886.95K **Privately Held**
Web: www.rjacobsfph.com
SIC: 3261 5074 Vitreous plumbing fixtures;
Plumbing fittings and supplies

(G-10418)
R N LEA INC
Also Called: Lea R N
707 N West St Ste 104 (27603-1135)
PHONE..............................919 247-5998
Karl Rectanus, *CEO*
EMP: 4 EST: 2014
SALES (est): 1.7MM **Privately Held**
Web: www.learnplatform.com
SIC: 7372 7379 8748 Educational computer
software; Online services technology
consultants; Test development and
evaluation service

(G-10419)
RACHEL DUBOIS
Also Called: Moondance Soaps & More
6013 Old Horseman Trl (27613-8104)
PHONE..............................919 870-8063
Rachel Dubois, *Owner*
EMP: 6 EST: 1999
SALES (est): 77.26K **Privately Held**
Web: www.moondancesoaps.com
SIC: 2841 7215 Soap: granulated, liquid,
cake, flaked, or chip; Coin-operated
laundries and cleaning

(G-10420)
RACKWISE INC
Also Called: Rackwise
4020 Westchase Blvd Ste 470
(27607-3938)
PHONE..............................919 533-5533
Doug Macrae, *Brnch Mgr*
EMP: 10
Web: www.rackwise.com
SIC: 7372 Business oriented computer
software
PA: Rackwise, Inc.
1610 Wynkoop St Ste 400
Denver CO 80202

(G-10421)
RAINFOREST NUTRITIONALS INC
9201 Leesville Rd Ste 120c (27613-7540)
PHONE..............................919 847-2221
Paul J Bobrowski, *Pr*
Donna Theriot, *Sec*
EMP: 7 EST: 2002
SALES (est): 204.94K **Privately Held**
Web: www.rainforest-inc.com
SIC: 2023 2834 Dietary supplements, dairy
and non-dairy based; Pharmaceutical
preparations

(G-10422)
RALEIGH DOWNTOWNER
Also Called: Downtown Raleigh Publishing
12 E Hargett St (27601-1426)
P.O. Box 27603 (27611-7603)
PHONE..............................919 821-9000
Crash Gregg, *Prin*
EMP: 8 EST: 2007
SALES (est): 85.87K **Privately Held**
Web: www.welovedowntown.com
SIC: 2711 5994 Newspapers, publishing and
printing; Newsstand

(G-10423)
RALEIGH ENGRAVING CO
Also Called: Raleigh Engraving Press
806 N West St (27603-1138)
P.O. Box 2854 (27602-2854)
PHONE..............................919 832-5557
Edwin G Brandle, *Pr*
Jacqueline Brandle, *Prin*
Greg Brandle, *VP*
EMP: 5 EST: 1955
SQ FT: 6,000
SALES (est): 91.32K **Privately Held**
Web: www.ostlingslasercraft.com
SIC: 2791 2759 Typesetting; Engraving, nec

(G-10424)
RALEIGH MAGAZINE
6511 Creedmoor Rd Ste 207 (27613-1687)
PHONE..............................919 307-3047
EMP: 5 EST: 2019
SALES (est): 178.02K **Privately Held**
Web: www.raleighmag.com
SIC: 2721 Magazines: publishing only, not
printed on site

(G-10425)
RALEIGH MECHANICAL & MTLS INC
7405 Acc Blvd (27617-8406)
PHONE..............................919 598-4601
Peter Manuel, *Pr*
EMP: 12 EST: 1984
SQ FT: 15,000
SALES (est): 2.04MM **Privately Held**
Web: www.raleighmech.com
SIC: 1711 1761 3444 Mechanical contractor;
Sheet metal work, nec; Awnings and
canopies

(G-10426)
RALEIGH POWDER COATING CO
2100 Garner Rd (27610-6890)
PHONE..............................919 301-8065
EMP: 4 EST: 2019
SALES (est): 93.93K **Privately Held**
Web: www.raleighpowdercoating.com
SIC: 3479 Coating of metals and formed
products

(G-10427)
RALEIGH PRINTING & TYPING INC
Also Called: Raleigh Printing
5415 Fayetteville Rd (27603-4182)
PHONE..............................919 662-8001
Patricia Simmons, *Pr*
Clyde E Simmons, *VP*
EMP: 9 EST: 1972
SQ FT: 3,000
SALES (est): 386.42K **Privately Held**
Web: www.raleighprintinginc.com
SIC: 2752 7338 Offset printing; Secretarial
and typing service

(G-10428)
RALEIGH RINGERS INC
2200 E Millbrook Rd Ste 113 (27604-1788)
PHONE..............................919 847-7574
David Harris, *Admn*
David Harris, *Dir*
EMP: 9 EST: 1990
SALES (est): 262.34K **Privately Held**
Web: www.rr.org
SIC: 3931 Bells (musical instruments)

(G-10429)
RALEIGH SAW CO INC
5805 Departure Dr Ste C (27616-1859)
PHONE..............................919 832-2248
William J Shields, *Pr*
▲ EMP: 8 EST: 1950
SQ FT: 9,600

SALES (est): 498.48K **Privately Held**
Web: www.raleighsaw.com
SIC: 7699 3425 Knife, saw and tool
sharpening and repair; Saw blades, for
hand or power saws

(G-10430)
RALEIGH TEES LLC
Also Called: Raleigh Tees
4909 Alpinis Dr Ste 113 (27616-1957)
PHONE..............................919 850-3378
Roland Jones, *Pr*
Willie Sinclair, *Pt*
Geraldine Jones, *Pr*
EMP: 5 EST: 1988
SQ FT: 6,000
SALES (est): 113.71K **Privately Held**
Web: www.123raleightees.com
SIC: 7389 2261 Embroidery advertising;
Screen printing of cotton broadwoven
fabrics

(G-10431)
RALEIGH WORKSHOP INC
Also Called: Raleigh Denim
319 W Martin St (27601-1352)
PHONE..............................919 917-8969
Victor Lytvinenko, *Pr*
Sarah Lytvinenko, *
◆ EMP: 24 EST: 2012
SQ FT: 7,000
SALES (est): 2.42MM **Privately Held**
Web: www.raleighdenimworkshop.com
SIC: 2211 5651 5137 5136 Denims; Family
clothing stores; Women's and children's
clothing; Men's and boy's clothing

(G-10432)
RANPAK CORP
3401 Gresham Lake Rd (27615-4243)
PHONE..............................919 790-8225
EMP: 5
SALES (corp-wide): 94.08MM **Privately**
Held
Web: www.ranpak.com
SIC: 2621 Packaging paper
HQ: Ranpak Corp.
7990 Auburn Rd
Concord Township OH 44077
440 354-4445

(G-10433)
RDD PHARMA INC
8480 Honeycutt Rd Ste 120 (27615-2261)
PHONE..............................302 319-9970
John Temperato, *CEO*
Mark Sirgo, *Ch Bd*
Arie Giniger, *Bd of Dir*
Nir Barak, *Prin*
EMP: 5 EST: 2013
SQ FT: 150
SALES (est): 429.84K **Privately Held**
Web: www.rddpharma.com
SIC: 3841 Surgical and medical instruments

(G-10434)
READABLE COMMUNICATIONS INC
Also Called: Poole Printing Company
2609 Spring Forest Rd (27616-1825)
PHONE..............................919 876-5260
Mory Read, *Pr*
EMP: 8 EST: 2015
SQ FT: 8,400
SALES (est): 1.06MM **Privately Held**
SIC: 2731 2752 Pamphlets: publishing and
printing; Offset and photolithographic
printing

(G-10435)
READILITE & BARRICADE INC (PA)
708 Freedom Dr (27610-1402)
P.O. Box 58280 (27658-8280)
PHONE..............................919 231-8309
Larry J Cashwell, *Pr*
Deborah Cashwell, *VP*
EMP: 18 **EST:** 1965
SQ FT: 5,000
SALES (est): 461.38K
SALES (corp-wide): 461.38K **Privately Held**
Web: www.unitedsiteservices.com
SIC: 7519 3993 3431 2451 Trailer rental; Signs and advertising specialties; Metal sanitary ware; Mobile homes

(G-10436)
RED HAT INC (HQ)
Also Called: Centos Project
100 E Davie St (27601-1806)
PHONE..............................919 754-3700
Matt Hicks, *Pr*
Paul Cormier, *
Laurie Krebs, *
Delisa K Alexander, *CPO**
Michael A Kelly, *CIO**
EMP: 610 **EST:** 1998
SQ FT: 380,000
SALES (est): 2.72B
SALES (corp-wide): 62.75B **Publicly Held**
Web: www.redhat.com
SIC: 7371 7372 Computer software development; Prepackaged software
PA: International Business Machines Corporation
1 New Orchard Rd
Armonk NY 10504
914 499-1900

(G-10437)
RED HOUSE CABINETS LLC
9660 Falls Of Neuse Rd (27615-2473)
PHONE..............................919 201-2101
John Jones, *Prin*
EMP: 5 **EST:** 2016
SALES (est): 53.79K **Privately Held**
Web: www.redhousecabinets.com
SIC: 2434 Wood kitchen cabinets

(G-10438)
REDBIRD SCREEN PRINTING LLC
8711 Owl Roost Pl (27617-8731)
PHONE..............................919 946-0005
EMP: 5 **EST:** 2014
SALES (est): 81.6K **Privately Held**
Web: www.redbirdscreenprinting.com
SIC: 2752 Offset printing

(G-10439)
REDDY ICE LLC
8700 Ice Dr (27613)
P.O. Box 90518 (27675-0518)
PHONE..............................919 782-9358
David Young, *Mgr*
EMP: 9
SALES (corp-wide): 3.82B **Privately Held**
Web: www.reddyice.com
SIC: 2097 Manufactured ice
HQ: Reddy Ice Llc
5710 Lbj Fwy Ste 300
Dallas TX 75240
214 526-6740

(G-10440)
REDHILL BIOPHARMA INC
8045 Arco Corporate Dr (27617-2025)
PHONE..............................984 444-7010
Rick Scruggs, *Pr*
Guy Goldberg, *Chief Business Officer**
June Almenoff, *CSO**

EMP: 74 **EST:** 2017
SALES (est): 15.43MM **Privately Held**
Web: www.redhillbio.com
SIC: 2834 Pharmaceutical preparations

(G-10441)
RESIDEO LLC
Also Called: ADI Global Distribution
2741 Noblin Rd Ste 101 (27604-3381)
PHONE..............................919 872-5556
Johnny Hudson, *Brnch Mgr*
EMP: 8
SALES (corp-wide): 6.76B **Publicly Held**
Web: www.adiglobaldistribution.us
SIC: 5063 3669 3822 Electrical apparatus and equipment; Emergency alarms; Environmental controls
HQ: Resideo Llc
275 Bradhollow Rd Ste 400
Melville NY 11747
631 692-1000

(G-10442)
REVWARE INC
1645 Old Louisburg Rd (27604-1376)
P.O. Box 90786 (27675-0786)
PHONE..............................919 790-0000
Thomas Welsh, *Pr*
EMP: 7 **EST:** 1992
SQ FT: 6,000
SALES (est): 1.45MM **Privately Held**
Web: www.revware.net
SIC: 3577 7372 3829 Computer peripheral equipment, nec; Prepackaged software; Measuring and controlling devices, nec

(G-10443)
REYES PRDCTOS MXCNOS REYES LLC
2905 Benjamin Hill Cir (27610-6617)
PHONE..............................704 777-5805
EMP: 4 **EST:** 2014
SALES (est): 208.18K **Privately Held**
SIC: 2096 Potato chips and similar snacks

(G-10444)
RFMD INFRSTRCTURE PDT GROUP IN
327 Hillsborough St (27603-1725)
PHONE..............................704 996-2997
Robert A Bruggeworth, *Pr*
William A Priddy Junior, *CFO*
Alan Hallberg, *
J Forrest Moore, *
EMP: 6 **EST:** 2004
SALES (est): 1.61MM
SALES (corp-wide): 3.77B **Publicly Held**
SIC: 3674 Semiconductors and related devices
HQ: Qorvo Us, Inc.
2300 Ne Brookwood Pkwy
Hillsboro OR 97124
503 615-9000

(G-10445)
ROBERT ST CLAIR CO INC
7701 Leesville Rd (27613-4028)
PHONE..............................919 847-8611
Robert Stclaire, *Pr*
Toni Stclaire, *VP*
▲ **EMP:** 10 **EST:** 1986
SALES (est): 162.78K **Privately Held**
SIC: 2426 Flooring, hardwood

(G-10446)
ROBERTS FAMILY ENTERPRISES LLP
7101 Ebenezer Church Rd (27612-1856)
PHONE..............................919 785-3111
Roy Roberts, *Mng Pt*

EMP: 7 **EST:** 2005
SALES (est): 219.88K **Privately Held**
SIC: 3312 Blast furnaces and steel mills

(G-10447)
ROCKY MOUNT MILL LLC
2619 Western Blvd (27606-2125)
PHONE..............................919 890-6000
James F Goodmon, *CEO*
EMP: 5 **EST:** 2012
SALES (est): 105.71K **Privately Held**
Web: www.capitolbroadcasting.com
SIC: 2281 Cotton yarn, spun

(G-10448)
ROYAL BLUNTS CONNECTIONS INC
4900 Thornton Rd Ste 109 (27616-5879)
PHONE..............................919 961-4910
Louis Wilson, *Pr*
EMP: 4 **EST:** 2002
SQ FT: 8,800
SALES (est): 117.03K **Privately Held**
Web: www.royalbc.com
SIC: 5194 3634 Smokeless tobacco; Vaporizers, electric: household

(G-10449)
ROYAL OAK STAIRS INC
3201 Wellington Ct Ste 104 (27615-5494)
PHONE..............................919 855-8988
Christopher Morley, *Pr*
Cathy Morley, *VP*
EMP: 6 **EST:** 2000
SQ FT: 4,900
SALES (est): 454.23K **Privately Held**
Web: www.royaloakstairs.net
SIC: 2431 Staircases and stairs, wood

(G-10450)
RSR FITNESS INC
Also Called: Batca Fitness Systems
1207 N New Hope Rd (27610-1413)
P.O. Box 28328 (27611-8328)
PHONE..............................919 255-1233
Ron Batca, *Pr*
▲ **EMP:** 10 **EST:** 1994
SQ FT: 30,000
SALES (est): 2.21MM **Privately Held**
Web: www.batcafitness.com
SIC: 3949 Exercise equipment

(G-10451)
RT CARDIAC SYSTEMS INC
5420 Deer Forest Trl (27614-8221)
PHONE..............................954 908-1074
Jeffrey Larose, *CEO*
Al Basilico, *Prin*
Ernie Baker, *Sec*
Daiga Koenig, *Mgr*
EMP: 9 **EST:** 1998
SQ FT: 8,100
SALES (est): 305.74K **Privately Held**
Web: www.rtcardiacsystems.us
SIC: 3674 Microcircuits, integrated (semiconductor)

(G-10452)
S CHAMBLEE INCORPORATED
Also Called: Chamblee Graphics
1300 Hodges St (27604-1414)
P.O. Box 40727 (27629-0727)
PHONE..............................919 833-7561
EMP: 22 **EST:** 1966
SALES (est): 2.38MM **Privately Held**
Web: www.chambleeinc.com
SIC: 2752 2791 2789 Offset printing; Typesetting; Bookbinding and related work

(G-10453)
S P CO INC
Also Called: Spco.
200 W Millbrook Rd (27609-4304)
PHONE..............................919 848-3599
Roy Avent, *Pr*
Brenda Avent, *Sec*
▼ **EMP:** 4 **EST:** 1983
SALES (est): 246.27K **Privately Held**
SIC: 7389 2048 Brokers' services; Feed supplements

(G-10454)
S T WOOTEN CORPORATION
Rdu Airport Concrete Plant
9001 Fortune Way (27613)
PHONE..............................919 783-5507
Eric Henderson, *Mgr*
EMP: 10
SALES (corp-wide): 319.83MM **Privately Held**
Web: www.stwcorp.com
SIC: 3272 Concrete products, nec
PA: S. T. Wooten Corporation
3801 Black Creek Rd Se
Wilson NC 27894
252 291-5165

(G-10455)
S T WOOTEN CORPORATION
Also Called: Gresham Lake Concrete Plant
6937 Capital Blvd (27616-3029)
PHONE..............................252 291-5165
Eric Henderson, *Mgr*
EMP: 23
SALES (corp-wide): 319.83MM **Privately Held**
Web: www.stwcorp.com
SIC: 3531 Concrete plants
PA: S. T. Wooten Corporation
3801 Black Creek Rd Se
Wilson NC 27894
252 291-5165

(G-10456)
SANTARUS INC
8510 Colonnade Center Dr (27615-5860)
PHONE..............................919 862-1000
Gerald T Proehl, *Pr*
Debra P Crawford, *Sr VP*
Carey J Fox, *Sr VP*
Michael D Step, *Senior Vice President Corporate Development*
Teri L Chuppe, *Corporate Controller*
EMP: 290 **EST:** 1998
SQ FT: 40,000
SALES (est): 4.47MM
SALES (corp-wide): 8.76B **Privately Held**
Web: www.salix.com
SIC: 2834 Pharmaceutical preparations
HQ: Salix Pharmaceuticals, Ltd.
400 Smrset Corp Blvd Unit
Bridgewater NJ 08807

(G-10457)
SASH AND SABER CASTINGS
119 Dublin Rd (27609-3822)
PHONE..............................919 870-5513
EMP: 4 **EST:** 2011
SALES (est): 231.59K **Privately Held**
Web: www.sashandsaber.com
SIC: 3812 Defense systems and equipment

(G-10458)
SAVOYE SOLUTIONS INC
5408 Von Hoyt Dr (27613-6820)
PHONE..............................919 466-9784
Steve C Savoye, *Prin*
EMP: 5 **EST:** 2009
SALES (est): 117.88K **Privately Held**

SIC: **3577** Computer peripheral equipment, nec

(G-10459)
SBM INDUSTRIES LLC
3948 Browning Pl Ste 208 (27609-6512)
PHONE..........................919 625-3672
Gustavo Velazquez, *Admn*
EMP: 5 **EST:** 2016
SALES (est): 921.53K **Privately Held**
SIC: **3999** Manufacturing industries, nec

(G-10460)
SCATTERED WRENCHES INC
Also Called: Matt's Auto Shop
130 Annaron Ct (27603-3640)
PHONE..........................919 480-1605
Matt Simmons, *Pr*
EMP: 7
SALES (corp-wide): 197.46K **Privately Held**
Web: www.raleighev.com
SIC: **7539 7699 3694** Automotive repair shops, nec; Miscellaneous automotive repair services; Automotive electrical equipment, nec
PA: Scattered Wrenches Inc.
267 Timber Dr Unit 1248
Garner NC
919 454-4782

(G-10461)
SCHMALZ INC
5850 Oak Forest Dr (27616)
PHONE..........................919 713-0880
Volker Schmitz, *Pr*
Gary Vickerson, *
▲ **EMP:** 110 **EST:** 1999
SQ FT: 5,000
SALES (est): 44.46MM
SALES (corp-wide): 163.73MM **Privately Held**
Web: www.schmalz.com
SIC: **5084 3563** Materials handling machinery; Vacuum (air extraction) systems, industrial
PA: Schmalz-International Gmbh
Johannes-Schmalz-Str. 1
Glatten BW 72293
744324030

(G-10462)
SCHNEIDER AUTOMATION INC
2641 Sumner Blvd (27616-3234)
PHONE..........................919 855-1262
Grerg Odiheim, *Brnch Mgr*
EMP: 133
SALES (corp-wide): 1.09K **Privately Held**
Web: www.schneider-electric.com
SIC: **3699** Electrical equipment and supplies, nec
HQ: Schneider Automation Inc.
800 Federal St
Andover MA 01810
978 794-0800

(G-10463)
SCINOVIA CORP
8801 Fast Park Dr Ste 301 (27617-4853)
PHONE..........................703 957-0396
Scinovia Address, *CEO*
James Sund, *CEO*
EMP: 12 **EST:** 2014
SQ FT: 2,300
SALES (est): 3.4MM **Privately Held**
Web: www.scinovia.com
SIC: **3841** Diagnostic apparatus, medical

(G-10464)
SEAL INNOVATION INC
2520 Kenmore Dr (27608-1420)
PHONE..........................919 302-7870
Graham Snyder, *CEO*
Cassandra Taylor, *Contrlr*
EMP: 4 **EST:** 2013
SALES (est): 795.38K **Privately Held**
Web: www.sealswimsafe.com
SIC: **3669** Emergency alarms

(G-10465)
SEAS PUBLICATIONS
3608 Ladywood Ct (27616-9769)
PHONE..........................919 266-0035
EMP: 5 **EST:** 2014
SALES (est): 65.22K **Privately Held**
SIC: **2741** Miscellaneous publishing

(G-10466)
SECURED SHRED
Also Called: Shred Instead
3901 Barrett Dr Ste 306 (27609-6653)
PHONE..........................443 288-6375
James Knight, *Owner*
EMP: 7 **EST:** 2006
SALES (est): 461.12K **Privately Held**
Web: www.shredinstead.com
SIC: **3589 7389** Shredders, industrial and commercial; Business Activities at Non-Commercial Site

(G-10467)
SELECTBUILD CONSTRUCTION INC
Also Called: BMC Construction
4800 Falls Of Neuse Rd Ste 400 (27609-8141)
PHONE..........................208 331-4300
Stanley M Wilson, *Pr*
EMP: 13 **EST:** 1999
SALES (est): 981.45K
SALES (corp-wide): 16.4B **Publicly Held**
SIC: **1521 1771 1751 2431** Single-family housing construction; Concrete work; Framing contractor; Windows and window parts and trim, wood
PA: Builders Firstsource, Inc.
6031 Cnnection Dr Ste 400
Irving TX 75039
214 880-3500

(G-10468)
SHEET METAL PRODUCTS INC
3728 Overlook Rd (27616-3039)
PHONE..........................919 954-9950
Ryan Wilson, *Mgr*
EMP: 6 **EST:** 2004
SALES (est): 332.69K **Privately Held**
Web: www.smpnc.com
SIC: **3444** Sheet metalwork

(G-10469)
SHERWIN-WILLIAMS COMPANY
Also Called: Sherwin-Williams
5301 Capital Blvd (27616-2956)
PHONE..........................919 436-2460
Jeff Allen, *Prin*
EMP: 6
SALES (corp-wide): 23.1B **Publicly Held**
Web: www.sherwin-williams.com
SIC: **2851 5198** Paints and allied products; Paint brushes, rollers, sprayers
PA: The Sherwin-Williams Company
101 W Prospect Ave
Cleveland OH 44115
216 566-2000

(G-10470)
SHIBUMI SHADE INC
4039 Atlantic Ave (27604)

PHONE..........................336 816-9903
Dane Barnes, *Pr*
Scott Barnes, *Pr*
Alex Slater, *Prin*
EMP: 10 **EST:** 2016
SALES (est): 1.05MM **Privately Held**
Web: www.shibumishade.com
SIC: **5331 2394** Variety stores; Shades, canvas: made from purchased materials

(G-10471)
SHOWLINE INC (PA)
Also Called: US Soaps Manufacturing Co
2114 Atlantic Ave Ste 160 (27604-1555)
PHONE..........................919 255-9160
Patrick Diehl, *Pr*
▲ **EMP:** 17 **EST:** 2009
SQ FT: 65,000
SALES (est): 985.34K
SALES (corp-wide): 985.34K **Privately Held**
SIC: **2841** Soap and other detergents

(G-10472)
SHOWLINE AUTOMOTIVE PDTS INC (PA)
1108 N New Hope Rd (27610-1416)
PHONE..........................919 255-9160
Patrick Diehl, *CEO*
Robert Patrick Diehl Junior, *Pr*
EMP: 9 **EST:** 1999
SQ FT: 16,000
SALES (est): 1.82MM
SALES (corp-wide): 1.82MM **Privately Held**
SIC: **2841** Detergents, synthetic organic or inorganic alkaline

(G-10473)
SHRED-TECH USA LLC
4701 Trademark Dr (27610-3051)
PHONE..........................919 387-8220
Tim Fields, *Managing Member*
EMP: 4 **EST:** 2007
SQ FT: 5,000
SALES (est): 5.63MM **Privately Held**
Web: www.shred-tech.com
SIC: **3559** Recycling machinery
HQ: Shred-Tech Corporation
295 Pinebush Rd
Cambridge ON N1T 1
519 621-3560

(G-10474)
SIGN-A-RAMA
Also Called: Sign A Rama
972 Trinity Rd (27607-4940)
P.O. Box 51004 (27717-1004)
PHONE..........................919 383-5561
Thomas Zelaney, *Pr*
Brian Cox, *Sec*
EMP: 8 **EST:** 1990
SALES (est): 350.48K **Privately Held**
Web: www.signarama.com
SIC: **3993** Signs and advertising specialties

(G-10475)
SIGNS NOW
2424 Atlantic Ave (27604-1410)
PHONE..........................919 546-0006
David R Dalzell, *Owner*
EMP: 6 **EST:** 1995
SALES (est): 198.93K **Privately Held**
Web: www.signsnow.com
SIC: **3993** Signs and advertising specialties

(G-10476)
SILANNA SEMICDTR N AMER INC
1130 Situs Ct Ste 100 (27606-3372)
PHONE..........................984 444-6500
EMP: 84

Web: www.silanna.com
SIC: **3674 3625 3679** Semiconductor circuit networks; Switches, electronic applications; Electronic switches
HQ: Silanna Semiconductor North America, Inc.
4795 Estgate Mall Ste 100
San Diego CA 92121
858 373-0440

(G-10477)
SIMON INDUSTRIES INC
Also Called: Wakefield Solutions
2910 Industrial Dr (27609-7529)
PHONE..........................919 469-2004
David Stone, *Pr*
Wayne Frerichs, *
James J Polakiewicz, *
EMP: 42 **EST:** 1997
SQ FT: 50,000
SALES (est): 3.84MM **Privately Held**
Web: www.wakefieldthermal.com
SIC: **3444 8711** Forming machine work, sheet metal; Engineering services
HQ: Wakefield Thermal Solutions, Inc.
120 Northwest Blvd
Nashua NH 03063
603 635-2800

(G-10478)
SIMPLIFYBER INC
625 Hutton St Ste 106 (27606-6321)
PHONE..........................919 396-8355
Philip Cohen, *Prin*
EMP: 11 **EST:** 2022
SALES (est): 1.08MM **Privately Held**
Web: www.simplifyber.com
SIC: **2221** Bedspreads, silk and manmade fiber

(G-10479)
SINNOVATEK INC
2609 Discovery Dr Ste 115 (27616-1905)
PHONE..........................919 694-0974
Michael Druga, *Pr*
Amanda Vargochik, *VP*
Josip Simunovic, *CSO*
EMP: 7 **EST:** 2016
SALES (est): 9.55MM **Privately Held**
Web: www.sinnovatek.com
SIC: **5084 3499 3589 3556** Food product manufacturing machinery; Fire- or burglary-resistive products; Commercial cooking and foodwarming equipment; Food products machinery

(G-10480)
SINNOVITA INC
2609 Discovery Dr Ste 115 (27616-1905)
PHONE..........................919 694-0974
Michael Druga, *Pr*
EMP: 8 **EST:** 2016
SALES (est): 385.65K **Privately Held**
Web: www.sinnovatek.com
SIC: **2099** Food preparations, nec

(G-10481)
SINOWEST MFG LLC
5915 Oak Forest Dr Ste 103 (27616-1967)
PHONE..........................919 289-9337
Abdulhameed Manadath, *Prin*
EMP: 4 **EST:** 2017
SALES (est): 209.17K **Privately Held**
SIC: **2911** Diesel fuels

(G-10482)
SIRE TEES
6104 Westgate Rd Ste 115 (27617-4618)
PHONE..........................919 787-6843
Brian Unger, *Prin*
EMP: 4 **EST:** 2011

SALES (est): 199.91K **Privately Held**
Web: www.sirescreenprinting.com
SIC: 2752 Offset printing

(G-10483)
SIROCCO MARINE LLC
Also Called: Fluid Watercraft
5100 N Glen Dr (27609-4453)
PHONE..............................954 692-8333
Boyd Tomkies, *Managing Member*
EMP: 6 EST: 2015
SALES (est): 405.28K **Privately Held**
Web: www.fluidboats.com
SIC: 3732 Boatbuilding and repairing

(G-10484)
SITELINK SOFTWARE LLC
3301 Atlantic Ave (27604-1658)
P.O. Box 19744 (27619-9744)
PHONE..............................919 865-0789
Chuck Gordon, *CEO*
Ross Lampe, *
Luke Lenzen, *
EMP: 96 EST: 2006
SALES (est): 10.93MM
SALES (corp-wide): 39.72MM **Privately Held**
Web: www.sitelink.com
SIC: 7372 Prepackaged software
PA: Sparefoot, Llc
11000 N Mpac Expy Ste 300
Austin TX 78759
844 264-4136

(G-10485)
SKAN US INC
7409 Acc Blvd Ste 200 (27617-1920)
PHONE..............................919 354-6380
Sonia White, *Prin*
◆ **EMP:** 12 EST: 2011
SALES (est): 17.41MM **Privately Held**
Web: www.skan.com
SIC: 3674 Semiconductors and related devices
HQ: Skan Ag
Kreuzstrasse 5
Allschwil BL 4123

(G-10486)
SMALL BUSINESS SOFTWARE LLC
5117 Wickham Rd (27606-2547)
PHONE..............................919 400-8298
Brett J Stephenson, *Admn*
EMP: 5 EST: 2010
SALES (est): 106.54K **Privately Held**
SIC: 7372 Prepackaged software

(G-10487)
SMART CAST GROUP
Also Called: Fortis Track
5540 Centerview Dr Ste 204 (27606-3363)
PHONE..............................855 971-2287
Puia Purkyan, *Brnch Mgr*
EMP: 10 EST: 2017
SALES (est): 533.6K **Privately Held**
SIC: 3011 3531 Industrial tires, pneumatic; Tractors, tracklaying

(G-10488)
SMT INC
7300 Acc Blvd (27617-8407)
PHONE..............................919 782-4804
EMP: 64 EST: 1969
SALES (est): 14.18MM **Privately Held**
Web: www.smtcoinc.com
SIC: 3444 Sheet metalwork

(G-10489)
SOFTWARE PROFESSIONALS INC
8529 Six Forks Rd Ste 400 (27615-4972)

PHONE..............................503 860-4507
EMP: 9 EST: 2018
SALES (est): 3.13MM **Privately Held**
SIC: 7372 Prepackaged software

(G-10490)
SOLAR HOT LIMITED
Also Called: Solar Hot USA
1105 Transport Dr (27603-4146)
PHONE..............................919 439-2387
Dan Gretsch, *VP*
EMP: 7 EST: 2007
SALES (est): 1.6MM **Privately Held**
Web: www.solarhotusa.com
SIC: 3433 5074 Solar heaters and collectors; Heating equipment and panels, solar

(G-10491)
SOLAR PACK
Also Called: Solarpack
1791 Varsity Dr (27606-5241)
PHONE..............................919 515-2194
Bryon Spells, *VP*
Hannah Schauer, *
EMP: 42 EST: 2016
SQ FT: 78,022
SALES (est): 456.3K **Privately Held**
SIC: 3711 Cars, electric, assembly of

(G-10492)
SOLARBROOK WATER AND PWR CORP (PA)
1220 Corporation Pkwy Ste 103 (27610-1360)
PHONE..............................919 231-3205
George A Moore, *CEO*
Shane Traveller, *Dir*
Ross W Smith, *Dir*
Michael Griffith, *COO*
EMP: 4 EST: 1999
SQ FT: 4,550
SALES (est): 501.06K
SALES (corp-wide): 501.06K **Privately Held**
Web:
www.solarbrookwaterandpower.com
SIC: 3589 6799 3823 5999 Water treatment equipment, industrial; Investors, nec; Process control instruments; Water purification equipment

(G-10493)
SOLARH2OT LTD
Also Called: Solarhot
1105 Transport Dr (27603-4146)
PHONE..............................919 439-2387
Jeanette Gretsch, *Pr*
Daniel Gretsch, *VP*
Dan Gretsch, *VP*
▲ **EMP:** 6 EST: 2006
SQ FT: 8,750
SALES (est): 199.91K **Privately Held**
Web: www.solarhotusa.com
SIC: 3433 6531 Solar heaters and collectors; Real estate managers

(G-10494)
SOUTHERN WICKED DISTILLERY INC
3211 Imperial Oaks Dr (27614-7881)
PHONE..............................919 539-1620
Tolan Lucas, *Prin*
EMP: 4 EST: 2015
SALES (est): 169.8K **Privately Held**
SIC: 2082 Malt beverages

(G-10495)
SPECGX LLC
8801 Capital Blvd (27616-3116)
PHONE..............................919 878-4706
Keitha Buckingham, *Brnch Mgr*

EMP: 250
Web: www.mallinckrodt.com
SIC: 2834 2899 Analgesics; Chemical preparations, nec
HQ: Specgx Llc
385 Marshall Ave
Webster Groves MO 63119
314 654-2000

(G-10496)
SPECTRA INTEGRATED SYSTEMS INC
4805 Green Rd Ste 110 (27616-2848)
PHONE..............................919 876-3666
Elsa Mcnamara, *Mgr*
EMP: 5
SALES (corp-wide): 4.54MM **Privately Held**
SIC: 3699 Laser systems and equipment
PA: Spectra Integrated Systems, Inc.
8100 Arrowridge Blvd G
Charlotte NC 28273
704 525-7099

(G-10497)
SPECTRUM NEWS
2505 Atlantic Ave Ste 102 (27604-1593)
PHONE..............................919 882-4009
EMP: 4 EST: 2019
SALES (est): 232.97K **Privately Held**
SIC: 2721 Periodicals

(G-10498)
SPEEDPRO IMAGING
2400 Sumner Blvd Ste 110 (27616-6676)
PHONE..............................919 578-4338
EMP: 4 EST: 2017
SALES (est): 648.21K **Privately Held**
Web: www.speedpro.com
SIC: 3993 Signs and advertising specialties

(G-10499)
SPIRAL GRAPHICS INC
8821 Gulf Ct Ste A (27617-4612)
PHONE..............................919 571-3371
Donnie Williams, *Owner*
EMP: 9 EST: 1993
SQ FT: 3,500
SALES (est): 97.64K **Privately Held**
Web: www.spiralgraphics.com
SIC: 2759 Screen printing

(G-10500)
SPROUT PHARMACEUTICALS INC
4350 Lassiter At North Hills Ave Ste 260 (27609-5743)
PHONE..............................919 882-0850
Cynthia Whitehead, *CEO*
Robert Whitehead, *COO*
Eric Atkins, *CFO*
EMP: 10 EST: 2011
SALES (est): 20.97MM
SALES (corp-wide): 20.97MM **Privately Held**
Web: www.sproutpharmaceuticals.com
SIC: 2834 Pharmaceutical preparations
PA: Sprout2 Inc.
4208 Six Forks Rd # 1010
Raleigh NC 27609
844 746-5745

(G-10501)
SSI SERVICES INC
7231 Acc Blvd Ste 107 (27617-4886)
PHONE..............................919 867-1450
Bryan Johnson, *Pr*
Cindy Anderson, *CFO*
EMP: 5 EST: 2012
SQ FT: 2,000
SALES (est): 2.34MM **Privately Held**
Web: www.ssiservicesusa.com

SIC: 4783 8711 3613 Crating goods for shipping; Engineering services; Control panels, electric

(G-10502)
STACLEAR INC
7250 Acc Blvd (27617-8736)
PHONE..............................919 838-2844
Vinay Sakhrani, *Pr*
EMP: 4
SALES (est): 701.73K **Privately Held**
SIC: 3841 Surgical and medical instruments

(G-10503)
STAINLESS STEEL SPC INC
2025 Carr Pur Dr (27603-8885)
PHONE..............................919 779-4290
Ricky Ennis, *Pr*
Brenda Ennis, *Sec*
Amanda Daley, *Brnch Mgr*
EMP: 12 EST: 1989
SQ FT: 9,500
SALES (est): 2.64MM **Privately Held**
Web: www.ssspec.com
SIC: 3441 Fabricated structural metal

(G-10504)
STAINLESS STL FABRICATORS INC
5325 Departure Dr (27616-1835)
P.O. Box 58459 (27658-8459)
PHONE..............................919 833-3520
William E Bolton Iii, *Pr*
EMP: 9 EST: 2000
SQ FT: 30,000
SALES (est): 3.66MM **Privately Held**
Web: www.sstlf.com
SIC: 3441 Fabricated structural metal

(G-10505)
STARTA DEVELOPMENT INC
Also Called: Cstruct
2610 Wycliff Rd Ste 19 (27607-3073)
PHONE..............................919 865-7700
Gordon Blackwell, *Prin*
Dave Demski, *Prin*
EMP: 7 EST: 2000
SQ FT: 5,000
SALES (est): 346.5K **Privately Held**
Web: www.startadev.com
SIC: 7372 Business oriented computer software

(G-10506)
STAY ALERT SAFETY SERVICES LLC
1240 Kirkland Rd (27603-2850)
P.O. Box 467 (27285-0467)
PHONE..............................919 828-5399
Melissa Babcock, *Brnch Mgr*
EMP: 40
SALES (corp-wide): 530.93MM **Privately Held**
Web: www.stayalertsafety.com
SIC: 3993 Signs and advertising specialties
HQ: Stay Alert Safety Services, Llc
272 Clayton Forest Rd
Kernersville NC 27284
336 993-2828

(G-10507)
STEELFAB OF VIRGINIA INC (HQ)
4909 Western Blvd Ste 100 (27606-1772)
PHONE..............................919 828-9545
EMP: 21 EST: 1990
SALES (est): 44.16MM
SALES (corp-wide): 408.94MM **Privately Held**
SIC: 3449 3441 Miscellaneous metalwork; Fabricated structural metal
PA: Steelfab, Inc.
3025 Westport Rd
Charlotte NC 28208

704 394-5376

(G-10508)
STEVENS FOODSERVICE
8392 Six Forks Rd Ste 202 (27615-3061)
PHONE..................................919 322-5470
Robert Stevens, *Owner*
EMP: 6 **EST:** 2010
SALES (est): 355.93K **Privately Held**
SIC: 2032 Canned specialties

(G-10509)
**STOCK BUILDING SUPPLY
HOLDINGS LLC**
8020 Arco Corporate Dr Ste 400
(27617-2037)
P.O. Box 90068 (27675-0068)
PHONE..................................919 431-1000
▲ **EMP:** 2557
SIC: 5211 2431 5031 5713 Millwork and
lumber; Millwork; Lumber: rough, dressed,
and finished; Floor covering stores

(G-10510)
STOWE WOODWARD LICENSCO LLC
8537 Six Forks Rd Ste 300 (27615-6545)
PHONE..................................919 526-1400
EMP: 4 **EST:** 1988
SALES (est): 151.47K **Privately Held**
SIC: 2221 Broadwoven fabric mills,
manmade

(G-10511)
STOWE WOODWARD LLC
8521 Six Forks Rd (27615-5278)
PHONE..................................919 556-7235
Dave Pretty, *Pr*
EMP: 65
SALES (corp-wide): 1.13B **Privately Held**
SIC: 3069 Roll coverings, rubber
HQ: Stowe Woodward Llc
8537 Six Forks Rd Ste 300
Raleigh NC 27615

(G-10512)
STRATEGIC 3D SOLUTIONS INC
Also Called: Strategic3dsolutions
4805 Green Rd Ste 114 (27616-2848)
PHONE..................................919 451-5963
EMP: 4 **EST:** 2011
SALES (est): 745.51K **Privately Held**
Web: www.strategic3dsolutions.com
SIC: 3577 Printers and plotters

(G-10513)
STROMASYS CORPORATION
2840 Plaza Pl Ste 450 (27612-2156)
PHONE..................................617 500-4556
John Prot, *CEO*
EMP: 18 **EST:** 2022
SALES (est): 4.31MM **Privately Held**
SIC: 7372 Prepackaged software

(G-10514)
STRONGER BY SCIENCE TECH LLC
514 Daniels St 101 (27605-1317)
PHONE..................................336 391-9377
EMP: 5 **EST:** 2021
SALES (est): 333.18K **Privately Held**
Web: www.strongerbyscience.com
SIC: 7372 Application computer software

(G-10515)
STRUCTURAL PLANNERS INC
312 Dalton Dr (27615-1654)
PHONE..................................919 848-8964
Thomas J Vassallo, *Pr*
Pauline Vassallo, *Sec*
EMP: 10 **EST:** 1977
SALES (est): 335.97K **Privately Held**

Web: www.structuralplannersinc.com
SIC: 3441 Fabricated structural metal

(G-10516)
STRYKER CORP
525 Pylon Dr (27606-1414)
PHONE..................................919 455-6755
EMP: 8 **EST:** 2019
SALES (est): 916.67K **Privately Held**
Web: www.stryker.com
SIC: 3841 Surgical and medical instruments

(G-10517)
SUCCESS PUBLISHING INC
Also Called: Success Magazine
150 Fayetteville St M (27601-1395)
PHONE..................................919 807-1100
Victoria Conte, *Pr*
Chris Reid, *
EMP: 109 **EST:** 1999
SALES (est): 915.1K **Privately Held**
Web: www.waltermagazine.com
SIC: 2741 Miscellaneous publishing
PA: The Successful Company Llc
150 Fayetteville St
Raleigh NC 27601

(G-10518)
**SUMITOMO ELC LIGHTWAVE CORP
(HQ)**
201 S Rogers Ln Ste 100 (27610-4336)
PHONE..................................919 541-8100
Koji Niikura, *Pr*
Junichiro Hanai, *Ex VP*
Barrett Mills, *Sr VP*
Kevin Mistele, *Marketing*
Patria Smith, *Corporate Secretary*
▼ **EMP:** 52 **EST:** 1994
SALES (est): 46.92MM **Privately Held**
Web:
www.sumitomoelectriclightwave.com
SIC: 3357 Communication wire
PA: Sumitomo Electric Industries, Ltd.
4-5-33, Kitahama, Chuo-Ku
Osaka OSK 541-0

(G-10519)
SUNDAY DRIVE HOLDINGS INC
421 Fayetteville St Ste 1100 (27601-1792)
P.O. Box 98084 (27624-8084)
PHONE..................................919 825-5613
Francesco Gozzo, *Pr*
Robert Woodruff, *Prin*
EMP: 7 **EST:** 2002
SALES (est): 431.58K **Privately Held**
SIC: 7372 Business oriented computer
software

(G-10520)
**SUNROCK GROUP HOLDINGS CORP
(PA)**
200 Horizon Dr Ste 100 (27615-4947)
PHONE..................................919 747-6400
Bryan M Pfohl, *Ch*
Gregg W Bowler, *
Katherine Pfohl Tejano, *
Elisabeth A Pfohl Sasser, *
John A Tankard Iii, *General Vice President*
EMP: 80 **EST:** 2004
SALES (est): 51.02MM
SALES (corp-wide): 51.02MM **Privately
Held**
Web: www.thesunrockgroup.com
SIC: 1429 3273 2951 1411 Trap rock,
crushed and broken-quarrying; Ready-
mixed concrete; Asphalt paving mixtures
and blocks; Dimension stone

(G-10521)
SUNTORY INTERNATIONAL (DH)
4141 Parklake Ave Ste 600 (27612-2380)
PHONE..................................917 756-2747
Tsuyoshi Nishizaki, *Pr*
Yoshihiko Kunimoto, *Ex VP*
Tsutomu Santoki, *CFO*
Yoshito Shihara, *Treas*
Masaru Ijima, *Sec*
◆ **EMP:** 13 **EST:** 1967
SQ FT: 5,100
SALES (est): 1.26B **Privately Held**
Web: www.beamsuntory.com
SIC: 5149 2084 2086 5499 Mineral or spring
water bottling; Wines, brandy, and brandy
spirits; Bottled and canned soft drinks;
Health and dietetic food stores
HQ: Suntory Spirits Limited
2-3-3, Daiba
Minato-Ku TKY 135-0

(G-10522)
SUPREME T-SHIRTS & APPAREL
2813 Banks Rd (27603-8943)
PHONE..................................919 772-9040
Paulette Disbrow, *Pr*
EMP: 20 **EST:** 2017
SALES (est): 157.5K **Privately Held**
Web: www.shopsupremets.com
SIC: 2759 Screen printing

(G-10523)
SURFACE BUFF LLC
9013 Duval Hill St (27603-7522)
P.O. Box 857 (27529-0857)
PHONE..................................919 341-2873
Georgia Rivera, *Prin*
EMP: 5 **EST:** 2008
SALES (est): 87K **Privately Held**
Web: www.surfacebuff.com
SIC: 5032 1389 7349 3531 Stone, crushed
or broken; Construction, repair, and
dismantling services; Janitorial service,
contract basis; Surfacers, concrete grinding

(G-10524)
SURTRONICS INC
4001 Beryl Rd (27606-1451)
P.O. Box 33459 (27636-3459)
PHONE..................................919 834-8027
Angela D Stanley, *CEO*
EMP: 47 **EST:** 1965
SQ FT: 41,000
SALES (est): 4.48MM **Privately Held**
Web: www.surtronics.com
SIC: 3471 Electroplating of metals or formed
products

(G-10525)
SYMBRIUM INC (PA)
Also Called: Factory Systems
6021 Triangle Dr (27617-4744)
P.O. Box 90514 (27675)
PHONE..................................919 879-2470
Alicia A Blankenship, *Prin*
G Wesley Blankenship, *COO*
EMP: 15 **EST:** 2013
SQ FT: 25,000
SALES (est): 3.62MM
SALES (corp-wide): 3.62MM **Privately
Held**
Web: www.symbrium.com
SIC: 7372 3823 Application computer
software; Computer interface equipment,
for industrial process control

(G-10526)
SYNCHRONO GROUP INC
8601 Six Forks Rd Ste 400 (27615-2965)
PHONE..................................888 389-0439
EMP: 12 **EST:** 2019

SALES (est): 806.83K **Privately Held**
Web: www.synchronosure.com
SIC: 3695 Computer software tape and
disks: blank, rigid, and floppy

(G-10527)
**SYNTEGON TECHNOLOGY SVCS
LLC (PA)**
2440 Sumner Blvd (27616-3275)
PHONE..................................919 877-0886
Gary Anderton, *Pr*
Brian Dieter, *
Shane Larsen, *
▲ **EMP:** 44 **EST:** 2000
SALES (est): 22.55MM
SALES (corp-wide): 22.55MM **Privately
Held**
Web: www.syntegon.com
SIC: 3599 3565 Machine shop, jobbing and
repair; Packaging machinery

(G-10528)
**T HOFF MANUFACTURING CORP
(PA)**
4500 Preslyn Dr D (27603)
PHONE..................................919 833-8671
Theodore C Hoffman, *Pr*
Bill White, *CFO*
EMP: 4 **EST:** 1968
SQ FT: 19,000
SALES (est): 389.12K
SALES (corp-wide): 389.12K **Privately
Held**
Web: www.t-hoff.com
SIC: 3599 Machine shop, jobbing and repair

(G-10529)
TAB INDEX INC
2708 Discovery Dr Ste J (27616-1961)
PHONE..................................919 876-8988
Dianne Puryear, *Pr*
Don Puryear, *VP*
EMP: 8 **EST:** 1990
SQ FT: 10,000
SALES (est): 1.5MM **Privately Held**
Web: www.tabindex.com
SIC: 2679 8322 Tags and labels, paper;
Individual and family services

(G-10530)
TACTILE WORKSHOP LLC
1001 S Saunders St (27603-2201)
PHONE..................................919 738-9924
EMP: 4 **EST:** 2014
SALES (est): 1.19MM **Privately Held**
Web: www.tactilewksp.com
SIC: 3541 Home workshop machine tools,
metalworking

(G-10531)
TAGOIO INC ○
1017 Main Campus Dr Ste 2300
(27606-5512)
PHONE..................................984 263-4376
EMP: 4 **EST:** 2024
SALES (est): 1.48MM **Privately Held**
SIC: 7372 Prepackaged software

(G-10532)
TALLAHASSEE DEMOCRAT
4600 Trinity Rd (27607-3924)
PHONE..................................919 832-9430
Steve Clark, *Prin*
EMP: 4 **EST:** 2007
SALES (est): 98.33K **Privately Held**
Web: www.tallahassee.com
SIC: 2711 Newspapers, publishing and
printing

(G-10533)

TANNIS ROOT PRODUCTIONS INC

Also Called: Cognito Promo
1720 Capital Blvd (27604-1362)
PHONE...............................919 832-8552
Barbara Herring, *Pr*
William Mooney, *VP*
▲ **EMP**: 9 **EST**: 1992
SQ FT: 4,600
SALES (est): 802.31K **Privately Held**
Web: www.tannisroot.com
SIC: 2759 5199 7336 Screen printing;
    Advertising specialties; Graphic arts and
    related design

(G-10534)

TC2 LABS LLC

3948 Browning Pl Ste 334 (27609-6534)
PHONE...............................919 380-2171
EMP: 5 **EST**: 2015
SALES (est): 1.49MM **Privately Held**
Web: www.tc2.com
SIC: 3823 7371 Infrared instruments,
    industrial process type; Software
    programming applications

(G-10535)

TD CLOUD SERVICES

Also Called: Td Cloud
3129 Oaklyn Springs Dr (27606-8311)
PHONE...............................518 258-6788
Christopher Groff, *Mng Pt*
EMP: 5 **EST**: 2013
SALES (est): 394.9K **Privately Held**
SIC: 7372 7389 Business oriented computer
    software; Business Activities at Non-
    Commercial Site

(G-10536)

TEA AND HONEY BLENDS LLC

444 S Blount St Ste 115b (27601-2087)
PHONE...............................919 673-4273
Tashni-ann Dubroy, *Managing Member*
Tashni-ann Coote, *Managing Member*
EMP: 5 **EST**: 2008
SALES (est): 236.34K **Privately Held**
SIC: 2844 Perfumes, cosmetics and other
    toilet preparations

(G-10537)

TEBO DISPLAYS LLC

2609 Discovery Dr Ste 105 (27616-1905)
PHONE...............................919 832-8525
Joseph White, *Managing Member*
EMP: 6 **EST**: 2012
SALES (est): 482.2K **Privately Held**
Web: www.jwimageco.com
SIC: 3993 Signs and advertising specialties

(G-10538)

TEKTRONIX INC

Also Called: Tektronix
5608 Pine Dr (27606-8944)
PHONE...............................919 233-9490
Richard Willis, *CEO*
EMP: 5
SALES (corp-wide): 6.23B **Publicly Held**
Web: www.tek.com
SIC: 3825 Test equipment for electronic and
    electric measurement
HQ: Tektronix, Inc.
    14150 Sw Karl Braun Dr
    Beaverton OR 97077
    800 833-9200

(G-10539)

TELECMMNCTONS RESOURCE MGT INC

Also Called: TRM
156 Annaron Ct (27603-3640)

PHONE...............................919 779-0776
Thomas Mcdowell, *Pr*
Thomas Mcdowell, *Pr*
Tammy Mcdowell, *Sec*
Kevin Sullivan, *VP*
EMP: 12 **EST**: 1997
SQ FT: 45,000
SALES (est): 2.43MM **Privately Held**
Web: www.trminc.net
SIC: 5999 1731 3429 5065 Telephone
    equipment and systems; Fiber optic cable
    installation; Security cable locking systems;
    Security control equipment and systems

(G-10540)

TELEPATHIC GRAPHICS INC (PA)

6001 Chapel Hill Rd Ste 106 (27607-0119)
PHONE...............................919 342-4603
Bob Boyle, *Pr*
Mark Gauley, *

EMP: 35 **EST**: 2004
SQ FT: 9,700
SALES (est): 5.91MM **Privately Held**
Web: www.telepathicgraphics.com
SIC: 2759 7374 Publication printing;
    Computer graphics service

(G-10541)

TELETEC CORPORATION

5617 Departure Dr Ste 107 (27616-1913)
PHONE...............................919 954-7300
Nader Al Farouqi, *Pr*
Harry F Taji, *Pr*
EMP: 18 **EST**: 1983
SQ FT: 3,000
SALES (est): 1.45MM **Privately Held**
Web: www.teleteccorporation.com
SIC: 8748 7382 3663 Telecommunications
    consultant; Security systems services;
    Encryption devices

(G-10542)

TERADATA CORPORATION

5565 Centerview Dr Ste 300 (27606-3563)
PHONE...............................919 816-1900
Charles Douthart, *Brnch Mgr*
EMP: 19
Web: www.teradata.com
SIC: 3571 Electronic computers
PA: Teradata Corporation
    17095 Via Del Campo
    San Diego CA 92127

(G-10543)

TETHIS INC

3401 Spring Forest Rd (27616-2948)
PHONE...............................919 808-2866
Robin Weitkamp, *CEO*
EMP: 40 **EST**: 2012
SQ FT: 1,200
SALES (est): 2.55MM **Privately Held**
Web: www.tethis.com
SIC: 2822 Ethylene-propylene rubbers,
    EPDM polymers

(G-10544)

THE TARHEEL ELECTRIC MEMBERSHIP ASSOCIATION INCORPORATED

Also Called: T E M A
8730 Wadford Dr (27616-9027)
P.O. Box 61050 (27661-1050)
PHONE...............................919 876-4603
EMP: 17 **EST**: 1950
SALES (est): 3.88MM **Privately Held**
Web: www.tema.coop
SIC: 3264 5722 Porcelain electrical supplies;
    Electric ranges

(G-10545)

THERMO FISHER SCIENTIFIC INC

3315 Atlantic Ave (27604-1680)
PHONE...............................919 876-2352
EMP: 22
SALES (corp-wide): 42.86B **Publicly Held**
Web: www.thermofisher.com
SIC: 3826 Analytical instruments
PA: Thermo Fisher Scientific Inc.
    168 3rd Ave
    Waltham MA 02451
    781 622-1000

(G-10546)

THOMAS CONCRETE CAROLINA INC (DH)

1131 Nw Street (27603)
P.O. Box 12544 (27605-2544)
PHONE...............................919 832-0451
John N Holding Junior, *Pr*
EMP: 10 **EST**: 1959
SQ FT: 3,000
SALES (est): 15.43MM
SALES (corp-wide): 1.15B **Privately Held**
Web: www.thomasconcrete.com
SIC: 3273 Ready-mixed concrete
HQ: Thomas Concrete, Inc.
    2500 Cumberland Pkwy Se # 200
    Atlanta GA 30339
    770 431-3300

(G-10547)

THORWORKS INDUSTRIES INC

Also Called: Sealmaster
550 Corporate Center Dr (27607-0153)
PHONE...............................919 852-3714
Paul Cappabianca, *Brnch Mgr*
EMP: 5
Web: www.sealmaster.net
SIC: 2951 Asphalt paving mixtures and
    blocks
PA: Thorworks Industries, Inc.
    2520 Campbell St
    Sandusky OH 44870

(G-10548)

THUNDERBIRD TECHNOLOGIES INC

5540 Centerview Dr Ste 200 (27606-3386)
PHONE...............................919 481-3239
Andrew C Vinal, *Pr*
Michael W Dennen, *Ex VP*
Laura Perry, *CFO*
EMP: 5 **EST**: 1989
SQ FT: 3,200
SALES (est): 2.16MM **Privately Held**
SIC: 3674 Semiconductors and related
    devices

(G-10549)

TICE KITCHENS & INTERIORS LLC

1504 Capital Blvd (27603-1122)
PHONE...............................919 366-4117
EMP: 10 **EST**: 2014
SQ FT: 700
SALES (est): 776.49K **Privately Held**
Web: www.ticekitchensandinteriors.com
SIC: 1799 2599 5211 2434 Kitchen and
    bathroom remodeling; Cabinets, factory;
    Cabinets, kitchen; Wood kitchen cabinets

(G-10550)

TKM GLOBAL LLC

Also Called: Bimbo Bkeries Authorized Distr
8041 Brier Creek Pkwy (27617-7596)
PHONE...............................732 694-0311
Kamel Conde, *Managing Member*
EMP: 5 **EST**: 2019
SALES (est): 205.99K **Privately Held**
Web: www.tkmglobal.net

SIC: 2051 4212 Bakery: wholesale or
    wholesale/retail combined; Moving services

(G-10551)

TOBACCO MRCHNTS ASSN OF US INC

Also Called: Tobacco Merchants Association
    of The United States Inc.
901 Jones Franklin Rd Ste 102
    (27606-5441)
PHONE...............................919 872-5040
EMP: 13
SALES (corp-wide): 4.72MM **Privately Held**
Web: www.tma.org
SIC: 2721 Magazines: publishing only, not
    printed on site
PA: Tobacco Merchants Association Of
    The United States Inc.
    231 Clarksville Rd Ste 6
    Princeton Junction NJ 08550
    609 275-4900

(G-10552)

TOPQUADRANT INC

930 Main Campus Dr Ste 300
    (27606-5560)
PHONE...............................919 300-7945
Nimit Mehta, *CEO*
Irene Polikoff, *Pr*
Robert Coyne, *VP*
Ralph Hodgson, *Ex VP*
EMP: 20 **EST**: 2001
SQ FT: 4,400
SALES (est): 2.63MM **Privately Held**
Web: www.topquadrant.com
SIC: 7372 Prepackaged software

(G-10553)

TOUCH TONE TEES LLC

3316c Capital Blvd Ste 8 (27604-3340)
PHONE...............................919 358-5536
Antonio Blanding, *CEO*
EMP: 5 **EST**: 2022
SALES (est): 73.28K **Privately Held**
SIC: 2759 Screen printing

(G-10554)

TOWER ENGRG PROFESSIONALS INC (PA)

Also Called: Southern Environmental Cons
326 Tryon Rd (27603-3530)
PHONE...............................919 661-6351
Pete Jernigan, *Pr*
Andrew Haldane, *
Michael L Gardner, *
EMP: 223 **EST**: 1997
SQ FT: 29,000
SALES (est): 31.28MM
SALES (corp-wide): 31.28MM **Privately Held**
Web: www.tepgroup.net
SIC: 8711 3441 Consulting engineer;
    Fabricated structural metal

(G-10555)

TRAINING INDUSTRY INC

Also Called: TRAININGINDUSTRY.COM
110 Horizon Dr Ste 110 (27615-4927)
PHONE...............................919 653-4990
William Douglas Harward, *CEO*
Doug Harward, *CEO*
Ken Taylor, *Pr*
EMP: 74 **EST**: 2005
SQ FT: 6,000
SALES (est): 363.43K **Privately Held**
Web: www.trainingindustry.com
SIC: 8742 8249 2741 Marketing consulting
    services; Business training services;
    Internet publishing and broadcasting

(G-10556)
TRAJAN INC
2942 Imperial Oaks Dr (27614-6919)
PHONE..................................919 435-1105
EMP: 4 EST: 2017
SALES (est): 419.05K Privately Held
Web: www.trajanwealthetf.com
SIC: 3826 Analytical instruments

(G-10557)
TREKLITE INC
904 Dorothea Dr (27603-2140)
PHONE..................................919 610-1788
Joseph Huberman, Pr
Ruth Bromer, Sec
EMP: 6 EST: 1977
SQ FT: 2,000
SALES (est): 138.18K Privately Held
Web: www.treklite.com
SIC: 3299 3949 2399 Architectural
   sculptures: gypsum, clay, papier mache, etc.
   ; Sporting and athletic goods, nec; Sleeping
   bags

(G-10558)
TRIANGLE MICROSYSTEMS INC
Also Called: T M S
   1807 Garner Station Blvd (27603-3644)
PHONE..................................919 878-1880
Tommy Goodson, Pr
George King, Pr
Earl Parks, VP
Jeffrey Luther, VP
EMP: 10 EST: 1979
SQ FT: 11,500
SALES (est): 1.46MM Privately Held
Web: www.trianglemicrosystems.net
SIC: 3824 3823 3625 Gasoline dispensing
   meters; Process control instruments;
   Relays and industrial controls

(G-10559)
TRIANGLE MICROWORKS INC
2840 Plaza Pl Ste 205 (27612-6343)
PHONE..................................919 870-5101
Jim Coats, Pr
Robin Treadway, Treas
EMP: 10 EST: 1994
SALES (est): 1.52MM Privately Held
Web: www.trianglemicroworks.com
SIC: 7372 Application computer software

(G-10560)
TRIANGLE PLASTICS INC
6435 Mount Herman Rd (27617-8962)
P.O. Box 32222 (27622-2222)
PHONE..................................919 598-8839
Jeanene Rose Martin, CEO
Eric Martin, Pr
◆ EMP: 5 EST: 1991
SQ FT: 20,000
SALES (est): 737.98K Privately Held
Web: www.accu-steel.com
SIC: 3089 Injection molding of plastics

(G-10561)
TRIANGLE REGULATORY PUBG LLC
7780 Brier Creek Pkwy (27617-7849)
P.O. Box 91594 (27675-1594)
PHONE..................................919 886-4587
Irisha Johnson, Prin
EMP: 5 EST: 2010
SALES (est): 254.9K Privately Held
Web:
www.triangleregulatorypublishing.com
SIC: 2741 8748 Miscellaneous publishing;
   Publishing consultant

(G-10562)
TRIANGLE TRGGR-PINT THRAPY INC
184 Wind Chime Ct Ste 202 (27615-6485)
PHONE..................................919 845-1818
Terrie Mendenhall, Pr
EMP: 4 EST: 1989
SALES (est): 241.72K Privately Held
Web: www.triangletrigger.com
SIC: 7299 3999 Massage parlor; Massage
   machines, electric: barber and beauty shops

(G-10563)
TRIBOFILM RESEARCH INC
7250 Acc Blvd (27617-8736)
PHONE..................................919 838-2844
Vinay Sakhrani, CEO
Robert A Mineo Esq, VP Legal
EMP: 7 EST: 1997
SALES (est): 987.82K Privately Held
Web: www.tribofilmresearch.com
SIC: 3999 8731 Barber and beauty shop
   equipment; Commercial physical research

(G-10564)
TRIMED LLC
7429 Acc Blvd Ste 105 (27617-8401)
PHONE..................................919 615-2784
Michael Jones, Managing Member
EMP: 9 EST: 2011
SALES (est): 468.7K Privately Held
SIC: 3842 3841 7699 Ligatures, medical;
   Surgical and medical instruments; Medical
   equipment repair, non-electric

(G-10565)
TROPHY ON MAYWOOD LLC
656 Maywood Ave (27603-2340)
PHONE..................................919 803-1333
EMP: 15 EST: 2014
SQ FT: 11,000
SALES (est): 3.41MM Privately Held
Web: www.trophybrewing.com
SIC: 2082 Beer (alcoholic beverage)

(G-10566)
TRTL INC
120 Penmarc Dr Ste 118 (27603-2400)
PHONE..................................844 811-5816
Micheal Corrigan, CEO
Cara Hunt, Brand Relations
◆ EMP: 7 EST: 2016
SALES (est): 169.38K Privately Held
Web: www.trtltravel.com
SIC: 2392 Cushions and pillows

(G-10567)
TRUSWOOD INC (PA)
8816 Running Oak Dr (27617-4617)
P.O. Box 90035 (27675-0035)
PHONE..................................800 473-8787
Richard Watts, Pr
Jeff Landon, *
▲ EMP: 50 EST: 1980
SQ FT: 30,000
SALES (est): 8.77MM
SALES (corp-wide): 8.77MM Privately
Held
Web: www.truswood.com
SIC: 2439 Trusses, wooden roof

(G-10568)
TRYTON MEDICAL INC
1 Floretta Pl Rm 208 (27676-9803)
PHONE..................................919 226-1490
Carl J St Bernard, Pr
Brett Farabaugh, CFO
H Richard Davis, COO
EMP: 8 EST: 2008
SALES (est): 1.01MM Privately Held
Web: www.trytonmedical.com

SIC: 3841 Surgical and medical instruments

(G-10569)
TURNER BOYS CARRIER SVC LLC
1012 Southern Living Dr (27610-9301)
PHONE..................................919 946-7553
EMP: 4 EST: 2021
SALES (est): 65K Privately Held
SIC: 3799 Transportation equipment, nec

(G-10570)
UDM SYSTEMS LLC
6621 Fleetwood Dr (27612-1838)
PHONE..................................919 789-0777
Andre Cates, Mgr
EMP: 4
Web: www.udmsystems.com
SIC: 2891 Adhesives
PA: Udm Systems Llc
   8311 Brier Creek Pkwy Ste
   Raleigh NC 27617

(G-10571)
UDM SYSTEMS LLC (PA)
Also Called: Fleetwood
   8311 Brier Creek Pkwy Ste 105-159
   (27617-7328)
PHONE..................................919 789-0777
▲ EMP: 6 EST: 2005
SALES (est): 15.82MM Privately Held
Web: www.udmsystems.com
SIC: 2891 Adhesives

(G-10572)
UGLY ESSENTIALS LLC
8601 Six Forks Rd Ste 400 (27615)
PHONE..................................910 319-9945
EMP: 15 EST: 2020
SALES (est): 522.12K Privately Held
SIC: 8743 5087 2844 5122 Sales promotion;
   Beauty salon and barber shop equipment
   and supplies; Face creams or lotions;
   Cosmetics, perfumes, and hair products

(G-10573)
ULTIMATE PRODUCTS INC (PA)
3201 Wellington Ct Ste 115 (27615-5494)
PHONE..................................919 836-1627
Carey Dean Debnam, Pr
Stephanie Fanjul, Sec
▲ EMP: 15 EST: 1989
SQ FT: 28,000
SALES (est): 763.81K
SALES (corp-wide): 763.81K Privately
Held
SIC: 5075 5031 3442 Warm air heating
   equipment and supplies; Doors, garage;
   Metal doors, sash, and trim

(G-10574)
UMETHOD HEALTH INC
9660 Falls Of Neuse Rd Ste 138-146
   (27615-2473)
PHONE..................................984 232-6699
Vikas Chandra, CEO
EMP: 19 EST: 2014
SALES (est): 870.23K Privately Held
Web: www.umethod.com
SIC: 2834 Pharmaceutical preparations

(G-10575)
UMICORE USA INC (HQ)
3600 Glenwood Ave Ste 250 (27612-4945)
PHONE..................................919 874-7171
Ravila Gupta, Pr
Richard Laird, Ex VP
Jacques Dandoy, Treas
Alan Godfroid, Sec
J Hovey Kemp, Sec
◆ EMP: 23 EST: 1993

SQ FT: 9,000
SALES (est): 199.37MM
SALES (corp-wide): 4.6B Privately Held
Web: www.umicore.com
SIC: 5052 5051 5093 5169 Metallic ores;
   Nonferrous metal sheets, bars, rods, etc.,
   nec; Metal scrap and waste materials;
   Industrial chemicals
PA: Umicore
   Rue Du Marais 31
   Brussels 1000
   22277111

(G-10576)
UNION MASONRY INC
4708 Forestville Rd (27616-9678)
PHONE..................................919 217-7806
Mardelo Adueoar, Pr
EMP: 4 EST: 2001
SALES (est): 193.37K Privately Held
SIC: 3271 Blocks, concrete or cinder:
   standard

(G-10577)
UNIVERSAL TIRE SERVICE INC
4608 Fayetteville Rd (27603-3616)
PHONE..................................919 779-8798
Ray Sears, Pr
EMP: 9 EST: 1989
SALES (est): 513.95K Privately Held
Web: www.universaltireservice.com
SIC: 5531 7538 7534 Automotive tires;
   General automotive repair shops; Tire
   retreading and repair shops

(G-10578)
US PRINT INC
1665 N Market Dr (27609-2502)
P.O. Box 58278 (27658-8278)
PHONE..................................919 878-0981
John Lem, Pr
EMP: 8 EST: 2012
SQ FT: 6,000
SALES (est): 360.38K Privately Held
Web: www.usprint-usa.com
SIC: 2752 2754 2679 Offset printing; Post
   cards, picture: gravure printing; Tags and
   labels, paper

(G-10579)
US TOBACCO COOPERATIVE INC
(PA)
1304 Annapolis Dr (27608)
PHONE..................................919 821-4560
Keith H Merrick, CFO
Stuart Thompson, *
Tommy Bunn, *
Kenneth M Bopp, *
Wayne Crawford, *
◆ EMP: 75 EST: 1946
SQ FT: 35,000
SALES (est): 7.65MM
SALES (corp-wide): 7.65MM Privately
Held
Web: www.usleaf.com
SIC: 8611 2111 Growers' associations;
   Cigarettes

(G-10580)
V1 PHARMA LLC (PA)
Also Called: V1 Pharma
   353 E Six Forks Rd Ste 220 (27609-7881)
PHONE..................................919 338-5744
Luis Banks, Managing Member
EMP: 5 EST: 2015
SALES (est): 134K
SALES (corp-wide): 134K Privately Held
SIC: 2834 5122 Druggists' preparations
   (pharmaceuticals); Drugs and drug
   proprietaries

▲ = Import ▼ = Export
◆ = Import/Export

(G-10581)
VALENCELL INC
4601 Six Forks Rd Ste 103 (27609-5272)
PHONE....................919 747-3668
Kent Novak, *CEO*
Steven Leboeuf, *Pr*
Jesse Tucker, *VP*
Michael Aumer, *VP*
Todd Ackman, *VP*
EMP: 9 EST: 2006
SALES (est): 5.49MM Privately Held
Web: www.valencell.com
SIC: 3841 Diagnostic apparatus, medical

(G-10582)
VAN PRODUCTS INC (PA)
2521 Noblin Rd (27604-2415)
PHONE....................919 878-7110
David H Wendt, *Ch Bd*
Libby Wendt, *
W H Wendt Iii, *VP*
EMP: 26 EST: 1975
SQ FT: 21,000
SALES (est): 4.95MM
SALES (corp-wide): 4.95MM Privately
Held
Web: www.vanproducts.com
SIC: 7514 5531 3716 Passenger car rental;
Automotive accessories; Motor homes

(G-10583)
VANS INC
5959 Triangle Town Blvd Ste 1152
(27616-3268)
PHONE....................919 792-2555
Crystal Pool, *Brnch Mgr*
EMP: 6
SALES (corp-wide): 10.45B Publicly Held
Web: www.vans.com
SIC: 3021 Rubber and plastics footwear
HQ: Vans, Inc.
1588 S Coast Dr
Costa Mesa CA 92626
714 755-4000

(G-10584)
VAUGHAN ENTERPRISES INC
Also Called: Toddler Tables
834 Purser Dr Ste 102 (27603-4177)
PHONE....................919 772-4765
Tom Vaughan, *Pr*
▼ EMP: 4 EST: 1982
SQ FT: 2,500
SALES (est): 150.15K Privately Held
SIC: 2531 Chairs, table and arm

(G-10585)
VENTILATION DIRECT
14460 Falls Of Neuse Rd # 14
(27614-8227)
PHONE....................919 573-1522
Bob Luddy, *Owner*
▼ EMP: 5 EST: 2004
SALES (est): 306.24K Privately Held
Web: www.ventilationdirect.com
SIC: 3444 Sheet metalwork

(G-10586)
VERADIGM LLC (HQ)
Also Called: Veradigm
305 Church At North Hills St Ste 100
(27609-2667)
PHONE....................919 847-8102
Melinda Whittington, *CFO*
Dennis Olis Senior, *VP*
John P Mcconnell, *Pt*
Eric Jacobson, *Sec*
EMP: 1150 EST: 1982
SALES (est): 325.76MM
SALES (corp-wide): 1.5B Publicly Held
Web: www.allscripts.com

SIC: 7372 Prepackaged software
PA: Veradigm Inc.
222 Mrchndise Mart Plz St
Chicago IL 60654
800 334-8534

(G-10587)
VIDEO FUEL
6417 Lakeland Dr (27612-6524)
PHONE....................919 676-9940
Alain Tartevet, *Prin*
EMP: 5 EST: 2011
SALES (est): 248.24K Privately Held
Web: www.mainehealthalliance.com
SIC: 2869 Fuels

(G-10588)
VILLAGE TIRE CENTER INC
Also Called: Duty Tire and Service Center
5220 Atlantic Ave (27616-1870)
PHONE....................919 862-8500
David Duty, *Pr*
Steve Duty, *VP*
EMP: 9 EST: 1975
SQ FT: 5,000
SALES (est): 696.56K Privately Held
Web: www.dutytire.net
SIC: 5531 7534 Automotive tires; Tire repair
shop

(G-10589)
VIM PRODUCTS INC
5060 Trademark Dr (27610-3054)
PHONE....................919 277-0267
Gary Phillips, *Pr*
EMP: 4 EST: 2012
SALES (est): 207.06K Privately Held
Web: www.vimproducts.com
SIC: 3272 Shower receptors, concrete

(G-10590)
VIRTUE LABS LLC (PA)
426 S Dawson St (27601-1723)
PHONE....................844 782-4247
Melisse Shavan, *Pr*
Julieanne Danniels, *VP*
EMP: 5 EST: 2013
SALES (est): 9.24MM
SALES (corp-wide): 9.24MM Privately
Held
Web: www.virtuelabs.com
SIC: 2844 Hair preparations, including
shampoos

(G-10591)
VISHAY PRECISION GROUP INC
Micro-Measurements (27611)
P.O. Box 2777 (27602-2777)
PHONE....................919 374-5555
EMP: 10
SALES (corp-wide): 306.52MM Publicly
Held
Web: www.vpgsensors.com
SIC: 3823 Pressure measurement
instruments, industrial
PA: Vishay Precision Group, Inc.
3 Great Vly Pkwy Ste 150
Malvern PA 19355
484 321-5300

(G-10592)
VISION STAIRWAYS & MLLWK LLC
2200 Westinghouse Blvd Ste 108
(27604-2491)
PHONE....................919 878-5622
Andrew F Lund, *Admn*
EMP: 10
SALES (corp-wide): 7.93MM Privately
Held
Web:
www.visionstairwaysandmillwork.com

SIC: 2431 Millwork
PA: Vision Stairways & Millwork, Llc
105 Smoke Hill Ln Ste 180
Woodstock GA 30188
678 701-5520

(G-10593)
VOLTA GROUP CORPORATION LLC
Also Called: Consulting & Management Svcs
300 Fayetteville St Unit 1344 (27602-0915)
PHONE....................919 637-0273
Nana Ansah, *CEO*
Anan Ansah, *Pr*
Joan Atkins, *VP*
EMP: 21 EST: 2008
SALES (est): 367.11K Privately Held
SIC: 8711 5172 2911 1709 Engineering
services; Crude oil; Petroleum refining;
Petroleum storage tanks, pumping and
draining

(G-10594)
VONTIER CORPORATION (PA)
Also Called: Vontier
5438 Wade Park Blvd Ste 601 (27607)
PHONE....................984 275-6000
Mark D Morelli, *Pr*
Anshooman Aga, *Sr VP*
Kathryn K Rowen, *CAO*
EMP: 249 EST: 2019
SALES (est): 2.98B
SALES (corp-wide): 2.98B Publicly Held
Web: www.vontier.com
SIC: 3824 Fluid meters and counting devices

(G-10595)
VORTEX-CYCLONE TECHNOLOGIES
Also Called: Vortex
4400 Blossom Hill Ct (27613-6323)
PHONE....................919 225-1724
Jason Janet, *Prin*
EMP: 10 EST: 2006
SALES (est): 677.72K Privately Held
SIC: 3699 Electrical equipment and supplies,
nec

(G-10596)
VOTE OWL LLC ✪
932 Stone Falls Trl (27614-9389)
PHONE....................919 264-1796
EMP: 6 EST: 2023
SALES (est): 1.12MM Privately Held
SIC: 7372 7389 Educational computer
software; Business Activities at Non-
Commercial Site

(G-10597)
**WAKE CROSS ROADS EXPRESS
LLC**
3501 Forestville Rd (27616-9531)
PHONE....................919 266-7966
Charlotte Thaxton, *Pr*
EMP: 4 EST: 2006
SQ FT: 6,356
SALES (est): 330.78K Privately Held
Web: www.wakecrossroads.com
SIC: 2741 Miscellaneous publishing

(G-10598)
WASTE INDUSTRIES USA LLC (DH)
Also Called: Gfl Environmental Company
3301 Benson Dr Ste 601 (27609-7331)
PHONE....................919 325-3000
Patrick Dovigi, *CEO*
Ven Poole, *
Lonnie C Poole Junior, *Ch Bd*
Stephen Grissom, *
Harrell J Auten Iii, *S&M/VP*
EMP: 114 EST: 1970
SQ FT: 33,730
SALES (est): 547.68MM

SALES (corp-wide): 5.47B Privately Held
Web: www.gflenv.com
SIC: 4953 3443 Rubbish collection and
disposal; Dumpsters, garbage
HQ: Wrangler Super Holdco Corp.
3301 Benson Dr Ste 601
Raleigh NC 27609
919 325-3000

(G-10599)
WASTEZERO INC (PA)
8396 Six Forks Rd Ste 103 (27615-3058)
PHONE....................919 322-1208
Mark A Dancy, *Pr*
Mark A Dancy, *Pr*
James Calvin Cunningham, *VP*
William J Easton, *VP*
▲ EMP: 20 EST: 1998
SALES (est): 15.31MM Privately Held
Web: www.wastezero.com
SIC: 4953 2673 Refuse systems; Bags:
plastic, laminated, and coated

(G-10600)
WAVE FRONT COMPUTERS LLC
Also Called: Wave Front Studios
8015 Creedmoor Rd Ste 201 (27613-4397)
PHONE....................919 896-6121
EMP: 4 EST: 2011
SQ FT: 1,800
SALES (est): 243.19K Privately Held
SIC: 7372 Home entertainment computer
software

(G-10601)
WAVETHERM CORPORATION
5995 Chapel Hill Rd Ste 119 (27607-5148)
PHONE....................919 307-8071
David Mosier, *Pr*
Rodney Bame, *
EMP: 26 EST: 2008
SQ FT: 1,500
SALES (est): 2.48MM Privately Held
Web: shop.wavetherm.com
SIC: 3429 Hardware, nec

(G-10602)
WEAVEXX LLC
8521 Six Forks Rd (27615-5278)
PHONE....................919 556-7235
Stephen R Light, *CEO*
Miguel Quionez, *
▲ EMP: 900 EST: 1890
SALES (est): 12.86MM
SALES (corp-wide): 1.13B Privately Held
Web: www.andritz.com
SIC: 2221 Specialty broadwoven fabrics,
including twisted weaves
HQ: Andritz Fabrics And Rolls Inc.
8521 Six Forks Rd
Raleigh NC 27615
919 526-1400

(G-10603)
WEDPICS
6413 Rushingbrook Dr (27612-6547)
PHONE....................919 699-5676
EMP: 4 EST: 2018
SALES (est): 336.24K Privately Held
SIC: 2741 Miscellaneous publishing

(G-10604)
WELLOYT ENTERPRISES INC
Also Called: International Minute Press
221 W Martin St (27601-1323)
PHONE....................919 821-7897
George Wells, *Pr*
Linda D Wells, *VP*
EMP: 4 EST: 1985
SQ FT: 1,900
SALES (est): 89.74K Privately Held

(PA)=Parent Co (HQ)=Headquarters
✪ = New Business established in last 2 years

2025 Harris North Carolina
Manufacturers Directory

465

GEOGRAPHIC

SIC: 2752 Offset printing

(G-10605)
WESTROCK COMPANY
7605b Welborn St (27615-4115)
PHONE...............................919 861-8760
Dean Robinson, *Brnch Mgr*
EMP: 11
Web: www.westrock.com
SIC: 2671 Paper; coated and laminated packaging
HQ: Westrock Company
1000 Abernathy Rd Ne
Atlanta GA 30328
770 448-2193

(G-10606)
WESTROCK MWV LLC
Also Called: Meadwestvaco Research Center
1021 Main Campus Dr (27606-5238)
PHONE...............................919 334-3200
James Wright, *Brnch Mgr*
EMP: 5
Web: www.westrock.com
SIC: 2631 2671 2678 2677 Linerboard; Paper; coated and laminated packaging; Stationery products; Envelopes
HQ: Westrock Mwv, Llc
3500 45th St Sw
Lanett AL 36863
804 444-1000

(G-10607)
WHATS YOUR SIGN LLC
720 Sawmill Rd (27615-4847)
PHONE...............................919 274-5703
Jennifer Aubut, *Prin*
EMP: 5 EST: 2017
SALES (est): 93.64K **Privately Held**
Web: www.signsofnc.com
SIC: 3993 Signs and advertising specialties

(G-10608)
WHITAKER MILL WORKS LLC
3801 Beryl Rd (27607-5244)
PHONE...............................919 772-3030
Richard Stephenson, *Pt*
Tom Rickman, *Pt*
EMP: 8 EST: 2013
SALES (est): 1.4MM **Privately Held**
Web: www.whitakermillworks.com
SIC: 2431 Millwork

(G-10609)
WHITE PACKING CO INC -VA
5404 Hillsborough St Ste A (27606-1339)
P.O. Box 7067 (22404-7067)
PHONE...............................540 373-9883
Karl White, *Pr*
Kris White, *Sec*
Collin White, *CFO*
EMP: 7 EST: 1971
SQ FT: 60,000
SALES (est): 1.02MM **Privately Held**
SIC: 2013 2011 Bacon, side and sliced: from purchased meat; Meat packing plants

(G-10610)
WILLIAMS INDUSTRIES INC (PA)
1128 Tyler Farms Dr (27603-7949)
P.O. Box 1770 (20108-1770)
PHONE...............................919 604-1746
Frank E Williams Iii, *Ch Bd*
Danny C Dunlap, *
Marianne Pastor, *
▲ EMP: 200 EST: 1970
SALES (est): 49.93MM
SALES (corp-wide): 49.93MM **Privately Held**
Web: www.wmsi.com

SIC: 3441 1531 1541 3315 Fabricated structural metal for bridges; Operative builders; Steel building construction; Steel wire and related products

(G-10611)
WISER SYSTEMS INC
819 W Hargett St (27603-1603)
PHONE...............................919 551-5566
Elaine Rideout, *CEO*
Jeff Shelden, *Dir*
Margaret Hostetler, *Dir*
EMP: 10 EST: 2007
SALES (est): 7.17MM **Privately Held**
Web: www.wisersystems.com
SIC: 5065 3829 Electronic parts and equipment, nec; Measuring and controlling devices, nec

(G-10612)
WMB OF WAKE COUNTY INC
Also Called: Glenwood Village Exxon
2601 Glenwood Ave (27608)
PHONE...............................919 782-0419
William Barker, *Pr*
Bryan Barker, *VP*
EMP: 6 EST: 2006
SALES (est): 865.13K **Privately Held**
Web: www.glenwoodvillageexxon.com
SIC: 3011 5014 Tires and inner tubes; Tires and tubes

(G-10613)
WORKDAY INC
4801 Glenwood Ave Ste 300 (27612-3857)
PHONE...............................919 703-2559
EMP: 5
Web: www.workday.com
SIC: 7372 Prepackaged software
PA: Workday, Inc.
6110 Stoneridge Mall Rd
Pleasanton CA 94588

(G-10614)
WORLDGRANITE & STONEART INC
4600 Twisted Oaks Dr Apt 1505 (27612-2505)
PHONE...............................919 871-0078
Mel Neale, *Pr*
Emily Rosevage, *VP*
EMP: 4 EST: 2001
SQ FT: 7,000
SALES (est): 801.51K **Privately Held**
Web: www.worldgranite.biz
SIC: 1411 Granite, dimension-quarrying

(G-10615)
WPMHJ LLC
4216 Atlantic Ave (27612)
PHONE...............................919 601-5445
Lamar Jones, *Managing Member*
◆ EMP: 8 EST: 2010
SQ FT: 5,000
SALES (est): 3.38MM **Privately Held**
Web: www.palparts.com
SIC: 3821 5049 Laboratory equipment: fume hoods, distillation racks, etc.; Laboratory equipment, except medical or dental

(G-10616)
X-JET TECHNOLOGIES INC
146 Annaron Ct (27603-3640)
PHONE...............................800 983-7467
Kenneth L Sapic Ii, *Pr*
Dana Sapic, *VP*
EMP: 9 EST: 2015
SALES (est): 514.28K **Privately Held**
Web: www.xjetnozzle.com
SIC: 3429 Hardware, nec

(G-10617)
XANDERGLASSES INC
1 Glenwood Ave Ste 500 (27603-2580)
PHONE...............................617 286-3012
Alex Westner, *CEO*
Alex Westner, *Pr*
EMP: 6 EST: 2020
SALES (est): 533.35K **Privately Held**
Web: www.xanderglasses.com
SIC: 3842 Hearing aids

(G-10618)
XELAQUA INC
404b Glenwood Ave (27603-1220)
PHONE...............................919 964-4181
Graham A Crispin, *CEO*
EMP: 4 EST: 2013
SALES (est): 372.73K **Privately Held**
Web: www.xelaqua.com
SIC: 3589 Sewage and water treatment equipment

(G-10619)
XILINX INC
220 Horizon Dr Ste 114 (27615-4928)
PHONE...............................919 846-3922
Tony Scarangella, *Brnch Mgr*
EMP: 10
SALES (corp-wide): 25.79B **Publicly Held**
Web: www.xilinx.com
SIC: 3674 Microcircuits, integrated (semiconductor)
HQ: Xilinx, Inc.
2100 Logic Dr
San Jose CA 95124
408 559-7778

(G-10620)
XPC CORPORATION
3070 Business Park Dr Ste 108 (27610-3592)
PHONE...............................919 210-1756
EMP: 8
Web: www.xpcc.com
SIC: 3629 Power conversion units, a.c. to d.c.: static-electric
PA: Xpc Corporation
230 Yuma St
Denver CO 80223

(G-10621)
XPC CORPORATION
Also Called: Xtreme Power Conversion
7239 Acc Blvd (27617-4881)
PHONE...............................800 582-4524
EMP: 8
Web: www.xpcc.com
SIC: 3629 Power conversion units, a.c. to d.c.: static-electric
PA: Xpc Corporation
230 Yuma St
Denver CO 80223

(G-10622)
YES REAL ESTATE CNSTR GROUP IN
4805 Green Rd Ste 103 (27616-2848)
PHONE...............................919 389-4104
Antwane Yelverton, *Managing Member*
EMP: 25 EST: 2012
SQ FT: 1,500
SALES (est): 2.27MM **Privately Held**
Web: www.yesrecg.com
SIC: 1521 1389 1799 1522 Single-family housing construction; Construction, repair, and dismantling services; Construction site cleanup; Hotel/motel and multi-family home construction

(G-10623)
ZENECAR LLC
Also Called: Enwood Structures
10224 Durant Rd Ste 201 (27614-6468)
PHONE...............................919 518-0464
EMP: 8 EST: 2011
SALES (est): 465.06K **Privately Held**
Web: www.enwood.com
SIC: 2426 Frames for upholstered furniture, wood

(G-10624)
ZONKD LLC
2419 Atlantic Ave (27604)
P.O. Box 6492 (27628)
PHONE...............................919 977-6463
Ryan Martin Graven, *CEO*
Steve Martin Graven, *Pr*
Ashley Holder, *Sec*
EMP: 49 EST: 2013
SALES (est): 4.55MM **Privately Held**
Web: www.zonkd.com
SIC: 2299 Upholstery filling, textile

Ramseur
Randolph County

(G-10625)
AUTO-SYSTEMS AND SERVICE INC
839 Crestwick Rd (27316-8726)
P.O. Box 1180 (27316-1180)
PHONE...............................336 824-3580
Jimmy Wayne Harris, *Pr*
EMP: 14 EST: 1976
SQ FT: 24,000
SALES (est): 1.47MM **Privately Held**
SIC: 3559 Brick making machinery

(G-10626)
KN FURNITURE INC
244 Nc Highway 22 N (27316-8774)
PHONE...............................336 953-3259
Kevin Arevalo, *Pr*
EMP: 24 EST: 2018
SALES (est): 668.71K **Privately Held**
SIC: 2511 2522 2512 Bed frames, except water bed frames: wood; Office furniture, except wood; Upholstered household furniture

(G-10627)
KRAFTSMAN INC
10051 Us Highway 64 E (27316-8699)
PHONE...............................336 824-1114
Paul Kaufman, *Pr*
Jenatte Kaufman, *
EMP: 52 EST: 2000
SQ FT: 9,000
SALES (est): 2.85MM **Privately Held**
Web: www.kraftsmantrailers.com
SIC: 5599 3715 Utility trailers; Bus trailers, tractor type

(G-10628)
LINE DRIVE SPORTS CENTER INC
Also Called: Beet River Traders
161 Crestwick Rd (27316-8720)
P.O. Box 346 (27316-0346)
PHONE...............................336 824-1692
Doug Langley, *Pr*
Doug Langley, *Pr*
Pat Pate, *Genl Mgr*
EMP: 7 EST: 1992
SQ FT: 40,000
SALES (est): 166.16K **Privately Held**
Web: www.linedrivegraphics.com
SIC: 5941 7374 2396 Sporting goods and bicycle shops; Computer graphics service; Screen printing on fabric articles

(G-10629)
MARCH FURNITURE MANUFACTURING INC
447 Reed Creek Rd (27316-8890)
P.O. Box 875 (27316-0875)
PHONE..............................336 824-4413
◆ **EMP:** 240
SIC: 2512 Living room furniture: upholstered on wood frames

(G-10630)
QUICK N EASY 12 NC739
8112 Us Highway 64 E (27316-8649)
PHONE..............................336 824-3832
Donna Woodard, *Mgr*
Burnan Major, *Owner*
EMP: 4 **EST:** 2003
SALES (est): 288.1K **Privately Held**
SIC: 1389 Gas field services, nec

(G-10631)
SILVER DOLLAR GUN PAWN SP INC
6787 Jordan Rd (27316-9529)
PHONE..............................336 824-8989
Shawn Dong, *CEO*
EMP: 7 **EST:** 1989
SQ FT: 10,000
SALES (est): 551.9K **Privately Held**
Web: www.silverdollargunandpawn.com
SIC: 3999 Education aids, devices and supplies

(G-10632)
TOWER COMPONENTS INC
Also Called: TCI
5960 Us Highway 64 E (27316-8858)
PHONE..............................336 824-2102
William G Bartley, *Pr*
▼ **EMP:** 90 **EST:** 1990
SQ FT: 250,000
SALES (est): 10.81MM
SALES (corp-wide): 608.8MM **Privately Held**
Web: www.towercomponentsinc.com
SIC: 3443 Fabricated plate work (boiler shop)
PA: Evapco, Inc.
5151 Allendale Ln
Taneytown MD 21787
410 756-2600

(G-10633)
UNIFIED SCRNING CRSHING - NC I (PA)
136 Crestwick Rd (27316-8720)
P.O. Box 486 (27316-0486)
PHONE..............................336 824-2151
Troy Hartman, *Pr*
Pete Smith, *Dir*
◆ **EMP:** 6 **EST:** 1997
SALES (est): 1.14MM
SALES (corp-wide): 1.14MM **Privately Held**
Web: www.unifiedscreening.com
SIC: 3496 Miscellaneous fabricated wire products

Randleman
Randolph County

(G-10634)
BUTLER TRAILER MFG CO INC
259 Hockett Dairy Rd (27317-8037)
PHONE..............................336 674-8850
Cornelius Butler Junior, *Pr*
EMP: 10 **EST:** 1965
SQ FT: 900
SALES (est): 2.03MM **Privately Held**

SIC: 3537 5031 Truck trailers, used in plants, docks, terminals, etc.; Lumber: rough, dressed, and finished

(G-10635)
BWH FOAM AND FIBER INC
605 Sunset Dr (27317-1917)
P.O. Box 370 (27317-0370)
PHONE..............................336 498-6949
Bruce W Hughes, *Pr*
EMP: 4 **EST:** 2005
SALES (est): 99.86K **Privately Held**
SIC: 3086 Plastics foam products

(G-10636)
CARAUSTAR CSTM PACKG GROUP INC
Also Called: Randleman Carton Plant
4139 Us Highway 311 (27317-7314)
P.O. Box 609 (27317-0609)
PHONE..............................336 498-2631
Doris Rigud, *Brnch Mgr*
EMP: 234
SALES (corp-wide): 5.45B **Publicly Held**
SIC: 2652 2657 Setup paperboard boxes; Folding paperboard boxes
HQ: Caraustar Custom Packaging Group, Inc.
5000 Austell Powder Sprin
Austell GA 30106

(G-10637)
CARAUSTAR INDUSTRIES INC
4139 Us Highway 311 (27317-7314)
PHONE..............................336 498-2631
Doug Wagner, *Genl Mgr*
EMP: 11
SALES (corp-wide): 5.45B **Publicly Held**
Web: www.greif.com
SIC: 2655 2631 2679 2656 Tubes, fiber or paper: made from purchased material; Paperboard mills; Paperboard products, converted, nec; Food containers (liquid tight), including milk cartons
HQ: Caraustar Industries, Inc.
5000 Astell Pwdr Sprng Rd
Austell GA 30106
770 948-3101

(G-10638)
COMMONWEALTH HOSIERY MILLS INC
Also Called: Commonwealth Hosiery
4964 Island Ford Rd (27317)
P.O. Box 939 (27317)
PHONE..............................336 498-2621
▲ **EMP:** 65 **EST:** 1916
SALES (est): 2.37MM **Privately Held**
Web: www.commonwealth-hosiery.com
SIC: 2251 2252 Panty hose; Socks

(G-10639)
CUSTOM STEEL FABRICATORS INC
362 Providence Church Rd (27317-7876)
P.O. Box 128 (27317-0128)
PHONE..............................336 498-5099
Marvin Tickle, *Pr*
J R Criscoe, *VP*
EMP: 8 **EST:** 1992
SQ FT: 4,000
SALES (est): 1.72MM **Privately Held**
SIC: 3441 Fabricated structural metal

(G-10640)
D & D ENTPS GREENSBORO INC
10458 Us Highway 220 Bus N (27317-8121)
PHONE..............................336 495-3407
Ralph Davis, *Pr*
Harold Davis, *

EMP: 40 **EST:** 1976
SQ FT: 38,000
SALES (est): 5.4MM **Privately Held**
Web: www.ddent-usa.com
SIC: 3599 Machine shop, jobbing and repair

(G-10641)
DART CONTAINER CORP GEORGIA
3219 Wesleyan Rd (27317-7667)
PHONE..............................336 495-1101
Steve Ridgill, *Mgr*
EMP: 233
SQ FT: 507,092
SALES (corp-wide): 72MM **Privately Held**
SIC: 3086 Plastics foam products
PA: Dart Container Corporation Of Georgia
500 Hogsback Rd
Mason MI 48854
517 676-3800

(G-10642)
DIGGER SPECIALTIES INC
Also Called: Polyvnyl Fnce By Digger Spc In
4256 Heath Dairy Rd (27317-7489)
PHONE..............................336 495-1517
David Atkins, *Mgr*
EMP: 9
SALES (corp-wide): 22.11MM **Privately Held**
Web: www.diggerspecialties.com
SIC: 3089 1799 Plastics hardware and building products; Fence construction
PA: Digger Specialties, Inc.
3446 Us Hwy 6
Bremen IN 46506
574 546-5999

(G-10643)
DST MANUFACTURING LLC
166 Regal Dr (27317-8148)
P.O. Box 295 (27317-0295)
PHONE..............................336 676-6096
EMP: 5 **EST:** 2010
SALES (est): 799.04K **Privately Held**
Web: www.nviroclean.net
SIC: 2899 Chemical preparations, nec

(G-10644)
DWD INDUSTRIES LLC
151 Southern Dr (27317-8261)
PHONE..............................336 498-6327
Mike Schoolcraft, *Mgr*
EMP: 47
Web: www.estevesgroup.com
SIC: 5084 3544 Industrial machinery and equipment; Special dies, tools, jigs, and fixtures
HQ: Dwd Industries, Llc
1921 Patterson St
Decatur IN 46733
260 728-9272

(G-10645)
E F P INC
8013 Adams Farm Rd (27317-7384)
PHONE..............................336 498-4134
Frank Moore, *Pr*
Glenda Moore, *VP*
EMP: 11 **EST:** 1983
SQ FT: 40,000
SALES (est): 862.69K **Privately Held**
Web: www.efpfactorydirect.com
SIC: 3599 Machine shop, jobbing and repair

(G-10646)
EAST COAST FAB LLC
195 Labrador Dr (27317-8050)
PHONE..............................336 285-7444
EMP: 10 **EST:** 2016
SALES (est): 2.8MM **Privately Held**

SIC: 3441 Fabricated structural metal

(G-10647)
ESCO INDUSTRIES INC
4717 Island Ford Rd (27317-7208)
PHONE..............................336 495-3772
James Cossee, *Genl Mgr*
EMP: 13
SALES (corp-wide): 24.08MM **Privately Held**
Web: www.escoindustries.com
SIC: 3275 7389 2451 2435 Wallboard, gypsum; Laminating service; Mobile homes ; Hardwood veneer and plywood
PA: Esco Industries, Inc.
185 Sink Hole Road
Douglas GA 31533
912 384-1417

(G-10648)
GERALD HARTSOE
Also Called: Precision Enterprises
3109 Tom Brown Rd (27317)
PHONE..............................336 498-3233
Gerald Hartsoe, *Owner*
EMP: 4 **EST:** 1984
SALES (est): 207.96K **Privately Held**
SIC: 3544 3823 3469 Special dies and tools; Process control instruments; Metal stampings, nec

(G-10649)
HITECH CONTROLS INC
1348 Plantation Ct (27317-8186)
PHONE..............................336 498-1534
Jack Phan, *Owner*
EMP: 4 **EST:** 2003
SALES (est): 240.4K **Privately Held**
Web: www.hitechcontrols.com
SIC: 3625 Industrial controls: push button, selector switches, pilot

(G-10650)
HUGHES FURNITURE INDS INC (PA)
Also Called: H F I
952 S Stout Rd (27317-7638)
P.O. Box 486 (27317-0486)
PHONE..............................336 498-8700
Bruce W Hughes, *Pr*
Steve Hunsucker, *
◆ **EMP:** 250 **EST:** 1963
SQ FT: 140,000
SALES (est): 14.59MM **Privately Held**
Web: www.hughesfurniture.com
SIC: 2512 7641 2426 Living room furniture: upholstered on wood frames; Upholstery work; Furniture stock and parts, hardwood

(G-10651)
MARTIN MARIETTA MATERIALS INC
Also Called: Martin Marietta Aggregates
2757 Hopewood Rd (27317-7518)
PHONE..............................336 672-1501
Doyle Carlise, *Brnch Mgr*
EMP: 5
Web: www.martinmarietta.com
SIC: 1422 Crushed and broken limestone
PA: Martin Marietta Materials Inc
4123 Parklake Ave
Raleigh NC 27612

(G-10652)
MARTIN MARIETTA MATERIALS INC
Also Called: Martin Marietta
2757 Hopewood Rd (27317-7518)
P.O. Box 1084 (27317-1084)
PHONE..............................336 672-1501
Frank Mobley, *Prin*
EMP: 5
Web: www.martinmarietta.com

GEOGRAPHIC

SIC: **1422** Crushed and broken limestone
PA: Martin Marietta Materials Inc
　　4123 Parklake Ave
　　Raleigh NC 27612

(G-10653)
MMJ MACHINING AND FABG INC
1332 Gene Allred Dr　(27317-7769)
PHONE..............................336 495-1029
Michael Allred, *Pr*
Mark Allred, *VP*
EMP: 10 EST: 1993
SALES (est): 2.48MM **Privately Held**
Web: www.mmjmachine.com
SIC: **5084** 3599　Textile machinery and
　equipment; Machine shop, jobbing and
　repair

(G-10654)
**NORTH CAROLINA LUMBER
COMPANY**
Also Called: Motion-Eaze
　1 Parrish Dr　(27317-9598)
　P.O. Box 486　(27317-0486)
PHONE..............................336 498-6600
Bruce W Hughes, *Pr*
R Wilbur Hughes, *
A Stephen Hunsucker, *
◆ EMP: 6 EST: 1985
SQ FT: 156,000
SALES (est): 446.85K **Privately Held**
SIC: **2426** 2392 2512　Lumber, hardwood
　dimension; Cushions and pillows;
　Upholstered household furniture

(G-10655)
PILGRIM TRACT SOCIETY INC
105 Depot St　(27317-1705)
P.O. Box 126　(27317)
PHONE..............................336 495-1241
Chris Hancock, *Pr*
Sandra Hancock, *Sec*
John Henderson, *Mgr*
EMP: 8 EST: 1938
SQ FT: 7,400
SALES (est): 439.78K **Privately Held**
Web: www.pilgrimtract.org
SIC: **2752** Offset printing

(G-10656)
POLYMER CONCEPTS INC
124 Regal Dr　(27317-8148)
PHONE..............................336 495-7713
Larry A Draughn, *Pr*
Rickey Barker, *VP*
◆ EMP: 6 EST: 1999
SQ FT: 9,000
SALES (est): 427.16K **Privately Held**
Web: www.polymerconcepts.com
SIC: **3089** Injection molding of plastics

(G-10657)
RANDOLPH MACHINE INC
498 Pointe South Dr　(27317-9502)
PHONE..............................336 799-1039
EMP: 4
Web: www.randolphmachine.com
SIC: **3479** Coating of metals and formed
　products
PA: Randolph Machine, Inc.
　　1206 Uwharrie St
　　Asheboro NC 27203

(G-10658)
**RHEEM MANUFACTURING
COMPANY**
Also Called: Rheem Sales Company
4744 Island Ford Rd　(27317-7208)
PHONE..............................336 495-6800
Don Harter, *Dir*

EMP: 162
Web: www.rheem.com
SIC: **5075** 3585　Electrical heating equipment
　; Air conditioning condensers and
　condensing units
HQ: Rheem Manufacturing Company Inc
　　1100 Abrnathy Rd Ste 1700
　　Atlanta GA 30328
　　770 351-3000

(G-10659)
SAFE AIR SYSTEMS INC
210 Labrador Dr　(27317-8165)
PHONE..............................336 674-0749
Joseph C Smith, *Pr*
EMP: 20 EST: 1992
SALES (est): 3.29MM **Privately Held**
Web: www.safeairsystems.com
SIC: **7699** 3563　Industrial equipment services
　; Air and gas compressors including
　vacuum pumps

(G-10660)
SKIDRIL INDUSTRIES LLC
235 Labrador Dr　(27317-8165)
P.O. Box 8041　(27419-0041)
PHONE..............................800 843-3745
Mark T Salman, *Admn*
▲ EMP: 8 EST: 2008
SALES (est): 254.86K **Privately Held**
Web: www.skidril.com
SIC: **3999** Barber and beauty shop
　equipment

(G-10661)
SUB-AQUATICS INC
Also Called: Breathingair Systems
210 Labrador Dr　(27317-8165)
PHONE..............................336 674-0749
EMP: 20
SALES (corp-wide): 32.82MM **Privately
Held**
Web: www.breathingair.com
SIC: **7699** 3563　Industrial equipment services
　; Air and gas compressors including
　vacuum pumps
PA: Sub-Aquatics, Inc.
　　8855 E Broad St
　　Reynoldsburg OH
　　614 864-1235

(G-10662)
TECHNIMARK
208 Nc Highway 62 W　(27317-9774)
PHONE..............................336 736-9366
EMP: 6 EST: 2018
SALES (est): 83.71K **Privately Held**
Web: www.technimark.com
SIC: **3089** Injection molding of plastics

(G-10663)
UNITED BRASS WORKS INC (HQ)
Also Called: United Brass Works
714 S Main St　(27317-2100)
PHONE..............................336 498-2661
Michael Berkelhammer, *CEO*
Anthony Forman, *
▲ EMP: 153 EST: 1910
SQ FT: 70,000
SALES (est): 21.48MM
SALES (corp-wide): 29.03MM **Privately
Held**
Web: www.ubw.com
SIC: **3491** 3494 3369　Industrial valves;
　Valves and pipe fittings, nec; Nonferrous
　foundries, nec
PA: Bradford Equities Management Llc
　　360 Hamilton Ave Ste 425
　　White Plains NY 10601
　　914 922-7171

Red Springs
Robeson County

(G-10664)
AMERICAN PLUSH TEX MILLS LLC
213 S Edinborough St　(28377-1233)
PHONE..............................765 609-0456
Virgil E Stanley, *Prin*
EMP: 15 EST: 2011
SALES (est): 700.22K **Privately Held**
Web: www.americanplush.com
SIC: **5199** 2326　Fabrics, yarns, and knit
　goods; Aprons, work, except rubberized
　and plastic: men's

(G-10665)
**CAROLINA TEXTILE SERVICES INC
(PA)**
Off Hwy 211　(28377)
P.O. Box 205　(28377-0205)
PHONE..............................910 843-3033
Morris Pounds, *Pr*
EMP: 7 EST: 1992
SALES (est): 190.56K **Privately Held**
SIC: **7699** 3552 8748　Industrial machinery
　and equipment repair; Textile machinery;
　Business consulting, nec

(G-10666)
DESIGNTEK FABRICATION INC
16824 A Hwy 211　(28377)
PHONE..............................910 359-0130
Kevin Mauldin, *Pr*
EMP: 17 EST: 2012
SALES (est): 706.55K **Privately Held**
SIC: **3556** 3559　Food products machinery;
　Pharmaceutical machinery

(G-10667)
ECO BUILDING CORPORATION
Also Called: Emerging Technology Institute
16824 A Nc-211　(28377)
PHONE..............................910 736-1540
James Freeman, *Pr*
Jeff Collins, *Ex VP*
EMP: 4 EST: 2017
SALES (est): 1.44MM **Privately Held**
Web: www.eticommunity.com
SIC: **3812** 8742　Acceleration indicators and
　systems components, aerospace;
　Management consulting services

(G-10668)
**INDUSTRIAL AND AGRICULTURAL
CHEMICALS INCORPORATED**
Also Called: I A C
2042 Buie Philadelphus Rd　(28377-6052)
PHONE..............................910 843-2121
◆ EMP: 20 EST: 1972
SALES (est): 2MM **Privately Held**
Web:
www.industrial-agricultural-chemicals-inc.com
SIC: **2819** 5191　Industrial inorganic
　chemicals, nec; Chemicals, agricultural

(G-10669)
**MCCABES INDUS MLLWRGHT MFG
INC**
9502 Nc Highway 71 N　(28377-7608)
P.O. Box 32　(28377-0032)
PHONE..............................910 843-8699
Robert Mccabe, *Pr*
EMP: 6 EST: 2001
SALES (est): 823.14K **Privately Held**
SIC: **3441** Fabricated structural metal

(G-10670)
MUVIQ USA LLC
Also Called: Red Springs Distribution Ctr
16824 Nc Highway 211 W　(28377-8887)
PHONE..............................910 843-1024
Anna Contoleon, *Brnch Mgr*
EMP: 41
Web: www.muviqofficial.com
SIC: **3052** Rubber and plastics hose and
　beltings
PA: Muviq Usa, Llc
　　16000 Common Rd
　　Roseville MI 48066

Reidsville
Rockingham County

(G-10671)
ALBAAD USA INC
Also Called: Albaad Fem US
1900 Barnes St　(27320-6410)
P.O. Box 1825　(27323-1825)
PHONE..............................336 634-0091
Boaz Roseman, *CEO*
Adi Maor, *CFO*
◆ EMP: 350 EST: 2003
SQ FT: 146,622
SALES (est): 20.26MM **Privately Held**
Web: www.albaad.com
SIC: **2844** Towelettes, premoistened
HQ: Albaad Massuot Yitzhak Ltd
　　Moshav
　　Massuot Itzhak 79858

(G-10672)
**ALCORNS CUSTOM
WOODWORKING INC**
941 Flat Rock Rd　(27320-7645)
PHONE..............................336 342-0908
Richie Alcorn, *Owner*
EMP: 4 EST: 1990
SALES (est): 136.84K **Privately Held**
Web: www.alcornswoodworking.com
SIC: **1751** 2499　Cabinet building and
　installation; Applicators, wood

(G-10673)
ALTIUM PACKAGING LP
Envision Ecoplast Group
606 Walters St Unit B　(27320-2609)
PHONE..............................336 342-4749
EMP: 62
SALES (corp-wide): 17.51B **Publicly Held**
Web: www.altiumpkg.com
SIC: **3089** Plastics containers, except foam
HQ: Altium Packaging Lp
　　3101 Towercreek Pkwy
　　Atlanta GA 30339
　　678 742-4600

(G-10674)
**BALL METAL BEVERAGE CONT
CORP**
Also Called: Ball Metal Beverage Cont Div
1900 Barnes St　(27320-6410)
P.O. Box 1170　(27323-1170)
PHONE..............................336 342-4711
Joseph Corbett, *Mgr*
EMP: 251
SALES (corp-wide): 11.79B **Publicly Held**
Web: www.ball.com
SIC: **3411** Beer cans, metal
HQ: Ball Metal Beverage Container Corp.
　　9300 W 108th Cir
　　Westminster CO 80021

(G-10675)
BEJEWELED CREATIONS
386 River Run Dr (27320-9037)
PHONE....................................336 552-0841
Barbara Conroy, *Prin*
EMP: 5 **EST:** 2010
SALES (est): 90K **Privately Held**
SIC: 3911 Jewelry apparel

(G-10676)
BETA FUELING SYSTEMS LLC
Also Called: Beta Fluid Systems
1209 Freeway Dr (27320-7103)
P.O. Box 1737 (27323-1737)
PHONE....................................336 342-0306
Jonathan Deline, *Managing Member*
John Ingold, *
Marcel Haar, *
▲ **EMP:** 51 **EST:** 1972
SQ FT: 76,000
SALES (est): 18.47MM **Privately Held**
Web: www.betafueling.com
SIC: 3728 Aircraft parts and equipment, nec

(G-10677)
BOEHME-FILATEX INC
209 Watlington Industrial Dr (27320-8147)
PHONE....................................336 342-4507
Rene A Eckert, *CEO*
Phil Goodman, *
George Sembert, *
Judy Pope, *
◆ **EMP:** 140 **EST:** 1981
SQ FT: 40,000
SALES (est): 4.49MM
SALES (corp-wide): 3.16MM **Privately Held**
Web: boehme.lookchem.com
SIC: 2869 Industrial organic chemicals, nec
PA: Boehme Systems Ohg
An Der Triebe 12-14
Moritzburg SN 01468
351 838-2603

(G-10678)
CAMCO MANUFACTURING INC
Also Called: CAMCO MANUFACTURING, INC.
2900 Vance Street Ext (27320-9499)
PHONE....................................336 348-6609
Todd Powell, *Mgr*
EMP: 5
SALES (corp-wide): 86.27MM **Privately Held**
Web: www.camco.net
SIC: 2899 3714 3822 5013 Antifreeze compounds; Motor vehicle parts and accessories; Water heater controls; Motor vehicle supplies and new parts
PA: Camco Manufacturing, Llc
121 Landmark Dr
Greensboro NC 27409
336 668-7661

(G-10679)
CAROLINA CORE MACHINE LLC
638 Tamco Rd (27320-8690)
PHONE....................................336 342-1141
Brent Allen, *Managing Member*
EMP: 25 **EST:** 2021
SALES (est): 1.13MM **Privately Held**
SIC: 3599 Machine and other job shop work

(G-10680)
CONTINENTAL STONE COMPANY
159 Harvest Rd (27320-8820)
PHONE....................................336 951-2945
Lloyd C Prontaut Junior, *Owner*
EMP: 4 **EST:** 1982
SALES (est): 214.4K **Privately Held**
Web: www.continentalstone.com

SIC: 3272 Concrete products, precast, nec

(G-10681)
CREIGHTON AB INC
205 Watlington Industrial Dr (27320-8147)
P.O. Box 1797 (27323-1797)
PHONE....................................336 349-8275
Steve Mcmichael, *Pr*
EMP: 5 **EST:** 2010
SALES (est): 558.62K **Privately Held**
Web: www.abelectricalserv.com
SIC: 2326 Men's and boy's work clothing

(G-10682)
DAVID ROTHSCHILD CO INC
618 Grooms Rd (27320-8673)
PHONE....................................336 342-0035
Walter Rothschild, *Pr*
EMP: 65
SALES (corp-wide): 9.11MM **Privately Held**
Web: www.davidrothschildco.com
SIC: 2221 Acetate broadwoven fabrics
PA: David Rothschild Co., Inc.
512 12th St
Columbus GA 31901
706 324-2411

(G-10683)
DYSTAR LP
209 Watlington Industrial Dr (27320-8147)
PHONE....................................336 342-6631
Marc Bumgarner, *Manager*
EMP: 137
Web: www.dystar.com
SIC: 2865 Dyes and pigments
HQ: Dystar L.P.
9844 A Southern Pine Blvd
Charlotte NC 28273

(G-10684)
GENERAL MACHINING INC
37 W Plymouth (27320)
PHONE....................................336 342-2759
James Putnam, *Pr*
EMP: 4 **EST:** 1980
SQ FT: 4,000
SALES (est): 392.98K **Privately Held**
SIC: 3599 Custom machinery

(G-10685)
GLOBAL TEXTILE ALLIANCE INC (PA)
Also Called: G.T.a
2361 Holiday Loop (27320-8684)
PHONE....................................336 347-7601
Remy Tack, *CEO*
Rich Roper, *
Michael Swerbinsky, *
Gregory Tack, *
Timothy M Dolan, *
◆ **EMP:** 8 **EST:** 2001
SALES (est): 9.96MM
SALES (corp-wide): 9.96MM **Privately Held**
Web: www.globaltextileallianceinc.com
SIC: 2299 5131 Broadwoven fabrics: linen, jute, hemp, and ramie; Piece goods and notions

(G-10686)
GP FABRICATION INC
9968 Us 158 (27320-9543)
PHONE....................................336 361-0410
Gerald Pruitt, *Pr*
EMP: 11 **EST:** 2001
SQ FT: 800
SALES (est): 2.45MM **Privately Held**
Web: www.gpfabrication.com

SIC: 3441 Fabricated structural metal

(G-10687)
GRAILGAME INC ✪
301 N Scales St (27320-2906)
P.O. Box 3003 (23228-9701)
PHONE....................................804 517-3102
Evans Richards, *Pr*
Christopher Farrar, *CFO*
EMP: 5 **EST:** 2023
SALES (est): 222K **Privately Held**
SIC: 5961 3944 Electronic shopping; Electronic games and toys

(G-10688)
HENNIGES AUTOMOTIVE N AMER INC (DH)
226 Watlington Industrial Dr (27320-8147)
PHONE....................................336 342-9300
Mark Drumheller, *Pr*
Larry Williams, *VP*
▲ **EMP:** 156 **EST:** 1994
SQ FT: 250,000
SALES (est): 46.29MM **Privately Held**
Web: www.hennigesautomotive.com
SIC: 3053 Gaskets and sealing devices
HQ: Schlegel Corporation
2750 High Meadow Cir
Auburn Hills MI 48326
248 340-4100

(G-10689)
ISOMETRICS INC (PA)
1266 N Scales St (27320-8306)
P.O. Box 660 (27323-0660)
PHONE....................................336 349-2329
Dennis Bracy, *Ch Bd*
David Mccollum, *VP*
Gail Martin, *
◆ **EMP:** 40 **EST:** 1973
SQ FT: 80,000
SALES (est): 10.34MM
SALES (corp-wide): 10.34MM **Privately Held**
Web: www.isometrics-inc.com
SIC: 3714 3728 Gas tanks, motor vehicle; Fuel tanks, aircraft

(G-10690)
ISOMETRICS INC
7537 Nc Highway 87 (27320-8803)
PHONE....................................336 342-4150
Gary Mcgrath, *Mgr*
EMP: 10
SALES (corp-wide): 10.34MM **Privately Held**
Web: www.isometrics-inc.com
SIC: 3728 3714 Fuel tanks, aircraft; Gas tanks, motor vehicle
PA: Isometrics, Inc.
1266 N Scales St
Reidsville NC 27320
336 349-2329

(G-10691)
KEYSTONE FOODS LLC
Equity Group
227 Equity Dr (27320-7000)
P.O. Box 1436 (27323-1436)
PHONE....................................336 342-6601
Tom Harris, *Manager*
EMP: 150
SALES (corp-wide): 53.31B **Publicly Held**
Web: www.tysonfoods.com
SIC: 2015 Chicken, processed, nsk
HQ: Keystone Foods Llc
905 Airport Rd Ste 400
West Chester PA 19380
610 667-6700

(G-10692)
MARIETTA MARTIN MATERIALS INC
Also Called: Martin Marietta Aggregates
7639 Nc Highway 87 (27320-8818)
PHONE....................................336 349-3333
Kenneth Roberts, *Brnch Mgr*
EMP: 6
Web: www.martinmarietta.com
SIC: 1422 Crushed and broken limestone
PA: Martin Marietta Materials Inc
4123 Parklake Ave
Raleigh NC 27612

(G-10693)
MIRROR TECH INC
1011 Freeway Dr (27320-7101)
P.O. Box 468 (27357-0468)
PHONE....................................336 342-6041
Paul Potter, *Pr*
▲ **EMP:** 6 **EST:** 1991
SQ FT: 1,200
SALES (est): 146.11K **Privately Held**
SIC: 2869 Industrial organic chemicals, nec

(G-10694)
MORRISETTE PAPER COMPANY INC
Also Called: Paper Development
105 E Harrison St (27320-3901)
P.O. Box 786 (27323-0786)
PHONE....................................336 342-5570
Rodney Martin, *Brnch Mgr*
EMP: 8
SALES (corp-wide): 100.46MM **Privately Held**
Web: www.morrisette.com
SIC: 2621 2675 2631 Paper mills; Die-cut paper and board; Paperboard mills
PA: Morrisette Packaging, Inc.
5925 Summit Ave
Browns Summit NC 27214
336 375-1515

(G-10695)
MY THREESONS GOURMET
2138 Wentworth St (27320-7304)
PHONE....................................336 324-5638
Cheryl Bennett, *Owner*
EMP: 5 **EST:** 2011
SALES (est): 230.45K **Privately Held**
SIC: 2099 Food preparations, nec

(G-10696)
NEWS & RECORD
1921 Vance St (27320-3254)
PHONE....................................336 627-1781
Karl Miller, *Prin*
EMP: 5 **EST:** 2011
SALES (est): 158.19K **Privately Held**
Web: www.greensboro.com
SIC: 2711 Newspapers, publishing and printing

(G-10697)
PIPELINE ENTERPRISES LLC
Also Called: AEL Locate Services
1543 Barnes St (27320-5750)
PHONE....................................804 593-6999
David Perry, *Managing Member*
EMP: 65 **EST:** 2021
SALES (est): 2.2MM **Privately Held**
SIC: 3669 Pedestrian traffic control equipment

(G-10698)
SMITH-CAROLINA CORPORATION
Also Called: S C C
654 Freeway Dr (27320-7207)
PHONE....................................336 349-2905
Wes Taylor, *Sec*
EMP: 27 **EST:** 1977

SALES (est): 4.39MM Publicly Held
Web: www.smithmidland.com
SIC: 3272 Concrete products, precast, nec
PA: Smith-Midland Corporation
    5119 Catlett Rd
    Midland VA 22728

(G-10699)
TOYMAKERZ LLC
2358 Holiday Loop (27320-8684)
PHONE.............................843 267-3477
David Ankin, *CEO*
David Young, *Prin*
EMP: 10 EST: 2017
SALES (est): 501.97K Privately Held
Web: www.toymakerz.com
SIC: 3711 7922 Motor vehicles and car
  bodies; Television program, including
  commercial producers

(G-10700)
UNIFI INC
Also Called: Unifi Plant 2
2920 Vance Street Ext (27320-9499)
P.O. Box 1437 (27323-1437)
PHONE.............................336 348-6539
Ron Mangrun, *Mgr*
EMP: 63
**SALES (corp-wide): 582.21MM Publicly
Held**
Web: www.unifi.com
SIC: 2269 2281 Finishing: raw stock, yarn,
  and narrow fabrics; Yarn spinning mills
PA: Unifi, Inc.
    7201 W Friendly Ave
    Greensboro NC 27410
    336 294-4410

(G-10701)
WLC FORKLIFT SERVICES LLC
2433 Freeway Dr (27320-7209)
PHONE.............................336 345-2571
William Conklin, *Managing Member*
EMP: 9 EST: 2014
SALES (est): 3.59MM Privately Held
Web: www.wlcforkliftservicesllc.com
SIC: 3537 Forklift trucks

(G-10702)
WP REIDSVILLE LLC
109 Sands Rd (27320-6521)
P.O. Box 368 (46507-0368)
PHONE.............................336 342-1200
▼ **EMP: 125**
SIC: 2821 Molding compounds, plastics

Research Triangle Pa
Durham County

(G-10703)
**ASKLEPIOS BOPHARMACEUTICAL
INC (HQ)**
Also Called: Askbio
20 Tw Alexander Dr Ste 110 (27709)
PHONE.............................919 561-6210
Gustavo Pesquin, *CEO*
Philippe Moullier, *CSO*
Martin K Childers, *CMO*
Don Haut, *Chief Business Officer*
EMP: 238 EST: 2001
SALES (est): 54.58MM
SALES (corp-wide): 49.29B Privately Held
Web: www.askbio.com
SIC: 2834 Pharmaceutical preparations
PA: Bayer Ag
    Kaiser-Wilhelm-Allee 1
    Leverkusen NW 51373
    214301

(G-10704)
AUTOMATIONCOM LLC
67 Tw Alexander Dr (27709-0185)
PHONE.............................952 563-5448
Patrick Gouhin, *CEO*
EMP: 5 EST: 2015
SQ FT: 25,000
SALES (est): 146.73K Privately Held
Web: www.automation.com
SIC: 2721 Statistical reports (periodicals):
  publishing only

(G-10705)
AVAYA LLC
4001 E Chapel Hl (27709)
PHONE.............................919 425-8268
EMP: 255
Web: www.avaya.com
SIC: 3661 Telephone and telegraph
  apparatus
HQ: Avaya Llc
    350 Mount Kemble Ave # 1
    Morristown NJ 07960
    908 953-6000

(G-10706)
B3 BIO INC
6 Davis Dr (27709-0003)
PHONE.............................919 226-3079
Robert Bonczek, *Pr*
EMP: 9 EST: 2008
SALES (est): 223.42K Privately Held
SIC: 2834 Pharmaceutical preparations

(G-10707)
CYBERLUX CORPORATION (PA)
800 Park Offices Dr Ste 3209 (27709-1014)
PHONE.............................984 363-6894
Mark Schmidt, *CEO*
Mark D Schmidt, *CEO*
David D Downing, *Treas*
EMP: 16 EST: 2000
SQ FT: 7,472
SALES (est): 49.54MM
**SALES (corp-wide): 49.54MM Publicly
Held**
Web: www.cyberlux.com
SIC: 3728 3721 3648 7371 Target drones;
  Aircraft; Arc lighting fixtures; Computer
  software development and applications

(G-10708)
DZONE INC
Also Called: Devada
600 Park Offices Dr Ste 150 (27709-1009)
P.O. Box 12077 (27709-2077)
PHONE.............................919 678-0300
Terry Walters, *Pr*
EMP: 15 EST: 2005
SQ FT: 6,000
SALES (est): 2.67MM Privately Held
Web: www.dzone.com
SIC: 7319 7372 Media buying service;
  Publisher's computer software

(G-10709)
**FENNEC PHARMACEUTICALS INC
(PA)**
Also Called: Pedmark
68 Tw Alexander Dr (27709)
P.O. Box 13628 (27709)
PHONE.............................919 636-4530
Jeffrey Hackman, *CEO*
Khalid Islam, *Ch Bd*
Robert Andrade, *CFO*
Pierre Sayad, *CMO*
Terry Evans, *CCO*
EMP: 23 EST: 1996
SALES (est): 21.25MM
**SALES (corp-wide): 21.25MM Publicly
Held**

Web: www.fennecpharma.com
SIC: 2834 Pharmaceutical preparations

(G-10710)
GLAXOSMITHKLINE LLC
52069 Five Moore Dr (27709)
P.O. Box 13358 (27709-3358)
PHONE.............................919 483-5006
EMP: 30
SALES (corp-wide): 39.77B Privately Held
Web: us.gsk.com
SIC: 2834 Pharmaceutical preparations
HQ: Glaxosmithkline Llc
    2929 Walnut St Ste 1700
    Philadelphia PA 19112
    888 825-5249

(G-10711)
GRIFOLS THERAPEUTICS LLC (DH)
79 Tw Alexander Dr (27709-0152)
P.O. Box 110526 (27709-5526)
PHONE.............................919 316-6300
David Bell, *
Max Debrouwer, *
▲ **EMP: 300 EST: 2004**
SALES (est): 489.6MM Privately Held
Web: www.discovertheplasma.com
SIC: 2834 2836 Pharmaceutical preparations
  ; Agar culture media
HQ: Grifols Shared Services North
    America, Inc.
    2410 Lillyvale Ave
    Los Angeles CA 90032
    323 225-2221

(G-10712)
INSTROTEK INC (PA)
1 Triangle Dr (27709-0005)
P.O. Box 13944 (27709-3944)
PHONE.............................919 875-8371
Al Regimand, *Pr*
Lawrence James, *VP*
Maurice Arbelaez, *Dir*
▲ **EMP: 23 EST: 1997**
SQ FT: 23,000
SALES (est): 11.53MM
**SALES (corp-wide): 11.53MM Privately
Held**
Web: www.instrotek.com
SIC: 3531 Construction machinery

(G-10713)
**INTERNATIONAL SOCIETY
AUTOMTN (PA)**
Also Called: I S A
67 T W Alexander Dr (27709)
P.O. Box 12277 (27709-2277)
PHONE.............................919 206-4176
Patrick Gouhin, *Ex Dir*
Leo Staples, *
James Keaveney, *
Mary Ramsey, *
EMP: 50 EST: 1945
SQ FT: 43,000
SALES (est): 16.48MM
**SALES (corp-wide): 16.48MM Privately
Held**
Web: www.isa.org
SIC: 8621 2721 2731 Scientific membership
  association; Magazines: publishing only,
  not printed on site; Books, publishing and
  printing

(G-10714)
**MICROSS ADVNCED INTRCNNECT
TEC**
Also Called: Micross Components
3021 Cornwallis Rd (27709-0146)
P.O. Box 110283 (27709-5283)
PHONE.............................919 248-1872
John Lannon, *Genl Mgr*

Anna Khlebnikova Ctrl, *Prin*
Michael Rooney, *
EMP: 30 EST: 1998
SQ FT: 95,000
SALES (est): 4.72MM
**SALES (corp-wide): 340.38MM Privately
Held**
SIC: 3674 Microcircuits, integrated
  (semiconductor)
PA: Micross Inc.
    225 Bradhollow Rd Ste 305
    Melville NY 11747
    407 298-7100

(G-10715)
STIEFEL LABORATORIES INC (DH)
5 Moore Dr (27709-0143)
PHONE.............................888 784-3335
Charles W Stiefel, *Ch Bd*
William D Humphries, *
Gavin Corcoran, *
Michael T Cornelius, *
Simon Jose, *
EMP: 40 EST: 1944
SQ FT: 13,000
SALES (est): 21.34MM
SALES (corp-wide): 39.77B Privately Held
SIC: 5122 2834 Pharmaceuticals;
  Pharmaceutical preparations
HQ: Glaxosmithkline Sl Holdings, Inc.
    1500 Spring Garden St
    Philadelphia PA 19130

(G-10716)
**TROXLER ELECTRONIC LABS INC
(PA)**
3008 Cornwallis Rd (27709)
P.O. Box 12057 (27709)
PHONE.............................919 549-8661
William F Troxler, *Pr*
James H Boylan Junior, *Sec*
▲ **EMP: 85 EST: 1956**
SQ FT: 64,000
SALES (est): 29.45MM
**SALES (corp-wide): 29.45MM Privately
Held**
Web: www.troxlerlabs.com
SIC: 8731 3823 3825 3829 Commercial
  research laboratory; Density and specific
  gravity instruments, industrial process; Test
  equipment for electronic and electric
  measurement; Measuring and controlling
  devices, nec

(G-10717)
UNITED THERAPEUTICS CORP
Also Called: United Therapeatics
55 Tw Alexander Dr (27709-0152)
P.O. Box 14186 (27709-4186)
PHONE.............................919 485-8350
Roger Jess, *Brnch Mgr*
EMP: 90
Web: www.unither.com
SIC: 2834 Pharmaceutical preparations
PA: United Therapeutics Corporation
    1000 Spring St
    Silver Spring MD 20910

(G-10718)
XONA MICROFLUIDICS INC
76 Tw Alexander Dr (27709-0152)
P.O. Box 14205 (27709)
PHONE.............................951 553-6400
Anne Taylor, *Ex Dir*
Anne Taylor, *Pr*
Brad Taylor, *CEO*
Joseph Harris, *Managing Member*
EMP: 6 EST: 2008
SQ FT: 1,400
SALES (est): 536.19K Privately Held
Web: www.xonamicrofluidics.com

SIC: **8999** 2869 3821 Scientific consulting; Silicones; Laboratory apparatus, except heating and measuring

Richfield
Stanly County

(G-10719)
MAGNA MACHINING INC
111 3rd Park Dr (28137-7500)
PHONE.............................704 463-9904
George Williams Junior, *Pr*
Nancy Williams, *VP*
EMP: 21 **EST:** 1998
SQ FT: 5,000
SALES (est): 2.2MM **Privately Held**
Web: www.magnamachining.com
SIC: 3599 Machine shop, jobbing and repair

Richlands
Onslow County

(G-10720)
DP HILL INC
Also Called: Dp Hill Manufacturing
1439 Hwy 258 (28574-9414)
PHONE.............................252 568-4282
David Hill, *Pr*
Juliann Hill, *Sec*
EMP: 4 **EST:** 1991
SQ FT: 2,000
SALES (est): 824.15K **Privately Held**
Web: www.dphill.com
SIC: 3554 Paper forming machines

(G-10721)
MARTIN MARIETTA MATERIALS INC
Also Called: Martin Marietta Aggregates
131 Duffy Field Rd (28574-2300)
P.O. Box 67 (28574-0067)
PHONE.............................910 324-7430
Greg Meadows, *Mgr*
EMP: 4
Web: www.martinmarietta.com
SIC: 3273 Ready-mixed concrete
PA: Martin Marietta Materials Inc
4123 Parklake Ave
Raleigh NC 27612

(G-10722)
WAR HORSE NEWS INC
8404 Richlands Hwy (28574-7475)
PHONE.............................910 430-0868
Richlands Brennan, *Prin*
EMP: 11 **EST:** 2016
SALES (est): 96.24K **Privately Held**
Web: www.thewarhorse.org
SIC: 2711 Newspapers

Riegelwood
Columbus County

(G-10723)
BEST WORKERS COMPANY
5494 Port Royal Rd Ne (28456-9314)
PHONE.............................336 665-0076
Rufus Grainger, *Owner*
EMP: 5 **EST:** 1987
SALES (est): 173.81K **Privately Held**
SIC: 3272 Burial vaults, concrete or precast terrazzo

(G-10724)
FRASER WEST INC
361 Federal Rd (28456)
PHONE.............................910 655-4106

Kelly Hoffman, *Dir Opers*
EMP: 25 **EST:** 2000
SALES (est): 6.21MM **Privately Held**
SIC: 2421 Sawmills and planing mills, general

(G-10725)
INTERNATIONAL PAPER COMPANY
Also Called: International Paper
1865 John Riegel Rd (28456)
PHONE.............................910 655-2211
EMP: 5
SALES (corp-wide): 18.62B **Publicly Held**
Web: www.internationalpaper.com
SIC: 2621 Paper mills
PA: International Paper Company
6400 Poplar Ave
Memphis TN 38197
901 419-7000

(G-10726)
INTERNATIONAL PAPER COMPANY
Also Called: International Paper
865 John L Regel Rd (28456-9581)
P.O. Box 825 (28456-0825)
PHONE.............................910 362-4900
Scott Grimes, *Mgr*
EMP: 243
SALES (corp-wide): 18.62B **Publicly Held**
Web: www.internationalpaper.com
SIC: 2621 2631 Paper mills; Paperboard mills
PA: International Paper Company
6400 Poplar Ave
Memphis TN 38197
901 419-7000

(G-10727)
OAK-BARK CORPORATION
Also Called: Wright
1507 Cronly Dr (28456-9504)
PHONE.............................910 655-2263
William Oakley, *Brnch Mgr*
EMP: 20
SALES (corp-wide): 2.2MM **Privately Held**
Web: www.oakbark12.com
SIC: 2869 Industrial organic chemicals, nec
PA: Oak-Bark Corporation
514 Wayne Dr
Wilmington NC 28403

(G-10728)
SILAR LLC (DH)
Also Called: Silar Laboratories
333 Neils Eddy Rd (28456-9570)
PHONE.............................910 655-4212
Martha Neely, *Prin*
◆ **EMP:** 35 **EST:** 2008
SALES (est): 8.97MM
SALES (corp-wide): 3.24B **Publicly Held**
Web: www.entegris.com
SIC: 2869 Industrial organic chemicals, nec
HQ: Mpd Holdings, Llc
340 Mathers Rd
Ambler PA 19002

Roanoke Rapids
Halifax County

(G-10729)
ALLIE M POWELL III
Also Called: Powell's Ready-Mix
3692 Nc Highway 48 (27870-8474)
P.O. Box 395 (27870-0395)
PHONE.............................252 535-9717
Allie M Powell Iii, *Owner*
EMP: 4 **EST:** 1994
SQ FT: 1,200
SALES (est): 252.05K **Privately Held**

SIC: **3273** Ready-mixed concrete

(G-10730)
ARGOS USA LLC
Also Called: Ready Mixed Concrete Co
75 W 13th St (27870-3725)
P.O. Box 2065 (27533-2065)
PHONE.............................252 443-5046
Robert Porter, *Mgr*
EMP: 4
Web: www.argos-us.com
SIC: 3273 Ready-mixed concrete
HQ: Argos Usa Llc
3015 Windward Plz Ste 300
Alpharetta GA 30005
678 368-4300

(G-10731)
AUTOVERTERS INC
2212 W 10th St (27870-9295)
P.O. Box 850 (27870-0850)
PHONE.............................252 537-0426
Barbara A Dickens, *Pr*
Shawn Burke, *Sec*
▲ **EMP:** 16 **EST:** 1976
SQ FT: 87,700
SALES (est): 1.01MM **Privately Held**
Web: www.autovertersinc.com
SIC: 7389 3999 Textile folding and packing services; Advertising curtains

(G-10732)
BUCK LUCAS LOGGING COMPANIES
812 W Hawkins Rd (27870-9519)
PHONE.............................252 410-0160
Jonathan Vance Lucas, *Prin*
EMP: 5 **EST:** 2007
SALES (est): 395.87K **Privately Held**
SIC: 2411 Logging camps and contractors

(G-10733)
BUTCHERS BEST INC
944 Raleigh St (27870-2923)
PHONE.............................252 533-0961
Chris Rice, *Owner*
EMP: 4 **EST:** 2002
SALES (est): 210.64K **Privately Held**
SIC: 3421 Cutlery

(G-10734)
C&A HOCKADAY TRANSPORT LLC
1660 Hill St (27870-4210)
PHONE.............................252 676-5956
EMP: 4
SALES (est): 182.43K **Privately Held**
SIC: 3537 7389 Trucks: freight, baggage, etc.: industrial, except mining; Business Activities at Non-Commercial Site

(G-10735)
COASTAL TREATED PRODUCTS LLC
1433 Georgia Ave (27870-4653)
PHONE.............................252 410-0180
EMP: 13 **EST:** 2012
SALES (est): 445.33K
SALES (corp-wide): 6.84B **Publicly Held**
SIC: 2491 Wood preserving
PA: Boise Cascade Company
1111 W Jffrson St Ste 300
Boise ID 83702
208 384-6161

(G-10736)
CULPEPER ROANOKE RAPIDS LLC
2262 W 10th St (27870-9295)
PHONE.............................252 678-3804
EMP: 6 **EST:** 2017
SALES (est): 279.72K **Privately Held**
Web: www.culpeperwood.com

SIC: **2491** Wood preserving

(G-10737)
FRANKLIN BAKING COMPANY LLC
610 Julian R Allsbrook Hwy (27870-4613)
PHONE.............................252 410-0255
Tim Hales, *Mgr*
EMP: 10
SALES (corp-wide): 5.1B **Publicly Held**
Web: franklin-co4goldsboro.edan.io
SIC: 2051 Bread, all types (white, wheat, rye, etc); fresh or frozen
HQ: Franklin Baking Company, Llc
500 W Grantham St
Goldsboro NC 27530
919 735-0344

(G-10738)
HERALD PRINTING CO INC
916 Roanoke Ave (27870-2720)
PHONE.............................252 537-2505
Stephen Woody, *VP*
Walter M Wick, *
Robert J Wick, *Treas*
EMP: 5 **EST:** 1947
SQ FT: 9,000
SALES (est): 220.52K **Privately Held**
Web: www.rrdailyherald.com
SIC: 2711 Newspapers, publishing and printing

(G-10739)
J E KERR TIMBER CO CORP
1005 Old Halifax Rd (27870-8572)
PHONE.............................252 537-0544
James Kerr, *Pr*
Charlotte Kerr, *
Joan Kerr, *
EMP: 8 **EST:** 1975
SQ FT: 1,500
SALES (est): 999.29K **Privately Held**
SIC: 5031 2411 Lumber: rough, dressed, and finished; Logging

(G-10740)
LYNCHS OFFICE SUPPLY CO INC (PA)
921 Roanoke Ave (27870-2719)
PHONE.............................252 537-6041
TOLL FREE: 800
Cecil T Lynch Junior, *Pr*
Lynne S Lynch, *VP*
Christian T Lynch, *VP*
Kevin S Lynch, *VP*
EMP: 10 **EST:** 1961
SALES (est): 937.16K
SALES (corp-wide): 937.16K **Privately Held**
Web: www.lynchsofficesupply.com
SIC: 5943 5999 2752 Office forms and supplies; Business machines and equipment; Offset printing

(G-10741)
MCPHERSON BEVERAGES INC
Also Called: Pepsico
1330 Stancell St (27870-4824)
PHONE.............................252 537-3571
Russell M Hull, *Pr*
EMP: 47 **EST:** 1932
SQ FT: 15,000
SALES (est): 3.62MM **Privately Held**
Web: www.pepsico.com
SIC: 2086 Bottled and canned soft drinks

(G-10742)
ROANOKE TRUSS INC
711 E 15th St (27870-4441)
PHONE.............................252 537-0012
James D Cagle, *Pr*
Linda Mozingo, *VP*

GEOGRAPHIC

EMP: 8 **EST:** 1984
SQ FT: 3,500
SALES (est): 336.4K **Privately Held**
SIC: 2439 Trusses, wooden roof

(G-10743)
WELLS MECHANICAL SERVICES
LLC
628 Raleigh Dr (27870-3915)
PHONE..............................252 532-2632
Michael Wells, *Prin*
EMP: 6 **EST:** 2013
SALES (est): 1.01MM **Privately Held**
SIC: 7692 Welding repair

(G-10744)
WESTROCK KRAFT PAPER LLC
100 Gaston Rd (27870-1900)
PHONE..............................252 533-6000
EMP: 5
Web: www.westrock.com
SIC: 2621 Specialty papers
HQ: Westrock Kraft Paper, Llc
1000 Abernathy Rd
Atlanta GA 30328
770 448-2193

(G-10745)
WESTROCK PAPER AND PACKG LLC
Also Called: Kapstone Kraft Paper
100 Gaston Rd (27870-1900)
PHONE..............................252 533-6000
Anitra Collins, *Brnch Mgr*
EMP: 500
Web: www.westrock.com
SIC: 2631 2611 2621 Paperboard mills; Pulp
mills; Paper mills
HQ: Westrock Paper And Packaging, Llc
1000 Abernathy Rd Ne
Atlanta GA 30328

(G-10746)
WHIPPOORWILL HILLS INC
1509 E 10th St (27870-4101)
P.O. Box 56 (27832-0056)
PHONE..............................252 537-2765
Philipp Moncure, *Pr*
EMP: 4 **EST:** 2010
SALES (est): 192.11K **Privately Held**
SIC: 2519 Household furniture, nec

(G-10747)
WICK COMMUNICATIONS CO
Also Called: Daily Herald
1025 Roanoke Ave (27870-3701)
P.O. Box 520 (27870-0520)
PHONE..............................252 537-2505
Stephen Woody, *Publisher*
EMP: 22
SALES (corp-wide): 37.72MM **Privately**
Held
Web: www.wickcommunications.com
SIC: 2711 2752 Newspapers, publishing and
printing; Commercial printing, lithographic
HQ: Wick Communications Co.
333 W Wilcox Dr Ste 302
Sierra Vista AZ 85635
520 458-0200

(G-10748)
WRIGHT & HOBBS INC
105 W Becker Dr (27870-4800)
P.O. Box 696 (27832-0696)
PHONE..............................252 537-5817
Leslie Wright Junior, *Pr*
EMP: 26 **EST:** 1967
SQ FT: 4,000
SALES (est): 2.33MM **Privately Held**

SIC: 2411 2426 2421 Timber, cut at logging
camp; Hardwood dimension and flooring
mills; Sawmills and planing mills, general

Roaring River
Wilkes County

(G-10749)
GENTRYS CABNT DOORS
2872 Austin Little Mtn Rd (28669-9190)
PHONE..............................336 957-8787
Scott Gentry, *Prin*
EMP: 4 **EST:** 2010
SALES (est): 191K **Privately Held**
SIC: 2434 7389 Wood kitchen cabinets;
Business Activities at Non-Commercial Site

(G-10750)
LOUISIANA-PACIFIC CORPORATION
1151 Abtco Rd (28669)
PHONE..............................336 696-2751
EMP: 8
SALES (corp-wide): 2.94B **Publicly Held**
Web: www.lpcorp.com
SIC: 2493 Strandboard, oriented
PA: Louisiana-Pacific Corporation
1610 West End Ave Ste 200
Nashville TN 37203
615 986-5600

Robbins
Moore County

(G-10751)
AMERICAN GROWLER INC (PA)
121 N Green St (27325-9480)
P.O. Box 430 (27325-0430)
PHONE..............................352 671-5393
Terry Crews, *Pr*
EMP: 30 **EST:** 1992
SALES (est): 1.01MM
SALES (corp-wide): 1.01MM **Privately**
Held
Web: www.growlerme.com
SIC: 3799 Off-road automobiles, except
recreational vehicles

(G-10752)
CAROLINA GROWLER INC
Also Called: Growler Manufacturing & Engrg
121 N Green St (27325-9480)
PHONE..............................910 948-2114
Curtis Crews, *CEO*
Terry Crews, *
John Crews, *
EMP: 30 **EST:** 2007
SALES (est): 6.65MM **Privately Held**
Web: www.growlerme.com
SIC: 3699 Security devices

(G-10753)
KEY PACKING COMPANY INC
596 Maness Rd (27325-8243)
PHONE..............................910 464-5054
Gilbert M Key, *Pr*
Elizabeth Key, *Sec*
Mitchell Key, *VP*
EMP: 8 **EST:** 1975
SALES (est): 243.48K **Privately Held**
Web: www.keypackingcompany.com
SIC: 2011 Beef products, from beef
slaughtered on site

(G-10754)
MINHAS FURNITURE HOUSE INC
Also Called: Flair Designs
6844 Nc 705 Hwy (27325-7828)
PHONE..............................910 898-0808

Bill Minhas, *Pr*
Kamanjeet Minhas, *
◆ **EMP:** 30 **EST:** 2012
SQ FT: 125,000
SALES (est): 5.25MM
SALES (corp-wide): 17.39MM **Privately**
Held
SIC: 2512 5021 Upholstered household
furniture; Furniture
PA: Minhas Furniture House Ltd
3916 72 Ave Se
Calgary AB T2C 2
403 219-1006

(G-10755)
VANDERBILT MINERALS LLC
Also Called: Standard Mineral Division
400 Spies Rd (27325-7395)
P.O. Box 279 (27325-0279)
PHONE..............................910 948-2266
James Faile, *Genl Mgr*
EMP: 26
SALES (corp-wide): 266.87MM **Privately**
Held
Web: www.vanderbiltminerals.com
SIC: 1499 3295 Pyrophyllite mining;
Minerals, ground or treated
HQ: Vanderbilt Minerals, Llc
33 Winfield St
Norwalk CT 06855
203 295-2140

Robbinsville
Graham County

(G-10756)
BEASLEY CONTRACTING
756 Gladdens Creek Rd (28771-6909)
PHONE..............................828 479-3775
Gary Beasley, *Owner*
EMP: 4 **EST:** 2009
SALES (est): 178.92K **Privately Held**
SIC: 3531 Construction machinery

(G-10757)
BLUE ROCK MATERIALS LLC
750 Tallulah Rd (28771-9461)
PHONE..............................828 479-3581
Randy Jordan, *Managing Member*
EMP: 10 **EST:** 2010
SALES (est): 991.26K **Privately Held**
Web: www.bluerockllc.com
SIC: 1423 1442 Crushed and broken granite;
Construction sand and gravel

(G-10758)
COMMUNITY NEWSPAPERS INC
Also Called: The Graham Star
720 Tallulah Rd (28771-9461)
P.O. Box 69 (28771-0069)
PHONE..............................828 479-3383
Gary Corsair, *Mgr*
EMP: 4
SALES (corp-wide): 40.95MM **Privately**
Held
Web: www.cninewspapers.com
SIC: 2711 Newspapers, publishing and
printing
PA: Community Newspapers, Inc.
2365 Prince Ave # A
Athens GA 30606
706 548-0010

(G-10759)
HOLDER MACHINE & MFG CO
1483 Fontana Rd (28771-5661)
PHONE..............................828 479-8627
Tony Holder, *Pr*
EMP: 5 **EST:** 1985

SQ FT: 7,000
SALES (est): 267.67K **Privately Held**
SIC: 7699 3599 Industrial machinery and
equipment repair; Custom machinery

(G-10760)
MEDACCESS INC
1236 Gladdens Creek Rd (28771-6913)
PHONE..............................828 264-4085
Daniel K Stover, *Pr*
EMP: 4 **EST:** 2001
SALES (est): 243.85K **Privately Held**
Web: www.medaccessinc.com
SIC: 5999 7352 7359 8099 Wheelchair lifts;
Medical equipment rental; Equipment rental
and leasing, nec; Medical services
organization

(G-10761)
ROBBINSVILLE CSTM MOLDING INC
Also Called: CM Supply
1450 Old Hwy 129 (28771-6807)
P.O. Box 817 (28771-0817)
PHONE..............................828 479-2317
John Garland, *Pr*
EMP: 10 **EST:** 1987
SQ FT: 5,000
SALES (est): 1.46MM **Privately Held**
Web: www.custommoulding.com
SIC: 1521 2434 2435 2431 New
construction, single-family houses; Wood
kitchen cabinets; Panels, hardwood plywood
; Moldings, wood: unfinished and
prefinished

(G-10762)
SMOKEY MOUNTAIN AMUSEMENTS
5660 Tallulah Rd (28771-7535)
PHONE..............................828 479-2814
Billy J Clark, *Prin*
▲ **EMP:** 4 **EST:** 2002
SALES (est): 466.57K **Privately Held**
SIC: 3599 Industrial machinery, nec

(G-10763)
SMOKY MTN NATIV PLANT ASSN
546 Upper Tuskeegee Rd (28771-9012)
P.O. Box 761 (28771-0761)
PHONE..............................828 479-8788
Beverley Whitehead, *Dir*
EMP: 4 **EST:** 2008
SALES (est): 243.23K **Privately Held**
Web: www.smnpa.org
SIC: 8731 3523 Environmental research;
Incubators and brooders, farm

(G-10764)
SNOWBIRD LOGGING LLC
270 Dick Branch Rd (28771-7951)
PHONE..............................828 479-6635
Walter Hooper, *Pt*
Tommy Cable, *Pt*
Jason Hooper, *Pt*
Lucas Hooper, *Pt*
EMP: 7 **EST:** 1994
SALES (est): 655.99K **Privately Held**
SIC: 2411 Logging camps and contractors

Robersonville
Martin County

(G-10765)
ANNS HOUSE OF NUTS
1159 Robersonville Products Rd (27871)
PHONE..............................252 795-6500
EMP: 7 **EST:** 2020
SALES (est): 1.02MM **Privately Held**
SIC: 2034 Soup mixes

▲ = Import ▼ = Export
◆ = Import/Export

(G-10766)
CAROLINA EASTERN INC
Also Called: Eastern Crlina Agrculture Svcs
6940 Us Highway 64 (27871-9654)
P.O. Box 989 (27871-0989)
PHONE.................................252 795-3128
Bill Van Derford, *Mgr*
EMP: 5
SALES (corp-wide): 90.16MM **Privately Held**
Web: www.carolina-eastern.com
SIC: 2873 Nitrogenous fertilizers
PA: Carolina Eastern, Inc.
1820 Savannah Hwy Ste G1
Charleston SC 29407
843 571-0411

(G-10767)
FLAGSTONE FOODS LLC
201 E 3rd St (27871-9756)
PHONE.................................252 795-6500
Steve Gandy, *Mgr*
EMP: 421
SALES (corp-wide): 920.58MM **Privately Held**
Web: www.flagstonefoods.com
SIC: 3556 Food products machinery
HQ: Flagstone Foods Llc
323 N Wash Ave Ste 400
Minneapolis MN 55401
612 222-3800

Rockingham
Richmond County

(G-10768)
ADVANCED MACHINE SERVICES
835 N Us Highway 220 (28379-6809)
PHONE.................................910 410-0099
Jermey Festheran, *Owner*
EMP: 4 EST: 2007
SALES (est): 354.18K **Privately Held**
SIC: 3365 Machinery castings, aluminum

(G-10769)
ADVANCED MACHINE SERVICES LLC
128 Industrial Park Dr (28379-3536)
P.O. Box 2512 (28380-2512)
PHONE.................................910 410-0099
EMP: 7 EST: 2020
SALES (est): 1.02MM **Privately Held**
SIC: 7692 Welding repair

(G-10770)
ALLEN BROTHERS TIMBER COMPANY
Also Called: Crestview Trading Post
723 N Us Highway 220 (28379-6807)
PHONE.................................910 997-6412
Bruce G Allen, *Pr*
Craig Allen, *Sec*
Clay Allen, *VP*
EMP: 6 EST: 1968
SALES (est): 434.7K **Privately Held**
SIC: 2411 Logging camps and contractors

(G-10771)
CASCADES MOULDED PULP INC
112 Cascades Way (28379-3689)
P.O. Box 609 (28380-0609)
PHONE.................................910 997-2775
Gary A Hayden, *Pr*
Alain Lemaire, *
Guy Prenevost, *
Debbie Lear, *
Shannon Willart, *
EMP: 30 EST: 1986
SQ FT: 250,000

SALES (est): 9.93MM
SALES (corp-wide): 3.32B **Privately Held**
Web: www.cascades.com
SIC: 2621 Paper mills
PA: Cascades Inc
404 Boul Marie-Victorin
Kingsey Falls QC J0A 1
819 363-5100

(G-10772)
CASCADES TISSUE GROUP - NC INC
Also Called: Cascades Tissue Group
805 Midway Rd (28379-4101)
P.O. Box 578 (28380-0578)
PHONE.................................910 895-4033
Alain Lemaire, *Pr*
Suzanne Blanchet, *
◆ EMP: 130 EST: 1983
SQ FT: 155,000
SALES (est): 24.19MM **Privately Held**
Web: www.cascades.com
SIC: 2676 2621 Toilet paper: made from
purchased paper; Tissue paper
HQ: Cascades Fine Papers Group Inc
7280 West Credit Ave
Mississauga ON L5N 5
905 813-9400

(G-10773)
CENTRE INGREDIENT TECH INC
Also Called: CIT
101 Commerce Pl (28379-3969)
PHONE.................................910 895-9277
Atsuto Yasui, *Pr*
Mohamad Farbood, *Pr*
EMP: 9 EST: 1998
SALES (est): 1.74MM **Privately Held**
SIC: 2869 Perfumes, flavorings, and food
additives

(G-10774)
DIRECT PACK EAST LLC
612 Airport Rd (28379-7494)
PHONE.................................910 331-0071
EMP: 25 EST: 2017
SALES (est): 12MM
SALES (corp-wide): 1.71B **Privately Held**
Web: www.directpackinc.com
SIC: 3565 Aerating machines, for beverages
PA: Pmc Global, Inc.
12243 Branford St
Sun Valley CA 91352
818 896-1101

(G-10775)
DORSETT PRINTING COMPANY
1203 Rockingham Rd (28379-4958)
P.O. Box 428 (28380-0428)
PHONE.................................910 895-3520
Karen Dunn, *Pt*
Susan Martin, *Pt*
EMP: 5 EST: 1966
SQ FT: 6,000
SALES (est): 141.12K **Privately Held**
SIC: 2752 Offset printing

(G-10776)
ELEKTRAN INC
220 River Rd (28379-4219)
P.O. Box 1027 (28380-1027)
PHONE.................................910 997-6640
Richard Adams, *Pr*
Brian Fournier, *VP*
EMP: 6 EST: 1977
SQ FT: 9,900
SALES (est): 2.15MM **Privately Held**
Web: www.elektran.com
SIC: 5063 7694 Power transmission
equipment, electric; Electric motor repair

(G-10777)
GGI GLASS DISTRIBUTORS CORP
Also Called: General Glass International
208 Silver Grove Church Rd (28379-5401)
PHONE.................................910 895-2022
Terry Miller, *Mgr*
EMP: 30
Web: www.generalglass.com
SIC: 3231 Products of purchased glass
PA: Ggi Glass Distributors Corp.
101 Venture Way
Secaucus NJ 07094

(G-10778)
HENSON FAMILY INVESTMENTS LLC
Also Called: Unique Stone
395 Ledbetter Rd (28379-7819)
PHONE.................................910 817-9450
Douglas Henson, *Managing Member*
EMP: 20 EST: 2015
SALES (est): 788.49K **Privately Held**
Web: www.uniquestone.com
SIC: 3272 Art marble, concrete

(G-10779)
HILDRETH READY MIX LLC
518 W Us Highway 74 (28379-7006)
P.O. Box 1098 (28170-1098)
PHONE.................................704 694-2034
Melissa Renea Hildreth, *Managing Member*
EMP: 9 EST: 2008
SALES (est): 261.39K **Privately Held**
SIC: 3273 Ready-mixed concrete

(G-10780)
HUDSON PAVING INC
120 Yates Hill Rd (28379-3374)
P.O. Box 1232 (28380-1232)
PHONE.................................910 895-5910
Eugene Tom Hudson Junior, *Pr*
Ronnie Hudson, *
Brenda W Herring, *
EMP: 53 EST: 1961
SALES (est): 14.46MM
SALES (corp-wide): 1.82B **Publicly Held**
Web:
www.hudsonpavingrockinghamnc.com
SIC: 1611 2951 1771 Surfacing and paving;
Asphalt paving mixtures and blocks;
Concrete work
PA: Construction Partners, Inc.
290 Healthwest Dr Ste 2
Dothan AL 36303
334 673-9763

(G-10781)
K & W WELDING LLC
180 Old 74 Hwy (28379)
P.O. Box 430 (28380-0430)
PHONE.................................910 895-9220
EMP: 6 EST: 2006
SALES (est): 5.32MM **Privately Held**
Web: www.kandwwelding.com
SIC: 7692 Welding repair

(G-10782)
LEGACY VULCAN LLC
Mideast Division
353 Galestown Rd (28379-7486)
P.O. Box 547 (28380-0547)
PHONE.................................910 895-2415
TOLL FREE: 800
Charles Heatherly, *Mgr*
EMP: 6
Web: www.vulcanmaterials.com
SIC: 3273 Ready-mixed concrete
HQ: Legacy Vulcan, Llc
1200 Urban Center Dr
Birmingham AL 35242
205 298-3000

(G-10783)
MOSS BROTHERS TIRES & SVC INC
190 W Us Highway 74 (28379-3488)
PHONE.................................910 895-4572
William Moss, *Pr*
Elaine N Moss, *Sec*
EMP: 5 EST: 1988
SALES (est): 297.02K **Privately Held**
Web: www.mossbrotherstires.com
SIC: 5531 5014 7534 Automotive tires;
Automobile tires and tubes; Tire retreading
and repair shops

(G-10784)
NPX ONE LLC
112 Sonoco Paper Mill Rd (28379-9535)
P.O. Box 1747 (28380-1747)
PHONE.................................910 997-2217
Michael Hardy, *Brnch Mgr*
EMP: 198
SALES (corp-wide): 231.02MM **Privately Held**
Web: www.novipax.com
SIC: 3086 2671 Packaging and shipping
materials, foamed plastics; Paper; coated
and laminated packaging
PA: Npx One Llc
4275 Reading Crest Ave
Reading PA 19605
866 764-8338

(G-10785)
PERDUE FARMS INCORPORATED
Also Called: Rockingham Plant
416 S Long Dr (28379-3965)
P.O. Box 1357 (28380-1357)
PHONE.................................910 997-8600
Jim Booth, *Brnch Mgr*
EMP: 851
SALES (corp-wide): 1.24B **Privately Held**
Web: www.perdue.com
SIC: 2015 Poultry, slaughtered and dressed
PA: Perdue Farms Incorporated
31149 Old Ocean City Rd
Salisbury MD 21804
800 473-7383

(G-10786)
PLASTEK GROUP
206 Enterprise Dr (28379-6997)
PHONE.................................910 895-2089
EMP: 7 EST: 2019
SALES (est): 1.19MM **Privately Held**
Web: www.plastekgroup.com
SIC: 3089 Injection molding of plastics

(G-10787)
RICHMOND INVESTMENT (PA)
611 Airport Rd (28379-7495)
PHONE.................................910 410-8200
William D Maness, *Pr*
Terence B Lewis, *
Patsy Maness, *
Mandy Luther, *
EMP: 30 EST: 1956
SALES (est): 670.33K **Privately Held**
SIC: 7534 5531 Tire recapping; Automotive
tires

(G-10788)
RICHMOND MILLWORK LLC
707 Haywood St (28379-4216)
PHONE.................................910 331-1009
EMP: 5 EST: 2000
SALES (est): 99.97K **Privately Held**
Web: www.richmondmillwork.com
SIC: 2431 Millwork

(G-10789)
RICHMOND OBSERVER LLP
505 Rockingham Rd (28379-3615)
P.O. Box 2662 (28380-2662)
PHONE..............................910 817-3169
Charles Melvin, *Prin*
EMP: 8 EST: 2017
SALES (est): 119.15K Privately Held
Web: www.richmondobserver.com
SIC: 2711 Newspapers, publishing and
printing

(G-10790)
RICHMOND STEEL WELDING
895 Airport Rd (28379-4707)
PHONE..............................910 582-4026
EMP: 4 EST: 2020
SALES (est): 27.6K Privately Held
SIC: 3441 Fabricated structural metal

(G-10791)
THOMPSON SUNNY ACRES INC
150 Thompson Farm Rd (28379-8976)
PHONE..............................910 206-1801
William Thompson, *Pr*
Dewey Thompson, *VP*
Dianne Thompson, *Sec*
Kris Thompson, *Treas*
EMP: 4 EST: 1975
SALES (est): 401.68K Privately Held
Web: www.thompsonsunnyacres.com
SIC: 3663 5191 0139 Satellites,
communications; Farm supplies; Hay farm

(G-10792)
UNIQUE STONE INCORPORATED
222 Lakeshore Dr (28379-9709)
P.O. Box 460 (28380-0460)
PHONE..............................910 817-9450
Alex Perakis, *Pr*
Jason Perakis, *VP*
EMP: 7 EST: 1992
SALES (est): 977.59K Privately Held
Web: www.uniquestone.com
SIC: 3281 5199 Monument or burial stone,
cut and shaped; Statuary

Rockwell
Rowan County

(G-10793)
CMH MANUFACTURING INC
Also Called: CMH
508 Palmer Rd (28138-9318)
P.O. Box 700 (28138-0700)
PHONE..............................704 279-4659
Joe Earnhadt, *Genl Mgr*
EMP: 708
SALES (corp-wide): 424.23B Publicly
Held
Web: www.claytonhomes.com
SIC: 2451 Mobile homes, except recreational
HQ: Cmh Manufacturing, Inc.
5000 Clayton Rd
Maryville TN 37804
865 380-3000

(G-10794)
CONSOLIDATED TRUCK PARTS INC
7665 Hwy 52 North (28138)
P.O. Box 697 (28138-0697)
PHONE..............................704 279-5543
EMP: 7 EST: 1985
SALES (est): 944.92K Privately Held
Web: www.consolidatedtruckparts.com
SIC: 5531 5013 7694 Truck equipment and
parts; Truck parts and accessories; Electric
motor repair

(G-10795)
DAILY MANUFACTURING INC
4820 Pless Rd (28138-8921)
P.O. Box 7 (28138-0007)
PHONE..............................704 782-0700
James Daily Iii, *Pr*
EMP: 15 EST: 1979
SQ FT: 7,000
SALES (est): 2.23MM Privately Held
Web: www.dailymfg.com
SIC: 5499 2834 Vitamin food stores; Adrenal
pharmaceutical preparations

(G-10796)
FILLTECH INC
228 W Main St (28138-8582)
P.O. Box 1209 (28138-1209)
PHONE..............................704 279-4300
EMP: 22 EST: 2019
SALES (est): 2.03MM Privately Held
Web: www.filltechusa.com
SIC: 2844 Perfumes, cosmetics and other
toilet preparations

(G-10797)
FILLTECH USA LLC
380 Palmer Cir (28138-6501)
P.O. Box 1209 (28138-1209)
PHONE..............................704 279-4300
Dennis R Jones, *CEO*
Cookie Jones, *
Elizabeth P Noble, *
Scott Hughes, *
Benjamin Weisensel, *
EMP: 47 EST: 1995
SQ FT: 9,300
SALES (est): 2.35MM Privately Held
Web: www.filltechusa.com
SIC: 2844 Perfumes, cosmetics and other
toilet preparations

(G-10798)
INX INTERNATIONAL INK CO
Also Called: INX INTERNATIONAL INK CO
75 Coral St (28138-9527)
PHONE..............................704 414-6428
Henry Mullis, *Brnch Mgr*
EMP: 17
Web: www.inxinternational.com
SIC: 2893 Printing ink
HQ: Inx International Ink Co.
150 N Mrtngale Rd Ste 700
Schaumburg IL 60173
630 382-1800

(G-10799)
LIME-CHEM INC
8135 Red Rd (28138-8557)
PHONE..............................910 843-2121
Randall Andrews, *Brnch Mgr*
EMP: 5
SIC: 2899 Chemical preparations, nec
PA: Lime-Chem Inc
2042 Buie Philadelphus Rd
Red Springs NC 28377

(G-10800)
RED MAPLE LOGGING COMPANY INC
10007 Meismer Ln (28138-9753)
PHONE..............................704 279-6379
Danny Scott, *Prin*
EMP: 6 EST: 2000
SALES (est): 664.41K Privately Held
SIC: 2411 Logging camps and contractors

(G-10801)
SNIDERS MACHINE SHOP INC
8025 Highway 52 (28138-8543)
PHONE..............................704 279-6129
Michael Snider, *Pr*
EMP: 4 EST: 1996
SALES (est): 232.9K Privately Held
SIC: 3599 Machine shop, jobbing and repair

(G-10802)
SUNSHINE MNFCTRED STRCTRES INC
850 Gold Hill Ave (28138-7763)
P.O. Box 1000 (28138-1000)
PHONE..............................704 279-6600
Dean Bodine, *Pr*
John D Bodine, *
Nancy Bodine, *
EMP: 7 EST: 1984
SQ FT: 55,000
SALES (est): 347.99K Privately Held
Web: www.sunshinemodulars.com
SIC: 2452 3448 2451 Prefabricated
buildings, wood; Buildings, portable:
prefabricated metal; Mobile homes

(G-10803)
SUPPLYONE ROCKWELL INC
729 Palmer Rd (28138-8578)
P.O. Box 1469 (28138-1469)
PHONE..............................704 279-5650
William T Leith, *CEO*
Kevin M O'brien, *Pr*
George Ruth, *
Ryan S Northington, *
EMP: 150 EST: 1985
SQ FT: 85,000
SALES (est): 21.57MM
SALES (corp-wide): 841.65MM Privately
Held
Web: www.supplyone.com
SIC: 2631 2653 Container, packaging, and
boxboard; Display items, corrugated: made
from purchased materials
PA: Supplyone Holdings Company, Inc.
11 Campus Blvd Ste 150
Newtown Square PA 19073
484 582-5005

(G-10804)
THOMPSON SCREEN PRINTS INC
712 Palmer Rd (28138-8578)
P.O. Box 1325 (28138-1325)
PHONE..............................704 209-6161
Mark Harrison, *Pr*
Troy Thompson, *
EMP: 40 EST: 1977
SQ FT: 17,000
SALES (est): 3.64MM Privately Held
Web: www.thompsonscreenprints.com
SIC: 2759 Screen printing

(G-10805)
THORNEBURG HOSIERY MILLS INC
Also Called: Thor.lo
319 Link St (28138-7500)
PHONE..............................704 279-7247
Kevin Goodden, *Mgr*
EMP: 26
SALES (corp-wide): 20.05MM Privately
Held
Web: www.thmills.com
SIC: 2252 2251 Socks; Women's hosiery,
except socks
PA: Thorneburg Hosiery Mills, Inc.
2210 Newton Dr
Statesville NC 28677
704 872-6522

(G-10806)
UFP ROCKWELL LLC
Also Called: Ufp Rockwell
175 Old Mail Rd (28138-6823)
PHONE..............................704 279-0744
Jeff Richards, *Mgr*
EMP: 9 EST: 2016
SALES (est): 1.62MM
SALES (corp-wide): 6.65B Publicly Held
Web: www.prowoodlumber.com
SIC: 2491 Millwork, treated wood
HQ: Prowood, Llc
2801 E Beltline Ave Ne
Grand Rapids MI

Rocky Mount
Edgecombe County

(G-10807)
ACME UNITED CORPORATION
2280 Tanner Rd (27801-2731)
P.O. Box 458 (27830-0458)
PHONE..............................252 822-5051
Larry Buchkmann, *Brnch Mgr*
EMP: 29
SALES (corp-wide): 194.49MM Publicly
Held
Web: www.acmeunited.com
SIC: 3841 5112 Surgical and medical
instruments; Office supplies, nec
PA: Acme United Corporation
1 Waterview Dr Ste 200
Shelton CT 06484
203 254-6060

(G-10808)
BERRY GLOBAL INC
6941 Corporation Pkwy (27801)
PHONE..............................252 984-4104
Mark Powell, *Genl Mgr*
EMP: 65
Web: www.berryglobal.com
SIC: 3089 Plastics containers, except foam
HQ: Berry Global, Inc.
101 Oakley St
Evansville IN 47710

(G-10809)
DAUGHTRIDGE ENTERPRISES INC
Also Called: Tharrington Parts
1200 East St (27801-5484)
P.O. Box 1680 (27802-1680)
PHONE..............................252 977-7775
Tony Gay, *Brnch Mgr*
EMP: 5
SALES (corp-wide): 3.16MM Privately
Held
Web: www.citgo.com
SIC: 3523 Tobacco curers
PA: Daughtridge Enterprises Inc
1200 East St
Rocky Mount NC 27801
252 446-6137

(G-10810)
DOZIER INDUSTRIAL ELECTRIC INC
1151 Atlantic Ave (27801-2707)
PHONE..............................252 451-0020
Blake Dozier, *Pr*
Janie Houfe, *
EMP: 4 EST: 2005
SQ FT: 5,000
SALES (est): 619.61K Privately Held
SIC: 3625 Industrial electrical relays and
switches

(G-10811)
ENC CONVEYANCE LLC
Also Called: Enc Conveyance
4314 Bulluck School Rd (27801-9190)
PHONE..............................252 378-9990
EMP: 6 EST: 2019
SALES (est): 715.73K Privately Held
SIC: 3711 Truck and tractor truck assembly

(G-10812)
GUY N LANGLEY
2026 Leggett Rd (27801-2810)
PHONE..............................252 972-9875
Guy N Langley, *Prin*
EMP: 4 **EST:** 2001
SALES (est): 578.9K **Privately Held**
SIC: 3713 Dump truck bodies

(G-10813)
HOSPIRA INC
Highway 301 North (27801)
P.O. Box 2226 (27802-2226)
PHONE..............................252 977-5500
Marty Nealey, *Prin*
EMP: 211
SALES (corp-wide): 63.63B **Publicly Held**
Web: www.pfizer.com
SIC: 2834 Pharmaceutical preparations
HQ: Hospira, Inc.
275 N Field Dr
Lake Forest IL 60045
224 212-2000

(G-10814)
NUTRIEN AG SOLUTIONS INC
CPS
1160 Brake Rd (27801-8347)
PHONE..............................252 977-2025
Jeff Griffin, *Mgr*
EMP: 10
SALES (corp-wide): 29.06B **Privately Held**
Web: www.nutrienagsolutions.com
SIC: 2875 5191 2048 2874 Fertilizers,
mixing only; Pesticides; Prepared feeds, nec
; Phosphatic fertilizers
HQ: Nutrien Ag Solutions, Inc.
3005 Rocky Mountain Ave
Loveland CO 80538
970 685-3300

(G-10815)
TELEPATHIC GRAPHICS INC
1131 Atlantic Ave (27801-2707)
P.O. Box 91709 (27675-1709)
PHONE..............................919 342-4603
Bob Boyle, *CEO*
EMP: 12
Web: www.telepathicgraphics.com
SIC: 2752 Offset printing
PA: Telepathic Graphics, Inc.
6001 Chapel Hill Rd # 106
Raleigh NC 27607

(G-10816)
TO THE TOP TIRES AND SVC LLC
327 E Raleigh Blvd Ste 943 (27801-5773)
P.O. Box 943 (27802-0943)
PHONE..............................252 886-3286
Shabere Dorsett, *Managing Member*
EMP: 6 **EST:** 2018
SALES (est): 679.36K **Privately Held**
Web: tothetoptires.business.site
SIC: 7534 Tire retreading and repair shops

(G-10817)
TRANS-TECH ENERGY INC (PA)
Also Called: T 2 E
14527 Us Highway 64 Alt W (27801)
P.O. Box 8197 (27804)
PHONE..............................252 446-4357
Greg Ezzell, *Pr*
◆ **EMP:** 7 **EST:** 1998
SQ FT: 2,500
SALES (est): 97.36MM
SALES (corp-wide): 97.36MM **Privately Held**
Web: www.transtechenergy.com
SIC: 1389 Gas field services, nec

(G-10818)
TRANS-TECH ENERGY LLC
14527 Us Highway 64 Alt W (27801-9806)
PHONE..............................254 840-3355
EMP: 12 **EST:** 2012
SALES (est): 5.81MM **Privately Held**
Web: www.transtechenergy.com
SIC: 1311 Natural gas production

(G-10819)
TRI-COUNTY INDUSTRIES INC
1250 Atlantic Ave (27801-2710)
PHONE..............................252 977-3800
Brenda Cogdell, *Pr*
EMP: 140 **EST:** 1966
SQ FT: 43,500
SALES (est): 2.76MM **Privately Held**
Web: www.tricountyind.com
SIC: 8331 2448 Vocational rehabilitation
agency; Wood pallets and skids

(G-10820)
WILSON IRON WORKS INCORPORATED (PA)
Also Called: Eastern Hydraulic & Pwr Transm
600 S Washington St (27801-5669)
P.O. Box 552 (27802-0552)
PHONE..............................252 291-4465
C Ray Pittman, *CEO*
C Sarvis Bass, *
Kenneth L Dollar, *
Reba Welfare, *
Elaine Goff, *
EMP: 69 **EST:** 1933
SQ FT: 40,500
SALES (est): 25.3MM **Privately Held**
Web: www.wilsonironworks.com
SIC: 3599 Machine shop, jobbing and repair

Rocky Mount
Nash County

(G-10821)
ACS ADVNCED CLOR SOLUTIONS INC
120 S Business Ct (27804-6543)
PHONE..............................252 442-0098
Franco Furlin, *Owner*
▲ **EMP:** 9 **EST:** 2005
SALES (est): 714.72K **Privately Held**
SIC: 3429 Keys, locks, and related hardware

(G-10822)
AMERICAN PRINTERS INC
120 Sorsbys Aly (27804-5723)
PHONE..............................252 977-7468
John S Taylor, *Pr*
Everett K Nightingale, *Sec*
EMP: 6 **EST:** 2000
SQ FT: 10,000
SALES (est): 481.98K **Privately Held**
SIC: 2752 Offset printing

(G-10823)
BABINGTON TECHNOLOGY INC (PA)
159 Fabrication Way (27804-9356)
PHONE..............................252 984-0349
Andrew Babington, *CEO*
Robert Babington, *Prin*
Andrew Babington, *Prin*
EMP: 6 **EST:** 1965
SALES (est): 8.63MM
SALES (corp-wide): 8.63MM **Privately Held**
Web: www.babingtontechnology.com
SIC: 5084 3556 Food product manufacturing
machinery; Food products machinery

(G-10824)
BEFCO INC
1781 S Wesleyan Blvd (27803-5629)
P.O. Box 6036 (27802-6036)
PHONE..............................252 977-9920
Pio Figna, *Pr*
Francesco Figna, *
Rina Figna, *
Merle Hendricks, *
Bobby Davis, *
◆ **EMP:** 45 **EST:** 1980
SQ FT: 80,000
SALES (est): 9.75MM
SALES (corp-wide): 7.84MM **Privately Held**
Web: www.befco.com
SIC: 3523 3531 3524 Grounds mowing
equipment; Posthole diggers, powered;
Lawn and garden equipment
PA: Rotomec Spa
Via Molino Di Sopra 56
Nogara VR 37054
044 251-0400

(G-10825)
BOWDEN ELECTRIC MOTOR SVC INC
1681 S Wesleyan Blvd (27803-5627)
P.O. Box 1874 (27802-1874)
PHONE..............................252 446-4203
David E Bowden, *Pr*
Richard E Bowden, *VP*
Charlotte Briley, *Sec*
EMP: 6 **EST:** 1965
SQ FT: 12,500
SALES (est): 445.65K **Privately Held**
SIC: 7694 5063 Electric motor repair;
Motors, electric

(G-10826)
C D J & P INC
Also Called: PIP Printing
1911 N Wesleyan Blvd (27804-6634)
PHONE..............................252 446-3611
Laura Friedrich, *Pr*
Peter Friedrich, *Sec*
EMP: 4 **EST:** 1990
SQ FT: 1,600
SALES (est): 384.94K **Privately Held**
Web: www.pip.com
SIC: 2752 Offset printing

(G-10827)
CENTRAL EAST SERVICES INC
4352 N Old Carriage Rd (27804-8261)
PHONE..............................252 883-9629
Kemp Pridgen, *CEO*
EMP: 9 **EST:** 2012
SALES (est): 613.63K **Privately Held**
SIC: 3561 Pumps and pumping equipment

(G-10828)
CINTERS INC
501 Woods Walk Ln (27804-7473)
PHONE..............................336 267-3051
Jacob Adelowo, *Owner*
Jacob Adelowo, *Pr*
Emmanuel Adelowo, *Sec*
Christy Adelowo, *Treas*
Howard Williams, *VP*
EMP: 14 **EST:** 2002
SQ FT: 6,000
SALES (est): 343.59K **Privately Held**
SIC: 3061 Mechanical rubber goods

(G-10829)
COLONY TIRE CORPORATION
1463 N Wesleyan Blvd (27804-1843)
PHONE..............................252 973-0004
Lee Hadison, *Brnch Mgr*
EMP: 8

SALES (corp-wide): 138.19MM **Privately Held**
Web: locations.mrtire.com
SIC: 5531 7534 Automotive tires; Tire
retreading and repair shops
PA: Colony Tire Corporation
1429 N Broad St
Edenton NC 27932
252 482-5521

(G-10830)
DAVIS DAVIS MCH & WLDG CO INC
4956 Community Dr (27804-3065)
P.O. Box 8558 (27804-1558)
PHONE..............................252 443-2652
Michael Davis, *Pr*
Phil Davis, *VP*
Robert K Davis, *Treas*
Tim Davis, *Sec*
John S Davis Junior, *Stockholder*
EMP: 14 **EST:** 1972
SQ FT: 6,000
SALES (est): 2.16MM **Privately Held**
SIC: 3599 7692 Machine shop, jobbing and
repair; Welding repair

(G-10831)
DRAKA ELEVATOR PRODUCTS INC (DH)
2151 N Church St (27804-2026)
PHONE..............................252 446-8113
Richard Parvesse, *Pr*
◆ **EMP:** 160 **EST:** 1999
SQ FT: 158,000
SALES (est): 61.98MM **Privately Held**
Web: www.prysmian.com
SIC: 3315 3357 Cable, steel: insulated or
armored; Nonferrous wiredrawing and
insulating
HQ: Prysmian Cables And Systems Usa,
Llc
4 Tesseneer Dr
Highland Heights KY 41076
859 572-8000

(G-10832)
DRILL & FILL MFG LLC
5484 S Old Carriage Rd (27803-8372)
PHONE..............................252 937-4555
EMP: 4 **EST:** 2006
SQ FT: 5,000
SALES (est): 990.18K **Privately Held**
Web: www.drillandfillmfg.com
SIC: 3541 Drilling and boring machines

(G-10833)
DUNCAN-PARNELL INC
2741 N Wesleyan Blvd (27804-8664)
P.O. Box 7517 (27804-0517)
PHONE..............................252 977-7832
James May, *Mgr*
EMP: 7
SALES (corp-wide): 34.27MM **Privately Held**
Web: www.duncan-parnell.com
SIC: 5049 5999 2752 Scientific and
engineering equipment and supplies;
Drafting equipment and supplies; Offset
printing
PA: Duncan-Parnell, Inc.
900 S Mcdowell St
Charlotte NC 28204
704 372-7766

(G-10834)
EAST INDUSTRIES INC
1114 Instrument Dr (27804-9002)
P.O. Box 7724 (27804-0724)
PHONE..............................252 442-9662
David W Wilson, *Pr*
EMP: 55 **EST:** 1975

G E O G R A P H I C

SQ FT: 63,000
SALES (est): 6.79MM **Privately Held**
Web: www.eastindustries.com
SIC: 5031 2448 Pallets, wood; Pallets, wood

(G-10835)
ELECTRIC MTR SP WAKE FREST INC
Also Called: Electric Motor Shop
2421 W Raleigh Blvd (27803-2757)
PHONE.............................252 446-4173
Kevin Lee, *Brnch Mgr*
EMP: 33
SALES (corp-wide): 15.64MM **Privately
Held**
Web: www.electricmotorshopnc.com
SIC: 7694 Electric motor repair
PA: Electric Motor Shop Of Wake Forest,
　Inc.
　1225 N White St
　Wake Forest NC 27587
　919 556-3229

(G-10836)
ENGINE SYSTEMS INC (HQ)
175 Freight Rd (27804-8002)
PHONE.............................252 977-2720
Dorman L Strahan, *Pr*
J H Pyne, *Ex VP*
Norman Nolen, *VP*
◆ EMP: 80 EST: 1984
SALES (est): 18.54MM
SALES (corp-wide): 3.27B **Publicly Held**
Web: www.kirbycorp.com
SIC: 5084 3519 Engines and parts, diesel;
　Diesel engine rebuilding
PA: Kirby Corporation
　55 Waugh Dr Ste 1000
　Houston TX 77007
　713 435-1000

(G-10837)
ESSAY OPERATIONS INC (PA)
Also Called: Essay Polyfab
3701 Winchester Rd (27804-3340)
PHONE.............................252 443-6010
FAX: 252 443-6529
EMP: 4
SALES (est): 511.73K
SALES (corp-wide): 511.73K **Privately
Held**
SIC: 3061 2821 3949 Appliance rubber
　goods (mechanical); Plastics materials and
　resins; Sporting and athletic goods, nec

(G-10838)
EVELYN T BURNEY
Also Called: Plott Bakery Products
2551 N Church St (27804-2040)
PHONE.............................336 473-9794
Evelyn Burney, *Owner*
EMP: 5 EST: 1983
SALES (est): 177.04K **Privately Held**
SIC: 5142 2052 2051 2521 Bakery products,
　frozen; Bakery products, dry; Bread, cake,
　and related products; Tables, office: wood

(G-10839)
FREEDOM INDUSTRIES INC
4000 E Old Spring Hope Rd (27804-7727)
P.O. Box 7099 (27804-0099)
PHONE.............................252 984-0007
Derrick Vick, *CEO*
Douglas Ezzell, *
EMP: 150 EST: 2003
SQ FT: 40,000
SALES (est): 27.12MM **Privately Held**
Web: www.freedomind.us
SIC: 3449 1731 1711 Bars, concrete
　reinforcing: fabricated steel; Electrical work;
　Mechanical contractor

(G-10840)
HINSON INDUSTRIES INC
Also Called: Allegra Print & Imaging
109 Zebulon Ct (27804-2420)
P.O. Box 8003 (27804-1003)
PHONE.............................252 937-7171
Henry Hinson, *Pr*
Mark Hinson, *VP*
Todd Hinson, *VP*
Lucy Hinson, *Sec*
EMP: 9 EST: 1956
SQ FT: 4,800
SALES (est): 1.24MM **Privately Held**
Web: www.allegramarketingprint.com
SIC: 2752 6411 Offset printing; Insurance
　agents, brokers, and service

(G-10841)
HONEYWELL INTERNATIONAL INC
Honeywell
3475 N Wesleyan Blvd (27804-8677)
PHONE.............................252 977-2100
Juergen Heller, *Mgr*
EMP: 48
SALES (corp-wide): 38.5B **Publicly Held**
Web: www.honeywell.com
SIC: 3812 3728 Search and navigation
　equipment; Aircraft parts and equipment,
　nec
PA: Honeywell International Inc.
　855 S Mint St
　Charlotte NC 28202
　704 627-6200

(G-10842)
HOSPIRA INC
4285 N Wesleyan Blvd (27804-8612)
PHONE.............................252 977-5111
Rick Isaza, *Pr*
EMP: 762
SALES (corp-wide): 63.63B **Publicly Held**
Web: www.pfizer.com
SIC: 2834 Pharmaceutical preparations
HQ: Hospira, Inc.
　275 N Field Dr
　Lake Forest IL 60045
　224 212-2000

(G-10843)
ILCO UNICAN HOLDING CORP
400 Jeffreys Rd (27804-6624)
P.O. Box 2627 (27802-2627)
PHONE.............................252 446-3321
Aaron M Fish, *Ch Bd*
▲ EMP: 9 EST: 1988
SALES (est): 3.28MM **Privately Held**
Web: www.ilco.us
SIC: 3429 Keys, locks, and related hardware
HQ: Dormakaba Schweiz Ag
　Kempten
　Wetzikon ZH 8623

(G-10844)
KABA ILCO CORP (HQ)
400 Jeffreys Rd (27804)
P.O. Box 2627 (27802)
PHONE.............................252 446-3321
Frank Belflower, *Pr*
Tom Boswell, *
◆ EMP: 700 EST: 1981
SQ FT: 323,000
SALES (est): 71.52MM **Privately Held**
Web: www.ilco.us
SIC: 3429 Keys, locks, and related hardware
PA: Dormakaba Holding Ag
　Hofwisenstrasse 24
　Rumlang ZH 8153

(G-10845)
KAMLAR CORPORATION (PA)
444 Kamlar Rd (27804-8175)
PHONE.............................252 443-2576
Richard C Seale, *Pr*
Albert Oettinger Junior, *VP*
EMP: 20 EST: 1966
SQ FT: 6,500
SALES (est): 4.05MM
SALES (corp-wide): 4.05MM **Privately
Held**
Web: www.kamlar.com
SIC: 2499 2873 2421 Mulch, wood and bark;
　Nitrogenous fertilizers; Sawmills and
　planing mills, general

(G-10846)
KBK CSTOM DSGNS ESSNTIAL OILS
1384 Northridge Dr (27804-8324)
PHONE.............................252 886-3315
Malinda Rackley, *Mgr*
EMP: 4 EST: 2021
SALES (est): 100K **Privately Held**
SIC: 1389 Construction, repair, and
　dismantling services

(G-10847)
KOI POND BREWING COMPANY LLC
1107 Falls Rd (27804-4407)
P.O. Box 4307 (27803-0307)
PHONE.............................252 231-1660
EMP: 7 EST: 2014
SQ FT: 1,823
SALES (est): 233.42K **Privately Held**
Web: www.koipondbrewingcompany.com
SIC: 5813 2082 5181 5921 Bars and lounges
　; Beer (alcoholic beverage); Beer and ale;
　Beer (packaged)

(G-10848)
LARRY S CABINET SHOP INC
4217 S Church St (27803-5710)
PHONE.............................252 442-4330
Larry Gupton, *Pr*
EMP: 5 EST: 1976
SQ FT: 2,000
SALES (est): 190.11K **Privately Held**
SIC: 2434 Wood kitchen cabinets

(G-10849)
LOG CABIN HOMES LTD (PA)
Also Called: Cabin Craft American Homes
513 Keen St # 515 (27804-4824)
P.O. Box 1457 (27802-1457)
PHONE.............................252 454-1500
Thomas Vesce, *Pr*
◆ EMP: 60 EST: 1987
SALES (est): 7.91MM
SALES (corp-wide): 7.91MM **Privately
Held**
Web: www.logcabinhomes.com
SIC: 2452 5031 Log cabins, prefabricated,
　wood; Lumber: rough, dressed, and finished

(G-10850)
MARTIN MANUFACTURING CO LLC
Also Called: Martin Innovations
2585 Eastern Ave (27804-8179)
PHONE.............................919 741-5439
EMP: 9 EST: 2004
SALES (est): 585.81K **Privately Held**
Web: www.martininnovations.com
SIC: 3841 Surgical and medical instruments

(G-10851)
MATTRESS FIRM
794 Sutters Creek Blvd (27804-8429)
PHONE.............................252 443-1259
EMP: 5 EST: 2016
SALES (est): 84.07K **Privately Held**

Web: www.mattressfirm.com
SIC: 5712 5021 2515 Mattresses; Mattresses
　; Mattresses and bedsprings

(G-10852)
MIJO ENTERPRISES INC
Also Called: Natures Own Gallery
2220 N Wesleyan Blvd (27804-8636)
PHONE.............................252 442-6806
Tom Minges, *Pr*
Morrie Minges, *Sec*
EMP: 8 EST: 1982
SQ FT: 12,000
SALES (est): 204.83K **Privately Held**
Web: www.mbuddies.com
SIC: 7389 2542 Interior designer; Counters
　or counter display cases, except wood

(G-10853)
MILWAUKEE INSTRUMENTS INC
2950 Business Park Dr (27804-2818)
PHONE.............................252 443-3630
Bryan Moore, *Prin*
Bryan Moore, *Genl Mgr*
EMP: 5 EST: 1998
SALES (est): 1.9MM **Privately Held**
Web: www.milwaukeeinstruments.co.nz
SIC: 3829 Measuring and controlling
　devices, nec

(G-10854)
NEW STANDARD CORPORATION
3883 S Church St (27803-5702)
PHONE.............................252 446-5481
C Meckley, *Pr*
EMP: 173
SALES (corp-wide): 82.32MM **Privately
Held**
Web: www.newstandard.com
SIC: 3469 Stamping metal for the trade
PA: New Standard Corporation
　74 Commerce Way
　York PA 17406
　717 757-9450

(G-10855)
NORTH STATE MILLWORK
2950 Raleigh Rd (27803-4626)
PHONE.............................252 442-9090
EMP: 5 EST: 2020
SALES (est): 215.79K **Privately Held**
SIC: 2431 Millwork

(G-10856)
O D EYECARECENTER P A
Also Called: Opticare
3044 Sunset Ave (27804-3647)
PHONE.............................252 443-7011
Rick Adams, *Mgr*
EMP: 6
SALES (corp-wide): 19.86MM **Privately
Held**
Web: www.eyecarecenter.com
SIC: 8042 5995 3851 Offices and clinics of
　optometrists; Optical goods stores;
　Ophthalmic goods
PA: O D Eyecarecenter P A
　2325 Sunset Ave
　Rocky Mount NC

(G-10857)
O R PRDGEN SONS SPTIC TANK I
4824 S Halifax Rd (27803-5897)
PHONE.............................252 442-3338
Dale M Pridgen, *Pr*
Cindy Pridgen, *VP*
EMP: 5 EST: 1973
SALES (est): 559.2K **Privately Held**
SIC: 3272 1711 Septic tanks, concrete;
　Septic system construction

(G-10858)
PEN-CELL PLASTICS INC
546 English Rd (27804-9517)
PHONE..................................252 467-2210
Robert R Schlegel, *Pr*
◆ EMP: 50 EST: 2010
SQ FT: 90,000
SALES (est): 2.25MM
SALES (corp-wide): 5.63B **Publicly Held**
Web: www.hubbell.com
SIC: 3089 Injection molding of plastics
PA: Hubbell Incorporated
40 Waterview Dr
Shelton CT 06484
800 626-0005

(G-10859)
PEPSI BOTTLING VENTURES LLC
Also Called: Pepsi-Cola
620 Health Dr (27804-9445)
PHONE..................................252 451-1811
Evelyn Cowan, *Off Mgr*
EMP: 46
Web: www.pepsibottlingventures.com
SIC: 2086 5149 Carbonated soft drinks,
bottled and canned; Groceries and related
products, nec
HQ: Pepsi Bottling Ventures Llc
4141 Parklake Ave
Raleigh NC 27612
919 865-2300

(G-10860)
PEPSI-COLA METRO BTLG CO INC
Also Called: Pepsi-Cola
620 Health Dr (27804-9445)
PHONE..................................252 446-7181
Alan Sleischer, *Mgr*
EMP: 6
SALES (corp-wide): 91.47B **Publicly Held**
Web: www.pepsico.com
SIC: 2086 Soft drinks: packaged in cans,
bottles, etc.
HQ: Pepsi-Cola Metropolitan Bottling
Company, Inc.
700 Anderson Hill Rd
Purchase NY 10577
914 767-6000

(G-10861)
PFIZER INC
4285 N Wesleyan Blvd (27804-8612)
PHONE..................................252 977-5111
EMP: 56
SALES (corp-wide): 63.63B **Publicly Held**
Web: www.pfizercentreone.com
SIC: 2834 Pharmaceutical preparations
PA: Pfizer Inc.
66 Hudson Blvd E
New York NY 10001
212 733-2323

(G-10862)
PRINT SHOPPE OF ROCKY MT INC
140 S Business Ct (27804-6543)
PHONE..................................252 442-9912
Andy Dickerson, *Pr*
Randall Pridgen, *Sec*
EMP: 4 EST: 1999
SQ FT: 4,000
SALES (est): 435.6K **Privately Held**
Web:
www.printshoppeofrockymount.com
SIC: 2752 Offset printing

(G-10863)
QCS ACQUISITION CORPORATION
Also Called: Quality Conveyor Solutions
130 N Business Ct (27804-6546)
PHONE..................................252 446-5000
EMP: 6

SALES (corp-wide): 4.71B **Privately Held**
Web:
www.qualityconveyorsolutions.com
SIC: 3535 Belt conveyor systems, general
industrial use
HQ: Qcs Acquisition Corporation
971 B Russell Dr
Salem VA 24153
540 427-7705

(G-10864)
R/W CONNECTION INC
Also Called: Virginia Carolina Belting
136 S Business Ct (27804-6543)
PHONE..................................252 446-0114
Al Blonberg, *Brnch Mgr*
EMP: 4
SALES (corp-wide): 4.71B **Privately Held**
Web: www.rwconnection.com
SIC: 2399 Belting and belt products
HQ: R/W Connection, Inc.
936 Links Ave
Landisville PA 17538

(G-10865)
RBI MANUFACTURING INC
Also Called: Rbi Precision
4642 S Us Highway 301 (27803-8641)
P.O. Box 250 (27878-0250)
PHONE..................................252 977-6704
Edward Bunch Junior, *Pr*
EMP: 12 EST: 1994
SQ FT: 12,000
SALES (est): 11.34MM **Privately Held**
Web: www.rbimfg.com
SIC: 3599 Machine shop, jobbing and repair

(G-10866)
ROCKY MOUNT AWNING & TENT CO
Also Called: Carolina Awning and Tent
602 N Church St (27804-4910)
PHONE..................................252 442-0184
TOLL FREE: 800
Joseph R Daniel Iii, *Pr*
Bobby Pridgen, *Sec*
EMP: 6 EST: 1925
SQ FT: 10,000
SALES (est): 534.63K **Privately Held**
Web: www.rockymountawning.com
SIC: 2394 3444 Awnings, fabric: made from
purchased materials; Sheet metalwork

(G-10867)
ROCKY MOUNT CORD COMPANY
Also Called: Romoco
381 N Grace St (27804-5317)
P.O. Box 4304 (27803-0304)
PHONE..................................252 977-9130
Louis Hinson, *Pr*
Joseph E Bunn, *
Thomas B Battle, *
Andrew K Barker, *
Dawn Fowler, *
▲ EMP: 75 EST: 1946
SQ FT: 110,000
SALES (est): 4.72MM **Privately Held**
Web: www.rmcord.com
SIC: 2298 Cord, braided

(G-10868)
ROCKY MOUNT ELECTRIC MOTOR LLC
3870 S Church St (27803-5701)
P.O. Box 1063 (27802-1063)
PHONE..................................252 446-1510
Timmy Thorne, *VP*
Deborah Vick, *Off Mgr*
EMP: 8 EST: 1972
SQ FT: 3,300
SALES (est): 4.15MM **Privately Held**
Web: www.rmemnc.com

SIC: 5063 7694 Motors, electric; Electric
motor repair

(G-10869)
STEEL TECHNOLOGY INC (PA)
2620 Business Park Dr (27804-8459)
P.O. Box 7217 (27804-0217)
PHONE..................................252 937-7122
William H Pruden Iii, *Pr*
Lillian M Pruden, *Sec*
EMP: 8 EST: 1999
SALES (est): 4.13MM
SALES (corp-wide): 4.13MM **Privately Held**
Web: www.steeltechnc.com
SIC: 3441 Fabricated structural metal

(G-10870)
STONEWORX INC
7015 Stanley Park Dr (27804-3046)
P.O. Box 109 (15376-0109)
PHONE..................................252 937-8080
Elizabeth S Hunt, *Pr*
Frank Hunt, *VP*
EMP: 7 EST: 2003
SQ FT: 6,000
SALES (est): 214.11K **Privately Held**
SIC: 3281 Marble, building: cut and shaped

(G-10871)
SUN-DROP BTLG ROCKY MT NC INC
Also Called: Sun Drop Bottling
2406 W Raleigh Blvd (27803-2751)
PHONE..................................252 977-4586
Michael K Berry, *Sec*
John D Berry, *Pr*
Stephen L Berry, *VP*
EMP: 9 EST: 1955
SQ FT: 20,000
SALES (est): 907.41K **Privately Held**
SIC: 2086 Soft drinks: packaged in cans,
bottles, etc.

(G-10872)
TORPEDO SPECIALTY WIRE INC
1115 Instrument Dr (27804-9003)
P.O. Box 21 (27868-0021)
PHONE..................................252 977-3900
▲ EMP: 100
Web: www.summitplating.com
SIC: 3315 3351 3356 Wire and fabricated
wire products; Copper rolling and drawing;
Nickel and nickel alloy: rolling, drawing, or
extruding

(G-10873)
TRIPLE R MBL CIGR LOUNGE LLC
163 S Winstead Ave Ste A (27804-1000)
PHONE..................................252 281-7738
EMP: 6
SALES (est): 490.11K **Privately Held**
SIC: 3711 Mobile lounges (motor vehicle),
assembly of

(G-10874)
WATERS BROTHERS CONTRS INC
511 Instrument Dr (27804-8614)
PHONE..................................252 446-7141
Trudy Waters, *Pr*
Lou Carson, *Treasurer Finance*
EMP: 11 EST: 1921
SQ FT: 22,500
SALES (est): 1.3MM **Privately Held**
Web: www.watersbros.com
SIC: 3441 Fabricated structural metal

(G-10875)
WILDWOOD LAMPS & ACCENTS INC (PA)
516 Paul St (27803-3545)

P.O. Box 672 (27802-0672)
PHONE..................................252 446-3266
William H Kincheloe, *Pr*
Russ Barnes, *
John B Kincheloe, *
◆ EMP: 40 EST: 1968
SQ FT: 150,000
SALES (est): 9.06MM **Privately Held**
Web: www.wildwoodhome.com
SIC: 3645 Table lamps

(G-10876)
WOOD MACHINE SERVICE INC
2 Great State Ln (27803-8747)
PHONE..................................252 446-2142
William T Wood, *Pr*
EMP: 10 EST: 1983
SALES (est): 1.7MM **Privately Held**
Web: www.woodsmachine.com
SIC: 3599 Machine shop, jobbing and repair

Rocky Point
Pender County

(G-10877)
CARLTON ENTERPRIZES LLC
Also Called: General Contracting
195 Rocky Point Trng Sch Rd
(28457-7321)
P.O. Box 986 (28457-0986)
PHONE..................................919 534-5424
Terrell Carlton, *Admn*
EMP: 8 EST: 2012
SALES (est): 289.71K **Privately Held**
SIC: 1611 0782 1389 7389 General
contractor, highway and street construction;
Landscape contractors; Construction,
repair, and dismantling services; Business
services, nec

(G-10878)
CINCINNATI THERMAL SPRAY INC
Also Called: CTS
11766 Nc Hwy 210 (28457-8560)
PHONE..................................910 675-2909
Will Reed, *Brnch Mgr*
EMP: 50
Web: www.cts-inc.net
SIC: 3479 Coating of metals and formed
products
PA: Cincinnati Thermal Spray, Inc.
10904 Deerfield Rd
Cincinnati OH 45242

(G-10879)
FUSION WELDING
37 Brandon Ln (28457-7673)
PHONE..................................508 320-3525
EMP: 5 EST: 2016
SALES (est): 55.68K **Privately Held**
SIC: 7692 Welding repair

(G-10880)
H & P WOOD TURNINGS INC
9375 Us Hwy 117 S (28457-8028)
P.O. Box 505 (28457-0505)
PHONE..................................910 675-2784
Neal Cavanaugh, *Pr*
Richard Cavanaugh, *VP*
EMP: 7 EST: 1965
SQ FT: 13,000
SALES (est): 724.88K **Privately Held**
Web: www.hpwoodturnings.com
SIC: 2499 Decorative wood and woodwork

(G-10881)
HEATH AND SONS MGT SVCS LLC
Also Called: Heath and Sons Management
514 Complex Rd (28457-7724)

P.O. Box 11280 (28404-1280)
PHONE..............................910 679-6142
Micheal Heath, *Managing Member*
EMP: 12 **EST:** 2018
SALES (est): 1.64MM **Privately Held**
Web: www.handsmgmt.com
SIC: 1771 1629 1711 1389 Concrete work;
Drainage system construction; Plumbing
contractors; Construction, repair, and
dismantling services

(G-10882)
SEA MARK BOATS INC
Also Called: Entropy
13991 Nc Hwy 210 (28457-8523)
PHONE..............................910 675-1877
J P Klingenberger, *Pr*
EMP: 6 **EST:** 1969
SALES (est): 399.02K **Privately Held**
Web: www.seamarkboats.com
SIC: 3732 Boatbuilding and repairing

(G-10883)
SOUTHERN STYLE LOGGING LLC
3595 Little Kelly Rd (28457-8659)
PHONE..............................910 259-9897
EMP: 8 **EST:** 2014
SALES (est): 474.59K **Privately Held**
SIC: 2411 Logging

(G-10884)
STROUDCRAFT MARINE LLC
13991 Nc Hwy 210 (28457-8523)
PHONE..............................910 623-4055
EMP: 10
SALES (est): 340.14K **Privately Held**
Web: www.stroudcraft.com
SIC: 3732 Boatbuilding and repairing

(G-10885)
SUPERIOR MACHINE SHOP INC
354 Sawdust Rd (28457-9379)
P.O. Box 308 (28457-0308)
PHONE..............................910 675-1336
Ronald D Graves, *Pr*
John O Keel Iii, *VP*
EMP: 5 **EST:** 1969
SQ FT: 9,000
SALES (est): 485.52K **Privately Held**
SIC: 3599 Machine shop, jobbing and repair

(G-10886)
TANK FAB INC
8787 Us Hwy 117 S (28457-6001)
P.O. Box 680 (28457-0680)
PHONE..............................910 675-8999
Thomas Lippincott, *Pr*
Jeff Lippincott, *Sec*
EMP: 10 **EST:** 1995
SQ FT: 30,000
SALES (est): 1.96MM **Privately Held**
Web: www.tankfab.com
SIC: 3441 3443 Fabricated structural metal;
Tanks, standard or custom fabricated: metal
plate

(G-10887)
WOODTREATERS INC
224 Sawdust Rd (28457)
P.O. Box 557 (28457-0557)
PHONE..............................910 675-0038
Ronnie Graves, *Pr*
John Keel, *Sec*
EMP: 7 **EST:** 1976
SQ FT: 4,000
SALES (est): 792.61K **Privately Held**
SIC: 2491 Wood preserving

Rodanthe
Dare County

(G-10888)
RIDE BEST LLC
Also Called: Best Kiteboarding
24267 Hwy 12 (27968)
P.O. Box 571 (11561-0571)
PHONE..............................252 489-2959
◆ **EMP:** 6 **EST:** 2003
SQ FT: 5,000
SALES (est): 2.1MM **Privately Held**
SIC: 3721 Hang gliders
PA: Pure Action Sports Worldwide, Inc.
2016 Autumn Dr Nw
Alexandria MN 56308

Rolesville
Wake County

(G-10889)
POLYONE DISTRIBUTION
118 Brandi Dr (27571-9432)
PHONE..............................919 413-4547
Abel Salgado, *Prin*
EMP: 4 **EST:** 2018
SALES (est): 74.42K **Privately Held**
SIC: 2821 Thermoplastic materials

(G-10890)
TEAM X-TREME LLC
600 S Main St Ste C (27571-9309)
PHONE..............................919 562-8100
EMP: 8 **EST:** 1983
SQ FT: 4,800
SALES (est): 234.85K **Privately Held**
SIC: 7538 5531 7534 General automotive
repair shops; Automotive tires; Tire
retreading and repair shops

(G-10891)
**WAKE MONUMENT COMPANY INC
(PA)**
213 N Main St (27571-9646)
P.O. Box 130 (27571-0130)
PHONE..............................919 556-3422
Carolyn Bartholomew, *Pr*
Ron Bartholomew, *VP*
Cathy Batts, *Sec*
EMP: 9 **EST:** 1934
SALES: 1.1MM
SALES (corp-wide): 1.1MM **Privately Held**
Web: www.wakemonument.com
SIC: 3281 5999 Monuments, cut stone (not
finishing or lettering only); Monuments,
finished to custom order

(G-10892)
WIGGINS NORTH STATE CO INC (PA)
204 S Main St (27571-8702)
P.O. Box 70 (27571-0070)
PHONE..............................919 556-3231
Bertie Wiggins, *Pr*
Alvin T Wiggins Junior, *VP*
James W Wiggins, *Treas*
EMP: 5 **EST:** 1962
SALES (est): 597.8K
SALES (corp-wide): 597.8K **Privately Held**
SIC: 3281 7261 Tombstones, cut stone (not
finishing or lettering only); Funeral service
and crematories

Ronda
Wilkes County

(G-10893)
**CAROLINA PRCSION FBERS SPV
LLC**
145 Factory St (28670-9236)
PHONE..............................336 527-4140
Alfred Vincelli, *Pr*
EMP: 24 **EST:** 2017
SALES (est): 8.22MM **Privately Held**
Web: www.carolinafibers.com
SIC: 2823 5039 Cellulosic manmade fibers;
Soil erosion control fabrics

(G-10894)
CAROLINA PRECISION FIBERS INC
145 Factory St (28670-9236)
P.O. Box 624 (28621-0624)
PHONE..............................336 527-4140
EMP: 30
Web: www.carolinafibers.com
SIC: 2679 Paper products, converted, nec

(G-10895)
**NORTHWEST MACHINE AND
SUPPLY**
204 3rd St (28670-9324)
P.O. Box 157 (28670-0157)
PHONE..............................336 526-2029
Michael Johnson, *Pr*
Peggy Johnson, *VP*
EMP: 10 **EST:** 1985
SQ FT: 6,000
SALES (est): 345.67K **Privately Held**
Web: www.thenorthwestcompany.com
SIC: 3599 Machine shop, jobbing and repair

(G-10896)
PICCIONE VINYARDS
2364 Cedar Forest Rd (28670-9107)
PHONE..............................312 342-0181
William Piccione, *Prin*
EMP: 7 **EST:** 2017
SALES (est): 94.11K **Privately Held**
Web: www.piccionevineyards.com
SIC: 2084 Wines

(G-10897)
PRECISION FABRICATORS INC (PA)
Hwy 268 (28670)
P.O. Box 69 (28670-0069)
PHONE..............................336 835-4763
James K Willis, *Pr*
Brenda P Willis, *Sec*
EMP: 6 **EST:** 1980
SQ FT: 1,700
SALES (est): 500K
SALES (corp-wide): 500K **Privately Held**
Web: www.precision-fab.com
SIC: 3599 1796 7692 3444 Custom
machinery; Millwright; Welding repair;
Sheet metalwork

(G-10898)
**RAFFALDINI VNEYARDS WINERY
LLC**
450 Groce Rd (28670-9134)
PHONE..............................336 835-9463
Jerome Raffaldini, *Managing Member*
▲ **EMP:** 15 **EST:** 2001
SALES (est): 957.16K **Privately Held**
Web: www.raffaldini.com
SIC: 2084 Wines

Roper
Washington County

(G-10899)
PC SATELLITE SOLUTIONS
325 Jones White Rd (27970-9598)
PHONE..............................252 217-7237
Keith Patrick, *Pt*
EMP: 8 **EST:** 2009
SALES (est): 416.37K **Privately Held**
SIC: 3651 Household audio and video
equipment

(G-10900)
TIM CON WOOD PRODUCTS INC
1438 Cross Rd (27970-9406)
P.O. Box 600 (27846-0600)
PHONE..............................252 793-4819
Billy Corey, *Pr*
Sharon Corey, *Sec*
EMP: 15 **EST:** 1985
SALES (est): 1.88MM **Privately Held**
SIC: 2411 Logging camps and contractors

(G-10901)
TYLERIAS CLOSET LLC
1250 Jones White Rd (27970-9683)
PHONE..............................252 325-6639
Sharon Meniefield, *Managing Member*
EMP: 4 **EST:** 2021
SALES (est): 119.68K **Privately Held**
SIC: 3911 3161 Jewelry apparel; Clothing
and apparel carrying cases

Rose Hill
Duplin County

(G-10902)
**AMERICAN MATERIALS COMPANY
LLC**
9763 Taylors Bridge Hwy (28458-8661)
PHONE..............................910 532-6659
EMP: 50
Web: www.americanmaterialsco.com
SIC: 3599 Machine shop, jobbing and repair
HQ: American Materials Company, Llc
1410 Commwl Dr Ste 201
Wilmington NC 28403
910 799-1411

(G-10903)
COOPER TECHNICAL SERVICES INC
4527 S Us Highway 117 (28458-8910)
P.O. Box 398 (28458-0398)
PHONE..............................910 285-2925
John C Cooper Iii, *Pr*
Deborah Cooper, *Sec*
EMP: 8 **EST:** 1989
SQ FT: 4,500
SALES (est): 957.12K **Privately Held**
Web: www.coopertechnicalservices.com
SIC: 3821 Laboratory equipment: fume
hoods, distillation racks, etc.

(G-10904)
DARLING INGREDIENTS INC
469 Yellowcut Rd (28458)
P.O. Box 1026 (28458-1026)
PHONE..............................910 289-2083
Stan Rutherford, *Brnch Mgr*
EMP: 5
SQ FT: 10,000
SALES (corp-wide): 6.79B **Publicly Held**
Web: www.darpro-solutions.com
SIC: 2077 Animal and marine fats and oils
PA: Darling Ingredients Inc.
5601 N Macarthur Blvd

Irving TX 75038
972 717-0300

(G-10905)
DUPLIN WINE CELLARS INC (PA)
Also Called: Cape Fear Vineyards
505 N Sycamore St (28458-8423)
P.O. Box 756 (28458-0756)
PHONE....................910 289-3888
David G Fussell Junior, *Pr*
Jonathan Fussell, *
Jeff Craft, *
EMP: 30 **EST:** 1972
SQ FT: 20,000
SALES (est): 14.84MM
SALES (corp-wide): 14.84MM **Privately
Held**
Web: www.duplinwinery.com
SIC: 2084 Wines

(G-10906)
**HOUSE OF RAEFORD FARMS INC
(HQ)**
3333 S Us 117 Hwy (28458)
P.O. Box 3628 (29070)
PHONE....................912 222-4090
Robert Johnson, *CEO*
Donald Taber, *
Ken Qualls, *
Marvin Johnson, *
◆ **EMP:** 1500 **EST:** 1925
SQ FT: 400,000
SALES (est): 648.38MM
SALES (corp-wide): 1.79B **Privately Held**
Web: www.houseofraeford.com
SIC: 2015 Turkey, slaughtered and dressed
PA: Nash Johnson & Sons Farms, Inc.
3385 Us Hwy 117 S
Rose Hill NC 28458
910 289-3113

(G-10907)
**JOHNSON NASH & SONS FARMS
INC (PA)**
3385 S Us 117 Hwy (28458)
P.O. Box 699 (28458)
PHONE....................910 289-3113
Robert C Johnson, *CEO*
E Marvin Johnson, *
Don Taber, *
Dennis E Abraczinskas, *
Glenn Fox, *
◆ **EMP:** 400 **EST:** 1934
SQ FT: 2,000
SALES (est): 1.79B
SALES (corp-wide): 1.79B **Privately Held**
Web: www.houseofraeford.com
SIC: 2015 0254 0253 0251 Poultry,
slaughtered and dressed; Poultry hatcheries
; Turkey farm; Broiler, fryer, and roaster
chickens

(G-10908)
MURPHY-BROWN LLC
Also Called: Chief Feed Mill
210 Chief Ln (28458)
PHONE....................910 293-3434
Greg Ewing, *Mgr*
EMP: 50
Web: www.smithfieldfoods.com
SIC: 2048 Prepared feeds, nec
HQ: Murphy-Brown Llc
2822 W Nc 24 Hwy
Warsaw NC 28398
910 293-3434

(G-10909)
MURPHY-BROWN LLC
Smithfield Hog Prodn S Cntl Div
152 Farrow To Finish Ln (28458-1500)
P.O. Box 759 (28458-0759)

PHONE....................910 282-4264
Jaz Kydes, *Mgr*
EMP: 151
Web: www.smithfieldfoods.com
SIC: 0213 2048 Hogs; Prepared feeds, nec
HQ: Murphy-Brown Llc
2822 W Nc 24 Hwy
Warsaw NC 28398
910 293-3434

(G-10910)
SHUTTER PRODUCTION INC
227 First St (28458-0106)
P.O. Box 446 (28458-0446)
PHONE....................910 289-2620
Patrick Byrd, *Pr*
EMP: 8 **EST:** 1997
SALES (est): 492.62K **Privately Held**
Web: www.shutterproduction.com
SIC: 5211 2431 Door and window products;
Awnings, blinds and shutters: wood

Roseboro
Sampson County

(G-10911)
CAROLINA CUSTOM CABINETS
104 Andrews Chapel Rd (28382-8611)
PHONE....................910 525-3096
Roger Faircloth, *Owner*
EMP: 5 **EST:** 1995
SQ FT: 2,400
SALES (est): 282.15K **Privately Held**
Web: www.carolinacustomcabinet.com
SIC: 2434 Wood kitchen cabinets

(G-10912)
CRUMPLER PLASTIC PIPE INC
852 Autry Hwy 24 (28382-8307)
P.O. Box 2068 (28382-2068)
PHONE....................910 525-4046
Houston Crumpler Junior, *Pr*
Houston Temple Iii, *VP*
Richard Brian Temple, *
▼ **EMP:** 65 **EST:** 1975
SALES (est): 10MM **Privately Held**
Web: www.cpp-pipe.com
SIC: 3084 Plastics pipe

Rosman
Transylvania County

(G-10913)
M-B INDUSTRIES INC
Also Called: Sunbelt Spring & Stamping
9205 Rosman Hwy (28772-0378)
PHONE....................828 862-4201
Edwin E Morrow, *Pr*
Carla Morrow, *
▲ **EMP:** 130 **EST:** 1894
SQ FT: 110,000
SALES (est): 20.14MM **Privately Held**
Web: www.mb-industries.com
SIC: 3495 3469 3552 3496 Wire springs;
Stamping metal for the trade; Textile
machinery; Miscellaneous fabricated wire
products

Rougemont
Durham County

(G-10914)
MOVING SCREENS INCORPORATED
7807 Helena Moriah Rd (27572-7522)
PHONE....................336 364-9259
Wesley Winstead, *Pr*

Greg Fogleman, *Treas*
EMP: 4 **EST:** 1989
SQ FT: 6,000
SALES (est): 364.5K **Privately Held**
Web: www.blsales.net
SIC: 7336 2395 2759 Silk screen design;
Embroidery products, except Schiffli
machine; Screen printing

Rowland
Robeson County

(G-10915)
HELENA AGRI-ENTERPRISES LLC
13866 Hwy 301 S (28383)
P.O. Box 1027 (28383-1027)
PHONE....................910 422-8901
William Bates, *Brnch Mgr*
EMP: 10
Web: www.helenaagri.com
SIC: 2873 5191 Fertilizers: natural (organic),
except compost; Fertilizers and agricultural
chemicals
HQ: Helena Agri-Enterprises, Llc
225 Schilling Blvd
Collierville TN 38017
901 761-0050

(G-10916)
**LOCKLEAR CABINETS WDWRK SP
INC**
Also Called: Locklear Cabinet and Woodworks
4659 Cabinet Shop Rd (28383-9257)
PHONE....................910 521-4463
Harold B Locklear, *Pr*
Janie Locklear Davis, *VP*
EMP: 5 **EST:** 1949
SQ FT: 4,500
SALES (est): 431.75K **Privately Held**
Web: www.locklearcabinets.com
SIC: 5712 2591 Cabinet work, custom;
Curtain and drapery rods, poles, and
fixtures

Roxboro
Person County

(G-10917)
ABSOLUTE SECURITY & LOCK INC
216 S Main St (27573-5546)
P.O. Box 3250 (27573-3250)
PHONE....................336 322-4598
Scott Spencer, *Pr*
EMP: 5 **EST:** 2003
SALES (est): 364.53K **Privately Held**
Web: www.absolutesecurityandlock.com
SIC: 7699 3429 7382 1731 Locksmith shop;
Door opening and closing devices, except
electrical; Burglar alarm maintenance and
monitoring; Access control systems
specialization

(G-10918)
**ACCELERATED MEDIA
TECHNOLOGIES**
4400 Semora Rd (27574-6624)
PHONE....................336 599-2070
Wilbur Brann, *Mgr*
EMP: 4 **EST:** 2018
SALES (est): 423.07K **Privately Held**
Web: www.acceleratedmt.com
SIC: 3441 Fabricated structural metal

(G-10919)
B & B DISTRIBUTING INC
Also Called: Brady's Baked Goods
2888 Durham Rd Ste 102 (27573-6178)
PHONE....................336 592-5665

Tr Brady, *Pr*
EMP: 6 **EST:** 1978
SALES (est): 73.36K **Privately Held**
SIC: 2011 Pork products, from pork
slaughtered on site

(G-10920)
BOISE CASCADE WOOD PDTS LLC
Also Called: Roxboro Ewp Mill
1000 N Park Dr (27573-2474)
PHONE....................336 598-3001
Ralph Cook, *Mgr*
EMP: 29
SALES (corp-wide): 6.84B **Publicly Held**
Web: www.bc.com
SIC: 2491 Structural lumber and timber,
treated wood
HQ: Boise Cascade Wood Products, L.L.C.
1111 W Jefferson St # 300
Boise ID 83728
208 384-6161

(G-10921)
**CAMP CHEMICAL CORPORATION
(PA)**
200 Hester St (27573-5957)
P.O. Box 521 (27573-0521)
PHONE....................336 597-2214
EMP: 19 **EST:** 1929
SALES (est): 13.91MM
SALES (corp-wide): 13.91MM **Privately
Held**
Web: www.campchemical.com
SIC: 2875 5999 5191 Fertilizers, mixing only;
Feed and farm supply; Seeds: field, garden,
and flower

(G-10922)
CENTEREDGE SOFTWARE
5050 Durham Rd (27574-9811)
P.O. Box 1359 (27573-1359)
PHONE....................336 598-5934
EMP: 8 **EST:** 2013
SALES (est): 3.63MM **Privately Held**
Web: www.centeredgesoftware.com
SIC: 7372 Business oriented computer
software

(G-10923)
CHANDLER CONCRETE INC
Also Called: CHANDLER CONCRETE INC
121 Burch Ave (27573-4738)
P.O. Box 1732 (27573-1732)
PHONE....................336 599-8343
Michael Owen, *Genl Mgr*
EMP: 9
Web: www.chandlerconcrete.com
SIC: 3273 Ready-mixed concrete
PA: Chandler Concrete Co., Inc.
1006 S Church Street
Burlington NC 27215

(G-10924)
EATON CORPORATION
Also Called: Air Controls Division
2564 Durham Rd (27573-6172)
P.O. Box 241 (27573-0241)
PHONE....................336 322-0696
David Sintson, *Brnch Mgr*
EMP: 440
Web: www.dix-eaton.com
SIC: 3714 Motor vehicle parts and
accessories
HQ: Eaton Corporation
1000 Eaton Blvd
Cleveland OH 44122
440 523-5000

(G-10925)
EPIC RESTORATIONS LLC
118 Commerce Dr (27573-3812)
P.O. Box 3010 (27573-3010)
PHONE...................................866 597-2733
EMP: 4 EST: 2003
SALES (est): 4.36MM **Privately Held**
Web: www.strutmasters.com
SIC: 3714 Motor vehicle parts and
    accessories

(G-10926)
FORCE PROTECTION INC
3300 Jim Thorpe Hwy (27574-5445)
PHONE...................................336 597-2381
Ernie Nagy, *Dir*
EMP: 10
SALES (corp-wide): 47.72B **Publicly Held**
SIC: 3711 Motor vehicles and car bodies
HQ: Force Protection, Inc.
    9801 Hwy 78 Bldg Ste 1
    Ladson SC 29456

(G-10927)
GO ASK ERIN LLC
328 Virgilina Rd (27573-4422)
PHONE...................................336 747-3777
Erin Miller, *Pr*
EMP: 5 EST: 2018
SALES (est): 48.16K **Privately Held**
Web: www.goaskerinllc.com
SIC: 3448 Prefabricated metal buildings and
    components

(G-10928)
JH LOGGING
1300 Virgilina Rd (27573-4461)
PHONE...................................336 599-0278
James H Heath, *Owner*
James Heath, *Owner*
EMP: 5 EST: 1993
SALES (est): 109.2K **Privately Held**
SIC: 2411 Logging camps and contractors

(G-10929)
LOUISIANA-PACIFIC CORPORATION
Also Called: Louisiana-Pacific Southern Div
10475 Boston Rd (27574-6774)
PHONE...................................336 599-8080
Wayne Young, *Mgr*
EMP: 117
SALES (corp-wide): 2.94B **Publicly Held**
Web: www.lpcorp.com
SIC: 2431 2493 Millwork; Reconstituted
    wood products
PA: Louisiana-Pacific Corporation
    1610 West End Ave Ste 200
    Nashville TN 37203
    615 986-5600

(G-10930)
NEWELL & SONS INC
Also Called: Newell
211 Clayton Ave (27573-4641)
P.O. Box 1098 (27573-1098)
PHONE...................................336 597-2248
David Newell, *Pr*
Linda Newell Garza, *Sec*
EMP: 9 EST: 1967
SQ FT: 15,000
SALES (est): 467.66K **Privately Held**
Web: www.newellandsons.com
SIC: 2392 Mops, floor and dust

(G-10931)
NEWELL NOVELTY CO INC
Also Called: Roxboro Broom Works
25 Weeks Dr (27573-5954)
P.O. Box 949 (27573)
PHONE...................................336 597-2246

Henry Newell Junior, *Pr*
David Newell, *VP*
Jean Newell, *Prin*
▲ **EMP: 4 EST:** 1920
SQ FT: 20,000
SALES (est): 244.7K **Privately Held**
Web: www.roxborobroom.com
SIC: 3991 5169 Brooms; Chemicals and
    allied products, nec

(G-10932)
**NORTH AMERCN AERODYNAMICS
INC (PA)**
1803 N Main St (27573-4047)
PHONE...................................336 599-9266
John P Higgins, *Pr*
Jim Barker, *
EMP: 82 EST: 1964
SQ FT: 56,000
SALES (est): 4.71MM
SALES (corp-wide): 4.71MM **Privately
Held**
Web: www.naaero.com
SIC: 2399 Parachutes

(G-10933)
NORTH CRLINA DEPT CRIME CTRL P
Also Called: State Hwy Patrol-Troop D
3434 Burlington Rd (27574-7742)
PHONE...................................336 599-9233
Robert Pearson, *Prin*
EMP: 6
SALES (corp-wide): 74.26B **Privately Held**
Web: www.ncdps.gov
SIC: 3711 9229 Patrol wagons (motor
    vehicles), assembly of; Public order and
    safety, State government
HQ: North Carolina Department Of Crime
    Control And Public Safety
    512 N Salisbury St
    Raleigh NC 27604

(G-10934)
OLD BELT EXTRACTS LLC
Also Called: Open Book Extracts
317 Lucy Garrett Rd (27574-9789)
P.O. Box 1328 (27573-1328)
PHONE...................................336 530-5784
Oscar Hackett, *Pr*
David Neundorfer, *
EMP: 50 EST: 2019
SALES (est): 15.28MM **Privately Held**
Web: www.openbookextracts.com
SIC: 2899 Oils and essential oils

(G-10935)
OLIVE HL WLDG FABRICATION INC
Also Called: Olive Hill Wldg & Fabrication
1940 Semora Rd (27574-6654)
PHONE...................................336 597-0737
Charles Dickerson, *Pr*
Charles E Dickerson, *
EMP: 32 EST: 1982
SQ FT: 4,500
SALES (est): 4.18MM **Privately Held**
Web: www.olivehillwelding.com
SIC: 7692 Welding repair

(G-10936)
OUR PRIDE FOODS ROXBORO INC
Also Called: Our Pride Foods
1128 N Main St (27573-4402)
PHONE...................................336 597-4978
Malcolm Wooten, *Pr*
Ray Dunlap, *VP*
Danny Hodge, *Sec*
EMP: 8 EST: 1990
SQ FT: 18,000
SALES (est): 244.6K **Privately Held**
Web: www.ourpridepimentocheese.com

SIC: 2022 Cheese spreads, dips, pastes,
    and other cheese products

(G-10937)
OWENS CORNING SALES LLC
Owens Corning
3321 Durham Rd (27573-2713)
P.O. Box 61 (27573-0061)
PHONE...................................419 248-8000
Tom Mc Elveen, *Mgr*
EMP: 26
SIC: 3442 3444 3354 Screen doors, metal;
    Sheet metalwork; Aluminum extruded
    products
HQ: Owens Corning Sales, Llc
    1 Owens Corning Pkwy
    Toledo OH 43659
    419 248-8000

(G-10938)
**P&A INDSTRIAL FABRICATIONS LLC
(HQ)**
Also Called: Epoch Solutions
1841 N Main St (27573)
P.O. Box 28 (27573)
PHONE...................................336 322-1766
Don Millwater, *Contrlr*
Brent C Hilleary, *Managing Member*
▲ **EMP: 34 EST:** 2006
SALES (est): 10.01MM
SALES (corp-wide): 486.1K **Privately Held**
Web: www.paifllc.com
SIC: 3991 3089 2221 Paint rollers; Watering
    pots, plastics; Automotive fabrics,
    manmade fiber
PA: The P&A Group Llc
    1413 Evans St Ste E
    Greenville NC 27834
    252 329-8881

(G-10939)
PANELS BY PAITH INC
2728 Allensville Rd (27574-7278)
PHONE...................................336 599-3437
Don C Paith, *Pr*
Greta S Paith, *Sec*
EMP: 5 EST: 1975
SALES (est): 380.44K **Privately Held**
SIC: 2541 5712 3442 Partitions for floor
    attachment, prefabricated: wood; Cabinet
    work, custom; Moldings and trim, except
    automobile: metal

(G-10940)
PERSON PRINTING COMPANY INC
Also Called: Taylor Printing & Office Sup
115 Clayton Ave (27573-4611)
P.O. Box 681 (27573-0681)
PHONE...................................336 599-2146
Donald Ray Wilkins, *Pr*
EMP: 20 EST: 1945
SQ FT: 7,950
SALES (est): 4.56MM **Privately Held**
Web: www.taylorbusinessproducts.com
SIC: 2752 2791 2789 5112 Offset printing;
    Typesetting; Bookbinding and related work;
    Stationery and office supplies

(G-10941)
PIEDMONT PARACHUTE INC
2712 Durham Rd (27573-6176)
PHONE...................................336 597-2225
Carolyn Oakley, *Pr*
EMP: 6 EST: 2008
SALES (est): 61.3K **Privately Held**
Web: www.triangleparachute.com
SIC: 2399 Parachutes

(G-10942)
R & S SPORTING GOODS CTR INC
Also Called: Sign and Graphics
515 S Morgan St (27573-5451)
PHONE...................................336 599-0248
Wayne T Roberts, *Pr*
Doris Winstead, *VP*
EMP: 4 EST: 1977
SQ FT: 3,200
SALES (est): 363K **Privately Held**
SIC: 2396 5941 Screen printing on fabric
    articles; Sporting goods and bicycle shops

(G-10943)
ROXBORO WELDING
3735 Cates Mill Rd (27574-7992)
PHONE...................................336 364-2307
Daniel Hutchinson, *Prin*
EMP: 5 EST: 2017
SALES (est): 62.77K **Privately Held**
Web: www.olivehillwelding.com
SIC: 7692 Welding repair

(G-10944)
S OAKLEY MACHINE SHOP INC
126 W Gordon St (27573-5211)
PHONE...................................336 599-6105
Charles R Oakley, *Pr*
Arthur R Oakley, *VP*
Marie Oakley, *Sec*
EMP: 6 EST: 1942
SQ FT: 10,000
SALES (est): 609.9K **Privately Held**
SIC: 7692 3599 Welding repair; Machine
    shop, jobbing and repair

(G-10945)
SOUTHERN STATES COOP INC
Also Called: S S C 7883-7
1112 N Main St (27573-4402)
PHONE...................................336 599-2185
Donald Bowes, *Mgr*
EMP: 10
SALES (corp-wide): 1.71B **Privately Held**
Web: www.southernstates.com
SIC: 2048 5261 Prepared feeds, nec; Retail
    nurseries and garden stores
PA: Southern States Cooperative,
    Incorporated
    6606 W Broad St Ste B
    Richmond VA 23230
    804 281-1000

(G-10946)
SPUNTECH INDUSTRIES INC
555 N Park Dr (27573)
PHONE...................................336 330-9000
Hezi Yeheskel Nissan, *Ch*
Tomer Duash, *
Moshe Zorea, *
Ilan Pickman, *
Yiftah Sharrown, *
◆ **EMP: 210 EST:** 2003
SQ FT: 250,000
SALES (est): 41.2MM **Privately Held**
Web: www.spuntech.com
SIC: 2299 2841 2241 Upholstery filling,
    textile; Textile soap; Lacings, textile
HQ: N.R. Spuntech Industries Ltd.
    Tiberias

(G-10947)
STOKES MFG LLC
140 Somerset Church Rd (27573-6069)
PHONE...................................336 270-8746
EMP: 4 EST: 2018
SALES (est): 504.26K **Privately Held**
Web: www.stokesmfg.com
SIC: 3999 Manufacturing industries, nec

(G-10948)
SUSPENSION EXPERTS LLC
Also Called: Strutmasters
118 Commerce Dr (27573-3812)
PHONE...............................855 419-3072
Chip Lofton, *Managing Member*
EMP: 24 **EST:** 1999
SALES (est): 3.08MM **Privately Held**
Web: www.strutmasters.com
SIC: 3751 Motorcycles and related parts

Roxobel
Bertie County

(G-10949)
BAKERS SOUTHERN TRADITIONS INC
Also Called: Bakers Sthern Trdtions Peanuts
704 E Church St (27872-9612)
P.O. Box 62 (27872-0062)
PHONE...............................252 344-2120
Danielle Baker, *Pr*
EMP: 4 **EST:** 2007
SALES (est): 1.19MM **Privately Held**
Web: www.bakerspeanuts.com
SIC: 2096 5963 5499 5149 Cheese curls and puffs; Snacks, direct sales; Gourmet food stores; Groceries and related products, nec

---

Rtp
Durham County

(G-10950)
VERINETICS INC
2 Davis Dr (27709-0003)
PHONE...............................919 354-1029
Thomas J Mercolino, *CEO*
EMP: 4 **EST:** 2011
SALES (est): 530.57K **Privately Held**
Web: www.verinetics.com
SIC: 2834 Pharmaceutical preparations

Rural Hall
Forsyth County

(G-10951)
A & J PALLETS INC
121 Anderson St (27045-9147)
PHONE...............................336 969-0265
Richard Scott, *Brnch Mgr*
EMP: 7
SALES (corp-wide): 1.21MM **Privately Held**
Web: www.ajpalletsandmulch.com
SIC: 2448 2499 Pallets, wood; Mulch, wood and bark
PA: A & J Pallets, Inc.
195 Apache Dr
Winston Salem NC 27107
336 407-4368

(G-10952)
BBF PRINTING SOLUTIONS
1190 Old Beltway (27045-9537)
PHONE...............................336 969-2323
EMP: 4 **EST:** 2017
SALES (est): 147.67K **Privately Held**
Web: www.bbfprinting.com
SIC: 2752 Offset printing

(G-10953)
BUSICK BROTHERS MACHINE INC
262 Northstar Dr (27045-9949)
P.O. Box 1009 (27045-1009)
PHONE...............................336 969-2717
Roy Busick, *Pr*
Barbara Busick, *Sec*
Wayne Busick, *VP*
Carl Busick, *VP*
EMP: 11 **EST:** 1990
SQ FT: 7,000
SALES (est): 2.01MM **Privately Held**
Web: www.busickmachine.com
SIC: 3599 Machine shop, jobbing and repair

(G-10954)
CAROLON COMPANY
601 Forum Pkwy (27045-8934)
P.O. Box 1329 (27045-1329)
PHONE...............................336 969-6001
▲ **EMP:** 100 **EST:** 1973
SALES (est): 9.13MM **Privately Held**
Web: www.carolon.com
SIC: 3842 Surgical appliances and supplies

(G-10955)
CASE SMITH INC
625 Montroyal Rd (27045-9550)
PHONE...............................336 969-9786
Anthony Smith, *Pr*
Randall Sorrells, *VP Opers*
Teresa Porter, *AR Vice President*
EMP: 16 **EST:** 2011
SQ FT: 30,000
SALES (est): 249.13K **Privately Held**
Web: www.smithcase.com
SIC: 3161 Cases, carrying, nec

(G-10956)
CAVERT WIRE COMPANY INC (HQ)
Also Called: Cavert Red Line Wire Division
620 Forum Pkwy (27045-8934)
P.O. Box 725 (27045)
PHONE...............................800 969-2601
▲ **EMP:** 45 **EST:** 1910
SALES (est): 20.93MM
SALES (corp-wide): 102.21MM **Privately Held**
Web: www.accentwiretie.com
SIC: 3315 3496 Wire products, ferrous/iron: made in wiredrawing plants; Miscellaneous fabricated wire products
PA: Accent Packaging, Inc.
10131 Fm 2920 Rd
Tomball TX 77375
281 255-4881

(G-10957)
CHERRY CONTRACTING INC
Also Called: Cherry Precast
8640 Broad St (27045-9458)
P.O. Box 368 (27023-0368)
PHONE...............................336 969-1825
Cherry K Fulcher, *Pr*
Nelson T Fulcher, *
EMP: 95 **EST:** 2001
SQ FT: 50,000
SALES (est): 827K **Privately Held**
Web: www.cherrycontracting.com
SIC: 3272 Concrete products, precast, nec

(G-10958)
DAC PRODUCTS INC
Also Called: D A C
625 Montroyal Rd (27045-9550)
PHONE...............................336 969-9786
Durward Smith Iii, *Pr*
Chris Smith, *
Chris Hodges, *
Squire Irwin, *
◆ **EMP:** 35 **EST:** 1987
SALES (est): 9.5MM **Privately Held**
Web: www.dacproducts.com
SIC: 2541 2431 2449 3442 Display fixtures, wood; Door frames, wood; Wood containers, nec; Metal doors, sash, and trim

(G-10959)
FORSYTH PRINTING COMPANY INC
627 Forum Pkwy (27045-8934)
PHONE...............................336 969-0383
Ricky Jones, *Pr*
Wiley R Jones Senior, *Sec*
EMP: 4 **EST:** 1977
SQ FT: 5,000
SALES (est): 178.98K **Privately Held**
Web: www.burkleeprinting.com
SIC: 2752 Offset printing

(G-10960)
GRAPHIC REWARDS INC
130 Northstar Dr Ste B (27045-9450)
P.O. Box 1166 (27021-1166)
PHONE...............................336 969-2733
Stanley John Cantrell Junior, *Pr*
Susan Cantrell, *Sec*
Kevin Williams, *Pr*
EMP: 4 **EST:** 1996
SQ FT: 10,000
SALES (est): 86.09K **Privately Held**
SIC: 2752 Business form and card printing, lithographic

(G-10961)
HANESBRANDS INC
710 Almondridge Dr (27045-9576)
PHONE...............................336 519-8080
EMP: 25 **EST:** 2006
SALES (est): 2.8MM **Privately Held**
SIC: 2252 Socks

(G-10962)
KEN GARNER MFG - RHO INC
Also Called: Ken Garner Mfg
8610 Chipboard Rd (27045-9503)
PHONE...............................336 969-0416
Jerry Prince, *Pr*
EMP: 47 **EST:** 2006
SALES (est): 4.93MM
SALES (corp-wide): 24.41MM **Privately Held**
Web: www.kgarnermfg.com
SIC: 3531 Aerial work platforms: hydraulic/elec. truck/carrier mounted
PA: Ken Garner Manufacturing, Inc.
1201 E 28th St
Chattanooga TN 37404
423 698-6200

(G-10963)
LANTAL TEXTILES INC (HQ)
1300 Langenthal Dr (27045-9800)
P.O. Box 965 (27045-0965)
PHONE...............................336 969-9551
Urs Baumann, *Ch Bd*
Scott C Walker, *Pr*
Kim Lawson, *Prin*
Jamey Hughes, *Treas*
▲ **EMP:** 147 **EST:** 1979
SQ FT: 50,000
SALES (est): 19.85MM **Privately Held**
Web: www.lantal.com
SIC: 2231 2211 5131 Upholstery fabrics, wool; Upholstery fabrics, cotton; Upholstery fabrics, woven
PA: Lantal Textiles Ag
Dorfgasse 5
Langenthal BE 4900

(G-10964)
LEISTRIZ ADVANCED TURBINE COMPONENTS INC
3050 Westinghouse Rd Ste 190 (27045-9570)
P.O. Box 790 (16117-0790)
PHONE...............................336 969-1352
▲ **EMP:** 165

SIC: 3511 Turbines and turbine generator set units, complete

(G-10965)
NORTHLINE NC LLC
262 Northstar Dr Ste 122 (27045-9180)
PHONE...............................336 283-4811
Tonya Morris, *Prin*
EMP: 9 **EST:** 2013
SALES (est): 6.03MM **Privately Held**
Web: www.northlinenc.com
SIC: 5084 3825 Industrial machinery and equipment; Test equipment for electronic and electrical circuits

(G-10966)
ROBERT H WAGER COMPANY INC
Also Called: Wager
570 Montroyal Rd (27045-9233)
PHONE...............................336 969-6909
Robert Wager Senior, *CEO*
Lynn Wager Powers, *Ex VP*
Mike Wager, *Pr*
▲ **EMP:** 18 **EST:** 1933
SQ FT: 20,000
SALES (est): 3.56MM **Privately Held**
Web: www.wagerusa.com
SIC: 3491 3823 Valves, automatic control; Process control instruments

(G-10967)
SIEMENS ENERGY INC
Also Called: Power Generation Mfg Oper Div
3050 Westinghouse Rd (27045-9570)
PHONE...............................336 969-1351
Amogh Bhonde, *Mgr*
EMP: 37
SALES (corp-wide): 38.48B **Privately Held**
Web: www.siemens.com
SIC: 3621 3511 Motors and generators; Turbines and turbine generator sets
HQ: Siemens Energy, Inc.
4400 N Alafaya Trl
Orlando FL 32826
407 736-2000

(G-10968)
WESTROCK SHARED SERVICES LLC
Also Called: Westrock Merchandising Display
520 Northridge Park Dr (27045-9575)
PHONE...............................336 642-4165
Stephanie W Bignon, *Mgr*
EMP: 840
Web: www.westrock.com
SIC: 2621 2631 Packaging paper; Container, packaging, and boxboard
HQ: Westrock Shared Services, Llc
1000 Abernathy Rd
Atlanta GA 30328

(G-10969)
WILLIAMS PRINTING LLC
510 Northridge Park Dr (27045-9575)
P.O. Box 866 (27045-0866)
PHONE...............................336 969-2733
David Sharpe, *CEO*
EMP: 20 **EST:** 2006
SALES (est): 2.84MM
SALES (corp-wide): 2.84MM **Privately Held**
Web: www.wpicolor.com
SIC: 2752 Offset printing
PA: Dzs Consulting, Llc
122 Meadows Edge Dr
Advance NC 27006
336 671-9118

Rutherford College
Burke County

(G-10970)
AQUAFIL OMARA INC
Also Called: Omtex
160 Fashion Ave (28671)
P.O. Box 970 (28671-0970)
PHONE..............................828 874-2100
Gary Bradley, *Pr*
Joseph Leirer, *
Andrea Pugnali, *
Angela Elliott, *
◆ **EMP:** 150 **EST:** 1970
SALES (est): 22.74MM
SALES (corp-wide): 623.74MM **Privately Held**
Web: www.aquafil.com
SIC: 2282 2281 5199 Textured yarn; Yarn spinning mills; Fabrics, yarns, and knit goods
HQ: Aquafil U.S.A., Inc.
1 Aquafil Dr
Cartersville GA 30120
678 605-8100

(G-10971)
FILTEX INC
160 Fashion Ave (28671)
P.O. Box 970 (28671-0970)
PHONE..............................828 874-2100
Joseph J O'mara Junior, *Pr*
Joe Leirer Junior, *Sec*
▲ **EMP:** 75 **EST:** 1987
SQ FT: 27,000
SALES (est): 2.91MM **Privately Held**
Web: www.aquafil.com
SIC: 2221 Shirting fabrics, manmade fiber and silk

Rutherfordton
Rutherford County

(G-10972)
3TEX INC
208 Laurel Hill Dr (28139-2599)
P.O. Box 97544 (27624-7544)
PHONE..............................919 481-2500
◆ **EMP:** 42
Web: www.3tex.com
SIC: 3297 Heat resistant mixtures

(G-10973)
ALLRAIL INC
289 Calton Hill Ln (28139-9181)
PHONE..............................828 287-3747
Thomas Calton, *Pr*
▲ **EMP:** 8 **EST:** 2008
SALES (est): 992.88K **Privately Held**
Web: www.allrail.us
SIC: 3317 Steel pipe and tubes

(G-10974)
AMERICAN MISO COMPANY INC
4225 Maple Creek Rd (28139-7521)
PHONE..............................828 287-2940
Barry Evans, *Pr*
Jan Paige, *VP*
EMP: 10 **EST:** 1982
SALES (est): 612.97K **Privately Held**
Web: www.greateasternsun.com
SIC: 2099 Sauces: dry mixes

(G-10975)
ASSOCIATED PRINTING & SVCS INC
905 N Main St (28139-2523)
P.O. Box 905 (28139-0905)
PHONE..............................828 286-9064
Ginny Wells, *Pr*
Eric Wells, *VP*
Joe Wells, *Sec*
EMP: 7 **EST:** 1967
SQ FT: 20,000
SALES (est): 1.14MM **Privately Held**
Web: www.associatedprinting.biz
SIC: 2752 2789 Offset printing; Swatches and samples

(G-10976)
BADGER WELDING INCORPORATED
387 Creek Rd (28139-6720)
PHONE..............................828 863-2078
Stanley Badger, *Pr*
Lori Badger, *VP*
EMP: 4 **EST:** 1985
SALES (est): 552.22K **Privately Held**
Web: www.badgerweld.net
SIC: 7692 Welding repair

(G-10977)
BLUE RIDGE ARMOR LLC
340 Industrial Park Rd (28139-2541)
PHONE..............................844 556-6855
James D Taylor, *Pr*
Dale Taylor, *Managing Member*
EMP: 7 **EST:** 2014
SALES (est): 2.86MM **Privately Held**
Web: www.blueridgearmor.com
SIC: 3812 Defense systems and equipment

(G-10978)
BOONES SAWMILL INC
182 Goldfinch Ln (28139-8386)
PHONE..............................828 287-8774
Jesse Boone, *Pr*
EMP: 5 **EST:** 2013
SALES (est): 449.55K **Privately Held**
Web: www.boonessawmill.com
SIC: 2421 Lumber: rough, sawed, or planed

(G-10979)
BROAD RIVER FOREST PRODUCTS
2250 Us 221 Hwy N (28139-8686)
PHONE..............................828 287-8003
Tim Parton, *Pr*
William Parton, *VP*
Mike Parton, *Treas*
EMP: 7 **EST:** 1998
SALES (est): 294.19K **Privately Held**
SIC: 2611 Pulp mills

(G-10980)
CARPENTER DESIGN INC
Also Called: Carpenter Design
330 Broyhill Rd (28139-9612)
PHONE..............................828 248-9070
Thomas Carpenter, *Pr*
EMP: 15 **EST:** 1989
SQ FT: 30,000
SALES (est): 4.5MM **Privately Held**
Web: www.carpenterpallet.com
SIC: 2448 Pallets, wood

(G-10981)
COUNTRY HEART BRAIDING
955 Hopper Rd (28139-8749)
PHONE..............................828 245-0562
Joyce Shires, *Owner*
EMP: 8 **EST:** 1988
SALES (est): 125.52K **Privately Held**
SIC: 2273 Rugs, braided and hooked

(G-10982)
DAILY COURIER
162 N Main St (28139-2502)
PHONE..............................828 245-6431
Jim Brown, *Mgr*
EMP: 5 **EST:** 1969
SALES (est): 245.61K **Privately Held**
Web: www.thedigitalcourier.com
SIC: 2711 Newspapers, publishing and printing

(G-10983)
GOOD EARTH MINISTRIES
156 River Ridge Pkwy (28139-8478)
PHONE..............................828 287-9826
Jeffery Wilkins, *Owner*
Pastor Jeffery Wilkins, *Prin*
Sylvia Wilkins, *Sec*
EMP: 6 **EST:** 1998
SALES (est): 452.07K **Privately Held**
SIC: 3271 Blocks, concrete: landscape or retaining wall

(G-10984)
GUERRERO ENTERPRISES INC
1621 Poors Ford Rd (28139-8728)
P.O. Box 103 (28139-0103)
PHONE..............................828 286-4900
Alejandro Guerrero, *Pr*
EMP: 4 **EST:** 2005
SALES (est): 181.44K **Privately Held**
Web: www.dssignsandgraphics.com
SIC: 3993 1799 Signs and advertising specialties; Sign installation and maintenance

(G-10985)
HARRIS LUMBER COMPANY INC
1266 Big Island Rd (28139-8761)
PHONE..............................828 245-2664
Dwayne Harris, *Pr*
EMP: 4 **EST:** 2000
SALES (est): 96.96K **Privately Held**
Web: www.broadriverhomes.com
SIC: 2421 Lumber: rough, sawed, or planed

(G-10986)
HEAL
Also Called: H.E.A.L. Marketplace
360 Carpenter Rd (28139-8552)
PHONE..............................828 287-8787
Michael Dietz, *Prin*
EMP: 4 **EST:** 2010
SALES (est): 67.15K **Privately Held**
Web: www.healmarketplace.shop
SIC: 3421 Table and food cutlery, including butchers'

(G-10987)
HENDRENS RACG ENGS CHASSIS INC
1310 Us 221 Hwy N (28139-9507)
PHONE..............................828 286-0780
Bill Hendren, *Pr*
Steve Hendren, *VP*
Bettie Hendren, *Sec*
▼ **EMP:** 6 **EST:** 1977
SQ FT: 7,500
SALES (est): 580.56K **Privately Held**
Web: www.hendrensracingengines.com
SIC: 3714 Motor vehicle parts and accessories

(G-10988)
PACKAGING CORPORATION AMERICA
Pca/Rutherfordton 373
321 Industrial Park Rd (28139-2542)
PHONE..............................828 286-9156
Peter Anzenberger, *Mgr*
EMP: 44
SALES (corp-wide): 7.73B **Publicly Held**
Web: www.packagingcorp.com
SIC: 2653 Boxes, corrugated: made from purchased materials
PA: Packaging Corporation Of America
1 N Field Ct
Lake Forest IL 60045
847 482-3000

(G-10989)
PARTON FOREST PRODUCTS INC
251 Parton Rd (28139-8116)
PHONE..............................828 287-4257
Furman Parton, *Pr*
Patrick Parton, *Sec*
▼ **EMP:** 4 **EST:** 1996
SALES (est): 473.47K
SALES (corp-wide): 10.97MM **Privately Held**
Web: www.partonlumber.com
SIC: 2421 Sawmills and planing mills, general
PA: Parton Lumber Company, Inc.
251 Parton Rd
Rutherfordton NC 28139
828 287-4257

(G-10990)
PARTON LUMBER COMPANY INC
(PA)
Also Called: Parton Export
251 Parton Rd (28139-8116)
PHONE..............................828 287-4257
Carl F Parton, *Pr*
Scott Hughes, *
▼ **EMP:** 72 **EST:** 1937
SQ FT: 1,500
SALES (est): 10.97MM
SALES (corp-wide): 10.97MM **Privately Held**
Web: www.partonlumber.com
SIC: 2421 2426 Planing mills, nec; Lumber, hardwood dimension

(G-10991)
RCM INDUSTRIES INC
Also Called: Aallied Die Casting of N C
401 Aallied Dr (28139-2990)
PHONE..............................828 286-4003
Mike Nowak, *Mgr*
EMP: 150
Web: www.aalliednc.com
SIC: 3363 3365 Aluminum die-castings; Aluminum foundries
PA: R.C.M. Industries, Inc.
3021 Cullerton Dr
Franklin Park IL 60131

(G-10992)
S RUPPE INC
Also Called: Liberty Press
137 Taylor St (28139-2558)
P.O. Box 837 (28139-0837)
PHONE..............................828 287-4936
Edward R Ruppe, *Pr*
Ethel Ruppe, *
Diane Ruppe, *
EMP: 8 **EST:** 1940
SALES (est): 2MM **Privately Held**
Web: www.libertypressonline.com
SIC: 5112 2752 2791 2789 Business forms; Offset printing; Typesetting; Bookbinding and related work

(G-10993)
SAVATECH CORP
715 Railroad Ave (28139-2207)
PHONE..............................386 760-0706
Izidor Debenc, *Pr*
David Lander, *Ex VP*
▲ **EMP:** 6 **EST:** 1999
SQ FT: 8,000
SALES (est): 1.95MM **Privately Held**
Web: www.savatrade.com
SIC: 3069 Hard rubber and molded rubber products

▲ = Import ▼ = Export
◆ = Import/Export

HQ: Sava, D.D.
Dunajska Cesta 152
Ljubljana 1000

(G-10994)
SUNRAY INC
4761 Us 64 74a Hwy (28139-6322)
PHONE.................................828 287-7030
EMP: 30 **EST:** 1976
SALES (est): 9.88MM **Privately Held**
Web: www.sunray-inc.com
SIC: 3089 2822 3429 Molding primary
plastics; Synthetic rubber; Hardware, nec

(G-10995)
TOOL-WELD LLC
180 Cross Ridge Dr (28139-6437)
PHONE.................................843 986-4931
Juhn Anthony Zucker Senior, *Pr*
Rose Mary Zucker, *VP*
▼ **EMP:** 4 **EST:** 1960
SALES (est): 900K **Privately Held**
Web: www.toolweld.com
SIC: 7692 Welding repair

(G-10996)
TRELLEBORG CTD SYSTEMS US INC
Also Called: Industrial Ctd Fabrics Group
715 Railroad Ave (28139-2207)
PHONE.................................828 286-9126
Mark Patterson, *Brnch Mgr*
EMP: 120
SALES (corp-wide): 276.11MM **Privately
Held**
Web: www.trelleborg.com
SIC: 3069 2824 Rubber coated fabrics and
clothing; Vinyl fibers
PA: Trelleborg Coated Systems Us, Inc.
715 Railroad Ave
Rutherfordton NC 28139
828 286-9126

(G-10997)
TRELLEBORG CTD SYSTEMS US INC
Also Called: Atg Division
715 Railroad Ave (28139-2207)
P.O. Box 929 (28139-0929)
PHONE.................................864 576-1210
Patrick Walsh, *Prin*
EMP: 149
SALES (corp-wide): 276.11MM **Privately
Held**
Web: www.trelleborg.com
SIC: 2261 2231 Finishing plants, cotton;
Fabric finishing: wool, mohair, or similar
fibers
PA: Trelleborg Coated Systems Us, Inc.
715 Railroad Ave
Rutherfordton NC 28139
828 286-9126

(G-10998)
TRELLEBORG CTD SYSTEMS US INC
Also Called: Engineered Coated Fabrics
631 Rock Rd (28139-8123)
PHONE.................................828 286-9126
EMP: 86
SALES (corp-wide): 276.11MM **Privately
Held**
Web: www.trelleborg.com
SIC: 2295 Coated fabrics, not rubberized
PA: Trelleborg Coated Systems Us, Inc.
715 Railroad Ave
Rutherfordton NC 28139
828 286-9126

(G-10999)
**TRELLEBORG CTD SYSTEMS US
INC (PA)**
715 Railroad Ave (28139)
PHONE.................................828 286-9126

Patric Vestlund, *Pr*
Jessie Marlowe, *
Jennifer Walker, *
Thomas Yaczik, *
▲ **EMP:** 170 **EST:** 1937
SQ FT: 43,000
SALES (est): 276.11MM
SALES (corp-wide): 276.11MM **Privately
Held**
Web: www.trelleborg.com
SIC: 2295 2221 2394 2396 Coated fabrics,
not rubberized; Manmade and synthetic
broadwoven fabrics; Tarpaulins, fabric:
made from purchased materials;
Automotive and apparel trimmings

(G-11000)
ULTIMATE TEXTILE INC
1437 Us 221 Hwy S (28139-7204)
P.O. Box 1465 (28139-1465)
PHONE.................................828 286-8880
Rocky R Guarriello, *Pr*
Anthony Guarriello, *
▲ **EMP:** 35 **EST:** 1994
SQ FT: 100,000
SALES (est): 9.62MM **Privately Held**
Web: www.ultimatetextileinc.com
SIC: 2269 2261 Finishing plants, nec;
Finishing plants, cotton

(G-11001)
URETEK LLC
715 Railroad Ave (28139-2207)
PHONE.................................203 468-0342
Milton Berlinski, *Managing Member*
Stuart Press, *
◆ **EMP:** 9 **EST:** 2006
SALES (est): 447.8K **Privately Held**
Web: www.trelleborg.com
SIC: 2295 Resin or plastic coated fabrics

(G-11002)
US PRECISION CABINETRY LLC
Also Called: Touchstone Fine Cabinetry
160 Executive Dr (28139-2929)
P.O. Box 2141 (28139-4341)
PHONE.................................828 351-2020
Chris Britton, *Managing Member*
EMP: 100 **EST:** 2018
SALES (est): 8MM **Privately Held**
SIC: 2434 Wood kitchen cabinets

(G-11003)
WRKCO INC
300 Broyhill Rd (28139-9612)
PHONE.................................828 287-9430
EMP: 28
SIC: 2653 Boxes, corrugated: made from
purchased materials
HQ: Wrkco Inc.
1000 Abrnthy Rd Ne Ste 12
Atlanta GA 30328
770 448-2193

Saint Pauls
Robeson County

(G-11004)
CORNEY TRANSPORTATION INC
19214 Us Highway 301 N (28384-7443)
P.O. Box 385 (28384-0385)
PHONE.................................800 354-9111
Bobby R Corney, *Pr*
EMP: 28 **EST:** 1996
SALES (est): 12.24MM **Privately Held**
Web: www.corneytransportation.com
SIC: 2653 Boxes, corrugated: made from
purchased materials

(G-11005)
MUELLER STEAM SPECIALTY (DH)
Also Called: Mueller Steam Specialty
1491 Nc Highway 20 W (28384-9209)
PHONE.................................910 865-8241
David Palmer, *CEO*
Cameron Sheets, *
◆ **EMP:** 89 **EST:** 1956
SALES (est): 9.57MM
SALES (corp-wide): 2.25B **Publicly Held**
Web: www.watts.com
SIC: 3491 Industrial valves
HQ: Watts Regulator Co.
815 Chestnut St
North Andover MA 01845
978 689-6000

(G-11006)
PEPSI BOTTLING VENTURES LLC
Also Called: Pepsico
137 Pepsi Way (28384-5400)
PHONE.................................910 865-1600
David Graham, *Mgr*
EMP: 100
Web: www.pepsibottlingventures.com
SIC: 2086 Carbonated soft drinks, bottled
and canned
HQ: Pepsi Bottling Ventures Llc
4141 Parklake Ave
Raleigh NC 27612
919 865-2300

(G-11007)
PRESTAGE FOODS INC
4470 Nc Hwy 20 E (28384)
PHONE.................................910 865-6611
John Prestage, *Pr*
John Hott, *
Scott Prestage, *
Ron Prestage, *
▼ **EMP:** 350 **EST:** 2000
SQ FT: 210,000
SALES (est): 43.76MM
SALES (corp-wide): 174.84MM **Privately
Held**
Web: www.prestagefarms.com
SIC: 2015 Turkey, processed, nsk
PA: Prestage Farms, Inc.
4651 Taylors Bridge Hwy
Clinton NC 28328
910 596-5700

(G-11008)
SANDERSON FARMS INC
Also Called: Sanderson Farms, Inc.
2076 Nc Highway 20 W (28384-5501)
PHONE.................................910 274-0220
EMP: 4
SALES (corp-wide): 4.8B **Privately Held**
Web: www.sandersonfarms.com
SIC: 2015 Chicken, slaughtered and dressed
HQ: Sanderson Farms, Llc
127 Flynt Rd
Laurel MS 39443
601 649-4030

(G-11009)
SANDERSON FARMS LLC PROC DIV
Also Called: St Pauls, NC Processing Plant
2076 Nc Highway 20 W (28384-5501)
PHONE.................................910 274-0220
EMP: 896
SALES (corp-wide): 4.8B **Privately Held**
Web: www.sandersonfarms.com
SIC: 2015 Chicken, slaughtered and dressed
HQ: Sanderson Farms, Llc (Processing
Division)
127 Flynt Rd
Laurel MS 39443
601 649-4030

Salisbury
Rowan County

(G-11010)
A-1 COATINGS
525 Linda St (28146-1158)
PHONE.................................704 790-9528
EMP: 5
SALES (est): 237.93K **Privately Held**
SIC: 3479 Metal coating and allied services

(G-11011)
ABILITY ORTHOPEDICS
209 Statesville Blvd (28144-2313)
P.O. Box 9526 (28603-9526)
PHONE.................................704 630-6789
James P Rubel, *Owner*
EMP: 4 **EST:** 2000
SQ FT: 1,260
SALES (est): 1.07MM **Privately Held**
Web: www.ncability.com
SIC: 3842 Orthopedic appliances

(G-11012)
ACCEL DISCOUNT TIRE (PA)
201 E Liberty St (28144-5040)
PHONE.................................704 636-0323
Darryl White, *Owner*
EMP: 6 **EST:** 1935
SQ FT: 7,000
SALES (est): 78.41K
SALES (corp-wide): 78.41K **Privately Held**
Web: www.micasakb.com
SIC: 5531 7389 7534 5722 Automotive tires;
Drive-a-way automobile service; Tire
recapping; Electric household appliances

(G-11013)
**ADVANCED MACHINING TOOLING
LLC**
Also Called: Advanced Machining
215 Forbes Ave (28147-6930)
PHONE.................................704 633-8157
Keith A Felts, *Pr*
Bobby L Miller, *VP*
EMP: 8 **EST:** 1985
SQ FT: 4,800
SALES (est): 2.29MM **Privately Held**
Web: www.advancedmachiningcnc.com
SIC: 3599 Machine shop, jobbing and repair

(G-11014)
AIRGAS USA LLC
Also Called: Airgas
1924 S Main St (28144-6714)
P.O. Box 2125 (28145-2125)
PHONE.................................704 636-5049
Steve Simpson, *Mgr*
EMP: 8
SALES (corp-wide): 114.13MM **Privately
Held**
Web: www.airgas.com
SIC: 5084 7692 Welding machinery and
equipment; Welding repair
HQ: Airgas Usa, Llc
259 N Rdnor Chster Rd Ste
Radnor PA 19087
216 642-6600

(G-11015)
ALLOYWORKS LLC
814 W Innes St (28144-4152)
PHONE.................................704 645-0511
William Russell Chinnis, *Pt*
▲ **EMP:** 15 **EST:** 2001
SALES (est): 2.55MM **Privately Held**
SIC: 3339 Precious metals

GEOGRAPHIC

(G-11016)
AMREP INC
1405 Julian Rd (28146-2322)
PHONE..........................704 949-2595
EMP: 51
Web: www.amrepproducts.com
SIC: 3713 Truck bodies (motor vehicles)
HQ: Amrep, Inc.
　　6525 Carnegie Blvd # 300
　　Charlotte NC 28211
　　909 923-0430

(G-11017)
APPLE BAKING COMPANY INC
4470 Hampton Rd (28144-1202)
PHONE..........................704 637-6800
Robert Watts, Pr
Jeff Haas, Contrlr
EMP: 20 EST: 1984
SALES (est): 952.36K Privately Held
Web: www.applebaking.com
SIC: 2051 Bread, cake, and related products

(G-11018)
ATHENA MARBLE INCORPORATED
7400 Bringle Ferry Rd (28146-7154)
PHONE..........................704 636-7810
Alan R Jones, Pr
Jean Jones, Treas
EMP: 6 EST: 1973
SQ FT: 6,000
SALES (est): 594.79K Privately Held
SIC: 3261 3281 Vitreous plumbing fixtures;
　　Bathroom fixtures, cut stone

(G-11019)
ATLANTIC MFG & FABRICATION INC
705 S Railroad St Unit 1 (28144-5665)
PHONE..........................704 647-6200
Felipe Castaneda, Mgr
EMP: 5 EST: 2009
SALES (est): 156.03K Privately Held
SIC: 3999 Manufacturing industries, nec

(G-11020)
B & B MACHINE CO INC
1890 Barringer Rd (28147-9518)
PHONE..........................704 637-2356
Danny Bogle, Pr
Rick Bogle, VP
EMP: 8 EST: 1986
SQ FT: 7,000
SALES (est): 1.5MM Privately Held
SIC: 3599 Machine shop, jobbing and repair

(G-11021)
B V HEDRICK GRAVEL & SAND CO (PA)
Also Called: Grove Stone & Sand Division
120 1/2 N Church St (28144)
P.O. Box 1040 (28145)
PHONE..........................704 633-5982
Jeffrey V Goodman, Pr
Frances H Johnson, *
Jane B Arnold, *
Joanne Johnson, *
Artie Hattaway, *
EMP: 50 EST: 1924
SQ FT: 2,000
SALES (est): 238.17MM
SALES (corp-wide): 238.17MM Privately Held
Web: www.hedrickind.com
SIC: 1442 7359 6512 3273 Construction
　　sand mining; Equipment rental and leasing,
　　nec; Commercial and industrial building
　　operation; Ready-mixed concrete

(G-11022)
BAILEYS QUICK COPY SHOP INC (PA)
Also Called: Quick Copy Print Shop
324 E Fisher St (28144-5002)
P.O. Box 1527 (28145-1527)
PHONE..........................704 637-2020
Robert R Bailey, Pr
Mary Ellen Bailey, Ex VP
EMP: 14 EST: 1973
SQ FT: 4,320
SALES (est): 1.3MM
SALES (corp-wide): 1.3MM Privately Held
SIC: 2752 Offset printing

(G-11023)
BOSMERE INC
Also Called: The Wynsum Gardener
2701 S Main St (28147-7901)
P.O. Box 2267 (28145-2267)
PHONE..........................704 784-1608
Patrick Rykens, Pr
Susan Rykens, VP
▲ EMP: 12 EST: 1988
SQ FT: 20,000
SALES (est): 4.9MM Privately Held
Web: www.bosmereusa.com
SIC: 3524 Lawn and garden equipment

(G-11024)
CAROLINA BEVERAGE CORPORATION (PA)
Also Called: Cheerwine
1413 Jake Alexander Blvd S (28146-8359)
P.O. Box 697 (28145-0697)
PHONE..........................704 636-2191
Cliff Ritchie, CEO
Mark Ritchie, *
Raymond Ritchie, *
Tommy Page, *
EMP: 25 EST: 1917
SQ FT: 35,000
SALES (est): 16.65MM
SALES (corp-wide): 16.65MM Privately Held
Web: www.cheerwine.com
SIC: 2086 Bottled and canned soft drinks

(G-11025)
CAROLINA BOTTLING COMPANY
1413 Jake Alexander Blvd S (28146-8359)
P.O. Box 697 (28145-0697)
PHONE..........................704 637-5869
Mark Ritchie, CEO
Cliff Ritchie, *
Tommy Page, *
EMP: 72 EST: 1994
SQ FT: 35,000
SALES (est): 9.1MM
SALES (corp-wide): 16.65MM Privately Held
Web: www.cheerwine.com
SIC: 2086 Bottled and canned soft drinks
PA: Carolina Beverage Corporation
　　1413 Jake Alxander Blvd S
　　Salisbury NC 28146
　　704 636-2191

(G-11026)
CAROLINA CUSTOM RUBBER INC
5415 Statesville Blvd (28147-7473)
P.O. Box 459 (27013-0459)
PHONE..........................704 636-6989
Bob Clester, Pr
Karen Clester, Sec
EMP: 8 EST: 1983
SQ FT: 2,000
SALES (est): 571.08K Privately Held
Web: www.carolinacustomrubber.com
SIC: 3069 3061 Foam rubber; Mechanical
　　rubber goods

(G-11027)
CAROLINA PRINT WORKS INC
Also Called: Lewis Frank Specialty Products
600 N Long St Ste B (28144-4421)
P.O. Box 2581 (28145-2581)
PHONE..........................704 637-6902
▲ EMP: 10 EST: 1992
SQ FT: 20,000
SALES (est): 869.39K Privately Held
Web: www.carolinaprintworks.com
SIC: 3089 Novelties, plastics

(G-11028)
CAROLINA QUARRIES INC (PA)
Also Called: Rock of Ages
805 Harris Granite Rd (28146-7810)
PHONE..........................704 633-0201
Doug Smith, Prin
Doug Smith, Pr
Helen Holshouser, *
EMP: 60 EST: 1991
SALES (est): 2.34MM Privately Held
SIC: 1411 3281 Dimension stone; Granite,
　　cut and shaped

(G-11029)
CAROLINA STALITE CO LTD PARTNR (PA)
205 Klumac Rd (28144-6723)
P.O. Box 1037 (28145-1037)
PHONE..........................704 637-1515
Frances H Johnson, Mng Pt
EMP: 10 EST: 1972
SALES (est): 7.41MM
SALES (corp-wide): 7.41MM Privately Held
Web: www.stalite.com
SIC: 3281 0711 Slate products; Soil
　　chemical treatment services

(G-11030)
CAROLINA STAMPING COMPANY
701 Corporate Cir (28147-7220)
PHONE..........................704 637-0260
Daniel Cronin, Pr
EMP: 55 EST: 1977
SQ FT: 27,000
SALES (est): 9.64MM
SALES (corp-wide): 10.51MM Privately Held
Web: www.carolinastamping.com
SIC: 3469 Stamping metal for the trade
PA: W.L.S. Stamping Co.
　　3292 E 80th St
　　Cleveland OH 44104
　　216 271-5100

(G-11031)
CHANDLER CONCRETE INC
Also Called: Chandler Concrete & Bldg Sup
400 N Long St (28144-4455)
P.O. Box 139 (28145-0139)
PHONE..........................704 636-4711
Ed Williams, Genl Mgr
EMP: 82
Web: www.chandlerconcrete.com
SIC: 3273 1771 Ready-mixed concrete;
　　Concrete work
PA: Chandler Concrete Co., Inc.
　　1006 S Church Street
　　Burlington NC 27215

(G-11032)
CHARTER DURA-BAR INC
Also Called: Durabar Metals Services Div
770 Cedar Springs Rd (28147-9252)
PHONE..........................704 637-1906
Jim Lewis, Opers Mgr
EMP: 19
SALES (corp-wide): 570.48MM Privately Held
Web: www.dura-barms.com
SIC: 5051 3599 Steel; Machine shop,
　　jobbing and repair
HQ: Charter Dura-Bar, Inc.
　　2100 W Lake Shore Dr
　　Woodstock IL 60098
　　815 338-3900

(G-11033)
CHROMA COLOR CORPORATION
100 E 17th St (28144-2980)
PHONE..........................704 637-7000
Matt Barr, Prin
EMP: 148
SALES (corp-wide): 78.23MM Privately Held
Web: www.chromacolors.com
SIC: 2821 Plastics materials and resins
PA: Chroma Color Corporation
　　3900 W Dayton St
　　Mc Henry IL 60050
　　877 385-8777

(G-11034)
CLAY TAYLOR PRODUCTS INC
1225 Chuck Taylor Ln (28147-9813)
P.O. Box 2128 (28145-2128)
PHONE..........................704 636-2411
Charles D Taylor Junior, Pr
Barbara Johnson, *
Burton Benfield, *
▲ EMP: 100 EST: 1949
SQ FT: 212,000
SALES (est): 15.2MM Privately Held
Web: www.taylorclaybrick.com
SIC: 3251 Brick and structural clay tile

(G-11035)
CMW MANUFACTURING LLC
1217 Speedway Blvd (28146-7448)
PHONE..........................704 216-0171
Scott Lowrie, Pr
EMP: 35 EST: 2014
SQ FT: 40,000
SALES (est): 7.6MM Privately Held
Web: www.cmwmfg.com
SIC: 3441 Fabricated structural metal

(G-11036)
CONCISE MANUFACTURING INC
630 Corporate Cir (28147-9004)
PHONE..........................704 796-8419
EMP: 6 EST: 2019
SALES (est): 3.18MM Privately Held
Web: www.concisecnc.com
SIC: 3999 Manufacturing industries, nec

(G-11037)
CONTEMPORARY FURNISHINGS CORP (PA)
Also Called: Carter Furniture
1000 N Long St (28144-3834)
P.O. Box 117 (28388-0117)
PHONE..........................704 633-8000
Robert Logan, Ch Bd
Lloyd Davis, *
Bill Ward, *
Luke Fisher, *
Michael Murray, *
◆ EMP: 85 EST: 1968
SQ FT: 121,000
SALES (est): 1.79MM
SALES (corp-wide): 1.79MM Privately Held
SIC: 2512 2599 Couches, sofas, and
　　davenports: upholstered on wood frames;
　　Hotel furniture

(G-11038)
CONVEYING SOLUTIONS LLC
Also Called: Conveying Solutions LLC NC
804 Julian Rd (28147-9080)
PHONE.....................704 636-4241
EMP: 12 EST: 2009
SALES (est): 1.64MM Privately Held
Web: www.csllc.us
SIC: 3535 Conveyors and conveying
    equipment

(G-11039)
CUMBERLAND GRAVEL & SAND CO
P.O. Box 1040 (28145-1040)
PHONE.....................704 633-4241
Donald B Hensley, Pr
Robert Settle Iii, VP
Anthony M Arnold, VP
F Joanne Johnson, Sec
Jeffrey V Goodman, Treas
EMP: 6 EST: 1949
SALES (est): 359.72K Privately Held
Web: www.hedrickind.com
SIC: 1442 Construction sand and gravel

(G-11040)
CUSTOM CABINETS BY LIVENGOOD
490 Parks Rd (28146-1189)
PHONE.....................704 279-3031
Billy Livengood, Owner
EMP: 6 EST: 1961
SQ FT: 15,000
SALES (est): 103.53K Privately Held
SIC: 2434 2521 Wood kitchen cabinets;
    Cabinets, office: wood

(G-11041)
CUSTOM DESIGN INC
2001 S Main St (28144-6833)
P.O. Box 835 (28145-0835)
PHONE.....................704 637-7110
Lynn Butler, Pr
EMP: 9 EST: 2006
SALES (est): 958.19K Privately Held
Web: www.hydraulicdepotnc.com
SIC: 3449 Miscellaneous metalwork

(G-11042)
CUSTOM GOLF CAR SUPPLY INC
Also Called: Custom Plastic Forming
1735 Heilig Rd (28146-2314)
PHONE.....................704 855-1130
William Canady, CEO
◆ EMP: 174 EST: 1991
SQ FT: 86,000
SALES (est): 21.53MM
SALES (corp-wide): 559.08MM Privately
Held
Web: www.doubletakegolfcar.com
SIC: 2394 3949 Canopies, fabric: made from
    purchased materials; Golf equipment
PA: Arrowhead Engineered Products, Inc.
    3705 95th Ave Ne
    Blaine MN 55014
    763 255-2555

(G-11043)
DIMENSIONAL METALS INC
819 S Salisbury Ave (28146)
PHONE.....................704 279-9691
Steve Wissman, Pr
EMP: 7
Web: www.dmimetals.com
SIC: 3531 1761 Roofing equipment; Roofing,
    siding, and sheetmetal work
PA: Dimensional Metals, Inc.
    58 Klema Dr N
    Reynoldsburg OH 43068

(G-11044)
DOWNTOWN GRAPHICS NETWORK INC
1409 S Fulton St (28144-6411)
P.O. Box 4216 (28145)
PHONE.....................704 637-0855
Diane M Young, Pr
Michael Young, VP
◆ EMP: 7 EST: 1988
SQ FT: 3,500
SALES (est): 388.02K Privately Held
Web: www.materialpromotions.com
SIC: 2399 2674 1521 Banners, made from
    fabric; Shopping bags: made from
    purchased materials; Single-family housing
    construction

(G-11045)
DUDLEY INC
Old Carolina Brick Company
475 Majolica Rd (28147-8010)
PHONE.....................704 636-8850
Art Burkhart, VP
EMP: 9
SALES (corp-wide): 5.39MM Privately
Held
Web: www.handmadebrick.com
SIC: 3251 Brick clay: common face, glazed,
    vitrified, or hollow
PA: Dudley Inc
    705 Quintard Ave
    Anniston AL 36207
    256 237-2890

(G-11046)
DURAFIBER TECHNOLOGIES DFT INC
7401 Statesville Blvd (28147-7493)
PHONE.....................704 639-2722
EMP: 7
SALES (corp-wide): 17.78B Privately Held
SIC: 2824 Organic fibers, noncellulosic
HQ: Durafiber Technologies (Dft), Inc.
    13620 Reese Blvd E # 400
    Huntersville NC 28078
    704 912-3700

(G-11047)
EASTERN WHOLESALE FENCE LLC
7401 Statesville Blvd (28147-1000)
PHONE.....................631 698-0975
EMP: 62
SALES (corp-wide): 162.07MM Privately
Held
Web: www.easternfence.com
SIC: 5039 3496 Wire fence, gates, and
    accessories; Barbed wire, made from
    purchased wire
PA: Eastern Wholesale Fence Llc
    266 Middle Island Rd
    Medford NY 11763
    631 698-0900

(G-11048)
EPK LLC
Also Called: Epk Industrial Solutions
425 Klumac Rd (28144-6727)
PHONE.....................980 643-4787
Paul Kennedy, VP Engg
EMP: 6 EST: 2018
SALES (est): 2.1MM Privately Held
SIC: 3711 Motor vehicles and car bodies

(G-11049)
EVER GLO SIGN CO INC
4975 S Main St (28147-9388)
P.O. Box 1349 (28145-1349)
PHONE.....................704 633-3324
Robert Gainer, Pr
Joseph J Gainer, Sec

EMP: 5 EST: 1920
SQ FT: 15,000
SALES (est): 247.16K Privately Held
SIC: 3993 3441 Electric signs; Fabricated
    structural metal

(G-11050)
EXTENSIVE BUILDERS LLC
2604 Old Wilkesboro Rd (28144-3073)
PHONE.....................980 621-3793
EMP: 5
SALES (est): 1.12MM Privately Held
SIC: 1389 7389 Construction, repair, and
    dismantling services; Business Activities at
    Non-Commercial Site

(G-11051)
FAB DESIGNS INCORPORATED
2231 Old Wilkesboro Rd (28144-3042)
PHONE.....................704 636-2349
Lee Gillespie, Pr
EMP: 5 EST: 2002
SALES (est): 892.24K Privately Held
Web: www.fabdesignsinc.com
SIC: 3441 Fabricated structural metal

(G-11052)
FAITH FARM INC
585 W Ritchie Rd Ste A (28147-8176)
PHONE.....................704 431-4566
Tim Ervin, Pr
Pam Ervin, VP
EMP: 4 EST: 1995
SALES (est): 952.42K Privately Held
Web: www.faithfarm.com
SIC: 3799 5999 Trailers and trailer
    equipment; Alarm and safety equipment
    stores

(G-11053)
FEE KEES WREATHS LLC
1047 Landsdown Dr (28147-9048)
PHONE.....................704 636-1008
EMP: 5 EST: 2020
SALES (est): 150.7K Privately Held
SIC: 3999 Wreaths, artificial

(G-11054)
FISHER ATHLETIC EQUIPMENT INC
2060 Cauble Rd (28144-1506)
P.O. Box 1985 (28145-1985)
PHONE.....................704 636-5713
Robert Pritchard, Pr
Brian Pritchard, *
EMP: 45 EST: 1959
SQ FT: 50,000
SALES (est): 7.89MM
SALES (corp-wide): 13.47MM Privately
Held
SIC: 3949 2393 Sporting and athletic goods,
    nec; Textile bags
PA: Pritchard Enterprises, Inc.
    2060 Cauble Rd
    Salisbury NC 28144
    704 636-5713

(G-11055)
FREIRICH FOODS INC
815 W Kerr St (28144-3241)
P.O. Box 1529 (28145-1529)
EMP: 105 EST: 1921
SQ FT: 50,000
SALES (est): 24.46MM Privately Held
Web: www.freirich.com
SIC: 2011 2013 Meat packing plants;
    Sausages and other prepared meats

(G-11056)
GILLESPIES FBRCTION DESIGN INC
Also Called: Gillespies Fabrication Design

110 Hidden Creek Dr (28147-7268)
PHONE.....................704 636-2349
Ligon Lee Gillespie, Pr
EMP: 5 EST: 1927
SALES (est): 212.14K Privately Held
Web: www.fabdesignsinc.com
SIC: 1799 3599 3949 Welding on site;
    Machine shop, jobbing and repair; Sporting
    and athletic goods, nec

(G-11057)
GOLF SHOP
747 Club Dr (28144)
PHONE.....................704 636-7070
Randy Padavic, Owner
EMP: 5 EST: 1983
SALES (est): 247.12K Privately Held
Web: www.ccofsalisbury.com
SIC: 3949 Golf equipment

(G-11058)
GOODMAN MILLWORK INC
201 Lumber St (28144-6553)
P.O. Box 859 (28145-0859)
PHONE.....................704 633-2421
Francis E Goodman, Pr
Brenda M Goodman, *
EMP: 16 EST: 1907
SQ FT: 67,000
SALES (est): 2.02MM Privately Held
Web: www.goodmanmillwork.com
SIC: 2431 5211 Millwork; Lumber and other
    building materials

(G-11059)
GRANGES AMERICAS INC
1709 Jake Alexander Blvd S (28146-8365)
PHONE.....................704 633-6020
Bean Stout, Mgr
EMP: 92
SQ FT: 11,310
SALES (corp-wide): 13.03MM Privately
Held
Web: www.granges.com
SIC: 3353 3497 Foil, aluminum; Metal foil
    and leaf
HQ: Granges Americas Inc.
    501 Crprate Cntre Dr Ste
    Franklin TN 37067
    615 778-2004

(G-11060)
GRINDTEC ENTERPRISES CORP
3402 Mooresville Rd (28147-8828)
PHONE.....................704 636-1825
Julius Waggoner, Pr
Dan Waggoner, Ex VP
▲ EMP: 9 EST: 1982
SQ FT: 4,500
SALES (est): 473.52K Privately Held
SIC: 3541 7699 Drilling and boring machines
    ; Industrial tool grinding

(G-11061)
HARVEST HOMES AND HANDI HOUSES
Also Called: Bunce Buildings
3711 Statesville Blvd (28147-7456)
PHONE.....................704 637-3878
Richard Smith, Mgr
EMP: 5
SALES (corp-wide): 2.27MM Privately
Held
Web: www.buncebuildings.com
SIC: 3448 5999 Buildings, portable:
    prefabricated metal; Awnings
PA: Harvest Homes And Handi Houses Inc
    2100 S Main St
    Lexington NC 27292
    336 243-2382

(G-11062)
HENKEL CORPORATION
Also Called: Henkel Corporation
485 Cedar Springs Rd (28147-9249)
PHONE.................................704 633-1731
EMP: 57
SALES (corp-wide): 22.83B **Privately Held**
Web: www.henkel.com
SIC: 2843 Surface active agents
HQ: Henkel Us Operations Corporation
   1 Henkel Way
   Rocky Hill CT 06067
   860 571-5100

(G-11063)
HENKEL US OPERATIONS CORP
Also Called: Henkel Electronic Materials
825 Cedar Springs Rd (28147-9253)
PHONE.................................704 647-3500
Katrina Brown, *Brnch Mgr*
EMP: 50
SQ FT: 111,824
SALES (corp-wide): 22.83B **Privately Held**
Web: www.henkel-northamerica.com
SIC: 2891 Adhesives
HQ: Henkel Us Operations Corporation
   1 Henkel Way
   Rocky Hill CT 06067
   860 571-5100

(G-11064)
HERITAGE STEEL LLC
3870 Statesville Blvd (28147-7457)
P.O. Box 217 (27013-0217)
PHONE.................................704 431-4097
Jadon Lavern Martin, *Managing Member*
EMP: 10 **EST:** 2018
SALES (est): 2.68MM **Privately Held**
Web: www.heritagecarports.com
SIC: 3448 Prefabricated metal buildings and
   components

(G-11065)
HESS MANUFACTURING INC
Also Called: Blast-It-All
185 Piper Ln (28147-7949)
P.O. Box 1615 (28145-1615)
PHONE.................................704 637-3300
TOLL FREE: 800
EMP: 29 **EST:** 1978
SALES (est): 6.28MM **Privately Held**
Web: www.blast-it-all.com
SIC: 3589 Sandblasting equipment

(G-11066)
IMS FABRICATION INC
150 Summit Park Dr (28146-6325)
PHONE.................................704 216-0255
Andrew Clayton, *Brnch Mgr*
EMP: 35
Web: www.imsfabrication.com
SIC: 3549 Metalworking machinery, nec
PA: Ims Fabrication, Inc.
   1278 Highway 461
   Somerset KY 42503

(G-11067)
INDUSTRIAL SUP SOLUTIONS INC
(PA)
Also Called: Issi
804 Julian Rd (28147-9080)
PHONE.................................704 636-4241
R Frank Carmazzi, *Pr*
Joe Carmazzi, *
Perry Bernhardt, *
Mike Lear, *
◆ **EMP:** 43 **EST:** 1988
SQ FT: 70,000
SALES (est): 105.69MM **Privately Held**
Web: www.issimro.com

SIC: 5084 5085 3535 3511 Hydraulic
   systems equipment and supplies; Industrial
   supplies; Belt conveyor systems, general
   industrial use; Turbines and turbine
   generator sets and parts

(G-11068)
INNOSPEC ACTIVE CHEMICALS LLC
Also Called: Innospec Performance
Chemicals
500 Hinkle Ln (28144-8574)
PHONE.................................704 633-8028
Vic Jamison, *Mgr*
EMP: 172
SALES (corp-wide): 1.85B **Publicly Held**
Web: www.innospec.com
SIC: 2869 Industrial organic chemicals, nec
HQ: Innospec Active Chemicals Llc
   510 W Grimes Ave
   High Point NC 27260
   336 882-3308

(G-11069)
INNOSPEC INC
Also Called: Innospec Performance
Chemicals
500 Hinkle Ln (28144-8574)
PHONE.................................704 633-8028
◆ **EMP:** 35
SIC: 2819 Catalysts, chemical

(G-11070)
INNOSPEC INC
Also Called: Innospec Performance
Chemicals
500 Hinkle Ln (28144-8574)
PHONE.................................704 633-8028
EMP: 35
SALES (corp-wide): 1.85B **Publicly Held**
Web: www.innospec.com
SIC: 2819 Catalysts, chemical
PA: Innospec Inc.
   8310 S Valley Hwy Ste 350
   Englewood CO 80112
   303 792-5554

(G-11071)
INVISTA CAPITAL MANAGEMENT
LLC
Hwy 70 W (28145)
PHONE.................................704 636-6000
Larry T Macon, *Brnch Mgr*
EMP: 136
SALES (corp-wide): 64.44B **Privately Held**
Web: www.invista.com
SIC: 2821 2823 2281 2284 Polyethylene
   resins; Cellulosic manmade fibers; Yarn
   spinning mills; Sewing thread
HQ: Invista Capital Management, Llc
   2801 Centerville Rd
   Wilmington DE 19808
   302 683-3000

(G-11072)
JESTINES JEWELS INC
512 Klumac Rd Ste 4 (28144-6752)
PHONE.................................704 904-0191
Tracey Bost, *Pr*
Keith Bost, *VP*
EMP: 5 **EST:** 2016
SQ FT: 1,000
SALES (est): 68.91K **Privately Held**
Web: www.jestinesjewels.com
SIC: 5621 2335 2389 8742 Boutiques;
   Women's, junior's, and misses' dresses;
   Men's miscellaneous accessories;
   Management consulting services

(G-11073)
JKA IDUSTRIES
353 Grayson Dr (28147-8111)
PHONE.................................980 225-5350
Stacey Blashfield, *Owner*
EMP: 6 **EST:** 2013
SALES (est): 210K **Privately Held**
SIC: 3993 2542 2531 Signs and advertising
   specialties; Postal lock boxes, mail racks,
   and related products; Public building and
   related furniture

(G-11074)
JOHNSON CONCRETE COMPANY
(PA)
Also Called: Johnson Concrete Products
217 Klumac Rd (28144-6723)
P.O. Box 1037 (28145-1037)
PHONE.................................704 636-5231
Judith Johnson, *Pr*
Joanne Johnson, *Sec*
Kathryn Johnson, *Treas*
◆ **EMP:** 30 **EST:** 1947
SQ FT: 4,000
SALES (est): 24.88MM
SALES (corp-wide): 24.88MM **Privately
Held**
Web: www.johnsonproductsusa.com
SIC: 3271 3272 Blocks, concrete or cinder:
   standard; Pipe, concrete or lined with
   concrete

(G-11075)
JONES MARINE INC
10285 Bringle Ferry Rd (28146-9566)
PHONE.................................704 639-0173
Brian Jones, *Pr*
Larry Jones, *Sec*
EMP: 4 **EST:** 2002
SALES (est): 943.32K **Privately Held**
Web: www.jonesmarine.net
SIC: 5551 3519 5088 3732 Marine supplies,
   nec; Marine engines; Marine crafts and
   supplies; Motorboats, inboard or outboard:
   building and repairing

(G-11076)
JPI COASTAL
1114 Old Concord Rd (28146-1353)
PHONE.................................704 310-5867
Henry Van Hoy Ii, *Admn*
EMP: 8 **EST:** 2015
SALES (est): 347.04K **Privately Held**
Web: www.jpindustrial.com
SIC: 2821 Plastics materials and resins

(G-11077)
JULIAN FREIRICH COMPANY INC
815 W Kerr St (28144-3241)
P.O. Box 1529 (28145-1529)
PHONE.................................704 636-2621
Jeff Freirich, *Pr*
EMP: 50
SALES (corp-wide): 1.68MM **Privately
Held**
SIC: 2013 Prepared beef products, from
   purchased beef
PA: Julian Freirich Company, Inc.
   4601 5th St
   Long Island City NY 11101
   718 361-9111

(G-11078)
JULIAN FREIRICH FOOD PRODUCTS
Also Called: Julian Freirich Co
815 W Kerr St (28144-3241)
P.O. Box 1529 (28145-1529)
PHONE.................................704 636-2621
Jerry Freirich, *Ch*
Jeff Freirich, *Pr*
Digna Freirich, *Sec*

EMP: 20 **EST:** 1957
SQ FT: 32,000
SALES (est): 969.1K **Privately Held**
Web: www.freirich.com
SIC: 5147 2013 2011 Meats and meat
   products; Sausages and other prepared
   meats; Meat packing plants

(G-11079)
KIMBALLS SCREEN PRINT INC
1315 Union Church Rd (28146-7979)
PHONE.................................704 636-0488
Tommy Kimball, *Pr*
Todd Kimball, *VP*
Carlen Kimball, *Sec*
EMP: 5 **EST:** 1988
SALES (est): 71.23K **Privately Held**
SIC: 2759 Screen printing

(G-11080)
KITCHEN MASTERS CHARLOTTE
LLC
504 Sarazen Way (28144-8426)
PHONE.................................704 375-3320
David Garst, *Owner*
EMP: 4 **EST:** 2004
SALES (est): 549.4K **Privately Held**
Web: www.kitchenmastersclt.com
SIC: 2434 Wood kitchen cabinets

(G-11081)
KNORR BRAKE TRUCK SYSTEMS
CO
115 Summit Park Dr (28146-6325)
PHONE.................................888 836-6922
EMP: 539
SALES (corp-wide): 144.19K **Privately
Held**
Web: www.nyab.com
SIC: 3743 Railroad equipment
HQ: Knorr Brake Truck Systems Company
   748 Starbuck Ave
   Watertown NY 13601

(G-11082)
KRIEGER CABINETS DEWAYNE
415 Sailboat Dr (28146-2539)
PHONE.................................704 630-0609
EMP: 4 **EST:** 2011
SALES (est): 63.58K **Privately Held**
SIC: 2434 Wood kitchen cabinets

(G-11083)
LGC CONSULTING INC
Also Called: Cmw Holding
1217 Speedway Blvd (28146-7448)
PHONE.................................704 216-0171
▼ **EMP:** 20
SIC: 3069 Rubber automotive products

(G-11084)
LINGLE ELECTRIC REPAIR INC
600 N Main St (28144-3644)
PHONE.................................704 636-5591
Mary Ann S Lingle, *Pr*
Hilton Lingle, *Mgr*
EMP: 12 **EST:** 1936
SQ FT: 9,000
SALES (est): 1.09MM **Privately Held**
Web: www.lingleelectric.com
SIC: 7694 5063 Electric motor repair;
   Motors, electric

(G-11085)
LOCKREY COMPANY LLC (PA)
Also Called: Liquid Moly
614 Emerald Bay Dr (28146-1595)
PHONE.................................856 665-4794
EMP: 8 **EST:** 1940
SALES (est): 269.56K

SALES (corp-wide): 269.56K **Privately Held**
SIC: 2992 Re-refining lubricating oils and greases, nec

(G-11086)
LOCUST PLASTICS INC
630 Industrial Ave (28144-3013)
PHONE...............................704 636-2742
Russell Hayes, *Pr*
Russell B Hayes, *
▲ EMP: 72 EST: 2008
SQ FT: 80,000
SALES (est): 14.49MM **Privately Held**
Web: www.locustplastics.com
SIC: 3089 Injection molding of plastics

(G-11087)
LOG HOME BUILDERS INC
Also Called: Locktite Log Systems
470 B Leazer Rd (28147-8261)
PHONE...............................704 638-0677
Jim Kilgore, *Pr*
Debra Kilgore, *VP*
EMP: 7 EST: 1991
SALES (est): 194.11K **Privately Held**
Web: www.loghomebuildersnc.com
SIC: 2411 2439 Timber, cut at logging camp;
Timbers, structural: laminated lumber

(G-11088)
MAGNA COMPOSITES LLC
6701 Statesville Blvd (28147-7486)
PHONE...............................704 797-8744
▲ EMP: 323
SIC: 3714 Motor vehicle parts and accessories

(G-11089)
MARIETTA MARTIN MATERIALS INC
Also Called: Martin Marietta Aggregates
3825 Trexler St (28147-8378)
PHONE...............................704 636-6372
Damon Allen, *Brnch Mgr*
EMP: 11
Web: www.martinmarietta.com
SIC: 1422 Crushed and broken limestone
PA: Martin Marietta Materials Inc
4123 Parklake Ave
Raleigh NC 27612

(G-11090)
MCDANIEL AWNING CO
Also Called: McDaniel Awning Manufacturing
225 White Farm Rd (28147-7730)
PHONE...............................704 636-8503
Joseph M Mcdaniel, *Pr*
Dale G Mcdaniel, *Admn*
EMP: 5 EST: 1966
SQ FT: 5,200
SALES (est): 178.68K **Privately Held**
Web: www.mcdanielawning.com
SIC: 1521 3446 3444 3442 Single-family
home remodeling, additions, and repairs;
Architectural metalwork; Sheet metalwork;
Metal doors, sash, and trim

(G-11091)
MCKENZIE SPORTS PRODUCTS LLC (PA)
Also Called: Mc Kenzie Taxidermy Supply
1910 Saint Luke Church Rd (28146-7956)
P.O. Box 480 (28072-0480)
PHONE...............................704 279-7985
◆ EMP: 125 EST: 1974
SQ FT: 120,000
SALES (est): 26.03MM
SALES (corp-wide): 26.03MM **Privately Held**
Web: www.mckenziesp.com

SIC: 3949 3423 Targets, archery and rifle
shooting; Taxidermist tools and equipment

(G-11092)
MDI SOLUTIONS LLC
760 Choate Rd (28146-3211)
PHONE...............................845 721-6758
Matthew Tomosivitch, *Pr*
EMP: 6 EST: 2014
SALES (est): 1.01MM **Privately Held**
SIC: 3999 Manufacturing industries, nec

(G-11093)
MERIDIAN BRICK LLC
700 S Long St (28144)
P.O. Box 1249 (28145-1249)
PHONE...............................704 636-0131
Bill Hughes, *Mgr*
EMP: 66
SALES (corp-wide): 4.59B **Privately Held**
Web: www.generalshale.com
SIC: 3251 Brick clay: common face, glazed,
vitrified, or hollow
HQ: Meridian Brick Llc
3015 Bristol Hwy
Johnson City TN 37601
770 645-4500

(G-11094)
MPX MANUFACTURING INC
1531 S Main St (28144-6705)
PHONE...............................704 762-9207
Jeffrey Goodman, *Pr*
EMP: 4 EST: 2019
SALES (est): 261.31K **Privately Held**
SIC: 3999 Manufacturing industries, nec

(G-11095)
NC DIESEL PERFORMANCE LLC
5213 Mooresville Rd (28147-7658)
PHONE...............................704 431-3257
Brandon Lottes, *Pr*
Brandon Lottes, *Managing Member*
EMP: 4 EST: 2018
SALES (est): 359.93K **Privately Held**
SIC: 7389 7538 3443 3519 Business
Activities at Non-Commercial Site; General
automotive repair shops; Tanks, standard
or custom fabricated: metal plate; Diesel
engine rebuilding

(G-11096)
NEW SARUM BREWING CO LLC
109 N Lee St (28144-5033)
PHONE...............................704 310-5048
Tony Hornick, *Pdt Mgr*
Gian-mauro Moscardini, *Sls Dir*
Gianni Moscardini, *CEO*
Edward Moscardini, *COO*
EMP: 6 EST: 2012
SALES (est): 1.73MM **Privately Held**
Web: www.newsarumbrewing.com
SIC: 2082 Beer (alcoholic beverage)

(G-11097)
NEW YORK AIR BRAKE LLC
Premtec Division
985 Whitney Dr (28147-8394)
P.O. Box 6760 (13601-6760)
PHONE...............................315 786-5200
EMP: 51
SALES (corp-wide): 144.19K **Privately Held**
Web: www.nyab.com
SIC: 3743 Brakes, air and vacuum: railway
HQ: New York Air Brake Llc
748 Starbuck Ave
Watertown NY 13601

(G-11098)
NORTH CAROLINA DEPT TRNSP
Also Called: Driver License
5780 S Main St (28147-9396)
PHONE...............................704 633-5873
R Crowe, *Brnch Mgr*
EMP: 28
SALES (corp-wide): 74.26B **Privately Held**
Web: www.nc.gov
SIC: 3469 Automobile license tags, stamped
metal
HQ: North Carolina Department Of
Transportation
1 S Wilmington St
Raleigh NC 27610

(G-11099)
P P KILN ERECTORS
5351 Faith Rd (28146-0365)
PHONE...............................980 825-2263
EMP: 5 EST: 2018
SALES (est): 122.52K **Privately Held**
SIC: 3559 Kilns

(G-11100)
PACKAGING CORPORATION AMERICA
Also Called: Pca/Salisbury 375
1302 N Salisbury Ave (28144-8543)
PHONE...............................704 633-3611
Pete Esenburger, *Mgr*
EMP: 74
SALES (corp-wide): 7.73B **Publicly Held**
Web: www.packagingcorp.com
SIC: 2653 Boxes, corrugated: made from
purchased materials
PA: Packaging Corporation Of America
1 N Field Ct
Lake Forest IL 60045
847 482-3000

(G-11101)
PERMA FLEX ROLLER TECHNOLOGY (PA)
1415 Jake Alexander Blvd S (28146-8359)
PHONE...............................704 633-1201
Michael Berwick, *Pr*
Linda Elkins, *
▲ EMP: 30 EST: 2001
SALES (est): 1.63MM
SALES (corp-wide): 1.63MM **Privately Held**
SIC: 3069 Rubber rolls and roll coverings

(G-11102)
PERMA-FLEX ROLLERS INC
Also Called: Perma Flex Rller Tchnlgy-Rgnge
1415 Jake Alexander Blvd S (28146-8359)
P.O. Box 2389 (28145-2389)
PHONE...............................704 633-1201
Michael Berwick, *Pr*
Doug Angel, *
▲ EMP: 75 EST: 1977
SQ FT: 22,000
SALES (est): 702.67K
SALES (corp-wide): 1.63MM **Privately Held**
SIC: 3069 Printers' rolls and blankets: rubber
or rubberized fabric
PA: Perma Flex Roller Technology-
Organge, Llc
1415 Jake Alxander Blvd S
Salisbury NC 28146
704 633-1201

(G-11103)
POST PUBLISHING COMPANY
Also Called: Salisbury Post
131 W Innes St (28144-4338)
P.O. Box 4639 (28145-4639)

PHONE...............................704 633-8950
EMP: 88 EST: 1905
SALES (est): 1.58MM
SALES (corp-wide): 93.4MM **Privately Held**
Web: www.salisburypost.com
SIC: 2711 Newspapers, publishing and
printing
PA: Epi Group, Llc.
4020 Stirrup Creek Dr
Durham NC 27703
843 577-7111

(G-11104)
POWER CURBERS INC (PA)
727 Bendix Dr (28146-5876)
P.O. Box 1639 (28145-1639)
PHONE...............................704 636-5871
Dwight F Messinger, *Pr*
Stephen B Bullock, *
Deborah W Messinger, *
◆ EMP: 82 EST: 1953
SQ FT: 90,500
SALES (est): 24.98MM
SALES (corp-wide): 24.98MM **Privately Held**
Web: www.powercurbers.com
SIC: 3531 Road construction and
maintenance machinery

(G-11105)
PPG ARCHITECTURAL FINISHES INC
Also Called: Glidden Professional Paint Ctr
1333 Klumac Rd (28147-9086)
PHONE...............................704 633-0673
Regina O'brien, *Mgr*
EMP: 4
SALES (corp-wide): 17.65B **Publicly Held**
Web: www.glidden.com
SIC: 2851 Paints and allied products
HQ: Ppg Architectural Finishes, Inc.
1 Ppg Pl
Pittsburgh PA 15272
412 434-3131

(G-11106)
PRETTY BABY HERBAL SOAPS
1050 Winding Brook Ln (28146-9428)
P.O. Box 555 (28023-0555)
PHONE...............................704 209-0669
Terrianne Taylor, *Owner*
EMP: 5 EST: 1992
SALES (est): 226.32K **Privately Held**
Web: www.nakedbarnaturals.com
SIC: 2841 Soap: granulated, liquid, cake,
flaked, or chip

(G-11107)
PROTEX SPORT PRODUCTS INC
1029 S Main St (28144-6421)
P.O. Box 106 (28159)
PHONE...............................336 956-2419
Tim Clancy, *Pr*
Dawn Clancy, *VP*
EMP: 14 EST: 1993
SQ FT: 4,000
SALES (est): 1.19MM **Privately Held**
Web: www.protexsportproducts.com
SIC: 3949 Sporting and athletic goods, nec

(G-11108)
PYROTEK INCORPORATED
Also Called: Neco Division
970 Grace Church Rd (28147-9694)
PHONE...............................704 642-1993
Denny Weis, *Mgr*
EMP: 48
SQ FT: 9,000
SALES (corp-wide): 462.43MM **Privately Held**
Web: www.pyrotek.com

SIC: 3255 3544 3264　Clay refractories;
Special dies, tools, jigs, and fixtures;
Porcelain electrical supplies
PA: Pyrotek Incorporated
705 W 1st Ave
Spokane WA 99201
509 926-6212

(G-11109)
QUALITY BEVERAGE LLC (PA)
Also Called: Quality Beverage Brands
1413 Jake Alexander Blvd S (28146-8359)
P.O. Box 778 (28145-0778)
PHONE.....................704 637-5881
EMP: 4 EST: 1998
SALES (est): 10.39MM
SALES (corp-wide): 10.39MM Privately
Held
Web: www.cheerwine.com
SIC: 2086 Bottled and canned soft drinks

(G-11110)
QUICK PRINT OF CONCORD
Also Called: Quick Print
700 N Long St Ste C (28144-4463)
PHONE.....................704 782-6634
Orbe A Garcia, Pr
Nina H Garcia, VP
EMP: 5 EST: 1985
SALES (est): 67.76K Privately Held
SIC: 2752 Offset printing

(G-11111)
RETROFIX SCREWS LLC
710 Mitchell Ave (28144-6251)
PHONE.....................980 432-8412
Teresa Miller, Managing Member
EMP: 5 EST: 2017
SALES (est): 1.59MM Privately Held
Web: www.retrofixscrews.com
SIC: 3841 Surgical and medical instruments

(G-11112)
ROYCE APPAREL INC
408 Long Meadow Dr (28147-8201)
PHONE.....................704 933-6000
James Whitney, Brnch Mgr
EMP: 25
SALES (corp-wide): 16.79MM Privately
Held
Web: www.royceapparel.com
SIC: 2331 T-shirts and tops, women's: made
from purchased materials
PA: Royce Apparel, Inc.
5800 Royce St
Kannapolis NC 28083
704 933-6000

(G-11113)
S LOFLIN ENTERPRISES INC
Also Called: Thread Shed Clothing Company
133 S Main St (28144-4941)
PHONE.....................704 633-1159
Alan D Loflin, Pr
Cynthia Loflin, VP
Adam D Loflin Field, Ofcr
Annalacy Loflin Field, Ofcr
EMP: 10 EST: 1963
SQ FT: 5,000
SALES (est): 558.48K Privately Held
SIC: 2326 2399 2499 Work uniforms; Military
insignia, textile; Shoe and boot products,
wood

(G-11114)
SALISBURY MTAL FABRICATION LLC
565 Trexler Loop (28144-9060)
P.O. Box 2591 (28145-2591)
PHONE.....................704 278-0785
Debi Malone, Managing Member
EMP: 12 EST: 2014

SALES (est): 447.91K Privately Held
SIC: 3441 Fabricated structural metal

(G-11115)
SHAT-R-SHIELD LIGHTING INC
116 Ryan Patrick Dr (28147-5624)
PHONE.....................800 223-0853
Robert Nolan, CEO
Karen Clause, *
Margaret Nolan, *
▲ EMP: 64 EST: 1968
SQ FT: 46,000
SALES (est): 13.59MM Privately Held
Web: www.shatrshield.com
SIC: 3646 Commercial lighting fixtures

(G-11116)
SHIELD & STEEL ENTERPRISES LLC
Also Called: Impeccable Improvements NC
417b Peach Orchard Rd (28147-8325)
PHONE.....................704 607-0869
Simon Wentzel, Prin
EMP: 4 EST: 2015
SALES (est): 468.53K Privately Held
Web: www.shatrshield.com
SIC: 3646 Commercial lighting fixtures

(G-11117)
SOUTHERN CONCRETE MTLS INC
1155 Chuck Taylor Ln (28147-9812)
PHONE.....................877 788-3001
EMP: 16
SALES (corp-wide): 238.17MM Privately
Held
Web: www.scmusa.com
SIC: 3273 1771 Ready-mixed concrete;
Concrete work
HQ: Southern Concrete Materials, Inc.
35 Meadow Rd
Asheville NC 28803
828 253-6421

(G-11118)
SPEED BRITE INC
Also Called: Windsor Gallery
1810 W Innes St (28144-2554)
P.O. Box 1766 (28145-1766)
PHONE.....................704 639-9771
Jim Rabon, Pr
Carol Rabon, Sec
EMP: 6 EST: 1991
SQ FT: 3,800
SALES (est): 486.28K Privately Held
Web: www.speedbrite.com
SIC: 2842 5944 Specialty cleaning; Jewelry
stores

(G-11119)
STACLEAN DIFFUSER COMPANY
LLC (PA)
Also Called: Staclean Diffuser
2205 Executive Dr (28147-9008)
P.O. Box 1147 (28145-1147)
PHONE.....................704 636-8697
EMP: 12 EST: 1980
SQ FT: 57,000
SALES (est): 3.59MM
SALES (corp-wide): 3.59MM Privately
Held
Web: www.staclean.com
SIC: 3564 3826 Air purification equipment;
Environmental testing equipment

(G-11120)
SUPERIOR WALLS SYSTEMS LLC
Also Called: Superior Walls
3570 S Main St (28147-7909)
PHONE.....................704 636-6200
David Varner, Brnch Mgr
EMP: 28
SALES (corp-wide): 16.38MM Privately
Held

Web: www.superiorwalls.com
SIC: 5211 3272 Masonry materials and
supplies; Concrete products, nec
PA: Superior Walls Systems, Llc
3570 S Main St
Salisbury NC 28147
704 636-6200

(G-11121)
SUPERIOR WALLS SYSTEMS LLC
(PA)
Also Called: Superior Walls
3570 S Main St (28147-7909)
PHONE.....................704 636-6200
David Varner, Managing Member
EMP: 70 EST: 1998
SALES (est): 16.38MM
SALES (corp-wide): 16.38MM Privately
Held
Web: www.superiorwalls.com
SIC: 1771 3272 Concrete work; Concrete
products, nec

(G-11122)
TARHEEL TOOL & GAUGE LLC
4665 Miller Rd (28147-7636)
PHONE.....................704 213-6924
Dale W Brown, Owner
EMP: 6 EST: 2016
SALES (est): 137.8K Privately Held
Web: www.tarheeltoolgauge.com
SIC: 3599 Machine shop, jobbing and repair

(G-11123)
TEIJIN AUTOMOTIVE TECH INC
Also Called: Salisbury Operations
6701 Statesville Blvd (28147-7486)
PHONE.....................704 797-8744
Nick Jockheck, Brnch Mgr
EMP: 350
Web: www.teijinautomotive.com
SIC: 3089 Injection molding of plastics
HQ: Teijin Automotive Technologies, Inc.
255 Rex Blvd
Auburn Hills MI 48326
248 237-7800

(G-11124)
TEXTILE PRODUCTS INC
119 121 N Main St (28144)
PHONE.....................704 636-6221
Linda Dukelow, Pr
Daryl Dukelow, VP
EMP: 21 EST: 1994
SQ FT: 10,000
SALES (est): 200.88K Privately Held
Web: www.textileproducts.com
SIC: 5714 7389 2392 2391 Drapery and
upholstery stores; Interior design services;
Household furnishings, nec; Curtains and
draperies

(G-11125)
TIVOLI WOODWORKS LLC
4850 Bringle Ferry Rd (28146-7108)
PHONE.....................336 602-3512
Tivoli Woodworks, Prin
EMP: 5 EST: 2011
SALES (est): 173.08K Privately Held
SIC: 2431 Millwork

(G-11126)
TOOL RENTAL DEPOT LLC
2001 S Main St (28144-6833)
PHONE.....................704 636-6400
Philip Butler, Owner
EMP: 4 EST: 2012
SQ FT: 72,000
SALES (est): 2.4MM Privately Held
Web: www.toolrentaldepot.com

SIC: 3599 7699 Machine shop, jobbing and
repair; Industrial machinery and equipment
repair
PA: Hydraulics Depot, L.L.C.
2001 S Main St
Salisbury NC 28144

(G-11127)
TRELLEBORG SALISBURY INC
510 Long Meadow Dr (28147-8202)
PHONE.....................704 797-8030
D C Howard, Pr
Denise Reid, *
◆ EMP: 45 EST: 1997
SQ FT: 5,600
SALES (est): 17.95MM
SALES (corp-wide): 60.4MM Privately
Held
SIC: 3089 Automotive parts, plastic
HQ: Trelleborg Corporation
200 Veterans Blvd Ste 3
South Haven MI 49090
269 639-9891

(G-11128)
TURNKEY TECHNOLOGIES INC
402 Bringle Ferry Rd (28144-4417)
PHONE.....................704 245-6437
Tony Ward, Pr
Michael Brusich, VP
Paul Galvin, VP
EMP: 9 EST: 1999
SQ FT: 6,100
SALES (est): 7.23MM Privately Held
Web: www.turnkeytechnologies.net
SIC: 3599 Custom machinery

(G-11129)
UFP SALISBURY LLC (DH)
Also Called: U F P
358 Woodmill Rd (28147)
P.O. Box 1635 (28145-1635)
PHONE.....................704 855-1600
EMP: 9 EST: 2012
SALES (est): 9.34MM
SALES (corp-wide): 6.65B Publicly Held
SIC: 2491 Wood preserving
HQ: Ufp Structural Packaging, Llc
5840 Wi-60
Hartford WI 53027
262 673-6090

(G-11130)
UFP SALISBURY LLC
520 Grace Church Rd (28147-9690)
PHONE.....................704 855-1600
EMP: 300
SALES (corp-wide): 6.65B Publicly Held
SIC: 2491 Wood preserving
HQ: Ufp Salisbury Llc
358 Woodmill Rd
Salisbury NC 28147
704 855-1600

(G-11131)
UNDERBRINKS LLC
705 Hedrick St (28144-3154)
P.O. Box 5194 (28117)
PHONE.....................866 495-4465
Billie Underbrink, Managing Member
EMP: 5 EST: 2018
SALES (est): 590.06K Privately Held
SIC: 3449 Bars, concrete reinforcing:
fabricated steel

(G-11132)
VALUE CLOTHING INC (PA)
Also Called: Value Clothing
1310 Richard St (28144-3732)
PHONE.....................704 638-6111
Doctor Richard Williams, Pr

Richard Williams Junior, *VP*
Elaine Williams, *Sec*
Wendy Workman, *Sec*
Candy Trivette, *Treas*
▼ **EMP:** 55 **EST:** 1968
SQ FT: 90,000
SALES (est): 4.11MM
SALES (corp-wide): 4.11MM **Privately
Held**
Web: www.valueclothing.us
SIC: 2211 1521 5141 Broadwoven fabric
mills, cotton; General remodeling, single-
family houses; Food brokers

(G-11133)
VIRGINIA CAROLINA REFR INC (PA)
Also Called: Refractory Construction
1123 Speedway Blvd (28146-8389)
P.O. Box 761 (28037-0761)
PHONE..............................704 216-0223
TOLL FREE: 800
Tony R Basinger, *Pr*
EMP: 7 **EST:** 1989
SQ FT: 6,000
SALES (est): 6.89MM **Privately Held**
Web: www.vcref.com
SIC: 3297 Nonclay refractories

(G-11134)
**W A BROWN & SON
INCORPORATED (PA)**
209 Long Meadow Dr (28147-9299)
PHONE..............................704 636-5131
Jacob Werner, *Pr*
Robert L Rouse, *
EMP: 40 **EST:** 1910
SQ FT: 111,000
SALES (est): 1.76MM
SALES (corp-wide): 1.76MM **Privately
Held**
Web: www.imperialbrown.com
SIC: 3585 3822 5078 Refrigeration
equipment, complete; Environmental
controls; Refrigerators, commercial (reach-
in and walk-in)

(G-11135)
WATKINS AGENCY INC
Also Called: Watkins Fitness & Sports Eqp
721 N Long St (28144-4468)
PHONE..............................704 213-6997
TOLL FREE: 800
John Watkins Senior, *Pr*
Helen Watkins, *VP*
John Watkins Junior, *VP Opers*
EMP: 8 **EST:** 1983
SALES (est): 388.33K **Privately Held**
SIC: 7699 5941 3949 5091 Recreational
sporting equipment repair services;
Exercise equipment; Exercise equipment;
Fitness equipment and supplies

(G-11136)
WOODSHED SOFTWARE
925 Mainsail Rd (28146-1459)
PHONE..............................941 240-1780
Stephen Wood, *Prin*
EMP: 5 **EST:** 2008
SALES (est): 435.25K **Privately Held**
SIC: 7372 Prepackaged software

(G-11137)
YALE ROPE TECHNOLOGIES INC
634 Industrial Ave (28144-3013)
PHONE..............................704 630-0331
Tom Yale, *Pr*
▲ **EMP:** 8 **EST:** 2006
SALES (est): 916.23K **Privately Held**
SIC: 2298 Cordage and twine

(G-11138)
ZEON TECHNOLOGIES INC
425 Lash Dr (28147-9153)
PHONE..............................704 680-9160
Richard F Zopf Junior, *Pr*
Michael A Burnett, *VP*
▲ **EMP:** 4 **EST:** 1990
SQ FT: 32,000
SALES (est): 1.18MM **Privately Held**
Web: www.zeontech.net
SIC: 3087 Custom compound purchased
resins

Saluda
Polk County

(G-11139)
JIM ALLRED TAXIDERMY SUPPLY
1309 Ozone Dr (28773-9665)
PHONE..............................828 749-5900
Jim Allred, *Owner*
EMP: 4 **EST:** 1986
SQ FT: 3,000
SALES (est): 438.5K **Privately Held**
Web: www.jimallred.com
SIC: 3423 5087 Taxidermist tools and
equipment; Taxidermist tools and equipment

(G-11140)
SALUDA YARN CO INC
Greenville & Walnut Streets (28773)
PHONE..............................828 749-2861
Ray P Reid, *Pr*
Ellen B Reid, *Sec*
EMP: 12 **EST:** 1962
SQ FT: 11,200
SALES (est): 129.18K **Privately Held**
SIC: 2299 Yarns, specialty and novelty

Sandy Ridge
Stokes County

(G-11141)
BHAKTIVEDANTA ARCHIVES
Also Called: BBT ARCHIVES
1453 Tom Shelton Rd (27046-7026)
P.O. Box 255 (27046-0255)
PHONE..............................336 871-3636
Eddy Gaasbeek, *Pr*
▲ **EMP:** 9 **EST:** 1989
SQ FT: 5,500
SALES (est): 138.92K **Privately Held**
Web: www.prabhupada.com
SIC: 2731 2741 3999 Books, publishing only
; Miscellaneous publishing; Education aids,
devices and supplies

(G-11142)
**CRISTAL DRAGON CANDLE
COMPANY**
3271 Moir Farm Rd (27046-7504)
PHONE..............................336 997-4210
EMP: 5 **EST:** 2014
SALES (est): 53.54K **Privately Held**
SIC: 3999 Candles

(G-11143)
DUNCAN JUNIOR D
Also Called: Duncan, JD Logging
1165 Troy Brown Rd (27046-7426)
PHONE..............................336 871-3599
Junior David Duncan, *Owner*
EMP: 4 **EST:** 1982
SALES (est): 238.03K **Privately Held**
SIC: 2411 Logging camps and contractors

Sanford
Lee County

(G-11144)
3M COMPANY
Also Called: 3M
3010 Lee Ave (27332-6210)
PHONE..............................919 774-3808
Michael Swartz, *Brnch Mgr*
EMP: 5
SALES (corp-wide): 32.68B **Publicly Held**
Web: www.3m.com
SIC: 3629 Static elimination equipment,
industrial
PA: 3m Company
3m Center
Saint Paul MN 55144
651 733-1110

(G-11145)
ACE LASER RECYCLING INC
1808 Rice Rd (27330-9045)
P.O. Box 151 (27331-0151)
PHONE..............................919 775-5521
Phillip C Kelly, *Pr*
EMP: 4 **EST:** 1998
SALES (est): 247.99K **Privately Held**
SIC: 3955 Print cartridges for laser and other
computer printers

(G-11146)
AIR SYSTEM COMPONENTS INC
Also Called: ASC
275 Pressly Foushee Rd (27330-7595)
PHONE..............................919 279-8868
EMP: 93
Web: www.airsysco.com
SIC: 3585 Air conditioning equipment,
complete
HQ: Air System Components, Inc.
605 Shiloh Rd
Plano TX 75074
972 212-4888

(G-11147)
AIR SYSTEM COMPONENTS INC
Also Called: Trion Iaq
101 Mcneill Rd (27330-9451)
PHONE..............................919 775-2201
William Crawford, *Contrlr*
EMP: 100
Web: www.trioniaq.com
SIC: 3585 Air conditioning equipment,
complete
HQ: Air System Components, Inc.
605 Shiloh Rd
Plano TX 75074
972 212-4888

(G-11148)
APEX INDUSTRIAL
2903 Lee Ave (27332)
P.O. Box 1216 (25560)
PHONE..............................877 676-2739
Jonathan Link, *Pr*
EMP: 15 **EST:** 2014
SALES (est): 4.34MM **Privately Held**
Web: www.apexmro.com
SIC: 3429 Clamps, couplings, nozzles, and
other metal hose fittings

(G-11149)
ARDEN COMPANIES LLC
Also Called: Arden
1611 Broadway Rd (27332-9795)
PHONE..............................919 258-3081
Alice Edmisten, *Brnch Mgr*
EMP: 29
SALES (corp-wide): 3.2B **Publicly Held**

Web: www.ardencompanies.com
SIC: 2392 3999 Cushions and pillows;
Umbrellas, canes, and parts
HQ: Arden Companies, Llc
30400 Telg Rd Ste 200
Bingham Farms MI 48025
248 415-8500

(G-11150)
ARDEN COMPANIES LLC
Also Called: Arden Companies
1611 Broadway Rd (27332-9795)
PHONE..............................919 258-3081
Al Smith, *Prin*
EMP: 52
SALES (corp-wide): 3.2B **Publicly Held**
Web: www.ardencompanies.com
SIC: 2519 2515 2392 Lawn and garden
furniture, except wood and metal;
Mattresses and bedsprings; Household
furnishings, nec
HQ: Arden Companies, Llc
30400 Telg Rd Ste 200
Bingham Farms MI 48025
248 415-8500

(G-11151)
ASTELLAS GENE THERAPIES INC
6074 Enterprise Park Dr (27330-9709)
PHONE..............................415 638-6561
EMP: 60
Web: www.audentestx.com
SIC: 2836 Biological products, except
diagnostic
HQ: Astellas Gene Therapies, Inc.
480 Forbes Blvd
South San Francisco CA 94080
415 818-1001

(G-11152)
ATLANTIC HYDRAULICS SVCS LLC
5225 Womack Rd (27330-9517)
P.O. Box 5225 (27331-5225)
PHONE..............................919 542-2985
Tiffany Roberts, *Pr*
▲ **EMP:** 30 **EST:** 1981
SQ FT: 8,000
SALES (est): 6.99MM **Privately Held**
Web: www.atlantic-hydraulics.com
SIC: 1799 3594 3541 3593 Hydraulic
equipment, installation and service; Motors:
hydraulic, fluid power, or air; Lathes, metal
cutting and polishing; Fluid power cylinders
and actuators

(G-11153)
BATTLE TRUCKING INC
Also Called: Battle Trucking Company
911 San Lee Dr (27330-9067)
PHONE..............................919 708-2288
Howard Battle, *Owner*
EMP: 4 **EST:** 1976
SALES (est): 217.82K **Privately Held**
Web: www.atticmoldremediation.com
SIC: 3715 Truck trailers

(G-11154)
BEAR CREEK ARSENAL LLC
310 Mcneill Rd (27330-6523)
PHONE..............................919 292-6000
EMP: 128 **EST:** 2010
SALES (est): 5.66MM **Privately Held**
Web: www.bearcreekarsenal.com
SIC: 5941 3489 Firearms; Artillery or artillery
parts, over 30 mm.

(G-11155)
**BHARAT FORGE ALUMINUM USA
INC (DH)**
777 Kalyani Way (27330)
PHONE..............................585 576-7483

EMP: 192 EST: 2019
SALES (est): 25.97MM **Privately Held**
SIC: 3353 Aluminum sheet and strip
HQ: Bharat Forge America Inc.
2105 Schmiede St
Surgoinsville TN 37873

(G-11156)
BLACK COLLECTION APPAREL LLC
Also Called: Manufacturing
1140 N Horner Blvd (27330-9444)
PHONE..............................919 716-5183
Betty Richardson, *CEO*
EMP: 4 EST: 2022
SALES (est): 74.79K **Privately Held**
SIC: 2759 2389 Promotional printing;
Apparel and accessories, nec

(G-11157)
BNP INC
Also Called: J M C Tool and Machine
5910 Elwin Buchanan Dr (27330-9525)
PHONE..............................919 775-7070
Glen Berry, *Pr*
Howard Nystrom, *VP*
Frank Patkunas, *VP*
EMP: 10 EST: 1993
SQ FT: 5,000
SALES (est): 4.04MM **Privately Held**
Web: www.jmctool.com
SIC: 3469 3544 Machine parts, stamped or
pressed metal; Special dies, tools, jigs, and
fixtures

(G-11158)
BOST DISTRIBUTING COMPANY INC
2209 Boone Trail Rd (27330-8641)
P.O. Box 447 (27331-0447)
PHONE..............................919 775-5931
James H Bost Junior, *Pr*
Jim Bost, *
EMP: 7 EST: 1987
SALES (est): 471.06K **Privately Held**
Web: www.bostdistributingcompany.com
SIC: 2032 2099 Chili, with or without meat:
packaged in cans, jars, etc.; Gravy mixes,
dry

(G-11159)
BROADWIND INDUS SOLUTIONS LLC
1824 Boone Trail Rd (27330-8662)
PHONE..............................919 777-2907
Gil Mayo, *Pr*
▲ **EMP: 40 EST:** 2007
SQ FT: 125,000
SALES (est): 24.73MM **Publicly Held**
Web: www.bwen.com
SIC: 4783 3599 8742 8734 Packing and
crating; Machine and other job shop work;
Materials mgmt. (purchasing, handling,
inventory) consultant; Calibration and
certification
PA: Broadwind, Inc.
3240 S Central Ave
Cicero IL 60804

(G-11160)
CATERPILLAR INC
Also Called: Caterpillar
5000 Womack Rd (27330-9594)
P.O. Box 3667 (27331-3667)
PHONE..............................919 777-2000
Bill Allenbough, *Brnch Mgr*
EMP: 39
SALES (corp-wide): 64.81B **Publicly Held**
Web: www.caterpillar.com
SIC: 3531 3519 3511 3537 Construction
machinery; Internal combustion engines,
nec; Turbines and turbine generator sets;
Industrial trucks and tractors

PA: Caterpillar Inc.
5205 N Ocnnor Blvd Ste 10
Irving TX 75039
972 891-7700

(G-11161)
CENTURY STONE LLC
624 Fairway Dr (27330-9267)
PHONE..............................919 774-3334
Kevin Noel, *Managing Member*
EMP: 5 EST: 2005
SALES (est): 379.83K **Privately Held**
SIC: 3281 Curbing, granite or stone

(G-11162)
CERTIFIED MACHINING INC
2710 Wilkins Dr (27330-9400)
PHONE..............................919 777-9608
Tim Coggins, *Pr*
Lisa Coggins, *Sec*
EMP: 10 EST: 1996
SQ FT: 9,600
SALES (est): 2.39MM **Privately Held**
Web: www.dnzproducts.com
SIC: 3599 Machine shop, jobbing and repair

(G-11163)
CHALLNGE PRTG OF CRLNAS INC TH
5905 Clyde Rhyne Dr (27330-9508)
PHONE..............................919 777-2820
Thomas Forrest, *Prin*
EMP: 4 EST: 2013
SALES (est): 199.27K **Privately Held**
Web:
www.carolinaballroomchallenge.com
SIC: 2671 Paper; coated and laminated
packaging

(G-11164)
CIRCOR PRECISION METERING LLC
Zenith Pumps Division
5910 Elwin Buchanan Dr (27330-9525)
PHONE..............................919 774-7667
Bill Roller, *Brnch Mgr*
EMP: 548
Web: www.zenithpumps.com
SIC: 3728 3724 3561 3541 Pumps, propeller
feathering; Lubricating systems, aircraft;
Pump jacks and other pumping equipment;
Drilling machine tools (metal cutting)
HQ: Circor Precision Metering, Llc
1710 Airport Rd
Monroe NC 28110
704 289-6511

(G-11165)
CONVEYOR TECHNOLOGIES OF SANFORD NC INC
Also Called: CTI Systems
5313 Womack Rd (27330-9517)
PHONE..............................919 776-7227
◆ **EMP:** 80
Web: www.conveyor-technologies.com
SIC: 3535 Conveyors and conveying
equipment

(G-11166)
COTY INC
Also Called: Coty Sanford Factory
1400 Broadway Rd (27332-7739)
PHONE..............................919 895-5000
EMP: 84
Web: www.coty.com
SIC: 2844 Perfumes, cosmetics and other
toilet preparations
PA: Coty Inc.
350 5th Ave
New York NY 10118

(G-11167)
COTY US LLC
Also Called: Coty
1400 Broadway Rd (27332-7713)
PHONE..............................919 895-5374
EMP: 850
SQ FT: 435,000
Web: www.coty.com
SIC: 2844 Perfumes, natural or synthetic
HQ: Coty Us Llc
350 5th Ave
New York NY 10016

(G-11168)
DESCO INDUSTRIES INC
Also Called: Jj Electronic Solutions Div
920 J R Industrial Dr (27332-9733)
PHONE..............................919 718-0000
Tommie Lee, *Mgr*
EMP: 11
SALES (corp-wide): 48.53MM **Privately Held**
Web: www.descoindustries.com
SIC: 3081 Plastics film and sheet
PA: Desco Industries, Inc.
3651 Walnut Ave
Chino CA 91710
909 627-8178

(G-11169)
DESCO INDUSTRIES INC
Electronic Solutions Division
926 J R Industrial Dr (27332-9733)
PHONE..............................919 718-0000
Vladimir Kraz, *Brnch Mgr*
EMP: 27
SALES (corp-wide): 48.53MM **Privately Held**
Web: www.descoindustries.com
SIC: 3829 Measuring and controlling
devices, nec
PA: Desco Industries, Inc.
3651 Walnut Ave
Chino CA 91710
909 627-8178

(G-11170)
DESCO INDUSTRIES INC
914 J R Industrial Dr (27332-9733)
PHONE..............................919 718-0000
Tommie Lee, *Mgr*
EMP: 17
SALES (corp-wide): 48.53MM **Privately Held**
Web: www.descoindustries.com
SIC: 3841 Surgical instruments and
apparatus
PA: Desco Industries, Inc.
3651 Walnut Ave
Chino CA 91710
909 627-8178

(G-11171)
DESCO INDUSTRIES INC
917 J R Industrial Dr (27332-9733)
PHONE..............................919 718-0000
Tommie Lee, *Mgr*
EMP: 15
SALES (corp-wide): 48.53MM **Privately Held**
Web: www.descoindustries.com
SIC: 3629 Static elimination equipment,
industrial
PA: Desco Industries, Inc.
3651 Walnut Ave
Chino CA 91710
909 627-8178

(G-11172)
DSE EXPRESS LLC
10 Valley View Ct (27332-2302)
PHONE..............................540 686-0981
EMP: 4
SALES (est): 1.83MM **Privately Held**
SIC: 3537 Trucks: freight, baggage, etc.:
industrial, except mining

(G-11173)
DURAFIBER TECHNOLOGIES DFT INC
672 Douglas Farm Rd (27332-1831)
PHONE..............................919 356-3824
EMP: 4
SALES (corp-wide): 17.78B **Privately Held**
SIC: 2824 Organic fibers, noncellulosic
HQ: Durafiber Technologies (Dft), Inc.
13620 Reese Blvd E # 400
Huntersville NC 28078
704 912-3700

(G-11174)
EARLS PRECISION MACHINING
365 Taylors Chapel Rd (27330-0988)
PHONE..............................919 542-1869
Robert Earl Junior, *Pr*
EMP: 4 EST: 1989
SALES (est): 378.71K **Privately Held**
Web: www.earlspm.com
SIC: 3599 Machine shop, jobbing and repair

(G-11175)
EDELBROCK LLC
5715 Clyde Rhyne Dr (27330-9563)
PHONE..............................919 718-9737
Terry Pattigno, *Manager*
EMP: 115
Web: www.edelbrock.com
SIC: 3751 3714 Motorcycle accessories;
Gas tanks, motor vehicle
HQ: Edelbrock, Llc
8649 Hacks Cross Rd
Olive Branch MS 38654
310 781-2222

(G-11176)
ELIZABETH S JAVA EXPRESS
120 S Moore St (27330-4224)
PHONE..............................919 777-5282
Jeff Sadlick, *Owner*
EMP: 4 EST: 2006
SALES (est): 142.36K **Privately Held**
SIC: 2741 Miscellaneous publishing

(G-11177)
ENVIRCO CORPORATION (PA)
101 Mcneill Rd (27330-9451)
PHONE..............................919 775-2201
Paul Christiansen, *Sls Dir*
▲ **EMP: 27 EST:** 1965
SQ FT: 45,000
SALES (est): 5.11MM
SALES (corp-wide): 5.11MM **Privately Held**
Web: www.envirco-hvac.com
SIC: 3564 Purification and dust collection
equipment

(G-11178)
FLOWERS BKG CO JAMESTOWN LLC
Also Called: Flowers Bakery
708 E Main St (27330)
PHONE..............................919 776-8932
Mike Waites, *Mgr*
EMP: 27
SALES (corp-wide): 5.1B **Publicly Held**
SIC: 2051 Bread, all types (white, wheat,
rye, etc); fresh or frozen

HQ: Flowers Baking Co. Of Jamestown, Llc
801 W Main St
Jamestown NC 27282
336 841-8840

(G-11179)
FOELL PACKING COMPANY OF NC
2209 Boone Trail Rd (27330-8641)
P.O. Box 2340 (27331-2340)
PHONE................................919 776-0592
Jim Bost, *Pr*
EMP: 6 **EST:** 1919
SQ FT: 32,000
SALES (est): 226.05K **Privately Held**
SIC: 2013 2099 Canned meats (except baby food), from purchased meat; Ready-to-eat meals, salads, and sandwiches

(G-11180)
FOILED AGIN CHOCLAT COINS LLC
1488 Mcneill Rd # A (27330-9526)
PHONE................................919 342-4601
Scott Wayne, *Pr*
EMP: 4 **EST:** 2011
SALES (est): 406.68K **Privately Held**
Web: www.foiledagainchocolate.com
SIC: 2064 Chocolate candy, except solid chocolate

(G-11181)
FRONTIER YARNS INC (HQ)
1823 Boone Trail Rd (27330-8662)
PHONE................................919 776-9940
Robin Perkins, *CEO*
EMP: 62 **EST:** 2019
SALES (est): 21.66MM
SALES (corp-wide): 3.2B **Privately Held**
Web: www.gildanyarns.com
SIC: 2281 Yarn spinning mills
PA: Les Vetements De Sport Gildan Inc
600 Boul De Maisonneuve O 33eme Etage
Montreal QC H3A 3
514 735-2023

(G-11182)
FRONTIER YARNS INC
1823 Boone Trail Rd (27330-8662)
PHONE................................919 776-9940
EMP: 68
SALES (corp-wide): 33.59MM **Privately Held**
SIC: 2281 Spinning yarn
PA: Frontier Yarns, Inc.
1823 Boone Trail Rd
Sanford NC 27330
919 776-9940

(G-11183)
FSM LIQUIDATION CORP
1823 Boone Trail Rd (27330-8662)
PHONE................................919 776-9940
◆ **EMP:** 1200
SIC: 2281 Spinning yarn

(G-11184)
GKN DRIVELINE NORTH AMER INC
Also Called: Plant 12
4901 Womack Rd (27330-9593)
PHONE................................919 708-4500
Bob Arble, *Brnch Mgr*
EMP: 116
SALES (corp-wide): 6.06B **Privately Held**
SIC: 3463 3469 3714 Nonferrous forgings; Metal stampings, nec; Motor vehicle parts and accessories
HQ: Gkn Driveline North America, Inc.
2200 N Opdyke Rd
Auburn Hills MI 48326
248 296-7000

(G-11185)
GLENDON PYROPHYLLITE INC
Also Called: Glendon Pyrophllite Rock Quar
1789 Clarence Mckeithen Rd (27330-8780)
PHONE................................919 464-5243
Benny Lee, *Mgr*
EMP: 6
SALES (corp-wide): 820.19K **Privately Held**
SIC: 3295 Pyrophyllite, ground or otherwise treated
PA: Glendon Pyrophyllite Inc
1789 Mckeithan Rd
Sanford NC
919 774-6602

(G-11186)
GORDON ENTERPRISES
3125 Hawkins Ave (27330-6916)
PHONE................................919 776-8784
William A Gordon, *Owner*
EMP: 6 **EST:** 1978
SALES (est): 814.98K **Privately Held**
SIC: 3599 Custom machinery

(G-11187)
GRP INC
1823 Boone Trail Rd (27330-8662)
PHONE................................919 776-9940
EMP: 6 **EST:** 2010
SALES (est): 215K **Privately Held**
SIC: 2281 Cotton yarn, spun

(G-11188)
HAWK DISTRIBUTORS INC
2980 Lee Ave (27332-6208)
PHONE................................888 334-1307
Terry Earle, *Pr*
EMP: 8 **EST:** 2012
SALES (est): 708.22K **Privately Held**
Web: www.hawkdistributors.com
SIC: 2337 2311 2387 3949 Women's and misses' suits and coats; Coats, overcoats and vests; Apparel belts; Hunting equipment

(G-11189)
HERITAGE CONCRETE SERVICE CORP (PA)
Also Called: Heritage Concrete
140 Deep River Rd (27330-6528)
P.O. Box 964 (27331-0964)
PHONE................................919 775-5014
Cliff Stephens, *Pr*
Ovide De St Aubin Junior, *Sec*
Dennis D Aubin, *Prin*
EMP: 19 **EST:** 1986
SQ FT: 5,000
SALES (est): 5.73MM
SALES (corp-wide): 5.73MM **Privately Held**
Web: www.heritageconcreteservice.com
SIC: 3273 Ready-mixed concrete

(G-11190)
HFC PRESTIGE PRODUCTS INC
1400 Broadway Rd (27332-7713)
PHONE................................919 895-5300
Mark Duncan, *Brnch Mgr*
EMP: 7
SIC: 2844 Perfumes, cosmetics and other toilet preparations
HQ: Hfc Prestige Products, Inc.
350 Fifth Ave 19th Fl
New York NY 10118

(G-11191)
HUGGER MUGGER LLC
Also Called: Brick City Phenomicon
229 Wicker St (27330-4253)
PHONE................................910 585-2749

Tim Emmert, *Managing Member*
EMP: 11 **EST:** 2015
SALES (est): 431.09K **Privately Held**
Web: www.huggermuggerbrewing.com
SIC: 2082 Beer (alcoholic beverage)

(G-11192)
HUMBER STREET FACILITY INC
105 E Humber St (27330-5844)
P.O. Box 2705 (27331-2705)
PHONE................................919 775-3628
Allen Heckle, *Genl Mgr*
Kirby Weisner, *
Martin Marks, *
EMP: 7 **EST:** 1946
SQ FT: 50,000
SALES (est): 990.51K **Privately Held**
Web: www.hallmanfoundryusa.com
SIC: 3321 Gray iron castings, nec

(G-11193)
HYDRO TUBE ENTERPRISES INC
2645 Mount Pisgah Church Rd (27332-8508)
PHONE................................919 258-3070
Barbara Reining, *Brnch Mgr*
EMP: 35
SALES (corp-wide): 22.56MM **Privately Held**
Web: www.hydrotube.com
SIC: 3292 Tubing and piping, asbestos and asbestos cement
PA: Hydro Tube Enterprises, Inc.
137 Artino St
Oberlin OH 44074
440 774-1022

(G-11194)
HYDRO TUBE SOUTH LLC
2645 Mount Pisgah Church Rd (27332-8508)
PHONE................................919 258-3070
Lawrence L Reining, *Managing Member*
EMP: 9 **EST:** 1997
SQ FT: 40,000
SALES (est): 1.6MM **Privately Held**
Web: www.hydrotube.com
SIC: 3498 Tube fabricating (contract bending and shaping)

(G-11195)
INGRAM WOODYARDS INC
1925 Jefferson Davis Hwy (27330-9123)
P.O. Box 828 (27209-0828)
PHONE................................910 556-1250
Wayne Ingram, *Pr*
Scott Ingram, *VP*
EMP: 10 **EST:** 1998
SALES (est): 720.04K **Privately Held**
SIC: 2611 Pulp mills

(G-11196)
JEFFERS LOGGING INC
279 Garner Rd (27330-9684)
PHONE................................919 708-2193
Johnny D Jeffers, *Pr*
EMP: 5 **EST:** 1992
SALES (est): 810.3K **Privately Held**
SIC: 2411 Logging camps and contractors

(G-11197)
JMC TOOL & MACHINE CO
5910 Elwin Buchanan Dr (27330-9525)
PHONE................................919 775-7070
Anthony Butler, *Managing Member*
Glenn Berry, *
EMP: 44 **EST:** 1997
SALES (est): 5.52MM **Privately Held**
Web: www.jmctool.com
SIC: 3599 Machine shop, jobbing and repair

(G-11198)
JONES PRINTING COMPANY INC
104 Hawkins Ave (27330-4322)
P.O. Box 1089 (27331-1089)
PHONE................................919 774-9442
Dale Harrison, *Pr*
John Lemon, *VP*
Michael Thomas, *Sec*
David G Spivey, *Treas*
P J Patterson, *Off Mgr*
EMP: 9 **EST:** 1924
SQ FT: 6,000
SALES (est): 905.67K **Privately Held**
Web: www.jonesprintingco.com
SIC: 2752 Offset printing

(G-11199)
KEEBLER COMPANY
Also Called: Keebler
5801 Mockingbird Ln (27332-7811)
PHONE................................919 774-6431
EMP: 121
SALES (corp-wide): 13.12B **Publicly Held**
Web: www.keebler.com
SIC: 2052 Cookies
HQ: Keebler Company
1 Kellogg Sq
Battle Creek MI 49017
269 961-2000

(G-11200)
KELLER COMPANIES INC
1600 Colon Rd (27330-9577)
PHONE................................919 776-4641
EMP: 6 **EST:** 2012
SALES (est): 111.37K **Privately Held**
SIC: 2421 Building and structural materials, wood

(G-11201)
L F I SERVICES INC
1136 Broadway Rd (27332-9793)
PHONE................................215 343-0411
Lucille Jones, *Pr*
Salvatore J Stea, *
Larry Jones, *
Virginia Stea, *Stockholder* *
EMP: 4 **EST:** 1978
SQ FT: 7,000
SALES (est): 208.74K **Privately Held**
SIC: 3567 Heating units and devices, industrial: electric

(G-11202)
LAUNCHMAGICCOM INC
Also Called: Bookingbuilder Technologies
500 Westover Dr Pmb 13081 (27330-8941)
PHONE................................845 234-4440
Seth Perelman, *CEO*
EMP: 9 **EST:** 1999
SALES (est): 236.89K **Privately Held**
SIC: 7372 Prepackaged software

(G-11203)
LEE BRICK & TILE COMPANY
3704 Hawkins Ave (27330-9519)
P.O. Box 1027 (27331-1027)
PHONE................................919 774-4800
Don Perry, *Pr*
Paul Perry, *
Gil Perry, *
Frank G Perry Junior, *VP*
Michael Lilly, *
EMP: 54 **EST:** 1946
SQ FT: 2,000
SALES (est): 5MM **Privately Held**
Web: www.leebrickonline.com
SIC: 3259 Adobe brick

(G-11204)
LEE BUILDER MART INC
1000 N Horner Blvd (27330-9401)
EMP: 23 **EST:** 1956
SALES (est): 654.54K **Privately Held**
Web: www.leebuildermart.com
SIC: 5211 2431 Home centers; Millwork

(G-11205)
LEE COUNTY INDUSTRIES INC
Also Called: LCI
2711 Tramway Rd (27332-7140)
P.O. Box 973 (27331-0973)
PHONE.....................................919 775-3439
Meg Moss, *Ex Dir*
Sue Marshburn, *Dir*
EMP: 8 **EST:** 1967
SQ FT: 30,000
SALES (est): 1.09MM **Privately Held**
Web: www.lciinc.org
SIC: 8331 3412 2796 2789 Vocational
rehabilitation agency; Metal barrels, drums,
and pails; Platemaking services;
Bookbinding and related work

(G-11206)
MAC-VANN INC
1650 Colon Rd (27330-9577)
P.O. Box 1030 (27526-1030)
PHONE.....................................919 577-0746
Michele M Freeman, *VP*
John M Van Nest Senior, *Pr*
Michael Freeman, *VP*
EMP: 5 **EST:** 2005
SALES (est): 981.16K **Privately Held**
Web: www.mac-vann.com
SIC: 2426 Hardwood dimension and flooring
mills

(G-11207)
MARTIN MARIETTA MATERIALS INC
Also Called: Martin Marietta Aggregates
1227 Willett Rd (27332-0805)
P.O. Box 247 (28355-0247)
PHONE.....................................919 788-4391
Ray Thatcher, *Mgr*
EMP: 5
Web: www.martinmarietta.com
SIC: 1422 Crushed and broken limestone
PA: Martin Marietta Materials Inc
4123 Parklake Ave
Raleigh NC 27612

(G-11208)
MATTHEW JOHNSON LOGGING
536 Farrell Rd (27330-7961)
PHONE.....................................919 291-0197
Matthew Johnson, *Owner*
EMP: 6 **EST:** 1999
SALES (est): 556.76K **Privately Held**
SIC: 2411 Logging

(G-11209)
MERTEK SOLUTIONS INC
3913 Hawkins Ave (27330-9419)
PHONE.....................................919 774-7827
Jerry L Pedley, *Prin*
Jeremy Pedley, *
EMP: 37 **EST:** 2010
SQ FT: 25,000
SALES (est): 7.98MM **Privately Held**
Web: www.merteknc.com
SIC: 3599 Machine shop, jobbing and repair

(G-11210)
MODERN MACHINING INC
115 Brady Rd (27330-9503)
PHONE.....................................919 775-7332
John Clark, *Pr*
EMP: 5 **EST:** 1986

SQ FT: 8,000
SALES (est): 671.11K **Privately Held**
Web: modern-machining.business.site
SIC: 3599 Machine shop, jobbing and repair

(G-11211)
NEW BOSTON FRUIT SLICE &
CONFE
Also Called: Boston Fruit Slice & Conf
2627 Watson Ave (27332-6146)
PHONE.....................................919 775-2471
Michael Hiera, *Pr*
EMP: 24 **EST:** 2001
SQ FT: 1,800
SALES (est): 4.74MM **Privately Held**
Web: www.bostonfruitslice.com
SIC: 2064 Candy and other confectionery
products

(G-11212)
NOBLE OIL SERVICES INC
5617 Clyde Rhyne Dr (27330-9562)
PHONE.....................................919 774-8180
James Noble, *Pr*
Richard Kalin, *
EMP: 120 **EST:** 1983
SQ FT: 1,800
SALES (est): 31.56MM
SALES (corp-wide): 5.89B **Publicly Held**
Web: www.nobleoil.com
SIC: 1799 4953 7699 1795 Decontamination
services; Recycling, waste materials; Tank
repair and cleaning services; Dismantling
steel oil tanks
HQ: Safety-Kleen Systems, Inc.
1255 W 15th St
Plano TX 75075
972 265-2000

(G-11213)
OLIVIA MACHINE & TOOL INC
815 Seawell Rosser Rd (27332-2411)
P.O. Box 351 (28368-0351)
PHONE.....................................919 499-6021
Terry W Thomas, *Pr*
Sam Thomas, *VP*
Waylon W Thomas, *Sec*
Sammy D Thomas, *Sec*
Wayne W Thomas, *Treas*
EMP: 18 **EST:** 1981
SQ FT: 30,000
SALES (est): 4.5MM **Privately Held**
Web: www.oliviamachine.com
SIC: 3599 Machine shop, jobbing and repair

(G-11214)
PACKET PUSHERS INTERACTIVE
LLC
500 Westover Dr Ste 16993 (27330-8941)
PHONE.....................................928 793-2450
Ethan Banks, *Managing Member*
EMP: 5 **EST:** 2012
SALES (est): 173.8K **Privately Held**
Web: www.packetpushers.net
SIC: 3545 Pushers

(G-11215)
PCC AIRFOILS LLC
Also Called: Sherwood Refractores
5105 Rex Mcleod Dr (27330)
PHONE.....................................919 774-4300
Steve Chance, *Mgr*
EMP: 366
SALES (corp-wide): 424.23B **Publicly**
Held
Web: www.pccairfoils.com
SIC: 3369 3728 3714 3297 Castings, except
die-castings, precision; Aircraft parts and
equipment, nec; Motor vehicle parts and
accessories; Castable refractories, nonclay
HQ: Pcc Airfoils, Llc

3401 Entp Pkwy Ste 200
Beachwood OH 44122
216 831-3590

(G-11216)
PEARSON TEXTILES INC
7975 Villanow Dr (27332-7595)
P.O. Box 1289 (27331-1289)
PHONE.....................................919 776-8730
Mike W Gonella, *Pr*
Cynthia Gonella, *
EMP: 6 **EST:** 1974
SQ FT: 40,000
SALES (est): 230.57K **Privately Held**
SIC: 5131 2281 Textiles, woven, nec;
Knitting yarn, spun

(G-11217)
PENTAIR WATER POOL AND SPA
INC (DH)
Also Called: Pentair Pool Products
1620 Hawkins Ave (27330-9501)
PHONE.....................................919 566-8000
Mario R D'ovidio, *Pr*
Karl Frykman, *
Robert D Miller, *
Dave Murray, *
◆ **EMP:** 600 **EST:** 1971
SALES (est): 380.97MM **Privately Held**
Web: www.pentairpool.com
SIC: 3589 3561 3569 3648 Swimming pool
filter and water conditioning systems;
Pumps, domestic: water or sump; Heaters,
swimming pool: electric; Underwater
lighting fixtures
HQ: Pentair, Inc.
5500 Wayzata Blvd Ste 900
Minneapolis MN 55416
763 545-1730

(G-11218)
PERRY BROTHERS TIRE SVC INC
(PA)
610 Wicker St (27330-4141)
P.O. Box 968 (27331-0968)
PHONE.....................................919 775-7225
Hugh P Perry, *CEO*
Paul Steven Perry, *Pr*
Charles Ross Perry, *VP*
Hal Chaplan Perry, *VP*
Paul Horton, *VP*
EMP: 21 **EST:** 1932
SQ FT: 8,000
SALES (est): 3.29MM
SALES (corp-wide): 3.29MM **Privately**
Held
Web: www.blackstire.com
SIC: 5531 5722 5014 7534 Automotive tires;
Household appliance stores; Automobile
tires and tubes; Tire recapping

(G-11219)
PFIZER INC
Wyeth
4300 Oak Park Rd (27330-9550)
PHONE.....................................919 775-7100
Bruce Kaylos, *Brnch Mgr*
EMP: 125
SALES (corp-wide): 63.63B **Publicly Held**
Web: www.pfizer.com
SIC: 2836 5122 2834 Biological products,
except diagnostic; Biologicals and allied
products; Pharmaceutical preparations
PA: Pfizer Inc.
66 Hudson Blvd E
New York NY 10001
212 733-2323

(G-11220)
PHILOSOPHY INC (HQ)
Also Called: Biotech Research Laboratories
1400 Broadway Rd (27332-7713)
PHONE.....................................602 794-8701
Michele Carlino, *VP*
Mark Harshbarger, *
▲ **EMP:** 40 **EST:** 1996
SQ FT: 55,000
SALES (est): 3.54MM **Publicly Held**
Web: www.philosophy.com
SIC: 5122 2844 Cosmetics; Perfumes,
cosmetics and other toilet preparations
PA: Coty Inc.
350 5th Ave
New York NY 10118

(G-11221)
PIEDMONT SALES & RENTALS LLC
Also Called: Piedmont Sales
5074 Nc 87 N (27332-2858)
P.O. Box 516 (28368-0516)
PHONE.....................................919 499-9888
Bobby D Holder, *Pr*
A J Gaster, *VP*
EMP: 6 **EST:** 1995
SQ FT: 5,750
SALES (est): 616.8K **Privately Held**
Web: www.piedmontutilitybuildings.com
SIC: 2452 Prefabricated buildings, wood

(G-11222)
PILGRIMS PRIDE CORPORATION
484 Zimmerman Rd (27330-0519)
PHONE.....................................919 774-7333
Phil Brooks, *Mgr*
EMP: 44
Web: www.pilgrims.com
SIC: 2015 Poultry slaughtering and
processing
HQ: Pilgrim's Pride Corporation
1770 Promontory Cir
Greeley CO 80634
970 506-8000

(G-11223)
RALPH B HALL
Also Called: M & G Screen Service
804 Cox Maddox Rd (27332-8505)
PHONE.....................................919 258-3634
Ralph B Hall, *Owner*
EMP: 8 **EST:** 1965
SALES (est): 487.38K **Privately Held**
SIC: 3569 Filters

(G-11224)
ROCTOOL INC
5900 Westover Dr #15609 (27330)
PHONE.....................................888 364-6321
Mathieu Boulanger, *Pr*
EMP: 7 **EST:** 2013
SALES (est): 743.02K
SALES (corp-wide): 8.76MM **Privately**
Held
Web: www.roctool.com
SIC: 3585 Parts for heating, cooling, and
refrigerating equipment
PA: Roctool
Modul R - Savoie Technolac
Le Bourget-Du-Lac ARA 73370
479262707

(G-11225)
RODECO COMPANY
5811 Elwin Buchanan Dr (27330-9541)
PHONE.....................................919 775-7149
Ryan Murphy, *Pr*
EMP: 19 **EST:** 1961
SQ FT: 28,000
SALES (est): 4.93MM **Privately Held**
Web: www.rodeco.com

SIC: 5084 3471 Metalworking machinery;
Anodizing (plating) of metals or formed
products

(G-11226)
ROGER D THOMAS
8313 Hillcrest Farm Rd (27330-9006)
PHONE..............................919 258-3148
Roger D Thomas, *Prin*
EMP: 7 EST: 2005
SALES (est): 132.59K Privately Held
SIC: 3827 Optical instruments and lenses

(G-11227)
S T WOOTEN CORPORATION
Also Called: Sanford Asphalt Plant
966 Rocky Fork Church Rd (27332-0838)
PHONE..............................919 776-2736
Scott Wooten, *Pr*
EMP: 40
SALES (corp-wide): 319.83MM Privately
Held
Web: www.stwcorp.com
SIC: 3531 Asphalt plant, including gravel-mix
type
PA: S. T. Wooten Corporation
3801 Black Creek Rd Se
Wilson NC 27894
252 291-5165

(G-11228)
SANDHILLS CNSLD SVCS INC
Also Called: Scs Wood Products
200 E Williams St (27332-6149)
P.O. Box 2592 (27331-2592)
PHONE..............................919 718-7909
Jerry Davis, *CEO*
Michelle Davis, *
EMP: 38 EST: 2009
SALES (est): 9.8MM Privately Held
Web: www.scswoodproducts.com
SIC: 2448 Pallets, wood

(G-11229)
**SANFORD COCA-COLA BOTTLING
CO**
Also Called: Coca-Cola
1605 Hawkins Ave (27330-9501)
P.O. Box 887 (27502-0887)
PHONE..............................919 774-4111
Charles A Ingram, *Pr*
Margaret Harrington, *
EMP: 19 EST: 1907
SQ FT: 30,000
SALES (est): 2.41MM Privately Held
Web: www.sanfordherald.com
SIC: 2086 Bottled and canned soft drinks

(G-11230)
**SANFORD TRANSITION COMPANY
INC**
5108 Rex Mcleod Dr (27330-9539)
P.O. Box 421 (28350)
PHONE..............................919 775-4989
Chuck Leuth, *Pr*
▲ EMP: 50 EST: 1995
SQ FT: 50,000
SALES (est): 3.94MM
SALES (corp-wide): 3.85B Privately Held
Web: www.fuchs.com
SIC: 2992 7389 Lubricating oils and greases
; Packaging and labeling services
HQ: Fuchs Lubricants Co.
17050 Lathrop Ave
Harvey IL 60426
708 333-8900

(G-11231)
SANTRONICS INC
Also Called: Santronics

3010 Lee Ave (27332)
P.O. Box 152 (27331)
PHONE..............................919 775-1223
Juan Carlos Bonell, *Pr*
EMP: 980 EST: 1987
SALES (est): 3.62MM Privately Held
Web: www.santronicsinc.com
SIC: 3679 3674 Electronic loads and power
supplies; Transistors

(G-11232)
SEAL IT SERVICES INC
3301 Industrial Dr (27332-6072)
PHONE..............................919 777-0374
David Moore, *Pr*
EMP: 12 EST: 2016
SQ FT: 30,000
SALES (est): 10.62MM
SALES (corp-wide): 502.14K Privately
Held
Web: www.sealitgroup.com
SIC: 2822 Silicone rubbers
PA: Bond It Limited
11b Enterprise House, Manchester
Science Park
Manchester M15 6
161 737-6270

(G-11233)
SILLAMAN & SONS INC
Also Called: PIP Printing
356 Wilson Rd (27332-9616)
PHONE..............................919 774-6324
Samuel W Sillaman, *Pr*
EMP: 4 EST: 1986
SQ FT: 3,500
SALES (est): 1.01MM Privately Held
Web: www.pip.com
SIC: 2752 7334 2741 Offset printing;
Photocopying and duplicating services;
Miscellaneous publishing

(G-11234)
SLOANS MACHINE SHOP
1186 Walker Rd (27332-9650)
P.O. Box 2261 (27331-2261)
PHONE..............................919 499-5655
Jerry Sloan, *Owner*
EMP: 6 EST: 1991
SALES (est): 177.89K Privately Held
SIC: 3599 Machine shop, jobbing and repair

(G-11235)
SOUTHERN ELC & AUTOMTN CORP
Also Called: Direct South Logistics
800 Hawkins Ave (27330-3312)
P.O. Box 733 (27331-0733)
PHONE..............................919 718-0122
David Griffith, *Pr*
◆ EMP: 13 EST: 2002
SQ FT: 1,500
SALES (est): 2.48MM Privately Held
Web: www.seacorpservices.com
SIC: 1731 3825 3661 General electrical
contractor; Integrating electricity meters;
Data sets, telephone or telegraph

(G-11236)
SPANSET INC (HQ)
3125 Industrial Dr (27332-6068)
P.O. Box 2828 (27331-2828)
PHONE..............................919 774-6316
Kenneth Milligan, *CEO*
William Lyn Roberts, *
◆ EMP: 36 EST: 1980
SQ FT: 42,000
SALES (est): 14.8MM Privately Held
Web: www.spanset.com
SIC: 2241 Fabric tapes
PA: Spanset Inter Ag
Samstagernstrasse 45

Wollerau SZ 8832

(G-11237)
SRI VENTURES INC
3415 Hawkins Ave (27330-6944)
PHONE..............................919 427-1681
Ashley Bethea, *Brnch Mgr*
EMP: 17
SALES (corp-wide): 5.31MM Privately
Held
Web: www.sri.com
SIC: 2741 Telephone and other directory
publishing
PA: Sri Ventures, Inc.
1071 Classic Rd
Apex NC 27539
919 465-2300

(G-11238)
**STATIC CONTROL COMPONENTS
INC (HQ)**
Also Called: Static Control
3010 Lee Ave (27332-6210)
P.O. Box 152 (27331-0152)
PHONE..............................919 774-3808
Juan Carlos Bonell, *Ch*
Michael L Swartz, *
◆ EMP: 1190 EST: 1987
SALES (est): 42.86MM Privately Held
Web: www.scc-inc.com
SIC: 3629 3955 Static elimination
equipment, industrial; Print cartridges for
laser and other computer printers
PA: Jihai Microelectronics Co., Ltd.
F1, F2 Area A, F3, F5, F6, F7, F8, F9,
Block 01, No.83 Guangwan
Zhuhai GD

(G-11239)
STATIC CONTROL IC-DISC INC
3010 Lee Ave (27332-6210)
P.O. Box 152 (27331-0152)
PHONE..............................919 774-3808
William London, *VP*
EMP: 15 EST: 1987
SALES (est): 529.75K Privately Held
Web: www.scc-inc.com
SIC: 3629 Blasting machines, electrical

(G-11240)
STEEL AND PIPE CORPORATION
3709 Hawkins Ave (27330-9519)
P.O. Box 700 (27331-0700)
PHONE..............................919 776-0751
EMP: 37 EST: 1961
SALES (est): 10.09MM Privately Held
Web: www.steelandpipecorp.com
SIC: 5051 3441 Steel; Fabricated structural
metal

(G-11241)
STI POLYMER INC
5618 Clyde Rhyne Dr (27330)
PHONE..............................800 874-5878
Jeffrey A Lamb, *Pr*
▲ EMP: 20 EST: 1978
SQ FT: 30,000
SALES (est): 12.53MM Privately Held
Web: www.stipolymer.com
SIC: 2891 Adhesives

(G-11242)
TRAMWAY VENEERS INC
2603 Tramway Rd (27332-9175)
P.O. Box 322 (27331-0322)
PHONE..............................919 776-7606
Lowell W Rickard, *Ch Bd*
Tim Mcfarland, *VP*
Linda Bryant, *Sec*
Carroll Rickard, *Sls Dir*
EMP: 6 EST: 1965

SQ FT: 26,000
SALES (est): 974.47K Privately Held
Web: www.yorkflowershop.com
SIC: 2435 Hardwood veneer and plywood

(G-11243)
TRANSDATA SOLUTIONS INC
221 N Horner Blvd (27330-3965)
P.O. Box 110021 (27709-5021)
PHONE..............................919 770-9329
Matthew Sakurad, *CEO*
EMP: 5 EST: 2017
SALES (est): 304.88K Privately Held
Web: www.transdatasolutions.com
SIC: 7372 Business oriented computer
software

(G-11244)
TRIAD CORRUGATED METAL INC
Also Called: Triad Corrugated Metal
109 Mcneill Rd (27330-9451)
PHONE..............................919 775-1663
EMP: 15
SALES (corp-wide): 23.91MM Privately
Held
Web: www.triadcorrugatedmetal.com
SIC: 3444 Sheet metalwork
PA: Triad Corrugated Metal, Inc.
208 Luck Rd
Asheboro NC 27205
336 625-9727

(G-11245)
TYSON FOODS INC
800 E Main St (27332-9746)
PHONE..............................919 774-7925
EMP: 5
SALES (corp-wide): 53.31B Publicly Held
Web: www.tyson.com
SIC: 2015 2032 2096 2048 Chicken
slaughtering and processing; Ethnic foods,
canned, jarred, etc.; Potato chips and
similar snacks; Feeds from meat and from
meat and vegetable meals
PA: Tyson Foods, Inc.
2200 W Don Tyson Pkwy
Springdale AR 72762
479 290-4000

(G-11246)
TYSON MEXICAN ORIGINAL INC
800 E Main St (27332-9708)
PHONE..............................919 777-9428
Richard Price, *Mgr*
EMP: 36
SALES (corp-wide): 53.31B Publicly Held
Web: www.tysonfoods.com
SIC: 2032 2099 2096 Mexican foods, nec:
packaged in cans, jars, etc.; Food
preparations, nec; Potato chips and similar
snacks
HQ: Tyson Mexican Original, Inc.
2200 W Don Tyson Pkwy
Springdale AR 72762
479 290-6111

(G-11247)
UNIFI INC
1921 Boone Trail Rd (27330-9414)
PHONE..............................919 774-7401
Ken Huggins, *Prin*
EMP: 4
SALES (corp-wide): 582.21MM Publicly
Held
Web: www.unifi.com
SIC: 2281 Cotton yarn, spun
PA: Unifi, Inc.
7201 W Friendly Ave
Greensboro NC 27410
336 294-4410

(G-11248)
VIOLET SANFORD HOLDINGS LLC
Also Called: Boone Brands
2209 Boone Trail Rd (27330-8641)
PHONE................................919 775-5931
EMP: 50 EST: 2014
SALES (est): 8.03MM **Privately Held**
Web: www.boonebrands.com
SIC: 2099 Sauce, gravy, dressing, and dip
mixes

(G-11249)
WHITE TIGER BTQ & CANDLE CO ☺
3206 Smokey Path (27330-0907)
PHONE................................919 610-7244
Keiomi Woodson, CEO
EMP: 5 EST: 2023
SALES (est): 1.02MM **Privately Held**
SIC: 3999 7389 Candles; Business services,
nec

(G-11250)
WILLIAMS ELECTRIC MTR REPR INC
2515 Cox Mill Rd Ste A (27332-7701)
PHONE................................919 859-9790
George Williams, Pr
EMP: 4 EST: 2008
SALES (est): 993.76K **Privately Held**
SIC: 7694 5531 Electric motor repair; Auto
and home supply stores

(G-11251)
WILSON MACHINE & TOOL INC
4956 Womack Rd (27330-9592)
P.O. Box 773 (27331-0773)
PHONE................................919 776-0043
F Ray Wilson, Pr
EMP: 8 EST: 1992
SQ FT: 10,000
SALES (est): 1.33MM **Privately Held**
Web: www.wmtusa.com
SIC: 3599 Machine shop, jobbing and repair

(G-11252)
WIND SOLUTIONS LLC
111 Rand St (27332-6211)
P.O. Box 57 (27331)
PHONE................................919 292-2096
Christopher Winslow, Managing Member
▲ EMP: 28 EST: 2010
SALES (est): 6MM **Privately Held**
Web: www.wind-solutions-llc.com
SIC: 5013 3511 Motor vehicle supplies and
new parts; Turbines and turbine generator
sets and parts
PA: Integrated Power Services Llc
250 Exctive Ctr Dr Ste 20
Greenville SC 29615

(G-11253)
**WOLVERINE MTAL STMPING
SLTONS**
Also Called: Metal Stamping Solutions
5720 Clyde Rhyne Dr (27330-9563)
PHONE................................919 774-4729
Rick Dresser, Managing Member
EMP: 10 EST: 2002
SQ FT: 38,000
SALES (est): 3.12MM **Privately Held**
Web: www.stampingsolutionsnc.com
SIC: 3469 Stamping metal for the trade

(G-11254)
WORLD STONE OF SANFORD LLC
3201 Industrial Dr (27332-6070)
PHONE................................919 468-8450
EMP: 12 EST: 2013
SALES (est): 924.49K **Privately Held**
Web: www.worldstoneonline.com

SIC: 3281 Cut stone and stone products

(G-11255)
WYETH HOLDINGS LLC
Also Called: Wyeth Pharmaceutical Division
4300 Oak Park Rd (27330-9550)
PHONE................................919 775-7100
Brian Frost, Mgr
EMP: 639
SALES (corp-wide): 63.63B **Publicly Held**
SIC: 2834 Pharmaceutical preparations
HQ: Wyeth Holdings Llc
5 Giralda Farms
Madison NJ 07940

(G-11256)
**ZURN ELKAY WTR SOLUTIONS
CORP**
5900 Elwin Buchanan Dr (27330-9525)
PHONE................................855 663-9876
EMP: 11
Web: www.zurnelkay.com
SIC: 3491 Water works valves
PA: Zurn Elkay Water Solutions Corporation
511 W Freshwater Way
Milwaukee WI 53204

(G-11257)
ZURN INDUSTRIES LLC
Zurn Commercial Brass
5900 Elwin Buchanan Dr (27330-9525)
PHONE................................919 775-2255
EMP: 22
Web: www.zurn.com
SIC: 5074 3499 Plumbing and hydronic
heating supplies; Aerosol valves, metal
HQ: Zurn Industries, Llc
511 W Freshwater Way
Milwaukee WI 53204
855 663-9876

Sapphire
Transylvania County

(G-11258)
LBM INDUSTRIES INC
Also Called: Toxaway Concrete
17668 Rosman Hwy (28774)
P.O. Box 40 (28774-0040)
PHONE................................828 966-4270
Bo Mccalu, Mgr
EMP: 10
SALES (corp-wide): 18.35MM **Privately
Held**
Web: www.mcneelycompanies.com
SIC: 3281 5032 1475 Stone, quarrying and
processing of own stone products; Stone,
crushed or broken; Phosphate rock
PA: Lbm Industries, Inc.
2000 Whitewater Rd
Sapphire NC 28774
828 966-4270

(G-11259)
LBM INDUSTRIES INC (PA)
Also Called: McNeelys Store Rental & Eqp
2000 Whitewater Rd (28774)
P.O. Box 40 (28774-0040)
PHONE................................828 966-4270
William L Mc Neely Junior, Pr
William L Mc Neely Iii, VP
Grace Mc Neely, Treas
Kathy Fisher, Sec
EMP: 11 EST: 1976
SQ FT: 8,000
SALES (est): 18.35MM
SALES (corp-wide): 18.35MM **Privately
Held**
Web: www.mcneelycompanies.com

SIC: 1411 5231 Dimension stone; Paint,
glass, and wallpaper stores

(G-11260)
MCNEELY TRUCKING CO
17692 Rosman Hwy (28774)
P.O. Box 40 (28774-0040)
PHONE................................828 966-4270
William L Mcneely Junior, Pr
Grace Mc Neely, Treas
EMP: 8 EST: 1971
SQ FT: 3,000
SALES (est): 3.99MM **Privately Held**
Web: www.mcneelycompanies.com
SIC: 1411 Dimension stone

Saratoga
Wilson County

(G-11261)
OLD SARATOGA INC
6351 Nc Hwy 222 (27873)
P.O. Box 270 (27873-0270)
PHONE................................252 238-2175
Christopher Hudson, CEO
Fitzgerald D Hudson, *
M Grady Golson, *
Christopher A Hudson, *
Keith Johnston, *
EMP: 25 EST: 1993
SQ FT: 45,000
SALES (est): 1.68MM **Privately Held**
Web: www.oldsaratogainc.com
SIC: 2086 5963 Bottled and canned soft
drinks; Bottled water delivery

Saxapahaw
Alamance County

(G-11262)
HAW RIVER FARMHOUSE ALES LLC
1713 Sax-Beth Church Rd (27340)
P.O. Box 390 (27340-0390)
PHONE................................336 525-9270
EMP: 9 EST: 2011
SALES (est): 1.73MM **Privately Held**
Web: www.hawriverstore.com
SIC: 2082 Beer (alcoholic beverage)

Scotland Neck
Halifax County

(G-11263)
**AIRBOSS RBR COMPOUNDING NC
LLC**
Also Called: Airboss Rubber Solutions
500 Airboss Pkwy (27874-1567)
PHONE................................252 826-4919
Robert Hagerman, Pr
Wendy Ford, *
Earl Laurie, *
Yvan Ambeault, *
Lisa Swartzman, *
▲ EMP: 40 EST: 2004
SALES (est): 10.55MM
SALES (corp-wide): 426.02MM **Privately
Held**
Web: www.airboss.com
SIC: 3011 Automobile tires, pneumatic
PA: Airboss Of America Corp
16441 Yonge St
Newmarket ON L3X 2
905 751-1188

(G-11264)
JOSEY LUMBER COMPANY INC
476 Lees Meadow Rd (27874-8778)
P.O. Box 447 (27874-0447)
PHONE................................252 826-5614
Joey Josey, Pr
Deborah G Josey, *
EMP: 40 EST: 1983
SQ FT: 1,200
SALES (est): 5.5MM **Privately Held**
SIC: 2421 2426 Lumber: rough, sawed, or
planed; Hardwood dimension and flooring
mills

(G-11265)
SCOTLAND NECK HEART PINE INC
25574 Hwy 125 (27874)
P.O. Box 536 (27874-0536)
PHONE................................252 826-2755
Hodge Kitchin, Owner
Hodge Kitchin, Pr
EMP: 9 EST: 2003
SALES (est): 488.19K **Privately Held**
Web: www.snheartpine.com
SIC: 2439 Arches, laminated lumber

(G-11266)
**SHENANDOAH WOOD
PRESERVERS INC**
301 E 16th St (27874-1707)
P.O. Box 310 (27874-0310)
PHONE................................252 826-4151
Courtney Hutcherson, Pr
J Eldrige Wimmer, Prin
Steve Michael, VP
Brenda Jones, Treas
Anthony Bailey, Dir
EMP: 4 EST: 1987
SQ FT: 2,000
SALES (est): 228.91K **Privately Held**
SIC: 2491 Wood preserving

(G-11267)
W H BUNTING THINNING
2305 Bynums Bridge Rd (27874-8970)
PHONE................................252 826-4025
William Bunting, Owner
EMP: 4 EST: 1995
SALES (est): 87K **Privately Held**
SIC: 2411 Logging

(G-11268)
WIGGINS DESIGN FABRICATION INC
140 Edwards Fork Rd (27874-8692)
P.O. Box 252 (27874-0252)
PHONE................................252 826-5239
James C Wiggins, Pr
Kelvin L Wiggins, VP
Lendo M Wiggins, Treas
Linda Wiggins, Pr
EMP: 9 EST: 1972
SQ FT: 21,000
SALES (est): 485.56K **Privately Held**
Web: www.wigginsdesign.com
SIC: 3443 Fabricated plate work (boiler shop)

Seaboard
Northampton County

(G-11269)
BLAST OFF INTL CHEM & MFG CO
199 Crocker St (27876-9713)
PHONE................................509 885-4525
Ellen Mclaughlin, Pr
Liana Mclaughlin, Pr
Shelley Van Dyk, VP
EMP: 4 EST: 1979
SALES (est): 1.3MM **Privately Held**

SIC: 2899 Chemical preparations, nec

(G-11270)
CAROLINA BARK PRODUCTS LLC
Hwy 186 E. (27876)
P.O. Box 395 (27876-0395)
PHONE...........................252 589-1324
EMP: 8 EST: 2002
SALES (est): 371.96K Privately Held
Web: www.carolinabarkproducts.com
SIC: 2499 Mulch, wood and bark

(G-11271)
ELSCO INC (PA)
199 Crocker St (27876-9713)
P.O. Box 99 (27876-0099)
PHONE...........................509 885-4525
Earl Smith, Pr
Liana Mclaughlin, Mgr
EMP: 4 EST: 1952
SQ FT: 1,488
SALES (est): 1.04MM
SALES (corp-wide): 1.04MM Privately
Held
SIC: 2842 Cleaning or polishing
preparations, nec

(G-11272)
WEST FRASER INC
4400 Nc Hwy 186 (27876)
P.O. Box 459 (27876-0459)
PHONE...........................252 589-2011
Carl Buck, Mgr
EMP: 187
SALES (corp-wide): 6.45B Privately Held
Web: www.westfraser.com
SIC: 2421 Sawmills and planing mills,
general
HQ: Fraser West Inc
57 Germantown Ct
Cordova TN 38018
901 620-4200

Seagrove
Randolph County

(G-11273)
CAROLINA BRONZE SCULPTURE INC
Also Called: Carolina Bronze
6108 Maple Springs Rd (27341-9047)
PHONE...........................336 873-8291
Ed Walker, Pr
EMP: 9 EST: 1990
SQ FT: 8,200
SALES (est): 2.04MM Privately Held
Web: www.carolinabronze.com
SIC: 3366 Copper foundries

(G-11274)
H & H FURNITURE MFRS INC
Also Called: Casual Crates
236 N Broad St (27341-9202)
P.O. Box 10 (27341-0010)
PHONE...........................336 873-7245
Ken H Hill, Pr
Jerry Hill, *
EMP: 120 EST: 1979
SQ FT: 290,000
SALES (est): 4.53MM Privately Held
Web: www.americanloftandlounge.com
SIC: 2511 3949 Wood household furniture;
Sporting and athletic goods, nec

(G-11275)
JOSH ALLRED
335 N Broad St (27341-8540)
PHONE...........................336 873-1006
Josh Allred, Prin

EMP: 7 EST: 2011
SALES (est): 177.24K Privately Held
SIC: 3621 Generators and sets, electric

(G-11276)
JUGTOWN POTTERY
330 Jugtown Rd (27341-7402)
PHONE...........................910 464-3266
Vernon Owens, Owner
EMP: 6 EST: 1920
SALES (est): 222.81K Privately Held
Web: www.jugtownware.com
SIC: 3269 5719 Pottery products, nec;
Pottery

(G-11277)
K & J ASHWORTH LOGGING LLC
8797 Erect Rd (27341-9098)
PHONE...........................336 879-2388
EMP: 5 EST: 2018
SALES (est): 215.26K Privately Held
SIC: 2411 Logging

(G-11278)
MCNEILL FRAME INC
3631 Alternate Rd (27341)
PHONE...........................336 873-7934
Gene Mcneill, Pr
EMP: 6 EST: 2001
SQ FT: 40,000
SALES (est): 533.85K Privately Held
SIC: 2426 Frames for upholstered furniture,
wood

(G-11279)
REEDER PALLET COMPANY INC
435 Reeder Rd (27341-7470)
P.O. Box 540 (27341-0540)
PHONE...........................336 879-3095
Cecil Reeder, Pr
EMP: 14 EST: 1989
SQ FT: 3,000
SALES (est): 1.45MM Privately Held
Web: www.reederpallet.com
SIC: 2448 Pallets, wood

(G-11280)
SAPONA PLASTIC LLC
798 Nc Highway 705 (27341-8665)
PHONE...........................336 873-7201
EMP: 4 EST: 2013
SALES (est): 975.49K Privately Held
Web: www.saponaplastics.com
SIC: 3089 Injection molding of plastics

(G-11281)
SEAGROVE LUMBER LLC
558 Little River Golf Dr (27341-9308)
PHONE...........................910 428-9663
Philip Sechrest, Mgr
EMP: 10 EST: 2010
SALES (est): 491.8K Privately Held
Web: www.discoverseagrove.com
SIC: 2511 Bed frames, except water bed
frames: wood

Selma
Johnston County

(G-11282)
3DDUCTCLEANING LLC
207 Merriman Dr (27576-3656)
PHONE...........................919 723-4512
EMP: 4 EST: 2022
SALES (est): 175.11K Privately Held
SIC: 3582 7389 Dryers, laundry:
commercial, including coin-operated;
Business services, nec

(G-11283)
AIRFLOW PRODUCTS COMPANY INC
100 Oak Tree Dr (27576-3540)
PHONE...........................919 975-0240
Roy Boswell, Pr
Jeff Holt, *
▲ EMP: 165 EST: 2002
SQ FT: 100,000
SALES (est): 23.65MM Privately Held
Web: viewer.zmags.com
SIC: 3564 Filters, air: furnaces, air
conditioning equipment, etc.

(G-11284)
APC LLC
Also Called: Atlantic Coast Protein Co
1451 W Noble St (27576-3639)
PHONE...........................919 965-2051
Matt Ruppert, Mgr
EMP: 32
SALES (corp-wide): 192.23MM Privately
Held
Web: www.apcproteins.com
SIC: 2048 Feed supplements
HQ: Apc, Llc
2425 Se Oak Tree Ct
Ankeny IA 50021
515 289-7600

(G-11285)
ATKINSON MILLING COMPANY
Also Called: Atkinson's Mill
95 Atkinson Mill Rd Intersection Hwy 42 &
39 (27576)
PHONE...........................919 965-3547
Glen R Wheeler Junior, Pr
Tim Wheeler, *
▲ EMP: 60 EST: 1951
SQ FT: 2,500
SALES (est): 9.24MM Privately Held
Web: www.atkinsonmilling.com
SIC: 2041 Corn meal

(G-11286)
DREWS CABINETS AND CASES
8100 Nc Highway 42 E (27576-7940)
PHONE...........................919 796-3985
Drew Roy, Owner
EMP: 4 EST: 1997
SALES (est): 152.37K Privately Held
Web: www.drewscabinets.com
SIC: 2599 Cabinets, factory

(G-11287)
EATON CORPORATION
Cuttler Hmmer Cmrcl Cntrls Div
1100 E Preston St (27576-3162)
P.O. Box 57 (27576-0057)
PHONE...........................919 965-2341
Michael K Carper, Brnch Mgr
EMP: 200
Web: www.dix-eaton.com
SIC: 3643 Electric switches
HQ: Eaton Corporation
1000 Eaton Blvd
Cleveland OH 44122
440 523-5000

(G-11288)
GUYCLEE MILLWORK
1251 S Pollock St (27576-3401)
PHONE...........................919 202-5738
Rodney Chambers, Genl Mgr
EMP: 10 EST: 2006
SALES (est): 570.72K Privately Held
Web: www.guyclee.com
SIC: 2431 Doors, wood

(G-11289)
JOHNSTON COUNTY INDUSTRIES INC
Also Called: J C I
1100 E Preston St (27576-3162)
PHONE...........................919 743-8700
C W Sharek, CEO
Lina Sanders-johnson, Sec
Durwood Woodall V, Ch Bd
EMP: 195 EST: 1975
SQ FT: 90,000
SALES (est): 8.05MM Privately Held
Web: www.jcindustries.com
SIC: 2448 3694 2452 Wood pallets and skids
; Engine electrical equipment; Prefabricated
wood buildings

(G-11290)
MIKE ATKINS & SON LOGGING INC
Also Called: Atkins, Mike & Son Logging
4336 Browns Pond Rd (27576-8119)
PHONE...........................919 965-8002
Mike Atkins, Pr
Jeff Atkins, VP
Betty Atkins, Sec
EMP: 4 EST: 1998
SALES (est): 401.06K Privately Held
SIC: 2411 Logging camps and contractors

(G-11291)
SONA AUTOCOMP USA LLC
500 Oak Tree Dr (27576-3544)
PHONE...........................919 965-5555
EMP: 165 EST: 2008
SALES (est): 1.3MM
SALES (corp-wide): 240.01MM Privately
Held
SIC: 3542 3462 Machine tools, metal
forming type; Automotive forgings, ferrous:
crankshaft, engine, axle, etc.
HQ: Sona Blw Prazisionsschmiede Gmbh
Papenberger Str. 37
Remscheid NW 42859
2191150

(G-11292)
SONA BLW PRECISION FORGE INC
500 Oak Tree Dr (27576-3544)
PHONE...........................919 828-3375
◆ EMP: 145
SIC: 3542 3462 Machine tools, metal
forming type; Automotive forgings, ferrous:
crankshaft, engine, axle, etc.

(G-11293)
TRANSMONTAIGNE TERMINALING INC
Also Called: TransMontaigne
2600 W Oak St (27576-9199)
PHONE...........................303 626-8200
EMP: 12 EST: 2020
SALES (est): 2.96MM Privately Held
Web: www.transmontaignepartners.com
SIC: 1389 Gas field services, nec

(G-11294)
WILLIAMSBURG WOODCRAFT INC
4901 Nc Highway 96 N (27576-6016)
PHONE...........................919 965-3363
Tim Stevens, Pr
Linda Stevens, VP
EMP: 7 EST: 1980
SQ FT: 22,400
SALES (est): 582.87K Privately Held
Web: www.williamsburgwoodcraft.com
SIC: 2431 Doors, wood

Semora
Person County

(G-11295)
PROASH LLC (HQ)
1514 Dunnaway Rd (27343-9057)
PHONE..............................336 597-8734
Jim Simon, *Mgr*
EMP: 8 **EST:** 1997
SALES (est): 990.69K **Privately Held**
SIC: 1481 Nonmetallic mineral services
PA: Separation Technologies, Llc
101 Hampton Ave
Needham MA

(G-11296)
SEPARATION TECHNOLOGIES LLC
1514 Dunnaway Rd (27343-9057)
PHONE..............................336 597-9814
Randy Dunlap, *Brnch Mgr*
EMP: 151
SALES (corp-wide): 8.01MM **Privately Held**
Web: www.proash.com
SIC: 3612 Transformers, except electric
HQ: Separation Technologies Llc
188 Summerfield Ct # 101
Roanoke VA 24019

Seven Springs
Wayne County

(G-11297)
GOALS IN SERVICE LLC
103 Richard Dupree Ln (28578-7604)
PHONE..............................919 440-2656
EMP: 4 **EST:** 2018
SALES (est): 1.77MM **Privately Held**
SIC: 3535 Conveyors and conveying equipment

Severn
Northampton County

(G-11298)
NORTHAMPTON PEANUT COMPANY
413 Main St (27877-9901)
P.O. Box 149 (27877-0149)
PHONE..............................252 585-0916
Dallas Barnes, *Pr*
William E Mckeown, *VP*
Jane Taylor, *
▼ **EMP:** 85 **EST:** 1989
SQ FT: 50,000
SALES (est): 20.31MM
SALES (corp-wide): 423.19MM **Privately Held**
Web: www.hamptonfarms.com
SIC: 5159 5441 2068 Peanuts (bulk), unroasted; Nuts; Nuts: dried, dehydrated, salted or roasted
HQ: Severn Peanut Company, Inc.
413 Main St
Severn NC 27877
252 585-0838

(G-11299)
RESINALL CORP
302 Water St (27877)
P.O. Box 195 (27877)
PHONE..............................252 585-1445
Paul Pierce, *Mgr*
EMP: 118
SALES (corp-wide): 1.44B **Privately Held**
Web: www.resinall.com

SIC: 2821 Plastics materials and resins
HQ: Resinall Corp
2829 Lakeland Dr
Flowood MS 39232
252 585-1445

Shallotte
Brunswick County

(G-11300)
BRUNSWICK BEACON INC
208 Smith Ave (28470-4458)
P.O. Box 2558 (28459-2558)
PHONE..............................910 754-6890
Edward M Sweatt, *Pr*
Carolyn Sweatt, *Sec*
EMP: 4 **EST:** 1962
SALES (est): 146.25K **Privately Held**
Web: www.newsargus.com
SIC: 2711 6531 Newspapers: publishing only, not printed on site; Real estate agents and managers

(G-11301)
COASTAL CABINETRY INC
5017 Songline St (28470-6700)
PHONE..............................910 367-8864
Laura Scinto, *Prin*
EMP: 4 **EST:** 2010
SALES (est): 116.38K **Privately Held**
SIC: 2434 Wood kitchen cabinets

(G-11302)
COASTAL MACHINE & WELDING INC
146 Wall St (28470-4510)
P.O. Box 617 (28462-0617)
PHONE..............................910 754-6476
Gene A Smith, *Pr*
Beverly A Smith, *Sec*
EMP: 6 **EST:** 1955
SQ FT: 15,000
SALES (est): 1.69MM **Privately Held**
Web: www.carolinacraneservice.com
SIC: 3448 3842 7692 Prefabricated metal buildings; Surgical appliances and supplies; Welding repair

(G-11303)
KART PRECISION BARREL CORP
3975 Garner St Sw (28470-5645)
PHONE..............................910 754-5212
Frederick Kart, *Pr*
Conrad Bulak, *Sec*
EMP: 4 **EST:** 1989
SQ FT: 5,000
SALES (est): 703.14K **Privately Held**
Web: www.kartbarrel.com
SIC: 3484 Small arms

(G-11304)
LLOYDS OYSTER HOUSE INC
Also Called: Milliken Calabash Seafood
1642 Village Point Rd Sw (28470-5581)
PHONE..............................910 754-6958
Lloyd R Milliken, *Pr*
Jeffrey Milliken, *
EMP: 30 **EST:** 1960
SQ FT: 6,000
SALES (est): 384.39K **Privately Held**
SIC: 0913 5146 2091 Oysters, dredging or tonging of; Seafoods; Canned and cured fish and seafoods

(G-11305)
SKIPPER GRAPHICS
209 Village Rd Sw (28470-4441)
P.O. Box 989 (28459-0989)
PHONE..............................910 754-8729
Barbara S Stanley, *Owner*

EMP: 4 **EST:** 1987
SQ FT: 2,400
SALES (est): 146.47K **Privately Held**
Web: www.skippergraphics.com
SIC: 7336 2759 3993 Commercial art and illustration; Letterpress printing; Signs, not made in custom sign painting shops

(G-11306)
SUN & SURF CONTAINERS INC
2589 Sun And Surf Ln Nw (28470-5978)
P.O. Box 67 (28459-0067)
PHONE..............................910 754-9600
Henry B Tonking Junior, *Pr*
Mary Lou Tonking, *Sec*
EMP: 8 **EST:** 1984
SQ FT: 20,000
SALES (est): 491.1K **Privately Held**
Web: www.sunandsurfcontainers.com
SIC: 2653 Boxes, corrugated: made from purchased materials

Sharpsburg
Nash County

(G-11307)
SCOGGINS INDUSTRIAL INC
Also Called: Langley Indus McHning Fbrction
4842 Us-301 (27878)
P.O. Box 1939 (27878-1939)
PHONE..............................252 977-9222
Gregory Scoggins, *Pr*
EMP: 17 **EST:** 2021
SALES (est): 1.5MM **Privately Held**
SIC: 3599 7389 Machine and other job shop work; Business Activities at Non-Commercial Site

Shelby
Cleveland County

(G-11308)
ABERCROMBIE TEXTILES INC (PA)
3051 River Rd (28152-8644)
PHONE..............................704 487-0935
Johnathan H Abercrombie, *Pr*
EMP: 6 **EST:** 1984
SALES (est): 147.73K
SALES (corp-wide): 147.73K **Privately Held**
SIC: 7349 3552 7389 Janitorial service, contract basis; Textile machinery; Business Activities at Non-Commercial Site

(G-11309)
ABERCROMBIE TEXTILES I LLC (PA)
1322 Mount Sinai Church Rd (28152-0755)
P.O. Box 427 (28024-0427)
PHONE..............................704 487-1245
John Regan, *CEO*
Kim Thompson, *
▲ **EMP:** 18 **EST:** 2006
SQ FT: 43,000
SALES (est): 4.79MM
SALES (corp-wide): 4.79MM **Privately Held**
Web: www.cryptonmills.com
SIC: 2221 2522 Automotive fabrics, manmade fiber; Office furniture, except wood

(G-11310)
ALPHA MAILING SERVICE INC
501 N Washington St (28150-4409)
P.O. Box 231 (28151-0231)
PHONE..............................704 484-1711
Oliver Emmert, *Pr*
EMP: 17 **EST:** 1978

SQ FT: 23,000
SALES (est): 1.45MM **Privately Held**
Web: www.alphamail.com
SIC: 7331 2782 Mailing service; Account books

(G-11311)
AMERICAN SAFETY UTILITY CORP
529 Caleb Rd (28152-7956)
P.O. Box 1740 (28151-1740)
PHONE..............................704 482-0601
Charles R Buddy Price, *Pr*
▼ **EMP:** 44 **EST:** 1982
SQ FT: 30,000
SALES (est): 9.84MM **Privately Held**
Web: www.americansafety.com
SIC: 5099 8734 2326 2311 Safety equipment and supplies; Testing laboratories; Men's and boy's work clothing; Men's and boy's suits and coats

(G-11312)
AMES COPPER GROUP LLC
125 Old Boiling Springs Rd (28152-0648)
PHONE..............................860 622-7626
Sean Meyer, *Managing Member*
EMP: 24 **EST:** 2020
SALES (est): 8.7MM **Privately Held**
Web: www.amescoppergroup.com
SIC: 1021 Copper ore mining and preparation

(G-11313)
BARRS COMPETITION
124 Drum Rd (28152-0907)
PHONE..............................704 482-5169
Robert L Barr, *Owner*
EMP: 10 **EST:** 1971
SQ FT: 6,000
SALES (est): 327.37K **Privately Held**
Web: www.barrscompetition.net
SIC: 3714 3751 5571 7538 Motor vehicle engines and parts; Motorcycles and related parts; Motorcycle dealers; General automotive repair shops

(G-11314)
BRADLEYS INC
Also Called: Bradley Screen Printing
2522 W Dixon Blvd (28152-9007)
PHONE..............................704 484-2077
Marty Bradley, *Pr*
EMP: 22 **EST:** 1990
SQ FT: 2,400
SALES (est): 2.2MM **Privately Held**
Web: www.bradleysinc.com
SIC: 2759 2395 Screen printing; Embroidery products, except Schiffli machine

(G-11315)
CAPITOL FUNDS INC
Also Called: Piedmont Components Division
649 Washburn Switch Rd (28150-7712)
P.O. Box 878 (28151-0878)
PHONE..............................704 482-0645
Joel Hoard, *Mgr*
EMP: 74
SALES (corp-wide): 6.94MM **Privately Held**
Web: www.capitolfundsinc.com
SIC: 2439 3441 2435 Trusses, wooden roof; Fabricated structural metal; Hardwood veneer and plywood
PA: Capitol Funds, Inc.
720 S Lafayette St
Shelby NC 28150
704 487-8547

▲ = Import ▼ = Export
◆ = Import/Export

(G-11316)
CAPITOL FUNDS INC (PA)
Also Called: Piedmont Components Division
720 S Lafayette St (28150-5860)
P.O. Box 146 (28151-0146)
PHONE............................704 487-8547
David W Royster Iii, Pr
James B Taylor, *
Ann R Taylor, *
EMP: 40 **EST:** 1949
SQ FT: 6,400
SALES (est): 6.94MM
SALES (corp-wide): 6.94MM **Privately Held**
Web: www.capitolfundsinc.com
SIC: 6552 5231 5251 2439 Land subdividers and developers, commercial; Paint; Hardware stores; Structural wood members, nec

(G-11317)
CHOICE USA BEVERAGE INC
Also Called: Sun Drop Bottling Co
2440 S Lafayette St (28152-7579)
P.O. Box 40 (28098-0040)
PHONE............................704 487-6951
Reggie Bean, Mgr
EMP: 5
SALES (corp-wide): 23.19MM **Privately Held**
Web: www.choiceusabeverage.com
SIC: 2086 5149 Bottled and canned soft drinks; Soft drinks
PA: Choice U.S.A. Beverage, Inc.
603 Grove St
Lowell NC 28098
704 823-1651

(G-11318)
CITY OF SHELBY
Also Called: Gas Dept
824 W Grover St (28150-2920)
P.O. Box 207 (28151-0207)
PHONE............................704 484-6840
EMP: 34
SALES (corp-wide): 36.64MM **Privately Held**
Web: www.cityofshelby.com
SIC: 1311 Natural gas production
PA: City Of Shelby
300 S Washington St
Shelby NC 28150
704 484-6801

(G-11319)
CLEVELAND COMPOUNDING INC
701 E Grover St # 2 (28150-4035)
PHONE............................704 487-1971
Gary Harden, Pr
EMP: 4 **EST:** 2008
SALES (est): 238.46K **Privately Held**
SIC: 8748 2834 Business consulting, nec; Pharmaceutical preparations

(G-11320)
CLEVELAND LUMBER COMPANY (PA)
Also Called: Benjamin Moore Authorized Ret
217 Arrowood Dr (28150-4300)
P.O. Box 1559 (28151-1559)
PHONE............................704 487-5263
M Garland Johnson Junior, Pr
Jane Hunter, *
EMP: 39 **EST:** 1937
SQ FT: 13,200
SALES (est): 2.24MM
SALES (corp-wide): 2.24MM **Privately Held**
Web:
www.clevelandlumbercompany.com

SIC: 5211 2431 2426 5231 Lumber products ; Millwork; Hardwood dimension and flooring mills; Paint, glass, and wallpaper stores

(G-11321)
CLEVELAND YUTAKA CORPORATION
2081 W Dixon Blvd (28152-9017)
PHONE............................704 480-9290
Mototsugu Watanabe, Pr
▲ **EMP:** 94 **EST:** 1995
SQ FT: 56,788
SALES (est): 4.53MM **Privately Held**
Web: www.clevelandyutaka.com
SIC: 3714 Acceleration equipment, motor vehicle
PA: Yutaka Industry Co.,Ltd.
1-17, Hiyoshi, Satocho
Anjo AIC 446-0

(G-11322)
COLORED METAL PRODUCTS INC
Also Called: Awning Shop
103 Cameron St (28152-6601)
P.O. Box 2572 (28151-2572)
PHONE............................704 482-1407
Jim Robinson, Pr
▼ **EMP:** 12 **EST:** 1983
SQ FT: 3,900
SALES (est): 839.39K **Privately Held**
Web: www.theawningshop.com
SIC: 2394 3444 3949 Awnings, fabric: made from purchased materials; Awnings, sheet metal; Soccer equipment and supplies

(G-11323)
COMMUNITY FIRST MEDIA INC
503 N Lafayette St (28150-4426)
PHONE............................704 482-4142
Greg Ledford, Prin
EMP: 5 **EST:** 2008
SALES (est): 169.39K **Privately Held**
Web: www.cfmedia.info
SIC: 2711 Newspapers, publishing and printing

(G-11324)
CONTROLLED RELEASE TECH INC
1016 Industry Dr (28152-8550)
PHONE............................704 487-0878
Rachelle Cunningham, Pr
EMP: 9 **EST:** 1985
SQ FT: 20,000
SALES (est): 4.15MM **Privately Held**
Web: www.cleanac.com
SIC: 2842 2841 5198 Polishes and sanitation goods; Soap and other detergents ; Paints

(G-11325)
CURTISS-WRIGHT CONTROLS INC
Flight Systms- PDT Support Div
201 Old Boiling Springs Rd (28152-0649)
PHONE............................704 869-2300
EMP: 50
SALES (corp-wide): 3.12B **Publicly Held**
Web: www.curtisswright.com
SIC: 3724 3812 3728 3625 Aircraft engines and engine parts; Search and navigation equipment; Aircraft parts and equipment, nec; Relays and industrial controls
HQ: Curtiss-Wright Controls, Inc.
15801 Brixham Hill Ave # 200
Charlotte NC 28277
704 869-4600

(G-11326)
CURTISS-WRIGHT CONTROLS INC
Actuation Division - Aerospace
201 Old Boiling Springs Rd (28152-0649)

PHONE............................704 481-1150
Mark Treffinger, Brnch Mgr
EMP: 25
SALES (corp-wide): 3.12B **Publicly Held**
Web: www.cwcontrols.com
SIC: 3593 Fluid power cylinders and actuators
HQ: Curtiss-Wright Controls, Inc.
15801 Brixham Hill Ave # 200
Charlotte NC 28277
704 869-4600

(G-11327)
CURTISS-WRIGHT CORPORATION
Actuation Division
201 Old Boiling Springs Rd (28152-0649)
PHONE............................704 481-1150
EMP: 12
SALES (corp-wide): 3.12B **Publicly Held**
Web: www.curtisswright.com
SIC: 3491 Industrial valves
PA: Curtiss-Wright Corporation
130 Harbour Pl Dr Ste 300
Davidson NC 28036
704 869-4600

(G-11328)
D M & E CORPORATION
833 S Post Rd (28152-6932)
P.O. Box 580 (28151-0580)
PHONE............................704 482-8876
Van D Durrett, VP
▲ **EMP:** 30 **EST:** 1976
SQ FT: 6,000
SALES (est): 4.51MM **Privately Held**
Web: www.dmecutter.com
SIC: 5085 3559 3552 Industrial supplies; Electronic component making machinery; Textile machinery

(G-11329)
DALE ADVERTISING INC
2523 Taylor Rd (28152-7942)
PHONE............................704 484-0971
Lanny R Newton, Pr
Cathy Newton, Sec
EMP: 4 **EST:** 1973
SQ FT: 3,000
SALES (est): 247.4K **Privately Held**
SIC: 2759 2395 5199 7311 Screen printing; Embroidery products, except Schiffli machine; Advertising specialties; Advertising agencies

(G-11330)
DAVIS RUG COMPANY
Also Called: Davis Rug
3938 Barclay Rd (28152-9562)
P.O. Box 217 (28017-0217)
PHONE............................704 434-7231
Harvey Davis, Pr
Brenda Davis, Sec
▲ **EMP:** 9 **EST:** 1976
SQ FT: 7,800
SALES (est): 322.51K **Privately Held**
SIC: 2273 Scatter rugs, except rubber or plastic

(G-11331)
DICEY MILLS INC
Also Called: Dicey Fabrics
430 Neisler St (Off Hwy 74 W) (28152-5000)
P.O. Box 1090 (28151-1090)
PHONE............................704 487-6324
◆ **EMP:** 6 **EST:** 1957
SALES (est): 182.8K **Privately Held**
SIC: 2221 Upholstery fabrics, manmade fiber and silk

(G-11332)
ELECTRIC GLASS FIBER AMER LLC (DH)
Also Called: Nippon Electric Glass
940 Washburn Switch Rd (28150)
PHONE............................704 434-2261
Shigeru Goto, CEO
▲ **EMP:** 500 **EST:** 1998
SQ FT: 1,001,880
SALES (est): 439.09MM **Privately Held**
Web: www.neg-us.com
SIC: 2851 Paints and allied products
HQ: Nippon Electric Glass America, Inc.
1515 E Wdfield Rd Ste 720
Schaumburg IL 60173
630 285-8500

(G-11333)
ELECTRIC MOTOR SERVICE OF SHELBY INC
1143 Airport Rd (28150-3723)
PHONE............................704 482-9979
EMP: 16
SIC: 7694 5999 7629 5063 Motor repair services; Motors, electric; Tool repair, electric; Motors, electric

(G-11334)
ELLIS LUMBER COMPANY INC
Also Called: Ellis Lumber Co and Logs
1681 S Lafayette St (28152-7152)
PHONE............................704 482-1414
Yancey Ellis, Pr
W Yancey Ellis, Pr
Scott Ellis, VP
Tim Ellis, VP
Brenda Arton, Mgr
EMP: 6 **EST:** 1946
SALES (est): 993.89K **Privately Held**
Web: www.ellislumbercompany.com
SIC: 2421 Lumber: rough, sawed, or planed

(G-11335)
EMERSON ELECTRIC CO
Also Called: Emerson
Plant 4I-32 4401 East Dix (28150)
PHONE............................704 480-8519
Eric Emerson, Mgr
EMP: 5
SALES (corp-wide): 17.49B **Publicly Held**
Web: www.emerson.com
SIC: 3823 Process control instruments
PA: Emerson Electric Co.
8027 Forsyth Boulevard
Saint Louis MO 63105
314 553-2000

(G-11336)
FITCH SIGN COMPANY INC
341 N Post Rd (28152-4948)
P.O. Box 1316 (28151-1316)
PHONE............................704 482-2916
Thomas Fitch, Pr
Charlene Fitch, VP
EMP: 4 **EST:** 1977
SQ FT: 1,500
SALES (est): 212.63K **Privately Held**
Web: www.fitchsigncoinc.com
SIC: 3993 7389 1799 Signs, not made in custom sign painting shops; Sign painting and lettering shop; Sign installation and maintenance

(G-11337)
FLINT HILL TEXTILES INC
2240 Flint Hill Church Rd (28152-8137)
PHONE............................704 434-9331
Billy E Pearson, Owner
Edith E Pearson, Owner
EMP: 5 **EST:** 1970

GEOGRAPHIC

SALES (est): 71.27K **Privately Held**
SIC: 2273 2399 Carpets and rugs; Seat covers, automobile

(G-11338)
GLENN LUMBER COMPANY INC
145 Rockford Rd (28152-0667)
P.O. Box 756 (28017-0756)
PHONE.................................704 434-7873
John C Glenn, *Pr*
EMP: 25 **EST:** 1948
SALES (est): 1.87MM **Privately Held**
Web: www.glennlumber.com
SIC: 5211 2448 2426 2421 Planing mill products and lumber; Wood pallets and skids; Hardwood dimension and flooring mills; Sawmills and planing mills, general

(G-11339)
GREENHECK FAN CORPORATION
2000 Partnership Dr (28150-9424)
PHONE.................................704 476-3700
EMP: 4
SALES (corp-wide): 1.29B **Privately Held**
Web: www.greenheck.com
SIC: 3564 Blowers and fans
PA: Greenheck Fan Corporation
1100 Greenheck Dr
Schofield WI 54476
715 359-6171

(G-11340)
HACKNER HOME LLC
806 W Warren St (28150-5024)
PHONE.................................980 552-9573
Jona Hackner, *CEO*
Cristoph Hackner, *Managing Member*
EMP: 7 **EST:** 2013
SALES (est): 361.75K **Privately Held**
Web: www.hacknerhome.com
SIC: 2211 Pillowcases

(G-11341)
HAMRICK PRECAST LLC
415 W College Ave (28152-8190)
P.O. Box 1052 (28017-1052)
PHONE.................................704 434-6551
Ryan Hamrick, *Managing Member*
EMP: 8 **EST:** 2022
SALES (est): 835.67K **Privately Held**
SIC: 3273 Ready-mixed concrete

(G-11342)
HANWHA ADVANCED MTLS AMER LLC
Also Called: Hanwha Shelby
925 Washburn Switch Rd (28150-7008)
PHONE.................................704 434-2271
Philip Welton, *Mgr*
EMP: 35
Web: www.hanwhaus.com
SIC: 3714 2821 Motor vehicle parts and accessories; Plastics materials and resins
HQ: Hanwha Advanced Materials America Llc
4400 Northpark Dr
Opelika AL 36801
334 741-7725

(G-11343)
HEADRICK OTDOOR MDIA OF CRLNAS
Also Called: Creative Outdoor Advertising
600 S Morgan St (28150-5832)
P.O. Box 248 (28151-0248)
PHONE.................................704 487-5971
Max Padgett Butler, *Pr*
Earnest Johnson, *VP*
Phyllis B Wortman, *Sec*
EMP: 4 **EST:** 1945

SQ FT: 20,000
SALES (est): 218.53K **Privately Held**
Web: www.creativesignservice.com
SIC: 3993 Signs and advertising specialties

(G-11344)
HUDSON INDUSTRIES LLC
439 Neisler St (28152-5001)
PHONE.................................704 480-0014
EMP: 4 **EST:** 2006
SALES (est): 236.96K **Privately Held**
SIC: 3999 Manufacturing industries, nec

(G-11345)
HURST JAWS OF LIFE INC (HQ)
711 N Post Rd (28150-4246)
PHONE.................................704 487-6961
Bruce Lear, *VP*
◆ **EMP:** 150 **EST:** 1917
SQ FT: 185,000
SALES (est): 24.89MM
SALES (corp-wide): 3.27B **Publicly Held**
Web: www.jawsoflife.com
SIC: 3569 3561 3594 Firefighting apparatus; Industrial pumps and parts; Fluid power pumps and motors
PA: Idex Corporation
3100 Sanders Rd Ste 301
Northbrook IL 60062
847 498-7070

(G-11346)
IF ARMOR INTERNATIONAL LLC
Also Called: Man Lift
2501 W Dixon Blvd (28152-9012)
PHONE.................................704 482-1399
Roger Bingham, *Managing Member*
EMP: 150 **EST:** 2019
SALES (est): 23.34MM
SALES (corp-wide): 23.95MM **Privately Held**
Web: www.if-armor.com
SIC: 3545 Measuring tools and machines, machinists' metalworking type
PA: The Armored Group Llc
5221 N Saddle Rock Dr
Phoenix AZ 85018
602 840-2271

(G-11347)
IMC-METALSAMERICA LLC (HQ)
Also Called: IMC
135 Old Boiling Springs Rd (28152-0648)
PHONE.................................704 482-8200
Bernard C Shilberg, *Managing Member*
Nathan B Shilberg, *
◆ **EMP:** 10 **EST:** 2009
SQ FT: 165,000
SALES (est): 3.3MM
SALES (corp-wide): 145.97MM **Privately Held**
Web: www.imc-ma.com
SIC: 3331 Primary copper smelter products
PA: Prime Materials Recovery Inc.
99 E River Dr
East Hartford CT 06108
860 622-7626

(G-11348)
IVARS DISPLAY
2001 Partnership Dr (28150-9424)
PHONE.................................909 923-2761
EMP: 27
SALES (corp-wide): 18.21MM **Privately Held**
Web: www.ivarsdisplay.com
SIC: 2541 Partitions for floor attachment, prefabricated: wood
PA: Ivar's Display
2314 E Locust Ct
Ontario CA 91761

909 923-2761

(G-11349)
JENKINS FOODS INC
2119 New House Rd (28150-7923)
PHONE.................................704 434-2347
Harry Mauney, *Pr*
Mark Mauney, *
Diane Mauney, *Stockholder**
Rachel Mauney, *Stockholder**
EMP: 16 **EST:** 1933
SQ FT: 24,000
SALES (est): 1.08MM **Privately Held**
SIC: 2013 2035 2099 Sausages, from purchased meat; Spreads, sandwich: salad dressing base; Food preparations, nec

(G-11350)
JOE ROBIN DARNELL
Also Called: First Choice Properties
2115 Chatfield Rd (28150-9491)
PHONE.................................704 482-1186
Joe R Darnell, *Prin*
EMP: 6 **EST:** 2011
SALES (est): 49K **Privately Held**
SIC: 7692 6531 Welding repair; Real estate brokers and agents

(G-11351)
KEMET ELECTRONICS CORPORATION
2501 W Dixon Blvd (28152-9012)
PHONE.................................864 963-6300
Bruce White, *Mgr*
EMP: 27
Web: www.kemet.com
SIC: 3675 Electronic capacitors
HQ: Kemet Electronics Corporation
1 E Broward Blvd Fl 2
Fort Lauderdale FL 33301
954 766-2800

(G-11352)
KSM CASTINGS USA INC (DH)
Also Called: Ksm
120 Blue Brook Dr (28150-1500)
PHONE.................................704 751-0559
Mark Bradley, *Pr*
John Rollins, *
▲ **EMP:** 40 **EST:** 2012
SALES (est): 18.75MM **Privately Held**
Web: www.ksmcastings.com
SIC: 3363 Aluminum die-castings
HQ: Dicastal North America, Inc.
1 Dicastal Dr
Greenville MI 48838
616 619-7500

(G-11353)
LEONARD MCSWAIN SPTIC TANK SVC
3020 Ramseur Church Rd (28150-9308)
PHONE.................................704 482-1380
Leonard L Mcswain, *Pr*
EMP: 5 **EST:** 1963
SALES (est): 245.58K **Privately Held**
Web: www.leonardmcswainseptic.com
SIC: 3272 1711 Septic tanks, concrete; Septic system construction

(G-11354)
LIZMERE CAVALIERS
403 S Washington St (28150-5902)
PHONE.................................704 418-2543
EMP: 4 **EST:** 2010
SALES (est): 49.9K **Privately Held**
Web: www.lizmere.com
SIC: 3999 Pet supplies

(G-11355)
MACHINE BUILDERS & DESIGN INC
806 N Post Rd (28150-4247)
PHONE.................................704 482-3456
Daryl Mims, *Pr*
Teresa Miller, *
Gonzalo Penya, *
Brad Hogan, *
◆ **EMP:** 40 **EST:** 1974
SQ FT: 15,000
SALES (est): 8.02MM **Privately Held**
Web: www.mbd-inc.com
SIC: 3599 Custom machinery

(G-11356)
MACK S LIVER MUSH INC
Also Called: Mack's Livermush & Meats
6126 Mckee Rd (28150-7102)
P.O. Box 227 (28136-0227)
PHONE.................................704 434-6188
B Ron Mckee, *Pr*
EMP: 6 **EST:** 1944
SQ FT: 8,000
SALES (est): 562.17K **Privately Held**
SIC: 2013 Puddings, meat, from purchased meat

(G-11357)
MACO INC
521 Plato Lee Rd (28150-9418)
PHONE.................................704 434-6800
EMP: 48 **EST:** 1979
SALES (est): 9.22MM **Privately Held**
Web: www.macoincorporated.com
SIC: 3441 Building components, structural steel

(G-11358)
MAFIC USA LLC
119 Metrolina Plz (28150-7708)
PHONE.................................704 967-8006
Mike Levine, *CEO*
Dwight Lacelle, *CFO*
EMP: 13 **EST:** 2015
SALES (est): 11.24MM **Privately Held**
Web: www.mafic.com
SIC: 1429 Basalt, crushed and broken-quarrying

(G-11359)
MAN LIFT MFG CO
2501 W Dixon Blvd (28152-9012)
P.O. Box 1466 (28151-1466)
PHONE.................................414 486-1760
Phil Sprio, *Pr*
EMP: 44 **EST:** 2000
SQ FT: 33,000
SALES (est): 4.62MM
SALES (corp-wide): 11.06MM **Privately Held**
SIC: 3531 8711 Aerial work platforms: hydraulic/elec. truck/carrier mounted; Professional engineer
PA: Universal Mfg. Co.
1128 Lincoln Mall Ste 301
Lincoln NE 68508
402 261-3851

(G-11360)
MAXXDRIVE LLC
1847 E Dixon Blvd (28152-6901)
PHONE.................................704 600-8684
EMP: 4 **EST:** 2016
SALES (est): 1.16MM **Privately Held**
Web: www.maxxdrive.us
SIC: 3711 Motor vehicles and car bodies

(G-11361)
MEDICAL ENGINEERING LABS
Also Called: Mel

3039 Longwood Dr (28152-8638)
P.O. Box 2423 (28151-2423)
PHONE..............................704 487-0166
William J Young Junior, *Pr*
EMP: 5 **EST:** 1973
SQ FT: 8,000
SALES (est): 221.24K **Privately Held**
SIC: 3841 Surgical instruments and
apparatus

(G-11362)
METAL WORKS MFG CO
2501 W Dixon Blvd (28152-9012)
PHONE..............................704 482-1399
Phil Sprio, *Pr*
EMP: 80 **EST:** 2015
SQ FT: 219,000
SALES (est): 2.38MM
SALES (corp-wide): 11.06MM **Privately
Held**
Web: www.metalworksmfg.com
SIC: 3441 Fabricated structural metal
PA: Universal Mfg. Co.
1128 Lincoln Mall Ste 301
Lincoln NE 68508
402 261-3851

(G-11363)
MODERN DENSIFYING INC
Also Called: M D I
662 Plato Lee Rd (28150-7769)
P.O. Box 2312 (28151-2312)
PHONE..............................704 434-8335
Andy Ball, *VP*
Joe Morgan, *Pr*
EMP: 12 **EST:** 1992
SALES (est): 2.5MM **Privately Held**
SIC: 2821 Plastics materials and resins

(G-11364)
**MOIRE CREATIONS AMERICA LLC
(PA)**
1808 Country Garden Dr (28150-6165)
PHONE..............................704 482-9860
John O Salazar, *Pr*
EMP: 40 **EST:** 1933
SALES (est): 2.6MM
SALES (corp-wide): 2.6MM **Privately Held**
SIC: 2221 2269 2262 2261 Broadwoven
fabric mills, manmade; Finishing plants, nec
; Finishing plants, manmade; Finishing
plants, cotton

(G-11365)
MR TIRE INC
315 S Dekalb St (28150-5403)
PHONE..............................704 484-0816
Darren Davis, *Brnch Mgr*
EMP: 7
SALES (corp-wide): 1.28B **Publicly Held**
Web: locations.mrtire.com
SIC: 5941 5531 5014 7534 Bicycle and
bicycle parts; Automotive tires; Tires and
tubes; Tire recapping
HQ: Mr. Tire Inc.
2078 New York Ave Unit 2
Huntington Station NY 11746
631 499-3700

(G-11366)
**NEWGRASS BREWING COMPANY
LLC**
101 Columns Cir (28150-4865)
PHONE..............................704 477-2795
EMP: 5 **EST:** 2015
SALES (est): 234.61K **Privately Held**
Web: www.newgrassbrewing.com
SIC: 2082 Beer (alcoholic beverage)

(G-11367)
OAKIE S TIRE & RECAPPING INC
800 W Warren St (28150-5024)
PHONE..............................704 482-5629
Oakie Canipe, *Pr*
Chris Canipe, *VP*
Ken Canipe, *VP*
Rachel Canipe, *Sec*
EMP: 6 **EST:** 1958
SQ FT: 7,000
SALES (est): 562.97K **Privately Held**
SIC: 5531 7534 5014 Automotive tires; Tire
recapping; Automobile tires and tubes

(G-11368)
OPERATING SHELBY LLC TAG
2501 W Dixon Blvd (28152-9012)
PHONE..............................704 482-1399
Robert Pazderka, *Managing Member*
EMP: 50 **EST:** 2022
SALES (est): 12.93MM **Privately Held**
Web: www.tagshelby.com
SIC: 3711 Military motor vehicle assembly
PA: The Armored Group Llc
5050 E Red Rock Dr
Phoenix AZ 85018

(G-11369)
PLASTIC ODDITIES INC
1701 Burke Rd (28152-8116)
PHONE..............................704 484-1830
Lewis B Izzi Senior, *Ch Bd*
Loretta B Izzi, *
Hilda Blanton, *
Bobby G Guffey, *
Thomas Clint Shuford Contl, *Prin*
EMP: 5 **EST:** 1975
SQ FT: 6,000
SALES (est): 448.31K **Privately Held**
SIC: 3088 5074 Plastics plumbing fixtures;
Plumbing and hydronic heating supplies

(G-11370)
PPG-DEVOLD LLC
940 Washburn Switch Rd (28150-9400)
PHONE..............................704 434-2261
▲ **EMP:** 8 **EST:** 2007
SALES (est): 1.18MM **Privately Held**
SIC: 3229 Pressed and blown glass, nec

(G-11371)
PRINTING & PACKAGING INC
1015 Buffalo St (28150-4047)
P.O. Box 1558 (28151-1558)
PHONE..............................704 482-3866
Boyce J Hanna, *Pr*
Joan Hanna, *
EMP: 27 **EST:** 1947
SQ FT: 26,000
SALES (est): 2.58MM **Privately Held**
Web: www.pandpinc.com
SIC: 2631 2752 2791 Folding boxboard;
Offset printing; Typesetting

(G-11372)
RAFTERS AND WALLS LLC
2312 W Randolph Rd (28150-7785)
PHONE..............................980 404-0209
Richard Peddy, *Managing Member*
EMP: 20 **EST:** 2015
SALES (est): 3.46MM **Privately Held**
Web: www.rafterswalls.com
SIC: 2439 5031 Structural wood members,
nec; Lumber, plywood, and millwork

(G-11373)
RIDDLEY METALS INC
639 Washburn Switch Rd (28150-7712)
P.O. Box 2406 (28151-2406)
PHONE..............................704 435-8829

EMP: 10 **EST:** 2020
SALES (est): 6.07MM **Privately Held**
Web: www.riddleyinc.com
SIC: 3441 Fabricated structural metal

(G-11374)
RUFUS N IVIE III
Also Called: Southern Machining
4007 Hillview Dr (28152-8978)
PHONE..............................704 482-2559
Rufus N Ivie Iii, *Owner*
EMP: 7 **EST:** 1990
SALES (est): 597.51K **Privately Held**
SIC: 3599 Machine shop, jobbing and repair

(G-11375)
SHELBY BUSINESS CARDS
2020 E Dixon Blvd (28152-6958)
P.O. Box 2344 (28151-2344)
PHONE..............................704 481-8341
Boyd H Hendrick, *Owner*
EMP: 4 **EST:** 1965
SQ FT: 1,800
SALES (est): 234.79K **Privately Held**
Web: www.westmorelandprinters.com
SIC: 2752 Offset printing

(G-11376)
**SHELBY ELASTICS OF NORTH
CAROLINA LLC**
Also Called: Shelby Elastics
639 N Post Rd (28150-4965)
P.O. Box 2405 (28151-2405)
PHONE..............................704 487-4301
EMP: 60
SIC: 2259 Convertors, knit goods

(G-11377)
SHELBY FREEDOM STAR INC
Also Called: Shelby Star The
315 E Graham St (28150-5452)
P.O. Box 48 (28151-0048)
PHONE..............................704 484-7000
Johnathan Segal, *Pr*
Richard Wallace, *
EMP: 53 **EST:** 1800
SALES (est): 1.32MM
SALES (corp-wide): 2.51B **Publicly Held**
Web: www.shelbystar.com
SIC: 2711 Newspapers, publishing and
printing
HQ: Gatehouse Media, Llc
175 Sllys Trl Fl 3 Corp C
Pittsford NY 14534
585 598-0030

(G-11378)
SILVER INK PUBLISHING INC
Also Called: Publishing/Education
917 Beau Rd (28152-9686)
PHONE..............................704 473-0192
Jill P Nolen, *Managing Member*
▲ **EMP:** 4 **EST:** 2003
SALES (est): 221.86K **Privately Held**
Web: www.silverinkpublishing.com
SIC: 2741 Miscellaneous publishing

(G-11379)
SOFIDEL SHELBY LLC
Also Called: Clearwater Paper Shelby, LLC
671 Washburn Switch Rd (28150-7712)
PHONE..............................704 476-3802
Michael Urlick, *Managing Member*
EMP: 300 **EST:** 2020
SALES (est): 23.08MM **Publicly Held**
Web: www.clearwaterpaper.com
SIC: 2621 Towels, tissues and napkins;
paper and stock
PA: Clearwater Paper Corporation
601 W Riverside Ste 1100
Spokane WA 99201

(G-11380)
**SOLERO TECHNOLOGIES SHELBY
LLC**
1100 Airport Rd (28150-3639)
PHONE..............................704 482-9582
Donald R James, *CEO*
Delon Hoffa Ctrl, *Prin*
◆ **EMP:** 118 **EST:** 2007
SQ FT: 180,000
SALES (est): 24.07MM
SALES (corp-wide): 98.22MM **Privately
Held**
Web: www.kendrion.com
SIC: 3822 3643 3625 3613 Built-in
thermostats, filled system and bimetal types
; Current-carrying wiring services; Relays
and industrial controls; Switchgear and
switchboard apparatus
HQ: Solero Technologies, Llc
2114 Austin Ave
Rochester MI 48309
248 410-3409

(G-11381)
SOUTHCO INDUSTRIES INC
1840 E Dixon Blvd (28152-6902)
PHONE..............................704 482-1477
J Steve Goforth, *Pr*
Dennis G Goforth, *
Richard Goforth, *
EMP: 130 **EST:** 1985
SQ FT: 15,000
SALES (est): 22.19MM **Privately Held**
Web: www.southcoindustries.com
SIC: 3713 3535 3711 3441 Truck bodies
(motor vehicles); Conveyors and conveying
equipment; Motor vehicles and car bodies;
Fabricated structural metal

(G-11382)
SPAKE CONCRETE PRODUCTS INC
1110 N Post Rd (28150-3399)
PHONE..............................704 482-2881
Faye Spake, *Pr*
Danny Spake, *VP*
Bobby I Spake, *Sec*
EMP: 18 **EST:** 1963
SALES (est): 2.35MM **Privately Held**
Web: www.spakeconcreteproducts.com
SIC: 3271 5032 5211 Blocks, concrete or
cinder: standard; Brick, stone, and related
material; Lumber and other building
materials

(G-11383)
SQUARE ONE MACHINE LLC
658 Washburn Switch Rd (28150-9480)
PHONE..............................704 600-6296
Terry Beck, *Owner*
EMP: 4 **EST:** 2018
SALES (est): 533.93K **Privately Held**
SIC: 3599 Machine shop, jobbing and repair

(G-11384)
TACTICAL COATINGS INC
1028 Railroad Ave (28152-6681)
P.O. Box 1042 (28151-1042)
PHONE..............................704 692-4511
David Bryant, *Pr*
Kelly Bryant, *VP*
EMP: 4 **EST:** 2009
SALES (est): 252.13K **Privately Held**
Web: www.tacticalcoatings.net
SIC: 3479 Metal coating and allied services

(G-11385)
TRIPLE D PUBLISHING INC
Also Called: Onsat Magazine
1300 S Dekalb St (28152-7210)
PHONE..............................704 482-9673
Douglas G Brown, *Pr*

▲ **EMP:** 7 **EST:** 1977
SQ FT: 100,000
SALES (est): 380.04K **Privately Held**
SIC: 2721 Magazines: publishing only, not
printed on site

(G-11386)
TUBE ENTERPRISES
INCORPORATED
Also Called: Integrity Medical Solutions
1028 Railroad Ave (28152-6681)
P.O. Box 2206 (28086-6206)
PHONE..............................941 629-9267
Robert A Wright, *Pr*
Alfred A Taylor, *VP*
EMP: 12 **EST:** 2004
SALES (est): 2.07MM **Privately Held**
Web:
www.integritymedicalsolutions.com
SIC: 2514 Lawn furniture: metal

(G-11387)
TWIN OAKS SERVICE SOUTH INC
1320 Stony Point Rd (28150-8198)
PHONE..............................704 914-7142
William Straight, *Pr*
Stacey Straight, *CFO*
EMP: 7 **EST:** 1996
SQ FT: 15,000
SALES (est): 1.98MM **Privately Held**
Web:
www.twinoaksservicessouthinc.com
SIC: 3743 Railroad equipment

(G-11388)
ULTRA MACHINE & FABRICATION
INC
Also Called: Ultra
2501 W Dixon Blvd (28152-9012)
P.O. Box 335 (28086-0335)
PHONE..............................704 482-1399
EMP: 103
SIC: 3542 3599 Machine tools, metal
forming type; Machine shop, jobbing and
repair

(G-11389)
VARIETY CONSULT LLC
3735 Robert Riding Rd (28150-7038)
PHONE..............................704 978-8108
Tamera Briscoe, *CEO*
EMP: 6 **EST:** 2003
SALES (est): 2.5K **Privately Held**
SIC: 3641 5015 Health lamps, infrared or
ultraviolet; Automotive supplies, used:
wholesale and retail

(G-11390)
WALKER WOODWORKING INC (PA)
Also Called: Greenbrook Design Center
112 N Lafayette St (28150-4446)
PHONE..............................704 434-0823
Travis Walker, *CEO*
EMP: 27 **EST:** 1997
SALES (est): 4.9MM
SALES (corp-wide): 4.9MM **Privately Held**
Web: www.walkerwoodworking.com
SIC: 2434 Wood kitchen cabinets

(G-11391)
WESTMORELAND PRINTERS INC
Also Called: Copyrite
2020 E Dixon Blvd (28152-6958)
PHONE..............................704 482-9100
Wes Westmoreland, *Pr*
EMP: 10 **EST:** 1999
SQ FT: 13,000
SALES (est): 439.46K **Privately Held**
Web: www.westmorelandprinters.com
SIC: 2759 5943 Screen printing; Office forms
and supplies

Sherrills Ford
Catawba County

(G-11392)
I-LEADR INC
2220 Lazy Ln (28673-9734)
P.O. Box 625 (28673-0625)
PHONE..............................910 431-5252
Brie Beane, *Prin*
EMP: 9 **EST:** 2014
SALES (est): 235.62K **Privately Held**
Web: www.ileadr.com
SIC: 8748 7372 Educational consultant;
Educational computer software

(G-11393)
NATIONAL SIGN & DECAL INC
2199 Lynmore Dr (28673-9740)
P.O. Box 189 (28673-0189)
PHONE..............................828 478-2123
Carin A Hooper, *Pr*
Meagan Suggs, *Opers Mgr*
EMP: 6 **EST:** 1971
SQ FT: 7,000
SALES (est): 226.44K **Privately Held**
Web: www.nationalsignanddecalinc.com
SIC: 2759 3953 Screen printing; Screens,
textile printing

Shiloh
Camden County

(G-11394)
RICKYS WELDING INC
899 S Sandy Hook Rd (27974-7213)
P.O. Box 336 (27974-0336)
PHONE..............................252 336-4437
Ricky Lee Edwards, *Pr*
Shelia Edwards, *Sec*
EMP: 9 **EST:** 1983
SQ FT: 5,000
SALES (est): 460.47K **Privately Held**
Web: www.rickyswelding.com
SIC: 7692 Welding repair

(G-11395)
STAIR TAMER LLC
Also Called: Stair Tamer Cargo Lifts
899 S Sandy Hook Rd (27974-7213)
PHONE..............................252 336-4437
Ricky Edwards, *Pr*
EMP: 4 **EST:** 2015
SALES (est): 729.69K **Privately Held**
Web: www.stairtamercargolifts.com
SIC: 3499 Stabilizing bars (cargo), metal

Siler City
Chatham County

(G-11396)
ACME - MCCRARY CORPORATION
Also Called: ACME - MCCRARY
CORPORATION
1311 E 11th St (27344-2772)
PHONE..............................336 625-2161
Neal Anderson, *Brnch Mgr*
EMP: 10
Web: www.acme-mccrary.com
SIC: 2251 Women's hosiery, except socks
HQ: Acme-Mccrary Corporation
162 N Cherry St
Asheboro NC 27203
336 625-2161

(G-11397)
ACME-MCCRARY CORPORATION
1200 E 3rd St (27344-2732)
P.O. Box 686 (27344-0686)
PHONE..............................919 663-2200
Dave Foster, *Mgr*
EMP: 124
Web: www.acme-mccrary.com
SIC: 2251 Panty hose
HQ: Acme-Mccrary Corporation
162 N Cherry St
Asheboro NC 27203
336 625-2161

(G-11398)
AXCHEM SOLUTIONS INC
1325 N 2nd Ave (27344-1841)
PHONE..............................919 742-9810
Richard Joy, *Mgr*
EMP: 6 **EST:** 2006
SALES (est): 200.12K **Privately Held**
Web: www.axchemgroup.com
SIC: 2822 Ethylene-propylene rubbers,
EPDM polymers

(G-11399)
BASIC MACHINERY COMPANY INC
Also Called: Basic Group, The
1220 Harold Andrews Rd (27344-9170)
P.O. Box 688 (27344-0688)
PHONE..............................919 663-2244
William F Milholen, *CEO*
William S Robinson, *
Harold J Milholon Junior, *VP*
William J Milholon, *
▲ **EMP:** 58 **EST:** 1975
SALES (est): 19.35MM **Privately Held**
Web: www.basicmachinery.com
SIC: 5084 3535 3537 Materials handling
machinery; Conveyors and conveying
equipment; Industrial trucks and tractors

(G-11400)
BOYD MANUFACTURING INC
222 W Raleigh St (27344-3420)
PHONE..............................336 301-6433
Paul D Thompson, *Prin*
EMP: 10 **EST:** 2012
SALES (est): 972.07K **Privately Held**
SIC: 3999 Barber and beauty shop
equipment

(G-11401)
BROOKWOOD FARMS INC
1015 Alston Bridge Rd (27344-9573)
P.O. Box 277 (27344-0277)
PHONE..............................919 663-3612
EMP: 68 **EST:** 1959
SALES (est): 17.59MM **Privately Held**
Web: www.brookwoodfarms.com
SIC: 2033 Barbecue sauce: packaged in
cans, jars, etc.

(G-11402)
CCO HOLDINGS LLC
466 Vineyard Rdg (27344-4366)
PHONE..............................919 200-6260
EMP: 168
SALES (corp-wide): 55.09MM **Publicly
Held**
SIC: 4841 3663 3651 Cable television
services; Radio and t.v. communications
equipment; Household audio and video
equipment
HQ: Cco Holdings, Llc
400 Atlantic St
Stamford CT 06901
203 905-7801

(G-11403)
CECIL BUDD TIRE COMPANY LLC
394 Pine Forest Dr (27344-7995)
PHONE..............................919 742-2322
Michael Budd, *Managing Member*
John Grimes, *Pt*
Ruth Budd, *Pt*
EMP: 10 **EST:** 1936
SALES (est): 232.18K **Privately Held**
SIC: 5531 7534 5014 Automotive tires; Tire
recapping; Automobile tires and tubes

(G-11404)
CELEBRITY DAIRY LLC
198 Celebrity Dairy Way (27344-6761)
PHONE..............................919 742-4931
EMP: 5 **EST:** 1987
SALES (est): 222.64K **Privately Held**
Web: www.celebritydairy.com
SIC: 7011 2022 5143 Bed and breakfast inn;
Cheese; natural and processed; Frozen
dairy desserts

(G-11405)
CHATHAM NEWS PUBLISHING CO
(PA)
Also Called: Chatham News
303 W Raleigh St (27344-3725)
P.O. Box 290 (27344-0290)
PHONE..............................919 663-4042
Alan D Resch, *Pr*
Mary L Resch, *Sec*
EMP: 4
SQ FT: 5,600
SALES (est): 510.6K
SALES (corp-wide): 510.6K **Privately Held**
Web: www.thechathamnews.com
SIC: 2711 5812 Newspapers, publishing and
printing; Eating places

(G-11406)
DAKOTA FAB & WELDING INC
1420 W 3rd St (27344-3626)
PHONE..............................919 881-0027
Chris Lonski, *Pr*
EMP: 4 **EST:** 1996
SALES (est): 639.64K **Privately Held**
Web: www.dakotafabwelding.com
SIC: 3446 Architectural metalwork

(G-11407)
DF FRAMING LLC
510 N Garden Ave (27344-2902)
PHONE..............................919 368-7903
EMP: 12 **EST:** 2021
SALES (est): 380.9K **Privately Held**
SIC: 2426 Frames for upholstered furniture,
wood

(G-11408)
FLOORAZZO
Also Called: Floor Azzo
215 W 3rd St (27344-3443)
P.O. Box 380 (27344-0380)
PHONE..............................919 663-1684
Donna Sich, *Managing Member*
EMP: 5 **EST:** 2002
SALES (est): 304.14K **Privately Held**
Web: www.floorazzo.com
SIC: 3253 Ceramic wall and floor tile

(G-11409)
FLOORAZZO TILE LLC
1217 Harold Andrews Rd (27344-9171)
P.O. Box 380 (27344-0380)
PHONE..............................919 663-1684
Donna Sich, *Managing Member*
EMP: 17 **EST:** 2002
SALES (est): 963.93K **Privately Held**
Web: www.floorazzo.com

SIC: 3272 Floor tile, precast terrazzo

(G-11410)
GATHERING PLACE PUBG CO LLC
274 Lambert Chapel Rd (27344-6307)
PHONE..............................919 742-5850
Timothy J Moore, *Prin*
EMP: 4 EST: 2011
SALES (est): 69.27K **Privately Held**
SIC: 2741 Miscellaneous publishing

(G-11411)
HOG SLAT INCORPORATED
17720 Us Highway 64 W (27344-1629)
PHONE..............................919 663-3321
Dwight Jenkins, *Brnch Mgr*
EMP: 24
SALES (corp-wide): 451.86MM **Privately Held**
Web: www.hogslat.com
SIC: 3523 Farm machinery and equipment
PA: Hog Slat, Incorporated
    206 Fayetteville St
    Newton Grove NC 28366
    800 949-4647

(G-11412)
IMMIXT LLC
9743 Silk Hope Liberty Rd (27344-4482)
PHONE..............................336 207-8679
EMP: 5 EST: 2009
SALES (est): 212.96K **Privately Held**
SIC: 3713 Truck and bus bodies

(G-11413)
INTERNATIONAL PRECAST INC
2469 Old Us 421 N (27344-1548)
PHONE..............................919 742-4241
Gregory M Lask, *Pr*
Stephen G Lask, *
▲ EMP: 25 EST: 2002
SALES (est): 6.4MM **Privately Held**
Web: www.international-precast.com
SIC: 3272 Concrete products, precast, nec

(G-11414)
JUAN J HERNANDEZ
4272 Piney Grove Church Rd (27344-5458)
PHONE..............................919 742-3381
Juan J Hernandez, *Owner*
EMP: 6 EST: 2015
SALES (est): 174.83K **Privately Held**
SIC: 2411 Logging

(G-11415)
LAZAR INDUSTRIES LLC (PA)
3025 Hamp Stone Rd (27344-1426)
PHONE..............................919 742-9303
Robert Luce, *Managing Member*
David Sowinski, *
James Baker, *
Wayne Gilman, *
Gary Piper, *
◆ EMP: 150 EST: 1983
SQ FT: 78,000
SALES (est): 24.46MM
SALES (corp-wide): 24.46MM **Privately Held**
Web: www.lazarind.com
SIC: 2512 Upholstered household furniture

(G-11416)
LAZAR INDUSTRIES EAST INC
Also Called: Textile Trends
3025 Hamp Stone Rd (27344-1426)
PHONE..............................919 742-9303
Barry Lazar, *Pr*
EMP: 6 EST: 1990
SALES (est): 466.05K **Privately Held**
Web: www.lazarind.com

SIC: 2512 Upholstered household furniture

(G-11417)
LODGING BY LIBERTY INC
Also Called: Charter Furniture
50 Industrial Park Dr (27344-1318)
PHONE..............................336 622-2201
Gene J Moriarty, *Pr*
Jeff Leonard, *
Frederick King, *
EMP: 200 EST: 2000
SALES (est): 2.56MM
SALES (corp-wide): 145.56MM **Privately Held**
SIC: 2512 5021 Upholstered household furniture; Furniture
HQ: Jordan Brown Inc
    475 W Town Pl Ste 200
    Saint Augustine FL 32092

(G-11418)
MOUNTAIRE FARMS LLC
Also Called: Master Hatchery
4555 Old Us Hwy 421 N (27344-7381)
P.O. Box 175 (27344-0175)
PHONE..............................919 663-1768
David Pogge, *Brnch Mgr*
EMP: 229
SALES (corp-wide): 2.07B **Privately Held**
Web: www.mountaire.com
SIC: 2015 Poultry slaughtering and processing
HQ: Mountaire Farms Inc.
    1901 Napa Valley Dr
    Little Rock AR 72212
    501 372-6524

(G-11419)
MOUNTAIRE FARMS INC
1101 E 3rd St (27344-2729)
PHONE..............................919 663-0848
EMP: 312
SALES (corp-wide): 2.07B **Privately Held**
Web: www.mountaire.com
SIC: 2015 Poultry slaughtering and processing
HQ: Mountaire Farms Inc.
    1901 Napa Valley Dr
    Little Rock AR 72212
    501 372-6524

(G-11420)
NATIONAL WDEN PLLET CONT ASSOC
2340 Ike Brooks Rd (27344-8769)
PHONE..............................919 837-2105
Kenny Reavis, *Prin*
EMP: 11 EST: 2014
SALES (est): 2.86MM **Privately Held**
Web: www.palletone.com
SIC: 2448 Pallets, wood

(G-11421)
ONEIDA MOLDED PLASTICS LLC
920 E Raleigh St (27344-2708)
PHONE..............................919 663-3141
Irvin Glasgow, *Brnch Mgr*
EMP: 10
SALES (corp-wide): 23.25MM **Privately Held**
Web: www.oneidamoldedplastics.com
SIC: 3089 Injection molding of plastics
PA: Oneida Molded Plastics, Llc
    104 S Warner St
    Oneida NY 13421
    315 363-7980

(G-11422)
ORARE INC
Also Called: Glass & Window Warehouse
812 E 3rd St (27344-2724)

PHONE..............................919 742-1003
Judy Harrelson, *Pr*
Michael Harrelson, *VP*
EMP: 5 EST: 2007
SALES (est): 490K **Privately Held**
Web: www.mikeharrelson.net
SIC: 1793 3231 5231 7536 Glass and glazing work; Products of purchased glass; Glass; Automotive glass replacement shops

(G-11423)
PALLETONE NORTH CAROLINA INC (HQ)
Also Called: Palletone
2340 Ike Brooks Rd (27344-8769)
PHONE..............................704 462-1882
Howe Wallace, *Pr*
Casey Fletcher, *
EMP: 93 EST: 1993
SALES (est): 23.07MM
SALES (corp-wide): 6.65B **Publicly Held**
Web: www.palletone.com
SIC: 2448 2426 2421 Pallets, wood; Hardwood dimension and flooring mills; Sawmills and planing-mills, general
PA: Ufp Industries, Inc.
    2801 E Beltline Ave Ne
    Grand Rapids MI 49525
    616 364-6161

(G-11424)
QUANTUM USA LLP
1405 E 11th St (27344)
PHONE..............................919 799-7171
Ovidiu Martin, *Managing Member*
EMP: 4 EST: 2014
SALES (est): 1.42MM **Privately Held**
SIC: 3572 Computer storage devices

(G-11425)
SOUTHERN TRADITIONS TWO INC
55 Industrial Park Dr (27344-1300)
P.O. Box 523 (27344-0523)
PHONE..............................919 742-4692
James Lloyd, *Prin*
EMP: 4 EST: 2010
SALES (est): 177.52K **Privately Held**
SIC: 2599 Furniture and fixtures, nec

(G-11426)
SOUTHERN TRUCKING & BACKHOE
165 Riverside Rd (27344-9416)
PHONE..............................919 548-9723
Gerald Palmer, *Prin*
EMP: 5 EST: 2013
SALES (est): 67.56K **Privately Held**
SIC: 3531 Backhoes

(G-11427)
WHOLESALE KENNEL SUPPLY CO
163 Stockyard Rd (27344)
P.O. Box 745 (27344-0745)
PHONE..............................919 742-2515
Thomas E Dewitt, *Owner*
EMP: 9 EST: 1959
SQ FT: 13,200
SALES (est): 94.89K **Privately Held**
Web: www.wholesalekennel.com
SIC: 5199 5999 2834 Pet supplies; Pet food; Veterinary pharmaceutical preparations

Sims
Wilson County

(G-11428)
ARGOS USA LLC
Also Called: Ready Mix Concrete Co
6823 Bruce Rd (27880-9208)
P.O. Box 280 (27880-0280)

PHONE..............................252 291-8888
Tim Jacobs, *Mgr*
EMP: 8
Web: www.argos-us.com
SIC: 3273 Ready-mixed concrete
HQ: Argos Usa Llc
    3015 Windward Plz Ste 300
    Alpharetta GA 30005
    678 368-4300

(G-11429)
DAVIS CABINET CO WILSON INC
6116 Green Pond Rd (27880-9672)
P.O. Box 295 (27880-0295)
PHONE..............................252 291-9052
Stanley G Davis, *Pr*
Keith Davis, *VP*
Susan Davis, *Sec*
EMP: 5 EST: 1981
SQ FT: 26,000
SALES (est): 447.41K **Privately Held**
Web: www.daviscabinet.com
SIC: 2434 2541 2431 Wood kitchen cabinets ; Cabinets, except refrigerated: show, display, etc.: wood; Millwork

(G-11430)
FLOWERS SLAUGHTERHOUSE LLC
5154a Saint Rose Church Rd (27880-9419)
PHONE..............................252 235-4106
Alan Sharp, *Prin*
Pender Sharp, *Prin*
EMP: 12 EST: 2019
SALES (est): 555.3K **Privately Held**
SIC: 2011 Meat packing plants

(G-11431)
HEIDELBERG MATERIALS US INC
Also Called: Neverson Quarry
7225 Neverson Rd (27880-9476)
PHONE..............................252 235-4162
Rodney Godwin, *Brnch Mgr*
EMP: 69
SALES (corp-wide): 23.02B **Privately Held**
Web: www.heidelbergmaterials.us
SIC: 3273 Ready-mixed concrete
HQ: Heidelberg Materials Us, Inc.
    300 E John Carpenter Fwy
    Irving TX 75062

(G-11432)
TRI-STEEL FABRICATORS INC
6864 Wagon Wheel Rd (27880-9694)
P.O. Box 250 (27880-0250)
PHONE..............................252 291-7900
Tom Robertson, *Pr*
Ronald Cook, *
Steve Gibbon, *
EMP: 35 EST: 1996
SQ FT: 40,000
SALES (est): 8.17MM **Privately Held**
Web: www.tri-steel.net
SIC: 3441 Fabricated structural metal

Smithfield
Johnston County

(G-11433)
ACE FABRICATION INC
Also Called: M & W Fab
2880 Us Highway 70 Bus W (27577-9360)
P.O. Box 2769 (27577-2769)
PHONE..............................919 934-3251
Michael Prince, *Pr*
Mike Munden, *Pr*
Mike Watkins, *VP*
EMP: 16 EST: 1966
SQ FT: 13,200
SALES (est): 3.01MM **Privately Held**

Web: www.acefab.com
SIC: 3441 Fabricated structural metal

(G-11434)
BAKERS STNLESS FABRICATION INC
1520 Freedom Rd (27577-8131)
PHONE..........................919 934-2707
Billy Baker, *Pr*
Sandy Baker, *VP*
Margie Crumley, *Sec*
EMP: 9 EST: 1996
SQ FT: 5,000
SALES (est): 1.08MM **Privately Held**
SIC: 3441 Fabricated structural metal

(G-11435)
CAROLINA ELCTRNIC ASSMBLERS IN
132 Citation Ln (27577-6969)
PHONE..........................919 938-1086
Steven S Yauch, *Pr*
Kimberly N Godfrey, *
◆ **EMP: 50 EST:** 2000
SQ FT: 50,000
SALES (est): 11.84MM **Privately Held**
Web: www.ceamanufacturing.com
SIC: 3679 3613 Electronic circuits;
Switchgear and switchboard apparatus

(G-11436)
CAROLINA PACKERS INC (PA)
2999 S Brightleaf Blvd (27577-5251)
Drawer 1109 (27577)
PHONE..........................919 934-2181
EMP: 80 EST: 1940
SQ FT: 100,000
SALES (est): 8.56MM
SALES (corp-wide): 8.56MM **Privately Held**
Web: www.carolinapackers.com
SIC: 2011 2013 Meat packing plants;
Sausages, from purchased meat

(G-11437)
CLARITY VISION OF SMITHFIELD
1680 E Booker Dairy Rd (27577-9405)
PHONE..........................919 938-6101
EMP: 4 EST: 2015
SALES (est): 1.12MM **Privately Held**
Web: www.findclarityvision.com
SIC: 3851 5995 Ophthalmic goods;
Eyeglasses, prescription

(G-11438)
CLASSIC INDUSTRIAL SERVICES
Also Called: Classic Industrial Services
1305 S Brightleaf Blvd Ste 103
(27577-4260)
PHONE..........................919 209-0909
Michael Landes, *Pr*
Mark Beuerle, *
EMP: 8 EST: 1987
SQ FT: 89,000
SALES (est): 2.06MM
SALES (corp-wide): 7.02B **Publicly Held**
Web: www.classicindustrial.com
SIC: 1499 7359 Corundum mining;
Equipment rental and leasing, nec
HQ: Api Group, Inc.
1100 Old Highway 8 Nw
New Brighton MN 55112
651 636-4320

(G-11439)
CMC SENCON INC (PA)
132 Citation Ln (27577-6969)
PHONE..........................919 938-3216
Steven S Yauch, *Pr*
▲ **EMP: 33 EST:** 1992

SQ FT: 4,000
SALES (est): 1.06MM **Privately Held**
SIC: 3625 Relays and industrial controls

(G-11440)
COMMSCOPE TECHNOLOGIES LLC
1315 Industrial Park Dr (27577)
PHONE..........................919 934-9711
Danny Ricker, *Brnch Mgr*
EMP: 8
SALES (corp-wide): 15.22B **Publicly Held**
Web: www.commscope.com
SIC: 3663 3357 3679 3812 Microwave
communication equipment; Coaxial cable,
nonferrous; Waveguides and fittings;
Search and navigation equipment
HQ: Commscope Technologies Llc
3642 E Us Highway 70
Claremont NC 28610
828 324-2200

(G-11441)
CREATIVE BREWING COMPANY LLC
809 S 2nd St (27577-4347)
PHONE..........................919 297-8182
EMP: 4 EST: 2013
SALES (est): 173.61K **Privately Held**
SIC: 7389 2082 Business Activities at Non-
Commercial Site; Ale (alcoholic beverage)

(G-11442)
ENVICOR ENTERPRISES LLC
207a Computer Dr (27577-3156)
PHONE..........................877 823-7231
Steve Arnold, *Pr*
EMP: 49 EST: 2011
SQ FT: 50,000
SALES (est): 5MM **Privately Held**
Web: envicor.esmarttank.com
SIC: 3089 Injection molding of plastics

(G-11443)
FLANDERS CORPORATION
Also Called: Flanders Precisionaire
2121 Wal Pat Rd (27577-8375)
PHONE..........................919 934-3020
Steve Young, *Mgr*
EMP: 99
Web: www.flanderscorp.com
SIC: 3569 Filters
HQ: Flanders Corporation
531 Flanders Filter Rd
Washington NC 27889

(G-11444)
FLANDERS FILTERS INC
1418 Wal Pat Rd (27577-8394)
PHONE..........................252 217-3978
EMP: 5
Web: www.aafintl.com
SIC: 3569 Filters
HQ: Flanders Filters, Inc.
531 Flanders Filter Rd
Washington NC 27889
252 946-8081

(G-11445)
GREAT WATERS COMPANY
Also Called: Craftsman Crate
1215 S Crescent Dr (27577-3607)
PHONE..........................919 818-4081
W Harral Young Iii, *Pr*
EMP: 5 EST: 2009
SALES (est): 160.06K **Privately Held**
SIC: 2731 Book publishing

(G-11446)
HINSONS TYPING & PRINTING
Also Called: Henson's Printing
1294 W Market St (27577-3337)

P.O. Box 87 (27577-0087)
PHONE..........................919 934-9036
Amy Stanley, *Pr*
Nolan Hinson, *Owner*
Joanne Hinson, *VP*
James L Stanley Junior, *Treas*
Jamie Stanley, *VP*
EMP: 7 EST: 1983
SALES (est): 405.8K **Privately Held**
Web: www.hinsprint.com
SIC: 2752 2389 8742 Offset printing;
Apparel for handicapped; Marketing
consulting services

(G-11447)
J & B LOGGING AND TIMBER CO
524 Brogden Rd (27577-4306)
P.O. Box 2430 (27577-2430)
PHONE..........................919 934-4115
John Mark Williams, *Pr*
Andy Lee, *Contrlr*
▼ **EMP: 6 EST:** 1987
SQ FT: 3,000
SALES (est): 126.9K **Privately Held**
Web: www.jerrygwilliamslumber.com
SIC: 2421 Sawmills and planing mills,
general

(G-11448)
JERRY G WILLIAMS & SONS INC
524 Brogden Rd (27577-4306)
P.O. Box 59 (27577-0059)
PHONE..........................919 934-4115
J Mark Williams, *Pr*
Virginia M Williams, *Sec*
Kevin D Williams, *VP*
EMP: 18 EST: 1986
SALES (est): 3.13MM **Privately Held**
Web: www.jerrygwilliamslumber.com
SIC: 2421 Sawmills and planing mills,
general

(G-11449)
JERRY WILLIAMS & SON INC
524 Brogden Rd (27577-4306)
P.O. Box 2430 (27577-2430)
PHONE..........................919 934-4115
John Mark Williams, *Pr*
Lynette Williams, *
EMP: 100 EST: 1938
SQ FT: 3,500
SALES (est): 4.62MM **Privately Held**
Web: www.jerrygwilliamslumber.com
SIC: 2421 Lumber: rough, sawed, or planed

(G-11450)
KEENER LUMBER COMPANY INC (PA)
1209 W Market St (27577-3338)
P.O. Box 2323 (27577-2323)
PHONE..........................919 934-1087
Wade M Stewart, *Pr*
Reid Stewart, *
Steve Clark, *CIO**
Wayne Stewart, *
Ralph Stewart, *
EMP: 95 EST: 1935
SQ FT: 1,800
SALES (est): 2.47MM
SALES (corp-wide): 2.47MM **Privately Held**
Web: www.keenerlumber.com
SIC: 2421 Sawmills and planing mills,
general

(G-11451)
KRATOS ANTENNA SOLUTIONS CORP
1315 Industrial Park Dr (27577)
PHONE..........................919 934-9711
Danny Ricker, *Mgr*

EMP: 5
Web: www.kratosdefense.com
SIC: 3679 Antennas, satellite: household use
HQ: Kratos Antenna Solutions Corporation
3801 E Plano Pkwy Ste 200
Plano TX 75074

(G-11452)
LAMPE & MALPHRUS LUMBER CO
37 E Peedin Rd (27577-4709)
P.O. Box 150 (27577-0150)
PHONE..........................919 934-6152
James Malphrus, *Pr*
EMP: 15
SALES (corp-wide): 10.05MM **Privately Held**
Web: www.lampemalphrus.com
SIC: 2421 Sawmills and planing mills,
general
PA: Lampe & Malphrus Lumber Company
37 E Peedin Rd
Smithfield NC 27577
919 934-6152

(G-11453)
LAMPE & MALPHRUS LUMBER CO (PA)
Also Called: Geecee
37 E Peedin Rd (27577-4709)
P.O. Box 150 (27577-0150)
PHONE..........................919 934-6152
James Malphrus, *Pr*
▼ **EMP: 84 EST:** 1986
SQ FT: 3,600
SALES (est): 10.05MM
SALES (corp-wide): 10.05MM **Privately Held**
Web: www.lampemalphrus.com
SIC: 2421 Sawmills and planing mills,
general

(G-11454)
LAMPE & MALPHRUS LUMBER CO
210 N 10th St (27577-4658)
P.O. Box 150 (27577-0150)
PHONE..........................919 934-1124
Jimmy Knight, *Mgr*
EMP: 15
SALES (corp-wide): 10.05MM **Privately Held**
Web: www.lampemalphrus.com
SIC: 2421 3543 Sawmills and planing mills,
general; Industrial patterns
PA: Lampe & Malphrus Lumber Company
37 E Peedin Rd
Smithfield NC 27577
919 934-6152

(G-11455)
MITCHELL CONCRETE PRODUCTS INC
490 W Market St (27577-3321)
P.O. Box 585 (27577-0585)
PHONE..........................919 934-4333
Nelson Mitchell, *Pr*
EMP: 9 EST: 1958
SQ FT: 85,000
SALES (est): 792.78K **Privately Held**
SIC: 3272 Concrete products, nec

(G-11456)
OLT LOGGING INC
451 Marshall Ln (27577-7492)
PHONE..........................919 894-4506
Donald Czysz, *Pr*
EMP: 7 EST: 1994
SALES (est): 960.66K **Privately Held**
SIC: 2411 Logging camps and contractors

▲ = Import ▼ = Export
◆ = Import/Export

(G-11457)
OPW FLING CNTNMENT SYSTEMS INC (DH)
3250 Us Highway 70 Bus W (27577-6954)
PHONE.............................919 209-2280
David Crouse, *Pr*
Susan Hathaway, *CFO*
◆ **EMP:** 24 **EST:** 2006
SQ FT: 190,000
SALES (est): 20.2MM
SALES (corp-wide): 7.75B **Publicly Held**
Web: www.opwglobal.com
SIC: 3089 3084 3561 Plastics processing; Plastics pipe; Pumps and pumping equipment
HQ: Opw Fluid Transfer Group
    4304 Mattox Rd
    Kansas City MO 64150

(G-11458)
OPW FUELING COMPONENTS INC
Also Called: Opw Feling Containment Systems
3250 Us Highway 70 Bus W (27577-6954)
PHONE.............................919 464-4569
EMP: 47
SALES (corp-wide): 7.75B **Publicly Held**
Web: www.opwglobal.com
SIC: 2899 Fuel treating compounds
HQ: Opw Fueling Components Inc.
    9393 Prnceton Glendale Rd
    West Chester OH 45011

(G-11459)
PENN COMPRESSION MOULDING INC (PA)
Also Called: Penn
309 Components Dr (27577-6030)
PHONE.............................919 934-5144
Richard S Robinson, *Pr*
EMP: 5 **EST:** 1995
SQ FT: 2,000
SALES (est): 21.24MM
SALES (corp-wide): 21.24MM **Privately Held**
Web: www.penncompression.com
SIC: 3089 3644 Molding primary plastics; Insulators and insulation materials, electrical

(G-11460)
POST EC HOLDINGS INC
207a Computer Dr (27577-3156)
PHONE.............................919 989-0175
G Steve Arnold, *CEO*
Stephen Butts, *
Francis Koh, *
▲ **EMP:** 35 **EST:** 2006
SQ FT: 40,000
SALES (est): 5.66MM **Privately Held**
Web: www.envicor.com
SIC: 3089 Injection molding of plastics

(G-11461)
RAVEN ANTENNA SYSTEMS INC
Also Called: Global Skyware
1315 Outlet Center Dr (27577-6024)
PHONE.............................919 934-9711
David C Mccourt, *Pr*
Michael Kevin Jackson, *
Hamid Moheb, *
◆ **EMP:** 200 **EST:** 2004
SQ FT: 75,200
SALES (est): 45.75MM **Privately Held**
Web: www.globalinvacom.com
SIC: 3663 Television antennas (transmitting) and ground equipment
PA: Global Invacom Group Limited
    7 Temasek Boulevard
    Singapore 03898

(G-11462)
RDC DEBRIS REMOVAL CNSTR LLC
149 Rainbow Ln (27577-6801)
PHONE.............................323 614-2353
EMP: 50 **EST:** 2019
SALES (est): 335.87K **Privately Held**
SIC: 1521 1771 0782 1081 Single-family housing construction; Stucco, gunite, and grouting contractors; Lawn and garden services; Metal mining exploration and development services

(G-11463)
RETAIL MARKET PLACE
950 W Market St (27577-3331)
PHONE.............................984 201-1948
Brian Parker, *Owner*
EMP: 4 **EST:** 2016
SQ FT: 10,000
SALES (est): 140.54K **Privately Held**
SIC: 2051 Bakery: wholesale or wholesale/retail combined

(G-11464)
SANDY RIDGE PORK
2080 Wilsons Mills Rd (27577-7657)
PHONE.............................919 989-8878
Whitley Stevenson, *Owner*
EMP: 4 **EST:** 2004
SALES (est): 315.39K **Privately Held**
SIC: 2011 Pork products, from pork slaughtered on site

(G-11465)
SHALLCO INC
308 Components Dr (27577-6029)
P.O. Box 1089 (27577-1089)
PHONE.............................919 934-3135
Jason Shallcross, *Pr*
▲ **EMP:** 40 **EST:** 1967
SQ FT: 15,000
SALES (est): 6.9MM **Privately Held**
Web: www.shallco.com
SIC: 3613 3679 Switches, electric power except snap, push button, etc.; Attenuators

(G-11466)
STEVENS SAUSAGE COMPANY INC
3411 Stevens Sausage Rd (27577-7539)
P.O. Box 2304 (27577-2304)
PHONE.............................919 934-3159
N S Stevens Junior, *Pr*
Carolyn Stevens, *
EMP: 72 **EST:** 1952
SQ FT: 46,000
SALES (est): 9.17MM **Privately Held**
Web: www.stevens-sausage.com
SIC: 2013 5812 2048 Sausages, from purchased meat; Eating places; Prepared feeds, nec

(G-11467)
TAR HEEL TLING PRCSION MCHNING
3290 Us Highway 70 E (27577-7771)
P.O. Box 1063 (27577-1063)
PHONE.............................919 965-6160
Bobby G Pilkington, *Pr*
Durwood D Woodall, *VP*
Charles L Pilkington, *Treas*
Cecil C Woodall, *Sec*
EMP: 13 **EST:** 1978
SQ FT: 15,000
SALES (est): 2.56MM **Privately Held**
Web: www.tarheeltooling.com
SIC: 3599 3545 Custom machinery; Tools and accessories for machine tools

(G-11468)
VIDA WOOD US INC
219 Peedin Rd Ste 102 (27577-4738)
PHONE.............................919 934-9904
Kenny W Woodard, *Pr*
EMP: 4 **EST:** 2008
SALES (est): 1.95MM **Privately Held**
Web: www.vidawoodus.com
SIC: 2421 Outdoor wood structural products

(G-11469)
WALLACE WELDING INC
403 W Market St (27577-3322)
PHONE.............................919 934-2488
Garrett Wallace, *Pr*
EMP: 10 **EST:** 1945
SQ FT: 3,500
SALES (est): 325.8K **Privately Held**
SIC: 3441 3599 7692 Fabricated structural metal; Machine shop, jobbing and repair; Welding repair

(G-11470)
WILSON BILLBOARD ADVG INC
Also Called: Wilson Signs
212 Bridge St (27577-3963)
P.O. Box 910 (27577-0910)
PHONE.............................919 934-2421
James E Wilson Iii, *Pr*
J E Wilson Iii, *Pr*
Pam Hanson, *Sec*
James E Wilson Junior, *Ch Bd*
Angela Wilson, *VP*
EMP: 8 **EST:** 1986
SALES (est): 244.57K **Privately Held**
SIC: 7312 3993 Billboard advertising; Signs and advertising specialties

Smyrna
Carteret County

(G-11471)
SAVVY - DISCOUNTSCOM NEWS LTR
195 Old Nassau Road Williston (28579-9519)
P.O. Box 117 (28579-0117)
PHONE.............................252 729-8691
Rick Doble, *Owner*
EMP: 10 **EST:** 1994
SALES (est): 72.47K **Privately Held**
Web: www.savvy-discounts.com
SIC: 2741 Business service newsletters: publishing and printing

Sneads Ferry
Onslow County

(G-11472)
MCLEAN PRECISION CABINETRY INC
2507 Nc Highway 172 (28460-6637)
PHONE.............................910 327-9217
John Mclean, *Prin*
EMP: 4 **EST:** 2007
SALES (est): 208.46K **Privately Held**
Web: www.mcleanprecisioncabinetry.com
SIC: 2434 Wood kitchen cabinets

Snow Camp
Alamance County

(G-11473)
CHARLIES HEATING & COOLING LLC
8277 Bethel South Fork Rd (27349-9879)
PHONE.............................336 260-1973
EMP: 4
SALES (est): 389.98K **Privately Held**
SIC: 7389 3585 Business Activities at Non-Commercial Site; Heating and air conditioning combination units

(G-11474)
COLE MACHINE INC
6144 Patterson Rd (27349-9911)
PHONE.............................336 222-8381
Harry Cole, *Pr*
Jason Cole, *VP*
EMP: 8 **EST:** 1990
SQ FT: 4,000
SALES (est): 583.26K **Privately Held**
SIC: 3599 Machine and other job shop work

Snow Hill
Greene County

(G-11475)
BOAT LIFT WAREHOUSE LLC
900 Hwy 258 S (28580-8964)
P.O. Box 798 (28580-0798)
PHONE.............................877 468-5438
▼ **EMP:** 6 **EST:** 2009
SQ FT: 7,000
SALES (est): 2.75MM **Privately Held**
Web: www.boatliftwarehouse.com
SIC: 3536 Boat lifts

(G-11476)
BUILDING ENVLOPE ERCTION SVCS (PA)
1441 Nahunta Rd (28580-7557)
PHONE.............................252 747-2015
John Taylor Iii, *Pr*
William R Brown, *VP*
Richard Logan, *Sec*
EMP: 12 **EST:** 2013
SQ FT: 30,000
SALES (est): 2.5MM
SALES (corp-wide): 2.5MM **Privately Held**
Web: www.beesinc.net
SIC: 1793 3442 Glass and glazing work; Baseboards, metal

(G-11477)
CAROLINA FARMSTEAD LLC
1012 Hardy Rd (28580-7389)
PHONE.............................800 822-6219
Wayne Noble, *Owner*
EMP: 6 **EST:** 2015
SALES (est): 112.56K **Privately Held**
Web: www.carolinafarmstead.com
SIC: 2511 Bed frames, except water bed frames: wood

(G-11478)
CD SNOW HILL LLC
Also Called: Nwl Capacitors
204 Carolina Dr (28580-1646)
PHONE.............................252 747-5943
James Kaplan, *CEO*
EMP: 85 **EST:** 2020
SALES (est): 4.91MM
SALES (corp-wide): 553.5MM **Publicly Held**
Web: www.nwl.com
SIC: 3679 Power supplies, all types: static
HQ: Cornell-Dubilier Electronics, Inc.
    140 Technology Pl
    Liberty SC 29657
    864 843-2277

(G-11479)
DEHYDRATION LLC
963 Hwy 258 S (28580-8964)
PHONE.............................252 747-8200

EMP: 7 **EST:** 2015
SALES: 168.52K **Privately Held**
Web: www.hamfarms.com
SIC: 2034 Dried and dehydrated fruits, vegetables and soup mixes

(G-11480)
HAPPY JACK INCORPORATED
Also Called: E- Stitch.com
2122 Hwy 258 S (28580-9016)
P.O. Box 475 (28580-0475)
PHONE.................................252 747-2911
EMP: 8 **EST:** 1946
SALES (est): 2.38MM **Privately Held**
Web: www.happyjackinc.com
SIC: 2834 5699 Veterinary pharmaceutical preparations; Sports apparel

(G-11481)
NWL INC
Also Called: N W L Capacitors
204 Carolina Dr (28580-1646)
P.O. Box 97 (28580-0097)
PHONE.................................252 747-5943
Stewart Irvin, *Opers Mgr*
EMP: 42
SQ FT: 35,000
SALES (corp-wide): 67.72MM **Privately Held**
Web: www.nwl.com
SIC: 3612 3675 3629 Power transformers, electric; Electronic capacitors; Capacitors and condensers
HQ: Nwl, Inc.
312 Rising Sun Rd
Bordentown NJ 08505
609 298-7300

(G-11482)
PARKERS EQUIPMENT COMPANY
3204 Hwy 258 S (28580-8914)
PHONE.................................252 560-0088
Richard Parker, *Owner*
Richard Dick Parker, *Prin*
EMP: 4 **EST:** 2001
SALES (est): 195.27K **Privately Held**
SIC: 3537 Forklift trucks

(G-11483)
VERTICAL ACCESS LLC
900 Hwy 258 S (28580-8964)
P.O. Box 737 (28580-0737)
PHONE.................................800 325-1116
Francis Shackelford, *Pr*
EMP: 7 **EST:** 2015
SALES (est): 797.65K **Privately Held**
Web: www.vertical-access.com
SIC: 3534 Elevators and equipment

(G-11484)
WORTH PRODUCTS LLC
856 Hwy 258 S (28580-8963)
P.O. Box 491 (28580-0491)
PHONE.................................252 747-9994
Kenneth Letchworth, *Owner*
EMP: 18 **EST:** 2004
SQ FT: 28,000
SALES (est): 2.3MM **Privately Held**
Web: www.worthproducts.com
SIC: 3544 3599 Jigs and fixtures; Custom machinery

(G-11485)
YAMCO LLC
310 Kingold Blvd (28580-1306)
P.O. Box 42 (28580-0042)
PHONE.................................252 747-9267
EMP: 4 **EST:** 2004
SALES (est): 3.66MM **Privately Held**
Web: www.yamco.net

Sophia
Randolph County

(G-11486)
COTNER CABINET
3004 Old County Farm Rd (27350-8862)
PHONE.................................336 672-1560
Raymond Dalton Cotner, *Owner*
EMP: 6 **EST:** 1978
SALES (est): 141.73K **Privately Held**
Web: www.cotnercabinet.com
SIC: 2434 Wood kitchen cabinets

(G-11487)
ENGINEERED STEEL PRODUCTS LLC
4977 Plainfield Rd (27350-8895)
PHONE.................................336 495-5266
Rick Ramsey, *Pr*
EMP: 30 **EST:** 1989
SALES (est): 2.66MM
SALES (corp-wide): 4.66MM **Privately Held**
Web: www.engineeredsteel.com
SIC: 3441 Fabricated structural metal
PA: New Page Capital, Llc
1404 Briarcliff Rd
Greensboro NC 27408
770 853-6748

(G-11488)
ENGINEERED STEEL PRODUCTS INC
4977 Plainfield Rd (27350-8895)
P.O. Box 967 (27317-0967)
PHONE.................................336 495-5266
EMP: 30
SIC: 3441 Fabricated structural metal

(G-11489)
G T RACING HEADS INC
2735 Banner Whitehead Rd (27350-9119)
PHONE.................................336 905-7988
Gregory B Burkhart, *Pr*
EMP: 4 **EST:** 2003
SQ FT: 7,200
SALES (est): 899.03K **Privately Held**
SIC: 3549 7539 3599 Metalworking machinery, nec; Machine shop, automotive; Machine shop, jobbing and repair

(G-11490)
RBC INC (PA)
Also Called: Braxton Culler
7310 Us Highway 311 (27350-8981)
P.O. Box 248 (27261)
PHONE.................................336 861-5800
Braxton Culler, *Pr*
Steve Greene, *
Ashley Culler, *
◆ **EMP:** 160 **EST:** 1975
SQ FT: 465,000
SALES (est): 23.83MM
SALES (corp-wide): 23.83MM **Privately Held**
Web: www.braxtonculler.com
SIC: 5021 2512 2519 Household furniture; Upholstered household furniture; Wicker and rattan furniture

(G-11491)
SOUTHERN CLASSIC SEATING LLC
7064 Us Highway 311 (27350-8978)
PHONE.................................336 498-3130
EMP: 11 **EST:** 1972
SQ FT: 20,000
SALES (est): 2.42MM **Privately Held**

SIC: 2033 Vegetable purees: packaged in cans, jars, etc.

(G-11492)
TAR HEEL FENCE & VINYL
5279 Branson Davis Rd (27350-9015)
PHONE.................................336 465-1297
Benny Cruthis, *Owner*
EMP: 6 **EST:** 2005
SALES (est): 90.81K **Privately Held**
SIC: 2865 Tar

South Mills
Camden County

(G-11493)
SWAIN & TEMPLE INC
149 Lilly Rd (27976-9533)
PHONE.................................252 771-8147
Tracy Swain, *Pr*
Douglas Temple, *
EMP: 10 **EST:** 1993
SALES (est): 929.54K **Privately Held**
SIC: 2411 Logging camps and contractors

Southern Pines
Moore County

(G-11494)
ARTISTIC KITCHENS & BATHS LLC
683 Sw Broad St (28387-5925)
PHONE.................................910 692-4000
John Wilson, *Pr*
EMP: 9 **EST:** 2009
SQ FT: 3,700
SALES (est): 393.61K **Privately Held**
Web: www.artistic-kitchens.com
SIC: 2434 Wood kitchen cabinets

(G-11495)
BIOMEDICAL INNOVATIONS INC
410 N Bennett St (28387-4815)
PHONE.................................910 603-0267
Melissa Justice, *Pr*
EMP: 4 **EST:** 2002
SALES (est): 275.99K **Privately Held**
SIC: 3842 Surgical appliances and supplies

(G-11496)
CAROLINA CANNERS INC
750 S Bennett St (28387-5922)
PHONE.................................843 537-5281
Brantley Burnett, *Prin*
EMP: 80
SALES (corp-wide): 42.01MM **Privately Held**
Web: www.carolinacanners.com
SIC: 2033 Canned fruits and specialties
PA: Carolina Canners, Inc.
300 Highway 1 S
Cheraw SC 29520
843 537-5281

(G-11497)
E-Z DUMPER PRODUCTS LLC
150 Vardon Ct (28387-2987)
PHONE.................................717 762-8432
EMP: 6 **EST:** 1972
SQ FT: 40,000
SALES (est): 1.51MM **Privately Held**
SIC: 3537 3594 Trucks, tractors, loaders, carriers, and similar equipment; Fluid power pumps and motors

SIC: 7532 2531 Customizing services, nonfactory basis; Seats, miscellaneous public conveyances

(G-11498)
EPIC ENTERPRISES INC (PA)
845 Valley View Rd (28387-2575)
P.O. Box 979 (28388-0979)
PHONE.................................910 692-5750
Edward P Crenshaw, *Pr*
John Shaw, *
▲ **EMP:** 47 **EST:** 1977
SQ FT: 37,000
SALES (est): 11.41MM
SALES (corp-wide): 11.41MM **Privately Held**
Web: www.epicenterprises.com
SIC: 5084 3499 Textile machinery and equipment; Aerosol valves, metal

(G-11499)
FLETCHER INDUSTRIES INC
1485 Central Dr 22 (28387-2105)
PHONE.................................910 692-7133
John H Taws, *Pr*
Carol F Prevatte, *
◆ **EMP:** 25 **EST:** 1960
SQ FT: 60,000
SALES (est): 3.07MM **Privately Held**
Web: www.fletcherindustries.com
SIC: 3552 Textile machinery

(G-11500)
HERITAGE FLAG LLC
230 S Bennett St (28387-5402)
PHONE.................................910 725-1540
Trigg Heath, *Prin*
EMP: 4 **EST:** 2015
SALES (est): 272.3K **Privately Held**
Web: www.theheritageflag.com
SIC: 5999 2499 Flags; Decorative wood and woodwork

(G-11501)
K2 SOLUTIONS INC
Also Called: K2 Canine, Inc.
5735 Us Hwy 1 N (28387)
P.O. Box 690 (28388-0690)
PHONE.................................910 692-6898
Lane Kjellsen, *Pr*
James A Lynch, *
Susan Kjellsen, *
Robert Spivey, *
EMP: 275 **EST:** 2003
SALES (est): 21.52MM **Privately Held**
Web: www.k2si.com
SIC: 8742 2892 8731 General management consultant; Explosives; Commercial physical research

(G-11502)
LONGWORTH INDUSTRIES INC (DH)
Also Called: Polarmax/Xgo
565 Air Tool Dr Ste K (28387-3469)
P.O. Box 2716 (28388-2716)
PHONE.................................910 673-5290
▼ **EMP:** 19 **EST:** 1985
SALES (est): 7.15MM
SALES (corp-wide): 99.5MM **Privately Held**
Web: www.proxgo.com
SIC: 2341 2322 Women's and children's undergarments; Underwear, men's and boys': made from purchased materials
HQ: Stanfield's Limited
1 Logan St
Truro NS B2N 5
902 895-5406

(G-11503)
PERFORMANCE APPAREL LLC
Also Called: Hot Chillys
565 Air Tool Dr Ste K (28387-3469)
P.O. Box 2716 (28388-2716)
PHONE.................................805 541-0989

▲ = Import ▼ = Export
◆ = Import/Export

Jon D F Stanfield, *Ch*
Traci Stapleton, *Sr VP*
▲ **EMP:** 10 **EST:** 1997
SALES (est): 2.17MM
SALES (corp-wide): 99.5MM **Privately Held**
Web: www.hotchillys.com
SIC: 2339 Athletic clothing: women's, misses', and juniors'
HQ: Stanfield's Limited
1 Logan St
Truro NS B2N 5
902 895-5406

(G-11504)
PILOT LLC
375 E Connecticut Ave (28387-5601)
P.O. Box 58 (28388-0058)
PHONE...............................864 430-6337
EMP: 4
SALES (corp-wide): 722.35K **Privately Held**
Web: www.thepilot.com
SIC: 2711 Newspapers, publishing and printing
PA: The Pilot Llc
145 W Pennsylvania Ave
Southern Pines NC 28387
910 692-7271

(G-11505)
PILOT LLC (PA)
145 W Pennsylvania Ave (28387-5428)
PHONE...............................910 692-7271
David Woronoff, *Managing Member*
Jack Andrews, *
Lee Dirks, *
EMP: 70 **EST:** 1996
SQ FT: 5,000
SALES (est): 4.45MM
SALES (corp-wide): 4.45MM **Privately Held**
Web: www.thepilot.com
SIC: 2711 2752 2791 Newspapers, publishing and printing; Offset printing; Typesetting

(G-11506)
PILOT PRESS LLC
175 Davis St (28387-7068)
PHONE...............................910 692-8366
Timothy E King, *Prin*
EMP: 6 **EST:** 1920
SALES (est): 284.5K **Privately Held**
SIC: 2741 Miscellaneous publishing

(G-11507)
RYJAK ENTERPRISES LLC
1050 N May St (28387-4206)
PHONE...............................910 638-0716
Rhonda Sweet, *Prin*
EMP: 4 **EST:** 2015
SALES (est): 437.75K **Privately Held**
SIC: 2711 Newspapers, publishing and printing

(G-11508)
SALON COUTURE
180 Council Way (28387-1000)
PHONE...............................910 693-1611
Lisa O Goneau, *Owner*
Lisa O Goneau Junior, *Owner*
EMP: 4 **EST:** 1997
SALES (est): 58.78K **Privately Held**
SIC: 7299 2361 Tanning salon; T-shirts and tops: girls', children's, and infants'

(G-11509)
SIERRA NEVADA CORPORATION
Also Called: SIERRA NEVADA
CORPORATION

795 Sw Broad St (28387-5926)
PHONE...............................775 331-0222
Fatih Ozmen, *CEO*
EMP: 15
SALES (corp-wide): 2.38B **Privately Held**
Web: www.sncorp.com
SIC: 3812 Search and navigation equipment
PA: Sierra Nevada Company, Llc
444 Salomon Cir
Sparks NV 89434
775 331-0222

(G-11510)
SOUTHERN SOFTWARE INC
150 Perry Dr (28387-7020)
PHONE...............................336 879-3350
Jennifer Maggs, *CEO*
John Roscoe, *
EMP: 70 **EST:** 1988
SQ FT: 10,000
SALES (est): 10.93MM **Privately Held**
Web: www.southernsoftware.com
SIC: 7372 Business oriented computer software

(G-11511)
SPARTAN BLADES LLC
625 Se Service Rd (28387-6062)
PHONE...............................910 757-0035
EMP: 4 **EST:** 2008
SALES (est): 260.05K **Privately Held**
Web: www.spartanbladesusa.com
SIC: 3421 Cutlery

(G-11512)
TRANE TECHNOLOGIES COMPANY LLC
Also Called: Ingersoll-Rand
1725 Us 1 Hwy N (28387-2362)
P.O. Box 8000 (28388)
PHONE...............................910 692-8700
Mark Amlot, *Brnch Mgr*
EMP: 250
Web: www.tranetechnologies.com
SIC: 3519 3714 3546 3423 Parts and accessories, internal combustion engines; Motor vehicle parts and accessories; Power-driven handtools; Hand and edge tools, nec
HQ: Trane Technologies Company Llc
800-E Beaty St
Davidson NC 28036
704 655-4000

(G-11513)
TURNBERRY PRESS
150 Crest Rd (28387-3149)
PHONE...............................860 670-4892
EMP: 4 **EST:** 2016
SALES (est): 46.57K **Privately Held**
SIC: 2741 Miscellaneous publishing

(G-11514)
WHISTLE STOP PRESS INC
175 Davis St (28387-7068)
PHONE...............................910 695-1403
Thomas L West, *Pr*
Sandra S West, *Sec*
▲ **EMP:** 10 **EST:** 1985
SQ FT: 13,000
SALES (est): 894.71K **Privately Held**
Web: www.gowhistlestop.com
SIC: 2752 Offset printing

Southport
Brunswick County

(G-11515)
ABOARD TRADE LLC
Also Called: Kalinka Arms

4705 Southport Supply Rd Se Ste 208 (28461-9035)
PHONE...............................919 341-7045
Jeffrey Letino, *Ch*
EMP: 5
SALES (corp-wide): 526.66K **Privately Held**
Web: www.aboardtrade.com
SIC: 3484 Small arms
PA: Aboard Trade, Llc
16192 Coastal Hwy
Lewes DE 19958
919 341-7045

(G-11516)
ARCHER-DANIELS-MIDLAND COMPANY
Also Called: ADM
1730 E Moore St (28461-9418)
P.O. Box 10640 (28461-0640)
PHONE...............................910 457-5011
Eric Warner, *Brnch Mgr*
EMP: 150
SQ FT: 16,463
SALES (corp-wide): 85.53B **Publicly Held**
Web: www.adm.com
SIC: 2041 2869 Flour and other grain mill products; Industrial organic chemicals, nec
PA: Archer-Daniels-Midland Company
77 W Wacker Dr Ste 4600
Chicago IL 60601
312 634-8100

(G-11517)
ASSOCIATED ARTISTS SOUTHPORT
130 E West St (28461-3950)
PHONE...............................910 457-5450
Donna Mandell, *Owner*
EMP: 4 **EST:** 1997
SALES (est): 123.67K **Privately Held**
Web: www.southport-oakisland.com
SIC: 2411 Logging

(G-11518)
CWI SERVICES LLC
3382 Willow Cir Se (28461-8545)
PHONE...............................704 560-9755
Barbara Clark, *Prin*
William Clark, *Prin*
EMP: 4
SALES (est): 101.56K **Privately Held**
SIC: 7692 Welding repair

(G-11519)
ENVIBOATS LLC
104 Sparkling Brook Way (28461)
PHONE...............................910 213-3200
EMP: 4 **EST:** 2013
SALES (est): 191.48K **Privately Held**
Web: www.enviboats.com
SIC: 3732 8711 Boatbuilding and repairing; Designing: ship, boat, machine, and product

(G-11520)
GTG ENGINEERING INC
4956 Long Beach Rd Se Ste 14 (28461-8498)
PHONE...............................910 457-0068
Michael Leblanc, *Pr*
EMP: 5
SALES (corp-wide): 901.19K **Privately Held**
Web: www.gtgengineering.com
SIC: 2899 Chemical preparations, nec
PA: Gtg Engineering, Inc.
766 Furnie Hammond Rd
Clarendon NC 28432
877 569-8572

(G-11521)
LEE CONTROLS LLC
8250 River Rd (28461-8911)
PHONE...............................732 752-5200
Glen Michalske, *Pr*
Jim Ashworth, *
▲ **EMP:** 7 **EST:** 1972
SQ FT: 42,000
SALES (est): 596.88K **Privately Held**
SIC: 3312 Primary finished or semifinished shapes

(G-11522)
LEE LINEAR
8250 River Rd (28461-8911)
P.O. Box 10100 (28461-0100)
PHONE...............................800 221-0811
EMP: 4 **EST:** 2015
SALES (est): 248.78K **Privately Held**
Web: www.leelinear.com
SIC: 3999 Manufacturing industries, nec

(G-11523)
LUTHERAN SVCS FOR THE AGING
4843 Southport Supply Rd Se (28461-8741)
PHONE...............................910 457-5604
William Sraver, *Ch*
EMP: 7 **EST:** 2008
SALES (est): 301.21K **Privately Held**
Web: www.brunswickcountync.gov
SIC: 3825 Instruments to measure electricity

(G-11524)
PARTY TIME INC
1658 N Howe St Ste 1 (28461-7940)
PHONE...............................910 454-4577
Beverly Mccloskey, *Pr*
Sharon Wilson, *Sec*
EMP: 6 **EST:** 1995
SQ FT: 6,100
SALES (est): 182.64K **Privately Held**
Web: www.partytime28461.com
SIC: 5947 2759 Party favors; Invitation and stationery printing and engraving

(G-11525)
PRINT DOC PACK AND
114 E Nash St (28461-3984)
PHONE...............................910 454-9104
Susan Davis, *Owner*
EMP: 4 **EST:** 2005
SALES (est): 122.06K **Privately Held**
SIC: 2752 Commercial printing, lithographic

(G-11526)
R E R SERVICES
55 N High Point Rd (28461-9757)
PHONE...............................818 993-1826
Rick Ray, *Owner*
EMP: 6 **EST:** 1989
SALES (est): 340.38K **Privately Held**
Web: www.rerservices.com
SIC: 7699 3565 Industrial machinery and equipment repair; Packaging machinery

(G-11527)
SEAWAY PRINTING COMPANY
Also Called: Seaway Printing & Mailing
4130 Long Beach Rd Se (28461-8653)
PHONE...............................910 457-6158
Gary Mattingry, *Owner*
EMP: 8 **EST:** 1967
SQ FT: 4,000
SALES (est): 372.85K **Privately Held**
Web: www.seawayprintingnc.com
SIC: 2752 Offset printing

(G-11528)
SINCERE SCENTS CO LLC
7300 River Rd Se Trlr 84 (28461-9608)
PHONE......................910 616-4697
EMP: 5 EST: 2022
SALES (est): 63.22K Privately Held
Web: www.sincerescentsco.com
SIC: 3999 Candles

(G-11529)
SOUTHPORT NC
5105 Bent Oak Ln (28461-3133)
PHONE......................910 524-7425
EMP: 5 EST: 2016
SALES (est): 99.09K Privately Held
Web: www.southportmag.com
SIC: 3519 Internal combustion engines, nec

(G-11530)
SPEED KING MANUFACTURING INC
8128 River Rd (28461-8972)
PHONE......................910 457-1995
Tammy C Johnston, Prin
EMP: 4 EST: 2012
SALES (est): 234.48K Privately Held
SIC: 3999 Manufacturing industries, nec

(G-11531)
SPOD INC
316 Cedar Rd (28461-7701)
PHONE......................910 477-6297
Christie Walker, Prin
EMP: 6 EST: 2016
SALES (est): 116.06K Privately Held
Web: www.4x4spod.com
SIC: 3714 Motor vehicle parts and
accessories

(G-11532)
STATE PORT PILOT
114 E Moore St (28461-3926)
P.O. Box 10548 (28461-0548)
PHONE......................910 457-4568
Edward T Harper, Pr
Margaret T Harper, Prin
EMP: 12 EST: 1935
SQ FT: 3,490
SALES (est): 761.08K Privately Held
Web: www.stateportpilot.com
SIC: 2711 Newspapers: publishing only, not
printed on site

Sparta
Alleghany County

(G-11533)
ALLEGHANY GARBAGE SERVICE INC
Also Called: Alleghany Garbage Service
453 N Main St (28675-8608)
P.O. Box 1538 (28675-1538)
PHONE......................336 372-4413
Kenneth Nichols, Pr
Don Nichols, VP
EMP: 4 EST: 1972
SALES (est): 479.56K Privately Held
Web: www.alleghanycounty-nc.gov
SIC: 4953 3469 Refuse collection and
disposal services; Garbage cans, stamped
and pressed metal

(G-11534)
AMANO PIONEER ECLIPSE CORP (DH)
Also Called: Pioneer
1 Eclipse Rd (28675-9233)
P.O. Box 909 (28675-0909)
PHONE......................336 372-8080
Thomas Benton, Pr

Byron Snyder, *
Thomas Ording, *
Robert Allen, Plant Operations*
Nurzat Jumukova, *
◆ EMP: 73 EST: 1978
SQ FT: 105,000
SALES (est): 25.55MM Privately Held
Web: www.pioneereclipse.com
SIC: 3589 2842 Floor washing and polishing
machines, commercial; Cleaning or
polishing preparations, nec
HQ: Amano Usa Holdings, Inc.
29j Commerce Way
Totowa NJ 07512

(G-11535)
BICKERSTAFF TREES INC
866 Nc Highway 18 S (28675-8477)
PHONE......................336 372-8866
Frank B Bickerstaff, Pr
Ruth Bickerstaff, *
EMP: 7 EST: 1978
SALES (est): 245.16K Privately Held
SIC: 0783 3999 5199 Planting, pruning, and
trimming services; Wreaths, artificial;
Christmas trees, including artificial

(G-11536)
CHANDLER CONCRETE INC
Also Called: CHANDLER CONCRETE INC
23 Birch Ln (28675-8741)
PHONE......................336 372-4348
Jess Millan, Mgr
EMP: 12
Web: www.chandlerconcrete.com
SIC: 3273 Ready-mixed concrete
PA: Chandler Concrete Co., Inc.
1006 S Church Street
Burlington NC 27215

(G-11537)
DAVID PRESNELL
Also Called: Presnells Prtg & Photography
1397 Us Highway 21 S (28675-8640)
P.O. Box 26 (28675)
PHONE......................336 372-5989
David Presnell, Owner
EMP: 6 EST: 1999
SQ FT: 1,500
SALES (est): 117.97K Privately Held
Web: www.offgridtogo.com
SIC: 7335 7221 2789 2759 Commercial
photography; Photographer, still or video;
Bookbinding and related work; Commercial
printing, nec

(G-11538)
DESIGNS IN WOOD
Also Called: Carolina Farm Table
122 E Doughton St (28675-9127)
P.O. Box 788 (28675-0788)
PHONE......................336 372-8995
John Ulery, Owner
Penny Ulery, Owner
EMP: 5 EST: 1973
SQ FT: 6,000
SALES (est): 221.25K Privately Held
Web: www.carolinafarmtable.com
SIC: 2426 Carvings, furniture: wood

(G-11539)
INTERNTNAL INSTLLTION GROUP LL
312 Riverside Dr (28675-9064)
P.O. Box 1057 (28675-1057)
PHONE......................704 231-1868
EMP: 10 EST: 2003
SALES (est): 976.73K Privately Held
Web:
www.internationalinstallationgroup.us
SIC: 1389 Construction, repair, and
dismantling services

(G-11540)
NAPCO INC (DH)
Also Called: Napco
120 Trojan Ave (28675-9073)
P.O. Box 1029 (28675-1029)
PHONE......................336 372-5214
James R Proffit, Pr
Henry Hayes, *
▲ EMP: 113 EST: 1977
SQ FT: 62,000
SALES (est): 39.76MM
SALES (corp-wide): 5.58B Privately Held
Web: www.napcousa.com
SIC: 2631 2782 Setup boxboard; Looseleaf
binders and devices
HQ: Ply Gem Holdings, Inc.
5020 Weston Pkwy Ste 400
Cary NC 27513
919 677-3900

(G-11541)
PERRYCRAFT INC
1549 Us Highway 21 S (28675-8924)
PHONE......................336 372-2545
Dan Epting, Pr
▲ EMP: 10 EST: 1982
SQ FT: 15,000
SALES (est): 947.57K Privately Held
Web: www.perrycraft.com
SIC: 3429 3069 Luggage racks, car top;
Grips or handles, rubber

(G-11542)
TRUSS SHOP INC
Also Called: Tri State Componenets
84 Buffalo Rd S (28675-9491)
P.O. Box 1795 (28675-1795)
PHONE......................336 372-6260
John Miller, Pr
EMP: 35 EST: 2000
SQ FT: 4,000
SALES (est): 12.7MM Privately Held
Web: www.tristatecomponents.com
SIC: 2439 Trusses, wooden roof

Spindale
Rutherford County

(G-11543)
ALLIANCE PRECISION PLAS CORP
171 Fairground Rd (28160-2209)
PHONE......................828 286-8631
EMP: 35
SALES (corp-wide): 46.31MM Privately
Held
SIC: 3089 3544 Injection molded finished
plastics products, nec; Dies, plastics forming
PA: Alliance Precision Plastics Corporation
1220 Lee Rd
Rochester NY 14606
585 426-5310

(G-11544)
BACKYARD ENTPS & SVCS LLC
281 Spindale St (28160-2415)
P.O. Box 888 (28139-0888)
PHONE......................828 755-4960
Michael M Galloway, Managing Member
David Russel, Managing Member
EMP: 4 EST: 2011
SALES (est): 1.94MM Privately Held
Web: www.backyardenterprisesnc.com
SIC: 3563 Air and gas compressors
including vacuum pumps

(G-11545)
BURNETT DARRILL STEPHEN
Also Called: Tri-City Tire Service
137 Williamsburg Dr (28160-1155)

PHONE......................828 287-8778
Darrill Stephen Burnett, Owner
EMP: 4 EST: 2012
SALES (est): 78.67K Privately Held
SIC: 7534 Tire repair shop

(G-11546)
CARDINAL TISSUE LLC
207 Oakland Rd (28160-2117)
PHONE......................815 503-2096
Steven Reese, Managing Member
EMP: 51 EST: 2017
SALES (est): 13.17MM Privately Held
Web: www.cardinal-tissue.com
SIC: 2676 Cleansing tissues: made from
purchased paper

(G-11547)
LAKESIDE MILLS INC (PA)
Also Called: Yelton Milling Co
398 W Main St (28160-1594)
P.O. Box 230 (28139-0230)
PHONE......................828 286-4866
Bryan A King, Pr
Aaron King, VP
Kim Allen King, Sec
EMP: 11 EST: 1936
SALES (est): 4.39MM
SALES (corp-wide): 4.39MM Privately
Held
Web:
lakeside-mills.mybigcommerce.com
SIC: 2041 Corn meal

(G-11548)
MANROY USA LLC
Also Called: Manroy Defense Systems
159 Yelton St (28160-1179)
PHONE......................828 286-9274
John P Buckner, Managing Member
EMP: 5 EST: 2009
SALES (est): 758.35K Privately Held
Web: www.manroy-usa.com
SIC: 3484 Small arms

(G-11549)
WATTS DRAINAGE PRODUCTS INC
Also Called: Enpoco
100 Watts Rd (28160-2211)
PHONE......................828 288-2179
William C Mccartney, Pr
Timothy M Macphee, CFO
Kristine Uttley, Treas
Lester J Taufen, Sec
◆ EMP: 10 EST: 1987
SALES (est): 2.89MM
SALES (corp-wide): 2.25B Publicly Held
SIC: 3432 Plumbing fixture fittings and trim
PA: Watts Water Technologies, Inc.
815 Chestnut St
North Andover MA 01845
978 688-1811

(G-11550)
WATTS REGULATOR CO
Regtrol Division
100 Watts Rd (28160-2211)
PHONE......................828 286-4151
Tommy Horton, Brnch Mgr
EMP: 700
SALES (corp-wide): 2.25B Publicly Held
Web: www.watts.com
SIC: 3491 Pressure valves and regulators,
industrial
HQ: Watts Regulator Co.
815 Chestnut St
North Andover MA 01845
978 689-6000

(G-11551)
WHITE OAK CARPET MILLS INC
Also Called: White Oak
1553 Old Ballpark Rd (28160-2177)
PHONE.....................828 287-8892
Steve Brandon, *Pr*
▲ **EMP:** 7 **EST:** 1996
SQ FT: 25,000
SALES (est): 415.94K **Privately Held**
SIC: 2273 Carpets and rugs

Spring Hope
Nash County

(G-11552)
BASS FARMS INC
Also Called: Bass Farm Sausage
6685 Highway 64 Alt East (27882)
P.O. Box 126 (27882-0126)
PHONE.....................252 478-4147
Kenneth Edwards, *Pr*
John Bass, *
Kenneth Edwards, *VP*
Brent Edwards, *
EMP: 15 **EST:** 1979
SALES (est): 2.69MM **Privately Held**
Web: www.bassfarmsausage.com
SIC: 2011 5147 2013 Meat packing plants; Meats, fresh; Sausages and other prepared meats

(G-11553)
BELT CONCEPTS AMERICA INC
605 N Pine St (27882-7875)
P.O. Box 340 (27882-0340)
PHONE.....................888 598-2358
Cris Balint, *Pr*
▲ **EMP:** 15 **EST:** 1993
SQ FT: 150,000
SALES (est): 7.04MM
SALES (corp-wide): 48.54MM **Privately Held**
Web: www.beltconcepts.com
SIC: 3496 3535 Conveyor belts; Conveyors and conveying equipment
PA: Right Lane Industries Llc
111 W Jckson Blvd Ste 170
Chicago IL 60604
857 869-4132

(G-11554)
BK SEAMLESS GUTTERS LLC
Also Called: Bk Seamless Gutters
1705 Old Us 64 (27882-7518)
PHONE.....................252 955-5414
Brandon King, *Owner*
EMP: 4 **EST:** 2011
SALES (est): 367.64K **Privately Held**
Web: www.bkroofingandgutters.com
SIC: 3589 High pressure cleaning equipment

(G-11555)
CAROLINA DUCT FABRICATION INC
360 Barbee St (27882-7957)
P.O. Box 820 (27882-0820)
PHONE.....................252 478-9955
J Derrill Edwards, *Pr*
Nathan Edward, *VP*
EMP: 4 **EST:** 2006
SALES (est): 947.52K **Privately Held**
Web: www.carolinaduct.com
SIC: 3441 Fabricated structural metal

(G-11556)
JHRG MANUFACTURING LLC
303 S Pine St (27882-9551)
P.O. Box D (27882-0930)
PHONE.....................252 478-4977
John Holland, *Managing Member*

EMP: 5 **EST:** 2012
SQ FT: 25,000
SALES (est): 469.58K **Privately Held**
SIC: 2298 3842 3537 Ropes and fiber cables; Life preservers, except cork and inflatable; Containers (metal), air cargo

(G-11557)
LEA AID ACQUISITION COMPANY
Also Called: Lea Aid
117 N Ash St (27882-7711)
P.O. Box 26688 (27611-6688)
PHONE.....................919 872-6210
Paige Briggs, *Pr*
EMP: 6 **EST:** 2012
SALES (est): 2MM **Privately Held**
Web: www.leacorp.com
SIC: 5099 3663 3577 5049 Video and audio equipment; Radio broadcasting and communications equipment; Encoders, computer peripheral equipment; Law enforcement equipment and supplies

(G-11558)
PURE WATER INNOVATIONS INC
272 Williams Rd (27882-7521)
P.O. Box 567 (27597-0567)
PHONE.....................919 301-8189
Vicky Hortman, *Pr*
Vicky Hortman, *Pr*
Bill Land, *VP*
Natalie Land, *Off Mgr*
EMP: 4 **EST:** 2009
SQ FT: 4,500
SALES (est): 175.04K **Privately Held**
Web: www.quenchwater.com
SIC: 2086 Pasteurized and mineral waters, bottled and canned

(G-11559)
SPRING HOPE ENTERPRISE INC
113 N Ash St (27882-7711)
P.O. Box 2447 (27894-2447)
PHONE.....................252 478-3651
Ken Ripley, *Pr*
Vickie Ripley, *VP*
EMP: 5 **EST:** 1947
SQ FT: 1,800
SALES (est): 154.73K **Privately Held**
Web: www.restorationnewsmedia.com
SIC: 2711 Job printing and newspaper publishing combined

(G-11560)
STRICKLAND BROS ENTPS INC
3622 Wiggins Rd (27882-8846)
P.O. Box 536 (27882-0536)
PHONE.....................252 478-3058
Terry Strickland, *Pr*
EMP: 19 **EST:** 1987
SQ FT: 10,000
SALES (est): 3.19MM **Privately Held**
Web: www.stricklandbros.com
SIC: 3523 7692 Farm machinery and equipment; Welding repair

Spring Lake
Cumberland County

(G-11561)
EXTERIORS INC LTD
650 W Manchester Rd (28390-2314)
PHONE.....................919 325-2251
Michelle Kettering, *CEO*
EMP: 8 **EST:** 2016
SALES (est): 714.23K **Privately Held**
Web: www.ltdexteriors.com

SIC: 1542 3259 7389 5033 Commercial and office buildings, renovation and repair; Roofing tile, clay; Business Activities at Non-Commercial Site; Roofing, asphalt and sheet metal

(G-11562)
RUHL INC
Also Called: Ruhl Tech Engineering
26 Mockingbird Ln (28390-8715)
PHONE.....................910 497-3172
Anita B Ruhland, *Pr*
Andrew S Ruhland, *VP*
EMP: 6 **EST:** 1999
SQ FT: 2,800
SALES (est): 2.41MM **Privately Held**
Web: www.ruhltech.us
SIC: 3441 Fabricated structural metal

(G-11563)
S & W READY MIX CON CO LLC
545 W Manchester Rd (28390-2311)
PHONE.....................910 496-3232
Tony Lee, *Mgr*
EMP: 19
SALES (corp-wide): 8.01MM **Privately Held**
Web: www.snwreadymix.com
SIC: 3273 Ready-mixed concrete
HQ: S & W Ready Mix Concrete Company Llc
217 Lisbon St
Clinton NC 28329
910 592-1733

(G-11564)
STITCH IN TIME INC
412 S Main St (28390-3907)
PHONE.....................910 497-4171
John Springer, *Pr*
Suk Hon Springer, *VP*
EMP: 6 **EST:** 1994
SQ FT: 6,000
SALES (est): 139.04K **Privately Held**
Web: www.customplaquesusa.com
SIC: 2395 7216 Embroidery products, except Schiffli machine; Drycleaning plants, except rugs

Spruce Pine
Mitchell County

(G-11565)
BRP US INC
Also Called: Brp Spruce Pine Distribution
12934 S 226 Hwy (28777-6345)
PHONE.....................828 766-1164
EMP: 5 **EST:** 2019
SALES (est): 790.96K **Privately Held**
Web: www.brp.com
SIC: 3732 Boatbuilding and repairing

(G-11566)
BRP US INC
Also Called: Brp Spruce Pine
1211 Greenwood Rd (28777-8808)
PHONE.....................828 766-1100
Bill Johnson, *Mgr*
EMP: 92
SALES (corp-wide): 7.38B **Privately Held**
Web: www.brp.com
SIC: 3732 Motorboats, inboard or outboard: building and repairing
HQ: Brp Us Inc.
10101 Science Dr
Sturtevant WI 53177
262 884-5000

(G-11567)
BUCHANAN GEM STONE MINES INC
Also Called: Gem Mountain
13780 S 226 Hwy (28777-6343)
P.O. Box 488 (28777-0488)
PHONE.....................828 765-6130
Madonna K Buchanan, *Pr*
Danyeale Forbes, *VP*
▲ **EMP:** 10 **EST:** 1985
SQ FT: 3,500
SALES (est): 535.08K **Privately Held**
Web: www.gemmountain.com
SIC: 1499 3915 5999 5944 Gemstone and industrial diamond mining; Gems, real and imitation: preparation for settings; Gems and precious stones; Jewelry stores

(G-11568)
COMMUNITY NEWSPAPERS INC
261 Locust St (28777-2713)
P.O. Box 339 (28777-0339)
PHONE.....................828 765-7169
Andy Ashuhet, *Mgr*
EMP: 7
SALES (corp-wide): 40.95MM **Privately Held**
Web: www.cninewspapers.com
SIC: 2711 Newspapers, publishing and printing
PA: Community Newspapers, Inc.
2365 Prince Ave # A
Athens GA 30606
706 548-0010

(G-11569)
COVIA HOLDINGS CORPORATION
Also Called: COVIA HOLDINGS CORPORATION
Rag Branch Rd (28777)
P.O. Box 588 (28777-0588)
PHONE.....................828 765-4823
Ian Larkins, *Mgr*
EMP: 8
SALES (corp-wide): 1.47B **Privately Held**
Web: www.coviacorp.com
SIC: 1446 Industrial sand
PA: Covia Holdings Llc
3 Summit Park Dr Ste 700
Independence OH 44131
800 243-9004

(G-11570)
COVIA HOLDINGS LLC
Also Called: Crystal Plant
136 Crystal Dr (28777-8726)
P.O. Box 588 (28777-0588)
PHONE.....................828 765-1114
Mike Bensill, *Mgr*
EMP: 4
SALES (corp-wide): 1.47B **Privately Held**
Web: www.coviacorp.com
SIC: 1446 Industrial sand
PA: Covia Holdings Llc
3 Summit Park Dr Ste 700
Independence OH 44131
800 243-9004

(G-11571)
COVIA HOLDINGS LLC
7638 S 226 Hwy (28777-0538)
PHONE.....................828 765-1215
EMP: 5
SALES (corp-wide): 1.47B **Privately Held**
Web: www.coviacorp.com
SIC: 1446 Industrial sand
PA: Covia Holdings Llc
3 Summit Park Dr Ste 700
Independence OH 44131
800 243-9004

(G-11572)
COVIA HOLDINGS LLC
Us Hwy 19 E (28777)
P.O. Box 588 (28777-0588)
PHONE...............................828 765-4251
Carl Horbat, *Mgr*
EMP: 9
SALES (corp-wide): 1.47B **Privately Held**
Web: www.coviacorp.com
SIC: 1446 Industrial sand
PA: Covia Holdings Llc
　　3 Summit Park Dr Ste 700
　　Independence OH 44131
　　800 243-9004

(G-11573)
COVIA HOLDINGS LLC
Bakersville Rd (28777)
P.O. Box 588 (28777-0588)
PHONE...............................828 765-4283
Karl Kuchta, *Mgr*
EMP: 64
SALES (corp-wide): 1.47B **Privately Held**
Web: www.coviacorp.com
SIC: 1459 3295 Feldspar mining; Minerals,
　　ground or treated
PA: Covia Holdings Llc
　　3 Summit Park Dr Ste 700
　　Independence OH 44131
　　800 243-9004

(G-11574)
DESIGNS BY RACHEL
Also Called: Graphic Design
220 Reservoir Rd (28777-2532)
PHONE...............................828 783-0698
Rachel Wheeler, *Owner*
EMP: 5 **EST:** 2016
SALES (est): 179.29K **Privately Held**
SIC: 7336 3952 Commercial art and graphic
　　design; Pastels, artists'

(G-11575)
**EXPLOSIVES SUPPLY COMPANY
(PA)**
167 Roan Rd (28777-2638)
P.O. Box 217 (28777-0217)
PHONE...............................828 765-2762
Robert H Boone, *Pr*
John H Boone, *VP*
Susan S Gardin, *Sec*
EMP: 15 **EST:** 1940
SQ FT: 800
SALES (est): 5.15MM
SALES (corp-wide): 5.15MM **Privately
Held**
Web:
www.explosivessupply-mcdowellcement.com
SIC: 5032 3273 5039 5169 Stone, crushed
　　or broken; Ready-mixed concrete; Septic
　　tanks; Explosives

(G-11576)
FEC INC
284 Roan Rd (28777-2624)
PHONE...............................828 765-4599
Scott Pearson, *Pr*
EMP: 6 **EST:** 2010
SALES (est): 3.94MM **Privately Held**
SIC: 3715 Truck trailers

(G-11577)
HIGHLAND CRAFTSMEN INC
534 Oak Ave (28777-2728)
PHONE...............................828 765-9010
Marty Mccurry, *CEO*
Chris Mccurry, *VP*
EMP: 10 **EST:** 2002
SALES (est): 3.48MM **Privately Held**
Web: www.barkhouse.com

SIC: 2499 Mulch, wood and bark

(G-11578)
**INNIAH PRODUCTION
INCORPORATED**
Also Called: Blue Ridge Christian News
152 Summit Ave (28777-2980)
PHONE...............................828 765-6800
Doug Harrell, *Pr*
Clint Pollard, *Editor*
Barbara Harrell, *Sec*
EMP: 4 **EST:** 2014
SALES (est): 206.59K **Privately Held**
Web: www.blueridgechristiannews.com
SIC: 2759 Publication printing

(G-11579)
**MCDOWELL CEMENT PRODUCTS
CO**
167 Roan Rd (28777-2638)
P.O. Box 217 (28777-0217)
PHONE...............................828 765-2762
Robert H Boone, *Pr*
EMP: 4
SALES (corp-wide): 5.15MM **Privately
Held**
Web: www.mcdowellnews.com
SIC: 3273 Ready-mixed concrete
HQ: Mcdowell Cement Products Company
　　S Garden St
　　Marion NC 28752
　　828 652-5721

(G-11580)
**MCGEE BROTHERS MACHINE &
WLDG**
Also Called: McGee Brothers Mch & Wldg Co
2585 Halltown Rd (28777-5461)
PHONE...............................828 766-9122
Donny Mcgee, *Pt*
Ted Mcgee, *Pt*
Jerry Mcgee, *Pt*
EMP: 6 **EST:** 1997
SALES (est): 5.66MM **Privately Held**
SIC: 3599 Machine shop, jobbing and repair

(G-11581)
MCKINNEY ELECTRIC & MCH CO INC
12923 S 226 Hwy (28777-6345)
PHONE...............................828 765-7910
Richard Mckinney, *Pr*
Angela Mckinney, *Sec*
Scott Mckinney, *Treas*
Bruce Mckinney, *VP*
EMP: 5 **EST:** 1978
SQ FT: 1,600
SALES (est): 609.11K **Privately Held**
SIC: 7694 5063 5999 7699 Electric motor
　　repair; Motors, electric; Motors, electric;
　　Pumps and pumping equipment repair

(G-11582)
**MCKINNEY LWNCARE GRBAGE SVC
LL**
Also Called: McKinney Garbage Service
1113 Dale Rd (28777-6301)
PHONE...............................828 766-9490
Tracey Mckinney, *Managing Member*
EMP: 6 **EST:** 2015
SALES (est): 263.17K **Privately Held**
SIC: 0782 3639 Lawn care services;
　　Garbage disposal units, household

(G-11583)
MITCHELL WELDING INC
7080 Us 19e (28777-5806)
PHONE...............................828 765-2620
John C Stout, *Pr*
Clarann S Dixon, *
Boyd W Dixon, *

EMP: 25 **EST:** 1983
SQ FT: 6,000
SALES (est): 977.04K **Privately Held**
Web: www.mitchellweldinginc.com
SIC: 7692 3444 Welding repair; Sheet
　　metalwork

(G-11584)
QUARTZ CORP USA (DH)
Also Called: Quartz
8342 S 226 Bypass (28777)
P.O. Box 309 (28777-0309)
PHONE...............................828 766-2104
Jeffrey Curtis, *Ex Dir*
Thomas Guillaume, *CEO*
Benny Hallam, *VP*
Robert Kolakowski, *CFO*
◆ **EMP:** 48 **EST:** 1957
SQ FT: 2,000
SALES (est): 26.42MM
SALES (corp-wide): 5.36MM **Privately
Held**
Web: www.thequartzcorp.com
SIC: 3295 Feldspar, ground or otherwise
　　treated
HQ: Imerys Usa, Inc.
　　100 Mansell Ct E Ste 300
　　Roswell GA 30076
　　770 645-3300

(G-11585)
SIBELCO
107 Harris Mining Company Rd
(28777-4506)
PHONE...............................828 765-1114
EMP: 15 **EST:** 2019
SALES (est): 6MM **Privately Held**
Web: www.sibelco.com
SIC: 2819 Industrial inorganic chemicals, nec

(G-11586)
SIBELCO NORTH AMERICA INC
74 Harris Mining Company Rd
(28777-4521)
PHONE...............................828 766-6050
EMP: 75
SALES (corp-wide): 118.92MM **Privately
Held**
Web: www.sibelco.com
SIC: 2851 Paints and allied products
HQ: Sibelco North America, Inc.
　　13024 Bllntyne Corp Pl St
　　Charlotte NC 28277
　　704 420-7905

(G-11587)
SIBELCO NORTH AMERICA INC
136 Crystal Dr (28777-8726)
PHONE...............................828 766-6050
EMP: 75
SALES (corp-wide): 118.92MM **Privately
Held**
Web: www.sibelco.com
SIC: 1499 Quartz crystal (pure) mining
HQ: Sibelco North America, Inc.
　　13024 Bllntyne Corp Pl St
　　Charlotte NC 28277
　　704 420-7905

(G-11588)
SPRUCE PINE BATCH INC
2490 Us 19e (28777-0517)
P.O. Box 159 (28777-0159)
PHONE...............................828 765-9876
Tom Littleton, *Pr*
◆ **EMP:** 6 **EST:** 1986
SQ FT: 11,000
SALES (est): 1.02MM **Privately Held**
Web: www.sprucepinebatch.com
SIC: 3229 Pressed and blown glass, nec

(G-11589)
SPRUCE PINE MICA COMPANY
132 Mountain Laurel Dr (28777-9231)
P.O. Box 219 (28777-0219)
PHONE...............................828 765-4241
Richard Montague, *Pr*
Linda Lonen, *Treas*
EMP: 15 **EST:** 1924
SQ FT: 16,000
SALES (est): 1.54MM **Privately Held**
Web: www.spruce-pine-mica.com
SIC: 3679 3469 Electronic circuits; Machine
　　parts, stamped or pressed metal

(G-11590)
WOODYS CHAIR SHOP
784 Dale Rd (28777-6314)
PHONE...............................828 765-9277
James Woody, *Owner*
EMP: 4 **EST:** 1944
SALES (est): 106.86K **Privately Held**
Web: www.woodyschairshop.com
SIC: 2511 Chairs, household, except
　　upholstered: wood

(G-11591)
ZEMEX INDUSTRIAL MINERALS INC
797 Altapass Hwy (28777-8927)
P.O. Box 99 (28777-0099)
PHONE...............................828 765-5500
Richard L Lister, *Dir*
EMP: 4 **EST:** 2000
SALES (est): 341.38K **Privately Held**
SIC: 1499 Talc mining

Staley
Randolph County

(G-11592)
CHAUDHRY MEAT COMPANY
380 Stockyard Rd (27355-8376)
P.O. Box 1019 (27344-1019)
PHONE...............................919 742-9292
Abdul Chaudhry, *Pr*
Shamin Chaudhry, *Sec*
EMP: 10 **EST:** 1996
SQ FT: 8,600
SALES (est): 700.64K **Privately Held**
SIC: 2011 Meat packing plants

(G-11593)
CLIFFORD W ESTES CO INC
2637 Old 421 Rd (27355-8244)
P.O. Box 127 (27355-0127)
PHONE...............................336 622-6410
Peter Osborne, *VP*
EMP: 50
SQ FT: 22,000
SALES (corp-wide): 9.35MM **Privately
Held**
Web: www.estesco.com
SIC: 3299 3281 1442 Gravel painting; Cut
　　stone and stone products; Construction
　　sand and gravel
PA: Clifford W. Estes Co., Inc.
　　182 Fairfield Rd
　　Fairfield NJ 07004
　　800 962-5128

(G-11594)
DISCOUNT BOX & PALLET INC (PA)
3174 Weeden St (27355-8305)
P.O. Box 459 (27298-0459)
PHONE...............................336 272-2220
Jeffrey W Coble, *Pr*
EMP: 31 **EST:** 1997
SQ FT: 20,000
SALES (est): 7.56MM **Privately Held**
Web: www.dboxpinc.com

SIC: 2448 5031 Pallets, wood; Lumber, plywood, and millwork

(G-11595)
JORDAN ELECTRIC MOTORS INC
1303 Stockyard Rd (27355-9107)
PHONE.....................919 708-7010
Don Jordan, *Pr*
EMP: 13 EST: 2004
SALES (est): 670.41K Privately Held
Web: www.djeminc.com
SIC: 7694 Electric motor repair

(G-11596)
MANHATTAN AMRCN TERRAZZO STRIP
2433 Us Hwy 421 (27355)
P.O. Box 7 (27355-0007)
PHONE.....................336 622-4247
Jim Behuniak, *Pr*
Tom Tassis, *
▲ EMP: 121
SQ FT: 25,000
SALES (est): 2.69MM
SALES (corp-wide): 19.54MM Privately Held
Web: www.manhattanamerican.com
SIC: 3272 3351 3316 Terrazzo products, precast, nec; Copper rolling and drawing; Cold finishing of steel shapes
PA: The Platt Brothers & Company
2670 S Main St
Waterbury CT 06706
203 753-4194

(G-11597)
MIDCOASTAL DEVELOPMENT CORP
Also Called: Southern Aggregates
2435 Old 421 Rd (27355-8242)
P.O. Box 70 (27355-0070)
PHONE.....................336 622-3091
Johnny Justice Iii, *Pr*
▲ EMP: 8 EST: 1981
SQ FT: 800
SALES (est): 2.35MM
SALES (corp-wide): 2.35MM Privately Held
SIC: 3281 Stone, quarrying and processing of own stone products
PA: Justice Products, Llc
301 Habersham St
Savannah GA 31401
855 720-2388

(G-11598)
PILGRIMS PRIDE CORPORATION
Also Called: Staley Feed Mill
2607 Old 421 Rd (27355-8244)
PHONE.....................336 622-4251
Dale Kidd, *Mgr*
EMP: 41
Web: www.pilgrims.com
SIC: 2015 Poultry slaughtering and processing
HQ: Pilgrim's Pride Corporation
1770 Promontory Cir
Greeley CO 80634
970 506-8000

(G-11599)
QUALITY FABRICATORS
1151 Langley Rd (27355-8068)
PHONE.....................336 622-3402
Curtis Coble, *Pt*
James Rex Johnson, *Pt*
EMP: 5 EST: 1984
SQ FT: 4,000
SALES (est): 498.97K Privately Held
Web: www.qfi-usa.com
SIC: 2426 Furniture stock and parts, hardwood

Stallings
Union County

(G-11600)
J MASSEY INC
3330 Smith Farm Rd (28104-5040)
PHONE.....................704 821-7084
James A Massey, *Pr*
EMP: 10 EST: 1972
SALES (est): 2.22MM Privately Held
Web: www.ipccorp.net
SIC: 3354 5051 Aluminum extruded products ; Aluminum bars, rods, ingots, sheets, pipes, plates, etc.

(G-11601)
METROLINA WOODWORKS INC
3475 Gribble Rd (28104-8114)
PHONE.....................704 821-9095
Fred W Crawford Ii, *Pr*
EMP: 10 EST: 2010
SALES (est): 476.31K Privately Held
Web: www.metrolinaww.com
SIC: 2431 Millwork

Stanfield
Stanly County

(G-11602)
AMERICAN RACG HDERS EXHUST INC (PA)
Also Called: Arh
120 Riverstone Dr (28163-0078)
PHONE.....................631 608-1986
Nicholas Filippides, *CEO*
Jose Cruz, *Pr*
Yaquelin Cruz, *VP*
Paul J Thau, *CFO*
EMP: 18 EST: 2005
SALES (est): 1.53MM Privately Held
Web: www.americanracingheaders.com
SIC: 3542 3714 Headers; Motor vehicle parts and accessories

(G-11603)
AVDEL USA LLC (HQ)
Also Called: Stanley Engineered Fastening
614 Nc Hwy 200 S (28163-6715)
PHONE.....................704 888-7100
John Wyatt, *Pr*
▲ EMP: 36 EST: 2005
SALES (est): 23.78MM
SALES (corp-wide): 15.78B Publicly Held
Web: www.stanleyengineeredfastening.com
SIC: 3965 3452 Fasteners, buttons, needles, and pins; Bolts, nuts, rivets, and washers
PA: Stanley Black & Decker, Inc.
1000 Stanley Dr
New Britain CT 06053
860 225-5111

(G-11604)
BONDO INNOVATIONS LLC
14904 Barbee Rd (28163-8539)
PHONE.....................704 888-9910
Timothy Bondurant, *Owner*
EMP: 4 EST: 2008
SALES (est): 892.17K Privately Held
Web: www.bondoinnovations.com
SIC: 3441 Fabricated structural metal

(G-11605)
EUDYS CABINET MANUFACTURING
Also Called: Kbs Sales Co
12303 Renee Ford Rd (28163-7692)
P.O. Box 639 (28163-0639)
PHONE.....................704 888-4454

Jeral Eudy, *Pr*
Rommie Gene Aldridge, *
Gary Eudy, *
Betty Eudy, *
EMP: 10 EST: 1964
SQ FT: 55,000
SALES (est): 902.82K Privately Held
Web: www.eudyscabinets.com
SIC: 2434 Wood kitchen cabinets

(G-11606)
GLH SYSTEMS & CONTROLS INC
4667 Love Mill Rd (28163-7625)
PHONE.....................980 581-1304
Lee Hallock, *Pr*
EMP: 5 EST: 2004
SQ FT: 1,500
SALES (est): 506.73K Privately Held
Web: www.kspanglerrealtor.com
SIC: 3613 1731 Control panels, electric; Electrical work

(G-11607)
GRAPHICAL CREATIONS INC
106 Conveyor Beltway Dr (28163-9528)
P.O. Box 850 (28097-0850)
PHONE.....................704 888-8870
David Schopler, *Pr*
Marla Schopler, *VP*
EMP: 17 EST: 1995
SQ FT: 12,000
SALES (est): 2.75MM Privately Held
Web: www.graphi-cal.com
SIC: 3993 2531 Signs, not made in custom sign painting shops; Public building and related furniture

(G-11608)
S EUDY CABINET SHOP INC
Also Called: Eudy's Cabinet Manufacturing
12303 Renee Ford Rd (28163-7692)
P.O. Box 639 (28163-0639)
PHONE.....................704 888-4454
Ernest L Eudy, *Ch Bd*
Jerel Eudy, *
Rommie G Aldridge, *
Betty Eudy, *
Gary Eudy, *
EMP: 7 EST: 1963
SQ FT: 185,000
SALES (est): 482.26K Privately Held
Web: www.eudyscabinets.com
SIC: 2434 Wood kitchen cabinets

Stanley
Gaston County

(G-11609)
AVIENT PROTECTIVE MTLS LLC
1101 S Highway 27 (28164-2206)
PHONE.....................704 862-5100
Ken Dooley, *Sr VP*
EMP: 92
SIC: 2834 Pharmaceutical preparations
HQ: Avient Protective Materials Llc
5750 Mrtin Lther King Jr
Greenville NC 27834
252 707-2547

(G-11610)
B & B STUCCO AND STONE LLC
816 Joseph Antoon Cir (28164-4112)
P.O. Box 119 (28164-0119)
PHONE.....................704 524-1230
Amy Brunner, *Prin*
EMP: 9 EST: 2010
SALES (est): 972.73K Privately Held
SIC: 3299 Stucco

(G-11611)
B V HEDRICK GRAVEL & SAND CO
Also Called: Hedrick Industries
6941 Quarry Ln (28164-6778)
PHONE.....................704 827-8114
Jeffrey Goodman, *Mgr*
EMP: 124
SALES (corp-wide): 238.17MM Privately Held
Web: www.hedrickind.com
SIC: 1442 Construction sand and gravel
PA: B. V. Hedrick Gravel & Sand Company
120 1/2 Church St
Salisbury NC 28144
704 633-5982

(G-11612)
BLUM INC
7733 Old Plank Rd (28164)
PHONE.....................704 827-1345
Shannon Lafferty, *Pr*
Stephen Regele, *
Donna Springs, *
◆ EMP: 400 EST: 1977
SQ FT: 300,000
SALES (est): 43.89MM
SALES (corp-wide): 2.52B Privately Held
Web: www.blum.com
SIC: 3429 Furniture hardware
HQ: Julius Blum Gmbh
IndustriestraBe 1
Hochst 6973
55787050

(G-11613)
DEB SBS INC
1100 S Highway 27 (28164-2205)
PHONE.....................704 263-4240
Allen Soden, *Pr*
EMP: 8 EST: 2015
SALES (est): 1.74MM Privately Held
SIC: 2844 Perfumes, cosmetics and other toilet preparations

(G-11614)
DSM DESOTECH INC
Also Called: Perkem Technology
1101 N Carolina 27 (28164)
PHONE.....................704 862-5000
John Aviles, *Brnch Mgr*
EMP: 5
SQ FT: 14,922
Web: www.dsm.com
SIC: 2893 Printing ink
HQ: Dsm Desotech Inc.
1122 Saint Charles St
Elgin IL 60120

(G-11615)
ENTERPRISE TWD
7482 Nc 73 Hwy (28164)
PHONE.....................704 822-6166
Tim Dellinger, *Owner*
EMP: 4 EST: 2007
SALES (est): 491.89K Privately Held
SIC: 3713 Dump truck bodies

(G-11616)
ERA POLYMERS CORPORATION
1101 S Highway 27 (28164-2206)
P.O. Box 548 (28164)
PHONE.....................704 931-3675
George Papamanuel, *Pr*
Alex Papamanuel, *VP*
John Eve, *Sec*
Tina Papamanuel, *Treas*
Reynaldo Lopez, *Prin*
EMP: 20 EST: 2018
SALES (est): 9.95MM Privately Held
Web: www.erapolymersusa.com

SIC: 2822 Ethylene-propylene rubbers, EPDM polymers

(G-11617)
GASTON SYSTEMS INC
200 S Main St (28164-2011)
PHONE..............................704 263-6000
Gary Harris, *Pr*
▲ EMP: 17 EST: 1997
SALES (est): 957.45K **Privately Held**
Web: www.gastonsystems.com
SIC: 2672 Chemically treated papers, made from purchased materials

(G-11618)
I C E S GASTON COUNTY INC
102 Mariposa Rd (28164-0049)
P.O. Box 89 (28164-0089)
PHONE..............................704 263-1418
Ronnie Lay, *Pr*
Jesse W Huffstickler, *Pr*
Jerry Haines, *Treas*
Darrell Kiser, *Sec*
EMP: 7 EST: 1985
SQ FT: 17,000
SALES (est): 418.39K **Privately Held**
Web: www.ices-inc.com
SIC: 5084 3625 Textile machinery and equipment; Electric controls and control accessories, industrial

(G-11619)
J&L MACHINE & FABRICATION INC
201 S Buckoak St (28164-1744)
P.O. Box 579 (28164-0579)
PHONE..............................704 755-5552
EMP: 22 EST: 2015
SALES (est): 4.32MM **Privately Held**
Web: www.jlmaf.com
SIC: 3599 Machine shop, jobbing and repair

(G-11620)
KETER US INC
2369 Charles Raper Jonas Hwy (28164-2246)
PHONE..............................704 263-1967
EMP: 64
SALES (corp-wide): 1.96MM **Privately Held**
Web: www.keter.com
SIC: 2519 Fiberglass and plastic furniture
HQ: Keter Us, Inc.
6435 S Scatterfield Rd
Anderson IN 46013
317 575-4700

(G-11621)
MACHINERY SALES
Also Called: Machinery Sales and Service
7659 Old Plank Rd (28164-7773)
PHONE..............................704 822-0110
Harvey Phillips, *Pt*
Curtis Philips, *Pt*
EMP: 7 EST: 1992
SALES (est): 570.3K **Privately Held**
SIC: 3089 Injection molding of plastics

(G-11622)
METAL ROOFING SYSTEMS LLC
Also Called: Central Carolina Steel
7687 Mikron Dr (28164-4500)
P.O. Box 1534 (28037-1534)
PHONE..............................704 820-3110
Gavin Seale, *
EMP: 30 EST: 2001
SQ FT: 40,000
SALES (est): 12.79MM
SALES (corp-wide): 102.45MM **Privately Held**
Web: www.metalroofingsystems.com

SIC: 1761 2952 3444 3531 Roofing contractor; Roofing materials; Metal roofing and roof drainage equipment; Roofing equipment
PA: Atlantic Squared Supply Llc
155 Professional Park Dr
Cumming GA 30040
470 598-1010

(G-11623)
ONYX ENVIRONMENTAL SOLUTIONS INC
Also Called: Onyx
7781 S Little Egypt Rd (28164-8732)
PHONE..............................800 858-3533
▲ EMP: 20
Web: www.onyxsolutions.com
SIC: 3589 Floor washing and polishing machines, commercial

(G-11624)
SC JOHNSON PROF USA INC
1100 S Highway 27 (28164-2205)
PHONE..............................704 263-4240
John Campbell, *Prin*
EMP: 93
Web: www.scjp.com
SIC: 2844 Face creams or lotions
HQ: Sc Johnson Professional Usa, Inc.
2815 Clseum Cntre Dr Ste
Charlotte NC 28217

(G-11625)
SC JOHNSON PROFESSIONAL
1100 S Hwy (28164)
PHONE..............................704 263-4240
Michael Bogdanski, *Pr*
◆ EMP: 23 EST: 2014
SQ FT: 60,000
SALES (est): 6.16MM **Privately Held**
Web: www.scjohnson.com
SIC: 2841 Textile soap
HQ: Sc Johnson Professional Usa, Inc.
2815 Clseum Cntre Dr Ste
Charlotte NC 28217

Stantonsburg
Wilson County

(G-11626)
NORTH CAROLINA TOBACCO MFG LLC
7427 N. Carolina Way (27883)
PHONE..............................252 238-6514
George Aguerriberry, *Managing Member*
EMP: 15 EST: 2014
SALES (est): 4.5MM **Privately Held**
Web: www.nctob.com
SIC: 2121 Cigars

Star
Montgomery County

(G-11627)
C & J CROSSPIECES LLC
126 S Lancer Rd (27356-7329)
P.O. Box 732 (27209-0732)
PHONE..............................910 652-4955
EMP: 5 EST: 2007
SALES (est): 138.64K **Privately Held**
SIC: 2421 Building and structural materials, wood

(G-11628)
JOHNSON CNC LLC
133 S Main St (27356-7961)
PHONE..............................910 428-1245

Ryan Johnson, *Managing Member*
EMP: 22 EST: 2011
SALES (est): 4.14MM **Privately Held**
Web: www.johnsoncnc.com
SIC: 3599 Machine shop, jobbing and repair

(G-11629)
JORDAN LUMBER & SUPPLY INC
Also Called: Cotton Creek Chip Company
4483 Spies Rd (27356-7938)
P.O. Box 822 (27356-0822)
PHONE..............................910 428-9048
Doug Richardson, *Brnch Mgr*
EMP: 6
SALES (corp-wide): 26.93MM **Privately Held**
Web: www.jordanlumber.com
SIC: 2421 Wood chips, produced at mill
PA: Jordan Lumber & Supply, Inc.
1939 Nc Hwy 109 S
Mount Gilead NC 27306
910 439-6121

(G-11630)
LANCER INCORPORATED
135 S Lancer Rd (27356-7329)
P.O. Box 848 (27356-0848)
PHONE..............................910 428-2181
Randy Deese, *Ch*
Peggy Thompson, *
Fred Ingle, *
EMP: 120 EST: 1969
SQ FT: 96,000
SALES (est): 4.67MM **Privately Held**
Web: www.lancerfurniture.com
SIC: 2512 Upholstered household furniture

(G-11631)
MAYNARD FRAME SHOP INC
306 Mcbride Lumber Rd (27356-7513)
P.O. Box 182 (27247-0182)
PHONE..............................910 428-2033
Johnny Maynard, *Pr*
Teresa Maynard, *
EMP: 5 EST: 1984
SQ FT: 50,000
SALES (est): 130.11K **Privately Held**
SIC: 2511 2426 Unassembled or unfinished furniture, household: wood; Hardwood dimension and flooring mills

(G-11632)
MCBRIDE LUMBER CO PARTNR LLC
668 Mcbride Lumber Rd (27356-7516)
P.O. Box 91 (27356-0091)
PHONE..............................910 428-2747
EMP: 7 EST: 1964
SALES (est): 1.29MM **Privately Held**
SIC: 2449 2448 Rectangular boxes and crates, wood; Wood pallets and skids

(G-11633)
PRESTIGE MILLWORK INC
671 Spies Rd (27356-7867)
P.O. Box 250 (27356-0250)
PHONE..............................910 428-2360
Stephen Bracey, *Pr*
David Allen, *VP*
EMP: 6 EST: 1992
SQ FT: 28,000
SALES (est): 941.11K **Privately Held**
Web: www.prestigemillworknc.com
SIC: 2431 2521 2434 Millwork; Wood office furniture; Wood kitchen cabinets

(G-11634)
SUTTON SCIENTICS INC
246 W College St (27356-7987)
P.O. Box 310 (27356-0310)
PHONE..............................910 428-1600
Steven Sutton, *Pr*

Elizabeth Sutton, *VP*
EMP: 5 EST: 2005
SQ FT: 36,000
SALES (est): 494.14K **Privately Held**
Web: www.suttonscientics.com
SIC: 8748 3999 Business consulting, nec; Barber and beauty shop equipment

(G-11635)
WET DOG GLASS LLC
100 Russell Dr (27356-7001)
P.O. Box 96 (27356-0096)
PHONE..............................910 428-4111
Edward B Bernard, *Managing Member*
▼ EMP: 8 EST: 2000
SQ FT: 7,000
SALES (est): 2.34MM **Privately Held**
Web: www.wdg-us.com
SIC: 3559 Glass making machinery: blowing, molding, forming, etc.

State Road
Surry County

(G-11636)
GRASSY CREEK VINEYARD & WINERY
235 Chatham Cottage Ln (28676-8836)
PHONE..............................336 835-2458
Cynthia Douthit, *Prin*
EMP: 4 EST: 2012
SALES (est): 244.23K **Privately Held**
Web: www.grassycreekvineyard.com
SIC: 2084 Wines

(G-11637)
HOT SHOT SERVICES LLC
2202 Us 21 (28676-9017)
PHONE..............................336 244-0331
Billy Hudspeth, *Prin*
EMP: 5 EST: 2016
SALES (est): 79.25K **Privately Held**
Web: hotshotservicesllc.business.site
SIC: 1389 Hot shot service

(G-11638)
PINE LOG CO INC
Also Called: Pine Log 118 Trdtnal Living Rd
118 Traditional Living Rd (28676-8708)
P.O. Box 858 (28621-0858)
PHONE..............................336 366-2770
Charles W Woodie, *Pt*
Randy Miller, *Pt*
EMP: 30 EST: 1992
SALES (est): 953.3K **Privately Held**
SIC: 2421 Sawmills and planing mills, general

(G-11639)
RALPH HARRIS LEATHER INC
219 Pat Nixon Rd (28676-9193)
PHONE..............................336 874-2100
Mabeline Harris, *Pr*
Phil Harris, *VP*
Edwin R Harris, *VP*
EMP: 5 EST: 1976
SQ FT: 2,400
SALES (est): 157.79K **Privately Held**
Web: www.harrisleather.com
SIC: 3199 Equestrian related leather articles

(G-11640)
WATSON METALS CO
2693 Poplar Springs Rd (28676-8842)
PHONE..............................336 366-4500
Hassell Watson, *Pr*
Nancy Watson, *VP*
EMP: 6 EST: 1988
SQ FT: 3,575

SALES (est): 476.76K **Privately Held**
SIC: 3441 Fabricated structural metal

Statesville
Iredell County

(G-11641)
3A COMPOSITES USA INC (HQ)
3480 Taylorsville Hwy (28625-2587)
P.O. Box 507 (42025-0507)
PHONE...............................704 872-8974
Brendan Cooper, *Pr*
◆ EMP: 125 EST: 1978
SQ FT: 6,000
SALES (est): 437.02MM **Privately Held**
Web: www.3acompositesusa.com
SIC: 3334 2679 3081 3449 Primary
  aluminum; Paper products, converted, nec;
  Unsupported plastics film and sheet;
  Curtain wall, metal
PA: Schweiter Technologies Ag
  Hinterbergstrasse 20
  Steinhausen ZG 6312

(G-11642)
A & A DRONE SERVICE LLC
166 Ralph Rd (28625-2135)
PHONE...............................704 928-5054
EMP: 5 EST: 2019
SALES (est): 86.08K **Privately Held**
SIC: 3728 Aircraft parts and equipment, nec

(G-11643)
ABT FOAM INC
Also Called: Multidrain Systems, Inc.
1405 Industrial Dr (28625-6263)
P.O. Box 88 (28010-0088)
PHONE...............................800 433-1119
Ralph Brafford, *Pr*
▲ EMP: 10 EST: 2002
SALES (est): 3.86MM **Privately Held**
Web: www.multidrainsystems.com
SIC: 3321 Cast iron pipe and fittings
PA: Abt, Inc.
  259 Murdock Rd
  Troutman NC 28166

(G-11644)
ABT FOAM LLC
Also Called: A B T
1405 Industrial Dr (28625-6263)
P.O. Box 7107 (28687-7107)
PHONE...............................704 508-1010
EMP: 7 EST: 2008
SALES (est): 3.07MM **Privately Held**
Web: www.abtfoam.com
SIC: 3086 Plastics foam products

(G-11645)
ABT MANUFACTURING LLC
Also Called: ABT
1903 Weinig St (28677-3190)
P.O. Box 188 (28106-0188)
PHONE...............................704 847-9188
Robert G Estridge, *Managing Member*
W Kress Query, *Managing Member*
EMP: 35 EST: 1954
SQ FT: 55,000
SALES (est): 5.3MM **Privately Held**
Web: www.abtmetals.com
SIC: 3469 3544 Stamping metal for the trade
  ; Special dies and tools

(G-11646)
ACCUMA CORPORATION (DH)
133 Fanjoy Rd (28625-8567)
PHONE...............................704 873-1488
Francesca Inzernizzi, *Ch*
Steve Lepow, *

Paolo Invernizzi, *
Matthew Gillespie, *
◆ EMP: 112 EST: 1985
SQ FT: 160,000
SALES (est): 30.82MM
SALES (corp-wide): 157.08MM **Privately Held**
Web: www.accuma.com
SIC: 3089 Injection molding of plastics
HQ: Accuma Plastics Limited
  26 Princewood Road
  Corby NORTHANTS NN17
  153 626-3461

(G-11647)
ACME LIQUIDATING COMPANY LLC
Also Called: Acme Metal Products
1784 Salisbury Rd (28677-6264)
PHONE...............................704 873-3731
David Barnes, *Managing Member*
▲ EMP: 20 EST: 2007
SALES (est): 4.63MM **Privately Held**
Web: www.acmemetalproducts.com
SIC: 3497 Metal foil and leaf

(G-11648)
ACME RENTAL COMPANY
1784 Salisbury Rd (28677-6264)
P.O. Box 1263 (28687-1263)
PHONE...............................704 873-3731
William B Raymer Senior, *Pr*
J T Alexander Junior, *VP*
▲ EMP: 6 EST: 1946
SQ FT: 32,000
SALES (est): 672.71K **Privately Held**
SIC: 3429 Furniture hardware

(G-11649)
AGROFUEL LLC
964 Snow Creek Rd (28625-2147)
PHONE...............................704 876-6667
Harry Mclain, *Mgr*
EMP: 5 EST: 2006
SALES (est): 445.77K **Privately Held**
SIC: 2911 Oils, fuel

(G-11650)
AIR CRAFTSMEN INC
2503 Northside Dr (28625-3182)
P.O. Box 5547 (28687-5547)
PHONE...............................336 248-5777
Ken Hodges, *Pr*
EMP: 15 EST: 1981
SQ FT: 6,500
SALES (est): 370.58K **Privately Held**
Web: www.aircraftsmen.com
SIC: 3564 Dust or fume collecting
  equipment, industrial

(G-11651)
AIRBOX INC
2668 Peachtree Rd (28625-8252)
PHONE...............................855 927-1386
Timothy Self, *Managing Member*
EMP: 20 EST: 2017
SALES (est): 4.85MM **Privately Held**
Web: www.airboxamerica.com
SIC: 3634 3564 3499 Air purifiers, portable;
  Air purification equipment; Fire- or burglary-
  resistive products

(G-11652)
ALLESON OF ROCHESTER INC (DH)
Also Called: Alleson Athletic
111 Badger Ln (28625-2758)
PHONE...............................585 272-0606
Todd Levine, *CEO*
Pete Palermo Iii, *COO*
Bob Baker, *CFO*
◆ EMP: 100 EST: 1966
SQ FT: 128,000

SALES (est): 21.92MM **Privately Held**
Web: www.foundersport.com
SIC: 2339 2329 Women's and misses'
  athletic clothing and sportswear; Athletic
  clothing, except uniforms: men's, youths'
  and boys'
HQ: Badger Sportswear, Llc
  111 Badger Ln
  Statesville NC 28625
  704 871-0990

(G-11653)
ALTIUM PACKAGING LLC
124 Commerce Blvd (28625-8526)
PHONE...............................704 873-6729
Les Smith, *Mgr*
EMP: 12
SALES (corp-wide): 17.51B **Publicly Held**
Web: www.altiumpkg.com
SIC: 3089 Plastics containers, except foam
HQ: Altium Packaging Llc
  2500 Windy Ridge Pkwy Se # 1400
  Atlanta GA 30339
  678 742-4600

(G-11654)
AMESBURY ACQSTION HLDNGS 2 INC (DH)
Also Called: Balance Systems
2061 Sherrill Dr (28625-9025)
PHONE...............................704 924-8586
Johnnthan Petromelis, *Pr*
Jeffrey Murphy, *Corporate Controller**
◆ EMP: 250 EST: 1980
SQ FT: 100,000
SALES (est): 264.28MM **Publicly Held**
SIC: 3429 Hardware, nec
HQ: Tyman Limited
  Flamstead House
  Ripley DE5 8
  207 976-8000

(G-11655)
AMESBURY GROUP INC
Amesbury Textile Division
125 Amesbury Truth Dr (28625-8578)
PHONE...............................704 978-2883
Rich Gustin, *Genl Mgr*
EMP: 92
SQ FT: 37,920
SIC: 3442 3089 2221 3086 Sash, door or
  window: metal; Boxes, plastics; Pile fabrics,
  manmade fiber and silk; Plastics foam
  products
HQ: Amesbury Group, Inc.
  5001 W Delbridge St
  Sioux Falls SD 57107
  978 388-0581

(G-11656)
AMESBURY GROUP INC
Amesbury Balance Systems Div
1920 Flintstone Dr (28677-2996)
PHONE...............................704 924-7694
Eddie Kistler, *Mgr*
EMP: 65
Web: www.amesburytruth.com
SIC: 3053 3442 3086 2221 Gaskets; packing
  and sealing devices; Sash, door or window:
  metal; Plastics foam products; Pile fabrics,
  manmade fiber and silk
HQ: Amesbury Group, Inc.
  5001 W Delbridge St
  Sioux Falls SD 57107
  978 388-0581

(G-11657)
AMESBURY INDUSTRIES INC
125 Amesbury Truth Dr (28625-8578)
PHONE...............................704 978-3250
Jeffrey Graby, *Pr*

Jeffrey Murphy, *Sec*
EMP: 32 EST: 1980
SALES (est): 1.57MM **Publicly Held**
Web: www.amesburytruth.com
SIC: 3272 Concrete window and door
  components, sills and frames
HQ: Tyman Limited
  Flamstead House
  Ripley DE5 8
  207 976-8000

(G-11658)
ANA GIZZI
124 Hatfield Rd (28625-8999)
PHONE...............................908 334-8733
Ana Gizzi, *Prin*
EMP: 6 EST: 2016
SALES (est): 298.46K **Privately Held**
Web: www.westsideindustries.us
SIC: 3599 Machine shop, jobbing and repair

(G-11659)
ARGOS USA LLC
Also Called: Unicon Concrete
2289 Salisbury Hwy (28677-2731)
P.O. Box 6388 (28687-6388)
PHONE...............................704 872-9566
Chet Miller, *Brnch Mgr*
EMP: 155
Web: www.argos-us.com
SIC: 3273 3271 3272 Ready-mixed concrete
  ; Blocks, concrete or cinder: standard;
  Septic tanks, concrete
HQ: Argos Usa Llc
  3015 Windward Plz Ste 300
  Alpharetta GA 30005
  678 368-4300

(G-11660)
ARMS RACE NUTRITION LLC
1415 Wilkesboro Hwy (28625-3262)
PHONE...............................888 978-2332
EMP: 5 EST: 2019
SALES (est): 454.82K **Privately Held**
Web: www.armsracenutrition.com
SIC: 2023 Dietary supplements, dairy and
  non-dairy based

(G-11661)
ASMO NORTH AMERICA LLC
470 Crawford Rd (28625-8545)
PHONE...............................704 872-2319
▲ EMP: 2000
SIC: 3089 3621 Plastics and fiberglass tanks
  ; Motors, electric

(G-11662)
AUGUSTA SPORTSWEAR INC
Also Called: Badgers Sports
111 Badger Ln (28625-2758)
PHONE...............................704 871-0990
David Elliot, *Pr*
EMP: 5
SIC: 2329 Men's and boys' sportswear and
  athletic clothing
HQ: Augusta Sportswear, Inc.
  425 Park W Dr
  Grovetown GA 30813
  800 237-6695

(G-11663)
AUTEC INC
2500 W Front St (28677-2998)
PHONE...............................704 871-9141
Thomas J Hobby, *Pr*
Lynn Hobby, *
◆ EMP: 50 EST: 1981
SQ FT: 104,000
SALES (est): 9.92MM **Privately Held**
Web: www.autec-carwash.com

SIC: 3559 2842 Automotive related machinery; Specialty cleaning

(G-11664)
B & J KNITS INC
3492 Wilkesboro Hwy (28625-1250)
PHONE.............................704 876-1498
Roger Mclelland, Pr
EMP: 4 EST: 1973
SQ FT: 16,000
SALES (est): 124.83K Privately Held
Web: www.bandjknits.com
SIC: 2253 Warm weather knit outerwear, including beachwear

(G-11665)
BADGER SPORTSWEAR LLC
Also Called: Taurus Textiles
111 Badger Ln (28625-2758)
PHONE.............................704 871-0990
Jeff Jones, Mgr
EMP: 62
Web: www.foundersport.com
SIC: 5199 5137 5136 2339 Knit goods; Women's and children's clothing; Men's and boy's clothing; Women's and misses' outerwear, nec
HQ: Badger Sportswear, Llc
111 Badger Ln
Statesville NC 28625
704 871-0990

(G-11666)
BADGER SPORTSWEAR LLC (HQ)
Also Called: Garb Athletics
111 Badger Ln (28625-2758)
P.O. Box 447 (28687-0447)
PHONE.............................704 871-0990
▲ EMP: 268 EST: 1971
SALES (est): 97MM Privately Held
Web: www.foundersport.com
SIC: 2329 2339 Men's and boys' sportswear and athletic clothing; Sportswear, women's
PA: Platinum Equity, Llc
360 N Crescent Dr Bldg S
Beverly Hills CA 90210

(G-11667)
BARTLETT MILLING COMPANY LP
701 S Center St (28677-6732)
P.O. Box 831 (28687-0831)
PHONE.............................704 872-9581
Joe Mitchell, Prin
EMP: 56
SALES (corp-wide): 1.73B Privately Held
Web: www.bartlettco.com
SIC: 2041 2048 Wheat flour; Prepared feeds, nec
HQ: Bartlett Milling Company, L.P.
4900 Main St Ste 1200
Kansas City MO 64112
816 753-6300

(G-11668)
BEBIDA BEVERAGE COMPANY
1304 N Barkley Rd (28677)
P.O. Box 125 F Trad (28117)
PHONE.............................704 660-0226
Brian Weber, CEO
▼ EMP: 21 EST: 2009
SALES (est): 699.06K Privately Held
Web: www.bebevco.com
SIC: 2086 Bottled and canned soft drinks

(G-11669)
BEC-CAR PRINTING CO INC (PA)
Also Called: Ber-Car Printing
970 Davie Ave (28677-5302)
P.O. Box 569 (28687-0569)
PHONE.............................704 873-1911
Delan White, Pr

Rebecca White Poplin, VP
Michelle White Baggarley, Treas
EMP: 12 EST: 1924
SQ FT: 4,000
SALES (est): 944.66K
SALES (corp-wide): 944.66K Privately Held
SIC: 2752 Offset printing

(G-11670)
BETCO INC (DH)
Also Called: Mini Storage of North Carolina
228 Commerce Blvd (28625-8549)
PHONE.............................704 872-2999
Samir Sabri, CEO
Fred Barnard, *
Chris Gilbert, *
◆ EMP: 95 EST: 1984
SQ FT: 40,000
SALES (est): 30.41MM
SALES (corp-wide): 1.07B Publicly Held
Web: www.betcoinc.com
SIC: 3448 Buildings, portable: prefabricated metal
HQ: Janus International Group, Llc
135 Janus Intl Blvd
Temple GA 30179
770 562-2850

(G-11671)
BILL MARTIN INC
106 Martin Ln (28625-2250)
PHONE.............................704 873-0241
Bill R Martin Senior, Pr
Bill Martin Junior, VP
John Martin, Sec
EMP: 8 EST: 1968
SQ FT: 4,141
SALES (est): 838.67K Privately Held
Web: www.billmartintires.com
SIC: 5531 7534 Automotive tires; Tire recapping

(G-11672)
BRUNING AND FEDERLE MFG CO (PA)
2503 Northside Dr (28625-3182)
P.O. Box 5547 (28687-5547)
PHONE.............................704 873-7237
Thomas H Bass, Pr
Michael D Hepler, General Vice President*
▲ EMP: 50 EST: 1963
SQ FT: 30,000
SALES (est): 9.25MM
SALES (corp-wide): 9.25MM Privately Held
Web: www.bruning-federle.com
SIC: 3564 Dust or fume collecting equipment, industrial

(G-11673)
BUSCH ENTERPRISES INC
908 Cochran St (28677-5655)
PHONE.............................704 878-2067
Ted Busch, Pr
Carolyn Busch, Sec
EMP: 6 EST: 1980
SQ FT: 12,000
SALES (est): 414.02K Privately Held
Web: www.buschpolishes.com
SIC: 2842 5999 Cleaning or polishing preparations, nec; Cleaning equipment and supplies

(G-11674)
CABINET MAKERS INC
534 Jane Sowers Rd (28625-8929)
PHONE.............................704 876-2808
Kenny Harris, Pr
Jonathan Baumgarner, *
Jodie Harris, *

Crystal Baumgarner, *
Jesse Barnett, Stockholder*
EMP: 5 EST: 1965
SQ FT: 54,000
SALES (est): 240.24K Privately Held
SIC: 2511 2434 Wood household furniture; Wood kitchen cabinets

(G-11675)
CARDINAL AMERICA INC
165 Commerce Blvd (28625-8526)
PHONE.............................704 810-1620
EMP: 6 EST: 2018
SALES (est): 1.32MM Privately Held
Web: www.cardinalamerica.com
SIC: 3452 Bolts, metal

(G-11676)
CCBCC OPERATIONS LLC
Also Called: Coca-Cola
2111 W Front St (28677-3650)
PHONE.............................704 872-3634
Richard Brogdon, Brnch Mgr
EMP: 37
SALES (corp-wide): 6.9B Publicly Held
Web: www.coca-cola.com
SIC: 2086 Bottled and canned soft drinks
HQ: Ccbcc Operations, Llc
4100 Coca-Cola Plz
Charlotte NC 28211
704 364-8728

(G-11677)
CEMEX CNSTR MTLS ATL LLC
2067 Salisbury Hwy (28677-2779)
PHONE.............................704 873-3263
Scott Matthews, Brnch Mgr
EMP: 5
SQ FT: 4,108
SIC: 3273 Ready-mixed concrete
HQ: Cemex Construction Materials Atlantic, Llc
1501 Belvedere Rd
West Palm Beach FL 33406
561 833-5555

(G-11678)
CONSTRUCTION METAL PDTS INC
2204 W Front St (28677-2917)
PHONE.............................704 871-8704
Michael J Morton, Ch Bd
Robert M Noble, *
Staci M Ivester, *
EMP: 30 EST: 1993
SQ FT: 43,000
SALES (est): 4.91MM Privately Held
Web: www.cmpmetalsystems.com
SIC: 3444 Metal roofing and roof drainage equipment

(G-11679)
CRAWFORD ROAD LIQUIDATING CO
174 Crawford Rd Ste A (28625-3002)
P.O. Box 249 (28687-0249)
PHONE.............................704 871-1830
Marvin W Mccombs Iii, Pr
Larry Harvey, VP
EMP: 16 EST: 1990
SQ FT: 20,000
SALES (est): 4.63MM Privately Held
Web: www.metalfabnc.com
SIC: 3441 Fabricated structural metal

(G-11680)
CREATIVE SIGN SOLUTIONS INC
563 Rimrock Rd (28625-1475)
PHONE.............................704 978-8499
Jonathan Elam, Pr
EMP: 8 EST: 2014
SALES (est): 138K Privately Held
Web: www.signsbycss.com

SIC: 3993 Signs and advertising specialties

(G-11681)
CROSSROADS COATINGS INC
Also Called: Crossroads Coatings
208 Bucks Industrial Rd (28625-2813)
P.O. Box 1508 (28687-1508)
PHONE.............................704 873-2244
William Lodgek, Pr
▲ EMP: 10 EST: 1958
SQ FT: 35,000
SALES (est): 7.58MM Privately Held
Web: www.crossroadscoatings.com
SIC: 2851 Paints and paint additives

(G-11682)
D & D MACHINE WORKS INC
Also Called: Machining
111 Dealwood Dr (28625-9143)
PHONE.............................704 878-0117
Aaron Jones, Pr
EMP: 8 EST: 1976
SQ FT: 5,500
SALES (est): 2.44MM Privately Held
Web: www.ddmachineworks.net
SIC: 3599 Machine shop, jobbing and repair

(G-11683)
D & F CONSOLIDATED INC
Also Called: Car-Mel Products
2205 Mocaro Dr (28677-3668)
P.O. Box 5877 (28687-5877)
PHONE.............................704 664-6660
William Greg Glasby, Pr
Melvin J Skerpon, Sr VP
Carl E Tompkins Junior, Sr VP
Terry L Skerpon, Sec
EMP: 5 EST: 2009
SQ FT: 15,000
SALES (est): 952.36K Privately Held
SIC: 5131 2269 Labels; Labels, cotton: printed

(G-11684)
DANDY LIGHT TRAPS INC
1256 N Barkley Rd (28677-9726)
PHONE.............................980 223-2744
Kenneth W Teeters, Pr
Beverly R Frye, Sec
EMP: 5 EST: 2015
SALES (est): 1.55MM Privately Held
Web: www.dandylighttraps.com
SIC: 3648 5046 Lighting equipment, nec; Commercial equipment, nec

(G-11685)
DAYTON BAG & BURLAP CO
233 Commerce Blvd (28625-8549)
PHONE.............................704 873-7271
Mitch Perkins, Brnch Mgr
EMP: 4
SALES (corp-wide): 19.35MM Privately Held
Web: www.daybag.com
SIC: 2396 2299 2393 2674 Automotive trimmings, fabric; Burlap, jute; Textile bags; Bags: uncoated paper and multiwall
PA: The Dayton Bag & Burlap Co
322 Davis Ave
Dayton OH 45403
937 258-8000

(G-11686)
DEAL MACHINE SHOP INC
400 Beulah Rd (28625-2537)
PHONE.............................704 872-7618
Wayne G Deal Senior, Pr
Wayne G Deal Junior, VP
Gary Deal, Sec
EMP: 6 EST: 1968
SQ FT: 6,000

SALES (est): 601.7K **Privately Held**
Web: www.dealmachineshop.com
SIC: 3599 Machine shop, jobbing and repair

(G-11687)
DEAL-RITE FEEDS INC
109 Anna Dr (28625)
P.O. Box 29 (28687)
PHONE..........................704 873-8646
Ronald Deal, *Pr*
Diane Williams, *
EMP: 30 **EST:** 1962
SQ FT: 6,400
SALES (est): 5.22MM **Privately Held**
Web: www.deal-ritefeeds.com
SIC: 2048 Cereal-, grain-, and seed-based
  feeds

(G-11688)
DENSO MANUFACTURING NC INC
(DH)
470 Crawford Rd (28625-8545)
PHONE..........................704 878-6663
Masanori Iyama, *Pr*
Daisuke Ishikawa, *
◆ **EMP:** 495 **EST:** 1988
SQ FT: 1,229,683
SALES (est): 68.09MM **Privately Held**
SIC: 3621 Motors and generators
HQ: Denso International America, Inc.
  24777 Denso Dr
  Southfield MI 48033
  248 350-7500

(G-11689)
DESCO EQUIPMENT COMPANY INC
1031 S Meeting St (28677-6655)
P.O. Box 6298 (28687-6298)
PHONE..........................704 873-2844
Nute H Shelton, *Pr*
Connie Shelton, *Sec*
EMP: 7 **EST:** 1983
SALES (est): 657.63K **Privately Held**
Web: www.descoequip.com
SIC: 3589 5169 High pressure cleaning
  equipment; Specialty cleaning and
  sanitation preparations

(G-11690)
DONALD AUTON
Also Called: Bill's Welding & Son
841 Reynolds Rd (28677-3062)
PHONE..........................704 872-7528
Donald Auton, *Owner*
EMP: 4 **EST:** 2016
SALES (est): 123.96K **Privately Held**
SIC: 7692 Automotive welding

(G-11691)
DOOSAN BOBCAT NORTH AMER INC
Doosan Infracore Portable Pwr
1293 Glenway Dr (28625-9218)
PHONE..........................704 883-3500
EMP: 152
Web: www.bobcat.com
SIC: 3714 Motor vehicle parts and
  accessories
HQ: Doosan Bobcat North America, Inc.
  250 E Beaton Dr
  West Fargo ND 58078
  701 241-8700

(G-11692)
DOT BLUE READI-MIX LLC
158 Intercraft Dr (28625-2737)
PHONE..........................704 978-2331
John Wood, *Manager*
EMP: 27
SALES (corp-wide): 23.52MM **Privately
Held**
Web: www.bluedotreadimix.com

SIC: 3273 Ready-mixed concrete
PA: Blue Dot Readi-Mix, Llc
  11330 Bain School Rd
  Mint Hill NC 28227
  704 971-7676

(G-11693)
DYNAMIC NUTRACEUTICALS LLC
(PA)
1441 Wilkesboro Hwy (28625-3262)
PHONE..........................704 380-2324
Jason Dean Wolff, *Pr*
EMP: 26 **EST:** 2018
SQ FT: 15,000
SALES (est): 10.1MM
SALES (corp-wide): 10.1MM **Privately
Held**
Web: www.dynamicnutraceuticals.com
SIC: 2834 Vitamin, nutrient, and hematinic
  preparations for human use

(G-11694)
ELITE METAL PERFORMANCE LLC
Also Called: Emp Services
132 Conifer Dr (28625-9020)
PHONE..........................704 660-0006
EMP: 10 **EST:** 2012
SALES (est): 3.18MM **Privately Held**
Web: www.elitemetalperformance.com
SIC: 3792 3841 3714 3599 Travel trailer
  chassis; Surgical and medical instruments;
  Motor vehicle parts and accessories;
  Machine and other job shop work

(G-11695)
ELLENBURG SHEET METAL
353 Stamey Farm Rd (28625-2531)
P.O. Box 5638 (28687-5638)
PHONE..........................704 872-2089
Tony Ellenburg, *Owner*
EMP: 4 **EST:** 1969
SALES (est): 322.63K **Privately Held**
Web: www.ellenburgs.com
SIC: 3444 1711 Sheet metalwork; Plumbing,
  heating, air-conditioning

(G-11696)
FIBRIX LLC
Also Called: Cumulus - Statesville West
166 Orbit Rd (28677-8634)
PHONE..........................704 872-5223
Gene Bardakjy, *Brnch Mgr*
EMP: 22
SALES (corp-wide): 46.63MM **Privately
Held**
Web: www.fibrix.com
SIC: 2297 Nonwoven fabrics
HQ: Fibrix, Llc
  1820 Evans St Ne
  Conover NC 28613

(G-11697)
FIBRIX LLC
Also Called: Cumulus Fibres - Statesville
1004 Bucks Industrial Rd (28625-2813)
PHONE..........................704 878-0027
Bucky Bradford, *Mgr*
EMP: 22
SALES (corp-wide): 46.63MM **Privately
Held**
Web: www.fibrix.com
SIC: 2297 2824 2221 2299 Nonwoven fabrics
  ; Organic fibers, noncellulosic; Broadwoven
  fabric mills, manmade; Batting, wadding,
  padding and fillings
HQ: Fibrix, Llc
  1820 Evans St Ne
  Conover NC 28613

SIC: 3273 Ready-mixed concrete
(G-11698)
FIRE FLY BALLONS 2006 LLC
850 Meacham Rd (28677-2982)
PHONE..........................704 878-9501
EMP: 5 **EST:** 1972
SQ FT: 28,000
SALES (est): 459.74K **Privately Held**
SIC: 3721 Balloons, hot air (aircraft)

(G-11699)
FIREFLY BALLOONS 2010 INC
850 Meacham Rd (28677-2982)
PHONE..........................704 878-9501
Brian K Gantt, *Admn*
EMP: 6 **EST:** 2010
SALES (est): 340K **Privately Held**
Web: www.fireflyballoons.net
SIC: 3721 Balloons, hot air (aircraft)

(G-11700)
FIREFLY BALLOONS INC
810 Salisbury Rd (28677-6224)
PHONE..........................704 878-9501
EMP: 4 **EST:** 2005
SALES (est): 99.49K **Privately Held**
Web: www.fireflyballoons.net
SIC: 3564 Blowers and fans

(G-11701)
G & M MILLING CO INC
4000 Taylorsville Hwy (28625-1842)
PHONE..........................704 873-5758
Jeffrey C Mcneely, *Pr*
Nancy S Mcneely, *Sec*
EMP: 11 **EST:** 1960
SQ FT: 6,400
SALES (est): 1.31MM **Privately Held**
Web: www.gmmillingco.com
SIC: 2048 5191 5451 Poultry feeds; Animal
  feeds; Dairy products stores

(G-11702)
GABDEN LLC
Also Called: Gabden Entertainment
232 N Center St (28677)
PHONE..........................704 451-8646
EMP: 6 **EST:** 2017
SALES (est): 120K **Privately Held**
SIC: 2024 Ices, flavored (frozen dessert)

(G-11703)
GLEMCO LLC
Also Called: Glemco Parts
1624 Northside Dr (28625-3163)
PHONE..........................866 619-6707
EMP: 8 **EST:** 2007
SALES (est): 3.55MM **Privately Held**
Web: www.glemcoparts.com
SIC: 3523 7699 3724 Cabs, tractors, and
  agricultural machinery; Tractor repair;
  Aircraft engines and engine parts

(G-11704)
GODFREY LUMBER COMPANY INC
(PA)
1715 Amity Hill Rd (28677-7201)
P.O. Box 615 (28687-0615)
PHONE..........................704 872-6366
Chester Godfrey, *Pr*
John Godfrey, *Treas*
William Godfrey, *VP*
Barry Godfrey, *VP*
▲ **EMP:** 16 **EST:** 1954
SQ FT: 75,000
SALES (est): 2.43MM
SALES (corp-wide): 2.43MM **Privately
Held**
Web: www.godfreylumber.com
SIC: 2421 Wood chips, produced at mill

(G-11705)
**GOODYEAR TIRE & RUBBER
COMPANY**
Also Called: Goodyear
108 Business Park Dr (28677-9133)
PHONE..........................704 928-4500
Chris Halleck, *Mgr*
EMP: 63
SALES (corp-wide): 18.88B **Publicly Held**
Web: www.goodyear.com
SIC: 3544 Forms (molds), for foundry and
  plastics working machinery
PA: The Goodyear Tire & Rubber Company
  200 Innovation Way
  Akron OH 44316
  330 796-2121

(G-11706)
HEINTZ BROS AUTOMOTIVES INC
1475 Old Mountain Rd (28677-2085)
PHONE..........................704 872-8081
Steve B Heintz, *Pr*
Shirley C Heintz, *Sec*
Scott Heintz, *VP*
EMP: 8 **EST:** 1965
SQ FT: 6,000
SALES (est): 437.25K **Privately Held**
Web: www.heintzbrothers.com
SIC: 5013 5531 3599 Automotive supplies
  and parts; Automotive parts; Machine shop,
  jobbing and repair

(G-11707)
HERFF JONES LLC
307 E Front St (28677-5906)
PHONE..........................704 873-5563
Joe Archibald, *Mgr*
EMP: 6
SALES (corp-wide): 8.23B **Privately Held**
Web: www.yearbookdiscoveries.com
SIC: 3911 Rings, finger: precious metal
HQ: Herff Jones, Llc
  4501 W 62nd St
  Indianapolis IN 46268
  317 297-3741

(G-11708)
HERITAGE BUILDING COMPANY LLC
114 N Center St Ste 300 (28677-5273)
PHONE..........................704 431-4494
James N Paquette, *Prin*
EMP: 8 **EST:** 2019
SALES (est): 3.53MM **Privately Held**
Web: www.heritagebuildings.com
SIC: 3448 Buildings, portable: prefabricated
  metal

(G-11709)
HERITAGE KNITTING CO LLC
240 Wilson Park Rd (28625-8525)
P.O. Box 1408 (28687-1408)
PHONE..........................704 872-7653
Charles S Dockery Junior, *Managing
Member*
EMP: 20 **EST:** 1994
SQ FT: 22,000
SALES (est): 599.92K **Privately Held**
Web: www.heritageknitting.com
SIC: 2257 2211 Pile fabrics, circular knit;
  Broadwoven fabric mills, cotton

(G-11710)
HEXPOL COMPOUNDING NC INC
Also Called: Hexpol
280 Crawford Rd (28625-8541)
PHONE..........................704 872-1585
Tracy Garrison, *Pr*
◆ **EMP:** 3100 **EST:** 1997
SQ FT: 44,000
SALES (est): 46.03MM
SALES (corp-wide): 6.47MM **Privately
Held**

Web: www.hexpol.com
SIC: **3069** 3087 2891　Rubber automotive products; Custom compound purchased resins; Adhesives and sealants
HQ: Hexpol Holding Inc.
　14330 Kinsman Rd
　Burton OH 44021
　440 834-4644

(G-11711)
HI-TEC PLATING INC
North Carolina Division
1603 Salisbury Rd (28677-6270)
PHONE..............................704 872-8969
Buddy G Bray, *Mgr*
EMP: 10
SQ FT: 7,123
SALES (corp-wide): 5.1MM **Privately Held**
Web: www.hitecplating.com
SIC: **3471**　Electroplating of metals or formed products
PA: Hi-Tec Plating, Inc.
　219 Hitec Rd
　Seneca SC 29678
　864 882-3311

(G-11712)
HILLGRAY INNOVATIONS LLC ✪
Also Called: General Contactor
119 Galley Ln (28677-8744)
PHONE..............................704 923-6618
Lonita Hilliard, *CEO*
Lonita Hilliard, *Managing Member*
EMP: 7 EST: 2023
SALES (est): 1.51MM **Privately Held**
SIC: **1389**　Construction, repair, and dismantling services

(G-11713)
HPC NC
280 Crawford Rd (28625-8541)
PHONE..............................704 978-0103
Ernie Ulmer, *Prin*
EMP: 5 EST: 2010
SALES (est): 1.07MM **Privately Held**
SIC: **3562**　Ball and roller bearings

(G-11714)
HUGHS SHEET MTAL STTSVLLE LLC
Also Called: Hugh's Sheet Metal
1312 N Barkley Rd (28677-9728)
PHONE..............................704 872-4621
Darrell Moose, *Pr*
Bonnie Moose, *Sec*
EMP: 12 EST: 1969
SQ FT: 8,000
SALES (est): 1.6MM **Privately Held**
Web: www.hughssheetmetal.com
SIC: **3441** 1761 3564 3444　Fabricated structural metal; Sheet metal work, nec; Blowers and fans; Sheet metalwork

(G-11715)
I-40 MACHINE AND TOOL INC
223 Commerce Blvd (28625-8549)
PHONE..............................704 881-0242
Alvin Anderson, *Pr*
Dan Anderson, *Sec*
EMP: 5 EST: 1987
SQ FT: 6,000
SALES (est): 424.15K **Privately Held**
Web: www.i40machine.com
SIC: **3599**　Machine shop, jobbing and repair

(G-11716)
IPS PERFORATING INC
1821 Weinig St (28677-3187)
PHONE..............................704 881-0050
Trish Idler, *Prin*
▲ EMP: 9 EST: 2005
SALES (est): 2.8MM **Privately Held**

Web: www.ipsperforating.com
SIC: **3443**　Perforating on heavy metal

(G-11717)
IREDELL FIBER INC
Also Called: Division of Leggett Platt
124 Fanjoy Rd (28625-8567)
P.O. Box 5728 (28687-5728)
PHONE..............................704 878-0884
Jerry Wahrmund, *Mgr*
▲ EMP: 12 EST: 1987
SALES (est): 2.49MM
SALES (corp-wide): 5.15B **Publicly Held**
SIC: **2515**　Mattresses and bedsprings
PA: Leggett & Platt, Incorporated
　1 Leggett Rd
　Carthage MO 64836
　417 358-8131

(G-11718)
JAX SPECIALTY WELDING LLC
621 Bristol Dr (28677-3011)
PHONE..............................704 380-3548
Michael T Jackson, *Prin*
EMP: 5 EST: 2019
SALES (est): 113.51K **Privately Held**
SIC: **7692**　Welding repair

(G-11719)
JMS SOUTHEAST INC
105 Temperature Ln (28677-9639)
PHONE..............................704 873-1835
Frank L Johnson, *CEO*
Mitchell Johnson, *Pr*
Linda Johnson, *VP*
Frank Phillips, *Sec*
▲ EMP: 50 EST: 1980
SQ FT: 40,000
SALES (est): 7.84MM **Privately Held**
Web: www.jms-se.com
SIC: **3822** 3829 3823 3812　Temperature controls, automatic; Measuring and controlling devices, nec; Process control instruments; Search and navigation equipment

(G-11720)
JPS COMPOSITE MATERIALS CORP
535 Connor St (28677-5757)
P.O. Box 871 (28687-0871)
PHONE..............................704 872-9831
Mike Marshall, *Brnch Mgr*
EMP: 107
SALES (corp-wide): 1.91B **Publicly Held**
Web: www.jpscm.com
SIC: **2821**　Plastics materials and resins
HQ: Jps Composite Materials Corp.
　2200 S Murray Ave
　Anderson SC 29624
　800 431-1110

(G-11721)
JS FIBER CO INC (PA)
290 Marble Rd (28625-2351)
PHONE..............................704 871-1582
Morris Long, *Pr*
Linda Long, *
◆ EMP: 44 EST: 1989
SQ FT: 70,000
SALES (est): 8.34MM **Privately Held**
Web: www.jsfiber.com
SIC: **3949** 2392　Sporting and athletic goods, nec; Cushions and pillows

(G-11722)
JS LINENS AND CURTAIN OUTLET (PA)
290 Marble Rd (28625-2351)
PHONE..............................704 871-1582
Morris Long, *Pr*
EMP: 18 EST: 2010

SALES (est): 239.4K
SALES (corp-wide): 239.4K **Privately Held**
Web: www.jslinenoutlet.com
SIC: **5999** 2392　Alcoholic beverage making equipment and supplies; Mattress pads

(G-11723)
KESELOWSKI ADVANCED MFG LLC
258 Aviation Dr (28677-2516)
PHONE..............................704 799-0206
EMP: 42 EST: 2018
SALES (est): 5.29MM **Privately Held**
Web: www.kamsolutions.com
SIC: **3291**　Abrasive metal and steel products

(G-11724)
KEWAUNEE SCIENTIFIC CORP (PA)
2700 W Front St (28677-2894)
P.O. Box 1842 (28687-1842)
PHONE..............................704 873-7202
Thomas D Hull Iii, *Pr*
Keith M Gehl, *
Donald T Gardner Iii, *VP Fin*
Elizabeth D Phillips, *Pers/VP*
Mandar Ranade, *VP*
EMP: 917 EST: 1906
SQ FT: 413,000
SALES (est): 203.75MM
SALES (corp-wide): 203.75MM **Publicly Held**
Web: www.kewaunee.com
SIC: **3821** 2599　Laboratory furniture; Factory furniture and fixtures

(G-11725)
KOOKS CUSTOM HEADERS
2333 Salisbury Hwy (28677-1129)
PHONE..............................704 838-1110
Auke De Pater, *Pr*
EMP: 6 EST: 2016
SALES (est): 1.14MM **Privately Held**
Web: www.kooksheaders.com
SIC: **3714**　Motor vehicle parts and accessories

(G-11726)
KOOKS CUSTOM HEADERS INC
141 Advantage Pl (28677-9793)
PHONE..............................704 768-2288
George Kryssing Junior, *CEO*
Carol Kryssing, *
▲ EMP: 30 EST: 1995
SQ FT: 45,000
SALES (est): 10.68MM **Privately Held**
Web: www.kooksheaders.com
SIC: **3498**　Fabricated pipe and fittings

(G-11727)
LEGGETT & PLATT INCORPORATED
Also Called: Super Sagless
178 Orbit Rd (28677-8634)
PHONE..............................704 380-6208
EMP: 4
SALES (corp-wide): 5.15B **Publicly Held**
Web: www.leggett.com
SIC: **2515** 2514 3495 2392　Furniture springs ; Frames for box springs or bedsprings; metal; Wire springs; Mattress pads
PA: Leggett & Platt, Incorporated
　1 Leggett Rd
　Carthage MO 64836
　417 358-8131

(G-11728)
MACK MOLDING COMPANY INC
149 Water Tank Rd (28677-8637)
PHONE..............................704 878-9641
Joe Carinci, *Mgr*
EMP: 150
SALES (corp-wide): 856.43MM **Privately Held**

Web: www.mack.com
SIC: **3089**　Injection molding of plastics
HQ: Mack Molding Company, Inc.
　608 Warm Brook Rd
　Arlington VT 05250
　802 375-2511

(G-11729)
MARIETTA MARTIN MATERIALS INC
Also Called: Martin Marietta Aggregates
220 Quarry Rd (28677)
PHONE..............................704 873-8191
Paul Wear, *Mgr*
EMP: 6
Web: www.martinmarietta.com
SIC: **1422**　Crushed and broken limestone
PA: Martin Marietta Materials Inc
　4123 Parklake Ave
　Raleigh NC 27612

(G-11730)
MCCOMBS STEEL COMPANY INC (PA)
117 Slingshot Rd (28677-8604)
PHONE..............................704 873-7563
Marvin W Mccombs Iii, *Pr*
John L Payne, *
Peggy Mccombs, *Sec*
EMP: 49 EST: 1915
SQ FT: 34,000
SALES (est): 12.78MM
SALES (corp-wide): 12.78MM **Privately Held**
Web: www.mccombs-steel.com
SIC: **3441** 5051　Building components, structural steel; Steel

(G-11731)
MERCHANTS METALS LLC
Also Called: Merchants Metals
165 Fanjoy Rd (28625-8567)
PHONE..............................704 878-8706
Harshad Londhe, *Mgr*
EMP: 115
SQ FT: 68,612
SALES (corp-wide): 1.09B **Privately Held**
Web: www.merchantsmetals.com
SIC: **3315** 3496　Chain link fencing; Miscellaneous fabricated wire products
HQ: Merchants Metals Llc
　3 Ravinia Dr Ste 1750
　Atlanta GA 30346
　770 741-0300

(G-11732)
MOCARO DYEING & FINISHING INC
2201 Mocaro Dr (28677-3668)
P.O. Box 6689 (28687-6689)
PHONE..............................704 878-6645
EMP: 100
SQ FT: 250,000
SALES (est): 13.86MM **Privately Held**
SIC: **2257**　Dyeing and finishing circular knit fabrics

(G-11733)
MOCARO INDUSTRIES INC
2201 Mocaro Dr (28677-3668)
P.O. Box 6689 (28687-6689)
PHONE..............................704 878-6645
T C Spell, *Pr*
George S Simon, *
Harry C Spell, *
EMP: 7 EST: 1987
SQ FT: 90,000
SALES (est): 491.44K **Privately Held**
Web: www.mocaro.com
SIC: **2257** 2269　Jersey cloth; Finishing plants, nec

▲ = Import ▼ = Export
◆ = Import/Export

(G-11734)
MODERN INFORMATION SVCS INC
Also Called: Sir Speedy
436 S Center St (28677-5841)
PHONE...................704 872-1020
Craig J Sudman, *Pr*
EMP: 8 EST: 1995
SQ FT: 1,300
SALES (est): 1.21MM Privately Held
Web: www.sirspeedy.com
SIC: 2752 Commercial printing, lithographic

(G-11735)
MOUNTAIRE FARMS INC
2206 W Front St (28677-2917)
PHONE...................704 978-3055
Dabbs Cavin, *CFO*
EMP: 8 EST: 2014
SALES (est): 1.29MM Privately Held
Web: www.mountaire.com
SIC: 2015 Poultry slaughtering and
processing

(G-11736)
MOUNTAIRE FARMS INC
Also Called: Statesville Breeder Feedmill
2206 W Front St (28677-2917)
PHONE...................704 978-3055
EMP: 125
SALES (corp-wide): 2.07B Privately Held
Web: www.mountaire.com
SIC: 2048 Livestock feeds
HQ: Mountaire Farms Inc.
1901 Napa Valley Dr
Little Rock AR 72212
501 372-6524

(G-11737)
MR TIRE INC
149 E Front St (28677-5851)
PHONE...................704 872-4127
Derek Jackson, *Brnch Mgr*
EMP: 8
SALES (corp-wide): 1.28B Publicly Held
Web: locations.mrtire.com
SIC: 5531 5941 5014 7534 Automotive tires;
Bicycle and bicycle parts; Tires and tubes;
Tire recapping
HQ: Mr. Tire Inc.
2078 New York Ave Unit 2
Huntington Station NY 11746
631 499-3700

(G-11738)
NATIONAL PEENING INC (DH)
Also Called: Wilmington National Peening
1902 Weinig St (28677-3189)
PHONE...................704 872-0113
Richard Stewart, *Pr*
Tom Wolf, *Prin*
Chuck Amaspas, *Prin*
EMP: 18 EST: 1986
SQ FT: 24,000
SALES (est): 24.3MM Privately Held
Web: www.sintoamerica.com
SIC: 3398 Shot peening (treating steel to
reduce fatigue)
HQ: Sinto America, Inc.
150 Orchard St
Grand Ledge MI 48837

(G-11739)
**NORTH CAROLINA CONVERTING
LLC**
1001 Bucks Industrial Rd (28625-2575)
P.O. Box 18493 (28218-0493)
PHONE...................704 871-2912
Michael J Dortch, *Managing Member*
EMP: 4 EST: 2008
SALES (est): 465.55K Privately Held
SIC: 2611 Pulp mills

(G-11740)
OHIO FOAM CORPORATION
Also Called: Ofc Fabricators
2185 Salisbury Hwy (28677-2780)
PHONE...................704 883-8402
Sam Ross, *Brnch Mgr*
EMP: 10
SALES (corp-wide): 8.08MM Privately
Held
Web: www.ohiofoam.com
SIC: 3069 Foam rubber
PA: Ohio Foam Corporation
820 Plymouth St
Bucyrus OH 44820
419 563-0399

(G-11741)
ORIGIN FOOD GROUP LLC
306 Stamey Farm Rd (28677-8326)
P.O. Box 7621 (28687-7621)
PHONE...................704 768-9000
Barbara Alarcon, *
David Stamey, *
▲ EMP: 24 EST: 2010
SQ FT: 34,000
SALES (est): 10.07MM Privately Held
Web: www.originfoodgroup.com
SIC: 2026 Yogurt

(G-11742)
PARKER-HANNIFIN CORPORATION
Precision Fluidics
149 Crawford Rd (28625-8546)
PHONE...................704 662-3500
Linnea Hargraves, *Mgr*
EMP: 26
SALES (corp-wide): 19.93B Publicly Held
Web: www.parker.com
SIC: 3339 Primary nonferrous metals, nec
PA: Parker-Hannifin Corporation
6035 Parkland Blvd
Cleveland OH 44124
216 896-3000

(G-11743)
PASHES LLC
328 E Broad St (28677-5327)
PHONE...................704 682-6535
Ernestina Peter, *Managing Member*
EMP: 6 EST: 2020
SALES (est): 379.93K Privately Held
SIC: 5641 3999 8742 Children's and infants'
wear stores; Hair and hair-based products;
Retail trade consultant

(G-11744)
PEPSI BOTTLING VENTURES LLC
Also Called: Pepsi-Cola
1703 Gregory Rd (28677-3162)
PHONE...................704 873-0249
Tom Byerly, *Mgr*
EMP: 48
Web: www.pepsibottlingventures.com
SIC: 2086 Carbonated soft drinks, bottled
and canned
HQ: Pepsi Bottling Ventures Llc
4141 Parklake Ave
Raleigh NC 27612
919 865-2300

(G-11745)
PIEDMONT FIBERGLASS INC
1166 Bunch Dr (28677-3261)
PHONE...................828 632-8883
EMP: 30
Web: www.piedmontcomposites.com
SIC: 5999 3544 7389 3949 Fiberglass
materials, except insulation; Forms (molds),
for foundry and plastics working machinery;
Crane and aerial lift service; Sporting and
athletic goods, nec

(G-11746)
PINE VIEW BUILDINGS LLC
933 Tomlin Mill Rd (28625-1597)
P.O. Box 120 (28688-0120)
PHONE...................704 876-1501
EMP: 85 EST: 2013
SALES (est): 7.15MM Privately Held
Web: www.pineviewbuildings.com
SIC: 3448 Prefabricated metal buildings and
components

(G-11747)
PLASGAD USA LLC
933 Meacham Rd (28677-2966)
PHONE...................980 223-2197
Ido Shifroni, *CEO*
EMP: 26 EST: 2019
SALES (est): 5.21MM Privately Held
Web: www.plasgad.com
SIC: 3089 Plastics containers, except foam

(G-11748)
PLASTIFLEX NORTH CAROLINA LLC
2101 Sherrill Dr (28625-9052)
PHONE...................704 871-8448
Peter Dirkx, *COO*
Hennie Kunneke, *
EMP: 53 EST: 2000
SALES (est): 19.12MM
SALES (corp-wide): 2.67MM Privately
Held
Web: www.plastiflex.com
SIC: 3052 Rubber and plastics hose and
beltings
HQ: Plastiflex Company Inc.
601 E Palomar St Ste 424
Chula Vista CA 91911

(G-11749)
POLY ONE DISTRIBUTION
114 Morehead Rd (28677-2744)
PHONE...................704 872-8168
Greg Mason, *Mgr*
EMP: 4 EST: 2014
SALES (est): 123.68K Privately Held
SIC: 2821 Thermoplastic materials

(G-11750)
POLYONE CORPORATION
POLYONE CORPORATION
114 Morehead Rd (28677-2744)
PHONE...................704 838-0457
Greg Mason, *Mgr*
EMP: 4
Web: www.avient.com
SIC: 2821 Plastics materials and resins
PA: Avient Corporation
33587 Walker Rd
Avon Lake OH 44012

(G-11751)
PRATT (JET CORR) INC
Also Called: Pratt Industries USA
185 Deer Ridge Dr (28625-2502)
PHONE...................704 878-6615
Bill Lefler, *Genl Mgr*
EMP: 688
Web: www.prattindustries.com
SIC: 2653 2631 Boxes, corrugated: made
from purchased materials; Paperboard mills
HQ: Pratt (Jet Corr), Inc.
1800 Sarasota Bus Pkwy Ne
Conyers GA 30013
770 929-1300

(G-11752)
PRATT INDUSTRIES INC
185 Deer Ridge Dr (28625-2502)
PHONE...................704 878-6615
Anthony Pratt, *Brnch Mgr*

EMP: 260
Web: www.prattindustries.com
SIC: 2653 Boxes, corrugated: made from
purchased materials
PA: Pratt Industries, Inc.
4004 Smmit Blvd Ne Ste 10
Atlanta GA 30319

(G-11753)
PRECISION MINDSET PLLC
130 April Showers Ln (28677-8003)
PHONE...................704 508-1314
Ronnie Fesperman, *Prin*
EMP: 4 EST: 2015
SALES (est): 541.95K Privately Held
Web: www.precisionmindsetllc.com
SIC: 3599 Industrial machinery, nec

(G-11754)
PRINTCRAFTERS INCORPORATED
115 W Water St (28677-5250)
P.O. Box 343 (28687-0343)
PHONE...................704 873-7387
Joseph Tomlin Junior, *Pr*
Sarah Tomlin, *Sec*
EMP: 6 EST: 1949
SQ FT: 8,000
SALES (est): 166.91K Privately Held
Web: www.printcraftersnc.com
SIC: 2752 Offset printing

(G-11755)
PRO-TECH INC
1256 N Barkley Rd (28677-9726)
PHONE...................704 872-6227
Jim Sutton, *Pr*
Keith Norris, *VP*
J Christopher Sutton, *VP*
▲ EMP: 7 EST: 1975
SALES (est): 3.17MM Privately Held
Web: www.pro-techinc.com
SIC: 3625 Control equipment, electric

(G-11756)
PROEDGE PRECISION LLC
113 Hatfield Rd (28625-8999)
PHONE...................704 872-3393
Joseph Chambers, *Pr*
EMP: 20 EST: 2012
SALES (est): 4.68MM Privately Held
Web: www.proedgeprecision.com
SIC: 3599 3728 Machine shop, jobbing and
repair; Aircraft parts and equipment, nec

(G-11757)
PURINA MILLS LLC
Also Called: Purina Mills
173 Mcness Rd (28677-2742)
PHONE...................704 872-0456
John Gherty, *CEO*
EMP: 59
SALES (corp-wide): 2.89B Privately Held
Web: www.purina-mills.com
SIC: 2047 Dog and cat food
HQ: Purina Mills, Llc
555 Mryvlle Univ Dr Ste 2
Saint Louis MO 63141

(G-11758)
R GREGORY JEWELERS INC (PA)
122 W Broad St (28677-5256)
PHONE...................704 872-6669
Rick Gregory, *Pr*
Pamela Gregory, *Sec*
EMP: 10 EST: 1981
SQ FT: 4,000
SALES (est): 1.12MM
SALES (corp-wide): 1.12MM Privately
Held
Web: www.rgregoryjewelers.com

SIC: **5944** 3911 7631 Jewelry, precious stones and precious metals; Jewelry, precious metal; Jewelry repair services

(G-11759)
ROTARY CLUB STATESVILLE
318 N Center St (28677-4064)
PHONE...............................704 872-6851
Dorothy M Reep, *Prin*
EMP: 10 **EST:** 2010
SALES (est): 89.95K **Privately Held**
Web: www.statesville.com
SIC: **2711** Newspapers, publishing and printing

(G-11760)
RPM PLASTICS LLC
933 Meacham Rd (28677-2985)
PHONE...............................704 871-0518
John Hobson, *Managing Member*
Kim Lookadoo, *
EMP: 50 **EST:** 2009
SALES (est): 9.89MM **Privately Held**
SIC: **3089** 1796 5084 Injection molding of plastics; Machine moving and rigging; Industrial machinery and equipment

(G-11761)
RPM PRODUCTS INC
2301 Speedball Rd (28677-2989)
PHONE...............................704 871-0518
John R Hobson, *Pr*
EMP: 5 **EST:** 2005
SQ FT: 4,000
SALES (est): 332.22K **Privately Held**
SIC: **5047** 3089 Medical and hospital equipment; Injection molding of plastics

(G-11762)
SACKNER PRODUCTS INC
178 Orbit Rd (28677-8634)
PHONE...............................704 380-6204
Zach Tigner, *CEO*
EMP: 45 **EST:** 1966
SALES (est): 1.98MM
SALES (corp-wide): 5.15B **Publicly Held**
SIC: **3357** Fiber optic cable (insulated)
PA: Leggett & Platt, Incorporated
1 Leggett Rd
Carthage MO 64836
417 358-8131

(G-11763)
SHADOW CREEK CONSULTING INC
124 Commerce Blvd (28625-8526)
PHONE...............................716 860-7397
Karen Erickson, *Pr*
Pauly Erickson, *VP*
EMP: 20 **EST:** 2012
SALES (est): 383.98K **Privately Held**
SIC: **2899** Essential oils

(G-11764)
SHERWIN-WILLIAMS COMPANY
Also Called: Sherwin-Williams
188 Side Track Dr (28625-2543)
PHONE...............................704 881-0245
Steve Schaffer, *Brnch Mgr*
EMP: 32
SALES (corp-wide): 23.1B **Publicly Held**
Web: www.sherwin-williams.com
SIC: **2851** Paints and paint additives
PA: The Sherwin-Williams Company
101 W Prospect Ave
Cleveland OH 44115
216 566-2000

(G-11765)
SKLAR BOV SOLUTIONS INC
Also Called: Bov Solutions

1105 E Garner Bagnal Blvd (28677-6967)
PHONE...............................704 872-7277
John Scheld, *Mgr*
EMP: 12
SALES (corp-wide): 12MM **Privately Held**
Web: www.bovsolutions.com
SIC: **2844** Concentrates, perfume
PA: Sklar Bov Solutions, Inc.
3137 E 26th St
Vernon CA 90058
352 746-6731

(G-11766)
SLADE OPERATING COMPANY LLC
Also Called: Slade
2030 Simonton Rd (28625-8205)
PHONE...............................704 873-1366
Greg Raty, *Pr*
EMP: 25 **EST:** 2021
SALES (est): 2.29MM
SALES (corp-wide): 10.55MM **Privately Held**
Web: www.egcgraphite.com
SIC: **3053** 3624 2891 Gaskets; packing and sealing devices; Carbon and graphite products; Adhesives and sealants
PA: Egc Operating Company, Llc
140 Parker Ct
Chardon OH 44024
440 285-5835

(G-11767)
SOUTHEAST TUBULAR PRODUCTS INC
Also Called: Stpi
1308 Industrial Dr (28625-6249)
PHONE...............................704 883-8883
Thomas O Loftin, *
Thomas O Loftin, *
Fred H Stubblefield Junior, *VP*
Neil Loftin, *
Brenda S Loftin, *
EMP: 45 **EST:** 2000
SQ FT: 55,000
SALES (est): 9.8MM **Privately Held**
Web: www.setube.com
SIC: **3312** Tubes, steel and iron

(G-11768)
SOUTHEASTERN CONCRETE PDTS CO
2325 Salisbury Hwy (28677-1129)
P.O. Box 5188 (28687-5188)
PHONE...............................704 873-2226
Herman Hammer, *Mgr*
EMP: 51 **EST:** 2002
SALES (est): 1.67MM
SALES (corp-wide): 24.3MM **Privately Held**
SIC: **3271** 3272 Concrete block and brick; Pipe, concrete or lined with concrete
PA: Southeastern Concrete Products Company
917 Frink St
Cayce SC 29033
803 794-7363

(G-11769)
SOUTHERN DISTILLING CO LLC
Also Called: Southern Distilling Company
211 Jennings Rd (28625-9447)
PHONE...............................704 677-4069
Stacey Barger, *Managing Member*
EMP: 4 **EST:** 2021
SALES (est): 6.09MM **Privately Held**
Web: www.southerndistillingcompany.com
SIC: **2429** 2085 Barrels and barrel parts; Distilled and blended liquors

(G-11770)
SOUTHERN PRESTIGE INDUSTRIES INC
Also Called: Precision Processing System
113 Hatfield Rd (28625-8999)
PHONE...............................704 872-9524
EMP: 50
SIC: **3599** Machine and other job shop work

(G-11771)
SOUTHERN PRESTIGE INTL LLC
113 Hatfield Rd (28625-8999)
PHONE...............................704 872-9524
Jeffrey Eidson, *
James Wilson, *
EMP: 14 **EST:** 2015
SALES (est): 4.09MM **Privately Held**
Web: www.southernprestige.com
SIC: **3081** 3599 3728 Polyvinyl film and sheet ; Electrical discharge machining (EDM); Aircraft parts and equipment, nec

(G-11772)
SOUTHERN STATES COOP INC
Also Called: S S C 7912-7
2504 Davie Ave (28625-9249)
PHONE...............................704 872-6364
Roger Clement, *Mgr*
EMP: 56
SQ FT: 9,270
SALES (corp-wide): 1.71B **Privately Held**
Web: www.southernstates.com
SIC: **2048** 2873 0181 2874 Prepared feeds, nec; Nitrogenous fertilizers; Bulbs and seeds; Phosphatic fertilizers
PA: Southern States Cooperative, Incorporated
6606 W Broad St Ste B
Richmond VA 23230
804 281-1000

(G-11773)
SPECIALTY PERF LLC
228 Crawford Rd (28625-8541)
PHONE...............................704 872-9980
EMP: 6 **EST:** 2015
SALES (est): 577.05K **Privately Held**
Web: www.specialtyperforating.com
SIC: **3081** 3599 3728 Polyvinyl film and sheet ; Electrical discharge machining (EDM); Aircraft parts and equipment, nec

(G-11774)
SPEEDBALL ART PRODUCTS CO LLC
Also Called: Speedball Art Products
2301 Speedball Rd (28677-2989)
PHONE...............................800 898-7224
Walt Glazer, *CEO*
Ben Lapin, *
◆ **EMP:** 55 **EST:** 1997
SQ FT: 224,000
SALES (est): 13.73MM **Privately Held**
Web: www.speedballart.com
SIC: **3952** Artists' materials, except pencils and leads

(G-11775)
SPINTECH LLC
159 Walker Rd (28625-2535)
PHONE...............................704 885-4758
Jian Weng, *Managing Member*
EMP: 40 **EST:** 2020
SALES (est): 5MM **Privately Held**
Web: www.spintech-usa.com
SIC: **3842** Personal safety equipment

(G-11776)
STAR MILLING COMPANY
247 Commerce Blvd Unit F (28625-8564)

P.O. Box 5067 (28687-5067)
PHONE...............................704 873-9561
James T Cashion Junior, *Pr*
James T Cashion Iii, *Sec*
Julia Cashion Johnson, *Stockholder*
EMP: 5 **EST:** 1910
SQ FT: 2,000
SALES (est): 1.15MM **Privately Held**
Web: www.starmilling.com
SIC: **2048** Prepared feeds, nec

(G-11777)
STATESVILLE BRICK COMPANY
391 Brick Yard Rd (28677-9383)
P.O. Box 471 (28687-0471)
PHONE...............................704 872-4123
EMP: 75 **EST:** 1903
SALES (est): 9.03MM **Privately Held**
Web: www.statesvillebrick.com
SIC: **3251** Brick clay: common face, glazed, vitrified, or hollow

(G-11778)
STATESVILLE HIGH
474 N Center St (28677-4022)
PHONE...............................704 873-3491
Ted Millsaps, *Prin*
EMP: 4 **EST:** 2008
SALES (est): 296.75K **Privately Held**
Web: www.issnc.org
SIC: **2711** Newspapers, publishing and printing

(G-11779)
STATESVILLE LLC
151 Walker Rd (28625-2535)
PHONE...............................704 872-3303
EMP: 6 **EST:** 2018
SALES (est): 197.72K **Privately Held**
Web: www.statesvillehousing.org
SIC: **2711** Newspapers, publishing and printing

(G-11780)
STATESVILLE MED MGT SVCS LLC
1503 E Broad St (28625-4301)
PHONE...............................704 996-6748
EMP: 6 **EST:** 2011
SALES (est): 2.05MM **Privately Held**
Web: www.statesvillechamber.org
SIC: **8062** 3841 8011 General medical and surgical hospitals; Surgical and medical instruments; Medical centers

(G-11781)
STEELCRAFT STRUCTURES LLC
1841 Amity Hill Rd (28677-7203)
P.O. Box 6177 (28687-6177)
PHONE...............................980 434-5400
James Paquette, *Managing Member*
EMP: 7 **EST:** 2020
SALES (est): 2.32MM **Privately Held**
Web: www.steelcraftmetal.com
SIC: **3441** Fabricated structural metal

(G-11782)
STOVERS PRECISION TOOLING INC
239 Treebark Rd (28625-1262)
PHONE...............................704 876-3673
David Stover, *Pr*
Carla Stover, *Sec*
EMP: 6 **EST:** 1994
SALES (est): 299.49K **Privately Held**
Web: www.lrprecisiontooling.com
SIC: **3599** Machine shop, jobbing and repair

(G-11783)
SUMTER PACKAGING CORPORATION
844 Meacham Rd (28677-2982)

2025 Harris North Carolina
Manufacturers Directory
▲ = Import ▼ = Export
◆ = Import/Export

PHONE....................704 873-0583
EMP: 5
SALES (corp-wide): 13.87MM **Privately Held**
Web: www.sumterpackaging.com
SIC: 2653 Boxes, corrugated: made from purchased materials
PA: Sumter Packaging Corporation
2341 Corporate Way
Sumter SC 29154
803 481-2003

(G-11784)
T & J PANEL SYSTEMS INC
269 Marble Rd (28625-2351)
PHONE....................704 924-8600
Timothy Johnson, *Pr*
EMP: 9 EST: 1997
SALES (est): 1.15MM **Privately Held**
Web: www.tjpanel.com
SIC: 2522 Panel systems and partitions, office: except wood

(G-11785)
TALLENT WOOD WORKS
113 Kammerer Dr (28625-1651)
PHONE....................704 592-2013
EMP: 4 EST: 2017
SALES (est): 54.13K **Privately Held**
SIC: 2431 Millwork

(G-11786)
THORNEBURG HOSIERY MILLS INC
1515 W Front St (28677-3638)
P.O. Box 5399 (28687-5399)
PHONE....................704 872-6522
James L Throneburg, *Mgr*
EMP: 27
SALES (corp-wide): 20.05MM **Privately Held**
Web: www.thmills.com
SIC: 2252 Socks
PA: Throneburg Hosiery Mills, Inc.
2210 Newton Dr
Statesville NC 28677
704 872-6522

(G-11787)
THORNEBURG HOSIERY MILLS INC (PA)
Also Called: Th Mills
2210 Newton Dr (28677-4850)
P.O. Box 5399 (28687-5399)
PHONE....................704 872-6522
James L Throneburg, *CEO*
Richard Oliver Junior, *Pr*
Robert B Tucker Junior, *Sec*
◆ EMP: 131 EST: 1952
SQ FT: 85,000
SALES (est): 20.05MM
SALES (corp-wide): 20.05MM **Privately Held**
Web: www.thmills.com
SIC: 2252 Socks

(G-11788)
THORNEBURG HOSIERY MILLS INC
1519 W Front St (28677-3638)
PHONE....................704 838-6329
Richard Oliver, *Mgr*
EMP: 26
SALES (corp-wide): 20.05MM **Privately Held**
Web: www.thmills.com
SIC: 2252 2251 Socks; Women's hosiery, except socks
PA: Throneburg Hosiery Mills, Inc.
2210 Newton Dr
Statesville NC 28677
704 872-6522

(G-11789)
TIMBER SPECIALISTS INC
2123 Shelton Ave (28677-2761)
PHONE....................704 902-5146
James E Johnson, *Pr*
EMP: 8 EST: 2005
SALES (est): 247.77K **Privately Held**
SIC: 2411 Timber, cut at logging camp

(G-11790)
TIMBER SPECIALISTS LLC
2511 Heritage Cir (28625-4411)
PHONE....................704 873-5756
James Johnson, *Prin*
EMP: 10 EST: 1999
SALES (est): 982.75K **Privately Held**
SIC: 2411 Logging camps and contractors

(G-11791)
TMGCR INC
Also Called: Piedmont First Aid
1002 Winston Ave (28677-6500)
P.O. Box 5386 (28687-5386)
PHONE....................704 872-4461
TOLL FREE: 800
James A Gardner Junior, *Pr*
A James Gardner Junior, *Pr*
Brenda Gardner, *
EMP: 38 EST: 1966
SQ FT: 24,000
SALES (est): 6.03MM **Privately Held**
Web: www.carpetrentals.com
SIC: 2679 Pressed fiber and molded pulp products, except food products

(G-11792)
TOTER LLC (DH)
841 Meacham Rd (28677-2983)
P.O. Box 5338 (28687-5338)
PHONE....................800 424-0422
John Scott, *Pr*
Steve Svetik, *
◆ EMP: 47 EST: 1983
SQ FT: 200,000
SALES (est): 46.17MM **Privately Held**
Web: www.toter.com
SIC: 3089 3536 3469 3412 Garbage containers, plastics; Hoists; Metal stampings, nec; Metal barrels, drums, and pails
HQ: Wastequip, Llc
6525 Crnegie Blvd Ste 300
Charlotte NC 28211

(G-11793)
TRICK KARTS INC
Also Called: Tubular Resources
935 Shelton Ave (28677-6726)
PHONE....................704 883-0089
Mark Mode, *Pr*
EMP: 4 EST: 1975
SALES (est): 253.76K **Privately Held**
Web: www.trickolimpic.com
SIC: 3799 5531 Go-carts, except children's; Auto and home supply stores

(G-11794)
TSAI WINDDOWN INC
607 Meacham Rd (28677-2979)
PHONE....................704 873-3106
▲ EMP: 21
SIC: 2511 Wood household furniture

(G-11795)
TUBE SPECIALTIES CO INC
Also Called: PS Cisco
1401 Industrial Dr (28625-6263)
PHONE....................704 818-8933
Gerald Mckley, *Brnch Mgr*
EMP: 150

Web: www.nelsongp.com
SIC: 3498 Tube fabricating (contract bending and shaping)
HQ: Tube Specialties Co., Inc.
1459 Nw Sundial Rd
Troutdale OR 97060
503 674-8705

(G-11796)
UNITED FINISHING SYSTEMS LLC
201 United Dr (28625-1609)
PHONE....................704 873-2475
Alwyn Otho Moody Iii, *Pr*
EMP: 6 EST: 2022
SALES (est): 758.28K **Privately Held**
Web: www.unitedfinishing.net
SIC: 2851 1799 Undercoatings, paint; Coating of metal structures at construction site

(G-11797)
VANDOR CORPORATION
2301 Speedball Rd (28677-2989)
PHONE....................980 392-8107
EMP: 44
SALES (corp-wide): 25.75MM **Privately Held**
SIC: 2655 3089 Fiber cans, drums, and similar products; Air mattresses, plastics
PA: Vandor Corporation
4251 W Industries Rd
Richmond IN 47374
765 966-7676

(G-11798)
WASTEQUIP
841 Meacham Rd (28677-2983)
PHONE....................800 255-4126
EMP: 11 EST: 2018
SALES (est): 3.5MM **Privately Held**
Web: www.wastequip.com
SIC: 3559 Special industry machinery, nec

(G-11799)
WEST SIDE INDUSTRIES LLC
124 Hatfield Rd (28625-8999)
PHONE....................980 223-8665
David Gizzi, *CEO*
David Gizzi, *Admn*
EMP: 8 EST: 2013
SALES (est): 772.76K **Privately Held**
Web: www.westsideindustries.us
SIC: 3499 3451 3728 Fire- or burglary-resistive products; Screw machine products ; Aircraft parts and equipment, nec

(G-11800)
WEST SIDE PRCSION MCH PDTS INC
124 Hatfield Rd (28625-8999)
PHONE....................908 647-4903
David Gizzi, *Pr*
Joseph Petitti, *VP*
▼ EMP: 10 EST: 1944
SQ FT: 5,000
SALES (est): 505.07K **Privately Held**
Web: www.westsideindustries.us
SIC: 3599 Machine shop, jobbing and repair

(G-11801)
WINECOFF MMRALS STTESVILLE INC
Also Called: Winecoff Memorials
2120 Newton Dr (28677-4848)
PHONE....................704 873-9661
Steve Bridle, *Pr*
Elizabeth Bridle, *VP*
EMP: 9 EST: 2000
SQ FT: 6,000
SALES (est): 230.86K **Privately Held**
Web: www.winecoff.com

SIC: 5999 3281 Gravestones, finished; Tombstones, cut stone (not finishing or lettering only)

(G-11802)
WWJ LLC (PA)
Also Called: Acoustek Nonwovens
1002 Bucks Industrial Rd (28625-2581)
P.O. Box 4846 (28117-4846)
PHONE....................704 871-8500
▼ EMP: 43 EST: 1990
SQ FT: 80,000
SALES (est): 4.2MM **Privately Held**
SIC: 3296 Fiberglass insulation

(G-11803)
YANJAN USA LLC
159 Walker Rd (28625-2535)
PHONE....................704 380-6230
Jian Weng, *Pr*
Gene Konzzal, *CFO*
▲ EMP: 115 EST: 2017
SQ FT: 50,000
SALES (est): 10.18MM **Privately Held**
SIC: 2297 Nonwoven fabrics
PA: Xiamen Yanjan New Material Co.,Ltd
No.666, Houdi Road, Industrial Cluster Zone, Xiang'an District
Xiamen FJ 36119

(G-11804)
ZNDUS INC (DH)
214 James Farm Rd (28625-2714)
PHONE....................704 981-8660
James Murphy, *Pr*
EMP: 4 EST: 2019
SALES (est): 6.14MM **Privately Held**
Web: www.znd.com
SIC: 3315 Fence gates, posts, and fittings: steel
HQ: Znd Group B.V.
John F. Kennedylaan 22
Valkenswaard NB

Stedman
Cumberland County

(G-11805)
AUTRY LOGGING INC
824 Magnolia Church Rd (28391-8677)
PHONE....................910 303-4943
Jamey Autry, *Pr*
EMP: 4 EST: 2012
SALES (est): 581.77K **Privately Held**
SIC: 2411 Logging

(G-11806)
CYNTHIA SAAR
Also Called: Cardinal Cabinets Distinction
5139 Front St (28391-9603)
PHONE....................910 480-2523
Cynthia Saar, *Owner*
EMP: 4 EST: 2010
SALES (est): 219.19K **Privately Held**
SIC: 2434 5712 2521 Wood kitchen cabinets ; Customized furniture and cabinets; Wood office filing cabinets and bookcases

(G-11807)
POSH PAD
700 Mill Bay Dr (28391-8453)
PHONE....................910 988-4800
Jacqueline Alphin, *Prin*
EMP: 5 EST: 2011
SALES (est): 170K **Privately Held**
SIC: 3699 Christmas tree lighting sets, electric

(G-11808)
TARHEEL ENVIROMENTAL LLC
633 Fred Hall Rd (28391-8408)
PHONE..............................910 425-4939
EMP: 4 **EST:** 2008
SALES (est): 113.91K **Privately Held**
SIC: 2875 Compost

Stella
Carteret County

(G-11809)
WETHERINGTON LOGGING INC
245 Walters Ln (28582-9744)
PHONE..............................252 393-8435
Walter Jon, *Pr*
Dora Wetherington, *Sec*
EMP: 4 **EST:** 1975
SALES (est): 231.36K **Privately Held**
SIC: 2411 Logging camps and contractors

Stokesdale
Guilford County

(G-11810)
CULP INC
Culps Knits
7209 Us Highway 158 (27357-9344)
P.O. Box 488 (27357-0488)
PHONE..............................336 885-2800
Denise Miles, *Mgr*
EMP: 85
SALES (corp-wide): 225.33MM **Publicly Held**
Web: www.culphomefashions.com
SIC: 2515 Mattresses and bedsprings
PA: Culp, Inc.
1823 Eastchester Dr
High Point NC 27265
336 889-5161

(G-11811)
CULP INC
Also Called: Culp Ticking
7209 Us Highway 158 (27357-9344)
P.O. Box 488 (27357-0488)
PHONE..............................336 643-7751
Elena Arnold Knit, *Dir*
EMP: 172
SALES (corp-wide): 225.33MM **Publicly Held**
Web: www.culphomefashions.com
SIC: 2211 2396 Tickings; Automotive and apparel trimmings
PA: Culp, Inc.
1823 Eastchester Dr
High Point NC 27265
336 889-5161

(G-11812)
KALO FOODS LLC
Also Called: Kalo Foods
119 Carlton Park Dr (27357-8578)
PHONE..............................336 949-4802
Michael Cusato, *Pt*
EMP: 8 **EST:** 2012
SQ FT: 7,800
SALES (est): 965.67K **Privately Held**
Web: www.kalofoods.com
SIC: 2038 2053 2052 Frozen specialties, nec ; Frozen bakery products, except bread; Cookies

(G-11813)
LAMINATION SERVICES INC
6919 Us Highway 158 (27357-9341)
P.O. Box 188 (27358-0188)
PHONE..............................336 643-7369

Mark Stroud, *Pr*
EMP: 24 **EST:** 1989
SQ FT: 25,000
SALES (est): 4.67MM **Privately Held**
Web: www.laminationservicesinc.com
SIC: 3089 Plastics processing

(G-11814)
ONTEX OPERATIONS USA LLC (HQ)
Also Called: Ontex North America
9300 Nc Highway 65 (27357)
PHONE..............................770 346-9250
James Alan Skinner, *Pr*
EMP: 53 **EST:** 2020
SALES (est): 25.58MM
SALES (corp-wide): 2.67MM **Privately Held**
SIC: 2676 Feminine hygiene paper products
PA: Ontex Group
Korte Keppestraat 21
Aalst VOV 9320
53333600

(G-11815)
SOUTHERN SPRING & STAMPING
2089 Us Highway 220 (27357-8540)
PHONE..............................336 548-3520
Jeff Artz, *Mgr*
EMP: 17
SALES (corp-wide): 12MM **Privately Held**
Web: www.southernspring.com
SIC: 3469 5085 Stamping metal for the trade ; Springs
PA: Southern Spring & Stamping Inc
401 Substation Rd
Venice FL 34285
941 488-2276

(G-11816)
STONEFIELD CELLARS LLC
8220 Nc Highway 68 N (27357-9330)
PHONE..............................336 632-2391
EMP: 4 **EST:** 2009
SALES (est): 502.01K **Privately Held**
Web: www.stonefieldcellars.com
SIC: 2084 Wines

(G-11817)
VALOR BRANDS LLC
Also Called: Ontex Stokesdale
9300 Nc Highway 65 (27357-8436)
PHONE..............................678 602-9268
Yvette Cooper, *Prin*
EMP: 12
SALES (corp-wide): 3.44MM **Privately Held**
Web: www.ontex.com
SIC: 2676 Sanitary paper products
PA: Valor Brands Llc
5900 Windward Pkwy # 100
Alpharetta GA 30005
770 346-9250

(G-11818)
WOODWIZARDS INC
4214 Ellisboro Rd (27357-8053)
PHONE..............................336 427-7698
Randy Neal, *Pr*
Pamela Neal, *Sec*
EMP: 5 **EST:** 2003
SALES (est): 98.17K **Privately Held**
SIC: 2431 Woodwork, interior and ornamental, nec

Stoneville
Rockingham County

(G-11819)
AMERICAN WOODMARK CORPORATION
300 S Henry St (27048-8070)
PHONE..............................540 665-9100
EMP: 13
SALES (corp-wide): 1.85B **Publicly Held**
Web: www.americanwoodmark.com
SIC: 2434 Vanities, bathroom: wood
PA: American Woodmark Corporation
561 Shady Elm Rd
Winchester VA 22602
540 665-9100

(G-11820)
CLAYBROOK TIRE INC
101 N Glenn St (27048-8641)
P.O. Box 92 (27048-0092)
PHONE..............................336 573-3135
L Mike Claybrook, *Pr*
Jessica Reeder, *Sec*
EMP: 10 **EST:** 1946
SQ FT: 1,800
SALES (est): 752.1K **Privately Held**
Web: www.claybrooktires.com
SIC: 5531 7534 7539 Automotive tires; Tire recapping; Wheel alignment, automotive

(G-11821)
GITSUM PRECISION LLC
390 Duggins Rd (27048-8134)
PHONE..............................336 453-3998
Sara Cutlip, *CEO*
Joshua Cutlip, *VP*
EMP: 5 **EST:** 2016
SALES (est): 305.04K **Privately Held**
SIC: 3484 3483 Small arms; Ammunition, except for small arms, nec

(G-11822)
GOINS SIGNS INC
1811 Victory Hill Church Rd (27048-8058)
PHONE..............................336 427-5783
Paula Goins, *Pr*
EMP: 5 **EST:** 2001
SALES (est): 205.83K **Privately Held**
SIC: 3993 Signs and advertising specialties

(G-11823)
NEAT FEET HOSIERY INC
304 Main St (27048-7663)
P.O. Box 23 (27048-0023)
PHONE..............................336 573-2177
Branch Bobbitt, *Pr*
Josh Bobbitt, *VP*
Patricia Bobbitt, *Sec*
EMP: 4 **EST:** 1992
SQ FT: 18,000
SALES (est): 237.7K **Privately Held**
SIC: 2252 2251 Socks; Women's hosiery, except socks

(G-11824)
NORMAN E CLARK
251 Duck Rd (27048-8130)
PHONE..............................336 573-9629
Norman Clark, *Prin*
EMP: 5 **EST:** 2005
SALES (est): 130.35K **Privately Held**
SIC: 2711 Newspapers, publishing and printing

(G-11825)
PAPA LONNIES INC
154 Dogwood Rd (27048-8424)
PHONE..............................336 573-9313

James M Bragdon, *Pr*
Carl S Bragdon, *VP*
EMP: 6 **EST:** 2002
SALES (est): 80.28K **Privately Held**
SIC: 2033 Barbecue sauce: packaged in cans, jars, etc.

(G-11826)
PRESS GLASS INC (HQ)
8901 Us Highway 220 (27048-8301)
P.O. Box 938 (27048-0938)
PHONE..............................336 573-2393
Michael Lankford, *Pr*
▲ **EMP:** 49 **EST:** 1985
SQ FT: 100,000
SALES (est): 47.66MM
SALES (corp-wide): 54.26MM **Privately Held**
Web: www.pressglass.us
SIC: 3231 Insulating glass: made from purchased glass
PA: Press Glass Na, Inc.
1345 Ave Of The Amrcas Fl
New York NY 10105
212 631-3044

(G-11827)
SHELTON LOGGING & CHIPPING INC
2861 Anglin Mill Rd (27048-7824)
PHONE..............................336 548-3860
David M Shelton, *Pr*
EMP: 7 **EST:** 1996
SALES (est): 83.19K **Privately Held**
SIC: 2411 Logging camps and contractors

(G-11828)
SOUTHERN FINISHING COMPANY INC (PA)
100 W Main St (27048)
P.O. Box 888 (27048-0888)
PHONE..............................336 573-3741
Ed Brown, *Pr*
Kathy Brown, *Sec*
◆ **EMP:** 16 **EST:** 1978
SQ FT: 10,000
SALES (est): 33.32MM
SALES (corp-wide): 33.32MM **Privately Held**
Web: www.southernfinishing.com
SIC: 2499 2511 Furniture inlays (veneers); Wood household furniture

(G-11829)
STITCH-A-DOOZY
140 Salems Ln (27048-8605)
PHONE..............................336 573-2339
Marla Joyce-nelson, *Prin*
EMP: 5 **EST:** 2010
SALES (est): 56.02K **Privately Held**
SIC: 2395 Embroidery and art needlework

(G-11830)
STONEVILLE LUMBER COMPANY INC
3442 Nc Highway 135 (27048-7578)
PHONE..............................336 623-4311
James Tuttle, *Pr*
EMP: 4 **EST:** 1998
SALES (est): 253.31K **Privately Held**
SIC: 2421 Lumber: rough, sawed, or planed

(G-11831)
SUTHERLAND PRODUCTS INC
Also Called: Charlie's Soap
301 S Henry St (27048)
P.O. Box 13 (27048)
PHONE..............................800 854-3541
Charles Sutherland Junior, *CEO*
C Taylor Sutherland, *VP*
▼ **EMP:** 17 **EST:** 1976

SQ FT: 5,500
SALES (est): 5.01MM **Privately Held**
Web: www.charliesoap.com
SIC: 2842 5169 Cleaning or polishing preparations, nec; Specialty cleaning and sanitation preparations

(G-11832)
TIGERTEK INDUSTRIAL SVCS LLC
Also Called: Tigertek Industrial Services
2741 Nc Highway 135 (27048-7570)
P.O. Box 5097 (27289-5097)
PHONE.............................336 623-1717
Hadi Sayess, *CEO*
EMP: 40 **EST:** 1983
SQ FT: 12,000
SALES (est): 4.34MM
SALES (corp-wide): 4.34MM **Privately Held**
Web: www.tigertek.com
SIC: 7694 3599 Electric motor repair; Machine shop, jobbing and repair
PA: Omninvest, Llc
4213 Abernathy Pl
Harrisburg NC 28075
336 623-1717

Stony Point
Alexander County

(G-11833)
EDDIES WELDING INC
213 Halyburton Rd (28678-9243)
PHONE.............................704 585-2024
Eddie Dillinger, *Prin*
EMP: 7 **EST:** 1994
SQ FT: 7,750
SALES (est): 922K **Privately Held**
Web: www.ewifab.com
SIC: 7692 Welding repair

Summerfield
Guilford County

(G-11834)
A STITCH TO REMEMBER
7621 Whitaker Dr (27358-9369)
PHONE.............................336 202-0026
Yigael Gavish, *Prin*
EMP: 5 **EST:** 2010
SALES (est): 47.39K **Privately Held**
SIC: 2395 Embroidery and art needlework

(G-11835)
ADPRESS PRINTING INCORPORATED
Also Called: Ad Press Printing
7000 Morganshire Ct (27358-7804)
PHONE.............................336 294-2244
Larry Swaney, *Pr*
Carl Swaney, *Sec*
EMP: 9 **EST:** 1986
SQ FT: 3,000
SALES (est): 971.42K **Privately Held**
Web: www.adpressprinting.com
SIC: 2752 2789 Offset printing; Bookbinding and related work

(G-11836)
CEMCO PARTITIONS INC
5340 Us Highway 220 N (27358-9727)
P.O. Box 839 (27358-0839)
PHONE.............................336 643-6316
Larry D Guinn, *Pr*
Marilyn Guinn, *Sec*
Brian Guinn, *VP*
EMP: 5 **EST:** 1971
SQ FT: 12,000

SALES (est): 503.63K **Privately Held**
Web: www.cemcopartitions.com
SIC: 2542 Partitions for floor attachment, prefabricated: except wood

(G-11837)
CURIOUS DISCOVERIES INC
7911 Windspray Dr (27358-9715)
PHONE.............................336 643-0432
Jane Hawthorne, *Pr*
Michael Hawthorne, *Sec*
EMP: 4 **EST:** 1995
SALES (est): 225K **Privately Held**
SIC: 3944 Board games, puzzles, and models, except electronic

(G-11838)
DOVE MEDICAL SUPPLY LLC
8164 Mabe Marshall Rd Bldg 2 (27358-9225)
PHONE.............................336 643-9367
Tammy Bridges, *CEO*
EMP: 32 **EST:** 2013
SALES (est): 7.75MM **Privately Held**
Web: www.mydovestore.com
SIC: 3069 5047 3821 Laboratory sundries: cases, covers, funnels, cups, etc.; Medical and hospital equipment; Laboratory apparatus and furniture

(G-11839)
EM2 MACHINE CORP
7939 Highfill Rd (27358-9707)
PHONE.............................336 297-4110
Vince Simmons, *Pr*
Tana Simmons, *Sec*
EMP: 5 **EST:** 2005
SALES (est): 899K **Privately Held**
SIC: 3545 Machine tool accessories

(G-11840)
FRED L BROWN
2913 Pleasant Ridge Rd (27358-9094)
PHONE.............................336 643-7523
Fred L Brown, *Owner*
EMP: 5 **EST:** 2010
SALES (est): 303.68K **Privately Held**
SIC: 3571 7379 Electronic computers; Computer related consulting services

(G-11841)
LOGO WEAR GRAPHICS LLC
300 Norman Farm Rd (27358-9525)
PHONE.............................336 382-0455
Angela Scott, *Managing Member*
EMP: 10 **EST:** 2010
SALES (est): 132.08K **Privately Held**
Web: www.logoweargraphics.com
SIC: 7336 2759 Graphic arts and related design; Letterpress and screen printing

(G-11842)
LONG ASP PAV TRCKG OF GRNSBURG
4349 Us Highway 220 N (27358-9401)
PHONE.............................336 643-4121
James Long, *Pr*
EMP: 6 **EST:** 1983
SALES (est): 257.4K **Privately Held**
Web: www.asphaltpavingofgso.com
SIC: 4212 2951 1771 1611 Dump truck haulage; Asphalt paving mixtures and blocks; Concrete work; Highway and street construction

(G-11843)
M & M TIRE AND AUTO INC
5570 Spotswood Cir (27358-9805)
P.O. Box 625 (27358-0625)
PHONE.............................336 643-7877

Mark Middleton, *Pr*
EMP: 6 **EST:** 1989
SALES (est): 414.09K **Privately Held**
Web: www.mmtiresummerfield.com
SIC: 5531 7534 Automotive tires; Tire retreading and repair shops

(G-11844)
MERCHANT 1 MANUFACTURING LLC
200 Starview Ln (27358-9606)
PHONE.............................336 617-3008
Clarence Lawrence, *Brnch Mgr*
EMP: 4
SALES (corp-wide): 1.42MM **Privately Held**
Web: www.merchant1manufacturing.com
SIC: 3499 7389 Nozzles, spray: aerosol, paint, or insecticide; Business services, nec
PA: Merchant 1 Manufacturing Llc
1203 Freeway Dr
Reidsville NC 27320
336 580-1873

(G-11845)
PACKAGING PLUS NORTH CAROLINA
8301 Sangor Dr (27358-9732)
PHONE.............................336 643-4097
Robert Wray, *Owner*
EMP: 10 **EST:** 1999
SALES (est): 87.79K **Privately Held**
SIC: 3053 Packing materials

Sunbury
Gates County

(G-11846)
CLASSIC STEEL BUILDINGS INC
530 Folly Rd (27979-9412)
PHONE.............................252 465-4184
Calvin R Eason, *Pr*
EMP: 6 **EST:** 2006
SALES (est): 820.51K **Privately Held**
SIC: 3448 Buildings, portable: prefabricated metal

(G-11847)
GEORGE P GATLING LOGGING
223 Nc Highway 32 S (27979-9545)
PHONE.............................252 465-8983
George P Gatling, *Owner*
EMP: 9 **EST:** 1977
SALES (est): 95.51K **Privately Held**
SIC: 2411 Logging

(G-11848)
HOFLER H S & SONS LUMBER CO
577 Nc Highway 32 N (27979-9418)
P.O. Box 130 (27979-0130)
PHONE.............................252 465-8603
James M Hofler, *Pr*
Bernard S Hofler Junior, *Sec*
James M Hofler, *Treas*
EMP: 4 **EST:** 1960
SQ FT: 570
SALES (est): 213.7K **Privately Held**
SIC: 2421 2426 Lumber: rough, sawed, or planed; Hardwood dimension and flooring mills

(G-11849)
HOFLER LOGGING INC
491 Nc Highway 32 S (27979-9550)
PHONE.............................252 465-8921
Charles T Hofler, *Pr*
Thomas Hofler, *VP*
Barbara Hofler, *Sec*
EMP: 9 **EST:** 1935
SALES (est): 365.15K **Privately Held**

SIC: 2411 Logging camps and contractors

Sunset Beach
Brunswick County

(G-11850)
HOME ELEVATORS & LIFT PDTS LLC
Also Called: Home Elevators & Lift
8311 Ocean Hwy W (28468-6118)
PHONE.............................910 427-0006
EMP: 20 **EST:** 2016
SQ FT: 8,000
SALES (est): 4.34MM **Privately Held**
Web: www.homeelevatorsandlift.com
SIC: 3534 1796 Elevators and equipment; Elevator installation and conversion

(G-11851)
MEDICAL SPCLTIES OF CRLNAS INC
565 Meadow Ridge (28468)
P.O. Box 6837 (28469-0837)
PHONE.............................910 575-4542
James W Hardie, *Pr*
EMP: 5 **EST:** 1998
SQ FT: 2,333
SALES (est): 248.52K **Privately Held**
SIC: 3842 Surgical appliances and supplies

(G-11852)
ROD JAHNER
157 Crooked Gulley Cir (28468-4438)
PHONE.............................919 435-7580
Rod Jahner, *Prin*
EMP: 4 **EST:** 2016
SALES (est): 50.37K **Privately Held**
Web: www.justrodbooks.com
SIC: 2741 Miscellaneous publishing

(G-11853)
WOOD WORKS
9040 Forest Dr Sw (28468-5020)
PHONE.............................910 579-1487
Kevin Scott, *Prin*
EMP: 5 **EST:** 2015
SALES (est): 105.11K **Privately Held**
SIC: 2431 Millwork

Supply
Brunswick County

(G-11854)
A-1 HITCH & TRAILORS SALES INC
360 Ocean Hwy E (28462-3348)
PHONE.............................910 755-6025
Don Carson, *Pr*
Cheryl Winans, *Sec*
EMP: 5 **EST:** 1996
SQ FT: 300
SALES (est): 490.5K **Privately Held**
Web: www.a1hitchandtrailers.com
SIC: 3799 5599 5013 Trailers and trailer equipment; Utility trailers; Trailer parts and accessories

(G-11855)
BCAC HOLDINGS LLC
Also Called: Brunswick Cabinets Countertops
674 Ocean Hwy W (28462-4048)
PHONE.............................910 754-5689
Chris Gibson, *Mgr*
Todd Stancombe, *Mgr*
EMP: 6 **EST:** 2019
SALES (est): 256.94K **Privately Held**
Web: www.brunswickcabinetsandcountertops.com
SIC: 2434 Wood kitchen cabinets

(G-11856)
CAROLINA PRTG WILMINGTON INC
2790 Sea Vista Dr Sw (28462-5612)
PHONE..............................910 762-2453
Kenneth Kalaher, *Owner*
EMP: 4 **EST:** 1995
SALES (est): 187.82K **Privately Held**
Web: www.printingwilmingtonnc.com
SIC: 2752 Offset printing

(G-11857)
PRECISION TIME SYSTEMS INC
959 Little Macedonia Rd Nw (28462-3749)
P.O. Box 171 (28422-0171)
PHONE..............................910 253-9850
Michael Costabile, *Pr*
▲ **EMP:** 4 **EST:** 1993
SALES (est): 764.96K **Privately Held**
Web: www.precisiontime.com
SIC: 3613 Time switches, electrical
switchgear apparatus

(G-11858)
S & S TRAWL SHOP INC
896 Stanbury Rd Sw (28462-6024)
P.O. Box 789 (28462-0789)
PHONE..............................910 842-9197
Steve Parrish, *Pr*
Sabrina Parrish, *Sec*
Henry Steven Parrish Junior, *VP*
EMP: 4 **EST:** 1980
SQ FT: 1,800
SALES (est): 242.22K **Privately Held**
SIC: 2399 5091 Fishing nets; Fishing
equipment and supplies

(G-11859)
SIGN SHOPPE INC
782 Ocean Hwy W (28462-4056)
P.O. Box 1037 (28462-1037)
PHONE..............................910 754-5144
Jerome Munna, *Prin*
EMP: 4 **EST:** 1987
SQ FT: 5,000
SALES (est): 208.75K **Privately Held**
Web: www.signshoppe.org
SIC: 3993 Signs and advertising specialties

(G-11860)
STUMP LOGGING
61 Supply St Se (28462-3367)
PHONE..............................910 620-7000
Tonia Twigg, *Prin*
EMP: 6 **EST:** 2016
SALES (est): 143.34K **Privately Held**
SIC: 2411 Logging

(G-11861)
TRADEMARK LANDSCAPE GROUP INC
Also Called: Trademark Ldscp Cntg Trdmark
O
360 Ocean Hwy E (28462-3348)
PHONE..............................910 253-0560
Tracy Dale Wheeler, *CEO*
EMP: 11 **EST:** 1999
SALES (est): 669.64K **Privately Held**
Web: www.trademarklandscaping.biz
SIC: 8741 3271 1629 Construction
management; Blocks, concrete: landscape
or retaining wall; Irrigation system
construction

Surf City
Onslow County

(G-11862)
DAILY GRIND LLC
114 N Topsail Dr (28445-6718)

P.O. Box 2519 (28445-0028)
PHONE..............................910 541-0471
Margaret Hutchison Allan, *Mgr*
EMP: 9 **EST:** 2011
SALES (est): 1.99MM **Privately Held**
Web: www.dailygrindsurfcity.com
SIC: 3599 Grinding castings for the trade

(G-11863)
SALTY TURTLE BEER COMPANY
103 Triton Ln (28445-6923)
PHONE..............................910 803-2019
Dan Callander, *Pr*
EMP: 20 **EST:** 2017
SALES (est): 524.07K **Privately Held**
Web: www.saltyturtlebeer.com
SIC: 5813 2082 5181 Bars and lounges;
Beer (alcoholic beverage); Beer and ale

Swannanoa
Buncombe County

(G-11864)
APPALACHIAN TOOL & MACHINE INC
121 Lytle Cove Rd (28778-3702)
PHONE..............................828 669-0142
Grace Frizsell, *Pr*
Ed Frizsell, *VP*
EMP: 20 **EST:** 1990
SQ FT: 10,000
SALES (est): 2.2MM **Privately Held**
Web: www.appalachiantool.com
SIC: 3599 Custom machinery

(G-11865)
AVADIM HOLDINGS INC (PA)
Also Called: Avadim Health
4 Old Patton Cove Rd (28778)
PHONE..............................877 677-2723
Keith Daniels, *CEO*
EMP: 25 **EST:** 2021
SALES (est): 24.62MM
SALES (corp-wide): 24.62MM **Privately Held**
Web: www.avadimhealth.com
SIC: 2834 Medicines, capsuled or ampuled

(G-11866)
B V HEDRICK GRAVEL & SAND CO
Also Called: Grove Stone & Sand
Old Us 70 (28778)
P.O. Box 425 (28778-0425)
PHONE..............................828 686-3844
Robert Graham, *Mgr*
EMP: 142
SALES (corp-wide): 238.17MM **Privately Held**
Web: www.hedrickind.com
SIC: 1429 1442 Igneus rock, crushed and
broken-quarrying; Construction sand and
gravel
PA: B. V. Hedrick Gravel & Sand Company
120 1/2 Church St
Salisbury NC 28144
704 633-5982

(G-11867)
CAROLINA CONCRETE MATERIALS
650 Old Us 70 Hwy (28778-2645)
PHONE..............................828 686-3040
Beth Wilson, *Pr*
Emmett Wilson, *Sec*
EMP: 8 **EST:** 1979
SQ FT: 250
SALES (est): 125.67K **Privately Held**
Web: www.carolinareadymixinc.com
SIC: 3273 Ready-mixed concrete

(G-11868)
CAROLINA READY MIX & BUILD (PA)
606 Old Us 70 Hwy (28778-2645)
PHONE..............................828 686-3041
Mark Mcmeans, *Prin*
EMP: 5 **EST:** 2008
SALES (est): 4.61MM
SALES (corp-wide): 4.61MM **Privately Held**
Web: www.carolinareadymixinc.com
SIC: 3273 Ready-mixed concrete

(G-11869)
COSMETIC CREATIONS INC
107 W Buckeye Rd (28778-2747)
PHONE..............................828 298-4625
Carolyn S Capps, *Pr*
David M Capps, *Sec*
EMP: 8 **EST:** 2014
SALES (est): 192.03K **Privately Held**
SIC: 2844 5122 Perfumes, cosmetics and
other toilet preparations; Cosmetics

(G-11870)
CUMBERLAND GRAV & SAND MIN CO (PA)
Also Called: Piedmont Sand
Old Us Highway 70 (28778)
PHONE..............................828 686-3844
Jeffrey V Goodman, *Pr*
Charles E Brady, *Ch Bd*
Don Hensley, *VP*
EMP: 10 **EST:** 1949
SQ FT: 3,000
SALES (est): 2.83MM
SALES (corp-wide): 2.83MM **Privately Held**
Web: www.hedrickind.com
SIC: 1442 Common sand mining

(G-11871)
GARNER WOODWORKS LLC
304 Patton Hill Rd (28778-2470)
P.O. Box 868 (28778-0868)
PHONE..............................828 775-1790
Micdalia Cairns, *Managing Member*
EMP: 4 **EST:** 2002
SALES (est): 245.51K **Privately Held**
Web: www.garnerwoodworks.com
SIC: 2431 Millwork

(G-11872)
JBS2 INC
Also Called: National Wiper Alliance
875 Warren Wilson Rd (28778-2039)
P.O. Box 367 (28778-0367)
PHONE..............................828 236-1300
Jeff Slosman, *Pr*
◆ **EMP:** 75 **EST:** 1996
SQ FT: 110,000
SALES (est): 47.68MM
SALES (corp-wide): 15.32B **Publicly Held**
Web: www.nationalwiper.com
SIC: 2392 Towels, dishcloths and dust cloths
PA: Ecolab Inc.
1 Ecolab Pl
Saint Paul MN 55102
800 232-6522

(G-11873)
MIXX-POINT 5 PROJECT LLC
Also Called: Mixx Pt 5
107 W Buckeye Rd (28778-2747)
PHONE..............................858 298-4625
Tom Dawson, *Prin*
Michele Dawson, *Prin*
EMP: 6 **EST:** 2021
SALES (est): 222.93K **Privately Held**
SIC: 2834 Pharmaceutical preparations

(G-11874)
NONWOVENS OF AMERICA INC
Also Called: Noa
875 Warren Wilson Rd (28778-2039)
P.O. Box 367 (28778-0367)
PHONE..............................828 236-1300
Jeffrey Slosman, *Pr*
EMP: 4 **EST:** 2012
SQ FT: 200,000
SALES (est): 237.92K **Privately Held**
Web: www.nationalwiper.com
SIC: 2679 Insulating paper: batts, fills, and
blankets

(G-11875)
ONIXX MANUFACTURING LLC
107 W Buckeye Rd (28778-2747)
PHONE..............................828 298-4625
EMP: 5
SALES (est): 229.77K **Privately Held**
SIC: 2844 Cosmetic preparations

(G-11876)
REDTAIL GROUP LLC
2131 Us 70 Hwy Unit C (28778-9201)
P.O. Box 1188 (28778-1188)
PHONE..............................828 539-4700
EMP: 5 **EST:** 2022
SALES (est): 1.09MM **Privately Held**
Web: www.redtailwire.com
SIC: 3496 Barbed wire, made from
purchased wire

(G-11877)
RISE OVER RUN INC (PA)
2131 Us 70 Hwy Unit C (28778-9201)
PHONE..............................303 819-1566
Ryan Brazell, *Pr*
EMP: 6 **EST:** 2017
SALES (est): 301.13K
SALES (corp-wide): 301.13K **Privately Held**
SIC: 2084 Wines

(G-11878)
SOUTHEASTERN HARDWOODS INC
Also Called: Bee Tree Hardwoods
734 Bee Tree Rd (28778-3403)
PHONE..............................828 581-0197
Phillip Long, *Pr*
EMP: 5 **EST:** 2003
SQ FT: 400
SALES (est): 452.18K **Privately Held**
Web: www.beetreehardwoods.com
SIC: 2421 5211 Kiln drying of lumber;
Lumber products

(G-11879)
WRIGHT MACHINE & TOOL CO INC
101 Jims Branch Rd (28778-3604)
PHONE..............................828 298-8440
Doris Wright, *Sec*
Frank A Wright, *
David Thomas, *
◆ **EMP:** 50 **EST:** 1970
SQ FT: 100,000
SALES (est): 3.78MM **Privately Held**
Web: www.wrightmachtool.com
SIC: 3599 3544 Machine shop, jobbing and
repair; Special dies and tools

Swanquarter
Hyde County

(G-11880)
MATTAMUSKEET SEAFOOD INC
24694 Us Highway 264 (27885-9536)
PHONE..............................252 926-2431
Robert Eugene Carawan, *Pr*

▲ = Import ▼ = Export
◆ = Import/Export

Gary Mayo, *
Patty Jarvis, *
Charles Carawan, *
EMP: 100 **EST:** 1984
SQ FT: 5,000
SALES (est): 914.36K **Privately Held**
Web: www.mattamuskeetseafoodnc.com
SIC: 2091 Bouillon, clam: packaged in cans, jars, etc.

(G-11881)
PAMLICO SHORES INC
14166 Us Highway 264 (27885-9661)
P.O. Box 218 (27824-0218)
PHONE....................252 926-0011
Hunter Gibbs, *Pr*
EMP: 40 **EST:** 2012
SALES (est): 3.68MM **Privately Held**
Web: www.pamlicoshores.com
SIC: 2499 Food handling and processing products, wood

Swansboro
Onslow County

(G-11882)
CAROLINA CABINETS OF CEDAR PT
136 Vfw Rd (28584-8085)
PHONE....................252 393-6236
Paul Westmeier, *Owner*
EMP: 4 **EST:** 2003
SALES (est): 249.58K **Privately Held**
Web: www.carolina-cabinets.com
SIC: 2434 Wood kitchen cabinets

(G-11883)
CARTERET PUBLISHING COMPANY
Also Called: Tideland News
774 W Corbett Ave (28584-8452)
P.O. Box 1000 (28584-1000)
PHONE....................910 326-5066
Jimmy Williams, *Mgr*
EMP: 6
SALES (corp-wide): 2.17MM **Privately Held**
Web: www.carolinacoastonline.com
SIC: 2711 Commercial printing and newspaper publishing combined
PA: Carteret Publishing Company
5039 Executive Dr Ste 300
Morehead City NC 28557
252 726-7081

(G-11884)
DEVILS KINDRED MC
310 S Chestnut St (28584-9538)
PHONE....................336 712-7689
James F Killian, *VP*
James F Killian, *VP*
EMP: 20 **EST:** 2016
SALES (est): 335.75K **Privately Held**
SIC: 3751 Motorcycles, bicycles and parts

(G-11885)
HIGH SPEED GEAR INC
Also Called: H S G
87 Old Hammock Rd (28584-8661)
P.O. Box 940 (28584-0940)
PHONE....................910 325-1000
Gene Higdon, *Ch*
Becky Higdon, *Pr*
EMP: 11 **EST:** 1999
SQ FT: 6,000
SALES (est): 5.67MM **Privately Held**
Web: www.highspeedgear.com
SIC: 2824 Nylon fibers

(G-11886)
HSG LLC (PA)
Also Called: Comp-TAC Operations
87 Old Hammock Rd (28584-8661)
PHONE....................910 325-1000
Matthew Gadams, *CEO*
Gary R Langford, *CFO*
EMP: 100 **EST:** 2012
SALES (est): 2.98MM
SALES (corp-wide): 2.98MM **Privately Held**
SIC: 3489 Guns, howitzers, mortars, and related equipment

(G-11887)
NC STEEL SERVICES INC
141 Seth Thomas Ln (28584-8538)
PHONE....................252 393-7888
Maria Parrish, *Pr*
Mark Parrish, *VP*
EMP: 10 **EST:** 2004
SQ FT: 40,000
SALES (est): 995.77K **Privately Held**
Web: www.ncsteelservicesinc.com
SIC: 3441 Fabricated structural metal

(G-11888)
OPTOMETRIC EYECARE CENTER INC
775 W Corbett Ave (28584-8562)
PHONE....................910 326-3050
Tina Siegel, *Pr*
EMP: 8 **EST:** 1996
SALES (est): 220.27K **Privately Held**
Web: www.eyecarecenter.com
SIC: 3211 Optical glass, flat

Swepsonville
Alamance County

(G-11889)
AMERICAN HONDA MOTOR CO INC
3721 Nc Hwy 119 (27359)
PHONE....................336 578-6300
Hiroki Chubachi, *Mgr*
EMP: 335
Web: www.honda.com
SIC: 3524 Lawn and garden mowers and accessories
HQ: American Honda Motor Co., Inc.
1919 Torrance Blvd
Torrance CA 90501
310 783-2000

Sylva
Jackson County

(G-11890)
BILLET SPEED INC
488 Fairview Rd (28779-9099)
PHONE....................828 226-8127
Matt Welsh, *Pr*
EMP: 4 **EST:** 2016
SALES (est): 152.64K **Privately Held**
Web: www.billet-speed.com
SIC: 3714 Motor vehicle parts and accessories

(G-11891)
DECOR GLASS SPECIALTIES INC
Also Called: Decor Glass
61 Timber Creek Cir (28779-5757)
PHONE....................828 586-8180
Thomas Grant Junior, *Pr*
Thomas A Grant Junior, *Pr*
EMP: 4 **EST:** 2008
SQ FT: 1,500

SALES (est): 460.58K **Privately Held**
Web: www.decorglassinc.com
SIC: 5231 3229 1793 Glass; Glass furnishings and accessories; Glass and glazing work

(G-11892)
GRAY WOLF LOG HOMES INC
538 Big Oak Springs Rd (28779-1223)
P.O. Box 636 (28725-0636)
PHONE....................828 586-4662
Larry Phillips, *Pr*
Pat Phillips, *Park Ranger*
EMP: 5 **EST:** 1992
SALES (est): 395.41K **Privately Held**
SIC: 2452 Log cabins, prefabricated, wood

(G-11893)
INNOVATION BREWING LLC
414 W Main St (28779-5548)
PHONE....................828 586-9678
Charles Owen, *Prin*
EMP: 7 **EST:** 2013
SALES (est): 979.65K **Privately Held**
Web: www.innovation-brewing.com
SIC: 5813 2082 Bars and lounges; Ale (alcoholic beverage)

(G-11894)
JACKSON PAPER MANUFACTURING CO (PA)
152 W Main St (28779-2928)
P.O. Box 667 (28779-0667)
PHONE....................828 586-5534
Tim Campbell, *CEO*
Nicki Slusser, *
Tim Campbell, *VP*
Jeff Murphy, *
Tammy Francis, *
▲ **EMP:** 41 **EST:** 1994
SALES (est): 102.27MM **Privately Held**
Web: www.jacksonpaper.net
SIC: 2621 Paper mills

(G-11895)
LBM INDUSTRIES INC
Also Called: Mc Neely's Store Rental & Eqpt
21 E Hall Hts (28779-2800)
PHONE....................828 631-1227
Luke Fisher, *Brnch Mgr*
EMP: 5
SALES (corp-wide): 18.35MM **Privately Held**
Web: www.mcneelycompanies.com
SIC: 1411 Dimension stone
PA: Lbm Industries, Inc.
2000 Whitewater Rd
Sapphire NC 28774
828 966-4270

(G-11896)
LUCY IN RYE LLC
612 W Main St (28779-5449)
PHONE....................828 586-4601
Constantinos Mitsides, *Mgr*
EMP: 4 **EST:** 2020
SALES (est): 483.35K **Privately Held**
SIC: 2099 Food preparations, nec

(G-11897)
Q C APPAREL INC
330 Scotts Creek Rd (28779-5237)
PHONE....................828 586-5663
Clemmey Queen, *Pr*
Carley Queen, *Sec*
▲ **EMP:** 5 **EST:** 1993
SQ FT: 70,000
SALES (est): 124.54K **Privately Held**
SIC: 2392 Household furnishings, nec

(G-11898)
QUARTZ MATRIX LLC
283 Winding Ridge Dr (28779-7616)
PHONE....................828 631-3207
Ofelia C Balta, *Prin*
EMP: 6 **EST:** 2012
SALES (est): 184.87K **Privately Held**
Web: www.quartzmatrixllc.com
SIC: 3599 Machine shop, jobbing and repair

(G-11899)
SOUTHERN CONCRETE MTLS INC
1362 W Main St (28779-5213)
PHONE....................828 586-5280
Ken Ewary, *Mgr*
EMP: 10
SALES (corp-wide): 238.17MM **Privately Held**
Web: www.scmusa.com
SIC: 3273 Ready-mixed concrete
HQ: Southern Concrete Materials, Inc.
35 Meadow Rd
Asheville NC 28803
828 253-6421

(G-11900)
SYLVA HERALD AND RURALITE
Also Called: Sylva Herald, The
539 W Main St (28779-5551)
P.O. Box 307 (28779-0307)
PHONE....................828 586-2611
Steve Gray, *Pr*
James A Gray, *VP*
EMP: 9 **EST:** 1926
SQ FT: 5,000
SALES (est): 475.4K **Privately Held**
Web: www.thesylvaherald.com
SIC: 2711 2752 Newspapers, publishing and printing; Commercial printing, lithographic

(G-11901)
SYLVA HERALD PUBG CO INCTHE
539 W Main St (28779-5551)
P.O. Box 307 (28779-0307)
PHONE....................828 586-2611
James A Gray Junior, *VP*
EMP: 10 **EST:** 2012
SALES (est): 1.08MM **Privately Held**
Web: www.thesylvaherald.com
SIC: 2711 Newspapers, publishing and printing

(G-11902)
T & S HARDWOODS INC
3635 Skyland Dr (28779-8359)
P.O. Box 1233 (31059-1233)
PHONE....................828 586-4044
Jack Swanner, *Mgr*
EMP: 90
SALES (corp-wide): 19.88MM **Privately Held**
Web: www.tshardwoods.com
SIC: 2421 2426 Lumber: rough, sawed, or planed; Hardwood dimension and flooring mills
PA: T & S Hardwoods, Inc.
293 Harrisburg Rd Sw
Milledgeville GA 31061
478 454-3400

(G-11903)
VISTA TRANQUILA PUBLISHERS LLC
53 Lands End Dr (28779-7037)
PHONE....................828 586-8401
Kimberly Mathis Pitts, *Prin*
EMP: 4 **EST:** 2019
SALES (est): 77.96K **Privately Held**
Web: www.vistatranquila.com
SIC: 2741 Miscellaneous publishing

(G-11904)
WEBSTER ENTPS JACKSON CNTY INC
140 Little Savannah Rd (28779-6852)
P.O. Box 220 (28788-0220)
PHONE.................................828 586-8981
Bob Cochran, *Treas*
EMP: 6 **EST:** 1976
SQ FT: 18,000
SALES (est): 2MM **Privately Held**
Web: www.websterenterprises.org
SIC: 3841 8331 Surgical and medical instruments; Skill training center

(G-11905)
WNC WHITE CORPORATION
Also Called: Industrial Construction
3563 Skyland Dr (28779-6146)
P.O. Box 630 (28779-0630)
PHONE.................................828 477-4895
Greg White, *CEO*
Greg White, *Pr*
Andy White, *VP*
EMP: 20 **EST:** 2007
SQ FT: 3,000
SALES (est): 4.28MM **Privately Held**
Web: www.wncwhitecorporation.com
SIC: 1629 1623 3443 Industrial plant construction; Water and sewer line construction; Fabricated plate work (boiler shop)

Tabor City
Columbus County

(G-11906)
ATLANTIC AUTOMOTIVE ENTPS LLC
Also Called: Atlantic Enterprises
1007 Pireway Rd Ste B (28463-9457)
PHONE.................................910 377-4108
Maria Treece, *Managing Member*
▲ **EMP:** 7 **EST:** 2002
SQ FT: 45,000
SALES (est): 1.07MM **Privately Held**
SIC: 3089 Automotive parts, plastic

(G-11907)
BYRON DALE SPIVEY
2009 Reynolds Rd (28463-7385)
PHONE.................................910 653-3128
Byron Dale Spivey, *Prin*
EMP: 4 **EST:** 2011
SALES (est): 76.79K **Privately Held**
Web: www.shamrockboxers.com
SIC: 3861 Tanks, photographic developing, fixing, and washing

(G-11908)
CAROLINA PACKING HOUSE SUPS
305 Green Sea Rd (28463-2499)
PHONE.................................910 653-3438
Paul Hathaway, *Pr*
EMP: 5 **EST:** 1954
SQ FT: 6,000
SALES (est): 345.04K **Privately Held**
SIC: 3556 Packing house machinery

(G-11909)
DOWN SOUTH LOGGING LLC
121 Lake Tabor Dr (28463-2268)
PHONE.................................843 333-1649
Steven Wayne Stanley, *Prin*
EMP: 4 **EST:** 2014
SALES (est): 418.45K **Privately Held**
SIC: 2411 Logging camps and contractors

(G-11910)
E A DUNCAN CNSTR CO INC
1475 Savannah Rd (28463-9156)
PHONE.................................910 653-3535
Edgar A Duncan, *Pr*
EMP: 4 **EST:** 2000
SALES (est): 1.14MM **Privately Held**
Web: www.eaduncanconstruction.com
SIC: 1521 3448 New construction, single-family houses; Prefabricated metal buildings and components

(G-11911)
FILTEC PRECISE INC
218 N Us Highway 701 Byp (28463-2238)
P.O. Box 755 (28463-0755)
PHONE.................................910 653-5200
James Bailey, *Pr*
Dieter Vande Kamp, *
▲ **EMP:** 40 **EST:** 1989
SQ FT: 48,000
SALES (est): 4.79MM
SALES (corp-wide): 19MM **Privately Held**
Web: www.filtec-precise.com
SIC: 2281 Yarn spinning mills
PA: Filament-Technik Gesellschaft Fur Technische Garne Mbh & Cie. Kg Hermann-Hollerith-Str. 13 Baesweiler NW 52499 240 193-3000

(G-11912)
KRS PLASTICS INC
26 Tabor Industrial Park Rd (28463)
P.O. Box 693 (28463-0693)
PHONE.................................910 653-3602
Billy Douglas, *Pr*
Charles Balkcum, *VP*
Lindsey Smith, *VP*
EMP: 15 **EST:** 1982
SQ FT: 9,000
SALES (est): 2.06MM **Privately Held**
Web: www.krsplastics.com
SIC: 3081 Vinyl film and sheet

(G-11913)
MILLIGAN HOUSE MOVERS INC (PA)
2115 Swamp Fox Hwy E (28463-7451)
PHONE.................................910 653-2272
Patrick Milligan, *Pr*
Charles Milligan, *Sec*
EMP: 4 **EST:** 1968
SALES (est): 386.86K **Privately Held**
Web: www.milliganhousemovers.com
SIC: 1799 3448 4212 Building mover, including houses; Prefabricated metal buildings and components; Moving services

(G-11914)
SMITHS LOGGING
13169 Swamp Fox Hwy E (28463-9166)
PHONE.................................910 653-4422
Leo Smith, *Owner*
EMP: 4 **EST:** 1984
SALES (est): 218.71K **Privately Held**
SIC: 2411 Logging camps and contractors

(G-11915)
TABOR CITY LUMBER COMPANY (PA)
510 N Main St (28463-8500)
P.O. Box 37 (28463-0037)
PHONE.................................910 653-3162
Roderick D Sanders, *Pr*
Daniel M Sanders, *
Anne M Sanders, *
EMP: 25 **EST:** 1946
SALES (est): 1.78MM
SALES (corp-wide): 1.78MM **Privately Held**
Web: www.taborcitylumber.com

SIC: 5031 2421 Lumber: rough, dressed, and finished; Lumber: rough, sawed, or planed

(G-11916)
TWIGS SCREEN PRINTING
5474 Sidney Cherry Grove Rd (28463-8714)
PHONE.................................910 770-1605
Justin Worley, *Prin*
EMP: 4 **EST:** 2017
SALES (est): 83.91K **Privately Held**
SIC: 2752 Commercial printing, lithographic

Tar Heel
Bladen County

(G-11917)
MARK III LOGGING INC
16324 Nc Highway 87 W (28392-9302)
PHONE.................................910 862-4820
Shannon Woodell, *Managing Member*
EMP: 6 **EST:** 2006
SALES (est): 236.99K **Privately Held**
SIC: 2411 Logging camps and contractors

(G-11918)
SMITHFELD FRESH MEATS SLS CORP
15855 Hwy 87 W (28392)
PHONE.................................910 862-7675
EMP: 364
Web: www.smithfieldculinary.com
SIC: 2011 Pork products, from pork slaughtered on site
HQ: Smithfield Fresh Meats Sales Corp. 200 Commerce St Smithfield VA 23430 757 357-3131

(G-11919)
SMITHFIELD FOODS INC
16261 Nc Highway 87 W (28392-9322)
PHONE.................................910 241-2022
EMP: 29
Web: www.smithfieldfoods.com
SIC: 2011 Meat packing plants
HQ: Smithfield Foods, Inc. 200 Commerce St Smithfield VA 23430 757 365-3000

(G-11920)
SMITHFIELD FOODS INC
15855 Nc Highway 87 W (28392-9307)
PHONE.................................910 862-7675
EMP: 45 **EST:** 1994
SALES (est): 13.04MM **Privately Held**
Web: smithfield.sfdbrands.com
SIC: 2011 Meat packing plants

Tarboro
Edgecombe County

(G-11921)
AIR SYSTEM COMPONENTS INC
Also Called: ASC
3301 N Main St (27886-1926)
PHONE.................................252 641-5900
EMP: 83
Web: www.airsysco.com
SIC: 3585 Air conditioning equipment, complete
HQ: Air System Components, Inc. 605 Shiloh Rd Plano TX 75074 972 212-4888

(G-11922)
AIR SYSTEM COMPONENTS INC
Also Called: Titus
3301 N Main St (27886-1926)
PHONE.................................252 641-0875
Barry Beyer, *Pr*
EMP: 224
Web: www.airsysco.com
SIC: 3585 Air conditioning equipment, complete
HQ: Air System Components, Inc. 605 Shiloh Rd Plano TX 75074 972 212-4888

(G-11923)
BIMBO BAKERIES USA INC
Also Called: Sara Lee Bakery Outlet
110 Sara Lee Rd (27886-5269)
PHONE.................................252 641-2200
Jim Dibble, *Mgr*
EMP: 1100
Web: www.arnoldbread.com
SIC: 2053 2051 Frozen bakery products, except bread; Bread, cake, and related products
HQ: Bimbo Bakeries Usa, Inc. 355 Business Center Drive Horsham PA 19044 215 347-5500

(G-11924)
CORNING INCORPORATED
Also Called: Corning
7708 Us Highway 64 Alternate W (27886-8229)
PHONE.................................252 316-4500
EMP: 19
SALES (corp-wide): 13.12B **Publicly Held**
Web: www.corning.com
SIC: 3229 3357 3661 3674 Glass fiber products; Fiber optic cable (insulated); Telephone and telegraph apparatus; Semiconductors and related devices
PA: Corning Incorporated 1 Riverfront Plz Corning NY 14831 607 974-9000

(G-11925)
DFA DAIRY BRANDS FLUID LLC
1079 W Saint James St (27886-4860)
PHONE.................................336 714-9032
Michael Hardcastle, *Brnch Mgr*
EMP: 6
SALES (corp-wide): 21.72B **Privately Held**
Web: www.dfamilk.com
SIC: 2026 Fluid milk
HQ: Dfa Dairy Brands Fluid, Llc 1405 N 98th St Kansas City KS 66111 816 801-6455

(G-11926)
FOCAL POINT PRODUCTS INC
Also Called: Focal Point Architectural Pdts
3006 Anaconda Rd (27886-8836)
PHONE.................................252 824-0015
▲ **EMP:** 100
SIC: 3271 Architectural concrete: block, split, fluted, screen, etc.

(G-11927)
GENERAL FOAM PLASTICS CORP
501 Daniel St (27886-2249)
P.O. Box 2196 (23450-2196)
PHONE.................................757 857-0153
EMP: 5 **EST:** 2019
SALES (est): 332.43K **Privately Held**
SIC: 3999 Manufacturing industries, nec

(G-11928)
HC COMPOSITES LLC
Also Called: Powercat Group
1090 W Saint James St (27886-4822)
PHONE..................252 641-8000
EMP: 166 EST: 2002
SQ FT: 145,000
SALES (est): 24.62MM Privately Held
Web: www.worldcat.com
SIC: 3732 Boatbuilding and repairing

(G-11929)
HOLLINGSWORTH HEATING AIR COND
1893 Mcnair Rd (27886-9054)
PHONE..................252 824-0355
Johnnie Hollingsworth, Prin
EMP: 4 EST: 2004
SALES (est): 280.96K Privately Held
Web: www.tarboroheatingandair.com
SIC: 3699 1711 Electrical equipment and supplies, nec; Heating systems repair and maintenance

(G-11930)
HORNET CAPITAL LLC (PA)
1090 W Saint James St (27886-4822)
PHONE..................252 641-8000
EMP: 10 EST: 1999
SALES (est): 2.48MM
SALES (corp-wide): 2.48MM Privately Held
Web: www.hornetcapital.com
SIC: 3089 Synthetic resin finished products, nec

(G-11931)
LONG TRAILER CO INC
313 Bass Ln (27886-7921)
PHONE..................252 823-8828
Lisa Gay, Pr
Linda Johnson, *
E L Elrod, Stockholder*
EMP: 6 EST: 1958
SQ FT: 3,000
SALES (est): 649.59K Privately Held
Web: www.longtrailer.com
SIC: 3799 Boat trailers

(G-11932)
LS CABLE & SYSTEM USA INC
2801 Anaconda Rd (27886-8833)
PHONE..................252 824-3553
David Han, Manager
EMP: 150
Web: www.lscsusa.com
SIC: 3357 2298 5063 Aircraft wire and cable, nonferrous; Ropes and fiber cables; Electrical apparatus and equipment
HQ: Ls Cable & System U.S.A., Inc.
6625 The Crners Pkwy Ste
Peachtree Corners GA 30092
770 657-6000

(G-11933)
MADEM-MOORECRAFT REELS USA INC
3006 Anaconda Rd (27886-8836)
P.O. Box 1528 (27886-1528)
PHONE..................252 823-2510
Stephen Redhage, Prin
Fatima Bellini, *
EMP: 107 EST: 2017
SALES (est): 21.25MM Privately Held
Web: madem.com.br
SIC: 2499 Reels, plywood

(G-11934)
MAYO KNITTING MILL INC (PA)
Also Called: Mayo

2204 W Austin St (27886-2467)
P.O. Box 160 (27886-0160)
PHONE..................252 823-3101
Ben C Mayo Ii, Pr
C W Mayo Iv, VP
Bryan T Mayo, *
▲ EMP: 101 EST: 1931
SQ FT: 100,000
SALES (est): 2.13MM
SALES (corp-wide): 2.13MM Privately Held
Web: www.mayoknitting.com
SIC: 2252 5949 2251 Socks; Sewing, needlework, and piece goods; Women's hosiery, except socks

(G-11935)
MOORECRAFT REELS INC
101 Royster St (27886-8845)
P.O. Box 1528 (27886-1528)
PHONE..................252 823-2510
Stephen J Redhage, Pr
Steve Redhage, *
Marvin Horton, *
Sharon Horton, *
Sharon H Redhage, *
EMP: 58 EST: 1992
SQ FT: 12,000
SALES (est): 4.9MM Privately Held
SIC: 2499 Spools, reels, and pulleys: wood

(G-11936)
MOORECRAFT WOOD PROUCTS INC
101 Royster St (27886-8845)
P.O. Box 1528 (27886-1528)
PHONE..................252 823-2510
Marvin V Horton, Pr
Sharon L Horton, Ch Bd
Sharon H Redhage, Sec
EMP: 8 EST: 1966
SQ FT: 80,000
SALES (est): 117.73K Privately Held
SIC: 6512 2449 Commercial and industrial building operation; Rectangular boxes and crates, wood

(G-11937)
MURDOCK WEBBING COMPANY INC
Also Called: Phoenix Trimming
1052 W Saint James St (27886-4822)
P.O. Box 609 (27886-0609)
PHONE..................252 823-1131
Vann Cummings, Off Mgr
EMP: 42
SALES (corp-wide): 23.07MM Privately Held
Web: www.murdockwebbing.com
SIC: 2241 Webbing, woven
PA: Murdock Webbing Company, Inc.
27 Foundry St
Central Falls RI 02863
401 724-3000

(G-11938)
NASH BUILDING SYSTEMS INC
1803 Anaconda Rd (27886-8811)
P.O. Box 1320 (27886-1320)
PHONE..................252 823-1905
EMP: 25 EST: 2014
SALES (est): 4.94MM Privately Held
Web: www.nashbuildingsystems.com
SIC: 3448 Prefabricated metal buildings and components

(G-11939)
NGX
3002 Anaconda Rd (27886-8836)
PHONE..................866 782-7749
Steve Thompson, Managing Member
▼ EMP: 29 EST: 2007
SALES (est): 2.2MM

SALES (corp-wide): 95.55MM Privately Held
SIC: 3086 Packaging and shipping materials, foamed plastics
PA: Noel Group, Llc
501 Nmc Dr
Zebulon NC 27597
919 269-6500

(G-11940)
S & W METAL WORKS INC
1813 Anaconda Rd (27886-8811)
PHONE..................252 641-0912
Ray Whitehurst, Pr
Kevin Comb, VP
EMP: 9 EST: 1987
SQ FT: 10,000
SALES (est): 1.7MM Privately Held
SIC: 3599 Machine shop, jobbing and repair

(G-11941)
SUPERIOR ESSEX INC
2801 Anaconda Rd (27886-8833)
PHONE..................252 823-5111
Jim Berry, Brnch Mgr
EMP: 87
Web: www.superioressex.com
SIC: 3357 Nonferrous wiredrawing and insulating
HQ: Superior Essex Inc.
5770 Pwers Frry Rd Nw Ste
Atlanta GA 30327
770 657-6000

(G-11942)
SUPERIOR ESSEX INTL INC
2801 Anaconda Rd (27886-8833)
PHONE..................252 823-5111
Paul Neuhart, Brnch Mgr
EMP: 196
Web: www.superioressex.com
SIC: 3357 Communication wire
HQ: Superior Essex International Inc.
5770 Pwers Frry Rd Ste 40
Atlanta GA 30327
770 657-6000

(G-11943)
SWIMWAYS
3002 Anaconda Rd (27886-8836)
PHONE..................252 563-1101
EMP: 13 EST: 2018
SALES (est): 6.79MM Privately Held
SIC: 3086 Plastics foam products

(G-11944)
TOWN OF TARBORO
Also Called: Waterplant
600 Albemarle Ave (27886-4300)
P.O. Box 220 (27886-0220)
PHONE..................252 641-4284
Harry Penwell, Brnch Mgr
EMP: 21
Web: www.tarboro-nc.com
SIC: 3589 Water treatment equipment, industrial
PA: Town Of Tarboro
500 N Main St
Tarboro NC 27886
252 641-4250

(G-11945)
TRITON INTERNATIONAL WOODS LLC
600 W James St (27886)
P.O. Box 1255 (27886-1255)
PHONE..................252 823-6675
Richard A Edwards Junior, Managing Member
▲ EMP: 60 EST: 2002
SQ FT: 365,000

SALES (est): 1.63MM Privately Held
Web: www.tritonwoods.com
SIC: 2491 2426 Flooring, treated wood block ; Hardwood dimension and flooring mills

(G-11946)
W R LONG INC
1607 Cedar St (27886-2464)
P.O. Box 460 (27886-0460)
PHONE..................252 823-4570
Z Vance Long, Pr
▲ EMP: 18 EST: 1987
SQ FT: 27,000
SALES (est): 4.76MM Privately Held
Web: www.wrlonginc.com
SIC: 3531 Buckets, excavating: clamshell, concrete, dragline, etc.

(G-11947)
YARD PRO SALES AND SERVICE LLC
105 W Howard Ave (27886-2561)
PHONE..................252 641-9776
June F Cherry, Managing Member
EMP: 6 EST: 2018
SALES (est): 1.4MM Privately Held
SIC: 3546 Chain saws, portable

Taylorsville
Alexander County

(G-11948)
ADVANTAGE NN-WVENS CNVRTING LL
173 Wittenburg Industrial Dr (28681-8259)
P.O. Box 996 (28613-0996)
PHONE..................828 635-1880
EMP: 4 EST: 2016
SALES (est): 757.16K Privately Held
Web: www.advantagenonwovens.com
SIC: 2297 Nonwoven fabrics

(G-11949)
ANCHOR-RICHEY EMERGENCY VEHICL
Also Called: Anchor Richey E V S
241 Advent Church Rd (28681-4622)
P.O. Box 6342 (28603-6342)
PHONE..................828 495-8145
Matthew Richey, Pr
Bill Mccormick, VP
EMP: 23 EST: 1979
SQ FT: 6,000
SALES (est): 3.24MM Privately Held
Web: www.anchor-richeyevs.com
SIC: 3713 Specialty motor vehicle bodies

(G-11950)
BOREALIS COMPOUNDS INC
401 We Baab Industrial Dr (28681-6027)
PHONE..................908 798-7497
Roland Janssen, Brnch Mgr
EMP: 30
SALES (corp-wide): 7.7B Privately Held
Web: www.borealisgroup.com
SIC: 3087 Custom compound purchased resins
HQ: Borealis Compounds Inc.
176 Thomas Rd
Port Murray NJ 07865

(G-11951)
BROWN BROTHERS LUMBER
1388 Little River Church Rd (28681-3644)
PHONE..................828 632-6486
Rickey Brown, Prin
EMP: 6 EST: 2012
SALES (est): 136.72K Privately Held

SIC: 2411 Logging camps and contractors

(G-11952)
CARPENTER CO
Hwy 90 E (28681)
P.O. Box 455 (28681-0455)
PHONE..............................828 632-7061
Tom Dunston, *Brnch Mgr*
EMP: 32
SALES (corp-wide): 506.96MM **Privately Held**
Web: www.carpenter.com
SIC: 3086 2821 2392 Insulation or cushioning material, foamed plastics; Plastics materials and resins; Household furnishings, nec
PA: Carpenter Co.
5016 Monument Ave
Richmond VA 23230
804 359-0800

(G-11953)
CHASE LAMINATING INC
138 Wittenburg Rd (28681-6515)
PHONE..............................828 632-6666
Al Stozer, *Mgr*
EMP: 4 EST: 2004
SALES (est): 283.92K **Publicly Held**
SIC: 2295 Coated fabrics, not rubberized
HQ: Chase Corporation
375 University Ave
Westwood MA 02090
781 332-0700

(G-11954)
COMPOSITE FABRICS AMERICA LLC
105 Pierpoint Ln (28681-3827)
P.O. Box 609 (28681-0609)
PHONE..............................828 632-5220
Matthew M Mcpherson, *Managing Member*
▲ EMP: 4 EST: 2009
SALES (est): 481.5K
SALES (corp-wide): 22.87MM **Privately Held**
Web: www.cfamills.com
SIC: 5949 2221 Fabric stores piece goods; Acetate broadwoven fabrics
PA: Schneider Mills, Inc.
1170 Nc Hwy 16 N
Taylorsville NC 28681
828 632-8181

(G-11955)
COUNTY OF ALEXANDER
Also Called: Department of Solid Waste
255 Liledoun Rd (28681-2576)
P.O. Box 12 (28681-0012)
PHONE..............................828 632-1101
Rick French, *Mgr*
EMP: 25
Web: www.alexandercountync.gov
SIC: 3089 Garbage containers, plastics
PA: County Of Alexander
151 W Main Ave # 1
Taylorsville NC 28681
828 632-9332

(G-11956)
CUSTOM EDUCATIONAL FURN LLC
Also Called: CEF
2696 Nc Highway 16 S (28681-8952)
PHONE..............................800 255-9189
Scott Mchugh, *Managing Member*
EMP: 15 EST: 2014
SALES (est): 2.11MM
SALES (corp-wide): 2.11MM **Privately Held**
Web: www.cefinc.com
SIC: 2531 2541 School furniture; Office fixtures, wood

PA: Precision Materials, Llc
6246 Nc Highway 16 S
Taylorsville NC 28681
828 632-8851

(G-11957)
D J ENVIRO SOLUTIONS
334 Riverview Rd (28681-7651)
PHONE..............................828 495-7448
Dennis Gillen, *Prin*
EMP: 6 EST: 2010
SALES (est): 85.48K **Privately Held**
SIC: 3564 Air cleaning systems

(G-11958)
DANIELS WOODCARVING CO INC
2325 Nc Highway 90 E (28681-3750)
PHONE..............................828 632-7336
David L Daniels, *Pr*
Paula Daniels, *
EMP: 10 EST: 1972
SQ FT: 45,000
SALES (est): 897.38K **Privately Held**
SIC: 2426 2512 Carvings, furniture: wood; Upholstered household furniture

(G-11959)
DURA-CRAFT DIE INC
1442 Liledoun Rd (28681-3090)
PHONE..............................828 632-1944
J Mark Warren, *Pr*
J M Warren, *Pr*
Ricky Bowman, *VP*
John C Warren, *Sec*
EMP: 4 EST: 1993
SQ FT: 400
SALES (est): 426.08K **Privately Held**
Web: www.duracraftdie.com
SIC: 3544 Special dies and tools

(G-11960)
FLAVOR SCIENCES INC
715 Houck Mountain Rd (28681-7714)
PHONE..............................828 758-2525
Roger E Kiley, *Pr*
Joyce Kiley, *VP*
EMP: 20 EST: 1969
SALES (est): 1.01MM **Privately Held**
Web: www.flavorsciences.com
SIC: 2087 Extracts, flavoring

(G-11961)
FRIENDSHIP UPHOLSTERY CO INC
6035 Church Rd (28681-8207)
PHONE..............................828 632-9836
Greg Hefner, *Pr*
EMP: 25 EST: 1972
SQ FT: 40,000
SALES (est): 1.42MM **Privately Held**
Web: www.friendshipupholstery.com
SIC: 2512 Upholstered household furniture

(G-11962)
HANCOCK & MOORE LLC (HQ)
Also Called: Cabot Wrenn
166 Hancock And Moore Ln (28681-7679)
P.O. Box 3444 (28603-3444)
PHONE..............................828 495-8235
John Glasheen, *CEO*
Timothy Rogers, *
Jimmy Moore, *
Brandon Hucks, *
EMP: 86 EST: 2015
SQ FT: 150,000
SALES (est): 23.39MM
SALES (corp-wide): 87.25MM **Privately Held**
Web: www.hancockandmoore.com
SIC: 2512 Upholstered household furniture
PA: Rhf Investments, Inc.
401 11th St Nw

Hickory NC 28601
828 326-8350

(G-11963)
HANCOCK & MOORE LLC
Also Called: Cabot Wrenn
405 Rink Dam Rd (28681-6726)
PHONE..............................828 495-8235
Bryan Craft, *Brnch Mgr*
EMP: 206
SALES (corp-wide): 87.25MM **Privately Held**
Web: www.hancockandmoore.com
SIC: 2512 2511 2521 Upholstered household furniture; Wood household furniture; Wood office furniture
HQ: Hancock & Moore, Llc
166 Hancock And Moore Ln
Taylorsville NC 28681
828 495-8235

(G-11964)
HEFNER REELS LLC
34 Wittenburg Industrial Dr (28681-8255)
PHONE..............................828 632-5717
Vicki Heffner, *
Hal Ray Hefner, *
Kim Ferguson, *
EMP: 45 EST: 2007
SALES (est): 8.71MM **Privately Held**
SIC: 2499 Spools, reels, and pulleys: wood

(G-11965)
HUNTINGTON HOUSE INC
210 Bethlehem Park Ln (28681-7682)
PHONE..............................828 495-4400
Monty Meadlock, *Mgr*
EMP: 50
SALES (corp-wide): 19.15MM **Privately Held**
Web: www.huntingtonhouse.com
SIC: 2512 Upholstered household furniture
PA: Huntington House, Inc.
661 Rink Dam Rd
Hickory NC 28601
828 495-4400

(G-11966)
ISENHOUR FURNITURE COMPANY (PA)
486 S Center St (28681-3027)
P.O. Box 1089 (28603-1089)
PHONE..............................828 632-8849
Dwight Isenhour, *Pr*
▲ EMP: 87 EST: 1989
SQ FT: 100,000
SALES (est): 2.16MM
SALES (corp-wide): 2.16MM **Privately Held**
Web: www.isenhourfurn.com
SIC: 2512 Upholstered household furniture

(G-11967)
MASTERFIELD FURNITURE CO INC
6463 Church Rd (28681-6413)
PHONE..............................828 632-8535
Jeffrey Hefner, *Pr*
Johnny Hefner, *
EMP: 50 EST: 1976
SQ FT: 95,000
SALES (est): 2.91MM **Privately Held**
Web: www.masterfieldfurniturecompany.com
SIC: 2512 Living room furniture: upholstered on wood frames

(G-11968)
PARAGON FILMS INC
255 We Baab Industrial Dr (28681-6013)
PHONE..............................828 632-5552
Michael J Baab, *Brnch Mgr*

EMP: 15
SALES (corp-wide): 111.43MM **Privately Held**
Web: www.paragon-films.com
SIC: 3081 2671 Polyethylene film; Plastic film, coated or laminated for packaging
PA: Paragon Films, Inc.
3500 W Tacoma St
Broken Arrow OK 74012
918 250-3456

(G-11969)
PAUL ROBERT CHAIR INC (PA)
Also Called: Paul Robert
266 Martin Luther King Dr (28681-3065)
P.O. Box 969 (28681-0969)
PHONE..............................828 632-7021
Paul Robert Dickinson, *Pr*
Daniel Y Dickinson, *
Patricia M Dickinson, *
◆ EMP: 69 EST: 1983
SQ FT: 125,000
SALES (est): 6.16MM
SALES (corp-wide): 6.16MM **Privately Held**
Web: www.paulrobert.com
SIC: 2512 Chairs: upholstered on wood frames

(G-11970)
PIEDMONT CMPOSITES TOOLING LLC
33 Lewittes Rd (28681-2873)
PHONE..............................828 632-8883
EMP: 55 EST: 2018
SALES (est): 12.18MM **Privately Held**
Web: www.piedmontcomposites.com
SIC: 2221 Fiberglass fabrics

(G-11971)
PIEDMONT WOOD PRODUCTS INC
1924 Black Oak Ridge Rd (28681-3309)
P.O. Box 307 (28681-0307)
PHONE..............................828 632-4077
Gary Coffey, *Pr*
Malcolm Reese, *VP*
EMP: 13 EST: 1972
SQ FT: 16,500
SALES (est): 1.16MM **Privately Held**
Web: www.piedmontwood.com
SIC: 2431 Millwork

(G-11972)
PRECISION MATERIALS LLC (PA)
6246 Nc Highway 16 S (28681-6354)
P.O. Box 848 (28681-0848)
PHONE..............................828 632-8851
EMP: 17 EST: 2009
SALES (est): 2.11MM
SALES (corp-wide): 2.11MM **Privately Held**
Web: www.pmatnc.com
SIC: 2521 2531 2511 Wood office furniture; School furniture; Wood household furniture

(G-11973)
RHF INVESTMENTS INC
165 Matheson Park Ave (28681-2435)
PHONE..............................828 632-7070
Dennis Lockhart, *Mgr*
EMP: 9
SALES (corp-wide): 87.25MM **Privately Held**
Web: www.centuryfurniture.com
SIC: 2426 Frames for upholstered furniture, wood
PA: Rhf Investments, Inc.
401 11th St Nw
Hickory NC 28601
828 326-8350

(G-11974)
ROYALE COMFORT SEATING INC
140 Alspaugh Dam Rd (28681-4632)
P.O. Box 235 (28681-0235)
PHONE...................828 352-9021
Clyde Goble, Pr
Harrison Reid Junior, VP
David Lawson, *
Fred Crump, *
EMP: 100 EST: 1987
SQ FT: 37,500
SALES (est): 5.22MM Privately Held
Web: www.royalekomfortbedding.com
SIC: 2392 3089 Cushions and pillows; Fiber, vulcanized

(G-11975)
ROYALE KOMFORT BEDDING INC
2320 All Healing Springs Rd (28681-7273)
P.O. Box 549 (28681-0549)
PHONE...................828 632-5631
Harrison Reid, Pr
EMP: 7 EST: 1997
SALES (est): 421.89K Privately Held
Web: www.royalekomfortbedding.com
SIC: 2515 Mattresses, innerspring or box spring

(G-11976)
RUSSELL LOUDERMILK LOGGING
330 Dee Loudermelk Ln (28681-8560)
PHONE...................828 632-4968
Russell Loudermilk, Owner
EMP: 4 EST: 1985
SALES (est): 245.64K Privately Held
Web: www.grandmarquis.com
SIC: 2411 Logging camps and contractors

(G-11977)
SCHNEIDER MILLS INC (PA)
1170 Nc Highway 16 N (28681-2468)
PHONE...................828 632-8181
Peter M Campanelli, Pr
Mark A Labbe, VP
EMP: 12 EST: 1921
SQ FT: 4,500
SALES (est): 22.87MM
SALES (corp-wide): 22.87MM Privately Held
Web: www.schneidermills.com
SIC: 2221 Manmade and synthetic broadwoven fabrics

(G-11978)
SIPE LUMBER COMPANY INC
2750 Us Highway 64 90 W (28681-7579)
PHONE...................828 632-4679
EMP: 28 EST: 1941
SALES (est): 4.97MM Privately Held
Web: www.sipelumber.com
SIC: 5031 5211 2421 Building materials, exterior; Lumber and other building materials; Lumber: rough, sawed, or planed

(G-11979)
STIKELEATHER INC
146 Windsor Dr (28681-6910)
PHONE...................828 352-9095
Timothy D Stikeleather, Prin
EMP: 6 EST: 2012
SALES (est): 225.16K Privately Held
SIC: 3199 Leather goods, nec

(G-11980)
TAILOR CUT WOOD PRODUCTS INC
35 Wittenburg Industrial Dr (28681-8250)
P.O. Box 99 (28681-0099)
PHONE...................828 632-2808
Ricky Price, Pr
Hal Hefner, VP
EMP: 4 EST: 1989
SQ FT: 31,500
SALES (est): 156.94K Privately Held
SIC: 2435 Panels, hardwood plywood

(G-11981)
TAYLOR KING FURNITURE INC
286 County Home Rd (28681-9375)
PHONE...................828 632-7731
John G Mullins, CEO
Del Starnes, *
Ron Downs, *
Dana Beach, *
Tanya Comer, *
▲ EMP: 120 EST: 1974
SQ FT: 160,000
SALES (est): 10.07MM Privately Held
Web: www.taylorking.com
SIC: 2512 Upholstered household furniture

(G-11982)
TAYLORSVILLE PRECAST MOLDS INC
128 Taylorsville Mfg Rd (28681-4005)
PHONE...................828 632-4608
David R Mecimore, Pr
Sharon Mecimore, Sec
EMP: 6 EST: 1989
SQ FT: 6,000
SALES (est): 727.48K Privately Held
SIC: 1761 3444 Sheet metal work, nec; Sheet metalwork

(G-11983)
TAYLORSVILLE TIMES
24 E Main Ave (28681-2541)
P.O. Box 279 (28681-0279)
PHONE...................828 632-2532
Walter Lee Sharpe, Owner
EMP: 6 EST: 1930
SQ FT: 8,000
SALES (est): 499.05K Privately Held
Web: www.taylorsvilletimes.com
SIC: 2711 Commercial printing and newspaper publishing combined

(G-11984)
THOMAS LEE FORTNER SAWMILL
70 Mount Olive Church Rd (28681-4335)
PHONE...................828 632-9525
Thomas Lee Fortner, Owner
EMP: 8 EST: 1983
SALES (est): 234.37K Privately Held
SIC: 2421 Sawmills and planing mills, general

(G-11985)
VINTAGE EDITIONS INC
88 Buff Ln (28681-3352)
PHONE...................828 632-4185
Perry L Austin, Pr
▲ EMP: 10 EST: 2002
SQ FT: 25,000
SALES (est): 475.31K Privately Held
Web: www.vintageeditions.com
SIC: 2499 3993 Decorative wood and woodwork; Signs and advertising specialties

(G-11986)
WATTS BUMGARNER & BROWN INC
9541 Us Highway 64 90 W (28681-7543)
PHONE...................828 632-4797
Greg Bumgarner, Pr
Danny Bumgarner, VP
Patsy Wilson, Sec
EMP: 4 EST: 1964
SALES (est): 221.06K Privately Held
SIC: 2421 Lumber: rough, sawed, or planed

Teachey
Duplin County

(G-11987)
HOUSE OF RAEFORD FARMS INC
253 Butterball Rd (28464-9638)
P.O. Box 669 (28466)
PHONE...................910 285-2349
Donald Taber, Brnch Mgr
EMP: 742
SALES (corp-wide): 1.79B Privately Held
Web: www.houseofraeford.com
SIC: 2015 Poultry slaughtering and processing
HQ: House Of Raeford Farms, Inc.
3333 S Us Highway 117
Rose Hill NC 28458
912 222-4090

(G-11988)
INDUSTRIAL METAL MAINT INC
164 John Deere Rd (28464-9446)
PHONE...................910 285-3240
Jennifer Crist, Pr
EMP: 5 EST: 2001
SALES (est): 257.44K Privately Held
Web: imm.embarqspace.com
SIC: 7692 Welding repair

Terrell
Catawba County

(G-11989)
GREENSTORY GLOBL GVRNMENT MLTA
3811 Gordon St (28682-9731)
PHONE...................828 446-9278
Meghan Stout, Ch Bd
EMP: 16 EST: 2019
SALES (est): 649.09K Privately Held
SIC: 3589 Water filters and softeners, household type

Thomasville
Davidson County

(G-11990)
ADVANCED MOTOR SPORTS COATINGS
17 High Tech Blvd (27360-5560)
PHONE...................336 472-5518
Brett Watkins, Genl Mgr
EMP: 8 EST: 2004
SALES (est): 105.89K Privately Held
Web:
www.advancedmaterialcoatings.com
SIC: 3471 Plating and polishing

(G-11991)
ALBRIGHT QULTY WD TURNING INC
193 Black Farm Rd (27360-6804)
PHONE...................336 475-1434
Fred Albright, Owner
EMP: 8 EST: 2001
SALES (est): 109.99K Privately Held
Web: www.lakesbci.com
SIC: 2499 Carved and turned wood

(G-11992)
ALTIUM PACKAGING LLC
1408 Unity St (27360-4957)
PHONE...................336 472-1500
Jeff Fay, Brnch Mgr
EMP: 75
SALES (corp-wide): 17.51B Publicly Held
Web: www.altiumpkg.com

SIC: 3089 Plastics containers, except foam
HQ: Altium Packaging Llc
2500 Windy Ridge Pkwy Se # 1400
Atlanta GA 30339
678 742-4600

(G-11993)
AM HAIRE MFG & SVC CORP
516 Pinewood Rd (27360-2763)
PHONE...................336 472-4444
Darrell K Haire, Pr
Rita C Haire, *
EMP: 175 EST: 2010
SQ FT: 68,300
SALES (est): 27.93MM Privately Held
Web: www.amhairecorp.com
SIC: 3713 Truck bodies (motor vehicles)

(G-11994)
AMERICAN RNOVATION SYSTEMS LLC
208 Bell Dr (27360-7960)
PHONE...................336 313-6210
EMP: 6 EST: 2013
SALES (est): 252.91K Privately Held
Web: www.arsfixit.com
SIC: 1389 7389 Construction, repair, and dismantling services; Business services, nec

(G-11995)
ATTL PRODUCTS INC
216 E Holly Hill Rd (27360-5820)
PHONE...................336 475-8101
Randy Ramsom, Owner
EMP: 4 EST: 2008
SALES (est): 248.49K Privately Held
Web: www.tracktac.com
SIC: 2899 Chemical preparations, nec

(G-11996)
BARTIMAEUS BY DESIGN INC
1010 Randolph St (27360-5877)
PHONE...................336 475-4346
Eddie Brinkley, Pr
Chadwick Brinkley, *
Gloria Brinkley, *
EMP: 110 EST: 2001
SALES (est): 19.18MM Privately Held
Web: www.bartbydesign.com
SIC: 2426 3441 Frames for upholstered furniture, wood; Fabricated structural metal

(G-11997)
BRASSCRAFT
1024 Randolph St (27360-5877)
PHONE...................336 475-2131
Don Woddy, Pr
▲ EMP: 131 EST: 1962
SQ FT: 200,000
SALES (est): 14.47MM
SALES (corp-wide): 7.83B Publicly Held
Web: www.brasscraft.com
SIC: 5074 3491 Plumbers' brass goods and fittings; Automatic regulating and control valves
HQ: Brasscraft Manufacturing Company
39600 Orchard Hill Pl
Novi MI 48375
248 305-6000

(G-11998)
BRASSCRAFT MANUFACTURING CO
Also Called: Brasscraft Brownstown
1024 Randolph St (27360-5877)
PHONE...................336 475-2131
EMP: 23
SALES (corp-wide): 7.83B Publicly Held
Web: www.brasscraft.com

SIC: 3432 Plumbing fixture fittings and trim
HQ: Brasscraft Manufacturing Company
　　39600 Orchard Hill Pl
　　Novi MI 48375
　　248 305-6000

(G-11999)
BRYSON INDUSTRIES INC
416 Albertson Rd (27360-8985)
PHONE.................................336 931-0026
David Lancaster, *Pr*
Tommy Lancaster, *Sr VP*
EMP: 14 **EST:** 2001
SQ FT: 10,000
SALES (est): 11.47MM **Privately Held**
Web: www.brysonusa.com
SIC: 2819 Industrial inorganic chemicals, nec

(G-12000)
C & D WOODWORKING INC
7139 Wright Rd (27360-8342)
P.O. Box 1913 (27361-1913)
PHONE.................................336 476-8722
David Trimnal, *Pr*
EMP: 5 **EST:** 1990
SQ FT: 15,000
SALES (est): 97.96K **Privately Held**
SIC: 2499 Laundry products, wood

(G-12001)
CAROLINA ATTACHMENTS LLC
704 Pineywood Rd (27360-2753)
PHONE.................................336 474-7309
Wesley C Blackburn, *Pr*
EMP: 7 **EST:** 2013
SALES (est): 2.84MM **Privately Held**
Web: www.carolinaattachments.com
SIC: 3714 Steering mechanisms, motor
　vehicle

(G-12002)
CAROLINA CONTAINER LLC
Also Called: Box Shop
1205 Trinity St (27360-8821)
P.O. Box 2166 (27261-2166)
PHONE.................................336 883-7146
EMP: 27
SALES (corp-wide): 644.8MM **Privately Held**
Web: www.carolinacontainer.com
SIC: 5999 2672 Packaging materials: boxes,
　padding, etc.; Adhesive backed films,
　foams and foils
HQ: Carolina Container Company
　　909 Prospect St
　　High Point NC 27260
　　336 883-7146

(G-12003)
**CAROLINA FAIRWAY CUSHIONS
LLC**
15 N Robbins St (27360-8970)
PHONE.................................336 434-4292
Nicole L Gardner, *Prin*
EMP: 8 **EST:** 2011
SALES (est): 859.74K **Privately Held**
Web: www.carolinafairwaycushions.com
SIC: 2392 Cushions and pillows

(G-12004)
CAROLINA MATTRESS GUILD INC
385 North Dr (27360-8944)
PHONE.................................336 841-8529
▲ **EMP:** 85
Web: www.carolinamattressguild.com
SIC: 2515 Mattresses and bedsprings

(G-12005)
CAROLINA MOVILE BUS SYSTEMS
771 Old Emanuel Church Rd (27360-7508)

PHONE.................................336 475-0983
Larry Shockley, *Owner*
▼ **EMP:** 5 **EST:** 2005
SQ FT: 10,000
SALES (est): 192.29K **Privately Held**
SIC: 3711 Motor vehicles and car bodies

(G-12006)
**CAROLINA UNDERWEAR COMPANY
(PA)**
110 W Guilford St (27360-3919)
PHONE.................................336 472-7788
N C English Iii, *Pr*
Walter Jones, *VP*
James W English, *Sec*
◆ **EMP:** 20 **EST:** 1928
SQ FT: 140,000
SALES (est): 2.97MM
SALES (corp-wide): 2.97MM **Privately
Held**
SIC: 2341 2322 Women's and children's
　undergarments; Nightwear, men's and
　boys': from purchased materials

(G-12007)
CELAND YARN DYERS INC
606 Davidson St (27360-3628)
P.O. Box 2127 (27361-2127)
PHONE.................................336 472-4400
Margaret Hill Norton, *Pr*
Rebecca Hill Leonard, *
Steve Yokeley, *
EMP: 4 **EST:** 1955
SQ FT: 49,500
SALES (est): 119.81K **Privately Held**
SIC: 2269 Dyeing: raw stock, yarn, and
　narrow fabrics

(G-12008)
CEMEX MATERIALS LLC
208 Randolph St (27360-4642)
PHONE.................................800 627-2986
Mike Shook, *Mgr*
EMP: 60
SIC: 3273 Ready-mixed concrete
HQ: Cemex Materials Llc
　　1720 Cntrpark Dr E Ste 10
　　West Palm Beach FL 33401
　　561 833-5555

(G-12009)
**COMBINTONS SCREEN PRTG EMB
INC**
Also Called: Combinations Embroidery
4 N Robbins St (27360-8970)
P.O. Box 1857 (27361-1857)
PHONE.................................336 472-4420
Mark Berrier, *Pr*
Douglas Berrier, *VP*
June Berrier, *Sec*
EMP: 6 **EST:** 1985
SQ FT: 10,000
SALES (est): 95.48K **Privately Held**
SIC: 2396 2395 Screen printing on fabric
　articles; Embroidery products, except
　Schiffli machine

(G-12010)
COMFORT SLEEP LLC
1100 National Hwy Ste L (27360-2342)
P.O. Box 1351 (27361-1351)
PHONE.................................336 267-5853
EMP: 4 **EST:** 2019
SALES (est): 942.09K **Privately Held**
Web: www.comfortsleepnc.com
SIC: 2515 Mattresses and foundations

(G-12011)
CON-TAB INC
4001 Ball Park Rd (27360-8976)

P.O. Box 1369 (27361-1369)
PHONE.................................336 476-0104
EMP: 16
SIC: 2522 5072 5021 Tables, office: except
　wood; Hardware; Office furniture, nec

(G-12012)
**CRAFTSMAN FOAM FABRICATORS
INC**
196 Mason Way (27360-4921)
PHONE.................................336 476-5655
Olin Hill, *Pr*
Michael Hill, *
EMP: 4 **EST:** 1985
SQ FT: 22,000
SALES (est): 678.93K **Privately Held**
SIC: 3069 Foam rubber

(G-12013)
**CUSTOM DESIGNS AND
UPHOLSTERY**
1372 Unity St # B (27360-3223)
PHONE.................................336 882-1516
Mitzi Marlowe, *Pr*
Missy Marlowe, *Pr*
David Marlowe, *VP*
Will Swain, *Treas*
EMP: 10 **EST:** 2005
SALES (est): 74.64K **Privately Held**
SIC: 2512 Upholstered household furniture

(G-12014)
CUSTOM FABRIC SAMPLES INC
261 Sunset Dr (27360-9190)
P.O. Box 6632 (27262-6632)
PHONE.................................336 472-1854
Brad Moser, *Pr*
▲ **EMP:** 8 **EST:** 2000
SALES (est): 139.6K **Privately Held**
Web: www.acmesample.com
SIC: 2241 Fabric tapes

(G-12015)
DAN MOORE INC
405 Albertson Rd (27360-8986)
PHONE.................................336 475-8350
A Daniel Moore Junior, *Pr*
Martha Moore, *Sec*
EMP: 6 **EST:** 1975
SQ FT: 9,000
SALES (est): 384.2K **Privately Held**
Web: www.danmooreinc.com
SIC: 1611 3531 Highway and street
　construction; Construction machinery

(G-12016)
DANTHERM FILTRATION INC
Also Called: Nordfab
150 Transit Ave (27360-8927)
P.O. Box 429 (27361-0429)
PHONE.................................336 889-5599
EMP: 13
SQ FT: 45,000
SIC: 3564 3444 Dust or fume collecting
　equipment, industrial; Ducts, sheet metal
HQ: Dantherm Filtration, Inc.
　　150 Transit Ave
　　Thomasville NC 27360
　　336 821-0800

(G-12017)
DESIGN PRINTING INC
1107 Trinity St (27360-8819)
PHONE.................................336 472-3333
Larry Utz, *Pr*
EMP: 8 **EST:** 1979
SQ FT: 20,000
SALES (est): 115.65K **Privately Held**
Web: www.dprintla.com
SIC: 2752 Offset printing

(G-12018)
DIE-TECH INC
4 Stanley Ave (27360-8969)
PHONE.................................336 475-9186
Russell Hall, *Pr*
Norma Hall, *
Russell Hall, *VP*
EMP: 8 **EST:** 1966
SALES (est): 579.41K **Privately Held**
Web: www.dietechonline.com
SIC: 3544 Special dies and tools

(G-12019)
DIRECTIONAL BUYING GROUP INC
Also Called: Directional
201 E Holly Hill Rd (27360-5819)
PHONE.................................336 472-6187
Tom Powell, *Pr*
EMP: 5 **EST:** 1965
SQ FT: 100,000
SALES (est): 238.25K **Privately Held**
Web: www.directionalinc.com
SIC: 2512 Chairs: upholstered on wood
　frames

(G-12020)
DSI INNOVATIONS LLC
42 High Tech Blvd (27360)
P.O. Box 1127 (27023)
PHONE.................................336 893-8385
Jason Dupre, *CEO*
Jason Dupre, *Managing Member*
Bobby Cole, *
Damien Johns, *
EMP: 45 **EST:** 2008
SALES (est): 8.62MM **Privately Held**
Web: www.dsiinnovations.com
SIC: 3625 3599 Relays and industrial
　controls; Custom machinery

(G-12021)
ELITE DISPLAYS & DESIGN INC
6771 Pikeview Dr (27360-8924)
P.O. Box 1949 (27361-1949)
PHONE.................................336 472-8200
Thomas Waterhouse, *Pr*
Rusty Slate, *
▲ **EMP:** 75 **EST:** 2002
SQ FT: 60,000
SALES (est): 8.01MM **Privately Held**
Web: www.elitedisplays.com
SIC: 2542 Bar fixtures, except wood

(G-12022)
ENNIS-FLINT INC
505 County Line Rd (27360-5979)
PHONE.................................336 477-8439
EMP: 6
SALES (corp-wide): 17.65B **Publicly Held**
Web: www.ennisflint.com
SIC: 2851 Paints and allied products
HQ: Ennis-Flint, Inc.
　　4161 Pedmont Pkwy Ste 370
　　Greensboro NC 27410
　　800 331-8118

(G-12023)
ENNIS-FLINT INC
115 Todd Ct (27360-3233)
PHONE.................................800 331-8118
EMP: 4
SALES (corp-wide): 17.65B **Publicly Held**
Web: www.ennisflintamericas.com
SIC: 2851 3953 Paints and allied products;
　Marking devices
HQ: Ennis-Flint, Inc.
　　4161 Pedmont Pkwy Ste 370
　　Greensboro NC 27410
　　800 331-8118

(G-12024)
FINCH INDUSTRIES INCORPORATED
104 Williams St (27360-3600)
P.O. Box 1847 (27361-1847)
PHONE..................336 472-4499
◆ **EMP:** 90 **EST:** 1978
SALES (est): 7.8MM **Privately Held**
Web: www.finchindustries.com
SIC: 3231 2759 2396 Products of purchased glass; Screen printing; Automotive and apparel trimmings

(G-12025)
FLINT ACQUISITION CORP
115 Todd Ct (27360-3233)
P.O. Box 160 (27361-0160)
PHONE..................336 475-6600
Steven Vetter, CEO
Michael Murren, *
EMP: 76 **EST:** 2004
SALES (est): 23.97MM
SALES (corp-wide): 17.65B **Publicly Held**
SIC: 2851 Paints and allied products
HQ: Road Infrastructure Investment Holdings, Inc.
115 Todd Ct
Thomasville NC 27360
336 475-6600

(G-12026)
FLINT TRADING INC
505 County Line Rd (27360-5979)
PHONE..................336 308-3770
EMP: 8 **EST:** 2017
SALES (est): 508.79K **Privately Held**
Web: www.ennisflint.com
SIC: 2851 Paints and allied products

(G-12027)
FLINT TRADING INC
Also Called: Ennis-Flint
115 Todd Ct (27360-3233)
P.O. Box 160 (27361-0160)
PHONE..................336 475-6600
▲ **EMP:** 73
Web: www.ennisflint.com
SIC: 3953 Marking devices

(G-12028)
GARY J YOUNTS MACHINE COMPANY
4786 Turnpike Ct (27360-8842)
PHONE..................336 476-7930
Gary J Younts, Pr
Pat Younts, Sec
EMP: 10 **EST:** 1987
SQ FT: 8,400
SALES (est): 916.43K **Privately Held**
Web: www.christmaswithelvis.com
SIC: 3451 Screw machine products

(G-12029)
GRESCO MANUFACTURING INC
216 E Holly Hill Rd (27360-5820)
PHONE..................336 475-8101
R E Ransom, Pr
R E Ransom, Pr
EMP: 7 **EST:** 1984
SQ FT: 30,000
SALES (est): 118.93K **Privately Held**
Web: www.tracktac.com
SIC: 2819 Industrial inorganic chemicals, nec

(G-12030)
HIGH POINT ENTERPRISE INC
Thomasville Times, The
512 Turner St (27360-2646)
PHONE..................336 472-9500
Sara Smith, Mgr
EMP: 15

SQ FT: 17,810
SALES (corp-wide): 147.64MM **Privately Held**
Web: www.hpenews.com
SIC: 2711 Commercial printing and newspaper publishing combined
HQ: The High Point Enterprise Llc
213 Woodbine St
High Point NC 27260
336 888-3500

(G-12031)
HILL HOSIERY MILL INC
Also Called: Hill Spinning Division
602 Davidson St (27360-3628)
P.O. Box 2127 (27361-2127)
PHONE..................336 472-7908
Chris Yokeley, Pr
Mark Leonard, *
Steve Yokeley, *
▼ **EMP:** 8 **EST:** 1941
SQ FT: 90,000
SALES (est): 908.98K **Privately Held**
SIC: 2252 Socks

(G-12032)
HILLIARD FABRICATORS LLC
501 Carolina Ave (27360-4807)
P.O. Box 239 (27370-0239)
PHONE..................336 861-8833
EMP: 10 **EST:** 1986
SALES (est): 387.76K **Privately Held**
SIC: 3069 Foam rubber

(G-12033)
HUGHES SUP OF THOMASVILLE INC
175 Kanoy Rd (27360-8703)
P.O. Box 1003 (27361-1003)
PHONE..................336 475-8146
Jeffrey T Hughes, Pr
Terri Saintsing, *
Crystal Brock, *
Melissa Lawrence, Stockholder*
Jimmy Saintsing, *
▲ **EMP:** 91 **EST:** 1973
SQ FT: 70,000
SALES (est): 15.09MM **Privately Held**
Web: www.hughessupplyco.com
SIC: 3089 Injection molding of plastics

(G-12034)
HUNT COUNTRY COMPONENT LLC
1120 Trinity St (27360-8818)
PHONE..................336 475-7000
▲ **EMP:** 5 **EST:** 2003
SALES (est): 899.89K **Privately Held**
Web: www.huntcc.com
SIC: 3469 Furniture components, porcelain enameled

(G-12035)
HYDRO CONDUIT LLC
Also Called: Randolph Street - Pipe
208 Randolph St (27360-4642)
PHONE..................336 475-1371
John Peter, Genl Mgr
EMP: 6
Web: www.rinkerpipe.com
SIC: 3272 Pipe, concrete or lined with concrete
HQ: Hydro Conduit, Llc
5 Concourse Pkwy Ste 1900
Atlanta GA 30328
404 926-3100

(G-12036)
IMAFLEX USA INC
7137 Prospect Church Rd (27360-8839)
P.O. Box 1719 (27361-1719)
PHONE..................336 885-8131
Daniel A Jones, Opers Mgr

EMP: 35
SALES (corp-wide): 68.14MM **Privately Held**
Web: www.imaflex.com
SIC: 2673 Plastic bags: made from purchased materials
HQ: Imaflex Usa, Inc.
1200 Unity St
Thomasville NC 27360

(G-12037)
IMAFLEX USA INC (HQ)
1200 Unity St (27360-3220)
P.O. Box 1550 (27261-1550)
PHONE..................336 474-1190
Joseph Abbandonato, Pr
EMP: 32 **EST:** 2005
SQ FT: 93,000
SALES (est): 25.62MM
SALES (corp-wide): 68.14MM **Privately Held**
Web: www.imaflex.com
SIC: 2821 Plastics materials and resins
PA: Imaflex Inc
5710 Rue Notre-Dame O
Montreal QC H4C 1
514 935-5710

(G-12038)
IMAGES OF AMERICA INC
Also Called: Ioa Healthcare Furniture
829 Blair St (27360-4302)
PHONE..................336 475-7106
▲ **EMP:** 60 **EST:** 1969
SALES (est): 23.93MM **Privately Held**
Web: www.ioa-hcf.com
SIC: 2522 2512 Office furniture, except wood ; Wood upholstered chairs and couches

(G-12039)
INTERNATIONAL FURNISHINGS INC
1506 Lexington Ave (27360-3329)
P.O. Box 722 (27361-0722)
PHONE..................336 472-8422
Jack W Medlin, Pt
Judy Medlin, Pt
EMP: 9 **EST:** 1984
SALES (est): 88.58K **Privately Held**
Web: www.internationalfurnishingsinc.com
SIC: 2512 Chairs: upholstered on wood frames

(G-12040)
ISON FURNITURE MFG INC
801 Trinity St Ste 3a (27360-4846)
P.O. Box 2271 (27361-2271)
PHONE..................336 476-4700
Philip Ison, CEO
Akira Ison, *
EMP: 35 **EST:** 2018
SQ FT: 45,000
SALES (est): 2.24MM **Privately Held**
Web: www.architecturalhomecollection.com
SIC: 2511 5021 Wood household furniture; Household furniture

(G-12041)
JOHN CONRAD INC
Also Called: Conrad Tire & Automotive
1028 Johnsontown Rd (27360-4416)
PHONE..................336 475-8144
Robert Bergsma, Pr
Robert Conrad, Pr
Carol Conrad, Sec
EMP: 7 **EST:** 1969
SQ FT: 1,500
SALES (est): 924.55K **Privately Held**
Web: www.conradtireandauto.com

SIC: 5531 7534 7539 Automotive tires; Tire recapping; Auto front end repair

(G-12042)
LATHAM-HALL CORPORATION
5003 Ball Park Rd (27360-7911)
PHONE..................336 475-9723
Gary Dellinger, Pr
Jeanna Latham Dellinger, Sec
EMP: 20 **EST:** 1972
SQ FT: 23,000
SALES (est): 1.6MM **Privately Held**
SIC: 3599 Machine shop, jobbing and repair

(G-12043)
LEXINGTON FURNITURE INDS INC (PA)
Also Called: Lexington Home Brands
1300 National Hwy (27360-2318)
PHONE..................336 474-5300
Phil Haney, Pr
◆ **EMP:** 250 **EST:** 1936
SQ FT: 25,000
SALES (est): 40.91MM
SALES (corp-wide): 40.91MM **Privately Held**
Web: www.lexington.com
SIC: 2512 5021 5712 Upholstered household furniture; Furniture; Furniture stores

(G-12044)
LILLYS INTERIORS CSTM QUILTING
Also Called: Lillies Intriors Cstm Quilting
1165 Hillside Dr (27360-0526)
PHONE..................336 475-1421
Marty Gallimore, Pr
Betty Gallimore, Sec
EMP: 6 **EST:** 1967
SQ FT: 6,000
SALES (est): 145.13K **Privately Held**
SIC: 2211 Bedspreads, cotton

(G-12045)
LLOYDS FABRICATING SOLUTIONS
5896 Denton Rd (27360-8270)
PHONE..................336 250-0154
Robert Lloyd, Admn
EMP: 12 **EST:** 2017
SALES (est): 648.03K **Privately Held**
SIC: 7692 Welding repair

(G-12046)
MCINTYRE MANUFACTURING GROUP INC
310 Kendall Mill Rd (27360)
PHONE..................336 476-3646
▲ **EMP:** 60 **EST:** 1985
SALES (est): 8MM **Privately Held**
Web: www.mcintyredisplays.com
SIC: 2542 3537 3496 Racks, merchandise display or storage: except wood; Industrial trucks and tractors; Miscellaneous fabricated wire products

(G-12047)
MICKEY TRUCK BODIES INC
Also Called: Reconditioning Dept
Hwy 29-70 (27360)
P.O. Box 2044 (27261-2044)
PHONE..................336 882-6806
Greg Mclaughlin, Mgr
EMP: 8
SALES (corp-wide): 488.43K **Privately Held**
Web: www.mickeybody.com
SIC: 3713 Truck and bus bodies
PA: Mickey Truck Bodies Inc.
1305 Trinity Ave
High Point NC 27261

GEOGRAPHIC

336 882-6806

(G-12048)
MIKES WELDING & FABRICATING
2871 Old Highway 29 (27360-0040)
PHONE...............................336 472-5804
Michael Hillard, *Pr*
EMP: 4 **EST:** 1975
SQ FT: 4,200
SALES (est): 370.31K **Privately Held**
SIC: 7692 Welding repair

(G-12049)
MILL-CHEM MANUFACTURING INC
650 Bassett Dr (27360-8991)
P.O. Box 1455 (27261-1455)
PHONE...............................336 889-8038
Ernest Miller, *Pr*
EMP: 25 **EST:** 1989
SQ FT: 21,000
SALES (est): 5.01MM **Privately Held**
Web: www.millchem.com
SIC: 2842 Specialty cleaning

(G-12050)
MINNEWAWA INC
130 Sunrise Center Dr (27360-4900)
PHONE...............................865 522-8103
Lloyd Horner, *CEO*
Robert Puvey, *Pr*
EMP: 17 **EST:** 1939
SALES (est): 749.08K **Privately Held**
Web: www.minnewawa.com
SIC: 2241 2269 Labels, woven; Labels,
　cotton: printed
PA: Ctc Holdings, Llc
　165 Bluedevil Dr
　Gastonia NC 28056

(G-12051)
MOHAWK INDUSTRIES INC
Also Called: Mohawk Laminate & Hardwood
550 Cloniger Dr (27360-4960)
PHONE...............................336 313-4156
EMP: 8
Web: careers.mohawkind.com
SIC: 3253 Ceramic wall and floor tile
PA: Mohawk Industries, Inc.
　160 S Industrial Blvd
　Calhoun GA 30701

(G-12052)
MOTORSPORTS MACHINING TECH LLC
37 High Tech Blvd (27360-5560)
P.O. Box 915 (27361-0915)
PHONE...............................336 475-3742
EMP: 5 **EST:** 1999
SALES (est): 456.35K **Privately Held**
SIC: 3599 3714 Machine shop, jobbing and
　repair; Motor vehicle parts and accessories

(G-12053)
NEDERMAN INC
150 Transit Ave (27360-8927)
PHONE...............................336 821-0827
◆ **EMP:** 92 **EST:** 1980
SQ FT: 28,000
SALES (est): 12.34MM **Privately Held**
Web: www.nederman.com
SIC: 5084 3564 Pollution control equipment,
　air (environmental); Blowers and fans
PA: Nederman Holding Ab
　Sydhamnsgatan 2
　Helsingborg 252 3

(G-12054)
NEXT WORLD DESIGN INC
Also Called: Cycra Racing Systems
42 High Tech Blvd (27360-5560)

PHONE...............................800 448-1223
Glen Laivins, *Pr*
Kenneth T Laivins, *VP*
▲ **EMP:** 6 **EST:** 1992
SALES (est): 534.48K **Privately Held**
SIC: 3751 7389 Motorcycles and related
　parts; Design services

(G-12055)
NORDFAB LLC
150 Transit Ave (27360-8927)
P.O. Box 190 (27361-0190)
PHONE...............................336 821-0829
Tomas Hagstrom, *CEO*
Henrik Bjerregaard, *＊*
EMP: 137 **EST:** 1979
SALES (est): 16.3MM **Privately Held**
Web: www.nordfab.com
SIC: 3443 Ducting, metal plate
HQ: Nederman Holding Usa, Inc.
　4404a Chesapeake Dr
　Charlotte NC 28216
　704 859-2723

(G-12056)
NORTH AMERICAN IMPLEMENTS INC
215 Washboard Rd (27360-7900)
P.O. Box 2840 (27361-2840)
PHONE...............................336 476-2904
Eric Garner, *Prin*
EMP: 7 **EST:** 2012
SALES (est): 5.17MM **Privately Held**
Web:
www.northamericanimplements.com
SIC: 5083 3531 3523 Agricultural machinery
　and equipment; Construction machinery;
　Farm machinery and equipment

(G-12057)
OTB MACHINERY INC
51 Proctor Rd (27360-9266)
PHONE...............................336 323-1035
Kevin J Arvin, *Pr*
Sallie Ann Church, *VP*
▲ **EMP:** 5 **EST:** 2003
SALES (est): 2.27MM **Privately Held**
Web: www.otbmachinery.com
SIC: 3553 Woodworking machinery

(G-12058)
PARKDALE MILLS INCORPORATED
Also Called: Plant 6 & 7
400 Carmalt St (27360-4611)
PHONE...............................336 476-3181
Charles Russell, *Brnch Mgr*
EMP: 130
SALES (corp-wide): 1.44B **Privately Held**
Web: www.parkdalemills.com
SIC: 2281 Yarn spinning mills
HQ: Parkdale Mills, Incorporated
　531 Cotton Blossom Cir
　Gastonia NC 28054
　704 874-5000

(G-12059)
PETROLIANCE LLC
Also Called: Rex Oil Company
814 Lexington Ave (27360-3518)
PHONE...............................336 472-3000
EMP: 190
Web: www.petroliance.com
SIC: 3569 Lubricating equipment
HQ: Petroliance Llc
　640 Frdom Bus Ctr Dr Ste
　King Of Prussia PA 19406

(G-12060)
PIEDMONT TURNING & WDWKG CO
328 Jarrett Rd (27360-6018)
PHONE...............................336 475-7161

Jimmy Jones, *Pr*
EMP: 5 **EST:** 2002
SQ FT: 12,002
SALES (est): 499.47K **Privately Held**
Web: turningandcarving.tripod.com
SIC: 2431 Millwork

(G-12061)
POWDER WORKS INC
6698 Pikeview Dr (27360-9223)
P.O. Box 65 (27361-0065)
PHONE...............................336 475-7715
Jonathan C Hall, *Pr*
EMP: 8 **EST:** 2000
SALES (est): 981.33K **Privately Held**
Web: www.powderworksinc.com
SIC: 3479 Painting of metal products

(G-12062)
PRIME SYNTEX LLC
6980 Pikeview Dr (27360-8803)
PHONE...............................828 324-5496
EMP: 23 **EST:** 2015
SALES (est): 461.63K **Privately Held**
Web: www.primesyntex.com
SIC: 2299 Upholstery filling, textile

(G-12063)
PROMINENCE FURNITURE INC
415 Commercial Park Dr (27360-9591)
PHONE...............................336 475-6505
Paul M Buch, *Prin*
EMP: 20 **EST:** 2007
SALES (est): 1.01MM **Privately Held**
Web: www.prominence-furniture.com
SIC: 2512 Chairs: upholstered on wood
　frames

(G-12064)
QUALITY MARBLE
416 Julian Ave (27360-4835)
PHONE...............................336 472-1000
Victor Chamorro, *Prin*
EMP: 5 **EST:** 2007
SALES (est): 78.33K **Privately Held**
SIC: 3281 Cut stone and stone products

(G-12065)
RAND ANGE ENTERPRISES INC
800 Bryan Rd (27360-5430)
PHONE...............................336 472-7313
Angie B Black, *Prin*
EMP: 6 **EST:** 2008
SALES (est): 227.09K **Privately Held**
SIC: 3131 Rands

(G-12066)
ROAD INFRSTRCTURE INV HLDNGS I (HQ)
Also Called: Ennis-Flint
115 Todd Ct (27360-3233)
PHONE...............................336 475-6600
Steve Vetter, *CEO*
Michael Murren, *CFO*
EMP: 23 **EST:** 2012
SQ FT: 70,000
SALES (est): 4.31MM
SALES (corp-wide): 17.65B **Publicly Held**
Web: www.ennisflint.com
SIC: 2851 Paints and allied products
PA: Ppg Industries, Inc.
　1 Ppg Pl
　Pittsburgh PA 15272
　412 434-3131

(G-12067)
ROYAL COLONY FURNITURE INC
20 Carolina Ave (27360-4760)
PHONE...............................336 472-8833
James Beck, *Pr*

EMP: 6 **EST:** 1979
SQ FT: 8,256
SALES (est): 61.65K **Privately Held**
SIC: 2511 5712 Wood household furniture;
　Furniture stores

(G-12068)
S & S SAMPLES INC
880 Whitehart School Rd (27360-8465)
PHONE...............................336 472-0402
Sharon H Stone, *Pr*
Don Stone, *Sec*
EMP: 6 **EST:** 1997
SALES (est): 109.69K **Privately Held**
SIC: 2299 Textile mill waste and remnant
　processing

(G-12069)
S AND R SHEET METAL INC
521 Broad St (27360-5359)
PHONE...............................336 476-1069
Sammy Strickland, *Pr*
EMP: 6 **EST:** 1997
SALES (est): 961.99K **Privately Held**
Web: www.sandrsheetmetal.com
SIC: 3444 Sheet metal specialties, not
　stamped

(G-12070)
S DORSETT UPHOLSTERY INC
406 Aycock St (27360-4804)
PHONE...............................336 472-7076
Ronald Dorsett, *Pr*
Teresa Dorsett Holt, *Sec*
EMP: 4 **EST:** 1978
SQ FT: 7,000
SALES (est): 178.92K **Privately Held**
Web: www.dorsettupholsteryinc.com
SIC: 2512 7641 Upholstered household
　furniture; Reupholstery and furniture repair

(G-12071)
SOUTHERN RESIN INC
3440 Denton Rd (27360-6168)
P.O. Box 4186 (28603-4186)
PHONE...............................336 475-1348
E J Temple Junior, *Pr*
E J Temple Iii, *VP*
EMP: 38 **EST:** 1987
SALES (est): 7.75MM **Privately Held**
Web: www.tailoredchemical.com
SIC: 2891 Adhesives and sealants

(G-12072)
SOUTHILL INDUSTRIAL CARVING
1861 N Nc Highway 109 (27360-7489)
P.O. Box 2126 (27361-2126)
PHONE...............................336 472-5311
Bob Hill, *Owner*
EMP: 4 **EST:** 1980
SALES (est): 100.13K **Privately Held**
SIC: 2426 7389 Carvings, furniture: wood;
　Furniture finishing

(G-12073)
SPRINKLE OF SUGAR LLC
11 E Main St (27360-4043)
PHONE...............................336 474-8620
Bobby Hall, *Prin*
Joy Hall Thompson, *Prin*
EMP: 4 **EST:** 2011
SALES (est): 218.66K **Privately Held**
SIC: 5461 2051 Retail bakeries; Bakery:
　wholesale or wholesale/retail combined

(G-12074)
STN CUSHION COMPANY
3 Regency Industrial Blvd (27360-4940)
P.O. Box 2510 (27361-2510)
PHONE...............................336 476-9100

Steve Cothran, *Pr*
EMP: 100 EST: 1994
SQ FT: 55,000
SALES (est): 5.05MM **Privately Held**
Web: www.stncushion.com
SIC: 2392 2515 Cushions and pillows;
Mattresses and bedsprings

(G-12075)
STONE MARBLE CO INC
Also Called: Stone International USA
7004 Pikeview Dr (27360-8875)
PHONE.....................773 227-1161
Katherine J Mark, *Pr*
Anselmo Mannelli, *VP*
Nate Grossman, *Sec*
▲ **EMP:** 6 **EST:** 1992
SQ FT: 700
SALES (est): 3.04MM **Privately Held**
Web: www.stoneinternational.it
SIC: 5021 7641 2512 2511 Furniture;
Reupholstery and furniture repair;
Upholstered household furniture; Wood
household furniture
HQ: Stone Italia Srl
Via Caravaggio 41/43
Barberino Tavarnelle FI 50028
055755657

(G-12076)
SUPERIOR WOOD PRODUCTS INC
10190 E Us Highway 64 (27360-7749)
PHONE.....................336 472-2237
Billy C Noah, *Pr*
EMP: 4 **EST:** 1961
SQ FT: 47,902
SALES (est): 241.44K **Privately Held**
Web: www.superiorwoodproducts.com
SIC: 2531 2511 2512 Public building and
related furniture; Wood household furniture;
Upholstered household furniture

(G-12077)
SV PLASTICS LLC
Also Called: Cycra Racing
42 High Tech Blvd (27360-5560)
P.O. Box 915 (27361-0915)
PHONE.....................336 472-2242
Jim Zoretich, *Managing Member*
▲ **EMP:** 4 **EST:** 2013
SALES (est): 1.5MM
SALES (corp-wide): 4.97MM **Privately
Held**
SIC: 3751 7389 Motorcycles and related
parts; Design services
PA: Xceldyne Group, Llc
37 High Tech Blvd
Thomasville NC 27360
336 472-2242

(G-12078)
TEMPLEX INC
3 Stanley Ave (27360-8969)
P.O. Box 5648 (27262-5648)
PHONE.....................336 472-5933
Chris R Jones, *Pr*
Erin Jones-keaton, *Sec*
▲ **EMP:** 20 **EST:** 1958
SQ FT: 18,000
SALES (est): 2.22MM **Privately Held**
Web: www.templexinc.com
SIC: 3083 3563 Laminated plastics plate and
sheet; Vacuum (air extraction) systems,
industrial

(G-12079)
TIMOTHY LEE BLACJMON
Also Called: 62 Woodworking
2658 Johnsontown Rd (27360-7597)
PHONE.....................336 481-9038
Timothy Lee Blacjmon, *Owner*

EMP: 5 **EST:** 2022
SALES (est): 154.86K **Privately Held**
SIC: 2426 Frames for upholstered furniture,
wood

(G-12080)
TOMLINSON OF ORLANDO INC
Also Called: Carter
201 E Holly Hill Rd (27360-5819)
PHONE.....................336 475-8000
William Lambeth, *Pr*
Howard Williams, *
EMP: 4 **EST:** 2015
SALES (est): 159.31K **Privately Held**
Web: www.tomlinsoncompanies.com
SIC: 2599 Boards: planning, display, notice

(G-12081)
TOMLINSON/ERWIN-LAMBETH INC
201 E Holly Hill Rd (27360-5819)
PHONE.....................336 472-5005
William Roderick Lambeth, *Pr*
Howard L Williams, *
▲ **EMP:** 85 **EST:** 1900
SQ FT: 90,000
SALES (est): 4.48MM **Privately Held**
Web: www.tomlinsonerwinlambeth.com
SIC: 2512 Upholstered household furniture

(G-12082)
TRANSCONTINENTAL TVL LLC
1308 Blair St (27360-3249)
PHONE.....................336 476-3131
EMP: 13 **EST:** 2003
SALES (est): 7.18MM
SALES (corp-wide): 2.09B **Privately Held**
SIC: 2673 Bags: plastic, laminated, and
coated
PA: Transcontinental Inc
1 Place Ville-Marie Bureau 3240
Montreal QC H3B 0
514 954-4000

(G-12083)
TRIAD PRECISION PRODUCTS INC
128 Sunrise Center Dr (27360-4900)
PHONE.....................336 474-0980
Ken Maines, *Pr*
Donald Maines, *VP*
Marcia Maines, *Sec*
EMP: 12 **EST:** 1991
SQ FT: 10,000
SALES (est): 2.9MM **Privately Held**
Web: www.triadpp.com
SIC: 3599 Machine shop, jobbing and repair

(G-12084)
TRIMFIT INC
605 Pineywood Rd (27360-2750)
P.O. Box 699 (27361-0699)
PHONE.....................336 476-6154
Marty Erdman, *Manager*
EMP: 110
SALES (corp-wide): 4.43MM **Privately
Held**
Web: www.trimfit.com
SIC: 2252 4226 Socks; Special warehousing
and storage, nec
PA: Trimfit, Inc.
463 Fashion Ave Rm 1501
New York NY 10018
215 245-1122

(G-12085)
UNIVERSAL STEEL NC LLC
630 Bassett Dr (27360-8991)
PHONE.....................336 476-3105
Bill Noethling, *Managing Member*
EMP: 50 **EST:** 1972
SQ FT: 40,000
SALES (est): 5.03MM **Privately Held**

Web: www.universalsteelinc.com
SIC: 3441 3449 3444 Joists, open web steel:
long-span series; Bars, concrete
reinforcing: fabricated steel; Roof deck,
sheet metal

(G-12086)
WHITEWOOD INDUSTRIES INC (PA)
Also Called: Whitewood
100 Liberty Dr (27360-4837)
P.O. Box 1087 (27361-1087)
PHONE.....................336 472-0303
◆ **EMP:** 75 **EST:** 1982
SALES (est): 20.02MM
SALES (corp-wide): 20.02MM **Privately
Held**
Web: www.whitewood.net
SIC: 5021 2511 Dining room furniture; Bed
frames, except water bed frames: wood

(G-12087)
WILDCAT TERRITORY INC
110 W Guilford St (27360-3919)
P.O. Box 2005 (27361)
PHONE.....................718 361-6726
Nancy F Reib, *Pr*
Ibrahim Coban, *VP*
▲ **EMP:** 5 **EST:** 1992
SQ FT: 10,000
SALES (est): 431.08K **Privately Held**
Web: www.wildcatterritory.com
SIC: 2392 2391 Household furnishings, nec;
Curtains and draperies

(G-12088)
WINSTON CONCEPT FURNITURE
1110 Lexington Ave (27360-3415)
PHONE.....................336 472-7839
Jerry Kearns, *Owner*
EMP: 5 **EST:** 1979
SQ FT: 5,000
SALES (est): 246.7K **Privately Held**
SIC: 2511 Wood household furniture

(G-12089)
**WOEMPNER MACHINE COMPANY
INC**
Also Called: Wmc
385 Lloyd Murphy Rd (27360-7447)
PHONE.....................336 475-2268
Scott Woempner, *Pr*
Peggy Woempner, *CEO*
Ken Woempner, *VP*
EMP: 8 **EST:** 1978
SQ FT: 13,000
SALES (est): 826.89K **Privately Held**
Web: www.woempner.com
SIC: 3599 Machine shop, jobbing and repair

(G-12090)
WOODLINE INC
4695 Turnpike Ct (27360-8841)
PHONE.....................336 476-7100
Gail Lewis, *Pr*
Nancy Lewis, *Sec*
EMP: 4 **EST:** 1978
SQ FT: 6,000
SALES (est): 221.32K **Privately Held**
Web: www.woodline.com
SIC: 2426 2491 Furniture stock and parts,
hardwood; Wood preserving

(G-12091)
WRIGHT OF THOMASVILLE INC (PA)
Also Called: Global Graphics Solution
5115 Prospect St (27360-8849)
P.O. Box 1069 (27361-1069)
PHONE.....................336 472-4200
▲ **EMP:** 10 **EST:** 1961
SALES (est): 9.48MM
SALES (corp-wide): 9.48MM **Privately
Held**

Web: www.wrightlabels.com
SIC: 2679 2759 2241 Tags, paper
(unprinted): made from purchased paper;
Commercial printing, nec; Narrow fabric
mills

(G-12092)
XCELDYNE LLC
37 High Tech Blvd (27360-5560)
PHONE.....................336 472-2242
Corey Smith, *Managing Member*
EMP: 84 **EST:** 2011
SALES (est): 11.5MM **Privately Held**
Web: www.xceldyne.com
SIC: 3714 Motor vehicle parts and
accessories

(G-12093)
XCELDYNE GROUP LLC (PA)
Also Called: C.V.products
37 High Tech Blvd (27360-5560)
P.O. Box 915 (27361)
PHONE.....................336 472-2242
Corey Smith, *Pt*
James Zoretich, *
Larry Nichols, *
Clyde Vickers, *
▲ **EMP:** 68 **EST:** 1988
SQ FT: 42,000
SALES (est): 4.97MM
SALES (corp-wide): 4.97MM **Privately
Held**
Web: xceldyne.com
SIC: 3599 3471 Crankshafts and camshafts,
machining; Electroplating and plating

(G-12094)
XCELDYNE TECHNOLOGIES LLC
37 High Tech Blvd (27360-5560)
P.O. Box 915 (27361-0915)
PHONE.....................336 475-0201
Larry W Nichols, *Managing Member*
EMP: 75 **EST:** 2004
SQ FT: 30,000
SALES (est): 5.81MM **Privately Held**
Web: www.cvproducts.com
SIC: 3714 Motor vehicle engines and parts

(G-12095)
XTREME FABRICATION LTD
25b High Tech Blvd (27360-5560)
PHONE.....................336 472-4562
Dan Kingen, *Pr*
Larry Nichols, *VP*
Clyde Vickers, *Sec*
EMP: 8 **EST:** 2001
SALES (est): 1.08MM **Privately Held**
Web: www.xtremefabrication.com
SIC: 3714 5013 Fuel pumps, motor vehicle;
Pumps, oil and gas

(G-12096)
YOUNGER FURNITURE INC
110 Todd Ct (27360-3233)
P.O. Box 5165 (27262-5165)
PHONE.....................336 476-0444
Michael H Younger, *CEO*
Meredith Spell, *
Dreama Causey, *
EMP: 87 **EST:** 1989
SQ FT: 5,000
SALES (est): 7.08MM **Privately Held**
Web: www.youngerfurniture.com
SIC: 2512 Living room furniture: upholstered
on wood frames

Thurmond
Wilkes County

(G-12097)
JONES VONDREHLE VINEYARDS LLC
Also Called: Jones Vndrhle Vineyards Winery
964 Old Railroad Grade Rd (28683-9709)
P.O. Box 25 (28683-0025)
PHONE...............................336 874-2800
EMP: 10 EST: 2008
SALES (est): 1.55MM **Privately Held**
Web: www.jonesvondrehle.com
SIC: 2084 Wines

(G-12098)
LYON LOGGING
3256 S Center Church Rd (28683-9770)
PHONE...............................336 957-3131
EMP: 5 EST: 2005
SALES (est): 182.76K **Privately Held**
SIC: 2411 Logging

Timberlake
Person County

(G-12099)
CARDEN PRINTING COMPANY
52 Hunters Ln (27583-8781)
PHONE...............................336 364-2923
Skip Carden, Prin
EMP: 6 EST: 2010
SALES (est): 244.25K **Privately Held**
SIC: 2752 Commercial printing, lithographic

(G-12100)
GKN DRIVELINE NORTH AMER INC
Also Called: GKN Driveline Roxboro
6400 Durham Rd (27583)
PHONE...............................336 364-6200
Sherry Folkestad, Brnch Mgr
EMP: 153
SALES (corp-wide): 6.06B **Privately Held**
SIC: 3694 3714 3568 Engine electrical equipment; Motor vehicle parts and accessories; Power transmission equipment, nec
HQ: Gkn Driveline North America, Inc.
2200 N Opdyke Rd
Auburn Hills MI 48326
248 296-7000

(G-12101)
MEDALLION COMPANY INC (HQ)
250 Crown Blvd (27583-8507)
PHONE...............................919 990-3500
Wayne Eugene Rice, Pr
EMP: 105 EST: 1996
SQ FT: 100,000
SALES (est): 24.05MM **Publicly Held**
SIC: 3999 2111 Cigarette and cigar products and accessories; Cigarettes
PA: Vector Group Ltd.
4400 Biscayne Blvd
Miami FL 33137

Tobaccoville
Forsyth County

(G-12102)
R J REYNOLDS TOBACCO COMPANY
100 Moore-Rjr Dr (27050-9816)
PHONE...............................336 741-0400
EMP: 95
Web: www.rjrt.com

SIC: 2131 Smoking tobacco
HQ: R. J. Reynolds Tobacco Company
401 N Main St
Winston Salem NC 27101
336 741-5000

(G-12103)
STEWARTS GARAGE AND WELDING CO
6544 Doral Dr (27050-9562)
P.O. Box 88 (27050-0088)
PHONE...............................336 983-5563
Daniel L Stewart, Pr
Jackie Stewart, Sec
Daniel L Stewart Junior, VP
EMP: 6 EST: 1962
SQ FT: 2,000
SALES (est): 232.38K **Privately Held**
SIC: 1799 7692 Welding on site; Welding repair

Todd
Ashe County

(G-12104)
M & M STONE SCULPTING & ENGRV
498 Carter Miller Rd (28684-9416)
PHONE...............................336 877-3842
David Mason, Owner
EMP: 5 EST: 2005
SALES (est): 116.64K **Privately Held**
SIC: 0781 1741 1799 3281 Landscape services; Stone masonry; Sandblasting of building exteriors; Cut stone and stone products

Topton
Cherokee County

(G-12105)
NANTAHALA TALC & LIMESTONE CO
Also Called: NANTAHALA TALC & LIMESTONE CO
720 Hewitts Rd (28781-7510)
P.O. Box 174 (28781-0174)
PHONE...............................828 321-4239
Johnathon Mcguire, Mgr
EMP: 17
SALES (corp-wide): 2.43MM **Privately Held**
Web: www.mcneelycompanies.com
SIC: 1411 Limestone, dimension-quarrying
PA: Nantahala Talc & Limestone Co Inc
840 Main St
Andrews NC
828 321-3284

Traphill
Wilkes County

(G-12106)
SMITH UTILITY BUILDINGS
Also Called: B & W Enterprises
13721 Longbottom Rd (28685-8724)
PHONE...............................336 957-8211
David Smith, Owner
Bert Smith, Owner
EMP: 6 EST: 1982
SALES (est): 388.22K **Privately Held**
Web: www.design1usa.com
SIC: 3691 4222 Storage batteries; Refrigerated warehousing and storage

Trent Woods
Craven County

(G-12107)
J E CARPENTER LOGGING CO INC
4911 Hermitage Rd (28562-7558)
PHONE...............................252 633-0037
Jerry E Carpenter, Pr
EMP: 7 EST: 1979
SALES (est): 454.05K **Privately Held**
SIC: 2411 Logging camps and contractors

(G-12108)
UNITED DECORATIVE PLAS NC INC
Also Called: Udp
812 Llewellyn Dr (28562-8339)
PHONE...............................252 637-1803
Robert H Barnhill, Pr
Susy Barnhill, VP
EMP: 4 EST: 1989
SQ FT: 6,000
SALES (est): 1.34MM **Privately Held**
SIC: 3089 Injection molding of plastics

Trenton
Jones County

(G-12109)
ANTHONY B ANDREWS LOGGING INC
1000 Phillips Rd (28585-9356)
PHONE...............................252 448-8901
Anthony B Andrews, Pr
Betty Andrews, Sec
EMP: 9 EST: 1987
SALES (est): 447.63K **Privately Held**
SIC: 2411 Logging camps and contractors

(G-12110)
ROWMARK LLC
Color Path Technologies
182 Industrial Park Dr (28585-9593)
PHONE...............................252 448-9900
Bill Luzzi, Brnch Mgr
EMP: 6
SALES (corp-wide): 95.17MM **Privately Held**
Web: www.rowlam.com
SIC: 3089 Extruded finished plastics products, nec
PA: Rowmark Llc
5409 Hamlet Dr
Findlay OH 45840
419 425-8974

(G-12111)
TRENTON EMERGENCY MED SVCS INC
Also Called: Trenton Ems
105 Cherry St (28585-7714)
P.O. Box 309 (28585-0309)
PHONE...............................252 448-2646
Edward V Eubanks, Prin
Michael Jarman, Prin
EMP: 6 EST: 1959
SALES (est): 183.65K **Privately Held**
SIC: 3711 Fire department vehicles (motor vehicles), assembly of

(G-12112)
TRIPLE E EQUIPMENT LLC
Also Called: A.E. Logging
3899 Nc Highway 58 N (28585-9415)
PHONE...............................252 448-1002
EMP: 7 EST: 2020
SALES (est): 466.79K **Privately Held**
SIC: 2411 Logging

Trinity
Randolph County

(G-12113)
BATT FABRICATORS INC
12957 Trinity Rd (27370-8306)
PHONE...............................336 431-9334
Robert T Hoover, Pr
Tara Hoover, Sec
EMP: 10 EST: 2006
SQ FT: 48,000
SALES (est): 124.28K **Privately Held**
SIC: 3357 Nonferrous wiredrawing and insulating

(G-12114)
FURNITURE AT WORK
6089 Kennedy Rd (27370-7365)
PHONE...............................336 472-6619
Abby Williams, Pr
EMP: 5 EST: 1998
SALES (est): 173.4K **Privately Held**
Web: www.trinityfurniture.com
SIC: 5021 3469 Furniture; Metal stampings, nec

(G-12115)
GRUBB & SON SAWMILL INC
1498 Summey Town Rd (27370-7155)
PHONE...............................336 241-2252
Ronald Grubb, Pr
EMP: 4 EST: 1995
SALES (est): 445.74K **Privately Held**
SIC: 2421 Sawmills and planing mills, general

(G-12116)
INDUSTRIAL ANODIZING
112 School Rd (27370-9425)
PHONE...............................336 434-2110
Bill Smith, Pr
EMP: 4 EST: 2017
SALES (est): 305.14K **Privately Held**
Web: www.industrialanodizinginc.com
SIC: 3471 Anodizing (plating) of metals or formed products

(G-12117)
L RANCHO INVESTMENTS INC
5740 Hopewell Church Rd (27370-7646)
P.O. Box 370 (27370-0370)
PHONE...............................336 431-1004
Terry Labonte, Pr
Kim Labonte, Sec
EMP: 6 EST: 1986
SQ FT: 16,000
SALES (est): 175.45K **Privately Held**
Web: www.justinlabonte.com
SIC: 7948 5651 3711 Motor vehicle racing and drivers; Unisex clothing stores; Motor vehicles and car bodies

(G-12118)
OHIO MAT LCNSING CMPNNTS GROUP (DH)
1 Office Parkway Rd (27370-9449)
PHONE...............................336 861-3500
Lawrence Rogers, Pr
Kenneth L Walker, VP
◆ EMP: 5 EST: 1933
SQ FT: 179,000
SALES (est): 85.8MM
SALES (corp-wide): 4.93MM **Publicly Held**
SIC: 2515 6794 Box springs, assembled; Franchises, selling or licensing
HQ: Sealy Mattress Company
1 Office Parkway Rd
Trinity NC 27370
336 861-3500

▲ = Import ▼ = Export
◆ = Import/Export

(G-12119)
OHIO-SEALY MATTRESS MFG CO
1 Office Parkway Rd (27370-9449)
PHONE..................................336 861-3500
EMP: 150 **EST:** 1936
SQ FT: 35,000
SALES (est): 5.08MM
SALES (corp-wide): 4.93MM **Publicly Held**
SIC: 2515 Mattresses, innerspring or box spring
HQ: Sealy Mattress Company
1 Office Parkway Rd
Trinity NC 27370
336 861-3500

(G-12120)
P P M CYCLE AND CUSTOM
112 School Rd (27370-9425)
PHONE..................................336 434-5243
Tom Zales, *Pt*
Bill Smith, *Pt*
EMP: 5 **EST:** 2005
SALES (est): 212.44K **Privately Held**
SIC: 3751 Motorcycle accessories

(G-12121)
PACKAGING CORPORATION AMERICA
Also Called: PCA/High Point 334
212 Roelee St (27370-8263)
PHONE..................................336 434-0600
Dean Carter, *Brnch Mgr*
EMP: 49
SQ FT: 102,458
SALES (corp-wide): 7.73B **Publicly Held**
Web: www.packagingcorp.com
SIC: 2653 Boxes, corrugated: made from purchased materials
PA: Packaging Corporation Of America
1 N Field Ct
Lake Forest IL 60045
847 482-3000

(G-12122)
PALLET PLUS INC
12990 Trinity Rd (27370-8306)
PHONE..................................336 887-1810
William E Mcbride Junior, *Pr*
Keith Fraley, *VP*
EMP: 4 **EST:** 1998
SQ FT: 6,500
SALES (est): 86.28K **Privately Held**
SIC: 2448 Pallets, wood

(G-12123)
SEALY CORPORATION (HQ)
Also Called: Sealy & Company
1 Office Parkway Rd (27370-9449)
PHONE..................................336 861-3500
Lawrence J Rogers, *Pr*
Jeffrey C Ackerman, *
Louis R Bachicha, *
Jodi Allen, *
Michael Q Murray, *
◆ **EMP:** 130 **EST:** 1907
SALES (est): 58.38MM
SALES (corp-wide): 4.93MM **Publicly Held**
Web: www.sealy.com
SIC: 2515 Mattresses, innerspring or box spring
PA: Somnigroup International Inc.
1000 Tempur Way
Lexington KY 40511
800 878-8889

(G-12124)
SEALY MATTRESS COMPANY (DH)
1 Office Parkway Rd (27370-9449)
PHONE..................................336 861-3500

Larry Rogers, *Pr*
Kenneth L Walker, *
Jim Hirshorn, *
Lawrence J Rogers, *
Jeffrey C Ackerman, *
◆ **EMP:** 150 **EST:** 1881
SALES (est): 447.35MM
SALES (corp-wide): 4.93MM **Publicly Held**
Web: www.sealy.com
SIC: 2515 Mattresses, innerspring or box spring
HQ: Sealy Mattress Corporation
1 Office Way
Trinity NC 27370
336 861-3500

(G-12125)
SEALY MATTRESS MFG CO LLC
Also Called: Sealy Mattress
239 Sealy Dr (27370-9405)
PHONE..................................336 861-2900
Tom Boggs, *Mgr*
EMP: 96
SQ FT: 97,400
SALES (corp-wide): 4.93MM **Publicly Held**
Web: www.sealy.com
SIC: 2515 Mattresses, containing felt, foam rubber, urethane, etc.
HQ: Sealy Mattress Manufacturing Company, Llc
1000 Tempur Way
Lexington KY 40511
859 455-1000

(G-12126)
SOMNIGROUP INTERNATIONAL INC
1 Office Parkway Rd (27370)
PHONE..................................336 861-2900
EMP: 155
SALES (corp-wide): 4.93MM **Publicly Held**
Web: www.tempursealy.com
SIC: 2515 2392 Mattresses and foundations; Pillows, bed: made from purchased materials
PA: Somnigroup International Inc.
1000 Tempur Way
Lexington KY 40511
800 878-8889

(G-12127)
STRUCTURAL 0201 LLC ✪
300 Roelee St (27370-9411)
PHONE..................................240 288-8607
Scott Austin, *
EMP: 30 **EST:** 2023
SALES (est): 1.44MM **Privately Held**
SIC: 7389 2421 Design services; Building and structural materials, wood

---

Troutman
Iredell County

(G-12128)
ABT INC
Sportsedge
259 Murdock Rd (28166-9695)
PHONE..................................314 610-8798
Cory Formyduval, *Mgr*
EMP: 5
Web: www.abtdrains.com
SIC: 3272 Concrete products used to facilitate drainage
PA: Abt, Inc.
259 Murdock Rd
Troutman NC 28166

(G-12129)
ABT INC (PA)
259 Murdock Rd (28166-9695)
P.O. Box 837 (28166-0837)
PHONE..................................704 528-9806
Ralph Brafford, *Pr*
◆ **EMP:** 40 **EST:** 1988
SQ FT: 32,000
SALES (est): 21.36MM **Privately Held**
Web: www.abtdrains.com
SIC: 2821 3272 Plastics materials and resins ; Concrete products used to facilitate drainage

(G-12130)
AE TECHNOLOGY INC
Also Called: Atlantic Engineering
150 Ostwalt Amity Rd (28166-8834)
PHONE..................................704 528-2000
Dennis Lauffenburger, *Pr*
Virginia Lauffenburger, *VP*
EMP: 10 **EST:** 1995
SQ FT: 5,000
SALES (est): 1.17MM **Privately Held**
SIC: 2899 Chemical preparations, nec

(G-12131)
C R ONSRUD INC (PA)
120 Technology Dr (28166-8537)
P.O. Box 419 (28166-0419)
PHONE..................................704 508-7000
Thomas Onsrud, *CEO*
Charles R Onsrud, *
Thomas C Onsrud, *
John Onsrud, *
Bill Onsrud, *
▲ **EMP:** 159 **EST:** 1976
SQ FT: 60,000
SALES (est): 29.97MM
SALES (corp-wide): 29.97MM **Privately Held**
Web: www.cronsrud.com
SIC: 5084 3545 Industrial machinery and equipment; Machine tool accessories

(G-12132)
CAROLINA CEMETERY PARK CORP
Also Called: Ostwalt-Vault Co
344 Field Dr (28166-9737)
PHONE..................................704 528-5543
Avory Tucker, *Mgr*
EMP: 8
SALES (corp-wide): 797.35K **Privately Held**
Web: www.carolinacemetery.com
SIC: 3272 Burial vaults, concrete or precast terrazzo
PA: Carolina Cemetery Park Corp
601 Mount Olivet Rd
Kannapolis NC
704 786-2161

(G-12133)
CASE FARMS LLC (PA)
Also Called: Case Foods
385 Pilch Rd (28166-8782)
P.O. Box 729 (28166-0729)
PHONE..................................704 528-4501
EMP: 15 **EST:** 1995
SQ FT: 4,500
SALES (est): 110.02MM **Privately Held**
Web: www.casefarms.com
SIC: 2015 8731 Poultry slaughtering and processing; Commercial physical research

(G-12134)
CASE FARMS PROCESSING INC (HQ)
385 Pilch Rd (28166)
P.O. Box 308 (28680)
PHONE..................................704 528-4501

Michael Popwycz, *CEO*
Joseph D Long, *
◆ **EMP:** 35 **EST:** 1955
SQ FT: 11,200
SALES (est): 10.28MM
SALES (corp-wide): 117.64MM **Privately Held**
Web: www.casefarms.com
SIC: 2015 Poultry slaughtering and processing
PA: Case Foods, Inc.
385 Pilch Rd
Troutman NC 28166
704 528-4501

(G-12135)
CASE FOODS INC (PA)
Also Called: Case Farms Chicken
385 Pilch Rd (28166-8782)
P.O. Box 729 (28166-0729)
PHONE..................................704 528-4501
Thomas Shelton, *Pr*
David Van Hoose, *
Michael Popowycz, *
Chuck Mcdaniel, *Pr*
Brian Roberts, *Chief Commercial Officer*
▼ **EMP:** 140 **EST:** 1986
SALES (est): 117.64MM
SALES (corp-wide): 117.64MM **Privately Held**
Web: www.casefarms.com
SIC: 2015 Poultry, processed, nsk

(G-12136)
CAST FIRST STONE MINISTRY
106 Justin Dr (28166-8797)
PHONE..................................704 437-1053
EMP: 5 **EST:** 2013
SALES (est): 74.27K **Privately Held**
SIC: 3272 Concrete products, nec

(G-12137)
FIBERLINK
151 Flower House Loop (28166-9569)
PHONE..................................901 826-8126
EMP: 9 **EST:** 2016
SALES (est): 2.87MM **Privately Held**
SIC: 3661 Data sets, telephone or telegraph

(G-12138)
FIVE STAR BODIES
177 Houston Rd (28166-8740)
PHONE..................................262 325-9126
EMP: 5 **EST:** 2015
SALES (est): 1.58MM **Privately Held**
Web: www.fivestarbodies.com
SIC: 3714 Motor vehicle parts and accessories

(G-12139)
GLOBAL EMSSONS SYSTEMS INC-USA
158 Houston Rd (28166-8740)
PHONE..................................704 585-8490
Eric Latino, *Pr*
EMP: 8 **EST:** 2021
SALES (est): 959.54K **Privately Held**
SIC: 3621 Frequency converters (electric generators)

(G-12140)
HLM LEGACY GROUP INC
129 Honeycutt Rd (28166-7610)
P.O. Box 909 (28166-0909)
PHONE..................................704 878-8823
Tommy Mccoy, *Pr*
Fred Lampe, *VP*
Maria Haughton, *Prin*
▼ **EMP:** 200 **EST:** 1994
SQ FT: 82,000
SALES (est): 22.08MM **Privately Held**

Web: www.asti-nc.com
SIC: 3317 6719 Tubing, mechanical or hypodermic sizes: cold drawn stainless; Personal holding companies, except banks

(G-12141)
J & S FAB INC
354 S Eastway Dr (28166-8614)
P.O. Box 240 (28166-0240)
PHONE......................704 528-4251
Joe N Fox, *Pr*
EMP: 5 **EST:** 2000
SQ FT: 18,560
SALES (est): 946K **Privately Held**
Web: www.jandsfab.com
SIC: 3441 Fabricated structural metal

(G-12142)
JASPER SEATING COMPANY INC
Also Called: Jasper Library Furniture
694 N Main St (28166-8529)
PHONE......................704 528-4506
Anthony Moore, *Brnch Mgr*
EMP: 169
SALES (corp-wide): 198.33MM **Privately Held**
Web: jaspergroup.us.com
SIC: 2521 Wood office furniture
PA: Jasper Seating Company Inc
225 Clay St
Jasper IN 47546
812 482-3204

(G-12143)
LEGACY PRE-FINISHING INC
450 S Eastway Dr (28166-8613)
P.O. Box 768 (28166-0768)
PHONE......................704 528-7136
Jonathan Myers, *Pr*
EMP: 11 **EST:** 2009
SALES (est): 1.86MM **Privately Held**
Web: www.legacyprefinishing.com
SIC: 2421 Cants, resawed (lumber)

(G-12144)
LIAT LLC
Also Called: Jasper Library Furniture
694 N Main St (28166-8529)
P.O. Box 70 (28010-0070)
PHONE......................704 528-4506
EMP: 53 **EST:** 2010
SALES (est): 4.14MM **Privately Held**
Web: www.liatfurniture.com
SIC: 2531 Library furniture

(G-12145)
MACHINING SOLUTIONS INC
102 Corporate Dr (28166-8508)
P.O. Box 300 (28166-0300)
PHONE......................704 528-5436
Curtis Goodman, *Pr*
Harold Knight, *VP*
EMP: 5 **EST:** 1988
SQ FT: 7,000
SALES (est): 919.05K **Privately Held**
Web: www.msiracingproducts.com
SIC: 3599 Machine shop, jobbing and repair

(G-12146)
OSTWALT LEASING CO INC
867 S Main St (28166-8739)
P.O. Box 419 (28166-0419)
PHONE......................704 528-4528
Charlie Onsrud, *Pr*
Tom Onsrud, *
John Onsrud, *
Bill Onsrud, *
EMP: 56 **EST:** 1990
SALES (est): 2.86MM
SALES (corp-wide): 29.97MM **Privately Held**

SIC: 3553 Woodworking machinery
PA: C. R. Onsrud, Inc.
120 Technology Dr
Troutman NC 28166
704 508-7000

(G-12147)
OSTWALT MACHINE COMPANY INC
140 Apple Hill Rd (28166-9570)
PHONE......................704 528-5730
Reginald K Ostwalt, *Pr*
Derek Ostwalt, *VP*
Melissa O Willis, *Sec*
Joanne Ostwalt, *Treas*
EMP: 5 **EST:** 1964
SQ FT: 5,500
SALES (est): 465.19K **Privately Held**
SIC: 3599 Machine shop, jobbing and repair

(G-12148)
ROCKET INSTALLATION LLC
329 Talley St (28166-7622)
PHONE......................704 657-9492
EMP: 12 **EST:** 2020
SALES (est): 400K **Privately Held**
SIC: 3446 Stairs, fire escapes, balconies, railings, and ladders

(G-12149)
SCHAFER MANUFACTURING CO LLC
551 N Main St (28166-8526)
P.O. Box 388 (28166-0388)
PHONE......................704 528-5321
Carlene C Schafer, *Managing Member*
EMP: 5 **EST:** 1955
SQ FT: 30,000
SALES (est): 464.6K **Privately Held**
Web: www.church-steeples.com
SIC: 3315 Staples, steel: wire or cut

(G-12150)
SERENITY HOME SERVICES LLC
767 Morrison Farm Rd (28166-7625)
PHONE......................910 233-8733
James Shields, *Managing Member*
EMP: 5 **EST:** 2019
SALES (est): 698.69K **Privately Held**
SIC: 1389 7389 Construction, repair, and dismantling services; Business Activities at Non-Commercial Site

(G-12151)
STOWE ENTERPRISES INC
140 Royal Oak Dr (28166-8527)
P.O. Box 421 (28668-0421)
PHONE......................800 315-6751
EMP: 6 **EST:** 1997
SALES (est): 991.18K **Privately Held**
Web: www.stoweenterprises.com
SIC: 1542 3599 Commercial and office building contractors; Machine and other job shop work

(G-12152)
TROUTMAN CARECONNECT CORP
191 Timber Lake Dr (28166-7687)
PHONE......................704 838-9389
EMP: 18 **EST:** 2019
SALES (est): 1.41MM **Privately Held**
Web: www.troutmanchairs.com
SIC: 2511 Wood household furniture

(G-12153)
TROUTMAN CHAIR COMPANY LLC
134 Rocker Ln (28166)
P.O. Box 208 (28166-0208)
PHONE......................704 872-7625
Edward Land, *
▲ **EMP:** 43 **EST:** 1924
SQ FT: 50,000

SALES (est): 1.52MM **Privately Held**
Web: www.troutmanchairs.com
SIC: 2511 Rockers, except upholstered: wood

(G-12154)
U S PROPELLER SERVICE INC
844 S Main St (28166-8514)
PHONE......................704 528-9515
Steve Rogers, *Pr*
Dee Dee Rogers, *Sec*
EMP: 5 **EST:** 1980
SALES (est): 162.32K **Privately Held**
Web: www.uspropellerservice.com
SIC: 7699 3732 Marine propeller repair; Boatbuilding and repairing

(G-12155)
UP ON HILL
Also Called: Precious Oils Up On The Hill
129 Fesperman Cir (28166-3401)
P.O. Box 2036 (28031-2036)
PHONE......................704 664-7971
Cynthia Hillson, *Owner*
EMP: 4 **EST:** 1989
SALES (est): 198.35K **Privately Held**
Web: preciousoils.wordpress.com
SIC: 2844 Perfumes, natural or synthetic

Troy
Montgomery County

(G-12156)
ALANDALE INDUSTRIES INC
208 Burnette St (27371-3067)
P.O. Box 804 (27371-0804)
PHONE......................910 576-1291
Laurie Gutschmit, *Pr*
▼ **EMP:** 8 **EST:** 1986
SALES (est): 2.42MM **Privately Held**
Web: www.alandale.net
SIC: 3552 Knitting machines

(G-12157)
AURIA TROY LLC
163 Glen Rd (27371-8320)
P.O. Box B (27371-0455)
PHONE......................910 572-3721
Brian Pour, *Pr*
EMP: 91 **EST:** 2007
SQ FT: 120,000
SALES (est): 3.58MM
SALES (corp-wide): 19K **Privately Held**
Web: www.auriasolutions.com
SIC: 3714 Motor vehicle parts and accessories
HQ: Auria Solutions Usa Inc.
26999 Cntl Pk Blvd Ste 30
Southfield MI 48076
248 728-8000

(G-12158)
CAPEL INCORPORATED (PA)
Also Called: Capel Rugs
831 N Main St (27371-2507)
P.O. Box 826 (27371-0826)
PHONE......................910 572-7000
John A Magee, *Pr*
Bud Young, *
Mary Clara Capel, *
N C Capel, *
Arron W E Capel Iii, *Dir*
◆ **EMP:** 60 **EST:** 1957
SQ FT: 80,000
SALES (est): 22.9MM
SALES (corp-wide): 22.9MM **Privately Held**
Web: www.capelrugs.com

SIC: 5023 2273 Rugs; Rugs, braided and hooked

(G-12159)
DEBERRY LAND & TIMBER INC
112 Leslie St (27371-2506)
P.O. Box 622 (27371-0622)
PHONE......................910 572-2698
Danny V Deberry, *Owner*
EMP: 6 **EST:** 1984
SALES (est): 471.5K **Privately Held**
SIC: 5099 2411 Pulpwood; Pulpwood contractors engaged in cutting

(G-12160)
DEX N DOX
225 Basswood Rd (27371-9765)
P.O. Box 618 (28009-0618)
PHONE......................910 576-4644
Georgia Inskeep, *Owner*
Rick Inskeep, *Mgr*
EMP: 4 **EST:** 1986
SQ FT: 3,200
SALES (est): 86.64K **Privately Held**
SIC: 5031 2452 Lumber: rough, dressed, and finished; Log cabins, prefabricated, wood

(G-12161)
HICKMAN OIL & ICE CO INC
Also Called: Hickman Oil & Ice
165 Lemonds Drywall Rd (27371-8587)
P.O. Box 563 (27371-0563)
PHONE......................910 576-2501
Ricky L Harris, *Pr*
Ivey H Harris, *Sec*
EMP: 4 **EST:** 1986
SQ FT: 2,184
SALES (est): 460.43K **Privately Held**
Web: www.patpoor.us
SIC: 2097 5983 Manufactured ice; Fuel oil dealers

(G-12162)
HURLEYS ORNAMENTAL IRON
2179 Love Joy Rd (27371-7205)
P.O. Box 502 (27371-0502)
PHONE......................910 576-4731
David Hurley, *Owner*
EMP: 4 **EST:** 1997
SALES (est): 179.03K **Privately Held**
Web: hurleysiron.wordpress.com
SIC: 3446 Architectural metalwork

(G-12163)
MONTGOMERY LOGGING INC
207 Atkins Dairy Rd (27371-8502)
PHONE......................910 572-2806
Bill Lynthacum, *Pr*
EMP: 8 **EST:** 1993
SALES (est): 249.56K **Privately Held**
Web: www.postroadliquors.com
SIC: 2411 7389 Logging; Brokers, contract services

(G-12164)
PRECISION TEXTILES LLC
Also Called: North Carolina Warehouse
163 Glen Rd (27371-8320)
PHONE......................910 515-6696
EMP: 105
SALES (corp-wide): 48.14MM **Privately Held**
Web: www.precisiontextiles-usa.com
SIC: 2295 Varnishing of textiles
PA: Precision Textiles Llc
90 New Dutch Ln
Fairfield NJ 07004
973 890-3873

▲ = Import ▼ = Export
◆ = Import/Export

(G-12165)
PRO PALLET SOUTH INC
105 Poole Rd (27371-9300)
PHONE..............................910 576-4902
Mark Collare, *Pr*
Kristen Pruitt, *
EMP: 110 **EST:** 2007
SQ FT: 42,000
SALES (est): 8.66MM **Privately Held**
Web: www.propalletsouth.com
SIC: 2448 Pallets, wood

(G-12166)
SAPUTO CHEESE USA INC
131 Wright Way (27371-8715)
PHONE..............................847 267-1100
Lino A Saputo Junior, *CEO*
EMP: 131
SALES (corp-wide): 3.79B **Privately Held**
Web: www.saputousafoodservice.com
SIC: 2022 Natural cheese
HQ: Saputo Cheese Usa Inc.
10700 W Res Dr Ste 400
Milwaukee WI 53226

(G-12167)
SHEPHERD FAMILY LOGGING LLC
138 Ivey St (27371-8437)
PHONE..............................910 572-4098
EMP: 6 **EST:** 2016
SALES (est): 859.32K **Privately Held**
SIC: 2411 Logging

(G-12168)
SUGARSHACK BAKERY AND EMB
275 Sugar Loaf Rd (27371-1978)
PHONE..............................803 920-3311
EMP: 4 **EST:** 2015
SALES (est): 69.51K **Privately Held**
SIC: 2395 Embroidery and art needlework

(G-12169)
TROY READY - MIX INC
1739 Nc Highway 24 27 109 W
(27371-8337)
P.O. Box 137 (27371-0137)
PHONE..............................910 572-1011
James Macon, *Pr*
Robert Foushee, *VP*
Jeff Macon, *Sec*
EMP: 9 **EST:** 1969
SQ FT: 7,000
SALES (est): 1.64MM **Privately Held**
SIC: 3272 5032 Concrete products, nec;
Concrete mixtures

(G-12170)
UWHARRIE LUMBER CO
335 Page St (27371-2837)
P.O. Box 533 (27371-0533)
PHONE..............................910 572-3731
Ray Allen, *Pr*
John Fred Allen, *
Kerry Anderson, *
Becky Saunders, *
EMP: 14 **EST:** 1983
SQ FT: 522,720
SALES (est): 2.02MM **Privately Held**
Web: www.uwharrielumber.com
SIC: 2426 2421 Hardwood dimension and
flooring mills; Sawmills and planing mills,
general

(G-12171)
WOOD RIGHT LUMBER COMPANY
225 Basswood Rd (27371-9765)
P.O. Box 618 (28009-0618)
PHONE..............................910 576-4642
Gergio Inskeep, *Owner*
Gergia Inskeep, *Owner*

Rick Inskeep, *Owner*
▲ **EMP:** 4 **EST:** 1985
SALES (est): 84.3K **Privately Held**
SIC: 5031 2452 Lumber, plywood, and
millwork; Prefabricated wood buildings

Tryon
Polk County

(G-12172)
CAROLINA YARN PROCESSORS INC
Also Called: Cyp
250 Screvens Rd (28782-2720)
PHONE..............................828 859-5891
Steve Silvia, *Pr*
EMP: 155 **EST:** 1957
SALES (est): 528.59K **Privately Held**
SIC: 2269 2389 Finishing: raw stock, yarn,
and narrow fabrics; Handkerchiefs, except
paper
HQ: Fendrich Industries, Inc.
7025 Augusta Rd
Greenville SC 29605
864 299-0600

(G-12173)
COMMUNITYS KITCHEN L3C
835 N Trade St Ste A (28782-5630)
PHONE..............................828 817-2308
Carol Lynn Jackson, *CEO*
EMP: 5 **EST:** 2013
SALES (est): 84.12K **Privately Held**
SIC: 0723 2099 5411 7299 Crop preparation
services for market; Food preparations, nec
; Cooperative food stores; Banquet hall
facilities

(G-12174)
D&S COMPANY INC
265 Hugh Champion Rd (28782-8888)
PHONE..............................828 894-2778
James Deck, *Pr*
Christopher Stott, *VP*
James Shehan, *Treas*
EMP: 6 **EST:** 1998
SALES (est): 415.93K **Privately Held**
SIC: 5032 2951 Asphalt mixture; Asphalt
and asphaltic paving mixtures (not from
refineries)

(G-12175)
MG12 LP
874 S Trade St (28782-3720)
P.O. Box 429 (27357-0429)
PHONE..............................828 440-1144
Thomas Strader, *Managing Member*
Rhett Greene, *Sls Dir*
EMP: 8 **EST:** 2014
SALES (est): 463.87K **Privately Held**
Web: www.mg12.com
SIC: 3356 Magnesium

(G-12176)
POLK SAWMILL LLC
206 Will Green Rd (28782-8879)
PHONE..............................828 863-0436
Patrick Parton, *Admn*
EMP: 6 **EST:** 2016
SALES (est): 269.82K **Privately Held**
SIC: 2421 Sawmills and planing mills,
general

(G-12177)
PURE COUNTRY INC
Also Called: Fine Art Tapestries
81 Skylar Dr (28782-6683)
P.O. Box 407 (28750-0407)
PHONE..............................828 871-2890
George Clark, *Pr*

Ann Wetherill, *
Mark Majewski, *
▲ **EMP:** 90 **EST:** 1988
SQ FT: 35,000
SALES (est): 7.07MM **Privately Held**
Web: www.purecountry.com
SIC: 2392 2211 Household furnishings, nec;
Broadwoven fabric mills, cotton

(G-12178)
TRYON FINISHING CORPORATION
250 Screvens Rd (28782-2720)
PHONE..............................828 859-5891
Naiden Kremenliev, *Pr*
EMP: 4 **EST:** 2020
SALES (est): 256.65K **Privately Held**
Web: www.tryonfinishing.com
SIC: 2261 Screen printing of cotton
broadwoven fabrics

(G-12179)
TRYON NEWSMEDIA LLC
Also Called: Appointments
16 N Trade St (28782-6656)
PHONE..............................828 859-9151
Teddy Ramsey, *Pr*
EMP: 9 **EST:** 1928
SQ FT: 6,000
SALES (est): 187.69K **Privately Held**
Web: www.tryondailybulletin.com
SIC: 2711 2752 Newspapers, publishing and
printing; Commercial printing, lithographic

(G-12180)
WOVENART INC
Also Called: Wovern Art
687 N Trade St (28782-5596)
P.O. Box 271 (28722-0271)
PHONE..............................828 859-6349
Caryn Cunningham, *Pr*
EMP: 10 **EST:** 1998
SALES (est): 169K **Privately Held**
Web: www.wovenart.net
SIC: 2399 5131 Hand woven and crocheted
products; Linen piece goods, woven

Turkey
Sampson County

(G-12181)
FABULOUS FIGUREZ LLC
7535 Old Warsaw Rd (28393-8853)
PHONE..............................336 894-6014
EMP: 5
SALES (est): 298.68K **Privately Held**
SIC: 2339 Athletic clothing: women's,
misses', and juniors'

Tyner
Chowan County

(G-12182)
BILLY HARRELL LOGGING INC
152 County Line Rd (27980-9690)
PHONE..............................252 221-4995
William H Harrell Senior, *Pr*
Doris Harrell, *Sec*
William H Harrell Junior, *VP*
EMP: 8 **EST:** 1990
SALES (est): 469.04K **Privately Held**
SIC: 2411 Logging camps and contractors

(G-12183)
J R NIXON WELDING
212 Center Hill Rd (27980-9774)
PHONE..............................252 221-4574
James R Nixon, *Owner*
EMP: 4 **EST:** 1980

SALES (est): 303.29K **Privately Held**
SIC: 7692 Welding repair

Union Grove
Iredell County

(G-12184)
CUTTING SYSTEMS INC
774 Zeb Rd (28689-9148)
PHONE..............................704 592-2451
Tony Johnson, *Pr*
John Johnson, *
Pauline Johnson, *
▲ **EMP:** 60 **EST:** 1995
SQ FT: 80,000
SALES (est): 9.55MM **Privately Held**
Web: www.cuttingsys.com
SIC: 5271 5082 3537 3531 Mobile home
equipment; Logging equipment and supplies
; Industrial trucks and tractors; Construction
machinery

(G-12185)
G & G FOREST PRODUCTS
147 Lumber Dr (28689)
P.O. Box 99 (28689-0099)
PHONE..............................704 539-5110
EMP: 7 **EST:** 2014
SALES (est): 658.26K **Privately Held**
Web: www.gandgforestproducts.com
SIC: 0831 2421 Forest products; Building
and structural materials, wood

(G-12186)
UNION GROVE SAW & KNIFE INC
157 Sawtooth Lane (28689)
PHONE..............................704 539-4442
Edward A Bissell, *Pr*
Shelba Bissell, *
▲ **EMP:** 67 **EST:** 1981
SQ FT: 20,400
SALES (est): 1.86MM **Privately Held**
Web: www.sawandknife.com
SIC: 3425 3541 7699 Saws, hand:
metalworking or woodworking; Machine
tools, metal cutting type; Knife, saw and
tool sharpening and repair

Union Mills
Rutherford County

(G-12187)
CABINETS AND THINGS
141 Bill Deck Rd (28167-7608)
PHONE..............................828 652-1734
Kenneth Smalley, *Prin*
EMP: 5 **EST:** 2010
SALES (est): 189.35K **Privately Held**
SIC: 2434 Wood kitchen cabinets

(G-12188)
CVMR (USA) INC
2702 Centennial Rd (28167-9617)
PHONE..............................828 288-3768
Michael C Hargett, *Pr*
Kamran M Khozan, *Ch*
John R Finley, *Sec*
Nanthakumar Victor Emmanuel, *VP*
John D Wagoner, *Dir*
EMP: 165 **EST:** 2007
SALES (est): 7.3B
SALES (corp-wide): 44.56MM **Privately
Held**
Web: www.cvmr.ca
SIC: 3339 7389 Primary nonferrous metals,
nec; Business services, nec
PA: Cvmr Corporation
35 Kenhar Dr

GEOGRAPHIC

North York ON M9L 1
416 743-2746

Valdese
Burke County

(G-12189)
BURKE MILLS INC
191 Sterling St Nw (28690-2649)
P.O. Box 190 (28690-0190)
PHONE.............................828 874-6341
Humayun N Shaikh, *Ch Bd*
Thomas I Nail, *
Richard F Byers, *
Pender R Mcelroy, *Sec*
William E Singleton, *VP Mfg*
◆ **EMP:** 7 **EST:** 1948
SALES (est): 471.81K **Privately Held**
SIC: 2299 Yarns and thread, made from non-
fabric materials
PA: Naseus Inc.
C/O: Franco Y Franco
Panama City

(G-12190)
BY-DESIGN BLACK OXIDE & TL LLC
1260 Margaret St Nw (28690-2148)
PHONE.............................828 874-0610
EMP: 10 **EST:** 2012
SALES (est): 241.19K **Privately Held**
Web:
www.bydesignblackoxideandtool.com
SIC: 7389 3398 Design services; Annealing
of metal

(G-12191)
C & S WOODWORKING
833 Summers Rd (28690-9547)
PHONE.............................828 437-5024
Howard Crump, *Owner*
EMP: 5 **EST:** 1976
SQ FT: 11,250
SALES (est): 250K **Privately Held**
SIC: 2426 Frames for upholstered furniture,
wood

(G-12192)
CCO HOLDINGS LLC
240 Main St W (28690-2835)
PHONE.............................828 368-4161
EMP: 112
SALES (corp-wide): 55.09MM **Publicly
Held**
SIC: 4841 3663 3651 Cable television
services; Radio and t.v. communications
equipment; Household audio and video
equipment
HQ: Cco Holdings, Llc
400 Atlantic St
Stamford CT 06901
203 905-7801

(G-12193)
CONTINENTAL AUTO SYSTEMS INC
1103 Johnstown Rd (28690)
PHONE.............................828 584-4500
EMP: 50
SALES (corp-wide): 45.02B **Privately Held**
Web: www.continental-automotive.com
SIC: 3714 Motor vehicle parts and
accessories
HQ: Continental Automotive Systems, Inc.
1 Continental Dr
Auburn Hills MI 48326
248 393-5300

(G-12194)
CUSTOM SEATINGS
3011 High Peak Rd (28690-9464)

P.O. Box 602 (28619-0602)
PHONE.............................828 879-1964
Ken Ramsey, *Owner*
EMP: 8 **EST:** 1983
SQ FT: 12,000
SALES (est): 471.32K **Privately Held**
SIC: 3429 Furniture, builders' and other
household hardware

(G-12195)
HUDDLE FURNITURE INC (PA)
1801 Main St E (28690-8733)
PHONE.............................828 874-8888
Gideon C Huddle, *CEO*
Candace H Payne, *
Damaris Huddle, *
John P Payne, *
▲ **EMP:** 50 **EST:** 1981
SQ FT: 50,000
SALES (est): 9.79MM
SALES (corp-wide): 9.79MM **Privately
Held**
Web: www.shenandoahfurniture.com
SIC: 2512 Upholstered household furniture

(G-12196)
KELLEX CORP
Kellex Seating
501 Hoyle St Sw (28690-2605)
PHONE.............................828 874-0389
Larry Parsons, *VP*
EMP: 148
SQ FT: 298,000
Web: www.kellex.com
SIC: 2512 Chairs: upholstered on wood
frames
PA: Kellex Corp.
33390 Liberty Pkwy
North Ridgeville OH 44039

(G-12197)
**MERIDIAN SPCALTY YRN GROUP
INC (HQ)**
312 Colombo St Sw (28690-2750)
P.O. Box 10 (28690-0010)
PHONE.............................828 874-2151
Tim Manson, *Pr*
Bruce Eben Pindyck, *
Mary Ellen Pindyck, *
Douglas C Miller, *
Joseph B Tyson, *
◆ **EMP:** 74 **EST:** 2006
SALES (est): 4.55MM
SALES (corp-wide): 331.16MM **Privately
Held**
Web: www.msyg.com
SIC: 5949 2282 Knitting goods and supplies;
Acetate filament yarn: throwing, twisting,
winding, spooling
PA: Meridian Industries, Inc.
735 N Water St Ste 630
Milwaukee WI 53202
414 224-0610

(G-12198)
**PIEDMONT CORRUGATED
SPECIALTY**
Also Called: Piedmont Corrugated
340 Morgan St Se (28690-2930)
P.O. Box 68 (28690-0068)
PHONE.............................828 874-1153
Boyd Baird, *Pr*
Charles Baird, *
Dorothy Bauguess, *
Frank Welch, *General Vice President*
EMP: 60 **EST:** 1974
SQ FT: 32,000
SALES (est): 4.56MM **Privately Held**
Web: www.piedmontcorrugated.com
SIC: 2653 Boxes, corrugated: made from
purchased materials

(G-12199)
ROBINSON HOSIERY MILL INC
113 Robinson St Se (28690-8813)
PHONE.............................828 874-2228
Kenneth Robinson, *Pr*
Alton Robinson, *
EMP: 6 **EST:** 1956
SQ FT: 1,500
SALES (est): 257.59K **Privately Held**
SIC: 2252 Socks

(G-12200)
SAFT AMERICA INC
Lithium Battery Div
313 Crescent St Ne (28690-9643)
PHONE.............................828 874-4111
John Lundeen, *Brnch Mgr*
EMP: 275
SQ FT: 20,346
SALES (corp-wide): 7.88B **Privately Held**
Web: www.saft.com
SIC: 3692 3691 Primary batteries, dry and
wet; Batteries, rechargeable
HQ: Saft America Inc
13575 Waterworks St
Jacksonville FL 32221
904 861-1501

(G-12201)
**VALDESE PACKAGING & LABEL INC
(PA)**
302 Saint Germain Ave Se (28690)
P.O. Box 1215 (28690-1215)
PHONE.............................828 879-9772
Darren Little, *Pr*
Doyle Little, *
David Little, *
▼ **EMP:** 25 **EST:** 1993
SQ FT: 40,000
SALES (est): 3.61MM **Privately Held**
Web: www.visitvaldese.com
SIC: 2671 2752 2759 Paper; coated and
laminated packaging; Offset and
photolithographic printing; Flexographic
printing

(G-12202)
VALDESE PACKAGING & LABEL INC
302 Saint Germain Ave Sw (28690-2734)
PHONE.............................828 879-9772
Darren Little, *Brnch Mgr*
EMP: 15
Web: www.visitvaldese.com
SIC: 2752 2759 Offset and photolithographic
printing; Flexographic printing
PA: Valdese Packaging & Label, Inc.
302 Saint Germain Ave Se
Valdese NC 28690

(G-12203)
VALDESE TEXTILES INC
1901 Main St E (28690-8734)
P.O. Box 490 (28690-0490)
PHONE.............................828 874-4216
Yasmine Safadi, *Pr*
EMP: 4 **EST:** 1987
SQ FT: 20,000
SALES (est): 258.52K **Privately Held**
Web: www.msyg.com
SIC: 2221 2211 Broadwoven fabric mills,
manmade; Broadwoven fabric mills, cotton

(G-12204)
VALDESE WEAVERS LLC
705 Lovelady Rd Ne (28690-8856)
P.O. Box 23000 (28603-0230)
PHONE.............................828 874-2181
Scott Malcolm, *Brnch Mgr*
▲ **EMP:** 4
SALES (corp-wide): 47.25MM **Privately
Held**

Web: www.valdeseweavers.com
SIC: 2211 Broadwoven fabric mills, cotton
PA: Valdese Weavers, Llc
1000 Perkins Rd Se
Valdese NC 28690
828 874-2181

(G-12205)
VALDESE WEAVERS LLC
Also Called: C V Industries
280 Crescent St Ne (28690-8914)
P.O. Box 70 (28690-0070)
PHONE.............................828 874-2181
EMP: 949
SALES (corp-wide): 47.25MM **Privately
Held**
Web: www.valdeseweavers.com
SIC: 2211 2221 Broadwoven fabric mills,
cotton; Broadwoven fabric mills, manmade
PA: Valdese Weavers, Llc
1000 Perkins Rd Se
Valdese NC 28690
828 874-2181

(G-12206)
VALDESE WEAVERS LLC (PA)
Also Called: Valdese Weavers
1000 Perkins Rd Se (28690)
P.O. Box 70 (28690)
PHONE.............................828 874-2181
Blake Millinor, *CEO*
Richard Reese, *
Snyder Garrison, *
◆ **EMP:** 450 **EST:** 1915
SALES (est): 47.25MM
SALES (corp-wide): 47.25MM **Privately
Held**
Web: www.valdeseweavers.com
SIC: 2675 2221 Jacquard (textile weaving)
cards: from purchased materials;
Upholstery fabrics, manmade fiber and silk

Vale
Lincoln County

(G-12207)
AMERICAN SAMPLE HOUSE INC
2105 Cat Square Rd (28168-8766)
P.O. Box 6 (28168-0006)
PHONE.............................704 276-1970
Thomas R Lackey, *Pr*
Judy Lackey, *Sec*
EMP: 6 **EST:** 1985
SQ FT: 8,268
SALES (est): 278.85K **Privately Held**
Web:
americansamplehouse.godaddysites.com
SIC: 2789 5087 2782 Swatches and samples
; Upholsterers' equipment and supplies;
Blankbooks and looseleaf binders

(G-12208)
ETHICS ARCHERY LLC
Also Called: Ethics Bullets
2664 Sam Houser Rd (28168-9365)
PHONE.............................980 429-2070
Scott Gizowski, *CEO*
Deborah Kelley, *VP Opers*
EMP: 5 **EST:** 2010
SALES (est): 615.91K **Privately Held**
Web: www.ethicsarchery.com
SIC: 3949 Sporting and athletic goods, nec

(G-12209)
MEGHAN BLAKE INDUSTRIES INC
Also Called: Hickory Leather Company
7514 W Nc 10 Hwy (28168-9511)
PHONE.............................704 462-2988
Brian Litten, *Pr*
Melinda M Litten, *

▲ **EMP:** 50 **EST:** 2007
SALES (est): 9.34MM **Privately Held**
Web: www.hickorycontract.com
SIC: 5047 3999 Hospital furniture;
   Wheelchair lifts

(G-12210)
PITMAN KNITS INC
7625 Palm Tree Church Rd (28168-7463)
PHONE.............................704 276-3262
Fred Pitman, *VP*
Fred L Pitman, *VP*
Tracy Pitman, *Sec*
EMP: 7 **EST:** 1997
SALES (est): 490K **Privately Held**
SIC: 2253 Knit outerwear mills

(G-12211)
WEST EXPRESS
4472 W Highway 27 (28168-9656)
PHONE.............................704 276-9001
Ronald Burton, *Pr*
EMP: 4 **EST:** 2006
SALES (est): 188.06K **Privately Held**
Web: www.westexpress.lt
SIC: 2741 Miscellaneous publishing

(G-12212)
WOODMILL WINERY INC
1350 Woodmill Winery Ln (28168-6796)
PHONE.............................704 276-9911
Larry Gene Cagle Junior, *Pr*
EMP: 7 **EST:** 2005
SALES (est): 493.76K **Privately Held**
Web: www.woodmillwinery.com
SIC: 2084 Wines

Vanceboro
Craven County

(G-12213)
A & J CANVAS INC
2450 Streets Ferry Rd (28586-8349)
PHONE.............................252 244-1509
Jerry L Shoe, *Pr*
Ada Shoe, *VP*
Georgia Kirkman, *Sec*
EMP: 22 **EST:** 1982
SQ FT: 960
SALES (est): 856.92K **Privately Held**
SIC: 2394 3732 Canvas and related products
   ; Boatbuilding and repairing

(G-12214)
ALL IN 1 HOME IMPROVEMENT
261 Streets Ferry Rd (28586-8306)
PHONE.............................252 725-4560
Marvin Alston, *Owner*
EMP: 5 **EST:** 2018
SALES (est): 365.55K **Privately Held**
SIC: 1389 Construction, repair, and
   dismantling services

(G-12215)
DPS MOLDING INC
276 Bailey Ln (28586-8226)
PHONE.............................732 763-4811
Roger Clark, *Pr*
◆ **EMP:** 5 **EST:** 2010
SALES (est): 709.31K **Privately Held**
Web: www.dpsmolding.com
SIC: 3089 Injection molding of plastics

(G-12216)
FUSION INCORPORATED
276 Bailey Ln (28586-8226)
PHONE.............................252 244-4300
David Gubb, *Pr*
Thomas Harris, *COO*

◆ **EMP:** 21 **EST:** 1994
SQ FT: 50,000
SALES (est): 475.54K **Privately Held**
Web: www.fusion-inc.com
SIC: 3069 Brushes, rubber

(G-12217)
IDUSTRIAL BURKETT SERVICES
2050 Nc Highway 43 (28586-8916)
PHONE.............................252 244-0143
EMP: 6 **EST:** 2013
SALES (est): 329.06K **Privately Held**
Web: www.burkettindustrial.com
SIC: 7692 Welding repair

(G-12218)
INTERNATIONAL PAPER COMPANY
Also Called: International Paper
1785 Weyerhaeuser Rd (28586-7606)
PHONE.............................252 633-7509
Donna Cannon, *Owner*
EMP: 53
SALES (corp-wide): 18.62B **Publicly Held**
Web: www.internationalpaper.com
SIC: 2621 Paper mills
PA: International Paper Company
   6400 Poplar Ave
   Memphis TN 38197
   901 419-7000

(G-12219)
MCKEEL & SONS LOGGING INC
170 Spruill Town Rd (28586-8086)
PHONE.............................252 244-3903
Edward W Mckeel, *Pr*
EMP: 4 **EST:** 1986
SALES (est): 219.1K **Privately Held**
SIC: 2411 Logging camps and contractors

(G-12220)
MILLER LOGGING CO INC
7901 Main St (28586-9151)
PHONE.............................252 229-9860
Gregory S Miller, *Pr*
Carol Harper, *Sec*
EMP: 5 **EST:** 1988
SQ FT: 1,200
SALES (est): 66.05K **Privately Held**
SIC: 2411 Logging camps and contractors

(G-12221)
NORALEX INC (PA)
Also Called: Noralex Timber
215 Wilmar Rd (28586-8961)
PHONE.............................252 974-1253
John Hines, *Pr*
EMP: 8 **EST:** 1985
SQ FT: 5,000
SALES (est): 206.8K **Privately Held**
SIC: 2411 Timber, cut at logging camp

(G-12222)
**STEVEN C HADDOCK DBA
HADDOCK**
4122 Leary Mills Rd (28586-9551)
PHONE.............................252 714-2431
Steven C Haddock, *Prin*
EMP: 6 **EST:** 2005
SQ FT: 1,782
SALES (est): 407.82K **Privately Held**
SIC: 2411 Logging

(G-12223)
WEYERHAEUSER COMPANY
Also Called: Pulp Mill
1785 Weyerhaeuser Rd (28586-7606)
PHONE.............................252 633-7100
John Ashley, *Manager*
EMP: 23
SALES (corp-wide): 7.12B **Publicly Held**

Web: www.weyerhaeuser.com
SIC: 2621 2421 2611 Paper mills; Sawmills
   and planing mills, general; Pulp mills
PA: Weyerhaeuser Company
   220 Occidental Ave S
   Seattle WA 98104
   206 539-3000

(G-12224)
WEYERHAEUSER NEW BERN
Also Called: Weyerhaeuser
1785 Weyerhaeuser Rd (28586-7606)
PHONE.............................252 633-7100
EMP: 21 **EST:** 2015
SALES (est): 9.22MM
SALES (corp-wide): 7.12B **Publicly Held**
SIC: 2631 Container, packaging, and
   boxboard
PA: Weyerhaeuser Company
   220 Occidental Ave S
   Seattle WA 98104
   206 539-3000

(G-12225)
WEYERHAEUSER NR COMPANY
1482 Weyerhaeuser Rd (28586-9244)
PHONE.............................252 633-7100
EMP: 100
SALES (corp-wide): 7.12B **Publicly Held**
Web: www.weyerhaeuser.com
SIC: 2421 Lumber: rough, sawed, or planed
HQ: Weyerhaeuser Nr Company
   220 Occidental Ave S
   Seattle WA 98104

Vandemere
Pamlico County

(G-12226)
PAMLICO PACKING CO INC
28 N First St (28587)
P.O. Box 336 (28529-0336)
PHONE.............................252 745-3688
Ed Cross, *Prin*
EMP: 10
SALES (corp-wide): 3.78MM **Privately
Held**
Web: www.bestseafood.com
SIC: 2092 2091 5146 Seafoods, fresh:
   prepared; Bouillon, clam: packaged in cans,
   jars, etc.; Fish and seafoods
PA: Pamlico Packing Co., Inc.
   66 Cross Rd S
   Grantsboro NC 28529
   252 745-3688

Vass
Moore County

(G-12227)
CAROLINA CRATE & PALLET INC
3281 Us 1 Hwy (28394-9314)
P.O. Box 279 (28394-0279)
PHONE.............................910 245-4001
Wallace Wilson, *Pr*
EMP: 35 **EST:** 1979
SQ FT: 40,000
SALES (est): 2.65MM **Privately Held**
Web: www.carolinacrate.com
SIC: 2441 2448 2499 2449 Boxes, wood;
   Pallets, wood; Reels, plywood; Wood
   containers, nec

(G-12228)
PACE INCORPORATED (PA)
Also Called: Pace Worldwide
346 Grant Rd (28394-9338)
PHONE.............................910 695-7223

Erick Siegel, *Ch Bd*
Eric Siegel, *
◆ **EMP:** 40 **EST:** 1958
SQ FT: 37,000
SALES (est): 10.84MM
SALES (corp-wide): 10.84MM **Privately
Held**
Web: www.paceworldwide.com
SIC: 3699 Electrical equipment and supplies,
   nec

(G-12229)
TIER 1 HEATING AND AIR LLC
3459 Us Hwy 1 (28394)
PHONE.............................910 556-1444
EMP: 12 **EST:** 2020
SALES (est): 2.72MM **Privately Held**
Web: www.tier1-hvac.com
SIC: 3585 Heating and air conditioning
   combination units

Vilas
Watauga County

(G-12230)
INTERSPORT GROUP INC
336 Willowdale Church Rd (28692-8961)
PHONE.............................814 968-3085
EMP: 4
SALES (est): 300.03K **Privately Held**
SIC: 2326 7389 Work uniforms; Business
   Activities at Non-Commercial Site

(G-12231)
MIXON MILLS INC
4965 Us Highway 421 N (28692-9489)
PHONE.............................828 297-5431
Ernest Mixon, *Pr*
Nancy Mixon, *Sec*
EMP: 5 **EST:** 1995
SALES (est): 65.6K **Privately Held**
SIC: 2421 5084 Sawmills and planing mills,
   general; Industrial machinery and
   equipment

(G-12232)
MW ENTERPRISES INC
Also Called: Muncy Winds
5014 Nc Highway 105 S (28692-9015)
P.O. Box 422 (28679-0422)
PHONE.............................828 963-7083
Philip Muncy, *Pr*
Pam Muncy, *VP*
◆ **EMP:** 6 **EST:** 1987
SQ FT: 4,000
SALES (est): 166.48K **Privately Held**
Web: www.muncywinds.com
SIC: 5736 3931 Pianos; Clarinets and parts

Wadesboro
Anson County

(G-12233)
ANSON EXPRESS
Also Called: Express, The
205 W Morgan St (28170-2147)
PHONE.............................704 694-2480
Alan Lyon Junior, *Owner*
EMP: 6 **EST:** 1993
SALES (est): 86.31K **Privately Held**
Web: www.ansonrecord.com
SIC: 2711 Newspapers, publishing and
   printing

(G-12234)
ANSON WOOD PRODUCTS
Parsons St (28170)
P.O. Box 247 (28170-0247)

PHONE....................704 694-5390
Bob Jordan, *Pt*
Jack Jordan, *Pt*
EMP: 6 **EST:** 1969
SALES (est): 88.55K **Privately Held**
SIC: 2411 Wood chips, produced in the field

(G-12235)
BILL RATLIFF JR LOGGING I
4437 Beck Rd (28170-6380)
PHONE....................704 694-5403
William H Ratliff Junior, *Prin*
EMP: 8 **EST:** 2005
SQ FT: 2,304
SALES (est): 134.74K **Privately Held**
SIC: 2411 Logging camps and contractors

(G-12236)
BRASINGTONS INC
1515 Us Highway 74 W (28170-7550)
P.O. Box 411 (28170-0411)
PHONE....................704 694-5191
B C Brasington Junior, *Pr*
B C Brasington Iii, *VP*
Patsy Brasington, *Sec*
EMP: 5 **EST:** 1953
SQ FT: 7,200
SALES (est): 173.61K **Privately Held**
SIC: 5331 7692 Variety stores; Welding
   repair

(G-12237)
**BROWN CREEK TIMBER COMPANY
INC**
2691 Nc 742 N (28170-8712)
PHONE....................704 694-3529
Edward Flake, *Pr*
EMP: 5 **EST:** 1989
SALES (est): 80.93K **Privately Held**
SIC: 2411 Logging camps and contractors

(G-12238)
BUDS LOGGING AND TRUCKING
1561 Stanbackfry Ice Plnt Rd (28170-9236)
PHONE....................704 465-8016
Buddy H Jarrell, *Pr*
Emily Jarrell, *Sec*
EMP: 6 **EST:** 2002
SALES (est): 218.61K **Privately Held**
SIC: 2411 Logging

(G-12239)
CAROLINA APPAREL GROUP INC
425 Us Highway 52 S (28170-6466)
P.O. Box 827 (28170-0827)
PHONE....................704 694-6544
Don W Trexler, *Pr*
Laurie G Trexler, *
Michael A Gutschmit, *
▼ **EMP:** 60 **EST:** 1999
SALES (est): 3.49MM
SALES (corp-wide): 14.26MM **Privately
Held**
SIC: 2322 Men's and boy's underwear and
   nightwear
PA: Coville, Inc.
   8065-O North Point Blvd
   Winston Salem NC 27106
   336 759-0115

(G-12240)
**COLUMBUS MCKINNON
CORPORATION**
Also Called: Columbus McKinnon
2020 Country Club Rd (28170-3204)
P.O. Box 779 (28170-0779)
PHONE....................704 694-2156
John Farnandez, *Brnch Mgr*
EMP: 98
SALES (corp-wide): 1.01B **Publicly Held**

Web: www.cmco.com
SIC: 3536 Hoists
PA: Columbus Mckinnon Corporation
   13320 Bllntyne Corp Pl St
   Charlotte NC 28277
   716 689-5400

(G-12241)
DARLING INGREDIENTS INC
656 Little Duncan Rd (28170)
P.O. Box 718 (28170)
PHONE....................704 694-3701
Dean Deivert, *Genl Mgr*
EMP: 12
SALES (corp-wide): 6.79B **Publicly Held**
Web: www.darlingii.com
SIC: 2048 2077 Feed supplements;
   Rendering
PA: Darling Ingredients Inc.
   5601 N Macarthur Blvd
   Irving TX 75038
   972 717-0300

(G-12242)
GLENN TREXLER & SONS LOG INC
1095 Bethel Rd (28170-7309)
PHONE....................704 694-5644
Franklin G Trexler, *Pr*
EMP: 6 **EST:** 1970
SALES (est): 486.37K **Privately Held**
SIC: 2411 Logging camps and contractors

(G-12243)
HILDRETH WOOD PRODUCTS INC
825 Mount Vernon Rd (28170-7108)
PHONE....................704 826-8326
Blake Hildreth Junior, *Pr*
EMP: 5 **EST:** 1968
SQ FT: 10,000
SALES (est): 492.13K **Privately Held**
Web: www.hildrethwoodproducts.com
SIC: 2448 2449 Pallets, wood; Shipping
   cases and drums, wood: wirebound and
   plywood

(G-12244)
HORNWOOD INC
204 E Wade St (28170-2265)
PHONE....................704 694-3009
Kenneth W Horne Senior, *Brnch Mgr*
EMP: 50
SALES (corp-wide): 46.97MM **Privately
Held**
Web: www.hornwoodinc.com
SIC: 2258 Cloth, warp knit
PA: Hornwood, Inc.
   766 Haileys Ferry Rd
   Lilesville NC 28091
   704 848-4121

(G-12245)
J4 CONSTRUCTION LLC
2634 W Hwy 74 W (28170-6108)
P.O. Box 756 (28097-0756)
PHONE....................704 550-7970
Adrian Kennedy, *Managing Member*
EMP: 5 **EST:** 2022
SALES (est): 789.26K **Privately Held**
SIC: 3446 Lintels, light gauge steel

(G-12246)
JAMES L JOHNSON
Also Called: Deep Creek Timber
2151 Beaver Rd (28170-7360)
PHONE....................704 694-0103
James L Johnson, *Prin*
EMP: 4 **EST:** 2012
SALES (est): 236.3K **Privately Held**
SIC: 2411 Logging

(G-12247)
LOBA-WAKOL LLC
2732 Us Highway 74 W (28170-7558)
P.O. Box 829 (28170-0829)
PHONE....................704 527-5919
Ashley Carter, *Managing Member*
▲ **EMP:** 22 **EST:** 2009
SALES (est): 11.84MM
SALES (corp-wide): 154.09MM **Privately
Held**
Web: www.loba-wakol.com
SIC: 2891 Adhesives and sealants
PA: Wakol Gmbh
   Bottenbacher Str. 30
   Pirmasens RP 66954
   633180010

(G-12248)
LYON COMPANY
Also Called: Lyon Apartments
208 S Rutherford St (28170-2686)
P.O. Box 886 (28170-0886)
PHONE....................919 787-0024
R A Lyon, *Pr*
Allen Lyon, *Sec*
Anne Lyon, *VP*
EMP: 11 **EST:** 1909
SQ FT: 2,500
SALES (est): 241.03K **Privately Held**
SIC: 4832 6531 3211 6513 Radio
   broadcasting stations; Real estate brokers
   and agents; Cathedral glass; Apartment
   hotel operation

(G-12249)
MEDICAL SPECIALTIES INC
308 Parson St (28170-9623)
P.O. Box 977 (28170-0977)
PHONE....................704 694-2434
Scott Gaylord, *Mgr*
EMP: 6
SALES (corp-wide): 8.49MM **Privately
Held**
Web: www.medspec.com
SIC: 3842 Orthopedic appliances
PA: Medical Specialties Incorporated
   4600 Lebanon Rd Ste K
   Mint Hill NC 28227
   704 573-4040

(G-12250)
TREXLER LOGGING INC
2292 Bethel Rd (28170-7321)
PHONE....................704 694-5272
Robert Trexler, *Pr*
EMP: 5 **EST:** 2006
SALES (est): 144.52K **Privately Held**
SIC: 2411 Logging camps and contractors

(G-12251)
TRIANGLE BRICK COMPANY
2960 Us Highway 52 N (28170-9122)
PHONE....................704 695-1420
Howard Brown, *Mgr*
EMP: 49
SALES (corp-wide): 31.97MM **Privately
Held**
Web: www.trianglebrick.com
SIC: 3251 5211 Brick and structural clay tile;
   Brick
PA: Triangle Brick Company
   6523 Nc Hwy 55
   Durham NC 27713
   919 544-1796

(G-12252)
**WADE MANUFACTURING COMPANY
(PA)**
76 Mill St (28170-2410)
P.O. Box 32 (28170-0032)
PHONE....................704 694-2131

Bernard M Hodges, *Pr*
Carl A Holt, *
Shelton Faulkner, *
▲ **EMP:** 29 **EST:** 1923
SQ FT: 300,000
SALES (est): 3.95MM
SALES (corp-wide): 3.95MM **Privately
Held**
Web: www.waremfg.com
SIC: 2211 2221 Cotton broad woven goods;
   Polyester broadwoven fabrics

(G-12253)
**XCEL HRMETIC MTR REWINDING
INC**
2356 Bethel Rd (28170-7322)
P.O. Box 799 (28170-0799)
PHONE....................704 694-6001
Cecil Meachum, *Pr*
Brenda Meachum, *VP*
EMP: 8 **EST:** 1996
SQ FT: 30,000
SALES (est): 939.35K **Privately Held**
Web: www.xcelhermeticmotors.com
SIC: 7694 Electric motor repair

Wagram
Scotland County

(G-12254)
**CASCADES TSSUE GROUP - ORE
INC**
Also Called: Cascades Tissue Group-Oregon
19320 Airbase Rd (28396-6102)
PHONE....................503 397-2900
Suzanne Blanchet, *Pr*
Craig Nelson, *
Guy Prenevost, *
EMP: 70 **EST:** 2002
SALES (est): 22.07MM
SALES (corp-wide): 3.32B **Privately Held**
Web: www.cascades.com
SIC: 2621 Paper mills
HQ: Cascades Canada Ulc
   404 Boul Marie-Victorin
   Kingsey Falls QC J0A 1
   819 363-5100

(G-12255)
CYPRESS BEND VINEYARDS INC
21904 Riverton Rd (28396-8700)
PHONE....................910 369-0411
Daniel Smith, *Pr*
Tina Smith, *VP*
EMP: 5 **EST:** 2003
SQ FT: 5,000
SALES (est): 1.9MM **Privately Held**
Web: www.cypressbendvineyards.com
SIC: 2084 Wines

(G-12256)
DIRECT DISTRIBUTION INDS INC
24581 Main St (28396-9465)
P.O. Box 947 (28396-0947)
PHONE....................910 217-0000
Neill Shaw, *Prin*
EMP: 4 **EST:** 2004
SALES (est): 250K **Privately Held**
SIC: 3999 Manufacturing industries, nec

(G-12257)
WESTPOINT HOME INC
Also Called: Biddeford Mill
19320 Airbase Rd (28396-6102)
PHONE....................910 369-2231
Roger F Carr Junior, *Brnch Mgr*
EMP: 13
Web: www.westpointhome.com

▲ = Import ▼ = Export
◆ = Import/Export

Brian Sandy, *Prin*
EMP: 4 **EST:** 2001
SALES (est): 106.88K **Privately Held**
SIC: 2431 Millwork

(G-12309)
TRICKFIT & SUEPACK TRAINING
Also Called: Gym 30
918 Gateway Commons Cir (27587-5992)
PHONE..............................919 737-2231
EMP: 4 **EST:** 2017
SALES (est): 155.24K **Privately Held**
Web: www.gymthirty.com
SIC: 7991 7372 Physical fitness facilities;
Application computer software

(G-12310)
TWIN ATTIC PUBLISHING HSE INC
1415 Cedar Branch Ct (27587-9208)
P.O. Box 51531 (27717-1531)
PHONE..............................919 426-0322
Crishna Murray, *Prin*
EMP: 6 **EST:** 2012
SALES (est): 9.74K **Privately Held**
Web: www.twinatticpublishinghouse.com
SIC: 2741 Miscellaneous publishing

(G-12311)
ULTRA ELEC OCEAN SYSTEMS INC
204 Capcom Ave (27587-6509)
PHONE..............................781 848-3400
EMP: 11
SALES (corp-wide): 2.67MM **Privately
Held**
Web: www.umaritime.com
SIC: 3812 Search and navigation equipment
HQ: Ultra Electronics Ocean Systems Inc.
115 Bay State Dr
Braintree MA 02184
781 848-3400

(G-12312)
VASILIY YAVDOSHNYAK
3517 Trawden Dr (27587-5073)
PHONE..............................919 995-9469
Vasiliy Yavdoshnyak, *Prin*
EMP: 4 **EST:** 2010
SALES (est): 135.08K **Privately Held**
Web: www.vintagewings-millersfield.com
SIC: 2741 Miscellaneous publishing

(G-12313)
WAKE FOREST GAZETTE
1255 S Main St (27587-9282)
PHONE..............................919 556-3409
EMP: 5 **EST:** 2017
SALES (est): 120.32K **Privately Held**
Web: www.wakeforestgazette.com
SIC: 2711 Newspapers, publishing and
printing

(G-12314)
**WELL-BEAN COFFEE & CRUMBS
LLC**
Also Called: Well-Bean Coffee Company
4154 Shearon Farms Ave Ste 106
(27587-4570)
PHONE..............................833 777-2326
Melissa Brown, *Pt*
Melissa Brown, *Genl Pt*
EMP: 5 **EST:** 2013
SALES (est): 832.61K **Privately Held**
Web: www.wellbean.com
SIC: 5499 2095 Coffee; Coffee roasting
(except by wholesale grocers)

Walkertown
Forsyth County

(G-12315)
**AMERICAN TCHNCAL SOLUTIONS
INC**
Also Called: Atsi
4790 Walkertown Plaza Blvd (27051-9772)
P.O. Box 10 (27051)
PHONE..............................336 595-2763
Robert Sandee, *Pr*
Gettys H Knox, *
EMP: 93 **EST:** 1994
SQ FT: 20,000
SALES (est): 2.12MM **Privately Held**
Web: www.atsi-online.com
SIC: 2221 Slip cover fabrics, manmade fiber
and silk

(G-12316)
ITS YOUR TIME BUSINESS CENTER
2735 Old Hollow Rd (27051-9529)
PHONE..............................336 754-4456
EMP: 4 **EST:** 2011
SALES (est): 77.45K **Privately Held**
SIC: 2752 Business form and card printing,
lithographic

(G-12317)
STOLTZ AUTOMOTIVE INC
4861 New Walkertown Rd (27051-9556)
P.O. Box 998 (27051-0998)
PHONE..............................336 595-4218
Aubrey Stoltz, *Owner*
Jean S Stoltz, *Pt*
James Eugene Stoltz, *Pt*
Michael R Stoltz, *Pt*
EMP: 5 **EST:** 1938
SQ FT: 2,400
SALES (est): 495.78K **Privately Held**
SIC: 7538 7534 7539 General automotive
repair shops; Tire repair shop; Frame and
front end repair services

Wallace
Duplin County

(G-12318)
360 FOREST PRODUCTS INC
113 N Rockfish St (28466-2917)
P.O. Box 157 (28466-0157)
PHONE..............................910 285-5838
Larry Batchelor, *Pr*
Ricky Pope, *VP*
EMP: 6 **EST:** 1997
SALES (est): 246.01K **Privately Held**
Web: www.360forestproducts.com
SIC: 2411 Logging camps and contractors

(G-12319)
CAPE FEAR NEWSPAPERS INC
107 N College St (28466-2707)
P.O. Box 69 (28349-0069)
PHONE..............................910 285-2178
Myrna Fountain Fusco, *Prin*
EMP: 4 **EST:** 2010
SALES (est): 134.79K **Privately Held**
SIC: 2711 Newspapers, publishing and
printing

(G-12320)
DUPLIN FOREST PRODUCTS INC
312 Jack Dale Rd (28466-6019)
PHONE..............................910 285-5381
Terry Hill Rivenbark, *Pr*
Ramona Rivenbark, *Sec*
EMP: 7 **EST:** 1970

SQ FT: 4,000
SALES (est): 463.27K **Privately Held**
SIC: 2411 2421 Logging camps and
contractors; Sawmills and planing mills,
general

(G-12321)
HOLMES LOGGING - WALLACE LLC
2788 Lightwood Bridge Rd (28466-7358)
PHONE..............................910 271-1216
Howard Feinman, *Admn*
EMP: 10 **EST:** 2010
SALES (est): 392.29K **Privately Held**
SIC: 2411 Logging camps and contractors

(G-12322)
LSG LLC
Also Called: Large & Small Graphics
268 Hc Powers Rd (28466-8263)
PHONE..............................919 878-5500
EMP: 15 **EST:** 2001
SQ FT: 3,300
SALES (est): 1.13MM **Privately Held**
SIC: 2759 Screen printing

(G-12323)
S & W READY MIX CON CO LLC
768 Sw Railroad St (28466-8210)
PHONE..............................910 285-2191
Robert Long, *Mgr*
EMP: 19
SALES (corp-wide): 8.01MM **Privately
Held**
Web: www.snwreadymix.com
SIC: 3273 Ready-mixed concrete
HQ: S & W Ready Mix Concrete Company
Llc
217 Lisbon St
Clinton NC 28329
910 592-1733

(G-12324)
SOUTHEAST WOOD PRODUCTS INC
444 Jack Dale Rd (28466-6021)
PHONE..............................910 285-4359
David Rivenbark Junior, *Pr*
Judy Rivenbark, *Sec*
▲ **EMP:** 10 **EST:** 1982
SALES (est): 438.64K **Privately Held**
SIC: 2411 4213 Logging camps and
contractors; Contract haulers

(G-12325)
SOUTHERN STATES COOP INC
939 Nw Railroad St (28466-5700)
PHONE..............................910 285-8213
EMP: 13
SALES (corp-wide): 1.71B **Privately Held**
Web: www.southernstates.com
SIC: 2048 0181 2873 2874 Prepared feeds,
nec; Bulbs and seeds; Nitrogenous
fertilizers; Phosphatic fertilizers
PA: Southern States Cooperative,
Incorporated
6606 W Broad St Ste B
Richmond VA 23230
804 281-1000

Walnut Cove
Stokes County

(G-12326)
AGRICLTRAL-INDUSTRIAL FABR INC
Also Called: Thrift-Tents
223 S Main St (27052-8306)
PHONE..............................336 591-3690
Donald C Brinkley, *Pr*
Charles Couch, *VP*
EMP: 5 **EST:** 1974

SALES (est): 195.61K **Privately Held**
SIC: 2394 Tents: made from purchased
materials

(G-12327)
CLARK STEEL FABRICATORS INC
870 Warren Farm Rd (27052-7299)
PHONE..............................336 595-9353
Steve Clark, *Pr*
Karen Clark, *Pr*
EMP: 10 **EST:** 1989
SQ FT: 6,000
SALES (est): 347.79K **Privately Held**
Web: clarksteelfab.wixsite.com
SIC: 3441 Fabricated structural metal

(G-12328)
MITCHELLS MEAT PROCESSING
Also Called: Mitchell Meat Processing
401 Mitchell St (27052-7321)
P.O. Box 421 (27052-0421)
PHONE..............................336 591-7420
EMP: 10 **EST:** 2018
SALES (est): 476.98K **Privately Held**
Web: www.mitchellsmeatnc.com
SIC: 5421 2011 0751 Meat and fish markets;
Meat packing plants; Slaughtering: custom
livestock services

(G-12329)
MONITOR ROLLER MILL INC
109 E 4th St (27052)
P.O. Box 393 (27052-0393)
PHONE..............................336 591-4126
William F Southern, *Pr*
Ron Southern, *Sec*
Patricia Southern, *VP*
EMP: 6 **EST:** 1909
SQ FT: 8,500
SALES (est): 99.73K **Privately Held**
SIC: 5999 2048 Feed and farm supply;
Prepared feeds, nec

(G-12330)
PARKDALE MILLS INCORPORATED
Also Called: Parkdale Plant 26
1660 Us 311 Hwy N (27052-6930)
PHONE..............................336 591-4644
Robert Lawrence, *Brnch Mgr*
EMP: 119
SALES (corp-wide): 1.44B **Privately Held**
Web: www.parkdalemills.com
SIC: 2281 Yarn spinning mills
HQ: Parkdale Mills, Incorporated
531 Cotton Blossom Cir
Gastonia NC 28054
704 874-5000

(G-12331)
WALNUT COVE FURNITURE INC
4730 Nc 89 Hwy E (27052-6904)
PHONE..............................336 591-8008
Douglas Stephens, *CEO*
Wendell Dodson, *Sec*
Douglas Stephens, *Pr*
EMP: 6 **EST:** 2003
SALES (est): 423.28K **Privately Held**
Web: www.walnutcovefurniture.com
SIC: 2599 5722 Factory furniture and fixtures
; Household appliance stores

Walstonburg
Greene County

(G-12332)
JAK MOULDING & SUPPLY INC
1565 Strickland Rd (27888-9478)
PHONE..............................252 753-5546
Tony Holloman, *Pr*

GEOGRAPHIC

John Holloman, *VP*
Rose Holloman, *Sec*
EMP: 12 **EST:** 2002
SQ FT: 20,000
SALES (est): 2.51MM **Privately Held**
Web: www.jakmoulding.com
SIC: 2491 5211 Millwork, treated wood;
　Lumber and other building materials

(G-12333)
KS CUSTOM WOODWORKS INC
3205 Fire Tower Rd (27888-9111)
P.O. Box 224 (27888-0224)
PHONE..............................252 714-3957
Kevin Holloman, *Prin*
EMP: 4 **EST:** 2015
SALES (est): 256.64K **Privately Held**
SIC: 2431 Millwork

(G-12334)
MOORES FIBERGLASS INC
926 Howell Swamp Church Rd
(27888-9517)
P.O. Box 219 (27888-0219)
PHONE..............................252 753-2583
Hardy Moore, *Pr*
Chris Moore, *VP*
EMP: 10 **EST:** 1986
SQ FT: 2,600
SALES (est): 2.51MM **Privately Held**
Web: www.mooresfiberglass.com
SIC: 1799 3088 Fiberglass work; Plastics
　plumbing fixtures

(G-12335)
S K BOWLING INC
1068 Fieldsboro Rd (27888-9427)
P.O. Box 8 (27894-0008)
PHONE..............................252 243-1803
Sam Bowling, *Pr*
Phil Sharitz, *VP*
EMP: 11 **EST:** 1984
SALES (est): 2.15MM **Privately Held**
Web: www.skbowling.com
SIC: 3444 Sheet metal specialties, not
　stamped

Wanchese
Dare County

(G-12336)
BAYLISS BOATWORKS INC
600 Harbor Rd (27981-9588)
P.O. Box 300 (27981-0300)
PHONE..............................252 473-9797
John Bayliss, *Pr*
▲ **EMP:** 45 **EST:** 2002
SQ FT: 10,000
SALES (est): 7.09MM **Privately Held**
Web: www.baylissboatworks.com
SIC: 3732 Boats, fiberglass: building and
　repairing

(G-12337)
BAYLISS BOATYARD INC
600 Harbor Rd (27981-9588)
P.O. Box 300 (27981-0300)
PHONE..............................252 473-9797
John Bayliss, *CEO*
Christopher Parker Ctrl, *Prin*
EMP: 15 **EST:** 2007
SQ FT: 1,500
SALES (est): 252.22K **Privately Held**
Web: www.baylissboatworks.com
SIC: 3732 Fishing boats: lobster, crab,
　oyster, etc.: small

(G-12338)
**BRIGGS BOAT WORKS
INCORPORATED**
370 Harbor Rd (27981-9648)
P.O. Box 277 (27981-0277)
PHONE..............................252 473-2393
Thomas H Briggs Iii, *Pr*
Deanna Briggs, *Sec*
◆ **EMP:** 5 **EST:** 1980
SQ FT: 4,800
SALES (est): 246.97K **Privately Held**
SIC: 3732 Boats, fiberglass: building and
　repairing

(G-12339)
CRAIG & SANDRA BLACKWELL INC
Also Called: Blackwell Boatwork
932 Harbor Rd (27981-9617)
P.O. Box 580 (27981-0580)
PHONE..............................252 473-1803
Craig Blackwell, *Owner*
EMP: 8 **EST:** 1989
SALES (est): 226.82K **Privately Held**
Web: www.blackwellboatworks.com
SIC: 3732 Motorized boat, building and
　repairing

(G-12340)
**CROSWAIT CUSTOM COMPOSITES
INC**
90 Dusty Ln (27981-9535)
P.O. Box 478 (27981-0478)
PHONE..............................252 423-1245
EMP: 6 **EST:** 2014
SALES (est): 725.74K **Privately Held**
Web: www.croswait.com
SIC: 3732 Boatbuilding and repairing

(G-12341)
DANIELS BOATWORKS INC
620 Harbor Rd (27981-9588)
PHONE..............................252 473-1400
EMP: 5 **EST:** 2017
SALES (est): 314.44K **Privately Held**
Web: www.danielsboatworks.com
SIC: 3732 Boatbuilding and repairing

(G-12342)
GUNBOAT INTERNATIONAL LTD
829 Harbor Rd (27981-9646)
PHONE..............................252 305-8700
Peter L Johnstone, *CEO*
◆ **EMP:** 12 **EST:** 2011
SQ FT: 30,000
SALES (est): 422.62K **Privately Held**
Web: www.gunboat.com
SIC: 3732 Boatbuilding and repairing

(G-12343)
HARBOR WELDING INC
935 Harbor Rd (27981-9617)
P.O. Box 720 (27981-0720)
PHONE..............................252 473-3777
Wayne Umphlett, *Pr*
EMP: 6 **EST:** 1986
SALES (est): 247.48K **Privately Held**
Web: www.harborwelding.com
SIC: 7692 Welding repair

(G-12344)
ISLAND WOOD CRAFTS LTD
776 Old Wharf Rd (27981-9600)
P.O. Box 448 (27981-0448)
PHONE..............................252 473-5363
Cliff Granitzki, *Pr*
Jeff Granitzki, *VP*
Linda Boyd, *Sec*
EMP: 4 **EST:** 1972
SALES (est): 474.94K **Privately Held**
Web: www.islandwoodcrafts.com

SIC: 2434 Wood kitchen cabinets

(G-12345)
MARINE FABRICATIONS LLC
31 Beverly Dr (27981-9652)
P.O. Box 240 (27981-0240)
PHONE..............................252 473-4767
Paul Spencer, *Mgr*
EMP: 6 **EST:** 2007
SALES (est): 467.62K **Privately Held**
SIC: 7692 3599 Welding repair; Machine
　shop, jobbing and repair

(G-12346)
**RICHARD SCARBOROUGH BOAT
WORKS**
Ficket Lump Rd (27981)
P.O. Box 191 (27981-0191)
PHONE..............................252 473-3646
Ricky Scarborough, *Pr*
Annette Scarborough, *Sec*
EMP: 4 **EST:** 1974
SALES (est): 365.55K **Privately Held**
Web: www.scarboroughboatworks.com
SIC: 3732 Boats, fiberglass: building and
　repairing

(G-12347)
WANCHESE DOCK AND HAUL LLC
593 Baumtown Rd (27981-9502)
P.O. Box 415 (27981-0415)
PHONE..............................252 473-6424
Winston Silver, *Prin*
EMP: 4 **EST:** 2008
SALES (est): 229.53K **Privately Held**
Web: www.wanchesefirearms.com
SIC: 3732 Boatbuilding and repairing

(G-12348)
WELDING SHOP LLC
102 Cb Daniels Sr Rd (27981-9557)
P.O. Box 668 (27981-0668)
PHONE..............................252 982-6567
EMP: 10 **EST:** 2007
SALES (est): 246.32K **Privately Held**
Web:
www.thewancheseweldingshop.com
SIC: 7692 Welding repair

Warrenton
Warren County

(G-12349)
**ARCOLA HARDWOOD COMPANY
INC**
2316 Nc Highway 43 (27589-9294)
PHONE..............................252 257-4484
Gary C Harris, *Pr*
EMP: 8 **EST:** 1966
SALES (est): 746.64K **Privately Held**
SIC: 2449 Wood containers, nec

(G-12350)
ARCOLA LUMBER COMPANY INC
2316 Nc Highway 43 (27589-9294)
PHONE..............................252 257-4923
Elmer W Harris Senior, *Pr*
Garry C Harris, *
EMP: 32 **EST:** 1952
SQ FT: 1,200
SALES (est): 2.49MM **Privately Held**
SIC: 2421 2449 2441 Tobacco hogshead
　stock; Wood containers, nec; Nailed wood
　boxes and shook

(G-12351)
CAST STONE SYSTEMS INC
532 N Main St (27589-1633)
PHONE..............................252 257-1599

Ted Echols, *Pr*
Thomas Edward Echols Junior, *Pr*
Margaret Echols, *
EMP: 25 **EST:** 1998
SQ FT: 600,000
SALES (est): 5.77MM **Privately Held**
Web: www.caststonesystems.com
SIC: 3272 Concrete products, nec

(G-12352)
ELBERTA CRATE & BOX CO
619 N Main St (27589-1634)
P.O. Box 760 (39818-0760)
PHONE..............................252 257-4659
EMP: 110
SALES (corp-wide): 20.39MM **Privately
Held**
Web: www.elbertacrate.com
SIC: 2449 Wood containers, nec
PA: Elberta Crate & Box Co.
　606 Dothan Rd
　Bainbridge GA 39817
　229 243-1268

(G-12353)
RABBIT BOTTOM LOGGING CO INC
Also Called: Rabbit Bottom Logging Co
Hc 151 (27589)
PHONE..............................252 257-3585
Johnny M Coleman, *Prin*
EMP: 8 **EST:** 1980
SALES (est): 681.75K **Privately Held**
Web: www.inezforest.com
SIC: 2411 Logging camps and contractors

(G-12354)
SIDNEY PERRY COOPER III
445 Nc Highway 58 (27589-9161)
PHONE..............................252 257-3886
Sidney Perry Cooper Iii, *Prin*
EMP: 4 **EST:** 2010
SALES (est): 120.47K **Privately Held**
SIC: 3993 Signs and advertising specialties

(G-12355)
SMOKE HOUSE LUMBER COMPANY
2711 Nc Highway 58 (27589-9284)
PHONE..............................252 257-3303
Warren Griffin, *Pr*
EMP: 32 **EST:** 1980
SALES (est): 2.56MM **Privately Held**
Web: www.smokehouselumber.com
SIC: 2421 Lumber: rough, sawed, or planed

(G-12356)
WOMACK PUBLISHING CO INC
Also Called: Warren Record, The
112 N Main St (27589-1922)
P.O. Box 70 (27589-0070)
PHONE..............................252 257-3341
Jennifer Harris, *Prin*
EMP: 6
SALES (corp-wide): 4.28MM **Privately
Held**
Web: www.warrenrecord.com
SIC: 2711 Newspapers: publishing only, not
　printed on site
PA: Womack Publishing Company, Inc.
　28 N Main St
　Chatham VA 24531
　434 432-2791

Warsaw
Duplin County

(G-12357)
ACCU-FORM POLYMERS INC
170 Water Tank Rd (28398-7821)
P.O. Box 445 (28398-0445)

▲ = Import ▼ = Export
◆ = Import/Export

(G-12405)
PAMLICO AIR INC (DH)
112 S Respess St (27889-4956)
P.O. Box 579 (27920)
PHONE....................252 995-6267
Harry Smith, *CEO*
EMP: 10 **EST:** 1990
SALES (est): 2.45MM
SALES (corp-wide): 5.11B **Privately Held**
Web: www.pamlicoair.com
SIC: 1711 3564 Warm air heating and air
conditioning contractor; Blowers and fans
HQ: Tri-Dim Filter Corporation
93 Industrial Dr
Louisa VA 23093
540 967-2600

(G-12406)
PAMLICO SCREEN PRINTING INC
7669 Broad Creek Rd (27889-7796)
PHONE....................252 944-6001
EMP: 4 **EST:** 2014
SALES (est): 81.95K **Privately Held**
SIC: 2752 Commercial printing, lithographic

(G-12407)
PAS USA INC
2010 W 15th St (27889-3590)
PHONE....................252 974-5500
Glenn Sparrow, *CEO*
Stefan Kaiser, *
David Greco, *
April Woolard, *
▲ **EMP:** 141 **EST:** 2003
SQ FT: 50,000
SALES (est): 22.89MM
SALES (corp-wide): 577.95MM **Privately
Held**
SIC: 3822 Appliance controls,except air-
conditioning and refrigeration
HQ: Pas Management Holding Gmbh
Wilhelm-Bartelt-Str. 10-14
Neuruppin BB 16816

(G-12408)
PRECISIONAIRE INC (DH)
Also Called: Precisionaire of Smithfield
531 Flanders Filter Rd (27889-7805)
PHONE....................252 946-8081
Ted Beneski, *Ch*
Harry Smith, *
Mark Sokolowski, *
Warren Bonham, *
Eliot Kerlin, *
◆ **EMP:** 119 **EST:** 1970
SQ FT: 25,000
SALES (est): 8.71MM **Privately Held**
SIC: 3564 Filters, air: furnaces, air
conditioning equipment, etc.
HQ: Flanders Corporation
531 Flanders Filter Rd
Washington NC 27889

(G-12409)
PRO-LINE NORTH CAROLINA INC
Also Called: Fountain Powerboats
1653 Whichards Beach Rd (27889)
PHONE....................252 975-2000
John Walker, *Pr*
William R Gates, *Prin*
Joseph Wortley, *Prin*
EMP: 95 **EST:** 1979
SQ FT: 235,000
SALES (est): 1.46MM **Privately Held**
Web: www.fountainpowerboats.com
SIC: 3732 Motorboats, inboard or outboard:
building and repairing

(G-12410)
PROTOTECH MANUFACTURING INC
✿
715 Page Rd (27889-9540)
PHONE....................508 646-8849
Brett Palaschak, *Pr*
Jesus Chavez Lopez, *VP*
EMP: 11 **EST:** 2024
SALES (est): 1.04MM **Privately Held**
SIC: 2821 3086 3069 7389 Plastics
materials and resins; Plastics foam products
; Floor coverings, rubber; Business
Activities at Non-Commercial Site

(G-12411)
RONDOL CORDON LOGGING INC
101 Raccoon Run (27889-7680)
P.O. Box 1746 (27889-1746)
PHONE....................252 944-9220
Rondol Cordon, *Pr*
EMP: 8 **EST:** 2010
SALES (est): 173.99K **Privately Held**
SIC: 2411 Logging camps and contractors

(G-12412)
SESAME TECHNOLOGIES INC
3718 River Rd (27889-7526)
P.O. Box 803 (27889-0803)
PHONE....................252 964-2205
Sue Faircloth, *Pr*
Ernest T Jefferson, *VP*
EMP: 10 **EST:** 1989
SQ FT: 3,200
SALES (est): 1.64MM **Privately Held**
Web: www.sesametech.com
SIC: 3052 Rubber and plastics hose and
beltings

(G-12413)
SHUTTER FACTORY INC
6139w Us Highway 264 W (27889-8028)
PHONE....................252 974-2795
Reed Boseman, *Pr*
EMP: 5 **EST:** 1997
SALES (est): 487.86K **Privately Held**
Web: www.theshutterfactory.ie
SIC: 3442 5023 Shutters, door or window:
metal; Vertical blinds

(G-12414)
SPINRITE YARNS LP
190 Plymouth St (27889-4291)
PHONE....................252 833-4970
EMP: 7 **EST:** 2018
SALES (est): 545.16K **Privately Held**
Web: www.spinriteyarns.com
SIC: 2281 Yarn spinning mills

(G-12415)
STARCRAFT DIAMONDS INC
444 Stewart Pkwy (27889-4974)
PHONE....................252 717-2548
James M Fortescue Senior, *Pr*
Elvira W Fortescue, *VP*
James M Fortescue Junior, *Treas*
Haywood P Fortescue, *Sec*
▲ **EMP:** 5 **EST:** 1962
SQ FT: 7,500
SALES (est): 262.37K **Privately Held**
Web: www.guyharveyjewelry.com
SIC: 5944 3911 Jewelry, precious stones
and precious metals; Jewelry, precious
metal

(G-12416)
TRANSPORTATION TECH INC (DH)
Also Called: Hackney
911 W 5th St (27889-4205)
P.O. Box 880 (27889)
PHONE....................252 946-6521

Michael A Tucker, *Pr*
Jeffery T Joyner, *
Sandra W Tankard, *
▲ **EMP:** 165 **EST:** 1989
SALES (est): 77.89MM **Privately Held**
Web: www.vthackney.com
SIC: 3713 Truck bodies (motor vehicles)
HQ: St Engineering North America, Inc.
99 Canal Ctr Plz Ste 220
Alexandria VA 22314
703 739-2610

(G-12417)
UNIFORMS GALORE
Also Called: Stitchworks Embroidery
628 River Rd (27889-3923)
PHONE....................252 975-5878
Zane G Buckman, *Pr*
Kent Buckman Senior, *Treas*
Sandra Buckman, *Sec*
EMP: 5 **EST:** 1992
SQ FT: 12,500
SALES (est): 239K **Privately Held**
Web: www.buyworkwearforless.com
SIC: 2395 2759 Embroidery and art
needlework; Commercial printing, nec

(G-12418)
VEON INC
Also Called: Adaptive Mobility Solutions
601 W 5th St (27889-4301)
PHONE....................252 623-2102
Michael Harragin, *Pr*
EMP: 10 **EST:** 2016
SQ FT: 1,500
SALES (est): 3.43MM **Privately Held**
Web: www.amslifts.com
SIC: 5047 3448 3536 3842 Medical
equipment and supplies; Ramps,
prefabricated metal; Boat lifts; Personal
safety equipment

(G-12419)
VT HACKNEY INC
Also Called: Hackney A Div VT Spclzed Vhcle
400 Hackney Ave (27889-4726)
P.O. Box 880 (27889-0880)
PHONE....................252 946-6521
Michael Tucker, *Brnch Mgr*
EMP: 101
Web: www.hackneyusa.com
SIC: 3713 Truck bodies (motor vehicles)
HQ: Transportation Technologies, Inc.
911 W 5th St
Washington NC 27889
252 946-6521

(G-12420)
WASHINGTON CABINET COMPANY
4799 Voa Rd (27889-7997)
PHONE....................252 946-3457
Alan Peele, *Pt*
Wayne Jackson, *Pt*
EMP: 5 **EST:** 1987
SQ FT: 1,200
SALES (est): 222.6K **Privately Held**
Web: www.wcabinet.com
SIC: 2541 5712 1751 Cabinets, except
refrigerated: show, display, etc.: wood;
Cabinet work, custom; Cabinet and finish
carpentry

(G-12421)
**WASHINGTON NEWS PUBLISHING
CO**
Also Called: Washington Daily News
217 N Market St (27889-4949)
P.O. Box 1788 (27889-1788)
PHONE....................252 946-2144
Ashley B Futrell Junior, *Pr*
Susan B Futrell, *

Rachel Futrell, *
Ashley B Futrell Senior, *Ch Bd*
EMP: 15 **EST:** 1909
SQ FT: 15,000
SALES (est): 470.73K **Privately Held**
Web: www.thewashingtondailynews.com
SIC: 2711 Newspapers, publishing and
printing

Waxhaw
Union County

(G-12422)
ABBOTT LABORATORIES
9108 Kingsmead Ln (28173-9075)
P.O. Box 75896 (28275-0896)
PHONE....................704 243-1832
EMP: 4
SALES (corp-wide): 41.95B **Publicly Held**
Web: www.abbott.com
SIC: 2834 Pharmaceutical preparations
PA: Abbott Laboratories
100 Abbott Park Rd
Abbott Park IL 60064
224 667-6100

(G-12423)
BIRCH BROS SOUTHERN INC
9510 New Town Rd (28173-8574)
P.O. Box 70 (28173-1038)
PHONE....................704 843-2111
Steven W Birch, *Pr*
EMP: 27 **EST:** 1883
SQ FT: 36,000
SALES (est): 4.89MM **Privately Held**
Web: www.birchbrothers.com
SIC: 5084 3559 Industrial machinery and
equipment; Ammunition and explosives,
loading machinery

(G-12424)
**BLACK MOUNTAIN CNSTR GROUP
INC**
Also Called: Waxhaw Cabinet Company
10704 Lancaster Hwy (28173-9156)
PHONE....................704 243-5593
Brandon Hilbert, *Pr*
Brandon Hilbert, *Owner*
EMP: 10 **EST:** 2015
SQ FT: 1,800
SALES (est): 98.23K **Privately Held**
SIC: 2434 1751 5712 1522 Wood kitchen
cabinets; Cabinet building and installation;
Cabinet work, custom; Residential
construction, nec

(G-12425)
BRAND FUEL PROMOTIONS
400 N Broome St Ste 203 (28173-7033)
PHONE....................704 256-4057
Steve Walker, *Mgr*
EMP: 5 **EST:** 2010
SALES (est): 119.48K **Privately Held**
Web: www.brandfuel.com
SIC: 2752 Commercial printing, lithographic

(G-12426)
CAPTIVE-AIRE SYSTEMS INC
516 Wyndham Ln (28173-6632)
PHONE....................704 843-7215
Robert Ludley, *Pr*
EMP: 9
SALES (corp-wide): 485.13MM **Privately
Held**
Web: www.captiveaire.com
SIC: 3444 Restaurant sheet metalwork
PA: Captive-Aire Systems, Inc.
4641 Pragon Pk Rd Ste 104
Raleigh NC 27616

---

919 882-2410

(G-12427)
CAROLINA CUSTOM CABINETRY
6823 Davis Rd (28173-8410)
PHONE...............................704 808-1225
EMP: 4 **EST:** 2013
SALES (est): 176.09K **Privately Held**
SIC: 2434 Wood kitchen cabinets

(G-12428)
DEMILO BROS NC LLC
Also Called: Demilo Bros.
1807 Palazzo Dr (28173-0033)
PHONE...............................704 771-0762
Robert Demilo, *Managing Member*
EMP: 5 **EST:** 2017
SALES (est): 167.1K **Privately Held**
Web: www.demilobros.com
SIC: 1771 3251 Concrete work; Paving
brick, clay

(G-12429)
DREAMWEAVERS BREWERY LLC
115 E North Main St (28173-6029)
PHONE...............................704 507-7773
Anita Gimon, *Pr*
EMP: 4 **EST:** 2014
SQ FT: 4,900
SALES (est): 393.63K **Privately Held**
Web: www.dreamchasersbrewery.com
SIC: 2082 Beer (alcoholic beverage)

(G-12430)
DUBOSE NATIONAL ENRGY SVCS INC
103 Waxhaw Professional Park Dr Ste D
(28173-5022)
PHONE...............................704 295-1060
Sam Lambert, *Mgr*
EMP: 9
SALES (corp-wide): 13.84B **Publicly Held**
Web: www.dubosenes.com
SIC: 3965 Fasteners
HQ: Dubose National Energy Services, Inc.
900 Industrial Dr
Clinton NC 28328

(G-12431)
FLORES CRANE SERVICES LLC
8705 Kentucky Derby Dr (28173-6592)
PHONE...............................704 243-4347
Maria Del Carmen Flores, *Admn*
EMP: 13 **EST:** 2014
SALES (est): 3.37MM **Privately Held**
SIC: 3531 7389 Crane carriers; Crane and
aerial lift service

(G-12432)
FRONTIER MEAT PROCESSING INC
8303 Lancaster Hwy (28173-9102)
PHONE...............................704 843-3921
Dale Walkup, *Pr*
Tim D Walkup, *VP*
Patty Liles, *Sec*
EMP: 7 **EST:** 1975
SQ FT: 1,500
SALES (est): 540.79K **Privately Held**
Web: www.frontiermeatswaxhawnc.com
SIC: 2011 Meat packing plants

(G-12433)
KBC OF NC LLC
4114 Western Union School Rd
(28173-9211)
PHONE...............................704 589-3711
EMP: 6 **EST:** 2014
SALES (est): 1.51MM **Privately Held**
SIC: 3272 Slabs, crossing: concrete

(G-12434)
KEYPOINT LLC
Also Called: Keypoint Fabrication
8002 New Town Rd (28173-9398)
PHONE...............................704 962-8110
EMP: 10 **EST:** 2012
SALES (est): 580.19K **Privately Held**
Web: www.keypointfab.com
SIC: 3449 Miscellaneous metalwork

(G-12435)
KLEIBERIT ADHESIVES USA INC
109b Howie Mine Rd (28173-6873)
P.O. Box 1319 (28173-1013)
PHONE...............................704 843-3339
Klause Becker Weimann, *Pr*
◆ **EMP:** 15 **EST:** 1996
SQ FT: 1,200
SALES (est): 5.03MM
SALES (corp-wide): 25.84MM **Privately
Held**
Web: www.kleiberit.com
SIC: 2891 Adhesives
PA: Kleiberit Se & Co. Kg
Max-Becker-Str. 4
Weingarten (Baden) BW 76356
7244620

(G-12436)
OASIS AKHAL-TEKES
6528 Rehobeth Rd (28173-7603)
PHONE...............................704 843-3139
EMP: 4 **EST:** 2016
SALES (est): 105.37K **Privately Held**
Web: www.oasisakhal-tekes.com
SIC: 7372 Prepackaged software

(G-12437)
PRESSURE WASHING NEAR ME LLC
Also Called: Mulch Magicians
10002 King George Ln (28173-6816)
PHONE...............................704 280-0351
EMP: 5 **EST:** 2020
SALES (est): 187K **Privately Held**
SIC: 2821 Plastics materials and resins

(G-12438)
QUALITY CUSTOM WOODWORKS INC
5019 Pleasant Springs Rd (28173-9785)
PHONE...............................704 843-1584
John Kronberger, *Pr*
EMP: 5 **EST:** 1993
SALES (est): 232.05K **Privately Held**
Web:
www.qualitycustomwoodworks.com
SIC: 5712 2517 Cabinet work, custom;
Wood television and radio cabinets

(G-12439)
RUTH HICKS ENTERPRISE INC
9417 Marvin School Rd (28173-8594)
PHONE...............................704 469-4741
Ruth Hicks, *Pr*
Ruth C Hicks, *Pr*
Elbert Glenn Hicks Junior, *VP*
▼ **EMP:** 11 **EST:** 2007
SALES (est): 1.47MM **Privately Held**
Web: www.ruthhicksenterprises.com
SIC: 3999 Hair, dressing of, for the trade

(G-12440)
SERUM SOURCE INTERNATIONAL INC
406 Belvedere Ln (28173-6581)
PHONE...............................704 588-6607
Maranda E Swoyer, *Pr*
EMP: 10 **EST:** 2006
SALES (est): 364.66K **Privately Held**
Web: www.serumsourceintl.com

SIC: 2836 Biological products, except
diagnostic

(G-12441)
SIRIUS TACTICAL ENTPS LLC
679 Brandy Ct (28173-9326)
PHONE...............................704 256-3660
EMP: 5 **EST:** 2012
SALES (est): 72.03K **Privately Held**
SIC: 3482 Small arms ammunition

(G-12442)
STACKS KITCHEN MATTHEWS
1315 N Broome St (28173-9380)
PHONE...............................704 243-2024
EMP: 6
SALES (corp-wide): 327.1K **Privately Held**
Web: www.stackskitchen.com
SIC: 3421 Table and food cutlery, including
butchers'
PA: Stacks Kitchen Matthews
11100 Monroe Rd
Matthews NC 28105
704 841-2025

(G-12443)
TANGLES KNITTING ON MAIN LLC
200 W North Main St (28173-6012)
PHONE...............................704 243-7150
EMP: 5 **EST:** 2009
SALES (est): 138.15K **Privately Held**
Web: www.tanglesyarn.com
SIC: 2284 Thread mills

(G-12444)
THERMODYNAMX LLC
Also Called: Thermodynamx
514 King St (28173-8950)
PHONE...............................704 622-1086
EMP: 4 **EST:** 2000
SQ FT: 2,300
SALES (est): 240.14K **Privately Held**
SIC: 3089 Thermoformed finished plastics
products, nec

(G-12445)
TOMMY SIGNS
8716 Maggie Robinson Rd (28173-7681)
PHONE...............................704 877-1234
Tommy Williams, *Prin*
EMP: 5 **EST:** 2011
SALES (est): 172.27K **Privately Held**
SIC: 3993 Signs and advertising specialties

(G-12446)
TOTAL SPORTS ENTERPRISES
9624 Belloak Ln (28173-6767)
PHONE...............................704 237-3930
EMP: 4 **EST:** 2018
SALES (est): 194.8K **Privately Held**
Web: www.tseshop.com
SIC: 3949 Sporting and athletic goods, nec

(G-12447)
V & B CONSTRUCTION SVCS INC
8413 Walkup Rd (28173-8613)
P.O. Box 77415 (28271-7009)
PHONE...............................704 641-9936
Gayla Haag, *Admn*
EMP: 6 **EST:** 2019
SALES (est): 1.06MM **Privately Held**
SIC: 1799 1389 Construction site cleanup;
Construction, repair, and dismantling
services

(G-12448)
VOCO AMERICA INC
1104 Real Quiet Ln (28173-6586)
PHONE...............................917 923-7698
EMP: 5 **EST:** 2018

SALES (est): 135.74K **Privately Held**
SIC: 3843 Dental equipment and supplies

(G-12449)
WAXHAW CREAMERY LLC
109 E North Main St (28173-6029)
PHONE...............................704 843-7927
Richard Geist, *Managing Member*
EMP: 13 **EST:** 2013
SALES (est): 284.52K **Privately Held**
Web: www.visitwaxhaw.com
SIC: 2021 Creamery butter

Waynesville
Haywood County

(G-12450)
ALP SYSTEMS INC
Also Called: Lightning Protection
46 Allegiance Ln (28786-0460)
PHONE...............................828 454-5164
Stacy Bean, *Pr*
EMP: 15 **EST:** 2006
SQ FT: 2,000
SALES (est): 1.23MM **Privately Held**
Web: www.alpsystemsinc.com
SIC: 1799 3643 Lightning conductor erection
; Lightning arrestors and coils

(G-12451)
BLUE RIDGE PAPER PRODUCTS LLC
Also Called: Evergreen Packaging
81 Old Howell Mill Rd (28786-0339)
PHONE...............................828 452-0834
Allen Denney, *Mgr*
EMP: 141
SQ FT: 27,666
Web: www.pactivevergreen.com
SIC: 2672 2621 Coated paper, except
photographic, carbon, or abrasive; Paper
mills
HQ: Blue Ridge Paper Products Llc
41 Main St
Canton NC 28716
828 454-0676

(G-12452)
CARAUSTAR INDUSTRIES INC
5095 Old River Rd (28786-7581)
PHONE...............................828 246-7234
EMP: 5
SALES (corp-wide): 5.45B **Publicly Held**
Web: www.greif.com
SIC: 2655 Tubes, fiber or paper: made from
purchased material
HQ: Caraustar Industries, Inc.
5000 Astell Pwdr Spmg Rd
Austell GA 30106
770 948-3101

(G-12453)
CEDAR HILL STUDIO & GALLERY
Also Called: Sonshine Promises
196 N Main St (28786-3810)
P.O. Box 328 (28786-0328)
PHONE...............................828 456-6344
Gretchen Clasby, *Owner*
Mark B Clasby, *Owner*
EMP: 8 **EST:** 1972
SQ FT: 17,500
SALES (est): 109.68K **Privately Held**
Web: www.cedarhillstudio.com
SIC: 5199 2741 Art goods; Art copy and
poster publishing

(G-12454)
CLASSY GLASS INC
39 Macs Ln (28786-6919)
PHONE...............................828 452-2242

▲ = Import ▼ = Export
◆ = Import/Export

TOLL FREE: 877
Gene Rainone, *Pr*
Gene Rainone, *Owner*
Alice Rainone, *Sec*
EMP: 7 **EST:** 1995
SALES (est): 595.87K **Privately Held**
Web: www.pelucida.com
SIC: 3231 5999 5231 Ornamental glass: cut, engraved or otherwise decorated; Trophies and plaques; Glass, leaded or stained

(G-12455)
DECEMBER DIAMONDS INC
3425 Dellwood Rd (28786-6218)
P.O. Box 1419 (28751-1419)
PHONE....................................828 926-3308
Scott Nielsen, *Pr*
▲ **EMP:** 4 **EST:** 1999
SALES (est): 227.63K **Privately Held**
Web: www.decemberdiamonds.com
SIC: 3961 Ornaments, costume, except precious metal and gems

(G-12456)
DISTINCTIVE BLDG & DESIGN INC
24 Chloe Ln (28786-0799)
P.O. Box 600 (28786-0600)
PHONE....................................828 456-4730
Tom Hines, *Pr*
EMP: 4 **EST:** 2000
SQ FT: 1,675
SALES (est): 3.15MM **Privately Held**
Web: www.distinctivecustomhomes.com
SIC: 2452 1521 Log cabins, prefabricated, wood; Single-family housing construction

(G-12457)
EDGE BROADBAND SOLUTIONS LLC
Also Called: Gogofiber
244 Lea Plant Rd (28786-4984)
PHONE....................................828 785-1420
Alan Gauvreau, *Managing Member*
Edward A Donnahoe, *Managing Member*
EMP: 20 **EST:** 2013
SALES (est): 5.82MM **Privately Held**
Web: www.edge-bbs.com
SIC: 7629 3661 3663 Telecommunication equipment repair (except telephones); Fiber optics communications equipment; Cable television equipment

(G-12458)
GILES CHEMICAL CORPORATION
75 Giles Pl (28786-1938)
PHONE....................................828 452-4784
Richard N Nwrenn Junior, *Pr*
EMP: 4
SALES (corp-wide): 93.25MM **Privately Held**
Web: www.premiermagnesia.com
SIC: 2819 2899 Magnesium compounds or salts, inorganic; Salt
HQ: Giles Chemical Corporation
102 Commerce St
Waynesville NC 28786
828 452-4784

(G-12459)
GILES CHEMICAL CORPORATION (HQ)
Also Called: Giles Chemical Industries
102 Commerce St (28786-5739)
P.O. Box 370 (28786-0370)
PHONE....................................828 452-4784
Richard N Wrenn Junior, *Pr*
Darrell H Clark, *Sec*
▲ **EMP:** 22 **EST:** 1950
SQ FT: 33,013
SALES (est): 26.47MM
SALES (corp-wide): 93.25MM **Privately Held**

Web: www.premiermagnesia.com
SIC: 2819 2899 Magnesium compounds or salts, inorganic; Salt
PA: Premier Magnesia, Llc
75 Giles Pl
Waynesville NC 28786
828 452-4784

(G-12460)
GREEN MOUNTAIN INTL LLC
235 Pigeon St (28786-4442)
PHONE....................................800 942-5151
EMP: 7 **EST:** 1987
SQ FT: 2,000
SALES (est): 4.42MM **Privately Held**
Web: www.mountaingrout.com
SIC: 5169 2821 Polyurethane products; Acrylic resins

(G-12461)
HAYWOOD VCTNAL OPPRTNITIES INC
Also Called: H V O
172 Riverbend St (28786-1969)
P.O. Box 7 (28738-0007)
PHONE....................................828 454-9682
George Marshall, *Pr*
◆ **EMP:** 416 **EST:** 1966
SQ FT: 75,000
SALES (est): 20.25MM **Privately Held**
Web: www.hvoinc.com
SIC: 3842 Abdominal supporters, braces, and trusses

(G-12462)
JOHN LAUGHTER JEWELRY INC
146 N Main St (28786-3810)
PHONE....................................828 456-4772
Tammy Mosely, *Mgr*
EMP: 6
SALES (corp-wide): 498.88K **Privately Held**
Web: www.grantljewelry.com
SIC: 5944 3911 7631 Jewelry, precious stones and precious metals; Jewelry, precious metal; Jewelry repair services
PA: John Laughter Jewelry, Inc.
1800 Hendersonville Rd # 2
Asheville NC 28803
828 274-5770

(G-12463)
METZGERS BURL WOOD GALLERY
101 N Main St (28786-3809)
PHONE....................................828 452-2550
Janet L Metzger, *Prin*
EMP: 4 **EST:** 2016
SALES (est): 90.51K **Privately Held**
Web: www.burlgallery.com
SIC: 2431 Millwork

(G-12464)
MOUNTAINEER INC
220 N Main St (28786-3812)
P.O. Box 129 (28786-0129)
PHONE....................................828 452-0661
Jonathan Key, *Pr*
Jeff Schumacher, *
EMP: 7 **EST:** 1887
SALES (est): 176.97K **Privately Held**
Web: www.themountaineer.com
SIC: 2759 2752 2711 Newspapers: printing, nsk; Commercial printing, lithographic; Newspapers

(G-12465)
OAKS UNLIMITED INC (PA)
3530 Jonathan Creek Rd (28785-9864)
P.O. Box 1070 (28201-1070)
PHONE....................................828 926-1621
Joe Pryor Ii, *Pr*

Trent Thomas, *
Nancy Pryor, *
▼ **EMP:** 25 **EST:** 1979
SALES (est): 4.9MM
SALES (corp-wide): 4.9MM **Privately Held**
Web: www.oaksunlimited.com
SIC: 2421 5031 Lumber: rough, sawed, or planed; Lumber: rough, dressed, and finished

(G-12466)
OLD STYLE PRINTING
1046 Sulphur Springs Rd (28786-4247)
PHONE....................................828 452-1122
J Lloyd Allen, *Owner*
EMP: 5 **EST:** 1992
SALES (est): 193.76K **Privately Held**
SIC: 2752 Offset printing

(G-12467)
POWELL INDUSTRIES INC (PA)
Also Called: Powell Wholesale Lumber
4595 Jonathan Creek Rd (28785-8302)
P.O. Box 65 (28786-0065)
PHONE....................................828 926-9114
Carl B Powell Junior, *Pr*
George G Powell, *
James M Powell, *
EMP: 55 **EST:** 1958
SQ FT: 20,000
SALES (est): 6.39MM
SALES (corp-wide): 6.39MM **Privately Held**
Web: www.powellind.com
SIC: 2426 5211 2421 Dimension, hardwood; Flooring, wood; Wood chips, produced at mill

(G-12468)
PREMIER MAGNESIA LLC (PA)
75 Giles Pl (28786)
P.O. Box 370 (28786)
PHONE....................................828 452-4784
John Gehret, *CEO*
Rick Wrenn Junior, *Pr*
◆ **EMP:** 20 **EST:** 2001
SALES (est): 93.25MM
SALES (corp-wide): 93.25MM **Privately Held**
Web: www.premiermagnesia.com
SIC: 3295 Minerals, ground or treated

(G-12469)
PRINT HAUS INC
641 N Main St (28786-3819)
PHONE....................................828 456-8622
Jeffrey Kuhlman, *CEO*
EMP: 7 **EST:** 1982
SQ FT: 3,500
SALES (est): 582.13K **Privately Held**
Web: www.theprinthaus.com
SIC: 2752 7334 2761 2759 Offset printing; Photocopying and duplicating services; Manifold business forms; Commercial printing, nec

(G-12470)
RIKKI TIKKI TEES
Also Called: Thomas Enterprises
546 Hazelwood Ave (28786-2067)
PHONE....................................828 454-0515
Richard Thomas, *Owner*
EMP: 5 **EST:** 1990
SALES (est): 249.1K **Privately Held**
Web: www.rikkitikkitees.com
SIC: 2759 2741 Screen printing; Miscellaneous publishing

(G-12471)
ROC-N-SOC INC
151 Kelly Park Ln (28786-2738)
PHONE....................................828 452-1736
Steven Mcintosh, *Pr*
◆ **EMP:** 9 **EST:** 1990
SQ FT: 3,500
SALES (est): 460.02K **Privately Held**
Web: www.rocnsoc.com
SIC: 3931 Drums, parts, and accessories (musical instruments)

(G-12472)
SANDERS INDUSTRIES INC
Also Called: CMC
559 Bow And Arrow Cv (28785-0210)
PHONE....................................410 277-8565
William Sanders, *Pr*
William N Sanders, *VP*
W Scott Sanders, *VP*
Carolyn Sanders, *VP*
▲ **EMP:** 9 **EST:** 1967
SALES (est): 330.82K **Privately Held**
SIC: 2392 5023 2369 5136 Tablecloths: made from purchased materials; Linens, table; Children's robes and housecoats; Robes, men's and boys'

(G-12473)
SBG DIGITAL INC
Also Called: Satellite & Cellular
1562 S Main St (28786-2155)
PHONE....................................828 476-0030
Sherry Garnes, *Pr*
EMP: 5 **EST:** 2001
SALES (est): 598.42K **Privately Held**
SIC: 3663 Satellites, communications

(G-12474)
SMOKY MOUNTAIN NEWS INC (PA)
144 Montgomery St (28786-3720)
P.O. Box 629 (28786-0629)
PHONE....................................828 452-4251
Scott Mccleod, *Prin*
Scott Mccloud, *Pr*
Greg Boothroyd, *VP*
EMP: 12 **EST:** 1999
SALES (est): 1.06MM
SALES (corp-wide): 1.06MM **Privately Held**
Web: www.smokymountainnews.com
SIC: 2711 Newspapers: publishing only, not printed on site

(G-12475)
SORRELLS SHEREE WHITE (PA)
Also Called: Whitewoven Handweaving Studio
1834 Cove Creek Rd (28785-2766)
PHONE....................................828 452-4864
Sheree White Sorrells, *Owner*
EMP: 4 **EST:** 1981
SALES (est): 84.61K **Privately Held**
Web: www.rugweaver.com
SIC: 2231 2273 Weaving mill, broadwoven fabrics: wool or similar fabric; Rugs, hand and machine made

(G-12476)
SOUTHERN CONCRETE MTLS INC
201 Boundary St (28786-5754)
PHONE....................................828 456-9048
Ronald Mahaley, *Mgr*
EMP: 19
SALES (corp-wide): 238.17MM **Privately Held**
Web: www.scmusa.com
SIC: 3273 Ready-mixed concrete
HQ: Southern Concrete Materials, Inc.
35 Meadow Rd
Asheville NC 28803
828 253-6421

GEOGRAPHIC

(G-12477)
TOP NOTCH LOG HOMES INC
3517 Jonathan Creek Rd (28785-9864)
PHONE......................................828 926-4300
Tom Blackburn, *Pr*
EMP: 5 EST: 1996
SALES (est): 167.23K **Privately Held**
SIC: 2411 Logging

(G-12478)
TOWN OF WAYNESVILLE
Also Called: Water Treatment Department
341 Rocky Branch Rd (28786-1850)
PHONE......................................828 456-8497
Kyle Cooke, *Dir*
EMP: 8
Web: www.waynesvillenc.gov
SIC: 3589 Water treatment equipment,
industrial
PA: Town Of Waynesville
16 S Main St
Waynesville NC 28786
828 456-2491

(G-12479)
WAYNESVILLE SODA JERKS LLC
Also Called: Waynesville Soda Jerks
35 Bridges St (28786-8890)
PHONE......................................828 278-8589
Christopher Allen, *Owner*
EMP: 4 EST: 2013
SALES (est): 253.84K **Privately Held**
Web: www.waynesvillesodajerks.com
SIC: 2086 Carbonated beverages,
nonalcoholic: pkged. in cans, bottles

(G-12480)
WMXF AM 1400
Also Called: Clear Channel Communications
54 N Main St (28786-3949)
PHONE......................................828 456-8661
EMP: 55
SALES (est): 2.19MM **Privately Held**
SIC: 2731 Book publishing

Weaverville
Buncombe County

(G-12481)
**ABB MOTORS AND MECHANICAL
INC**
Also Called: Baldor Dodge Reliance
70 Reems Creek Rd (28787-9211)
PHONE......................................828 645-1706
EMP: 157
Web: www.baldor.com
SIC: 5511 3566 3463 3366 Automobiles,
new and used; Speed changers, drives,
and gears; Pump, compressor, turbine, and
engine forgings, except auto; Bushings and
bearings
HQ: Abb Motors And Mechanical Inc.
5711 R S Boreham Jr St
Fort Smith AR 72901
479 646-4711

(G-12482)
B V HEDRICK GRAVEL & SAND CO
Also Called: North Buncombe Quarry
100 Gold View Rd (28787)
P.O. Box 610 (28787-0610)
PHONE......................................828 645-5560
J V Goodman, *Pr*
EMP: 33
SALES (corp-wide): 238.17MM **Privately
Held**
Web: www.hedrickind.com

SIC: 3281 1442 Stone, quarrying and
processing of own stone products;
Construction sand and gravel
PA: B. V. Hedrick Gravel & Sand Company
120 1/2 Church St
Salisbury NC 28144
704 633-5982

(G-12483)
BALCRANK CORPORATION
90 Monticello Rd (28787-9441)
PHONE......................................800 747-5300
C Roy Mendenhall, *CEO*
Donald Youman, *
Alberto G Moratiel, *
Ramon Noblejas, *
◆ EMP: 25 EST: 2009
SQ FT: 130,000
SALES (est): 8.1MM **Privately Held**
Web: www.balcrank.com
SIC: 3569 3586 3429 3089 Lubricating
equipment; Gasoline pumps, measuring or
dispensing; Hardware, nec; Handles, brush
or tool: plastics
HQ: Linter, North America Corporation
48 Patton Ave
Asheville NC 28801

(G-12484)
**BARKLEYS MILL ON SOUTHERN
CRO**
6 Barkley Pl (28787-8234)
PHONE......................................828 626-3344
Micah Stowe, *Genl Mgr*
EMP: 6 EST: 2013
SQ FT: 2,800
SALES (est): 236.1K **Privately Held**
SIC: 0139 2046 Broomcorn farm; Corn
milling by-products

(G-12485)
BROOKSTONE BAPTIST CHURCH
Also Called: Southern Baptist Church
90 Griffee Rd (28787-9619)
PHONE......................................828 658-9443
EMP: 23 EST: 1974
SQ FT: 5,400
SALES (est): 1.02MM **Privately Held**
Web: www.brookstonechurch.org
SIC: 8661 7372 Baptist Church; Application
computer software

(G-12486)
CLASSIC SCENT
72 Hillcrest Dr (28787-8921)
PHONE......................................828 645-5171
Denise Peters, *Owner*
EMP: 6 EST: 1989
SALES (est): 238.14K **Privately Held**
Web: www.theclassicscent.com
SIC: 3999 Handles, handbag and luggage

(G-12487)
**CONRAD EMBROIDERY COMPANY
LLC**
Also Called: C E C
22 A B Emblem Dr (28787-0258)
P.O. Box 695 (28787-0695)
PHONE......................................828 645-3015
Paul Conrad, *Managing Member*
EMP: 46 EST: 2013
SALES (est): 2.92MM
SALES (corp-wide): 11.19MM **Privately
Held**
Web: www.abemblem.com
SIC: 2395 Emblems, embroidered
PA: Conrad Industries, Inc.
22 A B Emblem Dr
Weaverville NC 28787
828 645-3015

(G-12488)
CONRAD INDUSTRIES INC (PA)
Also Called: A-B Emblem
22 A B Emblem Dr (28787-0258)
P.O. Box 695 (28787-0695)
PHONE......................................828 645-3015
Bernhard Conrad, *Pr*
Jerry Williams, *
▲ EMP: 83 EST: 1944
SQ FT: 140,000
SALES (est): 11.19MM
SALES (corp-wide): 11.19MM **Privately
Held**
Web: www.conrad-industries.com
SIC: 2395 Emblems, embroidered

(G-12489)
CORMARK INTERNATIONAL LLC
179 Reems Creek Rd (28787-8204)
PHONE......................................828 658-8455
Massimo Corte, *Prin*
▲ EMP: 9 EST: 2004
SALES (est): 2.29MM **Privately Held**
Web: www.cormarkint.com
SIC: 2499 Decorative wood and woodwork

(G-12490)
CREEK INDUSTRIES INC
87 Island In The Sky Trl (28787-0379)
PHONE......................................828 319-7490
Robert Breining, *Prin*
EMP: 7 EST: 2017
SALES (est): 1.44MM **Privately Held**
SIC: 3999 Manufacturing industries, nec

(G-12491)
FILLAUER NORTH CAROLINA INC
220 Merrimon Ave Ste A (28787-9113)
PHONE......................................828 658-8330
Richard Anderson, *Pr*
EMP: 25 EST: 1979
SQ FT: 35,000
SALES (est): 2.75MM **Privately Held**
Web: www.fillauer.com
SIC: 3842 5047 Orthopedic appliances;
Orthopedic equipment and supplies
PA: Fillauer, Inc.
2710 Amnicola Hwy
Chattanooga TN 37406

(G-12492)
HIGH FIVE ENTERPRISES INC
Also Called: Wnc Homes & Realstate
12 Strawberry Ln (28787-9270)
P.O. Box 8683 (28814-8683)
PHONE......................................828 279-5962
Alan Sheppard, *Pr*
EMP: 4 EST: 2012
SALES (est): 390.7K **Privately Held**
Web: www.rewnc.com
SIC: 2731 7389 Book publishing; Business
Activities at Non-Commercial Site

(G-12493)
**J STAHL SALES & SOURCING INC
(PA)**
81 Monticello Rd (28787-9441)
P.O. Box 1673 (28787-1673)
PHONE......................................828 645-3005
John Stahl, *CEO*
John Stahl, *Pr*
James Stahl, *VP Sls*
Elizabeth Stahl, *Sec*
▲ EMP: 23 EST: 1978
SQ FT: 15,000
SALES (est): 1.51MM
SALES (corp-wide): 1.51MM **Privately
Held**
Web: www.wolverinetuff.com

SIC: 2393 3949 Canvas bags; Skin diving
equipment, scuba type

(G-12494)
KRW PACKAGING MACHINERY INC
81 Monticello Rd (28787-9441)
PHONE......................................828 658-0912
Kenneth Wilkes, *Ofcr*
EMP: 10 EST: 2011
SALES (est): 2.54MM **Privately Held**
Web: www.smartbottleinc.com
SIC: 3565 Packaging machinery

(G-12495)
LASER PRECISION CUTTING INC
181 Reems Creek Rd Ste 3 (28787-8229)
P.O. Box 1654 (28787)
PHONE......................................828 658-0644
Joseph Karpen, *Pr*
▲ EMP: 8 EST: 1990
SQ FT: 15,000
SALES (est): 2.68MM **Privately Held**
Web: www.lpcutting.com
SIC: 3599 Machine shop, jobbing and repair

(G-12496)
MOUNTAIN HOMES OF WNC LLC
12 White Walnut Dr (28787-8259)
PHONE......................................828 216-2546
Jeffrey Allen, *Managing Member*
EMP: 10 EST: 2019
SALES (est): 904.61K **Privately Held**
Web: www.mountainhomesofwestnc.com
SIC: 1389 7389 Construction, repair, and
dismantling services; Business Activities at
Non-Commercial Site

(G-12497)
**MS WHLCHAIR N CA AM STATE
COOR**
61 Cheek Rd (28787-9635)
PHONE......................................828 230-1129
Brandee Ponder, *Prin*
EMP: 6 EST: 2011
SALES (est): 183.9K **Privately Held**
SIC: 3842 Wheelchairs

(G-12498)
MULTI-COLOR CORPORATION
15 Conrad Industrial Dr (28787-5505)
PHONE......................................828 658-6800
East Mark, *Brnch Mgr*
EMP: 23
SALES (corp-wide): 14.54B **Privately Held**
Web: www.mcclabel.com
SIC: 2759 Labels and seals: printing, nsk
HQ: Multi-Color Corporation
6111 N River Rd Fl 8
Rosemont IL 60018
847 427-5354

(G-12499)
MYRICKS CUSTOM FAB INC
181 Reems Creek Rd Ste 2 (28787-8229)
PHONE......................................828 645-5800
Anthony Myricks, *Pr*
EMP: 4 EST: 2005
SALES (est): 349.11K **Privately Held**
SIC: 3499 Fabricated metal products, nec

(G-12500)
NO EVIL FOODS LLC
108 Monticello Rd Ste 2000 (28787-0634)
P.O. Box 1199 (28787-1199)
PHONE......................................828 367-1536
Michael Woliansky, *CEO*
EMP: 70 EST: 2014
SALES (est): 5.88MM **Privately Held**
Web: www.noevilfoods.com

▲ = Import ▼ = Export
◆ = Import/Export

SIC: 2099 Food preparations, nec

(G-12501)
ROCKWELL AUTOMATION INC
70 Reems Creek Rd (28787-9211)
PHONE...............................828 645-4235
James Chlopek, *Mgr*
EMP: 19
Web: www.rockwellautomation.com
SIC: 3625 Relays and industrial controls
PA: Rockwell Automation, Inc.
   1201 S 2nd St
   Milwaukee WI 53204

(G-12502)
SAMOA CORPORATION
90 Monticello Rd (28787-9441)
PHONE...............................828 645-2290
Vicki O'shields, *Pr*
EMP: 30 EST: 2015
SQ FT: 90,000
SALES (est): 7.61MM Privately Held
Web: www.samoaindustrial.com
SIC: 3586 Oil pumps, measuring or
   dispensing

(G-12503)
SAMPLE GROUP INC (PA)
179 Merrimon Ave Ste 100 (28787-9675)
PHONE...............................828 658-9040
Gary Gottdiener, *Pr*
Pat Manente, *
▲ EMP: 350 EST: 1999
SQ FT: 160,000
SALES (est): 9.95MM
SALES (corp-wide): 9.95MM Privately
Held
Web: www.thesamplegroup.com
SIC: 2299 Batting, wadding, padding and
   fillings

(G-12504)
STAMPCO METAL PRODUCTS INC
108 Herron Cove Rd (28787-9221)
P.O. Box 8189 (28814-8189)
PHONE...............................828 645-4271
Marvin Eckerich, *Pr*
EMP: 7 EST: 1969
SQ FT: 23,000
SALES (est): 929.62K Privately Held
Web: www.stampcometal.com
SIC: 3544 Special dies and tools

(G-12505)
THERMO FSHER SCNTFIC ASHVLLE L
220 Merrimon Ave Ste A (28787-9113)
PHONE...............................828 658-2711
EMP: 271
SALES (corp-wide): 42.86B Publicly Held
Web: www.marysittonteam.com
SIC: 3826 Analytical instruments
HQ: Thermo Fisher Scientific (Asheville) Llc
   275 Aiken Rd
   Asheville NC 28804
   828 658-2711

(G-12506)
VORTANT TECHNOLOGIES LLC
88 High Country Rd (28787-9374)
PHONE...............................828 645-1026
Phil Schaefer, *Pr*
EMP: 7 EST: 1999
SALES (est): 122.16K Privately Held
Web: www.vortant.com
SIC: 8731 7371 8711 3845 Engineering
   laboratory, except testing; Computer
   software development and applications;
   Electrical or electronic engineering;
   Electromedical apparatus

(G-12507)
WNC MATERIAL SALES
351 Flat Creek Church Rd (28787-8519)
PHONE...............................828 658-8368
EMP: 7 EST: 2017
SALES (est): 209.65K Privately Held
Web: www.scmusa.com
SIC: 3273 Ready-mixed concrete

(G-12508)
WNC REFAB INC
125 Old Homestead Trl (28787-8757)
PHONE...............................828 658-8368
Steven Boone, *Pr*
EMP: 4 EST: 2013
SALES (est): 1.38MM Privately Held
Web: www.wncrefab.com
SIC: 3441 5051 Fabricated structural metal;
   Nonferrous metal sheets, bars, rods, etc.,
   nec

Welcome
Davidson County

(G-12509)
ASCO POWER TECHNOLOGIES LP
325 Welcome Center Blvd (27374)
PHONE...............................336 731-5009
EMP: 105
SALES (corp-wide): 1.09K Privately Held
Web: www.ascopower.com
SIC: 3699 High-energy particle physics
   equipment
HQ: Asco Power Technologies, L.P.
   160 Park Ave
   Florham Park NJ 07932

(G-12510)
ATRIUM EXTRUSION SYSTEMS INC
300 Welcome Center Blvd (27374)
PHONE...............................336 764-6400
Gregory T Faherty, *CEO*
EMP: 10 EST: 1993
SALES (est): 929.25K Privately Held
Web: www.atrium.com
SIC: 3442 Window and door frames

(G-12511)
AURORA PLASTICS INC
Also Called: Aurora Plastics, Inc.
180 Welcome Center Blvd (27374)
P.O. Box 849 (27374-0849)
PHONE...............................336 775-2640
Larry Medford, *Mgr*
EMP: 10
Web: www.auroramaterialsolutions.com
SIC: 2821 Plastics materials and resins
HQ: Aurora Plastics, Llc
   9280 Jefferson St
   Streetsboro OH 44241

(G-12512)
MORTON METALCRAFT COMPANY N
P.O. Box 729 (27374-0729)
PHONE...............................336 731-5700
Charles Crump, *Pr*
EMP: 9 EST: 2008
SALES (est): 241.22K Privately Held
SIC: 3399 Primary metal products

(G-12513)
RICHARD CHLDRESS RACG ENTPS IN
236 Industrial Dr (27374)
P.O. Box 1189 (27374-1189)
PHONE...............................336 731-3334
Richard R Childress, *Pr*
EMP: 22
SALES (corp-wide): 22.42MM Privately
Held

Web: www.rcrracing.com
SIC: 7549 3711 High performance auto
   repair and service; Automobile assembly,
   including specialty automobiles
PA: Richard Childress Racing Enterprises,
   Inc.
   425 Industrial Dr
   Welcome NC 27374
   336 731-3334

(G-12514)
RICHARD CHLDRESS RACG ENTPS IN (PA)
425 Industrial Dr (27374)
P.O. Box 1189 (27374-1189)
PHONE...............................336 731-3334
Richard Childress, *Pr*
Jean Wilson, *
Bill Patterson, *
▲ EMP: 475 EST: 1978
SQ FT: 83,000
SALES (est): 22.42MM
SALES (corp-wide): 22.42MM Privately
Held
Web: www.rcrracing.com
SIC: 7549 7941 3711 High performance auto
   repair and service; Sports clubs, managers,
   and promoters; Automobile assembly,
   including specialty automobiles

(G-12515)
SUMMER INDUSTRIES LLC
Also Called: Summer Industries
262 Welcome Center Court (27374)
P.O. Box 789 (27374-0789)
PHONE...............................336 731-9217
▲ EMP: 106
Web: www.summerindustries.net
SIC: 3554 2655 Paper industries machinery;
   Tubes, fiber or paper: made from
   purchased material

(G-12516)
TUBULAR TEXTILE LLC
4157 Old Highway 52 (27374)
PHONE...............................336 731-2860
EMP: 4 EST: 2004
SQ FT: 10,000
SALES (est): 268.39K Privately Held
SIC: 3441 Fabricated structural metal

(G-12517)
WOOTEN GRAPHICS INC
172 Hinkle Ln (27374)
P.O. Box 819 (27374-0819)
PHONE...............................336 731-4650
James Wooten, *
Jewel Wooten, *
Jordan Wooten, *
EMP: 6 EST: 1977
SQ FT: 30,000
SALES (est): 524.4K Privately Held
Web: www.wootengraphics.com
SIC: 2759 2396 Screen printing; Automotive
   and apparel trimmings

Weldon
Halifax County

(G-12518)
AGNATURAL LLC
802 Julian R Allsbrook Hwy (27890-1166)
PHONE...............................252 536-0322
Michael Dunlow, *Prin*
EMP: 4 EST: 2010
SALES (est): 178.33K Privately Held
SIC: 2074 Cottonseed oil, cake or meal

(G-12519)
BLAQ BEAUTY NATURALZ INC
Also Called: Blaq Beauty Naturalz
307 Woodlawn Ave (27890-1843)
PHONE...............................252 326-5621
Zeandra M Jones, *CEO*
EMP: 9 EST: 2017
SALES (est): 69.87K Privately Held
Web: www.blaqbeautynaturalz.com
SIC: 2844 5999 Hair preparations, including
   shampoos; Miscellaneous retail stores, nec

(G-12520)
HOOVER TREATED WOOD PDTS INC
1772 Trueblood Rd (27890-2000)
PHONE...............................866 587-8761
Rick Farnsam, *Brnch Mgr*
EMP: 23
SALES (corp-wide): 4.79B Publicly Held
Web: www.frtw.com
SIC: 2491 5031 Structural lumber and
   timber, treated wood; Lumber: rough,
   dressed, and finished
HQ: Hoover Treated Wood Products, Inc.
   154 Wire Rd
   Thomson GA 30824
   706 595-5058

(G-12521)
JBB PACKAGING LLC
100 Grace Dr (27890-1200)
PHONE...............................201 470-8501
Brendan Barba, *Managing Member*
Robert George Runz, *Contrlr*
EMP: 7 EST: 2018
SALES (est): 2.69MM Privately Held
Web: www.jbbpkg.com
SIC: 2671 Plastic film, coated or laminated
   for packaging

(G-12522)
KENNAMETAL INC
100 Kennametal Dr (27890-1174)
PHONE...............................252 536-5209
Glenn Faylor, *Brnch Mgr*
EMP: 77
SQ FT: 60,000
SALES (corp-wide): 2.05B Publicly Held
Web: www.kennametal.com
SIC: 3545 Cutting tools for machine tools
PA: Kennametal Inc.
   525 Wlliam Penn Pl Ste 33
   Pittsburgh PA 15219
   412 248-8000

(G-12523)
MEHERRIN RIVER FOREST PDTS INC
Also Called: Meherrin River International
1478 Trueblood Rd (27890-2040)
P.O. Box 100 (23821-0100)
PHONE...............................252 558-4238
Don Bright, *Pr*
EMP: 56
SALES (corp-wide): 2.56MM Privately
Held
Web: www.meherrinriver.com
SIC: 2421 Sawmills and planing mills,
   general
PA: Meherrin River Forest Products, Inc.
   71 N Oak St
   Alberta VA 23821
   434 949-7707

(G-12524)
NAES-OMS
1200 Julian R Allsbrook Hwy (27890-1170)
PHONE...............................252 536-4525
Edward Hardwell, *Prin*
EMP: 6 EST: 2011
SALES (est): 134.4K Privately Held
Web: www.naes.com

SIC: 3443 Boiler shop products: boilers, smokestacks, steel tanks

(G-12525)
PATCH RUBBER COMPANY
Also Called: Advanced Traffic Marking
100 Patch Rubber Rd (27890-1220)
P.O. Box H (27870-8082)
PHONE..............................252 536-2574
Stephen E Myers, *Pr*
John Orr, *
◆ EMP: 150 EST: 1947
SQ FT: 172,000
SALES (est): 22.24MM
SALES (corp-wide): 836.28MM **Publicly Held**
Web: www.patchrubber.com
SIC: 3069 Molded rubber products
PA: Myers Industries, Inc.
1293 S Main St
Akron OH 44301
330 253-5592

(G-12526)
ROANOKE VALLEY STEEL CORP
101 Kennametal Dr (27890-1175)
P.O. Box 661 (27890-0661)
PHONE..............................252 538-4137
William K Neal Junior, *Pr*
EMP: 10 EST: 2001
SQ FT: 2,000
SALES (est): 2.66MM **Privately Held**
Web: www.roanokevalleysteel.com
SIC: 3441 Fabricated structural metal

(G-12527)
WELDON MILLS DISTILLERY LLC
(PA)
Also Called: Weldon Mills Distillery
200 Rock Fish Dr (27890-2106)
PHONE..............................252 220-4235
Bruce Tyler, *Prin*
Michael Hinderliter, *Prin*
EMP: 5 EST: 2019
SALES (est): 530.48K
SALES (corp-wide): 530.48K **Privately Held**
Web: www.weldonmills.com
SIC: 2085 Distilled and blended liquors

(G-12528)
WELDON STEEL CORPORATION
101 Kennametal Dr (27890-1175)
P.O. Box 226 (27890-0226)
PHONE..............................252 536-2113
William K Neal Junior, *Pr*
EMP: 44 EST: 1988
SQ FT: 50,000
SALES (est): 8.29MM **Privately Held**
Web: www.weldonsteel.com
SIC: 3441 Fabricated structural metal

Wendell
Wake County

(G-12529)
AAA LOUVERS INC
7328 Siemens Rd (27591-8315)
P.O. Box 721 (27591-0721)
PHONE..............................919 365-7220
Larry Gower, *Pr*
EMP: 11 EST: 1988
SQ FT: 10,000
SALES (est): 2.42MM **Privately Held**
Web: www.aaalouvers.com
SIC: 2431 Doors and door parts and trim, wood

(G-12530)
CMS ASSOCIATES INC
7308 Siemens Rd Ste D (27591-6000)
P.O. Box 2139 (27591-2139)
PHONE..............................919 365-0881
Joseph T Hunt Junior, *Pr*
Elaine C Hunt, *Sec*
EMP: 7 EST: 1994
SQ FT: 6,000
SALES (est): 953.9K **Privately Held**
Web: www.cms-associates.com
SIC: 3679 Electronic circuits

(G-12531)
DARA HOLSTERS & GEAR INC
4120 Wendell Blvd (27591-6831)
PHONE..............................919 374-2170
Jonathan Dara, *Pr*
EMP: 22 EST: 2012
SALES (est): 937.23K **Privately Held**
Web: www.daraholsters.com
SIC: 5941 3999 Firearms; Manufacturing industries, nec

(G-12532)
DOGWOOD PRINT
400 Big Branch Ln (27591-6860)
PHONE..............................919 906-0617
Jonathan Priest, *Prin*
EMP: 4 EST: 2016
SALES (est): 85.35K **Privately Held**
Web: www.dogwoodprint.com
SIC: 2752 Commercial printing, lithographic

(G-12533)
DOUGLAS FABRICATION & MCH INC
430 Industrial Dr (27591-7714)
PHONE..............................919 365-7553
Sharon Douglas, *Pr*
Thomas Douglas, *Sec*
EMP: 11 EST: 1986
SQ FT: 30,000
SALES (est): 4.26MM **Privately Held**
Web: www.douglasfab.com
SIC: 3089 3599 Thermoformed finished plastics products, nec; Machine shop, jobbing and repair

(G-12534)
EAGLE SPORTSWEAR LLC
Also Called: Eagle USA
4251 Wendell Blvd (27591-8412)
P.O. Box 127 (27591-0127)
PHONE..............................919 365-9805
Brian Morrel, *Pr*
EMP: 4 EST: 2013
SALES (est): 133.12K **Privately Held**
SIC: 2389 Men's miscellaneous accessories

(G-12535)
ELECTRONIC PRODUCTS DESIGN INC
Also Called: E P D
2554 Lake Wendell Rd (27591-7164)
P.O. Box 1569 (27591-1569)
PHONE..............................919 365-9199
Devera Eggimann, *Pr*
Peter Eggimann, *VP*
Michelle Glidewell, *Com Operations Vice President*
EMP: 9 EST: 1983
SQ FT: 12,000
SALES (est): 935.37K **Privately Held**
Web: www.epd-inc.com
SIC: 3677 Coil windings, electronic

(G-12536)
FORTRANS INC
7400 Siemens Rd Ste B (27591-6756)
P.O. Box 40 (27591-0040)

PHONE..............................919 365-8004
Robert Cooke, *Pr*
Steven V Fiano, *CEO*
EMP: 4 EST: 1996
SQ FT: 5,000
SALES (est): 330.97K **Privately Held**
Web: www.fortransinc.com
SIC: 5169 2819 Industrial chemicals; Industrial inorganic chemicals, nec

(G-12537)
HENRY & RYE INCORPORATED
485 Old Wilson Rd Ste 1 (27591-6302)
PHONE..............................919 365-7045
Al Wayne Lucas, *Pr*
Al Wayne Lucas Senior, *Pr*
EMP: 4 EST: 1954
SQ FT: 20,000
SALES (est): 379.55K **Privately Held**
SIC: 3469 Kitchen fixtures and equipment: metal, except cast aluminum

(G-12538)
MAGNIFICENT CONCESSIONS LLC
Also Called: Food Industry
106 Northwinds North Dr (27591-7757)
PHONE..............................919 413-1558
Shaunetta Burk, *CEO*
EMP: 20 EST: 2019
SALES (est): 616.92K **Privately Held**
Web: www.magnificentconcessions.com
SIC: 2599 Food wagons, restaurant

(G-12539)
MODERN TOOL SERVICE
Also Called: Ideas Aesthetech
100 Walnut St (27591)
P.O. Box 220 (27591-0220)
PHONE..............................919 365-7470
Larry Liles, *Owner*
EMP: 10 EST: 1960
SQ FT: 3,600
SALES (est): 364.06K **Privately Held**
SIC: 3545 Measuring tools and machines, machinists' metalworking type

(G-12540)
POWER CHEM INC
7316b Siemens Rd (27591-8315)
PHONE..............................919 365-3400
Lawrence L Leonard, *Pr*
EMP: 6 EST: 1984
SALES (est): 98.3K **Privately Held**
SIC: 2833 Medicinals and botanicals

(G-12541)
PRECISION STAMPERS INC
Also Called: Stamp-Tech
480 Old Wilson Rd (27591-9355)
P.O. Box 1840 (27591-1840)
PHONE..............................919 366-3333
Douglas Parrish, *Pr*
Terry King, *VP*
EMP: 6 EST: 1999
SQ FT: 4,000
SALES (est): 1.02MM **Privately Held**
Web: www.stamptechinc.com
SIC: 3469 Stamping metal for the trade

(G-12542)
QUANTEX INC
280 W Haywood St (27591-9005)
P.O. Box 1388 (27591-1388)
PHONE..............................919 219-9604
Melissa Barker, *Pr*
James Barker, *VP*
EMP: 6 EST: 2002
SALES (est): 480.4K **Privately Held**
Web: quantexinc.com
SIC: 3532 Drills and drilling equipment, mining (except oil and gas)

(G-12543)
R J REYNOLDS TOBACCO COMPANY
7408 Siemens Rd Ste D (27591-8317)
PHONE..............................919 366-0220
Joe Dilger, *Prin*
EMP: 95
Web: www.rjrt.com
SIC: 2111 Cigarettes
HQ: R. J. Reynolds Tobacco Company
401 N Main St
Winston Salem NC 27101
336 741-5000

(G-12544)
RICHARDS WLDG MET FBRCTION LLC
7324 Siemens Rd (27591-8315)
PHONE..............................919 626-0134
Terry Richards, *Pr*
EMP: 16 EST: 2016
SALES (est): 2.28MM **Privately Held**
Web: www.richardsmetalfabrication.com
SIC: 7692 Welding repair

(G-12545)
RLS COMMERCIAL INTERIORS INC
7212 Siemens Rd (27591-8313)
PHONE..............................919 365-4086
Robert L Stout, *Pr*
Deborah Y Stout, *Sec*
EMP: 6 EST: 1983
SQ FT: 10,000
SALES (est): 329.73K **Privately Held**
Web: www.millcaseinteriors.com
SIC: 2431 Doors, wood

(G-12546)
SIEMENS ENERGY INC
7000 Siemens Rd (27591-8309)
PHONE..............................919 365-2200
Smith Macintosh, *Prin*
EMP: 21
SALES (corp-wide): 38.48B **Privately Held**
Web: www.siemens.com
SIC: 3621 Electric motor and generator parts
HQ: Siemens Energy, Inc.
4400 N Alafaya Trl
Orlando FL 32826
407 736-2000

(G-12547)
SIEMENS INDUSTRY INC
Engineered Products Division
7000 Siemens Rd (27591-8309)
PHONE..............................919 365-2200
Terry Royer, *Brnch Mgr*
EMP: 106
SQ FT: 35,000
SALES (corp-wide): 84.78B **Privately Held**
Web: www.siemens.com
SIC: 3625 3566 Motor control centers; Speed changers, drives, and gears
HQ: Siemens Industry, Inc.
1000 Deerfield Pkwy
Buffalo Grove IL 60089
847 215-1000

(G-12548)
SOUTHAG MFG INC
2023 Wendell Blvd (27591-6965)
PHONE..............................919 365-5111
Bill Thornton, *Pr*
▲ EMP: 6 EST: 1985
SQ FT: 17,000
SALES (est): 479.96K **Privately Held**
SIC: 3792 5084 5083 Trailer coaches, automobile; Trailers, industrial; Lawn and garden machinery and equipment

(G-12549)
SPC MECHANICAL CORPORATION (PA)
Also Called: Spc Heating & Cooling
1500 Wendell Rd (27591-7374)
P.O. Box 3006 (27895)
PHONE.............................252 237-9035
S Christopher Williford, *Pr*
Peggy Williford, *
Larry Bissette, *
George Dail, *
Mark Williford, *
EMP: 235 **EST:** 1970
SALES (est): 58.2MM
SALES (corp-wide): 58.2MM **Privately Held**
Web: www.spcmechanical.com
SIC: 3494 1711 3444 Valves and pipe fittings, nec; Plumbing contractors; Sheet metalwork

(G-12550)
THIRD STREET SCREEN PRINT INC
115 E Third St (27591-9791)
PHONE.............................919 365-2725
Eward Morrell, *Pr*
Kerry O'steen, *Sec*
EMP: 4 **EST:** 2014
SQ FT: 130,000
SALES (est): 233.59K **Privately Held**
Web: www.thirdstreetscreen.com
SIC: 2759 Screen printing

(G-12551)
TREE FROG INDUSTRIES LLC
246 Dogwood Trl (27591-9411)
PHONE.............................919 986-2229
Michael Firstbrook, *Admn*
EMP: 5 **EST:** 2016
SALES (est): 70.75K **Privately Held**
SIC: 3999 Manufacturing industries, nec

(G-12552)
VISHAY MEASUREMENTS GROUP INC (HQ)
Also Called: Micro Measurements
951 Wendell Blvd (27591-9515)
P.O. Box 27777 (27611-7777)
PHONE.............................919 365-3800
William M Clancy, *CEO*
Thomas P Kieffer, *Pr*
Steven Klausner, *Treas*
Jeffrey King, *Sec*
◆ **EMP:** 5 **EST:** 1962
SQ FT: 127,000
SALES (est): 38.59MM
SALES (corp-wide): 306.52MM **Publicly Held**
Web: www.micro-measurements.com
SIC: 3829 5065 Stress, strain, and flaw detecting/measuring equipment; Electronic parts and equipment, nec
PA: Vishay Precision Group, Inc.
3 Great Vly Pkwy Ste 150
Malvern PA 19355
484 321-5300

(G-12553)
VISHAY TRANSDUCERS LTD (HQ)
Also Called: Stress-Tek
951 Wendell Blvd (27591-9515)
PHONE.............................919 365-3800
Ziv Shoshani, *CEO*
Keith Reichow, *
▲ **EMP:** 31 **EST:** 1978
SQ FT: 35,000
SALES (est): 5.52MM
SALES (corp-wide): 306.52MM **Publicly Held**
Web: www.micro-measurements.com

SIC: 3545 3679 3596 Scales, measuring (machinists' precision tools); Loads, electronic; Scales and balances, except laboratory
PA: Vishay Precision Group, Inc.
3 Great Vly Pkwy Ste 150
Malvern PA 19355
484 321-5300

(G-12554)
YUKON INC
Also Called: Unique Concepts
485 Old Wilson Rd Ste 8 (27591-6302)
P.O. Box 56 (27591-0056)
PHONE.............................919 366-2001
Fred Leach, *Pr*
David Curry, *VP*
Lynne Leach, *Treas*
Greg Taylor, *Stockholder*
EMP: 12 **EST:** 1994
SQ FT: 10,000
SALES (est): 823.72K **Privately Held**
Web: www.uniqueconcepts.com
SIC: 2511 5712 Wood household furniture; Furniture stores

West End
Moore County

(G-12555)
JUBILEE SCREEN PRINTING INC
314 Grant St Ste F (27376-8388)
P.O. Box 485 (27376-0485)
PHONE.............................910 673-4240
William H Mcneill, *Pr*
Matt Mcneill, *VP*
Kim Mcneill, *VP*
Judy Mcneill, *Sec*
EMP: 5 **EST:** 1991
SALES (est): 188.79K **Privately Held**
Web: www.jubileescreenprint.com
SIC: 7389 2759 Textile designers; Screen printing

(G-12556)
LONGLEAF TRUSS COMPANY
4476 Nc Highway 211 (27376-8382)
P.O. Box 225 (27376-0225)
PHONE.............................910 673-4711
Frederick L Taylor Ii, *VP*
Robert Gravely, *
Ann Gravely, *
EMP: 29 **EST:** 2000
SQ FT: 10,000
SALES (est): 5.05MM **Privately Held**
SIC: 2439 Trusses, wooden roof

(G-12557)
MILITARY PRODUCTS INC
Also Called: TAC Shield
5425 Nc Highway 211 (27376-9248)
P.O. Box 4613 (28374-4613)
PHONE.............................910 637-0315
David Nau, *CEO*
Barry Bond, *VP*
▲ **EMP:** 9 **EST:** 2010
SALES (est): 2.08MM **Privately Held**
Web: www.tacshield.com
SIC: 2389 2387 2311 Men's miscellaneous accessories; Apparel belts; Military uniforms, men's and youths': purchased materials

(G-12558)
SANDHLLS FBRCTORS CRANE SVCS I
6536 7 Lakes Vlg (27376-9314)
PHONE.............................910 673-4573
Cliff Baldwin, *Pr*

EMP: 10 **EST:** 2005
SALES (est): 470.72K **Privately Held**
SIC: 3699 3599 Electrical equipment and supplies, nec; Machine shop, jobbing and repair

(G-12559)
SEVEN LAKES NEWS CORPORATION
Also Called: Carthage Gazette
2033 7 Lks S (27376-9609)
PHONE.............................910 685-0320
Victoria Levinger, *Prin*
Brandon Levinger, *Prin*
EMP: 4 **EST:** 2017
SALES (est): 231.32K **Privately Held**
Web: www.sevenlakesnews.com
SIC: 2711 Newspapers, publishing and printing

(G-12560)
WILSON MACHINE SHO
333 Hoffman Rd (27376-9025)
P.O. Box 685 (27376-0685)
PHONE.............................910 673-3505
EMP: 5 **EST:** 2013
SALES (est): 139.48K **Privately Held**
SIC: 3599 Machine shop, jobbing and repair

West Jefferson
Ashe County

(G-12561)
CAROLINA TIMBERWORKS LLC
210 Industrial Park Way (28694-7641)
PHONE.............................828 266-9663
Craig Kitson, *Prin*
EMP: 12 **EST:** 2003
SALES (est): 1.04MM **Privately Held**
Web: www.carolinatimberworks.com
SIC: 8712 2421 Architectural services; Sawmills and planing mills, general

(G-12562)
COBBLE CREEK LUMBER LLC
225 Hice Ave (28694-7059)
P.O. Box 1848 (28694-1848)
PHONE.............................336 844-2620
EMP: 23 **EST:** 2017
SALES (est): 5.24MM **Privately Held**
Web: www.cobblecreeklumber.com
SIC: 2421 Sawmills and planing mills, general

(G-12563)
CREATIVE PRINTERS INC
4 N 6th Ave (28694-9522)
P.O. Box 53 (28694-0053)
PHONE.............................336 246-7746
Steve Craven, *Owner*
EMP: 5 **EST:** 1993
SQ FT: 1,600
SALES (est): 213.97K **Privately Held**
Web: www.cpiprintgroup.com
SIC: 2752 2759 7389 Offset printing; Screen printing; Sign painting and lettering shop

(G-12564)
DR PPPER BTLG W JFFRSON NC IN
Also Called: Dr Pepper
109 W 3rd St (28694-9157)
P.O. Box 34 (28694-0034)
PHONE.............................336 846-2433
Michael Vannoy, *VP*
EMP: 42
SALES (corp-wide): 13.14MM **Privately Held**
Web: www.drpepper.com

SIC: 2086 Soft drinks: packaged in cans, bottles, etc.
PA: Dr. Pepper Bottling Company Of West Jefferson, North Carolina, Incorporated
2614 Nc Highway 163
West Jefferson NC
336 246-4591

(G-12565)
K & K STITCH & SCREEN
240 Helen Blevins Rd Unit 1 (28694-8465)
PHONE.............................336 246-5477
Kevin Hardy, *Owner*
EMP: 5 **EST:** 2003
SALES (est): 229.73K **Privately Held**
Web: www.explorations-unlimited.com
SIC: 2759 Screen printing

(G-12566)
LEVITON MANUFACTURING CO INC
618 S Jefferson Ave (28694-9739)
PHONE.............................336 846-3246
Van Shatley, *Mgr*
EMP: 5
SALES (corp-wide): 1.46B **Privately Held**
Web: www.leviton.com
SIC: 3643 3674 Plugs, electric; Diodes, solid state (germanium, silicon, etc.)
PA: Leviton Manufacturing Co., Inc.
201 N Service Rd
Melville NY 11747
800 323-8920

(G-12567)
MOUNTAIN TIMES INC
Also Called: Sundown Times
7 W Main St (28694-9121)
PHONE.............................336 246-6397
Tommy Wilson, *Pr*
EMP: 4 **EST:** 1993
SALES (est): 220.88K **Privately Held**
Web: www.wataugademocrat.com
SIC: 2711 Newspapers, publishing and printing

(G-12568)
MOUNTAIN TOP WOODWORKING
816 Old Obids Rd (28694-8204)
PHONE.............................336 982-4059
Alvin Day, *Owner*
EMP: 4 **EST:** 2005
SALES (est): 206.21K **Privately Held**
Web: www.mountaintopwoodworkingshop.com
SIC: 2431 Millwork

(G-12569)
OSAGE PECAN COMPANY
713 Claybank Rd (28694-7354)
PHONE.............................660 679-6137
Barbara Tippin, *Pr*
EMP: 10 **EST:** 1958
SALES (est): 142.96K **Privately Held**
Web: www.osagepecans.com
SIC: 0723 2099 2068 2034 Pecan hulling and shelling services; Food preparations, nec; Salted and roasted nuts and seeds; Dried and dehydrated fruits, vegetables and soup mixes

(G-12570)
SCREEN SPECIALTY SHOP INC
8406 Nc Highway 163 (28694-8128)
PHONE.............................336 982-4135
Gary C Prange, *Pr*
Debra Lynn Prange, *VP*
EMP: 6 **EST:** 1990
SALES (est): 985.5K **Privately Held**
Web: www.sssink.com
SIC: 2759 Screen printing

GEOGRAPHIC

(G-12571)
TOP DAWG LANDSCAPE INC
605 S Jefferson Ave # 1 (28694-9739)
P.O. Box 326 (28694-0326)
PHONE..................................336 877-7519
Robert Hodges, *Pr*
EMP: 4 **EST:** 2012
SALES (est): 72.39K **Privately Held**
Web: www.topdawgnc.com
SIC: 3271 3645 0782 Blocks, concrete: landscape or retaining wall; Garden, patio, walkway and yard lighting fixtures: electric; Lawn and garden services

Westfield
Surry County

(G-12572)
CHARLOTTE SHUTTER AND SHADES
1825 Pell Rd (27053-7555)
PHONE..................................336 351-3391
Richard Pell, *Prin*
EMP: 5 **EST:** 2016
SALES (est): 78.13K **Privately Held**
SIC: 3442 Shutters, door or window: metal

(G-12573)
JPS ELSTMERICS WESTFIELD PLANT
1535 Elastic Plant Rd (27053-8242)
PHONE..................................336 351-0938
Marvin Conner, *Pr*
EMP: 6 **EST:** 2011
SALES (est): 64.55K **Privately Held**
SIC: 2211 Broadwoven fabric mills, cotton

Whitakers
Nash County

(G-12574)
CONSOLIDATED DIESEL INC
9377 N Us Highway 301 (27891-8621)
P.O. Box 670 (27891-0670)
PHONE..................................252 437-6611
◆ **EMP:** 1400 **EST:** 1982
SALES (est): 10.8MM
SALES (corp-wide): 34.1B **Publicly Held**
SIC: 3519 Engines, diesel and semi-diesel or dual-fuel
PA: Cummins Inc.
500 Jackson St
Columbus IN 47201
812 377-5000

White Oak
Bladen County

(G-12575)
WOOD LOGGING
361 Gum Spring Rd (28399-9407)
P.O. Box 143 (28399-0143)
PHONE..................................910 866-4018
Mickey Wood, *Owner*
EMP: 7 **EST:** 1992
SALES (est): 313.61K **Privately Held**
SIC: 2411 Logging camps and contractors

Whiteville
Columbus County

(G-12576)
BALDWIN SIGN & AWNING
2 Whiteville Mini Mall (28472-2105)
PHONE..................................910 642-8812
Eric Baldwin, *Owner*
EMP: 4 **EST:** 2005
SALES (est): 253.27K **Privately Held**
Web: www.baldwinsigns.net
SIC: 3993 Signs and advertising specialties

(G-12577)
BUDGET PRINTING CO
1424 S Jk Powell Blvd Ste B (28472-9145)
P.O. Box 1175 (28472-1175)
PHONE..................................910 642-7306
Lynn Packer, *Pr*
Jimmy Packer, *VP*
EMP: 4 **EST:** 1980
SALES (est): 194.74K **Privately Held**
SIC: 2752 Offset printing

(G-12578)
CAROLINA RETREAD LLC
30 Bitmore Rd (28472-4928)
P.O. Box 919 (28472-0919)
PHONE..................................910 642-4123
Ricky Benton, *Pr*
EMP: 6 **EST:** 2010
SALES (est): 355.35K **Privately Held**
SIC: 7534 Rebuilding and retreading tires

(G-12579)
CCBCC OPERATIONS LLC
Also Called: Coca-Cola
239 Industrial Blvd (28472-5417)
PHONE..................................910 642-3002
Hugh Mcmillan, *Mgr*
EMP: 33
SALES (corp-wide): 6.9B **Publicly Held**
Web: www.cokeconsolidated.com
SIC: 2086 Bottled and canned soft drinks
HQ: Ccbcc Operations, Llc
4100 Coca-Cola Plz
Charlotte NC 28211
704 364-8728

(G-12580)
DONUT SHOP
1602 S Madison St (28472-4947)
PHONE..................................910 640-3317
Mary Harrelson, *Pt*
Elizabeth Kasitati, *Pt*
EMP: 8 **EST:** 1995
SALES (est): 458.35K **Privately Held**
Web: www.donutshopdiner.com
SIC: 2051 5812 Doughnuts, except frozen; Eating places

(G-12581)
GEORGIA-PACIFIC LLC
Also Called: Plywood Plant
1980 Georgia Pacific Rd (28472-3026)
PHONE..................................910 642-5041
Norman Haris, *Brnch Mgr*
EMP: 25
SALES (corp-wide): 64.44B **Privately Held**
Web: www.gp.com
SIC: 2435 Plywood, hardwood or hardwood faced
HQ: Georgia-Pacific Llc
133 Peachtree St Ne
Atlanta GA 30303
404 652-4000

(G-12582)
GORE S TRLR MANUFACTURER S INC
305 Gores Trailer Rd (28472-7541)
PHONE..................................910 642-2246
Daniel Jackson Gore, *Pr*
Janice Gore, *VP*
EMP: 6 **EST:** 1972
SQ FT: 49,019
SALES (est): 509.64K **Privately Held**
Web: www.goretrailers.com
SIC: 5599 3799 Utility trailers; Horse trailers, except fifth-wheel type

(G-12583)
H CLYDE MOORE JR
Also Called: Clyde Moore Logging
790 Honey Field Rd (28472-7952)
PHONE..................................910 642-3507
H Clyde Moore Junior, *Owner*
EMP: 5 **EST:** 1983
SALES (est): 99.77K **Privately Held**
SIC: 2411 Logging camps and contractors

(G-12584)
HIGHCORP INCORPORATED
Also Called: News Reporter
127 W Columbus St (28472-4023)
P.O. Box 707 (28472-0707)
PHONE..................................910 642-4104
James C High, *Pr*
Stuart High Nance, *
Leslie T High, *
EMP: 50 **EST:** 1896
SQ FT: 20,000
SALES (est): 674.48K **Privately Held**
Web: www.nrcolumbus.com
SIC: 2711 Newspapers, publishing and printing

(G-12585)
J L POWELL & CO INC (PA)
Also Called: Cinema III Theaters
135 E Main St (28472-4131)
PHONE..................................910 642-8989
Jesse C Fisher Junior, *Pr*
EMP: 8 **EST:** 1876
SALES (est): 495K
SALES (corp-wide): 495K **Privately Held**
Web: www.7-eleven.com
SIC: 6512 6513 2426 5411 Commercial and industrial building operation; Apartment building operators; Flooring, hardwood; Convenience stores

(G-12586)
JACKS MOTOR PARTS INC
Hwy 701 (28472)
P.O. Box 338 (28472-0338)
PHONE..................................910 642-4077
Yvonne Ellis, *Pr*
Keith Ellis, *VP*
EMP: 5 **EST:** 1963
SQ FT: 1,800
SALES (est): 226.86K **Privately Held**
SIC: 7538 3599 Engine repair, except diesel: automotive; Machine shop, jobbing and repair

(G-12587)
MAXPRO MANUFACTURING LLC
31 Industrial Blvd (28472-3867)
P.O. Box 567 (28472-0567)
PHONE..................................910 640-5505
Joe Cobbe, *Pr*
Ron Foley, *Sr VP*
Elizabeth Dillon, *Marketing*
Mike Newman, *VP Mfg*
Renee Mullins, *International Sales Vice President*
EMP: 11 **EST:** 2012
SALES (est): 2.47MM **Privately Held**
Web: www.maxprofilms.com
SIC: 3578 Accounting machines and cash registers

(G-12588)
METAL ARC
5547 James B White Hwy S (28472-6515)
PHONE..................................910 770-1180
EMP: 4 **EST:** 2018

SALES (est): 77.33K **Privately Held**
Web: metal-arc.business.site
SIC: 7692 Welding repair

(G-12589)
NATIONAL SPINNING CO INC
Hwy 130 240 Spinning Rd (28472)
P.O. Box 547 (28472-0547)
PHONE..................................910 642-4181
Rick Barton, *Brnch Mgr*
EMP: 114
SALES (corp-wide): 40.55MM **Privately Held**
Web: www.natspin.com
SIC: 2281 Knitting yarn, spun
PA: National Spinning Co., Inc.
1481 W 2nd St
Washington NC 27889
252 975-7111

(G-12590)
NICE BLENDS CORP
222 Industrial Blvd (28472-5417)
PHONE..................................910 640-1000
Barrie Nadi, *Pr*
EMP: 54 **EST:** 1993
SQ FT: 24,000
SALES (est): 3.86MM **Privately Held**
Web: www.niceblends.com
SIC: 2099 2037 Spices, including grinding; Frozen fruits and vegetables

(G-12591)
NORTH CAROLINA PLYWOOD LLC
512 E Main St (28472-4309)
P.O. Box 458 (32331-0458)
PHONE..................................850 948-2211
John Maultsby, *Managing Member*
John P Maultsby, *Managing Member*
EMP: 8 **EST:** 2013
SQ FT: 100,000
SALES (est): 330.83K **Privately Held**
Web: www.ncplywood.com
SIC: 2435 Plywood, hardwood or hardwood faced

(G-12592)
PRIDGEN WOODWORK INC
910 Jefferson St (28472-3701)
PHONE..................................910 642-7175
Linnwood Pridgen, *VP*
A Rudolph Pridgen, *
EMP: 47 **EST:** 1947
SQ FT: 50,200
SALES (est): 2.96MM **Privately Held**
Web: www.pridgenwoodwork.com
SIC: 2431 2521 Doors and door parts and trim, wood; Cabinets, office: wood

(G-12593)
SHODJA TEXTILES INC
Also Called: Whiteville Fabrick
68 Industrial Dr (28472-4545)
P.O. Box 3 (28472-0003)
PHONE..................................910 914-0456
Mohammad Shodja, *Pr*
Cameron Shodja, *VP*
EMP: 4 **EST:** 1972
SALES (est): 483.54K **Privately Held**
SIC: 2258 Lace and warp knit fabric mills

(G-12594)
W & W ELECTRIC MOTOR SHOP INC
5240 James B White Hwy N (28472)
PHONE..................................910 642-2369
Robert Ward, *Pr*
Annie Ward, *Sec*
EMP: 7 **EST:** 1955
SQ FT: 4,000
SALES (est): 91.72K **Privately Held**

SIC: 7694 Rewinding stators

(G-12595)
WHITEVILLE AG
3654 James B White Hwy S (28472-8684)
PHONE..................................910 914-0007
Timothy J Rausch Senior, *Prin*
EMP: 6 EST: 2012
SALES (est): 94.24K **Privately Held**
Web: www.whitevillenc.gov
SIC: 2711 Newspapers

(G-12596)
WHITEVILLE FABRICS LLC (PA)
68 Industrial Dr (28472-4545)
P.O. Box 3 (28472-0003)
PHONE..................................910 914-0456
Cameron Shodja, *Managing Member*
▲ **EMP: 17 EST:** 2000
SALES (est): 2.46MM **Privately Held**
SIC: 2258 Warp and flat knit products

(G-12597)
WHITEVILLE FABRICS LLC
68 Industrial Blvd (28472-3867)
PHONE..................................910 639-4444
Cameron Shodja, *Mgr*
EMP: 18
SIC: 2258 Warp and flat knit products
PA: Whiteville Fabrics, L.L.C.
68 Industrial Dr
Whiteville NC 28472

(G-12598)
WHITEVILLE FORKLIFT & EQP
Also Called: Whiteville Rentals
344 Vinson Blvd (28472-4999)
PHONE..................................910 642-6642
Ken Thomas, *Pr*
Ken Thomas, *Pr*
Roberta Thomas, *VP*
EMP: 6 EST: 1991
SQ FT: 2,000
SALES (est): 4.83MM **Privately Held**
Web: www.whitevillerentals.com
SIC: 3537 7699 Forklift trucks; Industrial
truck repair

Whitsett
Guilford County

(G-12599)
ASCENDING IRON LLC
6504 Burlington Rd (27377-9200)
PHONE..................................336 266-6462
EMP: 27 EST: 2019
SALES (est): 4.91MM **Privately Held**
SIC: 3441 Fabricated structural metal

(G-12600)
**BOXMOOR TRUCK BEDLINERS &
ACC**
1900 Buckminster Dr (27377-9331)
PHONE..................................336 447-4621
Pieter Swanepoel, *Owner*
EMP: 7 EST: 2011
SALES (est): 293.7K **Privately Held**
SIC: 3714 Pickup truck bed liners

(G-12601)
CAROLINA BIOLOGICAL SUPPLY CO
6537 Judge Adams Rd (27377-9718)
PHONE..................................336 446-7600
Ronald Simpson, *Mgr*
EMP: 150
SQ FT: 214,253
SALES (corp-wide): 29.35MM **Privately
Held**
Web: www.carolina.com

SIC: 2836 5049 Biological products, except
diagnostic; Laboratory equipment, except
medical or dental
PA: Carolina Biological Supply Company
2700 York Rd
Burlington NC 27215
336 584-0381

(G-12602)
CLAPP FERTILIZER AND TRCKG INC
2225 Herron Rd (27377-9801)
PHONE..................................336 449-6103
Wendell G Clapp, *CEO*
EMP: 8 EST: 1948
SQ FT: 11,520
SALES (est): 2.11MM **Privately Held**
Web: www.kzootms.com
SIC: 5191 2873 5153 Fertilizer and fertilizer
materials; Nitrogenous fertilizers; Grains

(G-12603)
CROSS TECHNOLOGIES INC
Cross Precision Measurement
6541c Franz Warner Pkwy (27377-9215)
PHONE..................................336 292-0511
Dave Thornhill, *Brnch Mgr*
EMP: 60
SALES (corp-wide): 197.14MM **Privately
Held**
Web: www.crossco.com
SIC: 5084 3492 Industrial machinery and
equipment; Fluid power valves and hose
fittings
PA: Cross Technologies, Inc.
4400 Piedmont Pkwy
Greensboro NC 27410
800 327-7727

(G-12604)
DREW ROBERTS LLC
Also Called: Can-Do Handyman Services
6627 Barton Creek Dr (27377-9277)
PHONE..................................336 497-1679
EMP: 7 EST: 2013
SALES (est): 426.45K **Privately Held**
Web: www.newnusedoutlet.com
SIC: 8741 3955 5734 5731 Management
services; Print cartridges for laser and other
computer printers; Modems, monitors,
terminals, and disk drives: computers;
Consumer electronic equipment, nec

(G-12605)
ENGINEERED CONTROLS INTL LLC
Also Called: Ecii
1239 Rock Creek Dairy Rd (27377-9116)
PHONE..................................336 449-7706
Chester Johnson, *Mgr*
EMP: 200
SALES (corp-wide): 7.75B **Publicly Held**
Web: www.regoproducts.com
SIC: 3491 3494 Industrial valves; Valves and
pipe fittings, nec
HQ: Engineered Controls International, Llc
100 Rego Dr
Elon NC 27244

(G-12606)
FOCKE & CO INC
5730 Millstream Rd (27377-9789)
PHONE..................................336 449-7200
Juergen Focke, *Pr*
Johann Betschart, *
▲ **EMP: 68 EST:** 1989
SQ FT: 100,000
SALES (est): 17.6MM
SALES (corp-wide): 447.2MM **Privately
Held**
Web: www.focke.com
SIC: 3565 Packaging machinery
PA: Focke & Co. (Gmbh & Co. Kg)

Siemensstr. 10
Verden (Aller) NI 27283
42318910

(G-12607)
GALVANIZING CONSULTANTS INC
687 Winners Pt (27377-8720)
PHONE..................................336 603-4218
John F Malone, *Pr*
Leana Malone, *VP*
Donald Wetzel, *Ex VP*
EMP: 5 EST: 1986
SALES (est): 90.38K **Privately Held**
Web: www.galvanizingconsulting.com
SIC: 3479 Coating of metals and formed
products

(G-12608)
GIBRALTAR PACKAGING INC
6530 Franz Warner Pkwy (27377-9215)
P.O. Box 700 (27306-0700)
PHONE..................................910 439-6137
Jim Downey, *Brnch Mgr*
EMP: 120
Web: www.onepaperworks.com
SIC: 2752 2759 Offset printing; Commercial
printing, nec
HQ: Gibraltar Packaging Inc.
2000 Summit Ave
Hastings NE 68901
402 463-1366

(G-12609)
HARRELL PROPER TRANSPORT LLC
205 Boling Springs Ct (27377-9828)
PHONE..................................336 202-7135
EMP: 6 EST: 2020
SALES (est): 1.66MM **Privately Held**
SIC: 3537 Trucks: freight, baggage, etc.:
industrial, except mining

(G-12610)
ICA MID-ATLANTIC INC
Also Called: Integrted Cble Assmbly Hldings
6532 Judge Adams Rd (27377-9835)
PHONE..................................336 447-4546
Jim Laird, *Mgr*
Jim Laird, *VP*
Mehdi Ali Junior, *Mgr*
Jesus Maldonado, *
▲ **EMP: 125 EST:** 2002
SQ FT: 70,000
SALES (est): 4.94MM
SALES (corp-wide): 15.22B **Publicly Held**
Web: www.icaholdings.com
SIC: 3496 Miscellaneous fabricated wire
products
HQ: Integrated Cable Assembly Holdings,
Inc.
6401 S Cntry Clb Ste 101
Tucson AZ 85706
520 290-9987

(G-12611)
J & W SERVICE INCORPORATED
7471 Danford Rd (27377)
P.O. Box 194 (27377-0194)
PHONE..................................336 449-4584
Jerry L Small, *Pr*
Wanda Small, *VP*
EMP: 6 EST: 1984
SALES (est): 509.41K **Privately Held**
Web: www.jandwservice.com
SIC: 7699 1711 1521 8711 Mobile home
repair; Heating systems repair and
maintenance; Mobile home repair, on site;
Heating and ventilation engineering

(G-12612)
LINDE GAS & EQUIPMENT INC
Also Called: Linde Gas North America
1304 Roosevelt Ct (27377-9121)
PHONE..................................866 543-3427
Timothy Allen, *Brnch Mgr*
EMP: 14
Web: www.lindedirect.com
SIC: 2813 Nitrogen
HQ: Linde Gas & Equipment Inc.
10 Riverview Dr
Danbury CT 06810
844 445-4633

(G-12613)
MACHINE SPECIALTIES LLC
6511 Franz Warner Pkwy (27377-9215)
PHONE..................................336 603-1919
Robert Simmons, *CEO*
Brent Allen, *
EMP: 160 EST: 1969
SQ FT: 150,000
SALES (est): 24.14MM
SALES (corp-wide): 47.96MM **Privately
Held**
Web: www.machspec.com
SIC: 3599 Machine shop, jobbing and repair
PA: Calvert Street Capital Partners, Inc.
1 Olympic Pl
Towson MD 21204
443 573-3700

(G-12614)
MARK/TRECE INC
6799 Leaf Crest Dr Apt 2c (27377-8740)
PHONE..................................336 292-3424
Bob Bauses, *Genl Mgr*
EMP: 25
SALES (corp-wide): 24.32MM **Privately
Held**
Web: www.marktrece.com
SIC: 3555 7336 2796 Printing plates;
Graphic arts and related design;
Platemaking services
PA: Mark/Trece, Inc.
2001 Stockton Rd
Joppa MD 21085
410 879-0060

(G-12615)
MEDI MANUFACTURING INC
6481 Franz Warner Pkwy (27377-9214)
PHONE..................................336 449-4440
Michael Weihermueller, *Pr*
Stefan Weihermueller, *Sec*
EMP: 30 EST: 1996
SQ FT: 15,000
SALES (est): 10.35MM **Privately Held**
Web: www.mediusa.com
SIC: 5047 3842 Medical equipment and
supplies; Abdominal supporters, braces,
and trusses

(G-12616)
PAPERWORKS INDUSTRIES INC
6530 Franz Warner Pkwy (27377-9215)
PHONE..................................336 447-7278
EMP: 112
Web: www.onepaperworks.com
SIC: 2653 Boxes, corrugated: made from
purchased materials
PA: Paperworks Industries, Inc.
1300 Virginia Dr Ste 220
Fort Washington PA 19034

(G-12617)
PREPAC MANUFACTURING US LLC
3031 Hendren Rd (27377-9144)
PHONE..................................800 665-1266
Michelle Mackinnon, *VP*
EMP: 15 EST: 2020

SALES (est): 13.12MM
SALES (corp-wide): 13.89MM **Privately Held**
SIC: 5021 2511 Furniture; Unassembled or unfinished furniture, household: wood
PA: Prepac Manufacturing Ltd.
6705 Dennett Pl
Delta BC V4G 1
604 940-2300

(G-12618)
QUALICAPS INC
6505 Franz Warner Pkwy (27377-9215)
PHONE...............................336 449-3900
Yogi Date, *Pr*
Paul J Verchick, *
◆ EMP: 175 EST: 1992
SQ FT: 94,000
SALES (est): 16.19MM
SALES (corp-wide): 3.18B **Privately Held**
Web: www.qualicaps.com
SIC: 2834 Pharmaceutical preparations
HQ: Qualicaps Co., Ltd.
321-5, Ikezawacho
Yamatokoriyama NAR 639-1

(G-12619)
ROTRON INCORPORATED
Also Called: Ametek Rtron Technical Mtr Div
1210 Nc Highway 61 (27377-9114)
PHONE...............................336 449-3400
Jim Liddle, *Genl Mgr*
EMP: 120
SQ FT: 104,467
SALES (corp-wide): 6.94B **Publicly.Held**
Web: www.rotron.com
SIC: 3564 5063 3621 Blowers and fans; Electrical apparatus and equipment; Motors and generators
HQ: Rotron Incorporated
55 Hasbrouck Ln
Woodstock NY 12498
845 679-2401

(G-12620)
SOUTHLAND LOG HOMES INC
5692 Millstream Rd (27377-9724)
PHONE...............................336 449-5388
Stacey Steelman, *Mgr*
EMP: 6
SQ FT: 4,173
SALES (corp-wide): 9.95MM **Privately Held**
Web: www.southlandloghomes.com
SIC: 2452 Log cabins, prefabricated, wood
PA: Southland Log Homes, Inc.
7521 Broad River Rd
Irmo SC 29063
803 781-5100

(G-12621)
TRUSSWAY MANUFACTURING INC
Also Called: Trussway
940 Golf House Rd W Ste 201
(27377-9299)
PHONE...............................336 883-6966
Greg Ausderher, *Mgr*
EMP: 35
SALES (corp-wide): 16.4B **Publicly Held**
Web: www.bldr.com
SIC: 2439 Trusses, wooden roof
HQ: Trussway Manufacturing, Llc
9411 Alcorn St
Houston TX 77093

(G-12622)
ZINK HOLDINGS LLC
6900 Konica Dr (27377-9787)
PHONE...............................336 449-8000
Rick Lewis, *Brnch Mgr*
EMP: 85

SALES (corp-wide): 22.6MM **Privately Held**
Web: www.zink.com
SIC: 3861 Photographic equipment and supplies
PA: Zink Holdings Llc
114 Tived Ln E
Edison NJ 08837
781 761-5400

(G-12623)
ZINK IMAGING INC
Also Called: Zink
6900 Konica Dr (27377-9787)
PHONE...............................336 449-8000
Mary Jeffries, *CEO*
Paul Baker, *
Stephen R Herchen, *
Gary Lortie, *
Scott Wicker, *
EMP: 49 EST: 2005
SALES (est): 4.29MM
SALES (corp-wide): 22.6MM **Privately Held**
Web: www.zink.com
SIC: 3861 Photographic equipment and supplies
PA: Zink Holdings Llc
114 Tived Ln E
Edison NJ 08837
781 761-5400

Whittier
Jackson County

(G-12624)
JAMES KEITH NATIONS
Also Called: Keith Nations Log Company
69 Thomas Valley Rd (28789-9198)
PHONE...............................828 421-5391
James Keith Nations, *Prin*
EMP: 8 EST: 2012
SALES (est): 184.92K **Privately Held**
SIC: 2411 Logging

(G-12625)
PEPSI-COLA BTLG HICKRY NC INC
Also Called: Pepsi-Cola
1060 Gateway Rd (28789-7640)
P.O. Box 1545 (28789-1545)
PHONE...............................828 497-1235
Teresa Leatherwood, *Off Mgr*
EMP: 53
SALES (corp-wide): 28.58MM **Privately Held**
Web: www.hickorync.gov
SIC: 2086 Carbonated soft drinks, bottled and canned
PA: Pepsi-Cola Bottling Company Of Hickory, N.C., Inc.
2401 14th Avenue Cir Nw
Hickory NC 28601
828 322-8090

Wilkesboro
Wilkes County

(G-12626)
A D SERVICES
402 S Cherry St (28697-2823)
PHONE...............................336 667-8190
EMP: 5 EST: 2018
SALES (est): 80.05K **Privately Held**
Web: www.journalpatriot.com
SIC: 2711 Newspapers: publishing only, not printed on site

(G-12627)
ACTION INSTALLS LLC
1202 Industrial Park Rd (28697-8490)
PHONE...............................704 787-3828
Michael Kerhoulas, *Prin*
EMP: 6 EST: 2013
SALES (est): 186.72K **Privately Held**
Web: www.actionsign.com
SIC: 3993 Signs and advertising specialties

(G-12628)
APPALACHIAN LUMBER COMPANY INC (PA)
Also Called: Appalachian Lumber
5879 W Us Highway 421 (28697-7905)
PHONE...............................336 973-7205
William B Church Junior, *Pr*
Robin Church, *
▲ EMP: 25 EST: 1988
SQ FT: 64,000
SALES (est): 6.01MM
SALES (corp-wide): 6.01MM **Privately Held**
Web: www.appalachianlumber.net
SIC: 2431 2426 Panel work, wood; Furniture stock and parts, hardwood

(G-12629)
BEST IMAGE SIGNS LLC
Also Called: Best Image Signs and Graphics
178 Nicholas Landing Dr (28697-7169)
P.O. Box 296 (28651-0296)
PHONE...............................336 973-7445
EMP: 5 EST: 2005
SALES (est): 373.19K **Privately Held**
Web: www.bestimagesigns.com
SIC: 3993 Signs, not made in custom sign painting shops

(G-12630)
CALL FAMILY DISTILLERS LLC
1611 Industrial Dr (28697-7344)
PHONE...............................336 990-0708
EMP: 4 EST: 2015
SALES (est): 647.7K **Privately Held**
Web: www.callfamilydistillers.com
SIC: 2085 Distilled and blended liquors

(G-12631)
CHURCH & CHURCH LUMBER LLC (PA)
863 New Browns Ford Rd (28697-7365)
P.O. Box 619 (28651-0619)
PHONE...............................336 973-5700
Bruce Church, *
Ken Church, *
Cindy Holcombe, *
EMP: 90 EST: 1979
SALES (est): 15.41MM
SALES (corp-wide): 15.41MM **Privately Held**
Web: www.churchandchurchlumber.com
SIC: 2426 2421 Dimension, hardwood; Sawmills and planing mills, general

(G-12632)
CHURCH & CHURCH LUMBER LLC
Brown Ford Rd (28697)
PHONE...............................336 973-4297
Mark Church, *Mgr*
EMP: 53
SALES (corp-wide): 15.41MM **Privately Held**
Web: www.churchandchurchlumber.com
SIC: 5031 2426 Lumber, plywood, and millwork; Hardwood dimension and flooring mills
PA: Church & Church Lumber, Llc
863 New Browns Ford Rd
Wilkesboro NC 28697

336 973-5700

(G-12633)
CJ PARTNERS LLC
1702 W Us Highway 421 Ste P
(28697-2377)
PHONE...............................336 838-3080
C James, *Dir*
EMP: 4 EST: 2007
SALES (est): 377.6K **Privately Held**
SIC: 3721 Aircraft

(G-12634)
EXTERIOR VINYL WHOLESALE
1808 Industrial Dr (28697-7346)
PHONE...............................336 838-7772
Patty Wells, *Pt*
James Brennan, *Pt*
Philip Brennan, *Pt*
Sergio Pezzotti, *Pt*
EMP: 5 EST: 1990
SQ FT: 11,000
SALES (est): 453.67K **Privately Held**
Web: www.exteriorvinyl.com
SIC: 3292 3441 Tile, vinyl asbestos; Fabricated structural metal

(G-12635)
FIRST PRRITY EMRGNCY VHCLES IN
1208 School St (28697-2625)
PHONE...............................908 645-0788
EMP: 27
SALES (corp-wide): 14.69MM **Privately Held**
Web: www.1fpg.com
SIC: 3711 Ambulances (motor vehicles), assembly of
HQ: First Priority Emergency Vehicles, Inc.
2444 Rdgway Blvd Bldg 500
Manchester NJ 08759
973 347-4321

(G-12636)
FLOWERS BAKING CO NEWTON LLC
Also Called: Flowers Baking Co. of Newton, LLC
802 N Moravian St (28697-2338)
PHONE...............................336 903-1345
John Johnston, *Mgr*
EMP: 9
SALES (corp-wide): 5.1B **Publicly Held**
SIC: 2051 Bread, cake, and related products
HQ: Flowers Baking Co. Of Jamestown, Llc
801 W Main St
Jamestown NC 27282
336 841-8840

(G-12637)
HAYES PRINT-STAMP CO INC
1150 Foster St (28697-8432)
PHONE...............................336 667-1116
David Eller, *Pr*
Teresa H Bowman, *Sec*
EMP: 6 EST: 1968
SQ FT: 6,000
SALES (est): 138.34K **Privately Held**
Web: www.hayesprint.net
SIC: 2752 3953 Offset printing; Time stamps, hand: rubber or metal

(G-12638)
HERBAL INNOVATIONS LLC
Also Called: Herbal Ingenuity
151 Herbal Ingenuity Way (28697-8868)
PHONE...............................336 818-2332
Rich Ahren, *
Daniel Dickers, *
◆ EMP: 30 EST: 2015
SALES (est): 2.88MM **Privately Held**
Web: www.herbalingenuity.com

SIC: **5499** 1541 2099 5191 Spices and herbs ; Food products manufacturing or packing plant construction; Almond pastes; Herbicides

(G-12639)
INDUSTRIAL PRCESS SLUTIONS INC
915 Germantown Rd (28697-8843)
P.O. Box 1391 (28659-1391)
PHONE..................336 926-1511
Sherman Aaron, *CEO*
Sherman Aaron, *Pr*
Theresa Aaron, *CFO*
▲ **EMP:** 4 **EST:** 2003
SALES (est): 326.85K **Privately Held**
Web:
www.industrialprocesssolutionsinc.com
SIC: **3567** 3398 Industrial furnaces and ovens; Metal heat treating

(G-12640)
INTERCONNECT PRODUCTS AND SERVICES INC (PA)
1206 Industrial Park Rd (28697-8490)
P.O. Box 55 (28697-0055)
PHONE..................336 667-3356
EMP: 23 **EST:** 1982
SALES (est): 8.33MM
SALES (corp-wide): 8.33MM **Privately Held**
Web: www.interconnect-inc.com
SIC: **3679** 4813 5045 5065 Harness assemblies, for electronic use: wire or cable ; Telephone cable service, land or submarine; Computers, peripherals, and software; Electronic parts and equipment, nec

(G-12641)
INTERFLEX ACQUISITION CO LLC (HQ)
Also Called: Interflex Group
3200 W Nc Highway 268 (28697-7459)
PHONE..................336 921-3505
EMP: 125 **EST:** 2012
SALES (est): 50.01MM **Privately Held**
Web: www.interflexgroup.com
SIC: **2752** Photolithographic printing
PA: Toppan Holdings Inc.
1-3-3, Suido
Bunkyo-Ku TKY 112-0

(G-12642)
INTERFLEX ACQUISITION CO LLC
3200 W Nc Highway 268 (28697-7459)
PHONE..................336 921-3505
Stephen Doyle, *Brnch Mgr*
EMP: 200
Web: www.interflexgroup.com
SIC: **3053** Packing materials
HQ: Interflex Acquisition Company, Llc
3200 W Nc Hwy 268
Wilkesboro NC 28697
336 921-3505

(G-12643)
JENKINS MILLWORK LLC
1603 Industrial Dr (28697-7344)
PHONE..................336 667-3344
James Carter, *Managing Member*
▲ **EMP:** 27 **EST:** 2012
SALES (est): 2.48MM
SALES (corp-wide): 8.62MM **Privately Held**
Web: www.jenkinsmillworkllc.com
SIC: **2431** Millwork
PA: Millwork Products, L.L.C.
1003 Monroe St
Paducah KY 42001
270 442-5481

(G-12644)
JERRY HUFFMAN SAWMILL
Also Called: Jerry Huffman Sawmill & Log
287 Cactus Ln (28697-8136)
PHONE..................336 973-3606
Jerry Huffman, *Owner*
EMP: 8 **EST:** 1970
SALES (est): 244.01K **Privately Held**
SIC: **2421** Sawmills and planing mills, general

(G-12645)
KEITH LAWS
1001 N Marley Ford Rd (28697-8183)
PHONE..................336 973-7220
Keith Laws, *Prin*
EMP: 5 **EST:** 2013
SALES (est): 126.69K **Privately Held**
SIC: **2411** Logging

(G-12646)
KEY CITY FURNITURE COMPANY INC
1804 River St (28697-7657)
P.O. Box 680 (28697-0680)
PHONE..................336 818-1161
▲ **EMP:** 105
Web: www.keycityfurn.com
SIC: **2512** Living room furniture: upholstered on wood frames

(G-12647)
KOTOHIRA
1206 River St (28697-2138)
PHONE..................336 667-0150
EMP: 4 **EST:** 2010
SALES (est): 274.31K **Privately Held**
SIC: **3421** Table and food cutlery, including butchers'

(G-12648)
OLLIS ENTERPRISES INC
Also Called: Precision Printing
1613 Industrial Dr (28697-7344)
PHONE..................828 265-0004
Paul Ollis, *Pr*
EMP: 20 **EST:** 1983
SALES (est): 1.8MM **Privately Held**
SIC: **2752** 2791 2789 Offset printing; Typesetting; Bookbinding and related work

(G-12649)
RANDY D MILLER LUMBER CO INC
538 Hwy 16 N (28697)
P.O. Box 1515 (28651-1515)
PHONE..................336 973-7515
Randy D Miller, *Pr*
Janet Miller, *
EMP: 26 **EST:** 1983
SQ FT: 22,000
SALES (est): 3.56MM **Privately Held**
SIC: **2421** Lumber: rough, sawed, or planed

(G-12650)
SCREEN PRINTERS UNLIMITED LLC
331 E Main St Ste 1 (28697-2529)
PHONE..................336 667-8737
Herbert Boehm, *Managing Member*
EMP: 4 **EST:** 1994
SQ FT: 12,000
SALES (est): 248.93K **Privately Held**
Web: www.shirtsandsigns.com
SIC: **2759** 7389 Screen printing; Embroidery advertising

(G-12651)
SIGNFACTORY DIRECT INC
1202 Industrial Park Rd (28697-8490)
PHONE..................336 903-0300
Mike Kerhoulas, *Owner*
EMP: 8 **EST:** 1992

SALES (est): 747.72K **Privately Held**
Web: www.esignz.com
SIC: **3993** Signs and advertising specialties

(G-12652)
SPECIALTY FABRICATORS INC
1806 Industrial Dr (28697-7346)
P.O. Box 1384 (28697-1384)
PHONE..................336 838-7704
Jody Caudill, *Sec*
EMP: 5 **EST:** 2001
SALES (est): 374.3K **Privately Held**
SIC: **3441** Fabricated structural metal

(G-12653)
SUN OVENS INTERNATIONAL INC
Also Called: Sun Oven
418 Wilkesboro Blvd Unit 1 (28697-2530)
PHONE..................630 208-7273
Forrest Garvin, *CEO*
George C Critz Iii, *Pr*
EMP: 6 **EST:** 1998
SQ FT: 10,000
SALES (est): 1.09MM **Privately Held**
Web: www.sunoven.com
SIC: **3634** Ovens, portable: household
PA: Virexit Technologies, Inc.
6428 W Wlknson Blvd St305
Belmont NC 28012

(G-12654)
SUNCREST FARMS CNTRY HAMS INC
Also Called: Junior Johnson Country Hams
1148 Foster St (28697-8432)
P.O. Box 634 (28697-0634)
PHONE..................336 667-4441
Randall Gambill, *Pr*
Odell White, *
Russell Gambill, *
EMP: 20 **EST:** 1995
SALES (est): 10.85MM **Privately Held**
Web: www.suncrestham.com
SIC: **2013** 5421 Prepared pork products, from purchased pork; Meat markets, including freezer provisioners

(G-12655)
THE INTERFLEX GROUP INC
3200 W Nc Highway 268 (28697-7459)
PHONE..................336 921-3505
▲ **EMP:** 205
SIC: **3053** Packing materials

(G-12656)
TYSON FOODS INC
1000 Spring St (28697-2753)
PHONE..................336 651-2866
EMP: 5
SALES (corp-wide): 53.31B **Publicly Held**
SIC: **2015** Poultry slaughtering and processing
PA: Tyson Foods, Inc.
2200 W Don Tyson Pkwy
Springdale AR 72762
479 290-4000

(G-12657)
TYSON FOODS INC
Also Called: Tyson
901 Wilkes St (28697-2889)
PHONE..................336 838-2171
Molly Adams, *Mgr*
EMP: 8
SALES (corp-wide): 53.31B **Publicly Held**
Web: www.tysonfoods.com
SIC: **2015** Poultry slaughtering and processing
PA: Tyson Foods, Inc.
2200 W Don Tyson Pkwy
Springdale AR 72762

479 290-4000

(G-12658)
TYSON FOODS INC
Tyson
706 Factory St (28697-2935)
PHONE..................336 838-2171
Kirk Church, *Mgr*
EMP: 123
SALES (corp-wide): 53.31B **Publicly Held**
Web: www.tyson.com
SIC: **2015** 2011 Poultry, slaughtered and dressed; Meat packing plants
PA: Tyson Foods, Inc.
2200 W Don Tyson Pkwy
Springdale AR 72762
479 290-4000

(G-12659)
TYSON FOODS INC
Also Called: Tyson
1600 River St (28697-7630)
PHONE..................336 838-0083
Lani Stevens, *Mgr*
EMP: 5
SALES (corp-wide): 53.31B **Publicly Held**
Web: www.tyson.com
SIC: **2011** Meat packing plants
PA: Tyson Foods, Inc.
2200 W Don Tyson Pkwy
Springdale AR 72762
479 290-4000

(G-12660)
TYSON FOODS INC
Also Called: Tyson
115 Factory St (28697-2896)
PHONE..................336 838-2171
Kirk Church, *Prin*
EMP: 2400
SALES (corp-wide): 53.31B **Publicly Held**
Web: www.tyson.com
SIC: **2011** Meat packing plants
PA: Tyson Foods, Inc.
2200 W Don Tyson Pkwy
Springdale AR 72762
479 290-4000

(G-12661)
US CHEMICAL STORAGE LLC
1806 River St (28697-7633)
PHONE..................828 264-6032
Mark Mcelhinny, *CEO*
EMP: 50 **EST:** 1998
SALES (est): 22.97MM
SALES (corp-wide): 472.72MM **Privately Held**
Web: www.uschemicalstorage.com
SIC: **3448** Buildings, portable: prefabricated metal
PA: Justrite Manufacturing Company, L.L.C.
3921 Dewitt Ave
Mattoon IL 61938
217 234-7486

(G-12662)
WELDING COMPANY
646 Old Us 421 Rd (28697-8214)
P.O. Box 1798 (28659-1798)
PHONE..................336 667-0265
Clifford Kemp, *Owner*
EMP: 5 **EST:** 1992
SQ FT: 1,200
SALES (est): 198.32K **Privately Held**
Web: www.welding.com
SIC: **7692** Welding repair

(G-12663)
WORLDWIDE PROTECTIVE PDTS LLC (DH)
Also Called: Worldwide Protective Products

GEOGRAPHIC

1409 World Wide Ln (28697-2270)
PHONE.....................................877 678-4568
▲ EMP: 30 EST: 2004
SALES (est): 28.31MM
SALES (corp-wide): 2.61B **Privately Held**
Web: www.pipglobal.com
SIC: 2381 Fabric dress and work gloves
HQ: Protective Industrial Products, Inc.
    25 British American Blvd
    Latham NY 12110
    518 861-0133

(G-12664)
**WORLDWIDE PROTECTIVE PDTS
LLC**
1404 River St (28697-2108)
PHONE.....................................336 933-8035
EMP: 80
SALES (corp-wide): 2.61B **Privately Held**
Web: www.pipglobal.com
SIC: 2381 Fabric dress and work gloves
HQ: Worldwide Protective Products Llc
    1409 World Wide Ln
    Wilkesboro NC 28697
    877 678-4568

Willard
Pender County

(G-12665)
DAVID WEST
9090 Us Hwy 117 N (28478-8462)
PHONE.....................................910 271-0757
David West, Admn
EMP: 4 EST: 2017
SALES (est): 479.74K **Privately Held**
Web:
www.westweldingandfabricating.com
SIC: 7692 Welding repair

(G-12666)
P & S WELDING INC
8414 Us Hwy 117 N (28478-8450)
PHONE.....................................910 285-3126
Fred Simpson, Pr
Dale Simpson, Sec
EMP: 7 EST: 1980
SQ FT: 1,800
SALES (est): 499.4K **Privately Held**
SIC: 3312 Structural shapes and pilings,
  steel

Williamston
Martin County

(G-12667)
ARGOS USA LLC
Also Called: Ready Mixed Concrete
741 Warren St (27892-2747)
P.O. Box 682 (27892-0682)
PHONE.....................................252 792-3148
Michael Odom, Mgr
EMP: 7
Web: www.argos-us.com
SIC: 3273 Ready-mixed concrete
HQ: Argos Usa Llc
    3015 Windward Plz Ste 300
    Alpharetta GA 30005
    678 368-4300

(G-12668)
BY FAITH LOGGING INC
1046 Cedar Hill Dr (27892-8689)
PHONE.....................................252 792-0019
David L Tadlock, Prin
EMP: 6 EST: 2010
SALES (est): 392.72K **Privately Held**
Web: www.horiuchianddamicodds.com

SIC: 2411 Logging camps and contractors

(G-12669)
COX NRTH CRLINA PBLCATIONS INC
Also Called: Enterprise, The
106 W Main St (27892-2471)
P.O. Box 387 (27892-0387)
PHONE.....................................252 792-1181
Dallas Coltrain, Prin
EMP: 74
SALES (corp-wide): 961.55MM **Privately
Held**
Web: www.reflector.com
SIC: 2711 Newspapers, publishing and
  printing
HQ: Cox North Carolina Publications, Inc.
    1150 Sugg Pkwy
    Greenville NC 27834
    252 329-9643

(G-12670)
GRAVES INC
1909 W Main St (27892-7611)
P.O. Box 71 (27892-0071)
PHONE.....................................252 792-1191
C Swanson Graves Iii, Pr
Lind C Graves, *
Jane C Griffin, *
Linda C Graves, *
EMP: 10 EST: 1965
SQ FT: 20,000
SALES (est): 2.33MM **Privately Held**
Web: www.reddickequipment.com
SIC: 3523 3563 Sprayers and spraying
  machines, agricultural; Spraying outfits:
  metals, paints, and chemicals (compressor)

(G-12671)
KEN WOOD CORP
1660 Arthur Corey Rd (27892-8731)
PHONE.....................................252 792-6481
S Ken Wilson Iii, Pr
Ann Wilson, VP
EMP: 9 EST: 1987
SALES (est): 498.89K **Privately Held**
SIC: 2411 Logging camps and contractors

(G-12672)
MILLERS SPORTS AND TROPHIES
101 Washington St (27892-2491)
P.O. Box 501 (27892-0501)
PHONE.....................................252 792-2050
Walter H Miller, Pt
John Miller Iii, Pt
EMP: 4 EST: 1937
SQ FT: 6,000
SALES (est): 113.57K **Privately Held**
SIC: 5941 2395 Specialty sport supplies, nec
  ; Embroidery and art needlework

(G-12673)
SOMETHING FOR YOUTH
503 E Main St (27892-2531)
P.O. Box 213 (27892-0213)
PHONE.....................................252 799-8837
Ricardo L Hardison Senior, Pastor
EMP: 10
SALES (est): 308.24K **Privately Held**
SIC: 2531 Public building and related
  furniture

(G-12674)
STEVE EVANS LOGGING INC
7096 Us Highway 17 (27892-7953)
PHONE.....................................252 792-1836
Steve Evans, Pr
EMP: 5 EST: 1983
SALES (est): 1.46MM **Privately Held**
SIC: 2411 Logging camps and contractors

(G-12675)
VIKING TRUSS INC
424 Railroad St (27892-2334)
PHONE.....................................252 792-1051
Jeffrey H Whitley, Pr
EMP: 4 EST: 2018
SALES (est): 277.58K **Privately Held**
Web: www.vikingtruss.com
SIC: 1761 2439 Roofing, siding, and
  sheetmetal work; Trusses, wooden roof

(G-12676)
VINCENT L TAYLOR
3930 Bear Grass Rd (27892-7226)
PHONE.....................................252 792-2987
Vincent L Taylor, Prin
EMP: 5 EST: 2005
SALES (est): 221.91K **Privately Held**
SIC: 2411 Logging

(G-12677)
W AND W TRUSS BUILDERS INC
424 Railroad St (27892-2334)
PHONE.....................................252 792-1051
Don H Whitley, Pr
EMP: 10 EST: 1983
SQ FT: 40,000
SALES (est): 534.31K **Privately Held**
Web: www.wwtbi.com
SIC: 2439 Trusses, wooden roof

Willow Spring
Wake County

(G-12678)
BAKERS QUALITY TRIM INC
1616 Kendall Hill Rd (27592-9069)
PHONE.....................................919 552-3621
Joseph Baker, Pr
Lori Baker, Sec
EMP: 4 EST: 1991
SALES (est): 59.14K **Privately Held**
SIC: 2431 Interior and ornamental woodwork
  and trim

(G-12679)
JOHNSON CONCRETE COMPANY
Johnson Concrete Products
1401 Nc 42 Hwy (27592-7879)
P.O. Box 188 (27592-0188)
PHONE.....................................704 636-5231
Rich Curney, Mgr
EMP: 34
SALES (corp-wide): 24.88MM **Privately
Held**
Web: www.johnsonproductsusa.com
SIC: 3271 3272 Blocks, concrete or cinder:
  standard; Pipe, concrete or lined with
  concrete
PA: Johnson Concrete Company
    217 Klumac Rd
    Salisbury NC 28144
    704 636-5231

(G-12680)
NC SAND AND ROCK INC
9520 Kennebec Rd (27592-9415)
PHONE.....................................919 538-9001
Valerie Gonzalez, Prin
EMP: 4 EST: 2018
SALES (est): 805.39K **Privately Held**
SIC: 1442 Construction sand and gravel

(G-12681)
RICHARD WILCOX
1400 Struble Cir (27592-7678)
P.O. Box 201 (27592-0201)
PHONE.....................................919 218-5907
Richard Wilcox, Owner

EMP: 7 EST: 2015
SALES (est): 208.84K **Privately Held**
SIC: 2741 Miscellaneous publishing

(G-12682)
WHITLEY METALS INC
769 Mount Pleasant Rd (27592-8000)
PHONE.....................................919 894-3326
Tommie Whitley, Pr
Bonnie Whitley, Sec
EMP: 5 EST: 1996
SALES (est): 810.13K **Privately Held**
Web: www.whitleymetal.com
SIC: 3441 Fabricated structural metal

(G-12683)
YOUNG LOGGING COMPANY INC
1517 Clayton Rd (27592-9351)
PHONE.....................................919 552-9753
Jim Young, Pr
EMP: 7 EST: 1978
SALES (est): 601.58K **Privately Held**
SIC: 2411 Logging

Wilmington
New Hanover County

(G-12684)
1 CLICK WEB SOLUTIONS LLC
3333 Wrightsville Ave M (28403-4115)
PHONE.....................................910 790-9330
Anthony Wunsh, Pr
Jack Tracht, *
EMP: 50 EST: 1996
SQ FT: 5,000
SALES (est): 2.16MM **Privately Held**
SIC: 2741 Telephone and other directory
  publishing

(G-12685)
123 PRECIOUS METAL REF LLC (PA)
Also Called: Www 123 Precious Metal Com
609a Piner Rd Ste 303 (28409-4201)
PHONE.....................................910 228-5403
Pricilla Olivolo, Managing Member
Alford Olivolo, Managing Member
EMP: 4 EST: 2004
SALES (est): 230.28K
SALES (corp-wide): 230.28K **Privately
Held**
Web: www.123preciousmetal.com
SIC: 3911 Jewelry, precious metal

(G-12686)
A&M SCREEN PRINTING NC INC
6404 Amsterdam Way Unit 4 (28405-2568)
PHONE.....................................910 792-1111
Tony Delcotto, Pr
EMP: 4 EST: 1998
SALES (est): 98.63K **Privately Held**
SIC: 2396 Screen printing on fabric articles

(G-12687)
A1 BIOCHEM LABS LLC
5598 Marvin K Moss Ln Ste 2017
(28409-3702)
P.O. Box 11337 (13218-1337)
PHONE.....................................315 299-4775
Rajendra Gadikota, Managing Member
◆ EMP: 5 EST: 2014
SALES (est): 2.1MM **Privately Held**
Web: www.a1biochemlabs.com
SIC: 2834 Pharmaceutical preparations

(G-12688)
AA CERAMICS
2002 Eastwood Rd (28403-7218)
PHONE.....................................910 632-3053
EMP: 5 EST: 2013

SALES (est): 115.53K **Privately Held**
SIC: 3269 Pottery products, nec

(G-12689)
ACCELERATED PRESS INC
616 Windchime Dr (28412-7521)
PHONE..............................248 524-1850
Gaylord Vince, *Pr*
EMP: 7
SALES (est): 301.17K **Privately Held**
Web: www.acceleratedpress.com
SIC: 2752 7334 Offset printing;
   Photocopying and duplicating services

(G-12690)
ACCUGENOMICS INC
1410 Commonwealth Dr Ste 105
(28403-0364)
PHONE..............................910 332-6522
Tom Morrison, *VP*
EMP: 7 EST: 2011
SALES (est): 1.12MM **Privately Held**
Web: www.accugenomics.com
SIC: 2835 Diagnostic substances

(G-12691)
ACTIVE HATS AND THINGS SUITE
2201 Inkberry Ct (28411-6502)
PHONE..............................888 352-9292
EMP: 4 EST: 2016
SALES (est): 84.69K **Privately Held**
SIC: 2353 Hats, caps, and millinery

(G-12692)
ADVANCED MARKETING INTERNATIONAL INC
Also Called: Admark
211 Racine Dr Ste 202 (28403-8842)
PHONE..............................910 392-0508
◆ EMP: 12 EST: 1989
SALES (est): 6.22MM **Privately Held**
Web: www.admarkintl.com
SIC: 5169 5162 2819 Chemicals, industrial
   and heavy; Plastics materials, nec;
   Catalysts, chemical

(G-12693)
AHLBERG CAMERAS INC
Also Called: Ahlberg Cameras
432 Landmark Dr (28412-6309)
PHONE..............................910 523-5876
Ulf Ahlberg, *CEO*
EMP: 10 EST: 2009
SALES (est): 114.77K **Privately Held**
Web: www.ahlbergcameras.com
SIC: 7389 3861 Design services; Cameras
   and related equipment
HQ: Ahlberg Cameras Ab
   Gosvagen 22
   NorrtAlje 761 4
   176205500

(G-12694)
AIRGAS USA LLC
Also Called: Airgas National Welders
2824 Carolina Beach Rd (28412-1810)
PHONE..............................910 392-2711
Aaron Wescott, *Brnch Mgr*
EMP: 8
SQ FT: 9,360
SALES (corp-wide): 114.13MM **Privately Held**
Web: www.airgas.com
SIC: 5084 2813 Welding machinery and
   equipment; Industrial gases
HQ: Airgas Usa, Llc
   259 N Rdnor Chster Rd Ste
   Radnor PA 19087
   216 642-6600

(G-12695)
ALBANY TOOL & DIE INC
315 Van Dyke Dr Ste A (28405-3765)
PHONE..............................910 392-1207
Andrew Kerekes, *Pr*
Andrew Kerekes Senior, *VP*
EMP: 5 EST: 1951
SQ FT: 4,000
SALES (est): 760.63K **Privately Held**
Web: www.albanytool.com
SIC: 3599 Machine shop, jobbing and repair

(G-12696)
ALCAMI CAROLINAS CORPORATION
Also Called: Alcami
1206 N 23rd St (28405-1810)
PHONE..............................910 254-7000
Stephan Kutzer, *Brnch Mgr*
EMP: 4
SALES (corp-wide): 418.48MM **Privately Held**
Web: www.alcami.com
SIC: 2834 8731 Pharmaceutical preparations
   ; Medical research, commercial
HQ: Alcami Carolinas Corporation
   2320 Scientific Park Dr
   Wilmington NC 28405

(G-12697)
ALCAMI CAROLINAS CORPORATION
1519 N 23rd St (28405-1827)
PHONE..............................910 254-7000
Stephan Kutzer, *CEO*
EMP: 4
SALES (corp-wide): 418.48MM **Privately Held**
Web: www.alcami.com
SIC: 2834 8731 Pharmaceutical preparations
   ; Medical research, commercial
HQ: Alcami Carolinas Corporation
   2320 Scientific Park Dr
   Wilmington NC 28405

(G-12698)
ALCAMI CAROLINAS CORPORATION (HQ)
Also Called: Alcami
2320 Scientific Park Dr (28405-1800)
PHONE..............................910 254-7000
Patrick Walsh, *CEO*
Adam Lauber, *
Scott Warner, *Corporate Secretary*
Ken Morgan, *
Burton Ely, *
EMP: 463 EST: 2009
SALES (est): 224.79MM
SALES (corp-wide): 418.48MM **Privately Held**
Web: www.alcami.com
SIC: 2834 8731 8734 Drugs affecting
   neoplasms and endrocrine systems;
   Biological research; Product testing
   laboratories
PA: Alcami Corporation
   2320 Scientific Park Dr
   Wilmington NC 28405
   910 254-7000

(G-12699)
ALCAMI CAROLINAS CORPORATION
Also Called: Alcami
1726 N 23rd St (28405-1822)
PHONE..............................910 254-7000
Stephan Kutzer, *CEO*
EMP: 7
SALES (corp-wide): 418.48MM **Privately Held**
Web: www.alcami.com
SIC: 8071 2834 Medical laboratories;
   Pharmaceutical preparations
HQ: Alcami Carolinas Corporation

2320 Scientific Park Dr
Wilmington NC 28405

(G-12700)
ALCAMI CORPORATION (PA)
2320 Scientific Park Dr (28405)
PHONE..............................910 254-7000
Stephan Kutzer, *CEO*
Syed Hyusain, *
Adam Lauber, *
Ted Dolan, *
Scott Warner, *
EMP: 600 EST: 2009
SQ FT: 100,000
SALES (est): 418.48MM
SALES (corp-wide): 418.48MM **Privately Held**
Web: www.alcami.com
SIC: 2834 Pharmaceutical preparations

(G-12701)
ALCAMI HOLDINGS LLC
2320 Scientific Park Dr (28405-1800)
PHONE..............................910 254-7000
Stephan Kutzer, *CEO*
EMP: 1038 EST: 2012
Web: www.alcami.com
SIC: 6719 2834 Investment holding
   companies, except banks; Pharmaceutical
   preparations

(G-12702)
ALLEN-GODWIN CONCRETE INC
8871 Sidbury Rd (28411-7923)
P.O. Box 11120 (28404-1120)
PHONE..............................910 686-4890
John D Allen, *Pr*
Janet B Allen, *
Ebew Godwin, *
EMP: 6 EST: 2004
SQ FT: 4,000
SALES (est): 242.77K **Privately Held**
SIC: 3273 Ready-mixed concrete

(G-12703)
AMERICAN MATERIALS COMPANY LLC (DH)
Also Called: Summit Materials
1410 Commonwealth Dr Ste 201 (28403)
PHONE..............................910 799-1411
Gary Bizzell, *Pr*
Daniel Roy, *Finance*
EMP: 18 EST: 1999
SQ FT: 2,500
SALES (est): 86.49MM **Privately Held**
Web: www.americanmaterialsco.com
SIC: 1442 Construction sand and gravel
HQ: Summit Materials, Inc.
   1801 Cal St Ste 3500
   Denver CO 80202
   303 893-0012

(G-12704)
AMERICAN STRIKING TOOLS INC
Also Called: American Hammer
1312 S 12th St (28401-5946)
PHONE..............................910 769-1318
Ted Leitter, *Pr*
EMP: 8 EST: 1957
SQ FT: 8,000
SALES (est): 1.99MM **Privately Held**
Web: www.americanhammer.com
SIC: 3423 Hammers (hand tools)

(G-12705)
AR CORP
7639 Myrtle Grove Rd (28409-4923)
P.O. Box 2555 (28402-2555)
PHONE..............................910 763-8530
Elizabeth Ann Ross, *Pr*
◆ EMP: 4 EST: 1985

2320 Scientific Park Dr
Wilmington NC 28405

SALES (est): 182.19K **Privately Held**
Web: www.qisglass.com
SIC: 2835 Diagnostic substances

(G-12706)
AREA 51 POWDER COATING INC
2721 Old Wrightsboro Rd (28405-8036)
PHONE..............................910 769-1724
Brett D Lenz, *Owner*
EMP: 7 EST: 2008
SALES (est): 1.02MM **Privately Held**
Web: www.area51powdercoating.com
SIC: 3479 Coating of metals and formed
   products

(G-12707)
ARGOS USA LLC
Also Called: Argos Ready Mix
8871 Sidbury Rd (28411-7923)
PHONE..............................910 686-4890
EMP: 4
Web: www.argos-us.com
SIC: 3273 Ready-mixed concrete
HQ: Argos Usa Llc
   3015 Windward Plz Ste 300
   Alpharetta GA 30005
   678 368-4300

(G-12708)
ARGOS USA LLC
Also Called: Argos Ready Mix
800 Sunnyvale Dr (28412-7031)
PHONE..............................910 796-3469
EMP: 30
Web: www.argos-us.com
SIC: 3273 Ready-mixed concrete
HQ: Argos Usa Llc
   3015 Windward Plz Ste 300
   Alpharetta GA 30005
   678 368-4300

(G-12709)
ARMA CO LLC
Also Called: Ripoff Holsters
4557 Technology Dr Ste 4 (28405-2145)
PHONE..............................717 295-6805
EMP: 4 EST: 2004
SALES (est): 975.02K **Privately Held**
SIC: 3842 Bulletproof vests

(G-12710)
ARW OPTICAL CORP
2021 Capital Dr (28405-6463)
PHONE..............................910 452-7373
Gunter Wolff, *Pr*
EMP: 9 EST: 1980
SQ FT: 8,700
SALES (est): 939.53K **Privately Held**
Web: www.arwoptical.com
SIC: 3827 Optical instruments and apparatus

(G-12711)
ATLANTIC CARIBBEAN LLC
806 N 23rd St (28405-1802)
PHONE..............................910 343-0624
EMP: 6 EST: 2006
SALES (est): 277.7K **Privately Held**
Web: www.atlanticpkg.com
SIC: 6799 2679 Investors, nec; Book covers,
   paper

(G-12712)
ATLANTIC CORP WILMINGTON INC (PA)
Also Called: Atlantic
806 N 23rd St (28405-1802)
PHONE..............................800 722-5841
Russell Carter, *Pr*
Livingston Sheats, *VP*
Henry Boon, *VP*

GEOGRAPHIC

Roger Teague, *Sec*
Susan Carter, *Treas*
◆ **EMP:** 95 **EST:** 1946
SQ FT: 100,000
SALES (est): 483.78MM
SALES (corp-wide): 483.78MM **Privately Held**
Web: www.atlanticpkg.com
SIC: 5113 2621 2679 Industrial and personal service paper; Paper mills; Paper products, converted, nec

(G-12713)
ATLANTIC CORPORATION (HQ)
Also Called: Packaging and Supply Solutions
806 N 23rd St (28405-1802)
PHONE.............................910 343-0624
Steven C Quidley, *Pr*
◆ **EMP:** 48 **EST:** 1946
SALES (est): 98.51MM
SALES (corp-wide): 483.78MM **Privately Held**
Web: www.atlanticpkg.com
SIC: 2671 Paper, coated or laminated for packaging
PA: Atlantic Corporation Of Wilmington Inc.
806 N 23rd St
Wilmington NC 28405
800 722-5841

(G-12714)
ATLANTIC SOFTWARE CO
607 S 13th St (28401-5410)
PHONE.............................910 763-3907
Richard Irving, *Owner*
EMP: 4 **EST:** 2002
SALES (est): 35K **Privately Held**
SIC: 7372 Prepackaged software

(G-12715)
ATMAX ENGINEERING
806 Morris Ct (28405-2626)
PHONE.............................910 233-4881
Andrew Allen, *Owner*
EMP: 9 **EST:** 1995
SQ FT: 10,000
SALES (est): 256.6K **Privately Held**
SIC: 1442 Construction sand and gravel

(G-12716)
AVIAN CETACEAN PRESS
1616 Jettys Reach (28409-4514)
P.O. Box 15643 (28408-5643)
PHONE.............................910 392-5537
Peter K Meyer, *Owner*
EMP: 4 **EST:** 1990
SALES (est): 159.47K **Privately Held**
Web: www.aviancetaceanpress.com
SIC: 2741 Miscellaneous publishing

(G-12717)
AZTECH PRODUCTS INC (PA)
Also Called: New Hanover Printing & Pubg
2145 Wrightsville Ave (28403-0270)
PHONE.............................910 763-5599
EMP: 6 **EST:** 1997
SALES (est): 846.52K
SALES (corp-wide): 846.52K **Privately Held**
SIC: 2752 Offset printing

(G-12718)
BACKWATER GUNS LLC
1024 S Kerr Ave (28403-4313)
PHONE.............................910 399-1451
Marlon Kirk Andrews, *Prin*
EMP: 6 **EST:** 2009
SALES (est): 1.22MM **Privately Held**
Web: www.backwaterguns.com

SIC: 7699 5099 3489 Gun services; Machine guns; Guns or gun parts, over 30 mm.

(G-12719)
BENNETT BROTHERS YACHTS INC
1701 Jel Wade Dr Ste 16 (28401-2826)
PHONE.............................910 772-9277
Patricia Bennett, *Pr*
EMP: 30 **EST:** 1986
SQ FT: 15,000
SALES (est): 842.47K **Privately Held**
Web: www.bbyachts.com
SIC: 3732 7389 Yachts, building and repairing; Yacht brokers

(G-12720)
BENTONS WLDG REPR & SVCS INC
1206 S 3rd St (28401-6108)
PHONE.............................910 343-8322
James A Tew, *Pr*
Amy Tew, *Sec*
EMP: 6 **EST:** 1975
SQ FT: 1,200
SALES (est): 244.71K **Privately Held**
SIC: 7692 Welding repair

(G-12721)
BMT MICRO INC
5019 Carolina Beach Rd (28412-7841)
P.O. Box 15016 (28408-5016)
PHONE.............................910 792-9100
Peter Nelson, *Pr*
Thomas Bradford, *Pr*
Marie Bradford, *VP*
EMP: 7 **EST:** 1992
SALES (est): 1.88MM **Privately Held**
Web: www.bmtmicro.com
SIC: 7372 7371 Publisher's computer software; Custom computer programming services

(G-12722)
BONE TRED BEDS SMMIT WOODWORKS
617 Creekwood Rd (28411-7963)
PHONE.............................910 319-7583
EMP: 4 **EST:** 2012
SALES (est): 62.53K **Privately Held**
SIC: 2431 Millwork

(G-12723)
BRILLIANT SOLE INC
1930 Senova Trce (28405-6226)
PHONE.............................339 222-8528
Jeffrey W Guard, *CEO*
Mike Bower, *Prin*
Andrew Keener, *Prin*
William Fleming, *Prin*
EMP: 4 **EST:** 2017
SALES (est): 238.48K **Privately Held**
Web: www.runonbrilliantsole.com
SIC: 3577 Computer peripheral equipment, nec

(G-12724)
BUILDERS FIRSTSOURCE - SE GRP
4151 Emerson St (28403-1414)
PHONE.............................910 313-3056
Matthew Willard, *Brnch Mgr*
EMP: 9
SALES (corp-wide): 16.4B **Publicly Held**
Web: www.bldr.com
SIC: 2431 5211 Doors and door parts and trim, wood; Millwork and lumber
HQ: Builders Firstsource - Southeast Group, Llc
6031 Connection Dr # 400
Irving TX 75039
844 487-8625

(G-12725)
BUSINESS BROKERAGE PRESS INC
2726 Warlick Dr (28409-2077)
PHONE.............................800 239-5085
EMP: 8 **EST:** 2018
SALES (est): 866.76K **Privately Held**
Web: www.businessbrokeragepress.com
SIC: 2741 Miscellaneous publishing

(G-12726)
C2C PLASTICS INC
3024 Hall Watters Dr Ste 101 (28405-8717)
PHONE.............................910 338-5260
Mark Pandozzi, *CEO*
EMP: 4 **EST:** 2019
SALES (est): 814.16K **Privately Held**
SIC: 3089 Injection molding of plastics

(G-12727)
CAMAG SCIENTIFIC INC
515 Cornelius Harnett Dr (28401-2856)
PHONE.............................910 343-1830
Don Oates, *VP*
EMP: 8 **EST:** 1984
SQ FT: 3,000
SALES (est): 2.43MM **Privately Held**
Web: www.botanical-id.com
SIC: 3826 Analytical instruments
HQ: Camag Chemie-Erzeugnisse Und Adsorptionstechnik Ag
Sonnenmattstrasse 11
Muttenz BL 4132

(G-12728)
CAPE FEAR CNSTR GROUP LLC
102 Autumn Hall Dr Ste 210 (28403-2056)
PHONE.............................910 344-1000
EMP: 4
SALES (est): 1.24MM **Privately Held**
Web: www.capefeardevelopmentgroup.com
SIC: 1389 Construction, repair, and dismantling services

(G-12729)
CAPE FEAR YACHT WORKS LLC
111 Bryan Rd (28412-7033)
PHONE.............................910 540-1685
EMP: 10 **EST:** 2000
SQ FT: 7,000
SALES (est): 132.14K **Privately Held**
Web: www.capefearyachtandboat.com
SIC: 3732 5551 Sailboats, building and repairing; Boat dealers

(G-12730)
CAPITAL VALUE CENTER SLS & SVC
5406 Market St (28405-3508)
PHONE.............................910 799-4060
Mark Newmoyer, *Prin*
EMP: 5 **EST:** 2014
SALES (est): 175.35K **Privately Held**
SIC: 7549 3751 High performance auto repair and service; Motorcycle accessories

(G-12731)
CAPRE OMNIMEDIA LLC
801 N 4th St Apt 404 (28401-3485)
PHONE.............................917 460-3572
Brian Klebash, *Pr*
EMP: 5 **EST:** 2010
SALES (est): 190.09K **Privately Held**
Web: www.shure.international
SIC: 7299 7319 8742 2721 Facility rental and party planning services; Media buying service; Marketing consulting services; Trade journals: publishing and printing

(G-12732)
CARDIOPHARMA INC
100-A Eastwood Center Dr Ste 117 (28403)
PHONE.............................910 791-1361
Daniel Gregory, *Pr*
EMP: 10 **EST:** 2006
SALES (est): 257.06K **Privately Held**
Web: www.cardio-pharma.com
SIC: 2834 Pharmaceutical preparations

(G-12733)
CAROLINA COMMERCIAL COATINGS
20 Wrights Aly (28401-4991)
PHONE.............................910 279-6045
Donald Lashley, *Owner*
EMP: 6 **EST:** 1993
SALES (est): 493.16K **Privately Held**
Web: www.qccommercial.com
SIC: 2851 Paints and allied products

(G-12734)
CASABLANCA 4 LLC
4805 Wrightsville Ave (28403-6918)
PHONE.............................910 702-4399
Clayton Gsell, *Prin*
Bruce Brawley, *Prin*
Chris Nesselroade, *Prin*
Steve Cobb, *Prin*
EMP: 4 **EST:** 2021
SALES (est): 156.69K **Privately Held**
SIC: 2842 Polishes and sanitation goods

(G-12735)
CASEWORK ETC INC
3116 Kitty Hawk Rd (28405-8621)
PHONE.............................910 763-7119
Mitchell Wayne Matthews, *Pr*
Claudia Matthews, *VP*
EMP: 7 **EST:** 2007
SQ FT: 12,000
SALES (est): 487.56K **Privately Held**
SIC: 2434 Wood kitchen cabinets

(G-12736)
CAVA DI PIETRA INC
1502 N 23rd St (28405-1816)
PHONE.............................910 338-5024
Christopher Mitscherlich, *Prin*
EMP: 5 **EST:** 2015
SALES (est): 145.63K **Privately Held**
SIC: 3272 Silo staves, cast stone or concrete

(G-12737)
CBR SIGNS LLC
Also Called: Souther Signs Company
5649 Carolina Beach Rd (28412-2609)
PHONE.............................910 794-8243
Andrea Wilson, *Managing Member*
EMP: 8 **EST:** 2015
SALES (est): 186.74K **Privately Held**
Web: www.southernsigncompany.com
SIC: 3993 Signs and advertising specialties

(G-12738)
CE KITCHEN INC
417 Raleigh St (28412-6368)
PHONE.............................910 399-2334
EMP: 37
SALES (corp-wide): 4.59MM **Privately Held**
SIC: 2038 Frozen specialties, nec
PA: Ce Kitchen Inc.
306 Old Dairy Rd
Wilmington NC 28405
910 399-2334

(G-12739)
CE KITCHEN INC (PA)
306 Old Dairy Rd (28405-3766)
PHONE.............................910 399-2334

▲ = Import ▼ = Export
◆ = Import/Export

Jason Nista, *CEO*
Evonne Varady, *Pr*
Samuel B Potter, *Prin*
EMP: 26 EST: 2017
SALES (est): 4.59MM
SALES (corp-wide): 4.59MM **Privately Held**
Web: www.cleaneatzkitchen.com
SIC: 2038 Dinners, frozen and packaged

(G-12740)
CELANESE
4600 Us Highway 421 N (28401-2225)
PHONE..............................910 343-5000
EMP: 6 **EST:** 2019
SALES (est): 930.06K **Privately Held**
SIC: 2819 Industrial inorganic chemicals, nec

(G-12741)
CERES TURF INC
Also Called: CTI
2312 N 23rd St (28401-8812)
P.O. Box 12447 (28405-0119)
PHONE..............................910 256-8974
Robert Merritt, *Pr*
Ruth Merritt, *VP*
◆ **EMP:** 4 **EST:** 2007
SQ FT: 15,000
SALES (est): 579.85K **Privately Held**
Web: www.ceresturf.com
SIC: 3523 Turf equipment, commercial

(G-12742)
CHADSWORTH INCORPORATED
Also Called: Polystone Columns
420 Raleigh St Ste A (28412-6335)
P.O. Box 2618 (28402-2618)
PHONE..............................910 763-7600
Jeff L Davis, *CEO*
◆ **EMP:** 8 **EST:** 1987
SALES (est): 794.89K **Privately Held**
Web: www.columns.com
SIC: 2431 3089 3281 Interior and
ornamental woodwork and trim; Plastics
hardware and building products; Cut stone
and stone products

(G-12743)
COASTAL MILLWORK SUPPLY CO
1301 S 13th St (28401-6404)
PHONE..............................910 763-3300
Jim Risley, *Pr*
Bob Padul, *
EMP: 30 **EST:** 2005
SALES (est): 6.41MM **Privately Held**
Web: www.coastalmillworksupply.com
SIC: 2431 Millwork

(G-12744)
COASTAL PRECAST SYSTEMS LLC
5125 Us Highway 421 N (28401-2251)
PHONE..............................910 444-4682
Paul F Ogorchock, *Managing Member*
EMP: 143
Web: www.cpsprecast.com
SIC: 3272 Concrete products, precast, nec
PA: Coastal Precast Systems, Llc
1316 Yacht Dr Ste 307
Chesapeake VA 23320

(G-12745)
COLUMBIA SILICA SAND LLC
Also Called: American Materials Company
1410 Commonwealth Dr Ste 201
(28403-0314)
PHONE..............................803 755-1036
Sophie Sagrera, *Pr*
Jean Toal, *Sec*
Lilla Hoefer Ii, *Treas*
EMP: 5 **EST:** 1990
SALES (est): 814.98K **Privately Held**

SIC: 1442 Common sand mining

(G-12746)
CONNECTIVITY GROUP LLC
Also Called: Apple Annie's Bake Shop
837 S Kerr Ave (28403-8427)
PHONE..............................910 799-9023
Robert Cooley Junior, *Managing Member*
Frank Lewis, *
EMP: 35 **EST:** 1999
SALES (est): 4.29MM **Privately Held**
SIC: 2051 Bakery: wholesale or wholesale/
retail combined

(G-12747)
CONROLL CORPORATION
3302 Kitty Hawk Rd Ste 100 (28405-8772)
PHONE..............................910 202-4292
▲ **EMP:** 10
SIC: 3535 Conveyors and conveying
equipment

(G-12748)
CONTAINER PRODUCTS CORPORATION (PA)
112 N College Rd (28405-3514)
P.O. Box 3767 (28406-0767)
PHONE..............................910 392-6100
Dwight Campbell, *Pr*
C S Johnston, *Pr*
Jeff Kahle, *Ex VP*
EMP: 65 **EST:** 1981
SQ FT: 52,000
SALES (est): 18.69MM
SALES (corp-wide): 18.69MM **Privately Held**
Web: www.c-p-c.net
SIC: 3411 3443 3354 Metal cans; Industrial
vessels, tanks, and containers; Aluminum
extruded products

(G-12749)
CONTAINER TECHNOLOGY INC
Also Called: Container Technology
430 Raleigh St (28412-6367)
PHONE..............................910 350-1303
Michael Causey, *Pr*
EMP: 6 **EST:** 1994
SALES (est): 527.98K **Privately Held**
Web: www.containertechnology.com
SIC: 7692 7538 Welding repair; General
truck repair

(G-12750)
CONVERT-A-STAIR LLC
3013 Hall Watters Dr Ste C (28405-8790)
PHONE..............................888 908-5657
Brian Estes, *Pr*
Frank Everett, *Managing Member*
EMP: 4 **EST:** 2014
SALES (est): 482.02K **Privately Held**
Web: www.convertastair.com
SIC: 2431 Staircases and stairs, wood

(G-12751)
COPYCAT PRINT SHOP INC
637 S Kerr Ave (28403-8423)
P.O. Box 3347 (28406-0347)
PHONE..............................910 799-1500
Betsy L Kahn, *Pr*
Marie S Kahn, *VP*
Max Kahn, *Treas*
EMP: 17 **EST:** 1970
SALES (est): 2.25MM **Privately Held**
Web: www.copycatprintshop.net
SIC: 7334 2752 Photocopying and
duplicating services; Offset printing

(G-12752)
CORBETT PACKAGE COMPANY
1200 Castle Hayne Rd (28401-8885)
P.O. Box 210 (28402-0210)
PHONE..............................910 763-9991
Edward M Corbett, *Pt*
James W Corbett, *Pt*
EMP: 55 **EST:** 2019
SALES (est): 3.52MM **Privately Held**
Web: www.thecorbettcompanies.com
SIC: 2435 Veneer stock, hardwood

(G-12753)
CORNING INCORPORATED
Also Called: Corning
310 N College Rd (28405-3590)
PHONE..............................910 784-7200
Thomas Nettleman, *Brnch Mgr*
EMP: 75
SALES (corp-wide): 13.12B **Publicly Held**
Web: www.corning.com
SIC: 3827 3229 Optical instruments and
lenses; Fiber optics strands
PA: Corning Incorporated
1 Riverfront Plz
Corning NY 14831
607 974-9000

(G-12754)
CREATIVE CUSTOM WOODWORKS INC
1290 S 15th St B (28401-6410)
PHONE..............................910 431-8544
John Andrew Salley, *Prin*
EMP: 5 **EST:** 2002
SALES (est): 622.33K **Privately Held**
Web:
www.wilmingtoncustomcabinet.com
SIC: 2431 Millwork

(G-12755)
CREATIVE SIGNS INC
Also Called: Fastsigns
4305 Oleander Dr (28403-5007)
PHONE..............................910 395-0100
Pete Spadafora, *Pr*
EMP: 6 **EST:** 2014
SALES (est): 700K **Privately Held**
Web: www.fastsigns.com
SIC: 3993 Signs and advertising specialties

(G-12756)
CRETE SOLUTIONS LLC
2005 Eastwood Rd Ste 200 (28403-7233)
PHONE..............................910 726-1686
Harry M Shaw, *Managing Member*
EMP: 48 **EST:** 2017
SALES (est): 5.84MM **Privately Held**
Web: www.cretesolutionsllc.com
SIC: 3273 Ready-mixed concrete

(G-12757)
CRS/LAS INC
Also Called: All Ways Graphics
120 Racine Dr Ste 3 (28403-8836)
PHONE..............................910 392-0883
Charles R Stone Junior, *Pr*
EMP: 16 **EST:** 1991
SQ FT: 5,800
SALES (est): 1.73MM **Privately Held**
Web: www.allwaysgraphics.com
SIC: 2752 Offset printing

(G-12758)
CUSTOM REHABILITATION SPC INC
7225 Anaca Point Rd (28411-9501)
PHONE..............................910 471-2962
William D Eno, *Pr*
Carl Thompson, *VP*
EMP: 4 **EST:** 1994

SALES (est): 186.91K **Privately Held**
SIC: 5999 3842 Medical apparatus and
supplies; Orthopedic appliances

(G-12759)
DARIUS ALL ACCESS LLC
Also Called: Darius All Access
1013 Glenlea Dr (28405-2203)
P.O. Box 105 (28402-0105)
PHONE..............................910 262-8567
Darius Brunson, *CEO*
EMP: 20 **EST:** 2020
SALES (est): 255.98K **Privately Held**
Web: www.dariusallaccess.com
SIC: 7299 7349 3524 Handyman service;
Cleaning service, industrial or commercial;
Lawnmowers, residential: hand or power

(G-12760)
DAVIS NEWELL COMPANY INC
2962 N Kerr Ave (28405-8677)
PHONE..............................910 762-3500
Teresa Mcgee, *Pr*
Robert Mcgee, *VP*
▲ **EMP:** 17 **EST:** 1997
SQ FT: 15,000
SALES (est): 972.71K **Privately Held**
Web: www.newelldavis.com
SIC: 3496 Woven wire products, nec

(G-12761)
DAZTECH INC
Also Called: Daztech Promotions
214 Walnut St (28401-3931)
P.O. Box 156 (28402-0156)
PHONE..............................800 862-6360
Kathy Bowen, *Pr*
Jon Spetrino, *VP*
▲ **EMP:** 4 **EST:** 1992
SQ FT: 4,000
SALES (est): 85.56K **Privately Held**
SIC: 2261 5199 Screen printing of cotton
broadwoven fabrics; Advertising specialties

(G-12762)
DDM INC
Also Called: Diversified Disposables Mfg
210 Sea Shell Ln (28411-7645)
PHONE..............................910 686-1481
W Harley Ford, *Pr*
EMP: 7 **EST:** 1976
SQ FT: 5,000
SALES (est): 67.42K **Privately Held**
SIC: 2389 5047 Disposable garments and
accessories; Medical and hospital
equipment

(G-12763)
DECKLE PAPERBOARD SALES INC
256 Osprey Pl (28411-6895)
PHONE..............................910 686-9145
William F Lee, *Prin*
EMP: 6 **EST:** 2015
SALES (est): 1.17MM **Privately Held**
SIC: 2631 Paperboard mills

(G-12764)
DIANE BRITT
Also Called: Design Workshop, The
3205 Kitty Hawk Rd Ste 1 (28405-8630)
PHONE..............................910 763-9600
Diane Britt, *Owner*
EMP: 4 **EST:** 1985
SQ FT: 2,500
SALES (est): 243.44K **Privately Held**
Web: www.pendercreek.com
SIC: 2391 2392 Draperies, plastic and
textile: from purchased materials;
Bedspreads and bed sets: made from
purchased materials

(G-12765)
DIGITAURUS INC
4605 Wrightsville Ave (28403-6914)
PHONE......................910 794-9243
Lisa Zupan, *Pr*
EMP: 4 EST: 1994
SQ FT: 3,000
SALES (est): 81.25K **Privately Held**
Web: www.digitaurus.com
SIC: 2759 Screen printing

(G-12766)
DORIAN CORPORATION
Also Called: Musicmedic.com
901 Martin St (28401-7827)
PHONE......................910 352-6939
Curt Altarac, *Prin*
EMP: 8 EST: 2009
SALES (est): 234.92K **Privately Held**
Web: www.musicmedic.com
SIC: 5736 3999 Musical instrument stores;
Advertising curtains

(G-12767)
DR PEPPER CO OF WILMINGTON
Also Called: Dr Pepper
415 Landmark Dr (28412-6303)
PHONE......................910 792-5400
Terry Dolwling, *Owner*
EMP: 7 EST: 2011
SALES (est): 81.6K **Privately Held**
Web: www.drpepper.com
SIC: 2086 Soft drinks: packaged in cans,
bottles, etc.

(G-12768)
DUSTCONTROL INC
6720 Amsterdam Way Ste 400
(28405-3777)
PHONE......................910 395-1808
▲ EMP: 16 EST: 2006
SQ FT: 15,302
SALES (est): 4.79MM **Privately Held**
Web: www.dustcontrol.us
SIC: 3564 1796 3589 Purification and dust
collection equipment; Machinery installation
; Vacuum cleaners and sweepers, electric:
industrial
HQ: Dustcontrol Ab
Kumla Gardsvag 14
Norsborg 145 6
853194000

(G-12769)
E W GODWIN S SONS INC (PA)
1207 Castle Hayne Rd (28401-8886)
P.O. Box 1806 (28402-1806)
PHONE......................910 762-7747
TOLL FREE: 800
James Z Godwin Ii, *Pr*
EMP: 22 EST: 1909
SQ FT: 6,400
SALES (est): 4.74MM
SALES (corp-wide): 4.74MM **Privately
Held**
Web: www.vistaprint.com
SIC: 2421 5211 Sawmills and planing mills,
general; Lumber and other building
materials

(G-12770)
EKC ADVANCED ELEC USA 4 LLC ✪
Also Called: Operating
1209 Orange St (28401-4853)
PHONE......................302 774-1000
EMP: 6 EST: 2024
SALES (est): 2.01MM
SALES (corp-wide): 12.39B **Publicly Held**
SIC: 3674 3629 Integrated circuits,
semiconductor networks, etc.; Electronic
generation equipment

HQ: Ddp Specialty Electronic Materials Us
9, Llc
974 Centre Rd
Wilmington DE 19805
302 774-1000

(G-12771)
EOD DISTILLERY LLC
Also Called: End of Days Distillery
1815 Castle St (28403-2103)
PHONE......................910 399-1133
Shane Faulkner, *Managing Member*
EMP: 30 EST: 2019
SALES (est): 1.97MM **Privately Held**
Web: www.eoddistillery.com
SIC: 2085 Distilled and blended liquors

(G-12772)
**EVERGREEN FOREST PRODUCTS
INC**
2605 Blue Clay Rd (28405-8613)
PHONE......................910 762-9156
Brian Benford, *Pr*
Cheryl Benford, *Sec*
EMP: 5 EST: 1998
SALES (est): 489.79K **Privately Held**
Web: www.evergreennc.us
SIC: 2411 Logging camps and contractors

(G-12773)
EXPOGO INC
Also Called: Expogo Displays & Graphics
411 Landmark Dr (28412-6303)
PHONE......................910 452-3976
Wallace T Carter, *Pr*
▲ EMP: 10 EST: 1988
SALES (est): 948K **Privately Held**
Web: www.expogo.com
SIC: 3993 Signs and advertising specialties

(G-12774)
F & M STEEL PRODUCTS INC
3314 Enterprise Dr (28405-2120)
PHONE......................910 793-1345
Nathan Edwards, *Pr*
Floyd Knowles, *Pr*
Maggie Knowles, *VP*
Chris Banks, *VP*
EMP: 9 EST: 1996
SALES (est): 1.67MM **Privately Held**
Web: www.wilmingtongrill.com
SIC: 3444 Sheet metalwork

(G-12775)
FAIRWAY OUTDOOR ADVG LLC
Also Called: FAIRWAY OUTDOOR
ADVERTISING LLC
1530 S College Rd Ste 600 (28403-7306)
PHONE......................910 343-1900
Mike Russell, *Mgr*
EMP: 5
SIC: 7312 3993 Billboard advertising; Signs
and advertising specialties
HQ: Fairway Outdoor Advertising Llc
420 The Pkwy Bldg H
Greer SC 29650

(G-12776)
**FATHOM OFFSHORE HOLDINGS
LLC**
Also Called: Fathom Offshore
3018 N Kerr Ave Ste A (28405-8679)
PHONE......................910 399-6882
Andrew I Holcomb, *Managing Member*
▲ EMP: 9 EST: 2006
SQ FT: 10,000
SALES (est): 690.46K **Privately Held**
Web: www.fathomoffshore.com

SIC: 3949 5941 5091 Fishing equipment;
Fishing equipment; Fishing equipment and
supplies

(G-12777)
FLOAT LIFTS OF CAROLINAS LLC
8012 Yellow Daisy Dr (28412-3275)
PHONE......................919 972-1082
Tim Holloway, *Brnch Mgr*
EMP: 6
SALES (corp-wide): 190.15K **Privately
Held**
Web: www.floatlifts.com
SIC: 3536 Boat lifts
PA: Float Lifts Of The Carolinas, Llc
2527 Hoot Owl Dr
Hillsborough NC

(G-12778)
FLOYD S BRACES AND LIMBS INC
709 Parkway Blvd (28412-6556)
PHONE......................910 763-0821
Michael Floyd, *Pr*
Nancy Floyd, *Prin*
EMP: 6 EST: 1953
SALES (est): 431.62K **Privately Held**
SIC: 3842 Limbs, artificial

(G-12779)
FRITO-LAY NORTH AMERICA INC
3215 Kitty Hawk Rd (28405-8620)
PHONE......................980 224-3730
Sidney Bletcher, *Mgr*
EMP: 4
SALES (corp-wide): 91.47B **Publicly Held**
Web: www.fritolay.com
SIC: 2086 Carbonated soft drinks, bottled
and canned
HQ: Frito-Lay North America, Inc.
7701 Legacy Dr
Plano TX 75024

(G-12780)
FTM ENTERPRISES INC
301 N Green Meadows Dr Ste C
(28405-4041)
PHONE......................910 798-2045
Dennis Shaw, *Pr*
EMP: 10 EST: 2005
SALES (est): 252.56K **Privately Held**
SIC: 3281 Cut stone and stone products

(G-12781)
FURNITURE COMPANY
822 Santa Maria Ave (28411-7641)
PHONE......................910 686-1937
Jim Huene, *Prin*
EMP: 4 EST: 2011
SALES (est): 130K **Privately Held**
SIC: 2511 Wood household furniture

(G-12782)
G & E SOFTWARE INC
1410 Commonwealth Dr Ste 102b
(28403-0375)
PHONE......................910 762-5608
EMP: 28 EST: 2015
SALES (est): 6.17MM **Privately Held**
SIC: 7372 Prepackaged software

(G-12783)
**GE-HITCHI NCLEAR ENRGY INTL LL
(HQ)**
Also Called: Nuclear Energy Ne US
3901 Castle Hayne Rd (28402)
PHONE......................518 433-4338
Mark R Sweeney, *
EMP: 35 EST: 2007
SALES (est): 13.56MM
SALES (corp-wide): 38.7B **Publicly Held**

Web: www.gevernova.com
SIC: 2819 Nuclear fuel and cores, inorganic
PA: General Electric Company
1 Aviation Way
Cincinnati OH 45215
617 443-3000

(G-12784)
GELARTO INC
18 S Water St (28401-4477)
PHONE......................646 795-3505
Sandy Auriti, *Genl Mgr*
EMP: 10 EST: 2016
SALES (est): 407.88K **Privately Held**
Web: www.gelarto.com
SIC: 2024 Ice cream and frozen deserts

(G-12785)
GENERAL ELECTRIC COMPANY
GE
3901 Castle Hayne Rd (28401)
PHONE......................910 675-5000
Andrew White, *Brnch Mgr*
EMP: 2436
SALES (corp-wide): 38.7B **Publicly Held**
Web: www.ge.com
SIC: 2819 3519 3812 3728 Nuclear fuels,
uranium slug (radioactive); Jet propulsion
engines; Search and navigation equipment;
Aircraft parts and equipment, nec
PA: General Electric Company
1 Aviation Way
Cincinnati OH 45215
617 443-3000

(G-12786)
GENERAL SHALE BRICK INC
Also Called: General Shale Brick
3750 Us Highway 421 N (28401-9022)
PHONE......................910 452-3498
Terry Wright, *Mgr*
EMP: 9
SALES (corp-wide): 4.59B **Privately Held**
Web: www.generalshale.com
SIC: 3251 5032 Brick clay: common face,
glazed, vitrified, or hollow; Brick, stone, and
related material
HQ: General Shale Brick, Inc.
3015 Bristol Hwy
Johnson City TN 37601
423 282-4661

(G-12787)
GLOBAL LASER ENRICHMENT LLC
4110 Us Highway 421 N # 100
(28401-9030)
P.O. Box 5117 (12301-5117)
PHONE......................910 819-7255
Stephen Long, *CEO*
Matthew Greene, *Treas*
James A Dobchuk, *CCO*
EMP: 51 EST: 2007
SALES (est): 12.24MM **Privately Held**
SIC: 2819 Nuclear fuel and cores, inorganic

(G-12788)
GLOBAL NUCLEAR FUEL LLC
3901 Castle Hayne Rd (28401)
PHONE......................910 819-6181
EMP: 11 EST: 1999
SALES (est): 5.83MM **Privately Held**
Web: www.gevernova.com
SIC: 2819 Nuclear fuel and cores, inorganic

(G-12789)
GLOBAL RESOURCE NC INC
Also Called: Sign-A-Rama
1001 Broomsedge Ter (28412-1054)
PHONE......................910 793-4770
Rebecca Kronfeld, *Pr*
EMP: 4 EST: 2001

▲ = Import ▼ = Export
◆ = Import/Export

SALES (est): 152.17K **Privately Held**
Web: www.signarama.com
SIC: 3993 Signs and advertising specialties

(G-12790)
GO ENERGIES LLC
1410 Commonwealth Dr Ste 102b
(28403-0375)
PHONE..............................877 712-5999
EMP: 15 EST: 2010
SQ FT: 6,000
SALES (est): 4.99MM
SALES (corp-wide): 4.99MM **Privately
Held**
Web: www.goenergies.com
SIC: 5983 7372 8742 Fuel oil dealers;
   Prepackaged software; Management
   consulting services
PA: Go Energies Holdings, Inc.
   1410 Commwl Dr Ste 102b
   Wilmington NC 28403
   910 762-5802

(G-12791)
GO ENERGIES HOLDINGS INC (PA)
1410 Commonwealth Dr Ste 102b
(28403-0375)
PHONE..............................910 762-5802
James Phillip Dorroll Ii, *Pr*
EMP: 9 EST: 2009
SALES (est): 4.99MM
SALES (corp-wide): 4.99MM **Privately
Held**
Web: www.goenergies.com
SIC: 8742 7372 5983 Management
   consulting services; Prepackaged software;
   Fuel oil dealers

(G-12792)
GOLD BOND BUILDING PDTS LLC
838 Sunnyvale Dr (28412-7031)
PHONE..............................910 799-3954
EMP: 7
SALES (corp-wide): 96.43MM **Privately
Held**
Web: www.nationalgypsum.com
SIC: 2621 Paper mills
HQ: Gold Bond Building Products, Llc
   2001 Rexford Rd
   Charlotte NC 28211
   704 365-7300

(G-12793)
GORE S MAR MET FABRICATION INC
302 N Channel Haven Dr (28409-3506)
PHONE..............................910 763-6066
Danny Gore, *Pr*
David Gore, *VP*
EMP: 5 EST: 1985
SALES (est): 591.33K **Privately Held**
Web: www.goremarineinc.com
SIC: 3441 7692 Boat and barge sections,
   prefabricated metal; Welding repair

(G-12794)
GRACIE GOODNESS INC
113 Portwatch Way Ste 101 (28412-7056)
P.O. Box 7701 (28406-7701)
PHONE..............................910 792-0800
Carter Price, *Pr*
Sallie Price, *VP*
EMP: 5 EST: 1995
SALES (est): 67.82K **Privately Held**
Web: www.goodnessgracie.com
SIC: 2052 Cookies

(G-12795)
GRAPHIC IMAGE OF CAPE FEAR INC
Also Called: Graphic Image
2840 S College Rd (28412-6827)
PHONE..............................910 313-6768

Calvin Barnes, *Pr*
Demetrius Barnes, *Sec*
EMP: 4 EST: 1987
SQ FT: 1,500
SALES (est): 768.05K **Privately Held**
Web: www.mailroomshipandprint.com
SIC: 2759 7336 Commercial printing, nec;
   Graphic arts and related design

(G-12796)
GREATER WILMINGTON BUSINESS
101 N 3rd St (28401-4034)
PHONE..............................910 343-8600
Joy B Allen, *Owner*
EMP: 5 EST: 2005
SALES (est): 242.42K **Privately Held**
Web: www.wilmingtonbiz.com
SIC: 2721 Magazines: publishing and printing

(G-12797)
GREEN COMPASS LLC (PA)
305 Raleigh St Ste D (28412-6304)
PHONE..............................833 336-9223
Sterling Cook, *CEO*
EMP: 6 EST: 2019
SALES (est): 5.05MM
SALES (corp-wide): 5.05MM **Privately
Held**
Web: www.greencompassglobal.com
SIC: 0139 2844 2099 Feeder crops;
   Cosmetic preparations; Food preparations,
   nec

(G-12798)
GUILFORD MILLS LLC
1001 Military Cutoff Rd Ste 300
(28405-4376)
PHONE..............................910 794-5810
◆ EMP: 2600
SIC: 2258 2399 Cloth, warp knit; Automotive
   covers, except seat and tire covers

(G-12799)
**HANOVER ELECTRIC MOTOR SVC
INC**
Also Called: Hanover Electric Motors & Sups
602 Wellington Ave (28401-7614)
PHONE..............................910 762-3702
Bradley E Dunn, *Pr*
Bradley Dunn, *Pr*
Richard A Wingo, *VP*
Misty Dunn, *Treas*
EMP: 9 EST: 1960
SQ FT: 4,100
SALES (est): 2.01MM **Privately Held**
Web: www.hanoverelectric.com
SIC: 5063 7694 Motors, electric; Electric
   motor repair

(G-12800)
HANOVER IRON WORKS INC
2602 Park Ave (28403-4027)
P.O. Box 7155 (28406-7155)
PHONE..............................910 763-7318
Horace T King Iii, *Pr*
Horace T King Iv, *VP*
William F King, *
EMP: 4 EST: 1903
SQ FT: 23,000
SALES (est): 880.58K **Privately Held**
Web: www.hiwsheetmetal.com
SIC: 3444 Sheet metalwork

(G-12801)
**HANOVER IRON WORKS SHTMTL
INC**
Also Called: Cnc Laser Shop
1861 Dawson St (28403-2328)
PHONE..............................910 399-1146
Thompson King, *Pr*

EMP: 7 EST: 2008
SALES (est): 711.15K **Privately Held**
Web: www.hiwsheetmetal.com
SIC: 3444 Sheet metalwork

(G-12802)
HARBOR LINES LLC
127 Northern Blvd (28401-6731)
P.O. Box 2151 (28402-2151)
PHONE..............................910 279-3796
Don Bordeaux, *Managing Member*
EMP: 5 EST: 1987
SALES (est): 470.02K **Privately Held**
Web: www.harborlines.com
SIC: 3731 7389 Shipbuilding and repairing;
   Courier or messenger service

(G-12803)
HARTLEY LOUDSPEAKERS INC
Also Called: The Audio Lab
5732 Oleander Dr (28403-4714)
PHONE..............................910 392-1200
Richard Schmetterer, *Pr*
▲ EMP: 5 EST: 1951
SALES (est): 234.42K **Privately Held**
Web: www.audiolab1.com
SIC: 3651 Speaker systems

(G-12804)
**HERAEUS QUARTZ NORTH AMER
LLC**
Also Called: Wholesale Glass Fabricators
3016 Boundary St (28405-8619)
PHONE..............................910 799-6230
Greg Little, *Mgr*
EMP: 28
SALES (corp-wide): 2.67MM **Privately
Held**
Web: www.heraeus-comvance.com
SIC: 3231 3229 Products of purchased glass
   ; Pressed and blown glass, nec
HQ: Heraeus Quartz North America Llc
   100 Heraeus Blvd
   Buford GA 30518
   770 945-2275

(G-12805)
HIGH SPEED WELDING LLC
1536 Castle Hayne Rd 6 (28405)
PHONE..............................910 632-4427
Staurt A Foreman, *Managing Member*
EMP: 10 EST: 2006
SALES (est): 612.64K **Privately Held**
Web: www.highspeedweld.com
SIC: 7692 Welding repair

(G-12806)
HIS COMPANY INC
All-Spec
2516 Independence Blvd Ste 201
(28412-7161)
PHONE..............................800 537-0351
Robert Dill, *Pr*
EMP: 6
SALES (corp-wide): 1.8B **Publicly Held**
Web: www.hisco.com
SIC: 2891 5063 5065 Adhesives and
   sealants; Electrical apparatus and
   equipment; Electronic parts and equipment,
   nec
HQ: His Company, Inc.
   6650 Concord Park Dr
   Houston TX 77040
   713 934-1600

(G-12807)
**HOMESTEAD COUNTRY BUILT
FURN (PA)**
4942 Tanbark Dr (28412-7718)
PHONE..............................910 799-6489

Russell L Hill, *Owner*
EMP: 5 EST: 1985
SALES (est): 85.25K **Privately Held**
SIC: 2511 Wood bedroom furniture

(G-12808)
HORIZON VISION RESEARCH INC
1717 Shipyard Blvd Ste 140 (28403-8023)
PHONE..............................910 796-8600
Tara Tatum, *Contrlr*
EMP: 4 EST: 2002
SALES (est): 360.75K **Privately Held**
Web: www.damsickles.com
SIC: 3841 Surgical and medical instruments

(G-12809)
HOUSE OF RAEFORD FARMS INC
118 Cardinal Drive Ext Ste 102
(28405-2481)
PHONE..............................910 763-0475
Ron Carlos, *Owner*
EMP: 456
SALES (corp-wide): 1.79B **Privately Held**
Web: www.houseofraeford.com
SIC: 2015 Poultry slaughtering and
   processing
HQ: House Of Raeford Farms, Inc.
   3333 S Us Highway 117
   Rose Hill NC 28458
   912 222-4090

(G-12810)
HUFF MJ LLC
5617 Carolina Beach Rd (28412-3376)
PHONE..............................910 313-3133
Ronnie Hufstedler, *Prin*
EMP: 6 EST: 2013
SALES (est): 616.65K **Privately Held**
SIC: 2024 Ice cream and frozen deserts

(G-12811)
ICE COMPANIES INC (PA)
Also Called: Industrial Cleaning Eqp Co
2820 Carolina Beach Rd (28412-1810)
P.O. Box 66 (28402-0066)
PHONE..............................910 791-1970
Frances C Gay, *CEO*
Larry Gay, *Pr*
Frances C Gay, *Treas*
Wayne Gay, *VP*
EMP: 8 EST: 1974
SQ FT: 18,800
SALES (est): 4.08MM
SALES (corp-wide): 4.08MM **Privately
Held**
Web: www.icenc.com
SIC: 2842 5087 Cleaning or polishing
   preparations, nec; Cleaning and
   maintenance equipment and supplies

(G-12812)
ICE CUBE RECORDING STUDIOS ✪
801 Greenfield St (28401-7916)
PHONE..............................910 260-7616
Laterria Davis, *Owner*
EMP: 4 EST: 2023
SALES (est): 125.39K **Privately Held**
SIC: 2097 Ice cubes

(G-12813)
ICON COOLERS LLC
7213 Ogden Business Ln (28411-7456)
PHONE..............................855 525-4266
Ian Titley, *Admn*
EMP: 4 EST: 2017
SALES (est): 217.3K **Privately Held**
Web: www.iconcoolers.com
SIC: 3949 Sporting and athletic goods, nec

(G-12814)
IKA-WORKS INC (HQ)
Also Called: Ika
2635 Northchase Pkwy Se (28405-7419)
PHONE.............................910 452-7059
Sarah Angel, *CEO*
Rene Stiegelmann, *
Michael Janssen, *
◆ EMP: 85 EST: 1985
SQ FT: 33,000
SALES (est): 46.98MM
SALES (corp-wide): 190.37MM **Privately Held**
Web: www.ikaprocess.com
SIC: 3821 Laboratory apparatus and furniture
PA: Ika-Werke Gmbh & Co. Kg
    Janke-Und-Kunkel-Str. 10
    Staufen Im Breisgau BW 79219
    76338310

(G-12815)
IMS USA LLC
Also Called: Wood Tooling Shop
110 Portwatch Way Ste 103 (28412-7008)
PHONE.............................910 796-2040
Emanuele Porro, *Ofcr*
▲ EMP: 5 EST: 2010
SALES (est): 3.02MM
SALES (corp-wide): 687.29K **Privately Held**
Web: www.imsusanc.com
SIC: 3451 Screw machine products
PA: I.M.S. Industrial Management Services Spa
    Via Antonio Tolomeo Trivulzio 1
    Milano MI 20146

(G-12816)
INDUSTRIAL MACHINE & WLDG INC
1918 Castle Hayne Rd (28401-2766)
PHONE.............................910 251-1393
Ronald Turner, *Pr*
EMP: 6 EST: 1992
SQ FT: 9,000
SALES (est): 844.95K **Privately Held**
Web: www.industrialmachineandwelding.com
SIC: 3599 Machine shop, jobbing and repair

(G-12817)
INMAN SEPTIC TANK SERVICE INC
2631 Blue Clay Rd (28405-8613)
PHONE.............................910 763-1146
William Inman, *Pr*
Michelle Inman, *Sec*
David Inman, *VP*
EMP: 6 EST: 1964
SQ FT: 6,218
SALES (est): 200.15K **Privately Held**
Web: www.mckinneylandscape.com
SIC: 1711 7699 3272 Septic system construction; Septic tank cleaning service; Septic tanks, concrete

(G-12818)
INSPIRE CREATIVE STUDIOS INC
Also Called: Port City Films
720 N 3rd St Ste 101 (28401-3474)
P.O. Box 1849 (28402-1849)
PHONE.............................910 395-0200
Jonathan Medford, *Pr*
Curtis Thieman, *Prin*
EMP: 6 EST: 2005
SALES (est): 461.1K **Privately Held**
Web: www.inspirecreativestudios.com
SIC: 7311 7371 7812 8743 Advertising consultant; Computer software development and applications; Video production; Public relations services

(G-12819)
INTERROLL CORPORATION
3000 Corporate Dr (28405-7422)
PHONE.............................910 799-1100
Paul Zumbuhl, *CEO*
◆ EMP: 110 EST: 2002
SQ FT: 210,000
SALES (est): 24.38MM **Privately Held**
Web: www.interroll.com
SIC: 3535 Conveyors and conveying equipment
PA: Interroll Holding Ag
    Via Gorelle 3
    S. Antonino TI

(G-12820)
INTERROLL USA HOLDING LLC
3000 Corporate Dr (28405-7422)
PHONE.............................910 799-1100
Richard Keely, *
Barry Dempsey, *
Bill Rooks, *
EMP: 75 EST: 1996
Web: www.interroll.com
SIC: 6719 3535 Investment holding companies, except banks; Conveyors and conveying equipment
PA: Interroll Holding Ag
    Via Gorelle 3
    S. Antonino TI

(G-12821)
J&R SERVICES/J&R LUMBER CO
1319 Military Cutoff Rd Ste Cc Pmb 173 (28405-3174)
PHONE.............................956 778-7005
John Vento, *Owner*
EMP: 4 EST: 2013
SALES (est): 347.39K **Privately Held**
SIC: 2449 5032 Berry crates, wood wirebound; Brick, stone, and related material

(G-12822)
JC PRINT
321 N Front St (28401-3908)
PHONE.............................910 556-9663
Daniel Pena, *Pr*
EMP: 4 EST: 2015
SALES (est): 163.51K **Privately Held**
Web: www.jcprintservices.com
SIC: 2752 Offset printing

(G-12823)
JOHNSON CONTROLS INC
Also Called: Johnson Controls
395 N Green Meadows Dr (28405-3749)
PHONE.............................910 392-2372
Sheldon Utz, *Mgr*
EMP: 30
Web: www.johnsoncontrols.com
SIC: 2531 Seats, automobile
HQ: Johnson Controls, Inc.
    5757 N Green Bay Ave
    Milwaukee WI 53209
    866 496-1999

(G-12824)
JOHNSON CUSTOM BOATS INC
6820a Market St (28405-9723)
PHONE.............................910 232-4594
Richard Johnson, *Pr*
EMP: 4 EST: 2011
SALES (est): 255.08K **Privately Held**
Web: www.johnsoncustomboats.com
SIC: 3732 Boatbuilding and repairing

(G-12825)
JUSTICE
3500 Oleander Dr Ste 1054 (28403-0854)
PHONE.............................910 392-1581
EMP: 24 EST: 2019
SALES (est): 114.16K **Privately Held**
Web: www.justice.gov
SIC: 2361 Girl's and children's dresses, blouses

(G-12826)
KENNETH MOORE SIGNS
Also Called: Moore Signs
6220 Riverwoods Dr Apt 103 (28412-2882)
PHONE.............................910 458-6428
Kenneth Moore, *Owner*
EMP: 1 EST: 1995
SALES (est): 121.08K **Privately Held**
Web: www.kennethmooresigns.com
SIC: 3993 5046 2499 Signs and advertising specialties; Signs, electrical; Signboards, wood

(G-12827)
KENNY FOWLER HEATING AND A INC (PA)
Also Called: Honeywell Authorized Dealer
711 Wellington Ave (28401-7615)
PHONE.............................910 508-4553
Kenny Fowler, *Pr*
James Lewis, *Sls Mgr*
Debra Fowler, *VP*
EMP: 12 EST: 2009
SQ FT: 1,600
SALES (est): 948.95K
SALES (corp-wide): 948.95K **Privately Held**
Web: www.hvacwilmingtonnc.com
SIC: 1711 3585 5075 Heating systems repair and maintenance; Heating and air conditioning combination units; Warm air heating and air conditioning

(G-12828)
KESSEBOHMER USA INC
4301 Us Highway 421 N (28401-9035)
PHONE.............................910 338-5080
David Ivey, *S&M/Dir*
◆ EMP: 10 EST: 2007
SALES (est): 2.35MM
SALES (corp-wide): 745.73MM **Privately Held**
Web: www.cleverstorage.com
SIC: 3469 Household cooking and kitchen utensils, metal
HQ: Kessebohmer Gmbh
    Mindener Str. 208
    Bad Essen NI 49152

(G-12829)
KNIGHT SAFETY COATINGS CO INC
201 Beval Rd (28401-9071)
PHONE.............................910 458-3145
Katherine C Tilley, *Pr*
EMP: 16 EST: 1996
SQ FT: 7,000
SALES (est): 242.06K **Privately Held**
SIC: 2891 Adhesives and sealants

(G-12830)
L TS GAS AND SNAKS
2461 Carolina Beach Rd (28401-7656)
PHONE.............................910 762-7130
David Spaller, *Owner*
EMP: 4 EST: 2017
SALES (est): 475.51K **Privately Held**
SIC: 1311 Crude petroleum and natural gas

(G-12831)
LEAR CORPORATION
Also Called: Guilford Performance Textiles
1001 Military Cutoff Rd Ste 300 (28405-4376)
PHONE.............................910 794-5810
EMP: 2600
SALES (corp-wide): 23.31B **Publicly Held**
Web: www.lear.com
SIC: 2258 2399 Cloth, warp knit; Automotive covers, except seat and tire covers
PA: Lear Corporation
    21557 Telegraph Rd
    Southfield MI 48033
    248 447-1500

(G-12832)
LEES TACKLE INC
5316 Us Highway 421 N (28401-2254)
P.O. Box 2478 (28402)
PHONE.............................910 386-5100
Roswell E Lee Junior, *Pr*
Brian Lee, *
▲ EMP: 8 EST: 1920
SQ FT: 40,000
SALES (est): 958.66K **Privately Held**
Web: www.leetackle.com
SIC: 3949 Rods and rod parts, fishing

(G-12833)
LEGACY KNITTING LLC
3310 Kitty Hawk Rd Ste 100 (28405-8637)
PHONE.............................844 762-2678
EMP: 6 EST: 2020
SALES (est): 402.53K **Privately Held**
Web: www.legacyknitting.com
SIC: 2252 Socks

(G-12834)
LEONARD ALUM UTLITY BLDNGS INC
Also Called: Leonard Building & Trck Cover
5705 Market St (28405-3501)
PHONE.............................910 392-4921
John Coiro, *Mgr*
EMP: 4
SALES (corp-wide): 98.91MM **Privately Held**
Web: www.leonardusa.com
SIC: 3448 3713 3089 3714 Prefabricated metal buildings; Truck tops; Molding primary plastics; Motor vehicle parts and accessories
PA: Leonard Aluminum Utility Buildings, Inc.
    630 W Indpndnce Blvd
    Mount Airy NC 27030
    336 789-5018

(G-12835)
LICENSE PLATE AGENCY
2390 Carolina Beach Rd (28401-7647)
PHONE.............................910 763-7076
Betty Smithson, *Owner*
EMP: 7 EST: 2012
SALES (est): 130.9K **Privately Held**
SIC: 3469 Automobile license tags, stamped metal

(G-12836)
LINDE INC
Also Called: Praxair
Hwy 421 N (28405)
P.O. Box 1169 (28402-1169)
PHONE.............................910 343-0241
Vincent R Gutierrez, *Brnch Mgr*
EMP: 5
Web: www.lindeus.com
SIC: 2813 Nitrogen
HQ: Linde Inc.
    10 Riverview Dr
    Danbury CT 06810
    203 837-2000

(G-12837)
LINPRINT COMPANY
3405 Market St Unit 2 (28403-1321)
PHONE..............................910 763-5103
Bradley G Donnell, *Pr*
Brenda Donnell, *Sec*
EMP: 19 EST: 1947
SQ FT: 11,500
SALES (est): 3.08MM **Privately Held**
Web: www.linprint.com
SIC: 2752 2754 Lithographing on metal;
Commercial printing, gravure

(G-12838)
LOGIC HYDRAULIC CONTROLS INC
6616 Windmill Way (28405-3745)
P.O. Box 11059 (28404-1059)
PHONE..............................910 791-9293
Michael Van Vekoven, *Pr*
Rodney Matthews, *
Lorraine Van Vekoven, *
Andrew Vankoven, *
EMP: 27 EST: 1983
SQ FT: 30,000
SALES (est): 2.78MM **Privately Held**
Web: www.logichyd.com
SIC: 3492 3728 3594 Control valves, fluid
power: hydraulic and pneumatic; Aircraft
parts and equipment, nec; Fluid power
pumps and motors

(G-12839)
LOGICOM COMPUTER SYSTEMS INC
1121 Military Cutoff Rd Ste C (28405-3658)
PHONE..............................910 256-5916
Donald G Parrish, *Pr*
EMP: 6 EST: 2004
SALES (est): 287.78K **Privately Held**
Web: www.logicomcomputers.com
SIC: 7372 Prepackaged software

(G-12840)
LOGOSDIRECT LLC
6303 Oleander Dr Ste 102b (28403-3577)
PHONE..............................866 273-2335
John Denison, *Managing Member*
EMP: 10 EST: 2007
SALES (est): 630.83K **Privately Held**
Web: www.logosdirect.com
SIC: 2395 Embroidery and art needlework

(G-12841)
LUMINA NEWS
7232 Wrightsville Ave (28403-7223)
PHONE..............................910 256-6569
Pat Lowe, *Owner*
EMP: 6 EST: 2006
SALES (est): 317.75K **Privately Held**
Web: www.luminanews.com
SIC: 2711 Newspapers, publishing and
printing

(G-12842)
LUMSDEN WELDING COMPANY
Also Called: Lumsden Steel
6736 Carolina Beach Rd (28412-3006)
PHONE..............................910 791-6336
Ricky Moore, *Pr*
Margaret Moore, *VP*
EMP: 8 EST: 1950
SQ FT: 4,000
SALES (est): 623.94K **Privately Held**
Web: www.lumsdenwelding.com
SIC: 7692 1799 Welding repair;
Sandblasting of building exteriors

(G-12843)
M & G POLYMERS USA LLC
1979 Eastwood Rd (28403-7214)

PHONE..............................910 509-4414
EMP: 4
SALES (est): 383.1K **Privately Held**
SIC: 2819 Industrial inorganic chemicals, nec

(G-12844)
M&N CONSTRUCTION SUPPLY INC
323 Eastwood Rd Ste A (28403-1738)
P.O. Box 2046 (28402-2046)
PHONE..............................910 791-0908
Sean Block, *Brnch Mgr*
EMP: 10
SALES (corp-wide): 1.92MM **Privately
Held**
Web: www.mnconstructionsupply.com
SIC: 3441 Fabricated structural metal
PA: M&N Construction Supply, Inc.
323 Eastwood Rd
Wilmington NC 28403
910 791-0908

(G-12845)
MARKRAFT CABINETS DIRECT SALES
2705 Castle Creek Ln (28401-2689)
PHONE..............................910 762-1986
EMP: 7 EST: 2019
SALES (est): 221.73K **Privately Held**
Web: www.markraft.com
SIC: 2434 Wood kitchen cabinets

(G-12846)
MARPAC LLC (PA)
Also Called: Yogasleep
3870 Us Highway 421 N (28401)
PHONE..............................910 602-1421
Mark Mangum, *Managing Member*
Gordon Wallace, *
◆ EMP: 60 EST: 1962
SALES (est): 9.71MM
SALES (corp-wide): 9.71MM **Privately
Held**
Web: www.yogasleep.com
SIC: 3699 Sound signaling devices, electrical

(G-12847)
MASON INLET DISTILLERY LLC
611 Everbreeze Ln (28411-6104)
PHONE..............................910 200-4584
Christopher Burney Smith, *Owner*
EMP: 5 EST: 2018
SALES (est): 233.66K **Privately Held**
Web: www.masoninlet.com
SIC: 2085 Distilled and blended liquors

(G-12848)
MASONBORO SOUND MACHINERY INC
4628 Northchase Pkwy Ne (28405)
P.O. Box 7308 (28406)
PHONE..............................910 452-5090
Russell J La Belle, *Pr*
Susan Bino, *
Jeff Newman, *
▲ EMP: 25 EST: 1973
SQ FT: 60,000
SALES (est): 7.38MM **Privately Held**
Web: www.wilmingtonmachinery.com
SIC: 3599 Machine shop, jobbing and repair

(G-12849)
MCCARTHY TIRE SERVICE COMPANY
118 Portwatch Way (28412-7010)
PHONE..............................910 791-0132
Kelly Mccarthy, *Prin*
EMP: 10
SALES (corp-wide): 636MM **Privately
Held**
Web: www.mccarthytire.com

SIC: 7534 5531 Tire retreading and repair
shops; Automotive tires
PA: Mccarthy Tire Service Company Inc
340 Kidder St
Wilkes Barre PA 18702
570 822-3151

(G-12850)
MCNAUGHTON-MCKAY SOUTHEAST INC
6719 Amsterdam Way (28405-3778)
P.O. Box 10400 (28404-0400)
PHONE..............................910 392-0940
Tim Curtis, *Brnch Mgr*
EMP: 10
SALES (corp-wide): 2.81B **Privately Held**
Web: www.mc-mc.com
SIC: 5063 3625 Electrical supplies, nec;
Motor control accessories, including
overload relays
HQ: Mcnaughton-Mckay Southeast, Inc.
1357 E Lincoln Ave
Madison Heights MI 48071
844 687-6262

(G-12851)
MEDIA WILIMINGTON CO
Also Called: Ad Pak, The
6700 Netherlands Dr Unit A (28405-4771)
P.O. Box 12430 (28405-0119)
PHONE..............................910 791-0688
Jeff Phenicie, *Pt*
Boykin Wright, *Pt*
EMP: 4 EST: 1990
SALES (est): 223.78K **Privately Held**
SIC: 2711 Newspapers, publishing and
printing

(G-12852)
METAL-CAD STL FRMNG SYSTEMS IN
Also Called: Custom Metal Products
150 Division Dr (28401-8849)
PHONE..............................910 343-3338
Larry W Prewitt, *Pr*
Ellen T Prewitt, *
EMP: 71 EST: 2000
SALES (est): 9.91MM **Privately Held**
Web: www.custommetalproductsnc.com
SIC: 3499 Aerosol valves, metal

(G-12853)
MICRONOVA SYSTEMS INC
Also Called: Multi Form
2038 Oleander Dr (28403-2336)
PHONE..............................910 202-0564
Lee Furr, *Pr*
Gene Burleson, *Dir*
EMP: 4 EST: 1980
SQ FT: 2,000
SALES (est): 280.63K **Privately Held**
Web: www.multiform.com
SIC: 7372 Home entertainment computer
software

(G-12854)
MIKE POWELL INC
Also Called: Coastal Cabinets
3407a Enterprise Dr (28405-6406)
PHONE..............................910 792-6152
Danny Michael Powell, *Pr*
EMP: 16 EST: 1983
SQ FT: 4,000
SALES (est): 2.48MM **Privately Held**
Web: www.coastalcabinets.com
SIC: 1521 2431 2434 New construction,
single-family houses; Millwork; Vanities,
bathroom: wood

(G-12855)
MKC85 INC (PA)
2705 Castle Creek Ln (28401-2689)
PHONE..............................910 762-1986
Joe Jacobus, *CEO*
Grover C Edwards, *Pr*
Steve Ezzel, *CFO*
EMP: 15 EST: 1985
SQ FT: 3,500
SALES (est): 24.83MM
SALES (corp-wide): 24.83MM **Privately
Held**
Web: www.markraft.com
SIC: 5211 2541 Cabinets, kitchen; Table or
counter tops, plastic laminated

(G-12856)
N2 COMPANY INC
5051 New Centre Dr Ste 210 (28403-1665)
PHONE..............................910 202-0917
Duane Hixon, *CEO*
Earl Seals, *Pr*
EMP: 34 EST: 2005
SALES (est): 3.5MM **Privately Held**
Web: www.strollmag.com
SIC: 2721 Magazines: publishing and printing

(G-12857)
NCINO INC (PA)
Also Called: Ncino
6770 Parker Farm Dr Ste 100 (28405)
PHONE..............................888 676-2466
Pierre Naude, *Ch Bd*
Joshua Glover, *CRO*
David Rudow, *CFO*
Sean Desmond, *CUSTOMER SUCCESS*
Greg Orenstein, *CORP Development*
EMP: 136 EST: 2011
SQ FT: 57,000
SALES: 476.54MM
SALES (corp-wide): 476.54MM **Publicly
Held**
Web: www.ncino.com
SIC: 7372 Prepackaged software

(G-12858)
NCINO OPCO INC (HQ)
6770 Parker Farm Dr Ste 200 (28405)
PHONE..............................888 676-2466
Pierre Naude, *CEO*
David Rudow, *CFO*
April Rieger, *
EMP: 760 EST: 2011
SQ FT: 57,000
SALES (est): 204.29MM
SALES (corp-wide): 476.54MM **Publicly
Held**
Web: www.ncino.com
SIC: 7372 Prepackaged software
PA: Ncino, Inc.
6770 Parker Farm Dr
Wilmington NC 28405
888 676-2466

(G-12859)
NEW ANTHEM LLC (PA)
110 Greenfield St (28401-6123)
PHONE..............................910 319-7430
EMP: 6 EST: 2015
SALES (est): 1.29MM
SALES (corp-wide): 1.29MM **Privately
Held**
SIC: 2082 Beer (alcoholic beverage)

(G-12860)
NEW HANOVER PRINTING AND PUBG
Also Called: New Hanover Printing
2145 Wrightsville Ave (28403-0270)
PHONE..............................910 520-7173
Cynthia Howell, *Pr*

Claude Howell, *Sec*
Charles Howell, *Prin*
EMP: 5 EST: 2015
SALES (est): 263.43K **Privately Held**
Web: www.newhanoverprinting.com
SIC: 2752 3993 Offset printing; Signs and
advertising specialties

(G-12861)
NONI BACCA WINERY
420 Eastwood Rd (28403-1869)
PHONE................................910 397-7617
Antoinette Incorvaia, *Prin*
EMP: 4 EST: 2007
SALES (est): 392.95K **Privately Held**
Web: www.nbwinery.com
SIC: 2084 Wines

(G-12862)
NORMANDIE BAKERY INC
7316 Market St (28411-8807)
PHONE................................910 686-1372
Phillippe Blondel, *Pr*
Bev Shuette, *VP*
Annette Blondel, *Sec*
Art Shuette, *Treas*
EMP: 6 EST: 1991
SALES (est): 305.51K **Privately Held**
SIC: 5461 2051 Retail bakeries; Bakery:
wholesale or wholesale/retail combined

(G-12863)
NORMTEX INCORPORATED
1700 Verrazzano Pl (28405-4040)
P.O. Box 12 (28650-0012)
PHONE................................828 428-3363
Henry T Lilly, *Pr*
Kathleen Lilly, *Sec*
◆ **EMP: 9 EST:** 1965
SQ FT: 114,644
SALES (est): 418.87K **Privately Held**
SIC: 2281 5199 Yarn spinning mills; Yarns,
nec

(G-12864)
OAK-BARK CORPORATION (PA)
514 Wayne Dr (28403-1255)
▼ **EMP: 10 EST:** 1959
SQ FT: 4,500
SALES (est): 2.2MM
SALES (corp-wide): 2.2MM **Privately Held**
Web: www.oakbark12.com
SIC: 2869 Formaldehyde (formalin)

(G-12865)
OLD GROWTH RIVERWOOD INC
1407b Castle Hayne Rd (28401-8890)
PHONE................................910 762-4077
Chris Metz, *Pr*
Terrie Metz, *VP*
EMP: 5 EST: 2007
SQ FT: 3,500
SALES (est): 214.44K **Privately Held**
Web: www.oldgrowthriverwood.com
SIC: 2511 2426 Camp furniture: wood;
Flooring, hardwood

(G-12866)
ONE ON ONE PRESS LLC
616 Princess St (28401-4133)
PHONE................................910 228-8821
Karen Doniere, *CEO*
EMP: 5 EST: 2019
SALES (est): 119.72K **Privately Held**
SIC: 2741 Miscellaneous publishing

(G-12867)
ORACLE HEARING GROUP
1016 Striking Island Dr (28403-4381)
PHONE................................732 349-6804

EMP: 6 EST: 2013
SALES (est): 260.25K **Privately Held**
SIC: 7372 Prepackaged software

(G-12868)
ORBITA CORPORATION
6740 Netherlands Dr Ste D (28405-4702)
PHONE................................910 256-5300
Charles Agnoff, *Pr*
Karen Lampkin, *
Mark Lampkin, *
Evelyn Agnoff, *
◆ **EMP: 25 EST:** 1997
SQ FT: 8,000
SALES (est): 2.27MM **Privately Held**
Web: www.orbita.com
SIC: 3873 Watches and parts, except
crystals and jewels

(G-12869)
OUTER BANKS HAMMOCKS INC
7228 Wrightsville Ave (28403-7223)
PHONE................................910 256-4001
Clark Helton, *Pr*
Sharon Helton, *Sec*
EMP: 10 EST: 1972
SQ FT: 1,000
SALES (est): 413.57K **Privately Held**
Web: www.obxhammocks.com
SIC: 2514 5021 5712 Hammocks: metal or
fabric and metal combination; Outdoor and
lawn furniture, nec; Outdoor and garden
furniture

(G-12870)
PAPERFOAM PACKAGING USA LLC
4220 Us Highway 421 N (28401-9032)
PHONE................................910 371-0480
Roel Groenveld, *Prin*
◆ **EMP: 4 EST:** 2007
SALES (est): 4.78MM **Privately Held**
Web: www.paperfoam.com
SIC: 5199 2679 Packaging materials; Paper
products, converted, nec

(G-12871)
PARADIGM SOLUTIONS INC
1213 Culbreth Dr (28405-3639)
PHONE................................910 392-2611
Frank E Gensemer Senior, *Prin*
EMP: 6 EST: 2006
SALES (est): 567.6K **Privately Held**
Web: www.rvpartfinder.com
SIC: 2759 Screen printing

(G-12872)
PATTERSON CUSTOM DRAPERY
4315 Deer Creek Ln (28405-2273)
PHONE................................910 791-4332
Donna Patterson, *Pr*
Christopher Patterson, *Sec*
EMP: 8 EST: 2005
SALES (est): 162.42K **Privately Held**
Web: www.pattersoncustomdrapery.com
SIC: 2391 5023 Draperies, plastic and
textile: from purchased materials; Window
furnishings

(G-12873)
PENCO PRECISION LLC
Also Called: Machine Shop
1901 Blue Clay Rd Ste I (28405)
PHONE................................910 292-6542
Vincenzo Campellone, *Pr*
EMP: 7 EST: 2019
SALES (est): 489.5K **Privately Held**
Web: www.pencoprecision.net
SIC: 3545 Precision tools, machinists'

(G-12874)
PEPSI BOTTLING VENTURES LLC
Also Called: Pepsi-Cola
415 Landmark Dr (28412-6303)
PHONE................................910 792-5400
Randy Kennedy, *Mgr*
EMP: 58
SQ FT: 45,872
Web: www.pepsibottlingventures.com
SIC: 2086 5149 Soft drinks: packaged in
cans, bottles, etc.; Groceries and related
products, nec
HQ: Pepsi Bottling Ventures Llc
4141 Parklake Ave
Raleigh NC 27612
919 865-2300

(G-12875)
PEVO SPORTS CO
212 Transcom Ct (28401-9006)
PHONE................................910 397-9388
Susan G Pevonka, *CEO*
Don Pevonka, *VP*
Frank Ensctin, *Prin*
EMP: 8 EST: 2001
SALES (est): 2.02MM **Privately Held**
Web: www.pevosports.com
SIC: 3949 Sporting and athletic goods, nec

(G-12876)
PHARMASONE LLC
1800 Sir Tyler Dr (28405-8305)
PHONE................................910 679-8364
Colin Gray, *Prin*
Douglas Rupp, *Prin*
EMP: 5 EST: 2019
SALES (est): 143.69K **Privately Held**
SIC: 2834 Pharmaceutical preparations

(G-12877)
PHARMGATE ANIMAL HEALTH LLC
1800 Sir Tyler Dr (28405-8305)
PHONE................................910 679-8364
Colin Gray, *Managing Member*
▲ **EMP: 7 EST:** 2010
SQ FT: 2,000
SALES (est): 437.66K **Privately Held**
Web: www.pharmgate.com
SIC: 2834 Veterinary pharmaceutical
preparations

(G-12878)
PHARMGATE INC (HQ)
1800 Sir Tyler Dr (28405-8305)
PHONE................................910 679-8364
Colin Gray, *CEO*
▲ **EMP: 10 EST:** 2008
SALES (est): 30.24MM **Privately Held**
Web: www.pharmgate.com
SIC: 2834 Veterinary pharmaceutical
preparations
PA: Jinhe Biotechnology Co., Ltd.
No.71, Xinping Road, Tuoketuo County
Hohhot NM 01029

(G-12879)
PLANET LOGO INC
23 N Front St # 3 (28401-4483)
PHONE................................910 763-2554
Frank L Thompson, *Pr*
EMP: 8 EST: 2006
SQ FT: 3,000
SALES (est): 392.27K **Privately Held**
Web: www.planetlogoinc.com
SIC: 7311 3993 Advertising agencies; Signs
and advertising specialties

(G-12880)
POLLY AND ASSOCIATES LLC
7426 Janice Ln (28411-9658)

PHONE................................910 319-7564
Elizabeth Simpson, *Prin*
EMP: 4 EST: 2016
SALES (est): 89.96K **Privately Held**
SIC: 2752 Commercial printing, lithographic

(G-12881)
POLYHOSE INCORPORATED
353 Acme Way (28401-2306)
PHONE................................732 512-9141
Fatema Mohammed, *Prin*
EMP: 24 EST: 2007
SALES (est): 989.82K **Privately Held**
Web: www.polyhose.com
SIC: 5661 3052 3492 Shoe stores; Air line or
air brake hose, rubber or rubberized fabric;
Fluid power valves and hose fittings

(G-12882)
POLYQUEST INCORPORATED (PA)
1979 Eastwood Rd Ste 201 (28403)
PHONE................................910 342-9554
John Marinelli, *CEO*
Thomas Durst, *Pr*
Brad Dutton, *VP*
Randy Bragg, *Treas*
Ryan Nettles, *Sr VP*
▲ **EMP: 11 EST:** 2000
SQ FT: 220,000
SALES (est): 170.07MM
SALES (corp-wide): 170.07MM **Privately
Held**
Web: www.polyquest.com
SIC: 2821 Plastics materials and resins

(G-12883)
PORT CITY SIGNS & GRAPHICS INC
4011 Oleander Dr (28403-6816)
P.O. Box 4053 (28406-1053)
PHONE................................910 350-8242
Fred Maurer, *Prin*
EMP: 6 EST: 2008
SALES (est): 465.87K **Privately Held**
Web: www.portcitysigns.com
SIC: 3993 Signs and advertising specialties

(G-12884)
POWERS BOATWORKS
2725 Old Wrightsboro Rd Unit 8a
(28405-8066)
PHONE................................910 762-3636
Chris Powers, *Owner*
EMP: 6 EST: 2005
SALES (est): 370.41K **Privately Held**
SIC: 3732 Boatbuilding and repairing

(G-12885)
POWERSIGNS INC
3617 1/2 Market St (28403-1325)
PHONE................................910 343-1789
Mark P Hicks, *Pr*
EMP: 4 EST: 2008
SALES (est): 204.55K **Privately Held**
Web: www.powersignsinc.com
SIC: 3993 Electric signs

(G-12886)
PPD INC (HQ)
Also Called: Ppd
929 N Front St (28401-3331)
PHONE................................910 251-0081
David Simmons, *CEO*
William J Sharbaugh, *COO*
Glen Donovan, *CAO*
Christopher G Scully, *Ex VP*
B Judd Hartman, *Ex VP*
EMP: 237 EST: 2017
SQ FT: 395,000
SALES (est): 4.68B
SALES (corp-wide): 42.86B **Publicly Held**
Web: www.ppd.com

▲ = Import ▼ = Export
◆ = Import/Export

EMP: 13 EST: 2015
SALES (est): 884.84K **Privately Held**
Web: www.budgetblinds.com
SIC: 2591 Window blinds

(G-12936)
TARHEEL MONITORING LLC
709 Princess St (28401-4146)
PHONE..............................910 763-1490
Grady Richardson, *Cncil Mbr*
EMP: 6 EST: 2009
SALES (est): 971.2K **Privately Held**
Web: www.tarheelmonitoring.com
SIC: 7359 8322 3663 Electronic equipment
   rental, except computers; Offender self-
   help agency; Global positioning systems
   (GPS) equipment

(G-12937)
TARHEEL WOOD DESIGNS INC
Also Called: Tarheel Solid Surfaces
6609b Windmill Way (28405-3746)
P.O. Box 10638 (28404-0638)
PHONE..............................910 395-2226
Earl Lee, *Pr*
Pamela Lee, *Sec*
EMP: 9 EST: 1987
SQ FT: 5,000
SALES (est): 299.67K **Privately Held**
Web: www.tarheelsolidsurfaces.com
SIC: 2434 Wood kitchen cabinets

(G-12938)
TCPRST LLC
Also Called: AlphaGraphics
3534 S College Rd Ste I (28412-0902)
PHONE..............................910 791-9767
Charles Stinson Junior, *Pr*
Gay Burke, *Ex Dir*
EMP: 7 EST: 2008
SQ FT: 2,700
SALES (est): 903.07K **Privately Held**
Web: www.alphagraphicsilm.com
SIC: 2752 Offset printing

(G-12939)
TIMA CAPITAL INC
800 Sunnyvale Dr (28412-7031)
PHONE..............................910 769-3273
Timurlan Aitaly, *Brnch Mgr*
EMP: 12
SALES (corp-wide): 2.21MM **Privately
Held**
Web: www.timacapitalinc.com
SIC: 2436 2426 Plywood, softwood; Lumber,
   hardwood dimension
PA: Tima Capital Inc.
   340 Shipyard Blvd
   Wilmington NC 28412
   910 769-3273

(G-12940)
TIMBERLAKE VENTURES INC
Also Called: Toxplanet
1908 Eastwood Rd Ste 327 (28403-7235)
P.O. Box 1603 (28031-1603)
PHONE..............................704 896-7499
Matthias Timberlake, *Pr*
EMP: 5 EST: 2015
SALES (est): 158.36K **Privately Held**
Web: www.enhesa.com
SIC: 2741 Internet publishing and
   broadcasting

(G-12941)
TRIDENT LURE
2153 Harrison St (28401-6921)
PHONE..............................910 520-4659
Marshall Davis, *Prin*
EMP: 4 EST: 2016
SALES (est): 78.49K **Privately Held**

SIC: 3949 Sporting and athletic goods, nec

(G-12942)
TWO FIFTY CLEANERS
Also Called: 250 Cyrstal Cleaner
5601 Carolina Beach Rd Ste C
(28412-3695)
PHONE..............................910 397-0071
Sek Seo, *Pr*
EMP: 10 EST: 2000
SALES (est): 218.8K **Privately Held**
SIC: 3582 Drycleaning equipment and
   machinery, commercial, nec

(G-12943)
US PROTOTYPE INC
Also Called: Rapid Cut
341 S College Rd Ste 11 Pmb 3004
(28403-1622)
P.O. Box 10433 (28404-0433)
PHONE..............................866 239-2848
Peter Lamporte, *Pr*
EMP: 20 EST: 2009
SQ FT: 2,500
SALES (est): 2.29MM **Privately Held**
Web: www.rapidcut.com
SIC: 3812 3714 3845 3679 Acceleration
   indicators and systems components,
   aerospace; Motor vehicle engines and parts
   ; Electrocardiographs; Electronic loads and
   power supplies

(G-12944)
US VALVE CORPORATION
Also Called: Champion Valves
3111 Kitty Hawk Rd (28405-8622)
PHONE..............................910 799-9913
EMP: 5
SALES (corp-wide): 3.27B **Publicly Held**
SIC: 3592 3491 Valves; Automatic regulating
   and control valves
HQ: Us Valve Corporation
   812 Oregon Ave Ste E
   Linthicum Heights MD 21090
   410 789-1009

(G-12945)
VILLARI FOOD GROUP LLC (PA)
1015 Ashes Dr Ste 102 (28405)
P.O. Box 485 (28398)
PHONE..............................910 293-2157
Salvatore Villari, *Managing Member*
Joseph P Villari, *Managing Member**
Rocco Villari, *Managing Member**
EMP: 39 EST: 2010
SQ FT: 35,000
SALES (est): 55.44MM
SALES (corp-wide): 55.44MM **Privately
Held**
Web: www.villarifood.com
SIC: 2011 Meat packing plants

(G-12946)
WE APPIT LLC
1319 Military Cutoff Rd Ste 184
(28405-3174)
PHONE..............................910 465-2722
Joshua O'hazza, *Managing Member*
EMP: 9 EST: 2019
SALES (est): 495.02K
SALES (corp-wide): 969.74K **Privately
Held**
Web: www.weappit.ai
SIC: 7379 7389 7372 8999 Computer
   related consulting services; Business
   oriented computer software; Scientific
   consulting
PA: Innovative Ai Solution Holdings Inc.
   1319 Military Cutoff Rd
   Wilmington NC

(G-12947)
WIELAND ELECTRIC INC (DH)
Also Called: Wieland
8207 Market St Ste P10680 (28404-0509)
PHONE..............................910 259-5050
Mark Matheny, *Pr*
Nicholas Fleming, *Pr*
Hana Radomil, *VP Fin*
▲ EMP: 10 EST: 1910
SQ FT: 200,000
SALES (est): 3.32MM
SALES (corp-wide): 386.66MM **Privately
Held**
Web: www.wieland-americas.com
SIC: 5063 3496 3679 5065 Wire and cable;
   Miscellaneous fabricated wire products;
   Electronic circuits; Electronic parts and
   equipment, nec
HQ: Wieland Electric Gmbh
   Brennerstr. 10-14
   Bamberg BY 96052
   95193240

(G-12948)
**WILMINGTON CAMERA SERVICE
LLC**
905 N 23rd St (28405-1803)
PHONE..............................910 343-1089
EMP: 5 EST: 2008
SALES (est): 607.45K **Privately Held**
Web: www.wilmingtoncamera.com
SIC: 3861 Cameras and related equipment

(G-12949)
WILMINGTON JOURNAL COMPANY
Also Called: Wilmington Journal, The
412 S 7th St (28401-5214)
P.O. Box 1020 (28402-1020)
PHONE..............................910 762-5502
Willy E Jervay, *Pr*
EMP: 8 EST: 1927
SALES (est): 232.87K **Privately Held**
Web: www.wilmingtonjournal.com
SIC: 2711 Newspapers, publishing and
   printing

(G-12950)
WILMINGTON MACHINE WORKS INC
Also Called: Ackermann Tool & Machine Co
3416 Enterprise Dr (28405-8893)
PHONE..............................910 343-8111
Kendall Wade Mccall, *Pr*
EMP: 6 EST: 1980
SQ FT: 9,700
SALES (est): 423.2K **Privately Held**
Web: www.wilmingtonmachinery.com
SIC: 3599 3544 Machine shop, jobbing and
   repair; Special dies, tools, jigs, and fixtures

(G-12951)
WILMINGTON MORTUARY SVC INC
Also Called: Wilmington Funeral & Cremation
1535 41st St (28403-7302)
PHONE..............................910 791-9099
John D Bevell Junior, *Pr*
EMP: 10 EST: 2005
SALES (est): 723.24K **Privately Held**
Web: www.wilmingtoncares.com
SIC: 3272 7261 Burial vaults, concrete or
   precast terrazzo; Crematory

(G-12952)
**WILMINGTON RBR & GASKET CO
INC**
321 Raleigh St (28412-6307)
P.O. Box 15249 (28408)
PHONE..............................910 762-4262
Howard Russell, *Pr*
EMP: 15 EST: 1985
SQ FT: 25,000

SALES (est): 2.97MM **Privately Held**
Web: www.wilmingtonrubber.com
SIC: 5085 3429 3053 Rubber goods,
   mechanical; Hardware, nec; Gaskets;
   packing and sealing devices

(G-12953)
WILMINGTON TODAY LLC
1213 Culbreth Dr (28405-3639)
PHONE..............................910 509-7195
▲ EMP: 6 EST: 2006
SALES (est): 216.45K **Privately Held**
Web: www.wilmingtontoday.com
SIC: 2721 Magazines: publishing only, not
   printed on site

(G-12954)
WORDEN BROTHERS INC
Also Called: Tc2000.com
6315 Boathouse Rd (28403-3576)
PHONE..............................919 202-8555
Christopher D Worden, *Pr*
Peter F Worden, *
Jon A Worden, *
EMP: 80 EST: 1988
SQ FT: 5,400
SALES (est): 4.81MM **Privately Held**
Web: www.worden.com
SIC: 7373 2731 Systems software
   development services; Books, publishing
   only

(G-12955)
XPERTEES PRFMCE SCREEN PRTG
1406 Castle Hayne Rd Ste 2 (28401-8889)
PHONE..............................910 763-7703
Rick Stefanick, *Pr*
EMP: 5 EST: 2005
SALES (est): 89.71K **Privately Held**
Web: www.xpertees.com
SIC: 2759 Screen printing

(G-12956)
YILDIZ ENTEGRE USA INC
1715 Woodbine St (28401-6559)
PHONE..............................910 763-4733
Fehmi Yildiz, *Pr*
Ismail Hakki Yildiz, *VP*
Taner Basaga, *Sec*
▼ EMP: 9 EST: 2011
SALES (est): 441.19K **Privately Held**
Web: www.yildizentegre.com
SIC: 2421 Wood chips, produced at mill

(G-12957)
YP ADVRTISING PUBG LLC NOT LLC
Also Called: BellSouth
2250 Shipyard Blvd (28403-8024)
PHONE..............................910 794-5151
Jackie Hooks, *Brnch Mgr*
EMP: 127
SALES (corp-wide): 824.16MM **Publicly
Held**
SIC: 2741 Miscellaneous publishing
HQ: Yp Advertising & Publishing Llc (Not
   Llc)
   2247 Northlake Pkwy
   Tucker GA 30084

(G-12958)
ZESKP LLC
Also Called: EZ Beverage Company
Wilmington
2027 Capital Dr (28405-6463)
PHONE..............................910 762-8300
Steven W Crouch, *CEO*
Ryan Tilworth, *Mgr*
EMP: 6 EST: 2010
SQ FT: 12,000
SALES (est): 906.33K **Privately Held**

GEOGRAPHIC

SIC: **2086** 5149 Water, natural: packaged in cans, bottles, etc.; Soft drinks

Wilson
Wilson County

(G-12959)
3C STORE FIXTURES INC
Also Called: 3 C
3363 Us Highway 301 N (27893-7990)
P.O. Box 219 (27894-0219)
PHONE.............................252 291-5181
Carolyn B Daniel, *CEO*
Michael Jones, *
▲ **EMP:** 81 **EST:** 1975
SQ FT: 400,000
SALES (est): 27.5MM **Privately Held**
Web: www.3cstorefixtures.com
SIC: **2521** 2541 Cabinets, office: wood; Wood partitions and fixtures

(G-12960)
A PLUS GRAPHICS INC
3101 Ward Blvd (27893-1729)
PHONE.............................252 243-0404
Bruce Jackson, *Pr*
Belinda Jackson, *VP*
EMP: 7 **EST:** 1991
SQ FT: 1,200
SALES (est): 220.71K **Privately Held**
Web: www.apluswilson.com
SIC: **2752** 7336 Offset printing; Graphic arts and related design

(G-12961)
ANITAS MARKETING CONCEPTS INC
437 Ward Blvd Unit B (27893-1750)
P.O. Box 2821 (27894-2821)
PHONE.............................252 243-3993
Anita Jones, *Pr*
EMP: 4
SALES (corp-wide): 185.36K **Privately Held**
Web: www.anitasmarketing.com
SIC: **7389** 2752 Advertising, promotional, and trade show services; Offset printing
PA: Anita's Marketing Concepts, Inc.
4773 Old Stantonsburg Rd
Wilson NC 27893
252 245-4206

(G-12962)
AOA SIGNS INC
Also Called: A O A Signs
2707 Wooten Blvd Sw (27893-4483)
P.O. Box 83 (27055-0083)
PHONE.............................336 679-3344
Joy A Kay, *Pr*
Wadonna Poindexter Managing, *Prin*
EMP: 8 **EST:** 1971
SALES (est): 907.01K **Privately Held**
Web: www.aoasigns.com
SIC: **3993** Electric signs

(G-12963)
AQWA INC
2604 Willis Ct N (27896-8962)
PHONE.............................252 243-7693
Steven M Barry, *Pr*
James M Barry, *VP*
EMP: 6 **EST:** 2002
SQ FT: 30,000
SALES (est): 2.67MM **Privately Held**
Web: www.aqwa.net
SIC: **3589** Sewage and water treatment equipment

(G-12964)
ARTISAN LEAF LLC
2231 Nash St Nw Ste E (27896-1712)
P.O. Box 1731 (27894-1731)
PHONE.............................252 674-1223
▼ **EMP:** 5 **EST:** 2014
SQ FT: 800
SALES (est): 199.69K **Privately Held**
Web: www.artisanleaf.com
SIC: **2541** Bar fixtures, wood

(G-12965)
ATLANTIC BEARING CO INC
321 Herring Ave Ne Bldg A (27893-4197)
P.O. Box 83 (27894-0083)
PHONE.............................252 243-0233
J Douglas Lamm, *Pr*
Wanda Lamm, *Sec*
EMP: 6 **EST:** 1987
SALES (est): 853.96K **Privately Held**
Web: www.atlantic-bearing.com
SIC: **3562** Ball and roller bearings

(G-12966)
AVERIX BIO LLC
3040 Black Creek Rd S (27893-9526)
PHONE.............................252 220-0887
Miles Wright, *CEO*
EMP: 20 **EST:** 2019
SALES (est): 4.39MM **Privately Held**
Web: www.averixbio.com
SIC: **2833** Medicinals and botanicals

(G-12967)
BALLISTICS TECHNOLOGY INTL LTD
511 Goldsboro St Ne (27893-4044)
P.O. Box 4763 (27893-0763)
PHONE.............................252 360-1650
Tyron Sutton, *Brnch Mgr*
EMP: 8
SALES (corp-wide): 138.97K **Privately Held**
SIC: **3272** Concrete products, precast, nec
PA: Ballistics Technology International Ltd.
2207 Concord Pike 657
Wilmington DE 19803
877 291-1111

(G-12968)
BARRETTS PRINTING HOUSE INC
131 Douglas St S (27893-4954)
P.O. Box 305 (27894-0305)
PHONE.............................252 243-2820
Childs D Barrett, *Pr*
Margaret Ward, *Sec*
EMP: 6 **EST:** 1896
SALES (est): 650.25K **Privately Held**
Web: www.barrettsprinting.com
SIC: **2752** Offset printing

(G-12969)
BB&P EMBROIDERY LLC
2801 Ward Blvd (27893-1733)
PHONE.............................252 206-1929
EMP: 5 **EST:** 2013
SALES (est): 230.21K **Privately Held**
SIC: **2395** Embroidery and art needlework

(G-12970)
BELLALOU DESIGNS LLC
3712 Stonehenge Ln W (27893-7791)
PHONE.............................252 360-7866
EMP: 6 **EST:** 2020
SALES (est): 144.59K **Privately Held**
SIC: **3944** Craft and hobby kits and sets

(G-12971)
BRETT MCHENRY LOGGING LLC
3204 Nash St N Ste C (27896-3002)
PHONE.............................252 243-7285

Brett Mchenry, *Prin*
EMP: 7 **EST:** 2015
SALES (est): 845.9K **Privately Held**
SIC: **2411** Logging

(G-12972)
BREWMASTERS INC
2117 Forest Hills Rd W (27893-3499)
PHONE.............................252 991-6035
Youssef Robert Morkos, *Prin*
EMP: 4 **EST:** 2013
SALES (est): 892.17K **Privately Held**
Web: www.brewmastersnc.com
SIC: **2082** Malt beverages

(G-12973)
BRIDGESTONE RET OPERATIONS LLC
Also Called: Firestone
1401 Ward Blvd (27893-3598)
P.O. Box 4 (27894-0004)
PHONE.............................252 243-5189
Reginald Reid, *Mgr*
EMP: 9
Web: www.bridgestoneamericas.com
SIC: **5531** 7534 Automotive tires; Rebuilding and retreading tires
HQ: Bridgestone Retail Operations, Llc
200 4th Ave S Ste 100
Nashville TN 37201
615 937-1000

(G-12974)
BRIDGESTONE AMRCAS TIRE OPRTONS
Also Called: Bridgestone
3001 Firestone Pkwy Ne (27893-7996)
P.O. Box 1139 (27893)
PHONE.............................252 291-4275
John Mcquade, *Manager*
EMP: 1694
Web: www.bridgestoneamericas.com
SIC: **5531** 3011 Automotive tires; Tires and inner tubes
HQ: Bridgestone Americas Tire Operations, Llc
200 4th Ave S Ste 100
Nashville TN 37201
615 937-1000

(G-12975)
BRUNSON MARINE GROUP LLC
4155 Dixie Inn Rd (27893-9000)
PHONE.............................252 291-0271
Robert R Brunson, *Managing Member*
EMP: 30 **EST:** 2014
SALES (est): 2.88MM **Privately Held**
Web: www.kencraftboats.com
SIC: **3089** Plastics boats and other marine equipment

(G-12976)
BUY SMART INC
Also Called: First Choice
1109 Brookside Dr Nw (27896-2134)
PHONE.............................252 293-4700
Pieter Van Den Berg, *Pr*
▲ **EMP:** 9 **EST:** 1999
SALES (est): 684.13K **Privately Held**
Web: www.buysmartnc.com
SIC: **5083** 3599 Agricultural machinery, nec; Amusement park equipment

(G-12977)
CAROLINA CLASSIC MANUFACTURING INC
510 Jones St S (27893-5032)
P.O. Box 159 (27894-0159)
PHONE.............................252 237-9105
EMP: 94

Brett Mchenry, *Prin*

SIC: **3088** Tubs (bath, shower, and laundry), plastics

(G-12978)
CAROLINA KELLER LLC
2401 Stantonsburg Rd Se (27893-8414)
P.O. Box 370 (27894-0370)
PHONE.............................252 237-8181
▲ **EMP:** 150
SIC: **3566** Gears, power transmission, except auto

(G-12979)
CEMEX MATERIALS LLC
1600 Thorne Ave S (27893-6043)
PHONE.............................252 243-6153
Ted Price, *Mgr*
EMP: 104
SIC: **3273** Ready-mixed concrete
HQ: Cemex Materials Llc
1720 Cntrpark Dr E Ste 10
West Palm Beach FL 33401
561 833-5555

(G-12980)
CLOTHES CLEANING SYSTEM LLC
4475 Technology Dr Nw (27896-8686)
PHONE.............................252 243-3752
Samuel Bowling, *Pr*
Amanda Sawrey, *VP*
EMP: 5 **EST:** 2007
SQ FT: 20,000
SALES (est): 354.77K **Privately Held**
Web: www.clothescleaningsystems.com
SIC: **3441** Fabricated structural metal

(G-12981)
COMPASS GROUP USA INC
2102 Industrial Park Dr Se (27893-9300)
PHONE.............................252 291-7733
EMP: 40
SALES (corp-wide): 42B **Privately Held**
Web: www.compass-usa.com
SIC: **5962** 2099 Food vending machines; Food preparations, nec
HQ: Compass Group Usa, Inc.
2400 Yorkmont Rd
Charlotte NC 28217

(G-12982)
CREEKSIDE CREATIVE DESIGN INC
206 Goldsboro St Sw (27893-4907)
PHONE.............................252 243-6272
Jimmy Sink, *Pr*
Alfred Sink, *Sec*
EMP: 9 **EST:** 1997
SQ FT: 16,000
SALES (est): 180.83K **Privately Held**
Web: www.creeksidecreativedesigns.com
SIC: **3446** Architectural metalwork

(G-12983)
DEGESCH AMERICA INC
1810 Firestone Pkwy Ne (27893-7991)
PHONE.............................800 548-2778
Chris Corvello, *Prin*
EMP: 36
SALES (corp-wide): 3.08MM **Privately Held**
Web: www.degeschamerica.com
SIC: **2879** Agricultural disinfectants
HQ: Degesch America, Inc.
153 Triangle Dr
Weyers Cave VA 24486
540 234-9281

(G-12984)
DOWN EAST OFFROAD INC
1425 Thorne Ave S (27893-6040)

▲ = Import ▼ = Export
◆ = Import/Export

PHONE.....................252 246-9440
Robert Bass, *Pr*
EMP: 10 **EST:** 1997
SQ FT: 8,000
SALES (est): 998.68K **Privately Held**
Web: www.downeastoffroad.com
SIC: 3799 5531 Off-road automobiles, except recreational vehicles; Automotive accessories

(G-12985)
EASTERN CABINET COMPANY INC
3100 Meteor Dr (27893-9029)
PHONE.....................252 237-5245
Troy Rouse, *Pr*
Thomas E Davis Junior, *Sec*
EMP: 5 **EST:** 1993
SQ FT: 4,000
SALES (est): 246.01K **Privately Held**
SIC: 2434 Wood kitchen cabinets

(G-12986)
EASTERN CAROLINA VAULT CO INC
1214 Queen St E (27893-5317)
P.O. Box 4202 (27893)
PHONE.....................252 243-5614
Louis Hall, *Owner*
EMP: 4 **EST:** 1950
SALES (est): 250.44K **Privately Held**
SIC: 3272 Burial vaults, concrete or precast terrazzo

(G-12987)
EMCO WHEATON RETAIL CORP
Also Called: Emco
2300 Industrial Park Dr Se (27893-9319)
PHONE.....................252 243-0150
Jim Lawrence, *Pr*
Charles Pearson, *
◆ **EMP:** 70 **EST:** 1996
SQ FT: 50,000
SALES (est): 9.13MM **Privately Held**
Web: www.emcoretail.com
SIC: 3491 3823 3494 Industrial valves; Process control instruments; Valves and pipe fittings, nec

(G-12988)
ENGINEERED PROCESSING EQP LLC
5036 Country Club Dr N (27896-9122)
P.O. Box 12322 (27709-2322)
PHONE.....................919 321-6891
EMP: 8 **EST:** 2003
SALES (est): 501.54K **Privately Held**
Web: www.epei.us
SIC: 2834 Pharmaceutical preparations

(G-12989)
EON LABS INC
4700 Sandoz Dr (27893-8143)
PHONE.....................252 234-2222
William F Holt, *VP*
▲ **EMP:** 436
Web: www.eonlabs.com
SIC: 2834 Pharmaceutical preparations
HQ: Eon Labs, Inc.
    1999 Marcus Ave Ste 300
    New Hyde Park NY 11042

(G-12990)
EVANS MACHINERY INC
5123 Ivy Ct (27893-7572)
P.O. Box 3408 (27895-3408)
PHONE.....................252 243-4006
Donald Evans, *Pr*
Bobby Evans, *
Charles Evans, *
Thomas Jackson, *SALES*
◆ **EMP:** 56 **EST:** 1979
SQ FT: 135,000

SALES (est): 9.71MM **Privately Held**
Web: www.evansmachinery.com
SIC: 3523 3441 Farm machinery and equipment; Fabricated structural metal

(G-12991)
FRESENIUS KABI USA LLC
5200 Corporate Pkwy (27893-9412)
PHONE.....................252 991-2692
Hector Gonzales, *Brnch Mgr*
EMP: 512
SALES (corp-wide): 24.24B **Privately Held**
Web: www.fresenius-kabi.com
SIC: 2834 Pharmaceutical preparations
HQ: Fresenius Kabi Usa, Llc
    3 Corporate Dr
    Lake Zurich IL 60047
    847 550-2300

(G-12992)
FULFORDS RESTORATIONS (PA)
320 Barnes St S (27893-5002)
PHONE.....................252 243-7727
Edward Fulford Junior, *Owner*
▲ **EMP:** 5 **EST:** 1983
SQ FT: 70,000
SALES (est): 340.6K **Privately Held**
Web: www.fulfords.us
SIC: 2511 7641 Wood household furniture; Antique furniture repair and restoration

(G-12993)
GODS SON PLUMBING INC
Also Called: God's Son Plumbing Repair
1711 Roxbury Dr N (27893-1859)
P.O. Box 571 (27894-0571)
PHONE.....................252 299-0983
William Pickett, *Prin*
EMP: 5 **EST:** 2007
SALES (est): 210.26K **Privately Held**
SIC: 3432 Plastic plumbing fixture fittings, assembly

(G-12994)
HYDRO CONDUIT LLC
1600 Thorne Ave S (27893-6043)
PHONE.....................252 243-6153
EMP: 5
Web: www.rinkerpipe.com
SIC: 3271 Concrete block and brick
HQ: Hydro Conduit, Llc
    5 Concourse Pkwy Ste 1900
    Atlanta GA 30328
    404 926-3100

(G-12995)
JAMES BUNN
4167 Black Creek Rd S (27893-9125)
PHONE.....................252 293-4867
EMP: 4 **EST:** 2016
SALES (est): 210.01K **Privately Held**
SIC: 3489 Ordnance and accessories, nec

(G-12996)
JUPITER BATHWARE INC
510 Jones St S (27893-5032)
P.O. Box 159 (27894-0159)
PHONE.....................800 343-8295
Hp Mc Coy, *Pr*
Brooks Davis, *Stockholder*
EMP: 6 **EST:** 2005
SQ FT: 115,000
SALES (est): 963.65K **Privately Held**
SIC: 3088 Plastics plumbing fixtures

(G-12997)
KATCHI TEES INCORPORATED
1108 Gold St N (27893-2514)
PHONE.....................252 315-4691
Teresa Jones, *CEO*

EMP: 4 **EST:** 2014
SALES (est): 183.45K **Privately Held**
SIC: 2759 7291 7389 5947 Screen printing; Tax return preparation services; Financial services; Gift baskets

(G-12998)
KENCRAFT MANUFACTURING INC
4078 Us Highway 117 (27893-0915)
PHONE.....................252 291-0271
Kenneth D Vick, *Pr*
EMP: 4 **EST:** 1975
SQ FT: 60,000
SALES (est): 459.85K **Privately Held**
Web: www.kencraftboats.com
SIC: 3732 5551 Boats, fiberglass: building and repairing; Boat dealers

(G-12999)
KIDDE TECHNOLOGIES INC
4200 Airport Dr Nw (27896-8630)
PHONE.....................252 237-7004
Brent Ehmke, *Brnch Mgr*
EMP: 325
SQ FT: 71,000
SALES (corp-wide): 80.74B **Publicly Held**
Web: www.kiddetechnologies.com
SIC: 3812 8611 Search and navigation equipment; Business associations
HQ: Kidde Technologies Inc.
    4200 Airport Dr Nw
    Wilson NC 27896

(G-13000)
KIDDE TECHNOLOGIES INC (HQ)
Also Called: Fenwal Safety Systems
4200 Airport Dr Nw (27896-8630)
PHONE.....................252 237-7004
Terry Hayden, *Pr*
Brent Ehmke, *
W Thomas Ramsey, *
John F Hannon, *
▼ **EMP:** 285 **EST:** 1935
SQ FT: 71,000
SALES (est): 47.25MM
SALES (corp-wide): 80.74B **Publicly Held**
Web: www.kiddetechnologies.com
SIC: 3669 Fire alarm apparatus, electric
PA: Rtx Corporation
    1000 Wilson Blvd
    Arlington VA 22209
    781 522-3000

(G-13001)
KIDDE TECHNOLOGIES INC
Kidde Dual Spectrum
4200 Airport Dr Nw (27896-8630)
PHONE.....................252 237-7004
Vincent Rowe, *Mgr*
EMP: 64
SALES (corp-wide): 80.74B **Publicly Held**
Web: www.kiddetechnologies.com
SIC: 3728 3674 Aircraft parts and equipment, nec; Semiconductors and related devices
HQ: Kidde Technologies Inc.
    4200 Airport Dr Nw
    Wilson NC 27896

(G-13002)
LELY MANUFACTURING INC
4608 Lely Rd (27893-8111)
P.O. Box 789 (27894-0789)
PHONE.....................252 291-7050
Brian Taylor, *Pr*
Peter Langebeeke, *Dir*
▼ **EMP:** 15 **EST:** 1975
SALES (est): 814.44K **Privately Held**
SIC: 3589 Sewage and water treatment equipment

(G-13003)
LINAMAR FORGINGS CAROLINA INC
2401 Old Stantonsburg Rd (27894)
P.O. Box 370 (27894-0370)
PHONE.....................252 237-8181
Jim Jarrell, *Pr*
Linda Hasenfratz, *VP*
Mark Stoddart, *VP*
Roger Fulton, *Sec*
Dale Schneider, *Treas*
▲ **EMP:** 100 **EST:** 2014
SQ FT: 245,000
SALES (est): 19.46MM
SALES (corp-wide): 7.09B **Privately Held**
SIC: 3562 3566 3462 Ball bearings and parts ; Gears, power transmission, except auto; Iron and steel forgings
HQ: Linamar Holding Nevada, Inc.
    32233 8 Mile Rd
    Livonia MI 48152
    248 477-6240

(G-13004)
LINKONE SRC LLC
2018 Beeler Rd S (27893-9591)
PHONE.....................252 206-0960
Melanie Foster, *Managing Member*
EMP: 5 **EST:** 1994
SALES (est): 193.64K **Privately Held**
Web: www.sunriverservice.com
SIC: 2048 Prepared feeds, nec

(G-13005)
LIVEDO USA INC
4925 Livedo Dr (27893)
PHONE.....................252 237-1373
Tadashi Hoshikawa, *Pr*
Keiichi Ishikawa, *
◆ **EMP:** 55 **EST:** 2004
SALES (est): 5.32MM **Privately Held**
Web: www.livedousa.com
SIC: 2676 Sanitary paper products
PA: Livedo Corporation
    45-2, Otsu, Kanadachohanda
    Shikokuchuo EHM 799-0

(G-13006)
MERCK SHARP & DOHME LLC
Merck
4633 Merck Rd W (27893-9633)
PHONE.....................252 243-2011
Ken Jones, *Brnch Mgr*
EMP: 285
SALES (corp-wide): 64.17B **Publicly Held**
Web: www.merck.com
SIC: 2834 Pharmaceutical preparations
PA: Merck & Co., Inc.
    126 E Lincoln Ave
    Rahway NJ 07065
    908 740-4000

(G-13007)
MORTON BUILDINGS INC
3042 Forest Hills Rd Sw Ste C (27893-9294)
PHONE.....................252 291-1300
Mark Smith, *Mgr*
EMP: 9
SALES (corp-wide): 89.89MM **Privately Held**
Web: www.mortonbuildings.com
SIC: 3448 Prefabricated metal buildings and components
PA: Morton Buildings, Inc.
    252 W Adams St
    Morton IL 61550
    800 447-7436

(G-13008)
NASHVILLE WLDG & MCH WORKS INC
2356 Firestone Pkwy Ne (27893-7736)
PHONE...................................252 243-0113
Oscar Ellis Junior, *Pr*
Janice Boone, *Off Mgr*
EMP: 20 **EST:** 1974
SQ FT: 15,000
SALES (est): 2.42MM **Privately Held**
Web: www.nashvillewelding.com
SIC: 7692 7389 3599 Welding repair; Crane and aerial lift service; Machine shop, jobbing and repair

(G-13009)
NEOPAC US INC
4940 Lamm Rd (27893-9693)
PHONE...................................908 342-0990
EMP: 6 **EST:** 2019
SALES (est): 13.3MM **Privately Held**
Web: www.neopac.com
SIC: 2671 Plastic film, coated or laminated for packaging
HQ: Hoffmann Neopac Beteiligungen Ag
Eisenbahnstrasse 71
Gwatt BE 3645

(G-13010)
OBRIAN TARPING SYSTEMS INC
110 Beacon St W (27893-3646)
PHONE...................................252 291-6710
Sean O'brian, *Prin*
EMP: 14
SALES (corp-wide): 5.25MM **Privately Held**
Web: www.obriantarping.com
SIC: 2394 Canvas and related products
PA: O'brian Tarping Systems, Inc.
2330 Womble Brooks Rd E
Wilson NC 27893
252 291-2141

(G-13011)
OBRIAN TARPING SYSTEMS INC (PA)
2330 Womble Brooks Rd E (27893-7947)
PHONE...................................252 291-2141
Woody V O'brian, *Pr*
Winnie O'brian, *Sec*
▼ **EMP:** 11 **EST:** 1961
SQ FT: 9,000
SALES (est): 5.25MM
SALES (corp-wide): 5.25MM **Privately Held**
Web: www.obriantarping.com
SIC: 2394 Tarpaulins, fabric: made from purchased materials

(G-13012)
PARKER-HANNIFIN CORPORATION
Also Called: Techseal Division
2600 Wilco Blvd S (27893-9022)
PHONE...................................252 237-6171
Patrick Donovan, *Brnch Mgr*
EMP: 11
SALES (corp-wide): 19.93B **Publicly Held**
Web: www.parker.com
SIC: 3061 3053 2296 Mechanical rubber goods; Gaskets; packing and sealing devices; Tire cord and fabrics
PA: Parker-Hannifin Corporation
6035 Parkland Blvd
Cleveland OH 44124
216 896-3000

(G-13013)
PEAK DEMAND INC
605 Tarboro Street Anx Sw (27893-4849)
P.O. Box 1668 (27894-1668)

PHONE...................................252 360-2777
Scott Bargoil, *CFO*
EMP: 11 **EST:** 2016
SALES (est): 3.77MM **Privately Held**
Web: www.peakdemand.com
SIC: 3677 Electronic coils and transformers

(G-13014)
PROTEIN FOR PETS OPCO LLC
Also Called: Sun River Service Company
2018 Beeler Rd S (27893-9591)
PHONE...................................252 206-0960
Jeff Ross, *Pr*
Watson Ross, *
Melanie Foster, *
▲ **EMP:** 29 **EST:** 2016
SQ FT: 15,000
SALES (est): 12.79MM **Privately Held**
Web: www.sunriverservice.com
SIC: 2048 Meat meal and tankage, prepared as animal feed

(G-13015)
PURDUE PHARMACEUTICALS LP
4701 International Blvd (27893-9664)
PHONE...................................252 265-1900
Edward Mahony, *Ex VP*
Stuart D Baker, *Ex VP*
David Long, *Sr VP*
Saeed Motahari, *Sr VP*
EMP: 11 **EST:** 1998
SALES (est): 19.54MM
SALES (corp-wide): 458.51MM **Privately Held**
Web: www.purduepharma.com
SIC: 5122 2834 Pharmaceuticals; Pharmaceutical preparations
HQ: Purdue Pharma L.P.
201 Tresser Blvd
Stamford CT 06901

(G-13016)
Q T CORPORATION
2700 Forest Hills Rd Sw (27893-4433)
PHONE...................................252 399-7600
Jimmy Sauls, *Pr*
EMP: 7 **EST:** 1993
SQ FT: 3,500
SALES (est): 4.56MM **Privately Held**
Web: www.qt-corporation.com
SIC: 3625 7373 8742 Relays and industrial controls; Computer integrated systems design; Industrial consultant

(G-13017)
R J REYNOLDS TOBACCO COMPANY
1500 Charleston St Se (27893-9035)
P.O. Box 636 (27894-0636)
PHONE...................................252 291-4700
Randy F Harris, *Mgr*
EMP: 133
Web: www.rjrt.com
SIC: 2141 Tobacco stemming and redrying
HQ: R. J. Reynolds Tobacco Company
401 N Main St
Winston Salem NC 27101
336 741-5000

(G-13018)
R R DONNELLEY & SONS COMPANY
Also Called: R R Donnelley
1900 Charleston St Se (27893-9032)
PHONE...................................252 243-0337
Bret Beach, *Brnch Mgr*
EMP: 57
SALES (corp-wide): 15B **Privately Held**
Web: www.rrd.com
SIC: 2759 2671 Screen printing; Paper; coated and laminated packaging
HQ: R. R. Donnelley & Sons Company

35 W Wacker Dr
Chicago IL 60601
312 326-8000

(G-13019)
RECON USA LLC
4744 Potato House Ct (27893-8592)
P.O. Box 498 (27813-0498)
PHONE...................................252 206-1391
EMP: 5 **EST:** 2010
SALES (est): 173.72K **Privately Held**
SIC: 2141 Tobacco stemming

(G-13020)
REFRESCO BEVERAGES US INC
Also Called: Refresco Wilson
4843 International Blvd (27893-9673)
PHONE...................................252 234-0493
Joyce August, *Off Mgr*
EMP: 33
Web: www.refresco-na.com
SIC: 2086 Carbonated beverages, nonalcoholic: pkged. in cans, bottles
HQ: Refresco Beverages Us Inc.
8112 Woodland Ctr Blvd
Tampa FL 33614

(G-13021)
REFRESCO BEVERAGES US INC
1805 Purina Cir S (27893-9590)
PHONE...................................252 234-0493
EMP: 13
Web: www.refresco-na.com
SIC: 2086 Soft drinks: packaged in cans, bottles, etc.
HQ: Refresco Beverages Us Inc.
8112 Woodland Ctr Blvd
Tampa FL 33614

(G-13022)
RHYNO ENTERPRISES
Also Called: Wilson Trophy & Hayes EMB
709 Tarboro St Sw (27893-4850)
P.O. Box 6170 (27894-6170)
PHONE...................................252 291-6700
Michael Hicks, *Owner*
EMP: 4 **EST:** 1994
SALES (est): 206.26K **Privately Held**
SIC: 2395 Embroidery and art needlework

(G-13023)
ROBERT RAPER WELDING INC
5326 Evansdale Rd (27893-8057)
P.O. Box 67 (27813-0067)
PHONE...................................252 399-0598
Robert K Raper, *Pr*
EMP: 5 **EST:** 2010
SALES (est): 313.4K **Privately Held**
SIC: 7692 Welding repair

(G-13024)
ROOFING TOOLS AND EQP INC (PA)
3710 Weaver Rd (27893-9441)
P.O. Box 126 (27894-0126)
PHONE...................................252 291-1800
John E Kent Junior, *Pr*
Elizabeth Kent Watson, *VP*
EMP: 9 **EST:** 1937
SQ FT: 36,000
SALES (est): 5.04MM
SALES (corp-wide): 5.04MM **Privately Held**
Web: www.roofingtool.com
SIC: 5033 5074 5075 3531 Roofing, asphalt and sheet metal; Heating equipment (hydronic); Air conditioning equipment, except room units, nec; Roofing equipment

(G-13025)
S STRICKLAND DIESEL SVC INC
5451 Old Raleigh Rd (27893-8322)
PHONE...................................252 291-6999
Brenda F Strickland, *Pr*
Kelly Strickland, *VP*
EMP: 7 **EST:** 1973
SQ FT: 9,600
SALES (est): 469.67K **Privately Held**
Web: www.stricklandsdieselservice.com
SIC: 7538 3599 5084 Diesel engine repair: automotive; Machine shop, jobbing and repair; Engines and parts, diesel

(G-13026)
S T WOOTEN CORPORATION
Also Called: Wilson Concrete Plant
2710 Commerce Rd S (27893-8122)
PHONE...................................252 291-5165
Scott Wooten, *Pr*
EMP: 22
SALES (corp-wide): 319.83MM **Privately Held**
Web: www.stwcorp.com
SIC: 3531 Concrete plants
PA: S. T. Wooten Corporation
3801 Black Creek Rd Se
Wilson NC 27894
252 291-5165

(G-13027)
S T WOOTEN CORPORATION (PA)
Also Called: S. T. Wooten
3801 Black Creek Rd Se (27894)
P.O. Box 2408 (27894)
PHONE...................................252 291-5165
Christopher Wooten, *Pr*
Nancy W Hammock, *
Keith H Merrick, *
George R Stickland, *
Gregory N Nelson, *
EMP: 45 **EST:** 1956
SQ FT: 15,000
SALES (est): 319.83MM
SALES (corp-wide): 319.83MM **Privately Held**
Web: www.stwcorp.com
SIC: 1611 3273 1623 General contractor, highway and street construction; Ready-mixed concrete; Water main construction

(G-13028)
SANDOZ INC
4700 Sandoz Dr (27893-8143)
PHONE...................................252 234-2222
Bill Coneber, *Mgr*
EMP: 305
Web: us.sandoz.com
SIC: 2834 Pharmaceutical preparations
HQ: Sandoz Inc.
100 College Rd W
Princeton NJ 08540
609 627-8500

(G-13029)
SCHWEITZER-MAUDUIT INTL INC
Also Called: Swm Intl
2711 Commerce Rd S (27893-8122)
PHONE...................................252 360-4666
Jeffrey Kramer, *Brnch Mgr*
EMP: 5
Web: www.mativ.com
SIC: 3081 Unsupported plastics film and sheet
PA: Mativ Holdings, Inc.
100 Kimball Pl Ste 600
Alpharetta GA 30009

(G-13030)
SOUTH EAST MANUFACTURING CO
Also Called: Barnes Metalcrafters
113 Walnut St W (27893-3628)
P.O. Box 2492 (27894-2492)
PHONE.................................252 291-0925
Tim Martin, *Pr*
EMP: 10 **EST:** 1996
SQ FT: 7,000
SALES (est): 3.2MM **Privately Held**
Web: www.barnesmetal.com
SIC: 3599 Machine shop, jobbing and repair

(G-13031)
STEPHENSON MILLWORK CO INC
210 Harper St Ne (27893-3307)
P.O. Box 699 (27894-0699)
PHONE.................................252 237-1141
Russell L Stephenson Junior, *Pr*
Russell L Stephenson Junior, *CEO*
Russell L Stephenson Iii, *Pr*
Lee Stephenson, *
EMP: 118 **EST:** 1945
SQ FT: 123,700
SALES (est): 10.04MM **Privately Held**
Web: www.stephensonmillwork.com
SIC: 2431 Millwork

(G-13032)
SUNSHINE PROSTHETICS INC
118 Nash St Sw Ste E (27893-3917)
PHONE.................................833 266-9781
John Clarke, *Pr*
EMP: 7 **EST:** 2018
SALES (est): 1.08MM **Privately Held**
Web: www.sunshineprosthetics.com
SIC: 3842 Surgical appliances and supplies

(G-13033)
SUPREME MURPHY TRCK BODIES INC
4000 Airport Dr Nw (27896-8648)
P.O. Box 463 (46527-0463)
PHONE.................................252 291-2191
Omer G Kropf, *Pr*
Herbert M Gardner, *
William J Barrett, *
Robert W Wilson, *
EMP: 104 **EST:** 1935
SQ FT: 120,000
SALES (est): 1.24MM
SALES (corp-wide): 1.95B **Publicly Held**
SIC: 3713 3711 3585 Truck bodies (motor vehicles); Motor vehicles and car bodies; Refrigeration and heating equipment
HQ: Supreme Corporation
2581 Kercher Rd
Goshen IN 46528
574 642-4888

(G-13034)
SWOFFORD INC
Also Called: Montrose Hanger Co
301 Railroad St S (27893-5135)
P.O. Box 1149 (27894-1149)
PHONE.................................252 478-5969
Faye Swofford, *Mgr*
EMP: 6
SQ FT: 125,000
SALES (corp-wide): 141.98K **Privately Held**
SIC: 2499 Washboards, wood and part wood
PA: Swofford, Inc.
6 Wisteria Ln
Bluffton SC 29909
843 379-8805

(G-13035)
TOBACCO RAG PROCESSORS INC
Also Called: T R P
4744 Potato House Ct (27893-8592)

PHONE.................................252 265-0081
EMP: 21
SALES (corp-wide): 22.75MM **Privately Held**
Web: www.tobaccorag.com
SIC: 2131 2141 Chewing and smoking tobacco; Tobacco stemming and redrying
PA: Tobacco Rag Processors, Inc.
4737 Yank Rd
Wilson NC 27893
252 265-0081

(G-13036)
TOBACCO RAG PROCESSORS INC
2105 Black Creek Rd Se Bldg 6 (27893-9536)
PHONE.................................252 237-8180
T Davis Miller, *Brnch Mgr*
EMP: 21
SALES (corp-wide): 22.75MM **Privately Held**
Web: www.tobaccorag.com
SIC: 2131 2141 Chewing and smoking tobacco; Tobacco stemming and redrying
PA: Tobacco Rag Processors, Inc.
4737 Yank Rd
Wilson NC 27893
252 265-0081

(G-13037)
TOBACCO RAG PROCESSORS INC (PA)
Also Called: T R P
4737 Yank Rd (27893-8528)
P.O. Box 498 (27813-0498)
PHONE.................................252 265-0081
T Davis Miller, *CEO*
Bobby Joe Johnson, *
Brian Tascher, *
◆ **EMP:** 33 **EST:** 2000
SALES (est): 22.75MM
SALES (corp-wide): 22.75MM **Privately Held**
Web: www.tobaccorag.com
SIC: 2141 2131 Tobacco stemming and redrying; Chewing and smoking tobacco

(G-13038)
TREGO INNOVATIONS LLC
2301 Wilco Blvd S (27893-9015)
PHONE.................................919 374-0089
Patrick Shelton, *Managing Member*
EMP: 5 **EST:** 2020
SALES (est): 262.05K **Privately Held**
Web: tregopartners.wordpress.com
SIC: 3086 Plastics foam products

(G-13039)
TRIAGA INC
1900 Stantonsburg Rd Se (27893-8406)
PHONE.................................919 412-6019
Darlene Quashie Henry, *Prin*
EMP: 9 **EST:** 2021
SALES (est): 1.97MM
SALES (corp-wide): 37.88B **Publicly Held**
Web: www.jobsinwilsonnc.com
SIC: 2111 Cigarettes
PA: Philip Morris International Inc.
677 Wshngton Blvd Ste 110
Stamford CT 06901
203 905-2410

(G-13040)
UNDER COVERS PUBLISHING
703 Glendale Dr W (27893-2707)
PHONE.................................704 965-8744
David Hager, *Prin*
EMP: 5 **EST:** 2018
SALES (est): 119.38K **Privately Held**
SIC: 2741 Miscellaneous publishing

(G-13041)
UPPER COASTL PLAIN BUS DEV CTR
121 Nash St W (27893-4012)
PHONE.................................252 234-5900
Greg Goddard, *Dir*
EMP: 7 **EST:** 2007
SALES (est): 519.42K **Privately Held**
Web: www.ucpcog.org
SIC: 3523 Incubators and brooders, farm

(G-13042)
VOITH FABRICS INC
3040 Black Creek Rd S (27893-9526)
P.O. Box 1411 (27894-1411)
PHONE.................................252 291-3800
▲ **EMP:** 350
SIC: 2231 Broadwoven fabric mills, wool

(G-13043)
WAINWRIGHT WAREHOUSE
2427 Us Highway 301 S (27893-6893)
P.O. Box 249 (27880-0249)
PHONE.................................252 237-5121
Donald Windbourne, *Owner*
EMP: 5 **EST:** 1930
SALES (est): 483.42K **Privately Held**
SIC: 2111 0191 Cigarettes; General farms, primarily crop

(G-13044)
WAKE SUPPLY COMPANY
3200 Turnage Rd (27893-7580)
PHONE.................................252 234-6012
Anthony Beedie, *Brnch Mgr*
EMP: 8
SALES (corp-wide): 17.51MM **Privately Held**
Web: www.wakesupply.com
SIC: 2952 5033 Siding materials; Siding, except wood
PA: Wake Supply Company
658 Maywood Ave Ste A
Raleigh NC 27603
252 234-6012

(G-13045)
WEENER PLASTICS INC
2201 Stantonsburg Rd Se (27893)
P.O. Box 2165 (27894)
PHONE.................................252 206-1400
Adam J Greenlee, *Ch Bd*
Joseph Vukcevich, *
Frank W Hogan Iii, *VP*
◆ **EMP:** 63 **EST:** 2006
SQ FT: 50,000
SALES (est): 11.59MM **Publicly Held**
Web: www.wppg.com
SIC: 3082 3949 Unsupported plastics profile shapes; Sporting and athletic goods, nec
PA: Silgan Holdings Inc.
4 Landmark Sq Ste 400
Stamford CT 06901

(G-13046)
WHITE S TIRE SVC WILSON INC
501 Goldsboro St S (27893-4924)
P.O. Box 1469 (27894-1469)
PHONE.................................252 237-0770
Robert W White, *VP*
EMP: 8
SALES (corp-wide): 5.78MM **Privately Held**
Web: www.whitestireservice.com
SIC: 5531 7534 3011 5014 Automotive tires; Tire recapping; Tread rubber, camelback for tire retreading; Automobile tires and tubes
PA: White S Tire Service Of Wilson, Inc.
701 Hines St S
Wilson NC 27893
252 237-5426

(G-13047)
WHITE S TIRE SVC WILSON INC (PA)
701 Hines St S (27893-5149)
P.O. Box 1469 (27894-1469)
PHONE.................................252 237-5426
James E White, *CEO*
Robert W White, *
EMP: 70 **EST:** 1951
SQ FT: 200,000
. **SALES (est):** 5.78MM
SALES (corp-wide): 5.78MM **Privately Held**
Web: www.whitestireservice.com
SIC: 5531 7534 3011 5014 Automotive tires; Tire recapping; Tread rubber, camelback for tire retreading; Automobile tires and tubes

(G-13048)
WILSON DAILY TIMES INC
126 Nash St. W (27893)
P.O. Box 2447 (27894-2447)
PHONE.................................252 243-5151
Morgan Dickerman, *Pr*
Margaret Dickerman, *
EMP: 25 **EST:** 1900
SQ FT: 30,000
SALES (est): 1.91MM **Privately Held**
Web: www.restorationnewsmedia.com
SIC: 2711 Commercial printing and newspaper publishing combined

(G-13049)
WILSON MOLD & MACHINE CORP
2131 Nc Highway 42 E (27893-8812)
PHONE.................................252 243-1831
Terry Dobbins, *Pr*
▲ **EMP:** 85 **EST:** 1989
SALES (est): 9.92MM **Privately Held**
Web: www.wilsonmoldandmachine.com
SIC: 3599 7692 Machine shop, jobbing and repair; Welding repair

(G-13050)
WILSON WOODWORKS INC
Also Called: Wilson Wood Works
2807 Crabtree St S (27893-6846)
P.O. Box 7092 (27895)
PHONE.................................252 237-3179
Ray Cunningham, *Pr*
EMP: 10 **EST:** 1979
SALES (est): 476.51K **Privately Held**
Web: wendellwilson.bigcartel.com
SIC: 2434 Wood kitchen cabinets

Windsor
Bertie County

(G-13051)
DELBERT WHITE LOGGING INC
452 White Oak Rd (27983-8006)
PHONE.................................252 209-4779
Delbert White, *Pr*
EMP: 7 **EST:** 1990
SALES (est): 635.87K **Privately Held**
SIC: 2411 Logging camps and contractors

(G-13052)
EAST COAST LOGGING INC
128 Mizelle Ln (27983-7228)
PHONE.................................252 794-4054
Neal Smith, *Owner*
EMP: 5 **EST:** 2002
SALES (est): 157.68K **Privately Held**
SIC: 2411 Logging camps and contractors

(G-13053)
EMANUEL HOGGARD
Also Called: Emanuel Hoggard Logging
837 Askewville Rd (27983-7967)

PHONE....................252 794-3724
Emanuel Hoggard, *Owner*
EMP: 18 **EST:** 1996
SALES (est): 390.62K **Privately Held**
SIC: 2411 5812 Logging; Eating places

(G-13054)
HTM CONCEPTS INC
118 County Farm Rd (27983-9078)
PHONE....................252 794-2122
John A Hughes, *Pr*
Harlan Hughes, *VP*
Marian W Hughes, *Sec*
EMP: 10 **EST:** 1971
SQ FT: 52,000
SALES (est): 262.99K **Privately Held**
Web: www.htmconcepts.com
SIC: 2396 2752 2631 Screen printing on
    fabric articles; Offset printing; Binders' board

(G-13055)
MORVEN PARTNERS LP
Gillam Brothers Peanut Sheller
406 Spring St (27983-6843)
P.O. Box 550 (27983-0550)
PHONE....................252 794-3435
David Cobb, *Genl Mgr*
EMP: 21
SIC: 2068 Salted and roasted nuts and seeds
PA: Morven Partners, L.P.
    11 Leigh Fisher Blvd
    El Paso TX 79906

(G-13056)
POWELL & STOKES INC
Also Called: Bertie County Peanuts
217 Us Highway 13 N (27983-8097)
PHONE....................252 794-2138
EMP: 9 **EST:** 1919
SALES (est): 3.94MM **Privately Held**
Web: www.pnuts.net
SIC: 5159 5999 2068 Peanuts (bulk),
    unroasted; Feed and farm supply; Nuts:
    dried, dehydrated, salted or roasted

(G-13057)
S & K LOGGING INC
1408 S King St (27983-9665)
PHONE....................252 794-2045
Kenneth S White Senior, *Pr*
Kenneth S White Junior, *VP*
Jason White, *VP*
Katherine White, *Sec*
EMP: 6 **EST:** 1993
SALES (est): 512.19K **Privately Held**
SIC: 2411 Logging camps and contractors

(G-13058)
SQUEAKS LOGGING INC
139 Republican Rd (27983-7501)
PHONE....................252 794-1531
William Capehart, *Prin*
EMP: 4 **EST:** 2015
SALES (est): 282.31K **Privately Held**
SIC: 2411 Logging camps and contractors

(G-13059)
W & T LOGGING LLC
118 Conner Ln (27983-9584)
PHONE....................252 209-4351
Tonyia Foy, *Prin*
EMP: 6 **EST:** 2013
SALES (est): 994.44K **Privately Held**
SIC: 2411 Logging camps and contractors

(G-13060)
W R WHITE INC
152 W Askewville St (27983-7238)
PHONE....................252 794-6577
William R White, *Pr*

Steve M White, *VP*
Connie S Cowan, *Sec*
William D White, *VP*
EMP: 11 **EST:** 2001
SALES (est): 961.53K **Privately Held**
SIC: 2411 Logging camps and contractors

(G-13061)
WILLARD RODNEY WHITE
142 E Askewville St (27983-9560)
PHONE....................252 794-3245
Willie R White, *Prin*
EMP: 6 **EST:** 2010
SALES (est): 151.64K **Privately Held**
SIC: 2741 Miscellaneous publishing

Wingate
Union County

(G-13062)
H & H WOOD PRODUCTS INC
3349 Us Hwy 74 E (28174)
P.O. Box 185 (28174-0185)
PHONE....................704 233-4148
Richard Herring, *Pr*
EMP: 4 **EST:** 1947
SQ FT: 30,000
SALES (est): 141.28K **Privately Held**
SIC: 2431 Moldings, wood: unfinished and
    prefinished

(G-13063)
PILGRIMS PRIDE CORPORATION
Pilgrim's Pride Feed Mills Div
205 Edgewood Dr (28174-6700)
P.O. Box 668 (28103-0668)
PHONE....................704 233-4047
Tommy Long, *Mgr*
EMP: 102
Web: www.pilgrims.com
SIC: 2015 Chicken, slaughtered and dressed
HQ: Pilgrim's Pride Corporation
    1770 Promontory Cir
    Greeley CO 80634
    970 506-8000

Winnabow
Brunswick County

(G-13064)
DIVERSIFIED INTL HOLDINGS INC ✪
107 Potomac Ct (28479-5174)
PHONE....................910 777-7122
William Slocumb, *Prin*
EMP: 5 **EST:** 2024
SALES (est): 925.27K **Privately Held**
SIC: 3679 7389 Electronic circuits; Business
    services, nec

(G-13065)
EVERY DAY CARRY LLC
Also Called: Sporting Goods
4716 Black Pine Ct (28479-0501)
PHONE....................203 231-0256
Marc Workiewicz, *Managing Member*
EMP: 10 **EST:** 2021
SALES (est): 114K **Privately Held**
SIC: 7389 3482 3484 5091 Business
    Activities at Non-Commercial Site; Small
    arms ammunition; Small arms; Firearms,
    sporting

(G-13066)
JLMADE LLC
2226 Jasper Forest Trl (28479-4401)
PHONE....................252 515-2195
Jacob Yount, *Managing Member*
EMP: 6 **EST:** 2012

SALES (est): 504.71K **Privately Held**
SIC: 3089 Injection molding of plastics

(G-13067)
KITCHEN MAN INC
6361 Ocean Hwy E Ste 1 (28479-5757)
PHONE....................910 408-1322
Chris Dabideen, *Pr*
EMP: 10 **EST:** 2015
SALES (est): 1.7MM **Privately Held**
Web: www.kitchenmannc.com
SIC: 3281 1799 Granite, cut and shaped;
    Counter top installation

Winston Salem
Forsyth County

(G-13068)
1A SMART START LLC
2453 Spaugh Industrial Dr (27103-6498)
PHONE....................336 765-7001
EMP: 7
Web: www.smartstartinc.com
SIC: 3694 Engine electrical equipment
PA: 1a Smart Start Llc
    500 E Dallas Rd Ste 100
    Grapevine TX 76051

(G-13069)
4TOPPS LLC
3135 Indiana Ave (27105-4343)
PHONE....................704 281-8451
EMP: 6 **EST:** 2011
SALES (est): 2.56MM **Privately Held**
Web: www.4topps.com
SIC: 2531 Stadium seating

(G-13070)
A L BECK & SONS INC
505 Jones Rd (27107-9406)
PHONE....................336 788-1896
Larry Beck, *CEO*
Steve Beck, *Sec*
EMP: 11 **EST:** 1973
SQ FT: 8,888
SALES (est): 1.01MM **Privately Held**
SIC: 2011 Meat packing plants

(G-13071)
ACCUSPORT INTERNATIONAL INC
(PA)
801 N Trade St (27101-1432)
PHONE....................336 759-3300
Randall Tuttle, *CEO*
Don Thoruk, *Pr*
James Kluttz, *Ch*
▲ **EMP:** 22 **EST:** 1989
SALES (est): 2.87MM **Privately Held**
Web: www.accusport.com
SIC: 3829 Measuring and controlling
    devices, nec

(G-13072)
ADELE KNITS INC
3304 Old Lexington Rd (27107-4119)
PHONE....................336 499-6010
Henry A Brown Junior, *Ch Bd*
Bruce T Brown, *
Patricia Brown, *
EMP: 150 **EST:** 1970
SQ FT: 160,000
SALES (est): 1.96MM **Privately Held**
Web: www.adeleknitsinc.com
SIC: 5131 2259 Piece goods and notions;
    Bags and bagging, knit

(G-13073)
ADSIGN CORP
6100 Gun Club Rd (27103-9716)
P.O. Box 280 (27012-0280)
PHONE....................336 766-3000
R Jack Perkins, *Pr*
Sue Perkins, *VP*
EMP: 8 **EST:** 1978
SQ FT: 5,500
SALES (est): 542.95K **Privately Held**
Web: www.adsigncorp.com
SIC: 3993 Signs, not made in custom sign
    painting shops

(G-13074)
**ADVANCED DRAINAGE SYSTEMS
INC**
Foltz Concrete Pipe
11875 N Nc Highway 150 (27127-9182)
PHONE....................336 764-0341
Jeff Leonards, *Genl Mgr*
EMP: 21
SALES (corp-wide): 2.87B **Publicly Held**
Web: www.adspipe.com
SIC: 3272 Pipe, concrete or lined with
    concrete
PA: Advanced Drainage Systems, Inc.
    4640 Trueman Blvd
    Hilliard OH 43026
    614 658-0050

(G-13075)
AFE VICTORY INC
3779 Champion Blvd (27105-2667)
PHONE....................856 428-4200
▲ **EMP:** 108
SIC: 3585 Refrigeration equipment, complete

(G-13076)
ALDERS POINT
590 Mock St (27127-2162)
PHONE....................336 725-9021
Darrell Hill, *Prin*
EMP: 4 **EST:** 2006
SALES (est): 635.32K **Privately Held**
SIC: 3553 Furniture makers machinery,
    woodworking

(G-13077)
**ALEXANDERS CBINETS
COUNTERTOPS**
4735 Kester Mill Rd (27103-1212)
P.O. Box 25445 (27114-5445)
PHONE....................336 774-2966
Crystal Cramer, *CEO*
EMP: 4 **EST:** 2006
SALES (est): 227.81K **Privately Held**
SIC: 2434 Wood kitchen cabinets

(G-13078)
ALI GROUP NORTH AMERICA CORP
Also Called: Champion Industries
3765 Champion Blvd (27105-2667)
PHONE....................336 661-1556
EMP: 100
SALES (corp-wide): 4.67B **Privately Held**
Web: www.aligroup.com
SIC: 3589 Dishwashing machines,
    commercial
HQ: Ali Group North America Corporation
    101 Corporate Woods Pkwy
    Vernon Hills IL 60061
    847 215-6565

(G-13079)
ALL OCCASION PRINTING
2408 Gardenia Rd (27107-2522)
PHONE....................336 926-7766
EMP: 4 **EST:** 2013
SALES (est): 56.97K **Privately Held**

SIC: 2752 Commercial printing, lithographic

(G-13080)
ALL STICK LABEL LLC
3929 Westpoint Blvd Ste B (27103-6761)
PHONE................................336 659-4660
EMP: 7 **EST:** 1997
SQ FT: 6,000
SALES (est): 474.3K **Privately Held**
Web: www.aslprintfx.com
SIC: 2759 Labels and seals: printing, nsk

(G-13081)
ALLIANCE ASSESSMENTS LLC
200 Northgate Park Dr (27106-3480)
PHONE................................336 283-9246
Kenneth Dutton, *Prin*
EMP: 5 **EST:** 2012
SALES (est): 520.88K **Privately Held**
Web: www.allianceassessments.com
SIC: 2899 Drug testing kits, blood and urine

(G-13082)
ALPHA ALUMINUM LLC
Also Called: Phoenix Aluminum
1300 Cunningham Ave (27107-2203)
PHONE................................336 777-5658
EMP: 6 **EST:** 2014
SALES (est): 1.6MM **Privately Held**
Web: www.alphaaluminum.net
SIC: 3353 Aluminum sheet, plate, and foil

(G-13083)
ALPHAGRAPHICS
8100 N Point Blvd Ste A (27105-2561)
P.O. Box 11643 (27116-1643)
PHONE................................336 759-8000
James Carpenter, *Pr*
EMP: 8 **EST:** 1998
SQ FT: 4,000
SALES (est): 295.19K **Privately Held**
Web: www.alphagraphics.com
SIC: 2752 Commercial printing, lithographic

(G-13084)
AMARR COMPANY (DH)
Also Called: Amarr Garage Doors
165 Carriage Ct (27105)
PHONE................................336 744-5100
Richard A Brenner, *Ch Bd*
Jeffrey D Mick, *
Richard S Sears, *
Matthew S Hukill, *
Stephen R Crawford, *
◆ **EMP:** 113 **EST:** 1951
SALES (est): 243.28MM **Privately Held**
Web: www.amarr.com
SIC: 5211 3442 2431 5031 Garage doors,
   sale and installation; Garage doors,
   overhead: metal; Garage doors, overhead,
   wood; Doors, garage
HQ: Assa Abloy Inc.
   110 Sargent Dr
   New Haven CT 06511

(G-13085)
AMERICAN SNUFF COMPANY LLC
Taylor Brothers
2415 S Stratford Rd (27103-6225)
P.O. Box 597 (27102-0597)
PHONE................................336 768-4630
Gregory Sawyers, *Genl Mgr*
EMP: 204
Web: www.americansnuffco.com
SIC: 2131 Chewing tobacco
HQ: American Snuff Company, Llc
   5106 Tradeport Dr
   Memphis TN 38141
   901 761-2050

(G-13086)
AMERICAN WEBBING FITTINGS INC
4959 Home Rd (27106-2802)
PHONE................................336 767-9390
Steve Schroeder, *Pr*
Steve Stewart, *Treas*
EMP: 18 **EST:** 1981
SALES (est): 1.92MM **Privately Held**
Web: www.americanwebbing.com
SIC: 2241 Narrow fabric mills

(G-13087)
APPLIED CATHETER TECH INC
113 Thomas St (27101-3628)
PHONE................................336 817-1005
Jon S Wilson, *CEO*
EMP: 4 **EST:** 2008
SQ FT: 12,000
SALES (est): 177.77K **Privately Held**
Web: www.appliedcatheter.com
SIC: 3841 Surgical and medical instruments

(G-13088)
ARGOS USA
1590 Williamson St (27107-1240)
PHONE................................336 784-5181
EMP: 11
SALES (est): 343.87K **Privately Held**
Web: www.argos-us.com
SIC: 3273 Ready-mixed concrete

(G-13089)
ARGOS USA LLC
Also Called: Redi-Mix Concrete
1590 Williamson St (27107-1240)
PHONE................................336 784-4888
Amy Radcliffe, *Brnch Mgr*
EMP: 55
Web: www.argos-us.com
SIC: 3273 Ready-mixed concrete
HQ: Argos Usa Llc
   3015 Windward Plz Ste 300
   Alpharetta GA 30005
   678 368-4300

(G-13090)
AWNING INNOVATIONS
1635 S Martin Luther King Jr Dr
(27107-1310)
PHONE................................336 831-8996
Brett Hodges, *Owner*
EMP: 15 **EST:** 2015
SALES (est): 437.79K **Privately Held**
Web: www.awninginnovations.com
SIC: 3993 Advertising artwork

(G-13091)
B/E AEROSPACE INC
2598 Empire Dr (27103-6762)
PHONE................................336 293-1823
Steve Franke, *Mgr*
▲ **EMP:** 5
SALES (corp-wide): 80.74B **Publicly Held**
Web: www.collinsaerospace.com
SIC: 3728 Aircraft parts and equipment, nec
HQ: B/E Aerospace, Inc.
   2730 West Tyvola Rd
   Charlotte NC 28217
   704 423-7000

(G-13092)
B/E AEROSPACE INC
175 Oak Plaza Blvd (27105-1471)
PHONE................................336 293-1823
Steve Franke, *Brnch Mgr*
▲ **EMP:** 8
SALES (corp-wide): 80.74B **Publicly Held**
Web: www.collinsaerospace.com
SIC: 3728 Aircraft parts and equipment, nec
HQ: B/E Aerospace, Inc.

2730 West Tyvola Rd
Charlotte NC 28217
704 423-7000

(G-13093)
B/E AEROSPACE INC
190 Oak Plaza Blvd (27105-1470)
PHONE................................336 744-6914
Alexander Pozzi, *Brnch Mgr*
EMP: 35
SALES (corp-wide): 80.74B **Publicly Held**
Web: www.collinsaerospace.com
SIC: 3728 Aircraft parts and equipment, nec
HQ: B/E Aerospace, Inc.
   2730 West Tyvola Rd
   Charlotte NC 28217
   704 423-7000

(G-13094)
B/E AEROSPACE INC
Also Called: Collins Aerospace
150 Oak Plaza Blvd Ste 200 (27105-1482)
PHONE................................336 767-2000
Werner Lieberherr, *Mgr*
EMP: 50
SALES (corp-wide): 80.74B **Publicly Held**
Web: www.collinsaerospace.com
SIC: 3728 Aircraft parts and equipment, nec
HQ: B/E Aerospace, Inc.
   2730 West Tyvola Rd
   Charlotte NC 28217
   704 423-7000

(G-13095)
B/E AEROSPACE INC
1455 Fairchild Rd # 1 (27105-4500)
PHONE................................520 733-1719
Doug Rasnussen, *Brnch Mgr*
EMP: 128
SALES (corp-wide): 80.74B **Publicly Held**
Web: www.collinsaerospace.com
SIC: 3728 Aircraft parts and equipment, nec
HQ: B/E Aerospace, Inc.
   2730 West Tyvola Rd
   Charlotte NC 28217
   704 423-7000

(G-13096)
B/E AEROSPACE INC
B/E Arspace Seating Pdts Group
2599 Empire Dr (27103-6709)
PHONE................................336 776-3500
Liam O'boyle, *Mgr*
EMP: 167
SALES (corp-wide): 80.74B **Publicly Held**
Web: www.collinsaerospace.com
SIC: 3728 Aircraft parts and equipment, nec
HQ: B/E Aerospace, Inc.
   2730 West Tyvola Rd
   Charlotte NC 28217
   704 423-7000

(G-13097)
B/E AEROSPACE INC
Also Called: Be Aerospace
1455 Fairchild Rd (27105-4500)
PHONE................................336 767-2000
Michael Baughns, *Brnch Mgr*
EMP: 235
SALES (corp-wide): 80.74B **Publicly Held**
Web: www.collinsaerospace.com
SIC: 3728 Aircraft parts and equipment, nec
HQ: B/E Aerospace, Inc.
   2730 West Tyvola Rd
   Charlotte NC 28217
   704 423-7000

(G-13098)
B/E AEROSPACE INC
Also Called: Collins Aerospace
4965 Indiana Ave (27106-2826)

2730 West Tyvola Rd
Charlotte NC 28217
704 423-7000

(G-13093) *(see above)*

PHONE................................336 692-8940
Brad Doss, *Logistics Leader*
EMP: 12
SALES (corp-wide): 80.74B **Publicly Held**
Web: www.collinsaerospace.com
SIC: 2531 3728 3647 Public building and
   related furniture; Aircraft parts and
   equipment, nec; Vehicular lighting
   equipment
HQ: B/E Aerospace, Inc.
   2730 West Tyvola Rd
   Charlotte NC 28217
   704 423-7000

(G-13099)
B/E AEROSPACE INC
Also Called: Collins Aerospace
150 Oak Plaza Blvd Ste 200 (27105-1482)
PHONE................................704 423-7000
Troy Brunk, *Pr*
EMP: 12
SALES (corp-wide): 80.74B **Publicly Held**
SIC: 2531 Seats, aircraft
HQ: B/E Aerospace, Inc.
   2730 West Tyvola Rd
   Charlotte NC 28217
   704 423-7000

(G-13100)
BA INTERNATIONAL LLC
1000 E Hanes Mill Rd (27105-1384)
PHONE................................336 519-8080
EMP: 4 **EST:** 2019
SALES (est): 2.75MM **Publicly Held**
Web: www.bachelorstudies.ng
SIC: 2253 T-shirts and tops, knit
PA: Hanesbrands Inc.
   1000 E Hanes Mill Rd
   Winston Salem NC 27105

(G-13101)
BAICY COMMUNICATIONS INC
Also Called: Immedia Print
1411 S Main St (27127-2705)
P.O. Box 26014 (27114-6014)
PHONE................................336 722-7768
John Baicy, *Pr*
Elizabeth Baicy, *Sec*
EMP: 7 **EST:** 1988
SQ FT: 6,000
SALES (est): 957.29K **Privately Held**
Web: www.immediaprint.com
SIC: 2752 2791 Offset printing; Hand
   composition typesetting

(G-13102)
BE HOUSE PUBLISHING LLC
400 Barnes Rd (27107-6860)
PHONE................................336 529-6143
Bridget Elam, *Owner*
EMP: 5 **EST:** 2018
SALES (est): 116.6K **Privately Held**
SIC: 2741 Miscellaneous publishing

(G-13103)
BEKAERTDESLEE USA INC
200 Business Park Dr (27107-6538)
PHONE................................336 747-4900
Rafael Rodriguez, *
Sam Sabbe, *
Dirk Verly, *Chief Human Resources Officer**
Jos Deslee, *Chief Strategic Officer**
EMP: 500 **EST:** 2002
SALES (est): 32.54MM
SALES (corp-wide): 4.82B **Privately Held**
Web: www.bekaertdeslee.com
SIC: 2211 5021 Tickings; Mattresses
HQ: Bekaertdeslee Holding
   Deerlijkseweg 22
   Waregem VWV 8790

(G-13104)
BEVERAGE-AIR CORPORATION (DH)
3779 Champion Blvd (27105-2667)
PHONE.....................336 245-6400
Filippo Berti, *CEO*
Oscar Villa, *
◆ **EMP:** 50 **EST:** 2008
SALES (est): 34.12MM
SALES (corp-wide): 4.67B **Privately Held**
Web: www.beverage-air.com
SIC: 3585 Refrigeration and heating
   equipment
HQ: Ali Group North America Corporation
   101 Corporate Woods Pkwy
   Vernon Hills IL 60061
   847 215-6565

(G-13105)
BIO-TECH PRSTHTICS ORTHTICS IN
1399 Westgate Center Dr (27103-2934)
PHONE.....................336 768-3666
Sherry Nisbet, *Mgr*
EMP: 9
SALES (corp-wide): 1.12B **Privately Held**
Web: www.hangerclinic.com
SIC: 3842 5999 Prosthetic appliances;
   Orthopedic and prosthesis applications
HQ: Bio-Tech Prosthetics And Orthotics,
   Inc.
   2301 N Church St
   Greensboro NC 27405

(G-13106)
BIRTH TISSUE RECOVERY LLC (PA)
3051 Trenwest Dr Ste A (27103-3230)
PHONE.....................336 448-1910
Kurt R Weber, *CEO*
Kurt R Weber, *Pr*
Leah A Weber Vp Tissue, *Bank Operations*
Anna Tirrell, *Quality Assurance Vice President*
EMP: 21 **EST:** 2011
SQ FT: 6,000
SALES (est): 6.96MM
SALES (corp-wide): 6.96MM **Privately Held**
Web: www.birthtissuerecovery.com
SIC: 8099 8731 3841 Organ bank; Medical
   research, commercial; Surgical and medical
   instruments

(G-13107)
BLACK SAND COMPANY INC
745 W Clemmonsville Rd (27127-5000)
PHONE.....................336 788-6411
Cynthia Black Shoaf, *Pr*
Mark Shoaf, *VP*
EMP: 5 **EST:** 1927
SALES (est): 909.15K **Privately Held**
Web: www.blacksandco.com
SIC: 1442 Construction sand and gravel

(G-13108)
BLOOMDAY GRANITE & MARBLE INC
3810 Indiana Ave (27105-3409)
P.O. Box 11906 (27116)
PHONE.....................336 724-0300
Frederick Cooke Junior, *CEO*
EMP: 26 **EST:** 1998
SALES (est): 4.99MM **Privately Held**
Web: www.bloomdaygranite.com
SIC: 5032 3281 Granite building stone;
   Granite, cut and shaped

(G-13109)
BLUE LIGHT WELDING OF TRIAD
2328 Pebble Creek Rd (27107-7602)
PHONE.....................336 442-9140
EMP: 5 **EST:** 2013
SALES (est): 55.72K **Privately Held**

SIC: 7692 Welding repair

(G-13110)
BRIDGESTONE RET OPERATIONS LLC
Also Called: Firestone
2743 Reynolda Rd (27106-3871)
PHONE.....................336 725-1580
David Bordeaux, *Mgr*
EMP: 8
SQ FT: 6,676
Web: www.bridgestoneamericas.com
SIC: 5531 7534 Automotive tires; Rebuilding
   and retreading tires
HQ: Bridgestone Retail Operations, Llc
   200 4th Ave S Ste 100
   Nashville TN 37201
   615 937-1000

(G-13111)
BROAD BRANCH DISTILLERY LLC
756 N Trade St (27101-1431)
PHONE.....................336 207-7855
John G Fragakis, *Managing Member*
EMP: 5 **EST:** 2014
SALES (est): 509.75K **Privately Held**
Web: www.broadbranchdistillery.com
SIC: 2085 Distilled and blended liquors

(G-13112)
BRUSHY MOUNTAIN BEE FARM INC (PA)
101 S Stratford Rd Ste 210 (27104-4224)
PHONE.....................336 921-3640
Steve Forrest, *Pr*
Sandra Forrest, *
◆ **EMP:** 45 **EST:** 1977
SALES (est): 3.83MM
SALES (corp-wide): 3.83MM **Privately Held**
Web: www.brushymountainbeefarm.com
SIC: 2499 5191 2326 Beekeeping supplies,
   wood; Beekeeping supplies (non-durable);
   Men's and boy's work clothing

(G-13113)
BUTTERCREME BAKERY INC
895 W Northwest Blvd (27101-1213)
PHONE.....................336 722-1022
Loland R Borton, *Pr*
EMP: 4 **EST:** 1977
SALES (est): 210.37K **Privately Held**
Web: www.rrpinsurance.com
SIC: 2051 Bread, cake, and related products

(G-13114)
BUZZISPACE INC (DH)
2880 Ridgewood Park Dr (27107-4581)
P.O. Box 2690 (27261-2690)
PHONE.....................336 821-3150
Tommaso Baldini, *CEO*
Wim Tytgat, *CFO*
▲ **EMP:** 8 **EST:** 2012
SALES (est): 8.45MM **Privately Held**
Web: www.buzzi.space
SIC: 2522 Office furniture, except wood
HQ: Buzzispace Group
   Italielei 8
   Antwerpen VAN 2000
   32573234

(G-13115)
C&J PUBLISHING
948 Sportsmans Dr (27101-6305)
PHONE.....................336 722-8005
EMP: 4 **EST:** 2014
SALES (est): 44.94K **Privately Held**
SIC: 2741 Miscellaneous publishing

(G-13116)
CAROLINA CUSTOM DRAPERIES INC
5723 Country Club Rd Ste D (27104-3385)
PHONE.....................336 945-5190
Sylvia G Marvelli, *Pr*
Marshall Marvelli, *Sec*
EMP: 7 **EST:** 1977
SALES (est): 119.43K **Privately Held**
Web: www.carolinacustomdraperies.com
SIC: 2391 7389 Draperies, plastic and
   textile: from purchased materials; Interior
   designer

(G-13117)
CAROLINA NARROW FABRIC COMPANY
1100 N Patterson Ave (27101-1530)
P.O. Box 1485 (27102-1485)
PHONE.....................336 631-3000
Horace L Freeman Junior, *CEO*
Jeffrey Freeman, *Pr*
Lee Laughlin, *CFO*
▲ **EMP:** 125 **EST:** 1928
SQ FT: 135,000
SALES (est): 22.24MM **Privately Held**
Web: www.carolinanarrowfabric.com
SIC: 2241 Fabric tapes

(G-13118)
CAROLINA RUBBER & SPC INC
4301 Idlewild Industrial Dr (27105-2659)
PHONE.....................336 744-5111
Keith Stauffer, *Pr*
Darlene Moore, *VP*
Charles H Cook, *Treas*
Michael C Lentz, *Sec*
EMP: 6 **EST:** 1994
SALES (est): 365.55K **Privately Held**
Web: www.carolinarubber.com
SIC: 5085 3492 Hose, belting, and packing;
   Hose and tube fittings and assemblies,
   hydraulic/pneumatic

(G-13119)
CAROLINA SCREW PRODUCTS
P.O. Box 24154 (27114-4154)
PHONE.....................336 760-7400
Tom Hicks, *Prin*
EMP: 5 **EST:** 2008
SALES (est): 163.83K **Privately Held**
SIC: 3451 Screw machine products

(G-13120)
CATHTEK LLC
3825 Reidsville Rd (27101-2166)
PHONE.....................336 748-0686
Mark Martel, *Pr*
Todd Cassidy, *VP*
▲ **EMP:** 6 **EST:** 2000
SQ FT: 2,500
SALES (est): 7.86MM **Privately Held**
Web: www.cathtek.com
SIC: 5047 3842 Medical equipment and
   supplies; Abdominal supporters, braces,
   and trusses

(G-13121)
CBG ACQUISITION COMPANY
3916 Westpoint Blvd (27103-6719)
PHONE.....................336 768-8872
Darrin Anderson, *CEO*
EMP: 2176 **EST:** 2018
SALES (est): 7.84MM **Privately Held**
SIC: 2431 Door frames, wood

(G-13122)
CHAMPION INDUSTRIES INC
3765 Champion Blvd (27105-2667)
PHONE.....................336 661-1556
▲ **EMP:** 100

Web: www.championindustries.com
SIC: 3589 Dishwashing machines,
   commercial

(G-13123)
CHARTER MEDICAL LLC
Also Called: Charter Medical, Ltd.
3948 Westpoint Blvd Ste A (27103-6770)
PHONE.....................336 768-6447
Gael Peron, *Pr*
Peter V Ferris, *
Paul G Igoe, *
◆ **EMP:** 90 **EST:** 1998
SALES (est): 24.48MM
SALES (corp-wide): 1.95B **Privately Held**
Web: www.chartermedical.com
SIC: 3841 Blood transfusion equipment
HQ: Fenner, Inc.
   187 W Airport Rd
   Lititz PA 17543
   717 665-2421

(G-13124)
CJR PRODUCTS INC
6206 Hacker Bend Ct (27103-9771)
PHONE.....................336 766-2710
John R Grayson, *Pr*
Jennie Grayson, *Owner*
EMP: 6 **EST:** 1988
SQ FT: 20,000
SALES (est): 437.69K **Privately Held**
Web: www.cjrproducts.com
SIC: 3714 Power steering equipment, motor
   vehicle

(G-13125)
CLOVERLEAF MIXING INC
Also Called: Yadkin Valley Paving
121 Cloverleaf Dr (27103-6715)
PHONE.....................336 765-7900
EMP: 8 **EST:** 1997
SALES (est): 987.81K **Privately Held**
SIC: 2951 Asphalt and asphaltic paving
   mixtures (not from refineries)

(G-13126)
CML MICRO CIRCUIT USA
486 N Patterson Ave Ste 301 (27101-4261)
PHONE.....................336 744-5050
George Gurry, *Ch Bd*
Mark Gunyuzlu, *Pr*
Nigel Clark, *Treas*
▲ **EMP:** 20 **EST:** 1980
SQ FT: 27,500
SALES (est): 2.22MM
SALES (corp-wide): 29.05MM **Privately Held**
Web: www.cmlmicro.com
SIC: 3674 3672 Microcircuits, integrated
   (semiconductor); Printed circuit boards
PA: Cml Microsystems Plc
   Oval Park
   Maldon CM9 6
   162 187-5500

(G-13127)
COOK & BOARDMAN GROUP LLC (HQ)
3064 Salem Industrial Dr (27127-8854)
PHONE.....................336 768-8872
Darrin Anderson, *CEO*
David Eisner, *
Lance Simpson, *
EMP: 99 **EST:** 2010
SQ FT: 24,000
SALES (est): 531.52MM **Privately Held**
Web: www.cookandboardman.com
SIC: 2431 Door frames, wood
PA: Platinum Equity, Llc
   360 N Crescent Dr Bldg S
   Beverly Hills CA 90210

(G-13128)
COOK & BOARDMAN NC LLC
Also Called: COOK & BOARDMAN NC, LLC
3916 Westpoint Blvd (27103-6719)
PHONE.................................336 768-8872
Tim Hutchen, *Mgr*
EMP: 20
Web: www.cookandboardman.com
SIC: 2431 Millwork
HQ: Cook & Boardman Llc
9347 D Dcks Ln Ste A Slve
Charlotte NC 28273
704 334-8683

(G-13129)
COOK GROUP INC
Also Called: Cook Medical Endoscopy Div
5941 Grassy Creek Blvd (27105-1206)
PHONE.................................336 744-0157
Bill Gibbons, *Prin*
EMP: 7 EST: 2010
SALES (est): 4.7MM Privately Held
Web: www.cookmedical.com
SIC: 3841 Surgical and medical instruments

(G-13130)
COOK INCORPORATED
Also Called: Wilson-Cook Medical Inc.
4900 Bethania Station Rd (27105-1203)
PHONE.................................336 744-0157
Tamisha Clark, *Genl Mgr*
EMP: 560
SALES (corp-wide): 1.61B Privately Held
Web: www.cookmedical.com
SIC: 3841 Catheters
HQ: Cook Incorporated
750 Daniels Way
Bloomington IN 47404
812 339-2235

(G-13131)
CORNING INCORPORATED
Also Called: Corning
3180 Centre Park Blvd (27107-4574)
PHONE.................................336 771-8000
Sandy Lion, *CEO*
EMP: 23
SALES (corp-wide): 13.12B Publicly Held
Web: www.corning.com
SIC: 3229 Glass fiber products
PA: Corning Incorporated
1 Riverfront Plz
Corning NY 14831
607 974-9000

(G-13132)
CORNING OPTCAL CMMNCATIONS LLC
Also Called: Corning
3180 Centre Park Blvd (27107-4574)
PHONE.................................336 771-8000
Sandy Lion, *Brnch Mgr*
EMP: 461
SALES (corp-wide): 13.12B Publicly Held
Web: www.corning.com
SIC: 3229 Pressed and blown glass, nec
HQ: Corning Optical Communications Llc
4200 Corning Pl
Charlotte NC 28216
828 901-5000

(G-13133)
COVILLE INC (PA)
8065 N Point Blvd Ste O (27106-3287)
P.O. Box 728 (27371-0728)
PHONE.................................336 759-0115
Don Trexler, *Pr*
Laurie Trexler, *VP*
EMP: 13 EST: 1975
SQ FT: 4,000
SALES (est): 14.26MM

SALES (corp-wide): 14.26MM Privately Held
Web: www.covilleinc.com
SIC: 2259 Bags and bagging, knit

(G-13134)
CRANIAL TECHNOLOGIES INC
1590 Westbrook Plaza Dr (27103-2965)
PHONE.................................336 760-5530
EMP: 4
Web: www.cranialtech.com
SIC: 3842 Surgical appliances and supplies
PA: Cranial Technologies, Inc.
1405 W Auto Dr Ste 201
Tempe AZ 85284

(G-13135)
CSC AWNINGS INC
3950 N Liberty St (27105-3810)
P.O. Box 21207 (27120)
PHONE.................................336 744-5006
Eric Gerhardt, *Pr*
EMP: 5 EST: 1999
SQ FT: 2,000
SALES (est): 1.84MM
SALES (corp-wide): 35.89MM Privately Held
Web: www.cscawnings.com
SIC: 2394 Awnings, fabric: made from purchased materials
PA: Bulldog Group, Inc.
758 Park Centre Dr
Kernersville NC 27284
336 724-2727

(G-13136)
DALTONS METAL WORKS INC
Also Called: Daltons Metal Works
2411 Gumtree Rd (27107-9325)
P.O. Box 1683 (27374-1683)
PHONE.................................336 731-1442
Jack Dalton, *Owner*
Jack Dalton, *Pr*
Debbie Dalton, *VP*
EMP: 8 EST: 1991
SALES (est): 307.4K Privately Held
SIC: 3441 Fabricated structural metal

(G-13137)
DAVIDSON STEEL SERVICES LLC
11075 Old Us Highway 52 # 100 (27107-9840)
PHONE.................................336 775-1234
Sheryl Waddell Whicker, *Managing Member*
EMP: 5 EST: 2004
SQ FT: 1,800
SALES (est): 1.18MM Privately Held
Web: www.davidsonsteel.com
SIC: 3441 Fabricated structural metal

(G-13138)
DAVIS SIGN COMPANY INC
208 Regent Dr (27103-6718)
P.O. Box 24264 (27114-4264)
PHONE.................................336 765-2990
William Davis Junior, *Pr*
William C Davis Senior, *Pr*
William C Davis Junior, *Pr*
Lee Hendrix, *Off Mgr*
EMP: 13 EST: 1986
SQ FT: 5,000
SALES (est): 1.01MM Privately Held
SIC: 3993 Signs, not made in custom sign painting shops

(G-13139)
DAYTECH SOLUTIONS LLC
101 N Chestnut St Ste 211 (27101-4046)
PHONE.................................336 918-4122
EMP: 5

SALES (est): 549.6K Privately Held
Web: www.daytechsolutions.com
SIC: 3083 Thermoplastics laminates: rods, tubes, plates, and sheet

(G-13140)
DB CUSTOM CRAFTS LLC
267 Kendall Farms Ct (27107-6894)
PHONE.................................336 867-4107
Donna Burgess, *CEO*
EMP: 11 EST: 2022
SALES (est): 752.65K Privately Held
SIC: 2759 7389 Screen printing; Business Activities at Non-Commercial Site

(G-13141)
DESIGN ENGNRED FBRICATIONS INC
2461 Spaugh Industrial Dr (27103-6498)
PHONE.................................336 768-8260
M Glenn Wells, *Pr*
Sheryl Wells, *
EMP: 25 EST: 1991
SQ FT: 15,000
SALES (est): 4.54MM Privately Held
Web: www.def-inc.com
SIC: 3444 3531 Sheet metalwork; Construction machinery

(G-13142)
DEVORA DESIGNS INC
Also Called: Papersassy Boutique
1315 Creekshire Way Apt 312 (27103-3088)
PHONE.................................336 782-0964
Devora Transou, *Pr*
EMP: 8 EST: 2006
SQ FT: 1,400
SALES (est): 475.84K Privately Held
Web: www.lavenderbelledesign.com
SIC: 5943 5112 2678 Stationery stores; Stationery; Stationery products

(G-13143)
DEWEY S BAKERY INC (PA)
Also Called: Salem Baking Company
3840 Kimwell Dr (27103)
PHONE.................................336 748-0230
Scott Livengood, *CEO*
Elizabeth Spencer Hood, *CFO*
EMP: 10 EST: 1930
SQ FT: 50,000
SALES (est): 24.69MM
SALES (corp-wide): 24.69MM Privately Held
Web: www.deweys.com
SIC: 2052 5461 5451 2051 Cookies and crackers; Retail bakeries; Dairy products stores; Bagels, fresh or frozen

(G-13144)
DIGITAL DESIGN & MODELING LLC
6201 Hacker Bend Ct (27103-9771)
PHONE.................................336 766-2155
Tom Mcguire, *Pr*
EMP: 9 EST: 1999
SALES (est): 1.32MM Privately Held
SIC: 3544 Special dies, tools, jigs, and fixtures

(G-13145)
DIGITS
306 S Stratford Rd (27103-1820)
PHONE.................................336 721-0209
Huong Nguyen, *Owner*
EMP: 4 EST: 2000
SALES (est): 91.42K Privately Held
SIC: 7299 2844 Tanning salon; Manicure preparations

(G-13146)
DIME EMB LLC
Also Called: Embroidery Store, The
3929 Westpoint Blvd Ste A (27103-6761)
PHONE.................................336 765-0910
William Fenimore Iii, *Brnch Mgr*
EMP: 10
SALES (corp-wide): 7.39MM Privately Held
Web: www.embstore.com
SIC: 2759 Commercial printing, nec
PA: Dime Emb Llc
10495 Olympic Dr Ste 100
Dallas TX 75220
888 739-0555

(G-13147)
DISCOUNT TIRES & AUTO REPAIR
812 Waughtown St (27107-2221)
PHONE.................................336 788-0057
Nazir Ahmed, *Prin*
EMP: 4 EST: 2008
SALES (est): 118.15K Privately Held
SIC: 5531 7538 7534 7539 Automotive tires; General automotive repair shops; Tire retreading and repair shops; Automotive repair shops, nec

(G-13148)
DIVISION 5 LLC
Also Called: Structural Steel of Carolina
1725 Vargrave St (27107-2205)
PHONE.................................336 725-0521
James Brewer, *Brnch Mgr*
EMP: 120
SALES (corp-wide): 31.95MM Privately Held
Web: www.division5inc.com
SIC: 3441 Fabricated structural metal
HQ: Division 5, Llc
2650 Strawn Rd
Winston GA 30187
770 577-0355

(G-13149)
DIZE COMPANY
Also Called: Dize Awning and Tent Company
1512 S Main St (27127-2707)
P.O. Box 937 (27102-0937)
PHONE.................................336 722-5181
TOLL FREE: 800
C R Skidmore Junior, *Pr*
Wanda Smith, *
▲ EMP: 60 EST: 1997
SQ FT: 80,000
SALES (est): 9.57MM Privately Held
Web: www.dizecompany.com
SIC: 2394 5023 3993 2591 Tarpaulins, fabric: made from purchased materials; Window furnishings; Signs and advertising specialties; Drapery hardware and window blinds and shades

(G-13150)
DNB HUMIDIFIER MFG INC
175 Dixie Club Rd (27107-9136)
PHONE.................................336 764-2076
James T Donley, *Pr*
T Craig Donley, *VP*
Nancy Donley, *Sec*
Marc Davis, *Genl Mgr*
EMP: 12 EST: 1987
SQ FT: 40,000
SALES (est): 2.21MM Privately Held
Web: www.dnbhumidifier.com
SIC: 3634 5999 Humidifiers, electric: household; Alcoholic beverage making equipment and supplies

(G-13151)
DOUGLAS BATTERY MFG CO
500 Battery Dr (27107-4137)
PHONE..................................336 650-7000
EMP: 7 **EST:** 2020
SALES (est): 911.83K **Privately Held**
SIC: 3999 Manufacturing industries, nec

(G-13152)
EAST PENN MANUFACTURING CO
Also Called: Deka Batteries & Cables
3117 Starlight Dr Ste 200 (27107-4123)
PHONE..................................336 771-1380
Michelle Allred, *Brnch Mgr*
EMP: 11
SQ FT: 12,500
SALES (corp-wide): 3.51B **Privately Held**
Web: www.eastpennmanufacturing.com
SIC: 3691 Storage batteries
PA: East Penn Manufacturing Co.
102 Deka Rd
Lyon Station PA 19536
610 682-6361

(G-13153)
EASTERN CABINET INSTALLERS INC
4735 Kester Mill Rd (27103-1212)
PHONE..................................336 774-2966
Crystal Cramer, *Owner*
EMP: 4 **EST:** 2007
SALES (est): 190.66K **Privately Held**
Web: www.acceci.com
SIC: 2434 Wood kitchen cabinets

(G-13154)
ECOLAB INC
Ecolab Kay Chemical Co
90 Piedmont Industrial Dr Ste 400
(27107-6876)
PHONE..................................336 931-2237
EMP: 30
SALES (corp-wide): 15.32B **Publicly Held**
Web: www.ecolab.com
SIC: 2841 Soap and other detergents
PA: Ecolab Inc.
1 Ecolab Pl
Saint Paul MN 55102
800 232-6522

(G-13155)
EI LLC
Also Called: Ei Solution Works
380 Knollwood St Ste 700 (27103-1862)
PHONE..................................704 857-0707
▲ **EMP:** 300
Web: www.eisolutionworks.com
SIC: 2834 2844 Pharmaceutical preparations
; Cosmetic preparations

(G-13156)
EL COMAL INC
2390 E Sprague St (27107-2441)
PHONE..................................336 788-8110
Guillarmo Mendoza, *Owner*
EMP: 6 **EST:** 1999
SALES (est): 222.24K **Privately Held**
Web: www.elcomal.com
SIC: 2099 Tortillas, fresh or refrigerated

(G-13157)
ENCORE GROUP INC
Also Called: Xpress Line
111 Cloverleaf Dr (27103-6715)
PHONE..................................336 768-7859
Lou Valente, *CFO*
EMP: 183
Web: www.encorecapital.com
SIC: 3999 3555 Novelties, bric-a-brac, and
hobby kits; Printing trades machinery
PA: The Encore Group Inc

80 E State Rt 4 Ste 290
Paramus NJ

(G-13158)
ENGINEERED ATTACHMENTS LLC
Also Called: North American Attachments
200 Kapp St (27105-2641)
PHONE..................................336 703-5266
Mike Miller, *Managing Member*
▼ **EMP:** 6 **EST:** 2002
SALES (est): 831.89K **Privately Held**
Web: www.na-attachments.com
SIC: 3531 Construction machinery

(G-13159)
ENVISION GLASS INC
3950 N Liberty St (27105-3810)
PHONE..................................336 283-9701
Craig Simmons, *Pr*
EMP: 6 **EST:** 2012
SALES (est): 1.33MM **Privately Held**
Web: www.envisionglassinc.com
SIC: 3231 3444 Doors, glass: made from
purchased glass; Door hoods, aluminum

(G-13160)
ERICSON FOODS INC
4143 Wycliff Dr (27106-2949)
PHONE..................................336 317-2199
Fred H Nelson, *Prin*
EMP: 10 **EST:** 2003
SALES (est): 300.99K **Privately Held**
SIC: 2099 Food preparations, nec

(G-13161)
EVERKEM DIVERSIFIED PDTS INC
120 Regent Dr (27103-6711)
PHONE..................................336 661-7801
Jason Lynch, *Pr*
Chin Lin, *VP*
EMP: 15 **EST:** 2011
SALES (est): 5.61MM **Privately Held**
Web: www.everkemproducts.com
SIC: 2891 3423 Adhesives; Caulking tools,
hand

(G-13162)
EVERYTHING INDUSTRIAL SUPPLY
164 N Hawthorne Rd (27104-4356)
P.O. Box 1476 (27012)
PHONE..................................743 333-2222
Austin York, *Managing Member*
EMP: 6 **EST:** 2018
SALES (est): 1.46MM **Privately Held**
SIC: 3562 3052 3496 3621 Ball and roller
bearings; V-belts, rubber; Conveyor belts;
Inverters, rotating: electrical

(G-13163)
FAIN ENTERPRISES INC
309 Deerglade Rd (27104-1860)
PHONE..................................336 724-0417
David Fain, *Pr*
Sherrie W Fain, *VP*
EMP: 6 **EST:** 1967
SQ FT: 8,000
SALES (est): 1.37MM **Privately Held**
Web: www.myfain.com
SIC: 2761 5112 Manifold business forms;
Office supplies, nec

(G-13164)
FAIRCHILD INDUSTRIAL PDTS CO (DH)
3920 Westpoint Blvd (27103-6719)
PHONE..................................336 659-3400
Alan G Paine, *Pr*
David C Velten, *
▲ **EMP:** 94 **EST:** 1955
SQ FT: 88,000

SALES (est): 20.73MM
SALES (corp-wide): 896.37MM **Privately Held**
Web: www.fairchildproducts.com
SIC: 2421 3568 Process control instruments;
Power transmission equipment, nec
HQ: Rotork Instruments Limited
Rotork House
Bath

(G-13165)
FAIRCLOTH MACHINE SHOP INC
2355 Farrington Point Dr (27107-2453)
PHONE..................................336 777-1529
Loris Pannell, *Prin*
Loris Pannell, *Pr*
David Pannell, *VP*
Judy Pannell, *Sec*
EMP: 13 **EST:** 1965
SALES (est): 3.59MM **Privately Held**
Web: www.fairclothmachine.com
SIC: 3599 Machine shop, jobbing and repair

(G-13166)
FALLS AUTOMOTIVE SERVICE INC
Also Called: Falls Automotive & Tire Svc
1548 S Main St (27127-2707)
PHONE..................................336 723-0521
Tim Falls, *Pr*
Debbie Falls, *VP*
EMP: 5 **EST:** 1958
SQ FT: 6,500
SALES (est): 176.02K **Privately Held**
Web: www.fallsautomotive.co
SIC: 7538 7534 General automotive repair
shops; Tire retreading and repair shops

(G-13167)
FIDDLIN FISH BREWING CO
Also Called: Fiddlin' Fish Brewing Company
772 N Trade St (27101-1431)
PHONE..................................336 999-8945
Stuart Barnhart, *Pr*
EMP: 15 **EST:** 2017
SALES (est): 549.33K **Privately Held**
Web: www.fiddlinfish.com
SIC: 2082 Malt beverages

(G-13168)
FIRESTOPPING PRODUCTS INC
Also Called: Flane Tech
120 Regent Dr (27103-6711)
PHONE..................................336 661-0102
Chin Chui Lin, *Pr*
Jason Lynch, *VP*
EMP: 10 **EST:** 1998
SALES (est): 300.84K **Privately Held**
Web: www.everkemproducts.com
SIC: 2891 Caulking compounds

(G-13169)
FISHEL STEEL COMPANY
760 Palmer Ln (27107-5297)
PHONE..................................336 788-2880
Roger Amstrong, *Pr*
EMP: 9 **EST:** 1930
SQ FT: 17,000
SALES (est): 2.07MM **Privately Held**
Web: www.fishelsteelws.com
SIC: 3315 4225 Wire and fabricated wire
products; General warehousing and storage

(G-13170)
FLAME TECH INC
120 Regent Dr (27103-6711)
PHONE..................................336 661-7801
Jason C Lynch, *Pr*
Chin C Lin, *VP*
EMP: 8 **EST:** 2002
SALES (est): 477.71K **Privately Held**
Web: www.everkemproducts.com

SIC: 2421 Building and structural materials,
wood

(G-13171)
FLOWERS BAKERY OF WINSTON-SALEM LLC
315 Cassell St (27107-4131)
PHONE..................................336 785-8700
▼ **EMP:** 190
SIC: 2051 2052 Cakes, bakery: except frozen
; Cookies and crackers

(G-13172)
FLOWERS BKG CO JAMESTOWN LLC
Also Called: Flowers Bakery Outlet
5610 Shattalon Dr (27105-1331)
PHONE..................................336 744-3525
Ronnie Chandler, *Mgr*
EMP: 27
SALES (corp-wide): 5.1B **Publicly Held**
SIC: 2051 Bread, cake, and related products
HQ: Flowers Baking Co. Of Jamestown, Llc
801 W Main St
Jamestown NC 27282
336 841-8840

(G-13173)
FOOTHILLS BREWING
3800 Kimwell Dr (27103-6708)
PHONE..................................336 997-9484
James Bartholomaus, *Pr*
▲ **EMP:** 7 **EST:** 2011
SALES (est): 3.15MM **Privately Held**
Web: www.foothillsbrewing.com
SIC: 2082 Ale (alcoholic beverage)

(G-13174)
FPS WIND DOWN INC
3820 N Liberty St (27105)
P.O. Box 11508 (27116)
PHONE..................................336 776-9165
Thomas W Ferrell, *CEO*
Barry J Orell, *Pr*
Ricky N Parnell, *VP*
Gordon H T Sheeran, *VP*
EMP: 11 **EST:** 2007
SQ FT: 800
SALES (est): 4.51MM **Privately Held**
Web: www.aero8.net
SIC: 3724 Aircraft engines and engine parts

(G-13175)
FREEDOM MAILING & MKTG INC
Also Called: Freedom Creative Solutions
427 W End Blvd (27101-1120)
P.O. Box 1464 (27051-1464)
PHONE..................................336 595-6300
Daniel Baird, *Pr*
EMP: 4 **EST:** 2000
SQ FT: 4,800
SALES (est): 510.71K **Privately Held**
Web:
www.freedomcreativesolutions.com
SIC: 2752 Offset printing

(G-13176)
GARDNER ASPHALT CO
Also Called: Gardner Gibson
1664 S Martin Luther King Jr Dr
(27107-1311)
PHONE..................................336 784-8924
Raymond T Hyer, *Ch Bd*
Chris Fontana, *Mgr*
EMP: 10 **EST:** 1973
SQ FT: 5,000
SALES (est): 894.26K
SALES (corp-wide): 715.86MM **Privately Held**
Web: www.gardner-gibson.com

▲ = Import ▼ = Export
◆ = Import/Export

SIC: **2951** Asphalt paving mixtures and blocks
HQ: Gardner-Gibson, Incorporated
4161 E 7th Ave
Tampa FL 33605
813 248-2101

(G-13177)
GFSI HOLDINGS LLC (HQ)
9700 Commerce Pkwy (27105)
PHONE...............................336 519-8080
Robert M Wolff, *Ch*
Robert G Shaw, *VP Fin*
Larry D Graveel, *Pr*
Michael H Gary, *VP Sls*
Jim Keaton, *Pers/VP*
EMP: 600 **EST:** 1996
SQ FT: 250,000
SALES (est): 45.03MM **Publicly Held**
SIC: **2339 2329** Sportswear, women's; Men's and boys' sportswear and athletic clothing
PA: Hanesbrands Inc.
1000 E Hanes Mill Rd
Winston Salem NC 27105

(G-13178)
GLG CORPORATION (PA)
Also Called: South Side Bargain Center
3410 Thomasville Rd (27107-5439)
Rural Route 4011 (27115)
PHONE...............................336 784-0396
Gordon L Greene, *Pr*
Edward F Greene, *Sec*
Jonathan Greene, *VP*
Evelyn Arndt Stcklhdr, *Prin*
▲ **EMP:** 16 **EST:** 1967
SQ FT: 100,000
SALES (est): 7.5MM
SALES (corp-wide): 7.5MM **Privately Held**
Web: www.southsidebargaincenter.com
SIC: **5211 1521 6162 2431** Lumber and other building materials; Single-family housing construction; Mortgage bankers and loan correspondents; Millwork

(G-13179)
GOLDING FARMS FOODS INC (PA)
Also Called: Golding Farms
6061 Gun Club Rd (27103-9727)
PHONE...............................336 766-6161
John Frostad, *CEO*
Chris Lischewski, *
Violet Golding, *
▲ **EMP:** 57 **EST:** 1955
SQ FT: 40,000
SALES (est): 84.18MM
SALES (corp-wide): 84.18MM **Privately Held**
Web: www.goldingblends.com
SIC: **2099 2035 2061** Honey, strained and bottled; Seasonings and sauces, except tomato and dry; Raw cane sugar

(G-13180)
GOODYEAR TIRE & RUBBER COMPANY
Also Called: Goodyear
130 Country Club Ln (27104-3786)
PHONE...............................336 794-0035
EMP: 4
SALES (corp-wide): 18.88B **Publicly Held**
Web: www.goodyear.com
SIC: **5531 3011** Automotive tires; Inner tubes, all types
PA: The Goodyear Tire & Rubber Company
200 Innovation Way
Akron OH 44316
330 796-2121

(G-13181)
GOSLEN PRINTING COMPANY
Also Called: Blums Almanac
3250 Healy Dr (27103-1436)
PHONE...............................336 768-5775
Mark A Goslen, *Pr*
Robyn Goslen, *Treas*
EMP: 13 **EST:** 1872
SALES (est): 532.2K **Privately Held**
Web: www.allegramarketingprint.com
SIC: **2752 2732** Offset printing; Book printing

(G-13182)
GRANDMAS SUGAR SHACK
209 S Gordon Dr (27104-3711)
PHONE...............................336 760-8822
EMP: 4 **EST:** 2011
SALES (est): 169.53K **Privately Held**
SIC: **2052** Cookies and crackers

(G-13183)
GRAPHIC PACKAGING INTL LLC
320 W Hanes Mill Rd (27105-9626)
PHONE...............................336 744-1222
James Kleinfield, *Genl Mgr*
EMP: 53
Web: www.americraft.com
SIC: **2657** Folding paperboard boxes
HQ: Graphic Packaging International, Llc
1500 Rvredge Pkwy Ste 100
Atlanta GA 30328

(G-13184)
GRAPHIC PRODUCTIONS INC
Also Called: Express Graphics
301 N Main St Ste 2104 (27101-3836)
PHONE...............................336 765-9335
Mitchell Termotto, *CEO*
Scott Dahlin, *Sec*
EMP: 4 **EST:** 1987
SQ FT: 8,500
SALES (est): 1.13MM **Privately Held**
Web: www.exgraphics.com
SIC: **3993** Signs and advertising specialties

(G-13185)
GRINS ENTERPRISES LLC
Also Called: Grins Beverages
1051 Arbor Rd (27104-1101)
PHONE...............................336 831-0534
EMP: 5 **EST:** 2011
SALES (est): 214K **Privately Held**
Web: www.grinsbev.com
SIC: **2086** Carbonated beverages, nonalcoholic: pkged. in cans, bottles

(G-13186)
HANES COMPANIES INC (HQ)
Also Called: Hanes Industries
815 Buxton St (27101-1310)
P.O. Box 202 (27102-0202)
PHONE...............................336 747-1600
Jerry W Greene Junior, *Pr*
Michael S Walters, *
Earnest Jett, *
Kenneth W Purser, *
Charles P Hutchins, *
◆ **EMP:** 160 **EST:** 1986
SQ FT: 709,921
SALES (est): 465.07MM
SALES (corp-wide): 5.15B **Publicly Held**
Web: www.hanescompanies.com
SIC: **2262 2261 2297** Dyeing: manmade fiber and silk broadwoven fabrics; Dyeing cotton broadwoven fabrics; Nonwoven fabrics
PA: Leggett & Platt, Incorporated
1 Leggett Rd
Carthage MO 64836
417 358-8131

(G-13187)
HANESBRANDS EXPORT CANADA LLC
1000 E Hanes Mill Rd (27105-1383)
PHONE...............................336 519-8080
Richard Noll, *CEO*
▼ **EMP:** 8 **EST:** 2013
SALES (est): 4.25MM **Publicly Held**
Web: ir.hanesbrands.com
SIC: **2389** Men's miscellaneous accessories
PA: Hanesbrands Inc.
1000 E Hanes Mill Rd
Winston Salem NC 27105

(G-13188)
HANESBRANDS INC (PA)
Also Called: Hanes
1000 E Hanes Mill Rd (27105)
PHONE...............................336 519-8080
Stephen B Bratspies, *CEO*
William S Simon, *
M Scott Lewis, *CAO*
Kristin L Oliver, *Chief Human Resources Officer Interim CAO*
Scott A Pleiman, *Ex VP*
EMP: 1800 **EST:** 1901
SQ FT: 470,000
SALES (est): 3.51B **Publicly Held**
Web: www.hanes.com
SIC: **2253 2322 2342 2341** T-shirts and tops, knit; Underwear, men's and boys': made from purchased materials; Bras, girdles, and allied garments; Panties: women's, misses', children's, and infants'

(G-13189)
HARCO PRINTING INCORPORATED
130 Back Forty Dr (27127-7404)
PHONE...............................336 771-0234
Ricky Corn, *Pr*
Lester Hargett, *Sec*
EMP: 4 **EST:** 1998
SALES (est): 218.06K **Privately Held**
Web: www.harcoprinting.com
SIC: **2752** Offset printing

(G-13190)
HARI KRUPA OIL AND GAS LLC
6031 Claudias Ln Apt 201 (27103-7178)
PHONE...............................860 805-1704
Ripal Patel, *Owner*
EMP: 4 **EST:** 2017
SALES (est): 1.27MM **Privately Held**
SIC: **1389** Oil and gas field services, nec

(G-13191)
HARTLEY READY MIX CON MFG INC (PA)
3510 Rothrock St (27107-5224)
P.O. Box 1719 (27374-1719)
PHONE...............................336 788-3928
Chad Hartley, *Pr*
EMP: 18 **EST:** 1950
SQ FT: 1,500
SALES (est): 6.36MM
SALES (corp-wide): 6.36MM **Privately Held**
Web: www.hartleyreadymix.com
SIC: **3273** Ready-mixed concrete

(G-13192)
HAUSER HVAC INSTALLATION
480 S Peace Haven Rd (27103-5973)
PHONE...............................336 416-2173
Darrell Hauser, *Owner*
EMP: 5 **EST:** 2015
SALES (est): 95.76K **Privately Held**
SIC: **1711 3272** Plumbing, heating, air-conditioning; Chimney caps, concrete

(G-13193)
HBI WH MINORITY HOLDINGS LLC
1000 E Hanes Mill Rd (27105-1384)
PHONE...............................336 519-8080
EMP: 4 **EST:** 2022
SALES (est): 1.75MM **Publicly Held**
SIC: **2253 2342** T-shirts and tops, knit; Bras, girdles, and allied garments
PA: Hanesbrands Inc.
1000 E Hanes Mill Rd
Winston Salem NC 27105

(G-13194)
HEARN GRAPHIC FINISHING INC
209 Regent Dr (27103-6718)
PHONE...............................336 760-1467
John Mullis, *Pr*
John C Mullis, *Pr*
Jon Lambertus, *Sec*
EMP: 6 **EST:** 1930
SQ FT: 10,000
SALES (est): 477.35K **Privately Held**
Web: www.hearngraphicfinishing.com
SIC: **2796 3554** Engraving on copper, steel, wood, or rubber: printing plates; Folding machines, paper

(G-13195)
HEAVENLY CHEESECAKES
11040 Old Us Highway 52 (27107-9840)
PHONE...............................336 577-9390
Becky Brown, *Owner*
EMP: 8 **EST:** 1999
SALES (est): 424.55K **Privately Held**
SIC: **2051** Cakes, bakery: except frozen

(G-13196)
HERBALIFE MANUFACTURING LLC
3200 Temple School Rd (27107-3628)
PHONE...............................336 970-6400
EMP: 8
Web: www.herbalife.com
SIC: **2087 2023** Beverage bases, concentrates, syrups, powders and mixes; Dietary supplements, dairy and non-dairy based
HQ: Herbalife Manufacturing Llc
800 W Olympic Blvd Ste 40
Los Angeles CA 90015

(G-13197)
HHH TEMPERING RESOURCES INC
5901 Gun Club Rd (27103-9732)
PHONE...............................336 201-5396
Mike Synon, *Pr*
EMP: 10 **EST:** 2019
SALES (est): 2.43MM
SALES (corp-wide): 30.43MM **Privately Held**
Web: www.hhhglassequipment.com
SIC: **3398** Tempering of metal
PA: Salem Fabrication Technologies Group, Inc.
5901 Gun Club Rd
Winston Salem NC 27103
800 234-1982

(G-13198)
HILLSHIRE BRANDS COMPANY
Also Called: Sara Lee
470 W Hanes Mill Rd Frnt Frnt (27105-9102)
P.O. Box 2760 (27102-2760)
PHONE...............................336 519-8080
Mike Gannaway, *Mgr*
EMP: 6
SALES (corp-wide): 53.31B **Publicly Held**
Web: www.tysonfoods.com
SIC: **2252 2254 2253** Hosiery, nec; Underwear, knit; Knit outerwear mills
HQ: The Hillshire Brands Company

400 S Jefferson St Ste 1n
Chicago IL 60607
312 614-6000

(G-13199)
HOH CORPORATION
Also Called: Carolina Pumps Instrumentation
1701 Vargrave St (27107-2205)
PHONE..............................336 723-9274
David A Bryant, *Pr*
▼ **EMP:** 10 **EST:** 1991
SALES (est): 2.21MM **Privately Held**
Web: www.hohcorp.com
SIC: 4953 3589 Nonhazardous waste
disposal sites; Water treatment equipment,
industrial

(G-13200)
HOOD CONTAINER CORPORATION
555 Aureole St (27107-3201)
PHONE..............................336 784-0445
Greg Hall, *Brnch Mgr*
EMP: 1200
Web: www.hoodcontainer.com
SIC: 3086 Packaging and shipping
materials, foamed plastics
HQ: Hood Container Corporation
2100 Rvredge Pkwy Ste 650
Atlanta GA 30328
855 605-6317

(G-13201)
HPFABRICS INC
Also Called: HP Textile
3821 Kimwell Dr (27103-6707)
PHONE..............................336 231-0278
Todd Lane, *Pr*
EMP: 5 **EST:** 2017
SALES (est): 462.32K **Privately Held**
SIC: 2211 2231 Upholstery, tapestry and
wall coverings: cotton; Felts, blanketing and
upholstery fabrics: wool

(G-13202)
HUGHES PRODUCTS CO INC
241 Emily Ann Dr (27107-8687)
P.O. Box 606 (27373-0606)
PHONE..............................336 769-3788
Jeffrey T Hughes, *Pr*
Lori Hughes, *Sec*
EMP: 8 **EST:** 1990
SQ FT: 11,475
SALES (est): 441.25K **Privately Held**
Web: www.hughesproductsco.com
SIC: 3949 Hunting equipment

(G-13203)
I-LUMENATE LLC
353 Jonestown Rd (27104-4620)
PHONE..............................336 448-0356
EMP: 4 **EST:** 2013
SALES (est): 256K **Privately Held**
Web: www.nocqua.com
SIC: 3949 Sporting and athletic goods, nec

(G-13204)
IN STYLE KITCHEN CABINETRY
8570 N Nc Highway 109 (27107-8400)
PHONE..............................336 769-9605
Harold Nash, *Prin*
EMP: 4 **EST:** 2011
SALES (est): 249.09K **Privately Held**
Web: www.instlyekitchens.com
SIC: 2434 Wood kitchen cabinets

(G-13205)
INDEPENDENCE PRINTING
130 Back Forty Dr (27127-7404)
PHONE..............................336 771-0234
Ricky Corn, *Owner*

EMP: 4 **EST:** 1993
SQ FT: 1,000
SALES (est): 211.01K **Privately Held**
Web: www.allegramarketingprint.com
SIC: 2752 Offset printing

(G-13206)
INDUSTRIAL CONTROL PANELS INC
Also Called: ICP
152 Capp St Ste A (27105)
PHONE..............................336 661-3037
Scott Inscore, *Pr*
Robert W Worth Junior, *VP*
EMP: 8 **EST:** 1995
SQ FT: 5,160
SALES (est): 785.79K **Privately Held**
Web: www.icppanelshop.com
SIC: 3613 Control panels, electric

(G-13207)
INDUSTRIAL LUBRICANTS INC
Also Called: Pro-Blend Chemical Co
1110 Fairchild Rd (27105-4528)
P.O. Box 17171 (27116-7171)
PHONE..............................336 767-0013
F Gaither Jenkins, *Pr*
EMP: 8 **EST:** 1981
SQ FT: 23,000
SALES (est): 440.71K **Privately Held**
SIC: 2869 Industrial organic chemicals, nec

(G-13208)
INGREDION INCORPORATED
Corn Prdcts-Wnston Salem Plant
4501 Overdale Rd (27107-6145)
P.O. Box 12939 (27117-2939)
PHONE..............................336 785-0100
Tony Kantor, *Mgr*
EMP: 100
SALES (corp-wide): 7.43B **Publicly Held**
Web: www.ingredion.com
SIC: 2046 Corn sugars and syrups
PA: Ingredion Incorporated
5 Westbrook Corporate Ctr
Westchester IL 60154
708 551-2600

(G-13209)
INK WELL
Also Called: Ink Well
1650 Hutton St (27127-3704)
PHONE..............................336 727-9750
Berry Walker, *Owner*
EMP: 8 **EST:** 1996
SALES (est): 462.97K **Privately Held**
Web: www.theinkwellusa.com
SIC: 2752 Offset printing

(G-13210)
INTERNATIONAL MCHY SLS INC
Also Called: IMS
8065 N Point Blvd Ste J (27106-3287)
P.O. Box 11276 (27116-1276)
PHONE..............................336 759-9548
Nicholas Sear, *Pr*
▲ **EMP:** 6 **EST:** 1977
SQ FT: 2,200
SALES (est): 980.59K **Privately Held**
SIC: 3552 Textile machinery

(G-13211)
J & P WOOD WORKS INC
Also Called: Watson Wood Works
780 Megahertz Dr (27107-4594)
PHONE..............................336 788-1881
John Watson, *Pr*
Parker Watson, *
EMP: 30 **EST:** 1984
SQ FT: 43,000
SALES (est): 4.84MM **Privately Held**
Web: www.watsonwood.com

SIC: 2431 Millwork

(G-13212)
J C ENTERPRISES
936 Washington Ave (27101-5753)
P.O. Box 11483 (27116-1483)
PHONE..............................336 986-1688
Rob Wolfe, *Prin*
EMP: 5 **EST:** 2016
SALES (est): 81.4K **Privately Held**
SIC: 2672 Paper; coated and laminated, nec

(G-13213)
J W HARRIS CO INC
Also Called: Harris Products Group, The
1690 Lowery St (27101-5603)
PHONE..............................336 831-8601
EMP: 7
SALES (corp-wide): 4.01B **Publicly Held**
Web: www.harrisproductsgroup.com
SIC: 3356 3548 2899 Solder: wire, bar, acid
core, and rosin core; Welding wire, bare
and coated; Fluxes: brazing, soldering,
galvanizing, and welding
HQ: J. W. Harris Co., Inc.
4501 Quality Pl
Mason OH 45040
513 754-2000

(G-13214)
J6 & COMPANY LLC
5077 Bismark St (27105-3148)
PHONE..............................336 997-4497
Jocelyn Dunston, *Managing Member*
EMP: 14 **EST:** 2016
SALES (est): 162.78K **Privately Held**
SIC: 7389 1389 Business Activities at Non-
Commercial Site; Construction, repair, and
dismantling services

(G-13215)
JABEC ENTERPRISE INC (PA)
5224 Mountain View Rd (27104-5116)
PHONE..............................336 655-8441
Jeffrey Trinh, *Prin*
EMP: 5 **EST:** 2015
SALES (est): 3.24MM
SALES (corp-wide): 3.24MM **Privately Held**
Web: www.stormguardrc.com
SIC: 3732 Boatbuilding and repairing

(G-13216)
JENNIFER MOWRER
Also Called: Painpathways Magazine
150 Kimel Park Dr Ste 100 (27103-6992)
PHONE..............................336 714-6462
Jennifer Mowrer, *Owner*
EMP: 6 **EST:** 2013
SALES (est): 241.55K **Privately Held**
SIC: 2721 7389 Magazines: publishing only,
not printed on site; Business Activities at
Non-Commercial Site

(G-13217)
JKS MOTORSPORTS INC (PA)
Also Called: JKS Incorporated
876 N Liberty St (27101-3042)
P.O. Box 450 (27374-0450)
PHONE..............................336 722-4129
Christy Cox Spencer, *Pr*
Will Spencer, *Pr*
EMP: 8 **EST:** 1984
SQ FT: 21,000
SALES (est): 2.24MM
SALES (corp-wide): 2.24MM **Privately Held**
Web: www.jksincorporated.com

SIC: 3993 7389 3577 7336 Signs and
advertising specialties; Sign painting and
lettering shop; Graphic displays, except
graphic terminals; Graphic arts and related
design

(G-13218)
JON KUHN INC
701 N Liberty St (27101-3001)
P.O. Box 20849 (27120-0849)
PHONE..............................336 722-2369
Jonathan D Kuhn, *Pr*
Sharon Kuhn, *
EMP: 30 **EST:** 1978
SQ FT: 9,000
SALES (est): 973.13K **Privately Held**
Web: www.kuhnstudio.com
SIC: 3231 Ornamental glass: cut, engraved
or otherwise decorated

(G-13219)
JOSEPH HALKER
Also Called: Al-Rite Manufacturing
481 Shady Grove Church Rd (27107-9665)
PHONE..............................336 769-4734
Joseph Halker, *Owner*
EMP: 4 **EST:** 1979
SQ FT: 4,800
SALES (est): 161.63K **Privately Held**
SIC: 2512 Couches, sofas, and davenports:
upholstered on wood frames

(G-13220)
JOSTENS INC
Also Called: Jostens
2505 Empire Dr (27103-6709)
PHONE..............................336 765-0070
Ron Sisk, *Brnch Mgr*
EMP: 350
SQ FT: 123,700
SALES (corp-wide): 250.27MM **Privately Held**
Web: www.jostens.com
SIC: 3911 Rings, finger: precious metal
HQ: Jostens, Inc.
7760 France Ave S Ste 400
Minneapolis MN 55435
952 830-3300

(G-13221)
JUAN PINO SIGNS INC
2041 Gumtree Rd (27107-9444)
PHONE..............................336 764-4422
Juan Pino, *Pr*
EMP: 4 **EST:** 1978
SQ FT: 5,000
SALES (est): 142.35K **Privately Held**
Web: www.juanpinosignsinc.com
SIC: 3993 Signs, not made in custom sign
painting shops

(G-13222)
KABA ILCO CORP
Also Called: Kaba Access Control
2941 Indiana Ave (27105-4425)
PHONE..............................336 725-1331
Michael Kincaid, *Mgr*
EMP: 325
Web: www.ilco.us
SIC: 3499 3429 Locks, safe and vault: metal;
Hardware, nec
HQ: Kaba Ilco Corp.
400 Jeffreys Rd
Rocky Mount NC 27804
252 446-3321

(G-13223)
KEIGER INC
Also Called: Keiger Printing Direct
3735 Kimwell Dr (27103-6705)
PHONE..............................336 760-0099

Louis Crockett, *Pr*
Julian Crockett, *
Barbara Crockett, *
Scott Crockett, *
▲ **EMP:** 34 **EST:** 1943
SQ FT: 32,250
SALES (est): 825.94K **Privately Held**
Web: www.salem-one.com
SIC: 2752 2791 2789 2759 Offset printing; Typesetting; Bookbinding and related work; Commercial printing, nec

(G-13224)
KENDALL JOHNSON CUSTOMS INC
Also Called: Kjc
3645 Indiana Ave (27105-3404)
P.O. Box 550 (27019-0550)
PHONE.............................336 748-3833
Kendall Johnson, *Pr*
Mellissa Johnson, *VP*
Zach Johnson, *Treas*
EMP: 5 **EST:** 2002
SQ FT: 8,000
SALES (est): 202.55K **Privately Held**
Web: www.kendalljohnsoncustoms.com
SIC: 3751 Motorcycles, bicycles and parts

(G-13225)
KERANETICS LLC
200 E 1st St Box 4 (27101-4165)
PHONE.............................336 725-0621
Luke Burnett, *CEO*
Rick Blank, *Ch Bd*
EMP: 6 **EST:** 2008
SALES (est): 2.31MM **Privately Held**
Web: www.keranetics.com
SIC: 2834 2836 Pharmaceutical preparations ; Biological products, except diagnostic

(G-13226)
KRISPY KREME DOUGHNUT CORP
Also Called: Krispy Kreme
259 S Stratford Rd (27103-1817)
PHONE.............................336 733-3780
Kevin Hoeing, *Mgr*
EMP: 29
SQ FT: 4,137
SALES (corp-wide): 1.69B **Publicly Held**
Web: www.krispykreme.com
SIC: 5461 2051 Doughnuts; Doughnuts, except frozen
HQ: Krispy Kreme Doughnut Corp
2116 Hawkins St Ste 102
Charlotte NC 28203
980 270-7117

(G-13227)
KRISPY KREME DOUGHNUT CORP
3190 Centre Park Blvd (27107-4574)
P.O. Box B (27102)
PHONE.............................336 726-8908
Patrick Cepson, *Brnch Mgr*
EMP: 27
SQ FT: 109,113
SALES (corp-wide): 1.69B **Publicly Held**
Web: www.krispykreme.com
SIC: 5461 3556 Doughnuts; Food products machinery
HQ: Krispy Kreme Doughnut Corp
2116 Hawkins St Ste 102
Charlotte NC 28203
980 270-7117

(G-13228)
KRISPY KREME DOUGHNUTS INC (HQ)
Also Called: Krispy Kreme
370 Knollwood St (27103-1835)
P.O. Box 83 (27102-0083)
PHONE.............................336 725-2981
G Price Cooper, *Ex VP*

◆ **EMP:** 200 **EST:** 1937
SQ FT: 86,000
SALES (est): 1.3B
SALES (corp-wide): 1.69B **Publicly Held**
Web: www.krispykreme.com
SIC: 5461 5149 2051 Doughnuts; Bakery products; Doughnuts, except frozen
PA: Krispy Kreme, Inc.
2116 Hawkins St
Charlotte NC 28203
800 457-4779

(G-13229)
LA TORTILLERIA LLC
Also Called: La Tortilleria
2900 Lowery St (27101)
PHONE.............................336 773-0010
Daniel Calhoun, *Pr*
Nathaniel Calhoun, *Stockholder*
J Phillip Calhoun, *Stockholder*
▲ **EMP:** 190 **EST:** 1995
SQ FT: 100,000
SALES (est): 46.72MM **Privately Held**
Web: www.purplecrow.com
SIC: 2099 5141 Tortillas, fresh or refrigerated ; Food brokers

(G-13230)
LABEL PRINTING SYSTEMS INC
Also Called: Lps Tag & Label
3937 Westpoint Blvd (27103-6721)
PHONE.............................336 760-3271
Richard Ebert, *Ch*
Greg Ebert, *Pr*
EMP: 20 **EST:** 1990
SQ FT: 25,000
SALES (est): 4.62MM **Privately Held**
Web: www.lpslabels.net
SIC: 2679 2759 Labels, paper: made from purchased material; Commercial printing, nec

(G-13231)
LATINO COMMUNICATIONS INC (PA)
Also Called: Que Pasa
3067 Waughtown St (27107-1634)
P.O. Box 12876 (27117-2876)
PHONE.............................336 714-2823
Jose Isasi, *Pr*
Flora Isasi, *
EMP: 55 **EST:** 1993
SALES (est): 1.2MM
SALES (corp-wide): 1.2MM **Privately Held**
Web: www.quepasamedia.com
SIC: 4832 2711 Radio broadcasting stations; Newspapers

(G-13232)
LEGACY VULCAN LLC
Mideast Division
4401 N Patterson Ave (27105-1638)
P.O. Box 4239 (27115-4239)
PHONE.............................336 767-0911
Gray Kimel Junior, *Pr*
EMP: 52
Web: www.vulcanmaterials.com
SIC: 3273 Ready-mixed concrete
HQ: Legacy Vulcan, Llc
1200 Urban Center Dr
Birmingham AL 35242
205 298-3000

(G-13233)
LEONARD BLOCK COMPANY
2390 Midway School Rd (27107-8701)
PHONE.............................336 764-0607
B Leonard, *Pr*
EMP: 9 **EST:** 1981
SQ FT: 5,000
SALES (est): 1.56MM **Privately Held**
Web: www.leonardblockcompany.com

SIC: 3271 5211 Blocks, concrete or cinder: standard; Masonry materials and supplies

(G-13234)
LEXINGTON ROAD PROPERTIES INC
500 Battery Dr (27107-4137)
PHONE.............................336 650-7209
▲ **EMP:** 125
SIC: 3691 3692 Storage batteries; Primary batteries, dry and wet

(G-13235)
LINOR TECHNOLOGY INC
4741 S Main St (27127-7427)
PHONE.............................336 485-6199
Gary Nalven, *CEO*
EMP: 15 **EST:** 2012
SALES (est): 5.95MM **Privately Held**
Web: www.linortek.com
SIC: 5084 3625 3823 3651 Instruments and control equipment; Relays and industrial controls; Data loggers, industrial process type; Audio electronic systems

(G-13236)
LIONSTAR TRANSPORT LLC
2597 Landmark Dr (27103-6717)
PHONE.............................336 448-0166
EMP: 4
SALES (est): 182.43K **Privately Held**
SIC: 3799 Transportation equipment, nec

(G-13237)
LLFLEX LLC
Also Called: Oracle Packaging
220 Polo Rd (27105-3441)
PHONE.............................336 777-5000
EMP: 120
Web: www.llflex.com
SIC: 2672 Paper; coated and laminated, nec
HQ: Llflex, Llc
1225 W Burnett Ave
Louisville KY 40210
502 636-8400

(G-13238)
LORILLARD LLC (DH)
401 N Main St (27101-3804)
PHONE.............................336 741-2000
Murray S Kessler, *Pr*
David H Taylor, *Ex VP*
Ronald S Milstein, *Ex VP*
Anthony B Petitt, *CAO*
EMP: 56 **EST:** 1997
SALES (est): 3.75MM **Privately Held**
Web: www.rjrt.com
SIC: 2111 Cigarettes
HQ: Reynolds American Inc.
401 N Main St
Winston Salem NC 27101
336 741-2000

(G-13239)
LOW COUNTRY STEEL SC LLC (PA)
2529 Viceroy Dr (27103-6713)
PHONE.............................336 283-9611
Bradley Mcmurray, *Pr*
EMP: 32 **EST:** 2011
SALES (est): 1.29MM
SALES (corp-wide): 1.29MM **Privately Held**
SIC: 3449 Bars, concrete reinforcing: fabricated steel

(G-13240)
LULULEMON
312 S Stratford Rd (27103-1820)
PHONE.............................336 723-3002
EMP: 4 **EST:** 1998
SALES (est): 42.55K **Privately Held**

SIC: 2389 Apparel and accessories, nec

(G-13241)
LYNDON STEEL COMPANY LLC (DH)
1947 Union Cross Rd (27107-6448)
PHONE.............................336 785-0848
David R Morgan, *Pr*
Sam Winters, *
Mike Carcieri, *
EMP: 150 **EST:** 1977
SQ FT: 53,000
SALES (est): 48.94MM
SALES (corp-wide): 586.31MM **Privately Held**
Web: www.lyndonsteel.com
SIC: 3441 Fabricated structural metal
HQ: Fabsouth Llc
721 Ne 44th St
Fort Lauderdale FL 33334
954 938-5800

(G-13242)
M T N OF PINELLAS INC
Also Called: Gallery of Cabinets, The
135 Crowne Chase Dr Apt 16 (27104-3580)
PHONE.............................727 823-1650
M Thomas Nelson, *Pr*
EMP: 6 **EST:** 1982
SQ FT: 2,390
SALES (est): 471.05K **Privately Held**
SIC: 1799 2521 Kitchen and bathroom remodeling; Cabinets, office: wood

(G-13243)
MAPLEWOOD IMAGING CTR
3155 Maplewood Ave (27103-3903)
PHONE.............................336 397-6000
Stephen Bower, *Prin*
EMP: 5 **EST:** 2002
SALES (est): 2.14MM **Privately Held**
SIC: 3861 Film, sensitized motion picture, X-ray, still camera, etc.

(G-13244)
MARANZ INC
Also Called: Archer Advanced Rbr Components
2860 Lowery St (27101-6128)
PHONE.............................336 996-7776
George Halages, *Pr*
George Halages, *Pr*
Alyssa White, *
▲ **EMP:** 85 **EST:** 1997
SQ FT: 22,500
SALES (est): 16.95MM **Privately Held**
Web: www.archerseal.com
SIC: 3069 Rubber automotive products

(G-13245)
MARTIN OBRIEN CABINETMAKER
1940 Brantley St (27103-3712)
PHONE.............................336 773-1334
Martin Obrien, *Owner*
EMP: 4 **EST:** 2010
SALES (est): 190.25K **Privately Held**
Web: www.martinobriencabinetmaker.com
SIC: 2511 Wood household furniture

(G-13246)
MAYO RESOURCES INC
2860 Lowery St (27101-6128)
PHONE.............................336 996-7776
EMP: 50
SALES (est): 3.67MM **Privately Held**
SIC: 5085 3053 Rubber goods, mechanical; Gaskets; packing and sealing devices

(G-13247)
MCDOWELLS MCH FABRICATION INC
2312a Cragmore Rd (27107-2458)
P.O. Box 12542 (27117-2542)
PHONE...............................336 720-9944
Rick Mcdowell, *Pr*
EMP: 5 **EST:** 1998
SALES (est): 1.18MM **Privately Held**
Web: www.mmfsteel.com
SIC: 3599 Machine shop, jobbing and repair

(G-13248)
MEL SCHLESINGER
1001 S Marshall St Ste 290 (27101-5852)
PHONE...............................336 525-6357
Mel Schlesinger, *Prin*
EMP: 5 **EST:** 2015
SALES (est): 55.05K **Privately Held**
Web: melschlesinger.medium.com
SIC: 2741 Miscellaneous publishing

(G-13249)
MG FOODS INC
3195 Centre Park Blvd (27107-4575)
PHONE...............................336 724-6327
Matthew Gallins, *Prin*
EMP: 11 **EST:** 2008
SALES (est): 299.57K **Privately Held**
SIC: 2099 Food preparations, nec

(G-13250)
MHS LTD
Also Called: Wear-Flex Slings
4961 Home Rd Ste A (27106-2802)
PHONE...............................336 767-2641
Earl Johnson, *Brnch Mgr*
EMP: 7
SALES (corp-wide): 2.58MM **Privately Held**
Web: www.wear-flex.com
SIC: 2298 Cordage and twine
PA: Mhs Ltd.
    4959 Home Rd
    Winston Salem NC 27106
    336 767-2641

(G-13251)
MHS LTD (PA)
Also Called: Wear-Flex Slings
4959 Home Rd (27106-2802)
P.O. Box 2379 (27021-2379)
PHONE...............................336 767-2641
Steve Schroeder, *Pr*
Steve Stewart, *Sec*
EMP: 10 **EST:** 1958
SQ FT: 6,000
SALES (est): 2.58MM
SALES (corp-wide): 2.58MM **Privately Held**
Web: www.wear-flex.com
SIC: 2298 Nets, seines, slings and insulator pads

(G-13252)
MICROFINE INC
Also Called: Poochpad Products
100 Cloverleaf Dr (27103-6714)
P.O. Box 516 (27040-0516)
PHONE...............................336 768-1480
John Martin, *Pr*
◆ **EMP:** 5 **EST:** 2000
SALES (est): 1.33MM **Privately Held**
Web: www.poochpad.com
SIC: 3999 5199 Pet supplies; Pet supplies

(G-13253)
MID-ATLANTIC CONCRETE PDTS INC
2460 Armstrong Dr (27103-6809)
PHONE...............................336 774-6544

Kenneth Armistead, *Pr*
EMP: 7 **EST:** 2005
SALES (est): 2.44MM **Privately Held**
Web: www.midatlanticcp.com
SIC: 3272 Concrete products, nec

(G-13254)
MINAS EQUITY PARTNERS LLC
2710 Boulder Park Ct (27101-4776)
PHONE...............................336 724-5152
EMP: 15 **EST:** 2020
SALES (est): 1.07MM **Privately Held**
SIC: 3599 Machine shop, jobbing and repair

(G-13255)
MINDFULLY MADE USA LLC
Also Called: Mindfully Made Brands
1976 Runnymede Rd (27104-3112)
PHONE...............................336 701-0377
Sonia Schilling, *CEO*
Michael Touby, *
EMP: 25 **EST:** 2017
SALES (est): 1.02MM **Privately Held**
Web: www.mariesharps.info
SIC: 2033 5137 5149 5199 Canned fruits and specialties; Hosiery: women's, children's, and infants'; Condiments; Pet supplies

(G-13256)
MOCK TIRE & AUTOMOTIVE INC
834 S Stratford Rd (27103-3202)
PHONE...............................336 774-0081
Frank Ward, *Mgr*
EMP: 36
SALES (corp-wide): 6.96MM **Privately Held**
Web: www.mockberothtire.com
SIC: 5531 7539 7534 Automotive tires; Auto front end repair; Tire repair shop
PA: Mock Tire & Automotive Inc
    4752 Country Club Rd
    Winston Salem NC 27104
    336 768-1010

(G-13257)
MOCK TIRE & AUTOMOTIVE INC (PA)
4752 Country Club Rd (27104-3599)
PHONE...............................336 768-1010
Carey W Mock, *VP*
Cecil G Mock, *
▲ **EMP:** 40 **EST:** 1973
SQ FT: 7,500
SALES (est): 6.96MM
SALES (corp-wide): 6.96MM **Privately Held**
Web: www.mockberothtire.com
SIC: 5531 7539 7534 Automotive tires; Auto front end repair; Tire repair shop

(G-13258)
MODERN MACHINE AND METAL FABRICATORS INC
3201 Centre Park Blvd (27107-4570)
PHONE...............................336 993-4808
EMP: 100 **EST:** 1966
SALES (est): 18.21MM **Privately Held**
SIC: 3444 3599 7692 Sheet metalwork; Machine shop, jobbing and repair; Welding repair

(G-13259)
MODORAL BRANDS INC
Also Called: Zonnic
401 N Main St (27101-3804)
P.O. Box 3000 (27102-3000)
PHONE...............................336 741-7230
Tommy Payne, *Pr*
Nils Siegbahn, *Prin*
EMP: 5 **EST:** 2010
SALES (est): 2.82MM **Privately Held**

Web: www.reynoldsamerican.com
SIC: 5912 8093 2111 2121 Drug stores; Drug clinic, outpatient; Cigarettes; Cigars
HQ: Reynolds American Inc.
    401 N Main St
    Winston Salem NC 27101
    336 741-2000

(G-13260)
MOE JT ENTERPRISES INC
Also Called: Paul Davis Restoration
130 Back Forty Dr (27127-7404)
PHONE...............................423 512-1427
Jeffrey Thomas Moe, *CEO*
EMP: 16 **EST:** 2022
SALES (est): 2.62MM **Privately Held**
Web: www.pauldavis.com
SIC: 2899 Water treating compounds

(G-13261)
MONUMENTAL CONTRACTORS INC
❂
4111 Field Crossing Dr (27107-6934)
PHONE...............................762 352-0564
Meggan Jones, *CEO*
EMP: 15 **EST:** 2023
SALES (est): 1.65MM **Privately Held**
SIC: 1389 Construction, repair, and dismantling services

(G-13262)
MOTSINGER BLOCK PLANT INC
199 Disher Rd (27107-8872)
PHONE...............................336 764-0350
F Smith Motsinger, *Pr*
Neal Motsinger, *VP*
EMP: 8 **EST:** 1953
SQ FT: 10,000
SALES (est): 1.14MM **Privately Held**
SIC: 3271 5032 Blocks, concrete or cinder: standard; Masons' materials

(G-13263)
NEW DAIRY OPCO LLC
Also Called: Dairy Fresh
800 E 21st St (27105-5354)
PHONE...............................336 725-8141
Larry Hughes, *Prin*
EMP: 69
SALES (corp-wide): 510.48MM **Privately Held**
SIC: 2026 Fluid milk
PA: New Dairy Opco, Llc
    12400 Coit Rd Ste 200
    Dallas TX 75251
    214 258-1200

(G-13264)
NEW VISION INVESTMENTS INC
4310 Enterprise Dr Ste I (27106-3260)
PHONE...............................336 757-1120
Chad Trater, *Pr*
Billie Litwin, *VP*
EMP: 7 **EST:** 2001
SALES (est): 446.16K **Privately Held**
SIC: 3827 Optical instruments and lenses

(G-13265)
NONE
1411 Plaza West Rd (27103-1482)
PHONE...............................336 408-6008
EMP: 4 **EST:** 2019
SALES (est): 123.22K **Privately Held**
Web: www.sanofi.com
SIC: 2834 Pharmaceutical preparations

(G-13266)
NORTHSTAR TRAVEL MEDIA
Also Called: Weissmann Travel Reports
331 High St (27101-5234)

PHONE...............................336 714-3328
David C Cox, *CEO*
Carolyn Wall, *
Arnie Weissmann, *
Frederick Moses, *
William Busch Junior, *Sec*
EMP: 23 **EST:** 1986
SALES (est): 648.87K **Privately Held**
Web: www.northstartravelgroup.com
SIC: 2721 Trade journals: publishing only, not printed on site

(G-13267)
NOVEX INNOVATIONS LLC
101 N Chestnut St Ste 303 (27101-4046)
PHONE...............................336 231-6693
EMP: 6 **EST:** 2014
SQ FT: 8,200
SALES (est): 4.58MM **Privately Held**
Web: www.novexinnovations.com
SIC: 3842 8731 Implants, surgical; Biotechnical research, commercial

(G-13268)
ODIGIA INC
300 S Liberty St Ste 210 (27101-5201)
PHONE...............................336 462-8056
Joshua Moe, *Pr*
EMP: 5 **EST:** 2010
SALES (est): 460.18K **Privately Held**
Web: www.odigia.com
SIC: 7372 Educational computer software

(G-13269)
OLD SALEM INCORPORATED
Also Called: Old Salem Town Merchant
730 S Poplar St (27101-5834)
P.O. Box 10400 (27108)
PHONE...............................336 721-7305
Skeebo Loveren, *Brnch Mgr*
EMP: 6
SALES (corp-wide): 7.06MM **Privately Held**
Web: www.oldsalem.org
SIC: 5961 2052 2051 2022 Catalog and mail-order houses; Cookies and crackers; Bread, cake, and related products; Cheese; natural and processed
PA: Old Salem, Incorporated
    600 S Main St
    Winston Salem NC 27101
    336 721-7300

(G-13270)
OMNI MOLD & DIE LLC
2710 Boulder Park Ct (27101-4776)
PHONE...............................336 724-5152
EMP: 16 **EST:** 2013
SQ FT: 18,000
SALES (est): 1.61MM **Privately Held**
Web: www.omnimoldnc.com
SIC: 3544 Forms (molds), for foundry and plastics working machinery

(G-13271)
ORACLE FLEXIBLE PACKAGING INC
220 Polo Rd (27105-3441)
P.O. Box 11137 (27116-1137)
PHONE...............................336 777-5000
◆ **EMP:** 285
SIC: 2672 Paper; coated and laminated, nec

(G-13272)
ORGANIZER LLC
274 Glen Eagles Dr (27104-5318)
PHONE...............................336 391-7591
EMP: 6 **EST:** 2019
SALES (est): 90K **Privately Held**
SIC: 2842 Cleaning or polishing preparations, nec

▲ = Import ▼ = Export
◆ = Import/Export

(G-13273)
ORTHOPEDIC SERVICES
3303 Healy Dr (27103-1498)
PHONE.................................336 716-3349
Jim Butts, *Pr*
EMP: 7 **EST:** 1964
SQ FT: 1,200
SALES (est): 225.34K **Privately Held**
SIC: 3842 8011 Orthopedic appliances;
   Offices and clinics of medical doctors

(G-13274)
PAGES SCREEN PRINTING LLC
4110 Cherry St (27105-2536)
P.O. Box 11196 (27116-1196)
PHONE.................................336 759-7979
Julia Page, *Sec*
EMP: 6 **EST:** 1983
SQ FT: 5,000
SALES (est): 248.34K **Privately Held**
Web: www.pagesscreenprinting.com
SIC: 2759 Screen printing

(G-13275)
**PANEL WHOLESALERS
INCORPORATED**
Also Called: P W I Computer Accessories
3841 Kimwell Dr (27103-6707)
PHONE.................................336 765-4040
Stephen W Harper, *Pr*
Lars Harper, *VP*
Sally Harper, *Sec*
EMP: 10 **EST:** 1960
SQ FT: 35,000
SALES (est): 381.85K **Privately Held**
Web: www.pwistratform.com
SIC: 3089 Thermoformed finished plastics
   products, nec

(G-13276)
PARRISH TIRE COMPANY (PA)
Also Called: Ptc
5130 Indiana Ave (27106-2822)
PHONE.................................800 849-8473
Logan Jackson, *Pr*
Bill Jackson, *
Michael Everhart, *
Charles Everhart, *
◆ **EMP:** 65 **EST:** 1946
SQ FT: 115,000
SALES (est): 378.88MM
SALES (corp-wide): 378.88MM **Privately
Held**
Web: www.parrishtire.com
SIC: 5014 5531 7534 Automobile tires and
   tubes; Automotive tires; Tire recapping

(G-13277)
PEACOAT MEDIA LLC
101 N Chestnut St Ste 203 (27101-4046)
PHONE.................................336 298-1133
EMP: 4 **EST:** 2020
SALES (est): 69.63K **Privately Held**
SIC: 2252 Socks

(G-13278)
PENN ENGINEERING & MFG CORP
Pennengineering
2400 Lowery St (27101-4725)
PHONE.................................336 631-8741
Bob Gentile, *Mgr*
EMP: 250
SQ FT: 133,396
Web: www.pemnet.com
SIC: 3429 Metal fasteners
HQ: Penn Engineering & Manufacturing
   Corp.
   5190 Old Easton Rd
   Danboro PA 18916
   800 237-4736

(G-13279)
PEPSI BOTTLING VENTURES LLC
Also Called: Pepsi-Cola
295 Business Park Dr (27107-6537)
PHONE.................................336 464-9227
EMP: 5
Web: www.pepsibottlingventures.com
SIC: 2086 Carbonated soft drinks, bottled
   and canned
HQ: Pepsi Bottling Ventures Llc
   4141 Parklake Ave
   Raleigh NC 27612
   919 865-2300

(G-13280)
PEPSI BOTTLING VENTURES LLC
Also Called: Pepsi-Cola Bottler
390 Business Park Dr (27107-6547)
PHONE.................................336 464-9227
Dan Stone, *Unit Manager*
EMP: 50
Web: www.pepsibottlingventures.com
SIC: 2086 Carbonated soft drinks, bottled
   and canned
HQ: Pepsi Bottling Ventures Llc
   4141 Parklake Ave
   Raleigh NC 27612
   919 865-2300

(G-13281)
PEPSI BOTTLING VENTURES LLC
Also Called: Pepsi-Cola
3425 Myer Lee Dr (27101-6209)
PHONE.................................336 724-4800
Jimmy Burns, *Mgr*
EMP: 200
Web: www.pepsibottlingventures.com
SIC: 2086 5149 Soft drinks: packaged in
   cans, bottles, etc.; Soft drinks
HQ: Pepsi Bottling Ventures Llc
   4141 Parklake Ave
   Raleigh NC 27612
   919 865-2300

(G-13282)
PEPSI-COLA METRO BTLG CO INC
Also Called: Pepsi-Cola
1100 Reynolds Blvd (27105-3400)
P.O. Box 10 (27102-0010)
PHONE.................................336 896-4000
Miah Gaudet, *Mgr*
EMP: 700
SALES (corp-wide): 91.47B **Publicly Held**
Web: www.pepsico.com
SIC: 2086 5149 Carbonated soft drinks,
   bottled and canned; Groceries and related
   products, nec
HQ: Pepsi-Cola Metropolitan Bottling
   Company, Inc.
   700 Anderson Hill Rd
   Purchase NY 10577
   914 767-6000

(G-13283)
PEPSICO INC
Also Called: Pepsico
P.O. Box 1800 (27102-1800)
PHONE.................................914 253-2000
EMP: 13
SALES (corp-wide): 91.47B **Publicly Held**
Web: www.pepsico.com
SIC: 2086 Carbonated soft drinks, bottled
   and canned
PA: Pepsico, Inc.
   700 Anderson Hill Rd
   Purchase NY 10577
   914 253-2000

(G-13284)
PERDUE FARMS INC
Also Called: Perdue Farms
7996 N Point Blvd (27106-3265)
PHONE.................................336 896-9121
EMP: 22
SALES (corp-wide): 1.24B **Privately Held**
Web: www.perdue.com
SIC: 2015 Poultry slaughtering and
   processing
PA: Perdue Farms Incorporated
   31149 Old Ocean City Rd
   Salisbury MD 21804
   800 473-7383

(G-13285)
**PERSONAL COMMUNICATION
SYSTEMS INC**
Also Called: P C S
301 N Main St (27101-3836)
PHONE.................................336 722-4917
▲ **EMP:** 58
Web: www.televox.com
SIC: 3661 Telephone and telegraph
   apparatus

(G-13286)
PETNET SOLUTIONS INC
3908 Westpoint Blvd Ste E (27103-6757)
PHONE.................................865 218-2000
EMP: 4
SALES (corp-wide): 84.78B **Privately Held**
Web: www.siemens.com
SIC: 2835 Radioactive diagnostic substances
HQ: Petnet Solutions, Inc.
   810 Innovation Dr
   Knoxville TN 37932
   865 218-2000

(G-13287)
PHARMACEUTIC LITHO LABEL INC
3360 Old Lexington Rd (27107-4119)
PHONE.................................336 785-4000
James Ladd, *Mgr*
EMP: 20
SALES (corp-wide): 4.27MM **Privately
Held**
Web: www.resourcelabel.com
SIC: 2759 2752 Letterpress printing;
   Commercial printing, lithographic
PA: Pharmaceutic Litho & Label Company,
   Inc.
   450 North Ave E
   Cranford NJ 07016
   336 785-4000

(G-13288)
PHILIP MORRIS USA INC
Also Called: Philip Morris
4338 Grove Ave (27105-2841)
PHONE.................................336 744-4401
Ceazer Swazay, *Brnch Mgr*
EMP: 99
SALES (corp-wide): 24.02B **Publicly Held**
Web: www.philipmorrisusa.com
SIC: 2111 Cigarettes
HQ: Philip Morris Usa Inc.
   6601 W Brd St
   Richmond VA 23230
   804 274-2000

(G-13289)
PHOENIX PACKAGING INC
111 E 10th St (27101-1509)
P.O. Box 15091 (27113-0091)
PHONE.................................336 724-1978
Tom Skinner, *Pr*
EMP: 25 **EST:** 1983
SALES (est): 2.08MM **Privately Held**
Web: www.purplepackaging.com

SIC: 2631 2653 Container, packaging, and
   boxboard; Corrugated boxes, partitions,
   display items, sheets, and pad

(G-13290)
PHOTO EMBLEM INCORPORATED
5010 S Main St (27107-6818)
PHONE.................................336 784-4000
Sherman Richardson, *Pr*
▲ **EMP:** 4 **EST:** 1978
SALES (est): 658.84K **Privately Held**
Web: www.photoemblem.com
SIC: 2399 Emblems, badges, and insignia:
   from purchased materials

(G-13291)
PIEDMONT FLIGHT INC
Also Called: Piedmont Flight Training
3789 N Liberty St (27105-3908)
PHONE.................................336 776-6070
F Houston Symmes, *Pr*
Sandra Symmes, *VP*
David Mount, *Prin*
Tara Connell, *Prin*
Kyle Mounts, *Prin*
EMP: 22 **EST:** 1991
SALES (est): 851.13K **Privately Held**
Web: www.flypft.com
SIC: 3728 8748 Link trainers (aircraft training
   mechanisms); Business consulting, nec

(G-13292)
PIEDMONT INDUS COATINGS INC
160 University Center Dr (27105-1395)
PHONE.................................336 377-3399
Thomas Ingram, *Pr*
Jim Ingram, *Ex VP*
EMP: 6 **EST:** 1994
SQ FT: 1,200
SALES (est): 103.32K **Privately Held**
Web: www.piedmontcoatings.com
SIC: 2851 Paints and allied products

(G-13293)
PIEDMONT PUBLISHING
418 N Marshall St (27101-2932)
PHONE.................................336 727-4099
Randy Noftle, *Prin*
EMP: 8 **EST:** 2005
SALES (est): 869.07K **Privately Held**
Web: www.wsjournal.com
SIC: 2741 2759 Miscellaneous publishing;
   Publication printing

(G-13294)
PIEDMONT STEEL COMPANY LLC
3480 Friendship Ledford Rd (27107-9906)
PHONE.................................336 875-5133
Nicki Cole, *Pr*
EMP: 65 **EST:** 2019
SALES (est): 7.31MM **Privately Held**
Web: www.piedmontsteelco.com
SIC: 3441 Fabricated structural metal

(G-13295)
PINE CREEK PRODUCTS LLC
2856 Country Club Rd (27104-3014)
PHONE.................................336 399-8806
EMP: 10 **EST:** 2017
SALES (est): 160.39K **Privately Held**
SIC: 2431 Millwork

(G-13296)
PINE HALL BRICK CO INC (PA)
Also Called: Riverside Brick & Supply
2701 Shorefair Dr (27105-4235)
P.O. Box 11044 (27116-1044)
PHONE.................................336 721-7500
Fletcher Steele Junior, *Pr*
Flake F Steele Junior, *Pr*

Ed Harrell, *CFO*
William P Steele Senior, *Sec*
Hugh Dowdle Junior, *VP Mfg*
◆ **EMP:** 25 **EST:** 1907
SQ FT: 10,000
SALES (est): 44.87MM
SALES (corp-wide): 44.87MM **Privately Held**
Web: www.pinehallbrick.com
SIC: 3251 5032 Brick and structural clay tile; Brick, except refractory

(G-13297)
PLAYTEX DORADO LLC
1000 E Hanes Mill Rd (27105-1384)
PHONE.............................336 519-8080
EMP: 5 **EST:** 1975
SALES (est): 2.1MM **Publicly Held**
SIC: 2253 T-shirts and tops, knit
PA: Hanesbrands Inc.
1000 E Hanes Mill Rd
Winston Salem NC 27105

(G-13298)
PLM INC
Also Called: Private Label Manufacturing
2371 Farrington Point Dr (27107-2453)
PHONE.............................336 788-7529
Dale Traxler, *Pr*
Kathy Traxler, *Sec*
EMP: 7 **EST:** 1985
SQ FT: 8,000
SALES (est): 2.73MM **Privately Held**
SIC: 2844 Perfumes, cosmetics and other toilet preparations

(G-13299)
POLYVLIES USA INC
260 Business Park Dr (27107-6538)
PHONE.............................336 769-0206
Gunnar Beyer, *CEO*
▲ **EMP:** 25 **EST:** 2014
SALES (est): 10.13MM
SALES (corp-wide): 110.3MM **Privately Held**
SIC: 2297 2299 5131 Nonwoven fabrics; Batting, wadding, padding and fillings; Synthetic fabrics, nec
HQ: Polyvlies Franz Beyer Gmbh
Rodder Str. 52
Horstel NW 48477
545993100

(G-13300)
POWERLAB INC
3352 Old Lexington Rd Bldg 43 (27107-4119)
PHONE.............................336 650-0706
Jeff Ward, *Brnch Mgr*
EMP: 21
SALES (corp-wide): 3MM **Privately Held**
Web: www.powerlabinc.com
SIC: 3356 2816 Nonferrous rolling and drawing, nec; Lead pigments: white lead, lead oxides, lead sulfate
PA: Powerlab, Inc.
1145 Highway 34 S
Terrell TX 75160
972 563-1477

(G-13301)
PPG INDUSTRIES INC
Also Called: PPG 9490
1455 Trademart Blvd (27127-5645)
PHONE.............................336 771-8878
Mark Cummings, *Mgr*
EMP: 4
SALES (corp-wide): 17.65B **Publicly Held**
Web: www.ppg.com
SIC: 2851 Paints and allied products
PA: Ppg Industries, Inc.

1 Ppg Pl
Pittsburgh PA 15272
412 434-3131

(G-13302)
PRECISION PART SYSTEMS WNSTN-S
Also Called: Precision Part Systems
1035 W Northwest Blvd (27101-1104)
P.O. Box 5565 (27113)
PHONE.............................336 723-5210
Nick Doumas, *Pr*
Klaul Hinrichsen, *
Tom Mc Caffrey, *
Rita Gallos, *
EMP: 27 **EST:** 1983
SALES (est): 1.46MM **Privately Held**
Web: www.precisionpartsystems.com
SIC: 3423 Hand and edge tools, nec

(G-13303)
PRIME SOURCE OPC LLC
320 Perimeter Point Blvd (27105-3542)
PHONE.............................336 661-3300
EMP: 35 **EST:** 2009
SALES (est): 4.64MM **Privately Held**
Web: www.primesourceopc.com
SIC: 2752 Offset printing

(G-13304)
PRIMESOURCE CORPORATION
320a Perimeter Point Blvd (27105-3542)
PHONE.............................336 661-3300
Richard B Trout, *Pr*
Diane Trout, *Sec*
EMP: 17 **EST:** 1984
SALES (est): 2.31MM **Privately Held**
Web: www.primesourceopc.com
SIC: 3577 Printers and plotters

(G-13305)
PRODUCT QUEST MANUFACTURING INC
380 Knollwood St Ste 700 (27103-1862)
PHONE.............................386 239-8787
EMP: 120
SIC: 2844 Face creams or lotions

(G-13306)
PRODUCT QUEST MANUFACTURING LLC
380 Knollwood St Ste 700 (27103-1862)
PHONE.............................386 239-8787
▲ **EMP:** 425
SIC: 2844 Face creams or lotions

(G-13307)
PROKIDNEY LLC
3929 Westpoint Blvd Ste G (27103-6761)
PHONE.............................336 448-2857
Depak Jain, *COO*
EMP: 20 **EST:** 2015
SALES (est): 10.08MM **Privately Held**
Web: www.prokidney.com
SIC: 2836 Biological products, except diagnostic

(G-13308)
PROKIDNEY CORP (PA)
2000 Frontis Plaza Blvd Ste 250 (27103-5682)
PHONE.............................336 999-7019
Bruce Culleton, *CEO*
Pablo Legorreta, *Non-Executive Chairman of the Board*
James Coulston, *CFO*
Todd C Girolamo, *CLO*
Ulrich Ernst, *Executive Technical Vice President*
EMP: 163 **EST:** 2015

SQ FT: 110,700
Web: www.prokidney.com
SIC: 2836 Biological products, except diagnostic

(G-13309)
PROSPECTIVE COMMUNICATIONS LLC
1959 N Peace Haven Rd (27106-4850)
PHONE.............................336 287-5535
EMP: 4 **EST:** 2017
SALES (est): 41.35K **Privately Held**
SIC: 2741 Miscellaneous publishing

(G-13310)
R AND R AUTO REPR & TIRES INC
2704 Old Lexington Rd (27107-3241)
PHONE.............................336 784-6893
Linda Sanders, *Owner*
EMP: 6 **EST:** 2008
SALES (est): 226.73K **Privately Held**
SIC: 5531 7538 7534 7539 Automotive tires; General automotive repair shops; Tire retreading and repair shops; Automotive repair shops, nec

(G-13311)
R J REYNOLDS TOBACCO COMPANY (DH)
401 N Main St (27101-3804)
P.O. Box 2959 (27102-2959)
PHONE.............................336 741-5000
◆ **EMP:** 100 **EST:** 2004
SALES (est): 1.36B **Privately Held**
Web: www.rjrt.com
SIC: 2131 Smoking tobacco
HQ: R. J. Reynolds Tobacco Holdings, Inc.
401 N Main St
Winston Salem NC 27102
336 741-5000

(G-13312)
R J REYNOLDS TOBACCO COMPANY
950 Reynolds Blvd Bldg 605-12 (27105-3450)
PHONE.............................336 741-2132
C Tinsley, *Brnch Mgr*
EMP: 208
Web: www.rjrt.com
SIC: 2111 2131 Cigarettes; Smoking tobacco
HQ: R. J. Reynolds Tobacco Company
401 N Main St
Winston Salem NC 27101
336 741-5000

(G-13313)
R J RYNOLDS TOB HOLDINGS INC (DH)
401 N Main St (27102)
P.O. Box Po Box2990 (27102-2990)
PHONE.............................336 741-5000
Susan Ivey, *Pr*
Dianne M Neal, *
Ann A Johnston, *
Tommy J Payne, *EXTERNAL Relations*
◆ **EMP:** 100 **EST:** 1999
SQ FT: 86,000
SALES (est): 1.85B **Privately Held**
Web: www.rjrt.com
SIC: 2111 Cigarettes
HQ: Reynolds American Inc.
401 N Main St
Winston Salem NC 27101
336 741-2000

(G-13314)
RADEL INC ✪
209 Mercantile Dr (27105-8618)
PHONE.............................336 245-8078

Francis Rademeyer, *CEO*
EMP: 5 **EST:** 2024
SALES (est): 1.41MM **Privately Held**
SIC: 3559 3694 Automotive maintenance equipment; Automotive electrical equipment, nec

(G-13315)
RAI SERVICES COMPANY
401 N Main St (27101-3804)
PHONE.............................336 741-6774
Luis Davila, *Pr*
EMP: 714 **EST:** 2009
SALES (est): 60.85MM **Privately Held**
Web: www.reynoldsamerican.com
SIC: 2111 Cigarettes
HQ: Reynolds American Inc.
401 N Main St
Winston Salem NC 27101
336 741-2000

(G-13316)
RAYLEN VINEYARDS INC
3055 Heather Meadow Dr (27106-5814)
PHONE.............................336 998-3100
Steve Shepard, *VP*
Joe Neely, *Pr*
EMP: 8 **EST:** 1999
SALES (est): 800.89K **Privately Held**
Web: www.raylenvineyards.com
SIC: 2084 Wines

(G-13317)
RENAISSANCE FIBER LLC
500 W 5th St Ste 400 (27101-2799)
PHONE.............................860 857-5987
Daniel Yohannes Ph.d. Mba, *CEO*
Andrew Hume, *CSO*
Bruce Maxwell, *CFO*
EMP: 5 **EST:** 2018
SALES (est): 253.79K **Privately Held**
Web: www.renaissance-fiber.com
SIC: 2299 Hemp yarn, thread, roving, and textiles

(G-13318)
REYNOLDS AMERICAN INC (HQ)
401 N Main St (27101)
P.O. Box 2990 (27101)
PHONE.............................336 741-2000
Ricardo Oberlander, *Pr*
Tony Hayward, *
Jeff Raborn, *
Priscilla Samuel, *SCIENTIFIC Research & Development*
Jonathan Reed, *Chief Commercial Officer*
◆ **EMP:** 39 **EST:** 2004
SALES (est): 2.77B **Privately Held**
Web: www.reynoldsamerican.com
SIC: 2111 2121 2131 Cigarettes; Cigars; Smoking tobacco
PA: British American Tobacco P.L.C.
Globe House
London WC2R

(G-13319)
RITE INSTANT PRINTING INC
Also Called: PIP Printing
1011 Burke St (27101-2412)
PHONE.............................336 768-5061
Charles Morgan, *Pr*
Kathy Morgan, *VP*
EMP: 7 **EST:** 1975
SALES (est): 114.87K **Privately Held**
Web: www.pip.com
SIC: 2752 7334 Offset printing; Photocopying and duplicating services

▲ = Import ▼ = Export
◆ = Import/Export

(G-13320)
ROCKWELL COLLINS INC
Also Called: Collins Aerospace
190 Oak Plaza Blvd (27105-1470)
PHONE.................336 744-3288
EMP: 5
SALES (corp-wide): 80.74B **Publicly Held**
Web: www.rockwellcollins.com
SIC: 3728 Aircraft parts and equipment, nec
HQ: Rockwell Collins, Inc.
    400 Collins Rd Ne
    Cedar Rapids IA 52498

(G-13321)
ROCKWELL COLLINS INC
2599 Empire Dr (27103-6709)
PHONE.................336 776-3444
EMP: 4
SALES (corp-wide): 80.74B **Publicly Held**
Web: www.rockwellcollins.com
SIC: 3812 Search and navigation equipment
HQ: Rockwell Collins, Inc.
    400 Collins Rd Ne
    Cedar Rapids IA 52498

(G-13322)
ROCKWELL COLLINS INC
Also Called: Collins Aerospace
1455 Fairchild Rd (27105-4549)
PHONE.................336 744-1097
EMP: 6
SALES (corp-wide): 80.74B **Publicly Held**
Web: www.rockwellcollins.com
SIC: 3812 Search and navigation equipment
HQ: Rockwell Collins, Inc.
    400 Collins Rd Ne
    Cedar Rapids IA 52498

(G-13323)
ROTORK-FAIRCHILD INDUS PDTS CO
3920 Westpoint Blvd (27103-6719)
PHONE.................336 659-3400
Alan G Paine, *Prin*
EMP: 11 EST: 2013
SALES (est): 3MM **Privately Held**
Web: www.fairchildproducts.com
SIC: 3823 Process control instruments

(G-13324)
ROYCE TOO LLC (HQ)
3330 Healy Dr Ste 200 (27103-2024)
P.O. Box 497 (25402-0497)
PHONE.................212 356-1627
Bob Boglioli, *Pr*
Ben Carson, *
◆ EMP: 30 EST: 2004
SQ FT: 200,000
SALES (est): 27.2MM **Privately Held**
Web: www.roycesocks.com
SIC: 7389 2252 Packaging and labeling
    services; Socks
PA: Okamoto Corporation
    1-11-9, Nishihonmachi, Nishi-Ku
    Osaka OSK 550-0

(G-13325)
SALEM ONE INC (PA)
Also Called: Salem Printing
5670 Shattalon Dr (27105)
PHONE.................336 744-9990
Philip Kelley Junior, *Pr*
Philip Kelley, *
Steve Yarbraugh, *
EMP: 127 EST: 1973
SQ FT: 45,500
SALES (est): 879.21K
SALES (corp-wide): 879.21K **Privately Held**
Web: www.salem-one.com

SIC: 7389 2752 2759 Packaging and
    labeling services; Commercial printing,
    lithographic; Commercial printing, nec

(G-13326)
SALEM SPORTS INC (PA)
1519 S Martin Luther King Jr Dr
(27107-1308)
PHONE.................336 722-2444
John Sullivan, *Pr*
Judith Sullivan, *Sec*
Jeff M Ickes, *Pr*
Kim G Ickes, *Sec*
▼ EMP: 4 EST: 1992
SQ FT: 14,000
SALES (est): 4.07MM
SALES (corp-wide): 4.07MM **Privately Held**
Web: www.salemsports.com
SIC: 3993 Signs and advertising specialties

(G-13327)
SALEM TECHNOLOGIES INC
Also Called: S T I
2580 Salem Point Ct (27103-6729)
PHONE.................336 777-3652
Robert Tribble, *Pr*
Robert O Bridges, *VP*
EMP: 17 EST: 1989
SQ FT: 15,300
SALES (est): 7.51MM **Privately Held**
Web: www.salemtechnologies.com
SIC: 3089 3699 3571 Plastics processing;
    Electrical equipment and supplies, nec;
    Electronic computers

(G-13328)
SALEM WOODWORKING COMPANY
4849 Kester Mill Rd (27103-1214)
PHONE.................336 768-7443
Dale Gramley, *Owner*
EMP: 6 EST: 1980
SQ FT: 10,500
SALES (est): 493K **Privately Held**
Web:
www.winstonsalemwoodworking.com
SIC: 2431 Millwork

(G-13329)
SANTA FE NATURAL TOBACCO COMPANY FOUNDATION (DH)
Also Called: Santa Fe Natural Tobacco
401 N Main St (27101-3804)
P.O. Box 2990 (87504-2990)
PHONE.................800 332-5595
▲ EMP: 150 EST: 1982
SALES (est): 397.84K **Privately Held**
Web: www.reynoldsamerican.com
SIC: 2131 Smoking tobacco
HQ: Reynolds American Inc.
    401 N Main St
    Winston Salem NC 27101
    336 741-2000

(G-13330)
SCHOENBERG SALT CO
4927 Home Rd (27106-2802)
P.O. Box 791 (27012-0791)
PHONE.................336 766-0600
▼ EMP: 5 EST: 2010
SALES (est): 977.3K **Privately Held**
Web: www.gosalt.com
SIC: 2899 Salt

(G-13331)
SG-CLW INC
Also Called: Smithgroup
1700 N Liberty St (27105-6186)
P.O. Box 20741 (27120-0741)
PHONE.................336 865-4980
Darius Smith, *CEO*

EMP: 10 EST: 2020
SALES (est): 498.93K **Privately Held**
SIC: 5172 2911 7389 1311 Petroleum
    brokers; Petroleum refining; Business
    Activities at Non-Commercial Site; Crude
    petroleum and natural gas

(G-13332)
SHARP STONE SUPPLY INC
126 Griffith Plaza Dr (27103-6826)
PHONE.................336 659-7777
Robert Fulton, *Prin*
EMP: 5 EST: 2002
SALES (est): 168.34K **Privately Held**
Web: www.sharpstonesupply.com
SIC: 3281 Cut stone and stone products

(G-13333)
SHARPE CO (PA)
230 Charlois Blvd (27103-1508)
P.O. Box 5716 (27113-5716)
PHONE.................336 724-2871
David G Sharpe, *Pr*
Buddy Sharpe Junior, *VP*
Burke Wilson Iii, *Treas*
Terri Sealey, *
▲ EMP: 30 EST: 1956
SQ FT: 38,000
SALES (est): 8.51MM **Privately Held**
Web: www.sharpeco.net
SIC: 2754 7359 Commercial printing, gravure
    ; Equipment rental and leasing, nec

(G-13334)
SHARPE IMAGES PROPERTIES INC (PA)
Also Called: Sharpe Images
230 Charlois Blvd (27103-1508)
P.O. Box 5716 (27113-5716)
PHONE.................336 724-2871
David Gregory Sharpe, *Pr*
B R Buddy Sharpe Junior, *VP*
Terri Sealey, *
Burke Wilson Iii, *Treas*
EMP: 29 EST: 1956
SQ FT: 11,000
SALES (est): 2.36MM
SALES (corp-wide): 2.36MM **Privately Held**
Web: www.sharpeco.net
SIC: 5999 5049 7334 7384 Architectural
    supplies; Engineers' equipment and
    supplies, nec; Photocopying and
    duplicating services; Photofinish
    laboratories

(G-13335)
SHEETS SMITH WEALTH MGT INC
120 Club Oaks Ct Ste 200 (27104-4769)
PHONE.................336 765-2020
John R Sheets, *Pr*
William G Smith, *Pt*
Dave Gilbert, *Ex VP*
EMP: 24 EST: 1982
SALES (est): 1.61MM **Privately Held**
Web: www.sheetssmith.com
SIC: 6282 2541 Investment counselors;
    Wood partitions and fixtures

(G-13336)
SIGNCASTER CORPORATION
6210 Hacker Bend Ct Ste B (27103-9501)
PHONE.................336 712-2525
Don Shaw, *Brnch Mgr*
EMP: 6
SALES (corp-wide): 95.17MM **Privately Held**
SIC: 7389 5087 2796 Engraving service;
    Engraving equipment and supplies;
    Engraving on copper, steel, wood, or
    rubber: printing plates

HQ: Signcaster Corporation
    12450 Oliver Ave S # 100
    Burnsville MN 55337
    800 869-7800

(G-13337)
SIGNS ETC
2432 Cherokee Ln (27103-4832)
PHONE.................336 722-9341
Susan B Davis, *Owner*
Shannon Davis, *Off Mgr*
EMP: 4 EST: 1984
SQ FT: 13,000
SALES (est): 107.45K **Privately Held**
Web: www.signsetcofcharlotte.com
SIC: 7389 7336 3993 Sign painting and
    lettering shop; Graphic arts and related
    design; Signs and advertising specialties

(G-13338)
SKETTIS WOODWORKS
2225 Sedgemont Dr (27103-9745)
PHONE.................336 671-9866
EMP: 5 EST: 2016
SALES (est): 58.29K **Privately Held**
SIC: 2431 Millwork

(G-13339)
SKIFAM LLC ✪
119 S Stratford Rd (27104-4213)
PHONE.................336 722-6111
Benjamin Holcomb, *Managing Member*
EMP: 10 EST: 2023
SALES (est): 222.97K **Privately Held**
Web: www.skiandtennisstation.com
SIC: 3949 Winter sports equipment

(G-13340)
SONICAIRE INC
3831 Kimwell Dr (27103-6707)
PHONE.................336 712-2437
William Bradley Carr, *Pr*
Jordan Newton, *
◆ EMP: 30 EST: 2004
SQ FT: 25,530
SALES (est): 3.93MM **Privately Held**
Web: www.sonicaire.com
SIC: 3564 Blowing fans: industrial or
    commercial

(G-13341)
SRB TECHNOLOGIES INC (PA)
2580 Landmark Dr (27103-6716)
P.O. Box 25267 (27114-5267)
PHONE.................336 659-2610
Brian Tullen, *Pr*
Michael Dougan, *
Stephane Levesque, *
EMP: 33 EST: 1979
SQ FT: 6,000
SALES (est): 1.31MM
SALES (corp-wide): 1.31MM **Privately Held**
Web: www.srbt.com
SIC: 3648 3993 Lighting equipment, nec;
    Signs and advertising specialties

(G-13342)
STAR READY-MIX INC
2865 Lowery St (27101-6127)
PHONE.................336 725-9401
Joe Wolfe, *CEO*
EMP: 5 EST: 2004
SALES (est): 239.72K **Privately Held**
SIC: 3273 Ready-mixed concrete

(G-13343)
STARDUST CELLARS LLC (PA)
Also Called: Stardust Cellars
1764 Camden Rd (27103-4510)

G
E
O
G
R
A
P
H
I
C

PHONE..................336 466-4454
Nicolas Von Cosmos, *CEO*
EMP: 4 **EST:** 2018
SALES (est): 1.45MM
SALES (corp-wide): 1.45MM **Privately Held**
Web: www.stardustcellars.com
SIC: 2084 5813 Wines; Tavern (drinking places)

(G-13344)
STOROPACK INC
2598 Empire Dr Ste G (27103-6763)
PHONE..................800 827-7225
EMP: 4
SALES (corp-wide): 655.85MM **Privately Held**
Web: www.storopack.in
SIC: 5199 3086 2671 Packaging materials; Packaging and shipping materials, foamed plastics; Paper; coated and laminated packaging
HQ: Storopack, Inc.
　4758 Devitt Dr
　Cincinnati OH 45246
　513 874-0314

(G-13345)
STRATFORD DIE CASTING INC
1665 S Martin Luther King Jr Dr Ste A (27107-1335)
PHONE..................336 784-0100
Norman Wallace, *Pr*
G Scott Wallace, *VP*
Virginia Lawson, *Sec*
EMP: 6 **EST:** 1980
SALES (est): 2.48MM **Privately Held**
SIC: 3364 Zinc and zinc-base alloy die-castings

(G-13346)
STRATFORD METALFINISHING INC
1681 S Martin Luther King Jr Dr (27107-1310)
PHONE..................336 723-7946
Scott Wallace, *Pr*
EMP: 48 **EST:** 1964
SALES (est): 3.8MM **Privately Held**
Web: www.stratfordmetal.com
SIC: 3471 Electroplating of metals or formed products

(G-13347)
STRATFORD TOOL & DIE CO INC
3841 Kimwell Dr (27103-6707)
PHONE..................336 765-2030
Stephen W Harper, *Pr*
Keith Smith, *VP*
Sally Harper, *Sec*
EMP: 7 **EST:** 1965
SQ FT: 31,200
SALES (est): 872.94K **Privately Held**
Web: www.stratfordtoolanddie.com
SIC: 3544 Special dies and tools

(G-13348)
STROUPE MIRROR CO
2661 Reynolds Dr (27104-1927)
PHONE..................336 475-2181
EMP: 5 **EST:** 1947
SALES (est): 65K **Privately Held**
Web: www.stroupemirror.com
SIC: 3231 Products of purchased glass

(G-13349)
SUNTEX INDUSTRIES
5000 S Main St (27107-6818)
PHONE..................336 784-1000
Tom Ahn, *Owner*
EMP: 10 **EST:** 2016
SALES (est): 749.91K **Privately Held**

Web: www.suntexindustries.com
SIC: 3999 Manufacturing industries, nec

(G-13350)
SUPERIOR MANUFACTURING COMPANY
4102 Indiana Ave (27105-3415)
P.O. Box 4048 (27115-4048)
PHONE..................336 661-1200
Bryan Peterson, *CEO*
Bryan S Peterson, *
Joe Brewster, *
Patricia Peterson, *
▲ **EMP:** 60 **EST:** 1945
SQ FT: 80,000
SALES (est): 5.16MM **Privately Held**
Web: www.superiormanufacturing.com
SIC: 3441 Fabricated structural metal

(G-13351)
SWAIM ORNAMENTAL IRON WORKS
2570 Landmark Dr (27103-6716)
PHONE..................336 765-5271
Don L Swaim, *Pr*
Gretchen Swaim, *Sec*
Trent Swaim, *VP*
EMP: 19 **EST:** 1951
SQ FT: 11,100
SALES (est): 3.08MM **Privately Held**
Web: www.swaimornamentalnc.com
SIC: 3446 Railings, banisters, guards, etc: made from metal pipe

(G-13352)
T W GARNER FOOD COMPANY
600 Northgate Park Dr (27106-3429)
PHONE..................336 661-1550
Ann Garner Riddle, *Brnch Mgr*
EMP: 4
SALES (corp-wide): 24.47MM **Privately Held**
Web: www.garnerfoods.com
SIC: 2033 Barbecue sauce: packaged in cans, jars, etc.
PA: T W Garner Food Company
　614 W 4th St
　Winston Salem NC 27101
　336 661-1550

(G-13353)
T W GARNER FOOD COMPANY (PA)
614 W 4th St (27101-2730)
PHONE..................336 661-1550
Ann Garner, *Pr*
Harold H Garner Junior, *Sec*
◆ **EMP:** 48 **EST:** 1929
SQ FT: 75,000
SALES (est): 24.47MM
SALES (corp-wide): 24.47MM **Privately Held**
Web: www.garnerfoods.com
SIC: 2033 2035 Barbecue sauce: packaged in cans, jars, etc.; Pickles, sauces, and salad dressings

(G-13354)
T W GARNER FOOD COMPANY
4045 Indiana Ave (27105-3412)
PHONE..................336 661-1550
Ann Garner Riddle, *Pr*
EMP: 4
SALES (corp-wide): 24.47MM **Privately Held**
Web: www.garnerfoods.com
SIC: 2033 Chili sauce, tomato: packaged in cans, jars, etc.
PA: T W Garner Food Company
　614 W 4th St
　Winston Salem NC 27101
　336 661-1550

(G-13355)
TAR HEEL MINI MOTORING CLUB
380 Knollwood St Ste H129 (27103-1884)
PHONE..................336 391-8084
EMP: 4 **EST:** 2010
SALES (est): 150K **Privately Held**
SIC: 2865 Tar

(G-13356)
TE CONNECTIVITY
3700 Reidsville Rd (27101-2165)
PHONE..................336 727-5295
EMP: 43 **EST:** 2014
SALES (est): 9.31MM **Privately Held**
SIC: 3678 Electronic connectors

(G-13357)
TE CONNECTIVITY CORPORATION
3900 Reidsville Rd (27101-2167)
PHONE..................336 664-7000
Randy Smith, *Brnch Mgr*
EMP: 69
SALES (corp-wide): 9.17B **Privately Held**
Web: www.te.com
SIC: 3678 3643 Electronic connectors; Current-carrying wiring services
HQ: Te Connectivity Corporation
　1050 Westlakes Dr
　Berwyn PA 19312
　610 893-9800

(G-13358)
TE CONNECTIVITY CORPORATION
3800 Reidsville Rd (27101-2166)
PHONE..................336 727-5122
Larry Novotny, *Mgr*
EMP: 165
SALES (corp-wide): 9.17B **Privately Held**
Web: www.te.com
SIC: 3678 8748 Electronic connectors; Testing services
HQ: Te Connectivity Corporation
　1050 Westlakes Dr
　Berwyn PA 19312
　610 893-9800

(G-13359)
TEAM CONNECTION
2508 Griffith Meadows Dr (27103-6329)
PHONE..................336 287-3892
Charmeka Foster, *Prin*
EMP: 8 **EST:** 2010
SALES (est): 114.72K **Privately Held**
Web: www.teamconnection.com
SIC: 2759 Screen printing

(G-13360)
TEDDY SOFT PAPER PRODUCTS INC
535 E Clemmonsville Rd Ste A (27107-5204)
PHONE..................336 784-5887
Sam Liontis, *Pr*
Bobby Laloudis, *Prin*
George Laloudis, *Prin*
EMP: 5 **EST:** 2015
SQ FT: 75,000
SALES (est): 1.15MM **Privately Held**
Web: www.teddysoftpaper.com
SIC: 2621 Paper mills

(G-13361)
TENGION INC
Also Called: Tengion
3929 Westpoint Blvd Ste G (27103-6761)
PHONE..................336 722-5855
EMP: 27
Web: www.tengion.com
SIC: 2836 8731 Biological products, except diagnostic; Biotechnical research, commercial

(G-13362)
THE COMPUTER SOLUTION COMPANY
Also Called: Tcsc
102 W 3rd St Ste 750 (27101-3902)
PHONE..................336 409-0782
Blaire Robinson, *Pr*
EMP: 13 **EST:** 1985
SALES (est): 883.12K **Privately Held**
SIC: 7372 7379 Business oriented computer software; Computer related consulting services

(G-13363)
THERMCRAFT HOLDING CO LLC
3950 Overdale Rd (27107-6106)
PHONE..................336 784-4800
Lee Watson, *CEO*
EMP: 65 **EST:** 2021
SALES (est): 9.8MM
SALES (corp-wide): 19.38MM **Privately Held**
Web: www.thermcraftinc.com
SIC: 3567 Heating units and devices, industrial: electric
PA: The Alloy Engineering Company
　844 Thacker St
　Berea OH 44017
　440 243-6800

(G-13364)
TINYPILOT LLC
5335 Robinhood Village Dr (27106-9820)
PHONE..................336 422-6525
EMP: 7
SALES (est): 1.44MM **Privately Held**
SIC: 3577 Computer peripheral equipment, nec

(G-13365)
TO THE POINT INC
130 Stratford Ct Ste E (27103-1852)
PHONE..................336 725-5303
Kevin Cope, *Pr*
Janice Stevens, *VP*
EMP: 8 **EST:** 1996
SQ FT: 5,000
SALES (est): 345.18K **Privately Held**
Web: www.ttpoint.com
SIC: 2395 Embroidery products, except Schiffli machine

(G-13366)
TOO HOTT CUSTOMS LLC
1249 W Academy St (27103-3812)
PHONE..................336 722-4919
Scott Walker, *Owner*
EMP: 7 **EST:** 2006
SALES (est): 717.09K **Privately Held**
Web: www.toohottcustoms.com
SIC: 3011 Tires and inner tubes

(G-13367)
TOOLMARX LLC
408 Ricks Dr (27103-1717)
PHONE..................919 725-0122
James Swing, *Prin*
EMP: 5 **EST:** 2018
SALES (est): 72.95K **Privately Held**
Web: www.toolmarx.com
SIC: 3999 Manufacturing industries, nec

(G-13368)
TRASH MASHER LLC
Also Called: Waste Smasher
1045 Burke St (27101-2412)
PHONE..................786 357-2697
Paul Chyrsson, *Pr*
Norman Thomas, *
EMP: 30 **EST:** 2015

SQ FT: 2,200
SALES (est): 1.17MM Privately Held
SIC: 3639 Trash compactors, household

(G-13369)
TRIAD AUTOMATION GROUP INC
Also Called: Triad Automation Group
4994 Indiana Ave Ste F (27106-2810)
P.O. Box 1065 (27012-1065)
PHONE..............................336 767-1379
Joe Collins, Pr
Jon Freeman, VP
EMP: 22 EST: 2000
SQ FT: 12,000
SALES (est): 4.72MM Privately Held
Web: www.trimantec.com
SIC: 3823 Industrial process measurement
equipment

(G-13370)
TRIAD SEMICONDUCTOR INC
1760 Jonestown Rd Ste 100 (27103-6993)
PHONE..............................336 774-2150
Lynn Hayden, Pr
David Bell, *
James Kemerling, VP
John Goode, CFO
EMP: 54 EST: 2002
SQ FT: 5,800
SALES (est): 10.25MM Privately Held
Web: www.triadsemi.com
SIC: 3674 Integrated circuits, semiconductor
networks, etc.

(G-13371)
TRIANGLE BODY WORKS INC
2014 Waughtown St (27107-2498)
PHONE..............................336 788-0631
Ronnie Lee Senior, Pr
EMP: 5 EST: 1927
SQ FT: 9,000
SALES (est): 728.29K Privately Held
Web: www.trianglebodyworks.com
SIC: 3713 7532 Truck bodies (motor
vehicles); Body shop, trucks

(G-13372)
TRIMANTEC
4994 Indiana Ave (27106-2810)
PHONE..............................336 767-1379
Joe Collins, Pr
Jon Freeman, VP
EMP: 20 EST: 2019
SALES (est): 5.34MM Privately Held
Web: www.trimantec.com
SIC: 3355 3613 Aluminum wire and cable;
Power switching equipment

(G-13373)
TRIVIUM PACKAGING USA INC
Also Called: Ardagh
4000 Old Milwaukee Ln (27107-6103)
PHONE..............................336 785-8500
Jerry Hubert, Brnch Mgr
EMP: 269
SALES (corp-wide): 1.42B Privately Held
Web: www.ardaghgroup.com
SIC: 3411 Aluminum cans
HQ: Trivium Packaging Usa Inc.
10255 W Higgins Rd
Rosemont IL 60018

(G-13374)
TRUELOOK INC
575 E 4th St (27101-4113)
PHONE..............................833 878-3566
Roger Yarrow, COO
EMP: 5 EST: 2000
SALES (est): 9.36MM Privately Held
Web: www.truelook.com

SIC: 3861 Cameras and related equipment

(G-13375)
TS KRUPA LLC
194 Briarcreek Dr (27107-9514)
PHONE..............................336 782-1515
Brian Shollenberger, Prin
EMP: 5 EST: 2014
SALES (est): 135.11K Privately Held
Web: www.tskrupa.com
SIC: 2741 Miscellaneous publishing

(G-13376)
TSQUARED CABINETS
118 Griffith Plaza Dr (27103-6824)
PHONE..............................336 655-0208
Troy Trinkle, Prin
EMP: 4 EST: 2013
SALES (est): 256.34K Privately Held
Web: www.t-squared-cabinets.com
SIC: 2434 Wood kitchen cabinets

(G-13377)
TWIN CITY CUSTOM CABINETS
1310 N Liberty St (27105-6626)
PHONE..............................336 773-7200
Steven Womble, Prin
EMP: 4 EST: 2007
SALES (est): 351.15K Privately Held
SIC: 2434 Wood kitchen cabinets

(G-13378)
TWIN CY KWNIS FNDTION WNSTN-SL
1 W 4th St (27101-3972)
PHONE..............................336 784-1649
EMP: 7 EST: 2011
SALES (est): 39.12K Privately Held
SIC: 2711 Newspapers, publishing and
printing

(G-13379)
UPEL INC
1000 E Hanes Mill Rd (27105-1384)
PHONE..............................336 519-8080
Gerald W Evans Junior, CEO
EMP: 8 EST: 1997
SALES (est): 2.33MM Publicly Held
SIC: 2253 2342 2341 2322 T-shirts and tops,
knit; Bras, girdles, and allied garments;
Panties: women's, misses', children's, and
infants'; Underwear, men's and boys': made
from purchased materials
PA: Hanesbrands Inc.
1000 E Hanes Mill Rd
Winston Salem NC 27105

(G-13380)
UPPER SOUTH STUDIO INC
330 S Main St (27101-5217)
PHONE..............................336 724-5480
Susan Rosen, Pr
Lawrence Rosen, VP
EMP: 12 EST: 1980
SQ FT: 7,000
SALES (est): 930.65K Privately Held
Web: www.uppersouthstudio.com
SIC: 2262 Dyeing: manmade fiber and silk
broadwoven fabrics

(G-13381)
VILLAGE PRODUCE & CNTRY STR IN
Also Called: Ogburn Village Solutions
4219 N Liberty St (27105-2817)
PHONE..............................336 661-8685
Paula Mccoy, Owner
EMP: 4 EST: 2010
SALES (est): 298.74K Privately Held
SIC: 3429 5399 Hardware, nec; Country
general stores

(G-13382)
VIRTUE LABS LLC
95 W 32nd St (27105-3615)
PHONE..............................781 316-5437
EMP: 21
SALES (corp-wide): 9.24MM Privately
Held
Web: www.virtuelabs.com
SIC: 2844 Perfumes, cosmetics and other
toilet preparations
PA: Virtue Labs, Llc
426 S Dawson St
Raleigh NC 27601
844 782-4247

(G-13383)
VISE & CO LLC
5063 Ramillie Run (27106-9641)
PHONE..............................336 354-3702
EMP: 5 EST: 2018
SALES (est): 64.54K Privately Held
Web: www.viseandco.com
SIC: 3949 Sporting and athletic goods, nec

(G-13384)
VULCAN CONSTRUCTION MTLS LLC
3651 Penn Ave (27105-3760)
P.O. Box 4007 (27115-4007)
PHONE..............................336 767-1201
Walter Speas, Mgr
EMP: 4
Web: www.vulcanmaterials.com
SIC: 3273 Ready-mixed concrete
HQ: Vulcan Construction Materials, Llc
1200 Urban Ctr Dr
Birmingham AL 35242
205 298-3000

(G-13385)
VULCAN CONSTRUCTION MTLS LLC
4401 N Patterson Ave (27105-1638)
PHONE..............................336 767-0911
Brad Ratledge, Brnch Mgr
EMP: 27
Web: www.vulcanmaterials.com
SIC: 3273 Ready-mixed concrete
HQ: Vulcan Construction Materials, Llc
1200 Urban Ctr Dr
Birmingham AL 35242
205 298-3000

(G-13386)
WALKER AND ASSOCIATES INC (DH)
Also Called: Netceed
110 Business Park Dr (27107-6539)
P.O. Box 639309 (45207)
PHONE..............................336 731-6391
Virginia M Walker, Ch Bd
Mark Walker, *
Douglas Leckie, *
Chrystie Walker Brown, *
Marshall Rick Walker, OF Development*
◆ EMP: 104 EST: 1970
SQ FT: 60,000
SALES (est): 125.79MM
SALES (corp-wide): 183.75K Privately
Held
Web: www.walkerfirst.com
SIC: 4813 5065 8731 8711 Telephone
communication, except radio; Electronic
parts and equipment, nec; Commercial
physical research; Engineering services
HQ: Ustc-United States Technologies
Communication Corp
225 Raritan Ctr Pkwy
Edison NJ 08837
732 902-2358

(G-13387)
WEBER AND WEBER INC (PA)
Also Called: Sir Speedy
1011 Burke St (27101-2412)
PHONE..............................336 722-4109
Arthur G Weber, Pr
Jody Weber Shaw, VP
J Dwight Shaw, VP
Susanne Weber, Sec
EMP: 18 EST: 1974
SQ FT: 6,000
SALES (est): 4.56MM
SALES (corp-wide): 4.56MM Privately
Held
Web: www.sirspeedy.com
SIC: 2752 7334 2791 2789 Commercial
printing, lithographic; Photocopying and
duplicating services; Typesetting;
Bookbinding and related work

(G-13388)
WERSUNSLLC ✪
615 Saint George Square Ct Ste 300
(27103-1356)
PHONE..............................857 209-8701
Michael Paolillo, Pr
EMP: 6 EST: 2023
SALES (est): 99.59K Privately Held
SIC: 5999 1795 6531 1531 Miscellaneous
retail stores, nec; Demolition, buildings and
other structures; Real estate leasing and
rentals; Condominium developers

(G-13389)
WESTBEND VINEYARDS INC
599 S Stratford Rd (27103-1806)
PHONE..............................336 768-7520
Jack Kroustalis, Pr
Lilian Kroustalis, Sec
EMP: 8 EST: 1987
SQ FT: 49,000
SALES (est): 584.51K Privately Held
SIC: 2084 Wine cellars, bonded: engaged in
blending wines

(G-13390)
WESTROCK COMPANY
8080 N Point Blvd (27106-3204)
PHONE..............................770 448-2193
EMP: 9
Web: www.westrock.com
SIC: 2899 2631 Chemical preparations, nec;
Paperboard mills
HQ: Westrock Company
1000 Abernathy Rd Ne
Atlanta GA 30328
770 448-2193

(G-13391)
WESTROCK CONVERTING LLC
5950 Grassy Creek Blvd (27105-1205)
PHONE..............................336 661-6736
Steve Voorhees, CEO
EMP: 12
Web: www.smurfitwestrock.com
SIC: 2631 Folding boxboard
HQ: Westrock Converting, Llc
1000 Abernathy Rd Ste 125
Atlanta GA 30328
770 448-2193

(G-13392)
WESTROCK CONVERTING LLC
Also Called: Rock-Tenn Converting
5900 Grassy Creek Blvd (27105-1205)
PHONE..............................336 661-1700
EMP: 18
Web: www.smurfitwestrock.com
SIC: 2653 Boxes, corrugated: made from
purchased materials
HQ: Westrock Converting, Llc

G
E
O
G
R
A
P
H
I
C

1000 Abernathy Rd Ste 125
Atlanta GA 30328
770 448-2193

(G-13393)
WESTROCK RKT LLC
Also Called: Westrock Merchandising Disp
5930 Grassy Creek Blvd (27105-1205)
PHONE..................................336 661-1700
EMP: 74
Web: www.westrock.com
SIC: 2653 Boxes, corrugated: made from
purchased materials
HQ: Westrock Rkt, Llc
1000 Abernathy Rd Ste 125
Atlanta GA 30328
770 448-2193

(G-13394)
WESTROCK RKT LLC
Alliance Display & Packg Div
5900a Grassy Creek Blvd (27105-1205)
PHONE..................................336 661-7180
John Dortch, Brnch Mgr
EMP: 161
Web: www.westrock.com
SIC: 2653 Hampers, solid fiber: made from
purchased materials
HQ: Westrock Rkt, Llc
1000 Abernathy Rd Ste 125
Atlanta GA 30328
770 448-2193

(G-13395)
WILSON-COOK MEDICAL INC
5941 Grassy Creek Blvd (27105-1206)
PHONE..................................336 744-0157
William Gibbons, Pr
EMP: 7 EST: 2016
SALES (est): 1.84MM Privately Held
Web: www.cookmedical.com
SIC: 3841 Surgical and medical instruments

(G-13396)
WILSON-COOK MEDICAL INC
Also Called: Cook Endoscopy
4900 Bethania Station Rd (27105-1203)
P.O. Box 489 (47402-0489)
PHONE..................................336 744-0157
EMP: 261
SIC: 3841 Diagnostic apparatus, medical

(G-13397)
WINSTN-SLEM CHRONICLE PUBG INC
1300 E 5th St (27101-4329)
P.O. Box 1636 (27102-1636)
PHONE..................................336 722-8624
Ernest H Pitt, Pr
Ndubrisi Egemonye, Stockholder
Elaine L Pitt, Sec
Mike Pitt, Genl Mgr
Kevin Walker, Prin
EMP: 5 EST: 1974
SALES (est): 239.07K Privately Held
Web: www.wschronicle.com
SIC: 2711 Newspapers, publishing and
printing

(G-13398)
WINSTN-SLEM INDS FOR BLIND INC (PA)
Also Called: Ifb Solutions
7730 N Point Blvd (27106)
PHONE..................................336 759-0551
David Horton, Ex Dir
Daniel Boucher, *
◆ EMP: 500 EST: 1963
SQ FT: 160,000
SALES (est): 16.74MM

SALES (corp-wide): 16.74MM Privately
Held
Web: www.ifbsolutions.org
SIC: 2515 3021 2392 2253 Mattresses,
containing felt, foam rubber, urethane, etc.;
Protective footwear, rubber or plastic; Bags,
laundry: made from purchased materials;
Shirts(outerwear), knit

(G-13399)
WINSTON PRINTING COMPANY (PA)
Also Called: Winston Packaging Division
8095 N Point Blvd (27106-3283)
P.O. Box 11026 (27116-1026)
PHONE..................................336 896-7631
James A Gordon, Pr
John Moore, *
Wayne Byrum, *
EMP: 97 EST: 1911
SQ FT: 75,000
SALES (est): 4.88MM
SALES (corp-wide): 4.88MM Privately
Held
Web: www.winstonpackaging.com
SIC: 2759 Commercial printing, nec

(G-13400)
WINSTON SALEM ENGRAVING CO
446 Brookstown Ave (27101-5026)
P.O. Box 20036 (27120-0036)
PHONE..................................336 725-4268
Richard M Mills, Pr
Glenn Mills, Treas
Trudy Sizemore, Sec
Glenda Mills, VP
EMP: 10 EST: 1964
SQ FT: 10,000
SALES (est): 569.21K Privately Held
Web: www.wsengraving.com
SIC: 2796 Platemaking services

(G-13401)
WINSTON SALEM JOURNAL
418 N Marshall St (27101-2979)
PHONE..................................336 727-7211
David Stanfield, Prin
◆ EMP: 36 EST: 1885
SALES (est): 1.97MM Privately Held
Web: www.journalnow.com
SIC: 2711 Newspapers, publishing and
printing

(G-13402)
WINSTON STEEL STAIR CO
216 Junia Ave (27127-3021)
PHONE..................................336 721-0020
Steve Darnell, Pr
Tom Craver, Treas
EMP: 4 EST: 2008
SALES (est): 234.82K Privately Held
SIC: 3441 3549 Fabricated structural metal;
Metalworking machinery, nec

(G-13403)
WINSTON-SALEM CASKET COMPANY
4340 Indiana Ave (27105-2512)
PHONE..................................336 661-1695
A W Bunch Iii, Pr
A W Bill Bunch Junior, Pr
EMP: 5 EST: 1948
SQ FT: 15,000
SALES (est): 386.3K Privately Held
SIC: 3995 5087 Grave vaults, metal; Caskets

(G-13404)
WORTHINGTON CYLINDER CORP
1690 Lowery St (27101-5603)
PHONE..................................336 777-8600
EMP: 112
SALES (corp-wide): 1.25B Publicly Held

Web: www.worthingtonenterprises.com
SIC: 3443 Containers, shipping (bombs,
etc.): metal plate
HQ: Worthington Cylinder Corporation
200 W Old Wlson Bridge Rd
Worthington OH 43085
614 840-3210

(G-13405)
WRKCO INC
8080 N Point Blvd (27106-3204)
PHONE..................................336 759-7501
EMP: 27
SIC: 2631 Paperboard mills
HQ: Wrkco Inc.
1000 Abrnthy Rd Ne Ste 12
Atlanta GA 30328
770 448-2193

(G-13406)
WRKCO INC
5900 Grassy Creek Blvd (27105-1205)
PHONE..................................770 448-2193
EMP: 106
SIC: 2631 Paperboard mills
HQ: Wrkco Inc.
1000 Abrnthy Rd Ne Ste 12
Atlanta GA 30328
770 448-2193

(G-13407)
WRKCO INC
3946 Westpoint Blvd (27103-6719)
PHONE..................................336 765-7004
EMP: 29
SIC: 2631 5113 Paperboard mills;
Corrugated and solid fiber boxes
HQ: Wrkco Inc.
1000 Abrnthy Rd Ne Ste 12
Atlanta GA 30328
770 448-2193

(G-13408)
XPRES LLC
111 Cloverleaf Dr (27103-6715)
PHONE..................................336 245-1596
Michael Wallach, *
◆ EMP: 40 EST: 2010
SQ FT: 30,000
SALES (est): 8.14MM Privately Held
Web: www.xpres.com
SIC: 2752 Commercial printing, lithographic

(G-13409)
YONTZ & SONS PAINTING INC
3803 S Main St (27127-6044)
P.O. Box 282 (27373-0282)
PHONE..................................336 784-7099
Paul Yontz Junior, Pr
EMP: 4 EST: 1970
SQ FT: 2,400
SALES (est): 271.76K Privately Held
SIC: 1721 3471 Commercial painting;
Plating and polishing

(G-13410)
ZIEHL-ABEGG INC
4971 Millennium Dr (27107-3736)
PHONE..................................336 934-9339
EMP: 162
SALES (corp-wide): 688.71MM Privately
Held
SIC: 3694 3443 3564 Battery charging
alternators and generators; Industrial
vessels, tanks, and containers; Purification
and dust collection equipment
HQ: Ziehl-Abegg, Inc.
719 N Regional Rd
Greensboro NC 27419
336 834-9339

(G-13411)
ZIM ARCRAFT CBIN SOLUTIONS LLC
Also Called: Haeco Americas Cabin Solutions
5568 Gumtree Rd (27107-9583)
PHONE..................................336 464-0122
Mark Lunsford, Brnch Mgr
EMP: 289
Web: www.haeco.aero
SIC: 2531 Seats, aircraft
HQ: Zim Aircraft Cabin Solutions Llc
8010 Piedmont Triad Pkwy
Greensboro NC 27409

(G-13412)
ZOES KITCHEN INC
205 S Stratford Rd (27103-1871)
PHONE..................................336 748-0587
EMP: 25
SALES (corp-wide): 963.71MM Publicly
Held
Web: www.zoeskitchen.com
SIC: 5812 3841 Restaurant, family:
independent; Catheters
HQ: Zoe's Kitchen, Inc.
5760 State Hwy 121 Ste 25
Plano TX 75024

(G-13413)
ZOOM APPAREL INC (PA)
303 S Broad St (27101-5022)
PHONE..................................336 993-9666
Jeffrey Federico, Pr
Christine Federico, VP
EMP: 4 EST: 2006
SQ FT: 6,000
SALES (est): 1.04MM Privately Held
Web: www.zoomapparel.com
SIC: 2759 2395 Screen printing; Embroidery
and art needlework

Winterville
Pitt County

(G-13414)
BUCK SUPPLY COMPANY INC
Also Called: Buck Marine Diesel
3060 Old Highway 11 (28590)
PHONE..................................252 215-1252
Kenneth Buck, Pr
Cindy Buck, Sec
EMP: 6 EST: 1952
SQ FT: 14,000
SALES (est): 359.34K Privately Held
Web: www.buckdiesel.com
SIC: 3519 Engines, diesel and semi-diesel
or dual-fuel

(G-13415)
CLARIOS LLC
Also Called: Johnson Controls
4125 Bayswater Rd (28590-9818)
PHONE..................................252 754-0782
EMP: 34
SALES (corp-wide): 69.83B Privately Held
Web: www.clarios.com
SIC: 2531 Seats, automobile
HQ: Clarios, Llc
5757 N Green Bay Ave Flor
Glendale WI 53209

(G-13416)
GREENVILLE READY MIX CONCRETE (PA)
Also Called: Greenville Rdymx Dpd Team Con
5039 Nc 11 S (28590-7764)
P.O. Box 131 (27216-0131)
PHONE..................................252 756-0119
Derek P Dunn, Pr
Elizabeth K Dunn, Sec

Cindy H Rhue, *Sec*
EMP: 20 **EST:** 1982
SQ FT: 3,000
SALES (est): 18.38MM
SALES (corp-wide): 18.38MM **Privately Held**
Web: www.dpdconcrete.com
SIC: 5032 3273 Concrete mixtures; Ready-mixed concrete

(G-13417)
JBR PROPERTIES OF GREENVILLE INC
Also Called: Roberts Company, The
133 Forlines Rd (28590-8508)
PHONE..............................252 355-9353
▲ **EMP:** 730 **EST:** 1977
SALES (est): 6.29MM **Privately Held**
SIC: 1541 3443 Industrial buildings, new construction, nec; Fabricated plate work (boiler shop)

(G-13418)
MIKE LUSZCZ
3424 Sagewood Ct (28590-5500)
PHONE..............................252 717-6282
Mike Luszcz, *Prin*
EMP: 5 **EST:** 2010
SALES (est): 73.46K **Privately Held**
Web: www.mlboatworksrc.com
SIC: 3732 Boatbuilding and repairing

(G-13419)
MORGAN PRINTERS INC
4120 Bayswater Rd (28590-9817)
P.O. Box 2126 (27836-0126)
PHONE..............................252 355-5588
Lydia Morgan, *CEO*
Jack Morgan, *Pr*
Parker Morgan, *Mgr*
EMP: 13 **EST:** 1964
SQ FT: 11,600
SALES (est): 852.06K **Privately Held**
Web: www.morganprinters.com
SIC: 2752 Offset printing

(G-13420)
NOBLE BROTHERS LOGGING COMPANY
237 W Meath Dr (28590-9184)
PHONE..............................252 355-2587
Larry Noble, *Pr*
Roger Noble, *Prin*
EMP: 4 **EST:** 1985
SALES (est): 148.45K **Privately Held**
SIC: 2411 Logging camps and contractors

(G-13421)
PHOENIX SIGN PROS INC
4409 Corey Rd (28590-9269)
PHONE..............................252 756-5685
Edward Lee Thornton, *Owner*
EMP: 4 **EST:** 2017
SALES (est): 50.69K **Privately Held**
Web: www.phoenixsignpros.net
SIC: 3993 Signs and advertising specialties

(G-13422)
ROYALKIND LLC
2131 Jubilee Ln (28590-9706)
PHONE..............................252 355-7484
Julia Lewis Fagundus, *Prin*
EMP: 5 **EST:** 2018
SALES (est): 105.09K **Privately Held**
SIC: 2741 Miscellaneous publishing

(G-13423)
S & S REPAIR SERVICE INC
1196 Pocosin Rd (28590-7137)
P.O. Box 102 (28590-0102)

PHONE..............................252 756-5989
George T Savage, *Pr*
Claudia Savage, *Prin*
EMP: 10 **EST:** 1969
SQ FT: 10,000
SALES (est): 989.86K **Privately Held**
Web: www.siteboxstorage.com
SIC: 7699 3599 Construction equipment repair; Machine shop, jobbing and repair

(G-13424)
TRC ACQUISITION LLC
133 Forlines Rd (28590-8508)
PHONE..............................252 355-9353
D Chris Bailey, *Managing Member*
Doyal Lee Barnett, *
Monty Glover, *
EMP: 505 **EST:** 2008
SALES (est): 25.83MM **Privately Held**
SIC: 1541 3443 Industrial buildings, new construction, nec; Fabricated plate work (boiler shop)

(G-13425)
VIATICUS INC
4104 Sterling Trace Dr (28590-9321)
PHONE..............................252 258-4679
Mark Weitzel, *Prin*
EMP: 7 **EST:** 2010
SALES (est): 153.84K **Privately Held**
Web: www.viaticusgroup.com
SIC: 2741 Miscellaneous publishing

(G-13426)
WINTERVILLE MACHINE WORKS INC
Also Called: Wmw Marine
2672 Mill St (28590-9228)
P.O. Box 520 (28590-0520)
PHONE..............................252 756-2130
John R Carroll, *Pr*
Ted Cox, *
Greis Lane, *
▲ **EMP:** 65 **EST:** 1957
SQ FT: 40,000
SALES (est): 5.66MM **Privately Held**
Web: www.wmwworks.com
SIC: 3429 3599 3732 Marine hardware; Machine shop, jobbing and repair; Boatbuilding and repairing

Winton
Hertford County

(G-13427)
ALFINITI INC
600 N Metcalf St (27986)
PHONE..............................252 358-5811
Jean Pare, *Pr*
Richard James, *
▲ **EMP:** 75 **EST:** 2006
SQ FT: 325,000
SALES (est): 8.55MM
SALES (corp-wide): 2.1MM **Privately Held**
Web: www.alfiniti.com
SIC: 3354 Aluminum extruded products
HQ: Spectube Inc.
1152 Rue De La Manic
Chicoutimi QC G7K 1
418 696-2545

(G-13428)
CRMP INC
115 Hwy 158 W (27986)
P.O. Box 189 (27986-0189)
PHONE..............................252 358-5461
Charles Harrell, *Genl Mgr*
EMP: 9 **EST:** 2005
SALES (est): 235.28K **Privately Held**
Web: www.crmpinc.com

SIC: 3273 Ready-mixed concrete

Woodleaf
Rowan County

(G-13429)
MARIETTA MARTIN MATERIALS INC
Also Called: Martin Marietta Aggregates
720 Quarry Rd (27054-9365)
PHONE..............................704 278-2218
Mike Cameron, *Mgr*
EMP: 5
Web: www.martinmarietta.com
SIC: 1422 1423 Crushed and broken limestone; Crushed and broken granite
PA: Martin Marietta Materials Inc
4123 Parklake Ave
Raleigh NC 27612

(G-13430)
PIEDMONT PALLET & CONT INC
667 Hendrix Farm Circle Ln (27054)
P.O. Box 400 (27054-0400)
PHONE..............................336 284-6302
Mark Lottes, *Pr*
Beverly Lottes, *VP*
EMP: 4 **EST:** 1995
SQ FT: 3,800
SALES (est): 243.82K **Privately Held**
SIC: 2448 Pallets, wood

Wrightsville Beach
New Hanover County

(G-13431)
GREENFIELD ENERGY LLC
213 Seacrest Dr (28480-1731)
PHONE..............................910 509-1805
Robin H Spinks, *Managing Member*
EMP: 10 **EST:** 2007
SALES (est): 1.4MM **Privately Held**
Web: www.consultgreenfield.net
SIC: 3621 7389 Frequency converters (electric generators); Business services, nec

(G-13432)
MARINEMAX OF NORTH CAROLINA
Also Called: Marinemax
130 Short St (28480-1764)
PHONE..............................910 256-8100
Bill Mcgill, *Pr*
EMP: 9 **EST:** 1992
SQ FT: 5,000
SALES (est): 237.9K
SALES (corp-wide): 2.43B **Publicly Held**
Web: www.marinemax.com
SIC: 5551 7699 3732 Motor boat dealers; Nautical repair services; Boatbuilding and repairing
PA: Marinemax, Inc.
501 Brooker Creek Blvd
Oldsmar FL 34677
727 531-1700

(G-13433)
STUMP PRINTING CO INC
Also Called: Stump's
525 Lumina Ave S (28480-6101)
PHONE..............................260 723-5171
N Shepard Moyle, *CEO*
Wendy Moyle, *
◆ **EMP:** 185 **EST:** 1926
SALES (est): 4.62MM **Privately Held**
SIC: 5199 2679 5961 2759 Novelties, paper; Novelties, paper: made from purchased material; Catalog sales; Commercial printing, nec

Yadkinville
Yadkin County

(G-13434)
ABBOTT PRODUCTS INC
1617 Fern Valley Rd (27055-6270)
PHONE..............................336 463-3135
Fred Smith, *Pr*
Richard Jacobson, *Ch Bd*
Glen Jacobson, *VP*
EMP: 20 **EST:** 1951
SQ FT: 15,000
SALES (est): 1.15MM **Privately Held**
Web: www.abbottbingoproducts.com
SIC: 3451 Screw machine products

(G-13435)
ADVANTAGE MACHINERY SVCS INC (PA)
Also Called: McLoud Trucking & Rigging
1407 Us 601 Hwy (27055-6358)
P.O. Box 1848 (27055-1848)
PHONE..............................336 463-4700
Robert D Gallimore, *Pr*
Chad Eller, *VP*
EMP: 32 **EST:** 1992
SALES (est): 9.71MM **Privately Held**
Web: www.amsrigging.com
SIC: 7699 4213 1799 1796 Industrial machinery and equipment repair; Heavy hauling, nec; Rigging and scaffolding; Machine moving and rigging

(G-13436)
AUSTIN COMPANY OF GREENSBORO
Also Called: Austin Company, The
2100 Hoots Rd (27055-6654)
P.O. Box 2320 (27055-2320)
PHONE..............................336 468-2851
James R Austin Iii, *Pr*
Dwayne Hunt, *
G Kevin Austin, *
Robin E Ludlow, *
Kristie Urbine Stkldr, *Prin*
EMP: 145 **EST:** 1964
SQ FT: 6,000
SALES (est): 8.03MM **Privately Held**
Web: www.austinenclosures.com
SIC: 3699 3644 Electrical equipment and supplies, nec; Junction boxes, electric

(G-13437)
B&G FOODS INC
500 Nonnis Way (27055)
P.O. Box 1489 (27055-1489)
PHONE..............................336 849-7000
Larry Fisk, *Mgr*
EMP: 50
SALES (corp-wide): 1.93B **Publicly Held**
Web: www.bgfoods.com
SIC: 2052 Cookies and crackers
PA: B&G Foods, Inc.
4 Gatehall Dr
Parsippany NJ 07054
973 401-6500

(G-13438)
BLUE RIDGE LBR LOG & TIMBER CO
2854 Old Us 421 Hwy W (27055-7146)
P.O. Box 2374 (27055-2374)
PHONE..............................336 961-5211
Thomas Perry, *Pr*
Dennis Billing, *Sec*
EMP: 4 **EST:** 1998
SALES (est): 474.36K **Privately Held**

SIC: **2491** 5211 2426 2421 Structural lumber and timber, treated wood; Lumber products; Hardwood dimension and flooring mills; Sawmills and planing mills, general

(G-13439)
BRIGGS-SHAFFNER ACQUISITION CO (PA)
Also Called: Briggs-Shaffner Company
1448 Us 601 Hwy (27055-6358)
P.O. Box 67 (27055-0067)
PHONE..........................336 463-4272
Emmitte Winslow, *Pr*
F John Mazur, *VP*
L Joe Bogan, *VP*
Carol M Winslow, *Sec*
◆ **EMP: 10 EST:** 1892
SQ FT: 80,000
SALES (est): 9.99MM **Privately Held**
Web: www.briggsbeams.com
SIC: **3552** 3365 3599 7699 Textile machinery ; Aluminum and aluminum-based alloy castings; Machine shop, jobbing and repair; Industrial machinery and equipment repair

(G-13440)
DIVERSIFIED FOAM INC (PA)
1813 Us 601 Hwy (27055-6347)
P.O. Box 1358 (27055-1358)
PHONE..........................336 463-5512
Brent Matthews, *Pr*
W Lawrence Green, *
Patricia Matthews, *
Bobby Holland, *
EMP: 34 **EST:** 1983
SQ FT: 5,400
SALES (est): 5.5MM
SALES (corp-wide): 5.5MM **Privately Held**
Web: www.diversifiedfoamusa.com
SIC: **3086** Packaging and shipping materials, foamed plastics

(G-13441)
DORSETT TECHNOLOGIES INC (PA)
100 Woodlyn Dr (27055-6673)
P.O. Box 1339 (27055-1339)
PHONE..........................855 387-2232
EMP: 43 **EST:** 1956
SALES (est): 17.43MM
SALES (corp-wide): 17.43MM **Privately Held**
Web: www.dorsett-tech.com
SIC: **3822** Air conditioning and refrigeration controls

(G-13442)
EVEREADY MIX CONCRETE CO INC
421 Old Hwy E (27055)
P.O. Box 577 (27055-0577)
PHONE..........................336 961-6688
David Adams, *Pr*
Charles Adams, *VP*
EMP: 8 **EST:** 1971
SQ FT: 400
SALES (est): 905.21K **Privately Held**
SIC: **3273** Ready-mixed concrete

(G-13443)
HIBCO PLASTICS INC
1820 Us 601 Hwy (27055-6347)
P.O. Box 157 (27055-0157)
PHONE..........................336 463-2391
Daniel S Pavlansky, *Ch*
Mark Pavlansky, *
Dan Pavlansky, *
Keith Pavlansky, *
Jon Pavlansky, *
▲ **EMP:** 45 **EST:** 1957
SQ FT: 120,000
SALES (est): 6.46MM **Privately Held**
Web: www.hibco.com

SIC: **3086** 5199 2679 3053 Insulation or cushioning material, foamed plastics; Automobile fabrics; Building, insulating, and packaging paper; Gaskets; packing and sealing devices

(G-13444)
IF DISHER MEAT PROCESSING
Also Called: Disher Packing Co
1437 Old Stage Rd (27055-6730)
PHONE..........................336 463-2907
Ida Mae Disher, *Owner*
Chris Disher, *Sec*
EMP: 5 **EST:** 1970
SALES (est): 98.79K **Privately Held**
SIC: **2011** Meat packing plants

(G-13445)
LOFLIN HANDLE CO INC
2837 Courtney Huntsville Rd (27055-6620)
PHONE..........................336 463-2422
J H Loflin Junior, *Pr*
Elizabeth Gonzales, *VP*
EMP: 4 **EST:** 1960
SALES (est): 230.32K **Privately Held**
SIC: **2499** 0132 5085 Handles, wood; Tobacco; Tools, nec

(G-13446)
LYDALL INC
2029 Anna Dr (27055)
PHONE..........................336 468-1323
EMP: 6
Web: www.lydall.com
SIC: **2297** Nonwoven fabrics
HQ: Lydall, Inc.
    180 Glstnbury Blvd Ste 12
    Glastonbury CT 06033
    860 646-1233

(G-13447)
PERDUE FARMS INC
Also Called: Perdue Farms
806 W Main St (27055-7806)
PHONE..........................336 679-7733
Clyde Weathers, *Brnch Mgr*
EMP: 90
SALES (corp-wide): 1.24B **Privately Held**
Web: www.perdue.com
SIC: **2015** Poultry slaughtering and processing
PA: Perdue Farms Incorporated
    31149 Old Ocean City Rd
    Salisbury MD 21804
    800 473-7383

(G-13448)
QUALITY STEEL FABRICATION INC
1301 Union Cross Church Rd (27055-7303)
P.O. Box 1902 (27055-1902)
PHONE..........................336 961-2670
Tim Doub, *Pr*
Avalon Doub, *VP*
Greg Miller, *Prin*
EMP: 7 **EST:** 1985
SALES (est): 879.32K **Privately Held**
SIC: **3441** Fabricated structural metal

(G-13449)
REBB INDUSTRIES INC
1617 Fern Valley Rd (27055-6270)
PHONE..........................336 463-2311
Richard Jacobson, *Pr*
EMP: 25 **EST:** 1978
SQ FT: 32,000
SALES (est): 1.76MM **Privately Held**
SIC: **3599** Machine shop, jobbing and repair
PA: Viewriver Machine Corporation
    1617 Fern Valley Rd
    Yadkinville NC 27055

(G-13450)
S H WOODWORKING
1316 Travis Rd (27055-6271)
PHONE..........................336 463-2885
EMP: 5 **EST:** 2011
SALES (est): 63.16K **Privately Held**
SIC: **2431** Millwork

(G-13451)
SHALLOWFORD FARMS POPCORN INC
Also Called: Shallowford Farms Popcorn
3732 Hartman Rd (27055-5638)
PHONE..........................336 463-5938
Booe Caswell, *Prin*
EMP: 6 **EST:** 1989
SALES (est): 498.57K **Privately Held**
Web: www.shallowfordfarmspopcorn.com
SIC: **5441** 2099 2096 Popcorn, including caramel corn; Food preparations, nec; Potato chips and similar snacks

(G-13452)
STEELMAN MILLING COMPANY INC
1517 Us 601 Hwy (27055-6344)
PHONE..........................336 463-5586
Max B Steelman, *Pr*
Betty Steelman, *Sec*
EMP: 6 **EST:** 1953
SQ FT: 7,000
SALES (est): 228.85K **Privately Held**
Web: www.steelmanmill.com
SIC: **5999** 2048 5251 Feed and farm supply; Prepared feeds, nec; Chainsaws

(G-13453)
TMP OF NC INC
1201 Old Stage Rd (27055-6728)
PHONE..........................336 463-3225
Randall Simmons, *Pr*
EMP: 6 **EST:** 2000
SQ FT: 6,000
SALES (est): 1.02MM **Privately Held**
SIC: **3599** Machine shop, jobbing and repair

(G-13454)
UNIFI INC
1032 Unifi Industrial Rd (27055)
P.O. Box 698 (27055-0698)
PHONE..........................336 679-3830
Robert Snider, *Mgr*
EMP: 142
SALES (corp-wide): 582.21MM **Publicly Held**
Web: www.unifi.com
SIC: **2282** 2281 Textured yarn; Yarn spinning mills
PA: Unifi, Inc.
    7201 W Friendly Ave
    Greensboro NC 27410
    336 294-4410

(G-13455)
UNIFI MANUFACTURING INC
Warehouse 2
601 E Main St (27055-8136)
PHONE..........................336 427-1515
Larry Fisk, *Pr*
EMP: 1139
SALES (corp-wide): 582.21MM **Publicly Held**
Web: www.unifi.com
SIC: **2281** Yarn spinning mills
HQ: Unifi Manufacturing, Inc.
    7201 W Friendly Ave
    Greensboro NC 27410

(G-13456)
UNIFI MANUFACTURING INC
1032 Unifi Industrial Rd (27055)
PHONE..........................336 679-8891
Larry Fisk, *Pr*
EMP: 1139
SALES (corp-wide): 582.21MM **Publicly Held**
Web: www.unifi.com
SIC: **2281** Nylon yarn, spinning of staple
HQ: Unifi Manufacturing, Inc.
    7201 W Friendly Ave
    Greensboro NC 27410

(G-13457)
VIEWRIVER MACHINE CORPORATION (PA)
Also Called: R E B B Industries
1617 Fern Valley Rd (27055-6270)
PHONE..........................336 463-2311
Richard Jacobson, *Pr*
Lee Wilmath, *
EMP: 25 **EST:** 1978
SALES (est): 2.51MM **Privately Held**
Web: nc-yadkinville.pacifica.org.au
SIC: **3599** Machine shop, jobbing and repair

(G-13458)
WILO INCORPORATED (DH)
350 W Maple St (27055-7700)
P.O. Box 309 (27055)
PHONE..........................336 679-4440
John W Willingham, *Pr*
▲ **EMP:** 30 **EST:** 1922
SQ FT: 135,000
SALES (est): 8.92MM
SALES (corp-wide): 74.45MM **Privately Held**
Web: www.inderamills.com
SIC: **2322** 2341 Men's and boy's underwear and nightwear; Women's and children's undergarments
HQ: Intradeco Apparel, Inc.
    9500 Nw 108th Ave
    Miami FL 33178
    305 264-8888

(G-13459)
YADKIN LUMBER COMPANY INC
800 N State St (27055-5258)
P.O. Box 729 (27055-0729)
PHONE..........................336 679-2432
Charles H Dinkins, *Pr*
Carolyn Long, *Sec*
EMP: 8 **EST:** 1949
SQ FT: 7,500
SALES (est): 901.86K **Privately Held**
SIC: **5211** 2421 Lumber and other building materials; Lumber: rough, sawed, or planed

Yanceyville
Caswell County

(G-13460)
ROYAL TEXTILE MILLS INC
Also Called: Duke Athletic Products
929 Firetower Rd (27379-9381)
P.O. Box 250 (27379-0250)
PHONE..........................336 694-4121
Mark V Atwater, *Pr*
W David Atwater, *
Jerry L Cole, *
EMP: 75 **EST:** 1948
SQ FT: 36,000
SALES (est): 5.64MM **Privately Held**
Web: www.dukeathletic-tactical.com

SIC: **2322** 2253 3949 2321 Underwear, men's and boys': made from purchased materials; T-shirts and tops, knit; Protective sporting equipment; Men's and boy's furnishings

Youngsville
Franklin County

(G-13461)
AMCOR PHRM PACKG USA LLC
Also Called: Wheaton Plastic Operations
111 Wheaton Ave (27596-9415)
P.O. Box 579 (27596-0579)
PHONE..............................919 556-9715
Julian Stewart, *Mgr*
EMP: 52
SALES (corp-wide): 14.69B **Privately Held**
SIC: **3085** Plastics bottles
HQ: Amcor Pharmaceutical Packaging Usa, Llc
625 Sharp St N
Millville NJ 08332
856 327-1540

(G-13462)
ATLANTIC COAST CABINET DISTRS
Also Called: ACC Distributors
150 Weathers Ct (27596-7844)
P.O. Box 1257 (27596-1257)
PHONE..............................919 554-8165
William A Konkle Iii, *Pr*
William A Konkle Junior, *VP*
Michelle Konkle, *
EMP: 25 EST: 1991
SQ FT: 68,000
SALES (est): 3.8MM **Privately Held**
Web: www.atlanticcoastcabinets.com
SIC: **2434** Wood kitchen cabinets

(G-13463)
BACHSTEIN CONSULTING LLC
70 Mosswood Blvd Ste 200 (27596-7990)
PHONE..............................410 322-4917
EMP: 6 EST: 2017
SALES (est): 514.7K **Privately Held**
Web: www.bachsteinconsulting.com
SIC: **8711** 8748 7373 3484 Consulting engineer; Systems engineering consultant, ex. computer or professional; Computer-aided engineering (CAE) systems service; Guns (firearms) or gun parts, 30 mm. and below

(G-13464)
BESI MACHINING LLC
95 Cypress Dr (27596-8795)
P.O. Box 40363 (27629-0363)
PHONE..............................919 218-9241
EMP: 10 EST: 2016
SALES (est): 1.59MM **Privately Held**
Web: www.besimachining.com
SIC: **7699** 3559 Industrial machinery and equipment repair; Special industry machinery, nec

(G-13465)
BUILDERS FIRSTSOURCE INC
45 Mosswood Blvd (27596-7802)
P.O. Box 1017 (27596-1017)
PHONE..............................919 562-6601
Craig Cornelius, *Genl Mgr*
EMP: 17
SALES (corp-wide): 16.4B **Publicly Held**
Web: www.bldr.com
SIC: **5211** 2431 5031 Millwork and lumber; Millwork; Lumber, plywood, and millwork
PA: Builders Firstsource, Inc.
6031 Cnnection Dr Ste 400

Irving TX 75039
214 880-3500

(G-13466)
C-TRON INCORPORATED
6473 Nc 96 Hwy W (27596-8621)
PHONE..............................919 494-7811
Donna Albright, *CEO*
Thomas Albright, *Pr*
EMP: 7 EST: 1991
SALES (est): 1.24MM **Privately Held**
Web: www.ctroninc.com
SIC: **3672** 3643 Printed circuit boards; Current-carrying wiring services

(G-13467)
CANYON STONE INC
409 Northbrook Dr (27596-7662)
PHONE..............................919 880-3273
Canyon Stone, *Brnch Mgr*
EMP: 12
SALES (corp-wide): 4.9MM **Privately Held**
Web: www.estoneworks.com
SIC: **3272** Stone, cast concrete
PA: Canyon Stone, Inc.
550 E Old Highway 56 B
Olathe KS 66061
913 254-9300

(G-13468)
CAPTIVE-AIRE SYSTEMS INC
360 Northbrook Dr (27596-7853)
PHONE..............................919 887-2721
Robert Luddy, *Prin*
EMP: 133
SALES (corp-wide): 485.13MM **Privately Held**
Web: www.captiveaire.com
SIC: **3444** Restaurant sheet metalwork
PA: Captive-Aire Systems, Inc.
4641 Pragon Pk Rd Ste 104
Raleigh NC 27616
919 882-2410

(G-13469)
CAROLINA MACHINING FABRICATION
Also Called: Cmfi
321 N Nassau St (27596-9209)
P.O. Box 1217 (27596-1217)
PHONE..............................919 554-9700
Muhammed Asim, *Pr*
EMP: 4 EST: 2009
SQ FT: 770
SALES (est): 1.9MM **Privately Held**
SIC: **3441** 7699 1761 Fabricated structural metal; Industrial machinery and equipment repair; Sheet metal work, nec

(G-13470)
CAROLINA RESOURCE CORP
850 Park Ave (27596-9472)
PHONE..............................919 562-0200
EMP: 16 EST: 1978
SALES (est): 2.32MM **Privately Held**
Web: www.carolinaresource.com
SIC: **3544** 3599 Special dies, tools, jigs, and fixtures; Machine shop, jobbing and repair

(G-13471)
CIRCUIT BOARD ASSEMBLERS INC
130 Mosswood Blvd (27596-8680)
PHONE..............................919 556-7881
Tom Albright, *Pr*
Tom Albright, *Ch*
Carol Albright, *
E C Sykes, *
EMP: 160 EST: 1985
SQ FT: 15,000
SALES (est): 1.11MM **Privately Held**

SIC: **3672** Printed circuit boards

(G-13472)
FRANKLIN LOGISTICAL SERVICES INC
Also Called: Welsh Paper Company
112 Franklin Park Dr (27596-9400)
P.O. Box 1529 (27588-1529)
PHONE..............................919 556-6711
▲ EMP: 100
SIC: **5113** 3086 Paper, wrapping or coarse, and products; Packaging and shipping materials, foamed plastics

(G-13473)
GRADY DISTRIBUTING CO INC
Also Called: ABC Hosiery
640 Park Ave (27596-9468)
P.O. Box 218 (27596-0218)
PHONE..............................919 556-5630
Anthony Grady, *Pr*
Pam Grady, *VP*
EMP: 12 EST: 1991
SALES (est): 1.25MM **Privately Held**
Web: www.abchosiery.com
SIC: **2252** Socks

(G-13474)
HVTE INC
90 Mosswood Blvd Ste 100 (27596-7804)
P.O. Box 1135 (27596-1135)
PHONE..............................919 274-8899
Alvin Kopp, *Prin*
EMP: 7 EST: 2006
SALES (est): 1.34MM **Privately Held**
SIC: **3825** Electrical power measuring equipment

(G-13475)
IMERYS PERLITE USA INC
Also Called: Harborlite
100 Robert Blunt Dr (27596-8524)
P.O. Box 727 (27596-0727)
PHONE..............................919 562-0031
Brandon Hedgecock, *Mgr*
EMP: 10
SALES (corp-wide): 5.36MM **Privately Held**
SIC: **3295** Perlite, aggregate or expanded
HQ: Imerys Perlite Usa, Inc.
1732 N First St Ste 450
San Jose CA 95112

(G-13476)
INTEGRATED INFO SYSTEMS INC
460 Boardwalk Dr (27596-3318)
P.O. Box 219 (27525-0219)
PHONE..............................919 488-5000
Richard K Washington, *CEO*
Deborah Washington, *Treas*
EMP: 10 EST: 2002
SQ FT: 2,500
SALES (est): 1.46MM **Privately Held**
Web: www.iisysinc.com
SIC: **3651** 7382 5999 Household audio and video equipment; Security systems services; Audio-visual equipment and supplies

(G-13477)
K-FLEX USA LLC
100 K Flex Way (27596)
PHONE..............................919 556-3475
Giuseppe Guarino, *Managing Member*
Carlo Spinelli, *
◆ EMP: 259 EST: 2001
SALES (est): 32.16MM
SALES (corp-wide): 355.83K **Privately Held**
Web: www.kflexusa.com

SIC: **3069** Hard rubber and molded rubber products
HQ: L'isolante K-Flex Spa
Via Don Giuseppe Locatelli 35
Roncello MB 20877

(G-13478)
LAYER27
205 Blue Heron Dr (27596-7674)
PHONE..............................919 909-9088
James Pierce, *Prin*
EMP: 5 EST: 2018
SALES (est): 130.29K **Privately Held**
Web: www.layer27.com
SIC: **3822** Hardware for environmental regulators

(G-13479)
OMEGA PRECIOUS METALS
40 Shorrey Pl (27596-7017)
PHONE..............................269 903-9330
Thomas Manley, *Owner*
EMP: 5 EST: 2013
SALES (est): 82.99K **Privately Held**
SIC: **3339** Precious metals

(G-13480)
PIEDMONT LOGGING LLC
870 Park Ave (27596-9472)
PHONE..............................919 562-1861
EMP: 5 EST: 2017
SALES (est): 167.57K **Privately Held**
SIC: **2411** Logging

(G-13481)
POWERGPU LLC
762 Park Ave (27596-9470)
PHONE..............................919 702-6757
Jese Martinez, *Managing Member*
Stephanie Ivette Martinez, *Managing Member*
EMP: 10 EST: 2019
SALES (est): 6.82MM **Privately Held**
Web: www.powergpu.com
SIC: **3629** Electronic generation equipment

(G-13482)
ROBLING MEDICAL LLC
Also Called: Robling Medical
90 Weathers Ct (27596)
PHONE..............................919 570-9605
Brent D Robling, *Pr*
Jodi Robling, *
▲ EMP: 70 EST: 1992
SQ FT: 18,000
SALES (est): 14.24MM **Privately Held**
Web: www.roblingmedical.com
SIC: **3841** Catheters

(G-13483)
ROOTS RUN DEEP LLC
90 Oak Leaf Trl (27596-7404)
PHONE..............................919 909-9117
Yan Garner, *Prin*
EMP: 4 EST: 2018
SALES (est): 498.63K **Privately Held**
Web: www.rootsrundeep.com
SIC: **2084** Wines

(G-13484)
SAND HAMMER FORGING INC
594 Bert Winston Rd (27596-8781)
PHONE..............................919 554-9554
Agnieszka Freer, *Admn*
Dustin Freer, *Pr*
Stan Wyrembak, *VP*
Agnieszka Freer, *Corporate Secretary*
Alica Wyrembak, *Treas*
EMP: 6 EST: 2017
SALES (est): 1.14MM **Privately Held**

Web: www.sandhammerforging.com
SIC: 3484 Small arms

(G-13485)
SILVERLINING SCREEN PRTRS INC
90 Mosswood Blvd Ste 600 (27596-7849)
P.O. Box 67 (27529)
PHONE..............................919 554-0340
Victoria Jaynes, *Pr*
Gabriel Schultz, *Sec*
EMP: 4 EST: 1981
SQ FT: 6,500
SALES (est): 78.09K **Privately Held**
Web:
www.silverliningscreenprinters.com
SIC: 2759 2261 5199 Screen printing;
    Screen printing of cotton broadwoven
    fabrics; Advertising specialties

(G-13486)
SIRCHIE ACQUISITION CO LLC (PA)
Also Called: Sirchie Finger Print Labs
100 Hunter Pl (27596)
PHONE..............................800 356-7311
Inez Neff, *Pr*
Gary L Monroe, *
Jennifer Walton, *
Anthony Saggiomo, *
◆ EMP: 113 EST: 1956
SQ FT: 172,978
SALES (est): 21.88MM
SALES (corp-wide): 21.88MM **Privately
Held**
Web: www.sirchie.com
SIC: 2899 Chemical preparations, nec

(G-13487)
SOUTHERN LITHOPLATE INC (PA)
105 Jeffrey Way (27596-9759)
P.O. Box 9400 (27588-6400)
PHONE..............................919 556-9400
Edward A Casson Iii, *Ch Bd*
Clark A Casson, *
Ronalda A Casson, *
◆ EMP: 110 EST: 1981
SQ FT: 135,000
SALES (est): 21.72MM
SALES (corp-wide): 21.72MM **Privately
Held**
Web: www.slp.com
SIC: 2796 Lithographic plates, positives or
    negatives

(G-13488)
SPECTRUM PRODUCTS INC
153 Mosswood Blvd (27596-8685)
P.O. Box 2075 (27588-2075)
PHONE..............................919 556-7797
Scott Cissel, *Pr*
EMP: 6 EST: 1991
SQ FT: 8,000
SALES (est): 2.34MM **Privately Held**
Web: www.treegator.com
SIC: 3523 Fertilizing, spraying, dusting, and
    irrigation machinery

(G-13489)
STOWE WOODWARD LLC
Also Called: Stove-Woodward Co
14101 Capital Blvd Ste 101 (27596-7854)
PHONE..............................360 636-0330
Robert L Deckon, *Mgr*
EMP: 34
SALES (corp-wide): 1.13B **Privately Held**
SIC: 3069 Roll coverings, rubber
HQ: Stowe Woodward Llc
    8537 Six Forks Rd Ste 300
    Raleigh NC 27615

(G-13490)
TAR RIVER TRADING POST LLC
Also Called: Distributor
385 Fleming Rd (27596-9698)
PHONE..............................919 589-3618
EMP: 5 EST: 2014
SQ FT: 5,400
SALES (est): 300.51K **Privately Held**
Web: www.tarrivertradingpost.com
SIC: 5083 3089 Farm and garden machinery
    ; Tubs, plastics (containers)

(G-13491)
TEAM MANUFACTURING - E W LLC
35 Weathers Ct (27596-7800)
P.O. Box 1218 (27596-1218)
PHONE..............................919 554-2442
EMP: 73
SALES (corp-wide): 460.52MM **Privately
Held**
Web: www.ewmfg.com
SIC: 3629 Electronic generation equipment
HQ: Team Manufacturing - East West, Llc
    4170 Ashford Dnwody Rd St
    Atlanta GA 30319
    919 554-2442

(G-13492)
TELECOMMUNICATIONS TECH INC
Also Called: TTI Wireless
14101 Capital Blvd Ste 201 (27596-0166)
PHONE..............................919 556-7100
Thomas G Albright, *Pr*
Dale Albright, *VP*
Carol Albright, *Sec*
EMP: 7 EST: 1989
SALES (est): 2.03MM **Privately Held**
Web: www.ttiwasp.com
SIC: 3823 Computer interface equipment, for
    industrial process control

(G-13493)
TOTAL FIRE SYSTEMS INC
30 Weathers Ct (27596-7801)
P.O. Box 1408 (27588-1408)
PHONE..............................919 556-9161
Mike Rohlik, *Pr*
Paul Collins, *
▼ EMP: 27 EST: 1990
SQ FT: 7,500
SALES (est): 5.11MM **Privately Held**
Web: www.totalfirenc.com
SIC: 3699 Fire control or bombing
    equipment, electronic

(G-13494)
TRIANGLE KITCHEN SUPPLY
336 Bert Winston Rd (27596-8726)
PHONE..............................919 562-3888
Andrew Hinton, *Owner*
EMP: 8 EST: 1973
SQ FT: 8,750
SALES (est): 79.1K **Privately Held**
SIC: 2434 Wood kitchen cabinets

(G-13495)
TRIANGLE METALWORKS INC
100 Moores Pond Rd (27596-9663)
PHONE..............................919 556-7786
Robbie Tilley, *Pr*
Sherri Tilley, *Sec*
EMP: 9 EST: 1995
SALES (est): 865.74K **Privately Held**
Web: www.trianglemetalworks.com
SIC: 3441 Fabricated structural metal

(G-13496)
TRIMM INTERNATIONAL INC
Also Called: Trimm
112 Franklin Park Dr (27596-9400)

PHONE..............................847 362-3700
G William Newton, *Pr*
Ayako M Newton, *Sec*
EMP: 20 EST: 1922
SALES (est): 6.36MM **Privately Held**
SIC: 3661 Telephone and telegraph
    apparatus

(G-13497)
VIA PRNTING GRAPHIC DESIGN INC
Also Called: Graphic Master
5841 Gentle Wind Dr (27596-8511)
PHONE..............................919 872-8688
Rodger Via, *Pt*
Chris Via, *Pt*
EMP: 5 EST: 1983
SQ FT: 1,697
SALES (est): 99.59K **Privately Held**
Web: www.graphicmaster.net
SIC: 2752 Offset printing

(G-13498)
WHITE STREET BREWING CO INC
400 Park Ave (27596-8688)
P.O. Box 2066 (27588-2066)
PHONE..............................919 647-9439
Dino Radosta, *Prin*
EMP: 13 EST: 2011
SALES (est): 938.75K **Privately Held**
Web: www.whitestreetbrewing.com
SIC: 5813 5181 2082 Bars and lounges;
    Beer and ale; Ale (alcoholic beverage)

(G-13499)
**WOODMASTER CUSTOM CABINETS
INC**
436 Park Ave (27596-8688)
P.O. Box 1206 (27596-1206)
PHONE..............................919 554-3707
Angela Ling, *Pr*
EMP: 12 EST: 2014
SALES (est): 938.71K **Privately Held**
Web: www.woodmasterwoodworks.com
SIC: 2434 2431 Wood kitchen cabinets;
    Millwork

Zebulon
Wake County

(G-13500)
ADVANCED PLASTIFORM INC (PA)
535 Mack Todd Rd (27597-2550)
PHONE..............................919 404-2080
Chris Jolly, *Pr*
EMP: 65 EST: 1987
SQ FT: 120,000
SALES (est): 24.4MM
SALES (corp-wide): 24.4MM **Privately
Held**
Web: www.advancedplastiform.com
SIC: 5162 3559 Plastics products, nec;
    Ammunition and explosives, loading
    machinery

(G-13501)
ADVANCED PLASTIFORM INC
113 Legacy Crest Ct (27597-9610)
PHONE..............................919 404-2080
EMP: 28
SALES (corp-wide): 24.4MM **Privately
Held**
Web: www.advancedplastiform.com
SIC: 3089 Injection molding of plastics
PA: Advanced Plastiform, Inc.
    535 Mack Todd Rd
    Zebulon NC 27597
    919 404-2080

(G-13502)
AIMET HOLDING INC
Also Called: Aimet Technologies
115 Legacy Crest Ct (27597-9610)
P.O. Box 1216 (27597-1216)
PHONE..............................919 887-5205
David Jackson, *Pr*
▲ EMP: 11 EST: 1993
SQ FT: 80,000
SALES (est): 1.5MM **Privately Held**
Web: www.aimet.com
SIC: 3089 Injection molding of plastics

(G-13503)
AIMET TECHNOLOGIES LLC
115 Legacy Crest Ct (27597-9610)
PHONE..............................919 887-5205
Tony Sturrus, *Prin*
EMP: 10 EST: 2014
SALES (est): 1.76MM **Privately Held**
SIC: 3089 Injection molding of plastics

(G-13504)
ASP HOLDINGS INC
Also Called: Power Pros
1014 N Arendell Ave (27597-2351)
P.O. Box 1585 (27545-1585)
PHONE..............................888 330-2538
Andy Young, *Pr*
Shelly Young, *VP*
EMP: 4 EST: 1994
SALES (est): 365.25K **Privately Held**
Web: www.powerprosinc.com
SIC: 3679 Power supplies, all types: static

(G-13505)
BROOKS MACHINE & DESIGN INC
1424 Old Us Highway 264 (27597-6921)
P.O. Box 65 (27597-0065)
PHONE..............................919 404-0901
Reginald G Brooks Iii, *Pr*
Ann S Brooks, *Sec*
EMP: 17 EST: 1994
SQ FT: 8,000
SALES (est): 6.83MM **Privately Held**
Web: www.brooksmachine.com
SIC: 3599 Machine shop, jobbing and repair

(G-13506)
CABLENC LLC
8012 Spiderlily Ct (27597-8952)
PHONE..............................919 307-9065
Justin Soustek, *CEO*
EMP: 9 EST: 2017
SALES (est): 1.09MM **Privately Held**
SIC: 3651 7389 Household audio and video
    equipment; Business services, nec

(G-13507)
**DEVIL DOG MANUFACTURING CO
INC**
400 E Gannon Ave (27597-2708)
P.O. Box 69 (27597-0069)
PHONE..............................919 269-7485
Tony Shannahan, *Brnch Mgr*
EMP: 194
SALES (corp-wide): 3.69MM **Privately
Held**
SIC: 2369 2361 2339 2325 Jeans: girls',
    children's, and infants'; Girl's and children's
    dresses, blouses; Women's and misses'
    outerwear, nec; Men's and boy's trousers
    and slacks
PA: Devil Dog Manufacturing Co., Inc.
    23 Market St
    Ellenville NY 12428
    845 647-4411

▲ = Import ▼ = Export
◆ = Import/Export

(G-13508)
ELECTRO MAGNETIC RESEARCH INC
Also Called: EMR Electric
9576 Covered Bridge Rd (27597-7410)
PHONE..................................919 365-3723
Rommel Edwards, *CEO*
EMP: 4 **EST:** 1986
SALES (est): 157.81K **Privately Held**
Web: www.emrelectric.com
SIC: 3625 8711 Industrial controls: push button, selector switches, pilot; Engineering services

(G-13509)
GLAXOSMITHKLINE LLC
Also Called: Glaxosmithkline
1011 N Arendell Ave (27597-2300)
P.O. Box 1217 (27597-1217)
PHONE..................................919 269-5000
Cliff Disbrow, *Genl Mgr*
EMP: 27
SALES (corp-wide): 39.77B **Privately Held**
Web: us.gsk.com
SIC: 2834 Pharmaceutical preparations
HQ: Glaxosmithkline Llc
2929 Walnut St Ste 1700
Philadelphia PA 19112
888 825-5249

(G-13510)
GREY AREA NEWS
70 Harrison St (27597-9307)
PHONE..................................919 637-6973
Carolyn Whatley, *Owner*
EMP: 4 **EST:** 2018
SALES (est): 74.87K **Privately Held**
Web: www.greyareanews.com
SIC: 2711 Newspapers, publishing and printing

(G-13511)
H BROTHERS FINE WDWKG LLC
1512 Earpsboro Rd (27597-7088)
PHONE..................................931 216-1955
EMP: 4 **EST:** 2019
SALES (est): 63.88K **Privately Held**
Web: www.millbrothersinc.com
SIC: 2434 Wood kitchen cabinets

(G-13512)
KAM TOOL & DIE INC
530 N Industrial Dr (27597-2748)
PHONE..................................919 269-5099
William Alford, *Pr*
Don Mitchell, *VP*
Jim Alford, *VP*
Addy Mitchell, *Stockholder*
EMP: 21 **EST:** 1995
SQ FT: 15,000
SALES (est): 3.6MM **Privately Held**
Web: www.kamtool.net
SIC: 3544 Special dies and tools

(G-13513)
LITTLE RIVER NATURALS LLC
7408 Riley Hill Rd (27597-8757)
PHONE..................................919 760-3708
EMP: 4 **EST:** 2019
SALES (est): 103.91K **Privately Held**
Web: www.littlerivernaturalsnc.com
SIC: 2844 Perfumes, cosmetics and other toilet preparations

(G-13514)
NOEL GROUP LLC (PA)
501 Innovative Way (27597-2661)
PHONE..................................919 269-6500
Marc Noel, *Managing Member*
EMP: 5 **EST:** 1996
SALES (est): 95.55MM
SALES (corp-wide): 95.55MM **Privately Held**
Web: www.noelgroup.net
SIC: 3086 Packaging and shipping materials, foamed plastics

(G-13515)
NOMACO INC (HQ)
501 Innovative Way (27597-2661)
PHONE..................................919 269-6500
Lars Von Kantzow, *Pr*
Steven Thompson, *
◆ **EMP:** 308 **EST:** 1979
SQ FT: 205,000
SALES (est): 49.45MM
SALES (corp-wide): 95.55MM **Privately Held**
Web: www.nomaco.com
SIC: 3086 Plastics foam products
PA: Noel Group, Llc
501 Nmc Dr
Zebulon NC 27597
919 269-6500

(G-13516)
NOMACORC HOLDINGS LLC
400 Vintage Park Dr (27597-3803)
PHONE..................................919 460-2200
Amy Bess Cook, *Prin*
EMP: 31 **EST:** 2014
SALES (est): 1.13MM **Privately Held**
Web: us.vinventions.com
SIC: 2084 Wines

(G-13517)
OAK CITY CUSTOMS LLC
501 Mack Todd Rd Ste 109 (27597-2550)
PHONE..................................919 995-5561
Dylan Selinger, *Pr*
EMP: 4 **EST:** 2016
SALES (est): 252.16K **Privately Held**
Web: www.oakcitycustoms.com
SIC: 7389 2426 2511 3499 Design services; Furniture stock and parts, hardwood; Wood household furniture; Fabricated metal products, nec

(G-13518)
OAK CITY METAL LLC
700 Pony Rd Ste C (27597-2656)
PHONE..................................919 375-4535
Melvin Brent Sanders, *Managing Member*
EMP: 6 **EST:** 2018
SALES (est): 1.09MM **Privately Held**
SIC: 3429 Metal fasteners

(G-13519)
OLDE RALEIGH DISTILLERY LLC
209 N Arendell Ave (27597-2603)
PHONE..................................919 208-0044
Jaime Mccraney, *CEO*
EMP: 10 **EST:** 2017
SALES (est): 256.95K **Privately Held**
SIC: 2085 Distilled and blended liquors

(G-13520)
PAUL CASPER INC
3533 Rosinburg Rd (27597-5300)
P.O. Box 9 (27597-0009)
PHONE..................................919 269-5362
Paul M Casper Junior, *Pr*
EMP: 6 **EST:** 1989
SQ FT: 5,000
SALES (est): 421.5K **Privately Held**
SIC: 7692 3441 3444 Welding repair; Fabricated structural metal; Sheet metalwork

(G-13521)
PINE GLO PRODUCTS INC
115 Legacy Crest Ct (27597-9610)
PHONE..................................919 556-7787
Matthew Diehl, *Pr*
Carolyn Diehl, *Sec*
◆ **EMP:** 19 **EST:** 1979
SALES (est): 4.38MM **Privately Held**
Web: www.pinegloproducts.com
SIC: 2842 2841 Polishes and sanitation goods; Soap and other detergents

(G-13522)
RTT MACHINE & WELDING SVC INC
12671 W Nc 97 (27597-6428)
PHONE..................................919 269-6863
Rodney Massey, *Pr*
EMP: 14 **EST:** 1996
SALES (est): 2.56MM **Privately Held**
Web: www.rttmachine.com
SIC: 3599 Machine shop, jobbing and repair

(G-13523)
THEO DAVIS SONS INCORPORATED
Also Called: Theo Davis Printing
1415 W Gannon Ave (27597-3306)
P.O. Box 277 (27597-0277)
PHONE..................................919 269-7401
Kenneth Carter, *Pr*
EMP: 28 **EST:** 1945
SQ FT: 28,000
SALES (est): 1.9MM
SALES (corp-wide): 15B **Privately Held**
SIC: 2752 2759 Offset printing; Laser printing
HQ: Consolidated Graphics, Inc.
5858 Westheimer Rd # 200
Houston TX 77057

(G-13524)
TRADEWINDS COFFEE CO INC
6308 Mitchell Mill Rd (27597-8407)
PHONE..................................919 556-1835
Art Watkins, *Pr*
Elaine Watkins, *VP*
EMP: 10 **EST:** 1987
SQ FT: 2,500
SALES (est): 394.99K **Privately Held**
Web: www.tradewindscoffee.com
SIC: 5149 5499 2095 Coffee, green or roasted; Coffee; Coffee roasting (except by wholesale grocers)

(G-13525)
VINVENTIONS USA LLC
Closure Innovations
505 Innovative Way (27597-2661)
PHONE..................................919 460-2200
Eric Dunkelberg, *Genl Mgr*
EMP: 170
SALES (corp-wide): 23.47MM **Privately Held**
Web: us.vinventions.com
SIC: 2499 Corks, bottle
PA: Vinventions Usa, Llc
888 Prospect St
La Jolla CA 92037
919 460-2200

(G-13526)
Z COLLECTION LLC
77 Gennessee Dr (27597-2164)
PHONE..................................919 247-1513
Zakeya Caldwell, *Managing Member*
EMP: 4 **EST:** 2017
SALES (est): 555.97K **Privately Held**
SIC: 3999 7389 5999 Hair and hair-based products; Business Activities at Non-Commercial Site; Alarm and safety equipment stores

Zionville
Watauga County

(G-13527)
BROWN BROTHERS CONSTRUCTION CO
10801 Us Highway 421 N (28698-9024)
PHONE..................................828 297-2131
EMP: 13 **EST:** 1948
SQ FT: 1,000
SALES (est): 505.5K **Privately Held**
SIC: 1611 1794 2951 General contractor, highway and street construction; Excavation work; Asphalt paving mixtures and blocks

Zirconia
Henderson County

(G-13528)
CAPPS NOBLE LOGGING
Bob's Creek Road (28790)
PHONE..................................828 696-9690
Noble Capps Junior, *Owner*
EMP: 4 **EST:** 1986
SALES (est): 478.2K **Privately Held**
SIC: 2411 Logging camps and contractors

(G-13529)
CAROLINA PAPER TUBES INC
Also Called: C P T
3932 Old Us 25 Hwy (28790-7907)
P.O. Box 219 (25423-0219)
PHONE..................................828 692-9686
Jerry Melton, *Pr*
Pennie Melton, *
▼ **EMP:** 32 **EST:** 1978
SQ FT: 40,000
SALES (est): 4.55MM **Privately Held**
Web: www.oxindustries.com
SIC: 2655 Tubes, fiber or paper: made from purchased material

(G-13530)
GREEN RIVER RESOURCE MGT
Also Called: Whole Log Lumber
195 Blueberry Farm Rd (28790-0265)
PHONE..................................828 697-0357
Jim Stowell, *Pr*
Loy Lauden, *VP*
EMP: 10 **EST:** 1984
SALES (est): 717.38K **Privately Held**
Web: www.wholeloglumber.com
SIC: 5211 5023 2426 Flooring, wood; Wood flooring; Flooring, hardwood

(G-13531)
MAYBIN EMERGENCY POWER INC
197 Mountain Valley Cemetery Rd (28790-6721)
PHONE..................................828 697-1195
Jim Maybin, *Pr*
Jessica Cox, *VP*
EMP: 7 **EST:** 1996
SQ FT: 3,500
SALES (est): 126.64K **Privately Held**
SIC: 7694 Electric motor repair

GEOGRAPHIC

SIC NO	PRODUCT

A

3291 Abrasive products
8721 Accounting, auditing, and bookkeeping
2891 Adhesives and sealants
7311 Advertising agencies
7319 Advertising, nec
2879 Agricultural chemicals, nec
3563 Air and gas compressors
4513 Air courier services
4522 Air transportation, nonscheduled
4512 Air transportation, scheduled
3721 Aircraft
3724 Aircraft engines and engine parts
3728 Aircraft parts and equipment, nec
4581 Airports, flying fields, and services
2812 Alkalies and chlorine
3363 Aluminum die-castings
3354 Aluminum extruded products
3365 Aluminum foundries
3355 Aluminum rolling and drawing, nec
3353 Aluminum sheet, plate, and foil
3483 Ammunition, except for small arms, nec
7999 Amusement and recreation, nec
3826 Analytical instruments
2077 Animal and marine fats and oils
0279 Animal specialties, nec
0752 Animal specialty services
6513 Apartment building operators
2389 Apparel and accessories, nec
2387 Apparel belts
3446 Architectural metalwork
8712 Architectural services
7694 Armature rewinding shops
3292 Asbestos products
2952 Asphalt felts and coatings
2951 Asphalt paving mixtures and blocks
5531 Auto and home supply stores
3581 Automatic vending machines
7521 Automobile parking
5012 Automobiles and other motor vehicles
2396 Automotive and apparel trimmings
5599 Automotive dealers, nec
7536 Automotive glass replacement shops
7539 Automotive repair shops, nec
7549 Automotive services, nec
3465 Automotive stampings
7537 Automotive transmission repair shops

B

2673 Bags: plastic, laminated, and coated
2674 Bags: uncoated paper and multiwall
3562 Ball and roller bearings
7241 Barber shops
7231 Beauty shops
0212 Beef cattle, except feedlots
5181 Beer and ale
2836 Biological products, except diagnostic
1221 Bituminous coal and lignite-surface mining
2782 Blankbooks and looseleaf binders
3312 Blast furnaces and steel mills
3564 Blowers and fans
5551 Boat dealers
3732 Boatbuilding and repairing
3452 Bolts, nuts, rivets, and washers
2732 Book printing
2731 Book publishing
5942 Book stores
2789 Bookbinding and related work
5192 Books, periodicals, and newspapers
2086 Bottled and canned soft drinks
2342 Bras, girdles, and allied garments
2051 Bread, cake, and related products
3251 Brick and structural clay tile
5032 Brick, stone, and related material
1622 Bridge, tunnel, and elevated highway
2211 Broadwoven fabric mills, cotton

2221 Broadwoven fabric mills, manmade
2231 Broadwoven fabric mills, wool
0251 Broiler, fryer, and roaster chickens
3991 Brooms and brushes
7349 Building maintenance services, nec
3995 Burial caskets
8611 Business associations
8748 Business consulting, nec
7389 Business services, nec

C

4841 Cable and other pay television services
3578 Calculating and accounting equipment
5946 Camera and photographic supply stores
2064 Candy and other confectionery products
5441 Candy, nut, and confectionery stores
2091 Canned and cured fish and seafoods
2033 Canned fruits and specialties
2032 Canned specialties
2394 Canvas and related products
3624 Carbon and graphite products
3955 Carbon paper and inked ribbons
3592 Carburetors, pistons, rings, valves
1751 Carpentry work
7217 Carpet and upholstery cleaning
2273 Carpets and rugs
7542 Carwashes
0119 Cash grains, nec
5961 Catalog and mail-order houses
2823 Cellulosic manmade fibers
3241 Cement, hydraulic
3253 Ceramic wall and floor tile
2043 Cereal breakfast foods
2022 Cheese; natural and processed
1479 Chemical and fertilizer mining
2899 Chemical preparations, nec
5169 Chemicals and allied products, nec
2131 Chewing and smoking tobacco
0252 Chicken eggs
5641 Children's and infants' wear stores
2066 Chocolate and cocoa products
2111 Cigarettes
2121 Cigars
0174 Citrus fruits
8641 Civic and social associations
1459 Clay and related minerals, nec
3255 Clay refractories
5052 Coal and other minerals and ores
1241 Coal mining services
2295 Coated fabrics, not rubberized
7993 Coin-operated amusement devices
7215 Coin-operated laundries and cleaning
3316 Cold finishing of steel shapes
8221 Colleges and universities
4939 Combination utilities, nec
7336 Commercial art and graphic design
5046 Commercial equipment, nec
3582 Commercial laundry equipment
3646 Commercial lighting fixtures
8732 Commercial nonphysical research
7335 Commercial photography
8731 Commercial physical research
2754 Commercial printing, gravure
2752 Commercial printing, lithographic
2759 Commercial printing, nec
6221 Commodity contracts brokers, dealers
4899 Communication services, nec
3669 Communications equipment, nec
5734 Computer and software stores
7376 Computer facilities management
7373 Computer integrated systems design
7378 Computer maintenance and repair
3577 Computer peripheral equipment, nec
7379 Computer related services, nec
3572 Computer storage devices
3575 Computer terminals

5045 Computers, peripherals, and software
3271 Concrete block and brick
3272 Concrete products, nec
1771 Concrete work
5145 Confectionery
5082 Construction and mining machinery
3531 Construction machinery
5039 Construction materials, nec
1442 Construction sand and gravel
2679 Converted paper products, nec
3535 Conveyors and conveying equipment
2052 Cookies and crackers
3366 Copper foundries
1021 Copper ores
3351 Copper rolling and drawing
2298 Cordage and twine
9223 Correctional institutions
2653 Corrugated and solid fiber boxes
3961 Costume jewelry
0131 Cotton
0724 Cotton ginning
2074 Cottonseed oil mills
4215 Courier services, except by air
2021 Creamery butter
0721 Crop planting and protection
0723 Crop preparation services for market
3466 Crowns and closures
1311 Crude petroleum and natural gas
1423 Crushed and broken granite
1422 Crushed and broken limestone
1429 Crushed and broken stone, nec
3643 Current-carrying wiring devices
2391 Curtains and draperies
3087 Custom compound purchased resins
7371 Custom computer programming services
3281 Cut stone and stone products
3421 Cutlery
2865 Cyclic crudes and intermediates

D

0241 Dairy farms
5451 Dairy products stores
5143 Dairy products, except dried or canned
7374 Data processing and preparation
8243 Data processing schools
0175 Deciduous tree fruits
2034 Dehydrated fruits, vegetables, soups
3843 Dental equipment and supplies
8072 Dental laboratories
5311 Department stores
7381 Detective and armored car services
2835 Diagnostic substances
2675 Die-cut paper and board
1411 Dimension stone
7331 Direct mail advertising services
5963 Direct selling establishments
7342 Disinfecting and pest control services
2085 Distilled and blended liquors
2047 Dog and cat food
3942 Dolls and stuffed toys
5714 Drapery and upholstery stores
2591 Drapery hardware and blinds and shades
1381 Drilling oil and gas wells
5813 Drinking places
5912 Drug stores and proprietary stores
5122 Drugs, proprietaries, and sundries
2023 Dry, condensed, evaporated products
7216 Drycleaning plants, except rugs
5099 Durable goods, nec

E

5812 Eating places
2079 Edible fats and oils
4931 Electric and other services combined
3634 Electric housewares and fans
3641 Electric lamps

S I C

SIC NO	PRODUCT
4911	Electric services
5063	Electrical apparatus and equipment
5064	Electrical appliances, television and radio
3699	Electrical equipment and supplies, nec
3629	Electrical industrial apparatus
7629	Electrical repair shops
1731	Electrical work
3845	Electromedical equipment
3313	Electrometallurgical products
3671	Electron tubes
3675	Electronic capacitors
3677	Electronic coils and transformers
3679	Electronic components, nec
3571	Electronic computers
3678	Electronic connectors
5065	Electronic parts and equipment, nec
3676	Electronic resistors
8211	Elementary and secondary schools
3534	Elevators and moving stairways
3694	Engine electrical equipment
8711	Engineering services
7929	Entertainers and entertainment groups
2677	Envelopes
3822	Environmental controls
7359	Equipment rental and leasing, nec
1794	Excavation work
2892	Explosives

F

SIC NO	PRODUCT
2381	Fabric dress and work gloves
3499	Fabricated metal products, nec
3498	Fabricated pipe and fittings
3443	Fabricated plate work (boiler shop)
3069	Fabricated rubber products, nec
3441	Fabricated structural metal
2399	Fabricated textile products, nec
8744	Facilities support services
5651	Family clothing stores
5083	Farm and garden machinery
3523	Farm machinery and equipment
0762	Farm management services
4221	Farm product warehousing and storage
5191	Farm supplies
5159	Farm-product raw materials, nec
3965	Fasteners, buttons, needles, and pins
2875	Fertilizers, mixing only
2655	Fiber cans, drums, and similar products
0139	Field crops, except cash grain
9311	Finance, taxation, and monetary policy
2261	Finishing plants, cotton
2262	Finishing plants, manmade
2269	Finishing plants, nec
6331	Fire, marine, and casualty insurance
5146	Fish and seafoods
3211	Flat glass
2087	Flavoring extracts and syrups, nec
5713	Floor covering stores
1752	Floor laying and floor work, nec
5992	Florists
2041	Flour and other grain mill products
5193	Flowers and florists supplies
3824	Fluid meters and counting devices
2026	Fluid milk
3593	Fluid power cylinders and actuators
3594	Fluid power pumps and motors
3492	Fluid power valves and hose fittings
2657	Folding paperboard boxes
2099	Food preparations, nec
3556	Food products machinery
5139	Footwear
3131	Footwear cut stock
3149	Footwear, except rubber, nec
0831	Forest products
0851	Forestry services
4731	Freight transportation arrangement
5148	Fresh fruits and vegetables
2092	Fresh or frozen packaged fish
2053	Frozen bakery products, except bread
2037	Frozen fruits and vegetables
2038	Frozen specialties, nec
0179	Fruits and tree nuts, nec
5989	Fuel dealers, nec

SIC NO	PRODUCT
5983	Fuel oil dealers
7261	Funeral service and crematories
2371	Fur goods
5021	Furniture
2599	Furniture and fixtures, nec
5712	Furniture stores

G

SIC NO	PRODUCT
3944	Games, toys, and children's vehicles
7212	Garment pressing and cleaners' agents
3053	Gaskets; packing and sealing devices
5541	Gasoline service stations
7538	General automotive repair shops
0191	General farms, primarily crop
3569	General industrial machinery,
8062	General medical and surgical hospitals
4225	General warehousing and storage
5947	Gift, novelty, and souvenir shop
2361	Girl's and children's dresses, blouses
2369	Girl's and children's outerwear, nec
1793	Glass and glazing work
3221	Glass containers
5153	Grain and field beans
0172	Grapes
3321	Gray and ductile iron foundries
2771	Greeting cards
5149	Groceries and related products, nec
5141	Groceries, general line
5411	Grocery stores
3761	Guided missiles and space vehicles
2861	Gum and wood chemicals
3275	Gypsum products

H

SIC NO	PRODUCT
3423	Hand and edge tools, nec
3996	Hard surface floor coverings, nec
5072	Hardware
5251	Hardware stores
3429	Hardware, nec
2426	Hardwood dimension and flooring mills
2435	Hardwood veneer and plywood
2353	Hats, caps, and millinery
8099	Health and allied services, nec
3433	Heating equipment, except electric
7353	Heavy construction equipment rental
1629	Heavy construction, nec
7363	Help supply services
1611	Highway and street construction
5945	Hobby, toy, and game shops
0213	Hogs
3536	Hoists, cranes, and monorails
6719	Holding companies, nec
8082	Home health care services
5023	Homefurnishings
2252	Hosiery, nec
7011	Hotels and motels
5722	Household appliance stores
3639	Household appliances, nec
3651	Household audio and video equipment
3631	Household cooking equipment
2392	Household furnishings, nec
2519	Household furniture, nec
3632	Household refrigerators and freezers
3635	Household vacuum cleaners

I

SIC NO	PRODUCT
2024	Ice cream and frozen deserts
8322	Individual and family services
5113	Industrial and personal service paper
1541	Industrial buildings and warehouses
3567	Industrial furnaces and ovens
2813	Industrial gases
2819	Industrial inorganic chemicals, nec
7218	Industrial launderers
5084	Industrial machinery and equipment
3599	Industrial machinery, nec
2869	Industrial organic chemicals, nec
3543	Industrial patterns
1446	Industrial sand
5085	Industrial supplies
3537	Industrial trucks and tractors
3491	Industrial valves

SIC NO	PRODUCT
7375	Information retrieval services
2816	Inorganic pigments
4785	Inspection and fixed facilities
1796	Installing building equipment
3825	Instruments to measure electricity
6411	Insurance agents, brokers, and service
3519	Internal combustion engines, nec
6282	Investment advice
6799	Investors, nec
3462	Iron and steel forgings

J

SIC NO	PRODUCT
3915	Jewelers' materials and lapidary work
5094	Jewelry and precious stones
5944	Jewelry stores
3911	Jewelry, precious metal
8331	Job training and related services

K

SIC NO	PRODUCT
2253	Knit outerwear mills
2254	Knit underwear mills
2259	Knitting mills, nec

L

SIC NO	PRODUCT
3821	Laboratory apparatus and furniture
2258	Lace and warp knit fabric mills
3083	Laminated plastics plate and sheet
9512	Land, mineral, and wildlife conservation
0781	Landscape counseling and planning
7219	Laundry and garment services, nec
3524	Lawn and garden equipment
0782	Lawn and garden services
3952	Lead pencils and art goods
2386	Leather and sheep-lined clothing
3151	Leather gloves and mittens
3199	Leather goods, nec
3111	Leather tanning and finishing
3648	Lighting equipment, nec
7213	Linen supply
5984	Liquefied petroleum gas dealers
5921	Liquor stores
0751	Livestock services, except veterinary
4111	Local and suburban transit
4214	Local trucking with storage
4212	Local trucking, without storage
2411	Logging
2992	Lubricating oils and greases
3161	Luggage
5211	Lumber and other building materials
5031	Lumber, plywood, and millwork

M

SIC NO	PRODUCT
2098	Macaroni and spaghetti
3545	Machine tool accessories
3541	Machine tools, metal cutting type
3542	Machine tools, metal forming type
3695	Magnetic and optical recording media
2083	Malt
2082	Malt beverages
8742	Management consulting services
8741	Management services
2761	Manifold business forms
2097	Manufactured ice
3999	Manufacturing industries, nec
4493	Marinas
3953	Marking devices
1741	Masonry and other stonework
2515	Mattresses and bedsprings
3829	Measuring and controlling devices, nec
3586	Measuring and dispensing pumps
5421	Meat and fish markets
2011	Meat packing plants
5147	Meats and meat products
3061	Mechanical rubber goods
5047	Medical and hospital equipment
7352	Medical equipment rental
8071	Medical laboratories
2833	Medicinals and botanicals
8699	Membership organizations, nec
5136	Men's and boy's clothing
2329	Men's and boy's clothing, nec
2321	Men's and boy's furnishings

SIC NO	PRODUCT
2323	Men's and boy's neckwear
2311	Men's and boy's suits and coats
2325	Men's and boy's trousers and slacks
2322	Men's and boy's underwear and nightwear
2326	Men's and boy's work clothing
5611	Men's and boys' clothing stores
3143	Men's footwear, except athletic
5962	Merchandising machine operators
3412	Metal barrels, drums, and pails
3411	Metal cans
3479	Metal coating and allied services
3442	Metal doors, sash, and trim
3497	Metal foil and leaf
3398	Metal heat treating
2514	Metal household furniture
1081	Metal mining services
1099	Metal ores, nec
3431	Metal sanitary ware
3469	Metal stampings, nec
5051	Metals service centers and offices
3549	Metalworking machinery, nec
2431	Millwork
3296	Mineral wool
3295	Minerals, ground or treated
3532	Mining machinery
5699	Miscellaneous apparel and accessories
6159	Miscellaneous business credit
3496	Miscellaneous fabricated wire products
5499	Miscellaneous food stores
5399	Miscellaneous general merchandise
5719	Miscellaneous homefurnishings
3449	Miscellaneous metalwork
1499	Miscellaneous nonmetallic mining
7299	Miscellaneous personal services
2741	Miscellaneous publishing
5999	Miscellaneous retail stores, nec
5271	Mobile home dealers
2451	Mobile homes
6162	Mortgage bankers and correspondents
7822	Motion picture and tape distribution
7812	Motion picture and video production
3716	Motor homes
3714	Motor vehicle parts and accessories
5015	Motor vehicle parts, used
5013	Motor vehicle supplies and new parts
3711	Motor vehicles and car bodies
5571	Motorcycle dealers
3751	Motorcycles, bicycles, and parts
3621	Motors and generators
8412	Museums and art galleries
5736	Musical instrument stores
3931	Musical instruments

N

SIC NO	PRODUCT
2441	Nailed wood boxes and shook
2241	Narrow fabric mills
9711	National security
4924	Natural gas distribution
1321	Natural gas liquids
4922	Natural gas transmission
5511	New and used car dealers
5994	News dealers and newsstands
2711	Newspapers
2873	Nitrogenous fertilizers
3297	Nonclay refractories
8733	Noncommercial research organizations
3644	Noncurrent-carrying wiring devices
5199	Nondurable goods, nec
3364	Nonferrous die-castings except aluminum
3463	Nonferrous forgings
3369	Nonferrous foundries, nec
3356	Nonferrous rolling and drawing, nec
3357	Nonferrous wiredrawing and insulating
3299	Nonmetallic mineral products,
1481	Nonmetallic mineral services
6512	Nonresidential building operators
1542	Nonresidential construction, nec
2297	Nonwoven fabrics

O

SIC NO	PRODUCT
5044	Office equipment
2522	Office furniture, except wood
3579	Office machines, nec
8021	Offices and clinics of dentists
8011	Offices and clinics of medical doctors
8042	Offices and clinics of optometrists
1382	Oil and gas exploration services
3533	Oil and gas field machinery
1389	Oil and gas field services, nec
1531	Operative builders
3851	Ophthalmic goods
5995	Optical goods stores
3827	Optical instruments and lenses
3489	Ordnance and accessories, nec
2824	Organic fibers, noncellulosic
0181	Ornamental nursery products
0783	Ornamental shrub and tree services
7312	Outdoor advertising services

P

SIC NO	PRODUCT
5142	Packaged frozen goods
3565	Packaging machinery
4783	Packing and crating
5231	Paint, glass, and wallpaper stores
1721	Painting and paper hanging
2851	Paints and allied products
5198	Paints, varnishes, and supplies
3554	Paper industries machinery
2621	Paper mills
2671	Paper; coated and laminated packaging
2672	Paper; coated and laminated, nec
2631	Paperboard mills
2542	Partitions and fixtures, except wood
7515	Passenger car leasing
7514	Passenger car rental
6794	Patent owners and lessors
3951	Pens and mechanical pencils
2721	Periodicals
6141	Personal credit institutions
3172	Personal leather goods, nec
2999	Petroleum and coal products, nec
5171	Petroleum bulk stations and terminals
5172	Petroleum products, nec
2911	Petroleum refining
2834	Pharmaceutical preparations
1475	Phosphate rock
2874	Phosphatic fertilizers
7334	Photocopying and duplicating services
7384	Photofinish laboratories
3861	Photographic equipment and supplies
7221	Photographic studios, portrait
7991	Physical fitness facilities
2035	Pickles, sauces, and salad dressings
5131	Piece goods and notions
1742	Plastering, drywall, and insulation
3085	Plastics bottles
3086	Plastics foam products
5162	Plastics materials and basic shapes
2821	Plastics materials and resins
3084	Plastics pipe
3088	Plastics plumbing fixtures
3089	Plastics products, nec
2796	Platemaking services
3471	Plating and polishing
2395	Pleating and stitching
5074	Plumbing and hydronic heating supplies
3432	Plumbing fixture fittings and trim
1711	Plumbing, heating, air-conditioning
2842	Polishes and sanitation goods
3264	Porcelain electrical supplies
1474	Potash, soda, and borate minerals
2096	Potato chips and similar snacks
3269	Pottery products, nec
5144	Poultry and poultry products
0254	Poultry hatcheries
2015	Poultry slaughtering and processing
3568	Power transmission equipment, nec
3546	Power-driven handtools
3448	Prefabricated metal buildings
2452	Prefabricated wood buildings
7372	Prepackaged software
2048	Prepared feeds, nec
2045	Prepared flour mixes and doughs
3652	Prerecorded records and tapes
3229	Pressed and blown glass, nec
3334	Primary aluminum
3692	Primary batteries, dry and wet
3331	Primary copper
3399	Primary metal products
3339	Primary nonferrous metals, nec
3672	Printed circuit boards
5111	Printing and writing paper
2893	Printing ink
3555	Printing trades machinery
3823	Process control instruments
3231	Products of purchased glass
5049	Professional equipment, nec
8621	Professional organizations
2531	Public building and related furniture
9229	Public order and safety, nec
8743	Public relations services
2611	Pulp mills
3561	Pumps and pumping equipment

R

SIC NO	PRODUCT
7948	Racing, including track operation
3663	Radio and t.v. communications equipment
7622	Radio and television repair
4832	Radio broadcasting stations
5731	Radio, television, and electronic stores
7313	Radio, television, publisher representatives
4812	Radiotelephone communication
3743	Railroad equipment
4011	Railroads, line-haul operating
2061	Raw cane sugar
3273	Ready-mixed concrete
6531	Real estate agents and managers
6798	Real estate investment trusts
2493	Reconstituted wood products
5735	Record and prerecorded tape stores
5561	Recreational vehicle dealers
4613	Refined petroleum pipelines
4222	Refrigerated warehousing and storage
3585	Refrigeration and heating equipment
5078	Refrigeration equipment and supplies
7623	Refrigeration service and repair
4953	Refuse systems
9621	Regulation, administration of transportation
3625	Relays and industrial controls
8661	Religious organizations
7699	Repair services, nec
8361	Residential care
1522	Residential construction, nec
3645	Residential lighting fixtures
5461	Retail bakeries
5261	Retail nurseries and garden stores
7641	Reupholstery and furniture repair
2095	Roasted coffee
2384	Robes and dressing gowns
3547	Rolling mill machinery
5033	Roofing, siding, and insulation
1761	Roofing, siding, and sheetmetal work
3021	Rubber and plastics footwear
3052	Rubber and plastics hose and beltings

S

SIC NO	PRODUCT
2068	Salted and roasted nuts and seeds
2656	Sanitary food containers
2676	Sanitary paper products
4959	Sanitary services, nec
2013	Sausages and other prepared meats
3425	Saw blades and handsaws
2421	Sawmills and planing mills, general
3596	Scales and balances, except laboratory
2397	Schiffli machine embroideries
4151	School buses
8299	Schools and educational services
5093	Scrap and waste materials
3451	Screw machine products
3812	Search and navigation equipment
3341	Secondary nonferrous metals
7338	Secretarial and court reporting
7382	Security systems services
3674	Semiconductors and related devices
3263	Semivitreous table and kitchenware
5087	Service establishment equipment

S I C

SIC NO	PRODUCT
3589	Service industry machinery, nec
7819	Services allied to motion pictures
8999	Services, nec
2652	Setup paperboard boxes
5949	Sewing, needlework, and piece goods
3444	Sheet metalwork
0913	Shellfish
3731	Shipbuilding and repairing
5661	Shoe stores
6153	Short-term business credit
3993	Signs and advertising specialties
3914	Silverware and plated ware
1521	Single-family housing construction
3484	Small arms
3482	Small arms ammunition
2841	Soap and other detergents
8399	Social services, nec
2436	Softwood veneer and plywood
0711	Soil preparation services
2075	Soybean oil mills
3764	Space propulsion units and parts
3769	Space vehicle equipment, nec
3544	Special dies, tools, jigs, and fixtures
3559	Special industry machinery, nec
2429	Special product sawmills, nec
1799	Special trade contractors, nec
4226	Special warehousing and storage, nec
8093	Specialty outpatient clinics, nec
3566	Speed changers, drives, and gears
3949	Sporting and athletic goods, nec
5091	Sporting and recreation goods
5941	Sporting goods and bicycle shops
7941	Sports clubs, managers, and promoters
5112	Stationery and office supplies
2678	Stationery products
5943	Stationery stores
4961	Steam and air-conditioning supply
3325	Steel foundries, nec
3324	Steel investment foundries
3317	Steel pipe and tubes
3493	Steel springs, except wire
3315	Steel wire and related products
3691	Storage batteries
3259	Structural clay products, nec
1791	Structural steel erection
2439	Structural wood members, nec
6552	Subdividers and developers, nec
2843	Surface active agents
3841	Surgical and medical instruments
3842	Surgical appliances and supplies
8713	Surveying services
3613	Switchgear and switchboard apparatus
2822	Synthetic rubber

T

SIC NO	PRODUCT
3795	Tanks and tank components
7291	Tax return preparation services
4822	Telegraph and other communications
3661	Telephone and telegraph apparatus
4813	Telephone communication, except radio
4833	Television broadcasting stations
1743	Terrazzo, tile, marble, mosaic work
8734	Testing laboratories
2393	Textile bags
2299	Textile goods, nec
3552	Textile machinery
7922	Theatrical producers and services
2284	Thread mills
2282	Throwing and winding mills
0811	Timber tracts
2296	Tire cord and fabrics
7534	Tire retreading and repair shops
3011	Tires and inner tubes
5014	Tires and tubes
0132	Tobacco
5194	Tobacco and tobacco products
2141	Tobacco stemming and redrying
5993	Tobacco stores and stands
2844	Toilet preparations
7532	Top and body repair and paint shops
5092	Toys and hobby goods and supplies
7033	Trailer parks and campsites
3612	Transformers, except electric
5088	Transportation equipment and supplies
3799	Transportation equipment, nec
4789	Transportation services, nec
3792	Travel trailers and campers
3713	Truck and bus bodies
7513	Truck rental and leasing, without drivers
3715	Truck trailers
4213	Trucking, except local
6733	Trusts, nec
3511	Turbines and turbine generator sets
0253	Turkeys and turkey eggs
2791	Typesetting

U

SIC NO	PRODUCT
3081	Unsupported plastics film and sheet
3082	Unsupported plastics profile shapes
2512	Upholstered household furniture
5521	Used car dealers
5932	Used merchandise stores
7519	Utility trailer rental

V

SIC NO	PRODUCT
3494	Valves and pipe fittings, nec
5331	Variety stores

SIC NO	PRODUCT
0161	Vegetables and melons
3647	Vehicular lighting equipment
7841	Video tape rental
3261	Vitreous plumbing fixtures
8249	Vocational schools, nec

W

SIC NO	PRODUCT
5075	Warm air heating and air conditioning
7631	Watch, clock, and jewelry repair
3873	Watches, clocks, watchcases, and parts
4489	Water passenger transportation
4941	Water supply
4449	Water transportation of freight
1781	Water well drilling
1623	Water, sewer, and utility lines
2385	Waterproof outerwear
2257	Weft knit fabric mills
3548	Welding apparatus
7692	Welding repair
2046	Wet corn milling
5182	Wine and distilled beverages
2084	Wines, brandy, and brandy spirits
3495	Wire springs
5632	Women's accessory and specialty stores
5137	Women's and children's clothing
2341	Women's and children's underwear
2331	Women's and misses' blouses and shirts
2339	Women's and misses' outerwear, nec
2337	Women's and misses' suits and coats
5621	Women's clothing stores
3144	Women's footwear, except athletic
3171	Women's handbags and purses
2251	Women's hosiery, except socks
2335	Women's, junior's, and misses' dresses
2449	Wood containers, nec
2511	Wood household furniture
2434	Wood kitchen cabinets
2521	Wood office furniture
2448	Wood pallets and skids
2541	Wood partitions and fixtures
2491	Wood preserving
2499	Wood products, nec
2517	Wood television and radio cabinets
3553	Woodworking machinery
1795	Wrecking and demolition work

X

SIC NO	PRODUCT
3844	X-ray apparatus and tubes

Y

SIC NO	PRODUCT
2281	Yarn spinning mills

SIC INDEX

SIC NO   **PRODUCT**

01 agricultural production - crops

0119 Cash grains, nec
0131 Cotton
0132 Tobacco
0139 Field crops, except cash grain
0161 Vegetables and melons
0172 Grapes
0174 Citrus fruits
0175 Deciduous tree fruits
0179 Fruits and tree nuts, nec
0181 Ornamental nursery products
0191 General farms, primarily crop

02 agricultural production - livestock and animal specialties

0212 Beef cattle, except feedlots
0213 Hogs
0241 Dairy farms
0251 Broiler, fryer, and roaster chickens
0252 Chicken eggs
0253 Turkeys and turkey eggs
0254 Poultry hatcheries
0279 Animal specialties, nec

07 agricultural services

0711 Soil preparation services
0721 Crop planting and protection
0723 Crop preparation services for market
0724 Cotton ginning
0751 Livestock services, except veterinary
0752 Animal specialty services
0762 Farm management services
0781 Landscape counseling and planning
0782 Lawn and garden services
0783 Ornamental shrub and tree services

08 forestry

0811 Timber tracts
0831 Forest products
0851 Forestry services

09 fishing, hunting and trapping

0913 Shellfish

10 metal mining

1021 Copper ores
1081 Metal mining services
1099 Metal ores, nec

12 coal mining

1221 Bituminous coal and lignite-surface mining
1241 Coal mining services

13 oil and gas extraction

1311 Crude petroleum and natural gas
1321 Natural gas liquids
1381 Drilling oil and gas wells
1382 Oil and gas exploration services
1389 Oil and gas field services, nec

14 mining and quarrying of nonmetallic minerals, except fuels

1411 Dimension stone
1422 Crushed and broken limestone
1423 Crushed and broken granite
1429 Crushed and broken stone, nec
1442 Construction sand and gravel
1446 Industrial sand
1459 Clay and related minerals, nec
1474 Potash, soda, and borate minerals
1475 Phosphate rock
1479 Chemical and fertilizer mining
1481 Nonmetallic mineral services
1499 Miscellaneous nonmetallic mining

15 construction - general contractors & operative builders

1521 Single-family housing construction
1522 Residential construction, nec
1531 Operative builders
1541 Industrial buildings and warehouses
1542 Nonresidential construction, nec

16 heamy construction, except building construction, contractor

1611 Highway and street construction
1622 Bridge, tunnel, and elevated highway
1623 Water, sewer, and utility lines
1629 Heavy construction, nec

17 construction - special trade contractors

1711 Plumbing, heating, air-conditioning
1721 Painting and paper hanging
1731 Electrical work
1741 Masonry and other stonework
1742 Plastering, drywall, and insulation
1743 Terrazzo, tile, marble, mosaic work
1751 Carpentry work
1752 Floor laying and floor work, nec
1761 Roofing, siding, and sheetmetal work
1771 Concrete work
1781 Water well drilling
1791 Structural steel erection
1793 Glass and glazing work
1794 Excavation work
1795 Wrecking and demolition work
1796 Installing building equipment
1799 Special trade contractors, nec

20 food and kindred products

2011 Meat packing plants
2013 Sausages and other prepared meats
2015 Poultry slaughtering and processing
2021 Creamery butter
2022 Cheese; natural and processed
2023 Dry, condensed, evaporated products
2024 Ice cream and frozen deserts
2026 Fluid milk
2032 Canned specialties
2033 Canned fruits and specialties
2034 Dehydrated fruits, vegetables, soups
2035 Pickles, sauces, and salad dressings
2037 Frozen fruits and vegetables
2038 Frozen specialties, nec
2041 Flour and other grain mill products
2043 Cereal breakfast foods
2045 Prepared flour mixes and doughs
2046 Wet corn milling
2047 Dog and cat food
2048 Prepared feeds, nec
2051 Bread, cake, and related products
2052 Cookies and crackers
2053 Frozen bakery products, except bread
2061 Raw cane sugar
2064 Candy and other confectionery products
2066 Chocolate and cocoa products
2068 Salted and roasted nuts and seeds
2074 Cottonseed oil mills
2075 Soybean oil mills
2077 Animal and marine fats and oils
2079 Edible fats and oils
2082 Malt beverages
2083 Malt
2084 Wines, brandy, and brandy spirits
2085 Distilled and blended liquors
2086 Bottled and canned soft drinks
2087 Flavoring extracts and syrups, nec
2091 Canned and cured fish and seafoods
2092 Fresh or frozen packaged fish
2095 Roasted coffee
2096 Potato chips and similar snacks
2097 Manufactured ice
2098 Macaroni and spaghetti
2099 Food preparations, nec

21 tobacco products

2111 Cigarettes
2121 Cigars
2131 Chewing and smoking tobacco
2141 Tobacco stemming and redrying

22 textile mill products

2211 Broadwoven fabric mills, cotton
2221 Broadwoven fabric mills, manmade
2231 Broadwoven fabric mills, wool
2241 Narrow fabric mills
2251 Women's hosiery, except socks
2252 Hosiery, nec
2253 Knit outerwear mills
2254 Knit underwear mills
2257 Weft knit fabric mills
2258 Lace and warp knit fabric mills
2259 Knitting mills, nec
2261 Finishing plants, cotton
2262 Finishing plants, manmade
2269 Finishing plants, nec
2273 Carpets and rugs
2281 Yarn spinning mills
2282 Throwing and winding mills
2284 Thread mills
2295 Coated fabrics, not rubberized
2296 Tire cord and fabrics
2297 Nonwoven fabrics
2298 Cordage and twine
2299 Textile goods, nec

23 apparel, finished products from fabrics & similar materials

2311 Men's and boy's suits and coats
2321 Men's and boy's furnishings
2322 Men's and boy's underwear and nightwear
2323 Men's and boy's neckwear
2325 Men's and boy's trousers and slacks
2326 Men's and boy's work clothing
2329 Men's and boy's clothing, nec
2331 Women's and misses' blouses and shirts
2335 Women's, junior's, and misses' dresses
2337 Women's and misses' suits and coats
2339 Women's and misses' outerwear, nec
2341 Women's and children's underwear
2342 Bras, girdles, and allied garments
2353 Hats, caps, and millinery
2361 Girl's and children's dresses, blouses
2369 Girl's and children's outerwear, nec
2371 Fur goods
2381 Fabric dress and work gloves
2384 Robes and dressing gowns
2385 Waterproof outerwear
2386 Leather and sheep-lined clothing
2387 Apparel belts
2389 Apparel and accessories, nec
2391 Curtains and draperies
2392 Household furnishings, nec
2393 Textile bags
2394 Canvas and related products
2395 Pleating and stitching
2396 Automotive and apparel trimmings
2397 Schiffli machine embroideries
2399 Fabricated textile products, nec

24 lumber and wood products, except furniture

2411 Logging
2421 Sawmills and planing mills, general
2426 Hardwood dimension and flooring mills
2429 Special product sawmills, nec

S
I
C

SIC NO	PRODUCT

2431 Millwork
2434 Wood kitchen cabinets
2435 Hardwood veneer and plywood
2436 Softwood veneer and plywood
2439 Structural wood members, nec
2441 Nailed wood boxes and shook
2448 Wood pallets and skids
2449 Wood containers, nec
2451 Mobile homes
2452 Prefabricated wood buildings
2491 Wood preserving
2493 Reconstituted wood products
2499 Wood products, nec

25 furniture and fixtures

2511 Wood household furniture
2512 Upholstered household furniture
2514 Metal household furniture
2515 Mattresses and bedsprings
2517 Wood television and radio cabinets
2519 Household furniture, nec
2521 Wood office furniture
2522 Office furniture, except wood
2531 Public building and related furniture
2541 Wood partitions and fixtures
2542 Partitions and fixtures, except wood
2591 Drapery hardware and blinds and shades
2599 Furniture and fixtures, nec

26 paper and allied products

2611 Pulp mills
2621 Paper mills
2631 Paperboard mills
2652 Setup paperboard boxes
2653 Corrugated and solid fiber boxes
2655 Fiber cans, drums, and similar products
2656 Sanitary food containers
2657 Folding paperboard boxes
2671 Paper; coated and laminated packaging
2672 Paper; coated and laminated, nec
2673 Bags: plastic, laminated, and coated
2674 Bags: uncoated paper and multiwall
2675 Die-cut paper and board
2676 Sanitary paper products
2677 Envelopes
2678 Stationery products
2679 Converted paper products, nec

27 printing, publishing and allied industries

2711 Newspapers
2721 Periodicals
2731 Book publishing
2732 Book printing
2741 Miscellaneous publishing
2752 Commercial printing, lithographic
2754 Commercial printing, gravure
2759 Commercial printing, nec
2761 Manifold business forms
2771 Greeting cards
2782 Blankbooks and looseleaf binders
2789 Bookbinding and related work
2791 Typesetting
2796 Platemaking services

28 chemicals and allied products

2812 Alkalies and chlorine
2813 Industrial gases
2816 Inorganic pigments
2819 Industrial inorganic chemicals, nec
2821 Plastics materials and resins
2822 Synthetic rubber
2823 Cellulosic manmade fibers
2824 Organic fibers, noncellulosic
2833 Medicinals and botanicals
2834 Pharmaceutical preparations
2835 Diagnostic substances
2836 Biological products, except diagnostic
2841 Soap and other detergents
2842 Polishes and sanitation goods
2843 Surface active agents
2844 Toilet preparations
2851 Paints and allied products

2861 Gum and wood chemicals
2865 Cyclic crudes and intermediates
2869 Industrial organic chemicals, nec
2873 Nitrogenous fertilizers
2874 Phosphatic fertilizers
2875 Fertilizers, mixing only
2879 Agricultural chemicals, nec
2891 Adhesives and sealants
2892 Explosives
2893 Printing ink
2899 Chemical preparations, nec

29 petroleum refining and related industries

2911 Petroleum refining
2951 Asphalt paving mixtures and blocks
2952 Asphalt felts and coatings
2992 Lubricating oils and greases
2999 Petroleum and coal products, nec

30 rubber and miscellaneous plastic products

3011 Tires and inner tubes
3021 Rubber and plastics footwear
3052 Rubber and plastics hose and beltings
3053 Gaskets; packing and sealing devices
3061 Mechanical rubber goods
3069 Fabricated rubber products, nec
3081 Unsupported plastics film and sheet
3082 Unsupported plastics profile shapes
3083 Laminated plastics plate and sheet
3084 Plastics pipe
3085 Plastics bottles
3086 Plastics foam products
3087 Custom compound purchased resins
3088 Plastics plumbing fixtures
3089 Plastics products, nec

31 leather and leather products

3111 Leather tanning and finishing
3131 Footwear cut stock
3143 Men's footwear, except athletic
3144 Women's footwear, except athletic
3149 Footwear, except rubber, nec
3151 Leather gloves and mittens
3161 Luggage
3171 Women's handbags and purses
3172 Personal leather goods, nec
3199 Leather goods, nec

32 stone, clay, glass, and concrete products

3211 Flat glass
3221 Glass containers
3229 Pressed and blown glass, nec
3231 Products of purchased glass
3241 Cement, hydraulic
3251 Brick and structural clay tile
3253 Ceramic wall and floor tile
3255 Clay refractories
3259 Structural clay products, nec
3261 Vitreous plumbing fixtures
3263 Semivitreous table and kitchenware
3264 Porcelain electrical supplies
3269 Pottery products, nec
3271 Concrete block and brick
3272 Concrete products, nec
3273 Ready-mixed concrete
3275 Gypsum products
3281 Cut stone and stone products
3291 Abrasive products
3292 Asbestos products
3295 Minerals, ground or treated
3296 Mineral wool
3297 Nonclay refractories
3299 Nonmetallic mineral products,

33 primary metal industries

3312 Blast furnaces and steel mills
3313 Electrometallurgical products
3315 Steel wire and related products
3316 Cold finishing of steel shapes
3317 Steel pipe and tubes
3321 Gray and ductile iron foundries
3324 Steel investment foundries

3325 Steel foundries, nec
3331 Primary copper
3334 Primary aluminum
3339 Primary nonferrous metals, nec
3341 Secondary nonferrous metals
3351 Copper rolling and drawing
3353 Aluminum sheet, plate, and foil
3354 Aluminum extruded products
3355 Aluminum rolling and drawing, nec
3356 Nonferrous rolling and drawing, nec
3357 Nonferrous wiredrawing and insulating
3363 Aluminum die-castings
3364 Nonferrous die-castings except aluminum
3365 Aluminum foundries
3366 Copper foundries
3369 Nonferrous foundries, nec
3398 Metal heat treating
3399 Primary metal products

34 fabricated metal products

3411 Metal cans
3412 Metal barrels, drums, and pails
3421 Cutlery
3423 Hand and edge tools, nec
3425 Saw blades and handsaws
3429 Hardware, nec
3431 Metal sanitary ware
3432 Plumbing fixture fittings and trim
3433 Heating equipment, except electric
3441 Fabricated structural metal
3442 Metal doors, sash, and trim
3443 Fabricated plate work (boiler shop)
3444 Sheet metalwork
3446 Architectural metalwork
3448 Prefabricated metal buildings
3449 Miscellaneous metalwork
3451 Screw machine products
3452 Bolts, nuts, rivets, and washers
3462 Iron and steel forgings
3463 Nonferrous forgings
3465 Automotive stampings
3466 Crowns and closures
3469 Metal stampings, nec
3471 Plating and polishing
3479 Metal coating and allied services
3482 Small arms ammunition
3483 Ammunition, except for small arms, nec
3484 Small arms
3489 Ordnance and accessories, nec
3491 Industrial valves
3492 Fluid power valves and hose fittings
3493 Steel springs, except wire
3494 Valves and pipe fittings, nec
3495 Wire springs
3496 Miscellaneous fabricated wire products
3497 Metal foil and leaf
3498 Fabricated pipe and fittings
3499 Fabricated metal products, nec

35 industrial and commercial machinery and computer equipment

3511 Turbines and turbine generator sets
3519 Internal combustion engines, nec
3523 Farm machinery and equipment
3524 Lawn and garden equipment
3531 Construction machinery
3532 Mining machinery
3533 Oil and gas field machinery
3534 Elevators and moving stairways
3535 Conveyors and conveying equipment
3536 Hoists, cranes, and monorails
3537 Industrial trucks and tractors
3541 Machine tools, metal cutting type
3542 Machine tools, metal forming type
3543 Industrial patterns
3544 Special dies, tools, jigs, and fixtures
3545 Machine tool accessories
3546 Power-driven handtools
3547 Rolling mill machinery
3548 Welding apparatus
3549 Metalworking machinery, nec
3552 Textile machinery

SIC NO	PRODUCT

3553 Woodworking machinery
3554 Paper industries machinery
3555 Printing trades machinery
3556 Food products machinery
3559 Special industry machinery, nec
3561 Pumps and pumping equipment
3562 Ball and roller bearings
3563 Air and gas compressors
3564 Blowers and fans
3565 Packaging machinery
3566 Speed changers, drives, and gears
3567 Industrial furnaces and ovens
3568 Power transmission equipment, nec
3569 General industrial machinery,
3571 Electronic computers
3572 Computer storage devices
3575 Computer terminals
3577 Computer peripheral equipment, nec
3578 Calculating and accounting equipment
3579 Office machines, nec
3581 Automatic vending machines
3582 Commercial laundry equipment
3585 Refrigeration and heating equipment
3586 Measuring and dispensing pumps
3589 Service industry machinery, nec
3592 Carburetors, pistons, rings, valves
3593 Fluid power cylinders and actuators
3594 Fluid power pumps and motors
3596 Scales and balances, except laboratory
3599 Industrial machinery, nec

36 electronic & other electrical equipment & components

3612 Transformers, except electric
3613 Switchgear and switchboard apparatus
3621 Motors and generators
3624 Carbon and graphite products
3625 Relays and industrial controls
3629 Electrical industrial apparatus
3631 Household cooking equipment
3632 Household refrigerators and freezers
3634 Electric housewares and fans
3635 Household vacuum cleaners
3639 Household appliances, nec
3641 Electric lamps
3643 Current-carrying wiring devices
3644 Noncurrent-carrying wiring devices
3645 Residential lighting fixtures
3646 Commercial lighting fixtures
3647 Vehicular lighting equipment
3648 Lighting equipment, nec
3651 Household audio and video equipment
3652 Prerecorded records and tapes
3661 Telephone and telegraph apparatus
3663 Radio and t.v. communications equipment
3669 Communications equipment, nec
3671 Electron tubes
3672 Printed circuit boards
3674 Semiconductors and related devices
3675 Electronic capacitors
3676 Electronic resistors
3677 Electronic coils and transformers
3678 Electronic connectors
3679 Electronic components, nec
3691 Storage batteries
3692 Primary batteries, dry and wet
3694 Engine electrical equipment
3695 Magnetic and optical recording media
3699 Electrical equipment and supplies, nec

37 transportation equipment

3711 Motor vehicles and car bodies
3713 Truck and bus bodies
3714 Motor vehicle parts and accessories
3715 Truck trailers
3716 Motor homes
3721 Aircraft
3724 Aircraft engines and engine parts
3728 Aircraft parts and equipment, nec
3731 Shipbuilding and repairing
3732 Boatbuilding and repairing
3743 Railroad equipment
3751 Motorcycles, bicycles, and parts

3761 Guided missiles and space vehicles
3764 Space propulsion units and parts
3769 Space vehicle equipment, nec
3792 Travel trailers and campers
3795 Tanks and tank components
3799 Transportation equipment, nec

38 measuring, photographic, medical, & optical goods, & clocks

3812 Search and navigation equipment
3821 Laboratory apparatus and furniture
3822 Environmental controls
3823 Process control instruments
3824 Fluid meters and counting devices
3825 Instruments to measure electricity
3826 Analytical instruments
3827 Optical instruments and lenses
3829 Measuring and controlling devices, nec
3841 Surgical and medical instruments
3842 Surgical appliances and supplies
3843 Dental equipment and supplies
3844 X-ray apparatus and tubes
3845 Electromedical equipment
3851 Ophthalmic goods
3861 Photographic equipment and supplies
3873 Watches, clocks, watchcases, and parts

39 miscellaneous manufacturing industries

3911 Jewelry, precious metal
3914 Silverware and plated ware
3915 Jewelers' materials and lapidary work
3931 Musical instruments
3942 Dolls and stuffed toys
3944 Games, toys, and children's vehicles
3949 Sporting and athletic goods, nec
3951 Pens and mechanical pencils
3952 Lead pencils and art goods
3953 Marking devices
3955 Carbon paper and inked ribbons
3961 Costume jewelry
3965 Fasteners, buttons, needles, and pins
3991 Brooms and brushes
3993 Signs and advertising specialties
3995 Burial caskets
3996 Hard surface floor coverings, nec
3999 Manufacturing industries, nec

40 railroad transportation

4011 Railroads, line-haul operating

41 local & suburban transit & interurban highway transportation

4111 Local and suburban transit
4151 School buses

42 motor freight transportation

4212 Local trucking, without storage
4213 Trucking, except local
4214 Local trucking with storage
4215 Courier services, except by air
4221 Farm product warehousing and storage
4222 Refrigerated warehousing and storage
4225 General warehousing and storage
4226 Special warehousing and storage, nec

44 water transportation

4449 Water transportation of freight
4489 Water passenger transportation
4493 Marinas

45 transportation by air

4512 Air transportation, scheduled
4513 Air courier services
4522 Air transportation, nonscheduled
4581 Airports, flying fields, and services

46 pipelines, except natural gas

4613 Refined petroleum pipelines

47 transportation services

4731 Freight transportation arrangement
4783 Packing and crating

4785 Inspection and fixed facilities
4789 Transportation services, nec

48 communications

4812 Radiotelephone communication
4813 Telephone communication, except radio
4822 Telegraph and other communications
4832 Radio broadcasting stations
4833 Television broadcasting stations
4841 Cable and other pay television services
4899 Communication services, nec

49 electric, gas and sanitary services

4911 Electric services
4922 Natural gas transmission
4924 Natural gas distribution
4931 Electric and other services combined
4939 Combination utilities, nec
4941 Water supply
4953 Refuse systems
4959 Sanitary services, nec
4961 Steam and air-conditioning supply

50 wholesale trade - durable goods

5012 Automobiles and other motor vehicles
5013 Motor vehicle supplies and new parts
5014 Tires and tubes
5015 Motor vehicle parts, used
5021 Furniture
5023 Homefurnishings
5031 Lumber, plywood, and millwork
5032 Brick, stone, and related material
5033 Roofing, siding, and insulation
5039 Construction materials, nec
5044 Office equipment
5045 Computers, peripherals, and software
5046 Commercial equipment, nec
5047 Medical and hospital equipment
5049 Professional equipment, nec
5051 Metals service centers and offices
5052 Coal and other minerals and ores
5063 Electrical apparatus and equipment
5064 Electrical appliances, television and radio
5065 Electronic parts and equipment, nec
5072 Hardware
5074 Plumbing and hydronic heating supplies
5075 Warm air heating and air conditioning
5078 Refrigeration equipment and supplies
5082 Construction and mining machinery
5083 Farm and garden machinery
5084 Industrial machinery and equipment
5085 Industrial supplies
5087 Service establishment equipment
5088 Transportation equipment and supplies
5091 Sporting and recreation goods
5092 Toys and hobby goods and supplies
5093 Scrap and waste materials
5094 Jewelry and precious stones
5099 Durable goods, nec

51 wholesale trade - nondurable goods

5111 Printing and writing paper
5112 Stationery and office supplies
5113 Industrial and personal service paper
5122 Drugs, proprietaries, and sundries
5131 Piece goods and notions
5136 Men's and boy's clothing
5137 Women's and children's clothing
5139 Footwear
5141 Groceries, general line
5142 Packaged frozen goods
5143 Dairy products, except dried or canned
5144 Poultry and poultry products
5145 Confectionery
5146 Fish and seafoods
5147 Meats and meat products
5148 Fresh fruits and vegetables
5149 Groceries and related products, nec
5153 Grain and field beans
5159 Farm-product raw materials, nec
5162 Plastics materials and basic shapes
5169 Chemicals and allied products, nec

S
I
C

SIC NO	PRODUCT

5171 Petroleum bulk stations and terminals
5172 Petroleum products, nec
5181 Beer and ale
5182 Wine and distilled beverages
5191 Farm supplies
5192 Books, periodicals, and newspapers
5193 Flowers and florists supplies
5194 Tobacco and tobacco products
5198 Paints, varnishes, and supplies
5199 Nondurable goods, nec

52 building materials, hardware, garden supplies & mobile homes

5211 Lumber and other building materials
5231 Paint, glass, and wallpaper stores
5251 Hardware stores
5261 Retail nurseries and garden stores
5271 Mobile home dealers

53 general merchandise stores

5311 Department stores
5331 Variety stores
5399 Miscellaneous general merchandise

54 food stores

5411 Grocery stores
5421 Meat and fish markets
5441 Candy, nut, and confectionery stores
5451 Dairy products stores
5461 Retail bakeries
5499 Miscellaneous food stores

55 automotive dealers and gasoline service stations

5511 New and used car dealers
5521 Used car dealers
5531 Auto and home supply stores
5541 Gasoline service stations
5551 Boat dealers
5561 Recreational vehicle dealers
5571 Motorcycle dealers
5599 Automotive dealers, nec

56 apparel and accessory stores

5611 Men's and boys' clothing stores
5621 Women's clothing stores
5632 Women's accessory and specialty stores
5641 Children's and infants' wear stores
5651 Family clothing stores
5661 Shoe stores
5699 Miscellaneous apparel and accessories

57 home furniture, furnishings and equipment stores

5712 Furniture stores
5713 Floor covering stores
5714 Drapery and upholstery stores
5719 Miscellaneous homefurnishings
5722 Household appliance stores
5731 Radio, television, and electronic stores
5734 Computer and software stores
5735 Record and prerecorded tape stores
5736 Musical instrument stores

58 eating and drinking places

5812 Eating places
5813 Drinking places

59 miscellaneous retail

5912 Drug stores and proprietary stores
5921 Liquor stores
5932 Used merchandise stores
5941 Sporting goods and bicycle shops
5942 Book stores
5943 Stationery stores
5944 Jewelry stores
5945 Hobby, toy, and game shops
5946 Camera and photographic supply stores
5947 Gift, novelty, and souvenir shop
5949 Sewing, needlework, and piece goods
5961 Catalog and mail-order houses
5962 Merchandising machine operators
5963 Direct selling establishments
5983 Fuel oil dealers

5984 Liquefied petroleum gas dealers
5989 Fuel dealers, nec
5992 Florists
5993 Tobacco stores and stands
5994 News dealers and newsstands
5995 Optical goods stores
5999 Miscellaneous retail stores, nec

61 nondepository credit institutions

6141 Personal credit institutions
6153 Short-term business credit
6159 Miscellaneous business credit
6162 Mortgage bankers and correspondents

62 security & commodity brokers, dealers, exchanges & services

6221 Commodity contracts brokers, dealers
6282 Investment advice

63 insurance carriers

6331 Fire, marine, and casualty insurance

64 insurance agents, brokers and service

6411 Insurance agents, brokers, and service

65 real estate

6512 Nonresidential building operators
6513 Apartment building operators
6531 Real estate agents and managers
6552 Subdividers and developers, nec

67 holding and other investment offices

6719 Holding companies, nec
6733 Trusts, nec
6794 Patent owners and lessors
6798 Real estate investment trusts
6799 Investors, nec

70 hotels, rooming houses, camps, and other lodging places

7011 Hotels and motels
7033 Trailer parks and campsites

72 personal services

7212 Garment pressing and cleaners' agents
7213 Linen supply
7215 Coin-operated laundries and cleaning
7216 Drycleaning plants, except rugs
7217 Carpet and upholstery cleaning
7218 Industrial launderers
7219 Laundry and garment services, nec
7221 Photographic studios, portrait
7231 Beauty shops
7241 Barber shops
7261 Funeral service and crematories
7291 Tax return preparation services
7299 Miscellaneous personal services

73 business services

7311 Advertising agencies
7312 Outdoor advertising services
7313 Radio, television, publisher representatives
7319 Advertising, nec
7331 Direct mail advertising services
7334 Photocopying and duplicating services
7335 Commercial photography
7336 Commercial art and graphic design
7338 Secretarial and court reporting
7342 Disinfecting and pest control services
7349 Building maintenance services, nec
7352 Medical equipment rental
7353 Heavy construction equipment rental
7359 Equipment rental and leasing, nec
7363 Help supply services
7371 Custom computer programming services
7372 Prepackaged software
7373 Computer integrated systems design
7374 Data processing and preparation
7375 Information retrieval services
7376 Computer facilities management
7378 Computer maintenance and repair
7379 Computer related services, nec

7381 Detective and armored car services
7382 Security systems services
7384 Photofinish laboratories
7389 Business services, nec

75 automotive repair, services and parking

7513 Truck rental and leasing, without drivers
7514 Passenger car rental
7515 Passenger car leasing
7519 Utility trailer rental
7521 Automobile parking
7532 Top and body repair and paint shops
7534 Tire retreading and repair shops
7536 Automotive glass replacement shops
7537 Automotive transmission repair shops
7538 General automotive repair shops
7539 Automotive repair shops, nec
7542 Carwashes
7549 Automotive services, nec

76 miscellaneous repair services

7622 Radio and television repair
7623 Refrigeration service and repair
7629 Electrical repair shops
7631 Watch, clock, and jewelry repair
7641 Reupholstery and furniture repair
7692 Welding repair
7694 Armature rewinding shops
7699 Repair services, nec

78 motion pictures

7812 Motion picture and video production
7819 Services allied to motion pictures
7822 Motion picture and tape distribution
7841 Video tape rental

79 amusement and recreation services

7922 Theatrical producers and services
7929 Entertainers and entertainment groups
7941 Sports clubs, managers, and promoters
7948 Racing, including track operation
7991 Physical fitness facilities
7993 Coin-operated amusement devices
7999 Amusement and recreation, nec

80 health services

8011 Offices and clinics of medical doctors
8021 Offices and clinics of dentists
8042 Offices and clinics of optometrists
8062 General medical and surgical hospitals
8071 Medical laboratories
8072 Dental laboratories
8082 Home health care services
8093 Specialty outpatient clinics, nec
8099 Health and allied services, nec

82 educational services

8211 Elementary and secondary schools
8221 Colleges and universities
8243 Data processing schools
8249 Vocational schools, nec
8299 Schools and educational services

83 social services

8322 Individual and family services
8331 Job training and related services
8361 Residential care
8399 Social services, nec

84 museums, art galleries and botanical and zoological gardens

8412 Museums and art galleries

86 membership organizations

8611 Business associations
8621 Professional organizations
8641 Civic and social associations
8661 Religious organizations
8699 Membership organizations, nec

87 engineering, accounting, research, and management services

SIC NO	PRODUCT
8711	Engineering services
8712	Architectural services
8713	Surveying services
8721	Accounting, auditing, and bookkeeping
8731	Commercial physical research
8732	Commercial nonphysical research
8733	Noncommercial research organizations
8734	Testing laboratories
8741	Management services
8742	Management consulting services
8743	Public relations services

SIC NO	PRODUCT
8744	Facilities support services
8748	Business consulting, nec

89 services, not elsewhere classified

SIC NO	PRODUCT
8999	Services, nec

92 justice, public order and safety

SIC NO	PRODUCT
9223	Correctional institutions
9229	Public order and safety, nec

93 public finance, taxation and monetary policy

SIC NO	PRODUCT
9311	Finance, taxation, and monetary policy

95 administration of environmental quality and housing programs

SIC NO	PRODUCT
9512	Land, mineral, and wildlife conservation

96 administration of economic programs

SIC NO	PRODUCT
9621	Regulation, administration of transportation

97 national security and international affairs

SIC NO	PRODUCT
9711	National security

S
I
C

SIC SECTION

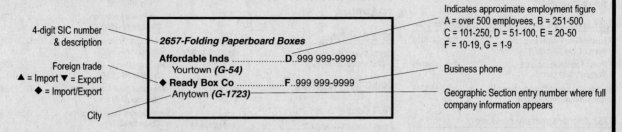

4-digit SIC number & description

Foreign trade
▲ = Import ▼ = Export
◆ = Import/Export

City

2657-Folding Paperboard Boxes

Affordable Inds ....**D**..999 999-9999
Yourtown **(G-54)**
◆ **Ready Box Co** ....**F**..999 999-9999
Anytown **(G-1723)**

Indicates approximate employment figure
A = over 500 employees, B = 251-500
C = 101-250, D = 51-100, E = 20-50
F = 10-19, G = 1-9

Business phone

Geographic Section entry number where full company information appears

See footnotes for symbols and codes identification.
- The SIC codes in this section are from the latest Standard Industrial Classification manual published by the U.S. Government's Office of Management and Budget. For more information regarding SICs, see the Explanatory Notes.
- Companies may be listed under multiple classifications.

01 AGRICULTURAL PRODUCTION - CROPS

0119 Cash grains, nec

Cogent Dynamics Inc.............................G..... 828 628-9025
Fletcher **(G-4730)**

0131 Cotton

Barnhardt Manufacturing Co..................C..... 704 331-0657
Charlotte **(G-1754)**

0132 Tobacco

Loflin Handle Co Inc..............................G..... 336 463-2422
Yadkinville **(G-13445)**

Top Tobacco LP.....................................C..... 910 646-3014
Lake Waccamaw **(G-7472)**

0139 Field crops, except cash grain

Barkleys Mill On Southern Cro...............G..... 828 626-3344
Weaverville **(G-12484)**

Green Compass LLC...............................G..... 833 336-9223
Wilmington **(G-12797)**

Thompson Sunny Acres Inc....................G..... 910 206-1801
Rockingham **(G-10791)**

0161 Vegetables and melons

◆ Dole Food Company Inc......................E 818 874-4000
Charlotte **(G-2061)**

0172 Grapes

Hinnant Farms Vineyard LLC................F..... 919 965-3350
Pine Level **(G-9681)**

Shelton Vineyards Inc............................E..... 336 366-4818
Dobson **(G-3825)**

0174 Citrus fruits

◆ Dole Food Company Inc......................E 818 874-4000
Charlotte **(G-2061)**

0175 Deciduous tree fruits

◆ Dole Food Company Inc......................E 818 874-4000
Charlotte **(G-2061)**

0179 Fruits and tree nuts, nec

◆ Dole Food Company Inc......................E 818 874-4000
Charlotte **(G-2061)**

0181 Ornamental nursery products

Southern States Coop Inc.......................G..... 336 246-3201
Creedmoor **(G-3654)**

Southern States Coop Inc.......................E..... 336 786-7545
Mount Airy **(G-9178)**

Southern States Coop Inc.......................E..... 919 658-5061
Mount Olive **(G-9259)**

Southern States Coop Inc.......................D..... 704 872-6364
Statesville **(G-11772)**

Southern States Coop Inc.......................F..... 910 285-8213
Wallace **(G-12325)**

Taylco Inc..E..... 910 739-0405
Lumberton **(G-7974)**

0191 General farms, primarily crop

Boggs Farm Center Inc...........................G..... 704 538-7176
Fallston **(G-4522)**

Catawba Farms Enterprises LLC............F..... 828 464-5780
Newton **(G-9452)**

Cauley Construction Company................G..... 252 522-1078
Kinston **(G-7401)**

Wainwright Warehouse...........................G..... 252 237-5121
Wilson **(G-13043)**

02 AGRICULTURAL PRODUCTION - LIVESTOCK AND ANIMAL SPECIALTIES

0212 Beef cattle, except feedlots

Boggs Farm Center Inc...........................G..... 704 538-7176
Fallston **(G-4522)**

Cauley Construction Company................G..... 252 522-1078
Kinston **(G-7401)**

0213 Hogs

Futrell Precasting LLC............................G..... 252 568-3481
Deep Run **(G-3732)**

◆ Hog Slat Incorporated.........................B..... 800 949-4647
Newton Grove **(G-9514)**

Murphy-Brown LLC................................C..... 910 282-4264
Rose Hill **(G-10909)**

▲ Murphy-Brown LLC.............................D..... 910 293-3434
Warsaw **(G-12363)**

0241 Dairy farms

Buffalo Creek Farm & Crmry LLC...........G..... 336 969-5698
Germanton **(G-5174)**

0251 Broiler, fryer, and roaster chickens

◆ Johnson Nash & Sons Farms Inc.........B..... 910 289-3113
Rose Hill **(G-10907)**

0252 Chicken eggs

Pilgrims Pride Corporation......................B..... 704 624-2171
Marshville **(G-8092)**

0253 Turkeys and turkey eggs

◆ Johnson Nash & Sons Farms Inc.........B..... 910 289-3113
Rose Hill **(G-10907)**

Sleepy Creek Turkeys LLC.....................C..... 919 778-3130
Goldsboro **(G-5244)**

0254 Poultry hatcheries

◆ Johnson Nash & Sons Farms Inc.........B..... 910 289-3113
Rose Hill **(G-10907)**

Pilgrims Pride Corporation......................B..... 704 624-2171
Marshville **(G-8092)**

0279 Animal specialties, nec

Archie Supply LLC.................................G..... 336 987-0895
Greensboro **(G-5368)**

07 AGRICULTURAL SERVICES

0711 Soil preparation services

Carolina Golfco Inc................................G..... 704 525-7846
Charlotte **(G-1848)**

Carolina Stalite Co Ltd Partnr.................E..... 704 279-2166
Gold Hill **(G-5190)**

Carolina Stalite Co Ltd Partnr.................F..... 704 637-1515
Salisbury **(G-11029)**

0721 Crop planting and protection

CPM of Nc Inc.......................................G..... 704 467-5819
Concord **(G-3347)**

0723 Crop preparation services for market

Communitys Kitchen L3c........................G..... 828 817-2308
Tryon **(G-12173)**

Garland Farm Supply Inc........................F..... 910 529-9731
Garland **(G-4909)**

Mineral Springs Fertilizer Inc.................G..... 704 843-2683
Mineral Springs **(G-8327)**

Osage Pecan Company...........................F..... 660 679-6137
West Jefferson **(G-12569)**

Renwood Mills LLC................................D..... 828 465-0302
Newton **(G-9490)**

Sandy Land Peanut Company Inc...........F..... 252 356-2679
Harrellsville **(G-6104)**

0724 Cotton ginning

Boggs Farm Center Inc...........................G..... 704 538-7176
Fallston **(G-4522)**

Coastal Carolina Gin LLC.......................F..... 252 943-6990
Pantego **(G-9642)**

S I C

Sampson Gin Company Inc.................. G 910 567-5111
Newton Grove *(G-9517)*

0751 Livestock services, except veterinary

Mitchells Meat Processing.................... F 336 591-7420
Walnut Cove *(G-12328)*

▼ Parks Family Meats LLC................... F 217 446-4600
Warsaw *(G-12364)*

Thomas Brothers Slaughter Hse........... G 336 667-1346
North Wilkesboro *(G-9551)*

0752 Animal specialty services

Farm Services Inc.................................. G 336 226-7381
Graham *(G-5268)*

0762 Farm management services

Sanders Ridge Inc................................ G 336 677-1700
Boonville *(G-958)*

0781 Landscape counseling and planning

Butler Trieu Inc................................... G 910 346-4929
Jacksonville *(G-7118)*

Carolina Lawnscape Inc........................ G 803 230-5570
Charlotte *(G-1849)*

M & M Stone Sculpting & Engrv............. G 336 877-3842
Todd *(G-12104)*

Native Naturalz Inc.............................. F 336 334-2984
Greensboro *(G-5704)*

0782 Lawn and garden services

Bemis Manufacturing Company............. C 828 754-1086
Lenoir *(G-7578)*

Butler Trieu Inc................................... G 910 346-4929
Jacksonville *(G-7118)*

Carlton Enterprizes LLC........................ G 919 534-5424
Rocky Point *(G-10877)*

Carolina Lawnscape Inc........................ G 803 230-5570
Charlotte *(G-1849)*

Classic Cleaning LLC........................... E 800 220-7101
Raleigh *(G-9998)*

Day 3 Lwncare Ldscpg Prfctnist............ G 910 574-8422
Fayetteville *(G-4584)*

McKinney Lwncare Grbage Svc LL........ G 828 766-9490
Spruce Pine *(G-11582)*

RDc Debris Removal Cnstr LLC............. E 323 614-2353
Smithfield *(G-11462)*

Taylco Inc... E 910 739-0405
Lumberton *(G-7974)*

Top Dawg Landscape Inc...................... G 336 877-7519
West Jefferson *(G-12571)*

0783 Ornamental shrub and tree services

Bickerstaff Trees Inc........................... G 336 372-8866
Sparta *(G-11535)*

CTI Property Services Inc..................... E 919 787-3789
Raleigh *(G-10025)*

08 FORESTRY

0811 Timber tracts

Lane Land & Timber Inc........................ G 252 443-1151
Battleboro *(G-700)*

0831 Forest products

G & G Forest Products.......................... G 704 539-5110
Union Grove *(G-12185)*

◆ Ivp Forest Products LLC.................... F 252 241-8126
Morehead City *(G-8836)*

0851 Forestry services

M & R Forestry Service Inc.................... G 980 439-1261
Albemarle *(G-80)*

09 FISHING, HUNTING AND TRAPPING

0913 Shellfish

Lloyds Oyster House Inc....................... E 910 754-6958
Shallotte *(G-11304)*

10 METAL MINING

1021 Copper ores

Ames Copper Group LLC....................... E 860 622-7626
Shelby *(G-11312)*

1081 Metal mining services

Charah LLC... C 704 731-2300
Charlotte *(G-1892)*

Charah LLC... C 502 873-6993
Mount Holly *(G-9223)*

Iperionx Critical Minerals LLC.............. E 980 237-8900
Charlotte *(G-2353)*

Iperionx Technology LLC...................... E 980 237-8900
Charlotte *(G-2355)*

RDc Debris Removal Cnstr LLC............. E 323 614-2353
Smithfield *(G-11462)*

1099 Metal ores, nec

Iperionx Limited.................................. E 980 237-8900
Charlotte *(G-2354)*

12 COAL MINING

1221 Bituminous coal and lignite-surface mining

Florida Progress Corporation................ C 704 382-3853
Raleigh *(G-10113)*

1241 Coal mining services

Aurum Capital Ventures Inc.................. F 877 467-7780
Cary *(G-1300)*

▲ Cowee Mountain Ruby Mine.............. G 828 369-5271
Franklin *(G-4823)*

13 OIL AND GAS EXTRACTION

1311 Crude petroleum and natural gas

City of Lexington................................. E 336 248-3945
Lexington *(G-7666)*

City of Shelby..................................... E 704 484-6840
Shelby *(G-11318)*

First Coast Energy LLP......................... G 828 667-0625
Asheville *(G-496)*

L TS Gas and Snaks............................ E 910 762-7130
Wilmington *(G-12830)*

Norcor Technologies Corp.................... G 704 309-4101
Greensboro *(G-5712)*

Renewco-Meadow Branch LLC.............. G 404 584-3552
Wake Forest *(G-12293)*

Sg-Clw Inc.. F 336 865-4980
Winston Salem *(G-13331)*

SRNg-T&w LLC.................................... G 704 271-9889
Charlotte *(G-2852)*

Trans-Tech Energy LLC........................ F 254 840-3355
Rocky Mount *(G-10818)*

1321 Natural gas liquids

Bi County Gas Producers LLC............... G 704 844-8990
Charlotte *(G-1778)*

Diversified Energy LLC......................... G 828 266-9800
Boone *(G-912)*

Euliss Oil Company Inc......................... G 336 622-3055
Liberty *(G-7766)*

Green Power Producers......................... G 704 844-8990
Charlotte *(G-2238)*

Landfill Gas Producers......................... G 704 844-8990
Charlotte *(G-2408)*

Panenergy Corp................................... F 704 594-6200
Charlotte *(G-2607)*

Renewable Power Producers LLC.......... G 704 844-8990
Charlotte *(G-2709)*

South Central Oil and Prpn Inc............. G 704 982-2173
Albemarle *(G-90)*

1381 Drilling oil and gas wells

Earth Matters Inc................................. G 410 747-4400
Denver *(G-3781)*

Integrity Envmtl Solutions LLC............. D 704 283-9765
Monroe *(G-8505)*

Terra Tech Inc..................................... G 906 399-0863
Concord *(G-3456)*

Vision Directional Drilling..................... G 336 570-4621
Burlington *(G-1174)*

1382 Oil and gas exploration services

BP Oil Corp Distributors....................... G 828 264-8516
Boone *(G-902)*

Citi Energy LLC................................... G 336 379-0800
Greensboro *(G-5445)*

▲ Das Oil Werks LLC........................... G 919 267-5781
New Hill *(G-9409)*

Energy and Entropy Inc........................ G 919 933-1365
Chapel Hill *(G-1544)*

EP Nisbet Company............................. G 704 332-7755
Charlotte *(G-2121)*

Maverick Biofuels................................ G 919 931-1434
Durham *(G-4120)*

Mpv Morganton Pressu......................... F 828 652-3704
Marion *(G-8056)*

1389 Oil and gas field services, nec

All In 1 Home Improvement................... G 252 725-4560
Vanceboro *(G-12214)*

American Rnovation Systems LLC......... G 336 313-6210
Thomasville *(G-11994)*

AMP Agency.. G 704 430-2313
Polkton *(G-9812)*

Anew Look Homes LLC......................... F 800 796-5152
Hickory *(G-6264)*

Atmox Inc... F 704 248-2858
Charlotte *(G-1715)*

Bcp East Land LLC.............................. G 704 248-2000
Charlotte *(G-1761)*

Bennett Elec Maint & Cnstr LLC........... G 910 231-0300
Raeford *(G-9832)*

Blue Ridge Contracting LLC.................. G 828 400-5194
Canton *(G-1243)*

Brown Building Corporation.................. F 919 782-1800
Morrisville *(G-8944)*

Cape Fear Cnstr Group LLC.................. G 910 344-1000
Wilmington *(G-12728)*

Carlton Enterprizes LLC........................ G 919 534-5424
Rocky Point *(G-10877)*

Carolina Housing Solutions LLC............ G 704 995-7078
Davidson *(G-3699)*

Carolina Siteworks Inc......................... E 704 855-7483
China Grove *(G-3072)*

Central Site Group LLC......................... G 336 380-4121
Ocean Isle Beach *(G-9587)*

CPM of Nc Inc..................................... G 704 467-5819
Concord *(G-3347)*

Danisson USA Trading Ltd LLC............. G 704 965-8317
Kernersville *(G-7264)*

Doble Engineering Company............... G..... 919 380-7461
Morrisville *(G-8966)*

Duke Energy Center............... F..... 919 464-0960
Raleigh *(G-10063)*

Edwin Reaves............... G..... 901 326-6382
Fayetteville *(G-4594)*

Enrg Brand LLC............... G..... 980 298-8519
Charlotte *(G-2116)*

Etbf LLC............... F..... 937 543-2223
Arden *(G-267)*

Extensive Builders LLC............... G..... 980 621-3793
Salisbury *(G-11050)*

Filter Srvcng of Chrltte 135............... G..... 704 619-3768
Charlotte *(G-2152)*

Fixed-NC LLC............... G..... 252 751-1911
Greenville *(G-5976)*

GP Technology LLC............... F..... 919 876-3666
Raleigh *(G-10141)*

Gt Rhyno Construction LLC............... G..... 919 737-3620
Raleigh *(G-10151)*

Hari Krupa Oil and Gas LLC............... G..... 860 805-1704
Winston Salem *(G-13190)*

Heath and Sons MGT Svcs LLC............... F..... 910 679-6142
Rocky Point *(G-10881)*

Hensel Phelps............... G..... 828 585-4689
Fletcher *(G-4741)*

Hillgray Innovations LLC............... G..... 704 923-6618
Statesville *(G-11712)*

Homeserve NC LLC............... G..... 740 552-8497
Pittsboro *(G-9784)*

Hot Shot Services LLC............... G..... 336 244-0331
State Road *(G-11637)*

Interntnal Instltion Group LL............... F..... 704 231-1868
Sparta *(G-11539)*

J & W Service Incorporated............... G..... 336 449-4584
Whitsett *(G-12611)*

J &D Contractor Service Inc............... G..... 919 427-0218
Angier *(G-122)*

J6 & Company LLC............... F..... 336 997-4497
Winston Salem *(G-13214)*

Johnson Controls Inc............... G..... 866 285-8345
Morrisville *(G-8995)*

Jordan Piping Inc............... G..... 336 818-9252
North Wilkesboro *(G-9539)*

K9 Installs Inc............... G..... 743 207-1507
Clemmons *(G-3195)*

KBK Cstom Dsgns Essntial Oils............... G..... 252 886-3315
Rocky Mount *(G-10846)*

Kcs Imprv & Cnstr Co Inc............... G..... 336 288-3865
Greensboro *(G-5645)*

Livengood Innovations LLC............... G..... 336 925-7604
Linwood *(G-7879)*

M and M Docks LLC............... F..... 336 537-0092
Lexington *(G-7714)*

M D Prevatt Inc............... F..... 919 796-4944
Clayton *(G-3158)*

M&S Enterprises Inc............... G..... 910 259-1763
Burgaw *(G-1027)*

McLean Sbsrface Utlity Engrg L............... F..... 336 340-0024
Greensboro *(G-5687)*

Midwest Modular Services Ltd............... F..... 847 417-0010
Moyock *(G-9279)*

Monumental Contractors Inc............... F..... 762 352-0564
Winston Salem *(G-13261)*

Mountain Homes of Wnc LLC............... F..... 828 216-2546
Weaverville *(G-12496)*

National Tank Monitor Inc............... F..... 704 335-8265
Charlotte *(G-2548)*

Parker Oil Inc............... G..... 828 253-7265
Asheville *(G-567)*

Prestige Cleaning Incorporated............... F..... 704 752-7747
Charlotte *(G-2662)*

Proven Prof Cnstr Svcs LLC............... F..... 919 821-2696
Garner *(G-4956)*

Quick N Easy 12 Nc739............... G..... 336 824-3832
Ramseur *(G-10630)*

RE Shads Group LLC............... G..... 704 299-8972
Charlotte *(G-2693)*

Reservoir Group LLC............... G..... 610 764-0269
Charlotte *(G-2713)*

Saybolt LP............... G..... 910 763-8444
Wilmington *(G-12912)*

Self Made Clt............... F..... 704 249-5263
Charlotte *(G-2785)*

Serenity Home Services LLC............... G..... 910 233-8733
Troutman *(G-12150)*

Simmie Bullard............... G..... 910 600-3191
Pembroke *(G-9659)*

Southern Estates Metal Roofing............... G..... 704 245-2023
Locust *(G-7902)*

Surface Buff LLC............... G..... 919 341-2873
Raleigh *(G-10523)*

◆ Trans-Tech Energy Inc............... G..... 252 446-4357
Rocky Mount *(G-10817)*

TransMontaigne Terminaling Inc............... F..... 303 626-8200
Selma *(G-11293)*

United Visions Corp............... G..... 704 953-4555
Davidson *(G-3724)*

V & B Construction Svcs Inc............... G..... 704 641-9936
Waxhaw *(G-12447)*

Well Doctor LLC............... G..... 704 909-9258
Charlotte *(G-3011)*

Wewoka Gas Producers LLC............... G..... 704 844-8990
Charlotte *(G-3014)*

William Brantley............... G..... 910 627-7286
Raeford *(G-9856)*

With Purpose Pressure Wshg LLC............... G..... 336 965-9473
Greensboro *(G-5921)*

WW&s Construction Inc............... G..... 217 620-4042
Dallas *(G-3693)*

Yes Real Estate Cnstr Group In............... E..... 919 389-4104
Raleigh *(G-10622)*

14 MINING AND QUARRYING OF NONMETALLIC MINERALS, EXCEPT FUELS

1411 Dimension stone

Carolina Quarries Inc............... D..... 704 633-0201
Salisbury *(G-11028)*

▲ Carolina Sunrock LLC............... E..... 919 575-4502
Butner *(G-1200)*

Jacobs Creek Stone Company Inc............... F..... 336 857-2602
Denton *(G-3751)*

Lbm Industries Inc............... G..... 828 631-1227
Sylva *(G-11895)*

Lbm Industries Inc............... F..... 828 966-4270
Sapphire *(G-11259)*

McNeely Trucking Co............... G..... 828 966-4270
Sapphire *(G-11260)*

Nantahala Talc & Limestone Co............... F..... 828 321-4239
Topton *(G-12105)*

Sunrock Group Holdings Corp............... D..... 919 747-6400
Raleigh *(G-10520)*

Tarheel Sand & Stone Inc............... G..... 336 468-4003
Hamptonville *(G-6093)*

Wilson Grading LLC............... F..... 919 778-1580
Goldsboro *(G-5254)*

Worldgranite & Stoneart Inc............... G..... 919 871-0078
Raleigh *(G-10614)*

1422 Crushed and broken limestone

Boyd Stone & Quarries............... G..... 828 659-6862
Marion *(G-8036)*

Buffalo Crushed Stone Inc............... F..... 919 688-6881
Durham *(G-3948)*

Bwi Etn LLC............... F..... 828 682-2645
Burnsville *(G-1184)*

Heidelberg Mtls Sthast Agg LLC............... E..... 919 936-4221
Princeton *(G-9824)*

Limestone Products Inc............... G..... 704 283-9492
Monroe *(G-8517)*

Marietta Martin Materials Inc............... E..... 704 525-7740
Charlotte *(G-2456)*

Marietta Martin Materials Inc............... G..... 252 749-2641
Fountain *(G-4806)*

Marietta Martin Materials Inc............... G..... 919 772-3563
Garner *(G-4938)*

Marietta Martin Materials Inc............... G..... 336 668-3253
Greensboro *(G-5673)*

Marietta Martin Materials Inc............... G..... 828 322-8386
Hickory *(G-6392)*

Marietta Martin Materials Inc............... G..... 336 886-5015
Jamestown *(G-7171)*

Marietta Martin Materials Inc............... G..... 336 769-3803
Kernersville *(G-7284)*

Marietta Martin Materials Inc............... G..... 704 739-4761
Kings Mountain *(G-7372)*

Marietta Martin Materials Inc............... G..... 910 743-6471
Maysville *(G-8211)*

Marietta Martin Materials Inc............... G..... 704 283-4915
Monroe *(G-8524)*

Marietta Martin Materials Inc............... F..... 919 788-4392
Raleigh *(G-10270)*

Marietta Martin Materials Inc............... G..... 336 349-3333
Reidsville *(G-10692)*

Marietta Martin Materials Inc............... F..... 704 636-6372
Salisbury *(G-11089)*

Marietta Martin Materials Inc............... G..... 704 873-8191
Statesville *(G-11729)*

Marietta Martin Materials Inc............... G..... 704 278-2218
Woodleaf *(G-13429)*

Martin Marietta Materials Inc............... G..... 919 894-2003
Benson *(G-794)*

Martin Marietta Materials Inc............... G..... 336 584-8875
Burlington *(G-1123)*

Martin Marietta Materials Inc............... G..... 910 675-2283
Castle Hayne *(G-1505)*

Martin Marietta Materials Inc............... G..... 704 547-9775
Charlotte *(G-2461)*

Martin Marietta Materials Inc............... G..... 704 588-1471
Charlotte *(G-2462)*

Martin Marietta Materials Inc............... G..... 704 932-4377
China Grove *(G-3076)*

Martin Marietta Materials Inc............... G..... 704 786-8415
Concord *(G-3398)*

Martin Marietta Materials Inc............... G..... 336 375-7584
Greensboro *(G-5678)*

Martin Marietta Materials Inc............... G..... 336 674-0836
Greensboro *(G-5679)*

Martin Marietta Materials Inc............... G..... 910 371-3848
Leland *(G-7554)*

Martin Marietta Materials Inc............... F..... 828 754-3077
Lenoir *(G-7625)*

Martin Marietta Materials Inc............... G..... 252 633-5308
New Bern *(G-9380)*

Martin Marietta Materials Inc............... F..... 360 424-3441
Raleigh *(G-10275)*

Martin Marietta Materials Inc............... G..... 336 672-1501
Randleman *(G-10651)*

Martin Marietta Materials Inc............... G..... 336 672-1501
Randleman *(G-10652)*

Martin Marietta Materials Inc............... G..... 919 788-4391
Sanford *(G-11207)*

◆ Martin Marietta Materials Inc...............C 919 781-4550
Raleigh *(G-10277)*

Quarries Petroleum................................G 919 387-0986
Apex *(G-190)*

Radford Quarries Inc..........................F 828 264-7008
Boone *(G-939)*

1423 Crushed and broken granite

Alamo North Texas Railroad Co..............G 919 787-9504
Raleigh *(G-9888)*

Blue Rock Materials LLC....................F 828 479-3581
Robbinsville *(G-10757)*

▲ Charlotte Instyle Inc........................E 704 665-8880
Charlotte *(G-1894)*

Georgia-Carolina Quarries Inc..............E 336 786-6978
Mount Airy *(G-9123)*

Heidelberg Mtls Sthast Agg LLC............E 910 893-8308
Bunnlevel *(G-1016)*

Heidelberg Mtls Sthast Agg LLC............F 910 893-2111
Lillington *(G-7797)*

Heidelberg Mtls Sthast Agg LLC............G 252 222-0812
Morehead City *(G-8834)*

Legacy Vulcan LLC.............................G 704 788-7833
Concord *(G-3391)*

Legacy Vulcan LLC.............................G 828 255-8561
Enka *(G-4487)*

Luck Stone Corporation.......................E 336 786-4693
Mount Airy *(G-9149)*

Marietta Martin Materials Inc...............G 704 278-2218
Woodleaf *(G-13429)*

Martin Marietta Materials Inc...............G 336 584-8875
Burlington *(G-1123)*

Martin Marietta Materials Inc...............G 919 863-4305
Raleigh *(G-10276)*

◆ Martin Marietta Materials Inc.............C 919 781-4550
Raleigh *(G-10277)*

Meridian Granite Company.....................G 919 781-4550
Raleigh *(G-10292)*

Wake Stone Corp................................G 252 985-4411
Battleboro *(G-708)*

Wake Stone Corporation.......................E 919 775-7349
Moncure *(G-8412)*

1429 Crushed and broken stone, nec

B V Hedrick Gravel & Sand Co..............C 828 686-3844
Swannanoa *(G-11866)*

Cardinal Stone Company Inc..................G 336 846-7191
Jefferson *(G-7187)*

▲ Carolina Sunrock LLC.......................E 919 575-4502
Butner *(G-1200)*

Heidelberg Mtls Sthast Agg LLC............F 252 235-4162
Bailey *(G-670)*

Heidelberg Mtls Sthast Agg LLC............E 919 787-0613
Raleigh *(G-10161)*

Luck Stone Corporation.......................D 919 545-0027
Moncure *(G-8408)*

Mafic USA LLC...................................F 704 967-8006
Shelby *(G-11358)*

Sunrock Group Holdings Corp...............D 919 747-6400
Raleigh *(G-10520)*

Wake Stone Corp................................G 252 985-4411
Battleboro *(G-708)*

Yancey Stone Inc...............................G 828 682-2645
Burnsville *(G-1194)*

Yancey Stone Inc...............................G 828 684-5522
Fletcher *(G-4782)*

1442 Construction sand and gravel

A-1 Sandrock Inc...............................E 336 855-8195
Greensboro *(G-5334)*

American Materials Company LLC..........G 252 752-2124
Greenville *(G-5935)*

American Materials Company LLC..........E 910 532-6070
Ivanhoe *(G-7109)*

American Materials Company LLC..........F 910 799-1411
Wilmington *(G-12703)*

Aquadale Query..................................G 704 474-3165
Norwood *(G-9553)*

Atmax Engineering.............................G 910 233-4881
Wilmington *(G-12715)*

B V Hedrick Gravel & Sand Co..............G 336 337-0706
Asheville *(G-450)*

B V Hedrick Gravel & Sand Co..............G 828 738-0332
Marion *(G-8032)*

B V Hedrick Gravel & Sand Co..............C 704 827-8114
Stanley *(G-11611)*

B V Hedrick Gravel & Sand Co..............G 828 686-3844
Swannanoa *(G-11866)*

B V Hedrick Gravel & Sand Co..............G 828 645-5560
Weaverville *(G-12482)*

B V Hedrick Gravel & Sand Co..............E 704 633-5982
Salisbury *(G-11021)*

Beazer East Inc.................................F 919 567-9512
Holly Springs *(G-6894)*

Black Sand Company Inc......................G 336 788-6411
Winston Salem *(G-13107)*

Blue Rock Materials LLC....................F 828 479-3581
Robbinsville *(G-10757)*

Bobby Cahoon Construction Inc............E 252 249-1617
Grantsboro *(G-5329)*

◆ Bonsal American Inc........................D 704 525-1621
Charlotte *(G-1799)*

Bulk Transport Service Inc..................G 910 329-0555
Holly Ridge *(G-6887)*

Carolina Stone LLC............................F 252 208-1633
Dover *(G-3828)*

Clifford W Estes Co Inc.....................E 336 622-6410
Staley *(G-11593)*

Columbia Silica Sand LLC....................G 803 755-1036
Wilmington *(G-12745)*

Crowder Trucking LLC.........................G 910 797-4163
Fayetteville *(G-4581)*

Cumberland Grav & Sand Min Co...........F 828 686-3844
Swannanoa *(G-11870)*

Cumberland Gravel & Sand Co..............G 704 633-4241
Salisbury *(G-11039)*

Cumberland Sand and Gravel................G 704 474-3165
Norwood *(G-9555)*

G S Materials Inc..............................E 336 584-1745
Burlington *(G-1093)*

Glover Materials Inc...........................G 252 536-2660
Pleasant Hill *(G-9797)*

Harrins Sand & Gravel Inc....................G 828 254-2744
Asheville *(G-516)*

Hedrick B V Gravel & Sand Co..............G 704 848-4165
Lilesville *(G-7785)*

Landsdown Mining Corporation.............F 704 753-5400
Leland *(G-7549)*

Long Branch Partners LLC....................G 828 837-1400
Brasstown *(G-965)*

Long J E & Sons Grading Inc................F 336 228-9706
Burlington *(G-1121)*

Martin Marietta Materials Inc...............F 360 424-3441
Raleigh *(G-10275)*

◆ Martin Marietta Materials Inc.............C 919 781-4550
Raleigh *(G-10277)*

Mugo Gravel & Grading Inc...................E 704 782-3478
Concord *(G-3406)*

NC Sand and Rock Inc.........................G 919 538-9001
Willow Spring *(G-12680)*

Parrish Contracting LLC......................G 828 524-9100
Franklin *(G-4838)*

Prize Management LLC.........................G 252 532-1939
Garysburg *(G-4977)*

Rogers Group Inc...............................G 828 657-9331
Mooresboro *(G-8585)*

Soundside Recycling & Mtls Inc...........G 252 491-8666
Jarvisburg *(G-7186)*

Tarheel Sand & Stone Inc.....................G 336 468-4003
Hamptonville *(G-6093)*

Thrills Hauling LLC............................F 407 383-3483
Arden *(G-310)*

Welbuilt Homes Inc............................G 910 323-0098
Fayetteville *(G-4699)*

1446 Industrial sand

Covia Holdings Corporation..................G 828 688-2169
Bakersville *(G-676)*

Covia Holdings Corporation..................G 980 495-2092
Huntersville *(G-6980)*

Covia Holdings Corporation..................G 828 765-4823
Spruce Pine *(G-11569)*

Covia Holdings LLC............................G 828 688-2169
Bakersville *(G-677)*

Covia Holdings LLC............................G 828 765-1114
Spruce Pine *(G-11570)*

Covia Holdings LLC............................G 828 765-1215
Spruce Pine *(G-11571)*

Covia Holdings LLC............................G 828 765-4251
Spruce Pine *(G-11572)*

Hammill Construction Co Inc................G 704 279-5309
Gold Hill *(G-5193)*

Next Generation Plastics Inc...............G 828 453-0221
Ellenboro *(G-4458)*

Taylor Timber Transport Inc.................G 252 943-1550
Chocowinity *(G-3085)*

1459 Clay and related minerals, nec

Covia Holdings LLC............................D 828 765-4283
Spruce Pine *(G-11573)*

Profile Products LLC...........................D 828 327-4165
Conover *(G-3552)*

1474 Potash, soda, and borate minerals

Pcs Phosphate Company Inc..................E 252 322-4111
Aurora *(G-645)*

1475 Phosphate rock

Lbm Industries Inc.............................F 828 966-4270
Sapphire *(G-11258)*

Pcs Phosphate Company Inc..................E 252 322-4111
Aurora *(G-645)*

1479 Chemical and fertilizer mining

Albemarle US Inc...............................G 980 299-5700
Charlotte *(G-1639)*

Piedmont Lithium Inc..........................F 704 461-8000
Belmont *(G-762)*

Verdesian Life Science US LLC.............E 919 825-1901
Cary *(G-1478)*

1481 Nonmetallic mineral services

Proash LLC.......................................G 336 597-8734
Semora *(G-11295)*

1499 Miscellaneous nonmetallic mining

▲ Buchanan Gem Stone Mines Inc........ F 828 765-6130
Spruce Pine *(G-11567)*

Classic Industrial Services...................G 919 209-0909
Smithfield *(G-11438)*

Comset Management Group....................G 910 574-6007
Hope Mills *(G-6926)*

Emerald Village Inc............................G 828 765-6463
Little Switzerland *(G-7882)*

Fsc II LLC..F 919 783-5700
Raleigh *(G-10122)*

Hiddenite Gems Inc.................................. G 828 632-3394
   Hiddenite *(G-6499)*

◆ Iluka Resources Inc.............................G 904 284-9832
   Raleigh *(G-10186)*

Johnson Paving Company Inc................. F 828 652-4911
   Marion *(G-8046)*

National Gypsum Services Co................. F 704 365-7300
   Charlotte *(G-2547)*

Sibelco North America Inc...................... D 828 766-6050
   Spruce Pine *(G-11587)*

Throwin Stones LLC................................ G 828 280-7870
   Asheville *(G-617)*

Vanderbilt Minerals LLC........................ E 910 948-2266
   Robbins *(G-10755)*

Zemex Industrial Minerals Inc................ G 828 765-5500
   Spruce Pine *(G-11591)*

15 CONSTRUCTION - GENERAL CONTRACTORS & OPERATIVE BUILDERS

1521 Single-family housing construction

Alamance Iron Works Inc........................ G 336 852-5940
   Greensboro *(G-5346)*

Around House Improvement LLC............. G 919 496-7029
   Bunn *(G-1013)*

Bennett Elec Maint & Cnstr LLC............. G 910 231-0300
   Raeford *(G-9832)*

Bridgport Restoration Svcs Inc............... G 336 996-1212
   Kernersville *(G-7248)*

Brown Building Corporation.................... F 919 782-1800
   Morrisville *(G-8944)*

Carolina Home Exteriors LLC................. F 252 637-6599
   New Bern *(G-9350)*

Champion Home Builders Inc................. B 910 893-5713
   Lillington *(G-7793)*

Distinctive Bldg & Design Inc................. G 828 456-4730
   Waynesville *(G-12456)*

◆ Downtown Graphics Network Inc.......G 704 637-0855
   Salisbury *(G-11044)*

E A Duncan Cnstr Co Inc........................ G 910 653-3535
   Tabor City *(G-11910)*

Fixed-NC LLC... G 252 751-1911
   Greenville *(G-5976)*

G A Lankford Construction..................... G 828 254-2467
   Alexander *(G-100)*

▲ GLG Corporation................................ F 336 784-0396
   Winston Salem *(G-13178)*

Goembel Inc... F 919 303-0485
   Apex *(G-159)*

Hamrick Fence Company........................ F 704 434-5011
   Boiling Springs *(G-884)*

Heidelberg Mtls Sthast Agg LLC............ E 919 936-4221
   Princeton *(G-9824)*

High Cntry Tmbrframe Gllery WD........... G 828 264-8971
   Boone *(G-921)*

Hope Renovations.................................. F 919 960-1957
   Chapel Hill *(G-1549)*

J & W Service Incorporated................... G 336 449-4584
   Whitsett *(G-12611)*

J &D Contractor Service Inc................... G 919 427-0218
   Angier *(G-122)*

Kcs Imprv & Cnstr Co Inc....................... G 336 288-3865
   Greensboro *(G-5645)*

Kitchen Tune-Up..................................... G 833 259-1838
   Matthews *(G-8123)*

▲ Lewtak Pipe Organ Builders Inc........ G 336 554-2251
   Mocksville *(G-8374)*

Lowder Steel Inc.................................... E 336 431-9000
   Archdale *(G-238)*

Marsh Furniture Company...................... F 336 273-8196
   Greensboro *(G-5676)*

McDaniel Awning Co.............................. G 704 636-8503
   Salisbury *(G-11090)*

Midway Blind & Awning Co Inc.............. G 336 226-4532
   Burlington *(G-1129)*

Mike Powell Inc..................................... F 910 792-6152
   Wilmington *(G-12854)*

Neals Carpentry & Cnstr........................ G 910 346-6154
   Jacksonville *(G-7135)*

Noble Bros Cabinets Mllwk LLC............ G 252 335-1213
   Elizabeth City *(G-4399)*

Noble Bros Cabinets Mllwk LLC............ G 252 482-9100
   Edenton *(G-4370)*

Nobscot Construction Co Inc.................. G 919 929-2075
   Chapel Hill *(G-1560)*

Nvr Inc... D 704 484-7170
   Kings Mountain *(G-7374)*

Old Hickory Log Homes Inc.................... G 704 489-8989
   Denver *(G-3795)*

Pro Choice Contractors Corp.................. G 919 696-7383
   Raleigh *(G-10398)*

RDc Debris Removal Cnstr LLC.............. E 323 614-2353
   Smithfield *(G-11462)*

Robbinsville Cstm Molding Inc............... F 828 479-2317
   Robbinsville *(G-10761)*

Rogers Manufacturing Company............ G 910 259-9898
   Burgaw *(G-1030)*

Safe Home Pro Inc................................. F 704 662-2299
   Cornelius *(G-3626)*

Selectbuild Construction Inc.................. F 208 331-4300
   Raleigh *(G-10467)*

▼ Value Clothing Inc.............................. D 704 638-6111
   Salisbury *(G-11132)*

W T Humphrey Inc.................................. E 910 455-3555
   Jacksonville *(G-7158)*

With Purpose Pressure Wshg LLC......... G 336 965-9473
   Greensboro *(G-5921)*

Yes Real Estate Cnstr Group In............. E 919 389-4104
   Raleigh *(G-10622)*

1522 Residential construction, nec

Atlantic Group Usa Inc........................... F 919 623-7824
   Raleigh *(G-9920)*

Black Mountain Cnstr Group Inc............. F 704 243-5593
   Waxhaw *(G-12424)*

Kitchen Tune-Up..................................... G 833 259-1838
   Matthews *(G-8123)*

Seashore Builders Inc............................ E 910 259-3404
   Maple Hill *(G-8026)*

Self Made Clt... F 704 249-5263
   Charlotte *(G-2785)*

United Visions Corp................................ G 704 953-4555
   Davidson *(G-3724)*

Yes Real Estate Cnstr Group In............. E 919 389-4104
   Raleigh *(G-10622)*

1531 Operative builders

Medaccess Inc.. G 828 264-4085
   Robbinsville *(G-10760)*

Smith Companies Lexington Inc............. G 336 249-4941
   Lexington *(G-7742)*

Wersunsllc... G 857 209-8701
   Winston Salem *(G-13388)*

▲ Williams Industries Inc...................... C 919 604-1746
   Raleigh *(G-10610)*

1541 Industrial buildings and warehouses

A R Byrd Company Inc........................... G 704 732-5675
   Lincolnton *(G-7807)*

Ansgar Industrial LLC............................ A 866 284-1931
   Charlotte *(G-1679)*

B V Hedrick Gravel & Sand Co............... E 704 633-5982
   Salisbury *(G-11021)*

Bwxt Investment Company..................... E 704 625-4900
   Charlotte *(G-1824)*

▲ Central Steel Buildings Inc................ F 336 789-7896
   Mount Airy *(G-9114)*

▲ Cornerstone Bldg Brands Inc............ B 281 897-7788
   Cary *(G-1336)*

Eagle Carports Inc................................. E 800 579-8589
   Mount Airy *(G-9117)*

◆ Herbal Innovations LLC.....................E 336 818-2332
   Wilkesboro *(G-12638)*

▲ Jbr Properties of Greenville Inc......... A 252 355-9353
   Winterville *(G-13417)*

▼ Millennium Mfg Structures LLC......... G 828 265-3737
   Boone *(G-934)*

Seashore Builders Inc............................ E 910 259-3404
   Maple Hill *(G-8026)*

Sonaron LLC... G 808 232-6168
   Fayetteville *(G-4672)*

TRC Acquisition LLC.............................. A 252 355-9353
   Winterville *(G-13424)*

▲ Williams Industries Inc...................... C 919 604-1746
   Raleigh *(G-10610)*

1542 Nonresidential construction, nec

A R Byrd Company Inc........................... G 704 732-5675
   Lincolnton *(G-7807)*

American Builders Anson Inc.................. E 704 272-7655
   Polkton *(G-9811)*

Atlantic Group Usa Inc........................... G 919 623-7824
   Raleigh *(G-9920)*

B V Hedrick Gravel & Sand Co............... E 704 633-5982
   Salisbury *(G-11021)*

Black Mountain Cnstr Group Inc............. F 704 243-5593
   Waxhaw *(G-12424)*

▲ Cornerstone Bldg Brands Inc............ B 281 897-7788
   Cary *(G-1336)*

Exteriors Inc Ltd.................................... G 919 325-2251
   Spring Lake *(G-11561)*

◆ Hog Slat Incorporated....................... B 800 949-4647
   Newton Grove *(G-9514)*

International Tela-Com Inc...................... G 828 651-9801
   Fletcher *(G-4743)*

J &D Contractor Service Inc................... G 919 427-0218
   Angier *(G-122)*

▲ Lock Drives Inc.................................. G 704 588-1844
   Pineville *(G-9740)*

M F C Inc... E 252 322-5004
   Aurora *(G-643)*

Pro Choice Contractors Corp.................. G 919 696-7383
   Raleigh *(G-10398)*

Reliable Construction Co Inc.................. G 704 289-1501
   Monroe *(G-8550)*

Retail Installation Svcs LLC................... G 336 818-1333
   Millers Creek *(G-8307)*

Robinsons Welding Service..................... G 336 622-3150
   Liberty *(G-7777)*

Seashore Builders Inc............................ E 910 259-3404
   Maple Hill *(G-8026)*

Sterling Cleora Corporation.................... F 919 563-5800
   Durham *(G-4250)*

Stowe Enterprises Inc............................ G 800 315-6751
   Troutman *(G-12151)*

Tigerswan LLC....................................... C 919 439-7110
   Apex *(G-197)*

United Visions Corp................................ G 704 953-4555
   Davidson *(G-3724)*

W T Humphrey Inc.................................. E 910 455-3555
   Jacksonville *(G-7158)*

16 HEAMY CONSTRUCTION, EXCEPT BUILDING CONSTRUCTION, CONTRACTOR

1611 Highway and street construction

Apac-Atlantic Inc................................. D 336 412-6800
Raleigh *(G-9907)*

Asheville Contracting Co Inc................. E 828 665-8900
Candler *(G-1217)*

Barnhill Contracting Company............... G 704 721-7500
Concord *(G-3317)*

Barnhill Contracting Company............... D 910 488-1319
Fayetteville *(G-4557)*

Barnhill Contracting Company............... E 252 752-7608
Greenville *(G-5946)*

Barnhill Contracting Company............... E 252 527-8021
Kinston *(G-7395)*

Batista Grading Inc............................... F 919 359-3449
Clayton *(G-3134)*

Blythe Construction Inc.......................... E 336 854-9003
Greensboro *(G-5396)*

▲ **Blythe Construction Inc**....................... B 704 375-8474
Charlotte *(G-1793)*

Brown Brothers Construction Co............ F 828 297-2131
Zionville *(G-13527)*

Brown Building Corporation................... F 919 782-1800
Morrisville *(G-8944)*

Carlton Enterprizes LLC........................ G 919 534-5424
Rocky Point *(G-10877)*

Carolina Paving Hickory Inc.................. G 828 328-3909
Hickory *(G-6285)*

Carolina Paving Hickory Inc.................. F 828 322-1706
Hickory *(G-6286)*

Chandler Concrete Inc........................... F 919 598-1424
Durham *(G-3969)*

Cjc Enterprises................................... E 919 266-3158
Wake Forest *(G-12270)*

Crowder Trucking LLC........................... G 910 797-4163
Fayetteville *(G-4581)*

Dan Moore Inc...................................... G 336 475-8350
Thomasville *(G-12015)*

Dickerson Group Inc............................. G 704 289-3111
Charlotte *(G-2042)*

Ferebee Corporation............................. C 704 509-2586
Charlotte *(G-2145)*

Garris Grading and Paving Inc............... F 252 749-1101
Farmville *(G-4529)*

Gelder & Associates Inc........................ C 919 772-6895
Raleigh *(G-10126)*

Heath and Sons MGT Svcs LLC............. F 910 679-6142
Rocky Point *(G-10881)*

Highland Paving Co LLC........................ D 910 482-0080
Fayetteville *(G-4613)*

Hudson Paving Inc................................ D 910 895-5910
Rockingham *(G-10780)*

Johnson Paving Company Inc................. F 828 652-4911
Marion *(G-8046)*

Lane Construction Corporation.............. C 919 876-4550
Raleigh *(G-10247)*

Long Asp Pav Trckg of Grnsburg........... G 336 643-4121
Summerfield *(G-11842)*

Macleod Construction Inc...................... C 704 483-3580
Charlotte *(G-2446)*

Mass Connection Inc............................. G 910 424-0940
Fayetteville *(G-4636)*

Moretz & Sipe Inc................................ G 828 327-8661
Hickory *(G-6397)*

Reliable Woodworks Inc........................ G 704 785-9663
Concord *(G-3431)*

Russell Standard Corporation................ F 336 292-6875
Greensboro *(G-5797)*

S T Wooten Corporation........................ E 919 965-9880
Princeton *(G-9826)*

S T Wooten Corporation........................ E 252 291-5165
Wilson *(G-13027)*

Stone Supply Inc.................................. G 828 678-9966
Burnsville *(G-1192)*

Young & McQueen Grading Co Inc.......... D 828 682-7714
Burnsville *(G-1196)*

1622 Bridge, tunnel, and elevated highway

▲ **Blythe Construction Inc**....................... B 704 375-8474
Charlotte *(G-1793)*

1623 Water, sewer, and utility lines

1st Choice Service Inc.......................... G 704 913-7685
Cherryville *(G-3058)*

Batista Grading Inc............................... F 919 359-3449
Clayton *(G-3134)*

Bolton Construction & Svc LLC............. D 919 861-1500
Raleigh *(G-9952)*

Cjc Enterprises................................... E 919 266-3158
Wake Forest *(G-12270)*

Davis Mechanical Inc............................ F 704 272-9366
Peachland *(G-9651)*

Ferebee Corporation............................. C 704 509-2586
Charlotte *(G-2145)*

Gillam & Mason Inc.............................. G 252 356-2874
Cofield *(G-3266)*

Hyper Networks LLC............................. G 704 837-8411
Pineville *(G-9734)*

Integrity Envmtl Solutions LLC.............. D 704 283-9765
Monroe *(G-8505)*

McLean Sbsrface Utility Engrg L............ F 336 340-0024
Greensboro *(G-5687)*

Merrill Resources Inc............................ E 828 877-4450
Penrose *(G-9662)*

Pipeline Plastics LLC............................ G 817 693-4100
Fair Bluff *(G-4499)*

S T Wooten Corporation........................ E 252 291-5165
Wilson *(G-13027)*

▲ **Spectrasite Communications LLC**......... E 919 468-0112
Cary *(G-1465)*

Terra Tech Inc...................................... G 906 399-0863
Concord *(G-3456)*

Vision Directional Drilling..................... G 336 570-4621
Burlington *(G-1174)*

Wirenet Inc.. F 513 774-7759
Huntersville *(G-7062)*

Wnc White Corporation......................... E 828 477-4895
Sylva *(G-11905)*

1629 Heavy construction, nec

A-1 Sandrock Inc.................................. E 336 855-8195
Greensboro *(G-5334)*

Barnhill Contracting Company............... D 910 488-1319
Fayetteville *(G-4557)*

Bobby Cahoon Construction Inc............. E 252 249-1617
Grantsboro *(G-5329)*

Bwxt Investment Company..................... E 704 625-4900
Charlotte *(G-1824)*

Component Sourcing Intl LLC................. E 704 843-9292
Charlotte *(G-1967)*

Dagenhart Pallet Inc............................. G 828 241-2374
Catawba *(G-1511)*

Harsco Rail LLC................................... G 980 960-2624
Charlotte *(G-2262)*

Heath and Sons MGT Svcs LLC............. F 910 679-6142
Rocky Point *(G-10881)*

JM Williams Timber Company................ G 919 362-1333
Apex *(G-172)*

Soundside Recycling & Mtls Inc............. G 252 491-8666
Jarvisburg *(G-7186)*

Stone Supply Inc.................................. G 828 678-9966
Burnsville *(G-1192)*

TNT Services Inc.................................. G 252 261-3073
Kitty Hawk *(G-7447)*

Trademark Landscape Group Inc............ F 910 253-0560
Supply *(G-11861)*

Triton Marine Services Inc..................... G 252 728-9958
Beaufort *(G-736)*

United Visions Corp.............................. G 704 953-4555
Davidson *(G-3724)*

Wnc White Corporation......................... E 828 477-4895
Sylva *(G-11905)*

Young & McQueen Grading Co Inc.......... D 828 682-7714
Burnsville *(G-1196)*

17 CONSTRUCTION - SPECIAL TRADE CONTRACTORS

1711 Plumbing, heating, air-conditioning

▲ **AC Corporation**.................................. B 336 273-4472
Greensboro *(G-5339)*

Accent Comfort Services LLC................ E 704 509-1200
Charlotte *(G-1614)*

Airboss Heating and Coolg Inc.............. G 252 586-0500
Littleton *(G-7883)*

Allen Kelly & Co Inc............................. D 919 779-4197
Raleigh *(G-9892)*

Ansonville Piping & Fabg Inc................. G 704 826-8403
Ansonville *(G-129)*

▲ **Attic Tent Inc**.................................... G 704 892-5399
Mooresville *(G-8601)*

Bahnson Holdings Inc........................... D 336 760-3111
Clemmons *(G-3178)*

Bolton Construction & Svc LLC............. D 919 861-1500
Raleigh *(G-9952)*

Carolina Fire Protection Inc................... E 910 892-1700
Dunn *(G-3847)*

Chichibone Inc..................................... G 919 785-0090
Morrisville *(G-8957)*

Comfort Engineers Inc........................... E 919 383-0158
Durham *(G-3985)*

Commercial Flter Svc of Triad................ G 336 272-1443
Greensboro *(G-5459)*

Dusty Rhoads Hvac Inc......................... G 252 261-5892
Kitty Hawk *(G-7444)*

Edwards Electronic Systems Inc............. E 919 359-2239
Clayton *(G-3146)*

Ellenburg Sheet Metal.......................... G 704 872-2089
Statesville *(G-11695)*

Envirnmntal Cmfort Sltions Inc.............. E 980 272-7327
Kannapolis *(G-7208)*

Fixed-NC LLC....................................... G 252 751-1911
Greenville *(G-5976)*

Franklin Sheet Metal Shop Inc............... G 828 524-2821
Franklin *(G-4829)*

Freedom Industries Inc.......................... C 252 984-0007
Rocky Mount *(G-10839)*

General Refrigeration Company.............. G 919 661-4727
Garner *(G-4929)*

Go Green Services LLC.......................... D 336 252-2999
Greensboro *(G-5565)*

GSM Services Inc.................................. D 704 864-0344
Gastonia *(G-5056)*

Harco Air LLC...................................... G 252 491-5220
Powells Point *(G-9821)*

Hauser Hvac Installation....................... G 336 416-2173
Winston Salem *(G-13192)*

Heath and Sons MGT Svcs LLC............. F 910 679-6142
Rocky Point *(G-10881)*

Hicks Wterstoves Solar Systems............F 336 789-4977
   Mount Airy (G-9129)

Hollingsworth Heating Air Cond........... G 252 824-0355
   Tarboro (G-11929)

Industrial Air Inc.......................... C 336 292-1030
   Greensboro (G-5616)

Industrial Mechanical Services............ G 828 397-3231
   Hildebran (G-6852)

Inman Septic Tank Service Inc.............. G 910 763-1146
   Wilmington (G-12817)

J & W Service Incorporated................ G 336 449-4584
   Whitsett (G-12611)

Jenkins Services Group LLC................ G 704 881-3210
   Catawba (G-1512)

Johnson Controls Inc...................... D 704 521-8889
   Charlotte (G-2375)

Kenny Fowler Heating and A Inc............F 910 508-4553
   Wilmington (G-12827)

Kinetic Systems Inc....................... D 919 322-7200
   Durham (G-4096)

Leonard McSwain Sptic Tank Svc........ G 704 482-1380
   Shelby (G-11353)

Lunar International Tech LLC.............. F 800 975-7153
   Charlotte (G-2441)

Mechanical Maintenance Inc.............. F 336 676-7133
   Climax (G-3227)

Mechanical Spc Contrs Inc.................D.... 919 829-9300
   Raleigh (G-10287)

Miller Sheet Metal Co Inc................. G 336 751-2304
   Mocksville (G-8378)

Muriel Harris Investments Inc............. F 800 932-3191
   Fayetteville (G-4644)

NC Solar Now Inc.......................... F 919 833-9096
   Raleigh (G-10327)

Norcor Technologies Corp................. G 704 309-4101
   Greensboro (G-5712)

O R Prdgen Sons Sptic Tank I............. G 252 442-3338
   Rocky Mount (G-10857)

Pamlico Air Inc........................... F 252 995-6267
   Washington (G-12405)

Prestige Cleaning Incorporated............ F 704 752-7747
   Charlotte (G-2662)

Prime Water Services Inc.................. G 919 504-1020
   Raleigh (G-10394)

◆ Progress Solar Solutions LLC...........F 919 363-3738
   Raleigh (G-10401)

Proven Prof Cnstr Svcs LLC............... F 919 821-2696
   Garner (G-4956)

Raleigh Mechanical & Mtls Inc............. F 919 598-4601
   Raleigh (G-10425)

▲ Saab Barracuda LLC.................... G 910 814-3088
   Lillington (G-7802)

Southern Pdmont Pping Fbrction.......... F 704 272-7936
   Peachland (G-9654)

Spc Mechanical Corporation............... C 252 237-9035
   Wendell (G-12549)

Taylco Inc................................ E 910 739-0405
   Lumberton (G-7974)

TNT Services Inc.......................... G 252 261-3073
   Kitty Hawk (G-7447)

Tony D Hildreth.......................... F 910 276-1803
   Laurel Hill (G-7488)

Trane US Inc.............................. F 704 697-9006
   Charlotte (G-2935)

Tri-City Mechanical Contrs Inc............ D 336 272-9495
   Greensboro (G-5872)

Triad Sheet Metal & Mech Inc............. F 336 379-9891
   Greensboro (G-5879)

W T Humphrey Inc......................... E 910 455-3555
   Jacksonville (G-7158)

Wen Bray Heating & AC.................... G 828 267-0635
   Hickory (G-6489)

1721 Painting and paper hanging

Auto Parts Fayetteville LLC.................. G 910 889-4026
   Fayetteville (G-4555)

Carlton Enterprizes LLC.................... G 919 534-5424
   Rocky Point (G-10877)

CTI Property Services Inc.................. E 919 787-3789
   Raleigh (G-10025)

Custom Steel Boats Inc.................... F 252 745-7447
   Merritt (G-8267)

Gemseal Pavement Products................ G 866 264-8273
   Charlotte (G-2198)

Hemco Wire Products Inc.................. G 336 454-7280
   Jamestown (G-7164)

Painting By Colors LLC.................... G 919 963-2300
   Clayton (G-3166)

Parrish Contracting LLC................... G 828 524-9100
   Franklin (G-4838)

Patricia Hall............................. G 704 729-6133
   Bessemer City (G-829)

Peaches Enterprises Inc................... G 910 868-5800
   Fayetteville (G-4653)

Yontz & Sons Painting Inc................. G 336 784-7099
   Winston Salem (G-13409)

1731 Electrical work

Absolute Security & Lock Inc.............. G 336 322-4598
   Roxboro (G-10917)

▲ AC Corporation....................... B 336 273-4472
   Greensboro (G-5339)

Allen Kelly & Co Inc...................... D 919 779-4197
   Raleigh (G-9892)

Amplified Elctronic Design Inc............ F 336 223-4811
   Greensboro (G-5362)

Atcom Inc................................ F 704 357-7900
   Charlotte (G-1708)

Audio Vdeo Concepts Design Inc........... R 704 821-2823
   Indian Trail (G-7069)

Automated Controls LLC................... G 704 724-7625
   Huntersville (G-6970)

Belham Management Ind LLC.............. G 704 815-4246
   Charlotte (G-1768)

Bennett Elec Maint & Cnstr LLC........... G 910 231-0300
   Raeford (G-9832)

Carolina Time Equipment Co Inc........... E 704 536-2700
   Charlotte (G-1859)

Cemco Electric Inc....................... F 704 504-0294
   Charlotte (G-1886)

Commscope Inc North Carolina............ A 828 459-5000
   Claremont (G-3094)

◆ Commscope Technologies LLC...........A 828 324-2200
   Claremont (G-3104)

Custom Controls Unlimited LLC........... F 919 812-6553
   Raleigh (G-10029)

Custom Light and Sound Inc.............. G 919 286-1122
   Durham (G-3994)

Diebold Nixdorf Incorporated............. E 704 599-3100
   Charlotte (G-2044)

DMC LLC................................. E 980 352-9806
   Concord (G-3355)

Edwards Electronic Systems Inc........... E 919 359-2239
   Clayton (G-3146)

Freedom Industries Inc................... C 252 984-0007
   Rocky Mount (G-10839)

Gillam & Mason Inc....................... G 252 356-2874
   Cofield (G-3266)

Glh Systems & Controls Inc................ G 980 581-1304
   Stanfield (G-11606)

International Tela-Com Inc................. G 828 651-9801
   Fletcher (G-4743)

JA Smith Inc............................. G 704 860-4910
   Lawndale (G-7517)

Jared Munday Electric Inc.................. G 828 355-9024
   Boone (G-927)

M & M Electric Service Inc................ E 704 867-0221
   Gastonia (G-5081)

M2 Optics Inc............................ G 919 342-5619
   Raleigh (G-10264)

Moss Sign Company Inc.................... F 828 299-7766
   Asheville (G-551)

Nkt Inc.................................. G 919 601-1970
   Cary (G-1408)

Pike Electric LLC......................... C 336 316-7068
   Greensboro (G-5748)

Power Integrity Corp...................... E 336 379-9773
   Greensboro (G-5752)

Power Support Engineering Inc............ G 813 909-1199
   Hayesville (G-6143)

Presley Group Ltd........................ D 828 254-9971
   Asheville (G-584)

Service Electric and Control.............. G 704 888-5100
   Locust (G-7901)

◆ Southern Elc & Automtn Corp..........F 919 718-0122
   Sanford (G-11235)

Telecmmnctons Resource MGT Inc....... F 919 779-0776
   Raleigh (G-10539)

Total Controls Inc........................ G 704 821-6341
   Matthews (G-8152)

▲ Unitape (usa) Inc...................... G 828 464-5695
   Conover (G-3568)

Watson Electrical Cnstr Co LLC........... D 252 756-4550
   Greenville (G-6033)

Yes Real Estate Cnstr Group In............ E 919 389-4104
   Raleigh (G-10622)

1741 Masonry and other stonework

John J Morton Company Inc................ F 704 332-6633
   Charlotte (G-2373)

M & M Stone Sculpting & Engrv............ G 336 877-3842
   Todd (G-12104)

▼ Stonemaster Inc....................... F 704 333-0353
   Concord (G-3449)

Taylco Inc................................ E 910 739-0405
   Lumberton (G-7974)

Vega Construction Company Inc........... E 336 756-3477
   Pilot Mountain (G-9675)

1742 Plastering, drywall, and insulation

ABS Southeast LLC....................... F 919 329-0014
   Raleigh (G-9869)

▲ Attic Tent Inc.......................... G 704 892-5399
   Mooresville (G-8601)

Delkote Machine Finishing Inc............. G 828 253-1023
   Asheville (G-485)

▲ Delve Interiors LLC.................... C 336 274-4661
   Greensboro (G-5495)

Precision Walls Inc....................... G 336 852-7710
   Greensboro (G-5759)

◆ Sika Corporation....................... E 704 810-0500
   Gastonia (G-5138)

Taylor Interiors LLC...................... F 980 207-3160
   Charlotte (G-2901)

1743 Terrazzo, tile, marble, mosaic work

Apex Marble and Granite Inc............... E 919 462-9202
   Morrisville (G-8929)

▲ David Allen Company Inc............... C 919 821-7100
   Raleigh (G-10039)

▲ Grancreations Inc..................... G 704 332-7625
   Charlotte (G-2230)

Precision Walls Inc....................... G 336 852-7710
   Greensboro (G-5759)

Sare Granite & Tile....................... G 828 676-2666
   Arden (G-305)

S I C

1751 Carpentry work

Alcorns Custom Woodworking Inc......... G 336 342-0908
Reidsville (G-10672)

Amarr Company..................................... G 336 936-0010
Mocksville (G-8347)

Andronics Construction Inc .... E 704 400-9562
Indian Trail (G-7068)

Architectural Craftsman Ltd.................. E 919 494-6911
Franklinton (G-4846)

Artistic Southern Inc............................ F 919 861-4695
Charlotte (G-1700)

Athol Arbor Corporation........................ F 919 643-1100
Hillsborough (G-6859)

Black Mountain Cnstr Group Inc........... F 704 243-5593
Waxhaw (G-12424)

Cabinet Solutions Usa Inc.................... E 828 358-2349
Hickory (G-6280)

Carolina Windows and Doors Inc.......... F 252 756-2585
Greenville (G-5951)

Classic Cleaning LLC........................... E 800 220-7101
Raleigh (G-9998)

Comm-Kab Inc..................................... F 336 873-8787
Asheboro (G-340)

Distinctive Cabinets Inc........................ F 704 529-6234
Charlotte (G-2053)

H & H Woodworking Inc .... G 336 884-5848
High Point (G-6637)

▲ Idx Impressions LLC......................... C 703 550-6902
Washington (G-12393)

Interior Trim Creations Inc................... G 704 821-1470
Charlotte (G-2342)

Jewers Doors Us Inc............................ E 888 510-5331
Greensboro (G-5636)

Marsh Furniture Company..................... F 336 273-8196
Greensboro (G-5676)

Mountain Showcase Group Inc .... E 828 692-9494
Hendersonville (G-6228)

Neals Carpentry & Cnstr...................... G 910 346-6154
Jacksonville (G-7135)

Riddley Retail Fixtures Inc.................... E 704 435-8829
Kings Mountain (G-7382)

Seashore Builders Inc.......................... E 910 259-3404
Maple Hill (G-8026)

Selectbuild Construction Inc................. F 208 331-4300
Raleigh (G-10467)

Ullman Group LLC................................ F 704 246-7333
Charlotte (G-2959)

Vaughn Woodworking Inc...................... G 828 963-6858
Banner Elk (G-690)

Washington Cabinet Company.............. G 252 946-3457
Washington (G-12420)

Wildwood Studios Inc........................... G 828 299-8696
Asheville (G-636)

1752 Floor laying and floor work, nec

Creative Stone Fyetteville Inc............... F 910 491-1225
Fayetteville (G-4580)

Mrrefinish LLC...................................... F 336 625-2400
Asheboro (G-379)

1761 Roofing, siding, and sheetmetal work

Allens Gutter Service............................ G 910 738-9509
Lumberton (G-7944)

ARS Extreme Construction Inc .... F 919 331-8024
Angier (G-111)

Budd-Piper Roofing Company............... G 919 682-2121
Durham (G-3947)

Carolina Custom Exteriors Inc.............. F 828 232-0402
Asheville (G-469)

Carolina Machining Fabrication............ G 919 554-9700
Youngsville (G-13469)

Carolina Windows and Doors Inc........... F 252 756-2585
Greenville (G-5951)

Cypress Mountain Company.................. G 252 758-2179
Greenville (G-5962)

Dimensional Metals Inc........................ G 704 279-9691
Salisbury (G-11043)

Exteriors Inc Ltd.................................. G 919 325-2251
Spring Lake (G-11561)

GSM Services Inc................................ D 704 864-0344
Gastonia (G-5056)

Herman Reeves Tex Shtmtl Inc............ E 704 865-2231
Gastonia (G-5059)

Hughs Sheet Mtal Sttsvlle LLC............. F 704 872-4621
Statesville (G-11714)

Larry Bissette Inc................................. F 919 773-2140
Apex (G-176)

Longhorn Roofing Inc........................... F 704 774-1080
Monroe (G-8520)

Metal Roofing Systems LLC................. E 704 820-3110
Stanley (G-11622)

Midway Blind & Awning Co Inc.............. G 336 226-4532
Burlington (G-1129)

Muriel Harris Investments Inc............... F 800 932-3191
Fayetteville (G-4644)

Oak Ridge Industries LLC..................... E 252 833-4061
Washington (G-12401)

On Time Metal LLC.............................. G 828 635-1001
Hiddenite (G-6503)

▲ Owens Crning Nn-Woven Tech LLC.. G 740 321-6131
Dallas (G-3681)

Protocase Mfg Usa Inc......................... E 866 849-3911
Wilmington (G-12892)

R E Bengel Sheet Metal Co.................. G 252 637-3404
New Bern (G-9390)

Raleigh Mechanical & Mtls Inc.............. F 919 598-4601
Raleigh (G-10425)

Ramsey Industries Inc.......................... F 704 827-3560
Belmont (G-763)

Ray Roofing Company Inc.................... E 704 372-0100
Charlotte (G-2692)

Service Rofg Shtmtl Wlmngton I............ F 910 343-9860
Wilmington (G-12918)

Service Roofing and Shtmtl Co.............. D 252 758-2179
Greenville (G-6021)

Southern Estates Metal Roofing............ G 704 245-2023
Locust (G-7902)

Taylorsville Precast Molds Inc.............. G 828 632-4608
Taylorsville (G-11982)

Triangle Installation Svc Inc................. G 919 363-7637
Apex (G-201)

Viking Truss Inc................................... G 252 792-1051
Williamston (G-12675)

Vinyl Windows & Doors Corp................. F 910 944-2100
Aberdeen (G-30)

1771 Concrete work

Apac-Atlantic Inc................................. D 336 412-6800
Raleigh (G-9907)

Barnhill Contracting Company............... F 336 584-1306
Burlington (G-1051)

Barnhill Contracting Company............... D 910 488-1319
Fayetteville (G-4557)

Barnhill Contracting Company............... E 252 527-8021
Kinston (G-7395)

Chandler Concrete Inc.......................... D 704 636-4711
Salisbury (G-11031)

Commercial Ready Mix Pdts Inc............ G 252 332-3590
Ahoskie (G-45)

Demilo Bros NC LLC............................ G 704 771-0762
Waxhaw (G-12428)

▲ Due Process Stable Trdg Co LLC...... E 910 608-0284
Lumberton (G-7949)

E & M Concrete Inc.............................. E 919 235-7221
Fuquay Varina (G-4880)

Ferebee Corporation............................. C 704 509-2586
Charlotte (G-2145)

Garris Grading and Paving Inc.............. F 252 749-1101
Farmville (G-4529)

Heath and Sons MGT Svcs LLC............ F 910 679-6142
Rocky Point (G-10881)

Heritage Design & Supply LLC............. E 919 453-1622
Morrisville (G-8987)

Hudson Paving Inc................................ D 910 895-5910
Rockingham (G-10780)

Long Asp Pav Trckg of Grnsburg.......... G 336 643-4121
Summerfield (G-11842)

RDc Debris Removal Cnstr LLC............ E 323 614-2353
Smithfield (G-11462)

Selectbuild Construction Inc................. F 208 331-4300
Raleigh (G-10467)

Solid Holdings LLC.............................. F 704 423-0260
Charlotte (G-2825)

Southern Concrete Mtls Inc.................. F 828 524-3555
Franklin (G-4840)

Southern Concrete Mtls Inc.................. F 877 788-3001
Salisbury (G-11117)

Superior Walls Systems LLC................. D 704 636-6200
Salisbury (G-11121)

TNT Services Inc................................. G 252 261-3073
Kitty Hawk (G-7447)

Vivet Inc.. E 909 390-1039
Greensboro (G-5904)

Young & McQueen Grading Co Inc........ D 828 682-7714
Burnsville (G-1196)

1781 Water well drilling

Camp S Well and Pump Co Inc.............. G 828 453-7322
Ellenboro (G-4456)

Merrill Resources Inc........................... G 828 877-4450
Penrose (G-9662)

Raymond Brown Well Company Inc....... G 336 374-4999
Danbury (G-3695)

1791 Structural steel erection

Ansonville Piping & Fabg Inc................ G 704 826-8403
Ansonville (G-129)

Apex Steel Corp.................................. E 919 362-6611
Raleigh (G-9908)

Asheville Maintenance and................... E 828 687-8110
Arden (G-254)

Burton Steel Company.......................... F 910 675-9241
Castle Hayne (G-1496)

Canalta Enterprises LLC...................... E 919 615-1570
Raleigh (G-9965)

Garden Metalwork................................ G 828 733-1077
Newland (G-9429)

King Stone Innovation LLC.................... G 704 352-1134
Charlotte (G-2398)

Oldcastle Infrastructure Inc.................. E 919 772-6269
Raleigh (G-10344)

Roderick Mch Erectors Wldg Inc........... G 910 343-0381
Wilmington (G-12901)

Steel Supply and Erection Co................ F 336 625-4830
Asheboro (G-399)

Watson Steel & Iron Works LLC............ E 704 821-7140
Matthews (G-8197)

▲ Williams Industries Inc...................... C 919 604-1746
Raleigh (G-10610)

1793 Glass and glazing work

A R Perry Corporation.......................... G 252 492-6181
Henderson (G-6146)

Albemarle Glass Company Inc.............. G 704 982-3323
Albemarle (G-58)

Building Envlope Erction Svcs................ F 252 747-2015
Snow Hill *(G-11476)*

Decor Glass Specialties Inc.................. G 828 586-8180
Sylva *(G-11891)*

Orare Inc.. G 919 742-1003
Siler City *(G-11422)*

Rice S Glass Company Inc................... E 919 967-9214
Carrboro *(G-1272)*

▲ **Sid Jenkins Inc**................................. G 336 632-0707
Greensboro *(G-5811)*

Triangle Glass Service Inc................... G 919 477-9508
Durham *(G-4279)*

1794 Excavation work

Bobby Cahoon Construction Inc........... E 252 249-1617
Grantsboro *(G-5329)*

Brown Brothers Construction Co.......... F 828 297-2131
Zionville *(G-13527)*

Garris Grading and Paving Inc............. F 252 749-1101
Farmville *(G-4529)*

J & L Bckh/Nvrnmental Svcs Inc.......... G 910 237-7351
Eastover *(G-4337)*

Mugo Gravel & Grading Inc................. E 704 782-3478
Concord *(G-3406)*

Privette Enterprises Inc...................... E 704 634-3291
Monroe *(G-8544)*

S T Wooten Corporation...................... E 919 965-9880
Princeton *(G-9826)*

Young & McQueen Grading Co Inc........ D 828 682-7714
Burnsville *(G-1196)*

1795 Wrecking and demolition work

Batista Grading Inc........................... F 919 359-3449
Clayton *(G-3134)*

Bobby Cahoon Construction Inc........... E 252 249-1617
Grantsboro *(G-5329)*

J & L Bckh/Nvrnmental Svcs Inc.......... G 910 237-7351
Eastover *(G-4337)*

Noble Oil Services Inc....................... C 919 774-8180
Sanford *(G-11212)*

Soundside Recycling & Mtls Inc........... G 252 491-8666
Jarvisburg *(G-7186)*

Wersunsllc....................................... G 857 209-8701
Winston Salem *(G-13388)*

1796 Installing building equipment

Advantage Machinery Svcs Inc............. E 336 463-4700
Yadkinville *(G-13435)*

Alpha 3d LLC.................................... G 704 277-6300
Charlotte *(G-1649)*

Asheville Maintenance and.................. E 828 687-8110
Arden *(G-254)*

◆ **Assa Abloy Entrnce Systems US**...... C 866 237-2687
Monroe *(G-8434)*

▲ **Cyrco Inc**...................................... E 336 668-0977
Greensboro *(G-5484)*

▲ **Dustcontrol Inc**.............................. F 910 395-1808
Wilmington *(G-12768)*

Home Elevators & Lift Pdts LLC........... E 910 427-0006
Sunset Beach *(G-11850)*

Jack A Farrior Inc............................. D 252 753-2020
Farmville *(G-4532)*

Johnson Industrial Mchy Svcs............. E 252 239-1944
Lucama *(G-7937)*

Ken Staley Co Inc.............................. G 336 685-4294
Franklinville *(G-4857)*

▲ **Mantissa Corporation**..................... E 704 525-1749
Charlotte *(G-2453)*

Otis Elevator Company....................... G 828 251-1248
Asheville *(G-563)*

Otis Elevator Company....................... C 704 519-0100
Charlotte *(G-2602)*

Park Manufacturing Company............... F 704 869-6128
Gastonia *(G-5115)*

Poehler Enterprises Inc...................... G 704 239-1166
Midland *(G-8292)*

Power Support Engineering Inc............. G 813 909-1199
Hayesville *(G-6143)*

Precision Fabricators Inc.................... G 336 835-4763
Ronda *(G-10897)*

RPM Plastics LLC.............................. E 704 871-0518
Statesville *(G-11760)*

Southeastern Elevator LLC.................. G 252 726-9983
Morehead City *(G-8845)*

Steel City Services LLC...................... F 919 698-2407
Durham *(G-4249)*

Thomas M Brown Inc.......................... F 704 597-0246
Charlotte *(G-2913)*

1799 Special trade contractors, nec

Accent Awnings Inc............................ F 828 321-4517
Andrews *(G-104)*

▲ **Acme Stone Company Inc**................. F 336 786-6978
Mount Airy *(G-9095)*

Advance Signs & Service Inc................ E 919 639-4666
Angier *(G-110)*

Advantage Machinery Svcs Inc............. E 336 463-4700
Yadkinville *(G-13435)*

Afsc LLC.. D 704 523-4936
Charlotte *(G-1627)*

Alamance Iron Works Inc.................... G 336 852-5940
Greensboro *(G-5346)*

Allens Environmental Cnstr LLC........... G 407 774-7100
Brevard *(G-967)*

Alp Systems Inc................................ F 828 454-5164
Waynesville *(G-12450)*

AP Granite Installation LLC.................. G 919 215-1795
Clayton *(G-3131)*

Apex Steel Corp................................ E 919 362-6611
Raleigh *(G-9908)*

Architectural Craftsman Ltd................. E 919 494-6911
Franklinton *(G-4846)*

Asheville Contracting Co Inc................ E 828 665-8900
Candler *(G-1217)*

▲ **Atlantic Hydraulics Svcs LLC**............ E 919 542-2985
Sanford *(G-11152)*

Automated Controls LLC..................... G 704 724-7625
Huntersville *(G-6970)*

Avery Machine & Welding Co............... G 828 733-4944
Fayetteville *(G-4556)*

Beacon Composites LLC...................... G 704 813-8408
Creedmoor *(G-3640)*

Black Mountain Cnstr Group Inc........... F 704 243-5593
Waxhaw *(G-12424)*

◆ **Bradford Products LLC**.................... D 910 791-2202
Leland *(G-7535)*

Bridgport Restoration Svcs Inc............. G 336 996-1212
Kernersville *(G-7248)*

Burchette Sign Company Inc................ F 336 996-6501
Colfax *(G-3274)*

Burkett Welding Services Inc............... F 252 635-2814
New Bern *(G-9345)*

Cabinet Solutions Usa Inc................... E 828 358-2349
Hickory *(G-6280)*

Carlton Enterprizes LLC...................... G 919 534-5424
Rocky Point *(G-10877)*

Carolina Marble & Granite................... G 704 523-2112
Charlotte *(G-1850)*

Carolina Sgns Grphic Dsgns Inc........... G 919 383-3344
Durham *(G-3962)*

Carolina Solar Structures Inc............... F 828 684-9900
Asheville *(G-471)*

Clark Art Shop Inc............................. G 919 832-8319
Raleigh *(G-9997)*

Classic Cleaning LLC.......................... E 800 220-7101
Raleigh *(G-9998)*

Closets By Design.............................. D 704 361-6424
Charlotte *(G-1931)*

Collins Fabrication & Wldg LLC............ G 704 861-9326
Gastonia *(G-5024)*

Connected 2k LLC.............................. G 910 321-7446
Fayetteville *(G-4578)*

Core Technology Molding Corp............. E 336 294-2018
Greensboro *(G-5469)*

Custom Steel Boats Inc...................... F 252 745-7447
Merritt *(G-8267)*

Cymbal LLC...................................... G 877 365-9622
Cary *(G-1342)*

Dbf Inc.. G 910 548-6725
Jacksonville *(G-7122)*

Digger Specialties Inc........................ G 336 495-1517
Randleman *(G-10642)*

Dimill Enterprises LLC........................ G 919 629-2011
Raleigh *(G-10046)*

Dna Services Inc............................... G 910 279-2775
Kure Beach *(G-7464)*

▲ **Drydog Barriers LLC**....................... G 704 334-8222
Indian Trail *(G-7077)*

Ebert Sign Company Inc..................... G 336 768-2867
Lexington *(G-7681)*

Englishs All Wood Homes Inc.............. F 252 524-5000
Grifton *(G-6036)*

Everglow Na Inc................................ E 704 841-2580
Matthews *(G-8111)*

Fence Quarter LLC............................. G 800 205-0128
Morganton *(G-8864)*

▼ **Filtration Technology Inc**.................. G 336 294-5655
Greensboro *(G-5531)*

Fitch Sign Company Inc...................... G 704 482-2916
Shelby *(G-11336)*

Four Points Recycling LLC................... F 910 333-5961
Jacksonville *(G-7123)*

▲ **Gainsborough Baths LLC**.................. F 336 357-0797
Lexington *(G-7691)*

Gastonia Ornamental Wldg Inc............. F 704 827-1146
Mount Holly *(G-9232)*

Gillespies Fbrction Design Inc.............. G 704 636-2349
Salisbury *(G-11056)*

▲ **Grancreations Inc**........................... G 704 332-7625
Charlotte *(G-2230)*

Guerrero Enterprises Inc..................... G 828 286-4900
Rutherfordton *(G-10984)*

Hamrick Fence Company..................... F 704 434-5011
Boiling Springs *(G-884)*

Harrison Fence Inc............................ G 919 244-6908
Apex *(G-162)*

Ie Furniture Inc................................. E 336 475-5050
Archdale *(G-227)*

Interstate Sign Company Inc................ E 336 789-3069
Mount Airy *(G-9135)*

Invisible Fencing of Mtn Reg................ G 828 667-8847
Candler *(G-1227)*

Ivey Ln Inc....................................... F 336 230-0062
Greensboro *(G-5631)*

J &D Contractor Service Inc................. G 919 427-0218
Angier *(G-122)*

James Iron & Steel Inc........................ G 704 283-2299
Monroe *(G-8508)*

King Stone Innovation LLC................... G 704 352-1134
Charlotte *(G-2398)*

Kitchen Man Inc................................ F 910 408-1322
Winnabow *(G-13067)*

Kitchen Tune-Up................................ G 833 259-1838
Matthews *(G-8123)*

Limitless Wldg Fabrication LLC............. G 252 753-0660
Farmville *(G-4534)*

Lockwood Identity Inc................................C 704 597-9801
Charlotte *(G-2430)*

Lumsden Welding Company..............G 910 791-6336
Wilmington *(G-12842)*

M & M Stone Sculpting & Engrv.............G 336 877-3842
Todd *(G-12104)*

M T N of Pinellas Inc...........................G 727 823-1650
Winston Salem *(G-13242)*

Marsh Furniture Company.....................F 336 273-8196
Greensboro *(G-5676)*

Maynard S Fabricators Inc..................G 336 230-1048
Greensboro *(G-5684)*

McCorkle Sign Company Inc ....E 919 687-7080
Durham *(G-4121)*

Mechanical Maintenance Inc................F 336 676-7133
Climax *(G-3227)*

Milligan House Movers Inc....................G 910 653-2272
Tabor City *(G-11913)*

Moores Fiberglass Inc...........................F 252 753-2583
Walstonburg *(G-12334)*

Mundy Machine Co Inc...........................F 704 922-8663
Dallas *(G-3679)*

Noble Oil Services Inc...........................E 919 774-8180
Sanford *(G-11212)*

Nova Enterprises Inc.............................E 828 687-8770
Arden *(G-290)*

Parish Sign & Service Inc....................E 910 875-6121
Raeford *(G-9846)*

Parrish Contracting LLC.......................G 828 524-9100
Franklin *(G-4838)*

Piedmont Weld & Pipe Inc....................G 704 782-7774
Concord *(G-3418)*

Piedmont Well Covers Inc.....................F 704 664-8488
Mount Ulla *(G-9270)*

Pro Choice Contractors Corp................G 919 696-7383
Raleigh *(G-10398)*

Retail Installation Svcs LLC..................G 336 818-1333
Millers Creek *(G-8307)*

◆ S Kivett Inc...F 910 592-0161
Clinton *(G-3243)*

Sare Granite & Tile...............................G 828 676-2666
Arden *(G-305)*

Satco Truck Equipment Inc...................F 919 383-5547
Durham *(G-4222)*

Sawyers Sign Service Inc.....................F
Mount Airy *(G-9175)*

Sign & Awning Systems Inc..................G 919 892-5900
Dunn *(G-3868)*

Sign Connection Inc..............................F 704 868-4500
Gastonia *(G-5136)*

Sign Systems Inc...................................F 828 322-5622
Hickory *(G-6446)*

Sign World Inc...G 704 529-4440
Charlotte *(G-2806)*

Signal Signs of Ga Inc..........................G 828 494-4913
Murphy *(G-9295)*

Specialty Welding & Mch Inc.................G 828 464-1104
Newton *(G-9499)*

Stamper Sheet Metal Inc......................G 336 476-5145
Archdale *(G-243)*

Stewarts Garage and Welding Co.........G 336 983-5563
Tobaccoville *(G-12103)*

Sunqest Inc...G 828 325-4910
Newton *(G-9501)*

Thomas Lcklars Cbnets Lrnburg............G 910 369-2094
Laurinburg *(G-7516)*

Tice Kitchens & Interiors LLC................F 919 366-4117
Raleigh *(G-10549)*

Tint Plus...G 910 229-5303
Fayetteville *(G-4681)*

Tony D Hildreth.....................................F 910 276-1803
Laurel Hill *(G-7488)*

Unique Office Solutions Inc..................F 336 854-0900
Greensboro *(G-5890)*

United Finishing Systems LLC...............G 704 873-2475
Statesville *(G-11796)*

V & B Construction Svcs Inc.................G 704 641-9936
Waxhaw *(G-12447)*

Viktors Gran MBL Kit Cnter Top............F 828 681-0713
Arden *(G-316)*

Volta Group Corporation LLC.................E 919 637-0273
Raleigh *(G-10593)*

Waldenwood Group Inc.........................F 704 313-8004
Charlotte *(G-2999)*

▲ Wandfluh of America Inc....................F 847 566-5700
Charlotte *(G-3003)*

Warsaw Welding Service Inc.................G 910 293-4261
Warsaw *(G-12368)*

Welcome Industrial Corp.......................D 336 329-9640
Burlington *(G-1178)*

With Purpose Pressure Wshg LLC.........G 336 965-9473
Greensboro *(G-5921)*

Yes Real Estate Cnstr Group In.............E 919 389-4104
Raleigh *(G-10622)*

20 FOOD AND KINDRED PRODUCTS

2011 Meat packing plants

A L Beck & Sons Inc.............................F 336 788-1896
Winston Salem *(G-13070)*

Acre Station Meat Farm Inc..................F 252 927-3700
Pinetown *(G-9707)*

Advancepierre Foods Inc.......................A 828 459-7626
Claremont *(G-3087)*

Alexanders Ham Company Inc...............F 704 857-9222
Mooresville *(G-8593)*

B & B Distributing Inc............................G 336 592-5665
Roxboro *(G-10919)*

Bass Farms Inc......................................F 252 478-4147
Spring Hope *(G-11552)*

Caldwells Mt Process Abattoirs.............G 828 428-8833
Maiden *(G-8009)*

Carolina Packers Inc..............................D 919 934-2181
Smithfield *(G-11436)*

Chaudhry Meat Company.......................F 919 742-9292
Staley *(G-11592)*

Curtis Packing Company.........................D 336 275-7684
Greensboro *(G-5478)*

D & M Packing Company.........................G 704 982-3716
Albemarle *(G-68)*

Flowers Slaughterhouse LLC..................F 252 235-4106
Sims *(G-11430)*

Foothills Sug Cured Cntry Hams.............F 336 835-2411
Jonesville *(G-7195)*

Freirich Foods Inc..................................C
Salisbury *(G-11055)*

Frontier Meat Processing Inc.................G 704 843-3921
Waxhaw *(G-12432)*

Ham Wayco Company..............................E 919 735-3962
Goldsboro *(G-5221)*

Hobes Country Hams Inc........................E 336 670-3401
North Wilkesboro *(G-9535)*

Huffman Sales and Service LLC...........G 828 234-0693
Burlington *(G-1106)*

If Disher Meat Processing......................G 336 463-2907
Yadkinville *(G-13444)*

Jbs USA LLC...F 828 855-9571
Hickory *(G-6375)*

▲ Jbs USA LLC.......................................E 828 725-7000
Lenoir *(G-7617)*

Jdh Capital LLC.......................................F 704 357-1220
Charlotte *(G-2365)*

Julian Freirich Food Products................E 704 636-2621
Salisbury *(G-11078)*

Key Packing Company Inc......................G 910 464-5054
Robbins *(G-10753)*

Meatinternational LLC............................G 910 628-8267
Fairmont *(G-4503)*

Mitchells Meat Processing.....................F 336 591-7420
Walnut Cove *(G-12328)*

Mt Airy Meat Center Inc.........................G 336 786-2023
Mount Airy *(G-9155)*

▲ Murphy-Brown LLC.............................D 910 293-3434
Warsaw *(G-12363)*

▼ Parks Family Meats LLC.....................F 217 446-4600
Warsaw *(G-12364)*

Piedmont Custom Meats Inc..................E 336 628-4949
Asheboro *(G-383)*

▲ Pork Company.....................................C 910 293-2157
Warsaw *(G-12365)*

R D Jones Packing Co Inc.......................G 910 267-2846
Faison *(G-4519)*

Randolph Packing Company....................D 336 672-1470
Asheboro *(G-390)*

Sandy Ridge Pork....................................G 919 989-8878
Smithfield *(G-11464)*

Smithfeld Fresh Meats Sls Corp.............B 910 862-7675
Tar Heel *(G-11918)*

Smithfield Foods Inc...............................C 910 299-3009
Clinton *(G-3246)*

Smithfield Foods Inc...............................F 704 298-0936
Kannapolis *(G-7220)*

Smithfield Foods Inc...............................D 252 208-4700
Kinston *(G-7428)*

Smithfield Foods Inc...............................E 910 241-2022
Tar Heel *(G-11919)*

Smithfield Foods Inc...............................E 910 862-7675
Tar Heel *(G-11920)*

Smithfield Packing Company Inc............E 910 592-2104
Clinton *(G-3247)*

Stevens Packing Inc...............................G 336 274-6033
Greensboro *(G-5840)*

Thomas Brothers Slaughter Hse............G 336 667-1346
North Wilkesboro *(G-9551)*

Tyson Foods Inc......................................G 919 774-7925
Sanford *(G-11245)*

Tyson Foods Inc......................................C 336 838-2171
Wilkesboro *(G-12658)*

Tyson Foods Inc......................................G 336 838-0083
Wilkesboro *(G-12659)*

Tyson Foods Inc......................................A 336 838-2171
Wilkesboro *(G-12660)*

Villari Bros Foods LLC............................E 910 293-2157
Warsaw *(G-12367)*

Villari Food Group LLC............................E 910 293-2157
Wilmington *(G-12945)*

Wells Jnkins Wells Mt Proc Inc..............G 828 245-5544
Forest City *(G-4800)*

Wells Pork and Beef Pdts Inc.................F 910 259-2523
Burgaw *(G-1038)*

White Packing Co Inc -Va.......................G 540 373-9883
Raleigh *(G-10609)*

2013 Sausages and other prepared meats

Advancepierre Foods Inc.......................A 828 459-7626
Claremont *(G-3087)*

Alexanders Ham Company Inc...............F 704 857-9222
Mooresville *(G-8593)*

American Skin Food Group LLC............E 910 259-2232
Burgaw *(G-1018)*

Ashe Hams Inc.......................................G 828 259-9426
Asheville *(G-432)*

▲ Bakkavor Foods Usa Inc....................C 704 522-1977
Charlotte *(G-1745)*

Bar-S Foods Co.. E 847 652-3238
Raleigh *(G-9932)*

Bass Farms Inc .... F 252 478-4147
Spring Hope *(G-11552)*

Bunge Oils Inc .... E 910 293-7917
Warsaw *(G-12358)*

Cangilosi Spcialty Sausage Inc............... G 336 665-5775
Greensboro *(G-5420)*

Carolina Packers Inc............................. D 919 934-2181
Smithfield *(G-11436)*

Chandler Foods Inc............................... E 336 299-1934
Greensboro *(G-5441)*

Country Snacks Mfg Inc......................... E 252 433-4644
Henderson *(G-6152)*

Foell Packing Company of NC................. G 919 776-0592
Sanford *(G-11179)*

Freirich Foods Inc................................. C
Salisbury *(G-11055)*

Goodnight Brothers Prod Co Inc............. E 828 264-8892
Boone *(G-918)*

Ham Wayco Company............................ E 919 735-3962
Goldsboro *(G-5221)*

Harris-Robinette Inc.............................. G 252 813-5794
Pinetops *(G-9706)*

Hormel Foods Corp Svcs LLC................ F 704 527-1535
Charlotte *(G-2287)*

Hunter Liver Mush Inc........................... G 828 652-7902
Marion *(G-8043)*

Jenkins Foods Inc................................. F 704 434-2347
Shelby *(G-11349)*

Julian Freirich Company Inc................... E 704 636-2621
Salisbury *(G-11077)*

Julian Freirich Food Products................ E 704 636-2621
Salisbury *(G-11078)*

Kansas City Sausage Co LLC................. G 910 567-5604
Godwin *(G-5189)*

Larry S Sausage Company..................... E 910 483-5148
Fayetteville *(G-4630)*

Lmb Corp .... G 704 547-8886
Charlotte *(G-2429)*

Mack S Liver Mush Inc........................... G 704 434-6188
Shelby *(G-11356)*

Macs Farms Sausage Co Inc.................. G 910 594-0095
Newton Grove *(G-9516)*

Skin Boys LLC....................................... F 910 259-2232
Burgaw *(G-1031)*

Smithfield Foods Inc............................. C 910 299-3009
Clinton *(G-3246)*

Smithfield Foods Inc............................. D 252 208-4700
Kinston *(G-7428)*

Stevens Packing Inc.............................. G 336 274-6033
Greensboro *(G-5840)*

Stevens Sausage Company Inc.............. D 919 934-3159
Smithfield *(G-11466)*

Suncrest Farms Cntry Hams Inc............. E 336 667-4441
Wilkesboro *(G-12654)*

Thomas Brothers Foods LLC.................. F 336 672-0337
Asheboro *(G-409)*

White Packing Co Inc -Va...................... G 540 373-9883
Raleigh *(G-10609)*

Williams Skin Co .... G 910 323-2628
Fayetteville *(G-4701)*

2015 Poultry slaughtering and processing

Advancepierre Foods Inc...................... A 828 459-7626
Claremont *(G-3087)*

Broomes Poultry Inc.............................. G 704 983-0965
Albemarle *(G-63)*

Butterball LLC....................................... E 919 658-6743
Goldsboro *(G-5203)*

Butterball LLC....................................... D 919 658-6743
Mount Olive *(G-9250)*

Butterball LLC....................................... B 910 875-8711
Raeford *(G-9833)*

▼ Butterball LLC.................................... E 919 255-7900
Garner *(G-4918)*

Calvin C Mooney Poultry........................ G 336 374-6690
Ararat *(G-210)*

Carolina Egg Companies Inc.................. D 252 459-2143
Nashville *(G-9314)*

Case Farms LLC.................................... D 919 735-5010
Dudley *(G-3835)*

Case Farms LLC.................................... E 919 658-2252
Goldsboro *(G-5204)*

Case Farms LLC.................................... D 919 635-2390
Mount Olive *(G-9252)*

Case Farms LLC.................................... F 704 528-4501
Troutman *(G-12133)*

◆ Case Farms Processing Inc................ E 704 528-4501
Troutman *(G-12134)*

Case Foods Inc..................................... A 919 736-4498
Goldsboro *(G-5205)*

▼ Case Foods Inc................................. C 704 528-4501
Troutman *(G-12135)*

▲ Charles Craft Inc.............................. G 910 844-3521
Laurinburg *(G-7497)*

Filet of Chicken.................................... F 336 751-4752
Mocksville *(G-8362)*

Hopkins Poultry Company...................... F 336 656-3361
Browns Summit *(G-998)*

House of Raeford Farms Inc.................. A 910 289-3191
Raeford *(G-9840)*

House of Raeford Farms Inc.................. A 910 285-2349
Teachey *(G-11987)*

House of Raeford Farms Inc.................. B 910 763-0475
Wilmington *(G-12809)*

◆ House of Raeford Farms Inc.............. A 912 222-4090
Rose Hill *(G-10906)*

House of Raeford Farms La LLC............. C 336 751-4752
Mocksville *(G-8369)*

Integra Foods LLC................................ F 910 984-2007
Bladenboro *(G-877)*

◆ Johnson Nash & Sons Farms Inc........ B 910 289-3113
Rose Hill *(G-10907)*

Keystone Foods LLC.............................. C 336 342-6601
Reidsville *(G-10691)*

Mountaire Farms LLC............................ G 910 843-3332
Lumber Bridge *(G-7939)*

Mountaire Farms LLC............................ B 910 843-5942
Lumber Bridge *(G-7940)*

Mountaire Farms LLC............................ C 919 663-1768
Siler City *(G-11418)*

Mountaire Farms Inc............................. A 910 843-5942
Lumber Bridge *(G-7941)*

Mountaire Farms Inc............................. B 919 663-0848
Siler City *(G-11419)*

Mountaire Farms Inc............................. G 704 978-3055
Statesville *(G-11735)*

Perdue Farms Inc................................. E 252 348-4287
Ahoskie *(G-51)*

Perdue Farms Inc................................. C 910 673-4148
Candor *(G-1240)*

Perdue Farms Inc................................. E 704 278-2228
Cleveland *(G-3218)*

Perdue Farms Inc................................. A 252 358-8245
Cofield *(G-3269)*

Perdue Farms Inc................................. A 704 789-2400
Concord *(G-3417)*

Perdue Farms Inc................................. E 252 338-1543
Elizabeth City *(G-4402)*

Perdue Farms Inc................................. C 336 366-2591
Elkin *(G-4450)*

Perdue Farms Inc................................. G 252 758-2141
Greenville *(G-6013)*

Perdue Farms Inc................................. D 252 583-5731
Halifax *(G-6047)*

Perdue Farms Inc................................. C 919 284-2033
Kenly *(G-7234)*

Perdue Farms Inc................................. A 252 348-4200
Lewiston Woodville *(G-7647)*

Perdue Farms Inc................................. E 910 738-8581
Lumberton *(G-7965)*

Perdue Farms Inc................................. C 252 398-5112
Murfreesboro *(G-9284)*

Perdue Farms Inc................................. C 252 459-9763
Nashville *(G-9323)*

Perdue Farms Inc................................. E 336 896-9121
Winston Salem *(G-13284)*

Perdue Farms Inc................................. D 336 679-7733
Yadkinville *(G-13447)*

Perdue Farms Incorporated................... A 910 997-8600
Rockingham *(G-10785)*

Pilgrims Pride Corporation.................... E 704 721-3585
Concord *(G-3419)*

Pilgrims Pride Corporation.................... B 704 624-2171
Marshville *(G-8092)*

Pilgrims Pride Corporation.................... E 919 774-7333
Sanford *(G-11222)*

Pilgrims Pride Corporation.................... E 336 622-4251
Staley *(G-11598)*

Pilgrims Pride Corporation.................... C 704 233-4047
Wingate *(G-13063)*

▼ Prestage Foods Inc........................... B 910 865-6611
Saint Pauls *(G-11007)*

Prestige Farms Inc............................... E 919 861-8867
Raleigh *(G-10393)*

Sanderson Farms Inc............................ F 252 208-0036
Kinston *(G-7427)*

Sanderson Farms Inc............................ G 910 274-0220
Saint Pauls *(G-11008)*

Sanderson Farms LLC........................... G 910 887-2284
Lumberton *(G-7972)*

Sanderson Farms LLC Proc Div............. A 910 274-0220
Saint Pauls *(G-11009)*

Tyson Foods Inc.................................... F 910 483-3282
Eastover *(G-4338)*

Tyson Foods Inc.................................... E 704 283-7571
Monroe *(G-8572)*

Tyson Foods Inc.................................... G 704 201-8654
Monroe *(G-8573)*

Tyson Foods Inc.................................... G 919 774-7925
Sanford *(G-11245)*

Tyson Foods Inc.................................... G 336 651-2866
Wilkesboro *(G-12656)*

Tyson Foods Inc.................................... G 336 838-2171
Wilkesboro *(G-12657)*

Tyson Foods Inc.................................... C 336 838-2171
Wilkesboro *(G-12658)*

Wayne Farms LLC................................. B 336 386-8151
Dobson *(G-3827)*

Wayne Farms LLC................................. B 336 366-4413
Elkin *(G-4454)*

Wayne Farms LLC................................. F 770 538-2120
Newton *(G-9511)*

2021 Creamery butter

Michaels Creamery Inc.......................... G 910 292-4172
Fayetteville *(G-4641)*

Waxhaw Creamery LLC........................... F 704 843-7927
Waxhaw *(G-12449)*

2022 Cheese; natural and processed

Big Delicious Brand Inc......................... F 919 270-7324
Raleigh *(G-9943)*

Buffalo Creek Farm & Crmry LLC........... G 336 969-5698
Germanton *(G-5174)*

Celebrity Dairy LLC...................................... G 919 742-4931
Siler City *(G-11404)*

Ethnicraft Usa LLC...................................... F 336 885-2055
High Point *(G-6615)*

▲ Looking Glass Creamery LLC........... G 828 458-0088
Columbus *(G-3302)*

Old Salem Incorporated........................ G 336 721-7305
Winston Salem *(G-13269)*

Our Pride Foods Roxboro Inc.............. G 336 597-4978
Roxboro *(G-10936)*

Saputo Cheese USA Inc........................ C 847 267-1100
Troy *(G-12166)*

Stans Quality Foods Inc........................ G 336 570-2572
Burlington *(G-1163)*

Tin Can Ventures LLC............................ G 919 732-9078
Cedar Grove *(G-1518)*

2023 Dry, condensed, evaporated products

Arms Race Nutrition LLC....................... G 888 978-2332
Statesville *(G-11660)*

Bestco LLC... E 704 664-4300
Mooresville *(G-8610)*

Bionutra Life Sciences LLC................... G 828 572-2838
Lenoir *(G-7587)*

Blue Ridge Silver Inc.............................. G 828 729-8610
Boone *(G-898)*

Body Engineering Inc............................. G 704 650-3434
Matthews *(G-8099)*

Chef Martini LLC..................................... A 919 327-3183
Raleigh *(G-9992)*

Disruptive Enterprises LLC................... G 336 567-0104
Burlington *(G-1084)*

Herbalife Manufacturing LLC............... G 336 970-6400
Winston Salem *(G-13196)*

Im8 (us) LLC.. G 862 485-8325
Charlotte *(G-2314)*

Ka-Ex LLC... G 704 343-5143
Charlotte *(G-2387)*

Muscadine Naturals Inc........................ G 888 628-5898
Clemmons *(G-3197)*

NPC Corporation..................................... G 336 998-2386
Mocksville *(G-8382)*

Rainforest Nutritionals Inc................... G 919 847-2221
Raleigh *(G-10421)*

2024 Ice cream and frozen deserts

▼ Alamance Foods Inc............................ C 336 226-6392
Burlington *(G-1043)*

Antkar LLC.. G 919 322-4100
Raleigh *(G-9905)*

Bilcat Inc... E 828 295-3088
Blowing Rock *(G-880)*

Brick & Mortar Grill................................ G 919 639-9700
Angier *(G-113)*

Cintoms Inc.. G 828 684-1317
Asheville *(G-476)*

▲ Delizza LLC.. F 252 442-0270
Battleboro *(G-696)*

Dream Kreams LLC................................. G 919 491-1984
Kernersville *(G-7269)*

Gabden LLC.. G 704 451-8646
Statesville *(G-11702)*

Gelarto Inc... F 646 795-3505
Wilmington *(G-12784)*

Good Vibrationz LLC.............................. G 919 820-3084
Greenville *(G-5982)*

Goodberry Creamery Inc....................... F 919 878-8870
Wake Forest *(G-12279)*

Homeland Creamery LLC...................... G 336 685-6455
Julian *(G-7201)*

Huff Mj LLC.. G 910 313-3133
Wilmington *(G-12810)*

Hunter Farms.. C 336 822-2300
High Point *(G-6664)*

Maola Milk and Ice Cream Co.............. E 252 756-3160
Greenville *(G-6002)*

Maple View Ice Cream........................... F 919 960-5535
Hillsborough *(G-6872)*

▲ Mooresville Ice Cream Com.............. E 704 664-5456
Mooresville *(G-8725)*

North Carolina State Univ..................... G 919 515-2760
Raleigh *(G-10336)*

Paletria La Mnrca McHacana LLC........ G 919 803-0636
Raleigh *(G-10354)*

Simply Natural Creamery LLC.............. E 252 746-3334
Ayden *(G-663)*

▲ Tony S Ice Cream Company Inc....... F 704 867-7085
Gastonia *(G-5156)*

Tonys Ice Cream Co Inc........................ G 704 853-0018
Gastonia *(G-5157)*

Yummy Tummy Ga LLC......................... G 704 658-0445
Mooresville *(G-8804)*

2026 Fluid milk

▼ Alamance Foods Inc............................ C 336 226-6392
Burlington *(G-1043)*

Carolina Dairy LLC................................. F 910 569-7070
Biscoe *(G-848)*

Carolina Yogurt Inc................................ G 828 754-9685
Lenoir *(G-7591)*

Dfa Dairy Brands Fluid LLC.................. G 704 341-2794
Charlotte *(G-2038)*

Dfa Dairy Brands Fluid LLC.................. G 336 714-9032
Tarboro *(G-11925)*

Maola Milk and Ice Cream Co.............. E 252 756-3160
Greenville *(G-6002)*

Maola Milk and Ice Cream Co.............. F 844 287-1970
New Bern *(G-9377)*

Milkco Inc... B 828 254-8428
Asheville *(G-547)*

New Dairy Opco LLC.............................. D 336 725-8141
Winston Salem *(G-13263)*

▲ Origin Food Group LLC...................... E 704 768-9000
Statesville *(G-11741)*

Saputo Cheese USA Inc........................ F 910 569-7070
Biscoe *(G-856)*

2032 Canned specialties

▲ Atlantic Natural Foods LLC............... D 888 491-0524
Nashville *(G-9309)*

Atlantis Foods Inc.................................. E 336 768-6101
Clemmons *(G-3177)*

Bost Distributing Company Inc............ G 919 775-5931
Sanford *(G-11158)*

Chandler Foods Inc................................ E 336 299-1934
Greensboro *(G-5441)*

Market Depot USA Nc Inc..................... F 888 417-8685
Greensboro *(G-5675)*

Papa Parusos Foods Inc....................... C 910 484-8999
Fayetteville *(G-4651)*

Plantation House Foods Inc................. G 919 381-5495
Durham *(G-4184)*

Ritas One Inc... G 919 650-2415
Cary *(G-1438)*

Soup Maven LLC.................................... G 727 919-5242
Asheville *(G-606)*

Stevens Foodservice............................. G 919 322-5470
Raleigh *(G-10508)*

Tortilleria Duvy LLC............................... G 336 497-1510
Kernersville *(G-7308)*

Tyson Foods Inc..................................... G 704 201-8654
Monroe *(G-8573)*

Tyson Foods Inc..................................... G 919 774-7925
Sanford *(G-11245)*

Tyson Mexican Original Inc.................. E 919 777-9428
Sanford *(G-11246)*

2033 Canned fruits and specialties

Arcadia Beverage LLC........................... G 828 684-3556
Arden *(G-252)*

Arcadia Farms LLC................................. D 828 684-3556
Arden *(G-253)*

Baileys Sauces Inc................................ G 252 756-7179
Greenville *(G-5944)*

Bevs & Bites LLC................................... G 704 247-7573
Charlotte *(G-1777)*

Blue Ridge Jams.................................... G 828 685-1783
Hendersonville *(G-6187)*

Brookwood Farms Inc............................ D 919 663-3612
Siler City *(G-11401)*

Cardinal Foods LLC............................... E 910 259-9407
Burgaw *(G-1020)*

Carolina Canners Inc............................. D 843 537-5281
Southern Pines *(G-11496)*

Clement Pappas Nc LLC....................... G 856 455-1000
Hendersonville *(G-6197)*

Cold Off Press LLC................................ G 984 444-9006
Raleigh *(G-10003)*

Dfa Dairy Brands Fluid LLC.................. G 704 341-2794
Charlotte *(G-2038)*

◆ Dole Food Company Inc.................... E 818 874-4000
Charlotte *(G-2061)*

Dunbar Foods Corporation.................... D 910 892-3175
Dunn *(G-3854)*

▲ Dutch Kettle LLC................................ G 336 468-8422
Hamptonville *(G-6083)*

DVine Foods.. G 910 862-2576
Elizabethtown *(G-4425)*

Kraft Heinz Foods Company................. G 704 565-5500
Charlotte *(G-2401)*

Lc Foods LLC... G 919 510-6688
Raleigh *(G-10250)*

McF Operating LLC................................ E 828 685-8821
Hendersonville *(G-6225)*

Mike DS Bbq LLC................................... G 866 960-8652
Durham *(G-4133)*

Mindfully Made Usa LLC....................... E 336 701-0377
Winston Salem *(G-13255)*

Palace Green LLC................................... G 919 827-7950
Raleigh *(G-10353)*

Pamela Stoeppelwerth............................ G 828 837-7293
Marble *(G-8027)*

Papa Lonnies Inc.................................... G 336 573-9313
Stoneville *(G-11825)*

T W Garner Food Company................... G 336 661-1550
Winston Salem *(G-13352)*

T W Garner Food Company................... G 336 661-1550
Winston Salem *(G-13354)*

◆ T W Garner Food Company............... E 336 661-1550
Winston Salem *(G-13353)*

Yamco LLC... G 252 747-9267
Snow Hill *(G-11485)*

2034 Dehydrated fruits, vegetables, soups

Anns House of Nuts............................... G 252 795-6500
Robersonville *(G-10765)*

Carolina Innvtive Fd Ingrdnts............... G 804 359-9311
Nashville *(G-9315)*

Dehydration LLC...................................... G 252 747-8200
Snow Hill *(G-11479)*

Interntnal Agrclture Group LLC............ F 908 323-3246
Mooresville *(G-8694)*

Naturesrules Inc..................................... G 336 427-2526
Madison *(G-7994)*

Osage Pecan Company.......................... F 660 679-6137
West Jefferson *(G-12569)*

2035 Pickles, sauces, and salad dressings

Bevs & Bites LLC .... G 704 247-7573
Charlotte *(G-1777)*

Chef Martini LLC .... A 919 327-3183
Raleigh *(G-9992)*

D C Thomas Group Inc .... E 252 433-0132
Henderson *(G-6153)*

D C Thomas Group Inc .... G 336 299-6263
Greensboro *(G-5486)*

Dana Fancy Foods .... G 828 685-2937
Hendersonville *(G-6201)*

Georges Sauces LLC .... G 252 459-3084
Nashville *(G-9320)*

▲ **Golding Farms Foods Inc** .... D 336 766-6161
Winston Salem *(G-13179)*

Jenkins Foods Inc .... F 704 434-2347
Shelby *(G-11349)*

Lusty Monk LLC .... G 828 645-5056
Asheville *(G-540)*

Mount Olive Pickle Company .... G 704 867-5585
Gastonia *(G-5104)*

Mount Olive Pickle Company Inc .... E 704 867-5585
Gastonia *(G-5105)*

◆ **Mount Olive Pickle Company Inc** .... C 919 658-2535
Mount Olive *(G-9257)*

◆ **T W Garner Food Company** .... E 336 661-1550
Winston Salem *(G-13353)*

Tracys Gourmet LLC .... G 919 672-1731
Asheville *(G-622)*

2037 Frozen fruits and vegetables

▲ **Alphin Brothers Inc** .... E 910 892-8751
Dunn *(G-3843)*

Caseiro International LLC .... G 919 530-8333
Durham *(G-3964)*

Milkco Inc .... B 828 254-8428
Asheville *(G-547)*

Neighborhood Smoothie LLC .... G 919 845-5513
Raleigh *(G-10329)*

Nice Blends Corp .... D 910 640-1000
Whiteville *(G-12590)*

Seal Seasons Inc .... F 919 245-3535
Durham *(G-4228)*

2038 Frozen specialties, nec

Advancepierre Foods Inc .... A 828 459-7626
Claremont *(G-3087)*

B Roberts Foods LLC .... E 704 522-1977
Charlotte *(G-1729)*

Ce Kitchen Inc .... E 910 399-2334
Wilmington *(G-12738)*

Ce Kitchen Inc .... E 910 399-2334
Wilmington *(G-12739)*

Chandler Foods Inc .... E 336 299-1934
Greensboro *(G-5441)*

ICEE Company .... G 910 346-3937
Jacksonville *(G-7127)*

James Fods Frnchise Corp Amer .... G 336 437-0393
Graham *(G-5272)*

Kalo Foods LLC .... G 336 949-4802
Stokesdale *(G-11812)*

McDonalds .... F 910 295-1112
Pinehurst *(G-9697)*

Orange Bakery Inc .... E 704 875-3003
Huntersville *(G-7029)*

▲ **Poppies International I Inc** .... D 252 442-4016
Battleboro *(G-707)*

Ricewrap Foods Corporation .... F 919 614-1179
Butner *(G-1206)*

▼ **Stefano Foods Inc** .... C 704 399-3935
Charlotte *(G-2865)*

2041 Flour and other grain mill products

Archer-Daniels-Midland Company .... E 704 332-3165
Charlotte *(G-1691)*

Archer-Daniels-Midland Company .... C 910 457-5011
Southport *(G-11516)*

▲ **Atkinson Milling Company** .... D 919 965-3547
Selma *(G-11285)*

Bartlett Milling Company LP .... D 704 872-9581
Statesville *(G-11667)*

Bay State Milling Company .... E 704 664-4873
Mooresville *(G-8606)*

Boonville Flour Feed Mill Inc .... G 336 367-7541
Boonville *(G-957)*

Buffaloe Milling Company Inc .... F 252 438-8637
Kittrell *(G-7439)*

◆ **Colony Gums LLC** .... E 704 226-9666
Monroe *(G-8464)*

House-Autry Mills Inc .... E 919 963-6200
Four Oaks *(G-4813)*

Lakeside Mills Inc .... F 828 286-4866
Spindale *(G-11547)*

Lindley Mills Inc .... D 336 376-6190
Graham *(G-5275)*

Midstate Mills Inc .... C 828 464-1611
Newton *(G-9482)*

Murphy-Brown LLC .... E 252 221-4463
Hobbsville *(G-6884)*

New Carbon Company LLC .... G 574 247-2270
Hickory *(G-6401)*

Old School Mill Inc .... G 704 781-5451
Albemarle *(G-83)*

Proximity Foods Corporation .... F 336 691-1700
Greensboro *(G-5769)*

Renwood Mills LLC .... D 828 465-0302
Newton *(G-9490)*

Romanos Pizza .... G 704 782-5020
Concord *(G-3434)*

Whitehat Seed Farms Inc .... G 252 264-2427
Hertford *(G-6257)*

2043 Cereal breakfast foods

Bakeboxx Company .... F 336 861-1212
High Point *(G-6536)*

Kellanova .... G 704 370-1658
Huntersville *(G-7006)*

Lrw Holdings Inc .... G 919 609-4172
Durham *(G-4110)*

Post Consumer Brands LLC .... F 336 672-0124
Asheboro *(G-384)*

2045 Prepared flour mixes and doughs

Dominos Pizza LLC .... F 910 424-4884
Fayetteville *(G-4588)*

Julias Southern Foods LLC .... G 919 609-6745
Raleigh *(G-10226)*

Lovegrass Kitchen Inc .... F 919 205-8426
Holly Springs *(G-6906)*

2046 Wet corn milling

Barkleys Mill On Southern Cro .... G 828 626-3344
Weaverville *(G-12484)*

Ingredion Incorporated .... D 336 785-0100
Winston Salem *(G-13208)*

Lc Foods LLC .... G 919 510-6688
Raleigh *(G-10250)*

2047 Dog and cat food

Barbaras Canine Catering Inc .... G 704 588-3647
Charlotte *(G-1749)*

Braswell Milling Company .... E 252 459-2143
Nashville *(G-9311)*

Carolina By-Products Co .... G 336 333-3030
Greensboro *(G-5424)*

▲ **Carolina Prime Pet Inc** .... E 888 370-2360
Lenoir *(G-7590)*

Crump Group USA Inc .... C 936 465-5870
Nashville *(G-9317)*

Mars Petcare Us Inc .... D 252 438-1600
Henderson *(G-6166)*

Nestle Purina Petcare Company .... C 314 982-1000
Eden *(G-4353)*

Purina Mills LLC .... D 704 872-0456
Statesville *(G-11757)*

2048 Prepared feeds, nec

Apc LLC .... E 919 965-2051
Selma *(G-11284)*

Bartlett Milling Company LP .... D 704 872-9581
Statesville *(G-11667)*

Bay State Milling Company .... E 704 664-4873
Mooresville *(G-8606)*

Boggs Farm Center Inc .... G 704 538-7176
Fallston *(G-4522)*

Boonville Flour Feed Mill Inc .... G 336 367-7541
Boonville *(G-957)*

Braswell Milling Company .... E 252 459-2143
Nashville *(G-9311)*

Cargill Incorporated .... D 704 523-0414
Charlotte *(G-1841)*

Cargill Incorporated .... G 704 278-2941
Cleveland *(G-3210)*

Cargill Incorporated .... E 252 752-1879
Greenville *(G-5949)*

Coker Feed Mill Inc .... F 919 778-3491
Goldsboro *(G-5207)*

Darling Ingredients Inc .... E 910 483-0473
Fayetteville *(G-4583)*

Darling Ingredients Inc .... F 704 864-9941
Gastonia *(G-5039)*

Darling Ingredients Inc .... F 704 694-3701
Wadesboro *(G-12241)*

Deal-Rite Feeds Inc .... E 704 873-8646
Statesville *(G-11687)*

G & M Milling Co Inc .... F 704 873-5758
Statesville *(G-11701)*

Garland Farm Supply Inc .... F 910 529-9731
Garland *(G-4909)*

Goldsboro Milling Company .... C 919 778-3130
Goldsboro *(G-5216)*

Griffin Industries LLC .... D 704 624-9140
Marshville *(G-8089)*

Hodge Farms LLC .... G 704 278-2684
Mount Ulla *(G-9269)*

Ifta Usa Inc .... G 919 659-8393
Durham *(G-4071)*

◆ **Johnson Nash & Sons Farms Inc** .... B 910 289-3113
Rose Hill *(G-10907)*

Linkone Src LLC .... G 252 206-0960
Wilson *(G-13004)*

Midstate Mills Inc .... C 828 464-1611
Newton *(G-9482)*

Monitor Roller Mill Inc .... G 336 591-4126
Walnut Cove *(G-12329)*

Mountaire Farms LLC .... B 910 974-3232
Candor *(G-1239)*

Mountaire Farms Inc .... D 910 844-3126
Maxton *(G-8204)*

Mountaire Farms Inc .... C 704 978-3055
Statesville *(G-11736)*

Murphy-Brown LLC .... D 910 277-8999
Laurinburg *(G-7510)*

Murphy-Brown LLC .... E 910 293-3434
Rose Hill *(G-10908)*

S
I
C

Murphy-Brown LLC .... C 910 282-4264
Rose Hill *(G-10909)*

Noahs Inc .... F 704 718-2354
Charlotte *(G-2570)*

Nutrien AG Solutions Inc .... F 252 977-2025
Rocky Mount *(G-10814)*

Nutrotonic LLC .... F 855 948-0008
Charlotte *(G-2590)*

Pilgrims Pride Corporation .... B 704 624-2171
Marshville *(G-8092)*

▲ Protein For Pets Opco LLC .... E 252 206-0960
Wilson *(G-13014)*

▼ S P Co Inc .... G 919 848-3599
Raleigh *(G-10453)*

Southeastern Minerals Inc .... E 252 492-0831
Henderson *(G-6179)*

Southern States Coop Inc .... G 336 629-3977
Asheboro *(G-397)*

Southern States Coop Inc .... G 336 246-3201
Creedmoor *(G-3654)*

Southern States Coop Inc .... E 919 528-1516
Creedmoor *(G-3655)*

Southern States Coop Inc .... E 336 786-7545
Mount Airy *(G-9178)*

Southern States Coop Inc .... E 919 658-5061
Mount Olive *(G-9259)*

Southern States Coop Inc .... E 919 693-6136
Oxford *(G-9636)*

Southern States Coop Inc .... G 252 823-2520
Princeville *(G-9828)*

Southern States Coop Inc .... F 336 599-2185
Roxboro *(G-10945)*

Southern States Coop Inc .... D 704 872-6364
Statesville *(G-11772)*

Southern States Coop Inc .... F 910 285-8213
Wallace *(G-12325)*

▼ Springmill Products Inc .... G 336 406-9050
Lawsonville *(G-7520)*

Star Milling Company .... G 704 873-9561
Statesville *(G-11776)*

Steelman Milling Company Inc .... G 336 463-5586
Yadkinville *(G-13452)*

Stevens Sausage Company Inc .... D 919 934-3159
Smithfield *(G-11466)*

Tuckaway Pines Inc .... G 704 979-3443
Concord *(G-3460)*

Two Percent LLC .... G 301 401-2750
Lincolnton *(G-7865)*

Tyson Foods Inc .... G 919 774-7925
Sanford *(G-11245)*

Valley Proteins (de) Inc .... B 336 333-3030
Greensboro *(G-5895)*

2051 Bread, cake, and related products

A Taste of Heavenly Sweetness .... G 336 825-7321
Greensboro *(G-5333)*

Accidental Baker .... G 919 732-6777
Hillsborough *(G-6857)*

All Baked Out Company .... F 336 861-1212
High Point *(G-6516)*

Apple Baking Company Inc .... E 704 637-6800
Salisbury *(G-11017)*

Artesias Swets Bnged By Dior L .... G 704 794-3792
Concord *(G-3312)*

Bakemark USA LLC .... D 336 848-9790
Greensboro *(G-5384)*

Bakkavor Foods Usa Inc .... C 704 522-1977
Charlotte *(G-1744)*

▲ Bakkavor Foods Usa Inc .... C 704 522-1977
Charlotte *(G-1745)*

Bimbo Bakeries Usa Inc .... A 252 641-2200
Tarboro *(G-11923)*

Bluebird Cupcakes .... G 919 616-7347
Raleigh *(G-9950)*

Burney Sweets & More Inc .... G 910 862-2099
Elizabethtown *(G-4419)*

Buttercreme Bakery Inc .... G 336 722-1022
Winston Salem *(G-13113)*

Carolina Foods LLC .... B 704 333-9812
Pineville *(G-9719)*

▲ Carolina Foods LLC .... B 704 333-9812
Charlotte *(G-1846)*

Connectivity Group LLC .... E 910 799-9023
Wilmington *(G-12746)*

Cupcake Bar .... G 919 816-2905
Durham *(G-3993)*

Cupcake Stop Shop LLC .... G 919 457-7900
Raleigh *(G-10026)*

Depalo Foods Inc .... E 704 827-0245
Belmont *(G-746)*

Dewey S Bakery Inc .... F 336 748-0230
Winston Salem *(G-13143)*

Donut Shop .... G 910 640-3317
Whiteville *(G-12580)*

Evelyn T Burney .... G 336 473-9794
Rocky Mount *(G-10838)*

Event Extravaganza LLC .... F 252 679-7004
Elizabeth City *(G-4388)*

▼ Flowers Bakery of Winston .... C 336 785-8700
Winston Salem *(G-13171)*

Flowers Baking Co Newton LLC .... G 336 903-1345
Wilkesboro *(G-12636)*

Flowers Bkg Co Jamestown LLC .... G 704 305-0766
Concord *(G-3365)*

Flowers Bkg Co Jamestown LLC .... E 704 305-0766
Eden *(G-4346)*

Flowers Bkg Co Jamestown LLC .... G 252 492-1519
Henderson *(G-6156)*

Flowers Bkg Co Jamestown LLC .... G 704 296-1000
Monroe *(G-8489)*

Flowers Bkg Co Jamestown LLC .... E 919 776-8932
Sanford *(G-11178)*

Flowers Bkg Co Jamestown LLC .... E 336 744-3525
Winston Salem *(G-13172)*

Flowers Bkg Co Jamestown LLC .... D 336 841-8840
Jamestown *(G-7161)*

Franklin Baking Company LLC .... F 252 752-4600
Greenville *(G-5978)*

Franklin Baking Company LLC .... F 252 752-4600
Greenville *(G-5979)*

Franklin Baking Company LLC .... F 910 425-5090
Hope Mills *(G-6927)*

Franklin Baking Company LLC .... G 919 832-7942
Raleigh *(G-10118)*

Franklin Baking Company LLC .... F 252 410-0255
Roanoke Rapids *(G-10737)*

Franklin Baking Company LLC .... G 252 946-3340
Washington *(G-12387)*

▲ Franklin Baking Company LLC .... B 919 735-0344
Goldsboro *(G-5214)*

Fuquay-Varina Baking Co Inc .... G 919 557-2237
Fuquay Varina *(G-4882)*

Harris Teeter LLC .... D 704 846-7117
Matthews *(G-8115)*

Harris Teeter LLC .... D 919 859-0110
Raleigh *(G-10156)*

Harvest Time Bread Company .... D
Mount Airy *(G-9128)*

Heavenly Cheesecakes .... G 336 577-9390
Winston Salem *(G-13195)*

Ingles Markets Incorporated .... D 704 434-0096
Boiling Springs *(G-885)*

Jps Cupcakery LLC .... F 919 894-5000
Benson *(G-793)*

Krispy Kreme Doughnut Corp .... E 919 669-6151
Gastonia *(G-5074)*

Krispy Kreme Doughnut Corp .... E 336 854-8275
Greensboro *(G-5655)*

Krispy Kreme Doughnut Corp .... E 336 733-3780
Winston Salem *(G-13226)*

◆ Krispy Kreme Doughnut Corp .... C 980 270-7117
Charlotte *(G-2402)*

◆ Krispy Kreme Doughnuts Inc .... C 336 725-2981
Winston Salem *(G-13228)*

La Estrella Inc .... G 919 639-6559
Angier *(G-124)*

La Farm Inc .... E 919 657-0657
Cary *(G-1385)*

Lc Foods LLC .... G 919 510-6688
Raleigh *(G-10250)*

Martins Fmous Pstry Shoppe Inc .... G 800 548-1200
Charlotte *(G-2465)*

Martins Fmous Pstry Shoppe Inc .... G 800 548-1200
Fayetteville *(G-4635)*

Martins Fmous Pstry Shoppe Inc .... G 800 548-1200
Kernersville *(G-7285)*

Mon Macaron LLC .... G 984 200-1387
Raleigh *(G-10312)*

Neomonde Baking Company .... E 919 469-8009
Morrisville *(G-9023)*

Normandie Bakery Inc .... G 910 686-1372
Wilmington *(G-12862)*

Northeast Foods Inc .... G 919 585-5178
Clayton *(G-3163)*

Novas Bakery Inc .... F 704 333-5566
Charlotte *(G-2579)*

Old Salem Incorporated .... G 336 721-7305
Winston Salem *(G-13269)*

Orange Bakery Inc .... E 704 875-3003
Huntersville *(G-7029)*

Patty Cakes .... G 828 696-8240
Hendersonville *(G-6235)*

Picassomoesllc .... G 216 703-4547
Hillsborough *(G-6875)*

Premier Cakes LLC .... G 919 274-8511
Raleigh *(G-10392)*

Queen City Pastry Llc .... E 704 660-5706
Mooresville *(G-8757)*

Retail Market Place .... G 984 201-1948
Smithfield *(G-11463)*

▲ Scotts & Associates Inc .... F 336 581-3141
Bear Creek *(G-718)*

Sls Baking Company .... G 704 421-2763
Charlotte *(G-2815)*

Sprinkle of Sugar LLC .... G 336 474-8620
Thomasville *(G-12073)*

Suarez Bakery Inc .... F 704 525-0145
Charlotte *(G-2876)*

Sweet Room LLC .... G 336 567-1620
High Point *(G-6799)*

Swirl Oakhurst LLC .... G 704 258-1209
Charlotte *(G-2889)*

Tkm Global LLC .... G 732 694-0311
Raleigh *(G-10550)*

Underground Baking Co LLC .... G 828 674-7494
Hendersonville *(G-6246)*

Yummi Factory Corporation .... E 980 248-1062
Concord *(G-3472)*

2052 Cookies and crackers

B&G Foods Inc .... E 336 849-7000
Yadkinville *(G-13437)*

Burney Sweets & More Inc .... G 910 862-2099
Elizabethtown *(G-4419)*

Dewey S Bakery Inc .... F 336 748-0230
Winston Salem *(G-13143)*

Divine South Baking Co LLC.................. G 828 421-2042
Highlands *(G-6845)*

Evelyn T Burney.............................. G 336 473-9794
Rocky Mount *(G-10838)*

▼ Flowers Bakery of Winston................ C 336 785-8700
Winston Salem *(G-13171)*

Gracie Goodness Inc......................... G 910 792-0800
Wilmington *(G-12794)*

Graham Cracker LLC......................... G 336 288-4440
Greensboro *(G-5571)*

Grandmas Sugar Shack........................ G 336 760-8822
Winston Salem *(G-13182)*

Imperial Falcon Group Inc.................... G 646 717-1128
Charlotte *(G-2315)*

Kalo Foods LLC............................... G 336 949-4802
Stokesdale *(G-11812)*

Keebler Company............................. C 919 774-6431
Sanford *(G-11199)*

Lotus Bakeries Us LLC....................... G 415 956-8956
Mebane *(G-8250)*

North Crolina Tortilla Mfg LLC............... D 270 861-5956
Lincolnton *(G-7848)*

Old Salem Incorporated...................... G 336 721-7305
Winston Salem *(G-13269)*

▼ S-L Snacks National LLC.................. E 704 554-1421
Charlotte *(G-2747)*

S-L Snacks Pa LLC........................... C 704 554-1421
Charlotte *(G-2748)*

▲ Scotts & Associates Inc.................. F 336 581-3141
Bear Creek *(G-718)*

SE Co-Brand Ventures LLC..................... G 704 598-9322
Charlotte *(G-2773)*

◆ Snyders-Lance Inc........................G 704 557-8013
Charlotte *(G-2821)*

Steven-Robert Originals LLC................. C 910 521-0199
Pembroke *(G-9660)*

Yummi Factory Corporation................... E 980 248-1062
Concord *(G-3472)*

2053 Frozen bakery products, except bread

Bimbo Bakeries Usa Inc....................... A 252 641-2200
Tarboro *(G-11923)*

Crumble Cups LLC............................. G 919 520-7414
Raleigh *(G-10023)*

Hais Kookies & More.......................... G 980 819-8256
Charlotte *(G-2251)*

Kalo Foods LLC.............................. G 336 949-4802
Stokesdale *(G-11812)*

Orange Bakery Inc........................... E 704 875-3003
Huntersville *(G-7029)*

▼ Stefano Foods Inc........................ C 704 399-3935
Charlotte *(G-2865)*

2061 Raw cane sugar

▲ Golding Farms Foods Inc................. D 336 766-6161
Winston Salem *(G-13179)*

2064 Candy and other confectionery products

American Sprinkle Co Inc..................... E 800 408-6708
Pineville *(G-9713)*

Bakeboxx Company............................ F 336 861-1212
High Point *(G-6536)*

◆ Bestco Holdings Inc.....................B 704 664-4300
Mooresville *(G-8609)*

Bilcat Inc.................................. E 828 295-3088
Blowing Rock *(G-880)*

Butterfields Candy LLC...................... G 252 459-2577
Nashville *(G-9313)*

Carolina Chocolatiers Inc.................... G 828 652-4496
Marion *(G-8038)*

Chocolate Fetish LLC......................... G 828 258-2353
Asheville *(G-475)*

Foiled Agin Choclat Coins LLC................ G 919 342-4601
Sanford *(G-11180)*

French Broad Chocolates LLC.................. G 828 252-4181
Asheville *(G-502)*

Fudgeboat Inc............................... G 910 617-9793
Carolina Beach *(G-1261)*

▲ Golden Grove Inc........................ F 910 293-4209
Warsaw *(G-12361)*

Hershey Company............................. F 919 284-0272
Kenly *(G-7233)*

Hospitality Mints LLC........................ E 828 262-0950
Boone *(G-925)*

▲ KLb Enterprises Incorporated............. F 336 605-0773
Greensboro *(G-5650)*

Lady May Swets Confections Inc............... G 704 749-9258
Charlotte *(G-2407)*

Lollipop Cenral............................. G 704 934-0015
Kannapolis *(G-7215)*

Lovegrass Kitchen Inc........................ F 919 205-8426
Holly Springs *(G-6906)*

▲ Lucky Country USA LLC.................... E 828 428-8313
Lincolnton *(G-7840)*

Mast General Store Inc...................... A 423 895-1632
Boone *(G-932)*

▲ Morinaga America Foods Inc.............. E 919 643-2439
Mebane *(G-8252)*

Mr Bs Fun Foods Inc.......................... E 828 879-1901
Connelly Springs *(G-3480)*

New Boston Fruit Slice & Confe............... E 919 775-2471
Sanford *(G-11211)*

Piedmont Candy Company....................... F 336 248-2477
Lexington *(G-7731)*

▲ Piedmont Candy Company.................... D 336 248-2477
Lexington *(G-7732)*

Tastebuds LLC............................... G 704 461-8755
Belmont *(G-771)*

Tnw Ventures Inc............................. G 828 216-4089
Pisgah Forest *(G-9773)*

2066 Chocolate and cocoa products

Barry Callebaut USA LLC...................... D 828 685-2443
Hendersonville *(G-6185)*

Beech Street Ventures LLC................... E 919 755-5053
Raleigh *(G-9938)*

Chocolate Fetish LLC......................... G 828 258-2353
Asheville *(G-475)*

Chocolate Smiles Village LLC................. G 919 469-5282
Cary *(G-1327)*

Escazu Artisan Chocolate LLC................ F 919 832-3433
Raleigh *(G-10091)*

Mountain Bear & Co Inc...................... G 828 631-0156
Dillsboro *(G-3819)*

◆ Nutkao USA Inc............................E 252 595-1000
Battleboro *(G-703)*

Secret Chocolatier LLC...................... G 704 323-8178
Charlotte *(G-2781)*

2068 Salted and roasted nuts and seeds

▼ Big Spoon Roasters LLC.................... F 919 309-9100
Hillsborough *(G-6860)*

Carolina Nut Inc............................ F 910 293-4209
Mount Olive *(G-9251)*

Innovative Business Growth LLC............... E 888 334-4367
Asheboro *(G-366)*

Morven Partners LP.......................... E 252 794-3435
Windsor *(G-13055)*

▼ Northampton Peanut Company............... D 252 585-0916
Severn *(G-11298)*

Osage Pecan Company.......................... F 660 679-6137
West Jefferson *(G-12569)*

Powell & Stokes Inc.......................... G 252 794-2138
Windsor *(G-13056)*

Sachs Peanuts LLC........................... E 910 647-4711
Clarkton *(G-3128)*

Sandy Land Peanut Company Inc................ F 252 356-2679
Harrellsville *(G-6104)*

See Clearly Inc.............................. G 929 464-6887
Greensboro *(G-5805)*

◆ Tropical Nut & Fruit Co...................C 800 438-4470
Charlotte *(G-2947)*

Universal Blanchers LLC...................... D 252 482-2112
Edenton *(G-4372)*

2074 Cottonseed oil mills

Agnatural LLC............................... G 252 536-0322
Weldon *(G-12518)*

Oil Mill Salvage Recyclers Inc............... G 910 268-2111
Gibson *(G-5175)*

Renew Life Formulas LLC..................... E 727 450-1061
Durham *(G-4212)*

2075 Soybean oil mills

Cargill Incorporated........................ E 800 227-4455
Fayetteville *(G-4569)*

Whitehat Seed Farms Inc..................... G 252 264-2427
Hertford *(G-6257)*

2077 Animal and marine fats and oils

Carolina By-Products Co...................... G 336 333-3030
Greensboro *(G-5424)*

Coastal Protein Products Inc................. G 910 567-6102
Godwin *(G-5188)*

Darling Ingredients Inc...................... E 910 483-0473
Fayetteville *(G-4583)*

Darling Ingredients Inc...................... F 704 864-9941
Gastonia *(G-5039)*

Darling Ingredients Inc...................... G 910 289-2083
Rose Hill *(G-10904)*

Darling Ingredients Inc...................... F 704 694-3701
Wadesboro *(G-12241)*

Enterprise Rendering Company................. G 704 485-3018
Oakboro *(G-9578)*

Neptune Hlth Wllness Innvtion................ C 888 664-9166
Conover *(G-3541)*

Valley Proteins.............................. F 252 348-4200
Lewiston Woodville *(G-7648)*

Valley Proteins (de) Inc.................... B 336 333-3030
Greensboro *(G-5895)*

Valley Proteins (de) Inc.................... C 540 877-2533
Oakboro *(G-9584)*

2079 Edible fats and oils

American Cltvtion Extrction Sv............... G 336 544-1072
Greensboro *(G-5355)*

Bunge Oils Inc.............................. E 910 293-7917
Warsaw *(G-12358)*

▲ Herbs Gaia Inc............................ D 828 884-4242
Brevard *(G-972)*

Olive Beaufort Oil Company................... G 252 504-2474
Beaufort *(G-731)*

Olive Euro Oil LLC........................... G 336 310-4624
Kernersville *(G-7290)*

Oliventures Inc............................. G 800 231-2619
Raleigh *(G-10345)*

Whole Harvest Foods LLC...................... E 910 293-7917
Warsaw *(G-12369)*

2082 Malt beverages

760 Craft Works LLC......................... F 704 274-5216
Huntersville *(G-6962)*

Anheuser-Busch LLC.......................... F 704 321-9319
Charlotte *(G-1677)*

S
I
C

Aviator Brewing Company Inc.............. G 919 601-5497
Holly Springs *(G-6893)*

Bearwaters Brewing Company.............. F 828 237-4200
Canton *(G-1242)*

Between Two Worlds LLC.................... G 828 774-5055
Asheville *(G-453)*

Beverage Innovation Corp.................. F 425 222-4900
Concord *(G-3320)*

Bombshell Beer Company LLC.............. F 919 823-1933
Holly Springs *(G-6895)*

Brew Publik Incorporated.................. G 704 231-2703
Charlotte *(G-1810)*

Brewmasters Inc............................. G 252 991-6035
Wilson *(G-12972)*

Bull Durham Beer Co LLC.................. G 919 744-3568
Durham *(G-3951)*

Cabarrus Brewing Company LLC.......... E 704 490-4487
Concord *(G-3326)*

Carolina Beverage Group LLC............. E 704 799-3627
Mooresville *(G-8629)*

Craft Brew Alliance Inc.................... G 828 263-1111
Boone *(G-908)*

Craft Revolution LLC...................... F 347 924-7540
Charlotte *(G-1994)*

Creative Brewing Company LLC.......... G 919 297-8182
Smithfield *(G-11441)*

Dreamweavers Brewery LLC............... G 704 507-7773
Waxhaw *(G-12429)*

Duck-Rabbit Craft Brewery Inc........... G 252 753-7745
Farmville *(G-4527)*

Fiddlin Fish Brewing Co.................... F 336 999-8945
Winston Salem *(G-13167)*

▲ Foothills Brewing......................... G 336 997-9484
Winston Salem *(G-13173)*

Fresh Point LLC............................. G 919 895-0790
Holly Springs *(G-6902)*

Gingers Revenge LLC...................... F 828 505-2462
Asheville *(G-506)*

Glass Jug.................................... F 919 818-6907
Durham *(G-4048)*

Glass Jug LLC.............................. F 919 813-0135
Durham *(G-4049)*

Goose and Monkey Brewhouse LLC...... F 336 239-0206
Lexington *(G-7693)*

Haw River Farmhouse Ales LLC.......... G 336 525-9270
Saxapahaw *(G-11262)*

Heckler Brewing Company................. G 910 748-0085
Fayetteville *(G-4609)*

Heist Brewing Company LLC.............. G 603 969-8012
Charlotte *(G-2270)*

▲ Highland Brewing Company Inc....... F 828 299-3370
Asheville *(G-517)*

House of Hops............................... G 919 819-0704
Raleigh *(G-10177)*

Hugger Mugger LLC........................ F 910 585-2749
Sanford *(G-11191)*

Innovation Brewing LLC.................... G 828 586-9678
Sylva *(G-11893)*

Koi Pond Brewing Company LLC.......... G 252 231-1660
Rocky Mount *(G-10847)*

Monster Brewing Company LLC........... D 828 883-2337
Brevard *(G-976)*

▲ Mother Earth Brewing LLC............. G 252 208-2437
Kinston *(G-7423)*

Nachos & Beer LLC........................ G 828 298-2280
Asheville *(G-553)*

New Anthem LLC.......................... G 910 319-7430
Wilmington *(G-12859)*

New Sarum Brewing Co LLC.............. G 704 310-5048
Salisbury *(G-11096)*

Newgrass Brewing Company LLC........ G 704 477-2795
Shelby *(G-11366)*

Ponysaurus Brewing LLC.................. F 919 455-3737
Durham *(G-4188)*

Resident Culture Brewing LLC............ E 704 333-1862
Charlotte *(G-2714)*

Salty Turtle Beer Company................ E 910 803-2019
Surf City *(G-11863)*

Salud LLC................................... E 980 495-6612
Charlotte *(G-2751)*

Shortway Brewing Company LLC......... G 252 777-3065
Newport *(G-9444)*

Southern Range Brewing LLC............. G 704 289-4049
Monroe *(G-8560)*

Southern Wicked Distillery Inc............ G 919 539-1620
Raleigh *(G-10494)*

▲ Stout Beverages LLC.................... E 704 293-7640
Kings Mountain *(G-7388)*

▲ Stout Brands LLC....................... G 704 293-7640
Kings Mountain *(G-7389)*

Sugar Creek Brewing Co LLC............. E 704 521-3333
Charlotte *(G-2878)*

Sycamore Brewing LLC.................... E 704 910-3821
Charlotte *(G-2891)*

▲ Triple C Brewing Company LLC....... F 704 372-3212
Charlotte *(G-2945)*

Trophy On Maywood LLC.................. F 919 803-1333
Raleigh *(G-10565)*

Trve-Avl LLC................................ G 303 909-1956
Asheville *(G-625)*

Wedge Brewing Co.......................... G 828 505-2792
Asheville *(G-632)*

Weeping Radish Farm Brewry LLC....... G 252 491-5205
Grandy *(G-5291)*

White Street Brewing Co Inc.............. F 919 647-9439
Youngsville *(G-13498)*

2083 Malt

Whitehat Seed Farms Inc.................. G 252 264-2427
Hertford *(G-6257)*

2084 Wines, brandy, and brandy spirits

Adams Beverages NC LLC................. D 910 763-6216
Leland *(G-7531)*

Adams Beverages NC LLC................. D 910 738-8165
Lumberton *(G-7942)*

Adams Beverages NC LLC................. F 704 509-3000
Charlotte *(G-1622)*

American Alcohollery LLC................. G 704 960-7243
Moravian Falls *(G-8807)*

Asheville Meadery LLC.................... G 828 454-6188
Asheville *(G-438)*

Autumn Creek Vineyards Inc............. G 336 548-9463
Greensboro *(G-5377)*

Banner Elk Winery Inc..................... G 828 898-9090
Banner Elk *(G-682)*

Battle Fermentables LLC.................. G 336 225-4585
Durham *(G-3917)*

▲ Biltmore Estate Wine Co LLC......... C 828 225-6776
Asheville *(G-454)*

Black Rock Landscaping LLC............. G 910 295-4470
Carthage *(G-1277)*

Botanist and Barrel........................ G 919 644-7777
Cedar Grove *(G-1516)*

Burntshirt Vineyards LLC.................. F 828 685-2402
Hendersonville *(G-6191)*

Cape Fear Vineyard Winery LLC......... F 844 846-3386
Elizabethtown *(G-4421)*

Cape Fear Vinyrd & Winery LLC......... G 910 645-4292
Elizabethtown *(G-4422)*

Carolina Coast Vineyard................... G 910 707-1777
Carolina Beach *(G-1258)*

Catawba Farms Enterprises LLC......... F 828 464-5780
Newton *(G-9452)*

Chateau Jourdain LLC..................... G 786 273-2869
Jonesville *(G-7194)*

▲ Childress Vineyards LLC............... E 336 236-9463
Lexington *(G-7663)*

▲ Childress Winery LLC.................. G 336 775-0522
Lexington *(G-7664)*

Cider Bros LLC............................. F 919 943-9692
Lexington *(G-7665)*

Coastal Carolina Winery................... G 843 443-9463
Cornelius *(G-3594)*

Cougar Run Winery......................... G 704 788-2746
Concord *(G-3346)*

Cypress Bend Vineyards Inc.............. G 910 369-0411
Wagram *(G-12255)*

Davidson Wine Co LLC.................... F 614 738-0051
Davidson *(G-3702)*

Dennis Vineyards Inc...................... G 704 982-6090
Albemarle *(G-70)*

Divine Llama Vineyards LLC.............. G 336 699-2525
East Bend *(G-4323)*

Drink A Bull LLC........................... G 919 818-3321
Durham *(G-4008)*

Duplin Wine Cellars Inc.................... E 910 289-3888
Rose Hill *(G-10905)*

Elkin Creek Vineyard LLC................. G 336 526-5119
Elkin *(G-4445)*

▲ Fair Game Beverage Company......... G 919 245-5434
Pittsboro *(G-9783)*

Grandfather Vinyrd Winery LLC.......... G 828 963-2400
Banner Elk *(G-685)*

Grassy Creek Vineyard & Winery........ G 336 835-2458
State Road *(G-11636)*

Gregory Vineyards.......................... G 919 427-9409
Angier *(G-119)*

Hertford ABC Board........................ G 252 426-5290
Hertford *(G-6254)*

Hilton Vineyards LLC...................... G 704 776-9656
Monroe *(G-8499)*

Hinnant Farms Vineyard LLC............. F 919 965-3350
Pine Level *(G-9681)*

Honeygirl Meadery LLC.................... G 919 399-3056
Durham *(G-4063)*

Hutton Vineyards LLC..................... G 336 374-2321
Dobson *(G-3822)*

Jackson Wine............................... G 828 508-9292
Brevard *(G-973)*

Jolo Winery & Vineyards LLC............. E 954 816-5649
Pilot Mountain *(G-9671)*

Jones Vondrehle Vineyards LLC.......... F 336 874-2800
Thurmond *(G-12097)*

Laurel Gray Vineyards Inc................. G 336 468-9463
Hamptonville *(G-6086)*

Linville Falls Winery....................... G 828 733-9021
Newland *(G-9431)*

Medaloni Cellars LLC...................... G 305 509-2004
Lewisville *(G-7652)*

Molley Chomper LLC....................... G 404 769-1439
Lansing *(G-7478)*

Nomacorc Holdings LLC................... E 919 460-2200
Zebulon *(G-13516)*

Noni Bacca Winery......................... G 910 397-7617
Wilmington *(G-12861)*

Oklawaha Brewing Company LLC........ F 828 595-9956
Hendersonville *(G-6233)*

Old North State Winery Inc............... F 336 789-9463
Mount Airy *(G-9161)*

Piccione Vinyards........................... G 312 342-0181
Ronda *(G-10896)*

Pig Pounder LLC........................... G 336 255-1306
Greensboro *(G-5747)*

Pleb Urban Winery......................... G 828 767-6445
Asheville *(G-578)*

Priscllas Crystal Cast Wnes In .... G 252 422-8336
Newport *(G-9442)*

Queen of Wines LLC .... F 919 348-6630
Durham *(G-4204)*

▲ Raffaldini Vneyards Winery LLC ...... F 336 835-9463
Ronda *(G-10898)*

Raylen Vineyards Inc .... G 336 998-3100
Winston Salem *(G-13316)*

Rise Over Run Inc .... G 303 819-1566
Swannanoa *(G-11877)*

Rockfish Creek Winery LLC .... G 910 729-0648
Raeford *(G-9851)*

Rocky River Vineyards LLC .... G 704 781-5035
Midland *(G-8295)*

Roots Run Deep LLC .... G 919 909-9117
Youngsville *(G-13483)*

Round Peak Vineyards LLC .... G 336 352-5595
Mount Airy *(G-9173)*

Saint Paul Mountain Vineyards .... F 828 685-4002
Hendersonville *(G-6239)*

Sanders Ridge Inc .... G 336 677-1700
Boonville *(G-958)*

Shelton Vineyards Inc .... E 336 366-4818
Dobson *(G-3825)*

Sommerville Enterprises LLC .... F 919 924-1594
Hillsborough *(G-6878)*

Southern Range Brewing LLC .... G 704 289-4049
Monroe *(G-8560)*

Stardust Cellars LLC .... G 336 466-4454
Winston Salem *(G-13343)*

Stonefield Cellars LLC .... G 336 632-2391
Stokesdale *(G-11816)*

◆ Suntory International .... F 917 756-2747
Raleigh *(G-10521)*

Thistle Meadow Winery Inc .... G 800 233-1505
Laurel Springs *(G-7490)*

Tom Burgiss .... G 336 359-2995
Laurel Springs *(G-7491)*

Urban Orchard Cider Company .... F 252 904-5135
Asheville *(G-628)*

Vineyard Bluffton LLC .... G 704 307-2737
Charlotte *(G-2985)*

Vineyards On Scuppernong LLC .... G 252 796-4727
Columbia *(G-3299)*

Weathervane Winery Inc .... G 336 793-3366
Lexington *(G-7757)*

Westbend Vineyards Inc .... G 336 768-7520
Winston Salem *(G-13389)*

Willowcroft .... F 704 540-0367
Charlotte *(G-3021)*

Woodmill Winery Inc .... G 704 276-9911
Vale *(G-12212)*

2085 Distilled and blended liquors

Asheville Distilling Company .... G 828 575-2000
Asheville *(G-436)*

◆ Azure Skye Beverages Inc .... G 704 909-7394
Charlotte *(G-1727)*

Barrister and Brewer LLC .... G 919 323-2777
Durham *(G-3913)*

Blue Ridge Distilling Co Inc .... G 828 245-2041
Bostic *(G-961)*

Bogue Sound Distillery Inc .... F 252 241-1606
Newport *(G-9438)*

▲ Bold Rock Partners LP .... F 828 595-9940
Mills River *(G-8312)*

Broad Branch Distillery LLC .... G 336 207-7855
Winston Salem *(G-13111)*

Buffalo City Distillery LLC .... G 252 256-1477
Point Harbor *(G-9809)*

Call Family Distillers LLC .... G 336 990-0708
Wilkesboro *(G-12630)*

Copper Barrel Distillery LLC .... G 336 262-6500
North Wilkesboro *(G-9526)*

Dark Moon Distileries LLC .... G 704 222-8063
Banner Elk *(G-683)*

Doc Porters Distillery LLC .... G 704 266-1399
Charlotte *(G-2060)*

Durham Distillery Llc .... G 919 937-2121
Durham *(G-4015)*

Eod Distillery LLC .... E 910 399-1133
Wilmington *(G-12771)*

Fainting Goat Spirits LLC .... G 336 273-6221
Greensboro *(G-5529)*

▲ Fair Game Beverage Company .... G 919 245-5434
Pittsboro *(G-9783)*

Graybeard Distillery Inc .... F 919 361-9980
Durham *(G-4056)*

Great Wagon Road Distlg Co LLC .... F 704 469-9330
Charlotte *(G-2236)*

Greensboro Distilling LLC .... G 336 273-6221
Greensboro *(G-5576)*

H&H Distillery LLC .... G 828 338-9779
Asheville *(G-514)*

Howling Moon Distillery Inc .... G 828 208-1469
Burnsville *(G-1187)*

Loud Lemon Beverage LLC .... G 919 949-7649
Bahama *(G-666)*

Mason Inlet Distillery LLC .... G 910 200-4584
Wilmington *(G-12847)*

Mayberry Distillery .... G 336 719-6860
Mount Airy *(G-9152)*

Muddy River Distillery LLC .... G 336 516-4190
Mount Holly *(G-9239)*

New River Distilling Co LLC .... G 732 673-4852
Deep Gap *(G-3728)*

Oak & Grist Distilling Co LLC .... G 914 450-0589
Asheville *(G-557)*

Oak & Grist Distilling Co LLC .... G 828 357-5750
Black Mountain *(G-869)*

Olde Raleigh Distillery LLC .... F 919 208-0044
Zebulon *(G-13519)*

Piedmont Distillers Inc .... D 336 445-0055
Madison *(G-7995)*

Southern Distilling Co LLC .... G 704 677-4069
Statesville *(G-11769)*

Three Stacks Distilling Co LLC .... G 252 468-0779
Kinston *(G-7431)*

Two Trees Distilling Co LLC .... G 803 767-1322
Fletcher *(G-4774)*

Waltons Distillery Inc .... G 910 347-7770
Jacksonville *(G-7159)*

Warehouse Distillery LLC .... G 828 464-5183
Newton *(G-9510)*

Weldon Mills Distillery LLC .... G 252 220-4235
Weldon *(G-12527)*

2086 Bottled and canned soft drinks

Aberdeen Coca-Cola Btlg Co Inc .... F 910 944-2305
Aberdeen *(G-1)*

▼ Alamance Foods Inc .... C 336 226-6392
Burlington *(G-1043)*

▼ Bebida Beverage Company .... E 704 660-0226
Statesville *(G-11668)*

Brewitt & Dreenkupp Inc .... G 704 525-3366
Charlotte *(G-1811)*

Carolina Beverage Corporation .... E 704 636-2191
Salisbury *(G-11024)*

▲ Carolina Beverage Group LLC .... E 704 799-2337
Mooresville *(G-8630)*

Carolina Bottling Company .... D 704 637-5869
Salisbury *(G-11025)*

Ccbcc Inc .... B 704 557-4000
Charlotte *(G-1871)*

Ccbcc Operations LLC .... E 704 557-4038
Charlotte *(G-1872)*

Ccbcc Operations LLC .... E 252 752-2446
Greenville *(G-5953)*

Ccbcc Operations LLC .... E 252 536-3611
Halifax *(G-6046)*

Ccbcc Operations LLC .... E 910 582-3543
Hamlet *(G-6053)*

Ccbcc Operations LLC .... E 252 637-3157
New Bern *(G-9352)*

Ccbcc Operations LLC .... D 252 671-4515
New Bern *(G-9353)*

Ccbcc Operations LLC .... E 704 872-3634
Statesville *(G-11676)*

Ccbcc Operations LLC .... E 910 642-3002
Whiteville *(G-12579)*

Ccbcc Operations LLC .... D 828 687-1300
Arden *(G-260)*

Ccbcc Operations LLC .... E 828 297-2141
Boone *(G-905)*

Ccbcc Operations LLC .... E 828 488-2874
Bryson City *(G-1009)*

Ccbcc Operations LLC .... F 704 359-5600
Charlotte *(G-1873)*

Ccbcc Operations LLC .... E 704 399-6043
Charlotte *(G-1875)*

Ccbcc Operations LLC .... C 980 321-3226
Charlotte *(G-1876)*

Ccbcc Operations LLC .... D 919 359-2966
Clayton *(G-3138)*

Ccbcc Operations LLC .... E 910 483-6158
Fayetteville *(G-4572)*

Ccbcc Operations LLC .... D 336 664-1116
Greensboro *(G-5434)*

Ccbcc Operations LLC .... E 828 322-5097
Hickory *(G-6292)*

Ccbcc Operations LLC .... E 704 225-1973
Monroe *(G-8455)*

Ccbcc Operations LLC .... E 336 789-7111
Mount Airy *(G-9112)*

Ccbcc Operations LLC .... E 704 364-8728
Charlotte *(G-1874)*

Central Carolina Btlg Co Inc .... G 919 542-3226
Bear Creek *(G-713)*

Choice USA Beverage Inc .... E 704 861-1029
Gastonia *(G-5020)*

Choice USA Beverage Inc .... G 704 487-6951
Shelby *(G-11317)*

Choice USA Beverage Inc .... D 704 823-1651
Lowell *(G-7930)*

Coca-Cola Bottling Co .... G 704 509-1812
Charlotte *(G-1946)*

Coca-Cola Consolidated Inc .... G 704 398-2252
Charlotte *(G-1947)*

Coca-Cola Consolidated Inc .... D 980 321-3001
Charlotte *(G-1948)*

Coca-Cola Consolidated Inc .... C 919 550-0611
Clayton *(G-3141)*

Coca-Cola Consolidated Inc .... D 252 334-1820
Elizabeth City *(G-4382)*

Coca-Cola Consolidated Inc .... E 704 551-4500
Kinston *(G-7402)*

Coca-Cola Consolidated Inc .... G 919 763-3172
Leland *(G-7539)*

Coca-Cola Consolidated Inc .... E 828 322-5096
Newton *(G-9455)*

▲ Coca-Cola Consolidated Inc .... A 980 392-8298
Charlotte *(G-1949)*

Dr Pepper Co of Wilmington .... G 910 792-5400
Wilmington *(G-12767)*

Dr Pepper/Seven-Up Bottling .... G 828 322-8090
Hickory *(G-6324)*

S
I
C

Dr Ppper Btlg W Jffrson NC In.............. E 336 846-2433
West Jefferson *(G-12564)*

Durham Coca-Cola Bottling Co.............. G 919 510-0574
Raleigh *(G-10066)*

Durham Coca-Cola Bottling Company... C 919 383-1531
Durham *(G-4014)*

Frito-Lay North America Inc................. G 980 224-3730
Wilmington *(G-12779)*

Ginger Supreme Inc.............................. G 919 812-8986
Apex *(G-158)*

Grins Enterprises LLC.......................... G 336 831-0534
Winston Salem *(G-13185)*

Ice River Springs Usa Inc..................... F 519 925-2929
Morganton *(G-8874)*

ICEE Company....................................... G 704 357-6865
Charlotte *(G-2308)*

◆ Independent Beverage Co LLC........... F 704 399-2504
Charlotte *(G-2320)*

Le Bleu Corporation.............................. G 828 254-5105
Arden *(G-280)*

McPherson Beverages Inc..................... E 252 537-3571
Roanoke Rapids *(G-10741)*

Midland Bottling LLC............................ G 919 865-2300
Raleigh *(G-10306)*

Milkco Inc... B 828 254-8428
Asheville *(G-547)*

Minges Bottling Group.......................... F 252 636-5898
New Bern *(G-9383)*

Niagara Bottling LLC............................ G 909 815-6310
Mooresville *(G-8734)*

Old Saratoga Inc................................... E 252 238-2175
Saratoga *(G-11261)*

Original New York Seltzer LLC.............. E 323 500-0757
Cornelius *(G-3617)*

◆ Packo Bottling Inc............................. E 919 496-4286
Louisburg *(G-7921)*

Pepsi Bottling Group Inc....................... G 704 507-4031
Midland *(G-8291)*

Pepsi Bottling Ventures LLC................. E 800 879-8884
Cary *(G-1418)*

Pepsi Bottling Ventures LLC................. E 828 264-7702
Deep Gap *(G-3729)*

Pepsi Bottling Ventures LLC................. E 252 335-4355
Elizabeth City *(G-4401)*

Pepsi Bottling Ventures LLC................. D 919 865-2388
Garner *(G-4952)*

Pepsi Bottling Ventures LLC................. C 919 863-4000
Garner *(G-4953)*

Pepsi Bottling Ventures LLC................. E 919 778-8300
Goldsboro *(G-5236)*

Pepsi Bottling Ventures LLC................. C 704 455-0800
Harrisburg *(G-6115)*

Pepsi Bottling Ventures LLC................. E 252 451-1811
Rocky Mount *(G-10859)*

Pepsi Bottling Ventures LLC................. D 910 865-1600
Saint Pauls *(G-11006)*

Pepsi Bottling Ventures LLC................. E 704 873-0249
Statesville *(G-11744)*

Pepsi Bottling Ventures LLC................. D 910 792-5400
Wilmington *(G-12874)*

Pepsi Bottling Ventures LLC................. G 336 464-9227
Winston Salem *(G-13279)*

Pepsi Bottling Ventures LLC................. E 336 464-9227
Winston Salem *(G-13280)*

Pepsi Bottling Ventures LLC................. C 336 724-4800
Winston Salem *(G-13281)*

▲ Pepsi Bottling Ventures LLC............. D 919 865-2300
Raleigh *(G-10366)*

Pepsi Cola Bottling Co.......................... D 828 650-7800
Fletcher *(G-4760)*

Pepsi Cola Co....................................... G 704 357-9166
Charlotte *(G-2625)*

Pepsi-Cola Btlg Hickry NC Inc.............. G 828 322-8090
Granite Falls *(G-5316)*

Pepsi-Cola Btlg Hickry NC Inc.............. D 828 322-8090
Hickory *(G-6409)*

Pepsi-Cola Btlg Hickry NC Inc.............. D 828 497-1235
Whittier *(G-12625)*

Pepsi-Cola Btlg Hickry NC Inc.............. C 828 322-8090
Hickory *(G-6410)*

Pepsi-Cola Metro Btlg Co Inc............... G 980 581-1099
Charlotte *(G-2626)*

Pepsi-Cola Metro Btlg Co Inc............... D 704 736-2640
Cherryville *(G-3068)*

Pepsi-Cola Metro Btlg Co Inc............... G 252 446-7181
Rocky Mount *(G-10860)*

Pepsi-Cola Metro Btlg Co Inc............... A 336 896-4000
Winston Salem *(G-13282)*

Pepsico Inc... G 828 756-4662
Marion *(G-8060)*

Pepsico Inc... F 914 253-2000
Winston Salem *(G-13283)*

Piedmont Cheerwine Bottling Co.......... D 336 993-7733
Colfax *(G-3287)*

Pure Water Innovations Inc................... G 919 301-8189
Spring Hope *(G-11558)*

Quality Beverage LLC........................... E 910 371-3596
Belville *(G-781)*

Quality Beverage LLC........................... G 704 637-5881
Salisbury *(G-11109)*

Raleigh Ventures Inc............................. N 910 350-0036
Wilmington *(G-12895)*

Red Bull Distribution Co Inc................. F 910 500-1566
Havelock *(G-6126)*

Redux Beverages LLC.......................... G 951 304-1144
Hillsborough *(G-6876)*

Refresco Beverages US Inc................... E 252 234-0493
Wilson *(G-13020)*

Refresco Beverages US Inc................... F 252 234-0493
Wilson *(G-13021)*

◆ S & D Coffee Inc.............................. A 704 782-3121
Concord *(G-3437)*

Sanford Coca-Cola Bottling Co............. F 919 774-4111
Sanford *(G-11229)*

Sun-Drop Btlg Rocky Mt NC Inc............ G 252 977-4586
Rocky Mount *(G-10871)*

◆ Suntory International.......................... F 917 756-2747
Raleigh *(G-10521)*

Unix Packaging LLC.............................. C 310 877-7979
Morganton *(G-8907)*

◆ USa Wholesale and Distrg Inc........... F 888 484-6872
Fayetteville *(G-4693)*

Waynesville Soda Jerks LLC.................. G 828 278-8589
Waynesville *(G-12479)*

Zeskp LLC... G 910 762-8300
Wilmington *(G-12958)*

2087 Flavoring extracts and syrups, nec

Alternative Ingredients Inc................... G 336 378-5368
Greensboro *(G-5351)*

▼ Blue Mountain Enterprises Inc.......... E 252 522-1544
Kinston *(G-7396)*

Bunge Oils Inc....................................... E 910 293-7917
Warsaw *(G-12358)*

Choice USA Beverage Inc...................... D 704 823-1651
Lowell *(G-7930)*

Crude LLC... G 919 391-8185
Raleigh *(G-10022)*

Flavor Sciences Inc............................... E 828 758-2525
Taylorsville *(G-11960)*

▲ Freedom Beverage Company............. G 336 316-1260
Greensboro *(G-5540)*

Fuji Foods Inc....................................... E 336 897-3373
Browns Summit *(G-994)*

Fuji Foods Inc....................................... G 336 226-8817
Burlington *(G-1091)*

▲ Fuji Foods Inc.................................. E 336 375-3111
Browns Summit *(G-995)*

GNT Usa LLC.. E 914 524-0600
Dallas *(G-3673)*

▲ Great Eastern Sun Trdg Co Inc.......... F 828 665-7790
Asheville *(G-511)*

Herbalife Manufacturing LLC................ G 336 970-6400
Winston Salem *(G-13196)*

▲ Larrys Beans Inc.............................. G 919 828-1234
Raleigh *(G-10248)*

Little Beekeeper LLC............................ G 704 215-9690
Lincolnton *(G-7839)*

▲ Mary Macks Inc................................ G 770 234-6333
Clinton *(G-3234)*

Mother Murphys Labs Inc...................... E 336 273-1737
Greensboro *(G-5697)*

Mother Murphys Labs Inc...................... D 336 273-1737
Greensboro *(G-5698)*

Prime Beverage Group LLC................... C 704 385-5451
Concord *(G-3423)*

Prime Beverage Group LLC................... D 704 385-5450
Huntersville *(G-7038)*

▲ Specialty Products Intl Ltd................ G 910 897-4706
Erwin *(G-4492)*

Speed Energy Drink LLC....................... G 704 949-1255
Concord *(G-3444)*

2091 Canned and cured fish and seafoods

Avon Seafood....................................... G 252 995-4553
Avon *(G-650)*

Bay Breeze Seafood Rest Inc................. F 828 697-7106
Hendersonville *(G-6186)*

Capt Neills Seafood Inc........................ C 252 796-0795
Columbia *(G-3295)*

Carolina ATL Seafood Entps.................. G 252 728-2552
Morehead City *(G-8822)*

◆ Classic Seafood Group Inc................ C 252 746-2818
Ayden *(G-654)*

Lloyds Oyster House Inc....................... E 910 754-6958
Shallotte *(G-11304)*

Mattamuskeet Seafood Inc.................... D 252 926-2431
Swanquarter *(G-11880)*

Pamlico Packing Co Inc........................ F 252 745-3688
Vandemere *(G-12226)*

Pamlico Packing Co Inc........................ F 252 745-3688
Grantsboro *(G-5331)*

▲ Quality Foods From Sea Inc.............. D 252 338-5455
Elizabeth City *(G-4405)*

Quality Seafood Co Inc......................... G 252 338-2800
Elizabeth City *(G-4406)*

Queens Creek Seafood.......................... G 910 326-4801
Hubert *(G-6936)*

2092 Fresh or frozen packaged fish

▲ Alphin Brothers Inc.......................... E 910 892-8751
Dunn *(G-3843)*

Aurora Packing Co Inc.......................... G 252 322-5232
Aurora *(G-641)*

B & J Seafood Co Inc............................ F 252 637-0483
New Bern *(G-9338)*

▲ Bakkavor Foods Usa Inc................... C 704 522-1977
Charlotte *(G-1745)*

Capt Charlies Seafood Inc.................... E 252 796-7278
Columbia *(G-3294)*

Capt Neills Seafood Inc........................ C 252 796-0795
Columbia *(G-3295)*

Carolina ATL Seafood Entps.................. G 252 728-2552
Morehead City *(G-8822)*

Carolina Catch Inc............................... D 252 946-5796
Washington *(G-12377)*

Hare Asian Trading Company LLC......... E 910 524-4667
Burgaw (G-1023)

Just Shrimp Holdings US Inc................. G 805 832-1828
Charlotte (G-2384)

Pamlico Packing Co Inc....................... F 252 745-3688
Vandemere (G-12226)

Pamlico Packing Co Inc....................... F 252 745-3688
Grantsboro (G-5331)

Quality Seafood Co Inc........................ G 252 338-2800
Elizabeth City (G-4406)

Ricewrap Foods Corporation................ F 919 614-1179
Butner (G-1206)

Sea Supreme Inc................................ G 919 556-1188
Wake Forest (G-12298)

Williams Seafood Arapahoe Inc .... D 252 249-0594
Arapahoe (G-208)

2095 Roasted coffee

Alamance Kaffee Werks LLC................. G 662 617-4573
Burlington (G-1044)

Anchor Coffee Co Inc.......................... G 336 265-7458
North Wilkesboro (G-9521)

Five Star Coffee Roasters LLC.............. G 919 671-0645
Holly Springs (G-6901)

Fryeday Coffee Roasters LLC............... G 704 879-9083
Lowell (G-7931)

▲ Larrys Beans Inc............................. G 919 828-1234
Raleigh (G-10248)

Muddy Dog LLC.................................. G 919 371-2818
New Hill (G-9411)

Royal Cup Inc.................................... F 704 597-5756
Charlotte (G-2734)

◆ S & D Coffee Inc.............................. A 704 782-3121
Concord (G-3437)

Tradewinds Coffee Co Inc.................... F 919 556-1835
Zebulon (G-13524)

▼ Wallingford Coffee Mills Inc.............. D 513 771-3131
Concord (G-3466)

Well-Bean Coffee & Crumbs LLC.......... G 833 777-2326
Wake Forest (G-12314)

2096 Potato chips and similar snacks

American Skin Food Group LLC............. E 910 259-2232
Burgaw (G-1018)

Bakers Southern Traditions Inc............. G 252 344-2120
Roxobel (G-10949)

Blazing Foods LLC.............................. G 336 865-2933
Charlotte (G-1789)

Frito-Lay North America Inc.................. C 704 588-4150
Charlotte (G-2181)

Ginny O s Inc.................................... F 919 816-7276
Warsaw (G-12360)

Golden Pop Shop LLC......................... G 704 236-9455
Charlotte (G-2224)

Gruma Corporation............................. E 919 778-5553
Goldsboro (G-5220)

▲ Igh Enterprises Inc.......................... F 704 372-6744
Charlotte (G-2310)

Julias Southern Foods LLC.................. G 919 609-6745
Raleigh (G-10226)

▲ KLb Enterprises Incorporated............ F 336 605-0773
Greensboro (G-5650)

▲ Lc America Inc................................ F 336 676-5129
Colfax (G-3282)

Mr Bs Fun Foods Inc........................... E 828 879-1901
Connelly Springs (G-3480)

North Crolina Tortilla Mfg LLC.............. D 270 861-5956
Lincolnton (G-7848)

R W Garcia Co Inc.............................. E 828 428-0115
Lincolnton (G-7850)

Reyes Prdctos Mxcnos Reyes LLC........ G 704 777-5805
Raleigh (G-10443)

S-L Snacks Pa LLC............................. C 704 554-1421
Charlotte (G-2748)

Shallowford Farms Popcorn Inc............ G 336 463-5938
Yadkinville (G-13451)

Skin Boys LLC................................... F 910 259-2232
Burgaw (G-1031)

Stormberg Foods LLC......................... E 919 947-6011
Goldsboro (G-5247)

Tyson Foods Inc................................. G 919 774-7925
Sanford (G-11245)

Tyson Mexican Original Inc.................. E 919 777-9428
Sanford (G-11246)

2097 Manufactured ice

Carolina Ice Inc................................. E 252 527-3178
Kinston (G-7399)

Dfa Dairy Brands Fluid LLC.................. G 704 341-2794
Charlotte (G-2038)

Herrin Bros Coal & Ice Co.................... G 704 332-2193
Charlotte (G-2275)

Hickman Oil & Ice Co Inc..................... G 910 576-2501
Troy (G-12161)

Ice Cube Recording Studios.................. G 910 260-7616
Wilmington (G-12812)

Reddy Ice LLC................................... G 704 824-4611
Gastonia (G-5132)

Reddy Ice LLC................................... G 910 738-9930
Lumberton (G-7968)

Reddy Ice LLC................................... G 919 782-9358
Raleigh (G-10439)

Robert D Starr.................................. G 336 697-0286
Greensboro (G-5790)

Rose Ice & Coal Company.................... G 910 762-2464
Wilmington (G-12902)

Taylor Products Inc............................ G 910 862-2576
Elizabethtown (G-4435)

Zippy Ice Inc.................................... E 980 355-9851
Charlotte (G-3049)

2098 Macaroni and spaghetti

▲ First Noodle Co Inc......................... G 704 393-3238
Charlotte (G-2157)

2099 Food preparations, nec

Advancepierre Foods Inc..................... A 828 459-7626
Claremont (G-3087)

Ajinomoto Hlth Ntrtn N Amer In............ C 919 231-0100
Raleigh (G-9887)

Alta Foods llc.................................... D 919 734-0233
Goldsboro (G-5197)

American Miso Company Inc................. F 828 287-2940
Rutherfordton (G-10974)

Apex Salsa Company.......................... G 919 363-1486
Apex (G-137)

▲ Avoca LLC..................................... D 252 482-2133
Merry Hill (G-8268)

Bay Valley Foods LLC......................... D 715 366-4511
Albertson (G-98)

▲ Bay Valley Foods LLC..................... E 910 267-4711
Faison (G-4515)

Bay Valley Foods LLC......................... G 704 476-7141
Kings Mountain (G-7349)

Big Show Foods Inc............................ G 919 242-7769
Fremont (G-4859)

Bost Distributing Company Inc.............. G 919 775-5931
Sanford (G-11158)

Cargill Incorporated........................... E 800 227-4455
Fayetteville (G-4569)

Carolina Innvtive Fd Ingrdnts................ G 804 359-9311
Nashville (G-9315)

Cary Keisler Inc................................. G 336 586-9333
Burlington (G-1065)

Chandler Foods Inc............................ E 336 299-1934
Greensboro (G-5441)

Clay County Food Pantry Inc................ G 828 389-1657
Hayesville (G-6138)

Clean Catch Fish Market LLC................ G 704 333-1212
Charlotte (G-1928)

Communitys Kitchen L3c...................... G 828 817-2308
Tryon (G-12173)

Compass Group Usa Inc...................... A 704 398-6515
Charlotte (G-1965)

Compass Group Usa Inc...................... B 919 381-9577
Garner (G-4924)

Compass Group Usa Inc...................... E 252 291-7733
Wilson (G-12981)

Cool Runnings Jamaican LLC................ G 919 818-9220
Raleigh (G-10015)

Dover Foods Inc................................. E 800 348-7416
Mills River (G-8313)

▲ Drake S Fresh Pasta Company........... E 336 861-5454
High Point (G-6597)

E2m Kitchen LLC............................... F 704 731-5070
Charlotte (G-2081)

El Comal Inc...................................... G 336 788-8110
Winston Salem (G-13156)

Equinom Enterprises LLC..................... G 704 817-8489
Charlotte (G-2125)

Ericson Foods Inc.............................. F 336 317-2199
Winston Salem (G-13160)

Foell Packing Company of NC............... G 919 776-0592
Sanford (G-11179)

Frito-Lay North America Inc.................. C 704 588-4150
Charlotte (G-2181)

Fuji Foods Inc.................................... G 336 226-8817
Burlington (G-1091)

▲ Fuji Foods Inc................................ E 336 375-3111
Browns Summit (G-995)

Gallo Lea Organics LLC....................... G 828 337-1037
Asheville (G-503)

▲ Golding Farms Foods Inc................. D 336 766-6161
Winston Salem (G-13179)

Gourmet Foods USA LLC...................... G 704 248-1724
Cornelius (G-3604)

▲ Great Eastern Sun Trdg Co Inc.......... F 828 665-7790
Asheville (G-511)

Green Compass LLC........................... G 833 336-9223
Wilmington (G-12797)

Hanor Co Inc..................................... G 252 977-0035
Battleboro (G-698)

Hans Kissle Company LLC................... C 980 500-1630
Dallas (G-3674)

Harmony House Foods Inc................... G 800 696-1395
Franklin (G-4831)

◆ Herbal Innovations LLC.................... E 336 818-2332
Wilkesboro (G-12638)

Horballs Inc...................................... G 919 925-0483
Raleigh (G-10174)

▲ Igh Enterprises Inc.......................... F 704 372-6744
Charlotte (G-2310)

Improved Nature LLC.......................... D 919 588-2299
Garner (G-4934)

James Foods Inc................................ E 336 437-0393
Graham (G-5273)

Jenkins Foods Inc.............................. F 704 434-2347
Shelby (G-11349)

Johnson Harn Vngar Gee GL Pllc.......... F 919 213-6163
Raleigh (G-10220)

Julias Southern Foods LLC.................. G 919 609-6745
Raleigh (G-10226)

Kimbees Inc...................................... G 336 323-8773
Greensboro (G-5647)

Kloud Hemp Co.................................. G 336 740-2528
Greensboro (G-5651)

▲ La Tortilleria LLC.............................C 336 773-0010
Winston Salem *(G-13229)*

Lc Foods LLC.....................................G 919 510-6688
Raleigh *(G-10250)*

◆ LCI Corporation International............E 704 399-7441
Charlotte *(G-2411)*

Lucy In Rye LLC................................G 828 586-4601
Sylva *(G-11896)*

▼ Mana Nutritive Aid Pdts Inc.............G 855 438-6262
Matthews *(G-8129)*

McF Operating LLC............................E 828 685-8821
Hendersonville *(G-6225)*

Mg Foods Inc.....................................F 336 724-6327
Winston Salem *(G-13249)*

▲ Miss Tortillas Inc...........................G 919 598-8646
Durham *(G-4138)*

Morven Partners LP...........................E 252 482-2193
Edenton *(G-4369)*

My Threesons Gourmet......................G 336 324-5638
Reidsville *(G-10695)*

Nafshi Enterprises LLC......................G 910 986-9888
Aberdeen *(G-17)*

Natures Cup LLC...............................G 910 795-2700
Raeford *(G-9843)*

Neu Spice and Seasonings Llc...........G 252 378-7912
Washington *(G-12400)*

Nice Blends Corp..............................D 910 640-1000
Whiteville *(G-12590)*

No Evil Foods LLC.............................D 828 367-1536
Weaverville *(G-12500)*

O-Taste-N-c LLC................................G 919 696-9547
Dunn *(G-3863)*

Ole Mexican Foods Inc......................E 704 587-1763
Charlotte *(G-2595)*

Osage Pecan Company......................F 660 679-6137
West Jefferson *(G-12569)*

Over Rainbow Inc..............................G 704 332-5521
Charlotte *(G-2604)*

Palmetto and Associate LLC...............G 336 382-7432
Greensboro *(G-5731)*

Panaceutics Nutrition Inc...................F 919 797-9623
Durham *(G-4164)*

Peanut Processors Inc.......................F 910 862-2136
Dublin *(G-3832)*

Peanut Processors Sherman Inc.........F 910 862-2136
Dublin *(G-3833)*

Pickles Manufacturing LLC.................C 910 267-4711
Faison *(G-4518)*

Poppy Handcrafted Popcorn Inc..........F 828 552-3149
Old Fort *(G-9597)*

Poppy Handcrafted Popcorn Inc..........F 828 552-3149
Asheville *(G-581)*

◆ Pregel America Inc.........................C 704 707-0300
Concord *(G-3421)*

▲ Rolls Enterprises Inc......................G 919 545-9401
Pittsboro *(G-9789)*

Roots Organic Gourmet LLC...............F 828 232-2828
Fairview *(G-4510)*

Rositas Tortillas Inc..........................G 910 944-0577
Aberdeen *(G-22)*

Sage Mule..G 336 209-9183
Greensboro *(G-5801)*

Sarahs Salsa Inc...............................G 336 508-3033
Greensboro *(G-5802)*

▲ Scotts & Associates Inc.................F 336 581-3141
Bear Creek *(G-718)*

Shallowford Farms Popcorn Inc...........G 336 463-5938
Yadkinville *(G-13451)*

Sideboard...G 910 612-4398
Wilmington *(G-12920)*

Signature Seasonings LLC..................G 252 746-1001
Ayden *(G-661)*

Sinnovita Inc.....................................G 919 694-0974
Raleigh *(G-10480)*

Smiling Hara LLC...............................G 828 545-4150
Barnardsville *(G-694)*

Solo Foods LLC.................................E 910 259-9407
Burgaw *(G-1032)*

▼ Star Food Products Inc...................D 336 227-4079
Burlington *(G-1164)*

◆ Star Snax LLC.................................D 828 261-0255
Conover *(G-3562)*

▼ Stefano Foods Inc...........................C 704 399-3935
Charlotte *(G-2865)*

Stony Gap Wholesale Co Inc...............G 704 982-5360
Albemarle *(G-93)*

Tate & Lyle Solutions USA LLC...........E 252 482-0402
Merry Hill *(G-8269)*

Ted Wheeler......................................G 252 438-0820
Oxford *(G-9638)*

◆ Tropical Nut & Fruit Co....................C 800 438-4470
Charlotte *(G-2947)*

Tyson Mexican Original Inc................E 919 777-9428
Sanford *(G-11246)*

Universal Blanchers LLC....................D 252 482-2112
Edenton *(G-4372)*

Urban Spiced LLC..............................G 704 741-1174
Charlotte *(G-2968)*

Vanguard Culinary Group Ltd...............D 910 484-8999
Fayetteville *(G-4695)*

Vintage South Inc..............................G 919 362-4079
Apex *(G-202)*

Violet Sanford Holdings LLC...............E 919 775-5931
Sanford *(G-11248)*

Vista Horticultural Group Inc...............F 828 633-6338
Arden *(G-317)*

▼ Wallingford Coffee Mills Inc............D 513 771-3131
Concord *(G-3466)*

Williams Skin Co...............................G 910 323-2628
Fayetteville *(G-4701)*

21 TOBACCO PRODUCTS

2111 Cigarettes

22nd Century Group Inc.....................F 716 270-1523
Mocksville *(G-8345)*

Commonwealth Brands Inc.................C 336 634-4200
Greensboro *(G-5460)*

▲ Fontem US LLC...............................G 888 207-4588
Greensboro *(G-5536)*

Itg Brands..D 336 335-6600
Greensboro *(G-5626)*

Itg Brands..D 919 366-0220
Raleigh *(G-10210)*

Itg Brands LLC..................................E 336 335-6669
Greensboro *(G-5627)*

▲ Liggett Group LLC...........................B 919 304-7700
Mebane *(G-8249)*

Lorillard LLC.....................................D 336 741-2000
Winston Salem *(G-13238)*

◆ Lorillard Tobacco Company LLC.......A 336 335-6600
Greensboro *(G-5665)*

Medallion Company Inc......................C 919 990-3500
Timberlake *(G-12101)*

Modoral Brands Inc...........................G 336 741-7230
Winston Salem *(G-13259)*

Mr Tobacco.......................................G 919 747-9052
Raleigh *(G-10316)*

Philip Morris USA Inc.........................D 336 744-4401
Winston Salem *(G-13288)*

R J Reynolds Tobacco Company..........D 919 366-0220
Wendell *(G-12543)*

R J Reynolds Tobacco Company..........C 336 741-2132
Winston Salem *(G-13312)*

◆ R J Rynolds Tob Holdings Inc..........D 336 741-5000
Winston Salem *(G-13313)*

Rai Services Company........................A 336 741-6774
Winston Salem *(G-13315)*

◆ Reynolds American Inc.....................E 336 741-2000
Winston Salem *(G-13318)*

Santa Fe Ntural Tob Foundation..........C 919 690-0880
Oxford *(G-9633)*

Triaga Inc...G 919 412-6019
Wilson *(G-13039)*

◆ US Tobacco Cooperative Inc............D 919 821-4560
Raleigh *(G-10579)*

Wainwright Warehouse.......................G 252 237-5121
Wilson *(G-13043)*

2121 Cigars

Modoral Brands Inc...........................G 336 741-7230
Winston Salem *(G-13259)*

North Carolina Tobacco Mfg LLC.........F 252 238-6514
Stantonsburg *(G-11626)*

◆ Reynolds American Inc.....................E 336 741-2000
Winston Salem *(G-13318)*

Santa Fe Natural Tob Co Inc...............G 919 690-1905
Oxford *(G-9632)*

2131 Chewing and smoking tobacco

American Snuff Company LLC.............C 336 768-4630
Winston Salem *(G-13085)*

▲ Cres Tobacco Company LLC.............E 336 983-7727
King *(G-7325)*

▲ Ioto Usa LLC..................................F 252 413-7343
Greenville *(G-5992)*

Itg Holdings USA Inc..........................F 954 772-9000
Greensboro *(G-5629)*

Modoral Brands Inc...........................G 336 741-7230
Winston Salem *(G-13259)*

R J Reynolds Tobacco Company..........D 336 741-0400
Tobaccoville *(G-12102)*

R J Reynolds Tobacco Company..........C 336 741-2132
Winston Salem *(G-13312)*

◆ R J Reynolds Tobacco Company.......D 336 741-5000
Winston Salem *(G-13311)*

◆ Reynolds American Inc.....................E 336 741-2000
Winston Salem *(G-13318)*

▲ Santa Fe Natural Tobacco...............E 800 332-5595
Winston Salem *(G-13329)*

Tobacco Rag Processors Inc..............E 252 265-0081
Wilson *(G-13035)*

Tobacco Rag Processors Inc..............E 252 237-8180
Wilson *(G-13036)*

◆ Tobacco Rag Processors Inc............E 252 265-0081
Wilson *(G-13037)*

Top Tobacco LP.................................C 910 646-3014
Lake Waccamaw *(G-7472)*

2141 Tobacco stemming and redrying

Pyxus International Inc.......................C 252 753-8000
Farmville *(G-4538)*

R J Reynolds Tobacco Company..........C 252 291-4700
Wilson *(G-13017)*

Recon Usa LLC.................................G 252 206-1391
Wilson *(G-13019)*

Tobacco Rag Processors Inc..............E 252 265-0081
Wilson *(G-13035)*

Tobacco Rag Processors Inc..............E 252 237-8180
Wilson *(G-13036)*

◆ Tobacco Rag Processors Inc............E 252 265-0081
Wilson *(G-13037)*

Top Tobacco LP.................................C 910 646-3014
Lake Waccamaw *(G-7472)*

22 TEXTILE MILL PRODUCTS

2211 Broadwoven fabric mills, cotton

◆ Alamac American Knits LLC .... C 910 618-2248
Lumberton *(G-7943)*

▲ American Fiber & Finishing Inc .... E 704 984-9256
Albemarle *(G-61)*

◆ American Silk Mills LLC .... F 570 822-7147
High Point *(G-6522)*

▲ Amerifab International Inc .... E 336 882-9010
High Point *(G-6523)*

Atlantic Trading LLC .... F
Charlotte *(G-1711)*

◆ Barnhardt Manufacturing Company .... C 800 277-0377
Charlotte *(G-1755)*

Bekaertdeslee USA Inc .... B 336 747-4900
Winston Salem *(G-13103)*

Belk Department Stores LP .... E 704 357-4000
Charlotte *(G-1769)*

Beverly Knits Inc .... E 704 964-0835
Gastonia *(G-4999)*

▲ Beverly Knits Inc .... E 704 861-1536
Gastonia *(G-5000)*

Brighton Weaving LLC .... G 336 665-3000
Greensboro *(G-5403)*

Burlington House LLC .... F 336 379-6220
Greensboro *(G-5412)*

◆ Burlington Industries LLC .... C 336 379-6220
Greensboro *(G-5414)*

Canvas Beauty Bar LLC .... F 828 355-9688
Boone *(G-903)*

◆ Carolina Mills Incorporated .... D 828 428-9911
Maiden *(G-8010)*

▲ Champion Thread Company .... G 704 867-6611
Gastonia *(G-5018)*

Circa 1801 .... G 828 397-7003
Connelly Springs *(G-3475)*

Cloth Barn Inc .... F 919 735-3643
Goldsboro *(G-5206)*

◆ Cone Denim LLC .... D 336 379-6165
Greensboro *(G-5462)*

◆ Copland Industries Inc .... B 336 226-0272
Burlington *(G-1076)*

◆ Creative Fabric Services LLC .... G 704 861-8383
Gastonia *(G-5031)*

◆ Ct-Nassau Ticking LLC .... E 336 570-0091
Burlington *(G-1079)*

Culp Inc .... E 662 844-7144
Burlington *(G-1080)*

Culp Inc .... C 336 643-7751
Stokesdale *(G-11811)*

◆ Cv Industries Inc .... G 828 328-1851
Hickory *(G-6316)*

Designer Fabrics Inc .... G 704 305-4144
Concord *(G-3354)*

Elevate Textiles Inc .... G 910 997-5001
Cordova *(G-3580)*

◆ Elevate Textiles Inc .... F 336 379-6220
Charlotte *(G-2098)*

Elevate Textiles Holding Corp .... D 336 379-6220
Charlotte *(G-2099)*

Faizon Global Inc .... G 704 774-1141
Monroe *(G-8487)*

▲ Ferncrest Fashions Inc .... D 704 283-6422
Monroe *(G-8488)*

◆ Fisher Textiles Inc .... E 800 554-8886
Matthews *(G-8170)*

Flint Spinning LLC .... G 336 665-3000
Greensboro *(G-5535)*

◆ Glen Raven Inc .... C 336 227-6211
Burlington *(G-1098)*

Gracefully Broken LLC .... G 980 474-0309
Gastonia *(G-5055)*

Hackner Home LLC .... G 980 552-9573
Shelby *(G-11340)*

Heritage Classic Wovens LLC .... G 828 247-6010
Forest City *(G-4791)*

Heritage Knitting Co LLC .... E 704 872-7653
Statesville *(G-11709)*

Highland Composites .... G 704 924-3090
Greensboro *(G-5596)*

Hpfabrics Inc .... G 336 231-0278
Winston Salem *(G-13201)*

Industrial Opportunities Inc .... B 828 321-4754
Andrews *(G-107)*

Interrs-Exteriors Asheboro Inc .... G 336 629-2148
Asheboro *(G-367)*

◆ Itg Holdings Inc .... A 336 379-6220
Greensboro *(G-5628)*

Ivy Brand LLC .... G 980 225-7866
Charlotte *(G-2359)*

JPS Elstmerics Westfield Plant .... G 336 351-0938
Westfield *(G-12573)*

Lanart International Inc .... G 704 875-1972
Huntersville *(G-7009)*

▲ Lantal Textiles Inc .... C 336 969-9551
Rural Hall *(G-10963)*

Lillys Interiors Cstm Quilting .... G 336 475-1421
Thomasville *(G-12044)*

Luray Textiles Inc .... F 336 670-3725
North Wilkesboro *(G-9544)*

Makemine Inc .... G 704 906-7164
Charlotte *(G-2449)*

Manning Fabrics Inc .... E 910 295-1970
Pinebluff *(G-9687)*

Manning Fabrics Inc .... G 910 295-1970
Pinehurst *(G-9696)*

▲ Marlatex Corporation .... E 704 829-7797
Charlotte *(G-2458)*

Mdkscrubs LLC .... G 980 250-4708
Charlotte *(G-2483)*

▼ Mfi Products Inc .... F 910 944-2128
Aberdeen *(G-16)*

Milliken & Company .... F 828 247-4300
Bostic *(G-963)*

Modena Southern Dyeing Corp .... G 704 866-9156
Gastonia *(G-5100)*

Paragon Global LLC .... G 336 899-8525
High Point *(G-6725)*

◆ Perfect Fit Industries LLC .... C 800 864-7618
Charlotte *(G-2627)*

▲ Pure Country Inc .... D 828 871-2890
Tryon *(G-12177)*

◆ Raleigh Workshop Inc .... E 919 917-8969
Raleigh *(G-10431)*

Ribbon Enterprises Inc .... G 828 264-6444
Boone *(G-941)*

▼ Riddle & Company LLC .... G 336 229-1856
Burlington *(G-1147)*

Ripstop By Roll LLC .... F 877 525-7210
Durham *(G-4215)*

Sampson Gin Company Inc .... G 910 567-5111
Newton Grove *(G-9517)*

◆ Sattler Corp .... D 828 759-2100
Hudson *(G-6958)*

Skeen Decorative Fabrics Inc .... G 336 884-4044
High Point *(G-6778)*

Star Wipers Inc .... E 888 511-2656
Gastonia *(G-5143)*

Swatch Works Inc .... G 336 626-9971
Asheboro *(G-400)*

Swatchworks Inc .... G 336 626-9971
Asheboro *(G-401)*

▲ Textile-Based Delivery Inc .... E 866 256-8420
Conover *(G-3565)*

Textum Opco LLC .... E 704 822-2400
Belmont *(G-773)*

▲ Trelleborg Ctd Systems US Inc .... C 828 286-9126
Rutherfordton *(G-10999)*

Valdese Textiles Inc .... G 828 874-4216
Valdese *(G-12203)*

▲ Valdese Weavers LLC .... G 828 874-2181
Valdese *(G-12204)*

Valdese Weavers LLC .... A 828 874-2181
Valdese *(G-12205)*

▼ Value Clothing Inc .... D 704 638-6111
Salisbury *(G-11132)*

VF Corporation .... G 336 424-6000
Greensboro *(G-5899)*

VF Corporation .... F 336 424-6000
Greensboro *(G-5900)*

Vlr LLC .... E 252 355-4610
Morganton *(G-8909)*

▲ Wade Manufacturing Company .... E 704 694-2131
Wadesboro *(G-12252)*

Westpoint Home Inc .... F 910 369-2231
Wagram *(G-12257)*

Zingerle Group Usa Inc .... E 704 312-1600
Charlotte *(G-3048)*

2221 Broadwoven fabric mills, manmade

▲ Abercrombie Textiles I LLC .... F 704 487-1245
Shelby *(G-11309)*

Admiral Marine Pdts & Svcs Inc .... G 704 489-8771
Denver *(G-3767)*

Advocacy To Allvate Hmlessness ...... G 919 810-3431
Raleigh *(G-9882)*

◆ American Silk Mills LLC .... F 570 822-7147
High Point *(G-6522)*

American Tchncal Solutions Inc .... D 336 595-2763
Walkertown *(G-12315)*

American Yarn Inc .... G 919 614-1542
Burlington *(G-1046)*

Amesbury Group Inc .... D 704 978-2883
Statesville *(G-11655)*

Amesbury Group Inc .... D 704 924-7694
Statesville *(G-11656)*

Andritz Fabrics and Rolls Inc .... D 919 526-1400
Raleigh *(G-9904)*

Asheboro Elastics Corp .... G 336 629-2626
Asheboro *(G-328)*

◆ Asheboro Elastics Corp .... D 336 629-2626
Asheboro *(G-327)*

Ashfar Enterprises Inc .... F 704 462-4672
Newton *(G-9449)*

Barcovvsion LLC .... F 704 392-9371
Charlotte *(G-1751)*

Bettys Drapery Design Workroom ...... G 828 264-2392
Boone *(G-897)*

◆ Burlington Industries LLC .... C 336 379-6220
Greensboro *(G-5414)*

◆ Carolina Mills Incorporated .... D 828 428-9911
Maiden *(G-8010)*

◆ Carriff Corporation Inc .... G 704 888-3330
Midland *(G-8282)*

Classical Elements .... G 828 575-9145
Asheville *(G-478)*

Collins & Aikman Europe Inc .... E 704 548-2350
Charlotte *(G-1953)*

Collins & Aikman Interiors .... E 704 548-2350
Charlotte *(G-1954)*

Collins & Aikman International .... E 704 548-2350
Charlotte *(G-1955)*

Collins & Aikman Prpts Inc .... E 704 548-2350
Charlotte *(G-1956)*

Collins Akman Canada Dom Holdg ..... E 704 548-2350
Charlotte *(G-1958)*

▲ Composite Fabrics America LLC..... G..... 828 632-5220
Taylorsville *(G-11954)*

Copland Fabrics Inc........................ B 336 226-0272
Burlington *(G-1075)*

◆ Copland Industries Inc..................B 336 226-0272
Burlington *(G-1076)*

Crypton Mills LLC........................... E 828 202-5875
Cliffside *(G-3225)*

◆ Ct-Nassau Ticking LLC.................E 336 570-0091
Burlington *(G-1079)*

Culp Inc.. C 336 889-5161
High Point *(G-6582)*

David Rothschild Co Inc................. D 336 342-0035
Reidsville *(G-10682)*

Design Concepts Incorporated.............. F 336 887-1932
High Point *(G-6590)*

◆ Dicey Mills Inc............................G..... 704 487-6324
Shelby *(G-11331)*

▼ Efa Inc.. C 336 378-2603
Greensboro *(G-5513)*

▼ Efa Inc.. C 336 275-9401
Greensboro *(G-5514)*

Elevate Textiles Inc...................... G 336 379-6220
Burlington *(G-1087)*

◆ Elevate Textiles Inc....................F 336 379-6220
Charlotte *(G-2098)*

Elevate Textiles Holding Corp............ D 336 379-6220
Charlotte *(G-2099)*

Everest Textile Usa LLC................ C 828 245-6755
Forest City *(G-4789)*

▲ Feinberg Enterprises Inc.............. F 704 822-2400
Belmont *(G-750)*

Fiber Company................................ G 336 725-5277
Lewisville *(G-7650)*

Fibrix LLC..E 704 878-0027
Statesville *(G-11697)*

▲ Filtex Inc.................................... D 828 874-2100
Rutherford College *(G-10971)*

◆ Flynt/Amtex Inc...........................E 336 226-0621
Burlington *(G-1090)*

Freudenberg Prfmce Mtls LP............ C 828 665-5000
Candler *(G-1225)*

▲ Gale Pacific Usa Inc..................... F 407 772-7900
Charlotte *(G-2185)*

◆ Glen Raven Inc.............................C 336 227-6211
Burlington *(G-1098)*

Glen Raven Mtl Solutions LLC............ C 828 682-2142
Burnsville *(G-1185)*

Glen Rven Tchnical Fabrics LLC............ C 336 229-5576
Burlington *(G-1100)*

Glen Rven Tchnical Fabrics LLC............ E 336 227-6211
Burlington *(G-1099)*

Hanes Companies Inc..................... B 828 464-4673
Conover *(G-3525)*

Hickory Heritage of Falling Creek Inc.....E
Hickory *(G-6351)*

Highland Industries Inc.................. E 336 547-1600
Greensboro *(G-5597)*

Highland Industries Inc.................. E 336 855-0625
Greensboro *(G-5598)*

Hs Hyosung Usa Inc...................... C 336 495-2202
Asheboro *(G-362)*

◆ Hs Hyosung Usa Inc....................E 704 790-6100
Charlotte *(G-2292)*

▲ Hs Hyosung USA Holdings Inc......... G 704 790-6134
Charlotte *(G-2293)*

◆ Itg Holdings Inc...........................A 336 379-6220
Greensboro *(G-5628)*

Ivy Brand LLC.................................G 980 225-7866
Charlotte *(G-2359)*

◆ King Textiles LLC........................F 336 861-3257
Archdale *(G-236)*

◆ Kings Plush Inc.............................C 704 739-9931
Kings Mountain *(G-7370)*

Kontoor Brands Inc........................ E 336 332-3577
Greensboro *(G-5654)*

Ledford Upholstery......................... G 704 732-0233
Lincolnton *(G-7836)*

Metyx USA Inc................................ D 704 824-1030
Gastonia *(G-5096)*

Moire Creations America LLC............ E 704 482-9860
Shelby *(G-11364)*

Nouveau Verre Holdings Inc............ F 336 545-0011
Greensboro *(G-5714)*

Nvh Inc... G 336 545-0011
Greensboro *(G-5717)*

▲ P&A Indstrial Fabrications LLC...... E 336 322-1766
Roxboro *(G-10938)*

Patricia Hall................................... G 704 729-6133
Bessemer City *(G-829)*

Performance Fibers......................... F 704 947-7193
Huntersville *(G-7032)*

Piedmont Cmposites Tooling LLC......... D 828 632-8883
Taylorsville *(G-11970)*

Plush Comforts................................ G 336 882-9185
High Point *(G-6737)*

Point Blank Enterprises Inc............ D 910 893-2071
Lillington *(G-7801)*

◆ Precision Fabrics Group Inc...............E 336 281-3049
Greensboro *(G-5757)*

Premier Quilting Corporation............ G 919 693-1151
Oxford *(G-9626)*

▲ Quantum Materials LLC.................. E 336 605-9002
Colfax *(G-3288)*

Schneider Mills Inc......................... F 828 632-8181
Taylorsville *(G-11977)*

▲ Seiren North America LLC.............. F 828 430-3456
Morganton *(G-8894)*

◆ Shuford Mills LLC..........................G 828 324-4265
Hickory *(G-6442)*

Simplifyber Inc................................ F 919 396-8355
Raleigh *(G-10478)*

Southline Converting LLC................ G 828 781-6414
Conover *(G-3560)*

Stowe Woodward Licensco LLC............ G 919 526-1400
Raleigh *(G-10510)*

Style Upholstering Inc.................... G 828 322-4882
Hickory *(G-6460)*

▲ Sunrise Development LLC.............. F 828 453-0590
Mooresboro *(G-8586)*

Svcm.. G 305 767-3595
Lincolnton *(G-7858)*

▲ Tapestries Ltd.............................. G 336 883-9864
Greensboro *(G-5851)*

Texinnovate Inc.............................. E 336 279-7800
Greensboro *(G-5860)*

▲ Trelleborg Ctd Systems US Inc...... C 828 286-9126
Rutherfordton *(G-10999)*

◆ Unifi Inc..D 336 294-4410
Greensboro *(G-5887)*

Uniquetex LLC................................. E 704 457-3003
Grover *(G-6045)*

Valdese Textiles Inc....................... G 828 874-4216
Valdese *(G-12203)*

Valdese Weavers LLC...................... A 828 874-2181
Valdese *(G-12205)*

Valdese Weavers LLC...................... B 828 874-2181
Valdese *(G-12206)*

▲ Wade Manufacturing Company......... E 704 694-2131
Wadesboro *(G-12252)*

◆ Weavexx LLC.................................A 919 556-7235
Raleigh *(G-10602)*

Wickes Manufacturing Company............ E 704 548-2350
Charlotte *(G-3018)*

Windsor Fiberglass Inc................... G 910 259-0057
Burgaw *(G-1040)*

2231 Broadwoven fabric mills, wool

Altus Finishing LLC........................ E 704 861-1536
Gastonia *(G-4987)*

▲ Barrday Corp................................. G 704 395-0311
Charlotte *(G-1756)*

Burlington Industries III LLC............ F 336 379-2000
Greensboro *(G-5413)*

◆ Burlington Industries LLC..............C 336 379-6220
Greensboro *(G-5414)*

Carlisle Finishing LLC..................... D 864 466-4173
Greensboro *(G-5423)*

Circa 1801...................................... G 828 397-7003
Connelly Springs *(G-3475)*

◆ Elevate Textiles Inc.....................F 336 379-6220
Charlotte *(G-2098)*

Elevate Textiles Holding Corp............ D 336 379-6220
Charlotte *(G-2099)*

▲ Finishing Partners Inc.................. G 704 583-7322
Charlotte *(G-2153)*

Hpfabrics Inc.................................. G 336 231-0278
Winston Salem *(G-13201)*

I T G Raeford................................. G 910 875-3736
Raeford *(G-9841)*

Idea Oven LLC................................. G 910 343-5280
Castle Hayne *(G-1503)*

◆ Itg Holdings Inc............................A 336 379-6220
Greensboro *(G-5628)*

Ivy Brand LLC.................................. G 980 225-7866
Charlotte *(G-2359)*

▲ Lantal Textiles Inc....................... C 336 969-9551
Rural Hall *(G-10963)*

Lustar Dyeing and Finshg Inc............ G 828 274-2440
Asheville *(G-539)*

Michelson Enterprises Inc................ G 828 693-5500
Hendersonville *(G-6227)*

Milliken & Company......................... F 828 247-4300
Bostic *(G-963)*

National Spinning Co Inc................. C 910 298-3131
Beulaville *(G-844)*

Sorrells Sheree White..................... G 828 452-4864
Waynesville *(G-12475)*

Trelleborg Ctd Systems US Inc............ C 864 576-1210
Rutherfordton *(G-10997)*

▲ Voith Fabrics Inc......................... B 252 291-3800
Wilson *(G-13042)*

▲ Xtinguish LLC............................... G 704 868-9500
Charlotte *(G-3034)*

2241 Narrow fabric mills

All American Braids Inc.................. E 704 852-4380
Gastonia *(G-4985)*

American Webbing Fittings Inc............ F 336 767-9390
Winston Salem *(G-13086)*

Asheboro Elastics Corp................... G 336 629-2626
Asheboro *(G-328)*

◆ Asheboro Elastics Corp................D 336 629-2626
Asheboro *(G-327)*

▲ Carolina Narrow Fabric Company..... C 336 631-3000
Winston Salem *(G-13117)*

Circa 1801...................................... G 828 397-7003
Connelly Springs *(G-3475)*

◆ Coats & Clark Inc..........................D 888 368-8401
Charlotte *(G-1942)*

▲ Coats N Amer De Rpblica Dmncan... C 800 242-8095
Charlotte *(G-1945)*

◆ Continental Ticking Corp Amer........D 336 570-0091
Alamance *(G-55)*

◆ Ct-Nassau Tape LLC......................D 336 570-0091
Alamance *(G-56)*

▲ Custom Fabric Samples Inc............ G 336 472-1854
Thomasville *(G-12014)*

Datamark Graphics Inc.................... E 336 629-0267
Asheboro *(G-345)*

◆ Dunn Manufacturing Corp............. C 704 283-2147
Monroe *(G-8479)*

▼ Efa Inc....................................... C 336 275-9401
Greensboro *(G-5514)*

◆ Hickory Brands Inc...................... D 828 322-2600
Hickory *(G-6347)*

Hickory Springs Mfg Co................... F 336 491-4131
High Point *(G-6648)*

▲ Interstate Narrow Fabrics Inc.......... D 336 578-1037
Haw River *(G-6132)*

McMichael Mills Inc....................... E 336 584-0134
Burlington *(G-1127)*

◆ McMichael Mills Inc..................... C 336 548-4242
Mayodan *(G-8207)*

Minnewawa Inc............................. F 865 522-8103
Thomasville *(G-12050)*

Murdock Webbing Company Inc......... E 252 823-1131
Tarboro *(G-11937)*

National Foam Inc.......................... C 919 639-6151
Angier *(G-125)*

Nouveau Verre Holdings Inc............. F 336 545-0011
Greensboro *(G-5714)*

Nvh Inc....................................... G 336 545-0011
Greensboro *(G-5717)*

◆ Parkdale Mills Incorporated........... D 704 874-5000
Gastonia *(G-5117)*

Parker-Hannifin Corporation............. D 336 373-1761
Greensboro *(G-5734)*

Quiknit Crafting Inc....................... G 704 861-1030
Gastonia *(G-5129)*

▲ Ramseur Inter-Lock Knitting Co....... G 336 824-2427
Asheboro *(G-388)*

◆ Spanset Inc............................... E 919 774-6316
Sanford *(G-11236)*

▲ Spt Technology Inc...................... F 612 332-1880
Monroe *(G-8561)*

◆ Spuntech Industries Inc................ C 336 330-9000
Roxboro *(G-10946)*

Standard Tytape Company Inc........... G 828 693-6594
Hendersonville *(G-6244)*

◆ Supreme Elastic Corporation.......... E 828 302-3836
Conover *(G-3563)*

US Cotton LLC............................. D 704 874-5000
Belmont *(G-774)*

◆ US Cotton LLC............................ C 216 676-6400
Gastonia *(G-5161)*

US Label Corporation..................... G 336 332-7000
Greensboro *(G-5894)*

▲ West & Associates of NC.............. G 919 479-5680
Durham *(G-4303)*

▲ World Elastic Corporation............. E 704 786-9508
Concord *(G-3469)*

▲ Wright of Thomasville Inc.............. F 336 472-4200
Thomasville *(G-12091)*

◆ Zimmermann - Dynayarn Usa LLC.... E 336 222-8129
Graham *(G-5290)*

2251 Women's hosiery, except socks

Acme - McCrary Corporation............ F 336 625-2161
Siler City *(G-11396)*

Acme-Mccrary Corporation.............. C 336 625-2161
Asheboro *(G-323)*

Acme-Mccrary Corporation.............. C 919 663-2200
Siler City *(G-11397)*

◆ Acme-Mccrary Corporation........... B 336 625-2161
Asheboro *(G-324)*

Bossong Corporation...................... G 336 625-2175
Asheboro *(G-332)*

▲ Cajah Corporation........................ C 828 728-7300
Hudson *(G-6944)*

Catawba Valley Finishing LLC.......... E 828 464-2252
Newton *(G-9453)*

▲ Central Carolina Hosiery Inc.......... E 910 428-9688
Biscoe *(G-849)*

▲ Commonwealth Hosiery Mills Inc..... D 336 498-2621
Randleman *(G-10638)*

Concord Trading Inc....................... E 704 375-3333
Concord *(G-3343)*

De Feet International Inc................. G 828 397-7025
Hildebran *(G-6848)*

Felice Hosiery Co Inc..................... E 336 996-2371
Kernersville *(G-7274)*

◆ Fine Line Hosiery Inc................... G 336 498-8022
Asheboro *(G-356)*

Fine Sheer Industries Inc................ B 704 375-3333
Concord *(G-3363)*

Glen Raven Inc............................. F 336 227-6211
Altamahaw *(G-103)*

◆ Goldtoemoretz LLC...................... B 828 464-0751
Newton *(G-9470)*

Hanesbrands Inc........................... G 336 789-6118
Mount Airy *(G-9126)*

Hanesbrands Inc........................... A 336 519-8080
Winston Salem *(G-13188)*

▲ Huffman Finishing Company Inc...... C 828 396-1741
Granite Falls *(G-5308)*

◆ Kayser-Roth Corporation.............. C 336 852-2030
Greensboro *(G-5643)*

Mas Acme USA.............................. G 336 625-2161
Asheboro *(G-376)*

▲ Mayo Knitting Mill Inc.................. C 252 823-3101
Tarboro *(G-11934)*

Neat Feet Hosiery Inc..................... G 336 573-2177
Stoneville *(G-11823)*

North Carolina Sock Inc.................. G 828 327-4664
Hickory *(G-6403)*

Rogers Knitting Inc........................ G 336 789-4155
Mount Airy *(G-9172)*

▲ Royal Hosiery Company Inc........... G 828 496-2200
Granite Falls *(G-5322)*

Simmons Hosiery Mill Inc................ G 828 327-4890
Hickory *(G-6448)*

◆ Slane Hosiery Mills Inc................. C 336 883-4136
High Point *(G-6781)*

Special T Hosiery Mills Inc.............. G 336 227-2858
Burlington *(G-1161)*

▲ Star America Inc......................... C 704 788-4700
Concord *(G-3448)*

Sue-Lynn Textiles Inc..................... E 336 578-0871
Haw River *(G-6135)*

Surratt Hosiery Mill Inc.................. G 336 859-4583
Denton *(G-3762)*

Teamwork Inc............................... G 336 578-3456
Elon *(G-4472)*

Thorneburg Hosiery Mills Inc........... E 704 279-7247
Rockwell *(G-10805)*

Thorneburg Hosiery Mills Inc........... E 704 838-6329
Statesville *(G-11788)*

Upel Inc...................................... G 336 519-8080
Winston Salem *(G-13379)*

◆ Zimmermann - Dynayarn Usa LLC.... E 336 222-8129
Graham *(G-5290)*

2252 Hosiery, nec

B & B Hosiery Mill......................... G 336 368-4849
Pinnacle *(G-9767)*

B & M Wholesale Inc...................... G 336 789-3916
Mount Airy *(G-9100)*

Beard Hosiery Co........................... D 828 758-1942
Lenoir *(G-7577)*

▲ Bossong Hosiery Mills Inc............. C 336 625-2175
Asheboro *(G-333)*

Carolina Hosiery Mills Inc............... G 336 226-5581
Burlington *(G-1062)*

Carolina Hosiery Mills Inc............... G 336 226-5581
Burlington *(G-1063)*

▲ Carolina Hosiery Mills Inc............. E 336 570-2129
Burlington *(G-1064)*

Catawba Valley Finishing LLC.......... E 828 464-2252
Newton *(G-9453)*

Cedar Valley Hosiery Mill Inc........... G 828 396-1804
Hudson *(G-6949)*

▲ Central Carolina Hosiery Inc.......... E 910 428-9688
Biscoe *(G-849)*

▲ Commonwealth Hosiery Mills Inc..... D 336 498-2621
Randleman *(G-10638)*

Concord Trading Inc....................... E 704 375-3333
Concord *(G-3343)*

Custom Socks Ink Inc..................... E 828 695-9869
Newton *(G-9463)*

De Feet International Inc................. G 828 397-7025
Hildebran *(G-6848)*

▲ Devmir Legwear Inc..................... G 919 545-5500
Pittsboro *(G-9781)*

Diabetic Sock Club....................... G 800 214-0218
Gastonia *(G-5041)*

Elder Hosiery Mills Inc................... G 336 226-0673
Burlington *(G-1086)*

Farr Knitting Company Inc............... G 336 625-5561
Asheboro *(G-354)*

Felice Hosiery Co Inc..................... E 336 996-2371
Kernersville *(G-7274)*

Fine Sheer Industries Inc................ B 704 375-3333
Concord *(G-3363)*

◆ Gold Toe Stores Inc..................... G 828 464-0751
Newton *(G-9469)*

◆ Goldtoemoretz LLC...................... B 828 464-0751
Newton *(G-9470)*

Grady Distributing Co Inc................ F 919 556-5630
Youngsville *(G-13473)*

◆ Graham Dyeing & Finishing Inc........ D 336 228-9981
Burlington *(G-1101)*

Hanesbrands Inc........................... G 336 789-6118
Mount Airy *(G-9126)*

Hanesbrands Inc........................... E 336 519-8080
Rural Hall *(G-10961)*

Hanesbrands Inc........................... A 336 519-8080
Winston Salem *(G-13188)*

Harriss & Covington Hsy Mills......... G 336 882-6811
High Point *(G-6638)*

◆ Harriss Cvington Hsy Mills Inc........ C 336 882-6811
High Point *(G-6639)*

▼ Hill Hosiery Mill Inc.................... G 336 472-7908
Thomasville *(G-12031)*

Hillshire Brands Company............... G 336 519-8080
Winston Salem *(G-13198)*

◆ Holt Hosiery Mills Inc................... C 336 227-1431
Burlington *(G-1103)*

▲ Huffman Finishing Company Inc...... C 828 396-1741
Granite Falls *(G-5308)*

Huitt Mills Inc............................. E 828 322-8628
Hildebran *(G-6851)*

Implus LLC.................................. F 828 485-3318
Hickory *(G-6367)*

▲ Iq Brands Inc............................. F 336 751-0040
Advance *(G-34)*

J R B and J Knitting Inc.................. G 910 439-4242
Mount Gilead *(G-9199)*

▲ Jefferies Socks LLC..................... F 336 226-7316
Burlington *(G-1112)*

▲ JI Hosiery LLC............................ F 910 974-7156
Candor *(G-1237)*

S I C

◆ Kayser-Roth Corporation.....................C 336 852-2030
  Greensboro *(G-5643)*

▲ Kayser-Roth Hosiery Inc.................. F 336 229-2269
  Graham *(G-5274)*

Kayser-Roth Hosiery Inc.................. E 336 852-2030
  Greensboro *(G-5644)*

KB Socks Inc.......................................G 336 719-8000
  Mount Airy *(G-9139)*

Kelly Hosiery Mill Inc.......................G 828 324-6456
  Hickory *(G-6376)*

L & R Knitting Inc.............................G 828 874-2960
  Hickory *(G-6383)*

Legacy Knitting LLC..........................G 844 762-2678
  Wilmington *(G-12833)*

▲ Lyons Hosiery Inc..........................G 336 789-2651
  Mount Airy *(G-9150)*

▲ Mayo Knitting Mill Inc...................C 252 823-3101
  Tarboro *(G-11934)*

Michael Tate.....................................G 336 374-4695
  Mount Airy *(G-9153)*

NC Quality Sales LLC........................F 336 786-7211
  Mount Airy *(G-9157)*

Neat Feet Hosiery Inc.......................G 336 573-2177
  Stoneville *(G-11823)*

Nester Hosiery Inc............................D 336 789-0026
  Mount Airy *(G-9159)*

▲ Nester Hosiery LLC....................... E 336 789-0026
  Mount Airy *(G-9160)*

North Carolina Sock Inc....................G 828 327-4664
  Hickory *(G-6403)*

◆ Parker Hosiery Company Inc.............E 828 668-7628
  Old Fort *(G-9596)*

Peacoat Media LLC............................G 336 298-1133
  Winston Salem *(G-13277)*

Pickett Hosiery Mills Inc...................E 336 227-2716
  Burlington *(G-1139)*

R Evans Hosiery LLC.........................E 828 397-3715
  Connelly Springs *(G-3482)*

Renfro LLC..F 336 786-3000
  Mount Airy *(G-9168)*

Renfro LLC..D 336 719-8290
  Mount Airy *(G-9169)*

◆ Renfro LLC.....................................C 336 719-8000
  Mount Airy *(G-9170)*

Renfro Mexico Holdings LLC..............G 336 786-3501
  Mount Airy *(G-9171)*

Robinson Hosiery Mill Inc..................G 828 874-2228
  Valdese *(G-12199)*

▲ Royal Hosiery Company Inc............. G 828 496-2200
  Granite Falls *(G-5322)*

Royal Textile Mills Inc......................D 336 694-4121
  Yanceyville *(G-13460)*

◆ Royce Too LLC...............................E 212 356-1627
  Winston Salem *(G-13324)*

Russell-Fshion Foot Hsy Mlls I............G 336 299-0741
  Greensboro *(G-5799)*

Sara Lee Socks................................G 336 789-6118
  Mount Airy *(G-9174)*

Simmons Hosiery Mill Inc..................G 828 327-4890
  Hickory *(G-6448)*

◆ Slane Hosiery Mills Inc...................C 336 883-4136
  High Point *(G-6781)*

Sock Factory Inc...............................E 828 328-5207
  Hickory *(G-6451)*

Sock Inc...G 561 254-2223
  Charlotte *(G-2823)*

Socks and Other Things LLC..............G 704 904-2472
  Charlotte *(G-2824)*

Special T Hosiery Mills Inc.................G 336 227-2858
  Burlington *(G-1161)*

Sports Solutions Inc..........................F 336 368-1100
  Pilot Mountain *(G-9674)*

▲ Star America Inc............................C 704 788-4700
  Concord *(G-3448)*

Surratt Hosiery Mill Inc.....................G 336 859-4583
  Denton *(G-3762)*

Teamwork Inc...................................G 336 578-3456
  Elon *(G-4472)*

Thorneburg Hosiery Mills Inc.............E 704 279-7247
  Rockwell *(G-10805)*

Thorneburg Hosiery Mills Inc.............E 704 872-6522
  Statesville *(G-11786)*

Thorneburg Hosiery Mills Inc.............E 704 838-6329
  Statesville *(G-11788)*

◆ Thorneburg Hosiery Mills Inc..........C 704 872-6522
  Statesville *(G-11787)*

Trimfit Inc..C 336 476-6154
  Thomasville *(G-12084)*

Tysinger Hosiery Mill Inc...................F 336 472-2148
  Lexington *(G-7755)*

Upel Inc...G 336 519-8080
  Winston Salem *(G-13379)*

US Custom Socks Co LLC...................G 336 549-1088
  Greensboro *(G-5893)*

◆ Wells Hosiery Mills Inc....................C 336 633-4881
  Asheboro *(G-420)*

▲ Wilson Brown Inc............................F 336 226-0237
  Burlington *(G-1180)*

Woodland Hosiery Inc........................G 910 439-4843
  Mount Gilead *(G-9212)*

2253 Knit outerwear mills

Associated Distributors Inc.................G 910 895-5800
  Hamlet *(G-6050)*

B & J Knits Inc.................................G 704 876-1498
  Statesville *(G-11664)*

Ba International LLC..........................G 336 519-8080
  Winston Salem *(G-13100)*

Belevation LLC..................................F 803 517-9030
  Biscoe *(G-847)*

Blue Bay Distributing Inc...................G 919 957-1300
  Durham *(G-3935)*

Blue Lagoon Inc................................G 828 324-2333
  Hickory *(G-6273)*

C & L Manufacturing.........................G 336 957-8359
  Hays *(G-6145)*

◆ Charlotte Trimming Company Inc......E 704 529-8427
  Charlotte *(G-1905)*

Contempora Fabrics Inc......................C 910 345-0150
  Lumberton *(G-7948)*

◆ Gerbings LLC.................................D 800 646-5916
  Greensboro *(G-5558)*

Hanesbrands Inc...............................G 910 462-2001
  Laurel Hill *(G-7483)*

Hanesbrands Inc...............................A 336 519-8080
  Winston Salem *(G-13188)*

Hbi Wh Minority Holdings LLC............G 336 519-8080
  Winston Salem *(G-13193)*

Hillshire Brands Company..................G 336 519-8080
  Winston Salem *(G-13198)*

Hugger Inc..C 704 735-7422
  Lincolnton *(G-7832)*

Innovaknits LLC.................................G 828 536-9348
  Conover *(G-3533)*

◆ Kamp Usa Inc................................F 336 668-1169
  High Point *(G-6682)*

Knitwear America Inc.........................G 704 396-1193
  Granite Falls *(G-5310)*

◆ L C Industries Inc...........................C 919 596-8277
  Durham *(G-4100)*

Mitt S Nitts Inc.................................E 919 596-6793
  Durham *(G-4139)*

Noble Wholesalers Inc.......................G 409 739-3803
  Clayton *(G-3162)*

▲ Park Shirt Company.........................G 931 879-5894
  Fayetteville *(G-4652)*

Pitman Knits Inc................................G 704 276-3262
  Vale *(G-12210)*

Playtex Dorado LLC...........................G 336 519-8080
  Winston Salem *(G-13297)*

Royal Textile Mills Inc......................D 336 694-4121
  Yanceyville *(G-13460)*

Slum Dog Head Gear LLC...................F 704 713-8125
  Charlotte *(G-2816)*

Textile Piece Dyeing Co Inc................C 704 732-4200
  Lincolnton *(G-7862)*

Upel Inc...G 336 519-8080
  Winston Salem *(G-13379)*

◆ Winstn-Slem Inds For Blind Inc........B 336 759-0551
  Winston Salem *(G-13398)*

▲ Xtinguish LLC.................................G 704 868-9500
  Charlotte *(G-3034)*

2254 Knit underwear mills

Hillshire Brands Company..................G 336 519-8080
  Winston Salem *(G-13198)*

Verena Designs Inc............................E 336 869-8235
  High Point *(G-6825)*

2257 Weft knit fabric mills

◆ Carolina Mills Incorporated...............D 828 428-9911
  Maiden *(G-8010)*

Century Textile Mfg Inc......................F 704 869-6660
  Gastonia *(G-5016)*

Contempora Fabrics Inc......................C 910 345-0150
  Lumberton *(G-7948)*

Early Bird Hosiery Mills Inc................G 828 324-6745
  Hickory *(G-6327)*

Everest Textile Usa LLC......................C 828 245-6755
  Forest City *(G-4789)*

▲ Flagship Brands LLC........................E 888 801-7227
  Newton *(G-9465)*

Heiq Chemtex Inc...............................G 704 795-9322
  Concord *(G-3373)*

Heritage Knitting Co LLC....................E 704 872-7653
  Statesville *(G-11709)*

◆ Innofa Usa LLC...............................E 336 635-2900
  Eden *(G-4348)*

Innovaknits LLC.................................G 828 536-9348
  Conover *(G-3533)*

Innovative Knitting LLC......................E 336 350-8122
  Burlington *(G-1110)*

Knit-Wear Fabrics Inc.........................E 336 226-4342
  Burlington *(G-1115)*

Luray Textiles Inc..............................F 336 670-3725
  North Wilkesboro *(G-9544)*

◆ McMurray Fabrics Inc......................C 910 944-2128
  Aberdeen *(G-12)*

Mocaro Dyeing & Finishing Inc............D 704 878-6645
  Statesville *(G-11732)*

Mocaro Industries Inc.........................G 704 878-6645
  Statesville *(G-11733)*

▲ Ramseur Inter-Lock Knitting Co........ G 336 824-2427
  Asheboro *(G-388)*

Russ Knits Inc...................................F 910 974-4114
  Candor *(G-1241)*

Sdfc LLC...F 704 878-6645
  Monroe *(G-8556)*

South Fork Industries Inc....................D 828 428-9921
  Maiden *(G-8017)*

Tommys Tubing & Stockenettes............F 336 449-6461
  Gibsonville *(G-5185)*

Toms Knit Fabrics..............................G 704 867-4236
  Gastonia *(G-5155)*

Unifour Finishers Inc..........................E 828 322-9435
  Hickory *(G-6478)*

Unifour Finishers Inc.................... E 828 322-9435
Hickory (G-6477)

2258 Lace and warp knit fabric mills

◆ Gildan Activewear (eden) Inc..........C 336 623-9555
Eden (G-4347)

◆ Guilford Mills LLC............................A 910 794-5810
Wilmington (G-12798)

Hornwood Inc................................. E 704 694-3009
Wadesboro (G-12244)

◆ Hornwood Inc...............................B 704 848-4121
Lilesville (G-7786)

Innovaknits LLC............................. G 828 536-9348
Conover (G-3533)

Knit-Wear Fabrics Inc.................... 336 226-4342
Burlington (G-1115)

Lear Corporation............................ E 910 296-8671
Kenansville (G-7226)

Lear Corporation............................ A 910 794-5810
Wilmington (G-12831)

▼ McComb Industries Lllp................ D 336 229-9139
Burlington (G-1126)

▼ Mohican Mills Inc......................... B 704 735-3343
Lincolnton (G-7844)

Shodja Textiles Inc....................... G 910 914-0456
Whiteville (G-12593)

▲ Supertex Inc................................. E 336 622-1000
Liberty (G-7781)

▲ Uwharrie Knits Inc....................... F 704 474-4123
Norwood (G-9563)

Warp Technologies Inc.................. C 919 552-2311
Holly Springs (G-6920)

Whiteville Fabrics LLC................... F 910 639-4444
Whiteville (G-12597)

▲ Whiteville Fabrics LLC................. F 910 914-0456
Whiteville (G-12596)

2259 Knitting mills, nec

Adele Knits Inc............................... C 336 499-6010
Winston Salem (G-13072)

Brookline Inc................................. G 704 824-1390
Cramerton (G-3634)

Compton Tape & Label Inc............ F 336 548-4400
Madison (G-7984)

Coville Inc..................................... F 336 759-0115
Winston Salem (G-13133)

◆ Fisher Textiles Inc........................E 800 554-8886
Matthews (G-8170)

▲ Gloves-Online Inc......................... G 919 468-4244
Cary (G-1367)

Griffin Tubing Company Inc........... G 336 449-4822
Gibsonville (G-5176)

Mitt S Nitts Inc.............................. E 919 596-6793
Durham (G-4139)

▲ Paceline Inc.................................. D 704 290-5007
Matthews (G-8140)

Shelby Elastics of North Carolina LLC..D 704 487-4301
Shelby (G-11376)

Tommys Tubing & Stockenettes........... F 336 449-6461
Gibsonville (G-5185)

◆ United Glove Inc............................E 828 464-2510
Newton (G-9508)

2261 Finishing plants, cotton

▲ Advanced Digital Textiles LLC.......... E 704 226-9600
Monroe (G-8417)

Barron Legacy Mgmt Group LLC........ G 301 367-4735
Charlotte (G-1757)

Bread & Butter Custom Scrn Prt.......... G 919 942-3198
Chapel Hill (G-1531)

◆ Burlington Industries LLC..................C 336 379-6220
Greensboro (G-5414)

Century Textile Mfg Inc.................. F 704 869-6660
Gastonia (G-5016)

▲ Daztech Inc.................................. G 800 862-6360
Wilmington (G-12761)

▲ Deep Rver Mlls Ctd Fabrics Inc......... F 910 464-3135
Greensboro (G-5492)

Gaston Screen Printing Inc............ G 704 399-0459
Charlotte (G-2191)

◆ Glen Raven Inc..............................C 336 227-6211
Burlington (G-1098)

Glen Rven Tchnical Fabrics LLC......... C 336 229-5576
Burlington (G-1100)

▼ Graphic Attack Inc........................ G 252 491-2174
Harbinger (G-6095)

◆ Hanes Companies Inc.....................C 336 747-1600
Winston Salem (G-13186)

▲ Hanes Companies - NJ LLC............ E 828 464-4673
Conover (G-3526)

◆ Holt Sublimation Printing...............G 336 222-3600
Burlington (G-1104)

▲ Huffman Finishing Company Inc........ C 828 396-1741
Granite Falls (G-5308)

◆ Hydromer Inc.................................. E 908 526-2828
Concord (G-3374)

◆ Itg Holdings Inc..............................A 336 379-6220
Greensboro (G-5628)

K Formula Enterprises Inc.............. G 910 323-3315
Fayetteville (G-4626)

Marvin Bailey Screen Printing......... G 252 335-1554
Elizabeth City (G-4397)

McMurray Fabrics Inc.................... D 704 732-9613
Lincolnton (G-7843)

Moire Creations America LLC......... E 704 482-9860
Shelby (G-11364)

Mojo Sportswear Inc...................... G 252 758-4176
Greenville (G-6006)

One Hundred Ten Percent Screen........ G 252 728-3848
Beaufort (G-732)

Raleigh Tees LLC........................... G 919 850-3378
Raleigh (G-10430)

Richard E Page............................... G 704 988-7090
Charlotte (G-2726)

S & L Creations Inc....................... G 704 824-1930
Lowell (G-7934)

Screen Master Inc.......................... G 252 492-8407
Henderson (G-6178)

Silverlining Screen Prtrs Inc........... G 919 554-0340
Youngsville (G-13485)

South Fork Industries Inc............... D 828 428-9921
Maiden (G-8017)

T & R Signs.................................... G 919 779-1185
Garner (G-4967)

Tex-Tech Coatings LLC.................. F 336 992-7500
Kernersville (G-7306)

Thermal Control Products Inc......... E 704 454-7605
Concord (G-3457)

Travis L Bunker............................. G 336 352-3289
Mount Airy (G-9187)

Trelleborg Ctd Systems US Inc........ G 864 576-1210
Rutherfordton (G-10997)

Tryon Finishing Corporation........... G 828 859-5891
Tryon (G-12178)

Tsg Finishing LLC.......................... E 828 328-5522
Hickory (G-6473)

Tsg Finishing LLC.......................... D 828 328-5535
Hickory (G-6474)

▲ Ultimate Textile Inc...................... E 828 286-8880
Rutherfordton (G-11000)

Unifour Finishers Inc...................... E 828 322-9435
Hickory (G-6478)

Unifour Finishers Inc...................... E 828 322-9435
Hickory (G-6477)

▲ Xtinguish LLC................................ G 704 868-9500
Charlotte (G-3034)

2262 Finishing plants, manmade

▲ Advanced Digital Textiles LLC.......... E 704 226-9600
Monroe (G-8417)

◆ Burlington Industries LLC.................C 336 379-6220
Greensboro (G-5414)

Cedar Valley Finishing Co Inc............ F 704 289-9546
Monroe (G-8456)

◆ Commercial Seaming Co Inc..............G 252 492-6178
Henderson (G-6151)

Custom Screens Inc....................... G 336 427-0265
Madison (G-7985)

Everest Textile Usa LLC................. C 828 245-6755
Forest City (G-4789)

Gaston Screen Printing Inc............ G 704 399-0459
Charlotte (G-2191)

◆ Hanes Companies Inc.....................C 336 747-1600
Winston Salem (G-13186)

◆ Holt Sublimation Printing...............G 336 222-3600
Burlington (G-1104)

▲ Huffman Finishing Company Inc........ C 828 396-1741
Granite Falls (G-5308)

◆ Itg Holdings Inc..............................A 336 379-6220
Greensboro (G-5628)

McMurray Fabrics Inc.................... D 704 732-9613
Lincolnton (G-7843)

Moire Creations America LLC......... E 704 482-9860
Shelby (G-11364)

◆ Precision Fabrics Group Inc...........E 336 281-3049
Greensboro (G-5757)

Printology Signs Graphics LLC........ G 843 473-4984
Davidson (G-3716)

▲ Spoonflower Inc............................ D 919 886-7885
Durham (G-4248)

Upper South Studio Inc.................. F 336 724-5480
Winston Salem (G-13380)

Visigraphix Inc............................... G 336 882-1935
Colfax (G-3292)

2269 Finishing plants, nec

▲ Advanced Digital Textiles LLC.......... E 704 226-9600
Monroe (G-8417)

Bridgport Restoration Svcs Inc........ G 336 996-1212
Kernersville (G-7248)

Carolina Dyeing and Finshg LLC........ E 336 227-2770
Burlington (G-1061)

Carolina Yarn Processors Inc......... C 828 859-5891
Tryon (G-12172)

Celand Yarn Dyers Inc................... G 336 472-4400
Thomasville (G-12007)

D & F Consolidated Inc.................. G 704 664-6660
Statesville (G-11683)

Dale Advertising Inc...................... G 704 484-0971
Shelby (G-11329)

Glen Rven Tchnical Fabrics LLC......... C 336 229-5576
Burlington (G-1100)

▲ Grover Industries Inc..................... F 828 859-9125
Grover (G-6044)

▲ Insect Shield LLC.......................... E 336 272-4157
Greensboro (G-5620)

Minnewawa Inc.............................. F 865 522-8103
Thomasville (G-12050)

Mocaro Industries Inc.................... G 704 878-6645
Statesville (G-11733)

Moire Creations America LLC......... E 704 482-9860
Shelby (G-11364)

South Fork Industries Inc............... D 828 428-9921
Maiden (G-8017)

▲ Spartan Dyers Inc.......................... D 704 829-0467
Belmont (G-767)

Tsg Finishing LLC.................................D 828 328-5535
Hickory (G-6474)

▲ Ultimate Textile Inc........................ E 828 286-8880
Rutherfordton (G-11000)

Unifi Inc..D 336 348-6539
Reidsville (G-10700)

US Label Corporation........................ G 336 332-7000
Greensboro (G-5894)

Westpoint Home Inc.......................... F 910 369-2231
Wagram (G-12257)

2273 Carpets and rugs

Aladdin Manufacturing Corp.................. A 336 623-6000
Eden (G-4340)

▲ Bellaire Dynamik LLC...................... G 704 779-3755
Charlotte (G-1770)

◆ Burlington Industries LLC................C 336 379-6220
Greensboro (G-5414)

◆ Capel Incorporated........................D 910 572-7000
Troy (G-12158)

Columbia Forest Products Inc.............. G 336 605-0429
Greensboro (G-5454)

Country Heart Braiding........................ G 828 245-0562
Rutherfordton (G-10981)

▲ Davis Rug Company........................ G 704 434-7231
Shelby (G-11330)

▲ Due Process Stable Trdg Co LLC...... E 910 608-0284
Lumberton (G-7949)

◆ Elevate Textiles Inc........................F 336 379-6220
Charlotte (G-2098)

Elevate Textiles Holding Corp.............. D 336 379-6220
Charlotte (G-2099)

Flint Hill Textiles Inc........................ G 704 434-9331
Shelby (G-11337)

Furniture Fair Inc.............................. E 910 455-4044
Jacksonville (G-7124)

▲ Hampton Capital Partners LLC.......... A
Aberdeen (G-6)

Horizon Home Imports Inc.................. G 704 859-5133
Clemmons (G-3190)

◆ Itg Holdings Inc..............................A 336 379-6220
Greensboro (G-5628)

Karastan.. G 336 627-7200
Eden (G-4349)

▲ Michaelian & Kohlberg Inc............... G 828 891-8511
Horse Shoe (G-6930)

Mohawk Industries Inc...................... F 919 661-5590
Garner (G-4944)

Mohawk Industries Inc...................... G 919 609-4759
Garner (G-4945)

Pasb Inc.. G 704 490-2556
Kannapolis (G-7218)

Royal Textile Mills Inc...................... D 336 694-4121
Yanceyville (G-13460)

Rug & Home Inc.................................. E 828 785-4480
Asheville (G-594)

Shaw Industries Inc.......................... B 828 369-1701
Franklin (G-4839)

Shaw Industries Group Inc................ G 877 996-5942
Charlotte (G-2795)

Shaw Industries Group Inc................ E 877 996-5942
Charlotte (G-2796)

Sorrells Sheree White........................ G 828 452-4864
Waynesville (G-12475)

▲ White Oak Carpet Mills Inc.............. G 828 287-8892
Spindale (G-11551)

2281 Yarn spinning mills

American & Efird LLC........................ F 704 864-0977
Gastonia (G-4990)

American & Efird LLC........................ F 828 754-9066
Lenoir (G-7571)

◆ Aquafil OMara Inc............................C 828 874-2100
Rutherford College (G-10970)

◆ Carolina Mills Incorporated.................D 828 428-9911
Maiden (G-8010)

◆ Charles Craft Inc.............................. G 910 844-3521
Laurinburg (G-7497)

◆ Coats & Clark Inc.............................D 888 368-8401
Charlotte (G-1942)

◆ Coats HP Inc.................................... B 704 824-9904
Mc Adenville (G-8213)

Coats HP Inc...................................... E 704 329-5800
Charlotte (G-1944)

Coats N Amer De Rpblica Dmncan.... C 800 242-8095
Charlotte (G-1945)

◆ Cs Carolina Inc................................G 336 578-0110
Burlington (G-1078)

Cumins Machinery Corp...................... G 336 622-1000
Liberty (G-7762)

Fiber-Line LLC.................................... D 828 326-8700
Hickory (G-6333)

▲ Filtec Precise Inc............................ E 910 653-5200
Tabor City (G-11911)

Frontier Yarns Inc.............................. D 919 776-9940
Sanford (G-11182)

Frontier Yarns Inc.............................. D 919 776-9940
Sanford (G-11181)

◆ Fsm Liquidation Corp.......................A 919 776-9940
Sanford (G-11183)

◆ Glen Raven Inc................................C 336 227-6211
Burlington (G-1079)

Glen Rven Tchnical Fabrics LLC........ C 336 229-5576
Burlington (G-1100)

Grateful Union Family Inc.................. F 828 622-3258
Asheville (G-510)

Grp Inc.. G 919 776-9940
Sanford (G-11187)

▲ Hampton Art Inc.............................. C 252 975-7207
Washington (G-12391)

▲ Hickory Dyg & Winding Co Inc.......... F 828 322-1550
Hickory (G-6350)

◆ Hickory Throwing Company..............E 828 322-1158
Hickory (G-6359)

Invista Capital Management LLC........... C 704 636-6000
Salisbury (G-11071)

Kordsa.. C 910 462-2051
Laurel Hill (G-7485)

Krodsa USA Inc.................................. G 910 462-2041
Laurel Hill (G-7486)

Mannington Mills Inc.......................... D 704 824-3551
Mc Adenville (G-8214)

Marilyn Cook...................................... G 704 735-4414
Lincolnton (G-7842)

Meridian Industries Inc...................... E 704 824-7880
Gastonia (G-5093)

Milliken & Company............................ F 828 247-4300
Bostic (G-963)

Milliken & Company............................ F 336 548-5680
Mayodan (G-8208)

National Spinning Co Inc.................... C 910 298-3131
Beulaville (G-844)

National Spinning Co Inc.................... C 336 226-0141
Burlington (G-1135)

National Spinning Co Inc.................... C 910 642-4181
Whiteville (G-12589)

◆ National Spinning Co Inc..................C 252 975-7111
Washington (G-12398)

▲ National Spnning Oprations LLC...... G 252 975-7111
Washington (G-12399)

◆ Normtex Incorporated......................G 828 428-3363
Wilmington (G-12863)

▲ North Crlina Spnning Mills Inc........ E 704 732-1171
Lincolnton (G-7847)

Oakdale Cotton Mills.......................... G 336 454-1144
Jamestown (G-7174)

◆ Parkdale Incorporated......................D 704 874-5000
Gastonia (G-5116)

Parkdale Mills Incorporated................ E 704 825-5324
Belmont (G-758)

Parkdale Mills Incorporated................ D 704 913-3917
Belmont (G-759)

Parkdale Mills Incorporated................ F 704 825-2529
Belmont (G-760)

Parkdale Mills Incorporated................ E 704 739-7411
Kings Mountain (G-7375)

Parkdale Mills Incorporated................ E 704 855-3164
Landis (G-7475)

Parkdale Mills Incorporated................ E 336 243-2141
Lexington (G-7729)

Parkdale Mills Incorporated................ E 704 292-1255
Mineral Springs (G-8328)

Parkdale Mills Incorporated................ E 704 822-0778
Mount Holly (G-9241)

Parkdale Mills Incorporated................ C 336 476-3181
Thomasville (G-12058)

Parkdale Mills Incorporated................ C 336 591-4644
Walnut Cove (G-12330)

◆ Parkdale Mills Incorporated..............D 704 874-5000
Gastonia (G-5117)

Parkdale Mills Inc.............................. E 704 857-3456
Landis (G-7476)

▲ Patrick Yarn Mill Inc........................ C 704 739-4119
Kings Mountain (G-7377)

Pearson Textiles Inc.......................... C 919 776-8730
Sanford (G-11216)

Pharr McAdenville Corporation.......... D 704 824-3551
Mc Adenville (G-8215)

▲ Richmond Specialty Yarns LLC........ C 910 652-5554
Ellerbe (G-4462)

Rocky Mount Mill LLC........................ G 919 890-6000
Raleigh (G-10447)

Sgrtex LLC.. G 336 635-9420
Eden (G-4356)

Shuford Yarns LLC............................ C 828 396-2342
Granite Falls (G-5323)

▲ Shuford Yarns LLC.......................... D 828 324-4265
Hickory (G-6443)

Shuford Yarns Management Inc.......... G 828 324-4265
Hickory (G-6444)

Spinrite Yarns LP.............................. G 252 833-4970
Washington (G-12414)

Summit Yarn LLC.............................. G 704 874-5000
Gastonia (G-5146)

◆ Supreme Elastic Corporation..............E 828 302-3836
Conover (G-3563)

◆ Tuscarora Yarns Inc........................B 704 436-6527
Mount Pleasant (G-9266)

Unifi Inc.. C 336 427-1890
Madison (G-8002)

Unifi Inc.. D 336 348-6539
Reidsville (G-10700)

Unifi Inc.. G 919 774-7401
Sanford (G-11247)

Unifi Inc.. C 336 679-3830
Yadkinville (G-13454)

◆ Unifi Inc..D 336 294-4410
Greensboro (G-5887)

Unifi Manufacturing Inc...................... A 336 427-1515
Yadkinville (G-13455)

Unifi Manufacturing Inc...................... A 336 679-8891
Yadkinville (G-13456)

◆ Unifi Manufacturing Inc..................C 336 294-4410
Greensboro (G-5888)

Universal Fibers Inc.......................... C 336 672-2600
Asheboro (G-415)

▲ World Elastic Corporation............... E 704 786-9508
Concord *(G-3469)*

◆ Zimmermann - Dynayarn Usa LLC..... E 336 222-8129
Graham *(G-5290)*

2282 Throwing and winding mills

◆ Aquafil OMara Inc..........................C 828 874-2100
Rutherford College *(G-10970)*

BA Robbins Company LLC.................G 828 466-3900
Newton *(G-9450)*

◆ C S America Inc.............................D 336 578-0110
Burlington *(G-1058)*

▲ Coats HP Inc................................ B 704 824-9904
Mc Adenville *(G-8213)*

Coats HP Inc.................................E 704 329-5800
Charlotte *(G-1944)*

Glen Raven Inc.............................. F 336 227-6211
Altamahaw *(G-103)*

▲ Hickory Dyg & Winding Co Inc......... F 828 322-1550
Hickory *(G-6350)*

◆ Hickory Throwing Company.............E 828 322-1158
Hickory *(G-6359)*

◆ J Charles Saunders Co Inc.............E 704 866-9156
Gastonia *(G-5070)*

Keel Labs Inc................................ G 917 848-9066
Morrisville *(G-8997)*

Lear Corporation........................... E 910 296-8671
Kenansville *(G-7226)*

Marilyn Cook.................................G 704 735-4414
Lincolnton *(G-7842)*

Material Return LLC........................G 828 234-5368
Morganton *(G-8880)*

◆ Meridian Spcalty Yrn Group Inc.......D 828 874-2151
Valdese *(G-12197)*

National Spinning Co Inc..................C 910 298-3131
Beulaville *(G-844)*

New Generation Yarn Corp.............. G 336 449-5607
Gibsonville *(G-5183)*

▲ Owens Crning Nn-Woven Tech LLC.. G 740 321-6131
Dallas *(G-3681)*

Parkdale Mills Incorporated............. F 704 825-2529
Belmont *(G-760)*

Pharr McAdenville Corporation.......... D 704 824-3551
Mc Adenville *(G-8215)*

◆ Premiere Fibers LLC......................C 704 826-8321
Ansonville *(G-131)*

Sack-UPS Corporation.................... F 828 584-4579
Morganton *(G-8893)*

Sam M Butler Inc........................... E 704 364-8647
Charlotte *(G-2753)*

Sam M Butler Inc........................... E 910 276-2360
Laurinburg *(G-7513)*

Sapona Manufacturing Co Inc............C 336 873-8700
Asheboro *(G-392)*

◆ Sapona Manufacturing Co Inc..........E 336 625-2727
Cedar Falls *(G-1515)*

Unifi Inc.......................................C 336 679-3830
Yadkinville *(G-13454)*

◆ Unifi Inc......................................G 336 294-4410
Greensboro *(G-5887)*

2284 Thread mills

American & Efird Global LLC............. E 704 827-4311
Mount Holly *(G-9213)*

American & Efird LLC...................... F 704 867-3664
Gastonia *(G-4989)*

American & Efird LLC...................... F 704 864-0977
Gastonia *(G-4990)*

American & Efird LLC...................... F 828 754-9066
Lenoir *(G-7571)*

American & Efird LLC...................... F 704 827-4311
Mount Holly *(G-9214)*

American & Efird LLC...................... F 704 823-2501
Mount Holly *(G-9216)*

◆ American & Efird LLC....................C 704 827-4311
Mount Holly *(G-9215)*

◆ Coats & Clark Inc..........................D 888 368-8401
Charlotte *(G-1942)*

◆ Coats American Inc....................... C 800 242-8095
Charlotte *(G-1943)*

◆ Coats N Amer De Rpblica Dmncan....C 800 242-8095
Charlotte *(G-1945)*

Ctc Holdings LLC........................... C 704 867-6611
Gastonia *(G-5034)*

Invista Capital Management LLC........ C 704 636-6000
Salisbury *(G-11071)*

◆ J Charles Saunders Co Inc.............E 704 866-9156
Gastonia *(G-5070)*

Ruddick Operating Company LLC....... A 704 372-5404
Charlotte *(G-2742)*

Sam M Butler Inc........................... E 704 364-8647
Charlotte *(G-2753)*

◆ Sam M Butler Inc..........................E 910 277-7456
Laurinburg *(G-7514)*

◆ Sans Technical Fibers LLC..............F 704 869-8311
Gastonia *(G-5134)*

◆ Supreme Elastic Corporation...........E 828 302-3836
Conover *(G-3563)*

Tangles Knitting On Main LLC........... G 704 243-7150
Waxhaw *(G-12443)*

2295 Coated fabrics, not rubberized

▲ Athol Manufacturing Corp.............. G 919 575-6523
Butner *(G-1197)*

◆ Carlisle Corporation......................A 704 501-1100
Charlotte *(G-1842)*

Chase Laminating Inc...................... G 828 632-6666
Taylorsville *(G-11953)*

CMI Enterprises............................. G 305 685-9651
Forest City *(G-4786)*

◆ Compmillennia LLC.......................G 252 628-8065
Washington *(G-12383)*

▲ Engineered Recycling Comp........... E 704 358-6700
Charlotte *(G-2114)*

Fiber-Line LLC...............................D 828 326-8700
Hickory *(G-6333)*

Fs LLC.. E 919 309-9727
Durham *(G-4039)*

▲ Morbern USA Inc.......................... E 336 883-4332
High Point *(G-6715)*

Nouveau Verre Holdings Inc............. F 336 545-0011
Greensboro *(G-5714)*

Nvh Inc....................................... G 336 545-0011
Greensboro *(G-5717)*

Omnia LLC................................... G 919 696-2193
Oxford *(G-9621)*

▲ Parker Medical Associates LLC........ F 704 344-9998
Charlotte *(G-2610)*

Precision Textiles LLC..................... C 336 861-0168
High Point *(G-6742)*

Precision Textiles LLC..................... G 910 515-6696
Troy *(G-12164)*

◆ Sam M Butler Inc..........................E 910 277-7456
Laurinburg *(G-7514)*

Shawmut Corporation..................... F 336 229-5576
Burlington *(G-1155)*

Taylor Interiors LLC....................... F 980 207-3160
Charlotte *(G-2901)*

Tosaf Aw Inc................................ D 980 533-3000
Bessemer City *(G-838)*

Trelleborg Ctd Systems US Inc.......... D 828 286-9126
Rutherfordton *(G-10998)*

▲ Trelleborg Ctd Systems US Inc......... E 828 286-9126
Rutherfordton *(G-10999)*

◆ Uretek LLC..................................G 203 468-0342
Rutherfordton *(G-11001)*

▲ Vescom America Inc...................... E 252 431-6200
Henderson *(G-6182)*

2296 Tire cord and fabrics

◆ Burlan Manufacturing LLC...............C 704 867-3548
Gastonia *(G-5007)*

Hs Hyosung Usa Inc....................... C 336 495-2202
Asheboro *(G-362)*

◆ Hs Hyosung Usa Inc......................E 704 790-6100
Charlotte *(G-2292)*

▲ Hs Hyosung USA Holdings Inc......... G 704 790-6134
Charlotte *(G-2293)*

Parker-Hannifin Corporation............. F 252 237-6171
Wilson *(G-13012)*

Tex-Tech Coatings LLC....................D 336 992-7500
Kernersville *(G-7305)*

Tex-Tech Coatings LLC.................... F 336 992-7500
Kernersville *(G-7306)*

2297 Nonwoven fabrics

Advantage Nn-Wvens Cnvrting LL..... G 828 635-1880
Taylorsville *(G-11948)*

Allyn International Trdg Corp............. G 877 858-2482
Marshville *(G-8085)*

◆ Avgol America Inc.........................C 336 936-2500
Mocksville *(G-8350)*

◆ Avintiv Inc..................................E 704 697-5100
Charlotte *(G-1724)*

Avintiv Specialty Mtls Inc................. C 704 660-6242
Mooresville *(G-8604)*

◆ Avintiv Specialty Mtls Inc...............A 704 697-5100
Charlotte *(G-1725)*

Berry Global Inc............................ A 704 697-5100
Charlotte *(G-1773)*

▲ Carolina Nonwovens LLC............... F 704 735-5600
Maiden *(G-8011)*

Chicopee Inc................................ G 919 894-4111
Benson *(G-786)*

◆ Chicopee Inc...............................E 704 697-5100
Charlotte *(G-1914)*

Cumulus Fibres Inc........................ B 704 394-2111
Charlotte *(G-2004)*

Dalco GF Technologies LLC..............D 828 459-2577
Conover *(G-3512)*

▲ Dalco Gft Nonwovens LLC..............D 828 459-2577
Conover *(G-3513)*

Fibrix LLC.................................... E 704 394-2111
Charlotte *(G-2150)*

Fibrix LLC.................................... E 704 872-5223
Statesville *(G-11696)*

Fibrix LLC.................................... E 704 878-0027
Statesville *(G-11697)*

▲ Freudenberg Nonwovens Lim........... A 919 620-3900
Durham *(G-4036)*

Freudenberg Prfmce Mtls LP.............C 828 665-5000
Candler *(G-1225)*

◆ Freudenberg Prfmce Mtls LP...........E 919 479-7443
Durham *(G-4037)*

▲ Glatfelter Inds Asheville Inc............. D 828 670-0041
Candler *(G-1226)*

Glatflter Sntara Old Hckry Inc............ F 615 526-2100
Charlotte *(G-2213)*

◆ Hanes Companies Inc....................C 336 747-1600
Winston Salem *(G-13186)*

▲ Hendrix Batting Company................ C 336 431-1181
High Point *(G-6644)*

Kem-Wove Inc.............................. E 704 588-0080
Charlotte *(G-2392)*

Lydall Inc.................................... G 336 468-8522
Hamptonville *(G-6087)*

Lydall Inc..G 336 468-1323
Yadkinville (G-13446)

Mitt S Nitts Inc.....................................E 919 596-6793
Durham (G-4139)

Mountain International LLC.................E 828 606-0194
Brevard (G-978)

◆ Nutex Concepts NC Corp..................E 828 726-8801
Lenoir (G-7631)

◆ Pgi Polymer Inc................................A 704 697-5100
Charlotte (G-2633)

▲ Polyvlies Usa Inc..............................E 336 769-0206
Winston Salem (G-13299)

◆ Saertex Usa LLC...............................C 704 464-5998
Huntersville (G-7050)

◆ Scorpio Acquisition Corp..................G 704 697-5100
Charlotte (G-2770)

▲ Shalag US Inc....................................D
Oxford (G-9634)

◆ Tenowo Inc..F 704 732-3525
Lincolnton (G-7860)

◆ Twe Nonwovens Us Inc......................E 336 431-7187
High Point (G-6815)

▲ Vitaflex LLC.......................................F 888 616-8848
Burlington (G-1175)

Warm Products Inc...............................F 425 248-2424
Hendersonville (G-6249)

Westpoint Home Inc.............................F 910 369-2231
Wagram (G-12257)

▲ Yanjan USA LLC.................................C 704 380-6230
Statesville (G-11803)

2298 Cordage and twine

◆ Ace Marine Rigging & Supply Inc......F 252 726-6620
Morehead City (G-8811)

All American Braids Inc.......................E 704 852-4380
Gastonia (G-4985)

Dayton Bag & Burlap Co......................G 704 873-7271
Statesville (G-11685)

Energy Management Insulation............F 828 894-3635
Columbus (G-3301)

Genevieve M Brownlee..........................G 336 226-5260
Burlington (G-1095)

◆ Hatteras Hammocks Inc......................C 252 758-0641
Greenville (G-5987)

Jhrg Manufacturing LLC......................G 252 478-4977
Spring Hope (G-11556)

Ls Cable & System USA Inc.................C 252 824-3553
Tarboro (G-11932)

MHS Ltd..G 336 767-2641
Winston Salem (G-13250)

MHS Ltd..F 336 767-2641
Winston Salem (G-13251)

Mills Manufacturing Corp....................C 828 645-3061
Asheville (G-548)

Moon Audio...G 919 649-5018
Cary (G-1402)

Oakdale Cotton Mills............................G 336 454-1144
Jamestown (G-7174)

▲ Rocky Mount Cord Company..............D 252 977-9130
Rocky Mount (G-10867)

Standard Tytape Company Inc.............G 828 693-6594
Hendersonville (G-6244)

Wound-About Inc...................................G 336 368-5001
Pilot Mountain (G-9676)

▲ Yale Rope Technologies Inc................G 704 630-0331
Salisbury (G-11137)

2299 Textile goods, nec

▲ A Land of Furniture Inc......................G 336 882-3866
High Point (G-6507)

▲ Atex Technologies Inc.........................C 910 255-2839
Pinebluff (G-9684)

▲ Azusa International Inc......................G 704 879-4464
Gastonia (G-4996)

◆ Barnhardt Manufacturing Company....C 800 277-0377
Charlotte (G-1755)

Brandspeed...G 410 204-1032
Mooresville (G-8619)

◆ Burke Mills Inc..................................G 828 874-6341
Valdese (G-12189)

Carbon Market Exchange LLC.............G 828 545-0140
Asheville (G-467)

Creative Textiles Inc............................G 919 693-4427
Oxford (G-9609)

Cumulus Fibres Inc..............................B 704 394-2111
Charlotte (G-2004)

Custom Gears Inc.................................G 704 735-6883
Lincolnton (G-7827)

D2 Government Solutions LLC..............E 662 655-4554
New Bern (G-9362)

Dayton Bag & Burlap Co......................G 704 873-7271
Statesville (G-11685)

E By Design LLC..................................G 980 231-5483
Cornelius (G-3598)

Fibrix LLC...E 704 394-2111
Charlotte (G-2150)

Fibrix LLC...E 704 878-0027
Statesville (G-11697)

Fimia Inc..G 828 697-8447
Hendersonville (G-6205)

◆ Firestone Fibers Textiles LLC...........A 704 734-2110
Kings Mountain (G-7364)

Global Products & Mfg Svcs Inc..........G 360 870-9876
Charlotte (G-2215)

◆ Global Textile Alliance Inc................G 336 347-7601
Reidsville (G-10685)

◆ Hendrix Batting Company...................C 336 431-1181
High Point (G-6644)

◆ Hickory Business Furniture LLC........B 828 328-2064
Hickory (G-6348)

▼ High Point Fibers Inc.........................E 336 887-8771
High Point (G-6652)

▼ J E Herndon Company........................E 704 739-4711
Kings Mountain (G-7366)

Kem-Wove Inc.......................................E 704 588-0080
Charlotte (G-2392)

Kemmler Products Inc..........................G 704 663-5678
Mooresville (G-8702)

Kids Playhouse LLC..............................G 704 299-4449
Charlotte (G-2395)

Kloud Hemp Co.....................................G 336 740-2528
Greensboro (G-5651)

Leighdeux LLC......................................G 704 965-4889
Charlotte (G-2418)

Northeast Textiles.................................G 704 799-2235
Mooresville (G-8737)

▲ Oakhurst Textiles Inc.........................E 336 668-0733
Greensboro (G-5718)

Opulence of Southern Pine...................G 919 467-1781
Raleigh (G-10348)

Performance Goods LLC.......................G 704 361-8600
Charlotte (G-2628)

▲ Polyvlies Usa Inc..............................E 336 769-0206
Winston Salem (G-13299)

Prime Syntex LLC.................................E 828 324-5496
Thomasville (G-12062)

Regency Fibers LLC..............................E 828 459-7645
Claremont (G-3119)

Renaissance Fiber LLC.........................G 860 857-5987
Winston Salem (G-13317)

S & S Samples Inc................................G 336 472-0402
Thomasville (G-12068)

Saluda Yarn Co Inc...............................F 828 749-2861
Saluda (G-11140)

▲ Sample Group Inc..............................B 828 658-9040
Weaverville (G-12503)

◆ Skeen Textiles Inc.............................F 336 884-4044
High Point (G-6779)

Skeen Txtiles Auto Fabrics Inc.............G 336 884-4044
High Point (G-6780)

South Point Hospitality Inc...................F 704 542-2304
Charlotte (G-2830)

Specialty Textiles Inc...........................G 704 710-8657
Kings Mountain (G-7386)

Specialty Textiles Inc...........................C 704 739-4503
Kings Mountain (G-7387)

▲ Spt Technology Inc............................F 612 332-1880
Monroe (G-8561)

◆ Spuntech Industries Inc.....................C 336 330-9000
Roxboro (G-10946)

▲ Sunrise Development LLC...................F 828 453-0590
Mooresboro (G-8586)

Svcm..G 305 767-3595
Lincolnton (G-7858)

▲ Tex-Tech Industries Inc......................C 207 756-8606
Kernersville (G-7307)

◆ Vmod Fiber LLC.................................F 704 525-6851
Charlotte (G-2988)

William Barnet & Son LLC....................C 252 522-2418
Kinston (G-7437)

▲ World Fibers Inc.................................G 704 786-9508
Concord (G-3470)

Zonkd LLC...E 919 977-6463
Raleigh (G-10624)

23 APPAREL, FINISHED PRODUCTS FROM FABRICS & SIMILAR MATERIALS

2311 Men's and boy's suits and coats

▼ American Safety Utility Corp.............E 704 482-0601
Shelby (G-11311)

Centric Brands LLC..............................B 646 582-6000
Greensboro (G-5438)

Greene Mountain Outdoors LLC...........F 336 670-2186
North Wilkesboro (G-9532)

Hawk Distributors Inc...........................G 888 334-1307
Sanford (G-11188)

Lelantos Group Inc...............................D 704 780-4127
Mooresville (G-8709)

McDaniel Delmar..................................E 336 284-6377
Mocksville (G-8375)

▲ Military Products Inc..........................G 910 637-0315
West End (G-12557)

Safety & Security Intl Inc......................G 336 285-8673
Greensboro (G-5800)

Salute Industries Inc............................G 844 937-2588
Archdale (G-242)

Tresmc LLC...G 919 900-0868
Knightdale (G-7461)

Trotters Sewing Company Inc...............D 336 629-4550
Asheboro (G-413)

US Patriot LLC......................................F 803 787-9398
Fort Bragg (G-4805)

2321 Men's and boy's furnishings

◆ Century Place II LLC..........................E 704 790-0970
Charlotte (G-1888)

Devil Dog Manufacturing Co Inc...........C 919 269-7485
Zebulon (G-13507)

Funco Inc..G 704 788-3003
Concord (G-3367)

▼ Granite Knitwear Inc..........................E 704 279-5526
Granite Quarry (G-5326)

◆ JD Apparel Inc..................................E 704 289-5600
  Monroe (G-8510)

Royal Textile Mills Inc........................D 336 694-4121
  Yanceyville (G-13460)

Wrangler Apparel Corp........................B 336 332-3400
  Greensboro (G-5925)

2322 Men's and boy's underwear and nightwear

▼ Carolina Apparel Group Inc.............D 704 694-6544
  Wadesboro (G-12239)

◆ Carolina Underwear Company..........E 336 472-7788
  Thomasville (G-12006)

Hanesbrands Inc.................................A 336 519-8080
  Winston Salem (G-13188)

Longworth Industries Inc.....................E 910 673-5290
  Aberdeen (G-11)

Longworth Industries Inc.....................E 910 974-3068
  Candor (G-1238)

▼ Longworth Industries Inc..................F 910 673-5290
  Southern Pines (G-11502)

Royal Textile Mills Inc........................D 336 694-4121
  Yanceyville (G-13460)

Upel Inc...G 336 519-8080
  Winston Salem (G-13379)

▲ Wilo Incorporated.............................E 336 679-4440
  Yadkinville (G-13458)

2323 Men's and boy's neckwear

Angunique..G 336 392-5866
  Greensboro (G-5364)

▲ Brown & Church Neck Wear Co........E 336 368-5502
  Pilot Mountain (G-9670)

Hbb Global LLC...................................G 615 306-1270
  Apex (G-163)

Hirsch Solutions LLC...........................G 631 701-2112
  Huntersville (G-6999)

HL James LLC.....................................G 516 398-3311
  Durham (G-4062)

Lizzys Logos Inc.................................G 704 321-2588
  Matthews (G-8127)

Mudgear LLC......................................G 347 674-9102
  Charlotte (G-2525)

Vf Jeanswear Inc................................F 336 332-3400
  Greensboro (G-5901)

Wicked Oceans....................................G 252 269-0488
  Nags Head (G-9306)

2325 Men's and boy's trousers and slacks

Brilliant You LLC.................................G 336 343-5535
  Greensboro (G-5404)

Centric Brands LLC.............................B 646 582-6000
  Greensboro (G-5438)

Devil Dog Manufacturing Co Inc...........C 919 269-7485
  Zebulon (G-13507)

Fox Apparel Inc..................................C 336 629-7641
  Asheboro (G-357)

Kontoor Brands Inc.............................D 336 332-3400
  Greensboro (G-5652)

Lee Apparel Company Inc....................B 336 332-3400
  Greensboro (G-5658)

Ralph Lauren Corporation....................G 336 632-5000
  Greensboro (G-5780)

Vf Receivables LP...............................G 336 424-6000
  Greensboro (G-5902)

Wrangler Apparel Corp........................B 336 332-3400
  Greensboro (G-5925)

2326 Men's and boy's work clothing

Aj & Raine Scrubs & More LLC.............G 646 374-5198
  Charlotte (G-1634)

American Plush Tex Mills LLC...............F 765 609-0456
  Red Springs (G-10664)

▼ American Safety Utility Corp............E 704 482-0601
  Shelby (G-11311)

▲ Belvoir Manufacturing Corp..............D 252 746-1274
  Greenville (G-5947)

◆ Bennett Uniform Mfg Inc..................F 336 232-5772
  Greensboro (G-5387)

◆ Brushy Mountain Bee Farm Inc.........E 336 921-3640
  Winston Salem (G-13112)

▲ Causa LLC..G 866 695-7022
  Charlotte (G-1868)

Creighton Ab Inc................................G 336 349-8275
  Reidsville (G-10681)

▲ Criticore Inc.....................................F 704 542-6876
  Charlotte (G-1996)

Evans and McClain LLC.......................G 919 374-5578
  Raleigh (G-10093)

Excelsior Sewing LLC..........................F 828 398-8056
  Fletcher (G-4735)

Garland Apparel Group LLC..................E 646 647-2790
  Garland (G-4908)

Hawk Distributors Inc..........................G 888 334-1307
  Sanford (G-11188)

High Ground Incorporated....................G 704 372-6620
  Charlotte (G-2278)

Home T LLC..F 646 797-4768
  Charlotte (G-2284)

Ican Clothes Company.........................F 910 670-1494
  Fayetteville (G-4614)

▲ Ics North America Corp.....................E 704 794-6620
  Concord (G-3375)

Intersport Group Inc...........................G 814 968-3085
  Vilas (G-12230)

Keani Furniture Inc.............................E 336 303-5484
  Asheboro (G-369)

Kontoor Brands Inc.............................A 336 332-3400
  Greensboro (G-5653)

Magnolia Linen Inc.............................F 336 449-0447
  Gibsonville (G-5182)

McDaniel Delmar.................................E 336 284-6377
  Mocksville (G-8375)

Riverside Adventure Company..............F 910 457-4944
  Wilmington (G-12899)

S Loflin Enterprises Inc.......................E 704 633-1159
  Salisbury (G-11113)

Seafarer LLC......................................G 704 624-3200
  Marshville (G-8094)

Smissons Inc......................................G 660 537-3219
  Clayton (G-3169)

Tafford Uniforms LLC..........................D 888 823-3673
  Charlotte (G-2897)

Tillery Accessories Inc........................G 704 474-3013
  Norwood (G-9562)

West Hllcrest Dda Group HM LLC.........F 336 478-7444
  Burlington (G-1179)

White Knght Engneered Pdts Inc..........E 828 687-0940
  Asheville (G-634)

Workwear Outfitters LLC......................E 877 824-0613
  Greensboro (G-5924)

2329 Men's and boy's clothing, nec

◆ Alleson of Rochester Inc...................D 585 272-0606
  Statesville (G-11652)

Augusta Sportswear Inc.......................G 704 871-0990
  Statesville (G-11662)

▲ Badger Sportswear LLC.....................B 704 871-0990
  Statesville (G-11666)

Castle Hayne Hardware LLC.................G 910 675-9205
  Castle Hayne (G-1497)

Eatumup Lure Company Inc..................G 336 218-0896
  Greensboro (G-5511)

Evolution of Style LLC.........................G 914 329-3078
  Charlotte (G-2132)

Fox Apparel Inc..................................C 336 629-7641
  Asheboro (G-357)

Gfsi Holdings LLC...............................A 336 519-8080
  Winston Salem (G-13177)

Hudson Overall Company Inc................G 336 314-5024
  Greensboro (G-5609)

Ican Clothes Company.........................F 910 670-1494
  Fayetteville (G-4614)

▲ Ics North America Corp.....................E 704 794-6620
  Concord (G-3375)

Levi Strauss International....................G 828 665-2417
  Asheville (G-534)

Mk Global Holdings LLC.......................E 704 334-1904
  Charlotte (G-2511)

Ralph Lauren Corporation....................G 336 632-5000
  High Point (G-6752)

Ramco...G 704 794-6620
  Concord (G-3430)

Salute Industries Inc...........................G 844 937-2588
  Archdale (G-242)

Walter Reynolds.................................G 704 735-6050
  Lincolnton (G-7870)

Wrangler Apparel Corp........................B 336 332-3400
  Greensboro (G-5925)

2331 Women's and misses' blouses and shirts

Grateful Union Family Inc....................F 828 622-3258
  Asheville (G-510)

Kontoor Brands Inc.............................D 336 332-3586
  Greensboro (G-5652)

Royce Apparel Inc..............................E 704 933-6000
  Salisbury (G-11112)

Wrangler Apparel Corp........................B 336 332-3400
  Greensboro (G-5925)

2335 Women's, junior's, and misses' dresses

▲ Bon Worth Inc..................................E 800 355-5131
  Hendersonville (G-6190)

Front Street Vlg Mstr Assn Inc..............G 252 838-1524
  Beaufort (G-727)

Gerson & Gerson Inc...........................E 252 235-2441
  Middlesex (G-8276)

▼ Granite Knitwear Inc.........................E 704 279-5526
  Granite Quarry (G-5326)

Hugger Inc...C 704 735-7422
  Lincolnton (G-7832)

Jestines Jewels Inc.............................G 704 904-0191
  Salisbury (G-11072)

2337 Women's and misses' suits and coats

◆ Bennett Uniform Mfg Inc..................F 336 232-5772
  Greensboro (G-5387)

▲ Bon Worth Inc..................................E 800 355-5131
  Hendersonville (G-6190)

Centric Brands LLC.............................B 646 582-6000
  Greensboro (G-5438)

Fox Apparel Inc..................................C 336 629-7641
  Asheboro (G-357)

Hawk Distributors Inc..........................G 888 334-1307
  Sanford (G-11188)

Salute Industries Inc...........................G 844 937-2588
  Archdale (G-242)

2339 Women's and misses' outerwear, nec

◆ Alleson of Rochester Inc...................D 585 272-0606
  Statesville (G-11652)

Apparel USA Inc.................................E 212 869-5495
  Fairmont (G-4500)

S
I
C

Badger Sportswear LLC.........................D 704 871-0990
   Statesville *(G-11665)*

▲ Badger Sportswear LLC........................B 704 871-0990
   Statesville *(G-11666)*

▲ Belvoir Manufacturing Corp..................D 252 746-1274
   Greenville *(G-5947)*

◆ Bennett Uniform Mfg Inc......................F... 336 232-5772
   Greensboro *(G-5387)*

Blacqueladi Styles LLC..........................G 877 977-7798
   Cary *(G-1308)*

▲ Bon Worth Inc.................................E 800 355-5131
   Hendersonville *(G-6190)*

Brilliant You LLC.................................G 336 343-5535
   Greensboro *(G-5404)*

Burlington Outlet................................G 910 278-3442
   Oak Island *(G-9564)*

Centric Brands LLC..............................B 646 582-6000
   Greensboro *(G-5438)*

Devil Dog Manufacturing Co Inc............C 919 269-7485
   Zebulon *(G-13507)*

Divine Creations................................G 704 364-5844
   Morehead City *(G-8829)*

Eagle Sportswear LLC..........................G 252 235-4082
   Middlesex *(G-8273)*

Eatumup Lure Company Inc...................G 336 218-0896
   Greensboro *(G-5511)*

Fabulous Figurez LLC...........................G 336 894-6014
   Turkey *(G-12181)*

Fox Apparel Inc.................................C 336 629-7641
   Asheboro *(G-357)*

Gfsi Holdings LLC...............................A 336 519-8080
   Winston Salem *(G-13177)*

▼ Granite Knitwear Inc..........................E 704 279-5526
   Granite Quarry *(G-5326)*

Headbands of Hope LLC........................G 919 323-4140
   Denver *(G-3786)*

Ican Clothes Company.........................F 910 670-1494
   Fayetteville *(G-4614)*

J C Custom Sewing Inc.........................G 336 449-4586
   Gibsonville *(G-5178)*

Kayla Jonise Bernhardt Crutch...............G 252 457-5367
   Elizabeth City *(G-4394)*

Kontoor Brands Inc.............................A 336 332-3400
   Greensboro *(G-5653)*

Lee Apparel Company Inc......................B 336 332-3400
   Greensboro *(G-5658)*

Levi Strauss International.......................G ... 828 665-2417
   Asheville *(G-534)*

Live It Boutique LLC.............................G 704 492-2402
   Charlotte *(G-2427)*

Lm Shea LLC.....................................G 919 608-1901
   Raleigh *(G-10259)*

McDaniel Delmar................................E 336 284-6377
   Mocksville *(G-8375)*

Mitt S Nitts Inc..................................E 919 596-6793
   Durham *(G-4139)*

Mk Global Holdings LLC........................E 704 334-1904
   Charlotte *(G-2511)*

▲ Performance Apparel LLC.....................F 805 541-0989
   Southern Pines *(G-11503)*

Seafarer LLC....................................G 704 624-3200
   Marshville *(G-8094)*

▲ Sorbe Ltd.......................................G 704 562-2991
   Matthews *(G-8193)*

Walter Reynolds.................................G 704 735-6050
   Lincolnton *(G-7870)*

Wrangler Apparel Corp.........................B 336 332-3400
   Greensboro *(G-5925)*

2341 Women's and children's underwear

◆ Carolina Underwear Company............E 336 472-7788
   Thomasville *(G-12006)*

Hanesbrands Inc................................A 336 519-8080
   Winston Salem *(G-13188)*

Longworth Industries Inc.......................E 910 673-5290
   Aberdeen *(G-11)*

Longworth Industries Inc.......................E 910 974-3068
   Candor *(G-1238)*

▼ Longworth Industries Inc......................F 910 673-5290
   Southern Pines *(G-11502)*

The Madison Company Inc......................G 336 548-9624
   Madison *(G-8001)*

Upel Inc...G 336 519-8080
   Winston Salem *(G-13379)*

Verena Designs Inc.............................E 336 869-8235
   High Point *(G-6825)*

▲ Wilo Incorporated..............................E 336 679-4440
   Yadkinville *(G-13458)*

2342 Bras, girdles, and allied garments

Hanesbrands Inc................................A 336 519-8080
   Winston Salem *(G-13188)*

Hbi Wh Minority Holdings LLC.................G 336 519-8080
   Winston Salem *(G-13193)*

In Pink...G 919 380-1487
   Cary *(G-1373)*

Remington 1816 Foundation...................G 866 686-7778
   Charlotte *(G-2707)*

Upel Inc...G 336 519-8080
   Winston Salem *(G-13379)*

2353 Hats, caps, and millinery

Active Hats and Things Suite..................G 888 352-9292
   Wilmington *(G-12691)*

▲ Americap Co Inc................................G 252 445-2388
   Enfield *(G-4481)*

Custom Patch Hats LLC........................E 919 424-7723
   Raleigh *(G-10030)*

2361 Girl's and children's dresses, blouses

▲ Cannon & Daughters Inc.....................D 828 254-9236
   Asheville *(G-466)*

Devil Dog Manufacturing Co Inc............C 919 269-7485
   Zebulon *(G-13507)*

Justice..E 910 392-1581
   Wilmington *(G-12825)*

Salon Couture..................................G 910 693-1611
   Southern Pines *(G-11508)*

Tiara Inc..G 828 484-8236
   Asheville *(G-619)*

2369 Girl's and children's outerwear, nec

Bonaventure Co LLC............................F 336 584-7530
   Burlington *(G-1053)*

Devil Dog Manufacturing Co Inc............C 919 269-7485
   Zebulon *(G-13507)*

▲ Sanders Industries Inc........................G 410 277-8565
   Waynesville *(G-12472)*

2371 Fur goods

Gmg International Inc...........................G 800 845-6051
   Charlotte *(G-2217)*

Jones Fabricare Inc.............................G 336 272-7261
   Greensboro *(G-5639)*

2381 Fabric dress and work gloves

American Made Products Inc..................F 252 747-2010
   Hookerton *(G-6921)*

▲ Carolina Glove Company......................E 828 464-1132
   Conover *(G-3500)*

Mitt S Nitts Inc..................................E 919 596-6793
   Durham *(G-4139)*

◆ Southern Glove Inc............................B 828 464-4884
   Newton *(G-9497)*

▼ United Glove Inc...............................E 828 464-2510
   Newton *(G-9508)*

Worldwide Protective Pdts LLC................D 336 933-8035
   Wilkesboro *(G-12664)*

▲ Worldwide Protective Pdts LLC.............E 877 678-4568
   Wilkesboro *(G-12663)*

2384 Robes and dressing gowns

Jocephus Originals Inc..........................F 336 229-9600
   Haw River *(G-6133)*

▲ Sanders Industries Inc........................G 410 277-8565
   Waynesville *(G-12472)*

2385 Waterproof outerwear

▲ Drydog Barriers LLC...........................G 704 334-8222
   Indian Trail *(G-7077)*

2386 Leather and sheep-lined clothing

Belt Shop Inc....................................F 704 865-3636
   Gastonia *(G-4997)*

▲ Gerbings LLC...................................D 800 646-5916
   Greensboro *(G-5558)*

Inspiration Leather Design Inc.................G 336 420-2265
   Jamestown *(G-7169)*

▲ JP Leather Company Inc.......................G 828 396-7728
   Hudson *(G-6951)*

▲ Madison Company Inc..........................E 336 548-9624
   Madison *(G-7992)*

Rmg Leather Usa LLC...........................G 828 466-5489
   Conover *(G-3555)*

2387 Apparel belts

Belt Shop Inc....................................F 704 865-3636
   Gastonia *(G-4997)*

Centric Brands LLC..............................B 646 582-6000
   Greensboro *(G-5438)*

Hawk Distributors Inc...........................G 888 334-1307
   Sanford *(G-11188)*

▲ Madison Company Inc..........................E 336 548-9624
   Madison *(G-7992)*

▲ Military Products Inc...........................G 910 637-0315
   West End *(G-12557)*

Point Blank Enterprises Inc....................D 910 893-2071
   Lillington *(G-7801)*

The Madison Company Inc......................E 336 548-9624
   Madison *(G-8001)*

▲ Wentworth Corporation........................G 336 548-1802
   Madison *(G-8003)*

2389 Apparel and accessories, nec

Apparel USA Inc.................................E 212 869-5495
   Fairmont *(G-4500)*

Atlantic Trading LLC.............................F
   Charlotte *(G-1711)*

▲ Belvoir Manufacturing Corp..................D 252 746-1274
   Greenville *(G-5947)*

Black Collection Apparel LLC..................G 919 716-5183
   Sanford *(G-11156)*

Burlington Coat Fctry Whse Cor.............E 919 468-9312
   Cary *(G-1317)*

Carolina Yarn Processors Inc..................C 828 859-5891
   Tryon *(G-12172)*

Custom Patch Hats LLC........................E 919 424-7723
   Raleigh *(G-10030)*

Ddm Inc..G 910 686-1481
   Wilmington *(G-12762)*

Duck Head LLC..................................G 855 457-1865
   Greensboro *(G-5508)*

Eagle Sportswear LLC...........................G 919 365-9805
   Wendell *(G-12534)*

▼ Hanesbrands Export Canada LLC.....G 336 519-8080
   Winston Salem *(G-13187)*

Healing Crafter............................G 336 567-1620
High Point *(G-6642)*

Health Supply Us LLC.....................F 888 408-1694
Mooresville *(G-8680)*

Hinsons Typing & Printing.............G 919 934-9036
Smithfield *(G-11446)*

Jestines Jewels Inc......................G 704 904-0191
Salisbury *(G-11072)*

Kayser-Roth Hosiery Inc...............E 336 852-2030
Greensboro *(G-5644)*

Lebos Shoe Store Inc....................F 704 987-6540
Cornelius *(G-3614)*

Lululemon....................................G 336 723-3002
Winston Salem *(G-13240)*

▲ Madison Company Inc.................G 336 548-9624
Madison *(G-7992)*

▲ Military Products Inc...................G 910 637-0315
West End *(G-12557)*

Mischief Makers Local 816 LLC.......E 336 763-2003
Greensboro *(G-5694)*

▲ Morris Family Theatrical Inc........E 704 332-3304
Charlotte *(G-2519)*

◆ Pearl River Group LLC.................G 704 283-4667
Monroe *(G-8541)*

▲ Precept Medical Products Inc.......F 828 681-0209
Arden *(G-298)*

Remington 1816 Foundation.............G 866 686-7778
Charlotte *(G-2707)*

◆ Royal Park Uniforms Inc.............G 336 562-3345
Prospect Hill *(G-9829)*

▼ Spiritus Systems Company...........E 910 637-0196
Aberdeen *(G-25)*

The Madison Company Inc..............E 336 548-9624
Madison *(G-8001)*

The McQuackins Company LLC.........G 980 254-2309
Gastonia *(G-5153)*

Whitewood Contracts LLC...............G 336 885-9300
High Point *(G-6834)*

Zoeys Btq Style Spclty Trats...........G 910 808-1778
Lillington *(G-7805)*

2391 Curtains and draperies

Atlantic Window Coverings Inc.........E 704 392-0043
Charlotte *(G-1712)*

Carolina Custom Draperies Inc.........G 336 945-5190
Winston Salem *(G-13116)*

Chf Industries Inc........................E 212 951-7800
Charlotte *(G-1912)*

Diane Britt..................................G 910 763-9600
Wilmington *(G-12764)*

▲ Ferncrest Fashions Inc...............D 704 283-6422
Monroe *(G-8488)*

Lichtenberg Inc............................G 336 949-9438
Madison *(G-7991)*

National Mastercraft Inds Inc..........G 919 896-8858
Raleigh *(G-10324)*

Patterson Custom Drapery.............G 910 791-4332
Wilmington *(G-12872)*

Smith Draperies Inc......................F 336 226-2183
Burlington *(G-1158)*

▲ Stage Decoration and Sups Inc.....G 336 621-5454
Greensboro *(G-5834)*

Textile Products Inc......................E 704 636-6221
Salisbury *(G-11124)*

Walker Draperies Inc.....................F 919 220-1424
Durham *(G-4301)*

▲ Wildcat Territory Inc...................G 718 361-6726
Thomasville *(G-12087)*

2392 Household furnishings, nec

▲ American Fiber & Finishing Inc......E 704 984-9256
Albemarle *(G-61)*

Arden Companies LLC....................E 919 258-3081
Sanford *(G-11149)*

Arden Companies LLC....................D 919 258-3081
Sanford *(G-11150)*

Artisans Guild Incorporated...........G 336 841-4140
High Point *(G-6530)*

◆ Avintiv Specialty Mtls Inc............A 704 697-5100
Charlotte *(G-1725)*

◆ Babine Lake Corporation.............E 910 285-7955
Hampstead *(G-6069)*

Bed In A Box...............................E 800 588-5720
Mount Airy *(G-9102)*

Berry Global Inc...........................A 704 697-5100
Charlotte *(G-1773)*

Blue Ridge Products Co Inc............G 828 322-7990
Hickory *(G-6274)*

◆ Bob Barker Company Inc.............C 800 334-9880
Fuquay Varina *(G-4870)*

Carolina Fairway Cushions LLC........G 336 434-4292
Thomasville *(G-12003)*

Carpenter Co...............................E 828 632-7061
Taylorsville *(G-11952)*

Chf Industries Inc........................E 212 951-7800
Charlotte *(G-1912)*

Creative Textiles Inc......................G 919 693-4427
Oxford *(G-9609)*

Dale Ray Fabrics LLC....................G 704 932-6411
Kannapolis *(G-7206)*

Deep River Fabricators Inc.............F 336 824-8881
Franklinville *(G-4856)*

▲ Dewoolfson Down Intl Inc............G 828 963-2750
Banner Elk *(G-684)*

Diane Britt..................................G 910 763-9600
Wilmington *(G-12764)*

Discover Night LLC........................F 888 825-6282
Raleigh *(G-10049)*

Fiber Cushioning Inc......................F 336 887-4782
High Point *(G-6620)*

▲ Fiber Cushioning Inc..................F 336 629-8442
Asheboro *(G-355)*

Hickory Springs Mfg Co..................D 336 861-4195
High Point *(G-6647)*

Image Matters Inc........................G 336 940-3000
Clemmons *(G-3191)*

Innovative Cushions LLC................G 336 861-2060
Archdale *(G-228)*

Innovative Fabrication Inc..............G 919 544-0254
Raleigh *(G-10196)*

J C Custom Sewing Inc..................G 336 449-4586
Gibsonville *(G-5178)*

◆ Jbs2 Inc..................................D 828 236-1300
Swannanoa *(G-11872)*

◆ Js Fiber Co Inc.........................E 704 871-1582
Statesville *(G-11721)*

Js Linens and Curtain Outlet...........F 704 871-1582
Statesville *(G-11722)*

▲ Js Royal Home Usa Inc...............E 704 542-2304
Charlotte *(G-2382)*

◆ L C Industries Inc.....................C 919 596-8277
Durham *(G-4100)*

Leggett & Platt Incorporated...........G 704 380-6208
Statesville *(G-11727)*

Lions Services Inc........................B 704 921-1527
Charlotte *(G-2425)*

▲ Lomar Specialty Advg Inc.............F 704 788-4380
Concord *(G-3396)*

◆ Manual Woodworkers Weavers Inc......C 828 692-7333
Hendersonville *(G-6224)*

Newell & Sons Inc........................G 336 597-2248
Roxboro *(G-10930)*

◆ North Carolina Lumber Company......G 336 498-6600
Randleman *(G-10654)*

Owens Quilting Inc........................G 828 695-1495
Newton *(G-9485)*

Pacific Coast Feather LLC...............G 252 492-0051
Henderson *(G-6169)*

Party Tables Land Co LLC...............G 919 596-3521
Durham *(G-4166)*

▲ Perfect Fit Industries LLC............C 800 864-7618
Charlotte *(G-2627)*

◆ Pgi Polymer Inc.........................A 704 697-5100
Charlotte *(G-2633)*

Premium Cushion Inc.....................E 828 464-4783
Conover *(G-3550)*

▲ Pure Country Inc.......................D 828 871-2890
Tryon *(G-12177)*

▲ Q C Apparel Inc........................G 828 586-5663
Sylva *(G-11897)*

Quality Home Fashions Inc.............G 704 983-5906
Albemarle *(G-85)*

Quickie Manufacturing Corp............C 910 737-6500
Lumberton *(G-7966)*

R & D Weaving Inc........................F 828 248-1910
Ellenboro *(G-4460)*

Richard Shew...............................F 828 781-3294
Conover *(G-3554)*

▼ Riddle & Company LLC.................G 336 229-1856
Burlington *(G-1147)*

Royale Comfort Seating Inc.............D 828 352-9021
Taylorsville *(G-11974)*

▲ Sanders Industries Inc...............G 410 277-8565
Waynesville *(G-12472)*

Signature Seating Inc.....................E 828 325-0174
Hickory *(G-6447)*

Smith Draperies Inc......................F 336 226-2183
Burlington *(G-1158)*

Snyder Paper Corporation...............E 336 884-1172
High Point *(G-6782)*

Snyder Paper Corporation...............E 828 464-1189
Newton *(G-9496)*

Somnigroup International Inc............C 336 861-2900
Trinity *(G-12126)*

Stn Cushion Company.....................D 336 476-9100
Thomasville *(G-12074)*

▲ Sunrise Development LLC.............F 828 453-0590
Mooresboro *(G-8586)*

▲ Tempo Products LLC...................E 336 434-8649
High Point *(G-6804)*

Textile Products Inc......................E 704 636-6221
Salisbury *(G-11124)*

◆ Trtl Inc...................................G 844 811-5816
Raleigh *(G-10566)*

▲ Watson Party Tables Inc..............F 919 294-9153
Durham *(G-4302)*

▲ Wayne Industries Inc..................E 336 434-5017
Archdale *(G-246)*

Westpoint Home Inc......................F 910 369-2231
Wagram *(G-12257)*

▲ Wildcat Territory Inc..................G 718 361-6726
Thomasville *(G-12087)*

◆ Winstn-Slem Inds For Blind Inc......B 336 759-0551
Winston Salem *(G-13398)*

2393 Textile bags

▲ American Pride Inc.....................E 828 697-8847
Hendersonville *(G-6184)*

◆ Cekal Specialties Inc..................E 704 822-6206
Mount Holly *(G-9222)*

Cross Canvas Company Inc.............E 828 252-0440
Asheville *(G-480)*

Cushion Manufacturing Inc.............G 828 324-9555
Hickory *(G-6315)*

Dayton Bag & Burlap Co.................G 704 873-7271
Statesville *(G-11685)*

▲ East Coast Umbrella Inc................... E 910 462-2500
   Laurel Hill *(G-7482)*

Fisher Athletic Equipment Inc................ E 704 636-5713
   Salisbury *(G-11054)*

Fuller Specialty Company Inc................ G 336 226-3446
   Burlington *(G-1092)*

Hdb Inc.. G 800 403-2247
   Greensboro *(G-5590)*

J C Custom Sewing Inc......................... G 336 449-4586
   Gibsonville *(G-5178)*

▲ J Stahl Sales & Sourcing Inc............ E 828 645-3005
   Weaverville *(G-12493)*

▲ Lomar Specialty Advg Inc................. F 704 788-4380
   Concord *(G-3396)*

Mountain International LLC................... E 828 606-0194
   Brevard *(G-978)*

Nyp Corp Frmrly New Yrkr-Pters.......... F 910 739-4403
   Lumberton *(G-7964)*

2394 Canvas and related products

A & J Canvas Inc.................................. E 252 244-1509
   Vanceboro *(G-12213)*

Accent Awnings Inc.............................. F 828 321-4517
   Andrews *(G-104)*

Agricltral-Industrial Fabr Inc................ G 336 591-3690
   Walnut Cove *(G-12326)*

Alpha Canvas and Awning Co Inc......... F 704 333-1581
   Charlotte *(G-1650)*

Canvasmasters LLC.............................. G 828 369-0406
   Franklin *(G-4820)*

Cape Lookout Canvas & Customs......... G 252 726-3751
   Morehead City *(G-8821)*

◆ Cdv LLC.. F 919 674-3460
   Morrisville *(G-8953)*

Clark Art Shop Inc................................ G 919 832-8319
   Raleigh *(G-9997)*

Coastal Awnings Inc............................. F 252 222-0707
   Morehead City *(G-8826)*

Coastal Canvas Mfg Inc........................ G 252 728-4946
   Beaufort *(G-723)*

▼ Colored Metal Products Inc.............. F 704 482-1407
   Shelby *(G-11322)*

Cross Canvas Company Inc................... E 828 252-0440
   Asheville *(G-480)*

CSC Awnings Inc.................................. G 336 744-5006
   Winston Salem *(G-13135)*

Custom Canvas Works Inc.................... G 919 662-4800
   Garner *(G-4928)*

◆ Custom Golf Car Supply Inc............. C 704 855-1130
   Salisbury *(G-11042)*

▲ Dize Company.................................... D 336 722-5181
   Winston Salem *(G-13149)*

DLM Sales Inc...................................... F 704 399-2776
   Charlotte *(G-2058)*

◆ Dunn Manufacturing Corp................. C 704 283-2147
   Monroe *(G-8479)*

◆ Hatteras Hammocks Inc.................... C 252 758-0641
   Greenville *(G-5987)*

Howell & Sons Canvas Repairs............ G 704 892-7913
   Cornelius *(G-3607)*

M & M Signs and Awnings Inc.............. F 336 352-4300
   Mount Airy *(G-9151)*

OBrian Tarping Systems Inc................. F 252 291-6710
   Wilson *(G-13010)*

▼ OBrian Tarping Systems Inc............. F 252 291-2141
   Wilson *(G-13011)*

▲ Prem Corp.. E 704 921-1799
   Charlotte *(G-2660)*

Red Sky Shelters LLC........................... G 828 258-8417
   Asheville *(G-589)*

Rocky Mount Awning & Tent Co............ G 252 442-0184
   Rocky Mount *(G-10866)*

Sawyers Sign Service Inc...................... F
   Mount Airy *(G-9175)*

Shibumi Shade Inc............................... F 336 816-9903
   Raleigh *(G-10470)*

Sign & Awning Systems Inc.................. G 919 892-5900
   Dunn *(G-3868)*

▲ Southbridge Inc................................. G 828 350-9112
   Asheville *(G-607)*

▲ Trelleborg Ctd Systems US Inc......... C 828 286-9126
   Rutherfordton *(G-10999)*

Trimaco Inc.. G 919 674-3460
   Morrisville *(G-9078)*

◆ Trivantage LLC.................................. D 800 786-1876
   Burlington *(G-1171)*

▲ WC&r Interests LLC.......................... C 828 684-9848
   Fletcher *(G-4777)*

◆ Winstn-Slem Inds For Blind Inc......... B 336 759-0551
   Winston Salem *(G-13398)*

2395 Pleating and stitching

822tees Inc.. G 910 822-8337
   Fayetteville *(G-4541)*

A Stitch To Remember........................... G 336 202-0026
   Summerfield *(G-11834)*

Amy Smith.. G 828 352-1001
   Burnsville *(G-1182)*

Apex Embroidery Inc............................ G 919 793-6083
   Apex *(G-135)*

Artex Group Inc.................................... G 866 845-1042
   Fairview *(G-4505)*

Artist S Needle Inc............................... G 336 294-5884
   Greensboro *(G-5371)*

Artwear Embroidery Inc........................ E 336 992-2166
   Kernersville *(G-7245)*

B6usa Inc... G 919 833-3851
   Raleigh *(G-9929)*

▲ Baysix USA.. F 919 833-3851
   Raleigh *(G-9935)*

BB&p Embroidery LLC.......................... G 252 206-1929
   Wilson *(G-12969)*

Body Billboards Inc.............................. G 919 544-4540
   Durham *(G-3936)*

Bradleys Inc... E 704 484-2077
   Shelby *(G-11314)*

Cintas Corporation No 2........................ E 336 632-4412
   Greensboro *(G-5444)*

Cold Water No Bleach LLC.................... G 336 505-9584
   Durham *(G-3981)*

▲ Colonial LLC...................................... E 336 434-5600
   High Point *(G-6572)*

Combintons Screen Prtg EMB Inc......... G 336 472-4420
   Thomasville *(G-12009)*

Conrad Embroidery Company LLC........ E 828 645-3015
   Weaverville *(G-12487)*

▲ Conrad Industries Inc....................... D 828 645-3015
   Weaverville *(G-12488)*

Consumer Concepts............................. F 252 247-7000
   Morehead City *(G-8828)*

▼ Crawford Industries Inc.................... G 336 884-8822
   High Point *(G-6579)*

Creative Caps Inc................................. G 919 701-1175
   Dunn *(G-3852)*

Dale Advertising Inc............................. G 704 484-0971
   Shelby *(G-11329)*

Emb Inc.. G 336 945-0759
   High Point *(G-6609)*

Embroid It... G 704 617-0357
   Charlotte *(G-2107)*

▲ Fabric Services Hickory Inc.............. G 828 397-7331
   Hildebran *(G-6849)*

Fines and Carriel Inc............................ G 919 929-0702
   Chapel Hill *(G-1547)*

Freeman Screen Printers Inc................. G 704 521-9148
   Charlotte *(G-2179)*

Funny Bone EMB & Screening............... G 704 663-4711
   Mooresville *(G-8668)*

Gaston Screen Printing Inc................... G 704 399-0459
   Charlotte *(G-2191)*

Grace Apparel Company Inc.................. G 828 242-8172
   Black Mountain *(G-865)*

▼ High Point Quilting Inc..................... F 336 861-4180
   High Point *(G-6655)*

Home Team Athletics Inc...................... G 910 938-0862
   Jacksonville *(G-7126)*

Hometown Sports Inc............................ G 919 732-7090
   Hillsborough *(G-6867)*

Industrial Opportunities Inc.................. B 828 321-4754
   Andrews *(G-107)*

Ink n Stitches LLC................................ G 336 633-3898
   Asheboro *(G-365)*

International Embroidery........................ G 704 792-0641
   Concord *(G-3379)*

Ivars Sportswear Inc............................ G 336 227-9683
   Graham *(G-5271)*

Kelleys Sports and Awards Inc.............. E 828 728-4600
   Hudson *(G-6952)*

Kraken-Skulls....................................... F 910 500-9100
   Fayetteville *(G-4627)*

Lake Norman EMB & Monogramming.... G 704 892-8450
   Cornelius *(G-3612)*

Lee Marks.. G 919 493-2208
   Durham *(G-4102)*

Liberty Embroidery Inc.......................... A 336 548-1802
   Madison *(G-7990)*

Logosdirect LLC................................... F 866 273-2335
   Wilmington *(G-12840)*

M-Prints Inc.. G 828 265-4929
   Boone *(G-931)*

Manna Corp North Carolina.................. G 828 696-3642
   Hendersonville *(G-6223)*

McCotter Industries Inc........................ F 704 282-2102
   Monroe *(G-8529)*

Millers Sports and Trophies.................. G 252 792-2050
   Williamston *(G-12672)*

Mojo Sportswear Inc............................. G 252 758-4176
   Greenville *(G-6006)*

Monogram Asheville.............................. G 828 707-8110
   Asheville *(G-549)*

Moving Screens Incorporated............... G 336 364-9259
   Rougemont *(G-10914)*

Pacific Coast Feather LLC.................... G 252 492-0051
   Henderson *(G-6169)*

Pine State Corporate AP LLC................ F 336 789-9437
   Mount Airy *(G-9164)*

Professnal Alterations EMB Inc............. G 910 577-8484
   Jacksonville *(G-7139)*

Quilt Lizzy.. G 252 257-3800
   Ayden *(G-658)*

Rhyno Enterprises................................ G 252 291-6700
   Wilson *(G-13022)*

Robert Citrano..................................... G 910 264-7746
   Wilmington *(G-12900)*

Rogers Screenprinting EMB Inc............ G 910 628-1983
   Fairmont *(G-4504)*

Southern Roots Monogramming............ G 706 599-5383
   Cleveland *(G-3222)*

◆ Ss Handcrafted Art LLC.................... G 704 664-2544
   Mooresville *(G-8775)*

Stanley E Dixon Jr Inc.......................... G 252 332-5004
   Ahoskie *(G-53)*

Steelcity LLC.. E 336 434-7000
   Archdale *(G-244)*

Stitch 98 Inc... F 704 235-5783
   Mooresville *(G-8777)*

Stitch In Time Inc................G 910 497-4171
Spring Lake *(G-11564)*

Stitch-A-Doozy.....................G 336 573-2339
Stoneville *(G-11829)*

Stitchcrafters Incorporated ....G 828 397-7656
Hickory *(G-6458)*

Stitchery Inc.......................G 336 248-5604
Lexington *(G-7746)*

Stitches On Critter Pond........G 919 624-5886
Wake Forest *(G-12305)*

Stitchmaster LLC..................F 336 852-6448
Greensboro *(G-5841)*

STS Screen Printing Inc.........G 704 821-8488
Matthews *(G-8195)*

Sugarshack Bakery and EMB...G 803 920-3311
Troy *(G-12168)*

Three Wishes Monogramming ...G 980 298-2981
Harrisburg *(G-6118)*

To The Point Inc..................G 336 725-5303
Winston Salem *(G-13365)*

Topsail Sportswear Inc..........G 910 270-4903
Hampstead *(G-6077)*

Twg Inc.............................G 336 998-9731
Advance *(G-40)*

Uniforms Galore...................G 252 975-5878
Washington *(G-12417)*

Vocatnal Sltons Hndrson Cnty I.....E 828 692-9626
East Flat Rock *(G-4335)*

WB Embroidery Inc................G 828 432-0076
Morganton *(G-8912)*

Wendys Embrdred Spc Screen Prt.....F 704 982-5978
Albemarle *(G-97)*

Zoom Apparel Inc..................G 336 993-9666
Winston Salem *(G-13413)*

2396 Automotive and apparel trimmings

A&M Screen Printing NC Inc.....G 910 792-1111
Wilmington *(G-12686)*

Amy Smith..........................G 828 352-1001
Burnsville *(G-1182)*

Boardwalk Inc......................G 252 240-1095
Morehead City *(G-8819)*

Body Billboards Inc...............G 919 544-4540
Durham *(G-3936)*

Brandrpm LLC......................D 704 225-1800
Charlotte *(G-1807)*

Broome Sign Company............G 704 782-0422
Concord *(G-3325)*

◆ Charlotte Trimming Company Inc.....E 704 529-8427
Charlotte *(G-1905)*

Combintons Screen Prtg EMB Inc.....G 336 472-4420
Thomasville *(G-12009)*

Consumer Concepts...............F 252 247-7000
Morehead City *(G-8828)*

Contagious Graphics Inc.........E 704 529-5600
Charlotte *(G-1977)*

Crystal Impressions Ltd.........F 704 821-7678
Indian Trail *(G-7076)*

Culp Inc.............................C 336 643-7751
Stokesdale *(G-11811)*

Custom Screens Inc...............G 336 427-0265
Madison *(G-7985)*

Dale Advertising Inc..............G 704 484-0971
Shelby *(G-11329)*

Dayton Bag & Burlap Co..........G 704 873-7271
Statesville *(G-11685)*

Dicks Store.........................G 336 548-9358
Madison *(G-7987)*

Domestic Fabrics Blankets Corp.....E 252 523-7948
Kinston *(G-7406)*

Expressive Screen Printing......G 910 739-3221
Lumberton *(G-7952)*

F & H Print Sign Design LLC......G 252 335-0181
Elizabeth City *(G-4389)*

◆ Finch Industries Incorporated.....D 336 472-4499
Thomasville *(G-12024)*

Flawless Touch Detailing LLC....G 910 987-8093
Fayetteville *(G-4602)*

◆ Fms Enterprises Usa Inc........D 704 735-4249
Lincolnton *(G-7831)*

Freeman Screen Printers Inc.....G 704 521-9148
Charlotte *(G-2179)*

G & G Enterprises.................G 336 764-2493
Clemmons *(G-3186)*

Gaston Screen Printing Inc.......G 704 399-0459
Charlotte *(G-2191)*

Glen Rven Tchnical Fabrics LLC....C 336 229-5576
Burlington *(G-1100)*

Grace Apparel Company Inc......G 828 242-8172
Black Mountain *(G-865)*

◆ Haeco Americas LLC.............A 336 668-4410
Greensboro *(G-5585)*

Hi-Tech Screens Inc..............G 828 452-5151
Mooresville *(G-8683)*

Htm Concepts Inc.................F 252 794-2122
Windsor *(G-13054)*

International Foam Pdts Inc......G 704 588-0080
Charlotte *(G-2343)*

Island Xprtees of Oter Bnks In....E 252 480-3990
Nags Head *(G-9298)*

Kelleys Sports and Awards Inc....G 828 728-4600
Hudson *(G-6952)*

▲ King International Corporation....E 336 983-5171
King *(G-7329)*

Lee County Industries Inc.......G 919 775-3439
Sanford *(G-11205)*

Lee Marks..........................G 919 493-2208
Durham *(G-4102)*

Line Drive Sports Center Inc.....G 336 824-1692
Ramseur *(G-10628)*

M-Prints Inc.......................G 828 265-4929
Boone *(G-931)*

Manna Corp North Carolina......G 828 696-3642
Hendersonville *(G-6223)*

Marketing One Sportswear Inc....G 704 334-9333
Charlotte *(G-2457)*

Marvin Bailey Screen Printing....G 252 335-1554
Elizabeth City *(G-4397)*

Motorsports Designs Inc.........F 336 454-1181
High Point *(G-6716)*

Premium Fabricators LLC........E 828 464-3818
Conover *(G-3551)*

Pro-System Inc....................F 704 799-8100
Mooresville *(G-8756)*

PSM Enterprises Inc..............F 336 789-8888
Mount Airy *(G-9167)*

Qst Industries Inc.................F 336 751-1000
Mocksville *(G-8386)*

R & S Sporting Goods Ctr Inc.....G 336 599-0248
Roxboro *(G-10942)*

Regimental Flag & T Shirts.......G 919 496-2888
Louisburg *(G-7925)*

Rogers Screenprinting EMB Inc....G 910 628-1983
Fairmont *(G-4504)*

Simple & Sentimental LLC........G 252 320-9458
Ayden *(G-662)*

Soisa Inc...........................G 336 940-4006
Mocksville *(G-8390)*

Standard Tytape Company Inc....G 828 693-6594
Hendersonville *(G-6244)*

Stitchcrafters Incorporated......G 828 397-7656
Hickory *(G-6458)*

T T S D Productions LLC..........G 704 829-6666
Belmont *(G-770)*

Tapped Tees LLC..................G 919 943-9692
Durham *(G-4259)*

TEC Graphics Inc..................F 919 567-2077
Fuquay Varina *(G-4901)*

▲ Textile Printing Inc.............G 704 521-8099
Charlotte *(G-2909)*

▲ Trelleborg Ctd Systems US Inc....C 828 286-9126
Rutherfordton *(G-10999)*

Vocatnal Sltons Hndrson Cnty I....E 828 692-9626
East Flat Rock *(G-4335)*

Wooten Graphics Inc..............G 336 731-4650
Welcome *(G-12517)*

2397 Schiffli machine embroideries

Collegate Clors Christn Colors....G 919 536-8179
Durham *(G-3982)*

2399 Fabricated textile products, nec

▲ Aircraft Belts Inc..............E 919 956-4395
Creedmoor *(G-3635)*

All-State Industries Inc..........G 704 588-4081
Charlotte *(G-1642)*

▲ Ballistic Recovery Systems Inc....E 651 457-7491
Pinebluff *(G-9685)*

◆ Beocare Group Inc..............C 828 728-7300
Hudson *(G-6943)*

Bymonetcrochet....................G 443 613-1736
Charlotte *(G-1826)*

Dickson Elberton Mill Inc.........G 336 226-3556
Burlington *(G-1083)*

◆ Downtown Graphics Network Inc....G 704 637-0855
Salisbury *(G-11044)*

◆ Dunn Manufacturing Corp.......C 704 283-2147
Monroe *(G-8479)*

▲ Fex Straw Manufacturing Inc....G 910 671-4141
Lumberton *(G-7954)*

Flexi North America LLC..........G 704 588-0785
Charlotte *(G-2163)*

Flint Hill Textiles Inc............G 704 434-9331
Shelby *(G-11337)*

◆ Guilford Mills LLC..............A 910 794-5810
Wilmington *(G-12798)*

Harvey & Sons Net & Twine.......G 252 729-1731
Davis *(G-3726)*

◆ Hatteras Hammocks Inc.........C 252 758-0641
Greenville *(G-5987)*

◆ Hickory Springs Manufactu......D 828 328-2201
Hickory *(G-6355)*

▲ Horseware Triple Crown Blanket....F 252 208-0080
Raleigh *(G-10176)*

Lear Corporation..................A 910 794-5810
Wilmington *(G-12831)*

▲ Lomar Specialty Advg Inc.......F 704 788-4380
Concord *(G-3396)*

Mills Manufacturing Corp.........C 828 645-3061
Asheville *(G-548)*

Nags Head Hammocks LLC........G 252 441-6115
Nags Head *(G-9301)*

North Amercn Aerodynamics Inc....D 336 599-9266
Roxboro *(G-10932)*

Oleksynprannyk LLC...............F 704 450-0182
Mooresville *(G-8738)*

▲ Photo Emblem Incorporated......G 336 784-4000
Winston Salem *(G-13290)*

Piedmont Parachute Inc..........G 336 597-2225
Roxboro *(G-10941)*

R/W Connection Inc................G 252 446-0114
Rocky Mount *(G-10864)*

Red Oak Sales Company...........G 704 483-8464
Denver *(G-3802)*

S & S Trawl Shop Inc..............G 910 842-9197
Supply *(G-11858)*

S I C

S Loflin Enterprises Inc............................ F 704 633-1159
　Salisbury *(G-11113)*

▲ Saab Barracuda LLC........................... E 910 814-3088
　Lillington *(G-7802)*

Spc-Usa Inc.. G 910 875-9002
　Raeford *(G-9852)*

Thin Line Saddle Pads Inc....................... G 919 680-6803
　Durham *(G-4271)*

Tonyas Crocheted Creations................... G 704 421-2143
　Charlotte *(G-2929)*

Treklite Inc.. G 919 610-1788
　Raleigh *(G-10557)*

Wovenart Inc.. F 828 859-6349
　Tryon *(G-12180)*

▲ Yellow Dog Design Inc......................... F 336 553-2172
　Greensboro *(G-5929)*

24 LUMBER AND WOOD PRODUCTS, EXCEPT FURNITURE

2411 Logging

360 Forest Products Inc........................ G 910 285-5838
　Wallace *(G-12318)*

Afsc LLC.. D 704 523-4936
　Charlotte *(G-1627)*

Alan Walsh Logging LLC........................ G 828 234-7500
　Lenoir *(G-7569)*

Allen Brothers Timber Company............. G 910 997-6412
　Rockingham *(G-10770)*

Allen R Goodson Logging Co................... G 910 455-4177
　Jacksonville *(G-7115)*

Alligood Brothers Logging...................... G 252 927-2358
　Washington *(G-12371)*

Anson Wood Products............................ G 704 694-5390
　Wadesboro *(G-12234)*

Anthony B Andrews Logging Inc............. G 252 448-8901
　Trenton *(G-12109)*

Arauco - NA.. G 910 569-7020
　Biscoe *(G-846)*

Arcola Logging Co Inc........................... G 252 257-3205
　Macon *(G-7982)*

Arrants Logging Inc.............................. F 252 792-1889
　Jamesville *(G-7182)*

Asheville Contracting Co Inc.................. E 828 665-8900
　Candler *(G-1217)*

Ashworth Logging................................. G 910 464-2136
　Carthage *(G-1275)*

Associated Artists Southport................. G 910 457-5450
　Southport *(G-11517)*

Atlantic Logging Inc.............................. G 252 229-9997
　New Bern *(G-9335)*

Autry Logging Inc.................................. G 910 303-4943
　Stedman *(G-11805)*

Backwoods Logging LLC........................ G 910 298-3786
　Pink Hill *(G-9764)*

Barnes Logging Co Inc.......................... F 252 799-6016
　Plymouth *(G-9798)*

Bateman Logging Co Inc........................ F 252 482-8959
　Edenton *(G-4362)*

Bill Ratliff Jr Logging I......................... G 704 694-5403
　Wadesboro *(G-12235)*

Billy Harrell Logging Inc....................... G 252 221-4995
　Tyner *(G-12182)*

Billy Harrell Logging Inc....................... G 252 426-1362
　Hertford *(G-6251)*

Black River Logging Inc......................... G 910 669-2850
　Ivanhoe *(G-7110)*

Blankenship Logging............................. G 828 652-2250
　Nebo *(G-9327)*

Bobby A Herring Logging....................... G 919 658-9768
　Mount Olive *(G-9249)*

Boone Logging Company Inc.................. G 252 443-7641
　Elm City *(G-4464)*

Bracey Bros Logging LLC....................... G 910 231-9543
　Delco *(G-3734)*

Bradley Todd Baugus............................ G 252 665-4901
　Maysville *(G-8210)*

Brett McHenry Logging LLC................... G 252 243-7285
　Wilson *(G-12971)*

Broadway Logging Co Inc....................... E 252 633-2693
　New Bern *(G-9341)*

Brown Brothers Lumber......................... G 828 632-6486
　Taylorsville *(G-11951)*

Brown Creek Timber Company Inc......... G 704 694-3529
　Wadesboro *(G-12237)*

Buck Lucas Logging Companies.............. G 252 410-0160
　Roanoke Rapids *(G-10732)*

Buds Logging and Trucking.................... G 704 465-8016
　Wadesboro *(G-12238)*

Bundy Logging Company Inc.................. G 252 357-0191
　Gatesville *(G-5170)*

By Faith Logging Inc............................. G 252 792-0019
　Williamston *(G-12668)*

Cahoon Brothers Logging LLC................ F 252 943-9901
　Pantego *(G-9641)*

Cahoon Logging Company Inc................ G 252 943-6805
　Pinetown *(G-9708)*

Capps Noble Logging............................ G 828 696-9690
　Zirconia *(G-13528)*

Caraway Logging Inc............................. G 252 633-1230
　New Bern *(G-9347)*

Carolina East Timber Inc....................... G 252 638-1914
　New Bern *(G-9348)*

Cauley Construction Company............... G 252 522-1078
　Kinston *(G-7401)*

Chapman Brothers Logging LLC............. G 828 437-6498
　Connelly Springs *(G-3474)*

Charles Ferguson Logging...................... G 336 921-3126
　Moravian Falls *(G-8809)*

CJ Stallings Logging Inc......................... F 252 297-2272
　Belvidere *(G-778)*

Cjc Enterprises.................................... E 919 266-3158
　Wake Forest *(G-12270)*

Claybourn Walters Log Co Inc................ F 910 628-7075
　Fairmont *(G-4501)*

Coastal Carolina Loggin......................... G 252 474-2165
　Ernul *(G-4490)*

▲ Columbia West Virginia Corp.............. E 336 605-0429
　Greensboro *(G-5456)*

Conetoe Land & Timber LLC.................. G 252 717-4648
　Goldsboro *(G-5208)*

D & M Logging of Wnc LLC.................... G 828 648-4366
　Canton *(G-1251)*

D & W Logging Inc................................ G 919 820-0826
　Four Oaks *(G-4810)*

D T Bracy Logging Inc........................... G 252 332-8332
　Ahoskie *(G-46)*

Dan Morton Logging.............................. G 919 693-1898
　Oxford *(G-9612)*

Dannies Logging Inc............................. G 919 528-2370
　Creedmoor *(G-3647)*

Darrell T Bracy.................................... G 252 358-1432
　Ahoskie *(G-47)*

David Raynor Logging Inc....................... E 910 980-0129
　Linden *(G-7873)*

Deberry Land & Timber Inc................... G 910 572-2698
　Troy *(G-12159)*

Delbert White Logging Inc..................... G 252 209-4779
　Windsor *(G-13051)*

Donald R Young Logging Inc.................. G 910 934-6769
　Lillington *(G-7795)*

Douglas Temple & Son Inc.................... G 252 771-5676
　Elizabeth City *(G-4386)*

Down South Logging LLC...................... G 843 333-1649
　Tabor City *(G-11909)*

Dr Logging LLC.................................... G 910 417-9643
　Hamlet *(G-6054)*

Duncan Junior D................................... G 336 871-3599
　Sandy Ridge *(G-11143)*

Duplin Forest Products Inc.................... G 910 285-5381
　Wallace *(G-12320)*

Dustin Ellis Logging............................. G 704 732-6027
　Lincolnton *(G-7829)*

E Z Stop Number Two........................... G 828 627-9081
　Clyde *(G-3259)*

East Coast Log & Timber Inc................. G 252 568-4344
　Albertson *(G-99)*

East Coast Logging Inc.......................... G 252 794-4054
　Windsor *(G-13052)*

Edsel G Barnes Jr Inc........................... F 252 793-4170
　Plymouth *(G-9803)*

Emanuel Hoggard................................. F 252 794-3724
　Windsor *(G-13053)*

Enterprise Loggers Company Inc........... F 252 586-4805
　Littleton *(G-7885)*

Eric Martin Jermey.............................. G 704 692-0389
　Bostic *(G-962)*

Evans Logging Inc................................ F 252 792-3865
　Jamesville *(G-7183)*

Evergreen Forest Products Inc............... G 910 762-9156
　Wilmington *(G-12772)*

Evergreen Logging LLC......................... G 910 654-1662
　Evergreen *(G-4498)*

Frankie York Logging Co........................ G 252 633-4825
　New Bern *(G-9368)*

Fred R Harrris Logging Inc..................... G 919 853-2266
　Louisburg *(G-7916)*

G & H Broadway Logging Inc.................. G 252 229-4594
　New Bern *(G-9369)*

General Wood Preserving Co Inc............ G 910 371-3131
　Leland *(G-7545)*

George P Gatling Logging...................... G 252 465-8983
　Sunbury *(G-11847)*

Glacier Forestry Inc.............................. G 704 902-2594
　Mooresville *(G-8673)*

Gladsons Logging LLC........................... G 252 670-8813
　Aurora *(G-642)*

Glenn Trexler & Sons Log Inc................ G 704 694-5644
　Wadesboro *(G-12242)*

Gmd Logging Inc.................................. G 704 985-5460
　Albemarle *(G-75)*

Gold Creek Inc..................................... G 336 468-4495
　Hamptonville *(G-6084)*

Goodson S All Terrain Log Inc................ G 910 347-7919
　Jacksonville *(G-7125)*

Gouge Logging..................................... G 828 675-9216
　Burnsville *(G-1186)*

Grady & Son Atkins Logging................... G 919 934-7785
　Four Oaks *(G-4812)*

Greene Logging.................................... G 336 667-6960
　Purlear *(G-9831)*

H & L Logging Inc................................. F 252 793-2778
　Plymouth *(G-9805)*

H Clyde Moore Jr.................................. G 910 642-3507
　Whiteville *(G-12583)*

Hardister Logging................................. G 336 857-2397
　Denton *(G-3749)*

Harris Logging LLC............................... G 336 859-2786
　Denton *(G-3750)*

Hofler Logging Inc................................ G 252 465-8921
　Sunbury *(G-11849)*

Holmes Logging - Wallace LLC.............. F 910 271-1216
　Wallace *(G-12321)*

Htc Logging Inc.................................... G 828 625-1601
　Mill Spring *(G-8301)*

Hunt Logging Co.................................... G 919 853-2850
Louisburg (G-7918)

Ivey Icenhour DBA................................ G 704 786-0676
Mount Pleasant (G-9262)

◆ Ivp Forest Products LLC..................F 252 241-8126
Morehead City (G-8836)

J & J Logging Inc................................ E 252 430-1110
Henderson (G-6162)

J E Carpenter Logging Co Inc................ G 252 633-0037
Trent Woods (G-12107)

J E Kerr Timber Co Corp........................ G 252 537-0544
Roanoke Rapids (G-10739)

J&R Cohoon Logging & Tidewater......... G 252 943-6300
Pantego (G-9645)

Jackson Logging.................................. G 919 658-2757
Mount Olive (G-9256)

James Keith Nations............................ G 828 421-5391
Whittier (G-12624)

James L Johnson.................................. G 704 694-0103
Wadesboro (G-12246)

James Moore & Son Logging.................. G 336 656-9858
Browns Summit (G-999)

Jared Sasnett Logging Co Inc................ G 252 939-6289
Kinston (G-7416)

Jeffers Logging Inc.............................. G 919 708-2193
Sanford (G-11196)

Jh Logging.. G 336 599-0278
Roxboro (G-10928)

Jif Logging Inc.................................... G 252 398-2249
Murfreesboro (G-9282)

Jimmy D Nelms Logging Inc.................. G 919 853-2597
Louisburg (G-7919)

JM Williams Timber Company................ G 919 362-1333
Apex (G-172)

Johnny Daniel.................................... G 336 859-2480
Denton (G-3752)

Juan J Hernandez................................ G 919 742-3381
Siler City (G-11414)

K & J Ashworth Logging LLC.................. G 336 879-2388
Seagrove (G-11277)

K L Butler Logging Inc.......................... G 910 648-6016
Bladenboro (G-878)

Keck Logging Company........................ G 336 538-6903
Gibsonville (G-5179)

Keith Call Logging LLC.......................... G 336 262-3681
Millers Creek (G-8305)

Keith Laws.. G 336 973-7220
Wilkesboro (G-12645)

Ken Horton Logging LLC........................ G 336 789-2849
Mount Airy (G-9140)

Ken Wood Corp.................................. G 252 792-6481
Williamston (G-12671)

Laceys Tree Service............................ G 910 330-2868
Jacksonville (G-7129)

Lake Creek Logging & Trckg Inc............ F 910 532-2041
Harrells (G-6101)

Lane Land & Timber Inc........................ G 252 443-1151
Battleboro (G-700)

Ledford Logging Co Inc........................ G 828 644-5410
Murphy (G-9291)

Leonard Logging Co............................ G 336 857-2776
Denton (G-3755)

Little Logging Inc................................ F 704 201-8185
Oakboro (G-9580)

Log Home Builders Inc........................ G 704 638-0677
Salisbury (G-11087)

Lyon Logging.................................... G 336 957-3131
Thurmond (G-12098)

M & K Logging LLC.............................. G 252 349-8975
New Bern (G-9376)

M M & D Harvesting Inc........................ G 252 793-4074
Plymouth (G-9806)

Mark III Logging Inc............................ G 910 862-4820
Tar Heel (G-11917)

Matthew Johnson Logging.................... G 919 291-0197
Sanford (G-11208)

McKeel & Sons Logging Inc.................. G 252 244-3903
Vanceboro (G-12219)

McKoys Logging Company Inc.............. G 910 862-2706
Elizabethtown (G-4429)

McLendon Logging Incorporated............ G 910 439-6223
Mount Gilead (G-9202)

Merritt Logging & Chipping Co.............. G 910 862-4905
Elizabethtown (G-4430)

Michael L Goodson Logging Inc............ G 910 346-8399
Jacksonville (G-7131)

Micheal Langdon Logging Inc................ G 910 890-5295
Erwin (G-4491)

Mike Atkins & Son Logging Inc.............. G 919 965-8002
Selma (G-11290)

Miller Logging Co Inc.......................... G 252 229-9860
Vanceboro (G-12220)

Montgomery Logging Inc...................... G 910 572-2806
Troy (G-12163)

Mud Duck Operations.......................... G 910 253-7669
Bolivia (G-886)

Nat Black Logging Inc.......................... G 704 826-8834
Ansonville (G-130)

Nathan Beiler.................................... G 252 935-5141
Pantego (G-9647)

Noble Brothers Logging Company.......... G 252 355-2587
Winterville (G-13420)

Noralex Inc...................................... G 252 974-1253
Vanceboro (G-12221)

North Cape Fear Logging LLC................ G 910 876-3197
Harrells (G-6102)

Nrfp Logging LLC................................ G 919 738-0989
Goldsboro (G-5232)

OBrien Logging Co.............................. G 910 655-3830
Delco (G-3738)

OLT Logging Inc.................................. G 919 894-4506
Smithfield (G-11456)

Pack Brothers Logging........................ G 828 894-2191
Mill Spring (G-8302)

Phillip Dunn Logging Co Inc.................. G 252 633-4577
New Bern (G-9388)

Piedmont Logging LLC.......................... G 919 562-1861
Youngsville (G-13480)

Potter Logging.................................. G 704 483-2738
Denver (G-3799)

Potts Logging Inc.............................. G 704 463-7549
New London (G-9420)

Preferred Logging.............................. G 910 471-4011
Delco (G-3739)

Price Logging Inc................................ F 252 792-5687
Jamesville (G-7184)

Puett Trucking & Logging...................... G 919 853-2071
Louisburg (G-7923)

R & R Logging Inc.............................. G 704 483-5733
Iron Station (G-7107)

R & S Logging Inc.............................. G 252 426-5880
Hertford (G-6256)

R R Mickey Logging Inc........................ G 910 205-0525
Hamlet (G-6061)

R W Britt Logging Inc.......................... G 252 799-7682
Pinetown (G-9709)

Rabbit Bottom Logging Co Inc.............. G 252 257-3585
Warrenton (G-12353)

Randolph Goodson Logging Inc............ G 910 347-5117
Jacksonville (G-7141)

Red Maple Logging Company Inc.......... G 704 279-6379
Rockwell (G-10800)

Richard C Jones................................ G 919 853-2096
Louisburg (G-7926)

Richard Lewis Von.............................. G 910 628-9292
Orrum (G-9605)

Robert L Rich Tmber Hrvstg Inc............ G 910 529-7321
Garland (G-4910)

Rondol Cordon Logging Inc.................. G 252 944-9220
Washington (G-12411)

Ronnie Andrews................................ G 336 921-4017
Boomer (G-893)

Ronnie Boyds Logging LLC.................... G 336 613-0229
Eden (G-4355)

Ronnie Garrett Logging........................ G 828 894-8413
Columbus (G-3304)

Ronnie L Poole.................................. G 336 657-3956
Ennice (G-4489)

Ross Phelps Logging Co Inc.................. F 252 356-2560
Colerain (G-3272)

Russell Loudermilk Logging.................. G 828 632-4968
Taylorsville (G-11976)

S & K Logging Inc.............................. G 252 794-2045
Windsor (G-13057)

Shelton Logging & Chipping Inc............ G 336 548-3860
Stoneville (G-11827)

Shepherd Family Logging LLC.............. G 910 572-4098
Troy (G-12167)

Simmons Logging & Trucking Inc.......... G 910 287-6344
Ash (G-322)

Smith Brothers Logging........................ G 828 265-1506
Deep Gap (G-3730)

Smiths Logging.................................. G 910 653-4422
Tabor City (G-11914)

Snowbird Logging LLC.......................... G 828 479-6635
Robbinsville (G-10764)

▲ Southeast Wood Products Inc............ F 910 285-4359
Wallace (G-12324)

Southern Logging Inc.......................... G 336 859-5057
Denton (G-3760)

Southern Style Logging LLC.................. G 910 259-9897
Rocky Point (G-10883)

Squeaks Logging Inc.......................... G 252 794-1531
Windsor (G-13058)

SSS Logging Inc................................ G 828 467-1155
Marion (G-8067)

Steve & Ray Banks Logging Inc............ G 910 743-3051
Maysville (G-8212)

Steve Evans Logging Inc...................... G 252 792-1836
Williamston (G-12674)

Steven C Haddock DBA Haddock.......... G 252 714-2431
Vanceboro (G-12222)

Stone House Creek Logging.................. G 252 586-4477
Littleton (G-7887)

Stump Logging.................................. G 910 620-7000
Supply (G-11860)

Summit Logging LLC............................ G 910 734-8787
Lumberton (G-7973)

Swain & Temple Inc............................ F 252 771-8147
South Mills (G-11493)

SWB Logging LLC................................ G 704 485-3411
Oakboro (G-9583)

T W Hathcock Logging Inc.................... G 704 485-9457
Locust (G-7905)

Tar River Thinning Inc.......................... G 919 497-1647
Louisburg (G-7927)

Terry Leggett Logging Co Inc................ E 252 927-4671
Pinetown (G-9710)

Terry Logging Company........................ G 919 477-9170
Bahama (G-667)

Thomas Timber Inc.............................. G 910 532-4542
Harrells (G-6103)

Tim Con Wood Products Inc.................. F 252 793-4819
Roper (G-10900)

Timber Harvester Inc.......................... G 910 346-9754
Jacksonville (G-7156)

Timber Specialists Inc.............................. G 704 902-5146
Statesville *(G-11789)*

Timber Specialists LLC.............................. F 704 873-5756
Statesville *(G-11790)*

Timber Stand Improvements Inc ..... G 910 439-6121
Mount Gilead *(G-9210)*

Top Notch Log Homes Inc...................... G 828 926-4300
Waynesville *(G-12477)*

Trexler Logging Inc.................................. G 704 694-5272
Wadesboro *(G-12250)*

Triple E Equipment LLC............................ G 252 448-1002
Trenton *(G-12112)*

Tucker Logging... G 336 857-2674
Denton *(G-3764)*

Turn Bull Lumber Company..................... F 336 272-5200
Greensboro *(G-5883)*

Vincent L Taylor....................................... G 252 792-2987
Williamston *(G-12676)*

W & T Logging LLC.................................. G 252 209-4351
Windsor *(G-13059)*

W H Bunting Thinning............................... G 252 826-4025
Scotland Neck *(G-11267)*

W R White Inc.. F 252 794-6577
Windsor *(G-13060)*

Wade Biggs Logging Inc........................... G 252 927-4470
Pinetown *(G-9711)*

Wetherington Logging Inc........................ G 252 393-8435
Stella *(G-11809)*

Whitener Sales Company......................... G 828 253-0518
Asheville *(G-635)*

William Shawn Staley............................... G 336 838-9193
Millers Creek *(G-8308)*

Williams Logging Inc................................ G 919 542-2740
Moncure *(G-8413)*

Wilson Bros Logging Inc.......................... F 252 445-5317
Enfield *(G-4486)*

Wood Logging.. G 910 866-4018
White Oak *(G-12575)*

Wright & Hobbs Inc................................. E 252 537-5817
Roanoke Rapids *(G-10748)*

Wst Logging LLC..................................... G 336 857-0147
Denton *(G-3766)*

Young Logging Company Inc.................... G 919 552-9753
Willow Spring *(G-12683)*

2421 Sawmills and planing mills, general

Alan Kimzey... G 828 891-8720
Mills River *(G-8310)*

Arcola Lumber Company Inc.................... E 252 257-4923
Warrenton *(G-12350)*

Ashton Lewis Lumber Co Inc................... D 252 357-0050
Gatesville *(G-5169)*

Beasley Flooring Products Inc................. E 828 524-3248
Bryson City *(G-1008)*

BII Innovations Inc................................... G 888 501-0678
Hickory *(G-6271)*

Blue Ridge Lbr Log & Timber Co............ G 336 961-5211
Yadkinville *(G-13438)*

Boones Sawmill Inc................................. G 828 287-8774
Rutherfordton *(G-10978)*

Builders Firstsource Inc.......................... F 336 884-5454
Greensboro *(G-5409)*

C & C Chipping Inc.................................. G 252 249-1617
Grantsboro *(G-5330)*

C & J Crosspieces LLC............................ G 910 652-4955
Star *(G-11627)*

Cagle Sawmill Inc.................................... G 336 857-2674
Denton *(G-3741)*

Canal Wood LLC...................................... G 910 733-7436
Lumberton *(G-7947)*

Canton Hardwood Company................... G 828 492-0715
Canton *(G-1247)*

Capital Wood Products Inc...................... G 704 982-2417
New London *(G-9414)*

Capitol City Lumber Company................. F 919 832-6492
Raleigh *(G-9970)*

Carolina Timberworks LLC....................... F 828 266-9663
West Jefferson *(G-12561)*

Church & Church Lumber LLC.................. F 336 838-1256
Millers Creek *(G-8304)*

Church & Church Lumber LLC.................. D 336 973-5700
Wilkesboro *(G-12631)*

Clary Lumber Company............................ D 252 537-2558
Gaston *(G-4978)*

Cobble Creek Lumber LLC...................... E 336 844-2620
West Jefferson *(G-12562)*

◆ Coco Lumber Company LLC.................. G 336 906-3754
Charlotte *(G-1950)*

Conover Lumber Company Inc................ F 828 464-4591
Conover *(G-3506)*

▼ Coxe-Lewis Corporation........................ G 252 357-0050
Gatesville *(G-5171)*

Creedmoor Forest Products.................... E 919 529-1779
Creedmoor *(G-3646)*

Dagenhart Pallet Inc............................... G 828 241-2374
Catawba *(G-1511)*

Daniels Lumber Sales Inc....................... G 336 622-5486
Liberty *(G-7763)*

David Raynor Logging Inc........................ E 910 980-0129
Linden *(G-7873)*

Delzer Construction................................ G 919 625-0755
Cary *(G-1345)*

Domtar Paper Company LLC................... B 252 793-8111
Plymouth *(G-9802)*

Donald Henley & Sons Sawmill............... G 336 625-5665
Asheboro *(G-346)*

Duplin Forest Products Inc..................... G 910 285-5381
Wallace *(G-12320)*

E W Godwin S Sons Inc.......................... E 910 762-7747
Wilmington *(G-12769)*

East Coast Firewood LLC........................ F 919 542-0792
Moncure *(G-8403)*

Edwards Timber Company Inc................. G 704 624-5098
Marshville *(G-8087)*

Edwards Wood Pdts Inc/Woodlawn........ G 828 756-4758
Marion *(G-8041)*

Edwards Wood Products Inc................... D 704 624-5098
Liberty *(G-7764)*

Edwards Wood Products Inc................... D 336 622-7537
Liberty *(G-7765)*

◆ Edwards Wood Products Inc.................C 704 624-3624
Marshville *(G-8088)*

Edwards Wood Products Inc................... D 910 276-6870
Laurinburg *(G-7499)*

Elkins Sawmill Inc................................... E 919 362-1235
Moncure *(G-8404)*

Ellis Lumber Company Inc....................... G 704 482-1414
Shelby *(G-11334)*

Enviva Pellets Ahoskie LLC..................... D 301 657-5560
Ahoskie *(G-49)*

Enviva Pellets Sampson LLC................... D 301 657-5560
Faison *(G-4516)*

F L Turlington Lumber Co Inc.................. E 910 592-7197
Clinton *(G-3233)*

Felts Lumber Co Inc................................ G 336 368-5667
Pinnacle *(G-9768)*

Flame Tech Inc.. G 336 661-7801
Winston Salem *(G-13170)*

Fraser West Inc....................................... E 910 655-4106
Riegelwood *(G-10724)*

Fred Winfield Lumber Co Inc................... F 828 648-3414
Canton *(G-1253)*

G & G Forest Products............................. G 704 539-5110
Union Grove *(G-12185)*

G & G Lumber Company Inc.................... G 704 539-5110
Harmony *(G-6098)*

Gates Custom Milling Inc........................ E 252 357-0116
Gatesville *(G-5172)*

Glenn Lumber Company Inc.................... E 704 434-7873
Shelby *(G-11338)*

▲ Godfrey Lumber Company Inc............... F 704 872-6366
Statesville *(G-11704)*

Grubb & Son Sawmill Inc........................ G 336 241-2252
Trinity *(G-12115)*

H Parsons Incorporated.......................... F 828 757-9191
Lenoir *(G-7611)*

H W Culp Lumber Company..................... D 704 463-7311
New London *(G-9417)*

Harris Lumber Company Inc.................... G 828 245-2664
Rutherfordton *(G-10985)*

Hartley Brothers Sawmill Inc.................. G 336 921-2955
Boomer *(G-892)*

Hedrick Brothers Lumber Co Inc............ F 336 746-5885
Lexington *(G-7697)*

Hewlin Brothers Lumber Co.................... G 252 586-6473
Enfield *(G-4484)*

High and High Inc................................... F 252 257-2390
Henderson *(G-6159)*

Hofler H S & Sons Lumber Co................ G 252 465-8603
Sunbury *(G-11848)*

Howard Brothers Mfg LLC....................... G 919 772-4800
Garner *(G-4932)*

Hull Brothers Lumber Co Inc.................. G 336 789-5252
Mount Airy *(G-9130)*

Ibx Lumber LLC....................................... G 252 935-4050
Pantego *(G-9644)*

Idaho Timber NC LLC.............................. E 910 654-5555
Chadbourn *(G-1520)*

Idaho Timber NC LLC.............................. E 252 430-0030
Henderson *(G-6161)*

Independence Lumber Inc....................... D 276 773-3744
Davidson *(G-3708)*

▲ Industrial Wood Products Inc............... E 336 333-5959
Climax *(G-3226)*

Itl Corp... F 828 659-9663
Marion *(G-8044)*

▼ J & B Logging and Timber Co.............. G 919 934-4115
Smithfield *(G-11447)*

J & D Wood Inc....................................... F 910 628-9000
Fairmont *(G-4502)*

J E Jones Lumber Company..................... E 336 472-3478
Lexington *(G-7700)*

▼ J W Jones Lumber Company Inc.......... D 252 771-2497
Elizabeth City *(G-4393)*

Jeld-Wen Inc... C 336 838-0292
North Wilkesboro *(G-9536)*

◆ Jeld-Wen Inc..B 800 535-3936
Charlotte *(G-2366)*

Jerry G Williams & Sons Inc................... F 919 934-4115
Smithfield *(G-11448)*

Jerry Huffman Sawmill............................ G 336 973-3606
Wilkesboro *(G-12644)*

Jerry Williams & Son Inc......................... D 919 934-4115
Smithfield *(G-11449)*

Jordan Lumber & Supply Inc................... C 910 439-6121
Mount Gilead *(G-9200)*

Jordan Lumber & Supply Inc................... G 910 428-9048
Star *(G-11629)*

Jordan Lumber & Supply Inc................... C 910 439-6121
Mount Gilead *(G-9201)*

Jordan-Holman Lumber Co Inc............... D 828 396-3101
Granite Falls *(G-5309)*

Josey Lumber Company Inc.................... E 252 826-5614
Scotland Neck *(G-11264)*

Kamlar Corporation................................. E 252 443-2576
Rocky Mount *(G-10845)*

Katesville Pallet Mill Inc........................F 919 496-3162
   Franklinton (G-4849)

Keener Lumber Company Inc................D 919 934-1087
   Smithfield (G-11450)

Keener Wood Products Inc....................G 828 428-1562
   Maiden (G-8015)

Keller Companies Inc............................G 919 776-4641
   Sanford (G-11200)

Kepley-Frank Hardwood Co Inc.............E 336 746-5419
   Lexington (G-7705)

Kiln-Directcom....................................G 910 259-9794
   Burgaw (G-1026)

L F Delp Lumber Co Inc........................G 336 359-8202
   Laurel Springs (G-7489)

Lampe & Malphrus Lumber Co.............F 919 934-6152
   Smithfield (G-11452)

Lampe & Malphrus Lumber Co.............F 919 934-1124
   Smithfield (G-11454)

▼ Lampe & Malphrus Lumber Co.........D 919 934-6152
   Smithfield (G-11453)

Legacy Pre-Finishing Inc......................F 704 528-7136
   Troutman (G-12143)

Liberty Dry Kiln Corp...........................G 336 622-5490
   Liberty (G-7771)

Liberty Lumber Company......................F 336 622-4901
   Liberty (G-7772)

▲ Marsh Furniture Company.................B 336 884-7363
   High Point (G-6703)

◆ McCreary Modern Inc......................B 828 464-6465
   Newton (G-9481)

Megawood Inc......................................G 910 572-3796
   Mount Gilead (G-9205)

Meherrin River Forest Pdts Inc.............D 252 558-4238
   Weldon (G-12523)

Miller Brothers Lumber Co Inc.............E 336 366-3400
   Elkin (G-4448)

Mixon Mills Inc....................................G 828 297-5431
   Vilas (G-12231)

Myers Forest Products Inc....................G 704 278-4532
   Cleveland (G-3217)

Nelson Logging Company Inc................F 919 849-2547
   Oxford (G-9620)

New South Lumber Company Inc...........C 336 376-3130
   Graham (G-5280)

▼ Oaks Unlimited Inc.........................E 828 926-1621
   Waynesville (G-12465)

Ossiriand Inc.......................................E 336 385-1100
   Creston (G-3658)

Palletone North Carolina Inc.................D 704 462-1882
   Siler City (G-11423)

▼ Parton Forest Products Inc...............G 828 287-4257
   Rutherfordton (G-10989)

▼ Parton Lumber Company Inc.............D 828 287-4257
   Rutherfordton (G-10990)

Peachtree Lumber Company Inc............E 828 837-0118
   Brasstown (G-966)

Piedmont Hardwood Lbr Co Inc............F 704 436-9311
   Mount Pleasant (G-9264)

Pine Log Co Inc...................................E 336 366-2770
   State Road (G-11638)

Pleasant Garden Dry Kiln......................G 336 674-2863
   Pleasant Garden (G-9793)

Polk Sawmill LLC.................................G 828 863-0436
   Tryon (G-12176)

Powell Industries Inc............................D 828 926-9114
   Waynesville (G-12467)

Price Logging Inc.................................F 252 792-5687
   Jamesville (G-7184)

Randy D Miller Lumber Co Inc..............E 336 973-7515
   Wilkesboro (G-12649)

Robert L Rich Tmber Hrvstg Inc...........G 910 529-7321
   Garland (G-4910)

Ross Phelps Logging Co Inc..................F 252 356-2560
   Colerain (G-3272)

S & L Sawmill Inc.................................F 704 483-3264
   Denver (G-3803)

Sawmill Catering LLC...........................F 910 769-7455
   Wilmington (G-12911)

Shaver Wood Products Inc....................D 704 278-1482
   Cleveland (G-3221)

Sipe Lumber Company Inc.....................E 828 632-4679
   Taylorsville (G-11978)

Smoke House Lumber Company.............E 252 257-3303
   Warrenton (G-12355)

Somers Lumber and Mfg Inc.................F 704 539-4751
   Harmony (G-6099)

Southeastern Hardwoods Inc.................G 828 581-0197
   Swannanoa (G-11878)

Southern Woods Lumber Inc..................G 919 963-2233
   Four Oaks (G-4816)

Stoneville Lumber Company Inc.............G 336 623-4311
   Stoneville (G-11830)

Structural 0201 LLC.............................E 240 288-8607
   Trinity (G-12127)

Sunrise Sawmill Inc..............................G 828 277-0120
   Asheville (G-612)

T & S Hardwoods Inc...........................D 828 586-4044
   Sylva (G-11902)

T E Johnson Lumber Co Inc..................G 919 963-2233
   Four Oaks (G-4817)

T H Blue Inc..E 910 673-3033
   Eagle Springs (G-4319)

Tabor City Lumber Company.................E 910 653-3162
   Tabor City (G-11915)

Thomas Lee Fortner Sawmill.................G 828 632-9525
   Taylorsville (G-11984)

Thomas Timber Inc..............................G 910 532-4542
   Harrells (G-6103)

Toney Lumber Company Inc..................D 919 496-5711
   Louisburg (G-7928)

United Visions Corp.............................G 704 953-4555
   Davidson (G-3724)

Uwharrie Lumber Co............................F 910 572-3731
   Troy (G-12170)

Valwood Corporation...........................G 828 321-4717
   Marble (G-8028)

▲ Veneer Technologies Inc..................C 252 223-5600
   Newport (G-9446)

Vida Wood Us Inc................................G 919 934-9904
   Smithfield (G-11468)

▲ W M Cramer Lumber Co...................D 828 397-7481
   Connelly Springs (G-3485)

W N C Pallet Forest Pdts Inc................F 828 667-5426
   Candler (G-1235)

▼ Warmack Lumber Co Inc..................G 252 638-1435
   Cove City (G-3632)

Watts Bumgarner & Brown Inc..............G 828 632-4797
   Taylorsville (G-11986)

West Fraser Inc...................................C 252 589-2011
   Seaboard (G-11272)

Weyerhaeuser Company........................F 252 746-7200
   Grifton (G-6039)

Weyerhaeuser Company........................F 252 791-3200
   Plymouth (G-9808)

Weyerhaeuser Company........................E 252 633-7100
   Vanceboro (G-12223)

Weyerhaeuser Nr Company....................D 252 633-7100
   Vanceboro (G-12225)

Wnc Dry Kiln Inc.................................F 828 652-0050
   Marion (G-8074)

Woodpecker Sawmill............................G 828 891-8720
   Mills River (G-8325)

World Wood Company...........................D 252 523-0021
   Cove City (G-3633)

Wright & Hobbs Inc.............................E 252 537-5817
   Roanoke Rapids (G-10748)

Yadkin Lumber Company Inc.................G 336 679-2432
   Yadkinville (G-13459)

▼ Yildiz Entegre Usa Inc.....................G 910 763-4733
   Wilmington (G-12956)

2426 Hardwood dimension and flooring mills

A C Furniture Company Inc...................B 336 623-3430
   Eden (G-4339)

▲ Adams Wood Turning Inc..................G 336 882-0196
   High Point (G-6509)

Ana Muf Corporation...........................G 336 653-3509
   Asheboro (G-326)

▲ Appalachian Lumber Company Inc.....E 336 973-7205
   Wilkesboro (G-12628)

▲ Ariston Hospitality Inc.....................E 626 458-8668
   High Point (G-6528)

Artistic Frame Corp.............................B 212 289-2100
   Kannapolis (G-7202)

▲ Associated Hardwoods Inc................E 828 396-3321
   Granite Falls (G-5295)

B & E Woodturning Inc.........................G 828 758-2843
   Lenoir (G-7575)

Bartimaeus By Design Inc.....................C 336 475-4346
   Thomasville (G-11996)

Beasley Flooring Products Inc...............E 828 349-7000
   Franklin (G-4818)

Blue Ridge Lbr Log & Timber Co...........G 336 961-5211
   Yadkinville (G-13438)

Blue Ridge Products Co Inc..................G 828 322-7990
   Hickory (G-6274)

Bona USA..F 704 220-6943
   Monroe (G-8443)

Bruex Inc..E 828 754-1186
   Lenoir (G-7589)

Bull City Designs LLC..........................E 919 908-6252
   Durham (G-3949)

C & S Woodworking..............................G 828 437-5024
   Valdese (G-12191)

Cagle Sawmill Inc................................G 336 857-2274
   Denton (G-3741)

Carolina Leg Supply LLC.......................G 828 446-6838
   Hudson (G-6947)

Catawba Frames Inc.............................G 828 459-7717
   Claremont (G-3091)

Cecil-Johnson Mfg Inc..........................E 336 431-5233
   High Point (G-6565)

Chris Isom Inc.....................................F 336 629-0240
   Asheboro (G-338)

Church & Church Lumber LLC...............F 336 838-1256
   Millers Creek (G-8304)

Church & Church Lumber LLC...............D 336 973-4297
   Wilkesboro (G-12632)

Church & Church Lumber LLC...............D 336 973-5700
   Wilkesboro (G-12631)

Clary Lumber Company........................D 252 537-2558
   Gaston (G-4978)

Cleveland Lumber Company..................E 704 487-5263
   Shelby (G-11320)

Columbia Forest Products Inc...............G 336 605-0429
   Greensboro (G-5454)

Columbia Plywood Corporation..............B 828 724-4191
   Old Fort (G-9592)

Contemporary Furnishings Corp............G 336 857-2988
   Denton (G-3744)

▼ Coxe-Lewis Corporation...................G 252 357-0050
   Gatesville (G-5171)

Curved Plywood Inc.............................G 336 249-6901
   Lexington (G-7674)

▲ Danbartex LLC................................G 704 323-8728
   Mooresville (G-8650)

S
I
C

Daniels Woodcarving Co Inc.............. F 828 632-7336
Taylorsville *(G-11958)*

David Raynor Logging Inc................... E 910 980-0129
Linden *(G-7873)*

▲ Delve Interiors LLC...................... C 336 274-4661
Greensboro *(G-5495)*

Designs In Wood.............................. G 336 372-8995
Sparta *(G-11538)*

Df Framing LLC................................. F 919 368-7903
Siler City *(G-11407)*

Dimension Milling Co Inc.................. G 336 983-2820
Denton *(G-3748)*

Dimension Wood Products Inc.......... F 828 459-9891
Claremont *(G-3107)*

◆ Edwards Wood Products Inc........... C 704 624-3624
Marshville *(G-8088)*

Eekkohart Floors & Lbr Co Inc.......... G 336 409-2672
Mocksville *(G-8361)*

Eskimo 7 Limited.............................. G 252 726-8181
Morehead City *(G-8832)*

Ethan Allen Retail Inc....................... E 828 428-9361
Maiden *(G-8012)*

F L Turlington Lumber Co Inc............ E 910 592-7197
Clinton *(G-3233)*

Fairgrove Furniture Co Inc............... G 828 322-8570
Hickory *(G-6331)*

Fortner Lumber Inc........................... G 704 585-2383
Hiddenite *(G-6496)*

Framewright Inc................................ G 828 459-2284
Conover *(G-3523)*

Franklin Veneers Inc......................... G 919 494-2284
Franklinton *(G-4848)*

Gates Custom Milling Inc.................. E 252 357-0116
Gatesville *(G-5172)*

Glenn Lumber Company Inc.............. E 704 434-7873
Shelby *(G-11338)*

Green River Resource MGT................ F 828 697-0357
Zirconia *(G-13530)*

Gregory Hill Frame........................... F 828 428-0007
Maiden *(G-8014)*

H T Jones Lumber Company.............. G 252 332-4135
Ahoskie *(G-50)*

Hfi Wind Down Inc............................ C 828 438-5767
Morganton *(G-8872)*

HM Frame Company Inc.................... E 828 428-3354
Newton *(G-9472)*

Hofler H S & Sons Lumber Co............ G 252 465-8603
Sunbury *(G-11848)*

Horizon Forest Products Co LP.......... G 336 993-9663
Colfax *(G-3280)*

Horizon Frest Pdts Wlmngton LP....... D 919 424-8265
Raleigh *(G-10175)*

◆ Hughes Furniture Inds Inc.............. C 336 498-8700
Randleman *(G-10650)*

Hull Brothers Lumber Co Inc............. G 336 789-5252
Mount Airy *(G-9130)*

▲ Ideaitlia Cntmporary Furn Corp...... C 828 464-1000
Conover *(G-3532)*

J & D Wood Inc................................. F 910 628-9000
Fairmont *(G-4502)*

J L Frame Shop Inc........................... G 828 256-6290
Conover *(G-3535)*

J L Powell & Co Inc........................... G 910 642-8989
Whiteville *(G-12585)*

Jerry Blevins.................................... G 336 384-3726
Lansing *(G-7477)*

Jones Frame Inc............................... E 336 434-2531
High Point *(G-6679)*

Josey Lumber Company Inc............... E 252 826-5614
Scotland Neck *(G-11264)*

L F Delp Lumber Co Inc..................... G 336 359-8202
Laurel Springs *(G-7489)*

La Barge Inc..................................... G 336 812-2400
High Point *(G-6688)*

▲ Lambeth Dimension Inc................. F 336 629-3838
Asheboro *(G-372)*

Latham Inc....................................... G 336 857-3702
Denton *(G-3754)*

Leisure Craft Holdings LLC............... D 828 693-8241
Flat Rock *(G-4708)*

Leisure Craft Inc.............................. C 828 693-8241
Flat Rock *(G-4709)*

M & M Frame Company Inc............... G 336 859-8166
Denton *(G-3757)*

◆ M & S Warehouse Inc.................... E 828 728-3733
Lenoir *(G-7622)*

Mac-Vann Inc................................... G 919 577-0746
Sanford *(G-11206)*

Mannington Mills Inc........................ E 336 884-5600
High Point *(G-6697)*

Maynard Frame Shop Inc.................. G 910 428-2033
Star *(G-11631)*

Mc Gees Crating Inc......................... E 828 758-4660
Lenoir *(G-7626)*

McNeill Frame Inc............................. G 336 873-7934
Seagrove *(G-11278)*

◆ North Carolina Lumber Company.... G 336 498-6600
Randleman *(G-10654)*

Oak City Customs LLC...................... G 919 995-5561
Zebulon *(G-13517)*

Oceania Hardwoods LLC................... G 910 862-4447
Elizabethtown *(G-4431)*

Old Growth Riverwood Inc................. G 910 762-4077
Wilmington *(G-12865)*

Palletone North Carolina Inc............. D 704 462-1882
Siler City *(G-11423)*

▼ Parton Lumber Company Inc.......... D 828 287-4257
Rutherfordton *(G-10990)*

Perrys Frame Inc.............................. F 828 327-4681
Newton *(G-9487)*

Piedmont Hardwood Lbr Co Inc........ F 704 436-9311
Mount Pleasant *(G-9264)*

Pilot View Wood Works Inc............... G 336 883-2511
High Point *(G-6733)*

Powell Industries Inc........................ D 828 926-9114
Waynesville *(G-12467)*

Price Logging Inc............................. F 252 792-5687
Jamesville *(G-7184)*

Quality Fabricators.......................... G 336 622-3402
Staley *(G-11599)*

Redi-Frame Inc................................. G 828 322-4227
Hickory *(G-6427)*

Rhf Investments Inc.......................... E 828 632-7070
Taylorsville *(G-11973)*

Ritch Face Veneer Company............. G 336 883-4184
High Point *(G-6758)*

▲ Robert St Clair Co Inc................... F 919 847-8611
Raleigh *(G-10445)*

Ross Phelps Logging Co Inc............. F 252 356-2560
Colerain *(G-3272)*

Rudisill Frame Shop Inc.................... E 828 464-7020
Newton *(G-9492)*

Ruskin Inc.. E 828 324-6500
Hickory *(G-6436)*

Select Frame Shop Inc...................... D 910 428-1225
Biscoe *(G-857)*

Shaver Wood Products Inc................ D 704 278-1482
Cleveland *(G-3221)*

Sipes Carving Shop Inc.................... E 828 327-3077
Hickory *(G-6449)*

Solid Frames Inc.............................. G 336 882-5082
High Point *(G-6784)*

Southill Industrial Carving............... G 336 472-5311
Thomasville *(G-12072)*

Sure Wood Products Inc................... G 828 261-0004
Hickory *(G-6461)*

T & S Hardwoods Inc........................ D 828 586-4044
Sylva *(G-11902)*

▲ The Southwood Furniture C............ G 828 465-1776
Hickory *(G-6465)*

Tima Capital Inc............................... F 910 769-3273
Wilmington *(G-12939)*

Timothy Lee Blacjmon...................... G 336 481-9038
Thomasville *(G-12079)*

▲ Triton International Woods LLC...... D 252 823-6675
Tarboro *(G-11945)*

◆ Turn Bull Lumber Company............ E 910 862-4447
Elizabethtown *(G-4436)*

Ufp Site Built LLC............................. F 910 590-3220
Clinton *(G-3252)*

▲ United Finishers Intl Inc................ G 336 883-3901
High Point *(G-6818)*

Universal Forest Products Inc........... F 252 338-0319
Elizabeth City *(G-4416)*

Uwharrie Frames Mfg LLC................ E 336 626-6649
Asheboro *(G-416)*

Uwharrie Lumber Co......................... F 910 572-3731
Troy *(G-12170)*

▲ Valendrawers Inc.......................... E 336 956-2118
Lexington *(G-7756)*

▲ Veneer Technologies Inc............... C 252 223-5600
Newport *(G-9446)*

Vivet Inc.. F 909 390-1039
Greensboro *(G-5904)*

W & S Frame Company Inc............... G 828 728-6078
Granite Falls *(G-5325)*

▲ W M Cramer Lumber Co................ D 828 397-7481
Connelly Springs *(G-3485)*

Walton Lumber Co............................ G 919 563-6565
Mebane *(G-8264)*

WB Frames Inc................................. G 828 459-2147
Hickory *(G-6488)*

Weyerhaeuser Company.................... F 252 746-7200
Grifton *(G-6039)*

Woodline Inc.................................... G 336 476-7100
Thomasville *(G-12090)*

Woodwright of Wilson Co Inc............ G 252 243-9663
Elm City *(G-4468)*

Wright & Hobbs Inc.......................... E 252 537-5817
Roanoke Rapids *(G-10748)*

Zenecar LLC..................................... G 919 518-0464
Raleigh *(G-10623)*

Zickgraf Enterprises Inc................... G 704 369-1200
Franklin *(G-4845)*

2429 Special product sawmills, nec

Southern Distilling Co LLC............... G 704 677-4069
Statesville *(G-11769)*

2431 Millwork

A and H Millwork Inc........................ F 704 983-2402
Albemarle *(G-57)*

AAA Louvers Inc............................... F 919 365-7220
Wendell *(G-12529)*

Acorn Woodworks NC LLC................ G 828 361-9953
Murphy *(G-9286)*

Against Grain Woodworking Inc........ G 704 309-5750
Charlotte *(G-1628)*

Ajs Dezigns Inc................................ G 828 652-6304
Marion *(G-8030)*

Amarr Company................................ G 704 599-5858
Charlotte *(G-1661)*

Amarr Company................................ G 336 936-0010
Mocksville *(G-8347)*

◆ Amarr Company............................ C 336 744-5100
Winston Salem *(G-13084)*

American Woodmark Corporation.......... E 704 947-3280
   Huntersville *(G-6964)*

American Woodworkery Inc................. G 910 916-8098
   Fayetteville *(G-4552)*

Andronics Construction Inc................. E 704 400-9562
   Indian Trail *(G-7068)*

▲ Appalachian Lumber Company Inc.. E 336 973-7205
   Wilkesboro *(G-12628)*

Archdale Millworks Inc.................... G 336 431-9019
   Archdale *(G-212)*

Architectural Craftsman Ltd............... E 919 494-6911
   Franklinton *(G-4846)*

Around House Improvement LLC......... G 919 496-7029
   Bunn *(G-1013)*

Artistic Southern Inc...................... F 919 861-4695
   Charlotte *(G-1700)*

Athol Arbor Corporation................... F 919 643-1100
   Hillsborough *(G-6859)*

B & B Wood Shop & Bldg Contrs........ G 828 488-2078
   Bryson City *(G-1007)*

B&H Millwork and Fixtures Inc............ E 336 431-0068
   High Point *(G-6534)*

Bakers Quality Trim Inc................... G 919 552-3621
   Willow Spring *(G-12678)*

Barber Furniture & Supply................ F 704 278-9367
   Cleveland *(G-3209)*

Barewoodworking Inc..................... F 828 758-0694
   Lenoir *(G-7576)*

▲ Bfs Asset Holdings LLC................ B 303 784-4288
   Raleigh *(G-9941)*

▲ Bfs Operations LLC.................... A 919 431-1000
   Raleigh *(G-9942)*

Black River Woodwork LLC................ G 919 757-4559
   Angier *(G-112)*

Blinds Plus Inc........................... G 910 487-5196
   Fayetteville *(G-4560)*

Blumer & Stanton Entps Inc.............. G 828 765-2800
   Newland *(G-9425)*

Bonakemi Usa Incorporated.............. D 704 218-3917
   Monroe *(G-8444)*

Bone Tred Beds Smmit Woodworks...... G 910 319-7583
   Wilmington *(G-12722)*

Brookshire Woodworking Inc.............. G 828 779-2119
   Asheville *(G-462)*

Browns Woodworking LLC................. G 704 983-5917
   Albemarle *(G-65)*

Builders Firstsource Inc.................. F 336 884-5454
   Greensboro *(G-5409)*

Builders Firstsource Inc.................. F 919 562-6601
   Youngsville *(G-13465)*

Builders Firstsource - SE Grp............ G 910 313-3056
   Wilmington *(G-12724)*

Builders Frstsrce - Sthast Gro........... C 910 944-2516
   Aberdeen *(G-2)*

Building Center Inc...................... D 704 889-8182
   Pineville *(G-9717)*

Built By Ben Woodworks LLC.............. G 336 438-1159
   Burlington *(G-1055)*

Cardinal Millwork & Supply Inc........... E 336 665-9811
   Greensboro *(G-5422)*

Carolina Building Services Inc............ F 704 664-7110
   Mooresville *(G-8631)*

Carolina Stairs Inc....................... F 704 664-5032
   Mount Ulla *(G-9267)*

Carolina Woodworks Trim of NC.......... G 252 492-9259
   Henderson *(G-6150)*

Carpathian Woodworks Inc............... G 919 669-7546
   Clayton *(G-3136)*

Carter Millwork Inc....................... D 800 861-0734
   Lexington *(G-7661)*

Cbg Acquisition Company................. A 336 768-8872
   Winston Salem *(G-13121)*

◆ Chadsworth Incorporated.............. G 910 763-7600
   Wilmington *(G-12742)*

Chesnick Corporation..................... F 919 231-2899
   Raleigh *(G-9993)*

Cleveland Lumber Company.............. E 704 487-5263
   Shelby *(G-11320)*

Coastal Custom Wood Works LLC........ G 252 675-8732
   New Bern *(G-9355)*

Coastal Millwork Supply Co............... G 910 763-3300
   Wilmington *(G-12743)*

Contemporary Design Co LLC............. F 704 375-6030
   Gastonia *(G-5030)*

Convert-A-Stair LLC...................... G 888 908-5657
   Wilmington *(G-12750)*

Cook & Boardman Group LLC............. D 336 768-8872
   Winston Salem *(G-13127)*

Cook & Boardman Nc LLC................ E 336 768-8872
   Winston Salem *(G-13128)*

Craft Doors Usa LLC..................... F 828 469-7029
   Newton *(G-9462)*

Creative Custom Woodworks Inc.......... G 910 431-8544
   Wilmington *(G-12754)*

Crown Heritage Inc...................... E 336 835-1424
   Elkin *(G-4443)*

Currier Woodworks Inc................... G 252 725-4233
   Beaufort *(G-725)*

Curvemakers Inc......................... G 919 690-1121
   Oxford *(G-9611)*

Curvemakers Inc......................... G 919 821-5792
   Raleigh *(G-10027)*

▲ Custom Doors Incorporated........... F 704 982-2885
   Albemarle *(G-67)*

◆ Dac Products Inc...................... E 336 969-9786
   Rural Hall *(G-10958)*

Davis Cabinet Co Wilson Inc.............. G 252 291-9052
   Sims *(G-11429)*

Davis Mechanical Inc..................... F 704 272-9366
   Peachland *(G-9651)*

Decore-Ative Spc NC LLC................ C 704 291-9669
   Monroe *(G-8475)*

Division Six Incorporated................. G 910 420-3305
   New Bern *(G-9365)*

▲ Door Store of America Inc............. F 919 781-3200
   Raleigh *(G-10056)*

Door Works Huntersville LLC.............. G 704 947-1900
   Huntersville *(G-6982)*

Double Hung LLC........................ E 888 235-8956
   Greensboro *(G-5501)*

East Coast Door & Hardware Inc.......... G 704 791-4128
   Concord *(G-3358)*

Ecmd Inc................................ C 336 835-1182
   Elkin *(G-4444)*

▲ Ecmd Inc.............................. D 336 667-5976
   North Wilkesboro *(G-9529)*

Elite Wood Classics Inc................... G 910 454-8745
   Oak Island *(G-9565)*

Endgrain Woodworks LLC................. G 980 237-2612
   Charlotte *(G-2113)*

Exley Custom Woodwork Inc.............. G 910 763-5445
   Castle Hayne *(G-1498)*

Flat Iron Mill Works LLC.................. G 828 768-7770
   Leicester *(G-7524)*

Forest Millwork Inc....................... F 828 251-5264
   Asheville *(G-499)*

Frederick and Frederick Entp.............. F 252 235-4849
   Middlesex *(G-8275)*

Freedom Enterprise LLC.................. G 502 510-7296
   Charlotte *(G-2177)*

Funder America Inc...................... F 336 751-3501
   Mocksville *(G-8364)*

◆ Funder America Inc.................... C 336 751-3501
   Mocksville *(G-8365)*

Garner Woodworks LLC................... G 828 775-1790
   Swannanoa *(G-11871)*

Gary Forte Woodworking Inc.............. G 704 780-0095
   Monroe *(G-8491)*

Gates Custom Milling Inc................. E 252 357-0116
   Gatesville *(G-5172)*

▲ GLG Corporation...................... F 336 784-0396
   Winston Salem *(G-13178)*

Goodman Millwork Inc.................... F 704 633-2421
   Salisbury *(G-11058)*

Guyclee Millwork........................ F 919 202-5738
   Selma *(G-11288)*

H & H Wood Products Inc................. G 704 233-4148
   Wingate *(G-13062)*

H & H Woodworking Inc.................. G 336 884-5848
   High Point *(G-6637)*

H T Jones Lumber Company.............. G 252 332-4135
   Ahoskie *(G-50)*

H&M Woodworks Inc..................... F 919 496-5993
   Louisburg *(G-7917)*

Harley S Woodworks Inc.................. G 828 776-0120
   Barnardsville *(G-692)*

Hedrick Construction..................... G 336 362-3443
   Kernersville *(G-7278)*

Hogan Cabinetry and Mllwk LLC.......... G 704 856-0425
   China Grove *(G-3075)*

Hunter Innovations Ltd................... G 919 848-8814
   Raleigh *(G-10181)*

Hunter Millwork Inc...................... F 704 821-0144
   Matthews *(G-8174)*

Idaho Wood Inc.......................... F 208 263-9521
   Oxford *(G-9617)*

▲ Idx Impressions LLC.................. C 703 550-6902
   Washington *(G-12393)*

Interior Trim Creations Inc............... G 704 821-1470
   Charlotte *(G-2342)*

Itc Millwork LLC......................... D 704 821-1470
   Matthews *(G-8176)*

▲ J & M Woodworking Inc............... F 828 728-3253
   Hudson *(G-6950)*

J & P Wood Works Inc.................... E 336 788-1881
   Winston Salem *(G-13211)*

Jeld-Wen Inc............................ D 828 724-9511
   Marion *(G-8045)*

Jeld-Wen Inc............................ C 336 838-0292
   North Wilkesboro *(G-9536)*

▲ Jeld-Wen Holding Inc................. B 704 378-5700
   Charlotte *(G-2367)*

▲ Jenkins Millwork LLC.................. E 336 667-3344
   Wilkesboro *(G-12643)*

Jody Stowe.............................. G 704 519-6560
   Matthews *(G-8119)*

John Lindenberger....................... G 919 337-6741
   Raleigh *(G-10217)*

Jones Doors & Windows Inc.............. F 336 998-8624
   Mocksville *(G-8372)*

Keglers Woodworks LLC.................. G 919 608-7220
   Raleigh *(G-10232)*

Kingdom Woodworks Inc.................. G 704 678-8134
   Kings Mountain *(G-7368)*

Kotek Holdings Inc....................... E 919 643-1100
   Hillsborough *(G-6870)*

KS Custom Woodworks Inc................ G 252 714-3957
   Walstonburg *(G-12333)*

Laborie Sons Cstm Wodworks LLC....... G 910 769-2524
   Castle Hayne *(G-1504)*

Lee Builder Mart Inc...................... E
   Sanford *(G-11204)*

Libasci Woodworks Inc................... G 828 524-7073
   Franklin *(G-4834)*

Liberty Wood Products Inc................ F 828 524-7958
   Franklin *(G-4835)*

Employee Codes: A=Over 500 employees, B=251-500
C=101-250, D=51-100, E=20-50, F=10-19, G=1-9   2025 Harris North Carolina
Manufacturers Directory   639

Louisiana-Pacific Corporation	C	336 599-8080	Roxboro *(G-10929)*
Lumberton Overhead Doors Inc	G	910 739-6426	Lumberton *(G-7961)*
Martin Wood Products Inc	G	336 548-3470	Madison *(G-7993)*
Martins Woodworking LLC	F	704 473-7617	Lattimore *(G-7481)*
Masonite International Corp	E	919 575-3700	Butner *(G-1202)*
Master Kraft Inc	E	704 234-2673	Matthews *(G-8183)*
▲ **Masterwrap Inc**	E	336 243-4515	Lexington *(G-7716)*
Matthews Building Supply Co	E	704 847-2106	Matthews *(G-8130)*
Matthews Millwork Inc	G	704 821-4499	Monroe *(G-8526)*
Mesa Quality Fenestration Inc	G	828 393-0132	Hendersonville *(G-6226)*
Metal Crafters of Goldsboro NC	G	919 778-7200	Goldsboro *(G-5228)*
Metalfab of North Carolina LLC	C	704 841-1090	Matthews *(G-8132)*
Metrolina Woodworks Inc	F	704 821-9095	Stallings *(G-11601)*
Metzgers Burl Wood Gallery	G	828 452-2550	Waynesville *(G-12463)*
Mh Libman Woodturning	G	828 360-5530	Asheville *(G-546)*
Mike Powell Inc	F	910 792-6152	Wilmington *(G-12854)*
Miters Touch Inc	G	828 963-4445	Banner Elk *(G-688)*
Morrison Mill Work	G	828 774-5415	Asheville *(G-550)*
▲ **Moulding Millwork LLC**	G	704 504-9880	Charlotte *(G-2522)*
Moulding Source Incorporated	G	704 658-1111	Mooresville *(G-8729)*
Mountain Top Woodworking	G	336 982-4059	West Jefferson *(G-12568)*
Mw Manufacturers Inc	E	919 677-3900	Cary *(G-1404)*
Normac Kitchens Inc	F	704 485-1911	Oakboro *(G-9582)*
North State Millwork	G	252 442-9090	Rocky Mount *(G-10855)*
Northside Millwork Inc	E	919 732-6100	Hillsborough *(G-6874)*
Old Mill Precision Gun Works &	G	704 284-2832	Bessemer City *(G-828)*
Olde Lexington Products Inc	G	336 956-2355	Linwood *(G-7880)*
Onsite Woodwork Corporation	F	704 523-1380	Charlotte *(G-2600)*
▲ **Ornamental Mouldings LLC**	F	336 431-9120	Archdale *(G-240)*
Oyama Cabinet Inc	G	828 327-2668	Conover *(G-3542)*
P & P Distributing Company	G	910 582-1968	Hamlet *(G-6060)*
P R Sparks Enterprises Inc	G	336 272-7200	Greensboro *(G-5728)*
Pegasus Builders Supply LLC	G	919 244-1586	Durham *(G-4172)*
Piedmont Joinery Inc	G	919 632-3703	Durham *(G-4182)*
Piedmont Stairworks LLC	G	704 483-3721	Denver *(G-3798)*
Piedmont Stairworks LLC	G	704 697-0259	Charlotte *(G-2637)*
Piedmont Turning & Wdwkg Co	G	336 475-7161	Thomasville *(G-12060)*
Piedmont Wood Products Inc	F	828 632-4077	Taylorsville *(G-11971)*
Pine Creek Products LLC	F	336 399-8806	Winston Salem *(G-13295)*
Ply Gem Holdings Inc	D	919 677-3900	Cary *(G-1421)*
Ply Gem Industries Inc	D	919 677-3900	Cary *(G-1422)*
Prestige Millwork Inc	G	910 428-2360	Star *(G-11633)*
Pridgen Woodwork Inc	E	910 642-7175	Whiteville *(G-12592)*
Pro-Kay Supply Inc	F	910 628-0882	Orrum *(G-9604)*
▲ **Profilform Us Inc**	E	252 430-0392	Henderson *(G-6170)*
R L Roten Woodworking LLC	G	336 982-3830	Crumpler *(G-3662)*
Red Shed Woodworks Inc	G	828 768-3854	Marshall *(G-8083)*
Reeb Millwork Corporation	F	336 751-4650	Mocksville *(G-8387)*
Reliable Construction Co Inc	G	704 289-1501	Monroe *(G-8550)*
Richmond Millwork LLC	G	910 331-1009	Rockingham *(G-10788)*
Rls Commercial Interiors Inc	G	919 365-4086	Wendell *(G-12545)*
Robbinsville Cstm Molding Inc	F	828 479-2317	Robbinsville *(G-10761)*
Rowland Woodworking Inc	E	336 887-0700	High Point *(G-6761)*
Royal Oak Stairs Inc	G	919 855-8988	Raleigh *(G-10449)*
S Banner Cabinets Incorporated	E	828 733-2031	Newland *(G-9434)*
S H Woodworking	G	336 463-2885	Yadkinville *(G-13450)*
Salem Woodworking Company	G	336 768-7443	Winston Salem *(G-13328)*
Sauder Woodworking Co	G	704 799-6782	Mooresville *(G-8766)*
▲ **Select Stainless Products LLC**	G	888 843-2345	Charlotte *(G-2783)*
Selectbuild Construction Inc	F	208 331-4300	Raleigh *(G-10467)*
Shep Berryhill Woodworking	G	828 242-3227	Asheville *(G-598)*
Shutter Production Inc	G	910 289-2620	Rose Hill *(G-10910)*
Signature Custom Wdwkg Inc	G	336 983-9905	King *(G-7337)*
Skettis Woodworks	G	336 671-9866	Winston Salem *(G-13338)*
Smith Companies Lexington Inc	G	336 249-4941	Lexington *(G-7742)*
▲ **Smith Millwork Inc**	E	800 222-8498	Lexington *(G-7743)*
Smokey Mountain Lumber Inc	G	828 298-3958	Asheville *(G-602)*
Southern Classic Stairs Inc	G	828 285-9828	Alexander *(G-101)*
Southern Staircase Inc	D	704 357-1221	Charlotte *(G-2839)*
Southern Staircase Inc	G	704 363-2123	Charlotte *(G-2840)*
Southern Woodcraft Design LLC	G	919 693-8995	Oxford *(G-9637)*
Southern Woodworking Inc	G	336 693-5892	Burlington *(G-1159)*
Southwood Doors LLC	G	704 625-2578	Conover *(G-3561)*
▲ **Spartacraft Inc**	E	828 397-4630	Connelly Springs *(G-3483)*
Stephenson Millwork Co Inc	C	252 237-1141	Wilson *(G-13031)*
Stevenson Woodworking	G	919 362-9121	Apex *(G-196)*
▲ **Stock Building Supply Hol**	A	919 431-1000	Raleigh *(G-10509)*
Sugar Mountain Woodworks Inc	G	423 292-6245	Newland *(G-9435)*
Summit Peak Pens and WD Works	G	336 404-8312	Liberty *(G-7780)*
Ta Lost Pines Woodwork	G	828 367-7517	Asheville *(G-614)*
Tallent Wood Works	G	704 592-2013	Statesville *(G-11785)*
▲ **Tiger Mountain Woodworks Inc**	F	828 526-5577	Highlands *(G-6846)*
Timber Wolf Forest Products	F	828 728-7500	Hudson *(G-6961)*
Timber Wolf Wood Creations Inc	G	704 309-5118	Charlotte *(G-2919)*
Tivoli Woodworks LLC	G	336 602-3512	Salisbury *(G-11125)*
Triad Prefinish & Lbr Sls Inc	G	336 375-4849	Greensboro *(G-5877)*
Triangle Custom Woodworks LLC	G	919 637-8857	Fuquay Varina *(G-4903)*
Triangle Woodworks Inc	G	919 570-0337	Wake Forest *(G-12308)*
Trim Inc	G	336 751-3591	Mocksville *(G-8395)*
Trimsters Inc	G	919 639-3126	Angier *(G-128)*
Trimworks Inc	G	704 753-4149	Monroe *(G-8570)*
TS Woodworks & RAD Design Inc	F	704 238-1015	Monroe *(G-8571)*
Tuckers Farm Inc	G	704 375-8199	Charlotte *(G-2952)*
▲ **United Finishers Intl Inc**	G	336 883-3901	High Point *(G-6818)*
United Wood Products Inc	G	336 626-2281	Asheboro *(G-414)*
Ventura Systems Inc	E	704 712-8630	Dallas *(G-3692)*
Vision Stairways & Mllwk LLC	F	919 878-5622	Raleigh *(G-10592)*
Western Crlina Cstm Cswork Inc	F	828 669-0459	Black Mountain *(G-872)*
Whitaker Mill Works LLC	G	919 772-3030	Raleigh *(G-10608)*
Wigal Wood Works	G	580 890-9723	Fayetteville *(G-4700)*
Williamsburg Woodcraft Inc	G	919 965-3363	Selma *(G-11294)*
Windsor Window Company	D	704 283-7459	Monroe *(G-8582)*
Wizards Wood Werks	G	252 813-3929	Macclesfield *(G-7981)*
Wood Barn Inc	E	919 496-6714	Louisburg *(G-7929)*
Wood Creations NC Inc	G	704 865-1822	Gastonia *(G-5166)*
Wood Surgeon	G	252 728-5767	Beaufort *(G-737)*
Wood Works	G	910 579-1487	Sunset Beach *(G-11853)*
Woodmaster Custom Cabinets Inc	F	919 554-3707	Youngsville *(G-13499)*

Woodtech/Interiors Inc............................ G 704 332-7215
Charlotte *(G-3024)*

Woodwizards Inc...................................... G 336 427-7698
Stokesdale *(G-11818)*

Woodworking Unlimited Inc.................... G 704 903-8080
Olin *(G-9598)*

▲ Zepsa Industries Inc.......................... D 704 583-9220
Charlotte *(G-3047)*

2434 Wood kitchen cabinets

Advance Cabinetry Inc............................ F 828 676-3550
Fletcher *(G-4718)*

Alexanders Cbinets Countertops.......... G 336 774-2966
Winston Salem *(G-13077)*

Allen & Son S Cabinet Shop Inc........... G 919 963-2196
Four Oaks *(G-4807)*

American Wood Reface of Triad............ G 336 345-2837
Kernersville *(G-7244)*

American Woodmark Corporation.......... D 828 428-6300
Lincolnton *(G-7813)*

American Woodmark Corporation.......... F 540 665-9100
Stoneville *(G-11819)*

Artistic Kitchens & Baths LLC............... G 910 692-4000
Southern Pines *(G-11494)*

Ashleys Kit Bath Dsign Stdio L............. F 828 669-5281
Black Mountain *(G-860)*

Aspen Cabinetry Inc............................... G 828 466-0216
Conover *(G-3492)*

Atlantic Coast Cabinet Distrs................ E 919 554-8165
Youngsville *(G-13462)*

Barber Furniture & Supply...................... F 704 278-9367
Cleveland *(G-3209)*

Bcac Holdings LLC................................. G 910 754-5689
Supply *(G-11855)*

Bill Truitt Wood Works Inc..................... G 704 398-8499
Charlotte *(G-1782)*

Black Mountain Cnstr Group Inc............ F 704 243-5593
Waxhaw *(G-12424)*

Black Rock Granite & Cabinetry............. G 828 787-1100
Highlands *(G-6843)*

Blue Ridge Cab Connection LLC........... G 828 891-2281
Mills River *(G-8311)*

Brown Cabinet Co.................................... G 704 933-2731
Kannapolis *(G-7205)*

Burlington Distributing Co...................... G 336 292-1415
Greensboro *(G-5411)*

C & F Custom Cabinets Inc................... E 910 424-7475
Hope Mills *(G-6923)*

Cabinet Creations Inc............................. G 919 542-3722
Moncure *(G-8401)*

Cabinet Door World LLC......................... F 877 929-2750
Hickory *(G-6279)*

Cabinet Makers Inc................................. G 704 876-2808
Statesville *(G-11674)*

Cabinet Shop Inc..................................... G 252 726-6965
Morehead City *(G-8820)*

Cabinet Solutions Usa Inc..................... E 828 358-2349
Hickory *(G-6280)*

Cabinet Transitions Inc........................... G 336 382-7154
Greensboro *(G-5418)*

Cabinets and Things................................ G 828 652-1734
Union Mills *(G-12187)*

Cabinets Plus Inc.................................... G 718 213-3300
Charlotte *(G-1828)*

Cabinetworks Group Mich LLC.............. E 803 984-2285
Charlotte *(G-1829)*

Cabinetworks Group Mich LLC.............. E 919 868-8174
Raleigh *(G-9964)*

Caldwell Cabinets NC LLC..................... E 828 212-0000
Hudson *(G-6945)*

Cape Fear Cabinet Co Inc...................... G 910 703-8760
Fayetteville *(G-4565)*

Cardinal Cabinetworks Inc..................... G 919 829-3634
Raleigh *(G-9973)*

Carocraft Cabinets Inc........................... E 704 376-0022
Charlotte *(G-1843)*

Carolina Cab Specialist LLC.................. G 919 818-4375
Cary *(G-1322)*

Carolina Cabinets of Cedar Pt.............. G 252 393-6236
Swansboro *(G-11882)*

Carolina Custom Cabinetry..................... G 704 808-1225
Waxhaw *(G-12427)*

Carolina Custom Cabinets...................... G 910 525-3096
Roseboro *(G-10911)*

Carolina Custom Cabinets Inc.............. G 252 491-5475
Powells Point *(G-9820)*

Carolina Surfaces LLC............................ G 910 874-1335
Elizabethtown *(G-4423)*

Carolinas Top Shelf Cstm Cbnets......... G 704 376-5844
Charlotte *(G-1862)*

Casework Etc Inc..................................... G 910 763-7119
Wilmington *(G-12735)*

Chesnick Corporation.............................. F 919 231-2899
Raleigh *(G-9993)*

Coastal Cabinetry Inc............................. G 910 367-8864
Shallotte *(G-11301)*

Colonial Cabinets LLC............................ G 910 579-2954
Calabash *(G-1209)*

Comm-Kab Inc.. F 336 873-8787
Asheboro *(G-340)*

Commercial Property LLC........................ E 336 818-1078
North Wilkesboro *(G-9525)*

Concord Custom Cabinets....................... G 704 773-0081
Concord *(G-3341)*

Conestoga Wood Spc Corp..................... D 919 284-2258
Kenly *(G-7229)*

▲ Corilam Fabricating Co........................ E 336 993-2371
Kernersville *(G-7259)*

Cornerstone Kitchens Inc....................... G 919 510-4200
Raleigh *(G-10017)*

Cotner Cabinet... G 336 672-1560
Sophia *(G-11486)*

Covenantmade LLC................................. G 336 434-4725
Archdale *(G-218)*

Creations Cabinetry Design LLC........... G 919 865-5979
Raleigh *(G-10019)*

Creative Woodcrafters Inc...................... G 828 252-9663
Leicester *(G-7522)*

Custom Cabinet Works............................ G 828 396-6348
Granite Falls *(G-5301)*

Custom Cabinets By Livengood............. G 704 279-3031
Salisbury *(G-11040)*

Custom Marble Corporation.................... G 910 215-0679
Pinehurst *(G-9690)*

Custom Surfaces Corporation................ G 252 638-3800
New Bern *(G-9361)*

Cut Above Construction.......................... G 828 758-8557
Lenoir *(G-7598)*

Cynthia Saar... G 910 480-2523
Stedman *(G-11806)*

D & L Cabinets Inc.................................. F 336 376-6009
Graham *(G-5267)*

Davis Cabinet Co Wilson Inc................ G 252 291-9052
Sims *(G-11429)*

Decima Corporation LLC........................ E 734 516-1535
Charlotte *(G-2025)*

Designer Woodwork.................................. G 910 521-1252
Pembroke *(G-9658)*

Distinctive Cabinets Inc.......................... F 704 529-6234
Charlotte *(G-2053)*

Dublin Woodwork Shop............................ G 910 862-2289
Dublin *(G-3831)*

Duocraft Cabinets & Dist Co.................. G 252 240-1476
Morehead City *(G-8830)*

Eastern Cabinet Company Inc............... G 252 237-5245
Wilson *(G-12985)*

Eastern Cabinet Installers Inc............... G 336 774-2966
Winston Salem *(G-13153)*

Eudys Cabinet Manufacturing................ F 704 888-4454
Stanfield *(G-11605)*

Ferguson Cabinet Works.......................... G 828 433-8710
Morganton *(G-8865)*

Firehouse Cabinets.................................. G 704 689-5243
Belmont *(G-752)*

▲ Gate City Kitchens LLC...................... G 336 378-0870
Greensboro *(G-5549)*

Gentrys Cabnt Doors............................... G 336 957-8787
Roaring River *(G-10749)*

Goembel Inc.. F 919 303-0485
Apex *(G-159)*

H Brothers Fine Wdwkg LLC.................. G 931 216-1955
Zebulon *(G-13511)*

Hans Krug... F 704 370-0809
Charlotte *(G-2254)*

Hargenrader Cstm Woodcraft LLC......... G 828 896-7182
Hickory *(G-6342)*

Heritage Design & Supply LLC.............. E 919 453-1622
Morrisville *(G-8987)*

High Cntry Cbnets Bnner Elk In............. G 828 898-3435
Banner Elk *(G-686)*

Hollingswrth Cbnets Intrors LL.............. F 910 251-1490
Castle Hayne *(G-1502)*

Honeycutt Custom Cabinets Inc............ E 910 567-6766
Autryville *(G-648)*

▲ Idx Impressions LLC............................ C 703 550-6902
Washington *(G-12393)*

In Style Kitchen Cabinetry...................... G 336 769-9605
Winston Salem *(G-13204)*

Innovative Custom Cabinets Inc............ G 813 748-0655
Kannapolis *(G-7212)*

Innovative Kitchens Baths Inc............... G 336 279-1188
Greensboro *(G-5619)*

Island Wood Crafts Ltd........................... G 252 473-5363
Wanchese *(G-12344)*

Kay & Sons Woodworks Inc................... F 919 556-1060
Wake Forest *(G-12284)*

Kc Stone Enterprise Inc.......................... G 704 907-1361
Indian Trail *(G-7085)*

▲ Kitchen Cabinet Designers LLC......... C 919 833-6532
Raleigh *(G-10238)*

Kitchen Masters Charlotte LLC............. G 704 375-3320
Salisbury *(G-11080)*

Kitchen Tune-Up...................................... G 833 259-1838
Matthews *(G-8123)*

Kkb Biltmore Inc...................................... G 828 274-6711
Asheville *(G-531)*

Kohnle Cabinetry..................................... G 828 640-2498
Hickory *(G-6381)*

Krieger Cabinets Dewayne...................... G 704 630-0609
Salisbury *(G-11082)*

Laborie Sons Cstm Wodworks LLC....... G 910 769-2524
Castle Hayne *(G-1504)*

Larry S Cabinet Shop Inc....................... G 252 442-4330
Rocky Mount *(G-10848)*

Luxemark Company.................................. G 919 863-0101
Raleigh *(G-10262)*

Markraft Cabinets Direct Sales............. G 910 762-1986
Wilmington *(G-12845)*

Marsh Furniture Company....................... G 336 229-5122
Graham *(G-5277)*

Marsh Furniture Company....................... F 336 273-8196
Greensboro *(G-5676)*

Marsh Furniture Company....................... F 336 884-7393
High Point *(G-6702)*

▲ Marsh Furniture Company................... B 336 884-7363
High Point *(G-6703)*

Masterbrand Cabinets Inc.......................... E 765 491-2385
   Lexington *(G-7715)*

Masterbrand Cabinets LLC.......................D 252 523-4131
   Kinston *(G-7422)*

McDowell County Millwork LLC.......... G 828 682-6215
   Marion *(G-8054)*

McLean Precision Cabinetry Inc............ G 910 327-9217
   Sneads Ferry *(G-11472)*

MDN Cabinets Inc..................................... G 919 662-1090
   Garner *(G-4940)*

Metro Woodcrafter of Nc Inc................. E 704 394-9622
   Charlotte *(G-2496)*

Mid Carolina Cabinets Inc...................... G 704 358-9950
   Matthews *(G-8134)*

Mike Powell Inc.. F 910 792-6152
   Wilmington *(G-12854)*

Mike S Custom Cabinets Inc.................. G 252 224-5351
   Pollocksville *(G-9818)*

Mint Hill Cabinet Shop Inc..................... E 704 821-9373
   Monroe *(G-8531)*

Miters Touch Inc...................................... G 828 963-4445
   Banner Elk *(G-688)*

Morgans Cabinets Inc.............................. F 704 485-8693
   Oakboro *(G-9581)*

Mountain Cabinetry Closets LLC........... G 828 966-9000
   Brevard *(G-977)*

Mountain Showcase Group Inc.............. E 828 692-9494
   Hendersonville *(G-6228)*

Murphy S Custom Cabinetry Inc........... G 828 891-3050
   Hendersonville *(G-6229)*

Myricks Cabinet Shop Inc...................... G 919 266-3720
   Knightdale *(G-7453)*

Noble Bros Cabinets Mllwk LLC........... G 252 335-1213
   Elizabeth City *(G-4399)*

Noble Bros Cabinets Mllwk LLC........... G 252 482-9100
   Edenton *(G-4370)*

Noles Cabinets Inc................................... G 919 552-4257
   Fuquay Varina *(G-4892)*

Norcraft Companies LP........................... C 336 622-4281
   Liberty *(G-7774)*

Normac Kitchens Inc............................... F 704 485-1911
   Oakboro *(G-9582)*

Oyama Cabinet Inc.................................. G 828 327-2668
   Conover *(G-3542)*

P R Sparks Enterprises Inc.................... G 336 272-7200
   Greensboro *(G-5728)*

Pb & J Industries Inc.............................. F 919 661-2738
   Raleigh *(G-10363)*

Precision Cabinets Inc............................ G 828 262-5080
   Boone *(G-938)*

Prestige Millwork Inc.............................. G 910 428-2360
   Star *(G-11633)*

Red House Cabinets LLC....................... G 919 201-2101
   Raleigh *(G-10437)*

Riverview Cabinet & Supply Inc............ G 336 228-1486
   Burlington *(G-1148)*

Robbinsville Cstm Molding Inc.............. F 828 479-2317
   Robbinsville *(G-10761)*

Rowan Custom Cabinets Inc.................. G 704 855-4778
   China Grove *(G-3079)*

Rugby Acquisition LLC...........................D 336 993-8686
   Kernersville *(G-7297)*

S Banner Cabinets Incorporated............ E 828 733-2031
   Newland *(G-9434)*

S Eudy Cabinet Shop Inc....................... G 704 888-4454
   Stanfield *(G-11608)*

S Zaytoun Custom Cabinets Inc............ G 252 638-8390
   New Bern *(G-9394)*

Seema Intl Custom Cabinetry................ G 917 703-0820
   Wake Forest *(G-12299)*

▲ Selpro LLC... G 336 513-0550
   Greensboro *(G-5806)*

Signature Custom Cabinets LLC........... G 704 753-4874
   Monroe *(G-8558)*

Sjr Incorporated....................................... F 828 254-8966
   Asheville *(G-601)*

Smiths Custom Kitchen Inc.................... G 828 652-9033
   Marion *(G-8065)*

Sorrells Cabinet Co Inc.......................... G 919 639-4320
   Lillington *(G-7803)*

Southern Cabinet Co Inc........................ G 704 373-2299
   Matthews *(G-8149)*

Southern Design Cabinetry LLC............ G 919 263-9414
   Wake Forest *(G-12301)*

Stallings Cabinets Inc............................. G 252 338-6747
   Elizabeth City *(G-4410)*

Sunhs Warehouse LLC............................ G 919 908-1523
   Durham *(G-4255)*

Sycamore Cabinetry Inc.......................... G 704 375-1617
   Dallas *(G-3691)*

Tarheel Wood Designs Inc...................... G 910 395-2226
   Wilmington *(G-12937)*

Tarheel Woodcrafters Inc........................ G 252 432-3035
   Henderson *(G-6180)*

Thomas Lcklars Cbnets Lrnburg............ G 910 369-2094
   Laurinburg *(G-7516)*

Tice Kitchens & Interiors LLC................. F 919 366-4117
   Raleigh *(G-10549)*

Tommy W Smith Inc................................. G 704 436-6616
   Mount Pleasant *(G-9265)*

Tonys Cabinets... G 910 592-2028
   Clinton *(G-3250)*

Travis Alfrey Woodworking Inc............... G 910 639-3553
   Aberdeen *(G-28)*

Triangle Cabinet Company...................... G 336 869-6401
   High Point *(G-6811)*

Triangle Kitchen Supply.......................... G 919 562-3888
   Youngsville *(G-13494)*

True Cabinet LLC..................................... G 828 855-9200
   Hickory *(G-6470)*

TS Woodworks & RAD Design Inc......... F 704 238-1015
   Monroe *(G-8571)*

Tsquared Cabinets................................... G 336 655-0208
   Winston Salem *(G-13376)*

Twin City Custom Cabinets..................... G 336 773-7200
   Winston Salem *(G-13377)*

US Precision Cabinetry LLC....................D 828 351-2020
   Rutherfordton *(G-11002)*

Verona Cabinets & Surfaces LLC........... G 704 755-5259
   Charlotte *(G-2979)*

Vine & Branch Woodworks LLC............. G 704 663-0077
   Mooresville *(G-8793)*

Walker Woodworking Inc......................... E 704 434-0823
   Shelby *(G-11390)*

Watkins Cabinets LLC............................. G 704 634-1724
   Matthews *(G-8157)*

Wilson Woodworks Inc............................ F 252 237-3179
   Wilson *(G-13050)*

Windsors Cbnetry For Kit Baths............ G 336 275-0190
   Greensboro *(G-5920)*

Winstons Woodworks............................... G 919 693-4120
   Oxford *(G-9640)*

Wood Done Right Inc............................... G 919 623-4557
   Chapel Hill *(G-1595)*

Wood Technology Inc............................... E 828 464-8049
   Conover *(G-3577)*

Woodmaster Custom Cabinets Inc......... F 919 554-3707
   Youngsville *(G-13499)*

Woodmasters Woodworking Inc............. G 336 985-4000
   King *(G-7341)*

Woodworking Unlimited............................ G 252 235-5285
   Bailey *(G-674)*

Xylem Inc.. G 919 772-4126
   Garner *(G-4976)*

Yadkin Valley Cabinet Co Inc................. G 336 786-9860
   Mount Airy *(G-9197)*

Your Cabinet Connection Inc.................. G 919 641-2877
   Morrisville *(G-9092)*

2435 Hardwood veneer and plywood

A-1 Face Inc.. G 336 248-5555
   Lexington *(G-7654)*

▲ Adwood Corporation........................... E 336 884-1846
   High Point *(G-6510)*

▼ Atlantic Veneer Company LLC........... C 252 728-3169
   Beaufort *(G-719)*

▲ Autumn House Inc..............................D 828 728-1121
   Granite Falls *(G-5297)*

Burke Veneers Inc................................... G 828 437-8510
   Morganton *(G-8854)*

Capitol Funds Inc....................................D 704 482-0645
   Shelby *(G-11315)*

Chesterfield Wood Products Inc............. F 828 433-0042
   Morganton *(G-8856)*

Columbia Forest Products Inc................ C 828 724-9495
   Old Fort *(G-9591)*

◆ Columbia Forest Products Inc.............D 336 605-0429
   Greensboro *(G-5455)*

Columbia Panel Mfg Co Inc...................D 336 861-4100
   High Point *(G-6573)*

Columbia Plywood Corporation............... B 828 724-4191
   Old Fort *(G-9592)*

Corbett Package Company......................D 910 763-9991
   Wilmington *(G-12752)*

▼ Coxe-Lewis Corporation...................... G 252 357-0050
   Gatesville *(G-5171)*

Custom Veneers Inc................................ G 828 758-7001
   Lenoir *(G-7597)*

David R Webb Company Inc................... G 336 605-3355
   Greensboro *(G-5488)*

Esco Industries Inc.................................. F 336 495-3772
   Randleman *(G-10647)*

Franklin Veneers Inc............................... G 919 494-2284
   Franklinton *(G-4848)*

G & G Lumber Company Inc.................. G 704 539-5110
   Harmony *(G-6098)*

Gates Custom Milling Inc........................ E 252 357-0116
   Gatesville *(G-5172)*

Georgia-Pacific LLC.................................D 919 580-1078
   Dudley *(G-3836)*

Georgia-Pacific LLC................................. E 910 642-5041
   Whiteville *(G-12581)*

HM Frame Company Inc.......................... E 828 428-3354
   Newton *(G-9472)*

Mannington Mills Inc................................ E 336 884-5600
   High Point *(G-6697)*

North Carolina Plywood LLC.................. G 850 948-2211
   Whiteville *(G-12591)*

Ritch Face Veneer Company................... G 336 883-4184
   High Point *(G-6758)*

Robbinsville Cstm Molding Inc.............. F 828 479-2317
   Robbinsville *(G-10761)*

▲ Sauers & Company Inc....................... F 336 956-1200
   Lexington *(G-7737)*

Southern Vneer Spclty Pdts LLC........... F 919 642-7004
   Moncure *(G-8409)*

Tailor Cut Wood Products Inc................. G 828 632-2808
   Taylorsville *(G-11980)*

Tramway Veneers Inc.............................. G 919 776-7606
   Sanford *(G-11242)*

Ufp New London LLC............................. F 704 463-1400
   New London *(G-9423)*

▲ Veneer Technologies Inc.................... C 252 223-5600
   Newport *(G-9446)*

2436 Softwood veneer and plywood

A-1 Face Inc.. G 336 248-5555
  Lexington *(G-7654)*

◆ Baltek Inc... C 336 398-1900
  Colfax *(G-3273)*

David R Webb Company Inc.................... G 336 605-3355
  Greensboro *(G-5488)*

Faces South Inc.. G 336 883-0647
  High Point *(G-6618)*

Georgia-Pacific LLC................................. D 919 580-1078
  Dudley *(G-3836)*

Tima Capital Inc.. F 910 769-3273
  Wilmington *(G-12939)*

Ufp New London LLC................................ F 704 463-1400
  New London *(G-9423)*

Weyerhaeuser Company........................... E 336 835-5100
  Elkin *(G-4455)*

2439 Structural wood members, nec

Anderson Truss Company Inc................. F 252 746-7726
  Ayden *(G-652)*

Andrews Truss Inc................................... E 828 321-3105
  Andrews *(G-105)*

▲ Bfs Asset Holdings LLC........................ B 303 784-4288
  Raleigh *(G-9941)*

Blue Ridge Bldg Components Inc........... G 828 685-0452
  Dana *(G-3694)*

Builders Frstsrce - Rleigh LLC............... D 919 363-4956
  Apex *(G-147)*

C & C Chipping Inc................................. G 252 249-1617
  Grantsboro *(G-5330)*

C & R Building Supply Inc....................... G 910 567-6293
  Autryville *(G-647)*

Capitol Funds Inc.................................... F 910 439-5275
  Mount Gilead *(G-9198)*

Capitol Funds Inc.................................... D 704 482-0645
  Shelby *(G-11315)*

Capitol Funds Inc.................................... E 704 487-8547
  Shelby *(G-11316)*

Carolina Custom Exteriors Inc............... F 828 232-0402
  Asheville *(G-469)*

Fast Arch of Carolinas Inc...................... G 336 431-2724
  Archdale *(G-221)*

High Cntry Tmbrframe Gllery WD........... G 828 264-8971
  Boone *(G-921)*

Idaho Timber NC LLC.............................. E 252 430-0030
  Henderson *(G-6161)*

Lignaterra Global LLC............................. G 970 481-6952
  Charlotte *(G-2422)*

Log Home Builders Inc............................ G 704 638-0677
  Salisbury *(G-11087)*

Longleaf Truss Company......................... E 910 673-4711
  West End *(G-12556)*

Nvr Inc... D 704 484-7170
  Kings Mountain *(G-7374)*

Peak Truss Builders LLC......................... G 919 552-5933
  Holly Springs *(G-6910)*

Rafters and Walls LLC............................. E 980 404-0209
  Shelby *(G-11372)*

Roanoke Truss Inc................................... G 252 537-0012
  Roanoke Rapids *(G-10742)*

Scotland Neck Heart Pine Inc................. G 252 826-2755
  Scotland Neck *(G-11265)*

Smokey Mountain Lumber Inc................. G 828 298-3958
  Asheville *(G-602)*

Truss Buildings LLC................................. G 919 377-0217
  Cary *(G-1475)*

Truss Shop Inc... E 336 372-6260
  Sparta *(G-11542)*

Trussway Manufacturing Inc................... E 336 883-6966
  Whitsett *(G-12621)*

▲ Truswood Inc... E 800 473-8787
  Raleigh *(G-10567)*

Ufp New London LLC................................ F 704 463-1400
  New London *(G-9423)*

Ufp Site Built LLC.................................... E 704 781-2520
  Locust *(G-7906)*

Universal Forest Products Inc................. F 252 338-0319
  Elizabeth City *(G-4416)*

US Lbm Operating Co 2009 LLC............. C 910 864-8787
  Fayetteville *(G-4690)*

Viking Truss Inc....................................... G 252 792-1051
  Williamston *(G-12675)*

W and W Truss Builders Inc.................... F 252 792-1051
  Williamston *(G-12677)*

2441 Nailed wood boxes and shook

A McGee Wood Products Inc.................. F 828 212-1700
  Granite Falls *(G-5293)*

Arcola Lumber Company Inc................... E 252 257-4923
  Warrenton *(G-12350)*

Carolina Crate & Pallet Inc..................... E 910 245-4001
  Vass *(G-12227)*

Carolina Crating Inc................................ E 910 276-7170
  Laurinburg *(G-7495)*

Carolina WD Pdts Mrshville Inc.............. D 704 624-2119
  Marshville *(G-8086)*

Clemmons Pallet Skid Works Inc............ E 336 766-5462
  Clemmons *(G-3180)*

Freedom Enterprise LLC.......................... G 502 510-7296
  Charlotte *(G-2177)*

▲ Kontane Logistics Inc........................... G 828 397-5501
  Hickory *(G-6382)*

Mc Gees Crating Inc................................ E 828 758-4660
  Lenoir *(G-7626)*

Millennium Packaging Svc LLC.............. G 775 353-5127
  Durham *(G-4135)*

▲ Spartacraft Inc...................................... E 828 397-4630
  Connelly Springs *(G-3483)*

Timberline Acquisition LLC..................... G 252 492-6144
  Henderson *(G-6181)*

Universal Forest Products Inc................. F 252 338-0319
  Elizabeth City *(G-4416)*

2448 Wood pallets and skids

48forty Solutions LLC.............................. A 910 891-1534
  Dunn *(G-3839)*

A & J Pallets Inc...................................... G 336 969-0265
  Rural Hall *(G-10951)*

Alan Kimzey... G 828 891-8720
  Mills River *(G-8310)*

Amware Pallet Services LLC................... G 919 207-2403
  Benson *(G-784)*

Atlas Box and Crating Co Inc................. G 919 941-1023
  Durham *(G-3905)*

Bastrop Skid Company............................ G 252 793-6600
  Plymouth *(G-9799)*

Blue Stone Industries Ltd....................... G 919 379-3986
  Cary *(G-1310)*

Bluewater Pallet Solutions...................... G 336 697-9109
  Mc Leansville *(G-8219)*

Bolivia Lumber Company LLC.................. G 910 371-2515
  Leland *(G-7533)*

Carolina Base - Pac Corp........................ E 828 728-7304
  Hudson *(G-6946)*

Carolina Crate & Pallet Inc..................... E 910 245-4001
  Vass *(G-12227)*

Carolina Crating Inc................................ E 910 276-7170
  Laurinburg *(G-7495)*

Carolina Mat Incorporated...................... F 252 793-1111
  Plymouth *(G-9800)*

Carolina Pallet Recycling Inc................. G 828 652-6818
  Marion *(G-8039)*

Carolina WD Pdts Mrshville Inc.............. D 704 624-2119
  Marshville *(G-8086)*

Carpenter Design Inc............................... F 828 248-9070
  Rutherfordton *(G-10980)*

Clary Lumber Company........................... D 252 537-2558
  Gaston *(G-4978)*

Clemmons Pallet Skid Works Inc............ E 336 766-5462
  Clemmons *(G-3180)*

Columbus Pallet Company Inc................ G 910 655-4513
  Delco *(G-3735)*

CP Liquidation Inc................................... D 704 921-1100
  Charlotte *(G-1992)*

Dagenhart Pallet Inc............................... G 828 241-2374
  Catawba *(G-1511)*

Dails Pallet & Produce Inc...................... G 252 717-1338
  Kinston *(G-7404)*

Direct Wood Products.............................. G 336 238-2516
  Lexington *(G-7679)*

Discount Box & Pallet Inc....................... E 336 272-2220
  Staley *(G-11594)*

Diversified Wood Products Inc................ F 252 793-6600
  Plymouth *(G-9801)*

East Industries Inc.................................. D 252 442-9662
  Rocky Mount *(G-10834)*

Eds Pallet World Inc................................ F 828 453-8986
  Ellenboro *(G-4457)*

◆ Edwards Wood Products Inc.................. C 704 624-3624
  Marshville *(G-8088)*

Evergreen Pallets LLC............................. F 828 313-0050
  Granite Falls *(G-5302)*

First Alance Logistics MGT LLC............. F 704 522-0233
  Charlotte *(G-2155)*

Forest City Pallett Co Inc....................... G 828 652-8432
  Nebo *(G-9328)*

Gamble Associates Inc........................... F 704 375-9301
  Charlotte *(G-2187)*

Glenn Lumber Company Inc.................... E 704 434-7873
  Shelby *(G-11338)*

Granville Pallet Co Inc............................ D 919 528-2347
  Oxford *(G-9616)*

H Parsons Incorporated.......................... F 828 757-9191
  Lenoir *(G-7611)*

Hildreth Wood Products Inc.................... G 704 826-8326
  Wadesboro *(G-12243)*

Industrial Recycling Services................. G 704 462-1882
  Newton *(G-9475)*

Jeld-Wen Inc.. C 336 838-0292
  North Wilkesboro *(G-9536)*

Johnston County Industries Inc............. C 919 743-8700
  Selma *(G-11289)*

Lucky Landports....................................... G 704 399-9880
  Charlotte *(G-2439)*

MAC Grading Co....................................... G 910 531-4642
  Autryville *(G-649)*

Mc Gees Crating Inc................................ E 828 758-4660
  Lenoir *(G-7626)*

McBride Lumber Co Partnr LLC.............. G 910 428-2747
  Star *(G-11632)*

Millwood Inc... F 704 817-7541
  Charlotte *(G-2506)*

Myers Forest Products Inc...................... G 704 278-4532
  Cleveland *(G-3217)*

National Wden Pllet Cont Assoc............ F 919 837-2105
  Siler City *(G-11420)*

Neal S Pallet Company Inc...................... E 704 393-8568
  Charlotte *(G-2551)*

P1 Catawba Development Co LLC........... G 704 462-1882
  Newton *(G-9486)*

Pallet Alliance Inc................................... F 919 442-1400
  Durham *(G-4163)*

Pallet Express Inc.................................... C 336 621-2266
  Liberty *(G-7775)*

Pallet Plus Inc... G 336 887-1810
  Trinity *(G-12122)*

S I C

Pallet Resource of NC Inc.............. D 336 731-8338
  Lexington *(G-7728)*

Pallet World........................... G 919 800-1113
  Dunn *(G-3864)*

Pallet World USA Inc................... G 828 298-7270
  Asheville *(G-564)*

Palletone North Carolina Inc.......... D 919 575-6491
  Butner *(G-1204)*

Palletone North Carolina Inc.......... D 336 492-5565
  Mocksville *(G-8384)*

Palletone North Carolina Inc.......... D 704 462-1882
  Siler City *(G-11423)*

Pallets and More....................... G 919 815-6134
  Franklinton *(G-4852)*

Piedmont Pallet & Cont Inc............. G 336 284-6302
  Woodleaf *(G-13430)*

Precision Pallet LLC................... F 252 935-5355
  Pantego *(G-9648)*

Pro Pallet South Inc................... C 910 576-4902
  Troy *(G-12165)*

Reeder Pallet Company Inc.............. F 336 879-3095
  Seagrove *(G-11279)*

Richard West Co Inc.................... G 252 793-4440
  Plymouth *(G-9807)*

Ross Skid Products Inc................. E 828 652-7450
  Marion *(G-8064)*

Ross Woodworking Inc................... G 704 629-4551
  Bessemer City *(G-832)*

Ross Woodworking Inc................... G 704 629-4551
  Bessemer City *(G-833)*

Sandhills Cnsld Svcs Inc............... E 919 718-7909
  Sanford *(G-11228)*

Somers Lumber and Mfg Inc.............. F 704 539-4751
  Harmony *(G-6099)*

Starnes Pallet Service Inc............. E 704 596-9006
  Charlotte *(G-2861)*

Statesville Pallet Company Inc......... G 828 632-0268
  Hiddenite *(G-6505)*

Steelman Lumber & Pallet LLC........... F 336 468-2757
  Hamptonville *(G-6092)*

Sunny View Pallet Company.............. G 828 625-9907
  Mill Spring *(G-8303)*

T P Supply Co Inc...................... E 336 789-2337
  Mount Airy *(G-9183)*

Timberline Acquisition LLC............. E 252 492-6144
  Henderson *(G-6181)*

Tree Brand Packaging Inc............... D 704 483-0719
  Newton *(G-9505)*

Tri-County Industries Inc.............. C 252 977-3800
  Rocky Mount *(G-10819)*

Triple C Companies LLC................. E 704 966-1999
  Denver *(G-3814)*

United Lumber Inc...................... G 919 575-6491
  Butner *(G-1208)*

Universal Forest Products Inc.......... F 252 338-0319
  Elizabeth City *(G-4416)*

W N C Pallet Forest Pdts Inc........... F 828 667-5426
  Candler *(G-1235)*

Walker Pallet Company Inc.............. F 910 259-2235
  Burgaw *(G-1037)*

Wheeler Industries Inc................. G 919 736-4256
  Pikeville *(G-9669)*

2449 Wood containers, nec

Arcola Hardwood Company Inc............ G 252 257-4484
  Warrenton *(G-12349)*

Arcola Lumber Company Inc.............. E 252 257-4923
  Warrenton *(G-12350)*

Carolina Crate & Pallet Inc............ E 910 245-4001
  Vass *(G-12227)*

Carolina WD Pdts Mrshville Inc......... D 704 624-2119
  Marshville *(G-8086)*

Case Specialists....................... G 919 818-4476
  Raleigh *(G-9986)*

Container Systems Incorporated......... D 919 496-6133
  Franklinton *(G-4847)*

Craftwood Veneers Inc.................. G 336 434-2158
  High Point *(G-6577)*

▼ Custom Air Trays Inc................. F 336 889-8729
  High Point *(G-6583)*

◆ Dac Products Inc..................... E 336 969-9786
  Rural Hall *(G-10958)*

Elberta Crate & Box Co................. C 252 257-4659
  Warrenton *(G-12352)*

Hildreth Wood Products Inc............. G 704 826-8326
  Wadesboro *(G-12243)*

J&R SERvices/J&r Lumber Co............. G 956 778-7005
  Wilmington *(G-12821)*

▲ Kontane Logistics Inc............... G 828 397-5501
  Hickory *(G-6382)*

Lee County Industries Inc.............. G 919 775-3439
  Sanford *(G-11205)*

M O Deviney Lumber Co Inc.............. G 704 538-9071
  Casar *(G-1489)*

McBride Lumber Co Partnr LLC........... G 910 428-2747
  Star *(G-11632)*

Moorecraft Wood Proucts Inc............ G 252 823-2510
  Tarboro *(G-11936)*

Pro Choice Contractors Corp............ G 919 696-7383
  Raleigh *(G-10398)*

Raleigh Road Box Corporation........... G 252 438-7401
  Henderson *(G-6174)*

2451 Mobile homes

Brig Homes NC.......................... G 252 459-7026
  Nashville *(G-9312)*

Cavalier Home Builders LLC............. C 252 459-7026
  Nashville *(G-9316)*

Champion Home Builders Inc............. B 910 893-5713
  Lillington *(G-7793)*

Clayton Homes Inc...................... G 828 667-8701
  Candler *(G-1221)*

Clayton Homes Inc...................... G 828 684-1550
  Fletcher *(G-4729)*

CMH Manufacturing Inc.................. A 704 279-4659
  Rockwell *(G-10793)*

Conway Entps Carteret Cnty LLC......... G 252 504-3518
  Beaufort *(G-724)*

Elite Mountain Business LLC............ G 828 349-0403
  Franklin *(G-4827)*

Esco Industries Inc.................... F 336 495-3772
  Randleman *(G-10647)*

Home City Ltd.......................... G 910 428-2196
  Biscoe *(G-853)*

R-Anell Custom Homes Inc............... G 704 483-5511
  Denver *(G-3801)*

R-Anell Housing Group LLC.............. D 704 445-9610
  Crouse *(G-3659)*

Readilite & Barricade Inc.............. F 919 231-8309
  Raleigh *(G-10435)*

Ridgewood Management LLC............... G 336 644-0006
  Greensboro *(G-5788)*

Sunshine Mnfctred Strctres Inc......... G 704 279-6600
  Rockwell *(G-10802)*

Two Brothers NC LLC.................... G 336 516-5181
  Burlington *(G-1172)*

2452 Prefabricated wood buildings

Bear Creek Log Tmber Homes LLC......... G 336 751-6180
  Mocksville *(G-8351)*

Braswell Realty........................ G 828 733-5800
  Newland *(G-9426)*

Cavco Industries Inc................... D 910 410-5050
  Hamlet *(G-6052)*

▼ Deltec Homes Inc.................... E 828 253-0483
  Asheville *(G-486)*

Dex n Dox.............................. G 910 576-4644
  Troy *(G-12160)*

Distinctive Bldg & Design Inc.......... G 828 456-4730
  Waynesville *(G-12456)*

Enertia Building Systems Inc........... G 919 556-2391
  Wake Forest *(G-12275)*

Gray Wolf Log Homes Inc................ G 828 586-4662
  Sylva *(G-11892)*

Hope Renovations....................... F 919 960-1957
  Chapel Hill *(G-1549)*

Johnston County Industries Inc......... C 919 743-8700
  Selma *(G-11289)*

Log Cabin Homes Ltd.................... G 252 454-1548
  Battleboro *(G-701)*

◆ Log Cabin Homes Ltd................. D 252 454-1500
  Rocky Mount *(G-10849)*

Log Homes of America Inc............... G 336 982-8989
  Jefferson *(G-7190)*

Manning Building Products LLC.......... G 919 662-9894
  Garner *(G-4937)*

Mast Woodworks......................... F 336 468-1194
  Hamptonville *(G-6090)*

Mountain Rcrtion Log Cbins LLC......... G 828 387-6688
  Newland *(G-9432)*

Old Hickory Log Homes Inc.............. G 704 489-8989
  Denver *(G-3795)*

Outlaw Step Co......................... G 252 568-4384
  Deep Run *(G-3733)*

Piedmont Sales & Rentals LLC........... G 919 499-9888
  Sanford *(G-11221)*

Quality Housing Corporation............ F 336 274-2622
  Greensboro *(G-5778)*

R-Anell Custom Homes Inc............... G 704 483-5511
  Denver *(G-3801)*

Rclgh Inc.............................. G 828 707-4383
  Asheville *(G-588)*

Salt Wood Products Inc................. G 252 830-8875
  Greenville *(G-6020)*

Seashore Builders Inc.................. E 910 259-3404
  Maple Hill *(G-8026)*

South-East Lumber Company.............. E 336 996-5322
  Kernersville *(G-7301)*

Southland Log Homes Inc................ G 336 449-5388
  Whitsett *(G-12620)*

Sunshine Mnfctred Strctres Inc......... G 704 279-6600
  Rockwell *(G-10802)*

▼ Topsider Building Systems Inc....... E 336 766-9300
  Clemmons *(G-3204)*

Tree Craft Log Homes Inc............... G 828 689-2240
  Mars Hill *(G-8078)*

Tuff Shed Inc.......................... G 919 413-2494
  Morrisville *(G-9081)*

Ufp New London LLC..................... F 704 463-1400
  New London *(G-9423)*

▲ Web-Don Incorporated................ E 800 532-0434
  Charlotte *(G-3009)*

▲ Wood Right Lumber Company........... G 910 576-4642
  Troy *(G-12171)*

2491 Wood preserving

Albemarle Wood Prsv Plant Inc.......... G 704 982-2516
  Albemarle *(G-60)*

Atlantic Wood & Timber LLC............. F 704 390-7479
  Charlotte *(G-1713)*

Blue Ridge Lbr Log & Timber Co......... G 336 961-5211
  Yadkinville *(G-13438)*

Boise Cascade Wood Pdts LLC............ E 336 598-3001
  Roxboro *(G-10920)*

Carolina Square Inc.................... G 336 793-3222
  Mocksville *(G-8356)*

Coastal Treated Products LLC............ F 252 410-0180
  Roanoke Rapids (G-10735)

Culpeper Roanoke Rapids LLC......... G 252 678-3804
  Roanoke Rapids (G-10736)

Durable Wood Preservers Inc............ G 704 537-3113
  Charlotte (G-2067)

Fiberon.. G 704 463-2955
  Concord (G-3362)

Fortress Wood Products Inc.............. F 336 854-5121
  High Point (G-6621)

General Wood Preserving Co Inc......... G 910 371-3131
  Leland (G-7545)

H & M Wood Preserving Inc.............. E 704 279-5188
  Gold Hill (G-5192)

Hoover Treated Wood Pdts Inc........... E 866 587-8761
  Weldon (G-12520)

Jak Moulding & Supply Inc............... F 252 753-5546
  Walstonburg (G-12332)

Shenandoah Wood Preservers Inc........ G 252 826-4151
  Scotland Neck (G-11266)

Soha Holdings LLC......................... E 828 264-2314
  Boone (G-942)

Tarheel Wood Treating Company......... F 919 467-9176
  Morrisville (G-9063)

Tri-H Molding Co........................... G 252 491-8530
  Harbinger (G-6096)

▲ Triton International Woods LLC......... D 252 823-6675
  Tarboro (G-11945)

Ufp Biscoe LLC............................. F 910 294-8179
  Biscoe (G-858)

Ufp Rockwell LLC.......................... G 704 279-0744
  Rockwell (G-10806)

Ufp Salisbury LLC.......................... B 704 855-1600
  Salisbury (G-11130)

Ufp Salisbury LLC.......................... G 704 855-1600
  Salisbury (G-11129)

Universal Forest Products Inc............ F 252 338-0319
  Elizabeth City (G-4416)

Woodline Inc................................ G 336 476-7100
  Thomasville (G-12090)

Woodtreaters Inc........................... G 910 675-0038
  Rocky Point (G-10887)

2493 Reconstituted wood products

◆ Aconcagua Timber Corp.................. B 919 542-2128
  Moncure (G-8398)

Arauco - NA................................. G 910 569-7020
  Biscoe (G-846)

Arauco North America Inc................. D 919 542-2128
  Moncure (G-8399)

◆ Atc Panels Inc.............................. G 919 653-6053
  Morrisville (G-8935)

▲ Attic Tent Inc.............................. G 704 892-5399
  Mooresville (G-8601)

Custom Finishers Inc...................... E 336 431-7141
  High Point (G-6584)

Egger Wood Products LLC................. B 336 843-7000
  Linwood (G-7876)

Georgia-Pacific LLC........................ D 919 580-1078
  Dudley (G-3836)

◆ Huber Engineered Woods LLC............ E 800 933-9220
  Charlotte (G-2297)

Industrial Timber LLC..................... D 704 919-1215
  Hiddenite (G-6500)

▲ Industrial Timber LLC..................... D 704 919-1215
  Charlotte (G-2326)

J R Craver & Associates Inc............... G 336 769-3330
  Clemmons (G-3193)

LL Cultured Marble Inc..................... G 336 789-3908
  Mount Airy (G-9147)

Louisiana-Pacific Corporation............ C 336 696-2751
  North Wilkesboro (G-9543)

Louisiana-Pacific Corporation............ G 336 696-2751
  Roaring River (G-10750)

Louisiana-Pacific Corporation............ C 336 599-8080
  Roxboro (G-10929)

Mohawk Industries Inc.................... C 910 439-6959
  Mount Gilead (G-9207)

Olon Industries Inc (us)................... F 630 232-4705
  Mocksville (G-8383)

Quality Insulation Company.............. G 252 438-3711
  Henderson (G-6171)

◆ Uniboard USA LLC......................... C 919 542-2128
  Moncure (G-8411)

Weyerhaeuser Company................... E 336 835-5100
  Elkin (G-4455)

2499 Wood products, nec

1st Time Contracting...................... G 774 289-3321
  Clemmons (G-3176)

A & J Pallets Inc............................ G 336 969-0265
  Rural Hall (G-10951)

▲ A M Moore and Company Inc............ G 336 294-6994
  Greensboro (G-5332)

A-1 Face Inc................................. G 336 248-5555
  Lexington (G-7654)

Albright Qulty WD Turning Inc........... G 336 475-1434
  Thomasville (G-11991)

Alcorns Custom Woodworking Inc........ G 336 342-0908
  Reidsville (G-10672)

American Soil and Mulch Inc............. G 919 460-1349
  Raleigh (G-9897)

▲ Apollo Designs LLC....................... E 336 886-0260
  High Point (G-6524)

Archdale Millworks Inc.................... G 336 431-9019
  Archdale (G-212)

Blind Nail and Company Inc.............. G 919 967-0388
  Chapel Hill (G-1530)

Boards and Bowls LLC..................... G 704 293-2004
  Mooresville (G-8617)

◆ Brushy Mountain Bee Farm Inc.......... E 336 921-3640
  Winston Salem (G-13112)

C & D Woodworking Inc................... G 336 476-8722
  Thomasville (G-12000)

Carolina Bark Products LLC............... G 252 589-1324
  Seaboard (G-11270)

Carolina Crate & Pallet Inc............... G 910 245-4001
  Vass (G-12227)

Carolina Stake and WD Pdts Inc.......... G 704 545-7774
  Mint Hill (G-8335)

Chesterfield Wood Products Inc.......... F 828 433-0042
  Morganton (G-8856)

Clausen Craftworks LLC................... G 704 252-5048
  Charlotte (G-1927)

▲ Cormark International LLC................ G 828 658-8455
  Weaverville (G-12489)

Cranberry Wood Works Inc............... G 336 877-8771
  Fleetwood (G-4715)

◆ Daramic LLC................................ D 704 587-8599
  Charlotte (G-2018)

▲ Design Surfaces Inc....................... G 919 781-0310
  Raleigh (G-10043)

Dilworth Custom Framing................. G 704 370-7660
  Charlotte (G-2048)

Fairview Woodcarving Inc................. G 828 428-9491
  Maiden (G-8013)

Fence Quarter LLC......................... G 800 205-0128
  Morganton (G-8864)

Four Corners Frmng Gallery Inc.......... G 704 662-7154
  Mooresville (G-8667)

G & G Management LLC.................... F 336 444-6271
  Greensboro (G-5544)

▲ G & G Moulding Inc....................... E 828 438-1112
  Morganton (G-8867)

Garick LLC.................................. G 704 455-6418
  Harrisburg (G-6109)

Gates Custom Milling Inc................. E 252 357-0116
  Gatesville (G-5172)

▲ Ges Industries............................. E 252 430-8851
  Kittrell (G-7441)

◆ Graphik Dimensions Limited............. D 800 332-8884
  High Point (G-6634)

H & P Wood Turnings Inc................. G 910 675-2784
  Rocky Point (G-10880)

▼ Heartwood Pine Floors Inc............... G 919 542-4394
  Moncure (G-8406)

Heartwood Refuge......................... G 828 513-5016
  Hendersonville (G-6213)

Hefner Reels LLC........................... E 828 632-5717
  Taylorsville (G-11964)

Heritage Flag LLC.......................... G 910 725-1540
  Southern Pines (G-11500)

Highland Craftsmen Inc................... F 828 765-9010
  Spruce Pine (G-11577)

Huneywood Inc............................. G 704 385-9785
  Monroe (G-8501)

Johnson Lumber Products Inc............ G 910 532-4201
  Ivanhoe (G-7111)

Jordan Group Corporation................ G 803 309-9988
  Charlotte (G-2378)

JRs Custom Framing....................... G 704 449-2830
  Charlotte (G-2381)

Kamlar Corporation........................ E 252 443-2576
  Rocky Mount (G-10845)

Keener Wood Products Inc................ G 828 428-1562
  Maiden (G-8015)

Kenneth Moore Signs...................... G 910 458-6428
  Wilmington (G-12826)

Kindled Provisions LLC.................... F 919 542-0792
  Moncure (G-8407)

◆ L G Sourcing Inc........................... E 704 758-1000
  Mooresville (G-8707)

Legends Countertops LLC................. G 980 230-4501
  Concord (G-3392)

Loflin Handle Co Inc....................... G 336 463-2422
  Yadkinville (G-13445)

Lynn Ladder Scaffolding Co Inc........... G 301 336-4700
  Charlotte (G-2443)

Madem-Moorecraft Reels USA Inc........ C 252 823-2510
  Tarboro (G-11933)

Marlinwoodworks LLC..................... G 919 343-2605
  Lillington (G-7800)

Martin Lumber & Mulch LLC.............. F 252 935-5294
  Pantego (G-9646)

McCrorie Group LLC....................... E 828 328-4538
  Hickory (G-6394)

Megawood Holdings Inc................... G 910 439-2124
  Mount Gilead (G-9206)

Miller Bee Supply Inc...................... F 336 670-2249
  North Wilkesboro (G-9548)

Minelli Usa LLC............................. G 828 578-6734
  Hickory (G-6396)

Mirrormate LLC............................. F 704 390-7377
  Charlotte (G-2508)

Moorecraft Reels Inc...................... D 252 823-2510
  Tarboro (G-11935)

Mulch Masters of NC Inc.................. G 919 676-0031
  Raleigh (G-10318)

Mulch Solutions LLC....................... F 704 956-2343
  Concord (G-3407)

National Salvage & Svc Corp.............. D 919 739-5633
  Dudley (G-3838)

NC Moulding Acquisition LLC............. F 336 249-7309
  Lexington (G-7721)

North Carolina Mulch Inc................. G 252 478-4609
  Middlesex (G-8278)

Pamlico Shores Inc................E.....252 926-0011
   Swanquarter *(G-11881)*

Phelps Wood Products LLC................G.....336 284-2149
   Cleveland *(G-3219)*

Privette Enterprises Inc................E.....704 634-3291
   Monroe *(G-8544)*

Quantico Tactical Incorporated................E.....910 944-5800
   Aberdeen *(G-20)*

Reel Solutions Inc................G.....910 947-3117
   Carthage *(G-1279)*

Reliable Woodworks Inc................G.....704 785-9663
   Concord *(G-3431)*

▲ Renner Usa Corp................G.....704 527-9261
   Charlotte *(G-2711)*

Robert Hamms LLC................G.....704 605-8057
   Monroe *(G-8552)*

Rodney S Cstm Cut Sign Co Inc................E.....919 362-9669
   Holly Springs *(G-6911)*

S Loflin Enterprises Inc................F.....704 633-1159
   Salisbury *(G-11113)*

Salazar Custom Framing LLC................G.....919 349-0830
   Dunn *(G-3867)*

Saluda Mountain Products Inc................F.....828 696-2296
   Flat Rock *(G-4713)*

Soundside Recycling & Mtls Inc................G.....252 491-8666
   Jarvisburg *(G-7186)*

◆ Southern Finishing Company Inc................F.....336 573-3741
   Stoneville *(G-11828)*

Square Peg Construction Inc................G.....828 277-5164
   Asheville *(G-610)*

Swofford Inc................G.....252 478-5969
   Wilson *(G-13034)*

T Distribution NC Inc................E.....828 438-1112
   Morganton *(G-8903)*

▼ Treeforms Inc................E.....336 292-8998
   Greensboro *(G-5871)*

◆ Turn Bull Lumber Company................E.....910 862-4447
   Elizabethtown *(G-4436)*

Universal Forest Products Inc................F.....252 338-0319
   Elizabeth City *(G-4416)*

Vaughn Woodworking Inc................G.....828 963-6858
   Banner Elk *(G-690)*

▲ Vintage Editions Inc................F.....828 632-4185
   Taylorsville *(G-11985)*

Vinventions Usa LLC................C.....919 460-2200
   Zebulon *(G-13525)*

▲ Whitley Holding Company................E.....704 888-2625
   Midland *(G-8298)*

◆ Whitley/Monahan Handle LLC................E.....704 888-2625
   Midland *(G-8299)*

Working Widget Technology LLC................G.....704 684-6277
   Charlotte *(G-3025)*

World Art Gallery Incorporated................G.....910 989-0203
   Jacksonville *(G-7160)*

25 FURNITURE AND FIXTURES

2511 Wood household furniture

A C Furniture Company Inc................B.....336 623-3430
   Eden *(G-4339)*

A E Nesbitt Woodwork................G.....828 625-2428
   Black Mountain *(G-859)*

American of High Point Inc................F.....336 431-1513
   High Point *(G-6521)*

▲ Apollo Designs LLC................E.....336 886-0260
   High Point *(G-6524)*

Artisans Guild Incorporated................G.....336 841-4140
   High Point *(G-6530)*

Ashley Furniture Inds LLC................E.....336 998-1066
   Advance *(G-31)*

Baker Interiors Furniture Co................G.....336 431-9115
   High Point *(G-6537)*

◆ Baker Interiors Furniture Co................D.....336 431-9115
   Connelly Springs *(G-3473)*

Barber Furniture & Supply................F.....704 278-9367
   Cleveland *(G-3209)*

Barker and Martin Inc................G.....336 275-5056
   Greensboro *(G-5385)*

Bassett Furniture Direct Inc................F.....704 979-5700
   Concord *(G-3318)*

Bernhardt Furniture Company................D.....828 759-6652
   Lenoir *(G-7580)*

Bernhardt Furniture Company................D.....828 758-9811
   Lenoir *(G-7581)*

Bernhardt Furniture Company................E.....828 759-6205
   Lenoir *(G-7584)*

◆ Bernhardt Furniture Company................C.....828 758-9811
   Lenoir *(G-7582)*

◆ Bernhardt Industries Inc................C.....828 758-9811
   Lenoir *(G-7585)*

▲ Boggs Collective Inc................G.....828 398-9701
   Asheville *(G-459)*

Bookcase Shop................G.....919 683-1922
   Durham *(G-3938)*

Bradington-Young LLC................C.....276 656-3335
   Cherryville *(G-3059)*

Brown Cabinet Co................G.....704 933-2731
   Kannapolis *(G-7205)*

Cabinet Makers Inc................G.....704 876-2808
   Statesville *(G-11674)*

▲ Carolina Business Furn Inc................A.....336 431-9400
   High Point *(G-6556)*

Carolina Csual Otdoor Furn Inc................F.....252 491-5171
   Jarvisburg *(G-7185)*

Carolina Farmstead LLC................G.....800 822-6219
   Snow Hill *(G-11477)*

◆ Carolina Mills Incorporated................D.....828 428-9911
   Maiden *(G-8010)*

Carroll Russell Mfg Inc................E.....919 779-2273
   Raleigh *(G-9982)*

Cashman Inc................G.....252 995-4319
   Frisco *(G-4863)*

Century Furniture LLC................D.....828 326-8410
   Hickory *(G-6295)*

Century Furniture LLC................C.....828 326-8201
   Hickory *(G-6296)*

Century Furniture LLC................D.....828 326-8535
   Hickory *(G-6297)*

Century Furniture LLC................D.....828 326-8458
   Hickory *(G-6298)*

Century Furniture LLC................G.....336 889-8286
   High Point *(G-6566)*

Chf Industries Inc................E.....212 951-7800
   Charlotte *(G-1912)*

Chris Isom Inc................F.....336 629-0240
   Asheboro *(G-338)*

▲ Classic Leather Inc................B.....828 328-2046
   Conover *(G-3504)*

Closets By Design................D.....704 361-6424
   Charlotte *(G-1931)*

▲ Councill Company LLC................G.....336 859-2155
   Denton *(G-3745)*

Craftmaster Furniture Inc................A.....828 632-8127
   Hiddenite *(G-6495)*

Cranberry Wood Works Inc................G.....336 877-8771
   Fleetwood *(G-4715)*

◆ Cv Industries Inc................G.....828 328-1851
   Hickory *(G-6316)*

◆ Davis Furniture Industries Inc................C.....336 889-2009
   High Point *(G-6589)*

◆ Dedon Inc................F.....336 790-1070
   Greensboro *(G-5491)*

◆ Design Workshop Incorporated................F.....910 293-7329
   Warsaw *(G-12359)*

▲ Designmaster Furniture Inc................E.....828 324-7992
   Hickory *(G-6322)*

Drexel Heritage Furnishings................G.....828 391-6400
   Lenoir *(G-7601)*

Ducduc LLC................G.....212 226-1868
   Raleigh *(G-10062)*

◆ E J Victor Inc................C.....828 437-1991
   Morganton *(G-8861)*

▲ Easyglass Inc................G.....336 786-1800
   Mount Airy *(G-9118)*

Ethan Allen Retail Inc................E.....828 428-9361
   Maiden *(G-8012)*

Fairfield Chair Company................E.....828 785-5571
   Lenoir *(G-7605)*

◆ Fairfield Chair Company................C.....828 758-5571
   Lenoir *(G-7606)*

▲ Fulfords Restorations................G.....252 243-7727
   Wilson *(G-12992)*

Furniture Company................G.....910 686-1937
   Wilmington *(G-12781)*

Furniture Concepts................F.....828 323-1590
   Hickory *(G-6336)*

G A Lankford Construction................G.....828 254-2467
   Alexander *(G-100)*

Gram Furniture................G.....828 241-2836
   Claremont *(G-3114)*

Guy Chaddock and Company LLC................C.....828 584-0664
   Morganton *(G-8869)*

H & H Furniture Mfrs Inc................C.....336 873-7245
   Seagrove *(G-11274)*

Hancock & Moore LLC................B.....828 495-8235
   Taylorsville *(G-11963)*

Hdm Furniture Industries Inc................C.....336 882-8135
   Hickory *(G-6343)*

Hdm Furniture Industries Inc................A.....800 349-4579
   Hickory *(G-6344)*

Hfi Wind Down Inc................C.....828 430-3355
   Morganton *(G-8873)*

◆ Hickory Chair Company................D.....800 225-0265
   Hickory *(G-6349)*

HM Frame Company Inc................E.....828 428-3354
   Newton *(G-9472)*

Hollingswrth Cbnets Intrors LL................F.....910 251-1490
   Castle Hayne *(G-1502)*

Home Meridian Group LLC................D.....336 819-7200
   High Point *(G-6660)*

▲ Home Meridian Holdings Inc................C.....336 887-1985
   High Point *(G-6661)*

Homestead Country Built Furn................G.....910 799-6489
   Wilmington *(G-12807)*

Hooker Furnishings Corporation................C.....336 819-7200
   High Point *(G-6662)*

Ison Furniture Mfg Inc................E.....336 476-4700
   Thomasville *(G-12040)*

▼ Johnston Casuals Furniture Inc................D.....336 838-5178
   North Wilkesboro *(G-9538)*

Jones Frame Inc................E.....336 434-2531
   High Point *(G-6679)*

Kenzie Layne Company................G.....704 485-2282
   Locust *(G-7894)*

▲ Kincaid Furniture Company Inc................D.....828 728-3261
   Hudson *(G-6953)*

Kn Furniture Inc................E.....336 953-3259
   Ramseur *(G-10626)*

Kolcraft Enterprises Inc................C.....910 944-9345
   Aberdeen *(G-10)*

Kustom Kraft Wdwrks Mt Airy In................G.....336 786-2831
   Mount Airy *(G-9143)*

◆ Lacquer Craft Hospitality Inc................C.....336 822-8086
   High Point *(G-6689)*

▲ Lea Industries Inc................C.....336 294-5233
   Hudson *(G-6954)*

◆ Leathercraft Inc................................C..... 828 322-3305
Conover (G-3536)

Leisure Craft Holdings LLC............ D..... 828 693-8241
Flat Rock (G-4708)

Leisure Craft Inc.............................. C..... 828 693-8241
Flat Rock (G-4709)

Liberty Hse Utility Buildings................ G..... 828 209-3390
Horse Shoe (G-6929)

▼ Linwood Inc.................................. G..... 336 300-8307
Lexington (G-7712)

Magnussen Home Furnishings Inc........ G..... 336 841-4424
Greensboro (G-5671)

Martin Obrien Cabinetmaker................. G..... 336 773-1334
Winston Salem (G-13245)

Maynard Frame Shop Inc................. G..... 910 428-2033
Star (G-11631)

Michael Parker Cabinetry................. G..... 919 833-5117
Raleigh (G-10298)

Nobscot Construction Co Inc............. G..... 919 929-2075
Chapel Hill (G-1560)

Oak City Customs LLC.................... G..... 919 995-5561
Zebulon (G-13517)

Old Growth Riverwood Inc................. G..... 910 762-4077
Wilmington (G-12865)

Old Wood Company.......................... G..... 828 259-9663
Asheville (G-559)

One Furniture Group Corp................. G..... 336 235-0221
Greensboro (G-5722)

P R Sparks Enterprises Inc............. G..... 336 272-7200
Greensboro (G-5728)

Philip Brady................................. G..... 336 581-3999
Bennett (G-782)

◆ Phoenix Home Furnishings Inc..........C
High Point (G-6730)

Precast Terrazzo Entps Inc............. E..... 919 231-6200
Raleigh (G-10388)

Precision Materials LLC.................. F..... 828 632-8851
Taylorsville (G-11972)

Prepac Manufacturing US LLC................ F..... 800 665-1266
Whitsett (G-12617)

Pricely Inc.................................. E..... 336 431-2055
High Point (G-6745)

Progressive Furniture Inc............... C..... 828 459-2151
Claremont (G-3118)

Quality Contemporary Furniture......... G..... 919 758-7277
Raleigh (G-10414)

Ralph S Frame Works Inc............... D..... 336 431-2168
High Point (G-6753)

Riverview Cabinet & Supply Inc............ G..... 336 228-1486
Burlington (G-1148)

Robert Bergelin Company................. E..... 828 437-6409
Morganton (G-8892)

Royal Colony Furniture Inc............. G..... 336 472-8833
Thomasville (G-12067)

Ruskin Inc................................... G..... 828 324-6500
Hickory (G-6436)

Seagrove Lumber LLC...................... F..... 910 428-9663
Seagrove (G-11281)

◆ Sherrill Furniture Company............... B..... 828 322-2640
Hickory (G-6441)

South Mountain Crafts..................... G..... 828 433-2607
Morganton (G-8899)

◆ Southern Finishing Company Inc........F..... 336 573-3741
Stoneville (G-11828)

Stanley Furniture Company LLC.......... C..... 336 884-7700
High Point (G-6791)

▲ Stone Marble Co Inc...................... G..... 773 227-1161
Thomasville (G-12075)

▲ Storagemotion Inc....................... G..... 704 746-3700
Mooresville (G-8779)

Style Upholstering Inc.................... G..... 828 322-4882
Hickory (G-6460)

Superior Wood Products Inc............... G..... 336 472-2237
Thomasville (G-12076)

Tatum Galleries Inc........................ G..... 828 963-6466
Banner Elk (G-689)

◆ Thayer Coggin Inc........................D..... 336 841-6000
High Point (G-6805)

▲ The Southwood Furniture C............. G..... 828 465-1776
Hickory (G-6465)

▲ Tiger Mountain Woodworks Inc........ F..... 828 526-5577
Highlands (G-6846)

▼ Treeforms Inc............................. E..... 336 292-8998
Greensboro (G-5871)

Troutman Careconnect Corp............. F..... 704 838-9389
Troutman (G-12152)

▲ Troutman Chair Company LLC........... E..... 704 872-7625
Troutman (G-12153)

▲ Tsai Winddown Inc....................... E..... 704 873-3106
Statesville (G-11794)

◆ Unigel Inc................................. G..... 828 228-2095
Hickory (G-6479)

Universal Furniture Intl Inc............. G..... 828 241-3191
Claremont (G-3123)

Universal Furniture Intl Inc............. G..... 828 464-0311
Conover (G-3570)

◆ Universal Furniture Limited..............D..... 336 822-8888
High Point (G-6819)

Uwharrie Chair Company LLC............. G..... 336 431-2055
High Point (G-6820)

Vaughan-Bassett Furn Co Inc............. A..... 336 835-2670
Elkin (G-4453)

Vaughan-Bassett Furn Co Inc............. A..... 336 889-9111
High Point (G-6822)

◆ Wdm Inc...................................E..... 704 283-7508
Monroe (G-8578)

Wesley Hall Inc............................. C..... 828 324-7466
Conover (G-3573)

◆ Whitewood Industries Inc................. D..... 336 472-0303
Thomasville (G-12086)

Willow Creek Furniture Inc............... G..... 336 889-0076
High Point (G-6835)

Winston Concept Furniture................ G..... 336 472-7839
Thomasville (G-12088)

Wise Living Inc............................. F..... 336 991-5346
High Point (G-6838)

Wood N Things.............................. G..... 910 990-4448
Clinton (G-3254)

Wood Technology Inc....................... E..... 828 464-8049
Conover (G-3577)

Woodsmiths Company........................ G..... 406 626-3102
Lenoir (G-7646)

Woodys Chair Shop.......................... G..... 828 765-9277
Spruce Pine (G-11590)

Xylem Inc................................... G..... 919 772-4126
Garner (G-4976)

▲ Yorkshire House Inc..................... G..... 336 869-9714
High Point (G-6841)

Yukon Inc................................... F..... 919 366-2001
Wendell (G-12554)

2512 Upholstered household furniture

A C Furniture Company Inc................. B..... 336 623-3430
Eden (G-4339)

▲ AB New Beginnings Inc.................. D..... 828 465-6953
Conover (G-3487)

Amor Furniture and Bedding LLC........ F..... 336 795-0044
Liberty (G-7760)

Archdale Furniture Distributor............ G..... 336 431-1081
Archdale (G-211)

▲ Aria Designs LLC........................ F..... 828 572-4303
Lenoir (G-7573)

Baker Interiors Furniture Co............. G..... 336 431-9115
High Point (G-6537)

Bassett Furniture Inds NC LLC............. A..... 828 465-7700
Newton (G-9451)

Berkeley Home Furniture LLC............. G..... 336 882-0012
High Point (G-6546)

Bernhardt Furniture Company............. D..... 828 759-6652
Lenoir (G-7580)

Bernhardt Furniture Company............. D..... 828 758-9811
Lenoir (G-7581)

Bernhardt Furniture Company............. D..... 828 572-4664
Lenoir (G-7583)

Bernhardt Furniture Company............. E..... 828 759-6205
Lenoir (G-7584)

◆ Bernhardt Furniture Company...........C..... 828 758-9811
Lenoir (G-7582)

◆ Bernhardt Industries Inc...............C..... 828 758-9811
Lenoir (G-7585)

Blackstone Furniture Inds Inc............. F..... 910 428-2833
Ether (G-4494)

Bradington-Young LLC...................... C..... 276 656-3335
Cherryville (G-3059)

▲ Bradington-Young LLC................... C..... 704 435-5881
Hickory (G-6275)

Brookline Furniture Co Inc............... D..... 336 841-8503
Archdale (G-214)

Burrough Furniture......................... G..... 336 841-3129
Archdale (G-215)

▲ C R Laine Furniture Co Inc............. C..... 828 328-1831
Hickory (G-6278)

Cargill & Pendleton Inc................. E..... 336 882-5510
High Point (G-6555)

Carolina Chair Inc........................ F..... 828 459-1330
Conover (G-3499)

◆ Carolina Mills Incorporated.............D..... 828 428-9911
Maiden (G-8010)

◆ Carolina Tape & Supply Corp............E..... 828 322-3991
Hickory (G-6289)

Cedar Rock Home Furnishings............. G..... 828 396-2361
Hudson (G-6948)

Century Furniture LLC..................... C..... 828 326-8201
Hickory (G-6296)

Century Furniture LLC..................... D..... 828 326-8458
Hickory (G-6298)

Century Furniture LLC..................... D..... 828 326-8410
Hickory (G-6299)

Century Furniture LLC..................... D..... 828 326-8650
Hickory (G-6300)

Century Furniture LLC..................... F..... 828 326-8495
Hickory (G-6301)

◆ Century Furniture LLC...................C..... 828 267-8739
Hickory (G-6302)

◆ Chateau DAx USA Ltd....................G..... 336 885-9777
High Point (G-6567)

▲ Classic Leather Inc..................... B..... 828 328-2046
Conover (G-3504)

◆ Contemporary Furnishings Corp.........D..... 704 633-8000
Salisbury (G-11037)

Contract Seating Inc....................... G..... 828 322-6662
Hickory (G-6310)

Cotton Belt Inc............................. D..... 252 689-6847
Greenville (G-5960)

▲ Councill Company LLC.................... C..... 336 859-2155
Denton (G-3745)

Country At Home Furniture Inc............. F..... 828 464-7498
Newton (G-9461)

▲ Cox Manufacturing Company Inc...... E..... 828 397-4123
Hickory (G-6313)

Craftmaster Furniture Inc................. A..... 828 632-8127
Hiddenite (G-6495)

◆ Craftmaster Furniture Inc...............B..... 828 632-9786
Hiddenite (G-6494)

Craymer McElwee Holdings Inc............ G..... 828 326-6100
Hickory (G-6314)

Creations By Taylor .... G 410 269-6430
Mount Pleasant *(G-9261)*

Custom Designs and Upholstery .... F 336 882-1516
Thomasville *(G-12013)*

◆ Cv Industries Inc .... G 828 328-1851
Hickory *(G-6316)*

▲ D R Kincaid Chair Co Inc .... E 828 754-0255
Lenoir *(G-7599)*

Dal Leather Inc .... G 828 302-1667
Conover *(G-3511)*

Daniels Woodcarving Co Inc .... F 828 632-7336
Taylorsville *(G-11958)*

Design Theory LLC .... F 336 912-0155
High Point *(G-6591)*

Dexter Inc .... G 828 459-7904
Claremont *(G-3106)*

Dexter Inc .... G 919 510-5050
Raleigh *(G-10045)*

▲ Dfp Inc .... D 336 841-3028
High Point *(G-6592)*

Directional Buying Group Inc .... G 336 472-6187
Thomasville *(G-12019)*

Distinctive Furniture Inc .... G 828 754-3947
Lenoir *(G-7600)*

Domenicks Furniture Mfr LLC .... E 336 442-3348
High Point *(G-6596)*

◆ E J Victor Inc .... C 828 437-1991
Morganton *(G-8861)*

Elite Furniture Mfg Inc .... G 336 882-0406
High Point *(G-6606)*

England Inc .... D 336 861-5266
High Point *(G-6612)*

Fairfield Chair Company .... E 828 785-5571
Lenoir *(G-7605)*

◆ Fairfield Chair Company .... C 828 758-5571
Lenoir *(G-7606)*

Framewright Inc .... G 828 459-2284
Conover *(G-3523)*

Friendship Upholstery Co Inc .... E 828 632-9836
Taylorsville *(G-11961)*

Furniture Concepts .... F 828 323-1590
Hickory *(G-6336)*

Geiger International Inc .... F 828 324-6500
Hildebran *(G-6850)*

Golden Rctangle Enteprises Inc .... E 828 389-3336
Hayesville *(G-6141)*

Grand Manor Furniture Inc .... D 828 758-5521
Lenoir *(G-7608)*

▲ H W S Company Inc .... B 828 322-8624
Hickory *(G-6341)*

Hancock & Moore LLC .... C 828 495-8235
Taylorsville *(G-11963)*

Hancock & Moore LLC .... D 828 495-8235
Taylorsville *(G-11962)*

Hdm Furniture Industries Inc .... A 800 349-4579
Hickory *(G-6344)*

Hdm Furniture Industries Inc .... E 336 812-4434
High Point *(G-6641)*

Hester Enterprises Inc .... E 704 865-4480
Gastonia *(G-5060)*

Hfi Wind Down Inc .... C 828 438-5767
Morganton *(G-8872)*

HM Frame Company Inc .... E 828 428-3354
Newton *(G-9472)*

HM Liquidation Inc .... G 828 495-8235
Hickory *(G-6361)*

▲ Huddle Furniture Inc .... E 828 874-8888
Valdese *(G-12195)*

◆ Hughes Furniture Inds Inc .... C 336 498-8700
Randleman *(G-10650)*

Huntington House Inc .... E 828 495-4400
Taylorsville *(G-11965)*

▲ Huntington House Inc .... C 828 495-4400
Hickory *(G-6363)*

▲ Images of America Inc .... D 336 475-7106
Thomasville *(G-12038)*

▲ Indiana Chair Frame Company .... G 574 825-9355
Liberty *(G-7768)*

▲ Intensa Inc .... G 336 884-4003
High Point *(G-6674)*

International Furnishings Inc .... G 336 472-8422
Thomasville *(G-12039)*

▲ Isenhour Furniture Company .... D 828 632-8849
Taylorsville *(G-11966)*

▲ Jack Cartwright Incorporated .... E 336 889-9400
High Point *(G-6676)*

▼ Jarrett Brothers .... G 828 433-8036
Morganton *(G-8876)*

▲ Jessica Charles LLC .... D 336 434-2124
High Point *(G-6678)*

Joerns Healthcare Parent LLC .... B 800 966-6662
Charlotte *(G-2372)*

Joseph Halker .... G 336 769-4734
Winston Salem *(G-13219)*

Keani Furniture Inc .... G 336 303-5484
Asheboro *(G-369)*

Kellex Corp .... C 828 874-0389
Valdese *(G-12196)*

▲ Key City Furniture Company Inc .... C 336 818-1161
Wilkesboro *(G-12646)*

▲ Kincaid Furniture Company Inc .... D 828 728-3261
Hudson *(G-6953)*

King Hickory Furniture Company .... G 828 324-0472
Hickory *(G-6378)*

King Hickory Furniture Company .... G 336 841-6140
High Point *(G-6685)*

▲ King Hickory Furniture Company .... C 828 322-6025
Hickory *(G-6379)*

Kn Furniture Inc .... E 336 953-3259
Ramseur *(G-10626)*

Kolcraft Enterprises Inc .... C 910 944-9345
Aberdeen *(G-10)*

Lancer Incorporated .... C 910 428-2181
Star *(G-11630)*

◆ Lazar Industries LLC .... C 919 742-9303
Siler City *(G-11415)*

Lazar Industries East Inc .... G 919 742-9303
Siler City *(G-11416)*

◆ Leathercraft Inc .... C 828 322-3305
Conover *(G-3536)*

Lee Industries LLC .... C 828 464-8318
Newton *(G-9479)*

Lee Industries LLC .... C 828 464-8318
Newton *(G-9480)*

◆ Lee Industries LLC .... B 828 464-8318
Conover *(G-3537)*

▲ Level 4 Designs Corp .... G 336 235-3450
Greensboro *(G-5662)*

◆ Lexington Furniture Inds Inc .... C 336 474-5300
Thomasville *(G-12043)*

◆ LLC Ferguson Copeland .... C 828 584-0664
Morganton *(G-8879)*

▲ Lloyds Chatham Ltd Partnership .... E 919 742-4692
High Point *(G-6693)*

Lodging By Liberty Inc .... C 336 622-2201
Siler City *(G-11417)*

M & M Frame Company Inc .... G 336 859-8166
Denton *(G-3757)*

◆ March Furniture Manufacturing Inc .... C 336 824-4413
Ramseur *(G-10629)*

▲ Marquis Contract Corporation .... E 336 884-8200
High Point *(G-6701)*

Masterfield Furniture Co Inc .... E 828 632-8535
Taylorsville *(G-11967)*

◆ McCreary Modern Inc .... B 828 464-6465
Newton *(G-9481)*

◆ McKinley Leather Hickory Inc .... E 828 459-2884
Claremont *(G-3115)*

McNeillys Inc .... E 704 300-1712
Lawndale *(G-7518)*

◆ Minhas Furniture House Inc .... E 910 898-0808
Robbins *(G-10754)*

Moores Upholstering Interiors .... G 704 240-8393
Lincolnton *(G-7845)*

NC Custom Leather Inc .... F 828 404-2973
Conover *(G-3540)*

Nobscot Construction Co Inc .... G 919 929-2075
Chapel Hill *(G-1560)*

◆ North Carolina Lumber Company .... G 336 498-6600
Randleman *(G-10654)*

O Henry House Ltd .... E 336 431-5350
Archdale *(G-239)*

▲ Old Hickory Tannery Inc .... E 828 465-6599
Newton *(G-9484)*

◆ Overnight Sofa Corporation .... E 828 324-2271
Hickory *(G-6408)*

◆ Paladin Industries Inc .... D 828 635-0448
Hiddenite *(G-6504)*

Parker Southern Inc .... F 828 428-3506
Maiden *(G-8016)*

◆ Paul Robert Chair Inc .... D 828 632-7021
Taylorsville *(G-11969)*

Plat LLC .... F 828 358-4564
Granite Falls *(G-5317)*

Popes Signature Gallery .... G 828 396-9494
Hudson *(G-6956)*

Prominence Furniture Inc .... E 336 475-6505
Thomasville *(G-12063)*

R & D Weaving Inc .... F 828 248-1910
Ellenboro *(G-4460)*

Rbc Inc .... G 336 889-7573
High Point *(G-6754)*

◆ Rbc Inc .... C 336 861-5800
Sophia *(G-11490)*

Restaurant Furniture Inc .... F 828 459-9992
Claremont *(G-3120)*

Rhf Investments Inc .... G 828 326-8350
Hickory *(G-6428)*

Richard Shew .... F 828 781-3294
Conover *(G-3554)*

Rowes .... G 828 241-2609
Catawba *(G-1513)*

Rufco Inc .... G 919 829-1332
Wake Forest *(G-12294)*

S Dorsett Upholstery Inc .... G 336 472-7076
Thomasville *(G-12070)*

Seam-Craft Inc .... G 336 861-4156
High Point *(G-6765)*

▲ Seam-Craft Inc .... F 336 861-4156
High Point *(G-6766)*

Select Furniture Company Inc .... F 336 886-3572
High Point *(G-6767)*

Sherrill Furniture Company .... F 828 322-8624
Hickory *(G-6439)*

Sherrill Furniture Company .... F 828 328-5241
Hickory *(G-6440)*

Sherrill Furniture Company .... F 336 884-0974
High Point *(G-6768)*

Sherrill Furniture Company .... F 828 437-2256
Morganton *(G-8896)*

Sherrill Furniture Company .... D 828 465-0844
Newton *(G-9494)*

◆ Sherrill Furniture Company .... B 828 322-2640
Hickory *(G-6441)*

Sides Furniture Inc .... G 336 869-5509
High Point *(G-6769)*

Simplicity Sofas Inc.............................. G 800 813-2889
High Point (G-6775)

Smith Novelty Company Inc................ G 704 982-7413
Albemarle (G-89)

Southandenglish LLC.......................... G 336 888-8333
High Point (G-6786)

Southfield Ltd....................................... F 336 434-6220
High Point (G-6789)

Stone & Leigh LLC............................... G 919 971-2096
Morganton (G-8901)

▲ Stone Marble Co Inc....................... G 773 227-1161
Thomasville (G-12075)

Style Upholstering Inc........................ G 828 322-4882
Hickory (G-6460)

Superior Wood Products Inc.............. 336 472-2237
Thomasville (G-12076)

◆ Swaim Inc.......................................C 336 885-6131
High Point (G-6797)

▲ Taylor King Furniture Inc................. C 828 632-7731
Taylorsville (G-11981)

Tb Arhaus LLC.................................... C 828 465-6953
Conover (G-3564)

TCS Designs Inc................................. F 828 324-9944
Hickory (G-6463)

Temple Inc.. D 828 428-8031
Maiden (G-8018)

▲ The Southwood Furniture C............ G 828 465-1776
Hickory (G-6465)

Thomasville Upholstery Inc................ C 828 345-6225
Hickory (G-6467)

▲ Tomlinson/Erwin-Lambeth Inc........ D 336 472-5005
Thomasville (G-12081)

Universal Furniture Intl Inc................ G 828 241-3191
Claremont (G-3123)

Universal Furniture Intl Inc................ C 828 464-0311
Conover (G-3570)

◆ Universal Furniture Limited............. D 336 822-8888
High Point (G-6819)

Upholstery Designs Hickory Inc........... G 828 324-2002
Hickory (G-6480)

◆ Vanguard Furniture Co Inc..............B 828 328-5601
Conover (G-3571)

Vaughan-Bassett Furn Co Inc.............. A 336 835-2670
Elkin (G-4453)

◆ Verellen Inc.....................................E 336 889-7379
High Point (G-6824)

Violino USA Ltd................................... E 336 889-6623
High Point (G-6826)

▲ Watauga Creek LLC......................... G 828 369-7881
Franklin (G-4842)

Wesley Hall Inc.................................... G 828 324-7466
Conover (G-3573)

Whitewood Contracts LLC................... E 336 885-9300
High Point (G-6834)

Wise Living Inc.................................... F 336 991-5346
High Point (G-6838)

▲ Woodmark Originals Inc.................. C 336 841-6409
High Point (G-6839)

Younger Furniture Inc......................... D 336 476-0444
Thomasville (G-12096)

2514 Metal household furniture

Biologics Inc.. G 919 546-9810
Raleigh (G-9945)

Bull City Designs LLC......................... E 919 908-6252
Durham (G-3949)

Conestoga Wood Spc Corp................. D 919 284-2258
Kenly (G-7229)

Creative Metal and Wood Inc............. G 336 475-9400
Colfax (G-3276)

Dorel Ecommerce Inc......................... G 828 378-0092
Asheville (G-488)

Four Corners Home Inc...................... G 828 398-4187
Asheville (G-500)

Greg Price.. G 847 778-4426
Hampstead (G-6073)

◆ Hickory Springs Manufactu.............D 828 328-2201
Hickory (G-6355)

Hickory Springs Mfg Co...................... G 828 325-4757
Hickory (G-6358)

Leggett & Platt Incorporated.............. G 704 380-6208
Statesville (G-11727)

Leisure Craft Holdings LLC................ D 828 693-8241
Flat Rock (G-4708)

Leisure Craft Inc.................................. C 828 693-8241
Flat Rock (G-4709)

Mlf Company LLC................................ F 919 231-9401
Raleigh (G-10311)

Outer Banks Hammocks Inc............... F 910 256-4001
Wilmington (G-12869)

Powder River Technologies Inc.......... G 828 465-2894
Newton (G-9489)

◆ Swaim Inc..C 336 885-6131
High Point (G-6797)

Timmerman Manufacturing Inc.......... E 828 464-1778
Conover (G-3566)

Tube Enterprises Incorporated............ F 941 629-9267
Shelby (G-11386)

2515 Mattresses and bedsprings

Affordable Bedding Inc........................ G 828 254-5555
Asheville (G-424)

Arden Companies LLC......................... D 919 258-3081
Sanford (G-11150)

Bedex LLC... E 336 617-6755
High Point (G-6544)

Bemco Sleep Products Inc.................. E 910 892-3107
Dunn (G-3846)

Bjmf Inc... E 704 554-6333
Charlotte (G-1787)

Blue Ridge Products Co Inc................ G 828 322-7990
Hickory (G-6274)

▲ Carolina Mattress Guild Inc............. D 336 841-8529
Thomasville (G-12004)

Comfort Bay Home Fashions Inc........ G 843 442-7477
Hickory (G-6305)

Comfort Sleep LLC.............................. G 336 267-5853
Thomasville (G-12010)

Cotton Belt Inc..................................... D 252 689-6847
Greenville (G-5960)

Culp Inc... D 336 885-2800
Stokesdale (G-11810)

Dilworth Mattress Company Inc........... G 704 333-6564
Charlotte (G-2049)

Elborn Holdings LLC........................... G 919 917-1419
Davidson (G-3704)

Hill-Rom Inc... E 919 854-3600
Cary (G-1372)

▲ Iredell Fiber Inc............................... F 704 878-0884
Statesville (G-11717)

Jones Frame Inc.................................. E 336 434-2531
High Point (G-6679)

◆ Kingsdown Incorporated..................E 919 563-3531
Mebane (G-8247)

Kingsdown Acquisition Corp............... G 919 563-3531
Mebane (G-8248)

L C Industries Inc................................ C 919 596-8277
Fayetteville (G-4629)

◆ L C Industries Inc........................... G 919 596-8277
Durham (G-4100)

Larlin Cushion Company...................... F 828 465-5599
Hickory (G-6384)

Leggett & Platt Incorporated.............. C 336 379-7777
Greensboro (G-5660)

Leggett & Platt Incorporated.............. D 336 884-4306
High Point (G-6690)

Leggett & Platt Incorporated.............. G 855 853-3539
Lexington (G-7709)

Leggett & Platt Incorporated.............. F 336 622-0121
Liberty (G-7770)

Leggett & Platt Incorporated.............. G 704 380-6208
Statesville (G-11727)

Leggett & Platt Incorporated.............. E 828 322-6855
Conover (G-3538)

Leggett & Platt Incorporated.............. C 336 889-2600
High Point (G-6691)

Mattress Firm....................................... G 252 443-1259
Rocky Mount (G-10851)

◆ Ohio Mat Lcnsing Cmpnnts Group.....G 336 861-3500
Trinity (G-12118)

Ohio-Sealy Mattress Mfg Co............... C 336 861-3500
Trinity (G-12119)

Reliable Bedding Company................. F 336 883-0648
Archdale (G-241)

Reliable Quilting Company.................. G 336 886-7036
High Point (G-6756)

Riverside Mattress Co Inc.................. E 910 483-0461
Fayetteville (G-4662)

Roadmster Trck Conversions Inc....... G 252 412-3980
Grifton (G-6038)

Royale Komfort Bedding Inc............... G 828 632-5631
Taylorsville (G-11975)

◆ Sealy Corporation...........................C 336 861-3500
Trinity (G-12123)

◆ Sealy Mattress Company.................C 336 861-3500
Trinity (G-12124)

Sealy Mattress Mfg Co LLC................ D 336 861-2900
Trinity (G-12125)

Somnigroup International Inc.............. C 336 861-2900
Trinity (G-12126)

Spring Air Mattress Corp.................... D 336 272-1141
Greensboro (G-5831)

Ssb Manufacturing Company............. C 704 596-4935
Charlotte (G-2853)

Stn Cushion Company......................... D 336 476-9100
Thomasville (G-12074)

▼ Timeless Bedding Inc...................... G 336 472-6603
Lexington (G-7752)

Vaughan-Bassett Furn Co Inc.............. A 336 835-2670
Elkin (G-4453)

◆ Winstn-Slem Inds For Blind Inc.........B 336 759-0551
Winston Salem (G-13398)

2517 Wood television and radio cabinets

Distinctive Cabinets Inc....................... F 704 529-6234
Charlotte (G-2053)

Mountain Showcase Group Inc............ E 828 692-9494
Hendersonville (G-6228)

Ocean Woodworking Inc...................... G 910 579-2233
Ocean Isle Beach (G-9588)

Philip Brady... G 336 581-3999
Bennett (G-782)

Quality Custom Woodworks Inc........... G 704 843-1584
Waxhaw (G-12438)

▲ Quality Musical Systems Inc........... E 828 667-5719
Candler (G-1231)

Wood Technology Inc.......................... E 828 464-8049
Conover (G-3577)

2519 Household furniture, nec

A N E Services LLC............................. G 704 882-1117
Charlotte (G-1605)

▲ Acacia Home & Garden Inc............. F 828 465-1700
Conover (G-3488)

Arden Companies LLC......................... D 919 258-3081
Sanford (G-11150)

S
I
C

Built To Last NC LLC......................F 252 232-0055
Moyock (G-9277)

Bull City Designs LLC.................E 919 908-6252
Durham (G-3949)

Carolina Casting Inc..................E 336 884-7311
High Point (G-6557)

Council Trnsp & Logistics LLC......G 910 322-7588
Fayetteville (G-4579)

Creative Metal and Wood Inc.......G 336 475-9400
Colfax (G-3276)

▲ French Heritage Inc.................F 336 882-3565
High Point (G-6622)

Joseph Sotanski.....................E 407 324-6187
Marion (G-8047)

Keter Us Inc........................D 704 263-1967
Stanley (G-11620)

Market of Raleigh LLC..............G 919 212-2100
Raleigh (G-10272)

Masters Moving Services Inc.......G 919 523-9836
Raleigh (G-10280)

▲ Millenia Usa LLC..................F
Hickory (G-6395)

Otto and Moore Inc.................F 336 887-0017
High Point (G-6722)

◆ Rbc Inc...........................C 336 861-5800
Sophia (G-11490)

Riverwood Inc.......................E 336 956-3034
Lexington (G-7735)

Stephanie Baxter....................G 803 203-8467
Lincolnton (G-7857)

Stephanies Mattress LLC............G 704 763-0705
Charlotte (G-2867)

Suncast Corporation.................E 704 274-5394
Huntersville (G-7059)

Val-U-King Group Inc...............G 980 306-5342
Gastonia (G-5162)

Whippoorwill Hills Inc..............G 252 537-2765
Roanoke Rapids (G-10746)

Wise Living Inc.....................F 323 541-0410
High Point (G-6837)

2521 Wood office furniture

▲ 3c Store Fixtures Inc.............D 252 291-5181
Wilson (G-12959)

A C Furniture Company Inc..........B 336 623-3430
Eden (G-4339)

A R Byrd Company Inc...............G 704 732-5675
Lincolnton (G-7807)

Amcase Inc..........................E 336 784-5992
High Point (G-6519)

Appalachian Cabinet Inc............G 828 265-0830
Deep Gap (G-3727)

B&H Millwork and Fixtures Inc......E 336 431-0068
High Point (G-6534)

Bernhardt Furniture Company........D 828 759-6245
Lenoir (G-7579)

Bernhardt Furniture Company........D 828 758-9811
Lenoir (G-7581)

Bernhardt Furniture Company........E 828 759-6205
Lenoir (G-7584)

◆ Bernhardt Furniture Company......C 828 758-9811
Lenoir (G-7582)

◆ Bernhardt Industries Inc.........C 828 758-9811
Lenoir (G-7585)

Boone Enterprises LLC..............G 910 859-8299
Leland (G-7534)

Boss Design US Inc.................G 844 353-7834
High Point (G-6550)

Bull City Designs LLC..............E 919 908-6252
Durham (G-3949)

▲ Carolina House Furniture Inc.....E 828 459-7400
Claremont (G-3090)

Cbt Supply..........................G 803 617-8230
Mooresville (G-8636)

▲ Classic Leather Inc..............B 828 328-2046
Conover (G-3504)

Comm-Kab Inc.......................F 336 873-8787
Asheboro (G-340)

▲ Corilam Fabricating Co...........E 336 993-2371
Kernersville (G-7259)

Custom Cabinets By Livengood.......G 704 279-3031
Salisbury (G-11040)

Cynthia Saar........................G 910 480-2523
Stedman (G-11806)

Darran Furniture Inds Inc..........C 336 861-2400
High Point (G-6588)

◆ Davis Furniture Industries Inc...C 336 889-2009
High Point (G-6589)

▲ Delve Interiors LLC..............C 336 274-4661
Greensboro (G-5495)

▲ Element Designs Inc..............D 704 332-3114
Charlotte (G-2096)

Evelyn T Burney.....................G 336 473-9794
Rocky Mount (G-10838)

Geiger International Inc............F 828 324-6500
Hildebran (G-6850)

Groupe Lacasse LLC.................G 336 778-2098
Clemmons (G-3187)

Hancock & Moore LLC...............C 828 495-8235
Taylorsville (G-11963)

Harris House Furn Inds Inc.........E 336 431-2802
Archdale (G-225)

Haworth Inc.........................E 828 328-5600
Conover (G-3527)

Haworth Inc.........................G 336 885-4021
High Point (G-6640)

Haworth Health Environments LLC....E 828 328-5600
Conover (G-3528)

▲ Hickory Business Furniture LLC...B 828 328-2064
Hickory (G-6348)

▲ High Point Furniture Inds Inc....D 336 431-7101
High Point (G-6653)

▲ Idx Impressions LLC..............C 703 550-6902
Washington (G-12393)

Ie Furniture Inc....................E 336 475-5050
Archdale (G-227)

Jasper Seating Company Inc.........C 704 528-4506
Troutman (G-12142)

◆ Leathercraft Inc.................C 828 322-3305
Conover (G-3536)

M T N of Pinellas Inc..............G 727 823-1650
Winston Salem (G-13242)

Michael Parker Cabinetry...........G 919 833-5117
Raleigh (G-10298)

Ocean Woodworking Inc..............G 910 579-2233
Ocean Isle Beach (G-9588)

▲ Ofm LLC..........................D 919 303-6389
Holly Springs (G-6909)

Parker Southern Inc................F 828 428-3506
Maiden (G-8016)

Precision Materials LLC............F 828 632-8851
Taylorsville (G-11972)

Prestige Millwork Inc..............G 910 428-2360
Star (G-11633)

Pridgen Woodwork Inc...............E 910 642-7175
Whiteville (G-12592)

Professinal Sales Associates.......G 336 210-2756
High Point (G-6748)

Rcws Inc............................F 919 680-2655
Durham (G-4208)

▲ Sbfi-North America Inc...........F 828 236-3993
Asheville (G-596)

Sdv Office Systems LLC.............F 844 968-9500
Fletcher (G-4766)

Thomasville Upholstery Inc.........C 828 345-6225
Hickory (G-6467)

Triune Business Furniture Inc......G 336 884-8341
High Point (G-6812)

Ullmanique Inc.....................G 336 885-5111
High Point (G-6816)

Upholstery Designs Hickory Inc.....G 828 324-2002
Hickory (G-6480)

Woodsmiths Company.................G 406 626-3102
Lenoir (G-7646)

Xylem Inc...........................G 919 772-4126
Garner (G-4976)

2522 Office furniture, except wood

A C Furniture Company Inc..........B 336 623-3430
Eden (G-4339)

A R Byrd Company Inc...............G 704 732-5675
Lincolnton (G-7807)

▲ Abercrombie Textiles I LLC.......F 704 487-1245
Shelby (G-11309)

Advocacy To Allvate Hmlessness.....G 919 810-3431
Raleigh (G-9882)

Bernhardt Furniture Company........D 828 759-6245
Lenoir (G-7579)

Bernhardt Furniture Company........E 828 759-6205
Lenoir (G-7584)

◆ Bernhardt Furniture Company......C 828 758-9811
Lenoir (G-7582)

◆ Bernhardt Industries Inc.........C 828 758-9811
Lenoir (G-7585)

Blue-Hen Inc........................G 407 322-2262
Asheville (G-458)

▲ Buzzispace Inc...................G 336 821-3150
Winston Salem (G-13114)

Con-Tab Inc.........................F 336 476-0104
Thomasville (G-12011)

Davidson House Inc.................F 704 791-0171
Davidson (G-3701)

◆ Davis Furniture Industries Inc...C 336 889-2009
High Point (G-6589)

▲ Delve Interiors LLC..............C 336 274-4661
Greensboro (G-5495)

Frazier Holdings LLC...............G 919 868-8651
Clayton (G-3148)

Haworth Inc.........................E 828 328-5600
Conover (G-3527)

HM Liquidation Inc.................G 828 495-8235
Hickory (G-6361)

▲ Images of America Inc............D 336 475-7106
Thomasville (G-12038)

▲ Intensa Inc......................G 336 884-4003
High Point (G-6674)

Kn Furniture Inc....................E 336 953-3259
Ramseur (G-10626)

▲ L B Plastics LLC.................D 704 663-1543
Mooresville (G-8706)

◆ Leathercraft Inc.................C 828 322-3305
Conover (G-3536)

▲ Old Hickory Tannery Inc..........E 828 465-6599
Newton (G-9484)

◆ Portable Displays LLC............E 919 544-6504
Cary (G-1424)

▲ Sbfi-North America Inc...........F 828 236-3993
Asheville (G-596)

Sdv Office Systems LLC.............F 844 968-9500
Fletcher (G-4766)

▲ Studio Tk LLC....................E 919 464-2920
Clayton (G-3172)

T & J Panel Systems Inc............G 704 924-8600
Statesville (G-11784)

Unique Office Solutions Inc........F 336 854-0900
Greensboro (G-5890)

▲ Wheatstone Corporation................ D 252 638-7000
New Bern (G-9405)

2531 Public building and related furniture

4topps LLC... G 704 281-8451
Winston Salem (G-13069)

A C Furniture Company Inc.............. B 336 623-3430
Eden (G-4339)

Amcase Inc... E 336 784-5992
High Point (G-6519)

Artisan LLC... G 855 582-3539
Concord (G-3313)

Artisans Guild Incorporated............ G 336 841-4140
High Point (G-6530)

B/E Aerospace Inc............................. F 336 692-8940
Winston Salem (G-13098)

B/E Aerospace Inc............................. F 704 423-7000
Winston Salem (G-13099)

▲ B/E Aerospace Inc......................... E 704 423-7000
Charlotte (G-1731)

◆ Beaufurn LLC................................. E 336 768-2544
High Point (G-6543)

Clarios LLC... E 866 589-8883
Charlotte (G-1926)

Clarios LLC... E 336 884-5832
High Point (G-6569)

Clarios LLC... C 336 761-1550
Kernersville (G-7257)

Clarios LLC... E 252 754-0782
Winterville (G-13415)

▲ Corilam Fabricating Co.................. E 336 993-2371
Kernersville (G-7259)

Custom Educational Furn LLC.......... F 800 255-9189
Taylorsville (G-11956)

▲ Custom Products Inc..................... D 704 663-4159
Mooresville (G-8647)

◆ Davis Furniture Industries Inc......C 336 889-2009
High Point (G-6589)

▲ Dfp Inc... D 336 841-3028
High Point (G-6592)

Gram Furniture.................................. G 828 241-2836
Claremont (G-3114)

Graphical Creations Inc.................... F 704 888-8870
Stanfield (G-11607)

H & T Chair Co Inc............................. G 828 264-7742
Boone (G-920)

Harris House Furn Inds Inc............... E 336 431-2802
Archdale (G-225)

Haworth Inc.. G 336 885-4021
High Point (G-6640)

Indiana Mills & Manufacturing......... C 336 862-7519
High Point (G-6669)

Interior Wood Specialties Inc........... E 336 431-0068
High Point (G-6675)

Jka Idustries..................................... G 980 225-5350
Salisbury (G-11073)

Johnson Controls Inc......................... F 828 225-3200
Asheville (G-528)

Johnson Controls Inc......................... F 919 905-5745
Durham (G-4089)

Johnson Controls Inc......................... D 919 743-3500
Raleigh (G-10219)

Johnson Controls Inc......................... E 910 392-2372
Wilmington (G-12823)

Johnson Controls Inc......................... E 704 521-8889
Charlotte (G-2376)

Joie of Seating Inc............................. G 704 795-7474
Concord (G-3387)

Ken Staley Co Inc............................... G 336 685-4294
Franklinville (G-4857)

Krueger International Inc................... F 336 434-5011
High Point (G-6687)

L & R Installations Inc....................... G 336 547-8998
Greensboro (G-5656)

Leisure Craft Holdings LLC............... D 828 693-8241
Flat Rock (G-4708)

Leisure Craft Inc................................ C 828 693-8241
Flat Rock (G-4709)

Liat LLC.. D 704 528-4506
Troutman (G-12144)

Marshall Group of NC Inc.................. G 252 638-8585
New Bern (G-9379)

Precision Materials LLC..................... F 828 632-8851
Taylorsville (G-11972)

◆ S Kivett Inc..................................... F 910 592-0161
Clinton (G-3243)

Sedia Systems Inc............................. G 336 887-3818
Asheboro (G-395)

Something For Youth........................... F 252 799-8837
Williamston (G-12673)

Southern Classic Seating LLC........... F 336 498-3130
Sophia (G-11491)

Superior Wood Products Inc.............. G 336 472-2237
Thomasville (G-12076)

◆ Syntec Inc.......................................D 336 861-9023
High Point (G-6800)

▼ Vaughan Enterprises Inc................ G 919 772-4765
Raleigh (G-10584)

Zim Arcraft Cbin Solutions LLC........ B 336 464-0122
Winston Salem (G-13411)

Zim Arcraft Cbin Solutions LLC........ F 336 862-1418
Greensboro (G-5932)

2541 Wood partitions and fixtures

▲ 3c Store Fixtures Inc...................... D 252 291-5181
Wilson (G-12959)

Ajs Dezigns Inc.................................. G 828 652-6304
Marion (G-8030)

Amcase Inc... E 336 784-5992
High Point (G-6519)

AP Granite Installation LLC............... G 919 215-1795
Clayton (G-3131)

Appalachian Cabinet Inc................... G 828 265-0830
Deep Gap (G-3727)

▼ Artisan Leaf LLC............................. G 252 674-1223
Wilson (G-12964)

Carolina Cab Specialist LLC.............. G 919 818-4375
Cary (G-1322)

Carolina Countertops of Garner........ F 919 832-3335
Raleigh (G-9974)

Carolnas Top Shelf Cstm Cbnets...... G 704 376-5844
Charlotte (G-1862)

▲ Corilam Fabricating Co.................. E 336 993-2371
Kernersville (G-7259)

Cub Creek Kitchens & Baths Inc....... G 336 651-8983
North Wilkesboro (G-9527)

Custom Educational Furn LLC.......... F 800 255-9189
Taylorsville (G-11956)

Custom Surfaces Corporation........... G 252 638-3800
New Bern (G-9361)

Cutting Edge Stoneworks Inc............ G 704 799-1227
Mooresville (G-8648)

D & B Concepts Inc........................... G 336 885-8292
High Point (G-6585)

◆ D & D Displays Inc..........................E 336 667-8765
North Wilkesboro (G-9528)

◆ Dac Products Inc.............................E 336 969-9786
Rural Hall (G-10958)

Dale Reynolds Cabinets Inc.............. G 704 890-5962
Charlotte (G-2017)

Davis Cabinet Co Wilson Inc............. G 252 291-9052
Sims (G-11429)

Display Options Woodwork Inc.......... G 704 599-6525
Belmont (G-747)

E T Sales Inc...................................... F 704 888-4010
Midland (G-8286)

Endeavour Fbrication Group Inc........ G 919 479-1453
Durham (G-4025)

Grice Showcase Display Mfg Inc....... G 704 423-8888
Charlotte (G-2242)

▼ Hardwood Store of NC Inc.............. F 336 449-9627
Gibsonville (G-5177)

Hargrove Countertops & ACC Inc...... E 919 981-0163
Raleigh (G-10155)

Harris Wood Products Inc.................. G 704 550-5494
New London (G-9418)

Hollingswrth Cbnets Intrors LL......... F 910 251-1490
Castle Hayne (G-1502)

Holt Group Inc.................................... F 336 668-2770
High Point (G-6659)

▲ Idx Impressions LLC...................... C 703 550-6902
Washington (G-12393)

◆ Interlam Corporation.......................E 336 786-6254
Mount Airy (G-9134)

◆ Intermarket Technology Inc............E 252 623-2199
Washington (G-12395)

Ivars Display..................................... E 909 923-2761
Shelby (G-11348)

Ivey Fixture & Design Inc.................. G 704 283-4398
Monroe (G-8506)

Marsh Furniture Company................. F 336 273-8196
Greensboro (G-5676)

McAd Inc.. E 336 299-3030
Greensboro (G-5686)

Medals To Honor Inc.......................... G 910 326-4275
Hubert (G-6935)

Michael Parker Cabinetry................... G 919 833-5117
Raleigh (G-10298)

Mkc85 Inc... F 910 762-1986
Wilmington (G-12855)

Normac Kitchens Inc.......................... F 704 485-1911
Oakboro (G-9582)

Old Castle Service Inc....................... G 336 992-1601
Kernersville (G-7289)

Oyama Cabinet Inc............................ G 828 327-2668
Conover (G-3542)

Panels By Paith Inc........................... G 336 599-3437
Roxboro (G-10939)

Reliable Construction Co Inc............. G 704 289-1501
Monroe (G-8550)

Riddley Retail Fixtures Inc................. E 704 435-8829
Kings Mountain (G-7382)

Rowland Woodworking Inc................. E 336 887-0700
High Point (G-6761)

RPM Installions Inc............................ G 704 907-0868
Cornelius (G-3624)

Rugby Acquisition LLC....................... D 336 993-8686
Kernersville (G-7297)

Rusco Fixture Company Inc................ E 704 474-3184
Norwood (G-9559)

S Zaytoun Custom Cabinets Inc........ G 252 638-8390
New Bern (G-9394)

Saluda Mountain Products Inc.......... F 828 696-2296
Flat Rock (G-4713)

Sare Granite & Tile............................ G 828 676-2666
Arden (G-305)

Sheets Smith Wealth MGT Inc........... E 336 765-2020
Winston Salem (G-13335)

▲ Spartacraft Inc............................... E 828 397-4630
Connelly Springs (G-3483)

Specialized Retail Svcs LLC............. G 727 639-0804
Garner (G-4965)

Stanly Fixs Acquisition LLC.............. G 704 474-3184
Norwood (G-9560)

Sterling Cleora Corporation............... F 919 563-5800
Durham (G-4250)

Employee Codes: A=Over 500 employees, B=251-500
C=101-250, D=51-100, E=20-50, F=10-19, G=1-9

2025 Harris North Carolina
Manufacturers Directory

651

S I C

Stonery LLC.. G 704 662-8702
Mooresville (G-8778)

▼ Treeforms Inc................................... E 336 292-8998
Greensboro (G-5871)

Triangle Custom Cabinets Inc.............. G 919 387-1133
Apex (G-200)

TS Woodworks & RAD Design Inc......... F 704 238-1015
Monroe (G-8571)

Ullman Group LLC............................... F 704 246-7333
Charlotte (G-2959)

Washington Cabinet Company............. G 252 946-3457
Washington (G-12420)

Wildwood Studios Inc......................... G 828 299-8696
Asheville (G-636)

▲ William Stone & Tile Inc.................. G 910 353-0914
Hubert (G-6938)

Wilsonart LLC.................................... G 866 267-7360
Fletcher (G-4779)

2542 Partitions and fixtures, except wood

Amcase Inc.. E 336 784-5992
High Point (G-6519)

B&H Millwork and Fixtures Inc............. E 336 431-0068
High Point (G-6534)

Cemco Partitions Inc.......................... G 336 643-6316
Summerfield (G-11836)

Chatsworth Products Inc..................... C 252 514-2779
New Bern (G-9354)

◆ Coregrp LLC..................................... F 845 876-5109
Mooresville (G-8643)

Cub Creek Kitchens & Baths Inc........... G 336 651-8983
North Wilkesboro (G-9527)

Ds Smith PLC..................................... E 919 557-3148
Holly Springs (G-6898)

E G A Products Inc.............................. F 704 664-1221
Mooresville (G-8657)

▲ Elite Displays & Design Inc............. D 336 472-8200
Thomasville (G-12021)

Endless Plastics LLC........................... F 336 346-1839
Greensboro (G-5520)

Forbes Custom Cabinets LLC............... E 919 362-4277
Apex (G-156)

▼ Friedrich Metal Pdts Co Inc............. E 336 375-3067
Browns Summit (G-993)

Grice Showcase Display Mfg Inc........... G 704 423-8888
Charlotte (G-2242)

Hemco Wire Products Inc.................... G 336 454-7280
Jamestown (G-7164)

Idx Corporation.................................. C 252 948-2048
Washington (G-12392)

Innovative Design Tech LLC................. G 919 331-0204
Angier (G-121)

Jka Idustries..................................... G 980 225-5350
Salisbury (G-11073)

Leggett & Platt Incorporated............... G 704 380-6208
Statesville (G-11727)

Leisure Craft Holdings LLC.................. D 828 693-8241
Flat Rock (G-4708)

Leisure Craft Inc................................ C 828 693-8241
Flat Rock (G-4709)

Madix.. G 804 456-3007
Raleigh (G-10265)

◆ Master Displays Inc........................ D 336 884-5575
High Point (G-6706)

▲ McIntyre Manufacturing Group Inc... D 336 476-3646
Thomasville (G-12046)

Mijo Enterprises Inc........................... G 252 442-6806
Rocky Mount (G-10852)

Oro Manufacturing Company............... E 704 283-2186
Monroe (G-8539)

Parker Brothers Incorporated............. G 910 564-4132
Clinton (G-3237)

◆ Penco Products Inc......................... E 252 917-5287
Greenville (G-6012)

▲ Sid Jenkins Inc.............................. G 336 632-0707
Greensboro (G-5811)

Stanly Fixtures Company Inc................ G 704 474-3184
Norwood (G-9561)

Sterling Rack Inc............................... G 704 866-9131
Gastonia (G-5144)

◆ Technibilt Ltd................................. E 828 464-7388
Newton (G-9502)

Thomasville Mtal Fbricators Inc........... E 336 248-4992
Lexington (G-7750)

▼ Treeforms Inc................................ E 336 292-8998
Greensboro (G-5871)

▼ Wireway/Husky Corp........................ C 704 483-1135
Denver (G-3817)

2591 Drapery hardware and blinds and shades

Carolina Blind Outlet Inc..................... G 828 697-8525
Hendersonville (G-6194)

Chf Industries Inc.............................. D 704 522-5000
Charlotte (G-1911)

Dbf Inc.. G 910 548-6725
Jacksonville (G-7122)

Decolux USA..................................... G 704 340-3532
Charlotte (G-2026)

▲ Dize Company................................ D 336 722-5181
Winston Salem (G-13149)

Elite Textiles Fabrication Inc............... F 888 337-0977
High Point (G-6608)

Empire Carpet & Blinds Inc................. G 704 541-3988
Charlotte (G-2111)

First Rate Blinds................................ G 800 655-1080
Cornelius (G-3601)

H2h Blinds....................................... G 704 628-5084
Matthews (G-8114)

Hunter Douglas Inc............................ C 704 629-6500
Bessemer City (G-822)

Locklear Cabinets Wdwrk Sp Inc.......... G 910 521-4463
Rowland (G-10916)

Mountaintop Cheesecakes LLC............. G 336 391-9127
Mocksville (G-8380)

Newell Brands Inc.............................. F 336 812-8181
High Point (G-6718)

Nova Wildcat Drapery Hdwr LLC.......... E 704 696-5110
Huntersville (G-7023)

Penrock LLC..................................... E 704 800-6722
Mooresville (G-8745)

Raven Rock Manufacturing Inc............. G 910 308-8430
Dunn (G-3865)

Rollease Acmeda Inc.......................... D 800 552-5100
Conover (G-3556)

Royal Textile Products Sw LLC............. G 602 276-4598
Charlotte (G-2735)

◆ Selective Enterprises Inc................. C 704 588-3310
Charlotte (G-2784)

Shuttercraft Inc................................. F 704 708-9079
Matthews (G-8148)

Synoptix Companies LLC..................... F 910 790-3630
Wilmington (G-12935)

Vertical Solutions of NC Inc................. G 919 285-2251
Holly Springs (G-6918)

Vista Products Inc............................. D 910 582-0130
Hamlet (G-6065)

2599 Furniture and fixtures, nec

Alexanders....................................... G 910 938-0013
Jacksonville (G-7114)

Alligood Cabinet Shop......................... G 252 927-3201
Washington (G-12372)

Amcase Inc.. E 336 784-5992
High Point (G-6519)

AMG Casework LLC............................. F 919 462-9203
Morrisville (G-8926)

Appalachian Cabinet Inc...................... G 828 265-0830
Deep Gap (G-3727)

▲ Ariston Hospitality Inc..................... E 626 458-8668
High Point (G-6528)

▲ Arper USA...................................... G 336 434-2376
High Point (G-6529)

Atelier Maison and Co LLC.................. F 828 277-7202
Asheville (G-446)

◆ Beaufurn LLC.................................. E 336 768-2544
High Point (G-6543)

Capital City Cuisine LLC...................... G 919 432-2126
Raleigh (G-9966)

▲ Carolina Business Furn Inc............... A 336 431-9400
High Point (G-6556)

Contemporary Design Co LLC............... F 704 375-6030
Gastonia (G-5030)

◆ Contemporary Furnishings Corp........ D 704 633-8000
Salisbury (G-11037)

Distinction Hospitality Inc................... F 336 875-3043
High Point (G-6594)

Distinctive Soul Creations LLC............. G 704 299-3269
Charlotte (G-2054)

Drews Cabinets and Cases.................. G 919 796-3985
Selma (G-11286)

Drexel Heritage Home Furnsngs........... G 336 812-4430
High Point (G-6598)

Epsilon Holdings LLC.......................... G 336 763-6147
Greensboro (G-5524)

Government Sales LLC......................... G 252 726-6315
Morehead City (G-8833)

▲ Hightower Group LLC....................... F 816 286-1051
High Point (G-6656)

Holders Restaurant Furniture.............. G 828 754-8383
Lenoir (G-7615)

Iv-S Metal Stamping Inc...................... E 336 861-2100
Archdale (G-229)

Kci LLC.. E 843 675-2626
Harrisburg (G-6111)

Kewaunee Scientific Corp.................... A 704 873-7202
Statesville (G-11724)

Kuntrys Soul-Food & Bbq LLC.............. G 910 797-0766
Fayetteville (G-4628)

◆ Lee Industries LLC.......................... B 828 464-8318
Conover (G-3537)

Magnificent Concessions LLC.............. E 919 413-1558
Wendell (G-12538)

Melt Your Heart LLC........................... G 828 989-6749
Leicester (G-7527)

Neil Allen Industries Inc...................... G 336 887-6500
High Point (G-6717)

Penco Products Inc............................ C 252 798-4000
Hamilton (G-6049)

◆ Penco Products Inc......................... E 252 917-5287
Greenville (G-6012)

▲ Pinnacle Furnishings Inc.................. E 910 944-0908
Aberdeen (G-19)

Rapp Productions Inc......................... F 919 913-0270
Carrboro (G-1271)

Rasin Haitian Restaurant LLC.............. G 704 780-5129
Charlotte (G-2691)

Restaurant Furniture Inc..................... F 828 459-9992
Claremont (G-3120)

Solace Healthcare Furn LLC................ F 336 884-0046
High Point (G-6783)

Southern Traditions Two Inc............... G 919 742-4692
Siler City (G-11425)

Tameka Burros.................................. G 330 338-8941
Concord (G-3451)

Tice Kitchens & Interiors LLC................ F 919 366-4117
Raleigh *(G-10549)*

Tomlinson of Orlando Inc............... G 336 475-8000
Thomasville *(G-12080)*

Touch Up Solutions Inc.................... E 828 428-9094
Maiden *(G-8019)*

Walnut Cove Furniture Inc............... G 336 591-8008
Walnut Cove *(G-12331)*

Wangs and Thangs LLC................ G 980 925-7010
Gastonia *(G-5164)*

Whatz Cookin LLC................ G 336 353-0227
Mount Airy *(G-9193)*

Woodsmiths Company................ G 406 626-3102
Lenoir *(G-7646)*

Zingerle Group Usa Inc................ E 704 312-1600
Charlotte *(G-3048)*

26 PAPER AND ALLIED PRODUCTS

2611 Pulp mills

Arauco - NA................ G 910 569-7020
Biscoe *(G-846)*

▲ Bft Lumberton Ops Corp................ E 910 737-3200
Lumberton *(G-7946)*

Broad River Forest Products................ G 828 287-8003
Rutherfordton *(G-10979)*

Buckeye Technologies Inc................ C 704 822-6400
Mount Holly *(G-9220)*

◆ Burrows Paper Corporation................C 800 272-7122
Charlotte *(G-1819)*

Collins Banks Investments Inc................ G 252 439-1200
Greenville *(G-5956)*

◆ Glatfelter Mt Holly LLC................D 704 812-2299
Mount Holly *(G-9233)*

Glycotech Inc................ G 910 371-2234
Leland *(G-7546)*

Ingram Woodyards Inc................ F 910 556-1250
Sanford *(G-11195)*

International Paper Company................ C 704 334-5222
Charlotte *(G-2348)*

Martin Materials Inc................ G 336 697-1800
Greensboro *(G-5680)*

North Carolina Converting LLC................ G 704 871-2912
Statesville *(G-11739)*

Old School Crushing Co Inc................ G 919 661-0011
Garner *(G-4950)*

Profile Products LLC................ D 828 327-4165
Conover *(G-3552)*

Todco Inc................ F 336 248-2001
Lexington *(G-7753)*

Westrock Mwv LLC................ G 919 334-3200
Raleigh *(G-10606)*

Westrock Paper and Packg LLC................ B 252 533-6000
Roanoke Rapids *(G-10745)*

Weyerhaeuser Company................ E 252 633-7100
Vanceboro *(G-12223)*

2621 Paper mills

Abzorbit Inc................ F 828 464-9944
Newton *(G-9447)*

Andrea L Grizzle................ G 252 202-3278
Moyock *(G-9275)*

Arauco - NA................ G 910 569-7020
Biscoe *(G-846)*

Atlantic Corp Wilmington Inc................ E 910 259-3600
Burgaw *(G-1019)*

Atlantic Corp Wilmington Inc................ D 704 588-1400
Charlotte *(G-1710)*

◆ Atlantic Corp Wilmington Inc................D 800 722-5841
Wilmington *(G-12712)*

Attindas Hygiene Partners Inc................ C 252 752-1100
Greenville *(G-5942)*

Attindas Hygiene Partners Inc................ F 919 237-4000
Raleigh *(G-9922)*

Blue Ridge Paper Products LLC................ C 828 235-3023
Canton *(G-1245)*

Blue Ridge Paper Products LLC................ C 828 452-0834
Waynesville *(G-12451)*

◆ Blue Ridge Paper Products LLC................D 828 454-0676
Canton *(G-1244)*

Buckeye Technologies Inc................ C 704 822-6400
Mount Holly *(G-9220)*

◆ Burrows Paper Corporation................C 800 272-7122
Charlotte *(G-1819)*

Carolina Paper Guys LLC................ G 704 980-3112
Charlotte *(G-1852)*

Cascades Moulded Pulp Inc................ E 910 997-2775
Rockingham *(G-10771)*

◆ Cascades Tissue Group - NC Inc................C 910 895-4033
Rockingham *(G-10772)*

Cascades Tssue Group - Ore Inc................ D 503 397-2900
Wagram *(G-12254)*

◆ Cdv LLC................F 919 674-3460
Morrisville *(G-8953)*

CT Commercial Paper LLC................ E 704 485-3212
Oakboro *(G-9577)*

Domtar Paper Company LLC................ D 252 752-1100
Greenville *(G-5966)*

Domtar Paper Company LLC................ B 252 793-8111
Plymouth *(G-9802)*

Ds Smith Packaging and Paper................ G 336 668-0871
Greensboro *(G-5505)*

▲ Encertec Inc................ G 336 288-7226
Greensboro *(G-5519)*

Enriched Abundance Entp LLC................ F 704 369-6363
Charlotte *(G-2117)*

Evergreen Packaging LLC................ A 828 454-0676
Canton *(G-1252)*

Evergreen Packaging LLC................ B 919 828-9134
Raleigh *(G-10095)*

Filtrona Filters Inc................ D 336 362-1333
Greensboro *(G-5533)*

Firm Ascend LLC................ G 704 464-3024
Charlotte *(G-2154)*

Geami Ltd................ E 919 654-7700
Raleigh *(G-10125)*

Georgia-Pacific LLC................ D 919 736-2722
Dudley *(G-3837)*

Georgia-Pacific LLC................ G 252 438-2238
Middleburg *(G-8271)*

Glatfelter Corporation................ G 828 877-2110
Pisgah Forest *(G-9769)*

Gold Bond Building Pdts LLC................ G 910 799-3954
Wilmington *(G-12792)*

Gold Bond Building Pdts LLC................ G 704 365-7300
Charlotte *(G-2223)*

▲ H & V Processing Inc................ G 336 224-2985
Lexington *(G-7694)*

Hollingsworth & Vose Company................ G 704 708-5913
Matthews *(G-8117)*

International Paper Company................ G 910 259-1723
Burgaw *(G-1024)*

International Paper Company................ G 704 393-8210
Charlotte *(G-2345)*

International Paper Company................ G 704 588-8522
Charlotte *(G-2346)*

International Paper Company................ G 704 398-8354
Charlotte *(G-2347)*

International Paper Company................ G 704 334-5222
Charlotte *(G-2348)*

International Paper Company................ G 910 738-8930
Lumberton *(G-7959)*

International Paper Company................ D 828 464-3841
Newton *(G-9478)*

International Paper Company................ G 919 831-4764
Raleigh *(G-10207)*

International Paper Company................ G 910 655-2211
Riegelwood *(G-10725)*

International Paper Company................ C 910 362-4900
Riegelwood *(G-10726)*

International Paper Company................ D 252 633-7509
Vanceboro *(G-12218)*

▲ Jackson Paper Manufacturing Co................ E 828 586-5534
Sylva *(G-11894)*

Kimberly-Clark Corporation................ C 828 698-5230
Hendersonville *(G-6218)*

◆ Laurel Hill Paper Co................G 910 997-4526
Cordova *(G-3581)*

Leapfrog Document Services Inc................ F 704 372-1078
Charlotte *(G-2412)*

Magnera Corporation................ A 866 744-7380
Charlotte *(G-2448)*

Morrisette Paper Company Inc................ G 336 342-5570
Reidsville *(G-10694)*

Nakos Paper Products Inc................ G 704 238-0717
Charlotte *(G-2541)*

Paper Perfector LLC................ G 910 695-1092
Pinehurst *(G-9698)*

▼ Poly Packaging Systems Inc................ D 336 889-8334
High Point *(G-6739)*

Pregis LLC................ E 828 396-2373
Granite Falls *(G-5319)*

Ranpak Corp................ G 919 790-8225
Raleigh *(G-10432)*

Reynolds Consumer Products Inc................ A 704 371-5550
Huntersville *(G-7042)*

Simply Btiful Events Decor LLC................ G 252 375-3839
Greenville *(G-6024)*

Skybien Press LLC................ G 919 544-1777
Durham *(G-4238)*

Snyder Paper Corporation................ G 800 222-8562
Asheville *(G-604)*

Sofidel Shelby LLC................ B 704 476-3802
Shelby *(G-11379)*

STS Packaging Charlotte LLC................ D 980 259-2290
Charlotte *(G-2874)*

Synthomer Inc................ D 704 225-1872
Monroe *(G-8567)*

Teddy Soft Paper Products Inc................ G 336 784-5887
Winston Salem *(G-13360)*

▲ Transcontinental AC US LLC................ F 704 847-9171
Matthews *(G-8153)*

Triangle Converting Corp................ E 919 596-6656
Durham *(G-4278)*

▲ Twisted Paper Products Inc................ E 336 393-0273
Greensboro *(G-5884)*

Westrock Kraft Paper LLC................ G 252 533-6000
Roanoke Rapids *(G-10744)*

Westrock Paper and Packg LLC................ B 252 533-6000
Roanoke Rapids *(G-10745)*

Westrock Shared Services LLC................ A 336 642-4165
Rural Hall *(G-10968)*

Weyerhaeuser Company................ E 252 633-7100
Vanceboro *(G-12223)*

◆ WR Rayson Co Inc................E 910 259-8100
Burgaw *(G-1041)*

2631 Paperboard mills

Berlin Packaging LLC................ G 704 612-4500
Charlotte *(G-1772)*

Box Company of America LLC................ E 910 582-0100
Hamlet *(G-6051)*

Caraustar Brlngton Rgid Box In................ G 336 226-1616
Burlington *(G-1059)*

Caraustar Industries Inc.............................. F 704 333-5488
Charlotte *(G-1838)*

Caraustar Industries Inc.............................. F 704 554-5796
Charlotte *(G-1839)*

Caraustar Industries Inc.............................. F 336 498-2631
Randleman *(G-10637)*

Dbt Coatings LLC....................................... G 336 834-9700
Greensboro *(G-5489)*

Deckle Paperboard Sales Inc.................... G 910 686-9145
Wilmington *(G-12763)*

Domtar Paper Company LLC..................... B 252 793-8111
Plymouth *(G-9802)*

◆ Edwards Wood Products Inc..................C 704 624-3624
Marshville *(G-8088)*

Graphic Packaging Intl LLC...................... C 704 588-1750
Pineville *(G-9730)*

Htm Concepts Inc..................................... F 252 794-2122
Windsor *(G-13054)*

International Paper Company..................... C 910 362-4900
Riegelwood *(G-10726)*

Kme Consolidated Inc............................... E 704 847-9888
Matthews *(G-8124)*

Morrisette Paper Company Inc.............. G 336 342-5570
Reidsville *(G-10694)*

▲ Napco Inc... C 336 372-5214
Sparta *(G-11540)*

Packaging Services.................................G 919 630-4145
Raleigh *(G-10352)*

Pactiv LLC... C 252 527-6300
Kinston *(G-7425)*

Parkwood Corporation.............................G 910 815-4300
Oak Island *(G-9567)*

Phoenix Packaging Inc............................. E 336 724-1978
Winston Salem *(G-13289)*

Pratt (jet Corr) Inc.................................... A 704 878-6615
Statesville *(G-11751)*

Precision Walls Inc................................... D 336 852-7710
Greensboro *(G-5759)*

Printing & Packaging Inc.......................... E 704 482-3866
Shelby *(G-11371)*

Sonoco Products Company...................... G 828 648-1987
Canton *(G-1256)*

Sonoco Products Company...................... G 910 455-6903
Jacksonville *(G-7148)*

▲ Southcorr LLC.. D 336 498-1700
Asheboro *(G-396)*

Southeastern Corrugated LLC.................. G 980 224-9551
Charlotte *(G-2831)*

Supplyone Rockwell Inc........................... C 704 279-5650
Rockwell *(G-10803)*

▲ Transcontinental AC US LLC.............. F 704 847-9171
Matthews *(G-8153)*

Westrock Company.................................. G 770 448-2193
Winston Salem *(G-13390)*

Westrock Converting LLC......................... F 336 661-6736
Winston Salem *(G-13391)*

Westrock Mwv LLC................................... G 919 334-3200
Raleigh *(G-10606)*

Westrock Paper and Packg LLC............... B 252 533-6000
Roanoke Rapids *(G-10745)*

Westrock Rkt LLC..................................... D 704 662-8494
Mooresville *(G-8798)*

Westrock Shared Services LLC.............. A 336 642-4165
Rural Hall *(G-10968)*

Weyerhaeuser New Bern.......................... E 252 633-7100
Vanceboro *(G-12224)*

Wrkco Inc... E 828 692-6254
East Flat Rock *(G-4336)*

Wrkco Inc... E 919 304-0300
Mebane *(G-8266)*

Wrkco Inc... E 336 759-7501
Winston Salem *(G-13405)*

Wrkco Inc... C 770 448-2193
Winston Salem *(G-13406)*

Wrkco Inc... E 336 765-7004
Winston Salem *(G-13407)*

2652 Setup paperboard boxes

A Klein & Co Inc.. C 828 459-9261
Claremont *(G-3086)*

Caraustar Cstm Packg Group Inc............ C 336 498-2631
Randleman *(G-10636)*

Caraustar Industries Inc.......................... F 336 498-2631
Randleman *(G-10637)*

▲ Eastcoast Packaging Inc....................... E 919 562-6060
Middlesex *(G-8274)*

Transylvnia Vcational Svcs Inc................. D 828 884-1548
Fletcher *(G-4773)*

Transylvnia Vcational Svcs Inc................. C 828 884-3195
Brevard *(G-983)*

Westrock Rkt LLC..................................... D 828 459-8006
Claremont *(G-3125)*

Westrock Rkt LLC..................................... D 704 662-8494
Mooresville *(G-8798)*

2653 Corrugated and solid fiber boxes

Axis Corrugated Container LLC.............. F 919 575-0500
Butner *(G-1198)*

C L Rabb Inc... E 704 865-0295
Gastonia *(G-5010)*

Caraustar Brlngton Rgid Box In............... G 336 226-1616
Burlington *(G-1059)*

◆ Carolina Container Company.............D 336 883-7146
High Point *(G-6558)*

Carolina Container LLC............................. E 828 322-3380
Hickory *(G-6284)*

Carolina Container LLC............................. E 910 277-0400
Laurinburg *(G-7494)*

Carolina Packaging & Sup Inc................. D 919 201-5592
Raleigh *(G-9978)*

Corney Transportation Inc........................ E 800 354-9111
Saint Pauls *(G-11004)*

Custom Corrugated Cntrs Inc.................. E 704 588-0371
Charlotte *(G-2008)*

Custom Packaging Inc............................. C 828 684-5060
Arden *(G-264)*

Ds Smith PLC... E 919 557-3148
Holly Springs *(G-6898)*

Ferguson & Company LLC........................ G 704 332-4396
Charlotte *(G-2146)*

Ferguson Box... E 704 597-0310
Charlotte *(G-2147)*

Ferguson Supply and Box Mfg Co........... D 704 597-0310
Charlotte *(G-2148)*

Freeman Container Company Inc............. G 704 922-7972
Dallas *(G-3672)*

Gbc Distribution LLC................................ G 704 341-8473
Charlotte *(G-2193)*

Georgia Pratt Box Inc............................... C 919 872-3007
Raleigh *(G-10129)*

Georgia-Pacific LLC.................................. D 336 629-2151
Asheboro *(G-361)*

Highland Containers Inc........................... C 336 887-5400
Jamestown *(G-7166)*

▲ Highland Containers Inc....................... C 336 887-5400
Jamestown *(G-7165)*

Hood Container Corporation..................... E 336 887-5400
Jamestown *(G-7167)*

Industrial Container Corp......................... F 336 886-7031
High Point *(G-6670)*

Industrial Container Inc............................ G 336 882-1310
High Point *(G-6671)*

▲ Inter-Continental Corporation............ D 828 464-8250
Newton *(G-9477)*

◆ Intermarket Technology Inc................E 252 623-2199
Washington *(G-12395)*

International Paper Company.................. G 704 588-8522
Charlotte *(G-2349)*

International Paper Company.................. D 910 738-6214
Lumberton *(G-7958)*

International Paper Company.................. G 252 456-3111
Manson *(G-8022)*

International Paper Company.................. G 252 633-7407
New Bern *(G-9372)*

Lls Investments Inc.................................. F 919 662-7283
Raleigh *(G-10258)*

Lone Star Container Sales Corp............... D 704 588-1737
Charlotte *(G-2433)*

Michigan Packaging Company.................. E 704 455-4206
Concord *(G-3402)*

Package Craft LLC.................................... E 252 825-0111
Bethel *(G-840)*

Package Crafters Incorporated................ D 336 431-9700
High Point *(G-6723)*

Packaging Corporation America............... G 252 753-8450
Farmville *(G-4537)*

Packaging Corporation America............... G 336 434-0600
Goldsboro *(G-5234)*

Packaging Corporation America............... G 704 664-5010
Mooresville *(G-8741)*

Packaging Corporation America............... E 828 584-1511
Morganton *(G-8887)*

Packaging Corporation America............... E 828 286-9156
Rutherfordton *(G-10988)*

Packaging Corporation America............... D 704 633-3611
Salisbury *(G-11100)*

Packaging Corporation America............... E 336 434-0600
Trinity *(G-12121)*

Paperworks Industries Inc........................ C 910 439-6137
Mount Gilead *(G-9209)*

Paperworks Industries Inc........................ C 336 447-7278
Whitsett *(G-12616)*

Phoenix Packaging Inc............................. E 336 724-1978
Winston Salem *(G-13289)*

Piedmont Corrugated Specialty............... D 828 874-1153
Valdese *(G-12198)*

Piedmont Packaging Inc........................... F 336 886-5043
High Point *(G-6732)*

Piranha Industries Inc.............................. G 704 248-7843
Charlotte *(G-2639)*

Pratt (jet Corr) Inc.................................... A 704 878-6615
Statesville *(G-11751)*

Pratt Industries....................................... G 704 864-4022
Gastonia *(G-5124)*

Pratt Industries Inc.................................. D 919 334-7400
Raleigh *(G-10387)*

Pratt Industries Inc.................................. B 704 878-6615
Statesville *(G-11752)*

RLM/Universal Packaging Inc................... F 336 644-6161
Greensboro *(G-5789)*

Rocktenn In-Store Solutions Inc.............. B 828 245-9871
Forest City *(G-4796)*

Schutz Container Systems Inc................. D 336 249-6816
Lexington *(G-7738)*

Sonoco Products Company...................... E 704 875-2685
Charlotte *(G-2827)*

Stronghaven Incorporated....................... D 770 739-6080
Matthews *(G-8151)*

Sumter Packaging Corporation................ G 704 873-0583
Statesville *(G-11783)*

Sun & Surf Containers Inc....................... G 910 754-9600
Shallotte *(G-11306)*

Supplyone Rockwell Inc........................... C 704 279-5650
Rockwell *(G-10803)*

Sustainable Corrugated LLC.................... D 828 608-0990
Morganton *(G-8902)*

Thomco Inc.................................. G..... 336 292-3300
Greensboro *(G-5863)*

Westrock - Southern Cont LLC.............. E..... 704 662-8496
Mooresville *(G-8797)*

Westrock Company....................... F..... 470 484-1183
Claremont *(G-3124)*

Westrock Company....................... F..... 828 248-4815
Forest City *(G-4801)*

Westrock Converting LLC............... B..... 828 245-9871
Forest City *(G-4802)*

Westrock Converting LLC............... F..... 336 661-1700
Winston Salem *(G-13392)*

Westrock Paper and Packg LLC........... B..... 919 463-3100
Morrisville *(G-9090)*

Westrock Rkt LLC........................ E..... 828 655-1303
Marion *(G-8072)*

Westrock Rkt LLC....................... D..... 704 662-8494
Mooresville *(G-8798)*

Westrock Rkt LLC....................... D..... 336 661-1700
Winston Salem *(G-13393)*

Westrock Rkt LLC....................... C..... 336 661-7180
Winston Salem *(G-13394)*

Weyerhaeuser Co......................... G..... 828 464-3841
Newton *(G-9512)*

Weyerhaeuser Company.................... G..... 253 924-2345
Charlotte *(G-3015)*

Wilmington Box Company.................. E..... 910 259-0402
Burgaw *(G-1039)*

Wrkco Inc............................... G..... 336 956-6000
Lexington *(G-7758)*

Wrkco Inc............................... E..... 828 287-9430
Rutherfordton *(G-11003)*

2655 Fiber cans, drums, and similar products

Atlantic Custom Container Inc........... G..... 336 437-9302
Graham *(G-5260)*

▲ Axjo America Inc...................... D..... 828 322-6046
Conover *(G-3493)*

C L Rabb Inc............................ E..... 704 865-0295
Gastonia *(G-5010)*

Caraustar Indus Cnsmr Pdts Gro......... G..... 336 564-2163
Kernersville *(G-7249)*

Caraustar Indus Cnsmr Pdts Gro......... E..... 336 996-4165
Kernersville *(G-7250)*

Caraustar Industries Inc............... E..... 336 992-1053
Kernersville *(G-7251)*

Caraustar Industries Inc............... F..... 336 498-2631
Randleman *(G-10637)*

Caraustar Industries Inc............... E..... 828 246-7234
Waynesville *(G-12452)*

▼ Carolina Paper Tubes Inc............ E..... 828 692-9686
Zirconia *(G-13529)*

◆ Conitex Sonoco Usa Inc.............. C..... 704 864-5406
Gastonia *(G-5028)*

Greif Inc............................... D..... 704 588-3895
Charlotte *(G-2241)*

Mauser Usa LLC......................... C..... 704 625-0737
Charlotte *(G-2472)*

Mm Clayton LLC.......................... B..... 919 553-4113
Clayton *(G-3160)*

Sonoco Products Company................. F..... 336 449-7731
Elon College *(G-4475)*

Sonoco Products Company................. F..... 828 322-8844
Hickory *(G-6454)*

▲ Summer Industries LLC................ C..... 336 731-9217
Welcome *(G-12515)*

Trident Fibers Inc.................... G..... 336 605-9002
Greensboro *(G-5880)*

Vandor Corporation...................... E..... 980 392-8107
Statesville *(G-11797)*

2656 Sanitary food containers

Candies Italian ICEE LLC................ G..... 980 475-7429
Charlotte *(G-1835)*

Caraustar Industries Inc.............. F..... 336 498-2631
Randleman *(G-10637)*

CKS Packaging Inc..................... E..... 704 663-6510
Mooresville *(G-8639)*

Thomco Inc............................ G..... 336 292-3300
Greensboro *(G-5863)*

Waddington Group Inc.................. E..... 800 845-6051
Charlotte *(G-2997)*

Yukon Packaging LLC................... G..... 704 214-0579
Mooresville *(G-8803)*

2657 Folding paperboard boxes

A Klein & Co Inc...................... C..... 828 459-9261
Claremont *(G-3086)*

Caraustar Brlngton Rgid Box In......... G..... 336 226-1616
Burlington *(G-1059)*

Caraustar Cstm Packg Group Inc......... C..... 336 498-2631
Randleman *(G-10636)*

Container Systems Incorporated......... D..... 919 496-6133
Franklinton *(G-4847)*

Graphic Packaging Intl LLC............. C..... 704 588-1750
Pineville *(G-9730)*

Graphic Packaging Intl LLC............. D..... 336 744-1222
Winston Salem *(G-13183)*

Kme Consolidated Inc.................. E..... 704 847-9888
Matthews *(G-8124)*

Max Solutions Inc..................... E..... 215 458-7050
Concord *(G-3400)*

Pactiv LLC.............................. G..... 910 944-1800
Aberdeen *(G-18)*

Pactiv LLC.............................. C..... 252 527-6300
Kinston *(G-7425)*

Snyder Packaging Inc.................. D..... 704 786-3111
Concord *(G-3441)*

Specialized Packaging Radisson LLC..... D..... 336 574-1513
Greensboro *(G-5829)*

Thomco Inc............................ G..... 336 292-3300
Greensboro *(G-5863)*

Westrock Rkt LLC....................... D..... 828 459-8006
Claremont *(G-3125)*

Westrock Rkt LLC....................... C..... 828 464-5560
Conover *(G-3574)*

Westrock Rkt LLC....................... B..... 770 448-2193
Marion *(G-8073)*

2671 Paper; coated and laminated packaging

Abx Innvtive Pckg Slutions LLC......... D..... 980 443-1100
Charlotte *(G-1613)*

◆ Atlantic Corporation................. E..... 910 343-0624
Wilmington *(G-12713)*

◆ Automated Solutions LLC............ F..... 828 396-9900
Granite Falls *(G-5296)*

▲ Bagcraftpapercon III LLC........... D..... 800 845-6051
Charlotte *(G-1739)*

▲ Box Board Products Inc............... C..... 336 668-3347
Greensboro *(G-5397)*

Box Company of America LLC........... E..... 910 582-0100
Hamlet *(G-6051)*

◆ Burrows Paper Corporation............ C..... 800 272-7122
Charlotte *(G-1819)*

Challnge Prtg of Crlnas Inc Th......... G..... 919 777-2820
Sanford *(G-11163)*

Datamark Graphics Inc................ E..... 336 629-0267
Asheboro *(G-345)*

Ds Smith PLC............................ E..... 919 557-3148
Holly Springs *(G-6898)*

◆ Dubose Strapping Inc............... D..... 910 590-1020
Clinton *(G-3232)*

▲ Eastcoast Packaging Inc.............. E..... 919 562-6060
Middlesex *(G-8274)*

◆ Goulston Technologies Inc.......... E..... 704 289-6464
Monroe *(G-8495)*

Graphic Packaging Intl LLC............. C..... 704 588-1750
Pineville *(G-9730)*

▲ Interntnal Tray Pads Packg Inc....... G..... 910 944-1800
Aberdeen *(G-8)*

Jbb Packaging LLC....................... G..... 201 470-8501
Weldon *(G-12521)*

Jd2 Company LLC......................... G..... 800 811-6441
Denver *(G-3791)*

Label Line Ltd.......................... D..... 336 857-3115
Asheboro *(G-371)*

Multi Packaging Solutions............... A..... 336 855-7142
Greensboro *(G-5699)*

Neopac Us Inc........................... G..... 908 342-0990
Wilson *(G-13009)*

Npx One LLC............................. C..... 910 997-2217
Rockingham *(G-10784)*

Pactiv LLC.............................. C..... 252 527-6300
Kinston *(G-7425)*

Paragon Films Inc..................... F..... 828 632-5552
Taylorsville *(G-11968)*

▼ Poly Packaging Systems Inc........... D..... 336 889-8334
High Point *(G-6739)*

Pregis Innovative Packg LLC............ E..... 847 597-2200
Granite Falls *(G-5318)*

Quality Packaging Corp................. G..... 336 881-5300
High Point *(G-6750)*

R R Donnelley & Sons Company........... D..... 252 243-0337
Wilson *(G-13018)*

▲ Rgees LLC............................ G..... 828 708-7178
Arden *(G-304)*

Sealed Air Corporation (us)............ A..... 201 791-7600
Charlotte *(G-2777)*

Shurtech Brands LLC................... G..... 704 799-0779
Mooresville *(G-8770)*

▲ St Johns Packaging Usa LLC.......... C..... 336 292-9911
Greensboro *(G-5833)*

Storopack Inc......................... G..... 800 827-7225
Winston Salem *(G-13344)*

Transcontinental AC US LLC............. F..... 704 847-9171
Matthews *(G-8154)*

▼ Valdese Packaging & Label Inc........ E..... 828 879-9772
Valdese *(G-12201)*

Westrock Company........................ F..... 919 861-8760
Raleigh *(G-10605)*

Westrock Mwv LLC...................... G..... 919 334-3200
Raleigh *(G-10606)*

2672 Paper; coated and laminated, nec

Achem Industry America Inc........... G..... 704 283-6144
Monroe *(G-8415)*

◆ Acucote Inc......................... C..... 336 578-1800
Graham *(G-5259)*

Avery Dennison Corporation............. D..... 336 621-2570
Greensboro *(G-5378)*

Avery Dennison Corporation............. G..... 336 553-2436
Greensboro *(G-5379)*

Avery Dennison Corporation............. G..... 336 856-8235
Greensboro *(G-5380)*

Avery Dennison Corporation............. G..... 864 938-1400
Greensboro *(G-5381)*

Avery Dennison Corporation............. F..... 336 665-6481
Greensboro *(G-5382)*

Avery Dennison Rfid Company............ G..... 626 304-2000
Greensboro *(G-5383)*

Bay Tech Label Inc................... G..... 828 296-8900
Asheville *(G-452)*

Blue Ridge Paper Products LLC.......... C..... 828 452-0834
Waynesville *(G-12451)*

Carolina Container LLC................. E..... 336 883-7146
Thomasville *(G-12002)*

◆ Carolina Tape & Supply Corp.............E 828 322-3991
Hickory *(G-6289)*

◆ Cdv LLC...F 919 674-3460
Morrisville *(G-8953)*

Datamark Graphics Inc..................... E 336 629-0267
Asheboro *(G-345)*

Draft DOT International LLC................ G 336 775-0525
Lexington *(G-7680)*

▲ Gaston Systems Inc........................ F 704 263-6000
Stanley *(G-11617)*

Granite Tape Co................................ G 828 396-5614
Granite Falls *(G-5305)*

Intertape Polymer Corp...................... D 980 907-4871
Midland *(G-8288)*

J C Enterprises................................ G 336 986-1688
Winston Salem *(G-13212)*

Label Line Ltd................................... D 336 857-3115
Asheboro *(G-371)*

Lakebrook Corporation....................... G 207 947-4051
Oak Island *(G-9566)*

Liflex LLC.. C 336 777-5000
Winston Salem *(G-13237)*

Loparex LLC..................................... C 336 635-0192
Eden *(G-4352)*

◆ Loparex LLC................................... D 919 678-7700
Cary *(G-1392)*

Marsh-Armfield Incorporated................ F 336 882-4175
High Point *(G-6704)*

▲ Maxim Label Packg High Pt Inc........ F 336 861-1666
High Point *(G-6708)*

Neptco Incorporated........................... C 828 313-0149
Granite Falls *(G-5314)*

Neptco Incorporated........................... C 828 728-5951
Lenoir *(G-7629)*

◆ Oracle Flexible Packaging Inc............ B 336 777-5000
Winston Salem *(G-13271)*

▼ Pocono Coated Products LLC............ G 704 445-7891
Cherryville *(G-3069)*

R T Barbee Company Inc.................... F 704 375-4421
Charlotte *(G-2687)*

▲ Reliance Packaging LLC................... E 910 944-2561
Aberdeen *(G-21)*

Shurtape Technologies LLC................. G 704 553-9441
Charlotte *(G-2800)*

Shurtape Technologies LLC................. G 828 304-8302
Hickory *(G-6445)*

◆ Stm Industries Inc........................... E 828 322-2700
Hickory *(G-6459)*

▲ T - Square Enterprises Inc............... G 704 846-8233
Charlotte *(G-2894)*

◆ Tailored Chemical Products Inc.......... D 828 322-6512
Hickory *(G-6462)*

TEC Graphics Inc.............................. F 919 567-2077
Fuquay Varina *(G-4901)*

◆ Technical Coating Intl Inc................. E 910 371-0860
Leland *(G-7559)*

Transcontinental AC US LLC................ F 704 847-9171
Matthews *(G-8154)*

Upm Raflatac Inc.............................. F 828 335-3289
Fletcher *(G-4775)*

Upm Raflatac Inc.............................. E 828 651-4800
Fletcher *(G-4776)*

◆ Upm Raflatac Inc............................ B 828 651-4800
Mills River *(G-8322)*

2673 Bags: plastic, laminated, and coated

Berry Global Films LLC..................... C 704 821-2316
Matthews *(G-8160)*

▲ Bioselect Inc................................. G 704 521-8585
Charlotte *(G-1784)*

Bulk Sak International Inc................... E 704 833-1361
Gastonia *(G-5006)*

▲ Classic Packaging Company.............. D 336 922-4224
Pfafftown *(G-9663)*

Cryovac Leasing Corporation............... G 980 430-7000
Charlotte *(G-2001)*

Dayton Bag & Burlap Co..................... G 704 873-7271
Statesville *(G-11685)*

◆ Hilex Poly Co LLC........................... D
Charlotte *(G-2280)*

Hood Packaging Corporation................ C 910 582-1842
Hamlet *(G-6057)*

Imaflex Usa Inc............................... E 336 885-8131
Thomasville *(G-12036)*

◆ Liqui-Box Corporation...................... D 804 325-1400
Charlotte *(G-2426)*

Maverick Enterprises Intl Inc............... G 704 291-9474
Monroe *(G-8527)*

▲ Novolex Heritage Bag LLC................ G 800 845-6051
Charlotte *(G-2582)*

▼ Poly Plastic Products NC Inc............ D 704 624-2555
Marshville *(G-8093)*

Printpack Inc.................................... C 828 693-1723
Hendersonville *(G-6237)*

Reynolds Consumer Products Inc.......... A 704 371-5550
Huntersville *(G-7042)*

◆ Rgees LLC.................................... G 828 708-7178
Arden *(G-304)*

◆ Rubbermaid Commercial Pdts LLC..... A 540 667-8700
Huntersville *(G-7045)*

Sealed Air Corporation....................... D 828 728-6610
Hudson *(G-6959)*

Sealed Air Corporation (us)................. A 201 791-7600
Charlotte *(G-2777)*

Sealed Air LLC................................. F 980 430-7000
Charlotte *(G-2779)*

Transcontinental Tvl LLC..................... F 336 476-3131
Thomasville *(G-12082)*

◆ Wastezero Inc................................ E 919 322-1208
Raleigh *(G-10599)*

2674 Bags: uncoated paper and multiwall

◆ Automated Solutions LLC.................. F 828 396-9900
Granite Falls *(G-5296)*

▲ Cardinal Bag & Envelope Co Inc....... E 704 225-9636
Monroe *(G-8450)*

Dayton Bag & Burlap Co..................... G 704 873-7271
Statesville *(G-11685)*

◆ Downtown Graphics Network Inc......... G 704 637-0855
Salisbury *(G-11044)*

Duro Hilex Poly LLC.......................... D 800 845-6051
Charlotte *(G-2069)*

Eagle Products Inc............................ G 336 886-5688
High Point *(G-6601)*

◆ Hilex Poly Co LLC........................... D
Charlotte *(G-2280)*

Hood Packaging Corporation................ C 910 582-1842
Hamlet *(G-6057)*

Pro Choice Contractors Corp............... G 919 696-7383
Raleigh *(G-10398)*

Sealed Air Corporation....................... D 828 728-6610
Hudson *(G-6959)*

Tsg2 Inc... G 704 347-4484
Charlotte *(G-2949)*

2675 Die-cut paper and board

Boingo Graphics Inc.......................... E 704 527-4963
Charlotte *(G-1797)*

Box Company of America LLC.............. A 910 582-0100
Hamlet *(G-6051)*

▲ Eastcoast Packaging Inc.................. E 919 562-6060
Middlesex *(G-8274)*

L C Industries Inc............................. C 919 596-8277
Fayetteville *(G-4629)*

◆ L C Industries Inc.......................... C 919 596-8277
Durham *(G-4100)*

Lakebrook Corporation....................... G 207 947-4051
Oak Island *(G-9566)*

Morrisette Paper Company Inc............. G 336 342-5570
Reidsville *(G-10694)*

◆ Mueller Die Cut Solutions Inc............ E 704 588-3900
Charlotte *(G-2526)*

Paper Specialties Inc........................ G 919 431-0028
Raleigh *(G-10357)*

Snyder Packaging Inc......................... D 704 786-3111
Concord *(G-3441)*

Subtle Impressions Inc....................... E
Gastonia *(G-5145)*

Triangle Converting Corp.................... E 919 596-6656
Durham *(G-4278)*

◆ Valdese Weavers LLC....................... B 828 874-2181
Valdese *(G-12206)*

2676 Sanitary paper products

▲ Associated Hygienic Pdts LLC........... D 770 497-9800
Greenville *(G-5940)*

Attends Healthcare Pdts Inc................ D 252 752-1100
Greenville *(G-5941)*

◆ Attends Healthcare Products Inc......... B 800 428-8363
Raleigh *(G-9921)*

Cardinal Tissue LLC.......................... D 815 503-2096
Spindale *(G-11546)*

◆ Cascades Tissue Group - NC Inc....... C 910 895-4033
Rockingham *(G-10772)*

Edtech Systems LLC.......................... G 919 341-0613
Raleigh *(G-10078)*

Hygiene Systems Inc.......................... E 910 462-2661
Laurel Hill *(G-7484)*

Kimberly-Clark Corporation.................. C 828 698-5230
Hendersonville *(G-6218)*

◆ L C Industries Inc.......................... C 919 596-8277
Durham *(G-4100)*

◆ Livedo Usa Inc.............................. D 252 237-1373
Wilson *(G-13005)*

Marcal Paper Mills LLC...................... B 828 322-1805
Hickory *(G-6391)*

◆ Merfin Systems LLC......................... D 800 874-6373
King *(G-7331)*

Ontex Operations Usa LLC.................. G 770 346-9250
Stokesdale *(G-11814)*

▲ Pacon Manufacturing Co LLC............ C 910 239-3001
Leland *(G-7556)*

Procter & Gamble Mfg Co................... D 336 954-0000
Greensboro *(G-5767)*

Sealed Air Corporation....................... D 828 728-6610
Hudson *(G-6959)*

Shower ME With Love LLC.................. F 704 302-1555
Charlotte *(G-2799)*

Top Tier Paper Products Inc............... G 828 994-2222
Conover *(G-3567)*

Valor Brands LLC.............................. F 678 602-9268
Stokesdale *(G-11817)*

2677 Envelopes

S Ruppe Inc.................................... G 828 287-4936
Rutherfordton *(G-10992)*

Westrock Mwv LLC............................ G 919 334-3200
Raleigh *(G-10606)*

2678 Stationery products

Devora Designs Inc........................... G 336 782-0964
Winston Salem *(G-13142)*

Kimberly Gordon Studios Inc............... E 980 287-6420
Charlotte *(G-2396)*

Texpack USA Inc.............................. G 704 864-5406
Gastonia *(G-5151)*

Westrock Mwv LLC.............................. G 919 334-3200
Raleigh *(G-10606)*

2679 Converted paper products, nec

◆ 3a Composites USA Inc..........................C 704 872-8974
Statesville *(G-11641)*

Abx Innvtive Pckg Slutions LLC............ D 980 443-1100
Charlotte *(G-1613)*

◆ Acucote Inc......................................C 336 578-1800
Graham *(G-5259)*

American Converting Co Ltd LLC........... E 704 479-5025
Lincolnton *(G-7812)*

Atlantic Caribbean LLC......................G 910 343-0624
Wilmington *(G-12711)*

Atlantic Corp Wilmington Inc............... E 910 259-3600
Burgaw *(G-1019)*

Atlantic Corp Wilmington Inc............... D 704 588-1400
Charlotte *(G-1710)*

◆ Atlantic Corp Wilmington Inc............D 800 722-5841
Wilmington *(G-12712)*

Bay Tech Label Inc............................G 828 296-8900
Asheville *(G-452)*

Box Company of America LLC............... E 910 582-0100
Hamlet *(G-6051)*

◆ Burrows Paper Corporation...............C 800 272-7122
Charlotte *(G-1819)*

Caraustar Industries Inc..................... F 336 498-2631
Randleman *(G-10637)*

◆ Carolina Container Company.............D 336 883-7146
High Point *(G-6558)*

Carolina Precision Fibers Inc................ E 336 527-4140
Ronda *(G-10894)*

◆ Cdv LLC...F 919 674-3460
Morrisville *(G-8953)*

Grand Encore Charlotte LLC................. E 513 482-7500
Charlotte *(G-2231)*

Graphic Finshg Solutions LLC............... G 336 255-7857
Greensboro *(G-5573)*

▲ Hibco Plastics Inc..........................E 336 463-2391
Yadkinville *(G-13443)*

Hill-Pak Inc.....................................G 336 431-3833
High Point *(G-6657)*

J R Cole Industries Inc....................... D 704 523-6622
Charlotte *(G-2362)*

Label & Printing Solutions Inc............... G 919 782-1242
Raleigh *(G-10243)*

Label Line Ltd...................................D 336 857-3115
Asheboro *(G-371)*

Label Printing Systems Inc.................. E 336 760-3271
Winston Salem *(G-13230)*

Lpm Inc..G 704 922-6137
Gastonia *(G-5078)*

Milpak Graphics Inc........................... E 336 347-8772
King *(G-7332)*

National Gyps Receivables LLC............ G 704 365-7300
Charlotte *(G-2546)*

Ng Corporate LLC.............................. E 704 365-7300
Charlotte *(G-2564)*

Ng Operations LLC............................ G 704 365-7300
Charlotte *(G-2565)*

Nonwovens of America Inc.................. G 828 236-1300
Swannanoa *(G-11874)*

NPS Holdings LLC.............................. E 828 757-7501
Lenoir *(G-7630)*

Pactiv LLC.......................................D 336 292-2796
Greensboro *(G-5730)*

◆ Paperfoam Packaging Usa LLC.........G 910 371-0480
Wilmington *(G-12870)*

Paperworks......................................G 704 548-9057
Charlotte *(G-2608)*

◆ Proform Finishing Products LLC........B 704 365-7300
Charlotte *(G-2674)*

Quality Packaging Corp....................... G 336 881-5300
High Point *(G-6750)*

Rapid Response Inc............................ G 704 588-8890
Charlotte *(G-2689)*

▲ Rgees LLC....................................G 828 708-7178
Arden *(G-304)*

◆ Stump Printing Co Inc.....................C 260 723-5171
Wrightsville Beach *(G-13433)*

Tab Index Inc................................... G 919 876-8988
Raleigh *(G-10529)*

◆ Technical Coating Intl Inc................E 910 371-0860
Leland *(G-7559)*

Tmgcr Inc....................................... E 704 872-4461
Statesville *(G-11791)*

Triangle Converting Corp.................... E 919 596-6656
Durham *(G-4278)*

US Print Inc..................................... G 919 878-0981
Raleigh *(G-10578)*

Veritiv Operating Company................. G 336 834-3488
Greensboro *(G-5898)*

▲ W R Rayson Export Ltd...................G 910 686-5802
Burgaw *(G-1036)*

▲ Welsh Cstm Sltting Rwnding LLC..... G 336 665-6481
Greensboro *(G-5915)*

▼ Winter Bell Company......................G 336 887-2651
High Point *(G-6836)*

▲ Wright of Thomasville Inc................ F 336 472-4200
Thomasville *(G-12091)*

27 PRINTING, PUBLISHING AND ALLIED INDUSTRIES

2711 Newspapers

A D Services.................................... G 336 667-8190
Wilkesboro *(G-12626)*

ACC Sports Journal........................... G 919 846-7502
Raleigh *(G-9871)*

Advantage Newspaper......................... E 910 323-0349
Fayetteville *(G-4545)*

Alameen A Haqq............................... G 336 965-8339
Greensboro *(G-5347)*

American City Bus Journals Inc............. D 336 271-6539
Greensboro *(G-5354)*

▲ American City Bus Journals Inc........ E 704 973-1000
Charlotte *(G-1664)*

Anson Express.................................. G 704 694-2480
Wadesboro *(G-12233)*

Apg/East LLC....................................C 252 329-9500
Greenville *(G-5937)*

Asheville Citizen-Times....................... F 828 252-5611
Asheville *(G-434)*

Asheville Global Report....................... G 828 236-3103
Asheville *(G-437)*

Asian (korean) Herald Inc.................... G 704 332-5656
Charlotte *(G-1705)*

Automail LLC.................................... G 704 677-0152
Mooresville *(G-8602)*

Benmot Publishing Company Inc........... G 919 658-9456
Mount Olive *(G-9247)*

Black Mountain News Inc..................... G 828 669-8727
Black Mountain *(G-861)*

Boone Newspapers Inc........................ G 252 332-2123
Ahoskie *(G-43)*

Bridgetower Media LLC....................... E 612 317-9420
Greensboro *(G-5402)*

Brunswick Beacon Inc......................... G 910 754-6890
Shallotte *(G-11300)*

Business Journals.............................. G 704 371-3248
Charlotte *(G-1820)*

Camp Lejeune Globe........................... F 910 939-0705
Jacksonville *(G-7119)*

Cape Fear Newspapers Inc................... G 910 285-2178
Wallace *(G-12319)*

Carolina Newspapers Inc..................... G 336 274-7829
Greensboro *(G-5431)*

Carolinian Pubg Group LLC.................. G 919 834-5558
Raleigh *(G-9980)*

Carter Publishing Company Inc............. F 336 993-2161
Kernersville *(G-7253)*

Carteret Publishing Company............... G 910 326-5066
Swansboro *(G-11883)*

Carteret Publishing Company............... D 252 726-7081
Morehead City *(G-8823)*

Catawba Vly Youth Soccer Assoc........... G 828 234-7082
Hickory *(G-6291)*

Catholic News and Herald.................... G 704 370-3333
Charlotte *(G-1867)*

Champion Media LLC...........................C 910 506-3021
Laurinburg *(G-7496)*

Champion Media LLC.......................... E 704 746-3955
Mooresville *(G-8637)*

Charlotte Observer.............................D 704 358-5000
Charlotte *(G-1896)*

Charlotte Observer Pubg Co................. E 704 987-3660
Charlotte *(G-1897)*

Charlotte Observer Pubg Co................. E 704 572-0747
Charlotte *(G-1898)*

Charlotte Observer Pubg Co................. E 704 358-6020
Matthews *(G-8105)*

Charlotte Observer Pubg Co................. A 704 358-5000
Charlotte *(G-1899)*

Charlotte Post Pubg Co Inc.................. F 704 376-0496
Charlotte *(G-1904)*

Charltte McKInburg Dream Ctr I........... G 704 421-4440
Charlotte *(G-1906)*

Chatham News Publishing Co............... G 919 663-4042
Siler City *(G-11405)*

Chronicle Mill Land LLC....................... G 704 527-3227
Gastonia *(G-5021)*

Chronicles....................................... G 252 617-1774
Jacksonville *(G-7121)*

Citizen Media Inc............................... G 704 363-6062
Huntersville *(G-6976)*

Coman Publishing Co Inc..................... F 919 688-0218
Durham *(G-3984)*

Community First Media Inc................... G 704 482-4142
Shelby *(G-11323)*

Community Newspapers Inc.................. G 828 743-5101
Cashiers *(G-1490)*

Community Newspapers Inc.................. G 828 369-3430
Franklin *(G-4822)*

Community Newspapers Inc.................. G 828 389-8431
Hayesville *(G-6140)*

Community Newspapers Inc.................. G 828 479-3383
Robbinsville *(G-10758)*

Community Newspapers Inc.................. G 828 765-7169
Spruce Pine *(G-11568)*

Cooke Communications NC LLC............. F 252 329-9500
Greenville *(G-5958)*

County Press Inc............................... G 919 894-2112
Benson *(G-787)*

Cox Nrth Crlina Pblcations Inc.............. G 252 482-4418
Edenton *(G-4364)*

Cox Nrth Crlina Pblcations Inc..............C 252 335-0841
Elizabeth City *(G-4385)*

Cox Nrth Crlina Pblcations Inc.............. G 910 296-0239
Kenansville *(G-7225)*

Cox Nrth Crlina Pblcations Inc..............D 252 792-1181
Williamston *(G-12669)*

Cox Nrth Crlina Pblcations Inc..............C 252 329-9643
Greenville *(G-5961)*

Daily Courier.................................... G 828 245-6431
Rutherfordton *(G-10982)*

Daily Living Solutions Inc	G	704 614-0977	Charlotte (G-2015)
Davie County Publishing Co	F	336 751-2120	Mocksville (G-8357)
Db North Carolina Holdings Inc	E	910 323-4848	Fayetteville (G-4585)
Denton Orator	G	336 859-3131	Denton (G-3746)
Dolan LLC	F	919 829-9333	Raleigh (G-10055)
Dth Publishing Inc	G	919 962-1163	Chapel Hill (G-1541)
Duke Student Publishing Co Inc	G	919 684-3811	Durham (G-4010)
Ellis Publishing Company Inc	G	252 444-1999	New Bern (G-9367)
▲ Epi Group Llc	B	843 577-7111	Durham (G-4029)
F B Publications Inc	F	910 484-6200	Fayetteville (G-4599)
▲ Fayetteville Publishing Co	E	910 323-4848	Fayetteville (G-4601)
Franklin County Newspapers Inc	G	919 496-6503	Louisburg (G-7915)
Fun Publications Inc	G	919 847-5263	Raleigh (G-10123)
Gannett Media Corp	G	828 649-1075	Marshall (G-8080)
Gannett Media Corp	F	919 467-1402	Morrisville (G-8981)
Gaston Gazette LLP	A	704 869-1700	Gastonia (G-5051)
Gastonia	G	704 377-3687	Gastonia (G-5052)
Gatehouse Media LLC	E	336 626-6103	Asheboro (G-360)
Granville Publishing Co Inc	G	919 528-2393	Creedmoor (G-3649)
Green Line Media Inc	E	828 251-1333	Asheville (G-512)
Greensboro News & Record LLC	A	336 373-7000	Greensboro (G-5577)
Greensboro Voice	F	336 255-1006	Greensboro (G-5579)
Grey Area News	G	919 637-6973	Zebulon (G-13510)
Halifax Media Group	F	704 869-1700	Gastonia (G-5057)
Halifax Media Holdings LLC	G	828 692-5763	Hendersonville (G-6211)
Hendersnvlle Affrdbl Hsing Cor	F	828 692-6175	Hendersonville (G-6215)
Henderson Newspapers Inc	F	252 436-2700	Henderson (G-6158)
Herald Huntersville	G	704 766-2100	Huntersville (G-6997)
Herald Printing Co Inc	G	252 537-2505	Roanoke Rapids (G-10738)
Hickory Publishing Co Inc	E	828 322-4510	Hickory (G-6352)
High Country Media LLC	G	828 733-2448	Newland (G-9430)
High Country News Inc	G	828 264-2262	Boone (G-922)
High Point Enterprise Inc	G	336 434-2716	High Point (G-6649)
High Point Enterprise Inc	F	336 883-2839	High Point (G-6650)
High Point Enterprise Inc	F	336 472-9500	Thomasville (G-12030)
High Point Enterprise Llc	C	336 888-3500	High Point (G-6651)

Highcorp Incorporated	E	910 642-4104	Whiteville (G-12584)
Horizon Publications Inc	F	828 464-0221	Newton (G-9473)
In Greensboro	G	336 621-0279	Greensboro (G-5615)
Indy Week	G	919 832-8774	Raleigh (G-10192)
Inform Inc	E	828 322-7766	Hickory (G-6368)
Jamestown News	G	336 841-4933	Jamestown (G-7170)
Jones Media	G	828 264-3612	Boone (G-928)
Journal Vacuum Science & Tech	G	919 361-2787	Cary (G-1381)
Kinston Free Press Company	E	252 527-3191	Kinston (G-7417)
La Noticia Inc	F	704 568-6966	Charlotte (G-2406)
Lantern of Hendersonville LLC	G	828 513-5033	Hendersonville (G-6220)
Latino Communications Inc	F	704 319-5044	Charlotte (G-2409)
Latino Communications Inc	F	919 645-1680	Raleigh (G-10249)
Latino Communications Inc	D	336 714-2823	Winston Salem (G-13231)
Ledger Publishing Company	G	919 693-2646	Oxford (G-9619)
Lincoln Herald LLC	G	704 735-3620	Lincolnton (G-7838)
Lumina News	G	910 256-6569	Wilmington (G-12841)
Magic Mile Media Inc	F	252 572-1330	Kinston (G-7421)
Mc Clatchy Interactive USA	G	919 861-1200	Raleigh (G-10284)
McDowell Lfac	F	828 289-5553	Marion (G-8055)
McLoud Media	G	828 837-9539	Murphy (G-9292)
Media Wilimington Co	G	910 791-0688	Wilmington (G-12851)
Mooresville NC	G	704 909-6459	Mooresville (G-8726)
Mountain Area Info Netwrk	F	828 255-0182	Asheville (G-552)
Mountain Times Inc	G	336 246-6397	West Jefferson (G-12567)
Mountaineer Inc	G	828 452-0661	Waynesville (G-12464)
Mullen Publications Inc	F	704 527-5111	Charlotte (G-2527)
Nash County Newspapers Inc	F	252 459-7101	Nashville (G-9322)
News & Record	G	336 627-1781	Reidsville (G-10696)
News & Record Commercial Prtg	F	336 373-7300	Greensboro (G-5708)
News 14 Carolina	G	704 973-5700	Charlotte (G-2559)
News and Observer Pubg Co	E	919 894-4170	Benson (G-795)
News and Observer Pubg Co	E	919 419-6500	Durham (G-4148)
News and Observer Pubg Co	E	919 829-8903	Garner (G-4949)
▲ News and Observer Pubg Co	A	919 829-4500	Raleigh (G-10331)
Next Magazine	G	910 609-0638	Fayetteville (G-4645)

Norman E Clark	G	336 573-9629	Stoneville (G-11824)
Observer News Enterprise Inc	G	828 464-0221	Newton (G-9483)
Paxton Media Group	G	704 289-1541	Monroe (G-8540)
Pilot LLC	G	864 430-6337	Southern Pines (G-11504)
Pilot LLC	D	910 692-7271	Southern Pines (G-11505)
PMG Acquisition Corp	D	828 758-7381	Lenoir (G-7634)
PMG-DH Company	C	919 419-6500	Durham (G-4185)
Post Publishing Company	D	704 633-8950	Salisbury (G-11103)
Pride Publishing & Typsg Inc	G	704 531-9988	Charlotte (G-2666)
Promiseland Media Inc	G	910 762-1337	Wilmington (G-12891)
Raleigh Downtowner	G	919 821-9000	Raleigh (G-10422)
Record Publishing Company	F	910 230-1948	Dunn (G-3866)
Rennasentient Inc	G	919 233-7710	Cary (G-1435)
Rhinoceros Times	G	336 763-4170	Greensboro (G-5787)
Richard D Stewart	G	919 284-2295	Kenly (G-7236)
Richmond Observer LLP	G	910 817-3169	Rockingham (G-10789)
Robert Laskowski	G	203 732-0846	New Bern (G-9391)
Rotary Club Statesville	F	704 872-6851	Statesville (G-11759)
Ryjak Enterprises LLC	G	910 638-0716	Southern Pines (G-11507)
Seaside Press Co Inc	G	910 458-8156	Carolina Beach (G-1264)
Sentinel Newspapers	F	828 389-8338	Hayesville (G-6144)
Seven Lakes News Corporation	G	910 685-0320	West End (G-12559)
Shelby Freedom Star Inc	D	704 484-7000	Shelby (G-11377)
Shopper	G	252 633-1153	New Bern (G-9396)
Skybien Press LLC	G	919 544-1777	Durham (G-4238)
Slam Publications LLC	F	252 480-2234	Nags Head (G-9303)
Smoky Mountain News Inc	F	828 452-4251	Waynesville (G-12474)
Snap Publications LLC	G	336 274-8531	Greensboro (G-5819)
Spectacular Publishing Inc	G	919 672-0289	Durham (G-4244)
Spring Hope Enterprise Inc	G	252 478-3651	Spring Hope (G-11559)
St Johns Museum of Art	G	910 763-0281	Wilmington (G-12929)
Star Fleet Communications Inc	G	828 252-6565	Asheville (G-611)
State Port Pilot	F	910 457-4568	Southport (G-11532)
Statesville High	G	704 873-3491	Statesville (G-11778)
Statesville LLC	G	704 872-3303	Statesville (G-11779)
Sun-Journal Incorporated	E	252 638-8101	New Bern (G-9398)

Sylva Herald and Ruralite.......................... G 828 586-2611
Sylva *(G-11900)*

Sylva Herald Pubg Co Incthe..................... F 828 586-2611
Sylva *(G-11901)*

Tallahassee Democrat................................. G 919 832-9430
Raleigh *(G-10532)*

Taylorsville Times...................................... G 828 632-2532
Taylorsville *(G-11983)*

Times Journal Inc....................................... G 828 682-4067
Burnsville *(G-1193)*

▲ Times News Publishing Company.... F 336 226-4414
Burlington *(G-1168)*

Times Printing Company............................ E 252 473-2105
Manteo *(G-8024)*

Times Printing Company Inc...................... G 252 441-2223
Kill Devil Hills *(G-7320)*

Topsail Voice LLC...................................... G 910 270-2944
Hampstead *(G-6078)*

Triangle Tribune... G 704 376-0496
Durham *(G-4282)*

Tribune Papers Inc.................................... G 828 606-5050
Asheville *(G-624)*

Tryon Newsmedia LLC............................... G 828 859-9151
Tryon *(G-12179)*

Tucker Production Incorporated............. G 828 322-1036
Hickory *(G-6475)*

Twin Cy Kwnis Fndtion Wnstn-SL......... G 336 784-1649
Winston Salem *(G-13378)*

Up & Coming Magazine............................ G 910 391-3859
Fayetteville *(G-4689)*

Virginn-Plot Mdia Cmpanies LLC........... G 252 441-3628
Nags Head *(G-9305)*

Wake Forest Gazette................................ G 919 556-3409
Wake Forest *(G-12313)*

War Horse News Inc................................. F 910 430-0868
Richlands *(G-10722)*

Washington News Publishing Co......... F 252 946-2144
Washington *(G-12421)*

▲ Wayne Printing Company Inc.......... F 919 778-2211
Goldsboro *(G-5252)*

West Stkes Wldcat Grdron CLB I........... G 336 985-6152
King *(G-7339)*

Whiteville AG... G 910 914-0007
Whiteville *(G-12595)*

Wick Communications Co....................... E 252 537-2505
Roanoke Rapids *(G-10747)*

Wilmington Journal Company................ G 910 762-5502
Wilmington *(G-12949)*

Wilson Daily Times Inc............................ E 252 243-5151
Wilson *(G-13048)*

Winstn-Slem Chronicle Pubg Inc.......... G 336 722-8624
Winston Salem *(G-13397)*

◆ Winston Salem Journal...................... E 336 727-7211
Winston Salem *(G-13401)*

Womack Newspaper Inc.......................... G 336 316-1231
Greensboro *(G-5923)*

Womack Publishing Co Inc...................... G 919 732-2171
Hillsborough *(G-6882)*

Womack Publishing Co Inc...................... G 252 586-2700
Littleton *(G-7888)*

Womack Publishing Co Inc...................... G 919 563-3555
Mebane *(G-8265)*

Womack Publishing Co Inc...................... D 252 480-2234
Nags Head *(G-9307)*

Womack Publishing Co Inc...................... G 252 257-3341
Warrenton *(G-12356)*

Womack Publishing Company Inc........ F 704 660-5520
Mooresville *(G-8800)*

Wtvd Television LLC.................................. C 919 683-1111
Durham *(G-4313)*

Yancy Common Times Journal................ G 828 682-2120
Burnsville *(G-1195)*

2721 Periodicals

Academy Association Inc........................ F 919 544-0835
Durham *(G-3877)*

American City Bus Journals Inc............. G 704 973-1100
Charlotte *(G-1665)*

▲ American City Bus Journals Inc........ E 704 973-1000
Charlotte *(G-1664)*

▲ American Inst Crtif Pub Accntn........ B 919 402-0682
Durham *(G-3890)*

Assoction Intl Crtif Prof Accn................ A 919 402-4500
Durham *(G-3901)*

Automationcom LLC................................. G 952 563-5448
Research Triangle Pa *(G-10704)*

Biosupplynet Inc...................................... F 919 659-2121
Morrisville *(G-8941)*

Business To Business Inc........................ G 919 872-7077
Raleigh *(G-9963)*

Capre Omnimedia LLC............................. G 917 460-3572
Wilmington *(G-12731)*

Carolina Home Garden............................ G 828 692-3230
Hendersonville *(G-6195)*

Carolina Parenting Inc............................. F 704 344-1980
Charlotte *(G-1853)*

Ceco Publishing Inc................................. G 828 253-2047
Asheville *(G-472)*

Charlotte Magazine.................................. G 980 207-5124
Charlotte *(G-1895)*

Cherokee Publishing Co Inc.................... F 919 674-6020
Cary *(G-1326)*

Christian Focus Magazine....................... G 252 240-1656
Morehead City *(G-8825)*

Cityview Publishing LLC.......................... F 910 423-6500
Fayetteville *(G-4575)*

Cline Printing Inc..................................... G 704 394-8144
Charlotte *(G-1929)*

Colefields Publishing Inc......................... G 704 661-1599
Charlotte *(G-1952)*

Duke University.. D 919 687-3600
Durham *(G-4011)*

Education Center LLC.............................. E 336 854-0309
Oak Ridge *(G-9571)*

Forsyth Family Magazine Inc.................. G 336 782-0331
Clemmons *(G-3183)*

Ft Media Holdings LLC............................ F 336 605-0121
Greensboro *(G-5542)*

Furniture Tday Media Group LLC........... D 336 605-0121
Greensboro *(G-5543)*

Grace Communion International.............. E 626 650-2300
Charlotte *(G-2229)*

Greater Wilmington Business................. G 910 343-8600
Wilmington *(G-12796)*

Hearst Corporation.................................. F 704 348-8000
Charlotte *(G-2268)*

Hearst Corporation.................................. F 704 348-8000
Charlotte *(G-2269)*

Hemispheres Magazine............................ F 336 255-0195
Greensboro *(G-5593)*

Ifpo - Ifmo/American Image Inc.............. G 336 945-9867
Hamptonville *(G-6085)*

International Society Automtn................. E 919 206-4176
Research Triangle Pa *(G-10713)*

ISA... G 919 549-8411
Durham *(G-4085)*

Jennifer Mowrer....................................... G 336 714-6462
Winston Salem *(G-13216)*

Jobs Magazine LLC.................................. G 919 319-6816
Cary *(G-1379)*

Knight Communications Inc.................... F 704 568-7804
Indian Trail *(G-7086)*

La Noticia Inc... F 704 568-6966
Charlotte *(G-2406)*

Lafauci.. G 919 244-5912
Holly Springs *(G-6905)*

▲ M&J Oldco Inc...................................... D 336 854-0309
Greensboro *(G-5669)*

Magazine Nakia Lashawn....................... G 919 875-1156
Raleigh *(G-10266)*

Mann Media Inc.. E 336 286-0600
Greensboro *(G-5672)*

Mathisen Ventures Inc............................ G 212 986-1025
Charlotte *(G-2468)*

Mb-F Inc.. D 336 379-9352
Greensboro *(G-5685)*

McKinnon Enterprise LLC........................ G 919 408-6365
Fayetteville *(G-4639)*

N2 Company Inc....................................... E 910 202-0917
Wilmington *(G-12856)*

Ncoast Communications.......................... F 252 247-7442
Morehead City *(G-8839)*

▲ News and Observer Pubg Co............. A 919 829-4500
Raleigh *(G-10331)*

Northstar Travel Media............................ E 336 714-3328
Winston Salem *(G-13266)*

▲ Obbc Inc.. G 252 261-0612
Kitty Hawk *(G-7446)*

▲ Pace Communications Inc.................. C 336 378-6065
Greensboro *(G-5729)*

Pride Communications Inc....................... G 704 375-9553
Charlotte *(G-2665)*

Prism Publishing Inc............................... F 919 319-6816
Cary *(G-1428)*

Raleigh Magazine..................................... G 919 307-3047
Raleigh *(G-10424)*

Randall-Reilly LLC.................................... C 704 814-1390
Charlotte *(G-2688)*

Red Hand Media LLC................................ F 704 523-6987
Charlotte *(G-2698)*

Rose Media Inc.. F 919 736-1154
Goldsboro *(G-5241)*

Scalawag... F 917 671-7240
Durham *(G-4224)*

Shannon Media Inc.................................. F 919 933-1551
Chapel Hill *(G-1570)*

Sigma Xi Scntfic RES Hnor Soc.............. E 919 549-4691
Durham *(G-4235)*

Southern Trade Publications Co............. G 336 454-3516
Greensboro *(G-5828)*

Spectrum News... G 919 882-4009
Raleigh *(G-10497)*

Stratton Publishing & Mktg Inc.............. G 703 914-9200
Wilmington *(G-12932)*

Tobacco Mrchnts Assn of US Inc........... F 919 872-5040
Raleigh *(G-10551)*

Todays Charlotte Woman......................... G 704 521-6872
Charlotte *(G-2925)*

Tourist Baseball Inc................................. E 828 258-0428
Asheville *(G-621)*

▲ Triple D Publishing Inc....................... G 704 482-9673
Shelby *(G-11385)*

Ty Brown.. G 828 264-6865
Boone *(G-948)*

Up & Coming Magazine............................ G 910 391-3859
Fayetteville *(G-4689)*

▲ Wilmington Today LLC......................... G 910 509-7195
Wilmington *(G-12953)*

2731 Book publishing

Ambassador Services Inc....................... C 800 576-8627
Gastonia *(G-4988)*

▲ Bhaktivedanta Archives....................... G 336 871-3636
Sandy Ridge *(G-11141)*

◆ C D Stampley Enterprises Inc............. F 704 333-6631
Charlotte *(G-1827)*

Carlina Shotwell LLC.............................. G 252 417-8688
Greenville (G-5950)

Carolina Wren Press Inc.......................... G 919 560-2738
Durham (G-3963)

◆ Carson-Dellosa Publishing LLC........ D 336 632-0084
Greensboro (G-5433)

▲ Celtic Ocean International Inc........... E 828 299-9005
Arden (G-261)

Center for Creative Leadership.............. B 336 288-7210
Greensboro (G-5436)

Cherokee Publications............................. G 828 627-2424
Cherokee (G-3051)

Church Initiative Inc.............................. E 919 562-2112
Wake Forest (G-12269)

Coding Institute LLC.............................. E 239 280-2300
Durham (G-3980)

Comfort Publishing Svcs LLC................ G 704 907-7848
Concord (G-3338)

Contemporary Concepts Inc.................. E 704 864-9572
Gastonia (G-5029)

Contemporary Publishing Co.................. G 919 834-4432
Raleigh (G-10013)

Dex Media East LLC.............................. F 919 297-1600
Cary (G-1347)

Duke University.. D 919 687-3600
Durham (G-4011)

Fidelity Associates Inc........................... E 704 864-3766
Gastonia (G-5047)

▲ Good Will Publishers Inc................... D 704 853-3237
Gastonia (G-5054)

Graedon Enterprises Inc......................... G 919 493-0448
Durham (G-4055)

Grateful Steps Foundation..................... G 828 277-0998
Asheville (G-509)

Great Waters Company............................ G 919 818-4081
Smithfield (G-11445)

▲ Gryphon House Inc............................. F 800 638-0928
Lewisville (G-7651)

Hatrack River Enterprises Inc................ G 336 282-9848
Greensboro (G-5588)

High Five Enterprises Inc....................... G 828 279-5962
Weaverville (G-12492)

How Great Thou Art Publication............ G 704 851-3117
Mc Farlan (G-8216)

International Society Automtn................. E 919 206-4176
Research Triangle Pa (G-10713)

ISA.. G 919 549-8411
Durham (G-4085)

JFK Conferences LLC............................ E 980 255-3336
Fayetteville (G-4623)

Jfl Enterprises Inc................................. G 704 786-7838
Concord (G-3385)

Kr Publications....................................... G 910 852-1525
Lumberton (G-7960)

Lees Press and Pubg Co LLC................ G 833 440-0770
Charlotte (G-2415)

▲ Light-Beams Publishing...................... F 603 659-1300
Carolina Beach (G-1262)

▼ Longleaf Services Inc......................... F 800 848-6224
Chapel Hill (G-1553)

Lulu Press Inc... D 919 447-3290
Durham (G-4111)

Lulu Technology Circus Inc.................... E 919 459-5858
Morrisville (G-9015)

Magic Factory LLC................................. E 919 585-5644
Durham (G-4116)

Marco Products Inc................................. F 215 956-0313
New Bern (G-9378)

Mathisen Ventures Inc............................ G 212 986-1025
Charlotte (G-2468)

Mc Farland & Company Inc.................... E 336 246-4460
Jefferson (G-7191)

New Growth Press LLC........................... G 336 378-7775
Greensboro (G-5707)

One Library At A Time Inc...................... G 704 578-1812
Charlotte (G-2598)

Payload Media Inc.................................. G 919 367-2969
Cary (G-1415)

Phoenix St Claire Pubg LLC................... G 919 303-3223
Cary (G-1420)

Plan Nine Publishing Inc........................ G 336 454-7766
High Point (G-6735)

Positive Prints Prof Svcs LLC................ G 336 701-2330
Durham (G-4189)

Readable Communications Inc................ G 919 876-5260
Raleigh (G-10434)

Royal Faires Inc..................................... F 704 896-5555
Huntersville (G-7044)

Sighttech LLC... G 855 997-4448
Charlotte (G-2805)

▲ Tan Books and Publishers Inc........... G 704 731-0651
Charlotte (G-2898)

Technica Editorial Services.................... G 919 918-3991
Carrboro (G-1274)

Two of A Kind Publishing LLC................ G 704 497-2879
Charlotte (G-2955)

University NC At Chapel Hl..................... G 919 962-0369
Chapel Hill (G-1585)

▲ University NC Press Inc..................... E 919 966-3561
Chapel Hill (G-1586)

Wisdom For Heart.................................. F 866 482-4253
Cary (G-1483)

Wisdom House Books Inc........................ G 919 883-4669
Chapel Hill (G-1594)

Wlc LLC.. G 336 852-6422
Greensboro (G-5922)

Wmxf AM 1400.. D 828 456-8661
Waynesville (G-12480)

Worden Brothers Inc.............................. D 919 202-8555
Wilmington (G-12954)

2732 Book printing

Goslen Printing Company........................ F 336 768-5775
Winston Salem (G-13181)

Herff Jones LLC..................................... G 704 845-3355
Charlotte (G-2271)

Hf Group LLC.. E 336 931-0800
Greensboro (G-5595)

Lsc Communications Inc......................... F 704 889-5800
Pineville (G-9741)

Rose Reprographics................................ G 336 222-0727
Burlington (G-1149)

▲ Tan Books and Publishers Inc........... G 704 731-0651
Charlotte (G-2898)

2741 Miscellaneous publishing

1 Click Web Solutions LLC.................... E 910 790-9330
Wilmington (G-12684)

Alphamed Company Inc........................... G 919 680-0011
Durham (G-3889)

Amber Brooks Publishing LLC............... G 704 582-1035
Raleigh (G-9896)

American Image Press............................. G 336 468-2796
Hamptonville (G-6081)

Appalachian State University.................. F 828 262-2047
Boone (G-896)

Ashville Postage Express....................... G 828 255-9250
Asheville (G-443)

Autosound 2000 Inc................................ G 336 227-3434
Burlington (G-1050)

Avian Cetacean Press............................ G 910 392-5537
Wilmington (G-12716)

Backstreets Publishing........................... G 919 968-9466
Carrboro (G-1266)

Barsina Publishing.................................. G 336 869-2849
High Point (G-6539)

Be House Publishing LLC....................... G 336 529-6143
Winston Salem (G-13102)

Beckett Media LP................................... G 800 508-2582
Durham (G-3921)

Better Publishing Inc.............................. G 828 688-9188
Bakersville (G-675)

▲ Bhaktivedanta Archives...................... G 336 871-3636
Sandy Ridge (G-11141)

Bold Life Publication.............................. G 828 692-3230
Hendersonville (G-6189)

Business Brokerage Press Inc................ G 800 239-5085
Wilmington (G-12725)

C&J Publishing....................................... G 336 722-8005
Winston Salem (G-13115)

Carolina Academic Press LLC................ D 919 489-7486
Durham (G-3959)

Carson-Dellosa Publishing LLC............. E 336 632-0084
Greensboro (G-5432)

Cedar Hill Studio & Gallery.................... G 828 456-6344
Waynesville (G-12453)

CFS Press Slim Ray................................ G 828 505-1030
Asheville (G-473)

Charlotte Observer Pubg Co................... E 704 358-6020
Matthews (G-8105)

Cherokee Publications Inc...................... G 828 627-2424
Clyde (G-3256)

Chief Corporation................................... G 704 916-4521
Charlotte (G-1915)

China Free Press Inc.............................. G 919 308-9826
Durham (G-3974)

Chiron Publications LLC.......................... G 828 285-0838
Asheville (G-474)

Church Initiative Inc............................... E 919 562-2112
Wake Forest (G-12269)

Clinton Press Inc.................................... F 336 275-8491
Greensboro (G-5451)

Cog Glbal Media/Consulting LLC........... E 980 239-8042
Matthews (G-8109)

Coman Publishing Co Inc........................ F 919 688-0218
Durham (G-3984)

Deverger Systems Inc............................ G 919 201-5146
Asheville (G-487)

Dex One Corporation.............................. A 919 297-1600
Cary (G-1348)

Direct Legal Mail LLC............................ G 919 353-9158
Raleigh (G-10047)

Document Imaging Systems Inc.............. G 919 460-9440
Raleigh (G-10054)

Domco Technology LLC........................... G 888 834-8541
Barnardsville (G-691)

E and J Publishing LLC.......................... G 877 882-2138
Charlotte (G-2079)

Eastonsweb Multimedia.......................... G 704 607-0941
Charlotte (G-2084)

Elizabeth S Java Express....................... G 919 777-5282
Sanford (G-11176)

Fastrack Publishing Co Inc..................... G 828 294-0544
Hickory (G-6332)

Fit1media LLC.. G 919 925-2200
Raleigh (G-10110)

Foothold Publications Inc....................... G 770 891-3423
Raleigh (G-10116)

Free Will Bptst Press Fndtion................ F 252 746-6128
Ayden (G-657)

Ft Media Holdings LLC............................ F 336 605-0121
Greensboro (G-5542)

Gathering Place Pubg Co LLC................ G 919 742-5850
Siler City (G-11410)

▲ Good Will Catholic Media LLC........... E 704 731-0651
Charlotte (G-2226)

Green Line Media Inc	E	828 251-1333	Asheville (G-512)
Grey House Publishing Inc	G	704 784-0051	Concord (G-3370)
Hardwood Publishing Co Inc	G	704 543-4408	Charlotte (G-2257)
Health Educator Publications	G	919 243-1299	Clayton (G-3153)
Hearsay Guides LLC	G	336 584-1440	Elon (G-4470)
Heaven & Earth Works	G	845 797-0902	Brevard (G-971)
Herff Jones LLC	G	704 845-3355	Charlotte (G-2271)
Hiddenite Conference Ctr LLC	G	828 352-9200	Hiddenite (G-6498)
Holy Cow Publications LLC	G	704 900-5779	Charlotte (G-2283)
Hope Tree Publishing LLC	G	336 858-5301	High Point (G-6663)
Imleagues LLC	F	919 617-1113	Wake Forest (G-12282)
Indie Services	G	336 524-6966	Burlington (G-1108)
Information Age Publishing Inc	G	704 752-9125	Charlotte (G-2332)
▲ Intereco USA Belt Filter Press	G	919 349-6041	Raleigh (G-10206)
Interntnal Chldbrth Edcatn Ass	G	919 863-9487	Raleigh (G-10208)
Journalistic Inc	E	919 945-0700	Chapel Hill (G-1550)
Keowee Publishing Co Inc	G	828 877-4742	Pisgah Forest (G-9770)
▲ Kindermusik International Inc	E	800 628-5687	Greensboro (G-5648)
Klazzy Magazine Inc	G	704 293-8321	Charlotte (G-2399)
Land and Loft LLC	G	315 560-7060	Raleigh (G-10244)
▲ Laser Ink Corporation	E	919 361-5822	Durham (G-4101)
Lighthouse Press Inc	E	919 371-8640	Cary (G-1388)
Likeable Press LLC	G	844 882-8340	Charlotte (G-2423)
Lookwhatqmade LLC	G	980 330-1995	Charlotte (G-2434)
Lovekin & Young PC	G	828 322-5435	Hickory (G-6388)
Main Street Rag Publishing Co	G	704 573-2516	Mint Hill (G-8339)
Map Shop LLC	G	704 332-5557	Charlotte (G-2454)
Map Supply Inc	G	336 731-3230	Flat Rock (G-4710)
Mathisen Ventures Inc	G	212 986-1025	Charlotte (G-2468)
McGill Advsory Pblications Inc	G	866 727-6100	Charlotte (G-2477)
Medical Missionary Press	G	828 649-3976	Marshall (G-8081)
Mel Schlesinger	G	336 525-6357	Winston Salem (G-13248)
Micro Scribe Publishing Inc	G	919 848-0388	Raleigh (G-10300)
Middle of Nowhere Music LLC	G	301 237-7290	Carrboro (G-1270)
Mocha Memoir Press	G	336 404-7445	Kernersville (G-7287)
Month9 Books LLC	G	919 645-5786	Raleigh (G-10313)
Moonshine Press	G	828 371-8519	Franklin (G-4837)
Mountaineer Yellowpages	G	866 758-0123	Huntersville (G-7018)
Mra Services Inc	F	704 933-4300	Kannapolis (G-7216)
▲ Music Matters Inc	G	336 272-5303	Greensboro (G-5702)
Musicland Express	G	828 627-9431	Clyde (G-3260)
My Alabaster Box LLC	G	919 873-1442	Raleigh (G-10319)
N2 Franchising Inc	F	844 353-5378	Raleigh (G-10321)
N2 Publishing	G	336 293-3845	Advance (G-36)
▲ News and Observer Pubg Co	A	919 829-4500	Raleigh (G-10331)
Norsan Media LLC	E	704 494-7181	Charlotte (G-2573)
One On One Press LLC	G	910 228-8821	Wilmington (G-12866)
Oslo Press Inc	G	919 606-2028	Raleigh (G-10351)
Outer Banks Internet Inc	G	252 441-6698	Kill Devil Hills (G-7318)
Oxford University Press LLC	D	919 677-0977	Cary (G-1412)
Oxford University Press LLC	B	919 677-0977	Cary (G-1413)
Pdf and Associates	G	252 332-7749	Colerain (G-3271)
Peaberry Press LLC	G	828 773-1489	Asheville (G-569)
Peace of Mind Publications	G	919 308-5137	Durham (G-4171)
Piedmont Publishing	G	336 727-4099	Winston Salem (G-13293)
Pilot Press LLC	G	910 692-8366	Southern Pines (G-11506)
Press Ganey Associates Inc	G	800 232-8032	Charlotte (G-2661)
Princeton Information	G	980 224-7114	Charlotte (G-2668)
Production Media Inc	F	919 325-0120	Raleigh (G-10400)
Prospective Communications LLC	G	336 287-5535	Winston Salem (G-13309)
Publishing Group Inc	G	704 847-7150	Matthews (G-8142)
Quinlan Publishing Company	G	229 886-7995	Wilmington (G-12894)
Rancho Park Publishing Inc	G	919 942-9493	Pittsboro (G-9787)
RC Boldt Publishing LLC	G	904 624-0033	Oak Island (G-9568)
Red Adept Publishing LLC	G	919 798-7410	Garner (G-4958)
Redrum Press	G	866 374-7881	Wilmington (G-12897)
Rehab Solutions Inc	G	800 273-3418	Matthews (G-8144)
Research Triangle Software Inc	G	919 233-8796	Cary (G-1436)
Research Trngle Edtrial Sltons	G	919 808-2719	Durham (G-4213)
Rhd Service LLC	E	919 297-1600	Cary (G-1437)
Richard Schwartz	G	914 358-4518	Wilmington (G-12898)
Richard Wilcox	G	919 218-5907	Willow Spring (G-12681)
Rikki Tikki Tees	G	828 454-0515	Waynesville (G-12470)
Riptide Publishing LLC	G	908 295-4517	Burnsville (G-1190)
Riteway Express Inc of NC	G	828 966-4822	Brevard (G-981)
▲ Roadrnner Mtrcycle Turing Trvl	G	336 765-7780	Clemmons (G-3202)
Roaring Lion Publishing	G	828 350-1454	Asheville (G-592)
Rod Jahner	G	919 435-7580	Sunset Beach (G-11852)
Rogers Express Lube LLC	G	828 648-7772	Canton (G-1255)
Roosterfish Media LLC	G	980 722-7454	Mooresville (G-8761)
Royalkind LLC	G	252 355-7484	Winterville (G-13422)
S & A Cherokee LLC	E	919 674-6020	Cary (G-1443)
Savvy - Discountscom News Ltr	F	252 729-8691	Smyrna (G-11471)
School Directorease LLC	G	240 206-6273	Charlotte (G-2768)
Seas Publications	G	919 266-0035	Raleigh (G-10465)
Security Self Storage	G	919 544-3969	Durham (G-4229)
Sillaman & Sons Inc	G	919 774-6324	Sanford (G-11233)
▲ Silver Ink Publishing Inc	G	704 473-0192	Shelby (G-11378)
Skybien Press LLC	G	919 544-1777	Durham (G-4238)
Sml Raleigh LLC	G	919 585-0100	Clayton (G-3170)
Sola Publishing	G	336 226-8240	Graham (G-5285)
SRI Ventures Inc	F	919 427-1681	Sanford (G-11237)
Stackhouse Publishing Inc	G	203 699-6571	Boone (G-944)
Stegall Petroleum Inc	G	704 283-5058	Monroe (G-8564)
Stephen J McCusker	G	336 884-1916	High Point (G-6792)
Stork News Tm of America	F	910 868-3065	Fayetteville (G-4675)
Strawbridge Studios Inc	D	919 286-9512	Durham (G-4252)
Success Publishing Inc	C	919 807-1100	Raleigh (G-10517)
Sun Publishing Company	F	919 942-5282	Chapel Hill (G-1575)
Tarheel Publishing Co	F	919 553-9042	Clayton (G-3173)
Teabar Publishing Inc	G	252 764-2453	Emerald Isle (G-4480)
Thinking Maps Inc	G	919 678-8778	Cary (G-1470)
Timberlake Ventures Inc	G	704 896-7499	Wilmington (G-12940)
Toplink Publishing	G	888 375-9818	Kelly (G-7223)
Training Industry Inc	D	919 653-4990	Raleigh (G-10555)
Triangle Pointer Inc	G	919 968-4801	Chapel Hill (G-1580)
Triangle Regulatory Pubg LLC	G	919 886-4587	Raleigh (G-10561)
TS Krupa LLC	G	336 782-1515	Winston Salem (G-13375)

S
I
C

Tudg Multimedia Firm............................ G 704 916-9819
Huntersville (G-7061)

Turnberry Press.................................... G 860 670-4892
Southern Pines (G-11513)

Twin Attic Publishing Hse Inc............... G 919 426-0322
Wake Forest (G-12310)

Uai Technology Inc............................... G 919 541-9339
Durham (G-4287)

Under Covers Publishing........................ G 704 965-8744
Wilson (G-13040)

United House Publishing........................ G 248 605-3787
Concord (G-3462)

University Directories LLC..................... D 800 743-5556
Durham (G-4290)

Uptown Publishing Inc.......................... G 704 543-0690
Charlotte (G-2967)

Vasiliy Yavdoshnyak............................. G 919 995-9469
Wake Forest (G-12312)

Viaticus Inc.. G 252 258-4679
Winterville (G-13425)

Vista Tranquila Publishers LLC.............. G 828 586-8401
Sylva (G-11903)

Wake Cross Roads Express LLC............ G 919 266-7966
Raleigh (G-10597)

◆ Webster Fine Art Limited.................. G 919 349-8455
Morrisville (G-9089)

Wedpics.. G 919 699-5676
Raleigh (G-10603)

West Express.. G 704 276-9001
Vale (G-12211)

White Picket Media Inc........................ G 773 769-8400
Cornelius (G-3630)

Willard Rodney White........................... G 252 794-3245
Windsor (G-13061)

Workcom Inc....................................... E 310 586-4000
Cary (G-1486)

Writ Press Inc...................................... G 815 988-7074
Durham (G-4311)

Writing Penn LLC................................. G 301 529-5324
Durham (G-4312)

Yackety Yack Publishing Inc.................. G 919 843-5092
Chapel Hill (G-1598)

Yeeka LLC.. G 919 308-9826
Durham (G-4316)

Yp Advrtising Pubg LLC Not LLC........... C 704 522-5500
Charlotte (G-3042)

Yp Advrtising Pubg LLC Not LLC........... C 910 794-5151
Wilmington (G-12957)

2752 Commercial printing, lithographic

3 Star Enterprises LLC.......................... E 704 821-7503
Indian Trail (G-7065)

4 Over LLC.. F 919 875-3187
Raleigh (G-9858)

A & M Paper and Printing..................... G 919 813-7852
Durham (G-3874)

A Better Image Printing Inc.................. F 919 967-0319
Durham (G-3875)

A Forbes Company................................ F
Lenoir (G-7565)

A Plus Graphics Inc.............................. G 252 243-0404
Wilson (G-12960)

Able Graphics Company LLC.................. G 336 753-1812
Mocksville (G-8346)

Abolder Image...................................... F 336 856-1300
Greensboro (G-5338)

Accelerated Press Inc........................... G 248 524-1850
Wilmington (G-12689)

Acme Sample Books Inc........................ E 336 883-4336
High Point (G-6508)

Ad Spice Marketing LLC....................... G 919 286-7110
Durham (G-3880)

Adpress Printing Incorporated.............. G 336 294-2244
Summerfield (G-11835)

ADS Printing Co Inc............................ G 919 834-0579
Raleigh (G-9879)

Advanced Teo Corp.............................. G 305 278-4474
Charlotte (G-1625)

Advantage Printing Inc......................... F 828 252-7667
Arden (G-248)

Advantage Printing & Design................ G 252 523-8133
Kinston (G-7392)

AEC Imaging & Graphics LLC................ G 910 693-1034
Hope Mills (G-6922)

AEL Services LLC................................ E 704 525-3710
Charlotte (G-1626)

Alexander Press Inc.............................. G 336 884-8063
High Point (G-6514)

All Occasion Printing........................... G 336 926-7766
Winston Salem (G-13079)

AlphaGraphics...................................... F 704 887-3430
Charlotte (G-1654)

AlphaGraphics...................................... G 336 759-8000
Winston Salem (G-13083)

AlphaGraphics Downtown Raleigh.......... G 919 832-2828
Garner (G-4914)

AlphaGraphics Pineville......................... G 704 541-3678
Charlotte (G-1655)

American Indian Printing Inc................ G 336 230-1551
Greensboro (G-5357)

American Multimedia Inc...................... D 336 229-7101
Burlington (G-1045)

American Printers Inc........................... G 252 977-7468
Rocky Mount (G-10822)

American Speedy Printing Ctrs.............. G 828 322-3981
Hickory (G-6263)

Anav Yofi Inc....................................... G 828 217-7746
Charlotte (G-1676)

Andrews Graphics LLC.......................... G 252 633-3199
New Bern (G-9334)

Anitas Marketing Concepts Inc.............. G 252 243-3993
Wilson (G-12961)

Apex Printing Company......................... G 919 362-9856
Apex (G-136)

Appalachian State University.................. F 828 262-2047
Boone (G-896)

Archdale Printing Company Inc.............. G 336 884-5312
High Point (G-6525)

Arrowhead Graphics Inc........................ G 336 274-2419
Greensboro (G-5370)

Artcraft Press Inc................................ G 828 397-8612
Icard (G-7064)

Artech Graphics Inc............................. G 704 545-9804
New London (G-9413)

Artesian Future Technology LLC........... G 919 904-4940
Chapel Hill (G-1529)

Arthur Demarest.................................. G 252 473-1449
Manteo (G-8023)

Arzberger Engravers Inc....................... E 704 376-1151
Charlotte (G-1702)

Asheville Print Shop............................. G 828 214-5286
Asheville (G-440)

Asheville Quickprint............................. G 828 252-7667
Fletcher (G-4720)

Associated Printing & Svcs Inc.............. G 828 286-9064
Rutherfordton (G-10975)

Atlantis Graphics Inc........................... E 919 361-5809
Durham (G-3904)

Austin Printing Company Inc................. G 704 289-1445
Monroe (G-8437)

Aztech Products Inc............................. G 910 763-5599
Wilmington (G-12717)

B F I Industries Inc............................. G 919 229-4509
Wake Forest (G-12262)

B P Printing and Copying Inc................ G 704 821-8219
Matthews (G-8159)

Babusci Crtive Prtg Imging LLC............ G 704 423-9864
Charlotte (G-1735)

Baicy Communications Inc..................... G 336 722-7768
Winston Salem (G-13101)

Baileys Quick Copy Shop Inc................ F 704 637-2020
Salisbury (G-11022)

Bakeshot Prtg & Graphics LLC.............. G 704 532-9326
Charlotte (G-1743)

Ballantyne One..................................... G 704 926-7009
Charlotte (G-1747)

Barefoot Press Inc.............................. G 919 283-6396
Raleigh (G-9933)

Barretts Printing House Inc.................. G 252 243-2820
Wilson (G-12968)

Bbf Printing Solutions........................... G 336 969-2323
Rural Hall (G-10952)

BEC-Car Printing Co Inc...................... F 704 873-1911
Statesville (G-11669)

Bennett & Associates Inc..................... G 919 477-7362
Durham (G-3925)

Better Business Printing Inc.................. G 704 867-3366
Gastonia (G-4998)

Blackleys Printing Co............................ G 919 553-6813
Clayton (G-3135)

Blue Ridge Printing Co Inc................... D 828 254-1000
Asheville (G-457)

Blue Ridge Quick Print Inc................... G 828 883-2420
Brevard (G-968)

Boingo Graphics Inc............................. E 704 527-4963
Charlotte (G-1797)

Boundless Inc....................................... G 919 622-9051
Four Oaks (G-4809)

BP Solutions Group Inc........................ E 828 252-4476
Asheville (G-460)

Brand Fuel Promotions.......................... G 704 256-4057
Waxhaw (G-12425)

Brandilly of Nc Inc.............................. G 919 278-7896
Raleigh (G-9957)

Brodie-Jones Printing Co Inc................ G 252 438-7992
Louisburg (G-7910)

Brown Printing Inc.............................. G 704 849-9292
Charlotte (G-1814)

Buchanan Prtg & Graphics Inc.............. G 336 299-6868
Greensboro (G-5408)

Budget Printing Co............................... G 910 642-7306
Whiteville (G-12577)

Burco International Inc......................... G 828 252-4481
Asheville (G-463)

Burrow Family Corporation.................... E 336 887-3173
Asheboro (G-334)

C B C Printing.................................... G 828 497-5510
Cherokee (G-3050)

C D J & P Inc.................................... G 252 446-3611
Rocky Mount (G-10826)

Call Printing & Copying........................ G 704 821-6554
Indian Trail (G-7073)

Canvas Giclee Printing.......................... G 910 458-4229
Carolina Beach (G-1257)

Carden Printing Company...................... G 336 364-2923
Timberlake (G-12099)

Cardinal Graphics Inc........................... G 704 545-4144
Mint Hill (G-8334)

Carolina Copy Services Inc.................... F 704 375-9099
Cornelius (G-3592)

Carolina Newspapers Inc....................... G 336 274-7829
Greensboro (G-5431)

Carolina Print Mill.............................. G 919 607-9452
Cary (G-1323)

Carolina Printing Co............................ G 919 834-0433
Princeton (G-9823)

Carolina Prtg Wilmington Inc................ G 910 762-2453
Supply (G-11856)

Carolina Vinyl Printing.......................... G 910 603-3036
Pinehurst (G-9689)

▲ Carolina Warp Prints Inc................... F 704 866-4763
Gastonia (G-5014)

Carroll Signs & Advertising................... G 336 983-3415
King (G-7324)

Carter Printing.................................... G 919 373-0531
Knightdale (G-7450)

Carter Printing & Graphics Inc............. F 919 266-5280
Knightdale (G-7451)

Cary Printing...................................... G 919 266-9005
Raleigh (G-9984)

Cascadas Nye Corporation.................... F 919 834-8128
Raleigh (G-9985)

Cashiers Printing Inc........................... G 828 787-1324
Highlands (G-6844)

◆ Causekeepers Inc.............................. E 336 824-2518
Franklinville (G-4855)

Cavu Printing Inc................................ G 336 818-9790
Elkin (G-4441)

Celestial Products Inc.......................... G 540 338-4040
Huntersville (G-6975)

Central Carolina Printing LLC............... G 910 572-3344
Asheboro (G-336)

Ceprint Solutions Inc........................... E 336 956-6327
Lexington (G-7662)

Chanmala Gallery Fine Art Prtg............ G 704 975-7695
Wake Forest (G-12268)

Charlotte Printing Company Inc............. F 704 888-5181
Concord (G-3334)

Choice Printing LLC............................. G 919 790-0680
Raleigh (G-9994)

City Prints LLC.................................... G 404 273-5741
Matthews (G-8106)

Clarks Printing Service Inc.................... E 828 254-1432
Asheville (G-477)

Cline Printing Inc................................ G 704 394-8144
Charlotte (G-1929)

Clinton Press Inc................................ F 336 275-8491
Greensboro (G-5451)

Clondalkin Pharma & Healthcare........... G 336 292-4555
Greensboro (G-5452)

Coastal Impressions Inc....................... G 252 480-1717
Nags Head (G-9297)

Coastal Press Inc................................ G 252 726-1549
Morehead City (G-8827)

Coble Printing Co Inc........................... G 919 693-4622
Oxford (G-9608)

Commercial Enterprises NC Inc............. G 910 592-8163
Clinton (G-3230)

Commercial Printing Company............... E 919 832-2828
Garner (G-4922)

Commercial Prtg Co of Clinton.............. G 910 592-8163
Clinton (G-3231)

◆ Commercial Prtg Lincolnton NC.......... G 704 735-6831
Lincolnton (G-7822)

Concord Printing Company Inc.............. G 704 786-3717
Concord (G-3342)

Connected 2k LLC.............................. G 910 321-7446
Fayetteville (G-4578)

▼ Consolidated Press Inc.................... G 704 372-6785
Charlotte (G-1975)

Copy Cat Instant Prtg Chrltte............... G 704 529-6606
Charlotte (G-1982)

Copy Express Charlotte Inc................... G 704 527-1750
Charlotte (G-1983)

Copy King Inc..................................... G 336 333-9900
Greensboro (G-5468)

Copy Works.. G 828 698-7622
Hendersonville (G-6199)

Copycat Print Shop Inc........................ F 910 799-1500
Wilmington (G-12751)

Copymasters Printing Svcs Inc............. G 828 324-0532
Hickory (G-6311)

Copymatic United Cerebral................... F 252 695-6155
Greenville (G-5959)

▲ CPS Resources Inc.......................... E 704 628-7678
Indian Trail (G-7075)

CRC Printing Co Inc............................ G 704 875-1804
Huntersville (G-6981)

Creative Printers Inc........................... G 336 246-7746
West Jefferson (G-12563)

Creative Printers & Brks Inc................. G 828 321-4663
Andrews (G-106)

Creative Printing Stanley Inc................. G 704 732-6398
Lincolnton (G-7825)

Creative Prtg Intrnet Svcs LLC............. G 828 265-2800
Boone (G-910)

Crisp Printers Inc............................... G 704 867-6663
Gastonia (G-5032)

CRS/Las Inc....................................... F 910 392-0883
Wilmington (G-12757)

Currie Motorsports Inc......................... G 910 580-1765
Raeford (G-9836)

Custom Marking & Printing Inc.............. G 704 866-8245
Gastonia (G-5036)

Custom Printing Solutions Inc............... G 336 992-1161
Kernersville (G-7262)

D & B Printing Co............................... G 919 876-3530
Raleigh (G-10032)

Daniels Business Services Inc............... E 828 277-8250
Asheville (G-483)

Davidson Printing Inc.......................... G 336 357-0555
Lexington (G-7675)

Dbw Print & Promo.............................. G 704 906-8551
Concord (G-3352)

Ddi Print... F 919 829-8810
Raleigh (G-10040)

▲ Decal Source Inc............................. E 336 574-3141
Mc Leansville (G-8221)

Del-Mark Inc...................................... F 828 322-6180
Hickory (G-6320)

Deluxe Printing Co Inc......................... E 828 322-1329
Hickory (G-6321)

Design Printing Inc.............................. G 336 472-3333
Thomasville (G-12017)

▼ Dew Group Enterprises Inc............... E 919 585-0100
Clayton (G-3144)

Digital AP Prtg DBA F4mily Mtt............. G 980 939-8066
Charlotte (G-2045)

Discount Printing Inc........................... G 704 365-3665
Charlotte (G-2052)

Docu Source of NC.............................. F 919 459-5900
Morrisville (G-8967)

Document Comm Solutions Inc............. G 336 856-1300
Greensboro (G-5498)

Dogwood Print................................... G 919 906-0617
Wendell (G-12532)

Dokja Inc... G 336 852-5190
Greensboro (G-5500)

Dorsett Printing Company..................... G 910 895-3520
Rockingham (G-10775)

Dove Communications Inc.................... G 336 855-5491
Greensboro (G-5502)

Downtown Raleigh............................... G 919 821-7897
Raleigh (G-10057)

Drake Enterprises Ltd.......................... G 828 524-7045
Franklin (G-4824)

▼ Dtbtla Inc...................................... F 336 769-0000
Greensboro (G-5506)

Duncan-Parnell Inc............................. G 252 977-7832
Rocky Mount (G-10833)

E C U Univ Prtg & Graphics.................. F 252 737-1301
Greenville (G-5971)

Eastern Offset Printing Co.................... G 252 247-6791
Atlantic Beach (G-639)

Ed Kemp Associates Inc....................... G 336 869-2155
High Point (G-6604)

Elledge Family Inc.............................. F 919 876-2300
Raleigh (G-10082)

Erleclair Inc....................................... E 919 233-7710
Cary (G-1355)

Fairway Printing Inc............................ G 919 779-4797
Raleigh (G-10102)

Fast Pro Media LLC............................. G 704 799-8040
Cornelius (G-3599)

Fast Pro Media LLC............................. G 704 799-8040
Cornelius (G-3600)

▲ Fayetteville Publishing Co................. E 910 323-4848
Fayetteville (G-4601)

Flanagan Printing Company Inc............. G 828 693-7380
Hendersonville (G-6207)

Flash Printing Company Inc.................. E 704 375-2474
Charlotte (G-2159)

Forsyth Printing Company Inc............... G 336 969-0383
Rural Hall (G-10959)

Forward Design & Print Co Inc.............. G 704 776-9304
Monroe (G-8490)

Free Will Bptst Press Fndtion................ F 252 746-6128
Ayden (G-657)

Freedom Mailing & Mktg Inc................. G 336 595-6300
Winston Salem (G-13175)

Galaxy Graphics Inc............................ G 704 724-9057
Matthews (G-8113)

Gaston Printing and Signs LLC............. G 702 267-5633
Belmont (G-753)

Geo-Lin Inc....................................... G 336 884-0648
Jamestown (G-7162)

Get Custom Print................................ G 336 682-3891
Kernersville (G-7275)

Gibraltar Packaging Inc........................ C 910 439-6137
Whitsett (G-12608)

Gik Inc... F 919 872-9498
Raleigh (G-10133)

◆ Gilbarco Inc................................... A 336 547-5000
Greensboro (G-5560)

Gilley Printers Inc............................... G 910 295-6317
Pinehurst (G-9692)

Gilmore Globl Lgstics Svcs Inc.............. D 919 277-2700
Morrisville (G-8982)

Ginas Processing & Prtg Ctr................. G 910 476-0037
Raeford (G-9839)

Ginkgo Print Studio LLC...................... G 828 275-6300
Asheville (G-507)

Glover Corporation Inc......................... E 919 821-5535
Raleigh (G-10139)

Goffstar Inc....................................... G 704 895-3878
Charlotte (G-2222)

◆ Golf Associates Advertising Co.......... E 828 252-6544
Asheville (G-508)

Goslen Printing Company..................... F 336 768-5775
Winston Salem (G-13181)

Graphic Finshg Solutions LLC............... G 336 255-7857
Greensboro (G-5573)

Graphic Impressions Inc....................... E 704 596-4921
Charlotte (G-2232)

Graphic Products Inc........................... G 919 894-3661
Benson (G-790)

Graphic Rewards Inc........................... G 336 969-2733
Rural Hall (G-10960)

Greencross Inc.................................... G 704 984-6700
Albemarle (G-76)

Greensboro News & Record LLC........... A 336 373-7000
Greensboro (G-5577)

Greybeard Printing Inc................G..... 828 252-3082	J R Cole Industries Inc................F..... 704 523-6622	Masters Hand Print Works Inc................G..... 828 652-5833
Asheville *(G-513)*	Charlotte *(G-2361)*	Marion *(G-8051)*
▲ Griffin Printing Inc................G..... 919 832-6931	Jag Graphics Inc................G..... 828 259-9020	▲ Maxim Label Packg High Pt Inc................F..... 336 861-1666
Raleigh *(G-10147)*	Asheville *(G-527)*	High Point *(G-6708)*
Gso Printing................G..... 336 292-1601	James G Gouge................G..... 336 854-1551	Mb-F Inc................D..... 336 379-9352
Greensboro *(G-5581)*	High Point *(G-6677)*	Greensboro *(G-5685)*
Gso Printing Inc................G..... 336 288-5778	JB II Printing LLC................E..... 336 222-0717	◆ McGrann Paper Corporation................E..... 800 240-9455
Greensboro *(G-5582)*	Burlington *(G-1111)*	Charlotte *(G-2478)*
Harco Printing Incorporated................G..... 336 771-0234	JC Print................G..... 910 556-9663	Measurement Incorporated................D..... 919 683-2413
Winston Salem *(G-13189)*	Wilmington *(G-12822)*	Durham *(G-4122)*
Hayes Print-Stamp Co Inc................G..... 336 667-1116	JM Graphics Inc................G..... 704 375-1147	Medlit Solutions................G..... 919 878-6789
Wilkesboro *(G-12637)*	Charlotte *(G-2371)*	Garner *(G-4941)*
Herald Printing Inc................G..... 252 726-3534	Jofra Graphics Inc................G..... 910 259-1717	▲ Medlit Solutions LLC................D..... 919 878-6789
Morehead City *(G-8835)*	Burgaw *(G-1025)*	Garner *(G-4942)*
Heritage Prtg & Graphics Inc................G..... 704 551-0700	Jones Media................G..... 828 264-3612	Mellineum Printing................F..... 919 267-5752
Charlotte *(G-2274)*	Boone *(G-928)*	Apex *(G-179)*
Hickory Printing Group Inc H................F..... 828 465-3431	Jones Printing Company Inc................G..... 919 774-9442	Meredith - Webb Prtg Co Inc................D..... 336 228-8378
Conover *(G-3529)*	Sanford *(G-11198)*	Burlington *(G-1128)*
Hickory Printing Solutions LLC................B..... 828 465-3431	Joseph C Woodard Prtg Co Inc................F..... 919 829-0634	Metro Productions Inc................F..... 919 851-6420
Conover *(G-3530)*	Raleigh *(G-10221)*	Raleigh *(G-10296)*
High Concepts LLC................G..... 704 377-3467	Js Printing LLC................G..... 919 773-1103	Minges Printing & Advg Co................G..... 704 867-6791
Denver *(G-3787)*	Raleigh *(G-10224)*	Gastonia *(G-5098)*
Hinson Industries Inc................G..... 252 937-7171	Kathie S Mc Daniel................G..... 336 835-1544	Minuteman Press of Gastonia................G..... 704 867-3366
Rocky Mount *(G-10840)*	Elkin *(G-4446)*	Gastonia *(G-5099)*
Hinsons Typing & Printing................G..... 919 934-9036	▲ Keiger Inc................E..... 336 760-0099	Minuteman Quick Copy Svc Inc................G..... 910 455-5353
Smithfield *(G-11446)*	Winston Salem *(G-13223)*	Jacksonville *(G-7132)*
Htm Concepts Inc................F..... 252 794-2122	Keller Cres U To Be Phrmgraphi................E..... 336 851-1150	Mjt Us Inc................G..... 704 826-7828
Windsor *(G-13054)*	Greensboro *(G-5646)*	Charlotte *(G-2510)*
Hunsucker Printing Co Inc................G..... 336 629-9125	Key Printing Inc................F..... 252 459-4783	Mlb Screen Printing................G..... 704 363-6124
Asheboro *(G-363)*	Nashville *(G-9321)*	Huntersville *(G-7016)*
Huntpack Inc................G..... 704 986-0684	Kieffer Starlite Company................G..... 800 659-2493	Modern Information Svcs Inc................G..... 704 872-1020
Albemarle *(G-78)*	Mount Airy *(G-9141)*	Statesville *(G-11734)*
Ideal Printing Services Inc................G..... 336 784-0074	▲ King International Corporation................E..... 336 983-5171	Monarch Printers................G..... 704 376-1533
Kernersville *(G-7279)*	King *(G-7329)*	Charlotte *(G-2517)*
▲ Image Works Inc................G..... 336 668-3338	Kinston Office Supply Co Inc................E..... 252 523-7654	Monk Lekeisha................G..... 910 385-0361
Jamestown *(G-7168)*	Kinston *(G-7419)*	Goldsboro *(G-5230)*
Imagemark Business Svcs Inc................G..... 704 865-4912	Kolb Boyette & Assoc Inc................E..... 919 544-7839	Monte Enterprises Inc................G..... 252 637-5803
Gastonia *(G-5062)*	Durham *(G-4097)*	New Bern *(G-9385)*
Imperial Printing Pdts Co Inc................G..... 704 554-1188	Kreber................D..... 336 861-2700	Moore Printing & Graphics Inc................F..... 919 821-3293
Lowell *(G-7932)*	High Point *(G-6686)*	Raleigh *(G-10314)*
Independence Printing................G..... 336 771-0234	Label & Printing Solutions Inc................G..... 919 782-1242	More Than Billboards Inc................E..... 336 723-1018
Winston Salem *(G-13205)*	Raleigh *(G-10243)*	Kernersville *(G-7288)*
Industrial Motions Inc................G..... 734 284-8944	Landmark Printing Inc................G..... 919 833-5151	Morgan Printers Inc................F..... 252 355-5588
Apex *(G-168)*	Raleigh *(G-10245)*	Winterville *(G-13419)*
▲ Industrial Sign & Graphics Inc................E..... 704 371-4985	Landmark Printing Co Inc................G..... 919 833-5151	Motorsports Designs Inc................F..... 336 454-1181
Charlotte *(G-2324)*	Raleigh *(G-10246)*	High Point *(G-6716)*
Infinity S End Inc................F..... 704 900-8355	▲ Laser Ink Corporation................E..... 919 361-5822	Mountaineer Inc................G..... 828 452-0661
Charlotte *(G-2328)*	Durham *(G-4101)*	Waynesville *(G-12464)*
Ingalls Alton................G..... 252 975-2056	Legacy Graphics Inc................F..... 919 741-6262	Multi Packaging Solutions................A..... 336 855-7142
Washington *(G-12394)*	Garner *(G-4936)*	Greensboro *(G-5699)*
Ink Well................G..... 336 727-9750	Lenoir Printing Inc................G..... 828 758-7260	Murphy Printing & Vinyl LLC................G..... 828 835-4848
Winston Salem *(G-13209)*	Lenoir *(G-7621)*	Murphy *(G-9294)*
Ink Well Inc................G..... 919 682-8279	Linprint Company................F..... 910 763-5103	Natel Inc................G..... 336 227-1227
Durham *(G-4078)*	Wilmington *(G-12837)*	Burlington *(G-1134)*
Inkwell................G..... 919 433-7539	Litho Priting Inc................G..... 919 755-9542	▲ National Print Services Inc................G..... 704 892-9209
Fayetteville *(G-4617)*	Raleigh *(G-10257)*	Mooresville *(G-8731)*
Inprimo Solutions Inc................G..... 919 390-7776	Loftin & Company Inc................E..... 704 393-9393	NC Imprints Inc................G..... 336 790-4546
Raleigh *(G-10199)*	Charlotte *(G-2431)*	Lexington *(G-7720)*
Insta Copy Shop Ltd................F..... 704 376-1350	Lynchs Office Supply Co Inc................F..... 252 537-6041	NC Printing LLC................G..... 828 393-4615
Charlotte *(G-2339)*	Roanoke Rapids *(G-10740)*	Hendersonville *(G-6230)*
Instant Imprints................G..... 704 864-1510	M & S Systems Inc................G..... 336 996-7118	New Hanover Printing and Pubg................G..... 910 520-7173
Gastonia *(G-5067)*	Kernersville *(G-7283)*	Wilmington *(G-12860)*
Interflex Acquisition Co LLC................C..... 336 921-3505	M C C of Laurinburg Inc................G..... 910 276-0519	▲ News and Observer Pubg Co................A..... 919 829-4500
Wilkesboro *(G-12641)*	Laurinburg *(G-7506)*	Raleigh *(G-10331)*
International Minute Press................G..... 919 762-0054	Mail Management Services LLC................F..... 828 236-0076	Nine Thirteen LLC................G..... 919 876-8070
Fuquay Varina *(G-4885)*	Asheville *(G-541)*	Raleigh *(G-10332)*
Inventive Graphics Inc................G..... 704 814-4900	Map Shop LLC................G..... 704 332-5557	Norman Lake Graphics Inc................G..... 704 896-8444
Charlotte *(G-2351)*	Charlotte *(G-2454)*	Huntersville *(G-7022)*
Itek Graphics LLC................E..... 704 357-6002	Markell Publishing Company Inc................G..... 336 226-7148	Notepad Enterprises LLC................G..... 704 377-3467
Concord *(G-3383)*	Burlington *(G-1122)*	Charlotte *(G-2576)*
Its Your Time Business Center................G..... 336 754-4456	Master Marketing Group LLC................G..... 870 932-4491	Observer News Enterprise Inc................G..... 828 464-0221
Walkertown *(G-12316)*	Raleigh *(G-10279)*	Newton *(G-9483)*

Occasions Group Inc.............................. G 919 751-2400
Goldsboro *(G-5233)*

Occasions Group Inc.............................. E 252 321-5805
Greenville *(G-6009)*

Office Sup Svcs Inc Charlotte............... E 704 786-4677
Concord *(G-3410)*

Old Style Printing.................................. G 828 452-1122
Waynesville *(G-12466)*

Ollis Enterprises Inc............................. E 828 265-0004
Wilkesboro *(G-12648)*

Omega Studios Inc................................ G 704 889-5800
Pineville *(G-9745)*

On Demand Printing & Desi................... G 828 252-0965
Asheville *(G-560)*

On Demand Screen Printing LLC........... G 704 661-0788
Concord *(G-3413)*

Os Press LLC... G 910 485-7955
Fayetteville *(G-4649)*

Owen G Dunn Co Inc............................. G 252 633-3197
New Bern *(G-9387)*

Pamela A Adams................................... G 919 876-5949
Raleigh *(G-10355)*

Pamela Taylor....................................... G 828 692-8599
Hendersonville *(G-6234)*

Pamlico Screen Printing Inc................. G 252 944-6001
Washington *(G-12406)*

Pamor Fine Print................................... G 919 559-2846
Raleigh *(G-10356)*

Paragon ID High Point Us Inc............... E 336 882-8115
High Point *(G-6726)*

Park Communications LLC.................... D 336 292-4000
Greensboro *(G-5732)*

PBM Graphics Inc................................. C 919 544-6222
Durham *(G-4169)*

PBM Graphics Inc................................. C 336 664-5800
Greensboro *(G-5737)*

◆ PBM Graphics Inc.............................. C 919 544-6222
Durham *(G-4170)*

Performance Print Services LLC........... G 919 957-9995
Durham *(G-4173)*

Perlman Inc... F 704 332-1164
Charlotte *(G-2629)*

Person Printing Company Inc............... E 336 599-2146
Roxboro *(G-10940)*

Pharmaceutic Litho Label Inc.............. E 336 785-4000
Winston Salem *(G-13287)*

Piedmont Business Forms Inc.............. G 828 464-0010
Newton *(G-9488)*

▲ Piedmont Graphics Inc...................... E 336 230-0040
Greensboro *(G-5742)*

Pilgrim Tract Society Inc...................... G 336 495-1241
Randleman *(G-10655)*

Pilot LLC.. D 910 692-7271
Southern Pines *(G-11505)*

Pioneer Printing Company Inc............. G 336 789-4011
Mount Airy *(G-9165)*

PIP Printing & Document Servic........... G 336 222-0717
Burlington *(G-1141)*

Platesetterscom................................... 888 380-7483
Greensboro *(G-5751)*

Plum Print Inc....................................... F 828 633-5535
Asheville *(G-579)*

PMG Acquisition Corp........................... D 828 758-7381
Lenoir *(G-7634)*

Polly and Associates LLC..................... G 910 319-7564
Wilmington *(G-12880)*

Polyprint Usa Inc.................................. G 888 389-8618
Charlotte *(G-2646)*

Poole Printing Company Inc................. G 919 876-5260
Raleigh *(G-10377)*

Pope Printing & Design Inc.................. G 828 274-5945
Asheville *(G-580)*

Postal Instant Press............................. G 336 222-0717
Burlington *(G-1142)*

Powell Ink Inc....................................... F 828 253-6886
Asheville *(G-582)*

Precision Printing................................ G 252 338-2450
Elizabeth City *(G-4404)*

Precision Printing................................ G 336 273-5794
Greensboro *(G-5758)*

Pretty Paid LLC..................................... G 980 443-3876
Kings Mountain *(G-7379)*

Prime Source Opc LLC.......................... E 336 661-3300
Winston Salem *(G-13303)*

▼ Primo Inc.. G 888 822-5815
Cornelius *(G-3620)*

Print Doc Pack and.............................. G 910 454-9104
Southport *(G-11525)*

Print Express Enterprises Inc.............. G 336 765-5505
Clemmons *(G-3199)*

Print Express Inc.................................. F 910 455-4554
Jacksonville *(G-7138)*

Print Haus Inc....................................... G 828 456-8622
Waynesville *(G-12469)*

Print Management Group LLC............... F 704 821-0114
Charlotte *(G-2669)*

Print Media Associates Inc.................. G 704 529-0555
Charlotte *(G-2670)*

Print Path LLC....................................... E 828 855-9966
Hickory *(G-6417)*

Print Professionals.............................. G 607 279-3335
Pinehurst *(G-9700)*

Print Shoppe of Rocky Mt Inc.............. G 252 442-9912
Rocky Mount *(G-10862)*

Print Social.. G 980 430-4483
Huntersville *(G-7039)*

Print Usa Inc.. G 910 485-2254
Fayetteville *(G-4658)*

Print Works Fayetteville Inc................. G 910 864-8100
Fayetteville *(G-4659)*

Printcrafters Incorporated................... G 704 873-7387
Statesville *(G-11754)*

Printery... F 336 852-9774
Greensboro *(G-5764)*

Printing & Packaging Inc..................... E 704 482-3866
Shelby *(G-11371)*

Printing Partners Inc........................... G 336 996-2268
Kernersville *(G-7293)*

Printing Press....................................... G 828 299-1234
Asheville *(G-585)*

Printing Pro.. G 704 748-9396
Iron Station *(G-7106)*

Printing Svcs Greensboro Inc.............. G 336 274-7663
Greensboro *(G-5765)*

Printlogic Inc.. G 336 626-6680
Asheboro *(G-387)*

Printmarketing LLC.............................. G 828 261-0063
Hickory *(G-6418)*

Printsurge Incorporated...................... G 919 854-4376
Raleigh *(G-10396)*

Prism Printing & Design Inc................. G 919 706-5977
Cary *(G-1427)*

Pro Cal Prof Decals Inc........................ F 704 795-6090
Concord *(G-3424)*

Professional Bus Systems Inc............. G 704 333-2444
Charlotte *(G-2673)*

Professional Laminating LLC............... G 919 465-0400
Cary *(G-1429)*

Proforma Print Source.......................... G 919 383-2070
Durham *(G-4198)*

▲ Promographix Inc.............................. F 919 846-1379
Carolina Beach *(G-1263)*

Quad/Graphics Inc............................... E 706 648-5456
Charlotte *(G-2680)*

Quality Prtg Cartridge Fctry................ G 336 852-2505
Greensboro *(G-5779)*

Quick Color Solutions.......................... G 336 698-0951
Mc Leansville *(G-8226)*

Quick Color Solutions Inc.................... G 336 282-3900
Chapel Hill *(G-1564)*

Quick Print Henderson Inc................... G 252 492-8905
Henderson *(G-6173)*

Quick Print of Concord......................... G 704 782-6634
Salisbury *(G-11110)*

Quik Print Inc....................................... G 910 738-6775
Lumberton *(G-7967)*

R & D Label LLC.................................... G 336 889-2900
Jamestown *(G-7177)*

R L Lasater Printing............................. G 919 639-6662
Angier *(G-127)*

R R Donnelley & Sons Company.......... G 704 864-5717
Gastonia *(G-5131)*

R T Barbee Company Inc...................... F 704 375-4421
Charlotte *(G-2687)*

Raleigh Printing & Typing Inc.............. G 919 662-8001
Raleigh *(G-10427)*

Randall Printing Inc............................. G 336 272-3333
Greensboro *(G-5781)*

Readable Communications Inc............. G 919 876-5260
Raleigh *(G-10434)*

Red 5 Printing LLC............................... G 704 996-3848
Cornelius *(G-3623)*

Redbird Screen Printing LLC................ G 919 946-0005
Raleigh *(G-10438)*

Renascence Inc.................................... G 252 355-1636
Greenville *(G-6018)*

Richa Inc... G 704 944-0230
Charlotte *(G-2724)*

Richa Inc... F 704 331-9744
Charlotte *(G-2725)*

Rite Instant Printing Inc...................... G 336 768-5061
Winston Salem *(G-13319)*

Rodney Tyler... G 336 629-0951
Asheboro *(G-391)*

Russell Printing Inc............................. G 404 366-0552
Burlington *(G-1151)*

S Chamblee Incorporated.................... E 919 833-7561
Raleigh *(G-10452)*

S Ruppe Inc... G 828 287-4936
Rutherfordton *(G-10992)*

S&A Marketing Inc............................... G 704 376-0938
Charlotte *(G-2746)*

Salem One Inc....................................... F 336 722-2886
Kernersville *(G-7299)*

Salem One Inc....................................... C 336 744-9990
Winston Salem *(G-13325)*

Scriptorium Pubg Svcs Inc.................. G 919 481-2701
Durham *(G-4227)*

Seaside Press Co Inc............................ G 910 458-8156
Carolina Beach *(G-1264)*

Seaway Printing Company.................... G 910 457-6158
Southport *(G-11527)*

Sennett Security Products LLC............ D 336 375-1134
Browns Summit *(G-1005)*

▲ Sennett Security Products LLC......... G 336 404-3284
Greensboro *(G-5807)*

Shelby Business Cards......................... G 704 481-8341
Shelby *(G-11375)*

Sillaman & Sons Inc............................. G 919 774-6324
Sanford *(G-11233)*

Simple & Sentimental LLC................... G 252 320-9458
Ayden *(G-662)*

Sir Speedy Printing.............................. G 704 664-1911
Mooresville *(G-8771)*

Sire Tees.. G 919 787-6843
Raleigh *(G-10482)*

Smith & Fox Inc .... F 828 684-4512
Arden (G-307)

Smith Family Screen Printing .... G 336 317-4849
Pleasant Garden (G-9794)

Southern Printing Company Inc .... G 910 259-4807
Burgaw (G-1033)

Southport Graphics LLC .... G 919 650-3822
Morrisville (G-9057)

Spee Dee Que Instant Prtg Inc .... G 919 683-1307
Durham (G-4245)

Speediprint Inc .... F 910 483-2553
Fayetteville (G-4674)

Sundrop Printing .... G 704 960-1592
Kannapolis (G-7221)

Swatchcraft LLC .... G 336 434-5095
High Point (G-6798)

Sylva Herald and Ruralite .... G 828 586-2611
Sylva (G-11900)

Systel Business Eqp Co Inc .... E 336 808-8000
Greensboro (G-5849)

T & R Signs .... G 919 779-1185
Garner (G-4967)

Table Rock Printers LLC .... G 828 433-1377
Morganton (G-8904)

Tcprst LLC .... G 910 791-9767
Wilmington (G-12938)

Telepathic Graphics Inc .... F 919 342-4603
Rocky Mount (G-10815)

Theo Davis Sons Incorporated .... E 919 269-7401
Zebulon (G-13523)

Thompson Printing & Packg Inc .... G 704 313-7323
Mooresboro (G-8587)

Trejo Soccer Academy LLC .... G 336 899-7910
Asheboro (G-410)

Triad Business Card Assoc .... G 336 706-2729
Greensboro (G-5875)

Triangle Inner Vision Company .... G 919 460-6013
Morrisville (G-9076)

Triangle Solutions Inc .... G 919 481-1235
Cary (G-1473)

Tryon Newsmedia LLC .... G 828 859-9151
Tryon (G-12179)

Twigs Screen Printing .... G 910 770-1605
Tabor City (G-11916)

Twyford Printing Company Inc .... G 910 892-3271
Dunn (G-3870)

Unlimted Potential Sanford Inc .... E 919 852-1117
Morrisville (G-9083)

US Print Inc .... G 919 878-0981
Raleigh (G-10578)

Valassis Communications Inc .... D 919 544-4511
Durham (G-4294)

Valassis Communications Inc .... D 919 361-7900
Durham (G-4295)

Valdese Packaging & Label Inc .... F 828 879-9772
Valdese (G-12202)

▼ Valdese Packaging & Label Inc .... E 828 879-9772
Valdese (G-12201)

Value Printing Inc .... G 919 380-9883
Cary (G-1477)

Verticalfx Inc .... G 704 594-5000
Mooresville (G-8790)

Via Prnting Graphic Design Inc .... G 919 872-8688
Youngsville (G-13497)

Victory Press LLC .... G 704 660-0348
Mooresville (G-8792)

Village Graphics .... G 252 745-4600
Oriental (G-9603)

Village Instant Printing Inc .... G 919 968-0000
Chapel Hill (G-1591)

Village Printing Co .... F 336 629-0951
Asheboro (G-417)

W B Mason Co Inc .... E 888 926-2766
Charlotte (G-2994)

Wallace Printing Inc .... F 828 466-3300
Newton (G-9509)

Walter Printing Company Inc .... G 704 982-8899
Albemarle (G-96)

Wayne Trademark Prtg Packg LLC .... E 800 327-1290
Asheboro (G-419)

Weber and Weber Inc .... G 336 889-6322
High Point (G-6833)

Weber and Weber Inc .... F 336 722-4109
Winston Salem (G-13387)

Welloyt Enterprises Inc .... G 919 821-7897
Raleigh (G-10604)

Westrock Rkt LLC .... B 770 448-2193
Marion (G-8073)

Whatever You Need Screen Print .... G 704 287-8603
Concord (G-3467)

Whimsical Prints Paper & Gifts .... G 919 544-8491
Durham (G-4304)

▲ Whistle Stop Press Inc .... F 910 695-1403
Southern Pines (G-11514)

Whitney Screen Printing .... G 910 673-0309
Eagle Springs (G-4321)

Wick Communications Co .... E 252 537-2505
Roanoke Rapids (G-10747)

▲ William George Printing LLC .... E 910 221-2700
Hope Mills (G-6928)

Williams Printing LLC .... E 336 969-2733
Rural Hall (G-10969)

Wilsons Planning & Consulting .... G 919 592-0935
Garner (G-4974)

Wright Printing Service Inc .... G 336 427-4768
Madison (G-8004)

◆ Xpres LLC .... E 336 245-1596
Winston Salem (G-13408)

Xtreme Postcard Profits System .... G 919 894-8886
Benson (G-800)

Your Source For Printing .... G 704 957-5922
Charlotte (G-3041)

Zebra Communications Inc .... E 919 314-3700
Morrisville (G-9093)

2754 Commercial printing, gravure

AEL Services LLC .... E 704 525-3710
Charlotte (G-1626)

Amber Alert International Tm .... G 919 641-8773
Raleigh (G-9895)

Appalachian State University .... G 828 262-7497
Boone (G-895)

Arzberger Engravers Inc .... E 704 376-1151
Charlotte (G-1702)

Big Fish Dpi .... G 704 545-8112
Mint Hill (G-8331)

Business Wise Inc .... G 704 554-4112
Charlotte (G-1822)

Executive Promotions Inc .... F 704 663-4000
Mooresville (G-8661)

Huntpack Inc .... G 704 986-0684
Albemarle (G-78)

Linprint Company .... F 910 763-5103
Wilmington (G-12837)

▲ Master Screens South LLC .... G 704 226-9600
Monroe (G-8525)

◆ Shamrock Corporation .... C 336 574-4200
Greensboro (G-5809)

▲ Sharpe Co .... E 336 724-2871
Winston Salem (G-13333)

Synthomer Inc .... D 704 225-1872
Monroe (G-8567)

US Print Inc .... G 919 878-0981
Raleigh (G-10578)

2759 Commercial printing, nec

1st Choice Activewear II LLC .... E 704 528-7814
Mooresville (G-8588)

822tees Inc .... G 910 822-8337
Fayetteville (G-4541)

A A Logo Gear .... G 704 795-7100
Concord (G-3307)

A B C Screenprinting and EMB .... G 704 937-3452
Grover (G-6041)

Aardvark Screen Printing .... G 919 829-9058
Raleigh (G-9861)

Abe Entercom Holdings LLC .... G 336 691-4337
Greensboro (G-5337)

AC Valor Reyes LLC .... G 910 431-3256
Castle Hayne (G-1493)

Acculink .... F 252 321-5805
Greenville (G-5934)

Acorn Printing .... G 704 868-4522
Bessemer City (G-801)

ADS N Art Screenprinting & EMB .... G 919 453-0400
Wake Forest (G-12258)

Advantage Marketing .... G 919 872-8610
Louisburg (G-7908)

AEL Services LLC .... E 704 525-3710
Charlotte (G-1626)

All Stick Label LLC .... G 336 659-4660
Winston Salem (G-13080)

Ambrose Signs Inc .... G 252 338-8522
Camden (G-1210)

American Label Tech LLC .... F 984 269-5078
Garner (G-4915)

American Multimedia Inc .... D 336 229-7101
Burlington (G-1045)

American Solutions For Bu .... G 919 848-2442
Raleigh (G-9898)

Amped Events LLC .... F 888 683-4386
Gastonia (G-4994)

▲ Anilox Roll Company Inc .... G 704 588-1809
Charlotte (G-1678)

Appalachian State University .... F 828 262-2047
Boone (G-896)

Aquarius Designs & Logo Wear .... G 919 821-4646
Raleigh (G-9909)

Arden Engraving US Inc .... G 704 547-4581
Charlotte (G-1694)

Armac Inc .... F 919 878-9836
Raleigh (G-9916)

Arrowhead Graphics Inc .... G 336 274-2419
Greensboro (G-5370)

Art Enterprises Inc .... G 828 277-1211
Asheville (G-431)

Art House .... G 919 552-7327
Fuquay Varina (G-4867)

Artcraft Press Inc .... G 828 397-8612
Icard (G-7064)

Arzberger Engravers Inc .... E 704 376-1151
Charlotte (G-1702)

Asheville Color & Imaging Inc .... G 828 774-5040
Asheville (G-435)

Asheville Promo LLC .... G 828 575-2767
Asheville (G-441)

Austin Business Forms Inc .... F 704 821-6165
Indian Trail (G-7070)

Avant Publications LLC .... G 704 897-6048
Mooresville (G-8603)

▲ Banknote Corp America Inc .... C 336 375-1134
Browns Summit (G-990)

Bender Apparel & Signs Inc .... G 252 636-8337
New Bern (G-9340)

Black Collection Apparel LLC .... G 919 716-5183
Sanford (G-11156)

Blp Products and Services Inc	G	704 899-5505	
Pineville *(G-9716)*			
Body Billboards Inc	G	919 544-4540	
Durham *(G-3936)*			
Bradleys Inc	E	704 484-2077	
Shelby *(G-11314)*			
Brunswick Screen Prtg & EMB	G	910 579-1234	
Ocean Isle Beach *(G-9586)*			
Bryan Austin	336 841-6573	
High Point *(G-6551)*			
Business Mogul LLC	G	919 605-2165	
Raleigh *(G-9962)*			
C & M Enterprise Inc	G	704 545-1180	
Mint Hill *(G-8333)*			
Carolina Classifiedscom LLC	D	704 246-0900	
Monroe *(G-8452)*			
Carolina Printing Co	G	919 834-0433	
Princeton *(G-9823)*			
Carolina Sgns Grphic Dsgns Inc	G	919 383-3344	
Durham *(G-3962)*			
Carolina Tailors Inc	G	252 247-6469	
Newport *(G-9439)*			
Carter Publishing Company Inc	F	336 993-2161	
Kernersville *(G-7253)*			
▲ Castle Shirt Company LLC	G	336 992-7727	
Kernersville *(G-7254)*			
◆ Causekeepers Inc	E	336 824-2518	
Franklinville *(G-4855)*			
▲ CCL Label	F	919 713-0388	
Raleigh *(G-9988)*			
CCL Label Inc	C	704 714-4800	
Charlotte *(G-1877)*			
CCL Label Inc	D	919 713-0388	
Fuquay Varina *(G-4872)*			
Circle Graphics Inc	C	919 864-4518	
Raleigh *(G-9995)*			
Comedycd	336 273-0077	
Greensboro *(G-5458)*			
Concord Printing Company Inc	G	704 786-3717	
Concord *(G-3342)*			
Consumer Concepts	F	252 247-7000	
Morehead City *(G-8828)*			
Contagious Graphics Inc	E	704 529-5600	
Charlotte *(G-1977)*			
Contract Printing & Graphics	G	919 832-7178	
Raleigh *(G-10014)*			
Cranford Silk Screen Prcess In	F	336 434-6544	
Archdale *(G-219)*			
Crazie Tees	G	704 898-2272	
Mount Holly *(G-9226)*			
Creative Printers Inc	336 246-7746	
West Jefferson *(G-12563)*			
Creative Screening	G	919 467-5081	
Cary *(G-1338)*			
Creative T-Shirts Imaging LLC	G	919 828-0204	
Raleigh *(G-10020)*			
Crystal Impressions Ltd	F	704 821-7678	
Indian Trail *(G-7076)*			
Dale Advertising Inc	G	704 484-0971	
Shelby *(G-11329)*			
Daniels Business Services Inc	E	828 277-8250	
Asheville *(G-483)*			
Datamark Graphics Inc	E	336 629-0267	
Asheboro *(G-345)*			
David Presnell	336 372-5989	
Sparta *(G-11537)*			
Davis Vogler Enterprises LLC	G	402 257-7188	
Charlotte *(G-2022)*			
DB CUSTOM CRAFTS LLC	F	336 867-4107	
Winston Salem *(G-13140)*			
Dbt Coatings LLC	G	336 834-9700	
Greensboro *(G-5489)*			

▲ Deep South Holding Company Inc	D	336 427-0265	
Madison *(G-7986)*			
Digital Print & Imaging Inc	G	910 341-3005	
Greenville *(G-5965)*			
Digital Printing Systems Inc	E	704 525-0190	
Charlotte *(G-2047)*			
Digitaurus Inc	G	910 794-9243	
Wilmington *(G-12765)*			
Dime EMB LLC	F	336 765-0910	
Winston Salem *(G-13146)*			
Document Directs Inc	G	919 829-8810	
Raleigh *(G-10053)*			
Docusource North Carolina LLC	E	919 459-5900	
Morrisville *(G-8968)*			
Draft DOT International LLC	G	336 775-0525	
Lexington *(G-7680)*			
▼ Dtbtla Inc	F	336 769-0000	
Greensboro *(G-5506)*			
Dynagraphics Screenprintng	G	919 212-2898	
Holly Springs *(G-6899)*			
East Coast Designs LLC	G	910 865-1070	
Fayetteville *(G-4592)*			
Easter Seals Ucp NC & VA Inc	D	919 856-0250	
Raleigh *(G-10070)*			
Eatumup Lure Company Inc	G	336 218-0896	
Greensboro *(G-5511)*			
Edge Promo Team LLC	E	919 946-4218	
Clayton *(G-3145)*			
Electronic Imaging Svcs Inc	F	704 587-3323	
Charlotte *(G-2095)*			
Endaxi Company Inc	G	919 467-8895	
Morrisville *(G-8972)*			
Epic Apparel	G	980 335-0463	
Charlotte *(G-2123)*			
Expressive Screen Printing	G	910 739-3221	
Lumberton *(G-7952)*			
EZ Custom Screen Printing	E	704 821-8488	
Matthews *(G-8167)*			
EZ Custom Scrnprinting EMB Inc	G	704 821-9641	
Matthews *(G-8168)*			
F C C LLC	G	336 883-7314	
High Point *(G-6617)*			
Fabrix Inc	G	704 953-1239	
Charlotte *(G-2141)*			
▲ Fayetteville Publishing Co	E	910 323-4848	
Fayetteville *(G-4601)*			
◆ Finch Industries Incorporated	D	336 472-4499	
Thomasville *(G-12024)*			
First Impressions Ltd	F	704 536-3622	
Charlotte *(G-2156)*			
Flint Group US LLC	F	828 687-2485	
Arden *(G-272)*			
Funny Bone EMB & Screening	G	704 663-4711	
Mooresville *(G-8668)*			
Galloreecom	G	704 644-0978	
Charlotte *(G-2186)*			
Garage Shop LLC	F	980 500-0583	
Denver *(G-3784)*			
Geographics Screenprinting Inc	G	704 357-3300	
Charlotte *(G-2209)*			
Gibraltar Packaging Inc	C	910 439-6137	
Whitsett *(G-12608)*			
Gilmore Globl Lgstics Svcs Inc	D	919 277-2700	
Morrisville *(G-8982)*			
Gmg Group LLC	G	252 441-8374	
Kill Devil Hills *(G-7317)*			
Go Postal In Boone Inc	F	828 262-0027	
Boone *(G-917)*			
◆ Golf Associates Advertising Co	G	828 252-6544	
Asheville *(G-508)*			
Graphic Image of Cape Fear Inc	G	910 313-6768	
Wilmington *(G-12795)*			

Graphixx Screen Printing Inc	G	919 736-3995	
Goldsboro *(G-5219)*			
Graveoke Inc	E	704 534-3480	
Charlotte *(G-2233)*			
Herald Printing Inc	G	252 726-3534	
Morehead City *(G-8835)*			
Hickory Printing Solutions LLC	B	828 465-3431	
Conover *(G-3530)*			
High Performance Marketing Inc	G	919 870-9915	
Raleigh *(G-10167)*			
Home Team Athletics Inc	G	910 938-0862	
Jacksonville *(G-7126)*			
Hunsucker Printing Co Inc	G	336 629-9125	
Asheboro *(G-363)*			
▲ Ics North America Corp	E	704 794-6620	
Concord *(G-3375)*			
ID Images LLC	G	704 494-0444	
Charlotte *(G-2309)*			
Identify Yourself LLC	F	252 202-1452	
Kitty Hawk *(G-7445)*			
Image Designs Ink LLC	G	252 235-1964	
Bailey *(G-671)*			
Imagemark Business Svcs Inc	G	704 865-4912	
Gastonia *(G-5062)*			
Imprinting Systems Spcalty Inc	G	704 527-4545	
Charlotte *(G-2317)*			
Infinity S End Inc	F	704 900-8355	
Charlotte *(G-2328)*			
Ingalls Alton	G	252 975-2056	
Washington *(G-12394)*			
Ink n Stitches LLC	G	336 633-3898	
Asheboro *(G-365)*			
Inniah Production Incorporated	G	828 765-6800	
Spruce Pine *(G-11578)*			
Inspire Creative Studios Inc	G	910 395-0200	
Wilmington *(G-12818)*			
J C Lawrence Co	G	919 553-3044	
Oriental *(G-9600)*			
Jax Brothers Inc	G	704 732-3351	
Lincolnton *(G-7834)*			
Jubilee Screen Printing Inc	G	910 673-4240	
West End *(G-12555)*			
K & K Stitch & Screen	G	336 246-5477	
West Jefferson *(G-12565)*			
▲ Kalajdzic Inc	F	855 465-4225	
Clemmons *(G-3196)*			
Kannapolis Awards and Graphics	G	704 224-3695	
Kannapolis *(G-7213)*			
Katchi Tees Incorporated	G	252 315-4691	
Wilson *(G-12997)*			
Kathie S Mc Daniel	G	336 835-1544	
Elkin *(G-4446)*			
▲ Keiger Inc	E	336 760-0099	
Winston Salem *(G-13223)*			
Kelleys Sports and Awards Inc	G	828 728-4600	
Hudson *(G-6952)*			
Kimballs Screen Print Inc	G	704 636-0488	
Salisbury *(G-11079)*			
King Business Service Inc	G	910 610-1030	
Laurinburg *(G-7504)*			
Kna	G	704 847-4280	
Charlotte *(G-2400)*			
Kraftsman Tactical Inc	G	336 465-3576	
Albemarle *(G-79)*			
Kraken-Skulls	F	910 500-9100	
Fayetteville *(G-4627)*			
Label & Printing Solutions Inc	G	919 782-1242	
Raleigh *(G-10243)*			
Label Printing Systems Inc	E	336 760-3271	
Winston Salem *(G-13230)*			
Labels Tags & Inserts Inc	F	336 227-8485	
Burlington *(G-1117)*			

Lake Norman EMB & Monogramming.... G ..... 704 892-8450 Cornelius *(G-3612)*	Multi Packaging Solutions......................A ..... 336 855-7142 Greensboro *(G-5699)*	Pro Cal Prof Decals Inc......................... F ..... 704 795-6090 Concord *(G-3424)*
Lakeside Cstm Tees & Embroider....... G ..... 704 274-3730 Cornelius *(G-3613)*	Multi-Color Corporation......................E ..... 828 658-6800 Weaverville *(G-12498)*	Product Identification Inc......................E ..... 919 544-4136 Durham *(G-4197)*
Laniers Screen Printing......................... G ..... 336 857-2699 Denton *(G-3753)*	Mundo Uniformes LLC......................... G ..... 704 287-1527 Charlotte *(G-2531)*	Professional Laminating LLC................ G ..... 919 465-0400 Cary *(G-1430)*
Laru Industries Inc............................... G ..... 704 821-7503 Indian Trail *(G-7087)*	Napoleon James................................. G ..... 413 331-9560 Charlotte *(G-2542)*	Proforma Hanson Branding................. G ..... 210 437-3061 High Point *(G-6749)*
▲ Laser Ink Corporation......................E ..... 919 361-5822 Durham *(G-4101)*	National Sign & Decal Inc.................... G ..... 828 478-2123 Sherrills Ford *(G-11393)*	Progressive Graphics Inc..................... F ..... 919 821-3223 Raleigh *(G-10402)*
Laurel of Asheville LLC...................... F ..... 828 670-7503 Asheville *(G-533)*	New Drections Screen Prtrs Inc........... G ..... 704 393-1769 Charlotte *(G-2556)*	Promothreads Inc................................ G ..... 704 248-0942 Cornelius *(G-3621)*
LDR Designs...................................... G ..... 252 375-4484 Greenville *(G-6001)*	News & Record Commercial Prtg........... F ..... 336 373-7300 Greensboro *(G-5708)*	Queen City Screen Printers................. G ..... 980 335-2334 Charlotte *(G-2685)*
Legend-Tees...................................... G ..... 828 585-2066 Arden *(G-282)*	Nvizion Inc.. G ..... 336 985-3862 King *(G-7334)*	▲ Queensboro Industries Inc............... C ..... 910 251-1251 Wilmington *(G-12893)*
Living Intntionally For Excell.............E ..... 810 600-3425 Cary *(G-1391)*	One Source Document Solutions........... G ..... 336 482-2360 Greensboro *(G-5723)*	Quik Print Inc.................................... G ..... 910 738-6775 Lumberton *(G-7967)*
Logo Dogz.. G ..... 888 827-8866 Monroe *(G-8519)*	Orlandos Cstm Design T-Shirts............ G ..... 919 220-5515 Durham *(G-4160)*	R R Donnelley & Sons Company........... E ..... 919 596-8942 Durham *(G-4205)*
Logo Label Printing Company.............. G ..... 919 309-0007 Durham *(G-4109)*	Owen G Dunn Co Inc.......................... G ..... 252 633-3197 New Bern *(G-9387)*	R R Donnelley & Sons Company........... D ..... 252 243-0337 Wilson *(G-13018)*
Logo Wear Graphics LLC..................... F ..... 336 382-0455 Summerfield *(G-11841)*	Pages Screen Printing LLC.................. G ..... 336 759-7979 Winston Salem *(G-13274)*	Ragg Co Inc....................................... G ..... 336 838-4895 North Wilkesboro *(G-9550)*
Logonation Inc.................................E ..... 704 799-0612 Mooresville *(G-8714)*	Paraclete Xp Sky Venture LLC.............. F ..... 910 848-2600 Raeford *(G-9844)*	Raleigh Engraving Co......................... G ..... 919 832-5557 Raleigh *(G-10423)*
Lsg LLC... F ..... 919 878-5500 Wallace *(G-12322)*	Paraclete Xp Skyventure LLC.............E ..... 910 904-0027 Raeford *(G-9845)*	Reliance Management Group Inc........... F ..... 704 282-2255 Monroe *(G-8551)*
M-Prints Inc....................................... G ..... 828 265-4929 Boone *(G-931)*	Paradigm Solutions Inc....................... G ..... 910 392-2611 Wilmington *(G-12871)*	Rikki Tikki Tees................................. G ..... 828 454-0515 Waynesville *(G-12470)*
Magnet America Intl Inc......................E ..... 336 985-0320 King *(G-7330)*	Paradise Printers................................ G ..... 336 570-2922 Burlington *(G-1138)*	Rogers Screenprinting EMB Inc............ G ..... 910 738-6208 Lumberton *(G-7971)*
Magnet Guys..................................... G ..... 855 624-4897 Asheboro *(G-375)*	Paragon ID High Point Us Inc.............E ..... 336 882-8115 High Point *(G-6726)*	Russell Printing Inc............................ G ..... 404 366-0552 Burlington *(G-1151)*
Make An Impression Inc...................... G ..... 919 557-7400 Holly Springs *(G-6907)*	Park Communications LLC.................. D ..... 336 292-4000 Greensboro *(G-5732)*	Salem One Inc.................................... C ..... 336 744-9990 Winston Salem *(G-13325)*
Mass Connection Inc.......................... G ..... 910 424-0940 Fayetteville *(G-4636)*	Park Communications LLC.................. G ..... 919 852-1117 Raleigh *(G-10358)*	Screen Printers Unlimited LLC............. G ..... 336 667-8737 Wilkesboro *(G-12650)*
Masters Hand Print Works Inc.............. G ..... 828 652-5833 Marion *(G-8051)*	Party Time Inc.................................... G ..... 910 454-4577 Southport *(G-11524)*	Screen Specialty Shop Inc.................. G ..... 336 982-4135 West Jefferson *(G-12570)*
Max B Smith Jr.................................. G ..... 828 434-0238 Boone *(G-933)*	Pharmaceutic Litho Label Inc.............E ..... 336 785-4000 Winston Salem *(G-13287)*	Sharpe Images Properties Inc.............E ..... 336 724-2871 Winston Salem *(G-13334)*
▲ Maxim Label Packg High Pt Inc......... F ..... 336 861-1666 High Point *(G-6708)*	Piedmont Business Forms Inc.............. G ..... 828 464-0010 Newton *(G-9488)*	Silkscreen Specialists........................ G ..... 910 353-8859 Jacksonville *(G-7144)*
Mb-F Inc... D ..... 336 379-9352 Greensboro *(G-5685)*	Piedmont Publishing........................... G ..... 336 727-4099 Winston Salem *(G-13293)*	Silverlining Screen Prtrs Inc................ G ..... 919 554-0340 Youngsville *(G-13485)*
McCotter Industries Inc...................... F ..... 704 282-2102 Monroe *(G-8529)*	Pinkston Properties LLC...................... G ..... 828 252-9867 Asheville *(G-575)*	Skipper Graphics............................... G ..... 910 754-8729 Shallotte *(G-11305)*
McLamb Group Inc............................. G ..... 704 333-1171 Charlotte *(G-2480)*	Plasticard Products Inc...................... F ..... 828 665-7774 Asheville *(G-576)*	Sml Raleigh LLC................................ G ..... 919 585-0100 Clayton *(G-3170)*
Measurement Incorporated................. D ..... 919 683-2413 Durham *(G-4122)*	Poole Printing Company Inc................. G ..... 919 876-5260 Raleigh *(G-10377)*	Southern Engraving Company.............. G ..... 336 656-0084 High Point *(G-6787)*
▲ Medlit Solutions LLC....................... D ..... 919 878-6789 Garner *(G-4942)*	Pop Designs Mktg Solutions LLC........... G ..... 336 444-4033 Mount Airy *(G-9166)*	Spectrum Screen Prtg Svc Inc............. F ..... 919 481-9905 Garner *(G-4966)*
▼ Mega Media Concepts Ltd Lblty....... G ..... 973 919-5661 Brevard *(G-975)*	Poteet Printing Systems LLC.............. D ..... 704 588-0005 Charlotte *(G-2647)*	Spiral Graphics Inc............................ G ..... 919 571-3371 Raleigh *(G-10499)*
Memories of Orangeburg Inc................ G ..... 803 533-0035 Mooresville *(G-8722)*	Pre Flight Inc.................................... G ..... 828 758-1138 Lenoir *(G-7636)*	Squeegee Tees & More Inc................. G ..... 704 888-0336 Midland *(G-8297)*
Merch Connect Studios Inc.................. G ..... 336 501-6722 Greensboro *(G-5690)*	Prince Manufacturing Corp.................. G ..... 828 681-8860 Mills River *(G-8320)*	▲ St Johns Packaging Usa LLC........... C ..... 336 292-9911 Greensboro *(G-5833)*
Millenium Print Group......................... G ..... 919 818-1229 Greensboro *(G-5693)*	Print Express Inc............................... F ..... 910 455-4554 Jacksonville *(G-7138)*	Steves TS & Uniforms Inc................... G ..... 919 554-4221 Wake Forest *(G-12304)*
Miller Products Inc............................E ..... 704 587-1870 Charlotte *(G-2505)*	Print Haus Inc.................................... G ..... 828 456-8622 Waynesville *(G-12469)*	STS Screen Printing Inc...................... G ..... 704 821-8488 Matthews *(G-8195)*
More Than Just Art Inc........................ G ..... 910 864-7797 Fayetteville *(G-4643)*	Printcraft Company Inc...................... D ..... 336 248-2544 Lexington *(G-7734)*	◆ Stump Printing Co Inc......................C ..... 260 723-5171 Wrightsville Beach *(G-13433)*
Motorsports Designs Inc..................... F ..... 336 454-1181 High Point *(G-6716)*	Printful Inc.. F ..... 818 351-7181 Charlotte *(G-2671)*	Substance Incorporated...................... G ..... 800 985-9485 Claremont *(G-3122)*
Mountaineer Inc................................ G ..... 828 452-0661 Waynesville *(G-12464)*	Printing Press.................................... G ..... 828 299-1234 Asheville *(G-585)*	Subtle Impressions Inc......................E Gastonia *(G-5145)*
Moving Screens Incorporated.............. G ..... 336 364-9259 Rougemont *(G-10914)*	Printing Svcs Greensboro Inc.............. G ..... 336 274-7663 Greensboro *(G-5765)*	Supreme T-Shirts & Apparel................E ..... 919 772-9040 Raleigh *(G-10522)*

T S Designs Incorporated...................E 336 226-5694
Burlington (G-1167)

T T S D Productions LLC........................G 704 829-6666
Belmont (G-770)

▲ Tannis Root Productions Inc............G 919 832-8552
Raleigh (G-10533)

Team Connection.................................G 336 287-3892
Winston Salem (G-13359)

TEC Graphics Inc.................................F 919 567-2077
Fuquay Varina (G-4901)

Tef Inc..G 704 786-9577
Concord (G-3455)

Telepathic Graphics Inc.......................E 919 342-4603
Raleigh (G-10540)

Tennessee Nedgraphics Inc.................F 704 414-4224
Charlotte (G-2908)

Theo Davis Sons Incorporated............E 919 269-7401
Zebulon (G-13523)

Third Street Screen Print Inc...............G 919 365-2725
Wendell (G-12550)

Thomco Inc..G 336 292-3300
Greensboro (G-5863)

Thompson Screen Prints Inc................E 704 209-6161
Rockwell (G-10804)

Tickets Plus Inc....................................E 616 222-4000
Morrisville (G-9072)

▲ Timeplanner Calendars Inc.............C 704 377-0024
Charlotte (G-2920)

Times Printing Company Inc................G 252 441-2223
Kill Devil Hills (G-7320)

TNT Web & Grafix LLC.........................G 252 289-8846
Nashville (G-9324)

Touch Tone Tees LLC...........................G 919 358-5536
Raleigh (G-10553)

Triad Printing NC Inc...........................G 336 422-8752
Greensboro (G-5878)

Twyford Printing Company Inc............G 910 892-3271
Dunn (G-3870)

Uniforms Galore...................................G 252 975-5878
Washington (G-12417)

Valassis Communications Inc.............D 919 544-4511
Durham (G-4294)

Valassis Communications Inc.............D 919 361-7900
Durham (G-4295)

Valdese Packaging & Label Inc...........F 828 879-9772
Valdese (G-12202)

▼ Valdese Packaging & Label Inc.......E 828 879-9772
Valdese (G-12201)

Visigraphix Inc.....................................G 336 882-1935
Colfax (G-3292)

Vision Envelope Inc.............................F 704 392-9090
Charlotte (G-2986)

Walgreen Co...G 704 525-2628
Charlotte (G-3001)

We Print T-Shirts Inc............................G 910 822-8337
Fayetteville (G-4698)

Western Roto Engravers Incorporated..E 336 275-9821
Greensboro (G-5916)

Westmoreland Printers Inc...................F 704 482-9100
Shelby (G-11391)

Winso Dsgns Screenprinting LLC.........G 704 967-5776
Charlotte (G-3022)

Winston Printing Company...................D 336 896-7631
Winston Salem (G-13399)

Wooten Graphics Inc............................G 336 731-4650
Welcome (G-12517)

▲ Wright of Thomasville Inc...............F 336 472-4200
Thomasville (G-12091)

Xpertees Prfmce Screen Prtg...............G 910 763-7703
Wilmington (G-12955)

Yourlogowear.......................................G 704 664-1290
Cornelius (G-3631)

Zoom Apparel Inc.................................G 336 993-9666
Winston Salem (G-13413)

2761 Manifold business forms

▲ American Forms Mfg Inc..................E 704 866-9139
Gastonia (G-4991)

Apperson Inc..E 704 399-2571
Charlotte (G-1685)

Fain Enterprises Inc.............................G 336 724-0417
Winston Salem (G-13163)

◆ Golf Associates Advertising Co.........E 828 252-6544
Asheville (G-508)

Holley Selinda......................................G 919 351-9466
Raleigh (G-10171)

Print Haus Inc......................................G 828 456-8622
Waynesville (G-12469)

R R Donnelley & Sons Company...........G 704 864-5717
Gastonia (G-5131)

Reynolds and Reynolds Company........G 321 287-3939
Charlotte (G-2721)

S Ruppe Inc..G 828 287-4936
Rutherfordton (G-10992)

Taylor Communications Inc.................F 336 841-7700
High Point (G-6803)

Taylor Communications Inc.................E 704 282-0989
Monroe (G-8568)

2771 Greeting cards

Walgreen Co...G 704 525-2628
Charlotte (G-3001)

Wit & Whistle.......................................G 919 609-5309
Cary (G-1485)

2782 Blankbooks and looseleaf binders

Alpha Mailing Service Inc....................F 704 484-1711
Shelby (G-11310)

American Sample House Inc.................G 704 276-1970
Vale (G-12207)

Binders Incorporated...........................F 704 377-9704
Charlotte (G-1783)

Blissfull Memories...............................G 336 903-1835
North Wilkesboro (G-9523)

Carolina Swatching Inc........................F 828 327-9499
Hickory (G-6288)

Clarke Harland Corp.............................G 210 697-8888
High Point (G-6570)

Deluxe Corporation..............................F 336 851-4600
Greensboro (G-5494)

Design Concepts Incorporated............F 336 887-1932
High Point (G-6590)

▲ E Feibusch Company Inc.................E 336 434-5095
High Point (G-6600)

Focusales Inc.......................................G 919 614-3076
Raleigh (G-10115)

▲ Napco Inc...C 336 372-5214
Sparta (G-11540)

Premedia Group LLC............................F 336 274-2421
Greensboro (G-5761)

Printing Press.......................................G 828 299-1234
Asheville (G-585)

Stamping & Scrapbooking Rm Inc.......G 336 389-9538
Greensboro (G-5835)

Swatchworks Inc..................................G 336 626-9971
Asheboro (G-401)

Synq Marketing Group LLC..................F 800 380-6360
Charlotte (G-2892)

Visual Products Inc..............................F 336 883-0156
High Point (G-6828)

2789 Bookbinding and related work

Adpress Printing Incorporated.............G 336 294-2244
Summerfield (G-11835)

American Multimedia Inc.....................D 336 229-7101
Burlington (G-1045)

American Sample House Inc.................G 704 276-1970
Vale (G-12207)

Appalachian State University...............F 828 262-2047
Boone (G-896)

Arzberger Engravers Inc......................E 704 376-1151
Charlotte (G-1702)

Associated Printing & Svcs Inc...........G 828 286-9064
Rutherfordton (G-10975)

Atlantis Graphics Inc...........................E 919 361-5809
Durham (G-3904)

Bennett & Associates Inc....................G 919 477-7362
Durham (G-3925)

Boingo Graphics Inc............................E 704 527-4963
Charlotte (G-1797)

Book Lover Search................................G 336 889-6127
High Point (G-6549)

BP Solutions Group Inc........................E 828 252-4476
Asheville (G-460)

Carolina Swatching Inc........................F 828 327-9499
Hickory (G-6288)

Coastal Press Inc.................................G 252 726-1549
Morehead City (G-8827)

Creative Services Usa Inc....................G 336 887-1958
High Point (G-6580)

David Presnell......................................G 336 372-5989
Sparta (G-11537)

Docusource North Carolina LLC..........E 919 459-5900
Morrisville (G-8968)

Dokja Inc..G 336 852-5190
Greensboro (G-5500)

▲ E Feibusch Company Inc.................E 336 434-5095
High Point (G-6600)

Etherngton Cnservation Ctr Inc............E 336 665-1317
Greensboro (G-5525)

Flash Printing Company Inc.................E 704 375-2474
Charlotte (G-2159)

Flex Finishing Inc................................G 704 342-3600
Charlotte (G-2162)

Free Will Bptst Press Fndtion...............F 252 746-6128
Ayden (G-657)

Gik Inc..F 919 872-9498
Raleigh (G-10133)

Hickory Printing Solutions LLC............B 828 465-3431
Conover (G-3530)

◆ Holt Sublimation Printing................G 336 222-3600
Burlington (G-1104)

Itek Graphics LLC.................................E 704 357-6002
Concord (G-3383)

Jag Graphics Inc...................................G 828 259-9020
Asheville (G-527)

Joseph C Woodard Prtg Co Inc............F 919 829-0634
Raleigh (G-10221)

▲ Keiger Inc...E 336 760-0099
Winston Salem (G-13223)

Kreber...D 336 861-2700
High Point (G-6686)

Lee County Industries Inc....................G 919 775-3439
Sanford (G-11205)

Loftin & Company Inc..........................E 704 393-9393
Charlotte (G-2431)

Measurement Incorporated..................D 919 683-2413
Durham (G-4122)

▲ Medlit Solutions LLC........................D 919 878-6789
Garner (G-4942)

Occasions Group Inc............................E 252 321-5805
Greenville (G-6009)

Ollis Enterprises Inc.............................E 828 265-0004
Wilkesboro (G-12648)

Owen G Dunn Co Inc............................G 252 633-3197
New Bern (G-9387)

S
I
C

Pamela A Adams................................ G 919 876-5949
   Raleigh (G-10355)

Park Communications LLC................ D 336 292-4000
   Greensboro (G-5732)

Person Printing Company Inc............ E 336 599-2146
   Roxboro (G-10940)

Piedmont Business Forms Inc........... G 828 464-0010
   Newton (G-9488)

Postal Instant Press......................... G 336 222-0717
   Burlington (G-1142)

Powell Ink Inc.................................. F 828 253-6886
   Asheville (G-582)

Printing Svcs Greensboro Inc........... G 336 274-7663
   Greensboro (G-5765)

Quality Prtg Cartridge Fctry.............. G 336 852-2505
   Greensboro (G-5779)

S Chamblee Incorporated................. E 919 833-7561
   Raleigh (G-10452)

S Ruppe Inc..................................... G 828 287-4936
   Rutherfordton (G-10992)

▲ Sampletech Inc............................ F 336 882-1717
   High Point (G-6763)

Subtle Impressions Inc..................... E
   Gastonia (G-5145)

Three Trees Bindery......................... G 704 724-9409
   Charlotte (G-2917)

Trejo Soccer Academy LLC.............. G 336 899-7910
   Asheboro (G-410)

▲ Unique Collating & Bindery Svc........ E 336 664-0960
   Greensboro (G-5889)

Weber and Weber Inc....................... F 336 722-4109
   Winston Salem (G-13387)

2791 Typesetting

Advertising Design Systems Inc........ G 828 264-8060
   Boone (G-894)

American Multimedia Inc.................. D 336 229-7101
   Burlington (G-1045)

Appalachian State University............ F 828 262-2047
   Boone (G-896)

Atlantis Graphics Inc........................ E 919 361-5809
   Durham (G-3904)

Austin Printing Company Inc............ G 704 289-1445
   Monroe (G-8437)

Baicy Communications Inc................ G 336 722-7768
   Winston Salem (G-13101)

Bennett & Associates Inc................. G 919 477-7362
   Durham (G-3925)

Boingo Graphics Inc......................... E 704 527-4963
   Charlotte (G-1797)

BP Solutions Group Inc.................... E 828 252-4476
   Asheville (G-460)

Coastal Press Inc............................. G 252 726-1549
   Morehead City (G-8827)

▲ CPS Resources Inc....................... E 704 628-7678
   Indian Trail (G-7075)

Creative Printing Inc......................... G 828 265-2800
   Boone (G-909)

Dokja Inc... G 336 852-5190
   Greensboro (G-5500)

F C C LLC....................................... G 336 883-7314
   High Point (G-6617)

▲ Fayetteville Publishing Co............. E 910 323-4848
   Fayetteville (G-4601)

Flash Printing Company Inc............. E 704 375-2474
   Charlotte (G-2159)

Free Will Bptst Press Fndtion........... F 252 746-6128
   Ayden (G-657)

Gik Inc... F 919 872-9498
   Raleigh (G-10133)

Greensboro News & Record LLC...... A 336 373-7000
   Greensboro (G-5577)

Hickory Printing Solutions LLC......... B 828 465-3431
   Conover (G-3530)

Ips.. G 704 788-3327
   Concord (G-3381)

Jag Graphics Inc.............................. G 828 259-9020
   Asheville (G-527)

Jones Media..................................... G 828 264-3612
   Boone (G-928)

Joseph C Woodard Prtg Co Inc........ F 919 829-0634
   Raleigh (G-10221)

Kathie S Mc Daniel.......................... G 336 835-1544
   Elkin (G-4446)

▲ Keiger Inc.................................... E 336 760-0099
   Winston Salem (G-13223)

Loftin & Company Inc....................... E 704 393-9393
   Charlotte (G-2431)

Measurement Incorporated............... D 919 683-2413
   Durham (G-4122)

▲ Medlit Solutions LLC.................... D 919 878-6789
   Garner (G-4942)

Ollis Enterprises Inc........................ E 828 265-0004
   Wilkesboro (G-12648)

Owen G Dunn Co Inc....................... G 252 633-3197
   New Bern (G-9387)

Pamela A Adams.............................. G 919 876-5949
   Raleigh (G-10355)

Park Communications LLC................ D 336 292-4000
   Greensboro (G-5732)

Person Printing Company Inc............ E 336 599-2146
   Roxboro (G-10940)

Pilot LLC... D 910 692-7271
   Southern Pines (G-11505)

Powell Ink Inc.................................. F 828 253-6886
   Asheville (G-582)

Printery.. F 336 852-9774
   Greensboro (G-5764)

Printing & Packaging Inc.................. E 704 482-3866
   Shelby (G-11371)

Printing Partners Inc........................ G 336 996-2268
   Kernersville (G-7293)

Printing Svcs Greensboro Inc........... G 336 274-7663
   Greensboro (G-5765)

Quality Prtg Cartridge Fctry.............. G 336 852-2505
   Greensboro (G-5779)

Raleigh Engraving Co....................... G 919 832-5557
   Raleigh (G-10423)

Richard D Stewart............................ G 919 284-2295
   Kenly (G-7236)

S Chamblee Incorporated................. E 919 833-7561
   Raleigh (G-10452)

S Ruppe Inc..................................... G 828 287-4936
   Rutherfordton (G-10992)

Trejo Soccer Academy LLC.............. G 336 899-7910
   Asheboro (G-410)

Tseng Information Systems Inc.......... G 919 682-9197
   Durham (G-4284)

Weber and Weber Inc....................... F 336 722-4109
   Winston Salem (G-13387)

2796 Platemaking services

Container Graphics Corp................... E 704 588-7230
   Pineville (G-9720)

Docusource North Carolina LLC........ E 919 459-5900
   Morrisville (G-8968)

Dtp Inc.. G 336 272-5122
   Greensboro (G-5507)

F C C LLC....................................... G 336 883-7314
   High Point (G-6617)

GA Communications Inc.................... E 704 360-1860
   Mooresville (G-8670)

Greensboro News & Record LLC...... A 336 373-7000
   Greensboro (G-5577)

Hearn Graphic Finishing Inc............. G 336 760-1467
   Winston Salem (G-13194)

Image Matters Inc............................ G 336 940-3000
   Clemmons (G-3191)

Jones Media..................................... G 828 264-3612
   Boone (G-928)

Lee County Industries Inc................. G 919 775-3439
   Sanford (G-11205)

Mark/Trece Inc................................. E 336 292-3424
   Whitsett (G-12614)

Motor Vhcles Lcense Plate Agcy...... G 252 338-6965
   Elizabeth City (G-4398)

Pre Flight Inc................................... G 828 758-1138
   Lenoir (G-7636)

Roto-Plate Inc.................................. G 336 226-4965
   Burlington (G-1150)

Signcaster Corporation..................... G 336 712-2525
   Winston Salem (G-13336)

◆ Southern Lithoplate Inc................ C 919 556-9400
   Youngsville (G-13487)

Subtle Impressions Inc..................... E
   Gastonia (G-5145)

Winston Salem Engraving Co............ F 336 725-4268
   Winston Salem (G-13400)

Xsys North America Corporation........ E 828 654-6805
   Arden (G-320)

Xsys North America Corporation........ F 704 504-2626
   Charlotte (G-3033)

28 CHEMICALS AND ALLIED PRODUCTS

2812 Alkalies and chlorine

▼ Albemarle Corporation.................. A 980 299-5700
   Charlotte (G-1638)

Buckeye International Inc.................. G 704 523-9400
   Charlotte (G-1817)

Global Ecosciences Inc.................... G 252 631-6266
   Wake Forest (G-12278)

Jci Jones Chemicals Inc................... F 704 392-9767
   Charlotte (G-2363)

Occidental Chemical Corp................ F 910 675-7200
   Castle Hayne (G-1508)

▲ Pavco Inc..................................... E 704 496-6800
   Charlotte (G-2619)

PPG Industries Inc........................... G 919 772-3093
   Greensboro (G-5755)

2813 Industrial gases

Airgas Usa LLC............................... F 704 333-5475
   Charlotte (G-1632)

Airgas Usa LLC............................... G 704 394-1420
   Charlotte (G-1633)

Airgas Usa LLC............................... G 919 544-1056
   Durham (G-3884)

Airgas Usa LLC............................... G 919 544-3773
   Durham (G-3885)

Airgas Usa LLC............................... G 919 735-5276
   Goldsboro (G-5196)

Airgas Usa LLC............................... G 910 392-2711
   Wilmington (G-12694)

Andy-OXY Co Inc............................. E 828 258-0271
   Asheville (G-426)

Arc3 Gases Inc................................ G 919 772-9500
   Durham (G-3897)

Arc3 Gases Inc................................ G 336 275-3333
   Greensboro (G-5367)

Arc3 Gases Inc................................ G 704 220-1029
   Monroe (G-8429)

Arc3 Gases Inc................................ E 910 892-4016
   Dunn (G-3844)

CMC Industrial Services LLC................ F 980 565-5224
Concord (G-3337)

East Coast Oxygen Inc...................... G 828 252-7770
Asheville (G-490)

Helium Agency LLC.......................... G 919 833-1358
Raleigh (G-10162)

Helium Brands LLC.......................... G.... 561 350-1328
Cary (G-1370)

James Oxygen and Supply Co............... E 704 322-5438
Hickory (G-6374)

Legacy Biogas LLC.......................... G 713 253-9013
Goldsboro (G-5223)

Linde Gas & Equipment Inc............. F 919 380-7411
Cary (G-1389)

Linde Gas & Equipment Inc............. F 704 587-7096
Charlotte (G-2424)

Linde Gas & Equipment Inc............. D 919 549-0633
Durham (G-4105)

Linde Gas & Equipment Inc............. F 866 543-3427
Whitsett (G-12612)

Linde Inc.................................... G 910 343-0241
Wilmington (G-12836)

Matheson Tri-Gas Inc...................... F 919 556-6461
Wake Forest (G-12286)

Messer LLC.................................. G 704 583-0313
Charlotte (G-2494)

Messer LLC.................................. E 908 464-8100
Midland (G-8290)

Noahs Inc.................................... F 704 718-2354
Charlotte (G-2570)

Panenergy Corp............................. F 704 594-6200
Charlotte (G-2607)

2816 Inorganic pigments

Americhem Inc.............................. E 704 782-6411
Concord (G-3311)

Avient Colorants USA LLC.................. D 704 331-7000
Charlotte (G-1723)

Powerlab Inc................................ E 336 650-0706
Winston Salem (G-13300)

Ultra Coatings Incorporated............... F 336 883-8853
High Point (G-6817)

2819 Industrial inorganic chemicals, nec

Access Technologies LLC................... G 574 286-1255
Mooresville (G-8590)

◆ Advanced Marketing International Inc F 910 392-0508
Wilmington (G-12692)

Airgas Usa LLC.............................. G 704 394-1420
Charlotte (G-1633)

Airgas Usa LLC.............................. G 919 544-3773
Durham (G-3885)

Airgas Usa LLC.............................. F 919 735-5276
Goldsboro (G-5196)

Akuratemp LLC.............................. F 828 708-7178
Arden (G-249)

Albemarle Amendments LLC................ F 800 535-3030
Charlotte (G-1637)

Albemarle Corporation..................... C 704 739-2501
Kings Mountain (G-7345)

▼ Albemarle Corporation................... A 980 299-5700
Charlotte (G-1638)

◆ Albemarle US Inc.......................... C 704 739-2501
Kings Mountain (G-7346)

▼ American Ripener LLC.................... G 704 527-8813
Charlotte (G-1666)

◆ Apollo Chemical Corp..................... D 336 226-1161
Burlington (G-1047)

◆ Archroma US Inc........................... E 704 353-4100
Charlotte (G-1692)

Arkema Inc.................................. D 919 469-6700
Cary (G-1294)

▲ Baikowski International Corp............ F 704 587-7100
Charlotte (G-1741)

Blue Nano Inc............................... F 888 508-6266
Cornelius (G-3589)

Bluestone Metals & Chem LLC............. G 704 662-8632
Cornelius (G-3590)

Bluestone Specialty Chem LLC............ F 704 662-8632
Cornelius (G-3591)

Borden Chemical............................ G 828 584-3800
Morganton (G-8853)

Bryson Industries Inc...................... F 336 931-0026
Thomasville (G-11999)

Carus LLC................................... E 704 822-1441
Belmont (G-741)

Celanese................................... G 910 343-5000
Wilmington (G-12740)

Cheltec Inc................................. G 941 355-1045
Morganton (G-8855)

Chemol Company Inc........................ E 336 333-3050
Greensboro (G-5443)

Chemtrade Logistics (us) Inc.............. G 773 646-2500
Charlotte (G-1910)

◆ Clariant Corporation...................... G 704 331-7000
Charlotte (G-1925)

Clift Industries Inc....................... G 704 752-0031
Mount Holly (G-9225)

Coalogix Inc................................ C 704 827-8933
Charlotte (G-1940)

Conference Inc.............................. G 704 349-0203
Gastonia (G-5027)

◆ Cormetech Inc............................. C 704 827-8933
Charlotte (G-1985)

Corrtrac Systems Corporation.............. G 252 232-3975
Currituck (G-3663)

Dupont Specialty Pdts USA LLC............ E 919 248-5109
Durham (G-4013)

◆ Dystar LP................................. A 704 561-3000
Charlotte (G-2078)

Eidp Inc.................................... C 910 483-4681
Fayetteville (G-4595)

Eidp Inc.................................... D 252 522-6111
Grifton (G-6035)

Eidp Inc.................................... G 252 522-6896
Kinston (G-7408)

Eidp Inc.................................... G 910 371-4000
Leland (G-7540)

Element West LLC........................... G 336 853-6118
Lexington (G-7683)

Elements Brands LLC........................ F 503 230-8008
Charlotte (G-2097)

Energy Solutions (us) LLC................. C 919 786-4555
Raleigh (G-10087)

Fil-Chem Inc............................... G 919 878-1270
Raleigh (G-10108)

FMC Corporation............................ D 704 868-5300
Bessemer City (G-818)

FMC Corporation............................ B 704 426-5336
Bessemer City (G-819)

Fortrans Inc............................... G 919 365-8004
Wendell (G-12536)

Fuji Silysia Chemical Ltd.................. F 919 484-4158
Greenville (G-5980)

▲ Fuji Silysia Chemical USA Ltd.......... E 252 413-0003
Greenville (G-5981)

◆ Ge-Hitchi Nclear Enrgy Amrcas......... A 910 819-5000
Castle Hayne (G-1500)

Ge-Hitchi Nclear Enrgy Intl LL........... G 518 433-4338
Wilmington (G-12783)

General Electric Company................... A 910 675-5000
Wilmington (G-12785)

Geo Specialty Chemicals Inc.............. G 252 793-2121
Plymouth (G-9804)

Giles Chemical Corporation................ G 828 452-4784
Waynesville (G-12458)

▲ Giles Chemical Corporation............. E 828 452-4784
Waynesville (G-12459)

Global Laser Enrichment LLC.............. D 910 819-7255
Wilmington (G-12787)

Global Nuclear Fuel LLC................... F 910 819-6181
Wilmington (G-12788)

◆ Global Nuclear Fuel-Americas LLC..... E 910 819-5950
Castle Hayne (G-1501)

Gresco Manufacturing Inc.................. G 336 475-8101
Thomasville (G-12029)

◆ Hemo Bioscience Inc...................... G 919 313-2888
Durham (G-4059)

Highland International...................... F 828 265-2513
Boone (G-923)

◆ Industrial and Agricultur............... E 910 843-2121
Red Springs (G-10668)

◆ Innospec Inc.............................. E 704 633-8028
Salisbury (G-11069)

Innospec Inc................................ E 704 633-8028
Salisbury (G-11070)

Leke LLC.................................... E 704 523-1452
Pineville (G-9739)

M & G Polymers Usa LLC.................... G 910 509-4414
Wilmington (G-12843)

Marlowe-Van Loan Corporation............. G 336 886-7126
High Point (G-6699)

Metallix Refining Inc...................... E 252 413-0346
Greenville (G-6003)

▲ Microban Products Company.............. E 704 766-4267
Huntersville (G-7013)

Mount Vernon Chemicals LLC............... D 336 226-1161
Burlington (G-1131)

Mount Vernon Mills Inc..................... A 336 226-1161
Burlington (G-1132)

▲ Netqem LLC............................... G 919 544-4122
Durham (G-4146)

New Element................................ G 704 890-7292
Charlotte (G-2557)

▼ Novalent Ltd............................. F 336 375-7555
Greensboro (G-5715)

Oneh2 Inc.................................. E 844 996-6342
Hickory (G-6406)

▲ Pavco Inc................................. E 704 496-6800
Charlotte (G-2619)

Pcs Phosphate Company Inc................ E 252 322-4111
Aurora (G-645)

Pencco Inc................................. F 252 235-5300
Middlesex (G-8279)

Piedmont Lithium Carolinas Inc........... F 434 664-7643
Belmont (G-761)

◆ Qc LLC................................... E 800 883-0010
Cary (G-1432)

Reagents Holdings LLC..................... E 800 732-8484
Charlotte (G-2695)

Rockwood Lithium........................... E 704 739-2501
Kings Mountain (G-7383)

Sciepharm LLC.............................. F 307 352-9559
Durham (G-4225)

Sciepharm LLC.............................. G 307 352-9559
Apex (G-193)

Sciteck Diagnostics Inc................... G 828 650-0409
Fletcher (G-4765)

Sibelco.................................... F 828 765-1114
Spruce Pine (G-11585)

▲ Sostram Corporation..................... G 919 226-1195
Durham (G-4242)

Southern States Chemical Inc............. E 910 762-5054
Wilmington (G-12926)

Steag SCR-Tech Inc......................... E 704 827-8933
Charlotte (G-2863)

Stepan Company...................................C..... 316 828-1000
Wilmington (G-12930)

Synnovator Inc.................................G..... 919 360-0518
Durham (G-4257)

Tecgrachem Inc..................................G..... 336 993-6785
Kernersville (G-7304)

▲ Techmet Carbides Inc......................D..... 828 624-0222
Hickory (G-6464)

Tutcu-Farnam Custom Products...........E..... 828 684-3766
Arden (G-315)

◆ Unichem IV Ltd................................F..... 336 578-5476
Haw River (G-6136)

▲ US Specialty Color Corp...................G..... 704 292-1476
Monroe (G-8574)

Venator Chemicals LLC.......................D..... 704 454-4811
Harrisburg (G-6120)

2821 Plastics materials and resins

3a Composites Holding Inc...................D..... 704 658-3527
Davidson (G-3696)

◆ Abt Inc...E..... 704 528-9806
Troutman (G-12129)

Albemarle Corporation.........................G..... 252 482-7423
Edenton (G-4360)

▼ Albemarle Corporation......................A..... 980 299-5700
Charlotte (G-1638)

Allotropica Technologies Inc................G..... 919 522-4374
Chapel Hill (G-1524)

Alpek Polyester Miss Inc.....................C..... 228 533-4000
Charlotte (G-1647)

Alpek Polyester Usa LLC....................C..... 910 433-8200
Fayetteville (G-4550)

◆ Alpek Polyester Usa LLC.................D..... 704 940-7500
Charlotte (G-1648)

American Durafilm Co Inc....................G..... 704 895-7701
Mooresville (G-8595)

◆ Aqua Plastics Inc............................F..... 828 324-6284
Hickory (G-6266)

Arclin USA LLC..................................G..... 919 542-2526
Moncure (G-8400)

◆ Auriga Polymers Inc.........................C..... 864 579-5570
Charlotte (G-1717)

Aurora Plastics Inc............................F..... 336 775-2640
Welcome (G-12511)

◆ Avient Protective Mtls LLC...............D..... 252 707-2547
Greenville (G-5943)

Bluesky Polymers LLC........................G..... 919 522-4374
Cary (G-1311)

Canplast Usa Inc...............................G..... 336 668-9555
Greensboro (G-5421)

Carpenter Co.....................................D..... 828 464-9470
Conover (G-3501)

Carpenter Co.....................................E..... 828 322-6545
Hickory (G-6290)

Carpenter Co.....................................D..... 336 861-5730
High Point (G-6560)

Carpenter Co.....................................E..... 828 632-7061
Taylorsville (G-11952)

Celanese Intl Corp.............................G..... 704 480-5798
Grover (G-6042)

Celgard LLC......................................D..... 704 588-5310
Charlotte (G-1884)

◆ Celgard LLC....................................D..... 800 235-4273
Charlotte (G-1885)

Chase Corporation..............................G..... 828 855-9316
Hickory (G-6303)

Chroma Color Corporation...................D..... 336 629-9184
Asheboro (G-339)

Chroma Color Corporation...................C..... 704 637-7000
Salisbury (G-11033)

Coates Designers & Craftsmen............G..... 828 349-9700
Franklin (G-4821)

Consolidated Pipe & Sup Co Inc...........F..... 336 294-8577
Greensboro (G-5463)

Cs Systems Company Inc....................F..... 800 525-9878
Candler (G-1222)

◆ Custom Polymers Inc........................F..... 704 332-6070
Charlotte (G-2011)

▲ Custom Polymers Pet LLC.................D..... 866 717-0716
Charlotte (G-2012)

◆ Darnel Inc.......................................G..... 704 625-9869
Monroe (G-8474)

Ddp Spclty Elctric Mtls US 9...............E..... 336 547-7112
Greensboro (G-5490)

Delcor Polymers Inc...........................G..... 704 847-0640
Matthews (G-8110)

Dow Silicones Corporation..................C..... 336 547-7100
Greensboro (G-5503)

Dupont Teijin Films............................G..... 910 433-8200
Fayetteville (G-4589)

▲ Eastern Plastics Company.................G..... 704 542-7786
Charlotte (G-2082)

Eidp Inc..G..... 252 522-6286
Kinston (G-7409)

Essay Operations Inc..........................G..... 252 443-6010
Rocky Mount (G-10837)

Freudenberg Prfmce Mtls LP................F..... 919 620-3900
Durham (G-4038)

Future Foam Inc.................................D..... 336 885-4121
High Point (G-6625)

Genpak LLC.......................................D..... 704 588-6202
Charlotte (G-2207)

Gersan Industries Incorporated............G..... 336 886-5455
High Point (G-6628)

Green Mountain Intl LLC......................G..... 800 942-5151
Waynesville (G-12460)

Hanwha Advanced Mtls Amer LLC.........E..... 704 434-2271
Shelby (G-11342)

Hexion Inc...E..... 910 483-1311
Fayetteville (G-4612)

Hexion Inc...G..... 336 884-8918
High Point (G-6646)

Hexion Inc...E..... 828 584-3800
Morganton (G-8871)

Huntsman Corporation.........................F..... 706 272-4020
Charlotte (G-2298)

Huntsman International LLC...................E..... 704 588-6082
Charlotte (G-2299)

▲ Huntsman Textile Effects..................E..... 704 587-5000
Charlotte (G-2300)

Imaflex Usa Inc..................................E..... 336 474-1190
Thomasville (G-12037)

Intertape Polymer Corp.......................D..... 252 792-2083
Everetts (G-4497)

Intrinsic Advanced Mtls LLC................G..... 704 874-5000
Gastonia (G-5068)

Invista Capital Management LLC...........C..... 704 636-6000
Salisbury (G-11071)

J-M Manufacturing Company Inc...........D..... 919 575-6515
Creedmoor (G-3650)

Jpi Coastal......................................G..... 704 310-5867
Salisbury (G-11076)

JPS Composite Materials Corp.............C..... 704 872-9831
Statesville (G-11720)

▲ Kattermann Ventures Inc..................E..... 828 651-8737
Fletcher (G-4744)

Kestrel I Acquisition Corporation..........A..... 919 990-7500
Durham (G-4095)

Lanxess Corporation...........................G..... 704 923-0121
Dallas (G-3678)

Lanxess Corporation...........................E..... 704 868-7200
Gastonia (G-5077)

◆ Liquidating Reichhold Inc.................A..... 919 990-7500
Durham (G-4106)

Mallard Creek Polymers LLC................G..... 704 547-0622
Charlotte (G-2450)

Mallard Creek Polymers LLC................G..... 877 240-0171
Charlotte (G-2452)

Mallard Creek Polymers LLC................G..... 704 547-0622
Harrisburg (G-6112)

◆ Mallard Creek Polymers LLC.............E..... 704 547-0622
Charlotte (G-2451)

Mdt Bromley LLC................................E..... 828 651-8737
Fletcher (G-4752)

Mexichem Spcalty Compounds Inc........D..... 704 889-7821
Pineville (G-9742)

▲ Microban Products Company.............E..... 704 766-4267
Huntersville (G-7013)

Modern Densifying Inc........................F..... 704 434-8335
Shelby (G-11363)

▼ Modern Polymers Inc.......................E..... 704 435-5825
Cherryville (G-3067)

Norell Inc..G..... 828 584-2600
Morganton (G-8885)

Olympic Products LLC.........................D..... 336 378-9620
Greensboro (G-5721)

Olympic Products LLC.........................D..... 336 378-9620
Greensboro (G-5720)

Parkway Products LLC........................C..... 828 684-1362
Arden (G-294)

▲ Performance Additives LLC...............F..... 215 321-4388
Pinehurst (G-9699)

Phase II Creations Inc........................G..... 336 249-0673
Lexington (G-7730)

Plaskolite LLC...................................C..... 704 588-3800
Charlotte (G-2640)

◆ Plaskolite North Carolina LLC...........F..... 704 588-3800
Charlotte (G-2641)

Plastic Products Inc...........................E..... 704 739-7463
Bessemer City (G-830)

Plastic Solutions Inc..........................F..... 678 353-2100
Ellenboro (G-4459)

Plastiexports TN LLC..........................E..... 423 735-2207
Charlotte (G-2643)

Poly One Distribution..........................G..... 704 872-8168
Statesville (G-11749)

▲ Polychem Alloy Inc..........................E..... 828 754-7570
Lenoir (G-7635)

Polyone Corporation............................G..... 704 838-0457
Statesville (G-11750)

Polyone Distribution............................G..... 919 413-4547
Rolesville (G-10889)

▲ Polyquest Incorporated.....................F..... 910 342-9554
Wilmington (G-12882)

◆ Poppelmann Plastics USA LLC...........E..... 828 466-9500
Claremont (G-3116)

PPG Industries Inc.............................G..... 919 772-3093
Greensboro (G-5755)

PQ Recycling LLC...............................E..... 910 342-9554
Wilmington (G-12889)

Pressure Washing Near Me LLC............G..... 704 280-0351
Waxhaw (G-12437)

Prototech Manufacturing Inc................F..... 508 646-8849
Washington (G-12410)

◆ Reichhold Holdings Us Inc................A..... 919 990-7500
Durham (G-4210)

▲ Repi LLC..E..... 704 648-0252
Dallas (G-3685)

Resinall Corp....................................C..... 252 585-1445
Severn (G-11299)

▲ Robix America Inc...........................C..... 336 668-9555
Greensboro (G-5791)

Rugby Acquisition LLC........................D..... 336 993-8686
Kernersville (G-7297)

◆ Rutland Group Inc............................C..... 704 553-0046
Pineville (G-9752)

◆ Rutland Holdings LLC.................E 704 553-0046
Pineville *(G-9753)*

Sanctuary Systems LLC............. D 305 989-0953
Fremont *(G-4860)*

▲ Scentair Technologies LLC............. C 704 504-2320
Charlotte *(G-2762)*

▲ Schlaadt USA Limited.................F 252 634-9494
New Bern *(G-9395)*

Sealed Air Corporation..................A 980 221-3235
Charlotte *(G-2776)*

▲ Spt Technology Inc.................F 612 332-1880
Monroe *(G-8561)*

Spt Technology Inc.................G 704 290-5007
Monroe *(G-8562)*

Ssd Designs LLC.................F 980 245-2988
Charlotte *(G-2854)*

▲ Starpet Inc.................C 336 672-0101
Asheboro *(G-398)*

Stepan Company.................C 316 828-1000
Wilmington *(G-12930)*

Stockhausen Superabsorber LLC........ E 336 333-7540
Greensboro *(G-5842)*

Superskinsystems Inc.................G 336 601-6005
Greensboro *(G-5845)*

▲ Syncot Plastics LLC.................D 704 967-0010
Belmont *(G-769)*

◆ Tailored Chemical Products Inc..........D 828 322-6512
Hickory *(G-6462)*

Tosaf Inc.................G 704 396-7097
Bessemer City *(G-836)*

◆ Tosaf Inc.................F 980 533-3000
Bessemer City *(G-837)*

◆ Toter LLC.................E 800 424-0422
Statesville *(G-11792)*

▲ Unifi Kinston LLC.................G 252 522-6518
Kinston *(G-7432)*

▲ W M Plastics Inc.................F 704 599-0511
Charlotte *(G-2996)*

◆ Wilsonart LLC.................D 828 684-2351
Fletcher *(G-4780)*

▼ Wp Reidsville LLC.................C 336 342-1200
Reidsville *(G-10702)*

2822 Synthetic rubber

Axchem Solutions Inc.................G 919 742-9810
Siler City *(G-11398)*

Bridgestone Americas Inc.................C 984 888-0413
Durham *(G-3940)*

◆ Custom Polymers Inc.................F 704 332-6070
Charlotte *(G-2011)*

Dupont Electronic Polymers L P..........F 919 248-5135
Durham *(G-4012)*

ERA Polymers Corporation.................E 704 931-3675
Stanley *(G-11616)*

Fibex LLC.................G 336 358-5014
Greensboro *(G-5530)*

◆ Goulston Technologies Inc.................E 704 289-6464
Monroe *(G-8495)*

▲ Indulor America LP.................D 336 578-6855
Graham *(G-5270)*

Kestrel I Acquisition Corporation.........A 919 990-7500
Durham *(G-4095)*

Lanxess Corporation.................E 704 868-7200
Gastonia *(G-5077)*

◆ Liquidating Reichhold Inc.................A 919 990-7500
Durham *(G-4106)*

◆ M & P Polymers Inc.................G 910 246-6585
Pinehurst *(G-9695)*

◆ Reichhold Holdings Us Inc.................A 919 990-7500
Durham *(G-4210)*

Seal It Services Inc.................F 919 777-0374
Sanford *(G-11232)*

Sunray Inc.................E 828 287-7030
Rutherfordton *(G-10994)*

Tethis Inc.................E 919 808-2866
Raleigh *(G-10543)*

Wellco Two Inc.................G 828 667-4662
Asheville *(G-633)*

2823 Cellulosic manmade fibers

A Oliver Arthur & Son Inc.................F 828 459-8000
Conover *(G-3486)*

Carolina Prcsion Fbers Spv LLC.........E 336 527-4140
Ronda *(G-10893)*

Invista Capital Management LLC..........C 704 636-6000
Salisbury *(G-11071)*

Neptco Incorporated.................C 828 313-0149
Granite Falls *(G-5314)*

Profile Products LLC.................D 828 327-4165
Conover *(G-3552)*

▼ Thanet Inc.................G 704 483-4175
Denver *(G-3812)*

2824 Organic fibers, noncellulosic

◆ Auriga Polymers Inc.................C 864 579-5570
Charlotte *(G-1717)*

▼ Basofil Fibers LLC.................E 828 304-2307
Charlotte *(G-1759)*

◆ Coats HP Inc.................B 704 824-9904
Mc Adenville *(G-8213)*

Coats HP Inc.................E 704 329-5800
Charlotte *(G-1944)*

Covation Biomaterials LLC.................C 252 643-7000
Grifton *(G-6034)*

Durafiber Technologies.................A 704 912-3700
Huntersville *(G-6983)*

▲ Durafiber Technologies (dft) Inc........ A 704 912-3700
Huntersville *(G-6984)*

◆ Durafiber Technologies (d.................A 704 912-3770
Huntersville *(G-6985)*

Durafiber Technologies DFT Inc.........G 704 639-2722
Salisbury *(G-11046)*

Durafiber Technologies DFT Inc.........G 919 356-3824
Sanford *(G-11173)*

Fibrix LLC.................E 704 878-0027
Statesville *(G-11697)*

◆ Fibrix LLC.................E 828 459-7064
Conover *(G-3521)*

◆ High Speed Gear Inc.................F 910 325-1000
Swansboro *(G-11885)*

◆ Innofa Usa LLC.................E 336 635-2900
Eden *(G-4348)*

Mannington Mills Inc.................D 704 824-3551
Mc Adenville *(G-8214)*

Military Wraps Inc.................G 910 671-0008
Lumberton *(G-7962)*

Morbern LLC.................F 336 883-4332
High Point *(G-6714)*

Omnia Products LLC.................G 919 514-3977
Oxford *(G-9622)*

◆ Pbi Performance Products Inc.................D 704 554-3378
Charlotte *(G-2621)*

Pharr McAdenville Corporation.................D 704 824-3551
Mc Adenville *(G-8215)*

▼ Polycor Holdings Inc.................D 828 459-7064
Conover *(G-3547)*

◆ Snp Inc.................F 919 598-0400
Durham *(G-4241)*

▼ Southern Fiber Inc.................C 704 736-0011
Lincolnton *(G-7854)*

Stein Fibers Ltd.................D 704 599-2804
Charlotte *(G-2866)*

Thomasville-Dexel Incorporated.................E 336 819-5550
High Point *(G-6808)*

Trelleborg Ctd Systems US Inc.................C 828 286-9126
Rutherfordton *(G-10996)*

Warp Technologies Inc.................C 919 552-2311
Holly Springs *(G-6920)*

2833 Medicinals and botanicals

A House of Hemp LLC.................G 910 984-1441
Linden *(G-7872)*

Alternative Health Dist LLC.................F 336 465-6618
Mooresville *(G-8594)*

Averix Bio LLC.................E 252 220-0887
Wilson *(G-12966)*

Cbdmd Inc.................F 704 445-3060
Charlotte *(G-1869)*

Direct Digital LLC.................F 704 557-0987
Charlotte *(G-2051)*

Emergo Therapeutics Inc.................G 919 649-5544
Durham *(G-4022)*

Guerbet LLC.................F 919 878-2930
Raleigh *(G-10152)*

Healing Springs Farmacy.................G 336 549-6159
Greensboro *(G-5591)*

▲ Herbs Gaia Inc.................D 828 884-4242
Brevard *(G-972)*

Inneroptic Technology Inc.................G 919 732-2090
Hillsborough *(G-6868)*

Interntnal Agrclture Group LLC.................F 908 323-3246
Mooresville *(G-8694)*

Mallinckrodt LLC.................G 919 878-2900
Raleigh *(G-10269)*

Medkoo Inc.................G 919 636-5577
Durham *(G-4124)*

▲ Pisgah Laboratories Inc.................E 828 884-2789
Pisgah Forest *(G-9772)*

Power Chem Inc.................G 919 365-3400
Wendell *(G-12540)*

White Stone Labs Inc.................G 704 775-5274
Mooresville *(G-8799)*

2834 Pharmaceutical preparations

◆ A1 Biochem Labs LLC.................G 315 299-4775
Wilmington *(G-12687)*

▼ A2a Integrated Logistics Inc.................G 800 493-3736
Fayetteville *(G-4542)*

Abbott Laboratories.................G 704 243-1832
Waxhaw *(G-12422)*

▼ Accord Healthcare Inc.................E 919 941-7878
Raleigh *(G-9873)*

Aceragen Inc.................F 919 271-1032
Durham *(G-3878)*

Achelios Therapeutics LLC.................G 919 354-6233
Durham *(G-3879)*

Aer Therapeutics Inc.................G 919 345-4256
Raleigh *(G-9883)*

Aerami Therapeutics Inc.................F 650 773-5926
Durham *(G-3882)*

Aerie Pharmaceuticals Inc.................G 919 237-5300
Durham *(G-3883)*

▼ Albemarle Corporation.................A 980 299-5700
Charlotte *(G-1638)*

Albion Medical Holdings Inc.................F 800 378-3906
Lenoir *(G-7570)*

Alcami Carolinas Corporation.................E 919 957-5500
Durham *(G-3887)*

Alcami Carolinas Corporation.................G 910 619-3952
Garner *(G-4913)*

Alcami Carolinas Corporation.................F 910 254-7000
Morrisville *(G-8922)*

Alcami Carolinas Corporation.................G 910 254-7000
Morrisville *(G-8923)*

Alcami Carolinas Corporation.................G 910 254-7000
Morrisville *(G-8924)*

Alcami Carolinas Corporation.................G..... 910 254-7000
Wilmington *(G-12696)*

Alcami Carolinas Corporation.................G..... 910 254-7000
Wilmington *(G-12697)*

Alcami Carolinas Corporation.................G..... 910 254-7000
Wilmington *(G-12699)*

Alcami Carolinas Corporation.................B..... 910 254-7000
Wilmington *(G-12698)*

Alcami Corporation...............................A..... 910 254-7000
Wilmington *(G-12700)*

Alcami Holdings LLC..............................A..... 910 254-7000
Wilmington *(G-12701)*

AMO Pharma Services Corp...................G..... 215 826-7420
Durham *(G-3893)*

Amryt Pharmaceuticals Inc....................F..... 877 764-3131
Cary *(G-1289)*

Anelleo Inc...G..... 919 448-4008
Chapel Hill *(G-1526)*

Arbor Organic Technologies LLC...........E..... 704 276-7100
Lincolnton *(G-7816)*

Arbor Pharmaceuticals Inc.....................G..... 919 792-1700
Raleigh *(G-9910)*

Areteia Therapeutics Inc.......................F..... 973 985-0597
Chapel Hill *(G-1527)*

Array Biopharma Inc.............................D..... 303 381-6600
Morrisville *(G-8931)*

Arrivo Management LLC.........................G..... 919 460-9500
Morrisville *(G-8932)*

Asklepios Bopharmaceutical Inc............C..... 919 561-6210
Research Triangle Pa *(G-10703)*

Astrazeneca Pharmaceuticals LP...........C..... 919 647-4990
Durham *(G-3902)*

Atsena Therapeutics Inc.......................F..... 352 273-9342
Durham *(G-3906)*

Aurobindo Pharma USA Inc....................E..... 732 839-9400
Durham *(G-3907)*

Aurolife Pharma LLC.............................E..... 732 839-9408
Durham *(G-3908)*

Avadim Holdings Inc.............................E..... 877 677-2723
Asheville *(G-447)*

Avadim Holdings Inc.............................E..... 877 677-2723
Charlotte *(G-1720)*

Avadim Holdings Inc.............................E..... 877 677-2723
Swannanoa *(G-11865)*

Avient Protective Mtls LLC.....................D..... 704 862-5100
Stanley *(G-11609)*

Avior Inc...G..... 919 234-0068
Cary *(G-1303)*

Avista Pharma Solutions Inc..................E..... 919 544-8600
Durham *(G-3910)*

Axitare Corporation..............................G..... 919 256-8196
Raleigh *(G-9925)*

B3 Bio Inc...G..... 919 226-3079
Research Triangle Pa *(G-10706)*

Balanced Pharma Incorporated..............G..... 704 278-7054
Cornelius *(G-3588)*

Banner Life Sciences LLC......................E..... 336 812-8700
High Point *(G-6538)*

Battery Watering Systems LLC...............G..... 336 714-0448
Clemmons *(G-3179)*

Bausch Health Americas Inc..................F..... 949 461-6000
Durham *(G-3918)*

Baxter Healthcare Corporation...............F..... 828 756-6623
Marion *(G-8034)*

Baxter Healthcare Corporation...............B..... 828 756-6600
Marion *(G-8035)*

Bayer Corp..F..... 704 373-0991
Charlotte *(G-1760)*

Bayer Corporation................................E..... 800 242-5897
Durham *(G-3919)*

◆ Bayer Cropscience Inc......................E..... 412 777-2000
Durham *(G-3920)*

Bayer Healthcare LLC...........................F..... 919 461-6525
Morrisville *(G-8938)*

Bayer Hlthcare Pharmaceuticals............G..... 602 469-6846
Raleigh *(G-9934)*

▲ Be Pharmaceuticals Inc....................G..... 704 560-1444
Cary *(G-1305)*

Beaker Inc...F..... 919 803-7422
Raleigh *(G-9936)*

Bespak Laboratories Inc........................E..... 919 884-2064
Morrisville *(G-8940)*

Bestco LLC...E..... 704 664-4300
Mooresville *(G-8611)*

Bestco LLC...C..... 704 664-4300
Mooresville *(G-8612)*

Bestco LLC...C..... 704 664-4300
Mooresville *(G-8613)*

◆ Bestco LLC.......................................C..... 704 664-4300
Mooresville *(G-8614)*

▲ Biocryst Pharmaceuticals Inc............B..... 919 859-1302
Durham *(G-3928)*

Biogen MA Inc......................................C..... 919 941-1100
Durham *(G-3929)*

Biolex Therapeutics Inc.........................E..... 919 542-9901
Pittsboro *(G-9776)*

Bioresource International Inc..................G..... 919 267-3758
Apex *(G-145)*

Bpc Plasma Inc....................................F..... 910 463-2603
Jacksonville *(G-7117)*

Bright Holdings Usa Inc........................C..... 919 327-5500
Raleigh *(G-9960)*

Bright Path Laboratories Inc..................G..... 858 281-8121
Kannapolis *(G-7204)*

Brii Biosciences Inc..............................F..... 919 240-5605
Durham *(G-3943)*

Bristol-Myers Squibb Company...............G..... 800 321-1335
Charlotte *(G-1812)*

Bristol-Myers Squibb Company...............B..... 336 855-5500
Greensboro *(G-5406)*

Camargo Phrm Svcs LLC.......................G..... 513 618-0325
Durham *(G-3955)*

Cambrex High Point Inc.........................D..... 336 841-5250
High Point *(G-6553)*

Capnostics LLC.....................................G..... 610 442-1363
Concord *(G-3329)*

Cardinal Health 414 LLC........................G..... 704 644-7989
Charlotte *(G-1840)*

Cardiopharma Inc.................................F..... 910 791-1361
Wilmington *(G-12732)*

Cardioxyl Pharmaceuticals Inc...............G..... 919 869-8586
Chapel Hill *(G-1534)*

Catalent Greenville Inc.........................D..... 252 752-3800
Greenville *(G-5952)*

Catalent Pharma Solutions LLC.............G..... 919 481-4855
Morrisville *(G-8949)*

Catalent Pharma Solutions LLC.............G..... 919 465-8101
Morrisville *(G-8950)*

Catalent Pharma Solutions Inc...............F..... 919 465-8206
Durham *(G-3965)*

Catalent Pharma Solutions Inc...............G..... 919 481-2614
Morrisville *(G-8951)*

Catalent Pharma Solutions LLC.............F..... 919 481-4855
Morrisville *(G-8952)*

Cell Microsystems Inc...........................G..... 919 608-2035
Durham *(G-3966)*

Cem-102 Pharmaceuticals Inc...............F..... 919 576-2306
Chapel Hill *(G-1536)*

Cempra Pharmaceuticals Inc.................F..... 919 803-6882
Chapel Hill *(G-1537)*

Cenerx Biopharma Inc..........................G..... 919 234-4072
Cary *(G-1325)*

Chemogenics Biopharma LLC................G..... 919 323-8133
Durham *(G-3972)*

Chimerix Inc...E..... 919 806-1074
Durham *(G-3973)*

Civentichem Usa LLC............................G..... 919 672-8865
Cary *(G-1329)*

Cleveland Compounding Inc...................G..... 704 487-1971
Shelby *(G-11319)*

Closure Medical Corporation..................C..... 919 876-7800
Raleigh *(G-10001)*

Cloud Pharmaceuticals Inc....................G..... 919 558-1254
Durham *(G-3978)*

Cmp Pharma Inc...................................E..... 252 753-7111
Farmville *(G-4525)*

Cornerstone Biopharma Inc....................F..... 919 678-6507
Cary *(G-1335)*

Cosette Pharmaceuticals Inc..................C..... 704 735-5700
Lincolnton *(G-7823)*

▲ Cosette Phrmctcals NC Labs LLC.....C..... 908 753-2000
Lincolnton *(G-7824)*

Daily Manufacturing Inc........................F..... 704 782-0700
Rockwell *(G-10795)*

Dataspectrum......................................G..... 919 341-3300
Raleigh *(G-10036)*

Debmed Usa LLC..................................G..... 704 263-4240
Charlotte *(G-2024)*

Diagnostic Devices...............................G..... 704 599-5908
Charlotte *(G-2039)*

Dignify Therapeutics LLC.......................G..... 919 371-8138
Durham *(G-4001)*

Dova Pharmaceuticals Inc......................E..... 919 748-5975
Morrisville *(G-8969)*

Dpi Newco LLC.....................................A..... 252 758-3436
Greenville *(G-5967)*

DSM..F..... 408 582-2610
Greenville *(G-5968)*

Dsm Inc..G..... 919 876-2802
Raleigh *(G-10061)*

▲ DSM Pharmaceuticals Inc.................D..... 252 758-3436
Greenville *(G-5969)*

▲ DSM Pharmaceuticals Inc.................A..... 252 758-3436
Greenville *(G-5970)*

Dynamic Nutraceuticals LLC..................E..... 704 380-2324
Statesville *(G-11693)*

East Coast Biologics.............................G..... 717 919-9980
Fayetteville *(G-4591)*

Effipharma Inc......................................G..... 919 338-2628
Chapel Hill *(G-1543)*

▲ Ei LLC...B..... 704 857-0707
Winston Salem *(G-13155)*

Eisai Inc..F..... 919 941-6920
Raleigh *(G-10079)*

Elanco US Inc.......................................F..... 812 230-2745
Greensboro *(G-5515)*

Eli Lilly and Company............................F..... 317 296-1226
Durham *(G-4017)*

Embrex Poultry Health LLC....................G..... 910 844-5566
Maxton *(G-8200)*

Encube Ethicals Inc..............................G..... 919 767-3292
Durham *(G-4024)*

Engineered Processing Eqp LLC.............G..... 919 321-6891
Wilson *(G-12988)*

▲ Environmental Science US LLC.........F..... 800 331-2867
Cary *(G-1354)*

Envisia Therapeutics Inc.......................E..... 919 973-1440
Durham *(G-4028)*

▲ Eon Labs Inc...................................B..... 252 234-2222
Wilson *(G-12989)*

Esc Brands LLC....................................G..... 888 331-8332
Lexington *(G-7685)*

Evoqua Water Technologies LLC............E..... 919 477-2161
Durham *(G-4031)*

Exela Drug Substance LLC.....................G..... 828 758-5474
Lenoir *(G-7603)*

Exela Pharma Sciences LLC .... E 828 758-5474
 Lenoir (G-7604)

Exemplar Laboratories LLC .... G 336 817-6794
 Lexington (G-7686)

Fennec Pharmaceuticals Inc .... E 919 636-4530
 Research Triangle Pa (G-10709)

Fervent Pharmaceuticals LLC .... G 252 558-9700
 Greenville (G-5975)

Fidelity Pharmaceuticals LLC .... G 704 274-3192
 Huntersville (G-6989)

Fortovia Therapeutics Inc .... G 919 872-5578
 Raleigh (G-10117)

Fortrea Holdings Inc .... E 480 295-7600
 Durham (G-4035)

Fresenius Kabi Usa LLC .... A 252 991-2692
 Wilson (G-12991)

Fsc Therapeutics LLC .... F 704 941-2500
 Charlotte (G-2182)

Fujifilm Diosynth Biotechnolog .... G 919 337-4400
 Durham (G-4040)

Fujifilm Dsynth Btchnlgies USA .... D 919 337-4400
 Morrisville (G-8977)

Furiex Pharmaceuticals LLC .... F 919 456-7800
 Morrisville (G-8978)

G1 Therapeutics Inc .... C 919 213-9835
 Durham (G-4042)

Gale Global Research Inc .... G 910 795-8595
 Leland (G-7544)

▲ Gb Biosciences LLC .... D 336 632-6000
 Greensboro (G-5550)

Generics Bidco II LLC .... G 980 389-2501
 Charlotte (G-2202)

◆ Generics Bidco II LLC .... D 704 612-8830
 Charlotte (G-2203)

Genixus Corp .... G 877 436-4987
 Concord (G-3368)

Genixus Corp .... F 877 436-4987
 Kannapolis (G-7209)

George Clinical Inc .... G 919 789-2022
 Raleigh (G-10128)

Gilead Sciences Inc .... G 650 574-3000
 Raleigh (G-10134)

Gingras Sleep Medicine PA .... G 704 944-0562
 Charlotte (G-2211)

Glaxosmithkline LLC .... G 704 962-5786
 Cornelius (G-3602)

Glaxosmithkline LLC .... E 919 483-5302
 Durham (G-4050)

Glaxosmithkline LLC .... E 919 483-2100
 Durham (G-4051)

Glaxosmithkline LLC .... G 252 315-9774
 Durham (G-4052)

Glaxosmithkline LLC .... F 919 483-2100
 Durham (G-4053)

Glaxosmithkline LLC .... G 336 392-3058
 Greensboro (G-5562)

Glaxosmithkline LLC .... G 919 628-3630
 Morrisville (G-8983)

Glaxosmithkline LLC .... E 919 483-5006
 Research Triangle Pa (G-10710)

Glaxosmithkline LLC .... E 919 269-5000
 Zebulon (G-13509)

Glaxosmithkline Services Inc .... B 919 483-2100
 Durham (G-4054)

Glenmark Phrmceuticals Inc USA .... D 704 218-2600
 Monroe (G-8492)

GNH Pharmaceuticals USA LLC .... G 704 585-8769
 Charlotte (G-2219)

▲ Greer Laboratories Inc .... C 828 754-5327
 Lenoir (G-7610)

Grifols Inc .... E 919 553-5011
 Clayton (G-3150)

Grifols Therapeutics LLC .... D 919 359-7069
 Clayton (G-3151)

Grifols Therapeutics LLC .... C 919 553-0172
 Clayton (G-3152)

▲ Grifols Therapeutics LLC .... B 919 316-6300
 Research Triangle Pa (G-10711)

Hammock Pharmaceuticals Inc .... G 704 727-7926
 Charlotte (G-2253)

Happy Jack Incorporated .... G 252 747-2911
 Snow Hill (G-11480)

Health Choice Pharmacy .... G 281 741-8358
 Arden (G-273)

Heron Therapeutics Inc .... C 858 251-4400
 Cary (G-1371)

High Point Pharmaceuticals LLC .... F 336 841-0300
 High Point (G-6654)

Hipra Scientific USA .... G 919 605-8256
 Garner (G-4931)

Hospira Inc .... E 252 977-5111
 Battleboro (G-699)

Hospira Inc .... F 704 335-1300
 Charlotte (G-2288)

Hospira Inc .... B 919 553-3831
 Clayton (G-3154)

Hospira Inc .... C 252 977-5500
 Rocky Mount (G-10813)

Hospira Inc .... A 252 977-5111
 Rocky Mount (G-10842)

Huvepharma Inc .... F 910 506-4649
 Maxton (G-8201)

Icagen LLC .... D 919 941-5206
 Durham (G-4068)

Idexx Pharmaceuticals Inc .... G 336 834-6500
 Greensboro (G-5614)

Imbrium Therapeutics LP .... F 984 439-1075
 Morrisville (G-8992)

Indivior Manufacturing LLC .... D 804 594-0974
 Raleigh (G-10187)

Inhalon Biopharma Inc .... G 650 439-0110
 Durham (G-4077)

▲ Innobioactives LLC .... G 336 235-0838
 Greensboro (G-5618)

Innocrin Pharmaceuticals Inc .... G 919 467-8539
 Fuquay Varina (G-4884)

Intas Pharmaceuticals Limited .... E 919 941-7878
 Raleigh (G-10204)

Interpace Pharma Solutions Inc .... G 919 678-7024
 Morrisville (G-8994)

▲ Ioto Usa LLC .... F 252 413-7343
 Greenville (G-5992)

Iqvia Pharma Inc .... D 919 998-2000
 Durham (G-4084)

Ixc Discovery Inc .... C 919 941-5206
 Durham (G-4086)

Kbi Biopharma Inc .... G 919 479-9898
 Durham (G-4093)

Kbi Biopharma Inc .... D 919 479-9898
 Durham (G-4094)

Keranetics LLC .... G 336 725-0621
 Winston Salem (G-13225)

King Bio Inc .... D 828 255-0201
 Asheville (G-530)

King Phrmceuticals RES Dev LLC .... C 919 653-7001
 Cary (G-1383)

Kowa Research Institute Inc .... E 919 433-1600
 Morrisville (G-9000)

Krenitsky Pharmaceuticals Inc .... G 919 493-4631
 Chapel Hill (G-1551)

Krigen Pharmaceuticals LLC .... G 919 523-7530
 Lillington (G-7799)

Ksep Systems LLC .... G 919 339-1850
 Morrisville (G-9001)

Lexitas Pharma Services Inc .... E 919 205-0012
 Durham (G-4104)

Lonza Rtp .... G 800 748-8979
 Morrisville (G-9013)

Lq3 Pharmaceuticals Inc .... G 919 794-7391
 Morrisville (G-9014)

Mallinckrodt LLC .... D 919 878-2800
 Raleigh (G-10268)

Mallinckrodt LLC .... G 919 878-2900
 Raleigh (G-10269)

Marius Pharmaceuticals LLC .... G 919 374-1913
 Raleigh (G-10271)

Mayne Pharma Commercial LLC .... B 984 242-1400
 Raleigh (G-10281)

Mayne Pharma LLC .... C 252 752-3800
 Raleigh (G-10282)

Mayne Pharma Ventures LLC .... G 252 752-3800
 Raleigh (G-10283)

Melinta Therapeutics LLC .... F 919 313-6601
 Chapel Hill (G-1555)

Merck & Co Inc .... E 908 423-3000
 Charlotte (G-2492)

Merck Sharp & Dohme LLC .... C 919 425-4000
 Durham (G-4128)

Merck Sharp & Dohme LLC .... B 252 243-2011
 Wilson (G-13006)

Merck Teknika LLC .... E 919 620-7200
 Durham (G-4129)

▲ Merz Incorporated .... C 919 582-8196
 Raleigh (G-10293)

Merz North America Inc .... F 919 582-8000
 Raleigh (G-10294)

▲ Merz Pharmaceuticals LLC .... C 919 582-8000
 Raleigh (G-10295)

Millennium Pharmaceuticals Inc .... D 866 466-7779
 Charlotte (G-2503)

Mixx-Point 5 Project LLC .... G 858 298-4625
 Swannanoa (G-11873)

Musa Gold LLC .... F 704 579-7894
 Charlotte (G-2536)

Mylan Pharmaceuticals Inc .... E 336 271-6571
 Greensboro (G-5703)

Nationwide Analgesics LLC .... G 704 651-5551
 Matthews (G-8135)

Natures Pharmacy Inc .... G 828 251-0094
 Asheville (G-555)

Neptune Hlth Wllness Innvtion .... C 888 664-9166
 Conover (G-3541)

Neuronex Inc .... G 919 460-9500
 Morrisville (G-9024)

Neurotronik Inc .... E 919 883-4155
 Durham (G-4147)

New Paradigm Therapeutics Inc .... G 919 259-0026
 Chapel Hill (G-1559)

Niras Inc .... G 919 439-4562
 Cary (G-1407)

None .... G 336 408-6008
 Winston Salem (G-13265)

Nontoxic Pthgen Erdction Cons .... G 800 308-1094
 Matthews (G-8136)

Nortria Inc .... F 919 440-3253
 Raleigh (G-10340)

▲ Novartis Vccnes Dagnostics Inc .... B 617 871-7000
 Holly Springs (G-6908)

Novo Nordisk Phrm Inds LP .... D 919 820-9985
 Clayton (G-3164)

Novo Nordisk Phrm Inds LP .... C 919 820-9985
 Clayton (G-3165)

Novo Nordisk Phrm Inds LP .... E 919 550-2200
 Durham (G-4151)

Nucleus Radiopharma Inc .... E 980 483-1766
 Davidson (G-3715)

Nutra-Pharma Mfg Corp NC .... D 631 846-2500
Lexington *(G-7726)*

Nutraceutical Lf Sciences Inc .... C 336 956-0800
Lexington *(G-7727)*

Nvn Liquidation Inc .... E 212 765-9100
Durham *(G-4154)*

Oncoceutics Inc .... F 678 897-0563
Durham *(G-4156)*

OnTarget Labs Inc .... G 919 846-3877
Raleigh *(G-10346)*

Oriel Therapeutics Inc .... G 919 313-1290
Durham *(G-4159)*

Patheon Calculus Merger LLC .... G 919 226-3200
Morrisville *(G-9034)*

Patheon Inc .... G 919 226-3200
Durham *(G-4167)*

Patheon Inc .... A 919 226-3200
Durham *(G-4168)*

▲ Patheon Manufacturing Svcs LLC ..... D 252 758-3436
Greenville *(G-6010)*

Patheon Pharmaceuticals Inc .... A 866 728-4366
High Point *(G-6727)*

◆ Patheon Pharmaceuticals Inc .... D 919 226-3200
Morrisville *(G-9035)*

Patheon Phrmceuticals Svcs Inc .... E 919 226-3200
Morrisville *(G-9036)*

Patheon Softgels Inc .... F 336 812-8700
Greensboro *(G-5736)*

◆ Patheon Softgels Inc .... E 336 812-8700
High Point *(G-6728)*

Pfizer Inc .... G 252 382-3309
Battleboro *(G-705)*

Pfizer Inc .... F 919 941-5185
Durham *(G-4176)*

Pfizer Inc .... D 252 977-5111
Rocky Mount *(G-10861)*

Pfizer Inc .... C 919 775-7100
Sanford *(G-11219)*

▲ Pharmaceutical Dimensions .... G 336 297-4851
Greensboro *(G-5739)*

Pharmaceutical Equipment Svcs .... G 239 699-9120
Asheville *(G-571)*

Pharmagra Holding Company LLC .... G 828 884-8656
Brevard *(G-979)*

Pharmasone LLC .... G 910 679-8364
Wilmington *(G-12876)*

▲ Pharmgate Animal Health LLC .... G 910 679-8364
Wilmington *(G-12877)*

▲ Pharmgate Inc .... F 910 679-8364
Wilmington *(G-12878)*

Piedmont Animal Health Inc .... E 336 544-0320
Greensboro *(G-5740)*

Pozen Inc .... F 919 913-1030
Raleigh *(G-10382)*

Ppd Inc .... C 910 251-0081
Wilmington *(G-12886)*

Ppd International Holdings LLC .... G 910 251-0081
Wilmington *(G-12887)*

Praetego Inc .... G 919 237-7969
Durham *(G-4193)*

◆ Premex Inc .... F 561 962-4128
Durham *(G-4196)*

Promethera Biosciences LLC .... F 919 354-1930
Durham *(G-4199)*

Promethera Biosciences LLC .... G 919 354-1933
Raleigh *(G-10403)*

Propella Therapeutics Inc .... G 703 631-7523
Pittsboro *(G-9786)*

PSI Pharma Support America Inc .... E 919 249-2660
Durham *(G-4200)*

Purdue Pharmaceuticals LP .... F 252 265-1900
Wilson *(G-13015)*

Qualicaps Inc .... C 336 449-3900
Whitsett *(G-12618)*

Quatrobio LLC .... G 919 460-9500
Morrisville *(G-9041)*

Rainforest Nutritionals Inc .... G 919 847-2221
Raleigh *(G-10421)*

Raybow Usa Inc .... F 828 884-8656
Brevard *(G-980)*

Redhill Biopharma Inc .... D 984 444-7010
Raleigh *(G-10440)*

Salubrent Phrma Solutions Corp .... G 301 980-7224
Kannapolis *(G-7219)*

Sandoz Inc .... B 252 234-2222
Wilson *(G-13028)*

Santarus Inc .... B 919 862-1000
Raleigh *(G-10456)*

Satsuma Pharmaceuticals Inc .... F 650 410-3200
Durham *(G-4223)*

Scipher Medicine Corporation .... G 781 755-2063
Durham *(G-4226)*

Scorpius Holdings Inc .... E 919 240-7133
Morrisville *(G-9049)*

Sobi Inc .... G 844 506-3682
Morrisville *(G-9056)*

Solvekta LLC .... G 336 944-4677
Greensboro *(G-5821)*

Specgx LLC .... C 919 878-4706
Raleigh *(G-10495)*

Sprout Pharmaceuticals Inc .... F 919 882-0850
Raleigh *(G-10500)*

Sterling Pharma Usa LLC .... E 919 678-0702
Cary *(G-1467)*

Stiefel Laboratories Inc .... C 888 784-3335
Durham *(G-4251)*

Stiefel Laboratories Inc .... E 888 784-3335
Research Triangle Pa *(G-10715)*

Syneos Health Consulting Inc .... F 919 876-9300
Morrisville *(G-9061)*

Synereca Pharmaceuticals Inc .... G 919 966-3929
Chapel Hill *(G-1576)*

Synthon Pharmaceuticals Inc .... E 919 493-6006
Durham *(G-4258)*

Synthonix Inc .... F 919 875-9277
Wake Forest *(G-12307)*

Tarheel Solutions LLC .... G 336 420-9265
Pleasant Garden *(G-9795)*

Tavros Therapeutics Inc .... F 919 602-2631
Durham *(G-4260)*

Tergus Pharma LLC .... E 919 549-9700
Durham *(G-4268)*

Teva Pharmaceuticals Usa Inc .... D 336 316-4132
Greensboro *(G-5859)*

Tg Therapeutics Inc .... D 877 575-8489
Morrisville *(G-9069)*

Tomorrowmed Pharma LLC .... E 832 615-2880
Morrisville *(G-9073)*

Transtech Pharma LLC .... C 336 841-0300
High Point *(G-6810)*

Tripharm Services Inc .... F 984 243-0800
Morrisville *(G-9080)*

Turbomed LLC .... F 973 527-5299
Fayetteville *(G-4684)*

Umethod Health Inc .... F 984 232-6699
Raleigh *(G-10574)*

United Therapeutics Corp .... E 919 246-9389
Durham *(G-4289)*

United Therapeutics Corp .... D 919 485-8350
Research Triangle Pa *(G-10717)*

◆ Universal Preservachem Inc .... D 732 568-1266
Mebane *(G-8262)*

Urovant Sciences Inc .... F 919 323-8528
Durham *(G-4293)*

V1 Pharma LLC .... G 919 338-5744
Raleigh *(G-10580)*

Vascular Pharmaceuticals Inc .... G 919 345-7933
Chapel Hill *(G-1588)*

Vast Therapeutics Inc .... G 919 321-1403
Morrisville *(G-9085)*

Verinetics Inc .... G 919 354-1029
Rtp *(G-10950)*

Viiv Healthcare Company .... G 919 445-2770
Chapel Hill *(G-1590)*

Viiv Healthcare Company .... A 919 483-2100
Durham *(G-4298)*

Vogenx Inc .... G 919 659-5677
Durham *(G-4299)*

Vtv Therapeutics LLC .... G 336 841-0300
High Point *(G-6830)*

We Pharma Inc .... D 919 389-1478
Morrisville *(G-9088)*

West Pharmaceutical Svcs Inc .... G 252 522-8956
Kinston *(G-7436)*

Wholesale Kennel Supply Co .... G 919 742-2515
Siler City *(G-11427)*

Wyeth Holdings LLC .... A 919 775-7100
Sanford *(G-11255)*

Zoetis Inc .... C 919 941-5185
Durham *(G-4318)*

Zoetis Products LLC .... G 336 333-9356
Greensboro *(G-5933)*

2835 Diagnostic substances

Accugenomics Inc .... G 910 332-6522
Wilmington *(G-12690)*

◆ AR Corp .... G 910 763-8530
Wilmington *(G-12705)*

Baebies Inc .... D 919 891-0432
Durham *(G-3912)*

Cardinal Health 414 LLC .... G 704 644-7989
Charlotte *(G-1840)*

Celplor LLC .... G 919 961-1961
Cary *(G-1324)*

Datar Cancer Genetics Inc .... F 919 377-2119
Morrisville *(G-8962)*

Gateway Campus .... G 919 833-0096
Raleigh *(G-10124)*

Gbf Inc .... D 336 665-0205
High Point *(G-6627)*

Liebel-Flarsheim Company LLC .... C 919 878-2930
Raleigh *(G-10255)*

Liposcience Inc .... C 919 212-1999
Morrisville *(G-9012)*

Molecular Toxicology Inc .... F 828 264-9099
Boone *(G-935)*

Multigen Diagnostics LLC .... G 336 510-1120
Greensboro *(G-5700)*

North Carolina Department of A .... G 828 684-8188
Arden *(G-289)*

▲ Novartis Vccnes Dagnostics Inc .... B 617 871-7000
Holly Springs *(G-6908)*

Petnet Solutions Inc .... G 919 572-5544
Durham *(G-4175)*

Petnet Solutions Inc .... G 865 218-2000
Winston Salem *(G-13286)*

Pregnancy Support Services .... G 919 490-0203
Chapel Hill *(G-1563)*

Sapere Bio Inc .... G 919 260-2565
Durham *(G-4220)*

Sciteck Diagnostics Inc .... G 828 650-0409
Fletcher *(G-4765)*

Thurston Genomics LLC .... G 980 237-7547
Charlotte *(G-2918)*

Triangle Prcsion Dgnostics Inc .... G 919 345-0110
Durham *(G-4280)*

◆ Tripath Imaging Inc..............................D 336 222-9707
Burlington *(G-1170)*

Your Choice Pregnancy Clinic.............. G 919 577-9050
Fuquay Varina *(G-4907)*

2836 Biological products, except diagnostic

Albion Medical Holdings Inc................. F 800 378-3906
Lenoir *(G-7570)*

Anatech Ltd... F 704 489-1488
Denver *(G-3770)*

Astellas Gene Therapies Inc............... D 415 638-6561
Sanford *(G-11151)*

Biologix of The Triangle Inc................. G 919 696-4544
Cary *(G-1307)*

Boehrnger Inglheim Anmal Hlth........... D 919 577-9020
Fuquay Varina *(G-4871)*

Business Mogul LLC............................ G 919 605-2165
Raleigh *(G-9962)*

Carolina Biological Supply Co............. C 336 446-7600
Whitsett *(G-12601)*

◆ Carolina Biological Supply Company.C 336 584-0381
Burlington *(G-1060)*

Cedarlane Laboratories USA................ E 336 513-5135
Burlington *(G-1067)*

Chelsea Therapeutics International Ltd. F 704 341-1516
Charlotte *(G-1908)*

Cytonet LLC.. F
Durham *(G-3997)*

Duke Human Vaccine Institute............. G 919 684-5384
Durham *(G-4009)*

▲ Embrex LLC...................................... C 919 941-5185
Durham *(G-4019)*

Epicypher Inc..................................... F 855 374-2461
Durham *(G-4030)*

Greer Laboratories Inc....................... E 828 758-2388
Lenoir *(G-7609)*

▲ Greer Laboratories Inc.................... C 828 754-5327
Lenoir *(G-7610)*

Grifols Therapeutics LLC.................... F 919 316-6214
Durham *(G-4057)*

Grifols Therapeutics LLC.................... A 919 316-6612
Raleigh *(G-10148)*

▲ Grifols Therapeutics LLC................. B 919 316-6300
Research Triangle Pa *(G-10711)*

Immunotek Bio Centers LLC............... E 828 569-6264
Hickory *(G-6366)*

Immunotek Bio Centers LLC............... E 336 781-4901
High Point *(G-6668)*

Keranetics LLC................................... G 336 725-0621
Winston Salem *(G-13225)*

▲ Microban Products Company............. E 704 766-4267
Huntersville *(G-7013)*

Molecular Toxicology Inc.................... F 828 264-9099
Boone *(G-935)*

▲ Novartis Vccnes Dagnostics Inc....... B 617 871-7000
Holly Springs *(G-6908)*

Passport Health Triangle..................... G 919 781-0053
Cary *(G-1414)*

Pfizer Inc... F 919 775-7100
Sanford *(G-11219)*

Plasma Games.................................... G 252 721-3294
Raleigh *(G-10370)*

Plasma Games Inc.............................. E 919 627-1252
Raleigh *(G-10371)*

Precision Biosciences Inc................... E 919 314-5512
Durham *(G-4194)*

Prokidney LLC.................................... E 336 448-2857
Winston Salem *(G-13307)*

Prokidney Corp................................... C 336 999-7019
Winston Salem *(G-13308)*

Quo Vademus LLC.............................. G 910 296-1632
Kenansville *(G-7227)*

Seqirus Inc... F 919 577-5000
Holly Springs *(G-6914)*

Serum Source International Inc............ F 704 588-6607
Waxhaw *(G-12440)*

Tengion Inc.. E 336 722-5855
Winston Salem *(G-13361)*

2841 Soap and other detergents

Ada Marketing Inc.............................. E 910 221-2189
Dunn *(G-3841)*

▲ AG Provision LLC............................. E 910 296-0302
Kenansville *(G-7224)*

Anders Natural Soap Co Inc................ G 919 678-9393
Cary *(G-1290)*

Bottom Line Technologies Inc.............. F 919 472-0541
Durham *(G-3939)*

Buckeye International Inc.................... G 704 523-9400
Charlotte *(G-1817)*

C & C Chemical Company Inc.............. G 828 255-7639
Asheville *(G-464)*

Controlled Release Tech Inc................ G 704 487-0878
Shelby *(G-11324)*

Country Lotus Soaps LLC.................... G 786 384-4174
Charlotte *(G-1991)*

CTS Cleaning Systems Inc.................. G 910 483-5349
Fayetteville *(G-4582)*

Ecolab Inc.. F 336 931-3423
High Point *(G-6603)*

Ecolab Inc.. E 336 931-2237
Winston Salem *(G-13154)*

Freakin Pekin...................................... G 828 705-3313
Morganton *(G-8866)*

▼ Greenology Products LLC................. E 877 473-3650
Raleigh *(G-10144)*

Greenwich Bay Trading Co Inc............ E 919 781-5008
Raleigh *(G-10145)*

▲ Innovasource LLC............................ F 704 584-0072
Huntersville *(G-7001)*

Luxuriously Natural Soaps LLC........... G 910 378-9064
Jacksonville *(G-7130)*

Marlin Company Inc............................ G 828 758-9999
Lenoir *(G-7623)*

◆ Marlin Company Inc......................... E 828 754-0980
Lenoir *(G-7624)*

Metrotech Chemicals Inc.................... D 704 343-9315
Charlotte *(G-2497)*

Naturally ME Boutique Inc.................. G 919 519-0783
Durham *(G-4143)*

Old Town Soap Co.............................. F 704 796-8775
China Grove *(G-3077)*

◆ Pine Glo Products Inc...................... F 919 556-7787
Zebulon *(G-13521)*

Pretty Baby Herbal Soaps................... G 704 209-0669
Salisbury *(G-11106)*

Procter & Gamble Mfg Co.................... D 336 954-0000
Greensboro *(G-5767)*

▲ Qualpak LLC..................................... G 910 610-1213
Laurinburg *(G-7512)*

Rachel Dubois..................................... G 919 870-8063
Raleigh *(G-10419)*

SC Johnson Prof USA Inc.................... D 704 263-4240
Greensboro *(G-5803)*

◆ SC Johnson Professional................. E 704 263-4240
Stanley *(G-11625)*

Sheets Laundry Club Inc..................... G 704 662-8696
Mooresville *(G-8768)*

▲ Showline Inc.................................... G 919 255-9160
Raleigh *(G-10471)*

Showline Automotive Pdts Inc............. G 919 255-9160
Raleigh *(G-10472)*

South / Win LLC................................. D 336 398-5650
Greensboro *(G-5822)*

Specialty National Inc........................ G 336 996-8783
Kernersville *(G-7303)*

◆ Spuntech Industries Inc................... C 336 330-9000
Roxboro *(G-10946)*

◆ Surry Chemicals Incorporated......... E 336 786-4607
Mount Airy *(G-9181)*

◆ Syntha Group Inc............................. D 336 885-5131
High Point *(G-6801)*

Unx-Christeyns LLC............................ G 252 355-8433
Greenville *(G-6031)*

Unx-Christeyns LLC............................ E 252 756-8616
Greenville *(G-6030)*

Wepak Corporation............................ E 704 334-5781
Charlotte *(G-3013)*

Whispering Willow Soap Co LLC.......... G 828 455-0322
Denver *(G-3816)*

2842 Polishes and sanitation goods

3M Company....................................... G 704 588-4782
Charlotte *(G-1601)*

A & B Chem-Dry.................................. F 919 878-0288
Raleigh *(G-9859)*

A Cleaner Tomorrow Dry Clg LLC......... G 919 639-6396
Dunn *(G-3840)*

Abzorbit Inc.. F 828 464-9944
Newton *(G-9447)*

Ace Industries Inc.............................. G 336 427-5316
Madison *(G-7983)*

AEC Consumer Products LLC.............. F 704 904-0578
Fayetteville *(G-4546)*

◆ Amano Pioneer Eclipse Corp........... D 336 372-8080
Sparta *(G-11534)*

Annihilare Medical Systems Inc.......... F 855 545-5677
Lincolnton *(G-7814)*

◆ Autec Inc.. E 704 871-9141
Statesville *(G-11663)*

Awesome Products Inc........................ G 336 374-5900
Mount Airy *(G-9099)*

Buckeye International Inc.................... G 704 523-9400
Charlotte *(G-1817)*

Busch Enterprises Inc......................... G 704 878-2067
Statesville *(G-11673)*

Casablanca 4 LLC.............................. G 910 702-4399
Wilmington *(G-12734)*

Chem-Tech Solutions Inc.................... E 704 829-9202
Gastonia *(G-5019)*

Cherryville Distrg Co Inc..................... G 704 435-9692
Cherryville *(G-3060)*

Controlled Release Tech Inc................ G 704 487-0878
Shelby *(G-11324)*

Dewill Inc... G 919 426-9550
Cary *(G-1346)*

Ecolab Inc.. G 704 527-5912
Charlotte *(G-2088)*

Ecolab Inc.. E 336 931-2289
Greensboro *(G-5512)*

Economy Clrs Lillington LLC............... G 910 893-3927
Coats *(G-3261)*

Elevate Cleaning Service.................... G 347 928-4030
Fayetteville *(G-4596)*

Elsco Inc.. G 509 885-4525
Seaboard *(G-11271)*

Eminess Technologies Inc.................. E 704 283-2600
Monroe *(G-8482)*

Entrust Services LLC.......................... F 336 274-5175
Greensboro *(G-5523)*

Fresh As A Daisy Inc.......................... G 336 869-3002
High Point *(G-6623)*

Fresh-N-Mobile LLC............................ G 704 251-4643
Charlotte *(G-2180)*

Global Ecosciences Inc...................... G 252 631-6266
Wake Forest *(G-12278)*

H & H Products Incorporated................. G..... 910 891-4276
Dunn *(G-3860)*

◆ Harper Corporation of America..........C..... 704 588-3371
Charlotte *(G-2259)*

◆ Hickory Brands Inc.........................D..... 828 322-2600
Hickory *(G-6347)*

Ice Companies Inc.............................. G..... 910 791-1970
Wilmington *(G-12811)*

Illinois Tool Works Inc........................C..... 336 996-7046
Kernersville *(G-7280)*

Jci Jones Chemicals Inc...................... F..... 704 392-9767
Charlotte *(G-2363)*

◆ Kay Chemical Company...................A..... 336 668-7290
Greensboro *(G-5642)*

M and R Inc.. G..... 704 332-5999
Charlotte *(G-2444)*

Metrotech Chemicals Inc..................... D..... 704 343-9315
Charlotte *(G-2497)*

▲ Microban Products Company............ E..... 704 766-4267
Huntersville *(G-7013)*

Mill-Chem Manufacturing Inc................ E..... 336 889-8038
Thomasville *(G-12049)*

Mooresvlle Pub Wrks Snttion De.......... G..... 704 664-4278
Mooresville *(G-8727)*

▼ Novalent Ltd.................................... F..... 336 375-7555
Greensboro *(G-5715)*

Organizer Llc...................................... G..... 336 391-7591
Winston Salem *(G-13272)*

Patel Deepal...................................... G..... 704 634-5141
Concord *(G-3416)*

Piece of Pie LLC................................ G..... 919 286-7421
Durham *(G-4181)*

◆ Pine Glo Products Inc......................F..... 919 556-7787
Zebulon *(G-13521)*

Procter & Gamble Mfg Co................... D..... 336 954-0000
Greensboro *(G-5767)*

Public Health Corps Inc...................... G..... 336 545-2999
Greensboro *(G-5770)*

Pureon Inc.. D..... 480 505-3409
Monroe *(G-8545)*

Quail Dry Cleaning.............................. G..... 704 947-7335
Charlotte *(G-2681)*

Remodeez LLC.................................... F..... 704 428-9050
Charlotte *(G-2708)*

Rga Enterprises Inc............................Cbmd..... 704 398-0487
Charlotte *(G-2723)*

Speed Brite Inc.................................. G..... 704 639-9771
Salisbury *(G-11118)*

Sun Cleaners & Laundry Inc................ G..... 704 325-3722
Newton *(G-9500)*

▼ Sutherland Products Inc................... F..... 800 854-3541
Stoneville *(G-11831)*

Unx-Christeyns Inc.............................. G..... 252 355-8433
Greenville *(G-6031)*

Unx-Christeyns LLC............................ D..... 252 756-8616
Greenville *(G-6032)*

W G of Southwest Raleigh Inc.............. G..... 919 629-7327
Holly Springs *(G-6919)*

◆ Walex Products Company Inc...........F..... 910 371-2242
Leland *(G-7564)*

Wepak Corporation............................. E..... 704 334-5781
Charlotte *(G-3013)*

2843 Surface active agents

Arrochem Inc...................................... F..... 704 827-0216
Mount Holly *(G-9217)*

◆ Cht R Beitlich Corporation...............E..... 704 523-4242
Charlotte *(G-1917)*

Cliffside Technologies Inc................... G..... 828 657-4477
Mooresboro *(G-8583)*

Diarkis LLC.. G..... 704 888-5244
Locust *(G-7891)*

◆ Fine Line Hosiery Inc.......................G..... 336 498-8022
Asheboro *(G-356)*

Henkel Corporation............................. D..... 704 633-1731
Salisbury *(G-11062)*

▼ Lindley Laboratories Inc.................. F..... 336 449-7521
Gibsonville *(G-5181)*

◆ Surry Chemicals Incorporated..........E..... 336 786-4607
Mount Airy *(G-9181)*

◆ Syntha Group Inc.............................D..... 336 885-5131
High Point *(G-6801)*

2844 Toilet preparations

▲ 3rd Phaze Bdy Oils Urban Lnks........ G..... 704 344-1138
Charlotte *(G-1603)*

A M P Laboratories Ltd....................... G..... 704 894-9721
Cornelius *(G-3582)*

▲ Active Concepts LLC....................... G..... 704 276-7372
Lincolnton *(G-7809)*

▲ Active Concepts LLC...................... E..... 704 276-7100
Lincolnton *(G-7810)*

Adoratherapy Inc................................ F..... 917 297-8904
Asheville *(G-423)*

◆ Albaad Usa Inc................................B..... 336 634-0091
Reidsville *(G-10671)*

Alywillow.. G..... 919 454-4826
Raleigh *(G-9894)*

▲ American Fiber & Finishing Inc......... E..... 704 984-9256
Albemarle *(G-61)*

Artisan Aromatics............................... G..... 800 456-6675
Burnsville *(G-1183)*

Beauty 4 Love LLC............................. G..... 704 802-2844
Charlotte *(G-1766)*

Blaq Beauty Naturalz Inc.................... G..... 252 326-5621
Weldon *(G-12519)*

◆ Body Shop Inc.................................C..... 919 554-4900
Wake Forest *(G-12265)*

Burts Bees Inc.................................. B..... 919 998-5200
Durham *(G-3954)*

Burts Bees Inc.................................. C..... 919 238-6450
Morrisville *(G-8946)*

◆ Burts Bees Inc...............................C..... 919 998-5200
Durham *(G-3953)*

Carolina Perfumer Inc......................... G..... 910 295-5600
Pinehurst *(G-9688)*

Cbdmd Inc... F..... 704 445-3060
Charlotte *(G-1869)*

Clutch Inc.. F..... 919 448-8654
Durham *(G-3979)*

Cocoa Botanics Corporation................ F..... 980 565-7739
Matthews *(G-8108)*

Conopco Inc...................................... B..... 910 875-4121
Raeford *(G-9834)*

Cosmetic Creations Inc....................... G..... 828 298-4625
Swannanoa *(G-11869)*

Coty Inc.. D..... 919 895-5000
Sanford *(G-11166)*

Coty US LLC...................................... A..... 919 895-5374
Sanford *(G-11167)*

Cryogen LLC...................................... F..... 919 649-7027
Raleigh *(G-10024)*

Deb SBS Inc...................................... G..... 704 263-4240
Stanley *(G-11613)*

Dexios Services LLC.......................... G..... 704 946-5101
Cornelius *(G-3597)*

Digits.. G..... 336 721-0209
Winston Salem *(G-13145)*

▲ Ei LLC.. B..... 704 857-0707
Winston Salem *(G-13155)*

Emage Medical LLC............................ G..... 704 904-1873
Charlotte *(G-2106)*

Filltech Inc.. E..... 704 279-4300
Rockwell *(G-10796)*

Filltech USA LLC................................ E..... 704 279-4300
Rockwell *(G-10797)*

Go Green Miracle Balm....................... G..... 630 209-0226
Cornelius *(G-3603)*

Green Compass LLC........................... G..... 833 336-9223
Wilmington *(G-12797)*

Greenwich Bay Trading Co Inc............. E..... 919 781-5008
Raleigh *(G-10145)*

Haircutters of Raleigh Inc................... G..... 919 781-3465
Raleigh *(G-10153)*

HFC Prestige Products Inc.................. G..... 919 895-5300
Sanford *(G-11190)*

Johnny Slicks Inc............................... G..... 910 803-2159
Holly Ridge *(G-6890)*

Keller Cosmetics Inc.......................... G..... 704 399-2226
Monroe *(G-8512)*

Lash Out Inc...................................... G..... 919 342-0221
Clayton *(G-3156)*

Litex Industries Inc............................ G..... 704 799-3758
Mooresville *(G-8713)*

Little River Naturals LLC.................... G..... 919 760-3708
Zebulon *(G-13513)*

Narayana Inc..................................... G..... 828 708-0954
Asheville *(G-554)*

Naturally ME Boutique Inc.................. G..... 919 519-0783
Durham *(G-4143)*

▲ O Grayson Company......................... E..... 704 932-6195
Kannapolis *(G-7217)*

Oakstone Associates LLC................... F..... 704 946-5101
Cornelius *(G-3615)*

Onixx Manufacturing LLC.................... G..... 828 298-4625
Swannanoa *(G-11875)*

◆ Parkdale Mills Incorporated.............D..... 704 874-5000
Gastonia *(G-5117)*

Perfect 10 Brands LLC....................... G..... 702 738-0183
Cary *(G-1419)*

▲ Philosophy Inc............................... E..... 602 794-8701
Sanford *(G-11220)*

Plm Inc.. G..... 336 788-7529
Winston Salem *(G-13298)*

Procter & Gamble Mfg Co................... B..... 336 954-0000
Browns Summit *(G-1004)*

Procter & Gamble Mfg Co................... D..... 336 954-0000
Greensboro *(G-5767)*

Product Quest Manufacturing Inc......... C..... 386 239-8787
Winston Salem *(G-13305)*

▲ Product Quest Manufacturing LLC... B..... 386 239-8787
Winston Salem *(G-13306)*

Rebecca Trickey................................ G..... 910 584-5549
Raeford *(G-9850)*

Revlon Inc.. C..... 919 603-2782
Oxford *(G-9628)*

Revlon Inc.. E..... 919 603-2000
Oxford *(G-9629)*

Revlon Consumer Products Corp..........D..... 919 603-2000
Oxford *(G-9630)*

Salonexclusive Beauty LLC................. G..... 704 488-3909
Charlotte *(G-2750)*

SC Johnson Prof USA Inc................... D..... 704 263-4240
Stanley *(G-11624)*

◆ SC Johnson Prof USA Inc................C..... 443 521-1606
Charlotte *(G-2760)*

▲ Scentair Technologies LLC.............. C..... 704 504-2320
Charlotte *(G-2762)*

Skin So Soft Spa Inc.......................... G..... 800 674-7554
Charlotte *(G-2811)*

Sklar Bov Solutions Inc...................... F..... 704 872-7277
Statesville *(G-11765)*

▲ Steve Henry Woodcraft LLC............. G..... 919 489-7325
Chapel Hill *(G-1573)*

Tea and Honey Blends LLC................. G..... 919 673-4273
Raleigh *(G-10536)*

UGLy Essentials LLC................................ F 910 319-9945
Raleigh (G-10572)

Unilever.. F 910 988-1054
Raeford (G-9855)

Unique Body Blends Inc........................ G 910 302-5484
Fayetteville (G-4686)

◆ Universal Preservachem Inc ....D 732 568-1266
Mebane (G-8262)

Up On Hill.. G 704 664-7971
Troutman (G-12155)

US Cotton LLC.. D 704 874-5000
Belmont (G-774)

◆ US Cotton LLC......................................C 216 676-6400
Gastonia (G-5161)

▼ Usrx LLC.. E 980 221-1200
Charlotte (G-2969)

Virtue Labs LLC .... E 781 316-5437
Winston Salem (G-13382)

Virtue Labs LLC .... G 844 782-4247
Raleigh (G-10590)

◆ Walex Products Company Inc...............F 910 371-2242
Leland (G-7564)

2851 Paints and allied products

ACC Coatings LLC................................. F 336 701-0080
Elkin (G-4438)

Actega North America Inc .... G 704 736-9389
Kings Mountain (G-7343)

Akzo Nobel Coatings Inc....................... F 704 366-8435
Charlotte (G-1635)

Akzo Nobel Coatings Inc....................... G 336 665-9897
Greensboro (G-5345)

Akzo Nobel Coatings Inc....................... E 336 841-5111
High Point (G-6512)

◆ Alberdingk Boley Inc.............................D 336 454-5000
Greensboro (G-5348)

▼ Allied Pressroom Products Inc............. E 954 920-0909
Monroe (G-8421)

Americhem Inc.. E 704 782-6411
Concord (G-3311)

Atec Coatings LLC................................. G 336 753-8888
Mocksville (G-8348)

Atec Wind Energy Products LLC........... G 336 753-8888
Mocksville (G-8349)

Auto Parts Fayetteville LLC.................... G 910 889-4026
Fayetteville (G-4555)

Axalta Coating Systems LLC................. G 855 629-2582
Concord (G-3315)

Axalta Coating Systems Ltd................... F 336 802-5701
High Point (G-6531)

Axalta Coating Systems Ltd................... E 336 802-4392
High Point (G-6532)

Bay Painting Contractors .... G 252 435-5374
Moyock (G-9276)

Bonakemi Usa Incorporated.................D 704 220-6943
Monroe (G-8445)

Carolina Commercial Coatings.............. G 910 279-6045
Wilmington (G-12733)

Cast Iron Elegance Inc.......................... F 919 662-8777
Raleigh (G-9987)

◆ Cdv LLC...F 919 674-3460
Morrisville (G-8953)

▲ Crossroads Coatings Inc...................... F 704 873-2244
Statesville (G-11681)

Delta Contractors Inc............................. F 817 410-9481
Linden (G-7874)

Electric Glass Fiber Amer LLC...............C 336 357-8151
Lexington (G-7682)

▲ Electric Glass Fiber Amer LLC.......... B 704 434-2261
Shelby (G-11332)

Ennis-Flint Inc.. G 800 331-8118
High Point (G-6613)

Ennis-Flint Inc.. G 336 477-8439
Thomasville (G-12022)

Ennis-Flint Inc.. G 800 331-8118
Thomasville (G-12023)

◆ Ennis-Flint Inc.......................................F 800 331-8118
Greensboro (G-5522)

Eoncoat LLC... G 941 928-9401
Fuquay Varina (G-4881)

Fixxus Indus Holdings Co LLC .... E 336 674-3088
Archdale (G-222)

Flint Acquisition Corp............................. D 336 475-6600
Thomasville (G-12025)

Flint Trading Inc...................................... G 336 308-3770
Thomasville (G-12026)

Highland International LLC...................... F 828 265-2513
Boone (G-924)

◆ IGM Resins USA Inc.............................D 704 588-2500
Charlotte (G-2311)

Igm Specialties Holding Inc .... F 704 945-8702
Charlotte (G-2312)

◆ Keim Mineral Coatings Amer Inc.......... F 704 588-4811
Charlotte (G-2391)

Kestrel I Acquisition Corporation........... A 919 990-7500
Durham (G-4095)

◆ Liquidating Reichhold Inc ....A 919 990-7500
Durham (G-4106)

◆ Lord Corporation ....B 919 468-5979
Cary (G-1394)

Lord Far East Inc .... G 919 468-5979
Cary (G-1397)

Lubrizol Global Management Inc............D 704 865-7451
Gastonia (G-5080)

▲ Matlab Inc..F 336 629-4161
Asheboro (G-377)

◆ Meridian Zero Degrees LLC.................E 866 454-6757
Aberdeen (G-13)

Modern Recreational Tech Inc...............D 847 272-2278
Greensboro (G-5695)

Modern Recreational Tech Inc............... E 800 221-4466
Greensboro (G-5696)

New Finish Inc... E 704 474-4116
Norwood (G-9557)

Northwest Coatings Systems Inc........... G 336 924-1459
Pfafftown (G-9664)

Oerlikon AM US Inc................................ E 980 260-2827
Huntersville (G-7027)

Paint Company of NC............................. G 336 764-1648
Clemmons (G-3198)

Piedmont Indus Coatings Inc................. G 336 377-3399
Winston Salem (G-13292)

PMG SM Holdings LLC........................... G 336 548-3250
Madison (G-7997)

PPG Architectural Finishes Inc.............. G 910 484-5161
Fayetteville (G-4655)

PPG Architectural Finishes Inc.............. G 704 864-6783
Gastonia (G-5123)

PPG Architectural Finishes Inc.............. G 336 273-9761
Greensboro (G-5754)

PPG Architectural Finishes Inc.............. G 704 847-7251
Matthews (G-8141)

PPG Architectural Finishes Inc.............. G 704 658-9250
Mooresville (G-8751)

PPG Architectural Finishes Inc.............. G 828 438-9210
Morganton (G-8888)

PPG Architectural Finishes Inc.............. G 919 872-6500
Raleigh (G-10383)

PPG Architectural Finishes Inc.............. G 919 779-5400
Raleigh (G-10384)

PPG Architectural Finishes Inc.............. G 704 633-0673
Salisbury (G-11105)

PPG Industries Inc.................................. G 919 319-0113
Cary (G-1425)

PPG Industries Inc.................................. G 704 542-8880
Charlotte (G-2653)

PPG Industries Inc.................................. G 704 523-0888
Charlotte (G-2654)

PPG Industries Inc.................................. G 919 382-3100
Durham (G-4192)

PPG Industries Inc.................................. G 919 772-3093
Greensboro (G-5755)

PPG Industries Inc.................................. C 336 856-9280
Greensboro (G-5756)

PPG Industries Inc.................................. G 252 480-1970
Kill Devil Hills (G-7319)

PPG Industries Inc.................................. G 704 658-9250
Mooresville (G-8752)

PPG Industries Inc.................................. G 919 981-0600
Raleigh (G-10385)

PPG Industries Inc.................................. G 910 452-3289
Wilmington (G-12888)

PPG Industries Inc.................................. G 336 771-8878
Winston Salem (G-13301)

Rack Works Inc....................................... E 336 368-1302
Pilot Mountain (G-9673)

Renaissance Innovations LLC .... G 774 901-4642
Durham (G-4211)

Renner Wood Companies....................... F 704 527-9261
Charlotte (G-2712)

Road Infrstrcture Inv Hldngs I................ E 336 475-6600
Thomasville (G-12066)

RPM Indstrial Ctings Group Inc.............. C 828 261-0325
Hickory (G-6434)

RPM Indstrial Ctings Group Inc.............. C 828 261-0325
Hickory (G-6435)

RPM Indstrial Ctings Group Inc.............. C 828 728-8266
Hudson (G-6957)

▲ RPM Indstrial Ctings Group Inc.......... B 828 261-0325
Hickory (G-6433)

Rust-Oleum Corporation......................... G 704 662-7730
Mooresville (G-8765)

S Choice Baker Inc................................. G 919 556-1188
Wake Forest (G-12295)

◆ S&F Products...G 714 412-1298
Holly Springs (G-6913)

Sherwin-Williams Company.................... D 704 548-2820
Charlotte (G-2798)

Sherwin-Williams Company.................... E 336 292-3000
Greensboro (G-5810)

Sherwin-Williams Company.................... G 919 436-2460
Raleigh (G-10469)

Sherwin-Williams Company.................... E 704 881-0245
Statesville (G-11764)

Sibelco North America Inc...................... D 828 766-6050
Spruce Pine (G-11586)

Strobels Supply Inc................................ F 607 324-1721
Linwood (G-7881)

Transcontinental AC US LLC.................. F 704 847-9171
Matthews (G-8154)

United Finishing Systems LLC............... G 704 873-2475
Statesville (G-11796)

Valspar Corporation................................ G 704 897-5700
Davidson (G-3725)

2861 Gum and wood chemicals

Soto Industries LLC................................ G 706 643-5011
Charlotte (G-2828)

Westrock Mwv LLC................................. G 919 334-3200
Raleigh (G-10606)

2865 Cyclic crudes and intermediates

Americhem Inc.. E 704 782-6411
Concord (G-3311)

◆ Burlington Chemical Co LLC................G 336 584-0111
Greensboro (G-5410)

Clariant Corporation................. D 704 331-7000
Charlotte *(G-1923)*

Dystar Americas Holding Corp.............. G 561-3000
Charlotte *(G-2076)*

Dystar Carolina Chemical Corp............. D 704 391-6322
Charlotte *(G-2077)*

Dystar LP................................ C 336 342-6631
Reidsville *(G-10683)*

◆ Dystar LP............................. E 704 561-3000
Charlotte *(G-2078)*

Heubach Colorants USA LLC.......... E 408 686-2935
Charlotte *(G-2276)*

Marlowe-Van Loan Corporation....... G 336 886-7126
High Point *(G-6699)*

▲ Melatex Incorporated............... F 704 332-5046
Charlotte *(G-2489)*

▲ Repi LLC.............................. E 704 648-0252
Dallas *(G-3685)*

Tar Heel Credit Counciling............ G 336 254-0348
Greensboro *(G-5852)*

Tar Heel Cuisine Inc.................... G 704 435-6979
Cherryville *(G-3070)*

Tar Heel Fence & Vinyl................ G 336 465-1297
Sophia *(G-11492)*

Tar Heel Grnd Cmmndery Order K.......... G 910 867-6764
Fayetteville *(G-4678)*

Tar Heel Landworks LLC................ G 336 941-3009
Mocksville *(G-8393)*

Tar Heel Materials & Hdlg LLC........ G 704 659-5143
Cleveland *(G-3223)*

Tar Heel Mini Motoring Club........... G 336 391-8084
Winston Salem *(G-13355)*

▲ US Specialty Color Corp............ G 704 292-1476
Monroe *(G-8574)*

2869 Industrial organic chemicals, nec

▼ Albemarle Corporation............. A 980 299-5700
Charlotte *(G-1638)*

Alltech Inc............................. E 336 635-5190
Eden *(G-4341)*

Altech-Eco Corporation............... F 828 654-8300
Arden *(G-250)*

Archer-Daniels-Midland Company.......... C 910 457-5011
Southport *(G-11516)*

Aurorium LLC........................... D 336 292-1781
Greensboro *(G-5375)*

BASF.................................... G 919 731-1700
Pikeville *(G-9666)*

BASF Corporation...................... C 704 588-5280
Charlotte *(G-1758)*

BASF Corporation...................... C 919 433-6773
Durham *(G-3914)*

BASF Corporation...................... A 919 547-2000
Durham *(G-3915)*

BASF Corporation...................... E 919 461-6500
Morrisville *(G-8937)*

BASF Plant Science LP................. C 919 547-2000
Durham *(G-3916)*

◆ Boehme-Filatex Inc................. C 336 342-4507
Reidsville *(G-10677)*

Carbon Conversion Systems LLC....... G 919 883-4238
Chapel Hill *(G-1533)*

Centre Ingredient Tech Inc........... G 910 895-9277
Rockingham *(G-10773)*

Chemol Company Inc................... E 336 333-3050
Greensboro *(G-5443)*

Chemtech Industrial Inc.............. G 919 400-5743
Louisburg *(G-7912)*

Clariant Corporation................. D 704 371-3272
Charlotte *(G-1924)*

Clariant Corporation................. E 704 235-5700
Mooresville *(G-8640)*

Clariant Corporation................. E 704 822-2100
Mount Holly *(G-9224)*

◆ Clariant Corporation............... D 704 331-7000
Charlotte *(G-1925)*

Compagnie Parento Inc................ G 828 758-2525
Lenoir *(G-7595)*

Ddp Spclty Elctrnic Mtls US 9........ E 336 547-7112
Greensboro *(G-5490)*

◆ Dystar LP............................ E 704 561-3000
Charlotte *(G-2078)*

Enzyme Customs....................... G 704 888-8278
Locust *(G-7892)*

Evonik Corporation................... D 336 333-3565
Greensboro *(G-5526)*

FCC Butner............................ G 919 575-3900
Butner *(G-1201)*

Heiq Chemtex Inc..................... G 704 795-9322
Concord *(G-3373)*

Hexion Inc............................ E 910 483-1311
Fayetteville *(G-4612)*

Hospira Inc........................... B 919 553-3831
Clayton *(G-3154)*

Imperial Falcon Group Inc............ G 646 717-1128
Charlotte *(G-2315)*

Industrial Lubricants Inc............ G 336 767-0013
Winston Salem *(G-13207)*

Innospec Active Chemicals LLC........ C 704 633-8028
Salisbury *(G-11068)*

▲ Innospec Active Chemicals LLC..... D 336 882-3308
High Point *(G-6672)*

◆ KAO Specialties Americas LLC....... C 336 884-2214
High Point *(G-6683)*

Kestrel I Acquisition Corporation.... A 919 990-7500
Durham *(G-4095)*

Leke LLC.............................. G 704 523-1452
Pineville *(G-9739)*

▼ Lindley Laboratories Inc........... F 336 449-7521
Gibsonville *(G-5181)*

◆ Liquidating Reichhold Inc.......... A 919 990-7500
Durham *(G-4106)*

Marlowe-Van Loan Corporation........ G 336 886-7126
High Point *(G-6699)*

Maverick Biofeuls.................... G 919 749-8717
Durham *(G-4119)*

Mid Town Dixie Express Fuel.......... G 336 318-1200
Asheboro *(G-378)*

▲ Mirror Tech Inc.................... G 336 342-6041
Reidsville *(G-10693)*

Momentive Performance Mtls Inc...... C 704 805-6252
Charlotte *(G-2514)*

Momentive Performance Mtls Inc...... E 704 805-6200
Huntersville *(G-7017)*

▼ Norag Technology LLC............... G 336 316-0417
Pelham *(G-9655)*

Novozymes North America Inc......... E 919 494-3220
Morrisville *(G-9030)*

◆ Novozymes North America Inc....... D 919 494-2014
Franklinton *(G-4851)*

Oak-Bark Corporation................. G 910 655-2263
Riegelwood *(G-10727)*

▼ Oak-Bark Corporation............... F
Wilmington *(G-12864)*

▼ Piedmont Chemical Inds I LLC....... D 336 885-5131
High Point *(G-6731)*

▲ Pisgah Laboratories Inc............ E 828 884-2789
Pisgah Forest *(G-9772)*

Reagents Holdings LLC................ E 800 732-8484
Charlotte *(G-2695)*

Seacon Corp........................... G 704 331-3920
Charlotte *(G-2774)*

◆ Silar LLC............................ E 910 655-4212
Riegelwood *(G-10728)*

▲ Silicones Inc....................... F 336 886-5018
High Point *(G-6774)*

Sovereign Technologies LLC........... G 828 358-5355
Hickory *(G-6455)*

▲ Stewart Superabsorbents LLC........ G 828 855-9316
Hickory *(G-6457)*

Transeco Energy Corporation.......... G 828 684-6400
Arden *(G-311)*

Triangle Chemical Company............ G 919 942-3237
Chapel Hill *(G-1579)*

◆ Trinity Manufacturing Inc.......... D 910 582-5650
Hamlet *(G-6064)*

Tyton NC Biofuels LLC................ E 910 878-7820
Raeford *(G-9854)*

Video Fuel............................ G 919 676-9940
Raleigh *(G-10587)*

◆ Vpm Liquidating Inc................ F 336 292-1781
Greensboro *(G-5912)*

Wright Chemicals LLC................. G 919 296-1771
Durham *(G-4310)*

Xona Microfluidics Inc............... G 951 553-6400
Research Triangle Pa *(G-10718)*

2873 Nitrogenous fertilizers

Acton Corporation.................... G 434 728-4491
Greensboro *(G-5340)*

Carolina Eastern Inc................. G 252 795-3128
Robersonville *(G-10766)*

Clapp Fertilizer and Trckg Inc....... G 336 449-6103
Whitsett *(G-12602)*

▲ Farm Chemicals Inc................. F 910 875-4277
Raeford *(G-9837)*

Harvey Fertilizer and Gas Co......... F 919 731-2474
Goldsboro *(G-5222)*

Harvey Fertilizer and Gas Co......... F 252 523-9090
Kinston *(G-7414)*

▲ Harvey Fertilizer and Gas Co....... E 252 526-4150
Kinston *(G-7415)*

Helena Agri-Enterprises LLC.......... F 910 422-8901
Rowland *(G-10915)*

Kamlar Corporation................... E 252 443-2576
Rocky Mount *(G-10845)*

Mineral Springs Fertilizer Inc....... G 704 843-2683
Mineral Springs *(G-8327)*

Nutrien AG Solutions Inc............. A 252 322-4111
Aurora *(G-644)*

Nutrien AG Solutions Inc............. G 252 235-4161
Bailey *(G-672)*

Scotts Company LLC................... G 704 663-6088
Mooresville *(G-8767)*

Southern States Coop Inc............. G 336 246-3201
Creedmoor *(G-3654)*

Southern States Coop Inc............. E 336 786-7545
Mount Airy *(G-9178)*

Southern States Coop Inc............. E 919 658-5061
Mount Olive *(G-9259)*

Southern States Coop Inc............. D 704 872-6364
Statesville *(G-11772)*

Southern States Coop Inc............. F 910 285-8213
Wallace *(G-12325)*

2874 Phosphatic fertilizers

Nutrien AG Solutions Inc............. F 252 977-2025
Rocky Mount *(G-10814)*

Pcs Phosphate Company Inc............ E 252 322-4111
Aurora *(G-645)*

Potash Corp Saskatchewan Inc......... E 252 322-4111
Aurora *(G-646)*

Scotts Company LLC................... G 704 663-6088
Mooresville *(G-8767)*

Southern States Coop Inc............. G 336 246-3201
Creedmoor *(G-3654)*

Southern States Coop Inc.......................... E 336 786-7545
Mount Airy *(G-9178)*

Southern States Coop Inc.......................... E 919 658-5061
Mount Olive *(G-9259)*

Southern States Coop Inc.......................... D 704 872-6364
Statesville *(G-11772)*

Southern States Coop Inc.......................... F 910 285-8213
Wallace *(G-12325)*

2875 Fertilizers, mixing only

C A Perry & Son Inc.................................. G 252 330-2323
Elizabeth City *(G-4380)*

C A Perry & Son Inc.................................. E 252 221-4463
Hobbsville *(G-6883)*

Camp Chemical Corporation..................... F 336 597-2214
Roxboro *(G-10921)*

Charles Hill Enterprises............................ F 828 665-2116
Candler *(G-1220)*

Cmd Land Services LLC............................ G 919 554-2281
Wake Forest *(G-12271)*

Eastern Compost LLC................................ G 252 446-3636
Elm City *(G-4465)*

Gillam & Mason Inc.................................. G 252 356-2874
Cofield *(G-3266)*

Harvey Fertilizer and Gas Co.................... F 919 731-2474
Goldsboro *(G-5222)*

Harvey Fertilizer and Gas Co.................... F 252 523-9090
Kinston *(G-7414)*

▲ Harvey Fertilizer and Gas Co.................. E 252 526-4150
Kinston *(G-7415)*

McGill Environmental Gp LLC..................... F 919 362-1161
New Hill *(G-9410)*

Northwest AG Product.............................. G 509 547-8234
Cary *(G-1409)*

Nutrien AG Solutions Inc.......................... G 252 585-0282
Conway *(G-3578)*

Nutrien AG Solutions Inc.......................... F 252 977-2025
Rocky Mount *(G-10814)*

Southern AG Insecticides Inc.................... E 828 692-2233
Hendersonville *(G-6242)*

Southern States Coop Inc.......................... D 704 872-6364
Statesville *(G-11772)*

T H Blue Inc.. E 910 673-3033
Eagle Springs *(G-4319)*

Tarheel Enviromental LLC........................ G 910 425-4939
Stedman *(G-11808)*

2879 Agricultural chemicals, nec

Amika LLC.. G 984 664-9804
Cary *(G-1288)*

Aqua 10 Corporation................................ G 252 726-5421
Morehead City *(G-8813)*

Arysta Lifescience Inc.............................. E 919 678-4900
Cary *(G-1295)*

▲ Arysta Lifescience N Amer LLC........ E 919 678-4900
Cary *(G-1296)*

Atticus LLC.. E 984 465-4754
Cary *(G-1299)*

Cape Fear Chemicals Inc.......................... G 910 862-3139
Elizabethtown *(G-4420)*

Chemours Company.................................. E 910 483-4681
Fayetteville *(G-4573)*

Chemours Company Fc LLC..................... D 910 678-1314
Fayetteville *(G-4574)*

Degesch America Inc................................ E 800 548-2778
Wilson *(G-12983)*

Dupont.. G 919 414-0089
Raleigh *(G-10065)*

◆ Ensystex Inc..E.... 888 398-3772
Fayetteville *(G-4598)*

Fair Products Inc...................................... G 919 467-1599
Cary *(G-1361)*

▲ Gb Biosciences LLC.............................. D 336 632-6000
Greensboro *(G-5550)*

Harvey Fertilizer and Gas Co.................... E 252 753-2063
Farmville *(G-4530)*

Helena Agri-Enterprises LLC................... G 828 685-1182
Hendersonville *(G-6214)*

▲ Homs LLC.. G 919 533-4752
Pittsboro *(G-9785)*

▲ I Must Garden LLC.................................. G 919 929-2299
Raleigh *(G-10182)*

Jabb of Carolinas Inc.............................. G 919 965-9007
Pine Level *(G-9682)*

Lanxess Corporation................................ E 704 868-7200
Gastonia *(G-5077)*

◆ Makhteshim Agan North Amer Inc......E.... 919 256-9300
Raleigh *(G-10267)*

◆ Mey Corporation.................................... G 919 932-5800
Chapel Hill *(G-1557)*

Monsanto Company.................................. G 252 212-5421
Battleboro *(G-702)*

Privette Enterprises Inc.......................... E 704 634-3291
Monroe *(G-8544)*

Scotts Company LLC................................ E 704 663-6088
Mooresville *(G-8767)*

Southeastern Minerals Inc....................... E 252 492-0831
Henderson *(G-6179)*

Southern AG Insecticides Inc.................... E 828 264-8843
Boone *(G-943)*

Southern AG Insecticides Inc.................... E 828 692-2233
Hendersonville *(G-6242)*

▲ Summit Agro Usa LLC............................ G 984 260-0407
Durham *(G-4254)*

◆ Trinity Manufacturing Inc....................D.... 910 582-5650
Hamlet *(G-6064)*

Tyratech Inc.. E 919 415-4275
Morrisville *(G-9082)*

▲ Upl NA Inc.. G 800 358-7642
Cary *(G-1476)*

Vestaron Corporation.............................. G 919 694-1022
Durham *(G-4296)*

◆ Vpm Liquidating Inc..............................F.... 336 292-1781
Greensboro *(G-5912)*

2891 Adhesives and sealants

Arclin USA LLC.. G 919 542-2526
Moncure *(G-8400)*

▲ Beardowadams Inc................................ F 704 359-8443
Charlotte *(G-1764)*

Bio-Adhesive Alliance Inc....................... G 336 285-3676
Mount Olive *(G-9248)*

Bostik Inc.. F 864 535-3759
Greenville *(G-5948)*

Capital City Sealants LLC....................... G 919 427-4077
Raleigh *(G-9967)*

Carolina Solvents Inc.............................. E 828 322-1920
Hickory *(G-6287)*

Carroll-Baccari Inc.................................. G 561 585-2227
Flat Rock *(G-4705)*

Clesters Auto Rubber Seals LLC............. F 704 637-9979
Cleveland *(G-3211)*

Colquimica Adhesives Inc....................... E 704 318-4750
Charlotte *(G-1959)*

Dap Products Inc..................................... F 704 799-9640
Mooresville *(G-8651)*

Daystar Materials Inc.............................. G 919 734-0460
Goldsboro *(G-5211)*

Dbt Coatings LLC.................................... G 336 834-9700
Greensboro *(G-5489)*

Ddp Spclty Elctrnic Mtls US 9................ E 336 547-7112
Greensboro *(G-5490)*

Everkem Diversified Pdts Inc................... F 336 661-7801
Winston Salem *(G-13161)*

Firestopping Products Inc....................... F 336 661-0102
Winston Salem *(G-13168)*

GLS Products LLC.................................... G 704 334-2425
Charlotte *(G-2216)*

◆ Harper-Love Adhesives Corp..............D.... 704 588-4395
Charlotte *(G-2260)*

HB Fuller Adhesives LLC......................... E 415 878-7202
Morrisville *(G-8986)*

HB Fuller Company.................................. G 336 294-5939
Greensboro *(G-5589)*

Henkel US Operations Corp..................... G 704 799-0385
Mooresville *(G-8681)*

Henkel US Operations Corp..................... E 704 647-3500
Salisbury *(G-11063)*

Hexion Inc.. G 336 884-8918
High Point *(G-6646)*

◆ Hexpol Compounding NC Inc...............A.... 704 872-1585
Statesville *(G-11710)*

Hickory Adchem Inc................................ G 828 327-0936
Hickory *(G-6346)*

His Company Inc...................................... G 800 537-0351
Wilmington *(G-12806)*

Impact Technologies LLC....................... G 704 400-5364
Concord *(G-3376)*

INX Intrntnal Ctings Adhesives............... C 910 371-3184
Leland *(G-7548)*

Ips Corporation.. E 919 598-2400
Durham *(G-4083)*

Jowat Corporation.................................... G 336 434-9356
Archdale *(G-231)*

Jowat Corporation....................................D.... 336 442-5834
Archdale *(G-232)*

◆ Jowat Corporation................................E.... 336 434-9000
Archdale *(G-233)*

Jowat International Corp......................... E 336 434-9000
Archdale *(G-234)*

Jowat Properties Corp............................ G 336 434-9000
Archdale *(G-235)*

Kestrel I Acquisition Corporation............. A 919 990-7500
Durham *(G-4095)*

◆ Kleiberit Adhesives USA Inc.................F.... 704 843-3339
Waxhaw *(G-12435)*

Knight Safety Coatings Co Inc................. F 910 458-3145
Wilmington *(G-12829)*

Laticrete International Inc........................F.... 910 582-2252
Hamlet *(G-6059)*

LD Davis Industries Inc........................... E 704 289-4551
Monroe *(G-8514)*

◆ Liquidating Reichhold Inc.....................A.... 919 990-7500
Durham *(G-4106)*

▲ Loba-Wakol LLC.................................... E 704 527-5919
Wadesboro *(G-12247)*

Lord Corporation....................................D.... 919 469-2500
Cary *(G-1395)*

◆ Lord Corporation..................................B.... 919 468-5979
Cary *(G-1394)*

Lord Far East Inc.................................... G 919 468-5979
Cary *(G-1397)*

Manning Fabrics Inc................................ G 910 295-1970
Pinehurst *(G-9696)*

Marlin Company Inc................................ G 828 758-9999
Lenoir *(G-7623)*

◆ Marlin Company Inc..............................E.... 828 754-0980
Lenoir *(G-7624)*

Modern Recreational Tech Inc................. E 800 221-4466
Greensboro *(G-5696)*

◆ Phoenix Tapes Usa LLC.......................G.... 704 588-3090
Charlotte *(G-2635)*

Power Adhesives Ltd............................... G 704 578-9984
Charlotte *(G-2648)*

Pregis LLC.. E 828 465-9197
Conover *(G-3549)*

Psa Incorporated................................ G 910 371-1115
Belville *(G-780)*

◆ Reichhold Holdings Us Inc............A 919 990-7500
Durham *(G-4210)*

▲ Robix America Inc.......................... C 336 668-9555
Greensboro *(G-5791)*

◆ Rpoc Inc..C 910 371-3184
Wilmington *(G-12904)*

Rutland Fire Clay Company............ G 802 775-5519
Chapel Hill *(G-1569)*

Scott Bader Inc............................... E 330 920-4410
Mocksville *(G-8388)*

Sensus USA Inc.............................. C 919 576-6185
Morrisville *(G-9052)*

◆ Sensus USA Inc.............................. E 919 845-4000
Morrisville *(G-9051)*

◆ Sika Corporation............................E 704 810-0500
Gastonia *(G-5138)*

Slade Operating Company LLC...... E 704 873-1366
Statesville *(G-11766)*

Southern Resin Inc.......................... E 336 475-1348
Thomasville *(G-12071)*

Spectrum Adhesives Inc.................. E 828 396-4200
Granite Falls *(G-5324)*

▲ STI Polymer Inc.............................. E 800 874-5878
Sanford *(G-11241)*

◆ Tailored Chemical Products Inc..........D 828 322-6512
Hickory *(G-6462)*

Textile Rubber and Chem Co Inc...... G 704 376-3582
Indian Trail *(G-7103)*

◆ Tosaf Inc.......................................F 980 533-3000
Bessemer City *(G-837)*

Udm Systems LLC........................... G 919 789-0777
Raleigh *(G-10570)*

▲ Udm Systems LLC........................... G 919 789-0777
Raleigh *(G-10571)*

▲ Web-Don Incorporated.................... E 800 532-0434
Charlotte *(G-3009)*

▲ Weiss USA LLC............................... G 704 282-4496
Monroe *(G-8579)*

2892 Explosives

Austin Powder Company.................. E 828 645-4291
Denton *(G-3740)*

K2 Solutions Inc.............................. B 910 692-6898
Southern Pines *(G-11501)*

◆ Maxam North America Inc..........F 214 736-8100
Mooresville *(G-8721)*

2893 Printing ink

▲ Actega Wit Inc............................... C 704 735-8282
Lincolnton *(G-7808)*

▼ Allied Pressroom Products Inc........ E 954 920-0909
Monroe *(G-8421)*

▲ American Water Graphics Inc.......... G 828 247-0700
Forest City *(G-4783)*

Archie Supply LLC............................ G 336 987-0895
Greensboro *(G-5368)*

Arpro M-Tec Inc.............................. F 828 433-0699
Morganton *(G-8851)*

Crossroads Fuel Service Inc............ E 252 426-5216
Hertford *(G-6252)*

DSM Desotech Inc............................ G 704 862-5000
Stanley *(G-11614)*

▲ Environmental Inks and Co............ C 828 433-1922
Morganton *(G-8863)*

Flint Group Inc................................. E 828 687-4363
Arden *(G-269)*

Flint Group US LLC.......................... G 828 687-4309
Arden *(G-270)*

Flint Group US LLC.......................... G 828 687-4291
Arden *(G-271)*

Flint Group US LLC.......................... G 704 504-2626
Charlotte *(G-2166)*

Hubergroup USA Inc......................... F 336 292-5501
Greensboro *(G-5608)*

▲ Ink Tec Inc..................................... F 828 465-6411
Newton *(G-9476)*

INX International Ink Co.................... E 704 372-2080
Charlotte *(G-2352)*

INX International Ink Co.................... G 910 371-3184
Leland *(G-7547)*

INX International Ink Co.................... F 704 414-6428
Rockwell *(G-10798)*

Mirchandani Inc............................... G 919 872-8871
Raleigh *(G-10309)*

◆ Mitsubishi Chemical Amer Inc..........D 980 580-2839
Charlotte *(G-2509)*

◆ Monarch Color Corporation............E 704 394-4626
Charlotte *(G-2515)*

RPM Indstrial Ctings Group Inc.......... C 828 261-0325
Hickory *(G-6434)*

RPM Indstrial Ctings Group Inc.......... C 828 728-8266
Hudson *(G-6957)*

Rutland Group Inc............................ G 704 553-0046
Charlotte *(G-2744)*

◆ Siegwerk Eic LLC............................ F 800 368-4657
Morganton *(G-8897)*

Sun Chemical Corporation................ D 704 587-4531
Charlotte *(G-2880)*

Wikoff Color Corporation.................. E 704 392-4657
Charlotte *(G-3019)*

Wikoff Color Corporation.................. E 336 668-3423
Greensboro *(G-5918)*

Xsys North America Corporation.......... E 828 687-2485
Arden *(G-321)*

2899 Chemical preparations, nec

Ae Technology Inc............................ F 704 528-2000
Troutman *(G-12130)*

Akuratemp LLC................................ F 828 708-7178
Arden *(G-249)*

▼ Alamance Foods Inc........................ C 336 226-6392
Burlington *(G-1043)*

▼ Albemarle Corporation.................... A 980 299-5700
Charlotte *(G-1638)*

Alliance Assessments LLC................ G 336 283-9246
Winston Salem *(G-13081)*

American Chrome & Chem NA Inc.......... F 910 675-7200
Castle Hayne *(G-1494)*

American Phoenix Inc....................... C 910 484-4007
Fayetteville *(G-4551)*

Attl Products Inc.............................. G 336 475-8101
Thomasville *(G-11995)*

▲ Barker Industries Inc....................... G 704 391-1023
Charlotte *(G-1753)*

Blast Off Intl Chem & Mfg Co............ G 509 885-4525
Seaboard *(G-11269)*

Bnnano Inc...................................... F 844 926-6266
Burlington *(G-1052)*

◆ Bonsal American Inc........................D 704 525-1621
Charlotte *(G-1799)*

Buckeye International Inc.................. G 704 523-9400
Charlotte *(G-1817)*

◆ Burlington Chemical Co LLC............G 336 584-0111
Greensboro *(G-5410)*

Camco Manufacturing Inc................ G 336 348-6609
Reidsville *(G-10678)*

◆ Camco Manufacturing LLC............... C 336 668-7661
Greensboro *(G-5419)*

◆ Carlisle Corporation........................A 704 501-1100
Charlotte *(G-1842)*

Carolina Bottle Mfr LLC.................... G 704 635-8759
Monroe *(G-8451)*

Carolina Connections Inc.................. G 336 786-7030
Mount Airy *(G-9107)*

Celcore Inc..................................... G 828 669-4875
Black Mountain *(G-863)*

Championx LLC................................ G 704 506-4830
Belmont *(G-743)*

Chem-Tech Solutions Inc.................. E 704 829-9202
Gastonia *(G-5019)*

▲ Chem-Tex Laboratories Inc.............. E 706 602-8600
Concord *(G-3335)*

Chemtech North Carolina LLC.......... E 910 514-9575
Lillington *(G-7794)*

Clariant Corporation........................ D 704 331-7000
Charlotte *(G-1923)*

◆ Clariant Corporation........................D 704 331-7000
Charlotte *(G-1925)*

Continental Manufacturing Co............ G 336 697-2591
Mc Leansville *(G-8220)*

Copia Labs Inc................................. G 910 904-1000
Raeford *(G-9835)*

Dst Manufacturing LLC..................... G 336 676-6096
Randleman *(G-10643)*

Emerald Carolina Chemical LLC........ F 704 393-0089
Charlotte *(G-2109)*

Enviroserve Chemicals Inc................ F 910 892-1791
Dunn *(G-3856)*

Eoncoat LLC.................................... G 941 928-9401
Lenoir *(G-7602)*

Euclid Chemical Company................ G 704 283-2544
Monroe *(G-8486)*

◆ Fiber Composites LLC......................B 704 463-7120
New London *(G-9415)*

Fire Retardant Chem Tech LLC.......... G 980 253-8880
Matthews *(G-8169)*

FMC Corporation.............................. D 704 868-5300
Bessemer City *(G-818)*

FMC Corporation.............................. B 704 426-5336
Bessemer City *(G-819)*

Freudenberg Prfmce Mtls LP.............. C 828 665-5000
Candler *(G-1225)*

▲ Gb Biosciences LLC......................... D 336 632-6000
Greensboro *(G-5550)*

Gbf Inc.. D 336 665-0205
High Point *(G-6627)*

Giles Chemical Corporation.............. G 828 452-4784
Waynesville *(G-12458)*

▲ Giles Chemical Corporation.............. E 828 452-4784
Waynesville *(G-12459)*

Global Bioprotect LLC...................... F 336 861-0162
High Point *(G-6630)*

◆ Goulston Technologies Inc................E 704 289-6464
Monroe *(G-8495)*

Gtg Engineering Inc.......................... G 910 457-0068
Southport *(G-11520)*

◆ Gtg Engineering Inc.........................G 877 569-8572
Clarendon *(G-3127)*

Hexion Inc...................................... E 910 483-1311
Fayetteville *(G-4612)*

Hospira Inc..................................... B 919 553-3831
Clayton *(G-3154)*

Hzo Inc.. E 919 439-0505
Morrisville *(G-8989)*

Ifs Industries Inc............................. E 919 234-1397
Morrisville *(G-8991)*

▲ Info-Gel LLC................................... G 704 599-5770
Charlotte *(G-2330)*

Ivm Chemicals Inc........................... E 407 506-4913
Charlotte *(G-2358)*

J W Harris Co Inc............................. G 336 831-8601
Winston Salem *(G-13213)*

Jci Jones Chemicals Inc.................... F 704 392-9767
Charlotte *(G-2363)*

Jeskri Associates Inc............................ G 704 291-9991
 Monroe (G-8511)

Kestrel I Acquisition Corporation.......... A 919 990-7500
 Durham (G-4095)

Keystone Powdered Metal Co............ D 704 730-8805
 Kings Mountain (G-7367)

Lanxess Corporation............................ E 704 868-7200
 Gastonia (G-5077)

Laticrete International Inc................... F 910 582-2252
 Hamlet (G-6059)

◆ LCI Corporation International.............E 704 399-7441
 Charlotte (G-2411)

Lime-Chem Inc.................................... G 910 843-2121
 Rockwell (G-10799)

Liquid Ice Corporation......................... F 704 882-3505
 Matthews (G-8179)

◆ Liquidating Reichhold Inc....................A 919 990-7500
 Durham (G-4106)

Lord Corporation................................. D 919 342-3380
 Cary (G-1393)

Loy & Loy Inc...................................... G 919 942-6356
 Graham (G-5276)

Lubrizol Advanced Mtls Inc................. E 704 587-5583
 Charlotte (G-2437)

Lubrizol Global Management Inc......... D 704 865-7451
 Gastonia (G-5080)

Marlowe-Van Loan Sales Co............... G 336 882-3351
 High Point (G-6700)

Matchem Inc.. G 336 886-5000
 High Point (G-6707)

Metal & Materials Proc LLC................. G 260 438-8901
 Aberdeen (G-14)

▲ Microban Products Company............. E 704 766-4267
 Huntersville (G-7013)

Moe Jt Enterprises Inc........................ F 423 512-1427
 Winston Salem (G-13260)

Molecular Toxicology Inc.................... G 828 264-9099
 Boone (G-935)

◆ National Foam Inc..............................E 919 639-6100
 Angier (G-126)

Nitta Gelatin Holdings Inc.................. E 919 238-3300
 Morrisville (G-9027)

▲ Nitta Gelatin Usa Inc......................... E 910 484-0457
 Morrisville (G-9028)

▼ Novalent Ltd...................................... F 336 375-7555
 Greensboro (G-5715)

Nsi Lab Solutions Inc.......................... F 919 789-3000
 Raleigh (G-10342)

Old Belt Extracts LLC.......................... E 336 530-5784
 Roxboro (G-10934)

Opw Fueling Components Inc.............. E 919 464-4569
 Smithfield (G-11458)

Patriot Clean Fuel LLC........................ F 704 896-3600
 Mooresville (G-8743)

▲ Pavco Inc.. E 704 496-6800
 Charlotte (G-2619)

Pencco Inc.. F 252 235-5300
 Middlesex (G-8279)

▲ Polytec Inc.. E 704 277-3960
 Mooresville (G-8750)

Protek Services LLC............................ G 910 556-4121
 Cameron (G-1215)

◆ Radiator Specialty Company..............D 704 688-2302
 Indian Trail (G-7097)

RSC Bio Solutions LLC........................ G 800 661-3558
 Charlotte (G-2737)

RSC Chemical Solutions LLC.............. F 704 821-7643
 Indian Trail (G-7098)

Rust911 Inc... G 607 425-2882
 Hickory (G-6437)

▼ Schoenberg Salt Co........................... G 336 766-0600
 Winston Salem (G-13330)

▲ Seacon Corporation........................... F 704 333-6000
 Charlotte (G-2775)

Second Earth Inc................................. G 336 740-9333
 Greensboro (G-5804)

Shadow Creek Consulting Inc.............. E 716 860-7397
 Statesville (G-11763)

Silver Moon Nutraceuticals LLC.......... G 828 698-5795
 Fletcher (G-4768)

◆ Sirchie Acquisition Co LLC.................C 800 356-7311
 Youngsville (G-13486)

Soto Industries LLC............................ G 706 643-5011
 Charlotte (G-2828)

Specgx LLC.. C 919 878-4706
 Raleigh (G-10495)

◆ Surry Chemicals Incorporated...........E 336 786-4607
 Mount Airy (G-9181)

◆ Tailored Chemical Products Inc...........D 828 322-6512
 Hickory (G-6462)

Thunder Eagle Enterprises Inc............ G 828 242-0267
 Asheville (G-618)

Tribodyn Technologies Inc................... G 859 750-6299
 Mooresville (G-8788)

◆ Unitex Chemical Corp........................ G 336 378-0965
 Greensboro (G-5892)

Venator Chemicals LLC....................... D 704 454-4811
 Harrisburg (G-6120)

Vyse Gelatin LLC................................. G 919 238-3300
 Morrisville (G-9087)

Westrock Company............................... G 770 448-2193
 Winston Salem (G-13390)

William Bostic..................................... G 336 629-5243
 Asheboro (G-421)

Winton Products Company.................. F 704 399-5151
 Charlotte (G-3023)

Xelera Inc.. G 855 493-5372
 Charlotte (G-3030)

Xelera Inc.. G 540 915-6181
 Denver (G-3818)

Xylem Water Solutions USA Inc.......... D 704 409-9700
 Charlotte (G-3037)

29 PETROLEUM REFINING AND RELATED INDUSTRIES

2911 Petroleum refining

Agrofuel LLC.. G 704 876-6667
 Statesville (G-11649)

Balanced Health Plus LLC................... F 704 604-9524
 Charlotte (G-1746)

Carolina Bg... G 704 847-8840
 Matthews (G-8101)

Harvey Fertilizer and Gas Co.............. F 919 731-2474
 Goldsboro (G-5222)

Murphy USA Inc................................... E 828 758-7055
 Lenoir (G-7628)

Native Naturalz Inc............................. F 336 334-2984
 Greensboro (G-5704)

Norcor Technologies Corp................... G 704 309-4101
 Greensboro (G-5712)

▲ Parker Gas Company Inc.................... F 800 354-7250
 Clinton (G-3238)

Pitt Road LLC...................................... G 252 331-5818
 Elizabeth City (G-4403)

Sg-Clw Inc... F 336 865-4980
 Winston Salem (G-13331)

Sinowest Mfg LLC............................... G 919 289-9337
 Raleigh (G-10481)

Stop N Go LLC..................................... G 919 523-7355
 Morrisville (G-9059)

Volta Group Corporation LLC.............. E 919 637-0273
 Raleigh (G-10593)

▼ Warren Oil Company LLC.................... D 910 892-6456
 Dunn (G-3871)

2951 Asphalt paving mixtures and blocks

Barnhill Contracting Company............. F 336 584-1306
 Burlington (G-1051)

Barnhill Contracting Company............. G 704 721-7500
 Concord (G-3317)

Barnhill Contracting Company............. D 910 488-1319
 Fayetteville (G-4557)

Barnhill Contracting Company............. E 252 752-7608
 Greenville (G-5946)

Blythe Construction Inc...................... G 704 788-9733
 Concord (G-3322)

Blythe Construction Inc...................... E 336 854-9003
 Greensboro (G-5396)

▲ Blythe Construction Inc...................... B 704 375-8474
 Charlotte (G-1793)

Boggs Materials Inc............................ G 704 289-8482
 Monroe (G-8441)

Boggs Transport Inc............................ G 704 289-8482
 Monroe (G-8442)

Brown Brothers Construction Co......... F 828 297-2131
 Zionville (G-13527)

Carolina Asphalt Maintenance............ G 828 944-0425
 Maggie Valley (G-8005)

▲ Carolina Sunrock LLC......................... E 919 575-4502
 Butner (G-1200)

Cloverleaf Mixing Inc.......................... G 336 765-7900
 Winston Salem (G-13125)

Custom Brick Company Inc.................. E 919 832-2804
 Raleigh (G-10028)

D&S Company Inc................................ G 828 894-2778
 Tryon (G-12174)

Dickerson Group Inc............................ G 704 289-3111
 Charlotte (G-2042)

Fibrecrete Pprsrvtion Tech Inc............ G 336 789-7259
 Mount Airy (G-9121)

Fsc Holdings Inc.................................. G 919 782-1247
 Raleigh (G-10121)

Gardner Asphalt Co............................. F 336 784-8924
 Winston Salem (G-13176)

Garris Grading and Paving Inc............. F 252 749-1101
 Farmville (G-4529)

Gelder & Associates Inc...................... C 919 772-6895
 Raleigh (G-10126)

Gem Asset Acquisition LLC................. G 919 851-0799
 Cary (G-1365)

Gem Asset Acquisition LLC................. G 704 697-9577
 Charlotte (G-2197)

Gem Asset Acquisition LLC................. G 336 854-8200
 Greensboro (G-5551)

Gem Asset Acquisition LLC................. G 704 225-3321
 Charlotte (G-2196)

Highland Paving Co LLC...................... D 910 482-0080
 Fayetteville (G-4613)

Hudson Paving Inc............................... D 910 895-5910
 Rockingham (G-10780)

Johnson Paving Company Inc.............. F 828 652-4911
 Marion (G-8046)

Krebs Corporation............................... G 336 548-3250
 Madison (G-7989)

Lane Construction Corporation............ C 919 876-4550
 Raleigh (G-10247)

Long Asp Pav Trckg of Grnsburg.......... G 336 643-4121
 Summerfield (G-11842)

Russell Standard Corporation.............. F 336 292-6875
 Greensboro (G-5797)

Russell Standard Nc LLC..................... D 336 292-6875
 Greensboro (G-5798)

S T Wooten Corporation...................... E 919 965-9880
 Princeton (G-9826)

S
I
C

Sunrock Group Holdings Corp............... D 919 747-6400
Raleigh *(G-10520)*

Thorworks Industries Inc....................... G 919 852-3714
Raleigh *(G-10547)*

Vulcan Materials Company..................... G 704 545-5687
Charlotte *(G-2992)*

2952 Asphalt felts and coatings

Actega North America Inc..................... G 704 736-9389
Kings Mountain *(G-7343)*

Axalta Coating Systems USA LLC........ F 336 802-5701
High Point *(G-6533)*

Bridgestone Americas Inc..................... C 984 888-0413
Durham *(G-3940)*

◆ Carlisle Corporation............................A 704 501-1100
Charlotte *(G-1842)*

Carolina Solvents Inc........................... E 828 322-1920
Hickory *(G-6287)*

Certainteed LLC.................................... C 919 603-1971
Oxford *(G-9607)*

Gemseal Pavement Products................. G 866 264-8273
Charlotte *(G-2198)*

Longhorn Roofing Inc........................... F 704 774-1080
Monroe *(G-8520)*

Metal Roofing Systems LLC................. E 704 820-3110
Stanley *(G-11622)*

Ply Gem Holdings Inc.......................... D 919 677-3900
Cary *(G-1421)*

Plycem USA LLC.................................. C 336 696-2007
North Wilkesboro *(G-9549)*

Solid Holdings LLC.............................. F 704 423-0260
Charlotte *(G-2825)*

Texture Plus Inc................................... E 631 218-9200
Lincolnton *(G-7863)*

Triad Corrugated Metal Inc................... E 336 625-9727
Asheboro *(G-411)*

Wake Supply Company.......................... G 252 234-6012
Wilson *(G-13044)*

2992 Lubricating oils and greases

Blumenthal Holdings LLC..................... G 704 688-2302
Charlotte *(G-1792)*

Citgo Quik Lube of Clayton.................. G 919 550-0935
Clayton *(G-3140)*

Lockrey Company LLC........................... G 856 665-4794
Salisbury *(G-11085)*

Lord Corporation.................................. D 919 342-3380
Cary *(G-1393)*

▲ Lubrimetal Corporation...................... F 828 212-1083
Granite Falls *(G-5311)*

▼ Moroil Corp...................................... F 704 795-9595
Concord *(G-3405)*

Noble Oil Services Inc.......................... C 919 774-8180
Sanford *(G-11212)*

Revoultion Oil Inc................................ G 704 577-2546
Mooresville *(G-8758)*

▲ Sanford Transition Company Inc....... E 919 775-4989
Sanford *(G-11230)*

2999 Petroleum and coal products, nec

Carolina Golfco Inc.............................. G 704 525-7846
Charlotte *(G-1848)*

30 RUBBER AND MISCELLANEOUS PLASTIC PRODUCTS

3011 Tires and inner tubes

▲ Airboss Rbr Compounding NC LLC.. E 252 826-4919
Scotland Neck *(G-11263)*

Bestdrive LLC....................................... E 800 450-3187
Charlotte *(G-1774)*

▲ Black Tire Service Inc........................ G 919 908-6347
Durham *(G-3934)*

Bridgestone Americas Inc..................... C 984 888-0413
Durham *(G-3940)*

Bridgestone Amrcas Tire Oprtons......... A 252 291-4275
Wilson *(G-12974)*

◆ Carlisle Corporation............................ A 704 501-1100
Charlotte *(G-1842)*

Carolina Giant Tires Inc....................... F 919 609-9077
Henderson *(G-6149)*

Derrow Enterprises Inc......................... G 252 635-3375
New Bern *(G-9364)*

Diagnostic Shop Inc............................. G 704 933-3435
Kannapolis *(G-7207)*

Goodyear Tire & Rubber Company........ D 910 488-9295
Fayetteville *(G-4605)*

Goodyear Tire & Rubber Company........ G 919 552-9340
Holly Springs *(G-6903)*

Goodyear Tire & Rubber Company........ G 336 794-0035
Winston Salem *(G-13180)*

Mr Tire Inc.. G 704 735-8024
Lincolnton *(G-7846)*

Oliver Rubber Company LLC................. B 336 629-1436
Asheboro *(G-380)*

◆ Roll-Tech Molding Products LLC......... E 828 431-4515
Hickory *(G-6432)*

Smart Cast Group................................ F 855 971-2287
Raleigh *(G-10487)*

Too Hott Customs LLC......................... G 336 722-4919
Winston Salem *(G-13366)*

Tyrata Inc.. F 919 210-8992
Durham *(G-4286)*

White S Tire Svc Wilson Inc................. G 252 237-0770
Wilson *(G-13046)*

White S Tire Svc Wilson Inc................. D 252 237-5426
Wilson *(G-13047)*

Wmb of Wake County Inc..................... G 919 782-0419
Raleigh *(G-10612)*

3021 Rubber and plastics footwear

▲ CBA Productions Inc......................... G 703 568-4758
Fayetteville *(G-4571)*

McRae Industries Inc........................... C 910 439-6149
Mount Gilead *(G-9203)*

Vans Inc.. G 704 364-3811
Charlotte *(G-2973)*

Vans Inc.. G 919 792-2555
Raleigh *(G-10583)*

◆ Winstn-Slem Inds For Blind Inc.......... B 336 759-0551
Winston Salem *(G-13398)*

3052 Rubber and plastics hose and beltings

Belt Shop Inc...................................... F 704 865-3636
Gastonia *(G-4997)*

Beltservice Corporation........................ E 704 947-2264
Huntersville *(G-6973)*

Eaton Corporation................................ D 828 286-4157
Forest City *(G-4788)*

Everything Industrial Supply.................. G 743 333-2222
Winston Salem *(G-13162)*

Flextrol Corporation............................. F 704 888-1120
Locust *(G-7893)*

Forbo Belting...................................... E 704 948-0800
Huntersville *(G-6992)*

Forbo Siegling LLC.............................. F 704 948-0800
Huntersville *(G-6993)*

Forbo Siegling LLC.............................. F 704 948-0800
Huntersville *(G-6994)*

▲ Forbo Siegling LLC........................... B 704 948-0800
Huntersville *(G-6995)*

Ghx Industrial LLC............................... G 336 996-7271
Kernersville *(G-7276)*

▼ Industrial Power Inc.......................... G 910 483-4230
Fayetteville *(G-4615)*

▲ Mmb One Inc.................................... F 704 523-8163
Charlotte *(G-2512)*

Muviq Usa LLC..................................... E 910 843-1024
Red Springs *(G-10670)*

National Foam Inc................................ C 919 639-6151
Angier *(G-125)*

Plastiflex North Carolina LLC............... D 704 871-8448
Statesville *(G-11748)*

Polyhose Incorporated.......................... E 732 512-9141
Wilmington *(G-12881)*

Sesame Technologies Inc..................... F 252 964-2205
Washington *(G-12412)*

◆ Splawn Belting Inc............................ E 336 227-4277
Burlington *(G-1162)*

◆ Steele Rubber Products Inc............... D 704 483-9343
Denver *(G-3807)*

▲ Superior Fire Hose Corp................... E 704 643-5888
Pineville *(G-9762)*

Titeflex Corporation............................. D 647 638-7160
Charlotte *(G-2921)*

Transtex Belting.................................. G 704 334-5353
Charlotte *(G-2937)*

Triangle Indus Sup Hldings LLC........... G 704 395-0600
Charlotte *(G-2942)*

3053 Gaskets; packing and sealing devices

Amesbury Group Inc............................. D 704 924-7694
Statesville *(G-11656)*

Carolina Components Group Inc............ E 919 635-8438
Durham *(G-3960)*

◆ CGR Products Inc.............................. D 336 621-4568
Greensboro *(G-5439)*

▲ Coltec Industries Inc......................... A 704 731-1500
Charlotte *(G-1961)*

◆ Enpro Inc.. C 704 731-1500
Charlotte *(G-2115)*

Ghx Industrial LLC............................... G 336 996-7271
Kernersville *(G-7276)*

▲ Henniges Automotive N Amer Inc..... C 336 342-9300
Reidsville *(G-10688)*

▲ Hibco Plastics Inc............................. E 336 463-2391
Yadkinville *(G-13443)*

Interflex Acquisition Co LLC................. C 336 921-3505
Wilkesboro *(G-12642)*

Mayo Resources Inc............................. E 336 996-7776
Winston Salem *(G-13246)*

Michael Simmons................................ G 704 298-1103
Concord *(G-3401)*

◆ Mueller Die Cut Solutions Inc............ E 704 588-3900
Charlotte *(G-2526)*

Packaging Plus North Carolina.............. F 336 643-4097
Summerfield *(G-11845)*

Parker-Hannifin Corporation................. F 252 237-6171
Wilson *(G-13012)*

▲ Pfaff Molds Ltd Partnership.............. F 704 423-9484
Charlotte *(G-2631)*

Qualiseal Technology LLC.................... G 704 731-1522
Charlotte *(G-2682)*

Rempac LLC... G 910 737-6557
Lumberton *(G-7969)*

▲ Rubber Mill Inc.................................. E 336 622-1680
Liberty *(G-7778)*

▲ SAS Industries Inc............................ F 631 727-1441
Elizabeth City *(G-4409)*

Slade Operating Company LLC............. E 704 873-1366
Statesville *(G-11766)*

Southern Rubber Company Inc.............. E 336 299-2456
Greensboro *(G-5827)*

▲ The Interflex Group Inc..................... C 336 921-3505
Wilkesboro *(G-12655)*

▲ Universal Rubber Products Inc........... G 704 483-1249
  Denver *(G-3815)*

Victaulic Company.............................. E 910 371-5588
  Leland *(G-7563)*

Wilmington Rbr & Gasket Co Inc........... F 910 762-4262
  Wilmington *(G-12952)*

3061 Mechanical rubber goods

Carolina Custom Rubber Inc................. G 704 636-6989
  Salisbury *(G-11026)*

Cinters Inc....................................... F 336 267-3051
  Rocky Mount *(G-10828)*

Easth20 Holdings Llc......................... G 919 313-2100
  Greensboro *(G-5510)*

Essay Operations Inc......................... G 252 443-6010
  Rocky Mount *(G-10837)*

▲ Novaflex Hose Inc........................... D 336 578-2161
  Haw River *(G-6134)*

Oliver Rubber Company LLC................. B 336 629-1436
  Asheboro *(G-380)*

Parker-Hannifin Corporation................ F 252 237-6171
  Wilson *(G-13012)*

3069 Fabricated rubber products, nec

American Phoenix Inc......................... C 910 484-4007
  Fayetteville *(G-4551)*

Andritz Fabrics and Rolls Inc............... F 919 556-7235
  Raleigh *(G-9903)*

Andritz Fabrics and Rolls Inc............... D 919 526-1400
  Raleigh *(G-9904)*

Bear Pages...................................... G 828 837-0785
  Murphy *(G-9288)*

▲ Blachford Rbr Acquisition Corp......... E 704 730-1005
  Kings Mountain *(G-7350)*

▲ Bsci Inc....................................... G 704 664-3005
  Mooresville *(G-8623)*

C & M Industrial Supply Co................. G 704 483-4001
  Mill Spring *(G-8300)*

Carolina Custom Rubber Inc................. G 704 636-6989
  Salisbury *(G-11026)*

Catawba Valley Fabrication Inc............. F 828 459-1191
  Conover *(G-3503)*

Comfort Tech Inc.............................. G 910 428-1779
  Biscoe *(G-851)*

Contour Enterprises LLC..................... D 828 328-1550
  Hildebran *(G-6847)*

Cooper Crouse-Hinds LLC.................... D 252 566-3014
  La Grange *(G-7466)*

Core Technology Molding Corp............. E 336 294-2018
  Greensboro *(G-5469)*

Craftsman Foam Fabricators Inc........... G 336 476-5655
  Thomasville *(G-12012)*

Custom Assemblies Inc....................... E 919 202-4533
  Pine Level *(G-9678)*

Custom Marking & Printing Inc............. G 704 866-8245
  Gastonia *(G-5036)*

◆ Daramic LLC.................................. D 704 587-8599
  Charlotte *(G-2018)*

Daughters & Ryan Inc........................ G 919 284-0153
  Kenly *(G-7232)*

Dove Medical Supply LLC..................... E 336 643-9367
  Summerfield *(G-11838)*

Earth Edge LLC................................. F 828 624-0252
  Hickory *(G-6328)*

Eastern Crlina Vctonal Ctr Inc............. D 252 758-4188
  Greenville *(G-5972)*

Easth20 Holdings Llc......................... G 919 313-2100
  Greensboro *(G-5510)*

Eaton Corporation............................. D 910 695-2900
  Pinehurst *(G-9691)*

Elite Comfort Solutions LLC................. C 828 328-2201
  Conover *(G-3518)*

Flint Group US LLC............................ F 828 687-2485
  Arden *(G-272)*

Frenzelit Inc.................................... E 336 814-4317
  Lexington *(G-7690)*

◆ Fusion Incorporated......................... E 252 244-4300
  Vanceboro *(G-12216)*

GP Foam Fabricators Inc..................... F 336 434-3600
  High Point *(G-6633)*

◆ Hexpol Compounding NC Inc.............. A 704 872-1585
  Statesville *(G-11710)*

◆ Hickory Springs Manufactu............... D 828 328-2201
  Hickory *(G-6355)*

Hickory Springs Mfg Co...................... G 828 322-7994
  Hickory *(G-6356)*

Hickory Springs Mfg Co...................... D 828 728-9274
  Lenoir *(G-7614)*

Highland Foam Inc............................ G 828 327-0400
  Conover *(G-3531)*

Hilliard Fabricators LLC...................... F 336 861-8833
  Thomasville *(G-12032)*

Hygeia Marketing Corporation.............. G 704 933-5190
  Kannapolis *(G-7211)*

▲ Interstate Foam & Supply Inc............ C 828 459-9700
  Conover *(G-3534)*

◆ K-Flex USA LLC.............................. B 919 556-3475
  Youngsville *(G-13477)*

▲ L B Plastics LLC............................. D 704 663-1543
  Mooresville *(G-8706)*

▼ Lgc Consulting Inc.......................... E 704 216-0171
  Salisbury *(G-11083)*

Longhorn Roofing Inc......................... F 704 774-1080
  Monroe *(G-8520)*

▲ Longwood Industries Inc................... F 336 272-3710
  Greensboro *(G-5664)*

▲ Maranz Inc.................................... D 336 996-7776
  Winston Salem *(G-13244)*

Marx Industries Incorporated............... E 828 396-6700
  Hudson *(G-6955)*

▲ Maxime Knitting International............. G 803 627-2768
  Charlotte *(G-2473)*

Medaccess Inc.................................. G 828 264-4085
  Robbinsville *(G-10760)*

▲ Mount Hope Machinery Co................. F
  Charlotte *(G-2523)*

Mrrefinish LLC.................................. F 336 625-2400
  Asheboro *(G-379)*

▲ Mustang Reproductions Inc............... F 704 786-0990
  Concord *(G-3408)*

Nu-Tech Enterprises Inc...................... E 336 725-1691
  East Bend *(G-4324)*

Ohio Foam Corporation....................... F 704 883-8402
  Statesville *(G-11740)*

◆ Patch Rubber Company..................... C 252 536-2574
  Weldon *(G-12525)*

▲ Perma Flex Roller Technology............. E 704 633-1201
  Salisbury *(G-11101)*

▲ Perma-Flex Rollers Inc..................... D 704 633-1201
  Salisbury *(G-11102)*

▲ Perrycraft Inc................................ F 336 372-2545
  Sparta *(G-11541)*

Prototech Manufacturing Inc................ F 508 646-8849
  Washington *(G-12410)*

▲ Qrmc Ltd...................................... G 828 696-2000
  Hendersonville *(G-6238)*

Rempac LLC..................................... E 910 737-6557
  Lumberton *(G-7969)*

▲ Rp Fletcher Machine Co Inc............... D 336 249-6101
  Lexington *(G-7736)*

▲ Rubber Mill Inc.............................. E 336 622-1680
  Liberty *(G-7778)*

Russo Mike DBA Lrger Than Lf I........... G 760 942-0289
  Oriental *(G-9602)*

▲ Savatech Corp................................ G 386 760-0706
  Rutherfordton *(G-10993)*

Skelly Inc....................................... F 828 433-7070
  Morganton *(G-8898)*

▲ Spota LLC..................................... F 919 569-6765
  Wake Forest *(G-12303)*

Stowe Woodward LLC......................... D 919 556-7235
  Raleigh *(G-10511)*

Stowe Woodward LLC......................... E 360 636-0330
  Youngsville *(G-13489)*

Sun Fabricators Inc........................... E 336 885-0095
  High Point *(G-6795)*

Tekni-Plex Inc.................................. D 919 553-4151
  Clayton *(G-3174)*

Trelleborg Ctd Systems US Inc............. C 828 286-9126
  Rutherfordton *(G-10996)*

▲ William Goodyear Co....................... F 704 283-7824
  Monroe *(G-8580)*

Wright Roller Company....................... G 336 852-8393
  Greensboro *(G-5926)*

3081 Unsupported plastics film and sheet

◆ 3a Composites USA Inc..................... C 704 872-8974
  Statesville *(G-11641)*

Abx Innvtive Pckg Slutions LLC............ D 980 443-1100
  Charlotte *(G-1613)*

◆ Aqua Plastics Inc............................ F 828 324-6284
  Hickory *(G-6266)*

Berry Global Inc............................... G 336 841-1723
  High Point *(G-6547)*

Berry Global Inc............................... C 704 289-1526
  Monroe *(G-8439)*

Berry Global Films LLC....................... C 704 821-2316
  Matthews *(G-8160)*

◆ Bonset America Corporation............... C 336 375-0234
  Browns Summit *(G-991)*

Bright View Technologies Corp............. E 919 228-4370
  Durham *(G-3942)*

Cardinal Plastics Inc.......................... G 704 739-9420
  Kings Mountain *(G-7354)*

◆ Celgard LLC................................... D 800 235-4273
  Charlotte *(G-1885)*

Clear Defense LLC............................. G 336 370-1699
  Greensboro *(G-5450)*

Daliah Plastics Corp.......................... E 336 629-0551
  Asheboro *(G-344)*

Desco Industries Inc.......................... F 919 718-0000
  Sanford *(G-11168)*

◆ Dymetrol Company Inc...................... F 866 964-8632
  Bladenboro *(G-876)*

Gaylord Inc..................................... D 704 694-2434
  Charlotte *(G-2192)*

Icons America LLC............................ D 704 922-0041
  Dallas *(G-3676)*

Inteplast Group Corporation................ E 704 504-3200
  Charlotte *(G-2340)*

Krs Plastics Inc................................ F 910 653-3602
  Tabor City *(G-11912)*

◆ Liqui-Box Corporation...................... D 804 325-1400
  Charlotte *(G-2426)*

▲ Longwood Industries Inc................... F 336 272-3710
  Greensboro *(G-5664)*

Marine & Industrial Plastics................ G 252 224-1000
  Pollocksville *(G-9817)*

▲ Mastic Home Exteriors Inc................ E 816 426-8200
  Cary *(G-1399)*

Novolex Shields LLC.......................... B 800 845-6051
  Charlotte *(G-2584)*

Olon Industries Inc (us)...................... F 630 232-4705
  Mocksville *(G-8383)*

Paragon Films Inc............................. F 828 632-5552
  Taylorsville *(G-11968)*

**S
I
C**

◆ Piedmont Plastics Inc.................D 704 597-8200
Charlotte *(G-2636)*

Plastic Ingenuity Inc....................D 919 693-2009
Oxford *(G-9625)*

Printpack Inc................................C 828 649-3800
Marshall *(G-8082)*

Rays Classic Vinyl Repair Inc.......G 910 520-1626
Hampstead *(G-6075)*

Ready Solutions Inc.....................G 704 534-9221
Davidson *(G-3718)*

◆ Roechling Indus Gastonia LP........C 704 922-7814
Dallas *(G-3686)*

Schweitzer-Mauduit Intl Inc...........G 252 360-4666
Wilson *(G-13029)*

Southern Film Extruders Inc..........C 336 885-8091
High Point *(G-6788)*

Southern Prestige Intl LLC.............F 704 872-9524
Statesville *(G-11771)*

Specialty Perf LLC.......................G 704 872-9980
Statesville *(G-11773)*

3082 Unsupported plastics profile shapes

American Extruded Plastics Inc......E 336 274-1131
Greensboro *(G-5356)*

M2 Optics Inc..............................G 919 342-5619
Raleigh *(G-10264)*

◆ Piedmont Plastics Inc.................D 704 597-8200
Charlotte *(G-2636)*

Plastic Technology Inc..................E 828 328-8570
Conover *(G-3545)*

Plastic Technology Inc..................F 828 328-2201
Hickory *(G-6414)*

Precise Technology Inc.................G 704 576-9527
Charlotte *(G-2656)*

▲ Robetex Inc...............................F 910 671-8787
Lumberton *(G-7970)*

◆ Roechling Indus Gastonia LP........C 704 922-7814
Dallas *(G-3686)*

▲ United Plastics Corporation..........C 336 786-2127
Mount Airy *(G-9192)*

◆ Weener Plastics Inc....................D 252 206-1400
Wilson *(G-13045)*

3083 Laminated plastics plate and sheet

Bemis Manufacturing Company.......C 828 754-1086
Lenoir *(G-7578)*

Clear Defense LLC.......................G 336 370-1699
Greensboro *(G-5450)*

Crawford Composites LLC..............E 704 483-4175
Denver *(G-3778)*

Daytech Solutions LLC..................G 336 918-4122
Winston Salem *(G-13139)*

▲ Dynacast LLC............................E 704 927-2790
Charlotte *(G-2072)*

Innovative Laminations Company.....F 252 745-8133
New Bern *(G-9371)*

Manning Fabrics Inc.....................G 910 295-1970
Pinehurst *(G-9696)*

▲ Ram Industries Inc......................E 704 982-4015
Albemarle *(G-87)*

▲ Rk Enterprises LLC.....................G 910 481-0777
Fayetteville *(G-4663)*

▲ Robetex Inc...............................F 910 671-8787
Lumberton *(G-7970)*

Tech Medical Plastics Inc..............G 919 563-9272
Mebane *(G-8261)*

Tekni-Plex Inc.............................D 919 553-4151
Clayton *(G-3174)*

▲ Templex Inc...............................E 336 472-5933
Thomasville *(G-12078)*

Transcontinental AC US LLC...........F 704 847-9171
Matthews *(G-8154)*

◆ Upm Raflatac Inc........................B 828 651-4800
Mills River *(G-8322)*

Wilsonart LLC..............................E 828 684-2351
Fletcher *(G-4781)*

3084 Plastics pipe

Advanced Drainage Systems Inc......D 704 629-4151
Bessemer City *(G-803)*

Charlotte Pipe and Foundry Co........B 704 348-5416
Charlotte *(G-1901)*

Charlotte Pipe and Foundry Co........A 704 372-3650
Monroe *(G-8457)*

Charlotte Pipe and Foundry Co........A 704 887-8015
Oakboro *(G-9575)*

Charlotte Pipe and Foundry Com......F 704 379-0700
Charlotte *(G-1902)*

Consolidated Pipe & Sup Co Inc.......F 336 294-8577
Greensboro *(G-5463)*

▼ Crumpler Plastic Pipe Inc............D 910 525-4046
Roseboro *(G-10912)*

Fitt Usa Inc................................F 866 348-8872
Mooresville *(G-8665)*

Ipex USA LLC.............................F 704 889-2431
Pineville *(G-9736)*

◆ Ipex USA LLC............................C 704 889-2431
Pineville *(G-9735)*

J-M Manufacturing Company Inc.......D 919 575-6515
Creedmoor *(G-3650)*

National Pipe & Plastics Inc............C 336 996-2711
Colfax *(G-3284)*

◆ Opw Fling Cntnment Systems Inc.....E 919 209-2280
Smithfield *(G-11457)*

Performance Plastics Pdts Inc.........D 336 454-0350
Jamestown *(G-7175)*

◆ Silver-Line Plastics LLC...............C 828 252-8755
Asheville *(G-599)*

Southern Pipe Inc........................F 704 550-5935
Albemarle *(G-92)*

◆ Southern Pipe Inc.......................E 704 463-5202
New London *(G-9422)*

Teknor Apex Company..................D 401 642-3598
Jamestown *(G-7180)*

3085 Plastics bottles

Amcor Phrm Packg USA LLC............D 919 556-9715
Youngsville *(G-13461)*

CKS Packaging Inc.......................D 336 578-5800
Graham *(G-5265)*

Intertech Corporation...................D 336 621-1891
Greensboro *(G-5621)*

Precision Concepts Intl LLC............G 704 360-8923
Huntersville *(G-7037)*

Sonoco Products Company.............G 910 455-6903
Jacksonville *(G-7148)*

Southeastern Container Inc.............E 704 710-4200
Kings Mountain *(G-7385)*

◆ Southeastern Container Inc...........C 828 350-7200
Enka *(G-4488)*

Vav Plastics Nc LLC....................G 704 325-9332
Charlotte *(G-2974)*

3086 Plastics foam products

A Plus Service Inc.......................G 828 324-4397
Hickory *(G-6259)*

ABT Foam LLC............................G 704 508-1010
Statesville *(G-11644)*

Amesbury Group Inc.....................D 704 978-2883
Statesville *(G-11655)*

Amesbury Group Inc.....................D 704 924-7694
Statesville *(G-11656)*

▲ Apex Packaging Corporation LLC.....E 704 847-7274
Charlotte *(G-1682)*

Armacell LLC..............................D 828 464-5880
Conover *(G-3491)*

◆ Armacell LLC.............................C 919 913-0555
Chapel Hill *(G-1528)*

Armacell US Holdings LLC..............C 919 304-3846
Mebane *(G-8231)*

Barnhardt Manufacturing Co...........C 704 331-0657
Charlotte *(G-1754)*

Barnhardt Manufacturing Co...........C 336 789-9161
Mount Airy *(G-9101)*

◆ Barnhardt Manufacturing Company...C 800 277-0377
Charlotte *(G-1755)*

Berlin Packaging LLC....................G 704 612-4500
Charlotte *(G-1772)*

Blue Stone Industries Ltd...............G 919 379-3986
Cary *(G-1310)*

Bwh Foam and Fiber Inc................G 336 498-6949
Randleman *(G-10635)*

Carpenter Co..............................E 828 322-6545
Hickory *(G-6290)*

Carpenter Co..............................D 336 861-5730
High Point *(G-6560)*

Carpenter Co..............................C 336 789-9161
Mount Airy *(G-9110)*

Carpenter Co..............................E 828 632-7061
Taylorsville *(G-11952)*

▲ Classic Packaging Company...........D 336 922-4224
Pfafftown *(G-9663)*

Crown Foam Products Inc...............F 336 434-4024
High Point *(G-6581)*

▲ Cryovac LLC..............................A 980 430-7000
Charlotte *(G-1999)*

Cryovac Intl Holdings Inc................E 980 430-7000
Charlotte *(G-2000)*

Dart Container Corp Georgia............C 336 495-1101
Randleman *(G-10641)*

Deep River Fabricators Inc..............F 336 824-8881
Franklinville *(G-4856)*

Diversified Foam Inc.....................E 336 463-5512
Yadkinville *(G-13440)*

▲ Dynamic Systems Inc...................E 828 683-3523
Leicester *(G-7523)*

◆ Ffnc Inc...................................D 336 885-4121
High Point *(G-6619)*

▲ Franklin Logistical Services Inc.......D 919 556-6711
Youngsville *(G-13472)*

Frisby Technologies Inc.................F 336 998-6652
Advance *(G-32)*

Future Foam Inc..........................E 336 861-8095
Archdale *(G-223)*

Future Foam Inc..........................D 336 885-4121
High Point *(G-6625)*

Fxi Inc.....................................D 336 431-1171
High Point *(G-6626)*

Gaylord Inc................................D 704 694-2434
Charlotte *(G-2192)*

▲ Guilford Fabricators Inc.................F 336 434-3163
High Point *(G-6635)*

▲ Hibco Plastics Inc.......................E 336 463-2391
Yadkinville *(G-13443)*

▲ Hickory Springs California LLC........A 828 328-2201
Hickory *(G-6354)*

Hickory Springs Mfg Co.................E 828 632-9733
Hiddenite *(G-6497)*

Hickory Springs Mfg Co.................D 336 861-4195
High Point *(G-6647)*

Hood Container Corporation............A 336 784-0445
Winston Salem *(G-13200)*

Janesville LLC............................C 828 668-9251
Old Fort *(G-9594)*

▲ Kidkusion Inc.............................F 252 946-7162
Washington *(G-12396)*

Marves Industries Inc.....................D 828 397-4400
Hildebran **(G-6854)**

Marx LLC....................................D 828 396-6700
Granite Falls **(G-5312)**

Marx Industries Incorporated.............E 828 396-6700
Hudson **(G-6955)**

◆ Ncfi Polyurethanes.....................C 336 789-9161
Mount Airy **(G-9158)**

▼ Ngx...................................E 866 782-7749
Tarboro **(G-11939)**

Noel Group LLC..........................G 919 269-6500
Zebulon **(G-13514)**

◆ Nomaco Inc............................B 919 269-6500
Zebulon **(G-13515)**

Novolex Bagcraft Inc....................D 800 845-6051
Charlotte **(G-2581)**

Npx One LLC.............................C 910 997-2217
Rockingham **(G-10784)**

Pactiv LLC..............................F 828 396-2373
Granite Falls **(G-5315)**

Pactiv LLC..............................F 828 758-7580
Lenoir **(G-7632)**

Pak-Lite Inc............................G 919 563-1097
Mebane **(G-8254)**

▲ Palziv North America Inc..............C 919 497-0010
Louisburg **(G-7922)**

Piranha Industries Inc..................G 704 248-7843
Charlotte **(G-2639)**

▼ Poly Packaging Systems Inc............D 336 889-8334
High Point **(G-6739)**

Prestige Fabricators Inc................B 336 626-4595
Asheboro **(G-386)**

Prototech Manufacturing Inc.............F 508 646-8849
Washington **(G-12410)**

▼ Reedy International Corp..............F 980 819-6930
Charlotte **(G-2701)**

Ritchie Foam Company Inc................G 704 663-2533
Mooresville **(G-8760)**

Sealed Air Corporation..................D 336 883-9184
High Point **(G-6764)**

Sealed Air Corporation..................D 828 728-6610
Hudson **(G-6959)**

Sealed Air Corporation..................D 828 726-2100
Lenoir **(G-7639)**

Sealed Air Corporation (us).............A 201 791-7600
Charlotte **(G-2777)**

Sealed Air Intl Holdings LLC............D 980 221-3235
Charlotte **(G-2778)**

Shaw Industries Group Inc...............E 877 996-5942
Charlotte **(G-2796)**

Storopack Inc...........................G 800 827-7225
Winston Salem **(G-13344)**

Swimways................................F 252 563-1101
Tarboro **(G-11943)**

Technicon Industries Inc................E 704 788-1131
Concord **(G-3453)**

Thompson Printing & Packg Inc...........G 704 313-7323
Mooresboro **(G-8587)**

Trego Innovations LLC...................G 919 374-0089
Wilson **(G-13038)**

Unified2 Globl Packg Group LLC..........C 774 696-3643
Durham **(G-4288)**

Vpc Foam USA Inc........................E 336 626-4595
Asheboro **(G-418)**

Vpc Foam USA Inc........................E 704 622-0552
Conover **(G-3572)**

Watauga Opportunities Inc...............E 828 264-5009
Boone **(G-951)**

Wood Products Packg Intl Inc............G 704 279-3011
Faith **(G-4520)**

3087 Custom compound purchased resins

Avient Colorants USA LLC................D 704 331-7000
Charlotte **(G-1723)**

Borealis Compounds Inc..................E 908 798-7497
Taylorsville **(G-11950)**

Crp Usa LLC.............................F 704 660-0258
Mooresville **(G-8645)**

◆ Hexpol Compounding NC Inc.............A 704 872-1585
Statesville **(G-11710)**

Lubrizol Global Management Inc..........D 704 865-7451
Gastonia **(G-5080)**

Premix North Carolina LLC...............G 704 412-7922
Dallas **(G-3682)**

◆ Rutland Group Inc.....................C 704 553-0046
Pineville **(G-9752)**

◆ Rutland Holdings LLC..................G 704 553-0046
Pineville **(G-9753)**

Sealed Air Corporation..................D 828 728-6610
Hudson **(G-6959)**

Sealed Air Corporation (us).............A 201 791-7600
Charlotte **(G-2777)**

Teknor Apex Company.....................D 401 642-3598
Jamestown **(G-7180)**

Tru-Contour Inc.........................G 704 455-8700
Concord **(G-3459)**

▲ Zeon Technologies Inc.................G 704 680-9160
Salisbury **(G-11138)**

3088 Plastics plumbing fixtures

Accent Comfort Services LLC.............E 704 509-1200
Charlotte **(G-1614)**

Carolina Classic Manufacturing Inc......D 252 237-9105
Wilson **(G-12977)**

Creekraft Cultured Marble Inc...........G 252 636-5488
New Bern **(G-9358)**

Custom Marble Corporation...............G 910 215-0679
Pinehurst **(G-9690)**

▲ Gainsborough Baths LLC................F 336 357-0797
Lexington **(G-7691)**

Jupiter Bathware Inc....................G 800 343-8295
Wilson **(G-12996)**

LL Cultured Marble Inc..................G 336 789-3908
Mount Airy **(G-9147)**

Marion Cultured Marble Inc..............G 828 724-4782
Marion **(G-8049)**

Moen Incorporated.......................D 252 638-3300
New Bern **(G-9384)**

Moores Fiberglass Inc...................F 252 753-2583
Walstonburg **(G-12334)**

Plastic Oddities Inc....................G 704 484-1830
Shelby **(G-11369)**

3089 Plastics products, nec

ABS Southeast LLC.......................F 919 329-0014
Raleigh **(G-9869)**

▲ Accu-Form Polymers Inc................E 910 293-6961
Warsaw **(G-12357)**

◆ Accuma Corporation....................C 704 873-1488
Statesville **(G-11646)**

▲ Ace Plastics Inc......................G 704 527-5752
Charlotte **(G-1615)**

Acme Nameplate & Mfg Inc................G 704 283-8175
Monroe **(G-8416)**

Advanced Drainage Systems...............F 704 629-4151
Bessemer City **(G-802)**

Advanced Plastic Extrusion LLC..........G 252 224-1444
Pollocksville **(G-9816)**

Advanced Plastiform Inc.................E 919 404-2080
Zebulon **(G-13501)**

Afsc LLC................................D 704 523-4936
Charlotte **(G-1627)**

Aim Molding & Door LLC..................G 704 913-7211
Charlotte **(G-1630)**

▲ Aimet Holding Inc.....................F 919 887-5205
Zebulon **(G-13502)**

Aimet Technologies LLC..................F 919 887-5205
Zebulon **(G-13503)**

▼ All Source Security Cont Cal..........G 704 504-9908
Charlotte **(G-1641)**

Alliance Precision Plas Corp............E 828 286-8631
Spindale **(G-11543)**

Altium Packaging LLC....................F 704 873-6729
Statesville **(G-11653)**

Altium Packaging LLC....................D 336 472-1500
Thomasville **(G-11992)**

Altium Packaging LP.....................D 336 342-4749
Reidsville **(G-10673)**

◆ Amcor Tob Packg Americas Inc..........D 828 274-1611
Asheville **(G-425)**

American Plastic Inc....................G 828 652-3511
Marion **(G-8031)**

▼ American Wick Drain Corp..............E 704 296-5801
Monroe **(G-8424)**

Amesbury Group Inc......................D 704 978-2883
Statesville **(G-11655)**

Amesbury Group Inc......................D 704 924-7694
Statesville **(G-11656)**

Applied Plastic Services Inc............E 910 655-2156
Bolton **(G-888)**

◆ Aqua Plastics Inc.....................F 828 324-6284
Hickory **(G-6266)**

Asheville Thermoform Plas Inc...........F 828 684-8440
Fletcher **(G-4721)**

▲ Ashland Products Inc..................C 815 266-0250
Huntersville **(G-6968)**

▲ Asmo North America LLC................A 704 872-2319
Statesville **(G-11661)**

▲ Atlantic Automotive Entps LLC.........G 910 377-4108
Tabor City **(G-11906)**

Atlas Precision Inc.....................C 828 687-9900
Arden **(G-255)**

Auto Parts Fayetteville LLC.............G 910 889-4026
Fayetteville **(G-4555)**

AWC Holding Company.....................F 919 677-3900
Cary **(G-1304)**

Baily Enterprises LLC...................F 704 587-0109
Charlotte **(G-1742)**

◆ Balcrank Corporation..................E 800 747-5300
Weaverville **(G-12483)**

Beacon Composites LLC...................G 704 813-8408
Creedmoor **(G-3640)**

Beacon Roofing Supply Inc...............G 704 886-1555
Charlotte **(G-1763)**

Beaufort Composite Tech Inc.............G 252 728-1547
Beaufort **(G-721)**

Berry Global Inc........................E 252 332-7270
Ahoskie **(G-42)**

Berry Global Inc........................G 252 984-4100
Battleboro **(G-695)**

Berry Global Inc........................E 919 207-3202
Benson **(G-785)**

Berry Global Inc........................G 336 841-1723
High Point **(G-6547)**

Berry Global Inc........................C 704 289-1526
Monroe **(G-8439)**

Berry Global Inc........................C 704 664-3733
Mooresville **(G-8608)**

Berry Global Inc........................D 252 984-4104
Rocky Mount **(G-10808)**

Best Machine & Fabrication Inc..........G 919 731-7101
Dudley **(G-3834)**

Biomerics LLC...........................G 336 810-7178
Mebane **(G-8232)**

▲ Bioselect Inc.........................G 704 521-8585
Charlotte **(G-1784)**

S
I
C

Blue Ridge................................G 828 325-4705
Conover *(G-3495)*

Blue Ridge Molding LLC.......................D 828 485-2017
Conover *(G-3496)*

▼ Bms Investment Holdings LLC.........E 336 949-4107
Mayodan *(G-8206)*

▲ Borgwarner Turbo Systems LLC.......D 828 684-4000
Arden *(G-258)*

Borneo Inc.................................G 252 398-3100
Murfreesboro *(G-9281)*

Boyd Gmn Inc.............................D 206 284-2200
Monroe *(G-8446)*

◆ Braiform Enterprises Inc.................C 828 277-6420
Asheville *(G-461)*

▲ Brispa Investments Inc ....C 336 668-3636
Greensboro *(G-5405)*

Brunson Marine Group LLC ....E 252 291-0271
Wilson *(G-12975)*

▲ Bull Engineered Products Inc...........E 704 504-0300
Charlotte *(G-1818)*

C&K Plastics Nc LLC.....................G 833 232-4848
Mooresville *(G-8626)*

C2c Plastics Inc..........................G 910 338-5260
Wilmington *(G-12726)*

Cabarrus Plastics Inc....................C 704 784-2100
Concord *(G-3328)*

◆ Carlisle Corporation.....................A 704 501-1100
Charlotte *(G-1842)*

Caro-Polymers Inc........................F 704 629-5319
Bessemer City *(G-808)*

Carolina Base - Pac Corp................E 828 728-7304
Hudson *(G-6946)*

◆ Carolina Extruded Plastics Inc.........E 336 272-1191
Greensboro *(G-5426)*

Carolina Home Exteriors LLC............F 252 637-6599
New Bern *(G-9350)*

Carolina Moldings Inc....................F 704 523-7471
Charlotte *(G-1851)*

Carolina Precision Plas LLC.............D 336 283-4700
Mocksville *(G-8355)*

◆ Carolina Precision Plastics L...........C 336 498-2654
Asheboro *(G-335)*

▲ Carolina Print Works Inc................F 704 637-6902
Salisbury *(G-11027)*

Central Carolina Products Inc............C 336 226-1449
Burlington *(G-1068)*

Central Carolina Products Inc............C 336 226-0005
Burlington *(G-1069)*

Centro Inc.................................D 319 626-3200
Claremont *(G-3092)*

Certainteed LLC..........................D 828 459-0556
Claremont *(G-3093)*

◆ Chadsworth Incorporated...............G 910 763-7600
Wilmington *(G-12742)*

◆ Charlotte Pipe and Foundry Co........C 800 438-6091
Charlotte *(G-1900)*

Cks Packaging...........................F 704 663-6510
Mooresville *(G-8638)*

CKS Packaging Inc.......................D 336 578-5800
Graham *(G-5265)*

CKS Packaging Inc.......................E 704 663-6510
Mooresville *(G-8639)*

Clt 2016 Inc..............................D 704 886-1555
Charlotte *(G-1933)*

Clydesdle Acq Hld Inc...................D 843 857-4800
Charlotte *(G-1935)*

CMI Plastics Inc..........................E 252 746-2171
Ayden *(G-655)*

◆ Coats & Clark Inc.......................D 888 368-8401
Charlotte *(G-1942)*

▲ Coats N Amer De Rpblica Dmncan.....C 800 242-8095
Charlotte *(G-1945)*

Coeur Inc.................................G 252 946-1963
Washington *(G-12382)*

▲ Coltec Industries Inc....................A 704 731-1500
Charlotte *(G-1961)*

Concept Plastics Inc.....................C 336 889-2001
High Point *(G-6576)*

Consolidated Metco Inc..................E 360 828-2689
Arden *(G-263)*

Consolidated Models Inc.................E 252 746-2171
Ayden *(G-656)*

Core Technology Molding Corp..........E 336 294-2018
Greensboro *(G-5470)*

Corner Stone Plastics Inc................G 336 629-1828
Asheboro *(G-341)*

County of Alexander......................E 828 632-1101
Taylorsville *(G-11955)*

◆ CPS Resources Inc.....................E 704 628-7678
Indian Trail *(G-7075)*

Creative Liquid Coatings Inc.............D 336 415-6214
Mount Airy *(G-9116)*

Cross Technology Inc....................E 336 725-4700
East Bend *(G-4322)*

CT Commercial Paper LLC...............E 704 485-3212
Oakboro *(G-9577)*

Custom Extrusion Inc....................G 336 495-7070
Asheboro *(G-343)*

▼ Debotech Inc.............................C 704 664-1361
Mooresville *(G-8653)*

◆ Delta Mold Inc...........................D 704 588-6600
Charlotte *(G-2029)*

Dexterity LLC.............................F 919 524-7732
Greenville *(G-5964)*

Digger Specialties Inc...................F 919 255-2533
Fuquay Varina *(G-4879)*

Digger Specialties Inc...................G 336 495-1517
Randleman *(G-10642)*

▲ Diverse Corporate Tech Inc.............E 828 245-3717
Forest City *(G-4787)*

Double O Plastics Inc....................E 704 788-8517
Concord *(G-3357)*

Douglas Fabrication & Mch Inc..........F 919 365-7553
Wendell *(G-12533)*

◆ Dps Molding Inc.........................G 732 763-4811
Vanceboro *(G-12215)*

Duramax Holdings LLC...................C 704 588-9191
Charlotte *(G-2068)*

▲ Dynacast LLC............................E 704 927-2790
Charlotte *(G-2072)*

Easth20 Holdings Llc....................G 919 313-2100
Greensboro *(G-5510)*

◆ Elkamet Inc..............................C 828 233-4001
East Flat Rock *(G-4330)*

Englshs All Wood Homes Inc............F 252 524-5000
Grifton *(G-6036)*

◆ Enpro Inc.................................C 704 731-1500
Charlotte *(G-2115)*

Envicor Enterprises LLC.................E 877 823-7231
Smithfield *(G-11442)*

▲ Etimex USA Inc..........................D 704 583-0002
Charlotte *(G-2128)*

Exlon Extrusion Inc......................F 336 621-1295
Asheboro *(G-353)*

Fawn Industries Inc......................C 252 462-4700
Nashville *(G-9319)*

Fiber Composites LLC....................D 704 463-7118
New London *(G-9416)*

Fibreworks Composites LLC.............E 704 696-1084
Mooresville *(G-8663)*

Fineline Prototyping Inc..................D 919 781-7702
Morrisville *(G-8974)*

Fourshare LLC...........................F 336 714-0448
Clemmons *(G-3184)*

Genpak Industries Inc....................E 518 798-9511
Charlotte *(G-2205)*

◆ Genpak LLC..............................E 800 626-6695
Charlotte *(G-2206)*

▲ Gentry Plastics Inc......................E 704 864-4300
Gastonia *(G-5053)*

▲ Geo Plastics.............................F 704 588-8585
Charlotte *(G-2208)*

Glenn Mauser Company Inc..............F 828 464-8996
Newton *(G-9468)*

Global Packaging Inc.....................D 610 666-1608
Hamlet *(G-6056)*

▲ Gloves-Online Inc........................G 919 468-4244
Cary *(G-1367)*

▲ Great Pacific Entps US Inc..............E 980 256-7729
Charlotte *(G-2235)*

◆ Hayward Industrial Products............C 704 837-8002
Charlotte *(G-2264)*

Hayward Industries Inc...................D 336 712-9900
Clemmons *(G-3188)*

◆ Hayward Industries Inc...................B 704 837-8002
Charlotte *(G-2265)*

Heyco Werk USA Inc......................E 434 634-8810
Dallas *(G-3675)*

Hoffman Plasti-Form Company..........G 336 431-2934
High Point *(G-6658)*

Hornet Capital LLC.......................F 252 641-8000
Tarboro *(G-11930)*

▲ Hughes Sup of Thomasville Inc.........D 336 475-8146
Thomasville *(G-12033)*

Identigraph Signs & Awnings............G 704 635-7911
Monroe *(G-8502)*

Impact Plastics Inc.......................G 910 205-1493
Hamlet *(G-6058)*

Injection Technology Corporation........C 828 684-1362
Arden *(G-276)*

▲ Inplac North America Inc.................G 704 587-1151
Charlotte *(G-2338)*

Intertech Corporation.....................D 336 621-1891
Greensboro *(G-5621)*

Jeld-Wen Inc..............................C 336 838-0292
North Wilkesboro *(G-9536)*

Jlmade LLC...............................G 252 515-2195
Winnabow *(G-13066)*

Kennys Components Inc..................F 704 662-0777
Mooresville *(G-8703)*

▲ L B Plastics LLC.........................D 704 663-1543
Mooresville *(G-8706)*

Lamco Machine Tool Inc..................F 252 247-4360
Morehead City *(G-8838)*

Lamination Services Inc..................E 336 643-7369
Stokesdale *(G-11813)*

Leonard Alum Utlity Bldngs Inc..........G 919 872-4442
Raleigh *(G-10254)*

Leonard Alum Utlity Bldngs Inc..........G 910 392-4921
Wilmington *(G-12834)*

◆ Liqui-Box Corporation...................D 804 325-1400
Charlotte *(G-2426)*

▲ Locust Plastics Inc......................D 704 636-2742
Salisbury *(G-11086)*

Machinery Sales..........................G 704 822-0110
Stanley *(G-11621)*

Mack Molding Company Inc..............C 704 878-9641
Statesville *(G-11728)*

Mainetti Usa Inc..........................G 828 844-0105
Fletcher *(G-4751)*

Manning Fabrics Inc......................G 910 295-1970
Pinehurst *(G-9696)*

Manufacturing Services Inc..............E 704 629-4163
Bessemer City *(G-826)*

Marine & Industrial Plastics.............G 252 224-1000
Pollocksville *(G-9817)*

▲ Mastic Home Exteriors Inc................. E 816 426-8200
   Cary (G-1399)

Medical Cable Specialists Inc................ E 828 890-2888
   Mills River (G-8317)

Micro Lens Technology Inc.................. G 704 893-2109
   Indian Trail (G-7091)

▲ Micro Lens Technology Inc................ G 704 847-9234
   Matthews (G-8133)

Millar Industries Inc........................ E 828 687-0639
   Arden (G-285)

Molded Fibr GL Cmpny/Nrth Crli........... C 828 584-4974
   Morganton (G-8882)

▲ Mpe Usa Inc................................ E 704 340-4910
   Pineville (G-9743)

▲ New Innovative Products Inc............. G 919 631-6759
   Pine Level (G-9683)

Newell Brands Distribution LLC............. D 770 418-7000
   Gastonia (G-5110)

Newell Brands Inc.......................... E 704 987-4760
   Huntersville (G-7019)

Newell Brands Inc.......................... E 704 895-8082
   Huntersville (G-7020)

▲ Novolex Holdings LLC................... E 800 845-6051
   Charlotte (G-2583)

▲ Nypro Asheville Inc..................... C 828 684-3141
   Arden (G-291)

Nypro Inc.................................. A 919 304-1400
   Mebane (G-8253)

▲ Nypro Oregon Inc........................ B 541 753-4700
   Arden (G-292)

Oneida Molded Plastics LLC............... G 919 663-3141
   Siler City (G-11421)

◆ Opw Fling Cntnment Systems Inc......E 919 209-2280
   Smithfield (G-11457)

▲ P&A Indstrial Fabrications LLC........ E 336 322-1766
   Roxboro (G-10938)

▲ Pam Trading Corporation............... E 336 668-0901
   Kernersville (G-7292)

Panel Wholesalers Incorporated........... F 336 765-4040
   Winston Salem (G-13275)

Parkway Products LLC..................... C 828 684-1362
   Arden (G-293)

Pbs Ventures Inc.......................... G 252 235-2001
   Bailey (G-673)

PCI of North Carolina LLC................ E 919 467-5151
   Cary (G-1416)

◆ Pen-Cell Plastics Inc...................E 252 467-2210
   Rocky Mount (G-10858)

Penn Compression Moulding Inc........... G 919 934-5144
   Smithfield (G-11459)

Performance Plastics Pdts Inc............ D 336 454-0350
   Jamestown (G-7175)

▲ Phoenix Technology Ltd................ E 910 259-6804
   Burgaw (G-1029)

Pipeline Plastics LLC..................... G 817 693-4100
   Fair Bluff (G-4499)

Plasgad Usa LLC.......................... E 980 223-2197
   Statesville (G-11747)

Plastek Group............................. G 910 895-2089
   Rockingham (G-10786)

Plastic Ingenuity Inc..................... D 919 693-2009
   Oxford (G-9625)

Plastic Products Inc...................... F 704 739-7463
   Kings Mountain (G-7378)

Plastics Family Holdings Inc.............. E 704 597-8555
   Charlotte (G-2642)

Plastics Mlding Dsign Plus LLC........... G 828 459-7853
   Conover (G-3546)

Poly-Tech Industrial Inc.................. G 704 992-8100
   Huntersville (G-7034)

Poly-Tech Industrial Inc.................. E 704 948-8055
   Huntersville (G-7035)

◆ Polymer Concepts Inc...................G 336 495-7713
   Randleman (G-10656)

▲ Poppelmann Properties USA LLC.... G 828 466-9500
   Claremont (G-3117)

▲ Post EC Holdings Inc................... E 919 989-0175
   Smithfield (G-11460)

Precise Technology Inc.................... G 704 576-9527
   Charlotte (G-2656)

▲ Precision Concepts Mebane LLC...... D 919 563-9292
   Mebane (G-8257)

Pretium Packaging LLC.................... E 336 621-1891
   Greensboro (G-5762)

Prime Mill LLC............................ F 336 819-4300
   High Point (G-6746)

Proplastic Designs Inc.................... F 866 649-8665
   Charlotte (G-2675)

Proto Labs Inc............................ D 833 245-8827
   Morrisville (G-9040)

◆ Pucuda Inc...............................F 860 526-8004
   New Bern (G-9389)

R & D Plastics Inc........................ E 828 684-2692
   Flat Rock (G-4712)

R&D Plastics of Hickory Ltd.............. E 828 431-4660
   Hickory (G-6426)

Ramsey Industries Inc.................... F 704 827-3560
   Belmont (G-763)

◆ Reichhold Holdings Us Inc.............A 919 990-7500
   Durham (G-4210)

Resinart East Inc......................... F 828 687-0215
   Fletcher (G-4763)

Revolution Pd LLC........................ G 919 949-0241
   Pittsboro (G-9788)

▲ Rexam Beauty and Closures Inc...... A 704 551-1500
   Charlotte (G-2718)

Reynolds Consumer Products Inc........ A 704 371-5550
   Huntersville (G-7042)

▲ Robotex Inc.............................. F 910 671-8787
   Lumberton (G-7970)

Rowmark LLC............................. G 252 448-9900
   Trenton (G-12110)

Royale Comfort Seating Inc.............. D 828 352-9021
   Taylorsville (G-11974)

RPM Plastics Inc.......................... F 704 871-0518
   Conover (G-3557)

RPM Plastics LLC......................... E 704 871-0518
   Statesville (G-11760)

RPM Products Inc......................... G 704 871-0518
   Statesville (G-11761)

Rpp Acquisition LLC...................... E 919 248-9001
   Kenly (G-7237)

Rs Industries Inc......................... G 704 289-2734
   Cornelius (G-3625)

◆ Rubbermaid Commercial Pdts LLC....A 540 667-8700
   Huntersville (G-7045)

Rubbermaid Incorporated................. A 704 987-4339
   Huntersville (G-7046)

Rubbermaid Incorporated................. A 888 859-8294
   Huntersville (G-7053)

Saint-Gobain Vetrotex Amer Inc.......... C 704 895-5906
   Huntersville (G-7053)

Salem Technologies Inc................... F 336 777-3652
   Winston Salem (G-13327)

Sapona Manufacturing Co Inc............ C 336 873-8700
   Asheboro (G-392)

Sapona Plastic LLC....................... G 336 873-7201
   Seagrove (G-11280)

▲ Sapona Plastics LLC.................... D 336 873-8700
   Asheboro (G-394)

◆ Schaefer Systems International Inc....C 704 944-4500
   Charlotte (G-2763)

Schaefer Systems Intl Inc................ G 704 944-4500
   Charlotte (G-2764)

Schaefer Systems Intl Inc................ G 704 944-4550
   Charlotte (G-2765)

Sealed Air Corporation................... D 828 728-6610
   Hudson (G-6959)

Sealed Air Corporation (us).............. A 201 791-7600
   Charlotte (G-2777)

Senox Corporation........................ E 704 371-5043
   Charlotte (G-2786)

Sherri Gossett........................... G 910 367-0099
   Wilmington (G-12919)

Siena Plastics LLC....................... F 704 323-5252
   Charlotte (G-2804)

Sigma Plastics Group.................... E 336 885-8091
   High Point (G-6770)

Skyline Plastic Systems Inc.............. F 828 891-2515
   Mills River (G-4763)

◆ Sonoco Hickory Inc.................... D 828 328-2466
   Hickory (G-6453)

Sonoco Products Company............... D 828 245-0118
   Forest City (G-4797)

Southeaster Plastic Inc.................. F 336 275-6616
   Greensboro (G-5823)

Southern Vinyl Mfg Inc................... F 252 523-2520
   Kinston (G-7429)

▲ Spnc Associates Inc................... D 919 467-5151
   Cary (G-1466)

▲ Sspc Inc................................. E
   Charlotte (G-2855)

Stanford Manufacturing LLC.............. F 336 999-8799
   Clemmons (G-3203)

Sunray Inc............................... E 828 287-7030
   Rutherfordton (G-10994)

▲ Superior Plastics Inc................... F 704 864-5472
   Gastonia (G-5147)

▲ Surteco USA Inc........................ E 336 668-9555
   Greensboro (G-5846)

Sysmetric USA........................... G 704 522-8778
   Mooresville (G-8783)

Tar River Trading Post LLC............... G 919 589-3618
   Youngsville (G-13490)

Tarheel Plastics LLC..................... E
   Lexington (G-7748)

Team Gsg LLC........................... G 252 830-1032
   Greenville (G-6026)

Tech Medical Plastics Inc................ G 919 563-9272
   Mebane (G-8261)

◆ Technical Coating Intl Inc..............E 910 371-0860
   Leland (G-7559)

Technimark Inc........................... G 336 736-9366
   Randleman (G-10662)

Technimark LLC.......................... G 336 498-4171
   Asheboro (G-402)

Technimark LLC.......................... E 336 498-4171
   Asheboro (G-403)

◆ Technimark LLC.........................C 336 498-4171
   Asheboro (G-404)

Technimark Reynosa LLC................. G 336 498-4171
   Asheboro (G-405)

▲ Technimark Reynosa LLC............... B 336 498-4171
   Asheboro (G-406)

Teijin Automotive Tech Inc............... G 828 757-8313
   Lenoir (G-7641)

Teijin Automotive Tech Inc............... B 704 797-8744
   Salisbury (G-11123)

Tenn-Tex Plastics Inc.................... E 336 931-1100
   Colfax (G-3291)

Texlon Plastics Corp..................... E 704 866-8785
   Gastonia (G-5150)

TFS Management Group LLC............. G 704 399-3999
   Charlotte (G-2910)

▼ Thanet Inc............................... G 704 483-4175
   Denver (G-3812)

▼ THEM International Inc...................... G 336 855-7880
Greensboro *(G-5862)*

Thermodynamx LLC.............................. G 704 622-1086
Waxhaw *(G-12444)*

Thomson Plastics Inc......................... D 336 843-4255
Lexington *(G-7751)*

Thundrbird Mlding Grnsboro LLC........ F 336 668-3636
Greensboro *(G-5865)*

Thundrbird Mlding Grnsboro LLC........ E 336 668-3636
Greensboro *(G-5866)*

◆ Tosaf Inc.. F 980 533-3000
Bessemer City *(G-837)*

Toter LLC... D 704 936-5610
Charlotte *(G-2931)*

◆ Toter LLC... E 800 424-0422
Statesville *(G-11792)*

Trac Plastics Inc................................. F 704 864-9140
Gastonia *(G-5158)*

Treg Tool Inc....................................... G 828 676-0035
Arden *(G-312)*

◆ Trelleborg Salisbury Inc................... E 704 797-8030
Salisbury *(G-11127)*

Tri-Star Plastics Corp......................... E 704 598-2800
Denver *(G-3813)*

◆ Triangle Plastics Inc........................ G 919 598-8839
Raleigh *(G-10560)*

United Decorative Plas NC Inc............ G 252 637-1803
Trent Woods *(G-12108)*

▲ United Southern Industries Inc......... D 866 273-1810
Forest City *(G-4799)*

Universal Plastic Products Inc............. G 336 856-0882
Jamestown *(G-7181)*

US Drainage Systems LLC.................. G 828 855-1906
Hickory *(G-6483)*

▲ V and E Components Inc.................. F 336 884-0088
High Point *(G-6821)*

Vandor Corporation............................. E 980 392-8107
Statesville *(G-11797)*

Variform Inc... D 828 277-6420
Asheville *(G-630)*

Vault LLC... F 336 698-3796
High Point *(G-6823)*

Veka East Inc....................................... B 800 654-5589
Morganton *(G-8908)*

Volex Inc.. E 828 485-4500
Hickory *(G-6486)*

Volex Inc.. E 828 485-4500
Hickory *(G-6487)*

Waddington Group Inc......................... E 800 845-6051
Charlotte *(G-2997)*

◆ Waddington North America Inc.......... F 800 845-6051
Charlotte *(G-2998)*

Wambam Fence Inc.............................. G 877 778-5733
Charlotte *(G-3002)*

Warren Plastics Inc............................. G 704 827-9887
Mount Holly *(G-9245)*

▲ Wilbert Inc.. E 704 247-3850
Belmont *(G-775)*

Wilbert Plastic Services Inc................ G 866 273-1810
Belmont *(G-776)*

▲ Wilbert Plstic Svcs Acqstion L........ E 704 455-5191
Harrisburg *(G-6121)*

▲ Wilbert Plstic Svcs Acqstion L........ C 704 822-1423
Belmont *(G-777)*

Wilsonart LLC...................................... E 828 684-2351
Fletcher *(G-4781)*

◆ Wirthwein New Bern Corp................. C 252 634-2871
New Bern *(G-9408)*

31 LEATHER AND LEATHER PRODUCTS

3111 Leather tanning and finishing

▲ Arcona Leather Company LLC.......... G 828 396-7728
Hudson *(G-6941)*

◆ Automated Solutions LLC................. F 828 396-9900
Granite Falls *(G-5296)*

▲ Carolina Fur Dressing Company....... E 919 231-0086
Raleigh *(G-9976)*

Carroll Companies Inc......................... F 828 466-5489
Conover *(G-3502)*

Coast To Coast Lea & Vinyl Inc.......... G 336 886-5050
High Point *(G-6571)*

▲ Dani Leather USA Inc....................... G 973 598-0890
High Point *(G-6587)*

Distinction Leather Company.............. G
Conover *(G-3516)*

Greene Mountain Outdoors LLC........ F 336 670-2186
North Wilkesboro *(G-9532)*

Inspiration Leather Design Inc............ G 336 420-2265
Jamestown *(G-7169)*

Leather Magic Inc............................... G 704 283-5078
Monroe *(G-8515)*

◆ Leather Miracles LLC....................... E 828 464-7448
Hickory *(G-6386)*

Oowee Incorporated............................ F 828 633-0289
Candler *(G-1230)*

Tasman Industries Inc......................... F 502 587-0701
High Point *(G-6802)*

▲ Willow Tex LLC................................. E 336 789-1009
Mount Airy *(G-9195)*

3131 Footwear cut stock

A Bean Counter Inc.............................. G 919 359-9586
Garner *(G-4912)*

Barlin Ranch & Pets Inc...................... G 910 814-1930
Lillington *(G-7789)*

Counter Effect..................................... G 252 636-0080
New Bern *(G-9356)*

Green Bean Counters LLC.................. G 919 545-2324
Chapel Hill *(G-1548)*

Quarter Turn LLC................................ G 336 712-0811
Clemmons *(G-3201)*

Rand Ange Enterprises Inc................. G 336 472-7313
Thomasville *(G-12065)*

Upper Deck Company.......................... G 760 496-9149
Durham *(G-4292)*

3143 Men's footwear, except athletic

Allbirds Inc.. F 980 296-0006
Charlotte *(G-1643)*

Century Hosiery Inc............................ C 336 859-3806
Denton *(G-3742)*

▲ McRae Industries Inc....................... E 910 439-6147
Mount Gilead *(G-9204)*

3144 Women's footwear, except athletic

Century Hosiery Inc............................ C 336 859-3806
Denton *(G-3742)*

▲ McRae Industries Inc....................... E 910 439-6147
Mount Gilead *(G-9204)*

3149 Footwear, except rubber, nec

Century Hosiery Inc............................ C 336 859-3806
Denton *(G-3742)*

3151 Leather gloves and mittens

▲ Gloves-Online Inc............................ G 919 468-4244
Cary *(G-1367)*

3161 Luggage

Case Smith Inc.................................... F 336 969-9786
Rural Hall *(G-10955)*

Conn-Selmer Inc.................................. D 704 289-6459
Monroe *(G-8465)*

Cross Canvas Company Inc................. E 828 252-0440
Asheville *(G-480)*

Cursed Society LLC............................. G 702 445-5601
Greensboro *(G-5477)*

Glaser Designs Inc.............................. F 415 552-3188
Raleigh *(G-10136)*

Jfl LLC... G 919 440-3517
Farmville *(G-4533)*

Lilas Trunk... G 919 548-0784
Bear Creek *(G-715)*

Picassomoesllc................................... G 216 703-4547
Hillsborough *(G-6875)*

Random & Kind LLC............................ G 919 249-8809
Durham *(G-4207)*

Saundra D Hall................................... G 828 251-9859
Asheville *(G-595)*

Tumi Store - Chrltte Dglas Int............ F 704 359-8771
Charlotte *(G-2953)*

Tylerias Closet LLC............................. G 252 325-6639
Roper *(G-10901)*

3171 Women's handbags and purses

Blacqueladi Styles LLC....................... G 877 977-7798
Cary *(G-1308)*

Designed For Joy................................ F 919 395-2884
Apex *(G-150)*

Glaser Designs Inc.............................. F 415 552-3188
Raleigh *(G-10136)*

3172 Personal leather goods, nec

Glaser Designs Inc.............................. F 415 552-3188
Raleigh *(G-10136)*

◆ McKinley Leather Hickory Inc.......... E 828 459-2884
Claremont *(G-3115)*

Pioneer Square Brands Inc................. G 360 733-5608
High Point *(G-6734)*

Point Blank Enterprises Inc................ D 910 893-2071
Lillington *(G-7801)*

3199 Leather goods, nec

AC Valor Reyes LLC............................ G 910 431-3256
Castle Hayne *(G-1493)*

B & B Leather Co Inc........................... F 704 598-9080
Charlotte *(G-1728)*

◆ Carroll Companies Inc...................... E 828 264-2521
Boone *(G-904)*

Coast To Coast Lea & Vinyl Inc.......... G 336 886-5050
High Point *(G-6571)*

Colsenkeane Leather LLC................... G 704 750-9887
Charlotte *(G-1960)*

Doggies r US....................................... G 336 455-1113
Greensboro *(G-5499)*

Ellison Company Inc........................... C 704 889-7518
Charlotte *(G-2102)*

Greene Mountain Outdoors LLC......... F 336 670-2186
North Wilkesboro *(G-9532)*

In Blue Handmade Inc......................... G 828 774-5094
Asheville *(G-522)*

Mva Leatherwood LLC......................... G 704 519-4200
Charlotte *(G-2537)*

Oleksynprannyk LLC........................... F 704 450-0182
Mooresville *(G-8738)*

Oowee Incorporated............................ F 828 633-0289
Candler *(G-1230)*

Point Blank Enterprises Inc................ D 910 893-2071
Lillington *(G-7801)*

Ralph Harris Leather Inc.................... G 336 874-2100
State Road *(G-11639)*

◆ Splawn Belting Inc........................... E 336 227-4277
Burlington *(G-1162)*

Stikeleather Inc .... G 828 352-9095
Taylorsville (G-11979)

Taylor Made Cases Inc .... F 919 209-0555
Benson (G-797)

Thin Line Saddle Pads Inc .... G 919 680-6803
Durham (G-4271)

▲ VH Industries Inc .... G 704 743-2400
Concord (G-3464)

Voltage LLC .... F 919 391-9405
Chapel Hill (G-1592)

32 STONE, CLAY, GLASS, AND CONCRETE PRODUCTS

3211 Flat glass

A R Perry Corporation .... G 252 492-6181
Henderson (G-6146)

Cardinal CT Company .... E 336 719-6857
Mount Airy (G-9106)

Cardinal Glass Industries Inc .... C 704 660-0900
Mooresville (G-8628)

Corning Incorporated .... D 704 569-6000
Midland (G-8284)

▲ Industrial Glass Tech LLC .... F 704 853-2429
Gastonia (G-5065)

Lyon Company .... F 919 787-0024
Wadesboro (G-12248)

Optometric Eyecare Center Inc .... G 910 326-3050
Swansboro (G-11888)

Pgw Auto Glass LLC .... B 336 258-4950
Elkin (G-4451)

Pilkington North America Inc .... E 910 276-5630
Laurinburg (G-7511)

PPG Industries Inc .... G 919 772-3093
Greensboro (G-5755)

Tint Plus .... G 910 229-5303
Fayetteville (G-4681)

3221 Glass containers

Carolina Copacking LLC .... E 252 433-0130
Henderson (G-6148)

CHI Resources .... G 828 835-7878
Murphy (9-9289)

Gerresheimer Glass Inc .... F 828 433-5000
Morganton (G-8868)

King Bio Inc .... E 828 398-6058
Asheville (G-529)

Precision Concepts Intl LLC .... G 704 360-8923
Huntersville (G-7037)

3229 Pressed and blown glass, nec

Bridgestone Americas Inc .... C 984 888-0413
Durham (G-3940)

Carolina York LLC .... F 704 237-0873
Charlotte (G-1861)

Connexion Technologies .... F 919 674-0036
Cary (G-1332)

Corning Incorporated .... F 828 465-0016
Newton (G-9460)

Corning Incorporated .... F 252 316-4500
Tarboro (G-11924)

Corning Incorporated .... D 910 784-7200
Wilmington (G-12753)

Corning Incorporated .... E 336 771-8000
Winston Salem (G-13131)

Corning Optcal Cmmncations LLC .... B 336 771-8000
Winston Salem (G-13132)

Decor Glass Specialties Inc .... G 828 586-8180
Sylva (G-11891)

▲ Easyglass Inc .... G 336 786-1800
Mount Airy (G-9118)

Heraeus Quartz North Amer LLC .... E 910 799-6230
Wilmington (G-12804)

Incantare Art By Marilyn LLC .... F 704 713-8846
Charlotte (G-2319)

M 5 Scentific Glassblowing Inc .... G 704 663-0101
Mooresville (G-8716)

M2 Optics Inc .... G 919 342-5619
Raleigh (G-10264)

Mateenbar USA Inc .... E 704 662-2005
Concord (G-3399)

Nippon Electric Glass Co Ltd .... G 336 357-8151
Lexington (G-7722)

Piedmont Well Covers Inc .... F 704 664-8488
Mount Ulla (G-9270)

PPG Industries Inc .... G 919 772-3093
Greensboro (G-5755)

▲ PPG-Devold LLC .... G 704 434-2261
Shelby (G-11370)

Preformed Line Products Co .... C 704 983-6161
Albemarle (G-84)

Roblon US Inc .... D 828 396-2121
Granite Falls (G-5321)

▼ Royal Carolina Corporation .... E 336 292-8845
Greensboro (G-5796)

◆ Spruce Pine Batch Inc .... G 828 765-9876
Spruce Pine (G-11588)

▲ Spt Technology Inc .... F 612 332-1880
Monroe (G-8561)

3231 Products of purchased glass

A R Perry Corporation .... G 252 492-6181
Henderson (G-6146)

Albemarle Glass Company Inc .... G 704 982-3323
Albemarle (G-58)

All Glass Inc .... G 828 324-8609
Hickory (G-6262)

Cgmi Acquisition Company LLC .... F 919 533-6123
Kernersville (G-7255)

Classy Glass Inc .... G 828 452-2242
Waynesville (G-12454)

Custom Glass Works Inc .... G 704 597-0290
Charlotte (G-2009)

Done-Gone Adios Inc .... F 336 993-7300
Kernersville (G-7268)

Eastern Band Cherokee Indians .... E 828 497-6824
Cherokee (G-3053)

▲ Easyglass Inc .... G 336 786-1800
Mount Airy (G-9118)

Envision Glass Inc .... G 336 283-9701
Winston Salem (G-13159)

◆ Finch Industries Incorporated .... D 336 472-4499
Thomasville (G-12024)

◆ Florida Marine Tanks Inc .... F 305 620-9030
Henderson (G-6155)

Gardner Glass Products Inc .... F 336 838-2151
North Wilkesboro (G-9530)

◆ Gardner Glass Products Inc .... C 336 651-9300
North Wilkesboro (G-9531)

Gerresheimer Glass Inc .... F 828 433-5000
Morganton (G-8868)

Ggi Glass Distributors Corp .... E 910 895-2022
Rockingham (G-10777)

▲ Glass Unlimited High Point Inc .... D 336 889-4551
High Point (G-6629)

Glass Works of Hickory Inc .... G 828 322-2122
Hickory (G-6339)

Heraeus Quartz North Amer LLC .... E 910 799-6230
Wilmington (G-12804)

James Lammers .... G 252 491-2303
Powells Point (G-9822)

Jon Kuhn Inc .... E 336 722-2369
Winston Salem (G-13218)

▲ Lenoir Mirror Company .... C 828 728-3271
Lenoir (G-7620)

M 5 Scentific Glassblowing Inc .... G 704 663-0101
Mooresville (G-8716)

Merge Scientific Solutions LLC .... G 919 346-0999
Fuquay Varina (G-4890)

Miller Glass .... G 828 681-8083
Arden (G-286)

Norell Inc .... G 828 584-2600
Morganton (G-8885)

Orare Inc .... G 919 742-1003
Siler City (G-11422)

PPG Industries Inc .... G 919 772-3093
Greensboro (G-5755)

▲ Press Glass Inc .... E 336 573-2393
Stoneville (G-11826)

▲ Prism Research Glass Inc .... F 919 571-0078
Raleigh (G-10397)

Shed Brand Inc .... G 704 523-0096
Charlotte (G-2797)

▲ Sid Jenkins Inc .... G 336 632-0707
Greensboro (G-5811)

Stroupe Mirror Co .... G 336 475-2181
Winston Salem (G-13348)

Triangle Glass Service Inc .... G 919 477-9508
Durham (G-4279)

Triton Glass LLC .... G 704 982-4333
Albemarle (G-95)

◆ Van Wingerden Grnhse Co Inc .... E 828 891-7389
Mills River (G-8323)

3241 Cement, hydraulic

Argos USA LLC .... G 919 942-0381
Carrboro (G-1265)

Beazer East Inc .... F 919 567-9512
Holly Springs (G-6894)

Vega Construction Company Inc .... E 336 756-3477
Pilot Mountain (G-9675)

3251 Brick and structural clay tile

▲ Clay Taylor Products Inc .... D 704 636-2411
Salisbury (G-11034)

Cunningham Brick Company .... C 336 248-8541
Lexington (G-7673)

Demilo Bros NC LLC .... G 704 771-0762
Waxhaw (G-12428)

Dudley Inc .... G 704 636-8850
Salisbury (G-11045)

▲ Forterra Brick LLC .... C 704 341-8750
Charlotte (G-2175)

General Shale Brick Inc .... F 704 937-7431
Grover (G-6043)

General Shale Brick Inc .... E 919 775-2121
Moncure (G-8405)

General Shale Brick Inc .... E 919 775-2121
Raleigh (G-10127)

General Shale Brick Inc .... G 910 452-3498
Wilmington (G-12786)

J L Anderson Co Inc .... G 704 289-9599
Monroe (G-8507)

Meridian Brick LLC .... D 704 636-0131
Salisbury (G-11093)

Nash Brick Company .... F 252 443-4965
Enfield (G-4485)

◆ Pine Hall Brick Co Inc .... E 336 721-7500
Winston Salem (G-13296)

Statesville Brick Company .... D 704 872-4123
Statesville (G-11777)

Triangle Brick Company .... D 919 387-9257
Moncure (G-8410)

Triangle Brick Company .... E 704 695-1420
Wadesboro (G-12251)

▲ Triangle Brick Company..................... E 919 544-1796
Durham *(G-4277)*

3253 Ceramic wall and floor tile

◆ Bonsal American Inc.......................D 704 525-1621
Charlotte *(G-1799)*

Floorazzo.. G 919 663-1684
Siler City *(G-11408)*

Gray Ox Inc .... F 704 662-8247
Mooresville *(G-8676)*

Mohawk Industries Inc .... G 336 313-4156
Thomasville *(G-12051)*

Precast Terrazzo Entps Inc .... E 919 231-6200
Raleigh *(G-10388)*

Viktors Gran MBL Kit Cnter Top........ F 828 681-0713
Arden *(G-316)*

3255 Clay refractories

Harbisonwalker Intl Inc .... G 704 599-6540
Charlotte *(G-2255)*

Oldcastle Retail Inc............................ B 704 799-8083
Cornelius *(G-3616)*

Pyrotek Incorporated .... E 704 642-1993
Salisbury *(G-11108)*

Resco Products Inc............................ E 336 299-1441
Greensboro *(G-5782)*

Resco Products Inc............................ F 336 299-1441
Greensboro *(G-5783)*

Vesuvius Penn Corporation............... E 724 535-4374
Charlotte *(G-2981)*

3259 Structural clay products, nec

Allfuel Hst Inc .... F 919 868-9410
Hampstead *(G-6066)*

Exteriors Inc Ltd................................. G 919 325-2251
Spring Lake *(G-11561)*

Hearth & Home Technologies LLC........ C 336 274-1663
Greensboro *(G-5592)*

High Temperature Tech Inc................ F 704 375-2111
Charlotte *(G-2279)*

Lee Brick & Tile Company................. D 919 774-4800
Sanford *(G-11203)*

Pine Hall Brick Co Inc .... F 336 721-7500
Madison *(G-7996)*

3261 Vitreous plumbing fixtures

As America Inc.................................... F 704 398-4602
Charlotte *(G-1703)*

Athena Marble Incorporated............... G 704 636-7810
Salisbury *(G-11018)*

Custom Marble Corporation............... G 910 215-0679
Pinehurst *(G-9690)*

Division Eight Inc............................... F 336 852-1275
Greensboro *(G-5497)*

R Jacobs Fine Plbg & Hdwr Inc............ G 919 720-4202
Raleigh *(G-10417)*

▲ Tileware Global LLC........................ G 828 322-9273
Hickory *(G-6469)*

Welcome Industrial Corp .... D 336 329-9640
Burlington *(G-1178)*

3263 Semivitreous table and kitchenware

▲ Swiss Made Brands USA Inc.............. G 704 900-6622
Charlotte *(G-2890)*

3264 Porcelain electrical supplies

Duco-SCI Inc .... F 704 289-9502
Monroe *(G-8478)*

Greenleaf Corporation........................ E 828 693-0461
East Flat Rock *(G-4332)*

◆ Proterial North Carolina Ltd...............C 704 855-2800
China Grove *(G-3078)*

Pyrotek Incorporated.......................... E 704 642-1993
Salisbury *(G-11108)*

▲ Reuel Inc .... E 919 734-0460
Goldsboro *(G-5240)*

The Tarheel Electric Memb................. F 919 876-4603
Raleigh *(G-10544)*

3269 Pottery products, nec

AA Ceramics... G 910 632-3053
Wilmington *(G-12688)*

◆ Border Concepts Inc........................G 704 541-5509
Charlotte *(G-1800)*

Buffer Zone Ceramics......................... G 828 863-2000
Columbus *(G-3300)*

Cairn Studio Ltd.................................. G 704 664-7128
Mooresville *(G-8627)*

Ceder Creek Gallery & Pottery........... G 919 528-1041
Creedmoor *(G-3645)*

Celtic Ceramics.................................. G 919 510-6817
Raleigh *(G-9989)*

◆ Daramic LLC......................................D 704 587-8599
Charlotte *(G-2018)*

East Fork Pottery LLC......................... G 828 237-7200
Asheville *(G-491)*

East Fork Pottery LLC......................... G 828 237-7200
Asheville *(G-492)*

Haand Inc... F 336 350-7597
Burlington *(G-1102)*

Jugtown Pottery.................................. G 910 464-3266
Seagrove *(G-11276)*

◆ Selee Corporation.............................C 828 697-2411
Hendersonville *(G-6240)*

Shed Brand Inc................................... G 704 523-0096
Charlotte *(G-2797)*

Timothy L Griffin .... G 336 317-8314
Greenville *(G-6028)*

3271 Concrete block and brick

▲ Adams Products Company................. C 919 467-2218
Morrisville *(G-8919)*

Argos USA LLC.................................... C 704 872-9566
Statesville *(G-11659)*

Carolina Lawnscape Inc..................... G 803 230-5570
Charlotte *(G-1849)*

CTI Property Services Inc................... E 919 787-3789
Raleigh *(G-10025)*

Custom Brick Company Inc .... E 919 832-2804
Raleigh *(G-10028)*

Dnl Services LLC................................ G 910 689-8759
Harrells *(G-6100)*

East Fork Pottery LLC......................... G 828 575-2150
Asheville *(G-493)*

▼ Fayblock Materials Inc...................... D 910 323-9198
Fayetteville *(G-4600)*

▲ Focal Point Products Inc .... D 252 824-0015
Tarboro *(G-11926)*

General Shale Brick Inc..................... E 919 775-2121
Moncure *(G-8405)*

Global Stone Impex LLC .... G 336 609-1113
Greensboro *(G-5564)*

Good Earth Ministries......................... G 828 287-9826
Rutherfordton *(G-10983)*

Greystone Concrete Pdts Inc............. E 252 438-5144
Henderson *(G-6157)*

Hefty Concrete Inc.............................. G 910 483-1598
Fayetteville *(G-4610)*

Hydro Conduit LLC............................. G 252 243-6153
Wilson *(G-12994)*

Johnson Concrete Company............... E 704 786-4204
Concord *(G-3386)*

Johnson Concrete Company............... E 336 248-2918
Lexington *(G-7702)*

Johnson Concrete Company............... E 704 636-5231
Willow Spring *(G-12679)*

◆ Johnson Concrete Company.............E 704 636-5231
Salisbury *(G-11074)*

Leonard Block Company...................... G 336 764-0607
Winston Salem *(G-13233)*

Motsinger Block Plant Inc.................. G 336 764-0350
Winston Salem *(G-13262)*

▲ Mystic Lifestyle Inc.......................... G 704 960-4530
Concord *(G-3409)*

Old Castle Apg South Inc .... G 919 383-2521
Durham *(G-4155)*

Oldcastle Adams................................ G 336 310-0542
Colfax *(G-3285)*

Oldcastle Retail Inc............................ B 704 799-8083
Cornelius *(G-3616)*

Southeastern Concrete Pdts Co .... D 704 873-2226
Statesville *(G-11768)*

Southern Block Company.................... F 910 293-7844
Warsaw *(G-12366)*

Spake Concrete Products Inc .... F 704 482-2881
Shelby *(G-11382)*

Taylco Inc.. G 910 739-0405
Lumberton *(G-7974)*

Top Dawg Landscape Inc.................... G 336 877-7519
West Jefferson *(G-12571)*

Trademark Landscape Group Inc........... F 910 253-0560
Supply *(G-11861)*

Union Masonry Inc.............................. G 919 217-7806
Raleigh *(G-10576)*

3272 Concrete products, nec

360 Ballistics LLC.............................. G 919 883-8338
Cary *(G-1282)*

A & D Precast Inc............................... G 704 735-3337
Lincolnton *(G-7806)*

Abt Inc... G 314 610-8798
Troutman *(G-12128)*

◆ Abt Inc...E 704 528-9806
Troutman *(G-12129)*

▲ Adams Products Company................. C 919 467-2218
Morrisville *(G-8919)*

Advanced Drainage Systems Inc........... E 336 764-0341
Winston Salem *(G-13074)*

Alcrete Pell City LLC........................... G 910 455-7040
Jacksonville *(G-7113)*

Amesbury Industries Inc.................... E 704 978-3250
Statesville *(G-11657)*

▲ Apollo Designs LLC.......................... E 336 886-0260
High Point *(G-6524)*

Argos USA LLC.................................... C 704 872-9566
Statesville *(G-11659)*

Arnold-Wilbert Corporation............... D 919 735-5008
Goldsboro *(G-5200)*

Asheville Vault Service Inc................ E 828 665-6799
Candler *(G-1218)*

Autry Con Pdts & Bldrs Sup Co........... G 704 504-8830
Charlotte *(G-1719)*

B & C Concrete Products Inc............. G 336 838-4201
North Wilkesboro *(G-9522)*

Ballistics Technology Intl Ltd............. G 252 360-1650
Wilson *(G-12967)*

Beazer East Inc.................................. G 919 380-2610
Morrisville *(G-8939)*

Best Workers Company........................ G 336 665-0076
Riegelwood *(G-10723)*

Blue Rdge Elc Mmbers Fndtion I........... D 828 754-9071
Lenoir *(G-7588)*

◆ Bonsal American Inc.........................D 704 525-1621
Charlotte *(G-1799)*

Brant & Lassiter Septic Tank................ G 252 587-4321
Potecasi *(G-9819)*

Bryant Grant Mutual Burial Asn............ G 828 524-2411
Franklin *(G-4819)*

Canyon Stone Inc.............................. F 919 880-3273
Youngsville *(G-13467)*

Carolina Cemetery Park Corp.............. G 704 528-5543
Troutman *(G-12132)*

Carolina Precast Concrete.................. G 910 230-0028
Dunn *(G-3848)*

Carolina Traffic Devices Inc............... F 704 588-7055
Charlotte *(G-1860)*

Carr Precast Concrete Inc.................. F 910 892-1151
Dunn *(G-3849)*

Cast First Stone Ministry.................... G 704 437-1053
Troutman *(G-12136)*

Cast Stone Systems Inc..................... E 252 257-1599
Warrenton *(G-12351)*

Cava Di Pietra Inc............................... G 910 338-5024
Wilmington *(G-12736)*

Cherry Contracting Inc....................... D 336 969-1825
Rural Hall *(G-10957)*

Coastal Precast Systems LLC........... C 910 444-4682
Wilmington *(G-12744)*

Column & Post Inc............................. G 919 255-1533
Fuquay Varina *(G-4874)*

Concrete Pipe & Precast LLC............ F 910 892-6411
Dunn *(G-3851)*

Concrete Pipe & Precast LLC............ F 704 485-4614
Oakboro *(G-9576)*

Continental Stone Company............... G 336 951-2945
Reidsville *(G-10680)*

Craven Tire Inc.................................. G 252 633-0200
New Bern *(G-9357)*

Custom Brick Company Inc................ E 919 832-2804
Raleigh *(G-10028)*

▲ **David Allen Company Inc**................ C 919 821-7100
Raleigh *(G-10039)*

Eastern Carolina Vault Co Inc............ G 252 243-5614
Wilson *(G-12986)*

Easy Stones Corp.............................. G 980 201-9506
Charlotte *(G-2085)*

▼ **Fayblock Materials Inc**.................... D 910 323-9198
Fayetteville *(G-4600)*

Fletcher Limestone Company Inc........ G 828 684-6701
Fletcher *(G-4737)*

Floorazzo Tile LLC............................. F 919 663-1684
Siler City *(G-11409)*

Forterra Pipe & Precast LLC............. G 910 892-6411
Dunn *(G-3857)*

Futrell Precasting LLC........................ G 252 568-3481
Deep Run *(G-3732)*

Garners Septic Tank Inc..................... G 919 718-5181
Raeford *(G-9838)*

Gate Precast Company....................... C 919 603-1633
Oxford *(G-9614)*

Greystone Concrete Pdts Inc............. E 252 438-5144
Henderson *(G-6157)*

Hairfield Wilbert Burial Vlt.................. G 828 437-4319
Morganton *(G-8870)*

Hauser Hvac Installation................... G 336 416-2173
Winston Salem *(G-13192)*

Henson Family Investments LLC........ E 910 817-9450
Rockingham *(G-10778)*

High Point Precast Pdts Inc............... G 336 434-1815
Lexington *(G-7698)*

◆ **Hog Slat Incorporated**..................... B 800 949-4647
Newton Grove *(G-9514)*

Hydro Conduit LLC............................. G 336 475-1371
Thomasville *(G-12035)*

Ideal Precast Inc................................ G 919 801-8287
Durham *(G-4070)*

Imagine That Creations LLC............... G 480 528-6775
Black Mountain *(G-867)*

Imperial Vault Company...................... F 336 983-6343
King *(G-7328)*

Inman Septic Tank Service Inc............ G 910 763-1146
Wilmington *(G-12817)*

▲ **International Precast Inc**.................. E 919 742-4241
Siler City *(G-11413)*

Johnson Concrete Company............... E 704 636-5231
Willow Spring *(G-12679)*

◆ **Johnson Concrete Company**............ E 704 636-5231
Salisbury *(G-11074)*

Kbc of Nc LLC................................... G 704 589-3711
Waxhaw *(G-12433)*

Leonard McSwain Sptic Tank Svc........ G 704 482-1380
Shelby *(G-11353)*

Lindsay Precast Inc............................ E 919 494-7600
Franklinton *(G-4850)*

Lucas Concrete Products Inc............. E 704 525-9622
Charlotte *(G-2438)*

▲ **Manhattan Amrcn Terrazzo Strip**...... C 336 622-4247
Staley *(G-11596)*

MC Precast Concrete Inc................... G 919 367-3636
Apex *(G-178)*

Merchants Metals Inc........................ G 704 921-9192
Charlotte *(G-2491)*

Mid-Atlantic Concrete Pdts Inc........... G 336 774-6544
Winston Salem *(G-13253)*

Mitchell Concrete Products Inc........... G 919 934-4333
Smithfield *(G-11455)*

Moretz & Sipe Inc............................. G 828 327-8661
Hickory *(G-6397)*

Northeastern Ready Mix..................... G 252 335-1931
Elizabeth City *(G-4400)*

O R Prdgen Sons Sptic Tank I........... G 252 442-3338
Rocky Mount *(G-10857)*

Old Castle Apg South Inc.................. G 919 383-2521
Durham *(G-4155)*

Oldcastle Apg South Inc.................... G 336 854-8200
Greensboro *(G-5719)*

Oldcastle Infrastructure Inc............... E 704 788-4050
Concord *(G-3412)*

Oldcastle Infrastructure Inc............... F 910 433-2931
Fayetteville *(G-4648)*

Oldcastle Infrastructure Inc............... E 919 552-2252
Fuquay Varina *(G-4894)*

Oldcastle Infrastructure Inc............... E 919 772-6269
Raleigh *(G-10344)*

Oldcastle Retail Inc........................... B 704 799-8083
Cornelius *(G-3616)*

◆ **Oldcastle Retail Inc**........................ F 704 525-1621
Charlotte *(G-2594)*

P & D Archtectural Precast Inc........... F 252 566-9811
La Grange *(G-7470)*

Piedmont Surfaces of Triad LLC......... G 336 627-7790
Eden *(G-4354)*

Pipe Bridge Products Inc.................... G 919 786-4499
Raleigh *(G-10368)*

▲ **Precast Solutions Inc**...................... F 336 656-7991
Browns Summit *(G-1003)*

Precast Terrazzo Entps Inc................ E 919 231-6200
Raleigh *(G-10388)*

Prestress of Carolinas LLC................ G 704 587-4273
Charlotte *(G-2663)*

Quality Precast Inc............................ G 919 497-0660
Louisburg *(G-7924)*

Quikrete Companies LLC................... E 704 272-7677
Peachland *(G-9653)*

S T Wooten Corporation.................... F 919 783-5507
Raleigh *(G-10454)*

Sentry Vault Service Inc.................... G 252 243-2241
Elm City *(G-4467)*

Shoaf Precast Septic Tank Inc........... G 336 787-5826
Lexington *(G-7740)*

Smith-Carolina Corporation............... E 336 349-2905
Reidsville *(G-10698)*

Southeastern Concrete Pdts Co......... D 704 873-2226
Statesville *(G-11768)*

Southern Block Company................... F 910 293-7844
Warsaw *(G-12366)*

Speer Concrete Inc........................... E 910 947-3144
Carthage *(G-1280)*

Stay-Right Pre-Cast Concrete Inc....... D 919 494-7600
Franklinton *(G-4854)*

Superior Walls Systems LLC.............. E 704 636-6200
Salisbury *(G-11120)*

Superior Walls Systems LLC.............. D 704 636-6200
Salisbury *(G-11121)*

TNT Services Inc............................... G 252 261-3073
Kitty Hawk *(G-7447)*

Troy Ready - Mix Inc......................... G 910 572-1011
Troy *(G-12169)*

Tru-Contour Inc................................. G 704 455-8700
Concord *(G-3459)*

Utility Precast Inc.............................. E 704 721-0106
Concord *(G-3463)*

Vim Products Inc............................... G 919 277-0267
Raleigh *(G-10589)*

Watson Concrete Pipe Company......... G 828 754-6476
Lenoir *(G-7645)*

Wilbert Burial Vault Company............. G 910 739-7276
Lumberton *(G-7976)*

Wilbert Funeral Services Inc.............. E 800 828-5879
Greensboro *(G-5919)*

Wilbert Yates Vault Co Inc................. F 704 399-8453
Charlotte *(G-3020)*

Wilmington Mortuary Svc Inc.............. F 910 791-9099
Wilmington *(G-12951)*

3273 Ready-mixed concrete

Abhw Concrete Co............................. G 252 940-1002
Washington *(G-12370)*

Adams Oldcastle............................... G 980 229-7678
Charlotte *(G-1623)*

Allen-Godwin Concrete Inc................ G 910 686-4890
Wilmington *(G-12702)*

Allie M Powell III.............................. G 252 535-9717
Roanoke Rapids *(G-10729)*

Argos Ready Mix (carolinas) Corp....... B 919 790-1520
Raleigh *(G-9912)*

Argos USA.. F 336 784-5181
Winston Salem *(G-13088)*

Argos USA LLC................................. E 910 675-1262
Castle Hayne *(G-1495)*

Argos USA LLC................................. G 704 679-9431
Charlotte *(G-1695)*

Argos USA LLC................................. E 910 299-5046
Clinton *(G-3228)*

Argos USA LLC................................. F 704 483-4013
Denver *(G-3772)*

Argos USA LLC................................. G 910 892-3188
Dunn *(G-3845)*

Argos USA LLC................................. G 919 552-2294
Fuquay Varina *(G-4866)*

Argos USA LLC................................. E 919 772-4188
Garner *(G-4916)*

Argos USA LLC................................. D 828 322-9325
Hickory *(G-6267)*

Argos USA LLC................................. E 336 841-3379
High Point *(G-6527)*

Argos USA LLC................................. G 919 732-7509
Hillsborough *(G-6858)*

Argos USA LLC................................. E 252 527-8008
Kinston *(G-7394)*

Argos USA LLC................................. G 704 872-9566
Mooresville *(G-8600)*

Argos USA LLC........................... G 252 223-4348	CFI Ready Mix LLC........................ G 910 814-4238	Eagle Rock Concrete LLC.................... E 919 596-7077
Newport (G-9437)	Lillington (G-7792)	Apex (G-152)
Argos USA LLC........................... F 919 828-3695	Chandler Con Pdts of Chrstnber........... G 336 226-1181	Eagle Rock Concrete LLC.................... E 919 281-0120
Raleigh (G-9913)	Burlington (G-1070)	Raleigh (G-10068)
Argos USA LLC........................... F 919 775-5441	Chandler Concrete Co Inc.................. G 910 974-4744	Eagle Rock Concrete LLC.................... E 919 781-3744
Raleigh (G-9914)	Biscoe (G-850)	Raleigh (G-10067)
Argos USA LLC........................... E 919 790-1520	Chandler Concrete Co Inc.................. G 336 635-0975	Eastern Ready Mix LLC...................... F 919 207-2722
Raleigh (G-9915)	Eden (G-4343)	Benson (G-788)
Argos USA LLC........................... G 252 443-5046	Chandler Concrete Co Inc.................. D 336 272-6127	Eveready Mix Concrete Co Inc.............. G 336 961-6688
Roanoke Rapids (G-10730)	Burlington (G-1071)	Yadkinville (G-13442)
Argos USA LLC........................... G 252 291-8888	Chandler Concrete High Co................. G 828 264-8694	Explosives Supply Company................. F 828 765-2762
Sims (G-11428)	Boone (G-907)	Spruce Pine (G-11575)
Argos USA LLC........................... C 704 872-9566	Chandler Concrete Inc..................... F 336 625-1070	Greenville Ready Mix Concrete............. E 252 756-0119
Statesville (G-11659)	Asheboro (G-337)	Winterville (G-13416)
Argos USA LLC........................... E 919 554-2087	Chandler Concrete Inc..................... F 336 982-8760	Greystone Concrete Pdts Inc............... E 252 438-5144
Wake Forest (G-12261)	Crumpler (G-3660)	Henderson (G-6157)
Argos USA LLC........................... G 252 946-4704	Chandler Concrete Inc..................... F 919 598-1424	Hamby Brother S Incorporated............. F 336 667-1154
Washington (G-12373)	Durham (G-3969)	North Wilkesboro (G-9533)
Argos USA LLC........................... G 252 792-3148	Chandler Concrete Inc..................... G 336 342-5771	Hamby Brothers Concrete Inc.............. F 828 754-2176
Williamston (G-12667)	Eden (G-4344)	Lenoir (G-7613)
Argos USA LLC........................... G 910 686-4890	Chandler Concrete Inc..................... G 336 222-9716	Hamrick Precast LLC...................... G 704 434-6551
Wilmington (G-12707)	Graham (G-5263)	Shelby (G-11341)
Argos USA LLC........................... G 910 796-3469	Chandler Concrete Inc..................... F 336 297-1179	Hartley Ready Mix Con Mfg Inc........... G 336 294-5995
Wilmington (G-12708)	Greensboro (G-5440)	Greensboro (G-5587)
Argos USA LLC........................... D 336 784-4888	Chandler Concrete Inc..................... E 919 644-1058	Hartley Ready Mix Con Mfg Inc........... F 336 788-3928
Winston Salem (G-13089)	Hillsborough (G-6863)	Winston Salem (G-13191)
Asheboro Ready-Mix Inc................... G 336 672-0957	Chandler Concrete Inc..................... G 919 542-4242	Heidelberg Materials Us Inc............... D 252 235-4162
Asheboro (G-330)	Pittsboro (G-9779)	Sims (G-11431)
B V Hedrick Gravel & Sand Co............. E 704 633-5982	Chandler Concrete Inc..................... G 336 599-8343	Heidelberg Mtls Sthast Agg LLC........... E 919 556-4011
Salisbury (G-11021)	Roxboro (G-10923)	Wake Forest (G-12281)
Black Concrete Inc....................... G 336 243-1388	Chandler Concrete Inc..................... D 704 636-4711	Heidelberg Mtls US Cem LLC.............. G 919 682-5791
Lexington (G-7659)	Salisbury (G-11031)	Durham (G-4058)
Blue DOT Readi-Mix LLC.................. F 704 971-7676	Chandler Concrete Inc..................... F 336 372-4348	Heritage Concrete Service Corp........... G 910 892-4445
Mint Hill (G-8332)	Sparta (G-11536)	Dunn (G-3861)
Cabarrus Concrete Co.................... F 704 788-3000	Childers Concrete Company................ F 336 841-3111	Heritage Concrete Service Corp........... F 919 775-5014
Concord (G-3327)	High Point (G-6568)	Sanford (G-11189)
Capital Rdymx Pittsboro LLC.............. E 919 217-0222	Commercial Ready Mix Pdts Inc........... G 252 332-3590	Hildreth Ready Mix LLC................... G 704 694-2034
Moncure (G-8402)	Ahoskie (G-45)	Rockingham (G-10779)
Capitol Funds Inc....................... F 910 439-5275	Commercial Ready Mix Pdts Inc........... F 252 335-9740	Kerrs Hickry Ready-Mixed Con............ E 828 322-3157
Mount Gilead (G-9198)	Elizabeth City (G-4383)	Hickory (G-6377)
Capitol Funds Inc....................... E 704 487-8547	Commercial Ready Mix Pdts Inc........... G 252 232-1250	Legacy Vulcan LLC....................... G 828 963-7100
Shelby (G-11316)	Moyock (G-9278)	Boone (G-929)
Carolina Concrete Inc.................... F 704 596-6511	Commercial Ready Mix Pdts Inc........... F 252 585-1777	Legacy Vulcan LLC....................... G 704 788-7833
Charlotte (G-1845)	Pendleton (G-9661)	Concord (G-3391)
Carolina Concrete Inc.................... E 704 821-7645	Commercial Spclty Trck Hldngs........... C 859 234-1100	Legacy Vulcan LLC....................... G 252 338-2201
Matthews (G-8102)	Burlington (G-1074)	Elizabeth City (G-4396)
Carolina Concrete Materials.............. G 828 686-3040	Concrete Service Co Inc................... E 910 483-0396	Legacy Vulcan LLC....................... G 336 835-1439
Swannanoa (G-11867)	Fayetteville (G-4577)	Elkin (G-4447)
Carolina Ready Mix & Build............... G 828 686-3041	Concrete Supply Co LLC.................. G 864 517-4055	Legacy Vulcan LLC....................... G 828 255-8561
Swannanoa (G-11868)	Charlotte (G-1970)	Enka (G-4487)
Carolina Ready-Mix LLC.................. G 704 225-1112	Concrete Supply Co LLC.................. E 704 372-2930	Legacy Vulcan LLC....................... G 704 279-5566
Monroe (G-8454)	Charlotte (G-1971)	Gold Hill (G-5194)
Carolina Sunrock LLC.................... G 919 201-4201	Concrete Supply Holdings Inc............. B 704 372-2930	Legacy Vulcan LLC....................... G 252 438-3161
Creedmoor (G-3644)	Charlotte (G-1972)	Henderson (G-6164)
Carolina Sunrock LLC.................... E 252 433-4617	Crete Solutions LLC...................... E 910 726-1686	Legacy Vulcan LLC....................... G 828 692-0254
Kittrell (G-7440)	Wilmington (G-12756)	Hendersonville (G-6221)
Carolina Sunrock LLC.................... E 919 861-1860	Crh Americas Inc........................ C 704 282-8443	Legacy Vulcan LLC....................... G 828 754-5348
Raleigh (G-9979)	Monroe (G-8471)	Lenoir (G-7618)
Carolina Sunrock LLC.................... E 919 554-0500	Crmp Inc................................ G 252 358-5461	Legacy Vulcan LLC....................... G 828 437-2616
Wake Forest (G-12267)	Winton (G-13428)	Morganton (G-8877)
▲ Carolina Sunrock LLC.................. E 919 575-4502	Dean S Ready Mixed Inc.................. G 704 982-5520	Legacy Vulcan LLC....................... G 336 838-8072
Butner (G-1200)	Albemarle (G-69)	North Wilkesboro (G-9540)
Cemex Cnstr Mtls ATL LLC............... G 704 873-3263	DOT Blue Readi-Mix LLC.................. E 704 391-3000	Legacy Vulcan LLC....................... G 910 895-2415
Statesville (G-11677)	Charlotte (G-2063)	Rockingham (G-10782)
Cemex Materials LLC.................... C 704 455-1100	DOT Blue Readi-Mix LLC.................. E 704 247-2778	Legacy Vulcan LLC....................... D 336 767-0911
Harrisburg (G-6106)	Harrisburg (G-6107)	Winston Salem (G-13232)
Cemex Materials LLC.................... D 800 627-2986	DOT Blue Readi-Mix LLC.................. E 704 247-2777	Lenoir Concrete Cnstr Co.................. G 828 759-0449
Thomasville (G-12008)	Monroe (G-8477)	Lenoir (G-7619)
Cemex Materials LLC.................... C 252 243-6153	DOT Blue Readi-Mix LLC.................. E 704 978-2331	Loflin Concrete Co Inc.................... E 336 904-2788
Wilson (G-12979)	Statesville (G-11692)	Kernersville (G-7282)
Central Carolina Concrete LLC............ F 704 372-2930	E & M Concrete Inc...................... E 919 235-7221	Loven Ready Mix LLC..................... G 828 265-4671
Greensboro (G-5437)	Fuquay Varina (G-4880)	Boone (G-930)

Macleod Construction Inc............... C 704 483-3580
Charlotte *(G-2446)*

Martin Marietta Materials Inc............... G 910 602-6058
Castle Hayne *(G-1506)*

Martin Marietta Materials Inc............... G 919 929-7131
Chapel Hill *(G-1554)*

Martin Marietta Materials Inc............... G 704 392-1333
Charlotte *(G-2463)*

Martin Marietta Materials Inc............... F 919 557-7412
Fuquay Varina *(G-4888)*

Martin Marietta Materials Inc............... F 704 932-4379
Landis *(G-7474)*

Martin Marietta Materials Inc............... G 919 664-1700
Raleigh *(G-10274)*

Martin Marietta Materials Inc............... G 910 324-7430
Richlands *(G-10721)*

Massey Ready-Mix Concrete Inc............... G 336 221-8100
Burlington *(G-1125)*

McDowell Cement Products Co............... G 828 765-2762
Spruce Pine *(G-11579)*

McDowell Cement Products Co............... F 828 652-5721
Marion *(G-8053)*

Mulls Con & Septic Tanks Inc............... G 828 437-0959
Morganton *(G-8883)*

Northeastern Ready Mix............... G 252 335-1931
Elizabeth City *(G-4400)*

Old Rm Co LLC............... D 919 217-0222
Knightdale *(G-7454)*

Oldcastle Retail Inc............... B 704 799-8083
Cornelius *(G-3616)*

Pea Creek Mine LLC............... G 252 814-1388
Greenville *(G-6011)*

Quality Concrete Co Inc............... F 910 483-7155
Fayetteville *(G-4660)*

Quikrete Companies LLC............... E 704 272-7677
Peachland *(G-9653)*

Ready Mix of Carolinas Inc............... E 704 888-3027
Locust *(G-7899)*

Ready Mixed Concrete............... G 252 758-1181
Ayden *(G-659)*

Redy Mix of Carolinas Inc............... G 704 888-2224
Locust *(G-7900)*

Rinker Materials............... F 704 455-1100
Harrisburg *(G-6116)*

Rinker Materials............... G 704 827-8175
Mount Holly *(G-9244)*

Roanoke Chowan Ready Mix Inc............... G 252 332-7995
Ahoskie *(G-52)*

Robert S Concrete Service Inc............... G 910 391-3973
Fayetteville *(G-4664)*

S & W Ready Mix Con Co LLC............... F 910 592-2191
Clinton *(G-3241)*

S & W Ready Mix Con Co LLC............... G 910 645-6868
Elizabethtown *(G-4432)*

S & W Ready Mix Con Co LLC............... F 910 864-0939
Fayetteville *(G-4665)*

S & W Ready Mix Con Co LLC............... F 919 751-1796
Goldsboro *(G-5243)*

S & W Ready Mix Con Co LLC............... F 910 329-1201
Holly Ridge *(G-6891)*

S & W Ready Mix Con Co LLC............... F 252 527-1881
Kinston *(G-7426)*

S & W Ready Mix Con Co LLC............... F 252 726-2566
Morehead City *(G-8842)*

S & W Ready Mix Con Co LLC............... F 252 633-2115
New Bern *(G-9392)*

S & W Ready Mix Con Co LLC............... F 910 496-3232
Spring Lake *(G-11563)*

S & W Ready Mix Con Co LLC............... F 910 285-2191
Wallace *(G-12323)*

S & W Ready Mix Con Co LLC............... F 910 592-1733
Clinton *(G-3242)*

S T Wooten Corporation............... E 252 291-5165
Wilson *(G-13027)*

Smyrna Ready Mix Concrete LLC............... G 252 447-5356
Havelock *(G-6127)*

Smyrna Ready Mix Concrete LLC............... F 252 637-4155
New Bern *(G-9397)*

Southern Concrete Incorporated............... F 919 906-4069
Broadway *(G-987)*

Southern Concrete Materials............... G 704 641-9604
Concord *(G-3443)*

Southern Concrete Materials Inc............... C 828 253-6421
Asheville *(G-608)*

Southern Concrete Mtls Inc............... E 828 684-3636
Arden *(G-308)*

Southern Concrete Mtls Inc............... F 828 670-6450
Asheville *(G-609)*

Southern Concrete Mtls Inc............... G 828 682-2298
Burnsville *(G-1191)*

Southern Concrete Mtls Inc............... F 704 394-2346
Charlotte *(G-2834)*

Southern Concrete Mtls Inc............... E 704 394-2344
Charlotte *(G-2835)*

Southern Concrete Mtls Inc............... E 828 681-5178
Fletcher *(G-4771)*

Southern Concrete Mtls Inc............... F 828 524-3555
Franklin *(G-4840)*

Southern Concrete Mtls Inc............... E 828 692-6517
Hendersonville *(G-6243)*

Southern Concrete Mtls Inc............... F 877 788-3001
Salisbury *(G-11117)*

Southern Concrete Mtls Inc............... F 828 586-5280
Sylva *(G-11899)*

Southern Concrete Mtls Inc............... F 828 456-9048
Waynesville *(G-12476)*

Southern Hldings Goldsboro Inc............... G 919 920-6998
Goldsboro *(G-5245)*

Speer Concrete Inc............... E 910 947-3144
Carthage *(G-1280)*

Star Ready-Mix Inc............... G 336 725-9401
Winston Salem *(G-13342)*

Sunrock Group Holdings Corp............... D 919 747-6400
Raleigh *(G-10520)*

Thomas Concrete Carolina Inc............... F 704 333-0390
Charlotte *(G-2911)*

Thomas Concrete Carolina Inc............... F 919 557-3144
Fuquay Varina *(G-4902)*

Thomas Concrete Carolina Inc............... F 919 460-5317
Morrisville *(G-9071)*

Thomas Concrete Carolina Inc............... F 919 832-0451
Raleigh *(G-10546)*

Thomas Concrete SC Inc............... F 704 868-4545
Gastonia *(G-5154)*

Three Sisters Ready Mix LLC............... G 919 217-0222
Knightdale *(G-7459)*

Titan America LLC............... G 336 754-0143
Belews Creek *(G-739)*

TNT Services Inc............... G 252 261-3073
Kitty Hawk *(G-7447)*

Toxaway Concrete Inc............... F 828 966-4270
Cashiers *(G-1491)*

Tri City Concrete Co LLC............... F 828 245-2011
Forest City *(G-4798)*

Tri-City Concrete LLC............... G 704 372-2930
Charlotte *(G-2940)*

Triangle Ready Mix LLC............... E 919 859-4190
Morrisville *(G-9077)*

Tyrrell Ready Mix Inc............... G 252 796-0265
Columbia *(G-3298)*

Vulcan Construction Mtls LLC............... G 336 767-1201
Winston Salem *(G-13384)*

Vulcan Construction Mtls LLC............... E 336 767-0911
Winston Salem *(G-13385)*

Vulcan Materials Company............... G 828 963-7100
Boone *(G-950)*

Vulcan Materials Company............... G 704 549-1540
Charlotte *(G-2991)*

Vulcan Materials Company............... G 704 545-5687
Charlotte *(G-2992)*

Vulcan Materials Company............... G 828 692-0039
Hendersonville *(G-6248)*

Vulcan Materials Company............... G 336 869-2148
Kernersville *(G-7313)*

Watauga Ready Mixed............... G 336 246-6441
Boone *(G-952)*

White Cap LP............... G 704 921-4420
Charlotte *(G-3017)*

Williams Ready Mix Pdts Inc............... F 704 283-1137
Monroe *(G-8581)*

Wnc Material Sales............... G 828 658-8368
Weaverville *(G-12507)*

3275 Gypsum products

Esco Industries Inc............... F 336 495-3772
Randleman *(G-10647)*

Mbp Acquisition LLC............... E 704 349-5055
Monroe *(G-8528)*

Ng Operations LLC............... D 704 916-2082
Charlotte *(G-2566)*

Precision Walls Inc............... G 336 852-7710
Greensboro *(G-5759)*

Proform Finishing Products LLC............... E 704 398-3900
Mount Holly *(G-9243)*

Proform Finishing Products LLC............... D 910 799-3954
Wilmington *(G-12890)*

◆ Proform Finishing Products LLC............... B 704 365-7300
Charlotte *(G-2674)*

3281 Cut stone and stone products

▲ Acme Stone Company Inc............... F 336 786-6978
Mount Airy *(G-9095)*

Amanzi Marble & Granite LLC............... G 336 993-9998
Kernersville *(G-7242)*

American Stone Company............... G 919 929-7131
Chapel Hill *(G-1525)*

Apex Marble and Granite Inc............... E 919 462-9202
Morrisville *(G-8929)*

Asp Distribution Inc............... F 336 375-5672
Greensboro *(G-5373)*

Athena Marble Incorporated............... G 704 636-7810
Salisbury *(G-11018)*

B V Hedrick Gravel & Sand Co............... E 828 645-5560
Weaverville *(G-12482)*

Beautimar Manufactured MBL Inc............... G 919 779-1181
Raleigh *(G-9937)*

Bloomday Granite & Marble Inc............... E 336 724-0300
Winston Salem *(G-13108)*

Boone-Woody Mining Company Inc............... G 828 675-5188
Micaville *(G-8270)*

Buechel Stone Corp............... D 800 236-4474
Marion *(G-8037)*

▲ Caesarstone Tech USA Inc............... G 818 779-0999
Charlotte *(G-1831)*

Capital Marble Creations Inc............... G 910 893-2462
Lillington *(G-7791)*

Carolina Marble & Granite............... G 704 523-2112
Charlotte *(G-1850)*

◆ Carolina North Granite Corp............... D 336 719-2600
Mount Airy *(G-9109)*

Carolina Quarries Inc............... D 704 633-0201
Salisbury *(G-11028)*

Carolina Stalite Co Ltd Partnr............... E 704 279-2166
Gold Hill *(G-5190)*

Carolina Stalite Co Ltd Partnr............... F 704 474-3165
Norwood *(G-9554)*

Carolina Stalite Co Ltd Partnr................. F 704 637-1515
Salisbury *(G-11029)*

Century Stone LLC................................ G 919 774-3334
Sanford *(G-11161)*

◆ Chadsworth Incorporated.....................G 910 763-7600
Wilmington *(G-12742)*

Clifford W Estes Co Inc........................ E 336 622-6410
Staley *(G-11593)*

Conway Development Inc....................... F 252 756-2168
Greenville *(G-5957)*

Creative Stone Fyetteville Inc................ F 910 491-1225
Fayetteville *(G-4580)*

Custom Marble Corporation.................. G 910 215-0679
Pinehurst *(G-9690)*

E T Sales Inc..................................... F 704 888-4010
Midland *(G-8286)*

Exquisite Granite and MBL Inc............. G 336 851-8890
Greensboro *(G-5528)*

FTM Enterprises Inc............................ F 910 798-2045
Wilmington *(G-12780)*

Georgia-Carolina Quarries Inc............. E 336 786-6978
Mount Airy *(G-9123)*

Ginkgo Stone LLC.............................. G 704 451-8678
Charlotte *(G-2212)*

▲ Grancreations Inc............................ G 704 332-7625
Charlotte *(G-2230)*

Granite Memorials Inc......................... G 336 786-6596
Mount Airy *(G-9124)*

Heidelberg Mtls Sthast Agg LLC.......... E 910 893-8308
Bunnlevel *(G-1016)*

Ivey Ln Inc....................................... F 336 230-0062
Greensboro *(G-5631)*

Jacobs Creek Stone Company Inc........ F 336 857-2602
Denton *(G-3751)*

John J Morton Company Inc................. F 704 332-6633
Charlotte *(G-2373)*

King Stone Innovation LLC.................. G 704 352-1134
Charlotte *(G-2398)*

Kitchen Man Inc................................. F 910 408-1322
Winnabow *(G-13067)*

Lawing Marble Co Inc......................... G 704 732-0360
Lincolnton *(G-7835)*

Lbm Industries Inc............................. F 828 966-4270
Sapphire *(G-11258)*

Locust Monument LLC......................... G 704 888-5600
Locust *(G-7895)*

M & M Stone Sculpting & Engrv........... G 336 877-3842
Todd *(G-12104)*

Mables Headstone & Monu Co LLP....... G 919 724-8705
Creedmoor *(G-3652)*

Marion Cultured Marble Inc.................. G 828 724-4782
Marion *(G-8049)*

Master Tesh Stone Works.................... G 828 898-8333
Banner Elk *(G-687)*

McAd Inc.. E 336 299-3030
Greensboro *(G-5686)*

Meridian Granite Company................... G 919 781-4550
Raleigh *(G-10292)*

▲ Midcoastal Development Corp........... G 336 622-3091
Staley *(G-11597)*

Mongoose LLC................................... F 919 400-0772
Burlington *(G-1130)*

National Marble Products Inc.............. G 910 326-3005
Emerald Isle *(G-4478)*

▲ Natural Granite & Marble Inc............ G 919 872-1508
Raleigh *(G-10326)*

Nova Enterprises Inc.......................... E 828 687-8770
Arden *(G-290)*

Piedmont Marble Inc........................... G 336 274-1800
Oak Ridge *(G-9574)*

Quality Marble................................... G 336 472-1000
Thomasville *(G-12064)*

Royal Baths Manufacturing Co............. E 704 837-1701
Charlotte *(G-2733)*

RSI Home Products Inc........................ C 828 428-6300
Lincolnton *(G-7852)*

Sharp Stone Supply Inc....................... G 336 659-7777
Winston Salem *(G-13332)*

▲ Sid Jenkins Inc............................... G 336 632-0707
Greensboro *(G-5811)*

Southern Marble Co LLC...................... G 704 982-4142
Albemarle *(G-91)*

◆ Stone Resource Inc.......................... E 336 889-7800
High Point *(G-6794)*

▼ Stonemaster Inc.............................. F 704 333-0353
Concord *(G-3449)*

Stoneworx Inc.................................... G 252 937-8080
Rocky Mount *(G-10870)*

▲ Trade Venture Stones LLC................ G 919 803-3923
Knightdale *(G-7460)*

▲ Turmar Marble Inc........................... G 704 391-1800
Charlotte *(G-2954)*

Unique Stone Incorporated.................. G 910 817-9450
Rockingham *(G-10792)*

USA Dreamstone LLC.......................... G 919 615-4329
Garner *(G-4970)*

Wake Monument Company Inc.............. G 919 556-3422
Rolesville *(G-10891)*

Wake Stone Corporation...................... E 919 677-0050
Cary *(G-1481)*

Wake Stone Corporation...................... E 919 266-1100
Knightdale *(G-7462)*

▲ Web-Don Incorporated...................... E 800 532-0434
Charlotte *(G-3009)*

Wholesale Monument Company............. G 336 789-2031
Mount Airy *(G-9194)*

Wiggins North State Co Inc.................. G 919 556-3231
Rolesville *(G-10892)*

Winecoff Mmrals Sttesville Inc............. G 704 873-9661
Statesville *(G-11801)*

Woodsmiths Company.......................... G 406 626-3102
Lenoir *(G-7646)*

World Stone Fabricators Inc................. E 704 372-9968
Charlotte *(G-3026)*

World Stone of Sanford LLC................. F 919 468-8450
Sanford *(G-11254)*

3291 Abrasive products

3M Company....................................... G 704 588-4782
Charlotte *(G-1601)*

Advanced Superabrasives Inc.............. E 828 689-3200
Mars Hill *(G-8076)*

Eagle Superabrasives Inc................... G 828 261-7281
Hickory *(G-6326)*

▲ Farris Belt & Saw Company.............. F 704 527-6166
Charlotte *(G-2143)*

Gulfstream Steel & Supply Inc............. E 910 329-5100
Holly Ridge *(G-6888)*

▼ His Glassworks Inc.......................... G 828 254-2559
Asheville *(G-518)*

Keselowski Advanced Mfg LLC............. E 704 799-0206
Statesville *(G-11723)*

◆ Klingspor Abrasives Inc....................C 828 322-3030
Hickory *(G-6380)*

▲ Sia Abrasives Inc USA..................... D 704 587-7355
Lincolnton *(G-7853)*

▲ Starcke Abrasives Usa Inc............... E 704 583-3338
Charlotte *(G-2860)*

Sunbelt Abrasives Inc........................ G 336 882-6837
High Point *(G-6796)*

Syntech Abrasives Inc......................... F 704 525-8030
Charlotte *(G-2893)*

Tiger Steel Inc................................... G 336 624-4481
Mount Airy *(G-9186)*

W G Cannon Paint Co Inc..................... G 828 754-5376
Lenoir *(G-7644)*

3292 Asbestos products

Certainteed LLC................................. F 336 696-2007
North Wilkesboro *(G-9524)*

Exterior Vinyl Wholesale..................... G 336 838-7772
Wilkesboro *(G-12634)*

Hydro Tube Enterprises Inc................. E 919 258-3070
Sanford *(G-11193)*

Plycem USA LLC................................. C 336 696-2007
North Wilkesboro *(G-9549)*

3295 Minerals, ground or treated

3M Company....................................... D 919 642-0006
Moncure *(G-8397)*

Carolina Stalite Co Ltd Partnr.............. E 704 279-2166
Gold Hill *(G-5191)*

◆ Cormetech Inc.................................C 704 827-8933
Charlotte *(G-1985)*

Covia Holdings LLC............................ D 828 765-4283
Spruce Pine *(G-11573)*

Glendon Pyrophyllite Inc..................... G 919 464-5243
Sanford *(G-11185)*

Imerys Clays Inc................................ G 828 648-2668
Canton *(G-1254)*

◆ Imerys Mica Kings Mountain Inc.........F 704 739-3616
Kings Mountain *(G-7365)*

Imerys Perlite Usa Inc........................ F 919 562-0031
Youngsville *(G-13475)*

Iperionx Limited................................ E 980 237-8900
Charlotte *(G-2354)*

▲ Martin Marietta Magnesia .... D 800 648-7400
Raleigh *(G-10273)*

◆ Martin Marietta Materials Inc.............C 919 781-4550
Raleigh *(G-10277)*

Mathis Quarries Inc............................ G 336 984-4010
North Wilkesboro *(G-9545)*

◆ Premier Magnesia LLC.....................E 828 452-4784
Waynesville *(G-12468)*

◆ Quartz Corp USA.............................E 828 766-2104
Spruce Pine *(G-11584)*

Southeastern Minerals Inc................... E 252 492-0831
Henderson *(G-6179)*

Southern Products Company Inc........... E 910 281-3189
Hoffman *(G-6885)*

Vanderbilt Minerals LLC...................... E 910 948-2266
Robbins *(G-10755)*

3296 Mineral wool

Dfa US Inc.. E 336 756-0590
Mocksville *(G-8358)*

Freudenberg Prfmce Mtls LP............... C 828 665-5000
Candler *(G-1225)*

JPS Communications Inc..................... D 919 534-1168
Raleigh *(G-10222)*

Mid-Atlantic Specialties Inc................ G 919 212-1939
Raleigh *(G-10305)*

▲ Owens Corning Glass Metal Svcs..... D 704 721-2000
Concord *(G-3414)*

▼ Wwj LLC.. E 704 871-8500
Statesville *(G-11802)*

3297 Nonclay refractories

◆ 3tex Inc...E 919 481-2500
Rutherfordton *(G-10972)*

General Electric Company.................... A 910 675-5000
Wilmington *(G-12785)*

◆ Martin Marietta Materials Inc.............C 919 781-4550
Raleigh *(G-10277)*

PCC Airfoils LLC................................ B 919 774-4300
Sanford *(G-11215)*

Resco Products Inc.............................. F 336 299-1441
Greensboro *(G-5783)*

◆ Vesuvius Nc LLC...............................D 336 578-7728
Graham *(G-5288)*

◆ Vesuvius USA Corporation.................D 412 429-1800
Charlotte *(G-2982)*

Virginia Carolina Refr Inc............... G 704 216-0223
Salisbury *(G-11133)*

3299 Nonmetallic mineral products,

B & B Stucco and Stone LLC............. G 704 524-1230
Stanley *(G-11610)*

▲ Cairn Studio Ltd............................ G 704 892-3581
Davidson *(G-3698)*

Carolina Specialties Inc................... G 704 525-9599
Charlotte *(G-1857)*

Cje Construction Inc....................... G 828 650-6600
Arden *(G-262)*

Clifford W Estes Co Inc................... E 336 622-6410
Staley *(G-11593)*

▲ Lab Designs LLC............................ G 336 429-4114
Mount Airy *(G-9144)*

M & J Stucco LLC............................ G 704 634-2249
Monroe *(G-8521)*

Sanher Stucco & Lather Inc............. F 704 241-8517
Charlotte *(G-2754)*

Timothy L Griffin............................ G 336 317-8314
Greenville *(G-6028)*

Treklite Inc...................................... G 919 610-1788
Raleigh *(G-10557)*

33 PRIMARY METAL INDUSTRIES

3312 Blast furnaces and steel mills

ABB Installation Products Inc.......... E 828 322-1855
Hickory *(G-6260)*

▲ Bessemer City Machine Shop Inc...... G 704 629-4111
Bessemer City *(G-806)*

Charlotte Pipe and Foundry Co............. B 704 348-5416
Charlotte *(G-1901)*

◆ Charlotte Pipe and Foundry Co...........C 800 438-6091
Charlotte *(G-1900)*

Cleveland-Cliffs Plate LLC............... A 828 464-9214
Newton *(G-9454)*

Commercial Metals Company............. G 336 584-0333
Burlington *(G-1073)*

Commercial Metals Company............. G 919 833-9737
Gastonia *(G-5025)*

Component Sourcing Intl LLC............ E 704 843-9292
Charlotte *(G-1967)*

◆ Controls Southeast Inc.....................C 704 644-5000
Pineville *(G-9721)*

Dallas Fabrication............................ G 704 629-4000
Bessemer City *(G-812)*

Davis Equipment Handlers Inc........... G 704 792-9176
Charlotte *(G-2021)*

Eizi Group Llc.................................. G 919 397-3638
Raleigh *(G-10080)*

Garage Guys.................................... G 704 494-8841
Charlotte *(G-2188)*

Gerdau Ameristeel US Inc................. G 704 596-0361
Charlotte *(G-2210)*

GKN Sinter Metals LLC.....................C 828 464-0642
Conover *(G-3524)*

Greene Precision Products Inc........... G 828 262-0116
Boone *(G-919)*

Gulfstream Steel & Supply Inc........... E 910 329-5100
Holly Ridge *(G-6888)*

Industrial Alloys Inc......................... F 704 882-2887
Indian Trail *(G-7084)*

▲ Interntonal Specialty Pdts Inc........... G 828 326-9053
Hickory *(G-6371)*

Jack A Farrior Inc............................ D 252 753-2020
Farmville *(G-4532)*

Kinetic Systems Inc......................... D 919 322-7200
Durham *(G-4096)*

▲ Lee Controls LLC............................ G 732 752-5200
Southport *(G-11521)*

Lelantos Group Inc.......................... D 704 780-4127
Mooresville *(G-8709)*

Mechanical Spc Contrs Inc............... D 919 829-9300
Raleigh *(G-10287)*

Meritor Inc......................................C 828 433-4600
Morganton *(G-8881)*

Metallus Inc................................... D 330 471-6293
Columbus *(G-3303)*

Moes Hndy Svcs Fnce Instl Mno......... G 910 712-1402
Raeford *(G-9842)*

▲ Mount Hope Machinery Co................ F
Charlotte *(G-2523)*

Muriel Harris Investments Inc............ F 800 932-3191
Fayetteville *(G-4644)*

Nucor Castrip Arkansas LLC............. G 704 366-7000
Charlotte *(G-2585)*

Nucor Corporation.......................... D 252 356-3700
Cofield *(G-3268)*

Nucor Corporation...........................C 336 481-7924
Lexington *(G-7725)*

◆ Nucor Corporation...........................C 704 366-7000
Charlotte *(G-2586)*

Nucor Energy Holdings Inc............... G 704 366-7000
Charlotte *(G-2587)*

Nucor Steel Sales Corporation.......... F 302 622-4066
Charlotte *(G-2588)*

▲ Okaya Shinnichi Corp America......... E 704 588-3131
Charlotte *(G-2592)*

P & S Welding Inc............................ G 910 285-3126
Willard *(G-12666)*

Performance Plastics Pdts Inc........... D 336 454-0350
Jamestown *(G-7175)*

Quality Mechanical Contrs LLC......... D 336 228-0638
Burlington *(G-1143)*

Roberts Family Enterprises LLP......... G 919 785-3111
Raleigh *(G-10446)*

Saertex Multicom LP........................ E 704 946-9229
Huntersville *(G-7049)*

▲ Saertex Multicom LP........................ F 704 946-9229
Huntersville *(G-7048)*

Southeast Tubular Products Inc......... E 704 883-8883
Statesville *(G-11767)*

Spantek Expanded Metal Inc............. E 704 479-6210
Lincolnton *(G-7855)*

Steel City Services LLC..................... F 919 698-2407
Durham *(G-4249)*

Steel Technologies LLC..................... F 910 592-1266
Clinton *(G-3248)*

Structural Materials Inc................... G 828 754-6413
Lenoir *(G-7640)*

Thermochem Recovery Intl................ G 919 606-3282
Durham *(G-4270)*

Tms International LLC....................... F 704 604-0287
Charlotte *(G-2923)*

Vulcraft Carrier Corp........................ F 704 367-8674
Charlotte *(G-2993)*

Wheel Pros LLC............................... G 336 851-6705
Greensboro *(G-5917)*

3313 Electrometallurgical products

▲ Betek Tools Inc............................... F 980 498-2523
Charlotte *(G-1775)*

3315 Steel wire and related products

▲ A B Carter Inc................................ D 704 865-1201
Gastonia *(G-4982)*

Afsc LLC... D 704 523-4936
Charlotte *(G-1627)*

▲ Blue Ridge Metals Corporation.......... C 828 687-2525
Fletcher *(G-4725)*

▲ Cavert Wire Company Inc................. E 800 969-2601
Rural Hall *(G-10956)*

Classic Cleaning LLC........................ E 800 220-7101
Raleigh *(G-9998)*

Coleman Cable LLC.......................... D 828 389-8013
Hayesville *(G-6139)*

◆ Draka Elevator Products Inc.............C 252 446-8113
Rocky Mount *(G-10831)*

Fishel Steel Company........................ G 336 788-2880
Winston Salem *(G-13169)*

Granite Falls Furnaces LLC............... E 828 324-4394
Granite Falls *(G-5304)*

Harrison Fence Inc........................... G 919 244-6908
Apex *(G-162)*

▲ Haynes Wire Company..................... D 828 692-5791
Mountain Home *(G-9274)*

◆ Insteel Wire Products Company.........E 336 719-9000
Mount Airy *(G-9132)*

Lee Spring Company LLC................... E 336 275-3631
Greensboro *(G-5659)*

Masonite Corporation...................... A 704 599-0235
Charlotte *(G-2466)*

Merchants Metals LLC......................C 704 878-8706
Statesville *(G-11731)*

Rack Works Inc................................ E 336 368-1302
Pilot Mountain *(G-9673)*

◆ Sandvik Inc.....................................C 919 563-5008
Mebane *(G-8258)*

Schafer Manufacturing Co LLC.......... G 704 528-5321
Troutman *(G-12149)*

Southern Steel and Wire Inc............. D 336 548-9611
Madison *(G-8000)*

Specialty Nails Company................... G 336 883-0135
High Point *(G-6790)*

▲ Torpedo Specialty Wire Inc............... D 252 977-3900
Rocky Mount *(G-10872)*

Turner & Reeves Fence Co LLC.......... G 910 671-8851
Clayton *(G-3175)*

Van Blake Dixon.............................. F 336 282-1861
Greensboro *(G-5896)*

▲ Williams Industries Inc....................C 919 604-1746
Raleigh *(G-10610)*

▼ Wireway/Husky Corp.......................C 704 483-1135
Denver *(G-3817)*

Zndus Inc.. G 704 981-8660
Statesville *(G-11804)*

3316 Cold finishing of steel shapes

▲ Manhattan Amrcn Terrazzo Strip....... C 336 622-4247
Staley *(G-11596)*

◆ Sandvik Inc.....................................C 919 563-5008
Mebane *(G-8258)*

Southern Metals Company................. E 704 394-3161
Charlotte *(G-2837)*

3317 Steel pipe and tubes

▲ Allrail Inc....................................... G 828 287-3747
Rutherfordton *(G-10973)*

Appalachian Pipe Distrs LLC............. G 704 688-5703
Charlotte *(G-1684)*

Blacksand Metal Works LLC............. F 703 489-8282
Fayetteville *(G-4558)*

Border Concepts Inc........................ G 336 248-2419
Lexington *(G-7660)*

◆ Border Concepts Inc........................G 704 541-5509
Charlotte *(G-1800)*

▲ East Coast Stl Fabrication Inc........... E 757 351-2601
Hertford *(G-6253)*

▼ Fortiline LLC.................................... E 704 788-9800
  Concord (G-3366)

▲ Global Forming Tech Ltd .... G 919 234-1384
  Cary (G-1366)

▲ Heatmaster LLC............................... E 919 639-4568
  Angier (G-120)

▼ Hlm Legacy Group Inc.................... C 704 878-8823
  Troutman (G-12140)

▲ Lander Tubular Pdts USA Inc .... C 828 369-6682
  Franklin (G-4833)

Maysteel Porters LLC....................... B 704 864-1313
  Gastonia (G-5092)

Piedmont Pipe Mfg LLC .... G 704 489-0911
  Denver (G-3797)

▲ Porters Group LLC............................ B 704 864-1313
  Gastonia (G-5121)

◆ Sandvik Inc....................................C 919 563-5008
  Mebane (G-8258)

Zekelman Industries Inc .... F 704 560-6768
  Mooresville (G-8805)

3321 Gray and ductile iron foundries

▲ ABT Foam Inc.................................. F 800 433-1119
  Statesville (G-11643)

◆ Charlotte Pipe and Foundry Co..........C 800 438-6091
  Charlotte (G-1900)

Ej Usa Inc.. G 919 362-7744
  Apex (G-154)

Humber Street Facility Inc .... G 919 775-3628
  Sanford (G-11192)

Modacam Incorporated...................... G 704 489-8500
  Denver (G-3793)

Southern Cast Inc............................. E 704 335-0692
  Charlotte (G-2833)

▲ Venture Products Intl Inc................. G 828 285-0495
  Asheville (G-631)

3324 Steel investment foundries

Cold Mountain Capital LLC .... F 828 210-8129
  Asheville (G-479)

3325 Steel foundries, nec

American Builders Anson Inc.............. E 704 272-7655
  Polkton (G-9811)

Coder Foundry .... G 704 910-3077
  Charlotte (G-1951)

Harris Rebar Inc................................. G 919 528-8333
  Benson (G-792)

Norca Engineered Products LLC........... E 919 846-2010
  Raleigh (G-10334)

Nucor Corporation.............................. C 252 356-3700
  Cofield (G-3268)

Seven Cast... G 704 335-0692
  Charlotte (G-2791)

3331 Primary copper

◆ Imc-Metalsamerica LLC.....................F 704 482-8200
  Shelby (G-11347)

Rfr Metal Fabrication Inc................... D 919 693-1354
  Oxford (G-9631)

▲ Stillwood Ammun Systems LLC........ G 919 721-9096
  Burlington (G-1165)

3334 Primary aluminum

◆ 3a Composites USA Inc....................C 704 872-8974
  Statesville (G-11641)

▲ AGM Carolina Inc............................. G 336 431-4100
  High Point (G-6511)

Alcoa Power Generating Inc............... E 704 422-5691
  Badin (G-665)

Essex Group Inc................................. G 704 921-9605
  Charlotte (G-2127)

Kymera International LLC...................... E 919 544-8090
  Durham (G-4099)

Muriel Harris Investments Inc.............. F 800 932-3191
  Fayetteville (G-4644)

3339 Primary nonferrous metals, nec

▲ Alloyworks LLC.................................. F 704 645-0511
  Salisbury (G-11015)

Cvmr (usa) Inc................................... C 828 288-3768
  Union Mills (G-12188)

KS Precious Metals LLC.................... G 910 687-0244
  Pinehurst (G-9694)

Metallix Refining Inc.......................... E 252 413-0346
  Greenville (G-6003)

▲ Metchem Inc...................................... G 910 944-1405
  Aberdeen (G-15)

Omega Precious Metals........................ G 269 903-9330
  Youngsville (G-13479)

Parker-Hannifin Corporation............... E 704 662-3500
  Statesville (G-11742)

◆ Umicore USA Inc...............................E 919 874-7171
  Raleigh (G-10575)

3341 Secondary nonferrous metals

◆ Elan Trading Inc................................E 704 342-1696
  Charlotte (G-2094)

Renew Recycling LLC......................... D 919 550-8012
  Clayton (G-3168)

S Foil Incorporated............................. F 704 455-5134
  Harrisburg (G-6117)

3351 Copper rolling and drawing

Essex Group Inc................................. G 704 921-9605
  Charlotte (G-2127)

Hickory Wire Inc................................ F 828 322-9473
  Hickory (G-6360)

▲ Manhattan Amrcn Terrazzo Strip....... C 336 622-4247
  Staley (G-11596)

▲ Torpedo Specialty Wire Inc............... D 252 977-3900
  Rocky Mount (G-10872)

▲ Wieland Copper Products LLC......... B 336 445-4500
  Pine Hall (G-9677)

3353 Aluminum sheet, plate, and foil

Alpha Aluminum LLC.......................... G 336 777-5658
  Winston Salem (G-13082)

▲ Aviation Metals NC Inc..................... F 704 264-1647
  Charlotte (G-1721)

Bharat Forge Aluminum USA Inc....... C 585 576-7483
  Sanford (G-11155)

Central States Mfg Inc....................... C 336 719-3280
  Mount Airy (G-9113)

Granges Americas Inc........................ D 704 633-6020
  Salisbury (G-11059)

Hardcoatings Inc................................ F 704 377-2996
  Charlotte (G-2256)

Howmet Aerospace Inc....................... C 704 334-7276
  Charlotte (G-2290)

Wyda Packaging Corp......................... F 980 403-3346
  Charlotte (G-3029)

3354 Aluminum extruded products

▲ Alfiniti Inc... D 252 358-5811
  Winton (G-13427)

▲ Aviation Metals NC Inc..................... F 704 264-1647
  Charlotte (G-1721)

▲ CCL Metal Science LLC..................... D 910 299-0911
  Clinton (G-3229)

Container Products Corporation........... D 910 392-6100
  Wilmington (G-12748)

Hydro Extrusion Usa LLC.................. D 336 227-8826
  Burlington (G-1107)

J Massey Inc...................................... F 704 821-7084
  Stallings (G-11600)

Metal Impact East LLC...................... C 336 578-4515
  Graham (G-5278)

Owens Corning Sales LLC.................. E 419 248-8000
  Roxboro (G-10937)

Pexco LLC.. D 336 493-7500
  Asheboro (G-382)

Seg Systems LLC............................... F 704 579-5800
  Huntersville (G-7054)

3355 Aluminum rolling and drawing, nec

Design Specialties Inc........................ G 919 772-6955
  Raleigh (G-10042)

Mark Stoddard................................... G 910 797-7214
  Fayetteville (G-4634)

◆ Mitsubishi Chemical Amer Inc.............D 980 580-2839
  Charlotte (G-2509)

Nkt Inc... G 919 601-1970
  Cary (G-1408)

Southwire Company LLC..................... E 704 379-9600
  Huntersville (G-7056)

Trimantec.. E 336 767-1379
  Winston Salem (G-13372)

3356 Nonferrous rolling and drawing, nec

Advanced Plating Technologies............ G 704 291-9325
  Monroe (G-8418)

Aseptia Inc.. C 678 373-6751
  Raleigh (G-9919)

ATI Allvac .... F 541 967-9000
  Monroe (G-8436)

▲ Aviation Metals NC Inc..................... F 704 264-1647
  Charlotte (G-1721)

Haynes International Inc.................... E 765 456-6000
  Hendersonville (G-6212)

J W Harris Co Inc.............................. G 336 831-8601
  Winston Salem (G-13213)

Metal & Materials Proc LLC.............. G 260 438-8901
  Aberdeen (G-14)

Metallix Refining Inc.......................... E 252 413-0346
  Greenville (G-6003)

Mg12 LP.. G 828 440-1144
  Tryon (G-12175)

Peter J Hamann .... G 910 484-7877
  Fayetteville (G-4654)

Powerlab Inc...................................... E 336 650-0706
  Winston Salem (G-13300)

◆ Sandvik Inc.......................................C 919 563-5008
  Mebane (G-8258)

Southern Metals Company.................. E 704 394-3161
  Charlotte (G-2837)

▲ Stainless & Nickel Alloys LLC......... G 704 201-2898
  Charlotte (G-2857)

▲ Torpedo Specialty Wire Inc............... D 252 977-3900
  Rocky Mount (G-10872)

Wanda Nickel..................................... G 828 265-3246
  Deep Gap (G-3731)

3357 Nonferrous wiredrawing and insulating

Abl Electronics Supply Inc................. G 704 784-4225
  Concord (G-3308)

AFL Network Services Inc.................. E 704 289-5522
  Mint Hill (G-8329)

AFL Network Services Inc.................. E 919 658-2311
  Mount Olive (G-9246)

◆ Arris Solutions LLC...........................A 678 473-2000
  Claremont (G-3088)

Batt Fabricators Inc........................... F 336 431-9334
  Trinity (G-12113)

C O Jelliff Corporation....................... G 828 428-3672
  Maiden (G-8008)

Coleman Cable LLC......................... D 828 389-8013
   Hayesville (G-6139)

Commscope Inc North Carolina........... A 828 459-5000
   Claremont (G-3094)

◆ Commscope Inc North Carolina....... E 828 324-2200
   Claremont (G-3096)

Commscope Technologies LLC............ G 919 934-9711
   Smithfield (G-11440)

◆ Commscope Technologies LLC........ A 828 324-2200
   Claremont (G-3104)

▲ Cordset Designs Inc..................... G 252 568-4001
   Pink Hill (G-9765)

Corning Incorporated....................... D 704 569-6000
   Midland (G-8284)

Corning Incorporated....................... F 252 316-4500
   Tarboro (G-11924)

Corning Optcal Cmmncations LLC........ A 828 327-5290
   Hickory (G-6312)

Crww Specialty Composites Inc........... F 828 548-5002
   Claremont (G-3105)

▲ Draka Communications Amer........... B 828 459-8456
   Claremont (G-3108)

◆ Draka Elevator Products Inc...........C 252 446-8113
   Rocky Mount (G-10831)

▲ Draka Holdings Usa Inc................. A 828 383-0020
   Claremont (G-3109)

Draka Transport USA LLC.................. G 828 459-8895
   Claremont (G-3110)

Draka Usa Inc................................ F 828 459-9787
   Claremont (G-3111)

Emtelle USA Inc............................. E 828 707-9970
   Fletcher (G-4733)

Essex Group Inc............................. G 704 921-9605
   Charlotte (G-2127)

Frenzelit Inc................................. E 336 814-4317
   Lexington (G-7690)

▲ Huber + Suhner Inc.................... E 704 790-7300
   Charlotte (G-2295)

▲ Huber + Suhner North Amer Corp.... D 704 790-7300
   Charlotte (G-2296)

Infinite Blue Inc............................. G 919 744-7704
   Raleigh (G-10194)

Kaotic Parts LLC............................ G 919 766-6040
   Raleigh (G-10229)

Leviton Manufacturing Co Inc............. E 828 584-1611
   Morganton (G-8878)

Ls Cable & System USA Inc............... C 252 824-3553
   Tarboro (G-11932)

Neptco Incorporated........................ C 828 728-5951
   Lenoir (G-7629)

Opticoncepts Inc............................. G 828 320-0138
   Morganton (G-8886)

Ruckus Wireless LLC....................... A 503 495-9240
   Claremont (G-3121)

Sackner Products Inc....................... E 704 380-6204
   Statesville (G-11762)

▼ Sumitomo Elc Lightwave Corp......... D 919 541-8100
   Raleigh (G-10518)

Superior Essex Inc.......................... D 252 823-5111
   Tarboro (G-11941)

Superior Essex Intl Inc..................... C 252 823-5111
   Tarboro (G-11942)

▲ Unitape (usa) Inc....................... G 828 464-5695
   Conover (G-3568)

US Conec Ltd................................ E 828 323-8883
   Hickory (G-6481)

US Conec Ltd................................ D 828 323-8883
   Hickory (G-6482)

3363 Aluminum die-castings

Carolina Foundry Inc....................... G 704 376-3145
   Charlotte (G-1847)

Cascade Die Casting Group Inc........... C 336 882-0186
   High Point (G-6564)

Cs Alloys.................................... G 704 675-5810
   Gastonia (G-5033)

▲ Dynacast LLC.......................... E 704 927-2790
   Charlotte (G-2072)

Dynacast International LLC................. G 704 927-2790
   Charlotte (G-2073)

▲ Ksm Castings USA Inc................. E 704 751-0559
   Shelby (G-11352)

Leggett & Platt Incorporated.............. C 704 380-6208
   Statesville (G-11727)

Linamar Light Metal S-Mr LLC............ A 828 348-4010
   Fletcher (G-4748)

RCM Industries Inc......................... C 828 286-4003
   Rutherfordton (G-10991)

Sensus USA Inc............................. C 919 576-6185
   Morrisville (G-9052)

◆ Sensus USA Inc........................ E 919 845-4000
   Morrisville (G-9051)

3364 Nonferrous die-castings except aluminum

Carolina Foundry Inc....................... G 704 376-3145
   Charlotte (G-1847)

Cascade Die Casting Group Inc........... C 336 882-0186
   High Point (G-6564)

◆ Coats & Clark Inc......................D 888 368-8401
   Charlotte (G-1942)

▲ Coats N Amer De Rpblica Dmncan... C 800 242-8095
   Charlotte (G-1945)

▲ Dynacast LLC.......................... E 704 927-2790
   Charlotte (G-2072)

Dynacast International LLC................. G 704 927-2790
   Charlotte (G-2073)

Dynacast US Holdings Inc................. F 704 927-2786
   Charlotte (G-2074)

Form Technologies Inc..................... E 704 927-2790
   Charlotte (G-2173)

Stratford Die Casting Inc.................. G 336 784-0100
   Winston Salem (G-13345)

3365 Aluminum foundries

Advanced Machine Services................ G 910 410-0099
   Rockingham (G-10768)

◆ Briggs-Shaffner Acquisition Co.......F 336 463-4272
   Yadkinville (G-13439)

Cascade Die Casting Group Inc........... C 336 882-0186
   High Point (G-6564)

CAT Logistics Inc........................... F 252 447-2490
   New Bern (G-9351)

Consolidated Metco Inc.................... F 704 289-6492
   Monroe (G-8466)

Consolidated Metco Inc.................... E 704 289-6491
   Monroe (G-8467)

▲ Dynacast LLC.......................... E 704 927-2790
   Charlotte (G-2072)

RCM Industries Inc......................... C 828 286-4003
   Rutherfordton (G-10991)

3366 Copper foundries

ABB Motors and Mechanical Inc........... C 828 645-1706
   Weaverville (G-12481)

Carolina Bronze Sculpture Inc............. G 336 873-8291
   Seagrove (G-11273)

CSC Bearing North America Inc........... E 734 456-6206
   Lincolnton (G-7826)

Foundry Commercial........................ G 704 348-6875
   Charlotte (G-2176)

▲ Kayne & Son Custom Hdwr Inc........ G 828 665-1988
   Candler (G-1228)

▲ Saueressig North America Inc.......... E 336 395-6200
   Burlington (G-1154)

3369 Nonferrous foundries, nec

Dynacast International LLC................. G 704 927-2790
   Charlotte (G-2073)

PCC Airfoils LLC............................ B 919 774-4300
   Sanford (G-11215)

Tru-Cast Inc................................. E 336 294-2370
   Greensboro (G-5881)

▲ United Brass Works Inc................ C 336 498-2661
   Randleman (G-10663)

3398 Metal heat treating

American Metallurgy Inc.................... G 336 889-3277
   High Point (G-6520)

Bodycote Thermal Proc Inc................ F 704 664-1808
   Mooresville (G-8618)

By-Design Black Oxide & TI LLC.......... F 828 874-0610
   Valdese (G-12190)

East Crlina Metal Treating Inc............. E 919 834-2100
   Raleigh (G-10069)

Furnace Rebuilders Inc..................... F 704 483-4025
   Denver (G-3783)

Hhh Tempering Resources Inc............. F 336 201-5396
   Winston Salem (G-13197)

▲ Industrial Prcess Slutions Inc.......... G 336 926-1511
   Wilkesboro (G-12639)

J F Heat Treating Inc...................... G 704 864-0998
   Gastonia (G-5071)

▲ M-B Industries Inc..................... C 828 862-4201
   Rosman (G-10913)

Metal Improvement Company LLC........ D 704 525-3818
   Charlotte (G-2495)

Metal Improvement Company LLC........ G 414 536-1573
   Gastonia (G-5094)

National Peening Inc........................ F 704 872-0113
   Statesville (G-11738)

▲ Powerlyte Paintball Game Pdts........ G 919 713-4317
   Raleigh (G-10381)

Thermal Metal Treating Inc................ E 910 944-3636
   Aberdeen (G-27)

United TI & Stamping Co NC Inc.......... D 910 323-8588
   Fayetteville (G-4687)

Zion Industries Inc......................... E 828 397-2701
   Hildebran (G-6856)

3399 Primary metal products

▲ Airspeed LLC........................... E 919 644-1222
   Mebane (G-8227)

▲ Blue Ridge Metals Corporation........ C 828 687-2525
   Fletcher (G-4725)

Cross Technology Inc....................... E 336 725-4700
   East Bend (G-4322)

D Block Metals LLC........................ G 980 238-2600
   Lincolnton (G-7828)

▲ D Block Metals LLC.................... F 704 705-5895
   Gastonia (G-5037)

Keystone Powdered Metal Co............. D 704 435-4036
   Cherryville (G-3065)

Kymera International LLC................... E 919 544-8090
   Durham (G-4099)

Metal Structures Plus LLC................. G 704 896-7155
   Mooresville (G-8723)

Morton Metalcraft Company N............. G 336 731-5700
   Welcome (G-12512)

Oerlikon Metco (us) Inc.................... F 713 715-6300
   Huntersville (G-7028)

Piranha Nail and Staple Inc................ G 336 852-8358
   Greensboro (G-5749)

Wurth Revcar Fasteners Inc............... E 919 772-9930
   Garner (G-4975)

34 FABRICATED METAL PRODUCTS

3411 Metal cans

Ball Metal Beverage Cont Corp.............. B 336 342-4711
Reidsville (G-10674)

Container Products Corporation............ D 910 392-6100
Wilmington (G-12748)

▼ Fleetgenius of Nc Inc........................ C 828 726-3001
Lenoir (G-7607)

Leisure Craft Holdings LLC.................... D 828 693-8241
Flat Rock (G-4708)

Leisure Craft Inc................................ C 828 693-8241
Flat Rock (G-4709)

Tin Can Ventures LLC.......................... G 919 732-9078
Cedar Grove (G-1518)

Tin Cans LLC...................................... G 910 322-2626
Lillington (G-7804)

Trivium Packaging USA Inc..................... B 336 785-8500
Winston Salem (G-13373)

Waste Container Services LLC.............. G 910 257-4474
Fayetteville (G-4697)

3412 Metal barrels, drums, and pails

General Steel Drum LLC...................... F 704 525-7160
Charlotte (G-2201)

Greif Inc... D 704 588-3895
Charlotte (G-2241)

▲ Inter-Continental Corporation.......... D 828 464-8250
Newton (G-9477)

Lee County Industries Inc.................... G 919 775-3439
Sanford (G-11205)

Mauser Usa LLC................................ E 704 398-2325
Charlotte (G-2471)

Mauser Usa LLC................................ C 704 625-0737
Charlotte (G-2472)

Mauser Usa LLC................................ D 704 455-2111
Harrisburg (G-6114)

South Boulevard Associates Inc........... D 704 525-7160
Charlotte (G-2829)

◆ Toter LLC.....................................E 800 424-0422
Statesville (G-11792)

Waste Container Services LLC.............. G 910 257-4474
Fayetteville (G-4697)

3421 Cutlery

Bic Corporation................................. D 704 598-7700
Charlotte (G-1779)

Butchers Best Inc.............................. G 252 533-0961
Roanoke Rapids (G-10733)

Daniel Winkler Knifemaker LLC............ G 828 262-3691
Boone (G-911)

Edge-Works Manufacturing Co............. G 910 455-9834
Burgaw (G-1022)

Edgewell Per Care Brands LLC............. E 336 672-4500
Asheboro (G-347)

Edgewell Per Care Brands LLC............. E 336 629-1581
Asheboro (G-348)

Edgewell Per Care Brands LLC............. G 336 672-4500
Asheboro (G-349)

▲ Forveson Corp................................ G 336 292-6237
Greensboro (G-5537)

▲ Fred Marvin and Associates Inc........ G 330 784-9211
Greensboro (G-5539)

Generations L LLC............................. G 336 835-3095
Jonesville (G-7196)

Hao WEI Lai Inc................................ G 336 789-9969
Mount Airy (G-9127)

Heal.. G 828 287-8787
Rutherfordton (G-10986)

◆ Irwin Industrial Tool Company..............C 704 987-4555
Huntersville (G-7004)

▲ J Culpepper & Co........................... G 828 524-6842
Otto (G-9606)

Kotohira... G 336 667-0150
Wilkesboro (G-12647)

Procter & Gamble Mfg Co..................... D 336 954-0000
Greensboro (G-5767)

Singsa... G 336 882-9160
High Point (G-6777)

Spartan Blades LLC............................ G 910 757-0035
Southern Pines (G-11511)

Stacks Kitchen Matthews..................... G 704 243-2024
Waxhaw (G-12442)

Sugar Pops....................................... G 704 799-0959
Mooresville (G-8782)

Sword Conservatory Inc....................... G 919 557-4465
Holly Springs (G-6917)

3423 Hand and edge tools, nec

Allegion Access Tech LLC.................... E 704 789-7000
Concord (G-3309)

American Striking Tools Inc.................. G 910 769-1318
Wilmington (G-12704)

Apex Tool Group LLC.......................... D 410 773-7800
Huntersville (G-6966)

▲ Asheville Bit & Steel Company.......... F 828 274-3766
Asheville (G-433)

Belkoz Inc.. G 919 703-0694
Raleigh (G-9939)

Coconut Paradise Inc.......................... G 704 662-3443
Mooresville (G-8641)

Contemporary Products Inc.................. G 919 779-4228
Garner (G-4925)

Cooke Rentals Mt Airy NC Inc.............. G 336 789-5068
Cornelius (G-3595)

◆ Council Tool Company Inc................. E 910 646-3011
Lake Waccamaw (G-7471)

DCS USA Corporation........................ G 919 535-8000
Morrisville (G-8963)

Equipment & Supply Inc...................... E 704 289-6565
Monroe (G-8485)

Everkem Diversified Pdts Inc................ F 336 661-7801
Winston Salem (G-13161)

Fiskars Brands Inc............................. E 336 292-6237
Greensboro (G-5534)

G P Kittrell & Son Inc......................... G 252 465-8929
Corapeake (G-3579)

▲ Great Star Industrial Usa LLC........... G 704 892-4965
Huntersville (G-6996)

◆ Greenworks North America LLC........D 888 909-6757
Mooresville (G-8677)

Hamilton Indus Grinding Inc................. E 828 253-6796
Asheville (G-515)

Hayward Industries Inc....................... D 336 712-9900
Clemmons (G-3188)

◆ Hayward Industries Inc....................B 704 837-8002
Charlotte (G-2265)

▲ Horizon Tool Inc............................. C 336 299-4182
Greensboro (G-5607)

Irwin.. G 704 987-4339
Huntersville (G-7003)

◆ Irwin Industrial Tool Company..............C 704 987-4555
Huntersville (G-7004)

Jim Allred Taxidermy Supply................. G 828 749-5900
Saluda (G-11139)

Lidseen North Carolina Inc.................. G 828 389-8082
Hayesville (G-6142)

▲ Marbach America Inc........................ E 704 644-4900
Charlotte (G-2455)

Masonite Corporation......................... A 704 599-0235
Charlotte (G-2466)

◆ McKenzie Sports Products LLC............C 704 279-7985
Salisbury (G-11091)

Microtech Knives Inc.......................... D 828 684-4355
Mills River (G-8318)

Mil3 Inc... G 919 362-1217
Apex (G-181)

Origami Ink LLC................................ G 828 225-2300
Asheville (G-561)

Peco Inc..E 828 684-1234
Arden (G-296)

Precision Part Systems Wnstn-S............ E 336 723-5210
Winston Salem (G-13302)

Robert Bosch Tool Corporation............. F 252 551-7512
Greenville (G-6019)

Rush Masonry Management LLC............ G 910 787-9100
Jacksonville (G-7142)

S Duff Fabricating Inc......................... G 910 298-3060
Beulaville (G-845)

Stanley Black & Decker Inc.................. C 704 789-7000
Concord (G-3446)

Trane Technologies Company LLC......... C 910 692-8700
Southern Pines (G-11512)

▲ United Southern Industries Inc.......... D 866 273-1810
Forest City (G-4799)

▲ Wall-Lenk Corporation..................... E 252 527-4186
Kinston (G-7435)

3425 Saw blades and handsaws

▲ Grasche USA Inc............................. E 828 322-1226
Hickory (G-6340)

Leitz Tooling Systems LP..................... G 336 861-3367
Archdale (G-237)

Quality Saw Shop Inc.......................... G 336 882-1722
High Point (G-6751)

▲ Raleigh Saw Co Inc.......................... G 919 832-2248
Raleigh (G-10429)

Robert Bosch Tool Corporation............. E 704 735-7464
Lincolnton (G-7851)

▲ Union Grove Saw & Knife Inc............ D 704 539-4442
Union Grove (G-12186)

3429 Hardware, nec

Absolute Security & Lock Inc................ G 336 322-4598
Roxboro (G-10917)

◆ Ace Marine Rigging & Supply Inc........F 252 726-6620
Morehead City (G-8811)

▲ Acme Rental Company....................... G 704 873-3731
Statesville (G-11648)

▲ ACS Advnced Clor Solutions Inc........ G 252 442-0098
Rocky Mount (G-10821)

Alloy Fabricators Inc.......................... E 704 263-2281
Alexis (G-102)

▲ Amerock LLC.................................. F 800 435-6959
Huntersville (G-6965)

◆ Amesbury Acqstion Hldngs 2 Inc........C 704 924-8586
Statesville (G-11654)

Amesbury Group Inc........................... D 704 924-7694
Statesville (G-11656)

Apex Industrial.................................. F 877 676 2730
Sanford (G-11148)

▲ Appalachian Technology LLC............. E 828 210-8888
Asheville (G-427)

▲ Appalchian Stove Fbrcators Inc.......... G 828 253-0164
Asheville (G-428)

◆ Assa Abloy ACC Door Cntrls Gro........C 877 974-2255
Monroe (G-8432)

Assa Abloy Accessories and.................. B 704 233-4011
Monroe (G-8433)

◆ Balcrank Corporation........................E 800 747-5300
Weaverville (G-12483)

Belwith Products LLC......................... G 336 841-3899
High Point (G-6545)

Blue Ridge Global Inc .... G 828 252-5225
Asheville *(G-456)*

Blum Inc .... G 919 345-6214
Oak Ridge *(G-9570)*

◆ Blum Inc .... B 704 827-1345
Stanley *(G-11612)*

Buie Manufacturing Company .... E 910 610-3504
Laurinburg *(G-7493)*

Cabinet Solutions Usa Inc .... E 828 358-2349
Hickory *(G-6280)*

▲ Carolina North Mfg Inc .... G 336 992-0082
Kernersville *(G-7252)*

CSC Family Holdings Inc .... G 336 993-2680
Colfax *(G-3278)*

▲ Custom Industries Inc .... E 336 299-2885
Greensboro *(G-5481)*

Custom Seatings .... G 828 879-1964
Valdese *(G-12194)*

Division Eight Inc .... F 336 852-1275
Greensboro *(G-5497)*

Easykeyscom Inc .... F 877 839-5397
Charlotte *(G-2086)*

Endura Products LLC .... E 336 991-8818
High Point *(G-6610)*

▲ Endura Products LLC .... B 336 668-2472
Colfax *(G-3279)*

▼ Fireresq Incorporated .... F 888 975-0858
Mooresville *(G-8664)*

Fortress International Corp NC .... G 336 645-9365
Conover *(G-3522)*

◆ Grass America Inc .... C 336 996-4041
Kernersville *(G-7277)*

◆ Hafele America Co .... C 800 423-3531
Archdale *(G-224)*

Hearth & Home Technologies LLC .... C 336 274-1663
Greensboro *(G-5592)*

▲ Hickory Springs California LLC .... A 828 328-2201
Hickory *(G-6354)*

Hickory Springs Mfg Co .... D 828 328-2201
Hickory *(G-6357)*

▲ Ilco Unican Holding Corp .... G 252 446-3321
Rocky Mount *(G-10843)*

◆ Imperial Usa Ltd .... E 704 596-2444
Charlotte *(G-2316)*

Industrial Mtal Pdts Abrdeen I .... F 910 944-8110
Aberdeen *(G-7)*

Ingersoll-Rand Indus US Inc .... D 704 896-4000
Davidson *(G-3710)*

Jacob Holtz Company LLC .... E 828 328-1003
Hickory *(G-6373)*

Kaba Ilco Corp .... B 336 725-1331
Winston Salem *(G-13222)*

◆ Kaba Ilco Corp .... A 252 446-3321
Rocky Mount *(G-10844)*

Kdy Automation Solutions Inc .... G 888 219-0049
Morrisville *(G-8996)*

Kearfott Corporation .... B 828 350-5300
Black Mountain *(G-868)*

▲ Ketchie-Houston Inc .... E 704 786-5101
Concord *(G-3390)*

Kitchen Bath Gllries N Hlls LL .... G 919 600-6200
Raleigh *(G-10237)*

▲ Marcon International Inc .... E 704 455-9400
Harrisburg *(G-6113)*

Marine Tooling Technology Inc .... G 336 887-9577
High Point *(G-6698)*

Masonite Corporation .... A 704 599-0235
Charlotte *(G-2466)*

▼ Mepla-Alfit Incorporated .... E 336 289-2300
Kernersville *(G-7286)*

◆ Norton Door Controls .... F 704 233-4011
Monroe *(G-8538)*

Nova Mobility Systems Inc .... G 800 797-9861
Charlotte *(G-2577)*

Nuclamp System LLC .... G 336 643-1766
Oak Ridge *(G-9572)*

Oak City Metal LLC .... G 919 375-4535
Zebulon *(G-13518)*

Omnia Industries LLC .... G 704 707-6062
Matthews *(G-8138)*

Parker-Hannifin Corporation .... E 704 664-1922
Mooresville *(G-8742)*

Penn Engineering & Mfg Corp .... C 336 631-8741
Winston Salem *(G-13278)*

▲ Perrycraft Inc .... F 336 372-2545
Sparta *(G-11541)*

▲ Sentinel Door Controls LLC .... F 704 921-4627
Charlotte *(G-2788)*

Skinner Company .... G 336 580-4716
Greensboro *(G-5815)*

Stanley Black & Decker Inc .... G 704 509-0844
Charlotte *(G-2858)*

Stanley Black & Decker Inc .... C 704 789-7000
Concord *(G-3446)*

Sun Path Products Inc .... D 910 875-9002
Raeford *(G-9853)*

Sunray Inc .... E 828 287-7030
Rutherfordton *(G-10994)*

Telecmmnctons Resource MGT Inc ...... F 919 779-0776
Raleigh *(G-10539)*

◆ Ultra-Mek Inc .... D 336 859-4552
Denton *(G-3765)*

Village Produce & Cntry Str In .... G 336 661-8685
Winston Salem *(G-13381)*

Volvo Group North America LLC .... A 731 968-0151
Greensboro *(G-5909)*

WaveTherm Corporation .... E 919 307-8071
Raleigh *(G-10601)*

Wilmington Rbr & Gasket Co Inc .... F 910 762-4262
Wilmington *(G-12952)*

▲ Winterville Machine Works Inc .... D 252 756-2130
Winterville *(G-13426)*

◆ Woodlane Envmtl Tech Inc .... G 828 894-8383
Columbus *(G-3305)*

X-Jet Technologies Inc .... G 800 983-7467
Raleigh *(G-10616)*

3431 Metal sanitary ware

Americh Corporation .... D 704 588-3075
Charlotte *(G-1671)*

Capital Marble Creations Inc .... G 910 893-2462
Lillington *(G-7791)*

Comer Sanitary Service Inc .... G 336 629-8311
Lexington *(G-7668)*

Croscill Home LLC .... C 919 735-7111
Oxford *(G-9610)*

Custom Marble Corporation .... G 910 215-0679
Pinehurst *(G-9690)*

Elkay Ohio Plumbing Pdts Co .... A 910 739-8181
Lumberton *(G-7950)*

Elkay Plumbing Products Co .... A 910 739-8181
Lumberton *(G-7951)*

▲ Grancreations Inc .... G 704 332-7625
Charlotte *(G-2230)*

Metalfab of North Carolina LLC .... C 704 841-1090
Matthews *(G-8132)*

Readilite & Barricade Inc .... F 919 231-8309
Raleigh *(G-10435)*

▲ Select Stainless Products LLC .... G 888 843-2345
Charlotte *(G-2783)*

◆ Thompson Traders Inc .... F 336 272-3003
Greensboro *(G-5864)*

Tubs-Usa LLC .... F 336 884-5737
High Point *(G-6814)*

3432 Plumbing fixture fittings and trim

B & B Building Maintenance LLC .... G 910 494-2715
Bunnlevel *(G-1015)*

Brasscraft Manufacturing Co .... E 336 475-2131
Thomasville *(G-11998)*

▼ Flologic Inc .... G 919 878-1808
Morrisville *(G-8976)*

Gods Son Plumbing Inc .... G 252 299-0983
Wilson *(G-12993)*

H & H Representatives Inc .... G 704 596-6950
Charlotte *(G-2246)*

▲ Key Gas Components Inc .... E 828 655-1700
Marion *(G-8048)*

Masco Corporation .... G 704 658-9646
Mooresville *(G-8719)*

Piedmont Well Covers Inc .... F 704 664-8488
Mount Ulla *(G-9270)*

Romac Industries Inc .... D 704 915-3317
Dallas *(G-3688)*

Royal Baths Manufacturing Co .... E 704 837-1701
Charlotte *(G-2733)*

SL Liquidation LLC .... B 910 353-3666
Jacksonville *(G-7147)*

Union Plastics Company .... G 704 624-2112
Marshville *(G-8096)*

Victaulic Company .... E 910 371-5588
Leland *(G-7563)*

◆ Watts Drainage Products Inc .... F 828 288-2179
Spindale *(G-11549)*

3433 Heating equipment, except electric

▲ Appalchian Stove Fbrcators Inc .... G 828 253-0164
Asheville *(G-428)*

Canvas Mw LLC .... C 336 627-6000
Eden *(G-4342)*

Dna Services Inc .... G 910 279-2775
Kure Beach *(G-7464)*

Edco Products Inc .... F 828 264-1490
Boone *(G-915)*

◆ Flynn Burner Corporation .... E 704 660-1500
Mooresville *(G-8666)*

Gamma Js Inc .... F 336 294-3838
Greensboro *(G-5547)*

◆ Gas-Fired Products Inc .... D 704 372-3485
Charlotte *(G-2190)*

Hearth & Home Technologies LLC .... C 336 274-1663
Greensboro *(G-5592)*

Hicks Wterstoves Solar Systems .... F 336 789-4977
Mount Airy *(G-9129)*

Hoffman Hydronics LLC .... D 800 842-3328
Greensboro *(G-5602)*

Hoffman Hydronics LLC .... F 336 294-3838
Greensboro *(G-5603)*

Low Impact Tech USA Inc .... G 828 428-6310
Fletcher *(G-4749)*

Machining Technology Services .... G 704 282-1071
Monroe *(G-8522)*

▲ Marley Company LLC .... C 704 752-4400
Charlotte *(G-2459)*

Mestek Inc .... C 252 753-5323
Farmville *(G-4535)*

Norcor Technologies Corp .... G 704 309-4101
Greensboro *(G-5712)*

Romac Industries Inc .... D 704 915-3317
Dallas *(G-3688)*

▲ Smg Hearth and Home LLC .... E 919 973-4079
Durham *(G-4240)*

Snap Rite Manufacturing Inc .... E 910 897-4080
Coats *(G-3265)*

Solar Hot Limited .... G 919 439-2387
Raleigh *(G-10490)*

▲ Solarh2ot Ltd.. G 919 439-2387
Raleigh *(G-10493)*

Sunqest Inc... G 828 325-4910
Newton *(G-9501)*

Sunstar Heating Products Inc................ G 704 372-3486
Charlotte *(G-2883)*

Taylor Manufacturing Inc...................... E 910 862-2576
Elizabethtown *(G-4434)*

Thermo Products LLC........................... E 800 348-5130
Denton *(G-3763)*

3441 Fabricated structural metal

Accelerated Media Technologies........... G 336 599-2070
Roxboro *(G-10918)*

Ace Fabrication Inc............................... F 919 934-3251
Smithfield *(G-11433)*

Alamance Steel Fabricators................... G 336 887-3015
High Point *(G-6513)*

▼ Alamo Distribution LLC....................... C 704 398-5600
Belmont *(G-740)*

Alco Metal Fabricators Inc.................... F 704 739-1168
Kings Mountain *(G-7347)*

Alliance Mch & Fabrication LLC............ G 704 629-5677
Gastonia *(G-4986)*

American Trutzschler Inc....................... E 704 399-4521
Charlotte *(G-1669)*

Amt/Bcu Inc.. E 336 622-6200
Liberty *(G-7761)*

ARS Extreme Construction Inc.............. F 919 331-8024
Angier *(G-111)*

Ascending Iron LLC............................... E 336 266-6462
Whitsett *(G-12599)*

Asheville Maintenance and................... E 828 687-8110
Arden *(G-254)*

Ashley Welding & Machine Co............... F 252 482-3321
Edenton *(G-4361)*

Bakers Stnless Fabrication Inc.............. G 919 934-2707
Smithfield *(G-11434)*

Bartimaeus By Design Inc..................... C 336 475-4346
Thomasville *(G-11996)*

Bear Creek Fabrication LLC.................. F 919 837-2444
Bear Creek *(G-712)*

Bet-Mac Wilson Steel Inc...................... G 919 528-1540
Creedmoor *(G-3641)*

Bevans Steel Fabrication Inc................. F 704 395-0200
Charlotte *(G-1776)*

Bill S Iron Shop Inc.............................. G 919 596-8360
Durham *(G-3926)*

Blacksand Metal Works LLC................. F 703 489-8282
Fayetteville *(G-4558)*

◆ BMA America Inc................................. F 970 353-3770
Charlotte *(G-1794)*

◆ Bob Barker Company Inc..................... C 800 334-9880
Fuquay Varina *(G-4870)*

Bondo Innovations LLC......................... G 704 888-9910
Stanfield *(G-11604)*

Border Concepts Inc............................. G 336 248-2419
Lexington *(G-7660)*

BP Associates Inc................................ G 704 833-1494
Gastonia *(G-5004)*

◆ BP Associates Inc............................... C 704 864-3032
Gastonia *(G-5003)*

Bulldurhamfabrications Com................. G 919 479-1919
Durham *(G-3952)*

Burkett Welding Services Inc................. F 252 635-2814
New Bern *(G-9345)*

Burton Steel Company.......................... F 910 675-9241
Castle Hayne *(G-1496)*

◆ C Tek Lean Solutions Inc..................... E 704 895-0090
Mooresville *(G-8625)*

Capitol Funds Inc................................. D 704 482-0645
Shelby *(G-11315)*

▲ Cardinal Metalworks LLC..................... D 910 259-9990
Burgaw *(G-1021)*

Carolina Duct Fabrication Inc................ G 252 478-9955
Spring Hope *(G-11555)*

Carolina Fab Inc................................... F 704 820-8694
Mount Holly *(G-9221)*

Carolina Fabricators LLC....................... F 919 510-8410
Raleigh *(G-9975)*

Carolina Machining Fabrication............. G 919 554-9700
Youngsville *(G-13469)*

▲ Carver Machine Works Inc.................. D 252 975-3101
Washington *(G-12378)*

Chatsworth Products Inc....................... C 252 514-2779
New Bern *(G-9354)*

City Machine Company Inc.................... E 828 754-9661
Lenoir *(G-7594)*

Cives Corp... G 919 518-2140
Raleigh *(G-9996)*

Clark Steel Fabricators Inc.................... F 336 595-9353
Walnut Cove *(G-12327)*

Clothes Cleaning System LLC................ G 252 243-3752
Wilson *(G-12980)*

▲ CMC Rebar... G 704 865-8571
Gastonia *(G-5023)*

Cmw Manufacturing LLC....................... E 704 216-0171
Salisbury *(G-11035)*

Cochrane Steel Industries Inc............... F 704 291-9330
Monroe *(G-8462)*

Colliers Welding LLC............................. G 910 818-5728
Fayetteville *(G-4576)*

Collins Fabrication & Wldg LLC............. G 704 861-9326
Gastonia *(G-5024)*

Columbus Industries LLC...................... F 910 872-1625
Bladenboro *(G-875)*

Comfort Engineers Inc........................... E 919 383-0158
Durham *(G-3985)*

Commercial Fabricators Inc.................... E 828 465-1010
Newton *(G-9456)*

Commercial Metals Company.................. E 704 375-5937
Charlotte *(G-1963)*

Commercial Metals Company.................. E 704 399-9020
Charlotte *(G-1964)*

▲ Common Part Groupings LLC............... F 704 948-0097
Huntersville *(G-6978)*

Concept Frames Inc.............................. D 828 465-2015
Newton *(G-9459)*

Concept Steel Inc................................. E 704 874-0414
Gastonia *(G-5026)*

Confab Manufacturing Co LLC............... F 704 366-7140
Charlotte *(G-1973)*

Conover Metal Products Inc.................. F 828 464-9414
Conover *(G-3507)*

Cooper B-Line Inc................................. D 704 522-6272
Charlotte *(G-1981)*

Crawford Road Liquidating Co............... F 704 871-1830
Statesville *(G-11679)*

Cricket Forge LLC................................ G 919 680-3513
Durham *(G-3990)*

CSC Family Holdings Inc....................... G 336 993-2680
Colfax *(G-3278)*

CSC Family Holdings Inc....................... G 252 459-7116
Nashville *(G-9318)*

CSC Family Holdings Inc....................... E 336 275-9711
Greensboro *(G-5475)*

▲ Custom Enterprises Inc........................ G 336 226-8296
Burlington *(G-1081)*

Custom Steel Incorporated.................... G 919 383-9170
Durham *(G-3996)*

Custom Steel Fabricators Inc................ G 336 498-5099
Randleman *(G-10639)*

CWC Fabricating................................... G 704 360-8264
Mount Ulla *(G-9268)*

Daltons Metal Works Inc....................... G 336 731-1442
Winston Salem *(G-13136)*

Dave Steel Company Inc........................ D 828 252-2771
Asheville *(G-484)*

Davidson Steel Services LLC................. G 336 775-1234
Winston Salem *(G-13137)*

Davis Steel and Iron Co Inc.................. G 704 821-7676
Matthews *(G-8165)*

Diamondback Industries LLC................. E 336 956-8871
Lexington *(G-7677)*

Directus Holdings LLC.......................... G 919 510-8410
Raleigh *(G-10048)*

Division 5 LLC...................................... C 336 725-0521
Winston Salem *(G-13148)*

Dunavants Welding & Steel Inc.............. G 252 338-6533
Camden *(G-1211)*

Dwiggins Metal Masters Inc.................. G 336 751-2379
Mocksville *(G-8360)*

East Coast Fab LLC.............................. F 336 285-7444
Randleman *(G-10646)*

▲ East Coast Stl Fabrication Inc............. E 757 351-2601
Hertford *(G-6253)*

Edwards Unlimited Inc.......................... G 252 226-4583
Henderson *(G-6154)*

Engineered Steel Products LLC............. E 336 495-5266
Sophia *(G-11487)*

Engineered Steel Products Inc.............. E 336 495-5266
Sophia *(G-11488)*

▲ Equipment Dsign Fbrication Inc........... G 704 372-4513
Gastonia *(G-5046)*

◆ Evans Machinery Inc............................ D 252 243-4006
Wilson *(G-12990)*

Ever Glo Sign Co Inc............................ G 704 633-3324
Salisbury *(G-11049)*

Everettes Industrial Repr Svc............... F 252 527-4269
Goldsboro *(G-5213)*

Exterior Vinyl Wholesale....................... G 336 838-7772
Wilkesboro *(G-12634)*

Fab Designs Incorporated..................... G 704 636-2349
Salisbury *(G-11051)*

Fabco Industries.................................. G 919 481-3010
Cary *(G-1359)*

Fabricated Solutions LLC...................... G 704 982-7789
Albemarle *(G-72)*

Fabrication Associates Inc.................... D 704 535-8050
Charlotte *(G-2140)*

Fabrication Automation LLC.................. G 704 785-2120
Concord *(G-3360)*

Fabrineering LLC.................................. G 704 999-9906
Mooresville *(G-8662)*

Farris Fab & Machine Inc...................... G 704 629-4879
Bessemer City *(G-816)*

Farris Fab & Machine Inc...................... C 704 629-4879
Bessemer City *(G-817)*

▲ Farris Fab & Machine Inc..................... D 704 629-4879
Cherryville *(G-3064)*

▲ Ferrofab Inc....................................... E 910 557-5624
Hamlet *(G-6055)*

Forged Cstm Met Fbrication LLC........... G 910 274-8300
Castle Hayne *(G-1499)*

Forma-Fab Metals Inc........................... E 919 563-5630
Mebane *(G-8240)*

Freedom Metals Inc.............................. F 704 333-1214
Charlotte *(G-2178)*

Fuller Wldg & Fabricators Inc............... E 336 751-3712
Mocksville *(G-8363)*

Gamma Js Inc...................................... F 336 294-3838
Greensboro *(G-5547)*

Gb Industries...................................... G 828 692-9163
East Flat Rock *(G-4331)*

Gerdau Ameristeel US Inc..................... E 919 833-9737
Raleigh *(G-10131)*

Glovers Welding LLC .... F 252 586-7692
Littleton (G-7886)

Gore S Mar Met Fabrication Inc .... G 910 763-6066
Wilmington (G-12793)

GP Fabrication Inc .... F 336 361-0410
Reidsville (G-10686)

H T Wade Enterprises Inc .... F 336 375-8900
Browns Summit (G-997)

Ham Brothers Inc .... F 704 827-1303
Gastonia (G-5058)

Harris Rebar Inc .... G 919 528-8333
Benson (G-792)

Hercules Steel Company Inc .... E 910 488-5110
Fayetteville (G-4611)

Heyel Custom Metal .... F 919 957-8442
Raleigh (G-10164)

Heyel Custom Metal Inc .... F 919 957-8442
Raleigh (G-10165)

Hicks Wterstoves Solar Systems .... F 336 789-4977
Mount Airy (G-9129)

High-Tech Fabrications Inc .... F 336 871-2990
Lawsonville (G-7519)

Hirschfeld Industries Brdg LLC .... A 336 271-8252
Greensboro (G-5600)

Hsi Legacy Inc .... G 704 376-9631
Charlotte (G-2294)

Hughes Metal Works LLC .... E 336 297-0808
Greensboro (G-5610)

Hughs Sheet Mtal Sttsvlle LLC .... F 704 872-4621
Statesville (G-11714)

Ifab Corp .... F 704 864-3032
Gastonia (G-5061)

Industrial Mechanical Services .... G 828 397-3231
Hildebran (G-6852)

Industrial Mechatronics Inc .... G 704 900-2407
Charlotte (G-2322)

Industrial Mtal Pdts Abrdeen I .... F 910 944-8110
Aberdeen (G-7)

◆ Insteel Industries Inc .... C 336 786-2141
Mount Airy (G-9131)

J & S Fab Inc .... G 704 528-4251
Troutman (G-12141)

John Jenkins Company .... E 336 375-3717
Browns Summit (G-1001)

Jordan Innvtive Fbrication LLC .... F 910 428-2368
Biscoe (G-854)

◆ K & S Tool & Manufacturing Co .... E 336 410-7260
High Point (G-6681)

Kisner Corporation .... F 919 510-8410
Raleigh (G-10236)

Limitless Wldg Fabrication LLC .... G 252 753-0660
Farmville (G-4534)

▼ Lincoln County Fabricators Inc .... E 704 735-1398
Lincolnton (G-7837)

Llewellyn Mtal Fabricators Inc .... G 704 283-4816
Monroe (G-8518)

Lydech Thermal Acoustical Inc .... A 336 468-8522
Hamptonville (G-6089)

▲ Lydech Thermal Acoustical Inc .... D 248 277-4900
Hamptonville (G-6088)

Lyerlys Wldg & Fabrication Inc .... G 704 680-2317
Gold Hill (G-5195)

Lyndon Steel Company LLC .... C 336 785-0848
Winston Salem (G-13241)

M F C Inc .... E 252 322-5004
Aurora (G-643)

M&N Construction Supply Inc .... F 910 791-0908
Wilmington (G-12844)

Maco Inc .... E 704 434-6800
Shelby (G-11357)

Manufacturing Methods LLC .... E 910 371-1700
Leland (G-7553)

Martinez Wldg Fabrication Corp .... F 919 957-8904
Raleigh (G-10278)

▲ Master Form Inc .... G 704 292-1041
Matthews (G-8182)

Maysteel Porters LLC .... B 704 864-1313
Gastonia (G-5092)

McCabes Indus Mllwrght Mfg Inc .... G 910 843-8699
Red Springs (G-10669)

McCombs Steel Company Inc .... E 704 873-7563
Statesville (G-11730)

McCune Technology Inc .... G 910 424-2978
Fayetteville (G-4638)

▼ McGee Corporation .... D 704 882-1500
Matthews (G-8131)

▲ Metal Tech Murfreesboro Inc .... E 252 398-4041
Murfreesboro (G-9283)

Metal Works Mfg Co .... D 704 482-1399
Shelby (G-11362)

Metalcraft Fabricating Company .... F 919 477-2117
Durham (G-4131)

▼ Millennium Mfg Structures LLC .... G 828 265-3737
Boone (G-934)

Minda North America LLC .... E 828 313-0092
Granite Falls (G-5313)

Mmdi Inc .... D 704 882-4550
Matthews (G-8186)

▲ MTS Holdings Corp Inc .... E 336 227-0151
Burlington (G-1133)

Mundy Machine Co Inc .... F 704 922-8663
Dallas (G-3679)

NC Steel Services Inc .... F 252 393-7888
Swansboro (G-11887)

New South Fabricator LLC .... G 704 922-2072
Dallas (G-3680)

North State Steel Inc .... F 919 496-2506
Louisburg (G-7920)

North State Steel Inc .... E 252 830-8884
Greenville (G-6008)

Nucor Corporation .... C 336 481-7924
Lexington (G-7725)

◆ Nucor Corporation .... C 704 366-7000
Charlotte (G-2586)

Nucor Rebar Fabrication NC Inc .... C 910 739-9747
Lumberton (G-7963)

Ottenweller Co Inc .... E 336 783-6959
Mount Airy (G-9162)

Packiq LLC .... E 910 964-4331
Fayetteville (G-4650)

Parsons Metal Fabricators Inc .... F 828 758-7521
Lenoir (G-7633)

Paul Casper Inc .... G 919 269-5362
Zebulon (G-13520)

Peachland Dsign Fbrication LLC .... F 704 272-9296
Peachland (G-9652)

Peak Steel LLC .... F 919 362-5955
Apex (G-185)

Piedmont Metals Burlington Inc .... E 336 584-7742
Burlington (G-1140)

Piedmont Metalworks LLC .... G 919 598-6500
Mebane (G-8256)

Piedmont Steel Company LLC .... G 336 875-5133
Winston Salem (G-13294)

▲ Porters Group LLC .... B 704 864-1313
Gastonia (G-5121)

Precision Fabrication Inc .... F 336 885-6091
High Point (G-6741)

Production Wldg Fbrication Inc .... G 828 687-7466
Arden (G-302)

Protech Fabrication Inc .... F 704 663-1721
Mount Ulla (G-9271)

Quality Steel Fabrication Inc .... G 336 961-2670
Yadkinville (G-13448)

R & R Ironworks Inc .... G 828 448-0524
Morganton (G-8890)

Ramco Fabricators LLC .... F 336 996-6073
Colfax (G-3289)

Richmond Steel Welding .... G 910 582-4026
Rockingham (G-10790)

Riddley Metals Inc .... F 704 435-8829
Shelby (G-11373)

Roanoke Valley Steel Corp .... F 252 538-4137
Weldon (G-12526)

Roderick Mch Erectors Wldg Inc .... G 910 343-0381
Wilmington (G-12901)

Rovertym .... G 704 635-7305
Monroe (G-8553)

Rugged Metal Designs Inc .... G 336 352-5150
Dobson (G-3824)

Ruhl Inc .... G 910 497-3172
Spring Lake (G-11562)

Salisbury Mtal Fabrication LLC .... F 704 278-0785
Salisbury (G-11114)

Sanford Steel Corporation .... F 919 898-4799
Goldston (G-5258)

Sieber Industrial Inc .... F 252 746-2003
Ayden (G-660)

Smith Architectural Metals LLC .... E 336 273-1970
Greensboro (G-5818)

Southco Industries Inc .... C 704 482-1477
Shelby (G-11381)

Southeastern Steel Cnstr Inc .... F 910 346-4462
Jacksonville (G-7150)

◆ Southeastern Tool & Die Inc .... D 910 944-7677
Aberdeen (G-24)

Specialty Fabricators Inc .... G 336 838-7704
Wilkesboro (G-12652)

◆ Specialty Manufacturing Inc .... D 704 247-9300
Charlotte (G-2841)

Specialty Welding & Mch Inc .... G 828 464-1104
Newton (G-9499)

Stainless Steel Spc Inc .... F 919 779-4290
Raleigh (G-10503)

Stainless Stl Fabricators Inc .... G 919 833-3520
Raleigh (G-10504)

Steel and Pipe Corporation .... E 919 776-0751
Sanford (G-11240)

Steel Construct Systems LLC .... E 704 781-5575
Locust (G-7903)

Steel Specialty Co Belmont Inc .... E 704 825-4745
Belmont (G-768)

Steel Technology Inc .... G 252 937-7122
Rocky Mount (G-10869)

Steelco Inc .... F 704 896-1207
Matthews (G-8194)

Steelcraft Structures LLC .... G 980 434-5400
Statesville (G-11781)

Steelfab Inc .... B 704 394-5376
Charlotte (G-2864)

Steelfab of Virginia Inc .... E 919 828-9545
Raleigh (G-10507)

Stephens Mechanical .... G 336 998-2141
Mocksville (G-8392)

Structural Planners Inc .... F 919 848-8964
Raleigh (G-10515)

Structural Steel Products Corp .... D 919 359-2811
Clayton (G-3171)

▲ Superior Manufacturing Company .... D 336 661-1200
Winston Salem (G-13350)

T Cs Services Inc .... G 910 655-2796
Bolton (G-889)

Tab Steel & Fabricating Inc .... G 828 323-8300
Hildebran (G-6855)

Tank Fab Inc .... F 910 675-8999
Rocky Point (G-10886)

S
I
C

Tce Manufacturing LLC.............................G 252 330-9919
Elizabeth City *(G-4412)*

Thieman Manufacturing Tech LLC.........F 828 453-1866
Ellenboro *(G-4461)*

Thomasvlle Mtal Fbricators Inc..............E 336 248-4992
Lexington *(G-7750)*

Threadline Products Inc..........................F 704 527-9052
Charlotte *(G-2914)*

Timmons Fabrications Inc........................F 919 688-8998
Durham *(G-4274)*

Tower Engrg Professionals Inc................C 919 661-6351
Raleigh *(G-10554)*

Towerco LLC...F 919 653-5700
Cary *(G-1472)*

Trane Technologies Company LLC.........B 336 751-3561
Mocksville *(G-8394)*

Tri-City Mechanical Contrs Inc...............D 336 272-9495
Greensboro *(G-5872)*

Tri-Steel Fabricators Inc.........................E 252 291-7900
Sims *(G-11432)*

Triangle Metalworks Inc..........................G 919 556-7786
Youngsville *(G-13495)*

Triangle Steel Systems LLC....................G 919 615-0282
Garner *(G-4968)*

Truefab LLC..F 919 620-8158
Durham *(G-4283)*

Tubular Textile LLC..................................G 336 731-2860
Welcome *(G-12516)*

United Machine & Metal Fab Inc............E 828 464-5167
Conover *(G-3569)*

Universal Steel NC LLC............................E 336 476-3105
Thomasville *(G-12085)*

▼ US Buildings LLC.................................D 828 264-6198
Boone *(G-949)*

US Metal Crafters LLC.............................E 336 861-2100
Archdale *(G-245)*

USA Metal Structure LLP..........................G 336 717-2884
Dobson *(G-3826)*

Vann S Wldg & Orna Works Inc..............F 704 289-6056
Monroe *(G-8576)*

W&W-Afco Steel LLC................................D 336 993-2680
Colfax *(G-3293)*

W&W-Afco Steel LLC................................E 336 275-9711
Greensboro *(G-5913)*

W&W-Afco Steel LLC................................E 252 459-7116
Nashville *(G-9325)*

Waldenwood Group Inc...........................F 704 313-8004
Charlotte *(G-2999)*

Waldenwood Group LLC...........................F 704 331-8004
Charlotte *(G-3000)*

Wallace Welding Inc.................................F 919 934-2488
Smithfield *(G-11469)*

Waters Brothers Contrs Inc......................F 252 446-7141
Rocky Mount *(G-10874)*

Watson Metals Co....................................G 336 366-4500
State Road *(G-11640)*

Wede Corporation.....................................G 704 864-1313
Kings Mountain *(G-7390)*

Welding Solutions LLC.............................E 828 665-4363
Fletcher *(G-4778)*

Weldon Steel Corporation........................E 252 536-2113
Weldon *(G-12528)*

Whitley Metals Inc....................................G 919 894-3326
Willow Spring *(G-12682)*

▲ Williams Industries Inc........................C 919 604-1746
Raleigh *(G-10610)*

Winston Steel Stair Co.............................G 336 721-0020
Winston Salem *(G-13402)*

Wirenet Inc...F 513 774-7759
Huntersville *(G-7062)*

Wnc Refab Inc..G 828 658-8368
Weaverville *(G-12508)*

◆ Zarges Inc..F 704 357-6285
Charlotte *(G-3044)*

3442 Metal doors, sash, and trim

A R Perry Corporation.............................G 252 492-6181
Henderson *(G-6146)*

▲ Airspeed LLC.......................................E 919 644-1222
Mebane *(G-8227)*

Alside Window Co.....................................G 407 293-9010
Kinston *(G-7393)*

Amarr Company.......................................G 704 599-5858
Charlotte *(G-1661)*

Amarr Company.......................................G 336 936-0010
Mocksville *(G-8347)*

◆ Amarr Company....................................C 336 744-5100
Winston Salem *(G-13084)*

Amesbury Group Inc................................D 704 978-2883
Statesville *(G-11655)*

Amesbury Group Inc................................D 704 924-7694
Statesville *(G-11656)*

◆ Assa Abloy Entrnce Systems US.........C 866 237-2687
Monroe *(G-8434)*

Atlantic Coastal Shutters LLC...................G 252 441-4358
Kill Devil Hills *(G-7314)*

Atrium Extrusion Systems Inc...................F 336 764-6400
Welcome *(G-12510)*

Building Envlope Erction Svcs...................F 252 747-2015
Snow Hill *(G-11476)*

Champion Win Co of Charlotte..................G 704 398-0085
Charlotte *(G-1891)*

Charlotte Shutter and Shades...................G 336 351-3391
Westfield *(G-12572)*

Coastal Awnings Inc.................................F 252 222-0707
Morehead City *(G-8826)*

▲ Cornerstone Bldg Brands Inc...............B 281 897-7788
Cary *(G-1336)*

◆ Dac Products Inc..................................E 336 969-9786
Rural Hall *(G-10958)*

Energy Svers Windows Doors Inc............G 252 758-8700
Greenville *(G-5974)*

Envirnmental Win Solutions LLC...............G 704 200-2001
Charlotte *(G-2118)*

Garden Metalwork....................................G 828 733-1077
Newland *(G-9429)*

Him Inc...F 336 409-7795
King *(G-7327)*

Jeld-Wen Inc..C 336 838-0292
North Wilkesboro *(G-9536)*

◆ Jeld-Wen Inc...B 800 535-3936
Charlotte *(G-2366)*

▲ Jeld-Wen Holding Inc...........................B 704 378-5700
Charlotte *(G-2367)*

Jewers Doors Us Inc................................E 888 510-5331
Greensboro *(G-5636)*

Kennys Components Inc...........................F 704 662-0777
Mooresville *(G-8703)*

Kindred Rolling Doors LLC.......................G 704 905-3806
Gastonia *(G-5073)*

McDaniel Awning Co.................................G 704 636-8503
Salisbury *(G-11090)*

Moss Supply Company.............................C 704 596-8717
Charlotte *(G-2521)*

Ora Inc...G 540 903-7177
Marion *(G-8059)*

Owens Corning Sales LLC.......................E 419 248-8000
Roxboro *(G-10937)*

Panels By Paith Inc.................................G 336 599-3437
Roxboro *(G-10939)*

Peelle Company.......................................G 631 231-6000
Monroe *(G-8542)*

Ramsey Industries Inc.............................F 704 827-3560
Belmont *(G-763)*

Reynaers Inc..E 480 272-9688
Charlotte *(G-2719)*

Reynolds Advanced Mtls Inc....................G 704 357-0600
Charlotte *(G-2720)*

Rice S Glass Company Inc.......................E 919 967-9214
Carrboro *(G-1272)*

Shutter Factory Inc..................................G 252 974-2795
Washington *(G-12413)*

Sonaron LLC..G 808 232-6168
Fayetteville *(G-4672)*

Tompkins Industries Inc...........................C 828 254-2351
Asheville *(G-620)*

Trim Inc...G 336 751-3591
Mocksville *(G-8395)*

▲ Ultimate Products Inc..........................F 919 836-1627
Raleigh *(G-10573)*

Vinyl Windows & Doors Corp....................F 910 944-2100
Aberdeen *(G-30)*

YKK AP America Inc................................F 336 665-1963
Greensboro *(G-5930)*

3443 Fabricated plate work (boiler shop)

A O Smith Water Products Co..................F 704 597-8910
Charlotte *(G-1606)*

Adamson Global Technology Corp...........G 252 523-5200
Kinston *(G-7391)*

◆ Akg North America Inc..........................E 919 563-4286
Mebane *(G-8228)*

◆ Akg Nrth Amercn Operations Inc..........F 919 563-4286
Mebane *(G-8229)*

◆ Akg of America Inc...............................E 919 563-4286
Mebane *(G-8230)*

▼ Alamo Distribution LLC.........................C 704 398-5600
Belmont *(G-740)*

Alloy Fabricators Inc................................E 704 263-2281
Alexis *(G-102)*

American Metal Fabricators Inc.................E 704 824-8585
Gastonia *(G-4993)*

▲ Applied Medical Tech Inc.....................E 919 255-3220
Creedmoor *(G-3639)*

B&B Cap Liners LLC.................................G 585 598-1828
Raleigh *(G-9927)*

Bendel Tank Heat Exchanger LLC............E 704 596-5112
Charlotte *(G-1771)*

◆ Bfs Industries LLC................................E 919 575-6711
Butner *(G-1199)*

◆ BMA America Inc..................................F 970 353-3770
Charlotte *(G-1794)*

Bthec Inc...E 704 596-5112
Charlotte *(G-1816)*

Bwxt Mpower Inc.....................................F 980 365-4000
Charlotte *(G-1825)*

◆ Canvas Sx LLC.....................................C 980 474-3700
Charlotte *(G-1836)*

Carolina Piping Services Inc....................G 704 405-0297
Kings Mountain *(G-7356)*

Carolina Products Inc..............................E 704 364-9029
Charlotte *(G-1854)*

Cherokee Transfer Station........................G 828 497-4519
Cherokee *(G-3052)*

Chicago Tube and Iron Company..............D 704 781-2060
Locust *(G-7890)*

Columbiana Hi Tech LLC..........................G 336 497-3600
Kernersville *(G-7258)*

Commscope Technologies LLC.................G 919 934-9711
Smithfield *(G-11440)*

Container Products Corporation................D 910 392-6100
Wilmington *(G-12748)*

Contech Engnered Solutions LLC.............E 704 596-4226
Charlotte *(G-1978)*

Contech Engnered Solutions LLC.............G 919 858-7820
Raleigh *(G-10010)*

Contech Engnered Solutions LLC......... G..... 919 851-2880
Raleigh *(G-10011)*

Crown Case Co......... G..... 704 453-1542
Charlotte *(G-1998)*

Fabrication Associates Inc......... D..... 704 535-8050
Charlotte *(G-2140)*

▼ Fleetgenius of Nc Inc......... C..... 828 726-3001
Lenoir *(G-7607)*

◆ Florida Marine Tanks Inc......... F..... 305 620-9030
Henderson *(G-6155)*

▼ Friedrich Metal Pdts Co Inc......... E..... 336 375-3067
Browns Summit *(G-993)*

▼ Gaston County Dyeing Mach......... D..... 704 822-5000
Mount Holly *(G-9231)*

General Industries Inc......... E..... 919 751-1791
Goldsboro *(G-5215)*

Highland Tank NC Inc......... C..... 336 218-0801
Greensboro *(G-5599)*

Hockmeyer Equipment Corp......... D..... 252 338-4705
Elizabeth City *(G-4390)*

Icon Boiler Inc......... E..... 844 562-4266
Greensboro *(G-5612)*

Industrial Air Inc......... C..... 336 292-1030
Greensboro *(G-5616)*

▲ Ips Perforating Inc......... G..... 704 881-0050
Statesville *(G-11716)*

J & L Bckh/Nvrnmental Svcs Inc......... G..... 910 237-7351
Eastover *(G-4337)*

▲ Jbr Properties of Greenville Inc......... A..... 252 355-9353
Winterville *(G-13417)*

Job Shop Fabricators Inc......... G..... 336 427-7300
Madison *(G-7988)*

Kings Prtble Wldg Fbrction LLC......... G..... 336 789-2372
Mount Airy *(G-9142)*

Kirk & Blum Manufacturing Co......... D..... 801 728-6533
Greensboro *(G-5649)*

M M M Inc......... G..... 252 527-0229
La Grange *(G-7469)*

▲ Marley Company LLC......... C..... 704 752-4400
Charlotte *(G-2459)*

McCune Technology Inc......... G..... 910 424-2978
Fayetteville *(G-4638)*

Miller Dumpster Service LLC......... G..... 704 504-9300
Charlotte *(G-2504)*

◆ Mitsubishi Chemical Amer Inc......... D..... 980 580-2839
Charlotte *(G-2509)*

Mrr Southern LLC......... G..... 919 436-3571
Raleigh *(G-10317)*

Naes-Oms......... G..... 252 536-4525
Weldon *(G-12524)*

NC Diesel Performance LLC......... G..... 704 431-3257
Salisbury *(G-11095)*

Nordfab LLC......... C..... 336 821-0829
Thomasville *(G-12055)*

Piedmont Fiberglass Inc......... E..... 828 632-8883
Statesville *(G-11745)*

Piedmont Well Covers Inc......... F..... 704 664-8488
Mount Ulla *(G-9270)*

Poppe Inc......... E..... 828 345-6036
Hickory *(G-6415)*

Purthermal LLC......... G..... 828 855-0108
Hickory *(G-6422)*

Rack Works Inc......... E..... 336 368-1302
Pilot Mountain *(G-9673)*

Royall Development Co Inc......... G..... 336 889-2569
High Point *(G-6762)*

Second Green Holdings Inc......... F..... 336 996-6073
Colfax *(G-3290)*

Southeastern Mch & Wldg Co Inc......... E..... 910 791-6661
Wilmington *(G-12925)*

SPX Cooling Tech LLC......... F..... 630 881-9777
Charlotte *(G-2846)*

SPX Corporation......... F..... 336 627-6020
Eden *(G-4357)*

SPX Flow Us LLC......... C..... 919 735-4570
Goldsboro *(G-5246)*

SPX Technologies Inc......... D..... 980 474-3700
Charlotte *(G-2851)*

Tank Fab Inc......... F..... 910 675-8999
Rocky Point *(G-10886)*

Thieman Manufacturing Tech LLC......... F..... 828 453-1866
Ellenboro *(G-4461)*

▼ Tower Components Inc......... D..... 336 824-2102
Ramseur *(G-10632)*

TRC Acquisition LLC......... A..... 252 355-9353
Winterville *(G-13424)*

Turner Equipment Company Inc......... E..... 919 734-8328
Goldsboro *(G-5250)*

▲ Ward Vessel and Exchanger Corp......... D..... 704 568-3001
Charlotte *(G-3004)*

Waste Container Repair Svcs......... G..... 910 257-4474
Fayetteville *(G-4696)*

Waste Industries Usa LLC......... C..... 919 325-3000
Raleigh *(G-10598)*

◆ Wastequip LLC......... F..... 704 366-7140
Charlotte *(G-3005)*

◆ Wastequip Manufacturing Co LLC......... G..... 704 366-7140
Charlotte *(G-3006)*

Wiggins Design Fabrication Inc......... G..... 252 826-5239
Scotland Neck *(G-11268)*

Wnc White Corporation......... E..... 828 477-4895
Sylva *(G-11905)*

Worthington Cylinder Corp......... C..... 336 777-8600
Winston Salem *(G-13404)*

Ziehl-Abegg Inc......... C..... 336 934-9339
Winston Salem *(G-13410)*

▲ Ziehl-Abegg Inc......... E..... 336 834-9339
Greensboro *(G-5931)*

3444 Sheet metalwork

A B Metals of Polkton LLC......... G..... 704 694-6635
Polkton *(G-9810)*

A C S Enterprises NC Inc......... G..... 704 226-9898
Monroe *(G-8414)*

A Plus Carports......... G..... 336 367-1261
Boonville *(G-956)*

Abco Automation Inc......... C..... 336 375-6490
Browns Summit *(G-988)*

Able Metal Fabricators Inc......... C..... 704 394-8972
Charlotte *(G-1611)*

Advanced Mfg Solutions NC Inc......... F..... 828 633-2633
Candler *(G-1216)*

▼ Afi Capital Inc......... C..... 919 212-6400
Raleigh *(G-9885)*

Air Control Inc......... E..... 252 492-2300
Henderson *(G-6147)*

▼ Alamo Distribution LLC......... C..... 704 398-5600
Belmont *(G-740)*

Alert Metal Works Inc......... G..... 704 922-3152
Dallas *(G-3664)*

Allen Kelly & Co Inc......... D..... 919 779-4197
Raleigh *(G-9892)*

Allens Gutter Service......... G..... 910 738-9509
Lumberton *(G-7944)*

Allied Sheet Metal Works Inc......... F..... 704 376-8469
Charlotte *(G-1645)*

Allied Tool and Machine Co......... G..... 336 993-2131
Kernersville *(G-7240)*

Alloy Fabricators Inc......... E..... 704 263-2281
Alexis *(G-102)*

▼ American Wick Drain Corp......... E..... 704 296-5801
Monroe *(G-8424)*

APT Industries Inc......... F..... 704 598-9100
Charlotte *(G-1689)*

Axccellus LLC......... F..... 919 589-9800
Apex *(G-143)*

Beacon Roofing Supply Inc......... G..... 704 886-1555
Charlotte *(G-1763)*

Benton & Sons Fabrication Inc......... E..... 919 734-1700
Pikeville *(G-9667)*

Bolton Construction & Svc LLC......... D..... 919 861-1500
Raleigh *(G-9952)*

Budd-Piper Roofing Company......... G..... 919 682-2121
Durham *(G-3947)*

Bull City Sheet Metal LLC......... G..... 919 354-0993
Durham *(G-3950)*

Bulldog Industries Inc......... E..... 919 217-6170
Knightdale *(G-7449)*

▲ Byers Prcision Fabricators Inc......... E..... 828 693-4088
Hendersonville *(G-6192)*

C P Eakes Company......... F..... 336 574-1800
Greensboro *(G-5417)*

Calco Enterprises Inc......... F..... 910 695-0089
Aberdeen *(G-3)*

Camco Manufacturing Inc......... G..... 336 348-6609
Reidsville *(G-10678)*

Captive-Aire Systems Inc......... G..... 704 844-9088
Charlotte *(G-1837)*

Captive-Aire Systems Inc......... G..... 704 843-7215
Waxhaw *(G-12426)*

Captive-Aire Systems Inc......... C..... 919 887-2721
Youngsville *(G-13468)*

◆ Captive-Aire Systems Inc......... C..... 919 882-2410
Raleigh *(G-9972)*

◆ Carolina Custom Booth Co LLC......... E..... 336 886-3127
High Point *(G-6559)*

Carolina Spral Duct Fbrction L......... G..... 704 395-3289
Charlotte *(G-1858)*

Centria Inc......... G..... 704 341-0202
Charlotte *(G-1887)*

Centurion Industries Inc......... D..... 704 867-2304
Gastonia *(G-5015)*

Champion Win Co of Charlotte......... G..... 704 398-0085
Charlotte *(G-1891)*

Chatsworth Products Inc......... C..... 252 514-2779
New Bern *(G-9354)*

Clt 2016 Inc......... D..... 704 886-1555
Charlotte *(G-1933)*

Collins Fabrication & Wldg LLC......... G..... 704 861-9326
Gastonia *(G-5024)*

▼ Colored Metal Products Inc......... F..... 704 482-1407
Shelby *(G-11322)*

Comfort Engineers Inc......... E..... 919 383-0158
Durham *(G-3985)*

Construction Metal Pdts Inc......... E..... 704 871-8704
Statesville *(G-11678)*

▲ Cornerstone Bldg Brands Inc......... B..... 281 897-7788
Cary *(G-1336)*

Cox Machine Co Inc......... G..... 704 296-0118
Monroe *(G-8470)*

CPI Satcom & Antenna Tech Inc......... C..... 704 462-7330
Conover *(G-3508)*

▲ CSC Sheet Metal Inc......... F..... 919 544-8887
Durham *(G-3992)*

▲ Custom Industries Inc......... E..... 336 299-2885
Greensboro *(G-5481)*

Custom Sheetmetal Services Inc......... G..... 919 282-1088
Durham *(G-3995)*

Cypress Mountain Company......... G..... 252 758-2179
Greenville *(G-5962)*

Dantherm Filtration Inc......... F..... 336 889-5599
Thomasville *(G-12016)*

Design Engnred Fbrications Inc......... E..... 336 768-8260
Winston Salem *(G-13141)*

DOT Blue Services Inc......... G..... 704 342-2970
Charlotte *(G-2064)*

Dunavants Welding & Steel Inc............... G 252 338-6533
  Camden *(G-1211)*

Dusty Rhoads Hvac Inc........................ G 252 261-5892
  Kitty Hawk *(G-7444)*

Dwiggins Metal Masters Inc.................. G 336 751-2379
  Mocksville *(G-8360)*

▲ Effikal LLC.................................... F 252 522-3031
  Kinston *(G-7407)*

Ellenburg Sheet Metal......................... G 704 872-2089
  Statesville *(G-11695)*

Envision Glass Inc.............................. G 336 283-9701
  Winston Salem *(G-13159)*

Ep Custom Products Inc....................... G 704 483-8793
  Denver *(G-3782)*

Erdle Perforating Holdings Inc............... F 704 588-4380
  Charlotte *(G-2126)*

F & M Steel Products Inc..................... G 910 793-1345
  Wilmington *(G-12774)*

Fabrication Associates Inc.................... D 704 535-8050
  Charlotte *(G-2140)*

▲ Field Controls LLC.......................... D 252 208-7300
  Kinston *(G-7413)*

Form Tech Concrete Forms Inc.............. E 704 395-9910
  Charlotte *(G-2172)*

Franklin Sheet Metal Shop Inc............... G 828 524-2821
  Franklin *(G-4829)*

Garnett Component Sales Inc................. G 919 562-5158
  Wake Forest *(G-12277)*

General Metals Inc.............................. E 919 202-0100
  Pine Level *(G-9680)*

Gibbs Machine Company Incorporated. E 336 856-1907
  Greensboro *(G-5559)*

Gray Flex Systems Inc........................ D 910 897-3539
  Coats *(G-3262)*

Gray Metal South Inc.......................... D 910 892-2119
  Dunn *(G-3859)*

Griffiths Corporation........................... D 704 554-5657
  Pineville *(G-9732)*

GSM Services Inc.............................. D 704 864-0344
  Gastonia *(G-5056)*

H&S Autoshot LLC............................. E 847 662-8500
  Mooresville *(G-8679)*

Hamlin Sheet Metal Company Inc........... D 919 894-2224
  Benson *(G-791)*

◆ Hamlin Sheet Metal Compan........... E 919 772-8780
  Garner *(G-4930)*

Hanover Iron Works Inc....................... G 910 763-7318
  Wilmington *(G-12800)*

Hanover Iron Works Shtmtl Inc.............. G 910 399-1146
  Wilmington *(G-12801)*

Harco Air LLC................................... G 252 491-5220
  Powells Point *(G-9821)*

Herman Reeves Tex Shtmtl Inc.............. E 704 865-2231
  Gastonia *(G-5059)*

▲ Hi-Tech Fabrication Inc.................... C 919 781-6150
  Raleigh *(G-10166)*

Hughs Sheet Mtal Sttsvlle LLC.............. F 704 872-4621
  Statesville *(G-11714)*

Hunter Douglas Inc............................. C 704 629-6500
  Bessemer City *(G-822)*

Industrial Metal Craft Inc..................... F 704 864-3416
  Gastonia *(G-5066)*

Industrial Mtal Pdts Abrdeen I.............. F 910 944-8110
  Aberdeen *(G-7)*

Industrial Sheet Metal Works................. G 828 654-9655
  Arden *(G-275)*

Ism Inc.. E
  Arden *(G-277)*

Iv-S Metal Stamping Inc....................... E 336 861-2100
  Archdale *(G-229)*

◆ J & D Managements LLC................. G 910 321-7373
  Fayetteville *(G-4618)*

Jack A Farrior Inc.............................. D 252 753-2020
  Farmville *(G-4532)*

Jacksonville Metal Mfg Inc................... G 910 938-7635
  Jacksonville *(G-7128)*

Joe and La Inc................................... F 336 585-0313
  Burlington *(G-1113)*

John Jenkins Company......................... E 336 375-3717
  Browns Summit *(G-1001)*

Joseph F Decker................................ G 704 335-0021
  Charlotte *(G-2379)*

K&H Acquisition Company LLC.............. G 704 788-1128
  Concord *(G-3388)*

K&M Sheet Metal LLC......................... F 919 544-8887
  Durham *(G-4091)*

Kirk & Blum Manufacturing Co.............. D 801 728-6533
  Greensboro *(G-5649)*

Larry Bissette Inc.............................. F 919 773-2140
  Apex *(G-176)*

Len Corporation................................ F 919 876-2964
  Knightdale *(G-7452)*

▲ Loflin Fabrication LLC..................... E 336 859-4333
  Denton *(G-3756)*

Lyon Roofing Inc............................... F 828 397-2301
  Hildebran *(G-6853)*

M&N Construction Supply Inc................ G 336 996-7740
  Colfax *(G-3283)*

Mac/Fab Company Inc......................... E 704 822-1103
  Mount Holly *(G-9236)*

▲ Master Form Inc............................. G 704 292-1041
  Matthews *(G-8182)*

McCune Technology Inc....................... G 910 424-2978
  Fayetteville *(G-4638)*

McDaniel Awning Co........................... G 704 636-8503
  Salisbury *(G-11090)*

▼ McGee Corporation........................ D 704 882-1500
  Matthews *(G-8131)*

McGill Corporation............................. F 919 467-1993
  Cary *(G-1400)*

Metal Roofing Systems LLC................. E 704 820-3110
  Stanley *(G-11622)*

Metal Sales Manufacturing Corp........... E 704 859-0550
  Mocksville *(G-8377)*

Metal Structures Plus LLC................... G 704 896-7155
  Mooresville *(G-8723)*

Midway Blind & Awning Co Inc.............. G 336 226-4532
  Burlington *(G-1129)*

Mincar Group Inc............................... G 919 772-7170
  Raleigh *(G-10308)*

Mitchell Welding Inc........................... E 828 765-2620
  Spruce Pine *(G-11583)*

◆ Mitsubishi Chemical Amer Inc.......... D 980 580-2839
  Charlotte *(G-2509)*

Modern Machine and Metal.................. D 336 993-4808
  Winston Salem *(G-13258)*

▼ Monroe Metal Manufacturing Inc....... D 800 366-1391
  Monroe *(G-8536)*

▲ MTS Holdings Corp Inc................... E 336 227-0151
  Burlington *(G-1133)*

Muriel Harris Investments Inc............... F 800 932-3191
  Fayetteville *(G-4644)*

Mw Industries Inc.............................. E 704 837-0331
  Charlotte *(G-2538)*

▲ New Peco Inc................................ E 828 684-1234
  Arden *(G-288)*

Nitro Manufacturing Inc....................... F 704 663-3155
  Mooresville *(G-8736)*

Nordfab Ducting................................ G 336 821-0840
  Charlotte *(G-2572)*

Northeast Tool and Mfg Company.......... E 704 882-1187
  Matthews *(G-8187)*

Northern Star Technologies Inc.............. G 516 353-3333
  Indian Trail *(G-7092)*

Oak Ridge Industries LLC..................... E 252 833-4061
  Washington *(G-12401)*

On Time Metal LLC............................. G 828 635-1001
  Hiddenite *(G-6503)*

Oro Manufacturing Company................ E 704 283-2186
  Monroe *(G-8539)*

Owens Corning Sales LLC.................... E 419 248-8000
  Roxboro *(G-10937)*

P&S Machining Fabrication LLC............ E 336 227-0151
  Burlington *(G-1137)*

Paul Casper Inc................................ G 919 269-5362
  Zebulon *(G-13520)*

Penco Products Inc............................ C 252 798-4000
  Hamilton *(G-6049)*

Peter J Hamann................................ G 910 484-7877
  Fayetteville *(G-4654)*

Precise Sheet Metal Mech LLC............. G 336 693-3246
  Raeford *(G-9848)*

Precision Fabricators Inc..................... G 336 835-4763
  Ronda *(G-10897)*

Precision Machine Products Inc............. D 704 865-7490
  Gastonia *(G-5126)*

▲ Precision Mch Fabrication Inc........... D 919 231-8648
  Raleigh *(G-10390)*

▲ Production Systems Inc.................... E 336 886-7161
  High Point *(G-6747)*

Protocase Mfg Usa Inc....................... E 866 849-3911
  Wilmington *(G-12892)*

▲ QMF Mtal Elctrnic Slutions Inc......... D 336 992-8002
  Kernersville *(G-7295)*

▲ Quality Musical Systems Inc............. E 828 667-5719
  Candler *(G-1231)*

Queen City Engrg & Design Pllc............ G 704 918-5851
  Concord *(G-3428)*

R E Bengel Sheet Metal Co.................. G 252 637-3404
  New Bern *(G-9390)*

Raleigh Mechanical & Mtls Inc.............. G 919 598-4601
  Raleigh *(G-10425)*

Ray Roofing Company Inc.................... E 704 372-0100
  Charlotte *(G-2692)*

Rfr Metal Fabrication Inc..................... D 919 693-1354
  Oxford *(G-9631)*

Rocky Mount Awning & Tent Co............ G 252 442-0184
  Rocky Mount *(G-10866)*

S and R Sheet Metal Inc...................... G 336 476-1069
  Thomasville *(G-12069)*

S Duff Fabricating Inc......................... G 910 298-3060
  Beulaville *(G-845)*

S K Bowling Inc................................. F 252 243-1803
  Walstonburg *(G-12335)*

Schwartz Steel Service Inc................... E 704 865-9576
  Gastonia *(G-5135)*

Service Rofg Shtmtl Wlmngton I............ F 910 343-9860
  Wilmington *(G-12918)*

Service Roofing and Shtmtl Co.............. D 252 758-2179
  Greenville *(G-6021)*

Sheet Metal Duct Suppliers LLC............ G 919 732-4362
  Hillsborough *(G-6877)*

Sheet Metal Products Inc..................... G 919 954-9950
  Raleigh *(G-10468)*

Simon Industries Inc.......................... E 919 469-2004
  Raleigh *(G-10477)*

Smith Fabrication Inc......................... G 704 660-5170
  Mooresville *(G-8772)*

Smt Inc... D 919 782-4804
  Raleigh *(G-10488)*

▲ Southern Fabricators Inc.................. D 704 272-7615
  Polkton *(G-9815)*

Southern Pdmont Pping Fbrction........... F 704 272-7936
  Peachland *(G-9654)*

Spc Mechanical Corporation................. C 252 237-9035
  Wendell *(G-12549)*

◆ Specialty Manufacturing Inc..............D 704 247-9300
  Charlotte *(G-2841)*

Specified Metals Inc..............................G 336 786-6254
  Mount Airy *(G-9179)*

Stainless Supply Inc............................F 704 635-2064
  Monroe *(G-8563)*

Stamper Sheet Metal Inc.....................G 336 476-5145
  Archdale *(G-243)*

◆ Standard Tools and Eqp Co..............E 336 697-7177
  Greensboro *(G-5836)*

Superior Finishing Systems LLC..........G 336 956-2000
  Lexington *(G-7747)*

Superior Machine Co SC Inc................E 828 652-6141
  Marion *(G-8068)*

Suppliers To Wholesalers Inc............G 704 375-7406
  Charlotte *(G-2884)*

Swanson Sheetmetal Inc......................F 704 283-3955
  Monroe *(G-8566)*

Taylorsville Precast Molds Inc.............G 828 632-4608
  Taylorsville *(G-11982)*

Tfam Solutions LLC.............................G 910 637-0266
  Aberdeen *(G-26)*

Thieman Manufacturing Tech LLC........F 828 453-1866
  Ellenboro *(G-4461)*

Thomasvlle Mtal Fbricators Inc...........E 336 248-4992
  Lexington *(G-7750)*

Triad Corrugated Metal Inc.................F 919 775-1663
  Sanford *(G-11244)*

Triad Corrugated Metal Inc.................E 336 625-9727
  Asheboro *(G-411)*

Triad Fabrication and Mch Inc............G 336 993-6042
  Kernersville *(G-7309)*

Triad Sheet Metal & Mech Inc.............F 336 379-9891
  Greensboro *(G-5879)*

Triad Welding Contractors Inc............G 336 882-3902
  Clemmons *(G-3205)*

Triangle Installation Svc Inc...............G 919 363-7637
  Apex *(G-201)*

Triangle Stainless Inc.........................G 919 596-1335
  Butner *(G-1207)*

◆ Union Corrugating Company..............E 910 483-0479
  Fayetteville *(G-4685)*

Universal Steel NC LLC........................E 336 476-3105
  Thomasville *(G-12085)*

US Metal Crafters LLC.........................E 336 861-2100
  Archdale *(G-245)*

USA Dutch Inc.....................................E 336 227-8600
  Graham *(G-5287)*

USA Dutch Inc.....................................E 919 732-6956
  Efland *(G-4376)*

▼ Ventilation Direct..............................G 919 573-1522
  Raleigh *(G-10585)*

W H Rgers Shtmtl Ir Wrks Inc.............E 704 394-2191
  Charlotte *(G-2995)*

W T Humphrey Inc...............................E 910 455-3555
  Jacksonville *(G-7158)*

Waste Container Services LLC..............G 910 257-4474
  Fayetteville *(G-4697)*

Wede Corporation................................G 704 864-1313
  Kings Mountain *(G-7390)*

▼ Wph Ventures Inc..............................E 828 676-1700
  Arden *(G-319)*

WV Holdings Inc..................................G 704 853-8338
  Gastonia *(G-5168)*

3446 Architectural metalwork

◆ Advanced Technology Inc..................E 336 668-0488
  Greensboro *(G-5344)*

Afsc LLC..D 704 523-4936
  Charlotte *(G-1627)*

Alamance Iron Works Inc.....................G 336 852-5940
  Greensboro *(G-5346)*

Alamance Steel Fabricators..................G 336 887-3015
  High Point *(G-6513)*

▼ Alamo Distribution LLC......................C 704 398-5600
  Belmont *(G-740)*

Apex Steel Corp...................................E 919 362-6611
  Raleigh *(G-9908)*

Automated Controls LLC......................G 704 724-7625
  Huntersville *(G-6970)*

◆ Border Concepts Inc..........................G 704 541-5509
  Charlotte *(G-1800)*

Burlington Mscllneous Mtls LLC..........F 336 376-1264
  Graham *(G-5262)*

C P Eakes Company.............................F 336 574-1800
  Greensboro *(G-5417)*

Carolina Time Equipment Co Inc.........E 704 536-2700
  Charlotte *(G-1859)*

Cast Iron Elegance Inc.........................F 919 662-8777
  Raleigh *(G-9987)*

Commercial Fabricators Inc.................E 828 465-1010
  Newton *(G-9456)*

Concept Fusion LLC............................G 252 406-7052
  Middlesex *(G-8272)*

Creekside Creative Design Inc.............G 252 243-6272
  Wilson *(G-12982)*

Dakota Fab & Welding Inc....................G 919 881-0027
  Siler City *(G-11406)*

Davis Steel and Iron Co Inc.................G 704 821-7676
  Matthews *(G-8165)*

Dlss Manufacturing LLC.......................G 919 619-7594
  Pittsboro *(G-9782)*

Dudleys Fence Company.......................G 252 566-5759
  La Grange *(G-7467)*

Dwiggins Metal Masters Inc.................G 336 751-2379
  Mocksville *(G-8360)*

Eaton-Schultz Inc................................F 704 331-8004
  Charlotte *(G-2087)*

Esher LLC..G 704 975-1463
  Huntersville *(G-6987)*

Hotchkis Performance Mfg Inc.............G 704 660-3060
  Mooresville *(G-8688)*

Hurleys Ornamental Iron......................G 910 576-4731
  Troy *(G-12162)*

Ism Inc..E
  Arden *(G-277)*

J4 Construction LLC............................G 704 550-7970
  Wadesboro *(G-12245)*

James Cotter Ironworks.......................F 919 644-2664
  Cedar Grove *(G-1517)*

James Iron & Steel Inc.........................G 704 283-2299
  Monroe *(G-8508)*

Joseph F Decker..................................G 704 335-0021
  Charlotte *(G-2379)*

Leo Gaev Metalworks Inc......................G 919 883-4666
  Chapel Hill *(G-1552)*

Little River Metalworks LLC..................G 919 920-0292
  Goldsboro *(G-5225)*

Marine Systems Inc.............................F 828 254-5354
  Asheville *(G-543)*

McDaniel Awning Co.............................G 704 636-8503
  Salisbury *(G-11090)*

Mlf Company LLC.................................F 919 231-9401
  Raleigh *(G-10311)*

Nci Group Inc......................................G 919 926-4800
  Raleigh *(G-10328)*

◆ Nci Group Inc....................................B 281 897-7788
  Cary *(G-1405)*

Ornamental Specialties Inc..................F 704 821-9154
  Matthews *(G-8189)*

Poehler Enterprises Inc.......................G 704 239-1166
  Midland *(G-8292)*

Power-Utility Products Company..........F 704 375-0776
  Charlotte *(G-2651)*

▲ Prem Corp...E 704 921-1799
  Charlotte *(G-2660)*

Protech Metals LLC..............................F 910 295-6905
  Pinehurst *(G-9701)*

Rocket Installation LLC........................F 704 657-9492
  Troutman *(G-12148)*

Southern Staircase Inc........................D 704 357-1221
  Charlotte *(G-2839)*

Steel Smart Incorporated....................E 919 736-0681
  Pikeville *(G-9668)*

Steel Specialty Co Belmont Inc............E 704 825-4745
  Belmont *(G-768)*

Stony Knoll Forge................................G 704 507-0179
  Marshville *(G-8095)*

Swaim Ornamental Iron Works.............F 336 765-5271
  Winston Salem *(G-13351)*

Tampco Inc..D 336 835-1895
  Elkin *(G-4452)*

Timmerman Manufacturing Inc............F 828 464-1778
  Conover *(G-3566)*

Vann S Wldg & Orna Works Inc............F 704 289-6056
  Monroe *(G-8576)*

Watson Steel & Iron Works LLC............E 704 821-7140
  Matthews *(G-8197)*

3448 Prefabricated metal buildings

A Plus Carports..................................G 336 367-1261
  Boonville *(G-956)*

Alaska Structures Inc..........................D 910 323-0562
  Fayetteville *(G-4548)*

American Carports Structures..............G 336 710-1091
  Mount Airy *(G-9098)*

Amt/Bcu Inc...E 336 622-6200
  Liberty *(G-7761)*

◆ Betco Inc...D 704 872-2999
  Statesville *(G-11670)*

Bluescope Buildings N Amer Inc...........C 336 996-4801
  Greensboro *(G-5394)*

Bonitz Inc..D 803 799-0181
  Concord *(G-3323)*

Boondock S Manufacturing Inc............G 828 891-4242
  Etowah *(G-4495)*

Boxman Studios LLC............................G 704 333-3733
  Mount Holly *(G-9219)*

Camelot Rturn Intrmdate Hldngs..........D 866 419-0042
  Cary *(G-1320)*

◆ Carolina Carports Inc........................D 336 367-6400
  Dobson *(G-3820)*

Carolina Greenhouse Plants Inc...........G 252 523-9300
  Kinston *(G-7398)*

Carolina Solar Structures Inc..............F 828 684-9900
  Asheville *(G-471)*

Carolina Windows and Doors Inc..........F 252 756-2585
  Greenville *(G-5951)*

Carport Central Inc.............................E 336 673-6020
  Mount Airy *(G-9111)*

Central States Mfg Inc.........................C 336 719-3280
  Mount Airy *(G-9113)*

▲ Central Steel Buildings Inc................F 336 789-7896
  Mount Airy *(G-9114)*

CF Steel LLC.......................................G 704 516-1750
  Midland *(G-8283)*

Classic Steel Buildings Inc..................G 252 465-4184
  Sunbury *(G-11846)*

Coast To Coast Carports Inc................E 336 783-3015
  Mount Airy *(G-9115)*

Coastal Machine & Welding Inc............G 910 754-6476
  Shallotte *(G-11302)*

Component Sourcing Intl LLC...............E 704 843-9292
  Charlotte *(G-1967)*

▲ Cornerstone Bldg Brands Inc............B 281 897-7788
  Cary *(G-1336)*

E A Duncan Cnstr Co Inc.......................... G 910 653-3535
  Tabor City *(G-11910)*

Eagle Carports Inc................................... E 800 579-8589
  Mount Airy *(G-9117)*

▼ Friedrich Metal Pdts Co Inc .... E 336 375-3067
  Browns Summit *(G-993)*

Go Ask Erin LLC..................................... G 336 747-3777
  Roxboro *(G-10927)*

Harvest Homes and Handi Houses .... G 704 637-3878
  Salisbury *(G-11061)*

Harvest Homes and Handi Houses .... G 336 243-2382
  Lexington *(G-7696)*

Heritage Building Company LLC............ G 704 431-4494
  Statesville *(G-11708)*

Heritage Steel LLC................................ F 704 431-4097
  Salisbury *(G-11064)*

Innovative Awngs & Screens LLC.......... F 833 337-4233
  Cornelius *(G-3610)*

J&J Outdoor Accessories....................... G 910 742-1969
  Delco *(G-3736)*

Leonard Alum Utlty Bldngs Inc.............. G 336 226-9410
  Burlington *(G-1119)*

Leonard Alum Utlty Bldngs Inc.............. G 919 872-4442
  Raleigh *(G-10254)*

Leonard Alum Utlty Bldngs Inc.............. G 910 392-4921
  Wilmington *(G-12834)*

Leonard Alum Utlty Bldngs Inc.............. D 336 789-5018
  Mount Airy *(G-9146)*

▲ Lock Drives Inc.................................. G 704 588-1844
  Pineville *(G-9740)*

M & R Forestry Service Inc .... G 980 439-1261
  Albemarle *(G-80)*

Mast Woodworks..................................... F 336 468-1194
  Hamptonville *(G-6090)*

Mayse Manufacturing Co Inc................. G 828 245-1891
  Forest City *(G-4793)*

▼ McGee Corporation............................ D 704 882-1500
  Matthews *(G-8131)*

Millennium Buildings Inc....................... G 866 216-8499
  Dobson *(G-3823)*

▼ Millennium Mfg Structures LLC.......... G 828 265-3737
  Boone *(G-934)*

Milligan House Movers Inc..................... G 910 653-2272
  Tabor City *(G-11913)*

Morton Buildings Inc............................. G 252 291-1300
  Wilson *(G-13007)*

Nash Building Systems Inc .... E 252 823-1905
  Tarboro *(G-11938)*

Nci Group Inc.. G 919 926-4800
  Raleigh *(G-10328)*

◆ Nci Group Inc.....................................B 281 897-7788
  Cary *(G-1405)*

Neals Carpentry & Cnstr....................... G 910 346-6154
  Jacksonville *(G-7135)*

Norwood Manufacturing Inc.................. E 704 474-0505
  Norwood *(G-9558)*

Nucor Corporation................................ C 336 481-7924
  Lexington *(G-7725)*

◆ Nucor Corporation.............................C 704 366-7000
  Charlotte *(G-2586)*

OSteel Buildings Inc.............................. F 704 824-6061
  Gastonia *(G-5113)*

Pine View Buildings LLC........................ D 704 876-1501
  Statesville *(G-11746)*

Quick-Deck Inc...................................... E 704 888-0327
  Locust *(G-7898)*

▲ Remedios LLC..................................... G 203 453-6000
  Charlotte *(G-2706)*

RMC Advanced Technologies Inc........... D 704 325-7100
  Newton *(G-9491)*

▲ Robco Manufacturing Inc................... E 252 438-7399
  Henderson *(G-6175)*

▼ Robertson-Ceco II Corporation.......... C 281 897-7788
  Cary *(G-1439)*

Rogers Manufacturing Company............ G 910 259-9898
  Burgaw *(G-1030)*

Simonton Windows & Doors Inc............ F 919 677-3938
  Cary *(G-1456)*

Southern Leisure Builders Inc............... G 910 381-0426
  Jacksonville *(G-7151)*

Sunshine Mnfctred Strctres Inc............ G 704 279-6600
  Rockwell *(G-10802)*

T-N-T Carports Inc................................ G 336 789-3818
  Mount Airy *(G-9184)*

▼ T-N-T Carports Inc............................. E 336 789-3818
  Mount Airy *(G-9185)*

Tri-State Carports Inc........................... G 276 755-2081
  Mount Airy *(G-9188)*

Triton Industries LLC............................ F 336 816-3794
  Mount Airy *(G-9190)*

Truesteel Structures LLC...................... E 336 789-3818
  Mount Airy *(G-9191)*

Turner Equipment Company Inc........... E 919 734-8328
  Goldsboro *(G-5250)*

Twin Carports LLC................................ G 336 790-8284
  East Bend *(G-4327)*

US Chemical Storage LLC...................... E 828 264-6032
  Wilkesboro *(G-12661)*

◆ Van Wingerden Grnhse Co Inc........... E 828 891-7389
  Mills River *(G-8323)*

Veon Inc.. F 252 623-2102
  Washington *(G-12418)*

Viking Steel Structures LLC.................. G 877 623-7549
  Boonville *(G-959)*

Vinyl Structures LLC............................. G 336 468-4311
  Hamptonville *(G-6094)*

▲ Williamson Greenhouses Inc.............. G 910 592-7072
  Clinton *(G-3253)*

3449 Miscellaneous metalwork

◆ 3a Composites USA Inc.......................C 704 872-8974
  Statesville *(G-11641)*

Canalta Enterprises LLC....................... E 919 615-1570
  Raleigh *(G-9965)*

Composite Factory LLC......................... F 484 264-3306
  Mooresville *(G-8642)*

Concept Steel Inc.................................. E 704 874-0414
  Gastonia *(G-5026)*

Custom Design Inc................................ G 704 637-7110
  Salisbury *(G-11041)*

Dave Steel Company Inc........................ D 828 252-2771
  Asheville *(G-484)*

Davis Steel and Iron Co Inc.................. E 704 821-7676
  Matthews *(G-8165)*

Dwiggins Metal Masters Inc .... G 336 751-2379
  Mocksville *(G-8360)*

Eland Industries Inc.............................. E 910 304-5353
  Hampstead *(G-6071)*

Freedom Industries Inc......................... C 252 984-0007
  Rocky Mount *(G-10839)*

Gastonia Ornamental Wldg Inc.............. F 704 827-1146
  Mount Holly *(G-9232)*

Gerdau Ameristeel US Inc..................... E 919 833-9737
  Raleigh *(G-10131)*

Gulfstream Steel & Supply Inc.............. E 910 329-5100
  Holly Ridge *(G-6888)*

Ifab Corp.. F 704 864-3032
  Gastonia *(G-5061)*

J F Fabricators LLC............................... G 704 454-7224
  Harrisburg *(G-6110)*

Keypoint LLC... F 704 962-8110
  Waxhaw *(G-12434)*

Kontek Industries Inc............................ F 704 273-5040
  Kannapolis *(G-7214)*

Low Country Steel SC LLC.................... E 336 283-9611
  Winston Salem *(G-13239)*

Lowder Steel Inc................................... E 336 431-9000
  Archdale *(G-238)*

Mechanical Spc Contrs Inc.................... D 919 829-9300
  Raleigh *(G-10287)*

Paul Charles Englert.............................. G 704 824-2102
  Gastonia *(G-5118)*

Protech Metals LLC............................... F 910 295-6905
  Pinehurst *(G-9701)*

Simpson Strong-Tie Company Inc.......... G 336 841-1338
  High Point *(G-6776)*

Steel Smart Incorporated...................... E 919 736-0681
  Pikeville *(G-9668)*

Steelfab Inc.. B 704 394-5376
  Charlotte *(G-2864)*

Steelfab of Virginia Inc........................ E 919 828-9545
  Raleigh *(G-10507)*

Umi Company Inc.................................. G 704 479-6210
  Lincolnton *(G-7867)*

Underbrinks LLC................................... G 866 495-4465
  Salisbury *(G-11131)*

Universal Steel NC LLC......................... E 336 476-3105
  Thomasville *(G-12085)*

3451 Screw machine products

Abbott Products Inc.............................. E 336 463-3135
  Yadkinville *(G-13434)*

Accuking Inc... G 252 649-2323
  New Bern *(G-9330)*

Angels Path Ventures Inc...................... E 828 654-9530
  Arden *(G-251)*

B & Y Machining Co Inc......................... E 252 235-2180
  Bailey *(G-668)*

Barefoot Cnc Inc.................................., G 828 438-5038
  Morganton *(G-8852)*

Black Mtn Mch Fabrication Inc.............. E 828 669-9557
  Black Mountain *(G-862)*

Bravo Team LLC................................... E 704 309-1918
  Mooresville *(G-8621)*

Carolina Screw Products........................ G 336 760-7400
  Winston Salem *(G-13119)*

Conner Brothers Machine Co Inc........... D 704 864-6084
  Bessemer City *(G-809)*

Curtis L Maclean L C............................ C 704 940-5531
  Mooresville *(G-8646)*

Edward Heil Screw Products.................. G 828 345-6140
  Conover *(G-3517)*

Ellison Technologies Inc........................ D 704 545-7362
  Charlotte *(G-2103)*

Gamma Technologies Inc....................... G 919 319-5272
  Morrisville *(G-8980)*

Gary J Younts Machine Company.......... F 336 476-7930
  Thomasville *(G-12028)*

Griffiths Corporation............................. D 704 554-5657
  Pineville *(G-9732)*

▲ IMS Usa LLC...................................... G 910 796-2040
  Wilmington *(G-12815)*

Manufacturing Services Inc .... E 704 629-4163
  Bessemer City *(G-826)*

Mw Industries Inc................................. E 704 837-0331
  Charlotte *(G-2538)*

West Side Industries LLC...................... G 980 223-8665
  Statesville *(G-11799)*

3452 Bolts, nuts, rivets, and washers

▲ Avdel USA LLC................................... E 704 888-7100
  Stanfield *(G-11603)*

Belwith Products LLC............................ G 336 841-3899
  High Point *(G-6545)*

▲ C E Smith Co Inc............................... E 336 273-0166
  Greensboro *(G-5416)*

Cardinal America Inc.............................G..... 704 810-1620
Statesville *(G-11675)*

Derita Precision Mch Co Inc...................F..... 704 392-7285
Charlotte *(G-2034)*

Gesipa Fasteners Usa Inc.......................E..... 336 751-1555
Mocksville *(G-8367)*

Lightning Bolt Ink LLC...........................G..... 828 281-1274
Asheville *(G-536)*

Magnum Manufacturing LLC...................F..... 704 983-1340
New London *(G-9419)*

Masonite Corporation............................A..... 704 599-0235
Charlotte *(G-2466)*

McJast Inc...F..... 828 884-4809
Pisgah Forest *(G-9771)*

Moore S Welding Service Inc..................G..... 919 837-5769
Bear Creek *(G-716)*

◆ Pan American Screw LLC....................D..... 828 466-0060
Conover *(G-3543)*

Stanley Black & Decker Inc....................C..... 704 789-7000
Concord *(G-3446)*

3462 Iron and steel forgings

Altra Industrial Motion Corp...................C..... 704 588-5610
Charlotte *(G-1657)*

Artistic Ironworks LLC............................G..... 919 908-6888
Durham *(G-3900)*

Authentic Iron LLC................................G..... 910 648-6989
Bladenboro *(G-873)*

Blue Horseshoe....................................G..... 980 312-8202
Charlotte *(G-1790)*

Carroll Co..F..... 919 779-1900
Garner *(G-4920)*

Chatham Steel Corporation.....................E..... 912 233-4182
Durham *(G-3970)*

Consolidated Pipe & Sup Co Inc.............F..... 336 294-8577
Greensboro *(G-5463)*

◆ GKN Driveline Newton LLC..................A..... 828 428-3711
Newton *(G-9466)*

H Horseshoe..G..... 336 853-5913
Lexington *(G-7695)*

▲ Ketchie-Houston Inc..........................E..... 704 786-5101
Concord *(G-3390)*

▲ Liechti America................................G..... 704 948-1277
Huntersville *(G-7011)*

▲ Linamar Forgings Carolina Inc............D..... 252 237-8181
Wilson *(G-13003)*

Minute-Man Products Inc.......................E..... 828 692-0256
East Flat Rock *(G-4333)*

Pierce Farrier Supply Inc........................G..... 704 753-4358
Indian Trail *(G-7095)*

Roush & Yates Racing Engs LLC.............D..... 704 799-6216
Mooresville *(G-8762)*

▲ Roush & Yates Racing Engs LLC.........C..... 704 799-6216
Mooresville *(G-8763)*

S Duff Fabricating Inc.............................G..... 910 298-3060
Beulaville *(G-845)*

Sona Autocomp USA LLC.......................C..... 919 965-5555
Selma *(G-11291)*

◆ Sona Blw Precision Forge Inc..............C..... 919 828-3375
Selma *(G-11292)*

◆ Tim Conner Enterprises Inc.................E..... 704 629-4327
Bessemer City *(G-835)*

Victory 1 Performance Inc.......................F..... 704 799-1955
Mooresville *(G-8791)*

Volvo Motor Graders Inc.........................G..... 704 609-3604
Charlotte *(G-2990)*

Yates Precision Machining LLC................G..... 704 662-7165
Mooresville *(G-8802)*

3463 Nonferrous forgings

ABB Motors and Mechanical Inc.............C..... 828 645-1706
Weaverville *(G-12481)*

Accudyne Industries LLC........................A..... 469 518-4777
Davidson *(G-3697)*

Entrust Services LLC..............................F..... 336 274-5175
Greensboro *(G-5523)*

GKN Driveline North Amer Inc.................C..... 919 708-4500
Sanford *(G-11184)*

3465 Automotive stampings

AMF-NC Enterprise Company LLC...........F..... 704 489-2206
Denver *(G-3769)*

Belwith Products LLC.............................G..... 336 841-3899
High Point *(G-6545)*

▲ Borgwarner Turbo Systems LLC..........D..... 828 684-4000
Arden *(G-258)*

Continental Auto Systems Inc..................B..... 828 654-2000
Fletcher *(G-4731)*

Dutch Miller Charlotte Inc.......................F..... 704 522-8422
Charlotte *(G-2070)*

Gray Manufacturing Tech LLC.................F..... 704 489-2206
Denver *(G-3785)*

Harrah Enterprise Ltd.............................G..... 336 253-3963
Cornelius *(G-3605)*

▲ Irvan-Smith Inc................................F..... 704 788-2554
Concord *(G-3382)*

Performance Entps & Parts Inc................G..... 336 621-6572
Greensboro *(G-5738)*

Revmax Performance LLC.......................F..... 877 780-4334
Charlotte *(G-2717)*

Revolution Pd LLC.................................G..... 919 949-0241
Pittsboro *(G-9788)*

Vibration Solutions LLC..........................G..... 704 896-7535
Charlotte *(G-2983)*

3466 Crowns and closures

◆ Assa Abloy ACC Door Cntrls Gro.........C..... 877 974-2255
Monroe *(G-8432)*

3469 Metal stampings, nec

ABT Manufacturing LLC..........................E..... 704 847-9188
Statesville *(G-11645)*

Acme Aerofab LLC.................................G..... 704 806-3582
Charlotte *(G-1618)*

Alleghany Garbage Service Inc................G..... 336 372-4413
Sparta *(G-11533)*

Allied Tool and Machine Co.....................G..... 336 993-2131
Kernersville *(G-7240)*

Allred Metal Stamping Works Inc.............E..... 336 886-5221
High Point *(G-6517)*

Ashdan Enterprises................................G..... 336 375-9698
Greensboro *(G-5372)*

Atlantic Tool & Die Co Inc.......................G..... 910 270-2888
Hampstead *(G-6068)*

Belwith Products LLC.............................G..... 336 841-3899
High Point *(G-6545)*

Bnp Inc..F..... 919 775-7070
Sanford *(G-11157)*

Border Concepts Inc..............................G..... 336 248-2419
Lexington *(G-7660)*

Burris Machine Company Inc...................G..... 828 322-6914
Hickory *(G-6277)*

C E Smith Co Inc...................................E..... 336 273-0166
Greensboro *(G-5415)*

▲ C E Smith Co Inc..............................E..... 336 273-0166
Greensboro *(G-5416)*

Carolina Metals Inc...............................F..... 828 667-0876
Asheville *(G-470)*

Carolina Stamping Company....................D..... 704 637-0260
Salisbury *(G-11030)*

◆ Ceramco Incorporated.......................E..... 704 588-4814
Charlotte *(G-1889)*

City of Graham......................................F..... 336 570-6811
Graham *(G-5264)*

CMS Tool and Die Inc.............................F..... 910 458-3322
Carolina Beach *(G-1260)*

Col-Eve Metal Products Co......................G..... 336 472-7039
Lexington *(G-7667)*

Component Sourcing Intl LLC...................E..... 704 843-9292
Charlotte *(G-1967)*

▲ Custom Cnverting Solutions Inc...........E..... 336 292-2616
Greensboro *(G-5480)*

Derita Precision Mch Co Inc.....................F..... 704 392-7285
Charlotte *(G-2034)*

Dynamic Stampings NC Inc......................G..... 704 509-2501
Gastonia *(G-5044)*

Erdle Perforating Holdings Inc..................F..... 704 588-4380
Charlotte *(G-2126)*

▼ Friedrich Metal Pdts Co Inc.................E..... 336 375-3067
Browns Summit *(G-993)*

Furniture At Work.................................G..... 336 472-6619
Trinity *(G-12114)*

Gerald Hartsoe.....................................G..... 336 498-3233
Randleman *(G-10648)*

GKN Driveline North Amer Inc..................C..... 919 708-4500
Sanford *(G-11184)*

Gold Medal North Carolina II....................G..... 336 665-4997
Greensboro *(G-5567)*

Griffiths Corporation..............................D..... 704 552-6793
Pineville *(G-9731)*

Griffiths Corporation..............................D..... 704 554-5657
Pineville *(G-9732)*

Henry & Rye Incorporated.......................G..... 919 365-7045
Wendell *(G-12537)*

▲ Hi-Tech Fabrication Inc.......................C..... 919 781-6150
Raleigh *(G-10166)*

▲ Home Impressions Inc........................B..... 828 328-1142
Hickory *(G-6362)*

▲ Hunt Country Component LLC..............G..... 336 475-7000
Thomasville *(G-12034)*

Innovative Mfg Solutions Inc....................G..... 919 219-2424
Apex *(G-170)*

▲ Interactive Safety Pdts Inc..................G..... 704 664-7377
Huntersville *(G-7002)*

Iv-S Metal Stamping Inc.........................E..... 336 861-2100
Archdale *(G-229)*

Jacob Holtz Company LLC.......................E..... 828 328-1003
Hickory *(G-6373)*

◆ K & S Tool & Manufacturing Co............E..... 336 410-7260
High Point *(G-6681)*

◆ Kessebohmer USA Inc.......................F..... 910 338-5080
Wilmington *(G-12828)*

Leesona Corp.......................................E..... 336 226-5511
Burlington *(G-1118)*

License Plate Agency.............................G..... 910 763-7076
Wilmington *(G-12835)*

Lidseen North Carolina Inc......................G..... 828 389-8082
Hayesville *(G-6142)*

▲ M-B Industries Inc.............................C..... 828 862-4201
Rosman *(G-10913)*

Mac/Fab Company Inc............................E..... 704 822-1103
Mount Holly *(G-9236)*

Matt Bieneman Enterprises LLC...............G..... 704 856-0200
Mooresville *(G-8720)*

McJast Inc..F..... 828 884-4809
Pisgah Forest *(G-9771)*

Metal Works High Point Inc......................D..... 336 886-4612
High Point *(G-6709)*

Metalfab of North Carolina LLC.................C..... 704 841-1090
Matthews *(G-8132)*

▲ Moores Mch Co Fayetteville Inc............D..... 919 837-5354
Bear Creek *(G-717)*

NC License Plate Agency.........................G..... 910 347-1000
Jacksonville *(G-7134)*

NC Motor Vhcl Lcnse Plate Agcy..............G..... 336 228-7152
Burlington *(G-1136)*

New Can Company Inc..............G 704 853-3711
Gastonia *(G-5108)*

New Standard Corporation..............C 252 446-5481
Rocky Mount *(G-10854)*

North Carolina Dept Trnsp..............E 704 633-5873
Salisbury *(G-11098)*

North Crlina Lcense Plate Agcy..............G 910 485-1590
Fayetteville *(G-4646)*

Parker Industries Inc..............D 828 437-7779
Connelly Springs *(G-3481)*

Precision Partners LLC..............E 800 545-3121
Charlotte *(G-2658)*

Precision Stampers Inc..............G 919 366-3333
Wendell *(G-12541)*

Precision Tool & Stamping Inc..............E 910 592-0174
Clinton *(G-3239)*

Protocase Mfg Usa Inc..............E 866 849-3911
Wilmington *(G-12892)*

Rfr Metal Fabrication Inc..............D 919 693-1354
Oxford *(G-9631)*

▲ Select Stainless Products LLC..............G 888 843-2345
Charlotte *(G-2783)*

Singer Equipment Company Inc..............E 910 484-1128
Fayetteville *(G-4671)*

▲ Smart Machine Technologies Inc..............D 276 632-9853
Greensboro *(G-5817)*

SMC Holdco Inc..............C 910 844-3956
Laurinburg *(G-7515)*

Southern Spring & Stamping..............F 336 548-3520
Stokesdale *(G-11815)*

Spruce Pine Mica Company..............F 828 765-4241
Spruce Pine *(G-11589)*

Stroup Machine & Mfg Inc..............G 704 394-0023
Charlotte *(G-2873)*

Team 21st..............G 910 826-3676
Fayetteville *(G-4679)*

Thompson & Little Inc..............E 910 484-1128
Fayetteville *(G-4680)*

Toner Machining Tech Inc..............D 828 432-8007
Morganton *(G-8905)*

Toolcraft Inc North Carolina..............F 828 659-7379
Marion *(G-8070)*

◆ Toter LLC..............E 800 424-0422
Statesville *(G-11792)*

Umi Company Inc..............G 704 479-6210
Lincolnton *(G-7867)*

United TI & Stamping Co NC Inc..............D 910 323-8588
Fayetteville *(G-4687)*

◆ Vrush Industries Inc..............G 336 886-7700
High Point *(G-6829)*

Wolverine Mtal Stmping Sltons..............F 919 774-4729
Sanford *(G-11253)*

Youngs Welding & Machine Svcs..............G 910 488-1190
Fayetteville *(G-4702)*

3471 Plating and polishing

Advanced Motor Sports Coatings..............G 336 472-5518
Thomasville *(G-11990)*

Advanced Plating Technologies..............G 704 291-9325
Monroe *(G-8418)*

Advplating LLC..............G 704 291-9325
Monroe *(G-8419)*

Allied Metal Finishing Inc..............G 704 347-1477
Charlotte *(G-1644)*

Amplate Inc..............E 704 607-0191
Charlotte *(G-1672)*

Asheville Metal Finishing Inc..............E 828 253-1476
Asheville *(G-439)*

Blue Ridge Plating Company..............G 828 274-1795
Hendersonville *(G-6188)*

C & R Hard Chrome Service Inc..............G 704 861-8831
Gastonia *(G-5009)*

Capitol Bumper..............G 919 772-7330
Fayetteville *(G-4568)*

Capitol Bumper..............G 919 772-7330
Fayetteville *(G-4567)*

Carolina Finshg & Coating Inc..............F 704 730-8233
Kings Mountain *(G-7355)*

Champion Enterprises LLC..............E 704 866-8148
Gastonia *(G-5017)*

Charlotte Metal Finishing Inc..............F 704 732-7570
Lincolnton *(G-7821)*

Charlotte Plating Inc..............G 704 552-2100
Charlotte *(G-1903)*

Custom Metal Finishing..............G 704 445-1710
Cherryville *(G-3062)*

Dave Steel Company Inc..............D 828 252-2771
Asheville *(G-484)*

Fairmont Metal Finishing Inc..............G 336 434-4188
Archdale *(G-220)*

H & H Polishing Inc..............F 704 393-8728
Charlotte *(G-2245)*

Hardcoatings Inc..............F 704 377-2996
Charlotte *(G-2256)*

Hi-TEC Plating Inc..............F 704 872-8969
Statesville *(G-11711)*

▲ Hi-Tech Fabrication Inc..............C 919 781-6150
Raleigh *(G-10166)*

Industrial Anodizing..............G 336 434-2110
Trinity *(G-12116)*

Industrial Elcpltg Co Inc..............G 704 867-4547
Gastonia *(G-5063)*

Industrial Elcpltg Co Inc..............D 704 867-4547
Gastonia *(G-5064)*

▲ Kayne & Son Custom Hdwr Inc..............G 828 665-1988
Candler *(G-1228)*

◆ Kings Mountain Intl Inc..............D 704 739-4227
Kings Mountain *(G-7369)*

L F T Inc..............G 828 253-6830
Asheville *(G-532)*

▲ Master Form Inc..............G 704 292-1041
Matthews *(G-8182)*

Nb Corporation..............F 336 852-8786
Greensboro *(G-5705)*

Nb Corporation..............E 336 274-7654
Greensboro *(G-5706)*

Parker Metal Finishing Company..............G 336 275-9657
Greensboro *(G-5733)*

Phillips Plating Co Inc..............G 252 637-2695
Bridgeton *(G-985)*

Piedmont Plating Corporation..............E 336 272-2311
Greensboro *(G-5745)*

Precision Alloys Inc..............G 919 231-6329
Raleigh *(G-10389)*

Precision Metal Finishing Inc..............G 704 799-0250
Mooresville *(G-8754)*

Prince Group LLC..............D 828 681-8860
Mills River *(G-8319)*

Rodeco Company..............F 919 775-7149
Sanford *(G-11225)*

▼ Short Run Pro LLC..............F 704 825-1599
Belmont *(G-765)*

Sterling Rack Inc..............G 704 866-9131
Gastonia *(G-5144)*

Stratford Metalfinishing Inc..............E 336 723-7946
Winston Salem *(G-13346)*

Surtronics Inc..............E 919 834-8027
Raleigh *(G-10524)*

Te Connectivity Corporation..............C 336 665-4400
Greensboro *(G-5857)*

Tico Polishing..............G 704 788-2466
Concord *(G-3458)*

Triad Anodizing & Plating Inc..............G 336 292-7028
Greensboro *(G-5874)*

United Mtal Fnshg Inc Grnsboro..............G 336 272-8107
Greensboro *(G-5891)*

United TI & Stamping Co NC Inc..............D 910 323-8588
Fayetteville *(G-4687)*

Universal Black Oxide Inc..............G 704 867-1772
Gastonia *(G-5160)*

Williams Plating Company Inc..............F 828 681-0301
Arden *(G-318)*

▲ Xceldyne Group LLC..............D 336 472-2242
Thomasville *(G-12093)*

Yontz & Sons Painting Inc..............G 336 784-7099
Winston Salem *(G-13409)*

3479 Metal coating and allied services

A-1 Coatings..............G 704 790-9528
Salisbury *(G-11010)*

Abcor Supply Inc..............F 919 468-0856
Chapel Hill *(G-1523)*

Acme Nameplate & Mfg Inc..............G 704 283-8175
Monroe *(G-8416)*

Anatech Ltd..............F 704 489-1488
Denver *(G-3770)*

Area 51 Powder Coating Inc..............G 910 769-1724
Wilmington *(G-12706)*

As Inc..............G 704 225-1700
Monroe *(G-8430)*

Auto Parts Fayetteville LLC..............G 910 889-4026
Fayetteville *(G-4555)*

Boyd Gmn Inc..............C 206 284-2200
Monroe *(G-8446)*

C&V Powder Coating..............G 910 228-1173
Leland *(G-7536)*

Calico Technologies Inc..............E 704 483-2202
Denver *(G-3777)*

Carolina Coastal Coatings..............F 910 346-9607
Jacksonville *(G-7120)*

Carolina Coastal Coatings Inc..............F 910 346-9607
Maple Hill *(G-8025)*

Cincinnati Thermal Spray Inc..............E 910 675-2909
Rocky Point *(G-10878)*

Coating Concepts Inc..............G 704 391-0499
Charlotte *(G-1941)*

Coatings Technologies Inc..............G 704 821-8231
Indian Trail *(G-7074)*

CRC..............G 704 664-1242
Mooresville *(G-8644)*

Crown Trophy Inc..............G 336 851-1011
Greensboro *(G-5474)*

Dj Powdercoating Ironwork LLC..............G 336 310-4725
Kernersville *(G-7267)*

Dotson Metal Finishing Inc..............F 828 298-9844
Asheville *(G-489)*

Eric Arnold Klein..............F 828 464-0001
Newton *(G-9464)*

Exotics Power Coat..............G 336 831-3865
Kernersville *(G-7273)*

◆ Galvan Industries Inc..............C 704 455-5102
Harrisburg *(G-6108)*

Galvanizing Consultants Inc..............G 336 603-4218
Whitsett *(G-12607)*

Greg Price..............G 847 778-4426
Hampstead *(G-6073)*

▲ H M Elliott Inc..............G 704 663-8226
Mooresville *(G-8678)*

Hemco Wire Products Inc..............G 336 454-7280
Jamestown *(G-7164)*

▲ Hi-Tech Fabrication Inc..............C 919 781-6150
Raleigh *(G-10166)*

Hot Box Power Coating Inc..............G 704 398-8224
Charlotte *(G-2289)*

Jimmys Coating Unlimited Inc..............G 704 915-2420
Gastonia *(G-5072)*

Kelleys Sports and Awards Inc............ G 828 728-4600
  Hudson (G-6952)

Landmark Coatings LLC...................... G 336 492-2492
  Mocksville (G-8373)

Made By Custom LLC.......................... G 704 980-9840
  Charlotte (G-2447)

NC Graphic Pros LLC.......................... G 252 492-7326
  Kittrell (G-7442)

Oerlikon Metco (us) Inc...................... F 713 715-6300
  Huntersville (G-7028)

Overwith Inc....................................... G 704 866-8148
  Gastonia (G-5114)

Pages Hydro Dipping Coatings.............. G 910 322-2077
  Linden (G-7875)

Piedmont Lminating Coating Inc.......... F 336 272-1600
  Greensboro (G-5743)

Powder Coat USA............................... G 919 954-7170
  Raleigh (G-10378)

Powder Coating By 3 S X..................... G 704 784-3724
  Concord (G-3420)

Powder Coating Services Inc............... E 704 349-4100
  Gastonia (G-5122)

Powder Works Inc.............................. G 336 475-7715
  Thomasville (G-12061)

Powdertek.. G 828 225-3250
  Arden (G-297)

Premier Powder Coating Inc................ G 336 672-3828
  Asheboro (G-385)

Prime Coatings LLC........................... G 828 855-1136
  Hickory (G-6416)

Prince Group LLC............................... D 828 681-8860
  Mills River (G-8319)

Prince Manufacturing Corp.................. C 828 681-8860
  Mills River (G-8320)

Procoaters Inc.................................. F 336 992-0012
  Kernersville (G-7294)

Product Identification Inc.................. E 919 544-4136
  Durham (G-4197)

Professional Laminating LLC............... G 919 465-0400
  Cary (G-1430)

Protech Metals LLC........................... F 910 295-6905
  Pinehurst (G-9701)

Purthermal LLC................................. G 828 855-0108
  Hickory (G-6422)

Quad City High Prfmce Coatings......... G 937 623-2282
  Leland (G-7557)

R & R Powder Coating Inc................... F 704 853-0727
  Dallas (G-3684)

Raleigh Powder Coating Co................. G 919 301-8065
  Raleigh (G-10426)

Randolph Machine Inc........................ G 336 799-1039
  Randleman (G-10657)

RPM Indstrial Ctings Group Inc........... C 828 261-0325
  Hickory (G-6434)

RPM Indstrial Ctings Group Inc........... C 828 728-8266
  Hudson (G-6957)

Russell T Bundy Associates Inc........... F 704 523-6132
  Charlotte (G-2743)

South Atlantic LLC............................. F 336 376-0410
  Graham (G-5286)

◆ South Atlantic LLC.......................... F 910 332-1900
  Wilmington (G-12923)

Strobels Supply Inc........................... F 607 324-1721
  Linwood (G-7881)

Structral Catings Hertford LLC............ F 919 553-3034
  Cofield (G-3270)

Superior Powder Coating LLC.............. G 704 869-0004
  Gastonia (G-5148)

Tactical Coatings Inc......................... G 704 692-4511
  Shelby (G-11384)

▲ TEC Coat....................................... E 412 215-0152
  Charlotte (G-2903)

Tpt Coating Inc................................. G 919 479-0758
  Chapel Hill (G-1577)

Triangle Coatings Inc......................... G 919 781-6108
  Morrisville (G-9075)

▲ Turbocoating Corp.......................... E 828 328-8726
  Hickory (G-6476)

Ultra Coatings Incorporated............... F 336 883-8853
  High Point (G-6817)

United TI & Stamping Co NC Inc........... D 910 323-8588
  Fayetteville (G-4687)

Universal Black Oxide Inc................... G 704 867-1772
  Gastonia (G-5160)

Waste Container Repair Svcs............... G 910 257-4474
  Fayetteville (G-4696)

Weapon Works LLC............................ G 800 556-9498
  Burlington (G-1177)

Weapon Works LLC............................ G 800 556-9498
  Burlington (G-1176)

3482 Small arms ammunition

Every Day Carry LLc.......................... F 203 231-0256
  Winnabow (G-13065)

Global Synergy Group Inc................... G 704 254-9886
  Matthews (G-8172)

North American Trade LLC.................. G 828 712-3004
  Fletcher (G-4759)

R & S Precision Customs LLC.............. G 704 984-3480
  Albemarle (G-86)

Riley Defense Inc.............................. G 704 507-9224
  Hickory (G-6429)

Sirius Tactical Entps LLC.................... G 704 256-3660
  Waxhaw (G-12441)

▲ Stillwood Ammun Systems LLC.......... G 919 721-9096
  Burlington (G-1165)

3483 Ammunition, except for small arms, nec

Custom Armor Group Inc..................... G 336 617-4667
  Greensboro (G-5479)

Gitsum Precision LLC......................... G 336 453-3998
  Stoneville (G-11821)

North American Trade LLC.................. G 828 712-3004
  Fletcher (G-4759)

War Sport LLC.................................. G 910 948-2237
  Eagle Springs (G-4320)

3484 Small arms

Aboard Trade LLC............................. G 919 341-7045
  Southport (G-11515)

◆ Alotech Inc.................................... E 919 774-1297
  Goldston (G-5255)

Arisaka LLC..................................... F 919 601-5625
  Apex (G-139)

Bachstein Consulting LLC................... G 410 322-4917
  Youngsville (G-13463)

Every Day Carry LLc.......................... F 203 231-0256
  Winnabow (G-13065)

Gitsum Precision LLC......................... G 336 453-3998
  Stoneville (G-11821)

Grip Pod Systems Intl LLC.................. G 239 233-3694
  Raleigh (G-10149)

Kart Precision Barrel Corp.................. G 910 754-5212
  Shallotte (G-11303)

Manroy Usa LLC............................... G 828 286-9274
  Spindale (G-11548)

Microtech Defense Inds Inc................. G 828 684-4355
  Fletcher (G-4756)

Remington Arms Company LLC............. C 800 544-8892
  Madison (G-7998)

Remington Arms Company LLC............. C 800 544-8892
  Madison (G-7999)

Riley Defense Inc.............................. G 704 507-9224
  Hickory (G-6429)

Sand Hammer Forging Inc................... G 919 554-9554
  Youngsville (G-13484)

Urban Tactical and Cstm Armory.......... G 252 686-0122
  Kinston (G-7433)

US Arms & Ammunition LLC................. G 252 652-7400
  New Bern (G-9404)

Weapon Works LLC............................ G 800 556-9498
  Burlington (G-1177)

Weapon Works LLC............................ G 800 556-9498
  Burlington (G-1176)

3489 Ordnance and accessories, nec

Advanced Non-Lethal Tech Inc............ G 847 812-6450
  Raleigh (G-9880)

Agile Ventures LLC............................ G 202 716-7958
  East Flat Rock (G-4328)

Backwater Guns LLC.......................... G 910 399-1451
  Wilmington (G-12718)

Bear Creek Arsenal LLC..................... C 919 292-6000
  Sanford (G-11154)

Hsg LLC... D 910 325-1000
  Swansboro (G-11886)

James Bunn..................................... G 252 293-4867
  Wilson (G-12995)

Loading Republic Inc......................... G 704 561-1077
  Concord (G-3395)

Sturm Ruger & Company Inc............... B 336 427-0286
  Mayodan (G-8209)

3491 Industrial valves

ADC Industries Inc............................ G 919 550-9515
  Clayton (G-3130)

▲ Bonomi North America Inc................ F 704 412-9031
  Charlotte (G-1798)

▲ Brasscraft.................................... C 336 475-2131
  Thomasville (G-11997)

Burkert USA Corporation.................... C 800 325-1405
  Huntersville (G-6974)

▲ Carolina Conveying Inc.................... G 828 235-1005
  Canton (G-1248)

Celeros Flow Technology LLC.............. C 704 752-3100
  Charlotte (G-1883)

Circor Pumps North America LLC......... C 877 853-7867
  Monroe (G-8460)

Curtiss-Wright Corporation................. G 973 541-3700
  Charlotte (G-2006)

Curtiss-Wright Corporation................. G 704 869-4675
  Charlotte (G-2007)

Curtiss-Wright Corporation................. F 704 481-1150
  Shelby (G-11327)

Curtiss-Wright Corporation................. B 704 869-4600
  Davidson (G-3700)

Eizi Group Llc.................................. G 919 397-3638
  Raleigh (G-10080)

◆ Emco Wheaton Retail Corp.............. D 252 243-0150
  Wilson (G-12987)

Engineered Controls Intl LLC.............. C 336 226-3244
  Burlington (G-1088)

Engineered Controls Intl LLC.............. C 828 466-2153
  Conover (G-3519)

Engineered Controls Intl LLC.............. C 336 449-7706
  Whitsett (G-12605)

▲ Engineered Controls Intl LLC........... C 336 449-7707
  Elon (G-4469)

Engineering Mfg Svcs Co..................... F 704 821-7325
  Monroe (G-8483)

Equilibar LLC................................... E 828 650-6590
  Fletcher (G-4734)

▲ General Control Equipment Co.......... F 704 588-0484
  Charlotte (G-2199)

◆ Hayward Industrial Products............. C 704 837-8002
  Charlotte (G-2264)

S
I
C

Hersey Meters Co LLC .... G 704 278-2221
Cleveland *(G-3214)*

▲ Huber Technology Inc .... E 704 949-1010
Denver *(G-3788)*

▲ Key Gas Components Inc .... E 828 655-1700
Marion *(G-8048)*

▲ Mpv Mrgnton Prssure Vssels NC ...... C 828 652-3704
Marion *(G-8057)*

◆ Mueller Steam Specialty .... D 910 865-8241
Saint Pauls *(G-11005)*

Parker-Hannifin Corporation .... D 828 245-3233
Forest City *(G-4795)*

▲ Robert H Wager Company Inc .... F 336 969-6909
Rural Hall *(G-10966)*

Romac Industries Inc .... D 704 922-9595
Dallas *(G-3687)*

Romac Industries Inc .... D 704 915-3317
Dallas *(G-3688)*

Sensus USA Inc .... C 919 576-6185
Morrisville *(G-9052)*

◆ Sensus USA Inc .... E 919 845-4000
Morrisville *(G-9051)*

▲ Spanglercv Inc .... G 910 794-5547
Wilmington *(G-12928)*

SPX Flow Inc .... C 704 752-4400
Charlotte *(G-2847)*

▲ Tvl International LLC .... G 704 814-0930
Matthews *(G-8155)*

▲ United Brass Works Inc .... C 336 498-2661
Randleman *(G-10663)*

US Valve Corporation .... G 910 799-9913
Wilmington *(G-12944)*

Watts Regulator Co .... A 828 286-4151
Spindale *(G-11550)*

Zurn Elkay Wtr Solutions Corp .... G 910 501-1853
Lumberton *(G-7978)*

Zurn Elkay Wtr Solutions Corp .... F 855 663-9876
Sanford *(G-11256)*

3492 Fluid power valves and hose fittings

Anchor Coupling Inc .... B 919 739-8000
Goldsboro *(G-5198)*

Bulldog Hose Company LLC .... E 919 639-6151
Angier *(G-114)*

Carolina Components Group Inc .... E 919 635-8438
Durham *(G-3960)*

Carolina Rubber & Spc Inc .... G 336 744-5111
Winston Salem *(G-13118)*

Cross Technologies Inc .... G 336 370-4673
Greensboro *(G-5473)*

Cross Technologies Inc .... D 336 292-0511
Whitsett *(G-12603)*

Cross Technologies Inc .... E 800 327-7727
Greensboro *(G-5472)*

▲ Custom Hydraulics & Design .... F 704 347-0023
Cherryville *(G-3061)*

▲ Deetag USA Inc .... G 828 465-2644
Conover *(G-3514)*

Dickie Jones .... G 828 733-5084
Newland *(G-9428)*

▲ Dixon Valve & Coupling Co LLC .... F 704 334-9175
Dallas *(G-3668)*

Eagle Assembly Unlimited Inc .... G 252 462-0408
Castalia *(G-1492)*

Eaton Corporation .... D 828 286-4157
Forest City *(G-4788)*

Engineered Controls Intl LLC .... C 828 466-2153
Conover *(G-3519)*

▲ Flo-Tite Inc Valves & Contrls .... E 910 738-8904
Lumberton *(G-7955)*

▼ George W Dahl Company Inc .... E 336 668-4444
Greensboro *(G-5557)*

◆ Hayward Industrial Products .... C 704 837-8002
Charlotte *(G-2264)*

Hydac Technology Corp .... D 610 266-0100
Denver *(G-3789)*

Hydraulic Hose Depot Inc .... G 252 356-1862
Cofield *(G-3267)*

Logic Hydraulic Controls Inc .... E 910 791-9293
Wilmington *(G-12838)*

McC Holdings Inc .... C 828 724-4000
Marion *(G-8052)*

Metrohose Incorporated .... G 252 329-9891
Greenville *(G-6004)*

On-Site Hose Inc .... G 919 303-3840
Apex *(G-183)*

Polyhose Incorporated .... E 732 512-9141
Wilmington *(G-12881)*

Romac Industries Inc .... D 704 915-3317
Dallas *(G-3688)*

SCI Sharp Controls Inc .... G 704 394-1395
Pineville *(G-9755)*

▲ Stanadyne Intrmdate Hldngs LLC ..... C 860 525-0821
Jacksonville *(G-7152)*

Talladega Mchy & Sup Co NC .... G 256 362-4124
Fayetteville *(G-4677)*

▲ Wandfluh of America Inc .... F 847 566-5700
Charlotte *(G-3003)*

3493 Steel springs, except wire

Bridgestone Americas Inc .... C 984 888-0413
Durham *(G-3940)*

Lee Spring Company LLC .... E 336 275-3631
Greensboro *(G-5659)*

Matthew Warren Inc .... E
Charlotte *(G-2470)*

Southern ATL Spring Mfg Sls LL .... E 704 279-1331
Granite Quarry *(G-5328)*

◆ Stabilus Inc .... D 704 865-7444
Gastonia *(G-5141)*

Stable Holdco Inc .... B 704 866-7140
Gastonia *(G-5142)*

3494 Valves and pipe fittings, nec

◆ Aalberts Integrated Pipin .... E 704 841-6000
Charlotte *(G-1608)*

▲ American Valve Inc .... D 336 668-0554
Greensboro *(G-5358)*

Appalachian Pipe Distrs LLC .... G 704 688-5703
Charlotte *(G-1684)*

Atlantic Tube & Fitting LLC .... G 704 545-6166
Mint Hill *(G-8330)*

▲ Bonomi North America Inc .... F 704 412-9031
Charlotte *(G-1798)*

◆ Controls Southeast Inc .... C 704 644-5000
Pineville *(G-9721)*

◆ Emco Wheaton Retail Corp .... D 252 243-0150
Wilson *(G-12987)*

Engineered Controls Intl LLC .... C 336 226-3244
Burlington *(G-1088)*

Engineered Controls Intl LLC .... C 828 466-2153
Conover *(G-3519)*

Engineered Controls Intl LLC .... C 336 449-7706
Whitsett *(G-12605)*

General Refrigeration Company .... G 919 661-4727
Garner *(G-4929)*

◆ Hayward Industrial Products .... C 704 837-8002
Charlotte *(G-2264)*

Hayward Industries Inc .... D 336 712-9900
Clemmons *(G-3188)*

◆ Hayward Industries Inc .... B 704 837-8002
Charlotte *(G-2265)*

James M Pleasants Company Inc .... F 888 902-8324
Greensboro *(G-5634)*

James M Pleasants Company Inc .... E 800 365-9010
Greensboro *(G-5633)*

▲ Key Gas Components Inc .... E 828 655-1700
Marion *(G-8048)*

Mid-Atlantic Drainage Inc .... F 828 324-0808
Conover *(G-3539)*

Mosack Group LLC .... D 888 229-2874
Mint Hill *(G-8342)*

National Foam Inc .... C 919 639-6151
Angier *(G-125)*

Romac Industries Inc .... D 704 915-3317
Dallas *(G-3688)*

SCI Sharp Controls Inc .... G 704 394-1395
Pineville *(G-9755)*

Spc Mechanical Corporation .... C 252 237-9035
Wendell *(G-12549)*

◆ Titan Flow Control Inc .... E 910 735-0000
Lumberton *(G-7975)*

▲ Tlv Corporation .... E 704 597-9070
Charlotte *(G-2922)*

▲ United Brass Works Inc .... C 336 498-2661
Randleman *(G-10663)*

Victaulic Company .... E 910 371-5588
Leland *(G-7563)*

3495 Wire springs

▲ Cox Precision Springs Inc .... F 336 629-8500
Asheboro *(G-342)*

◆ Hickory Springs Manufactu .... D 828 328-2201
Hickory *(G-6355)*

Lee Spring Company LLC .... E 336 275-3631
Greensboro *(G-5659)*

Leggett & Platt Incorporated .... G 704 380-6208
Statesville *(G-11727)*

Leggett & Platt Incorporated .... D 336 889-2600
High Point *(G-6692)*

▲ M-B Industries Inc .... C 828 862-4201
Rosman *(G-10913)*

N C Coil Inc .... G 336 983-4440
King *(G-7333)*

Newcomb Spring Corp .... E 704 588-2043
Gastonia *(G-5109)*

Northeast Tool and Mfg Company .... E 704 882-1187
Matthews *(G-8187)*

Piedmont Springs Company Inc .... G 828 322-5347
Hickory *(G-6413)*

▲ Southern Precision Spring Inc .... E 704 392-4393
Charlotte *(G-2838)*

3496 Miscellaneous fabricated wire products

Aluminum Screen Manufacturing .... G 336 605-8080
Greensboro *(G-5352)*

American Fabricators .... G 252 637-2600
New Bern *(G-9332)*

Ashley Sling Inc .... E 704 347-0071
Charlotte *(G-1704)*

◆ Automated Solutions LLC .... F 828 396-9900
Granite Falls *(G-5296)*

▲ Belt Concepts America Inc .... F 888 598-2358
Spring Hope *(G-11553)*

Belt Shop Inc .... F 704 865-3636
Gastonia *(G-4997)*

Carolina Material Handling Inc .... F 336 294-2346
Greensboro *(G-5430)*

▲ Cavert Wire Company Inc .... E 800 969-2601
Rural Hall *(G-10956)*

Ceramawire .... G 252 335-7411
Elizabeth City *(G-4381)*

Chatsworth Products Inc .... C 252 514-2779
New Bern *(G-9354)*

Coleman Cable LLC .... D 828 389-8013
Hayesville *(G-6139)*

◆ Columbus McKinnon Corporation......C..... 716 689-5400
Charlotte *(G-1962)*

▲ Davis Newell Company Inc............... F..... 910 762-3500
Wilmington *(G-12760)*

▲ Dradura USA Corp........................ D..... 252 637-9660
New Bern *(G-9366)*

Eastern Wholesale Fence LLC............ D..... 631 698-0975
Salisbury *(G-11047)*

◆ Elevate Textiles Inc......................F..... 336 379-6220
Charlotte *(G-2098)*

Elevate Textiles Holding Corp........... D..... 336 379-6220
Charlotte *(G-2099)*

Essex Group Inc........................... G..... 704 921-9605
Charlotte *(G-2127)*

Everything Industrial Supply.............. G..... 743 333-2222
Winston Salem *(G-13162)*

Express Wire Services Inc................ G..... 704 393-5156
Charlotte *(G-2136)*

◆ Forbo Movement Systems................E..... 704 334-5353
Charlotte *(G-2171)*

Fuller Specialty Company Inc............ G..... 336 226-3446
Burlington *(G-1092)*

Hemco Wire Products Inc................. G..... 336 454-7280
Jamestown *(G-7164)*

I & I Sling Inc............................. G..... 336 323-1532
Greensboro *(G-5611)*

▲ Ica Mid-Atlantic Inc..................... C..... 336 447-4546
Whitsett *(G-12610)*

Intercontinental Metals Corp............. D..... 336 786-2141
Mount Airy *(G-9133)*

Leggett & Platt Incorporated............. D..... 336 889-2600
High Point *(G-6692)*

▲ M-B Industries Inc....................... C..... 828 862-4201
Rosman *(G-10913)*

▲ Masonry Reinforcing Corp Amer....... C..... 704 525-5554
Charlotte *(G-2467)*

▲ McIntyre Manufacturing Group Inc... D..... 336 476-3646
Thomasville *(G-12046)*

McJast Inc................................. F..... 828 884-4809
Pisgah Forest *(G-9771)*

Merchants Metals LLC.................... G..... 919 598-8471
Raleigh *(G-10290)*

Merchants Metals LLC.................... C..... 704 878-8706
Statesville *(G-11731)*

Preformed Line Products Co............. C..... 704 983-6161
Albemarle *(G-84)*

Prysmian Cbles Systems USA LLC..... E..... 828 322-9473
Hickory *(G-6421)*

Rack Works Inc........................... E..... 336 368-1302
Pilot Mountain *(G-9673)*

Redtail Group LLC........................ G..... 828 539-4700
Swannanoa *(G-11876)*

◆ Rolf Koerner LLC........................ G..... 704 714-8866
Charlotte *(G-2732)*

Royal Wire Products Inc................. E..... 704 596-2110
Charlotte *(G-2736)*

▲ Sid Jenkins Inc.......................... G..... 336 632-0707
Greensboro *(G-5811)*

Sunbelt Enterprises Inc.................. E..... 704 788-4749
Concord *(G-3450)*

◆ Technibilt Ltd............................E..... 828 464-7388
Newton *(G-9502)*

◆ Unified Scrning Crshing - NC I.........G..... 336 824-2151
Ramseur *(G-10633)*

Voltage LLC...............................F..... 919 391-9405
Chapel Hill *(G-1592)*

▲ Wieland Electric Inc.................... F..... 910 259-5050
Wilmington *(G-12947)*

▼ Wireway/Husky Corp.................... C..... 704 483-1135
Denver *(G-3817)*

3497 Metal foil and leaf

▲ Acme Liquidating Company LLC..... E..... 704 873-3731
Statesville *(G-11647)*

Granges Americas Inc.................... D..... 704 633-6020
Salisbury *(G-11059)*

Kurz Transfer Products LP............... D..... 336 764-4128
Lexington *(G-7706)*

▲ Kurz Transfer Products LP............. D..... 704 927-3700
Huntersville *(G-7008)*

Reynolds Consumer Products Inc....... A..... 704 371-5550
Huntersville *(G-7042)*

3498 Fabricated pipe and fittings

Advanced Systems Intgrtion LLC.......... G..... 260 447-5555
Wake Forest *(G-12259)*

Ansgar Industrial LLC.................... A..... 866 284-1931
Charlotte *(G-1679)*

ASC Engineered Solutions LLC.......... F..... 919 395-5222
Raleigh *(G-9917)*

Charlotte Pipe and Foundry Co.......... B..... 704 348-5416
Charlotte *(G-1901)*

Chicago Tube and Iron Company......... D..... 704 781-2060
Locust *(G-7890)*

◆ Controls Southeast Inc.................C..... 704 644-5000
Pineville *(G-9721)*

▲ Custom Enterprises Inc................. G..... 336 226-8296
Burlington *(G-1081)*

Erdle Perforating Holdings Inc............ F..... 704 588-4380
Charlotte *(G-2126)*

Hydro Tube South LLC................... G..... 919 258-3070
Sanford *(G-11194)*

Ipex USA LLC............................. F..... 704 889-2431
Pineville *(G-9736)*

Jim Fab of North Carolina Inc............ E..... 704 278-1000
Cleveland *(G-3215)*

Kds Fabricating and Mch Sp LLC.......... F..... 828 632-5091
Hiddenite *(G-6501)*

◆ Key Gas Components Inc............... E..... 828 655-1700
Marion *(G-8048)*

▲ Kooks Custom Headers Inc............. E..... 704 768-2288
Statesville *(G-11726)*

North Star Fbrication Repr Inc............ G..... 704 393-5243
Charlotte *(G-2574)*

Performance Plastics Pdts Inc............ D..... 336 454-0350
Jamestown *(G-7175)*

Protech Fabrication Inc................... F..... 704 663-1721
Mount Ulla *(G-9271)*

Purthermal LLC........................... G..... 828 855-0108
Hickory *(G-6422)*

Tube Specialties Co Inc.................. C..... 704 818-8933
Statesville *(G-11795)*

US Industrial Piping Inc.................. D..... 336 993-9505
Kernersville *(G-7311)*

Victaulic Company........................ E..... 910 371-5588
Leland *(G-7563)*

Waggoner Manufacturing Co.............. E..... 704 278-2000
Mount Ulla *(G-9272)*

3499 Fabricated metal products, nec

Airbox Inc................................. E..... 855 927-1386
Statesville *(G-11651)*

Alco Metal Fabricato..................... G..... 704 739-1168
Bessemer City *(G-804)*

◆ AP&t North America Inc................F..... 704 292-2900
Monroe *(G-8427)*

ARC Steel Fabrication LLC............... F..... 980 533-8302
Bessemer City *(G-805)*

Artistic Ironworks LLC................... G..... 919 908-6888
Durham *(G-3900)*

Avl Custom Fabrication................... G..... 828 713-0333
Asheville *(G-448)*

Babco Inc................................. G..... 888 376-5083
Ayden *(G-653)*

Barrier1 Systems Inc.....................F..... 336 617-8478
Greensboro *(G-5386)*

Black Mtn Mch Fabrication Inc........... E..... 828 669-9557
Black Mountain *(G-862)*

C & D Fabrications Inc................... G..... 919 639-2489
Angier *(G-115)*

Chatsworth Products Inc................. C..... 252 514-2779
New Bern *(G-9354)*

▲ Colonial Tin Works Inc................. E..... 336 668-4126
Greensboro *(G-5453)*

Concierge Transit LLC................... G..... 704 778-0755
Charlotte *(G-1969)*

Contemporary Products Inc.............. G..... 919 779-4228
Garner *(G-4925)*

Custom Cnc LLC......................... G..... 828 734-8293
Clyde *(G-3257)*

▲ Cyrco Inc................................ E..... 336 668-0977
Greensboro *(G-5484)*

Davis Brothers Roofing................... G..... 828 578-8561
Hickory *(G-6317)*

Diversfied Holdings Dallas Inc............ G..... 704 922-5293
Mount Holly *(G-9228)*

▲ Docmagnet Inc.......................... G..... 919 788-7999
Raleigh *(G-10052)*

◆ Dubose Strapping Inc...................D..... 910 590-1020
Clinton *(G-3232)*

Em2 Machine Corporation................ G..... 336 707-8409
Greensboro *(G-5518)*

▲ Epic Enterprises Inc.................... E..... 910 692-5750
Southern Pines *(G-11498)*

Four Corners Frmng Gallery Inc........... G..... 704 662-7154
Mooresville *(G-8667)*

◆ Graphik Dimensions Limited............D..... 800 332-8884
High Point *(G-6634)*

Gray Manufacturing Co................... G..... 615 841-3066
Charlotte *(G-2234)*

Ism Inc.................................... E
Arden *(G-277)*

Iv-S Metal Stamping Inc.................. E..... 336 861-2100
Archdale *(G-229)*

Jeffrey Sheffer........................... G..... 919 861-9126
Raleigh *(G-10214)*

JMS Rebar Inc........................... G..... 336 273-9084
Greensboro *(G-5637)*

Kaba Ilco Corp........................... B..... 336 725-1331
Winston Salem *(G-13222)*

M & M Frame Company Inc.............. G..... 336 859-8166
Denton *(G-3757)*

Mecha Inc................................ F..... 919 858-0372
Raleigh *(G-10286)*

Merchant 1 Manufacturing LLC............ G..... 336 617-3008
Summerfield *(G-11844)*

Metal Works High Point Inc.............. D..... 336 886-4612
High Point *(G-6709)*

Metal-Cad Stl Frmng Systems In........... D..... 910 343-3338
Wilmington *(G-12852)*

Mma Manufacturing Inc.................. E..... 828 692-0256
East Flat Rock *(G-4334)*

Myricks Custom Fab Inc................. G..... 828 645-5800
Weaverville *(G-12499)*

North Star Fbrication Repr Inc............ G..... 704 393-5243
Charlotte *(G-2574)*

Oak City Customs LLC................... G..... 919 995-5561
Zebulon *(G-13517)*

Oro Manufacturing Company.............. E..... 704 283-2186
Monroe *(G-8539)*

Pauls Cstm Fbrication Mch LLC.......... G..... 757 746-2743
Camden *(G-1212)*

Penco Products Inc.......................C..... 252 798-4000
Hamilton *(G-6049)*

Precision Partners LLC................... G..... 704 560-6442
Charlotte *(G-2657)*

SIC

Prezioso Ventures LLC.............................G..... 704 793-1602
Concord *(G-3422)*

▼ Problem Solver Inc.............................F..... 919 596-5555
Raleigh *(G-10399)*

◆ Ramsey Products Corporation............D..... 704 394-0322
Belmont *(G-764)*

Royce Company LLC.............................G..... 910 395-0046
Wilmington *(G-12903)*

Sinnovatek Inc.....................................G..... 919 694-0974
Raleigh *(G-10479)*

Spraying Systems Co.............................G..... 704 357-6499
Charlotte *(G-2845)*

Stair Tamer LLC....................................G..... 252 336-4437
Shiloh *(G-11395)*

Timmerman Manufacturing Inc.............F..... 828 464-1778
Conover *(G-3566)*

Truefab LLC..F..... 919 620-8158
Durham *(G-4283)*

◆ Usw-Menard Inc.................................G..... 910 371-1899
Leland *(G-7562)*

West Side Industries LLC......................G..... 980 223-8665
Statesville *(G-11799)*

Zurn Industries LLC..............................E..... 919 775-2255
Sanford *(G-11257)*

35 INDUSTRIAL AND COMMERCIAL MACHINERY AND COMPUTER EQUIPMENT

3511 Turbines and turbine generator sets

ABB Inc..E..... 704 587-1362
Charlotte *(G-1609)*

◆ ABB Inc...C..... 919 856-2360
Cary *(G-1285)*

Babcock Wlcox Eqity Invstmnts............G..... 704 625-4900
Charlotte *(G-1733)*

Babcock Wlcox Intl Sls Svc Cor............G..... 704 625-4900
Charlotte *(G-1734)*

Bwxt Investment Company....................E..... 704 625-4900
Charlotte *(G-1824)*

Caterpillar Inc......................................E..... 919 777-2000
Sanford *(G-11160)*

Diamond Power Intl LLC........................G..... 704 625-4900
Charlotte *(G-2040)*

Diamond Pwr Eqity Invstmnts In...........G..... 704 625-4900
Charlotte *(G-2041)*

◆ Industrial Sup Solutions Inc...............E..... 704 636-4241
Salisbury *(G-11067)*

▲ Leistriz Advanced Turbine.................C..... 336 969-1352
Rural Hall *(G-10964)*

Megtec India Holdings LLC....................G..... 704 625-4900
Charlotte *(G-2487)*

Megtec Turbosonic Tech Inc..................G..... 704 625-4900
Charlotte *(G-2488)*

Revloc Reclamation Service Inc.............G..... 704 625-4900
Charlotte *(G-2716)*

Siemens Energy Inc..............................C..... 704 551-5100
Charlotte *(G-2802)*

Siemens Energy Inc..............................E..... 336 969-1351
Rural Hall *(G-10967)*

Waterwheel Factory..............................G..... 828 369-5928
Franklin *(G-4843)*

▲ Wind Solutions LLC...........................E..... 919 292-2096
Sanford *(G-11252)*

Windlift Inc...G..... 919 490-8575
Durham *(G-4306)*

▲ Xylem Lnc..E..... 704 409-9700
Charlotte *(G-3035)*

3519 Internal combustion engines, nec

Blue Gas Marine Inc.............................F..... 919 238-3427
Apex *(G-146)*

Buck Supply Company Inc.....................G..... 252 215-1252
Winterville *(G-13414)*

Caterpillar Inc......................................E..... 919 777-2000
Sanford *(G-11160)*

▲ Coltec Industries Inc.........................A..... 704 731-1500
Charlotte *(G-1961)*

◆ Consolidated Diesel Inc.....................A..... 252 437-6611
Whitakers *(G-12574)*

Cummins Inc...F..... 704 596-7690
Charlotte *(G-2003)*

Cummins Inc...E..... 336 275-4531
Greensboro *(G-5476)*

Cummins Inc...G..... 919 284-9111
Kenly *(G-7230)*

Cummins Inc...G..... 704 588-1240
Pineville *(G-9723)*

Daimler Truck North Amer LLC..............A..... 704 645-5000
Cleveland *(G-3213)*

◆ Engine Systems Inc...........................D..... 252 977-2720
Rocky Mount *(G-10836)*

◆ Enpro Inc...C..... 704 731-1500
Charlotte *(G-2115)*

Farm Services Inc................................G..... 336 226-7381
Graham *(G-5268)*

General Electric Company.....................A..... 910 675-5000
Wilmington *(G-12785)*

Griffin Automotive Marine Inc...............G..... 252 940-0714
Washington *(G-12388)*

▲ Holman & Moody Inc.........................G..... 704 394-4141
Charlotte *(G-2281)*

Holman Automotive Inc.........................G..... 704 583-2888
Charlotte *(G-2282)*

▲ Ilmor Marine LLC...............................E..... 704 360-1901
Mooresville *(G-8691)*

Jasper Penske Engines.........................F..... 704 788-8996
Concord *(G-3384)*

Jones Marine Inc..................................G..... 704 639-0173
Salisbury *(G-11075)*

Lehr LLC...F..... 704 827-9368
Huntersville *(G-7010)*

NC Diesel Performance LLC...................G..... 704 431-3257
Salisbury *(G-11095)*

Pcai Inc..D..... 704 588-1240
Charlotte *(G-2622)*

Southport NC...G..... 910 524-7425
Southport *(G-11529)*

Trane Technologies Company LLC.........C..... 910 692-8700
Southern Pines *(G-11512)*

White River Marine Group LLC...............C..... 252 633-3101
New Bern *(G-9406)*

3523 Farm machinery and equipment

Airborn Industries Inc..........................E..... 704 483-5000
Lincolnton *(G-7811)*

◆ Befco Inc...E..... 252 977-9920
Rocky Mount *(G-10824)*

Carolina Golfco Inc..............................G..... 704 525-7846
Charlotte *(G-1848)*

Case Basket Creations.........................G..... 828 381-4908
Granite Falls *(G-5299)*

Case-Closed Investigations..................G..... 336 794-2274
Morehead City *(G-8824)*

◆ Ceres Turf Inc....................................G..... 910 256-8974
Wilmington *(G-12741)*

Coastal Agrobusiness Inc.....................G..... 828 697-2220
Flat Rock *(G-4706)*

Coastal Agrobusiness Inc.....................G..... 252 798-3481
Hamilton *(G-6048)*

◆ Coastal Agrobusiness Inc..................D..... 252 238-7391
Greenville *(G-5955)*

Dairy Services.......................................G..... 919 303-2442
Raleigh *(G-10033)*

Daughtridge Enterprises Inc.................G..... 252 977-7775
Rocky Mount *(G-10809)*

Deere & Company..................................B..... 919 567-6400
Fuquay Varina *(G-4878)*

Deere & Company..................................G..... 336 996-8100
Kernersville *(G-7265)*

◆ Evans Machinery Inc.........................D..... 252 243-4006
Wilson *(G-12990)*

◆ Gas-Fired Products Inc......................D..... 704 372-3485
Charlotte *(G-2190)*

General Fertilizer Eqp Inc.....................F..... 336 299-4711
Greensboro *(G-5554)*

Glemco LLC...G..... 866 619-6707
Statesville *(G-11703)*

▲ Granville Equipment LLC....................F..... 919 693-1425
Oxford *(G-9615)*

Graves Inc..F..... 252 792-1191
Williamston *(G-12670)*

Gum Drop Cases LLC.............................G..... 206 805-0818
High Point *(G-6636)*

H & H Farm Machine Co Inc..................F..... 704 753-1555
Monroe *(G-8497)*

Hog Slat Incorporated..........................F..... 252 209-0092
Aulander *(G-640)*

Hog Slat Incorporated..........................G..... 910 862-7081
Elizabethtown *(G-4427)*

Hog Slat Incorporated..........................F..... 800 949-4647
Newton Grove *(G-9515)*

Hog Slat Incorporated..........................E..... 919 663-3321
Siler City *(G-11411)*

◆ Hog Slat Incorporated......................B..... 800 949-4647
Newton Grove *(G-9514)*

James River Equipment........................F..... 704 821-7399
Monroe *(G-8509)*

Jo-Mar Group LLC.................................E
Belmont *(G-755)*

Johnson Industrial Mchy Svcs..............E..... 252 239-1944
Lucama *(G-7937)*

▲ Lock Drives Inc..................................G..... 704 588-1844
Pineville *(G-9740)*

North American Implements Inc............G..... 336 476-2904
Thomasville *(G-12056)*

▲ Pasture Management Systems Inc.....F..... 704 436-6401
Mount Pleasant *(G-9263)*

Sleepy Creek Turkeys LLC.....................C..... 919 778-3130
Goldsboro *(G-5244)*

Smoky Mtn Nativ Plant Assn.................G..... 828 479-8788
Robbinsville *(G-10763)*

▼ Sound Heavy Machinery Inc..............F..... 910 782-2477
Wilmington *(G-12922)*

Spectrum Products Inc..........................G..... 919 556-7797
Youngsville *(G-13488)*

STI Turf Equipment LLC.........................E..... 704 393-8873
Charlotte *(G-2868)*

Strickland Bros Entps Inc......................F..... 252 478-3058
Spring Hope *(G-11560)*

Taylor Manufacturing Inc......................E..... 910 862-2576
Elizabethtown *(G-4434)*

Tractor Country Inc..............................G..... 252 523-3007
Dover *(G-3829)*

Tri-W Farms Inc....................................G..... 910 533-3596
Clinton *(G-3251)*

Upper Coastl Plain Bus Dev Ctr............G..... 252 234-5900
Wilson *(G-13041)*

3524 Lawn and garden equipment

American Honda Motor Co Inc...............B..... 336 578-6300
Swepsonville *(G-11889)*

◆ Befco Inc...E..... 252 977-9920
Rocky Mount *(G-10824)*

▲ Bosmere Inc...................... F 704 784-1608
   Salisbury *(G-11023)*

CAM Enterprises Inc..................... G 252 946-4877
   Washington *(G-12375)*

Certified Lawnmower Inc.................. G 704 527-2765
   Belmont *(G-742)*

Daphne Lawson Espino.................. G 910 290-2762
   Beulaville *(G-841)*

Darius All Access LLC.................. E 910 262-8567
   Wilmington *(G-12759)*

Day 3 Lwncare Ldscpg Prfctnist........... G 910 574-8422
   Fayetteville *(G-4584)*

Deere & Company...................... B 919 567-6400
   Fuquay Varina *(G-4878)*

Green Pastures Lawn Care.................. G 828 758-9265
   Boomer *(G-891)*

H & H Farm Machine Co Inc............ F 704 753-1555
   Monroe *(G-8497)*

Husqvrna Cnsmr Otdoor Pdts NA......... A 704 597-5000
   Charlotte *(G-2302)*

Husqvrna Cnsmr Otdoor Pdts NA......... A 704 494-4810
   Charlotte *(G-2303)*

◆ Husqvrna Cnsmr Otdoor Pdts NA......D 704 597-5000
   Charlotte *(G-2301)*

John Deere Consumer Pdts Inc.......... G 919 804-2000
   Cary *(G-1380)*

Jrm Inc................................. E 888 576-7007
   Clemmons *(G-3194)*

Miller Saws & Supplies Inc.............. G 252 636-3347
   New Bern *(G-9382)*

▲ New Peco Inc......................... E 828 684-1234
   Arden *(G-288)*

Peco Inc................................ E 828 684-1234
   Arden *(G-296)*

▼ Root Spring Scraper Co.............. G 269 382-2025
   Pinehurst *(G-9702)*

S Duff Fabricating Inc.................. G 910 298-3060
   Beulaville *(G-845)*

Sunseeker North America Inc............. F 704 684-5709
   Indian Trail *(G-7101)*

Sunseeker US Inc....................... G 443 253-1546
   Indian Trail *(G-7102)*

Swell Home Solutions Inc............... G 919 440-4692
   Mount Olive *(G-9260)*

▲ Trailmate Inc......................... G 941 739-5743
   Chapel Hill *(G-1578)*

▲ United Southern Industries Inc........ D 866 273-1810
   Forest City *(G-4799)*

▲ Vegherb LLC.......................... F 800 914-9835
   Erwin *(G-4493)*

3531 Construction machinery

A-1 Concrete & Cnstr LLC.............. G 828 712-1160
   Arden *(G-247)*

Advanced Grading & Excvtg LLC........ G 828 320-7465
   Newton *(G-9448)*

Advantage Machinery Svcs Inc......... E 336 463-4700
   Yadkinville *(G-13435)*

Allied Marine Contractors LLC.......... G 910 367-2159
   Hampstead *(G-6067)*

Altec Industries Inc.................... D 828 678-5500
   Burnsville *(G-1181)*

Altec Industries Inc.................... B 919 528-2535
   Creedmoor *(G-3637)*

Altec Industries Inc.................... E 336 786-3623
   Mount Airy *(G-9097)*

▲ Altec Northeast LLC.................. E 508 320-9041
   Creedmoor *(G-3638)*

American Attachments Inc.............. G 336 859-2002
   Lexington *(G-7655)*

Ampac Machinery LLC.................. F 919 596-5320
   Durham *(G-3894)*

Apac-Atlantic Inc...................... D 336 412-6800
   Raleigh *(G-9907)*

Arrow Equipment LLC.................. G 803 765-2040
   Charlotte *(G-1698)*

Asphalt Emulsion Inds LLC............. G 252 726-0653
   Morehead City *(G-8814)*

Automated Designs Inc................ F 828 696-9625
   Flat Rock *(G-4703)*

Barnhill Contracting Company........... E 252 527-8021
   Kinston *(G-7395)*

Beasley Contracting................... G 828 479-3775
   Robbinsville *(G-10756)*

◆ Befco Inc............................. E 252 977-9920
   Rocky Mount *(G-10824)*

Berco of America Inc.................. E 336 931-1415
   Greensboro *(G-5388)*

Bgi Recovery Llc...................... G 336 429-6976
   Mount Airy *(G-9103)*

◆ Bromma Inc.......................... E 919 620-8039
   Durham *(G-3945)*

Cardinal Stone Company Inc............ G 336 846-7191
   Jefferson *(G-7187)*

Carolina Paving Hickory Inc............ G 828 328-3909
   Hickory *(G-6285)*

Carolina Paving Hickory Inc............ F 828 322-1706
   Hickory *(G-6286)*

Caterpillar Inc......................... D 919 550-1100
   Clayton *(G-3137)*

Caterpillar Inc......................... E 919 777-2000
   Sanford *(G-11160)*

Champion LLC......................... F 704 392-1038
   Charlotte *(G-1890)*

Conjet Inc............................. G 636 485-4724
   Charlotte *(G-1974)*

▲ Construction Attachments Inc.......... D 828 758-2674
   Lenoir *(G-7596)*

Construction Impts Depo Inc............ E 336 859-2002
   Denton *(G-3743)*

▲ Cutting Systems Inc.................. D 704 592-2451
   Union Grove *(G-12184)*

Dan Moore Inc........................ G 336 475-8350
   Thomasville *(G-12015)*

Design Engnred Fbrications Inc.......... E 336 768-8260
   Winston Salem *(G-13141)*

Dimensional Metals Inc................ G 704 279-9691
   Salisbury *(G-11043)*

Engcon North America Inc............. F 203 691-5920
   High Point *(G-6611)*

▼ Engineered Attachments LLC.......... G 336 703-5266
   Winston Salem *(G-13158)*

Everything Attachments................ F 828 464-0161
   Conover *(G-3520)*

Ferebee Inc........................... C 704 509-2586
   Charlotte *(G-2145)*

Ferguson Highway Products Inc......... F 704 320-3087
   Indian Trail *(G-7081)*

Flores Crane Services LLC............. F 704 243-4347
   Waxhaw *(G-12431)*

Four Points Recycling LLC............. F 910 333-5961
   Jacksonville *(G-7123)*

General Fertilizer Eqp Inc............. F 336 299-4711
   Greensboro *(G-5554)*

Harsco Metro Rail LLC................ G 980 960-2624
   Charlotte *(G-2261)*

Harsco Rail LLC....................... G 980 960-2624
   Charlotte *(G-2262)*

Hills Machinery Company LLC.......... E 828 820-5265
   Mills River *(G-8315)*

Hockmeyer Equipment Corp............ D 252 338-4705
   Elizabeth City *(G-4390)*

Holder Backhoe & Hauling Inc.......... G 336 622-7388
   Liberty *(G-7767)*

Hyper Networks LLC................... E 704 837-8411
   Pineville *(G-9734)*

Infrastrcture Sltons Group Inc.......... F 704 833-8048
   Mooresville *(G-8692)*

Ingersoll-Rand Indus US Inc............ D 704 896-4000
   Davidson *(G-3710)*

Ingersoll-Rand Intl Holdg.............. B 704 655-4000
   Davidson *(G-3711)*

▲ Instrotek Inc......................... E 919 875-8371
   Research Triangle Pa *(G-10712)*

◆ International Cnstr Eqp Inc...........E 704 821-8200
   Matthews *(G-8175)*

▲ John Deere Kernersville LLC.......... A 336 996-8100
   Kernersville *(G-7281)*

Ken Garner Mfg - RHO Inc............. E 336 969-0416
   Rural Hall *(G-10962)*

Linder Industrial Machinery Co.......... F 980 777-8345
   Concord *(G-3393)*

▲ Loflin Fabrication LLC................ E 336 859-4333
   Denton *(G-3756)*

Man Lift Mfg Co....................... E 414 486-1760
   Shelby *(G-11359)*

▼ Meadows Mills Inc................... E 336 838-2282
   North Wilkesboro *(G-9546)*

Metal Roofing Systems LLC............ E 704 820-3110
   Stanley *(G-11622)*

▲ Mid-Atlantic Crane and Eqp Co....... E 919 790-3535
   Raleigh *(G-10304)*

North American Implements Inc......... G 336 476-2904
   Thomasville *(G-12056)*

Paladin Custom Works................. G 336 996-2796
   Kernersville *(G-7291)*

Peco Inc.............................. E 828 684-1234
   Arden *(G-296)*

◆ Power Curbers Inc...................D 704 636-5871
   Salisbury *(G-11104)*

Redi-Mix LP.......................... D 704 596-6511
   Charlotte *(G-2699)*

Roadsafe Traffic Systems Inc.......... G 919 772-9401
   High Point *(G-6759)*

Rol-Mol Inc........................... G 828 328-1210
   Hickory *(G-6431)*

Ronny D Phelps...................... G 828 206-6339
   Hot Springs *(G-6934)*

Roofing Supply........................ G 919 779-6223
   Garner *(G-4959)*

Roofing Tools and Eqp Inc............. G 252 291-1800
   Wilson *(G-13024)*

▼ Root Spring Scraper Co.............. G 269 382-2025
   Pinehurst *(G-9702)*

S T Wooten Corporation................ E 919 363-3141
   Apex *(G-192)*

S T Wooten Corporation................ E 919 562-1851
   Franklinton *(G-4853)*

S T Wooten Corporation................ E 919 772-7991
   Fuquay Varina *(G-4897)*

S T Wooten Corporation................ E 252 393-2206
   Garner *(G-4961)*

S T Wooten Corporation................ E 919 779-6089
   Garner *(G-4962)*

S T Wooten Corporation................ E 919 779-7589
   Garner *(G-4963)*

S T Wooten Corporation................ E 252 636-2568
   New Bern *(G-9393)*

S T Wooten Corporation................ E 919 965-7176
   Princeton *(G-9827)*

S T Wooten Corporation................ E 252 291-5165
   Raleigh *(G-10455)*

S T Wooten Corporation................ E 919 776-2736
   Sanford *(G-11227)*

S T Wooten Corporation................ E 910 762-1940
   Wilmington *(G-12908)*

S T Wooten Corporation.................. E 252 291-5165
Wilson (G-13026)

Smart Cast Group.................. F 855 971-2287
Raleigh (G-10487)

Southern Trucking & Backhoe.............. G 919 548-9723
Siler City (G-11426)

St Engineering Leeboy Inc.................. B 704 966-3300
Lincolnton (G-7856)

Stone Supply Inc.................. G 828 678-9966
Burnsville (G-1192)

Strickland Backhoe.................. G 910 893-5274
Bunnlevel (G-1017)

▲ Sturdy Corporation.................. C 910 763-2500
Wilmington (G-12933)

Superior Dry Kilns Inc.................. E 828 754-7001
Hudson (G-6960)

Surface Buff LLC.................. G 919 341-2873
Raleigh (G-10523)

Tandemloc Inc.................. D 252 447-7155
Havelock (G-6128)

Tcom Ground Systems LP.................. F 252 338-3200
Elizabeth City (G-4414)

Tom Rochester & Associates Inc.......... G 704 896-5805
Charlotte (G-2928)

▼ USA Attachments Inc.................. E 336 983-0763
King (G-7338)

Vermeer Manufacturing Company.......... F 410 285-0200
Charlotte (G-2978)

◆ VT Leeboy Inc.................. B 704 966-3300
Lincolnton (G-7869)

▲ W R Long Inc.................. F 252 823-4570
Tarboro (G-11946)

Young & McQueen Grading Co Inc........ D 828 682-7714
Burnsville (G-1196)

3532 Mining machinery

80 Acres Urban Agriculture Inc.............. G 704 437-6115
Granite Falls (G-5292)

Batista Grading Inc.................. F 919 359-3449
Clayton (G-3134)

Brunner & Lay Inc.................. G 828 274-2770
Flat Rock (G-4704)

Junaluska Mill Engineering.................. G 828 321-3693
Andrews (G-108)

Omni Group LLC.................. G 828 404-3104
Hickory (G-6405)

Paschal Associates Ltd.................. F 336 625-2535
Raleigh (G-10359)

Quantex Inc.................. G 919 219-9604
Wendell (G-12542)

▼ Sound Heavy Machinery Inc............ F 910 782-2477
Wilmington (G-12922)

Stone Supply Inc.................. G 828 678-9966
Burnsville (G-1192)

3533 Oil and gas field machinery

Patty Knio.................. G 919 995-2670
Raleigh (G-10362)

◆ Sandvik Inc.................. C 919 563-5008
Mebane (G-8258)

3534 Elevators and moving stairways

Citilift Company.................. G 704 241-6477
Charlotte (G-1919)

Crockers Inc.................. F 336 366-2005
Elkin (G-4442)

Eastern Elevator Inc.................. G 877 840-2638
Raleigh (G-10071)

Ecs Group-NC LLC.................. G 919 830-1171
Wake Forest (G-12273)

Home Elevators & Lift Pdts LLC.......... E 910 427-0006
Sunset Beach (G-11850)

Liftavator Inc.................. E 252 634-1717
New Bern (G-9375)

▲ Nussbaum Auto Solutions LP.......... G 704 864-2470
Gastonia (G-5112)

Otis Elevator Company.................. G 828 251-1248
Asheville (G-563)

Otis Elevator Company.................. C 704 519-0100
Charlotte (G-2602)

Park Manufacturing Company.............. F 704 869-6128
Gastonia (G-5115)

Poehler Enterprises Inc.................. G 704 239-1166
Midland (G-8292)

Port City Elevator Inc.................. E 910 790-9300
Castle Hayne (G-1509)

Resolute Elevator LLC.................. E 919 903-0189
Burlington (G-1145)

Schindler Elevator Corporation.......... F 910 590-5590
Clinton (G-3245)

Southeastern Elevator LLC.................. G 252 726-9983
Morehead City (G-8845)

Vertical Access LLC.................. G 800 325-1116
Snow Hill (G-11483)

3535 Conveyors and conveying equipment

▲ AC Corporation.................. B 336 273-4472
Greensboro (G-5339)

Advance Conveying Tech LLC.............. E 704 710-4001
Kings Mountain (G-7344)

Advantage Conveyor Inc.................. F 919 781-0055
Raleigh (G-9881)

Altec Industries Inc.................. B 919 528-2535
Creedmoor (G-3637)

Automated Lumber Handling Inc.......... G 828 754-4662
Lenoir (G-7574)

▲ Basic Machinery Company Inc........ D 919 663-2244
Siler City (G-11399)

▲ Belt Concepts America Inc.............. F 888 598-2358
Spring Hope (G-11553)

Beltservice Corporation.................. E 704 947-2264
Huntersville (G-6973)

◆ Columbus McKinnon Corporation..... C 716 689-5400
Charlotte (G-1962)

▲ Conroll Corporation.................. F 910 202-4292
Wilmington (G-12747)

Conveying Solutions LLC.................. F 704 636-4241
Salisbury (G-11038)

◆ Conveyor Tech LLC.................. C 919 776-7227
Goldston (G-5257)

Conveyor Technologies Inc.................. G 919 732-8291
Efland (G-4375)

◆ Conveyor Technologies of .... D 919 776-7227
Sanford (G-11165)

Esco Group LLC.................. G 919 900-8226
Raleigh (G-10092)

◆ Forbo Movement Systems.................. E 704 334-5353
Charlotte (G-2171)

▲ Forbo Siegling LLC.................. B 704 948-0800
Huntersville (G-6995)

Gardner Machinery Corporation.......... F 704 372-3890
Charlotte (G-2189)

Goals In Service LLC.................. G 919 440-2656
Seven Springs (G-11297)

▲ Gough Econ Inc.................. E 704 399-4501
Charlotte (G-2228)

Greenline Corporation.................. G 704 333-3377
Charlotte (G-2240)

◆ Industrial Sup Solutions Inc.............. E 704 636-4241
Salisbury (G-11067)

◆ Interroll Corporation.................. C 910 799-1100
Wilmington (G-12819)

Interroll USA Holding LLC.................. D 910 799-1100
Wilmington (G-12820)

Ism Inc.................. E
Arden (G-277)

Jack A Farrior Inc.................. D 252 753-2020
Farmville (G-4532)

▲ Jayson Concepts Inc.................. G 828 654-8900
Arden (G-279)

▲ Lns Turbo Inc.................. D 704 739-7111
Kings Mountain (G-7371)

Machinex Technologies Inc.................. F 773 867-8801
High Point (G-6696)

▲ Mantissa Corporation.................. E 704 525-1749
Charlotte (G-2453)

Material Handling Technologies Inc...... D 919 388-0050
Morrisville (G-9018)

Memios LLC.................. D 336 664-5256
Greensboro (G-5689)

▲ National Conveyors Company Inc...... G 860 325-4011
Charlotte (G-2545)

Niels Jorgensen Company Inc.............. G 910 259-1624
Burgaw (G-1028)

Nunn Probst Installations Inc.............. G 704 822-9443
Belmont (G-757)

Process Automation Tech Inc.............. G 828 298-1055
Asheville (G-586)

▲ Production Systems Inc.................. E 336 886-7161
High Point (G-6747)

Qcs Acquisition Corporation.............. G 252 446-5000
Rocky Mount (G-10863)

RSI Leasing Inc NS Tbt.................. G 704 587-9300
Charlotte (G-2738)

▲ Rulmeca Corporation.................. G 910 794-9294
Wilmington (G-12905)

Sherrill Contract Mfg Inc.................. F 704 922-7871
Dallas (G-3689)

▲ Smart Machine Technologies Inc...... D 276 632-9853
Greensboro (G-5817)

Southco Industries Inc.................. C 704 482-1477
Shelby (G-11381)

Sunco Powder Systems Inc.................. E 704 545-3922
Charlotte (G-2881)

Superior Finishing Systems LLC.......... G 336 956-2000
Lexington (G-7747)

▲ Transbotics Corporation.................. E 704 362-1115
Charlotte (G-2936)

▲ Westwood Manufacturing Inc.......... G 910 862-9992
Elizabethtown (G-4437)

3536 Hoists, cranes, and monorails

Altec Industries Inc.................. B 919 528-2535
Creedmoor (G-3637)

▲ Altec Northeast LLC.................. E 508 320-9041
Creedmoor (G-3638)

▲ Boat Lift US Inc.................. G 239 283-9040
Leland (G-7532)

Boat Lift Store Inc.................. G 252 586-5437
Littleton (G-7884)

▼ Boat Lift Warehouse LLC.................. G 877 468-5438
Snow Hill (G-11475)

Columbus McKinnon Corporation.......... D 704 694-2156
Wadesboro (G-12240)

◆ Columbus McKinnon Corporation..... C 716 689-5400
Charlotte (G-1962)

Crane South LLC.................. G 980 422-5874
Charlotte (G-1995)

Float Lifts of Carolinas LLC.................. G 919 972-1082
Wilmington (G-12777)

HI & Dri Boat Lift Systems Inc.............. G 704 663-5438
Mooresville (G-8682)

Hydrohoist of North Carolina.............. G 704 799-1910
Mooresville (G-8689)

▲ Kuenz America Inc.................. F 984 255-1018
Raleigh (G-10241)

▲ Mias Inc .... G 704 665-1098
  Charlotte (G-2498)

Thomas M Brown Inc .... F 704 597-0246
  Charlotte (G-2913)

◆ Toter LLC .... E 800 424-0422
  Statesville (G-11792)

Veon Inc .... F 252 623-2102
  Washington (G-12418)

◆ Yale Industrial Products Inc .... E 704 588-4610
  Charlotte (G-3038)

3537 Industrial trucks and tractors

A+ Pro Transport Inc .... G 980 215-8694
  Charlotte (G-1607)

Altec Industries Inc .... B 919 528-2535
  Creedmoor (G-3637)

Arbon Equipment Corporation .... F 414 355-2600
  Charlotte (G-1690)

At Your Service Express LLC .... E 704 270-9918
  Charlotte (G-1707)

▲ Basic Machinery Company Inc .... D 919 663-2244
  Siler City (G-11399)

Bethlehem Manufacturing Co .... F 828 495-7731
  Hickory (G-6270)

Bottomley Enterprises Inc .... D 336 657-6400
  Mount Airy (G-9104)

◆ Bromma Inc .... E 919 620-8039
  Durham (G-3945)

Buck Racing Engines Inc .... G 336 983-6562
  King (G-7322)

Burton Global Logistics LLC .... E 336 663-6449
  Burlington (G-1057)

Butler Trailer Mfg Co Inc .... F 336 674-8850
  Randleman (G-10634)

C&A Hockaday Transport LLC .... G&G .. 252 676-5956
  Roanoke Rapids (G-10734)

Carolina Expediters LLC .... G 888 537-5330
  Mount Airy (G-9108)

Carolina Material Handling Inc .... F 336 294-2346
  Greensboro (G-5430)

Caterpillar Inc .... E 919 777-2000
  Sanford (G-11160)

Cbj Transit LLC .... D 252 417-9972
  Garner (G-4921)

◆ Columbus McKinnon Corporation ...... C 716 689-5400
  Charlotte (G-1962)

▲ Combilift USA LLC .... F 336 378-8884
  Greensboro (G-5457)

Crown Equipment Corporation .... E 336 291-2500
  Colfax (G-3277)

Crown Equipment Corporation .... D 704 721-4000
  Concord (G-3348)

Crown Equipment Corporation .... E 919 773-4160
  Garner (G-4927)

Crown Equipment Corporation .... B 252 522-3088
  Kinston (G-7403)

CSM Logistics LLC .... G 980 800-2621
  Charlotte (G-2002)

▲ Cutting Systems Inc .... D 704 592-2451
  Union Grove (G-12184)

D&E Freight LLC .... F 704 977-4847
  Charlotte (G-2013)

Daimler Truck North Amer LLC .... A 704 645-5000
  Cleveland (G-3213)

Discount Pallet Services LLC .... G 910 892-3760
  Dunn (G-3853)

Driveco Inc .... G 704 615-2111
  Charlotte (G-2065)

Drs Transportation Inc .... G 919 215-2770
  Raleigh (G-10060)

Dse Express LLC .... G 540 686-0981
  Sanford (G-11172)

E-Z Dumper Products LLC .... G 717 762-8432
  Southern Pines (G-11497)

Elektrikredd LLC .... G 704 805-0110
  Matthews (G-8166)

Fastlife Transport LLC .... G 484 350-6754
  Charlotte (G-2144)

Fleet Fixers Inc .... G 704 986-0066
  Albemarle (G-73)

◆ Forklift Pro Inc .... F 704 716-3636
  Pineville (G-9728)

Forward Dsptching Lgistics LLC .... G 252 907-9797
  Greenville (G-5977)

General Electric Company .... F 919 563-7445
  Mebane (G-8241)

General Electric Company .... B 919 563-5561
  Mebane (G-8242)

Go For Green Fleet Svcs LLC .... G 803 306-3683
  Charlotte (G-2221)

Good Grief Marketing LLC .... G 336 989-1984
  Greensboro (G-5569)

Gregory Poole Equipment Co .... G 252 931-5100
  Greenville (G-5984)

Hanging C Farms .... F 704 239-6691
  Kannapolis (G-7210)

Harrell Proper Transport LLC .... G 336 202-7135
  Whitsett (G-12609)

Hc Forklift America Corp .... F 980 888-8335
  Charlotte (G-2266)

Hyster-Yale Group Inc .... E 252 931-5100
  Greenville (G-5988)

Hyster-Yale Group Inc .... G 252 931-5100
  Greenville (G-5989)

◆ Hyster-Yale Materials Hdlg Inc .... D 252 931-5100
  Greenville (G-5990)

Jhrg Manufacturing LLC .... G 252 478-4977
  Spring Hope (G-11556)

Just n Tyme Trucking LLC .... G 704 804-9519
  Charlotte (G-2383)

▼ Kaufman Trailers Inc .... E 336 790-6800
  Lexington (G-7704)

◆ Kinston Neuse Corporation .... C 252 522-3088
  Kinston (G-7418)

▲ Master Tow Inc .... E 910 630-2000
  Fayetteville (G-4637)

Maxson & Associates .... G 336 632-0524
  Greensboro (G-5683)

▲ McIntyre Manufacturing Group Inc .... D 336 476-3646
  Thomasville (G-12046)

Mlg Trnscndent Trckg Trnsp Svc .... G 336 905-1192
  High Point (G-6713)

MMS Logistics Incorporated .... G 336 214-3552
  Mc Leansville (G-8225)

Moon N Sea Nc LLC .... G 704 588-1963
  Charlotte (G-2518)

▼ Multi-Shifter Inc .... F 704 588-9611
  Charlotte (G-2528)

New Vision Momentum Entp LLC .... G 800 575-1244
  Charlotte (G-2558)

Nexxt Level Trucking LLC .... G 980 205-4425
  Charlotte (G-2562)

Nolan Manufacturing LLC .... G 336 490-0086
  Denton (G-3758)

North American Implements .... E 336 476-2904
  Lexington (G-7723)

Otto Envmtl Systems NC LLC .... B 800 227-5885
  Charlotte (G-2603)

Parkers Equipment Company .... G 252 560-0088
  Snow Hill (G-11482)

Port City Elevator Inc .... E 910 790-9300
  Castle Hayne (G-1509)

Propane Trucks & Tanks Inc .... F 919 362-5000
  Apex (G-188)

Quick-Deck Inc .... E 704 888-0327
  Locust (G-7898)

Rainey and Wilson Logistics .... G 910 736-8540
  Raeford (G-9849)

Rapid Run Transport LLC .... F 704 615-3458
  Charlotte (G-2690)

Reginald DWayne Dillard .... G 980 254-5505
  Charlotte (G-2704)

RSI Leasing Inc NS Tbt .... G 704 587-9300
  Charlotte (G-2738)

Rucker Intrgrted Logistics LLC .... G 704 352-2018
  Charlotte (G-2741)

Scootatrailertm .... G 336 671-0444
  Lexington (G-7739)

Smithway Inc .... G 828 628-1756
  Fairview (G-4511)

▼ Smithway Inc .... E 828 628-1756
  Fairview (G-4512)

▼ Sound Heavy Machinery Inc .... F 910 782-2477
  Wilmington (G-12922)

Sterling Rack Inc .... G 704 866-9131
  Gastonia (G-5144)

Superior Dry Kilns Inc .... E 828 754-7001
  Hudson (G-6960)

Swing Kurve Logistic Trckg LLC .... G 704 506-7371
  Charlotte (G-2888)

▼ TCI Mobility Inc .... F 704 867-8331
  Gastonia (G-5149)

Tcom Limited Partnership .... B 252 330-5555
  Elizabeth City (G-4413)

Three Ladies and A Male LLC .... G 704 287-1584
  Charlotte (G-2916)

Trunorth Wrrnty Plans N Amer L .... E 800 903-7489
  Huntersville (G-7060)

V M Trucking Inc .... G 984 239-4853
  Morehead City (G-8848)

◆ Wastequip LLC .... F 704 366-7140
  Charlotte (G-3005)

Webbs Logistics LLC .... F 919 591-4308
  Garner (G-4972)

Westlift LLC .... F 919 242-4379
  Goldsboro (G-5253)

Whiteville Forklift & Eqp .... G 910 642-6642
  Whiteville (G-12598)

Wlc Forklift Services LLC .... G 336 345-2571
  Reidsville (G-10701)

3541 Machine tools, metal cutting type

Achilli USA Inc .... G 704 940-0115
  Charlotte (G-1617)

Amada America Inc .... G 877 262-3287
  High Point (G-6518)

▲ Atlantic Hydraulics Svcs LLC .... E 919 542-2985
  Sanford (G-11152)

Belkoz Inc .... G 919 703-0694
  Raleigh (G-9939)

▲ Betek Tools Inc .... F 980 498-2523
  Charlotte (G-1775)

Blue Inc Usa LLC .... E 828 346-8660
  Conover (G-3494)

Brown Equipment and Capitl Inc .... F 704 921-4644
  Monroe (G-8448)

C & J Machine Company Inc .... G 704 922-5913
  Dallas (G-3667)

▲ Casetec Precision Machine LLC .... G 704 663-6043
  Mooresville (G-8634)

Central Tool & Mfg Co Inc .... G 828 328-2383
  Hickory (G-6294)

Circor Precision Metering LLC .... A 919 774-7667
  Sanford (G-11164)

Delta Phoenix Inc .... E 336 621-3960
  Greensboro (G-5493)

▼ Design Tool Inc.................................. E 828 328-6414
Conover (G-3515)

Drill & Fill Mfg LLC............................. G 252 937-4555
Rocky Mount (G-10832)

▲ Efco USA Inc................................... G 800 332-6872
Charlotte (G-2092)

Exact Cut Inc.................................... G 336 207-4022
Greensboro (G-5527)

▲ Grindtec Enterprises Corp................. G 704 636-1825
Salisbury (G-11060)

Hamilton Indus Grinding Inc................ E 828 253-6796
Asheville (G-515)

▼ His Glassworks Inc.......................... G 828 254-2559
Asheville (G-518)

Industrial Mch Solutions Inc................ G 919 872-0016
Raleigh (G-10191)

J & B Tool Making Inc........................ G 704 827-4805
Mount Holly (G-9234)

▲ Kyocera Precision Tools Inc............. G 800 823-7284
Fletcher (G-4745)

L & R Specialties Inc.......................... F 704 853-3296
Gastonia (G-5075)

Lynn Electronics Corporation.............. G 704 369-0093
Concord (G-3397)

▲ Matcor Mtal Fbrction Wlcome In....... C 336 731-5700
Lexington (G-7717)

◆ Normac Incorporated....................... E 828 209-9000
Hendersonville (G-6231)

Northeast Tool and Mfg Company........ E 704 882-1187
Matthews (G-8187)

▲ Okuma America Corporation............. C 704 588-7000
Charlotte (G-2593)

Precision Industries Inc...................... F 828 465-3418
Conover (G-3548)

Protocase Mfg Usa Inc....................... E 866 849-3911
Wilmington (G-12892)

▲ Putsch & Company Inc..................... E 828 684-0671
Fletcher (G-4762)

Sandvik Tooling................................. G 919 563-5008
Mebane (G-8260)

▲ Schelling America Inc...................... E 919 544-0430
Morrisville (G-9044)

Schenck USA Corp............................. G 704 529-5300
Conover (G-3558)

Slack & Parr International................... G 704 527-2975
Dallas (G-3690)

Superior Dry Kilns Inc........................ E 828 754-7001
Hudson (G-6960)

Tactile Workshop LLC......................... G 919 738-9924
Raleigh (G-10530)

▲ Tigra Usa Inc.................................. E 828 324-8227
Hickory (G-6468)

Triad Cutting Tools Inc....................... G 336 873-8708
Asheboro (G-412)

▲ Union Grove Saw & Knife Inc........... D 704 539-4442
Union Grove (G-12186)

▼ Whiteside Mch & Repr Co Inc........... E 828 459-2141
Claremont (G-3126)

▲ Wieland Electric Inc........................ F 910 259-5050
Wilmington (G-12947)

Willis Manufacturing Inc..................... F 828 244-0435
Conover (G-3575)

Windco LLC....................................... G 704 846-6029
Indian Trail (G-7104)

3542 Machine tools, metal forming type

American Racg Hders Exhust Inc.......... F 631 608-1986
Stanfield (G-11602)

Arnolds Welding Service Inc................ E 910 323-3822
Fayetteville (G-4553)

CPM Wolverine Proctor LLC................ F 336 479-2983
Lexington (G-7670)

CPM Wolverine Proctor LLC................ D 336 248-5181
Lexington (G-7671)

◆ Cyril Bath Company.......................... F 704 289-8531
Monroe (G-8473)

Delta Phoenix Inc............................... E 336 621-3960
Greensboro (G-5493)

E G A Products Inc............................. F 704 664-1221
Mooresville (G-8657)

◆ Emery Corporation............................ D 828 433-1536
Morganton (G-8862)

Gesipa Fasteners Usa Inc................... E 336 751-1555
Mocksville (G-8367)

◆ Gesipa Fasteners Usa Inc................. F 609 208-1740
Mocksville (G-8368)

▼ Grey Holdings Inc............................ E 828 862-4772
Brevard (G-970)

▲ Legacy Mechanical.......................... F 704 225-8558
Monroe (G-8516)

Linde Advanced Mtl Tech Inc............... C 828 862-4772
Brevard (G-974)

▲ M & A Equipment Inc....................... G 704 703-9400
Mooresville (G-8715)

▲ Moores Mch Co Fayetteville Inc........ D 919 837-5354
Bear Creek (G-717)

◆ Murata Machinery Usa Inc................ C 704 875-9280
Charlotte (G-2532)

◆ Murata McHy USA Holdings Inc......... F 704 394-8331
Charlotte (G-2533)

Ora Inc... G 540 903-7177
Marion (G-8059)

▲ Price Metal Spinning Inc.................. G 704 922-3195
Dallas (G-3683)

Rollforming LLC................................. G 336 468-4317
Hamptonville (G-6091)

◆ Schunk Intec Inc.............................. D 919 572-2705
Morrisville (G-9046)

Sona Autocomp USA LLC.................... C 919 965-5555
Selma (G-11291)

◆ Sona Blw Precision Forge Inc........... C 919 828-3375
Selma (G-11292)

Ultra Machine & Fabrication Inc........... C 704 482-1399
Shelby (G-11388)

Wuko Inc... G 980 938-0512
Greensboro (G-5927)

Wysong and Miles Company............... E 336 621-3960
Greensboro (G-5928)

3543 Industrial patterns

Lampe & Malphrus Lumber Co............. F 919 934-1124
Smithfield (G-11454)

Pattern Box....................................... G 704 535-8743
Charlotte (G-2616)

3544 Special dies, tools, jigs, and fixtures

A & M Tool Inc................................... F 828 891-9990
Mills River (G-8309)

ABT Manufacturing LLC...................... E 704 847-9188
Statesville (G-11645)

Acme Die & Machine Corporation......... F 704 864-8426
Gastonia (G-4983)

Advance Machining Co Gastonia.......... G 704 866-7411
Gastonia (G-4984)

Alliance Precision Plas Corp............... E 828 286-8631
Spindale (G-11543)

Ameritech Die & Mold Inc................... E 704 664-0801
Mooresville (G-8596)

Ameritech Die & Mold South Inc.......... F 704 664-0801
Mooresville (G-8597)

Ameritek Lasercut Dies Inc................. G 336 292-1165
Greensboro (G-5360)

Atlantic Mold Inc............................... G 919 832-8151
Fuquay Varina (G-4868)

Atlantic Tool & Die Co Inc................... G 910 270-2888
Hampstead (G-6068)

Bethlehem Manufacturing Co.............. F 828 495-7731
Hickory (G-6270)

Bnp Inc... F 919 775-7070
Sanford (G-11157)

Brooks of Dallas Inc.......................... E 704 922-5219
Dallas (G-3666)

Brooks Tool Inc................................. G 704 283-0112
Monroe (G-8447)

Brothers Precision Tool Co.................. G 704 982-5667
Albemarle (G-64)

Cairn Studio Ltd................................ E 704 664-7128
Mooresville (G-8627)

Carolina Resource Corp...................... F 919 562-0200
Youngsville (G-13470)

Cascade Die Casting Group Inc........... E 336 882-0186
High Point (G-6563)

Container Graphics Corp..................... E 704 588-7230
Pineville (G-9720)

▲ Container Graphics Corp.................. F 919 481-4200
Cary (G-1333)

Continental Tool Works Inc.................. G 828 692-2578
Hendersonville (G-6198)

Converting Technology Inc.................. G 336 333-2386
Greensboro (G-5466)

Cross Technology Inc......................... E 336 725-4700
East Bend (G-4322)

DEB Manufacturing Inc....................... G 704 703-6618
Concord (G-3353)

Die-Tech Inc...................................... G 336 475-9186
Thomasville (G-12018)

Digital Design & Modeling LLC............ G 336 766-2155
Winston Salem (G-13144)

Dura-Craft Die Inc............................. G 828 632-1944
Taylorsville (G-11959)

Dwd Industries LLC............................ E 336 498-6327
Randleman (G-10644)

▲ Dynacast US Holdings Inc................ G 704 927-2790
Charlotte (G-2075)

Elizabeth Carbide NC Inc.................... G 336 472-5555
Lexington (G-7684)

▲ Emerald Tool and Mold Inc.............. F 336 996-6445
Kernersville (G-7271)

◆ Emery Corporation........................... D 828 433-1536
Morganton (G-8862)

Enplas Life Tech Inc.......................... G 828 633-2250
Asheville (G-494)

Flat Rock Tool & Mold Inc................... G 828 692-2578
Hendersonville (G-6208)

Foot To Die For.................................. G 704 577-2822
Charlotte (G-2170)

Gerald Hartsoe.................................. G 336 498-3233
Randleman (G-10648)

Goodyear Tire & Rubber Company........ D 704 928-4500
Statesville (G-11705)

Griffiths Corporation.......................... D 704 554-5657
Pineville (G-9732)

▲ H + M USA Management Co Inc......... G 704 599-9325
Charlotte (G-2247)

▲ Hasco America Inc.......................... G 828 650-2631
Fletcher (G-4740)

Industrial Mtal Flame Spryers............. G 919 596-9381
Durham (G-4074)

Industrial Mtal Pdts Abrdeen I............. F 910 944-8110
Aberdeen (G-7)

Its A Snap... G 828 254-3456
Asheville (G-525)

Jmk Tool & Die Inc............................. G 910 897-6373
Coats (G-3263)

KAM Tool & Die Inc............................ E 919 269-5099
Zebulon (G-13512)

Linden St Holdings Inc .... F 336 472-5555
Lexington *(G-7711)*

▲ Madern Usa Inc .... E 919 363-4248
Apex *(G-177)*

Marine Systems Inc .... F 828 254-5354
Asheville *(G-543)*

▲ Meusburger Us Inc .... E 704 526-0330
Mint Hill *(G-8340)*

Millar Industries Inc .... E 828 687-0639
Arden *(G-285)*

Modern Mold & Tool Company .... G 704 377-2300
Mount Holly *(G-9238)*

Northeast Tool and Mfg Company .... E 704 882-1187
Matthews *(G-8187)*

Omni Mold & Die LLC .... F 336 724-5152
Winston Salem *(G-13270)*

Palmer Senn .... G 704 451-3971
Charlotte *(G-2606)*

Parker Industries Inc .... D 828 437-7779
Connelly Springs *(G-3481)*

Piedmont Fiberglass Inc .... E 828 632-8883
Statesville *(G-11745)*

Precision Partners LLC .... E 800 545-3121
Charlotte *(G-2658)*

Precision Tool & Stamping Inc .... E 910 592-0174
Clinton *(G-3239)*

Precision Tool Dye and Mold .... F 828 687-2990
Arden *(G-301)*

Progressive Service Die Co .... F 910 353-4836
Jacksonville *(G-7140)*

Progressive Tool & Mfg Inc .... F 336 664-1130
Greensboro *(G-5768)*

Prototype Tooling Co .... G 704 864-7777
Gastonia *(G-5128)*

Pyrotek Incorporated .... E 704 642-1993
Salisbury *(G-11108)*

▲ Qrmc Ltd .... G 828 696-2000
Hendersonville *(G-6238)*

▼ R A Serafini Inc .... F 704 864-6763
Gastonia *(G-5130)*

▲ Rp Fletcher Machine Co Inc .... D 336 249-6101
Lexington *(G-7736)*

◆ Schunk Intec Inc .... D 919 572-2705
Morrisville *(G-9046)*

▲ Select Mold Service Inc .... G 910 323-1287
Fayetteville *(G-4667)*

Southeastern Die of NC .... G 336 275-5212
Greensboro *(G-5824)*

◆ Southeastern Tool & Die Inc .... D 910 944-7677
Aberdeen *(G-24)*

Southern Steel and Wire Inc .... D 336 548-9611
Madison *(G-8000)*

Speciality Cox Mfg LLC .... G 828 684-5762
Arden *(G-309)*

Specialty Machine Co Inc .... G 704 853-2102
Gastonia *(G-5139)*

▲ Spnc Associates Inc .... D 919 467-5151
Cary *(G-1466)*

Stafford Cutting Dies Inc .... D 704 821-6330
Indian Trail *(G-7100)*

Stampco Metal Products Inc .... G 828 645-4271
Weaverville *(G-12504)*

Stratford Tool & Die Co Inc .... G 336 765-2030
Winston Salem *(G-13347)*

Superior Tooling Inc .... E 919 570-9762
Wake Forest *(G-12306)*

T D M Corporation .... E
Fletcher *(G-4772)*

Tgr Enterprises Incorporated .... G 828 665-4427
Candler *(G-1234)*

Toner Machining Tech Inc .... D 828 432-8007
Morganton *(G-8905)*

Valmet Inc .... C 704 541-1453
Charlotte *(G-2972)*

Western Crlina TI Mold Corp In .... F 828 890-4448
Mills River *(G-8324)*

Wilmington Machine Works Inc .... G 910 343-8111
Wilmington *(G-12950)*

Wirtz Wire Edm LLC .... F 828 696-0830
Hendersonville *(G-6250)*

Worth Products LLC .... F 252 747-9994
Snow Hill *(G-11484)*

◆ Wright Machine & Tool Co Inc .... E 828 298-8440
Swannanoa *(G-11879)*

3545 Machine tool accessories

21st Century Tech of Amer .... F 910 826-3676
Fayetteville *(G-4540)*

Advanced Superabrasives Inc .... E 828 689-3200
Mars Hill *(G-8076)*

C & C Precision Machine Inc .... E 704 739-0505
Kings Mountain *(G-7352)*

▲ C R Onsrud Inc .... C 704 508-7000
Troutman *(G-12131)*

Calco Enterprises Inc .... F 910 695-0089
Aberdeen *(G-3)*

◆ Canvas Sx LLC .... C 980 474-3700
Charlotte *(G-1836)*

Carbo-Cut Inc .... G 828 685-7890
Hendersonville *(G-6193)*

Carolina Components Group Inc .... E 919 635-8438
Durham *(G-3960)*

Central Tool & Mfg Co Inc .... G 828 328-2383
Hickory *(G-6294)*

Cooper Bussmann LLC .... C 252 566-0278
La Grange *(G-7465)*

▲ Creative Tooling Solutions Inc .... G 704 504-5415
Pineville *(G-9722)*

Croft Precision Tools Inc .... G 704 399-4124
Charlotte *(G-1997)*

Cross Technology Inc .... E 336 725-4700
East Bend *(G-4322)*

◆ Diamond Dog Tools Inc .... D 828 687-3686
Arden *(G-265)*

◆ Dormer Pramet LLC .... C 800 877-3745
Mebane *(G-8238)*

Em2 Machine Corp .... G 336 297-4110
Summerfield *(G-11839)*

◆ Emery Corporation .... D 828 433-1536
Morganton *(G-8862)*

Eversharp Saw & Tool Inc .... G 828 345-1200
Hickory *(G-6330)*

◆ Freud America Inc .... C 800 334-4107
High Point *(G-6624)*

Greenleaf Corporation .... E 828 693-0461
East Flat Rock *(G-4332)*

▲ Hickory Saw & Tool Inc .... E 828 324-5585
Hickory *(G-6353)*

I G P .... G 828 728-5338
Lenoir *(G-7616)*

If Armor International LLC .... C 704 482-1399
Shelby *(G-11346)*

◆ Irwin Industrial Tool Company .... C 704 987-4555
Huntersville *(G-7004)*

Kenmar Inc .... F 336 884-8722
High Point *(G-6684)*

Kennametal Inc .... D 336 672-3313
Asheboro *(G-370)*

Kennametal Inc .... F 704 588-4777
Charlotte *(G-2393)*

Kennametal Inc .... D 252 492-4163
Henderson *(G-6163)*

Kennametal Inc .... D 252 536-5209
Weldon *(G-12522)*

▲ Kyocera Precision Tools Inc .... G 800 823-7284
Fletcher *(G-4745)*

▲ Linamar North Carolina Inc .... F 828 348-5343
Arden *(G-283)*

Lns Turbo North America .... G 704 435-6376
Cherryville *(G-3066)*

LS Starrett Company .... D 336 789-5141
Mount Airy *(G-9148)*

Mitsubishi Materials USA Corp .... G 980 312-3100
Mooresville *(G-8724)*

Modern Tool Service .... F 919 365-7470
Wendell *(G-12539)*

North Carolina Mfg Inc .... E 919 734-1115
Goldsboro *(G-5231)*

Packet Pushers Interactive LLC .... G 928 793-2450
Sanford *(G-11214)*

Penco Precision LLC .... G 910 292-6542
Wilmington *(G-12873)*

Pie Pushers .... G 919 901-0743
Durham *(G-4180)*

Premier Tool LLC .... G 704 895-8223
Cornelius *(G-3619)*

Production Tool and Die Co Inc .... F 704 525-0498
Charlotte *(G-2672)*

▲ Putsch & Company Inc .... E 828 684-0671
Fletcher *(G-4762)*

Robert Bosch Tool Corporation .... F 252 551-7512
Greenville *(G-6019)*

Rock-Weld Industries Inc .... G 336 375-6862
Greensboro *(G-5792)*

▲ Rp Fletcher Machine Co Inc .... D 336 249-6101
Lexington *(G-7736)*

◆ Salice America Inc .... E 704 841-7810
Charlotte *(G-2749)*

◆ Sandvik Inc .... C 919 563-5008
Mebane *(G-8258)*

Sandvik McHning Sltons USA LLC .... F 919 563-5008
Mebane *(G-8259)*

Selbach Machinery LLC .... G 910 794-9350
Wilmington *(G-12916)*

Smith Setzer and Sons Inc .... E 828 241-3161
Catawba *(G-1514)*

Speedwell Machine Works Inc .... E 704 866-7418
Gastonia *(G-5140)*

SPX Technologies Inc .... D 980 474-3700
Charlotte *(G-2851)*

Stanley Black & Decker Inc .... G 704 293-9392
Huntersville *(G-7058)*

Tar Heel Tling Prcsion McHning .... F 919 965-6160
Smithfield *(G-11467)*

▲ Techsouth Inc .... G 704 334-1100
Matthews *(G-8196)*

Tfam Solutions LLC .... G 910 637-0266
Aberdeen *(G-26)*

Toner Machining Tech Inc .... D 828 432-8007
Morganton *(G-8905)*

Toolcraft Inc North Carolina .... F 828 659-7379
Marion *(G-8070)*

Unique Tool and Mfg Co .... E 336 498-2614
Franklinville *(G-4858)*

United Machine & Metal Fab Inc .... E 828 464-5167
Conover *(G-3569)*

▲ Vishay Transducers Ltd .... E 919 365-3800
Wendell *(G-12553)*

W D Lee & Company .... G 704 864-0346
Gastonia *(G-5163)*

W T Mander & Son Inc .... G 336 562-5755
Prospect Hill *(G-9830)*

Wise Storage Solutions LLC .... E 336 789-5141
Mount Airy *(G-9196)*

Yat Usa Inc .... G 480 584-4096
Huntersville *(G-7063)*

SIC

▲ Yg-1 America Inc .... E 980 318-5348
Charlotte *(G-3040)*

3546 Power-driven handtools

Apex Tool Group LLC .... C 919 387-0099
Apex *(G-138)*

Black & Decker (us) Inc .... G 336 852-1300
Greensboro *(G-5391)*

Black & Decker Corporation .... G 803 396-3700
Charlotte *(G-1788)*

Black & Decker Corporation .... G 704 799-3929
Mooresville *(G-8616)*

Black & Decker Corporation .... G 919 878-0357
Raleigh *(G-9948)*

Bolton Investors Inc .... G 919 471-1197
Durham *(G-3937)*

Chicago Pneumatic Tool Co LLC .... F 704 504-6937
Charlotte *(G-1913)*

◆ Denver Global Products Inc .... D 704 665-1800
Charlotte *(G-2033)*

▲ Efco USA Inc .... G 800 332-6872
Charlotte *(G-2092)*

Farm Services Inc .... G 336 226-7381
Graham *(G-5268)*

◆ Freud America Inc .... C 800 334-4107
High Point *(G-6624)*

Ingersoll-Rand Indus US Inc .... D 704 896-4000
Davidson *(G-3710)*

John Deere Consumer Pdts Inc .... C 919 804-2000
Cary *(G-1380)*

Ledger Hardware Inc .... G 828 688-4798
Bakersville *(G-679)*

Leitz Tooling Systems LP .... G 336 861-3367
Archdale *(G-237)*

Masonite Corporation .... A 704 599-0235
Charlotte *(G-2466)*

Quality Equipment LLC .... G 919 493-3545
Durham *(G-4203)*

◆ Snap-On Power Tools Inc .... C 828 835-4400
Murphy *(G-9296)*

Stanley Black & Decker .... F 704 987-2271
Huntersville *(G-7057)*

Stanley Black & Decker Inc .... C 704 789-7000
Concord *(G-3446)*

Stanley Customer Support Divis .... G 704 789-7000
Concord *(G-3447)*

Trane Technologies Company LLC .... C 910 692-8700
Southern Pines *(G-11512)*

▲ Wall-Lenk Corporation .... E 252 527-4186
Kinston *(G-7435)*

Weber Screwdriving Systems Inc .... E 704 360-5820
Mooresville *(G-8795)*

Wto Inc .... F 704 714-7765
Charlotte *(G-3028)*

Yard Pro Sales and Service LLC .... G 252 641-9776
Tarboro *(G-11947)*

3547 Rolling mill machinery

Ew Jackson Transportation LLC .... G 919 586-2514
Holly Springs *(G-6900)*

South Atlantic LLC .... F 336 376-0410
Graham *(G-5286)*

Tecnofirma America Inc .... G 704 674-1296
Charlotte *(G-2905)*

3548 Welding apparatus

American Welding & Gas Inc .... G 984 222-2600
Raleigh *(G-9899)*

Fanuc America Corporation .... D 704 596-5121
Huntersville *(G-6988)*

Flawtech Inc .... E 704 795-4401
Concord *(G-3364)*

J W Harris Co Inc .... G 336 831-8601
Winston Salem *(G-13213)*

▲ Kincol Industries Incorporated .... G 704 372-8435
Charlotte *(G-2397)*

▲ Liburdi Dimetrics Corporation .... E 704 230-2510
Mooresville *(G-8711)*

Modlins Anonized Aluminum Wldg .... G 252 753-7274
Farmville *(G-4536)*

Qws LLC .... E 252 723-2106
Morehead City *(G-8841)*

U S Alloy Co .... F 888 522-8296
Lowell *(G-7935)*

3549 Metalworking machinery, nec

▲ Atlantic Hydraulics Svcs LLC .... E 919 542-2985
Sanford *(G-11152)*

DCS USA Corporation .... G 919 535-8000
Morrisville *(G-8963)*

▼ Design Tool Inc .... E 828 328-6414
Conover *(G-3515)*

▲ Efco USA Inc .... G 800 332-6872
Charlotte *(G-2092)*

Feeder Innovations Corporation .... G 910 276-3511
Laurinburg *(G-7502)*

G T Racing Heads Inc .... G 336 905-7988
Sophia *(G-11489)*

Gerringer Enterprises .... G 336 227-6535
Burlington *(G-1096)*

H C Production Co .... G 910 483-5267
Fayetteville *(G-4607)*

High Definition Tool Corp .... E 828 397-2467
Connelly Springs *(G-3478)*

IMS Fabrication Inc .... E 704 216-0255
Salisbury *(G-11066)*

J Wise Inc .... E 828 202-5563
Lincolnton *(G-7833)*

Joe and La Inc .... F 336 585-0313
Burlington *(G-1113)*

Kds Fabricating and Mch Sp LLC .... F 828 632-5091
Hiddenite *(G-6501)*

Manufacturing Methods LLC .... E 910 371-1700
Leland *(G-7553)*

Mestek Inc .... C 252 753-5323
Farmville *(G-4535)*

Nine-Ai Inc .... F 781 825-3267
Davidson *(G-3714)*

Obi Machine & Tool Inc .... G 252 946-1580
Chocowinity *(G-3084)*

Petty Machine Company Inc .... E 704 864-3254
Gastonia *(G-5119)*

Scott Systems Intl Inc .... F 704 362-1115
Charlotte *(G-2771)*

▲ Techmet Carbides Inc .... D 828 624-0222
Hickory *(G-6464)*

Winston Steel Stair Co .... G 336 721-0020
Winston Salem *(G-13402)*

3552 Textile machinery

▲ A B Carter Inc .... D 704 865-1201
Gastonia *(G-4982)*

Abercrombie Textiles Inc .... G 704 487-0935
Shelby *(G-11308)*

▼ Alandale Industries Inc .... G 910 576-1291
Troy *(G-12156)*

◆ American Linc Corporation .... E 704 861-9242
Gastonia *(G-4992)*

▲ American Trutzschler Inc .... D 704 399-4521
Charlotte *(G-1670)*

Barudan America Inc .... G 800 627-4776
High Point *(G-6540)*

▲ Belmont Textile Machinery Co .... E 704 827-5836
Mount Holly *(G-9218)*

▲ Bowman-Hollis Manufacturing Co .... E 704 374-1500
Charlotte *(G-1805)*

◆ Briggs-Shaffner Acquisition Co .... F 336 463-4272
Yadkinville *(G-13439)*

Burnett Machine Company Inc .... F 704 867-7786
Gastonia *(G-5008)*

C & J Machine Company Inc .... G 704 922-5913
Dallas *(G-3667)*

Carolina Loom Reed Company Inc .... G 336 274-7631
Greensboro *(G-5428)*

Carolina Tex Sls Gastonia Inc .... G 704 739-1646
Kings Mountain *(G-7357)*

Carolina Textile Services Inc .... G 910 843-3033
Red Springs *(G-10665)*

▲ Custom Enterprises Inc .... G 336 226-8296
Burlington *(G-1081)*

Custom Industries Inc .... F 704 825-3346
Belmont *(G-744)*

▲ Custom Industries Inc .... E 336 299-2885
Greensboro *(G-5481)*

◆ D & S International Inc .... F 336 578-3800
Mebane *(G-8237)*

▲ D M & E Corporation .... E 704 482-8876
Shelby *(G-11328)*

Diversified Textile Mchy Corp .... G 704 739-2121
Kings Mountain *(G-7360)*

Ellerre Tech Inc .... G 704 524-9096
Dallas *(G-3669)*

Elmarco Inc .... G 919 334-6495
Morrisville *(G-8970)*

▼ Excel Inc .... G 704 735-6535
Lincolnton *(G-7830)*

◆ Fab-Con Machinery Dev Corp .... D 704 486-7120
Oakboro *(G-9579)*

▲ Ferguson Companies .... G
Linwood *(G-7878)*

◆ Fletcher Industries Inc .... E 910 692-7133
Southern Pines *(G-11499)*

French Apron Manufacturing Co .... G 704 865-7666
Gastonia *(G-5049)*

Gastex LLC .... G 704 824-9861
Gastonia *(G-5050)*

▼ Gaston County Dyeing Mach .... D 704 822-5000
Mount Holly *(G-9231)*

Imperial Machine Company Inc .... E 704 739-8038
Bessemer City *(G-823)*

▲ International McHy Sls Inc .... G 336 759-9548
Winston Salem *(G-13210)*

◆ Itm Ltd South .... G 336 883-2400
Greensboro *(G-5630)*

▲ J & P Entrprses of Crlinas Inc .... E 704 861-1867
Gastonia *(G-5069)*

J J Jenkins Incorporated .... E 704 821-6648
Matthews *(G-8177)*

▲ Kern-Liebers USA Textile Inc .... E 704 329-7153
Matthews *(G-8122)*

▲ M-B Industries Inc .... C 828 862-4201
Rosman *(G-10913)*

Monarch Knitting McHy Corp .... E 704 283-8171
Monroe *(G-8533)*

◆ Monarch Knitting McHy Corp .... F 704 291-3300
Monroe *(G-8534)*

◆ Monarch Manufacturing Corp .... F 704 283-8171
Monroe *(G-8535)*

▲ Mount Hope Machinery Co .... F
Charlotte *(G-2523)*

◆ Murata McHy USA Holdings Inc .... F 704 394-8331
Charlotte *(G-2533)*

▲ Parts and Systems Company Inc .... F 828 684-7070
Arden *(G-295)*

Petty Machine Company Inc .... E 704 864-3254
Gastonia *(G-5119)*

▲ Pinco Usa Inc.. G..... 704 895-5766
Cornelius (G-3618)

Precision Comb Works Inc....................... G..... 704 864-2761
Gastonia (G-5125)

Precision Machine Products Inc............. D..... 704 865-7490
Gastonia (G-5126)

◆ Sam M Butler Inc...................................E..... 910 277-7456
Laurinburg (G-7514)

Sherrill Contract Mfg Inc........................... F..... 704 922-7871
Dallas (G-3689)

▲ Smart Machine Technologies Inc...... D..... 276 632-9853
Greensboro (G-5817)

▲ Spgprints America Inc........................... D..... 704 598-7171
Charlotte (G-2844)

▲ Stork United Corporation...................... A..... 704 598-7171
Charlotte (G-2870)

▼ TCI Mobility Inc.. F..... 704 867-8331
Gastonia (G-5149)

Textile Sales Intl Inc................................. G..... 704 483-7966
Denver (G-3811)

▲ Textrol Laboratories Inc..................... E..... 704 764-3400
Monroe (G-8569)

Tri State Plastics Inc................................. G..... 704 865-7431
Gastonia (G-5159)

Tsg Finishing LLC.................................... G..... 828 328-5522
Hickory (G-6471)

Tsg Finishing LLC.................................... E..... 828 328-5541
Hickory (G-6472)

Tsg Finishing LLC.................................... E..... 828 328-5522
Hickory (G-6473)

▲ Tubular Textile Machinery................. G..... 336 956-6444
Lexington (G-7754)

◆ Vanguard Pai Lung LLC......................G..... 704 283-8171
Monroe (G-8575)

Woolfoam Corporation............................. G..... 336 886-4964
High Point (G-6840)

3553 Woodworking machinery

Alders Point... G..... 336 725-9021
Winston Salem (G-13076)

Atlantic Commercial Caseworks............. G..... 704 393-9500
Charlotte (G-1709)

Automated Lumber Handling Inc............ G..... 828 754-4662
Lenoir (G-7574)

▲ Bacci America Inc................................. F..... 704 375-5044
Charlotte (G-1736)

Bmi Wood Products Inc............................ G..... 919 829-9505
Raleigh (G-9951)

Carbide Saws Incorporated.................... G..... 336 882-6835
High Point (G-6554)

Caterpillar Inc.. D..... 919 550-1100
Clayton (G-3137)

▲ Cefla North America Inc...................... E..... 704 598-0020
Charlotte (G-1882)

Dixon Custom Cabinetry LLC................. F..... 336 992-3306
Kernersville (G-7266)

Edmiston Hydrlic Swmill Eqp In............. G..... 336 921-2304
Boomer (G-890)

▲ Etk International Inc............................. G..... 704 819-1541
Indian Trail (G-7079)

▲ Eurohansa Inc...................................... G..... 336 885-1010
High Point (G-6616)

▲ Farris Belt & Saw Company................ F..... 704 527-6166
Charlotte (G-2143)

Fletcher Machine Inds Inc....................... D..... 336 249-6101
Lexington (G-7687)

▲ Grecon Dimter Inc............................... G..... 828 397-5139
Connelly Springs (G-3477)

◆ Holz-Her Us Inc................................... D..... 704 587-3400
Mooresville (G-8686)

◆ Jly Invstmnts Inc Fka Nwman Mc......E..... 336 273-8261
Browns Summit (G-1000)

◆ Karl Ogden Enterprises Inc.................G..... 704 845-2785
Matthews (G-8121)

Leitz Tooling Systems LP......................... G..... 336 861-3367
Archdale (G-237)

▲ Ligna Machinery Inc............................ G..... 336 584-0030
Burlington (G-1120)

▼ Meadows Mills Inc............................... E..... 336 838-2282
North Wilkesboro (G-9546)

Mill Art Wood.. G..... 919 828-7376
Raleigh (G-10307)

Normac Kitchens Inc................................ D..... 704 485-1911
Locust (G-7896)

◆ Ogden Sales Group LLC.....................G..... 704 845-2785
Matthews (G-8137)

Ostwalt Leasing Co Inc............................ D..... 704 528-4528
Troutman (G-12146)

▲ Otb Machinery Inc............................... G..... 336 323-1035
Thomasville (G-12057)

Peco Inc.. E..... 828 684-1234
Arden (G-296)

▼ Rfsprotech LLC.................................... E..... 704 845-2785
Matthews (G-8145)

Router Bit Service Company Inc............. F..... 336 431-5535
High Point (G-6760)

▲ Rp Fletcher Machine Co Inc................ D..... 336 249-6101
Lexington (G-7736)

Singley Specialty Co Inc.......................... G..... 336 852-8581
Greensboro (G-5814)

Smith Woodturning Inc............................. G..... 828 464-2230
Newton (G-9495)

Tawnico LLC... G..... 704 606-2345
Charlotte (G-2900)

Ventura Inc... G..... 252 291-7125
Fremont (G-4861)

Venture Cabinets...................................... G..... 252 299-0051
Fremont (G-4862)

3554 Paper industries machinery

Ameritek Inc... F..... 336 292-1165
Greensboro (G-5359)

DP Hill Inc.. G..... 252 568-4282
Richlands (G-10720)

Hearn Graphic Finishing Inc.................... G..... 336 760-1467
Winston Salem (G-13194)

Metso USA Inc.. D..... 877 677-2005
Bessemer City (G-827)

▲ Summer Industries LLC....................... C..... 336 731-9217
Welcome (G-12515)

◆ Triple Crown International LLC..........G..... 704 846-4983
Charlotte (G-2946)

Valmet Inc... G..... 803 289-4900
Charlotte (G-2971)

W V Doyle Enterprises Inc....................... G..... 336 885-2035
High Point (G-6831)

3555 Printing trades machinery

▲ Anilox Roll Company Inc..................... G..... 704 588-1809
Charlotte (G-1678)

◆ Cary Manufacturing Corporation.......G..... 704 527-4402
Charlotte (G-1864)

Coastal Press Inc..................................... G..... 252 726-1549
Morehead City (G-8827)

Cogent Dynamics Inc............................... G..... 828 628-9025
Fletcher (G-4730)

▲ Container Graphics Corp..................... F..... 919 481-4200
Cary (G-1333)

Creative Printing Inc................................ G..... 828 265-2800
Boone (G-909)

CTX Builders Supply................................ G..... 704 983-6748
Albemarle (G-66)

Diazit Company Inc.................................. G..... 919 556-5188
Wake Forest (G-12272)

Digital Highpoint LLC............................... C..... 336 883-7146
High Point (G-6593)

▲ Diversfied Prtg Techniques Inc........ E..... 704 583-9433
Charlotte (G-2055)

Encore Group Inc..................................... C..... 336 768-7859
Winston Salem (G-13157)

H F Kinney Co Inc.................................... E..... 704 540-9367
Charlotte (G-2248)

Harper Companies Intl Inc....................... G..... 800 438-3111
Charlotte (G-2258)

◆ Harper Corporation of America..........C..... 704 588-3371
Charlotte (G-2259)

Lazeredge LLC... F..... 336 480-7934
Mount Airy (G-9145)

Mark/Trece Inc... F..... 973 884-1005
Greensboro (G-5674)

Mark/Trece Inc... E..... 336 292-3424
Whitsett (G-12614)

National Color Graphics Inc.................... G..... 704 263-3187
Mount Holly (G-9240)

National Roller Supply Inc....................... G..... 704 853-1174
Gastonia (G-5107)

North Crlina Dept Adult Crrcto................ G..... 919 733-0867
Raleigh (G-10337)

▲ Spgprints America Inc........................ D..... 704 598-7171
Charlotte (G-2844)

Trio Labs Inc.. F..... 919 818-9646
Morrisville (G-9079)

3556 Food products machinery

A1gumballs... G..... 919 494-1322
Raleigh (G-9860)

▲ AC Corporation.................................... B..... 336 273-4472
Greensboro (G-5339)

▲ Are Management LLC........................... E..... 336 855-7800
High Point (G-6526)

Babington Technology Inc....................... G..... 252 984-0349
Rocky Mount (G-10823)

▲ Baker Thermal Solutions LLC............ G..... 919 674-3750
Clayton (G-3133)

Booneshine Brewing Co Inc.................... G..... 828 263-4305
Boone (G-901)

Buhler Inc... C..... 800 722-7483
Cary (G-1316)

Carolina Packing House Sups................. G..... 910 653-3438
Tabor City (G-11908)

Cates Mechanical Corporation................ G..... 704 458-5163
Charlotte (G-1866)

Community Brewing Ventures LLC......... G..... 800 579-6539
Newton (G-9458)

Corporate Place LLC................................ G..... 704 808-3848
Charlotte (G-1989)

▲ Dbt Holdings LLC................................ D..... 704 900-6606
Charlotte (G-2023)

Dean St Processing LLC.......................... G..... 252 235-0401
Bailey (G-669)

Delaney Holdings Co............................... G..... 704 808-3848
Charlotte (G-2027)

Designtek Fabrication Inc......................... F..... 910 359-0130
Red Springs (G-10666)

East Crlina Olseed Prcssors LL.............. D..... 252 935-5553
Pantego (G-9643)

▲ Embrex LLC.. C..... 919 941-5185
Durham (G-4019)

Ezbrew Inc.. G..... 833 233-2739
Cary (G-1358)

Flagstone Foods LLC............................... B..... 252 795-6500
Robersonville (G-10767)

Fmp Equipment Corp................................ G..... 336 621-2882
Browns Summit (G-992)

▼ Friedrich Metal Pdts Co Inc............... E..... 336 375-3067
Browns Summit (G-993)

S
I
C

▲ Gea Intec LLC .... E 919 433-0131
  Durham *(G-4044)*

Griffin Marketing Group .... G 336 558-5802
  Greensboro *(G-5580)*

Induction Food Systems Inc .... G 919 907-0179
  Raleigh *(G-10188)*

Industrial Tech Svcs Amrcas In .... D 704 808-3848
  Charlotte *(G-2325)*

Jbt Aerotech Services .... G 336 740-3737
  Greensboro *(G-5635)*

Jbt Marel Corporation .... G 919 362-8811
  Apex *(G-171)*

Krispy Kreme Doughnut Corp .... E 336 726-8908
  Winston Salem *(G-13227)*

M G Newell Corporation .... D 336 393-0100
  Greensboro *(G-5668)*

Marshall Middleby Inc .... D 919 762-1000
  Fuquay Varina *(G-4887)*

▼ Meadows Mills Inc .... E 336 838-2282
  North Wilkesboro *(G-9546)*

▲ Microthermics Inc .... F 919 878-8045
  Raleigh *(G-10303)*

◆ Middleby Marshall Inc .... C 919 762-1000
  Fuquay Varina *(G-4891)*

Prima Elements LLC .... G 910 483-8406
  Fayetteville *(G-4657)*

▲ Putsch & Company Inc .... E 828 684-0671
  Fletcher *(G-4762)*

Roi Industries Group Inc .... G 919 788-7728
  Durham *(G-4218)*

Sinnovatek Inc .... G 919 694-0974
  Raleigh *(G-10479)*

▲ Smart Machine Technologies Inc .... D 276 632-9853
  Greensboro *(G-5817)*

SPX Flow Inc .... C 704 752-4400
  Charlotte *(G-2847)*

SPX Flow Holdings Inc .... G 704 808-3848
  Charlotte *(G-2848)*

SPX Flow Tech Systems Inc .... A 704 752-4400
  Charlotte *(G-2849)*

SPX Latin America Corporation .... G 704 808-3848
  Charlotte *(G-2850)*

▲ Stanza Machinery Inc .... E 704 599-0623
  Charlotte *(G-2859)*

▲ Stork United Corporation .... A 704 598-7171
  Charlotte *(G-2870)*

◆ Tipper Tie Inc .... C 919 362-8811
  Apex *(G-198)*

Utsey Duskie & Associates .... G 704 663-0036
  Mooresville *(G-8789)*

▲ Weidenmiller Co .... F 630 250-2500
  Apex *(G-206)*

Wins Smokehouse Services Ltd .... G 828 884-7476
  Pisgah Forest *(G-9775)*

3559 Special industry machinery, nec

Advanced Plastiform Inc .... D 919 404-2080
  Zebulon *(G-13500)*

Apb Wrecker Service LLC .... G 704 400-0857
  Charlotte *(G-1681)*

Atmosphric Plsma Solutions Inc .... G 919 341-8325
  Cary *(G-1298)*

◆ Autec Inc .... E 704 871-9141
  Statesville *(G-11663)*

Auto-Systems and Service Inc .... F 336 824-3580
  Ramseur *(G-10625)*

▲ Autopark Logistics LLC .... G 704 365-3544
  Charlotte *(G-1718)*

Aylward Enterprises LLC .... E 252 639-9242
  New Bern *(G-9337)*

Bayatronics LLC .... E 980 432-0438
  Concord *(G-3319)*

◆ Besana-Lovati Inc .... F 336 768-6064
  Hamptonville *(G-6082)*

Besi Machining LLC .... F 919 218-9241
  Youngsville *(G-13464)*

Biesse America Inc .... F 704 357-3131
  Charlotte *(G-1780)*

Birch Bros Southern Inc .... E 704 843-2111
  Waxhaw *(G-12423)*

◆ Canvas Sx LLC .... C 980 474-3700
  Charlotte *(G-1836)*

Carolina Mechanical Services Inc .... E 919 477-7100
  Durham *(G-3961)*

Clean Green Inc .... G 919 596-3500
  Durham *(G-3977)*

Coastal Carolina Gin LLC .... F 252 943-6990
  Pantego *(G-9642)*

◆ Corob North America Inc .... F 704 588-8408
  Charlotte *(G-1988)*

Corporate Place LLC .... G 704 808-3848
  Charlotte *(G-1989)*

Cox Machine Co Inc .... G 704 296-0118
  Monroe *(G-8470)*

CVC Equipment Company .... G 704 300-6242
  Cherryville *(G-3063)*

▲ D M & E Corporation .... E 704 482-8876
  Shelby *(G-11328)*

Delaney Holdings Co .... G 704 808-3848
  Charlotte *(G-2027)*

Designtek Fabrication Inc .... F 910 359-0130
  Red Springs *(G-10666)*

◆ Dymetrol Company Inc .... F 866 964-8632
  Bladenboro *(G-876)*

▲ Encertec Inc .... F 336 288-7226
  Greensboro *(G-5519)*

Enforge LLC .... E 704 983-4146
  Albemarle *(G-71)*

Enplas Life Tech Inc .... G 828 633-2250
  Asheville *(G-494)*

Envirotek Worldwide LLC .... F 704 285-6400
  Charlotte *(G-2120)*

Falls of Neuse Management LLC .... A 919 573-2900
  Raleigh *(G-10103)*

Fanuc America Corporation .... D 704 596-5121
  Huntersville *(G-6988)*

Fil-Chem Inc .... G 919 878-1270
  Raleigh *(G-10108)*

Fireline Shields Llc .... G 704 948-3680
  Huntersville *(G-6991)*

G & E Investments Inc .... F 704 395-2155
  Charlotte *(G-2183)*

Gardner Machinery Corporation .... F 704 372-3890
  Charlotte *(G-2189)*

Gladiator Enterprises Inc .... G 336 944-6932
  Greensboro *(G-5561)*

▲ Global Resource Corporation .... G 919 972-7803
  Morrisville *(G-8984)*

Gold Refinery .... G 336 501-2977
  Browns Summit *(G-996)*

Gold Refinery .... G 336 471-4817
  High Point *(G-6632)*

Hockmeyer Equipment Corp .... D 252 338-4705
  Elizabeth City *(G-4390)*

▲ Ilsemann Corp .... G 610 323-4143
  Charlotte *(G-2313)*

Indian Tff-Tank Greensboro Inc .... G 336 625-2629
  Asheboro *(G-364)*

Industrial Mtal Pdts Abrdeen I .... F 910 944-8110
  Aberdeen *(G-7)*

Industrial Tech Svcs Amrcas In .... D 704 808-3848
  Charlotte *(G-2325)*

Industry Choice Solutions LLC .... G 828 628-1991
  Fairview *(G-4508)*

Jt International USA Inc .... E 201 871-1210
  Raleigh *(G-10225)*

▲ Kanthal Thermal Process Inc .... E 704 784-3001
  Concord *(G-3389)*

▲ Kiln Drying Systems Cmpnnts In .... E 828 891-8115
  Etowah *(G-4496)*

LCI Corporation International .... G 704 399-7441
  Charlotte *(G-2410)*

◆ LCI Corporation International .... E 704 399-7441
  Charlotte *(G-2411)*

McDonald Services Inc .... E 704 597-0590
  Charlotte *(G-2476)*

McDonald Services Inc .... G 704 753-9669
  Monroe *(G-8530)*

Mdsi Inc .... G 919 783-8730
  Browns Summit *(G-1002)*

Merchant 1 Marketing LLC .... G 888 853-9992
  Greensboro *(G-5691)*

Micropore Technologies Inc .... F 984 344-7499
  Morrisville *(G-9020)*

Mono Plate Inc .... G 631 643-3100
  Apex *(G-182)*

◆ NGK Ceramics Usa Inc .... G 704 664-7000
  Mooresville *(G-8733)*

P P Kiln Erectors .... G 980 825-2263
  Salisbury *(G-11099)*

Petty Machine Company Inc .... E 704 864-3254
  Gastonia *(G-5119)*

Power Components Inc .... G 704 321-9481
  Charlotte *(G-2650)*

Powerhouse Resources Intl LLC .... D 919 291-1783
  Raleigh *(G-10380)*

Progressive Elc Greenville LLC .... G 252 413-6957
  Emerald Isle *(G-4479)*

▲ Psi-Polymer Systems Inc .... E 828 468-2600
  Conover *(G-3553)*

Quarry & Kiln LLC .... G 704 888-0775
  Midland *(G-8294)*

Radel Inc .... G 336 245-8078
  Winston Salem *(G-13314)*

Shred-Tech Usa LLC .... G 919 387-8220
  Raleigh *(G-10473)*

▲ Single Temperature Contrls Inc .... G 704 504-4800
  Charlotte *(G-2810)*

SL - Laser Systems LLC .... G 704 561-9990
  Charlotte *(G-2813)*

Southeastern Installation Inc .... E 704 352-7146
  Lexington *(G-7744)*

SPX Flow Holdings Inc .... G 704 808-3848
  Charlotte *(G-2848)*

SPX Latin America Corporation .... G 704 808-3848
  Charlotte *(G-2850)*

SPX Technologies Inc .... D 980 474-3700
  Charlotte *(G-2851)*

Superior Dry Kilns Inc .... E 828 754-7001
  Hudson *(G-6960)*

Ultraloop Technologies Inc .... G 919 636-2842
  Chapel Hill *(G-1583)*

Wastequip .... F 800 255-4126
  Statesville *(G-11798)*

▼ Wet Dog Glass LLC .... G 910 428-4111
  Star *(G-11635)*

▲ Williams Performance Inc .... G 704 603-4431
  Mount Ulla *(G-9273)*

Wispry Inc .... G 919 854-7500
  Cary *(G-1484)*

3561 Pumps and pumping equipment

1st Choice Service Inc .... G 704 913-7685
  Cherryville *(G-3058)*

Air Control Inc .... E 252 492-2300
  Henderson *(G-6147)*

Allied/Carter Machining Inc....................... G 704 784-1253
Concord *(G-3310)*

◆ Bfs Industries LLC............................E 919 575-6711
Butner *(G-1199)*

Bornemann Pumps Inc............................ G 704 849-8636
Matthews *(G-8100)*

Camp S Well and Pump Co Inc .... G 828 453-7322
Ellenboro *(G-4456)*

Central East Services Inc.................. G 252 883-9629
Rocky Mount *(G-10827)*

Chichibone Inc.. G 919 785-0090
Morrisville *(G-8957)*

Chichibone Inc....................................... F 919 785-0090
Kernersville *(G-7256)*

Circor Precision Metering LLC............. A 919 774-7667
Sanford *(G-11164)*

▲ Circor Precision Metering LLC........ D 704 289-6511
Monroe *(G-8458)*

Circor Pumps North America LLC........ D 704 289-6511
Monroe *(G-8459)*

◆ Clyde Union (us) Inc.........................C 704 808-3000
Charlotte *(G-1934)*

Clydeunion Pumps Inc......................... E 704 808-3848
Charlotte *(G-1936)*

▲ Colfax Pump Group............................. C 704 289-6511
Monroe *(G-8463)*

Dynisco Instruments LLC.................... E 828 326-9888
Hickory *(G-6325)*

Enovis Corporation............................... F 704 289-6511
Monroe *(G-8484)*

Flowserve Corporation......................... E 704 494-0497
Charlotte *(G-2168)*

Flowserve Corporation......................... G 910 371-9011
Leland *(G-7543)*

Flowserve US Inc.................................... F 972 443-6500
Raleigh *(G-10114)*

◆ G Denver and Co LLC.........................E 704 896-4000
Davidson *(G-3705)*

Haldex Inc.. C 828 652-9308
Marion *(G-8042)*

Hayward Industries Inc....................... D 336 712-9900
Clemmons *(G-3188)*

Hayward Industries Inc....................... A 336 712-9900
Clemmons *(G-3189)*

◆ Hayward Industries Inc......................B 704 837-8002
Charlotte *(G-2265)*

◆ Hurst Jaws of Life Inc.......................C 704 487-6961
Shelby *(G-11345)*

IMO Industries Inc................................ C 704 289-6511
Monroe *(G-8504)*

▲ IMO Industries Inc............................. D 301 323-9000
Monroe *(G-8503)*

Ingersoll Rand Inc................................. G 828 375-8240
Mocksville *(G-8371)*

INGERSOLL RAND INC......................... A 704 896-4000
Davidson *(G-3709)*

Ingersoll-Rand Company...................... D 704 655-4836
Charlotte *(G-2336)*

Ingersoll-Rand Indus US Inc.............. D 704 896-4000
Davidson *(G-3710)*

James M Pleasants Company Inc........ E 800 365-9010
Greensboro *(G-5633)*

▲ Kral USA Inc.. G 704 814-6164
Matthews *(G-8125)*

▲ Maag Reduction Inc............................ E 704 716-9000
Charlotte *(G-2445)*

▲ Marley Company LLC.......................... C 704 752-4400
Charlotte *(G-2459)*

Merrill Resources Inc........................... G 828 877-4450
Penrose *(G-9662)*

◆ Opw Flng Cntnment Systems Inc.......E 919 209-2280
Smithfield *(G-11457)*

Pentair Water Pool and Spa Inc............. D 919 463-4640
Cary *(G-1417)*

◆ Pentair Water Pool and Spa Inc.........A 919 566-8000
Sanford *(G-11217)*

▲ Primax Usa Inc.................................... G 704 587-3377
Charlotte *(G-2667)*

Raymond Brown Well Company Inc....... G 336 374-4999
Danbury *(G-3695)*

SL Liquidation LLC............................. G 910 353-3666
Jacksonville *(G-7147)*

SPX Flow Inc.. C 704 752-4400
Charlotte *(G-2847)*

▲ Stockholm Corporation...................... E 704 552-9314
Charlotte *(G-2869)*

Trs-Sesco LLC..................................... D 336 996-2220
Kernersville *(G-7310)*

◆ Truflo Pumps Inc................................F 336 664-9225
Greensboro *(G-5882)*

◆ Xaloy Extrusion LLC...........................E 828 326-9888
Hickory *(G-6492)*

▲ Xylem Water Solutions USA Inc........ D 704 409-9700
Charlotte *(G-3036)*

3562 Ball and roller bearings

American Roller Bearing Inc................. C 828 624-1460
Hiddenite *(G-6493)*

American Roller Bearing Inc................. F 828 624-1460
Morganton *(G-8850)*

Atlantic Bearing Co Inc...................... G 252 243-0233
Wilson *(G-12965)*

▲ Baldor Dodge Reliance....................... E 828 652-0074
Marion *(G-8033)*

Coc USA Inc... G 888 706-0059
Matthews *(G-8107)*

Everything Industrial Supply................. G 743 333-2222
Winston Salem *(G-13162)*

Hpc NC... G 704 978-0103
Statesville *(G-11713)*

Justice Bearing LLC............................ G 800 355-2500
Mooresville *(G-8701)*

▲ Ketchie-Houston Inc.......................... E 704 786-5101
Concord *(G-3390)*

▲ Linamar Forgings Carolina Inc.......... D 252 237-8181
Wilson *(G-13003)*

◆ Lsrwm Corp...E 704 866-8533
Gastonia *(G-5079)*

Ltlb Holding Company.......................... D 704 585-2908
Hiddenite *(G-6502)*

▲ Ltlb Holding Company........................ F 828 624-1460
Hickory *(G-6389)*

▲ Nn Inc.. G 980 264-4300
Charlotte *(G-2569)*

▼ Problem Solver Inc............................. F 919 596-5555
Raleigh *(G-10399)*

◆ Reich LLC..C 828 651-9019
Arden *(G-303)*

Staunton Capital Inc............................ E 704 866-8533
Greensboro *(G-5838)*

Timken Company................................... C 704 736-2700
Iron Station *(G-7108)*

▲ Urethane Innovators Inc..................... E 252 637-7110
New Bern *(G-9403)*

3563 Air and gas compressors

Air & Gas Solutions LLC...................... E 704 897-2182
Charlotte *(G-1631)*

Atlas Copco Compressors LLC............ F 704 525-0124
Charlotte *(G-1714)*

Backyard Entps & Svcs LLC................ G 828 755-4960
Spindale *(G-11544)*

▲ Eagle Compressors Inc...................... E 336 370-4159
Greensboro *(G-5509)*

Edmac Compressor Parts..................... E 800 866-2959
Charlotte *(G-2091)*

▲ Elgi Compressors USA Inc................. G 704 943-7966
Charlotte *(G-2100)*

Fresh Air Technologies LLC................. F 704 622-7877
Matthews *(G-8171)*

◆ G Denver and Co LLC.........................E 704 896-4000
Davidson *(G-3705)*

Graves Inc... F 252 792-1191
Williamston *(G-12670)*

Hayward Industries Inc....................... A 336 712-9900
Clemmons *(G-3189)*

Hertz Kompressoren USA Inc............. G 704 579-5900
Huntersville *(G-6998)*

Ingersoll Rand Inc................................ E 704 774-4290
Charlotte *(G-2335)*

INGERSOLL RAND INC......................... A 704 896-4000
Davidson *(G-3709)*

Ingersoll-Rand Indus US Inc.............. D 704 896-4000
Davidson *(G-3710)*

Metal Impact East LLC......................... G 743 205-1900
Graham *(G-5279)*

Nordson Corporation............................ F 724 656-5600
Hickory *(G-6402)*

▲ Pattons Medical LLC.......................... E 704 529-5442
Charlotte *(G-2617)*

Peco Inc.. E 828 684-1234
Arden *(G-296)*

▲ Production Systems Inc...................... E 336 886-7161
High Point *(G-6747)*

Safe Air Systems Inc............................ E 336 674-0749
Randleman *(G-10659)*

▲ Schmalz Inc... C 919 713-0880
Raleigh *(G-10461)*

Sub-Aquatics Inc................................... E 336 674-0749
Randleman *(G-10661)*

Superior Finishing Systems LLC........ G 336 956-2000
Lexington *(G-7747)*

▲ Templex Inc... E 336 472-5933
Thomasville *(G-12078)*

Trane Technologies Company LLC....... B 336 751-3561
Mocksville *(G-8394)*

Universal Air Products Corp................. G 704 374-0600
Charlotte *(G-2965)*

3564 Blowers and fans

▲ 3nine USA Inc..................................... F 512 210-4005
Charlotte *(G-1602)*

▲ Absolent Inc.. F 919 570-2862
Raleigh *(G-9870)*

Acculabs Technologies Inc.................. G 919 468-8780
Morrisville *(G-8917)*

Air Control Inc...................................... E 252 492-2300
Henderson *(G-6147)*

Air Craftsmen Inc................................. F 336 248-5777
Statesville *(G-11650)*

Air Purification Inc............................... F 919 783-6161
Raleigh *(G-9886)*

Air Systems Mfg of Lenoir Inc............ E 828 757-3500
Lenoir *(G-7568)*

Airbox Inc.. E 855 927-1386
Statesville *(G-11651)*

▲ Airflow Products Company Inc.......... C 919 975-0240
Selma *(G-11283)*

Associated Metal Works Inc................. E 704 546-7002
Harmony *(G-6097)*

Bahnson Holdings Inc.......................... D 336 760-3111
Clemmons *(G-3178)*

◆ Breezer Holdings LLC.........................D 844 233-5673
Charlotte *(G-1809)*

▲ Bruning and Federle Mfg Co............. E 704 873-7237
Statesville *(G-11672)*

Employee Codes: A=Over 500 employees, B=251-500
C=101-250, D=51-100, E=20-50, F=10-19, G=1-9   2025 Harris North Carolina
Manufacturers Directory   723

Bwxt Investment Company...................... E 704 625-4900
Charlotte *(G-1824)*

Camfil Usa Inc.................................. E 828 465-2880
Conover *(G-3498)*

Camfil Usa Inc.................................. D 252 975-1141
Washington *(G-12376)*

▲ Cleanaire Inc.............................. B 252 623-4010
Washington *(G-12381)*

Commercial Flter Svc of Triad................ G 336 272-1443
Greensboro *(G-5459)*

Cosatron... G 704 785-8145
Concord *(G-3345)*

D J Enviro Solutions........................ G 828 495-7448
Taylorsville *(G-11957)*

Dantherm Filtration Inc..................... F 336 889-5599
Thomasville *(G-12016)*

▲ Dustcontrol Inc............................ F 910 395-1808
Wilmington *(G-12768)*

Dynamic Air Engineering Inc............... E 714 540-1000
Claremont *(G-3112)*

Eas Incorporated............................... G 704 734-4945
Kings Mountain *(G-7361)*

▲ Envirco Corporation..................... E 919 775-2201
Sanford *(G-11177)*

Environmental Specialties LLC............ D 919 829-9300
Raleigh *(G-10088)*

Ffi Holdings III Corp........................ E 800 690-3650
Charlotte *(G-2149)*

▲ Field Controls LLC...................... D 252 208-7300
Kinston *(G-7413)*

Filter Shop LLC................................ D 704 860-4822
Gastonia *(G-5048)*

Filtration Technology Inc.................... G 336 509-9960
Greensboro *(G-5532)*

▼ Filtration Technology Inc.............. G 336 294-5655
Greensboro *(G-5531)*

Firefly Balloons Inc........................... G 704 878-9501
Statesville *(G-11700)*

◆ Flanders Corporation.................... F 252 946-8081
Washington *(G-12385)*

◆ Flanders Filters Inc..................... C 252 946-8081
Washington *(G-12386)*

◆ G Denver and Co LLC.................. E 704 896-4000
Davidson *(G-3705)*

▲ Global Plasma Solutions Inc.......... E 980 279-5622
Charlotte *(G-2214)*

Greenheck Fan Co............................. G 336 852-5788
Greensboro *(G-5575)*

Greenheck Fan Corporation................ G 704 476-3700
Shelby *(G-11339)*

◆ Hayward Industrial Products.......... C 704 837-8002
Charlotte *(G-2264)*

Hughs Sheet Mtal Sttsvlle LLC........... F 704 872-4621
Statesville *(G-11714)*

Hunter Fan Company......................... G 704 896-9250
Cornelius *(G-3609)*

Jorlink Usa Inc................................. F 336 288-1613
Greensboro *(G-5640)*

Kch Services Inc.............................. E 828 245-9836
Forest City *(G-4792)*

Kirk & Blum Manufacturing Co............ D 801 728-6533
Greensboro *(G-5649)*

▼ Meadows Mills Inc....................... E 336 838-2282
North Wilkesboro *(G-9546)*

◆ Mikropor America Inc.................... F
Charlotte *(G-2501)*

Mikropul LLC.................................... G 704 998-2600
Charlotte *(G-2502)*

Miller Ctrl Mfg Inc Clinton NC............ G 910 592-5112
Clinton *(G-3235)*

National Air Filters Inc...................... F 919 231-8596
Raleigh *(G-10322)*

NC Filtration of Florida LLC............... D 704 822-4444
Belmont *(G-756)*

◆ Nederman Inc.............................. D 336 821-0827
Thomasville *(G-12053)*

Nederman Mikropul LLC..................... E 704 998-2600
Charlotte *(G-2553)*

Novaerus US Inc.............................. G 813 304-2468
Charlotte *(G-2578)*

P & G Manufacturing Wash Inc........... G 252 946-9110
Washington *(G-12402)*

Pamlico Air Inc................................. F 252 995-6267
Washington *(G-12405)*

Patholdco Inc................................... G 919 369-0345
Raleigh *(G-10360)*

Patholdco Inc................................... G 919 212-1300
Morrisville *(G-9037)*

◆ Precisionaire Inc.......................... C 252 946-8081
Washington *(G-12408)*

▲ Punker LLC................................. F 828 322-1951
Lincolnton *(G-7849)*

▲ Purolator Facet Inc...................... E 336 668-4444
Greensboro *(G-5771)*

▲ Ricura Corporation....................... F 704 875-0366
Huntersville *(G-7043)*

Rotron Incorporated.......................... C 336 449-3400
Whitsett *(G-12619)*

Schletter NA Inc.............................. F 704 595-4200
Charlotte *(G-2767)*

SCR-Tech LLC.................................. C 704 504-0191
Charlotte *(G-2772)*

Select Air Systems Usa Inc................ E 704 289-1122
Monroe *(G-8557)*

◆ Sonicaire Inc.............................. E 336 712-2437
Winston Salem *(G-13340)*

Staclean Diffuser Company LLC........... F 704 636-8697
Salisbury *(G-11119)*

Sunco Powder Systems Inc................. E 704 545-3922
Charlotte *(G-2881)*

◆ Trane Technologies Company LLC..... A 704 655-4000
Davidson *(G-3721)*

◆ Trane US Inc.............................. A 704 655-4000
Davidson *(G-3723)*

United Air Filter Company Corp........... E 704 334-5311
Charlotte *(G-2961)*

Universal Air Products Corp................ G 704 374-0600
Charlotte *(G-2965)*

WV Holdings Inc.............................. G 704 853-8338
Gastonia *(G-5168)*

Ziehl-Abegg Inc............................... C 336 934-9339
Winston Salem *(G-13410)*

▲ Ziehl-Abegg Inc........................... E 336 834-9339
Greensboro *(G-5931)*

3565 Packaging machinery

Abco Automation Inc......................... C 336 375-6400
Browns Summit *(G-988)*

◆ Alotech Inc................................. E 919 774-1297
Goldston *(G-5255)*

Automated Machine Technologies......... G 919 361-0121
Morrisville *(G-8936)*

Awcnc LLC...................................... G 252 633-5757
New Bern *(G-9336)*

▲ Axon LLC................................... E 919 772-8383
Raleigh *(G-9926)*

Aylward Enterprises LLC.................... E 252 639-9242
New Bern *(G-9337)*

▲ Bamal Corporation....................... F 980 225-7700
Charlotte *(G-1748)*

Cates Mechanical Corporation............. G 704 458-5163
Charlotte *(G-1866)*

Chase-Logeman Corporation............... F 336 665-0754
Greensboro *(G-5442)*

▲ Chudy Group LLC......................... D 262 279-5307
Durham *(G-3975)*

Container Systems Incorporated........... D 919 496-6133
Franklinton *(G-4847)*

Danby Barcoding LLC........................ G 770 416-9845
Kernersville *(G-7263)*

Direct Pack East LLC........................ E 910 331-0071
Rockingham *(G-10774)*

▲ Focke & Co Inc............................ D 336 449-7200
Whitsett *(G-12606)*

Gb Labs LLC.................................... G 919 606-7253
Lexington *(G-7692)*

Groninger USA LLC.......................... E 704 588-3873
Charlotte *(G-2243)*

▲ Keymac USA LLC......................... G 704 877-5137
Charlotte *(G-2394)*

Korber Pharma Inc........................... E 727 538-4644
Cary *(G-1384)*

Korber Pharma Inc........................... E 727 538-4644
Morrisville *(G-8999)*

▲ Korber Pharma Inc....................... D 727 538-4644
Apex *(G-175)*

Krw Packaging Machinery Inc.............. F 828 658-0912
Weaverville *(G-12494)*

▲ Ossid LLC.................................. D 252 446-6177
Battleboro *(G-704)*

Petty Machine Company Inc................ E 704 864-3254
Gastonia *(G-5119)*

R E R Services................................. G 818 993-1826
Southport *(G-11526)*

◆ Roberts Polypro Inc...................... E 704 588-1794
Charlotte *(G-2730)*

Roi Industries Group Inc.................... G 919 788-7728
Durham *(G-4218)*

▲ Syntegon Technology Svcs LLC...... E 919 877-0886
Raleigh *(G-10527)*

▲ U S Bottlers McHy Co Inc............. D 704 588-4750
Charlotte *(G-2957)*

◆ Windak Inc................................. F 828 322-2292
Conover *(G-3576)*

3566 Speed changers, drives, and gears

ABB Motors and Mechanical Inc........... C 828 645-1706
Weaverville *(G-12481)*

▲ Carolina Keller LLC...................... C 252 237-8181
Wilson *(G-12978)*

Gefran Inc....................................... F 501 442-1521
Charlotte *(G-2195)*

Hydreco Inc..................................... F 704 295-7575
Charlotte *(G-2306)*

Joe and Kitty Brown Inc.................... G 704 629-4327
Bessemer City *(G-824)*

▲ Linamar Forgings Carolina Inc........ D 252 237-8181
Wilson *(G-13003)*

Martin Sprocket & Gear Inc................ F 817 258-3000
Albemarle *(G-81)*

Martin Sprocket & Gear Inc................ E 704 394-9111
Charlotte *(G-2464)*

Nord Gear Corporation....................... G 888 314-6673
Charlotte *(G-2571)*

Parker-Hannifin Corporation............... C 704 588-3246
Charlotte *(G-2612)*

▲ Perfection Gear Inc....................... D 828 253-0000
Asheville *(G-570)*

Regal Rexnord Corporation................. G 800 825-6544
Charlotte *(G-2703)*

Siemens Industry Inc........................ C 919 365-2200
Wendell *(G-12547)*

◆ Solero Technologies Shelby LLC....... C 704 482-9582
Shelby *(G-11380)*

3567 Industrial furnaces and ovens

ABB Installation Products Inc.............. E 828 322-1855
  Hickory (G-6260)

Buhler Inc.. C 800 722-7483
  Cary (G-1316)

Custom Electric Mfg LLC.................... E 248 305-7700
  Concord (G-3350)

▲ Industrial Prcess Slutions Inc........ G 336 926-1511
  Wilkesboro (G-12639)

L F I Services Inc............................... G 215 343-0411
  Sanford (G-11201)

▲ Lambda Technologies Inc.............. E 919 462-1919
  Morrisville (G-9003)

Nutec Inc.. E 877 318-2430
  Huntersville (G-7025)

▲ Production Systems Inc................. G 336 886-7161
  High Point (G-6747)

Southeastern Installation Inc............. E 704 352-7146
  Lexington (G-7744)

Superior Finishing Systems LLC......... G 336 956-2000
  Lexington (G-7747)

Thermcraft Holding Co LLC................ D 336 784-4800
  Winston Salem (G-13363)

Tutco Inc.. D 828 654-1665
  Arden (G-314)

3568 Power transmission equipment, nec

Altra Industrial Motion Corp............... F 704 588-5610
  Charlotte (G-1658)

Assa Abloy Inc.................................... F 704 776-8773
  Monroe (G-8435)

Boston Gear LLC................................ B 704 588-5610
  Charlotte (G-1802)

◆ Cavotec USA Inc............................ E 704 873-3009
  Mooresville (G-8635)

Component Technology Intl Inc.......... G 704 331-0888
  Charlotte (G-1968)

Eaton Corporation.............................. D 910 695-2900
  Pinehurst (G-9691)

▲ Emrise Corporation........................ C 408 200-3040
  Durham (G-4023)

▲ Fairchild Industrial Pdts Co........... D 336 659-3400
  Winston Salem (G-13164)

Flextrol Corporation........................... F 704 888-1120
  Locust (G-7893)

GKN Driveline North Amer Inc........... C 336 364-6200
  Timberlake (G-12100)

Haldex Inc.. C 828 652-9308
  Marion (G-8042)

▲ Ketchie-Houston Inc...................... E 704 786-5101
  Concord (G-3390)

Keystone Powdered Metal Co............ D 704 435-4036
  Cherryville (G-3065)

Lovejoy Corporation Inc..................... F 336 472-0674
  Greensboro (G-5667)

Martin Sprocket & Gear Inc............... F 817 258-3000
  Albemarle (G-81)

Meritor Inc.. D 910 844-9401
  Maxton (G-8203)

▲ Oiles America Corporation............. F 704 784-4500
  Concord (G-3411)

Tb Woods Incorporated...................... D 704 588-5610
  Charlotte (G-2902)

3569 General industrial machinery,

Aae North America LLC...................... F 919 534-1500
  Morrisville (G-8916)

Abco Automation Inc.......................... C 336 375-6400
  Browns Summit (G-988)

◆ Balcrank Corporation...................... E 800 747-5300
  Weaverville (G-12483)

▼ Beacon Industrial Mfg LLC............ A 704 399-7441
  Charlotte (G-1762)

Beco Holding Company Inc................ C 800 826-3473
  Charlotte (G-1767)

▲ Bijur Delimon Intl Inc..................... E 919 465-4448
  Raleigh (G-9944)

Blueskye Automation LLC................... E 404 998-1320
  Charlotte (G-1791)

◆ Buckeye Fire Equipment Company...E 704 739-7415
  Kings Mountain (G-7351)

Carolina Fire Protection Inc............... E 910 892-1700
  Dunn (G-3847)

Catamount Energy Corporation.......... F 802 773-6684
  Charlotte (G-1865)

Cemco Electric Inc............................. F 704 504-0294
  Charlotte (G-1886)

City of Morganton.............................. F 828 584-1460
  Morganton (G-8857)

Combat Support Products Inc............ G 919 552-0205
  Fuquay Varina (G-4875)

Ddp Spclty Elctrnic Mtls US 9........... E 336 547-7112
  Greensboro (G-5490)

Dellinger Enterprises Ltd.................... E 704 825-9687
  Belmont (G-745)

Descher LLC....................................... G 919 828-7708
  Raleigh (G-10041)

▼ Design Tool Inc.............................. E 828 328-6414
  Conover (G-3515)

Deurotech America Inc....................... G 980 272-6827
  Charlotte (G-2037)

Drum Filter Media Inc........................ G 336 434-4195
  High Point (G-6599)

Elxsi Corporation............................... B 407 849-1090
  Charlotte (G-2105)

Erdle Perforating Holdings Inc........... F 704 588-4380
  Charlotte (G-2126)

Fagus Grecon Inc.............................. E 503 641-7731
  Charlotte (G-2142)

Fanuc America Corporation................ D 704 596-5121
  Huntersville (G-6988)

Farval Lubrication Systems................ E 252 527-6001
  Kinston (G-7411)

▲ Farval Lubrication Systems........... E 252 527-6001
  Kinston (G-7412)

Ffi Holdings III Corp........................... E 800 690-3650
  Charlotte (G-2149)

▼ Fireresq Incorporated.................... F 888 975-0858
  Mooresville (G-8664)

Flameoff Coatings Inc........................ G 888 816-7468
  Raleigh (G-10111)

Flanders Corporation......................... D 919 934-3020
  Smithfield (G-11443)

Flanders Filters Inc............................ E 252 217-3978
  Smithfield (G-11444)

Flash Technology LLC........................ G 980 474-3700
  Charlotte (G-2160)

Foss Industrial Recycling LLC............ E 336 342-4812
  La Grange (G-7468)

Genesis Water Technologies Inc........ E 704 360-5165
  Charlotte (G-2204)

Gibson Accumulator LLC.................... F 336 449-4753
  Burlington (G-1097)

Global Filter Source LLC.................... G 919 571-4945
  Raleigh (G-10137)

GNB Ventures LLC............................. F 704 488-4468
  Charlotte (G-2218)

Gregory Poole Equipment Co............ F 919 872-2691
  Raleigh (G-10146)

Hayward Holdings Inc........................ C 704 837-8002
  Charlotte (G-2263)

Hayward Industries Inc...................... D 336 712-9900
  Clemmons (G-3188)

◆ Hayward Industries Inc.................. B 704 837-8002
  Charlotte (G-2265)

◆ Hurst Jaws of Life Inc.................... C 704 487-6961
  Shelby (G-11345)

Industrial Automation Company......... F 877 727-8757
  Raleigh (G-10189)

▲ Industrial Piping Inc...................... A 704 588-1100
  Charlotte (G-2323)

Ingersoll-Rand US Holdco Inc............ G 704 655-4000
  Davidson (G-3712)

Ipi Acquisition LLC............................. A 704 588-1100
  Charlotte (G-2356)

Irsi Automation Inc............................. G 336 303-5320
  Mc Leansville (G-8224)

Ism Inc... E
  Arden (G-277)

John W Foster Sales Inc..................... G 704 821-3822
  Matthews (G-8178)

Keller Technology Corporation........... E 704 875-1605
  Huntersville (G-7007)

Kenmar Inc... F 336 884-8722
  High Point (G-6684)

Lightning X Products Inc.................... G 704 295-0299
  Charlotte (G-2421)

Linter North America Corp.................. G 828 645-4261
  Asheville (G-537)

▼ Liquid Process Systems Inc........... G 704 821-1115
  Indian Trail (G-7088)

▲ Ltd Industries LLC.......................... E 704 897-2182
  Charlotte (G-2436)

Main Filter LLC.................................. E 704 735-0009
  Lincolnton (G-7841)

◆ Mann+hmmel Fltrtion Tech US LL...C 704 869-3300
  Gastonia (G-5085)

Mann+hummel Filtration Technol....... G 704 869-3952
  Gastonia (G-5088)

Mann+hummel Filtration Technol....... C 704 869-3501
  Gastonia (G-5089)

Metro Fire Lifesafety LLC................... G 704 529-7348
  Gastonia (G-5095)

NAPA Filters....................................... G 704 864-6748
  Gastonia (G-5106)

◆ National Foam Inc.......................... E 919 639-6100
  Angier (G-126)

Noahs Inc... F 704 718-2354
  Charlotte (G-2570)

Ora Inc... G 540 903-7177
  Marion (G-8059)

Pentair Water Pool and Spa Inc......... D 919 463-4640
  Cary (G-1417)

◆ Pentair Water Pool and Spa Inc.....A 919 566-8000
  Sanford (G-11217)

Petroliance LLC.................................. C 336 472-3000
  Thomasville (G-12059)

Phoenix Assembly NC LLC................. G 252 801-4250
  Battleboro (G-706)

Ralph B Hall....................................... G 919 258-3634
  Sanford (G-11223)

Reclaim Filters and Systems.............. G 919 528-1787
  Wake Forest (G-12292)

Recoupl Inc.. G 704 544-0202
  Charlotte (G-2697)

▲ Rubber Mill Inc.............................. E 336 622-1680
  Liberty (G-7778)

◆ Russell Finex Inc........................... F 704 588-9808
  Pineville (G-9751)

◆ Scott Technologies Inc................... E 704 291-8300
  Monroe (G-8555)

▼ South-Tek Systems LLC................. D 910 332-4173
  Wilmington (G-12924)

Southern Machine Services................ G 919 658-9300
  Mount Olive (G-9258)

Southern Products Company Inc........ E 910 281-3189
  Hoffman (G-6885)

Superior Finishing Systems LLC............ G 336 956-2000
　Lexington *(G-7747)*

Supreme Sweepers LLC......................... G 888 698-9996
　Charlotte *(G-2885)*

Surelift Inc.. G 828 963-6899
　Boone *(G-945)*

Textile Parts and Mch Co Inc.................. G 704 865-5003
　Gastonia *(G-5152)*

US Filter... G 828 274-8282
　Asheville *(G-629)*

Verity America LLC................................. G 347 960-4198
　Chapel Hill *(G-1589)*

West Dynamics Us Inc............................ E 704 735-0009
　Lincolnton *(G-7871)*

◆ Yale Industrial Products Inc...............E 704 588-4610
　Charlotte *(G-3038)*

3571 Electronic computers

Albert E Mann.. G 919 497-0815
　Louisburg *(G-7909)*

Axtra3d Inc... E 888 315-5103
　Charlotte *(G-1726)*

Barcovvsion LLC.................................... F 704 392-9371
　Charlotte *(G-1751)*

Digital Audio Corporation....................... F 919 572-6767
　Hendersonville *(G-6202)*

Dimill Enterprises LLC........................... G 919 629-2011
　Raleigh *(G-10046)*

Fred L Brown... G 336 643-7523
　Summerfield *(G-11840)*

General Dynmics Mssion Systems........ F 910 497-7900
　Fort Bragg *(G-4803)*

Green Apple Studio................................ G 919 377-2239
　Cary *(G-1368)*

HP Inc.. G 704 523-3548
　Charlotte *(G-2291)*

Hypernova Inc.. G 704 360-0096
　Charlotte *(G-2307)*

I2e Group LLC....................................... G 336 884-2014
　High Point *(G-6665)*

International Bus Mchs Corp.................. B 919 543-6919
　Durham *(G-4080)*

Itron Inc... D 919 876-2600
　Raleigh *(G-10211)*

K12 Computers....................................... G 336 754-6111
　Lexington *(G-7703)*

Lenovo (united States) Inc..................... G 919 486-9627
　Morrisville *(G-9004)*

Lenovo (united States) Inc..................... C 919 237-8389
　Morrisville *(G-9005)*

▲ Lenovo (united States) Inc................. A 855 253-6686
　Morrisville *(G-9006)*

Lenovo Global Tech US Inc.................... A 855 253-6686
　Morrisville *(G-9007)*

Lenovo Holding Company Inc................ F 855 253-6686
　Morrisville *(G-9008)*

▲ Lenovo US Fulfillment Ctr LLC........... F 855 253-6686
　Morrisville *(G-9009)*

McKelvey Fulks...................................... G 704 357-1550
　Charlotte *(G-2479)*

▲ Pro-Face America LLC........................ E 734 477-0600
　Greensboro *(G-5766)*

Salem Technologies Inc......................... F 336 777-3652
　Winston Salem *(G-13327)*

Serra Wireless Inc................................. G 980 318-0873
　Charlotte *(G-2789)*

Shiftwizard Inc....................................... F 866 828-3318
　Morrisville *(G-9053)*

Silver Knight Pcs LLC............................ G 910 824-2054
　Fayetteville *(G-4670)*

▲ Teguar Corporation............................. E 704 960-1761
　Charlotte *(G-2906)*

Teradata Corporation............................. F 919 816-1900
　Raleigh *(G-10542)*

Usat LLC.. E 919 942-4214
　Chapel Hill *(G-1587)*

Utd Technology Corp.............................. G 704 612-0121
　Mint Hill *(G-8344)*

◆ Walker and Associates Inc..................C 336 731-6391
　Winston Salem *(G-13386)*

Zelaya Bros LLC.................................... G 980 833-0099
　Charlotte *(G-3046)*

3572 Computer storage devices

EMC Corporation................................... G 720 341-3274
　Charlotte *(G-2108)*

EMC Corporation................................... F 919 767-0641
　Durham *(G-4021)*

EMC Corporation................................... G 919 851-3241
　Raleigh *(G-10085)*

Halifax EMC.. F 252 445-5111
　Enfield *(G-4483)*

Netapp Inc.. D 919 476-4571
　Durham *(G-4145)*

Quantum Newswire................................ G 919 439-8800
　Raleigh *(G-10416)*

Quantum Solutions................................ G 828 615-7500
　Hickory *(G-6423)*

Quantum Usa LLP................................. G 919 799-7171
　Siler City *(G-11424)*

Raleigh Ventures Inc............................. G 910 350-0036
　Wilmington *(G-12895)*

Seagate Technology LLC........................ G 910 821-8310
　Wilmington *(G-12913)*

Verbatim Americas LLC......................... G 704 547-6551
　Charlotte *(G-2975)*

▲ Verbatim Americas LLC...................... D 704 547-6500
　Charlotte *(G-2976)*

◆ Verbatim Corporation..........................D 704 547-6500
　Charlotte *(G-2977)*

◆ Walker and Associates Inc..................C 336 731-6391
　Winston Salem *(G-13386)*

3575 Computer terminals

NCR Voyix Corporation.......................... G 937 445-5000
　Cary *(G-1406)*

Phynix Pc Inc.. F 503 890-1444
　Middlesex *(G-8280)*

▲ Pro-Face America LLC........................ E 734 477-0600
　Greensboro *(G-5766)*

3577 Computer peripheral equipment, nec

Altera Corporation................................. G 919 852-1004
　Raleigh *(G-9893)*

Amt Datasouth Corp............................... E 704 523-8500
　Charlotte *(G-1675)*

Black Box Corporation........................... G 704 248-6430
　Pineville *(G-9715)*

Branch Office Solutions Inc................... G 800 743-1047
　Indian Trail *(G-7072)*

Brilliant Sole Inc................................... G 339 222-8528
　Wilmington *(G-12723)*

▲ Cable Devices Incorporated................ C 714 554-4370
　Hickory *(G-6281)*

◆ Carlisle Corporation............................A 704 501-1100
　Charlotte *(G-1842)*

Cisco Systems Inc................................. G 910 707-1052
　Carolina Beach *(G-1259)*

Cisco Systems Inc................................. G 704 338-7350
　Charlotte *(G-1918)*

Cisco Systems Inc................................. E 919 392-2000
　Morrisville *(G-8958)*

Cisco Systems Inc................................. A 919 392-2000
　Morrisville *(G-8959)*

Commscope Technologies LLC............... G 919 934-9711
　Smithfield *(G-11440)*

Covington Barcoding Inc........................ G 336 996-5759
　Kernersville *(G-7260)*

Faith Computer Repairs.......................... G 910 730-1731
　Lumberton *(G-7953)*

Garrettcom Inc....................................... D 510 438-9071
　Mooresville *(G-8671)*

▲ H&A Scientific Inc.............................. G 252 752-4315
　Greenville *(G-5986)*

Hema Online Indian Btq LLC................. G 919 771-4374
　Apex *(G-164)*

Hermes Medical Solutions Inc............... G 252 355-4373
　Farmville *(G-4531)*

International Bus Mchs Corp.................. B 919 543-6919
　Durham *(G-4080)*

JKS Motorsports Inc.............................. G 336 722-4129
　Winston Salem *(G-13217)*

JPS Communications Inc....................... D 919 534-1168
　Raleigh *(G-10222)*

Lea Aid Acquisition Company................ G 919 872-6210
　Spring Hope *(G-11557)*

Lynn Electronics Corporation................. G 704 369-0093
　Concord *(G-3397)*

NCR Voyix Corporation.......................... G 937 445-5000
　Cary *(G-1406)*

Pendulum Inc... G 704 491-6320
　Charlotte *(G-2624)*

Primesource Corporation....................... F 336 661-3300
　Winston Salem *(G-13304)*

▲ Pro-Face America LLC........................ E 734 477-0600
　Greensboro *(G-5766)*

Revware Inc... G 919 790-0000
　Raleigh *(G-10442)*

Riverbed Technology LLC....................... E 415 247-8800
　Durham *(G-4216)*

Rsa Security LLC................................... E 704 847-4725
　Matthews *(G-8146)*

Sato Global Solutions Inc...................... G 954 261-3279
　Charlotte *(G-2758)*

Savoye Solutions Inc............................. G 919 466-9784
　Raleigh *(G-10458)*

Sighttech LLC.. G 855 997-4448
　Charlotte *(G-2805)*

Southern Data Systems Inc................... F 919 781-7603
　Oxford *(G-9635)*

St Investors Inc..................................... D 704 969-7500
　Charlotte *(G-2856)*

Strategic 3d Solutions Inc..................... G 919 451-5963
　Raleigh *(G-10512)*

Technology Partners LLC....................... D 704 553-1004
　Charlotte *(G-2904)*

▲ Terarecon Inc..................................... D 650 372-1100
　Durham *(G-4267)*

Thomco Inc.. G 336 292-3300
　Greensboro *(G-5863)*

Tinypilot LLC... G 336 422-6525
　Winston Salem *(G-13364)*

Toshiba Globl Cmmrce Sltons In........... E 919 544-8427
　Durham *(G-4275)*

Vocollect Inc.. E 980 279-4119
　Charlotte *(G-2989)*

Xerox Corporation.................................. E 919 428-9718
　Cary *(G-1487)*

Xeroxdata Center................................... G 704 329-7245
　Charlotte *(G-3031)*

Zebra Technologies Corporation............ G 704 517-5271
　Charlotte *(G-3045)*

3578 Calculating and accounting equipment

Add-On Technologies Inc....................... F 704 882-2227
　Indian Trail *(G-7066)*

Atlantic Bankcard Center Inc............... G..... 336 855-9250
  Greensboro *(G-5374)*

Buvic LLC.. G..... 910 302-7950
  Fayetteville *(G-4563)*

Cisco Systems Inc........................... E..... 919 392-2000
  Morrisville *(G-8958)*

Diebold Nixdorf Incorporated............... E..... 704 599-3100
  Charlotte *(G-2044)*

Extron Electronics........................... G..... 919 850-1000
  Raleigh *(G-10100)*

◆ Gilbarco Inc......................................A..... 336 547-5000
  Greensboro *(G-5560)*

Maxpro Manufacturing LLC.................. F..... 910 640-5505
  Whiteville *(G-12587)*

NCR Voyix Corporation....................... G..... 937 445-5000
  Cary *(G-1406)*

Noregon Systems Inc........................ C..... 336 615-8555
  Greensboro *(G-5713)*

One Source SEC & Sound Inc............. G..... 281 850-9487
  Mooresville *(G-8739)*

3579 Office machines, nec

▲ Bell and Howell LLC....................... A..... 919 767-4401
  Durham *(G-3923)*

Bell and Howell LLC.......................... E..... 919 767-6400
  Durham *(G-3924)*

Carolina Time Equipment Co Inc........... E..... 704 536-2700
  Charlotte *(G-1859)*

Pitney Bowes Inc.............................. F..... 336 805-3320
  Greensboro *(G-5750)*

Pitney Bowes Inc.............................. G..... 919 785-3480
  Raleigh *(G-10369)*

Postal Liquidation Inc........................ C
  Durham *(G-4190)*

3581 Automatic vending machines

Country Corner................................. G..... 919 444-9663
  Pittsboro *(G-9780)*

Jb-Isecurity LLC............................... G..... 910 824-7601
  Fayetteville *(G-4622)*

Microtronic Us LLC........................... G..... 336 869-0429
  High Point *(G-6712)*

3582 Commercial laundry equipment

3dductcleaning LLC........................... G..... 919 723-4512
  Selma *(G-11282)*

Hockmeyer Equipment Corp.................. D..... 252 338-4705
  Elizabeth City *(G-4390)*

Laundry Svc Tech Ltd Lblty Co............. G..... 908 327-1997
  Matthews *(G-8126)*

▼ Leonard Automatics Inc.................... E..... 704 483-9316
  Denver *(G-3792)*

Perfection Fabrics Inc........................ G..... 828 328-3322
  Hickory *(G-6411)*

◆ Talley Machinery Corporation.............G..... 336 664-0012
  Greensboro *(G-5850)*

Two Fifty Cleaners............................ F..... 910 397-0071
  Wilmington *(G-12942)*

3585 Refrigeration and heating equipment

▲ Afe Victory Inc.............................. C..... 856 428-4200
  Winston Salem *(G-13075)*

Air System Components Inc.................. D..... 919 279-8868
  Sanford *(G-11146)*

Air System Components Inc.................. D..... 919 775-2201
  Sanford *(G-11147)*

Air System Components Inc.................. D..... 252 641-5900
  Tarboro *(G-11921)*

Air System Components Inc.................. C..... 252 641-0875
  Tarboro *(G-11922)*

Airboss Heating and Coolg Inc............. G..... 252 586-0500
  Littleton *(G-7883)*

▲ American Coil Inc............................ G..... 310 515-1215
  Bostic *(G-960)*

American Moistening Co Inc................. F..... 704 889-7281
  Pineville *(G-9712)*

▼ Aqua Logic Inc.............................. E..... 858 292-4773
  Monroe *(G-8428)*

◆ Arneg LLC..................................... D..... 336 956-5300
  Lexington *(G-7656)*

Bahnson Holdings Inc........................ D..... 336 760-3111
  Clemmons *(G-3178)*

◆ Bally Refrigerated Boxes Inc............C..... 252 240-2829
  Morehead City *(G-8815)*

◆ Beverage-Air Corporation.................E..... 336 245-6400
  Winston Salem *(G-13104)*

Boles Holding Inc............................. C..... 828 264-4200
  Boone *(G-899)*

Buhler Inc....................................... C..... 800 722-7483
  Cary *(G-1316)*

Carolina Products Inc........................ E..... 704 364-9029
  Charlotte *(G-1854)*

Carrier Corporation........................... C..... 704 921-3800
  Charlotte *(G-1863)*

Carrier Corporation........................... E..... 704 494-2600
  Morrisville *(G-8948)*

Charlies Heating & Cooling LLC............ G..... 336 260-1973
  Snow Camp *(G-11473)*

Chichibone Inc................................. F..... 919 785-0090
  Kernersville *(G-7256)*

City Compressor Rebuilders.................. G..... 704 947-1811
  Charlotte *(G-1921)*

City Compressor Rebuilders.................. E..... 704 947-1811
  Charlotte *(G-1920)*

▲ Cooling Technology Inc.................... G..... 704 596-4109
  Cornelius *(G-3596)*

Daikin Applied Americas Inc................. G..... 704 588-0087
  Charlotte *(G-2014)*

▲ Dienes Apparatus Inc...................... G..... 704 525-3770
  Pineville *(G-9724)*

Dynamic Air Engineering Inc................. E..... 714 540-1000
  Claremont *(G-3112)*

Eneco East Inc................................ G..... 828 322-6008
  Hickory *(G-6329)*

Freudnberg Rsdntial Fltrtion T............. E..... 828 328-1142
  Hickory *(G-6335)*

Go Green Services LLC....................... D..... 336 252-2999
  Greensboro *(G-5565)*

Hoffman Hydronics LLC....................... F..... 336 294-3838
  Greensboro *(G-5603)*

J&R Precision Heating and Air.............. G..... 910 480-8322
  Fayetteville *(G-4619)*

James M Pleasants Company Inc........... E..... 800 365-9010
  Greensboro *(G-5633)*

Jenkins Services Group LLC................. E..... 704 881-3210
  Catawba *(G-1512)*

Kenny Fowler Heating and A Inc........... F..... 910 508-4553
  Wilmington *(G-12827)*

Lennox International Inc...................... C..... 828 633-4805
  Candler *(G-1229)*

◆ Liqui-Box Corporation......................D..... 804 325-1400
  Charlotte *(G-2426)*

Mestek Inc...................................... C..... 252 753-5323
  Farmville *(G-4535)*

◆ Middleby Marshall Inc......................C..... 919 762-1000
  Fuquay Varina *(G-4891)*

◆ Morris & Associates Inc...................D..... 919 582-9200
  Garner *(G-4947)*

Nissens Cooling Solutions Inc.............. F..... 704 696-8575
  Mooresville *(G-8735)*

▼ Parameter Generation Ctrl Inc........... E..... 828 669-8717
  Black Mountain *(G-870)*

Pro Refrigeration Inc......................... E..... 336 283-7281
  Mocksville *(G-8385)*

Rheem Manufacturing Company............. C..... 336 495-6800
  Randleman *(G-10658)*

Rifled Air Conditioning Inc................... E..... 800 627-1707
  High Point *(G-6757)*

Roctool Inc...................................... G..... 888 364-6321
  Sanford *(G-11224)*

Snap Rite Manufacturing Inc................. E..... 910 897-4080
  Coats *(G-3265)*

Spartan Systems LLC......................... F..... 336 946-1244
  Advance *(G-39)*

Supreme Murphy Trck Bodies Inc.......... C..... 252 291-2191
  Wilson *(G-13033)*

Thermo King Corporation..................... E..... 732 652-6774
  Davidson *(G-3720)*

Thermo Products LLC......................... E..... 800 348-5130
  Denton *(G-3763)*

Tier 1 Heating and Air LLC.................. F..... 910 556-1444
  Vass *(G-12229)*

▲ Trane Company.............................. E..... 704 398-4600
  Charlotte *(G-2933)*

◆ Trane Technologies Company LLC.....A..... 704 655-4000
  Davidson *(G-3721)*

Trane Technologies Mfg LLC................ G..... 704 655-4000
  Davidson *(G-3722)*

Trane US Inc................................... G..... 828 277-8664
  Asheville *(G-623)*

Trane US Inc................................... C..... 704 525-9600
  Charlotte *(G-2934)*

Trane US Inc................................... F..... 704 697-9006
  Charlotte *(G-2935)*

Trane US Inc................................... G..... 336 273-6353
  Greensboro *(G-5868)*

Trane US Inc................................... F..... 336 378-0670
  Greensboro *(G-5869)*

Trane US Inc................................... G..... 336 387-1735
  Greensboro *(G-5870)*

Trane US Inc................................... G..... 919 781-0458
  Morrisville *(G-9074)*

◆ Trane US Inc.................................A..... 704 655-4000
  Davidson *(G-3723)*

Transarctic North Carolina Inc.............. E..... 336 861-6116
  High Point *(G-6809)*

Trs-Sesco LLC................................. D..... 336 996-2220
  Kernersville *(G-7310)*

United Air Filter Company Corp............ E..... 704 334-5311
  Charlotte *(G-2961)*

W A Brown & Son Incorporated............ E..... 704 636-5131
  Salisbury *(G-11134)*

Wen Bray Heating & AC...................... G..... 828 267-0635
  Hickory *(G-6489)*

Work Well Hydrtion Systems LLC........... G..... 704 853-7788
  Gastonia *(G-5167)*

Xp Climate Control LLC....................... G..... 828 266-2006
  Boone *(G-955)*

3586 Measuring and dispensing pumps

Aptargroup Inc................................. C..... 828 970-6300
  Lincolnton *(G-7815)*

◆ Balcrank Corporation.......................E..... 800 747-5300
  Weaverville *(G-12483)*

Circor Precision Metering LLC.............. A..... 919 774-7667
  Sanford *(G-11164)*

Gasboy International Inc...................... F..... 336 547-5000
  Greensboro *(G-5548)*

◆ Gilbarco Inc..................................A..... 336 547-5000
  Greensboro *(G-5560)*

▲ Marley Company LLC....................... C..... 704 752-4400
  Charlotte *(G-2459)*

Nelson Holdings Nc Inc...................... F..... 828 322-9226
  Hickory *(G-6399)*

Samoa Corporation............................ E..... 828 645-2290
  Weaverville *(G-12502)*

3589 Service industry machinery, nec

A3-Usa Inc................................G 724 871-7170
  Chinquapin *(G-3081)*

Adr Hydro-Cut Inc........................G 919 388-2251
  Morrisville *(G-8920)*

Ali Group North America Corp...........E 800 648-4389
  High Point *(G-6515)*

Ali Group North America Corp...........D 336 661-1556
  Winston Salem *(G-13078)*

Allens Environmental Cnstr LLC...........G 407 774-7100
  Brevard *(G-967)*

Alpha-Advantage Inc.....................G 252 441-3766
  Kitty Hawk *(G-7443)*

◆ Amano Pioneer Eclipse Corp..........D 336 372-8080
  Sparta *(G-11534)*

Amerochem Corporation..................E 252 634-9344
  New Bern *(G-9333)*

◆ Amiad Filtration Systems Ltd..........E 805 377-0288
  Mooresville *(G-8598)*

▲ Amiad USA Inc........................F 704 662-3133
  Mooresville *(G-8599)*

Aquapro Solutions LLC...................G 828 255-0772
  Asheville *(G-430)*

Aqwa Inc................................G 252 243-7693
  Wilson *(G-12963)*

Ats Service Company LLC.................G 512 905-9005
  Godwin *(G-5186)*

B&C Xterior Cleaning Svc Inc............G 919 779-7905
  Raleigh *(G-9928)*

Bk Seamless Gutters LLC.................G 252 955-5414
  Spring Hope *(G-11554)*

Butler Trieu Inc.........................G 910 346-4929
  Jacksonville *(G-7118)*

Caldwells Water Conditioning............G 828 253-6605
  Asheville *(G-465)*

▲ Cary Manufacturing Corporation.......G 704 527-4402
  Charlotte *(G-1864)*

▲ Champion Industries Inc...............D 336 661-1556
  Winston Salem *(G-13122)*

City of Greensboro......................D 336 373-5855
  Greensboro *(G-5446)*

Columbus Industries LLC.................F 910 872-1625
  Bladenboro *(G-875)*

County of Anson.........................G 704 848-4849
  Lilesville *(G-7784)*

County of Dare..........................C 252 475-5990
  Kill Devil Hills *(G-7315)*

Desco Equipment Company Inc...........G 704 873-2844
  Statesville *(G-11689)*

Drch Inc................................G 919 383-9421
  Durham *(G-4007)*

▲ Dustcontrol Inc.......................F 910 395-1808
  Wilmington *(G-12768)*

Eizi Group Llc..........................G 919 397-3638
  Raleigh *(G-10080)*

◆ Entex Technologies Inc...............F 919 933-1380
  Chapel Hill *(G-1546)*

Envirnmntal Prcess Systems Inc..........G 704 827-0740
  Mount Holly *(G-9229)*

Epsiusa................................G 704 827-0740
  Mount Holly *(G-9230)*

Ew2 Environmental Inc...................G 704 542-2444
  Charlotte *(G-2133)*

▲ Ferguson Companies...................G
  Linwood *(G-7878)*

Ferguson Waterworks.....................G 704 540-7225
  Pineville *(G-9727)*

Galaxy Pressure Washing Inc.............G 888 299-3129
  Pineville *(G-9729)*

Gold Medal Products Co..................G 336 665-4997
  Greensboro *(G-5568)*

◆ Great Products Inc....................G 910 944-2020
  Aberdeen *(G-5)*

Green Waste Management LLC.............G 704 289-0720
  Charlotte *(G-2239)*

Greenstory Globl Gvrnment Mlta...........F 828 446-9278
  Terrell *(G-11989)*

Hayward Holdings Inc....................C 704 837-8002
  Charlotte *(G-2263)*

Hayward Industries Inc..................D 336 712-9900
  Clemmons *(G-3188)*

Hayward Industries Inc..................A 336 712-9900
  Clemmons *(G-3189)*

◆ Hayward Industries Inc...............B 704 837-8002
  Charlotte *(G-2265)*

Hess Manufacturing Inc..................E 704 637-3300
  Salisbury *(G-11065)*

▼ Hoh Corporation......................F 336 723-9274
  Winston Salem *(G-13199)*

▲ Hydro Service & Supplies Inc.........E 919 544-3744
  Durham *(G-4066)*

Imagine One LLC.........................G 828 324-6454
  Hickory *(G-6364)*

Imagine One Resources LLC...............G 828 328-1142
  Hickory *(G-6365)*

Jim Myers & Sons Inc....................D 704 554-8397
  Charlotte *(G-2370)*

▲ Kuenz America Inc....................F 984 255-1018
  Raleigh *(G-10241)*

Legacy Commercial Service LLC...........G 757 831-5291
  Charlotte *(G-2416)*

▼ Lely Manufacturing Inc...............F 252 291-7050
  Wilson *(G-13002)*

Majestic Xpress Handwash Inc............G 919 440-7611
  Goldsboro *(G-5227)*

◆ Mann+hmmel Fltrtion Tech US LL......C 704 869-3300
  Gastonia *(G-5085)*

▼ Marshall Air Systems Inc.............D 704 525-6230
  Charlotte *(G-2460)*

Marshall Middleby Inc...................D 919 762-1000
  Fuquay Varina *(G-4887)*

Meco Inc................................G 919 557-7330
  Fuquay Varina *(G-4889)*

Midsouth Power Eqp Co Inc..............F 336 389-0515
  Greensboro *(G-5692)*

◆ Mikropor America Inc.................F
  Charlotte *(G-2501)*

Miller S Utility MGT Inc.................G 910 298-3847
  Beulaville *(G-843)*

Nala Membranes Inc.....................G 540 230-5606
  Durham *(G-4142)*

Nunnery-Freeman Inc....................G 252 438-3149
  Henderson *(G-6167)*

▲ Onyx Environmental Solutions Inc....E 800 858-3533
  Stanley *(G-11623)*

Painting By Colors LLC..................G 919 963-2300
  Clayton *(G-3166)*

▲ Pauls Water Treatment LLC...........G 336 886-5600
  High Point *(G-6729)*

Pentair Water Pool and Spa Inc..........D 919 463-4640
  Cary *(G-1417)*

◆ Pentair Water Pool and Spa Inc......A 919 566-8000
  Sanford *(G-11217)*

▲ Pep Filters Inc.......................E 704 662-3133
  Mooresville *(G-8747)*

Piedmont Paper Stock LLC................F 336 285-8592
  Greensboro *(G-5744)*

Protect Plus Pro LLC....................F 828 328-1142
  Hickory *(G-6419)*

Pure Flow Inc...........................D 336 532-0300
  Graham *(G-5283)*

Quality Cleaning Services LLC............F 919 638-4969
  Durham *(G-4202)*

Scaltrol Inc.............................G 678 990-0858
  Charlotte *(G-2761)*

Secured Shred...........................G 443 288-6375
  Raleigh *(G-10466)*

Semper Fi Water LLC.....................G 910 381-3569
  Jacksonville *(G-7143)*

Sinnovatek Inc..........................G 919 694-0974
  Raleigh *(G-10479)*

Skyview Commercial Cleaning.............G 704 858-0134
  Charlotte *(G-2812)*

Solarbrook Water and Pwr Corp...........G 919 231-3205
  Raleigh *(G-10492)*

Supreme Sweepers LLC...................G 888 698-9996
  Charlotte *(G-2885)*

Sweep 24 LLC...........................F 980 428-5624
  Charlotte *(G-2887)*

Tempest Environmental Corp.............G 919 973-1609
  Durham *(G-4265)*

▼ Tempest Envmtl Systems Inc..........G 919 973-1609
  Durham *(G-4266)*

Town of Ahoskie........................G 252 332-3840
  Ahoskie *(G-54)*

Town of Jonesville......................G 336 835-2250
  Jonesville *(G-7199)*

Town of Maggie Valley Inc...............F 828 926-0145
  Maggie Valley *(G-8006)*

Town of Tarboro........................E 252 641-4284
  Tarboro *(G-11944)*

Town of Waynesville.....................G 828 456-8497
  Waynesville *(G-12478)*

Vacs America Inc........................G 910 259-9854
  Burgaw *(G-1035)*

Water-Gen Inc..........................G 888 492-8370
  Charlotte *(G-3007)*

▲ Water-Revolution LLC.................G 336 525-1015
  Blanch *(G-879)*

▲ Wedeco Uv Technologies Inc..........D 704 716-7600
  Charlotte *(G-3010)*

Wine To Water..........................E 828 355-9655
  Boone *(G-954)*

◆ Wmf Americas Inc.....................E 704 882-3898
  Indian Trail *(G-7105)*

Wnc Blue Ridge Fd Ventures LLC.........F 828 348-0130
  Candler *(G-1236)*

Xelaqua Inc.............................G 919 964-4181
  Raleigh *(G-10618)*

3592 Carburetors, pistons, rings, valves

Bill Pink Carburetors LLC................G 704 575-1645
  Denver *(G-3774)*

Classic Carburetor Rebuilders............G 336 613-5715
  Eden *(G-4345)*

Marvel-Schbler Arcft Crbrtors............G 336 446-0002
  Burlington *(G-1124)*

Robert Blake............................G 704 720-9341
  Concord *(G-3433)*

US Valve Corporation....................G 910 799-9913
  Wilmington *(G-12944)*

3593 Fluid power cylinders and actuators

Allied Mobile Systems LLC...............G 888 503-1501
  Dunn *(G-3842)*

▲ Atlantic Hydraulics Svcs LLC..........E 919 542-2985
  Sanford *(G-11152)*

▲ Bonomi North America Inc.............F 704 412-9031
  Charlotte *(G-1798)*

Curtiss-Wright Controls Inc.............E 704 481-1150
  Shelby *(G-11326)*

◆ Indian Head Industries Inc............E 704 547-7411
  Charlotte *(G-2321)*

Lord Corporation........................D 919 342-3380
  Cary *(G-1393)*

Parmer International Inc .... G 704 374-0066
Charlotte *(G-2613)*

◆ Solero Technologies Shelby LLC .... C 704 482-9582
Shelby *(G-11380)*

▲ Triumph Actuation Systems LLC ..... C 336 766-9036
Clemmons *(G-3206)*

◆ Yale Industrial Products Inc .... E 704 588-4610
Charlotte *(G-3038)*

3594 Fluid power pumps and motors

▲ Asmo Greenville of North .... B 252 754-1000
Greenville *(G-5939)*

▲ Atlantic Hydraulics Svcs LLC .... E 919 542-2985
Sanford *(G-11152)*

Caterpillar Inc .... D 919 550-1100
Clayton *(G-3137)*

Denso Manufacturing NC Inc .... B 252 754-1000
Greenville *(G-5963)*

E-Z Dumper Products LLC .... G 717 762-8432
Southern Pines *(G-11497)*

◆ Hurst Jaws of Life Inc .... C 704 487-6961
Shelby *(G-11345)*

▲ Hyde Park Partners Inc .... D 704 587-4819
Charlotte *(G-2304)*

Hydralic Engnered Pdts Svc Inc .... G 704 374-1306
Charlotte *(G-2305)*

Livingston & Haven LLC .... C 704 588-3670
Charlotte *(G-2428)*

Logic Hydraulic Controls Inc .... E 910 791-9293
Wilmington *(G-12838)*

Parker-Hannifin Corporation .... G 252 652-6592
Havelock *(G-6125)*

Parker-Hannifin Corporation .... B 704 739-9781
Kings Mountain *(G-7376)*

◆ Schunk Intec Inc .... D 919 572-2705
Morrisville *(G-9046)*

SCI Sharp Controls Inc .... G 704 394-1395
Pineville *(G-9755)*

3596 Scales and balances, except laboratory

American Scale Company LLC .... F 704 921-4556
Charlotte *(G-1667)*

Computerway Food Systems Inc .... E 336 841-7289
High Point *(G-6575)*

True Portion Inc .... F 336 362-6326
High Point *(G-6813)*

▲ Vishay Transducers Ltd .... E 919 365-3800
Wendell *(G-12553)*

Vision Metals Inc .... G 336 622-7300
Liberty *(G-7783)*

3599 Industrial machinery, nec

A & G Machining LLC .... G 919 329-7207
Garner *(G-4911)*

A & S Tool & Die Co Inc .... G 336 993-3440
Kernersville *(G-7238)*

Abco Automation Inc .... C 336 375-6400
Browns Summit *(G-988)*

Accu-Tool LLC .... F 919 363-2600
Apex *(G-132)*

Accurate Machine & Tool LLC .... F 919 212-0266
Raleigh *(G-9875)*

Acme Die & Machine Corporation .... F 704 864-8426
Gastonia *(G-4983)*

Acme Machine LLC .... F 828 483-6440
Hendersonville *(G-6183)*

Advance Machining Co Gastonia .... G 704 866-7411
Gastonia *(G-4984)*

Advanced Cutting Tech Inc .... G 910 944-3028
Maxton *(G-8199)*

Advanced Machining Tooling LLC .... G 704 633-8157
Salisbury *(G-11013)*

Advanced Mch & Fabrication Inc .... G 704 489-0096
Denver *(G-3768)*

Aero Precision Machine Inc .... F 336 685-0016
Liberty *(G-7759)*

Albany Tool & Die Inc .... G 910 392-1207
Wilmington *(G-12695)*

Allen Mch & Fabrication LLC .... F 336 521-4409
Asheboro *(G-325)*

◆ Alotech Inc .... E 919 774-1297
Goldston *(G-5255)*

Alotech North .... G 919 774-1297
Goldston *(G-5256)*

Alpha 3d LLC .... G 704 277-6300
Charlotte *(G-1649)*

Alphatech Inc .... E 828 684-9709
Fletcher *(G-4719)*

American Cylinder Products Inc .... G 336 993-7722
Kernersville *(G-7243)*

◆ American Linc Corporation .... G 704 861-9242
Gastonia *(G-4992)*

American Materials Company LLC .... E 910 532-6659
Rose Hill *(G-10902)*

American Rewinding Nc Inc .... G 704 289-4177
Monroe *(G-8422)*

Ana Gizzi .... G 908 334-8733
Statesville *(G-11658)*

Angels Path Ventures Inc .... G 828 654-9530
Arden *(G-251)*

Annas Machine Shop Inc .... G 828 754-4184
Lenoir *(G-7572)*

Anson Machine Works Inc .... E 704 272-7657
Polkton *(G-9813)*

Anson Metals LLC .... F 704 272-7878
Peachland *(G-9650)*

Apjet Inc .... G 919 595-5538
Morrisville *(G-8930)*

Appalachian Tool & Machine Inc .... E 828 669-0142
Swannanoa *(G-11864)*

Asheboro Machine Shop Inc .... G 336 625-6322
Asheboro *(G-329)*

Auto Machine Shop Inc .... G 910 483-6016
Fayetteville *(G-4554)*

Automated Machine Technologies .... G 919 361-0121
Morrisville *(G-8936)*

Avery Machine & Welding Co .... G 828 733-4944
Fayetteville *(G-4556)*

Axcellus LLC .... F 919 589-9800
Apex *(G-143)*

B & B Industries Inc .... G 704 882-4688
Indian Trail *(G-7071)*

B & B Machine Co Inc .... G 704 637-2356
Salisbury *(G-11020)*

B+e Manufacturing Co Inc .... G 704 236-8439
Monroe *(G-8438)*

Bace LLC .... F 704 394-2230
Charlotte *(G-1737)*

Ball S Machine & Mfg Co Inc .... F 828 667-0411
Candler *(G-1219)*

Bannister Inc .... G 252 638-6611
New Bern *(G-9339)*

Barbour S Marine Supply Co Inc .... G 252 728-2136
Beaufort *(G-720)*

Barnes Precision Machine Inc .... F 919 362-6805
Apex *(G-144)*

Benton & Sons Fabrication Inc .... E 919 734-1700
Pikeville *(G-9667)*

▲ Bessemer City Machine Shop Inc ..... G 704 629-4111
Bessemer City *(G-806)*

Betech Inc .... G 828 687-9917
Fletcher *(G-4723)*

Bibey Machine Company Inc .... E 336 275-9421
Greensboro *(G-5389)*

Bircher Incorporated .... G 252 726-5470
Morehead City *(G-8817)*

Black Mtn Mch Fabrication Inc .... E 828 669-9557
Black Mountain *(G-862)*

Blount Precision Machining Inc .... G 252 825-3701
Bethel *(G-839)*

Blue Ridge Tool Inc .... G 336 993-8111
High Point *(G-6548)*

Blue Steel Inc .... G 704 864-2583
Gastonia *(G-5001)*

Bond Technologies .... G 919 866-0075
Raleigh *(G-9954)*

Boone Iron Works Inc .... G 828 264-5284
Boone *(G-900)*

Bowen Machine Company Inc .... F 704 922-0423
Dallas *(G-3665)*

Bowen Machine Company Inc .... G 704 629-9111
Gastonia *(G-5002)*

◆ Briggs-Shaffner Acquisition Co .... F 336 463-4272
Yadkinville *(G-13439)*

▲ Broadsight Systems Inc .... G 336 837-1272
Mebane *(G-8233)*

▲ Broadwind Indus Solutions LLC .... E 919 777-2907
Sanford *(G-11159)*

Brock and Triplett Machine Sp .... G 336 667-6951
Moravian Falls *(G-8808)*

Brooks Machine & Design Inc .... F 919 404-0901
Zebulon *(G-13505)*

Bulldog Machine Inc .... G 704 200-7838
Matthews *(G-8161)*

Burlington Machine Service .... G 336 228-6758
Burlington *(G-1056)*

Burnett Machine Company Inc .... F 704 867-7786
Gastonia *(G-5008)*

Burris Machine Company Inc .... G 828 322-6914
Hickory *(G-6276)*

Burris Machine Company Inc .... G 828 322-6914
Hickory *(G-6277)*

Busick Brothers Machine Inc .... F 336 969-2717
Rural Hall *(G-10953)*

▲ Buy Smart Inc .... G 252 293-4700
Wilson *(G-12976)*

C & B Salvage Company Inc .... G 336 374-3946
Ararat *(G-209)*

C & C Precision Machine Inc .... E 704 739-0505
Kings Mountain *(G-7352)*

C & C Tool and Machine Inc .... G 704 226-1363
Monroe *(G-8449)*

CA Foy Machine Co .... E 704 734-4833
Kings Mountain *(G-7353)*

Campbell & Sons Machining Co .... G 704 394-0291
Lincolnton *(G-7818)*

◆ Canvas Sx LLC .... C 980 474-3700
Charlotte *(G-1836)*

Capper McCall Co .... G 919 270-8813
Raleigh *(G-9971)*

Carnes-Miller Gear Company Inc .... F 704 888-4448
Locust *(G-7889)*

Carolina .... G 919 851-0906
Cary *(G-1321)*

Carolina Core Machine LLC .... E 336 342-1141
Reidsville *(G-10679)*

Carolina Laser Cutting Inc .... E 336 292-1474
Greensboro *(G-5427)*

Carolina Mch Fayetteville Inc .... G 910 425-9115
Hope Mills *(G-6924)*

Carolina Prcsion Cmponents Inc .... E 828 496-1045
Granite Falls *(G-5298)*

Carolina Prcsion Machining Inc .... E 336 751-7788
Mocksville *(G-8353)*

Carolina Precision Machining .... G 336 751-7788
Mocksville *(G-8354)*

Carolina Precision Mfg LLC.................... E 704 662-3480
   Mooresville *(G-8632)*

Carolina Resource Corp....................... F 919 562-0200
   Youngsville *(G-13470)*

Carolina Tex Sls Gastonia Inc............... G 704 739-1646
   Kings Mountain *(G-7357)*

Carr Mill Supplies Inc........................... G 336 883-0135
   High Point *(G-6561)*

Carters Machine Company Inc............... G 704 784-3106
   Concord *(G-3332)*

▲ Casetec Precision Machine LLC....... G 704 663-6043
   Mooresville *(G-8634)*

Central Carolina Products Inc............... D 336 226-0005
   Burlington *(G-1069)*

Central Machine Company.................... G 336 855-0022
   Archdale *(G-216)*

Certified Machining Inc....................... F 919 777-9608
   Sanford *(G-11162)*

Chapman Machine............................... G 704 739-1834
   Kings Mountain *(G-7358)*

Charter Dura-Bar Inc........................... F 704 637-1906
   Salisbury *(G-11032)*

▲ Chiron America Inc.......................... D 704 587-9526
   Charlotte *(G-1916)*

City Machine Company Inc.................. E 828 754-9661
   Lenoir *(G-7594)*

Cjt Machine Inc.................................. G 828 376-3693
   Hendersonville *(G-6196)*

CMS Tool and Die Inc......................... F 910 458-3322
   Carolina Beach *(G-1260)*

Cnc Performance Eng LLC................... G 704 599-2555
   Charlotte *(G-1938)*

Cole Machine Inc................................ G 336 222-8381
   Snow Camp *(G-11474)*

Compass Precision LLC....................... F 704 790-6764
   Charlotte *(G-1966)*

Competition Tooling Inc....................... G 336 887-4414
   High Point *(G-6574)*

Component Technology Intl Inc............. G 704 331-0888
   Charlotte *(G-1968)*

Conner Brothers Machine Co Inc.......... D 704 864-6084
   Bessemer City *(G-809)*

Conover Machine and Design Inc......... G 828 328-6737
   Hickory *(G-6309)*

Consolidated Inspections Inc............... G 919 658-5800
   Mount Olive *(G-9253)*

CRC Machine & Fabrication Inc............ F 980 522-1361
   Bessemer City *(G-810)*

Crystal Coast Machine LLC.................. G 252 876-3859
   New Bern *(G-9359)*

CSM Manufacturing Inc........................ F 336 570-2282
   Graham *(G-5266)*

Current Enterprises Inc....................... G 919 469-1227
   Morrisville *(G-8961)*

Curti USA Corporation......................... G 910 769-1977
   Belville *(G-779)*

Custom Automated Machines Inc.......... G 704 289-7038
   Monroe *(G-8472)*

Custom Industries Inc......................... F 704 825-3346
   Belmont *(G-744)*

▲ Custom Industries Inc..................... E 336 299-2885
   Greensboro *(G-5481)*

Custom Machine Company Inc............. F 704 629-5326
   Bessemer City *(G-811)*

Custom Machining Inc......................... G 336 996-0855
   Kernersville *(G-7261)*

D & D Entps Greensboro Inc............... G 336 495-3407
   Greensboro *(G-5485)*

D & D Entps Greensboro Inc............... E 336 495-3407
   Randleman *(G-10640)*

D & D Machine Works Inc.................... G 704 878-0117
   Statesville *(G-11682)*

Daily Grind LLC................................... G 910 541-0471
   Surf City *(G-11862)*

Dallas Machine and............................ G 704 629-5611
   Bessemer City *(G-813)*

Damco Inc.. F 252 633-1404
   New Bern *(G-9363)*

Davis Davis Mch & Wldg Co Inc.......... F 252 443-2652
   Rocky Mount *(G-10830)*

Davis Machine Co Inc.......................... G 704 865-2863
   Gastonia *(G-5040)*

Dayco Manufacturing Inc..................... F 919 989-1820
   Clayton *(G-3143)*

◆ Daystar Machining Tech Inc............. E 828 684-1316
   Fletcher *(G-4732)*

Deal Machine Shop Inc........................ G 704 872-7618
   Statesville *(G-11686)*

Dellinger Enterprises Ltd...................... E 704 825-9687
   Belmont *(G-745)*

Denver Waterjet LLC............................ G 980 222-7447
   Denver *(G-3780)*

Dexco McHining Fabrication LLC.......... E 336 584-0260
   Burlington *(G-1082)*

Diamond Enterprises........................... G 828 495-4448
   Hickory *(G-6323)*

Diversfied McHning Cncepts Inc.......... G 828 665-2465
   Candler *(G-1224)*

Diversified Specialties Inc.................... E 704 825-3671
   Belmont *(G-748)*

Dma Inc.. G 704 527-0992
   Charlotte *(G-2059)*

Douglas Fabrication & Mch Inc............ F 919 365-7553
   Wendell *(G-12533)*

Dramar Machine Devices Inc............... E 704 866-0904
   Gastonia *(G-5043)*

DSI Innovations LLC............................ E 336 893-8385
   Thomasville *(G-12020)*

Dyna-Tech Manufacturing Inc.............. F 704 839-0203
   Monroe *(G-8480)*

Dynamic Machine Works LLC............... G 336 462-7370
   Clemmons *(G-3182)*

Dynamic Machining X Mfg LLC............ E 336 362-3425
   King *(G-7326)*

E F P Inc.. F 336 498-4134
   Randleman *(G-10645)*

Eagle Machining Usa Inc..................... F 717 235-9383
   Huntersville *(G-6986)*

Eaglestone Technology Inc................... F 336 476-0244
   High Point *(G-6602)*

Earls Precision Machining.................... G 919 542-1869
   Sanford *(G-11174)*

Economy Grinding Straightening........... G 704 400-2500
   Charlotte *(G-2089)*

Eddie Hsr S Prcsion McHning In........... G 704 750-4244
   Kings Mountain *(G-7363)*

Eddie S Mountain Machine Inc............. G 828 685-0733
   Hendersonville *(G-6204)*

Edwards Unlimited Inc......................... G 252 226-4583
   Henderson *(G-6154)*

▲ Electrical Apparatus & Mch Co.......... F 704 333-2987
   Gastonia *(G-5045)*

Elite Metal Performance LLC............... F 704 660-0006
   Statesville *(G-11694)*

Elomi Inc.. E 904 591-0095
   Concord *(G-3359)*

Equipment Parts Inc............................ E 704 827-7545
   Belmont *(G-749)*

Erecto Mch & Fabrication Inc............... G 704 922-8621
   Dallas *(G-3670)*

Estes Machine Co............................... F 336 786-7680
   Mount Airy *(G-9119)*

Everettes Company Inc........................ G 336 956-2097
   Linwood *(G-7877)*

Everettes Industrial Repr Svc............... F 252 527-4269
   Goldsboro *(G-5213)*

Fab-Tec Inc.. D 704 864-6872
   Dallas *(G-3671)*

Faircloth Machine Shop Inc.................. F 336 777-1529
   Winston Salem *(G-13165)*

Falcon Industries LLC.......................... G 336 229-1048
   Burlington *(G-1089)*

Farmer Machine Group LLC................. F 704 629-5133
   Bessemer City *(G-815)*

Farris Fab & Machine Inc..................... G 704 629-4879
   Bessemer City *(G-816)*

Farris Fab & Machine Inc..................... C 704 629-4879
   Bessemer City *(G-817)*

▲ Farris Fab & Machine Inc.................. D 704 629-4879
   Cherryville *(G-3064)*

Fieldco Machining Inc.......................... G 828 891-4100
   Fletcher *(G-4736)*

Foo Machine & Tool Precision.............. F 919 258-5099
   Broadway *(G-986)*

Franklin Machine Company LLC............ G 828 524-2313
   Franklin *(G-4828)*

Fulton Technology Corporation............. G 828 657-1611
   Mooresboro *(G-8584)*

G & J Machine Shop Inc...................... E 336 668-0996
   Greensboro *(G-5545)*

G T Racing Heads Inc......................... G 336 905-7988
   Sophia *(G-11489)*

Gamma Technologies Inc..................... G 919 319-5272
   Morrisville *(G-8980)*

Gaston Indus Machining LLC................ G 704 825-3346
   Bessemer City *(G-820)*

General Machining Inc......................... G 336 342-2759
   Reidsville *(G-10684)*

General Mch Wldg of Burlington........... G 336 227-5400
   Burlington *(G-1094)*

General Precision Svc.......................... G 919 553-2604
   Clayton *(G-3149)*

Gentle Machine and Tool Inc............... G 336 492-5055
   Mocksville *(G-8366)*

Gesipa Fasteners Usa Inc.................... E 336 751-1555
   Mocksville *(G-8367)*

◆ Gesipa Fasteners Usa Inc................. F 609 208-1740
   Mocksville *(G-8368)*

Gibbs Machine Company Incorporated. E 336 856-1907
   Greensboro *(G-5559)*

Gillespies Fbrction Design Inc.............. G 704 636-2349
   Salisbury *(G-11056)*

Gordon Enterprises.............................. G 919 776-8784
   Sanford *(G-11186)*

Goshen Engineering Inc....................... G 919 429-9798
   Mount Olive *(G-9254)*

Grandeur Manufacturing Inc................. E 336 526-2468
   Jonesville *(G-7197)*

Greens Machine & Tool Inc.................. G 828 654-0042
   Fletcher *(G-4739)*

Gunmar Machine Corporation............... F 910 738-6295
   Lumberton *(G-7956)*

H & B Tool & Die Supply Co................. G 704 376-8531
   Charlotte *(G-2244)*

H & R Mullis Machine Inc..................... G 704 791-4149
   Midland *(G-8287)*

Hamilton Machine Works LLC............... G 919 779-6892
   Raleigh *(G-10154)*

Hancock & Grandson Inc..................... G 252 728-2416
   Beaufort *(G-729)*

Heintz Bros Automotives Inc................ G 704 872-8081
   Statesville *(G-11706)*

Helms Machine Company...................... G 704 289-5571
   Monroe *(G-8498)*

Hi-TEC Machine Corp.......................... E 828 652-1060
   Old Fort *(G-9593)*

Highland Tool and Gauge Inc .... G .... 828 891-8557 Mills River *(G-8314)*	Johnson Machine Co Inc .... G .... 252 638-2620 New Bern *(G-9374)*	▲ Masonboro Sound Machinery Inc ..... E .... 910 452-5090 Wilmington *(G-12848)*
Hmf Inc .... G .... 704 821-6765 Matthews *(G-8173)*	K & C Machine Co Inc .... G .... 336 373-0745 Greensboro *(G-5641)*	Master Machining Inc .... E .... 910 675-3660 Castle Hayne *(G-1507)*
Hodges Precision Machine .... G .... 336 366-3024 Dobson *(G-3821)*	K & S Tool & Manufacturing Co .... F .... 336 410-7260 High Point *(G-6680)*	◆ Max Daetwyler Corp .... E .... 704 875-1200 Huntersville *(G-7012)*
Holder Machine & Mfg Co .... G .... 828 479-8627 Robbinsville *(G-10759)*	▲ K-M Machine Company Inc .... D .... 910 428-2368 Biscoe *(G-855)*	McDowells Mch Fabrication Inc .... G .... 336 720-9944 Winston Salem *(G-13247)*
▲ Holman & Moody Inc .... G .... 704 394-4141 Charlotte *(G-2281)*	Kennys Components Inc .... F .... 704 662-0777 Mooresville *(G-8703)*	McGee Brothers Machine & Wldg ...... G .... 828 766-9122 Spruce Pine *(G-11580)*
Hoser Inc .... G .... 704 989-7151 Monroe *(G-8500)*	L & K Machining Inc .... F .... 336 222-9444 Burlington *(G-1116)*	McJast Inc .... F .... 828 884-4809 Pisgah Forest *(G-9771)*
Hydraulics Express .... G .... 828 251-2500 Asheville *(G-519)*	L and L Machine Co Inc .... F .... 704 864-5521 Gastonia *(G-5076)*	Mdm Mfg LLC .... G .... 919 908-6574 Hillsborough *(G-6873)*
I-40 Machine and Tool Inc .... G .... 704 881-0242 Statesville *(G-11715)*	Lacy J Miller Machine .... G .... 336 764-0518 Lexington *(G-7707)*	▼ Meadows Mills Inc .... E .... 336 838-2282 North Wilkesboro *(G-9546)*
I2e Group LLC .... G .... 336 884-2014 High Point *(G-6665)*	Laser Dynamics Inc .... G .... 704 658-9769 Mooresville *(G-8708)*	Mecha Inc .... F .... 919 858-0372 Raleigh *(G-10286)*
Imperial Machine Company Inc .... E .... 704 739-8038 Bessemer City *(G-823)*	▲ Laser Precision Cutting Inc .... G .... 828 658-0644 Weaverville *(G-12495)*	Mechanical Specialty Inc .... G .... 336 272-5606 Greensboro *(G-5688)*
Indaux Usa Inc .... G .... 336 861-0740 Advance *(G-33)*	Latham-Hall Corporation .... E .... 336 475-9723 Thomasville *(G-12042)*	Mega Machine Shop Inc .... G .... 336 492-2728 Mocksville *(G-8376)*
Indtool Inc .... E .... 336 226-4923 Burlington *(G-1109)*	Laurinburg Machine Company .... G .... 910 276-0360 Laurinburg *(G-7505)*	Mertek Solutions Inc .... E .... 919 774-7827 Sanford *(G-11209)*
Industrial Machine & Wldg Inc .... G .... 910 251-1393 Wilmington *(G-12816)*	Lawrence Williams .... G .... 910 462-2332 Laurel Hill *(G-7487)*	Mid-Atlantic Tool and Die Inc .... F .... 252 946-2598 Washington *(G-12397)*
Industrial Machine Company .... F .... 704 922-9750 Dallas *(G-3677)*	Legacy Manufacturing LLC .... G .... 704 525-0498 Charlotte *(G-2417)*	Mik All Machine Co Inc .... F .... 704 866-4302 Gastonia *(G-5097)*
Industrial Mch Solutions Inc .... G .... 919 872-0016 Raleigh *(G-10191)*	Leland Machine Shop Inc .... G .... 910 371-0360 Leland *(G-7550)*	Minas Equity Partners LLC .... F .... 336 724-5152 Winston Salem *(G-13254)*
Industrial Mtal Flame Spryers .... G .... 919 596-9381 Durham *(G-4074)*	Levi Innovations Inc .... G .... 828 684-6640 Fletcher *(G-4747)*	Mitchell Medlin Machine Shop .... G .... 704 289-2840 Monroe *(G-8532)*
Industrial Mtal Pdts Abrdeen I .... F .... 910 944-8110 Aberdeen *(G-7)*	Lewis Machine Company Inc .... G .... 828 668-7752 Old Fort *(G-9595)*	Mmj Machining and Fabg Inc .... F .... 336 495-1029 Randleman *(G-10653)*
▲ Industrial Piping Inc .... A .... 704 588-1100 Charlotte *(G-2323)*	Ljm Machine Co Inc .... G .... 336 764-0518 Lexington *(G-7713)*	Modern Machine and Metal .... D .... 336 993-4808 Winston Salem *(G-13258)*
Industrial Tling Svcs Ashvlle .... G .... 828 683-4168 Leicester *(G-7526)*	Logic Manufacturing Inc .... E .... 704 821-0535 Indian Trail *(G-7089)*	Modern Machining Inc .... G .... 919 775-7332 Sanford *(G-11210)*
Ingram Machine & Balancing .... G .... 828 254-3420 Asheville *(G-524)*	Lucid Innovative Tech LLC .... G .... 910 233-5214 Leland *(G-7552)*	Moffitt Machine Company Inc .... G .... 910 485-2159 Fayetteville *(G-4642)*
Intelligent Tool Corp .... F .... 704 799-0449 Concord *(G-3378)*	M S I Precision Machine Inc .... G .... 704 629-9375 Bessemer City *(G-825)*	Moore Machine Products Inc .... G .... 910 592-2718 Clinton *(G-3236)*
Ipi Acquisition LLC .... A .... 704 588-1100 Charlotte *(G-2356)*	▲ Mabry Industries Inc .... E .... 336 584-1311 Elon College *(G-4474)*	Morris Machine Company Inc .... G .... 704 824-4242 Gastonia *(G-5102)*
Island Machining LLC .... G .... 704 278-3553 Mooresville *(G-8697)*	Mac/Fab Company Inc .... E .... 704 822-1103 Mount Holly *(G-9236)*	Morris South LLC .... D .... 704 523-6008 Charlotte *(G-2520)*
J & J Machine Works Inc .... G .... 336 434-4081 Archdale *(G-230)*	◆ Machine Builders & Design Inc .... E .... 704 482-3456 Shelby *(G-11355)*	Motorsports Machining Tech LLC ...... G .... 336 475-3742 Thomasville *(G-12052)*
J & K Tools LLC .... G .... 828 299-0589 Asheville *(G-526)*	Machine Consulting Svcs Inc .... G .... 919 596-3033 Durham *(G-4114)*	Mundy Machine Co Inc .... F .... 704 922-8663 Dallas *(G-3679)*
J & P Machine Works Inc .... G .... 252 758-1719 Greenville *(G-5993)*	Machine Specialties LLC .... C .... 336 603-1919 Whitsett *(G-12613)*	Myers Tool and Machine Co Inc .... D .... 336 956-1324 Lexington *(G-7719)*
J&L Machine & Fabrication Inc .... E .... 704 755-5552 Stanley *(G-11619)*	Machinex .... G .... 336 665-5030 High Point *(G-6695)*	▲ Nabell USA Corporation .... E .... 704 986-2455 Albemarle *(G-82)*
Jacks Motor Parts Inc .... G .... 910 642-4077 Whiteville *(G-12586)*	Machining Solutions Inc .... G .... 704 528-5436 Troutman *(G-12145)*	Nashville Wldg & Mch Works Inc ...... E .... 252 243-0113 Wilson *(G-13008)*
Jaeco Precision Inc .... G .... 336 633-1025 Asheboro *(G-368)*	Magna Machining Inc .... E .... 704 463-9904 Richfield *(G-10719)*	New World Technologies Inc .... G .... 828 652-8662 Marion *(G-8058)*
▲ James Tool Machine & Engrg Inc ...... C .... 828 584-8722 Morganton *(G-8875)*	Mammoth Machine and Design LLC ...... G .... 704 727-3330 Mooresville *(G-8718)*	▲ Newton Machine Co Inc .... F .... 704 394-2099 Charlotte *(G-2560)*
Jimbuilt Machines Inc .... G .... 828 874-3530 Connelly Springs *(G-3479)*	Mang Systems Inc .... G .... 704 292-1041 Matthews *(G-8181)*	Nolen Machine Co Inc .... G .... 704 867-7851 Gastonia *(G-5111)*
Jmc Tool & Machine Co .... E .... 919 775-7070 Sanford *(G-11197)*	Manufacturing Services Inc .... E .... 704 629-4163 Bessemer City *(G-826)*	North Carolina Dept Labor .... F .... 919 807-2770 Raleigh *(G-10335)*
Joe and La Inc .... F .... 336 585-0313 Burlington *(G-1113)*	Marc Machine Works Inc .... F .... 704 865-3625 Gastonia *(G-5091)*	North Carolina Mfg Inc .... E .... 919 734-1115 Goldsboro *(G-5231)*
John West Auto Service Inc .... G .... 919 250-0825 Raleigh *(G-10218)*	Marine Fabrications LLC .... G .... 252 473-4767 Wanchese *(G-12345)*	North State Machine Inc .... F .... 336 956-1441 Lexington *(G-7724)*
Johnson Cnc LLC .... E .... 910 428-1245 Star *(G-11628)*	Marion Machine LLC .... E .... 800 627-1639 Marion *(G-8050)*	Northwest Machine and Supply .... F .... 336 526-2029 Ronda *(G-10895)*
Johnson Industrial Mchy Svcs .... E .... 252 239-1944 Lucama *(G-7937)*	Mary Kay Inc .... G .... 336 998-1663 Advance *(G-35)*	Noxon Automation USA LLC .... G .... 919 390-1560 Morrisville *(G-9031)*

Employee Codes: A=Over 500 employees, B=251-500   2025 Harris North Carolina
C=101-250, D=51-100, E=20-50, F=10-19, G=1-9   Manufacturers Directory

731

SIC

Nu-Tech Enterprises Inc.......................... E 336 725-1691
  East Bend *(G-4324)*

Olivia Machine & Tool Inc................... F 919 499-6021
  Sanford *(G-11213)*

▲ Omega Manufacturing Corp............... F 704 597-0418
  Charlotte *(G-2596)*

Ora Inc.. G 540 903-7177
  Marion *(G-8059)*

Ostec Industries Corp........................... G 704 488-3841
  Denver *(G-3796)*

Ostwalt Machine Company Inc............... G 704 528-5730
  Troutman *(G-12147)*

Paul Norman Company Inc..................... G 704 399-4221
  Charlotte *(G-2618)*

Pemmco Manufacturing Inc..................... D 336 625-1122
  Asheboro *(G-381)*

Performance Machine & Fab Inc............. G 336 983-0414
  King *(G-7335)*

Petra Precision Machining..................... G 919 751-3461
  Goldsboro *(G-5237)*

Petteway Body Shop Inc....................... G 910 455-3272
  Jacksonville *(G-7137)*

Piedmont Precision Products................... G 828 304-0791
  Hickory *(G-6412)*

Piedmont Technical Services................... G 770 530-8313
  Charlotte *(G-2638)*

Pinnacle Converting Eqp & Svcs............. E 704 376-3855
  Pineville *(G-9747)*

Pinnacle Converting Eqp Inc................... E 704 376-3855
  Pineville *(G-9748)*

Pioneer Machine Works Inc................... G 704 864-5528
  Gastonia *(G-5120)*

Pleasant Gardens Machine Inc............... F 828 724-4173
  Marion *(G-8061)*

Poplin & Sons Machine Co Inc............... F 704 289-2079
  Monroe *(G-8543)*

Precision Design Machinery................... G 336 889-8157
  High Point *(G-6740)*

Precision Fabricators Inc....................... G 336 835-4763
  Ronda *(G-10897)*

Precision Machine Tech Inc................... F 910 678-8665
  Fayetteville *(G-4656)*

Precision Machine Tools Corp............... G 704 882-3700
  Matthews *(G-8190)*

▲ Precision Mch Components Inc......... G 704 201-8482
  Denver *(G-3800)*

▲ Precision Mch Fabrication Inc........... D 919 231-8648
  Raleigh *(G-10390)*

Precision Mindset Pllc........................... G 704 508-1314
  Statesville *(G-11753)*

Precision Partners LLC......................... E 800 545-3121
  Charlotte *(G-2658)*

Precision Pdts Asheville Inc................... E 828 684-4207
  Arden *(G-299)*

Precision Tool Dye and Mold................... F 828 687-2990
  Arden *(G-301)*

Precision Wldg Mch Charlotte................... G 704 357-1288
  Charlotte *(G-2659)*

Premier Mfg Co..................................... E 704 781-4001
  Midland *(G-8293)*

Pro Tool Company Inc........................... F 336 998-9212
  Advance *(G-37)*

Production Wldg Fbrication Inc............... G 828 687-7466
  Arden *(G-302)*

Proedge Precision LLC......................... E 704 872-3393
  Statesville *(G-11756)*

Promatic Automation Inc....................... F 828 684-1700
  Fletcher *(G-4761)*

Prometals Inc....................................... G 919 693-8884
  Oxford *(G-9627)*

Protech Metals LLC............................... F 910 295-6905
  Pinehurst *(G-9701)*

PSI Liquidating Inc............................... G 704 888-9930
  Locust *(G-7897)*

Quality Machine & Tool......................... G 336 769-9131
  Kernersville *(G-7296)*

Quality Mch & Fabrication Inc............... G 252 435-6041
  Moyock *(G-9280)*

Quality Products & Machine LLC............. E 704 504-3330
  Charlotte *(G-2684)*

Quartz Matrix LLC............................... G 828 631-3207
  Sylva *(G-11898)*

▲ R H Bolick & Company Inc............... G 828 322-7847
  Hickory *(G-6425)*

R&H Machining Fabrication Inc............... G 828 253-8930
  Asheville *(G-587)*

Ramco Machine & Pump Svc Inc............. G 910 371-3388
  Leland *(G-7558)*

Randolph Machine Inc........................... G 336 625-0411
  Asheboro *(G-389)*

Rawco LLC... G 908 832-7700
  Cornelius *(G-3622)*

Ray Houses Machine Shop..................... G 919 553-1249
  Clayton *(G-3167)*

Rbi Manufacturing Inc........................... F 252 977-6764
  Rocky Mount *(G-10865)*

Rbw LLC... G 919 319-1289
  Cary *(G-1434)*

Rebb Industries Inc............................... E 336 463-2311
  Yadkinville *(G-13449)*

Reel-Tex Inc... F 704 868-4419
  Gastonia *(G-5133)*

Reynolda Mfg Solutions Inc................... G 336 699-4204
  East Bend *(G-4325)*

Reynolda Mfg Solutions Inc................... E 336 699-4204
  East Bend *(G-4326)*

Robinson & Son Machine Inc............... G 910 592-4779
  Clinton *(G-3240)*

Rock Industrial Services Inc................... F 910 652-6267
  Ellerbe *(G-4463)*

Rowan Precision Machining Inc............... G 704 279-6092
  Granite Quarry *(G-5327)*

Rowdy Manufacturing LLC..................... G 704 662-0000
  Mooresville *(G-8764)*

Roy Dunn... G 919 963-3700
  Four Oaks *(G-4815)*

Rtt Machine & Welding Svc Inc............... G 919 269-6863
  Zebulon *(G-13522)*

Rufus N Ivie III..................................... G 704 482-2559
  Shelby *(G-11374)*

S & D Machine & Tool Inc....................... E 919 479-8433
  Durham *(G-4219)*

S & S Repair Service Inc....................... F 252 756-5989
  Winterville *(G-13423)*

S & W Metal Works Inc......................... G 252 641-0912
  Tarboro *(G-11940)*

S Oakley Machine Shop Inc................... G 336 599-6105
  Roxboro *(G-10944)*

S Strickland Diesel Svc Inc................... G 252 291-6999
  Wilson *(G-13025)*

Sanders Company Inc........................... F 252 338-3995
  Elizabeth City *(G-4408)*

Sandhlls Fbrctors Crane Svcs I............. F 910 673-4573
  West End *(G-12558)*

Scoggins Industrial Inc......................... F 252 977-9222
  Sharpsburg *(G-11307)*

Seymour Advanced Tech LLC............... G 704 709-9070
  Denver *(G-3804)*

Sloans Machine Shop........................... G 919 499-5655
  Sanford *(G-11234)*

Smith Fabrication Inc........................... G 704 660-5170
  Mooresville *(G-8772)*

▲ Smokey Mountain Amusements........ G 828 479-2814
  Robbinsville *(G-10762)*

Smoky Mountain Machining Inc............. D 828 665-1193
  Asheville *(G-603)*

Sniders Machine Shop Inc..................... G 704 279-6129
  Rockwell *(G-10801)*

Solomon Engineering Inc....................... E 828 855-1652
  Hickory *(G-6452)*

South East Manufacturing Co............... F 252 291-0925
  Wilson *(G-13030)*

Southeastern Enterprises..................... F 704 373-1750
  Charlotte *(G-2832)*

Southeastern Mch & Wldg Co Inc........... E 910 791-6661
  Wilmington *(G-12925)*

◆ Southeastern Tool & Die Inc............... D 910 944-7677
  Aberdeen *(G-24)*

Southern Machine Services..................... G 919 658-9300
  Mount Olive *(G-9258)*

Southern Prestige Industries Inc............. E 704 872-9524
  Statesville *(G-11770)*

Southern Prestige Intl LLC................... F 704 872-9524
  Statesville *(G-11771)*

Special Fab & Machine Inc..................... E 336 956-2121
  Lexington *(G-7745)*

Specialty Perf LLC............................... G 704 872-9980
  Statesville *(G-11773)*

Speedwell Machine Works Inc............... E 704 866-7418
  Gastonia *(G-5140)*

Sphenodon Tool Co Inc......................... G 252 757-3460
  Greenville *(G-6025)*

Spm Machine Works Inc......................... G 252 321-2134
  Ayden *(G-664)*

SPX Technologies Inc........................... D 980 474-3700
  Charlotte *(G-2851)*

Square One Machine LLC....................... G 704 600-6296
  Shelby *(G-11383)*

Stine Gear & Machine Company............. F 704 445-1245
  Bessemer City *(G-834)*

Stovers Precision Tooling Inc................... G 704 876-3673
  Statesville *(G-11782)*

Stowe Enterprises Inc........................... G 800 315-6751
  Troutman *(G-12151)*

Stump and Grind LLC........................... G 704 488-2271
  Charlotte *(G-2875)*

Sun Valley Stl Fabrication Inc............... F 704 289-5830
  Monroe *(G-8565)*

Superior Machine Co SC Inc................... E 828 652-6141
  Marion *(G-8068)*

Superior Machine Shop Inc................... G 910 675-1336
  Rocky Point *(G-10885)*

▲ Syntegon Technology Svcs LLC......... E 919 877-0886
  Raleigh *(G-10527)*

T D M Corporation............................... E
  Fletcher *(G-4772)*

T Hoff Manufacturing Corp................... G 919 833-8671
  Raleigh *(G-10528)*

▲ T Precision Machining Inc............... F 828 250-0993
  Asheville *(G-613)*

Tar Heel Tling Prcsion McHning............. F 919 965-6160
  Smithfield *(G-11467)*

Tarheel Tool & Gauge LLC..................... G 704 213-6924
  Salisbury *(G-11122)*

Taylor Manufacturing Inc....................... E 910 862-2576
  Elizabethtown *(G-4434)*

▲ Tdc International LLC......................... G 704 875-1198
  Concord *(G-3452)*

Team Industries Inc............................... D 828 837-5377
  Andrews *(G-109)*

Tech-Tool Inc....................................... G 919 906-6229
  Hampstead *(G-6076)*

Textile Designed Machine Co............... F 704 664-1374
  Mooresville *(G-8784)*

Thornburg Machine & Sup Co Inc........... E 704 735-5421
  Lincolnton *(G-7864)*

Tigertek Industrial Svcs LLC .... E 336 623-1717
Stoneville (G-11832)

Tilson Machine Inc .... D 828 668-4416
Marion (G-8069)

Titeflex Corporation .... D 647 638-7160
Charlotte (G-2921)

Tmp of Nc Inc .... G 336 463-3225
Yadkinville (G-13453)

Tobe Manufacturing Inc .... F 910 439-6203
Mount Gilead (G-9211)

Toner Machining Technologies .... F 828 432-8007
Morganton (G-8906)

Tony D Hildreth .... F 910 276-1803
Laurel Hill (G-7488)

Tool Rental Depot LLC .... G 704 636-6400
Salisbury (G-11126)

Tri-TEC Ind Inc .... G 704 424-5995
Charlotte (G-2941)

Triad Fabrication and Mch Inc .... G 336 993-6042
Kernersville (G-7309)

Triad Precision Products Inc .... F 336 474-0980
Thomasville (G-12083)

Triplett & Coffey Inc .... F 828 263-0561
Boone (G-947)

Triumph Tool Nc Inc .... E 828 676-3677
Arden (G-313)

Tru-Cast Inc .... E 336 294-2370
Greensboro (G-5881)

True Machine LLC .... G 919 270-2552
Oxford (G-9639)

Turnamics Inc .... E 828 254-1059
Asheville (G-626)

Turnkey Technologies Inc .... G 704 245-6437
Salisbury (G-11128)

Tyndall Machine Tool Inc .... G 919 542-4014
Pittsboro (G-9790)

Ultra Machine & Fabrication Inc .... C 704 482-1399
Shelby (G-11388)

Unique Concepts .... G 919 366-2001
Garner (G-4969)

United Machine Works Inc .... E 252 752-7434
Greenville (G-6029)

United Technical Services LLC .... F 980 237-1335
Charlotte (G-2963)

Universal Machine and Tool Inc .... G 828 659-2002
Marion (G-8071)

Upchurch Machine Co Inc .... G 704 588-2895
Charlotte (G-2966)

US Metal Crafters LLC .... E 336 861-2100
Archdale (G-245)

Viewriver Machine Corporation .... E 336 463-2311
Yadkinville (G-13457)

Vortex USA Inc .... F 972 410-3619
Cornelius (G-3629)

W D Lee & Company .... G 704 864-0346
Gastonia (G-5163)

W H Rgers Shtmtl Ir Wrks Inc .... E 704 394-2191
Charlotte (G-2995)

Wallace Welding Inc .... F 919 934-2488
Smithfield (G-11469)

Weathers Machine Mfg Inc .... F 919 552-5945
Fuquay Varina (G-4906)

▼ West Side Prcsion Mch Pdts Inc .... F 908 647-4903
Statesville (G-11800)

Wilkes Welding and Mch Co Inc .... G 336 670-2742
Mc Grady (G-8217)

Wilmington Machine Works Inc .... G 910 343-8111
Wilmington (G-12950)

Wilson Iron Works Incorporated .... D 252 291-4465
Rocky Mount (G-10820)

Wilson Machine & Tool Inc .... G 919 776-0043
Sanford (G-11251)

Wilson Machine Sho .... G 910 673-3505
West End (G-12560)

▲ Wilson Mold & Machine Corp .... D 252 243-1831
Wilson (G-13049)

Winston Tool Company Inc .... G 336 983-3722
King (G-7340)

▲ Winterville Machine Works Inc .... D 252 756-2130
Winterville (G-13426)

Woempner Machine Company Inc .... G 336 475-2268
Thomasville (G-12089)

Wood Machine Service Inc .... F 252 446-2142
Rocky Mount (G-10876)

Wooten John .... G 828 322-4031
Hickory (G-6490)

Worth Products LLC .... F 252 747-9994
Snow Hill (G-11484)

◆ Wright Machine & Tool Co Inc .... E 828 298-8440
Swannanoa (G-11879)

Wyrick Machine and Tool Co .... G 336 841-8261
Pleasant Garden (G-9796)

▲ Xceldyne Group LLC .... D 336 472-2242
Thomasville (G-12093)

Zumco Inc .... G 828 891-3300
Horse Shoe (G-6931)

36 ELECTRONIC & OTHER ELECTRICAL EQUIPMENT & COMPONENTS

3612 Transformers, except electric

ABB Enterprise Software Inc .... C 919 582-3283
Raleigh (G-9862)

▲ ABB Holdings Inc .... D 919 856-2360
Cary (G-1284)

ABB Inc .... E 704 587-1362
Charlotte (G-1609)

ABB Inc .... G 919 856-3920
Raleigh (G-9863)

ABB Inc .... D 919 856-2360
Raleigh (G-9864)

◆ ABB Inc .... C 919 856-2360
Cary (G-1285)

ABB Power Systems Inc .... G 919 856-2389
Raleigh (G-9865)

▼ ABB Power T & D Company Inc .... A 919 856-3806
Raleigh (G-9866)

Abundant Power Solutions LLC .... G 704 271-9890
Charlotte (G-1612)

Alk Investments LLC .... G 984 233-5353
Raleigh (G-9891)

Aprotech Powertrain LLC .... E 828 253-1350
Asheville (G-429)

Ced Incorporated .... F 336 378-0044
Greensboro (G-5435)

Eaton Corporation .... B 828 684-2381
Arden (G-266)

▲ Impulse NC LLC .... E 919 658-2311
Mount Olive (G-9255)

▲ Liburdi Dimetrics Corporation .... E 704 230-2510
Mooresville (G-8711)

▲ Manufacturing Systems Eqp Inc .... F 704 283-2086
Monroe (G-8523)

Nwl Inc .... E 252 747-5943
Snow Hill (G-11481)

Pennsylvania Trans Tech Inc .... D 910 875-7600
Raeford (G-9847)

Philpott Motors Ltd .... F 704 566-2400
Charlotte (G-2634)

Power Integrity Corp .... E 336 379-9773
Greensboro (G-5752)

Power Support Engineering Inc .... G 813 909-1199
Hayesville (G-6143)

Separation Technologies LLC .... C 336 597-9814
Semora (G-11296)

◆ Smartrac Tech Fletcher Inc .... C 828 651-6051
Fletcher (G-4770)

Trans East Inc .... D 910 892-1081
Dunn (G-3869)

Transformer Sales & Service .... G 910 594-1495
Newton Grove (G-9519)

3613 Switchgear and switchboard apparatus

ABB Enterprise Software Inc .... C 919 582-3283
Raleigh (G-9862)

ABB Inc .... E 704 587-1362
Charlotte (G-1609)

ABB Inc .... C 252 827-2121
Pinetops (G-9705)

ABB Inc .... D 919 856-2360
Raleigh (G-9864)

◆ ABB Inc .... C 919 856-2360
Cary (G-1285)

Acroplis Cntrls Engineers Pllc .... F 919 275-3884
Raleigh (G-9876)

American Moistening Co Inc .... F 704 889-7281
Pineville (G-9712)

Brooks Manufacturing Solutions .... F 336 438-1280
Graham (G-5261)

Brooks Mfg Solutions Inc .... F 336 438-1280
Burlington (G-1054)

◆ Carolina Elctrnic Assmblers In .... E 919 938-1086
Smithfield (G-11435)

Carolina Products Inc .... E 704 364-9029
Charlotte (G-1854)

Cooper Bussmann LLC .... C 252 566-0278
La Grange (G-7465)

Dg Matrix Inc .... G 724 877-7773
Cary (G-1349)

▲ Dna Group Inc .... E 919 881-0889
Raleigh (G-10051)

Eaton Corporation .... B 828 684-2381
Arden (G-266)

Electro Switch Corp .... C 919 833-0707
Raleigh (G-10081)

◆ Elster American Meter Company LLC ..... F 402 873-8200
Charlotte (G-2104)

Gasp Inc .... G 828 891-1628
Fletcher (G-4738)

General Electric Company .... G 704 561-5700
Charlotte (G-2200)

General Electric Company .... B 919 563-5561
Mebane (G-8242)

Glh Systems & Controls Inc .... G 980 581-1304
Stanfield (G-11606)

▲ Grecon Inc .... F 503 641-7731
Charlotte (G-2237)

Industrial Cnnctons Sltons LLC .... E 203 229-3932
Cary (G-1374)

Industrial Control Panels Inc .... G 336 661-3037
Winston Salem (G-13206)

Interstate All Batteries Ctr .... G 704 979-3430
Concord (G-3380)

JA Smith Inc .... G 704 860-4910
Lawndale (G-7517)

▲ JMS Southeast Inc .... E 704 873-1835
Statesville (G-11719)

Miller Ctrl Mfg Inc Clinton NC .... G 910 592-5112
Clinton (G-3235)

▲ Precision Mch Fabrication Inc .... D 919 231-8648
Raleigh (G-10390)

▲ Precision Time Systems Inc .... G 910 253-9850
Supply (G-11857)

PSI Control Solutions LLC .... E 704 596-5617
Charlotte (G-2676)

SIC

R S Integrators Inc.. G 704 588-8288
  Pineville (G-9749)

▲ Reuel Inc .... E 919 734-0460
  Goldsboro (G-5240)

Schneider Electric Usa Inc .... B 919 266-3671
  Knightdale (G-7458)

Schneider Electric Usa Inc .... C 888 778-2733
  Morrisville (G-9045)

▲ Shallco Inc .... E 919 934-3135
  Smithfield (G-11465)

▲ Siemens Power Transmissio .... A 919 463-8702
  Cary (G-1454)

◆ Solero Technologies Shelby LLC .... C 704 482-9582
  Shelby (G-11380)

Southern Electrical Eqp Co Inc .... G 704 392-1396
  Indian Trail (G-7099)

Ssi Services Inc .... G 919 867-1450
  Raleigh (G-10501)

Tencarva Machinery Company LLC .... G 336 665-1435
  Greensboro (G-5858)

Trimantec... E 336 767-1379
  Winston Salem (G-13372)

▲ Xylem Lnc .... E 704 409-9700
  Charlotte (G-3035)

3621 Motors and generators

057 Technology LLC .... G 855 557-7057
  Hickory (G-6258)

ABB Motors and Mechanical Inc .... G 336 272-6104
  Greensboro (G-5336)

ABB Motors and Mechanical Inc .... B 704 734-2500
  Kings Mountain (G-7342)

ABB Motors and Mechanical Inc .... G 479 646-4711
  Marion (G-8029)

Allan Drth Sons Gnrtor Sls Svc .... G 828 526-9325
  Highlands (G-6842)

Alternative Pwr Sls & Rent LLP .... G 919 467-8001
  Morrisville (G-8925)

Altom Fuel Cells LLC .... G 828 231-6889
  Leicester (G-7521)

Ao Smith Chatlotte .... G 704 597-8910
  Charlotte (G-1680)

▲ Ashbran LLC .... G 919 215-3567
  Clayton (G-3132)

▲ Asmo North America LLC .... A 704 872-2319
  Statesville (G-11661)

Battlgrund Strter Gnerator Inc .... G 336 685-4511
  Julian (G-7200)

◆ Buehler Motor Inc .... E 919 380-3333
  Morrisville (G-8945)

Bwx Technologies Inc .... D 980 365-4000
  Charlotte (G-1823)

Cummins Inc .... G 704 588-1240
  Pineville (G-9723)

Curtiss-Wright Corporation .... B 704 869-4600
  Davidson (G-3700)

DCS USA Corporation .... G 919 535-8000
  Morrisville (G-8963)

◆ Denso Manufacturing NC Inc .... B 704 878-6663
  Statesville (G-11688)

▲ Dna Group Inc .... E 919 881-0889
  Raleigh (G-10051)

Eaton Corporation .... B 828 684-2381
  Arden (G-266)

Elnik Systems LLC .... E 973 239-6066
  Pineville (G-9726)

Everything Industrial Supply .... G 743 333-2222
  Winston Salem (G-13162)

GE Vernova International LLC .... E 704 587-1300
  Charlotte (G-2194)

Genelect Services Inc .... F 828 255-7999
  Asheville (G-505)

Global Emssons Systems Inc-USA .... G 704 585-8490
  Troutman (G-12139)

Goldsboro Strter Altrntor Svc .... G 919 735-6745
  Goldsboro (G-5218)

Greenfield Energy LLC .... F 910 509-1805
  Wrightsville Beach (G-13431)

Hitachi Energy USA Inc .... C 919 856-2360
  Raleigh (G-10170)

Hlmf Logistics Inc .... G 704 782-0356
  Pineville (G-9733)

Ini Power Systems Inc .... F 919 677-7112
  Morrisville (G-8993)

Josh Allred .... G 336 873-1006
  Seagrove (G-11275)

Lennox International Inc .... C 828 633-4805
  Candler (G-1229)

Li-Ion Motors Corp .... G 704 662-0827
  Mooresville (G-8710)

Motor Rite Inc .... G 919 625-3653
  Raleigh (G-10315)

◆ Ohio Electric Motors Inc .... D 828 626-2901
  Barnardsville (G-693)

Peak Clean Energy LLC .... G 303 588-2789
  Huntersville (G-7031)

Petty Machine Company Inc .... E 704 864-3254
  Gastonia (G-5119)

Pinnacle Converting Eqp Inc .... E 704 376-3855
  Pineville (G-9748)

Powersecure Inc .... G 919 818-8700
  Princeton (G-9825)

▲ Powertec Industrial Motors Inc .... F 704 227-1580
  Charlotte (G-2652)

◆ Progress Solar Solutions LLC .... F 919 363-3738
  Raleigh (G-10401)

R D Tillson & Associates Inc .... G 336 454-1410
  Jamestown (G-7178)

Regal Rexnord Corporation .... G 800 825-6544
  Charlotte (G-2703)

Rotron Incorporated .... C 336 449-3400
  Whitsett (G-12619)

Sag Harbor Industries Inc .... E 252 753-7175
  Farmville (G-4539)

SCR Controls Inc .... F 704 821-6651
  Matthews (G-8192)

Siemens Energy Inc .... E 336 969-1351
  Rural Hall (G-10967)

Siemens Energy Inc .... G 919 365-2200
  Wendell (G-12546)

Siemens Med Solutions USA Inc .... E 919 468-7400
  Cary (G-1453)

▼ Sirius Energies Corporation .... G 704 425-6272
  Concord (G-3440)

Trane Technologies Company LLC .... B 336 751-3561
  Mocksville (G-8394)

Xavier Power Systems .... F 910 734-7813
  Lumberton (G-7977)

▲ Xylem Lnc .... E 704 409-9700
  Charlotte (G-3035)

3624 Carbon and graphite products

Asbury Graphite Mills .... G 910 671-4141
  Lumberton (G-7945)

▼ Debotech Inc .... C 704 664-1361
  Mooresville (G-8653)

Energy Conversion Syste .... G 910 892-8081
  Dunn (G-3855)

Morgan Advanced Mtls Tech Inc .... C 910 892-9677
  Dunn (G-3862)

Nouveau Verre Holdings Inc .... F 336 545-0011
  Greensboro (G-5714)

Nvh Inc .... G 336 545-0011
  Greensboro (G-5717)

◆ Pbi Performance Products Inc .... D 704 554-3378
  Charlotte (G-2621)

Sgl Carbon LLC .... G 828 437-3221
  Morganton (G-8895)

◆ Sgl Carbon LLC .... E 704 593-5100
  Charlotte (G-2792)

Sgl Composites Inc .... F 704 593-5100
  Charlotte (G-2793)

Sgl Technologies LLC .... G 704 593-5100
  Charlotte (G-2794)

Slade Operating Company LLC .... E 704 873-1366
  Statesville (G-11766)

▼ Thanet Inc .... G 704 483-4175
  Denver (G-3812)

Tokai Carbon GE LLC .... E 980 260-1130
  Charlotte (G-2927)

3625 Relays and industrial controls

2391 Eatons Ferry Rd Assoc LLC .... G 919 844-0565
  Raleigh (G-9857)

◆ Aalberts Integrated Pipin .... E 704 841-6000
  Charlotte (G-1608)

ABB Enterprise Software Inc .... C 919 582-3283
  Raleigh (G-9862)

ABB Inc .... E 704 587-1362
  Charlotte (G-1609)

◆ ABB Inc .... C 919 856-2360
  Cary (G-1285)

Abco Automation Inc .... C 336 375-6400
  Browns Summit (G-988)

Abco Controls and Eqp Inc .... G 704 394-2424
  Charlotte (G-1610)

▲ AC Corporation .... B 336 273-4472
  Greensboro (G-5339)

Aiken Development LLC .... G 828 572-4040
  Lenoir (G-7567)

Alan R Williams Inc .... E 704 372-8281
  Charlotte (G-1636)

Alcon Components Usa Inc .... G 704 799-2723
  Mooresville (G-8592)

Assembly Tech Components Inc .... G 919 773-0388
  Garner (G-4917)

▲ CMC Sencon Inc .... E 919 938-3216
  Smithfield (G-11439)

Cross Technologies Inc .... E 800 327-7727
  Greensboro (G-5472)

Curtiss-Wright Controls Inc .... E 704 869-2300
  Shelby (G-11325)

Custom Controls Unlimited LLC .... F 919 812-6553
  Raleigh (G-10029)

Dozier Industrial Electric Inc .... E 252 451-0020
  Rocky Mount (G-10810)

DSI Innovations LLC .... E 336 893-8385
  Thomasville (G-12020)

Eaton Corporation .... B 828 684-2381
  Arden (G-266)

Eaton Corporation .... A 910 677-5375
  Fayetteville (G-4593)

Eaton Corporation .... C 919 870-3000
  Raleigh (G-10072)

Electro Magnetic Research Inc .... G 919 365-3723
  Zebulon (G-13508)

Envirnmntal Cmfort Sltions Inc .... E 980 272-7327
  Kannapolis (G-7208)

Fortech Inc .... F 704 333-0621
  Charlotte (G-2174)

General Electric Company .... F 919 563-7445
  Mebane (G-8241)

General Electric Company .... B 919 563-5561
  Mebane (G-8242)

▲ Griffin Motion LLC .... F 919 577-6333
  Apex (G-161)

Hitech Controls Inc............................ G 336 498-1534
　Randleman (G-10649)

◆ Hubbell Industrial Contrls Inc............C 336 434-2800
　Archdale (G-226)

I C E S Gaston County Inc.................. G 704 263-1418
　Stanley (G-11618)

ITT LLC... F 704 716-7600
　Charlotte (G-2357)

ITT LLC... G 336 662-0113
　Colfax (G-3281)

J&L Manufacturing Inc...................... F 919 801-3219
　Fuquay Varina (G-4886)

JA Smith Inc..................................... G 704 860-4910
　Lawndale (G-7517)

Linor Technology Inc......................... F 336 485-6199
　Winston Salem (G-13235)

Lynn Electronics Corporation............. G 704 369-0093
　Concord (G-3397)

Masonite Corporation........................ A 704 599-0235
　Charlotte (G-2466)

McKenzie Supply Company................. G 910 276-1691
　Laurinburg (G-7509)

McNaughton-Mckay Southeast Inc........ F 910 392-0940
　Wilmington (G-12850)

Melltronics Industrial Inc................... G 704 821-6651
　Matthews (G-8185)

Middlesex Plant................................. G 252 235-2121
　Middlesex (G-8277)

Miller Ctrl Mfg Inc Clinton NC............ G 910 592-5112
　Clinton (G-3235)

Moog Inc... B 828 837-5115
　Murphy (G-9293)

Nexjen Systems LLC.......................... E 704 969-7070
　Charlotte (G-2561)

Nsi Industries................................... D 800 321-5847
　Huntersville (G-7024)

▲ Pro-Tech Inc.................................. G 704 872-6227
　Statesville (G-11755)

Q T Corporation................................ G 252 399-7600
　Wilson (G-13016)

Rockwell Automation Inc.................... G 919 804-0200
　Cary (G-1440)

Rockwell Automation Inc.................... E 704 665-6000
　Charlotte (G-2731)

Rockwell Automation Inc.................... F 828 652-0074
　Marion (G-8063)

Rockwell Automation Inc.................... F 828 645-4235
　Weaverville (G-12501)

Schneider Electric Usa Inc................. B 919 266-3671
　Knightdale (G-7458)

▲ Shopbot Tools Inc.......................... E 919 680-4800
　Durham (G-4233)

Siemens Industry Inc......................... C 919 365-2200
　Wendell (G-12547)

▲ Siemens Power Transmissio........... A 919 463-8702
　Cary (G-1454)

Silanna Semicdtr N Amer Inc............. D 984 444-6500
　Raleigh (G-10476)

◆ Solero Technologies Shelby LLC........ C 704 482-9582
　Shelby (G-11380)

Solvere LLC...................................... E 704 829-1015
　Belmont (G-766)

Southern Electrical Eqp Co Inc........... G 704 392-1396
　Indian Trail (G-7099)

◆ Southern Electrical Eqp Co Inc......... E 704 392-1396
　Charlotte (G-2836)

State Electric Supply Company........... F 336 855-8200
　Greensboro (G-5837)

▲ Stay Online LLC............................. E 888 346-4688
　Creedmoor (G-3656)

Strandberg Engrg Labs Inc................ F 336 274-3775
　Greensboro (G-5843)

Sure Trip Inc.................................... F 704 983-4651
　Albemarle (G-94)

Te Connectivity Corporation............... F 828 338-1000
　Fairview (G-4514)

▲ Textrol Laboratories Inc................. E 704 764-3400
　Monroe (G-8569)

Total Controls Inc............................. G 704 821-6341
　Matthews (G-8152)

Trane Technologies Company LLC........ C 910 692-8700
　Southern Pines (G-11512)

Triac Corporation.............................. F 336 297-1130
　Greensboro (G-5873)

Triangle Microsystems Inc................. F 919 878-1880
　Raleigh (G-10558)

Unifour Tech Inc................................ G 828 256-4962
　Newton (G-9507)

Vance Industrial Elec Inc................... G 336 570-1992
　Burlington (G-1173)

◆ Yale Industrial Products Inc............ E 704 588-4610
　Charlotte (G-3038)

3629 Electrical industrial apparatus

3M Company..................................... G 919 774-3808
　Sanford (G-11144)

Ametek Electronics Systems.............. F 800 645-9721
　Knightdale (G-7448)

Desco Industries Inc......................... F 919 718-0000
　Sanford (G-11171)

Eaton Corporation............................. D 864 433-1603
　Raleigh (G-10073)

Eaton Corporation............................. C 919 872-3020
　Raleigh (G-10074)

Eaton Power Quality Corp.................. F 919 872-3020
　Raleigh (G-10075)

▲ Eaton Power Quality Group Inc........ G 919 872-3020
　Raleigh (G-10076)

Ekc Advanced Elec USA 4 LLC............ G 302 774-1000
　Wilmington (G-12770)

Ensales Electrical Assoc Inc.............. F 910 298-3305
　Beulaville (G-842)

Equagen Engineers Pllc..................... E 919 444-5442
　Raleigh (G-10090)

Exide Technologies LLC...................... G 704 521-8016
　Charlotte (G-2135)

Exide Technologies LLC...................... G 919 553-3578
　Clayton (G-3147)

H C Production Co............................. G 910 483-5267
　Fayetteville (G-4607)

▲ Ifanatic LLC.................................. G 919 387-6062
　Apex (G-166)

◆ Laird Thermal Systems Inc............ E 919 597-7300
　Morrisville (G-9002)

▲ Majorpower Corporation................. E 919 563-6610
　Mebane (G-8251)

▲ North Fork Electric Inc................... G 336 982-4020
　Crumpler (G-3661)

Nwl Inc.. E 252 747-5943
　Snow Hill (G-11481)

Polypore Inc..................................... D 704 587-8409
　Charlotte (G-2644)

Power Integrity Corp.......................... E 336 379-9773
　Greensboro (G-5752)

Powergpu LLC................................... F 919 702-6757
　Youngsville (G-13481)

▲ Powersecure International Inc.......... A 919 556-3056
　Wake Forest (G-12289)

◆ Static Control Components Inc.......... A 919 774-3808
　Sanford (G-11238)

Static Control Ic-Disc Inc.................. F 919 774-3808
　Sanford (G-11239)

Team Manufacturing - E W LLC........... D 919 554-2442
　Youngsville (G-13491)

Xpc Corporation................................ G 919 210-1756
　Raleigh (G-10620)

Xpc Corporation................................ G 800 582-4524
　Raleigh (G-10621)

3631 Household cooking equipment

Bsh Home Appliances Corp................ E 252 636-4454
　New Bern (G-9342)

Electrolux Home Products Inc............ B 252 527-5100
　Kinston (G-7410)

Jebco Inc... E 919 557-2001
　Holly Springs (G-6904)

Marshall Middleby Inc........................ D 919 762-1000
　Fuquay Varina (G-4887)

◆ Middleby Marshall Inc.................... C 919 762-1000
　Fuquay Varina (G-4891)

Weber Stephen Products LLC.............. F 704 662-0335
　Mooresville (G-8796)

Whaley Foodservice LLC..................... D 704 529-6242
　Charlotte (G-3016)

3632 Household refrigerators and freezers

Bsh Home Appliances Corp................ B 252 672-9155
　New Bern (G-9343)

K2 Scientific LLC............................... F 800 218-7613
　Charlotte (G-2386)

3634 Electric housewares and fans

Airbox Inc.. E 855 927-1386
　Statesville (G-11651)

Blossman Propane Gas & Appl............ F 828 396-0144
　Hickory (G-6272)

CPM Acquisition Corp........................ F 972 243-8070
　Lexington (G-7669)

▲ Dampp-Chaser Electronics Corp....... E 828 692-8271
　Hendersonville (G-6200)

DNB Humidifier Mfg Inc..................... F 336 764-2076
　Winston Salem (G-13150)

Hamilton Beach Brands Inc................ G 252 975-0444
　Washington (G-12390)

▲ Madison Manufacturing Company...... D 828 622-7500
　Hot Springs (G-6933)

▲ Marley Company LLC...................... C 704 752-4400
　Charlotte (G-2459)

Mestek Inc.. C 252 753-5323
　Farmville (G-4535)

Minka Lighting Inc............................ D 704 785-9200
　Concord (G-3403)

Puffing Monkey................................. G 919 556-7779
　Wake Forest (G-12290)

Royal Blunts Connections Inc............. G 919 961-4910
　Raleigh (G-10448)

Sun Ovens International Inc................ G 630 208-7273
　Wilkesboro (G-12653)

◆ Trane US Inc................................. A 704 655-4000
　Davidson (G-3723)

▲ Trick Tank Inc............................... G 980 406-3200
　Charlotte (G-2943)

TTI Floor Care North Amer Inc............ D 440 996-2000
　Charlotte (G-2950)

3635 Household vacuum cleaners

Clean and Vac.................................. G 919 753-7951
　Fuquay Varina (G-4873)

▲ Vacuum Handling North Amer LLC.... E 828 327-2290
　Hickory (G-6485)

3639 Household appliances, nec

Airborn Industries Inc....................... E 704 483-5000
　Lincolnton (G-7811)

Big Vac.. G 910 947-3654
　Carthage (G-1276)

S
I
C

Bsh Home Appls A Ltd Partnr..............B 252 636-4200
  New Bern *(G-9344)*

Crizaf Inc..............G 919 251-7661
  Durham *(G-3991)*

McKinney Lwncare Grbage Svc LL........G 828 766-9490
  Spruce Pine *(G-11582)*

Mt Gilead Cut & Sew Inc..............F 910 439-9909
  Mount Gilead *(G-9208)*

Prime Water Services Inc..............G 919 504-1020
  Raleigh *(G-10394)*

Psnc Energy..............G 919 367-2735
  Apex *(G-189)*

Smartway of Carolinas LLC..............G 704 900-7877
  Charlotte *(G-2817)*

State Industries Inc..............G 704 597-8910
  Charlotte *(G-2862)*

Trash Masher LLC..............E 786 357-2697
  Winston Salem *(G-13368)*

3641 Electric lamps

Acquionics Inc..............G 980 256-5700
  Charlotte *(G-1619)*

▲ Adams Wood Turning Inc..............G 336 882-0196
  High Point *(G-6509)*

Alk Investments LLC..............G 984 233-5353
  Raleigh *(G-9891)*

▲ Arva LLC..............G 803 336-2230
  Charlotte *(G-1701)*

▲ Fintronx LLC..............F 919 324-3960
  Raleigh *(G-10109)*

Greenlights LLC..............E 919 766-8900
  Cary *(G-1369)*

Hiviz Lighting Inc..............G 703 382-5675
  Hendersonville *(G-6217)*

Invictus Lighting LLC..............G 828 855-9324
  Hickory *(G-6372)*

◆ Robert Abbey Inc..............C 828 322-3480
  Hickory *(G-6430)*

Sol-Rex Miniature Lamp Works..............G 845 292-1510
  Beaufort *(G-734)*

◆ Specialty Manufacturing Inc..............D 704 247-9300
  Charlotte *(G-2841)*

◆ Sunnex Inc..............F 800 445-7869
  Charlotte *(G-2882)*

Traxon Technologies LLC..............G 201 508-1570
  Charlotte *(G-2938)*

Variety Consult LLC..............G 704 978-8108
  Shelby *(G-11389)*

3643 Current-carrying wiring devices

ABB Installation Products Inc..............E 828 322-1855
  Hickory *(G-6260)*

Alp Systems Inc..............F 828 454-5164
  Waynesville *(G-12450)*

Amphenol Procom Inc..............D 888 262-7542
  Conover *(G-3490)*

C-Tron Incorporated..............G 919 494-7811
  Youngsville *(G-13466)*

Capital Lghtning Prtection Inc..............G 919 832-5574
  Raleigh *(G-9968)*

Coleman Cable LLC..............D 828 389-8013
  Hayesville *(G-6139)*

Commscope Technologies LLC..............E 828 324-2200
  Hickory *(G-6308)*

Dehn Inc..............F 772 460-9315
  Mooresville *(G-8654)*

Deringer-Ney Inc..............E 828 649-3232
  Marshall *(G-8079)*

▲ Dna Group Inc..............E 919 881-0889
  Raleigh *(G-10051)*

Eaton Corporation..............B 828 684-2381
  Arden *(G-266)*

Eaton Corporation..............C 919 965-2341
  Selma *(G-11287)*

Erico International Corp..............G 910 944-3355
  Aberdeen *(G-4)*

Hubbell Incorporated..............E 828 687-8505
  Arden *(G-274)*

Infinite Blue Inc..............G 919 744-7704
  Raleigh *(G-10194)*

International Tela-Com Inc..............G 828 651-9801
  Fletcher *(G-4743)*

Kearfott Corporation..............B 828 350-5300
  Black Mountain *(G-868)*

Leviton Manufacturing Co Inc..............E 828 584-1611
  Morganton *(G-8878)*

Leviton Manufacturing Co Inc..............G 336 846-3246
  West Jefferson *(G-12566)*

Lightning Prtction Systems LLC..............D 252 213-9900
  Raleigh *(G-10256)*

M & M Electric Service Inc..............E 704 867-0221
  Gastonia *(G-5081)*

Modern Lightning Protection Co..............F 252 756-3006
  Greenville *(G-6005)*

Pass & Seymour Inc..............A 315 468-6211
  Concord *(G-3415)*

Preformed Line Products Co..............C 704 983-6161
  Albemarle *(G-84)*

Quality Lghtning Prtection Inc..............F 919 832-9399
  Raleigh *(G-10415)*

▲ Quiktron Inc..............G 828 327-6009
  Hickory *(G-6424)*

◆ Solero Technologies Shelby LLC........C 704 482-9582
  Shelby *(G-11380)*

Southern Devices Inc..............G 828 584-1611
  Morganton *(G-8900)*

▲ Stay Online LLC..............E 888 346-4688
  Creedmoor *(G-3656)*

Te Connectivity Corporation..............B 828 338-1000
  Fairview *(G-4513)*

Te Connectivity Corporation..............G 919 557-8425
  Fuquay Varina *(G-4899)*

Te Connectivity Corporation..............F 919 552-3811
  Fuquay Varina *(G-4900)*

Te Connectivity Corporation..............D 336 664-7000
  Winston Salem *(G-13357)*

TEC Graphics Inc..............F 919 567-2077
  Fuquay Varina *(G-4901)*

Tri-City Mechanical Contrs Inc..............D 336 272-9495
  Greensboro *(G-5872)*

Triad Power & Controls Inc..............G 336 375-9780
  Greensboro *(G-5876)*

Vision Technologies Inc..............F 919 387-7878
  Apex *(G-203)*

▲ Wieland Electric Inc..............F 910 259-5050
  Wilmington *(G-12947)*

Wright Electric Inc..............G 704 435-6988
  Cherryville *(G-3071)*

3644 Noncurrent-carrying wiring devices

Austin Company of Greensboro..............C 336 468-2851
  Yadkinville *(G-13436)*

Basalt Specialty Products Inc..............G 336 835-5153
  Elkin *(G-4439)*

Carolina Products Inc..............E 704 364-9029
  Charlotte *(G-1854)*

Chase Corporation..............G 828 396-2121
  Granite Falls *(G-5300)*

Chase Corporation..............F 828 726-6023
  Lenoir *(G-7593)*

DMC LLC..............E 980 352-9806
  Concord *(G-3355)*

Essex Group Inc..............G 704 921-9605
  Charlotte *(G-2127)*

Hydro Extrusion Usa LLC..............D 336 227-8826
  Burlington *(G-1107)*

Maa Umiya Inc..............G 410 818-6811
  Hickory *(G-6390)*

Pcore..............F 919 734-0460
  Goldsboro *(G-5235)*

Penn Compression Moulding Inc..............G 919 934-5144
  Smithfield *(G-11459)*

Preformed Line Products Co..............C 704 983-6161
  Albemarle *(G-84)*

Preformed Line Products Co..............G 336 461-3513
  New London *(G-9421)*

▲ Sigma Engineered Solutions PC........D 919 773-0011
  Garner *(G-4964)*

3645 Residential lighting fixtures

▲ A M Moore and Company Inc..............G 336 294-6994
  Greensboro *(G-5332)*

▲ Adams Wood Turning Inc..............G 336 882-0196
  High Point *(G-6509)*

◆ Atlas Lighting Products Inc..............C 336 222-9258
  Burlington *(G-1049)*

▲ Clarolux Inc..............E 336 378-6800
  Greensboro *(G-5447)*

◆ Coast Lamp Manufacturing Inc..............G 828 648-7876
  Canton *(G-1249)*

Egi Associates Inc..............F 704 561-3337
  Charlotte *(G-2093)*

▲ Furnlite Inc..............E 704 538-3193
  Fallston *(G-4523)*

Kings Chandelier Company..............G 336 623-6188
  Eden *(G-4351)*

▲ Oakhurst Company Inc..............G 336 474-4600
  High Point *(G-6719)*

◆ Progress Solar Solutions LLC........F 919 363-3738
  Raleigh *(G-10401)*

◆ Robert Abbey Inc..............C 828 322-3480
  Hickory *(G-6430)*

Stevens Lighting Inc..............F 910 944-7187
  Carthage *(G-1281)*

◆ Sunnex Inc..............F 800 445-7869
  Charlotte *(G-2882)*

Top Dawg Landscape Inc..............G 336 877-7519
  West Jefferson *(G-12571)*

Ultimate Floor Cleaning..............G 704 912-8978
  Charlotte *(G-2960)*

Visual Comfort..............G 980 666-4120
  Charlotte *(G-2987)*

▲ W F Harris Lighting Inc..............F 704 283-7477
  Monroe *(G-8577)*

◆ Wildwood Lamps & Accents Inc........E 252 446-3266
  Rocky Mount *(G-10875)*

3646 Commercial lighting fixtures

▲ A M Moore and Company Inc..............G 336 294-6994
  Greensboro *(G-5332)*

▲ Arva LLC..............G 803 336-2230
  Charlotte *(G-1701)*

◆ Atlas Lighting Products Inc..............C 336 222-9258
  Burlington *(G-1049)*

Avcon Inc..............E 919 388-0203
  Cary *(G-1302)*

Biologcal Innvtion Optmztion S..............F 321 260-2467
  Wake Forest *(G-12264)*

Conservation Station Inc..............G 919 932-9201
  Chapel Hill *(G-1539)*

Enttec Americas LLC..............F 919 200-6468
  Durham *(G-4026)*

Idaho Wood Inc..............F 208 263-9521
  Oxford *(G-9617)*

Invictus Lighting LLC..............G 828 855-9324
  Hickory *(G-6372)*

Kings Chandelier Company..............G.....336 623-6188
 Eden *(G-4351)*

Lumenfocus LLC...............................F.....252 430-6970
 Henderson *(G-6165)*

Optimum Lighting LLC.......................E.....508 646-3324
 Henderson *(G-6168)*

◆ Progress Solar Solutions LLC.........F.....919 363-3738
 Raleigh *(G-10401)*

▲ Shat-R-Shield Lighting Inc.............D.....800 223-0853
 Salisbury *(G-11115)*

Shield & Steel Enterprises LLC.........G.....704 607-0869
 Salisbury *(G-11116)*

▲ Specialty Lighting LLC..................F.....704 538-6522
 Fallston *(G-4524)*

Stevens Lighting Inc.........................F.....910 944-7187
 Carthage *(G-1281)*

▲ W F Harris Lighting Inc.................F.....704 283-7477
 Monroe *(G-8577)*

3647 Vehicular lighting equipment

B/E Aerospace Inc............................F.....336 692-8940
 Winston Salem *(G-13098)*

▲ B/E Aerospace Inc........................E.....704 423-7000
 Charlotte *(G-1731)*

Go Ev and Go Green Corp..................G.....704 327-9040
 Charlotte *(G-2220)*

Three GS Enterprises Inc...................F.....828 696-2060
 Flat Rock *(G-4714)*

3648 Lighting equipment, nec

▲ Blue Sun Energy Inc.....................G.....336 218-6707
 Greensboro *(G-5393)*

Bright Light Technologies LLC...........G.....910 212-6869
 Lillington *(G-7790)*

▲ Busiapp Corporation.....................G.....877 558-2518
 Morrisville *(G-8947)*

Curlee Machinery Company................G.....919 467-9311
 Cary *(G-1341)*

Cyberlux Corporation........................F.....984 363-6894
 Research Triangle Pa *(G-10707)*

Dandy Light Traps Inc.......................G.....980 223-2744
 Statesville *(G-11684)*

Energizer Holdings Inc......................C.....336 672-3526
 Asheboro *(G-352)*

Enttec Americas LLC.........................F.....919 200-6468
 Durham *(G-4026)*

Epl & Solar Corp..............................G.....201 577-8966
 Wake Forest *(G-12276)*

Eye Dialogue...................................G.....704 567-7789
 Charlotte *(G-2137)*

▲ Furnlite Inc.................................E.....704 538-3193
 Fallston *(G-4523)*

Hayward Holdings Inc........................C.....704 837-8002
 Charlotte *(G-2263)*

Light Source Usa Inc.........................E.....704 504-8399
 Charlotte *(G-2420)*

Lightjunction...................................G.....919 607-9717
 Morrisville *(G-9011)*

▲ M-B Industries Inc.......................C.....828 862-4201
 Rosman *(G-10913)*

Nexxus Lighting Inc..........................F.....704 405-0416
 Charlotte *(G-2563)*

Parhelion Incorporated......................F.....866 409-1839
 Apex *(G-184)*

PDM Lighting LLC.............................G.....919 771-3230
 Raleigh *(G-10364)*

Pelican Ventures LLC........................G.....919 518-8203
 Raleigh *(G-10365)*

Pentair Water Pool and Spa Inc..........D.....919 463-4640
 Cary *(G-1417)*

◆ Pentair Water Pool and Spa Inc......A.....919 566-8000
 Sanford *(G-11217)*

Powertac Usa Inc.............................G.....919 239-4470
 Greensboro *(G-5753)*

◆ Progress Solar Solutions LLC.........F.....919 363-3738
 Raleigh *(G-10401)*

S C I A Inc......................................G.....919 387-7000
 Cary *(G-1444)*

◆ Specialty Manufacturing Inc...........D.....704 247-9300
 Charlotte *(G-2841)*

Srb Technologies Inc........................E.....336 659-2610
 Winston Salem *(G-13341)*

◆ Sunnex Inc..................................F.....800 445-7869
 Charlotte *(G-2882)*

▲ W F Harris Lighting Inc.................F.....704 283-7477
 Monroe *(G-8577)*

3651 Household audio and video equipment

Advanced Tech Systems Inc...............F.....336 299-6695
 Greensboro *(G-5343)*

Anthony Demaria Labs Inc.................F.....845 255-4695
 Cary *(G-1291)*

Cablenc LLC....................................G.....919 307-9065
 Zebulon *(G-13506)*

Carr Amplifiers Inc...........................F.....919 545-0747
 Pittsboro *(G-9778)*

▲ Cary Audio Design LLC.................E.....919 355-0010
 Raleigh *(G-9983)*

Cco Holdings LLC.............................C.....828 414-4238
 Blowing Rock *(G-881)*

Cco Holdings LLC.............................C.....828 355-4149
 Boone *(G-906)*

Cco Holdings LLC.............................C.....910 292-4083
 Dunn *(G-3850)*

Cco Holdings LLC.............................B.....828 270-7016
 Hickory *(G-6293)*

Cco Holdings LLC.............................C.....919 502-4007
 Kenly *(G-7228)*

Cco Holdings LLC.............................C.....828 394-0635
 Lenoir *(G-7592)*

Cco Holdings LLC.............................C.....704 308-3361
 Lincolnton *(G-7820)*

Cco Holdings LLC.............................C.....828 528-4004
 Newland *(G-9427)*

Cco Holdings LLC.............................G.....919 200-6260
 Siler City *(G-11402)*

Cco Holdings LLC.............................C.....828 368-4161
 Valdese *(G-12192)*

Cymbal LLC.....................................G.....877 365-9622
 Cary *(G-1342)*

Danley Sound Labs Inc......................G.....877 419-5805
 Candler *(G-1223)*

East Coast Digital Inc........................F.....919 304-1142
 Mebane *(G-8239)*

Eastern Sun Communications Inc.........G.....704 408-7668
 Charlotte *(G-2083)*

▼ Evolution Technologies Inc.............G.....919 544-3777
 Raleigh *(G-10097)*

Eye Trax Inc....................................G.....800 594-4157
 Charlotte *(G-2138)*

▲ Hartley Loudspeakers Inc..............G.....910 392-1200
 Wilmington *(G-12803)*

Huso Inc...G.....845 553-0100
 Black Mountain *(G-866)*

Integrated Info Systems Inc................F.....919 488-5000
 Youngsville *(G-13476)*

JPS Communications Inc....................G.....919 534-1168
 Raleigh *(G-10222)*

Linor Technology Inc.........................F.....336 485-6199
 Winston Salem *(G-13235)*

Moon Audio......................................G.....919 649-5018
 Cary *(G-1402)*

▲ Multi Technical Services Inc...........G.....919 553-2995
 Clayton *(G-3161)*

Ocean 10 Security LLC......................F.....828 484-1481
 Asheville *(G-558)*

Palmer Senn....................................G.....704 451-3971
 Charlotte *(G-2606)*

PC Satellite Solutions.......................G.....252 217-7237
 Roper *(G-10899)*

▲ Quality Musical Systems Inc...........E.....828 667-5719
 Candler *(G-1231)*

Secure Canopy LLC..........................G.....980 322-0590
 Albemarle *(G-88)*

SES Integration...............................G
 Concord *(G-3439)*

Unique Home Theater Inc..................G.....704 787-3239
 Concord *(G-3461)*

▲ Wheatstone Corporation................D.....252 638-7000
 New Bern *(G-9405)*

Worldwide Entrmt Mltimedia LLC.........G.....704 208-6113
 Charlotte *(G-3027)*

3652 Prerecorded records and tapes

American Multimedia Inc....................D.....336 229-7101
 Burlington *(G-1045)*

▲ Cda Inc......................................C
 Charlotte *(G-1879)*

Digital Recorders Inc........................C.....919 361-2155
 Morrisville *(G-8964)*

Merge Media Ltd..............................F.....919 688-9969
 Chapel Hill *(G-1556)*

Operable Inc....................................G.....757 617-0935
 Wake Forest *(G-12288)*

Puny Human LLC..............................G.....919 420-4538
 Raleigh *(G-10409)*

Reel-Scout Inc.................................F.....704 348-1484
 Charlotte *(G-2702)*

SMC Corporation of America...............F.....704 947-7556
 Huntersville *(G-7055)*

Sony Music Holdings Inc....................G.....336 886-1807
 High Point *(G-6785)*

Turnsmith LLC..................................G.....919 667-9804
 Chapel Hill *(G-1582)*

Ultimix Records................................G.....336 288-7566
 Greensboro *(G-5886)*

Xdri Inc..G.....919 361-2155
 Durham *(G-4315)*

3661 Telephone and telegraph apparatus

Abacon Telecommunications LLC........E.....336 855-1179
 Greensboro *(G-5335)*

Amphenol Procom Inc........................D.....888 262-7542
 Conover *(G-3490)*

Andrea L Grizzle..............................G.....252 202-3278
 Moyock *(G-9275)*

◆ Arris Solutions LLC.......................A.....678 473-2000
 Claremont *(G-3088)*

Atcom Inc..F.....704 357-7900
 Charlotte *(G-1708)*

Avaya LLC.......................................B.....919 425-8268
 Research Triangle Pa *(G-10705)*

Code LLC..E.....828 328-6004
 Hickory *(G-6304)*

◆ Conversant Products Inc.................G.....919 465-3456
 Cary *(G-1334)*

Corning Incorporated........................F.....252 316-4500
 Tarboro *(G-11924)*

Corning Optcal Cmmncations LLC........A.....828 901-5000
 Charlotte *(G-1987)*

◆ Corning Optcal Cmmncations LLC....A.....828 901-5000
 Charlotte *(G-1986)*

Edge Broadband Solutions LLC............E.....828 785-1420
 Waynesville *(G-12457)*

▲ Emrise Corporation.......................C.....408 200-3040
 Durham *(G-4023)*

◆ Extreme Networks Inc............B 408 579-2800
Morrisville *(G-8973)*

Fiberlink..........................G.... 901 826-8126
Troutman *(G-12137)*

Fiberlink Inc.....................G.... 828 274-5629
Asheville *(G-495)*

▲ Hatteras Networks Inc.........F 919 991-5440
Morrisville *(G-8985)*

JPS Communications Inc........D 919 534-1168
Raleigh *(G-10222)*

Lba Group Inc....................E 252 329-9243
Greenville *(G-5999)*

◆ Lba Technology Inc............E 252 757-0279
Greenville *(G-6000)*

▲ Newton Instrument Company....C 919 575-6426
Butner *(G-1203)*

Nvent Thermal LLC...............B 919 552-3811
Fuquay Varina *(G-4893)*

▲ Personal Communication Sy....D 336 722-4917
Winston Salem *(G-13285)*

Photon Energy Corp..............G 888 336-8128
Asheville *(G-572)*

R E Mason Enterprises Inc.......G 910 483-5016
Fayetteville *(G-4661)*

Ruckus Wireless LLC.............A 503 495-9240
Claremont *(G-3121)*

Siemens Airport.................G 704 359-5551
Charlotte *(G-2801)*

Siemens Corporation.............F 919 465-1287
Cary *(G-1452)*

◆ Southern Elc & Automtn Corp....F 919 718-0122
Sanford *(G-11235)*

▲ Spectrasite Communications LLC....E 919 468-0112
Cary *(G-1465)*

Tabur Services LLC..............G 704 483-1650
Denver *(G-3810)*

▲ Tekelec Inc....................C
Morrisville *(G-9065)*

Tekelec Global Inc..............A 919 460-5500
Morrisville *(G-9066)*

Trimm International Inc.........E 847 362-3700
Youngsville *(G-13496)*

Usat LLC........................E 919 942-4214
Chapel Hill *(G-1587)*

Uteck..........................F 910 483-5016
Fayetteville *(G-4694)*

3663 Radio and t.v. communications equipment

Akoustis Technologies Inc.......G 704 997-5735
Huntersville *(G-6963)*

▲ Amphenol Antenna Solutions Inc.....E 828 324-6971
Conover *(G-3489)*

◆ Arris Solutions LLC............A 678 473-2000
Claremont *(G-3088)*

Ascom (us) Inc..................C 877 712-7266
Morrisville *(G-8933)*

Audio Advice LLC................D 919 881-2005
Raleigh *(G-9923)*

▲ Avl Technologies Inc...........D 828 250-9950
Asheville *(G-449)*

Bae Systems Info Elctrnic Syst.....E 919 323-5800
Durham *(G-3911)*

Bahakel Communications Ltd LLC.....B 704 372-4434
Charlotte *(G-1740)*

Cable Devices Incorporated......F 704 588-0859
Charlotte *(G-1830)*

Cable Devices Incorporated......F 704 588-0859
Pineville *(G-9718)*

Carolina Design & Mfg Inc.......G 919 554-1823
Louisburg *(G-7911)*

CBS Radio Holdings Inc..........E 704 319-9369
Charlotte *(G-1870)*

Cco Holdings LLC................C 828 414-4238
Blowing Rock *(G-881)*

Cco Holdings LLC................C 828 355-4149
Boone *(G-906)*

Cco Holdings LLC................C 910 292-4083
Dunn *(G-3850)*

Cco Holdings LLC................B 828 270-7016
Hickory *(G-6293)*

Cco Holdings LLC................C 919 502-4007
Kenly *(G-7228)*

Cco Holdings LLC................C 828 394-0635
Lenoir *(G-7592)*

Cco Holdings LLC................C 704 308-3361
Lincolnton *(G-7820)*

Cco Holdings LLC................C 828 528-4004
Newland *(G-9427)*

Cco Holdings LLC................C 919 200-6260
Siler City *(G-11402)*

Cco Holdings LLC................C 828 368-4161
Valdese *(G-12192)*

Commscope Inc North Carolina....F 828 459-5001
Claremont *(G-3095)*

Commscope Inc North Carolina....F 828 324-2200
Hickory *(G-6306)*

Commscope Inc North Carolina....F 828 466-8600
Newton *(G-9457)*

◆ Commscope Inc North Carolina....E 828 324-2200
Claremont *(G-3096)*

Commscope LLC...................C 828 324-2200
Claremont *(G-3097)*

Commscope Cnnctvty Sltons LLC....F 828 324-2200
Hickory *(G-6307)*

Commscope Connectivity LLC......E 828 324-2200
Claremont *(G-3098)*

Commscope Dsl Systems LLC.......F 828 324-2200
Claremont *(G-3099)*

Commscope Holding Company Inc....F 919 677-2422
Cary *(G-1331)*

Commscope Holding Company Inc....A 828 459-5000
Claremont *(G-3100)*

Commscope Intl Holdings LLC......F 828 324-2200
Claremont *(G-3101)*

Commscope Solutions Intl Inc....E 828 324-2200
Claremont *(G-3102)*

Commscope Technologies Fin LLC....G 828 323-4970
Claremont *(G-3103)*

Commscope Technologies LLC......G 919 329-8700
Garner *(G-4923)*

Commscope Technologies LLC......E 336 665-6000
Greensboro *(G-5461)*

Commscope Technologies LLC......G 919 934-9711
Smithfield *(G-11440)*

◆ Commscope Technologies LLC....A 828 324-2200
Claremont *(G-3104)*

CPI Satcom & Antenna Tech Inc....C 704 462-7330
Conover *(G-3508)*

◆ CPI Satcom & Antenna Tech Inc....E 704 462-7330
Conover *(G-3509)*

▲ Crest Electronics Inc..........G 336 855-6422
Greensboro *(G-5471)*

Dexterity LLC...................F 919 524-7732
Greenville *(G-5964)*

Edge Broadband Solutions LLC....E 828 785-1420
Waynesville *(G-12457)*

General Dynmics Mssion Systems....C 336 323-9752
Greensboro *(G-5553)*

Gigabeam Corporation............G 919 206-4426
Durham *(G-4046)*

Golfstar Technology LLC.........G 910 420-3122
Pinehurst *(G-9693)*

Gpx Intelligence Inc............E 888 260-0706
Greensboro *(G-5570)*

Itron Inc.......................D 919 876-2600
Raleigh *(G-10211)*

JPS Communications Inc..........D 919 534-1168
Raleigh *(G-10222)*

JPS Intrprbility Solutions Inc....E 919 332-5009
Raleigh *(G-10223)*

Lba Group Inc...................E 252 329-9243
Greenville *(G-5999)*

◆ Lba Technology Inc............E 252 757-0279
Greenville *(G-6000)*

Lcf Enterprise..................G 208 415-4300
Hickory *(G-6385)*

Lea Aid Acquisition Company.....G 919 872-6210
Spring Hope *(G-11557)*

▼ Leonardo US Cyber SEC Sltons L....D 336 379-7135
Greensboro *(G-5661)*

Lets Talk Some Shit.............G 704 264-6212
Paw Creek *(G-9649)*

Little River Yachts LLC.........G 828 323-4955
Hickory *(G-6387)*

Lunar International Tech LLC.....F 800 975-7153
Charlotte *(G-2441)*

Macom Technology Solutions Inc....D 919 407-4768
Durham *(G-4115)*

McShan Inc......................G 980 355-9790
Charlotte *(G-2481)*

Motorola Mobility LLC...........E 919 294-1289
Morrisville *(G-9021)*

▲ Multi Technical Services Inc....G 919 553-2995
Clayton *(G-3161)*

Ni4l Antennas and Elec LLC......G 828 738-6445
Moravian Falls *(G-8810)*

Qualcomm Incorporated...........F 336 323-3300
Clemmons *(G-3200)*

Qualia Networks Inc.............G 805 637-2083
Raleigh *(G-10413)*

◆ Raven Antenna Systems Inc.....C 919 934-9711
Smithfield *(G-11461)*

Rf Das Systems Inc..............G 980 279-2388
Charlotte *(G-2722)*

Richmond County Gmrs Inc........G 910 461-0260
Hamlet *(G-6062)*

Ruckus Wireless LLC.............B 919 677-0571
Cary *(G-1442)*

Ruckus Wireless LLC.............A 503 495-9240
Claremont *(G-3121)*

Sbg Digital Inc.................G 828 476-0030
Waynesville *(G-12473)*

Serra Wireless Inc..............G 980 318-0873
Charlotte *(G-2789)*

Shadowtrack 247 LLC.............F 828 398-0980
Fletcher *(G-4767)*

Sierra Nevada Corporation.......F 910 307-0362
Fayetteville *(G-4668)*

Swir Vision Systems Inc.........E 919 248-0032
Durham *(G-4256)*

T-Metrics Inc...................E 704 523-9583
Charlotte *(G-2896)*

Tabur Services..................G 704 483-1650
Denver *(G-3809)*

Tarheel Monitoring LLC..........G 910 763-1490
Wilmington *(G-12936)*

Teletec Corporation.............F 919 954-7300
Raleigh *(G-10541)*

Thompson Sunny Acres Inc........G 910 206-1801
Rockingham *(G-10791)*

Triton Marine Services Inc......G 252 728-9958
Beaufort *(G-736)*

Universal Mania Inc.............G 866 903-0852
Fayetteville *(G-4688)*

▲ Wheatstone Corporation.................. D 252 638-7000
　New Bern (G-9405)

Wirenet Inc.................................... F 513 774-7759
　Huntersville (G-7062)

3669 Communications equipment, nec

Acterna LLC...................................... F 919 388-5100
　Morrisville (G-8918)

AFA Billing Services......................... G 910 868-8324
　Fayetteville (G-4547)

Amplified Elctronic Design Inc.......... F 336 223-4811
　Greensboro (G-5362)

▲ Argus Fire CONtrol-Pf&s Inc.......... E 704 372-1228
　Charlotte (G-1696)

▲ C & S Antennas Inc..................... F 828 324-2454
　Conover (G-3497)

Carolina Pwr Signalization LLC......... E 910 323-5589
　Fayetteville (G-4570)

▲ Elk Products Inc.......................... E 828 397-4200
　Connelly Springs (G-3476)

Envision Inc...................................... G 919 832-8962
　Raleigh (G-10089)

Flat Water Corp................................ G 704 584-7764
　Charlotte (G-2161)

Fulcher Elc Fayetteville Inc............... E 910 483-7772
　Fayetteville (G-4604)

General Dynmics Mssion Systems........ C 336 698-8000
　Mc Leansville (G-8223)

Honeywell SEC Americas LLC............ E 919 563-5911
　Mebane (G-8246)

Johnson Controls.............................. C 704 501-0500
　Charlotte (G-2374)

▼ Kidde Technologies Inc................. B 252 237-7004
　Wilson (G-13000)

▲ New Innovative Products Inc......... G 919 631-6759
　Pine Level (G-9683)

Pipeline Enterprises LLC................... D 804 593-6999
　Reidsville (G-10697)

Pomdevices LLC............................... F 919 200-6538
　Durham (G-4187)

Preferred Communication Inc............ E 919 575-4600
　Butner (G-1205)

R & J Road Service Inc..................... G 252 239-1404
　Lucama (G-7938)

Resideo LLC..................................... G 704 525-8899
　Charlotte (G-2715)

Resideo LLC..................................... G 336 668-3644
　Greensboro (G-5784)

Resideo LLC..................................... G 919 872-5556
　Raleigh (G-10441)

Romeo Six LLC................................. F 919 589-7150
　Holly Springs (G-6912)

▲ Safe Fire Detection Inc................. F 704 821-7920
　Monroe (G-8554)

Safeguard Medical Alarms Inc........... F 312 506-2900
　Huntersville (G-7052)

Seal Innovation Inc........................... G 919 302-7870
　Raleigh (G-10464)

Secured Traffic Control LLC.............. G 910 233-8148
　Wilmington (G-12915)

Simplyhome LLC............................... F 828 684-8441
　Arden (G-306)

Squarehead Technology LLC.............. G 571 299-4849
　Hickory (G-6456)

◆ Tektone Sound & Signal Mfg Inc.....D 828 524-9967
　Franklin (G-4841)

Telephonics Corporation................... E 631 755-7446
　Elizabeth City (G-4415)

◆ Walter Kidde Portable Eqp Inc..........B 919 563-5911
　Mebane (G-8263)

3671 Electron tubes

▲ Advanced Digital Cable Inc............ E 828 389-1652
　Hayesville (G-6137)

Communications & Pwr Inds LLC........ E 650 846-2900
　Conover (G-3505)

Ecoatm LLC...................................... E 858 324-4111
　Boone (G-913)

Electropin Technologies LLC............. G 919 288-1203
　Goldsboro (G-5212)

Tactical Support Equipment Inc......... F 910 425-3360
　Fayetteville (G-4676)

Xintek Inc.. G 919 449-5799
　Chapel Hill (G-1597)

3672 Printed circuit boards

615 Alton Place LLC.......................... G 336 431-4487
　High Point (G-6506)

American Circuits Inc........................ E 704 376-2800
　Charlotte (G-1663)

▲ Assembly Technologies Inc............ F 704 596-3903
　Charlotte (G-1706)

Asteelflash USA Corp....................... C 919 882-5400
　Morrisville (G-8934)

C-Tron Incorporated......................... G 919 494-7811
　Youngsville (G-13466)

Circuit Board Assemblers Inc............ C 919 556-7881
　Youngsville (G-13471)

▲ Cml Micro Circuit USA................. E 336 744-5050
　Winston Salem (G-13126)

Flextronics Corporation.................... G 704 598-3300
　Charlotte (G-2164)

Flextronics Intl USA Inc.................... B 704 509-8700
　Charlotte (G-2165)

Flextronics Intl USA Inc.................... C 919 998-4000
　Morrisville (G-8975)

Galaxy Electronics Inc...................... F 704 343-9881
　Charlotte (G-2184)

▲ Grt Electronics LLC...................... F 919 821-1996
　Raleigh (G-10150)

Hitech Circuits Inc........................... G 336 838-3420
　Indian Trail (G-7083)

Jabil Inc.. E 828 684-3141
　Arden (G-278)

Jabil Inc.. G 828 209-4202
　Mills River (G-8316)

▲ M & M Technology Inc.................. E 704 882-9432
　Indian Trail (G-7090)

▲ Mac Panel Company LLC............... E 336 861-3100
　High Point (G-6694)

Mathis Elec Sls & Svc Inc................. F 828 274-5925
　Asheville (G-544)

Plexus Corp..................................... D 919 807-8000
　Raleigh (G-10373)

Protronics Inc.................................. F 919 217-0007
　Knightdale (G-7457)

SBS Diversified Tech Inc................... F 336 884-5564
　Jamestown (G-7179)

▲ Wolfspeed Inc.............................. C 919 407-5300
　Durham (G-4308)

3674 Semiconductors and related devices

510nano Inc..................................... F 919 521-5982
　Durham (G-3873)

Advanced Micro Devices Inc.............. G 919 840-8080
　Morrisville (G-8921)

Agile Microwave Technology Inc......... G 984 228-8001
　Cary (G-1287)

Air Control Inc................................. E 252 492-2300
　Henderson (G-6147)

Altera Corporation........................... G 919 852-1004
　Raleigh (G-9893)

Amalfi Semiconductor Inc................. G 336 664-1233
　Greensboro (G-5353)

Amkor Technology Inc...................... G 919 248-1800
　Durham (G-3892)

Amkor Technology Inc...................... G 336 605-8009
　Greensboro (G-5361)

AMS USA Inc.................................... G 919 755-2889
　Raleigh (G-9900)

Analog Devices Inc........................... F 336 202-6503
　Durham (G-3895)

Analog Devices Inc........................... E 336 668-9511
　Greensboro (G-5363)

Analog Devices Inc........................... F 919 831-2790
　Raleigh (G-9902)

▲ Arva LLC..................................... G 803 336-2230
　Charlotte (G-1701)

ATI Industrial Automation Inc............ D 919 772-0115
　Apex (G-141)

Broadcom Corporation..................... D 919 865-2954
　Durham (G-3944)

▲ Brumley/South Inc....................... G 704 664-9251
　Mooresville (G-8622)

◆ Centrotherm Usa Inc.................... G 360 626-4445
　Durham (G-3968)

▲ Cml Micro Circuit USA................. E 336 744-5050
　Winston Salem (G-13126)

Convergent Integration Inc............... G 704 516-5922
　Charlotte (G-1979)

Corning Incorporated....................... F 252 316-4500
　Tarboro (G-11924)

Cortina Systems............................... G 919 226-1800
　Morrisville (G-8960)

Creeled Inc...................................... B 919 313-5330
　Durham (G-3989)

Disco Hi-TEC America Inc................. G 919 468-6003
　Morrisville (G-8965)

Ekc Advanced Elec USA 4 LLC.......... G 302 774-1000
　Wilmington (G-12770)

Flexgen Power Systems Inc.............. G 855 327-5674
　Durham (G-4033)

Flexgen Power Systems Inc.............. F 855 327-5674
　Durham (G-4034)

Gainspan Corporation...................... D 408 627-6500
　Morrisville (G-8979)

Galaxy Electronics Inc...................... F 704 343-9881
　Charlotte (G-2184)

Guerrilla Rf Inc................................ D 336 510-7840
　Greensboro (G-5583)

Harris Solar Inc............................... G 704 490-8374
　Concord (G-3371)

▲ Hexatech Inc................................ F 919 481-4412
　Morrisville (G-8988)

Hexatech Inc.................................... G 919 633-0583
　Raleigh (G-10163)

Hiviz Led Lighting LLC..................... F 703 662-3458
　Hendersonville (G-6216)

Hoffman Materials LLC..................... F 717 243-2011
　Granite Falls (G-5306)

◆ Industrial Hard Carbon LLC.............E 704 489-1488
　Denver (G-3790)

▲ Iqe Inc.. D 610 861-6930
　Greensboro (G-5622)

Iqe North Carolina LLC.................... F 336 609-6270
　Greensboro (G-5623)

Kidde Technologies Inc..................... D 252 237-7004
　Wilson (G-13001)

Kidsvidz Productions........................ G 704 663-4487
　Mooresville (G-8705)

▼ Kyma Technologies Inc.................. F 919 789-8880
　Raleigh (G-10242)

Larry Shackelford............................ G 919 467-8817
　Cary (G-1386)

Leviton Manufacturing Co Inc............ G 336 846-3246
　West Jefferson (G-12566)

Lullicoin LLC...................................... G 336 955-1159
　Charlotte *(G-2440)*

Lumenlux LLC...................................... G 704 222-7787
　Mint Hill *(G-8338)*

Lumeova Inc.. G 908 229-4651
　Raleigh *(G-10261)*

Macom Technology Solutions Inc........ D 919 807-9100
　Morrisville *(G-9016)*

Marvell Semiconductor Inc.................. D 408 222-2500
　Morrisville *(G-9017)*

Maxtronic Technologies LLC................ G 704 756-5354
　Charlotte *(G-2474)*

Memscap Inc.. E 919 248-4102
　Durham *(G-4126)*

Micro-OHM Corporation....................... G 800 845-5167
　Raleigh *(G-10301)*

Microchip Technology Inc.................... F 919 844-7510
　Raleigh *(G-10302)*

Micross Advnced Intrcnnect TEC........ E 919 248-1872
　Research Triangle Pa *(G-10714)*

Multisite Led LLC................................. G 650 823-7247
　Charlotte *(G-2529)*

Nhanced Semiconductors Inc.............. E 630 561-6813
　Morrisville *(G-9025)*

Nitronex LLC.. E 919 807-9100
　Morrisville *(G-9026)*

Nokia of America Corporation............. G 919 850-6000
　Raleigh *(G-10333)*

North Crlina Rnwable Prpts LLC......... G 407 536-5346
　Raleigh *(G-10338)*

Northrop Grmman Gdnce Elec Inc...... E 704 588-2340
　Charlotte *(G-2575)*

Northstar Computer Tech Inc.............. G 980 272-1969
　Monroe *(G-8537)*

Nvidia Corporation............................... F 408 486-2000
　Durham *(G-4153)*

Nxp Usa Inc... G 919 468-3251
　Cary *(G-1410)*

▲ Phononic Inc.................................... D 919 908-6300
　Durham *(G-4178)*

Pink Hill Wellness Edu Center............. G 252 568-2425
　Pink Hill *(G-9766)*

Poweramerica Institute........................ F 919 515-6013
　Raleigh *(G-10379)*

Powersecure Solar LLC....................... C 919 213-0798
　Durham *(G-4191)*

Qorvo Inc... C 336 664-1233
　Greensboro *(G-5772)*

Qorvo Inc... A 336 664-1233
　Greensboro *(G-5773)*

Qorvo International Holdg Inc.............. F 336 664-1233
　Greensboro *(G-5774)*

Qorvo International Svcs Inc............... G 336 664-1233
　Greensboro *(G-5775)*

Qorvo Us Inc.. G 336 662-1150
　Greensboro *(G-5776)*

Qorvo Us Inc.. E 336 931-8298
　Greensboro *(G-5777)*

Qorvo Us Inc.. G 503 615-9000
　Jamestown *(G-7176)*

Qualcomm Datacenter Tech Inc.......... D 858 567-1121
　Raleigh *(G-10412)*

Qualia Networks Inc............................ G 805 637-2083
　Raleigh *(G-10413)*

Rambus Inc.. F 919 960-6600
　Chapel Hill *(G-1566)*

▲ Reuel Inc... E 919 734-0460
　Goldsboro *(G-5240)*

▲ Rf Micro Devices Inc....................... A 336 664-1233
　Greensboro *(G-5785)*

Rfhic US Corporation........................... G 919 677-8780
　Morrisville *(G-9043)*

Rfmd LLC.. C 336 664-1233
　Greensboro *(G-5786)*

Rfmd Infrstrcture PDT Group In.......... G 704 996-2997
　Raleigh *(G-10444)*

Rhino Networks LLC............................. E 855 462-9434
　Asheville *(G-590)*

Rt Cardiac Systems Inc....................... G 954 908-1074
　Raleigh *(G-10451)*

Samsung Semiconductor Inc............... G 919 380-8483
　Cary *(G-1445)*

Santronics Inc..................................... A 919 775-1223
　Sanford *(G-11231)*

Sarda Technologies Inc....................... G 919 757-6825
　Durham *(G-4221)*

Silanna Semicdtr N Amer Inc.............. D 984 444-6500
　Raleigh *(G-10476)*

◆ Skan US Inc..................................... F 919 354-6380
　Raleigh *(G-10485)*

Skyworks Solutions Inc....................... E 336 291-4200
　Greensboro *(G-5816)*

Telit Wireless Solutions Inc................ D 919 439-7977
　Durham *(G-4264)*

Thunderbird Technologies Inc............. G 919 481-3239
　Raleigh *(G-10548)*

Triad Semiconductor Inc..................... D 336 774-2150
　Winston Salem *(G-13370)*

Viavi Solutions Inc.............................. G 919 388-5100
　Morrisville *(G-9086)*

Vrg Components Inc............................. G 980 244-3862
　Matthews *(G-8156)*

Wolfspeed Inc...................................... G 919 407-5300
　Durham *(G-4307)*

▲ Wolfspeed Inc.................................. C 919 407-5300
　Durham *(G-4308)*

Wolfspeed Employee Services Co........ G 919 313-5300
　Durham *(G-4309)*

X-Celeprint Inc.................................... F 919 248-0020
　Durham *(G-4314)*

Xilinx Inc... F 919 846-3922
　Raleigh *(G-10619)*

▲ Xylem Lnc.. E 704 409-9700
　Charlotte *(G-3035)*

Ziptronix Inc.. F 919 459-2400
　Morrisville *(G-9094)*

3675 Electronic capacitors

ABB Inc.. D 919 856-2360
　Raleigh *(G-9864)*

Hitachi Energy USA Inc........................ F 919 324-5403
　Raleigh *(G-10169)*

Hitachi Energy USA Inc........................ C 919 856-2360
　Raleigh *(G-10170)*

Kemet Electronics Corporation............ E 864 963-6300
　Shelby *(G-11351)*

M2 Optics Inc...................................... G 919 342-5619
　Raleigh *(G-10264)*

Nwl Inc... E 252 747-5943
　Snow Hill *(G-11481)*

▲ Reuel Inc... E 919 734-0460
　Goldsboro *(G-5240)*

United Chemi-Con Inc.......................... B 336 384-6903
　Lansing *(G-7479)*

3676 Electronic resistors

Invisible Fencing of Mtn Reg.............. G 828 667-8847
　Candler *(G-1227)*

K & L Resources.................................. G 910 494-3736
　Fayetteville *(G-4625)*

3677 Electronic coils and transformers

◆ Amiad Filtration Systems Ltd........... E 805 377-0288
　Mooresville *(G-8598)*

Branford Filtration LLC........................ D 704 394-2111
　Mooresville *(G-8620)*

Carolina Metals Inc............................. F 828 667-0876
　Asheville *(G-470)*

Coil Innovation Usa Inc....................... G 919 659-0300
　Cary *(G-1330)*

Electronic Products Design Inc............ G 919 365-9199
　Wendell *(G-12535)*

Fueltec Systems LLC........................... G 828 212-1141
　Granite Falls *(G-5303)*

Kwik Elc Mtr Sls & Svc Inc.................. G 252 335-2524
　Elizabeth City *(G-4395)*

▼ Liquid Process Systems Inc............. G 704 821-1115
　Indian Trail *(G-7088)*

◆ Mann+hmmel Fltrtion Tech US LL.....C 704 869-3300
　Gastonia *(G-5085)*

▲ Misonix Opco Inc............................. F 631 694-9555
　Durham *(G-4137)*

◆ Nederman Mikropul Canada Inc........G 704 998-2606
　Charlotte *(G-2554)*

Parkway Products LLC.......................... C 828 684-1362
　Arden *(G-294)*

Peak Demand Inc................................. F 252 360-2777
　Wilson *(G-13013)*

Prolec-GE Waukesha Inc...................... B 919 734-8900
　Goldsboro *(G-5238)*

▲ Purolator Facet Inc.......................... E 336 668-4444
　Greensboro *(G-5771)*

Smart Wires Inc................................... D 919 294-3999
　Durham *(G-4239)*

3678 Electronic connectors

Amphenol Procom Inc.......................... D 888 262-7542
　Conover *(G-3490)*

▲ Appalachian Technology LLC........... E 828 210-8888
　Asheville *(G-427)*

Coleman Cable LLC.............................. D 828 389-8013
　Hayesville *(G-6139)*

Crompton Instruments......................... G 919 557-8698
　Fuquay Varina *(G-4876)*

▲ Huber + Suhner Inc......................... E 704 790-7300
　Charlotte *(G-2295)*

▲ Southland Electrical Sup LLC.......... C 336 227-1486
　Burlington *(G-1160)*

Te Connectivity................................... E 336 727-5295
　Winston Salem *(G-13356)*

Te Connectivity Corporation................ B 828 338-1000
　Fairview *(G-4513)*

Te Connectivity Corporation................ E 919 552-3811
　Fuquay Varina *(G-4898)*

Te Connectivity Corporation................ G 919 557-8425
　Fuquay Varina *(G-4899)*

Te Connectivity Corporation................ F 919 552-3811
　Fuquay Varina *(G-4900)*

Te Connectivity Corporation................ F 336 428-7200
　Greensboro *(G-5855)*

Te Connectivity Corporation................ C 336 664-7000
　Greensboro *(G-5856)*

Te Connectivity Corporation................ C 336 665-4400
　Greensboro *(G-5857)*

Te Connectivity Corporation................ D 336 664-7000
　Winston Salem *(G-13357)*

Te Connectivity Corporation................ C 336 727-5122
　Winston Salem *(G-13358)*

US Conec Ltd....................................... D 828 323-8883
　Hickory *(G-6482)*

3679 Electronic components, nec

Acterna LLC... F 919 388-5100
　Morrisville *(G-8918)*

Advanced Substrate............................. F 336 285-5955
　Greensboro *(G-5342)*

▲ Anuva Services Inc.............................. F 919 468-6441
     Morrisville *(G-8928)*

Applied Drives Inc.............................. G 704 573-2324
     Charlotte *(G-1686)*

▲ Ashbran LLC.................................... G 919 215-3567
     Clayton *(G-3132)*

Asp Holdings Inc................................ G 888 330-2538
     Zebulon *(G-13504)*

◆ Carolina Elctrnic Assmblers In.......... E 919 938-1086
     Smithfield *(G-11435)*

CD Snow Hill LLC.............................. D 252 747-5943
     Snow Hill *(G-11478)*

◆ Cem Corporation............................... C 704 821-7015
     Matthews *(G-8162)*

Click Electronics LLC......................... F 704 840-6855
     Raleigh *(G-9999)*

CMS Associates Inc........................... G 919 365-0881
     Wendell *(G-12530)*

Cnc-Ke Inc....................................... D 704 333-0145
     Charlotte *(G-1939)*

◆ Commscope Inc North Carolina......... E 828 324-2200
     Claremont *(G-3096)*

Commscope Technologies LLC............ G 919 934-9711
     Smithfield *(G-11440)*

◆ Commscope Technologies LLC.......... A 828 324-2200
     Claremont *(G-3104)*

Communications & Pwr Inds LLC......... E 650 846-2900
     Conover *(G-3505)*

Cooper Crouse-Hinds LLC................. D 252 566-3014
     La Grange *(G-7466)*

Crackle Holdings LP.......................... A 704 927-7620
     Charlotte *(G-1993)*

Diversified Intl Holdings Inc............... G 910 777-7122
     Winnabow *(G-13064)*

Duotech Services LLC........................ E 828 369-5111
     Franklin *(G-4826)*

Eclipse Composite Engrg Inc.............. E 801 601-8559
     Mooresville *(G-8660)*

Edc Inc... D 336 993-0468
     Kernersville *(G-7270)*

▲ Emrise Corporation.......................... C 408 200-3040
     Durham *(G-4023)*

▲ Finnord North America Corp.............. F 704 723-4913
     Huntersville *(G-6990)*

Geotrak Incorporated......................... F 919 303-1467
     Apex *(G-157)*

Gocaissoncom.................................. G 336 454-4610
     Jamestown *(G-7163)*

High Vacuum Electronics Inc.............. G 910 738-1219
     Lumberton *(G-7957)*

Hoffman Materials Inc........................ G 717 243-2011
     Granite Falls *(G-5307)*

▲ Huber + Suhner Inc.......................... E 704 790-7300
     Charlotte *(G-2295)*

Infosense Inc.................................... G 704 644-1164
     Charlotte *(G-2333)*

Infosense Inc.................................... G 704 644-1164
     Charlotte *(G-2334)*

Innova-Con Incorporated.................... G 919 303-1467
     Apex *(G-169)*

Interconnect Products and.................. E 336 667-3356
     Wilkesboro *(G-12640)*

◆ Iqe Rf LLC...................................... D 732 271-5990
     Greensboro *(G-5624)*

Iqe Usa Inc...................................... G 610 861-6930
     Greensboro *(G-5625)*

▲ Iron Box LLC................................... E 919 890-0025
     Raleigh *(G-10209)*

James W McManus Inc....................... G 828 688-2560
     Bakersville *(G-678)*

Kratos Antenna Solutions Corp........... G 919 934-9711
     Smithfield *(G-11451)*

▲ Lutze Inc.. E 704 504-0222
     Charlotte *(G-2442)*

▲ Lxd Research & Display LLC.............. F 919 600-6440
     Raleigh *(G-10263)*

M2 Optics Inc.................................... G 919 342-5619
     Raleigh *(G-10264)*

Marmon Holdings Inc......................... G 910 291-2571
     Laurinburg *(G-7508)*

▲ Matsusada Precision Inc................... G 704 496-2644
     Charlotte *(G-2469)*

MTS Systems Corporation.................. C 919 677-2352
     Cary *(G-1403)*

Nuvotronics Inc................................. D 434 298-6940
     Durham *(G-4152)*

Parker-Hannifin Corporation............... C 704 588-3246
     Charlotte *(G-2612)*

▲ Protechnologies Inc......................... E 336 368-1375
     Pilot Mountain *(G-9672)*

Pt Marketing Incorporated.................. G 412 471-8995
     Raleigh *(G-10408)*

▲ QMF Mtal Elctrnic Slutions Inc......... D 336 992-8002
     Kernersville *(G-7295)*

▲ Rostra Precision Controls Inc........... D 910 291-2502
     Aberdeen *(G-23)*

Santronics Inc.................................. A 919 775-1223
     Sanford *(G-11231)*

Scion International US........................ G 919 570-9303
     Wake Forest *(G-12297)*

▲ Shallco Inc...................................... E 919 934-3135
     Smithfield *(G-11465)*

Silanna Semicdtr N Amer Inc.............. D 984 444-6500
     Raleigh *(G-10476)*

▲ Smallhd LLC................................... F 919 439-2166
     Cary *(G-1461)*

Smith Systems Inc............................. E 828 884-3490
     Brevard *(G-982)*

▲ Snap One LLC.................................. B 704 927-7620
     Charlotte *(G-2818)*

Snap One Holdings Corp.................... E 704 927-7620
     Charlotte *(G-2819)*

Spruce Pine Mica Company................ F 828 765-4241
     Spruce Pine *(G-11589)*

Tecworks Inc.................................... G 704 829-9700
     Belmont *(G-772)*

▲ Tresco.. C 361 985-3154
     Boone *(G-946)*

US Microwave Inc.............................. G 520 891-2444
     Pittsboro *(G-9791)*

US Prototype Inc............................... E 866 239-2848
     Wilmington *(G-12943)*

USA Dreamstone LLC......................... G 919 615-4329
     Garner *(G-4970)*

◆ Utility Solutions Inc......................... E 828 323-8914
     Hickory *(G-6484)*

▲ Vishay Transducers Ltd.................... E 919 365-3800
     Wendell *(G-12553)*

▲ Wieland Electric Inc......................... F 910 259-5050
     Wilmington *(G-12947)*

3691 Storage batteries

Associated Battery Company............... G 704 821-8311
     Matthews *(G-8158)*

Clarios LLC...................................... C 336 761-1550
     Kernersville *(G-7257)*

East Penn Manufacturing Co.............. F 336 771-1380
     Winston Salem *(G-13152)*

Energizer Holdings Inc....................... C 336 672-3526
     Asheboro *(G-352)*

Exide.. G 704 357-9845
     Charlotte *(G-2134)*

Infinite Blue Inc................................ G 919 744-7704
     Raleigh *(G-10194)*

▲ Lexington Road Properties Inc........... C 336 650-7209
     Winston Salem *(G-13234)*

Magnevolt Inc................................... F 919 553-2202
     Clayton *(G-3159)*

Polypore International LP.................... D 704 587-8409
     Charlotte *(G-2645)*

Saft America Inc................................ B 828 874-4111
     Valdese *(G-12200)*

Smith Utility Buildings........................ G 336 957-8211
     Traphill *(G-12106)*

Spectrum Brands Inc.......................... G 704 658-2060
     Mooresville *(G-8773)*

Toyota Battery Mfg Inc........................ E 469 292-6094
     Liberty *(G-7782)*

3692 Primary batteries, dry and wet

Clarios LLC...................................... C 336 761-1550
     Kernersville *(G-7257)*

Edgewell Per Care Brands LLC............ G 336 672-4500
     Asheboro *(G-349)*

Himcen Battery Inc............................ G 408 828-8744
     Apex *(G-165)*

L L C Batteries of N C......................... G 919 331-0241
     Angier *(G-123)*

▲ Lexington Road Properties Inc........... C 336 650-7209
     Winston Salem *(G-13234)*

Saft America Inc................................ B 828 874-4111
     Valdese *(G-12200)*

Spectrum Brands Inc.......................... G 800 854-3151
     Charlotte *(G-2842)*

3694 Engine electrical equipment

1a Smart Start LLC............................. G 336 765-7001
     Winston Salem *(G-13068)*

Cummins Inc..................................... G 704 588-1240
     Pineville *(G-9723)*

GKN Driveline North Amer Inc............. A 919 304-7200
     Mebane *(G-8244)*

GKN Driveline North Amer Inc............. C 336 364-6200
     Timberlake *(G-12100)*

Goldsboro Strter Altrntor Svc.............. G 919 735-6745
     Goldsboro *(G-5218)*

Hemco Wire Products Inc.................... G 336 454-7280
     Jamestown *(G-7164)*

Ineos Automotive Americas LLC.......... G 404 513-8577
     Raleigh *(G-10193)*

Johnston County Industries Inc........... C 919 743-8700
     Selma *(G-11289)*

Lmg Holdings Inc............................... F 919 653-0910
     Durham *(G-4107)*

▲ Manufacturing Systems Eqp Inc......... F 704 283-2086
     Monroe *(G-8523)*

Mc Cullough Auto Elc & Assoc............ G 704 376-5388
     Charlotte *(G-2475)*

Pass & Seymour Inc........................... A 315 468-6211
     Concord *(G-3415)*

Radel Inc... G 336 245-8078
     Winston Salem *(G-13314)*

▲ Reman Technologies Inc................... G 704 921-2293
     Charlotte *(G-2705)*

Scattered Wrenches Inc...................... G 919 480-1605
     Raleigh *(G-10460)*

Window Motor World Inc...................... G 800 252-2649
     Boone *(G-953)*

Ziehl-Abegg Inc................................. C 336 934-9339
     Winston Salem *(G-13410)*

▲ Ziehl-Abegg Inc............................... E 336 834-9339
     Greensboro *(G-5931)*

3695 Magnetic and optical recording media

▲ Assa Abloy AB................................. E 704 283-2101
     Monroe *(G-8431)*

Consolidated Sciences Inc...................... G 919 870-0344
Raleigh *(G-10009)*

High Mobility Solutions Inc................... G 704 849-8242
Matthews *(G-8116)*

Legalis Dms LLC................................ F 919 741-8260
Raleigh *(G-10252)*

Synchrono Group Inc........................... F 888 389-0439
Raleigh *(G-10526)*

3699 Electrical equipment and supplies, nec

A&B Integrators LLC........................... F 919 371-0750
Durham *(G-3876)*

▲ Acw Technology Inc.......................... A
Raleigh *(G-9877)*

▲ Advanced Electronic Svcs Inc............. E 336 789-0792
Mount Airy *(G-9096)*

Aegis Power Systems Inc..................... E 828 837-4029
Murphy *(G-9287)*

Alert Protection Systems Inc................ G 919 467-4357
Raleigh *(G-9890)*

Alpitronic Americas Inc........................ E 704 997-4201
Charlotte *(G-1656)*

American Physcl SEC Group LLC.......... G 919 363-1894
Apex *(G-134)*

AMP Services LLC.............................. G 828 313-1200
Granite Falls *(G-5294)*

Asco Power Technologies LP............... C 919 460-5200
Apex *(G-140)*

Asco Power Technologies LP............... F 336 731-5000
Lexington *(G-7657)*

Asco Power Technologies LP............... C 336 731-5009
Welcome *(G-12509)*

Assa Abloy Accessories and................ B 704 233-4011
Monroe *(G-8433)*

◆ Assa Abloy Entrnce Systems US........ C 866 237-2687
Monroe *(G-8434)*

Atom Power Inc.................................. D 844 704-2866
Huntersville *(G-6969)*

Audio Vdeo Concepts Design Inc.......... G 704 821-2823
Indian Trail *(G-7069)*

Austin Company of Greensboro............ C 336 468-2851
Yadkinville *(G-13436)*

Automated Controls LLC...................... G 704 724-7625
Huntersville *(G-6970)*

Campus Safety Products LLC............... G 919 321-1477
Durham *(G-3956)*

▲ Cargotec Port Security LLC............... G 919 620-1763
Durham *(G-3958)*

Carolina Electric Mtr Repr LLC............ G 704 289-3732
Monroe *(G-8453)*

Carolina Growler Inc........................... E 910 948-2114
Robbins *(G-10752)*

Carolina Tex Sls Gastonia Inc.............. G 704 739-1646
Kings Mountain *(G-7357)*

◆ Commscope Inc North Carolina.......... E 828 324-2200
Claremont *(G-3096)*

◆ Commscope Technologies LLC........... A 828 324-2200
Claremont *(G-3104)*

Communications & Pwr Inds LLC........... E 650 846-2900
Conover *(G-3505)*

Consoldted Elctrnic Rsrces Inc............. G 919 321-0004
Durham *(G-3987)*

Consolidated Elec Distrs Inc................ G 828 433-4689
Morganton *(G-8858)*

◆ Consolidated Mfg Intl LLC................. G 919 781-3411
Raleigh *(G-10008)*

▲ Cordset Designs Inc......................... G 252 568-4001
Pink Hill *(G-9765)*

Cortical Metrics LLC........................... G 919 903-9943
Carrboro *(G-1267)*

Crowdguard Inc.................................. G 919 605-1948
Cary *(G-1340)*

Custom Light and Sound Inc................ E 919 286-1122
Durham *(G-3994)*

Diverse Security Systems Inc............... G 919 848-9599
Raleigh *(G-10050)*

Eaton Corporation.............................. B 828 684-2381
Arden *(G-266)*

Eaton Corporation.............................. C 919 872-3020
Raleigh *(G-10074)*

Edwards Electronic Systems Inc........... E 919 359-2239
Clayton *(G-3146)*

◆ Feller LLC...................................... E 910 383-6920
Leland *(G-7541)*

Hamrick Fence Company..................... F 704 434-5011
Boiling Springs *(G-884)*

Hitachi Energy USA Inc....................... C 919 856-2360
Raleigh *(G-10170)*

Hollingsworth Heating Air Cond............ G 252 824-0355
Tarboro *(G-11929)*

Infinite Blue Inc................................ G 919 744-7704
Raleigh *(G-10194)*

International Thermodyne Inc................ G 704 579-8218
Charlotte *(G-2350)*

Jared Munday Electric Inc.................... G 828 355-9024
Boone *(G-927)*

◆ Jenkins Electric Company.................. D 800 438-3003
Charlotte *(G-2368)*

Jenkins Electric II LLC........................ E 704 392-7371
Charlotte *(G-2369)*

Kuebler Inc....................................... F 704 705-4711
Charlotte *(G-2403)*

L3harris Technologies Inc.................... G 704 588-7126
Charlotte *(G-2405)*

Lea Aid Acquisition Company............... G 919 872-6210
Spring Hope *(G-11557)*

▼ Leonardo US Cyber SEC Sltons L....... D 336 379-7135
Greensboro *(G-5661)*

Leonine Protection Systems LLC.......... G 704 296-2675
Mount Holly *(G-9235)*

M2 Optics Inc.................................... G 919 342-5619
Raleigh *(G-10264)*

Machine Control Company Inc.............. G 704 708-5782
Matthews *(G-8128)*

▲ Magnum Enterprize Inc..................... G 252 524-5391
Grifton *(G-6037)*

◆ Marpac LLC.................................... D 910 602-1421
Wilmington *(G-12846)*

Memscap Inc..................................... C 919 248-1441
Durham *(G-4127)*

NC Solar Now Inc............................... F 919 833-9096
Raleigh *(G-10327)*

Offshore Marine Elec LLC.................... G 252 504-2624
Newport *(G-9441)*

◆ Pace Incorporated........................... E 910 695-7223
Vass *(G-12228)*

Pathway Technologies Inc.................... E 919 847-2680
Raleigh *(G-10361)*

Pcx Holding LLC................................ D 919 550-2800
Knightdale *(G-7455)*

Pike Electric LLC.............................. C 336 316-7068
Greensboro *(G-5748)*

Plan B Enterprises LLC....................... G 919 387-4856
New Hill *(G-9412)*

Posh Pad.. G 910 988-4800
Stedman *(G-11807)*

Power and Ctrl Solutions LLC.............. G 704 609-9623
Charlotte *(G-2649)*

▲ Precision Drive Systems LLC............. G 704 922-1206
Bessemer City *(G-831)*

▲ Pro Ultrasonics Inc.......................... G 828 584-1005
Morganton *(G-8889)*

Process Electronics Corp..................... F 704 827-9019
Mount Holly *(G-9242)*

RDM Industrial Electronics Inc............. D 828 652-8346
Nebo *(G-9329)*

▲ Record Usa Inc............................... E 704 289-9212
Monroe *(G-8549)*

▲ Reuel Inc....................................... E 919 734-0460
Goldsboro *(G-5240)*

Salem Technologies Inc...................... F 336 777-3652
Winston Salem *(G-13327)*

Sandhlls Fbrctors Crane Svcs I............ F 910 673-4573
West End *(G-12558)*

Schneider Automation Inc.................... C 919 855-1262
Raleigh *(G-10462)*

Security Consult Inc........................... G 704 531-8399
Charlotte *(G-2782)*

▲ Sentinel Door Controls LLC............... F 704 921-4627
Charlotte *(G-2788)*

Service Electric and Control................. G 704 888-5100
Locust *(G-7901)*

Shipman Technologies Inc.................... G 919 294-8405
Durham *(G-4232)*

Sierra Nevada Corporation................... F 910 307-0362
Fayetteville *(G-4668)*

SL Laser Systems LP.......................... G 704 561-9990
Charlotte *(G-2814)*

▲ Smart Electric North Amer LLC........... G 828 323-1200
Conover *(G-3559)*

Sonaspection International.................... F 704 262-3384
Concord *(G-3442)*

Spartan Manufacturing Corp................ E 336 996-5585
Kernersville *(G-7302)*

Spectra Integrated Systems Inc............ G 919 876-3666
Raleigh *(G-10496)*

Stanley Black & Decker Inc.................. C 704 789-7000
Concord *(G-3446)*

▼ TCI Mobility Inc.............................. F 704 867-8331
Gastonia *(G-5149)*

▼ Total Fire Systems Inc..................... E 919 556-9161
Youngsville *(G-13493)*

Turbomed LLC................................... F 973 527-5299
Fayetteville *(G-4684)*

◆ Utility Solutions Inc......................... G 828 323-8914
Hickory *(G-6484)*

Vortex-Cyclone Technologies............... F 919 225-1724
Raleigh *(G-10595)*

Wilmore Electronics Company Inc......... D 919 732-9351
Hillsborough *(G-6881)*

▲ Zibra LLC...................................... G 704 271-4503
Mooresville *(G-8806)*

37 TRANSPORTATION EQUIPMENT

3711 Motor vehicles and car bodies

Ashville Wrecker Service Inc............... G 828 252-2388
Asheville *(G-444)*

B S R-Hess Race Cars Inc................... E 704 547-0901
Charlotte *(G-1730)*

Bobby Labonte Enterprises Inc............. F 336 434-1800
Archdale *(G-213)*

Brown Mitchell Hodges LLC................. G 800 477-8982
Charlotte *(G-1813)*

◆ Bucher Municipal N Amer Inc............. E 704 658-1333
Mooresville *(G-8624)*

Bus Safety Inc................................... G 336 671-0838
Mocksville *(G-8352)*

Can-AM Custom Trucks Inc.................. G 704 334-0322
Charlotte *(G-1834)*

▼ Carolina Movile Bus Systems............ G 336 475-0983
Thomasville *(G-12005)*

▲ Cleveland Freightliner Truck.............. F 704 645-5000
Cleveland *(G-3212)*

▼ Csi Armoring Inc................................. G 336 313-8561
  Lexington *(G-7672)*

▲ Custom Cnverting Solutions Inc........ E 336 292-2616
  Greensboro *(G-5480)*

Daimler Truck North Amer LLC.............. A 704 645-5000
  Cleveland *(G-3213)*

Dej Holdings LLC................................. E 704 799-4800
  Mooresville *(G-8655)*

◆ Demmel Inc...................................... D 828 585-6600
  East Flat Rock *(G-4329)*

▲ Designline Corporation.................... C 704 494-7800
  Charlotte *(G-2035)*

Designline Usa LLC............................. F 704 494-7800
  Charlotte *(G-2036)*

◆ Direct Chassislink Inc..................... E 704 594-3800
  Charlotte *(G-2050)*

E-N-G Mobile Systems LLC................... F 925 798-4060
  Fayetteville *(G-4590)*

Ecovehicle Enterprises Inc................... G 704 544-9907
  Charlotte *(G-2090)*

Enc Conveyance LLC............................ G 252 378-9990
  Rocky Mount *(G-10811)*

Epk LLC... G 980 643-4787
  Salisbury *(G-11048)*

Epv Corporation................................. D 704 494-7800
  Charlotte *(G-2124)*

Ev Fleet Inc...................................... G 704 425-6272
  Charlotte *(G-2130)*

First Prrity Emrgncy Vhcles In............. E 908 645-0788
  Wilkesboro *(G-12635)*

Force Protection Inc........................... F 336 597-2381
  Roxboro *(G-10926)*

Fortem Genus Inc............................... G 910 574-5214
  Fayetteville *(G-4603)*

GM Defense LLC................................. D 800 462-8782
  Concord *(G-3369)*

Go Green Racing................................ G 916 295-2621
  Mooresville *(G-8674)*

Grahams Transportation LLC................ G 910 627-6880
  Fayetteville *(G-4606)*

Granite Tactical Vehicles Inc............... F 336 789-5555
  Mount Airy *(G-9125)*

Halcore Group Inc.............................. E 336 982-9824
  Jefferson *(G-7188)*

◆ Halcore Group Inc.......................... B 336 846-8010
  Jefferson *(G-7189)*

Hedgecock Racing Entps Inc................. F 336 887-4221
  High Point *(G-6643)*

Highline Performance Group................ E 704 799-3500
  Mooresville *(G-8684)*

Holman Automotive Inc........................ G 704 583-2888
  Charlotte *(G-2282)*

International Motors LLC..................... G 704 596-3860
  Charlotte *(G-2344)*

▲ James Tool Machine & Engrg Inc...... C 828 584-8722
  Morganton *(G-8875)*

Jasper Engine Exchange Inc................. E 704 664-2300
  Mooresville *(G-8698)*

Jasper Penske Engines........................ F 704 788-8996
  Concord *(G-3384)*

L Rancho Investments Inc.................... G 336 431-1004
  Trinity *(G-12117)*

Lelantos Group Inc............................. D 704 780-4127
  Mooresville *(G-8709)*

Lynn Jones Race Cars......................... G 252 522-0705
  Kinston *(G-7420)*

◆ Mack Trucks Inc............................. A 336 291-9001
  Greensboro *(G-5670)*

Matthews Spcialty Vehicles Inc............ D 336 297-9600
  Greensboro *(G-5682)*

Maxxdrive LLC.................................... G 704 600-8684
  Shelby *(G-11360)*

▼ Mickey Truck Bodies Inc.................. B 336 882-6806
  High Point *(G-6711)*

North Crlina Dept Crime Ctrl P............. G 252 522-1511
  Kinston *(G-7424)*

North Crlina Dept Crime Ctrl P............. G 336 599-9233
  Roxboro *(G-10933)*

Operating Shelby LLC Tag..................... E 704 482-1399
  Shelby *(G-11368)*

▲ Penske Racing South Inc................. C 704 664-2300
  Mooresville *(G-8746)*

Performance Racing Whse Inc............... G 704 838-1400
  Mooresville *(G-8749)*

Pratt Mller Engrg Fbrction LLC............. C 704 977-0642
  Huntersville *(G-7036)*

Prevost Car (us) Inc........................... F 336 812-3504
  High Point *(G-6744)*

▲ Prevost Car (us) Inc....................... E 908 222-7211
  Greensboro *(G-5763)*

Propane Trucks & Tanks Inc................. F 919 362-5000
  Apex *(G-188)*

Race Tech Race Cars Cmpnnts In.......... G 336 538-4941
  Burlington *(G-1144)*

RFH Tactical Mobility Inc..................... F 910 916-0284
  Milton *(G-8326)*

Richard Chldress Racg Entps In............ E 336 731-3334
  Welcome *(G-12513)*

▲ Richard Chldress Racg Entps In....... B 336 731-3334
  Welcome *(G-12514)*

▲ Riley Technologies LLC.................... E 704 663-6319
  Mooresville *(G-8759)*

Rowdy Manufacturing LLC.................... G 704 662-0000
  Mooresville *(G-8764)*

Rp Motor Sports Inc........................... E 704 720-4200
  Concord *(G-3435)*

Smith Fabrication Inc.......................... G 704 660-5170
  Mooresville *(G-8772)*

Solar Pack.. E 919 515-2194
  Raleigh *(G-10491)*

Southco Industries Inc........................ C 704 482-1477
  Shelby *(G-11381)*

Spevco Inc.. D 336 924-8100
  Pfafftown *(G-9665)*

Streets Auto Sales & Four WD.............. G 704 888-8686
  Locust *(G-7904)*

Subaru Folger Automotive.................... F 704 531-8888
  Charlotte *(G-2877)*

Supreme Murphy Trck Bodies Inc.......... C 252 291-2191
  Wilson *(G-13033)*

Thomas Built Buses Inc........................ A 336 889-4871
  High Point *(G-6807)*

Toymakerz LLC................................... F 843 267-3477
  Reidsville *(G-10699)*

Trenton Emergency Med Svcs Inc........... G 252 448-2646
  Trenton *(G-12111)*

Triple R MBL Cigr Lounge LLC.............. G 252 281-7738
  Rocky Mount *(G-10875)*

◆ US Legend Cars Intl Inc................... E 704 455-3896
  Harrisburg *(G-6119)*

Vision Motor Cars Inc......................... G 704 425-6271
  Concord *(G-3465)*

3713 Truck and bus bodies

Adkins Truck Equipment Co.................. E 704 596-2299
  Charlotte *(G-1624)*

Altec Industries Inc............................ B 919 528-2535
  Creedmoor *(G-3637)*

▲ Altec Northeast LLC........................ E 508 320-9041
  Creedmoor *(G-3638)*

AM Haire Mfg & Svc Corp..................... C 336 472-4444
  Thomasville *(G-11993)*

Amrep Inc.. D 704 949-2595
  Salisbury *(G-11016)*

Amrep Inc.. E 909 923-0430
  Charlotte *(G-1674)*

Anchor-Richey Emergency Vehicl......... E 828 495-8145
  Taylorsville *(G-11949)*

Cabarrus Plastics Inc.......................... C 704 784-2100
  Concord *(G-3328)*

Can-AM Custom Trucks Inc................... G 704 334-0322
  Charlotte *(G-1834)*

Carroll Co... F 919 779-1900
  Garner *(G-4920)*

Courtesy Ford Inc............................... G 252 338-4783
  Elizabeth City *(G-4384)*

Daimler Truck North Amer LLC.............. A 704 868-5700
  Gastonia *(G-5038)*

Designline Usa LLC............................. F 704 494-7800
  Charlotte *(G-2036)*

Enterprise Twd................................... G 704 822-6166
  Stanley *(G-11615)*

Epv Corporation................................. D 704 494-7800
  Charlotte *(G-2124)*

Fontaine Modification Company............ F 704 392-8502
  Charlotte *(G-2169)*

◆ Godwin Manufacturing Co Inc........... C 910 897-4995
  Dunn *(G-3858)*

Guy N Langley.................................... G 252 972-9875
  Rocky Mount *(G-10812)*

Hackney & Sons Midwest Inc................ G 252 946-6521
  Washington *(G-12389)*

Immixt LLC.. G 336 207-8679
  Siler City *(G-11412)*

John Jenkins Company......................... E 336 375-3717
  Browns Summit *(G-1001)*

Johnie Gregory Trck Bodies Inc............ G 252 264-2626
  Hertford *(G-6255)*

Knapheide Trck Eqp Co Midsouth.......... E 910 484-0558
  Midland *(G-8289)*

Laurinburg Machine Company............... G 910 276-0360
  Laurinburg *(G-7505)*

Leonard Alum Utlity Bldngs Inc............ G 919 872-4442
  Raleigh *(G-10254)*

Leonard Alum Utlity Bldngs Inc............ G 910 392-4921
  Wilmington *(G-12834)*

Lift Bodies Inc.................................. G 336 667-2588
  North Wilkesboro *(G-9542)*

Matthews Spcialty Vehicles Inc............ D 336 297-9600
  Greensboro *(G-5682)*

Mdb Investors LLC.............................. F 704 507-6850
  Charlotte *(G-2482)*

Meritor Inc.. C 828 433-4600
  Morganton *(G-8881)*

Mickey Truck Bodies Inc...................... G 336 882-6806
  High Point *(G-6710)*

Mickey Truck Bodies Inc...................... G 336 882-6806
  Thomasville *(G-12047)*

▼ Mickey Truck Bodies Inc.................. B 336 882-6806
  High Point *(G-6711)*

Osprea Logistics Usa LLC.................... E 704 504-1677
  Charlotte *(G-2601)*

Petroleum Tank Corporation................ F 919 284-2418
  Kenly *(G-7235)*

▲ Prevost Car (us) Inc....................... E 908 222-7211
  Greensboro *(G-5763)*

Propane Trucks & Tanks Inc................. F 919 362-5000
  Apex *(G-188)*

Quality Trck Bodies & Repr Inc............ E 252 245-5100
  Elm City *(G-4466)*

R J Yeller Distribution Inc................... G 800 944-2589
  Charlotte *(G-2686)*

Satco Truck Equipment Inc................... F 919 383-5547
  Durham *(G-4222)*

Smithway Inc...................................... G 828 628-1756
  Fairview *(G-4511)*

S I C

▼ Smithway Inc.................................. E 828 628-1756
Fairview *(G-4512)*

Southco Industries Inc..................... C 704 482-1477
Shelby *(G-11381)*

Supreme Murphy Trck Bodies Inc......... C 252 291-2191
Wilson *(G-13033)*

Thomas Built Buses Inc..................... A 336 889-4871
High Point *(G-6807)*

▲ Transportation Tech Inc................. C 252 946-6521
Washington *(G-12416)*

Triangle Body Works Inc.................... G 336 788-0631
Winston Salem *(G-13371)*

◆ Vna Holding Inc........................... A 336 393-4890
Greensboro *(G-5905)*

Volvo Group North America LLC.......... A 336 393-2000
Greensboro *(G-5907)*

Volvo Group North America LLC.......... A 336 393-2000
Greensboro *(G-5908)*

◆ Volvo Group North America LLC......A 336 393-2000
Greensboro *(G-5906)*

◆ Volvo Logistics North America Inc......C 336 393-4746
Greensboro *(G-5910)*

◆ Volvo Trucks North America Inc........A 336 393-2000
Greensboro *(G-5911)*

VT Hackney Inc............................... C 252 946-6521
Washington *(G-12419)*

Waste Container Repair Svcs................ G 910 257-4474
Fayetteville *(G-4696)*

3714 Motor vehicle parts and accessories

Aerofabb LLC................................. G 919 793-8487
Raleigh *(G-9884)*

Aisin North Carolina Corp.................. C 919 529-0951
Creedmoor *(G-3636)*

◆ Aisin North Carolina Corp................A 919 479-6400
Durham *(G-3886)*

Altra Industrial Motion Corp............... C 704 588-5610
Charlotte *(G-1657)*

American Racg Hders Exhust Inc........ F 631 608-1986
Stanfield *(G-11602)*

Amsted Industries Incorporated............ G 704 226-5243
Monroe *(G-8425)*

◆ AP Emissions Technologies LLC.......A 919 580-2000
Goldsboro *(G-5199)*

▲ Atkinson International Inc................ E 704 865-7750
Gastonia *(G-4995)*

Auria Albemarle LLC........................ B 704 983-5166
Albemarle *(G-62)*

▲ Auria Old Fort LLC........................ C 828 668-7601
Old Fort *(G-9589)*

▲ Auria Old Fort II LLC..................... D 828 668-3277
Old Fort *(G-9590)*

Auria Troy LLC............................... D 910 572-3721
Troy *(G-12157)*

Autel New Energy US Inc................... F 336 810-7083
Greensboro *(G-5376)*

▼ Axle Holdings LLC........................ E 800 895-3276
Concord *(G-3316)*

▲ B & B Fabrication Inc..................... F 623 581-7600
Mooresville *(G-8605)*

Barrs Competition............................ F 704 482-5169
Shelby *(G-11313)*

Ben Huffman Enterprises LLC............. G 704 724-4705
Mooresville *(G-8607)*

Billet Speed Inc.............................. G 828 226-8127
Sylva *(G-11890)*

Borg-Warner Automotive Inc............... G 828 684-3501
Fletcher *(G-4726)*

Borgwarner Arden LLC...................... F 248 754-9200
Arden *(G-256)*

Borgwarner Inc............................... E 828 684-4000
Arden *(G-257)*

▲ Bosch Rexroth Corporation.............. E 704 583-4338
Charlotte *(G-1801)*

Boxmoor Truck Bedliners & ACC.......... G 336 447-4621
Whitsett *(G-12600)*

Brembo North America Inc.................. G 704 799-0530
Concord *(G-3324)*

▲ BT America Inc............................ G 704 434-8072
Boiling Springs *(G-883)*

CAM Craft LLC................................ G 828 681-5183
Arden *(G-259)*

Camco Manufacturing Inc................... G 336 348-6609
Reidsville *(G-10678)*

Can-AM Custom Trucks Inc................. G 704 334-0322
Charlotte *(G-1834)*

Carbotech USA Inc........................... G 704 481-8500
Concord *(G-3330)*

Carolina Attachments LLC................... G 336 474-7309
Thomasville *(G-12001)*

Carolina Cltch Brake Rbldrs In............. G 828 327-9358
Hickory *(G-6283)*

▲ Carpenter Industries Inc................. D 704 786-8139
Concord *(G-3331)*

▲ Cataler North America Corp.............. C 828 970-0026
Lincolnton *(G-7819)*

Ceco Friction Products Inc.................. F 704 857-1156
Landis *(G-7473)*

Certification Services In..................... G 828 458-1573
Fletcher *(G-4728)*

City of Charlotte-Atando.................... G 704 336-2722
Charlotte *(G-1922)*

Cjr Products Inc.............................. G 336 766-2710
Winston Salem *(G-13124)*

◆ Clarcor Eng MBL Solutions LLC........C 860 992-3496
Washington *(G-12379)*

Classic Wood Manufacturing............... G 336 691-1344
Greensboro *(G-5448)*

▲ Cleveland Yutaka Corporation........... D 704 480-9290
Shelby *(G-11321)*

Coconut Paradise Inc....................... G 704 662-3443
Mooresville *(G-8641)*

Commercial Vehicle Group Inc............. E 704 886-6407
Concord *(G-3340)*

Consolidated Metco Inc..................... D 828 488-5126
Bryson City *(G-1010)*

Consolidated Metco Inc..................... C 828 488-5114
Canton *(G-1250)*

Consolidated Metco Inc..................... E 704 226-5246
Monroe *(G-8468)*

Continental Auto Systems Inc.............. B 828 654-2000
Fletcher *(G-4731)*

Continental Auto Systems Inc.............. B 828 584-4500
Morganton *(G-8859)*

Continental Auto Systems Inc.............. E 828 584-4500
Valdese *(G-12193)*

Coolant & Cleaning Tech Inc............... G 704 753-1333
Monroe *(G-8469)*

Cooper-Standard Automotive Inc.......... D 919 735-5394
Goldsboro *(G-5209)*

Cox Machine Co Inc......................... G 704 296-0118
Monroe *(G-8470)*

Cummins Inc.................................. G 919 284-9111
Kenly *(G-7231)*

Cummins Inc.................................. G 704 588-1240
Pineville *(G-9723)*

Curtis L Maclean L C......................... C 704 940-5531
Mooresville *(G-8646)*

▲ Cycle Pro LLC............................. G 704 662-6682
Mooresville *(G-8649)*

Daimler Truck North Amer LLC............. A 704 868-5700
Gastonia *(G-5038)*

David Vizard Motortec Features............ G 865 850-0666
Mount Holly *(G-9227)*

◆ Dce Inc.................................... G 704 230-4649
Mooresville *(G-8652)*

Dhollandia Us Llc........................... G 909 251-7979
Bessemer City *(G-814)*

▲ Diamondback Products Inc.............. G 336 236-9800
Lexington *(G-7678)*

▲ Dill Air Controls Products LLC.......... C 919 692-2300
Oxford *(G-9613)*

Dnj Engine Comp Onents................... G 704 855-5505
China Grove *(G-3073)*

Doosan Bobcat North Amer Inc............ C 704 883-3500
Statesville *(G-11691)*

Eaton Corporation........................... C 704 937-7411
Kings Mountain *(G-7362)*

Eaton Corporation........................... B 336 322-0696
Roxboro *(G-10924)*

Edelbrock LLC............................... C 919 718-9737
Sanford *(G-11175)*

Elite Metal Performance LLC............... F 704 660-0006
Statesville *(G-11694)*

Epic Restorations LLC....................... G 866 597-2733
Roxboro *(G-10925)*

Fat Man Fabrications Inc.................... E 704 545-0369
Mint Hill *(G-8337)*

▲ FCC (north Carolina) LLC............... C 910 462-4465
Laurinburg *(G-7501)*

Five Star Bodies............................. G 262 325-9126
Troutman *(G-12138)*

Fox Factory Inc.............................. G 828 633-6840
Asheville *(G-501)*

G-Loc Brakes LLC........................... G 704 765-0213
Mooresville *(G-8669)*

GKN Dna Inc................................. G 919 304-7378
Mebane *(G-8243)*

GKN Driveline Newton LLC................. E 828 428-5292
Newton *(G-9467)*

◆ GKN Driveline Newton LLC..............A 828 428-3711
Newton *(G-9466)*

GKN Driveline North Amer Inc............. A 919 304-7200
Mebane *(G-8244)*

GKN Driveline North Amer Inc............. C 919 708-4500
Sanford *(G-11184)*

GKN Driveline North Amer Inc............. C 336 364-6200
Timberlake *(G-12100)*

Global Products LLC......................... G 336 227-7327
Greensboro *(G-5563)*

GM Defense LLC............................. D 800 462-8782
Concord *(G-3369)*

◆ Godwin Manufacturing Co Inc..........C 910 897-4995
Dunn *(G-3858)*

Goodyear Tire & Rubber Company......... G 919 552-9340
Holly Springs *(G-6903)*

Gracie & Lucas LLC......................... G 704 707-3207
Mooresville *(G-8675)*

Grede II LLC................................. B 910 428-2111
Biscoe *(G-852)*

Haldex Inc.................................... C 828 652-9308
Marion *(G-8042)*

Hamilton Sundstrand Corp.................. A 860 654-6000
Charlotte *(G-2252)*

Hanwha Advanced Mtls Amer LLC........ E 704 434-2271
Shelby *(G-11342)*

▼ Hendrens Racg Engs Chassis Inc...... G 828 286-0780
Rutherfordton *(G-10987)*

Hickory Springs Mfg Co..................... F 336 491-4131
High Point *(G-6648)*

Hitch Crafters LLC........................... G 336 859-3257
Lexington *(G-7699)*

Hogans Racing Manifolds Inc............... G 704 799-3424
Mooresville *(G-8685)*

▲ Holman & Moody Inc..................... G 704 394-4141
Charlotte *(G-2281)*

Holman Automotive Inc............................ G 704 583-2888
Charlotte *(G-2282)*

Hotchkis Bryde Incorporated.................... G 704 660-3060
Mooresville *(G-8687)*

Indian Head Industries Inc...................... D 704 547-7411
Murphy *(G-9290)*

◆ Indian Head Industries Inc.....................E 704 547-7411
Charlotte *(G-2321)*

▲ Inter-Continental Gear & Brake.......... G 704 599-3420
Charlotte *(G-2341)*

Isometrics Inc.. F 336 342-4150
Reidsville *(G-10690)*

◆ Isometrics Inc...E 336 349-2329
Reidsville *(G-10689)*

Jasper Engine Exchange Inc.................... E 704 664-2300
Mooresville *(G-8698)*

Jenkins Properties Inc.............................. E 336 667-4282
North Wilkesboro *(G-9537)*

▲ Jri Development Group LLC.............. F 704 660-8346
Mooresville *(G-8699)*

Jri Shocks LLC... F 704 660-8346
Mooresville *(G-8700)*

▲ Kck Holding Corp................................. E 336 513-0002
Burlington *(G-1114)*

Kee Auto Top Manufacturing Co............ E 704 332-8213
Charlotte *(G-2390)*

Kgt Enterprises Inc................................... E 704 662-3272
Mooresville *(G-8704)*

Kooks Custom Headers............................ G 704 838-1110
Statesville *(G-11725)*

Lake Shore Radiator Inc........................... F 336 271-2626
Greensboro *(G-5657)*

Lear Enterprises Inc................................. G 704 321-0027
Charlotte *(G-2413)*

Leonard Alum Utlity Bldngs Inc.............. G 919 872-4442
Raleigh *(G-10254)*

Leonard Alum Utlity Bldngs Inc.............. G 910 392-4921
Wilmington *(G-12834)*

Longs Machine & Tool Inc........................ E 336 625-3844
Asheboro *(G-374)*

Lord Corporation...................................... D 919 342-3380
Cary *(G-1393)*

◆ Mack Trucks Inc....................................A 336 291-9001
Greensboro *(G-5670)*

▲ Magna Composites LLC....................... B 704 797-8744
Salisbury *(G-11088)*

▲ Mahle Motorsports Inc......................... F 888 255-1942
Fletcher *(G-4750)*

▲ Mann+hmmel Fltrtion Tech Group..... G 704 869-3300
Gastonia *(G-5082)*

▼ Mann+hmmel Fltrtion Tech Intrm...... E 704 869-3300
Gastonia *(G-5083)*

Mann+hmmel Fltrtion Tech US LL......... C 704 869-3700
Gastonia *(G-5084)*

Mann+hmmel Prlator Filters LLC.......... C 910 425-4181
Fayetteville *(G-4633)*

Mann+hmmel Prlator Filters LLC.......... C 704 869-3441
Gastonia *(G-5086)*

◆ Mann+hmmel Prlator Filters LLC.....E 910 425-4181
Fayetteville *(G-4632)*

Mann+hummel Filtration Technol........... D 704 869-3500
Gastonia *(G-5087)*

Mann+hummel Filtration Technol........... G 704 869-3952
Gastonia *(G-5088)*

Mann+hummel Filtration Technol........... C 704 869-3501
Gastonia *(G-5089)*

◆ Mann+hummel Filtration Te.................A 704 869-3300
Gastonia *(G-5090)*

Marmon Engine Controls LLC................. E 843 701-5145
Laurinburg *(G-7507)*

Marmon Holdings Inc............................... G 910 291-2571
Laurinburg *(G-7508)*

▲ Master Tow Inc...................................... E 910 630-2000
Fayetteville *(G-4637)*

▲ MB Marketing & Mfg Inc...................... G 828 285-0882
Asheville *(G-545)*

Meritor Inc... F 910 425-4181
Fayetteville *(G-4640)*

Meritor Inc... F 828 687-2000
Fletcher *(G-4754)*

Meritor Inc... C 828 687-2000
Fletcher *(G-4755)*

Meritor Inc... C 828 247-0440
Forest City *(G-4794)*

Meritor Inc... F 910 844-9401
Maxton *(G-8202)*

Meritor Inc... D 910 844-9401
Maxton *(G-8203)*

Meritor Inc... C 828 433-4600
Morganton *(G-8881)*

Metalcraft & Mech Svc Inc...................... G 919 736-1029
Goldsboro *(G-5229)*

▲ Moores Cylinder Heads LLC............... E 704 786-8412
Concord *(G-3404)*

▲ Moores Mch Co Fayetteville Inc........ D 919 837-5354
Bear Creek *(G-717)*

Motoring Inc.. G 704 809-1265
Mooresville *(G-8728)*

Motorsport Innovations Inc...................... G 704 728-7837
Davidson *(G-3713)*

Motorsports Machining Tech LLC........... G 336 475-3742
Thomasville *(G-12052)*

Mr Tire Inc... F 828 322-8130
Hickory *(G-6398)*

MSI Defense Solutions LLC.................... D 704 660-8348
Mooresville *(G-8730)*

▲ Ohlins Usa Inc....................................... E 828 692-4525
Hendersonville *(G-6232)*

On Point Mobile Detailing LLC............... G 404 593-8882
Charlotte *(G-2597)*

P4rts LLC.. E 561 717-7580
Mooresville *(G-8740)*

▲ Parker Gas Company Inc.................... F 800 354-7250
Clinton *(G-3238)*

PCC Airfoils LLC...................................... B 919 774-4300
Sanford *(G-11215)*

Precision Pdts Prfmce Ctr Inc................ F 828 684-8569
Arden *(G-300)*

Pro-Fabrication Inc.................................. F 704 795-7563
Concord *(G-3425)*

Pro-Motor Engines Inc............................. G 704 664-6800
Mooresville *(G-8755)*

Race Technologies Concord NC............. G 704 799-0530
Concord *(G-3429)*

Reuben James Auto Electric.................... G 910 980-1056
Falcon *(G-4521)*

Richardson Racing Products Inc............ G 704 784-2602
Concord *(G-3432)*

Ripari Automotive LLC.............................. G 585 267-0228
Charlotte *(G-2727)*

▲ Roadactive Suspension Inc................ G 704 523-2646
Charlotte *(G-2729)*

▲ Rostra Precision Controls Inc........... D 910 291-2502
Aberdeen *(G-23)*

Rp Motor Sports Inc................................. E 704 720-4200
Concord *(G-3435)*

Saf-Holland Inc... G 336 310-4595
Kernersville *(G-7298)*

Satco Truck Equipment Inc...................... F 919 383-5547
Durham *(G-4222)*

Save-A-Load Inc....................................... G 704 650-4947
Charlotte *(G-2759)*

▲ Scorpion Products Inc......................... F 336 813-3241
King *(G-7336)*

SL Liquidation LLC................................... D 910 353-3666
Jacksonville *(G-7145)*

SL Liquidation LLC................................... B 910 353-3666
Jacksonville *(G-7147)*

◆ SL Liquidation LLC...............................E 860 525-0821
Jacksonville *(G-7146)*

Spod Inc.. G 910 477-6297
Southport *(G-11531)*

SRI Performance Inc................................ E 704 662-6982
Mooresville *(G-8774)*

▲ Stanadyne Intrmdate Hldngs LLC..... C 860 525-0821
Jacksonville *(G-7152)*

Stanadyne Jacksonville LLC.................... C 860 683-4553
Jacksonville *(G-7153)*

Stanadyne Operating Co LLC................... E 910 353-3666
Jacksonville *(G-7154)*

▲ Sturdy Corporation.............................. C 910 763-2500
Wilmington *(G-12933)*

Suspensions LLC..................................... F 704 809-1269
Denver *(G-3808)*

Teijin Automotive Tech Inc...................... C 828 754-8441
Lenoir *(G-7642)*

Teijin Automotive Tech Inc...................... C 828 466-7000
Newton *(G-9503)*

Tenowo Inc.. A 704 732-3525
Lincolnton *(G-7861)*

Thyssenkrupp Bilstein Amer Inc............ F 704 663-7563
Mooresville *(G-8786)*

Trane Technologies Company LLC.......... C 910 692-8700
Southern Pines *(G-11512)*

Trend Performance Products.................. G 828 862-8290
Pisgah Forest *(G-9774)*

Truck Parts Inc... F 704 332-7909
Charlotte *(G-2948)*

▲ Uchiyama Mfg Amer LLC...................... F 919 731-2364
Goldsboro *(G-5251)*

Unique Tool and Mfg Co.......................... E 336 498-2614
Franklinville *(G-4858)*

◆ US Legend Cars Intl Inc......................E 704 455-3896
Harrisburg *(G-6119)*

US Prototype Inc....................................... E 866 239-2848
Wilmington *(G-12943)*

Visual Impact Prfmce Systems L............ G 704 278-3552
Cleveland *(G-3224)*

Wenker Inc.. G 704 333-7790
Charlotte *(G-3012)*

Xceldyne LLC.. D 336 472-2242
Thomasville *(G-12092)*

Xceldyne Technologies LLC.................... D 336 475-0201
Thomasville *(G-12094)*

Xtreme Fabrication Ltd............................ G 336 472-4562
Thomasville *(G-12095)*

ZF Chassis Components LLC.................. C 828 468-3711
Newton *(G-9513)*

3715 Truck trailers

Battle Trucking Inc.................................. G 919 708-2288
Sanford *(G-11153)*

Bkc Industries Inc.................................... G 919 575-6699
Creedmoor *(G-3642)*

Daimler Truck North Amer LLC.............. A 704 645-5000
Cleveland *(G-3213)*

Ecovehicle Enterprises Inc..................... G 704 544-9907
Charlotte *(G-2090)*

Eugenes Trucking Inc.............................. G 910 267-0555
Faison *(G-4517)*

F & C Repair and Sales LLC.................... F 704 907-2461
Charlotte *(G-2139)*

FEC Inc.. G 828 765-4599
Spruce Pine *(G-11576)*

Gaines Motor Lines Inc............................ C 828 322-2000
Hickory *(G-6337)*

S
I
C

Kraftsman Inc.......................... D 336 824-1114	Textron Aviation Inc........................ C 336 605-7000	B/E Aerospace Inc........................ G 336 841-7698
Ramseur (G-10627)	Greensboro (G-5861)	High Point (G-6535)
L & S Automotive Inc................... G 704 391-7657	United States Dept of Navy.............. G 252 464-7228	▲ B/E Aerospace Inc........................ G 336 293-1823
Charlotte (G-2404)	Cherry Point (G-3056)	Winston Salem (G-13091)
Liberty Trailers LLC.................... G 219 866-7141	Vx Aerospace Corporation.............. F 828 433-5353	▲ B/E Aerospace Inc........................ G 336 293-1823
Liberty (G-7773)	Morganton (G-8910)	Winston Salem (G-13092)
▲ Master Tow Inc........................... E 910 630-2000	Vx Aerospace Holdings Inc............. F 828 433-5353	B/E Aerospace Inc........................ E 336 744-6914
Fayetteville (G-4637)	Morganton (G-8911)	Winston Salem (G-13093)
▼ Mickey Truck Bodies Inc.............. B 336 882-6806	Windlift Inc................................... G 919 490-8575	B/E Aerospace Inc........................ E 336 767-2000
High Point (G-6711)	Durham (G-4306)	Winston Salem (G-13094)
Road King Trailers Inc.................. E 828 670-8012		B/E Aerospace Inc........................ C 520 733-1719
Candler (G-1232)	**3724 Aircraft engines and engine parts**	Winston Salem (G-13095)
Smithway Inc................................ G 828 628-1756	Carolina Precision Tech LLC............ E 215 675-4590	B/E Aerospace Inc........................ C 336 776-3500
Fairview (G-4511)	Mooresville (G-8633)	Winston Salem (G-13096)
▼ Smithway Inc............................... E 828 628-1756	Circor Precision Metering LLC.......... A 919 774-7667	B/E Aerospace Inc........................ C 336 767-2000
Fairview (G-4512)	Sanford (G-11164)	Winston Salem (G-13097)
Speedway Link Inc........................ G 704 338-2028	Curtiss-Wright Controls Inc............. E 704 869-2300	B/E Aerospace Inc........................ F 336 692-8940
Matthews (G-8150)	Shelby (G-11325)	Winston Salem (G-13098)
Spring Repair Service Inc.............. G 336 299-5660	Fps Wind Down Inc........................ F 336 776-9165	▲ B/E Aerospace Inc........................ E 704 423-7000
Greensboro (G-5832)	Winston Salem (G-13174)	Charlotte (G-1731)
Vision Metals Inc.......................... G 336 622-7300	▲ GE Aircraft Engs Holdings Inc......... A 919 361-4400	▲ Ballistic Recovery Systems Inc....... E 651 457-7491
Liberty (G-7783)	Durham (G-4043)	Pinebluff (G-9685)
	Glemco LLC.................................. G 866 619-6707	▲ Beta Fueling Systems LLC............. D 336 342-0306
3716 Motor homes	Statesville (G-11703)	Reidsville (G-10676)
Hunckler Fabrication LLC............... F 336 753-0905	◆ Goodrich Corporation.....................C 704 423-7000	Blanket Aero LLC.......................... G 704 591-2878
Mocksville (G-8370)	Charlotte (G-2227)	Concord (G-3321)
Matthews Spcialty Vehicles Inc....... D 336 297-9600	Hiab USA Inc................................ F 704 896-9089	Blue Force Technologies LLC.......... D 919 443-1660
Greensboro (G-5682)	Cornelius (G-3606)	Morrisville (G-8942)
Van Products Inc.......................... E 919 878-7110	Honda Aero LLC........................... D 336 226-2376	▲ Brice Manufacturing Co Inc........... E 818 896-2938
Raleigh (G-10582)	Burlington (G-1105)	Greensboro (G-5398)
	Honeywell.................................... E 734 942-5823	Carolina Ground Svc Eqp Inc.......... F 252 565-0288
3721 Aircraft	Charlotte (G-2285)	New Bern (G-9349)
Anuma Aerospace LLC................... G 919 600-0142	Honeywell International Inc.............. G 910 436-5144	Carolina Metals Inc....................... F 828 667-0876
Raleigh (G-9906)	Fort Bragg (G-4804)	Asheville (G-470)
BEC-Faye LLC.............................. G 252 714-8700	Honeywell International Inc.............. A 919 662-7539	Circor Precision Metering LLC.......... A 919 774-7667
Grimesland (G-6040)	Raleigh (G-10173)	Sanford (G-11164)
Boeing Arospc Operations Inc......... F 919 722-4351	◆ Honeywell International Inc..............A 704 627-6200	Collins Aerospace........................ F 704 423-7000
Goldsboro (G-5201)	Charlotte (G-2286)	Charlotte (G-1957)
Boeing Company........................... G 704 572-8280	▲ James Tool Machine & Engrg Inc...... C 828 584-8722	Curtiss-Wright Controls Inc............. F 704 869-2320
Charlotte (G-1796)	Morganton (G-8875)	Gastonia (G-5035)
Charter Jet Transport Inc............... G 704 359-8833	◆ Lord Corporation...........................B 919 468-5979	Curtiss-Wright Controls Inc............. E 704 869-2300
Charlotte (G-1907)	Cary (G-1394)	Shelby (G-11325)
CJ Partners LLC............................ G 336 838-3080	Lord Far East Inc.......................... G 919 468-5979	▲ Curtiss-Wright Controls Inc............. E 704 869-4600
Wilkesboro (G-12633)	Cary (G-1397)	Charlotte (G-2005)
Cyberlux Corporation..................... F 984 363-6894	Pratt & Whitney Eng Svcs Inc.......... A 860 565-4321	Cyberlux Corporation..................... F 984 363-6894
Research Triangle Pa (G-10707)	Asheville (G-583)	Research Triangle Pa (G-10707)
Fire Fly Ballons 2006 LLC............... G 704 878-9501	Pratt & Whitney Eng Svcs Inc.......... B 704 660-9999	D2 Government Solutions LLC.......... E 662 655-4554
Statesville (G-11698)	Mooresville (G-8753)	New Bern (G-9362)
Firefly Balloons 2010 Inc................ G 704 878-9501	Precision Metals LLC..................... G 919 762-7481	DEB Manufacturing Inc................... G 704 703-6618
Statesville (G-11699)	Benson (G-796)	Concord (G-3353)
Hawthorne Services....................... G 910 436-9013	Tat Technologies Group.................. A 704 910-2215	Dronescape Pllc............................ G 704 953-3798
Fayetteville (G-4608)	Charlotte (G-2899)	Charlotte (G-2066)
Honda Aircraft Company LLC........... E 336 662-0246	Thermal Pane Inc.......................... G 336 722-9977	Equipment & Supply Inc.................. E 704 289-6565
Greensboro (G-5604)	Lexington (G-7749)	Monroe (G-8485)
Honda Aircraft Company LLC........... E 336 662-0246	Triad Engines Parts & Svcs Inc........ G 800 334-6437	Esterline Technologies Corp............ G 910 814-1222
Greensboro (G-5605)	Burlington (G-1169)	Lillington (G-7796)
◆ Honda Aircraft Company LLC...........B 336 662-0246	Unique Tool and Mfg Co.................. E 336 498-2614	Frisby Aerospace Inc..................... G 336 712-8004
Greensboro (G-5606)	Franklinville (G-4858)	Clemmons (G-3185)
Iomax USA LLC............................. E 704 662-1840		GE Aviation Systems LLC............... C 828 210-5076
Mooresville (G-8695)	**3728 Aircraft parts and equipment, nec**	Asheville (G-504)
Marshall USA LLC......................... G 301 481-1241	A & A Drone Service LLC................ G 704 928-5054	General Electric Company................ A 910 675-5000
Greensboro (G-5677)	Statesville (G-11642)	Wilmington (G-12785)
Piedmont AVI Cmponent Svcs LLC.... C 336 423-5100	Acme Aerofab LLC........................ G 704 806-3582	Goaero LLC.................................. G 815 713-1190
Greensboro (G-5741)	Charlotte (G-1618)	Greensboro (G-5566)
◆ Ride Best LLC..............................G 252 489-2959	Air-We-Go LLC............................. E 704 289-6565	Goodrich Corporation..................... G 704 282-2500
Rodanthe (G-10888)	Monroe (G-8420)	Monroe (G-8493)
Signature Flight Air Inc.................. E 919 840-4400	Aircraft Parts Solutions LLC............ G 843 300-1725	Goodrich Corporation..................... C 704 282-2500
Morrisville (G-9055)	Apex (G-133)	Monroe (G-8494)
Summit Aviation Inc...................... F 302 834-5400	AMF-NC Enterprise Company LLC...... F 704 489-2206	◆ Goodrich Corporation.....................C 704 423-7000
Greensboro (G-5844)	Denver (G-3769)	Charlotte (G-2227)
Tcom Limited Partnership............... B 252 330-5555	Ark Aviation Inc............................ G 336 379-0900	Gounmanned LLC.......................... G 919 835-2140
Elizabeth City (G-4413)	Greensboro (G-5369)	Raleigh (G-10140)

Gray Manufacturing Tech LLC.............. F 704 489-2206
Denver (G-3785)

Honeywell International Inc..................... E 252 977-2100
Rocky Mount (G-10841)

Isometrics Inc.. F 336 342-4150
Reidsville (G-10690)

◆ Isometrics Inc.....................................E 336 349-2329
Reidsville (G-10689)

▲ James Tool Machine & Engrg Inc...... C 828 584-8722
Morganton (G-8875)

Kearfott Corporation............................. B 828 350-5300
Black Mountain (G-868)

Kidde Technologies Inc......................... D 252 237-7004
Wilson (G-13001)

Legacy Aerospace and Def LLC.......... G 828 398-0981
Arden (G-281)

Logic Hydraulic Controls Inc............... E 910 791-9293
Wilmington (G-12838)

◆ Lord Corporation................................B 919 468-5979
Cary (G-1394)

Lord Far East Inc.................................. G 919 468-5979
Cary (G-1397)

Ontic Engineering and Mfg Inc............. B 919 395-3908
Creedmoor (G-3653)

Oro Manufacturing Company................. E 704 283-2186
Monroe (G-8539)

PCC Airfoils LLC................................... B 919 774-4300
Sanford (G-11215)

Piedmont Flight Inc............................... E 336 776-6070
Winston Salem (G-13291)

Pma Products Inc.................................. G 800 762-0844
Liberty (G-7776)

Proedge Precision LLC......................... E 704 872-3393
Statesville (G-11756)

▲ Purolator Facet Inc............................ E 336 668-4444
Greensboro (G-5771)

R S Skillen.. G 828 433-5353
Morganton (G-8891)

Rockwell Collins Inc............................. G 336 744-3288
Winston Salem (G-13320)

Rtx Corporation..................................... G 704 423-7000
Charlotte (G-2740)

Safety & Security Intl Inc...................... G 336 285-8673
Greensboro (G-5800)

Sierra Nevada Corporation.................... E 919 595-8551
Durham (G-4234)

Soisa Inc.. G 336 940-4006
Mocksville (G-8390)

Southern Prestige Intl LLC.................... F 704 872-9524
Statesville (G-11771)

Specialty Perf LLC................................ G 704 872-9980
Statesville (G-11773)

◆ Spirit Aerosystems NC Inc................F 252 208-4645
Kinston (G-7430)

◆ Starhgen Arospc Components LLC....F 704 660-1001
Mooresville (G-8776)

T Air Inc.. D 980 595-2840
Charlotte (G-2895)

Tcom Limited Partnership..................... B 252 330-5555
Elizabeth City (G-4413)

Telair US LLC.. C 919 705-2400
Goldsboro (G-5249)

Tempest Aero Group.............................. E 336 449-5054
Gibsonville (G-5184)

Tigerswan LLC....................................... C 919 439-7110
Apex (G-197)

▲ Triumph Actuation Systems LLC....... C 336 766-9036
Clemmons (G-3206)

◆ Unison Engine Components Inc......... B 828 274-4540
Asheville (G-627)

United States Dept of Navy................... E 252 466-4415
Cherry Point (G-3057)

Vannoy Construction Arcft LLC............ G 336 846-7191
Jefferson (G-7193)

Vx Aerospace Corporation..................... F 828 433-5353
Morganton (G-8910)

West Side Industries LLC..................... G 980 223-8665
Statesville (G-11799)

▲ Weststar Precision Inc....................... E 919 557-2820
Cary (G-1482)

Wildcat Petroleum Service Inc............. G 704 379-0132
Matthews (G-8198)

3731 Shipbuilding and repairing

Big Rock Industries Inc......................... G 252 222-3618
Morehead City (G-8816)

Edenton Boatworks LLC....................... E 252 482-7600
Edenton (G-4366)

Harbor Lines LLC.................................. G 910 279-3796
Wilmington (G-12802)

Lighthouse of Wayne County Inc.......... G 919 736-1313
Goldsboro (G-5224)

M & J Marine LLC................................. F 252 249-0522
Oriental (G-9601)

Vigor LLC... G 980 474-1124
Charlotte (G-2984)

Waterline Systems Inc.......................... G 910 708-1000
Hubert (G-6937)

Yang Ming America Corporation........... G 704 357-3817
Charlotte (G-3039)

3732 Boatbuilding and repairing

2topia Cycles Inc.................................. G 704 778-7849
Charlotte (G-1600)

▲ 33rd Strike Group LLC....................... G 910 371-9688
Leland (G-7530)

A & J Canvas Inc.................................. E 252 244-1509
Vanceboro (G-12213)

▼ Alb Boats... G 252 482-7600
Edenton (G-4359)

Baja Marine Inc..................................... G 252 975-2000
Washington (G-12374)

Barrs Competition................................. F 704 482-5169
Shelby (G-11313)

▲ Bayliss Boatworks Inc....................... E 252 473-9797
Wanchese (G-12336)

Bayliss Boatyard Inc............................. G 252 473-9797
Wanchese (G-12337)

Bennett Brothers Yachts Inc................. E 910 772-9277
Wilmington (G-12719)

Bilge Masters Inc.................................. G 704 995-4293
Charlotte (G-1781)

Blackbeards Boatworks......................... G 252 726-6161
Morehead City (G-8818)

◆ Briggs Boat Works Incorporated........G 252 473-2393
Wanchese (G-12338)

Brp US Inc... G 828 766-1164
Spruce Pine (G-11565)

Brp US Inc... D 828 766-1100
Spruce Pine (G-11566)

Budsin Wood Craft................................ G 252 729-1540
Marshallberg (G-8084)

C E Hicks Enterprises Inc.................... F 919 772-5131
Garner (G-4919)

Caison Yachts Inc................................. G 910 270-6394
Hampstead (G-6070)

Cape Fear Boat Works Inc.................... F 910 371-3460
Navassa (G-9326)

Cape Fear Yacht Works LLC................ F 910 540-1685
Wilmington (G-12729)

▼ CC Boats Inc...................................... G 252 482-3699
Edenton (G-4363)

Coastal Trimworks Inc.......................... G 910 231-8532
Leland (G-7538)

Craig & Sandra Blackwell Inc.............. G 252 473-1803
Wanchese (G-12339)

Croswait Custom Composites Inc........ G 252 423-1245
Wanchese (G-12340)

Custom Marine Fabrication Inc............ G 252 638-5422
New Bern (G-9360)

Custom Steel Boats Inc........................ F 252 745-7447
Merritt (G-8267)

◆ Daedalus Composites LLC................F 252 368-9000
Edenton (G-4365)

Daniels Boatworks Inc.......................... G 252 473-1400
Wanchese (G-12341)

Donzi Marine LLC................................. G 252 975-2000
Washington (G-12384)

Elite Marine LLC................................... E 919 495-6388
Benson (G-789)

Enviboats LLC....................................... G 910 213-3200
Southport (G-11519)

Gillikin Marine Railways Inc................. G 252 726-7284
Beaufort (G-728)

▼ Grady-White Boats Inc....................... C 252 752-2111
Greenville (G-5983)

◆ Gunboat International Ltd..................F 252 305-8700
Wanchese (G-12342)

Harding Enterprise Inc.......................... G 252 725-9785
Beaufort (G-730)

◆ Hatteras Yachts Inc...........................A 252 633-3101
New Bern (G-9370)

Hc Composites LLC.............................. C 252 641-8000
Tarboro (G-11928)

Hermes Marine LLC.............................. E 252 368-9000
Edenton (G-4367)

Hurricane Aqua Sports Inc................... G 910 293-2941
Warsaw (G-12362)

Iconic Marine Group LLC...................... B 252 975-2000
Chocowinity (G-3083)

Jabec Enterprise Inc............................. G 336 655-8441
Winston Salem (G-13215)

Jarrett Bay Offshore............................. G 919 803-1990
Raleigh (G-10213)

Johnson Custom Boats Inc................... G 910 232-4594
Wilmington (G-12824)

Jones Brothers Marine Mfg Inc............ G 252 240-1995
Morehead City (G-8837)

Jones Marine Inc.................................. G 704 639-0173
Salisbury (G-11075)

Kencraft Manufacturing Inc.................. G 252 291-0271
Wilson (G-12998)

Laytons Custom Boatworks LLC........... G 252 482-1504
Edenton (G-4368)

◆ Legacy Paddlesports LLC..................C 828 684-1933
Fletcher (G-4746)

M & J Marine LLC................................. F 252 249-0522
Oriental (G-9601)

Mann Custom Boats Inc........................ E 252 473-1716
Manns Harbor (G-8020)

Marine Tooling Technology Inc.............. G 336 887-9577
High Point (G-6698)

Marinemax of North Carolina................ G 910 256-8100
Wrightsville Beach (G-13432)

Mass Enterprises LLC........................... F 443 585-0732
New Bern (G-9381)

▼ May-Craft Fiberglass Pdts Inc........... G 919 934-3000
Four Oaks (G-4814)

Mike Luszcz... G 252 717-6282
Winterville (G-13418)

Nomad Houseboats Inc.......................... G 252 288-5670
New Bern (G-9386)

Obx Boatworks LLC.............................. G 336 878-9490
High Point (G-6720)

Onslow Bay Boatworks & Marine.......... G 910 270-3703
Hampstead (G-6074)

S
I
C

Pacific Seacraft LLC.................................. G 252 948-1421
Washington (G-12403)

Pair Marine Inc.................................... F 252 717-7009
Washington (G-12404)

▼ Parker Marine Enterprises Inc........... D 252 728-5621
Beaufort (G-733)

Powers Boatworks.................................. G 910 762-3636
Wilmington (G-12884)

Pro-Line North Carolina Inc................. D 252 975-2000
Washington (G-12409)

Rapid Response Technology LLC........ G 910 763-3856
Wilmington (G-12896)

▼ Regulator Marine Inc........................ D 252 482-3837
Edenton (G-4371)

Richard Scarborough Boat Works......... G 252 473-3646
Wanchese (G-12346)

Rings True LLC..................................... G 919 265-7600
Carrboro (G-1273)

Sea Mark Boats Inc.............................. G 910 675-1877
Rocky Point (G-10882)

Shearline Boatworks LLC..................... G 252 726-6916
Morehead City (G-8844)

Sirocco Marine LLC.............................. G 954 692-8333
Raleigh (G-10483)

Smoky Mountain Jet Boats LLC........ F 828 488-0522
Bryson City (G-1011)

Spencer Yachts Inc.............................. E 252 473-2660
Manns Harbor (G-8021)

▼ Starflite Companies Inc................... C 252 728-2690
Beaufort (G-735)

Stroudcraft Marine LLC........................ F 910 623-4055
Rocky Point (G-10884)

Taylor Boat Works................................ G 252 726-6374
Morehead City (G-8847)

Taylor Manufacturing Inc.................... E 910 862-2576
Elizabethtown (G-4434)

Todds Rv & Marine Inc........................ G 828 651-0007
Hendersonville (G-6245)

Trawler Incorporated............................ G 252 745-3751
Lowland (G-7936)

Triad Marine Center Inc....................... G 252 634-1880
New Bern (G-9401)

Twin Troller Boats Inc.......................... G 919 207-2622
Benson (G-798)

U S Propeller Service Inc.................... G 704 528-9515
Troutman (G-12154)

Wanchese Dock and Haul LLC........... G 252 473-6424
Wanchese (G-12347)

Warrior Boats....................................... G 336 885-2628
High Point (G-6832)

White River Marine Group LLC........... C 252 633-3101
New Bern (G-9406)

Winter Custom Yachts Inc.................. F 910 325-7583
Hubert (G-6939)

▲ Winterville Machine Works Inc......... D 252 756-2130
Winterville (G-13426)

3743 Railroad equipment

▲ Dellner Inc.. E 704 527-2121
Charlotte (G-2028)

Frit Car Inc... E 252 638-2675
Bridgeton (G-984)

▲ Kck Holding Corp.............................. E 336 513-0002
Burlington (G-1114)

Knorr Brake Truck Systems Co........... A 888 836-6922
Salisbury (G-11081)

New York Air Brake LLC..................... D 315 786-5200
Salisbury (G-11097)

◆ Railroad Friction Pdts Corp.............. C 910 844-9709
Maxton (G-8205)

Twin Oaks Service South Inc.............. G 704 914-7142
Shelby (G-11387)

3751 Motorcycles, bicycles, and parts

B & B Welding Inc................................ G 336 643-5702
Oak Ridge (G-9569)

Barrs Competition................................ F 704 482-5169
Shelby (G-11313)

▲ Cane Creek Cycling Cmpnnts Inc..... E 828 684-3551
Fletcher (G-4727)

Capital Value Center Sls & Svc........... G 910 799-4060
Wilmington (G-12730)

Devils Kindred MC............................... E 336 712-7689
Swansboro (G-11884)

Driver Distribution Inc......................... G 984 204-2929
Raleigh (G-10059)

Edelbrock LLC..................................... C 919 718-9737
Sanford (G-11175)

Ffr Electrics LLC................................. F 828 654-7555
Mars Hill (G-8077)

Huck Cycles Corporation..................... G 704 275-1735
Cornelius (G-3608)

Indian Motorcycle Company................ G 704 879-4560
Lowell (G-7933)

▲ Industry Nine LLC............................. G 828 210-5113
Asheville (G-523)

James King... G 910 308-8818
Fayetteville (G-4620)

Kendall Johnson Customs Inc............. G 336 748-3833
Winston Salem (G-13224)

Moto Group LLC.................................. E 828 350-7653
Fletcher (G-4757)

▲ Next World Design Inc...................... G 800 448-1223
Thomasville (G-12054)

P P M Cycle and Custom.................... G 336 434-5243
Trinity (G-12120)

Performance Parts Intl LLC................. F 704 660-1084
Mooresville (G-8748)

Rinehart Racing Inc............................. E 828 350-7653
Fletcher (G-4764)

Suspension Experts LLC..................... E 855 419-3072
Roxboro (G-10948)

▲ Sv Plastics LLC................................ G 336 472-2242
Thomasville (G-12077)

▲ Trailmate Inc.................................... G 941 739-5743
Chapel Hill (G-1578)

Vexea Mx LLC..................................... G 910 787-9391
Jacksonville (G-7157)

3761 Guided missiles and space vehicles

End Camp North.................................. F 980 337-4600
Charlotte (G-2112)

3764 Space propulsion units and parts

▲ James Tool Machine & Engrg Inc...... C 828 584-8722
Morganton (G-8875)

3769 Space vehicle equipment, nec

Carolina Metals Inc............................. F 828 667-0876
Asheville (G-470)

Firstmark Aerospace Corp................... D 919 956-4200
Creedmoor (G-3648)

Kearfott Corporation............................ B 828 350-5300
Black Mountain (G-868)

3792 Travel trailers and campers

Allison Globl Mnufacturing Inc............ G 704 392-7883
Charlotte (G-1646)

Boondock S Manufacturing Inc........... G 828 891-4242
Etowah (G-4495)

Cold Mountain Capital LLC................. F 828 210-8129
Asheville (G-479)

Derrow Enterprises Inc........................ G 252 635-3375
New Bern (G-9364)

Elite Metal Performance LLC.............. F 704 660-0006
Statesville (G-11694)

Greene Mountain Outdoors LLC......... F 336 670-2186
North Wilkesboro (G-9532)

▲ Southag Mfg Inc............................... G 919 365-5111
Wendell (G-12548)

3795 Tanks and tank components

▲ Carolina Custom Tank LLC............... G 980 406-3200
Gastonia (G-5013)

Crown Defense Ltd.............................. G 202 800-8848
Denver (G-3779)

▲ Parker Gas Company Inc................... F 800 354-7250
Clinton (G-3238)

3799 Transportation equipment, nec

A-1 Hitch & Trailors Sales Inc............ G 910 755-6025
Supply (G-11854)

American Growler Inc........................... E 352 671-5393
Robbins (G-10751)

BOB Trailers Inc.................................. E 208 375-5171
Charlotte (G-1795)

Brisk Transport 910 LLC..................... G 910 527-7398
Cameron (G-1214)

Colfax Trailer & Repair LLC................ G 336 993-8511
Colfax (G-3275)

Crown Defense Ltd.............................. G 202 800-8848
Denver (G-3779)

Dallas Trans LLC................................. G 704 965-6057
Raleigh (G-10035)

Down East Offroad Inc........................ F 252 246-9440
Wilson (G-12984)

Faith Farm Inc..................................... G 704 431-4566
Salisbury (G-11052)

Front Line Express LLC....................... G 800 260-1357
Greensboro (G-5541)

Gore S Trlr Manufacturer S Inc........... G 910 642-2246
Whiteville (G-12582)

Jo-Natta Transportation LLC............... G 888 424-8789
Fayetteville (G-4624)

▼ Kaufman Trailers Inc........................ E 336 790-6800
Lexington (G-7704)

Kenn M LLC.. G 678 755-6607
Raleigh (G-10233)

Libra Life Group Llc............................ G 910 550-8664
Leland (G-7551)

Lionstar Transport LLC....................... G 336 448-0166
Winston Salem (G-13236)

Long Trailer Co Inc.............................. G 252 823-8828
Tarboro (G-11931)

Mk Pro Logistics LLC.......................... G 980 420-8156
Huntersville (G-7015)

Naarva.. G 704 333-3070
Charlotte (G-2540)

New Beginnings Trnsp LLC................. G 704 293-0493
Charlotte (G-2555)

North Carolina Dept Trnsp.................. G 828 733-9002
Newland (G-9433)

Rapid Response Technology LLC........ G 910 763-3856
Wilmington (G-12896)

Sanford S Atv Repair LLC................... G 252 438-2730
Henderson (G-6177)

Seans Transportation LLC................... G 646 603-8128
Charlotte (G-2780)

Speed Utv LLC.................................... E 704 949-1255
Concord (G-3445)

◆ Technibilt Ltd................................... E 828 464-7388
Newton (G-9502)

Trick Karts Inc.................................... G 704 883-0089
Statesville (G-11793)

Turner Boys Carrier Svc LLC.............. G 919 946-7553
Raleigh (G-10569)

▲ Wiggins Kart Shop Inc........................ F 704 855-3165
China Grove (G-3080)

Williams Easy Hitch Inc..................... G 919 302-0062
Durham (G-4305)

Xxxtreme Motorsport............................ G 704 663-1500
Mooresville (G-8801)

38 MEASURING, PHOTOGRAPHIC, MEDICAL, & OPTICAL GOODS, & CLOCKS

3812 Search and navigation equipment

◆ Accurate Technology Inc.................G 828 654-7920
Fletcher (G-4717)

Advanced Detection Tech LLC............. E 704 663-1949
Mooresville (G-8591)

Assa Abloy Accessories and.............. B 704 233-4011
Monroe (G-8433)

Bae Systems Inc.................................. D 855 223-8363
Charlotte (G-1738)

Beyond Electronics Corp.................... G 919 231-8000
Raleigh (G-9940)

Blue Maiden Defense.......................... G 678 292-8342
Pinebluff (G-9686)

Blue Ridge Armor LLC......................... G 844 556-6855
Rutherfordton (G-10977)

Btc Electronic Components LLC.......... E 919 229-2162
Wake Forest (G-12266)

Chemring Snsors Elctrnic Syste........ G 980 235-2200
Charlotte (G-1909)

◆ Commscope Inc North Carolina......E 828 324-2200
Claremont (G-3096)

Commscope Technologies LLC........... G 919 934-9711
Smithfield (G-11440)

◆ Commscope Technologies LLC........A 828 324-2200
Claremont (G-3104)

Curtiss-Wright Controls Inc .... E 704 869-2300
Shelby (G-11325)

Curtiss-Wright Corporation................. B 704 869-4600
Davidson (G-3700)

Cyber Defense Advisors....................... G 336 899-6072
Greensboro (G-5482)

Damsel In Defense.............................. G 919 744-8776
Clayton (G-3142)

Defense Logistics Services LLC......... D 703 449-1620
Fayetteville (G-4586)

Dodson Defense LLC........................... G 336 421-9649
Burlington (G-1085)

Eco Building Corporation.................... G 910 736-1540
Red Springs (G-10667)

Fil-Chem Inc....................................... G 919 878-1270
Raleigh (G-10108)

Firstmark Aerospace Corp.................. D 919 956-4200
Creedmoor (G-3648)

Garmin International Inc...................... A 919 337-0116
Cary (G-1364)

General Dynmics Mssion Systems...... C 336 698-8000
Mc Leansville (G-8223)

General Electric Company................... A 910 675-5000
Wilmington (G-12785)

Green Line Defense LLC...................... G 828 707-5236
Leicester (G-7525)

Honeywell International Inc................. E 252 977-2100
Rocky Mount (G-10841)

Ickler Manufacturing LLC................... G 704 658-1195
Mooresville (G-8690)

James W McManus Inc........................ G 828 688-2560
Bakersville (G-678)

▲ JMS Southeast Inc........................... E 704 873-1835
Statesville (G-11719)

Kdh Defense Systems Inc................... C 336 635-4158
Eden (G-4350)

Kearfott Corporation........................... B 828 350-5300
Black Mountain (G-868)

Kidde Technologies Inc...................... B 252 237-7004
Wilson (G-12999)

Navelite LLC....................................... G 336 509-9924
Jamestown (G-7172)

New Phoenix Aerospace Inc.............. F 919 380-8500
Raleigh (G-10330)

Northrop Grmman Gdnce Elec Inc...... E 704 588-2340
Charlotte (G-2575)

Northrop Grmman Tchncal Svcs I....... E 252 447-7575
Havelock (G-6124)

Northrop Grumman Systems Corp...... D 252 225-0911
Atlantic (G-638)

Northrop Grumman Systems Corp...... D 252 447-7557
Cherry Point (G-3054)

Northrop Grumman Systems Corp...... C 919 465-5020
Morrisville (G-9029)

Northstar Computer Tech Inc............. G 980 272-1969
Monroe (G-8537)

Plane Defense Ltd.............................. G 828 254-6061
Hendersonville (G-6236)

Qualia Networks Inc........................... G 805 637-2083
Raleigh (G-10413)

Rockwell Collins Inc........................... G 336 776-3444
Winston Salem (G-13321)

Rockwell Collins Inc........................... G 336 744-1097
Winston Salem (G-13322)

Roy Bridgmohan.................................. G 804 426-9652
Henderson (G-6176)

Sash and Saber Castings.................... G 919 870-5513
Raleigh (G-10457)

Sierra Nevada Corporation.................. E 919 595-8551
Durham (G-4234)

Sierra Nevada Corporation.................. F 910 307-0362
Fayetteville (G-4668)

Sierra Nevada Corporation.................. F 775 331-0222
Southern Pines (G-11509)

Spatial Light LLC................................ G 617 213-0314
Cary (G-1464)

Tempest Aero Group........................... E 336 449-5054
Gibsonville (G-5184)

Ultra Elec Ocean Systems Inc............ F 781 848-3400
Wake Forest (G-12311)

United States Dept of Navy................. G 252 466-4514
Cherry Point (G-3055)

US Prototype Inc................................. E 866 239-2848
Wilmington (G-12943)

Usat LLC... E 919 942-4214
Chapel Hill (G-1587)

3821 Laboratory apparatus and furniture

Air Control Inc.................................... E 252 492-2300
Henderson (G-6147)

Aisthesis Products Inc........................ G 828 627-6555
Clyde (G-3255)

Biovind LLC.. G 512 217-3077
Charlotte (G-1786)

◆ Carolina Biological Supply Company.C 336 584-0381
Burlington (G-1060)

Clinicians Advocacy Group Inc........... G 704 751-9515
Charlotte (G-1930)

Cooper Technical Services Inc........... G 910 285-2925
Rose Hill (G-10903)

▲ Corilam Fabricating Co.................... E 336 993-2371
Kernersville (G-7259)

Corning Incorporated.......................... C 919 620-6200
Durham (G-3988)

Dove Medical Supply LLC................... E 336 643-9367
Summerfield (G-11838)

Ecodyst Inc.. G 919 599-4963
Apex (G-153)

Fisher Scientific Company LLC.......... D 800 252-7100
Asheville (G-498)

◆ Flow Sciences Inc...........................E 910 763-1717
Leland (G-7542)

Gems Frst Stop Med Sltions LLC........ G 336 965-9500
Greensboro (G-5552)

◆ Ika-Works Inc..................................D 910 452-7059
Wilmington (G-12814)

Intensa Inc... E 336 884-4096
High Point (G-6673)

Kewaunee Scientific Corp.................. A 704 873-7202
Statesville (G-11724)

Misonix LLC.. D 631 694-9555
Durham (G-4136)

▲ Pacon Manufacturing Co LLC.......... C 910 239-3001
Leland (G-7556)

▼ Parameter Generation Ctrl Inc......... E 828 669-8717
Black Mountain (G-870)

Primevigilance Inc.............................. G 781 703-5540
Raleigh (G-10395)

▲ S E Lab Group Inc........................... G 707 253-8852
Hickory (G-6438)

▲ Sarstedt Inc.................................... C 828 465-4000
Newton (G-9493)

▲ Thermo Fsher Scntfic Ashvlle L....... B 828 658-2711
Asheville (G-616)

▲ Wall-Lenk Corporation.................... E 252 527-4186
Kinston (G-7435)

◆ Wpmhj LLC......................................G 919 601-5445
Raleigh (G-10615)

Xona Microfluidics Inc........................ G 951 553-6400
Research Triangle Pa (G-10718)

3822 Environmental controls

AMR Systems LLC............................... G 704 980-9072
Charlotte (G-1673)

Belham Management Ind LLC.............. G 704 815-4246
Charlotte (G-1768)

Building Automation Svcs LLC............ F 336 884-4026
High Point (G-6552)

Camco Manufacturing Inc................... G 336 348-6609
Reidsville (G-10678)

Cooke Companies Intl......................... F 919 968-0848
Chapel Hill (G-1540)

▲ Dampp-Chaser Electronics Corp...... E 828 692-8271
Hendersonville (G-6200)

Delkote Machine Finishing Inc............ G 828 253-1023
Asheville (G-485)

▲ Dna Group Inc................................. E 919 881-0889
Raleigh (G-10051)

Dorsett Technologies Inc.................... E 855 387-2232
Yadkinville (G-13441)

Dynamac Corporation.......................... E 919 544-6428
Durham (G-4016)

▲ Effikal LLC...................................... F 252 522-3031
Kinston (G-7407)

Flame-Tec LLC.................................... F 844 352-6383
Hendersonville (G-6206)

Green Stream Technologies Inc.......... G 844 499-8880
Wake Forest (G-12280)

Hoffman Building Tech Inc.................. C 336 292-8777
Greensboro (G-5601)

Huber Usa Inc..................................... F 919 674-4266
Raleigh (G-10179)

Icare Usa Inc...................................... G 919 877-9607
Raleigh (G-10183)

Industrial Heat LLC............................ G 919 743-5727
Raleigh (G-10190)

▲ JMS Southeast Inc.......................... E 704 873-1835
Statesville (G-11719)

Johnson Controls Inc.................... D 704 521-8889
Charlotte *(G-2375)*

Johnson Global Cmplnce Contrls.......... G 704 552-1119
Charlotte *(G-2377)*

Layer27............................ G 919 909-9088
Youngsville *(G-13478)*

Miller Ctrl Mfg Inc Clinton NC............ G 910 592-5112
Clinton *(G-3235)*

▲ Nascent Technology LLC............. F 704 654-3035
Charlotte *(G-2543)*

▼ Parameter Generation Ctrl Inc....... E 828 669-8717
Black Mountain *(G-870)*

▲ Pas USA Inc...................... C 252 974-5500
Washington *(G-12407)*

Qualia Networks Inc................. G 805 637-2083
Raleigh *(G-10413)*

Realxperience LLC.................. G 512 775-4386
Durham *(G-4209)*

Resideo LLC........................ G 919 872-5556
Raleigh *(G-10441)*

Ruskin LLC......................... G 919 583-5444
Goldsboro *(G-5242)*

◆ Salice America Inc.................E 704 841-7810
Charlotte *(G-2749)*

◆ Solero Technologies Shelby LLC........C 704 482-9582
Shelby *(G-11380)*

Strandberg Engrg Labs Inc............ F 336 274-3775
Greensboro *(G-5843)*

Thermik Corporation................. E 252 636-5720
New Bern *(G-9400)*

◆ Trane US Inc......................A 704 655-4000
Davidson *(G-3723)*

▲ TRf Manufacturing NC Inc.......... E 252 223-1112
Newport *(G-9445)*

Ultratech Industries Inc............. G 919 779-2004
Benson *(G-799)*

W A Brown & Son Incorporated........ E 704 636-5131
Salisbury *(G-11134)*

3823 Process control instruments

▲ AC Corporation.................. B 336 273-4472
Greensboro *(G-5339)*

Acucal Inc......................... G 252 337-9975
Elizabeth City *(G-4377)*

Areva.............................. G 704 805-2935
Huntersville *(G-6967)*

Armtec Esterline Corp............... F 910 814-3029
Lillington *(G-7788)*

Asco LP............................ G 919 460-5200
Cary *(G-1297)*

ATI Industrial Automation Inc.......... D 919 772-0115
Apex *(G-141)*

B G V Inc.......................... G 704 588-3047
Pineville *(G-9714)*

Barcovision LLC.................... G 704 392-9371
Charlotte *(G-1750)*

Bergman Enterprises Inc............. E 252 335-7294
Elizabeth City *(G-4379)*

Bluetick Inc....................... F 336 294-4102
Greensboro *(G-5395)*

Centice Corporation................ F 919 653-0424
Raleigh *(G-9991)*

Cordex Instruments Inc.............. G 877 836-0764
Charlotte *(G-1984)*

Czechmate Enterprises LLC.......... G 704 784-6547
Concord *(G-3351)*

Dana Industries.................... G 919 496-3262
Louisburg *(G-7913)*

Delta Msrment Cmbstn Cntrls LL...... E 919 623-7133
Cary *(G-1344)*

Electrical Panel & Contrls Inc......... G 336 434-4445
High Point *(G-6605)*

◆ Emco Wheaton Retail Corp................D 252 243-0150
Wilson *(G-12987)*

Emerson Electric Co................. G 704 480-8519
Shelby *(G-11335)*

Emerson Prcess MGT Pwr Wtr Slt..... F 704 357-0294
Charlotte *(G-2110)*

Eng Solutions Inc................... E 919 831-1830
Chapel Hill *(G-1545)*

▲ Eno Scientific LLC................ G 910 778-2660
Hillsborough *(G-6865)*

◆ Fairchild Industrial Pdts Co.......... D 336 659-3400
Winston Salem *(G-13164)*

Gerald Hartsoe..................... G 336 498-3233
Randleman *(G-10648)*

◆ Global Sensors LLC................G 704 827-4331
Belmont *(G-754)*

Grover Gaming Inc.................. D 252 329-7900
Greenville *(G-5985)*

Hoffer Calibration Svcs LLC.......... G 252 338-6379
Elizabeth City *(G-4391)*

▼ Hoffer Flow Controls Inc........... D 252 331-1997
Elizabeth City *(G-4392)*

▲ JMS Southeast Inc................ E 704 873-1835
Statesville *(G-11719)*

Kdy Automation Solutions Inc......... G 888 219-0049
Morrisville *(G-8996)*

▲ Liburdi Turbine Services LLC........ F 704 230-2510
Mooresville *(G-8712)*

Linor Technology Inc................ F 336 485-6199
Winston Salem *(G-13235)*

▲ Mac Panel Company LLC........... E 336 861-3100
High Point *(G-6694)*

MTS Systems Corporation............ C 919 677-2352
Cary *(G-1403)*

▲ Multi Technical Services Inc......... G 919 553-2995
Clayton *(G-3161)*

Nexjen Systems LLC................ G 704 969-7070
Charlotte *(G-2561)*

Oryx Systems Inc................... G 704 519-8803
Indian Trail *(G-7094)*

▲ Palmer Instruments Inc............ E 828 658-3131
Asheville *(G-565)*

▲ Palmer Wahl Instruments Inc........ E 828 658-3131
Asheville *(G-566)*

Park Court Properties RE Inc.......... F 919 304-3110
Mebane *(G-8255)*

Progressive Intl Elec Inc............. G 919 266-4442
Knightdale *(G-7456)*

QMAX Industries LLC................ G 704 643-7299
Charlotte *(G-2679)*

▲ Robert H Wager Company Inc........ F 336 969-6909
Rural Hall *(G-10966)*

Rotork-Fairchild Indus Pdts Co........ F 336 659-3400
Winston Salem *(G-13323)*

Sapphire Tchncal Solutions LLC........ G 704 561-3100
Pineville *(G-9754)*

Sgl Carbon LLC.................... G 828 437-3221
Morganton *(G-8895)*

Signalscape Inc.................... E 919 859-4565
Cary *(G-1455)*

Solarbrook Water and Pwr Corp........ G 919 231-3205
Raleigh *(G-10492)*

Sota Vision Inc..................... E 800 807-7187
Midland *(G-8296)*

Southstern Prcess Eqp Cntrls I........ F 704 483-1141
Denver *(G-3806)*

Strandberg Engrg Labs Inc............ F 336 274-3775
Greensboro *(G-5843)*

Symbrium Inc...................... F 919 879-2470
Raleigh *(G-10525)*

Tc2 Labs LLC...................... G 919 380-2171
Raleigh *(G-10534)*

Telecommunications Tech Inc.......... G 919 556-7100
Youngsville *(G-13492)*

Temposonics LLC................... G 470 380-5103
Cary *(G-1469)*

Thermaco Incorporated.............. G 336 629-4651
Asheboro *(G-408)*

Trafag Inc......................... G 704 343-6339
Charlotte *(G-2932)*

Triad Automation Group Inc........... E 336 767-1379
Winston Salem *(G-13369)*

Triangle Microsystems Inc............ F 919 878-1880
Raleigh *(G-10558)*

▲ Troxler Electronic Labs Inc.......... D 919 549-8661
Research Triangle Pa *(G-10716)*

Vishay Precision Group Inc........... F 919 374-5555
Raleigh *(G-10591)*

Water Tech Solutions Inc............. G 704 408-8391
Mooresville *(G-8794)*

◆ Woodlane Envmtl Tech Inc..............G 828 894-8383
Columbus *(G-3305)*

3824 Fluid meters and counting devices

Danaher Indus Sensors Contrls.......... G 910 862-5426
Elizabethtown *(G-4424)*

▲ Dynapar Corporation.............. C 800 873-8731
Elizabethtown *(G-4426)*

◆ Elster American Meter Company LLCF 402 873-8200
Charlotte *(G-2104)*

▲ Measurement Controls Inc........... F 704 921-1101
Charlotte *(G-2484)*

▲ Mueller Systems LLC.............. C 704 278-2221
Cleveland *(G-3216)*

Nichols Spdmtr & Instr Co Inc......... G 336 273-2881
Greensboro *(G-5709)*

Romac Industries Inc................ D 704 915-3317
Dallas *(G-3688)*

Sensus............................ E 919 376-2617
Cary *(G-1451)*

Sensus USA Inc.................... C 919 879-3200
Morrisville *(G-9050)*

Sensus USA Inc.................... C 919 576-6185
Morrisville *(G-9052)*

◆ Sensus USA Inc...................E 919 845-4000
Morrisville *(G-9051)*

Triangle Microsystems Inc............ F 919 878-1880
Raleigh *(G-10558)*

Utility Metering Solutions Inc.......... G 910 270-2885
Hampstead *(G-6079)*

Vontier Corporation................. C 984 275-6000
Raleigh *(G-10594)*

3825 Instruments to measure electricity

Acterna LLC....................... F 919 388-5100
Morrisville *(G-8918)*

◆ Arris Technology Inc...............D 828 324-2200
Claremont *(G-3089)*

Breezeplay LLC.................... F 980 297-0885
Charlotte *(G-1808)*

C O Jelliff Corporation.............. G 828 428-3672
Maiden *(G-8008)*

Clairvoyant Technology Inc........... G 919 491-5062
Durham *(G-3976)*

Comtech Group Inc.................. G 919 313-4800
Durham *(G-3986)*

Controls Instrumentation Inc.......... F 704 786-1700
Concord *(G-3344)*

Delta Msrment Cmbstn Cntrls LL...... E 919 623-7133
Cary *(G-1344)*

Educated Design & Develop........... E 919 469-9434
Cary *(G-1351)*

Elster Solutions LLC................ B 919 212-4819
Raleigh *(G-10083)*

◆ Elster Solutions LLC...................B 919 212-4800
Raleigh *(G-10084)*

▲ Emrise Corporation.....................C 408 200-3040
Durham *(G-4023)*

Firstmark Aerospace Corp............D 919 956-4200
Creedmoor *(G-3648)*

▲ Grecon Inc..................................F 503 641-7731
Charlotte *(G-2237)*

Hvte Inc.....................................G 919 274-8899
Youngsville *(G-13474)*

Ideal Precision Meter Inc.............G 919 571-2000
Raleigh *(G-10185)*

Infinity Communications LLC........E 919 797-2334
Durham *(G-4076)*

International Instrumentation.......G 919 496-4208
Bunn *(G-1014)*

Konica Mnlta Hlthcare Amrcas I.....E 919 792-6420
Garner *(G-4935)*

Linor Technology Inc...................F 336 485-6199
Winston Salem *(G-13235)*

Lutheran Svcs For The Aging.........G 910 457-5604
Southport *(G-11523)*

Minipro LLC................................G 844 517-4776
Chapel Hill *(G-1558)*

MTS Systems Corporation.............C 919 677-2352
Cary *(G-1403)*

▲ Multitrode Inc...........................G 561 994-8090
Charlotte *(G-2530)*

▲ Ndsl Inc...................................E 919 790-7877
Durham *(G-4144)*

Network Integrity Systems Inc.......G 828 322-2181
Hickory *(G-6400)*

Nexjen Systems LLC.....................E 704 969-7070
Charlotte *(G-2561)*

Northline Nc LLC.........................G 336 283-4811
Rural Hall *(G-10965)*

▲ Palmer Instruments Inc.............E 828 658-3131
Asheville *(G-565)*

Qorvo Inc...................................A 336 664-1233
Greensboro *(G-5773)*

Radon Control Inc........................G 828 265-9534
Boone *(G-940)*

Renewble Enrgy Intgrtion Group....G 704 596-6186
Charlotte *(G-2710)*

RNS International Inc....................E 704 329-0444
Charlotte *(G-2728)*

◆ Southern Elc & Automtn Corp.......F 919 718-0122
Sanford *(G-11235)*

▲ Tekelec Inc...............................C
Morrisville *(G-9065)*

Tekelec Global Inc.......................A 919 460-5500
Morrisville *(G-9066)*

Tektronix Inc..............................G 704 527-5000
Charlotte *(G-2907)*

Tektronix Inc..............................G 919 233-9490
Raleigh *(G-10538)*

▲ Todaytec LLC............................E 704 790-2440
Charlotte *(G-2926)*

▲ Troxler Electronic Labs Inc.........G 919 549-8661
Research Triangle Pa *(G-10716)*

◆ TTI Floor Care North Amer Inc......B 888 321-1134
Charlotte *(G-2951)*

Viztek LLC..................................E 919 792-6420
Garner *(G-4971)*

3826 Analytical instruments

Apex Waves LLC...........................G 919 809-5227
Cary *(G-1292)*

Biofluidica Inc............................G 858 535-6493
Cary *(G-1306)*

▲ Biomerieux Inc.........................B 919 620-2000
Durham *(G-3930)*

Bmg Labtech Inc..........................F 919 678-1633
Cary *(G-1313)*

Camag Scientific Inc....................G 910 343-1830
Wilmington *(G-12727)*

◆ Carolina Biological Supply Company.C 336 584-0381
Burlington *(G-1060)*

◆ Cem Corporation.......................C 704 821-7015
Matthews *(G-8162)*

Cem Holdings Corporation............E 704 821-7015
Matthews *(G-8163)*

Centice Corporation.....................F 919 653-0424
Raleigh *(G-9991)*

Cooke Companies Intl...................F 919 968-0848
Chapel Hill *(G-1540)*

DOE & Ingalls Investors Inc..........E 919 598-1986
Durham *(G-4003)*

DOE & Ingalls Management LLC......F 919 598-1986
Durham *(G-4004)*

▲ DOE & Inglls Nrth Crlina Opti......E 919 282-1792
Durham *(G-4005)*

Environmental Specialties LLC.......D 919 829-9300
Raleigh *(G-10088)*

▲ Environmental Supply Co Inc........F 919 956-9688
Durham *(G-4027)*

Fisher Scientific Company LLC.......D 800 252-7100
Asheville *(G-498)*

Green Stream Technologies Inc......G 844 499-8880
Wake Forest *(G-12280)*

Hamilton.....................................N 704 896-1427
Davidson *(G-3706)*

Horiba Instruments Inc.................F 828 676-2801
Fletcher *(G-4742)*

Htx Technologies LLC....................F 919 928-5688
Carrboro *(G-1269)*

Institute For Resch Biotecnoly.......G 252 689-2205
Greenville *(G-5991)*

Microsolv Technology Corp............F 720 949-1302
Leland *(G-7555)*

Parata Systems LLC......................C 888 727-2821
Durham *(G-4165)*

Phitonex Inc...............................G 855 874-4866
Durham *(G-4177)*

Pine RES Instrumentation Inc.........F 919 782-8320
Durham *(G-4183)*

Practichem LLC............................G 919 714-8430
Morrisville *(G-9038)*

Sapphire Tchncal Solutions LLC......G 704 561-3100
Pineville *(G-9754)*

Sciteck Diagnostics Inc................G 828 650-0409
Fletcher *(G-4765)*

Sensory Analytics LLC...................G 336 315-6090
Greensboro *(G-5808)*

Shimadzu Scientific Instrs Inc........G 919 425-1010
Durham *(G-4231)*

Staclean Diffuser Company LLC......F 704 636-8697
Salisbury *(G-11119)*

Thermo Elctron Scntfic Instrs........G 828 281-2651
Asheville *(G-615)*

Thermo Fisher Scientific Inc..........F 800 955-6288
Durham *(G-4269)*

Thermo Fisher Scientific Inc..........G 800 955-6288
High Point *(G-6806)*

Thermo Fisher Scientific Inc..........G 919 380-2000
Morrisville *(G-9070)*

Thermo Fisher Scientific Inc..........E 919 876-2352
Raleigh *(G-10545)*

Thermo Fsher Scntfic Ashvlle L........B 828 658-2711
Weaverville *(G-12505)*

▲ Thermo Fsher Scntfic Ashvlle L......B 828 658-2711
Asheville *(G-616)*

Trajan Inc..................................G 919 435-1105
Raleigh *(G-10556)*

▼ Warren Oil Company LLC.............D 910 892-6456
Dunn *(G-3871)*

Waters Corporation......................G 910 270-3137
Hampstead *(G-6080)*

Zysense LLC................................G 215 485-1955
Chapel Hill *(G-1599)*

3827 Optical instruments and lenses

Advanced Photonic Crystals LLC......G 803 547-0881
Cornelius *(G-3583)*

ARW Optical Corp.........................G 910 452-7373
Wilmington *(G-12710)*

C M M..G 919 619-1716
Chapel Hill *(G-1532)*

Corning Incorporated...................D 910 784-7200
Wilmington *(G-12753)*

Imagineoptix Corporation.............F 919 757-4945
Durham *(G-4072)*

Klearoptics Inc............................G 760 224-6770
Lattimore *(G-7480)*

Leica Microsystems Nc Inc.............F 919 428-9661
Durham *(G-4103)*

Lightform....................................G 908 281-9098
Asheville *(G-535)*

M3 Products Com.........................G 631 938-1245
Matthews *(G-8180)*

New Vision Investments Inc...........G 336 757-1120
Winston Salem *(G-13264)*

Optics Inc...................................G 336 288-9504
Greensboro *(G-5726)*

Optics Inc...................................G 336 884-5677
High Point *(G-6721)*

▲ Opto Alignment Technology Inc.....E 704 893-0399
Indian Trail *(G-7093)*

▲ Rk Enterprises LLC....................G 910 481-0777
Fayetteville *(G-4663)*

Roger D Thomas...........................G 919 258-3148
Sanford *(G-11226)*

US Optics....................................G 828 874-2242
Connelly Springs *(G-3484)*

3829 Measuring and controlling devices, nec

▲ Accusport International Inc..........E 336 759-3300
Winston Salem *(G-13071)*

▲ Apex Instruments Incorporated.....E 919 557-7300
Fuquay Varina *(G-4865)*

Applied Roller Technology Inc........F 704 598-9500
Charlotte *(G-1687)*

Biomerieux Inc............................G 800 682-2666
Raleigh *(G-9946)*

▲ Biotage LLC.............................D 704 654-4900
Charlotte *(G-1785)*

◆ Boon Edam Inc..........................E 910 814-3800
Raleigh *(G-9955)*

C W Lawley Incorporated..............G 919 467-7782
Cary *(G-1318)*

◆ Canvas Sx LLC...........................C 980 474-3700
Charlotte *(G-1836)*

◆ Carolina Biological Supply Company.C 336 584-0381
Burlington *(G-1060)*

Carolina Lasers............................G 919 872-8001
Raleigh *(G-9977)*

Ceast USA Inc..............................G 704 423-0081
Charlotte *(G-1880)*

Cherokee Instruments Inc..............F 919 552-0554
Angier *(G-117)*

Circor Pumps North America LLC......D 704 289-6511
Monroe *(G-8459)*

Desco Industries Inc.....................E 919 718-0000
Sanford *(G-11169)*

Direct Diagnostic Services LLC........F 843 708-3891
Morganton *(G-8860)*

Dynisco Instruments LLC....................... E 828 326-9888
Hickory (G-6325)

Educated Design & Develop................... E 919 469-9434
Cary (G-1351)

▲ Efco USA Inc....................................... G 800 332-6872
Charlotte (G-2092)

Elsag North America LLC....................... E 336 379-7135
Greensboro (G-5517)

▲ Field Controls LLC............................... D 252 208-7300
Kinston (G-7413)

Fisher Scientific Company LLC.............. D 800 252-7100
Asheville (G-498)

Froehling & Robertson Inc.................... E 804 264-2701
Raleigh (G-10120)

General Electric Company...................... F 704 821-8260
Indian Trail (G-7082)

Geosonics Inc....................................... G 919 790-9500
Raleigh (G-10130)

Hemosonics LLC.................................... F 800 280-5589
Durham (G-4060)

Hemosonics LLC.................................... E 800 280-5589
Durham (G-4061)

▲ IMO Industries Inc............................... D 301 323-9000
Monroe (G-8503)

Inotec AMD Inc..................................... G 888 354-9772
Hickory (G-6370)

▲ James Tool Machine & Engrg Inc........ C 828 584-8722
Morganton (G-8875)

▲ JMS Southeast Inc............................... E 704 873-1835
Statesville (G-11719)

K & M Products of NC Inc..................... G 828 524-5905
Franklin (G-4832)

Lord Corporation................................... G 877 275-5673
Cary (G-1396)

Los Vientos Windpower Ib LLC............. G 704 594-6200
Charlotte (G-2435)

Mallinckrodt LLC.................................... G 919 878-2900
Raleigh (G-10269)

▲ Micro Epsilon Amer Ltd Partnr............ G 919 787-9707
Raleigh (G-10299)

Milwaukee Instruments Inc................... G 252 443-3630
Rocky Mount (G-10853)

Orpak Usa Inc....................................... F 201 441-9820
Greensboro (G-5727)

Pace Scientific Inc................................ G 704 799-0688
Boone (G-937)

▲ Palmer Instruments Inc....................... E 828 658-3131
Asheville (G-565)

▲ Pretoria Transit Interiors Inc............... D 615 867-8515
Charlotte (G-2664)

Qualitrol Company LLC.......................... G 704 587-9267
Charlotte (G-2683)

Revware Inc... G 919 790-0000
Raleigh (G-10442)

RG Convergence Tech LLC.................... G 336 953-2796
Burlington (G-1146)

RNS International Inc............................. E 704 329-0444
Charlotte (G-2728)

Roehrig Engineering Inc........................ G 336 956-3800
Greensboro (G-5793)

Russ Simmons....................................... G 910 686-1656
Wilmington (G-12906)

Sapphire Tchncal Solutions LLC........... G 704 561-3100
Pineville (G-9754)

Spencer Health Solutions Inc............... E 866 971-8564
Morrisville (G-9058)

SPX Technologies Inc............................ D 980 474-3700
Charlotte (G-2851)

Tcom Limited Partnership..................... B 252 330-5555
Elizabeth City (G-4413)

▲ Thermo Fsher Scntfic Ashvlle L........ B 828 658-2711
Asheville (G-616)

Trafag Inc.. G 704 343-6339
Charlotte (G-2932)

▲ Troxler Electronic Labs Inc................. D 919 549-8661
Research Triangle Pa (G-10716)

Usat LLC.. E 919 942-4214
Chapel Hill (G-1587)

Vinatoru Enterprises Inc....................... G 336 227-4300
Graham (G-5289)

◆ Vishay Measurements Group Inc........ G 919 365-3800
Wendell (G-12552)

Wiser Systems Inc................................. F 919 551-5566
Raleigh (G-10611)

3841 Surgical and medical instruments

3M Company.. G 704 588-4782
Charlotte (G-1601)

623 Medical LLC.................................... F 877 455-0112
Morrisville (G-8913)

Accumed Corp....................................... D 800 278-6796
Raleigh (G-9874)

Acme United Corporation...................... E 252 822-5051
Rocky Mount (G-10807)

▲ Acw Technology Inc............................. A
Raleigh (G-9877)

Adhezion Biomedical LLC..................... G 828 728-6116
Hudson (G-6940)

Alcon.. G 919 624-5868
Raleigh (G-9889)

Aldagen Inc... F 919 484-2571
Durham (G-3888)

Alveolus Inc.. E 704 921-2215
Charlotte (G-1659)

American Labor Inc............................... G 919 286-0726
Durham (G-3891)

Andersen Energy Inc............................. G 336 376-0107
Haw River (G-6129)

▼ Andersen Products Inc......................... G 336 376-3000
Haw River (G-6130)

Andersen Sterilizers Inc....................... E 336 376-8622
Haw River (G-6131)

Angstrom Medica Inc............................ F 781 933-6121
Greenville (G-5936)

Applied Catheter Tech Inc.................... G 336 817-1005
Winston Salem (G-13087)

Arcus Medical LLC................................ G 704 332-3424
Charlotte (G-1693)

Ascepi Medical Group LLC................... G 919 336-4246
Raleigh (G-9918)

▲ AVIOQ Inc.. F 919 314-5535
Durham (G-3909)

Bariatric Partners Inc........................... G 704 542-2256
Charlotte (G-1752)

Becton Dickinson and Company........... B 201 847-6800
Durham (G-3922)

Becton Dickinson and Company........... E 919 963-1307
Four Oaks (G-4808)

Biogeniv Inc.. G 828 850-1007
Lenoir (G-7586)

Biomedinnovations Inc......................... G 704 489-1290
Denver (G-3775)

▲ Biomerieux Inc.................................... B 919 620-2000
Durham (G-3930)

Bioventus Inc.. D 919 474-6700
Durham (G-3932)

Birth Tissue Recovery LLC................... E 336 448-1910
Winston Salem (G-13106)

Brandel LLC.. G 704 525-4548
Charlotte (G-1806)

▲ Cancer Diagnostics Inc....................... E 877 846-5393
Durham (G-3957)

Carefusion 303 Inc............................... G 919 528-5253
Creedmoor (G-3643)

◆ Carolina Lquid Chmistries Corp......... E 336 722-8910
Greensboro (G-5429)

Carolina Precision Tech LLC................. E 215 675-4590
Mooresville (G-8633)

◆ Charter Medical LLC........................... D 336 768-6447
Winston Salem (G-13123)

Colowrap LLC.. F 888 815-3376
Durham (G-3983)

Contego Medical Inc............................. E 919 606-3917
Raleigh (G-10012)

Convatec Inc.. G 336 297-3021
Greensboro (G-5464)

Convatec Inc.. C 336 855-5500
Greensboro (G-5465)

Cook Group Inc..................................... G 336 744-0157
Winston Salem (G-13129)

Cook Incorporated................................ A 336 744-0157
Winston Salem (G-13130)

Core Sound Imaging Inc....................... E 919 277-0636
Raleigh (G-10016)

Corning Incorporated............................ C 919 620-6200
Durham (G-3988)

Covidien Holding Inc............................ C 919 878-2930
Raleigh (G-10018)

Custom Assemblies Inc......................... E 919 202-4533
Pine Level (G-9678)

D R Burton Healthcare LLC.................. F 252 228-7038
Farmville (G-4526)

Desco Industries Inc............................ F 919 718-0000
Sanford (G-11170)

Diamond Orthopedic LLC...................... G 704 585-8258
Gastonia (G-5042)

Elite Metal Performance LLC................ F 704 660-0006
Statesville (G-11694)

Emitbio Inc... G 919 321-1726
Morrisville (G-8971)

Eye Glass Lady LLC.............................. F 828 669-2154
Black Mountain (G-864)

Genco.. G 919 963-4227
Four Oaks (G-4811)

Gilero LLC... B 919 595-8220
Durham (G-4047)

◆ Greiner Bio-One North Amer Inc......... B 704 261-7800
Monroe (G-8496)

Health Supply Us LLC........................... F 888 408-1694
Mooresville (G-8680)

Healthlink Europe.................................. F 919 368-2187
Raleigh (G-10158)

Healthlink Europe.................................. F 919 783-4142
Raleigh (G-10159)

Healthlink International Inc................... G 877 324-2837
Raleigh (G-10160)

Horizon Vision Research Inc................. G 910 796-8600
Wilmington (G-12808)

Hyperbranch Medical Tech Inc............. F 919 433-3325
Durham (G-4067)

Ickler Manufacturing LLC...................... G 704 658-1195
Mooresville (G-8690)

Innavasc Medical Inc............................ F 813 902-2228
Durham (G-4079)

Intelligent Endoscopy LLC.................... E 336 608-4375
Clemmons (G-3192)

Intuitive Surgical Inc............................ G 408 523-2100
Durham (G-4081)

Jaguar Gene Therapy LLC..................... F 919 465-6400
Cary (G-1377)

Janus Development Group Inc.............. G 252 551-9042
Greenville (G-5994)

Karamedica Inc...................................... G 919 302-1325
Raleigh (G-10230)

Kashif Mazhar....................................... G 919 314-2891
Durham (G-4092)

▲ Kyocera Precision Tools Inc............ G 800 823-7284
Fletcher *(G-4745)*

Liebel-Flarsheim Company LLC............ C 919 878-2930
Raleigh *(G-10255)*

Logiksavvy Solutions LLC.................. G 336 392-6149
Greensboro *(G-5663)*

Lucerno Dynamics LLC.................... G 317 294-1395
Cary *(G-1398)*

Luxor Hydration LLC...................... F 919 568-5047
Durham *(G-4113)*

Mallinckrodt LLC.......................... G 919 878-2900
Raleigh *(G-10269)*

Martin Manufacturing Co LLC............. G 919 741-5439
Rocky Mount *(G-10850)*

Maximum Asp............................. G 919 544-7900
Morrisville *(G-9019)*

Med Express/Medical Spc Inc............ F 919 572-2568
Durham *(G-4123)*

Medcor Inc................................ G 888 579-1050
Lexington *(G-7718)*

◆ Medi Mall Inc........................... G 877 501-6334
Fletcher *(G-4753)*

Medical Engineering Labs................ G 704 487-0166
Shelby *(G-11361)*

Micell Technologies Inc.................. E 919 313-2102
Durham *(G-4132)*

▲ Misonix Opco Inc....................... F 631 694-9555
Durham *(G-4137)*

Mission Srgcal Innovations LLC.......... G 678 699-6057
Raleigh *(G-10310)*

MTI Medical Cables LLC.................. G 828 890-2888
Fletcher *(G-4758)*

Multigen Diagnostics LLC................ G 336 510-1120
Greensboro *(G-5700)*

Murray Inc................................ E 704 329-0400
Charlotte *(G-2534)*

Murray Inc................................ E 847 620-7990
Charlotte *(G-2535)*

Ncontact Surgical LLC.................... F
Morrisville *(G-9022)*

Next Safety Inc........................... F 336 246-7700
Jefferson *(G-7192)*

Nocturnal Product Dev LLC............... G 919 321-1331
Durham *(G-4149)*

Nuvasive Inc.............................. G 336 430-3169
Greensboro *(G-5716)*

Odin Technologies LLC................... G 408 309-1925
Charlotte *(G-2591)*

Optopol Usa Inc.......................... G 833 678-6765
Raleigh *(G-10347)*

Oyster Merger Sub II LLC................ G 919 474-6700
Durham *(G-4162)*

▲ Parker Medical Associates LLC....... F 704 344-9998
Charlotte *(G-2611)*

▲ Pattons Medical LLC................... E 704 529-5442
Charlotte *(G-2617)*

▲ Pelton & Crane Company.............. B 704 588-2126
Charlotte *(G-2623)*

Perfusio Corp............................. G 252 656-0404
Greenville *(G-6014)*

Perseus Intermediate Inc................ E 919 474-6700
Durham *(G-4174)*

Photonicare Inc........................... E 866 411-3277
Durham *(G-4179)*

Pioneer Srgcal Orthblogics Inc.......... F 252 355-4405
Greenville *(G-6015)*

Plexus Corp............................... D 919 807-8000
Raleigh *(G-10373)*

Polyzen LLC............................... D 919 319-9599
Apex *(G-186)*

Polyzen Inc............................... G 919 319-9599
Cary *(G-1423)*

Rdd Pharma Inc........................... G 302 319-9970
Raleigh *(G-10433)*

React Innovations LLC.................... G 704 773-1276
Charlotte *(G-2694)*

Retrofix Screws LLC...................... G 980 432-8412
Salisbury *(G-11111)*

Retroject Inc.............................. G 919 619-3042
Chapel Hill *(G-1567)*

Rm Liquidation Inc........................ D 828 274-7996
Asheville *(G-591)*

▲ Robling Medical LLC................... D 919 570-9605
Youngsville *(G-13482)*

Safeguard Medical........................ D 855 428-6074
Huntersville *(G-7051)*

Salem Professional Anesthesia.......... G 336 998-3396
Advance *(G-38)*

Scinovia Corp............................. F 703 957-0396
Raleigh *(G-10463)*

Sfp Research Inc.......................... G 336 622-5266
Liberty *(G-7779)*

Sicel Technologies Inc.................... E 919 465-2236
Morrisville *(G-9054)*

Sonablate Corp............................ E 888 874-4384
Charlotte *(G-2826)*

Staclear Inc............................... G 919 838-2844
Raleigh *(G-10502)*

Statesville Med MGT Svcs LLC........... G 704 996-6748
Statesville *(G-11780)*

Strong Medical Partners LLC............. D 716 507-4476
Pineville *(G-9760)*

Strong Medical Partners LLC............. E 716 626-9400
Pineville *(G-9759)*

Stryker Corp.............................. G 919 455-6755
Raleigh *(G-10516)*

Stryker Corporation....................... F 919 433-3325
Durham *(G-4253)*

▼ Suntech Medical Inc................... D 919 654-2300
Morrisville *(G-9060)*

Surgilum LLC............................. G 910 202-2202
Wilmington *(G-12934)*

Teleflex Incorporated..................... G 919 433-2575
Durham *(G-4261)*

Teleflex Incorporated..................... E 919 544-8000
Morrisville *(G-9067)*

Teleflex Medical Incorporated............ G 336 498-4153
Asheboro *(G-407)*

Teleflex Medical Incorporated............ G 919 544-8000
Durham *(G-4263)*

◆ Teleflex Medical Incorporated........ D 919 544-8000
Morrisville *(G-9068)*

◆ Touchamerica Inc...................... G 919 732-6968
Hillsborough *(G-6879)*

▲ Transenterix Surgical Inc.............. D 919 765-8400
Durham *(G-4276)*

Traumtic Drect Trnsfsion Dvcs........... G 423 364-5828
Apex *(G-199)*

Trimed LLC............................... G 919 615-2784
Raleigh *(G-10564)*

◆ Tripath Imaging Inc.................... D 336 222-9707
Burlington *(G-1170)*

Tryton Medical Inc........................ G 919 226-1490
Raleigh *(G-10568)*

Valencell Inc.............................. G 919 747-3668
Raleigh *(G-10581)*

▲ Vasonova Inc........................... F 650 327-1412
Morrisville *(G-9084)*

Visitech Systems Inc..................... G 919 387-0524
Apex *(G-204)*

Webster Entps Jackson Cnty Inc......... G 828 586-8981
Sylva *(G-11904)*

Weslacova Corp........................... G 336 838-2614
North Wilkesboro *(G-9552)*

Wilson-Cook Medical Inc.................. G 336 744-0157
Winston Salem *(G-13395)*

Wilson-Cook Medical Inc.................. B 336 744-0157
Winston Salem *(G-13396)*

▲ Wnyh LLC............................... C 716 853-1800
Mocksville *(G-8396)*

Yukon Medical LLC....................... G 919 595-8250
Durham *(G-4317)*

Zoes Kitchen Inc.......................... E 336 748-0587
Winston Salem *(G-13412)*

3842 Surgical appliances and supplies

410 Medical Inc........................... F 919 241-7900
Durham *(G-3872)*

Ability Orthopedics....................... G 704 630-6789
Salisbury *(G-11011)*

Adaptive Technologies LLC............... G 919 231-6890
Raleigh *(G-9878)*

Advanced Brace & Limb Inc.............. G 910 483-5737
Fayetteville *(G-4543)*

Albemrle Orthotics Prosthetics........... E 252 338-3002
Elizabeth City *(G-4378)*

Albemrle Orthotics Prosthetics........... G 252 332-4334
Ahoskie *(G-41)*

All 4 U Home Medical LLC................ G 828 437-0684
Morganton *(G-8849)*

Allyn International Trdg Corp.............. G 877 858-2482
Marshville *(G-8085)*

Alternative Care Group LLC............... G 336 499-5644
Kernersville *(G-7241)*

▲ Ambra Le Roy LLC..................... G 704 392-7080
Charlotte *(G-1662)*

▲ American Fiber & Finishing Inc........ E 704 984-9256
Albemarle *(G-61)*

▲ Amtai Medical Equipment Inc.......... F 919 872-1803
Raleigh *(G-9901)*

▼ Andersen Products Inc................. E 336 376-3000
Haw River *(G-6130)*

Andersen Sterilizers Inc.................. E 336 376-8622
Haw River *(G-6131)*

Arma Co LLC.............................. G 717 295-6805
Wilmington *(G-12709)*

▲ Astral Buoyancy Company............. G 828 255-2638
Asheville *(G-445)*

Atlantic Prosthetics Orthtcs............... G 919 806-3260
Durham *(G-3903)*

Bar Squared Inc.......................... F 919 878-0578
Raleigh *(G-9931)*

▲ Beocare Inc............................. C 828 728-7300
Hudson *(G-6942)*

Bio-Tech Prsthtics Orthtics In............ G 336 768-3666
Winston Salem *(G-13105)*

Bio-Tech Prsthtics Orthtics In............ G 336 333-9081
Greensboro *(G-5390)*

Biomedical Innovations Inc............... G 910 603-0267
Southern Pines *(G-11495)*

Biotech Prsthtics Orthtics Drh............ G 919 471-4994
Durham *(G-3931)*

◆ BSN Medical Inc........................ C 704 554-9933
Charlotte *(G-1815)*

Cape Fear Orthtics Prsthtics I............ G 910 483-0933
Fayetteville *(G-4566)*

▲ Carolon Company....................... D 336 969-6001
Rural Hall *(G-10954)*

Caromed International Inc................. G 919 878-0578
Raleigh *(G-9981)*

▲ Cathtek LLC............................. G 336 748-0686
Winston Salem *(G-13120)*

Center For Orthotic & Prosthet........... D 919 585-4173
Clayton *(G-3139)*

Center For Orthtic Prsthtic CA............ E 919 797-1230
Durham *(G-3967)*

Coastal Machine & Welding Inc .... G 910 754-6476
Shallotte (G-11302)

◆ Comfortland International LLC .... F 866 277-3135
Mebane (G-8236)

Cranial Technologies Inc .... G 336 760-5530
Winston Salem (G-13134)

Creative Prosthetics and Ortho .... G 828 994-4808
Conover (G-3510)

▼ Custom Medical Specialties Inc .... G 919 202-8462
Pine Level (G-9679)

Custom Rehabilitation Spc Inc .... G 910 471-2962
Wilmington (G-12758)

Delaby Brace and Limb Co .... G 910 484-2509
Fayetteville (G-4587)

East Carolina Brace Limb Inc .... G 252 726-8068
Morehead City (G-8831)

◆ Elastic Therapy LLC .... E 336 625-0529
Asheboro (G-350)

Ethicon Inc .... G 919 234-2124
Cary (G-1356)

Faith Prsthtc-Rthotic Svcs Inc .... F 704 782-0908
Concord (G-3361)

Fillauer North Carolina Inc .... E 828 658-8330
Weaverville (G-12491)

Fla Orthopedics Inc .... D 800 327-4110
Charlotte (G-2158)

Floyd S Braces and Limbs Inc .... G 910 763-0821
Wilmington (G-12778)

▲ Gloves-Online Inc .... G 919 468-4244
Cary (G-1367)

Greene Mountain Outdoors LLC .... F 336 670-2186
North Wilkesboro (G-9532)

Guilford Orthtic Prothetic Inc .... G 336 676-5394
Greensboro (G-5584)

◆ Haywood Vctnal Opprtnities Inc .... B 828 454-9682
Waynesville (G-12461)

Health Supply Us LLC .... F 888 408-1694
Mooresville (G-8680)

Hollister Incorporated .... G 919 792-2095
Raleigh (G-10172)

Hyperbranch Medical Tech Inc .... F 919 433-3325
Durham (G-4067)

▲ Ing Source LLC .... F 828 855-0481
Hickory (G-6369)

Ingle Protective Systems Inc .... G 704 788-3327
Concord (G-3377)

Ipas .... C 919 967-7052
Durham (G-4082)

Jackson Products Inc .... F 704 598-4949
Wake Forest (G-12283)

Jhrg Manufacturing LLC .... G 252 478-4977
Spring Hope (G-11556)

◆ Kaye Products Inc .... E 919 732-6444
Hillsborough (G-6869)

◆ Kayser-Roth Corporation .... C 336 852-2030
Greensboro (G-5643)

Lifespan Incorporated .... D 336 838-2614
North Wilkesboro (G-9541)

Lifespan Incorporated .... E 704 944-5100
Charlotte (G-2419)

Medi Manufacturing Inc .... E 336 449-4440
Whitsett (G-12615)

◆ Medical Action Industries Inc .... D 631 404-3700
Arden (G-284)

Medical Device Bus Svcs Inc .... F 704 423-0033
Charlotte (G-2485)

Medical Spclties of Crlnas Inc .... G 910 575-4542
Sunset Beach (G-11851)

Medical Specialties Inc .... G 704 694-2434
Wadesboro (G-12249)

Medtrnic Sofamor Danek USA Inc .... G 919 457-9982
Cary (G-1401)

Michael H Branch Inc .... G 252 532-0930
Gaston (G-4979)

Mign Inc .... G 609 304-1617
Charlotte (G-2500)

Ms Whlchair N CA AM State Coor .... G 828 230-1129
Weaverville (G-12497)

MSA Safety Sales LLC .... D 910 353-1540
Jacksonville (G-7133)

North Crlina Orthtics Prsthtic .... E 919 210-0906
Wake Forest (G-12287)

Novex Innovations LLC .... G 336 231-6693
Winston Salem (G-13267)

Nufabrx LLC .... G 888 683-2279
Charlotte (G-2589)

Orthopedic Appliance Company .... D 828 254-6305
Asheville (G-562)

Orthopedic Appliance Company .... G 828 348-1960
Hickory (G-6407)

Orthopedic Services .... G 336 716-3349
Winston Salem (G-13273)

Orthorx Inc .... G 919 929-5550
Chapel Hill (G-1562)

▲ Paceline Inc .... D 704 290-5007
Matthews (G-8140)

▲ Pacon Manufacturing Co LLC .... C 910 239-3001
Leland (G-7556)

▲ Precept Medical Products Inc .... F 828 681-0209
Arden (G-298)

Premier Body Armor LLC .... F 704 750-3118
Gastonia (G-5127)

▲ Project Bean LLC .... D 201 438-1598
Huntersville (G-7040)

Prophysics Innovations Inc .... G 919 245-0406
Cary (G-1431)

▲ Protection Products Inc .... E 828 324-2173
Hickory (G-6420)

▲ R82 Inc .... E 704 882-0668
Matthews (G-8143)

Random Rues Botanical LLC .... G 252 214-2759
Greenville (G-6017)

Royal Baths Manufacturing Co .... E 704 837-1701
Charlotte (G-2733)

Safe Home Pro Inc .... F 704 662-2299
Cornelius (G-3626)

▲ Safewaze LLC .... D 704 262-7893
Concord (G-3438)

▲ Scivolutions Inc .... G 704 853-0100
Kings Mountain (G-7384)

Skyland Prsthtics Orthtics Inc .... E 828 684-1644
Fletcher (G-4769)

Soundside Orthtics Prsthtics L .... G 910 238-2026
Jacksonville (G-7149)

▲ Spenco Medical Corporation .... E 919 544-7900
Durham (G-4247)

Spintech LLC .... E 704 885-4758
Statesville (G-11775)

Structure Medical LLC .... D 704 799-3450
Mooresville (G-8780)

Structure Medical LLC .... D 256 461-0900
Mooresville (G-8781)

Stryker Corporation .... F 919 433-3325
Durham (G-4253)

Suits Usa Inc .... G 336 786-8808
Mount Airy (G-9180)

Sunshine Prosthetics Inc .... G 833 266-9781
Wilson (G-13032)

Surgical Center of Morehea .... E 252 247-0314
Morehead City (G-8846)

Taiji Medical Supplies Inc .... G 888 667-6658
Lincolnton (G-7859)

Teleflex Incorporated .... G 919 433-2575
Durham (G-4261)

Teleflex Incorporated .... G 919 433-2575
Durham (G-4262)

Test ME Out Inc .... G 252 635-6770
New Bern (G-9399)

The Wheelchair Place LLC .... G 828 855-9099
Hickory (G-6466)

Thuasne LLC .... C 910 557-5378
Hamlet (G-6063)

Trimed LLC .... G 919 615-2784
Raleigh (G-10564)

United Protective Tech LLC .... E 704 888-2470
Locust (G-7907)

Veon Inc .... F 252 623-2102
Washington (G-12418)

▲ VH Industries Inc .... G 704 743-2400
Concord (G-3464)

Village Ceramics Inc .... G 828 685-9491
Hendersonville (G-6247)

Walker Street LLC .... G 919 880-3959
Fuquay Varina (G-4905)

Xanderglasses Inc .... G 617 286-3012
Raleigh (G-10617)

3843 Dental equipment and supplies

◆ Amann Girrbach North Amer LP .... F 704 837-1404
Charlotte (G-1660)

Anutra Medical Inc .... E 919 648-1215
Morrisville (G-8927)

Aribex Inc .... E 866 340-5522
Charlotte (G-1697)

Bioventus Inc .... D 919 474-6700
Durham (G-3932)

▲ Cdb Corporation .... E 910 383-6464
Leland (G-7537)

▲ Cefla Dental Group America .... G 704 731-5293
Charlotte (G-1881)

Custom Smiles Inc .... F 919 331-2090
Angier (G-118)

▲ Dental Equipment LLC .... B 704 588-2126
Charlotte (G-2030)

▲ Dentonics Inc .... F 704 238-0245
Monroe (G-8476)

Dentsply North America LLC .... G 844 848-0137
Charlotte (G-2031)

◆ Dentsply Sirona Inc .... A 844 848-0137
Charlotte (G-2032)

Kavo Kerr Group .... F 704 927-0617
Charlotte (G-2389)

▲ Kyocera Precision Tools Inc .... G 800 823-7284
Fletcher (G-4745)

Nelson Rodriguez .... G 828 433-1223
Morganton (G-8884)

▲ Pelton & Crane Company .... B 704 588-2126
Charlotte (G-2623)

Preventive Technologies Inc .... G 704 684-1211
Indian Trail (G-7096)

◆ Salvin Dental Specialties LLC .... D 704 442-5400
Charlotte (G-2752)

Village Ceramics Inc .... G 828 685-9491
Hendersonville (G-6247)

Voco America Inc .... G 917 923-7698
Waxhaw (G-12448)

3844 X-ray apparatus and tubes

Digitome Corporation .... G 860 651-5560
Davidson (G-3703)

▲ Flow X Ray Corporation .... D 631 242-9729
Battleboro (G-697)

▲ Wolf X-Ray Corporation .... D 631 242-9729
Battleboro (G-710)

Xinray Systems Inc .... F 919 701-4100
Chapel Hill (G-1596)

3845 Electromedical equipment

Albemrle Orthotics Prosthetics............ G..... 252 332-4334
Ahoskie *(G-41)*

Automedx LLC.. G.... 888 617-2904
Huntersville *(G-6971)*

▲ Biomerieux Inc....................................... B..... 919 620-2000
Durham *(G-3930)*

▲ Bioventus LLC.. D..... 800 396-4325
Durham *(G-3933)*

Combat Medical Systems LLC................ E..... 704 705-1222
Huntersville *(G-6977)*

Fernel Therapeutics Inc......................... G..... 919 614-2375
Apex *(G-155)*

Hemosonics LLC...................................... F..... 800 280-5589
Durham *(G-4060)*

Hemosonics LLC...................................... E..... 800 280-5589
Durham *(G-4061)*

Inneroptic Technology Inc..................... G..... 919 732-2090
Hillsborough *(G-6868)*

▲ Kyocera Precision Tools Inc.................. G..... 800 823-7284
Fletcher *(G-4745)*

Lumedica Inc.. G..... 919 886-1863
Durham *(G-4112)*

◆ Medi Mall Inc...G..... 877 501-6334
Fletcher *(G-4753)*

▲ Misonix Opco Inc.................................. F.... 631 694-9555
Durham *(G-4137)*

Mobius Imaging LLC............................... E..... 704 773-7652
Charlotte *(G-2513)*

Odin Technologies LLC........................... G..... 408 309-1925
Charlotte *(G-2591)*

Polarean Inc... F..... 919 206-7900
Durham *(G-4186)*

Ribometrix... G..... 919 744-9634
Durham *(G-4214)*

Size Stream LLC..................................... G..... 919 355-5708
Cary *(G-1459)*

▲ Tearscience Inc.................................... D..... 919 459-4880
Morrisville *(G-9064)*

Telephys Inc... G..... 312 625-9128
Davidson *(G-3719)*

Thomas Mendolia MD.............................. G..... 336 835-5688
Mooresville *(G-8785)*

Trackx Technology LLC.......................... F..... 888 787-2259
Hillsborough *(G-6880)*

United Mobile Imaging Inc..................... G..... 800 983-9840
Clemmons *(G-3207)*

US Prototype Inc.................................... E..... 866 239-2848
Wilmington *(G-12943)*

Vald Group Inc....................................... G..... 704 345-5145
Charlotte *(G-2970)*

Volumetrics Med Systems LLC............... G..... 800 472-0900
Durham *(G-4300)*

Vortant Technologies LLC...................... G..... 828 645-1026
Weaverville *(G-12506)*

3851 Ophthalmic goods

Chentech Corp... G..... 919 749-8765
Holly Springs *(G-6897)*

Clarity Vision of Smithfield..................... G..... 919 938-6101
Smithfield *(G-11437)*

Eye Glass Lady LLC................................ F..... 828 669-2154
Black Mountain *(G-864)*

Kroops Brands LLC................................. G..... 704 635-7963
Monroe *(G-8513)*

Luxottica of America Inc......................... G..... 910 867-0200
Fayetteville *(G-4631)*

Luxottica of America Inc......................... G..... 919 778-5692
Goldsboro *(G-5226)*

O D Eyecarecenter P A........................... G..... 252 443-7011
Rocky Mount *(G-10856)*

◆ Ocutech Inc...G..... 919 967-6460
Chapel Hill *(G-1561)*

Optical Place Inc.................................... E..... 336 274-1300
Greensboro *(G-5725)*

◆ Winstn-Slem Inds For Blind Inc...........B..... 336 759-0551
Winston Salem *(G-13398)*

3861 Photographic equipment and supplies

Above Topsail LLC................................. G..... 910 803-1759
Holly Ridge *(G-6886)*

Ahlberg Cameras Inc.............................. F..... 910 523-5876
Wilmington *(G-12693)*

Applied Technologies Group.................. G..... 618 977-9872
Cornelius *(G-3584)*

Ball Photo Supply Inc............................. G..... 828 252-2443
Asheville *(G-451)*

Byron Dale Spivey.................................. G..... 910 653-3128
Tabor City *(G-11907)*

Carolina Cartridge Systems Inc............. E..... 704 347-2447
Charlotte *(G-1844)*

▲ Crest Electronics Inc............................ G..... 336 855-6422
Greensboro *(G-5471)*

Digital Progressions Inc......................... G..... 336 676-6570
Greensboro *(G-5496)*

Dmarcian... E..... 828 767-7588
Brevard *(G-969)*

Jason Case Corp..................................... G..... 212 786-2288
Durham *(G-4088)*

Kliersolutions... G..... 919 806-1287
Apex *(G-174)*

Kodak.. G..... 919 559-7232
Morrisville *(G-8998)*

Laser Recharge Carolina Inc................. F..... 919 467-5902
Cary *(G-1387)*

M T Industries Inc.................................. F..... 828 697-2864
Hendersonville *(G-6222)*

Maplewood Imaging Ctr.......................... G..... 336 397-6000
Winston Salem *(G-13243)*

▲ Nabell USA Corporation....................... E..... 704 986-2455
Albemarle *(G-82)*

Rb3 Enterprises Inc............................... G..... 919 795-5822
Wake Forest *(G-12291)*

◆ Smallhd LLC... F..... 919 439-2166
Cary *(G-1461)*

Strong Global Entrmt Inc........................ C..... 704 994-8279
Charlotte *(G-2872)*

Subsea Video Systems Inc..................... G..... 252 338-1001
Elizabeth City *(G-4411)*

Tehan Company Inc................................ G..... 800 283-7290
Burgaw *(G-1034)*

Truelook Inc.. G..... 833 878-3566
Winston Salem *(G-13374)*

Videndum Prod Solutions Inc................ G..... 919 244-0760
Cary *(G-1479)*

Wilmington Camera Service LLC........... G..... 910 343-1089
Wilmington *(G-12948)*

Zink Holdings LLC.................................. D..... 336 449-8000
Whitsett *(G-12622)*

Zink Imaging Inc.................................... E..... 336 449-8000
Whitsett *(G-12623)*

3873 Watches, clocks, watchcases, and parts

Ben Pushpa Inc...................................... G..... 828 428-8590
Maiden *(G-8007)*

◆ Orbita Corporation................................E..... 910 256-5300
Wilmington *(G-12868)*

Southern Digital Watch Repair.............. G..... 336 299-6718
Greensboro *(G-5825)*

39 MISCELLANEOUS MANUFACTURING INDUSTRIES

3911 Jewelry, precious metal

123 Precious Metal Ref LLC................... G..... 910 228-5403
Wilmington *(G-12685)*

Acme General Design Group LLC.......... G..... 843 466-6000
Benson *(G-783)*

Alex and Ani LLC................................... G..... 704 366-6029
Charlotte *(G-1640)*

Barnes Dmnd Gllery Jwly Mfrs I............ G..... 910 347-4300
Jacksonville *(G-7116)*

Bejeweled Creations.............................. G..... 336 552-0841
Reidsville *(G-10675)*

Blacqueladi Styles LLC.......................... G..... 877 977-7798
Cary *(G-1308)*

Byrd Designs Inc................................... G..... 828 628-0151
Fairview *(G-4506)*

▲ Charles & Colvard Ltd.......................... F..... 919 468-0399
Morrisville *(G-8954)*

Classy Sassy 5 Jewels Boutique........... G..... 252 481-8144
Greenville *(G-5954)*

▲ Cygany Inc... G..... 773 293-2999
Greensboro *(G-5483)*

D C Crsman Mfr Fine Jwly Inc............... G..... 828 252-9891
Asheville *(G-482)*

Dallas L Pridgen Inc.............................. G..... 919 732-4422
Carrboro *(G-1268)*

David Yurman Enterprises LLC.............. G..... 704 366-7259
Charlotte *(G-2020)*

Diamond Outdoor Entps Inc................... G..... 336 857-1450
Denton *(G-3747)*

Donald Haack Diamonds Inc.................. G..... 704 365-4400
Charlotte *(G-2062)*

Dons Fine Jewelry Inc............................ G..... 336 724-7826
Clemmons *(G-3181)*

Duncan Design Ltd................................. G..... 919 834-7713
Raleigh *(G-10064)*

Eurogold Art.. G..... 336 989-6205
Kernersville *(G-7272)*

Goldsmith By Rudi Ltd........................... G..... 828 693-1030
Hendersonville *(G-6210)*

Haydon & Company................................ G..... 919 781-1293
Raleigh *(G-10157)*

Herff Jones LLC..................................... G..... 704 962-1483
Charlotte *(G-2272)*

Herff Jones LLC..................................... G..... 704 873-5563
Statesville *(G-11707)*

Jewelry By Gail Inc................................ G..... 252 441-5387
Nags Head *(G-9299)*

Jkl Inc.. F..... 252 355-6714
Greenville *(G-5996)*

John Laughter Jewelry Inc..................... G..... 828 456-4772
Waynesville *(G-12462)*

Jostens Inc... B..... 336 765-0070
Winston Salem *(G-13220)*

Michael S North Wilkesboro Inc............ G..... 336 838-5964
North Wilkesboro *(G-9547)*

NCSMJ Inc.. F..... 704 544-1118
Pineville *(G-9744)*

R Gregory Jewelers Inc.......................... F..... 704 872-6669
Statesville *(G-11758)*

Soulku LLC.. F..... 828 273-4278
Asheville *(G-605)*

▲ Starcraft Diamonds Inc......................... G..... 252 717-2548
Washington *(G-12415)*

Sumpters Jwly & Collectibles................ G..... 704 399-5348
Charlotte *(G-2879)*

Tylerias Closet LLC................................ G..... 252 325-6639
Roper *(G-10901)*

William Travis Jewelry Ltd..................... G..... 919 968-0011
Chapel Hill *(G-1593)*

3914 Silverware and plated ware

◆ DWM INTERNATIONAL INC................E..... 646 290-7448
Charlotte *(G-2071)*

3915 Jewelers' materials and lapidary work

Alex and Ani LLC................................G..... 704 366-6029
Charlotte *(G-1640)*

▲ Buchanan Gem Stone Mines Inc...... F..... 828 765-6130
Spruce Pine *(G-11567)*

Charles & Colvard Direct LLC...............F..... 919 468-0399
Morrisville *(G-8955)*

Charlesandcolvardcom LLC...................E..... 877 202-5467
Morrisville *(G-8956)*

▲ Jewel Masters Inc.............................F..... 336 243-2711
Lexington *(G-7701)*

Steven Smoakes..................................G..... 910 352-4287
Wilmington *(G-12931)*

Stonehaven Jewelry Gallery Ltd............G..... 919 462-8888
Cary *(G-1468)*

3931 Musical instruments

Andrews Violinist.................................G..... 910 458-1226
Kure Beach *(G-7463)*

C A Zimmer Inc....................................G..... 704 483-4560
Denver *(G-3776)*

Conn-Selmer Inc..................................D..... 704 289-6459
Monroe *(G-8465)*

Epi Centre Sundries.............................G..... 704 650-9575
Charlotte *(G-2122)*

J L Smith & Co Inc...............................F..... 704 521-1088
Charlotte *(G-2360)*

Kelhorn Corporation.............................G..... 828 837-5833
Brasstown *(G-964)*

▲ Lewtak Pipe Organ Builders Inc........G..... 336 554-2251
Mocksville *(G-8374)*

▲ Lucky Man Inc...................................E.... 828 251-0090
Asheville *(G-538)*

Luthiers Workshop LLC........................G..... 919 241-4578
Hillsborough *(G-6871)*

Music & Arts..G..... 919 329-6069
Garner *(G-4948)*

◆ MW Enterprises Inc...........................G..... 828 963-7083
Vilas *(G-12232)*

Oneaka Dance Company......................G..... 704 299-7432
Charlotte *(G-2599)*

Raleigh Ringers Inc.............................G..... 919 847-7574
Raleigh *(G-10428)*

◆ ROC-N-Soc Inc..................................G..... 828 452-1736
Waynesville *(G-12471)*

Song of Wood Ltd................................G..... 828 669-7675
Black Mountain *(G-871)*

Southern Organ Services Ltd................G..... 828 667-8230
Candler *(G-1233)*

3942 Dolls and stuffed toys

A Stitch In Time...................................G..... 828 274-5193
Asheville *(G-422)*

PCS Collectibles LLC...........................G..... 805 306-1140
Huntersville *(G-7030)*

3944 Games, toys, and children's vehicles

All Signs & Graphics LLC.....................G..... 910 323-3115
Fayetteville *(G-4549)*

Banilla Games Inc................................G..... 252 329-7977
Greenville *(G-5945)*

Bellalou Designs LLC...........................G..... 252 360-7866
Wilson *(G-12970)*

Bougiejones..G..... 704 492-3029
Charlotte *(G-1804)*

▲ Cannon & Daughters Inc...................D..... 828 254-9236
Asheville *(G-466)*

Curious Discoveries Inc.......................G..... 336 643-0432
Summerfield *(G-11837)*

▲ Epic Kites LLC...................................G..... 203 209-6831
Kill Devil Hills *(G-7316)*

Game Box LLC....................................G..... 866 241-1882
Greensboro *(G-5546)*

Gracefully Gifted Hands LLC................G..... 845 248-8743
Raleigh *(G-10142)*

Grailgame Inc......................................G..... 804 517-3102
Reidsville *(G-10687)*

Hartford Products Inc...........................G..... 919 471-5937
Hillsborough *(G-6866)*

Imperial Falcon Group Inc....................G..... 646 717-1128
Charlotte *(G-2315)*

▲ Jasie Blanks LLC..............................F..... 910 485-0016
Fayetteville *(G-4621)*

Kenson Parenting Solutions..................G..... 919 637-1499
Wake Forest *(G-12285)*

Kitty Hawk Kites Inc............................F..... 252 441-4124
Nags Head *(G-9300)*

◆ Lionel LLC...D.... 704 454-4371
Concord *(G-3394)*

Puzzle Piece LLC.................................G..... 910 688-7119
Carthage *(G-1278)*

▲ Schleich USA Inc..............................G..... 704 659-7997
Charlotte *(G-2766)*

South Mountain Crafts..........................G..... 828 433-2607
Morganton *(G-8899)*

◆ US Legend Cars Intl Inc.....................E..... 704 455-3896
Harrisburg *(G-6119)*

Wersunsllc...G..... 857 209-8701
Winston Salem *(G-13388)*

3949 Sporting and athletic goods, nec

▲ ABC Fitness Products LLC.................G..... 704 649-0000
Raleigh *(G-9867)*

Action Surfboards.................................G..... 252 240-1818
Morehead City *(G-8812)*

Advantage Fitness Products Inc............G..... 336 643-8810
Kernersville *(G-7239)*

▲ American Netting Corp......................F.... 919 567-3737
Fuquay Varina *(G-4864)*

Archangel Arms LLC............................G..... 984 235-2536
Raleigh *(G-9911)*

Arnolds Welding Service Inc................E..... 910 323-3822
Fayetteville *(G-4553)*

Becwill Corp..G..... 919 552-8266
Fuquay Varina *(G-4869)*

Bluff Mountain Outfitters Inc................G..... 828 622-7162
Hot Springs *(G-6932)*

Bommerang Imprints............................G..... 704 933-9075
Kannapolis *(G-7203)*

Boomerang Water LLC.........................F..... 833 266-6420
Midland *(G-8281)*

Brookhurst Associates..........................G..... 919 792-0987
Raleigh *(G-9961)*

▲ Carolina Gym Supply Corp................G..... 919 732-6999
Hillsborough *(G-6862)*

Claypro LLC...G..... 828 301-6309
Norlina *(G-9520)*

▼ Colored Metal Products Inc...............F..... 704 482-1407
Shelby *(G-11322)*

◆ Custom Golf Car Supply Inc..............C..... 704 855-1130
Salisbury *(G-11042)*

Db Power Sports..................................G..... 828 324-1500
Hickory *(G-6318)*

Deerhunter Tree Stands Inc..................G..... 704 462-1116
Hickory *(G-6319)*

Dix Enterprises Inc..............................F..... 336 558-9512
High Point *(G-6595)*

▲ Electric Fshing Reel Systems I..........G..... 336 273-9101
Greensboro *(G-5516)*

Essay Operations Inc...........................G..... 252 443-6010
Rocky Mount *(G-10837)*

Ethics Archery LLC..............................G..... 980 429-2070
Vale *(G-12208)*

▲ Everyday Edisons LLC.......................G..... 704 369-7333
Charlotte *(G-2131)*

Family Industries Inc............................G..... 919 875-4499
Raleigh *(G-10104)*

▲ Fathom Offshore Holdings LLC.........G..... 910 399-6882
Wilmington *(G-12776)*

Fish Getter Lure Co LLC.......................G..... 704 538-9863
Casar *(G-1488)*

Fisher Athletic Equipment Inc...............E..... 704 636-5713
Salisbury *(G-11054)*

Frostie Bottom Tree Stand LLC............G..... 828 466-1708
Claremont *(G-3113)*

Geosurfaces Southeast Inc...................E..... 704 660-3000
Mooresville *(G-8672)*

Gillespies Fbrction Design Inc..............G..... 704 636-2349
Salisbury *(G-11056)*

Gladiator Enterprises Inc......................G..... 336 944-6932
Greensboro *(G-5561)*

Golf Shop...G..... 704 636-7070
Salisbury *(G-11057)*

Greene Precision Products Inc..............G..... 828 262-0116
Boone *(G-919)*

H & H Furniture Mfrs Inc......................C..... 336 873-7245
Seagrove *(G-11274)*

▲ H-T-L Perma USA Ltd Partnr..............E..... 704 377-3100
Charlotte *(G-2249)*

Hawk Distributors Inc...........................G..... 888 334-1307
Sanford *(G-11188)*

◆ Hayward Industrial Products..............C..... 704 837-8002
Charlotte *(G-2264)*

Hughes Products Co Inc.......................G..... 336 769-3788
Winston Salem *(G-13202)*

I-Lumenate LLC...................................G..... 336 448-0356
Winston Salem *(G-13203)*

Icon Coolers LLC.................................G..... 855 525-4266
Wilmington *(G-12813)*

◆ Implus Footcare LLC..........................B..... 800 446-7587
Durham *(G-4073)*

▲ J Stahl Sales & Sourcing Inc.............E..... 828 645-3005
Weaverville *(G-12493)*

◆ Js Fiber Co Inc..................................E.... 704 871-1582
Statesville *(G-11721)*

Kask America Inc.................................E..... 704 960-4851
Charlotte *(G-2388)*

Kelken Enterprises LLC........................G..... 910 890-7211
Lillington *(G-7798)*

Kol Incorporated..................................G..... 919 872-2340
Raleigh *(G-10240)*

▲ Lees Tackle Inc.................................G..... 910 386-5100
Wilmington *(G-12832)*

▲ Liberty Investment & MGT Corp........F..... 919 544-0344
Morrisville *(G-9010)*

◆ McKenzie Sports Products LLC.........C..... 704 279-7985
Salisbury *(G-11091)*

McNeely Motorsports Inc......................G..... 704 426-7430
Matthews *(G-8184)*

▲ Mettech Inc.......................................G..... 919 833-9460
Raleigh *(G-10297)*

Miracle Recreation Eqp Co...................C..... 704 875-6550
Huntersville *(G-7014)*

NC Softball Sales.................................G..... 704 663-2134
Mooresville *(G-8732)*

North Sports Inc...................................G..... 252 995-4970
Avon *(G-651)*

Not Just Archery..................................G..... 828 294-7727
Hickory *(G-6404)*

Openfire Systems.................................G..... 336 251-3991
Millers Creek *(G-8306)*

Parker Athletic Products LLC................G..... 704 370-0400
Charlotte *(G-2609)*

▲ Parker Medical Associates LLC....... F 704 344-9998
  Charlotte *(G-2610)*

Peggs Recreation Inc....................... G 704 660-0007
  Mooresville *(G-8744)*

Pevo Sports Co............................... G 910 397-9388
  Wilmington *(G-12875)*

Piedmont Fiberglass Inc.................... E 828 632-8883
  Statesville *(G-11745)*

◆ Playpower Inc................................ E 704 949-1600
  Huntersville *(G-7033)*

Precor Incorporated......................... C 336 603-1000
  Greensboro *(G-5760)*

Pretty Paid LLC............................... G 980 443-3876
  Kings Mountain *(G-7379)*

Protex Sport Products Inc................. F 336 956-2419
  Salisbury *(G-11107)*

▲ Revels Turf and Tractor LLC............. E 919 552-5697
  Fuquay Varina *(G-4896)*

▲ Rigem Right................................... G 252 726-9508
  Newport *(G-9443)*

Royal Baths Manufacturing Co........... E 704 837-1701
  Charlotte *(G-2733)*

Royal Textile Mills Inc...................... D 336 694-4121
  Yanceyville *(G-13460)*

▲ RSR Fitness Inc............................. F 919 255-1233
  Raleigh *(G-10450)*

◆ Sea Striker Inc.............................. G 252 247-4113
  Morehead City *(G-8843)*

▲ Secret Spot Inc............................. G 252 441-4030
  Nags Head *(G-9302)*

Simpleshot Inc................................ G 888 202-7475
  Asheville *(G-600)*

Skifam LLC..................................... F 336 722-6111
  Winston Salem *(G-13339)*

▲ Sports Products LLC....................... G 919 723-7470
  Wake Forest *(G-12302)*

Sportsedge Inc................................ F 704 528-0188
  Greensboro *(G-5830)*

Sportsfield Specialties Inc................ E 704 637-2140
  Mocksville *(G-8391)*

Surfline Inc.................................... G 252 715-1630
  Nags Head *(G-9304)*

Syntech of Burlington Inc................. F 336 570-2035
  Burlington *(G-1166)*

Thomas Golf Inc.............................. G 704 461-1342
  Charlotte *(G-2912)*

Thomson Plastics Inc....................... D 336 843-4255
  Lexington *(G-7751)*

Thunder Alley Enterprises................. G 910 371-0119
  Leland *(G-7560)*

Topgolf.. D 704 612-4745
  Charlotte *(G-2930)*

Total Sports Enterprises................... G 704 237-3930
  Waxhaw *(G-12446)*

Treklite Inc.................................... G 919 610-1788
  Raleigh *(G-10557)*

Trident Lure................................... G 910 520-4659
  Wilmington *(G-12941)*

▲ Triplette Fencing Supply Inc............ G 336 835-1205
  Mount Airy *(G-9189)*

◆ Ucs Inc... D 704 732-9922
  Lincolnton *(G-7866)*

◆ United Canvas & Sling Inc............... E 704 732-9922
  Lincolnton *(G-7868)*

VA Composites Inc........................... G 844 474-2387
  Aberdeen *(G-29)*

Vise & Co LLC................................. G 336 354-3702
  Winston Salem *(G-13383)*

Watkins Agency Inc.......................... G 704 213-6997
  Salisbury *(G-11135)*

◆ Weener Plastics Inc......................... D 252 206-1400
  Wilson *(G-13045)*

Wilder Tactical LLC.......................... G 704 750-7141
  Gastonia *(G-5165)*

3951 Pens and mechanical pencils

Bic Corporation............................... D 704 598-7700
  Charlotte *(G-1779)*

Industries of Blind Inc..................... C 336 274-1591
  Greensboro *(G-5617)*

3952 Lead pencils and art goods

Designs By Rachel........................... G 828 783-0698
  Spruce Pine *(G-11574)*

Eco-Kids LLC................................... F 207 899-2752
  Raleigh *(G-10077)*

◆ Speedball Art Products Co LLC......... D 800 898-7224
  Statesville *(G-11774)*

3953 Marking devices

Bear Pages..................................... G 828 837-0785
  Murphy *(G-9288)*

Ennis-Flint Inc................................ G 800 331-8118
  Thomasville *(G-12023)*

▲ Flint Trading Inc............................ D 336 475-6600
  Thomasville *(G-12027)*

H F Kinney Co Inc............................ E 704 540-9367
  Charlotte *(G-2248)*

Hayes Print-Stamp Co Inc................. G 336 667-1116
  Wilkesboro *(G-12637)*

Mass Connection Inc........................ G 910 424-0940
  Fayetteville *(G-4636)*

National Sign & Decal Inc................. G 828 478-2123
  Sherrills Ford *(G-11393)*

▲ Trophy House Inc........................... F 910 323-1791
  Fayetteville *(G-4683)*

3955 Carbon paper and inked ribbons

Ace Laser Recycling Inc.................... G 919 775-5521
  Sanford *(G-11145)*

Branch Office Solutions Inc.............. G 800 743-1047
  Indian Trail *(G-7072)*

Cartridge World............................... G 336 885-0989
  High Point *(G-6562)*

Complete Comp St of Ralgh Inc......... E 919 828-5227
  Raleigh *(G-10005)*

Digital Highpoint LLC....................... C 336 883-7146
  High Point *(G-6593)*

▲ Dnp Imagingcomm America Corp...... B 704 784-8100
  Concord *(G-3356)*

Drew Roberts LLC............................ G 336 497-1679
  Whitsett *(G-12604)*

Duraline Imaging Inc........................ G 828 692-1301
  Flat Rock *(G-4707)*

Filmon Process Corp........................ G 828 684-1360
  Arden *(G-268)*

▲ Image Industries NC Inc................. F 828 464-8882
  Newton *(G-9474)*

New East Cartridge Inc..................... G 252 329-0837
  Greenville *(G-6007)*

Sato Global Solutions Inc................. G 954 261-3279
  Charlotte *(G-2758)*

◆ Static Control Components Inc......... A 919 774-3808
  Sanford *(G-11238)*

3961 Costume jewelry

Byrd Designs Inc............................. G 828 628-0151
  Fairview *(G-4506)*

◆ Causekeepers Inc........................... E 336 824-2518
  Franklinville *(G-4855)*

▲ December Diamonds Inc.................. G 828 926-3308
  Waynesville *(G-12455)*

3965 Fasteners, buttons, needles, and pins

◆ Aplix Inc....................................... B 704 588-1920
  Charlotte *(G-1683)*

▲ Avdel USA LLC............................... E 704 888-7100
  Stanfield *(G-11603)*

◆ Coats & Clark Inc........................... D 888 368-8401
  Charlotte *(G-1942)*

▲ Coats N Amer De Rpblica Dmncan.... C 800 242-8095
  Charlotte *(G-1945)*

Dubose National Enrgy Svcs Inc......... G 704 295-1060
  Waxhaw *(G-12430)*

Gesipa Fasteners Usa Inc.................. E 336 751-1555
  Mocksville *(G-8367)*

◆ Gesipa Fasteners Usa Inc............... F 609 208-1740
  Mocksville *(G-8368)*

◆ Heico Fasteners Inc........................ E 828 261-0184
  Hickory *(G-6345)*

◆ Ideal Fastener Corporation.............. C 919 693-3115
  Oxford *(G-9618)*

Magnum Manufacturing LLC.............. F 704 983-1340
  New London *(G-9419)*

ND Southeastern Fastener................. G 704 329-0033
  Charlotte *(G-2550)*

Selbach Machinery LLC..................... G 910 794-9350
  Wilmington *(G-12916)*

3991 Brooms and brushes

▲ Carolina Brush Company................. E 704 867-0286
  Gastonia *(G-5011)*

▲ Carolina Brush Mfg Co.................... E 704 867-0286
  Gastonia *(G-5012)*

▲ Newell Novelty Co Inc..................... G 336 597-2246
  Roxboro *(G-10931)*

▲ P&A Indstrial Fabrications LLC......... E 336 322-1766
  Roxboro *(G-10938)*

Quickie Manufacturing Corp.............. C 910 737-6500
  Lumberton *(G-7966)*

Shur Line Inc.................................. E 317 442-8850
  Mooresville *(G-8769)*

Tarheel Pavement Clg Svcs Inc.......... E 704 895-8015
  Cornelius *(G-3627)*

▲ Zibra LLC..................................... G 704 271-4503
  Mooresville *(G-8806)*

3993 Signs and advertising specialties

310 Sign Company........................... G 704 910-2242
  Gastonia *(G-4981)*

910 Sign Co LLC.............................. G 910 353-2298
  Jacksonville *(G-7112)*

AAA Mobile Signs LLC...................... G 919 463-9768
  Morrisville *(G-8915)*

Aarons Quality Signs........................ G 704 841-7733
  Matthews *(G-8098)*

ABC Signs...................................... G 252 223-5900
  Newport *(G-9436)*

ABC Signs and Graphics LLC............. G 252 652-6620
  Havelock *(G-6122)*

Abee Custom Signs Inc..................... G 336 229-1554
  Burlington *(G-1042)*

Acsm Inc.. G 704 910-0243
  Charlotte *(G-1620)*

Action Graphics and Signs Inc........... G 919 690-1260
  Bullock *(G-1012)*

Action Installs LLC.......................... G 704 787-3828
  Wilkesboro *(G-12627)*

Action Sign Company Lenoir Inc......... G 828 754-4116
  Lenoir *(G-7566)*

Ad Runner MBL Outdoor Advg Inc....... G 336 945-1190
  Lewisville *(G-7649)*

Ad-Art Signs Inc............................. G 704 377-5369
  Charlotte *(G-1621)*

Adsign Corp.................................... G 336 766-3000
  Winston Salem *(G-13073)*

S
I
C

Advance Signs & Service Inc .... E 919 639-4666
Angier (G-110)

All Signs & Graphics LLC .... G 910 323-3115
Fayetteville (G-4549)

Allen Industries Inc .... C 336 294-4777
Greensboro (G-5350)

▼ Allen Industries Inc .... D 336 668-2791
Greensboro (G-5349)

American Sign Shop Inc .... G 704 527-6100
Charlotte (G-1668)

Ancient Mariner Inc .... F 704 635-7911
Monroe (G-8426)

Andark Graphics Inc .... G 704 882-1400
Indian Trail (G-7067)

Anthem Displays LLC .... F 910 746-8988
Elizabethtown (G-4417)

Anthem Displays LLC .... G 910 862-3550
Elizabethtown (G-4418)

Aoa Signs Inc .... G 336 679-3344
Wilson (G-12962)

Apple Rock Advg & Prom Inc .... E 336 232-4800
Greensboro (G-5366)

Art Sign Co .... G 919 596-8681
Durham (G-3899)

Artisan Direct LLC .... G 704 655-9100
Cornelius (G-3586)

▲ Artisan Signs and Graphics Inc .... F 704 655-9100
Cornelius (G-3587)

Artistic Images Inc .... G 704 332-6225
Charlotte (G-1699)

Asi Signage North Carolina .... E 919 362-9669
Holly Springs (G-6892)

Atlantic Sign Media Inc .... G 336 584-1375
Burlington (G-1048)

Atlas Sign Industries Nc LLC .... E 704 788-3733
Concord (G-3314)

Awning Innovations .... F 336 831-8996
Winston Salem (G-13090)

B&P Enterprise NC Inc .... G 727 669-6877
Hickory (G-6269)

Baac Business Solutions Inc .... G 704 333-4321
Charlotte (G-1732)

Baldwin Sign & Awning .... G 910 642-8812
Whiteville (G-12576)

Beane Signs Inc .... G 336 629-6748
Asheboro (G-331)

Beaty Corporation .... G 704 599-4949
Charlotte (G-1765)

Beeson Sign Co Inc .... G 336 993-5617
Kernersville (G-7247)

Best Image Signs LLC .... G 336 973-7445
Wilkesboro (G-12629)

Blashfield Sign Company Inc .... G 910 485-7200
Fayetteville (G-4559)

Blue Light Images Company Inc .... F 336 983-4986
King (G-7321)

Bobbitt Signs Inc .... G 252 492-7326
Kittrell (G-7438)

Boyd Gmn Inc .... C 206 284-2200
Monroe (G-8446)

Boyles Sign Shop Inc .... G 336 782-1189
Germanton (G-5173)

Burchette Sign Company Inc .... F 336 996-6501
Colfax (G-3274)

Buzz Saw Inc .... G 910 321-7446
Fayetteville (G-4564)

Camco Manufacturing Inc .... G 336 348-6609
Reidsville (G-10678)

Capital Sign Solutions LLC .... E 919 789-1452
Raleigh (G-9969)

Carolina Cstm Signs & Graphics .... G 336 681-4337
Greensboro (G-5425)

Carolina Sgns Grphic Dsgns Inc .... G 919 383-3344
Durham (G-3962)

Carolina Sign Co Inc .... G 704 399-3995
Charlotte (G-1855)

Carolina Sign Svc .... G 919 247-0927
Angier (G-116)

Carolina Signs & Lighting Inc .... G 336 399-1400
King (G-7323)

Carolina Signs and Wonders Inc .... F 704 286-1343
Charlotte (G-1856)

Casco Signs Inc .... E 704 788-9055
Concord (G-3333)

Cbr Signs LLC .... G 910 794-8243
Wilmington (G-12737)

Ccbs & Sign Shop Inc .... G 252 728-4866
Beaufort (G-722)

CD Dickie & Associates Inc .... F 704 527-9102
Charlotte (G-1878)

Choice Awards & Signs .... G 704 844-0860
Matthews (G-8164)

Clark Sign Corporation .... G 336 431-4944
Archdale (G-217)

Classic Sign Services LLC .... G 704 401-1466
Monroe (G-8461)

CMA Signs LLC .... F 919 245-8339
Hillsborough (G-6864)

Coates Designers & Crafstmen .... G 828 349-9700
Franklin (G-4821)

Cobb Sign Company Incorporated .... G 336 227-0181
Burlington (G-1072)

Connected 2k LLC .... G 910 321-7446
Fayetteville (G-4578)

Consumer Concepts .... F 252 247-7000
Morehead City (G-8828)

Contagious Graphics Inc .... E 704 529-5600
Charlotte (G-1977)

Craven Sign Services Inc .... G 336 883-7306
High Point (G-6578)

Creative Images Inc .... G 919 467-2188
Cary (G-1337)

Creative Sign Solutions Inc .... G 704 978-8499
Statesville (G-11680)

Creative Signs Inc .... G 910 395-0100
Wilmington (G-12755)

Custom Neon & Graphics Inc .... G 704 344-1715
Charlotte (G-2010)

Davcom Enterprises Inc .... G 919 872-9522
Raleigh (G-10038)

Davis Sign Company Inc .... F 336 765-2990
Winston Salem (G-13138)

Designelement .... F 919 383-5561
Raleigh (G-10044)

Dickie CD & Associates Inc .... F 704 527-9102
Charlotte (G-2043)

Digital Printing Systems Inc .... E 704 525-0190
Charlotte (G-2047)

Direct Wholesale Signs LLC .... G 704 750-2842
Kings Mountain (G-7359)

Diversified Signs Graphics Inc .... F 704 392-8165
Charlotte (G-2056)

▲ Dize Company .... D 336 722-5181
Winston Salem (G-13149)

Ebert Sign Company Inc .... G 336 768-2867
Lexington (G-7681)

Elite Graphics Inc .... G 336 887-2923
High Point (G-6607)

Embroidme .... G 919 316-1538
Durham (G-4020)

Endless Plastics LLC .... F 336 346-1839
Greensboro (G-5520)

Ever Glo Sign Co Inc .... G 704 633-3324
Salisbury (G-11049)

Everglow Na Inc .... E 704 841-2580
Matthews (G-8111)

Exhibit World Inc .... G 704 882-2272
Indian Trail (G-7080)

▲ Expogo Inc .... F 910 452-3976
Wilmington (G-12773)

Fairway Outdoor Advg LLC .... G 919 755-1900
Raleigh (G-10101)

Fairway Outdoor Advg LLC .... G 910 343-1900
Wilmington (G-12775)

Ferguson Design Inc .... E 704 394-0120
Belmont (G-751)

Fines and Carriel Inc .... G 919 929-0702
Chapel Hill (G-1547)

Fitch Sign Company Inc .... G 704 482-2916
Shelby (G-11336)

Global Resource NC Inc .... G 910 793-4770
Wilmington (G-12789)

Gmg Group LLC .... G 252 441-8374
Kill Devil Hills (G-7317)

Goins Signs Inc .... G 336 427-5783
Stoneville (G-11822)

Goldsboro Neon Sign Co Inc .... G 919 735-2035
Goldsboro (G-5217)

Gooder Grafix Inc .... G 828 349-4097
Franklin (G-4830)

▲ Grandwell Industries Inc .... E 919 557-1221
Fuquay Varina (G-4883)

Graphic Components LLC .... E 336 542-2128
Greensboro (G-5572)

Graphic Productions Inc .... G 336 765-9335
Winston Salem (G-13184)

▼ Graphic Systems Intl Inc .... E 336 662-8686
Greensboro (G-5574)

Graphical Creations Inc .... F 704 888-8870
Stanfield (G-11607)

Graphix Solution Inc .... F 919 213-0371
Apex (G-160)

Greene Imaging & Design Inc .... G 919 787-3737
Raleigh (G-10143)

Guerrero Enterprises Inc .... G 828 286-4900
Rutherfordton (G-10984)

H F Kinney Co Inc .... E 704 540-9367
Charlotte (G-2248)

Harwood Signs .... G 704 857-6203
China Grove (G-3074)

Hatleys Signs & Service Inc .... G 704 723-4027
Concord (G-3372)

Headrick Otdoor Mdia of Crlnas .... G 704 487-5971
Shelby (G-11343)

Heritage Custom Signs & Disp .... E 704 655-1465
Charlotte (G-2273)

Icon Sign Systems Inc .... G 828 253-4266
Asheville (G-520)

Identity Custom Signage Inc .... G 336 882-7446
High Point (G-6666)

▲ Image Design .... F 910 862-8988
Elizabethtown (G-4428)

Image Innovation Group Inc .... G 336 883-6010
High Point (G-6667)

Image Matters Inc .... G 336 940-3000
Clemmons (G-3191)

▲ Industrial Sign & Graphics Inc .... E 704 371-4985
Charlotte (G-2324)

Infinity S End Inc .... F 704 900-8355
Charlotte (G-2328)

Interstate Sign Company Inc .... E 336 789-3069
Mount Airy (G-9135)

Island Xprtees of Oter Bnks In .... E 252 480-3990
Nags Head (G-9298)

J & D Thorpe Enterprises Inc .... G 919 553-0918
Clayton (G-3155)

J Morgan Signs Inc................................ F 336 274-6509
Greensboro *(G-5632)*

J R Craver & Associates Inc................... G 336 769-3330
Clemmons *(G-3193)*

▲ J Signs and Graphics LLC................. G 910 315-2657
Aberdeen *(G-9)*

Jantec Sign Group LLC......................... E 336 429-5010
Mount Airy *(G-9136)*

Jaxonsigns... G 910 467-3409
Holly Ridge *(G-6889)*

JB II Printing LLC................................. E 336 222-0717
Burlington *(G-1111)*

Jeremy Weitzel...................................... G 919 878-4474
Raleigh *(G-10215)*

Jester-Crown Inc................................... G 919 872-1070
Raleigh *(G-10216)*

Jgi Inc.. E 704 522-8860
Pineville *(G-9737)*

Jka Idustries... G 980 225-5350
Salisbury *(G-11073)*

JKS Motorsports Inc............................. G 336 722-4129
Winston Salem *(G-13217)*

Joesigns Inc.. G 252 638-1622
New Bern *(G-9373)*

Juan Pino Signs Inc............................. G 336 764-4422
Winston Salem *(G-13221)*

K & D Signs LLC.................................. F 336 786-1111
Mount Airy *(G-9137)*

K&K Holdings Inc................................. G 704 341-5567
Charlotte *(G-2385)*

Kat Designs Inc................................... G 336 789-7288
Mount Airy *(G-9138)*

Kenneth Moore Signs............................ G 910 458-6428
Wilmington *(G-12826)*

Ki Agency LLC...................................... G 919 977-7075
Raleigh *(G-10234)*

King Tutt Graphics LLC......................... E 877 546-4888
Raleigh *(G-10235)*

Kranken Signs Vehicle Wraps................ G 704 339-0059
Pineville *(G-9738)*

▼ Leonardo US Cyber SEC Sltons L..... D 336 379-7135
Greensboro *(G-5661)*

Liberty Sign and Lighting LLC................ G 336 703-7465
Lexington *(G-7710)*

Lights-Lights LLC................................. G 919 798-2317
Coats *(G-3264)*

Lockwood Identity Inc........................... C 704 597-9801
Charlotte *(G-2430)*

M & M Signs and Awnings Inc............... F 336 352-4300
Mount Airy *(G-9151)*

Major Display Inc................................. G 800 260-1067
Franklin *(G-4836)*

Matthews Mobile Media LLC.................. G 336 303-4982
Greensboro *(G-5681)*

McCorkle Sign Company Inc.................. E 919 687-7080
Durham *(G-4121)*

McKnight15 Inc..................................... G 919 326-6488
Raleigh *(G-10285)*

▼ Mega Media Concepts Ltd Lblty......... G 973 919-5661
Brevard *(G-975)*

Mercury Signs Inc................................ G 919 808-1205
Apex *(G-180)*

Meredith Media Co............................... G 919 748-4808
Durham *(G-4130)*

Merge LLC.. G 919 832-3924
Raleigh *(G-10291)*

Metro Print Inc..................................... F 704 827-3796
Mount Holly *(G-9237)*

Moretz Signs Inc.................................. G 828 387-4600
Beech Mountain *(G-738)*

Morningstar Signs and Banners............. G 704 861-0020
Gastonia *(G-5101)*

Moss Sign Company Inc........................ F 828 299-7766
Asheville *(G-551)*

Motorsports Designs Inc....................... F 336 454-1181
High Point *(G-6716)*

Mount Airy Signs & Letters Inc.............. F 336 786-5777
Mount Airy *(G-9154)*

NC Graphic Pros LLC............................ G 252 492-7326
Kittrell *(G-7442)*

NC Sign and Lighting Svc LLC.............. F 586 764-0563
Jamestown *(G-7173)*

New Hanover Printing and Pubg............. G 910 520-7173
Wilmington *(G-12860)*

Newton Sign Co Inc.............................. G 910 347-1661
Jacksonville *(G-7136)*

Nomadic Display LLC............................ G 800 336-5019
Greensboro *(G-5710)*

▲ Nomadic North America LLC............. E 703 866-9200
Greensboro *(G-5711)*

North State Signs Inc........................... G 919 977-7053
Raleigh *(G-10339)*

▲ Oramental Post.................................. G 704 376-8111
Pineville *(G-9746)*

Overstreet Sign Contrs Inc.................... G 919 596-7300
Durham *(G-4161)*

Parish Sign & Service Inc..................... E 910 875-6121
Raeford *(G-9846)*

PC Signs & Graphics LLC..................... G 919 661-5801
Garner *(G-4951)*

Peaches Enterprises Inc........................ G 910 868-5800
Fayetteville *(G-4653)*

PFC Group LLC..................................... D 704 393-4040
Charlotte *(G-2632)*

Phoenix Sign Pros Inc.......................... G 252 756-5685
Winterville *(G-13421)*

Piedmont Mediaworks Inc...................... F 828 575-2250
Asheville *(G-573)*

Piranha Industries Inc.......................... G 704 248-7843
Charlotte *(G-2639)*

Planet Logo Inc.................................... G 910 763-2554
Wilmington *(G-12879)*

Plastic Art Design Inc.......................... G 919 878-1672
Raleigh *(G-10372)*

Playrace Inc... E 828 251-2211
Asheville *(G-577)*

Port City Signs & Graphics Inc.............. G 910 350-8242
Wilmington *(G-12883)*

◆ Portable Displays LLC........................ E 919 544-6504
Cary *(G-1424)*

Powersigns Inc..................................... G 910 343-1789
Wilmington *(G-12885)*

Precision Signs Inc.............................. G 919 615-0979
Garner *(G-4955)*

Print Management Group LLC................ F 704 821-0114
Charlotte *(G-2669)*

Printology Signs Graphics LLC.............. G 843 473-4984
Davidson *(G-3716)*

Professional Bus Systems Inc............... G 704 333-2444
Charlotte *(G-2673)*

Professional Laminating LLC................. G 919 465-0400
Cary *(G-1430)*

▲ Promographix Inc............................... F 919 846-1379
Carolina Beach *(G-1263)*

Purple Star Graphics Inc....................... G 704 723-4020
Concord *(G-3426)*

Qasioun LLC.. F 704 531-8000
Charlotte *(G-2678)*

R and L Collision Center Inc................. F 704 739-2500
Kings Mountain *(G-7381)*

R O Givens Signs Inc........................... G 252 338-6578
Elizabeth City *(G-4407)*

Readilite & Barricade Inc...................... F 919 231-8309
Raleigh *(G-10435)*

Rec Plus Inc... E 704 375-9098
Charlotte *(G-2696)*

Reese Sign Service Inc......................... G 919 580-0705
Goldsboro *(G-5239)*

Retail Installation Svcs LLC.................. G 336 818-1333
Millers Creek *(G-8307)*

RLM/Universal Packaging Inc................ F 336 644-6161
Greensboro *(G-5789)*

Rodney S Cstm Cut Sign Co Inc........... E 919 362-9669
Holly Springs *(G-6911)*

Routh Sign Service............................... G 336 272-0895
Greensboro *(G-5795)*

Ruth Arnold Graphics & Signs............... G 910 793-9087
Wilmington *(G-12907)*

S Tri Inc.. G 704 542-8186
Charlotte *(G-2745)*

▼ Salem Sports Inc............................. G 336 722-2444
Winston Salem *(G-13326)*

Saltwater Signworks Inc........................ G 910 212-5020
Wilmington *(G-12909)*

Sawyers Sign Service Inc..................... F
Mount Airy *(G-9175)*

Seaward Action Inc.............................. G 252 671-1684
Wilmington *(G-12914)*

Sensational Signs................................ G 704 358-1099
Charlotte *(G-2787)*

September Signs & Graphics LLC.......... G 910 791-9084
Wilmington *(G-12917)*

Shop Dawg Signs LLC.......................... E 919 556-2672
Wake Forest *(G-12300)*

Shutterbug Grafix & Signs..................... G 910 315-1556
Pinehurst *(G-9703)*

Sidney Perry Cooper III......................... G 252 257-3886
Warrenton *(G-12354)*

Sign & Awning Systems Inc.................. G 919 892-5900
Dunn *(G-3868)*

Sign A Rama Inc.................................. G 336 893-8042
Lewisville *(G-7653)*

Sign Company of Wilmington Inc........... F 910 392-1414
Wilmington *(G-12921)*

Sign Connection Inc............................. F 704 868-4500
Gastonia *(G-5136)*

Sign Here of Lake Norman Inc.............. G 704 483-6454
Denver *(G-3805)*

▼ Sign Medic Inc................................ G 336 789-5972
Mount Airy *(G-9176)*

Sign Mine Inc...................................... G 336 884-5780
High Point *(G-6771)*

Sign Resources of NC........................... G 336 310-4611
Kernersville *(G-7300)*

Sign Shop of The Triangle Inc............... G 919 363-3930
Apex *(G-194)*

Sign Shoppe Inc.................................. G 910 754-5144
Supply *(G-11859)*

Sign Systems Inc................................. F 828 322-5622
Hickory *(G-6446)*

Sign Technology Inc............................. G 336 887-3211
High Point *(G-6772)*

Sign World Inc..................................... G 704 529-4440
Charlotte *(G-2806)*

Sign Worxpress.................................... G 336 437-9889
Burlington *(G-1157)*

Sign-A-Rama.. G 919 383-5561
Raleigh *(G-10474)*

Signal Signs of Ga Inc......................... G 828 494-4913
Murphy *(G-9295)*

Signature Signs Inc.............................. G 336 431-2072
High Point *(G-6773)*

Signfactory Direct Inc........................... G 336 903-0300
Wilkesboro *(G-12651)*

Signify It Inc.. F 910 678-8111
Fayetteville *(G-4669)*

S
I
C

Signlite Services Inc.................................. G 336 751-9543
Mocksville *(G-8389)*

Signlogic Inc .... G 910 862-8965
Elizabethtown *(G-4433)*

Signs By Tomorrow.................................... G 704 527-6100
Charlotte *(G-2807)*

Signs Etc... G 336 722-9341
Winston Salem *(G-13337)*

Signs Etc of Charlotte .... E 704 522-8860
Charlotte *(G-2809)*

Signs Etc of Charlotte .... F 704 522-8860
Charlotte *(G-2808)*

Signs Now.. G 919 546-0006
Raleigh *(G-10475)*

Signs Now 103 LLC................................... G 252 355-0768
Greenville *(G-6022)*

Signs Now Charlotte .... G 704 844-0552
Pineville *(G-9757)*

Signs Sealed Delivered .... G 919 213-1280
Durham *(G-4236)*

Signs Unlimited Inc.................................. F 919 596-7612
Durham *(G-4237)*

Signsations Ltd.. G 571 340-3330
Chapel Hill *(G-1571)*

Signsmith Custom Signs & Awnin........ F 252 752-4321
Greenville *(G-6023)*

Signworks North Carolina Inc................ G 336 956-7446
Lexington *(G-7741)*

Signz Inc.. G 704 824-7446
Gastonia *(G-5137)*

Siqnarama Pinevillw................................ G 704 835-1123
Pineville *(G-9758)*

Sitzer & Spuria Inc.................................. G 919 929-0299
Chapel Hill *(G-1572)*

Skipper Graphics...................................... G 910 754-8729
Shallotte *(G-11305)*

Southeastern Sign Works Inc................ G 336 789-5516
Mount Airy *(G-9177)*

Southern Signworks................................. G 828 683-8726
Leicester *(G-7529)*

Speedpro Imaging .... G 704 321-1200
Charlotte *(G-2843)*

Speedpro Imaging .... G 919 578-4338
Raleigh *(G-10498)*

Speedpro Imaging Durham..................... G 919 278-7964
Durham *(G-4246)*

Srb Technologies Inc.............................. E 336 659-2610
Winston Salem *(G-13341)*

Stay Alert Safety Services LLC............ E 919 828-5399
Raleigh *(G-10506)*

Sterling Products Corporation.............. G 646 423-3175
Greensboro *(G-5839)*

Sticky Life .... G 910 817-4531
Newton Grove *(G-9518)*

Stonetree Signs.. G 336 625-0938
Denton *(G-3761)*

Studio Displays Inc................................ F 704 588-6590
Pineville *(G-9761)*

Syd Inc.. G 336 294-8807
Greensboro *(G-5848)*

Syntech of Burlington Inc...................... F 336 570-2035
Burlington *(G-1166)*

T & R Signs... G 919 779-1185
Garner *(G-4967)*

Tebo Displays LLC................................... G 919 832-8525
Raleigh *(G-10537)*

TEC Graphics Inc..................................... F 919 567-2077
Fuquay Varina *(G-4901)*

Thats A Good Sign Inc............................ G 301 870-0299
Bolivia *(G-887)*

Tier 1 Graphics LLC................................. G 704 625-6880
Cornelius *(G-3628)*

Timothy L Griffin...................................... G 336 317-8314
Greenville *(G-6028)*

Tommy Signs... G 704 877-1234
Waxhaw *(G-12445)*

Triangle Solutions Inc............................ G 919 481-1235
Cary *(G-1473)*

▲ Twinvision North America Inc........... C 919 361-2155
Durham *(G-4285)*

US Logoworks LLC................................... F 910 307-0312
Fayetteville *(G-4691)*

Vic Inc.. F 336 545-1124
Greensboro *(G-5903)*

Victory Signs LLC.................................... G 919 642-3091
Fuquay Varina *(G-4904)*

▲ Vintage Editions Inc........................... F 828 632-4185
Taylorsville *(G-11985)*

Vittro Sign Studio.................................... G 917 698-1594
Apex *(G-205)*

Web 4 Half LLC... E 855 762-4638
Greensboro *(G-5914)*

Whats Your Sign LLC.............................. G 919 274-5703
Raleigh *(G-10607)*

Wilson Billboard Advg Inc..................... G 919 934-2421
Smithfield *(G-11470)*

Wright Business Concepts Inc.............. G 828 466-1044
Hickory *(G-6491)*

3995 Burial caskets

Winston-Salem Casket Company.......... G 336 661-1695
Winston Salem *(G-13403)*

3996 Hard surface floor coverings, nec

Tarheel Mats Inc...................................... G 252 325-1903
Camden *(G-1213)*

3999 Manufacturing industries, nec

26 Industries Inc..................................... G 704 839-3218
Concord *(G-3306)*

A Cleaner Tomorrow Dry Clg LLC......... G 919 639-6396
Dunn *(G-3840)*

A Plus Five Star Trnsp LLC................... G 919 771-4820
Clayton *(G-3129)*

AIM Industries Inc................................... G 336 656-9990
Browns Summit *(G-989)*

American Eagle Mfg LLC........................ G 252 633-0603
New Bern *(G-9331)*

Andy Maylish Fabrication Inc............... G 704 785-1491
Denver *(G-3771)*

Apollonias Candles Things LLC............ G 910 408-2508
Durham *(G-3896)*

Applied Components Mfg LLC............... G 828 323-8915
Hickory *(G-6265)*

Aqua Blue Inc.. G 704 896-9007
Cornelius *(G-3585)*

Arden Companies LLC............................ E 919 258-3081
Sanford *(G-11149)*

Asterra Labs LLC..................................... G 800 430-9074
Nashville *(G-9308)*

Atlantic Group Usa Inc........................... F 919 623-7824
Raleigh *(G-9920)*

Atlantic Manufacturing LLC.................. G 336 497-5500
Kernersville *(G-7246)*

Atlantic Mfg & Fabrication Inc............. G 704 647-6200
Salisbury *(G-11019)*

Auralites Inc... G 828 687-7990
Fletcher *(G-4722)*

▲ Autoverters Inc.................................... F 252 537-0426
Roanoke Rapids *(G-10731)*

Beast Chains... G 336 346-9081
High Point *(G-6542)*

Belev En U Water Mfg Co....................... G 704 458-9950
Huntersville *(G-6972)*

▲ Bhaktivedanta Archives...................... G 336 871-3636
Sandy Ridge *(G-11141)*

Bickerstaff Trees Inc.............................. G 336 372-8866
Sparta *(G-11535)*

Biganodes LLC... G 828 245-1115
Forest City *(G-4784)*

Blue Ridge Bracket Inc.......................... G 828 808-3273
Fletcher *(G-4724)*

Blur Development Group LLC................ D 919 701-4213
Cary *(G-1312)*

Bonaventure Group Inc.......................... F 919 781-6610
Raleigh *(G-9953)*

Bouncers and Slides Inc........................ G 252 908-2292
Nashville *(G-9310)*

Boyd Manufacturing Inc......................... F 336 301-6433
Siler City *(G-11400)*

BR Lee Industries Inc............................. G 704 966-3317
Lincolnton *(G-7817)*

◆ Bradford Products LLC........................ D 910 791-2202
Leland *(G-7535)*

Brandy Thompson..................................... F 321 252-2911
Fayetteville *(G-4561)*

Brian McGregor Enterprise.................... G 919 732-2317
Hillsborough *(G-6861)*

Brite Sky LLC.. G 757 589-4676
Godwin *(G-5187)*

Brittany Smith... G 912 313-0588
Greensboro *(G-5407)*

Brooks Manufacturing Solutions.......... F 336 438-1280
Graham *(G-5261)*

Buddy Cut Inc... G 888 608-4701
Pittsboro *(G-9777)*

Cambbro Manufacturing Company....... F 919 568-8506
Mebane *(G-8234)*

Cambro.. G 919 563-0761
Mebane *(G-8235)*

Carbon-Less Industries Inc................... G 704 361-1231
Harrisburg *(G-6105)*

Carolina Candle... G 336 835-6020
Elkin *(G-4440)*

Carolina Gyps Reclamation LLC........... G 704 895-4506
Cornelius *(G-3593)*

Carolina Perfumer Inc............................. G 910 295-5600
Pinehurst *(G-9688)*

Carolina Windows and Doors Inc......... F 252 756-2585
Greenville *(G-5951)*

CCI Hair Boutique LLC............................ F 407 216-9213
Hope Mills *(G-6925)*

Chatter Free Tling Sltions Inc.............. G 828 659-7379
Marion *(G-8040)*

Classic Scent.. G 828 645-5171
Weaverville *(G-12486)*

Clean Green Sustainable Lf LLC.......... F 855 946-8785
Greensboro *(G-5449)*

Coates Designers & Crafstmen.......... G 828 349-9700
Franklin *(G-4821)*

Collin Mfg Inc... G 919 917-6264
Oriental *(G-9599)*

Commdoor Inc... G 800 565-1851
Concord *(G-3339)*

Concise Manufacturing Inc.................... G 704 796-8419
Salisbury *(G-11036)*

Conmech Industries LLC........................ G 919 306-6228
Apex *(G-149)*

Continental Manufacturing Co.............. G 336 697-2591
Mc Leansville *(G-8220)*

Cooper Industries LLC............................ G 304 545-1482
Greensboro *(G-5467)*

Corsan LLC... F 704 765-9979
Huntersville *(G-6979)*

Cosmopros.. G 704 717-7420
Charlotte *(G-1990)*

Creek Industries Inc	G	828 319-7490	
Weaverville *(G-12490)*			
Creek Life LLC	G	910 892-9337	
Garner *(G-4926)*			
Cristal Dragon Candle Company	G	336 997-4210	
Sandy Ridge *(G-11142)*			
Cross Manufacturing LLC	G	336 269-6542	
Burlington *(G-1077)*			
Crown Town Industries LLC	G	704 579-0387	
Concord *(G-3349)*			
D & T Soy Candles	G	704 320-2804	
Polkton *(G-9814)*			
Daisy Pink Co	G	704 907-3526	
Charlotte *(G-2016)*			
Dale Reynolds Cabinets Inc	G	704 890-5962	
Charlotte *(G-2017)*			
Dara Holsters & Gear Inc	E	919 374-2170	
Wendell *(G-12531)*			
David Oreck Candle	G	336 375-8411	
Greensboro *(G-5487)*			
▲ Daydream Education LLC	G	800 591-6150	
Clyde *(G-3258)*			
Direct Distribution Inds Inc	G	910 217-0000	
Wagram *(G-12256)*			
Dorian Corporation	G	910 352-6939	
Wilmington *(G-12766)*			
Douglas Battery Mfg Co	G	336 650-7000	
Winston Salem *(G-13151)*			
Draxlor Industries Inc	G	757 274-6771	
Durham *(G-4006)*			
Dynamic Mounting	G	704 978-8723	
Mooresville *(G-8656)*			
E Cache & Co LLC	F	919 590-0779	
Charlotte *(G-2080)*			
E-Liquid Brands LLC	E	828 385-5090	
Mooresville *(G-8658)*			
Earth-Kind Inc	G	701 751-4456	
Mooresville *(G-8659)*			
▲ East Coast Umbrella Inc	E	910 462-2500	
Laurel Hill *(G-7482)*			
Ella B Candles LLC	E	980 339-8898	
Charlotte *(G-2101)*			
Encore Group Inc	C	336 768-7859	
Winston Salem *(G-13157)*			
Enepay Corporation	G	919 788-1454	
Raleigh *(G-10086)*			
Energizer Battery Mfg	G	336 736-7936	
Asheboro *(G-351)*			
Equagen Engineers Pllc	E	919 444-5442	
Raleigh *(G-10090)*			
Evergreen Silks NC Inc	F	704 845-5577	
Matthews *(G-8112)*			
Fee Kees Wreaths LLC	G	704 636-1008	
Salisbury *(G-11053)*			
▲ Fill Pac LLC	F	828 322-1916	
Hickory *(G-6334)*			
Filter Shop LLC	D	704 860-4822	
Gastonia *(G-5048)*			
Filtrona Filters Inc	D	336 362-1333	
Greensboro *(G-5533)*			
Fisherman Creations Inc	E	252 725-0138	
Beaufort *(G-726)*			
▲ Fragrant Passage Candle Co LP	E	336 375-8411	
Greensboro *(G-5538)*			
Gallimore Fmly Investments Inc	F	336 625-5138	
Asheboro *(G-359)*			
General Foam Plastics Corp	G	757 857-0153	
Tarboro *(G-11927)*			
▲ Gentry Mills Inc	D	704 983-5555	
Albemarle *(G-74)*			
Gifted Hands Styling Salon	G	828 781-2781	
Hickory *(G-6338)*			

GNB Ventures LLC	F	704 488-4468	
Charlotte *(G-2218)*			
H&H Metal Fab	G	828 757-3747	
Lenoir *(G-7612)*			
▲ Hanes Industries-Newton	G	828 469-2000	
Newton *(G-9471)*			
Health At Home Inc	F	850 543-4482	
Charlotte *(G-2267)*			
Henry Williams Jr	G	336 897-8714	
High Point *(G-6645)*			
Hensley Corporation	G	828 230-9447	
Fairview *(G-4507)*			
Hershey Group LLC	G	336 855-3888	
Greensboro *(G-5594)*			
Hoodoo Honey LLC	G	252 548-0697	
Durham *(G-4064)*			
Hudson Industries LLC	G	704 480-0014	
Shelby *(G-11344)*			
▲ Hudson S Hardware Inc	E	919 553-3030	
Garner *(G-4933)*			
Humboldt Mfg Co Inc	G	919 832-6509	
Raleigh *(G-10180)*			
Innovative Technology Mfg LLC	G	980 248-3731	
Mooresville *(G-8693)*			
Inovative Vapes of Boone	G	828 386-1041	
Boone *(G-926)*			
Jag Industries LLC	G	704 655-2507	
Huntersville *(G-7005)*			
Jefferson Group Inc	E	252 752-6195	
Greenville *(G-5995)*			
Jhd Enterprise LLC	G	919 612-1787	
Creedmoor *(G-3651)*			
Jochum Industries	G	336 288-7975	
Greensboro *(G-5638)*			
Johnny Slicks Inc	G	910 803-2159	
Holly Ridge *(G-6890)*			
Joseph Sotanski	E	407 324-6187	
Marion *(G-8047)*			
◆ Justneem LLC	G	919 414-8826	
Apex *(G-173)*			
Karl Rl Manufacturing	G	919 846-3801	
Raleigh *(G-10231)*			
Kerdea Technologies Inc	F	971 900-1113	
Greenville *(G-5998)*			
King Charles Industries LLC	G	704 848-4121	
Lilesville *(G-7787)*			
L & B Jandrew Enterprises	G	828 687-8927	
Hendersonville *(G-6219)*			
Laura Gaskin	G	828 628-5891	
Fairview *(G-4509)*			
Lee Linear	G	800 221-0811	
Southport *(G-11522)*			
Lizmere Cavaliers	G	704 418-2543	
Shelby *(G-11354)*			
Love Knot Candles	G	336 456-1619	
Greensboro *(G-5666)*			
Lr Manufacturing Inc	G	910 399-1410	
Delco *(G-3737)*			
Luxuriously Natural Soaps LLC	G	910 378-9064	
Jacksonville *(G-7130)*			
Mammoth Machine and Design LLC	G	704 727-3330	
Mooresville *(G-8718)*			
Manufactur LLC	G	919 937-2090	
Durham *(G-4117)*			
Marties Miniatures	G	336 869-5952	
High Point *(G-6705)*			
Maximizer Systems Inc	G	828 345-6036	
Hickory *(G-6393)*			
Mdi Solutions LLC	G	845 721-6758	
Salisbury *(G-11092)*			
Medallion Company Inc	C	919 990-3500	
Timberlake *(G-12101)*			

▲ Meghan Blake Industries Inc	E	704 462-2988	
Vale *(G-12209)*			
◆ Microfine Inc	H	336 768-1480	
Winston Salem *(G-13252)*			
Mikron Industries	G	253 398-1382	
Durham *(G-4134)*			
Miller Bee Supply Inc	F	336 670-2249	
North Wilkesboro *(G-9548)*			
Minnewawa Inc	G	865 522-8103	
Charlotte *(G-2507)*			
Mint Hill Industries	G	704 545-8852	
Mint Hill *(G-8341)*			
Mountain Leisure Hot Tubs LLC	G	828 649-7727	
Arden *(G-287)*			
Mpx Manufacturing Inc	G	704 762-9207	
Salisbury *(G-11094)*			
Mvp Group International Inc	E	336 527-2238	
Mount Airy *(G-9156)*			
◆ Mvp Group International Inc	E	843 216-8380	
Elkin *(G-4449)*			
Myfuturenc Inc	F	919 649-7834	
Raleigh *(G-10320)*			
Nacho Industries Inc	G	919 937-9471	
Durham *(G-4141)*			
National Container Group LLC	G	704 393-9050	
Charlotte *(G-2544)*			
National Ctr For Social Impact	G	984 212-2285	
Raleigh *(G-10323)*			
National Voctnl Tech Honor Soc	G	828 698-8011	
Flat Rock *(G-4711)*			
Natrx Inc	E	919 263-0667	
Raleigh *(G-10325)*			
Nederman Manufacturing	G	704 898-7945	
Charlotte *(G-2552)*			
Neptune Hlth Wllness Innvtion	C	888 664-9166	
Conover *(G-3541)*			
Novem Industries Inc	G	704 660-6460	
Charlotte *(G-2580)*			
Oleksynprannyk LLC	F	704 450-0182	
Mooresville *(G-8738)*			
Optomill Solutions LLC	G	704 560-4037	
Matthews *(G-8188)*			
Pag Asb LLC	G	336 883-4187	
High Point *(G-6724)*			
Pashes LLC	G	704 682-6535	
Statesville *(G-11743)*			
Patrice Brent	G	980 999-7217	
Charlotte *(G-2615)*			
◆ Paul Hoge Creations Inc	F	704 624-6860	
Marshville *(G-8091)*			
Phillips Corporation	E	336 665-1080	
Colfax *(G-3286)*			
Plantd Inc	D	434 906-3445	
Oxford *(G-9624)*			
Plushh LLC	G	919 647-7911	
Raleigh *(G-10374)*			
Pmb Industries Inc	G	336 453-3121	
Lexington *(G-7733)*			
Pnb Manufacturing	G	336 883-0021	
High Point *(G-6738)*			
Precision Boat Mfg	G	336 395-8795	
Graham *(G-5282)*			
Prezioso Ventures LLC	G	704 793-1602	
Concord *(G-3422)*			
Producers Gin Murfreesboro LLC	G	252 398-3762	
Murfreesboro *(G-9285)*			
Professional Laminating LLC	G	919 465-0400	
Cary *(G-1430)*			
Progressive Industries Inc	G	919 267-6948	
Apex *(G-187)*			
Purilum LLC	E	252 931-8020	
Greenville *(G-6016)*			

Qspac Industries Inc .... E 704 635-7815
Monroe (G-8546)

Qualtech Industries Inc .... G 704 734-0345
Kings Mountain (G-7380)

Ratoon Agroprocessing LLC .... G 828 273-9114
Marion (G-8062)

Red Wolfe Industries LLC .... F 336 570-2282
Graham (G-5284)

Rockgeist LLC 518 461-2009
Asheville (G-593)

Rolling Umbrellas Inc .... G 828 754-4200
Lenoir (G-7637)

Rq Industries Inc .... G 704 701-1071
Concord (G-3436)

▼ Ruth Hicks Enterprise Inc .... F 704 469-4741
Waxhaw (G-12439)

Ryder Integrated Logistics Inc .... G 336 227-1130
Burlington (G-1152)

Ryder Integrated Logistics Inc .... F 336 227-1130
Burlington (G-1153)

S Y Shop Inc .... G 704 545-7710
Mint Hill (G-8343)

Salon & Spa Design Services .... G 919 556-6380
Wake Forest (G-12296)

Sapona Manufacturing Co Inc .... G 336 625-2161
Asheboro (G-393)

Sbm Industries LLC .... G 919 625-3672
Raleigh (G-10459)

Seneca Devices Inc .... F 301 412-3576
Durham (G-4230)

Sesmfg LLC .... G 803 917-3248
Charlotte (G-2790)

Shoffner Industries Inc .... G 336 226-9356
Burlington (G-1156)

Silver Dollar Gun Pawn Sp Inc .... G 336 824-8989
Ramseur (G-10631)

Simontic Composite Inc .... E 336 897-9885
Greensboro (G-5813)

Sincere Scents Co LLC .... G 910 616-4697
Southport (G-11528)

▲ Skidril Industries LLC .... G 800 843-3745
Randleman (G-10660)

Southern Home Spa and Wtr Pdts .... G 336 286-3564
Greensboro (G-5826)

Southland Amusements Vend Inc .... E 910 343-1809
Wilmington (G-12927)

Specialty Trnsp Systems Inc .... G 828 464-9738
Newton (G-9498)

Speed King Manufacturing Inc .... G 910 457-1995
Southport (G-11530)

Speer Operational Tech LLC .... G 864 631-2512
Marion (G-8066)

▲ Stage Decoration and Sups Inc .... G 336 621-5454
Greensboro (G-5834)

Steri-Air LLC .... G 336 434-1166
High Point (G-6793)

Stiletto Manufacturing Inc .... G 252 564-4877
Columbia (G-3297)

Stitchmaster LLC .... F 336 852-6448
Greensboro (G-5841)

Stokes Mfg LLC .... G 336 270-8746
Roxboro (G-10947)

Suntex Industries .... F 336 784-1000
Winston Salem (G-13349)

Sutton Scientifics Inc .... G 910 428-1600
Star (G-11634)

Taxation Station LLC .... G 336 209-3933
Greensboro (G-5853)

Tk Elevator Corporation .... D 336 272-4563
Greensboro (G-5867)

Tobacco Outlet Products LLC .... G 704 341-9388
Charlotte (G-2924)

Toolmarx LLC .... G 919 725-0122
Winston Salem (G-13367)

Tree Frog Industries LLC .... G 919 986-2229
Wendell (G-12551)

◆ Tree Masters Inc .... E 828 464-9443
Newton (G-9506)

Tri-Tech Forensics Inc .... D 910 457-6600
Leland (G-7561)

Triangle Trggr-Pint Thrapy Inc .... G 919 845-1818
Raleigh (G-10562)

Tribofilm Research Inc .... G 919 838-2844
Raleigh (G-10563)

Unity Hlthcare Lab Billing LLP .... G 980 209-0402
Charlotte (G-2964)

Urban Industries Corp .... G 980 209-9471
Pineville (G-9763)

◆ USa Wholesale and Distrg Inc .... F 888 484-6872
Fayetteville (G-4693)

◆ Vecoplan LLC .... E 336 861-6070
Greensboro (G-5897)

Velocita Inc .... G 336 764-8513
Clemmons (G-3208)

Veon Inc .... F 252 623-2102
Washington (G-12418)

Vision Contract Mfg LLC .... E 336 405-8784
High Point (G-6827)

Walco International .... G 704 624-2473
Marshville (G-8097)

Waxhaw Candle Company LLC .... G 980 245-2827
Charlotte (G-3008)

Web 4 Half LLC .... E 855 762-4638
Greensboro (G-5914)

White Tiger Btq & Candle Co .... G 919 610-7244
Sanford (G-11249)

Wildflwers Btq of Blowing Rock .... G 828 295-9655
Blowing Rock (G-882)

Xtra Light Manufacturing .... G 919 422-7281
Apex (G-207)

Z Collection LLC .... G 919 247-1513
Zebulon (G-13526)

Zeal Industries LLC .... G 828 575-9894
Asheville (G-637)

40 RAILROAD TRANSPORTATION

4011 Railroads, line-haul operating

Florida Progress Corporation .... C 704 382-3853
Raleigh (G-10113)

41 LOCAL & SUBURBAN TRANSIT & INTERURBAN HIGHWAY TRANSPORTATION

4111 Local and suburban transit

Concierge Transit LLC .... G 704 778-0755
Charlotte (G-1969)

4151 School buses

◆ Hickory Springs Manufactu .... D 828 328-2201
Hickory (G-6355)

42 MOTOR FREIGHT TRANSPORTATION

4212 Local trucking, without storage

A Plus Five Star Trnsp LLC .... G 919 771-4820
Clayton (G-3129)

Bobby Cahoon Construction Inc .... E 252 249-1617
Grantsboro (G-5329)

Central Carolina Concrete LLC .... F 704 372-2930
Greensboro (G-5437)

Comer Sanitary Service Inc .... G 336 629-8311
Lexington (G-7668)

Crowder Trucking LLC .... G 910 797-4163
Fayetteville (G-4581)

▼ Fayblock Materials Inc .... D 910 323-9198
Fayetteville (G-4600)

Fresh-N-Mobile LLC .... G 704 251-4643
Charlotte (G-2180)

H & M Wood Preserving Inc .... E 704 279-5188
Gold Hill (G-5192)

Hammill Construction Co Inc .... G 704 279-5309
Gold Hill (G-5193)

Long Asp Pav Trckg of Grnsburg .... G 336 643-4121
Summerfield (G-11842)

McLean Sbsrface Utlity Engrg L .... F 336 340-0024
Greensboro (G-5687)

Milligan House Movers Inc .... G 910 653-2272
Tabor City (G-11913)

New Finish Inc .... E 704 474-4116
Norwood (G-9557)

Privette Enterprises Inc .... E 704 634-3291
Monroe (G-8544)

Raleigh Road Box Corporation .... G 252 438-7401
Henderson (G-6174)

Stone Supply Inc .... G 828 678-9966
Burnsville (G-1192)

T H Blue Inc .... E 910 673-3033
Eagle Springs (G-4319)

Tkm Global LLC .... G 732 694-0311
Raleigh (G-10550)

V M Trucking Inc .... G 984 239-4853
Morehead City (G-8848)

4213 Trucking, except local

Advantage Machinery Svcs Inc .... E 336 463-4700
Yadkinville (G-13435)

Bundy Logging Company Inc .... G 252 357-0191
Gatesville (G-5170)

Firm Ascend LLC .... G 704 464-3024
Charlotte (G-2154)

J & L Bckh/Nvrnmental Svcs Inc .... G 910 237-7351
Eastover (G-4337)

RSI Leasing Inc NS Tbt .... SIC 704 587-9300
Charlotte (G-2738)

▲ Southeast Wood Products Inc .... F 910 285-4359
Wallace (G-12324)

T H Blue Inc .... E 910 673-3033
Eagle Springs (G-4319)

4214 Local trucking with storage

Bundy Logging Company Inc .... G 252 357-0191
Gatesville (G-5170)

Comer Sanitary Service Inc .... G 336 629-8311
Lexington (G-7668)

Elizabeth Logistic LLC .... D 803 920-3931
Indian Trail (G-7078)

Loflin Concrete Co Inc .... E 336 904-2788
Kernersville (G-7282)

Lunar International Tech LLC .... F 800 975-7153
Charlotte (G-2441)

Wheeler Industries Inc .... G 919 736-4256
Pikeville (G-9669)

4215 Courier services, except by air

Go Postal In Boone Inc .... F 828 262-0027
Boone (G-917)

Rapid Run Transport LLC .... F 704 615-3458
Charlotte (G-2690)

Yumitos Corporation .... E 786 952-6202
Charlotte (G-3043)

4221 Farm product warehousing and storage

C A Perry & Son Inc................................ G 252 330-2323
Elizabeth City (G-4380)

C A Perry & Son Inc................................ E 252 221-4463
Hobbsville (G-6883)

4222 Refrigerated warehousing and storage

Smith Utility Buildings........................... G 336 957-8211
Traphill (G-12106)

4225 General warehousing and storage

▲ Airspeed LLC..................................... E 919 644-1222
Mebane (G-8227)

Ashley Furniture Inds LLC...................... E 336 998-1066
Advance (G-31)

Burton Global Logistics LLC.................. E 336 663-6449
Burlington (G-1057)

Fishel Steel Company............................ G 336 788-2880
Winston Salem (G-13169)

◆ Hafele America Co.............................. C 800 423-3531
Archdale (G-224)

Metrohose Incorporated......................... G 252 329-9891
Greenville (G-6004)

Pactiv LLC.. F 828 396-2373
Granite Falls (G-5315)

Parkdale Mills Incorporated................... F 704 825-2529
Belmont (G-760)

Patheon Softgels Inc.............................. F 336 812-8700
Greensboro (G-5736)

Phoenix Assembly NC LLC..................... G 252 801-4250
Battleboro (G-706)

Warehouse Distillery LLC....................... G 828 464-5183
Newton (G-9510)

4226 Special warehousing and storage, nec

Cairn Studio Ltd..................................... E 704 664-7128
Mooresville (G-8627)

▲ Ideaitlia Cntmporary Furn Corp........ C 828 464-1000
Conover (G-3532)

Legalis Dms LLC.................................... F 919 741-8260
Raleigh (G-10252)

Svcm.. G 305 767-3595
Lincolnton (G-7858)

Trimfit Inc... C 336 476-6154
Thomasville (G-12084)

Weyerhaeuser Company......................... F 252 746-7200
Grifton (G-6039)

44 WATER TRANSPORTATION

4449 Water transportation of freight

Florida Progress Corporation................. C 704 382-3853
Raleigh (G-10113)

4489 Water passenger transportation

Amerochem Corporation......................... E 252 634-9344
New Bern (G-9333)

4493 Marinas

Cape Fear Boat Works Inc..................... F 910 371-3460
Navassa (G-9326)

45 TRANSPORTATION BY AIR

4512 Air transportation, scheduled

Charter Jet Transport Inc....................... G 704 359-8833
Charlotte (G-1907)

D2 Government Solutions LLC............... E 662 655-4554
New Bern (G-9362)

T Air Inc... D 980 595-2840
Charlotte (G-2895)

4513 Air courier services

Concierge Transit LLC........................... G 704 778-0755
Charlotte (G-1969)

T Air Inc... D 980 595-2840
Charlotte (G-2895)

4522 Air transportation, nonscheduled

D2 Government Solutions LLC............... E 662 655-4554
New Bern (G-9362)

4581 Airports, flying fields, and services

D2 Government Solutions LLC............... E 662 655-4554
New Bern (G-9362)

◆ Haeco Americas LLC.......................... A 336 668-4410
Greensboro (G-5585)

Piedmont AVI Cmponent Svcs LLC....... C 336 423-5100
Greensboro (G-5741)

Powerhouse Resources Intl LLC........... D 919 291-1783
Raleigh (G-10380)

Summit Aviation Inc............................... F 302 834-5400
Greensboro (G-5844)

Textron Aviation Inc.............................. C 336 605-7000
Greensboro (G-5861)

Zim Arcraft Cbin Solutions LLC............ F 336 862-1418
Greensboro (G-5932)

46 PIPELINES, EXCEPT NATURAL GAS

4613 Refined petroleum pipelines

Panenergy Corp..................................... F 704 594-6200
Charlotte (G-2607)

47 TRANSPORTATION SERVICES

4731 Freight transportation arrangement

Deliveright Logistics Inc........................ C 862 279-7332
Lexington (G-7676)

Elizabeth Logistic LLC........................... D 803 920-3931
Indian Trail (G-7078)

Gaines Motor Lines Inc......................... C 828 322-2000
Hickory (G-6337)

Kenn M LLC... E 678 755-6607
Raleigh (G-10233)

Lls Investments Inc............................... F 919 662-7283
Raleigh (G-10258)

Phoenix Assembly NC LLC..................... G 252 801-4250
Battleboro (G-706)

Rapid Run Transport LLC....................... F 704 615-3458
Charlotte (G-2690)

4783 Packing and crating

Berlin Packaging LLC............................ G 704 612-4500
Charlotte (G-1772)

▲ Broadwind Indus Solutions LLC....... E 919 777-2907
Sanford (G-11159)

Hershey Group LLC................................ G 336 855-3888
Greensboro (G-5594)

Lls Investments Inc............................... F 919 662-7283
Raleigh (G-10258)

Ssi Services Inc.................................... G 919 867-1450
Raleigh (G-10501)

4785 Inspection and fixed facilities

Surelift Inc... G 828 963-6899
Boone (G-945)

4789 Transportation services, nec

At Your Service Express LLC................. E 704 270-9918
Charlotte (G-1707)

Carolina Expediters LLC........................ G 888 537-5330
Mount Airy (G-9108)

Cymbal LLC.. G 877 365-9622
Cary (G-1342)

D&E Freight LLC.................................... F 704 977-4847
Charlotte (G-2013)

Harsco Rail LLC.................................... G 980 960-2624
Charlotte (G-2262)

MMS Logistics Incorporated.................. G 336 214-3552
Mc Leansville (G-8225)

Speedway Link Inc................................ G 704 338-2028
Matthews (G-8150)

48 COMMUNICATIONS

4812 Radiotelephone communication

Infinity Communications LLC................. E 919 797-2334
Durham (G-4076)

McShan Inc.. G 980 355-9790
Charlotte (G-2481)

▲ Spectrasite Communications LLC..... E 919 468-0112
Cary (G-1465)

4813 Telephone communication, except radio

Cengage Learning Inc........................... E 919 829-8181
Raleigh (G-9990)

Charlotte Observer Pubg Co.................. A 704 358-5000
Charlotte (G-1899)

Interconnect Products and..................... E 336 667-3356
Wilkesboro (G-12640)

M I Connection...................................... F 704 662-3255
Mooresville (G-8717)

Mountain Area Info Netwrk.................... F 828 255-0182
Asheville (G-552)

▲ Spectrasite Communications LLC..... E 919 468-0112
Cary (G-1465)

Telit Wireless Solutions Inc.................. D 919 439-7977
Durham (G-4264)

◆ Walker and Associates Inc................ C 336 731-6391
Winston Salem (G-13386)

4822 Telegraph and other communications

King Business Service Inc..................... G 910 610-1030
Laurinburg (G-7504)

4832 Radio broadcasting stations

Latino Communications Inc................... F 704 319-5044
Charlotte (G-2409)

Latino Communications Inc................... F 919 645-1680
Raleigh (G-10249)

Latino Communications Inc................... D 336 714-2823
Winston Salem (G-13231)

Lyon Company... F 919 787-0024
Wadesboro (G-12248)

National Ctr For Social Impact.............. G 984 212-2285
Raleigh (G-10323)

Wtvd Television LLC............................... C 919 683-1111
Durham (G-4313)

4833 Television broadcasting stations

News 14 Carolina.................................. G 704 973-5700
Charlotte (G-2559)

Wtvd Television LLC............................... C 919 683-1111
Durham (G-4313)

4841 Cable and other pay television services

Cco Holdings LLC.................................. C 828 414-4238
Blowing Rock (G-881)

Cco Holdings LLC.................................. C 828 355-4149
Boone (G-906)

Cco Holdings LLC.................................. C 910 292-4083
Dunn (G-3850)

S I C

Cco Holdings LLC.................................... B 828 270-7016
Hickory *(G-6293)*

Cco Holdings LLC.................................... C 919 502-4007
Kenly *(G-7228)*

Cco Holdings LLC.................................... C 828 394-0635
Lenoir *(G-7592)*

Cco Holdings LLC.................................... C 704 308-3361
Lincolnton *(G-7820)*

Cco Holdings LLC.................................... C 828 528-4004
Newland *(G-9427)*

Cco Holdings LLC.................................... C 919 200-6260
Siler City *(G-11402)*

Cco Holdings LLC.................................... C 828 368-4161
Valdese *(G-12192)*

Cog Glbal Media/Consulting LLC.... E 980 239-8042
Matthews *(G-8109)*

M I Connection....................................... F 704 662-3255
Mooresville *(G-8717)*

4899 Communication services, nec

Bluetick Inc.. F 336 294-4102
Greensboro *(G-5395)*

Commscope LLC..................................... C 828 324-2200
Claremont *(G-3097)*

Commscope Holding Company Inc........ F 919 677-2422
Cary *(G-1331)*

Commscope Holding Company Inc........ A 828 459-5000
Claremont *(G-3100)*

Fast Pro Media LLC................................ G 704 799-8040
Cornelius *(G-3600)*

Gpx Intelligence Inc.............................. E 888 260-0706
Greensboro *(G-5570)*

▲ Spectrasite Communications LLC.... E 919 468-0112
Cary *(G-1465)*

49 ELECTRIC, GAS AND SANITARY SERVICES

4911 Electric services

Florida Progress Corporation................. C 704 382-3853
Raleigh *(G-10113)*

Go Ev and Go Green Corp..................... G 704 327-9040
Charlotte *(G-2220)*

Johnson Controls Inc............................ G 866 285-8345
Morrisville *(G-8995)*

Livingston & Haven LLC........................ C 704 588-3670
Charlotte *(G-2428)*

Panenergy Corp..................................... F 704 594-6200
Charlotte *(G-2607)*

Pike Electric LLC................................... C 336 316-7068
Greensboro *(G-5748)*

Windlift Inc... G 919 490-8575
Durham *(G-4306)*

4922 Natural gas transmission

Panenergy Corp..................................... F 704 594-6200
Charlotte *(G-2607)*

4924 Natural gas distribution

Blue Gas Marine Inc.............................. F 919 238-3427
Apex *(G-146)*

Bolton Construction & Svc LLC.............. D 919 861-1500
Raleigh *(G-9952)*

4931 Electric and other services combined

Flexgen Power Systems Inc................... G 855 327-5674
Durham *(G-4033)*

Flexgen Power Systems Inc................... F 855 327-5674
Durham *(G-4034)*

▲ Powersecure International Inc.......... A 919 556-3056
Wake Forest *(G-12289)*

4939 Combination utilities, nec

Noahs Inc.. F 704 718-2354
Charlotte *(G-2570)*

4941 Water supply

Bolton Construction & Svc LLC.............. D 919 861-1500
Raleigh *(G-9952)*

County of Anson.................................... G 704 848-4849
Lilesville *(G-7784)*

Prime Water Services Inc...................... G 919 504-1020
Raleigh *(G-10394)*

Tempest Environmental Corp................ G 919 973-1609
Durham *(G-4265)*

4953 Refuse systems

A-1 Sandrock Inc................................... E 336 855-8195
Greensboro *(G-5334)*

Alleghany Garbage Service Inc.............. G 336 372-4413
Sparta *(G-11533)*

Clean Green Inc..................................... G 919 596-3500
Durham *(G-3977)*

Crizaf Inc.. G 919 251-7661
Durham *(G-3991)*

◆ Custom Polymers Inc........................ F 704 332-6070
Charlotte *(G-2011)*

Duramax Holdings LLC.......................... C 704 588-9191
Charlotte *(G-2068)*

Eastern Crlina Vctonal Ctr Inc............... D 252 758-4188
Greenville *(G-5972)*

◆ Elan Trading Inc............................... E 704 342-1696
Charlotte *(G-2094)*

Fiber Composites LLC............................ D 704 463-7118
New London *(G-9416)*

Global Ecosciences Inc......................... G 252 631-6266
Wake Forest *(G-12278)*

▼ Hoh Corporation................................ F 336 723-9274
Winston Salem *(G-13199)*

National Container Group LLC............... G 704 393-9050
Charlotte *(G-2544)*

Noble Oil Services Inc........................... C 919 774-8180
Sanford *(G-11212)*

Parkdale Mills Incorporated.................. F 704 825-2529
Belmont *(G-760)*

RDc Debris Removal Cnstr LLC.............. E 323 614-2353
Smithfield *(G-11462)*

Soundside Recycling & Mtls Inc............. G 252 491-8666
Jarvisburg *(G-7186)*

Steelman Lumber & Pallet LLC.............. F 336 468-2757
Hamptonville *(G-6092)*

Todco Inc.. F 336 248-2001
Lexington *(G-7753)*

Waste Industries Usa LLC...................... C 919 325-3000
Raleigh *(G-10598)*

▲ Wastezero Inc.................................. E 919 322-1208
Raleigh *(G-10599)*

4959 Sanitary services, nec

Big Vac.. G 910 947-3654
Carthage *(G-1276)*

Butler Trieu Inc..................................... G 910 346-4929
Jacksonville *(G-7118)*

Global Ecosciences Inc......................... G 252 631-6266
Wake Forest *(G-12278)*

Integrity Envmtl Solutions LLC.............. D 704 283-9765
Monroe *(G-8505)*

Noble Oil Services Inc........................... C 919 774-8180
Sanford *(G-11212)*

Protek Services LLC.............................. G 910 556-4121
Cameron *(G-1215)*

4961 Steam and air-conditioning supply

Bolton Construction & Svc LLC.............. D 919 861-1500
Raleigh *(G-9952)*

50 WHOLESALE TRADE - DURABLE GOODS

5012 Automobiles and other motor vehicles

▼ Axle Holdings LLC............................. E 800 895-3276
Concord *(G-3316)*

◆ Mack Trucks Inc................................ A 336 291-9001
Greensboro *(G-5670)*

◆ National Foam Inc............................. E 919 639-6100
Angier *(G-126)*

Parker-Hannifin Corporation................. E 704 664-1922
Mooresville *(G-8742)*

Pro-System Inc...................................... F 704 799-8100
Mooresville *(G-8756)*

Streets Auto Sales & Four WD............... G 704 888-8686
Locust *(G-7904)*

◆ Vna Holding Inc................................ A 336 393-4890
Greensboro *(G-5905)*

Volvo Group North America LLC........... A 336 393-2000
Greensboro *(G-5907)*

Volvo Group North America LLC........... A 336 393-2000
Greensboro *(G-5908)*

◆ Volvo Group North America LLC....... A 336 393-2000
Greensboro *(G-5906)*

◆ Volvo Trucks North America Inc........ A 336 393-2000
Greensboro *(G-5911)*

5013 Motor vehicle supplies and new parts

A-1 Hitch & Trailors Sales Inc................ G 910 755-6025
Supply *(G-11854)*

Auto Machine Shop Inc.......................... G 910 483-6016
Fayetteville *(G-4554)*

Camco Manufacturing Inc...................... G 336 348-6609
Reidsville *(G-10678)*

Capitol Bumper....................................... G 919 772-7330
Fayetteville *(G-4568)*

Consolidated Truck Parts Inc................. C 704 279-5543
Rockwell *(G-10794)*

Cummins Inc.. E 336 275-4531
Greensboro *(G-5476)*

Fontaine Modification Company............. F 704 392-8502
Charlotte *(G-2169)*

Heintz Bros Automotives Inc................. G 704 872-8081
Statesville *(G-11706)*

Johnson Machine Co Inc........................ G 252 638-2620
New Bern *(G-9374)*

Lake Shore Radiator Inc........................ F 336 271-2626
Greensboro *(G-5657)*

▲ Mann+hmmel Fltrtion Tech Group..... G 704 869-3300
Gastonia *(G-5082)*

Mc Cullough Auto Elc & Assoc............... G 704 376-5388
Charlotte *(G-2475)*

Merchant 1 Marketing LLC..................... G 888 853-9992
Greensboro *(G-5691)*

▼ Mfi Products Inc................................ F 910 944-2128
Aberdeen *(G-16)*

Nichols Spdmtr & Instr Co Inc................ G 336 273-2881
Greensboro *(G-5709)*

Oldcastle Infrastructure Inc................... E 919 772-6269
Raleigh *(G-10344)*

Patty Knio.. G 919 995-2670
Raleigh *(G-10362)*

Perry Brothers Tire Svc Inc................... F 919 693-2128
Oxford *(G-9623)*

▲ Pfaff Molds Ltd Partnership.............. F 704 423-9484
Charlotte *(G-2631)*

Pgw Auto Glass LLC............................... B 336 258-4950
Elkin *(G-4451)*

▲ Adams Products Company............... C 919 467-2218
   Morrisville (G-8919)

Apac-Atlantic Inc................................. D 336 412-6800
   Raleigh (G-9907)

Asphalt Emulsion Inds LLC.................. G 252 726-0653
   Morehead City (G-8814)

Barnhill Contracting Company.......... E 252 527-8021
   Kinston (G-7395)

Bloomday Granite & Marble Inc......... E 336 724-0300
   Winston Salem (G-13108)

Concrete Service Co Inc..................... E 910 483-0396
   Fayetteville (G-4577)

Custom Brick Company Inc................ E 919 832-2804
   Raleigh (G-10028)

D&S Company Inc............................... G 828 894-2778
   Tryon (G-12174)

Design Specialties Inc....................... G 919 772-6955
   Raleigh (G-10042)

Explosives Supply Company.............. F 828 765-2762
   Spruce Pine (G-11575)

Fletcher Limestone Company Inc.......... G 828 684-6701
   Fletcher (G-4737)

Fsc II LLC.. F 919 783-5700
   Raleigh (G-10122)

General Shale Brick Inc..................... E 919 775-2121
   Raleigh (G-10127)

General Shale Brick Inc..................... G 910 452-3498
   Wilmington (G-12786)

Greenville Ready Mix Concrete.......... E 252 756-0119
   Winterville (G-13416)

Heidelberg Mtls Sthast Agg LLC.......... E 910 893-8308
   Bunnlevel (G-1016)

J&R SERvices/J&r Lumber Co............ G 956 778-7005
   Wilmington (G-12821)

Lbm Industries Inc............................. F 828 966-4270
   Sapphire (G-11258)

Marietta Martin Materials Inc.............. G 336 769-3803
   Kernersville (G-7284)

Martin Marietta Materials Inc.............. G 336 674-0836
   Greensboro (G-5679)

Merchants Metals Inc......................... G 704 921-9192
   Charlotte (G-2491)

Motsinger Block Plant Inc................... G 336 764-0350
   Winston Salem (G-13262)

Old Castle Apg South Inc................... G 919 383-2521
   Durham (G-4155)

◆ Pine Hall Brick Co Inc.....................E 336 721-7500
   Winston Salem (G-13296)

Plycem USA LLC................................. C 336 696-2007
   North Wilkesboro (G-9549)

Radford Quarries Inc..........................F 828 264-7008
   Boone (G-939)

▲ Sid Jenkins Inc................................ G 336 632-0707
   Greensboro (G-5811)

Southern Marble Co LLC..................... G 704 982-4142
   Albemarle (G-91)

Spake Concrete Products Inc.............. F 704 482-2881
   Shelby (G-11382)

Speer Concrete Inc............................ E 910 947-3144
   Carthage (G-1280)

Stone & Leigh LLC............................. G 919 971-2096
   Morganton (G-8901)

Surface Buff LLC............................... G 919 341-2873
   Raleigh (G-10523)

▲ Trade Venture Stones LLC................ G 919 803-3923
   Knightdale (G-7460)

Troy Ready - Mix Inc.......................... G 910 572-1011
   Troy (G-12169)

Viktors Gran MBL Kit Cnter Top............F 828 681-0713
   Arden (G-316)

Wake Stone Corporation..................... E 919 775-7349
   Moncure (G-8412)

Welbuilt Homes Inc............................ G 910 323-0098
   Fayetteville (G-4699)

5033 Roofing, siding, and insulation

Carolina Home Exteriors LLC.............. F 252 637-6599
   New Bern (G-9350)

Exteriors Inc Ltd................................ G 919 325-2251
   Spring Lake (G-11561)

Longhorn Roofing Inc......................... F 704 774-1080
   Monroe (G-8520)

Mid-Atlantic Specialties Inc................ G 919 212-1939
   Raleigh (G-10305)

Roofing Tools and Eqp Inc.................. G 252 291-1800
   Wilson (G-13024)

Triad Corrugated Metal Inc................. E 336 625-9727
   Asheboro (G-411)

◆ Union Corrugating Company...............E 910 483-0479
   Fayetteville (G-4685)

Vinyl Windows & Doors Corp.............. F 910 944-2100
   Aberdeen (G-30)

Wake Supply Company....................... G 252 234-6012
   Wilson (G-13044)

5039 Construction materials, nec

1st Choice Service Inc....................... G 704 913-7635
   Cherryville (G-3058)

Afsc LLC.. D 704 523-4936
   Charlotte (G-1627)

Asheville Contracting Co Inc.............. E 828 665-8900
   Candler (G-1217)

Bobby Cahoon Construction Inc.......... E 252 249-1617
   Grantsboro (G-5329)

Carolina Prcsion Fbers Spv LLC.......... E 336 527-4140
   Ronda (G-10893)

Cymbal LLC.. G 877 365-9622
   Cary (G-1342)

Design Specialties Inc....................... G 919 772-6955
   Raleigh (G-10042)

Eastern Wholesale Fence LLC............ D 631 698-0975
   Salisbury (G-11047)

Explosives Supply Company............... F 828 765-2762
   Spruce Pine (G-11575)

Maxson & Associates.......................... G 336 632-0524
   Greensboro (G-5683)

Outlaw Step Co.................................. G 252 568-4384
   Deep Run (G-3733)

Southern Concrete Mtls Inc................ G 828 681-5178
   Fletcher (G-4771)

Southern Concrete Mtls Inc................ E 828 692-6517
   Hendersonville (G-6243)

5044 Office equipment

Branch Office Solutions Inc................ G 800 743-1047
   Indian Trail (G-7072)

Bryan Austin..................................... G 336 841-6573
   High Point (G-6551)

Digital Print & Imaging Inc................. G 910 341-3005
   Greenville (G-5965)

Systel Business Eqp Co Inc................. E 336 808-8000
   Greensboro (G-5849)

5045 Computers, peripherals, and software

Amt Datasouth Corp........................... E 704 523-8500
   Charlotte (G-1675)

Clairvoyant Technology Inc................. G 919 491-5062
   Durham (G-3976)

Database Incorporated........................ G 202 684-6252
   Durham (G-3999)

Dimill Enterprises LLC........................ G 919 629-2011
   Raleigh (G-10046)

EMC Corporation................................ G 720 341-3274
   Charlotte (G-2108)

Envirnmntal Systems RES Inst I............ E 704 541-9810
   Charlotte (G-2119)

Glover Corporation Inc....................... E 919 821-5535
   Raleigh (G-10139)

Interconnect Products and................. E 336 667-3356
   Wilkesboro (G-12640)

Iqe North Carolina LLC....................... F 336 609-6270
   Greensboro (G-5623)

Logiksavvy Solutions LLC................... G 336 392-6149
   Greensboro (G-5663)

McKelvey Fulks.................................. G 704 357-1550
   Charlotte (G-2479)

Medicor Imaging Inc........................... G 704 332-5532
   Charlotte (G-2486)

NCSMJ Inc.. F 704 544-1118
   Pineville (G-9744)

Reynolds and Reynolds Company.......... G 321 287-3939
   Charlotte (G-2721)

▲ Sato America LLC............................ C 704 644-1650
   Charlotte (G-2757)

Sighttech LLC.................................... G 855 997-4448
   Charlotte (G-2805)

Smartway of Carolinas LLC................. G 704 900-7877
   Charlotte (G-2817)

St Investors Inc.................................. D 704 969-7500
   Charlotte (G-2856)

▲ Teguar Corporation.......................... E 704 960-1761
   Charlotte (G-2906)

◆ Vrush Industries Inc.........................G 336 886-7700
   High Point (G-6829)

5046 Commercial equipment, nec

Chef Martini LLC................................A 919 327-3183
   Raleigh (G-9992)

Custom Neon & Graphics Inc.............. G 704 344-1715
   Charlotte (G-2010)

Dandy Light Traps Inc........................ G 980 223-2744
   Statesville (G-11684)

Elxsi Corporation............................... B 407 849-1090
   Charlotte (G-2105)

Gold Medal Products Co...................... G 336 665-4997
   Greensboro (G-5568)

Government Sales LLC........................ G 252 726-6315
   Morehead City (G-8833)

Innovative Design Tech LLC................ G 919 331-0204
   Angier (G-121)

Kenneth Moore Signs.......................... G 910 458-6428
   Wilmington (G-12826)

Maxson & Associates.......................... G 336 632-0524
   Greensboro (G-5683)

Picassomoesllc.................................. G 216 703-4547
   Hillsborough (G-6875)

Precision Walls Inc............................ G 336 852-7710
   Greensboro (G-5759)

Restaurant Furniture Inc.................... F 828 459-9992
   Claremont (G-3120)

Riddley Retail Fixtures Inc................. E 704 435-8829
   Kings Mountain (G-7382)

Satco Truck Equipment Inc................. F 919 383-5547
   Durham (G-4222)

◆ Schaefer Systems International Inc...C 704 944-4500
   Charlotte (G-2763)

Schaefer Systems Intl Inc................... G 704 944-4550
   Charlotte (G-2765)

Signature Signs Inc............................ G 336 431-2072
   High Point (G-6773)

Singer Equipment Company Inc............ E 910 484-1128
   Fayetteville (G-4671)

Southeastern Sign Works Inc............... G 336 789-5516
   Mount Airy (G-9177)

◆ Technibilt Ltd..................................E 828 464-7388
   Newton (G-9502)

S
I
C

Thompson & Little Inc.................................E 910 484-1128
  Fayetteville *(G-4680)*

True Portion Inc.......................................F 336 362-6326
  High Point *(G-6813)*

5047 Medical and hospital equipment

Aj & Raine Scrubs & More LLC..............G 646 374-5198
  Charlotte *(G-1634)*

Albemrle Orthotics Prosthetics.............E 252 338-3002
  Elizabeth City *(G-4378)*

▲ Amtai Medical Equipment Inc...........F 919 872-1803
  Raleigh *(G-9901)*

▲ Cathtek LLC...G 336 748-0686
  Winston Salem *(G-13120)*

Colowrap LLC...F 888 815-3376
  Durham *(G-3983)*

Combat Medical Systems LLC..............E 704 705-1222
  Huntersville *(G-6977)*

▲ Custom Industries Inc........................E 336 299-2885
  Greensboro *(G-5481)*

Ddm Inc..G 910 686-1481
  Wilmington *(G-12762)*

▲ Dentonics Inc.....................................F 704 238-0245
  Monroe *(G-8476)*

Dove Medical Supply LLC.......................E 336 643-9367
  Summerfield *(G-11838)*

Fidelity Pharmaceuticals LLC...............G 704 274-3192
  Huntersville *(G-6989)*

Fillauer North Carolina Inc....................E 828 658-8330
  Weaverville *(G-12491)*

Fla Orthopedics Inc...............................D 800 327-4110
  Charlotte *(G-2158)*

GNB Ventures LLC...................................F 704 488-4468
  Charlotte *(G-2218)*

◆ Greiner Bio-One North Amer Inc.......B 704 261-7800
  Monroe *(G-8496)*

Health Supply Us LLC.............................F 888 408-1694
  Mooresville *(G-8680)*

Jaguar Gene Therapy LLC......................F 919 465-6400
  Cary *(G-1377)*

Janus Development Group Inc...............G 252 551-9042
  Greenville *(G-5994)*

Joerns Healthcare Parent LLC...............B 800 966-6662
  Charlotte *(G-2372)*

Keani Furniture Inc..................................E 336 303-5484
  Asheboro *(G-369)*

Med Express/Medical Spc Inc................F 919 572-2568
  Durham *(G-4123)*

Medcor Inc...G 888 579-1050
  Lexington *(G-7718)*

◆ Medi Mall Inc.....................................G..... 877 501-6334
  Fletcher *(G-4753)*

Medi Manufacturing Inc.........................E 336 449-4440
  Whitsett *(G-12615)*

Medtrnic Sofamor Danek USA Inc.........G 919 457-9982
  Cary *(G-1401)*

▲ Meghan Blake Industries Inc............E 704 462-2988
  Vale *(G-12209)*

▲ Protection Products Inc.....................E 828 324-2173
  Hickory *(G-6420)*

Rm Liquidation Inc..................................D 828 274-7996
  Asheville *(G-591)*

RPM Products Inc....................................G 704 871-0518
  Statesville *(G-11761)*

▲ Sarstedt Inc...C 828 465-4000
  Newton *(G-9493)*

Sdv Office Systems LLC.........................F 844 968-9500
  Fletcher *(G-4766)*

Sg-Clw Inc...F 336 865-4980
  Winston Salem *(G-13331)*

Smissons Inc..G 660 537-3219
  Clayton *(G-3169)*

Specialty Trnsp Systems Inc..................G 828 464-9738
  Newton *(G-9498)*

Speer Operational Tech LLC...................G 864 631-2512
  Marion *(G-8066)*

▼ Suntech Medical Inc...........................D 919 654-2300
  Morrisville *(G-9060)*

Taiji Medical Supplies Inc......................G 888 667-6658
  Lincolnton *(G-7859)*

Test ME Out Inc.......................................G 252 635-6770
  New Bern *(G-9399)*

◆ Tripath Imaging Inc............................D 336 222-9707
  Burlington *(G-1170)*

Turbomed LLC..F 973 527-5299
  Fayetteville *(G-4684)*

United Mobile Imaging Inc......................G 800 983-9840
  Clemmons *(G-3207)*

Veon Inc...F 252 623-2102
  Washington *(G-12418)*

Yukon Medical LLC..................................G 919 595-8250
  Durham *(G-4317)*

5049 Professional equipment, nec

AEC Imaging & Graphics LLC.................G 910 693-1034
  Hope Mills *(G-6922)*

Biosupplynet Inc......................................F 919 659-2121
  Morrisville *(G-8941)*

Carolina Biological Supply Co................C 336 446-7600
  Whitsett *(G-12601)*

◆ Carolina Biological Supply Company.C 336 584-0381
  Burlington *(G-1060)*

Centice Corporation...............................F 919 653-0424
  Raleigh *(G-9991)*

◆ Diamond Dog Tools Inc......................D 828 687-3686
  Arden *(G-265)*

Diebold Nixdorf Incorporated................E 704 599-3100
  Charlotte *(G-2044)*

Duncan-Parnell Inc.................................G 252 977-7832
  Rocky Mount *(G-10833)*

Fisher Scientific Company LLC...............D 800 252-7100
  Asheville *(G-498)*

Lea Aid Acquisition Company.................G 919 872-6210
  Spring Hope *(G-11557)*

Optical Place Inc.....................................E 336 274-1300
  Greensboro *(G-5725)*

Piranha Nail and Staple Inc....................G 336 852-8358
  Greensboro *(G-5749)*

Sharpe Images Properties Inc................E 336 724-2871
  Winston Salem *(G-13334)*

Squarehead Technology LLC..................G 571 299-4849
  Hickory *(G-6456)*

Trafag Inc..G 704 343-6339
  Charlotte *(G-2932)*

Tri-Tech Forensics Inc............................D 910 457-6600
  Leland *(G-7561)*

Turbomed LLC..F 973 527-5299
  Fayetteville *(G-4684)*

◆ Wpmhj LLC..G..... 919 601-5445
  Raleigh *(G-10615)*

5051 Metals service centers and offices

Advanced Drainage Systems Inc............D 704 629-4151
  Bessemer City *(G-803)*

▲ Airspeed LLC.......................................E 919 644-1222
  Mebane *(G-8227)*

▼ Alamo Distribution LLC.......................C 704 398-5600
  Belmont *(G-740)*

Allens Gutter Service.............................G 910 738-9509
  Lumberton *(G-7944)*

▲ Asheville Bit & Steel Company.........F 828 274-3766
  Asheville *(G-433)*

▲ Aviation Metals NC Inc......................F 704 264-1647
  Charlotte *(G-1721)*

▲ Bessemer City Machine Shop Inc.....G 704 629-4111
  Bessemer City *(G-806)*

Biganodes LLC...G 828 245-1115
  Forest City *(G-4784)*

C & B Salvage Company Inc...................G 336 374-3946
  Ararat *(G-209)*

Charter Dura-Bar Inc..............................F 704 637-1906
  Salisbury *(G-11032)*

Chatham Steel Corporation....................E 912 233-4182
  Durham *(G-3970)*

Chicago Tube and Iron Company...........D 704 781-2060
  Locust *(G-7890)*

Component Sourcing Intl LLC.................E 704 843-9292
  Charlotte *(G-1967)*

Consolidated Pipe & Sup Co Inc............F 336 294-8577
  Greensboro *(G-5463)*

Corsan LLC..F 704 765-9979
  Huntersville *(G-6979)*

Dave Steel Company Inc.........................D 828 252-2771
  Asheville *(G-484)*

Dunavants Welding & Steel Inc..............G 252 338-6533
  Camden *(G-1211)*

Freedom Metals Inc.................................F 704 333-1214
  Charlotte *(G-2178)*

Gulfstream Steel & Supply Inc...............E 910 329-5100
  Holly Ridge *(G-6888)*

Harris Rebar Inc......................................G 919 528-8333
  Benson *(G-792)*

Hercules Steel Company Inc...................E 910 488-5110
  Fayetteville *(G-4611)*

Hsi Legacy Inc...G 704 376-9631
  Charlotte *(G-2294)*

Industrial Alloys Inc................................F 704 882-2887
  Indian Trail *(G-7084)*

▲ Iron Box LLC.......................................E 919 890-0025
  Raleigh *(G-10209)*

J Massey Inc..F 704 821-7084
  Stallings *(G-11600)*

McCombs Steel Company Inc.................E 704 873-7563
  Statesville *(G-11730)*

McCune Technology Inc..........................G 910 424-2978
  Fayetteville *(G-4638)*

▲ Pavco Inc...E 704 496-6800
  Charlotte *(G-2619)*

Reynolds Advanced Mtls Inc..................G 704 357-0600
  Charlotte *(G-2720)*

Sanders Company Inc.............................F 252 338-3995
  Elizabeth City *(G-4408)*

Schwartz Steel Service Inc....................E 704 865-9576
  Gastonia *(G-5135)*

Steel and Pipe Corporation....................E 919 776-0751
  Sanford *(G-11240)*

Sun Valley Stl Fabrication Inc.................F 704 289-5830
  Monroe *(G-8565)*

Triad Sheet Metal & Mech Inc.................F 336 379-9891
  Greensboro *(G-5879)*

◆ Umicore USA Inc..................................E 919 874-7171
  Raleigh *(G-10575)*

Wnc Refab Inc...G 828 658-8368
  Weaverville *(G-12508)*

5052 Coal and other minerals and ores

Daystar Materials Inc.............................E 919 734-0460
  Goldsboro *(G-5211)*

Norcor Technologies Corp......................G 704 309-4101
  Greensboro *(G-5712)*

◆ Umicore USA Inc..................................E 919 874-7171
  Raleigh *(G-10575)*

5063 Electrical apparatus and equipment

ABB Inc..E 704 587-1362
  Charlotte *(G-1609)*

ABB Inc... C 252 827-2121
　Pinetops (G-9705)

◆ ABB Inc..C 919 856-2360
　Cary (G-1285)

ABB Motors and Mechanical Inc............ G 336 272-6104
　Greensboro (G-5336)

Abl Electronics Supply Inc..................... G 704 784-4225
　Concord (G-3308)

Advance Stores Company Inc................. F 336 545-9091
　Greensboro (G-5341)

Alk Investments LLC............................. G 984 233-5353
　Raleigh (G-9891)

Automated Controls LLC........................ G 704 724-7625
　Huntersville (G-6970)

Blue Ridge Elc Mtr Repr Inc................... G 828 258-0800
　Asheville (G-455)

▲ Blue Sun Energy Inc........................... G 336 218-6707
　Greensboro (G-5393)

Bolton Investors Inc.............................. G 919 471-1197
　Durham (G-3937)

Bowden Electric Motor Svc Inc.............. G 252 446-4203
　Rocky Mount (G-10825)

Carolina Time Equipment Co Inc............ E 704 536-2700
　Charlotte (G-1859)

Cemco Electric Inc............................... F 704 504-0294
　Charlotte (G-1886)

▲ Clarolux Inc....................................... E 336 378-6800
　Greensboro (G-5447)

Clayton Electric Mtr Repr Inc................ F 336 584-3756
　Elon College (G-4473)

Code LLC.. E 828 328-6004
　Hickory (G-6304)

Conservation Station Inc....................... G 919 932-9201
　Chapel Hill (G-1539)

Cornell & Ferencz Inc........................... G 919 736-7373
　Goldsboro (G-5210)

Cummins Inc....................................... F 704 596-7690
　Charlotte (G-2003)

Dehn Inc.. F 772 460-9315
　Mooresville (G-8654)

Dixie Electro Mech Svcs Inc................. F 704 332-1116
　Charlotte (G-2057)

▲ Dna Group Inc.................................. E 919 881-0889
　Raleigh (G-10051)

Edgewell Per Care Brands LLC............. G 336 672-4500
　Asheboro (G-349)

Edwards Electronic Systems Inc........... E 919 359-2239
　Clayton (G-3146)

Egi Associates Inc.............................. F 704 561-3337
　Charlotte (G-2093)

Eizi Group Llc.................................... G 919 397-3638
　Raleigh (G-10080)

Electric Motor Service of Shelby Inc...... F 704 482-9979
　Shelby (G-11333)

Electric Motor Svc Ahoskie Inc............. G 252 332-4364
　Ahoskie (G-48)

Electric Mtr Sls Svc Pitt Cnty................ G 252 752-3170
　Greenville (G-5973)

Electric Mtr Sp Wake Frest Inc............. E 919 556-3229
　Wake Forest (G-12274)

Electrical Equipment Company.............. E 910 276-2141
　Laurinburg (G-7500)

Elektran Inc....................................... G 910 997-6640
　Rockingham (G-10776)

Envirnmntal Cmfort Sltions Inc............. E 980 272-7327
　Kannapolis (G-7208)

Epl & Solar Corp................................. G 201 577-8966
　Wake Forest (G-12276)

Exide Technologies LLC....................... G 704 521-8016
　Charlotte (G-2135)

Exide Technologies LLC....................... G 919 553-3578
　Clayton (G-3147)

▲ Fintronx LLC..................................... F 919 324-3960
　Raleigh (G-10109)

G-4 Electric Inc.................................. F 336 495-0500
　Asheboro (G-358)

General Motor Repair & Svc Inc............ G 336 292-1715
　Greensboro (G-5555)

Hammond Electric Motor Company........ F 704 983-3178
　Albemarle (G-77)

Hanover Electric Motor Svc Inc............ G 910 762-3702
　Wilmington (G-12799)

His Company Inc................................ G 800 537-0351
　Wilmington (G-12806)

Holland Supply Company..................... E 252 492-7541
　Henderson (G-6160)

◆ Hubbell Industrial Contrls Inc..............C 336 434-2800
　Archdale (G-226)

Interstate All Batteries Ctr................... G 704 979-3430
　Concord (G-3380)

▲ Iron Box LLC.................................... E 919 890-0025
　Raleigh (G-10209)

JA Smith Inc..................................... G 704 860-4910
　Lawndale (G-7517)

◆ Jenkins Electric Company....................D 800 438-3003
　Charlotte (G-2368)

Johnson Controls Inc.......................... D 704 521-8889
　Charlotte (G-2375)

L L C Batteries of N C........................ G 919 331-0241
　Angier (G-123)

Lingle Electric Repair Inc..................... F 704 636-5591
　Salisbury (G-11084)

Ls Cable & System USA Inc................. C 252 824-3553
　Tarboro (G-11932)

▲ Lutze Inc.. E 704 504-0222
　Charlotte (G-2442)

▲ Manufacturing Systems Eqp Inc......... F 704 283-2086
　Monroe (G-8523)

McKenzie Supply Company.................. G 910 276-1691
　Laurinburg (G-7509)

McKinney Electric & Mch Co Inc........... G 828 765-7910
　Spruce Pine (G-11581)

McNaughton-Mckay Southeast Inc........ F 910 392-0940
　Wilmington (G-12850)

Minka Lighting Inc.............................. D 704 785-9200
　Concord (G-3403)

Motor Shop Inc.................................. G 704 867-8488
　Gastonia (G-5103)

Ni4I Antennas and Elec LLC................ G 828 738-6445
　Moravian Falls (G-8810)

Pcai Inc... D 704 588-1240
　Charlotte (G-2622)

Power-Utility Products Company........... F 704 375-0776
　Charlotte (G-2651)

Randall Supply Inc............................. E 704 289-6479
　Monroe (G-8548)

Resideo LLC..................................... G 704 525-8899
　Charlotte (G-2715)

Resideo LLC..................................... G 336 668-3644
　Greensboro (G-5784)

Resideo LLC..................................... G 919 872-5556
　Raleigh (G-10441)

Rocky Mount Electric Motor LLC........... G 252 446-1510
　Rocky Mount (G-10868)

Rotron Incorporated........................... C 336 449-3400
　Whitsett (G-12619)

Sanders Electric Motor Svc Inc............ E 828 754-0513
　Lenoir (G-7638)

▲ Sigma Engineered Solutions PC......... D 919 773-0011
　Garner (G-4964)

▲ Smart Electric North Amer LLC.......... G 828 323-1200
　Conover (G-3559)

Southern Electric Motor Co.................. G 919 688-7879
　Durham (G-4243)

▲ Southland Electrical Sup LLC............. C 336 227-1486
　Burlington (G-1160)

State Electric Supply Company............. F 336 855-8200
　Greensboro (G-5837)

Stone Cllins Mtr Rewinding Inc............. G 910 347-2775
　Jacksonville (G-7155)

Tencarva Machinery Company LLC........ G 336 665-1435
　Greensboro (G-5858)

▲ Wieland Electric Inc.......................... F 910 259-5050
　Wilmington (G-12947)

5064 Electrical appliances, television and radio

McKenzie Supply Company.................. G 910 276-1691
　Laurinburg (G-7509)

Psnc Energy...................................... G 919 367-2735
　Apex (G-189)

5065 Electronic parts and equipment, nec

A&B Integrators LLC........................... F 919 371-0750
　Durham (G-3876)

Abacon Telecommunications LLC.......... E 336 855-1179
　Greensboro (G-5335)

Acterna LLC..................................... F 919 388-5100
　Morrisville (G-8918)

Alert Protection Systems Inc................ G 919 467-4357
　Raleigh (G-9890)

Bright Light Technologies LLC.............. G 910 212-6869
　Lillington (G-7790)

Btc Electronic Components LLC............ E 919 229-2162
　Wake Forest (G-12266)

▲ Cargotec Port Security LLC............... G 919 620-1763
　Durham (G-3958)

Commscope Technologies LLC............. G 919 329-8700
　Garner (G-4923)

Custom Light and Sound Inc................ E 919 286-1122
　Durham (G-3994)

Disco Hi-TEC America Inc................... G 919 468-6003
　Morrisville (G-8965)

Dupont Specialty Pdts USA LLC........... E 919 248-5109
　Durham (G-4013)

Edwards Electronic Systems Inc........... E 919 359-2239
　Clayton (G-3146)

Extron Electronics.............................. G 919 850-1000
　Raleigh (G-10100)

His Company Inc................................ G 800 537-0351
　Wilmington (G-12806)

▲ Huber + Suhner Inc.......................... E 704 790-7300
　Charlotte (G-2295)

▲ Huber + Suhner North Amer Corp...... D 704 790-7300
　Charlotte (G-2296)

Interconnect Products and................... E 336 667-3356
　Wilkesboro (G-12640)

Kuebler Inc....................................... F 704 705-4711
　Charlotte (G-2403)

Lea Aid Acquisition Company............... G 919 872-6210
　Spring Hope (G-11557)

▲ Lutze Inc.. E 704 504-0222
　Charlotte (G-2442)

▲ Majorpower Corporation.................... E 919 563-6610
　Mebane (G-8251)

◆ Murata McHy USA Holdings Inc..........F 704 394-8331
　Charlotte (G-2533)

Serra Wireless Inc............................. G 980 318-0873
　Charlotte (G-2789)

Synopsys Inc.................................... G 919 941-6600
　Morrisville (G-9062)

Tactical Support Equipment Inc............ F 910 425-3360
　Fayetteville (G-4676)

Telecmmnctons Resource MGT Inc...... F 919 779-0776
　Raleigh (G-10539)

United Chemi-Con Inc...................... B 336 384-6903
Lansing (G-7479)

US Microwave Inc.......................... G 520 891-2444
Pittsboro (G-9791)

◆ Vishay Measurements Group Inc........G 919 365-3800
Wendell (G-12552)

Vrg Components Inc........................ G 980 244-3862
Matthews (G-8156)

◆ Walker and Associates Inc..............C 336 731-6391
Winston Salem (G-13386)

▲ Wieland Electric Inc .... F 910 259-5050
Wilmington (G-12947)

Wiser Systems Inc......................... F 919 551-5566
Raleigh (G-10611)

5072 Hardware

A&B Integrators LLC...................... F 919 371-0750
Durham (G-3876)

▲ AGM Carolina Inc .... G 336 431-4100
High Point (G-6511)

Allegion Access Tech LLC................ E 704 789-7000
Concord (G-3309)

▲ Bamal Corporation .... F 980 225-7700
Charlotte (G-1748)

Belwith Products LLC..................... G 336 841-3899
High Point (G-6545)

Con-Tab Inc.................................. F 336 476-0104
Thomasville (G-12011)

◆ Freud America Inc.........................C 800 334-4107
High Point (G-6624)

◆ Grass America Inc.........................C 336 996-4041
Kernersville (G-7277)

◆ Greenworks North America LLC........D 888 909-6757
Mooresville (G-8677)

◆ Hafele America Co........................C 800 423-3531
Archdale (G-224)

◆ Hickory Springs Manufactu...............D 828 328-2201
Hickory (G-6355)

◆ Imperial Usa Ltd..........................E 704 596-2444
Charlotte (G-2316)

Roots Organic Gourmet LLC............... F 828 232-2828
Fairview (G-4510)

RPM Indstrial Ctings Group Inc .... C 828 261-0325
Hickory (G-6435)

◆ Salice America Inc........................E 704 841-7810
Charlotte (G-2749)

▲ Sentinel Door Controls LLC............. F 704 921-4627
Charlotte (G-2788)

Triangle Indus Sup Hldings LLC.......... G 704 395-0600
Charlotte (G-2942)

◆ TTI Floor Care North Amer Inc..........B 888 321-1134
Charlotte (G-2951)

Vista Products Inc.......................... D 910 582-0130
Hamlet (G-6065)

Yat Usa Inc.................................. G 480 584-4096
Huntersville (G-7063)

5074 Plumbing and hydronic heating supplies

510nano Inc.................................. F 919 521-5982
Durham (G-3873)

▲ American Valve Inc .... D 336 668-0554
Greensboro (G-5358)

▲ Brasscraft................................. C 336 475-2131
Thomasville (G-11997)

CTS Cleaning Systems Inc .... G 910 483-5349
Fayetteville (G-4582)

Drch Inc...................................... G 919 383-9421
Durham (G-4007)

Ffi Holdings III Corp....................... E 800 690-3650
Charlotte (G-2149)

▼ Flologic Inc................................. G 919 878-1808
Morrisville (G-8976)

Gamma Js Inc............................... F 336 294-3838
Greensboro (G-5547)

Genesis Water Technologies Inc............ E 704 360-5165
Charlotte (G-2204)

High Point Precast Pdts Inc............... G 336 434-1815
Lexington (G-7698)

Jim Fab of North Carolina Inc............. E 704 278-1000
Cleveland (G-3215)

Johnson Controls Inc...................... D 704 521-8889
Charlotte (G-2375)

McKenzie Supply Company................ G 910 276-1691
Laurinburg (G-7509)

Mid-Atlantic Drainage Inc................. F 828 324-0808
Conover (G-3539)

Plastic Oddities Inc........................ G 704 484-1830
Shelby (G-11369)

R Jacobs Fine Plbg & Hdwr Inc........... G 919 720-4202
Raleigh (G-10417)

Roofing Tools and Eqp Inc................ G 252 291-1800
Wilson (G-13024)

Scaltrol Inc.................................. G 678 990-0858
Charlotte (G-2761)

Solar Hot Limited........................... G 919 439-2387
Raleigh (G-10490)

Sunqest Inc.................................. G 828 325-4910
Newton (G-9501)

Water-Gen Inc............................... G 888 492-8370
Charlotte (G-3007)

Work Well Hydrtion Systems LLC.......... G 704 853-7788
Gastonia (G-5167)

Zurn Industries LLC........................ E 919 775-2255
Sanford (G-11257)

5075 Warm air heating and air conditioning

▲ Appalchian Stove Fbrcators Inc........ G 828 253-0164
Asheville (G-428)

Boles Holding Inc........................... G 828 264-4200
Boone (G-899)

Envirnmntal Cmfort Sltions Inc............ E 980 272-7327
Kannapolis (G-7208)

Ffi Holdings III Corp....................... E 800 690-3650
Charlotte (G-2149)

▼ Filtration Technology Inc................. G 336 294-5655
Greensboro (G-5531)

Freudnberg Rsdntial Fltrtion T............ E 828 328-1142
Hickory (G-6335)

Gamma Js Inc............................... F 336 294-3838
Greensboro (G-5547)

James M Pleasants Company Inc.......... E 800 365-9010
Greensboro (G-5633)

Johnson Controls Inc...................... D 704 521-8889
Charlotte (G-2375)

Kenny Fowler Heating and A Inc.......... F 910 508-4553
Wilmington (G-12827)

Kirk & Blum Manufacturing Co............ D 801 728-6533
Greensboro (G-5649)

Mestek Inc................................... C 252 753-5323
Farmville (G-4535)

Nederman Mikropul LLC................... E 704 998-2600
Charlotte (G-2553)

Rheem Manufacturing Company.......... C 336 495-6800
Randleman (G-10658)

▲ Ricura Corporation .... F 704 875-0366
Huntersville (G-7043)

Roofing Tools and Eqp Inc................ G 252 291-1800
Wilson (G-13024)

Spartan Systems LLC...................... F 336 946-1244
Advance (G-39)

Tfam Solutions LLC........................ G 910 637-0266
Aberdeen (G-26)

▲ Ultimate Products Inc................... F 919 836-1627
Raleigh (G-10573)

5078 Refrigeration equipment and supplies

◆ Bally Refrigerated Boxes Inc.............C 252 240-2829
Morehead City (G-8815)

Metalfab of North Carolina LLC........... C 704 841-1090
Matthews (G-8132)

▲ Select Stainless Products LLC........ G 888 843-2345
Charlotte (G-2783)

▲ TRf Manufacturing NC Inc.............. E 252 223-1112
Newport (G-9445)

W A Brown & Son Incorporated........... E 704 636-5131
Salisbury (G-11134)

Water-Gen Inc............................... G 888 492-8370
Charlotte (G-3007)

5082 Construction and mining machinery

Berco of America Inc...................... E 336 931-1415
Greensboro (G-5388)

Carolina Traffic Devices Inc............... F 704 588-7055
Charlotte (G-1860)

◆ Cavotec USA Inc..........................E 704 873-3009
Mooresville (G-8635)

Component Sourcing Intl LLC............. E 704 843-9292
Charlotte (G-1967)

▲ Cutting Systems Inc..................... D 704 592-2451
Union Grove (G-12184)

Gregory Poole Equipment Co............. F 919 872-2691
Raleigh (G-10146)

James River Equipment.................... F 704 821-7399
Monroe (G-8509)

Lynn Ladder Scaffolding Co Inc........... G 301 336-4700
Charlotte (G-2443)

M&N Construction Supply Inc............. G 336 996-7740
Colfax (G-3283)

Quality Equipment LLC.................... G 919 493-3545
Durham (G-4203)

▼ Sound Heavy Machinery Inc............ F 910 782-2477
Wilmington (G-12922)

5083 Farm and garden machinery

▲ Buy Smart Inc............................. G 252 293-4700
Wilson (G-12976)

Farm Services Inc.......................... G 336 226-7381
Graham (G-5268)

General Fertilizer Eqp Inc................. F 336 299-4711
Greensboro (G-5554)

Griffin Industries LLC..................... D 704 624-9140
Marshville (G-8089)

North American Implements Inc.......... G 336 476-2904
Thomasville (G-12056)

▲ Southag Mfg Inc .... G 919 365-5111
Wendell (G-12548)

Tar River Trading Post LLC............... G 919 589-3618
Youngsville (G-13490)

5084 Industrial machinery and equipment

▲ 3nine USA Inc............................ F 512 210-4005
Charlotte (G-1602)

▲ Adwood Corporation .... E 336 884-1846
High Point (G-6510)

Airgas Usa LLC............................. F 704 333-5475
Charlotte (G-1632)

Airgas Usa LLC............................. G 704 394-1420
Charlotte (G-1633)

Airgas Usa LLC............................. G 919 544-3773
Durham (G-3885)

Airgas Usa LLC............................. G 919 735-5276
Goldsboro (G-5196)

Airgas Usa LLC............................. G 704 636-5049
Salisbury (G-11014)

Airgas Usa LLC.................................... G 910 392-2711
Wilmington *(G-12694)*

▼ Alamo Distribution LLC.................... C 704 398-5600
Belmont *(G-740)*

Amada America Inc.............................. G 877 262-3287
High Point *(G-6518)*

◆ American Linc Corporation.............. E 704 861-9242
Gastonia *(G-4992)*

▲ American Trutzschler Inc................. D 704 399-4521
Charlotte *(G-1670)*

Andy-OXY Co Inc................................ E 828 258-0271
Asheville *(G-426)*

◆ AP&t North America Inc................... F 704 292-2900
Monroe *(G-8427)*

Arbon Equipment Corporation........... F 414 355-2600
Charlotte *(G-1690)*

Arc3 Gases Inc.................................... G 704 220-1029
Monroe *(G-8429)*

Arc3 Gases Inc.................................... E 910 892-4016
Dunn *(G-3844)*

Arnolds Welding Service Inc............. E 910 323-3822
Fayetteville *(G-4553)*

Automated Machine Technologies....... G 919 361-0121
Morrisville *(G-8936)*

Babington Technology Inc.................. G 252 984-0349
Rocky Mount *(G-10823)*

▲ Basic Machinery Company Inc........ D 919 663-2244
Siler City *(G-11399)*

Bear Pages.. G 828 837-0785
Murphy *(G-9288)*

Birch Bros Southern Inc.................... E 704 843-2111
Waxhaw *(G-12423)*

▲ Bosch Rexroth Corporation............ E 704 583-4338
Charlotte *(G-1801)*

Burris Machine Company Inc............ G 828 322-6914
Hickory *(G-6277)*

▲ C R Onsrud Inc............................... E 704 508-7000
Troutman *(G-12131)*

Carolina Material Handling Inc.......... F 336 294-2346
Greensboro *(G-5430)*

Carolina Moldings Inc........................ F 704 523-7471
Charlotte *(G-1851)*

▲ Carotek Inc..................................... E 704 844-1100
Matthews *(G-8103)*

▲ Cefla North America Inc................. E 704 598-0020
Charlotte *(G-1882)*

Chase-Logeman Corporation............. F 336 665-0754
Greensboro *(G-5442)*

▲ Chiron America Inc......................... D 704 587-9526
Charlotte *(G-1916)*

Cintas Corporation No 2.................... E 336 632-4412
Greensboro *(G-5444)*

◆ Clyde Union (us) Inc...................... C 704 808-3000
Charlotte *(G-1934)*

Community Brewing Ventures LLC........ G 800 579-6539
Newton *(G-9458)*

Container Graphics Corp.................... E 704 588-7230
Pineville *(G-9720)*

▲ Container Graphics Corp................ F 919 481-4200
Cary *(G-1333)*

▲ CPS Resources Inc......................... E 704 628-7678
Indian Trail *(G-7075)*

Crizaf Inc.. G 919 251-7661
Durham *(G-3991)*

Cross Technologies Inc..................... D 336 292-0511
Whitsett *(G-12603)*

Cross Technologies Inc..................... E 800 327-7727
Greensboro *(G-5472)*

Crown Equipment Corporation........... E 336 291-2500
Colfax *(G-3277)*

Cumins Machinery Corp..................... G 336 622-1000
Liberty *(G-7762)*

Cummins Inc.. F 704 596-7690
Charlotte *(G-2003)*

Cummins Inc.. E 336 275-4531
Greensboro *(G-5476)*

Cummins Inc.. G 919 284-9111
Kenly *(G-7230)*

▲ Custom Hydraulics & Design.......... F 704 347-0023
Cherryville *(G-3061)*

Custom Machine Company Inc........... F 704 629-5326
Bessemer City *(G-811)*

▲ Dbt Holdings LLC........................... D 704 900-6606
Charlotte *(G-2023)*

▲ Deetag USA Inc.............................. G 828 465-2644
Conover *(G-3514)*

Deurotech America Inc....................... G 980 272-6827
Charlotte *(G-2037)*

Digital Highpoint LLC......................... C 336 883-7146
High Point *(G-6593)*

▲ Diversfied Prtg Techniques Inc........ E 704 583-9433
Charlotte *(G-2055)*

Diversified Energy LLC....................... G 828 266-9800
Boone *(G-912)*

Drum Filter Media Inc......................... G 336 434-4195
High Point *(G-6599)*

Dudleys Fence Company.................... G 252 566-5759
La Grange *(G-7467)*

Dwd Industries LLC............................ E 336 498-6327
Randleman *(G-10644)*

Ellison Technologies Inc.................... D 704 545-7362
Charlotte *(G-2103)*

▲ Encertec Inc.................................... G 336 288-7226
Greensboro *(G-5519)*

◆ Engine Systems Inc........................ D 252 977-2720
Rocky Mount *(G-10836)*

▲ Epic Enterprises Inc....................... E 910 692-5750
Southern Pines *(G-11498)*

◆ Fab-Con Machinery Dev Corp.......... D 704 486-7120
Oakboro *(G-9579)*

Filter Shop LLC................................... D 704 860-4822
Gastonia *(G-5048)*

Gamma Js Inc..................................... F 336 294-3838
Greensboro *(G-5547)*

Glover Corporation Inc....................... E 919 821-5535
Raleigh *(G-10139)*

▲ Grecon Dimter Inc.......................... E 828 397-5139
Connelly Springs *(G-3477)*

▲ Grecon Inc...................................... F 503 641-7731
Charlotte *(G-2237)*

Gregory Poole Equipment Co............. G 252 931-5100
Greenville *(G-5984)*

Gregory Poole Equipment Co............. F 919 872-2691
Raleigh *(G-10146)*

Hargrove Countertops & ACC Inc....... G 919 981-0163
Raleigh *(G-10155)*

Hester Enterprises Inc....................... E 704 865-4480
Gastonia *(G-5060)*

Hiab USA Inc....................................... F 704 896-9089
Cornelius *(G-3606)*

▼ His Glassworks Inc.......................... G 828 254-2559
Asheville *(G-518)*

▲ Huber Technology Inc..................... E 704 949-1010
Denver *(G-3788)*

Hunter Douglas Inc............................ C 704 629-6500
Bessemer City *(G-822)*

Hunter Fan Company.......................... G 704 896-9250
Cornelius *(G-3609)*

▲ Hyde Park Partners Inc.................. D 704 587-4819
Charlotte *(G-2304)*

Hydralic Engnered Pdts Svc Inc......... G 704 374-1306
Charlotte *(G-2305)*

I C E S Gaston County Inc................. G 704 263-1418
Stanley *(G-11618)*

IMO Industries Inc.............................. C 704 289-6511
Monroe *(G-8504)*

◆ Industrial Sup Solutions Inc........... E 704 636-4241
Salisbury *(G-11067)*

▲ J & P Entrprses of Crlinas Inc........ E 704 861-1867
Gastonia *(G-5069)*

J J Jenkins Incorporated................... E 704 821-6648
Matthews *(G-8177)*

James Oxygen and Supply Co............ E 704 322-5438
Hickory *(G-6374)*

▼ Kaufman Trailers Inc....................... E 336 790-6800
Lexington *(G-7704)*

◆ LCI Corporation International.......... E 704 399-7441
Charlotte *(G-2411)*

Ledger Hardware Inc.......................... G 828 688-4798
Bakersville *(G-679)*

▲ Ligna Machinery Inc....................... G 336 584-0030
Burlington *(G-1120)*

Linor Technology Inc......................... F 336 485-6199
Winston Salem *(G-13235)*

Livingston & Haven LLC.................... C 704 588-3670
Charlotte *(G-2428)*

▲ Lock Drives Inc............................... G 704 588-1844
Pineville *(G-9740)*

▲ Maag Reduction Inc........................ E 704 716-9000
Charlotte *(G-2445)*

Machinex.. G 336 665-5030
High Point *(G-6695)*

Machinex Technologies Inc................ F 773 867-8801
High Point *(G-6696)*

Mang Systems Inc.............................. E 704 292-1041
Matthews *(G-8181)*

Material Handling Technologies Inc....... D 919 388-0050
Morrisville *(G-9018)*

Matheson Tri-Gas Inc......................... F 919 556-6461
Wake Forest *(G-12286)*

Maxson & Associates......................... G 336 632-0524
Greensboro *(G-5683)*

McDonald Services Inc...................... G 704 753-9669
Monroe *(G-8530)*

▲ Mid-Atlantic Crane and Eqp Co...... E 919 790-3535
Raleigh *(G-10304)*

Mixon Mills Inc................................... G 828 297-5431
Vilas *(G-12231)*

Mmj Machining and Fabg Inc............. F 336 495-1029
Randleman *(G-10653)*

◆ Monarch Knitting McHy Corp.......... F 704 291-3300
Monroe *(G-8534)*

Morris Machine Company Inc............ G 704 824-4242
Gastonia *(G-5102)*

▲ Mount Hope Machinery Co.............. F
Charlotte *(G-2523)*

◆ Mueller Die Cut Solutions Inc......... E 704 588-3900
Charlotte *(G-2526)*

◆ Murata Machinery Usa Inc.............. C 704 875-9280
Charlotte *(G-2532)*

◆ Nederman Inc.................................. D 336 821-0827
Thomasville *(G-12053)*

Northline Nc LLC................................ G 336 283-4811
Rural Hall *(G-10965)*

Oerlikon AM US Inc............................ E 980 260-2827
Huntersville *(G-7027)*

Oerlikon Metco (us) Inc..................... F 713 715-6300
Huntersville *(G-7028)*

▲ Okuma America Corporation............ C 704 588-7000
Charlotte *(G-2593)*

Otis Elevator Company....................... G 828 251-1248
Asheville *(G-563)*

Otis Elevator Company....................... C 704 519-0100
Charlotte *(G-2602)*

▲ Palmer Wahl Instruments Inc.......... E 828 658-3131
Asheville *(G-566)*

▲ Pam Trading Corporation................. E 336 668-0901
Kernersville *(G-7292)*

Parker-Hannifin Corporation.............. D 828 245-3233
Forest City *(G-4795)*

▲ Pavco Inc.. E 704 496-6800
Charlotte *(G-2619)*

Pcai Inc.. D 704 588-1240
Charlotte *(G-2622)*

Petroleum Tank Corporation.............. F 919 284-2418
Kenly *(G-7235)*

Pharmaceutical Equipment Svcs.......... G 239 699-9120
Asheville *(G-571)*

Phillips Corporation........................... E 336 665-1080
Colfax *(G-3286)*

Port City Elevator Inc........................ E 910 790-9300
Castle Hayne *(G-1509)*

Print Management Group LLC............... F 704 821-0114
Charlotte *(G-2669)*

▲ Psi-Polymer Systems Inc................. E 828 468-2600
Conover *(G-3553)*

Rapid Response Inc............................ G 704 588-8890
Charlotte *(G-2689)*

Rock-Weld Industries Inc.................... G 336 375-6862
Greensboro *(G-5792)*

Rodeco Company................................ F 919 775-7149
Sanford *(G-11225)*

Roi Industries Group Inc.................... G 919 788-7728
Durham *(G-4218)*

Rose Welding & Crane Service I........... G 252 796-9171
Columbia *(G-3296)*

RPM Plastics LLC............................... E 704 871-0518
Statesville *(G-11760)*

◆ Russell Finex Inc............................ F 704 588-9808
Pineville *(G-9751)*

Rvb Systems Group Inc...................... G 919 362-5211
Garner *(G-4960)*

S Strickland Diesel Svc Inc................. G 252 291-6999
Wilson *(G-13025)*

◆ Schaefer Systems International Inc....C 704 944-4500
Charlotte *(G-2763)*

Schaefer Systems Intl Inc................... G 704 944-4550
Charlotte *(G-2765)*

▲ Schelling America Inc...................... E 919 544-0430
Morrisville *(G-9044)*

▲ Schmalz Inc.................................... C 919 713-0880
Raleigh *(G-10461)*

◆ Schunk Intec Inc.............................D 919 572-2705
Morrisville *(G-9046)*

Sinnovatek Inc................................... G 919 694-0974
Raleigh *(G-10479)*

Slack & Parr International.................... G 704 527-2975
Dallas *(G-3690)*

▲ Smart Machine Technologies Inc....... D 276 632-9853
Greensboro *(G-5817)*

▲ Southag Mfg Inc.............................. G 919 365-5111
Wendell *(G-12548)*

▲ Stanza Machinery Inc...................... E 704 599-0623
Charlotte *(G-2859)*

▲ Stork United Corporation................. A 704 598-7171
Charlotte *(G-2870)*

Svcm... G 305 767-3595
Lincolnton *(G-7858)*

T P Supply Co Inc.............................. E 336 789-2337
Mount Airy *(G-9183)*

Talladega Mchy & Sup Co NC............... G 256 362-4124
Fayetteville *(G-4677)*

▼ TCI Mobility Inc.............................. F 704 867-8331
Gastonia *(G-5149)*

Thomas M Brown Inc.......................... F 704 597-0246
Charlotte *(G-2913)*

Tk Elevator Corporation...................... D 336 272-4563
Greensboro *(G-5867)*

Triangle Glass Service Inc................... G 919 477-9508
Durham *(G-4279)*

◆ Truflo Pumps Inc............................F 336 664-9225
Greensboro *(G-5882)*

▲ U S Bottlers McHy Co Inc................. D 704 588-4750
Charlotte *(G-2957)*

◆ Vanguard Pai Lung LLC....................G 704 283-8171
Monroe *(G-8575)*

Vrg Components Inc........................... G 980 244-3862
Matthews *(G-8156)*

Waste Container Repair Svcs............... G 910 257-4474
Fayetteville *(G-4696)*

Weathers Machine Mfg Inc.................. F 919 552-5945
Fuquay Varina *(G-4906)*

West Dynamics Us Inc........................ E 704 735-0009
Lincolnton *(G-7871)*

◆ Xaloy Extrusion LLC.........................E 828 326-9888
Hickory *(G-6492)*

5085 Industrial supplies

A R Perry Corporation......................... G 252 492-6181
Henderson *(G-6146)*

Airgas Usa LLC................................... G 704 394-1420
Charlotte *(G-1633)*

Airgas Usa LLC................................... G 919 544-3773
Durham *(G-3885)*

Airgas Usa LLC................................... G 919 735-5276
Goldsboro *(G-5196)*

Alan R Williams Inc............................ E 704 372-8281
Charlotte *(G-1636)*

Allyn International Trdg Corp............... G 877 858-2482
Marshville *(G-8085)*

Altra Industrial Motion Corp............... F 704 588-5610
Charlotte *(G-1658)*

▲ Apex Packaging Corporation LLC..... E 704 847-7274
Charlotte *(G-1682)*

Automated Designs Inc....................... F 828 696-9625
Flat Rock *(G-4703)*

B & M Wholesale Inc.......................... G 336 789-3916
Mount Airy *(G-9100)*

Biganodes LLC................................... G 828 245-1115
Forest City *(G-4784)*

▲ Bonomi North America Inc............... F 704 412-9031
Charlotte *(G-1798)*

Boston Gear LLC................................ B 704 588-5610
Charlotte *(G-1802)*

Boxman Studios LLC........................... G 704 333-3733
Mount Holly *(G-9219)*

▲ Carolina Brush Company.................. E 704 867-0286
Gastonia *(G-5011)*

Carolina Rubber & Spc Inc.................. G 336 744-5111
Winston Salem *(G-13118)*

Carr Mill Supplies Inc......................... G 336 883-0135
High Point *(G-6561)*

Consolidated Pipe & Sup Co Inc.......... F 336 294-8577
Greensboro *(G-5463)*

Cross Technologies Inc....................... G 336 370-4673
Greensboro *(G-5473)*

▲ Custom Hydraulics & Design............ F 704 347-0023
Cherryville *(G-3061)*

▲ D M & E Corporation....................... E 704 482-8876
Shelby *(G-11328)*

▲ Dixon Valve & Coupling Co LLC........ F 704 334-9175
Dallas *(G-3668)*

Easth20 Holdings Llc.......................... G 919 313-2100
Greensboro *(G-5510)*

▲ Flo-Tite Inc Valves & Contrls........... E 910 738-8904
Lumberton *(G-7955)*

▼ Fortiline LLC.................................. E 704 788-9800
Concord *(G-3366)*

Genevieve M Brownlee.......................... G 336 226-5260
Burlington *(G-1095)*

Ghx Industrial LLC............................. G 336 996-7271
Kernersville *(G-7276)*

▲ Grasche USA Inc............................. E 828 322-1226
Hickory *(G-6340)*

◆ Great Products Inc..........................G 910 944-2020
Aberdeen *(G-5)*

▲ H-T-L Perma USA Ltd Partnr............. E 704 377-3100
Charlotte *(G-2249)*

Hamilton Indus Grinding Inc............... E 828 253-6796
Asheville *(G-515)*

Harbisonwalker Intl Inc....................... G 704 599-6540
Charlotte *(G-2255)*

Holland Supply Company.................... E 252 492-7541
Henderson *(G-6160)*

◆ Ideal Fastener Corporation...............C 919 693-3115
Oxford *(G-9618)*

◆ Industrial Sup Solutions Inc.............E 704 636-4241
Salisbury *(G-11067)*

Ips Corporation................................. E 919 598-2400
Durham *(G-4083)*

Justice Bearing LLC............................ G 800 355-2500
Mooresville *(G-8701)*

Laurinburg Machine Company............. G 910 276-0360
Laurinburg *(G-7505)*

Lee Spring Company LLC..................... E 336 275-3631
Greensboro *(G-5659)*

Loflin Handle Co Inc.......................... G 336 463-2422
Yadkinville *(G-13445)*

▲ Ltd Industries LLC........................... E 704 897-2182
Charlotte *(G-2436)*

Mayo Resources Inc........................... E 336 996-7776
Winston Salem *(G-13246)*

▲ Measurement Controls Inc............... F 704 921-1101
Charlotte *(G-2484)*

▲ Mmb One Inc.................................. F 704 523-8163
Charlotte *(G-2512)*

▲ Mount Hope Machinery Co............... F
Charlotte *(G-2523)*

◆ Murata Machinery Usa Inc................C 704 875-9280
Charlotte *(G-2532)*

National Container Group LLC............. G 704 393-9050
Charlotte *(G-2544)*

▲ Novaflex Hose Inc........................... D 336 578-2161
Haw River *(G-6134)*

◆ Oiles America Corporation............... F 704 784-4500
Concord *(G-3411)*

Parker-Hannifin Corporation............... D 336 373-1761
Greensboro *(G-5734)*

Person Printing Company Inc.............. E 336 599-2146
Roxboro *(G-10940)*

▲ Purolator Facet Inc......................... E 336 668-4444
Greensboro *(G-5771)*

Purser Centl Rewinding Co Inc............ F 704 786-3131
Concord *(G-3427)*

Reclaim Filters and Systems............... G 919 528-1787
Wake Forest *(G-12292)*

Robert Bosch Tool Corporation........... E 704 735-7464
Lincolnton *(G-7851)*

Roots Organic Gourmet LLC................ F 828 232-2828
Fairview *(G-4510)*

▲ Rubber Mill Inc............................... E 336 622-1680
Liberty *(G-7778)*

Sanders Company Inc......................... F 252 338-3995
Elizabeth City *(G-4408)*

▲ SAS Industries Inc.......................... F 631 727-1441
Elizabeth City *(G-4409)*

Sherrill Contract Mfg Inc.................... F 704 922-7871
Dallas *(G-3689)*

Southern Rubber Company Inc............ E 336 299-2456
Greensboro *(G-5827)*

Southern Spring & Stamping.............. F 336 548-3520
Stokesdale *(G-11815)*

◆ Splawn Belting Inc.................................E 336 227-4277
Burlington *(G-1162)*

Strobels Supply Inc.................................F 607 324-1721
Linwood *(G-7881)*

Structural Materials Inc..........................G 828 754-6413
Lenoir *(G-7640)*

T P Supply Co Inc...................................E 336 789-2337
Mount Airy *(G-9183)*

Talladega Mchy & Sup Co NC..................G 256 362-4124
Fayetteville *(G-4677)*

Triangle Indus Sup Hldings LLC..............G 704 395-0600
Charlotte *(G-2942)*

▲ Uchiyama Mfg Amer LLC......................F 919 731-2364
Goldsboro *(G-5251)*

Wilmington Rbr & Gasket Co Inc..............F 910 762-4262
Wilmington *(G-12952)*

5087 Service establishment equipment

A Oliver Arthur & Son Inc.......................F 828 459-8000
Conover *(G-3486)*

Ace Industries Inc..................................G 336 427-5316
Madison *(G-7983)*

American Sample House Inc....................G 704 276-1970
Vale *(G-12207)*

Asheville Vault Service Inc....................E 828 665-6799
Candler *(G-1218)*

Beco Holding Company Inc.....................C 800 826-3473
Charlotte *(G-1767)*

◆ Burts Bees Inc....................................C 919 998-5200
Durham *(G-3953)*

Cherryville Distrg Co Inc........................G 704 435-9692
Cherryville *(G-3060)*

Cosmopros...G 704 717-7420
Charlotte *(G-1990)*

CTS Cleaning Systems Inc.....................G 910 483-5349
Fayetteville *(G-4582)*

▼ Fireresq Incorporated.........................F 888 975-0858
Mooresville *(G-8664)*

Gardner Machinery Corporation..............F 704 372-3890
Charlotte *(G-2189)*

Ice Companies Inc.................................G 910 791-1970
Wilmington *(G-12811)*

Imperial Vault Company.........................F 336 983-6343
King *(G-7328)*

Jim Allred Taxidermy Supply...................G 828 749-5900
Saluda *(G-11139)*

Johnny Slicks Inc...................................G 910 803-2159
Holly Ridge *(G-6890)*

Jorlink Usa Inc.......................................F 336 288-1613
Greensboro *(G-5640)*

King Business Service Inc......................G 910 610-1030
Laurinburg *(G-7504)*

Laundry Svc Tech Ltd Lblty Co...............G 908 327-1997
Matthews *(G-8126)*

Lightning X Products Inc........................G 704 295-0299
Charlotte *(G-2421)*

National Foam Inc..................................C 919 639-6151
Angier *(G-125)*

Signcaster Corporation..........................G 336 712-2525
Winston Salem *(G-13336)*

◆ Talley Machinery Corporation...............G 336 664-0012
Greensboro *(G-5850)*

UGLy Essentials LLC.............................F 910 319-9945
Raleigh *(G-10572)*

Winston-Salem Casket Company.............G 336 661-1695
Winston Salem *(G-13403)*

5088 Transportation equipment and supplies

At Your Service Express LLC..................E 704 270-9918
Charlotte *(G-1707)*

Barbour S Marine Supply Co Inc.............G 252 728-2136
Beaufort *(G-720)*

Carolina Ground Svc Eqp Inc..................F 252 565-0288
New Bern *(G-9349)*

Foxster Opco LLC..................................E 910 297-6996
Hampstead *(G-6072)*

◆ Haeco Americas LLC...........................A 336 668-4410
Greensboro *(G-5585)*

Harsco Rail LLC.....................................G 980 960-2624
Charlotte *(G-2262)*

Jones Marine Inc...................................G 704 639-0173
Salisbury *(G-11075)*

▲ Kck Holding Corp................................E 336 513-0002
Burlington *(G-1114)*

Ontic Engineering and Mfg Inc................B 919 395-3908
Creedmoor *(G-3653)*

Rapid Response Technology LLC............G 910 763-3856
Wilmington *(G-12896)*

◆ Trivantage LLC...................................D 800 786-1876
Burlington *(G-1171)*

5091 Sporting and recreation goods

Aqua Blue Inc..G 704 896-9007
Cornelius *(G-3585)*

Bic Corporation......................................D 704 598-7700
Charlotte *(G-1779)*

Custom Marine Fabrication Inc................G 252 638-5422
New Bern *(G-9360)*

Every Day Carry LLc..............................F 203 231-0256
Winnabow *(G-13065)*

▲ Fathom Offshore Holdings LLC............G 910 399-6882
Wilmington *(G-12776)*

Golfstar Technology LLC.........................G 910 420-3122
Pinehurst *(G-9693)*

Iconic Marine Group LLC........................B 252 975-2000
Chocowinity *(G-3083)*

▲ Mettech Inc...G 919 833-9460
Raleigh *(G-10297)*

North American Trade LLC......................G 828 712-3004
Fletcher *(G-4759)*

S & S Trawl Shop Inc.............................G 910 842-9197
Supply *(G-11858)*

Thomas Golf Inc....................................G 704 461-1342
Charlotte *(G-2912)*

▲ Triplette Fencing Supply Inc................G 336 835-1205
Mount Airy *(G-9189)*

◆ Trivantage LLC...................................D 800 786-1876
Burlington *(G-1171)*

◆ US Legend Cars Intl Inc......................E 704 455-3896
Harrisburg *(G-6119)*

Watkins Agency Inc................................G 704 213-6997
Salisbury *(G-11135)*

5092 Toys and hobby goods and supplies

Grateful Union Family Inc.......................F 828 622-3258
Asheville *(G-510)*

5093 Scrap and waste materials

Allyn International Trdg Corp...................G 877 858-2482
Marshville *(G-8085)*

Boomerang Water LLC...........................F 833 266-6420
Midland *(G-8281)*

◆ Elan Trading Inc.................................E 704 342-1696
Charlotte *(G-2094)*

Fisherman Creations Inc........................E 252 725-0138
Beaufort *(G-726)*

Piedmont Paper Stock LLC....................F 336 285-8592
Greensboro *(G-5744)*

Renew Recycling LLC............................D 919 550-8012
Clayton *(G-3168)*

S Foil Incorporated................................F 704 455-5134
Harrisburg *(G-6117)*

◆ Umicore USA Inc.................................E 919 874-7171
Raleigh *(G-10575)*

Wnc Dry Kiln Inc....................................F 828 652-0050
Marion *(G-8074)*

5094 Jewelry and precious stones

Duncan Design Ltd.................................G 919 834-7713
Raleigh *(G-10064)*

Made By Custom LLC.............................G 704 980-9840
Charlotte *(G-2447)*

NCSMJ..F 704 544-1118
Pineville *(G-9744)*

Soulku LLC..F 828 273-4278
Asheville *(G-605)*

Sumpters Jwly & Collectibles..................G 704 399-5348
Charlotte *(G-2879)*

▲ Trophy House Inc................................F 910 323-1791
Fayetteville *(G-4683)*

5099 Durable goods, nec

Allyn International Trdg Corp...................G 877 858-2482
Marshville *(G-8085)*

▼ American Safety Utility Corp................E 704 482-0601
Shelby *(G-11311)*

B & M Wholesale Inc.............................G 336 789-3916
Mount Airy *(G-9100)*

Backwater Guns LLC.............................G 910 399-1451
Wilmington *(G-12718)*

Beco Holding Company Inc.....................C 800 826-3473
Charlotte *(G-1767)*

▲ Cda Inc...C
Charlotte *(G-1879)*

Consolidated Elec Distrs Inc..................G 828 433-4689
Morganton *(G-8858)*

Conway Development Inc.......................F 252 756-2168
Greenville *(G-5957)*

Deberry Land & Timber Inc....................G 910 572-2698
Troy *(G-12159)*

Decima Corporation LLC........................E 734 516-1535
Charlotte *(G-2025)*

Domtar Paper Company LLC...................D 252 752-1100
Greenville *(G-5966)*

GNB Ventures LLC................................F 704 488-4468
Charlotte *(G-2218)*

▲ Home Impressions Inc........................B 828 328-1142
Hickory *(G-6362)*

J L Smith & Co Inc.................................F 704 521-1088
Charlotte *(G-2360)*

Lea Aid Acquisition Company..................G 919 872-6210
Spring Hope *(G-11557)*

Memories of Orangeburg Inc...................G 803 533-0035
Mooresville *(G-8722)*

◆ Norton Door Controls..........................F 704 233-4011
Monroe *(G-8538)*

◆ Schaefer Systems International Inc....C 704 944-4500
Charlotte *(G-2763)*

Schaefer Systems Intl Inc......................G 704 944-4550
Charlotte *(G-2765)*

Signature Signs Inc...............................G 336 431-2072
High Point *(G-6773)*

Song of Wood Ltd.................................G 828 669-7675
Black Mountain *(G-871)*

Sony Music Holdings Inc........................G 336 886-1807
High Point *(G-6785)*

Speer Operational Tech LLC..................G 864 631-2512
Marion *(G-8066)*

◆ Trivantage LLC...................................D 800 786-1876
Burlington *(G-1171)*

▲ VH Industries Inc...............................G 704 743-2400
Concord *(G-3464)*

◆ Walter Kidde Portable Eqp Inc............B 919 563-5911
Mebane *(G-8263)*

Zingerle Group Usa Inc.........................E 704 312-1600
Charlotte *(G-3048)*

S
I
C

51 WHOLESALE TRADE - NONDURABLE GOODS

5111 Printing and writing paper

Archie Supply LLC .... G 336 987-0895
   Greensboro (G-5368)

▲ Jasie Blanks LLC .... F 910 485-0016
   Fayetteville (G-4621)

◆ McGrann Paper Corporation .... E 800 240-9455
   Charlotte (G-2478)

5112 Stationery and office supplies

Acme United Corporation .... E 252 822-5051
   Rocky Mount (G-10807)

Archie Supply LLC .... G 336 987-0895
   Greensboro (G-5368)

Austin Business Forms Inc .... F 704 821-6165
   Indian Trail (G-7070)

Bic Corporation .... D 704 598-7700
   Charlotte (G-1779)

Cartridge World .... G 336 885-0989
   High Point (G-6562)

▼ Consolidated Press Inc .... G 704 372-6785
   Charlotte (G-1975)

Devora Designs Inc .... G 336 782-0964
   Winston Salem (G-13142)

Digital Print & Imaging Inc .... G 910 341-3005
   Greenville (G-5965)

Fain Enterprises Inc .... G 336 724-0417
   Winston Salem (G-13163)

Gbf Inc .... D 336 665-0205
   High Point (G-6627)

Laser Recharge Carolina Inc .... F 919 467-5902
   Cary (G-1387)

Person Printing Company Inc .... E 336 599-2146
   Roxboro (G-10940)

Printing Press .... G 828 299-1234
   Asheville (G-585)

S Ruppe Inc .... G 828 287-4936
   Rutherfordton (G-10992)

Sdv Office Systems LLC .... F 844 968-9500
   Fletcher (G-4766)

▲ Wall-Lenk Corporation .... E 252 527-4186
   Kinston (G-7435)

Wit & Whistle .... G 919 609-5309
   Cary (G-1485)

5113 Industrial and personal service paper

Atlantic Corp Wilmington Inc .... E 910 259-3600
   Burgaw (G-1019)

◆ Atlantic Corp Wilmington Inc .... D 800 722-5841
   Wilmington (G-12712)

▲ Axjo America Inc .... D 828 322-6046
   Conover (G-3493)

▲ Box Board Products Inc .... C 336 668-3347
   Greensboro (G-5397)

Box Company of America LLC .... E 910 582-0100
   Hamlet (G-6051)

C L Rabb Inc .... E 704 865-0295
   Gastonia (G-5010)

◆ Carolina Tape & Supply Corp .... E 828 322-3991
   Hickory (G-6289)

Custom Packaging Inc .... C 828 684-5060
   Arden (G-264)

▲ Eastcoast Packaging Inc .... E 919 562-6060
   Middlesex (G-8274)

Ferguson Supply and Box Mfg Co .... D 704 597-0310
   Charlotte (G-2148)

▲ Franklin Logistical Services Inc .... D 919 556-6711
   Youngsville (G-13472)

Freeman Container Company Inc .... G 704 922-7972
   Dallas (G-3672)

Genpak LLC .... D 704 588-6202
   Charlotte (G-2207)

Georgia-Pacific LLC .... D 336 629-2151
   Asheboro (G-361)

Gold Medal Products Co .... G 336 665-4997
   Greensboro (G-5568)

▲ Inplac North America Inc .... G 704 587-1151
   Charlotte (G-2338)

Lls Investments Inc .... F 919 662-7283
   Raleigh (G-10258)

Packaging Corporation America .... G 704 664-5010
   Mooresville (G-8741)

Pactiv LLC .... D 336 292-2796
   Greensboro (G-5730)

Pactiv LLC .... F 828 758-7580
   Lenoir (G-7632)

Pratt Industries Inc .... D 919 334-7400
   Raleigh (G-10387)

RLM/Universal Packaging Inc .... F 336 644-6161
   Greensboro (G-5789)

Thomco Inc .... G 336 292-3300
   Greensboro (G-5863)

Veritiv Operating Company .... G 336 834-3488
   Greensboro (G-5898)

Westrock Rkt LLC .... C 828 464-5560
   Conover (G-3574)

Wrkco Inc .... E 336 765-7004
   Winston Salem (G-13407)

5122 Drugs, proprietaries, and sundries

A M P Laboratories Ltd .... G 704 894-9721
   Cornelius (G-3582)

▲ Ambra Le Roy LLC .... G 704 392-7080
   Charlotte (G-1662)

▲ Bioventus LLC .... D 800 396-4325
   Durham (G-3933)

◆ Bob Barker Company Inc .... C 800 334-9880
   Fuquay Varina (G-4870)

Burts Bees Inc .... B 919 998-5200
   Durham (G-3954)

Burts Bees Inc .... C 919 238-6450
   Morrisville (G-8946)

◆ Burts Bees Inc .... C 919 998-5200
   Durham (G-3953)

Cosmetic Creations Inc .... G 828 298-4625
   Swannanoa (G-11869)

Fidelity Pharmaceuticals LLC .... G 704 274-3192
   Huntersville (G-6989)

Glaxosmithkline LLC .... G 252 315-9774
   Durham (G-4052)

Glaxosmithkline LLC .... F 919 483-2100
   Durham (G-4053)

Glenmark Phrmceuticals Inc USA .... D 704 218-2600
   Monroe (G-8492)

Guerbet LLC .... F 919 878-2930
   Raleigh (G-10152)

Interntnal Agrclture Group LLC .... F 908 323-3246
   Mooresville (G-8694)

Karamedica Inc .... G 919 302-1325
   Raleigh (G-10230)

Keller Cosmetics Inc .... G 704 399-2226
   Monroe (G-8512)

King Bio Inc .... D 828 255-0201
   Asheville (G-530)

◆ Mvp Group International Inc .... E 843 216-8380
   Elkin (G-4449)

Old Town Soap Co .... F 704 796-8775
   China Grove (G-3077)

Pfizer Inc .... C 919 775-7100
   Sanford (G-11219)

▲ Philosophy Inc .... E 602 794-8701
   Sanford (G-11220)

◆ Premex Inc .... F 561 962-4128
   Durham (G-4196)

Purdue Pharmaceuticals LP .... F 252 265-1900
   Wilson (G-13015)

Random Rues Botanical LLC .... G 252 214-2759
   Greenville (G-6017)

Revlon Inc .... G 919 603-2000
   Oxford (G-9629)

Stiefel Laboratories Inc .... C 888 784-3335
   Durham (G-4251)

Stiefel Laboratories Inc .... E 888 784-3335
   Research Triangle Pa (G-10715)

UGLy Essentials LLC .... F 910 319-9945
   Raleigh (G-10572)

▼ Usrx LLC .... E 980 221-1200
   Charlotte (G-2969)

V1 Pharma LLC .... G 919 338-5744
   Raleigh (G-10580)

5131 Piece goods and notions

Adele Knits Inc .... C 336 499-6010
   Winston Salem (G-13072)

◆ Bob Barker Company Inc .... C 800 334-9880
   Fuquay Varina (G-4870)

▲ Champion Thread Company .... G 704 867-6611
   Gastonia (G-5018)

Classical Elements .... G 828 575-9145
   Asheville (G-478)

Cloth Barn Inc .... F 919 735-3643
   Goldsboro (G-5206)

◆ Continental Ticking Corp Amer .... D 336 570-0091
   Alamance (G-55)

◆ Copland Industries Inc .... B 336 226-0272
   Burlington (G-1076)

Culp Inc .... E 662 844-7144
   Burlington (G-1080)

D & F Consolidated Inc .... G 704 664-6660
   Statesville (G-11683)

Distinctive Furniture Inc .... G 828 754-3947
   Lenoir (G-7600)

Domestic Fabrics Blankets Corp .... E 252 523-7948
   Kinston (G-7406)

◆ Freudenberg Prfmce Mtls LP .... E 919 479-7443
   Durham (G-4037)

▲ Gentry Mills Inc .... D 704 983-5555
   Albemarle (G-74)

◆ Global Textile Alliance Inc .... G 336 347-7601
   Reidsville (G-10685)

Heritage Prtg & Graphics Inc .... G 704 551-0700
   Charlotte (G-2274)

▲ Lantal Textiles Inc .... C 336 969-9551
   Rural Hall (G-10963)

▲ Morbern USA Inc .... E 336 883-4332
   High Point (G-6715)

NC Graphic Pros LLC .... G 252 492-7326
   Kittrell (G-7442)

▲ Oakhurst Textiles Inc .... G 336 668-0733
   Greensboro (G-5718)

Omnia LLC .... G 919 696-2193
   Oxford (G-9621)

Pearson Textiles Inc .... G 919 776-8730
   Sanford (G-11216)

▲ Polyvlies Usa Inc .... E 336 769-0206
   Winston Salem (G-13299)

Ripstop By Roll LLC .... F 877 525-7210
   Durham (G-4215)

Sam M Butler Inc .... E 704 364-8647
   Charlotte (G-2753)

◆ Selective Enterprises Inc .... C 704 588-3310
   Charlotte (G-2784)

Sml Raleigh LLC .... G 919 585-0100
Clayton (G-3170)

Svcm .... G 305 767-3595
Lincolnton (G-7858)

Warm Products Inc .... F 425 248-2424
Hendersonville (G-6249)

Wovenart Inc .... F 828 859-6349
Tryon (G-12180)

5136 Men's and boy's clothing

Apparel USA Inc .... E 212 869-5495
Fairmont (G-4500)

Associated Distributors Inc .... G 910 895-5800
Hamlet (G-6050)

Badger Sportswear LLC .... D 704 871-0990
Statesville (G-11665)

◆ Bob Barker Company Inc .... C 800 334-9880
Fuquay Varina (G-4870)

Burlington Coat Fctry Whse Cor ...... E 919 468-9312
Cary (G-1317)

Carolina Tailors Inc .... G 252 247-6469
Newport (G-9439)

▲ Flagship Brands LLC .... E 888 801-7227
Newton (G-9465)

◆ Gildan Activewear (eden) Inc ...... C 336 623-9555
Eden (G-4347)

◆ Gold Toe Stores Inc .... G 828 464-0751
Newton (G-9469)

Home T LLC .... F 646 797-4768
Charlotte (G-2284)

▲ Ics North America Corp .... E 704 794-6620
Concord (G-3375)

▲ Madison Company Inc .... E 336 548-9624
Madison (G-7992)

Marketing One Sportswear Inc .... G 704 334-9333
Charlotte (G-2457)

◆ Raleigh Workshop Inc .... E 919 917-8969
Raleigh (G-10431)

▲ Sanders Industries Inc .... G 410 277-8565
Waynesville (G-12472)

Seafarer LLC .... G 704 624-3200
Marshville (G-8094)

Simmons Hosiery Mill Inc .... G 828 327-4890
Hickory (G-6448)

Walter Reynolds .... G 704 735-6050
Lincolnton (G-7870)

5137 Women's and children's clothing

AC Valor Reyes LLC .... G 910 431-3256
Castle Hayne (G-1493)

Apparel USA Inc .... E 212 869-5495
Fairmont (G-4500)

Badger Sportswear LLC .... D 704 871-0990
Statesville (G-11665)

Burlington Coat Fctry Whse Cor ...... E 919 468-9312
Cary (G-1317)

Gerson & Gerson Inc .... E 252 235-2441
Middlesex (G-8276)

▲ Ics North America Corp .... E 704 794-6620
Concord (G-3375)

Marketing One Sportswear Inc .... G 704 334-9333
Charlotte (G-2457)

Mindfully Made Usa LLC .... E 336 701-0377
Winston Salem (G-13255)

◆ Parker Hosiery Company Inc .... E 828 668-7628
Old Fort (G-9596)

◆ Raleigh Workshop Inc .... E 919 917-8969
Raleigh (G-10431)

▲ Sanders Industries Inc .... G 410 277-8565
Waynesville (G-12472)

Seafarer LLC .... G 704 624-3200
Marshville (G-8094)

Simmons Hosiery Mill Inc .... G 828 327-4890
Hickory (G-6448)

▲ Sorbe Ltd .... G 704 562-2991
Matthews (G-8193)

Sue-Lynn Textiles Inc .... E 336 578-0871
Haw River (G-6135)

▲ Sunrise Development LLC .... F 828 453-0590
Mooresboro (G-8586)

Tiara Inc .... G 828 484-8236
Asheville (G-619)

Tresmc LLC .... G 919 900-0868
Knightdale (G-7461)

Walter Reynolds .... G 704 735-6050
Lincolnton (G-7870)

5139 Footwear

◆ Implus Footcare LLC ....B 800 446-7587
Durham (G-4073)

McRae Industries Inc .... C 910 439-6149
Mount Gilead (G-9203)

VF Corporation .... G 336 424-6000
Greensboro (G-5899)

VF Corporation .... F 336 424-6000
Greensboro (G-5900)

5141 Groceries, general line

Alta Foods llc .... D 919 734-0233
Goldsboro (G-5197)

▲ La Tortilleria LLC .... C 336 773-0010
Winston Salem (G-13229)

◆ USa Wholesale and Distrg Inc .....F 888 484-6872
Fayetteville (G-4693)

▼ Value Clothing Inc .... D 704 638-6111
Salisbury (G-11132)

5142 Packaged frozen goods

Evelyn T Burney .... G 336 473-9794
Rocky Mount (G-10838)

Thomas Brothers Foods LLC .... F 336 672-0337
Asheboro (G-409)

5143 Dairy products, except dried or canned

Celebrity Dairy LLC .... G 919 742-4931
Siler City (G-11404)

Dfa Dairy Brands Fluid LLC .... G 704 341-2794
Charlotte (G-2038)

Hershey Company .... F 919 284-0272
Kenly (G-7233)

Lc Foods LLC .... G 919 510-6688
Raleigh (G-10250)

Queen City Pastry Llc .... E 704 660-5706
Mooresville (G-8757)

Tonys Ice Cream Co Inc .... G 704 853-0018
Gastonia (G-5157)

5144 Poultry and poultry products

Carolina Egg Companies Inc .... D 252 459-2143
Nashville (G-9314)

5145 Confectionery

Bilcat Inc .... E 828 295-3088
Blowing Rock (G-880)

Gold Medal Products Co .... G 336 665-4997
Greensboro (G-5568)

▲ Lc America Inc .... F 336 676-5129
Colfax (G-3282)

Lotus Bakeries Us LLC .... G 415 956-8956
Mebane (G-8250)

Lrw Holdings Inc .... G 919 609-4172
Durham (G-4110)

Tastebuds LLC .... G 704 461-8755
Belmont (G-771)

◆ Tropical Nut & Fruit Co ....C 800 438-4470
Charlotte (G-2947)

5146 Fish and seafoods

Atlantis Foods Inc .... E 336 768-6101
Clemmons (G-3177)

B & J Seafood Co Inc .... F 252 637-0483
New Bern (G-9338)

Bay Breeze Seafood Rest Inc .... F 828 697-7106
Hendersonville (G-6186)

Capt Charlies Seafood Inc .... E 252 796-7278
Columbia (G-3294)

Carolina ATL Seafood Entps .... G 252 728-2552
Morehead City (G-8822)

◆ Classic Seafood Group Inc ....C 252 746-2818
Ayden (G-654)

Gillikin Marine Railways Inc .... G 252 726-7284
Beaufort (G-728)

Lloyds Oyster House Inc .... E 910 754-6958
Shallotte (G-11304)

Pamlico Packing Co Inc .... F 252 745-3688
Vandemere (G-12226)

Pamlico Packing Co Inc .... F 252 745-3688
Grantsboro (G-5331)

▲ Quality Foods From Sea Inc .... D 252 338-5455
Elizabeth City (G-4405)

Quality Seafood Co Inc .... G 252 338-2800
Elizabeth City (G-4406)

5147 Meats and meat products

Alexanders Ham Company Inc .... F 704 857-9222
Mooresville (G-8593)

Bass Farms Inc .... F 252 478-4147
Spring Hope (G-11552)

Goodnight Brothers Prod Co Inc ..... E 828 264-8892
Boone (G-918)

Julian Freirich Food Products .... E 704 636-2621
Salisbury (G-11078)

▼ Star Food Products Inc .... D 336 227-4079
Burlington (G-1164)

Stevens Packing Inc .... G 336 274-6033
Greensboro (G-5840)

Thomas Brothers Foods LLC .... F 336 672-0337
Asheboro (G-409)

5148 Fresh fruits and vegetables

Aseptia Inc .... C 678 373-6751
Raleigh (G-9919)

◆ Dole Food Company Inc ....E 818 874-4000
Charlotte (G-2061)

5149 Groceries and related products, nec

◆ Azure Skye Beverages Inc ....G 704 909-7394
Charlotte (G-1727)

Bakeboxx Company .... F 336 861-1212
High Point (G-6536)

Bakers Southern Traditions Inc ...... G 252 344-2120
Roxobel (G-10949)

▲ Celtic Ocean International Inc ...... E 828 299-9005
Arden (G-261)

Chef Martini LLC .... A 919 327-3183
Raleigh (G-9992)

Chocolate Fetish LLC .... G 828 258-2353
Asheville (G-475)

Chocolate Smiles Village LLC .... G 919 469-5282
Cary (G-1327)

Choice USA Beverage Inc .... G 704 487-6951
Shelby (G-11317)

Clay County Food Pantry Inc .... G 828 389-1657
Hayesville (G-6138)

Coca Cola Bottling Co .... G 704 509-1812
Charlotte (G-1946)

Coca-Cola Consolidated Inc.................... C 919 550-0611
 Clayton (G-3141)

Coca-Cola Consolidated Inc.................... D 252 334-1820
 Elizabeth City (G-4382)

Dfa Dairy Brands Fluid LLC................... G 704 341-2794
 Charlotte (G-2038)

Escazu Artisan Chocolate LLC.............. F 919 832-3433
 Raleigh (G-10091)

▲ Great Eastern Sun Trdg Co Inc......... F 828 665-7790
 Asheville (G-511)

Hare Asian Trading Company LLC........ E 910 524-4667
 Burgaw (G-1023)

Interntnal Agrclture Group LLC............ F 908 323-3246
 Mooresville (G-8694)

◆ Krispy Kreme Doughnuts Inc............C 336 725-2981
 Winston Salem (G-13228)

▲ Larrys Beans Inc................................ G 919 828-1234
 Raleigh (G-10248)

◆ Liqui-Box Corporation.....................D 804 325-1400
 Charlotte (G-2426)

Lotus Bakeries Us LLC........................ G 415 956-8956
 Mebane (G-8250)

Mindfully Made Usa LLC...................... E 336 701-0377
 Winston Salem (G-13255)

Novas Bakery Inc................................. F 704 333-5566
 Charlotte (G-2579)

Pepsi Bottling Ventures LLC................. C 919 863-4000
 Garner (G-4953)

Pepsi Bottling Ventures LLC................. E 252 451-1811
 Rocky Mount (G-10859)

Pepsi Bottling Ventures LLC................. D 910 792-5400
 Wilmington (G-12874)

Pepsi Bottling Ventures LLC................. C 336 724-4800
 Winston Salem (G-13281)

Pepsi-Cola Btlg Hickry NC Inc............. G 828 322-8090
 Granite Falls (G-5316)

Pepsi-Cola Btlg Hickry NC Inc............. D 828 322-8090
 Hickory (G-6409)

Pepsi-Cola Btlg Hickry NC Inc............. C 828 322-8090
 Hickory (G-6410)

Pepsi-Cola Metro Btlg Co Inc............... A 336 896-4000
 Winston Salem (G-13282)

Random Rues Botanical LLC................. G 252 214-2759
 Greenville (G-6017)

Royal Cup Inc...................................... F 704 597-5756
 Charlotte (G-2734)

◆ S & D Coffee Inc.............................A 704 782-3121
 Concord (G-3437)

Stony Gap Wholesale Co Inc................ G 704 982-5360
 Albemarle (G-93)

◆ Suntory International.......................F 917 756-2747
 Raleigh (G-10521)

Tracys Gourmet LLC............................ G 919 672-1731
 Asheville (G-622)

Tradewinds Coffee Co Inc.................... F 919 556-1835
 Zebulon (G-13524)

◆ Tropical Nut & Fruit Co....................C 800 438-4470
 Charlotte (G-2947)

Vintage South Inc............................... G 919 362-4079
 Apex (G-202)

Zeskp LLC... G 910 762-8300
 Wilmington (G-12958)

5153 Grain and field beans

C A Perry & Son Inc............................ G 252 330-2323
 Elizabeth City (G-4380)

C A Perry & Son Inc............................ E 252 221-4463
 Hobbsville (G-6883)

Catawba Farms Enterprises LLC........... F 828 464-5780
 Newton (G-9452)

▲ Celtic Ocean International Inc.......... E 828 299-9005
 Arden (G-261)

Clapp Fertilizer and Trckg Inc............. G 336 449-6103
 Whitsett (G-12602)

▲ Farm Chemicals Inc....................... F 910 875-4277
 Raeford (G-9837)

Murphy-Brown LLC.............................. G 252 221-4463
 Hobbsville (G-6884)

▲ Murphy-Brown LLC........................ D 910 293-3434
 Warsaw (G-12363)

5159 Farm-product raw materials, nec

C A Perry & Son Inc............................ G 252 330-2323
 Elizabeth City (G-4380)

C A Perry & Son Inc............................ E 252 221-4463
 Hobbsville (G-6883)

East Crlina Olseed Prcssors LL........... D 252 935-5553
 Pantego (G-9643)

Idea Oven LLC..................................... G 910 343-5280
 Castle Hayne (G-1503)

▼ Northampton Peanut Company........ D 252 585-0916
 Severn (G-11298)

Powell & Stokes Inc............................. G 252 794-2138
 Windsor (G-13056)

Pyxus International Inc......................... C 252 753-8000
 Farmville (G-4538)

◆ USa Wholesale and Distrg Inc........F 888 484-6872
 Fayetteville (G-4693)

5162 Plastics materials and basic shapes

▲ Ace Plastics Inc............................. G 704 527-5752
 Charlotte (G-1615)

◆ Advanced Marketing International IncF 910 392-0508
 Wilmington (G-12692)

Advanced Plastiform Inc...................... D 919 404-2080
 Zebulon (G-13500)

◆ Advanced Technology Inc.................E 336 668-0488
 Greensboro (G-5344)

Cardinal Plastics Inc........................... G 704 739-9420
 Kings Mountain (G-7354)

Custom Extrusion Inc.......................... G 336 495-7070
 Asheboro (G-343)

Easth20 Holdings Llc........................... G 919 313-2100
 Greensboro (G-5510)

Endless Plastics LLC........................... F 336 346-1839
 Greensboro (G-5520)

◆ Interlam Corporation......................E 336 786-6254
 Mount Airy (G-9134)

Mdsi Inc... G 919 783-8730
 Browns Summit (G-1002)

Mdt Bromley LLC.................................. E 828 651-8737
 Fletcher (G-4752)

◆ Mpe Usa Inc.................................. E 704 340-4910
 Pineville (G-9743)

◆ Piedmont Plastics Inc.....................D 704 597-8200
 Charlotte (G-2636)

Poly-Tech Industrial Inc....................... E 704 948-8055
 Huntersville (G-7035)

◆ Reichhold Holdings Us Inc.............. A 919 990-7500
 Durham (G-4210)

▲ Repi LLC....................................... E 704 648-0252
 Dallas (G-3685)

Tri-Star Plastics Corp.......................... E 704 598-2800
 Denver (G-3813)

▲ United Plastics Corporation............ C 336 786-2127
 Mount Airy (G-9192)

▲ Wilbert Plstic Svcs Acqstion L........ E 704 455-5191
 Harrisburg (G-6121)

5169 Chemicals and allied products, nec

A House of Hemp LLC.......................... G 910 984-1441
 Linden (G-7872)

Access Technologies LLC..................... G 574 286-1255
 Mooresville (G-8590)

Ada Marketing Inc............................... E 910 221-2189
 Dunn (G-3841)

◆ Advanced Marketing International IncF 910 392-0508
 Wilmington (G-12692)

Air & Gas Solutions LLC....................... E 704 897-2182
 Charlotte (G-1631)

Airgas Usa LLC................................... G 704 394-1420
 Charlotte (G-1633)

Airgas Usa LLC................................... G 919 544-1056
 Durham (G-3884)

Airgas Usa LLC................................... G 919 544-3773
 Durham (G-3885)

Airgas Usa LLC................................... G 919 735-5276
 Goldsboro (G-5196)

American Chrome & Chem NA Inc........ F 910 675-7200
 Castle Hayne (G-1494)

Arc3 Gases Inc.................................... G 336 275-3333
 Greensboro (G-5367)

Arc3 Gases Inc.................................... G 704 220-1029
 Monroe (G-8429)

Arc3 Gases Inc.................................... E 910 892-4016
 Dunn (G-3844)

Bonakemi Usa Incorporated................. D 704 220-6943
 Monroe (G-8445)

◆ Burlington Chemical Co LLC............G 336 584-0111
 Greensboro (G-5410)

Carolina Bg... G 704 847-8840
 Matthews (G-8101)

▲ Chem-Tex Laboratories Inc............. E 706 602-8600
 Concord (G-3335)

Desco Equipment Company Inc............ G 704 873-2844
 Statesville (G-11689)

Eminess Technologies Inc.................... E 704 283-2600
 Monroe (G-8482)

Explosives Supply Company................. F 828 765-2762
 Spruce Pine (G-11575)

Fil-Chem Inc....................................... G 919 878-1270
 Raleigh (G-10108)

Fortrans Inc.. G 919 365-8004
 Wendell (G-12536)

Green Mountain Intl LLC....................... G 800 942-5151
 Waynesville (G-12460)

▼ Greenology Products LLC................ E 877 473-3650
 Raleigh (G-10144)

Heiq Chemtex Inc................................ G 704 795-9322
 Concord (G-3373)

James Oxygen and Supply Co.............. E 704 322-5438
 Hickory (G-6374)

Jci Jones Chemicals Inc....................... F 704 392-9767
 Charlotte (G-2363)

◆ Jowat Corporation..........................E 336 434-9000
 Archdale (G-233)

Jowat International Corp...................... E 336 434-9000
 Archdale (G-234)

▲ Kincol Industries Incorporated......... G 704 372-8435
 Charlotte (G-2397)

Kymera International LLC...................... E 919 544-8090
 Durham (G-4099)

Leke LLC... G 704 523-1452
 Pineville (G-9739)

Marlowe-Van Loan Sales Co................. G 336 882-3351
 High Point (G-6700)

◆ Maxam North America Inc...............F 214 736-8100
 Mooresville (G-8721)

▲ Melatex Incorporated..................... F 704 332-5046
 Charlotte (G-2489)

▲ Newell Novelty Co Inc.................... G 336 597-2246
 Roxboro (G-10931)

▲ Pavco Inc...................................... E 704 496-6800
 Charlotte (G-2619)

Pencco Inc.. F 252 235-5300
 Middlesex (G-8279)

▲ Polytec Inc.................................. E 704 277-3960
Mooresville (G-8750)

Reagents Holdings LLC.................. E 800 732-8484
Charlotte (G-2695)

▼ Reedy International Corp................. F 980 819-6930
Charlotte (G-2701)

◆ Reichhold Holdings Us Inc.............. A 919 990-7500
Durham (G-4210)

◆ Rpoc Inc...................................... C 910 371-3184
Wilmington (G-12904)

▲ Sostram Corporation..................... G 919 226-1195
Durham (G-4242)

South / Win LLC............................ D 336 398-5650
Greensboro (G-5822)

▼ Sutherland Products Inc................. F 800 854-3541
Stoneville (G-11831)

▲ T - Square Enterprises Inc............. G 704 846-8233
Charlotte (G-2894)

Textile Rubber and Chem Co Inc......... G 704 376-3582
Indian Trail (G-7103)

◆ Umicore USA Inc.......................... E 919 874-7171
Raleigh (G-10575)

◆ Universal Preservachem Inc............ D 732 568-1266
Mebane (G-8262)

5171 Petroleum bulk stations and terminals

▼ Warren Oil Company LLC................. D 910 892-6456
Dunn (G-3871)

5172 Petroleum products, nec

Crossroads Fuel Service Inc.............. E 252 426-5216
Hertford (G-6252)

Danisson USA Trading Ltd LLC.......... G 704 965-8317
Kernersville (G-7264)

Euliss Oil Company Inc.................... G 336 622-3055
Liberty (G-7766)

Herrin Bros Coal & Ice Co................ G 704 332-2193
Charlotte (G-2275)

▼ Moroil Corp................................ F 704 795-9595
Concord (G-3405)

Nelson Holdings Nc Inc................... F 828 322-9226
Hickory (G-6399)

Panenergy Corp............................. F 704 594-6200
Charlotte (G-2607)

Sg-Clw Inc................................... F 336 865-4980
Winston Salem (G-13331)

South Central Oil and Prpn Inc.......... G 704 982-2173
Albemarle (G-90)

Southern States Coop Inc................. F 910 285-8213
Wallace (G-12325)

Volta Group Corporation LLC............ E 919 637-0273
Raleigh (G-10593)

▼ Warren Oil Company LLC................. D 910 892-6456
Dunn (G-3871)

5181 Beer and ale

Glass Jug..................................... F 919 818-6907
Durham (G-4048)

Glass Jug LLC............................... F 919 813-0135
Durham (G-4049)

Koi Pond Brewing Company LLC......... G 252 231-1660
Rocky Mount (G-10847)

Salty Turtle Beer Company................ E 910 803-2019
Surf City (G-11863)

White Street Brewing Co Inc.............. F 919 647-9439
Youngsville (G-13498)

5182 Wine and distilled beverages

Aviator Brewing Company Inc............ G 919 601-5497
Holly Springs (G-6893)

Drink A Bull LLC............................ G 919 818-3321
Durham (G-4008)

5191 Farm supplies

▲ AG Provision LLC......................... E 910 296-0302
Kenansville (G-7224)

Boggs Farm Center Inc.................... G 704 538-7176
Fallston (G-4522)

◆ Brushy Mountain Bee Farm Inc......... E 336 921-3610
Winston Salem (G-13112)

C A Perry & Son Inc....................... G 252 330-2323
Elizabeth City (G-4380)

C A Perry & Son Inc....................... E 252 221-4463
Hobbsville (G-6883)

Camp Chemical Corporation.............. F 336 597-2214
Roxboro (G-10921)

Carolina Greenhouse Plants Inc.......... G 252 523-9300
Kinston (G-7398)

Clapp Fertilizer and Trckg Inc........... G 336 449-6103
Whitsett (G-12602)

Coastal Agrobusiness Inc................. G 828 697-2220
Flat Rock (G-4706)

Coastal Agrobusiness Inc................. G 252 798-3481
Hamilton (G-6048)

◆ Coastal Agrobusiness Inc................. D 252 238-7391
Greenville (G-5955)

G & M Milling Co Inc...................... F 704 873-5758
Statesville (G-11701)

G P Kittrell & Son Inc..................... G 252 465-8929
Corapeake (G-3579)

Goodnight Brothers Prod Co Inc.......... E 828 264-8892
Boone (G-918)

Harvey Fertilizer and Gas Co............ E 252 753-2063
Farmville (G-4530)

Harvey Fertilizer and Gas Co............ F 252 523-9090
Kinston (G-7414)

▲ Harvey Fertilizer and Gas Co............ E 252 526-4150
Kinston (G-7415)

Helena Agri-Enterprises LLC............. G 828 685-1182
Hendersonville (G-6214)

Helena Agri-Enterprises LLC............. F 910 422-8901
Rowland (G-10915)

◆ Herbal Innovations LLC.................. G 336 818-2332
Wilkesboro (G-12638)

◆ Industrial and Agricultur................. E 910 843-2121
Red Springs (G-10668)

Mountaire Farms LLC...................... B 910 974-3232
Candor (G-1239)

Mountaire Farms Inc....................... D 910 844-3126
Maxton (G-8204)

Nutrien AG Solutions Inc................. G 252 585-0282
Conway (G-3578)

Nutrien AG Solutions Inc................. F 252 977-2025
Rocky Mount (G-10814)

Southern AG Insecticides Inc............. E 828 264-8843
Boone (G-943)

Southern AG Insecticides Inc............. E 828 692-2233
Hendersonville (G-6242)

Southern States Coop Inc................. D 704 872-6364
Statesville (G-11772)

Southern States Coop Inc................. F 910 285-8213
Wallace (G-12325)

Thompson Sunny Acres Inc............... G 910 206-1801
Rockingham (G-10791)

▲ Upl NA Inc.................................. E 800 358-7642
Cary (G-1476)

5192 Books, periodicals, and newspapers

Book Lover Search......................... G 336 889-6127
High Point (G-6549)

Cherokee Publications..................... G 828 627-2424
Cherokee (G-3051)

Comfort Publishing Svcs LLC............ G 704 907-7848
Concord (G-3338)

▲ Gryphon House Inc........................ F 800 638-0928
Lewisville (G-7651)

Oxford University Press LLC............. D 919 677-0977
Cary (G-1412)

Oxford University Press LLC............. B 919 677-0977
Cary (G-1413)

Wisdom House Books Inc................. G 919 883-4669
Chapel Hill (G-1594)

5193 Flowers and florists supplies

Government Sales LLC.................... G 252 726-6315
Morehead City (G-8833)

Jefferson Group Inc....................... E 252 752-6195
Greenville (G-5995)

5194 Tobacco and tobacco products

Mr Tobacco.................................. G 919 747-9052
Raleigh (G-10316)

Royal Blunts Connections Inc............ G 919 961-4910
Raleigh (G-10448)

5198 Paints, varnishes, and supplies

Akzo Nobel Coatings Inc.................. G 336 665-9897
Greensboro (G-5345)

Bonakemi Usa Incorporated.............. D 704 218-3917
Monroe (G-8444)

Bonakemi Usa Incorporated.............. D 704 220-6943
Monroe (G-8445)

Controlled Release Tech Inc.............. G 704 487-0878
Shelby (G-11324)

Highland International LLC................ F 828 265-2513
Boone (G-924)

◆ Keim Mineral Coatings Amer Inc........ F 704 588-4811
Charlotte (G-2391)

Modern Recreational Tech Inc............ E 800 221-4466
Greensboro (G-5696)

Sherwin-Williams Company............... E 336 292-3000
Greensboro (G-5810)

Sherwin-Williams Company............... G 919 436-2460
Raleigh (G-10469)

5199 Nondurable goods, nec

American Plush Tex Mills LLC............ F 765 609-0456
Red Springs (G-10664)

◆ Aquafil OMara Inc......................... C 828 874-2100
Rutherford College (G-10970)

▲ Arcona Leather Company LLC........... G 828 396-7728
Hudson (G-6941)

Aseptia Inc.................................. C 678 373-6751
Raleigh (G-9919)

Atlantic Corp Wilmington Inc............. D 704 588-1400
Charlotte (G-1710)

B & B Leather Co Inc...................... F 704 598-9080
Charlotte (G-1728)

B F I Industries Inc........................ G 919 229-4509
Wake Forest (G-12262)

Badger Sportswear LLC................... D 704 871-0990
Statesville (G-11665)

▲ Bagcraftpapercon III LLC................ D 800 845-6051
Charlotte (G-1739)

Berlin Packaging LLC...................... G 704 612-4500
Charlotte (G-1772)

Bickerstaff Trees Inc...................... G 336 372-8866
Sparta (G-11535)

Blue Stone Industries Ltd................. G 919 379-3986
Cary (G-1310)

C & M Enterprise Inc...................... G 704 545-1180
Mint Hill (G-8333)

Carroll Companies Inc..................... F 828 466-5489
Conover (G-3502)

◆ Carroll Companies Inc.................... E 828 264-2521
Boone (G-904)

S
I
C

Carroll Signs & Advertising................G..... 336 983-3415
King *(G-7324)*

◆ Causekeepers Inc......................E..... 336 824-2518
Franklinville *(G-4855)*

Cedar Hill Studio & Gallery.............G..... 828 456-6344
Waynesville *(G-12453)*

◆ Conitex Sonoco Usa Inc............C..... 704 864-5406
Gastonia *(G-5028)*

Consumer Concepts......................F..... 252 247-7000
Morehead City *(G-8828)*

Crown Trophy Inc...........................G..... 336 851-1011
Greensboro *(G-5474)*

Dale Advertising Inc......................G..... 704 484-0971
Shelby *(G-11329)*

▲ Daztech Inc...............................G..... 800 862-6360
Wilmington *(G-12761)*

Dicks Store...................................G..... 336 548-9358
Madison *(G-7987)*

Freudenberg Prfmce Mtls LP............C..... 828 665-5000
Candler *(G-1225)*

Geami Ltd.....................................E..... 919 654-7700
Raleigh *(G-10125)*

Global Packaging Inc.....................D..... 610 666-1608
Hamlet *(G-6056)*

Gourmet Foods USA LLC.................G..... 704 248-1724
Cornelius *(G-3604)*

Hans Kissle Company LLC..............C..... 980 500-1630
Dallas *(G-3674)*

Heritage Prtg & Graphics Inc...........G..... 704 551-0700
Charlotte *(G-2274)*

▲ Hibco Plastics Inc.......................E..... 336 463-2391
Yadkinville *(G-13443)*

◆ Hs Hyosung Usa Inc...................E..... 704 790-6100
Charlotte *(G-2292)*

▲ Hs Hyosung USA Holdings Inc.......G..... 704 790-6134
Charlotte *(G-2293)*

Identify Yourself LLC.....................F..... 252 202-1452
Kitty Hawk *(G-7445)*

Ink n Stitches LLC.........................G..... 336 633-3898
Asheboro *(G-365)*

International Foam Pdts Inc.............G..... 704 588-0080
Charlotte *(G-2343)*

▲ Interntnal Tray Pads Packg Inc.......G..... 910 944-1800
Aberdeen *(G-8)*

▲ J & P Entrprses of Crlinas Inc.......E..... 704 861-1867
Gastonia *(G-5069)*

J R Craver & Associates Inc............G..... 336 769-3330
Clemmons *(G-3193)*

Jenkins Properties Inc...................E..... 336 667-4282
North Wilkesboro *(G-9537)*

◆ Leather Miracles LLC..................E..... 828 464-7448
Hickory *(G-6386)*

Loparex LLC.................................C..... 336 635-0192
Eden *(G-4352)*

Map Supply Inc.............................G..... 336 731-3230
Flat Rock *(G-4710)*

Markell Publishing Company Inc.......G..... 336 226-7148
Burlington *(G-1122)*

Marketing One Sportswear Inc.........G..... 704 334-9333
Charlotte *(G-2457)*

Memories of Orangeburg Inc...........G..... 803 533-0035
Mooresville *(G-8722)*

◆ Microfine Inc.............................G..... 336 768-1480
Winston Salem *(G-13252)*

Mindfully Made Usa LLC.................E..... 336 701-0377
Winston Salem *(G-13255)*

Mm Clayton LLC............................B..... 919 553-4113
Clayton *(G-3160)*

◆ Normtex Incorporated.................G..... 828 428-3363
Wilmington *(G-12863)*

Office Sup Svcs Inc Charlotte..........E..... 704 786-4677
Concord *(G-3410)*

Olympic Products LLC....................D..... 336 378-9620
Greensboro *(G-5721)*

Pactiv LLC....................................G..... 910 944-1800
Aberdeen *(G-18)*

◆ Paperfoam Packaging Usa LLC......G..... 910 371-0480
Wilmington *(G-12870)*

▼ Poly Packaging Systems Inc.........D..... 336 889-8334
High Point *(G-6739)*

Pregis Innovative Packg LLC............E..... 847 597-2200
Granite Falls *(G-5318)*

Pretium Packaging LLC...................E..... 336 621-1891
Greensboro *(G-5762)*

▲ Project Bean LLC.......................D..... 201 438-1598
Huntersville *(G-7040)*

PSM Enterprises Inc......................F..... 336 789-8888
Mount Airy *(G-9167)*

Quiknit Crafting Inc.......................G..... 704 861-1030
Gastonia *(G-5129)*

▲ Reliance Packaging LLC..............E..... 910 944-2561
Aberdeen *(G-21)*

Richa Inc......................................G..... 704 944-0230
Charlotte *(G-2724)*

Richa Inc......................................F..... 704 331-9744
Charlotte *(G-2725)*

RLM/Universal Packaging Inc...........F..... 336 644-6161
Greensboro *(G-5789)*

Schutz Container Systems Inc..........D..... 336 249-6816
Lexington *(G-7738)*

Silverlining Screen Prtrs Inc............G..... 919 554-0340
Youngsville *(G-13485)*

Snyder Paper Corporation...............E..... 828 464-1189
Newton *(G-9496)*

◆ Sonoco Hickory Inc....................D..... 828 328-2466
Hickory *(G-6453)*

Storopack Inc...............................G..... 800 827-7225
Winston Salem *(G-13344)*

◆ Stump Printing Co Inc.................C..... 260 723-5171
Wrightsville Beach *(G-13433)*

T & R Signs..................................G..... 919 779-1185
Garner *(G-4967)*

▲ Tannis Root Productions Inc.........G..... 919 832-8552
Raleigh *(G-10533)*

Thompson Printing & Packg Inc........G..... 704 313-7323
Mooresboro *(G-8587)*

Tobacco Outlet Products LLC...........G..... 704 341-9388
Charlotte *(G-2924)*

◆ Trivantage LLC..........................D..... 800 786-1876
Burlington *(G-1171)*

Unified2 Globl Packg Group LLC.......C..... 774 696-3643
Durham *(G-4288)*

Unique Stone Incorporated.............G..... 910 817-9450
Rockingham *(G-10792)*

Wholesale Kennel Supply Co...........G..... 919 742-2515
Siler City *(G-11427)*

52 BUILDING MATERIALS, HARDWARE, GARDEN SUPPLIES & MOBILE HOMES

5211 Lumber and other building materials

All Glass Inc................................G..... 828 324-8609
Hickory *(G-6262)*

Alligood Cabinet Shop....................G..... 252 927-3201
Washington *(G-12372)*

◆ Amarr Company.........................C..... 336 744-5100
Winston Salem *(G-13084)*

Authentic Iron LLC........................G..... 910 648-6989
Bladenboro *(G-873)*

Barber Furniture & Supply..............F..... 704 278-9367
Cleveland *(G-3209)*

▲ Bfs Asset Holdings LLC...............B..... 303 784-4288
Raleigh *(G-9941)*

▲ Bfs Operations LLC....................A..... 919 431-1000
Raleigh *(G-9942)*

Blue Ridge Lbr Log & Timber Co.......G..... 336 961-5211
Yadkinville *(G-13438)*

Builders Firstsource Inc.................F..... 336 884-5454
Greensboro *(G-5409)*

Builders Firstsource Inc.................F..... 919 562-6601
Youngsville *(G-13465)*

Builders Firstsource - SE Grp..........G..... 910 313-3056
Wilmington *(G-12724)*

Builders Frstsrce - Rleigh LLC..........D..... 919 363-4956
Apex *(G-147)*

Builders Frstsrce - Sthast Gro.........C..... 910 944-2516
Aberdeen *(G-2)*

C & M Industrial Supply Co..............G..... 704 483-4001
Mill Spring *(G-8300)*

C & R Building Supply Inc...............G..... 910 567-6293
Autryville *(G-647)*

Capitol City Lumber Company..........F..... 919 832-6492
Raleigh *(G-9970)*

Carolina Cab Specialist LLC............G..... 919 818-4375
Cary *(G-1322)*

Carolina Windows and Doors Inc......F..... 252 756-2585
Greenville *(G-5951)*

Carport Central Inc.......................E..... 336 673-6020
Mount Airy *(G-9111)*

Cleveland Lumber Company.............E..... 704 487-5263
Shelby *(G-11320)*

▲ Design Surfaces Inc...................G..... 919 781-0310
Raleigh *(G-10043)*

E W Godwin S Sons Inc..................E..... 910 762-7747
Wilmington *(G-12769)*

Energy Svers Windows Doors Inc......G..... 252 758-8700
Greenville *(G-5974)*

General Shale Brick Inc..................F..... 704 937-7431
Grover *(G-6043)*

Glenn Lumber Company Inc............E..... 704 434-7873
Shelby *(G-11338)*

▲ GLG Corporation........................F..... 336 784-0396
Winston Salem *(G-13178)*

Glover Materials Inc......................G..... 252 536-2660
Pleasant Hill *(G-9797)*

Goodman Millwork Inc...................F..... 704 633-2421
Salisbury *(G-11058)*

Green River Resource MGT..............F..... 828 697-0357
Zirconia *(G-13530)*

▼ Hardwood Store of NC Inc............F..... 336 449-9627
Gibsonville *(G-5177)*

Hargrove Countertops & ACC Inc......E..... 919 981-0163
Raleigh *(G-10155)*

Hewlin Brothers Lumber Co.............G..... 252 586-6473
Enfield *(G-4484)*

Hunter Millwork Inc......................F..... 704 821-0144
Matthews *(G-8174)*

Interrs-Exteriors Asheboro Inc.........G..... 336 629-2148
Asheboro *(G-367)*

Ivey Ln Inc...................................F..... 336 230-0062
Greensboro *(G-5631)*

Jak Moulding & Supply Inc..............F..... 252 753-5546
Walstonburg *(G-12332)*

Lee Builder Mart Inc......................E
Sanford *(G-11204)*

Leonard Block Company..................G..... 336 764-0607
Winston Salem *(G-13233)*

M O Deviney Lumber Co Inc.............G..... 704 538-9071
Casar *(G-1489)*

Marsh Furniture Company................F..... 336 273-8196
Greensboro *(G-5676)*

Master Tesh Stone Works................G..... 828 898-8333
Banner Elk *(G-687)*

Matthews Building Supply Co .... E 704 847-2106
Matthews (G-8130)

Maxson & Associates .... G 336 632-0524
Greensboro (G-5683)

Mint Hill Cabinet Shop Inc .... E 704 821-9373
Monroe (G-8531)

Mkc85 Inc .... F 910 762-1986
Wilmington (G-12855)

Mountain Showcase Group Inc .... E 828 692-9494
Hendersonville (G-6228)

Native Naturalz Inc .... F 336 334-2984
Greensboro (G-5704)

Pine Hall Brick Co Inc .... F 336 721-7500
Madison (G-7996)

Powell Industries Inc .... D 828 926-9114
Waynesville (G-12467)

Precision Cabinets Inc .... G 828 262-5080
Boone (G-938)

Privette Enterprises Inc .... E 704 634-3291
Monroe (G-8544)

Robbinsville Cstm Molding Inc .... F 828 479-2317
Robbinsville (G-10761)

Salt Wood Products Inc .... G 252 830-8875
Greenville (G-6020)

Selectbuild Construction Inc .... F 208 331-4300
Raleigh (G-10467)

Shutter Production Inc .... G 910 289-2620
Rose Hill (G-10910)

Sipe Lumber Company Inc .... E 828 632-4679
Taylorsville (G-11978)

Smith Companies Lexington Inc .... G 336 249-4941
Lexington (G-7742)

Smokey Mountain Lumber Inc .... G 828 298-3958
Asheville (G-602)

Sorrells Cabinet Co Inc .... G 919 639-4320
Lillington (G-7803)

Southeastern Hardwoods Inc .... G 828 581-0197
Swannanoa (G-11878)

Southern Concrete Materials Inc .... C 828 253-6421
Asheville (G-608)

▲ Southland Electrical Sup LLC .... C 336 227-1486
Burlington (G-1160)

Spake Concrete Products Inc .... F 704 482-2881
Shelby (G-11382)

▲ Stock Building Supply Hol .... A 919 431-1000
Raleigh (G-10509)

Superior Walls Systems LLC .... E 704 636-6200
Salisbury (G-11120)

T E Johnson Lumber Co Inc .... G 919 963-2233
Four Oaks (G-4817)

Thomas Concrete SC Inc .... G 704 868-4545
Gastonia (G-5154)

Tice Kitchens & Interiors LLC .... F 919 366-4117
Raleigh (G-10549)

▲ TRf Manufacturing NC Inc .... E 252 223-1112
Newport (G-9445)

Triad Corrugated Metal Inc .... E 336 625-9727
Asheboro (G-411)

Triad Prefinish & Lbr Sls Inc .... G 336 375-4849
Greensboro (G-5877)

Triangle Brick Company .... E 704 695-1420
Wadesboro (G-12251)

▲ Triangle Brick Company .... E 919 544-1796
Durham (G-4277)

Ufp Site Built LLC .... F 910 590-3220
Clinton (G-3252)

Viktors Gran MBL Kit Cnter Top .... F 828 681-0713
Arden (G-316)

Walton Lumber Co .... G 919 563-6565
Mebane (G-8264)

▲ William Stone & Tile Inc .... G 910 353-0914
Hubert (G-6938)

Yadkin Lumber Company Inc .... G 336 679-2432
Yadkinville (G-13459)

5231 Paint, glass, and wallpaper stores

Capitol Funds Inc .... F 910 439-5275
Mount Gilead (G-9198)

Capitol Funds Inc .... E 704 487-8547
Shelby (G-11316)

Classy Glass Inc .... G 828 452-2242
Waynesville (G-12454)

Cleveland Lumber Company .... E 704 487-5263
Shelby (G-11320)

Decor Glass Specialties Inc .... G 828 586-8180
Sylva (G-11891)

Done-Gone Adios Inc .... F 336 993-7300
Kernersville (G-7268)

▲ Industrial Glass Tech LLC .... F 704 853-2429
Gastonia (G-5065)

Lbm Industries Inc .... F 828 966-4270
Sapphire (G-11259)

Ledger Hardware Inc .... G 828 688-4798
Bakersville (G-679)

Orare Inc .... G 919 742-1003
Siler City (G-11422)

Pgw Auto Glass LLC .... B 336 258-4950
Elkin (G-4451)

Sherwin-Williams Company .... E 336 292-3000
Greensboro (G-5810)

Triangle Glass Service Inc .... G 919 477-9508
Durham (G-4279)

W G Cannon Paint Co Inc .... G 828 754-5376
Lenoir (G-7644)

5251 Hardware stores

◆ Ace Marine Rigging & Supply Inc ...... F 252 726-6620
Morehead City (G-8811)

▲ AGM Carolina Inc .... G 336 431-4100
High Point (G-6511)

B&C Xterior Cleaning Svc Inc .... G 919 779-7905
Raleigh (G-9928)

▲ Bfs Operations LLC .... A 919 431-1000
Raleigh (G-9942)

Bolton Investors Inc .... G 919 471-1197
Durham (G-3937)

C & M Industrial Supply Co .... G 704 483-4001
Mill Spring (G-8300)

Capitol Funds Inc .... F 910 439-5275
Mount Gilead (G-9198)

Capitol Funds Inc .... E 704 487-8547
Shelby (G-11316)

Castle Hayne Hardware LLC .... G 910 675-9205
Castle Hayne (G-1497)

Discount Pallet Services LLC .... G 910 892-3760
Dunn (G-3853)

◆ Gesipa Fasteners Usa Inc .... F 609 208-1740
Mocksville (G-8368)

▲ Hudson S Hardware Inc .... E 919 553-3030
Garner (G-4933)

Ledger Hardware Inc .... G 828 688-4798
Bakersville (G-679)

Matthews Building Supply Co .... E 704 847-2106
Matthews (G-8130)

Merrill Resources Inc .... G 828 877-4450
Penrose (G-9662)

Quality Equipment LLC .... G 919 493-3545
Durham (G-4203)

▲ Shopbot Tools Inc .... E 919 680-4800
Durham (G-4233)

◆ Snap-On Power Tools Inc .... C 828 835-4400
Murphy (G-9296)

Steelman Milling Company Inc .... G 336 463-5586
Yadkinville (G-13452)

▲ Stock Building Supply Hol .... A 919 431-1000
Raleigh (G-10509)

Triad Cutting Tools Inc .... G 336 873-8708
Asheboro (G-412)

W E Nixons Wldg & Hdwr Inc .... G 252 221-4348
Edenton (G-4373)

Yat Usa Inc .... G 480 584-4096
Huntersville (G-7063)

5261 Retail nurseries and garden stores

American Soil and Mulch Inc .... G 919 460-1349
Raleigh (G-9897)

Certified Lawnmower Inc .... G 704 527-2765
Belmont (G-742)

Farm Services Inc .... G 336 226-7381
Graham (G-5268)

G P Kittrell & Son Inc .... G 252 465-8929
Corapeake (G-3579)

▲ I Must Garden LLC .... G 919 929-2299
Raleigh (G-10182)

Mineral Springs Fertilizer Inc .... G 704 843-2683
Mineral Springs (G-8327)

Quality Equipment LLC .... G 919 493-3545
Durham (G-4203)

R E Mason Enterprises Inc .... G 910 483-5016
Fayetteville (G-4661)

Southern States Coop Inc .... F 336 599-2185
Roxboro (G-10945)

▲ Vegherb LLC .... F 800 914-9835
Erwin (G-4493)

5271 Mobile home dealers

▲ Cutting Systems Inc .... D 704 592-2451
Union Grove (G-12184)

▼ Deltec Homes Inc .... E 828 253-0483
Asheville (G-486)

Home City Ltd .... G 910 428-2196
Biscoe (G-853)

53 GENERAL MERCHANDISE STORES

5311 Department stores

Belk Department Stores LP .... E 704 357-4000
Charlotte (G-1769)

Burlington Coat Fctry Whse Cor .... E 919 468-9312
Cary (G-1317)

◆ Gildan Activewear (eden) Inc .... C 336 623-9555
Eden (G-4347)

Val-U-King Group Inc .... G 980 306-5342
Gastonia (G-5162)

5331 Variety stores

Atlantic Trading LLC .... F
Charlotte (G-1711)

Brasingtons Inc .... G 704 694-5191
Wadesboro (G-12236)

Infinity S End Inc .... F 704 900-8355
Charlotte (G-2328)

Shibumi Shade Inc .... F 336 816-9903
Raleigh (G-10470)

5399 Miscellaneous general merchandise

Village Produce & Cntry Str In .... G 336 661-8685
Winston Salem (G-13381)

54 FOOD STORES

5411 Grocery stores

B & D Enterprises Inc .... G 704 739-2958
Kings Mountain (G-7348)

S I C

Bluff Mountain Outfitters Inc................... G 828 622-7162
　Hot Springs *(G-6932)*

Cardinal Foods LLC............................. E 910 259-9407
　Burgaw *(G-1020)*

Clean Catch Fish Market LLC.............. G 704 333-1212
　Charlotte *(G-1928)*

Coker Feed Mill Inc............................. F 919 778-3491
　Goldsboro *(G-5207)*

Communitys Kitchen L3c........................ G 828 817-2308
　Tryon *(G-12173)*

Harris Teeter LLC............................... D 704 846-7117
　Matthews *(G-8115)*

Harris Teeter LLC............................... D 919 859-0110
　Raleigh *(G-10156)*

Ingles Markets Incorporated................. D 704 434-0096
　Boiling Springs *(G-885)*

J L Powell & Co Inc............................. G 910 642-8989
　Whiteville *(G-12585)*

James Fods Frnchise Corp Amer.......... G 336 437-0393
　Graham *(G-5272)*

Kol Incorporated................................. G 919 872-2340
　Raleigh *(G-10240)*

Rose Ice & Coal Company..................... G 910 762-2464
　Wilmington *(G-12902)*

Ruddick Operating Company LLC......... A 704 372-5404
　Charlotte *(G-2742)*

Stevens Packing Inc............................ G 336 274-6033
　Greensboro *(G-5840)*

Whole Harvest Foods LLC.................... E 910 293-7917
　Warsaw *(G-12369)*

5421 Meat and fish markets

Acre Station Meat Farm Inc................. F 252 927-3700
　Pinetown *(G-9707)*

Ashe Hams Inc.................................... G 828 259-9426
　Asheville *(G-432)*

Carolina ATL Seafood Entps.................. G 252 728-2552
　Morehead City *(G-8822)*

Clean Catch Fish Market LLC.............. G 704 333-1212
　Charlotte *(G-1928)*

Hobes Country Hams Inc...................... E 336 670-3401
　North Wilkesboro *(G-9535)*

Mitchells Meat Processing..................... F 336 591-7420
　Walnut Cove *(G-12328)*

Mt Airy Meat Center Inc....................... G 336 786-2023
　Mount Airy *(G-9155)*

Stevens Packing Inc............................ G 336 274-6033
　Greensboro *(G-5840)*

Suncrest Farms Cntry Hams Inc............ E 336 667-4441
　Wilkesboro *(G-12654)*

Wells Jnkins Wells Mt Proc Inc.............. G 828 245-5544
　Forest City *(G-4800)*

5441 Candy, nut, and confectionery stores

Beech Street Ventures LLC.................. E 919 755-5053
　Raleigh *(G-9938)*

Bilcat Inc.. E 828 295-3088
　Blowing Rock *(G-880)*

Butterfields Candy LLC........................ G 252 459-2577
　Nashville *(G-9313)*

Chocolate Fetish LLC............................ G 828 258-2353
　Asheville *(G-475)*

Chocolate Smiles Village LLC................ G 919 469-5282
　Cary *(G-1327)*

French Broad Chocolates LLC............... G 828 252-4181
　Asheville *(G-502)*

▼ Northampton Peanut Company........... D 252 585-0916
　Severn *(G-11298)*

Sachs Peanuts LLC............................ E 910 647-4711
　Clarkton *(G-3128)*

Secret Chocolatier LLC....................... G 704 323-8178
　Charlotte *(G-2781)*

Shallowford Farms Popcorn Inc............. G 336 463-5938
　Yadkinville *(G-13451)*

Sugar Pops.. G 704 799-0959
　Mooresville *(G-8782)*

Tastebuds LLC.................................... G 704 461-8755
　Belmont *(G-771)*

5451 Dairy products stores

Bilcat Inc.. E 828 295-3088
　Blowing Rock *(G-880)*

Buffalo Creek Farm & Crmry LLC.......... G 336 969-5698
　Germanton *(G-5174)*

Dewey S Bakery Inc............................ F 336 748-0230
　Winston Salem *(G-13143)*

G & M Milling Co Inc............................ F 704 873-5758
　Statesville *(G-11701)*

Goodberry Creamery Inc....................... F 919 878-8870
　Wake Forest *(G-12279)*

▲ Mooresville Ice Cream Com............... E 704 664-5456
　Mooresville *(G-8725)*

Paletria La Mnrca McHacana LLC.......... G 919 803-0636
　Raleigh *(G-10354)*

▲ Tony S Ice Cream Company Inc......... F 704 867-7085
　Gastonia *(G-5156)*

5461 Retail bakeries

Bakeboxx Company.............................. F 336 861-1212
　High Point *(G-6536)*

Dewey S Bakery Inc............................ F 336 748-0230
　Winston Salem *(G-13143)*

Ingles Markets Incorporated................. D 704 434-0096
　Boiling Springs *(G-885)*

Krispy Kreme Doughnut Corp................ E 919 669-6151
　Gastonia *(G-5074)*

Krispy Kreme Doughnut Corp................ E 336 854-8275
　Greensboro *(G-5655)*

Krispy Kreme Doughnut Corp................ E 336 733-3780
　Winston Salem *(G-13226)*

Krispy Kreme Doughnut Corp................ E 336 726-8908
　Winston Salem *(G-13227)*

◆ Krispy Kreme Doughnut Corp............. C 980 270-7117
　Charlotte *(G-2402)*

◆ Krispy Kreme Doughnuts Inc.............. C 336 725-2981
　Winston Salem *(G-13228)*

Normandie Bakery Inc.......................... G 910 686-1372
　Wilmington *(G-12862)*

Novas Bakery Inc............................... F 704 333-5566
　Charlotte *(G-2579)*

SE Co-Brand Ventures LLC.................. G 704 598-9322
　Charlotte *(G-2773)*

Sprinkle of Sugar LLC.......................... G 336 474-8620
　Thomasville *(G-12073)*

Swirl Oakhurst LLC.............................. G 704 258-1209
　Charlotte *(G-2889)*

Yummi Factory Corporation................... E 980 248-1062
　Concord *(G-3472)*

5499 Miscellaneous food stores

▲ Atlantic Natural Foods LLC............... D 888 491-0524
　Nashville *(G-9309)*

Bakers Southern Traditions Inc.............. G 252 344-2120
　Roxobel *(G-10949)*

Blazing Foods LLC.............................. G 336 865-2933
　Charlotte *(G-1789)*

Blue Ridge Jams................................. G 828 685-1783
　Hendersonville *(G-6187)*

Cold Off Press LLC.............................. G 984 444-9006
　Raleigh *(G-10003)*

Daily Manufacturing Inc........................ F 704 782-0700
　Rockwell *(G-10795)*

◆ Herbal Innovations LLC..................... E 336 818-2332
　Wilkesboro *(G-12638)*

Induction Food Systems Inc................. G 919 907-0179
　Raleigh *(G-10188)*

Lc Foods LLC..................................... G 919 510-6688
　Raleigh *(G-10250)*

McDonalds... F 910 295-1112
　Pinehurst *(G-9697)*

Natures Pharmacy Inc.......................... G 828 251-0094
　Asheville *(G-555)*

Nutrotonic LLC................................... F 855 948-0008
　Charlotte *(G-2590)*

Random Rues Botanical LLC................. G 252 214-2759
　Greenville *(G-6017)*

Stormberg Foods LLC.......................... E 919 947-6011
　Goldsboro *(G-5247)*

◆ Suntory International........................... F 917 756-2747
　Raleigh *(G-10521)*

Tradewinds Coffee Co Inc.................... F 919 556-1835
　Zebulon *(G-13524)*

Well-Bean Coffee & Crumbs LLC........... G 833 777-2326
　Wake Forest *(G-12314)*

55 AUTOMOTIVE DEALERS AND GASOLINE SERVICE STATIONS

5511 New and used car dealers

ABB Motors and Mechanical Inc............ C 828 645-1706
　Weaverville *(G-12481)*

▼ Axle Holdings LLC............................ E 800 895-3276
　Concord *(G-3316)*

Courtesy Ford Inc................................ G 252 338-4783
　Elizabeth City *(G-4384)*

Daimler Truck North Amer LLC.............. A 704 645-5000
　Cleveland *(G-3213)*

Dutch Miller Charlotte Inc.................... F 704 522-8422
　Charlotte *(G-2070)*

Goodyear Tire & Rubber Company........ G 984 983-0161
　Mebane *(G-8245)*

▲ Saab Barracuda LLC......................... E 910 814-3088
　Lillington *(G-7802)*

Streets Auto Sales & Four WD.............. G 704 888-8686
　Locust *(G-7904)*

Subaru Folger Automotive..................... F 704 531-8888
　Charlotte *(G-2877)*

Vestal Buick Gmc Inc........................... D 336 310-0261
　Kernersville *(G-7312)*

◆ Volvo Trucks North America Inc.......... A 336 393-2000
　Greensboro *(G-5911)*

Window Motor World Inc....................... G 800 252-2649
　Boone *(G-953)*

5521 Used car dealers

Courtesy Ford Inc................................ G 252 338-4783
　Elizabeth City *(G-4384)*

G A Lankford Construction..................... G 828 254-2467
　Alexander *(G-100)*

Quality Investments Inc......................... E 252 492-8777
　Henderson *(G-6172)*

5531 Auto and home supply stores

A 1 Tire Service Inc............................. G 828 684-1860
　Fletcher *(G-4716)*

Accel Discount Tire.............................. G 704 636-0323
　Salisbury *(G-11012)*

Advance Stores Company Inc................ F 336 545-9091
　Greensboro *(G-5341)*

Aiken-Black Tire Service Inc................. E 828 322-3736
　Hickory *(G-6261)*

Albemarle Tire Retreading Inc............... G 704 982-4113
　Albemarle *(G-59)*

Alk Investments LLC............................ G 984 233-5353
　Raleigh *(G-9891)*

Avery County Recapping Co Inc............ G 828 733-0161
Newland *(G-9424)*

Barnharts Tech Tire Repair Inc.............. G 336 337-1569
Lexington *(G-7658)*

Beamer Tire & Auto Repair Inc............. F 336 882-7043
High Point *(G-6541)*

Bill Martin Inc............................... G 704 873-0241
Statesville *(G-11671)*

Boondock S Manufacturing Inc............ G 828 891-4242
Etowah *(G-4495)*

Bray S Recapping Service Inc.............. E 336 786-6182
Mount Airy *(G-9105)*

Bridgestone Ret Operations LLC........... G 919 471-4468
Durham *(G-3941)*

Bridgestone Ret Operations LLC........... G 910 864-4106
Fayetteville *(G-4562)*

Bridgestone Ret Operations LLC........... F 704 861-8146
Gastonia *(G-5005)*

Bridgestone Ret Operations LLC........... G 919 778-0230
Goldsboro *(G-5202)*

Bridgestone Ret Operations LLC........... G 336 282-6646
Greensboro *(G-5399)*

Bridgestone Ret Operations LLC........... F 336 852-8524
Greensboro *(G-5400)*

Bridgestone Ret Operations LLC........... G 336 282-4695
Greensboro *(G-5401)*

Bridgestone Ret Operations LLC........... G 252 522-5126
Kinston *(G-7397)*

Bridgestone Ret Operations LLC........... G 919 872-6402
Raleigh *(G-9958)*

Bridgestone Ret Operations LLC........... G 919 872-6566
Raleigh *(G-9959)*

Bridgestone Ret Operations LLC........... G 252 243-5189
Wilson *(G-12973)*

Bridgestone Ret Operations LLC........... G 336 725-1580
Winston Salem *(G-13110)*

Bridgestone Amrcas Tire Oprtons.......... A 252 291-4275
Wilson *(G-12974)*

▲ Carpenter Industries Inc................. D 704 786-8139
Concord *(G-3331)*

Cecil Budd Tire Company LLC.............. F 919 742-2322
Siler City *(G-11403)*

Claybrook Tire Inc.......................... F 336 573-3135
Stoneville *(G-11820)*

Closed Tire Company Inc................... F 704 864-5464
Gastonia *(G-5022)*

Colony Tire Corporation.................... G 252 973-0004
Rocky Mount *(G-10829)*

Consolidated Truck Parts Inc............... G 704 279-5543
Rockwell *(G-10794)*

Courtesy Ford Inc.......................... G 252 338-4783
Elizabeth City *(G-4384)*

Crossroads Tire Store Inc.................. G 704 888-2064
Midland *(G-8285)*

Cummins Inc................................ E 336 275-4531
Greensboro *(G-5476)*

Dfa US Inc................................. E 336 756-0590
Mocksville *(G-8358)*

Diagnostic Shop Inc........................ G 704 933-3435
Kannapolis *(G-7207)*

Discount Tires & Auto Repair.............. G 336 788-0057
Winston Salem *(G-13147)*

Down East Offroad Inc..................... F 252 246-9440
Wilson *(G-12984)*

Ed S Tire Laurinburg Inc................... G 910 277-0565
Laurinburg *(G-7498)*

Enfield Tire Service Inc.................... G 252 445-5016
Enfield *(G-4482)*

Foster Tire Sales Inc...................... G 336 248-6726
Lexington *(G-7688)*

Garage Shop LLC........................... F 980 500-0583
Denver *(G-3784)*

Goodyear Tire & Rubber Company........ G 919 552-9340
Holly Springs *(G-6903)*

Goodyear Tire & Rubber Company........ G 984 983-0161
Mebane *(G-8245)*

Goodyear Tire & Rubber Company........ G 336 794-0035
Winston Salem *(G-13180)*

Greensboro Tire & Auto Service........... G 336 294-9495
Greensboro *(G-5578)*

Hall Tire and Battery Co Inc............... G 336 275-3812
Greensboro *(G-5586)*

Haneys Tire Recapping Svc LLC........... G 910 276-2636
Laurinburg *(G-7503)*

Heintz Bros Automotives Inc............... G 704 872-8081
Statesville *(G-11706)*

▲ Irvan-Smith Inc........................... F 704 788-2554
Concord *(G-3382)*

John Conrad Inc............................ G 336 475-8144
Thomasville *(G-12041)*

Johnnys Tire Sales and Svc Inc........... F 252 353-8473
Greenville *(G-5997)*

Kerdea Technologies Inc................... F 971 900-1113
Greenville *(G-5998)*

Kgt Enterprises Inc........................ E 704 662-3272
Mooresville *(G-8704)*

L L C Batteries of N C..................... G 919 331-0241
Angier *(G-123)*

Leonard Alum Utlty Bldngs Inc............ G 336 226-9410
Burlington *(G-1119)*

Leonard Alum Utlty Bldngs Inc............ G 919 872-4442
Raleigh *(G-10254)*

Leonard Alum Utlty Bldngs Inc............ D 336 789-5018
Mount Airy *(G-9146)*

M & M Tire and Auto Inc................... G 336 643-7877
Summerfield *(G-11843)*

M & R Retreading & Oil Co Inc............ G 704 474-4101
Norwood *(G-9556)*

McCarthy Tire Service Company.......... F 910 791-0132
Wilmington *(G-12849)*

Merchants Inc.............................. G 252 447-2121
Havelock *(G-6123)*

Mock Tire & Automotive Inc............... E 336 753-8473
Mocksville *(G-8379)*

Mock Tire & Automotive Inc............... E 336 774-0081
Winston Salem *(G-13256)*

▲ Mock Tire & Automotive Inc............. E 336 768-1010
Winston Salem *(G-13257)*

Moss Brothers Tires & Svc Inc............ G 910 895-4572
Rockingham *(G-10783)*

Mr Tire Inc................................. G 828 262-3555
Boone *(G-936)*

Mr Tire Inc................................. F 704 483-1500
Denver *(G-3794)*

Mr Tire Inc................................. F 828 322-8130
Hickory *(G-6398)*

Mr Tire Inc................................. G 704 739-6456
Kings Mountain *(G-7373)*

Mr Tire Inc................................. G 828 758-0047
Lenoir *(G-7627)*

Mr Tire Inc................................. G 704 735-8024
Lincolnton *(G-7846)*

Mr Tire Inc................................. G 704 484-0816
Shelby *(G-11365)*

Mr Tire Inc................................. G 704 872-4127
Statesville *(G-11737)*

Oakie S Tire & Recapping Inc............. G 704 482-5629
Shelby *(G-11367)*

Parrish Tire Company...................... E 704 372-2013
Charlotte *(G-2614)*

Parrish Tire Company...................... E 336 334-9979
Greensboro *(G-5735)*

Parrish Tire Company...................... E 704 872-6565
Jonesville *(G-7198)*

◆ Parrish Tire Company.................... D 800 849-8473
Winston Salem *(G-13276)*

Perry Brothers Tire Svc Inc............... F 919 693-2128
Oxford *(G-9623)*

Perry Brothers Tire Svc Inc............... E 919 775-7225
Sanford *(G-11218)*

Phil S Tire Service Inc..................... G 828 682-2421
Burnsville *(G-1189)*

Piedmont Truck Tires Inc.................. F 828 277-1549
Asheville *(G-574)*

Piedmont Truck Tires Inc.................. F 828 202-5337
Conover *(G-3544)*

Piedmont Truck Tires Inc.................. F 336 223-9412
Graham *(G-5281)*

Piedmont Truck Tires Inc.................. E 336 668-0091
Greensboro *(G-5746)*

▲ Prem Corp................................ E 704 921-1799
Charlotte *(G-2660)*

Quality Investments Inc.................... E 252 492-8777
Henderson *(G-6172)*

R and R Auto Repr & Tires Inc............ G 336 784-6893
Winston Salem *(G-13310)*

Rabuns Trlr Repr Tire Svc Inc............. G 704 764-7841
Monroe *(G-8547)*

Richmond Investment....................... E 910 410-8200
Rockingham *(G-10787)*

Roy Dunn.................................. G 919 963-3700
Four Oaks *(G-4815)*

Satco Truck Equipment Inc................. F 919 383-5547
Durham *(G-4222)*

◆ Sika Corporation......................... E 704 810-0500
Gastonia *(G-5138)*

Small Brothers Tire Co Inc................ G 704 289-3531
Monroe *(G-8559)*

Snider Tire Inc............................. D 704 373-2910
Charlotte *(G-2820)*

Snider Tire Inc............................. F 336 691-5480
Greensboro *(G-5820)*

Snider Tire Inc............................. G 828 324-9955
Hickory *(G-6450)*

Super Retread Center Inc.................. F 919 734-0073
Goldsboro *(G-5248)*

Team X-Treme LLC.......................... G 919 562-8100
Rolesville *(G-10890)*

Thrifty Tire............................... G 919 220-7800
Durham *(G-4273)*

Tire Sls Svc Inc Fytteville NC............. E 910 485-1121
Fayetteville *(G-4682)*

Tires Incorporated of Clinton............. F 910 592-4741
Clinton *(G-3249)*

Towel City Tire & Wheel LLC.............. G 704 933-2143
Kannapolis *(G-7222)*

Toyota Battery Mfg Inc.................... E 469 292-6094
Liberty *(G-7782)*

Treadz LLC................................. G 704 664-0995
Mooresville *(G-8787)*

Trick Karts Inc............................ G 704 883-0089
Statesville *(G-11793)*

Universal Tire Service Inc................. G 919 779-8798
Raleigh *(G-10577)*

Van Products Inc........................... E 919 878-7110
Raleigh *(G-10582)*

Village Tire Center Inc.................... G 919 862-8500
Raleigh *(G-10588)*

Whitaker S Tire Service Inc............... G 704 786-6174
Concord *(G-3468)*

White S Tire Svc Wilson Inc............... G 252 237-0770
Wilson *(G-13046)*

White S Tire Svc Wilson Inc............... D 252 237-5426
Wilson *(G-13047)*

Whites Tire Svc New Bern Inc............. G 252 633-1170
New Bern *(G-9407)*

S I C

Williams Electric Mtr Repr Inc................ G 919 859-9790
   Sanford *(G-11250)*

Wilson Tire and Automotive Inc............ G 336 584-9638
   Elon College *(G-4476)*

5541 Gasoline service stations

City of Greensboro.............................. D 336 373-5855
   Greensboro *(G-5446)*

College Sun Do................................... G 910 521-9189
   Pembroke *(G-9657)*

E Z Stop Number Two......................... G 828 627-9081
   Clyde *(G-3259)*

Hardison Tire Co Inc........................... F 252 745-4561
   Bayboro *(G-711)*

Murphy USA Inc................................... E 828 758-7055
   Lenoir *(G-7628)*

5551 Boat dealers

◆ Ace Marine Rigging & Supply Inc....... F 252 726-6620
   Morehead City *(G-8811)*

Barbour S Marine Supply Co Inc........... G 252 728-2136
   Beaufort *(G-720)*

Cape Fear Yacht Works LLC.................. F 910 540-1685
   Wilmington *(G-12729)*

Jones Marine Inc................................. G 704 639-0173
   Salisbury *(G-11075)*

Kencraft Manufacturing Inc................. G 252 291-0271
   Wilson *(G-12998)*

M & J Marine LLC................................. F 252 249-0522
   Oriental *(G-9601)*

Mann Custom Boats Inc....................... E 252 473-1716
   Manns Harbor *(G-8020)*

Marinemax of North Carolina................ G 910 256-8100
   Wrightsville Beach *(G-13432)*

Nomad Houseboats Inc....................... G 252 288-5670
   New Bern *(G-9386)*

Todds Rv & Marine Inc........................ G 828 651-0007
   Hendersonville *(G-6245)*

Triad Marine Center Inc....................... G 252 634-1880
   New Bern *(G-9401)*

5561 Recreational vehicle dealers

Derrow Enterprises Inc........................ G 252 635-3375
   New Bern *(G-9364)*

Todds Rv & Marine Inc........................ G 828 651-0007
   Hendersonville *(G-6245)*

5571 Motorcycle dealers

Barrs Competition................................ F 704 482-5169
   Shelby *(G-11313)*

Smoky Mountain Machining Inc............ D 828 665-1193
   Asheville *(G-603)*

5599 Automotive dealers, nec

A-1 Hitch & Trailors Sales Inc............... G 910 755-6025
   Supply *(G-11854)*

Gore S Trlr Manufacturer S Inc............. G 910 642-2246
   Whiteville *(G-12582)*

▼ Kaufman Trailers Inc........................ E 336 790-6800
   Lexington *(G-7704)*

Kraftsman Inc..................................... D 336 824-1114
   Ramseur *(G-10627)*

Leonard Alum Utlity Bldngs Inc............ G 919 872-4442
   Raleigh *(G-10254)*

Road King Trailers Inc......................... E 828 670-8012
   Candler *(G-1232)*

56 APPAREL AND ACCESSORY STORES

5611 Men's and boys' clothing stores

Hudson Overall Company Inc............... G 336 314-5024
   Greensboro *(G-5609)*

5621 Women's clothing stores

Belevation LLC................................... F 803 517-9030
   Biscoe *(G-847)*

▲ Bon Worth Inc................................ E 800 355-5131
   Hendersonville *(G-6190)*

G & G Enterprises.............................. G 336 764-2493
   Clemmons *(G-3186)*

Grace Apparel Company Inc................ G 828 242-8172
   Black Mountain *(G-865)*

Hanesbrands Inc................................ G 910 462-2001
   Laurel Hill *(G-7483)*

Jestines Jewels Inc............................ G 704 904-0191
   Salisbury *(G-11072)*

Live It Boutique LLC........................... G 704 492-2402
   Charlotte *(G-2427)*

Pine State Corporate AP LLC................ F 336 789-9437
   Mount Airy *(G-9164)*

Pretty Paid LLC.................................. G 980 443-3876
   Kings Mountain *(G-7379)*

W E Nixons Wldg & Hdwr Inc............... G 252 221-4348
   Edenton *(G-4373)*

5632 Women's accessory and specialty stores

◆ Fine Line Hosiery Inc....................... G 336 498-8022
   Asheboro *(G-356)*

Jones Fabricare Inc............................ G 336 272-7261
   Greensboro *(G-5639)*

▲ Morris Family Theatrical Inc.............. E 704 332-3304
   Charlotte *(G-2519)*

Sweet Room LLC................................ G 336 567-1620
   High Point *(G-6799)*

Tafford Uniforms LLC.......................... D 888 823-3673
   Charlotte *(G-2897)*

5641 Children's and infants' wear stores

▲ Cannon & Daughters Inc.................. D 828 254-9236
   Asheville *(G-466)*

Pashes LLC....................................... G 704 682-6535
   Statesville *(G-11743)*

Stork News Tm of America................... F 910 868-3065
   Fayetteville *(G-4675)*

W E Nixons Wldg & Hdwr Inc............... G 252 221-4348
   Edenton *(G-4373)*

5651 Family clothing stores

L Rancho Investments Inc................... G 336 431-1004
   Trinity *(G-12117)*

Pdf and Associates............................ G 252 332-7749
   Colerain *(G-3271)*

Pretty Paid LLC.................................. G 980 443-3876
   Kings Mountain *(G-7379)*

◆ Raleigh Workshop Inc...................... E 919 917-8969
   Raleigh *(G-10431)*

Ralph Lauren Corporation................... G 336 632-5000
   High Point *(G-6752)*

▲ Secret Spot Inc............................... G 252 441-4030
   Nags Head *(G-9302)*

5661 Shoe stores

Bio-Tech Prsthtics Orthtics In.............. G 336 333-9081
   Greensboro *(G-5390)*

Lebos Shoe Store Inc......................... F 704 987-6540
   Cornelius *(G-3614)*

Polyhose Incorporated........................ E 732 512-9141
   Wilmington *(G-12881)*

W E Nixons Wldg & Hdwr Inc............... G 252 221-4348
   Edenton *(G-4373)*

5699 Miscellaneous apparel and accessories

Acorn Printing................................... G 704 868-4522
   Bessemer City *(G-801)*

Funny Bone EMB & Screening............. G 704 663-4711
   Mooresville *(G-8668)*

Global Products & Mfg Svcs Inc........... G 360 870-9876
   Charlotte *(G-2215)*

Gmg Group LLC................................. G 252 441-8374
   Kill Devil Hills *(G-7317)*

Happy Jack Incorporated.................... G 252 747-2911
   Snow Hill *(G-11480)*

▲ Ics North America Corp.................... E 704 794-6620
   Concord *(G-3375)*

K Formula Enterprises Inc................... G 910 323-3315
   Fayetteville *(G-4626)*

Kontoor Brands Inc............................. A 336 332-3400
   Greensboro *(G-5653)*

Manna Corp North Carolina.................. G 828 696-3642
   Hendersonville *(G-6223)*

McDaniel Delmar................................. E 336 284-6377
   Mocksville *(G-8375)*

▲ Morris Family Theatrical Inc.............. E 704 332-3304
   Charlotte *(G-2519)*

Plushh LLC.. G 919 647-7911
   Raleigh *(G-10374)*

Rec Plus Inc...................................... E 704 375-9098
   Charlotte *(G-2696)*

Screen Master................................... G 252 492-8407
   Henderson *(G-6178)*

Tresmc LLC....................................... G 919 900-0868
   Knightdale *(G-7461)*

57 HOME FURNITURE, FURNISHINGS AND EQUIPMENT STORES

5712 Furniture stores

A R Byrd Company Inc........................ G 704 732-5675
   Lincolnton *(G-7807)*

▲ Acacia Home & Garden Inc.............. F 828 465-1700
   Conover *(G-3488)*

Alligood Cabinet Shop........................ G 252 927-3201
   Washington *(G-12372)*

Archie Supply LLC.............................. G 336 987-0895
   Greensboro *(G-5368)*

▲ Aria Designs LLC............................ F 828 572-4303
   Lenoir *(G-7573)*

B & B Wood Shop & Bldg Contrs.......... G 828 488-2078
   Bryson City *(G-1007)*

Bassett Furniture Inds NC LLC............. A 828 465-7700
   Newton *(G-9451)*

Bernhardt Furniture Company............. E 828 759-6205
   Lenoir *(G-7584)*

Bjmf Inc.. E 704 554-6333
   Charlotte *(G-1787)*

Black Mountain Cnstr Group Inc........... F 704 243-5593
   Waxhaw *(G-12424)*

Blue-Hen Inc...................................... G 407 322-2262
   Asheville *(G-458)*

Browns Woodworking LLC.................... G 704 983-5917
   Albemarle *(G-65)*

Burroough Furniture............................ G 336 841-3129
   Archdale *(G-215)*

Carolina Chair Inc.............................. F 828 459-1330
   Conover *(G-3499)*

Cedar Rock Home Furnishings............. G 828 396-2361
   Hudson *(G-6948)*

Comm-Kab Inc................................... F 336 873-8787
   Asheboro *(G-340)*

Cynthia Saar..................................... G 910 480-2523
   Stedman *(G-11806)*

◆ Dedon Inc..............................F 336 790-1070
Greensboro *(G-5491)*

Dexter Inc............................... G 919 510-5050
Raleigh *(G-10045)*

Digital Printing Systems Inc................... E 704 525-0190
Charlotte *(G-2047)*

Dilworth Mattress Company Inc............... G 704 333-6564
Charlotte *(G-2049)*

Distinctive Furniture Inc................... G 828 754-3947
Lenoir *(G-7600)*

▲ East Coast Umbrella Inc .... E 910 462-2500
Laurel Hill *(G-7482)*

Ethan Allen Retail Inc................... E 828 428-9361
Maiden *(G-8012)*

Furniture Fair Inc........................ E 910 455-4044
Jacksonville *(G-7124)*

Hfi Wind Down Inc................... C 828 438-5767
Morganton *(G-8872)*

▲ Ideaitlia Cntmporary Furn Corp........ C 828 464-1000
Conover *(G-3532)*

Innovative Awngs & Screens LLC.......... F 833 337-4233
Cornelius *(G-3610)*

Keani Furniture Inc...................... E 336 303-5484
Asheboro *(G-369)*

◆ Kingsdown Incorporated................... E 919 563-3531
Mebane *(G-8247)*

Kinston Office Supply Co Inc............... E 252 523-7654
Kinston *(G-7419)*

▲ Kitchen Cabinet Designers LLC......... C 919 833-6532
Raleigh *(G-10238)*

◆ Lexington Furniture Inds Inc..........C 336 474-5300
Thomasville *(G-12043)*

Locklear Cabinets Wdwrk Sp Inc........... G 910 521-4463
Rowland *(G-10916)*

◆ M & S Warehouse Inc................. E 828 728-3733
Lenoir *(G-7622)*

M C C of Laurinburg Inc.................G 910 276-0519
Laurinburg *(G-7506)*

▲ Marsh Furniture Company................. B 336 884-7363
High Point *(G-6703)*

Mattress Firm........................ G 252 443-1259
Rocky Mount *(G-10851)*

McNeillys Inc........................... E 704 300-1712
Lawndale *(G-7518)*

Miters Touch Inc....................... G 828 963-4445
Banner Elk *(G-688)*

Murphy S Custom Cabinetry Inc........... G 828 891-3050
Hendersonville *(G-6229)*

Nags Head Hammocks LLC............ G 252 441-6115
Nags Head *(G-9301)*

Neil Allen Industries Inc.................. G 336 887-6500
High Point *(G-6717)*

Nobscot Construction Co Inc............... G 919 929-2075
Chapel Hill *(G-1560)*

O Henry House Ltd..................... E 336 431-5350
Archdale *(G-239)*

Olde Lexington Products Inc............... G 336 956-2355
Linwood *(G-7880)*

Outer Banks Hammocks Inc............... F 910 256-4001
Wilmington *(G-12869)*

Panels By Paith Inc..................... G 336 599-3437
Roxboro *(G-10939)*

▲ Perfect Fit Industries LLC................. C 800 864-7618
Charlotte *(G-2627)*

Plastic Art Design Inc.................... G 919 878-1672
Raleigh *(G-10372)*

Quality Custom Woodworks Inc........... G 704 843-1584
Waxhaw *(G-12438)*

Reliable Bedding Company................. F 336 883-0648
Archdale *(G-241)*

Royal Colony Furniture Inc................ G 336 472-8833
Thomasville *(G-12067)*

S Banner Cabinets Incorporated.......... E 828 733-2031
Newland *(G-9434)*

Sides Furniture Inc..................... G 336 869-5509
High Point *(G-6769)*

Smartway of Carolinas LLC............... G 704 900-7877
Charlotte *(G-2817)*

Stephanies Mattress LLC................. G 704 763-0705
Charlotte *(G-2867)*

Tatum Galleries Inc..................... G 828 963-6466
Banner Elk *(G-689)*

▲ Tiger Mountain Woodworks Inc........ F 828 526-5577
Highlands *(G-6846)*

Unique Office Solutions Inc.............. F 336 854-0900
Greensboro *(G-5890)*

◆ Verellen Inc...........................E 336 889-7379
High Point *(G-6824)*

◆ Vrush Industries Inc................... G 336 886-7700
High Point *(G-6829)*

W B Mason Co Inc..................... E 888 926-2766
Charlotte *(G-2994)*

Washington Cabinet Company............ G 252 946-3457
Washington *(G-12420)*

▲ Watauga Creek LLC.................. G 828 369-7881
Franklin *(G-4842)*

Wildwood Studios Inc................... G 828 299-8696
Asheville *(G-636)*

Woodwright of Wilson Co Inc.............. G 252 243-9663
Elm City *(G-4468)*

World Art Gallery Incorporated........... G 910 989-0203
Jacksonville *(G-7160)*

Yukon Inc.............................. F 919 366-2001
Wendell *(G-12554)*

5713 Floor covering stores

▲ Bfs Operations LLC.................... A 919 431-1000
Raleigh *(G-9942)*

▼ Heartwood Pine Floors Inc............... G 919 542-4394
Moncure *(G-8406)*

Interrs-Exteriors Asheboro Inc............ G 336 629-2148
Asheboro *(G-367)*

Mongoose LLC........................ F 919 400-0772
Burlington *(G-1130)*

▲ Stock Building Supply Hol.............. A 919 431-1000
Raleigh *(G-10509)*

5714 Drapery and upholstery stores

Bettys Drapery Design Workroom.......... G 828 264-2392
Boone *(G-897)*

Cloth Barn Inc........................ F 919 735-3643
Goldsboro *(G-5206)*

Dale Ray Fabrics LLC................... G 704 932-6411
Kannapolis *(G-7206)*

Distinctive Furniture Inc................. G 828 754-3947
Lenoir *(G-7600)*

Simplicity Sofas Inc.................... G 800 813-2889
High Point *(G-6775)*

Textile Products Inc................... E 704 636-6221
Salisbury *(G-11124)*

Walker Draperies Inc................... F 919 220-1424
Durham *(G-4301)*

5719 Miscellaneous homefurnishings

Ashdan Enterprises.................... G 336 375-9698
Greensboro *(G-5372)*

Blinds Plus Inc........................ G 910 487-5196
Fayetteville *(G-4560)*

Carolina Blind Outlet Inc................. G 828 697-8525
Hendersonville *(G-6194)*

Ceder Creek Gallery & Pottery............. G 919 528-1041
Creedmoor *(G-3645)*

Dale Ray Fabrics Inc................... G 704 932-6411
Kannapolis *(G-7206)*

Dbf Inc............................... G 910 548-6725
Jacksonville *(G-7122)*

Designer Fabrics Inc................... G 704 305-4144
Concord *(G-3354)*

▲ Dewoolfson Down Intl Inc............... G 828 963-2750
Banner Elk *(G-684)*

▲ Fintronx LLC.......................... F 919 324-3960
Raleigh *(G-10109)*

▲ G & G Moulding Inc................... E 828 438-1112
Morganton *(G-8867)*

Glass Works of Hickory Inc............... G 828 322-2122
Hickory *(G-6339)*

Hunckler Fabrication LLC................ F 336 753-0905
Mocksville *(G-8370)*

Interrs-Exteriors Asheboro Inc............ G 336 629-2148
Asheboro *(G-367)*

Jugtown Pottery........................ G 910 464-3266
Seagrove *(G-11276)*

Lawing Marble Co Inc................... G 704 732-0360
Lincolnton *(G-7835)*

Leighdeux LLC........................ G 704 965-4889
Charlotte *(G-2418)*

Shuttercraft Inc....................... F 704 708-9079
Matthews *(G-8148)*

Southern Marble Co LLC................ G 704 982-4142
Albemarle *(G-91)*

5722 Household appliance stores

Accel Discount Tire..................... G 704 636-0323
Salisbury *(G-11012)*

Creative Stone Fyetteville Inc............ F 910 491-1225
Fayetteville *(G-4580)*

Electrolux Home Products Inc............ B 252 527-5100
Kinston *(G-7410)*

▲ Grancreations Inc..................... G 704 332-7625
Charlotte *(G-2230)*

Lyon Company......................... F 919 787-0024
Wadesboro *(G-12248)*

Mr Tire Inc............................ F 704 483-1500
Denver *(G-3794)*

Mr Tire Inc............................ G 704 739-6456
Kings Mountain *(G-7373)*

Mr Tire Inc............................ G 704 484-0816
Shelby *(G-11365)*

Mr Tire Inc............................ G 704 872-4127
Statesville *(G-11737)*

Oowee Incorporated.................... F 828 633-0289
Candler *(G-1230)*

Perry Brothers Tire Svc Inc............... E 919 775-7225
Sanford *(G-11218)*

Psnc Energy........................... G 919 367-2735
Apex *(G-189)*

The Tarheel Electric Memb............... F 919 876-4603
Raleigh *(G-10544)*

TTI Floor Care North Amer Inc............. D 440 996-2000
Charlotte *(G-2950)*

Walnut Cove Furniture Inc............... G 336 591-8008
Walnut Cove *(G-12331)*

▲ Web-Don Incorporated................. E 800 532-0434
Charlotte *(G-3009)*

Wen Bray Heating & AC.................. G 828 267-0635
Hickory *(G-6489)*

5731 Radio, television, and electronic stores

▲ C & S Antennas Inc................... F 828 324-2454
Conover *(G-3497)*

▲ Crest Electronics Inc.................. G 336 855-6422
Greensboro *(G-5471)*

Drew Roberts LLC...................... G 336 497-1679
Whitsett *(G-12604)*

Ni4I Antennas and Elec LLC.............. G 828 738-6445
Moravian Falls *(G-8810)*

S
I
C

Perry Brothers Tire Svc Inc...................... F 919 693-2128
Oxford (G-9623)

Perry Brothers Tire Svc Inc...................... E 919 775-7225
Sanford (G-11218)

Serra Wireless Inc.................................... G 980 318-0873
Charlotte (G-2789)

Southern Printing Company Inc............. G 910 259-4807
Burgaw (G-1033)

5734 Computer and software stores

Barefoot Cnc Inc..................................... G 828 438-5038
Morganton (G-8852)

Branch Office Solutions Inc................... G 800 743-1047
Indian Trail (G-7072)

Complete Comp St of Ralgh Inc............ E 919 828-5227
Raleigh (G-10005)

Drew Roberts LLC................................. G 336 497-1679
Whitsett (G-12604)

Global Products & Mfg Svcs Inc........... G 360 870-9876
Charlotte (G-2215)

Grover Gaming Inc................................ D 252 329-7900
Greenville (G-5985)

Ideacode Inc... G 919 341-5170
Greensboro (G-5613)

Infisoft Software.................................... G 704 307-2619
Charlotte (G-2329)

Information Tech Works LLC................... G 919 232-5332
Raleigh (G-10195)

Northstar Computer Tech Inc................. G 980 272-1969
Monroe (G-8537)

Payload Media Inc................................. G 919 367-2969
Cary (G-1415)

Preferred Data Corporation................... G 336 886-3282
High Point (G-6743)

Silver Knight Pcs LLC........................... G 910 824-2054
Fayetteville (G-4670)

▲ Terarecon Inc.................................... D 650 372-1100
Durham (G-4267)

5735 Record and prerecorded tape stores

Davie County Publishing Co.................. F 336 751-2120
Mocksville (G-8357)

Mohawk Industries Inc.......................... G 919 609-4759
Garner (G-4945)

Song of Wood Ltd................................. G 828 669-7675
Black Mountain (G-871)

Ultimix Records.................................... G 336 288-7566
Greensboro (G-5886)

5736 Musical instrument stores

Classical Elements............................... G 828 575-9145
Asheville (G-478)

Dorian Corporation............................... G 910 352-6939
Wilmington (G-12766)

J L Smith & Co Inc............................... F 704 521-1088
Charlotte (G-2360)

Kelhorn Corporation............................. G 828 837-5833
Brasstown (G-964)

Music & Arts.. G 919 329-6069
Garner (G-4948)

▲ Music Matters Inc............................. G 336 272-5303
Greensboro (G-5702)

◆ MW Enterprises Inc..........................G 828 963-7083
Vilas (G-12232)

Song of Wood Ltd................................. G 828 669-7675
Black Mountain (G-871)

58 EATING AND DRINKING PLACES

5812 Eating places

Alamance Kaffee Werks LLC.................G 662 617-4573
Burlington (G-1044)

Anchor Coffee Co Inc........................... G 336 265-7458
North Wilkesboro (G-9521)

Bilcat Inc... E 828 295-3088
Blowing Rock (G-880)

Booneshine Brewing Co Inc.................. G 828 263-4305
Boone (G-901)

Brewitt & Dreenkupp Inc....................... G 704 525-3366
Charlotte (G-1811)

Brick & Mortar Grill............................... G 919 639-9700
Angier (G-113)

Cabarrus Brewing Company LLC........... E 704 490-4487
Concord (G-3326)

Carolina Yogurt Inc............................... G 828 754-9685
Lenoir (G-7591)

Chatham News Publishing Co................ G 919 663-4042
Siler City (G-11405)

Cintoms Inc.. G 828 684-1317
Asheville (G-476)

Cupcake Bar.. G 919 816-2905
Durham (G-3993)

Dominos Pizza LLC............................... F 910 424-4884
Fayetteville (G-4588)

Donut Shop.. G 910 640-3317
Whiteville (G-12580)

Elxsi Corporation.................................. B 407 849-1090
Charlotte (G-2105)

Emanuel Hoggard................................. F 252 794-3724
Windsor (G-13053)

Jebco Inc... E 919 557-2001
Holly Springs (G-6904)

Lmb Corp... G 704 547-8886
Charlotte (G-2429)

Lovegrass Kitchen Inc........................... F 919 205-8426
Holly Springs (G-6906)

McDonalds.. F 910 295-1112
Pinehurst (G-9697)

Mike DS Bbq LLC................................. G 866 960-8652
Durham (G-4133)

Neomonde Baking Company.................. E 919 469-8009
Morrisville (G-9023)

Nunnery-Freeman Inc........................... G 252 438-3149
Henderson (G-6167)

▲ Obbc Inc... G 252 261-0612
Kitty Hawk (G-7446)

Over Rainbow Inc................................. G 704 332-5521
Charlotte (G-2604)

Sawmill Catering LLC........................... F 910 769-7455
Wilmington (G-12911)

Stevens Sausage Company Inc.............. D 919 934-3159
Smithfield (G-11466)

Sugar Creek Brewing Co LLC................ E 704 521-3333
Charlotte (G-2878)

◆ Suntory International..........................F 917 756-2747
Raleigh (G-10521)

Sweet Room LLC.................................. G 336 567-1620
High Point (G-6799)

Swirl Oakhurst LLC............................... G 704 258-1209
Charlotte (G-2889)

Tonys Ice Cream Co Inc........................ G 704 853-0018
Gastonia (G-5157)

◆ USa Wholesale and Distrg Inc...........F 888 484-6872
Fayetteville (G-4693)

Yummy Tummy Ga LLC......................... G 704 658-0445
Mooresville (G-8804)

Zoes Kitchen Inc.................................. E 336 748-0587
Winston Salem (G-13412)

5813 Drinking places

760 Craft Works LLC............................. F 704 274-5216
Huntersville (G-6962)

Bearwaters Brewing Company............... F 828 237-4200
Canton (G-1242)

▲ Bold Rock Partners LP....................... F 828 595-9940
Mills River (G-8312)

Bombshell Beer Company LLC............... F 919 823-1933
Holly Springs (G-6895)

Booneshine Brewing Co Inc.................. G 828 263-4305
Boone (G-901)

Cabarrus Brewing Company LLC........... E 704 490-4487
Concord (G-3326)

Glass Jug... F 919 818-6907
Durham (G-4048)

Glass Jug LLC...................................... F 919 813-0135
Durham (G-4049)

▲ Highland Brewing Company Inc........ F 828 299-3370
Asheville (G-517)

Innovation Brewing LLC........................ G 828 586-9678
Sylva (G-11893)

Koi Pond Brewing Company LLC........... G 252 231-1660
Rocky Mount (G-10847)

McDonalds.. F 910 295-1112
Pinehurst (G-9697)

Oklawaha Brewing Company LLC.......... F 828 595-9956
Hendersonville (G-6233)

Resident Culture Brewing LLC............... E 704 333-1862
Charlotte (G-2714)

Salty Turtle Beer Company.................... E 910 803-2019
Surf City (G-11863)

Shortway Brewing Company LLC........... G 252 777-3065
Newport (G-9444)

Stardust Cellars LLC............................ G 336 466-4454
Winston Salem (G-13343)

Sugar Creek Brewing Co LLC................ E 704 521-3333
Charlotte (G-2878)

Sweet Room LLC.................................. G 336 567-1620
High Point (G-6799)

Sycamore Brewing LLC......................... E 704 910-3821
Charlotte (G-2891)

▲ Triple C Brewing Company LLC.......... F 704 372-3212
Charlotte (G-2945)

White Street Brewing Co Inc.................. F 919 647-9439
Youngsville (G-13498)

59 MISCELLANEOUS RETAIL

5912 Drug stores and proprietary stores

Bausch Health Americas Inc.................. F 949 461-6000
Durham (G-3918)

Harris Teeter LLC................................. D 704 846-7117
Matthews (G-8115)

King Bio Inc... D 828 255-0201
Asheville (G-530)

Modoral Brands Inc.............................. G 336 741-7230
Winston Salem (G-13259)

Natures Pharmacy Inc........................... G 828 251-0094
Asheville (G-555)

Walgreen Co... G 704 525-2628
Charlotte (G-3001)

5921 Liquor stores

Aviator Brewing Company Inc................ G 919 601-5497
Holly Springs (G-6893)

Drink A Bull LLC.................................. G 919 818-3321
Durham (G-4008)

Glass Jug... G 919 818-6907
Durham (G-4048)

Glass Jug LLC...................................... F 919 813-0135
Durham (G-4049)

Jkl Inc.. F 252 355-6714
Greenville (G-5996)

Koi Pond Brewing Company LLC........... G 252 231-1660
Rocky Mount (G-10847)

Sanders Ridge Inc..................................... G 336 677-1700
Boonville *(G-958)*

5932 Used merchandise stores

Barker and Martin Inc............................. G 336 275-5056
Greensboro *(G-5385)*

Etherngton Cnservation Ctr Inc.............. E 336 665-1317
Greensboro *(G-5525)*

J C Lawrence Co...................................... G 919 553-3044
Oriental *(G-9600)*

Microtronic Us LLC................................. G 336 869-0429
High Point *(G-6712)*

Sumpters Jwly & Collectibles.................. G 704 399-5348
Charlotte *(G-2879)*

5941 Sporting goods and bicycle shops

Action Surfboards.................................... G 252 240-1818
Morehead City *(G-8812)*

Bear Creek Arsenal LLC.......................... C 919 292-6000
Sanford *(G-11154)*

Brandrpm LLC.. D 704 225-1800
Charlotte *(G-1807)*

▲ Cane Creek Cycling Cmpnnts Inc...... E 828 684-3551
Fletcher *(G-4727)*

▲ Carolina Gym Supply Corp................. G 919 732-6999
Hillsborough *(G-6862)*

Custom Marine Fabrication Inc............... G 252 638-5422
New Bern *(G-9360)*

Dara Holsters & Gear Inc........................ E 919 374-2170
Wendell *(G-12531)*

▲ Electric Fshing Reel Systems I........... G 336 273-9101
Greensboro *(G-5516)*

▲ Fathom Offshore Holdings LLC.......... G 910 399-6882
Wilmington *(G-12776)*

Ffr Electrics LLC...................................... F 828 654-7555
Mars Hill *(G-8077)*

Fusion Sport Inc...................................... E 720 987-4403
Durham *(G-4041)*

Gmg Group LLC....................................... G 252 441-8374
Kill Devil Hills *(G-7317)*

Home Team Athletics Inc........................ G 910 938-0862
Jacksonville *(G-7126)*

▲ I Must Garden LLC............................. G 919 929-2299
Raleigh *(G-10182)*

Kelleys Sports and Awards Inc............... G 828 728-4600
Hudson *(G-6952)*

Ken Staley Co Inc.................................... G 336 685-4294
Franklinville *(G-4857)*

Land and Loft LLC................................... G 315 560-7060
Raleigh *(G-10244)*

Line Drive Sports Center Inc.................. G 336 824-1692
Ramseur *(G-10628)*

▲ Mettech Inc.. G 919 833-9460
Raleigh *(G-10297)*

Millers Sports and Trophies.................... G 252 792-2050
Williamston *(G-12672)*

Mr Tire Inc.. G 828 262-3555
Boone *(G-936)*

Mr Tire Inc.. F 704 483-1500
Denver *(G-3794)*

Mr Tire Inc.. F 828 322-8130
Hickory *(G-6398)*

Mr Tire Inc.. G 704 739-6456
Kings Mountain *(G-7373)*

Mr Tire Inc.. G 828 758-0047
Lenoir *(G-7627)*

Mr Tire Inc.. G 704 735-8024
Lincolnton *(G-7846)*

Mr Tire Inc.. G 704 484-0816
Shelby *(G-11365)*

Mr Tire Inc.. G 704 872-4127
Statesville *(G-11737)*

R & S Sporting Goods Ctr Inc................. G 336 599-0248
Roxboro *(G-10942)*

Rockgeist LLC.. G 518 461-2009
Asheville *(G-593)*

Screen Master.. G 252 492-8407
Henderson *(G-6178)*

Sturm Ruger & Company Inc.................. B 336 427-0286
Mayodan *(G-8209)*

▲ Triplette Fencing Supply Inc.............. G 336 835-1205
Mount Airy *(G-9189)*

Watkins Agency Inc................................. G 704 213-6997
Salisbury *(G-11135)*

5942 Book stores

Free Will Bptst Press Fndtion................. F 252 746-6128
Ayden *(G-657)*

▲ Good Will Publishers Inc.................... D 704 853-3237
Gastonia *(G-5054)*

Grateful Steps Foundation...................... G 828 277-0998
Asheville *(G-509)*

Idea People Inc.. G 704 398-4437
Huntersville *(G-7000)*

Kinston Office Supply Co Inc.................. E 252 523-7654
Kinston *(G-7419)*

5943 Stationery stores

▲ American Forms Mfg Inc.................... E 704 866-9139
Gastonia *(G-4991)*

◆ Carson-Dellosa Publishing LLC........ D 336 632-0084
Greensboro *(G-5433)*

Carter Publishing Company Inc.............. F 336 993-2161
Kernersville *(G-7253)*

Devora Designs Inc................................. G 336 782-0964
Winston Salem *(G-13142)*

Good Grief Marketing LLC...................... G 336 989-1984
Greensboro *(G-5569)*

Jofra Graphics Inc................................... G 910 259-1717
Burgaw *(G-1025)*

King Business Service Inc....................... G 910 610-1030
Laurinburg *(G-7504)*

L C Industries Inc.................................... C 919 596-8277
Fayetteville *(G-4629)*

◆ L C Industries Inc.............................. G 919 596-8277
Durham *(G-4100)*

Leapfrog Document Services Inc............ F 704 372-1078
Charlotte *(G-2412)*

Lynchs Office Supply Co Inc................... F 252 537-6041
Roanoke Rapids *(G-10740)*

M C C of Laurinburg Inc......................... G 910 276-0519
Laurinburg *(G-7506)*

Office Sup Svcs Inc Charlotte................. E 704 786-4677
Concord *(G-3410)*

Owen G Dunn Co Inc............................. G 252 633-3197
New Bern *(G-9387)*

Print Management Group LLC................ F 704 821-0114
Charlotte *(G-2669)*

Printing Press.. G 828 299-1234
Asheville *(G-585)*

Southern Printing Company Inc.............. G 910 259-4807
Burgaw *(G-1033)*

Times Printing Company......................... E 252 473-2105
Manteo *(G-8024)*

Times Printing Company Inc................... G 252 441-2223
Kill Devil Hills *(G-7320)*

W B Mason Co Inc.................................. E 888 926-2766
Charlotte *(G-2994)*

Westmoreland Printers Inc...................... F 704 482-9100
Shelby *(G-11391)*

Wright Printing Service Inc..................... G 336 427-4768
Madison *(G-8004)*

5944 Jewelry stores

Barnes Dmnd Gllery Jwly Mfrs I............ G 910 347-4300
Jacksonville *(G-7116)*

▲ Buchanan Gem Stone Mines Inc...... F 828 765-6130
Spruce Pine *(G-11567)*

Byrd Designs Inc..................................... G 828 628-0151
Fairview *(G-4506)*

D C Crsman Mfr Fine Jwly Inc............... G 828 252-9891
Asheville *(G-482)*

Donald Haack Diamonds Inc.................. G 704 365-4400
Charlotte *(G-2062)*

Dons Fine Jewelry Inc............................ G 336 724-7826
Clemmons *(G-3181)*

Duncan Design Ltd.................................. G 919 834-7713
Raleigh *(G-10064)*

Haydon & Company................................. G 919 781-1293
Raleigh *(G-10157)*

▲ Jewel Masters Inc.............................. F 336 243-2711
Lexington *(G-7701)*

Jewelry By Gail Inc................................. G 252 441-5387
Nags Head *(G-9299)*

Jkl Inc... F 252 355-6714
Greenville *(G-5996)*

John Laughter Jewelry Inc...................... G 828 456-4772
Waynesville *(G-12462)*

Made By Custom LLC.............................. G 704 980-9840
Charlotte *(G-2447)*

Michael S North Wilkesboro Inc............ G 336 838-5964
North Wilkesboro *(G-9547)*

NCSMJ Inc... F 704 544-1118
Pineville *(G-9744)*

R Gregory Jewelers Inc........................... F 704 872-6669
Statesville *(G-11758)*

Speed Brite Inc....................................... G 704 639-9771
Salisbury *(G-11118)*

▲ Starcraft Diamonds Inc...................... G 252 717-2548
Washington *(G-12415)*

William Travis Jewelry Ltd...................... G 919 968-0011
Chapel Hill *(G-1593)*

5945 Hobby, toy, and game shops

Bear Pages.. G 828 837-0785
Murphy *(G-9288)*

Bluff Mountain Outfitters Inc................. G 828 622-7162
Hot Springs *(G-6932)*

Burlington Outlet..................................... G 910 278-3442
Oak Island *(G-9564)*

Grateful Union Family Inc....................... F 828 622-3258
Asheville *(G-510)*

5946 Camera and photographic supply stores

Ball Photo Supply Inc............................. G 828 252-2443
Asheville *(G-451)*

5947 Gift, novelty, and souvenir shop

A Stitch In Time...................................... G 828 274-5193
Asheville *(G-422)*

Bakers Southern Traditions Inc.............. G 252 344-2120
Roxobel *(G-10949)*

Burlington Outlet..................................... G 910 278-3442
Oak Island *(G-9564)*

Carolina Perfumer Inc............................. G 910 295-5600
Pinehurst *(G-9688)*

Ceder Creek Gallery & Pottery............... G 919 528-1041
Creedmoor *(G-3645)*

▲ Colonial Tin Works Inc...................... E 336 668-4126
Greensboro *(G-5453)*

James Lammers....................................... G 252 491-2303
Powells Point *(G-9822)*

Jkl Inc... F 252 355-6714
Greenville *(G-5996)*

Joie of Seating Inc.................................. G 704 795-7474
Concord (G-3387)

Katchi Tees Incorporated...................... G 252 315-4691
Wilson (G-12997)

Michael S North Wilkesboro Inc............ G 336 838-5964
North Wilkesboro (G-9547)

Oleksynprannyk LLC............................. F 704 450-0182
Mooresville (G-8738)

Party Time Inc...................................... G 910 454-4577
Southport (G-11524)

Simple & Sentimental LLC.................... G 252 320-9458
Ayden (G-662)

▼ Starflite Companies Inc..................... C 252 728-2690
Beaufort (G-735)

◆ USa Wholesale and Distrg Inc............ F 888 484-6872
Fayetteville (G-4693)

Wit & Whistle....................................... G 919 609-5309
Cary (G-1485)

5949 Sewing, needlework, and piece goods

Artist S Needle Inc............................... G 336 294-5884
Greensboro (G-5371)

Cloth Barn Inc...................................... F 919 735-3643
Goldsboro (G-5206)

▲ Composite Fabrics America LLC......... G 828 632-5220
Taylorsville (G-11954)

Contempora Fabrics Inc........................ C 910 345-0150
Lumberton (G-7948)

Designer Fabrics Inc............................. G 704 305-4144
Concord (G-3354)

Distinctive Furniture Inc....................... G 828 754-3947
Lenoir (G-7600)

Embroidme.. G 919 316-1538
Durham (G-4020)

▲ Hampton Art Inc............................... C 252 975-7207
Washington (G-12391)

Innovaknits LLC.................................... G 828 536-9348
Conover (G-3533)

Ledford Upholstery................................ G 704 732-0233
Lincolnton (G-7836)

▲ Mayo Knitting Mill Inc...................... C 252 823-3101
Tarboro (G-11934)

McMurray Fabrics Inc........................... D 704 732-9613
Lincolnton (G-7843)

◆ Meridian Spcalty Yrn Group Inc.........D 828 874-2151
Valdese (G-12197)

▲ Uwharrie Knits Inc........................... F 704 474-4123
Norwood (G-9563)

5961 Catalog and mail-order houses

Apex Waves LLC................................... G..... 919 809-5227
Cary (G-1292)

Buddy Cut Inc....................................... G.... 888 608-4701
Pittsboro (G-9777)

Cbdmd Inc.. F 704 445-3060
Charlotte (G-1869)

▲ Celtic Ocean International Inc............ E 828 299-9005
Arden (G-261)

Cherokee Publications........................... G 828 627-2424
Cherokee (G-3051)

Dallas L Pridgen Inc............................. G 919 732-4422
Carrboro (G-1268)

▼ Fireresq Incorporated....................... F 888 975-0858
Mooresville (G-8664)

Glen Raven Mtl Solutions LLC............... C 828 682-2142
Burnsville (G-1185)

Grailgame Inc.. G.... 804 517-3102
Reidsville (G-10687)

Grateful Union Family Inc...................... F 828 622-3258
Asheville (G-510)

Hometown Sports Inc............................ G 919 732-7090
Hillsborough (G-6867)

◆ Kayser-Roth Corporation...................C 336 852-2030
Greensboro (G-5643)

Nutrotonic LLC...................................... F 855 948-0008
Charlotte (G-2590)

Old Salem Incorporated......................... G 336 721-7305
Winston Salem (G-13269)

Owen G Dunn Co Inc............................. G 252 633-3197
New Bern (G-9387)

Simple & Sentimental LLC.................... G 252 320-9458
Ayden (G-662)

Speed Utv LLC...................................... E 704 949-1255
Concord (G-3445)

◆ Stump Printing Co Inc......................C 260 723-5171
Wrightsville Beach (G-13433)

▲ Trophy House Inc............................. F 910 323-1791
Fayetteville (G-4683)

5962 Merchandising machine operators

Coca-Cola Consolidated Inc...................C 919 550-0611
Clayton (G-3141)

Compass Group Usa Inc........................ A 704 398-6515
Charlotte (G-1965)

Compass Group Usa Inc........................B 919 381-9577
Garner (G-4924)

Compass Group Usa Inc........................ E 252 291-7733
Wilson (G-12981)

Durham Coca-Cola Bottling Company... C 919 383-1531
Durham (G-4014)

5963 Direct selling establishments

Bakers Southern Traditions Inc.............. G 252 344-2120
Roxobel (G-10949)

Lotus Bakeries Us LLC.......................... G 415 956-8956
Mebane (G-8250)

Old Saratoga Inc................................... E 252 238-2175
Saratoga (G-11261)

Over Rainbow Inc.................................. G 704 332-5521
Charlotte (G-2604)

Picassomoesllc..................................... G 216 703-4547
Hillsborough (G-6875)

Random Rues Botanical LLC.................. G 252 214-2759
Greenville (G-6017)

5983 Fuel oil dealers

Euliss Oil Company Inc......................... G 336 622-3055
Liberty (G-7766)

Go Energies LLC................................... F 877 712-5999
Wilmington (G-12790)

Go Energies Holdings Inc...................... G 910 762-5802
Wilmington (G-12791)

Herrin Bros Coal & Ice Co..................... G 704 332-2193
Charlotte (G-2275)

Hickman Oil & Ice Co Inc...................... G 910 576-2501
Troy (G-12161)

M & R Retreading & Oil Co Inc.............. G 704 474-4101
Norwood (G-9556)

▲ Parker Gas Company Inc................... F 800 354-7250
Clinton (G-3238)

▼ Starflite Companies Inc..................... C 252 728-2690
Beaufort (G-735)

5984 Liquefied petroleum gas dealers

Blossman Propane Gas & Appl.............. F 828 396-0144
Hickory (G-6272)

Euliss Oil Company Inc......................... G 336 622-3055
Liberty (G-7766)

▲ Parker Gas Company Inc................... F 800 354-7250
Clinton (G-3238)

5989 Fuel dealers, nec

Herrin Bros Coal & Ice Co..................... G 704 332-2193
Charlotte (G-2275)

5992 Florists

Harris Teeter LLC................................. D 704 846-7117
Matthews (G-8115)

5993 Tobacco stores and stands

▲ Fontem US LLC................................ G 888 207-4588
Greensboro (G-5536)

J Wise Inc.. E 828 202-5563
Lincolnton (G-7833)

Jim Fab of North Carolina Inc............... E 704 278-1000
Cleveland (G-3215)

5994 News dealers and newsstands

Raleigh Downtowner.............................. G 919 821-9000
Raleigh (G-10422)

5995 Optical goods stores

Clarity Vision of Smithfield.................... G 919 938-6101
Smithfield (G-11437)

Luxottica of America Inc........................ G 910 867-0200
Fayetteville (G-4631)

Luxottica of America Inc........................ G 919 778-5692
Goldsboro (G-5226)

O D Eyecarecenter P A.......................... G 252 443-7011
Rocky Mount (G-10856)

Optical Place Inc.................................. E 336 274-1300
Greensboro (G-5725)

Optics Inc.. G 336 288-9504
Greensboro (G-5726)

5999 Miscellaneous retail stores, nec

A House of Hemp LLC........................... G 910 984-1441
Linden (G-7872)

▲ Acme Stone Company Inc................. F 336 786-6978
Mount Airy (G-9095)

Admiral Marine Pdts & Svcs Inc............ G..... 704 489-8771
Denver (G-3767)

Airgas Usa LLC.................................... G 919 544-1056
Durham (G-3884)

All 4 U Home Medical LLC..................... G 828 437-0684
Morganton (G-8849)

All Glass Inc... G 828 324-8609
Hickory (G-6262)

Applied Drives Inc................................ G 704 573-2324
Charlotte (G-1686)

Bio-Tech Prsthtics Orthtics In................ G 336 768-3666
Winston Salem (G-13105)

Bio-Tech Prsthtics Orthtics In................ G 336 333-9081
Greensboro (G-5390)

Blaq Beauty Naturalz Inc...................... G 252 326-5621
Weldon (G-12519)

Blue Ridge Elc Mtr Repr Inc.................. G 828 258-0800
Asheville (G-455)

Blue Ridge Quick Print Inc.................... G 828 883-2420
Brevard (G-968)

Boardwalk Inc....................................... G 252 240-1095
Morehead City (G-8819)

◆ Body Shop Inc.................................C 919 554-4900
Wake Forest (G-12265)

Boonville Flour Feed Mill Inc................. G 336 367-7541
Boonville (G-957)

Bright Light Technologies LLC............... G 910 212-6869
Lillington (G-7790)

Brigman Electric Motors Inc................... G 828 492-0568
Canton (G-1246)

▲ Buchanan Gem Stone Mines Inc........ F 828 765-6130
Spruce Pine (G-11567)

Busch Enterprises Inc........................... G 704 878-2067
Statesville (G-11673)

C & S Repair Center Inc........................ G 610 524-9724
New Bern (G-9346)

CAM Enterprises Inc.............................. G 252 946-4877
Washington *(G-12375)*

Camp Chemical Corporation................. F 336 597-2214
Roxboro *(G-10921)*

Canipe & Lynn Elc Mtr Repr Inc............ G 828 322-9052
Hickory *(G-6282)*

Cape Fear Orthtics Prsthtics I............... G 910 483-0933
Fayetteville *(G-4566)*

Carolina Container LLC......................... E 336 883-7146
Thomasville *(G-12002)*

Carolina Sgns Grphic Dsgns Inc........... G 919 383-3344
Durham *(G-3962)*

Carpenter Co... D 828 464-9470
Conover *(G-3501)*

Classy Glass Inc................................... G 828 452-2242
Waynesville *(G-12454)*

Connected 2k LLC................................ G 910 321-7446
Fayetteville *(G-4578)*

Conway Development Inc....................... F 252 756-2168
Greenville *(G-5957)*

Craven Tire Inc..................................... G 252 633-0200
New Bern *(G-9357)*

Crown Trophy Inc.................................. G 336 851-1011
Greensboro *(G-5474)*

Custom Rehabilitation Spc Inc.............. G 910 471-2962
Wilmington *(G-12758)*

▲ Danbartex LLC.................................. G 704 323-8728
Mooresville *(G-8650)*

Dixie Electro Mech Svcs Inc................. F 704 332-1116
Charlotte *(G-2057)*

DLM Sales Inc...................................... F 704 399-2776
Charlotte *(G-2058)*

DNB Humidifier Mfg Inc......................... F 336 764-2076
Winston Salem *(G-13150)*

Duncan-Parnell Inc............................... G 252 977-7832
Rocky Mount *(G-10833)*

Electric Motor Service of Shelby Inc...... F 704 482-9979
Shelby *(G-11333)*

Evoqua Water Technologies LLC........... E 919 477-2161
Durham *(G-4031)*

Faith Farm Inc...................................... G 704 431-4566
Salisbury *(G-11052)*

Faith Prsthtc-Rthotic Svcs Inc.............. F 704 782-0908
Concord *(G-3361)*

Farm Services Inc................................. G 336 226-7381
Graham *(G-5268)*

Fines and Carriel Inc............................ G 919 929-0702
Chapel Hill *(G-1547)*

▼ Fireresq Incorporated....................... F 888 975-0858
Mooresville *(G-8664)*

▼ Flologic Inc....................................... G 919 878-1808
Morrisville *(G-8976)*

Four Corners Frmng Gallery Inc............ G 704 662-7154
Mooresville *(G-8667)*

Free Will Bptst Press Fndtion................ F 252 746-6128
Ayden *(G-657)*

G & G Management LLC........................ F 336 444-6271
Greensboro *(G-5544)*

Gillam & Mason Inc.............................. G 252 356-2874
Cofield *(G-3266)*

GNB Ventures LLC................................ F 704 488-4468
Charlotte *(G-2218)*

Granite Memorials Inc........................... G 336 786-6596
Mount Airy *(G-9124)*

▲ Guilford Fabricators Inc..................... G 336 434-3163
High Point *(G-6635)*

Harvest Homes and Handi Houses........ G 704 637-3878
Salisbury *(G-11061)*

Heart Electric Motor Service................. G 704 922-4720
Bessemer City *(G-821)*

Heritage Flag LLC................................. G 910 725-1540
Southern Pines *(G-11500)*

Heritage Prtg & Graphics Inc................ G 704 551-0700
Charlotte *(G-2274)*

Herrin Bros Coal & Ice Co..................... G 704 332-2193
Charlotte *(G-2275)*

High Country Electric Mtrs LLC............. G 336 838-4808
North Wilkesboro *(G-9534)*

Infinity S End Inc.................................. F 704 900-8355
Charlotte *(G-2328)*

Innovative Awngs & Screens LLC.......... F 833 337-4233
Cornelius *(G-3610)*

Integrated Info Systems Inc.................. F 919 488-5000
Youngsville *(G-13476)*

J & D Thorpe Enterprises Inc................ G 919 553-0918
Clayton *(G-3155)*

Johnny Slicks Inc.................................. G 910 803-2159
Holly Ridge *(G-6890)*

Js Linens and Curtain Outlet................. F 704 871-1582
Statesville *(G-11722)*

Kelleys Sports and Awards Inc.............. G 828 728-4600
Hudson *(G-6952)*

Kloud Hemp Co..................................... G 336 740-2528
Greensboro *(G-5651)*

Kroops Brands LLC............................... G 704 635-7963
Monroe *(G-8513)*

Kwik Elc Mtr Sls & Svc Inc................... G 252 335-2524
Elizabeth City *(G-4395)*

L & B Jandrew Enterprises.................... G 828 687-8927
Hendersonville *(G-6219)*

Luxuriously Natural Soaps LLC............. G 910 378-9064
Jacksonville *(G-7130)*

Lynchs Office Supply Co Inc................. F 252 537-6041
Roanoke Rapids *(G-10740)*

M & S Systems Inc............................... G 336 996-7118
Kernersville *(G-7283)*

Mables Headstone & Monu Co LLP....... G 919 724-8705
Creedmoor *(G-3652)*

McKinney Electric & Mch Co Inc........... G 828 765-7910
Spruce Pine *(G-11581)*

Medaccess Inc...................................... G 828 264-4085
Robbinsville *(G-10760)*

◆ Medi Mall Inc.................................... G 877 501-6334
Fletcher *(G-4753)*

Mid-Atlantic Drainage Inc..................... F 828 324-0808
Conover *(G-3539)*

Mike DS Bbq LLC.................................. G 866 960-8652
Durham *(G-4133)*

Mirrormate LLC..................................... F 704 390-7377
Charlotte *(G-2508)*

Monitor Roller Mill Inc.......................... G 336 591-4126
Walnut Cove *(G-12329)*

Moon Audio... G 919 649-5018
Cary *(G-1402)*

More Than Just Art Inc......................... G 910 864-7797
Fayetteville *(G-4643)*

Morningstar Signs and Banners............ G 704 861-0020
Gastonia *(G-5101)*

Motor Shop Inc..................................... G 704 867-8488
Gastonia *(G-5103)*

NC Graphic Pros LLC............................ G 252 492-7326
Kittrell *(G-7442)*

Neptune Hlth Wllness Innvtion............... C 888 664-9166
Conover *(G-3541)*

Picassomoesllc.................................... G 216 703-4547
Hillsborough *(G-6875)*

Piedmont Fiberglass Inc....................... E 828 632-8883
Statesville *(G-11745)*

Pilgrims Pride Corporation.................... B 704 624-2171
Marshville *(G-8092)*

Powell & Stokes Inc.............................. G 252 794-2138
Windsor *(G-13056)*

Pregis LLC.. E 828 396-2373
Granite Falls *(G-5319)*

▲ Prem Corp... E 704 921-1799
Charlotte *(G-2660)*

Rec Plus Inc... E 704 375-9098
Charlotte *(G-2696)*

Rm Liquidation Inc............................... D 828 274-7996
Asheville *(G-591)*

S & L Creations Inc.............................. G 704 824-1930
Lowell *(G-7934)*

Safeguard Medical Alarms Inc.............. F 312 506-2900
Huntersville *(G-7052)*

Sanders Electric Motor Svc Inc............. E 828 754-0513
Lenoir *(G-7638)*

Scaltrol Inc.. G 678 990-0858
Charlotte *(G-2761)*

Screen Master....................................... G 252 492-8407
Henderson *(G-6178)*

Second Earth Inc.................................. G 336 740-9333
Greensboro *(G-5804)*

Sharpe Images Properties Inc............... E 336 724-2871
Winston Salem *(G-13334)*

Solarbrook Water and Pwr Corp............ G 919 231-3205
Raleigh *(G-10492)*

South Mountain Crafts.......................... G 828 433-2607
Morganton *(G-8899)*

Southern Electric Motor Co.................. G 919 688-7879
Durham *(G-4243)*

Southern States Coop Inc..................... G 336 629-3977
Asheboro *(G-397)*

Southern States Coop Inc..................... E 919 528-1516
Creedmoor *(G-3655)*

Southern States Coop Inc..................... E 919 693-6136
Oxford *(G-9636)*

Southern States Coop Inc..................... G 252 823-2520
Princeville *(G-9828)*

Speer Operational Tech LLC................. G 864 631-2512
Marion *(G-8066)*

Steelman Milling Company Inc.............. G 336 463-5586
Yadkinville *(G-13452)*

Tekni-Plex Inc...................................... D 919 553-4151
Clayton *(G-3174)*

Telecmmnctons Resource MGT Inc....... F 919 779-0776
Raleigh *(G-10539)*

Tractor Country Inc.............................. G 252 523-3007
Dover *(G-3829)*

▲ Trophy House Inc.............................. F 910 323-1791
Fayetteville *(G-4683)*

United Mobile Imaging Inc.................... G 800 983-9840
Clemmons *(G-3207)*

▼ Usrx LLC... E 980 221-1200
Charlotte *(G-2969)*

Utd Technology Corp............................ G 704 612-0121
Mint Hill *(G-8344)*

Veon Inc... F 252 623-2102
Washington *(G-12418)*

W E Nixons Wldg & Hdwr Inc................ G 252 221-4348
Edenton *(G-4373)*

Wake Monument Company Inc.............. G 919 556-3422
Rolesville *(G-10891)*

Walgreen Co... G 704 525-2628
Charlotte *(G-3001)*

We Appit LLC.. G 910 465-2722
Wilmington *(G-12946)*

Wersunsllc.. G 857 209-8701
Winston Salem *(G-13388)*

Wholesale Kennel Supply Co................. G 919 742-2515
Siler City *(G-11427)*

Wildflwers Btq of Blowing Rock............. G 828 295-9655
Blowing Rock *(G-882)*

Winecoff Mmrals Sttesville Inc.............. G 704 873-9661
Statesville *(G-11801)*

World Art Gallery Incorporated.............. G 910 989-0203
Jacksonville *(G-7160)*

S
I
C

Z Collection LLC.............................. G 919 247-1513
 Zebulon *(G-13526)*

Zingerle Group Usa Inc .... E 704 312-1600
 Charlotte *(G-3048)*

61 NONDEPOSITORY CREDIT INSTITUTIONS

6141 Personal credit institutions

◆ Mack Trucks Inc................................A 336 291-9001
 Greensboro *(G-5670)*

6153 Short-term business credit

◆ Mack Trucks Inc................................A 336 291-9001
 Greensboro *(G-5670)*

McRae Industries Inc .... C 910 439-6149
 Mount Gilead *(G-9203)*

6159 Miscellaneous business credit

◆ Vna Holding Inc................................A 336 393-4890
 Greensboro *(G-5905)*

6162 Mortgage bankers and correspondents

▲ GLG Corporation............................ F 336 784-0396
 Winston Salem *(G-13178)*

Ramsey Industries Inc...................... F 704 827-3560
 Belmont *(G-763)*

62 SECURITY & COMMODITY BROKERS, DEALERS, EXCHANGES & SERVICES

6221 Commodity contracts brokers, dealers

Smissons Inc.................................... G 660 537-3219
 Clayton *(G-3169)*

6282 Investment advice

Sheets Smith Wealth MGT Inc.............. E 336 765-2020
 Winston Salem *(G-13335)*

63 INSURANCE CARRIERS

6331 Fire, marine, and casualty insurance

Discovery Insurance Company.............. E 800 876-1492
 Kinston *(G-7405)*

64 INSURANCE AGENTS, BROKERS AND SERVICE

6411 Insurance agents, brokers, and service

Atlantic Group Usa Inc .... F 919 623-7824
 Raleigh *(G-9920)*

Donald Haack Diamonds Inc............... G 704 365-4400
 Charlotte *(G-2062)*

Hinson Industries Inc .... G 252 937-7171
 Rocky Mount *(G-10840)*

Katchi Tees Incorporated.................... G 252 315-4691
 Wilson *(G-12997)*

Motor Vhcles Lcense Plate Agcy .... G 252 338-6965
 Elizabeth City *(G-4398)*

65 REAL ESTATE

6512 Nonresidential building operators

B V Hedrick Gravel & Sand Co.............. E 704 633-5982
 Salisbury *(G-11021)*

Industrial Container Inc...................... G 336 882-1310
 High Point *(G-6671)*

J L Powell & Co Inc............................ G 910 642-8989
 Whiteville *(G-12585)*

Jenkins Properties Inc....................... E 336 667-4282
 North Wilkesboro *(G-9537)*

Moorecraft Wood Proucts Inc............... G 252 823-2510
 Tarboro *(G-11936)*

6513 Apartment building operators

J L Powell & Co Inc............................ G 910 642-8989
 Whiteville *(G-12585)*

Lyon Company.................................. F 919 787-0024
 Wadesboro *(G-12248)*

6531 Real estate agents and managers

Anew Look Homes LLC........................ F 800 796-5152
 Hickory *(G-6264)*

Braswell Realty .... G 828 733-5800
 Newland *(G-9426)*

Brookhurst Associates....................... G 919 792-0987
 Raleigh *(G-9961)*

Brunswick Beacon Inc........................ G 910 754-6890
 Shallotte *(G-11300)*

Fathom Holdings Inc.......................... E 888 455-6040
 Cary *(G-1362)*

Green Waste Management LLC.............. G 704 289-0720
 Charlotte *(G-2239)*

Jdh Capital LLC................................ F 704 357-1220
 Charlotte *(G-2365)*

Joe Robin Darnell.............................. G 704 482-1186
 Shelby *(G-11350)*

▼ Lindley Laboratories Inc .... F 336 449-7521
 Gibsonville *(G-5181)*

Lyon Company.................................. F 919 787-0024
 Wadesboro *(G-12248)*

▲ Solarh2ot Ltd................................ G 919 439-2387
 Raleigh *(G-10493)*

Town of Maggie Valley Inc.................... F 828 926-0145
 Maggie Valley *(G-8006)*

Wersunsllc....................................... G 857 209-8701
 Winston Salem *(G-13388)*

6552 Subdividers and developers, nec

Capitol Funds Inc.............................. F 910 439-5275
 Mount Gilead *(G-9198)*

Capitol Funds Inc.............................. E 704 487-8547
 Shelby *(G-11316)*

67 HOLDING AND OTHER INVESTMENT OFFICES

6719 Holding companies, nec

Alcami Holdings LLC........................... A 910 254-7000
 Wilmington *(G-12701)*

Atticus LLC...................................... E 984 465-4754
 Cary *(G-1299)*

▼ Hlm Legacy Group Inc..................... C 704 878-8823
 Troutman *(G-12140)*

Interroll USA Holding LLC.................... D 910 799-1100
 Wilmington *(G-12820)*

Ipi Acquisition LLC............................ A 704 588-1100
 Charlotte *(G-2356)*

K&K Holdings Inc.............................. G 704 341-5567
 Charlotte *(G-2385)*

Pharr McAdenville Corporation............. D 704 824-3551
 Mc Adenville *(G-8215)*

6733 Trusts, nec

Pinkston Properties LLC...................... G 828 252-9867
 Asheville *(G-575)*

6794 Patent owners and lessors

22nd Century Group Inc...................... F 716 270-1523
 Mocksville *(G-8345)*

◆ Body Shop Inc...............................C 919 554-4900
 Wake Forest *(G-12265)*

◆ Ohio Mat Lcnsing Cmpnnts Group.....G 336 861-3500
 Trinity *(G-12118)*

6798 Real estate investment trusts

Anew Look Homes LLC........................ F 800 796-5152
 Hickory *(G-6264)*

6799 Investors, nec

Atlantic Caribbean LLC....................... G 910 343-0624
 Wilmington *(G-12711)*

Igm Specialties Holding Inc................. F 704 945-8702
 Charlotte *(G-2312)*

Lm Shea LLC.................................... G 919 608-1901
 Raleigh *(G-10259)*

Rhf Investments Inc........................... G 828 326-8350
 Hickory *(G-6428)*

Solarbrook Water and Pwr Corp............ G 919 231-3205
 Raleigh *(G-10492)*

70 HOTELS, ROOMING HOUSES, CAMPS, AND OTHER LODGING PLACES

7011 Hotels and motels

Catawba Farms Enterprises LLC............ F 828 464-5780
 Newton *(G-9452)*

Celebrity Dairy LLC........................... G 919 742-4931
 Siler City *(G-11404)*

Tom Burgiss.....................................G 336 359-2995
 Laurel Springs *(G-7491)*

7033 Trailer parks and campsites

B & D Enterprises Inc......................... G 704 739-2958
 Kings Mountain *(G-7348)*

72 PERSONAL SERVICES

7212 Garment pressing and cleaners' agents

A Cleaner Tomorrow Dry Clg LLC........... G 919 639-6396
 Dunn *(G-3840)*

7213 Linen supply

Magnolia Linen Inc............................ F 336 449-0447
 Gibsonville *(G-5182)*

7215 Coin-operated laundries and cleaning

A Cleaner Tomorrow Dry Clg LLC........... G 919 639-6396
 Dunn *(G-3840)*

Rachel Dubois.................................. G 919 870-8063
 Raleigh *(G-10419)*

7216 Drycleaning plants, except rugs

A Cleaner Tomorrow Dry Clg LLC........... G 919 639-6396
 Dunn *(G-3840)*

Bridgport Restoration Svcs Inc............. G 336 996-1212
 Kernersville *(G-7248)*

Stitch In Time Inc.............................. G 910 497-4171
 Spring Lake *(G-11564)*

7217 Carpet and upholstery cleaning

Bridgport Restoration Svcs Inc............. G 336 996-1212
 Kernersville *(G-7248)*

7218 Industrial launderers

Ican Clothes Company........................ F 910 670-1494
 Fayetteville *(G-4614)*

7219 Laundry and garment services, nec

A Stitch In Time..................................... G 828 274-5193
Asheville *(G-422)*

Howell & Sons Canvas Repairs............. G 704 892-7913
Cornelius *(G-3607)*

Jones Fabricare Inc................................ G 336 272-7261
Greensboro *(G-5639)*

Professnal Alterations EMB Inc............. G 910 577-8484
Jacksonville *(G-7139)*

7221 Photographic studios, portrait

David Presnell.. G 336 372-5989
Sparta *(G-11537)*

Strawbridge Studios Inc......................... D 919 286-9512
Durham *(G-4252)*

7231 Beauty shops

Brandy Thompson.................................. F 321 252-2911
Fayetteville *(G-4561)*

Gifted Hands Styling Salon.................... G 828 781-2781
Hickory *(G-6338)*

Haircutters of Raleigh Inc..................... G 919 781-3465
Raleigh *(G-10153)*

Katchi Tees Incorporated....................... G 252 315-4691
Wilson *(G-12997)*

7241 Barber shops

Executive Grooming LLC........................ G 919 706-5382
Raleigh *(G-10098)*

Kraken-Skulls.. F 910 500-9100
Fayetteville *(G-4627)*

7261 Funeral service and crematories

▼ **Custom Air Trays Inc**........................ F 336 889-8729
High Point *(G-6583)*

Gooder Grafix Inc.................................. G 828 349-4097
Franklin *(G-4830)*

Wiggins North State Co Inc.................... G 919 556-3231
Rolesville *(G-10892)*

Wilmington Mortuary Svc Inc................. F 910 791-9099
Wilmington *(G-12951)*

7291 Tax return preparation services

Katchi Tees Incorporated....................... G 252 315-4691
Wilson *(G-12997)*

7299 Miscellaneous personal services

A Stitch In Time..................................... G 828 274-5193
Asheville *(G-422)*

Agingo Corporation............................... G 888 298-0777
Charlotte *(G-1629)*

Brandy Thompson.................................. F 321 252-2911
Fayetteville *(G-4561)*

Capre Omnimedia LLC.......................... G 917 460-3572
Wilmington *(G-12731)*

Communitys Kitchen L3c....................... G 828 817-2308
Tryon *(G-12173)*

Creative Stone Fyetteville Inc............... F 910 491-1225
Fayetteville *(G-4580)*

Darius All Access LLC........................... E 910 262-8567
Wilmington *(G-12759)*

Digits... G 336 721-0209
Winston Salem *(G-13145)*

Fixed-NC LLC.. G 252 751-1911
Greenville *(G-5976)*

Kraken-Skulls.. F 910 500-9100
Fayetteville *(G-4627)*

Owens Quilting Inc................................ G 828 695-1495
Newton *(G-9485)*

Salon Couture.. G 910 693-1611
Southern Pines *(G-11508)*

Sugar Pops.. G 704 799-0959
Mooresville *(G-8782)*

Telephys Inc... G 312 625-9128
Davidson *(G-3719)*

Triangle Trggr-Pint Thrapy Inc............... G 919 845-1818
Raleigh *(G-10562)*

73 BUSINESS SERVICES

7311 Advertising agencies

822tees Inc.. G 910 822-8337
Fayetteville *(G-4541)*

Advertising Design Systems Inc............ G 828 264-8060
Boone *(G-894)*

B&P Enterprise NC Inc.......................... G 727 669-6877
Hickory *(G-6269)*

Clarks Printing Service Inc................... E 828 254-1432
Asheville *(G-477)*

Dale Advertising Inc.............................. G 704 484-0971
Shelby *(G-11329)*

Ed Kemp Associates Inc........................ G 336 869-2155
High Point *(G-6604)*

Executive Promotions Inc...................... F 704 663-4000
Mooresville *(G-8661)*

Fit1media LLC.. G 919 925-2200
Raleigh *(G-10110)*

◆ **Golf Associates Advertising Co**.......... E 828 252-6544
Asheville *(G-508)*

Idea People Inc...................................... G 704 398-4437
Huntersville *(G-7000)*

Ifpo - Ifmo/American Image Inc............. G 336 945-9867
Hamptonville *(G-6085)*

Inform Inc.. F 828 322-7766
Hickory *(G-6368)*

Inspire Creative Studios Inc.................. G 910 395-0200
Wilmington *(G-12818)*

JB II Printing LLC.................................. G 336 222-0717
Burlington *(G-1111)*

▲ **Lomar Specialty Advg Inc**.................. F 704 788-4380
Concord *(G-3396)*

Planet Logo Inc...................................... G 910 763-2554
Wilmington *(G-12879)*

Shannon Media Inc................................ F 919 933-1551
Chapel Hill *(G-1570)*

Yp Advrtising Pubg LLC Not LLC........... C 704 522-5500
Charlotte *(G-3042)*

7312 Outdoor advertising services

Action Sign Company Lenoir Inc........... G 828 754-4116
Lenoir *(G-7566)*

Fairway Outdoor Advg LLC.................... G 919 755-1900
Raleigh *(G-10101)*

Fairway Outdoor Advg LLC.................... G 910 343-1900
Wilmington *(G-12775)*

Signlite Services Inc............................. G 336 751-9543
Mocksville *(G-8389)*

Sweatnet LLC... G 847 331-7287
Charlotte *(G-2886)*

Wilson Billboard Advg Inc..................... G 919 934-2421
Smithfield *(G-11470)*

7313 Radio, television, publisher representatives

Gatehouse Media LLC............................ E 336 626-6103
Asheboro *(G-360)*

Latino Communications Inc.................... F 919 645-1680
Raleigh *(G-10249)*

Yp Advrtising Pubg LLC Not LLC........... C 704 522-5500
Charlotte *(G-3042)*

7319 Advertising, nec

Apple Rock Advg & Prom Inc................. E 336 232-4800
Greensboro *(G-5366)*

Capre Omnimedia LLC.......................... G 917 460-3572
Wilmington *(G-12731)*

Dzone Inc... F 919 678-0300
Research Triangle Pa *(G-10708)*

Good Grief Marketing LLC..................... G 336 989-1984
Greensboro *(G-5569)*

La Noticia Inc.. F 704 568-6966
Charlotte *(G-2406)*

NC Diesel Performance LLC.................. G 704 431-3257
Salisbury *(G-11095)*

RLM/Universal Packaging Inc................ F 336 644-6161
Greensboro *(G-5789)*

7331 Direct mail advertising services

Alpha Mailing Service Inc...................... F 704 484-1711
Shelby *(G-11310)*

Heritage Prtg & Graphics Inc................. G 704 551-0700
Charlotte *(G-2274)*

King Business Service Inc...................... G 910 610-1030
Laurinburg *(G-7504)*

▲ **Laser Ink Corporation**....................... E 919 361-5822
Durham *(G-4101)*

Mb-F Inc.. D 336 379-9352
Greensboro *(G-5685)*

Meredith - Webb Prtg Co Inc................. D 336 228-8378
Burlington *(G-1128)*

Metro Productions Inc........................... F 919 851-6420
Raleigh *(G-10296)*

Mjt Us Inc.. G 704 826-7828
Charlotte *(G-2510)*

Professional Laminating LLC................. G 919 465-0400
Cary *(G-1430)*

Randall-Reilly LLC................................. C 704 814-1390
Charlotte *(G-2688)*

Salem One Inc.. F 336 722-2886
Kernersville *(G-7299)*

▲ **William George Printing LLC**............. E 910 221-2700
Hope Mills *(G-6928)*

Yp Advrtising Pubg LLC Not LLC........... C 704 522-5500
Charlotte *(G-3042)*

7334 Photocopying and duplicating services

Accelerated Press Inc........................... G 248 524-1850
Wilmington *(G-12689)*

AEC Imaging & Graphics LLC................ G 910 693-1034
Hope Mills *(G-6922)*

Asheville Quickprint.............................. G 828 252-7667
Fletcher *(G-4720)*

Better Business Printing Inc.................. G 704 867-3366
Gastonia *(G-4998)*

Branch Office Solutions Inc................... G 800 743-1047
Indian Trail *(G-7072)*

Carolina Copy Services Inc.................... F 704 375-9099
Cornelius *(G-3592)*

Copy King Inc.. G 336 333-9900
Greensboro *(G-5468)*

Copycat Print Shop Inc.......................... F 910 799-1500
Wilmington *(G-12751)*

Document Imaging Systems Inc............. G 919 460-9440
Raleigh *(G-10054)*

Gik Inc... F 919 872-9498
Raleigh *(G-10133)*

Kathie S Mc Daniel............................... G 336 835-1544
Elkin *(G-4446)*

Legalis Dms LLC................................... F 919 741-8260
Raleigh *(G-10252)*

Make An Impression Inc......................... G 919 557-7400
Holly Springs *(G-6907)*

Moore Printing & Graphics Inc.............. F 919 821-3293
Raleigh *(G-10314)*

Occasions Group Inc............................G..... 919 751-2400
Goldsboro *(G-5233)*

Occasions Group Inc............................E..... 252 321-5805
Greenville *(G-6009)*

Print Express Inc............................F..... 910 455-4554
Jacksonville *(G-7138)*

Print Haus Inc............................G..... 828 456-8622
Waynesville *(G-12469)*

Printing Svcs Greensboro Inc............G..... 336 274-7663
Greensboro *(G-5765)*

Richa Inc............................G..... 704 944-0230
Charlotte *(G-2724)*

Richa Inc............................F..... 704 331-9744
Charlotte *(G-2725)*

Rite Instant Printing Inc............................G..... 336 768-5061
Winston Salem *(G-13319)*

Sharpe Images Properties Inc............E..... 336 724-2871
Winston Salem *(G-13334)*

Sillaman & Sons Inc............................G..... 919 774-6324
Sanford *(G-11233)*

Triangle Solutions Inc............................G..... 919 481-1235
Cary *(G-1473)*

Unlimted Potential Sanford Inc............E..... 919 852-1117
Morrisville *(G-9083)*

Village Instant Printing Inc............G..... 919 968-0000
Chapel Hill *(G-1591)*

Weber and Weber Inc............................F..... 336 722-4109
Winston Salem *(G-13387)*

Zebra Communications Inc............E..... 919 314-3700
Morrisville *(G-9093)*

7335 Commercial photography

Above Topsail LLC............................G..... 910 803-1759
Holly Ridge *(G-6886)*

Advertising Design Systems Inc............G..... 828 264-8060
Boone *(G-894)*

David Presnell............................G..... 336 372-5989
Sparta *(G-11537)*

Kreber............................D..... 336 861-2700
High Point *(G-6686)*

Timothy L Griffin............................G..... 336 317-8314
Greenville *(G-6028)*

7336 Commercial art and graphic design

A Plus Graphics Inc............................G..... 252 243-0404
Wilson *(G-12960)*

Advertising Design Systems Inc............G..... 828 264-8060
Boone *(G-894)*

Barron Legacy Mgmt Group LLC............G..... 301 367-4735
Charlotte *(G-1757)*

Big Fish Dpi............................G..... 704 545-8112
Mint Hill *(G-8331)*

Body Billboards Inc............................G..... 919 544-4540
Durham *(G-3936)*

Boundless Inc............................G..... 919 622-9051
Four Oaks *(G-4809)*

Brandilly of Nc Inc............................G..... 919 278-7896
Raleigh *(G-9957)*

◆ Causekeepers Inc............................E..... 336 824-2518
Franklinville *(G-4855)*

CD Dickie & Associates Inc............F..... 704 527-9102
Charlotte *(G-1878)*

Coastal Press Inc............................G..... 252 726-1549
Morehead City *(G-8827)*

Cold Water No Bleach LLC............G..... 336 505-9584
Durham *(G-3981)*

Connected 2k LLC............................G..... 910 321-7446
Fayetteville *(G-4578)*

Contract Printing & Graphics............G..... 919 832-7178
Raleigh *(G-10014)*

Designs By Rachel............................G..... 828 783-0698
Spruce Pine *(G-11574)*

◆ DWM INTERNATIONAL INC............E..... 646 290-7448
Charlotte *(G-2071)*

Family Industries Inc............................G..... 919 875-4499
Raleigh *(G-10104)*

Fast Pro Media LLC............................G..... 704 799-8040
Cornelius *(G-3599)*

Fast Pro Media LLC............................G..... 704 799-8040
Cornelius *(G-3600)*

Fiber Company............................G..... 336 725-5277
Lewisville *(G-7650)*

Fiestic Inc............................F..... 888 935-3999
Raleigh *(G-10107)*

Gmg Group LLC............................G..... 252 441-8374
Kill Devil Hills *(G-7317)*

Graphic Components LLC............E..... 336 542-2128
Greensboro *(G-5572)*

Graphic Image of Cape Fear Inc............G..... 910 313-6768
Wilmington *(G-12795)*

Heritage Prtg & Graphics Inc............G..... 704 551-0700
Charlotte *(G-2274)*

High Performance Marketing Inc............G..... 919 870-9915
Raleigh *(G-10167)*

▲ Idx Impressions LLC............................C..... 703 550-6902
Washington *(G-12393)*

JKS Motorsports Inc............................G..... 336 722-4129
Winston Salem *(G-13217)*

Kathie S Mc Daniel............................G..... 336 835-1544
Elkin *(G-4446)*

Kreber............................D..... 336 861-2700
High Point *(G-6686)*

LDR Designs............................G..... 252 375-4484
Greenville *(G-6001)*

Logo Wear Graphics LLC............F..... 336 382-0455
Summerfield *(G-11841)*

Mark/Trece Inc............................E..... 336 292-3424
Whitsett *(G-12614)*

Max B Smith Jr............................G..... 828 434-0238
Boone *(G-933)*

Merge LLC............................G..... 919 832-3924
Raleigh *(G-10291)*

Metro Productions Inc............................F..... 919 851-6420
Raleigh *(G-10296)*

Moving Screens Incorporated............G..... 336 364-9259
Rougemont *(G-10914)*

Multi Packaging Solutions............................A..... 336 855-7142
Greensboro *(G-5699)*

NC Graphic Pros LLC............................G..... 252 492-7326
Kittrell *(G-7442)*

Piranha Industries Inc............................G..... 704 248-7843
Charlotte *(G-2639)*

Precision Concepts Intl LLC............G..... 704 360-8923
Huntersville *(G-7037)*

Prism Publishing Inc............................F..... 919 319-6816
Cary *(G-1428)*

Rapp Productions Inc............................F..... 919 913-0270
Carrboro *(G-1271)*

Signs Etc............................G..... 336 722-9341
Winston Salem *(G-13337)*

Skipper Graphics............................G..... 910 754-8729
Shallotte *(G-11305)*

▲ St Johns Packaging Usa LLC............C..... 336 292-9911
Greensboro *(G-5833)*

Studio Displays Inc............................F..... 704 588-6590
Pineville *(G-9761)*

▲ Tannis Root Productions Inc............G..... 919 832-8552
Raleigh *(G-10533)*

Timothy L Griffin............................G..... 336 317-8314
Greenville *(G-6028)*

Triangle Solutions Inc............................G..... 919 481-1235
Cary *(G-1473)*

Village Graphics............................G..... 252 745-4600
Oriental *(G-9603)*

Zebra Communications Inc............E..... 919 314-3700
Morrisville *(G-9093)*

7338 Secretarial and court reporting

Dtp Inc............................G..... 336 272-5122
Greensboro *(G-5507)*

Jones Media............................G..... 828 264-3612
Boone *(G-928)*

Raleigh Printing & Typing Inc............G..... 919 662-8001
Raleigh *(G-10427)*

7342 Disinfecting and pest control services

Bridgport Restoration Svcs Inc............G..... 336 996-1212
Kernersville *(G-7248)*

7349 Building maintenance services, nec

A & B Chem-Dry............................F..... 919 878-0288
Raleigh *(G-9859)*

Abercrombie Textiles Inc............................G..... 704 487-0935
Shelby *(G-11308)*

Asheville Maintenance and............E..... 828 687-8110
Arden *(G-254)*

Classic Cleaning LLC............................E..... 800 220-7101
Raleigh *(G-9998)*

Cymbal LLC............................G..... 877 365-9622
Cary *(G-1342)*

Darius All Access LLC............................E..... 910 262-8567
Wilmington *(G-12759)*

Galaxy Pressure Washing Inc............G..... 888 299-3129
Pineville *(G-9729)*

Green Waste Management LLC............G..... 704 289-0720
Charlotte *(G-2239)*

K & L Resources............................G..... 910 494-3736
Fayetteville *(G-4625)*

Patel Deepal............................G..... 704 634-5141
Concord *(G-3416)*

Prestige Cleaning Incorporated............F..... 704 752-7747
Charlotte *(G-2662)*

Surface Buff LLC............................G..... 919 341-2873
Raleigh *(G-10523)*

W G of Southwest Raleigh Inc............G..... 919 629-7327
Holly Springs *(G-6919)*

7352 Medical equipment rental

Medaccess Inc............................G..... 828 264-4085
Robbinsville *(G-10760)*

Quick-Deck Inc............................E..... 704 888-0327
Locust *(G-7898)*

7353 Heavy construction equipment rental

◆ International Cnstr Eqp Inc............E..... 704 821-8200
Matthews *(G-8175)*

▼ Sound Heavy Machinery Inc............F..... 910 782-2477
Wilmington *(G-12922)*

7359 Equipment rental and leasing, nec

Arc3 Gases Inc............................G..... 336 275-3333
Greensboro *(G-5367)*

Arc3 Gases Inc............................G..... 704 220-1029
Monroe *(G-8429)*

Arc3 Gases Inc............................E..... 910 892-4016
Dunn *(G-3844)*

B V Hedrick Gravel & Sand Co............E..... 704 633-5982
Salisbury *(G-11021)*

Cherokee Instruments Inc............................F..... 919 552-0554
Angier *(G-117)*

Classic Industrial Services............G..... 919 209-0909
Smithfield *(G-11438)*

Comer Sanitary Service Inc............G..... 336 629-8311
Lexington *(G-7668)*

Form Tech Concrete Forms Inc............E..... 704 395-9910
Charlotte *(G-2172)*

Gregory Poole Equipment Co.............. F 919 872-2691
Raleigh *(G-10146)*

Kids Playhouse LLC.......................... G 704 299-4449
Charlotte *(G-2395)*

Lynn Ladder Scaffolding Co Inc............ G 301 336-4700
Charlotte *(G-2443)*

M&N Construction Supply Inc............ G 336 996-7740
Colfax *(G-3283)*

Medaccess Inc................................. G 828 264-4085
Robbinsville *(G-10760)*

R O Givens Signs Inc........................ G 252 338-6578
Elizabeth City *(G-4407)*

Readilite & Barricade Inc.................. F 919 231-8309
Raleigh *(G-10435)*

▲ Sharpe Co.................................. E 336 724-2871
Winston Salem *(G-13333)*

Tarheel Monitoring LLC................... G 910 763-1490
Wilmington *(G-12936)*

Ultimate Floor Cleaning.................... G 704 912-8978
Charlotte *(G-2960)*

▲ Watson Party Tables Inc................ F 919 294-9153
Durham *(G-4302)*

7363 Help supply services

Delta Contractors Inc....................... F 817 410-9481
Linden *(G-7874)*

7371 Custom computer programming services

27 Software US Inc.......................... F 704 968-2879
Mooresville *(G-8589)*

Able Softsystems Corp...................... G 919 241-7907
Raleigh *(G-9868)*

Add-On Technologies Inc................... F 704 882-2227
Indian Trail *(G-7066)*

Advanced Computer Lrng Co LLC........ E 910 779-2254
Fayetteville *(G-4544)*

Advanced Digital Systems Inc............. F 919 485-4819
Durham *(G-3881)*

Agingo Corporation.......................... G 888 298-0777
Charlotte *(G-1629)*

Aiken Development LLC..................... G 828 572-4040
Lenoir *(G-7567)*

Applied Strategies Inc...................... G 704 525-4478
Charlotte *(G-1688)*

Bae Systems Info Elctrnic Syst........... E 919 323-5800
Durham *(G-3911)*

Bluetick Inc................................... F 336 294-4102
Greensboro *(G-5395)*

Bmt Micro Inc................................ G 910 792-9100
Wilmington *(G-12721)*

Bravo Team LLC.............................. E 704 309-1918
Mooresville *(G-8621)*

Camelot Computers Inc.................... F 704 554-1670
Charlotte *(G-1832)*

Carolina Housing Solutions LLC.......... G 704 995-7078
Davidson *(G-3699)*

Champion Media LLC....................... E 704 746-3955
Mooresville *(G-8637)*

Cmisolutions Inc............................. E 704 759-9950
Charlotte *(G-1937)*

Computational Engrg Intl Inc............. E 919 363-0883
Apex *(G-148)*

Computer Task Group Inc................. E 919 677-1313
Raleigh *(G-10006)*

Cyberlux Corporation....................... F 984 363-6894
Research Triangle Pa *(G-10707)*

Czechmate Enterprises LLC.............. G 704 784-6547
Concord *(G-3351)*

Deverger Systems Inc...................... G 919 201-5146
Asheville *(G-487)*

Digital Designs Inc.......................... E 704 790-7100
Charlotte *(G-2046)*

Digital Turbine Media Inc.................. E 866 254-2453
Durham *(G-4000)*

Dynamac Corporation....................... E 919 544-6428
Durham *(G-4016)*

Fics America Inc............................. D 704 329-7391
Charlotte *(G-2151)*

Fiestic Inc.................................... F 888 935-3999
Raleigh *(G-10107)*

Firstreport Software Inc.................... G 828 441-0404
Asheville *(G-497)*

Flameoff Coatings Inc...................... G 888 816-7468
Raleigh *(G-10111)*

Goldmine Software.......................... G 704 944-3579
Charlotte *(G-2225)*

▲ H&A Scientific Inc........................ G 252 752-4315
Greenville *(G-5986)*

Ideacode Inc.................................. G 919 341-5170
Greensboro *(G-5613)*

Infisoft Software............................ G 704 307-2619
Charlotte *(G-2329)*

Infobelt LLC.................................. F 980 223-4000
Charlotte *(G-2331)*

Information Tech Works LLC............... G 919 232-5332
Raleigh *(G-10195)*

Innait Inc..................................... G 406 241-5245
Charlotte *(G-2337)*

Inneroptic Technology Inc................. G 919 732-2090
Hillsborough *(G-6868)*

Insightsoftware LLC......................... E 919 872-7800
Raleigh *(G-10200)*

Inspectionxpert Corporation.............. F 919 249-6442
Raleigh *(G-10201)*

Inspire Creative Studios Inc.............. G 910 395-0200
Wilmington *(G-12818)*

Intelligent Apps LLC........................ G 919 628-6256
Raleigh *(G-10205)*

International Bus Mchs Corp.............. B 919 543-6919
Durham *(G-4080)*

Iqe North Carolina LLC..................... F 336 609-6270
Greensboro *(G-5623)*

▲ Jasie Blanks LLC.......................... F 910 485-0016
Fayetteville *(G-4621)*

Jctm LLC...................................... D 252 571-8678
Charlotte *(G-2364)*

Kdy Automation Solutions Inc............. G 888 219-0049
Morrisville *(G-8996)*

▲ Lenovo (united States) Inc.............. A 855 253-6686
Morrisville *(G-9006)*

Logicbit Software LLC...................... E 888 366-2280
Durham *(G-4108)*

Logiksavvy Solutions LLC.................. G 336 392-6149
Greensboro *(G-5663)*

Makemine Inc................................. G 704 906-7164
Charlotte *(G-2449)*

Medicor Imaging Inc........................ G 704 332-5532
Charlotte *(G-2486)*

Natrx Inc...................................... E 919 263-0667
Raleigh *(G-10325)*

Noregon Systems Inc....................... C 336 615-8555
Greensboro *(G-5713)*

Novisystems Inc............................. G 919 205-5005
Raleigh *(G-10341)*

Onion Peel Software Inc................... G 919 460-1789
Morrisville *(G-9032)*

Openfire Systems........................... G 336 251-3991
Millers Creek *(G-8306)*

Pai Services LLC............................. E 856 231-4667
Charlotte *(G-2605)*

▲ Phononic Inc............................... D 919 908-6300
Durham *(G-4178)*

Pogo Software Inc.......................... G 407 267-4864
Raleigh *(G-10375)*

Predatar Inc.................................. G 919 827-4516
Raleigh *(G-10391)*

Preferred Data Corporation............... G 336 886-3282
High Point *(G-6743)*

Proctorfree Inc.............................. F 704 759-6569
Davidson *(G-3717)*

Qplot Corporation........................... G 949 302-7928
Raleigh *(G-10410)*

Red Hat Inc.................................. A 919 754-3700
Raleigh *(G-10436)*

Rvb Systems Group Inc.................... G 919 362-5211
Garner *(G-4960)*

S C I A Inc................................... G 919 387-7000
Cary *(G-1444)*

▲ Sas Institute Inc.......................... C 919 677-8000
Cary *(G-1450)*

Sato Global Solutions Inc................. G 954 261-3279
Charlotte *(G-2758)*

School Directorease LLC.................. G 240 206-6273
Charlotte *(G-2768)*

Scriptorium Pubg Svcs Inc................ G 919 481-2701
Durham *(G-4227)*

Signalscape Inc............................. E 919 859-4565
Cary *(G-1455)*

Splendidcrm Software Inc................. G 919 604-1258
Holly Springs *(G-6916)*

Synopsys Inc................................. G 919 941-6600
Morrisville *(G-9062)*

Tc2 Labs LLC................................ G 919 380-2171
Raleigh *(G-10534)*

▲ Tekelec Inc................................ C
Morrisville *(G-9065)*

Tekelec Global Inc.......................... A 919 460-5500
Morrisville *(G-9066)*

Telephys Inc................................. G 312 625-9128
Davidson *(G-3719)*

Terida LLC.................................... F 910 693-1633
Pinehurst *(G-9704)*

Twork Technology Inc...................... G 704 218-9675
Charlotte *(G-2956)*

USA Metal Structure LLP.................. G 336 717-2884
Dobson *(G-3826)*

Vortant Technologies LLC................. G 828 645-1026
Weaverville *(G-12506)*

Web 4 Half LLC.............................. E 855 762-4638
Greensboro *(G-5914)*

Xsport Global Inc........................... F 212 541-6222
Charlotte *(G-3032)*

7372 Prepackaged software

/N Software Inc.............................. E 919 544-7070
Chapel Hill *(G-1521)*

27 Software US Inc.......................... F 704 968-2879
Mooresville *(G-8589)*

2u NC.. F 919 525-5075
Chapel Hill *(G-1522)*

6th Sense Analytics........................ G 919 439-4740
Morrisville *(G-8914)*

A4 Health Systems Inc..................... B 919 851-6177
Cary *(G-1283)*

Able Softsystems Corp...................... G 919 241-7907
Raleigh *(G-9868)*

Access Newswire Inc....................... C 919 481-4000
Raleigh *(G-9872)*

Aceyus Inc.................................... E 704 443-7900
Charlotte *(G-1616)*

Admissionpros LLC.......................... F 919 256-3889
Cary *(G-1286)*

Advanced Computer Lrng Co LLC........ E 910 779-2254
Fayetteville *(G-4544)*

Advanced Digital Systems Inc	F	919 485-4819	Durham *(G-3881)*
Agingo Corporation	G	888 298-0777	Charlotte *(G-1629)*
Alpha Theory LLC	G	704 844-1018	Charlotte *(G-1651)*
Alpha Theory LLC	G	212 235-2180	Charlotte *(G-1652)*
Alpha Theory LLC	G	212 235-2180	Charlotte *(G-1653)*
Altera Corporation	G	919 852-1004	Raleigh *(G-9893)*
AMS Software Inc	G	919 570-6001	Wake Forest *(G-12260)*
Apex Analytix LLC	C	336 272-4669	Greensboro *(G-5365)*
Applied Strategies Inc	G	704 525-4478	Charlotte *(G-1688)*
Appsense Incorporated	C	919 666-0080	Cary *(G-1293)*
Archivesocial Inc	E	888 558-6032	Durham *(G-3898)*
◆ Arris Technology Inc	D	828 324-2200	Claremont *(G-3089)*
Arrow Educational Products Inc	G	910 521-0840	Pembroke *(G-9656)*
Atlantic Software Co	G	910 763-3907	Wilmington *(G-12714)*
Attus Technologies Inc	E	704 341-5750	Charlotte *(G-1716)*
Automotive MGT Solutions	G	919 481-2439	Cary *(G-1301)*
Avercast LLC	F	208 538-5380	Emerald Isle *(G-4477)*
Avidxchange Holdings Inc	E	800 560-9305	Charlotte *(G-1722)*
Axial Exchange Inc	G	919 576-9988	Raleigh *(G-9924)*
Bandwidth Inc	B	800 808-5150	Raleigh *(G-9930)*
Biker Software	G	919 761-1681	Wake Forest *(G-12263)*
Bill Perfect Inc	F	954 889-6699	Denver *(G-3773)*
Billsoft Inc	F	913 859-9674	Durham *(G-3927)*
Biz Technology Solutions LLC	E	704 658-1707	Mooresville *(G-8615)*
Biznet Software Inc	F	919 872-7800	Raleigh *(G-9947)*
Blacktip Solutions	G	336 303-1580	Greensboro *(G-5392)*
Bloom Ai Inc	G	704 620-2886	Cary *(G-1309)*
Blue Wolf Technologies LLP	G	919 810-1508	Raleigh *(G-9949)*
BMC Software Inc	G	704 283-8179	Monroe *(G-8440)*
Bmt Micro Inc	G	910 792-9100	Wilmington *(G-12721)*
Boss Key Productions Inc	D	919 659-5704	Raleigh *(G-9956)*
Bottomline Medical	G	704 527-0919	Charlotte *(G-1803)*
▲ Bravosolution Us Inc	E	312 373-3100	Morrisville *(G-8943)*
Brick City Gaming Inc	F	919 297-2081	Cary *(G-1314)*
Brightly Software Inc	C	919 816-8237	Cary *(G-1315)*
Bronto Software LLC	C	919 595-2500	Durham *(G-3946)*

Brookstone Baptist Church	E	828 658-9443	Weaverville *(G-12485)*
Business Systems of America	G	704 766-2755	Charlotte *(G-1821)*
Cadence Design Systems Inc	G	919 380-3900	Cary *(G-1319)*
Camelot Computers Inc	F	704 554-1670	Charlotte *(G-1832)*
Camstar Systems Inc	C	704 227-6600	Charlotte *(G-1833)*
Cdata Software Inc	F	919 928-5214	Chapel Hill *(G-1535)*
Cdp Inc	G	336 270-6151	Burlington *(G-1066)*
Cengage Learning Inc	E	919 829-8181	Raleigh *(G-9990)*
Centeredge Software	G	336 598-5934	Roxboro *(G-10922)*
Channeltivity LLC	F	704 408-3560	Matthews *(G-8104)*
Charge Onsite LLC	G	888 343-2688	Charlotte *(G-1893)*
Checkfree Services Corporation	B	919 941-2640	Durham *(G-3971)*
Cicero Inc	G	919 380-5000	Cary *(G-1328)*
Client Care Web Inc	E	704 787-9901	Concord *(G-3336)*
Clinetic Inc	F	513 295-1332	Raleigh *(G-10000)*
Cloud Sftwr Group Holdings Inc	A	919 839-6139	Raleigh *(G-10002)*
Cloud Software Group Inc	G	919 969-6500	Chapel Hill *(G-1538)*
Cloudgenera Inc	E	980 332-4040	Charlotte *(G-1932)*
Cmisolutions Inc	E	704 759-9950	Charlotte *(G-1937)*
Competitive Solutions Inc	E	919 851-0058	Raleigh *(G-10004)*
Computational Engrg Intl Inc	E	919 363-0883	Apex *(G-148)*
Computer Task Group Inc	E	919 677-1313	Raleigh *(G-10006)*
Connectmedia Ventures LLC	G	773 551-7446	Raleigh *(G-10007)*
Consultants In Data Proc Inc	G	704 542-6339	Charlotte *(G-1976)*
Conxit Technology Group Inc	G	877 998-4227	Charlotte *(G-1980)*
Crm A LLC	F	888 600-7567	Cary *(G-1339)*
Crmnext Inc	E	415 424-4644	Raleigh *(G-10021)*
Csit Group	G	828 233-5750	Asheville *(G-481)*
Cyber Imaging Systems Inc	F	919 872-5179	Raleigh *(G-10031)*
D3 Software Inc	G	336 870-9138	High Point *(G-6586)*
Data443 Risk Mitigation Inc	E	919 858-6542	Durham *(G-3998)*
Database Incorporated	G	202 684-6252	Durham *(G-3999)*
Datascope North America Inc	E	980 819-5244	Mint Hill *(G-8336)*
Datawise LLC	G	704 293-1482	Charlotte *(G-2019)*
Dauntless Discovery LLC	C	610 909-7383	Raleigh *(G-10037)*
Definitive Media Corp	F	714 730-4958	Cary *(G-1343)*

Deliveright Logistics Inc	C	862 279-7332	Lexington *(G-7676)*
Digital Audio Corporation	F	919 572-6767	Hendersonville *(G-6202)*
Digital Designs Inc	E	704 790-7100	Charlotte *(G-2046)*
Digital Printing Systems Inc	E	704 525-0190	Charlotte *(G-2047)*
Digital Turbine Media Inc	E	866 254-2453	Durham *(G-4000)*
Digitome Corporation	G	860 651-5560	Davidson *(G-3703)*
Dilisym Services Inc	G	919 558-1323	Durham *(G-4002)*
Discovery Insurance Company	E	800 876-1492	Kinston *(G-7405)*
DL Hopper & Associates Inc	G	252 838-1062	Newport *(G-9440)*
Dp Solutions Inc	F	336 854-7700	Greensboro *(G-5504)*
Drake Software LLC	B	828 524-2922	Franklin *(G-4825)*
Dreamship Inc	G	908 601-8152	Raleigh *(G-10058)*
Dzone Inc	F	919 678-0300	Research Triangle Pa *(G-10708)*
E&C Medical Intelligence Inc	E	609 228-7898	Cary *(G-1350)*
Eatclub Inc	G	609 578-7942	Chapel Hill *(G-1542)*
◆ ECR Software Corporation	E	828 265-2907	Boone *(G-914)*
Educatrx Inc	G	980 328-0013	Monroe *(G-8481)*
Elizabeth Logistic LLC	D	803 920-3931	Indian Trail *(G-7078)*
Elxr Health Inc	E	919 917-8484	Durham *(G-4018)*
Emath360 LLC	F	919 744-4944	Cary *(G-1352)*
EMC Corporation	G	720 341-3274	Charlotte *(G-2108)*
Employus Inc	F	919 706-4008	Cary *(G-1353)*
En Fleur Corporation	G	919 556-1623	Louisburg *(G-7914)*
Engineered Software	G	336 299-4843	Greensboro *(G-5521)*
Envirnmntal Systems RES Inst I	E	704 541-9810	Charlotte *(G-2119)*
Estate Mentors Inc	G	877 378-7567	High Point *(G-6614)*
Euclid Innovations Inc	F	877 382-5431	Charlotte *(G-2129)*
Event 1 Software Inc	G	360 567-3752	Raleigh *(G-10094)*
Everview	G	800 549-4722	Mount Airy *(G-9120)*
▼ Eview Technology Inc	G	919 878-5199	Raleigh *(G-10096)*
Executive Grooming LLC	G	919 706-5382	Raleigh *(G-10098)*
Expersis Software Inc	G	919 874-0608	Cary *(G-1357)*
Exposure Software LLC	F	919 832-4124	Raleigh *(G-10099)*
◆ Extreme Networks Inc	B	408 579-2800	Morrisville *(G-8973)*
Facilitydudecom Inc	G	919 459-6430	Cary *(G-1360)*
Fathom Holdings Inc	E	888 455-6040	Cary *(G-1362)*

Feedtrail Incorporated.............................. F 757 618-7760
   Raleigh *(G-10105)*

Fics America Inc.................................... D 704 329-7391
   Charlotte *(G-2151)*

Fieldx Inc... G 919 926-7001
   Raleigh *(G-10106)*

Fiestic Inc.. F 888 935-3999
   Raleigh *(G-10107)*

First Leads Inc..................................... G 919 672-5329
   Durham *(G-4032)*

Firstreport Software Inc........................... G 828 441-0404
   Asheville *(G-497)*

Flow Rhythm Inc.................................. G 704 737-2178
   Charlotte *(G-2167)*

Fogle Computing Corporation................. G 828 697-9080
   Hendersonville *(G-6209)*

Foxster Opco LLC.................................. E 910 297-6996
   Hampstead *(G-6072)*

Fusion Sport Inc.................................... E 720 987-4403
   Durham *(G-4041)*

G & E Software Inc................................ E 910 762-5608
   Wilmington *(G-12782)*

Galvix Inc... G 925 434-6243
   Cary *(G-1363)*

General Dynamics Corporation............... E 336 698-8571
   Mc Leansville *(G-8222)*

Genesys Cloud Services Inc................... F 317 872-3000
   Durham *(G-4045)*

Genesys Technology Inc......................... G 336 789-0763
   Mount Airy *(G-9122)*

Geneva Software Company Inc............... G 336 275-8887
   Greensboro *(G-5556)*

Getbridge LLC..................................... C 919 645-2800
   Raleigh *(G-10132)*

◆ Gilbarco Inc......................................A 336 547-5000
   Greensboro *(G-5560)*

GK Software Usa Inc.............................. E 984 255-7995
   Raleigh *(G-10135)*

Global Software LLC.............................. G 919 872-7800
   Raleigh *(G-10138)*

Go Energies LLC................................... F 877 712-5999
   Wilmington *(G-12790)*

Go Energies Holdings Inc...................... G 910 762-5802
   Wilmington *(G-12791)*

Goldmine Software................................ G 704 944-3579
   Charlotte *(G-2225)*

◆ Goodrich Corporation........................C 704 423-7000
   Charlotte *(G-2227)*

HackEDU Inc....................................... D 804 742-2533
   Charlotte *(G-2250)*

Healthline Info Systems Inc.................... F 704 655-0447
   Davidson *(G-3707)*

Hiatus Inc... E 844 572-6185
   Charlotte *(G-2277)*

Hitachi Energy USA Inc.......................... F 919 649-7022
   Raleigh *(G-10168)*

Hortonworks Inc................................... G 855 846-7866
   Durham *(G-4065)*

Hrtms Incorporated............................... G 919 741-5099
   Raleigh *(G-10178)*

Hype World Inc..................................... G 336 588-8666
   Matthews *(G-8118)*

I-Leadr Inc.. G 910 431-5252
   Sherrills Ford *(G-11392)*

Icontact LLC.. D 919 957-6150
   Morrisville *(G-8990)*

Idea People Inc.................................... G 704 398-4437
   Huntersville *(G-7000)*

Idea Software Inc................................. G 407 453-3883
   Raleigh *(G-10184)*

Ideablock LLC..................................... G 919 551-5054
   Durham *(G-4069)*

Ideacode Inc....................................... G 919 341-5170
   Greensboro *(G-5613)*

Ientertainment Network Inc.................... G 919 238-4090
   Burnsville *(G-1188)*

Ilumivu Inc.. G 410 570-8846
   Asheville *(G-521)*

IMR Holdings LLC................................ G 980 287-8139
   Charlotte *(G-2318)*

Inferensys Inc...................................... G 910 398-1200
   Durham *(G-4075)*

Infinite Software Resorces LLC............... G 704 509-0031
   Charlotte *(G-2327)*

Infisoft Software.................................. G 704 307-2619
   Charlotte *(G-2329)*

Infobelt LLC.. F 980 223-4000
   Charlotte *(G-2331)*

Information Tech Works LLC.................... G 919 232-5332
   Raleigh *(G-10195)*

Informtion Rtrvval Cmpanies Inc............. E 919 460-7447
   Cary *(G-1375)*

Inn-Flow LLC....................................... E 919 277-9027
   Cary *(G-1376)*

Innait Inc.. G 406 241-5245
   Charlotte *(G-2337)*

Innowera Ltd Liability Company.............. G 214 295-9508
   Raleigh *(G-10197)*

Inovaetion Inc..................................... F 919 651-1628
   Raleigh *(G-10198)*

Insightsoftware LLC.............................. E 919 872-7800
   Raleigh *(G-10200)*

Insource Sftwr Solutions Inc................... G 704 895-1052
   Cornelius *(G-3611)*

Inspectionxpert Corporation................... F 919 249-6442
   Raleigh *(G-10201)*

Instantiations Inc................................. F 855 476-2558
   Raleigh *(G-10202)*

Insurance Systems Group Inc................. F 919 834-4907
   Raleigh *(G-10203)*

Intelligent Apps LLC............................. G 919 628-6256
   Raleigh *(G-10205)*

Iqmetrix USA Inc.................................. D 704 987-9903
   Mooresville *(G-8696)*

Jaggaer LLC.. D 919 659-2100
   Durham *(G-4087)*

Jctm LLC.. D 252 571-8678
   Charlotte *(G-2364)*

Jenesis Software Inc............................. G 828 245-1171
   Elon *(G-4471)*

Jfl Enterprises Inc................................ G 704 786-7838
   Concord *(G-3385)*

JMP Statistical Discovery Llc.................. F 877 594-6567
   Cary *(G-1378)*

Johnson Controls Inc............................ G 866 285-8345
   Morrisville *(G-8995)*

Jrg Technologies Corp........................... D 850 362-4310
   Charlotte *(G-2380)*

Juniper Networks Inc............................ F 888 586-4737
   Raleigh *(G-10227)*

Justenough Software Corp Inc................ G 800 949-3432
   Durham *(G-4090)*

Justi LLC.. F 919 434-5002
   Cary *(G-1382)*

Kaleida Systems Inc............................. G 704 814-4429
   Matthews *(G-8120)*

Kaleido Inc.. F 984 205-9436
   Raleigh *(G-10228)*

▼ Knowledge Management Asso.......... G 781 250-2001
   Raleigh *(G-10239)*

Konami Digital Entrmt Inc...................... E 310 220-8100
   Durham *(G-4098)*

Laser Recharge Carolina Inc.................. F 919 467-5902
   Cary *(G-1387)*

Launchmagiccom Inc............................ G 845 234-4440
   Sanford *(G-11202)*

Learningstationcom Inc......................... F 704 926-5400
   Charlotte *(G-2414)*

Leaseaccelerator Inc............................. F 866 446-0980
   Raleigh *(G-10251)*

Leoforce LLC....................................... E 919 539-5434
   Raleigh *(G-10253)*

Liquidehr Inc....................................... E 866 618-1531
   Cary *(G-1390)*

Lobbyguard Solutions LLC..................... F 919 785-3301
   Raleigh *(G-10260)*

Logicbit Software LLC........................... E 888 366-2280
   Durham *(G-4108)*

Logicom Computer Systems Inc............. G 910 256-5916
   Wilmington *(G-12839)*

London Luxury LLC.............................. G 980 819-1966
   Charlotte *(G-2432)*

M I Connection.................................... F 704 662-3255
   Mooresville *(G-8717)*

Make Solutions Inc............................... F 623 444-0098
   Asheville *(G-542)*

Mapjoy LLC... G 919 450-8360
   Durham *(G-4118)*

Medaptus Inc...................................... F 617 896-4000
   Raleigh *(G-10288)*

Medicor Imaging Inc............................. G 704 332-5532
   Charlotte *(G-2486)*

Medlio Inc.. G 919 599-4870
   Durham *(G-4125)*

Medvertical LLC.................................. G 919 867-4268
   Raleigh *(G-10289)*

Merchant Cash Systems LLC.................. G 336 499-9937
   Charlotte *(G-2490)*

Meridian Prfmce Systems Inc................. G 706 905-5637
   Charlotte *(G-2493)*

Micronova Systems Inc.......................... G 910 202-0564
   Wilmington *(G-12853)*

Microsoft Corporation...........................A 704 527-2987
   Charlotte *(G-2499)*

Moduslink Corporation.......................... E 781 663-5000
   Garner *(G-4943)*

Monarch Medical Tech LLC.................... F 704 335-1300
   Charlotte *(G-2516)*

Movers and Shakers LLC....................... G 980 771-0505
   Charlotte *(G-2524)*

Munibilling... E 800 259-7020
   Greensboro *(G-5701)*

Murano Corporation.............................. F 919 294-8233
   Durham *(G-4140)*

N3xt Inc... G 704 905-2209
   Charlotte *(G-2539)*

Navex Global Inc.................................. G 866 297-0224
   Charlotte *(G-2549)*

Ncino Inc.. C 888 676-2466
   Wilmington *(G-12857)*

Ncino Opco Inc....................................A 888 676-2466
   Wilmington *(G-12858)*

Neurametrix Inc................................... G 408 507-2366
   Asheville *(G-556)*

Nite Crawlers LLC................................ G 980 229-8706
   Charlotte *(G-2568)*

Notemeal Inc....................................... E 312 550-2049
   Durham *(G-4150)*

Novisystems Inc.................................. G 919 205-5005
   Raleigh *(G-10341)*

Oakbrook Solutions Inc......................... E 336 714-0321
   Oak Ridge *(G-9573)*

Oasis Akhal-Tekes................................ G 704 843-3139
   Waxhaw *(G-12436)*

Oasys Mobile Inc................................. G 919 807-5600
   Cary *(G-1411)*

S
I
C

Objective Security Corporation	F	415 997-9967
Raleigh (G-10343)		
Ocufii Inc	G	804 874-4036
Huntersville (G-7026)		
Odigia Inc	G	336 462-8056
Winston Salem (G-13268)		
One Srce Dcument Solutions Inc	E	800 401-9544
Greensboro (G-5724)		
Onion Peel Software Inc	G	919 460-1789
Morrisville (G-9032)		
Oracle Corporation	D	919 595-2500
Morrisville (G-9033)		
Oracle Hearing Group	G	732 349-6804
Wilmington (G-12867)		
Oracle of God Ministries Nc	G	919 522-2113
Raleigh (G-10349)		
Oracle Systems Corporation	G	704 423-1426
Matthews (G-8139)		
Oracle Systems Corporation	F	919 257-2300
Raleigh (G-10350)		
Orgbook Inc	G	615 483-5410
Durham (G-4157)		
Orgspan Inc	G	855 674-7726
Durham (G-4158)		
Output Services Group Inc	E	336 783-5948
Mount Airy (G-9163)		
Pai Services LLC	E	856 231-4667
Charlotte (G-2605)		
Payment Collect LLC	G	828 214-5550
Asheville (G-568)		
Payzer LLC	F	866 488-6525
Charlotte (G-2620)		
Pf2 Eis LLC	C	704 549-6931
Charlotte (G-2630)		
Photolynx Inc	G	760 787-1177
Raleigh (G-10367)		
Plataine Inc	G	336 883-7657
High Point (G-6736)		
Pogo Software Inc	G	407 267-4864
Raleigh (G-10375)		
Pogomaxy Inc	G	919 623-0118
Raleigh (G-10376)		
Powersolve Corporation LLC	F	919 662-8515
Garner (G-4954)		
▲ Practice Fusion Inc	C	415 346-7700
Raleigh (G-10386)		
Practicepro Sftwr Systems Inc	G	212 244-2100
Charlotte (G-2655)		
Pramana LLC	G	910 233-5118
Cary (G-1426)		
Precision Fermentations Inc	E	919 717-3983
Durham (G-4195)		
Predatar Inc	G	919 827-4516
Raleigh (G-10391)		
Preferred Data Corporation	G	336 886-3282
High Point (G-6743)		
Priority Backgrounds LLC	G	919 557-3247
Fuquay Varina (G-4895)		
Proctorfree Inc	F	704 759-6569
Davidson (G-3717)		
Progress Software Corp	F	919 461-4200
Morrisville (G-9039)		
Prometheus Group Holdings LLC	D	919 835-0810
Raleigh (G-10404)		
Propharma Group LLC	D	888 242-0559
Raleigh (G-10405)		
Prosapient Inc	G	984 282-2823
Raleigh (G-10406)		
Proximal Design Labs LLC	G	919 599-5742
Raleigh (G-10407)		
Qplot Corporation	G	949 302-7928
Raleigh (G-10410)		

Quadron Holdings Inc	G	919 523-5376
Raleigh (G-10411)		
Quest Software Inc	G	919 337-4719
Morrisville (G-9042)		
Quinsite LLC Fka Mile 5 Anlyti	F	317 313-5152
Chapel Hill (G-1565)		
R N Lea Inc	G	919 247-5998
Raleigh (G-10418)		
R65 Labs Inc	G	919 219-1983
Durham (G-4206)		
Rackwise Inc	F	919 533-5533
Raleigh (G-10420)		
Rapidform Inc	G	408 856-6200
Cary (G-1433)		
Reacredence It Solutions Inc	G	980 399-4071
Huntersville (G-7041)		
Red Hat Inc	A	919 754-3700
Raleigh (G-10436)		
Redtruc LLC	G	704 968-7888
Charlotte (G-2700)		
Revware Inc	G	919 790-0000
Raleigh (G-10442)		
Reynolds and Reynolds Company	G	321 287-3939
Charlotte (G-2721)		
Rivet Solutions Inc	G	888 487-3849
Matthews (G-8191)		
Rocketprint Software LLC	G	336 267-7272
Denton (G-3759)		
Ronak LLC	G	781 589-1973
Cary (G-1441)		
Roobrik Inc	G	919 667-7750
Greensboro (G-5794)		
Rssbus Inc	G	919 969-7675
Chapel Hill (G-1568)		
Rstack Solutions LLC	F	980 337-1295
Charlotte (G-2739)		
Rvb Systems Group Inc	G	919 362-5211
Garner (G-4960)		
Sam Software Corp	G	910 233-9924
Wilmington (G-12910)		
Sas Federal LLC	G	919 531-7505
Cary (G-1446)		
Sas Institute Inc	G	954 494-8189
Cary (G-1447)		
Sas Institute Inc	G	919 677-8000
Cary (G-1448)		
Sas Institute Inc	G	919 531-4153
Cary (G-1449)		
Sas Institute Inc	G	704 831-5595
Charlotte (G-2755)		
Sas Institute Inc	G	704 331-3956
Charlotte (G-2756)		
▲ Sas Institute Inc	C	919 677-8000
Cary (G-1450)		
▲ Sato America LLC	C	704 644-1650
Charlotte (G-2757)		
◆ Schaefer Systems International Inc	C	704 944-4500
Charlotte (G-2763)		
Science Applications Intl Corp	G	910 822-2100
Fayetteville (G-4666)		
Scientigo Inc	G	704 837-0500
Charlotte (G-2769)		
Sciolytix Inc	E	877 321-2451
Asheville (G-597)		
Sciquest Holdings Inc	D	919 659-2100
Morrisville (G-9047)		
Sciquest Parent LLC	F	919 659-2100
Morrisville (G-9048)		
Scribbles Software LLC	E	704 390-5690
Pineville (G-9756)		
Second Main Phase Slutions LLC	G	704 303-0090
Matthews (G-8147)		

Siemens Industry Software Inc	F	704 227-6600
Charlotte (G-2803)		
Sierra Software LLC	G	877 285-2867
Greensboro (G-5812)		
Simplecertifiedmailcom LLC	G	888 462-1750
Cary (G-1457)		
Simplicti Sftwr Solutions Inc	G	919 858-8898
Cary (G-1458)		
Sitelink Software LLC	D	919 865-0789
Raleigh (G-10484)		
Slickedit Inc	E	919 473-0070
Cary (G-1460)		
Small Business Software LLC	G	919 400-8298
Raleigh (G-10486)		
Smartlink Mobile Systems LLC	E	919 674-8400
Cary (G-1462)		
Smartware Group Inc	G	866 858-7800
Cary (G-1463)		
Socialtopias LLC	F	704 910-1713
Charlotte (G-2822)		
Software Goldsmith Inc	F	919 346-0403
Holly Springs (G-6915)		
Software Professionals Inc	G	503 860-4507
Raleigh (G-10489)		
Sofware LLC	G	828 820-2810
Hendersonville (G-6241)		
Southern Software Inc	D	336 879-3350
Southern Pines (G-11510)		
Southern Software Inc	G	910 638-8700
Fayetteville (G-4673)		
Splendidcrm Software Inc	G	919 604-1258
Holly Springs (G-6916)		
Spranto America Inc	G	919 741-5095
Apex (G-195)		
Starta Development Inc	G	919 865-7700
Raleigh (G-10505)		
Strategy	F	704 331-6521
Charlotte (G-2871)		
Stromasys Corporation	F	617 500-4556
Raleigh (G-10513)		
Stronger By Science Tech LLC	G	336 391-9377
Raleigh (G-10514)		
Sunday Drive Holdings Inc	G	919 825-5613
Raleigh (G-10519)		
Sweatnet LLC	G	847 331-7287
Charlotte (G-2886)		
Swk Technologies Inc	F	336 230-0200
Greensboro (G-5847)		
Symbrium Inc	F	919 879-2470
Raleigh (G-10525)		
Synergem Technologies Inc	E	866 859-0911
Mount Airy (G-9182)		
Synopsys Inc	G	919 941-6600
Morrisville (G-9062)		
Tagoio Inc	G	984 263-4376
Raleigh (G-10531)		
Td Cloud Services	G	518 258-6788
Raleigh (G-10535)		
Technology Partners LLC	D	704 553-1004
Charlotte (G-2904)		
Temprano Techvestors Inc	F	877 545-1509
Newton (G-9504)		
Terida LLC	F	910 693-1633
Pinehurst (G-9704)		
The Computer Solution Company	F	336 409-0782
Winston Salem (G-13362)		
Thorco LLC	F	919 363-6234
Cary (G-1471)		
Threatswitch Inc	E	877 449-3220
Charlotte (G-2915)		
Topquadrant Inc	E	919 300-7945
Raleigh (G-10552)		

▲ Transbotics Corporation...............E 704 362-1115
Charlotte *(G-2936)*

Transdata Solutions Inc....................G 919 770-9329
Sanford *(G-11243)*

Tresata Inc...E 980 224-2097
Charlotte *(G-2939)*

Triangle Microworks Inc....................F 919 870-5101
Raleigh *(G-10559)*

Triangle Systems Inc.........................G 919 544-0090
Durham *(G-4281)*

Triangle Systems Inc.........................G 919 544-0090
Chapel Hill *(G-1581)*

Trickfit & Suepack Training................G 919 737-2231
Wake Forest *(G-12309)*

Triggermesh Inc.................................G 919 228-8049
Cary *(G-1474)*

Trimech Solutions LLC......................G 704 503-6644
Charlotte *(G-2944)*

Tryhard Infinity LLC...........................G 252 269-0985
New Bern *(G-9402)*

Twork Technology Inc........................G 704 218-9675
Charlotte *(G-2956)*

Ukg Kronos Systems LLC..................G 800 225-1561
Charlotte *(G-2958)*

Ukg Kronos Systems LLC..................G 800 225-1561
Greensboro *(G-5885)*

UNC Campus Health Services.............D 919 966-2281
Chapel Hill *(G-1584)*

Unspecified Inc..................................G 919 907-2726
Durham *(G-4291)*

Usat LLC..E 919 942-4214
Chapel Hill *(G-1587)*

Utd Technology Corp.........................G 704 612-0121
Mint Hill *(G-8344)*

Veradigm LLC....................................A 919 847-8102
Raleigh *(G-10586)*

Verdante Bioenergy Svcs LLC...........G 828 394-1246
Lenoir *(G-7643)*

Vestige Group LLC.............................E 704 321-4960
Charlotte *(G-2980)*

Viasic Inc...G 336 774-2150
Durham *(G-4297)*

Virtus Entertainment Inc....................E 919 467-9700
Cary *(G-1480)*

Visionair Inc......................................A 910 675-9117
Castle Hayne *(G-1510)*

Vote Owl LLC.....................................G 919 264-1796
Raleigh *(G-10596)*

Wave Front Computers LLC................G 919 896-6121
Raleigh *(G-10600)*

We Appit LLC.....................................G 910 465-2722
Wilmington *(G-12946)*

Wispry Inc..G 919 854-7500
Cary *(G-1484)*

Woodshed Software............................G 941 240-1780
Salisbury *(G-11136)*

Workday Inc.......................................G 919 703-2559
Raleigh *(G-10613)*

Xschem Inc..E 919 379-3500
Morrisville *(G-9091)*

Xsport Global Inc...............................F 212 541-6222
Charlotte *(G-3032)*

Yepzy Inc...F 855 461-2678
Concord *(G-3471)*

Yumitos Corporation..........................E 786 952-6202
Charlotte *(G-3043)*

7373 Computer integrated systems design

057 Technology LLC..........................G 855 557-7057
Hickory *(G-6258)*

Acroplis Cntrls Engineers Pllc...........F 919 275-3884
Raleigh *(G-9876)*

Advanced Mfg Solutions NC Inc...........F 828 633-2633
Candler *(G-1216)*

Bachstein Consulting LLC..................G 410 322-4917
Youngsville *(G-13463)*

Billsoft Inc...F 913 859-9674
Durham *(G-3927)*

Blue Wolf Technologies LLP...............G 919 810-1508
Raleigh *(G-9949)*

Cicero Inc..G 919 380-5000
Cary *(G-1328)*

Computerway Food Systems Inc..........E 336 841-7289
High Point *(G-6575)*

Custom Controls Unlimited LLC..........F 919 812-6553
Raleigh *(G-10029)*

Descher LLC......................................G 919 828-7708
Raleigh *(G-10041)*

◆ Extreme Networks Inc.....................B 408 579-2800
Morrisville *(G-8973)*

General Dynmics Mssion Systems........C 336 698-8000
Mc Leansville *(G-8223)*

Infobelt LLC.......................................F 980 223-4000
Charlotte *(G-2331)*

Innait Inc..G 406 241-5245
Charlotte *(G-2337)*

International Bus Mchs Corp...............B 919 543-6919
Durham *(G-4080)*

Juniper Networks Inc.........................F 888 586-4737
Raleigh *(G-10227)*

Medicor Imaging Inc..........................G 704 332-5532
Charlotte *(G-2486)*

◆ Meridian Zero Degrees LLC.............E 866 454-6757
Aberdeen *(G-13)*

Q T Corporation.................................G 252 399-7600
Wilson *(G-13016)*

Qplot Corporation..............................G 949 302-7928
Raleigh *(G-10410)*

Romeo Six LLC...................................F 919 589-7150
Holly Springs *(G-6912)*

S C I A Inc...G 919 387-7000
Cary *(G-1444)*

Sato Global Solutions Inc...................G 954 261-3279
Charlotte *(G-2758)*

Science Applications Intl Corp.............G 910 822-2100
Fayetteville *(G-4666)*

Silver Knight Pcs LLC........................G 910 824-2054
Fayetteville *(G-4670)*

▲ Sostram Corporation.......................G 919 226-1195
Durham *(G-4242)*

St Investors Inc.................................D 704 969-7500
Charlotte *(G-2856)*

Trimech Solutions LLC......................G 704 503-6644
Charlotte *(G-2944)*

Twork Technology Inc........................G 704 218-9675
Charlotte *(G-2956)*

Utd Technology Corp.........................G 704 612-0121
Mint Hill *(G-8344)*

Worden Brothers Inc..........................D 919 202-8555
Wilmington *(G-12954)*

7374 Data processing and preparation

Big Fish Dpi.......................................G 704 545-8112
Mint Hill *(G-8331)*

Checkfree Services Corporation..........B 919 941-2640
Durham *(G-3971)*

Computer Task Group Inc...................E 919 677-1313
Raleigh *(G-10006)*

Consultants In Data Proc Inc..............G 704 542-6339
Charlotte *(G-1976)*

Elxr Health Inc...................................G 919 917-8484
Durham *(G-4018)*

Infobelt LLC.......................................F 980 223-4000
Charlotte *(G-2331)*

Innait Inc..G 406 241-5245
Charlotte *(G-2337)*

Legalis Dms LLC................................F 919 741-8260
Raleigh *(G-10252)*

Line Drive Sports Center Inc..............G 336 824-1692
Ramseur *(G-10628)*

Mjt Us Inc..G 704 826-7828
Charlotte *(G-2510)*

NCR Voyix Corporation......................G 937 445-5000
Cary *(G-1406)*

Northrop Grumman Systems Corp.......D 252 225-0911
Atlantic *(G-638)*

Outer Banks Internet Inc....................G 252 441-6698
Kill Devil Hills *(G-7318)*

Quinsite LLC Fka Mile 5 Anlyti.............F 317 313-5152
Chapel Hill *(G-1565)*

Raleigh Ventures Inc..........................G 910 350-0036
Wilmington *(G-12895)*

Richa Inc..G 704 944-0230
Charlotte *(G-2724)*

Richa Inc..F 704 331-9744
Charlotte *(G-2725)*

S & A Cherokee LLC..........................E 919 674-6020
Cary *(G-1443)*

Stitchmaster LLC...............................F 336 852-6448
Greensboro *(G-5841)*

Telepathic Graphics Inc.....................E 919 342-4603
Raleigh *(G-10540)*

7375 Information retrieval services

Bluetick Inc.......................................F 336 294-4102
Greensboro *(G-5395)*

Carolina Connections Inc...................G 336 786-7030
Mount Airy *(G-9107)*

Elxr Health Inc...................................G 919 917-8484
Durham *(G-4018)*

Quinsite LLC Fka Mile 5 Anlyti.............F 317 313-5152
Chapel Hill *(G-1565)*

◆ Vrush Industries Inc.......................G 336 886-7700
High Point *(G-6829)*

7376 Computer facilities management

Infobelt LLC.......................................F 980 223-4000
Charlotte *(G-2331)*

7378 Computer maintenance and repair

Artesian Future Technology LLC.........G 919 904-4940
Chapel Hill *(G-1529)*

Biz Technology Solutions LLC.............E 704 658-1707
Mooresville *(G-8615)*

Carolina Cartridge Systems Inc..........E 704 347-2447
Charlotte *(G-1844)*

Complete Comp St of Ralgh Inc..........E 919 828-5227
Raleigh *(G-10005)*

Comtech Group Inc.............................G 919 313-4800
Durham *(G-3986)*

Innait Inc..G 406 241-5245
Charlotte *(G-2337)*

Northrop Grumman Systems Corp.......D 252 225-0911
Atlantic *(G-638)*

Silver Knight Pcs LLC........................G 910 824-2054
Fayetteville *(G-4670)*

St Investors Inc.................................D 704 969-7500
Charlotte *(G-2856)*

7379 Computer related services, nec

A4 Health Systems Inc.......................B 919 851-6177
Cary *(G-1283)*

Acterna LLC.......................................F 919 388-5100
Morrisville *(G-8918)*

Agingo Corporation............................G 888 298-0777
Charlotte *(G-1629)*

Blue Wolf Technologies LLP.................. G..... 919 810-1508
Raleigh *(G-9949)*

Bluetick Inc............................. F..... 336 294-4102
Greensboro *(G-5395)*

Champion Media LLC...................... E..... 704 746-3955
Mooresville *(G-8637)*

Computer Task Group Inc................. E..... 919 677-1313
Raleigh *(G-10006)*

Comtech Group Inc........................ G..... 919 313-4800
Durham *(G-3986)*

Consultants In Data Proc Inc............ G..... 704 542-6339
Charlotte *(G-1976)*

Digital Designs Inc...................... E..... 704 790-7100
Charlotte *(G-2046)*

Fred L Brown........................... G..... 336 643-7523
Summerfield *(G-11840)*

◆ Graphik Dimensions Limited.............. D..... 800 332-8884
High Point *(G-6634)*

Informtion Rtrval Cmpanies Inc......... E..... 919 460-7447
Cary *(G-1375)*

LDR Designs.............................. G..... 252 375-4484
Greenville *(G-6001)*

Logiksavvy Solutions LLC............... G..... 336 392-6149
Greensboro *(G-5663)*

Magic Mile Media Inc.................... F..... 252 572-1330
Kinston *(G-7421)*

NCR Voyix Corporation.................. G..... 937 445-5000
Cary *(G-1406)*

Onion Peel Software Inc................. G..... 919 460-1789
Morrisville *(G-9032)*

R N Lea Inc............................. G..... 919 247-5998
Raleigh *(G-10418)*

Romeo Six LLC........................... F..... 919 589-7150
Holly Springs *(G-6912)*

Sighttech LLC........................... G..... 855 997-4448
Charlotte *(G-2805)*

Southern Data Systems Inc.............. F..... 919 781-7603
Oxford *(G-9635)*

Synergem Technologies Inc............. E..... 866 859-0911
Mount Airy *(G-9182)*

Terida LLC.............................. F..... 910 693-1633
Pinehurst *(G-9704)*

The Computer Solution Company......... F..... 336 409-0782
Winston Salem *(G-13362)*

Thorco LLC.............................. F..... 919 363-6234
Cary *(G-1471)*

Twork Technology Inc.................... G..... 704 218-9675
Charlotte *(G-2956)*

Usat LLC................................ E..... 919 942-4214
Chapel Hill *(G-1587)*

Verdante Bioenergy Svcs LLC............ G..... 828 394-1246
Lenoir *(G-7643)*

◆ Vrush Industries Inc.................... G..... 336 886-7700
High Point *(G-6829)*

We Appit LLC............................ G..... 910 465-2722
Wilmington *(G-12946)*

7381 Detective and armored car services

A&B Integrators LLC..................... F..... 919 371-0750
Durham *(G-3876)*

Diebold Nixdorf Incorporated........... E..... 704 599-3100
Charlotte *(G-2044)*

7382 Security systems services

A&B Integrators LLC..................... F..... 919 371-0750
Durham *(G-3876)*

Absolute Security & Lock Inc........... G..... 336 322-4598
Roxboro *(G-10917)*

Advanced Detection Tech LLC............ E..... 704 663-1949
Mooresville *(G-8591)*

American Physcl SEC Group LLC......... G..... 919 363-1894
Apex *(G-134)*

Amplified Elctronic Design Inc......... F..... 336 223-4811
Greensboro *(G-5362)*

Automated Controls LLC................. G..... 704 724-7625
Huntersville *(G-6970)*

Campus Safety Products LLC............. G..... 919 321-1477
Durham *(G-3956)*

▲ Crest Electronics Inc................. G..... 336 855-6422
Greensboro *(G-5471)*

Diebold Nixdorf Incorporated........... E..... 704 599-3100
Charlotte *(G-2044)*

GNB Ventures LLC........................ F..... 704 488-4468
Charlotte *(G-2218)*

Integrated Info Systems Inc............ F..... 919 488-5000
Youngsville *(G-13476)*

Lelantos Group Inc...................... D..... 704 780-4127
Mooresville *(G-8709)*

Lunar International Tech LLC............ G..... 800 975-7153
Charlotte *(G-2441)*

▲ Marcon International Inc.............. E..... 704 455-9400
Harrisburg *(G-6113)*

Modern Lightning Protection Co......... F..... 252 756-3006
Greenville *(G-6005)*

One Source SEC & Sound Inc............. G..... 281 850-9487
Mooresville *(G-8739)*

Security Consult Inc.................... G..... 704 531-8399
Charlotte *(G-2782)*

◆ Tektone Sound & Signal Mfg Inc........ D..... 828 524-9967
Franklin *(G-4841)*

Teletec Corporation.................... F..... 919 954-7300
Raleigh *(G-10541)*

7384 Photofinish laboratories

Dtp Inc................................. G..... 336 272-5122
Greensboro *(G-5507)*

Sharpe Images Properties Inc........... E..... 336 724-2871
Winston Salem *(G-13334)*

7389 Business services, nec

3dductcleaning LLC...................... G..... 919 723-4512
Selma *(G-11282)*

760 Craft Works LLC..................... F..... 704 274-5216
Huntersville *(G-6962)*

A Stitch In Time........................ G..... 828 274-5193
Asheville *(G-422)*

Abercrombie Textiles Inc............... G..... 704 487-0935
Shelby *(G-11308)*

Accel Discount Tire.................... G..... 704 636-0323
Salisbury *(G-11012)*

Ad Spice Marketing LLC................. G..... 919 286-7110
Durham *(G-3880)*

Adoratherapy Inc....................... F..... 917 297-8904
Asheville *(G-423)*

Advanced Non-Lethal Tech Inc........... G..... 847 812-6450
Raleigh *(G-9880)*

Ahlberg Cameras Inc.................... F..... 910 523-5876
Wilmington *(G-12693)*

Aj & Raine Scrubs & More LLC........... G..... 646 374-5198
Charlotte *(G-1634)*

Akuratemp LLC.......................... G..... 828 708-7178
Arden *(G-249)*

Allfuel Hst Inc........................ F..... 919 868-9410
Hampstead *(G-6066)*

AlphaGraphics Pineville................ G..... 704 541-3678
Charlotte *(G-1655)*

American Rnovation Systems LLC......... G..... 336 313-6210
Thomasville *(G-11994)*

AMP Agency............................. G..... 704 430-2313
Polkton *(G-9812)*

Amy Smith.............................. G..... 828 352-1001
Burnsville *(G-1182)*

Anitas Marketing Concepts Inc.......... G..... 252 243-3993
Wilson *(G-12961)*

Apex Analytix LLC...................... C..... 336 272-4669
Greensboro *(G-5365)*

Appalachian Pipe Distrs LLC............ G..... 704 688-5703
Charlotte *(G-1684)*

▲ Aria Designs LLC..................... F..... 828 572-4303
Lenoir *(G-7573)*

Arisaka LLC............................ F..... 919 601-5625
Apex *(G-139)*

Asheville Color & Imaging Inc.......... G..... 828 774-5040
Asheville *(G-435)*

Atlantic Bankcard Center Inc........... G..... 336 855-9250
Greensboro *(G-5374)*

Ats Service Company LLC................ G..... 512 905-9005
Godwin *(G-5186)*

▲ Autoverters Inc...................... F..... 252 537-0426
Roanoke Rapids *(G-10731)*

▲ Bamal Corporation.................... F..... 980 225-7700
Charlotte *(G-1748)*

Bennett Brothers Yachts Inc............ E..... 910 772-9277
Wilmington *(G-12719)*

Bloom Ai Inc........................... G..... 704 620-2886
Cary *(G-1309)*

Blue Ridge Quick Print Inc............. G..... 828 883-2420
Brevard *(G-968)*

Brite Sky LLC.......................... G..... 757 589-4676
Godwin *(G-5187)*

Broome Sign Company.................... G..... 704 782-0422
Concord *(G-3325)*

Bryan Austin........................... G..... 336 841-6573
High Point *(G-6551)*

Bull City Designs LLC.................. E..... 919 908-6252
Durham *(G-3949)*

By-Design Black Oxide & TI LLC......... F..... 828 874-0610
Valdese *(G-12190)*

C&A Hockaday Transport LLC............. G..... 252 676-5956
Roanoke Rapids *(G-10734)*

Cablenc LLC............................ G..... 919 307-9065
Zebulon *(G-13506)*

Capital City Cuisine LLC............... G..... 919 432-2126
Raleigh *(G-9966)*

Carlton Enterprizes LLC................ G..... 919 534-5424
Rocky Point *(G-10877)*

Carolina Coastal Coatings Inc.......... F..... 910 346-9607
Maple Hill *(G-8025)*

Carolina Connections Inc............... G..... 336 786-7030
Mount Airy *(G-9107)*

Carolina Custom Draperies Inc.......... G..... 336 945-5190
Winston Salem *(G-13116)*

CBS Radio Holdings Inc................. E..... 704 319-9369
Charlotte *(G-1870)*

CD Dickie & Associates Inc............. F..... 704 527-9102
Charlotte *(G-1878)*

▲ Champion Thread Company.............. G..... 704 867-6611
Gastonia *(G-5018)*

Charlies Heating & Cooling LLC......... G..... 336 260-1973
Snow Camp *(G-11473)*

Chicopee Inc........................... G..... 919 894-4111
Benson *(G-786)*

Classy Sassy 5 Jewels Boutique......... G..... 252 481-8144
Greenville *(G-5954)*

Coding Institute LLC................... E..... 239 280-2300
Durham *(G-3980)*

Council Trnsp & Logistics LLC.......... G..... 910 322-7588
Fayetteville *(G-4579)*

Covington Barcoding Inc................ G..... 336 996-5759
Kernersville *(G-7260)*

Creative Brewing Company LLC........... G..... 919 297-8182
Smithfield *(G-11441)*

Creative Printers Inc.................. G..... 336 246-7746
West Jefferson *(G-12563)*

Creative Printers & Brks Inc........... G..... 828 321-4663
Andrews *(G-106)*

Crump Group USA Inc	C	936 465-5870	Nashville (G-9317)
Crypton Mills LLC	E	828 202-5875	Cliffside (G-3225)
Cupcake Stop Shop LLC	G	919 457-7900	Raleigh (G-10026)
Custom Finishers Inc	E	336 431-7141	High Point (G-6584)
CVC Equipment Company	G	704 300-6242	Cherryville (G-3063)
Cvmr (usa) Inc	C	828 288-3768	Union Mills (G-12188)
Danby Barcoding LLC	G	770 416-9845	Kernersville (G-7263)
Daniels Business Services Inc	E	828 277-8250	Asheville (G-483)
Day 3 Lwncare Ldscpg Prfctnist	G	910 574-8422	Fayetteville (G-4584)
DB CUSTOM CRAFTS LLC	F	336 867-4107	Winston Salem (G-13140)
Decolux USA	G	704 340-3532	Charlotte (G-2026)
▲ Delve Interiors LLC	C	336 274-4661	Greensboro (G-5495)
Designed For Joy	F	919 395-2884	Apex (G-150)
Dg Matrix Inc	G	724 877-7773	Cary (G-1349)
Distinctive Furniture Inc	G	828 754-3947	Lenoir (G-7600)
Diversified Intl Holdings Inc	G	910 777-7122	Winnabow (G-13064)
Dix Enterprises Inc	F	336 558-9512	High Point (G-6595)
Dreamship Inc	G	908 601-8152	Raleigh (G-10058)
Dronescape Pllc	G	704 953-3798	Charlotte (G-2066)
Drs Transportation Inc	G	919 215-2770	Raleigh (G-10060)
Eatclub Inc	G	609 578-7942	Chapel Hill (G-1542)
Educatrx Inc	G	980 328-0013	Monroe (G-8481)
Envirnmntal Cmfort Sltions Inc	E	980 272-7327	Kannapolis (G-7208)
▲ Environmental Supply Co Inc	F	919 956-9688	Durham (G-4027)
Esco Industries Inc	F	336 495-3772	Randleman (G-10647)
Every Day Carry LLc	F	203 231-0256	Winnabow (G-13065)
Evolution of Style LLC	G	914 329-3078	Charlotte (G-2132)
Exhibit World Inc	G	704 882-2272	Indian Trail (G-7080)
Extensive Builders LLC	G	980 621-3793	Salisbury (G-11050)
Exteriors Inc Ltd	G	919 325-2251	Spring Lake (G-11561)
Fast Pro Media LLC	G	704 799-8040	Cornelius (G-3599)
Fast Pro Media LLC	G	704 799-8040	Cornelius (G-3600)
Fines and Carriel Inc	G	919 929-0702	Chapel Hill (G-1547)
Firm Ascend LLC	G	704 464-3024	Charlotte (G-2154)
Fitch Sign Company Inc	G	704 482-2916	Shelby (G-11336)
Flores Crane Services LLC	F	704 243-4347	Waxhaw (G-12431)

Forward Dsptching Lgistics LLC	G	252 907-9797	Greenville (G-5977)
Franks Millwright Services	G	336 248-6692	Lexington (G-7689)
Fresh Point LLC	G	919 895-0790	Holly Springs (G-6902)
Froehling & Robertson Inc	E	804 264-2701	Raleigh (G-10120)
Frostie Bottom Tree Stand LLC	G	828 466-1708	Claremont (G-3113)
Galaxy Pressure Washing Inc	G	888 299-3129	Pineville (G-9729)
Galvix Inc	G	925 434-6243	Cary (G-1363)
Garage Shop LLC	F	980 500-0583	Denver (G-3784)
Gentrys Cabnt Doors	G	336 957-8787	Roaring River (G-10749)
Georges Sauces LLC	G	252 459-3084	Nashville (G-9320)
Gilmore Globl Lgstics Svcs Inc	D	919 277-2700	Morrisville (G-8982)
Go For Green Fleet Svcs LLC	G	803 306-3683	Charlotte (G-2221)
Goldsboro Neon Sign Co Inc	G	919 735-2035	Goldsboro (G-5217)
Gracefully Broken LLC	G	980 474-0309	Gastonia (G-5055)
Grahams Transportation LLC	G	910 627-6880	Fayetteville (G-4606)
Greenfield Energy LLC	F	910 509-1805	Wrightsville Beach (G-13431)
Gt Rhyno Construction LLC	G	919 737-3620	Raleigh (G-10151)
Harbor Lines LLC	G	910 279-3796	Wilmington (G-12802)
Hema Online Indian Btq LLC	G	919 771-4374	Apex (G-164)
High Five Enterprises Inc	G	828 279-5962	Weaverville (G-12492)
Hrtms Incorporated	G	919 741-5099	Raleigh (G-10178)
Imperial Falcon Group Inc	G	646 717-1128	Charlotte (G-2315)
◆ Implus Footcare LLC	B	800 446-7587	Durham (G-4073)
IMR Holdings LLC	G	980 287-8139	Charlotte (G-2318)
Inspiration Leather Design Inc	G	336 420-2265	Jamestown (G-7169)
Intelligent Apps LLC	G	919 628-6256	Raleigh (G-10205)
Intelligent Tool Corp	F	704 799-0449	Concord (G-3378)
Intersport Group Inc	G	814 968-3085	Vilas (G-12230)
J &D Contractor Service Inc	G	919 427-0218	Angier (G-122)
J R Cole Industries Inc	D	704 523-6622	Charlotte (G-2362)
J6 & Company LLC	F	336 997-4497	Winston Salem (G-13214)
▲ Jasie Blanks LLC	F	910 485-0016	Fayetteville (G-4621)
Jeld-Wen Inc	C	336 838-0292	North Wilkesboro (G-9536)
Jenkins Services Group LLC	G	704 881-3210	Catawba (G-1512)
Jennifer Mowrer	G	336 714-6462	Winston Salem (G-13216)
JFK Conferences LLC	E	980 255-3336	Fayetteville (G-4623)

Jfl LLC	G	919 440-3517	Farmville (G-4533)
JKS Motorsports Inc	G	336 722-4129	Winston Salem (G-13217)
Jubilee Screen Printing Inc	G	910 673-4240	West End (G-12555)
Just n Tyme Trucking LLC	G	704 804-9519	Charlotte (G-2383)
Justice Bearing LLC	G	800 355-2500	Mooresville (G-8701)
▲ K-M Machine Company Inc	D	910 428-2368	Biscoe (G-855)
K&K Holdings Inc	G	704 341-5567	Charlotte (G-2385)
Kaotic Parts LLC	G	919 766-6040	Raleigh (G-10229)
Katchi Tees Incorporated	G	252 315-4691	Wilson (G-12997)
Keel Labs Inc	G	917 848-9066	Morrisville (G-8997)
Kenn M LLC	G	678 755-6607	Raleigh (G-10233)
Kindled Provisions LLC	F	919 542-0792	Moncure (G-8407)
King Business Service Inc	G	910 610-1030	Laurinburg (G-7504)
Klearoptics Inc	G	760 224-6770	Lattimore (G-7480)
Knight Communications Inc	F	704 568-7804	Indian Trail (G-7086)
Label & Printing Solutions Inc	G	919 782-1242	Raleigh (G-10243)
LDR Designs	G	252 375-4484	Greenville (G-6001)
Legalis Dms LLC	F	919 741-8260	Raleigh (G-10252)
Lions Services Inc	B	704 921-1527	Charlotte (G-2425)
Livengood Innovations LLC	G	336 925-7604	Linwood (G-7879)
Livingston & Haven LLC	C	704 588-3670	Charlotte (G-2428)
Lucerno Dynamics LLC	G	317 294-1395	Cary (G-1398)
Luxor Hydration LLC	F	919 568-5047	Durham (G-4113)
◆ M & S Warehouse Inc	E	828 728-3733	Lenoir (G-7622)
M I Connection	F	704 662-3255	Mooresville (G-8717)
Make Solutions Inc	F	623 444-0098	Asheville (G-542)
Mark Stoddard	G	910 797-7214	Fayetteville (G-4634)
Marketing One Sportswear Inc	G	704 334-9333	Charlotte (G-2457)
Mdkscrubs LLC	G	980 250-4708	Charlotte (G-2483)
Merchant 1 Manufacturing LLC	G	336 617-3008	Summerfield (G-11844)
Meridian Prfmce Systems Inc	G	706 905-5637	Charlotte (G-2493)
Mijo Enterprises Inc	G	252 442-6806	Rocky Mount (G-10852)
Minges Printing & Advg Co	G	704 867-6791	Gastonia (G-5098)
Mjt Us Inc	G	704 826-7828	Charlotte (G-2510)
Mk Pro Logistics LLC	G	980 420-8156	Huntersville (G-7015)
Monk Lekeisha	G	910 385-0361	Goldsboro (G-5230)

Montgomery Logging Inc	G	910 572-2806
Troy (G-12163)		
Moore S Welding Service Inc	G	919 837-5769
Bear Creek (G-716)		
Mountain Homes of Wnc LLC	F	828 216-2546
Weaverville (G-12496)		
N3xt Inc	G	704 905-2209
Charlotte (G-2539)		
Nafshi Enterprises LLC	G	910 986-9888
Aberdeen (G-17)		
Nashville Wldg & Mch Works Inc	E	252 243-0113
Wilson (G-13008)		
NC Diesel Performance LLC	G	704 431-3257
Salisbury (G-11095)		
Neurametrix Inc	G	408 507-2366
Asheville (G-556)		
▲ Next World Design Inc	G	800 448-1223
Thomasville (G-12054)		
Ni4l Antennas and Elec LLC	G	828 738-6445
Moravian Falls (G-8810)		
North American Trade LLC	G	828 712-3004
Fletcher (G-4759)		
Northern Star Technologies Inc	G	516 353-3333
Indian Trail (G-7092)		
Nucleus Radiopharma Inc	E	980 483-1766
Davidson (G-3715)		
Nutrotonic LLC	F	855 948-0008
Charlotte (G-2590)		
Oak City Customs LLC	G	919 995-5561
Zebulon (G-13517)		
Occasions Group Inc	E	252 321-5805
Greenville (G-6009)		
Ocufii Inc	G	804 874-4036
Huntersville (G-7026)		
On Point Mobile Detailing LLC	G	404 593-8882
Charlotte (G-2597)		
Orlandos Cstm Design T-Shirts	G	919 220-5515
Durham (G-4160)		
Panaceutics Nutrition Inc	F	919 797-9623
Durham (G-4164)		
Patrice Brent	G	980 999-7217
Charlotte (G-2615)		
PC Signs & Graphics LLC	G	919 661-5801
Garner (G-4951)		
▲ Performance Additives LLC	F	215 321-4388
Pinehurst (G-9699)		
Performance Parts Intl LLC	F	704 660-1084
Mooresville (G-8748)		
Phynix Pc Inc	F	503 890-1444
Middlesex (G-8280)		
Piedmont Fiberglass Inc	E	828 632-8883
Statesville (G-11745)		
Piranha Industries Inc	G	704 248-7843
Charlotte (G-2639)		
Power and Ctrl Solutions LLC	G	704 609-9623
Charlotte (G-2649)		
▲ Powerlyte Paintball Game Pdts	G	919 713-4317
Raleigh (G-10381)		
Pramana LLC	G	910 233-5118
Cary (G-1426)		
Production Media Inc	F	919 325-0120
Raleigh (G-10400)		
Professnal Alterations EMB Inc	G	910 577-8484
Jacksonville (G-7139)		
▲ Promographix Inc	F	919 846-1379
Carolina Beach (G-1263)		
Prototech Manufacturing Inc	F	508 646-8849
Washington (G-12410)		
Quadron Holdings Inc	G	919 523-5376
Raleigh (G-10411)		
Quinlan Publishing Company	G	229 886-7995
Wilmington (G-12894)		

Raleigh Tees LLC	G	919 850-3378
Raleigh (G-10430)		
Randall Printing Inc	G	336 272-3333
Greensboro (G-5781)		
Random & Kind LLC	G	919 249-8809
Durham (G-4207)		
Rebecca Trickey	G	910 584-5549
Raeford (G-9850)		
Redtruc LLC	G	704 968-7888
Charlotte (G-2700)		
Retroject Inc	G	919 619-3042
Chapel Hill (G-1567)		
Richmond County Gmrs Inc	G	910 461-0260
Hamlet (G-6062)		
▲ Riley Technologies LLC	E	704 663-6319
Mooresville (G-8759)		
Rockgeist LLC	G	518 461-2009
Asheville (G-593)		
Rogers Knitting Inc	G	336 789-4155
Mount Airy (G-9172)		
Royal Textile Products Sw LLC	G	602 276-4598
Charlotte (G-2735)		
◆ Royce Too LLC	E	212 356-1627
Winston Salem (G-13324)		
Rucker Intrgrted Logistics LLC	G	704 352-2018
Charlotte (G-2741)		
S C I A Inc	G	919 387-7000
Cary (G-1444)		
▼ S P Co Inc	G	919 848-3599
Raleigh (G-10453)		
Salem One Inc	C	336 744-9990
Winston Salem (G-13325)		
Salon & Spa Design Services	G	919 556-6380
Wake Forest (G-12296)		
Salonexclusive Beauty LLC	G	704 488-3909
Charlotte (G-2750)		
▲ Sanford Transition Company Inc	E	919 775-4989
Sanford (G-11230)		
Scoggins Industrial Inc	F	252 977-9222
Sharpsburg (G-11307)		
SCR-Tech LLC	C	704 504-0191
Charlotte (G-2772)		
Screen Printers Unlimited LLC	G	336 667-8737
Wilkesboro (G-12650)		
Secured Shred	G	443 288-6375
Raleigh (G-10466)		
Serenity Home Services LLC	G	910 233-8733
Troutman (G-12150)		
Sg-Clw Inc	F	336 865-4980
Winston Salem (G-13331)		
Sign Shop of The Triangle Inc	G	919 363-3930
Apex (G-194)		
Signcaster Corporation	G	336 712-2525
Winston Salem (G-13336)		
Signs Etc	G	336 722-9341
Winston Salem (G-13337)		
Sitzer & Spuria Inc	G	919 929-0299
Chapel Hill (G-1572)		
Skyview Commercial Cleaning	G	704 858-0134
Charlotte (G-2812)		
Smissons Inc	C	660 537-3219
Clayton (G-3169)		
Southill Industrial Carving	G	336 472-5311
Thomasville (G-12072)		
Steel Supply and Erection Co	F	336 625-4830
Asheboro (G-399)		
Stephanie Baxter	G	803 203-8467
Lincolnton (G-7857)		
Structural 0201 LLC	E	240 288-8607
Trinity (G-12127)		
▲ Sv Plastics LLC	G	336 472-2242
Thomasville (G-12077)		

Tatum Galleries Inc	G	828 963-6466
Banner Elk (G-689)		
Tawnico LLC	G	704 606-2345
Charlotte (G-2900)		
Taylor Interiors LLC	F	980 207-3160
Charlotte (G-2901)		
Td Cloud Services	G	518 258-6788
Raleigh (G-10535)		
Textile Products Inc	E	704 636-6221
Salisbury (G-11124)		
The McQuackins Company LLC	G	980 254-2309
Gastonia (G-5153)		
Thompson Printing & Packg Inc	G	704 313-7323
Mooresboro (G-8587)		
Three Ladies and A Male LLC	G	704 287-1584
Charlotte (G-2916)		
Tony D Hildreth	F	910 276-1803
Laurel Hill (G-7488)		
Triangle Prcsion Dgnostics Inc	G	919 345-0110
Durham (G-4280)		
◆ Triple Crown International LLC	G	704 846-4983
Charlotte (G-2946)		
Tryhard Infinity LLC	G	252 269-0985
New Bern (G-9402)		
UGLy Essentials LLC	F	910 319-9945
Raleigh (G-10572)		
Ultimate Floor Cleaning	G	704 912-8978
Charlotte (G-2960)		
US Logoworks LLC	F	910 307-0312
Fayetteville (G-4691)		
Viiv Healthcare Company	A	919 483-2100
Durham (G-4298)		
Vote Owl LLC	G	919 264-1796
Raleigh (G-10596)		
Watson Steel & Iron Works LLC	E	704 821-7140
Matthews (G-8197)		
We Appit LLC	G	910 465-2722
Wilmington (G-12946)		
Whatz Cookin LLC	G	336 353-0227
Mount Airy (G-9193)		
White Tiger Btq & Candle Co	G	919 610-7244
Sanford (G-11249)		
WW&s Construction Inc	G	217 620-4042
Dallas (G-3693)		
Z Collection LLC	G	919 247-1513
Zebulon (G-13526)		
Zelaya Bros LLC	G	980 833-0099
Charlotte (G-3046)		
Zysense LLC	G	215 485-1955
Chapel Hill (G-1599)		

75 AUTOMOTIVE REPAIR, SERVICES AND PARKING

7513 Truck rental and leasing, without drivers

Dutchman Creek Self-Storage	G	919 363-8878
Apex (G-151)		
Security Self Storage	G	919 544-3969
Durham (G-4229)		
V M Trucking Inc	G	984 239-4853
Morehead City (G-8848)		

7514 Passenger car rental

Van Products Inc	E	919 878-7110
Raleigh (G-10582)		

7515 Passenger car leasing

Courtesy Ford Inc	G	252 338-4783
Elizabeth City (G-4384)		

7519 Utility trailer rental

C & M Enterprise Inc.............................. G 704 545-1180
Mint Hill *(G-8333)*

Readilite & Barricade Inc.................... F 919 231-8309
Raleigh *(G-10435)*

Spring Repair Service Inc...................... G 336 299-5660
Greensboro *(G-5832)*

7521 Automobile parking

▲ Custom Doors Incorporated............. F 704 982-2885
Albemarle *(G-67)*

7532 Top and body repair and paint shops

Jenkins Properties Inc.......................... E 336 667-4282
North Wilkesboro *(G-9537)*

▼ Mickey Truck Bodies Inc.................. B 336 882-6806
High Point *(G-6711)*

Quality Trck Bodies & Repr Inc............ E 252 245-5100
Elm City *(G-4466)*

R and L Collision Center Inc................ F 704 739-2500
Kings Mountain *(G-7381)*

Southern Classic Seating LLC.............. F 336 498-3130
Sophia *(G-11491)*

Thats A Good Sign Inc......................... G 301 870-0299
Bolivia *(G-887)*

Triangle Body Works Inc....................... G 336 788-0631
Winston Salem *(G-13371)*

7534 Tire retreading and repair shops

A 1 Tire Service Inc.............................. G 828 684-1860
Fletcher *(G-4716)*

Accel Discount Tire............................. G 704 636-0323
Salisbury *(G-11012)*

Advance Stores Company Inc.............. F 336 545-9091
Greensboro *(G-5341)*

Aiken-Black Tire Service Inc................ E 828 322-3736
Hickory *(G-6261)*

Albemarle Tire Retreading Inc............. G 704 982-4113
Albemarle *(G-59)*

Autosmart Inc...................................... G 919 210-7936
Apex *(G-142)*

Avery County Recapping Co Inc........... G 828 733-0161
Newland *(G-9424)*

Barnharts Tech Tire Repair Inc............ G 336 337-1569
Lexington *(G-7658)*

Beamer Tire & Auto Repair Inc............ F 336 882-7043
High Point *(G-6541)*

Big Tire Outfitters................................ G 919 568-9605
Mc Leansville *(G-8218)*

Bill Martin Inc...................................... G 704 873-0241
Statesville *(G-11671)*

Bray S Recapping Service Inc.............. E 336 786-6182
Mount Airy *(G-9105)*

Bridgestone Ret Operations LLC........... G 919 471-4468
Durham *(G-3941)*

Bridgestone Ret Operations LLC........... G 910 864-4106
Fayetteville *(G-4562)*

Bridgestone Ret Operations LLC........... F 704 861-8146
Gastonia *(G-5005)*

Bridgestone Ret Operations LLC........... G 919 778-0230
Goldsboro *(G-5202)*

Bridgestone Ret Operations LLC........... G 336 282-6646
Greensboro *(G-5399)*

Bridgestone Ret Operations LLC........... F 336 852-8524
Greensboro *(G-5400)*

Bridgestone Ret Operations LLC........... G 336 282-4695
Greensboro *(G-5401)*

Bridgestone Ret Operations LLC........... G 252 522-5126
Kinston *(G-7397)*

Bridgestone Ret Operations LLC........... G 919 872-6402
Raleigh *(G-9958)*

Bridgestone Ret Operations LLC........... G 919 872-6566
Raleigh *(G-9959)*

Bridgestone Ret Operations LLC........... G 252 243-5189
Wilson *(G-12973)*

Bridgestone Ret Operations LLC........... G 336 725-1580
Winston Salem *(G-13110)*

Burnett Darrill Stephen......................... G 828 287-8778
Spindale *(G-11545)*

Carolina Giant Tires Inc....................... F 919 609-9077
Henderson *(G-6149)*

Carolina Retread LLC........................... G 910 642-4123
Whiteville *(G-12578)*

Cecil Budd Tire Company LLC.............. F 919 742-2322
Siler City *(G-11403)*

Claybrook Tire Inc................................ G 336 573-3135
Stoneville *(G-11820)*

Closed Tire Company Inc..................... F 704 864-5464
Gastonia *(G-5022)*

College Sun Do.................................... G 910 521-9189
Pembroke *(G-9657)*

Colony Tire Corporation....................... G 252 973-0004
Rocky Mount *(G-10829)*

Crossroads Tire Store Inc.................... G 704 888-2064
Midland *(G-8285)*

Discount Tires & Auto Repair............... G 336 788-0057
Winston Salem *(G-13147)*

Downtown Tire Center Inc..................... G 828 693-1676
Hendersonville *(G-6203)*

◆ Dunlop Aircraft Tyres Inc................. E 336 283-0979
Mocksville *(G-8359)*

Ed S Tire Laurinburg Inc...................... G 910 277-0565
Laurinburg *(G-7498)*

Enfield Tire Service Inc........................ G 252 445-5016
Enfield *(G-4482)*

Falls Automotive Service Inc................ G 336 723-0521
Winston Salem *(G-13166)*

Foster Tire Sales Inc........................... G 336 248-6726
Lexington *(G-7688)*

▲ Global Veneer Sales Inc.................. G 336 885-5061
High Point *(G-6631)*

Go Ev and Go Green Corp.................... G 704 327-9040
Charlotte *(G-2220)*

Goodyear Tire & Rubber Company........ G 984 983-0161
Mebane *(G-8245)*

Greensboro Tire & Auto Service........... G 336 294-9495
Greensboro *(G-5578)*

Hall Tire and Battery Co Inc................. F 336 275-3812
Greensboro *(G-5586)*

Haneys Tire Recapping Svc LLC.......... G 910 276-2636
Laurinburg *(G-7503)*

Hardison Tire Co Inc............................ G 252 745-4561
Bayboro *(G-711)*

John Conrad Inc.................................. G 336 475-8144
Thomasville *(G-12041)*

Johnnys Tire Sales and Svc Inc........... F 252 353-8473
Greenville *(G-5997)*

Lewis Brothers Tire & Algnmt.............. G 919 359-9050
Clayton *(G-3157)*

M & M Tire and Auto Inc...................... G 336 643-7877
Summerfield *(G-11843)*

M & R Retreading & Oil Co Inc............ G 704 474-4101
Norwood *(G-9556)*

McCarthy Tire Service Company........... F 910 791-0132
Wilmington *(G-12849)*

Merchants Inc...................................... G 252 447-2121
Havelock *(G-6123)*

Mock Tire & Automotive Inc................. E 336 753-8473
Mocksville *(G-8379)*

Mock Tire & Automotive Inc................. E 336 774-0081
Winston Salem *(G-13256)*

▲ Mock Tire & Automotive Inc............. E 336 768-1010
Winston Salem *(G-13257)*

Moss Brothers Tires & Svc Inc............ G 910 895-4572
Rockingham *(G-10783)*

Mr Tire Inc.. G 828 262-3555
Boone *(G-936)*

Mr Tire Inc.. F 704 483-1500
Denver *(G-3794)*

Mr Tire Inc.. F 828 322-8130
Hickory *(G-6398)*

Mr Tire Inc.. G 704 739-6456
Kings Mountain *(G-7373)*

Mr Tire Inc.. G 828 758-0047
Lenoir *(G-7627)*

Mr Tire Inc.. G 704 735-8024
Lincolnton *(G-7846)*

Mr Tire Inc.. G 704 484-0816
Shelby *(G-11365)*

Mr Tire Inc.. G 704 872-4127
Statesville *(G-11737)*

Newfound Tire & Quick Lube Inc.......... G 828 683-3232
Leicester *(G-7528)*

Oakie S Tire & Recapping Inc.............. G 704 482-5629
Shelby *(G-11367)*

Parrish Tire Company........................... E 704 372-2013
Charlotte *(G-2614)*

Parrish Tire Company........................... F 336 334-9979
Greensboro *(G-5735)*

Parrish Tire Company........................... E 704 872-6565
Jonesville *(G-7198)*

◆ Parrish Tire Company....................... D 800 849-8473
Winston Salem *(G-13276)*

Perry Brothers Tire Svc Inc.................. F 919 693-2128
Oxford *(G-9623)*

Perry Brothers Tire Svc Inc.................. E 919 775-7225
Sanford *(G-11218)*

Phil S Tire Service Inc......................... G 828 682-2421
Burnsville *(G-1189)*

Piedmont Truck Tires Inc..................... F 828 277-1549
Asheville *(G-574)*

Piedmont Truck Tires Inc..................... F 828 202-5337
Conover *(G-3544)*

Piedmont Truck Tires Inc..................... F 336 223-9412
Graham *(G-5281)*

Piedmont Truck Tires Inc..................... E 336 668-0091
Greensboro *(G-5746)*

Pumpkin Pacific LLC............................ G 704 226-4176
Charlotte *(G-2677)*

Quality Investments Inc....................... E 252 492-8777
Henderson *(G-6172)*

R and R Auto Repr & Tires Inc............. G 336 784-6893
Winston Salem *(G-13310)*

Rabuns Trlr Repr Tire Svc Inc.............. G 704 764-7841
Monroe *(G-8547)*

▲ RDh Tire and Retread Company........ D 980 368-4576
Cleveland *(G-3220)*

Richmond Investment............................ E 910 410-8200
Rockingham *(G-10787)*

Safe Tire & Autos LLC......................... G 910 590-3101
Clinton *(G-3244)*

Small Brothers Tire Co Inc................... G 704 289-3531
Monroe *(G-8559)*

Snider Tire Inc..................................... D 704 373-2910
Charlotte *(G-2820)*

Snider Tire Inc..................................... F 336 691-5480
Greensboro *(G-5820)*

Snider Tire Inc..................................... G 828 324-9955
Hickory *(G-6450)*

Stoltz Automotive Inc........................... G 336 595-4218
Walkertown *(G-12317)*

Super Retread Center Inc..................... F 919 734-0073
Goldsboro *(G-5248)*

Tbc Retail Group Inc............................ G 336 540-8066
Greensboro *(G-5854)*

Team X-Treme LLC................................ G 919 562-8100
Rolesville *(G-10890)*

Thrifty Tire... G 919 220-7800
Durham *(G-4273)*

Tire Sls Svc Inc Fytteville NC................ E 910 485-1121
Fayetteville *(G-4682)*

Tires Incorporated of Clinton................. F 910 592-4741
Clinton *(G-3249)*

To The Top Tires and Svc LLC............... G 252 886-3286
Rocky Mount *(G-10816)*

Toe River Service Station LLC............... G 828 688-6385
Bakersville *(G-681)*

Towel City Tire & Wheel LLC................. G 704 933-2143
Kannapolis *(G-7222)*

Treadz LLC.. G 704 664-0995
Mooresville *(G-8787)*

Universal Tire Service Inc..................... G 919 779-8798
Raleigh *(G-10577)*

USA Tire Sales and Storage LLC........... G 910 424-5330
Fayetteville *(G-4692)*

Vestal Buick Gmc Inc........................... D 336 310-0261
Kernersville *(G-7312)*

Village Tire Center Inc.......................... G 919 862-8500
Raleigh *(G-10588)*

Whitaker S Tire Service Inc................... G 704 786-6174
Concord *(G-3468)*

White S Tire Svc Wilson Inc.................. G 252 237-0770
Wilson *(G-13046)*

White S Tire Svc Wilson Inc.................. D 252 237-5426
Wilson *(G-13047)*

Whites Tire Svc New Bern Inc............... G 252 633-1170
New Bern *(G-9407)*

Wilson Tire and Automotive Inc............. G 336 584-9638
Elon College *(G-4476)*

Woodlawn Tire and Algnmt Inc.............. G 828 756-4212
Marion *(G-8075)*

7536 Automotive glass replacement shops

A R Perry Corporation........................... G 252 492-6181
Henderson *(G-6146)*

Orare Inc.. G 919 742-1003
Siler City *(G-11422)*

Rice S Glass Company Inc.................... E 919 967-9214
Carrboro *(G-1272)*

7537 Automotive transmission repair shops

Bridgestone Ret Operations LLC........... G 336 282-4695
Greensboro *(G-5401)*

Parrish Tire Company........................... E 336 334-9979
Greensboro *(G-5735)*

7538 General automotive repair shops

Aiken-Black Tire Service Inc................. E 828 322-3736
Hickory *(G-6261)*

B & B Welding Inc................................ G 336 643-5702
Oak Ridge *(G-9569)*

Barnharts Tech Tire Repair Inc.............. G 336 337-1569
Lexington *(G-7658)*

Barrs Competition................................ F 704 482-5169
Shelby *(G-11313)*

Beamer Tire & Auto Repair Inc.............. F 336 882-7043
High Point *(G-6541)*

Bridgestone Ret Operations LLC........... G 336 282-4695
Greensboro *(G-5401)*

Container Technology Inc...................... G 910 350-1303
Wilmington *(G-12749)*

Courtesy Ford Inc................................ G 252 338-4783
Elizabeth City *(G-4384)*

Cummins Inc.. F 704 596-7690
Charlotte *(G-2003)*

Diagnostic Shop Inc............................. G 704 933-3435
Kannapolis *(G-7207)*

Discount Tires & Auto Repair................. G 336 788-0057
Winston Salem *(G-13147)*

F & C Repair and Sales LLC................. F 704 907-2461
Charlotte *(G-2139)*

Falls Automotive Service Inc................. G 336 723-0521
Winston Salem *(G-13166)*

Greensboro Tire & Auto Service............ G 336 294-9495
Greensboro *(G-5578)*

Griffin Automotive Marine Inc................ G 252 940-0714
Washington *(G-12388)*

Haneys Tire Recapping Svc LLC........... G 910 276-2636
Laurinburg *(G-7503)*

Jacks Motor Parts Inc........................... G 910 642-4077
Whiteville *(G-12586)*

John West Auto Service Inc.................. G 919 250-0825
Raleigh *(G-10218)*

Johnson Machine Co Inc....................... G 252 638-2620
New Bern *(G-9374)*

L & S Automotive Inc............................ G 704 391-7657
Charlotte *(G-2404)*

Lewis Brothers Tire & Algnmt................ G 919 359-9050
Clayton *(G-3157)*

◆ Mack Trucks Inc............................... A 336 291-9001
Greensboro *(G-5670)*

Mr Tire Inc... G 828 262-3555
Boone *(G-936)*

Mr Tire Inc... F 704 483-1500
Denver *(G-3794)*

Mr Tire Inc... F 828 322-8130
Hickory *(G-6398)*

Mr Tire Inc... G 704 739-6456
Kings Mountain *(G-7373)*

Mr Tire Inc... G 828 758-0047
Lenoir *(G-7627)*

Mr Tire Inc... G 704 735-8024
Lincolnton *(G-7846)*

Mr Tire Inc... G 704 484-0816
Shelby *(G-11365)*

Mr Tire Inc... G 704 872-4127
Statesville *(G-11737)*

NC Diesel Performance LLC.................. G 704 431-3257
Salisbury *(G-11095)*

Quality Investments Inc........................ E 252 492-8777
Henderson *(G-6172)*

R & J Mechanical & Welding LLC.......... G 919 362-6630
Apex *(G-191)*

R and R Auto Repr & Tires Inc.............. G 336 784-6893
Winston Salem *(G-13310)*

Rabuns Trlr Repr Tire Svc Inc............... G 704 764-7841
Monroe *(G-8547)*

S Strickland Diesel Svc Inc................... G 252 291-6999
Wilson *(G-13025)*

Satco Truck Equipment Inc................... F 919 383-5547
Durham *(G-4222)*

Snider Tire Inc..................................... F 336 691-5480
Greensboro *(G-5820)*

Spring Repair Service Inc..................... G 336 299-5660
Greensboro *(G-5832)*

Stoltz Automotive Inc........................... G 336 595-4218
Walkertown *(G-12317)*

Team X-Treme LLC............................... G 919 562-8100
Rolesville *(G-10890)*

Universal Tire Service Inc..................... G 919 779-8798
Raleigh *(G-10577)*

Wooten John.. G 828 322-4031
Hickory *(G-6490)*

Zickgraf Enterprises Inc....................... G 828 524-2313
Franklin *(G-4844)*

7539 Automotive repair shops, nec

A 1 Tire Service Inc............................. G 828 684-1860
Fletcher *(G-4716)*

Avery County Recapping Co Inc............. G 828 733-0161
Newland *(G-9424)*

B S R-Hess Race Cars Inc.................... E 704 547-0901
Charlotte *(G-1730)*

Barnharts Tech Tire Repair Inc.............. G 336 337-1569
Lexington *(G-7658)*

Beamer Tire & Auto Repair Inc.............. F 336 882-7043
High Point *(G-6541)*

Bridgestone Ret Operations LLC........... F 336 852-8524
Greensboro *(G-5400)*

▲ Broadsight Systems Inc.................... G 336 837-1272
Mebane *(G-8233)*

Carolina.. G 919 851-0906
Cary *(G-1321)*

Carolina Precision Mfg LLC.................. E 704 662-3480
Mooresville *(G-8632)*

▲ Chiron America Inc......................... D 704 587-9526
Charlotte *(G-1916)*

Claybrook Tire Inc............................... F 336 573-3135
Stoneville *(G-11820)*

Colfax Trailer & Repair LLC.................. G 336 993-8511
Colfax *(G-3275)*

Diagnostic Shop Inc............................. G 704 933-3435
Kannapolis *(G-7207)*

Discount Tires & Auto Repair................. G 336 788-0057
Winston Salem *(G-13147)*

Downtown Tire Center Inc..................... G 828 693-1676
Hendersonville *(G-6203)*

G T Racing Heads Inc.......................... G 336 905-7988
Sophia *(G-11489)*

Goldsboro Strter Altrntor Svc................ G 919 735-6745
Goldsboro *(G-5218)*

Hall Tire and Battery Co Inc................. F 336 275-3812
Greensboro *(G-5586)*

John Conrad Inc.................................. G 336 475-8144
Thomasville *(G-12041)*

Kaotic Parts LLC................................. G 919 766-6040
Raleigh *(G-10229)*

Mc Cullough Auto Elc & Assoc............. G 704 376-5388
Charlotte *(G-2475)*

Mock Tire & Automotive Inc.................. E 336 753-8473
Mocksville *(G-8379)*

Mock Tire & Automotive Inc.................. E 336 774-0081
Winston Salem *(G-13256)*

▲ Mock Tire & Automotive Inc............. E 336 768-1010
Winston Salem *(G-13257)*

Nichols Spdmtr & Instr Co Inc.............. G 336 273-2881
Greensboro *(G-5709)*

One Source SEC & Sound Inc.............. G 281 850-9487
Mooresville *(G-8739)*

Parrish Tire Company........................... E 336 334-9979
Greensboro *(G-5735)*

Performance Entps & Parts Inc............. G 336 621-6572
Greensboro *(G-5738)*

▲ Prevost Car (us) Inc....................... E 908 222-7211
Greensboro *(G-5763)*

Pumpkin Pacific LLC............................ G 704 226-4176
Charlotte *(G-2677)*

R and R Auto Repr & Tires Inc.............. G 336 784-6893
Winston Salem *(G-13310)*

R S Integrators Inc.............................. G 704 588-8288
Pineville *(G-9749)*

Rabuns Trlr Repr Tire Svc Inc............... G 704 764-7841
Monroe *(G-8547)*

Scattered Wrenches Inc........................ G 919 480-1605
Raleigh *(G-10460)*

Sonaron LLC.. G 808 232-6168
Fayetteville *(G-4672)*

Spring Repair Service Inc..................... G 336 299-5660
Greensboro *(G-5832)*

Stoltz Automotive Inc........................... G 336 595-4218
Walkertown *(G-12317)*

Subaru Folger Automotive.................... F 704 531-8888
Charlotte (G-2877)

Tbc Retail Group Inc.......................... G 336 540-8066
Greensboro (G-5854)

Treadz LLC..................................... G 704 664-0995
Mooresville (G-8787)

Whitaker S Tire Service Inc.................. G 704 786-6174
Concord (G-3468)

7542 Carwashes

B & D Enterprises Inc......................... G 704 739-2958
Kings Mountain (G-7348)

B&C Xterior Cleaning Svc Inc............... G 919 779-7905
Raleigh (G-9928)

7549 Automotive services, nec

Apb Wrecker Service LLC.................... G 704 400-0857
Charlotte (G-1681)

Capital Value Center Sls & Svc............ G 910 799-4060
Wilmington (G-12730)

Diagnostic Shop Inc.......................... G 704 933-3435
Kannapolis (G-7207)

Garage Shop LLC.............................. F 980 500-0583
Denver (G-3784)

Kaotic Parts LLC.............................. G 919 766-6040
Raleigh (G-10229)

Mr Tire Inc.................................... G 828 758-0047
Lenoir (G-7627)

Newfound Tire & Quick Lube Inc........... G 828 683-3232
Leicester (G-7528)

Orpak Usa Inc................................. F 201 441-9820
Greensboro (G-5727)

Pro-Motor Engines Inc....................... G 704 664-6800
Mooresville (G-8755)

Pumpkin Pacific LLC.......................... G 704 226-4176
Charlotte (G-2677)

Richard Chldress Racg Entps In........... E 336 731-3334
Welcome (G-12513)

▲ Richard Chldress Racg Entps In...... B 336 731-3334
Welcome (G-12514)

Specialty Trnsp Systems Inc................ G 828 464-9738
Newton (G-9498)

76 MISCELLANEOUS REPAIR SERVICES

7622 Radio and television repair

Sonaron LLC................................... G 808 232-6168
Fayetteville (G-4672)

7623 Refrigeration service and repair

Chichibone Inc................................ F 919 785-0090
Kernersville (G-7256)

Daikin Applied Americas Inc................ G 704 588-0087
Charlotte (G-2014)

Diagnostic Shop Inc.......................... G 704 933-3435
Kannapolis (G-7207)

Environmental Specialties LLC............. D 919 829-9300
Raleigh (G-10088)

Johnson Controls Inc......................... D 919 743-3500
Raleigh (G-10219)

Trs-Sesco LLC................................. D 336 996-2220
Kernersville (G-7310)

7629 Electrical repair shops

A & W Electric Inc............................ E 704 333-4986
Charlotte (G-1604)

▲ Advanced Electronic Svcs Inc.......... E 336 789-0792
Mount Airy (G-9096)

Allan Drth Sons Gnrtor Sls Svc............ G 828 526-9325
Highlands (G-6842)

▲ Anuva Services Inc........................ F 919 468-6441
Morrisville (G-8928)

Applied Drives Inc............................ G 704 573-2324
Charlotte (G-1686)

Bsh Home Appliances Corp.................. B 252 672-9155
New Bern (G-9343)

◆ Conversant Products Inc..................G 919 465-3456
Cary (G-1334)

Eaton Corporation............................ D 864 433-1603
Raleigh (G-10073)

Eaton Corporation............................ C 919 872-3020
Raleigh (G-10074)

Eaton Power Quality Corp................... F 919 872-3020
Raleigh (G-10075)

▲ Eaton Power Quality Group Inc......... G 919 872-3020
Raleigh (G-10076)

Edge Broadband Solutions LLC............ E 828 785-1420
Waynesville (G-12457)

Electric Motor Service of Shelby Inc...... F 704 482-9979
Shelby (G-11333)

Electrical Equipment Company............. E 910 276-2141
Laurinburg (G-7500)

▲ Esco Electronic Services Inc............ F 252 753-4433
Farmville (G-4528)

Eversharp Saw & Tool Inc.................. G 828 345-1200
Hickory (G-6330)

GE Vernova International LLC............... E 704 587-1300
Charlotte (G-2194)

Genelect Services Inc........................ F 828 255-7999
Asheville (G-505)

Presley Group Ltd............................ D 828 254-9971
Asheville (G-584)

Protronics Inc................................. F 919 217-0007
Knightdale (G-7457)

SCR Controls Inc.............................. F 704 821-6651
Matthews (G-8192)

Superior Machine Co SC Inc................ E 828 652-6141
Marion (G-8068)

Trans East Inc................................. D 910 892-1081
Dunn (G-3869)

Transformer Sales & Service............... G 910 594-1495
Newton Grove (G-9519)

7631 Watch, clock, and jewelry repair

D C Crsman Mfr Fine Jwly Inc............. G 828 252-9891
Asheville (G-482)

Donald Haack Diamonds Inc................ G 704 365-4400
Charlotte (G-2062)

Dons Fine Jewelry Inc........................ G 336 724-7826
Clemmons (G-3181)

Jkl Inc... F 252 355-6714
Greenville (G-5996)

John Laughter Jewelry Inc.................. G 828 456-4772
Waynesville (G-12462)

Made By Custom LLC........................ G 704 980-9840
Charlotte (G-2447)

R Gregory Jewelers Inc...................... F 704 872-6669
Statesville (G-11758)

Southern Digital Watch Repair............. G 336 299-6718
Greensboro (G-5825)

Stonehaven Jewelry Gallery Ltd........... G 919 462-8888
Cary (G-1468)

Sumpters Jwly & Collectibles.............. G 704 399-5348
Charlotte (G-2879)

7641 Reupholstery and furniture repair

Barker and Martin Inc....................... G 336 275-5056
Greensboro (G-5385)

Bedex LLC..................................... E 336 617-6755
High Point (G-6544)

▲ Brice Manufacturing Co Inc.............. E 818 896-2938
Greensboro (G-5398)

Davidson House Inc.......................... F 704 791-0171
Davidson (G-3701)

Freedom Enterprise LLC..................... G 502 510-7296
Charlotte (G-2177)

▲ Fulfords Restorations...................... G 252 243-7727
Wilson (G-12992)

◆ Hughes Furniture Inds Inc................C 336 498-8700
Randleman (G-10650)

Ledford Upholstery........................... G 704 732-0233
Lincolnton (G-7836)

Moores Upholstering Interiors............. G 704 240-8393
Lincolnton (G-7845)

Otto and Moore Inc........................... F 336 887-0017
High Point (G-6722)

Rufco Inc...................................... G 919 829-1332
Wake Forest (G-12294)

S Dorsett Upholstery Inc.................... G 336 472-7076
Thomasville (G-12070)

◆ S Kivett Inc................................. F 910 592-0161
Clinton (G-3243)

▲ Stone Marble Co Inc...................... G 773 227-1161
Thomasville (G-12075)

Touch Up Solutions Inc...................... E 828 428-9094
Maiden (G-8019)

Unique Office Solutions Inc................. F 336 854-0900
Greensboro (G-5890)

7692 Welding repair

277 Metal Inc.................................. G 704 372-4513
Gastonia (G-4980)

A&W Welding Inc.............................. G 252 482-3233
Edenton (G-4358)

Advanced Machine Services LLC........... G 910 410-0099
Rockingham (G-10769)

Airgas Usa LLC................................ G 704 636-5049
Salisbury (G-11014)

Alloy Fabricators Inc......................... E 704 263-2281
Alexis (G-102)

Ansonville Piping & Fabg Inc............... G 704 826-8403
Ansonville (G-129)

Arc3 Gases Inc................................ G 336 275-3333
Greensboro (G-5367)

Arc3 Gases Inc................................ G 704 220-1029
Monroe (G-8429)

Arc3 Gases Inc................................ E 910 892-4016
Dunn (G-3844)

Archie S Steel Service Inc.................. G 252 355-5007
Greenville (G-5938)

Ashevlle Prcsion Mch Rblding I............ G 828 254-0884
Asheville (G-442)

Avery Machine & Welding Co............... G 828 733-4944
Fayetteville (G-4556)

B & D Enterprises Inc......................... G 704 739-2958
Kings Mountain (G-7348)

Badger Welding Incorporated............... G 828 863-2078
Rutherfordton (G-10976)

Bentons Wldg Repr & Svcs Inc............. G 910 343-8322
Wilmington (G-12720)

Blacksand Metal Works LLC................ F 703 489-8282
Fayetteville (G-4558)

Bladen Fabricators LLC...................... G 910 866-5225
Bladenboro (G-874)

Blue Light Welding of Triad................. G 336 442-9140
Winston Salem (G-13109)

▲ Boyd Welding and Mfg Inc............... F 828 247-0630
Forest City (G-4785)

Brasingtons Inc............................... G 704 694-5191
Wadesboro (G-12236)

C & B Welding & Fab Inc.................... G 704 435-6942
Bessemer City (G-807)

C & J Welding Inc............................ G 919 552-0275
Holly Springs (G-6896)

Calhoun Welding Inc........................ G 252 281-1455	Gibbs Machine Company Incorporated. E 336 856-1907	Mikes Welding & Fabricating.............. G 336 472-5804
Macclesfield *(G-7979)*	Greensboro *(G-5559)*	Thomasville *(G-12048)*
Carolina 1926 LLC.......................... G 828 251-2500	Glovers Welding LLC........................ F 252 586-7692	Miller Sheet Metal Co Inc................. G 336 751-2304
Asheville *(G-468)*	Littleton *(G-7886)*	Mocksville *(G-8378)*
Carolina Welding & Cnstr................. G 252 814-8740	Gonzalez Welding Inc....................... G 336 270-8179	Mitchell Welding Inc....................... E 828 765-2620
Kinston *(G-7400)*	Graham *(G-5269)*	Spruce Pine *(G-11583)*
▲ Carotek Inc.............................. D 704 844-1100	Gore S Mar Met Fabrication Inc.......... G 910 763-6066	Modern Machine and Metal .... D 336 993-4808
Matthews *(G-8103)*	Wilmington *(G-12793)*	Winston Salem *(G-13258)*
Chapman Welding LLC..................... G 919 951-8131	Gunmar Machine Corporation............ F 910 738-6295	Modlins Anonized Aluminum Wldg....... G 252 753-7274
Efland *(G-4374)*	Lumberton *(G-7956)*	Farmville *(G-4536)*
Clayton Welding............................ G 252 717-5909	Hales Welding and Fabrication........... G 252 907-5508	Montys Welding & Fabrication............ G 919 337-7859
Washington *(G-12380)*	Macclesfield *(G-7980)*	Garner *(G-4946)*
Coastal Machine & Welding Inc.......... G 910 754-6476	Hancock & Grandson Inc.................. G 252 728-2416	Moore S Welding Service Inc............. G 919 837-5769
Shallotte *(G-11302)*	Beaufort *(G-729)*	Bear Creek *(G-716)*
Collins Fabrication & Wldg LLC.......... G 704 861-9326	Harbor Welding Inc........................ G 252 473-3777	▲ Moores Mch Co Fayetteville Inc....... D 919 837-5354
Gastonia *(G-5024)*	Wanchese *(G-12343)*	Bear Creek *(G-717)*
Container Technology Inc................. G 910 350-1303	High Speed Welding LLC................... F 910 632-4427	▲ MTS Holdings Corp Inc................. E 336 227-0151
Wilmington *(G-12749)*	Wilmington *(G-12805)*	Burlington *(G-1133)*
▲ Custom Enterprises Inc................ G 336 226-8296	Highs Welding Shop........................ G 704 624-5707	Nashville Wldg & Mch Works Inc......... E 252 243-0113
Burlington *(G-1081)*	Marshville *(G-8090)*	Wilson *(G-13008)*
Custom Machine Company Inc........... F 704 629-5326	Idustrial Burkett Services................. G 252 244-0143	Newriverwelding............................ G 336 413-3040
Bessemer City *(G-811)*	Vanceboro *(G-12217)*	Mocksville *(G-8381)*
Cwi Services LLC........................... G 704 560-9755	▼ Imagination Fabrication................. G 919 280-4430	Nic Nac Welding Co........................ G 704 502-5178
Southport *(G-11518)*	Apex *(G-167)*	Charlotte *(G-2567)*
Dales Welding Service..................... G 919 872-6969	Industrial Mch Solutions Inc............. G 919 872-0016	Ninos Wldg & Cnstr Svcs LLC........... G 980 214-5804
Raleigh *(G-10034)*	Raleigh *(G-10191)*	Huntersville *(G-7021)*
David Bennett............................... G 919 798-3424	Industrial Metal Maint Inc................. G 910 285-3240	OHerns Welding Inc........................ G 910 484-2087
Fuquay Varina *(G-4877)*	Teachey *(G-11988)*	Fayetteville *(G-4647)*
David West................................... G 910 271-0757	Industrial Welding &....................... G 910 309-8540	Olive HI Wldg Fabrication Inc............ E 336 597-0737
Willard *(G-12665)*	Fayetteville *(G-4616)*	Roxboro *(G-10935)*
Davis Davis Mch & Wldg Co Inc......... F 252 443-2652	Iv-S Metal Stamping Inc................... E 336 861-2100	Paul Casper Inc............................ G 919 269-5362
Rocky Mount *(G-10830)*	Archdale *(G-229)*	Zebulon *(G-13520)*
Diversified Welding and Steel............ G 704 504-1111	J A King...................................... G 800 327-7727	Perkins Fabrications Inc.................. G 828 688-3157
Pineville *(G-9725)*	Raleigh *(G-10212)*	Bakersville *(G-680)*
Donald Auton............................... G 704 872-7528	J R Nixon Welding.......................... G 252 221-4574	Peter J Hamann............................ G 910 484-7877
Statesville *(G-11690)*	Tyner *(G-12183)*	Fayetteville *(G-4654)*
Donalds Welding Inc....................... F 910 298-5234	Jack A Farrior Inc.......................... D 252 753-2020	Piedmont Weld & Pipe Inc................ G 704 782-7774
Chinquapin *(G-3082)*	Farmville *(G-4532)*	Concord *(G-3418)*
Dunavants Welding & Steel Inc.......... G 252 338-6533	Jax Specialty Welding LLC............... G 704 380-3548	Powell Welding Inc......................... G 828 433-0831
Camden *(G-1211)*	Statesville *(G-11718)*	Drexel *(G-3830)*
Dutchman Creek Self-Storage........... G 919 363-8878	Joe Robin Darnell.......................... G 704 482-1186	Precision Fabricators Inc................. G 336 835-4763
Apex *(G-151)*	Shelby *(G-11350)*	Ronda *(G-10897)*
Eddies Welding Inc........................ G 704 585-2024	K & W Welding LLC........................ G 910 895-9220	Quillen Welding Services LLC............ G 252 269-4908
Stony Point *(G-11833)*	Rockingham *(G-10781)*	Morehead City *(G-8840)*
Estes Machine Co.......................... F 336 786-7680	Kenny Robinson S Wldg Svc Inc......... G 760 213-6454	R & H Welding LLC......................... G 919 763-7955
Mount Airy *(G-9119)*	Liberty *(G-7769)*	Garner *(G-4957)*
Everettes Industrial Repr Svc............ F 252 527-4269	Kings Prtble Wldg Fbrction LLC.......... G 336 789-2372	R & J Mechanical & Welding LLC........ G 919 362-6630
Goldsboro *(G-5213)*	Mount Airy *(G-9142)*	Apex *(G-191)*
Fabrication Associates Inc............... D 704 535-8050	Larry D Troxler............................. G 336 585-1141	Relentless Wldg & Fabrication............ G 336 402-3749
Charlotte *(G-2140)*	Gibsonville *(G-5180)*	High Point *(G-6755)*
Filer Micro Welding........................ G 828 248-1813	Limitless Wldg Fabrication LLC.......... G 252 753-0660	Richards Welding and Repr Inc.......... G 828 396-8705
Forest City *(G-4790)*	Farmville *(G-4534)*	Granite Falls *(G-5320)*
Flores Welding Inc......................... G 919 838-1060	Lloyds Fabricating Solutions............. F 336 250-0154	Richards Wldg Met Fbrction LLC......... F 919 626-0134
Raleigh *(G-10112)*	Thomasville *(G-12045)*	Wendell *(G-12544)*
Franks Millwright Services................ G 336 248-6692	Lumsden Welding Company............... G 910 791-6336	Rickys Welding Inc......................... G 252 336-4437
Lexington *(G-7689)*	Wilmington *(G-12842)*	Shiloh *(G-11394)*
Freeman Custom Welding Inc............ G 919 210-6267	Lyerlys Wldg & Fabrication Inc........... G 704 680-2317	Robert Raper Welding Inc................ G 252 399-0598
Raleigh *(G-10119)*	Gold Hill *(G-5195)*	Wilson *(G-13023)*
Full Throttle Fabrication LLC............. G 910 770-1180	Marc Machine Works Inc.................. F 704 865-3625	Robinsons Welding Service............... G 336 622-3150
Chadbourn *(G-1519)*	Gastonia *(G-5091)*	Liberty *(G-7777)*
Fusion Welding.............................. G 508 320-3525	Marine Fabrications LLC.................. G 252 473-4767	Rocas Welding LLC........................ G 252 290-2233
Rocky Point *(G-10879)*	Wanchese *(G-12345)*	Durham *(G-4217)*
Gamma Js Inc............................... F 336 294-3838	Martin Welding Inc......................... G 919 436-8805	Roderick Mch Erectors Wldg Inc........ G 910 343-0381
Greensboro *(G-5547)*	Garner *(G-4939)*	Wilmington *(G-12901)*
Gary Tucker................................. G 919 837-5724	Maynard S Fabricators Inc............... G 336 230-1048	Rose Welding & Crane Service I......... G 252 796-9171
Bear Creek *(G-714)*	Greensboro *(G-5684)*	Columbia *(G-3296)*
General Mch Wldg of Burlington......... G 336 227-5400	Mechanical Maintenance Inc............. F 336 676-7133	Roxboro Welding............................ G 336 364-2307
Burlington *(G-1094)*	Climax *(G-3227)*	Roxboro *(G-10943)*
General Refrigeration Company.......... G 919 661-4727	Medley S Garage Welding................. G 336 674-0422	Royal Welding LLC......................... G 704 750-9353
Garner *(G-4929)*	Pleasant Garden *(G-9792)*	Pineville *(G-9750)*
George F Wlson Wldg Fbrication......... G 828 262-1668	Metal ARC.................................... G 910 770-1180	S Oakley Machine Shop Inc............... G 336 599-6105
Boone *(G-916)*	Whiteville *(G-12588)*	Roxboro *(G-10944)*

Southeastern Mch & Wldg Co Inc............. E 910 791-6661
Wilmington *(G-12925)*

Steel Supply and Erection Co.................. F 336 625-4830
Asheboro *(G-399)*

Stewarts Garage and Welding Co.......... G 336 983-5563
Tobaccoville *(G-12103)*

Storybook Farm Metal Shop Inc............. G 919 967-9491
Chapel Hill *(G-1574)*

Strickland Bros Entps Inc...................... F 252 478-3058
Spring Hope *(G-11560)*

Technique Chassis LLC.......................... E 517 819-3579
Concord *(G-3454)*

Thomas Welding Service Inc................... G 919 471-6852
Durham *(G-4272)*

Thornburg Machine & Sup Co Inc........... E 704 735-5421
Lincolnton *(G-7864)*

Thurman Toler.. G 252 758-4082
Greenville *(G-6027)*

▼ Tool-Weld LLC.................................... G 843 986-4931
Rutherfordton *(G-10995)*

Trefena Welds.. G 203 551-1370
Browns Summit *(G-1006)*

Triplett & Coffey Inc............................... F 828 263-0561
Boone *(G-947)*

United Services Group LLC.................... G 980 237-1335
Charlotte *(G-2962)*

United Technical Services LLC............... F 980 237-1335
Charlotte *(G-2963)*

United TI & Stamping Co NC Inc............. D 910 323-8588
Fayetteville *(G-4687)*

Villabona Iron Works Inc........................ F 252 522-4005
Kinston *(G-7434)*

W D Lee & Company.............................. G 704 864-0346
Gastonia *(G-5163)*

W E Nixons Wldg & Hdwr Inc................. G 252 221-4348
Edenton *(G-4373)*

Wallace Welding Inc............................... F 919 934-2488
Smithfield *(G-11469)*

Walls Welding.. G 919 201-7544
Creedmoor *(G-3657)*

Warsaw Welding Service Inc.................. G 910 293-4261
Warsaw *(G-12368)*

Waste Container Repair Svcs.................. G 910 257-4474
Fayetteville *(G-4696)*

Webb S Maint & Piping Inc..................... F 252 972-2616
Battleboro *(G-709)*

Welding Company.................................. G 336 667-0265
Wilkesboro *(G-12662)*

Welding Shop LLC.................................. F 252 982-6567
Wanchese *(G-12348)*

Welding Solutions LLC........................... G 828 665-4363
Fletcher *(G-4778)*

Welding Spc & Mech Svcs Inc................ G 919 662-7898
Garner *(G-4973)*

Wells Mechanical Services LLC............. G 252 532-2632
Roanoke Rapids *(G-10743)*

West Stanly Fabrication Inc.................... G 704 254-2967
Oakboro *(G-9585)*

Wilkes Welding and Mch Co Inc............. G 336 670-2742
Mc Grady *(G-8217)*

▲ Wilson Mold & Machine Corp............. D 252 243-1831
Wilson *(G-13049)*

Youngs Welding & Machine Svcs.......... G 910 488-1190
Fayetteville *(G-4702)*

Zickgraf Enterprises Inc........................ G 828 524-2313
Franklin *(G-4844)*

7694 Armature rewinding shops

A & W Electric Inc................................. E 704 333-4986
Charlotte *(G-1604)*

American Rewinding Nc Inc.................... E 704 289-4177
Monroe *(G-8422)*

American Rewinding of NC Inc................ E 704 589-1020
Monroe *(G-8423)*

Averitt Enterprises Inc.......................... F 910 276-1294
Laurinburg *(G-7492)*

▲ B & M Electric Motor Service............ G 828 267-0829
Hickory *(G-6268)*

Blue Ridge Elc Mtr Repr Inc................... G 828 258-0800
Asheville *(G-455)*

Bowden Electric Motor Svc Inc............... G 252 446-4203
Rocky Mount *(G-10825)*

Brigman Electric Motors Inc................... G 828 492-0568
Canton *(G-1246)*

Brittenhams Rebuilding Service............ G 252 332-3181
Ahoskie *(G-44)*

C & S Repair Center Inc......................... G 610 524-9724
New Bern *(G-9346)*

Canipe & Lynn Elc Mtr Repr Inc............. G 828 322-9052
Hickory *(G-6282)*

Clayton Electric Mtr Repr Inc................. F 336 584-3756
Elon College *(G-4473)*

Consolidated Truck Parts Inc................. G 704 279-5543
Rockwell *(G-10794)*

Cornell & Ferencz Inc............................ G 919 736-7373
Goldsboro *(G-5210)*

▲ Custom Industries Inc....................... E 336 299-2885
Greensboro *(G-5481)*

Dixie Electro Mech Svcs Inc.................. F 704 332-1116
Charlotte *(G-2057)*

Electric Motor Rewinding Inc................. G 252 338-8856
Elizabeth City *(G-4387)*

Electric Motor Service of Shelby Inc...... F 704 482-9979
Shelby *(G-11333)*

Electric Motor Svc Ahoskie Inc.............. G 252 332-4364
Ahoskie *(G-48)*

Electric Mtr Sls Svc Pitt Cnty................ G 252 752-3170
Greenville *(G-5973)*

Electric Mtr Sp Wake Frest Inc.............. E 252 446-4173
Rocky Mount *(G-10835)*

Electric Mtr Sp Wake Frest Inc.............. E 919 556-3229
Wake Forest *(G-12274)*

Electrical Equipment Company............... E 910 276-2141
Laurinburg *(G-7500)*

Elektran Inc... G 910 997-6640
Rockingham *(G-10776)*

Energetics Inc....................................... G 910 483-2581
Fayetteville *(G-4597)*

▲ Esco Electronic Services Inc............ F 252 753-4433
Farmville *(G-4528)*

G-4 Electric Inc..................................... F 336 495-0500
Asheboro *(G-358)*

GE Vernova International LLC................. E 704 587-1300
Charlotte *(G-2194)*

General Motor Repair & Svc Inc............. G 336 292-1715
Greensboro *(G-5555)*

Hammond Electric Motor Company......... F 704 983-3178
Albemarle *(G-77)*

Hanover Electric Motor Svc Inc.............. G 910 762-3702
Wilmington *(G-12799)*

Heart Electric Motor Service.................. G 704 922-4720
Bessemer City *(G-821)*

High Country Electric Mtrs LLC.............. G 336 838-4808
North Wilkesboro *(G-9534)*

Holland Supply Company........................ E 252 492-7541
Henderson *(G-6160)*

◆ Jenkins Electric Company.................. D 800 438-3003
Charlotte *(G-2368)*

Jenkins Electric II LLC........................... E 704 392-7371
Charlotte *(G-2369)*

Jordan Electric Motors Inc..................... F 919 708-7010
Staley *(G-11595)*

Kwik Elc Mtr Sls & Svc Inc.................... G 252 335-2524
Elizabeth City *(G-4395)*

Lake City Electric Motor Repr................. G 336 248-2377
Lexington *(G-7708)*

Leonard Electric Mtr Repr Inc................ G 336 625-2375
Asheboro *(G-373)*

Lingle Electric Repair Inc...................... F 704 636-5591
Salisbury *(G-11084)*

Maybin Emergency Power Inc................. G 828 697-1195
Zirconia *(G-13531)*

McKinney Electric & Mch Co Inc............ G 828 765-7910
Spruce Pine *(G-11581)*

Motor Shop Inc...................................... G 704 867-8488
Gastonia *(G-5103)*

Presley Group Ltd.................................. D 828 254-9971
Asheville *(G-584)*

Pumps Blowers & Elc Mtrs LLC............. G 919 286-4975
Durham *(G-4201)*

Purser Centl Rewinding Co Inc.............. F 704 786-3131
Concord *(G-3427)*

Randall Supply Inc................................. E 704 289-6479
Monroe *(G-8548)*

Rocky Mount Electric Motor LLC............ G 252 446-1510
Rocky Mount *(G-10868)*

Sanders Electric Motor Svc Inc.............. E 828 754-0513
Lenoir *(G-7638)*

Southern Electric Motor Co.................... G 919 688-7879
Durham *(G-4243)*

Stone Cllins Mtr Rewinding Inc.............. G 910 347-2775
Jacksonville *(G-7155)*

Tencarva Machinery Company LLC......... G 336 665-1435
Greensboro *(G-5858)*

Tigertek Industrial Svcs LLC.................. E 336 623-1717
Stoneville *(G-11832)*

W & W Electric Motor Shop Inc.............. G 910 642-2369
Whiteville *(G-12594)*

Watson Electrical Cnstr Co LLC............. D 252 756-4550
Greenville *(G-6033)*

Williams Electric Mtr Repr Inc............... G 919 859-9790
Sanford *(G-11250)*

XCEL Hrmetic Mtr Rewinding Inc........... G 704 694-6001
Wadesboro *(G-12253)*

7699 Repair services, nec

Absolute Security & Lock Inc.................. G 336 322-4598
Roxboro *(G-10917)*

Admiral Marine Pdts & Svcs Inc............. G 704 489-8771
Denver *(G-3767)*

Advantage Machinery Svcs Inc.............. E 336 463-4700
Yadkinville *(G-13435)*

▲ Aircraft Belts Inc.............................. E 919 956-4395
Creedmoor *(G-3635)*

Ashevlle Prcsion Mch Rblding I............. G 828 254-0884
Asheville *(G-442)*

▲ Atlantic Hydraulics Svcs LLC........... E 919 542-2985
Sanford *(G-11152)*

Auto Parts Fayetteville LLC.................... G 910 889-4026
Fayetteville *(G-4555)*

Autry Con Pdts & Bldrs Sup Co.............. G 704 504-8830
Charlotte *(G-1719)*

B&C Xterior Cleaning Svc Inc................. G 919 779-7905
Raleigh *(G-9928)*

Backwater Guns LLC.............................. G 910 399-1451
Wilmington *(G-12718)*

Barrs Competition.................................. F 704 482-5169
Shelby *(G-11313)*

Besi Machining LLC............................... F 919 218-9241
Youngsville *(G-13464)*

Blinds Plus Inc...................................... G 910 487-5196
Fayetteville *(G-4560)*

▲ Bowman-Hollis Manufacturing Co..... E 704 374-1500
Charlotte *(G-1805)*

Brant & Lassiter Septic Tank.................. G 252 587-4321
Potecasi *(G-9819)*

◆ Briggs-Shaffner Acquisition Co..........F 336 463-4272
  Yadkinville *(G-13439)*

Bwxt Investment Company.....................E 704 625-4900
  Charlotte *(G-1824)*

Campbell & Sons Machining Co...........G 704 394-0291
  Lincolnton *(G-7818)*

Carbide Saws Incorporated..................G 336 882-6835
  High Point *(G-6554)*

Carolina Electric Mtr Repr LLC.............G 704 289-3732
  Monroe *(G-8453)*

Carolina Machining Fabrication.............G 919 554-9700
  Youngsville *(G-13469)*

Carolina Textile Services Inc................G 910 843-3033
  Red Springs *(G-10665)*

▲ Carver Machine Works Inc ....D 252 975-3101
  Washington *(G-12378)*

Central Tool & Mfg Co Inc....................G 828 328-2383
  Hickory *(G-6294)*

Certified Lawnmower Inc.......................G 704 527-2765
  Belmont *(G-742)*

Cherokee Instruments Inc.....................F 919 552-0554
  Angier *(G-117)*

Chicago Tube and Iron Company...........D 704 781-2060
  Locust *(G-7890)*

Classic Cleaning LLC............................E 800 220-7101
  Raleigh *(G-9998)*

Dimill Enterprises LLC..........................G 919 629-2011
  Raleigh *(G-10046)*

Galaxy Pressure Washing Inc................G 888 299-3129
  Pineville *(G-9729)*

Gamble Associates Inc.........................F 704 375-9301
  Charlotte *(G-2187)*

Gastex LLC..G 704 824-9861
  Gastonia *(G-5050)*

▲ GE Aircraft Engs Holdings Inc...........A 919 361-4400
  Durham *(G-4043)*

GE Vernova International LLC................E 704 587-1300
  Charlotte *(G-2194)*

Glemco LLC...G 866 619-6707
  Statesville *(G-11703)*

▲ Grindtec Enterprises Corp.................G 704 636-1825
  Salisbury *(G-11060)*

Hamilton Indus Grinding Inc..................E 828 253-6796
  Asheville *(G-515)*

▲ Hickory Saw & Tool Inc ....E 828 324-5585
  Hickory *(G-6353)*

Hlmf Logistics Inc.................................G 704 782-0356
  Pineville *(G-9733)*

Holder Machine & Mfg Co.....................G 828 479-8627
  Robbinsville *(G-10759)*

▲ Hydro Service & Supplies Inc ....E 919 544-3744
  Durham *(G-4066)*

Indian Motorcycle Company..................G 704 879-4560
  Lowell *(G-7933)*

Inman Septic Tank Service Inc..............G 910 763-1146
  Wilmington *(G-12817)*

Irsi Automation Inc...............................G 336 303-5320
  Mc Leansville *(G-8224)*

J & W Service Incorporated..................G 336 449-4584
  Whitsett *(G-12611)*

◆ Jly Invstmnts Inc Fka Nwman Mc......E 336 273-8261
  Browns Summit *(G-1000)*

▲ Kayne & Son Custom Hdwr Inc ....G 828 665-1988
  Candler *(G-1228)*

Limitless Wldg Fabrication LLC.............G 252 753-0660
  Farmville *(G-4534)*

M & J Marine LLC ....F 252 249-0522
  Oriental *(G-9601)*

MAC Grading Co...................................G 910 531-4642
  Autryville *(G-649)*

Marinemax of North Carolina.................G 910 256-8100
  Wrightsville Beach *(G-13432)*

Maxson & Associates...........................G 336 632-0524
  Greensboro *(G-5683)*

McKinney Electric & Mch Co Inc...........G 828 765-7910
  Spruce Pine *(G-11581)*

▲ Measurement Controls Inc.................F 704 921-1101
  Charlotte *(G-2484)*

Moes Hndy Svcs Fnce Instl Mno...........G 910 712-1402
  Raeford *(G-9842)*

Motor Shop Inc.....................................G 704 867-8488
  Gastonia *(G-5103)*

Mulls Con & Septic Tanks Inc ....G 828 437-0959
  Morganton *(G-8883)*

National Container Group LLC..............G 704 393-9050
  Charlotte *(G-2544)*

Neal S Pallet Company Inc....................E 704 393-8568
  Charlotte *(G-2551)*

Noble Oil Services Inc..........................C 919 774-8180
  Sanford *(G-11212)*

Not Just Archery..................................G 828 294-7727
  Hickory *(G-6404)*

Petroleum Tank Corporation..................F 919 284-2418
  Kenly *(G-7235)*

▲ Prem Corp...E 704 921-1799
  Charlotte *(G-2660)*

Pro-Motor Engines Inc..........................G 704 664-6800
  Mooresville *(G-8755)*

Quality Equipment LLC.........................G 919 493-3545
  Durham *(G-4203)*

R E R Services.......................................G 818 993-1826
  Southport *(G-11526)*

▲ Raleigh Saw Co Inc...........................G 919 832-2248
  Raleigh *(G-10429)*

▲ Rk Enterprises LLC............................G 910 481-0777
  Fayetteville *(G-4663)*

Robert Hamms LLC...............................G 704 605-8057
  Monroe *(G-8552)*

Roderick Mch Erectors Wldg Inc...........G 910 343-0381
  Wilmington *(G-12901)*

Router Bit Service Company Inc............F 336 431-5535
  High Point *(G-6760)*

S & S Repair Service Inc.......................F 252 756-5989
  Winterville *(G-13423)*

Safe Air Systems Inc............................E 336 674-0749
  Randleman *(G-10659)*

Scattered Wrenches Inc........................G 919 480-1605
  Raleigh *(G-10460)*

Schindler Elevator Corporation..............F 910 590-5590
  Clinton *(G-3245)*

Spring Repair Service Inc......................G 336 299-5660
  Greensboro *(G-5832)*

Storybook Farm Metal Shop Inc............G 919 967-9491
  Chapel Hill *(G-1574)*

Sub-Aquatics Inc..................................E 336 674-0749
  Randleman *(G-10661)*

T Air Inc...D 980 595-2840
  Charlotte *(G-2895)*

▲ Techsouth Inc...................................G 704 334-1100
  Matthews *(G-8196)*

Timothy L Griffin..................................G 336 317-8314
  Greenville *(G-6028)*

Tk Elevator Corporation........................D 336 272-4563
  Greensboro *(G-5867)*

Todds Rv & Marine Inc..........................G 828 651-0007
  Hendersonville *(G-6245)*

Tool Rental Depot LLC...........................G 704 636-6400
  Salisbury *(G-11126)*

Tractor Country Inc..............................G 252 523-3007
  Dover *(G-3829)*

Triad Cutting Tools Inc..........................G 336 873-8708
  Asheboro *(G-412)*

Triangle Glass Service Inc.....................G 919 477-9508
  Durham *(G-4279)*

Trimed LLC..G 919 615-2784
  Raleigh *(G-10564)*

Triton Marine Services Inc....................G 252 728-9958
  Beaufort *(G-736)*

Turbomed LLC.......................................F 973 527-5299
  Fayetteville *(G-4684)*

U S Propeller Service Inc.......................G 704 528-9515
  Troutman *(G-12154)*

Ultimate Floor Cleaning.........................G 704 912-8978
  Charlotte *(G-2960)*

▲ Union Grove Saw & Knife Inc............D 704 539-4442
  Union Grove *(G-12186)*

Valley Proteins (de) Inc........................B 336 333-3030
  Greensboro *(G-5895)*

Waggoner Manufacturing Co.................E 704 278-2000
  Mount Ulla *(G-9272)*

Waste Container Repair Svcs................G 910 257-4474
  Fayetteville *(G-4696)*

Watkins Agency Inc..............................G 704 213-6997
  Salisbury *(G-11135)*

Western Crlina TI Mold Corp In..............F 828 890-4448
  Mills River *(G-8324)*

Westlift Inc...F 919 242-4379
  Goldsboro *(G-5253)*

Whaley Foodservice LLC.......................D 704 529-6242
  Charlotte *(G-3016)*

Whiteville Forklift & Eqp.......................G 910 642-6642
  Whiteville *(G-12598)*

Zickgraf Enterprises Inc........................G 828 524-2313
  Franklin *(G-4844)*

78 MOTION PICTURES

7812 Motion picture and video production

Avcon Inc...E 919 388-0203
  Cary *(G-1302)*

Cog Glbal Media/Consulting LLC...........E 980 239-8042
  Matthews *(G-8109)*

Inspire Creative Studios Inc..................G 910 395-0200
  Wilmington *(G-12818)*

Magic Factory LLC................................E 919 585-5644
  Durham *(G-4116)*

Metro Productions Inc...........................F 919 851-6420
  Raleigh *(G-10296)*

Palmer Senn...G 704 451-3971
  Charlotte *(G-2606)*

7819 Services allied to motion pictures

American Multimedia Inc.......................D 336 229-7101
  Burlington *(G-1045)*

7822 Motion picture and tape distribution

AEC Consumer Products LLC...............F 704 904-0578
  Fayetteville *(G-4546)*

7841 Video tape rental

Wen Bray Heating & AC.........................G 828 267-0635
  Hickory *(G-6489)*

79 AMUSEMENT AND RECREATION SERVICES

7922 Theatrical producers and services

Oneaka Dance Company........................G 704 299-7432
  Charlotte *(G-2599)*

Royal Faires Inc....................................F 704 896-5555
  Huntersville *(G-7044)*

▲ Stage Decoration and Sups Inc.........G 336 621-5454
  Greensboro *(G-5834)*

Toymakerz LLC.....................................F 843 267-3477
  Reidsville *(G-10699)*

7929 Entertainers and entertainment groups

Brown Mitchell Hodges LLC.................. G 800 477-8982
Charlotte *(G-1813)*

Gracefully Broken LLC........................... G 980 474-0309
Gastonia *(G-5055)*

Oneaka Dance Company........................ G 704 299-7432
Charlotte *(G-2599)*

7941 Sports clubs, managers, and promoters

▲ Richard Chldress Racg Entps In....... B 336 731-3334
Welcome *(G-12514)*

Tourist Baseball Inc.............................. E 828 258-0428
Asheville *(G-621)*

7948 Racing, including track operation

Fibreworks Composites LLC................. E 704 696-1084
Mooresville *(G-8663)*

Garage Shop LLC.................................. F 980 500-0583
Denver *(G-3784)*

L Rancho Investments Inc.................... G 336 431-1004
Trinity *(G-12117)*

▲ Penske Racing South Inc.................. C 704 664-2300
Mooresville *(G-8746)*

Rp Motor Sports Inc.............................. E 704 720-4200
Concord *(G-3435)*

7991 Physical fitness facilities

Gladiator Enterprises Inc..................... G 336 944-6932
Greensboro *(G-5561)*

Southern Home Spa and Wtr Pdts........ G 336 286-3564
Greensboro *(G-5826)*

Trickfit & Suepack Training.................. G 919 737-2231
Wake Forest *(G-12309)*

7993 Coin-operated amusement devices

Brown Mitchell Hodges LLC.................. G 800 477-8982
Charlotte *(G-1813)*

Grover Gaming Inc................................ D 252 329-7900
Greenville *(G-5985)*

Southland Amusements Vend Inc.......... E 910 343-1809
Wilmington *(G-12927)*

7999 Amusement and recreation, nec

Clark Art Shop Inc............................... G 919 832-8319
Raleigh *(G-9997)*

Mb-F Inc... D 336 379-9352
Greensboro *(G-5685)*

Mk Global Holdings LLC....................... E 704 334-1904
Charlotte *(G-2511)*

Paraclete Xp Sky Venture LLC............. F 910 848-2600
Raeford *(G-9844)*

Paraclete Xp Skyventure LLC.............. E 910 904-0027
Raeford *(G-9845)*

Prima Elements LLC............................. G 910 483-8406
Fayetteville *(G-4657)*

Tickets Plus Inc................................... E 616 222-4000
Morrisville *(G-9072)*

80 HEALTH SERVICES

8011 Offices and clinics of medical doctors

▼ Accord Healthcare Inc....................... E 919 941-7878
Raleigh *(G-9873)*

Gems Frst Stop Med Sltions LLC.......... G 336 965-9500
Greensboro *(G-5552)*

▲ Herbs Gaia Inc................................... D 828 884-4242
Brevard *(G-972)*

Orthopedic Services............................. G 336 716-3349
Winston Salem *(G-13273)*

Statesville Med MGT Svcs LLC............ G 704 996-6748
Statesville *(G-11780)*

Surgical Center of Morehea.................. F 252 247-0314
Morehead City *(G-8846)*

Telephys Inc... G 312 625-9128
Davidson *(G-3719)*

Thomas Mendolia MD............................ G 336 835-5688
Mooresville *(G-8785)*

8021 Offices and clinics of dentists

Fidelity Associates Inc......................... E 704 864-3766
Gastonia *(G-5047)*

Preventive Technologies Inc................. G 704 684-1211
Indian Trail *(G-7096)*

8042 Offices and clinics of optometrists

O D Eyecarecenter P A........................ G 252 443-7011
Rocky Mount *(G-10856)*

Optics Inc... G 336 288-9504
Greensboro *(G-5726)*

Optics Inc... G 336 884-5677
High Point *(G-6721)*

8062 General medical and surgical hospitals

Statesville Med MGT Svcs LLC............ G 704 996-6748
Statesville *(G-11780)*

8071 Medical laboratories

Alcami Carolinas Corporation............... G 910 254-7000
Wilmington *(G-12699)*

▲ Biomerieux Inc.................................. B 919 620-2000
Durham *(G-3930)*

Liposcience Inc.................................... C 919 212-1999
Morrisville *(G-9012)*

Neurametrix Inc.................................... G 408 507-2366
Asheville *(G-556)*

Pregnancy Support Services................. G 919 490-0203
Chapel Hill *(G-1563)*

8072 Dental laboratories

▲ Cdb Corporation................................ E 910 383-6464
Leland *(G-7537)*

Village Ceramics Inc............................ G 828 685-9491
Hendersonville *(G-6247)*

8082 Home health care services

Allotropica Technologies Inc................. G 919 522-4374
Chapel Hill *(G-1524)*

Spencer Health Solutions Inc............... E 866 971-8564
Morrisville *(G-9058)*

8093 Specialty outpatient clinics, nec

Cape Fear Orthtics Prsthtics I.............. G 910 483-0933
Fayetteville *(G-4566)*

Modoral Brands Inc.............................. G 336 741-7230
Winston Salem *(G-13259)*

Transylvnia Vcational Svcs Inc............ D 828 884-1548
Fletcher *(G-4773)*

Transylvnia Vcational Svcs Inc............ C 828 884-3195
Brevard *(G-983)*

Unity Hlthcare Lab Billing LLP............. G 980 209-0402
Charlotte *(G-2964)*

8099 Health and allied services, nec

Annihilare Medical Systems Inc............ F 855 545-5677
Lincolnton *(G-7814)*

Birth Tissue Recovery LLC................... E 336 448-1910
Winston Salem *(G-13106)*

Gems Frst Stop Med Sltions LLC.......... G 336 965-9500
Greensboro *(G-5552)*

Health At Home Inc.............................. F 850 543-4482
Charlotte *(G-2267)*

Medaccess Inc..................................... G 828 264-4085
Robbinsville *(G-10760)*

Pink Hill Wellness Edu Center.............. G 252 568-2425
Pink Hill *(G-9766)*

◆ Premex Inc... F 561 962-4128
Durham *(G-4196)*

Unity Hlthcare Lab Billing LLP............. G 980 209-0402
Charlotte *(G-2964)*

West Hllcrest Dda Group HM LLC....... F 336 478-7444
Burlington *(G-1179)*

82 EDUCATIONAL SERVICES

8211 Elementary and secondary schools

Lifespan Incorporated........................... D 336 838-2614
North Wilkesboro *(G-9541)*

Lifespan Incorporated........................... E 704 944-5100
Charlotte *(G-2419)*

8221 Colleges and universities

Appalachian State University................. G 828 262-7497
Boone *(G-895)*

Appalachian State University................. F 828 262-2047
Boone *(G-896)*

North Carolina State Univ.................... G 919 515-2760
Raleigh *(G-10336)*

University NC At Chapel HI................. G 919 962-0369
Chapel Hill *(G-1585)*

8243 Data processing schools

Academy Association Inc..................... F 919 544-0835
Durham *(G-3877)*

Applied Strategies Inc......................... G 704 525-4478
Charlotte *(G-1688)*

Camstar Systems Inc.......................... C 704 227-6600
Charlotte *(G-1833)*

Emath360 LLC...................................... F 919 744-4944
Cary *(G-1352)*

Ideacode Inc.. G 919 341-5170
Greensboro *(G-5613)*

8249 Vocational schools, nec

Hope Renovations................................ F 919 960-1957
Chapel Hill *(G-1549)*

Training Industry Inc............................ D 919 653-4990
Raleigh *(G-10555)*

8299 Schools and educational services

Advanced Computer Lrng Co LLC........ E 910 779-2254
Fayetteville *(G-4544)*

▲ American Inst Crtif Pub Accntn........ B 919 402-0682
Durham *(G-3890)*

Assoction Intl Crtif Prof Accn.............. A 919 402-4500
Durham *(G-3901)*

Center for Creative Leadership............. B 336 288-7210
Greensboro *(G-5436)*

Communitys Kitchen L3c...................... G 828 817-2308
Tryon *(G-12173)*

Emath360 LLC...................................... F 919 744-4944
Cary *(G-1352)*

Jfl Enterprises Inc............................... G 704 786-7838
Concord *(G-3385)*

▲ Kindermusik International Inc........... E 800 628-5687
Greensboro *(G-5648)*

Lulu Technology Circus Inc................. E 919 459-5858
Morrisville *(G-9015)*

Music & Arts....................................... G 919 329-6069
Garner *(G-4948)*

National Ctr For Social Impact............ G 984 212-2285
Raleigh *(G-10323)*

Pdf and Associates.............................. G 252 332-7749
Colerain *(G-3271)*

Prima Elements LLC............................. G 910 483-8406
Fayetteville *(G-4657)*

RFH Tactical Mobility Inc......................... F 910 916-0284
  Milton *(G-8326)*

Stamping & Scrapbooking Rm Inc......... G 336 389-9538
  Greensboro *(G-5835)*

83 SOCIAL SERVICES

8322 Individual and family services

Clay County Food Pantry Inc................. G 828 389-1657
  Hayesville *(G-6138)*

Easter Seals Ucp NC & VA Inc................. D 919 856-0250
  Raleigh *(G-10070)*

Fixed-NC LLC.. G 252 751-1911
  Greenville *(G-5976)*

Hope Renovations.................................. F 919 960-1957
  Chapel Hill *(G-1549)*

Infinity Communications LLC................. E 919 797-2334
  Durham *(G-4076)*

Kenson Parenting Solutions................... G 919 637-1499
  Wake Forest *(G-12285)*

Lighthouse of Wayne County Inc............ G 919 736-1313
  Goldsboro *(G-5224)*

Oneaka Dance Company........................ G 704 299-7432
  Charlotte *(G-2599)*

Tab Index Inc...................................... G 919 876-8988
  Raleigh *(G-10529)*

Tarheel Monitoring LLC........................ G 910 763-1490
  Wilmington *(G-12936)*

8331 Job training and related services

Eastern Crlina Vctonal Ctr Inc................ D 252 758-4188
  Greenville *(G-5972)*

Hope Renovations.................................. F 919 960-1957
  Chapel Hill *(G-1549)*

Industrial Opportunities Inc................... B 828 321-4754
  Andrews *(G-107)*

Lee County Industries Inc..................... G 919 775-3439
  Sanford *(G-11205)*

Lions Services Inc................................ B 704 921-1527
  Charlotte *(G-2425)*

Sighttech LLC...................................... G 855 997-4448
  Charlotte *(G-2805)*

Transylvnia Vcational Svcs Inc.............. D 828 884-1548
  Fletcher *(G-4773)*

Transylvnia Vcational Svcs Inc.............. C 828 884-3195
  Brevard *(G-983)*

Tri-County Industries Inc....................... C 252 977-3800
  Rocky Mount *(G-10819)*

Vocatnal Sltons Hndrson Cnty I............ E 828 692-9626
  East Flat Rock *(G-4335)*

Watauga Opportunities Inc.................... E 828 264-5009
  Boone *(G-951)*

Webster Entps Jackson Cnty Inc............ E 828 586-8981
  Sylva *(G-11904)*

8361 Residential care

Gladiator Enterprises Inc...................... G 336 944-6932
  Greensboro *(G-5561)*

Lifespan Incorporated.......................... E 704 944-5100
  Charlotte *(G-2419)*

Watauga Opportunities Inc.................... E 828 264-5009
  Boone *(G-951)*

8399 Social services, nec

Ipas.. C 919 967-7052
  Durham *(G-4082)*

84 MUSEUMS, ART GALLERIES AND BOTANICAL AND ZOOLOGICAL GARDENS

8412 Museums and art galleries

Emerald Village Inc.............................. G 828 765-6463
  Little Switzerland *(G-7882)*

▼ Mega Media Concepts Ltd Lblty......... G 973 919-5661
  Brevard *(G-975)*

86 MEMBERSHIP ORGANIZATIONS

8611 Business associations

High Temperature Tech Inc.................... F 704 375-2111
  Charlotte *(G-2279)*

Kidde Technologies Inc......................... B 252 237-7004
  Wilson *(G-12999)*

◆ US Tobacco Cooperative Inc............... D 919 821-4560
  Raleigh *(G-10579)*

8621 Professional organizations

▲ American Inst Crtif Pub Accntn........... B 919 402-0682
  Durham *(G-3890)*

Assoction Intl Crtif Prof Accn............... A 919 402-4500
  Durham *(G-3901)*

Gems Frst Stop Med Sltions LLC............ G 336 965-9500
  Greensboro *(G-5552)*

International Society Automtn................ E 919 206-4176
  Research Triangle Pa *(G-10713)*

8641 Civic and social associations

◆ Clariant Corporation......................... D 704 331-7000
  Charlotte *(G-1925)*

Interntnal Chldbrth Edcatn Ass............. G 919 863-9487
  Raleigh *(G-10208)*

8661 Religious organizations

Brookstone Baptist Church.................... E 828 658-9443
  Weaverville *(G-12485)*

Church Initiative Inc............................ E 919 562-2112
  Wake Forest *(G-12269)*

Grace Communion International.............. E 626 650-2300
  Charlotte *(G-2229)*

8699 Membership organizations, nec

Oneaka Dance Company........................ G 704 299-7432
  Charlotte *(G-2599)*

Pregnancy Support Services.................. G 919 490-0203
  Chapel Hill *(G-1563)*

87 ENGINEERING, ACCOUNTING, RESEARCH, AND MANAGEMENT SERVICES

8711 Engineering services

ABB Enterprise Software Inc................. C 919 582-3283
  Raleigh *(G-9862)*

ABB Inc.. E 704 587-1362
  Charlotte *(G-1609)*

◆ ABB Inc.. C 919 856-2360
  Cary *(G-1285)*

Abco Automation Inc........................... G 336 375-6400
  Browns Summit *(G-988)*

Acroplis Cntrls Engineers Pllc............... F 919 275-3884
  Raleigh *(G-9876)*

Advanced Computer Lrng Co LLC......... E 910 779-2254
  Fayetteville *(G-4544)*

▲ Airspeed LLC.................................. E 919 644-1222
  Mebane *(G-8227)*

Automated Designs Inc........................ F 828 696-9625
  Flat Rock *(G-4703)*

Bachstein Consulting LLC..................... G 410 322-4917
  Youngsville *(G-13463)*

Bahnson Holdings Inc........................... D 336 760-3111
  Clemmons *(G-3178)*

Belham Management Ind LLC................. G 704 815-4246
  Charlotte *(G-1768)*

Belkoz Inc.. G 919 703-0694
  Raleigh *(G-9939)*

Big Rock Industries Inc......................... G 252 222-3618
  Morehead City *(G-8816)*

Boeing Arospc Operations Inc............... F 919 722-4351
  Goldsboro *(G-5201)*

◆ C Tek Lean Solutions Inc.................. E 704 895-0090
  Mooresville *(G-8625)*

◆ Centrotherm Usa Inc....................... G 360 626-4445
  Durham *(G-3968)*

Century Furniture LLC......................... D 828 326-8535
  Hickory *(G-6297)*

Cnc Performance Eng LLC.................... G 704 599-2555
  Charlotte *(G-1938)*

Coalogix Inc....................................... C 704 827-8933
  Charlotte *(G-1940)*

Collins Aerospace............................... F 704 423-7000
  Charlotte *(G-1957)*

Cross Technology Inc........................... E 336 725-4700
  East Bend *(G-4322)*

Custom Controls Unlimited LLC............. F 919 812-6553
  Raleigh *(G-10029)*

Descher LLC....................................... G 919 828-7708
  Raleigh *(G-10041)*

Doble Engineering Company.................. G 919 380-7461
  Morrisville *(G-8966)*

Dronescape Pllc.................................. G 704 953-3798
  Charlotte *(G-2066)*

Duotech Services LLC.......................... E 828 369-5111
  Franklin *(G-4826)*

Electro Magnetic Research Inc.............. G 919 365-3723
  Zebulon *(G-13508)*

Enviboats LLC..................................... G 910 213-3200
  Southport *(G-11519)*

Equagen Engineers Pllc........................ E 919 444-5442
  Raleigh *(G-10090)*

▲ Finnord North America Corp............. F 704 723-4913
  Huntersville *(G-6990)*

Flextronics Intl USA Inc........................ C 919 998-4000
  Morrisville *(G-8975)*

Froehling & Robertson Inc.................... E 804 264-2701
  Raleigh *(G-10120)*

General Dynmics Mssion Systems.......... C 336 698-8000
  Mc Leansville *(G-8223)*

Global Products & Mfg Svcs Inc............ G 360 870-9876
  Charlotte *(G-2215)*

Goshen Engineering Inc........................ G 919 429-9798
  Mount Olive *(G-9254)*

Integrity Envmtl Solutions LLC............... D 704 283-9765
  Monroe *(G-8505)*

Iomax USA LLC................................... E 704 662-1840
  Mooresville *(G-8695)*

Irsi Automation Inc............................. G 336 303-5320
  Mc Leansville *(G-8224)*

J & W Service Incorporated.................. G 336 449-4584
  Whitsett *(G-12611)*

J J Jenkins Incorporated....................... E 704 821-6648
  Matthews *(G-8177)*

JA Smith Inc....................................... G 704 860-4910
  Lawndale *(G-7517)*

John Deere Consumer Pdts Inc............. C 919 804-2000
  Cary *(G-1380)*

Kdy Automation Solutions Inc............... G 888 219-0049
  Morrisville *(G-8996)*

Keller Technology Corporation............... E 704 875-1605
  Huntersville *(G-7007)*

Lba Group Inc..................................... E 252 329-9243
  Greenville *(G-5999)*

Man Lift Mfg Co.................... E 414 486-1760
Shelby *(G-11359)*

McLean Sbsrface Utlity Engrg L........... F 336 340-0024
Greensboro *(G-5687)*

Motorsport Innovations Inc.................. G 704 728-7837
Davidson *(G-3713)*

Mra Services Inc........................... F 704 933-4300
Kannapolis *(G-7216)*

MSI Defense Solutions LLC........... D 704 660-8348
Mooresville *(G-8730)*

▲ **Multi Technical Services Inc**........... G 919 553-2995
Clayton *(G-3161)*

Peak Clean Energy LLC.................. G 303 588-2789
Huntersville *(G-7031)*

▲ **Penske Racing South Inc**............ C 704 664-2300
Mooresville *(G-8746)*

Plan B Enterprises LLC.................. G 919 387-4856
New Hill *(G-9412)*

Pratt Mller Engrg Fbrction LLC........ C 704 977-0642
Huntersville *(G-7036)*

Queen City Engrg & Design Pllc........... G 704 918-5851
Concord *(G-3428)*

R D Tillson & Associates Inc............... G 336 454-1410
Jamestown *(G-7178)*

Roehrig Engineering Inc................... G 336 956-3800
Greensboro *(G-5793)*

SCR Controls Inc........................ F 704 821-6651
Matthews *(G-8192)*

Simon Industries Inc...................... E 919 469-2004
Raleigh *(G-10477)*

Sitzer & Spuria Inc....................... G 919 929-0299
Chapel Hill *(G-1572)*

Ssi Services Inc.......................... G 919 867-1450
Raleigh *(G-10501)*

Subsea Video Systems Inc............ G 252 338-1001
Elizabeth City *(G-4411)*

Sunqest Inc.............................. G 828 325-4910
Newton *(G-9501)*

▲ **Tdc International LLC**................... G 704 875-1198
Concord *(G-3452)*

Team Industries Inc...................... D 828 837-5377
Andrews *(G-109)*

▲ **Textrol Laboratories Inc**................ E 704 764-3400
Monroe *(G-8569)*

Tower Engrg Professionals Inc........ C 919 661-6351
Raleigh *(G-10554)*

Volta Group Corporation LLC........ E 919 637-0273
Raleigh *(G-10593)*

Vortant Technologies LLC.................. G 828 645-1026
Weaverville *(G-12506)*

◆ **Walker and Associates Inc**..............C 336 731-6391
Winston Salem *(G-13386)*

Young & McQueen Grading Co Inc........ D 828 682-7714
Burnsville *(G-1196)*

8712 Architectural services

American Physcl SEC Group LLC........ G 919 363-1894
Apex *(G-134)*

Carolina Timberworks LLC................ F 828 266-9663
West Jefferson *(G-12561)*

Solid Holdings LLC...................... F 704 423-0260
Charlotte *(G-2825)*

Sterling Cleora Corporation........... F 919 563-5800
Durham *(G-4250)*

8713 Surveying services

McLean Sbsrface Utlity Engrg L............. F 336 340-0024
Greensboro *(G-5687)*

8721 Accounting, auditing, and bookkeeping

All Signs & Graphics LLC.................. G 910 323-3115
Fayetteville *(G-4549)*

Oxford University Press LLC................. D 919 677-0977
Cary *(G-1412)*

Oxford University Press LLC................. B 919 677-0977
Cary *(G-1413)*

8731 Commercial physical research

22nd Century Group Inc...................... F 716 270-1523
Mocksville *(G-8345)*

Advanced Non-Lethal Tech Inc........... G 847 812-6450
Raleigh *(G-9880)*

Alcami Carolinas Corporation.............. G 910 619-3952
Garner *(G-4913)*

Alcami Carolinas Corporation............. G 910 254-7000
Morrisville *(G-8924)*

Alcami Carolinas Corporation............. G 910 254-7000
Wilmington *(G-12696)*

Alcami Carolinas Corporation............. G 910 254-7000
Wilmington *(G-12697)*

Alcami Carolinas Corporation............. B 910 254-7000
Wilmington *(G-12698)*

▼ **Andersen Products Inc**..................... E 336 376-3000
Haw River *(G-6130)*

Birth Tissue Recovery LLC................. E 336 448-1910
Winston Salem *(G-13106)*

Case Farms LLC........................... D 919 735-5010
Dudley *(G-3835)*

Case Farms LLC........................... E 919 658-2252
Goldsboro *(G-5204)*

Case Farms LLC........................... F 704 528-4501
Troutman *(G-12133)*

Cedarlane Laboratories USA................. E 336 513-5135
Burlington *(G-1067)*

Cisco Systems Inc........................ A 919 392-2000
Morrisville *(G-8959)*

Core Technology Molding Corp........... E 336 294-2018
Greensboro *(G-5469)*

Epicypher Inc............................ F 855 374-2461
Durham *(G-4030)*

Gale Global Research Inc.................... G 910 795-8595
Leland *(G-7544)*

Greer Laboratories Inc...................... E 828 758-2388
Lenoir *(G-7609)*

Health Supply Us LLC...................... F 888 408-1694
Mooresville *(G-8680)*

◆ **Hydromer Inc**.............................E 908 526-2828
Concord *(G-3374)*

K2 Solutions Inc.......................... B 910 692-6898
Southern Pines *(G-11501)*

King Phrmceuticals RES Dev LLC.......... C 919 653-7001
Cary *(G-1383)*

Lexitas Pharma Services Inc................ E 919 205-0012
Durham *(G-4104)*

Linde Gas & Equipment Inc................. D 919 549-0633
Durham *(G-4105)*

Lord Corporation......................... D 919 469-2500
Cary *(G-1395)*

Neurametrix Inc.......................... G 408 507-2366
Asheville *(G-556)*

Novex Innovations LLC..................... G 336 231-6693
Winston Salem *(G-13267)*

Nuvotronics Inc.......................... D 434 298-6940
Durham *(G-4152)*

▲ **Penske Racing South Inc**................ C 704 664-2300
Mooresville *(G-8746)*

Pharmagra Holding Company LLC........ G 828 884-8656
Brevard *(G-979)*

Ppd Inc................................. C 910 251-0081
Wilmington *(G-12886)*

Praetego Inc............................. G 919 237-7969
Durham *(G-4193)*

Precision Biosciences Inc................... E 919 314-5512
Durham *(G-4194)*

Propharma Group LLC...................... D 888 242-0559
Raleigh *(G-10405)*

Raybow Usa Inc.......................... F 828 884-8656
Brevard *(G-980)*

▲ **Scentair Technologies LLC**............... C 704 504-2320
Charlotte *(G-2762)*

Signalscape Inc.......................... E 919 859-4565
Cary *(G-1455)*

Smoky Mtn Nativ Plant Assn.................. G 828 479-8788
Robbinsville *(G-10763)*

Squarehead Technology LLC................ G 571 299-4849
Hickory *(G-6456)*

Tengion Inc.............................. E 336 722-5855
Winston Salem *(G-13361)*

Transcontinental AC US LLC................ F 704 847-9171
Matthews *(G-8154)*

Tribofilm Research Inc..................... G 919 838-2844
Raleigh *(G-10563)*

▲ **Troxler Electronic Labs Inc**................ D 919 549-8661
Research Triangle Pa *(G-10716)*

Vacs America Inc......................... G 910 259-9854
Burgaw *(G-1035)*

Venator Chemicals LLC..................... D 704 454-4811
Harrisburg *(G-6120)*

Verdante Bioenergy Svcs LLC............ G 828 394-1246
Lenoir *(G-7643)*

Vortant Technologies LLC.................. G 828 645-1026
Weaverville *(G-12506)*

◆ **Walker and Associates Inc**..............C 336 731-6391
Winston Salem *(G-13386)*

8732 Commercial nonphysical research

Dex One Corporation....................... A 919 297-1600
Cary *(G-1348)*

Fuji Silysia Chemical Ltd.................... F 919 484-4158
Greenville *(G-5980)*

Konica Mnlta Hlthcare Amrcas I........... E 919 792-6420
Garner *(G-4935)*

Pro-Motor Engines Inc..................... G 704 664-6800
Mooresville *(G-8755)*

Sighttech LLC........................... G 855 997-4448
Charlotte *(G-2805)*

Viztek LLC.............................. E 919 792-6420
Garner *(G-4971)*

8733 Noncommercial research organizations

Biomedinnovations Inc..................... G 704 489-1290
Denver *(G-3775)*

Duke Human Vaccine Institute............... G 919 684-5384
Durham *(G-4009)*

Fire Retardant Chem Tech LLC............ G 980 253-8880
Matthews *(G-8169)*

Kbi Biopharma Inc........................ D 919 479-9898
Durham *(G-4094)*

King Phrmceuticals RES Dev LLC.......... C 919 653-7001
Cary *(G-1383)*

Parata Systems LLC...................... C 888 727-2821
Durham *(G-4165)*

Sigma Xi Scntfic RES Hnor Soc.............. E 919 549-4691
Durham *(G-4235)*

8734 Testing laboratories

Acterna LLC............................. F 919 388-5100
Morrisville *(G-8918)*

Albion Medical Holdings Inc.................. F 800 378-3906
Lenoir *(G-7570)*

Alcami Carolinas Corporation................ G 910 619-3952
Garner *(G-4913)*

Alcami Carolinas Corporation................ B 910 254-7000
Wilmington *(G-12698)*

▼ **American Safety Utility Corp**............. E 704 482-0601
Shelby *(G-11311)*

▲ Apex Instruments Incorporated........ E 919 557-7300
   Fuquay Varina *(G-4865)*

Avista Pharma Solutions Inc.............. E 919 544-8600
   Durham *(G-3910)*

Bachstein Consulting LLC..................... G 410 322-4917
   Youngsville *(G-13463)*

▲ Broadwind Indus Solutions LLC........ E 919 777-2907
   Sanford *(G-11159)*

Catalent Pharma Solutions LLC........... F 919 481-4855
   Morrisville *(G-8952)*

Cross Technologies Inc....................... E 800 327-7727
   Greensboro *(G-5472)*

Dynisco Instruments LLC..................... E 828 326-9888
   Hickory *(G-6325)*

Educated Design & Develop................. E 919 469-9434
   Cary *(G-1351)*

Froehling & Robertson Inc................... E 804 264-2701
   Raleigh *(G-10120)*

Greer Laboratories Inc........................ E 828 758-2388
   Lenoir *(G-7609)*

▲ Greer Laboratories Inc...................... C 828 754-5327
   Lenoir *(G-7610)*

Sapphire Tchncal Solutions LLC.......... G 704 561-3100
   Pineville *(G-9754)*

SCR-Tech LLC....................................... C 704 504-0191
   Charlotte *(G-2772)*

Tergus Pharma LLC.............................. E 919 549-9700
   Durham *(G-4268)*

Unity Hlthcare Lab Billing LLP.............. G 980 209-0402
   Charlotte *(G-2964)*

8741 Management services

Allyn International Trdg Corp................ G 877 858-2482
   Marshville *(G-8085)*

Competitive Solutions Inc.................... E 919 851-0058
   Raleigh *(G-10004)*

Drew Roberts LLC................................ G 336 497-1679
   Whitsett *(G-12604)*

Equagen Engineers Pllc....................... E 919 444-5442
   Raleigh *(G-10090)*

Integrity Envmtl Solutions LLC............ D 704 283-9765
   Monroe *(G-8505)*

◆ J & D Managements LLC..................... G 910 321-7373
   Fayetteville *(G-4618)*

Jebco Inc... E 919 557-2001
   Holly Springs *(G-6904)*

◆ Kayser-Roth Corporation.................. C 336 852-2030
   Greensboro *(G-5643)*

Phoenix Assembly NC LLC.................... G 252 801-4250
   Battleboro *(G-706)*

S & A Cherokee LLC.............................. E 919 674-6020
   Cary *(G-1443)*

Trademark Landscape Group Inc.......... F 910 253-0560
   Supply *(G-11861)*

▲ Triangle Brick Company.................... E 919 544-1796
   Durham *(G-4277)*

◆ Volvo Logistics North America Inc..... C 336 393-4746
   Greensboro *(G-5910)*

W T Humphrey Inc................................ E 910 455-3555
   Jacksonville *(G-7158)*

8742 Management consulting services

822tees Inc.. G 910 822-8337
   Fayetteville *(G-4541)*

Academy Association Inc..................... F 919 544-0835
   Durham *(G-3877)*

Access Newswire Inc........................... C 919 481-4000
   Raleigh *(G-9872)*

Anew Look Homes LLC......................... F 800 796-5152
   Hickory *(G-6264)*

Apex Analytix LLC................................ C 336 272-4669
   Greensboro *(G-5365)*

Archie Supply LLC................................ G 336 987-0895
   Greensboro *(G-5368)*

Barron Legacy Mgmt Group LLC.......... G 301 367-4735
   Charlotte *(G-1757)*

Blue Ridge Quick Print Inc................... G 828 883-2420
   Brevard *(G-968)*

▲ Broadwind Indus Solutions LLC........ E 919 777-2907
   Sanford *(G-11159)*

Camstar Systems Inc........................... C 704 227-6600
   Charlotte *(G-1833)*

Capre Omnimedia LLC.......................... G 917 460-3572
   Wilmington *(G-12731)*

Carolina By-Products Co...................... G 336 333-3030
   Greensboro *(G-5424)*

Competitive Solutions Inc.................... E 919 851-0058
   Raleigh *(G-10004)*

▼ Design Tool Inc.................................. E 828 328-6414
   Conover *(G-3515)*

DMC LLC... E 980 352-9806
   Concord *(G-3355)*

Eco Building Corporation...................... G 910 736-1540
   Red Springs *(G-10667)*

Educatrx Inc... G 980 328-0013
   Monroe *(G-8481)*

Electronic Imaging Svcs Inc................. F 704 587-3323
   Charlotte *(G-2095)*

Emath360 LLC...................................... F 919 744-4944
   Cary *(G-1352)*

Go Energies LLC................................... F 877 712-5999
   Wilmington *(G-12790)*

Go Energies Holdings Inc.................... G 910 762-5802
   Wilmington *(G-12791)*

Goshen Engineering Inc....................... G 919 429-9798
   Mount Olive *(G-9254)*

Hinsons Typing & Printing................... G 919 934-9036
   Smithfield *(G-11446)*

Intelligent Apps LLC............................ G 919 628-6256
   Raleigh *(G-10205)*

Irsi Automation Inc.............................. G 336 303-5320
   Mc Leansville *(G-8224)*

◆ J & D Managements LLC..................... G 910 321-7373
   Fayetteville *(G-4618)*

Jestines Jewels Inc............................. G 704 904-0191
   Salisbury *(G-11072)*

K2 Solutions Inc.................................. B 910 692-6898
   Southern Pines *(G-11501)*

LDR Designs.. G 252 375-4484
   Greenville *(G-6001)*

Logiksavvy Solutions LLC.................... G 336 392-6149
   Greensboro *(G-5663)*

Make Solutions Inc.............................. F 623 444-0098
   Asheville *(G-543)*

▲ Microthermics Inc............................. F 919 878-8045
   Raleigh *(G-10303)*

National Ctr For Social Impact............. G 984 212-2285
   Raleigh *(G-10323)*

Nexxt Level Trucking LLC.................... G 980 205-4425
   Charlotte *(G-2562)*

One Srce Dcument Solutions Inc.......... E 800 401-9544
   Greensboro *(G-5724)*

▲ Pace Communications Inc................. C 336 378-6065
   Greensboro *(G-5729)*

Pashes LLC.. G 704 682-6535
   Statesville *(G-11743)*

◆ Portable Displays LLC....................... E 919 544-6504
   Cary *(G-1424)*

Positive Prints Prof Svcs LLC.............. G 336 701-2330
   Durham *(G-4189)*

Propharma Group LLC.......................... D 888 242-0559
   Raleigh *(G-10405)*

Q T Corporation................................... G 252 399-7600
   Wilson *(G-13016)*

Red Oak Sales Company....................... G 704 483-8464
   Denver *(G-3802)*

Rennasentient Inc................................ G 919 233-7710
   Cary *(G-1435)*

Reynolds Consumer Products Inc......... A 704 371-5550
   Huntersville *(G-7042)*

Salem One Inc...................................... F 336 722-2886
   Kernersville *(G-7299)*

Scott Systems Intl Inc.......................... F 704 362-1115
   Charlotte *(G-2771)*

Sonaron LLC... G 808 232-6168
   Fayetteville *(G-4672)*

◆ Syntec Inc.. D 336 861-9023
   High Point *(G-6800)*

Training Industry Inc........................... D 919 653-4990
   Raleigh *(G-10555)*

◆ Triple Crown International LLC........... G 704 846-4983
   Charlotte *(G-2946)*

UNC Campus Health Services............... D 919 966-2281
   Chapel Hill *(G-1584)*

Wirenet Inc.. F 513 774-7759
   Huntersville *(G-7062)*

8743 Public relations services

822tees Inc.. G 910 822-8337
   Fayetteville *(G-4541)*

Apple Rock Advg & Prom Inc................ E 336 232-4800
   Greensboro *(G-5366)*

Ed Kemp Associates Inc....................... G 336 869-2155
   High Point *(G-6604)*

Inform Inc.. F 828 322-7766
   Hickory *(G-6368)*

Inspire Creative Studios Inc................. G 910 395-0200
   Wilmington *(G-12818)*

▲ Rulmeca Corporation........................ G 910 794-9294
   Wilmington *(G-12905)*

S & A Cherokee LLC.............................. E 919 674-6020
   Cary *(G-1443)*

UGLy Essentials LLC............................ F 910 319-9945
   Raleigh *(G-10572)*

8744 Facilities support services

Tempest Environmental Corp............... G 919 973-1609
   Durham *(G-4265)*

8748 Business consulting, nec

Aceyus Inc... E 704 443-7900
   Charlotte *(G-1616)*

Alpha Theory LLC................................. G 212 235-2180
   Charlotte *(G-1652)*

Alpha Theory LLC................................. G 212 235-2180
   Charlotte *(G-1653)*

Amplified Elctronic Design Inc............. F 336 223-4811
   Greensboro *(G-5362)*

Atlantic Group Usa Inc......................... F 919 623-7824
   Raleigh *(G-9920)*

Bachstein Consulting LLC..................... G 410 322-4917
   Youngsville *(G-13463)*

Brightly Software Inc.......................... C 919 816-8237
   Cary *(G-1315)*

Camstar Systems Inc........................... C 704 227-6600
   Charlotte *(G-1833)*

Carolina Textile Services Inc............... G 910 843-3033
   Red Springs *(G-10665)*

Cleveland Compounding Inc................. G 704 487-1971
   Shelby *(G-11319)*

Code LLC.. E 828 328-6004
   Hickory *(G-6304)*

Competitive Solutions Inc.................... E 919 851-0058
   Raleigh *(G-10004)*

▲ Cycle Pro LLC.................................... G 704 662-6682
   Mooresville *(G-8649)*

Emath360 LLC............................F 919 744-4944
Cary (G-1352)

Envirnmntal Cmfort Sltions Inc..............E 980 272-7327
Kannapolis (G-7208)

▲ Environmental Supply Co Inc............F 919 956-9688
Durham (G-4027)

I-Leadr Inc....................................G 910 431-5252
Sherrills Ford (G-11392)

Idea People Inc............................G 704 398-4437
Huntersville (G-7000)

Ideacode Inc................................G 919 341-5170
Greensboro (G-5613)

Infinite Software Resorces LLC............G 704 509-0031
Charlotte (G-2327)

Infinity Communications LLC................E 919 797-2334
Durham (G-4076)

Integrity Envmtl Solutions LLC............D 704 283-9765
Monroe (G-8505)

James King.....................................G 910 308-8818
Fayetteville (G-4620)

JPS Communications Inc....................D 919 534-1168
Raleigh (G-10222)

Measurement Incorporated..................D 919 683-2413
Durham (G-4122)

National Voctnl Tech Honor Soc............G 828 698-8011
Flat Rock (G-4711)

Native Naturalz Inc...........................F 336 334-2984
Greensboro (G-5704)

Noahs Inc.....................................F 704 718-2354
Charlotte (G-2570)

Picassomoesllc.............................G 216 703-4547
Hillsborough (G-6875)

Piedmont Flight Inc...........................E 336 776-6070
Winston Salem (G-13291)

Qplot Corporation...........................G 949 302-7928
Raleigh (G-10410)

R N Lea Inc....................................G 919 247-5998
Raleigh (G-10418)

Security Consult Inc.........................G 704 531-8399
Charlotte (G-2782)

▲ Spectrasite Communications LLC....E 919 468-0112
Cary (G-1465)

Stratton Publishing & Mktg Inc............G 703 914-9200
Wilmington (G-12932)

Sutton Scientifics Inc........................G 910 428-1600
Star (G-11634)

Te Connectivity Corporation..................C 336 727-5122
Winston Salem (G-13358)

Teletec Corporation..........................F 919 954-7300
Raleigh (G-10541)

Thinking Maps Inc............................G 919 678-8778
Cary (G-1470)

Triangle Regulatory Pubg LLC...............G 919 886-4587
Raleigh (G-10561)

89 SERVICES, NOT ELSEWHERE CLASSIFIED

8999 Services, nec

Cmd Land Services LLC....................G 919 554-2281
Wake Forest (G-12271)

Dimill Enterprises LLC.......................G 919 629-2011
Raleigh (G-10046)

Geosonics Inc.................................G 919 790-9500
Raleigh (G-10130)

Incantare Art By Marilyn LLC................F 704 713-8846
Charlotte (G-2319)

McLean Sbsrface Utlity Engrg L............F 336 340-0024
Greensboro (G-5687)

Native Naturalz Inc...........................F 336 334-2984
Greensboro (G-5704)

Prophysics Innovations Inc.................G 919 245-0406
Cary (G-1431)

Qplot Corporation...........................G 949 302-7928
Raleigh (G-10410)

Tempest Environmental Corp...............G 919 973-1609
Durham (G-4265)

We Appit LLC..................................G 910 465-2722
Wilmington (G-12946)

Xona Microfluidics Inc.......................G 951 553-6400
Research Triangle Pa (G-10718)

92 JUSTICE, PUBLIC ORDER AND SAFETY

9223 Correctional institutions

North Crlina Dept Adult Crrcto..............G 919 733-0867
Raleigh (G-10337)

9229 Public order and safety, nec

North Crlina Dept Crime Ctrl P............G 252 522-1511
Kinston (G-7424)

North Crlina Dept Crime Ctrl P............G 336 599-9233
Roxboro (G-10933)

93 PUBLIC FINANCE, TAXATION AND MONETARY POLICY

9311 Finance, taxation, and monetary policy

North Carolina Dept Labor..................F 919 807-2770
Raleigh (G-10335)

95 ADMINISTRATION OF ENVIRONMENTAL QUALITY AND HOUSING PROGRAMS

9512 Land, mineral, and wildlife conservation

North Carolina Department of A............G 828 684-8188
Arden (G-289)

96 ADMINISTRATION OF ECONOMIC PROGRAMS

9621 Regulation, administration of transportation

North Carolina Dept Trnsp..................G 828 733-9002
Newland (G-9433)

97 NATIONAL SECURITY AND INTERNATIONAL AFFAIRS

9711 National security

James King.....................................G 910 308-8818
Fayetteville (G-4620)

United States Dept of Navy...................G 252 466-4514
Cherry Point (G-3055)

United States Dept of Navy...................G 252 464-7228
Cherry Point (G-3056)

S
I
C

R & R Sealants (HQ)...999 999-9999
651 Tally Blvd, Yourtown (99999) *(G-458)*
Ready Box Co 999 999-9999
704 Lawrence Rd, Anytown (99999) *(G-1723)*
Rendall Mfg Inc, Anytown Also Called RMI *(G-1730)*

Designates this location as a headquarters
Business phone
Geographic Section entry number where full company information appears
Address, city & ZIP

See footnotes for symbols and codes identification.
- Companies listed alphabetically.
- Complete physical or mailing address.

(A Development Stage Company), Morrisville Also Called: Global Resource Corporation *(G-8984)*

/N Software Inc (PA)......................................919 544-7070
101 Europa Dr Ste 150 Chapel Hill (27517) *(G-1521)*

057 Technology LLC.......................................855 557-7057
728 11th Street Pl Nw Hickory (28601) *(G-6258)*

079948726, Colfax Also Called: W&W-Afco Steel LLC *(G-3293)*

1 Click Web Solutions LLC.........................910 790-9330
3333 Wrightsville Ave M Wilmington (28403) *(G-12684)*

123 Precious Metal Ref LLC (PA)..............910 228-5403
609a Piner Rd Ste 303 Wilmington (28409) *(G-12685)*

18 Chestnuts, Asheville Also Called: Soup Maven LLC *(G-606)*

1816, Charlotte Also Called: Remington 1816 Foundation *(G-2707)*

1a Smart Start LLC...336 765-7001
2453 Spaugh Industrial Dr Winston Salem (27103) *(G-13068)*

1st Choice Activewear II LLC....................704 528-7814
118 Overhill Dr Ste 101 Mooresville (28117) *(G-8588)*

1st Choice Service Inc.................................704 913-7685
3661 Eaker Rd Cherryville (28021) *(G-3058)*

1st Time Contracting....................................774 289-3321
104 Western Villa Dr Clemmons (27012) *(G-3176)*

21st Century Hosiery, Haw River Also Called: Sue-Lynn Textiles Inc *(G-6135)*

21st Century Tech of Amer.........................910 826-3676
6316 Yadkin Rd Fayetteville (28303) *(G-4540)*

21st Century Technologies Amer, Fayetteville Also Called: 21st Century Tech of Amer *(G-4540)*

22nd Century Group Inc (PA).....................716 270-1523
321 Farmington Rd Mocksville (27028) *(G-8345)*

2391 Eatons Ferry Rd Assoc LLC..............919 844-0565
7610 Six Forks Rd Ste 200 Raleigh (27615) *(G-9857)*

250 Cyrstal Cleaner, Wilmington Also Called: Two Fifty Cleaners *(G-12942)*

26 Industries Inc...704 839-3218
337 Sunnyside Dr Se Concord (28025) *(G-3306)*

27 Software US Inc.......................................704 968-2879
153 Farm Knoll Way Mooresville (28117) *(G-8589)*

277 Metal Inc...704 372-4513
201 Davis Heights Dr Gastonia (28052) *(G-4980)*

2topia Cycles Inc..704 778-7849
1512 Southwood Ave Charlotte (28203) *(G-1600)*

2u NC...919 525-5075
1210 Environ Way Chapel Hill (27517) *(G-1522)*

3 C, Wilson Also Called: 3c Store Fixtures Inc *(G-12959)*

3 Star Enterprises LLC................................704 821-7503
108 Business Park Dr Indian Trail (28079) *(G-7065)*

310 Sign Company..704 910-2242
5439 Candlewick Trl Gastonia (28056) *(G-4981)*

33rd Strike Group LLC.................................910 371-9688
9101 Lackey Rd Ne Ste 4 Leland (28451) *(G-7530)*

360 Ballistics LLC...919 883-8338
206 High House Rd Ste 102 Cary (27513) *(G-1282)*

360 Forest Products Inc..............................910 285-5838
113 N Rockfish St Wallace (28466) *(G-12318)*

3a Composites Holding Inc.........................704 658-3527
721 Jetton St Ste 325 Davidson (28036) *(G-3696)*

3a Composites USA Inc (HQ)......................704 872-8974
3480 Taylorsville Hwy Statesville (28625) *(G-11641)*

3c Store Fixtures Inc....................................252 291-5181
3363 Us Highway 301 N Wilson (27893) *(G-12959)*

3dductcleaning LLC......................................919 723-4512
207 Merriman Dr Selma (27576) *(G-11282)*

3M, Charlotte Also Called: 3M Company *(G-1601)*

3M, Sanford Also Called: 3M Company *(G-11144)*

3M Company..704 588-4782
13840 S Lakes Dr Charlotte (28273) *(G-1601)*

3M Company..919 642-0006
4191 Hwy 87 S Moncure (27559) *(G-8397)*

3M Company..919 774-3808
3010 Lee Ave Sanford (27332) *(G-11144)*

3nine USA Inc..512 210-4005
8325 Arrowridge Blvd Ste E Charlotte (28273) *(G-1602)*

3rd Phaze Bdy Oils Urban Lnks.................704 344-1138
3300 N Graham St Charlotte (28206) *(G-1603)*

3tex Inc..919 481-2500
208 Laurel Hill Dr Rutherfordton (28139) *(G-10972)*

4 Over LLC...919 875-3187
5609 Departure Dr Raleigh (27616) *(G-9858)*

4 Your Cause, Franklinville Also Called: Causekeepers Inc *(G-4855)*

410 Medical Inc...919 241-7900
68 Tw Alexander Dr Durham (27709) *(G-3872)*

48forty Solutions LLC..................................910 891-1534
2 Dinan Rd Dunn (28334) *(G-3839)*

4topps LLC..704 281-8451
3135 Indiana Ave Winston Salem (27105) *(G-13069)*

510nano Inc...919 521-5982
5441 Lumley Rd Ste 101 Durham (27703) *(G-3873)*

600 Racing Service, Harrisburg Also Called: US Legend Cars Intl Inc *(G-6119)*

615 Alton Place LLC.....................................336 431-4487
615 Alton Pl High Point (27263) *(G-6506)*

62 Woodworking, Thomasville Also Called: Timothy Lee Blacjmon *(G-12079)*

623 Medical, Morrisville Also Called: 623 Medical LLC *(G-8913)*

623 Medical LLC...877 455-0112
635 Davis Dr Ste 100 Morrisville (27560) *(G-8913)*

6th Sense Analytics.....................................919 439-4740
1 Copley Pkwy Ste 560 Morrisville (27560) *(G-8914)*

760 Craft Works LLC....................................704 274-5216
100 Gilead Rd Huntersville (28078) *(G-6962)*

80 Acres Urban Agriculture Inc..................704 437-6115
4141 Yorkview Ct Granite Falls (28630) *(G-5292)*

822tees Inc..910 822-8337
2598 Raeford Rd Fayetteville (28305) *(G-4541)*

910 Sign Co LLC...910 353-2298
614 Richlands Hwy Jacksonville (28540) *(G-7112)*

A & A Drone Service LLC.............................704 928-5054
166 Ralph Rd Statesville (28625) *(G-11642)*

A L P H A B E T I C

A & B Chem-Dry.. 919 878-0288
4208 Bertram Dr Raleigh (27604) *(G-9859)*

A & B Signs, Colfax *Also Called: Burchette Sign Company Inc (G-3274)*

A & D Precast Inc... 704 735-3337
1032 N Flint St Lincolnton (28092) *(G-7806)*

A & G Machining LLC.. 919 329-7207
333 Technical Ct Ste 33 Garner (27529) *(G-4911)*

A & J Canvas Inc... 252 244-1509
2450 Streets Ferry Rd Vanceboro (28586) *(G-12213)*

A & J Pallets Inc... 336 969-0265
121 Anderson St Rural Hall (27045) *(G-10951)*

A & M Paper and Printing..................................... 919 813-7852
4122 Bennett Memorial Rd Ste 108 Durham (27705) *(G-3874)*

A & M Tool Inc.. 828 891-9990
125 School House Rd Mills River (28759) *(G-8309)*

A & S Tool & Die Co Inc....................................... 336 993-3440
1510 Brookford Industrial Dr Kernersville (27284) *(G-7238)*

A & W Electric Inc... 704 333-4986
127 W 28th St Charlotte (28206) *(G-1604)*

A 1 Tire Service Inc... 828 684-1860
24 Cane Creek Rd Fletcher (28732) *(G-4716)*

A A Logo Gear... 704 795-7100
310 Church St N Concord (28025) *(G-3307)*

A and H Millwork Inc... 704 983-2402
509 Old Charlotte Rd Albemarle (28001) *(G-57)*

A B B Power Technolgies, Pinetops *Also Called: ABB Inc (G-9705)*

A B C Screenprinting and EMB............................... 704 937-3452
106 Sprouse Ln Grover (28073) *(G-6041)*

A B Carter Inc (PA)...704 865-1201
4801 York Hwy Gastonia (28052) *(G-4982)*

A B I, Creedmoor *Also Called: Aircraft Belts Inc (G-3635)*

A B Metals of Polkton LLC.................................... 704 694-6635
6245 Us Highway 74 W Polkton (28135) *(G-9810)*

A B T, Statesville *Also Called: ABT Foam LLC (G-11644)*

A Balloon For You, Asheville *Also Called: A Stitch In Time (G-422)*

A Bean Counter Inc... 919 359-9586
176 Foxglove Dr Garner (27529) *(G-4912)*

A Better Image Printing Inc.................................. 919 967-0319
4310 Garrett Rd Durham (27707) *(G-3875)*

A C Furniture Company Inc................................... 336 623-3430
724 Riverside Dr Eden (27288) *(G-4339)*

A C S Enterprises NC Inc...................................... 704 226-9898
307 N Secrest Ave Monroe (28110) *(G-8414)*

A Cleaner Tomorrow and Laundry, Dunn *Also Called: A Cleaner Tomorrow Dry Clg LLC (G-3840)*

A Cleaner Tomorrow Dry Clg LLC (PA)......................919 639-6396
102 S Wilson Ave Dunn (28334) *(G-3840)*

A D Services... 336 667-8190
402 S Cherry St Wilkesboro (28697) *(G-12626)*

A E Nesbitt Woodwork.. 828 625-2428
40 Bald Mountain Church Rd Black Mountain (28711) *(G-859)*

A Foodtruckqueen, Charlotte *Also Called: F & C Repair and Sales LLC (G-2139)*

A Forbes Company
1035 Harper Ave Sw Lenoir (28645) *(G-7565)*

A House of Hemp LLC... 910 984-1441
235 Shepard Dr Linden (28356) *(G-7872)*

A Klein & Co Inc.. 828 459-9261
1 Heart Dr Claremont (28610) *(G-3086)*

A L Beck & Sons Inc.. 336 788-1896
505 Jones Rd Winston Salem (27107) *(G-13070)*

A Land of Furniture Inc.. 336 882-3866
430 S Main St Ste 431 High Point (27260) *(G-6507)*

A M Moore and Company Inc (PA)........................... 336 294-6994
1207 Park Ter Greensboro (27403) *(G-5332)*

A M P Laboratories Ltd... 704 894-9721
20905 Torrence Chapel Rd Ste 204 Cornelius (28031) *(G-3582)*

A McGee Wood Products Inc.................................. 828 212-1700
171 N Main St Granite Falls (28630) *(G-5293)*

A N E Services LLC.. 704 882-1117
1716 Garette Rd Charlotte (28218) *(G-1605)*

A O A Signs, Wilson *Also Called: Aoa Signs Inc (G-12962)*

A O Smith Water Products Co................................. 704 597-8910
4302 Raleigh St Charlotte (28213) *(G-1606)*

A Oliver Arthur & Son Inc..................................... 828 459-8000
1904 Conover Blvd E Conover (28613) *(G-3486)*

A Palletone Company, Newton *Also Called: Industrial Recycling Services (G-9475)*

A Place To Copy, Raleigh *Also Called: Elledge Family Inc (G-10082)*

A Plus Carports.. 336 367-1261
6833 Us Highway 601 Boonville (27011) *(G-956)*

A Plus Five Star Trnsp LLC.................................... 919 771-4820
301 Mccarthy Dr Clayton (27527) *(G-3129)*

A Plus Graphics Inc... 252 243-0404
3101 Ward Blvd Wilson (27893) *(G-12960)*

A Plus Service Inc... 828 324-4397
2233a Highland Ave Ne Hickory (28601) *(G-6259)*

A R Byrd Company, Lincolnton *Also Called: A R Byrd Company Inc (G-7807)*

A R Byrd Company Inc.. 704 732-5675
171 Joshua Ct Lincolnton (28092) *(G-7807)*

A R Perry Corporation.. 252 492-6181
220 Old Epsom Rd Henderson (27536) *(G-6146)*

A S I, Pineville *Also Called: Leke LLC (G-9739)*

A Sign Co, Hickory *Also Called: Wright Business Concepts Inc (G-6491)*

A Stitch In Time.. 828 274-5193
1259 Sweeten Creek Rd 25a Asheville (28803) *(G-422)*

A Stitch To Remember... 336 202-0026
7621 Whitaker Dr Summerfield (27358) *(G-11834)*

A T Components, Garner *Also Called: Assembly Tech Components Inc (G-4917)*

A Taste of Heavenly Sweetness.............................. 336 825-7321
4518 W Market St Greensboro (27407) *(G-5333)*

A V E Parts & Accesories, Mooresville *Also Called: P4rts LLC (G-8740)*

A W S, Fayetteville *Also Called: Arnolds Welding Service Inc (G-4553)*

A-1 Coatings.. 704 790-9528
525 Linda St Salisbury (28146) *(G-11010)*

A-1 Concrete & Cnstr LLC..................................... 828 712-1160
42 Avery Creek Rd Arden (28704) *(G-247)*

A-1 Face Inc.. 336 248-5555
480 Dixon St Ste C Lexington (27292) *(G-7654)*

A-1 Hitch & Trailors Sales Inc............................... 910 755-6025
360 Ocean Hwy E Supply (28462) *(G-11854)*

A-1 Sandrock Inc (PA).. 336 855-8195
2606 Phoenix Dr Ste 518 Greensboro (27406) *(G-5334)*

A-1 Trucking, Greensboro *Also Called: A-1 Sandrock Inc (G-5334)*

A-B Emblem, Weaverville *Also Called: Conrad Industries Inc (G-12488)*

A-Line, Concord *Also Called: Prezioso Ventures LLC (G-3422)*

A.E. Logging, Trenton *Also Called: Triple E Equipment LLC (G-12112)*

A&B Integrators LLC.. 919 371-0750
2800 Meridian Pkwy Durham (27713) *(G-3876)*

A&M Screen Printing NC Inc.................................. 910 792-1111
6404 Amsterdam Way Unit 4 Wilmington (28405) *(G-12686)*

A&W Welding Inc.. 252 482-3233
1106 Haughton Rd 37 Edenton (27932) *(G-4358)*

A+ Pro Transport Inc... 980 215-8694
6201 Fairview Rd Charlotte (28210) *(G-1607)*

A1 Biochem Labs LLC.. 315 299-4775
5598 Marvin K Moss Ln Ste 2017 Wilmington (28409) *(G-12687)*

A1 Vending, Raleigh *Also Called: A1gumballs (G-9860)*

A1gumballs.. 919 494-1322
316 W Millbrook Rd Ste 113 Raleigh (27609) *(G-9860)*

A2a Integrated Logistics Inc................................. 800 493-3736
1830 Owen Dr Ste 102 Fayetteville (28304) *(G-4542)*

A3-Usa Inc... 724 871-7170
1674 Fountaintown Rd Chinquapin (28521) *(G-3081)*

A4 Health Systems Inc... 919 851-6177
5501 Dillard Dr Cary (27518) *(G-1283)*

AA Ceramics... 910 632-3053
2002 Eastwood Rd Wilmington (28403) *(G-12688)*

AAA Louvers Inc.. 919 365-7220
7328 Siemens Rd Wendell (27591) *(G-12529)*

AAA Mobile Signs LLC.. 919 463-9768
10404 Chapel Hill Rd Ste 110 Morrisville (27560) *(G-8915)*

Aae North America LLC... 919 534-1500
155 Kitty Hawk Dr Morrisville (27560) *(G-8916)*

2025 Harris North Carolina
Manufacturers Directory

(G-0000) Company's Geographic Section entry number

AAF Flanders, Washington *Also Called: Flanders Corporation (G-12385)*

Aalberts Integrated Piping Systems Americas Inc (HQ).................704 841-6000
10715 Sikes Pl Ste 200 Charlotte (28277) *(G-1608)*

Aallied Die Casting of N C, Rutherfordton *Also Called: RCM Industries Inc (G-10991)*

Aardvark Screen Printing.................919 829-9058
1600 Automotive Way Raleigh (27604) *(G-9861)*

Aarons Quality Signs.................704 841-7733
524 E Charles St Matthews (28105) *(G-8098)*

AB New Beginnings Inc.................828 465-6953
1211 Keisler Rd Se Conover (28613) *(G-3487)*

Abacon Telecommunications LLC (PA).................336 855-1179
4388 Federal Dr Greensboro (27410) *(G-5335)*

ABB Enterprise Software Inc.................919 582-3283
1021 Main Campus Dr Raleigh (27606) *(G-9862)*

ABB Holdings Inc (DH).................919 856-2360
305 Gregson Dr Cary (27511) *(G-1284)*

ABB Inc (DH).................919 856-2360
305 Gregson Dr Cary (27511) *(G-1285)*

ABB Inc.................704 587-1362
12037 Goodrich Dr Charlotte (28273) *(G-1609)*

ABB Inc.................252 827-2121
3022 Nc 43 N Pinetops (27864) *(G-9705)*

ABB Inc.................919 856-3920
901 Main Campus Dr Ste 300 Raleigh (27606) *(G-9863)*

ABB Inc.................919 856-2360
1021 Main Campus Dr Raleigh (27606) *(G-9864)*

ABB Installation Products Inc.................828 322-1855
415 19th Street Dr Se Hickory (28602) *(G-6260)*

ABB Motors and Mechanical Inc.................336 272-6104
1220 Rotherwood Rd Greensboro (27406) *(G-5336)*

ABB Motors and Mechanical Inc.................704 734-2500
101 Reliance Rd Kings Mountain (28086) *(G-7342)*

ABB Motors and Mechanical Inc.................479 646-4711
510 Rockwell Dr Marion (28752) *(G-8029)*

ABB Motors and Mechanical Inc.................828 645-1706
70 Reems Creek Rd Weaverville (28787) *(G-12481)*

ABB Power Systems, Raleigh *Also Called: ABB Inc (G-9864)*

ABB Power Systems Inc.................919 856-2389
901 Main Campus Dr Ste 300 Raleigh (27606) *(G-9865)*

ABB Power T & D Company Inc.................919 856-3806
1021 Main Campus Dr Raleigh (27606) *(G-9866)*

Abbott Laboratories.................704 243-1832
9108 Kingsmead Ln Waxhaw (28173) *(G-12422)*

Abbott Products Inc.................336 463-3135
1617 Fern Valley Rd Yadkinville (27055) *(G-13434)*

ABC 11, Durham *Also Called: Wtvd Television LLC (G-4313)*

ABC Fitness Products LLC (PA).................704 649-0000
8541 Glenwood Ave Raleigh (27612) *(G-9867)*

ABC Hosiery, Youngsville *Also Called: Grady Distributing Co Inc (G-13473)*

ABC Signs.................252 223-5900
214 Roberts Rd Newport (28570) *(G-9436)*

ABC Signs and Graphics LLC.................252 652-6620
160 Us Highway 70 W Havelock (28532) *(G-6122)*

Abco Automation Inc.................336 375-6400
6202 Technology Dr Browns Summit (27214) *(G-988)*

Abco Controls and Eqp Inc.................704 394-2424
4110 Monroe Rd Charlotte (28205) *(G-1610)*

Abcor Supply Inc (PA).................919 468-0856
811 Oxfordshire Ln Chapel Hill (27517) *(G-1523)*

Abe Entercom Holdings LLC.................336 691-4337
100 N Greene St Ste M Greensboro (27401) *(G-5337)*

Abee Custom Signs Inc.................336 229-1554
544 Chapel Hill Rd Burlington (27215) *(G-1042)*

Abercrombie Textiles Inc (PA).................704 487-0935
3051 River Rd Shelby (28152) *(G-11308)*

Abercrombie Textiles I LLC (PA).................704 487-1245
1322 Mount Sinai Church Rd Shelby (28152) *(G-11309)*

Aberdeen Coca-Cola Btlg Co Inc.................910 944-2305
203 W South St Aberdeen (28315) *(G-1)*

Abhw Concrete Co.................252 940-1002
347 S Wharton Station Rd Washington (27889) *(G-12370)*

Ability Orthopedics.................704 630-6789
209 Statesville Blvd Salisbury (28144) *(G-11011)*

Abl Electronics Supply Inc.................704 784-4225
1032 Central Dr Nw Ste A Concord (28027) *(G-3308)*

Able Graphics Company LLC.................336 753-1812
126 Horn St Mocksville (27028) *(G-8346)*

Able Metal Fabricators Inc.................704 394-8972
3441 Reno Ave Charlotte (28216) *(G-1611)*

Able Softsystems Corp.................919 241-7907
1017 Main Campus Dr Ste 1501 Raleigh (27606) *(G-9868)*

Aboard Trade LLC.................919 341-7045
4705 Southport Supply Rd Se Ste 208 Southport (28461) *(G-11515)*

Abolder Image.................336 856-1300
205 Aloe Rd Greensboro (27409) *(G-5338)*

Above Topsail LLC.................910 803-1759
301 Us Highway 17 S Holly Ridge (28445) *(G-6886)*

Abrasive Resource, Charlotte *Also Called: Starcke Abrasives Usa Inc (G-2860)*

Abrasives Industries AG, Lincolnton *Also Called: Sia Abrasives Inc USA (G-7853)*

ABS Southeast LLC (PA).................919 329-0014
5902 Fayetteville Rd Raleigh (27603) *(G-9869)*

Absolent Inc.................919 570-2862
6541 Meridien Dr Ste 125 Raleigh (27616) *(G-9870)*

Absolute Security & Lock Inc.................336 322-4598
216 S Main St Roxboro (27573) *(G-10917)*

ABT, Statesville *Also Called: ABT Manufacturing LLC (G-11645)*

Abt Inc.................314 610-8798
259 Murdock Rd Troutman (28166) *(G-12128)*

Abt Inc (PA).................704 528-9806
259 Murdock Rd Troutman (28166) *(G-12129)*

ABT Foam Inc.................800 433-1119
1405 Industrial Dr Statesville (28625) *(G-11643)*

ABT Foam LLC.................704 508-1010
1405 Industrial Dr Statesville (28625) *(G-11644)*

ABT Manufacturing LLC.................704 847-9188
1903 Weinig St Statesville (28677) *(G-11645)*

Abundant Power Solutions LLC.................704 271-9890
222 S Church St Ste 401 Charlotte (28202) *(G-1612)*

Abx Innvtive Pckg Slutions LLC (PA).................980 443-1100
2015 Ayrsley Town Blvd Ste 202 Charlotte (28273) *(G-1613)*

Abzorbit Inc.................828 464-9944
2628 Northwest Blvd Newton (28658) *(G-9447)*

AC Corporation (HQ).................336 273-4472
301 Creek Ridge Rd Greensboro (27406) *(G-5339)*

AC Corporation North Carolina, Greensboro *Also Called: AC Corporation (G-5339)*

AC Valor Reyes LLC.................910 431-3256
4610 College Rd N Castle Hayne (28429) *(G-1493)*

Acacia Home & Garden Inc.................828 465-1700
101 N Mclin Creek Rd Conover (28613) *(G-3488)*

Academy Association Inc.................919 544-0835
2222 Sedwick Rd Ste 101 Durham (27713) *(G-3877)*

Acadeus, Raleigh *Also Called: Propharma Group LLC (G-10405)*

ACC Coatings LLC.................336 701-0080
620 E Main St Elkin (28621) *(G-4438)*

ACC Distributors, Youngsville *Also Called: Atlantic Coast Cabinet Distrs (G-13462)*

ACC Sports Journal.................919 846-7502
3012 Highwoods Blvd Ste 200 Raleigh (27604) *(G-9871)*

Accel Discount Tire (PA).................704 636-0323
201 E Liberty St Salisbury (28144) *(G-11012)*

Accelerated Media Technologies.................336 599-2070
4400 Semora Rd Roxboro (27574) *(G-10918)*

Accelerated Press Inc.................248 524-1850
616 Windchime Dr Wilmington (28412) *(G-12689)*

Accent Awnings Inc (PA).................828 321-4517
91 Morgan Rd Andrews (28901) *(G-104)*

Accent Comfort Services LLC.................704 509-1200
8421 Old Statesville Rd Ste 17 Charlotte (28269) *(G-1614)*

Access Newswire Inc (PA).................919 481-4000
1 Glenwood Ave Ste 1001 Raleigh (27603) *(G-9872)*

Access Technologies LLC.................574 286-1255
163 Cooley Rd Mooresville (28117) *(G-8590)*

Accidental Baker.................919 732-6777
115 Boone Square St Hillsborough (27278) *(G-6857)*

Accord Healthcare Inc (HQ)..919 941-7878
  8041 Arco Corporate Dr Ste 200 Raleigh (27617) *(G-9873)*

Accord Ventilation Products, Greensboro *Also Called: American Valve Inc (G-5358)*

Accounting Office, Mooresville *Also Called: Bestco LLC (G-8610)*

Accu-Form Polymers Inc...910 293-6961
  170 Water Tank Rd Warsaw (28398) *(G-12357)*

Accu-Tool LLC..919 363-2600
  2490 Reliance Ave Apex (27539) *(G-132)*

Accudyne Industries LLC..469 518-4777
  800 Beaty St Ste A Davidson (28036) *(G-3697)*

Accugenomics Inc...910 332-6522
  1410 Commonwealth Dr Ste 105 Wilmington (28403) *(G-12690)*

Accuking Inc...252 649-2323
  3458 Martin Dr New Bern (28562) *(G-9330)*

Acculabs Technologies Inc..919 468-8780
  1018 Morrisville Pkwy Ste E Morrisville (27560) *(G-8917)*

Acculink...252 321-5805
  1055 Greenville Blvd Sw Greenville (27834) *(G-5934)*

Accuma Corporation (DH)...704 873-1488
  133 Fanjoy Rd Statesville (28625) *(G-11646)*

Accumed Corp (HQ)...800 278-6796
  160 Mine Lake Ct Ste 200 Raleigh (27615) *(G-9874)*

Accurate Machine & Tool LLC...919 212-0266
  5124 Trademark Dr Raleigh (27610) *(G-9875)*

Accurate Technology Inc (PA)..828 654-7920
  270 Rutledge Rd Fletcher (28732) *(G-4717)*

Accusport International Inc (PA)....................................336 759-3300
  801 N Trade St Winston Salem (27101) *(G-13071)*

Ace Fabrication Inc..919 934-3251
  2880 Us Highway 70 Bus W Smithfield (27577) *(G-11433)*

Ace Hardware, Bakersville *Also Called: Ledger Hardware Inc (G-679)*

Ace Industries Inc...336 427-5316
  213 Carlton Rd Madison (27025) *(G-7983)*

Ace Laser Recycling Inc...919 775-5521
  1808 Rice Rd Sanford (27330) *(G-11145)*

Ace Marine Rigging & Supply Inc (PA)..............................252 726-6620
  600 Arendell St Morehead City (28557) *(G-8811)*

Ace Plastics, Charlotte *Also Called: Ace Plastics Inc (G-1615)*

Ace Plastics Inc...704 527-5752
  5130 Hovis Rd Ste A Charlotte (28208) *(G-1615)*

Aceragen Inc...919 271-1032
  15 Tw Alexander Dr 418 Durham (27709) *(G-3878)*

Acetrace, Greensboro *Also Called: Sierra Software LLC (G-5812)*

Aceyus Inc...704 443-7900
  11111 Carmel Commons Blvd Ste 210 Charlotte (28226) *(G-1616)*

Achelios Therapeutics LLC..919 354-6233
  4364 S Alston Ave Ste 300 Durham (27713) *(G-3879)*

Achem Industry America Inc..704 283-6144
  2910 Stitt St Monroe (28110) *(G-8415)*

Achilli USA Inc..704 940-0115
  8610 Air Park West Dr Ste 100 Charlotte (28214) *(G-1617)*

Ackermann Tool & Machine Co, Wilmington *Also Called: Wilmington Machine Works Inc (G-12950)*

Aclc, Fayetteville *Also Called: Advanced Computer Lrng Co LLC (G-4544)*

Acme - McCrary Corporation...336 625-2161
  1311 E 11th St Siler City (27344) *(G-11396)*

ACME - MCCRARY CORPORATION, Siler City *Also Called: Acme - McCrary Corporation (G-11396)*

Acme Aerofab LLC...704 806-3582
  1907 Scott Futrell Dr Charlotte (28208) *(G-1618)*

Acme Die & Machine Corporation.....................................704 864-8426
  202 Trakas Blvd Gastonia (28052) *(G-4983)*

Acme General Design Group LLC......................................843 466-6000
  101 N Market St Benson (27504) *(G-783)*

Acme Liquidating Company LLC..704 873-3731
  1784 Salisbury Rd Statesville (28677) *(G-11647)*

Acme Machine LLC...828 483-6440
  95 Commercial Hill Dr Hendersonville (28792) *(G-6183)*

Acme Metal Products, Statesville *Also Called: Acme Liquidating Company LLC (G-11647)*

Acme Nameplate & Mfg Inc...704 283-8175
  300 Acme Dr (Off Hwy 74 E) Monroe (28112) *(G-8416)*

Acme Rental Company..704 873-3731
  1784 Salisbury Rd Statesville (28677) *(G-11648)*

Acme Sample Books, High Point *Also Called: Pag Asb LLC (G-6724)*

Acme Sample Books Inc..336 883-4336
  603 Fraley Rd High Point (27263) *(G-6508)*

Acme Stone Company Inc..336 786-6978
  1700 Fancy Gap Rd Mount Airy (27030) *(G-9095)*

Acme United Corporation..252 822-5051
  2280 Tanner Rd Rocky Mount (27801) *(G-10807)*

Acme-Mccrary Corporation..336 625-2161
  159 North St Asheboro (27203) *(G-323)*

Acme-Mccrary Corporation (DH).......................................336 625-2161
  162 N Cherry St Asheboro (27203) *(G-324)*

Acme-Mccrary Corporation..919 663-2200
  1200 E 3rd St Siler City (27344) *(G-11397)*

Aconcagua Timber Corp..919 542-2128
  985 Corinth Rd Moncure (27559) *(G-8398)*

Acorn Printing...704 868-4522
  4122 Kings Mountain Hwy Bessemer City (28016) *(G-801)*

Acorn Woodworks NC LLC...828 361-9953
  1221 Warren Dr Murphy (28906) *(G-9286)*

Acoustek Nonwovens, Statesville *Also Called: Wwj LLC (G-11802)*

Acquionics Inc...980 256-5700
  4215 Stuart Andrew Blvd Ste E Charlotte (28217) *(G-1619)*

Acre Station Meat Farm Inc...252 927-3700
  17076 Nc Highway 32 N Pinetown (27865) *(G-9707)*

Acroplis Cntrls Engineers Pllc.......................................919 275-3884
  313 S Blount St Ste 200d Raleigh (27601) *(G-9876)*

ACS Advnced Clor Solutions Inc......................................252 442-0098
  120 S Business Ct Rocky Mount (27804) *(G-10821)*

Acsm Inc...704 910-0243
  113 Freeland Ln Charlotte (28217) *(G-1620)*

Actega North America Inc...704 736-9389
  101 Reliance Rd Kings Mountain (28086) *(G-7343)*

Actega Wit, Kings Mountain *Also Called: Actega North America Inc (G-7343)*

Actega Wit Inc...704 735-8282
  125 Technolgy Dr Lincolnton (28092) *(G-7808)*

Acterna LLC..919 388-5100
  1100 Perimeter Park Dr Ste 101 Morrisville (27560) *(G-8918)*

Action Graphics, Charlotte *Also Called: Perlman Inc (G-2629)*

Action Graphics and Signs Inc.......................................919 690-1260
  8694b Us Highway 15 Bullock (27507) *(G-1012)*

Action Installs LLC..704 787-3828
  1202 Industrial Park Rd Wilkesboro (28697) *(G-12627)*

Action Sign Company Lenoir Inc......................................828 754-4116
  511 Creekway Dr Nw Lenoir (28645) *(G-7566)*

Action Surf Shop, Morehead City *Also Called: Action Surfboards (G-8812)*

Action Surfboards...252 240-1818
  4130 Arendell St Morehead City (28557) *(G-8812)*

Actionsign Group, Lenoir *Also Called: Action Sign Company Lenoir Inc (G-7566)*

Active Concepts LLC..704 276-7372
  110 Technolgy Dr Lincolnton (28092) *(G-7809)*

Active Concepts LLC (PA)...704 276-7100
  107 Technolgy Dr Lincolnton (28092) *(G-7810)*

Active Hats and Things Suite...888 352-9292
  2201 Inkberry Ct Wilmington (28411) *(G-12691)*

Acton Corporation...434 728-4491
  1451 S Elm Eugene St Greensboro (27406) *(G-5340)*

Acucal Inc...252 337-9975
  108 Enterprise Dr Elizabeth City (27909) *(G-4377)*

Acucote, Graham *Also Called: Acucote Inc (G-5259)*

Acucote Inc (DH)...336 578-1800
  910 E Elm St Graham (27253) *(G-5259)*

Acw Technology Inc
  3725 Althorp Dr Raleigh (27616) *(G-9877)*

Ad Pak, The, Wilmington *Also Called: Media Wilimington Co (G-12851)*

Ad Press Printing, Summerfield *Also Called: Adpress Printing Incorporated (G-11835)*

Ad Runner MBL Outdoor Advg Inc.....................................336 945-1190
  2555 Williams Rd Lewisville (27023) *(G-7649)*

Ad Spice Marketing LLC...919 286-7110
  4310 Garrett Rd Durham (27707) *(G-3880)*

Ad-Art Signs Inc.. 704 377-5369
2613 Lucena St Charlotte (28206) *(G-1621)*

Ada Marketing Inc... 910 221-2189
601 N Ashe Ave Dunn (28334) *(G-3841)*

Adama US, Raleigh *Also Called: Makhteshim Agan North Amer Inc (G-10267)*

Adams Beverages Leland, Leland *Also Called: Adams Beverages NC LLC (G-7531)*

Adams Beverages Lumberton, Lumberton *Also Called: Adams Beverages NC LLC (G-7942)*

Adams Beverages NC LLC (PA)........................ 704 509-3000
7505 Statesville Rd Charlotte (28269) *(G-1622)*

Adams Beverages NC LLC................................. 910 763-6216
2265 Mercantile Dr Leland (28451) *(G-7531)*

Adams Beverages NC LLC................................. 910 738-8165
797 Caton Rd Lumberton (28360) *(G-7942)*

Adams Handmade Soap, Dunn *Also Called: Ada Marketing Inc (G-3841)*

Adams Line Striping, Cornelius *Also Called: Safe Home Pro Inc (G-3626)*

Adams Oldcastle.. 980 229-7678
9968 Metromont Industrial Blvd Charlotte (28269) *(G-1623)*

Adams Products, Durham *Also Called: Old Castle Apg South Inc (G-4155)*

Adams Products Company................................. 919 467-2218
5701 Mccrimmon Pkwy Ste 201 Morrisville (27560) *(G-8919)*

Adams Wood Turning Inc.................................. 336 882-0196
216 Woodbine St High Point (27260) *(G-6509)*

Adamson Global Technology Corp (PA)............. 252 523-5200
2018 W Vernon Ave Kinston (28504) *(G-7391)*

Adaptive Health, Charlotte *Also Called: Direct Digital LLC (G-2051)*

Adaptive Mobility Solutions, Washington *Also Called: Veon Inc (G-12418)*

Adaptive Technologies LLC................................ 919 231-6890
3224 Lake Woodard Dr Ste 100 Raleigh (27604) *(G-9878)*

ADC, Hayesville *Also Called: Advanced Digital Cable Inc (G-6137)*

ADC Industries Inc... 919 550-9515
106 N Lombard St Clayton (27520) *(G-3130)*

Adcut, Maxton *Also Called: Advanced Cutting Tech Inc (G-8199)*

Add-On Technologies Inc.................................. 704 882-2227
7000 Stinson Hartis Rd Ste D Indian Trail (28079) *(G-7066)*

Adele Knits Inc... 336 499-6010
3304 Old Lexington Rd Winston Salem (27107) *(G-13072)*

Adhezion Biomedical LLC.................................. 828 728-6116
506 Pine Mountain Rd Hudson (28638) *(G-6940)*

ADI Global Distribution, Charlotte *Also Called: Resideo LLC (G-2715)*

ADI Global Distribution, Greensboro *Also Called: Resideo LLC (G-5784)*

ADI Global Distribution, Raleigh *Also Called: Resideo LLC (G-10441)*

ADI/PDM Trade Group, High Point *Also Called: Precision Design Machinery (G-6740)*

Adkins Truck Equipment Co............................. 704 596-2299
11300 Reames Rd Charlotte (28269) *(G-1624)*

ADM, Charlotte *Also Called: Archer-Daniels-Midland Company (G-1691)*

ADM, Southport *Also Called: Archer-Daniels-Midland Company (G-11516)*

Admark, Wilmington *Also Called: Advanced Marketing International Inc (G-12692)*

Admiral Marine Pdts & Svcs Inc....................... 704 489-8771
770 Crosspoint Dr Denver (28037) *(G-3767)*

Admissionpros LLC.. 919 256-3889
800 Pinner Weald Way Ste 101 Cary (27513) *(G-1286)*

Adoratherapy Inc... 917 297-8904
31 Mount Vernon Cir Asheville (28804) *(G-423)*

Adpress Printing Incorporated.......................... 336 294-2244
7000 Morganshire Ct Summerfield (27358) *(G-11835)*

Adr Hydro-Cut Inc... 919 388-2251
125 International Dr Ste E Morrisville (27560) *(G-8920)*

ADS, Bessemer City *Also Called: Advanced Drainage Systems Inc (G-803)*

ADS Graphic Design, Boone *Also Called: Advertising Design Systems Inc (G-894)*

ADS N Art Screenprinting & EMB...................... 919 453-0400
929 Heritage Lake Rd Ste 400 Wake Forest (27587) *(G-12258)*

ADS Printing Co Inc... 919 834-0579
733 W Hargett St Raleigh (27603) *(G-9879)*

Adsign Corp... 336 766-3000
6100 Gun Club Rd Winston Salem (27103) *(G-13073)*

Advance Auto Parts, Greensboro *Also Called: Advance Stores Company Inc (G-5341)*

Advance Cabinetry Inc..................................... 828 676-3550
15 Design Ave Unit 201 Fletcher (28732) *(G-4718)*

Advance Conveying Tech LLC........................... 704 710-4001
171 Kings Rd Kings Mountain (28086) *(G-7344)*

Advance Machining Co Gastonia....................... 704 866-7411
3517 W Franklin Blvd Gastonia (28052) *(G-4984)*

Advance Signs & Service Inc............................ 919 639-4666
596 W Church St Angier (27501) *(G-110)*

Advance Stores Company Inc........................... 336 545-9091
2514 Battleground Ave Ste A Greensboro (27408) *(G-5341)*

Advanced Brace & Limb Inc............................. 910 483-5737
4140 Ferncreek Dr Ste 803 Fayetteville (28314) *(G-4543)*

Advanced Brace and Limb, Fayetteville *Also Called: Advanced Brace & Limb Inc (G-4543)*

Advanced Computer Lrng Co LLC...................... 910 779-2254
208 Hay St Ste 2c Fayetteville (28301) *(G-4544)*

Advanced Cutting Tech Inc............................... 910 944-3028
12760 Airport Rd Maxton (28364) *(G-8199)*

Advanced Detection Tech LLC........................... 704 663-1949
215 Overhill Dr 1 Mooresville (28117) *(G-8591)*

Advanced Digital Cable Inc (PA)....................... 828 389-1652
94 Eagle Fork Rd Hayesville (28904) *(G-6137)*

Advanced Digital Systems Inc........................... 919 485-4819
4601 Creekstone Dr Ste 180 Durham (27703) *(G-3881)*

Advanced Digital Textiles LLC........................... 704 226-9600
600 Broome St Monroe (28110) *(G-8417)*

Advanced Drainage Systems.............................. 704 629-4151
333 Southridge Pkwy Bessemer City (28016) *(G-802)*

Advanced Drainage Systems Inc....................... 704 629-4151
902 E Maine Ave Bessemer City (28016) *(G-803)*

Advanced Drainage Systems Inc....................... 336 764-0341
11875 N Nc Highway 150 Winston Salem (27127) *(G-13074)*

Advanced Electronic Svcs Inc (PA).................... 336 789-0792
101 Technology Ln Mount Airy (27030) *(G-9096)*

Advanced Grading & Excvtg LLC....................... 828 320-7465
4360 Caldwell Rd Newton (28658) *(G-9448)*

Advanced Machine Services............................... 910 410-0099
835 N Us Highway 220 Rockingham (28379) *(G-10768)*

Advanced Machine Services LLC........................ 910 410-0099
128 Industrial Park Dr Rockingham (28379) *(G-10769)*

Advanced Machining, Salisbury *Also Called: Advanced Machining Tooling LLC (G-11013)*

Advanced Machining Co, Gastonia *Also Called: Advance Machining Co Gastonia (G-4984)*

Advanced Machining Tooling LLC....................... 704 633-8157
215 Forbes Ave Salisbury (28147) *(G-11013)*

Advanced Marketing International Inc................. 910 392-0508
211 Racine Dr Ste 202 Wilmington (28403) *(G-12692)*

Advanced Mch & Fabrication Inc....................... 704 489-0096
7842 Commerce Dr Denver (28037) *(G-3768)*

Advanced Mfg Solutions NC Inc........................ 828 633-2633
53 Rutherford Rd Candler (28715) *(G-1216)*

Advanced Micro Devices Inc............................. 919 840-8080
3000 Rdu Center Dr Ste 230 Morrisville (27560) *(G-8921)*

Advanced Motor Sports Coatings....................... 336 472-5518
17 High Tech Blvd Thomasville (27360) *(G-11990)*

Advanced Non-Lethal Tech Inc.......................... 847 812-6450
8311 Brier Creek Pkwy Ste 106-88 Raleigh (27617) *(G-9880)*

Advanced Photonic Crystals LLC....................... 803 547-0881
19825 North Cove Rd Ste 216 Cornelius (28031) *(G-3583)*

Advanced Plastic Extrusion LLC........................ 252 224-1444
213 Sermon Rd Pollocksville (28573) *(G-9816)*

Advanced Plastiform Inc (PA)............................ 919 404-2080
535 Mack Todd Rd Zebulon (27597) *(G-13500)*

Advanced Plastiform Inc................................... 919 404-2080
113 Legacy Crest Ct Zebulon (27597) *(G-13501)*

Advanced Plating Technologies........................... 704 291-9325
2600 Stitt St Monroe (28110) *(G-8418)*

Advanced Substrate... 336 285-5955
7860 Thorndike Rd Greensboro (27409) *(G-5342)*

Advanced Superabrasives Inc............................ 828 689-3200
1270 N Main St Mars Hill (28754) *(G-8076)*

Advanced Systems Intgrtion LLC (PA)................ 260 447-5555
8512 Mangum Hollow Dr Wake Forest (27587) *(G-12259)*

Advanced Tech Systems Inc.............................. 336 299-6695
2606 Phoenix Dr Ste 602 Greensboro (27406) *(G-5343)*

Advanced Technology Inc.................................. 336 668-0488
6106 W Market St Greensboro (27409) *(G-5344)*

A
L
P
H
A
B
E
T
I
C

Advanced Teo Corp...305 278-4474
5707 Hornet Dr Charlotte (28216) *(G-1625)*

Advanced Traffic Marking, Weldon *Also Called: Patch Rubber Company (G-12525)*

Advancepierre Foods Inc..828 459-7626
3437 E Main St Claremont (28610) *(G-3087)*

Advantage Conveyor Inc...919 781-0055
8816 Gulf Ct Ste C Raleigh (27617) *(G-9881)*

Advantage Fitness Products Inc.................................336 643-8810
115 Gralin St Kernersville (27284) *(G-7239)*

Advantage Machinery Svcs Inc (PA)...........................336 463-4700
1407 Us 601 Hwy Yadkinville (27055) *(G-13435)*

Advantage Manufacturing, Raleigh *Also Called: Advantage Conveyor Inc (G-9881)*

Advantage Marketing...919 872-8610
129 Bartholomew Rd Louisburg (27549) *(G-7908)*

Advantage Newspaper..910 323-0349
501 Executive Pl Ste B Fayetteville (28305) *(G-4545)*

Advantage Nn-Wvens Cnvrting LL..............................828 635-1880
173 Wittenburg Industrial Dr Taylorsville (28681) *(G-11948)*

Advantage Printing..828 252-7667
1848 Brevard Rd Arden (28704) *(G-248)*

Advantage Printing & Design.....................................252 523-8133
2425 N Herritage St Kinston (28501) *(G-7392)*

Advertising Design Systems Inc.................................828 264-8060
269 Grand Blvd Boone (28607) *(G-894)*

Advocacy To Allvate Hmlessness...............................919 810-3431
4000 Wake Forest Rd Ste 102 Raleigh (27609) *(G-9882)*

Advplating LLC...704 291-9325
2600 Stitt St Monroe (28110) *(G-8419)*

Adwood Corporation..336 884-1846
260 Durand Ave High Point (27263) *(G-6510)*

Ae Technology Inc...704 528-2000
150 Ostwalt Amity Rd Troutman (28166) *(G-12130)*

AEC Consumer Products, Fayetteville *Also Called: AEC Consumer Products LLC (G-4546)*

AEC Consumer Products LLC....................................704 904-0578
3005 Bankhead Dr Fayetteville (28306) *(G-4546)*

AEC Imaging & Graphics LLC (PA).............................910 693-1034
5755 Dove Dr Hope Mills (28348) *(G-6922)*

AEC Narrow Fabrics, Asheboro *Also Called: Asheboro Elastics Corp (G-327)*

AEC Narrow Fabrics, Asheboro *Also Called: Asheboro Elastics Corp (G-328)*

AEG International, Charlotte *Also Called: Livingston & Haven LLC (G-2428)*

Aegis Power Systems Inc...828 837-4029
805 Greenlawn Cemetery Rd Murphy (28906) *(G-9287)*

AEL Locate Services, Reidsville *Also Called: Pipeline Enterprises LLC (G-10697)*

AEL Services LLC..704 525-3710
8200 Arrowridge Blvd Ste A Charlotte (28273) *(G-1626)*

Aer Therapeutics Inc...919 345-4256
400 W North St Ste 112 Raleigh (27603) *(G-9883)*

Aerami Therapeutics Inc (PA)....................................650 773-5926
600 Park Offices Dr Durham (27709) *(G-3882)*

Aerie Pharmaceuticals Inc (HQ).................................919 237-5300
4301 Emperor Blvd Ste 400 Durham (27703) *(G-3883)*

Aero Precision Machine Inc.......................................336 685-0016
6024 Smithwood Rd Liberty (27298) *(G-7759)*

Aerofabb LLC...919 793-8487
3312 Marcony Way Raleigh (27610) *(G-9884)*

AF&f, Albemarle *Also Called: American Fiber & Finishing Inc (G-61)*

AFA Billing Services..910 868-8324
894 Elm St Ste D Fayetteville (28303) *(G-4547)*

Afe Victory Inc...856 428-4200
3779 Champion Blvd Winston Salem (27105) *(G-13075)*

Afex, Raleigh *Also Called: Bonaventure Group Inc (G-9953)*

Affordable Bedding Inc..828 254-5555
996 Patton Ave Ste A Asheville (28806) *(G-424)*

Afi Capital Inc...919 212-6400
801 Beacon Lake Dr Raleigh (27610) *(G-9885)*

AFL Network Services Inc...704 289-5522
11211 Allen Station Dr Mint Hill (28227) *(G-8329)*

AFL Network Services Inc...919 658-2311
100 Impulse Way Mount Olive (28365) *(G-9246)*

Afsc LLC...704 523-4936
3605 S Tryon St Charlotte (28217) *(G-1627)*

AG Provision LLC (PA)...910 296-0302
277 Faison W Mcgowan Rd Kenansville (28349) *(G-7224)*

Against Grain Woodworking Inc.................................704 309-5750
1015 Seigle Ave Charlotte (28205) *(G-1628)*

Agastat, Fairview *Also Called: Te Connectivity Corporation (G-4514)*

Agency Management Soluitons, Elon *Also Called: Jenesis Software Inc (G-4471)*

Aggregates Div, Raleigh *Also Called: Martin Marietta Materials Inc (G-10275)*

Agile Microwave Technology Inc................................984 228-8001
701 Cascade Pointe Ln Ste 101 Cary (27513) *(G-1287)*

Agile Mwt, Cary *Also Called: Agile Microwave Technology Inc (G-1287)*

Agile Ventures LLC...202 716-7958
2107 Spartanburg Hwy East Flat Rock (28726) *(G-4328)*

Agingo, Charlotte *Also Called: Agingo Corporation (G-1629)*

Agingo Corporation...888 298-0777
1401 W Morehead St Ste 150 Charlotte (28208) *(G-1629)*

AGM Carolina Inc..336 431-4100
1031 E Springfield Rd High Point (27263) *(G-6511)*

Agnatural LLC..252 536-0322
802 Julian R Allsbrook Hwy Weldon (27890) *(G-12518)*

Agricltral-Industrial Fabr Inc....................................336 591-3690
223 S Main St Walnut Cove (27052) *(G-12326)*

Agrofuel LLC..704 876-6667
964 Snow Creek Rd Statesville (28625) *(G-11649)*

Ahlberg Cameras, Wilmington *Also Called: Ahlberg Cameras Inc (G-12693)*

Ahlberg Cameras Inc...910 523-5876
432 Landmark Dr Wilmington (28412) *(G-12693)*

Aie We Go, Monroe *Also Called: Air-We-Go LLC (G-8420)*

Aiken Development LLC..828 572-4040
1028 West Ave Nw Lenoir (28645) *(G-7567)*

Aiken-Black Tire Service Inc.....................................828 322-3736
823 1st Ave Nw Hickory (28601) *(G-6261)*

Aikencontrols, Lenoir *Also Called: Aiken Development LLC (G-7567)*

AIM Industries Inc..336 656-9990
391 Brann Rd Browns Summit (27214) *(G-989)*

Aim Molding & Door LLC..704 913-7211
5431 Starflower Dr Charlotte (28215) *(G-1630)*

Aimet Holding Inc...919 887-5205
115 Legacy Crest Ct Zebulon (27597) *(G-13502)*

Aimet Technologies, Zebulon *Also Called: Aimet Holding Inc (G-13502)*

Aimet Technologies LLC...919 887-5205
115 Legacy Crest Ct Zebulon (27597) *(G-13503)*

Air & Gas Solutions LLC..704 897-2182
5509 David Cox Rd Charlotte (28269) *(G-1631)*

Air Control Inc...252 492-2300
237 Raleigh Rd Henderson (27536) *(G-6147)*

Air Controls Division, Roxboro *Also Called: Eaton Corporation (G-10924)*

Air Craftsmen Inc...336 248-5777
2503 Northside Dr Statesville (28625) *(G-11650)*

Air Force Fleet Readiness Ctr, Cherry Point *Also Called: United States Dept of Navy (G-3056)*

Air Purification Inc (PA)..919 783-6161
8121 Ebenezer Church Rd Raleigh (27612) *(G-9886)*

Air System Components Inc......................................919 279-8868
275 Pressly Foushee Rd Sanford (27330) *(G-11146)*

Air System Components Inc......................................919 775-2201
101 Mcneill Rd Sanford (27330) *(G-11147)*

Air System Components Inc......................................252 641-5900
3301 N Main St Tarboro (27886) *(G-11921)*

Air System Components Inc......................................252 641-0875
3301 N Main St Tarboro (27886) *(G-11922)*

Air Systems Mfg of Lenoir Inc..................................828 757-3500
2621 Hogan Dr Lenoir (28645) *(G-7568)*

Air-We-Go LLC...704 289-6565
4507 W Highway 74 Monroe (28110) *(G-8420)*

Airborn Industries Inc...704 483-5000
115 Industrial Park Rd Lincolnton (28092) *(G-7811)*

Airboss Heating and Coolg Inc..................................252 586-0500
127 W South Main St Littleton (27850) *(G-7883)*

Airboss Rbr Compounding NC LLC.............................252 826-4919
500 Airboss Pkwy Scotland Neck (27874) *(G-11263)*

Airboss Rubber Solutions, Scotland Neck *Also Called: Airboss Rbr Compounding NC LLC (G-11263)*

Airbox Inc..855 927-1386
2668 Peachtree Rd Statesville (28625) *(G-11651)*

Airclean Systems, Creedmoor Also Called: Applied Medical Tech Inc *(G-3639)*

Aircraft Belts Inc (DH)................................919 956-4395
1176 Telecom Dr Creedmoor (27522) *(G-3635)*

Aircraft Parts Solutions LLC........................843 300-1725
3378 Apex Peakway Apex (27502) *(G-133)*

Airdream.net, Davidson Also Called: Elborn Holdings LLC *(G-3704)*

Airflow Products Company Inc......................919 975-0240
100 Oak Tree Dr Selma (27576) *(G-11283)*

Airgas, Durham Also Called: Airgas Usa LLC *(G-3884)*

Airgas, Salisbury Also Called: Airgas Usa LLC *(G-11014)*

Airgas National Carbonation, Charlotte Also Called: Airgas Usa LLC *(G-1633)*

Airgas National Welders, Wilmington Also Called: Airgas Usa LLC *(G-12694)*

Airgas Usa LLC...704 333-5475
5311 77 Center Dr Charlotte (28217) *(G-1632)*

Airgas Usa LLC...704 394-1420
3101 Stafford Dr Charlotte (28208) *(G-1633)*

Airgas Usa LLC...919 544-1056
2810 S Miami Blvd Durham (27703) *(G-3884)*

Airgas Usa LLC...919 544-3773
630 United Dr Durham (27713) *(G-3885)*

Airgas Usa LLC...919 735-5276
109 Hinnant Rd Goldsboro (27530) *(G-5196)*

Airgas Usa LLC...704 636-5049
1924 S Main St Salisbury (28144) *(G-11014)*

Airgas Usa LLC...910 392-2711
2824 Carolina Beach Rd Wilmington (28412) *(G-12694)*

Airloom Furnishing, Bennett Also Called: Philip Brady *(G-782)*

Airspeed LLC..919 644-1222
1413 S Third Street Ext Mebane (27302) *(G-8227)*

Airt, Charlotte Also Called: T Air Inc *(G-2895)*

Airtek, Goldsboro Also Called: AP Emissions Technologies LLC *(G-5199)*

Aisin North Carolina Corp...........................919 529-0951
1187 Telecom Dr Creedmoor (27522) *(G-3636)*

Aisin North Carolina Corp (DH)....................919 479-6400
4112 Old Oxford Rd Durham (27712) *(G-3886)*

Aisthesis Products Inc...............................828 627-6555
70 Brigadoon Dr Clyde (28721) *(G-3255)*

Aj & Raine Scrubs & More LLC.....................646 374-5198
657 Fielding Rd Charlotte (28214) *(G-1634)*

Ajinomoto, Raleigh Also Called: Ajinomoto Hlth Ntrtn N Amer In *(G-9887)*

Ajinomoto Hlth Ntrtn N Amer In...................919 231-0100
4020 Ajinomoto Dr Raleigh (27610) *(G-9887)*

Ajs Dezigns Inc..828 652-6304
Ashworth Rd Marion (28752) *(G-8030)*

Akg North America Inc...............................919 563-4286
7315 Oakwood Street Ext Mebane (27302) *(G-8228)*

Akg Nrth Amercn Operations Inc (DH)...........919 563-4286
7315 Oakwood Street Ext Mebane (27302) *(G-8229)*

Akg of America Inc (DH)............................919 563-4286
7315 Oakwood Street Ext Mebane (27302) *(G-8230)*

Akoustis, Huntersville Also Called: Akoustis Technologies Inc *(G-6963)*

Akoustis Technologies Inc (PA)...................704 997-5735
9805 Northcross Center Ct Ste A Huntersville (28078) *(G-6963)*

Akuratemp LLC..828 708-7178
170 Bradley Branch Rd Ste 7 Arden (28704) *(G-249)*

Akzo Nobel Coatings, High Point Also Called: Akzo Nobel Coatings Inc *(G-6512)*

Akzo Nobel Coatings Inc............................704 366-8435
7506 E Independence Blvd Charlotte (28227) *(G-1635)*

Akzo Nobel Coatings Inc............................336 665-9897
4500 Green Point Dr Ste 104 Greensboro (27410) *(G-5345)*

Akzo Nobel Coatings Inc............................336 841-5111
1431 Progress Ave High Point (27260) *(G-6512)*

Al-Rite Manufacturing, Winston Salem Also Called: Joseph Halker *(G-13219)*

Aladdin Manufacturing Corp........................336 623-6000
712 Henry St Eden (27288) *(G-4340)*

Alamac American Knits LLC.........................910 618-2248
1885 Alamac Rd Lumberton (28358) *(G-7943)*

Alamance Cabinets, Graham Also Called: Marsh Furniture Company *(G-5277)*

Alamance Facility, Mebane Also Called: GKN Dna Inc *(G-8243)*

Alamance Foods Inc (PA)............................336 226-6392
840 Plantation Dr Burlington (27215) *(G-1043)*

Alamance Iron Works Inc............................336 852-5940
3900 Patterson St Greensboro (27407) *(G-5346)*

Alamance Kaffee Werks LLC.........................662 617-4573
3105 Midland Ct Burlington (27215) *(G-1044)*

Alamance Steel Fabricators.........................336 887-3015
5926 Prospect St High Point (27263) *(G-6513)*

Alameen A Haqq.......................................336 965-8339
4424 Gray Wolf Way Greensboro (27406) *(G-5347)*

Alamo Distribution LLC (DH).......................704 398-5600
2100 Oaks Pkwy Belmont (28012) *(G-740)*

Alamo Iron Works, Belmont Also Called: Alamo Distribution LLC *(G-740)*

Alamo North Texas Railroad Co....................919 787-9504
2710 Wycliff Rd Raleigh (27607) *(G-9888)*

Alan Kimzey..828 891-8720
42 Sawmill Rd Mills River (28759) *(G-8310)*

Alan R Williams Inc (HQ)............................704 372-8281
2318 Arty Ave Charlotte (28208) *(G-1636)*

Alan Walsh Logging, Lenoir Also Called: Alan Walsh Logging LLC *(G-7569)*

Alan Walsh Logging LLC.............................828 234-7500
2687 Nc Highway 268 Lenoir (28645) *(G-7569)*

Alandale Industries Inc..............................910 576-1291
208 Burnette St Troy (27371) *(G-12156)*

Alaska Structures Inc................................910 323-0562
2545 Ravenhill Dr Ste 101 Fayetteville (28303) *(G-4548)*

ALASKA STRUCTURES, INC., Fayetteville Also Called: Alaska Structures Inc *(G-4548)*

Alb Boats...252 482-7600
140 Midway Dr Edenton (27932) *(G-4359)*

Albaad Fem US, Reidsville Also Called: Albaad Usa Inc *(G-10671)*

Albaad Usa Inc..336 634-0091
1900 Barnes St Reidsville (27320) *(G-10671)*

Albany Tool & Die Inc................................910 392-1207
315 Van Dyke Dr Ste A Wilmington (28405) *(G-12695)*

ALBEMARLE, Charlotte Also Called: Albemarle Corporation *(G-1638)*

Albemarle Amendments LLC........................800 535-3030
4250 Congress St Charlotte (28209) *(G-1637)*

Albemarle Boats, Edenton Also Called: Edenton Boatworks LLC *(G-4366)*

Albemarle Corporation (PA).........................980 299-5700
4250 Congress St Ste 900 Charlotte (28209) *(G-1638)*

Albemarle Corporation...............................252 482-7423
140 Midway Dr Edenton (27932) *(G-4360)*

Albemarle Corporation...............................704 739-2501
348 Holiday Inn Dr Kings Mountain (28086) *(G-7345)*

Albemarle Glass and Stone, Albemarle Also Called: Albemarle Glass Company Inc *(G-58)*

Albemarle Glass Company Inc......................704 982-3323
1217 Pee Dee Ave Albemarle (28001) *(G-58)*

Albemarle Tire Retreading Inc.....................704 982-4113
542 W Main St Albemarle (28001) *(G-59)*

Albemarle US Inc......................................980 299-5700
4250 Congress St Ste 900 Charlotte (28209) *(G-1639)*

Albemarle US Inc (DH)...............................704 739-2501
348 Holiday Inn Dr Kings Mountain (28086) *(G-7346)*

Albemarle Wood Prsv Plant Inc....................704 982-2516
1509 Snuggs Park Rd Albemarle (28001) *(G-60)*

Albemrle Orthotics Prosthetics (PA)..............252 332-4334
103 Nc Highway 42 W Ahoskie (27910) *(G-41)*

Albemrle Orthotics Prosthetics....................252 338-3002
106 Medical Dr Elizabeth City (27909) *(G-4378)*

Alberdingk Boley Inc.................................336 454-5000
6008 W Gate City Blvd Greensboro (27407) *(G-5348)*

Albert E Mann...919 497-0815
106 Clifton Ridge Ct Louisburg (27549) *(G-7909)*

Albion Medical Holdings Inc (DH).................800 378-3906
639 Nuway Cir Lenoir (28645) *(G-7570)*

Albright Qulty WD Turning Inc.....................336 475-1434
193 Black Farm Rd Thomasville (27360) *(G-11991)*

Alcami, Durham Also Called: Alcami Carolinas Corporation *(G-3887)*

Alcami, Garner Also Called: Alcami Carolinas Corporation *(G-4913)*

A
L
P
H
A
B
E
T
I
C

Alcami, Wilmington *Also Called: Alcami Carolinas Corporation (G-12696)*

Alcami, Wilmington *Also Called: Alcami Carolinas Corporation (G-12698)*

Alcami, Wilmington *Also Called: Alcami Carolinas Corporation (G-12699)*

Alcami Carolinas Corporation.. 919 957-5500
4620 Creekstone Dr Ste 200 Durham (27703) *(G-3887)*

Alcami Carolinas Corporation.. 910 619-3952
5100 Jones Sausage Rd Ste 110 Garner (27529) *(G-4913)*

Alcami Carolinas Corporation.. 910 254-7000
627 Davis Dr Ste 100 Morrisville (27560) *(G-8922)*

Alcami Carolinas Corporation.. 910 254-7000
419 Davis Dr Ste 300 Morrisville (27560) *(G-8923)*

Alcami Carolinas Corporation.. 910 254-7000
200 Innovation Ave Ste 150 Morrisville (27560) *(G-8924)*

Alcami Carolinas Corporation.. 910 254-7000
1206 N 23rd St Wilmington (28405) *(G-12696)*

Alcami Carolinas Corporation.. 910 254-7000
1519 N 23rd St Wilmington (28405) *(G-12697)*

Alcami Carolinas Corporation (HQ)... 910 254-7000
2320 Scientific Park Dr Wilmington (28405) *(G-12698)*

Alcami Carolinas Corporation.. 910 254-7000
1726 N 23rd St Wilmington (28405) *(G-12699)*

Alcami Corporation (PA)... 910 254-7000
2320 Scientific Park Dr Wilmington (28405) *(G-12700)*

Alcami Holdings LLC... 910 254-7000
2320 Scientific Park Dr Wilmington (28405) *(G-12701)*

Alcatel-Lucent USA, Raleigh *Also Called: Nokia of America Corporation (G-10333)*

Alco Metal Fabricato... 704 739-1168
1111 Oates Rd Bessemer City (28016) *(G-804)*

Alco Metal Fabricators Inc.. 704 739-1168
307 S Cansler St Kings Mountain (28086) *(G-7347)*

Alcoa Badin Works, Badin *Also Called: Alcoa Power Generating Inc (G-665)*

Alcoa Power Generating Inc... 704 422-5691
293 Nc Hwy 740 Badin (28009) *(G-665)*

Alcon... 919 624-5868
6425 Belle Crest Dr Raleigh (27612) *(G-9889)*

Alcon Components, Mooresville *Also Called: Alcon Components Usa Inc (G-8592)*

Alcon Components Usa Inc.. 704 799-2723
121 Oakpark Dr Mooresville (28115) *(G-8592)*

Alcorns Custom Woodworking Inc.. 336 342-0908
941 Flat Rock Rd Reidsville (27320) *(G-10672)*

Alcrete Industries, Jacksonville *Also Called: Alcrete Pell City LLC (G-7113)*

Alcrete Pell City LLC... 910 455-7040
620 Mildred Thomas Ct Jacksonville (28540) *(G-7113)*

Aldagen Inc... 919 484-2571
2810 Meridian Pkwy Ste 148 Durham (27713) *(G-3888)*

Alders Point.. 336 725-9021
590 Mock St Winston Salem (27127) *(G-13076)*

Alert Metal Works Inc... 704 922-3152
105 Yates St Dallas (28034) *(G-3664)*

Alert Protection Systems Inc.. 919 467-4357
1401 Monkwood Pl Raleigh (27603) *(G-9890)*

Alex and Ani LLC.. 704 366-6029
4400 Sharon Rd Ste 201 Charlotte (28211) *(G-1640)*

Alexander Fabrics, Burlington *Also Called: McComb Industries Lllp (G-1126)*

Alexander Press Inc.. 336 884-8063
701 Greensboro Rd High Point (27260) *(G-6514)*

Alexanders... 910 938-0013
165 Blue Creek School Rd Jacksonville (28540) *(G-7114)*

Alexanders Cbinets Countertops.. 336 774-2966
4735 Kester Mill Rd Winston Salem (27103) *(G-13077)*

Alexanders Ham Company Inc... 704 857-9222
5920 Highway 152 W Mooresville (28115) *(G-8593)*

Alf Sjoberg, Chapel Hill *Also Called: Blind Nail and Company Inc (G-1530)*

Alfiniti Inc... 252 358-5811
600 N Metcalf St Winton (27986) *(G-13427)*

Ali Group North America Corp.. 800 648-4389
738 Gallimore Dairy Rd Ste 113 High Point (27265) *(G-6515)*

Ali Group North America Corp.. 336 661-1556
3765 Champion Blvd Winston Salem (27105) *(G-13078)*

Alk Investments LLC... 984 233-5353
6812 Glenwood Ave Ste 100 Raleigh (27612) *(G-9891)*

All 4 U Home Medical LLC.. 828 437-0684
617 S Green St Ste 100 Morganton (28655) *(G-8849)*

All American Braids Inc.. 704 852-4380
1613 Warren Ave Gastonia (28054) *(G-4985)*

All Baked Out Company... 336 861-1212
629 Mcway Dr High Point (27263) *(G-6516)*

All Decked Out, Frisco *Also Called: Cashman Inc (G-4863)*

All Glass Inc... 828 324-8609
1125 S Center St Hickory (28602) *(G-6262)*

All In 1 Home Improvement.. 252 725-4560
261 Streets Ferry Rd Vanceboro (28586) *(G-12214)*

All Occasion Printing.. 336 926-7766
2408 Gardenia Rd Winston Salem (27107) *(G-13079)*

All Signs & Graphics LLC... 910 323-3115
301 Hope Mills Rd Fayetteville (28304) *(G-4549)*

All Source Security Cont Cal.. 704 504-9908
1500 Continental Blvd Ste K Charlotte (28273) *(G-1641)*

All State Belting, Charlotte *Also Called: All-State Industries Inc (G-1642)*

All Stick Label LLC... 336 659-4660
3929 Westpoint Blvd Ste B Winston Salem (27103) *(G-13080)*

All Ways Graphics, Wilmington *Also Called: CRS/Las Inc (G-12757)*

All-State Industries Inc.. 704 588-4081
1400 Westinghouse Blvd Ste 100 Charlotte (28273) *(G-1642)*

Allan Dearth and Sons, Highlands *Also Called: Allan Drth Sons Gnrtor Sls Svc (G-6842)*

Allan Drth Sons Gnrtor Sls Svc... 828 526-9325
11259 Buck Creek Rd Highlands (28741) *(G-6842)*

Allbirds Inc... 980 296-0006
100 W Worthington Ave Charlotte (28203) *(G-1643)*

Alleghany Garbage Service, Sparta *Also Called: Alleghany Garbage Service Inc (G-11533)*

Alleghany Garbage Service Inc.. 336 372-4413
453 N Main St Sparta (28675) *(G-11533)*

Allegion Access Tech LLC.. 704 789-7000
1000 Stanley Dr Concord (28027) *(G-3309)*

Allegra Marketing, Asheville *Also Called: Mail Management Services LLC (G-541)*

Allegra Print & Imaging, Asheville *Also Called: Powell Ink Inc (G-582)*

Allegra Print & Imaging, Fayetteville *Also Called: Print Works Fayetteville Inc (G-4659)*

Allegra Print & Imaging, Rocky Mount *Also Called: Hinson Industries Inc (G-10840)*

Allen & Son S Cabinet Shop Inc.. 919 963-2196
5942 Us Highway 301 S Four Oaks (27524) *(G-4807)*

Allen Brothers Timber Company.. 910 997-6412
723 N Us Highway 220 Rockingham (28379) *(G-10770)*

Allen Goodson Logging Co, Jacksonville *Also Called: Allen R Goodson Logging Co (G-7115)*

Allen Industries Inc (PA).. 336 668-2791
6434 Burnt Poplar Rd Greensboro (27409) *(G-5349)*

Allen Industries Inc.. 336 294-4777
4100 Sheraton Ct Greensboro (27410) *(G-5350)*

Allen Kelly & Co Inc... 919 779-4197
220 Tryon Rd Ste A Raleigh (27603) *(G-9892)*

Allen Mch & Fabrication LLC.. 336 521-4409
420 Industrial Park Ave Asheboro (27205) *(G-325)*

Allen R Goodson Logging Co... 910 455-4177
1417 Kellum Loop Rd Jacksonville (28546) *(G-7115)*

Allen-Godwin Concrete Inc.. 910 686-4890
8871 Sidbury Rd Wilmington (28411) *(G-12702)*

Allens Environmental Cnstr LLC.. 407 774-7100
84 Greenfield Cir Brevard (28712) *(G-967)*

Allens Gutter Service... 910 738-9509
209 T P Rd Lumberton (28358) *(G-7944)*

Alleson Athletic, Statesville *Also Called: Alleson of Rochester Inc (G-11652)*

Alleson of Rochester Inc (DH)... 585 272-0606
111 Badger Ln Statesville (28625) *(G-11652)*

Allfuel Hst Inc.. 919 868-9410
109 W High Bluff Dr Hampstead (28443) *(G-6066)*

Alliance Assessments LLC... 336 283-9246
200 Northgate Park Dr Winston Salem (27106) *(G-13081)*

Alliance Mch & Fabrication LLC... 704 629-5677
3421 Fairview Dr Gastonia (28052) *(G-4986)*

Alliance One International, King *Also Called: Cres Tobacco Company LLC (G-7325)*

Alliance Precision Plas Corp.. 828 286-8631
171 Fairground Rd Spindale (28160) *(G-11543)*

Allie M Powell III...252 535-9717
3692 Nc Highway 48 Roanoke Rapids (27870) *(G-10729)*

Allied Industrial, Marion *Also Called: Ajs Dezigns Inc (G-8030)*

Allied Marine Contractors LLC...........................910 367-2159
92 Harold Ct Hampstead (28443) *(G-6067)*

Allied Metal Finishing Inc..................................704 347-1477
2525 Lucena St Charlotte (28206) *(G-1644)*

Allied Mobile Systems LLC.................................888 503-1501
17665 Us 421 S Dunn (28334) *(G-3842)*

Allied Pressroom Products Inc (PA)....................954 920-0909
4814 Persimmon Ct Monroe (28110) *(G-8421)*

Allied Sheet Metal Works Inc.............................704 376-8469
612 Charles Ave Charlotte (28205) *(G-1645)*

Allied Tool and Machine Co (PA).........................336 993-2131
115 Corum St Kernersville (27284) *(G-7240)*

Allied/Carter Machining Inc...............................704 784-1253
540 Lake Lynn Rd Concord (28025) *(G-3310)*

Alligood Brothers Logging.................................252 927-2358
436 Mill Hole Rd Washington (27889) *(G-12371)*

Alligood Cabinet Shop.......................................252 927-3201
121 Alligood Dr Washington (27889) *(G-12372)*

Alligood Cabinets, Washington *Also Called: Alligood Cabinet Shop (G-12372)*

Allison Globl Mnufacturing Inc...........................704 392-7883
3900 Sam Wilson Rd Charlotte (28214) *(G-1646)*

Allkindsa Signs, Raleigh *Also Called: Jeremy Weitzel (G-10215)*

Allotropica Technologies Inc..............................919 522-4374
601 W Rosemary St Unit 503 Chapel Hill (27516) *(G-1524)*

Alloy Fabricators Inc..704 263-2281
334 Alexis High Shoals Rd Alexis (28006) *(G-102)*

Alloyworks LLC..704 645-0511
814 W Innes St Salisbury (28144) *(G-11015)*

Allrail Inc..828 287-3747
289 Calton Hill Ln Rutherfordton (28139) *(G-10973)*

Allred Metal Stamping Works Inc.........................336 886-5221
1305 Old Thomasville Rd High Point (27260) *(G-6517)*

Alltech Inc..336 635-5190
11761 Hwy 770 E Eden (27288) *(G-4341)*

Allyn International Trdg Corp (PA).......................877 858-2482
412 College St Marshville (28103) *(G-8085)*

Alotech Inc...919 774-1297
751 S Church St Goldston (27252) *(G-5255)*

Alotech North...919 774-1297
751 S Church St Goldston (27252) *(G-5256)*

Alp Systems Inc..828 454-5164
46 Allegiance Ln Waynesville (28786) *(G-12450)*

Alpek Polyester Miss Inc (DH)............................228 533-4000
7621 Little Ave Ste 500 Charlotte (28226) *(G-1647)*

Alpek Polyester Usa LLC (DH)............................704 940-7500
7621 Little Ave Ste 500 Charlotte (28226) *(G-1648)*

Alpek Polyester Usa LLC....................................910 433-8200
3216 Cedar Creek Rd Fayetteville (28312) *(G-4550)*

Alpha 3d LLC..704 277-6300
1141 Homestead Glen Blvd Charlotte (28214) *(G-1649)*

Alpha Aluminum LLC...336 777-5658
1300 Cunningham Ave Winston Salem (27107) *(G-13082)*

Alpha Canvas and Awning Co Inc........................704 333-1581
411 E 13th St Charlotte (28206) *(G-1650)*

Alpha Mailing Service Inc...................................704 484-1711
501 N Washington St Shelby (28150) *(G-11310)*

Alpha Theory LLC..704 844-1018
2201 Coronation Blvd Ste 140 Charlotte (28227) *(G-1651)*

Alpha Theory LLC..212 235-2180
3537 Keithcastle Ct Charlotte (28210) *(G-1652)*

Alpha Theory LLC (PA).......................................212 235-2180
5701 Westpark Dr Ste 105 Charlotte (28217) *(G-1653)*

Alpha-Advantage Inc...252 441-3766
891 Emeline Ln Kitty Hawk (27949) *(G-7443)*

Alphagraphcis of New Bern, New Bern *Also Called: Andrews Graphics LLC (G-9334)*

AlphaGraphics..704 887-3430
13850 Ballantyne Corporate Pl Ste 500 Charlotte (28277) *(G-1654)*

AlphaGraphics..336 759-8000
8100 N Point Blvd Ste A Winston Salem (27105) *(G-13083)*

AlphaGraphics, Cary *Also Called: Erleclair Inc (G-1355)*

AlphaGraphics, Cary *Also Called: Rennasentient Inc (G-1435)*

AlphaGraphics, Charlotte *Also Called: AlphaGraphics Pineville (G-1655)*

AlphaGraphics, Charlotte *Also Called: Brown Printing Inc (G-1814)*

AlphaGraphics, Charlotte *Also Called: Inventive Graphics Inc (G-2351)*

AlphaGraphics, Garner *Also Called: AlphaGraphics Downtown Raleigh (G-4914)*

AlphaGraphics, Greensboro *Also Called: Document Comm Solutions Inc (G-5498)*

AlphaGraphics, Wilmington *Also Called: Tcprst LLC (G-12938)*

AlphaGraphics Downtown Raleigh.......................919 832-2828
3731 Centurion Dr Garner (27529) *(G-4914)*

AlphaGraphics Pineville.....................................704 541-3678
10100 Park Cedar Dr Ste 178 Charlotte (28210) *(G-1655)*

Alphamed Company Inc (PA)...............................919 680-0011
6100 Guess Rd Durham (27712) *(G-3889)*

Alphamed Press, Durham *Also Called: Alphamed Company Inc (G-3889)*

Alphatech Inc...828 684-9709
388 Cane Creek Rd Fletcher (28732) *(G-4719)*

Alphin Brothers Inc...910 892-8751
2302 Us 301 S Dunn (28334) *(G-3843)*

Alpitronic Americas Inc......................................704 997-4201
5815 Westpark Dr Charlotte (28217) *(G-1656)*

Alside Window Co...407 293-9010
3800 Window Way Kinston (28504) *(G-7393)*

Alta Foods llc...919 734-0233
105 Industry Ct Goldsboro (27530) *(G-5197)*

Altec Inds Mt Airy Operations, Mount Airy *Also Called: Altec Industries Inc (G-9097)*

Altec Industries Inc...828 678-5500
150 Altec Rd Burnsville (28714) *(G-1181)*

Altec Industries Inc...919 528-2535
1550 Aerial Ave Creedmoor (27522) *(G-3637)*

Altec Industries Inc...336 786-3623
200 Altec Way Mount Airy (27030) *(G-9097)*

Altec Northeast LLC..508 320-9041
1550 Aerial Ave Creedmoor (27522) *(G-3638)*

Altech-Eco Corporation......................................828 654-8300
101 Fair Oaks Rd Arden (28704) *(G-250)*

Altera Corporation...919 852-1004
5540 Centerview Dr Ste 318 Raleigh (27606) *(G-9893)*

Alternative Care Group LLC................................336 499-5644
931 S Main St Ste A Kernersville (27284) *(G-7241)*

Alternative Health Dist LLC................................336 465-6618
106 N Commercial Dr Ste A Mooresville (28115) *(G-8594)*

Alternative Ingredients Inc.................................336 378-5368
2826 S Elm Eugene St Greensboro (27406) *(G-5351)*

Alternative Pwr Sls & Rent LLP...........................919 467-8001
1000 Northgate Ct Morrisville (27560) *(G-8925)*

Altior Industries, Monroe *Also Called: Pearl River Group LLC (G-8541)*

Altium Packaging LLC..704 873-6729
124 Commerce Blvd Statesville (28625) *(G-11653)*

Altium Packaging LLC..336 472-1500
1408 Unity St Thomasville (27360) *(G-11992)*

Altium Packaging LP..336 342-4749
606 Walters St Unit B Reidsville (27320) *(G-10673)*

Altom Fuel Cells LLC...828 231-6889
117 Jones Rd Leicester (28748) *(G-7521)*

Altra Industrial Motion Corp...............................704 588-5610
701 N I-85 Service Rd Charlotte (28216) *(G-1657)*

Altra Industrial Motion Corp...............................704 588-5610
701 Carrier Dr Charlotte (28216) *(G-1658)*

Altus Finishing LLC...704 861-1536
1711 Sparta Ct Gastonia (28052) *(G-4987)*

Alumadock Marine Structure, Henderson *Also Called: Robco Manufacturing Inc (G-6175)*

Aluminum Screen Manufacturing.........................336 605-8080
4501 Green Point Dr Ste 104 Greensboro (27410) *(G-5352)*

Alveolus Inc..704 921-2215
9013 Perimeter Woods Dr Ste B Charlotte (28216) *(G-1659)*

Alywillow..919 454-4826
5301 Hillsborough St Ste 100 Raleigh (27606) *(G-9894)*

AM Haire Mfg & Svc Corp...................................336 472-4444
516 Pineywood Rd Thomasville (27360) *(G-11993)*

Amada America Inc..........877 262-3287
109 Penny Rd High Point (27260) *(G-6518)*

Amalfi Semiconductor Inc..........336 664-1233
7628 Thorndike Rd Greensboro (27409) *(G-5353)*

Amann Girrbach North Amer LP..........704 837-1404
13900 S Lakes Dr Ste D Charlotte (28273) *(G-1660)*

Amann Girrbach North America, Charlotte Also Called: Amann Girrbach North Amer LP *(G-1660)*

Amano Pioneer Eclipse Corp (DH)..........336 372-8080
1 Eclipse Rd Sparta (28675) *(G-11534)*

Amanzi Marble & Granite LLC..........336 993-9998
703 Park Lawn Ct Kernersville (27284) *(G-7242)*

Amarr Company..........704 599-5858
2801 Hutchison Mcdonald Rd Charlotte (28269) *(G-1661)*

Amarr Company..........336 936-0010
275 Enterprise Way Mocksville (27028) *(G-8347)*

Amarr Company (DH)..........336 744-5100
165 Carriage Ct Winston Salem (27105) *(G-13084)*

Amarr Garage Doors, Charlotte Also Called: Amarr Company *(G-1661)*

Amarr Garage Doors, Winston Salem Also Called: Amarr Company *(G-13084)*

Ambassador Services Inc..........800 576-8627
1520 S York Rd Gastonia (28052) *(G-4988)*

Amber Alert International Tm (PA)..........919 641-8773
6537 English Oaks Dr Raleigh (27615) *(G-9895)*

Amber Brooks Publishing LLC..........704 582-1035
7233 Mine Shaft Rd Raleigh (27615) *(G-9896)*

Ambra Le Roy LLC..........704 392-7080
8541 Crown Crescent Ct Charlotte (28227) *(G-1662)*

Ambra Leroy Medical Products, Charlotte Also Called: Ambra Le Roy LLC *(G-1662)*

Ambrose Signs Inc..........252 338-8522
123 Sawyers Creek Rd Camden (27921) *(G-1210)*

AMC, Arden Also Called: Asheville Maintenance and Construction Inc *(G-254)*

Amcase Inc..........336 784-5992
2214 Shore St High Point (27263) *(G-6519)*

Amcor Phrm Packg USA LLC..........919 556-9715
111 Wheaton Ave Youngsville (27596) *(G-13461)*

Amcor Tob Packg Americas Inc..........828 274-1611
3055 Sweeten Creek Rd Asheville (28803) *(G-425)*

American & Efird 56, Gastonia Also Called: American & Efird LLC *(G-4990)*

American & Efird Global LLC (DH)..........704 827-4311
22 American St Mount Holly (28120) *(G-9213)*

American & Efird LLC..........704 867-3664
401 Grover St Gastonia (28054) *(G-4989)*

American & Efird LLC..........704 864-0977
3200 York Hwy Gastonia (28056) *(G-4990)*

American & Efird LLC..........828 754-9066
619 Connelly Springs Rd Sw Lenoir (28645) *(G-7571)*

American & Efird LLC..........704 827-4311
22 American St Mount Holly (28120) *(G-9214)*

American & Efird LLC (DH)..........704 827-4311
24 American St Mount Holly (28120) *(G-9215)*

American & Efird LLC..........704 823-2501
101 Mill St Mount Holly (28120) *(G-9216)*

American Alcohollery LLC..........704 960-7243
385 Hose Rd Moravian Falls (28654) *(G-8807)*

American Attachments Inc..........336 859-2002
702 N Silver St Lexington (27292) *(G-7655)*

American Builders Anson Inc (PA)..........704 272-7655
8564 Hwy 74 W Polkton (28135) *(G-9811)*

American Carolina Lighting, Pisgah Forest Also Called: McJast Inc *(G-9771)*

American Carports Structures..........336 710-1091
152 Eastwind Ct Mount Airy (27030) *(G-9098)*

American Chrome & Chem NA Inc..........910 675-7200
5408 Holly Shelter Rd Castle Hayne (28429) *(G-1494)*

American Circuits Inc..........704 376-2800
10100 Sardis Crossing Dr Charlotte (28270) *(G-1663)*

American City Bus Journals Inc (HQ)..........704 973-1000
120 W Morehead St Ste 400 Charlotte (28202) *(G-1664)*

American City Bus Journals Inc..........704 973-1100
120 W Morehead St Charlotte (28202) *(G-1665)*

American City Bus Journals Inc..........336 271-6539
101 S Elm St Ste 100 Greensboro (27401) *(G-5354)*

American Cltvtion Extrction Sv..........336 544-1072
245 E Friendly Ave Ste 100 Greensboro (27401) *(G-5355)*

American Coil Inc..........310 515-1215
157 N Main St Bostic (28018) *(G-960)*

American Converting Co Ltd LLC..........704 479-5025
1161 Burris Blvd Lincolnton (28092) *(G-7812)*

American Cylinder Products Inc..........336 993-7722
115 Furlong Industrial Dr Kernersville (27284) *(G-7243)*

American Durafilm Co Inc..........704 895-7701
117 Infield Ct Mooresville (28117) *(G-8595)*

American Eagle Mfg LLC..........252 633-0603
3280 Us Highway 70 E New Bern (28560) *(G-9331)*

American Emergency Vehicles, Jefferson Also Called: Halcore Group Inc *(G-7189)*

American Extruded Plastics Inc..........336 274-1131
938 Reynolds Pl Greensboro (27403) *(G-5356)*

American Fabricators..........252 637-2600
4395 Us Highway 17 S New Bern (28562) *(G-9332)*

American Fence & Supply, Charlotte Also Called: Afsc LLC *(G-1627)*

American Fiber & Finishing Inc (PA)..........704 984-9256
225 N Depot St Albemarle (28001) *(G-61)*

American Forms Mfg Inc (PA)..........704 866-9139
170 Tarheel Dr Gastonia (28056) *(G-4991)*

American Growler Inc (PA)..........352 671-5393
121 N Green St Robbins (27325) *(G-10751)*

American Hammer, Wilmington Also Called: American Striking Tools Inc *(G-12704)*

American Honda Motor Co Inc..........336 578-6300
3721 Nc Hwy 119 Swepsonville (27359) *(G-11889)*

American Image Press..........336 468-2796
5043 Highland Grove Pl Hamptonville (27020) *(G-6081)*

American Indian Printing Inc..........336 230-1551
1310 Beaman Pl Greensboro (27408) *(G-5357)*

American Inst Crtif Pub Accntn (PA)..........919 402-0682
220 Leigh Farm Rd Durham (27707) *(G-3890)*

American Institute of Cpas, Durham Also Called: American Inst Crtif Pub Accntn *(G-3890)*

American Label Tech LLC..........984 269-5078
343 Technology Dr Ste 2106 Garner (27529) *(G-4915)*

American Labor Inc..........919 286-0726
1308 Broad St Durham (27705) *(G-3891)*

American Linc Corporation..........704 861-9242
159 Wolfpack Rd Gastonia (28056) *(G-4992)*

American Made Products Inc..........252 747-2010
606 5th St Hookerton (28538) *(G-6921)*

American Materials Company, Wilmington Also Called: Columbia Silica Sand LLC *(G-12745)*

American Materials Company LLC..........252 752-2124
2703 Nc Highway 222 Greenville (27834) *(G-5935)*

American Materials Company LLC..........910 532-6070
3596 Dr Kerr Rd Ivanhoe (28447) *(G-7109)*

American Materials Company LLC..........910 532-6659
9763 Taylors Bridge Hwy Rose Hill (28458) *(G-10902)*

American Materials Company LLC (DH)..........910 799-1411
1410 Commonwealth Dr Ste 201 Wilmington (28403) *(G-12703)*

American Media International, Burlington Also Called: American Multimedia Inc *(G-1045)*

American Metal Fabricators Inc..........704 824-8585
2608 Lowell Rd Gastonia (28054) *(G-4993)*

American Metal Treating, High Point Also Called: American Metallurgy Inc *(G-6520)*

American Metallurgy Inc..........336 889-3277
505 Garrison St High Point (27260) *(G-6520)*

American Miso Company Inc..........828 287-2940
4225 Maple Creek Rd Rutherfordton (28139) *(G-10974)*

American Modular Technologies, Liberty Also Called: Amt/Bcu Inc *(G-7761)*

American Moistening Co Inc..........704 889-7281
10402 Rodney St Pineville (28134) *(G-9712)*

American Multimedia Inc (PA)..........336 229-7101
2609 Tucker St Burlington (27215) *(G-1045)*

American Netting Corp..........919 567-3737
3209 Air Park Rd Fuquay Varina (27526) *(G-4864)*

American of High Point Inc..........336 431-1513
2224 Shore St High Point (27263) *(G-6521)*

American Phoenix Inc..........910 484-4007
318 Blount St Fayetteville (28301) *(G-4551)*

American Physcl SEC Group LLC..........919 363-1894
1030 Goodworth Dr Apex (27539) *(G-134)*

(G-0000) Company's Geographic Section entry number

American Plastic Inc.. 828 652-3511
  136 W Marion Business Park Marion (28752) *(G-8031)*

American Plush Tex Mills LLC... 765 609-0456
  213 S Edinborough St Red Springs (28377) *(G-10664)*

American Pride Inc.. 828 697-8847
  135 Sugarloaf Rd Hendersonville (28792) *(G-6184)*

American Printers Inc... 252 977-7468
  120 Sorsbys Aly Rocky Mount (27804) *(G-10822)*

American Quality Foods, Mills River Also Called: Dover Foods Inc *(G-8313)*

American Racg Hders Exhust Inc (PA).. 631 608-1986
  120 Riverstone Dr Stanfield (28163) *(G-11602)*

American Rewinding Co, Monroe Also Called: American Rewinding Nc Inc *(G-8422)*

American Rewinding Nc Inc.. 704 289-4177
  1825 N Rocky River Rd Monroe (28110) *(G-8422)*

American Rewinding of NC Inc.. 704 589-1020
  1825 N Rocky River Rd Monroe (28110) *(G-8423)*

American Ripener LLC.. 704 527-8813
  803 Pressley Rd Ste 106 Charlotte (28217) *(G-1666)*

American Rnovation Systems LLC.. 336 313-6210
  208 Bell Dr Thomasville (27360) *(G-11994)*

American Roller Bearing Co, Hickory Also Called: Ltlb Holding Company *(G-6389)*

American Roller Bearing Inc... 828 624-1460
  1095 Mcclain Rd Hiddenite (28636) *(G-6493)*

American Roller Bearing Inc (HQ)... 828 624-1460
  307 Burke Dr Morganton (28655) *(G-8850)*

American Safety Utility Corp.. 704 482-0601
  529 Caleb Rd Shelby (28152) *(G-11311)*

American Sample House Inc.. 704 276-1970
  2105 Cat Square Rd Vale (28168) *(G-12207)*

American Scale Company LLC.. 704 921-4556
  7231 Covecreek Dr Charlotte (28215) *(G-1667)*

American Sign, Greensboro Also Called: Syd Inc *(G-5848)*

American Sign Shop, Charlotte Also Called: American Sign Shop Inc *(G-1668)*

American Sign Shop Inc... 704 527-6100
  2440 Whitehall Park Dr Ste 100 Charlotte (28273) *(G-1668)*

American Silk Mills LLC (PA).. 570 822-7147
  329 S Wrenn St Ste 101 High Point (27260) *(G-6522)*

American Skin, Burgaw Also Called: Skin Boys LLC *(G-1031)*

American Skin Food Group LLC.. 910 259-2232
  140 Industrial Dr Burgaw (28425) *(G-1018)*

American Snuff Company LLC... 336 768-4630
  2415 S Stratford Rd Winston Salem (27103) *(G-13085)*

American Soil and Mulch Inc.. 919 460-1349
  1109 Athens Dr Raleigh (27606) *(G-9897)*

American Solutions For Bu... 919 848-2442
  9201 Leesville Rd Ste 120 Raleigh (27613) *(G-9898)*

American Speedy Printing, Asheville Also Called: Greybeard Printing Inc *(G-513)*

American Speedy Printing, Hickory Also Called: American Speedy Printing Ctrs *(G-6263)*

American Speedy Printing Ctrs.. 828 322-3981
  337 Main Ave Ne Hickory (28601) *(G-6263)*

American Sprinkle Co Inc... 800 408-6708
  11240 Rivers Edge Rd Pineville (28134) *(G-9713)*

American Stone Company... 919 929-7131
  1807 Nc Highway 54 W Chapel Hill (27516) *(G-1525)*

American Striking Tools Inc.. 910 769-1318
  1312 S 12th St Wilmington (28401) *(G-12704)*

American Tchncal Solutions Inc... 336 595-2763
  4790 Walkertown Plaza Blvd Walkertown (27051) *(G-12315)*

American Trayd, Wilmington Also Called: Sherri Gossett *(G-12919)*

American Truetzschler, Charlotte Also Called: American Trutzschler Inc *(G-1670)*

American Trutzschler Inc... 704 399-4521
  5315 Heavy Equipment School Rd Charlotte (28214) *(G-1669)*

American Trutzschler Inc (PA).. 704 399-4521
  12300 Moores Chapel Rd Charlotte (28214) *(G-1670)*

American Valve Inc (PA).. 336 668-0554
  4321 Piedmont Pkwy Greensboro (27410) *(G-5358)*

American Water Graphics Inc... 828 247-0700
  317 Vance St Forest City (28043) *(G-4783)*

American Webbing Fittings Inc.. 336 767-9390
  4959 Home Rd Winston Salem (27106) *(G-13086)*

American Welding & Gas Inc (PA).. 984 222-2600
  4900 Falls Of Neuse Rd Ste 150 Raleigh (27609) *(G-9899)*

American Wick Drain Corp.. 704 296-5801
  1209 Airport Rd Monroe (28110) *(G-8424)*

American Wood Reface of Triad.. 336 345-2837
  5339 Valleydale Rd Kernersville (27284) *(G-7244)*

American Woodmark Corporation.. 704 947-3280
  9825 Northcross Center Ct Ste N Huntersville (28078) *(G-6964)*

American Woodmark Corporation.. 828 428-6300
  838 Lincoln County Pkwy Lincolnton (28092) *(G-7813)*

American Woodmark Corporation.. 540 665-9100
  300 S Henry St Stoneville (27048) *(G-11819)*

American Woodworkery Inc.. 910 916-8098
  802 Bladen Cir Fayetteville (28312) *(G-4552)*

American Yarn LLC.. 919 614-1542
  1305 Graham St Burlington (27217) *(G-1046)*

Americap Co Inc.. 252 445-2388
  276 Daniels Bridge Rd Enfield (27823) *(G-4481)*

Americh Corporation... 704 588-3075
  10700 John Price Rd Charlotte (28273) *(G-1671)*

Americhem Inc... 704 782-6411
  723 Commerce Dr Concord (28025) *(G-3311)*

Amerifab International Inc... 336 882-9010
  203 Feld Ave High Point (27263) *(G-6523)*

Amerikrate, Lincolnton Also Called: American Converting Co Ltd LLC *(G-7812)*

Ameritech Die & Mold Inc... 704 664-0801
  107 Knob Hill Rd Mooresville (28117) *(G-8596)*

Ameritech Die & Mold South Inc (PA)... 704 664-0801
  107 Knob Hill Rd Mooresville (28117) *(G-8597)*

Ameritek, Greensboro Also Called: Ameritek Lasercut Dies Inc *(G-5360)*

Ameritek Inc.. 336 292-1165
  122 S Walnut Cir Ste B Greensboro (27401) *(G-5359)*

Ameritek Lasercut Dies Inc.. 336 292-1165
  122 S Walnut Cir Ste B Greensboro (27409) *(G-5360)*

Amerochem Corporation... 252 634-9344
  1885 Old Airport Rd New Bern (28562) *(G-9333)*

Amerock LLC (DH)... 800 435-6959
  10115 Kincey Ave Ste 210 Huntersville (28078) *(G-6965)*

Ames Copper Group LLC.. 860 622-7626
  125 Old Boiling Springs Rd Shelby (28152) *(G-11312)*

Amesbury Acqstion Hldngs 2 Inc (DH).. 704 924-8586
  2061 Sherrill Dr Statesville (28625) *(G-11654)*

Amesbury Group Inc... 704 978-2883
  125 Amesbury Truth Dr Statesville (28625) *(G-11655)*

Amesbury Group Inc... 704 924-7694
  1920 Flintstone Dr Statesville (28677) *(G-11656)*

Amesbury Industries Inc.. 704 978-3250
  125 Amesbury Truth Dr Statesville (28625) *(G-11657)*

Ametek Electronics Systems... 800 645-9721
  8001 Knightdale Blvd Ste 121 Knightdale (27545) *(G-7448)*

Ametek Rtron Technical Mtr Div, Whitsett Also Called: Rotron Incorporated *(G-12619)*

AMF Custom Upholstery, Lincolnton Also Called: Moores Upholstering Interiors *(G-7845)*

AMF-NC Enterprise Company LLC.. 704 489-2206
  3570 Denver Dr Denver (28037) *(G-3769)*

AMG Casework LLC.. 919 462-9203
  10315 Chapel Hill Rd Morrisville (27560) *(G-8926)*

Amiad Filtration Systems Ltd (PA).. 805 377-0288
  120 Talbert Rd Ste J Mooresville (28117) *(G-8598)*

Amiad USA Inc (DH)... 704 662-3133
  120 Talbert Rd Ste J Mooresville (28117) *(G-8599)*

Amiad Water Systems, Mooresville Also Called: Amiad Filtration Systems Ltd *(G-8598)*

Amidon Ballistic Concrete, Cary Also Called: 360 Ballistics LLC *(G-1282)*

Amika LLC.. 984 664-9804
  5000 Centre Green Way Cary (27513) *(G-1288)*

Amkor Technology Inc.. 919 248-1800
  3021 Cornwallis Rd Durham (27709) *(G-3892)*

Amkor Technology Inc.. 336 605-8009
  7870 Thorndike Rd Greensboro (27409) *(G-5361)*

AMO Pharma Services Corp... 215 826-7420
  321 E Chapel Hill St 3rd Fl Durham (27701) *(G-3893)*

Amoco, Pineville Also Called: American Moistening Co Inc *(G-9712)*

A
L
P
H
A
B
E
T
I
C

Amor Furniture, Liberty *Also Called: Amor Furniture and Bedding LLC (G-7760)*

Amor Furniture and Bedding LLC................................... 336 795-0044
   143 S Asheboro St Liberty (27298) *(G-7760)*

AMP Agency... 704 430-2313
   7550 Us Highway 74 W Polkton (28135) *(G-9812)*

AMP Services LLC.. 828 313-1200
   30 N Main St Granite Falls (28630) *(G-5294)*

Amp-Cherokee Envmtl Solutions, Angier *Also Called: Cherokee Instruments Inc (G-117)*

Ampac Machinery LLC.. 919 596-5320
   319 Us 70 Service Rd Durham (27703) *(G-3894)*

Amped, Greensboro *Also Called: Amplified Elctronic Design Inc (G-5362)*

Amped Events LLC... 888 683-4386
   401 S Marietta St Gastonia (28052) *(G-4994)*

Amphenol Antenna Solutions Inc................................. 828 324-6971
   1123 Industrial Dr Sw Conover (28613) *(G-3489)*

Amphenol Procom Inc... 888 262-7542
   1123 Industrial Dr Sw Conover (28613) *(G-3490)*

Amplate Inc... 704 607-0191
   7820 Tyner St Charlotte (28262) *(G-1672)*

Amplified Elctronic Design Inc..................................... 336 223-4811
   7617 Boeing Dr Greensboro (27409) *(G-5362)*

AMR Systems LLC.. 704 980-9072
   13850 Balntyn Corp Pl # 500 Charlotte (28277) *(G-1673)*

Amrep Inc (DH)..909 923-0430
   6525 Morrison Blvd Ste 300 Charlotte (28211) *(G-1674)*

Amrep Inc.. 704 949-2595
   1405 Julian Rd Salisbury (28146) *(G-11016)*

Amryt Pharmaceuticals Inc.. 877 764-3131
   175 Regency Woods Pl Cary (27518) *(G-1289)*

AMS, Raleigh *Also Called: AMS USA Inc (G-9900)*

AMS Software Inc.. 919 570-6001
   2012 S Main St Wake Forest (27587) *(G-12260)*

AMS USA Inc.. 919 755-2889
   353 E Six Forks Rd Ste 250 Raleigh (27609) *(G-9900)*

Amsted Industries Incorporated................................... 704 226-5243
   4515 Corporate Dr Monroe (28110) *(G-8425)*

Amt Datasouth Corp... 704 523-8500
   5033 Sirona Dr Ste 800 Charlotte (28273) *(G-1675)*

Amt/Bcu Inc.. 336 622-6200
   6306 Old 421 Rd Liberty (27298) *(G-7761)*

Amtai Medical Equipment Inc....................................... 919 872-1803
   5605 Primavera Ct Raleigh (27616) *(G-9901)*

Amware Pallet Services LLC.. 919 207-2403
   1700 Chicopee Rd Benson (27504) *(G-784)*

Amy Smith... 828 352-1001
   100 Club Dr Ste 270 Burnsville (28714) *(G-1182)*

Ana Gizzi.. 908 334-8733
   124 Hatfield Rd Statesville (28625) *(G-11658)*

Ana Muf Corporation.. 336 653-3509
   1046 Briles Dr Asheboro (27205) *(G-326)*

Analog Devices Inc.. 336 202-6503
   4001 Nc Hwy 54 Ste 3100 Durham (27709) *(G-3895)*

Analog Devices Inc.. 336 668-9511
   7910 Triad Center Dr Greensboro (27409) *(G-5363)*

Analog Devices Inc.. 919 831-2790
   223 S West St Ste 1400 Raleigh (27603) *(G-9902)*

Anatech, Durham *Also Called: Cancer Diagnostics Inc (G-3957)*

Anatech Ltd (PA)... 704 489-1488
   771 Crosspoint Dr Denver (28037) *(G-3770)*

Anav Yofi Inc.. 828 217-7746
   1501 Majestic Meadow Dr Charlotte (28216) *(G-1676)*

Anchor Coffee Co Inc... 336 265-7458
   313b 9th St Ste 1 North Wilkesboro (28659) *(G-9521)*

Anchor Coffee Co., North Wilkesboro *Also Called: Anchor Coffee Co Inc (G-9521)*

Anchor Coupling Inc... 919 739-8000
   106 Industry Ct Goldsboro (27530) *(G-5198)*

Anchor Richey E V S, Taylorsville *Also Called: Anchor-Richey Emergency Vehicl (G-11949)*

Anchor-Richey Emergency Vehicl................................. 828 495-8145
   241 Advent Church Rd Taylorsville (28681) *(G-11949)*

Ancient Mariner Inc... 704 635-7911
   1402 Walkup Ave Monroe (28110) *(G-8426)*

Andark Graphics Inc... 704 882-1400
   7204 Stinson Hartis Rd Ste A Indian Trail (28079) *(G-7067)*

Anders Natural Soap Co Inc.. 919 678-9393
   1943 Evans Rd Cary (27513) *(G-1290)*

Andersen Energy Inc.. 336 376-0107
   3151 Caroline Dr Haw River (27258) *(G-6129)*

Andersen Products, Haw River *Also Called: Andersen Sterilizers Inc (G-6131)*

Andersen Products Inc.. 336 376-3000
   3202 Caroline Dr Haw River (27258) *(G-6130)*

Andersen Sterilizers Inc.. 336 376-8622
   3202 Caroline Dr Haw River (27258) *(G-6131)*

Anderson Truss Company Inc...................................... 252 746-7726
   4825 Anderson Truss Rd Ayden (28513) *(G-652)*

Andrea L Grizzle... 252 202-3278
   101 Trinity Ln Box 751 Moyock (27958) *(G-9275)*

Andrew, Claremont *Also Called: Commscope Technologies LLC (G-3104)*

Andrew Pearson Design, Mount Airy *Also Called: Easyglass Inc (G-9118)*

Andrews Graphics LLC.. 252 633-3199
   3731 Trent Rd New Bern (28562) *(G-9334)*

Andrews Truss Inc... 828 321-3105
   47 Mcclelland Creek Rd Andrews (28901) *(G-105)*

Andrews Violinist... 910 458-1226
   546 Anchor Way Kure Beach (28449) *(G-7463)*

Andritz Fabrics and Rolls Inc....................................... 919 556-7235
   8521 Six Forks Rd Raleigh (27615) *(G-9903)*

Andritz Fabrics and Rolls Inc (HQ)............................... 919 526-1400
   8521 Six Forks Rd Ste 300 Raleigh (27615) *(G-9904)*

Andronics Construction Inc.. 704 400-9562
   110 Business Park Dr Indian Trail (28079) *(G-7068)*

Andronx, Indian Trail *Also Called: Andronics Construction Inc (G-7068)*

Andy Maylish Fabrication Inc....................................... 704 785-1491
   5384 Stone Henge Dr Denver (28037) *(G-3771)*

Andy-OXY Co Inc (PA)..828 258-0271
   27 Heritage Dr Asheville (28806) *(G-426)*

Anelleo Inc... 919 448-4008
   519 Dairy Glen Rd Chapel Hill (27516) *(G-1526)*

Anew Look Homes LLC... 800 796-5152
   1717 Highland Ave Ne Ste 102 Hickory (28601) *(G-6264)*

Angels Path Ventures Inc.. 828 654-9530
   21 Commerce Way Arden (28704) *(G-251)*

Angstrom Medica Inc.. 781 933-6121
   1800 N Greene St Ste A Greenville (27834) *(G-5936)*

Angunique.. 336 392-5866
   6190 Pine Cove Ct Greensboro (27410) *(G-5364)*

Angus Fire, Angier *Also Called: National Foam Inc (G-125)*

Angus Fire, Angier *Also Called: National Foam Inc (G-126)*

Anheuser-Busch, Charlotte *Also Called: Anheuser-Busch LLC (G-1677)*

Anheuser-Busch LLC.. 704 321-9319
   11325 N Community House Rd Charlotte (28277) *(G-1677)*

Anilox Roll Company Inc (PA).......................................704 588-1809
   10955 Withers Cove Park Dr Charlotte (28278) *(G-1678)*

Animal Supply House, Hendersonville *Also Called: L & B Jandrew Enterprises (G-6219)*

Anitas Marketing Concepts Inc..................................... 252 243-3993
   437 Ward Blvd Unit B Wilson (27893) *(G-12961)*

Annas Machine Shop Inc... 828 754-4184
   1751 Main St Nw Lenoir (28645) *(G-7572)*

Annihilare Medical Systems Inc.................................... 855 545-5677
   311 Motz Ave # E Lincolnton (28092) *(G-7814)*

Anns House of Nuts... 252 795-6500
   1159 Robersonville Products Rd Robersonville (27871) *(G-10765)*

Ansgar Industrial LLC (PA)..866 284-1931
   6000 Fairview Rd Ste 1200 Charlotte (28210) *(G-1679)*

Anson County Water Treatment, Lilesville *Also Called: County of Anson (G-7784)*

Anson Express.. 704 694-2480
   205 W Morgan St Wadesboro (28170) *(G-12233)*

Anson Machine Works Inc... 704 272-7657
   100 Efird Cir Polkton (28135) *(G-9813)*

Anson Metals LLC.. 704 272-7878
   2905 Hopewell Church Rd Peachland (28133) *(G-9650)*

Anson Wood Products.. 704 694-5390
   Parsons St Wadesboro (28170) *(G-12234)*

(G-0000) Company's Geographic Section entry number

Ansonville Piping & Fabg Inc...................................... 704 826-8403
122 Ansonville Polkton Rd Ansonville (28007) *(G-129)*

Anthem Displays LLC... 910 746-8988
518 Ben Green Industrial Park Rd Elizabethtown (28337) *(G-4417)*

Anthem Displays LLC... 910 862-3550
113 W Broad St Elizabethtown (28337) *(G-4418)*

Anthony B Andrews Logging Inc................................. 252 448-8901
1000 Phillips Rd Trenton (28585) *(G-12109)*

Anthony Demaria Labs Inc... 845 255-4695
122 Windbyrne Dr Cary (27513) *(G-1291)*

Antkar LLC.. 919 322-4100
2831 Jones Franklin Rd Raleigh (27606) *(G-9905)*

Anuma Aerospace LLC.. 919 600-0142
720 Pebblebrook Dr Raleigh (27609) *(G-9906)*

Anutra Medical Inc.. 919 648-1215
1000 Perimeter Park Dr Ste E Morrisville (27560) *(G-8927)*

Anuva, Morrisville *Also Called: Anuva Services Inc (G-8928)*

Anuva Services Inc... 919 468-6441
140 Southcenter Ct Ste 600 Morrisville (27560) *(G-8928)*

Ao Smith Chatlotte.. 704 597-8910
4302 Raleigh St Charlotte (28213) *(G-1680)*

Aoa Signs Inc.. 336 679-3344
2707 Wooten Blvd Sw Wilson (27893) *(G-12962)*

AP Emissions Technologies LLC................................ 919 580-2000
300 Dixie Trl Goldsboro (27530) *(G-5199)*

AP Granite Installation LLC...................................... 919 215-1795
2213 Stephanie Ln Clayton (27520) *(G-3131)*

AP Solutions, Cary *Also Called: Atmosphric Plsma Solutions Inc (G-1298)*

AP&t North America Inc.. 704 292-2900
4817 Persimmon Ct Monroe (28110) *(G-8427)*

APAC, Concord *Also Called: Barnhill Contracting Company (G-3317)*

APAC, Greenville *Also Called: Barnhill Contracting Company (G-5946)*

APAC, Raleigh *Also Called: Apac-Atlantic Inc (G-9907)*

Apac-Atlantic Inc (DH)... 336 412-6800
2626 Glenwood Ave Ste 550 Raleigh (27608) *(G-9907)*

Apara, Durham *Also Called: Implus Footcare LLC (G-4073)*

Apb Wrecker Service LLC... 704 400-0857
114 E 28th St Charlotte (28206) *(G-1681)*

Apc LLC.. 919 965-2051
1451 W Noble St Selma (27576) *(G-11284)*

APD, Charlotte *Also Called: Appalachian Pipe Distrs LLC (G-1684)*

Apex, Pollocksville *Also Called: Advanced Plastic Extrusion LLC (G-9816)*

Apex Analytix LLC (HQ).. 336 272-4669
1501 Highwoods Blvd Ste 200 Greensboro (27410) *(G-5365)*

Apex Embroidery Inc.. 919 793-6083
996 Ambergate Sta Apex (27502) *(G-135)*

Apex Facility and Dist Ctr, Apex *Also Called: Apex Tool Group LLC (G-138)*

Apex Industrial... 877 676-2739
2903 Lee Ave Sanford (27332) *(G-11148)*

Apex Instruments Incorporated................................. 919 557-7300
204 Technology Park Ln Fuquay Varina (27526) *(G-4865)*

Apex Manufacturing Facility, Apex *Also Called: Bioresource International Inc (G-145)*

Apex Marble and Granite Inc..................................... 919 462-9202
10315b Chapel Hill Rd Morrisville (27560) *(G-8929)*

Apex Packaging Corporation LLC............................... 704 847-7274
15105 John J Delaney Dr Charlotte (28277) *(G-1682)*

Apex Plant, Apex *Also Called: Eagle Rock Concrete LLC (G-152)*

Apex Printing Company... 919 362-9856
514 E Williams St Apex (27502) *(G-136)*

Apex Salsa Company... 919 363-1486
912 N York Ct Apex (27502) *(G-137)*

Apex Steel Corp... 919 362-6611
301 Petfinder Ln Raleigh (27603) *(G-9908)*

Apex Tool Group LLC.. 919 387-0099
1000 Lufkin Rd Apex (27539) *(G-138)*

Apex Tool Group LLC.. 410 773-7800
13620 Reese Blvrd Pkwy E Ste 410 Huntersville (28078) *(G-6966)*

Apex Waves LLC.. 919 809-5227
1624 Old Apex Rd Cary (27513) *(G-1292)*

Apex/Pittsboro Concrete Plant, Apex *Also Called: S T Wooten Corporation (G-192)*

Apg/East LLC.. 252 329-9500
1150 Sugg Pkwy Greenville (27834) *(G-5937)*

Apjet Inc (PA)... 919 595-5538
523 Davis Dr Ste 100 Morrisville (27560) *(G-8930)*

Aplix Inc (DH)... 704 588-1920
12300 Steele Creek Rd Charlotte (28273) *(G-1683)*

Apollo By Mosack Group, Mint Hill *Also Called: Mosack Group LLC (G-8342)*

Apollo Chemical Corp... 336 226-1161
2001 Willow Spring Ln Burlington (27215) *(G-1047)*

Apollo Designs, High Point *Also Called: Apollo Designs LLC (G-6524)*

Apollo Designs LLC (PA)... 336 886-0260
2147 Brevard Rd High Point (27263) *(G-6524)*

Apollo Valves, Charlotte *Also Called: Aalberts Integrated Piping Systems Americas Inc (G-1608)*

Apollonias Candles Things LLC................................. 910 408-2508
2112 Broad St Apt E8 Durham (27705) *(G-3896)*

Appalachian Cabinet Inc... 828 265-0830
7373 Old 421 S Deep Gap (28618) *(G-3727)*

Appalachian Lumber, Wilkesboro *Also Called: Appalachian Lumber Company Inc (G-12628)*

Appalachian Lumber Company Inc (PA)....................... 336 973-7205
5879 W Us Highway 421 Wilkesboro (28697) *(G-12628)*

Appalachian Mountain Brewery, Boone *Also Called: Craft Brew Alliance Inc (G-908)*

Appalachian Pipe Distrs LLC..................................... 704 688-5703
828 East Blvd Charlotte (28203) *(G-1684)*

Appalachian State University..................................... 828 262-7497
525 Rivers St Rm 221 Boone (28608) *(G-895)*

Appalachian State University..................................... 828 262-2047
169 Air Ln Boone (28608) *(G-896)*

Appalachian Technology, Asheville *Also Called: Appalachian Technology LLC (G-427)*

Appalachian Technology LLC..................................... 828 210-8888
187 Elk Mountain Rd Asheville (28804) *(G-427)*

Appalachian Tool & Machine Inc................................ 828 669-0142
121 Lytle Cove Rd Swannanoa (28778) *(G-11864)*

Appalchian Stove Fbrcators Inc................................. 828 253-0164
329 Emma Rd Asheville (28806) *(G-428)*

Apparel USA Inc.. 212 869-5495
102 Trinity St Fairmont (28340) *(G-4500)*

Apperson Inc.. 704 399-2571
2908 Stewart Creek Blvd Charlotte (28216) *(G-1685)*

Apple Annie's Bake Shop, Wilmington *Also Called: Connectivity Group LLC (G-12746)*

Apple Baking Company Inc.. 704 637-6800
4470 Hampton Rd Salisbury (28144) *(G-11017)*

Apple Rock Advg & Prom Inc (PA).............................. 336 232-4800
7602 Business Park Dr Greensboro (27409) *(G-5366)*

Apple Rock Displays, Greensboro *Also Called: Apple Rock Advg & Prom Inc (G-5366)*

Applied Catheter Tech Inc... 336 817-1005
113 Thomas St Winston Salem (27101) *(G-13087)*

Applied Components Mfg LLC.................................... 828 323-8915
101 33rd Street Dr Se Hickory (28602) *(G-6265)*

Applied Drives Inc... 704 573-2324
11016 Tara Oaks Dr Charlotte (28227) *(G-1686)*

Applied Medical Tech Inc (PA).................................... 919 255-3220
2179 E Lyon Station Rd Creedmoor (27522) *(G-3639)*

Applied Plastic Services Inc...................................... 910 655-2156
5932 Old Lake Rd Bolton (28423) *(G-888)*

Applied Roller Technology Inc................................... 704 598-9500
8800 Statesville Rd Charlotte (28269) *(G-1687)*

Applied Strategies Inc.. 704 525-4478
1515 Mockingbird Ln Ste 700 Charlotte (28209) *(G-1688)*

Applied Technologies Group...................................... 618 977-9872
19701 Bethel Church Rd Ste 103 Cornelius (28031) *(G-3584)*

Appointments, Tryon *Also Called: Tryon Newsmedia LLC (G-12179)*

Appsense, Cary *Also Called: Appsense Incorporated (G-1293)*

Appsense Incorporated... 919 666-0080
1100 Crescent Green Ste 206 Cary (27518) *(G-1293)*

Aprotech Powertrain Inc... 828 253-1350
31 Adams Hill Rd Asheville (28806) *(G-429)*

APT Industries Inc... 704 598-9100
601 E Sugar Creek Rd Charlotte (28213) *(G-1689)*

Aptargroup Inc.. 828 970-6300
3300 Finger Mill Rd Lincolnton (28092) *(G-7815)*

A L P H A B E T I C

APV Heat Exchanger PDT Group, Goldsboro *Also Called: SPX Flow Us LLC (G-5246)*

Aqua 10 Corporation... 252 726-5421
5112 Midyette Ave Morehead City (28557) *(G-8813)*

Aqua Blue Inc... 704 896-9007
9624 Bailey Rd Ste 270 Cornelius (28031) *(G-3585)*

Aqua Logic Inc... 858 292-4773
2806 Gray Fox Rd Monroe (28110) *(G-8428)*

Aqua Plastics Inc... 828 324-6284
1474 17th St Ne Hickory (28601) *(G-6266)*

Aqua-Matic, Raleigh *Also Called: Captive-Aire Systems Inc (G-9972)*

Aquadale Query.. 704 474-3165
12423 Old Aquadale Rd Norwood (28128) *(G-9553)*

Aquafil OMara Inc... 828 874-2100
160 Fashion Ave Rutherford College (28671) *(G-10970)*

Aquapro Solutions LLC.. 828 255-0772
46 New Leicester Hwy Ste 102 Asheville (28806) *(G-430)*

Aquarius Designs & Logo Wear...................................... 919 821-4646
4429 Beryl Rd Raleigh (27606) *(G-9909)*

Aqwa Inc... 252 243-7693
2604 Willis Ct N Wilson (27896) *(G-12963)*

AR Corp... 910 763-8530
7639 Myrtle Grove Rd Wilmington (28409) *(G-12705)*

AR Workshop Greensboro, Greensboro *Also Called: G & G Management LLC (G-5544)*

Arauco - NA... 910 569-7020
157 Atc Dr Biscoe (27209) *(G-846)*

Arauco North America Inc.. 919 542-2128
985 Corinth Rd Moncure (27559) *(G-8399)*

Arbon Equipment Corporation.. 414 355-2600
14100 S Lakes Dr Charlotte (28273) *(G-1690)*

Arbor Organic Technologies LLC.................................... 704 276-7100
107 Technolgy Dr Lincolnton (28092) *(G-7816)*

Arbor Pharmaceuticals Inc.. 919 792-1700
5511 Capital Center Dr Ste 224 Raleigh (27606) *(G-9910)*

ARC Steel Fabrication LLC.. 980 533-8302
649 Bess Town Rd Bessemer City (28016) *(G-805)*

ARC West, Charlotte *Also Called: Anilox Roll Company Inc (G-1678)*

Arc3 Gases Inc (PA).. 910 892-4016
1600 Us 301 S Dunn (28334) *(G-3844)*

Arc3 Gases Inc.. 919 772-9500
1001 Hill Dr Durham (27703) *(G-3897)*

Arc3 Gases Inc.. 336 275-3333
810 Post St Greensboro (27405) *(G-5367)*

Arc3 Gases Inc.. 704 220-1029
2411 Nelda Dr Monroe (28110) *(G-8429)*

Arcadia Beverage, Arden *Also Called: Arcadia Beverage LLC (G-252)*

Arcadia Beverage LLC (PA)... 828 684-3556
34 Arcadia Farms Rd Arden (28704) *(G-252)*

Arcadia Farms LLC... 828 684-3556
34 Arcadia Farms Rd Arden (28704) *(G-253)*

Archangel Arms LLC... 984 235-2536
3405 Banks Rd Raleigh (27603) *(G-9911)*

Archdale Furniture Distributor....................................... 336 431-1081
112 Englewood Dr Archdale (27263) *(G-211)*

Archdale Millworks Inc.. 336 431-9019
1204 Corporation Dr Archdale (27263) *(G-212)*

Archdale Printing Company Inc...................................... 336 884-5312
1316 Trinity Ave High Point (27260) *(G-6525)*

Archdale Trinity News, High Point *Also Called: High Point Enterprise Inc (G-6649)*

Archer Advanced Rbr Components, Winston Salem *Also Called: Maranz Inc (G-13244)*

Archer-Daniels-Midland Company................................... 704 332-3165
620 W 10th St Charlotte (28202) *(G-1691)*

Archer-Daniels-Midland Company................................... 910 457-5011
1730 E Moore St Southport (28461) *(G-11516)*

Archie S Steel Service Inc... 252 355-5007
4575 Us Highway 13 S Greenville (27834) *(G-5938)*

Archie Supply LLC (PA).. 336 987-0895
4762 Champion Ct Greensboro (27410) *(G-5368)*

Architectural Craftsman Ltd... 919 494-6911
315 Cedar Creek Rd Franklinton (27525) *(G-4846)*

Archivesocial, Durham *Also Called: Archivesocial Inc (G-3898)*

Archivesocial Inc... 888 558-6032
212 W Main St Ste 500 Durham (27701) *(G-3898)*

Archroma, Charlotte *Also Called: Archroma US Inc (G-1692)*

Archroma US Inc (DH).. 704 353-4100
5435 77 Center Dr Ste 10 Charlotte (28217) *(G-1692)*

Arclin USA LLC.. 919 542-2526
790 Corinth Rd Moncure (27559) *(G-8400)*

Arcola Hardwood Company Inc....................................... 252 257-4484
2316 Nc Highway 43 Warrenton (27589) *(G-12349)*

Arcola Logging Co Inc.. 252 257-3205
134 Chip Capps Rd Macon (27551) *(G-7982)*

Arcola Lumber Company Inc.. 252 257-4923
2316 Nc Highway 43 Warrenton (27589) *(G-12350)*

Arcona Leather Company LLC (PA)................................. 828 396-7728
2615 Mission Rd Hudson (28638) *(G-6941)*

Arcright Welding Service, Fayetteville *Also Called: Peter J Hamann (G-4654)*

Arcus Medical LLC.. 704 332-3424
4400 Stuart Andrew Blvd Ste A Charlotte (28217) *(G-1693)*

Ardagh, Winston Salem *Also Called: Trivium Packaging USA Inc (G-13373)*

Arden, Sanford *Also Called: Arden Companies LLC (G-11149)*

Arden Companies, Sanford *Also Called: Arden Companies LLC (G-11150)*

Arden Companies LLC... 919 258-3081
1611 Broadway Rd Sanford (27332) *(G-11149)*

Arden Companies LLC... 919 258-3081
1611 Broadway Rd Sanford (27332) *(G-11150)*

Arden Engraving US Inc.. 704 547-4581
100 Forsyth Hall Dr Charlotte (28273) *(G-1694)*

Are Management LLC.. 336 855-7800
1420 Lorraine Ave High Point (27263) *(G-6526)*

Area 51 Powder Coating Inc.. 910 769-1724
2721 Old Wrightsboro Rd Wilmington (28405) *(G-12706)*

Areteia Therapeutics Inc... 973 985-0597
101 Glen Lennox Dr Chapel Hill (27517) *(G-1527)*

Areva... 704 805-2935
11515 Vanstory Dr Ste 140 Huntersville (28078) *(G-6967)*

Argos Ready Mix, Raleigh *Also Called: Argos USA LLC (G-9915)*

Argos Ready Mix, Wilmington *Also Called: Argos USA LLC (G-12707)*

Argos Ready Mix, Wilmington *Also Called: Argos USA LLC (G-12708)*

Argos Ready Mix (carolinas) Corp.................................. 919 790-1520
3610 Bush St Raleigh (27609) *(G-9912)*

Argos USA... 336 784-5181
1590 Williamson St Winston Salem (27107) *(G-13088)*

Argos USA LLC.. 919 942-0381
219 Guthrie Ave Carrboro (27510) *(G-1265)*

Argos USA LLC.. 910 675-1262
5225 Holly Shelter Rd Castle Hayne (28429) *(G-1495)*

Argos USA LLC.. 704 679-9431
325 E Hebron St Charlotte (28273) *(G-1695)*

Argos USA LLC.. 910 299-5046
3095 Turkey Hwy Clinton (28328) *(G-3228)*

Argos USA LLC.. 704 483-4013
4451 N Nc 16 Business Hwy Denver (28037) *(G-3772)*

Argos USA LLC.. 910 892-3188
401 N Fayetteville Ave Dunn (28334) *(G-3845)*

Argos USA LLC.. 919 552-2294
1506 Holland Rd Fuquay Varina (27526) *(G-4866)*

Argos USA LLC.. 919 772-4188
1915 W Garner Rd Garner (27529) *(G-4916)*

Argos USA LLC.. 828 322-9325
2001 Main Ave Se Hickory (28602) *(G-6267)*

Argos USA LLC.. 336 841-3379
406 Tomlinson St High Point (27260) *(G-6527)*

Argos USA LLC.. 919 732-7509
411 Valley Forge Rd Hillsborough (27278) *(G-6858)*

Argos USA LLC.. 252 527-8008
3350 Nc Highway 11 N Kinston (28501) *(G-7394)*

Argos USA LLC.. 704 872-9566
Hwy 150 E Mooresville (28115) *(G-8600)*

Argos USA LLC.. 252 223-4348
247 Carl Garner Rd Newport (28570) *(G-9437)*

Argos USA LLC.. 919 828-3695
3200 Spring Forest Rd Ste 210 Raleigh (27616) *(G-9913)*

Argos USA LLC.. 919 775-5441
3200 Spring Forest Rd Ste 210 Raleigh (27616) *(G-9914)*

Argos USA LLC... 919 790-1520
3200 Spring Forest Rd Ste 210 Raleigh (27616) *(G-9915)*

Argos USA LLC... 252 443-5046
75 W 13th St Roanoke Rapids (27870) *(G-10730)*

Argos USA LLC... 252 291-8888
6823 Bruce Rd Sims (27880) *(G-11428)*

Argos USA LLC... 704 872-9566
2289 Salisbury Hwy Statesville (28677) *(G-11659)*

Argos USA LLC... 919 554-2087
5025 Unicon Dr Wake Forest (27587) *(G-12261)*

Argos USA LLC... 252 946-4704
1020 E 5th St Washington (27889) *(G-12373)*

Argos USA LLC... 252 792-3148
741 Warren St Williamston (27892) *(G-12667)*

Argos USA LLC... 910 686-4890
8871 Sidbury Rd Wilmington (28411) *(G-12707)*

Argos USA LLC... 910 796-3469
800 Sunnyvale Dr Wilmington (28412) *(G-12708)*

Argos USA LLC... 336 784-4888
1590 Williamson St Winston Salem (27107) *(G-13089)*

Argus Fire Control, Charlotte Also Called: Argus Fire CONtrol-Pf&s Inc *(G-1696)*

Argus Fire CONtrol-Pf&s Inc......................... 704 372-1228
2723 Interstate St Charlotte (28208) *(G-1696)*

Arh, Stanfield Also Called: American Racg Hders Exhust Inc *(G-11602)*

ARIA APPAREL, Mooresville Also Called: 1st Choice Activewear II LLC *(G-8588)*

Aria Designs LLC... 828 572-4303
800 Hickory Blvd Sw Lenoir (28645) *(G-7573)*

Aribex Inc.. 866 340-5522
11727 Fruehauf Dr Charlotte (28273) *(G-1697)*

Arisaka, Apex Also Called: Arisaka LLC *(G-139)*

Arisaka LLC... 919 601-5625
1600 Olive Chapel Rd Ste 260 Apex (27502) *(G-139)*

Ariston Hospitality Inc................................... 626 458-8668
1581 Prospect St High Point (27260) *(G-6528)*

Ark Aviation Inc... 336 379-0900
200 N Raleigh St Greensboro (27401) *(G-5369)*

Arkema Coating Resins, Cary Also Called: Arkema Inc *(G-1294)*

Arkema Inc.. 919 469-6700
410 Gregson Dr Cary (27511) *(G-1294)*

Arma Co LLC.. 717 295-6805
4557 Technology Dr Ste 4 Wilmington (28405) *(G-12709)*

Armac Inc.. 919 878-9836
4027 Atlantic Ave Raleigh (27604) *(G-9916)*

Armacell LLC (HQ).. 919 913-0555
55 Vilcom Center Dr Ste 200 Chapel Hill (27514) *(G-1528)*

Armacell LLC... 828 464-5880
1004 Keisler Rd Nw Conover (28613) *(G-3491)*

Armacell US Holdings LLC............................. 919 304-3846
7600 Oakwood Street Ext Mebane (27302) *(G-8231)*

Arms Race Nutrition LLC............................... 888 978-2332
1415 Wilkesboro Hwy Statesville (28625) *(G-11660)*

Armtec Esterline Corp.................................... 910 814-3029
608 E Mcneill St Lillington (27546) *(G-7788)*

Arneg LLC... 336 956-5300
750 Old Hargrave Rd Lexington (27295) *(G-7656)*

Arneg USA, Lexington Also Called: Arneg LLC *(G-7656)*

Arnold-Wilbert Corporation (PA).................... 919 735-5008
1401 W Grantham St Goldsboro (27530) *(G-5200)*

Arnolds Welding Service Inc (PA).................. 910 323-3822
1405 Waterless St Fayetteville (28306) *(G-4553)*

Around Campus Group, The, Durham Also Called: University Directories LLC *(G-4290)*

Around House Improvement LLC..................... 919 496-7029
75 Gus Mcghee Rd Bunn (27508) *(G-1013)*

Arper USA (PA).. 336 434-2376
660 Southwest St High Point (27260) *(G-6529)*

Arpro M-Tec LLC.. 828 433-0699
212 E Fleming Dr Morganton (28655) *(G-8851)*

Arrants Logging Inc....................................... 252 792-1889
3600 Jerden Thicket Rd Jamesville (27846) *(G-7182)*

Array Biopharma Inc...................................... 303 381-6600
3005 Carrington Mill Blvd Morrisville (27560) *(G-8931)*

Arris, Claremont Also Called: Arris Solutions LLC *(G-3088)*

Arris Group, Claremont Also Called: Ruckus Wireless LLC *(G-3121)*

Arris Solutions LLC (DH)............................... 678 473-2000
3642 E Us Highway 70 Claremont (28610) *(G-3088)*

Arris Technology Inc (DH)............................. 828 324-2200
3642 E Us Highway 70 Claremont (28610) *(G-3089)*

Arrivo Management LLC................................. 919 460-9500
3000 Rdu Center Dr Morrisville (27560) *(G-8932)*

Arrochem Inc... 704 827-0216
201 Westland Farm Rd Mount Holly (28120) *(G-9217)*

Arrow Educational Products Inc..................... 910 521-0840
208 Union Chapel Rd # 101 Pembroke (28372) *(G-9656)*

Arrow Equipment LLC (PA)............................ 803 765-2040
9000 Statesville Rd Charlotte (28269) *(G-1698)*

Arrowhead Graphics Inc................................ 336 274-2419
508 Houston St Greensboro (27401) *(G-5370)*

ARS Extreme Construction Inc....................... 919 331-8024
175 Medical Dr Angier (27501) *(G-111)*

Art Enterprises Inc.. 828 277-1211
1156 Sweeten Creek Rd Asheville (28803) *(G-431)*

Art House... 919 552-7327
3325 Air Park Rd Fuquay Varina (27526) *(G-4867)*

Art Press, Manteo Also Called: Arthur Demarest *(G-8023)*

Art Sign Co.. 919 596-8681
209 S Goley St Durham (27701) *(G-3899)*

Artcraft Press Inc.. 828 397-8612
7814 Old Hwy 10 Icard (28666) *(G-7064)*

Artech Graphics Inc....................................... 704 545-9804
176 Yadkin Falls Rd New London (28127) *(G-9413)*

Artesian Builds, Chapel Hill Also Called: Artesian Future Technology LLC *(G-1529)*

Artesian Future Technology LLC.................... 919 904-4940
5801 Cascade Dr Chapel Hill (27514) *(G-1529)*

Artesias Swets Bnged By Dior L.................... 704 794-3792
208 Church St Ne Ste 1 Concord (28025) *(G-3312)*

Artex Group Inc... 866 845-1042
1004 Charlotte Hwy Fairview (28730) *(G-4505)*

Artful Shelter, Asheville Also Called: Southbridge Inc *(G-607)*

Arthur Demarest.. 252 473-1449
419 Skyco Rd Manteo (27954) *(G-8023)*

Artisan LLC... 855 582-3539
8620 Westmoreland Dr Nw Concord (28027) *(G-3313)*

Artisan Aromatics.. 800 456-6675
517 Jim Creek Rd Burnsville (28714) *(G-1183)*

Artisan Direct LLC... 704 655-9100
18335 Old Statesville Rd Ste L Cornelius (28031) *(G-3586)*

Artisan Graphics, Cornelius Also Called: Artisan Signs and Graphics Inc *(G-3587)*

Artisan Leaf LLC... 252 674-1223
2231 Nash St Nw Ste E Wilson (27896) *(G-12964)*

Artisan Signs and Graphics Inc.................... 704 655-9100
18335 Old Statesville Rd Ste L Cornelius (28031) *(G-3587)*

Artisanal Brewing Ventures, Charlotte Also Called: Craft Revolution LLC *(G-1994)*

Artisans Guild Incorporated........................... 336 841-4140
639 Mcway Dr Ste 101 High Point (27263) *(G-6530)*

Artist S Needle Inc.. 336 294-5884
2611 Phoenix Dr Greensboro (27406) *(G-5371)*

Artistic Frame Corp....................................... 212 289-2100
401 N Little Texas Rd Kannapolis (28083) *(G-7202)*

Artistic Images Inc.. 704 332-6225
900 Remount Rd 920 Charlotte (28203) *(G-1699)*

Artistic Ironworks LLC................................... 919 908-6888
700 E Club Blvd Ste B Durham (27704) *(G-3900)*

Artistic Kitchens & Baths LLC....................... 910 692-4000
683 Sw Broad St Southern Pines (28387) *(G-11494)*

Artistic Quilting, High Point Also Called: Crawford Industries Inc *(G-6579)*

Artistic Southern Inc..................................... 919 861-4695
1108 Continental Blvd Charlotte (28273) *(G-1700)*

Artwear Embroidery Inc (PA)......................... 336 992-2166
621 Indeneer Dr Kernersville (27284) *(G-7245)*

Arva LLC.. 803 336-2230
1327 Wood Branch Dr Ste E Charlotte (28273) *(G-1701)*

Arvinmeritor Automotive, Maxton Also Called: Meritor Inc *(G-8202)*

Arvinmeritor Hvy Vhcl Systems, Fletcher *Also Called: Meritor Inc (G-4755)*

ARW Optical Corp..910 452-7373
2021 Capital Dr Wilmington (28405) *(G-12710)*

Arysta Lifescience Inc..919 678-4900
15401 Weston Pkwy Ste 150 Cary (27513) *(G-1295)*

Arysta Lifescience N Amer LLC (HQ)..........................919 678-4900
15401 Weston Pkwy Ste 150 Cary (27513) *(G-1296)*

Arzberger Engravers Inc..704 376-1151
2518 Dunavant St Charlotte (28203) *(G-1702)*

As Inc...704 225-1700
1920 Tower Industrial Dr Monroe (28110) *(G-8430)*

As America Inc..704 398-4602
4500 Morris Field Dr Charlotte (28208) *(G-1703)*

Asamo Co, Greenville *Also Called: Asmo Greenville of North Carolina Inc (G-5939)*

ASAP Embroideries, Morehead City *Also Called: Consumer Concepts (G-8828)*

ASAP Marketing, Greenville *Also Called: Carlina Shotwell LLC (G-5950)*

ASAP Printing, Raleigh *Also Called: 4 Over LLC (G-9858)*

Asb Graphics, High Point *Also Called: Acme Sample Books Inc (G-6508)*

Asbury Graphite Mills..910 671-4141
191 Magna Blvd Lumberton (28360) *(G-7945)*

ASC, Sanford *Also Called: Air System Components Inc (G-11146)*

ASC, Tarboro *Also Called: Air System Components Inc (G-11921)*

ASC Distribution, Asheville *Also Called: Appalchian Stove Fbrcators Inc (G-428)*

ASC Engineered Solutions LLC...................................919 395-5222
920 Friar Tuck Rd Raleigh (27610) *(G-9917)*

Ascending Iron LLC..336 266-6462
6504 Burlington Rd Whitsett (27377) *(G-12599)*

Ascepi Medical Group LLC..919 336-4246
3344 Hillsborough St Ste 100 Raleigh (27607) *(G-9918)*

Asco LP...919 460-5200
111 Corning Rd Ste 120 Cary (27518) *(G-1297)*

Asco Power Technologies LP.......................................919 460-5200
3412 Apex Peakway Apex (27502) *(G-140)*

Asco Power Technologies LP.......................................336 731-5000
325 Welcome Center Blvd Lexington (27295) *(G-7657)*

Asco Power Technologies LP.......................................336 731-5009
325 Welcome Center Blvd Welcome (27374) *(G-12509)*

Ascom (us) Inc..877 712-7266
300 Perimeter Park Dr Ste D Morrisville (27560) *(G-8933)*

Aseptia Inc..678 373-6751
723 W Johnson St Ste 100 Raleigh (27603) *(G-9919)*

Ashbran LLC..919 215-3567
700 Parkridge Dr Clayton (27527) *(G-3132)*

Ashdan Enterprises...336 375-9698
608 Summit Ave Ste 201 Greensboro (27405) *(G-5372)*

Ashe Hams Inc..828 259-9426
707 Merrimon Ave Asheville (28804) *(G-432)*

Asheboro Activewear, Asheboro *Also Called: Wells Hosiery Mills Inc (G-420)*

Asheboro Courrier Tribune, Asheboro *Also Called: Gatehouse Media LLC (G-360)*

Asheboro Elastics Corp (PA)......................................336 629-2626
150 N Park St Asheboro (27203) *(G-327)*

Asheboro Elastics Corp..336 629-2626
1947 N Fayetteville St Asheboro (27203) *(G-328)*

Asheboro Machine Shop Inc.......................................336 625-6322
3027 Us Business 220 S Asheboro (27204) *(G-329)*

Asheboro Maltomeal, Asheboro *Also Called: Post Consumer Brands LLC (G-384)*

Asheboro Ready-Mix Inc...336 672-0957
524 W Bailey St Asheboro (27203) *(G-330)*

Asheville Bit & Steel Company....................................828 274-3766
111 Edgewood Rd S Asheville (28803) *(G-433)*

Asheville Citizen-Times...828 252-5611
14 Ohenry Ave Asheville (28803) *(G-434)*

Asheville Color & Imaging Inc.....................................828 774-5040
611 Tunnel Rd Ste E Asheville (28805) *(G-435)*

Asheville Contracting Co Inc.......................................828 665-8900
1270 Smoky Park Hwy Candler (28715) *(G-1217)*

Asheville Daily Planet, The, Asheville *Also Called: Star Fleet Communications Inc (G-611)*

Asheville Distilling Company.......................................828 575-2000
45 S French Broad Ave Asheville (28801) *(G-436)*

Asheville Fence, Candler *Also Called: Asheville Contracting Co Inc (G-1217)*

Asheville Global Report...828 236-3103
20 Battery Park Ave Asheville (28801) *(G-437)*

Asheville Maintenance and Construction Inc...............828 687-8110
150 Glenn Bridge Rd Arden (28704) *(G-254)*

Asheville Meadery LLC..828 454-6188
155 Johnston Blvd Asheville (28806) *(G-438)*

Asheville Metal Finishing Inc.......................................828 253-1476
178 Clingman Ave Asheville (28801) *(G-439)*

Asheville Paint & Powder Coat, Asheville *Also Called: Dotson Metal Finishing Inc (G-489)*

Asheville Print Shop..828 214-5286
740 Haywood Rd Asheville (28806) *(G-440)*

Asheville Promo LLC...828 575-2767
202 Asheland Ave Asheville (28801) *(G-441)*

Asheville Quickprint..828 252-7667
8 Chanter Dr Fletcher (28732) *(G-4720)*

Asheville Thermoform Plas Inc....................................828 684-8440
200 Cane Creek Industrial Park Rd Fletcher (28732) *(G-4721)*

Asheville Tourist Baseball, Asheville *Also Called: Tourist Baseball Inc (G-621)*

Asheville Vault Service Inc (PA)..................................828 665-6799
2239 Smoky Park Hwy Candler (28715) *(G-1218)*

Asheville Wilbert Vault Svc, Candler *Also Called: Asheville Vault Service Inc (G-1218)*

Ashevlle Prcsion Mch Rblding I...................................828 254-0884
51 Haywood Rd Asheville (28806) *(G-442)*

Ashfar Enterprises Inc...704 462-4672
3772 Plateau Rd Newton (28658) *(G-9449)*

Ashland Hardware Systems, Huntersville *Also Called: Ashland Products Inc (G-6968)*

Ashland Products Inc..815 266-0250
8936 N Exec Dr S 250 Huntersville (28078) *(G-6968)*

Ashley Furniture, Advance *Also Called: Ashley Furniture Inds LLC (G-31)*

Ashley Furniture Inds LLC...336 998-1066
333 Ashley Furniture Way Advance (27006) *(G-31)*

Ashley Interiors, High Point *Also Called: Rbc Inc (G-6754)*

Ashley Sling Inc..704 347-0071
2401 N Graham St Charlotte (28206) *(G-1704)*

ASHLEY SLING, INC., Charlotte *Also Called: Ashley Sling Inc (G-1704)*

Ashley Welding & Machine Co.....................................252 482-3321
104 Tower Dr Edenton (27932) *(G-4361)*

Ashleys Kit Bath Dsign Stdio L....................................828 669-5281
2950 Us 70 Hwy Black Mountain (28711) *(G-860)*

Ashton Lewis Lumber, Gatesville *Also Called: Coxe-Lewis Corporation (G-5171)*

Ashton Lewis Lumber Co Inc.......................................252 357-0050
96 Lewis Mill Rd Gatesville (27938) *(G-5169)*

Ashville Postage Express..828 255-9250
22 New Leicester Hwy Ste C Asheville (28806) *(G-443)*

Ashville Wrecker Service Inc.......................................828 252-2388
80 Weaverville Rd Asheville (28804) *(G-444)*

Ashworth Logging...910 464-2136
249 Hunter Ridge Ln Carthage (28327) *(G-1275)*

Asi Signage North Carolina...919 362-9669
600 Irving Pkwy Holly Springs (27540) *(G-6892)*

Asian (korean) Herald Inc...704 332-5656
1300 Baxter St Ste 155 Charlotte (28204) *(G-1705)*

Askbio, Research Triangle Pa *Also Called: Asklepios Bopharmaceutical Inc (G-10703)*

Asklepios Bopharmaceutical Inc (HQ).........................919 561-6210
20 Tw Alexander Dr Ste 110 Research Triangle Pa (27709) *(G-10703)*

Asmo Greenville of North Carolina Inc........................252 754-1000
1125 Sugg Pkwy Greenville (27834) *(G-5939)*

Asmo North America LLC...704 872-2319
470 Crawford Rd Statesville (28625) *(G-11661)*

Asp Distribution Inc..336 375-5672
100 Bonita Dr Greensboro (27405) *(G-5373)*

Asp Holdings Inc...888 330-2538
1014 N Arendell Ave Zebulon (27597) *(G-13504)*

Aspen Cabinetry Inc...828 466-0216
908 Industrial Dr Sw Conover (28613) *(G-3492)*

Asphalt, Maggie Valley *Also Called: Carolina Asphalt Maintenance (G-8005)*

Asphalt Emulsion Inds LLC..252 726-0653
107 Arendell St Morehead City (28557) *(G-8814)*

Asphalt Plant 1, Raleigh *Also Called: Fsc Holdings Inc (G-10121)*

Assa Abloy, Monroe *Also Called: Assa Abloy ACC Door Cntrls Gro (G-8432)*

Assa Abloy AB.. 704 283-2101
1902 Airport Rd Monroe (28110) *(G-8431)*

Assa Abloy ACC Door Cntrls Gro (DH)..............877 974-2255
1902 Airport Rd Monroe (28110) *(G-8432)*

Assa Abloy Accessories and.......................... 704 233-4011
3000 E Highway 74 Monroe (28112) *(G-8433)*

Assa Abloy Entrnce Systems US (DH)............. 866 237-2687
1900 Airport Rd Monroe (28110) *(G-8434)*

Assa Abloy Inc.. 704 776-8773
3000 E Highway 74 Monroe (28112) *(G-8435)*

Assembly Tech Components Inc....................... 919 773-0388
467 Hein Dr Garner (27529) *(G-4917)*

Assembly Technologies Inc............................. 704 596-3903
6716 Orr Rd Charlotte (28213) *(G-1706)*

Associated Artists Southport.......................... 910 457-5450
130 E West St Southport (28461) *(G-11517)*

Associated Battery Company.......................... 704 821-8311
3469 Gribble Rd Matthews (28104) *(G-8158)*

Associated Distributors Inc............................ 910 895-5800
120 Doe Loop Hamlet (28345) *(G-6050)*

Associated Hardwoods Inc (PA).....................828 396-3321
650 N Main St Granite Falls (28630) *(G-5295)*

Associated Hygienic Pdts LLC (PA).................770 497-9800
1029 Old Creek Rd Greenville (27834) *(G-5940)*

Associated Hygienic Products, Greenville *Also Called: Associated Hygienic Pdts LLC (G-5940)*

Associated Metal Works Inc........................... 704 546-7002
137 E Memorial Hwy Harmony (28634) *(G-6097)*

Associated Posters, Kernersville *Also Called: More Than Billboards Inc (G-7288)*

Associated Printing & Svcs Inc...................... 828 286-9064
905 N Main St Rutherfordton (28139) *(G-10975)*

Assoction Intl Crtif Prof Accn (PA)................. 919 402-4500
220 Leigh Farm Rd Durham (27707) *(G-3901)*

Asteelflash USA Corp..................................... 919 882-5400
6833 Mount Herman Rd Morrisville (27560) *(G-8934)*

Astellas Gene Therapies Inc.......................... 415 638-6561
6074 Enterprise Park Dr Sanford (27330) *(G-11151)*

Asterra Labs LLC... 800 430-9074
800 Cooke Rd Nashville (27856) *(G-9308)*

Astral Buoyancy Company............................. 828 255-2638
347 Depot St # 201 Asheville (28801) *(G-445)*

Astral Designs, Asheville *Also Called: Astral Buoyancy Company (G-445)*

Astrazeneca Pharmaceuticals LP................... 919 647-4990
4222 Emperor Blvd Ste 560 Durham (27703) *(G-3902)*

At Your Service Express LLC.......................... 704 270-9918
101 N Tryon St Ste 112 Charlotte (28246) *(G-1707)*

Atc Conversions, Raleigh *Also Called: Jeffrey Sheffer (G-10214)*

Atc Panels Inc... 919 653-6053
2000 Aerial Center Pkwy Ste 113 Morrisville (27560) *(G-8935)*

Atcom Bus Telecom Solutions, Charlotte *Also Called: Atcom Inc (G-1708)*

Atcom Inc.. 704 357-7900
3330 Oak Lake Blvd Charlotte (28208) *(G-1708)*

Atec, Mocksville *Also Called: Atec Wind Energy Products LLC (G-8349)*

Atec Coatings LLC... 336 753-8888
111 Bailey St Mocksville (27028) *(G-8348)*

Atec Wind Energy Products LLC..................... 336 753-8888
111 Bailey St Mocksville (27028) *(G-8349)*

Atelier Maison and Co LLC............................ 828 277-7202
121 Sweeten Creek Rd Ste 50 Asheville (28803) *(G-446)*

Atex Technologies Inc.................................... 910 255-2839
120 W Monroe Ave Pinebluff (28373) *(G-9684)*

Atg Division, Rutherfordton *Also Called: Trelleborg Ctd Systems US Inc (G-10997)*

Athena Marble Incorporated........................... 704 636-7810
7400 Bringle Ferry Rd Salisbury (28146) *(G-11018)*

Athol Arbor Corporation................................. 919 643-1100
511 Valley Forge Rd Hillsborough (27278) *(G-6859)*

Athol Manufacturing Corp.............................. 919 575-6523
100 22nd St Butner (27509) *(G-1197)*

ATI, Charlotte *Also Called: Assembly Technologies Inc (G-1706)*

ATI Allvac.. 541 967-9000
6400 Alloy Way Monroe (28110) *(G-8436)*

ATI Industrial Automation Inc (DH)................. 919 772-0115
1031 Goodworth Dr Apex (27539) *(G-141)*

ATI Laminates, Greensboro *Also Called: Advanced Technology Inc (G-5344)*

Atkins, Mike & Son Logging, Selma *Also Called: Mike Atkins & Son Logging Inc (G-11290)*

Atkinson International Inc............................... 704 865-7750
3800 Little Mountain Rd Gastonia (28056) *(G-4995)*

Atkinson Milling Company.............................. 919 965-3547
95 Atkinson Mill Rd Intersection Hwy 42 & 39 Selma (27576) *(G-11285)*

Atkinson's Mill, Selma *Also Called: Atkinson Milling Company (G-11285)*

Atlantic, Wilmington *Also Called: Atlantic Corp Wilmington Inc (G-12712)*

Atlantic Automotive Entps LLC....................... 910 377-4108
1007 Pireway Rd Ste B Tabor City (28463) *(G-11906)*

Atlantic Bankcard Center Inc.......................... 336 855-9250
2920 Manufacturers Rd Greensboro (27406) *(G-5374)*

Atlantic Bearing Co Inc.................................. 252 243-0233
321 Herring Ave Ne Bldg A Wilson (27893) *(G-12965)*

Atlantic Caribbean LLC.................................. 910 343-0624
806 N 23rd St Wilmington (28405) *(G-12711)*

Atlantic Coast Cabinet Distrs......................... 919 554-8165
150 Weathers Ct Youngsville (27596) *(G-13462)*

Atlantic Coast Protein Co, Selma *Also Called: Apc LLC (G-11284)*

Atlantic Coastal Shutters LLC........................ 252 441-4358
2701 N Croatan Hwy Kill Devil Hills (27948) *(G-7314)*

Atlantic Commercial Caseworks..................... 704 393-9500
4700 Rozzelles Ferry Rd Charlotte (28216) *(G-1709)*

Atlantic Corp Wilmington Inc.......................... 910 259-3600
151 Industrial Dr Burgaw (28425) *(G-1019)*

Atlantic Corp Wilmington Inc.......................... 704 588-1400
12201 Steele Creek Rd Charlotte (28273) *(G-1710)*

Atlantic Corp Wilmington Inc (PA).................. 800 722-5841
806 N 23rd St Wilmington (28405) *(G-12712)*

Atlantic Corporation (HQ).............................. 910 343-0624
806 N 23rd St Wilmington (28405) *(G-12713)*

Atlantic Counter Top & ACC, Raleigh *Also Called: Hargrove Countertops & ACC Inc (G-10155)*

Atlantic Custom Container Inc........................ 336 437-9302
327 E Elm St Graham (27253) *(G-5260)*

Atlantic Division, High Point *Also Called: Cascade Die Casting Group Inc (G-6563)*

Atlantic Engineering, Troutman *Also Called: Ae Technology Inc (G-12130)*

Atlantic Enterprises, Tabor City *Also Called: Atlantic Automotive Entps LLC (G-11906)*

Atlantic Group Usa Inc (PA).......................... 919 623-7824
3401 Gresham Lake Rd Ste 118 Raleigh (27615) *(G-9920)*

Atlantic Hydraulics Svcs LLC......................... 919 542-2985
5225 Womack Rd Sanford (27330) *(G-11152)*

Atlantic Logging Inc....................................... 252 229-9997
232 Stony Branch Rd New Bern (28562) *(G-9335)*

Atlantic Manufacturing LLC............................ 336 497-5500
1322 S Park Dr Kernersville (27284) *(G-7246)*

Atlantic Mfg & Fabrication Inc........................ 704 647-6200
705 S Railroad St Unit 1 Salisbury (28144) *(G-11019)*

Atlantic Mold Inc... 919 832-8151
1000 N Main St Ste 221 Fuquay Varina (27526) *(G-4868)*

Atlantic Natural Foods LLC............................ 888 491-0524
110 Industry Ct Nashville (27856) *(G-9309)*

Atlantic Prosthetics Orthtcs........................... 919 806-3260
6208 Fayetteville Rd Ste 101 Durham (27713) *(G-3903)*

Atlantic Screen Print, Elizabeth City *Also Called: R O Givens Signs Inc (G-4407)*

Atlantic Sign Media Inc.................................. 336 584-1375
111 Trail One Ste 101 Burlington (27215) *(G-1048)*

Atlantic Software Co...................................... 910 763-3907
607 S 13th St Wilmington (28401) *(G-12714)*

Atlantic Tool & Die Co Inc.............................. 910 270-2888
2363 Nc Highway 210 W Hampstead (28443) *(G-6068)*

Atlantic Trading LLC
307 Ridgewood Ave Charlotte (28209) *(G-1711)*

Atlantic Tube & Fitting LLC............................ 704 545-6166
4475 Morris Park Dr Ste L Mint Hill (28227) *(G-8330)*

Atlantic Veneer Company LLC (HQ)................252 728-3169
2457 Lennoxville Rd Beaufort (28516) *(G-719)*

Atlantic Window Coverings Inc....................... 704 392-0043
6150 Brookshire Blvd Ste D Charlotte (28216) *(G-1712)*

Atlantic Wood & Timber LLC............................ 704 390-7479
  2200 Border Dr Charlotte (28208) *(G-1713)*

Atlantis Food Service, Clemmons Also Called: Atlantis Foods Inc *(G-3177)*

Atlantis Foods Inc... 336 768-6101
  4525 Hampton Rd Clemmons (27012) *(G-3177)*

Atlantis Graphics Inc (PA)................................919 361-5809
  2410 E Nc Highway 54 Durham (27713) *(G-3904)*

Atlas American Lighting, Burlington Also Called: Atlas Lighting Products Inc *(G-1049)*

Atlas Box and Crating Co Inc............................. 919 941-1023
  3829 S Miami Blvd Ste 100 Durham (27703) *(G-3905)*

Atlas Copco Compressors LLC............................ 704 525-0124
  2101 Westinghouse Blvd # D Charlotte (28273) *(G-1714)*

Atlas Lighting Products Inc................................ 336 222-9258
  1406 S Mebane St Burlington (27215) *(G-1049)*

Atlas Precision Inc.. 828 687-9900
  170 Clayton Rd Arden (28704) *(G-255)*

Atlas Sign Industries, Concord Also Called: Atlas Sign Industries Nc LLC *(G-3314)*

Atlas Sign Industries Nc LLC.............................. 704 788-3733
  707 Commerce Dr Concord (28025) *(G-3314)*

Atmax Engineering... 910 233-4881
  806 Morris Ct Wilmington (28405) *(G-12715)*

Atmosphric Plsma Solutions Inc......................... 919 341-8325
  11301 Penny Rd Ste D Cary (27518) *(G-1298)*

Atmox Inc.. 704 248-2858
  10612d Providence Rd Ste 229 Charlotte (28277) *(G-1715)*

Atom Power, Huntersville Also Called: Atom Power Inc *(G-6969)*

Atom Power Inc.. 844 704-2866
  13245 Reese Blvd W Ste 130 Huntersville (28078) *(G-6969)*

Atricure, Morrisville Also Called: Ncontact Surgical LLC *(G-9022)*

Atrium Extrusion Systems Inc............................ 336 764-6400
  300 Welcome Center Blvd Welcome (27374) *(G-12510)*

Ats Service Company LLC.................................... 512 905-9005
  8442 Fayetteville Rd Godwin (28344) *(G-5186)*

Atsena Therapeutics Inc..................................... 352 273-9342
  280 S Mangum St Ste 350 Durham (27701) *(G-3906)*

Atsi, Walkertown Also Called: American Tchncal Solutions Inc *(G-12315)*

Attends Healthcare Pdts Inc............................... 252 752-1100
  1029 Old Creek Rd Greenville (27834) *(G-5941)*

Attends Healthcare Products Inc (PA)................ 800 428-8363
  8020 Arco Corporate Dr Ste 200 Raleigh (27617) *(G-9921)*

Attic Tent Inc... 704 892-5399
  164 Mill Pond Ln Mooresville (28115) *(G-8601)*

Atticus LLC... 984 465-4754
  940 Nw Cary Pkwy Ste 200 Cary (27513) *(G-1299)*

Attindas Hygiene Partners Inc............................ 252 752-1100
  350 Industrial Blvd Greenville (27834) *(G-5942)*

Attindas Hygiene Partners Inc (PA)................... 919 237-4000
  8020 Arco Corporate Dr Ste 200 Raleigh (27617) *(G-9922)*

Attl Products Inc.. 336 475-8101
  216 E Holly Hill Rd Thomasville (27360) *(G-11995)*

Attus Technologies Inc....................................... 704 341-5750
  13860 Ballantyne Corporate Pl Ste 200 Charlotte (28277) *(G-1716)*

Audio Advice LLC... 919 881-2005
  8621 Glenwood Ave Ste 117 Raleigh (27617) *(G-9923)*

Audio Vdeo Concepts Design Inc........................ 704 821-2823
  1409 Babbage Ln Ste B Indian Trail (28079) *(G-7069)*

Augusta Sportswear Inc..................................... 704 871-0990
  111 Badger Ln Statesville (28625) *(G-11662)*

Auntie Anne's, Charlotte Also Called: SE Co-Brand Ventures LLC *(G-2773)*

Auralites Inc... 828 687-7990
  9a National Ave Fletcher (28732) *(G-4722)*

Auria Albemarle LLC.. 704 983-5166
  313 Bethany Rd Albemarle (28001) *(G-62)*

Auria Old Fort LLC (DH)....................................828 668-7601
  1506 E Main St Old Fort (28762) *(G-9589)*

Auria Old Fort II LLC.. 828 668-3277
  1542 E Main St Old Fort (28762) *(G-9590)*

Auria Troy LLC... 910 572-3721
  163 Glen Rd Troy (27371) *(G-12157)*

Auriga Polymers Inc (DH)..................................864 579-5570
  4235 Southstream Blvd Ste 450 Charlotte (28217) *(G-1717)*

Aurobindo Pharma USA Inc................................ 732 839-9400
  2929 Weck Dr Durham (27703) *(G-3907)*

Aurolife Pharma LLC... 732 839-9408
  2929 Weck Dr Durham (27709) *(G-3908)*

Aurora Packing Co Inc.. 252 322-5232
  655 Second St Aurora (27806) *(G-641)*

Aurora Plastics Inc... 336 775-2640
  180 Welcome Center Blvd Welcome (27374) *(G-12511)*

Aurora Plastics, Inc., Welcome Also Called: Aurora Plastics Inc *(G-12511)*

Aurorium, Greensboro Also Called: Aurorium LLC *(G-5375)*

Aurorium LLC... 336 292-1781
  2110 W Gate City Blvd Greensboro (27403) *(G-5375)*

Aurum Capital Ventures Inc............................... 877 467-7780
  270 Cornerstone Dr Ste 101c Cary (27519) *(G-1300)*

Austin Business Forms Inc.................................. 704 821-6165
  241 Post Office Dr Ste A5 Indian Trail (28079) *(G-7070)*

Austin Company of Greensboro.......................... 336 468-2851
  2100 Hoots Rd Yadkinville (27055) *(G-13436)*

Austin Company, The, Yadkinville Also Called: Austin Company of Greensboro *(G-13436)*

Austin Powder Company..................................... 828 645-4291
  372 Ernest Smith Rd Denton (27239) *(G-3740)*

Austin Powder South East, Denton Also Called: Austin Powder Company *(G-3740)*

Austin Print Solutions, Indian Trail Also Called: Austin Business Forms Inc *(G-7070)*

Austin Printing Company Inc.............................. 704 289-1445
  1823 Morgan Mill Rd Monroe (28110) *(G-8437)*

Austin Tarp & Cargo Control, Charlotte Also Called: Prem Corp *(G-2660)*

Autec Inc.. 704 871-9141
  2500 W Front St Statesville (28677) *(G-11663)*

Autel New Energy US Inc.................................... 336 810-7083
  8420 Triad Dr Greensboro (27409) *(G-5376)*

Authentic Iron LLC... 910 648-6989
  17838 Nc 131 Hwy Bladenboro (28320) *(G-873)*

Auto Machine Shop Inc...................................... 910 483-6016
  309 Winslow St Fayetteville (28301) *(G-4554)*

Auto Marine Boat Repairs, Garner Also Called: C E Hicks Enterprises Inc *(G-4919)*

Auto Parts Fayetteville LLC................................ 910 889-4026
  929 Bragg Blvd Ste 2 Fayetteville (28301) *(G-4555)*

Auto Parts USA, Fayetteville Also Called: Auto Parts Fayetteville LLC *(G-4555)*

Auto-Systems and Service Inc............................ 336 824-3580
  839 Crestwick Rd Ramseur (27316) *(G-10625)*

Automail LLC.. 704 677-0152
  2987 Charlotte Hwy Mooresville (28117) *(G-8602)*

Automated Controls LLC..................................... 704 724-7625
  13416 S Old Statesville Rd Huntersville (28078) *(G-6970)*

Automated Designs Inc....................................... 828 696-9625
  105 Education Dr Flat Rock (28731) *(G-4703)*

Automated Entrances, Clayton Also Called: ADC Industries Inc *(G-3130)*

Automated Lumber Handling Inc......................... 828 754-4662
  723 Virginia St Sw Lenoir (28645) *(G-7574)*

Automated Machine Technologies....................... 919 361-0121
  10404 Chapel Hill Rd Ste 100 Morrisville (27560) *(G-8936)*

Automated Solutions LLC (PA)........................... 828 396-9900
  4101 Us Highway 321a Granite Falls (28630) *(G-5296)*

Automationcom LLC.. 952 563-5448
  67 Tw Alexander Dr Research Triangle Pa (27709) *(G-10704)*

Automedx LLC.. 888 617-2904
  13359 Reese Blvd E Huntersville (28078) *(G-6971)*

Automotive MGT Solutions................................. 919 481-2439
  301 Birdwood Ct Cary (27519) *(G-1301)*

Autopark Logistics LLC....................................... 704 365-3544
  2703 Madison Oaks Ct Charlotte (28226) *(G-1718)*

Autosmart Inc.. 919 210-7936
  510 Fairview Rd Apex (27502) *(G-142)*

Autosound 2000 Inc... 336 227-3434
  2557 Faucette Ln Burlington (27217) *(G-1050)*

Autoverters Inc.. 252 537-0426
  2212 W 10th St Roanoke Rapids (27870) *(G-10731)*

Autry Con Pdts & Bldrs Sup Co.......................... 704 504-8830
  8918 Byrum Dr Charlotte (28217) *(G-1719)*

Autry Con Pdts & Septic Svcs, Charlotte Also Called: Autry Con Pdts & Bldrs Sup Co *(G-1719)*

2025 Harris North Carolina
Manufacturers Directory

(G-0000) Company's Geographic Section entry number

Autry Logging Inc..910 303-4943
824 Magnolia Church Rd Stedman (28391) *(G-11805)*

Autumn Creek Vineyards Inc....................................336 548-9463
2105 Lafayette Ave Greensboro (27408) *(G-5377)*

Autumn House Inc..828 728-1121
1206 Premier Rd Granite Falls (28630) *(G-5297)*

Autumn Wood Products, Granite Falls Also Called: Autumn House Inc *(G-5297)*

Avadim Health, Swannanoa Also Called: Avadim Holdings Inc *(G-11865)*

Avadim Holdings Inc..877 677-2723
600a Centrepark Dr Asheville (28805) *(G-447)*

Avadim Holdings Inc..877 677-2723
4944 Parkway Plaza Blvd Ste 480 Charlotte (28217) *(G-1720)*

Avadim Holdings Inc (PA)..877 677-2723
4 Old Patton Cove Rd Swannanoa (28778) *(G-11865)*

Avant Publications LLC..704 897-6048
116 Morlake Dr Ste 203 Mooresville (28117) *(G-8603)*

Avaya LLC..919 425-8268
4001 E Chapel HI Research Triangle Pa (27709) *(G-10705)*

Avcon Inc..919 388-0203
101 Triangle Trade Dr Ste 101 Cary (27513) *(G-1302)*

Avdel USA LLC (HQ)..704 888-7100
614 Nc Hwy 200 S Stanfield (28163) *(G-11603)*

Avercast LLC..208 538-5380
8921 Crew Dr Emerald Isle (28594) *(G-4477)*

Averitt Electric Motor Repair, Laurinburg Also Called: Averitt Enterprises Inc *(G-7492)*

Averitt Enterprises Inc..910 276-1294
14121 Highland Rd Laurinburg (28352) *(G-7492)*

Averix Bio LLC..252 220-0887
3040 Black Creek Rd S Wilson (27893) *(G-12966)*

Avery County Recapping Co Inc................................828 733-0161
405 Linville St Newland (28657) *(G-9424)*

Avery County Tire, Newland Also Called: Avery County Recapping Co Inc *(G-9424)*

Avery Dennison Corporation......................................336 621-2570
2100 Summit Ave Greensboro (27405) *(G-5378)*

Avery Dennison Corporation......................................336 553-2436
620 Green Valley Rd Ste 306 Greensboro (27408) *(G-5379)*

Avery Dennison Corporation......................................336 856-8235
1100 Revolution Mill Dr # 11 Greensboro (27405) *(G-5380)*

Avery Dennison Corporation......................................864 938-1400
1100 Revolution Mill Dr # 11 Greensboro (27405) *(G-5381)*

Avery Dennison Corporation......................................336 665-6481
200 Citation Ct Greensboro (27409) *(G-5382)*

Avery Dennison Rfid Company..................................626 304-2000
1100 Revolution Mill Dr # 11 Greensboro (27405) *(G-5383)*

Avery Journal Times, Newland Also Called: High Country Media LLC *(G-9430)*

Avery Machine & Welding Co....................................828 733-4944
1312 Longleaf Dr Fayetteville (28305) *(G-4556)*

Avgol America Inc..336 936-2500
178 Avgol Dr Mocksville (27028) *(G-8350)*

Avgol Nonwovens, Mocksville Also Called: Avgol America Inc *(G-8350)*

Avian Cetacean Press..910 392-5537
1616 Jettys Reach Wilmington (28409) *(G-12716)*

Aviation Metals, Charlotte Also Called: Aviation Metals NC Inc *(G-1721)*

Aviation Metals NC Inc..704 264-1647
1810 W Pointe Dr Ste D Charlotte (28214) *(G-1721)*

Aviator Brewing Company Inc....................................919 601-5497
5504 Caleb Knolls Dr Holly Springs (27540) *(G-6893)*

AVIDXCHANGE, Charlotte Also Called: Avidxchange Holdings Inc *(G-1722)*

Avidxchange Holdings Inc (PA)................................800 560-9305
1210 Avid Xchange Ln Charlotte (28206) *(G-1722)*

Avient Colorants USA LLC..704 331-7000
4000 Monroe Rd Charlotte (28205) *(G-1723)*

Avient Protective Mtls LLC (HQ)..............................252 707-2547
5750 Martin Luther King Jr Hwy Greenville (27834) *(G-5943)*

Avient Protective Mtls LLC..704 862-5100
1101 S Highway 27 Stanley (28164) *(G-11609)*

Avintiv Inc (HQ)..704 697-5100
9335 Harris Corners Pkwy Ste 300 Charlotte (28269) *(G-1724)*

Avintiv Specialty Mtls Inc (HQ)................................704 697-5100
9335 Harris Corners Pkwy Ste 300 Charlotte (28269) *(G-1725)*

Avintiv Specialty Mtls Inc..704 660-6242
111 Excellance Ln Mooresville (28115) *(G-8604)*

AVIOQ Inc (HQ)..919 314-5535
76 Tw Alexander Dr Durham (27709) *(G-3909)*

Avior Inc..919 234-0068
221 James Jackson Ave Cary (27513) *(G-1303)*

Avior Bio, Cary Also Called: Avior Inc *(G-1303)*

Avista Pharma Solutions Inc (HQ)............................919 544-8600
3501 Tricenter Blvd Ste C Durham (27713) *(G-3910)*

Avl Custom Fabrication..828 713-0333
250 Baird Cove Rd Asheville (28804) *(G-448)*

Avl Technologies, Asheville Also Called: Avl Technologies Inc *(G-449)*

Avl Technologies Inc..828 250-9950
15 N Merrimon Ave Asheville (28804) *(G-449)*

Avoca LLC (DH)..252 482-2133
841 Avoca Rd Merry Hill (27957) *(G-8268)*

Avon Seafood..252 995-4553
Harbor Rd Avon (27915) *(G-650)*

AWC, Charlotte Also Called: Atlantic Window Coverings Inc *(G-1712)*

AWC Holding Company..919 677-3900
5020 Weston Pkwy Ste 400 Cary (27513) *(G-1304)*

Awcnc LLC..252 633-5757
401 Industrial Dr New Bern (28562) *(G-9336)*

Awesome Products Inc..336 374-5900
1625 Sheep Farm Rd Mount Airy (27030) *(G-9099)*

Awning Innovations..336 831-8996
1635 S Martin Luther King Jr Dr Winston Salem (27107) *(G-13090)*

Awning Shop, Shelby Also Called: Colored Metal Products Inc *(G-11322)*

Awnings Etc, Garner Also Called: Custom Canvas Works Inc *(G-4928)*

Axalta Coating Systems LLC....................................855 629-2582
5388 Stowe Ln Concord (28027) *(G-3315)*

Axalta Coating Systems Ltd......................................336 802-5701
1717 W English Rd High Point (27262) *(G-6531)*

Axalta Coating Systems Ltd......................................336 802-4392
2137 Brevard Rd High Point (27263) *(G-6532)*

Axalta Coating Systems USA LLC............................336 802-5701
1717 W English Rd High Point (27262) *(G-6533)*

Axccellus LLC..919 589-9800
2501 Schieffelin Rd Apex (27502) *(G-143)*

Axchem Solutions Inc..919 742-9810
1325 N 2nd Ave Siler City (27344) *(G-11398)*

Axial Exchange Inc..919 576-9988
1111 Haynes St Ste 113 Raleigh (27604) *(G-9924)*

Axis Corrugated Container LLC (HQ)........................919 575-0500
201 Industrial Dr Butner (27509) *(G-1198)*

Axitare Corporation..919 256-8196
1717 Brassfield Rd Raleigh (27614) *(G-9925)*

Axjo America Inc..828 322-6046
221 S Mclin Creek Rd Ste A Conover (28613) *(G-3493)*

Axle Holdings LLC..800 895-3276
5051 Davidson Hwy Concord (28027) *(G-3316)*

Axon LLC..919 772-8383
3080 Business Park Dr Ste 103 Raleigh (27610) *(G-9926)*

Axon Styrotech, Raleigh Also Called: Axon LLC *(G-9926)*

Axtra3d, Charlotte Also Called: Axtra3d Inc *(G-1726)*

Axtra3d Inc..888 315-5103
5510 77 Center Dr Ste 150 Charlotte (28217) *(G-1726)*

Aylward Enterprises LLC (PA)..................................252 639-9242
401 Industrial Dr New Bern (28562) *(G-9337)*

Aztech Products Inc (PA)..910 763-5599
2145 Wrightsville Ave Wilmington (28403) *(G-12717)*

Azure Skye Beverages Inc..704 909-7394
5253 Old Dowd Rd Unit 3 Charlotte (28208) *(G-1727)*

Azusa International Inc..704 879-4464
2510 N Chester St Gastonia (28052) *(G-4996)*

B & B Building Maintenance LLC..............................910 494-2715
5318 Hwy 210 S Bunnlevel (28323) *(G-1015)*

B & B Distributing Inc..336 592-5665
2888 Durham Rd Ste 102 Roxboro (27573) *(G-10919)*

B & B Fabrication Inc..623 581-7600
125 Infield Ct Mooresville (28117) *(G-8605)*

B & B Hosiery Mill..336 368-4849
3608 Volunteer Rd Pinnacle (27043) *(G-9767)*

A
L
P
H
A
B
E
T
I
C

B & B Industries Inc.. 704 882-4688
4824 Unionville Indian Trail Rd W Ste A Indian Trail (28079) *(G-7071)*

B & B Leather Co Inc.. 704 598-9080
5518 Nevin Rd Charlotte (28269) *(G-1728)*

B & B Machine Co Inc...................................... 704 637-2356
1890 Barringer Rd Salisbury (28147) *(G-11020)*

B & B Stucco and Stone LLC.......................... 704 524-1230
816 Joseph Antoon Cir Stanley (28164) *(G-11610)*

B & B Welding Inc.. 336 643-5702
2900 Oak Ridge Rd Oak Ridge (27310) *(G-9569)*

B & B Wood Shop & Bldg Contrs.................... 828 488-2078
4829 Highway 19 W Bryson City (28713) *(G-1007)*

B & C Concrete Products Inc........................... 336 838-4201
228 New Brickyard Rd North Wilkesboro (28659) *(G-9522)*

B & D Enterprises Inc...................................... 704 739-2958
736 Stony Point Rd Kings Mountain (28086) *(G-7348)*

B & E Woodturning Inc..................................... 828 758-2843
2395 Howard Arnett Rd Lenoir (28645) *(G-7575)*

B & J Knits Inc... 704 876-1498
3492 Wilkesboro Hwy Statesville (28625) *(G-11664)*

B & J Seafood Co Inc....................................... 252 637-0483
1101 Us Highway 70 E New Bern (28560) *(G-9338)*

B & M Electric Motor Service........................... 828 267-0829
20 17th Street Pl Nw Hickory (28601) *(G-6268)*

B & M Wholesale, Mount Airy *Also Called: B & M Wholesale Inc (G-9100)*

B & M Wholesale Inc.. 336 789-3916
1800 Sparger Rd Mount Airy (27030) *(G-9100)*

B & W Enterprises, Traphill *Also Called: Smith Utility Buildings (G-12106)*

B & W Stone Company, Micaville *Also Called: Boone-Woody Mining Company Inc (G-8270)*

B & Y Machining Co Inc.................................... 252 235-2180
4495 Us Highway 264a Bailey (27807) *(G-668)*

B A S F Colors & Colorants, Charlotte *Also Called: BASF Corporation (G-1758)*

B C D, Durham *Also Called: Bull City Designs LLC (G-3949)*

B C I, Charlotte *Also Called: Border Concepts Inc (G-1800)*

B C M Company, Etowah *Also Called: Boondock S Manufacturing Inc (G-4495)*

B F I Industries Inc.. 919 229-4509
3650 Rogers Rd # 334 Wake Forest (27587) *(G-12262)*

B G V Inc.. 704 588-3047
12245 Nations Ford Rd Ste 503 Pineville (28134) *(G-9714)*

B J Logging, Louisburg *Also Called: Richard C Jones (G-7926)*

B P Printing and Copying Inc........................... 704 821-8219
3756 Pleasant Plains Rd Matthews (28104) *(G-8159)*

B Roberts Foods LLC....................................... 704 522-1977
2700 Westinghouse Blvd Ste A Charlotte (28273) *(G-1729)*

B S R-Hess Race Cars Inc............................... 704 547-0901
7701 N Tryon St Charlotte (28262) *(G-1730)*

B T C, Wake Forest *Also Called: Btc Electronic Components LLC (G-12266)*

B V Hedrick Gravel & Sand Co......................... 336 337-0706
15 Yorkshire St Asheville (28803) *(G-450)*

B V Hedrick Gravel & Sand Co......................... 828 738-0332
1182 Old Glenwood Rd Marion (28752) *(G-8032)*

B V Hedrick Gravel & Sand Co (PA)................. 704 633-5982
120 1/2 N Church St Salisbury (28144) *(G-11021)*

B V Hedrick Gravel & Sand Co......................... 704 827-8114
6941 Quarry Ln Stanley (28164) *(G-11611)*

B V Hedrick Gravel & Sand Co......................... 828 686-3844
Old Us 70 Swannanoa (28778) *(G-11866)*

B V Hedrick Gravel & Sand Co......................... 828 645-5560
100 Gold View Rd Weaverville (28787) *(G-12482)*

B. Robert's Prepared Foods, Charlotte *Also Called: B Roberts Foods LLC (G-1729)*

B/E Aerospace Inc (DH)................................... 704 423-7000
2730 W Tyvola Rd Charlotte (28217) *(G-1731)*

B/E Aerospace Inc... 336 841-7698
2376 Hickswood Rd Ste 106 High Point (27265) *(G-6535)*

B/E Aerospace Inc... 336 293-1823
2598 Empire Dr Winston Salem (27103) *(G-13091)*

B/E Aerospace Inc... 336 293-1823
175 Oak Plaza Blvd Winston Salem (27105) *(G-13092)*

B/E Aerospace Inc... 336 744-6914
190 Oak Plaza Blvd Winston Salem (27105) *(G-13093)*

B/E Aerospace Inc... 336 767-2000
150 Oak Plaza Blvd Ste 200 Winston Salem (27105) *(G-13094)*

B/E Aerospace Inc... 520 733-1719
1455 Fairchild Rd # 1 Winston Salem (27105) *(G-13095)*

B/E Aerospace Inc... 336 776-3500
2599 Empire Dr Winston Salem (27103) *(G-13096)*

B/E Aerospace Inc... 336 767-2000
1455 Fairchild Rd Winston Salem (27105) *(G-13097)*

B/E Aerospace Inc... 336 692-8940
4965 Indiana Ave Winston Salem (27106) *(G-13098)*

B/E Aerospace Inc... 704 423-7000
150 Oak Plaza Blvd Ste 200 Winston Salem (27105) *(G-13099)*

B&B Cap Liners LLC... 585 598-1828
3208 Spottswood St Ste 115 Raleigh (27615) *(G-9927)*

B&B Wood Shop Showroom, Bryson City *Also Called: B & B Wood Shop & Bldg Contrs (G-1007)*

B&C Xterior Cleaning Svc Inc.......................... 919 779-7905
142 Annaron Ct Raleigh (27603) *(G-9928)*

B&G Foods Inc... 336 849-7000
500 Nonnis Way Yadkinville (27055) *(G-13437)*

B&H Millwork and Fixtures Inc......................... 336 431-0068
1130 Bedford St High Point (27263) *(G-6534)*

B&P Enterprise NC Inc..................................... 727 669-6877
4128 Icard Ridge Rd Hickory (28601) *(G-6269)*

B&W, Charlotte *Also Called: Bwxt Investment Company (G-1824)*

B+e Manufacturing Co Inc............................... 704 236-8439
4811 Persimmon Ct Monroe (28110) *(G-8438)*

B3 Bio Inc.. 919 226-3079
6 Davis Dr Research Triangle Pa (27709) *(G-10706)*

B6usa Inc.. 919 833-3851
414 Dupont Cir Raleigh (27603) *(G-9929)*

Ba International LLC... 336 519-8080
1000 E Hanes Mill Rd Winston Salem (27105) *(G-13100)*

BA Robbins Company LLC................................ 828 466-3900
110 E 15th St Newton (28658) *(G-9450)*

Baac Business Solutions Inc........................... 704 333-4321
1701 South Blvd Charlotte (28203) *(G-1732)*

Babco Inc... 888 376-5083
639 Sumrell Rd Ayden (28513) *(G-653)*

Babcock Wlcox Eqity Invstmnts....................... 704 625-4900
13024 Ballantyne Corporate Pl Ste 700 Charlotte (28277) *(G-1733)*

Babcock Wlcox Intl Sls Svc Cor....................... 704 625-4900
13024 Ballantyne Corporate Pl Ste 700 Charlotte (28277) *(G-1734)*

Babeegreens, Asheville *Also Called: Tiara Inc (G-619)*

Babine Lake Corporation (PA).......................... 910 285-7955
113 Dogwood Cir Hampstead (28443) *(G-6069)*

Babington Technology Inc (PA)........................ 252 984-0349
159 Fabrication Way Rocky Mount (27804) *(G-10823)*

Babusci Crtive Prtg Imging LLC....................... 704 423-9864
4115 Rose Lake Dr Ste A Charlotte (28217) *(G-1735)*

Bacci America Inc.. 704 375-5044
1704 East Blvd Ste 101 Charlotte (28203) *(G-1736)*

Bace LLC... 704 394-2230
322 W 32nd St Charlotte (28206) *(G-1737)*

Bachstein Consulting LLC................................ 410 322-4917
70 Mosswood Blvd Ste 200 Youngsville (27596) *(G-13463)*

Backstreets Publishing.................................... 919 968-9466
200 N Greensboro St Ste D Carrboro (27510) *(G-1266)*

Backwater Guns LLC.. 910 399-1451
1024 S Kerr Ave Wilmington (28403) *(G-12718)*

Backwoods Logging LLC.................................. 910 298-3786
1066 Sumner Rd Pink Hill (28572) *(G-9764)*

Backyard Entps & Svcs LLC............................ 828 755-4960
281 Spindale St Spindale (28160) *(G-11544)*

Badger Sportswear LLC................................... 704 871-0990
111 Badger Ln Statesville (28625) *(G-11665)*

Badger Sportswear LLC (HQ)........................... 704 871-0990
111 Badger Ln Statesville (28625) *(G-11666)*

Badger Welding Incorporated........................... 828 863-2078
387 Creek Rd Rutherfordton (28139) *(G-10976)*

Badgers Sports, Statesville *Also Called: Augusta Sportswear Inc (G-11662)*

(G-0000) Company's Geographic Section entry number

Bae Systems Inc... 855 223-8363
  11215 Rushmore Dr Charlotte (28277) *(G-1738)*

Bae Systems Info Elctrnic Syst.......................... 919 323-5800
  4721 Emperor Blvd Ste 330 Durham (27703) *(G-3911)*

Baebies Inc.. 919 891-0432
  25 Alexandria Way Durham (27709) *(G-3912)*

Bagcraftpapercon III LLC (DH)........................... 800 845-6051
  3436 Toringdon Way Ste 100 Charlotte (28277) *(G-1739)*

Bahakel Communications Ltd LLC...................... 704 372-4434
  701 Television Pl Charlotte (28205) *(G-1740)*

Bahnson Holdings Inc (HQ)................................. 336 760-3111
  4731 Commercial Park Ct Clemmons (27012) *(G-3178)*

Bahnson Mechanical Specialties, Raleigh *Also Called: Mechanical Spc Contrs Inc (G-10287)*

Baicy Communications Inc.................................. 336 722-7768
  1411 S Main St Winston Salem (27127) *(G-13101)*

Baikowski International Corp (HQ)....................... 704 587-7100
  6601 Northpark Blvd Ste H Charlotte (28216) *(G-1741)*

Baileys Quick Copy Shop Inc (PA)...................... 704 637-2020
  324 E Fisher St Salisbury (28144) *(G-11022)*

Baileys Sauces Inc... 252 756-7179
  3765 Mills Rd Greenville (27858) *(G-5944)*

Baily Enterprises LLC.. 704 587-0109
  12016 Steele Creek Rd Charlotte (28273) *(G-1742)*

Baja Marine Inc... 252 975-2000
  1653 Whichards Beach Road Washington (27889) *(G-12374)*

Bakeboxx Company.. 336 861-1212
  629 Mcway Dr High Point (27263) *(G-6536)*

Bakemark USA LLC... 336 848-9790
  720 Pegg Rd Greensboro (27409) *(G-5384)*

Baker Furniture, High Point *Also Called: Baker Interiors Furniture Co (G-6537)*

Baker Interiors Furniture Co (DH)....................... 336 431-9115
  1 Baker Way Connelly Springs (28612) *(G-3473)*

Baker Interiors Furniture Co............................... 336 431-9115
  2219 Shore St High Point (27263) *(G-6537)*

Baker Thermal Solutions LLC............................. 919 674-3750
  8182 Us 70 Bus Hwy W Clayton (27520) *(G-3133)*

Bakers Quality Trim Inc...................................... 919 552-3621
  1616 Kendall Hill Rd Willow Spring (27592) *(G-12678)*

Bakers Southern Traditions Inc.......................... 252 344-2120
  704 E Church St Roxobel (27872) *(G-10949)*

Bakers Sthern Trdtions Peanuts, Roxobel *Also Called: Bakers Southern Traditions Inc (G-10949)*

Bakers Stnless Fabrication Inc............................ 919 934-2707
  1520 Freedom Rd Smithfield (27577) *(G-11434)*

Bakery Feeds, Marshville *Also Called: Griffin Industries LLC (G-8089)*

Bakeshot Prtg & Graphics LLC........................... 704 532-9326
  121 Greenwich Rd Ste 101 Charlotte (28211) *(G-1743)*

Bakkavor Foods Usa Inc..................................... 704 522-1977
  10220 Western Ridge Rd Ste P Charlotte (28273) *(G-1744)*

Bakkavor Foods Usa Inc (DH)............................. 704 522-1977
  2700 Westinghouse Blvd Charlotte (28273) *(G-1745)*

Balance Systems, Statesville *Also Called: Amesbury Acqstion Hldngs 2 Inc (G-11654)*

Balanced Health Plus LLC................................... 704 604-9524
  7804 Fairview Rd Box 275 Charlotte (28226) *(G-1746)*

Balanced Pharma Incorporated........................... 704 278-7054
  18204 Mainsail Pointe Dr Cornelius (28031) *(G-3588)*

Balcrank Corporation.. 800 747-5300
  90 Monticello Rd Weaverville (28787) *(G-12483)*

Baldor Dodge Reliance.. 828 652-0074
  510 Rockwell Dr Marion (28752) *(G-8033)*

Baldor Dodge Reliance, Weaverville *Also Called: ABB Motors and Mechanical Inc (G-12481)*

Baldor Motors & Drives, Greensboro *Also Called: ABB Motors and Mechanical Inc (G-5336)*

Baldwin Sign & Awning.. 910 642-8812
  2 Whiteville Mini Mall Whiteville (28472) *(G-12576)*

Ball Metal Beverage Cont Corp............................ 336 342-4711
  1900 Barnes St Reidsville (27320) *(G-10674)*

Ball Metal Beverage Cont Div, Reidsville *Also Called: Ball Metal Beverage Cont Corp (G-10674)*

Ball Photo, Asheville *Also Called: Ball Photo Supply Inc (G-451)*

Ball Photo Supply Inc.. 828 252-2443
  569 Merrimon Ave Asheville (28804) *(G-451)*

Ball S Machine, Candler *Also Called: Ball S Machine & Mfg Co Inc (G-1219)*

Ball S Machine & Mfg Co Inc............................... 828 667-0411
  2120 Smoky Park Hwy Candler (28715) *(G-1219)*

Ballabox, Matthews *Also Called: Kme Consolidated Inc (G-8124)*

Ballantyne One.. 704 926-7009
  15720 Brixham Hill Ave Ste 300 Charlotte (28277) *(G-1747)*

Ballistic Recovery Systems Inc (PA).................... 651 457-7491
  41383 Us 1 Hwy Pinebluff (28373) *(G-9685)*

Ballistics Technology Intl Ltd.............................. 252 360-1650
  511 Goldsboro St Ne Wilson (27893) *(G-12967)*

Bally Refrigerated Boxes Inc (PA)....................... 252 240-2829
  135 Little Nine Rd Morehead City (28557) *(G-8815)*

Baltek Inc (DH)... 336 398-1900
  5240 National Center Dr Colfax (27235) *(G-3273)*

Bamal Corporation (HQ)...................................... 980 225-7700
  13725 S Point Blvd Charlotte (28207) *(G-1748)*

Bamal Fastener, Charlotte *Also Called: Bamal Corporation (G-1748)*

Bandag, Charlotte *Also Called: Parrish Tire Company (G-2614)*

Bandag, Clinton *Also Called: Tires Incorporated of Clinton (G-3249)*

Bandag, Graham *Also Called: Piedmont Truck Tires Inc (G-5281)*

Bandwidth, Raleigh *Also Called: Bandwidth Inc (G-9930)*

Bandwidth Inc (PA).. 800 808-5150
  2230 Bandmate Way Raleigh (27607) *(G-9930)*

Banilla Games Inc... 252 329-7977
  3506 Greenville Blvd Ne Greenville (27834) *(G-5945)*

Banknote Corp America Inc................................. 336 375-1134
  6109 Corporate Park Dr Browns Summit (27214) *(G-990)*

Banknote Corporation America, Browns Summit *Also Called: Sennett Security Products LLC (G-1005)*

Banks Rd Concrete Plant, Fuquay Varina *Also Called: S T Wooten Corporation (G-4897)*

Banks, Steve and Ray Logging, Maysville *Also Called: Steve & Ray Banks Logging Inc (G-8212)*

Banner Elk Winery Inc... 828 898-9090
  135 Deer Run Ln Banner Elk (28604) *(G-682)*

Banner Life Sciences LLC.................................... 336 812-8700
  3980 Premier Dr Ste 110 High Point (27265) *(G-6538)*

Bannister Inc.. 252 638-6611
  303 Crescent St New Bern (28560) *(G-9339)*

Bar Squared Inc.. 919 878-0578
  5605 Spring Ct Raleigh (27616) *(G-9931)*

Bar-S Foods Co... 847 652-3238
  2101 Westinghouse Blvd Ste 109 Raleigh (27604) *(G-9932)*

Barbaras Canine Catering Inc.............................. 704 588-3647
  1447 S Tryon St Ste 101 Charlotte (28203) *(G-1749)*

Barber Furniture & Supply................................... 704 278-9367
  590 Mountain Rd Cleveland (27013) *(G-3209)*

Barber Shop AP Screen Prtg, Fayetteville *Also Called: Kraken-Skulls (G-4627)*

Barbour S Marine Supply Co Inc......................... 252 728-2136
  410 Hedrick St Beaufort (28516) *(G-720)*

Barcovision LLC.. 704 392-9371
  4420 Taggart Creek Rd Charlotte (28208) *(G-1750)*

Barcovvsion LLC (PA).. 704 392-9371
  4420 Taggart Creek Rd Ste 110 Charlotte (28208) *(G-1751)*

Barcy, D T Logging, Ahoskie *Also Called: Darrell T Bracy (G-47)*

Barefoot Cnc Inc.. 828 438-5038
  1004 Carbon City Rd Morganton (28655) *(G-8852)*

Barefoot Press Inc.. 919 283-6396
  731 Pershing Rd Raleigh (27608) *(G-9933)*

Barewoodworking Inc.. 828 758-0694
  4400 Fox Rd Lenoir (28645) *(G-7576)*

Bariatric Partners Inc... 704 542-2256
  7401 Carmel Executive Park Dr Charlotte (28226) *(G-1752)*

Barker and Martin Inc... 336 275-5056
  1316 Headquarters Dr Greensboro (27405) *(G-5385)*

Barker Industries Inc (PA)................................... 704 391-1023
  220 Crompton St Charlotte (28273) *(G-1753)*

Barkleys Mill On Southern Cro............................ 828 626-3344
  6 Barkley Pl Weaverville (28787) *(G-12484)*

Barlin Ranch & Pets Inc...................................... 910 814-1930
  390 D R Harvell Ln Lillington (27546) *(G-7789)*

A L P H A B E T I C

Barnes Dmnd Gllery Jwly Mfrs I.................................... 910 347-4300
   120 College Plz Jacksonville (28546) *(G-7116)*

Barnes Logging Co Inc.................................... 252 799-6016
   308 Golf Rd Plymouth (27962) *(G-9798)*

Barnes Metalcrafters, Wilson *Also Called: South East Manufacturing Co (G-13030)*

Barnes Precision Machine Inc.................................... 919 362-6805
   1434 Farrington Rd Ste 300 Apex (27523) *(G-144)*

Barnhardt Manufacturing Co.................................... 704 331-0657
   1300 Hawthorne Ln Charlotte (28205) *(G-1754)*

Barnhardt Manufacturing Co.................................... 336 789-9161
   1515 Carter St Mount Airy (27030) *(G-9101)*

Barnhardt Manufacturing Company (PA).................................... 800 277-0377
   1100 Hawthorne Ln Charlotte (28205) *(G-1755)*

Barnharts Tech Tire Repair Inc.................................... 336 337-1569
   278 Rocky Trail Rd Lexington (27292) *(G-7658)*

Barnhill Contracting Company.................................... 336 584-1306
   1858 Huffman Mill Rd Burlington (27215) *(G-1051)*

Barnhill Contracting Company.................................... 704 721-7500
   725 Derita Rd Concord (28027) *(G-3317)*

Barnhill Contracting Company.................................... 910 488-1319
   1100 Robeson St Fayetteville (28305) *(G-4557)*

Barnhill Contracting Company.................................... 252 752-7608
   562 Barrus Construction Rd Greenville (27834) *(G-5946)*

Barnhill Contracting Company.................................... 252 527-8021
   604 E New Bern Rd Kinston (28504) *(G-7395)*

Barrday Corp (HQ).................................... 704 395-0311
   1450 W Pointe Dr Ste C Charlotte (28214) *(G-1756)*

Barrday Protective Solutions, Charlotte *Also Called: Barrday Corp (G-1756)*

Barretts Printing House Inc.................................... 252 243-2820
   131 Douglas St S Wilson (27893) *(G-12968)*

Barrier1, Greensboro *Also Called: Barrier1 Systems Inc (G-5386)*

Barrier1 Systems Inc.................................... 336 617-8478
   8015 Thorndike Rd Greensboro (27409) *(G-5386)*

Barrister and Brewer LLC.................................... 919 323-2777
   1212 N Mineral Springs Rd Durham (27703) *(G-3913)*

Barron Legacy Mgmt Group LLC.................................... 301 367-4735
   1737 Arbor Vista Dr Charlotte (28262) *(G-1757)*

Barrs Competition.................................... 704 482-5169
   124 Drum Rd Shelby (28152) *(G-11313)*

Barry Callebaut USA LLC.................................... 828 685-2443
   51 Saint Pauls Rd Hendersonville (28792) *(G-6185)*

Barsina Publishing.................................... 336 869-2849
   3510 Pine Valley Rd High Point (27265) *(G-6539)*

Bartimaeus By Design Inc.................................... 336 475-4346
   1010 Randolph St Thomasville (27360) *(G-11996)*

Bartlett Milling Company LP.................................... 704 872-9581
   701 S Center St Statesville (28677) *(G-11667)*

Barudan America Inc.................................... 800 627-4776
   9826 Us Highway 311 Ste 4 High Point (27263) *(G-6540)*

Basalt Specialty Products Inc.................................... 336 835-5153
   600 E Main St Elkin (28621) *(G-4439)*

BASF.................................... 919 731-1700
   703 Nor Am Rd Pikeville (27863) *(G-9666)*

BASF Corporation.................................... 704 588-5280
   11501 Steele Creek Rd Charlotte (28273) *(G-1758)*

BASF Corporation.................................... 919 433-6773
   2 Tw Alexander Dr Durham (27709) *(G-3914)*

BASF Corporation.................................... 919 547-2000
   26 Davis Dr Durham (27709) *(G-3915)*

BASF Corporation.................................... 919 461-6500
   3500 Paramount Pkwy Morrisville (27560) *(G-8937)*

BASF Plant Science LP.................................... 919 547-2000
   26 Davis Dr Durham (27709) *(G-3916)*

Basic Group, The, Siler City *Also Called: Basic Machinery Company Inc (G-11399)*

Basic Machinery Company Inc.................................... 919 663-2244
   1220 Harold Andrews Rd Siler City (27344) *(G-11399)*

Basofil Fibers LLC.................................... 828 304-2307
   4824 Parkway Plaza Blvd Ste 250 Charlotte (28217) *(G-1759)*

Bass Farm Sausage, Spring Hope *Also Called: Bass Farms Inc (G-11552)*

Bass Farms Inc.................................... 252 478-4147
   6685 Highway 64 Alt East Spring Hope (27882) *(G-11552)*

Bassett Furniture Direct, Concord *Also Called: Bassett Furniture Direct Inc (G-3318)*

Bassett Furniture Direct Inc.................................... 704 979-5700
   7830 Lyles Ln Nw Concord (28027) *(G-3318)*

Bassett Furniture Inds NC LLC.................................... 828 465-7700
   1111 E 20th St Newton (28658) *(G-9451)*

Bassett Upholstery Division, Newton *Also Called: Bassett Furniture Inds NC LLC (G-9451)*

Bastrop Skid Company (PA).................................... 252 793-6600
   111 W Water St Plymouth (27962) *(G-9799)*

Batca Fitness Systems, Raleigh *Also Called: RSR Fitness Inc (G-10450)*

Bateman Logging Co Inc.................................... 252 482-8959
   1531 Virginia Rd Edenton (27932) *(G-4362)*

Batista Grading Inc.................................... 919 359-3449
   710 E Main St Clayton (27520) *(G-3134)*

Batt Fabricators Inc.................................... 336 431-9334
   12957 Trinity Rd Trinity (27370) *(G-12113)*

Batteries Plus, Raleigh *Also Called: Alk Investments LLC (G-9891)*

Battery Watering Systems LLC.................................... 336 714-0448
   6645 Holder Rd Clemmons (27012) *(G-3179)*

Battery Watering Technology, Clemmons *Also Called: Fourshare LLC (G-3184)*

Battle Fermentables LLC (PA).................................... 336 225-4585
   1604 Lathrop St Durham (27703) *(G-3917)*

Battle Trucking Inc.................................... 919 708-2288
   911 San Lee Dr Sanford (27330) *(G-11153)*

Battle Trucking Company, Sanford *Also Called: Battle Trucking Inc (G-11153)*

Battlgrund Strter Gnerator Inc.................................... 336 685-4511
   4497 Folger Rd Julian (27283) *(G-7200)*

Baumgartner Associates, Leland *Also Called: Pacon Manufacturing Co LLC (G-7556)*

Bausch Health Americas Inc.................................... 949 461-6000
   406 Blackwell St Ste 410 Durham (27701) *(G-3918)*

Baxter Healthcare Corporation.................................... 828 756-6623
   65 Pitts Station Rd Marion (28752) *(G-8034)*

Baxter Healthcare Corporation.................................... 828 756-6600
   65 Pitts Station Rd Marion (28752) *(G-8035)*

Baxter US, Marion *Also Called: Baxter Healthcare Corporation (G-8035)*

Bay Breeze Seafood, Hendersonville *Also Called: Bay Breeze Seafood Rest Inc (G-6186)*

Bay Breeze Seafood Rest Inc.................................... 828 697-7106
   1830 Asheville Hwy Hendersonville (28791) *(G-6186)*

Bay Painting Contractors.................................... 252 435-5374
   128 Bayside Dr Moyock (27958) *(G-9276)*

Bay Six, Raleigh *Also Called: B6usa Inc (G-9929)*

Bay State Milling Company.................................... 704 664-4873
   448 N Main St Mooresville (28115) *(G-8606)*

Bay Tech Label Inc.................................... 828 296-8900
   36 Old Charlotte Hwy Asheville (28803) *(G-452)*

Bay Valley Foods LLC.................................... 715 366-4511
   2953 N Nc 111 903 Hwy Albertson (28508) *(G-98)*

Bay Valley Foods LLC.................................... 910 267-4711
   354 N Faison Ave Faison (28341) *(G-4515)*

Bay Valley Foods LLC.................................... 704 476-7141
   120 Woodlake Pkwy Kings Mountain (28086) *(G-7349)*

Bayatronics LLC.................................... 980 432-0438
   7089 Weddington Rd Nw Concord (28027) *(G-3319)*

Bayer Agriculture, Durham *Also Called: Bayer Corporation (G-3919)*

Bayer Corp.................................... 704 373-0991
   2332 Croydon Rd Charlotte (28207) *(G-1760)*

Bayer Corporation.................................... 800 242-5897
   2 Tw Alexander Dr Durham (27709) *(G-3919)*

Bayer Cropscience, Cary *Also Called: Environmental Science US LLC (G-1354)*

Bayer Cropscience Inc.................................... 412 777-2000
   2400 Ellis Rd Durham (27703) *(G-3920)*

Bayer Healthcare LLC.................................... 919 461-6525
   3500 Paramount Pkwy Morrisville (27560) *(G-8938)*

Bayer Hlthcare Pharmaceuticals.................................... 602 469-6846
   1820 Liatris Ln Raleigh (27613) *(G-9934)*

Bayer Technology and Services, Morrisville *Also Called: Bayer Healthcare LLC (G-8938)*

Bayliss Boatworks Inc.................................... 252 473-9797
   600 Harbor Rd Wanchese (27981) *(G-12336)*

Bayliss Boatyard Inc.................................... 252 473-9797
   600 Harbor Rd Wanchese (27981) *(G-12337)*

Baysix USA.................................... 919 833-3851
   414 Dupont Cir Raleigh (27603) *(G-9935)*

BB&p Embroidery LLC.................................. 252 206-1929
2801 Ward Blvd Wilson (27893) *(G-12969)*

Bbf Printing Solutions.................................. 336 969-2323
1190 Old Beltway Rural Hall (27045) *(G-10952)*

BBT ARCHIVES, Sandy Ridge *Also Called: Bhaktivedanta Archives (G-11141)*

Bcac Holdings LLC...................................... 910 754-5689
674 Ocean Hwy W Supply (28462) *(G-11855)*

Bce South, Indian Trail *Also Called: 3 Star Enterprises LLC (G-7065)*

Bce South, Indian Trail *Also Called: Laru Industries Inc (G-7087)*

Bcp East Land LLC..................................... 704 248-2000
13860 Ballantyne Corporate Pl Charlotte (28277) *(G-1761)*

Bd Diagnostics Tripath, Burlington *Also Called: Tripath Imaging Inc (G-1170)*

Bd Medical Technology, Durham *Also Called: Becton Dickinson and Company (G-3922)*

Be Aerospace, Winston Salem *Also Called: B/E Aerospace Inc (G-13097)*

Be House Publishing LLC.............................. 336 529-6143
400 Barnes Rd Winston Salem (27107) *(G-13102)*

Be Pharmaceuticals Inc................................ 704 560-1444
203 New Edition Ct Cary (27511) *(G-1305)*

Beacon Composites LLC................................ 704 813-8408
4007 Estate Dr Ste C Creedmoor (27522) *(G-3640)*

Beacon Industrial Mfg LLC............................ 704 399-7441
4404a Chesapeake Dr Charlotte (28216) *(G-1762)*

Beacon Prosthetics & Orthotics, Raleigh *Also Called: Adaptive Technologies LLC (G-9878)*

Beacon Roofing Supply Inc............................ 704 886-1555
1836 Equitable Pl Charlotte (28213) *(G-1763)*

Beaker Inc.. 919 803-7422
700 Spring Forest Rd Ste 121 Raleigh (27609) *(G-9936)*

Beamer Tire & Auto Repair Inc....................... 336 882-7043
245 E Parris Ave High Point (27262) *(G-6541)*

Beane Signs Inc.. 336 629-6748
218 Vista Pkwy Asheboro (27205) *(G-331)*

Bear Creek Arsenal LLC............................... 919 292-6000
310 Mcneill Rd Sanford (27330) *(G-11154)*

Bear Creek Fabrication LLC........................... 919 837-2444
1930 Campbell Rd Bear Creek (27207) *(G-712)*

Bear Creek Log Tmber Homes LLC................... 336 751-6180
371 Valley Rd Mocksville (27028) *(G-8351)*

Bear Pages.. 828 837-0785
99 Smoke Rise Cir Murphy (28906) *(G-9288)*

Beard Hosiery Co....................................... 828 758-1942
652 Nuway Cir Lenoir (28645) *(G-7577)*

Beardowadams Inc...................................... 704 359-8443
3034 Horseshoe Ln Charlotte (28208) *(G-1764)*

Bearwaters Brewing Company......................... 828 237-4200
101 Park St Canton (28716) *(G-1242)*

Beasley Contracting................................... 828 479-3775
756 Gladdens Creek Rd Robbinsville (28771) *(G-10756)*

Beasley Flooring Products Inc........................ 828 524-3248
77 Industrial Park Rd Bryson City (28713) *(G-1008)*

Beasley Flooring Products Inc........................ 828 349-7000
41 Hardwood Dr Franklin (28734) *(G-4818)*

Beast Chains... 336 346-9081
733 Spinning Wheel Pt High Point (27265) *(G-6542)*

Beaty Corporation...................................... 704 599-4949
7407 N Tryon St Charlotte (28262) *(G-1765)*

Beaufort Composite Tech Inc......................... 252 728-1547
111 Safrit Dr Beaufort (28516) *(G-721)*

Beaufort Naval Armorers, Morehead City *Also Called: Bircher Incorporated (G-8817)*

Beaufurn, High Point *Also Called: Beaufurn LLC (G-6543)*

Beaufurn LLC... 336 768-2544
1005 W Fairfield Rd High Point (27263) *(G-6543)*

Beautimar Manufactured MBL Inc.................... 919 779-1181
1221 Home Ct Raleigh (27603) *(G-9937)*

Beauty 4 Love LLC..................................... 704 802-2844
1819 Sardis Rd N Ste 350 Charlotte (28270) *(G-1766)*

Beazer East Inc.. 919 567-9512
7000 Cass Holt Rd Holly Springs (27540) *(G-6894)*

Beazer East Inc.. 919 380-2610
3131 Rdu Center Dr Ste 220 Morrisville (27560) *(G-8939)*

Bebida Beverage Company............................. 704 660-0226
1304 N Barkley Rd Statesville (28677) *(G-11668)*

BEC, Raleigh *Also Called: Beyond Electronics Corp (G-9940)*

BEC-Car Printing Co Inc (PA)......................... 704 873-1911
970 Davie Ave Statesville (28677) *(G-11669)*

BEC-Faye LLC... 252 714-8700
3393 Mobleys Bridge Rd Grimesland (27837) *(G-6040)*

Beckett Media LP....................................... 800 508-2582
2222 Sedwick Rd Ste 102 Durham (27713) *(G-3921)*

Beco Holding Company Inc (PA)...................... 800 826-3473
10926 David Taylor Dr Ste 300 Charlotte (28262) *(G-1767)*

Becton Dickinson and Company....................... 201 847-6800
21 Davis Dr Durham (27709) *(G-3922)*

Becton Dickinson and Company....................... 919 963-1307
130 Four Oaks Pkwy Four Oaks (27524) *(G-4808)*

Becwill Corp... 919 552-8266
3209 Air Park Rd Fuquay Varina (27526) *(G-4869)*

Bed In A Box... 800 588-5720
199 Woltz St Mount Airy (27030) *(G-9102)*

Bedex LLC.. 336 617-6755
210 Swathmore Ave High Point (27263) *(G-6544)*

Bee Line Printing, Burgaw *Also Called: Jofra Graphics Inc (G-1025)*

Bee Tree Hardwoods, Swannanoa *Also Called: Southeastern Hardwoods Inc (G-11878)*

Beech Street Ventures LLC............................ 919 755-5053
327 W Davie St Ste 100 Raleigh (27601) *(G-9938)*

Beeson Sign Co Inc.................................... 336 993-5617
213 Berry Garden Rd Kernersville (27284) *(G-7247)*

Beet River Traders, Ramseur *Also Called: Line Drive Sports Center Inc (G-10628)*

Beewell, Raleigh *Also Called: Medvertical LLC (G-10289)*

Befco Inc.. 252 977-9920
1781 S Wesleyan Blvd Rocky Mount (27803) *(G-10824)*

Behappy.me, Charlotte *Also Called: Printful Inc (G-2671)*

Bejeweled Creations................................... 336 552-0841
386 River Run Dr Reidsville (27320) *(G-10675)*

Bekaertdeslee USA Inc................................ 336 747-4900
200 Business Park Dr Winston Salem (27107) *(G-13103)*

Belev En U Water Mfg Co.............................. 704 458-9950
13620 Reese Blvd E Ste 120 Huntersville (28078) *(G-6972)*

Belevation LLC... 803 517-9030
207 Shady Oak Dr Biscoe (27209) *(G-847)*

Belham Management Ind LLC.......................... 704 815-4246
9307 Monroe Rd Ste A Charlotte (28270) *(G-1768)*

Belk Department Stores LP............................ 704 357-4000
2801 W Tyvola Rd Charlotte (28217) *(G-1769)*

Belkoz Inc... 919 703-0694
4900 Thornton Rd Raleigh (27616) *(G-9939)*

Bell and Howell LLC (PA).............................. 919 767-4401
3791 S Alston Ave Durham (27713) *(G-3923)*

Bell and Howell LLC................................... 919 767-6400
3791 S Alston Ave Durham (27713) *(G-3924)*

Bellaire Dynamik LLC.................................. 704 779-3755
4714 Stockholm Ct Charlotte (28273) *(G-1770)*

Bellalou Designs LLC.................................. 252 360-7866
3712 Stonehenge Ln W Wilson (27893) *(G-12970)*

Bellatony, Pineville *Also Called: Forklift Pro Inc (G-9728)*

BellSouth, Charlotte *Also Called: Yp Advrtising Pubg LLC Not LLC (G-3042)*

BellSouth, Wilmington *Also Called: Yp Advrtising Pubg LLC Not LLC (G-12957)*

Belmont Textile Machinery Co......................... 704 827-5836
1212 W Catawba Ave Mount Holly (28120) *(G-9218)*

Belocal, Raleigh *Also Called: N2 Franchising Inc (G-10321)*

Belt Concepts America Inc............................ 888 598-2358
605 N Pine St Spring Hope (27882) *(G-11553)*

Belt Shop Inc.. 704 865-3636
1941 Chespark Dr Gastonia (28052) *(G-4997)*

Beltservice Corporation............................... 704 947-2264
9540 Julian Clark Ave Huntersville (28078) *(G-6973)*

Belvoir Manufacturing Corp (PA)...................... 252 746-1274
4081 Nc Highway 33 W Greenville (27834) *(G-5947)*

Belwith Products LLC.................................. 336 841-3899
1006 N Main St High Point (27262) *(G-6545)*

Bemco Sleep Products Inc............................ 910 892-3107
601 N Ashe Ave Dunn (28334) *(G-3846)*

A
L
P
H
A
B
E
T
I
C

Bemis Manufacturing Company.................................. 828 754-1086
201 Industrial Ct Lenoir (28645) *(G-7578)*

Ben Huffman Enterprises LLC................................... 704 724-4705
516 River Hwy Ste D Mooresville (28117) *(G-8607)*

Ben Pushpa Inc.. 828 428-8590
2896 E Maiden Rd Maiden (28650) *(G-8007)*

Bendel Tank Heat Exchanger LLC.............................. 704 596-5112
4823 N Graham St Charlotte (28269) *(G-1771)*

Bender Apparel & Signs Inc...................................... 252 636-8337
1841 Old Airport Rd New Bern (28562) *(G-9340)*

Benjamin Moore Authorized Ret, Shelby *Also Called: Cleveland Lumber Company (G-11320)*

Benmot Publishing Company Inc................................ 919 658-9456
214 N Center St Mount Olive (28365) *(G-9247)*

Bennett & Associates Inc... 919 477-7362
3312 Guess Rd Durham (27705) *(G-3925)*

Bennett Brothers Yachts Inc...................................... 910 772-9277
1701 Jel Wade Dr Ste 16 Wilmington (28401) *(G-12719)*

Bennett Elec Maint & Cnstr LLC................................ 910 231-0300
586 Allegiance St Raeford (28376) *(G-9832)*

Bennett Uniform Mfg Inc (PA).................................... 336 232-5772
4377 Federal Dr Greensboro (27410) *(G-5387)*

Benton & Sons Fabrication Inc................................... 919 734-1700
1921 N Nc 581 Hwy Pikeville (27863) *(G-9667)*

Benton Card, Benson *Also Called: Graphic Products Inc (G-790)*

Bentons Wldg Repr & Svcs Inc................................... 910 343-8322
1206 S 3rd St Wilmington (28401) *(G-12720)*

Benz Tling A Bus Unit Schnck U, Conover *Also Called: Schenck USA Corp (G-3558)*

Beocare Inc... 828 728-7300
1905 International Blvd Hudson (28638) *(G-6942)*

Beocare Group Inc (PA)... 828 728-7300
1905 International Blvd Hudson (28638) *(G-6943)*

Ber-Car Printing, Statesville *Also Called: BEC-Car Printing Co Inc (G-11669)*

Berco of America Inc... 336 931-1415
615 Pegg Rd Greensboro (27409) *(G-5388)*

Berenfield Containers, Harrisburg *Also Called: Mauser Usa LLC (G-6114)*

Bergman Enterprises Inc.. 252 335-7294
786 Pitts Chapel Rd Elizabeth City (27909) *(G-4379)*

Berkeley Home Furniture LLC..................................... 336 882-0012
2228 Shore St High Point (27263) *(G-6546)*

Berlin Packaging LLC... 704 612-4500
8008 Corporate Center Dr Ste 208 Charlotte (28226) *(G-1772)*

Bernhardt Design Plant 3, Lenoir *Also Called: Bernhardt Furniture Company (G-7579)*

Bernhardt Design Plant 7, Lenoir *Also Called: Bernhardt Furniture Company (G-7584)*

Bernhardt Furniture Company.................................... 828 759-6245
1502 Morganton Blvd Sw Lenoir (28645) *(G-7579)*

Bernhardt Furniture Company.................................... 828 759-6652
1828 Morganton Blvd Sw Lenoir (28645) *(G-7580)*

Bernhardt Furniture Company.................................... 828 758-9811
1840 Morganton Blvd Sw Lenoir (28645) *(G-7581)*

Bernhardt Furniture Company (HQ)............................ 828 758-9811
1839 Morganton Blvd Sw Lenoir (28645) *(G-7582)*

Bernhardt Furniture Company.................................... 828 572-4664
1814 Morganton Blvd Sw Lenoir (28645) *(G-7583)*

Bernhardt Furniture Company.................................... 828 759-6205
1402 Morganton Blvd Sw Lenoir (28645) *(G-7584)*

Bernhardt Furniture Company, Lenoir *Also Called: Bernhardt Industries Inc (G-7585)*

Bernhardt Industries Inc (PA).................................... 828 758-9811
1839 Morganton Blvd Sw Lenoir (28645) *(G-7585)*

Beroth Tire of Mocksville, Mocksville *Also Called: Mock Tire & Automotive Inc (G-8379)*

Berry Global Inc.. 252 332-7270
228 Johnny Mitchell Rd Ahoskie (27910) *(G-42)*

Berry Global Inc.. 252 984-4100
6941 Corporation Pkwy Battleboro (27809) *(G-695)*

Berry Global Inc.. 919 207-3202
1203 Chicopee Rd Benson (27504) *(G-785)*

Berry Global Inc.. 704 697-5100
9335 Harris Corners Pkwy Ste 300 Charlotte (28269) *(G-1773)*

Berry Global Inc.. 336 841-1723
314 Mandustry St High Point (27262) *(G-6547)*

Berry Global Inc.. 704 289-1526
3414 Wesley Chapel Stouts Rd Monroe (28110) *(G-8439)*

Berry Global Inc.. 704 664-3733
111 Excellance Ln Mooresville (28115) *(G-8608)*

Berry Global Inc.. 252 984-4104
6941 Corporation Pkwy Rocky Mount (27801) *(G-10808)*

Berry Global Films LLC.. 704 821-2316
303 Seaboard Dr Matthews (28104) *(G-8160)*

Berry Plastics, Ahoskie *Also Called: Berry Global Inc (G-42)*

Berry Plastics, Charlotte *Also Called: Berry Global Inc (G-1773)*

Berry Plastics, Mooresville *Also Called: Berry Global Inc (G-8608)*

Bertie County Peanuts, Windsor *Also Called: Powell & Stokes Inc (G-13056)*

Besam Entrance Solution, Monroe *Also Called: Assa Abloy Entrnce Systems US (G-8434)*

Besana-Lovati Inc (PA).. 336 768-6064
4112 W Old Us 421 Hwy Hamptonville (27020) *(G-6082)*

Besi Machining LLC... 919 218-9241
95 Cypress Dr Youngsville (27596) *(G-13464)*

Bespak Laboratories Inc.. 919 884-2064
511 Davis Dr Ste 100 Morrisville (27560) *(G-8940)*

Bessemer City Machinery Sales, Bessemer City *Also Called: Bessemer City Machine Shop Inc (G-806)*

Bessemer City Machine Shop Inc............................... 704 629-4111
524 Bess Town Rd Bessemer City (28016) *(G-806)*

Best Image Signs LLC.. 336 973-7445
178 Nicholas Landing Dr Wilkesboro (28697) *(G-12629)*

Best Image Signs and Graphics, Wilkesboro *Also Called: Best Image Signs LLC (G-12629)*

Best Kiteboarding, Rodanthe *Also Called: Ride Best LLC (G-10888)*

Best Machine & Fabrication Inc.................................. 919 731-7101
117 Sleepy Creek Rd Dudley (28333) *(G-3834)*

Best Workers Company... 336 665-0076
5494 Port Royal Rd Ne Riegelwood (28456) *(G-10723)*

Bestco Holdings Inc... 704 664-4300
288 Mazeppa Rd Mooresville (28115) *(G-8609)*

Bestco LLC.. 704 664-4300
137 Bestco Ln Mooresville (28115) *(G-8610)*

Bestco LLC.. 704 664-4300
119 E Super Sport Dr Mooresville (28117) *(G-8611)*

Bestco LLC.. 704 664-4300
139 Camp Ln Mooresville (28115) *(G-8612)*

Bestco LLC.. 704 664-4300
208 Manufacturers Blvd Mooresville (28115) *(G-8613)*

Bestco LLC (PA).. 704 664-4300
288 Mazeppa Rd Mooresville (28115) *(G-8614)*

Bestdrive LLC (DH).. 800 450-3187
9827 Mount Holly Rd Charlotte (28214) *(G-1774)*

Bet-Mac Wilson Steel Inc.. 919 528-1540
118 S Durham Ave Creedmoor (27522) *(G-3641)*

Beta Fluid Systems, Reidsville *Also Called: Beta Fueling Systems LLC (G-10676)*

Beta Fueling Systems LLC.. 336 342-0306
1209 Freeway Dr Reidsville (27320) *(G-10676)*

Betco Inc (DH).. 704 872-2999
228 Commerce Blvd Statesville (28625) *(G-11670)*

Betech Inc... 828 687-9917
190 Continuum Dr Fletcher (28732) *(G-4723)*

Betek Tools Inc... 980 498-2523
8325 Arrowridge Blvd Ste A Charlotte (28273) *(G-1775)*

Bethlehem Manufacturing Co (PA)............................. 828 495-7731
36 Bethlehem Manufacturing Ln Hickory (28601) *(G-6270)*

Better Business Printing Inc....................................... 704 867-3366
495 E Long Ave Gastonia (28054) *(G-4998)*

Better Publishing Inc... 828 688-9188
467 Byrd Rd Bakersville (28705) *(G-675)*

Bettys Drapery Design Workroom.............................. 828 264-2392
3207 Nc Highway 105 S Boone (28607) *(G-897)*

Between Two Worlds LLC... 828 774-5055
255 Short Coxe Ave Asheville (28801) *(G-453)*

Bevana, Newton *Also Called: Community Brewing Ventures LLC (G-9458)*

Bevans Steel Fabrication Inc...................................... 704 395-0200
4017 Hargrove Ave Charlotte (28208) *(G-1776)*

Beverage Innovation Corp.. 425 222-4900
1858 Kannapolis Pkwy Concord (28027) *(G-3320)*

Beverage-Air Corporation (DH).................................. 336 245-6400
3779 Champion Blvd Winston Salem (27105) *(G-13104)*

Beverly Knits Inc..704 964-0835
1640 Federal St Gastonia (28052) *(G-4999)*

Beverly Knits Inc (PA)..704 861-1536
1675 Garfield Dr Gastonia (28052) *(G-5000)*

Bevs & Bites LLC..704 247-7573
2913 Selwyn Ave Charlotte (28209) *(G-1777)*

Beyond Electronics Corp.....................................919 231-8000
12405 Cilcain Ct Raleigh (27614) *(G-9940)*

Beyond This Day, Gastonia Also Called: Ambassador Services Inc *(G-4988)*

Bfc Plant 2, Lenoir Also Called: Bernhardt Furniture Company *(G-7580)*

Bfc Plant 5a, Lenoir Also Called: Bernhardt Furniture Company *(G-7583)*

Bfs Asset Holdings LLC (HQ)...............................303 784-4288
4800 Falls Of Neuse Rd Ste 400 Raleigh (27609) *(G-9941)*

Bfs Industries LLC...919 575-6711
200 Industrial Dr Butner (27509) *(G-1199)*

Bfs Operations LLC (HQ).....................................919 431-1000
4800 Falls Of Neuse Rd Raleigh (27609) *(G-9942)*

Bft Lumberton, Lumberton Also Called: Bft Lumberton Ops Corp *(G-7946)*

Bft Lumberton Ops Corp......................................910 737-3200
1000 Noir St Lumberton (28358) *(G-7946)*

Bgi Recovery Llc...336 429-6976
127 Belvue Dr Mount Airy (27030) *(G-9103)*

Bh Holdings, Durham Also Called: Bell and Howell LLC *(G-3924)*

Bhaktivedanta Archives......................................336 871-3636
1453 Tom Shelton Rd Sandy Ridge (27046) *(G-11141)*

Bharat Forge Aluminum USA Inc (DH)...................585 576-7483
777 Kalyani Way Sanford (27330) *(G-11155)*

Bi County Gas Producers LLC..............................704 844-8990
10600 Nations Ford Rd Charlotte (28273) *(G-1778)*

Bibey Machine Company Inc................................336 275-9421
642 S Spring St Greensboro (27406) *(G-5389)*

Bic Corporation...704 598-7700
5900 Long Creek Park Dr Charlotte (28269) *(G-1779)*

Bickerstaff Trees Inc..336 372-8866
866 Nc Highway 18 S Sparta (28675) *(G-11535)*

Biddeford Mill, Wagram Also Called: Westpoint Home Inc *(G-12257)*

Biesse America Inc...704 357-3131
4110 Meadow Oak Dr Charlotte (28208) *(G-1780)*

Big Boss Baking Company, High Point Also Called: Bakeboxx Company *(G-6536)*

Big Delicious Brand Inc......................................919 270-7324
1632 Lorraine Rd Raleigh (27607) *(G-9943)*

Big Dipper, Asheboro Also Called: Thermaco Incorporated *(G-408)*

Big Fish Dpi..704 545-8112
9740 Lawyers Rd Mint Hill (28227) *(G-8331)*

Big Rock Industries Inc.......................................252 222-3618
111 Turners Dairy Rd Ste A Morehead City (28557) *(G-8816)*

Big Rock Propellers, Morehead City Also Called: Big Rock Industries Inc *(G-8816)*

Big Show Foods Inc..919 242-7769
588 Turner Swamp Rd Fremont (27830) *(G-4859)*

Big Spoon Roasters LLC......................................919 309-9100
500 Meadowlands Dr Hillsborough (27278) *(G-6860)*

Big Tire Outfitters...919 568-9605
5210 Cragganmore Dr Mc Leansville (27301) *(G-8218)*

Big Vac..910 947-3654
551 Priest Hill Rd Carthage (28327) *(G-1276)*

Biganodes LLC..828 245-1115
117 Westerly Hills Dr Forest City (28043) *(G-4784)*

Bijur Delimon Intl Inc (DH).................................919 465-4448
5909 Falls Of Neuse Rd Ste 201 Raleigh (27609) *(G-9944)*

Biker Software..919 761-1681
1165 Litchborough Way Wake Forest (27587) *(G-12263)*

Bilcat Inc (PA)..828 295-3088
1103 Main St Blowing Rock (28605) *(G-880)*

Bilge Masters Inc..704 995-4293
6239 River Cabin Ln Charlotte (28278) *(G-1781)*

Bill Martin Inc...704 873-0241
106 Martin Ln Statesville (28625) *(G-11671)*

Bill Perfect Inc..954 889-6699
4207 Burnwood Trl Denver (28037) *(G-3773)*

Bill Pink Carburetors LLC...................................704 575-1645
6137 Denver Industrial Park Rd Ste A Denver (28037) *(G-3774)*

Bill Ratliff Jr Logging I.......................................704 694-5403
4437 Beck Rd Wadesboro (28170) *(G-12235)*

Bill S Iron Shop Inc..919 596-8360
2243 Glover Rd Durham (27703) *(G-3926)*

Bill Truitt Wood Works Inc..................................704 398-8499
3124 W Trade St # B Charlotte (28208) *(G-1782)*

Bill's Ornamental Iron Shop, Durham Also Called: Bill S Iron Shop Inc *(G-3926)*

Bill's Welding & Son, Statesville Also Called: Donald Auton *(G-11690)*

Billet Speed Inc...828 226-8127
488 Fairview Rd Sylva (28779) *(G-11890)*

Billsoft Inc...913 859-9674
512 S Mangum St Ste 100 Durham (27701) *(G-3927)*

Billy Boat Performance Exhaust, Mooresville Also Called: B & B Fabrication Inc *(G-8605)*

Billy Harrell Logging Inc.....................................252 221-4995
152 County Line Rd Tyner (27980) *(G-12182)*

Billy Harrell Logging Inc.....................................252 426-1362
108 Ililda Dr Hertford (27944) *(G-6251)*

Bilt USA Manufacturing, Charlotte Also Called: Mdb Investors LLC *(G-2482)*

Biltmore Estate Wine Co LLC...............................828 225-6776
1 N Pack Sq Ste 400 Asheville (28801) *(G-454)*

Bimbo Bakeries Usa Inc......................................252 641-2200
110 Sara Lee Rd Tarboro (27886) *(G-11923)*

Bimbo Bkeries Authorized Distr, Raleigh Also Called: Tkm Global LLC *(G-10550)*

Binders Incorporated..704 377-9704
1303 Upper Asbury Ave Charlotte (28206) *(G-1783)*

Bio Air, Greensboro Also Called: Custom Industries Inc *(G-5481)*

Bio D, Morehead City Also Called: Aqua 10 Corporation *(G-8813)*

Bio-Adhesive Alliance Inc...................................336 285-3676
225 Daniel Chestnutt Rd Mount Olive (28365) *(G-9248)*

Bio-Tech Prsthtics Orthtics In (HQ)......................336 333-9081
2301 N Church St Greensboro (27405) *(G-5390)*

Bio-Tech Prsthtics Orthtics In..............................336 768-3666
1399 Westgate Center Dr Winston Salem (27103) *(G-13105)*

Biocryst, Durham Also Called: Biocryst Pharmaceuticals Inc *(G-3928)*

Biocryst Pharmaceuticals Inc (PA).......................919 859-1302
4505 Emperor Blvd Ste 200 Durham (27703) *(G-3928)*

Biofluidica Inc...858 535-6493
100 Conway Ct Cary (27513) *(G-1306)*

Biogen MA Inc...919 941-1100
5000 Davis Dr Durham (27709) *(G-3929)*

Biogeniv Inc..828 850-1007
640 Nuway Cir Lenoir (28645) *(G-7586)*

Biolex Therapeutics Inc......................................919 542-9901
158 Credle St Pittsboro (27312) *(G-9776)*

Biologcal Innvtion Optmztion S............................321 260-2467
224 E Holding Ave # 2116 Wake Forest (27587) *(G-12264)*

Biologics Inc...919 546-9810
625 Oberlin Rd Raleigh (27605) *(G-9945)*

Biologix of The Triangle Inc.................................919 696-4544
103 Hidden Rock Ct Cary (27513) *(G-1307)*

Biomedical Innovations Inc.................................910 603-0267
410 N Bennett St Southern Pines (28387) *(G-11495)*

Biomedinnovations Inc..704 489-1290
771 Crosspoint Dr Denver (28037) *(G-3775)*

Biomerics LLC...336 810-7178
1413 S Third Street Ext Mebane (27302) *(G-8232)*

Biomerieux Inc (DH)...919 620-2000
100 Rodolphe St Durham (27712) *(G-3930)*

Biomerieux Inc..800 682-2666
3300 Tarheel Dr Raleigh (27609) *(G-9946)*

Bionutra Life Sciences LLC..................................828 572-2838
2464 Norwood St Sw Lenoir (28645) *(G-7587)*

Bioresource International Inc...............................919 267-3758
2000 N Salem St Apex (27523) *(G-145)*

Bios Lighting, Wake Forest Also Called: Biologcal Innvtion Optmztion S *(G-12264)*

Bioselect Inc...704 521-8585
4740 Dwight Evans Rd Charlotte (28217) *(G-1784)*

Biosupplynet Inc..919 659-2121
3020 Carrington Mill Blvd Ste 100 Morrisville (27560) *(G-8941)*

Biotage LLC (HQ)...704 654-4900
10430 Harris Oak Blvd Ste C Charlotte (28269) *(G-1785)*

ALPHABETIC

Biotech Prsthtics Orthtics Drh.................... 919 471-4994
314 Crutchfield St Durham (27704) *(G-3931)*

Biotech Research Laboratories, Sanford *Also Called: Philosophy Inc (G-11220)*

Biotechnology, Charlotte *Also Called: Noahs Inc (G-2570)*

Biotechnology Center, Durham *Also Called: Intuitive Surgical Inc (G-4081)*

BIOVENTUS, Durham *Also Called: Bioventus Inc (G-3932)*

Bioventus Inc (PA)................................... 919 474-6700
4721 Emperor Blvd Ste 100 Durham (27703) *(G-3932)*

Bioventus LLC (HQ)................................ 800 396-4325
4721 Emperor Blvd Ste 100 Durham (27703) *(G-3933)*

Biovind LLC.. 512 217-3077
2219 Vail Ave Charlotte (28207) *(G-1786)*

Birch Bros Southern Inc............................ 704 843-2111
9510 New Town Rd Waxhaw (28173) *(G-12423)*

Bircher Incorporated................................. 252 726-5470
119 Industrial Dr Morehead City (28557) *(G-8817)*

Birth Tissue Recovery LLC (PA)..................336 448-1910
3051 Trenwest Dr Ste A Winston Salem (27103) *(G-13106)*

Biscoe Foundry, Biscoe *Also Called: Grede II LLC (G-852)*

Biz On Wheels, Charlotte *Also Called: R J Yeller Distribution Inc (G-2686)*

Biz Technology Solutions LLC....................704 658-1707
353 Oates Rd Mooresville (28117) *(G-8615)*

Biznet Software Inc................................. 919 872-7800
8529 Six Forks Rd Ste 400 Raleigh (27615) *(G-9947)*

BJ Williamson, Clinton *Also Called: Williamson Greenhouses Inc (G-3253)*

Bjmf Inc... 704 554-6333
8200 South Blvd Charlotte (28273) *(G-1787)*

Bk Seamless Gutters, Spring Hope *Also Called: Bk Seamless Gutters LLC (G-11554)*

Bk Seamless Gutters LLC........................ 252 955-5414
1705 Old Us 64 Spring Hope (27882) *(G-11554)*

Bkc Industries Inc................................... 919 575-6699
2117 Will Suitt Rd Creedmoor (27522) *(G-3642)*

Blachford Rbr Acquisition Corp....................704 730-1005
707 Broadview Dr Kings Mountain (28086) *(G-7350)*

Blachford Rp Corporation, Kings Mountain *Also Called: Blachford Rbr Acquisition Corp (G-7350)*

Black & Decker, Charlotte *Also Called: Black & Decker Corporation (G-1788)*

Black & Decker, Mooresville *Also Called: Black & Decker Corporation (G-8616)*

Black & Decker, Raleigh *Also Called: Black & Decker Corporation (G-9948)*

Black & Decker (us) Inc............................ 336 852-1300
4621 W Gate City Blvd Greensboro (27407) *(G-5391)*

Black & Decker Corporation....................... 803 396-3700
15040 Choate Cir Charlotte (28273) *(G-1788)*

Black & Decker Corporation....................... 704 799-3929
134 Talbert Pointe Dr Mooresville (28117) *(G-8616)*

Black & Decker Corporation....................... 919 878-0357
2930 Capital Blvd Raleigh (27604) *(G-9948)*

Black Box Corporation.............................. 704 248-6430
10817 Southern Loop Blvd Pineville (28134) *(G-9715)*

Black Collection Apparel LLC..................... 919 716-5183
1140 N Horner Blvd Sanford (27330) *(G-11156)*

Black Concrete Inc................................. 336 243-1388
705 Cotton Grove Rd Lexington (27292) *(G-7659)*

Black Mountain Cnstr Group Inc.................. 704 243-5593
10704 Lancaster Hwy Waxhaw (28173) *(G-12424)*

Black Mountain Machine & Tool, Black Mountain *Also Called: Black Mtn Mch Fabrication Inc (G-862)*

Black Mountain News Inc.......................... 828 669-8727
111 Richardson Blvd Black Mountain (28711) *(G-861)*

Black Mtn Mch Fabrication Inc.................... 828 669-9557
2988 Us 70 Hwy Black Mountain (28711) *(G-862)*

Black River Logging Inc............................ 910 669-2850
20289 North Carolina Hwy 210 E Ivanhoe (28447) *(G-7110)*

Black River Woodwork LLC........................ 919 757-4559
574 N Broad St E Angier (27501) *(G-112)*

Black Rock Granite & Cabinetry....................828 787-1100
2543 Cashiers Rd Highlands (28741) *(G-6843)*

Black Rock Landscaping LLC...................... 910 295-4470
6652 Us 15 501 Hwy Carthage (28327) *(G-1277)*

Black Sand Company Inc........................... 336 788-6411
745 W Clemmonsville Rd Winston Salem (27127) *(G-13107)*

Black Tire Service Inc............................... 919 908-6347
1400 E Geer St Durham (27704) *(G-3934)*

Blackbeards Boatworks............................. 252 726-6161
4531 Arendell St Morehead City (28557) *(G-8818)*

Blackleys Printing & Sign Shop, Clayton *Also Called: Blackleys Printing Co (G-3135)*

Blackleys Printing Co............................... 919 553-6813
229 E Main St Clayton (27520) *(G-3135)*

Blacksand Metal Works LLC........................703 489-8282
433 Delbert Dr Fayetteville (28306) *(G-4558)*

Blackstone Furniture Inds Inc..................... 910 428-2833
624 Hogan Farm Rd Ether (27247) *(G-4494)*

Blacktip Solutions.................................. 336 303-1580
3125 Kathleen Ave Ste 221 Greensboro (27408) *(G-5392)*

Blackwater, Concord *Also Called: Loading Republic Inc (G-3395)*

Blackwell Boatwork, Wanchese *Also Called: Craig & Sandra Blackwell Inc (G-12339)*

Blacqueladi Styles LLC............................. 877 977-7798
5000 Centre Green Way Ste 500 Cary (27513) *(G-1308)*

Bladen Fabricators LLC............................. 910 866-5225
2646 Old Hwy 41 Bladenboro (28320) *(G-874)*

BLAIR, Durham *Also Called: Carolina Wren Press Inc (G-3963)*

Blake Enterprises, Concord *Also Called: Robert Blake (G-3433)*

Blankenship Logging............................... 828 652-2250
397 Biggerstaff Loop Nebo (28761) *(G-9327)*

Blanket Aero LLC................................... 704 591-2878
9300 Aviation Blvd Nw Ste A Concord (28027) *(G-3321)*

Blaq Beauty Naturalz, Weldon *Also Called: Blaq Beauty Naturalz Inc (G-12519)*

Blaq Beauty Naturalz Inc.......................... 252 326-5621
307 Woodlawn Ave Weldon (27890) *(G-12519)*

Blashfield Sign Company Inc.......................910 485-7200
303 Williams St Fayetteville (28301) *(G-4559)*

Blast Off Intl Chem & Mfg Co...................... 509 885-4525
199 Crocker St Seaboard (27876) *(G-11269)*

Blast-It-All, Salisbury *Also Called: Hess Manufacturing Inc (G-11065)*

Blazing Foods LLC.................................. 336 865-2933
1520 West Blvd Charlotte (28208) *(G-1789)*

Blind Factory of Charlotte, Matthews *Also Called: Shuttercraft Inc (G-8148)*

Blind Nail and Company Inc........................919 967-0388
3027 Blueberry Ln Chapel Hill (27516) *(G-1530)*

Blinds Plus Inc...................................... 910 487-5196
5137 Raeford Rd Fayetteville (28304) *(G-4560)*

Blissfull Memories.................................. 336 903-1835
101 6th St North Wilkesboro (28659) *(G-9523)*

Bll Innovations Inc.................................. 888 501-0678
77 Pine Ridge Dr Hickory (28602) *(G-6271)*

Bloom Ai Inc... 704 620-2886
101 S Devimy Ct Cary (27511) *(G-1309)*

Bloomday Granite & Marble Inc.................... 336 724-0300
3810 Indiana Ave Winston Salem (27105) *(G-13108)*

Blossman Propane Gas & Appl..................... 828 396-0144
2315 Catawba Valley Blvd Se Hickory (28602) *(G-6272)*

Blount Precision Machining Inc.................... 252 825-3701
155 Railroad St W Bethel (27812) *(G-839)*

Blowing Rocket, Boone *Also Called: Jones Media (G-928)*

Blp Paper, Charlotte *Also Called: Nakos Paper Products Inc (G-2541)*

Blp Products and Services Inc.................... 704 899-5505
605 N Polk St Ste D Pineville (28134) *(G-9716)*

Blu Ecigs, Greensboro *Also Called: Fontem US LLC (G-5536)*

Blue Bay Distributing Inc.......................... 919 957-1300
3720 Appling Way Durham (27703) *(G-3935)*

Blue DOT Readi-Mix LLC (PA)..................... 704 971-7676
11330 Bain School Rd Mint Hill (28227) *(G-8332)*

Blue Force Technologies LLC...................... 919 443-1660
627 Distribution Dr Ste D Morrisville (27560) *(G-8942)*

Blue Gas Marine Inc................................ 919 238-3427
2528 Schieffelin Rd Apex (27502) *(G-146)*

Blue Horseshoe..................................... 980 312-8202
13024 Ballantyne Corporate Pl Charlotte (28277) *(G-1790)*

Blue Inc Usa LLC................................... 828 346-8660
1808 Emmanuel Church Rd Conover (28613) *(G-3494)*

Blue Lagoon Inc.................................... 828 324-2333
1011 10th Street Blvd Nw Hickory (28601) *(G-6273)*

2025 Harris North Carolina
Manufacturers Directory

(G-0000) Company's Geographic Section entry number

Blue Light Images Company Inc (PA)........................336 983-4986
428 Newsome Rd King (27021) *(G-7321)*

Blue Light Welding of Triad.........................336 442-9140
2328 Pebble Creek Rd Winston Salem (27107) *(G-13109)*

Blue Maiden Defense.........................678 292-8342
165 Laurel Oak Ln Pinebluff (28373) *(G-9686)*

Blue Mountain Enterprises Inc.........................252 522-1544
4000 Commerce Dr Kinston (28504) *(G-7396)*

Blue Mountain Flavors, Kinston Also Called: Blue Mountain Enterprises Inc *(G-7396)*

Blue Nano Inc.........................888 508-6266
18946 Brigadoon Pl Cornelius (28031) *(G-3589)*

Blue Rdge Elc Mmbers Fndtion I.........................828 754-9071
219 Nuway Cir Lenoir (28645) *(G-7588)*

Blue Ridge.........................828 325-4705
121 Fairgrove Church Rd Se Conover (28613) *(G-3495)*

Blue Ridge Armor LLC.........................844 556-6855
340 Industrial Park Rd Rutherfordton (28139) *(G-10977)*

Blue Ridge Bldg Components Inc.........................828 685-0452
208 Justice Hills Dr Dana (28724) *(G-3694)*

Blue Ridge Bracket Inc.........................828 808-3273
66 Fletcher Commercial Dr Fletcher (28732) *(G-4724)*

Blue Ridge Cab Connection LLC.........................828 891-2281
7 Brandy Branch Rd Mills River (28759) *(G-8311)*

Blue Ridge Christian News, Spruce Pine Also Called: Inniah Production Incorporated *(G-11578)*

Blue Ridge Contracting LLC.........................828 400-5194
14 New Clyde Hwy Canton (28716) *(G-1243)*

Blue Ridge Distilling Co Inc.........................828 245-2041
228 Redbud Ln Bostic (28018) *(G-961)*

Blue Ridge Elc Mtr Repr Inc.........................828 258-0800
629 Emma Rd Asheville (28806) *(G-455)*

BLUE RIDGE ELECTRIC MEMBERS FOUNDATION, INC., Lenoir Also Called: Blue Rdge Elc Mmbers Fndtion I *(G-7588)*

Blue Ridge Global Inc.........................828 252-5225
128 Bingham Rd Asheville (28806) *(G-456)*

Blue Ridge Jams.........................828 685-1783
75 Lytle Rd Hendersonville (28792) *(G-6187)*

Blue Ridge Lbr Log & Timber Co.........................336 961-5211
2854 Old Us 421 Hwy W Yadkinville (27055) *(G-13438)*

Blue Ridge Metals Corporation.........................828 687-2525
180 Mills Gap Rd Fletcher (28732) *(G-4725)*

Blue Ridge Molding LLC.........................828 485-2017
121a Fairgrove Church Rd Se Conover (28613) *(G-3496)*

Blue Ridge Paper Products LLC (DH).........................828 454-0676
41 Main St Canton (28716) *(G-1244)*

Blue Ridge Paper Products LLC.........................828 235-3023
119 Park St Canton (28716) *(G-1245)*

Blue Ridge Paper Products LLC.........................828 452-0834
81 Old Howell Mill Rd Waynesville (28786) *(G-12451)*

Blue Ridge Plastic Molding, Conover Also Called: Blue Ridge Molding LLC *(G-3496)*

Blue Ridge Plating Company.........................828 274-1795
127 Foxwood Dr Hendersonville (28791) *(G-6188)*

Blue Ridge Printing Co Inc.........................828 254-1000
544 Haywood Rd Asheville (28806) *(G-457)*

Blue Ridge Products Co Inc.........................828 322-7990
3050 Main Ave Nw Hickory (28601) *(G-6274)*

Blue Ridge Quick Print Inc.........................828 883-2420
82 E French Broad St Brevard (28712) *(G-968)*

Blue Ridge Silver Inc.........................828 729-8610
173 Marsh Lndg Boone (28607) *(G-898)*

Blue Ridge Tool Inc.........................336 993-8111
2546 Willard Dairy Rd High Point (27265) *(G-6548)*

Blue Rock Materials LLC.........................828 479-3581
750 Tallulah Rd Robbinsville (28771) *(G-10757)*

Blue Steel Inc.........................704 864-2583
4905 Sparrow Dairy Rd Gastonia (28056) *(G-5001)*

Blue Stone Block Supermarket, Burlington Also Called: Chandler Concrete Co Inc *(G-1071)*

Blue Stone Industries Ltd.........................919 379-3986
10030 Green Level Church Rd Cary (27519) *(G-1310)*

Blue Sun Energy Inc.........................336 218-6707
408 Gallimore Dairy Rd Ste C Greensboro (27409) *(G-5393)*

Blue Wolf Technologies LLP.........................919 810-1508
9650 Strickland Rd Ste 103 Raleigh (27615) *(G-9949)*

Blue Wtr Indstries-Yancey Quar, Burnsville Also Called: Bwi Etn LLC *(G-1184)*

Blue-Hen Inc.........................407 322-2262
60 N Market St Ste C200 Asheville (28801) *(G-458)*

Bluebird Cupcakes.........................919 616-7347
2524 Beech Gap Ct Raleigh (27603) *(G-9950)*

Bluescope Buildings N Amer Inc.........................336 996-4801
7031 Albert Pick Rd Ste 200 Greensboro (27409) *(G-5394)*

Bluesky Polymers LLC.........................919 522-4374
100 Woodsage Way Cary (27518) *(G-1311)*

Blueskye Automation LLC.........................404 998-1320
440 E Westinghouse Blvd Charlotte (28273) *(G-1791)*

Bluestone Metals & Chem LLC.........................704 662-8632
19720 Jetton Rd Ste 101 Cornelius (28031) *(G-3590)*

Bluestone Specialty Chem LLC.........................704 662-8632
19720 Jetton Rd Ste 101 Cornelius (28031) *(G-3591)*

Bluetick Inc.........................336 294-4102
1501 Highwoods Blvd Ste 104 Greensboro (27410) *(G-5395)*

Bluetick Services, Greensboro Also Called: Bluetick Inc *(G-5395)*

Bluewater Pallet Solutions.........................336 697-9109
5517 Burlington Rd Mc Leansville (27301) *(G-8219)*

Bluff Mountain Outfitters Inc.........................828 622-7162
152 Bridge St Hot Springs (28743) *(G-6932)*

Blum Inc.........................919 345-6214
594 Carson Ridge Dr Oak Ridge (27310) *(G-9570)*

Blum Inc.........................704 827-1345
7733 Old Plank Rd Stanley (28164) *(G-11612)*

Blumenthal Holdings LLC (PA).........................704 688-2302
1355 Greenwood Clfs Ste 200 Charlotte (28204) *(G-1792)*

Blumer & Stanton Entps Inc.........................828 765-2800
275 Bridge Ln Newland (28657) *(G-9425)*

Blums Almanac, Winston Salem Also Called: Goslen Printing Company *(G-13181)*

Blur Development Group LLC.........................919 701-4213
170 Weston Oaks Ct Cary (27513) *(G-1312)*

Blur Product Development, Cary Also Called: Blur Development Group LLC *(G-1312)*

Blythe Construction, Concord Also Called: Blythe Construction Inc *(G-3322)*

Blythe Construction Inc (DH).........................704 375-8474
2911 N Graham St Charlotte (28206) *(G-1793)*

Blythe Construction Inc.........................704 788-9733
7450 Poplar Tent Rd Concord (28027) *(G-3322)*

Blythe Construction Inc.........................336 854-9003
2606 Phoenix Dr Greensboro (27406) *(G-5396)*

BMA America Inc.........................970 353-3770
2020 Starita Rd Ste E Charlotte (28206) *(G-1794)*

BMC Construction, Raleigh Also Called: Selectbuild Construction Inc *(G-10467)*

BMC Software, Monroe Also Called: BMC Software Inc *(G-8440)*

BMC Software Inc.........................704 283-8179
2980 Mason St Monroe (28110) *(G-8440)*

Bmg Labtech Inc.........................919 678-1633
13000 Weston Pkwy Ste 109 Cary (27513) *(G-1313)*

Bmi Organbank, Denver Also Called: Biomedinnovations Inc *(G-3775)*

Bmi Wood Products Inc.........................919 829-9505
2506 Yonkers Rd Raleigh (27604) *(G-9951)*

Bms Investment Holdings LLC.........................336 949-4107
225 Commerce Ln Mayodan (27027) *(G-8206)*

Bmt Micro Inc.........................910 792-9100
5019 Carolina Beach Rd Wilmington (28412) *(G-12721)*

Bnnano Inc.........................844 926-6266
2119 W Webb Ave Burlington (27217) *(G-1052)*

Bnp Inc.........................919 775-7070
5910 Elwin Buchanan Dr Sanford (27330) *(G-11157)*

Boards and Bowls LLC.........................704 293-2004
141 Brookleaf Ln Mooresville (28115) *(G-8617)*

Boardwalk Inc.........................252 240-1095
4911 Bridges St Ext # A Morehead City (28557) *(G-8819)*

Boat Lift US Inc.........................239 283-9040
2216 Mercantile Dr Leland (28451) *(G-7532)*

Boat Lift Store Inc.........................252 586-5437
1557 Nc Highway 903 Littleton (27850) *(G-7884)*

Boat Lift Warehouse LLC.........................877 468-5438
900 Hwy 258 S Snow Hill (28580) *(G-11475)*

A
L
P
H
A
B
E
T
I
C

Boats Unlimited, New Bern *Also Called: Triad Marine Center Inc (G-9401)*

Bob Barker Company Inc (PA).............................800 334-9880
  7925 Purfoy Rd Fuquay Varina (27526) *(G-4870)*

BOB Trailers Inc...208 375-5171
  13501 S Ridge Dr Charlotte (28273) *(G-1795)*

Bobbees Bottling, Louisburg *Also Called: Packo Bottling Inc (G-7921)*

Bobbitt Signs Inc...252 492-7326
  2232 Rocky Ford Rd Kittrell (27544) *(G-7438)*

Bobby A Herring Logging..................................919 658-9768
  324 Alum Springs Rd Mount Olive (28365) *(G-9249)*

Bobby Cahoon Construction Inc.........................252 249-1617
  6003 Neuse Rd Grantsboro (28529) *(G-5329)*

Bobby Choon Mar Cnstr Land Dev, Grantsboro *Also Called: Bobby Cahoon Construction Inc (G-5329)*

Bobby Labonte Enterprises Inc..........................336 434-1800
  403 Interstate Dr Archdale (27263) *(G-213)*

Body Billboards Inc..919 544-4540
  4905 S Alston Ave Durham (27713) *(G-3936)*

Body Engineering Inc.......................................704 650-3434
  701 Matthews Mint Hill Rd Matthews (28105) *(G-8099)*

Body Shop, Wake Forest *Also Called: Body Shop Inc (G-12265)*

Body Shop Inc (DH)..919 554-4900
  5036 One World Way Wake Forest (27587) *(G-12265)*

Bodycote Thermal Proc Inc...............................704 664-1808
  128 Speedway Ln Mooresville (28117) *(G-8618)*

Bodycote Thermal Processing, Mooresville *Also Called: Bodycote Thermal Proc Inc (G-8618)*

Boehme-Filatex Inc..336 342-4507
  209 Watlington Industrial Dr Reidsville (27320) *(G-10677)*

Boehrnger Inglheim Anmal Hlth.........................919 577-9020
  3225 Air Park Rd Fuquay Varina (27526) *(G-4871)*

Boeing, Charlotte *Also Called: Boeing Company (G-1796)*

Boeing, Goldsboro *Also Called: Boeing Arospc Operations Inc (G-5201)*

Boeing Arospc Operations Inc...........................919 722-4351
  1950 Jabara Ave Bldg 4517 Goldsboro (27531) *(G-5201)*

Boeing Company..704 572-8280
  4930 Minuteman Way Charlotte (28208) *(G-1796)*

Boggs Collective Inc...828 398-9701
  239 Amboy Rd Asheville (28806) *(G-459)*

Boggs Farm Center Inc.....................................704 538-7176
  807 E Stagecoach Trl Fallston (28042) *(G-4522)*

Boggs Group, Monroe *Also Called: Boggs Transport Inc (G-8442)*

Boggs Materials Inc (PA)...................................704 289-8482
  1613 W Roosevelt Blvd Monroe (28110) *(G-8441)*

Boggs Transport Inc...704 289-8482
  2318 Concord Hwy Monroe (28110) *(G-8442)*

Bogue Sound Distillery Inc................................252 241-1606
  108 Bogue Commercial Dr Newport (28570) *(G-9438)*

Boingo Graphics Inc...704 527-4963
  656 Michael Wylie Dr Charlotte (28217) *(G-1797)*

Boise Cascade Wood Pdts LLC..........................336 598-3001
  1000 N Park Dr Roxboro (27573) *(G-10920)*

Bold Life Publication..828 692-3230
  105 S Main St Ste A Hendersonville (28792) *(G-6189)*

Bold Rock Hard Cider, Mills River *Also Called: Bold Rock Partners LP (G-8312)*

Bold Rock Partners LP......................................828 595-9940
  72 School House Rd Mills River (28759) *(G-8312)*

Boldesigns, Hudson *Also Called: Superior Dry Kilns Inc (G-6960)*

Boles Holding Inc..828 264-4200
  2165 Highway 105 Boone (28607) *(G-899)*

Bolivia Lumber Company LLC (PA)......................910 371-2515
  405 Old Mill Rd Ne Leland (28451) *(G-7533)*

Bolton, Raleigh *Also Called: Bolton Construction & Svc LLC (G-9952)*

Bolton Construction & Svc LLC...........................919 861-1500
  1623 Old Louisburg Rd Raleigh (27604) *(G-9952)*

Bolton Investors Inc...919 471-1197
  4914 N Roxboro St Ste 7 Durham (27704) *(G-3937)*

Bombshell Beer Company Inc.............................919 823-1933
  120 Quantum St Holly Springs (27540) *(G-6895)*

Bommerang Imprints...704 933-9075
  2305 Beaver Pond Rd Kannapolis (28083) *(G-7203)*

Bon Worth Inc (PA)..800 355-5131
  219 Commercial Hill Dr Hendersonville (28792) *(G-6190)*

Bon Worth Factory Outlets, Hendersonville *Also Called: Bon Worth Inc (G-6190)*

Bona US, Monroe *Also Called: Bonakemi Usa Incorporated (G-8444)*

Bona US Dc2, Monroe *Also Called: Bonakemi Usa Incorporated (G-8445)*

Bona USA..704 220-6943
  4275 Corporate Center Dr Monroe (28110) *(G-8443)*

Bonakemi Usa Incorporated..............................704 218-3917
  4275 Corporate Center Dr Monroe (28110) *(G-8444)*

Bonakemi Usa Incorporated..............................704 220-6943
  4110 Propel Way Monroe (28110) *(G-8445)*

Bonaventure Co LLC..336 584-7530
  1147 Saint Marks Church Rd Ste G Burlington (27215) *(G-1053)*

Bonaventure Group Inc.....................................919 781-6610
  6031 Oak Forest Dr Raleigh (27616) *(G-9953)*

Bond Technologies...919 866-0075
  909 Walkertown Dr Raleigh (27614) *(G-9954)*

Bondo Innovations LLC.....................................704 888-9910
  14904 Barbee Rd Stanfield (28163) *(G-11604)*

Bone Tred Beds Smmit Woodworks.....................910 319-7583
  617 Creekwood Rd Wilmington (28411) *(G-12722)*

Bonitz Inc..803 799-0181
  4539 Enterprise Dr Nw Concord (28027) *(G-3323)*

Bonomi North America Inc.................................704 412-9031
  306 Forsyth Hall Dr Charlotte (28273) *(G-1798)*

Bonsal American Inc (DH)..................................704 525-1621
  625 Griffith Rd Ste 100 Charlotte (28217) *(G-1799)*

Bonset America Corporation (PA)........................336 375-0234
  6107 Corporate Park Dr Browns Summit (27214) *(G-991)*

Boogs Materials Plant 1, Monroe *Also Called: Boggs Materials Inc (G-8441)*

Book Lover Search...336 889-6127
  High Point (27261) *(G-6549)*

Bookcase Shop (PA)...919 683-1922
  301 S Duke St Durham (27701) *(G-3938)*

Bookingbuilder Technologies, Sanford *Also Called: Launchmagiccom Inc (G-11202)*

Boomerang Water LLC......................................833 266-6420
  13570 Broadway Ave Midland (28107) *(G-8281)*

Boon Edam Inc (DH)...910 814-3800
  421 Northj Harrington St Raleigh (27603) *(G-9955)*

Boondock S Manufacturing Inc...........................828 891-4242
  6085 Brevard Rd Etowah (28729) *(G-4495)*

Boone Brands, Sanford *Also Called: Violet Sanford Holdings LLC (G-11248)*

Boone Enterprises LLC.....................................910 859-8299
  497 Olde Waterford Way Ste 103 Leland (28451) *(G-7534)*

Boone Iron Works Inc.......................................828 264-5284
  253 Ray Brown Rd Boone (28607) *(G-900)*

Boone Ironworks, Boone *Also Called: Boone Iron Works Inc (G-900)*

Boone Logging Company Inc.............................252 443-7641
  1996 Vaughan Rd Elm City (27822) *(G-4464)*

Boone Newspapers Inc.....................................252 332-2123
  801 Parker Ave E Ste 803 Ahoskie (27910) *(G-43)*

Boone-Woody Mining Company Inc.....................828 675-5188
  4456 E Us Hwy 19 E Micaville (28755) *(G-8270)*

Boones Sawmill Inc..828 287-8774
  182 Goldfinch Ln Rutherfordton (28139) *(G-10978)*

Booneshine Brewing Co Inc...............................828 263-4305
  465 Industrial Park Dr Boone (28607) *(G-901)*

Boonville Flour Feed Mill Inc.............................336 367-7541
  203 S Carolina Ave Boonville (27011) *(G-957)*

Borden, Fayetteville *Also Called: Hexion Inc (G-4612)*

Borden, High Point *Also Called: Hexion Inc (G-6646)*

Borden, Morganton *Also Called: Borden Chemical (G-8853)*

Borden Chemical..828 584-3800
  114 Industrial Blvd Morganton (28655) *(G-8853)*

Border Concepts Inc (PA)..................................704 541-5509
  15720 Brixham Hill Ave Ste 120 Charlotte (28277) *(G-1800)*

Border Concepts Inc..336 248-2419
  115 Lexington Pkwy Lexington (27295) *(G-7660)*

Borealis Compounds Inc....................................908 798-7497
  401 We Baab Industrial Dr Taylorsville (28681) *(G-11950)*

Borg-Warner Automotive Inc................................ 828 684-3501
  Cane Creek Ind Pk Fletcher (28732) *(G-4726)*

Borgwarner Arden LLC... 248 754-9200
  1849 Brevard Rd Arden (28704) *(G-256)*

Borgwarner Inc.. 828 684-4000
  1849 Brevard Rd Arden (28704) *(G-257)*

Borgwarner Turbo Systems LLC (DH)................... 828 684-4000
  1849 Brevard Rd Arden (28704) *(G-258)*

Bornemann Pumps Inc.. 704 849-8636
  901a Matthews Mint Hill Rd Matthews (28105) *(G-8100)*

Borneo Inc... 252 398-3100
  10 Commerce St Murfreesboro (27855) *(G-9281)*

Bosch Rexroth Corporation (DH)......................... 704 583-4338
  14001 S Lakes Dr South Point Business Park Charlotte (28273) *(G-1801)*

Bosmere Inc... 704 784-1608
  2701 S Main St Salisbury (28147) *(G-11023)*

Boss Design US Inc.. 844 353-7834
  2014 Chestnut Street Ext High Point (27262) *(G-6550)*

Boss Key Productions Inc.................................... 919 659-5704
  230 Fayetteville St Ste 300 Raleigh (27601) *(G-9956)*

Bossong Corporation... 336 625-2175
  840 W Salisbury St Asheboro (27203) *(G-332)*

Bossong Hosiery Mills Inc (PA)........................... 336 625-2175
  840 W Salisbury St Asheboro (27204) *(G-333)*

Bost Distributing Company Inc............................ 919 775-5931
  2209 Boone Trail Rd Sanford (27330) *(G-11158)*

Bostik Inc.. 864 535-3759
  130 Commerce St Greenville (27858) *(G-5948)*

Boston Fruit Slice & Conf, Sanford *Also Called: New Boston Fruit Slice & Confe (G-11211)*

Boston Gear, Charlotte *Also Called: Altra Industrial Motion Corp (G-1658)*

Boston Gear, Charlotte *Also Called: Tb Woods Incorporated (G-2902)*

Boston Gear LLC... 704 588-5610
  701 Carrier Dr Charlotte (28216) *(G-1802)*

Botanist and Barrel... 919 644-7777
  105 Persimmon Hill Ln Cedar Grove (27231) *(G-1516)*

Bottle Water Manufacture, Huntersville *Also Called: Belev En U Water Mfg Co (G-6972)*

Bottom Line Technologies Inc.............................. 919 472-0541
  1000 Parliament Ct Ste 310 Durham (27703) *(G-3939)*

Bottomley Enterprises Inc.................................... 336 657-6400
  452 Oak Grove Church Rd Mount Airy (27030) *(G-9104)*

Bottomline Medical.. 704 527-0919
  5200 Milford Rd Charlotte (28210) *(G-1803)*

Bougiejones... 704 492-3029
  5212 Galway Dr Charlotte (28215) *(G-1804)*

Bouncers and Slides Inc...................................... 252 908-2292
  2218 N Nc Highway 58 Nashville (27856) *(G-9310)*

Bouncing Brain Productions, Charlotte *Also Called: Everyday Edisons LLC (G-2131)*

Boundless Inc... 919 622-9051
  102 S Main St Four Oaks (27524) *(G-4809)*

Bov Solutions, Statesville *Also Called: Sklar Bov Solutions Inc (G-11765)*

Bowden Electric Motor Svc Inc............................ 252 446-4203
  1681 S Wesleyan Blvd Rocky Mount (27803) *(G-10825)*

Bowen Machine Company Inc.............................. 704 922-0423
  2006 Dallas Cherryville Hwy Dallas (28034) *(G-3665)*

Bowen Machine Company Inc.............................. 704 629-9111
  3421 Fairview Dr Gastonia (28052) *(G-5002)*

Bowman Distribution, Newland *Also Called: Dickie Jones (G-9428)*

Bowman-Hollis Manufacturing Co (PA)................ 704 374-1500
  2925 Old Steele Creek Rd Charlotte (28208) *(G-1805)*

Box Board Products Inc....................................... 336 668-3347
  8313 Triad Dr Greensboro (27409) *(G-5397)*

Box Company of America LLC............................. 910 582-0100
  12 Ev Hogan Dr Hamlet (28345) *(G-6051)*

Box Drop Furniture Whl NC, Greensboro *Also Called: Epsilon Holdings LLC (G-5524)*

Box Shop, Thomasville *Also Called: Carolina Container LLC (G-12002)*

Boxcarr Handmade Cheese, Cedar Grove *Also Called: Tin Can Ventures LLC (G-1518)*

Boxman Studios LLC.. 704 333-3733
  1310 Charles Raper Jonas Hwy Ste B Mount Holly (28120) *(G-9219)*

Boxmoor Truck Bedliners & ACC......................... 336 447-4621
  1900 Buckminster Dr Whitsett (27377) *(G-12600)*

Boyd Gmn Inc... 206 284-2200
  300 Acme Dr Monroe (28112) *(G-8446)*

Boyd Manufacturing Inc....................................... 336 301-6433
  222 W Raleigh St Siler City (27344) *(G-11400)*

Boyd Stone & Quarries.. 828 659-6862
  2207 Cannon Rd Marion (28752) *(G-8036)*

Boyd Welding and Mfg Inc................................... 828 247-0630
  324 Pine St Forest City (28043) *(G-4785)*

Boyd's Welding and Fabrication, Forest City *Also Called: Boyd Welding and Mfg Inc (G-4785)*

Boyles Sign Shop Inc.. 336 782-1189
  4050 Stafford Mill Rd Germanton (27019) *(G-5173)*

BP Associates Inc (PA).. 704 864-3032
  2408 Forbes Rd Gastonia (28056) *(G-5003)*

BP Associates Inc... 704 833-1494
  105 Wolfpack Rd Gastonia (28056) *(G-5004)*

BP Oil Corp Distributors...................................... 828 264-8516
  585 E King St Boone (28607) *(G-902)*

BP Solutions Group Inc....................................... 828 252-4476
  24 Wilmington St Asheville (28806) *(G-460)*

Bpc Plasma Inc.. 910 463-2603
  113 Yopp Rd Jacksonville (28540) *(G-7117)*

BR Lee Industries Inc... 704 966-3317
  500 Lincoln County Parkway Ext Lincolnton (28092) *(G-7817)*

Bracey Bros Logging LLC.................................... 910 231-9543
  418 Lennon Rd Delco (28436) *(G-3734)*

Bradford Products, Leland *Also Called: Bradford Products LLC (G-7535)*

Bradford Products LLC (PA)................................. 910 791-2202
  2101 Enterprise Dr Ne Leland (28451) *(G-7535)*

Bradington-Young LLC... 276 656-3335
  941 Tot Dellinger Rd Cherryville (28021) *(G-3059)*

Bradington-Young LLC (HQ).................................. 704 435-5881
  4040 10th Avenue Dr Sw Hickory (28602) *(G-6275)*

Bradley Screen Printing, Shelby *Also Called: Bradleys Inc (G-11314)*

Bradley Todd Baugus... 252 665-4901
  6444 White Oak River Rd Maysville (28555) *(G-8210)*

Bradleys Inc... 704 484-2077
  2522 W Dixon Blvd Shelby (28152) *(G-11314)*

Brady's Baked Goods, Roxboro *Also Called: B & B Distributing Inc (G-10919)*

Braiform Enterprises Inc...................................... 828 277-6420
  12 Gerber Rd Ste B Asheville (28803) *(G-461)*

Branch 0457, Hope Mills *Also Called: Franklin Baking Company LLC (G-6927)*

Branch Office Solutions Inc................................. 800 743-1047
  4391 Indian Trail Fairview Rd Ste A Indian Trail (28079) *(G-7072)*

Branch Welding Greensville Co, Gaston *Also Called: Michael H Branch Inc (G-4979)*

Brand Fuel Promotions.. 704 256-4057
  400 N Broome St Ste 203 Waxhaw (28173) *(G-12425)*

Brandel LLC... 704 525-4548
  2909 Rockbrook Dr Charlotte (28211) *(G-1806)*

Brandilly Marketing Creative, Raleigh *Also Called: Brandilly of Nc Inc (G-9957)*

Brandilly of Nc Inc... 919 278-7896
  1053 E Whitaker Mill Rd Ste 115 Raleigh (27604) *(G-9957)*

Brandrpm, Charlotte *Also Called: Brandrpm LLC (G-1807)*

Brandrpm LLC... 704 225-1800
  9555 Monroe Rd Charlotte (28270) *(G-1807)*

Brandspeed.. 410 204-1032
  915 River Hwy Mooresville (28117) *(G-8619)*

Brandy Thompson.. 321 252-2911
  6712 Bone Creek Dr Apt A Fayetteville (28314) *(G-4561)*

Branford Filtration LLC (PA)................................. 704 394-2111
  119 Poplar Pointe Dr Ste C Mooresville (28117) *(G-8620)*

Brant & Lassiter Septic Tank............................... 252 587-4321
  Hwy 35 Potecasi (27867) *(G-9819)*

Brasingtons Inc... 704 694-5191
  1515 Us Highway 74 W Wadesboro (28170) *(G-12236)*

Brasscraft... 336 475-2131
  1024 Randolph St Thomasville (27360) *(G-11997)*

Brasscraft Brownstown, Thomasville *Also Called: Brasscraft Manufacturing Co (G-11998)*

Brasscraft Manufacturing Co............................... 336 475-2131
  1024 Randolph St Thomasville (27360) *(G-11998)*

Braswell Foods, Nashville *Also Called: Braswell Milling Company (G-9311)*

Braswell Milling Company (PA)............................252 459-2143
104 E Cross St Nashville (27856) *(G-9311)*

Braswell Realty...828 733-5800
320 Linville St Newland (28657) *(G-9426)*

Bravo Team LLC...704 309-1918
603 N Church St Mooresville (28115) *(G-8621)*

Bravosolution Us Inc (DH).................................312 373-3100
3020 Carrington Mill Blvd Ste 100 Morrisville (27560) *(G-8943)*

Braxton Culler, Sophia Also Called: Rbc Inc *(G-11490)*

Bray S Recapping Service Inc (PA).....................336 786-6182
1120 W Lebanon St Mount Airy (27030) *(G-9105)*

Bread & Butter Custom Scrn Prt.........................919 942-3198
1201 Raleigh Rd Ste 100 Chapel Hill (27517) *(G-1531)*

Bread N Butter Screenprinting, Chapel Hill Also Called: Bread & Butter Custom Scrn Prt *(G-1531)*

Breathingair Systems, Randleman Also Called: Sub-Aquatics Inc *(G-10661)*

Breezeplay LLC..980 297-0885
8045 Corporate Center Dr Charlotte (28226) *(G-1808)*

Breezer Holdings LLC.......................................844 233-5673
4835 Sirona Dr Ste 400 Charlotte (28273) *(G-1809)*

Breezer Mobile Cooling, Charlotte Also Called: Breezer Holdings LLC *(G-1809)*

Brembo North America Inc.................................704 799-0530
7275 Westwinds Blvd Nw Concord (28027) *(G-3324)*

Bremeo North America, Concord Also Called: Brembo North America Inc *(G-3324)*

Brenthaven, High Point Also Called: Pioneer Square Brands Inc *(G-6734)*

Brett McHenry Logging LLC...............................252 243-7285
3204 Nash St N Ste C Wilson (27896) *(G-12971)*

Brew Publik Incorporated..................................704 231-2703
312 W Park Ave Charlotte (28203) *(G-1810)*

Brewitt & Dreenkupp Inc...................................704 525-3366
4321 Stuart Andrew Blvd Ste I Charlotte (28217) *(G-1811)*

Brewmasters Inc..252 991-6035
2117 Forest Hills Rd W Wilson (27893) *(G-12972)*

Brewpub, Charlotte Also Called: Salud LLC *(G-2751)*

Brian McGregor Enterprise................................919 732-2317
2207 Leah Dr Hillsborough (27278) *(G-6861)*

Brice Manufacturing Co Inc...............................818 896-2938
8010 Piedmont Triad Pkwy Greensboro (27409) *(G-5398)*

Brick & Mortar Grill...919 639-9700
8 N Broad St E Ste 200 Angier (27501) *(G-113)*

Brick City Gaming Inc.......................................919 297-2081
80 Hamilton Hedge Pl Cary (27519) *(G-1314)*

Brick City Phenomicon, Sanford Also Called: Hugger Mugger LLC *(G-11191)*

Bridge, Raleigh Also Called: Getbridge LLC *(G-10132)*

Bridgestone, Wilson Also Called: Bridgestone Amrcas Tire Oprtons *(G-12974)*

Bridgestone Americas Inc..................................984 888-0413
101 W Chapel Hill St Ste 200 Durham (27701) *(G-3940)*

Bridgestone Ret Operations LLC.........................919 471-4468
3809 N Duke St Durham (27704) *(G-3941)*

Bridgestone Ret Operations LLC.........................910 864-4106
660 Cross Creek Mall Fayetteville (28303) *(G-4562)*

Bridgestone Ret Operations LLC.........................704 861-8146
142 N New Hope Rd Gastonia (28054) *(G-5005)*

Bridgestone Ret Operations LLC.........................919 778-0230
507 N Berkeley Blvd Goldsboro (27534) *(G-5202)*

Bridgestone Ret Operations LLC.........................336 282-6646
3311 Battleground Ave Greensboro (27410) *(G-5399)*

Bridgestone Ret Operations LLC.........................336 852-8524
3937 W Gate City Blvd Greensboro (27407) *(G-5400)*

Bridgestone Ret Operations LLC.........................336 282-4695
512 Pisgah Church Rd Greensboro (27455) *(G-5401)*

Bridgestone Ret Operations LLC.........................252 522-5126
1901 W Vernon Ave Kinston (28504) *(G-7397)*

Bridgestone Ret Operations LLC.........................919 872-6402
5058 N New Hope Rd Raleigh (27604) *(G-9958)*

Bridgestone Ret Operations LLC.........................919 872-6566
4305 Wake Forest Rd Raleigh (27609) *(G-9959)*

Bridgestone Ret Operations LLC.........................252 243-5189
1401 Ward Blvd Wilson (27893) *(G-12973)*

Bridgestone Ret Operations LLC.........................336 725-1580
2743 Reynolda Rd Winston Salem (27106) *(G-13110)*

Bridgetower Media LLC (PA)..............................612 317-9420
7025 Albert Pick Rd Greensboro (27408) *(G-5402)*

Bridgport Restoration Svcs Inc...........................336 996-1212
742 Park Lawn Ct Kernersville (27284) *(G-7248)*

Bridgstone Amrcas Tire Oprtons.........................252 291-4275
3001 Firestone Pkwy Ne Wilson (27893) *(G-12974)*

Brig Homes NC...252 459-7026
1001 Eastern Ave Nashville (27856) *(G-9312)*

Briggs Boat Works Incorporated.........................252 473-2393
370 Harbor Rd Wanchese (27981) *(G-12338)*

Briggs-Shaffner Acquisition Co (PA)....................336 463-4272
1448 Us 601 Hwy Yadkinville (27055) *(G-13439)*

Briggs-Shaffner Company, Yadkinville Also Called: Briggs-Shaffner Acquisition Co *(G-13439)*

Bright Holdings Usa Inc....................................919 327-5500
8900 Capital Blvd Raleigh (27616) *(G-9960)*

Bright Light Technologies LLC............................910 212-6869
2217 Keith Hills Rd Lillington (27546) *(G-7790)*

Bright Path Laboratories Inc..............................858 281-8121
150 N Research Campus Dr Kannapolis (28081) *(G-7204)*

Bright Plastic, Greensboro Also Called: Thundrbird Mlding Grnsboro LLC *(G-5865)*

Bright View Technologies Corp...........................919 228-4370
4022 Stirrup Creek Dr Ste 301 Durham (27703) *(G-3942)*

Brightly Software Inc (HQ)................................919 816-8237
11000 Regency Pkwy Ste 110 Cary (27518) *(G-1315)*

Brighton Weaving LLC.......................................336 665-3000
7736 Mccloud Rd Ste 300 Greensboro (27409) *(G-5403)*

Brigman Electric Motors Inc...............................828 492-0568
6110 Old Clyde Rd Canton (28716) *(G-1246)*

Brii Biosciences Inc...919 240-5605
110 N Corcoran St Unit 5-130 Durham (27701) *(G-3943)*

Brilliant Sole Inc...339 222-8528
1930 Senova Trce Wilmington (28405) *(G-12723)*

Brilliant You LLC...336 343-5535
1451 S Elm Eugene St Ste 1102 Greensboro (27406) *(G-5404)*

Brisk Transport 910 LLC...................................910 527-7398
232 Old Montague Way Cameron (28326) *(G-1214)*

Brispa Investments Inc.....................................336 668-3636
4833 W Gate City Blvd Greensboro (27407) *(G-5405)*

Bristol-Myers Squibb, Charlotte Also Called: Bristol-Myers Squibb Company *(G-1812)*

Bristol-Myers Squibb Company...........................800 321-1335
Charlotte (28275) *(G-1812)*

Bristol-Myers Squibb Company...........................336 855-5500
211 American Ave Greensboro (27409) *(G-5406)*

Brite Sky LLC...757 589-4676
6461 Sherrill Baggett Rd Godwin (28344) *(G-5187)*

Brittany Smith..912 313-0588
2508 Glenhaven Dr Greensboro (27406) *(G-5407)*

Brittenhams Rebuilding Service..........................252 332-3181
2314 Us Hway13 S Ahoskie (27910) *(G-44)*

Broad Branch Distillery LLC...............................336 207-7855
756 N Trade St Winston Salem (27101) *(G-13111)*

Broad River Forest Products..............................828 287-8003
2250 Us 221 Hwy N Rutherfordton (28139) *(G-10979)*

Broadcom Corporation......................................919 865-2954
1030 Swabia Ct Ste 400 Durham (27703) *(G-3944)*

Broadsight Systems Inc.....................................336 837-1272
1023 Corporate Park Dr Mebane (27302) *(G-8233)*

Broadway Chipping Co., New Bern Also Called: Broadway Logging Co Inc *(G-9341)*

Broadway Logging Co Inc..................................252 633-2693
1525 Saints Delight Church Rd New Bern (28560) *(G-9341)*

Broadwick, Morrisville Also Called: Icontact LLC *(G-8990)*

Broadwind Indus Solutions LLC..........................919 777-2907
1824 Boone Trail Rd Sanford (27330) *(G-11159)*

Brock & Triplett Machine, Moravian Falls Also Called: Brock and Triplett Machine Sp *(G-8808)*

Brock and Triplett Machine Sp............................336 667-6951
285 E Meadows Rd Moravian Falls (28654) *(G-8808)*

Brodie-Jones Printing Co Inc..............................252 438-7992
253 Ronald Tharrington Rd Louisburg (27549) *(G-7910)*

Bromley Plastics, Fletcher Also Called: Mdt Bromley LLC *(G-4752)*

Bromma Inc...919 620-8039
4400 Ben Franklin Blvd Ste 200 Durham (27704) *(G-3945)*

(G-0000) Company's Geographic Section entry number

Bronto Software LLC.. 919 595-2500
324 Blackwell St Ste 410 Durham (27701) *(G-3946)*

Brookhurst Associates.. 919 792-0987
2400 Saint Pauls Sq Raleigh (27614) *(G-9961)*

Brookline Inc.. 704 824-1390
112 Cramer Mountain Woods Cramerton (28032) *(G-3634)*

Brookline Furniture, Archdale *Also Called: Brookline Furniture Co Inc (G-214)*

Brookline Furniture Co Inc.. 336 841-8503
4015 Cheyenne Dr Archdale (27263) *(G-214)*

Brooks Equipment, Charlotte *Also Called: Beco Holding Company Inc (G-1767)*

Brooks Machine & Design Inc.................................... 919 404-0901
1424 Old Us Highway 264 Zebulon (27597) *(G-13505)*

Brooks Manufacturing Solutions............................... 336 438-1280
1017 Davis Ln Graham (27253) *(G-5261)*

Brooks Mfg Solutions Inc.. 336 438-1280
418 N Main St Burlington (27217) *(G-1054)*

Brooks of Dallas Inc... 704 922-5219
203 E Lay St Dallas (28034) *(G-3666)*

Brooks Tool Inc... 704 283-0112
524 Marshall St Monroe (28112) *(G-8447)*

Brookshire Buiulders, Asheville *Also Called: Brookshire Woodworking Inc (G-462)*

Brookshire Woodworking Inc (PA)............................ 828 779-2119
355 Haywood Rd Asheville (28806) *(G-462)*

Brookstone Baptist Church....................................... 828 658-9443
90 Griffee Rd Weaverville (28787) *(G-12485)*

Brookwood Farms Inc... 919 663-3612
1015 Alston Bridge Rd Siler City (27344) *(G-11401)*

Broome Sign Company.. 704 782-0422
348 Spring St Nw Concord (28025) *(G-3325)*

Broomes Poultry Inc... 704 983-0965
24816 Austin Rd Albemarle (28001) *(G-63)*

Brothers Precision Tool Co.. 704 982-5667
310 S Broome St Albemarle (28001) *(G-64)*

Brown & Church Neck Wear Co................................. 336 368-5502
118 Mary Moore Ln Pilot Mountain (27041) *(G-9670)*

Brown Brothers Construction Co............................... 828 297-2131
10801 Us Highway 421 N Zionville (28698) *(G-13527)*

Brown Brothers Lumber.. 828 632-6486
1388 Little River Church Rd Taylorsville (28681) *(G-11951)*

Brown Building Corporation...................................... 919 782-1800
1111 Copeland Oaks Dr Morrisville (27560) *(G-8944)*

Brown Cabinet Co... 704 933-2731
1510 N Ridge Ave Kannapolis (28083) *(G-7205)*

Brown Creek Timber Company Inc............................ 704 694-3529
2691 Nc 742 N Wadesboro (28170) *(G-12237)*

Brown Equipment and Capitl Inc.............................. 704 921-4644
650 Broome St Monroe (28110) *(G-8448)*

Brown Mitchell Hodges LLC...................................... 800 477-8982
4111 Rose Lake Dr Ste E Pmb 678 Charlotte (28217) *(G-1813)*

Brown Printing Inc.. 704 849-9292
9129 Monroe Rd Ste 160 Charlotte (28270) *(G-1814)*

Browns Woodworking LLC... 704 983-5917
210 Charter St Albemarle (28001) *(G-65)*

Brp Spruce Pine, Spruce Pine *Also Called: Brp US Inc (G-11566)*

Brp Spruce Pine Distribution, Spruce Pine *Also Called: Brp US Inc (G-11565)*

Brp US Inc.. 828 766-1164
12934 S 226 Hwy Spruce Pine (28777) *(G-11565)*

Brp US Inc.. 828 766-1100
1211 Greenwood Rd Spruce Pine (28777) *(G-11566)*

Brs Aerospace, Pinebluff *Also Called: Ballistic Recovery Systems Inc (G-9685)*

Bruce Julian Heritage Foods, Charlotte *Also Called: Bevs & Bites LLC (G-1777)*

Bruex Inc.. 828 754-1186
312 Lutz St Sw Lenoir (28645) *(G-7589)*

Brumley-South, Mooresville *Also Called: Brumley/South Inc (G-8622)*

Brumley/South Inc.. 704 664-9251
422 N Broad St Mooresville (28115) *(G-8622)*

Bruning and Federle Mfg Co (PA)............................. 704 873-7237
2503 Northside Dr Statesville (28625) *(G-11672)*

Brunner & Lay Inc.. 828 274-2770
90 Reeds Way Flat Rock (28731) *(G-4704)*

Brunson Marine Group LLC....................................... 252 291-0271
4155 Dixie Inn Rd Wilson (27893) *(G-12975)*

Brunswick Beacon Inc.. 910 754-6890
208 Smith Ave Shallotte (28470) *(G-11300)*

Brunswick Cabinets Countertops, Supply *Also Called: Bcac Holdings LLC (G-11855)*

Brunswick Screen Prtg & EMB.................................. 910 579-1234
570 Meadow Summit Dr Ocean Isle Beach (28469) *(G-9586)*

Brushy Mountain Bee Farm Inc (PA)........................ 336 921-3640
101 S Stratford Rd Ste 210 Winston Salem (27104) *(G-13112)*

Bryan Austin... 336 841-6573
1589 Skeet Club Rd Ste 102 High Point (27265) *(G-6551)*

Bryant Grant Mutual Burial Asn................................ 828 524-2411
105 W Main St Franklin (28734) *(G-4819)*

Bryson Industries Inc... 336 931-0026
416 Albertson Rd Thomasville (27360) *(G-11999)*

Bsci Inc (PA).. 704 664-3005
170 Barley Park Ln Mooresville (28115) *(G-8623)*

Bsh Home Appliances Corp...................................... 252 636-4454
120 Bosch Blvd New Bern (28562) *(G-9342)*

Bsh Home Appliances Corp...................................... 252 672-9155
100 Bosch Blvd New Bern (28562) *(G-9343)*

Bsh Home Appls A Ltd Partnr................................... 252 636-4200
100 Bosch Blvd New Bern (28562) *(G-9344)*

Bsh International Trade, New Bern *Also Called: Bsh Home Appliances Corp (G-9343)*

BSN Medical Inc (DH)... 704 554-9933
5825 Carnegie Blvd Charlotte (28209) *(G-1815)*

BT America Inc... 704 434-8072
415 S Main St Boiling Springs (28017) *(G-883)*

Btc Electronic Components LLC (DH)........................ 919 229-2162
2709 Connector Dr Wake Forest (27587) *(G-12266)*

Bthec Inc... 704 596-5112
4823 N Graham St Charlotte (28269) *(G-1816)*

Buchanan Gem Stone Mines Inc.............................. 828 765-6130
13780 S 226 Hwy Spruce Pine (28777) *(G-11567)*

Buchanan Prtg & Graphics Inc................................. 336 299-6868
1088 Boulder Rd Greensboro (27409) *(G-5408)*

Bucher Municipal N Amer Inc................................... 704 658-1333
105 Motorsports Rd Mooresville (28115) *(G-8624)*

Buck Lucas Logging Companies............................... 252 410-0160
812 W Hawkins Rd Roanoke Rapids (27870) *(G-10732)*

Buck Marine Diesel, Winterville *Also Called: Buck Supply Company Inc (G-13414)*

Buck Racing Engines Inc.. 336 983-6562
205 Old Newsome Rd King (27021) *(G-7322)*

Buck Supply Company Inc.. 252 215-1252
3060 Old Highway 11 Winterville (28590) *(G-13414)*

Buckeye Cleaning Center, Charlotte *Also Called: Buckeye International Inc (G-1817)*

Buckeye Fire Equipment Company (PA)..................... 704 739-7415
110 Kings Rd Kings Mountain (28086) *(G-7351)*

Buckeye International Inc.. 704 523-9400
4123 Revolution Park Dr Ste A Charlotte (28217) *(G-1817)*

Buckeye Technologies Inc.. 704 822-6400
100 Buckeye Dr Mount Holly (28120) *(G-9220)*

BUCKEYE TECHNOLOGIES INC., Mount Holly *Also Called: Buckeye Technologies Inc (G-9220)*

Buckhorn Lumber and Wood Pdts, Brasstown *Also Called: Peachtree Lumber Company Inc (G-966)*

Budd-Piper Roofing Company................................... 919 682-2121
506 Ramseur St Durham (27701) *(G-3947)*

Buddy Cut Inc.. 888 608-4701
760 Redgate Rd Pittsboro (27312) *(G-9777)*

Budget Blinds, Wilmington *Also Called: Synoptix Companies LLC (G-12935)*

Budget Printing, Jamestown *Also Called: Geo-Lin Inc (G-7162)*

Budget Printing Co.. 910 642-7306
1424 S Jk Powell Blvd Ste B Whiteville (28472) *(G-12577)*

Buds Logging and Trucking....................................... 704 465-8016
1561 Stanbackfry Ice Plnt Rd Wadesboro (28170) *(G-12238)*

Budsin Wood Craft.. 252 729-1540
142 Moore Ln Marshallberg (28553) *(G-8084)*

Buechel Stone Corp.. 800 236-4474
7274 Us 221 N Marion (28752) *(G-8037)*

Buehler Motor Inc (HQ)... 919 380-3333
1100 Perimeter Park Dr Ste 118 Morrisville (27560) *(G-8945)*

Buffalo City Distillery LLC... 252 256-1477
8821 Caratoke Hwy Point Harbor (27964) *(G-9809)*

A
L
P
H
A
B
E
T
I
C

Buffalo Creek Farm, Germanton *Also Called: Buffalo Creek Farm & Crmry LLC (G-5174)*

Buffalo Creek Farm & Crmry LLC..336 969-5698
3241 Buffalo Creek Farm Rd Germanton (27019) *(G-5174)*

Buffalo Crushed Stone Inc...919 688-6881
1503 Camden Ave Durham (27704) *(G-3948)*

Buffaloe Milling Company Inc...252 438-8637
196 Buffalo Mill Rd Kittrell (27544) *(G-7439)*

Buffer Zone Ceramics...828 863-2000
655 John Weaver Rd Columbus (28722) *(G-3300)*

Buhler Inc..800 722-7483
100 Aeroglide Dr Cary (27511) *(G-1316)*

Buie and Company, Laurinburg *Also Called: Buie Manufacturing Company (G-7493)*

Buie Manufacturing Company...910 610-3504
105 Sterling Ln Laurinburg (28352) *(G-7493)*

Builders Firstsource, Raleigh *Also Called: Bfs Asset Holdings LLC (G-9941)*

Builders Firstsource Inc..336 884-5454
7601 Boeing Dr Greensboro (27409) *(G-5409)*

Builders Firstsource Inc..919 562-6601
45 Mosswood Blvd Youngsville (27596) *(G-13465)*

Builders Firstsource - SE Grp...910 313-3056
4151 Emerson St Wilmington (28403) *(G-12724)*

Builders Frstsrce - Rleigh LLC...919 363-4956
23 Red Cedar Way Apex (27502) *(G-147)*

Builders Frstsrce - Sthast Gro...910 944-2516
900 Pinehurst Dr Aberdeen (28315) *(G-2)*

Building Automation Svcs LLC...336 884-4026
1515 Bethel Dr High Point (27260) *(G-6552)*

Building Center Inc (PA)...704 889-8182
10201 Industrial Dr Pineville (28134) *(G-9717)*

Building Envlope Erction Svcs (PA).......................................252 747-2015
1441 Nahunta Rd Snow Hill (28580) *(G-11476)*

Building Stars of Charlotte, Charlotte *Also Called: Skyview Commercial Cleaning (G-2812)*

Built By Ben Woodworks LLC...336 438-1159
2232 Eric Ln Burlington (27215) *(G-1055)*

Built To Last NC LLC..252 232-0055
417h Caratoke Hwy Moyock (27958) *(G-9277)*

Bulk Sak International Inc..704 833-1361
1302 Industrial Pike Rd Gastonia (28052) *(G-5006)*

Bulk Transport Service Inc..910 329-0555
169 Preston Wells Rd Holly Ridge (28445) *(G-6887)*

Bull, Charlotte *Also Called: Bull Engineered Products Inc (G-1818)*

Bull City Ciderworks, Lexington *Also Called: Cider Bros LLC (G-7665)*

Bull City Designs LLC..919 908-6252
1111 Neville St Durham (27701) *(G-3949)*

Bull City Sheet Metal LLC...919 354-0993
4008 Comfort Ln Durham (27705) *(G-3950)*

Bull Durham Beer Co LLC...919 744-3568
409 Blackwell St Durham (27701) *(G-3951)*

Bull Engineered Products Inc (PA)..704 504-0300
12001 Steele Creek Rd Charlotte (28273) *(G-1818)*

Bulldog Hose Company LLC...919 639-6151
141 Junny Rd Angier (27501) *(G-114)*

Bulldog Industries Inc..919 217-6170
205 Forest Dr Knightdale (27545) *(G-7449)*

Bulldog Machine Inc...704 200-7838
3330 Smith Farm Rd Matthews (28104) *(G-8161)*

Bulldog Printing, Greensboro *Also Called: American Indian Printing Inc (G-5357)*

Bulldurhamfabrications Com..919 479-1919
5004 Mandel Rd Durham (27712) *(G-3952)*

Bunce Buildings, Salisbury *Also Called: Harvest Homes and Handi Houses (G-11061)*

Bundy Logging Company Inc..252 357-0191
37 Main St Gatesville (27938) *(G-5170)*

Bundy Trucking, Gatesville *Also Called: Bundy Logging Company Inc (G-5170)*

Bunge Oils Inc..910 293-7917
376 W Park Dr Warsaw (28398) *(G-12358)*

Burch Industries, Laurinburg *Also Called: Charles Craft Inc (G-7497)*

Burchette Sign Company Inc..336 996-6501
8705 Triad Dr Colfax (27235) *(G-3274)*

Burco International Inc...828 252-4481
1900 Hendersonville Rd Ste 10 Asheville (28803) *(G-463)*

Burgiss Farm Bed & Breakfast, Laurel Springs *Also Called: Tom Burgiss (G-7491)*

Burke Mills Inc...828 874-6341
191 Sterling St Nw Valdese (28690) *(G-12189)*

Burke Veneers Inc...828 437-8510
2170 Fr Coffey Rd Morganton (28655) *(G-8854)*

Burkert Fluid Control Systems, Huntersville *Also Called: Burkert USA Corporation (G-6974)*

Burkert USA Corporation..800 325-1405
11425 Mount Holly Hntrsvlle Rd Huntersville (28078) *(G-6974)*

Burkett Welding Services Inc...252 635-2814
1401 B St New Bern (28560) *(G-9345)*

Burlan Manufacturing LLC (PA)..704 867-3548
2740 W Franklin Blvd Gastonia (28052) *(G-5007)*

Burlington Chemical Co LLC..336 584-0111
8646 W Market St Ste 116 Greensboro (27409) *(G-5410)*

Burlington Coat Factory, Cary *Also Called: Burlington Coat Fctry Whse Cor (G-1317)*

Burlington Coat Fctry Whse Cor...919 468-9312
1741 Walnut St Cary (27511) *(G-1317)*

Burlington Distributing Co..336 292-1415
2232 Westbrook St Greensboro (27407) *(G-5411)*

Burlington House LLC..336 379-6220
804 Green Valley Rd Ste 300 Greensboro (27408) *(G-5412)*

Burlington Industries III LLC...336 379-2000
3330 W Friendly Ave Greensboro (27410) *(G-5413)*

Burlington Industries LLC (DH)..336 379-6220
804 Green Valley Rd Ste 300 Greensboro (27408) *(G-5414)*

Burlington Machine Service...336 228-6758
632 Chapel Hill Rd Burlington (27215) *(G-1056)*

Burlington Mscllneous Mtls LLC...336 376-1264
3406 William Newlin Dr Graham (27253) *(G-5262)*

Burlington Outlet (PA)...910 278-3442
5817 E Oak Island Dr Oak Island (28465) *(G-9564)*

Burlington Rigid Box Plant, Burlington *Also Called: Caraustar Brlngton Rgid Box In (G-1059)*

Burnett Darrill Stephen...828 287-8778
137 Williamsburg Dr Spindale (28160) *(G-11545)*

Burnett Machine Company Inc..704 867-7786
924 Hanover St Gastonia (28054) *(G-5008)*

Burney Sweets & More Inc (PA)..910 862-2099
106-B Martin Luther King Dr Elizabethtown (28337) *(G-4419)*

Burneys Sweets & More, Elizabethtown *Also Called: Burney Sweets & More Inc (G-4419)*

Burntshirt Vineyards LLC..828 685-2402
3737 Howard Gap Rd Hendersonville (28792) *(G-6191)*

Burris Machine Company Inc...828 322-6914
1631 Main Avenue Dr Nw Hickory (28601) *(G-6276)*

Burris Machine Company Inc (PA)...828 322-6914
3155 Highland Ave Ne Hickory (28601) *(G-6277)*

Burrough Furniture...336 841-3129
1302 Kersey Valley Rd Archdale (27263) *(G-215)*

Burrow Family Corporation (PA)...336 887-3173
5346 Nc Highway 49 S Asheboro (27205) *(G-334)*

Burrows Paper Corporation (DH)..800 272-7122
3436 Toringdon Way Ste 100 Charlotte (28277) *(G-1819)*

Burton Global Logistics LLC...336 663-6449
1603 Anthony Rd Burlington (27215) *(G-1057)*

Burton Steel Company (PA)...910 675-9241
102b Ritter Dr Castle Hayne (28429) *(G-1496)*

Burts Bees Inc (HQ)..919 998-5200
210 W Pettigrew St Durham (27701) *(G-3953)*

Burts Bees Inc...919 998-5200
701 Distribution Dr Durham (27709) *(G-3954)*

Burts Bees Inc...919 238-6450
900 Aviation Pkwy Ste 400 Morrisville (27560) *(G-8946)*

Bus Safety Inc...336 671-0838
133 Avgol Dr Mocksville (27028) *(G-8352)*

Bus Safety Solutions, Mocksville *Also Called: Bus Safety Inc (G-8352)*

Busch Enterprises Inc..704 878-2067
908 Cochran St Statesville (28677) *(G-11673)*

Busiapp Corporation...877 558-2518
400 Innovation Ave Ste 150 Morrisville (27560) *(G-8947)*

Busick Brothers Machine Inc...336 969-2717
262 Northstar Dr Rural Hall (27045) *(G-10953)*

Business Brokerage Press Inc..800 239-5085
2726 Warlick Dr Wilmington (28409) *(G-12725)*

(G-0000) Company's Geographic Section entry number

Business Card Express Raleigh, Morrisville *Also Called: Endaxi Company Inc* *(G-8972)*

Business Journals (DH)......................................704 371-3248
120 W Morehead St Ste 420 Charlotte (28202) *(G-1820)*

Business Leader, Raleigh *Also Called: Business To Business Inc* *(G-9963)*

Business Mogul LLC..919 605-2165
2120 Breezeway Dr Unit 112 Raleigh (27614) *(G-9962)*

Business North Carolina, Charlotte *Also Called: Red Hand Media LLC* *(G-2698)*

Business Systems of America.............................704 766-2755
3020 Prosperity Church Rd Charlotte (28269) *(G-1821)*

Business To Business Inc (PA)............................919 872-7077
3801 Wake Forest Rd Ste 102 Raleigh (27609) *(G-9963)*

Business Wise Inc..704 554-4112
615 S College St Ste 810 Charlotte (28202) *(G-1822)*

Butchers Best Inc..252 533-0961
944 Raleigh St Roanoke Rapids (27870) *(G-10733)*

Butler Trailer Mfg Co Inc...................................336 674-8850
259 Hockett Dairy Rd Randleman (27317) *(G-10634)*

Butler Trieu Inc...910 346-4929
1183 Kellum Loop Rd Jacksonville (28546) *(G-7118)*

Butner-Creedmoor News, Creedmoor *Also Called: Granville Publishing Co Inc* *(G-3649)*

Butterball LLC..919 658-6743
938 Millers Chapel Rd Goldsboro (27534) *(G-5203)*

Butterball LLC..919 658-6743
1628 Garner Chapel Rd Mount Olive (28365) *(G-9250)*

Butterball LLC..910 875-8711
1140 E Central Ave Raeford (28376) *(G-9833)*

Butterball LLC (HQ)..919 255-7900
1 Butterball Ln Garner (27529) *(G-4918)*

Buttercreme Bakery Inc.....................................336 722-1022
895 W Northwest Blvd Winston Salem (27101) *(G-13113)*

Butterfields Candies, Nashville *Also Called: Butterfields Candy LLC* *(G-9313)*

Butterfields Candy LLC.....................................252 459-2577
2155 S Old Franklin Rd Nashville (27856) *(G-9313)*

Buvic LLC...910 302-7950
6798 Weeping Water Run Fayetteville (28314) *(G-4563)*

Buy Smart Inc...252 293-4700
1109 Brookside Dr Nw Wilson (27896) *(G-12976)*

Buzz Saw Inc..910 321-7446
1015 Robeson St Ste 103 Fayetteville (28305) *(G-4564)*

Buzzispace Inc (DH)...336 821-3150
2880 Ridgewood Park Dr Winston Salem (27107) *(G-13114)*

Bw Trailer, Burlington *Also Called: Burton Global Logistics LLC* *(G-1057)*

Bwh Foam and Fiber Inc....................................336 498-6949
605 Sunset Dr Randleman (27317) *(G-10635)*

Bwi Etn LLC..828 682-2645
19 Crushing Rd Burnsville (28714) *(G-1184)*

Bwx Technologies Inc..980 365-4000
11525 N Community House Rd Ste 600 Charlotte (28277) *(G-1823)*

Bwxt Investment Company (HQ).........................704 625-4900
13024 Ballantyne Corporate Pl Ste 700 Charlotte (28277) *(G-1824)*

Bwxt Mpower Inc...980 365-4000
11525 N Community House Rd Ste 600 Charlotte (28277) *(G-1825)*

By Faith Logging Inc...252 792-0019
1046 Cedar Hill Dr Williamston (27892) *(G-12668)*

By-Design Black Oxide & TI LLC.........................828 874-0610
1260 Margaret St Nw Valdese (28690) *(G-12190)*

Byers Prcision Fabricators Inc...........................828 693-4088
675 Dana Rd Hendersonville (28792) *(G-6192)*

Bymonetcrochet..443 613-1736
8536 Caden Lee Way Apt 2208 Charlotte (28273) *(G-1826)*

Byrd Designs Inc...828 628-0151
140 Lee Dotson Rd Fairview (28730) *(G-4506)*

Byron Dale Spivey...910 653-3128
2009 Reynolds Rd Tabor City (28463) *(G-11907)*

C & B Salvage Company Inc................................336 374-3946
2882 Ararat Rd Ararat (27007) *(G-209)*

C & B Welding & Fab Inc....................................704 435-6942
2070 Mauney Rd Bessemer City (28016) *(G-807)*

C & C Chemical Company Inc..............................828 255-7639
119 Haywood Rd Asheville (28806) *(G-464)*

C & C Chipping Inc..252 249-1617
6003 Neuse Rd Grantsboro (28529) *(G-5330)*

C & C Precision Machine Inc...............................704 739-0505
418 Canterbury Rd Kings Mountain (28086) *(G-7352)*

C & C Tool and Machine Inc...............................704 226-1363
903 Icemorlee St Monroe (28110) *(G-8449)*

C & D Fabrications Inc.......................................919 639-2489
199 Fabrication Ln Angier (27501) *(G-115)*

C & D Woodworking Inc.....................................336 476-8722
7139 Wright Rd Thomasville (27360) *(G-12000)*

C & F Custom Cabinets Inc.................................910 424-7475
140 Sanders St Hope Mills (28348) *(G-6923)*

C & J Crosspieces LLC......................................910 652-4955
126 S Lancer Rd Star (27356) *(G-11627)*

C & J Machine Company Inc................................704 922-5913
3519 Philadelphia Church Rd Dallas (28034) *(G-3667)*

C & J Welding Inc..919 552-0275
136 Acorn Ridge Ln Holly Springs (27540) *(G-6896)*

C & L Manufacturing...336 957-8359
1519 Oak Ridge Church Rd Hays (28635) *(G-6145)*

C & M Enterprise Inc...704 545-1180
6808 Wilgrove Mint Hill Rd Mint Hill (28227) *(G-8333)*

C & M Industrial Supply Co.................................704 483-4001
748 N Hwy 16 Mill Spring (28756) *(G-8300)*

C & M Sawmill, Cleveland *Also Called: Myers Forest Products Inc* *(G-3217)*

C & M Tag, Mint Hill *Also Called: C & M Enterprise Inc* *(G-8333)*

C & R Building Supply Inc...................................910 567-6293
2300 Ernest Williams Rd Autryville (28318) *(G-647)*

C & R Hard Chrome Service Inc...........................704 861-8831
940 Hanover St Gastonia (28054) *(G-5009)*

C & S Antennas Inc...828 324-2454
1123 Industrial Dr Sw Conover (28613) *(G-3497)*

C & S Repair Center Inc.....................................610 524-9724
2081 Royal Pines Dr New Bern (28560) *(G-9346)*

C & S Woodworking...828 437-5024
833 Summers Rd Valdese (28690) *(G-12191)*

C A Perry & Son Inc..252 330-2323
683 Dry Ridge Rd Elizabeth City (27909) *(G-4380)*

C A Perry & Son Inc (DH)...................................252 221-4463
4033 Virginia Rd Hobbsville (27946) *(G-6883)*

C A Zimmer Inc...704 483-4560
731 Crosspoint Dr Denver (28037) *(G-3776)*

C B C Printing...828 497-5510
149 Childrens Home Rd Cherokee (28719) *(G-3050)*

C C S, Greensboro *Also Called: Custom Cnverting Solutions Inc* *(G-5480)*

C D J & P Inc...252 446-3611
1911 N Wesleyan Blvd Rocky Mount (27804) *(G-10826)*

C D Stampley Enterprises Inc.............................704 333-6631
6100 Orr Rd Charlotte (28213) *(G-1827)*

C E C, Weaverville *Also Called: Conrad Embroidery Company LLC* *(G-12487)*

C E Hicks Enterprises Inc...................................919 772-5131
230 Us 70 Hwy E Garner (27529) *(G-4919)*

C E I, Apex *Also Called: Computational Engrg Intl Inc* *(G-148)*

C E Smith Co Inc...336 273-0166
6396 Burnt Poplar Rd Greensboro (27409) *(G-5415)*

C E Smith Co Inc (PA)..336 273-0166
1001 Bitting St Greensboro (27403) *(G-5416)*

C G C, Cary *Also Called: Container Graphics Corp* *(G-1333)*

C G P, Clayton *Also Called: Dew Group Enterprises Inc* *(G-3144)*

C L Rabb Inc...704 865-0295
103 Wolfpack Rd Gastonia (28056) *(G-5010)*

C L S, Durham *Also Called: Custom Light and Sound Inc* *(G-3994)*

C M I, Raleigh *Also Called: Consolidated Mfg Intl LLC* *(G-10008)*

C M M...919 619-1716
2114 Damascus Church Rd Chapel Hill (27516) *(G-1532)*

C O Jelliff Corporation.......................................828 428-3672
4292 Providence Mill Rd Maiden (28650) *(G-8008)*

C P Eakes Company...336 574-1800
2012 Fairfax Rd Greensboro (27407) *(G-5417)*

C P T, Zirconia *Also Called: Carolina Paper Tubes Inc* *(G-13529)*

C R Laine Furniture Co Inc.................................828 328-1831
2829 Us Highway 70 Se Hickory (28602) *(G-6278)*

C R Onsrud Inc (PA).. 704 508-7000
120 Technology Dr Troutman (28166) *(G-12131)*

C S America Inc (HQ)...336 578-0110
1305 Graham St Burlington (27217) *(G-1058)*

C S I, Chapel Hill *Also Called: Conservation Station Inc (G-1539)*

C S I, Hickory *Also Called: Carolina Solvents Inc (G-6287)*

C T I, Indian Trail *Also Called: Coatings Technologies Inc (G-7074)*

C T I Pressure Washing, Raleigh *Also Called: CTI Property Services Inc (G-10025)*

C Tek Lean Solutions Inc................................. 704 895-0090
460 E Plaza Dr Ste A Mooresville (28115) *(G-8625)*

C V Industries, Valdese *Also Called: Valdese Weavers LLC (G-12205)*

C W Lawley Incorporated................................. 919 467-7782
201 Towerview Ct Cary (27513) *(G-1318)*

C Y Yard, Charlotte *Also Called: Lucky Landports (G-2439)*

C-Tron Incorporated... 919 494-7811
6473 Nc 96 Hwy W Youngsville (27596) *(G-13466)*

C.V.products, Thomasville *Also Called: Xceldyne Group LLC (G-12093)*

C&A Hockaday Transport LLC......................... 252 676-5956
1660 Hill St Roanoke Rapids (27870) *(G-10734)*

C&J Publishing... 336 722-8005
948 Sportsmans Dr Winston Salem (27101) *(G-13115)*

C&K Plastics Nc LLC....................................... 833 232-4848
164 Mckenzie Rd Mooresville (28115) *(G-8626)*

C&K Plastics North Carolina, Mooresville *Also Called: C&K Plastics Nc LLC (G-8626)*

C&V Powder Coating.. 910 228-1173
1068 Ashland Way Leland (28451) *(G-7536)*

C2c Plastics Inc.. 910 338-5260
3024 Hall Watters Dr Ste 101 Wilmington (28405) *(G-12726)*

CA Foy Machine Co... 704 734-4833
265 Kings Rd Kings Mountain (28086) *(G-7353)*

Cabarrus Brewing Company LLC..................... 704 490-4487
329 Mcgill Ave Nw Concord (28027) *(G-3326)*

Cabarrus Business Magazine, Concord *Also Called: Comfort Publishing Svcs LLC (G-3338)*

Cabarrus Concrete Co (PA)............................. 704 788-3000
2807 Armentrout Dr Concord (28025) *(G-3327)*

Cabarrus Plastics Inc...................................... 704 784-2100
2845 Armentrout Dr Concord (28025) *(G-3328)*

Cabin Craft American Homes, Rocky Mount *Also Called: Log Cabin Homes Ltd (G-10849)*

Cabinet Creations, Mount Pleasant *Also Called: Tommy W Smith Inc (G-9265)*

Cabinet Creations Inc...................................... 919 542-3722
585 Carl Foushee Rd Moncure (27559) *(G-8401)*

Cabinet Door World LLC................................... 877 929-2750
1711 11th Ave Sw Hickory (28602) *(G-6279)*

Cabinet Makers Inc.. 704 876-2808
534 Jane Sowers Rd Statesville (28625) *(G-11674)*

Cabinet Shop Inc.. 252 726-6965
4915 Arendell St Ste 309 Morehead City (28557) *(G-8820)*

Cabinet Solutions Usa Inc.............................. 828 358-2349
2001 Startown Rd Hickory (28602) *(G-6280)*

Cabinet Transitions Inc................................... 336 382-7154
5310 Solar Pl Greensboro (27406) *(G-5418)*

Cabinetry Div, Morrisville *Also Called: Heritage Design & Supply LLC (G-8987)*

Cabinets and Things.. 828 652-1734
141 Bill Deck Rd Union Mills (28167) *(G-12187)*

Cabinets Plus Inc... 718 213-3300
8431 Old Statesville Rd Charlotte (28269) *(G-1828)*

Cabinetworks Group Mich LLC........................ 803 984-2285
1200 Westinghouse Blvd Ste O Charlotte (28273) *(G-1829)*

Cabinetworks Group Mich LLC........................ 919 868-8174
6221 Westgate Rd Ste 100 Raleigh (27617) *(G-9964)*

Cable Devices Incorporated............................ 704 588-0859
10736 Nations Ford Rd Charlotte (28273) *(G-1830)*

Cable Devices Incorporated (HQ)................... 714 554-4370
3642 Us Highway 70 Sw Hickory (28602) *(G-6281)*

Cable Devices Incorporated............................ 704 588-0859
10540 Southern Loop Blvd Pineville (28134) *(G-9718)*

Cable Exchange, Hickory *Also Called: Cable Devices Incorporated (G-6281)*

Cable Exchange, Pineville *Also Called: Cable Devices Incorporated (G-9718)*

Cablenc LLC.. 919 307-9065
8012 Spiderlily Ct Zebulon (27597) *(G-13506)*

Cabot Wrenn, Hickory *Also Called: HM Liquidation Inc (G-6361)*

Cabot Wrenn, Taylorsville *Also Called: Hancock & Moore LLC (G-11962)*

Cabot Wrenn, Taylorsville *Also Called: Hancock & Moore LLC (G-11963)*

Cadence Design Systems Inc.......................... 919 380-3900
11000 Regency Pkwy Ste 401 Cary (27518) *(G-1319)*

Caesarstone Tech USA Inc (HQ).....................818 779-0999
1401 W Morehead St Ste 100 Charlotte (28208) *(G-1831)*

Cagle Sawmill Inc.. 336 857-2274
7065 Charles Mountain Rd Denton (27239) *(G-3741)*

Cahoon Brothers Logging LLC........................ 252 943-9901
26606 Us Highway 264 E Pantego (27860) *(G-9641)*

Cahoon Logging, Pinetown *Also Called: Cahoon Logging Company Inc (G-9708)*

Cahoon Logging Company Inc.......................... 252 943-6805
6848 Free Union Church Rd Pinetown (27865) *(G-9708)*

Cahoon, Bobby Logging, Grantsboro *Also Called: C & C Chipping Inc (G-5330)*

Cairn Studio Ltd (PA)......................................704 892-3581
121 N Main St Davidson (28036) *(G-3698)*

Cairn Studio Ltd.. 704 664-7128
200 Mckenzie Rd Mooresville (28115) *(G-8627)*

Caison Yachts Inc.. 910 270-6394
405 Lewis Rd Hampstead (28443) *(G-6070)*

Cajah Corporation.. 828 728-7300
1905 International Blvd Hudson (28638) *(G-6944)*

Cajah Mountain Hosiery Mills, Hudson *Also Called: Cajah Corporation (G-6944)*

Cakes, Charlotte *Also Called: Swirl Oakhurst LLC (G-2889)*

Cal-Cru, Granite Quarry *Also Called: Granite Knitwear Inc (G-5326)*

Cal-Van, Greensboro *Also Called: Horizon Tool Inc (G-5607)*

Calco Enterprises Inc (PA).............................910 695-0089
240 Crestline Ln Aberdeen (28315) *(G-3)*

Calco Sheet Metal Works, Aberdeen *Also Called: Calco Enterprises Inc (G-3)*

Caldwell Cabinets NC LLC.............................. 828 212-0000
3441 Hickory Blvd Hudson (28638) *(G-6945)*

Caldwells Mt Process Abattoirs...................... 828 428-8833
3726 Goodson Rd Maiden (28650) *(G-8009)*

Caldwells Water Conditioning.......................... 828 253-6605
22 Country Spring Dr Asheville (28804) *(G-465)*

Calhoun Welding Inc.. 252 281-1455
7367 Tory Pl Macclesfield (27852) *(G-7979)*

Calico Coatings, Denver *Also Called: Calico Technologies Inc (G-3777)*

Calico Technologies Inc (PA)...........................704 483-2202
5883 Balsom Ridge Rd Denver (28037) *(G-3777)*

Califrnia Grrett Cmmnctons Inc, Mooresville *Also Called: Garrettcom Inc (G-8671)*

Call Center, Cary *Also Called: Pepsi Bottling Ventures LLC (G-1418)*

Call Family Distillers LLC............................... 336 990-0708
1611 Industrial Dr Wilkesboro (28697) *(G-12630)*

Call Printing & Copying.................................... 704 821-6554
311 Indian Trail Rd S Indian Trail (28079) *(G-7073)*

Calsak Plastics, Charlotte *Also Called: Plastics Family Holdings Inc (G-2642)*

Calvin C Mooney Poultry.................................. 336 374-6690
4167 Nc 268 Ararat (27007) *(G-210)*

Calypso Feed Mill, Mount Olive *Also Called: Case Farms LLC (G-9252)*

CAM Craft LLC... 828 681-5183
54 Atrium Trl Arden (28704) *(G-259)*

CAM Enterprises Inc.. 252 946-4877
5601 Us Highway 264 W Washington (27889) *(G-12375)*

Camag Scientific Inc.. 910 343-1830
515 Cornelius Harnett Dr Wilmington (28401) *(G-12727)*

Camargo Phrm Svcs LLC................................. 513 618-0325
800 Taylor St Ste 101 Durham (27701) *(G-3955)*

Cambbro Manufacturing Company.................... 919 568-8506
1268 W Holt St Mebane (27302) *(G-8234)*

Cambrex, Durham *Also Called: Avista Pharma Solutions Inc (G-3910)*

Cambrex High Point Inc................................... 336 841-5250
4180 Mendenhall Oaks Pkwy High Point (27265) *(G-6553)*

Cambro (PA)... 919 563-0761
1268 Holt St Mebane (27302) *(G-8235)*

Camco Manufacturing Inc................................ 336 348-6609
2900 Vance Street Ext Reidsville (27320) *(G-10678)*

Camco Manufacturing LLC (PA).......................336 668-7661
121 Landmark Dr Greensboro (27409) *(G-5419)*

(G-0000) Company's Geographic Section entry number

CAMCO MANUFACTURING, INC., Reidsville Also Called: Camco Manufacturing Inc (G-10678)

Camel City Posters, King Also Called: Blue Light Images Company Inc (G-7321)

Camelot Computers Inc.. 704 554-1670
10020 Park Cedar Dr Ste 205 Charlotte (28210) **(G-1832)**

Camelot Rturn Intrmdate Hldngs (PA).......................... 866 419-0042
5020 Weston Pkwy Ste 400 Cary (27513) **(G-1320)**

Camelot Software Consulting, Charlotte Also Called: Camelot Computers Inc (G-1832)

Cameo Curtains Div, Charlotte Also Called: Chf Industries Inc (G-1912)

Cameo Fibers, Conover Also Called: Fibrix LLC (G-3521)

Camfil Usa Inc... 828 465-2880
1008 1st St W Conover (28613) **(G-3498)**

Camfil Usa Inc... 252 975-1141
200 Creekside Dr Washington (27889) **(G-12376)**

Camp Chemical Corporation (PA).................................. 336 597-2214
200 Hester St Roxboro (27573) **(G-10921)**

Camp Lejeune Globe.. 910 939-0705
149 Rea St Jacksonville (28546) **(G-7119)**

Camp S Well and Pump Co Inc...................................... 828 453-7322
149 Ola Dr Ellenboro (28040) **(G-4456)**

Campbell & Sons Machining Co..................................... 704 394-0291
230 W Congress St Lincolnton (28092) **(G-7818)**

Campus Safety Products LLC....................................... 919 321-1477
2530 Meridian Pkwy Ste 300 Durham (27713) **(G-3956)**

Camstar Systems Inc.. 704 227-6600
13024 Ballantyne Corporate Pl Charlotte (28277) **(G-1833)**

Can-AM Custom Trucks Inc.. 704 334-0322
1734 University Commercial Pl Charlotte (28213) **(G-1834)**

Can-Do Handyman Services, Whitsett Also Called: Drew Roberts LLC (G-12604)

Canal Wood LLC... 910 733-7436
1866 Hestertown Rd Lumberton (28358) **(G-7947)**

Canalta Enterprises LLC.. 919 615-1570
4809 Auburn Knightdale Rd Raleigh (27610) **(G-9965)**

Cancer Diagnostics Inc (PA).. 877 846-5393
116 Page Point Cir Durham (27703) **(G-3957)**

Candies Italian ICEE LLC.. 980 475-7429
3428 Nevin Brook Rd Ste 101 Charlotte (28269) **(G-1835)**

Cane Creek Cycling Cmpnnts Inc................................. 828 684-3551
355 Cane Creek Rd Fletcher (28732) **(G-4727)**

Cangilosi Spcialty Sausage Inc.................................... 336 665-5775
115 Landmark Dr Greensboro (27409) **(G-5420)**

Canine Cafe, Charlotte Also Called: Barbaras Canine Catering Inc (G-1749)

Canipe & Lynn Elc Mtr Repr Inc.................................... 828 322-9052
1909 1st Ave Sw Hickory (28602) **(G-6282)**

Cannon & Daughters Inc.. 828 254-9236
2000 Riverside Dr Ste 9 Asheville (28804) **(G-466)**

Cannon Paint and Abbraisives, Lenoir Also Called: W G Cannon Paint Co Inc (G-7644)

Canplast Usa Inc.. 336 668-9555
7104 Cessna Dr Greensboro (27409) **(G-5421)**

Canteen Raleigh/Durham, Garner Also Called: Compass Group Usa Inc (G-4924)

Canton Hardwood Company.. 828 492-0715
5373 Thickety Rd Canton (28716) **(G-1247)**

Canton Mill, Canton Also Called: Evergreen Packaging LLC (G-1252)

Canvas Beauty Bar LLC... 828 355-9688
181 Meadowview Dr Boone (28607) **(G-903)**

Canvas Giclee Printing... 910 458-4229
1018 Lake Park Blvd N Ste 19 Carolina Beach (28428) **(G-1257)**

Canvas Mw LLC.. 336 627-6000
523 S New St Eden (27288) **(G-4342)**

Canvas Sx LLC (HQ)... 980 474-3700
6325 Ardrey Kell Rd Ste 400 Charlotte (28277) **(G-1836)**

Canvasmasters LLC.. 828 369-0406
78 Cabe Cove Rd Franklin (28734) **(G-4820)**

Canyon Stone Inc... 919 880-3273
409 Northbrook Dr Youngsville (27596) **(G-13467)**

Cape Fear Boat Works Inc.. 910 371-3460
1690 Royster Rd Ne Navassa (28451) **(G-9326)**

Cape Fear Cabinet Co Inc... 910 703-8760
2908 Fort Bragg Rd Fayetteville (28303) **(G-4565)**

Cape Fear Chemicals Inc.. 910 862-3139
4271 Us Highway 701 N Elizabethtown (28337) **(G-4420)**

Cape Fear Cnstr Group LLC.. 910 344-1000
102 Autumn Hall Dr Ste 210 Wilmington (28403) **(G-12728)**

Cape Fear Designs, Wilmington Also Called: Robert Citrano (G-12900)

Cape Fear Newspapers Inc... 910 285-2178
107 N College St Wallace (28466) **(G-12319)**

Cape Fear Orthtics Prsthtics I...................................... 910 483-0933
435 W Russell St Fayetteville (28301) **(G-4566)**

Cape Fear Vineyard Winery LLC.................................... 844 846-3386
195 Vineyard Dr Elizabethtown (28337) **(G-4421)**

Cape Fear Vineyards, Rose Hill Also Called: Duplin Wine Cellars Inc (G-10905)

Cape Fear Vinyrd & Winery LLC.................................... 910 645-4292
218 Aviation Pkwy Ste C Elizabethtown (28337) **(G-4422)**

Cape Fear Yacht Works LLC.. 910 540-1685
111 Bryan Rd Wilmington (28412) **(G-12729)**

Cape Lookout Canvas & Customs................................. 252 726-3751
4444 Arendell St Ste D Morehead City (28557) **(G-8821)**

Capel Incorporated (PA)... 910 572-7000
831 N Main St Troy (27371) **(G-12158)**

Capel Rugs, Troy Also Called: Capel Incorporated (G-12158)

Capital Bumper, Fayetteville Also Called: Capitol Bumper (G-4568)

Capital City Cuisine LLC... 919 432-2126
4808 Wallingford Dr Raleigh (27616) **(G-9966)**

Capital City Sealants LLC... 919 427-4077
3101 Stony Brook Dr Ste 166 Raleigh (27604) **(G-9967)**

Capital Lghtning Prtection Inc....................................... 919 832-5574
743 Pershing Rd Raleigh (27608) **(G-9968)**

Capital Lightng Protection, Raleigh Also Called: Quality Lghtning Prtection Inc (G-10415)

Capital Marble Creations Inc... 910 893-2462
309 W Duncan St Lillington (27546) **(G-7791)**

Capital Rdymx Pittsboro LLC.. 919 217-0222
270 Moncure Pittsboro Rd Moncure (27559) **(G-8402)**

Capital Sign Solutions LLC... 919 789-1452
5800 Mchines Pl Ste 110 Raleigh (27616) **(G-9969)**

Capital Value Center Sls & Svc..................................... 910 799-4060
5406 Market St Wilmington (28405) **(G-12730)**

Capital Wood Products Inc.. 704 982-2417
38081 Saw Mill Rd New London (28127) **(G-9414)**

Capital Wraps, Raleigh Also Called: Ki Agency LLC (G-10234)

Capitol Bumper (PA)... 919 772-7330
126 Drake St Fayetteville (28301) **(G-4567)**

Capitol Bumper... 919 772-7330
126 Drake St Fayetteville (28301) **(G-4568)**

Capitol City Lumber Company....................................... 919 832-6492
4216 Beryl Rd Raleigh (27606) **(G-9970)**

Capitol Funds Inc... 910 439-5275
409 N Main St Mount Gilead (27306) **(G-9198)**

Capitol Funds Inc... 704 482-0645
649 Washburn Switch Rd Shelby (28150) **(G-11315)**

Capitol Funds Inc... 704 487-8547
720 S Lafayette St Shelby (28150) **(G-11316)**

Capnostics LLC.. 610 442-1363
9724 Colts Neck Ln Concord (28027) **(G-3329)**

Capper McCall Co... 919 270-8813
9650 Strickland Rd Ste 103420 Raleigh (27615) **(G-9971)**

Capps Noble Logging... 828 696-9690
Bob's Creek Road Zirconia (28790) **(G-13528)**

Capre Omnimedia LLC.. 917 460-3572
801 N 4th St Apt 404 Wilmington (28401) **(G-12731)**

Capt Charlies Seafood Inc.. 252 796-7278
508 N Road St Columbia (27925) **(G-3294)**

Capt Neills Seafood Inc.. 252 796-0795
508 N Road St Columbia (27925) **(G-3295)**

Captain Charlie's Seafood, Columbia Also Called: Capt Charlies Seafood Inc (G-3294)

Captive-Aire Systems Inc... 704 844-9088
6303 Carmel Rd Ste 105 Charlotte (28226) **(G-1837)**

Captive-Aire Systems Inc (PA)...................................... 919 882-2410
4641 Paragon Park Rd Ste 104 Raleigh (27616) **(G-9972)**

Captive-Aire Systems Inc... 704 843-7215
516 Wyndham Ln Waxhaw (28173) **(G-12426)**

Captive-Aire Systems Inc... 919 887-2721
360 Northbrook Dr Youngsville (27596) **(G-13468)**

A
L
P
H
A
B
E
T
I
C

Car RE Finish, Greensboro *Also Called: Akzo Nobel Coatings Inc (G-5345)*

Car-Mel Products, Statesville *Also Called: D & F Consolidated Inc (G-11683)*

Caraustar Brlngton Rgid Box In.. 336 226-1616
322 Fonville St Burlington (27217) *(G-1059)*

Caraustar Cstm Packg Group Inc... 336 498-2631
4139 Us Highway 311 Randleman (27317) *(G-10636)*

Caraustar Indus Cnsmr Pdts Gro... 336 564-2163
1485 Plaza South Dr Kernersville (27284) *(G-7249)*

Caraustar Indus Cnsmr Pdts Gro... 336 996-4165
1045 Industrial Park Dr Kernersville (27284) *(G-7250)*

Caraustar Industries Inc.. 704 333-5488
4915 Hovis Rd Charlotte (28208) *(G-1838)*

Caraustar Industries Inc.. 704 554-5796
8800 Crump Rd Charlotte (28273) *(G-1839)*

Caraustar Industries Inc.. 336 992-1053
1496 Plaza South Dr Kernersville (27284) *(G-7251)*

Caraustar Industries Inc.. 336 498-2631
4139 Us Highway 311 Randleman (27317) *(G-10637)*

Caraustar Industries Inc.. 828 246-7234
5095 Old River Rd Waynesville (28786) *(G-12452)*

Caraway Logging Inc.. 252 633-1230
1939 Olympia Rd New Bern (28560) *(G-9347)*

Carbide Saws Incorporated.. 336 882-6835
701 Garrison St High Point (27260) *(G-6554)*

Carbo-Cut Inc.. 828 685-7890
3937 Chimney Rock Rd Hendersonville (28792) *(G-6193)*

Carbon Conversion Systems LLC... 919 883-4238
95 Wood Laurel Ln Chapel Hill (27517) *(G-1533)*

Carbon Market Exchange LLC.. 828 545-0140
28 Schenck Pkwy Ste 200 Asheville (28803) *(G-467)*

Carbon-Less Industries Inc... 704 361-1231
12059 University City Blvd Harrisburg (28075) *(G-6105)*

Carbotech USA Inc.. 704 481-8500
4031 Dearborn Pl Nw Concord (28027) *(G-3330)*

Carden Printing Company.. 336 364-2923
52 Hunters Ln Timberlake (27583) *(G-12099)*

Cardinal Alaris Products, Creedmoor *Also Called: Carefusion 303 Inc (G-3643)*

Cardinal America Inc... 704 810-1620
165 Commerce Blvd Statesville (28625) *(G-11675)*

Cardinal Bag & Envelope Co Inc... 704 225-9636
2861 Gray Fox Rd Monroe (28110) *(G-8450)*

Cardinal Cabinets Distinction, Stedman *Also Called: Cynthia Saar (G-11806)*

Cardinal Cabinetworks Inc.. 919 829-3634
4900 Craftsman Dr Ste A Raleigh (27609) *(G-9973)*

Cardinal CT Company.. 336 719-6857
630 Derby St Mount Airy (27030) *(G-9106)*

Cardinal Fg, Mooresville *Also Called: Cardinal Glass Industries Inc (G-8628)*

Cardinal Foods LLC... 910 259-9407
201 Progress Dr Burgaw (28425) *(G-1020)*

Cardinal Glass Industries Inc.. 704 660-0900
342 Mooresville Blvd Mooresville (28115) *(G-8628)*

Cardinal Graphics Inc.. 704 545-4144
4475 Morris Park Dr Ste H Mint Hill (28227) *(G-8334)*

Cardinal Health 414, Charlotte *Also Called: Cardinal Health 414 LLC (G-1840)*

Cardinal Health 414 LLC.. 704 644-7989
3845 Shopton Rd Ste 18a Charlotte (28217) *(G-1840)*

Cardinal Metalworks LLC.. 910 259-9990
1090 E Wilmington Street Ext Burgaw (28425) *(G-1021)*

Cardinal Millwork & Supply Inc... 336 665-9811
7620 W Market St Greensboro (27409) *(G-5422)*

Cardinal Plastics Inc.. 704 739-9420
4910 Barrett Rd Kings Mountain (28086) *(G-7354)*

Cardinal Stone Company Inc... 336 846-7191
1608 Us Highway 221 N Jefferson (28640) *(G-7187)*

Cardinal Tissue LLC.. 815 503-2096
207 Oakland Rd Spindale (28160) *(G-11546)*

Cardiopharma Inc... 910 791-1361
100-A Eastwood Center Dr Ste 117 Wilmington (28403) *(G-12732)*

Cardioxyl Pharmaceuticals Inc.. 919 869-8586
1450 Raleigh Rd Ste 212 Chapel Hill (27517) *(G-1534)*

Cardservice of Carolinas, Greensboro *Also Called: Atlantic Bankcard Center Inc (G-5374)*

Carefusion 303 Inc... 919 528-5253
1515 Ivac Way Creedmoor (27522) *(G-3643)*

Cargill, Charlotte *Also Called: Cargill Incorporated (G-1841)*

Cargill, Cleveland *Also Called: Cargill Incorporated (G-3210)*

Cargill, Greenville *Also Called: Cargill Incorporated (G-5949)*

Cargill, High Point *Also Called: Cargill & Pendleton Inc (G-6555)*

Cargill Incorporated... 704 523-0414
5000 South Blvd Charlotte (28217) *(G-1841)*

Cargill Incorporated... 704 278-2941
9150 Statesville Blvd Cleveland (27013) *(G-3210)*

Cargill Incorporated... 800 227-4455
1754 River Rd Fayetteville (28312) *(G-4569)*

Cargill & Pendleton Inc.. 336 882-5510
330 N Hamilton St High Point (27260) *(G-6555)*

Cargill Incorporated... 252 752-1879
6 Miles East Farmville Greenville (27834) *(G-5949)*

Cargotec Port Security LLC (DH)... 919 620-1763
4400 Ben Franklin Blvd Ste 200a Durham (27704) *(G-3958)*

Carlina Shotwell LLC... 252 417-8688
204 E Arlington Blvd Ste C-103 Greenville (27858) *(G-5950)*

Carlisle Corporation... 704 501-1100
11605 N Community House Rd Charlotte (28277) *(G-1842)*

Carlisle Finishing LLC... 864 466-4173
804 Green Valley Rd Ste 300 Greensboro (27408) *(G-5423)*

Carlisle Syntec Systems A Div, Charlotte *Also Called: Carlisle Corporation (G-1842)*

Carlson Envmtl Cons Prof Corp, Monroe *Also Called: Integrity Envmtl Solutions LLC (G-8505)*

Carlton Enterprizes LLC.. 919 534-5424
195 Rocky Point Trng Sch Rd Rocky Point (28457) *(G-10877)*

Carnes-Miller Gear Company Inc... 704 888-4448
362 Browns Hill Rd Locust (28097) *(G-7889)*

Caro-Polymers Inc (PA)... 704 629-5319
611 Bess Town Rd Bessemer City (28016) *(G-808)*

Carocon, Laurinburg *Also Called: Carolina Container LLC (G-7494)*

Carocraft Cabinets Inc... 704 376-0022
1932 Statesville Ave Charlotte (28206) *(G-1843)*

Carolina.. 919 851-0906
8204 Tryon Woods Dr Cary (27518) *(G-1321)*

Carolina 1926 LLC.. 828 251-2500
40 Interstate Blvd Asheville (28806) *(G-468)*

Carolina Academic Press LLC.. 919 489-7486
700 Kent St Durham (27701) *(G-3959)*

Carolina Apparel Group Inc... 704 694-6544
425 Us Highway 52 S Wadesboro (28170) *(G-12239)*

Carolina Asphalt, Hickory *Also Called: Carolina Paving Hickory Inc (G-6285)*

Carolina Asphalt Maintenance... 828 944-0425
5490 Soco Rd Maggie Valley (28751) *(G-8005)*

Carolina ATL Seafood Entps... 252 728-2552
711 Shepard St Morehead City (28557) *(G-8822)*

Carolina Attachments LLC... 336 474-7309
704 Pineywood Rd Thomasville (27360) *(G-12001)*

Carolina Awning and Tent, Rocky Mount *Also Called: Rocky Mount Awning & Tent Co (G-10866)*

Carolina Bark Products LLC... 252 589-1324
Hwy 186 E Seaboard (27876) *(G-11270)*

Carolina Base - Pac Corp... 828 728-7304
3157 Freezer Locker Rd Hudson (28638) *(G-6946)*

Carolina Beer Company, Mooresville *Also Called: Carolina Beverage Group LLC (G-8630)*

Carolina Beverage Corporation (PA)... 704 636-2191
1413 Jake Alexander Blvd S Salisbury (28146) *(G-11024)*

Carolina Beverage Group LLC.. 704 799-3627
313 Mooresville Blvd Mooresville (28115) *(G-8629)*

Carolina Beverage Group LLC (HQ).. 704 799-2337
110 Barley Park Ln Mooresville (28115) *(G-8630)*

Carolina Bg.. 704 847-8840
624 Matthews Mint Hill Rd Ste B Matthews (28105) *(G-8101)*

Carolina Biological Supply Co.. 336 446-7600
6537 Judge Adams Rd Whitsett (27377) *(G-12601)*

Carolina Biological Supply Company (PA).................................... 336 584-0381
2700 York Rd Burlington (27215) *(G-1060)*

Carolina Blind Outlet Inc (PA)... 828 697-8525
225 Duncan Hill Rd Hendersonville (28792) *(G-6194)*

Carolina Bottle Mfr LLC..704 635-8759
2630 Nelda Dr Ste B Monroe (28110) *(G-8451)*

Carolina Bottling Company..704 637-5869
1413 Jake Alexander Blvd S Salisbury (28146) *(G-11025)*

Carolina Brace Systems, Chapel Hill *Also Called: Orthorx Inc (G-1562)*

Carolina Bronze, Seagrove *Also Called: Carolina Bronze Sculpture Inc (G-11273)*

Carolina Bronze Sculpture Inc....................................336 873-8291
6108 Maple Springs Rd Seagrove (27341) *(G-11273)*

Carolina Brush Company...704 867-0286
3093 Northwest Blvd Gastonia (28052) *(G-5011)*

Carolina Brush Mfg Co (PA)...704 867-0286
3093 Northwest Blvd Gastonia (28052) *(G-5012)*

Carolina Building Services Inc (PA)..............................704 664-7110
207 Timber Rd Mooresville (28115) *(G-8631)*

Carolina Business Furn Inc...336 431-9400
535 Archdale Blvd High Point (27263) *(G-6556)*

Carolina By-Products, Greensboro *Also Called: Valley Proteins (de) Inc (G-5895)*

Carolina By-Products Co...336 333-3030
2410 Randolph Ave Greensboro (27406) *(G-5424)*

Carolina Cab Specialist LLC..919 818-4375
311 Ashville Ave Ste K Cary (27518) *(G-1322)*

Carolina Cabinets of Cedar Pt.....................................252 393-6236
136 Vfw Rd Swansboro (28584) *(G-11882)*

Carolina Candle...336 835-6020
430 Gentry Rd Elkin (28621) *(G-4440)*

Carolina Canners Inc..843 537-5281
750 S Bennett St Southern Pines (28387) *(G-11496)*

Carolina Carports Inc (PA)..336 367-6400
187 Cardinal Ridge Ln Dobson (27017) *(G-3820)*

Carolina Carton Plant, Charlotte *Also Called: Caraustar Industries Inc (G-1839)*

Carolina Cartridge, Charlotte *Also Called: Carolina Cartridge Systems Inc (G-1844)*

Carolina Cartridge Systems Inc...................................704 347-2447
516 E Hebron St Charlotte (28273) *(G-1844)*

Carolina Casting Inc...336 884-7311
1416 Progress Ave High Point (27260) *(G-6557)*

Carolina Catch Inc...252 946-5796
321 N Pierce St Washington (27889) *(G-12377)*

Carolina Cemetery Park Corp......................................704 528-5543
344 Field Dr Troutman (28166) *(G-12132)*

Carolina Chair Inc..828 459-1330
1822 Brian Dr Ne Conover (28613) *(G-3499)*

Carolina Chocolatiers Inc...828 652-4496
20 N Main St Marion (28752) *(G-8038)*

Carolina Classic Manufacturing Inc.............................252 237-9105
510 Jones St S Wilson (27893) *(G-12977)*

Carolina Classifiedscom LLC (PA)...............................704 246-0900
1609 Airport Rd Monroe (28110) *(G-8452)*

Carolina Cltch Brake Rbldrs In...................................828 327-9358
430 Us Highway 70 Se Hickory (28602) *(G-6283)*

Carolina Co Packaging LLC, Henderson *Also Called: D C Thomas Group Inc (G-6153)*

Carolina Coast Vineyard...910 707-1777
1328 Lake Park Blvd N Carolina Beach (28428) *(G-1258)*

Carolina Coastal Coatings..910 346-9607
400 White St Jacksonville (28546) *(G-7120)*

Carolina Coastal Coatings Inc.....................................910 346-9607
375 Padgett Rd Maple Hill (28454) *(G-8025)*

Carolina Coating Solutions, Chapel Hill *Also Called: Abcor Supply Inc (G-1523)*

Carolina Commercial Coatings....................................910 279-6045
20 Wrights Aly Wilmington (28401) *(G-12733)*

Carolina Components Group, Durham *Also Called: Carolina Components Group Inc (G-3960)*

Carolina Components Group Inc..................................919 635-8438
1001 Hill Dr Durham (27703) *(G-3960)*

Carolina Concrete Inc...704 596-6511
11509 Reames Rd Charlotte (28269) *(G-1845)*

Carolina Concrete Inc (PA)..704 821-7645
1316 Waxhaw Rd Matthews (28105) *(G-8102)*

Carolina Concrete Materials..828 686-3040
650 Old Us 70 Hwy Swannanoa (28778) *(G-11867)*

Carolina Connections Inc..336 786-7030
805 Merita St Mount Airy (27030) *(G-9107)*

Carolina Container Company (HQ)...............................336 883-7146
909 Prospect St High Point (27260) *(G-6558)*

Carolina Container LLC...828 322-3380
61 30th St Nw Hickory (28601) *(G-6284)*

Carolina Container LLC...910 277-0400
16100 Joy St Laurinburg (28352) *(G-7494)*

Carolina Container LLC...336 883-7146
1205 Trinity St Thomasville (27360) *(G-12002)*

Carolina Conveying Inc...828 235-1005
162 Great Oak Dr Canton (28716) *(G-1248)*

Carolina Copacking LLC...252 433-0130
860 Commerce Dr Henderson (27537) *(G-6148)*

Carolina Copy Services Inc (PA)..................................704 375-9099
21300 Blakely Shores Dr Cornelius (28031) *(G-3592)*

Carolina Core Machine LLC..336 342-1141
638 Tamco Rd Reidsville (27320) *(G-10679)*

Carolina Counters, Midland *Also Called: E T Sales Inc (G-8286)*

Carolina Countertops of Garner..................................919 832-3335
3800 Tryon Rd Ste F Raleigh (27606) *(G-9974)*

Carolina Crate & Pallet Inc...910 245-4001
3281 Us 1 Hwy Vass (28394) *(G-12227)*

Carolina Crating Inc...910 276-7170
430 Hillside Ave Laurinburg (28352) *(G-7495)*

Carolina Cstm Cabinets & Furn, Powells Point *Also Called: Carolina Custom Cabinets Inc (G-9820)*

Carolina Cstm Signs & Graphics.................................336 681-4337
1023 Huffman St Greensboro (27405) *(G-5425)*

Carolina Csual Otdoor Furn Inc...................................252 491-5171
7359 Caratoke Hwy Jarvisburg (27947) *(G-7185)*

Carolina Custom Booth, High Point *Also Called: Carolina Custom Booth Co LLC (G-6559)*

Carolina Custom Booth Co LLC...................................336 886-3127
901 W Market Center Dr High Point (27260) *(G-6559)*

Carolina Custom Cabinetry...704 808-1225
6823 Davis Rd Waxhaw (28173) *(G-12427)*

Carolina Custom Cabinets..910 525-3096
104 Andrews Chapel Rd Roseboro (28382) *(G-10911)*

Carolina Custom Cabinets Inc.....................................252 491-5475
102 Park Dr Powells Point (27966) *(G-9820)*

Carolina Custom Draperies Inc....................................336 945-5190
5723 Country Club Rd Ste D Winston Salem (27104) *(G-13116)*

Carolina Custom Exteriors Inc.....................................828 232-0402
211 Amboy Rd Asheville (28806) *(G-469)*

Carolina Custom Leather, Conover *Also Called: NC Custom Leather Inc (G-3540)*

Carolina Custom Millwork, Gastonia *Also Called: Contemporary Design Co LLC (G-5030)*

Carolina Custom Pressing, Greensboro *Also Called: Ultimix Records (G-5886)*

Carolina Custom Rubber Inc.......................................704 636-6989
5415 Statesville Blvd Salisbury (28147) *(G-11026)*

Carolina Custom Surfaces, Greensboro *Also Called: McAd Inc (G-5686)*

Carolina Custom Tank LLC..980 406-3200
924 Dr Martin Luther King Jr Way Gastonia (28054) *(G-5013)*

Carolina Custom Windows, Belmont *Also Called: Ramsey Industries Inc (G-763)*

Carolina Dairy LLC...910 569-7070
116 Industrial Park Biscoe (27209) *(G-848)*

Carolina Design & Mfg Inc..919 554-1823
239 Wiggins Rd Louisburg (27549) *(G-7911)*

Carolina Dry Kiln, Lexington *Also Called: J E Jones Lumber Company (G-7700)*

Carolina Duct Fabrication Inc......................................252 478-9955
360 Barbee St Spring Hope (27882) *(G-11555)*

Carolina Dyeing and Finshg LLC.................................336 227-2770
220 Elmira St Burlington (27217) *(G-1061)*

Carolina East Timber Inc...252 638-1914
2145 Saints Delight Church Rd New Bern (28560) *(G-9348)*

Carolina Eastern Inc...252 795-3128
6940 Us Highway 64 Robersonville (27871) *(G-10766)*

Carolina Egg Companies Inc.......................................252 459-2143
10927 Cooper Rd Nashville (27856) *(G-9314)*

Carolina Elctrnic Assmblers In....................................919 938-1086
132 Citation Ln Smithfield (27577) *(G-11435)*

Carolina Electric Boats, Benson *Also Called: Twin Troller Boats Inc (G-798)*

Carolina Electric Mtr Repr LLC....................................704 289-3732
1812 Skyway Dr Monroe (28110) *(G-8453)*

Carolina Envelope, Lexington *Also Called: Ceprint Solutions Inc (G-7662)*

**A
L
P
H
A
B
E
T
I
C**

Carolina Expediters LLC................................888 537-5330
1415 Fancy Gap Rd Mount Airy (27030) *(G-9108)*

Carolina Extruded Plastics Inc.......................336 272-1191
728 Utility St Greensboro (27405) *(G-5426)*

Carolina Fab Inc..704 820-8694
2129 Charles Raper Jonas Hwy Mount Holly (28120) *(G-9221)*

Carolina Fabricators, Raleigh *Also Called: Carolina Fabricators LLC (G-9975)*

Carolina Fabricators, Raleigh *Also Called: Kisner Corporation (G-10236)*

Carolina Fabricators LLC...............................919 510-8410
6016 Triangle Dr Raleigh (27617) *(G-9975)*

Carolina Fairway Cushions LLC......................336 434-4292
15 N Robbins St Thomasville (27360) *(G-12003)*

Carolina Farm Table, Sparta *Also Called: Designs In Wood (G-11538)*

Carolina Farmstead LLC.................................800 822-6219
1012 Hardy Rd Snow Hill (28580) *(G-11477)*

Carolina Fine Snacks, Greensboro *Also Called: KLb Enterprises Incorporated (G-5650)*

Carolina Finshg & Coating Inc.......................704 730-8233
441 Countryside Rd Kings Mountain (28086) *(G-7355)*

Carolina Fire Journal, Indian Trail *Also Called: Knight Communications Inc (G-7086)*

Carolina Fire Protection Inc..........................910 892-1700
4055 Hodges Chapel Rd Dunn (28334) *(G-3847)*

Carolina Foods LLC (PA)................................704 333-9812
1807 S Tryon St Charlotte (28203) *(G-1846)*

Carolina Foods LLC.......................................704 333-9812
12031 Carolina Logistics Dr Pineville (28134) *(G-9719)*

Carolina Foundry Inc....................................704 376-3145
228 W Tremont Ave Charlotte (28203) *(G-1847)*

Carolina Frames, Asheboro *Also Called: Chris Isom Inc (G-338)*

Carolina Fur Dressing Company......................919 231-0086
900 Freedom Dr Raleigh (27610) *(G-9976)*

Carolina Giant Tires Inc................................919 609-9077
389 Americal Rd Henderson (27537) *(G-6149)*

Carolina Glove Company (PA).........................828 464-1132
116 S Mclin Creek Rd Conover (28613) *(G-3500)*

Carolina Gloves & Safety Co, Conover *Also Called: Carolina Glove Company (G-3500)*

Carolina Golfco Inc.......................................704 525-7846
209 E Exmore St Charlotte (28217) *(G-1848)*

Carolina Greenhouse Plants Inc.....................252 523-9300
1504 Cunningham Rd Kinston (28501) *(G-7398)*

Carolina Ground Svc Eqp Inc (PA)..................252 565-0288
430 Executive Pkwy New Bern (28562) *(G-9349)*

Carolina Growler Inc.....................................910 948-2114
121 N Green St Robbins (27325) *(G-10752)*

Carolina GSE, New Bern *Also Called: Carolina Ground Svc Eqp Inc (G-9349)*

Carolina Gym Supply Corp.............................919 732-6999
575 Dimmocks Mill Rd Hillsborough (27278) *(G-6862)*

Carolina Gyps Reclamation LLC.....................704 895-4506
19109 W Catawba Ave Cornelius (28031) *(G-3593)*

Carolina Heritage Cabinetry, North Wilkesboro *Also Called: Commercial Property LLC (G-9525)*

Carolina Home Exteriors LLC..........................252 637-6599
252 Kale Rd New Bern (28562) *(G-9350)*

Carolina Home Garden...................................828 692-3230
105 S Main St Hendersonville (28792) *(G-6195)*

Carolina Hosiery Mills Inc..............................336 226-5581
710 Koury Dr Burlington (27215) *(G-1062)*

Carolina Hosiery Mills Inc..............................336 226-5581
735 Koury Dr Burlington (27215) *(G-1063)*

Carolina Hosiery Mills Inc (PA).......................336 570-2129
2316 Tucker St. Extension Burlington (27215) *(G-1064)*

Carolina House Furniture Inc (PA)...................828 459-7400
5485 Herman Rd Claremont (28610) *(G-3090)*

Carolina Housing Solutions LLC......................704 995-7078
437 Hudson Pl Davidson (28036) *(G-3699)*

Carolina Ice Inc...252 527-3178
2466 Old Poole Rd Kinston (28504) *(G-7399)*

Carolina Innvtive Fd Ingrdnts........................804 359-9311
4626 Coleman Dr Nashville (27856) *(G-9315)*

Carolina Keller LLC.......................................252 237-8181
2401 Stantonsburg Rd Se Wilson (27893) *(G-12978)*

Carolina Knife Company, Asheville *Also Called: Hamilton Indus Grinding Inc (G-515)*

Carolina Laser Cutting Inc.............................336 292-1474
4400 S Holden Rd Greensboro (27406) *(G-5427)*

Carolina Lasers...919 872-8001
5508 Old Wake Forest Rd Raleigh (27609) *(G-9977)*

Carolina Lawnscape Inc................................803 230-5570
13105 Greencreek Dr Charlotte (28273) *(G-1849)*

Carolina Leatherwork, Fleetwood *Also Called: Cranberry Wood Works Inc (G-4715)*

Carolina Leg Supply LLC................................828 446-6838
111 Davis St Hudson (28638) *(G-6947)*

Carolina Loom Reed Company Inc...................336 274-7631
3503 Holts Chapel Rd Greensboro (27401) *(G-5428)*

Carolina Lquid Chmistries Corp (PA)...............336 722-8910
313 Gallimore Dairy Rd Greensboro (27409) *(G-5429)*

Carolina Machine Works, Belmont *Also Called: Equipment Parts Inc (G-749)*

Carolina Machining Fabrication.......................919 554-9700
321 N Nassau St Youngsville (27596) *(G-13469)*

Carolina Marble & Granite.............................704 523-2112
1924 Dilworth Rd W Charlotte (28203) *(G-1850)*

Carolina Mat Incorporated............................252 793-1111
193 Hwy 149 N Plymouth (27962) *(G-9800)*

Carolina Material Handling Inc.......................336 294-2346
2209 Patterson Ct Greensboro (27407) *(G-5430)*

Carolina Mattress Guild Inc...........................336 841-8529
385 North Dr Thomasville (27360) *(G-12004)*

Carolina Mch Fayetteville Inc.........................910 425-9115
3465 Black And Decker Rd Hope Mills (28348) *(G-6924)*

Carolina Mechanical Services Inc....................919 477-7100
5100 International Dr Durham (27712) *(G-3961)*

Carolina Metal Fabricators, Raleigh *Also Called: Directus Holdings LLC (G-10048)*

Carolina Metals Inc......................................828 667-0876
1398 Brevard Rd Asheville (28806) *(G-470)*

Carolina Meter and Supply, Hampstead *Also Called: Utility Metering Solutions Inc (G-6079)*

Carolina Mills Incorporated (PA).....................828 428-9911
618 N Carolina Ave Maiden (28650) *(G-8010)*

Carolina Moldings Inc...................................704 523-7471
4601 Macie St Charlotte (28217) *(G-1851)*

Carolina Money Saver, Monroe *Also Called: Carolina Classifiedscom LLC (G-8452)*

Carolina Movile Bus Systems.........................336 475-0983
771 Old Emanuel Church Rd Thomasville (27360) *(G-12005)*

Carolina Narrow Fabric Company.....................336 631-3000
1100 N Patterson Ave Winston Salem (27101) *(G-13117)*

Carolina Newspapers Inc..............................336 274-7829
807 Summit Ave Greensboro (27405) *(G-5431)*

Carolina Nonwovens LLC...............................704 735-5600
1106 Jw Abernathy Plant Rd Maiden (28650) *(G-8011)*

Carolina North Granite Corp..........................336 719-2600
151 Granite Quarry Trl Mount Airy (27030) *(G-9109)*

Carolina North Mfg Inc.................................336 992-0082
1161 S Park Dr Kernersville (27284) *(G-7252)*

Carolina Nut Inc..910 293-4209
1180 Stanley Chapel Church Rd Mount Olive (28365) *(G-9251)*

Carolina Packaging & Sup Inc (PA)..................919 201-5592
5609 Departure Dr Raleigh (27616) *(G-9978)*

Carolina Packers Inc (PA).............................919 934-2181
2999 S Brightleaf Blvd Smithfield (27577) *(G-11436)*

Carolina Packing House Sups.........................910 653-3438
305 Green Sea Rd Tabor City (28463) *(G-11908)*

Carolina Pallet Recycling Inc.........................828 652-6818
2855 Nc 226 I 40 Marion (28752) *(G-8039)*

Carolina Paper Guys LLC...............................704 980-3112
5800 Brookshire Blvd Charlotte (28216) *(G-1852)*

Carolina Paper Tubes Inc..............................828 692-9686
3932 Old Us 25 Hwy Zirconia (28790) *(G-13529)*

Carolina Parenting Inc (PA)...........................704 344-1980
214 W Tremont Ave Ste 302 Charlotte (28203) *(G-1853)*

Carolina Paving Hickory Inc...........................828 328-3909
445 9th St Se Hickory (28602) *(G-6285)*

Carolina Paving Hickory Inc (PA).....................828 322-1706
3203 Highland Ave Ne Hickory (28601) *(G-6286)*

Carolina Peacemaker, Greensboro *Also Called: Carolina Newspapers Inc (G-5431)*

Carolina Perfumer Inc (PA)............................910 295-5600
102 Berwick Ct Pinehurst (28374) *(G-9688)*

Carolina Piping Services Inc................................. 704 405-0297
307 S Cansler St Kings Mountain (28086) *(G-7356)*

Carolina Prcsion Cmponents Inc........................... 828 496-1045
4181 Us Highway 321a Granite Falls (28630) *(G-5298)*

Carolina Prcsion Fbers Spv LLC............................ 336 527-4140
145 Factory St Ronda (28670) *(G-10893)*

Carolina Prcsion Machining Inc............................. 336 751-7788
1500 N Main St Mocksville (27028) *(G-8353)*

Carolina Precast Concrete.................................... 910 230-0028
452 Webb Rd Dunn (28334) *(G-3848)*

Carolina Precision Fibers Inc................................ 336 527-4140
145 Factory St Ronda (28670) *(G-10894)*

Carolina Precision Machining............................... 336 751-7788
130 Funder Dr Mocksville (27028) *(G-8354)*

Carolina Precision Mfg LLC.................................. 704 662-3480
1138 Gateway Dr Mooresville (28115) *(G-8632)*

Carolina Precision Plas LLC.................................. 336 283-4700
111 Cpp Global Dr Mocksville (27028) *(G-8355)*

Carolina Precision Plastics L (HQ)........................ 336 498-2654
405 Commerce Pl Asheboro (27203) *(G-335)*

Carolina Precision Tech LLC................................. 215 675-4590
1055 Gateway Dr Ste A Mooresville (28115) *(G-8633)*

Carolina Press, Hendersonville *Also Called: Pamela Taylor (G-6234)*

Carolina Prime, Lenoir *Also Called: Carolina Prime Pet Inc (G-7590)*

Carolina Prime Pet Inc.. 888 370-2360
2040 Morganton Blvd Sw Lenoir (28645) *(G-7590)*

Carolina Print Mill.. 919 607-9452
527 E Chatham St Cary (27511) *(G-1323)*

Carolina Print Works Inc...................................... 704 637-6902
600 N Long St Ste B Salisbury (28144) *(G-11027)*

Carolina Printing Co... 919 834-0433
640 Quarterhorse Rd Princeton (27569) *(G-9823)*

Carolina Products Inc.. 704 364-9029
1132 Pro Am Dr Charlotte (28211) *(G-1854)*

Carolina Prtg Wilmington Inc............................... 910 762-2453
2790 Sea Vista Dr Sw Supply (28462) *(G-11856)*

Carolina Pumps Instrumentation, Winston Salem *Also Called: Hoh Corporation (G-13199)*

Carolina Pwr Signalization LLC............................ 910 323-5589
1416 Middle River Loop Fayetteville (28312) *(G-4570)*

Carolina Quarries Inc (PA)................................... 704 633-0201
805 Harris Granite Rd Salisbury (28146) *(G-11028)*

Carolina Ready Mix & Build (PA)........................... 828 686-3041
606 Old Us 70 Hwy Swannanoa (28778) *(G-11868)*

Carolina Ready-Mix LLC...................................... 704 225-1112
1901 Valley Pkwy Ste 100 Monroe (28110) *(G-8454)*

Carolina Resource Corp....................................... 919 562-0200
850 Park Ave Youngsville (27596) *(G-13470)*

Carolina Retread LLC.. 910 642-4123
30 Bitmore Rd Whiteville (28472) *(G-12578)*

Carolina Rubber & Spc Inc................................... 336 744-5111
4301 Idlewild Industrial Dr Winston Salem (27105) *(G-13118)*

Carolina Screw Products...................................... 336 760-7400
Winston Salem (27113) *(G-13119)*

Carolina Sgns Grphic Dsgns Inc............................ 919 383-3344
3535 Hillsborough Rd Durham (27705) *(G-3962)*

Carolina Sign Co Inc... 704 399-3995
2925 Beatties Ford Rd Charlotte (28216) *(G-1855)*

Carolina Sign Svc.. 919 247-0927
174 Kinnis Creek Dr Angier (27501) *(G-116)*

Carolina Signals and Lightings, Fayetteville *Also Called: Carolina Pwr Signalization LLC (G-4570)*

Carolina Signs & Lighting Inc............................... 336 399-1400
928 Spainhour Rd King (27021) *(G-7323)*

Carolina Signs and Graphics,, Durham *Also Called: Carolina Sgns Grphic Dsgns Inc (G-3962)*

Carolina Signs and Wonders Inc........................... 704 286-1343
1700 University Commercial Pl Charlotte (28213) *(G-1856)*

Carolina Siteworks Inc.. 704 855-7483
300 Wade Dr China Grove (28023) *(G-3072)*

Carolina Solar Structures Inc................................ 828 684-9900
1007 Tunnel Rd Asheville (28805) *(G-471)*

Carolina Solvents Inc.. 828 322-1920
2274 1st St Se Hickory (28602) *(G-6287)*

Carolina Specialties Inc....................................... 704 525-9599
4230 Barringer Dr Charlotte (28217) *(G-1857)*

Carolina Spral Duct Fbrction L............................. 704 395-3289
11524 Wilmar Blvd Charlotte (28273) *(G-1858)*

Carolina Sputter Solutions, Raleigh *Also Called: Kyma Technologies Inc (G-10242)*

Carolina Square Inc... 336 793-3222
1164 Cherry Hill Rd Mocksville (27028) *(G-8356)*

Carolina Stairs Inc... 704 664-5032
255 Belk Rd Mount Ulla (28125) *(G-9267)*

Carolina Stake and WD Pdts Inc............................ 704 545-7774
11223 Blair Rd Ste 4 Mint Hill (28227) *(G-8335)*

Carolina Stalite Co Ltd Partnr.............................. 704 279-2166
16815 Old Beatty Ford Rd Gold Hill (28071) *(G-5190)*

Carolina Stalite Co Ltd Partnr.............................. 704 279-2166
17700 Old Beatty Ford Rd Gold Hill (28071) *(G-5191)*

Carolina Stalite Co Ltd Partnr.............................. 704 474-3165
12423 Old Aquadale Rd Norwood (28128) *(G-9554)*

Carolina Stalite Co Ltd Partnr (PA)....................... 704 637-1515
205 Klumac Rd Salisbury (28144) *(G-11029)*

Carolina Stamping Company................................ 704 637-0260
701 Corporate Cir Salisbury (28147) *(G-11030)*

Carolina Stone LLC.. 252 208-1633
10600 Nc Highway 55 W Dover (28526) *(G-3828)*

Carolina Strapping Buckles Co, Gastonia *Also Called: Burlan Manufacturing LLC (G-5007)*

Carolina Sunrock, Durham *Also Called: Buffalo Crushed Stone Inc (G-3948)*

Carolina Sunrock LLC (HQ).................................. 919 575-4502
1001 W B St Butner (27509) *(G-1200)*

Carolina Sunrock LLC... 919 201-4201
3092 Rock Spring Church Rd Creedmoor (27522) *(G-3644)*

Carolina Sunrock LLC... 252 433-4617
214 Sunrock Rd Kittrell (27544) *(G-7440)*

Carolina Sunrock LLC... 919 861-1860
8620 Barefoot Industrial Rd Raleigh (27617) *(G-9979)*

Carolina Sunrock LLC... 919 554-0500
5043 Unicon Dr Wake Forest (27587) *(G-12267)*

Carolina Surfaces LLC.. 910 874-1335
242 Woodlief Dr Elizabethtown (28337) *(G-4423)*

Carolina Swatching Inc.. 828 327-9499
725 14th Street Dr Sw Hickory (28602) *(G-6288)*

Carolina Tailors Inc (PA)..................................... 252 247-6469
2896 Highway 24 Ste D Newport (28570) *(G-9439)*

Carolina Tape & Supply Corp............................... 828 322-3991
502 19th Street Pl Se Hickory (28602) *(G-6289)*

Carolina Tex Sls Gastonia Inc............................... 704 739-1646
521 N Sims St Kings Mountain (28086) *(G-7357)*

Carolina Textile Services Inc (PA)......................... 910 843-3033
Off Hwy 211 Red Springs (28377) *(G-10665)*

Carolina Textile Sls Gastonia, Kings Mountain *Also Called: Carolina Tex Sls Gastonia Inc (G-7357)*

Carolina Timberworks LLC................................... 828 266-9663
210 Industrial Park Way West Jefferson (28694) *(G-12561)*

Carolina Time, Charlotte *Also Called: Carolina Time Equipment Co Inc (G-1859)*

Carolina Time Equipment Co Inc (PA).................... 704 536-2700
1801 Norland Rd Charlotte (28205) *(G-1859)*

Carolina Traffic Devices Inc................................. 704 588-7055
11900 Goodrich Dr Charlotte (28278) *(G-1860)*

Carolina Turkeys, Mount Olive *Also Called: Butterball LLC (G-9250)*

Carolina Underwear Company (PA)........................ 336 472-7788
110 W Guilford St Thomasville (27360) *(G-12006)*

Carolina Vinyl Printing.. 910 603-3036
14 Troon Dr Pinehurst (28374) *(G-9689)*

Carolina Vinyl Products, Grifton *Also Called: Englishs All Wood Homes Inc (G-6036)*

Carolina Warp Prints Inc...................................... 704 866-4763
221 Meek Rd Gastonia (28056) *(G-5014)*

Carolina WD Pdts Mrshville Inc............................. 704 624-2119
1112 Doctor Blair Rd Marshville (28103) *(G-8086)*

Carolina Welding & Cnstr..................................... 252 814-8740
1806 N Herritage St Kinston (28501) *(G-7400)*

Carolina Windows and Doors Inc........................... 252 756-2585
3203 S Memorial Dr Greenville (27834) *(G-5951)*

Carolina Woodworks Trim of NC............................ 252 492-9259
625 Parham Rd Henderson (27536) *(G-6150)*

Carolina Wren Press Inc.......................................919 560-2738
811 9th St Ste 130-127 Durham (27705) *(G-3963)*

Carolina Yachts, Beaufort *Also Called: Harding Enterprise Inc (G-730)*

Carolina Yarn Processors Inc..............................828 859-5891
250 Screvens Rd Tryon (28782) *(G-12172)*

Carolina Yogurt Inc...828 754-9685
208 Morganton Blvd Sw Lenoir (28645) *(G-7591)*

Carolina York LLC..704 237-0873
1235 East Blvd Ste E Pmb 248 Charlotte (28203) *(G-1861)*

Carolinian Pubg Group LLC..................................919 834-5558
1504 New Bern Ave Raleigh (27610) *(G-9980)*

Carolnas Top Shelf Cstm Cbnets...........................704 376-5844
519 Armour Dr Charlotte (28206) *(G-1862)*

Carolnas Top Shelf Cstm Cbnets, Charlotte *Also Called: Carolnas Top Shelf Cstm Cbnets (G-1862)*

Carolon Company..336 969-6001
601 Forum Pkwy Rural Hall (27045) *(G-10954)*

Caromed, Raleigh *Also Called: Bar Squared Inc (G-9931)*

Caromed International Inc.....................................919 878-0578
5605 Spring Ct Raleigh (27616) *(G-9981)*

Carotek, Matthews *Also Called: Carotek Inc (G-8103)*

Carotek Inc (HQ)...704 844-1100
700 Sam Newell Rd Matthews (28105) *(G-8103)*

Carpathian Woodworks Inc...................................919 669-7546
46 Albemarle Dr Clayton (27527) *(G-3136)*

Carpe, Durham *Also Called: Clutch Inc (G-3979)*

Carpenter Co..828 464-9470
2009 Keisler Dairy Rd Conover (28613) *(G-3501)*

Carpenter Co..828 322-6545
30 29th St Nw Hickory (28601) *(G-6290)*

Carpenter Co..336 861-5730
1021 E Springfield Rd Ste 101 High Point (27263) *(G-6560)*

Carpenter Co..336 789-9161
220 Woltz St Mount Airy (27030) *(G-9110)*

Carpenter Co..828 632-7061
Hwy 90 E Taylorsville (28681) *(G-11952)*

Carpenter Design, Rutherfordton *Also Called: Carpenter Design Inc (G-10980)*

Carpenter Design Inc...828 248-9070
330 Broyhill Rd Rutherfordton (28139) *(G-10980)*

Carpenter Dnnis Rprdctns-Frd-C, Concord *Also Called: Carpenter Industries Inc (G-3331)*

Carpenter Industries Inc.......................................704 786-8139
21 Carpenter Ct Nw Concord (28027) *(G-3331)*

Carpet One, Asheboro *Also Called: Interrs-Exteriors Asheboro Inc (G-367)*

Carpigiani Corporation America, High Point *Also Called: Ali Group North America Corp (G-6515)*

Carport Central Inc (PA).......................................336 673-6020
1372 Boggs Dr Mount Airy (27030) *(G-9111)*

Carports.com, Mount Airy *Also Called: Truesteel Structures LLC (G-9191)*

Carr Amplifiers Inc...919 545-0747
433 W Salisbury St Pittsboro (27312) *(G-9778)*

Carr Mill Supplies Inc...336 883-0135
1015 Manley St High Point (27260) *(G-6561)*

Carr Precast Concrete Inc....................................910 892-1151
7519 Plain View Hwy Dunn (28334) *(G-3849)*

Carriage House Furniture Co, Jacksonville *Also Called: World Art Gallery Incorporated (G-7160)*

Carrier Chiller Op, Charlotte *Also Called: Carrier Corporation (G-1863)*

Carrier Corporation...704 921-3800
9701 Old Statesville Rd Charlotte (28269) *(G-1863)*

Carrier Corporation...704 494-2600
200 Perimeter Park Dr Ste A Morrisville (27560) *(G-8948)*

Carriff Corporation Inc (PA)..................................704 888-3330
3500 Fieldstone Trce Midland (28107) *(G-8282)*

Carriff Engineered Fabrics, Midland *Also Called: Carriff Corporation Inc (G-8282)*

Carroll Co...919 779-1900
5771 Nc Highway 42 W Garner (27529) *(G-4920)*

Carroll Companies Inc (PA)...................................828 264-2521
1640 Old 421 S Boone (28607) *(G-904)*

Carroll Companies Inc...828 466-5489
1226 Fedex Dr Sw Conover (28613) *(G-3502)*

Carroll Leather, Conover *Also Called: Carroll Companies Inc (G-3502)*

Carroll Russell Mfg Inc..919 779-2273
2009 Carr Pur Dr Raleigh (27603) *(G-9982)*

Carroll Signs & Advertising...................................336 983-3415
151 Jefferson Church Rd Ste B King (27021) *(G-7324)*

Carroll-Baccari Inc (PA).......................................561 585-2227
110 Commercial Blvd Flat Rock (28731) *(G-4705)*

Carson Dellosa Education, Greensboro *Also Called: Carson-Dellosa Publishing LLC (G-5432)*

Carson Dellosa Education, Greensboro *Also Called: Carson-Dellosa Publishing LLC (G-5433)*

Carson Dellosa Publishing, Greensboro *Also Called: Unique Collating & Bindery Svc (G-5889)*

Carson-Dellosa Publishing LLC.............................336 632-0084
657 Brigham Rd Ste A Greensboro (27409) *(G-5432)*

Carson-Dellosa Publishing LLC (PA).......................336 632-0084
7027 Albert Pick Rd Ste 300 Greensboro (27409) *(G-5433)*

Carter, Thomasville *Also Called: Tomlinson of Orlando Inc (G-12080)*

Carter Furniture, Salisbury *Also Called: Contemporary Furnishings Corp (G-11037)*

Carter Millwork Inc...800 861-0734
117 Cedar Lane Dr Lexington (27292) *(G-7661)*

Carter Printing...919 373-0531
1105 Great Falls Ct Ste A Knightdale (27545) *(G-7450)*

Carter Printing & Graphics Inc..............................919 266-5280
1001 Steeple Square Ct Knightdale (27545) *(G-7451)*

Carter Publishing Company Inc.............................336 993-2161
300 E Mountain St Kernersville (27284) *(G-7253)*

Carter Traveler Division, Gastonia *Also Called: A B Carter Inc (G-4982)*

Carteret Publishing Company (PA)..........................252 726-7081
5039 Executive Dr Ste 300 Morehead City (28557) *(G-8823)*

Carteret Publishing Company.................................910 326-5066
774 W Corbett Ave Swansboro (28584) *(G-11883)*

Carters Machine Company Inc...............................704 784-3106
540 Lake Lynn Rd Concord (28025) *(G-3332)*

Carthage Gazette, West End *Also Called: Seven Lakes News Corporation (G-12559)*

Cartridge World..336 885-0989
2640 Willard Dairy Rd Ste 114 High Point (27265) *(G-6562)*

Carus LLC...704 822-1441
181 Woodlawn St Belmont (28012) *(G-741)*

Carver Machine Works Inc....................................252 975-3101
129 Christian Service Camp Rd Washington (27889) *(G-12378)*

Cary Audio Design LLC..919 355-0010
6301 Chapel Hill Rd Raleigh (27607) *(G-9983)*

Cary Keisler Inc...336 586-9333
1372 Tiki Ln Burlington (27215) *(G-1065)*

Cary Manufacturing Corporation............................704 527-4402
10815 John Price Rd Ste E Charlotte (28273) *(G-1864)*

Cary Printing..919 266-9005
1528 Crickett Rd Raleigh (27610) *(G-9984)*

Casablanca 4 LLC..910 702-4399
4805 Wrightsville Ave Wilmington (28403) *(G-12734)*

Cascadas Nye Corporation....................................919 834-8128
2109 Avent Ferry Rd Ste 103 Raleigh (27606) *(G-9985)*

Cascade Die Casting, High Point *Also Called: Cascade Die Casting Group Inc (G-6564)*

Cascade Die Casting Group Inc.............................336 882-0186
501 Old Thomasville Rd High Point (27260) *(G-6563)*

Cascade Die Casting Group Inc.............................336 882-0186
1800 Albertson Rd High Point (27260) *(G-6564)*

Cascade Windows, Cary *Also Called: Mw Manufacturers Inc (G-1404)*

Cascades Moulded Pulp Inc..................................910 997-2775
112 Cascades Way Rockingham (28379) *(G-10771)*

Cascades Tissue Group, Rockingham *Also Called: Cascades Tissue Group - NC Inc (G-10772)*

Cascades Tissue Group - NC Inc............................910 895-4033
805 Midway Rd Rockingham (28379) *(G-10772)*

Cascades Tissue Group-Oregon, Wagram *Also Called: Cascades Tssue Group - Ore Inc (G-12254)*

Cascades Tssue Group - Ore Inc............................503 397-2900
19320 Airbase Rd Wagram (28396) *(G-12254)*

Casco Signs Inc...704 788-9055
199 Wilshire Ave Sw Concord (28025) *(G-3333)*

(G-0000) Company's Geographic Section entry number

Case Basket Creations.. 828 381-4908
4975 J M Craig Rd Granite Falls (28630) *(G-5299)*

Case Farms, Goldsboro *Also Called: Case Foods Inc (G-5205)*

Case Farms LLC... 919 735-5010
330 Pecan Rd Dudley (28333) *(G-3835)*

Case Farms LLC... 919 658-2252
330 Westbrook Rd Goldsboro (27530) *(G-5204)*

Case Farms LLC... 919 635-2390
188 Broadhurst Rd Mount Olive (28365) *(G-9252)*

Case Farms LLC (PA).. 704 528-4501
385 Pilch Rd Troutman (28166) *(G-12133)*

Case Farms Chicken, Troutman *Also Called: Case Foods Inc (G-12135)*

Case Farms Processing Inc (HQ)................................... 704 528-4501
385 Pilch Rd Troutman (28166) *(G-12134)*

Case Foods, Troutman *Also Called: Case Farms LLC (G-12133)*

Case Foods Inc.. 919 736-4498
259 Sandhill Dr Goldsboro (27530) *(G-5205)*

Case Foods Inc (PA)... 704 528-4501
385 Pilch Rd Troutman (28166) *(G-12135)*

Case Smith Inc.. 336 969-9786
625 Montroyal Rd Rural Hall (27045) *(G-10955)*

Case Specialists.. 919 818-4476
2033 Longwood Dr Raleigh (27612) *(G-9986)*

Case-Closed Investigations... 336 794-2274
5032 Hwy 70 W Morehead City (28557) *(G-8824)*

Caseiro International LLC.. 919 530-8333
105 Hood St Ste 7 Durham (27701) *(G-3964)*

Casetec, Mooresville *Also Called: Casetec Precision Machine LLC (G-8634)*

Casetec Precision Machine LLC..................................... 704 663-6043
178 Attleboro Pl Mooresville (28117) *(G-8634)*

Casework Etc Inc... 910 763-7119
3116 Kitty Hawk Rd Wilmington (28405) *(G-12735)*

Caseworx, Hudson *Also Called: Caldwell Cabinets NC LLC (G-6945)*

Cashiers Crossroads Chronicles, Cashiers *Also Called: Community Newspapers Inc (G-1490)*

Cashiers Printing Inc... 828 787-1324
68 Highlands Walk Highlands (28741) *(G-6844)*

Cashiers Printing & Graphics, Highlands *Also Called: Cashiers Printing Inc (G-6844)*

Cashman Inc... 252 995-4319
53392 Hwy 12 Frisco (27936) *(G-4863)*

Cast First Stone Ministry.. 704 437-1053
106 Justin Dr Troutman (28166) *(G-12136)*

Cast Iron Division, Charlotte *Also Called: Charlotte Pipe and Foundry Co (G-1901)*

Cast Iron Elegance Inc... 919 662-8777
831 Purser Dr Ste 103 Raleigh (27603) *(G-9987)*

Cast Stone Systems Inc... 252 257-1599
532 N Main St Warrenton (27589) *(G-12351)*

Caster House, Greensboro *Also Called: Carolina Material Handling Inc (G-5430)*

Castle Hayne Hardware LLC... 910 675-9205
6301 Castle Hayne Rd Castle Hayne (28429) *(G-1497)*

Castle Hayne Yard, Castle Hayne *Also Called: Martin Marietta Materials Inc (G-1506)*

Castle Shirt Company LLC.. 336 992-7727
621 Indeneer Dr Ste 1 Kernersville (27284) *(G-7254)*

Casual Crates, Seagrove *Also Called: H & H Furniture Mfrs Inc (G-11274)*

CAT Logistics Inc... 252 447-2490
7970 Hwy 70 E New Bern (28560) *(G-9351)*

Catalent Biologics, Morrisville *Also Called: Catalent Pharma Solutions LLC (G-8950)*

Catalent Greenville Inc.. 252 752-3800
1240 Sugg Pkwy Greenville (27834) *(G-5952)*

Catalent Pharma Solutions LLC.................................... 919 481-4855
140 Southcenter Ct Morrisville (27560) *(G-8949)*

Catalent Pharma Solutions LLC.................................... 919 465-8101
120 Southcenter Ct Ste 900 Morrisville (27560) *(G-8950)*

Catalent Pharma Solutions Inc..................................... 919 465-8206
160 N Pharma Dr Durham (27703) *(G-3965)*

Catalent Pharma Solutions Inc..................................... 919 481-2614
120 Southcenter Ct Ste 100 Morrisville (27560) *(G-8951)*

Catalent Pharma Solutions LLC.................................... 919 481-4855
160s N Pharma Dr Morrisville (27560) *(G-8952)*

Cataler North America Corp (DH)................................... 828 970-0026
2002 Cataler Dr Lincolnton (28092) *(G-7819)*

Catamount Energy Corporation (DH)............................. 802 773-6684
550 S Tryon St Charlotte (28202) *(G-1865)*

Catawba Farms Enterprises LLC................................... 828 464-5780
1670 Southwest Blvd Newton (28658) *(G-9452)*

Catawba Frames Inc.. 828 459-7717
4827 S Depot St Claremont (28610) *(G-3091)*

Catawba Plant, Claremont *Also Called: Universal Furniture Intl Inc (G-3123)*

Catawba Valley Fabrication Inc..................................... 828 459-1191
1823 Brian Dr Ne Conover (28613) *(G-3503)*

Catawba Valley Finishing LLC (PA)................................ 828 464-2252
1609 Northwest Blvd Newton (28658) *(G-9453)*

Catawba Valley Mills, Newton *Also Called: Ashfar Enterprises Inc (G-9449)*

Catawba Vly Youth Soccer Assoc.................................. 828 234-7082
3404 6th Street Dr Nw Hickory (28601) *(G-6291)*

Caterpillar, Clayton *Also Called: Caterpillar Inc (G-3137)*

Caterpillar, New Bern *Also Called: CAT Logistics Inc (G-9351)*

Caterpillar, Sanford *Also Called: Caterpillar Inc (G-11160)*

Caterpillar Authorized Dealer, Charlotte *Also Called: Arrow Equipment LLC (G-1698)*

Caterpillar Inc... 919 550-1100
954 Nc Highway 42 E Clayton (27527) *(G-3137)*

Caterpillar Inc... 919 777-2000
5000 Womack Rd Sanford (27330) *(G-11160)*

Cates Mechanical Corporation...................................... 704 458-5163
3901 Corporation Cir Charlotte (28216) *(G-1866)*

Cathedral Publishing, Charlotte *Also Called: Catholic News and Herald (G-1867)*

Catholic News and Herald.. 704 370-3333
1123 S Church St Charlotte (28203) *(G-1867)*

Cathtek LLC.. 336 748-0686
3825 Reidsville Rd Winston Salem (27101) *(G-13120)*

Cauley Construction Company...................................... 252 522-1078
2385 Westdowns Ter Kinston (28504) *(G-7401)*

Causa LLC.. 866 695-7022
9303 Monroe Rd Charlotte (28270) *(G-1868)*

Causekeepers Inc.. 336 824-2518
5068 Us Highway 64 E Franklinville (27248) *(G-4855)*

Cava Di Pietra Inc... 910 338-5024
1502 N 23rd St Wilmington (28405) *(G-12736)*

Cavalier Home Builders LLC... 252 459-7026
1001 Eastern Ave Nashville (27856) *(G-9316)*

Cavco Industries Inc.. 910 410-5050
106 Innovative Way Hamlet (28345) *(G-6052)*

Cavco of North Carolina, Hamlet *Also Called: Cavco Industries Inc (G-6052)*

Cavert Red Line Wire Division, Rural Hall *Also Called: Cavert Wire Company Inc (G-10956)*

Cavert Wire Company Inc (HQ)...................................... 800 969-2601
620 Forum Pkwy Rural Hall (27045) *(G-10956)*

Cavotec USA Inc (DH).. 704 873-3009
500 S Main St # 1 Mooresville (28115) *(G-8635)*

Cavu Printing Inc... 336 818-9790
339 Benham Church Rd Elkin (28621) *(G-4441)*

CBA Productions Inc.. 703 568-4758
579 Baywood Rd Fayetteville (28312) *(G-4571)*

Cbdmd, Charlotte *Also Called: Cbdmd Inc (G-1869)*

Cbdmd Inc (PA)... 704 445-3060
2101 Westinghouse Blvd Ste A Charlotte (28273) *(G-1869)*

Cbg Acquisition Company.. 336 768-8872
3916 Westpoint Blvd Winston Salem (27103) *(G-13121)*

Cbj Transit LLC... 252 417-9972
1220 Timber Dr E Garner (27529) *(G-4921)*

Cbm, Bessemer City *Also Called: Conner Brothers Machine Co Inc (G-809)*

Cbr Signs LLC... 910 794-8243
5649 Carolina Beach Rd Wilmington (28412) *(G-12737)*

CBS Radio Holdings Inc... 704 319-9369
1520 South Blvd Ste 300 Charlotte (28203) *(G-1870)*

CBS Windows & Doors, Mooresville *Also Called: Carolina Building Services Inc (G-8631)*

Cbt Supply.. 803 617-8230
109 Farmers Folly Dr Mooresville (28117) *(G-8636)*

CC, Durham *Also Called: Collegiate Clors Christn Colors (G-3982)*

CC Boats Inc... 252 482-3699
140 Midway Dr Edenton (27932) *(G-4363)*

Ccbcc Inc... 704 557-4000
4115 Coca Cola Plz Charlotte (28211) *(G-1871)*

Ccbcc Operations LLC...704 557-4038
　4115 Coca Cola Plz Charlotte (28211) *(G-1872)*

Ccbcc Operations LLC...252 752-2446
　1051 Staton Rd Greenville (27834) *(G-5953)*

Ccbcc Operations LLC...252 536-3611
　80 Industrial Dr Halifax (27839) *(G-6046)*

Ccbcc Operations LLC...910 582-3543
　1662 E Us 74 Hwy Hamlet (28345) *(G-6053)*

Ccbcc Operations LLC...252 637-3157
　3710 Dr M L King Jr Blvd New Bern (28562) *(G-9352)*

Ccbcc Operations LLC...252 671-4515
　3710 Dr M L King Jr Blvd New Bern (28562) *(G-9353)*

Ccbcc Operations LLC...704 872-3634
　2111 W Front St Statesville (28677) *(G-11676)*

Ccbcc Operations LLC...910 642-3002
　239 Industrial Blvd Whiteville (28472) *(G-12579)*

Ccbcc Operations LLC...828 687-1300
　36 Clayton Rd Arden (28704) *(G-260)*

Ccbcc Operations LLC...828 297-2141
　795 Nc Highway 105 Byp Boone (28607) *(G-905)*

Ccbcc Operations LLC...828 488-2874
　441 Industrial Park Rd Bryson City (28713) *(G-1009)*

Ccbcc Operations LLC...704 359-5600
　4690 First Flight Dr Charlotte (28208) *(G-1873)*

Ccbcc Operations LLC (HQ)...704 364-8728
　4100 Coca Cola Plz Charlotte (28211) *(G-1874)*

Ccbcc Operations LLC...704 399-6043
　801 Black Satchel Rd Charlotte (28216) *(G-1875)*

Ccbcc Operations LLC...980 321-3226
　920 Black Satchel Rd Charlotte (28216) *(G-1876)*

Ccbcc Operations LLC...919 359-2966
　977 Shotwell Rd Ste 104 Clayton (27520) *(G-3138)*

Ccbcc Operations LLC...910 483-6158
　800 Tom Starling Rd Fayetteville (28306) *(G-4572)*

Ccbcc Operations LLC...336 664-1116
　8200 Capital Dr 067 Greensboro (27409) *(G-5434)*

Ccbcc Operations LLC...828 322-5097
　820 1st Ave Nw Hickory (28601) *(G-6292)*

Ccbcc Operations LLC...704 225-1973
　4268 Capital Dr Monroe (28110) *(G-8455)*

Ccbcc Operations LLC...336 789-7111
　2516 W Pine St Mount Airy (27030) *(G-9112)*

Ccbs & Sign Shop Inc...252 728-4866
　1626 Live Oak St Beaufort (28516) *(G-722)*

CCI Hair Boutique LLC..407 216-9213
　3059 N Main St Hope Mills (28348) *(G-6925)*

CCL Label...919 713-0388
　308 S Rogers Ln Raleigh (27610) *(G-9988)*

CCL Label Inc..704 714-4800
　4000 Westinghouse Blvd Charlotte (28273) *(G-1877)*

CCL Label Inc..919 713-0388
　7924 Purfoy Rd Fuquay Varina (27526) *(G-4872)*

CCL Metal Science LLC...910 299-0911
　520 E Railroad St Clinton (28328) *(G-3229)*

Cco Holdings LLC...828 414-4238
　278 Shoppes On The Parkway Rd Blowing Rock (28605) *(G-881)*

Cco Holdings LLC...828 355-4149
　531 W King St Boone (28607) *(G-906)*

Cco Holdings LLC...910 292-4083
　102 W Divine St Dunn (28334) *(G-3850)*

Cco Holdings LLC...828 270-7016
　483 Us Highway 70 Sw Hickory (28602) *(G-6293)*

Cco Holdings LLC...919 502-4007
　607 W 2nd St Kenly (27542) *(G-7228)*

Cco Holdings LLC...828 394-0635
　1048 Harper Ave Nw Lenoir (28645) *(G-7592)*

Cco Holdings LLC...704 308-3361
　644 Center Dr Lincolnton (28092) *(G-7820)*

Cco Holdings LLC...828 528-4004
　520 Pineola St Newland (28657) *(G-9427)*

Cco Holdings LLC...919 200-6260
　466 Vineyard Rdg Siler City (27344) *(G-11402)*

Cco Holdings LLC...828 368-4161
　240 Main St W Valdese (28690) *(G-12192)*

Ccw, Concord *Also Called: Client Care Web Inc (G-3336)*

CD Dickie & Associates Inc..704 527-9102
　3400 S Tryon St Ste D Charlotte (28217) *(G-1878)*

CD Snow Hill LLC...252 747-5943
　204 Carolina Dr Snow Hill (28580) *(G-11478)*

Cda Inc...
　8500 S Tryon St Charlotte (28273) *(G-1879)*

Cdata Software Inc (PA)..919 928-5214
　101 Europa Dr Ste 110 Chapel Hill (27517) *(G-1535)*

Cdb Corporation..910 383-6464
　2304 Mercantile Dr Ne Leland (28451) *(G-7537)*

CDM Wireless, Louisburg *Also Called: Carolina Design & Mfg Inc (G-7911)*

Cdp, Charlotte *Also Called: Consultants In Data Proc Inc (G-1976)*

Cdp Inc..336 270-6151
　4014 Forbes Way Burlington (27215) *(G-1066)*

Cdv LLC (PA)..919 674-3460
　2300 Gateway Centre Blvd Ste 200 Morrisville (27560) *(G-8953)*

Ce Kitchen Inc...910 399-2334
　417 Raleigh St Wilmington (28412) *(G-12738)*

Ce Kitchen Inc (PA)...910 399-2334
　306 Old Dairy Rd Wilmington (28405) *(G-12739)*

Ceast USA Inc...704 423-0081
　4816 Sirus Ln Charlotte (28208) *(G-1880)*

Cecil Budd Tire Company LLC..919 742-2322
　394 Pine Forest Dr Siler City (27344) *(G-11403)*

Cecil-Johnson Mfg Inc...336 431-5233
　1445 Jackson Lake Rd High Point (27263) *(G-6565)*

Ceco Building Systems, Cary *Also Called: Robertson-Ceco II Corporation (G-1439)*

Ceco Friction Products Inc..704 857-1156
　2525 N Hwy 29 Landis (28088) *(G-7473)*

Ceco Publishing, Asheville *Also Called: Ceco Publishing Inc (G-472)*

Ceco Publishing Inc (PA)..828 253-2047
　208 Elk Park Dr Asheville (28804) *(G-472)*

Ced, Morganton *Also Called: Consolidated Elec Distrs Inc (G-8858)*

Ced Incorporated...336 378-0044
　7910 Industrial Village Rd Greensboro (27409) *(G-5435)*

Cedar Creek Pot & Cft Gallery, Creedmoor *Also Called: Ceder Creek Gallery & Pottery (G-3645)*

Cedar Hill Studio & Gallery...828 456-6344
　196 N Main St Waynesville (28786) *(G-12453)*

Cedar Rock Home Furnishings..828 396-2361
　3483 Hickory Blvd Hudson (28638) *(G-6948)*

Cedar Valley Finishing Co Inc..704 289-9546
　603 Broome St Monroe (28110) *(G-8456)*

Cedar Valley Hosiery Mill Inc...828 396-1804
　3074 Deal Mill Rd Hudson (28638) *(G-6949)*

Cedarlane, Burlington *Also Called: Cedarlane Laboratories USA (G-1067)*

Cedarlane Laboratories USA..336 513-5135
　1210 Turrentine St Burlington (27215) *(G-1067)*

Ceder Creek Gallery & Pottery..919 528-1041
　1150 Fleming Rd Creedmoor (27522) *(G-3645)*

CEF, Taylorsville *Also Called: Custom Educational Furn LLC (G-11956)*

Cefla Dental Group America...704 731-5293
　6125 Harris Technology Blvd Charlotte (28269) *(G-1881)*

Cefla North America Inc...704 598-0020
　6125 Harris Technology Blvd Charlotte (28269) *(G-1882)*

Cekal Specialties Inc..704 822-6206
　101 Brickyard Rd Mount Holly (28120) *(G-9222)*

Celand Yarn Dyers Inc...336 472-4400
　606 Davidson St Thomasville (27360) *(G-12007)*

Celanese...910 343-5000
　4600 Us Highway 421 N Wilmington (28401) *(G-12740)*

Celanese, Grover *Also Called: Celanese Intl Corp (G-6042)*

Celanese Intl Corp...704 480-5798
　2523 Blacksburg Rd Grover (28073) *(G-6042)*

Celcore Inc..828 669-4875
　3148 Us Highway 70 W Black Mountain (28711) *(G-863)*

Celebrity Dairy LLC..919 742-4931
　198 Celebrity Dairy Way Siler City (27344) *(G-11404)*

Celeros Flow Technology LLC (PA)................... 704 752-3100
   14045 Ballantyne Corporate Pl Ste 300 Charlotte (28277) *(G-1883)*

Celesta's, Asheville *Also Called: Monogram Asheville (G-549)*

Celestial Products Inc................................... 540 338-4040
   9632 Skybluff Cir Huntersville (28078) *(G-6975)*

Celgard LLC.. 704 588-5310
   13800 S Lakes Dr Charlotte (28273) *(G-1884)*

Celgard LLC (HQ).. 800 235-4273
   11430 N Community House Rd Ste 350 Charlotte (28277) *(G-1885)*

Cell Microsystems Inc.................................. 919 608-2035
   801 Capitola Dr Ste 10 Durham (27713) *(G-3966)*

Celplor LLC... 919 961-1961
   115 Centrewest Ct Ste B Cary (27513) *(G-1324)*

Celtic Ceramics... 919 510-6817
   4140 Mardella Dr Raleigh (27613) *(G-9989)*

Celtic Ocean International Inc........................ 828 299-9005
   4 Celtic Dr Arden (28704) *(G-261)*

Cem Corporation (HQ)................................. 704 821-7015
   3100 Smith Farm Rd Matthews (28104) *(G-8162)*

Cem Holdings Corporation (PA)..................... 704 821-7015
   3100 Smith Farm Rd Matthews (28104) *(G-8163)*

Cem-102 Pharmaceuticals Inc....................... 919 576-2306
   6320 Quadrangle Dr Ste 360 Chapel Hill (27517) *(G-1536)*

Cemco, Lincolnton *Also Called: Umi Company Inc (G-7867)*

Cemco Electric Inc....................................... 704 504-0294
   10913 Office Park Dr Charlotte (28273) *(G-1886)*

Cemco Partitions Inc.................................... 336 643-6316
   5340 Us Highway 220 N Summerfield (27358) *(G-11836)*

Cemco Systems, Charlotte *Also Called: Cemco Electric Inc (G-1886)*

Cemex, Harrisburg *Also Called: Cemex Materials LLC (G-6106)*

Cemex Cnstr Mtls ATL LLC............................ 704 873-3263
   2067 Salisbury Hwy Statesville (28677) *(G-11677)*

Cemex Materials LLC.................................... 704 455-1100
   5601 Pharr Mill Rd Harrisburg (28075) *(G-6106)*

Cemex Materials LLC.................................... 800 627-2986
   208 Randolph St Thomasville (27360) *(G-12008)*

Cemex Materials LLC.................................... 252 243-6153
   1600 Thorne Ave S Wilson (27893) *(G-12979)*

Cempra Pharmaceuticals Inc......................... 919 803-6882
   6320 Quadrangle Dr Ste 360 Chapel Hill (27517) *(G-1537)*

Cenerx Biopharma Inc.................................. 919 234-4072
   270 Cornerstone Dr Ste 103 Cary (27519) *(G-1325)*

Cengage Learning Inc................................... 919 829-8181
   1791 Varsity Dr Ste 200 Raleigh (27606) *(G-9990)*

Center for Creative Leadership (PA)............... 336 288-7210
   1 Leadership Pl Greensboro (27410) *(G-5436)*

Center For Orthotic & Prosthet...................... 919 585-4173
   166 Springbrook Ave Ste 203 Clayton (27520) *(G-3139)*

Center For Orthtic Prsthtic CA (HQ)............... 919 797-1230
   4702 Creekstone Dr Durham (27703) *(G-3967)*

Center For Orthtic Prsthtic Ca, Durham *Also Called: Center For Orthtic Prsthtic CA (G-3967)*

Centeredge Software................................... 336 598-5934
   5050 Durham Rd Roxboro (27574) *(G-10922)*

Centice Corporation..................................... 919 653-0424
   7283 Nc Highway 42 Ste 102 Raleigh (27603) *(G-9991)*

Centos Project, Raleigh *Also Called: Red Hat Inc (G-10436)*

Central Carolina Btlg Co Inc.......................... 919 542-3226
   1506 Mays Chapel Rd Bear Creek (27207) *(G-713)*

Central Carolina Concrete LLC (HQ)............... 704 372-2930
   296 Edwardia Dr Greensboro (27409) *(G-5437)*

Central Carolina Hosiery Inc (PA).................. 910 428-9688
   211 Shady Oak Dr Biscoe (27209) *(G-849)*

Central Carolina Printing LLC........................ 910 572-3344
   464 Cheshire Pl Asheboro (27205) *(G-336)*

Central Carolina Products Inc........................ 336 226-1449
   2804 Troxler Rd Burlington (27215) *(G-1068)*

Central Carolina Products Inc (PA)................. 336 226-0005
   250 W Old Glencoe Rd Burlington (27217) *(G-1069)*

Central Carolina Steel, Stanley *Also Called: Metal Roofing Systems LLC (G-11622)*

Central Concrete, Asheboro *Also Called: Chandler Concrete Inc (G-337)*

Central East Services Inc.............................. 252 883-9629
   4352 N Old Carriage Rd Rocky Mount (27804) *(G-10827)*

Central Machine Company............................. 336 855-0022
   2509 Surrett Dr Archdale (27263) *(G-216)*

Central Site Group LLC................................. 336 380-4121
   15 Scotland St Ocean Isle Beach (28469) *(G-9587)*

Central States Mfg Inc.................................. 336 719-3280
   751 Piedmont Triad West Dr Mount Airy (27030) *(G-9113)*

Central Steel Buildings Inc............................ 336 789-7896
   181 Woltz St Mount Airy (27030) *(G-9114)*

Central Tool & Mfg Co Inc............................. 828 328-2383
   1021 17th St Sw Hickory (28602) *(G-6294)*

Centre Ingredient Tech Inc............................ 910 895-9277
   101 Commerce Pl Rockingham (28379) *(G-10773)*

Centria Inc... 704 341-0202
   10801 Johnston Rd Ste 226 Charlotte (28226) *(G-1887)*

Centric Brands LLC...................................... 646 582-6000
   620 S Elm St Ste 395 Greensboro (27406) *(G-5438)*

Centro Inc.. 319 626-3200
   2725 Kelly Blvd Claremont (28610) *(G-3092)*

Centrotherm Usa Inc.................................... 360 626-4445
   3333 Durham Chapel Hill Blvd Ste D200 Durham (27707) *(G-3968)*

Centrtherm Phtvoltaics USA Inc, Durham *Also Called: Centrotherm Usa Inc (G-3968)*

Centurion Industries Inc................................ 704 867-2304
   1990 Industrial Pike Rd Gastonia (28052) *(G-5015)*

Century Case Goods Division, Hickory *Also Called: Century Furniture LLC (G-6296)*

Century Furniture LLC................................... 828 326-8410
   535 27th St Nw Hickory (28601) *(G-6295)*

Century Furniture LLC................................... 828 326-8201
   420 12th Street Dr Nw Hickory (28601) *(G-6296)*

Century Furniture LLC................................... 828 326-8535
   25 18th St Nw Hickory (28601) *(G-6297)*

Century Furniture LLC................................... 828 326-8458
   3086 Main Ave Nw Hickory (28601) *(G-6298)*

Century Furniture LLC................................... 828 326-8410
   420 27th St Nw Hickory (28601) *(G-6299)*

Century Furniture LLC................................... 828 326-8650
   820 21st St Nw Hickory (28601) *(G-6300)*

Century Furniture LLC................................... 828 326-8495
   126 33rd St Nw Hickory (28601) *(G-6301)*

Century Furniture LLC................................... 336 889-8286
   200 Steele St High Point (27260) *(G-6566)*

Century Furniture Industries, Hickory *Also Called: Cv Industries Inc (G-6316)*

Century Furniture LLC (HQ)........................... 828 267-8739
   401 11th St Nw Hickory (28601) *(G-6302)*

Century Furniture Uphl Plant, Hickory *Also Called: Century Furniture LLC (G-6295)*

Century Hosiery Inc (PA)............................... 336 859-3806
   651 Garner Rd Denton (27239) *(G-3742)*

Century Place Apparel, Charlotte *Also Called: Century Place II LLC (G-1888)*

Century Place II LLC..................................... 704 790-0970
   10220 Western Ridge Rd Ste A Charlotte (28273) *(G-1888)*

Century Stone LLC....................................... 919 774-3334
   624 Fairway Dr Sanford (27330) *(G-11161)*

Century Textile Mfg Inc................................. 704 869-6660
   803 N Oakland St Gastonia (28054) *(G-5016)*

Ceprint Solutions Inc.................................... 336 956-6327
   564 Dixon St Lexington (27292) *(G-7662)*

Ceramawire.. 252 335-7411
   786 Pitts Chapel Rd Elizabeth City (27909) *(G-4381)*

Ceramco Incorporated.................................. 704 588-4814
   11009 Carpet St Charlotte (28273) *(G-1889)*

Ceres Turf Inc... 910 256-8974
   2312 N 23rd St Wilmington (28401) *(G-12741)*

Certainteed LLC.. 828 459-0556
   2651 Penny Rd Claremont (28610) *(G-3093)*

Certainteed LLC.. 336 696-2007
   1149 Abtco Rd North Wilkesboro (28659) *(G-9524)*

Certainteed LLC.. 919 603-1971
   200 Certainteed Dr Oxford (27565) *(G-9607)*

Certification Services International LLC........... 828 458-1573
   510 La White Dr Bldg 12 Fletcher (28732) *(G-4728)*

Certified Lawnmower Inc............................... 704 527-2765
   124 Hubbard St Belmont (28012) *(G-742)*

Certified Machining Inc.................................... 919 777-9608
2710 Wilkins Dr Sanford (27330) *(G-11162)*

Ces, Mount Airy *Also Called: Advanced Electronic Svcs Inc (G-9096)*

Cessna Grnsboro Cttion Svc Ctr, Greensboro *Also Called: Textron Aviation Inc (G-5861)*

CF Steel LLC.. 704 516-1750
12322 Old Camden Rd Midland (28107) *(G-8283)*

CFI Ready Mix LLC... 910 814-4238
304 E Mcneill St Lillington (27546) *(G-7792)*

CFS Press Slim Ray.. 828 505-1030
8 Pelham Rd Asheville (28803) *(G-473)*

Cgc, Pineville *Also Called: Container Graphics Corp (G-9720)*

Cgmi Acquisition Company LLC........................ 919 533-6123
1318 Shields Rd Kernersville (27284) *(G-7255)*

CGR Products Inc (PA).................................... 336 621-4568
4655 Us Highway 29 N Greensboro (27405) *(G-5439)*

Chaddock, Morganton *Also Called: LLC Ferguson Copeland (G-8879)*

Chaddock Home, Morganton *Also Called: Guy Chaddock and Company LLC (G-8869)*

Chadsworth Incorporated................................ 910 763-7600
420 Raleigh St Ste A Wilmington (28412) *(G-12742)*

Challnge Prtg of Crlnas Inc Th........................ 919 777-2820
5905 Clyde Rhyne Dr Sanford (27330) *(G-11163)*

Chamblee Graphics, Raleigh *Also Called: S Chamblee Incorporated (G-10452)*

Champion, Charlotte *Also Called: Champion LLC (G-1890)*

Champion, Lillington *Also Called: Champion Home Builders Inc (G-7793)*

Champion Enterprises LLC.............................. 704 866-8148
1220 Industrial Ave Gastonia (28054) *(G-5017)*

Champion Home Builders Inc........................... 910 893-5713
4055 Us 401 S Lillington (27546) *(G-7793)*

Champion Industries, Winston Salem *Also Called: Ali Group North America Corp (G-13078)*

Champion Industries Inc.................................. 336 661-1556
3765 Champion Blvd Winston Salem (27105) *(G-13122)*

Champion LLC.. 704 392-1038
8844 Mount Holly Rd Charlotte (28214) *(G-1890)*

Champion Media LLC....................................... 910 506-3021
915 S Main St Ste H Laurinburg (28352) *(G-7496)*

Champion Media LLC (PA)................................ 704 746-3955
116 Morlake Dr Ste 203 Mooresville (28117) *(G-8637)*

Champion Powder Coating, Gastonia *Also Called: Champion Enterprises LLC (G-5017)*

Champion Products, Laurel Hill *Also Called: Hanesbrands Inc (G-7483)*

Champion Thread Company (PA)....................... 704 867-6611
165 Bluedevil Dr Gastonia (28056) *(G-5018)*

Champion Valves, Wilmington *Also Called: US Valve Corporation (G-12944)*

Champion Win Co of Charlotte......................... 704 398-0085
9100 Perimeter Woods Dr Ste C Charlotte (28216) *(G-1891)*

Champion Wndows Sding Ptio Rom, Charlotte *Also Called: Champion Win Co of Charlotte (G-1891)*

Championx LLC.. 704 506-4830
2000 Oaks Pkwy Belmont (28012) *(G-743)*

Chandler Con Pdts of Chrstnber...................... 336 226-1181
1006 S Church St Burlington (27215) *(G-1070)*

Chandler Concrete, Biscoe *Also Called: Chandler Concrete Co Inc (G-850)*

Chandler Concrete, Greensboro *Also Called: Chandler Concrete Inc (G-5440)*

Chandler Concrete & Bldg Sup, Salisbury *Also Called: Chandler Concrete Inc (G-11031)*

Chandler Concrete Co Inc................................ 910 974-4744
1517 Us Highway 220 Alt S Biscoe (27209) *(G-850)*

Chandler Concrete Co Inc (PA)........................ 336 272-6127
1006 S Church St Burlington (27215) *(G-1071)*

Chandler Concrete Co Inc................................ 336 635-0975
234 Main St Eden (27288) *(G-4343)*

Chandler Concrete Company, Pittsboro *Also Called: Chandler Concrete Inc (G-9779)*

Chandler Concrete High Co.............................. 828 264-8694
805 State Farm Rd Ste 203 Boone (28607) *(G-907)*

Chandler Concrete Inc..................................... 336 625-1070
205 W Academy St Asheboro (27203) *(G-337)*

Chandler Concrete Inc..................................... 336 982-8760
1992 Nc Highway 16 N Crumpler (28617) *(G-3660)*

Chandler Concrete Inc..................................... 919 598-1424
2700 E Pettigrew St Durham (27703) *(G-3969)*

Chandler Concrete Inc..................................... 336 342-5771
6354 Main St Eden (27288) *(G-4344)*

Chandler Concrete Inc..................................... 336 222-9716
301 W River St Graham (27253) *(G-5263)*

Chandler Concrete Inc..................................... 336 297-1179
300 S Swing Rd Greensboro (27409) *(G-5440)*

Chandler Concrete Inc..................................... 919 644-1058
1501 Old North Carolina Hwy 10 Hillsborough (27278) *(G-6863)*

Chandler Concrete Inc..................................... 919 542-4242
246 Chatham Forest Dr Pittsboro (27312) *(G-9779)*

Chandler Concrete Inc..................................... 336 599-8343
121 Burch Ave Roxboro (27573) *(G-10923)*

Chandler Concrete Inc..................................... 704 636-4711
400 N Long St Salisbury (28144) *(G-11031)*

Chandler Concrete Inc..................................... 336 372-4348
23 Birch Ln Sparta (28675) *(G-11536)*

CHANDLER CONCRETE INC, Eden *Also Called: Chandler Concrete Inc (G-4344)*

CHANDLER CONCRETE INC, Hillsborough *Also Called: Chandler Concrete Inc (G-6863)*

CHANDLER CONCRETE INC, Roxboro *Also Called: Chandler Concrete Inc (G-10923)*

CHANDLER CONCRETE INC, Sparta *Also Called: Chandler Concrete Inc (G-11536)*

Chandler Foods Inc... 336 299-1934
2727 Immanuel Rd Greensboro (27407) *(G-5441)*

Chanmala Gallery Fine Art Prtg........................ 704 975-7695
306 S White St Wake Forest (27587) *(G-12268)*

Channeltivity LLC.. 704 408-3560
301 E John St Matthews (28106) *(G-8104)*

Chapel Hill Magazine, Chapel Hill *Also Called: Shannon Media Inc (G-1570)*

Chapman Brothers Logging LLC....................... 828 437-6498
8849 Gus Peeler Rd Connelly Springs (28612) *(G-3474)*

Chapman Machine.. 704 739-1834
109 Joanne Dr Kings Mountain (28086) *(G-7358)*

Chapman Welding LLC..................................... 919 951-8131
4501 Gails Trl Efland (27243) *(G-4374)*

Charah LLC... 704 731-2300
4235 Southstream Blvd Ste 180 Charlotte (28217) *(G-1892)*

Charah LLC... 502 873-6993
175 Steam Plant Rd Mount Holly (28120) *(G-9223)*

Charge Onsite LLC.. 888 343-2688
1015 East Blvd Charlotte (28203) *(G-1893)*

Charles & Colvard, Morrisville *Also Called: Charles & Colvard Ltd (G-8954)*

Charles & Colvard Ltd (PA)............................. 919 468-0399
170 Southport Dr Morrisville (27560) *(G-8954)*

Charles & Colvard Direct LLC.......................... 919 468-0399
300 Perimeter Park Dr Ste A Morrisville (27560) *(G-8955)*

Charles Craft Inc (PA).................................... 910 844-3521
21381 Charles Craft Ln Laurinburg (28352) *(G-7497)*

Charles Ferguson Logging............................... 336 921-3126
245 Jack Russell Rd Moravian Falls (28654) *(G-8809)*

Charles Hill Enterprises.................................. 828 665-2116
145 Brooks Cove Rd Candler (28715) *(G-1220)*

Charlesandcolvardcom LLC............................. 877 202-5467
170 Southport Dr Morrisville (27560) *(G-8956)*

Charlie's Soap, Stoneville *Also Called: Sutherland Products Inc (G-11831)*

Charlies Heating & Cooling LLC....................... 336 260-1973
8277 Bethel South Fork Rd Snow Camp (27349) *(G-11473)*

Charlotte Branch, Charlotte *Also Called: Form Tech Concrete Forms Inc (G-2172)*

Charlotte Business Journal, Charlotte *Also Called: American City Bus Journals Inc (G-1665)*

Charlotte Instyle Inc...................................... 704 665-8880
801 Pressley Rd Ste 1071 Charlotte (28217) *(G-1894)*

Charlotte Magazine... 980 207-5124
214 W Tremont Ave Ste 303 Charlotte (28203) *(G-1895)*

Charlotte Metal Finishing Inc.......................... 704 732-7570
2708 E Main St Lincolnton (28092) *(G-7821)*

Charlotte Observer.. 704 358-5000
550 S Caldwell St Ste 1010 Charlotte (28202) *(G-1896)*

Charlotte Observer, Charlotte *Also Called: Charlotte Observer Pubg Co (G-1898)*

Charlotte Observer, Charlotte *Also Called: Charlotte Observer Pubg Co (G-1899)*

Charlotte Observer, Matthews *Also Called: Charlotte Observer Pubg Co (G-8105)*

Charlotte Observer Pubg Co............................ 704 987-3660
9140 Research Dr Ste C1 Charlotte (28262) *(G-1897)*

Charlotte Observer Pubg Co............................ 704 572-0747
724 Montana Dr Charlotte (28216) *(G-1898)*

Charlotte Observer Pubg Co (DH)............................704 358-5000
550 S Caldwell St Ste 1010 Charlotte (28202) *(G-1899)*

Charlotte Observer Pubg Co.................................704 358-6020
10810 Independence Pointe Pkwy Ste H Matthews (28105) *(G-8105)*

Charlotte Parent, Charlotte *Also Called: Carolina Parenting Inc (G-1853)*

Charlotte Pipe and Foundry Co (PA)....................800 438-6091
2109 Randolph Rd Charlotte (28207) *(G-1900)*

Charlotte Pipe and Foundry Co.............................704 348-5416
1335 S Clarkson St Charlotte (28208) *(G-1901)*

Charlotte Pipe and Foundry Co.............................704 372-3650
4210 Old Charlotte Hwy Monroe (28110) *(G-8457)*

Charlotte Pipe and Foundry Co.............................704 887-8015
10145 Lighthouse Rd Oakboro (28129) *(G-9575)*

Charlotte Pipe and Foundry Com...........................704 379-0700
2109 Randolph Rd Charlotte (28207) *(G-1902)*

Charlotte Plastics, Monroe *Also Called: Charlotte Pipe and Foundry Co (G-8457)*

Charlotte Plating Inc...704 552-2100
8421 Kirchenbaum Dr Charlotte (28210) *(G-1903)*

CHARLOTTE POST, Charlotte *Also Called: Charlotte Post Pubg Co Inc (G-1904)*

Charlotte Post Pubg Co Inc.................................704 376-0496
5118 Princess St Charlotte (28269) *(G-1904)*

Charlotte Printing Company Inc (PA)....................704 888-5181
3751 Dakeita Cir Concord (28025) *(G-3334)*

Charlotte Recycling Plant, Charlotte *Also Called: Caraustar Industries Inc (G-1838)*

Charlotte Shutter and Shades.............................336 351-3391
1825 Pell Rd Westfield (27053) *(G-12572)*

Charlotte T Shirt Authority, Charlotte *Also Called: Kna (G-2400)*

Charlotte Tent & Awning Co, Charlotte *Also Called: DLM Sales Inc (G-2058)*

Charlotte Trimming Company Inc (PA)..................704 529-8427
900 Pressley Rd Charlotte (28217) *(G-1905)*

Charlottes Crown, Matthews *Also Called: Jody Stowe (G-8119)*

Charltte McKInburg Dream Ctr I............................704 421-4440
129 W Trade St Charlotte (28202) *(G-1906)*

Charter Dura-Bar Inc...704 637-1906
770 Cedar Springs Rd Salisbury (28147) *(G-11032)*

Charter Furniture, Siler City *Also Called: Lodging By Liberty Inc (G-11417)*

Charter Jet Transport Inc.....................................704 359-8833
5400 Airport Dr Charlotte (28208) *(G-1907)*

Charter Medical LLC...336 768-6447
3948 Westpoint Blvd Ste A Winston Salem (27103) *(G-13123)*

Charter Medical, Ltd., Winston Salem *Also Called: Charter Medical LLC (G-13123)*

Chase Corporation..828 396-2121
3908 Hickory Blvd Granite Falls (28630) *(G-5300)*

Chase Corporation..828 855-9316
1954 Main Ave Se Hickory (28602) *(G-6303)*

Chase Corporation..828 726-6023
2012 Hickory Blvd Sw Lenoir (28645) *(G-7593)*

Chase Laminating Inc..828 632-6666
138 Wittenburg Rd Taylorsville (28681) *(G-11953)*

Chase-Logeman Corporation...............................336 665-0754
303 Friendship Dr Greensboro (27409) *(G-5442)*

Chateau DAx USA Ltd...336 885-9777
1838 Eastchester Dr Ste 106 High Point (27265) *(G-6567)*

Chateau Jourdain LLC...786 273-2869
2406 Swan Creek Rd Jonesville (28642) *(G-7194)*

Chatham News, Siler City *Also Called: Chatham News Publishing Co (G-11405)*

Chatham News Publishing Co (PA).......................919 663-4042
303 W Raleigh St Siler City (27344) *(G-11405)*

Chatham Steel Corporation..................................912 233-4182
2702 Cheek Rd Durham (27704) *(G-3970)*

Chatsworth Products Inc......................................252 514-2779
701 Industrial Dr New Bern (28562) *(G-9354)*

Chatter Free Tling Sltions Inc..............................828 659-7379
1877 Rutherford Rd Marion (28752) *(G-8040)*

Chaudhry Meat Company......................................919 742-9292
380 Stockyard Rd Staley (27355) *(G-11592)*

Chd, Cherryville *Also Called: Custom Hydraulics & Design (G-3061)*

Checkfree Mobius, Durham *Also Called: Checkfree Services Corporation (G-3971)*

Checkfree Services Corporation..........................919 941-2640
4819 Emperor Blvd Ste 300 Durham (27703) *(G-3971)*

Cheerwine, Salisbury *Also Called: Carolina Beverage Corporation (G-11024)*

Chef Martini LLC..919 327-3183
1908 Falls Of Neuse Rd Ste 215 Raleigh (27615) *(G-9992)*

Chelsea Therapeutics International Ltd................704 341-1516
3530 Toringdon Way Ste 200 Charlotte (28277) *(G-1908)*

Cheltec Inc..941 355-1045
647 Hopewell Rd Ste C Morganton (28655) *(G-8855)*

Chem-Tech Solutions Inc....................................704 829-9202
1932 Jordache Ct Gastonia (28052) *(G-5019)*

Chem-Tex Laboratories Inc.................................706 602-8600
180 Gee Rd Concord (28025) *(G-3335)*

Chemogenics Biopharma LLC (PA)......................919 323-8133
3325 Durham Chapel Hill Blvd Ste 250 Durham (27707) *(G-3972)*

Chemol Company Inc..336 333-3050
2300 Randolph Ave Greensboro (27406) *(G-5443)*

Chemours Company...910 483-4681
22828 Nc Highway 87 W Fayetteville (28306) *(G-4573)*

Chemours Company Fc LLC.................................910 678-1314
22828 Nc Highway 87 W Fayetteville (28306) *(G-4574)*

Chemring Detection Systems, Charlotte *Also Called: Chemring Snsors Elctrnic Syste* *(G-1909)*

Chemring Snsors Elctrnic Syste..........................980 235-2200
4205 Westinghouse Commons Dr Charlotte (28273) *(G-1909)*

Chemtech Industrial Inc.......................................919 400-5743
61 T Kemp Rd Louisburg (27549) *(G-7912)*

Chemtech North Carolina LLC.............................910 514-9575
1030 S Main St Lillington (27546) *(G-7794)*

Chemtrade Logistics (us) Inc (HQ)......................773 646-2500
814 Tyvola Rd Ste 126 Charlotte (28217) *(G-1910)*

Chentech Corp..919 749-8765
524 Texanna Way Holly Springs (27540) *(G-6897)*

Cherokee Instruments Inc (PA)...........................919 552-0554
100 Logan Ct Angier (27501) *(G-117)*

Cherokee Publications...828 627-2424
66 Luftee Lake Rd Cherokee (28719) *(G-3051)*

Cherokee Publications Inc...................................828 627-2424
186 Bobcat Trl Clyde (28721) *(G-3256)*

Cherokee Publishing Co Inc................................919 674-6020
301 Cascade Pointe Ln Cary (27513) *(G-1326)*

Cherokee Transfer Station..................................828 497-4519
Aloveit Church Rdd Cherokee (28719) *(G-3052)*

Cherry Contracting Inc..336 969-1825
8640 Broad St Rural Hall (27045) *(G-10957)*

Cherry Precast, Rural Hall *Also Called: Cherry Contracting Inc (G-10957)*

Cherryville Distrg Co Inc.....................................704 435-9692
322 E Main St Cherryville (28021) *(G-3060)*

Chesnick Corporation...919 231-2899
3236 Lake Woodard Dr Raleigh (27604) *(G-9993)*

Chesterfield Wood Products Inc..........................828 433-0042
1810 Us 64 Morganton (28655) *(G-8856)*

Chf Industries Inc..704 522-5000
8710 Red Oak Blvd Charlotte (28217) *(G-1911)*

Chf Industries Inc..212 951-7800
9741 Southern Pine Blvd Ste A Charlotte (28273) *(G-1912)*

CHI Resources...828 835-7878
1115 Horton Rd Murphy (28906) *(G-9289)*

Chicago Pneumatic Tool Co LLC.........................704 504-6937
11313 Steele Creek Rd Charlotte (28273) *(G-1913)*

Chicago Tube and Iron, Locust *Also Called: Chicago Tube and Iron Company (G-7890)*

Chicago Tube and Iron Company.........................704 781-2060
421 Browns Hill Rd Locust (28097) *(G-7890)*

Chichibone Inc (PA)...919 785-0090
1310 Grindelwald Dr Kernersville (27284) *(G-7256)*

Chichibone Inc...919 785-0090
600 Airport Blvd Ste 1400 Morrisville (27560) *(G-8957)*

Chicopee, Charlotte *Also Called: Pgi Polymer Inc (G-2633)*

Chicopee Inc..919 894-4111
1203 Chicopee Rd Benson (27504) *(G-786)*

Chicopee Inc (DH)..704 697-5100
9335 Harris Corners Pkwy Ste 300 Charlotte (28269) *(G-1914)*

Chief Corporation...704 916-4521
10926 David Taylor Dr Ste 300 Charlotte (28262) *(G-1915)*

Chief Feed Mill, Rose Hill *Also Called: Murphy-Brown LLC (G-10908)*

Childers Concrete Company.................... 336 841-3111
200 Wise Ave High Point (27260) *(G-6568)*

Childress Vineyards LLC.................... 336 236-9463
1000 Childress Vinyard Rd Lexington (27295) *(G-7663)*

Childress Winery LLC.................... 336 775-0522
9160 Hampton Rd Lexington (27295) *(G-7664)*

Chimerix Inc (PA).................... 919 806-1074
2505 Meridian Pkwy Ste 100 Durham (27713) *(G-3973)*

China Free Press Inc.................... 919 308-9826
4711 Hope Valley Rd # 122 Durham (27707) *(G-3974)*

Chiron America Inc (DH).................... 704 587-9526
10950 Withers Cove Park Dr Charlotte (28278) *(G-1916)*

Chiron Publications LLC.................... 828 285-0838
451 Beaucatcher Rd Asheville (28805) *(G-474)*

Chocolate Fetish LLC.................... 828 258-2353
36 Haywood St Asheville (28801) *(G-475)*

Chocolate Smiles Village LLC.................... 919 469-5282
312 W Chatham St Ste 101 Cary (27511) *(G-1327)*

Choice Awards & Signs.................... 704 844-0860
4036 Matthews Indian Trail Rd Matthews (28104) *(G-8164)*

Choice Printing LLC.................... 919 790-0680
4100 Wingate Dr Raleigh (27609) *(G-9994)*

Choice USA Beverage Inc.................... 704 861-1029
809 E Franklin Blvd Gastonia (28054) *(G-5020)*

Choice USA Beverage Inc (PA).................... 704 823-1651
603 Groves St Lowell (28098) *(G-7930)*

Choice USA Beverage Inc.................... 704 487-6951
2440 S Lafayette St Shelby (28152) *(G-11317)*

Chowan Herald, Edenton *Also Called: Cox Nrth Crlina Pblcations Inc (G-4364)*

Chris Isom Inc.................... 336 629-0240
1228 Green Farm Rd Asheboro (27205) *(G-338)*

Christian Focus Magazine.................... 252 240-1656
706 Wagon Cir Morehead City (28557) *(G-8825)*

Chroma Color Corporation.................... 336 629-9184
1134 Nc Highway 49 S Asheboro (27205) *(G-339)*

Chroma Color Corporation.................... 704 637-7000
100 E 17th St Salisbury (28144) *(G-11033)*

Chronicle Mill Land LLC.................... 704 527-3227
3826 S New Hope Rd Ste 4 Gastonia (28056) *(G-5021)*

Chronicles.................... 252 617-1774
121 Mendover Dr Jacksonville (28546) *(G-7121)*

Chrysalis, Morganton *Also Called: Material Return LLC (G-8880)*

Chrysler Freight Liner, Cleveland *Also Called: Daimler Truck North Amer LLC (G-3213)*

Cht R Beitlich Corporation.................... 704 523-4242
5046 Old Pineville Rd Charlotte (28217) *(G-1917)*

Chudy Group LLC.................... 262 279-5307
106 Roche Dr Durham (27703) *(G-3975)*

Church & Church Lumber LLC.................... 336 838-1256
185 Hensley Eller Rd Millers Creek (28651) *(G-8304)*

Church & Church Lumber LLC (PA).................... 336 973-5700
863 New Browns Ford Rd Wilkesboro (28697) *(G-12631)*

Church & Church Lumber LLC.................... 336 973-4297
Brown Ford Rd Wilkesboro (28697) *(G-12632)*

Church Initiative Inc.................... 919 562-2112
250 S Allen Rd Wake Forest (27587) *(G-12269)*

Church Production Magazine, Raleigh *Also Called: Production Media Inc (G-10400)*

Chushion Division, High Point *Also Called: Snyder Paper Corporation (G-6782)*

CIC, Concord *Also Called: Controls Instrumentation Inc (G-3344)*

Cicero Inc (PA).................... 919 380-5000
2500 Regency Pkwy Cary (27518) *(G-1328)*

Cider Bros LLC.................... 919 943-9692
599 S Railroad St Lexington (27292) *(G-7665)*

Cii Technologies, Fairview *Also Called: Te Connectivity Corporation (G-4513)*

Cincinnati Thermal Spray Inc.................... 910 675-2909
11766 Nc Hwy 210 Rocky Point (28457) *(G-10878)*

Cincro, Liberty *Also Called: Leggett & Platt Incorporated (G-7770)*

Cinema III Theaters, Whiteville *Also Called: J L Powell & Co Inc (G-12585)*

Cintas, Greensboro *Also Called: Cintas Corporation No 2 (G-5444)*

Cintas Corporation No 2.................... 336 632-4412
4345 Federal Dr Greensboro (27410) *(G-5444)*

Cinters Inc.................... 336 267-3051
501 Woods Walk Ln Rocky Mount (27804) *(G-10828)*

Cintoms Inc.................... 828 684-1317
3080 Sweeten Creek Rd Asheville (28803) *(G-476)*

Circa 1801.................... 828 397-7003
1 Jacquard Dr Connelly Springs (28612) *(G-3475)*

Circle Graphics Inc.................... 919 864-4518
10700 World Trade Blvd Raleigh (27617) *(G-9995)*

Circor Precision Metering LLC (DH).................... 704 289-6511
1710 Airport Rd Monroe (28110) *(G-8458)*

Circor Precision Metering LLC.................... 919 774-7667
5910 Elwin Buchanan Dr Sanford (27330) *(G-11164)*

Circor Pumping Technologies, Monroe *Also Called: Circor Pumps North America LLC (G-8460)*

Circor Pumps North America LLC (DH).................... 704 289-6511
1710 Airport Rd Monroe (28110) *(G-8459)*

Circor Pumps North America LLC.................... 877 853-7867
1710 Airport Rd Monroe (28110) *(G-8460)*

Circuit Board Assemblers Inc.................... 919 556-7881
130 Mosswood Blvd Youngsville (27596) *(G-13471)*

Circuits, Indian Trail *Also Called: Hitech Circuits Inc (G-7083)*

Cisco Systems, Carolina Beach *Also Called: Cisco Systems Inc (G-1259)*

Cisco Systems, Charlotte *Also Called: Cisco Systems Inc (G-1918)*

Cisco Systems, Morrisville *Also Called: Cisco Systems Inc (G-8958)*

Cisco Systems, Morrisville *Also Called: Cisco Systems Inc (G-8959)*

Cisco Systems Inc.................... 910 707-1052
1004 North Carolina Ave Carolina Beach (28428) *(G-1259)*

Cisco Systems Inc.................... 704 338-7350
1900 South Blvd Ste 200 Charlotte (28203) *(G-1918)*

Cisco Systems Inc.................... 919 392-2000
7100 Kit Creek Rd Morrisville (27560) *(G-8958)*

Cisco Systems Inc.................... 919 392-2000
7025 Kit Creek Rd Morrisville (27560) *(G-8959)*

CIT, Rockingham *Also Called: Centre Ingredient Tech Inc (G-10773)*

Citgo Quik Lube of Clayton.................... 919 550-0935
11133 Us 70 Business Hwy W Clayton (27520) *(G-3140)*

Citi Energy LLC.................... 336 379-0800
2309 W Cone Blvd Ste 200 Greensboro (27408) *(G-5445)*

Citilift Company.................... 704 241-6477
4732 West Blvd Ste D Charlotte (28208) *(G-1919)*

Citizen Media Inc.................... 704 363-6062
403 N Old Statesville Rd Huntersville (28078) *(G-6976)*

Citrix Sharefile, Raleigh *Also Called: Cloud Sftwr Group Holdings Inc (G-10002)*

City Compressor Rebuilders (PA).................... 704 947-1811
9750 Twin Lakes Pkwy Charlotte (28269) *(G-1920)*

City Compressor Rebuilders.................... 704 947-1811
9750 Twin Lakes Pkwy Charlotte (28269) *(G-1921)*

City Machine Company Inc.................... 828 754-9661
723 Virginia St Sw Lenoir (28645) *(G-7594)*

City of Charlotte-Atando.................... 704 336-2722
1031 Atando Ave Charlotte (28206) *(G-1922)*

City of Graham.................... 336 570-6811
111 E Crescent Square Dr Graham (27253) *(G-5264)*

City of Greensboro.................... 336 373-5855
1041 Battleground Ave Greensboro (27408) *(G-5446)*

City of Lexington.................... 336 248-3945
425 Carolina Ave Lexington (27292) *(G-7666)*

City of Morganton.................... 828 584-1460
100 Coulter St Morganton (28655) *(G-8857)*

City of Shelby.................... 704 484-6840
824 W Grover St Shelby (28150) *(G-11318)*

City Prints LLC.................... 404 273-5741
5008 Helena Park Ln Matthews (28105) *(G-8106)*

Cityview Magazine, Fayetteville *Also Called: Cityview Publishing LLC (G-4575)*

Cityview Publishing LLC.................... 910 423-6500
2533 Raeford Rd Ste A Fayetteville (28305) *(G-4575)*

Civentichem Usa LLC.................... 919 672-8865
329 Matilda Pl Cary (27513) *(G-1329)*

Cives Corp.................... 919 518-2140
1621 Morning Mountain Rd Raleigh (27614) *(G-9996)*

CJ Partners LLC.................... 336 838-3080
1702 W Us Highway 421 Ste P Wilkesboro (28697) *(G-12633)*

(G-0000) Company's Geographic Section entry number

CJ Stallings Logging Inc... 252 297-2272
1307 Acorn Hill Rd Belvidere (27919) *(G-778)*

Cjc Enterprises.. 919 266-3158
7608 Ligon Mill Rd Wake Forest (27587) *(G-12270)*

Cje Construction Inc... 828 650-6600
3869 Sweeten Creek Rd Arden (28704) *(G-262)*

Cjr Products Inc... 336 766-2710
6206 Hacker Bend Ct Winston Salem (27103) *(G-13124)*

Cjt Machine, Hendersonville *Also Called: Cjt Machine Inc (G-6196)*

Cjt Machine Inc... 828 376-3693
1172 Terrys Gap Rd Hendersonville (28792) *(G-6196)*

Cks Packaging... 704 663-6510
289 Rolling Hill Rd Mooresville (28117) *(G-8638)*

CKS Packaging Inc... 336 578-5800
943 Trollingwood Road Graham (27253) *(G-5265)*

CKS Packaging Inc... 704 663-6510
289 Rolling Hill Rd Mooresville (28117) *(G-8639)*

Clairvoyant Technology Inc.................................... 919 491-5062
3622 Lyckan Pkwy Ste 2006 Durham (27707) *(G-3976)*

Clapp Fertilizer and Trckg Inc................................ 336 449-6103
2225 Herron Rd Whitsett (27377) *(G-12602)*

Clarcor, Washington *Also Called: Clarcor Eng MBL Solutions LLC (G-12379)*

Clarcor Eng MBL Solutions LLC.............................. 860 992-3496
230 Clarks Neck Rd Washington (27889) *(G-12379)*

Clariant, Charlotte *Also Called: Clariant Corporation (G-1925)*

Clariant Corporation... 704 331-7000
4331 Chesapeake Dr Charlotte (28216) *(G-1923)*

Clariant Corporation... 704 371-3272
11701 Mount Holly Rd Charlotte (28214) *(G-1924)*

Clariant Corporation (HQ)...................................... 704 331-7000
500 E Morehead St Ste 400 Charlotte (28202) *(G-1925)*

Clariant Corporation... 704 235-5700
337 Timber Rd Mooresville (28115) *(G-8640)*

Clariant Corporation... 704 822-2100
625 E Catawba Ave Mount Holly (28120) *(G-9224)*

Clarios LLC.. 866 589-8883
9844 Southern Pine Blvd Charlotte (28273) *(G-1926)*

Clarios LLC.. 336 884-5832
211 S Hamilton St High Point (27260) *(G-6569)*

Clarios LLC.. 336 761-1550
2701 Johnson Controls Dr Kernersville (27284) *(G-7257)*

Clarios LLC.. 252 754-0782
4125 Bayswater Rd Winterville (28590) *(G-13415)*

Clarity Vision of Smithfield.................................... 919 938-6101
1680 E Booker Dairy Rd Smithfield (27577) *(G-11437)*

Clark Art Shop Inc... 919 832-8319
12705 Scenic Dr Raleigh (27614) *(G-9997)*

Clark Communications, Asheville *Also Called: Clarks Printing Service Inc (G-477)*

Clark Sign Corporation... 336 431-4944
11530 N Main St Archdale (27263) *(G-217)*

Clark Steel Fabricators Inc................................... 336 595-9353
870 Warren Farm Rd Walnut Cove (27052) *(G-12327)*

Clark Tire & Auto Service, Boone *Also Called: Mr Tire Inc (G-936)*

Clarke Harland Corp... 210 697-8888
4475 Premier Dr High Point (27265) *(G-6570)*

Clarks Printing Service Inc.................................... 828 254-1432
2 Westside Dr Asheville (28806) *(G-477)*

Clarolux Inc... 336 378-6800
2501 Greengate Dr Greensboro (27406) *(G-5447)*

Clary Lumber Company... 252 537-2558
204 Mitchell St Gaston (27832) *(G-4978)*

Classic Carburetor Rebuilders............................... 336 613-5715
1909 Stovall St Eden (27288) *(G-4345)*

Classic Cleaning LLC.. 800 220-7101
8601 Six Forks Rd Ste 400 Raleigh (27615) *(G-9998)*

Classic Industrial Services.................................... 919 209-0909
1305 S Brightleaf Blvd Ste 103 Smithfield (27577) *(G-11438)*

Classic Industrial Services, Smithfield *Also Called: Classic Industrial Services (G-11438)*

Classic Leather Inc (PA).. 828 328-2046
309 Simpson St Sw Conover (28613) *(G-3504)*

Classic Molders, Cornelius *Also Called: Rs Industries Inc (G-3625)*

Classic Packaging Company................................... 336 922-4224
5570 Bethania Rd Pfafftown (27040) *(G-9663)*

Classic Scent... 828 645-5171
72 Hillcrest Dr Weaverville (28787) *(G-12486)*

Classic Seafood Group Inc.................................... 252 746-2818
7178 Nc 11 S Ayden (28513) *(G-654)*

Classic Sign Services LLC..................................... 704 401-1466
2242 W Roosevelt Blvd Ste F Monroe (28110) *(G-8461)*

Classic Steel Buildings Inc.................................... 252 465-4184
530 Folly Rd Sunbury (27979) *(G-11846)*

Classic Wood Manufacturing.................................. 336 691-1344
1006 N Raleigh St Greensboro (27405) *(G-5448)*

Classical Elements.. 828 575-9145
9 Sweeten Creek Xing Asheville (28803) *(G-478)*

Classics, High Point *Also Called: Swaim Inc (G-6797)*

Classy Glass Inc... 828 452-2242
39 Macs Ln Waynesville (28786) *(G-12454)*

Classy Sassy 5 Jewels Boutique............................. 252 481-8144
Greenville (27836) *(G-5954)*

Clausen Carolina Lasers, Raleigh *Also Called: Carolina Lasers (G-9977)*

Clausen Craftworks LLC.. 704 252-5048
900 Pressley Rd Ste C Charlotte (28217) *(G-1927)*

Clay County Food Pantry Inc.................................. 828 389-1657
2278 Hinton Center Rd Hayesville (28904) *(G-6138)*

Clay County Progress, Hayesville *Also Called: Community Newspapers Inc (G-6140)*

Clay Creek Athletics, Burlington *Also Called: Fuller Specialty Company Inc (G-1092)*

Clay Taylor Products Inc....................................... 704 636-2411
1225 Chuck Taylor Ln Salisbury (28147) *(G-11034)*

Claybourn Walters Log Co Inc................................ 910 628-7075
16071 Nc Highway 130 E Fairmont (28340) *(G-4501)*

Claybrook Tire Inc... 336 573-3135
101 N Glenn St Stoneville (27048) *(G-11820)*

Claypro LLC.. 828 301-6309
343 Warren Plains Norlina Rd Norlina (27563) *(G-9520)*

Clayton & Co, High Point *Also Called: Oakhurst Company Inc (G-6719)*

Clayton Electric Mtr Repr Inc................................. 336 584-3756
1407 N Nc Highway 87 Elon College (27244) *(G-4473)*

Clayton Homes Inc.. 828 667-8701
651 Smokey Park Hwy Candler (28715) *(G-1221)*

Clayton Homes Inc.. 828 684-1550
5250 Hendersonville Rd Fletcher (28732) *(G-4729)*

Clayton Welding.. 252 717-5909
451 Barwick Dr Washington (27889) *(G-12380)*

Clean and Vac.. 919 753-7951
2013 Sterling Hill Dr Fuquay Varina (27526) *(G-4873)*

Clean Catch Fish Market LLC................................. 704 333-1212
2820 Selwyn Ave Ste 150 Charlotte (28209) *(G-1928)*

Clean Green Inc... 919 596-3500
928 Harvest Rd Durham (27704) *(G-3977)*

Clean Green Environmental Svcs, Durham *Also Called: Clean Green Inc (G-3977)*

Clean Green Sustainable Lf LLC............................. 855 946-8785
610 N Elam Ave Greensboro (27408) *(G-5449)*

Cleanaire Inc... 252 623-4010
112 S Respess St Washington (27889) *(G-12381)*

Clear Channel Communications, Waynesville *Also Called: Wmxf AM 1400 (G-12480)*

Clear Defense LLC... 336 370-1699
2000 N Church St Greensboro (27405) *(G-5450)*

Clear-Flo Air Filters, Charlotte *Also Called: United Air Filter Company Corp (G-2961)*

Clearlight Glass and Mirror, Kernersville *Also Called: Cgmi Acquisition Company LLC (G-7255)*

Clearwater Paper Shelby, LLC, Shelby *Also Called: Sofidel Shelby LLC (G-11379)*

Clement Pappas Nc LLC.. 856 455-1000
125 Industrial Park Rd Hendersonville (28792) *(G-6197)*

Clemmons Courier, Mocksville *Also Called: Davie County Publishing Co (G-8357)*

Clemmons Pallet Skid Works Inc............................ 336 766-5462
3449 Hwy 158 E Clemmons (27012) *(G-3180)*

Clesters Auto Rubber Seals LLC............................. 704 637-9979
5415 Statesville Blvd Cleveland (27013) *(G-3211)*

Cleveland Compounding Inc................................... 704 487-1971
701 E Grover St # 2 Shelby (28150) *(G-11319)*

A
L
P
H
A
B
E
T
I
C

Cleveland Freightliner Truck.................................704 645-5000
  11550 Statesville Blvd Cleveland (27013) *(G-3212)*

Cleveland Lumber Company (PA)...........................704 487-5263
  217 Arrowood Dr Shelby (28150) *(G-11320)*

Cleveland Yutaka Corporation................................704 480-9290
  2081 W Dixon Blvd Shelby (28152) *(G-11321)*

Cleveland-Cliffs Piedmont, Newton *Also Called: Cleveland-Cliffs Plate LLC (G-9454)*

Cleveland-Cliffs Plate LLC....................................828 464-9214
  2027 S Mclin Creek Rd Newton (28658) *(G-9454)*

Click Electronics LLC..704 840-6855
  4030 Wake Forest Rd Ste 349 Raleigh (27609) *(G-9999)*

Clickfold Plastics, Charlotte *Also Called: Proplastic Designs Inc (G-2675)*

Client Care Web Inc..704 787-9901
  4078 Morris Burn Dr Sw Concord (28027) *(G-3336)*

Clifford W Estes Co Inc.......................................336 622-6410
  2637 Old 421 Rd Staley (27355) *(G-11593)*

Cliffside Technologies Inc....................................828 657-4477
  4734 Us 221a Hwy Mooresboro (28114) *(G-8583)*

Clift Industries Inc...704 752-0031
  201 Westland Farm Rd Mount Holly (28120) *(G-9225)*

Climate Seal, Charlotte *Also Called: Envirnmental Win Solutions LLC (G-2118)*

Cline Printing Inc...704 394-8144
  3445 Carolina Ave Ste A Charlotte (28208) *(G-1929)*

Clinetic Inc..513 295-1332
  520 Guilford Cir Raleigh (27608) *(G-10000)*

Clinical Workflow Consulting, Cary *Also Called: Siemens Med Solutions USA Inc (G-1453)*

Clinicians Advocacy Group Inc..............................704 751-9515
  1433 Emerywood Dr Ste A Charlotte (28210) *(G-1930)*

Clinton Grains, Garland *Also Called: Garland Farm Supply Inc (G-4909)*

Clinton Press Inc...336 275-8491
  2100 Tennyson Dr Greensboro (27410) *(G-5451)*

Clondalkin Pharma & Healthcare............................336 292-4555
  1072 Boulder Rd Greensboro (27409) *(G-5452)*

Closed Tire Company Inc.....................................704 864-5464
  191 E Franklin Blvd Gastonia (28052) *(G-5022)*

Closets By Design..704 361-6424
  1108 Continental Blvd Ste A Charlotte (28273) *(G-1931)*

Closure Medical Corporation.................................919 876-7800
  5250 Greens Dairy Rd Raleigh (27616) *(G-10001)*

Cloth Barn Inc...919 735-3643
  1701 E Ash St Goldsboro (27530) *(G-5206)*

Clothes Cleaning System LLC................................252 243-3752
  4475 Technology Dr Nw Wilson (27896) *(G-12980)*

Cloud Pharmaceuticals Inc...................................919 558-1254
  6 Davis Dr Durham (27709) *(G-3978)*

Cloud Sftwr Group Holdings Inc............................919 839-6139
  120 S West St Raleigh (27603) *(G-10002)*

Cloud Software Group Inc....................................919 969-6500
  200 W Franklin St Ste 250 Chapel Hill (27516) *(G-1538)*

Cloudgenera Inc..980 332-4040
  1824 Statesville Ave Ste 103 Charlotte (28206) *(G-1932)*

Cloverdale Co Inc Roanoke Co, Newport *Also Called: Veneer Technologies Inc (G-9446)*

Cloverleaf Mixing Inc..336 765-7900
  121 Cloverleaf Dr Winston Salem (27103) *(G-13125)*

Clt 2016 Inc...704 886-1555
  1836 Equitable Pl Charlotte (28213) *(G-1933)*

Clutch Inc...919 448-8654
  120 W Parrish St Durham (27701) *(G-3979)*

Clyde Moore Logging, Whiteville *Also Called: H Clyde Moore Jr (G-12583)*

Clyde Union (us) Inc (HQ)....................................704 808-3000
  14045 Ballantyne Corporate Pl Ste 300 Charlotte (28277) *(G-1934)*

Clydesdle Acq Hld Inc (HQ).................................843 857-4800
  3436 Toringdon Way Ste 100 Charlotte (28277) *(G-1935)*

Clydeunion Pumps, Charlotte *Also Called: Clyde Union (us) Inc (G-1934)*

Clydeunion Pumps Inc...704 808-3848
  13320 Ballantyne Corporate Pl Charlotte (28277) *(G-1936)*

CM Supply, Robbinsville *Also Called: Robbinsville Cstm Molding Inc (G-10761)*

CMA Signs LLC...919 245-8339
  610 Meadowlands Dr Hillsborough (27278) *(G-6864)*

CMC, Waynesville *Also Called: Sanders Industries Inc (G-12472)*

CMC Industrial Services LLC.................................980 565-5224
  7160 Weddington Rd Nw Ste 136 Concord (28027) *(G-3337)*

CMC Rebar...704 865-8571
  2528 N Chester St Gastonia (28052) *(G-5023)*

CMC Rebar, Gastonia *Also Called: Commercial Metals Company (G-5025)*

CMC Sencon Inc (PA)..919 938-3216
  132 Citation Ln Smithfield (27577) *(G-11439)*

Cmd Land Services LLC.......................................919 554-2281
  532 S Wingate St Wake Forest (27587) *(G-12271)*

CMF, Lincolnton *Also Called: Charlotte Metal Finishing Inc (G-7821)*

Cmfi, Youngsville *Also Called: Carolina Machining Fabrication (G-13469)*

CMH, Rockwell *Also Called: CMH Manufacturing Inc (G-10793)*

CMH Manufacturing Inc.......................................704 279-4659
  508 Palmer Rd Rockwell (28138) *(G-10793)*

CMI Enterprises...305 685-9651
  135 Pine St Forest City (28043) *(G-4786)*

CMI Plastics, Ayden *Also Called: Consolidated Models Inc (G-656)*

CMI Plastics Inc..252 746-2171
  222 Pepsi Way Ayden (28513) *(G-655)*

Cmisolutions Inc...704 759-9950
  7520 E Independence Blvd Ste 400 Charlotte (28227) *(G-1937)*

Cml Micro Circuit USA...336 744-5050
  486 N Patterson Ave Ste 301 Winston Salem (27101) *(G-13126)*

Cmp Pharma Inc..252 753-7111
  8026 East Marlboro Rd Farmville (27828) *(G-4525)*

CMS Associates Inc..919 365-0881
  7308 Siemens Rd Ste D Wendell (27591) *(G-12530)*

CMS Printing Services, Raeford *Also Called: Currie Motorsports Inc (G-9836)*

CMS Tool and Die Inc...910 458-3322
  1331 Bridge Barrier Rd Carolina Beach (28428) *(G-1260)*

Cmw Global, Washington *Also Called: Carver Machine Works Inc (G-12378)*

Cmw Holding, Salisbury *Also Called: Lgc Consulting Inc (G-11083)*

Cmw Manufacturing LLC......................................704 216-0171
  1217 Speedway Blvd Salisbury (28146) *(G-11035)*

Cnc, Maiden *Also Called: Carolina Nonwovens LLC (G-8011)*

Cnc Laser Shop, Wilmington *Also Called: Hanover Iron Works Shtmtl Inc (G-12801)*

Cnc Performance Eng LLC....................................704 599-2555
  11125 Metromont Pkwy Charlotte (28269) *(G-1938)*

Cnc-Ke Inc...704 333-0145
  1340 Amble Dr Charlotte (28206) *(G-1939)*

Cnd, Oxford *Also Called: Revlon Consumer Products Corp (G-9630)*

Cni Regional, Franklin *Also Called: Community Newspapers Inc (G-4822)*

Co-Da, Indian Trail *Also Called: Audio Vdeo Concepts Design Inc (G-7069)*

Coalogix Inc...704 827-8933
  11707 Steele Creek Rd Charlotte (28273) *(G-1940)*

Coast Lamp Manufacturing Inc..............................828 648-7876
  35 Church St Canton (28716) *(G-1249)*

Coast To Coast Carports Inc.................................336 783-3015
  170 Holly Springs Rd Mount Airy (27030) *(G-9115)*

COAST TO COAST CARPORTS INC., Mount Airy *Also Called: Coast To Coast Carports Inc (G-9115)*

Coast To Coast Lea & Vinyl Inc.............................336 886-5050
  1022 Porter St High Point (27263) *(G-6571)*

Coastal Agrobusiness Inc.....................................828 697-2220
  814 Mcmurray Rd Flat Rock (28731) *(G-4706)*

Coastal Agrobusiness Inc (PA)..............................252 238-7391
  112 Staton Rd Greenville (27834) *(G-5955)*

Coastal Agrobusiness Inc.....................................252 798-3481
  12011 Nc 125 Hamilton (27840) *(G-6048)*

Coastal Awngs Hrrcane Shutters, Morehead City *Also Called: Coastal Awnings Inc (G-8826)*

Coastal Awnings Inc...252 222-0707
  5300 High St Unit 0 Morehead City (28557) *(G-8826)*

Coastal Cabinetry Inc...910 367-8864
  5017 Songline St Shallotte (28470) *(G-11301)*

Coastal Cabinets, Wilmington *Also Called: Mike Powell Inc (G-12854)*

Coastal Canvas, Beaufort *Also Called: Coastal Canvas Mfg Inc (G-723)*

Coastal Canvas Mfg Inc.......................................252 728-4946
  1403 Harkers Island Rd Beaufort (28516) *(G-723)*

Coastal Carolina Gin, Pantego *Also Called: Coastal Carolina Gin LLC (G-9642)*

(G-0000) Company's Geographic Section entry number

Coastal Carolina Gin LLC 252 943-6990
4851 Terra Ceia Rd Pantego (27860) *(G-9642)*

Coastal Carolina Loggin 252 474-2165
250 Aurora Rd Ernul (28527) *(G-4490)*

Coastal Carolina Winery 843 443-9463
10301 Carriage Ct Cornelius (28031) *(G-3594)*

Coastal Custom Wood Works LLC 252 675-8732
111 Premier Dr New Bern (28562) *(G-9355)*

Coastal Impressions Inc 252 480-1717
3022 S Croatan Hwy Nags Head (27959) *(G-9297)*

Coastal Machine & Welding Inc 910 754-6476
146 Wall St Shallotte (28470) *(G-11302)*

Coastal Millwork Supply Co 910 763-3300
1301 S 13th St Wilmington (28401) *(G-12743)*

Coastal Precast Systems LLC 910 444-4682
5125 Us Highway 421 N Wilmington (28401) *(G-12744)*

Coastal Press Inc 252 726-1549
1706 Arendell St Morehead City (28557) *(G-8827)*

Coastal Protein Products Inc 910 567-6102
1600 Martin Rd Godwin (28344) *(G-5188)*

Coastal Proteins, Godwin *Also Called: Kansas City Sausage Co LLC (G-5189)*

Coastal Treated Products LLC 252 410-0180
1433 Georgia Ave Roanoke Rapids (27870) *(G-10735)*

Coastal Trimworks Inc 910 231-8532
1114 Maplechase Dr Se Leland (28451) *(G-7538)*

Coaster Magazine Carteret Cnty, Morehead City *Also Called: Ncoast Communications (G-8839)*

Coastland Times, Manteo *Also Called: Times Printing Company (G-8024)*

Coates Designers & Crafstmen 828 349-9700
57 Mill St Franklin (28734) *(G-4821)*

Coating Concepts Inc 704 391-0499
8154 Westbourne Dr Charlotte (28216) *(G-1941)*

Coatings Technologies Inc 704 821-8231
214 Plyler Rd Indian Trail (28079) *(G-7074)*

Coats & Clark Inc (HQ) 888 368-8401
2550 W Tyvola Rd Ste 150 Charlotte (28217) *(G-1942)*

Coats American Inc (HQ) 800 242-8095
14120 Ballantyne Corporate Pl Ste 300 Charlotte (28277) *(G-1943)*

Coats HP Inc (DH) 704 329-5800
14120 Ballantyne Corporate Pl Ste 300 Charlotte (28277) *(G-1944)*

Coats HP Inc 704 824-9904
300 Dickson Rd Mc Adenville (28101) *(G-8213)*

Coats N Amer De Rpblica Dmncan (HQ) 800 242-8095
14120 Ballantyne Corporate Pl Ste 300 Charlotte (28277) *(G-1945)*

Coats N Amer De Rpblica Dmncan, Charlotte *Also Called: Coats & Clark Inc (G-1942)*

Coats North America, Charlotte *Also Called: Coats American Inc (G-1943)*

Coaxle Optical Device and Eqp, Hickory *Also Called: Code LLC (G-6304)*

Cobb Sign Company Incorporated 336 227-0181
528 Elmira St Burlington (27217) *(G-1072)*

Cobble Creek Lumber LLC 336 844-2620
225 Hice Ave West Jefferson (28694) *(G-12562)*

Coble Printing Co Inc 919 693-4622
120 Hillsboro St Oxford (27565) *(G-9608)*

Coc USA Inc 888 706-0059
624 Matthews Mint Hill Rd Ste C Matthews (28105) *(G-8107)*

Coca Cola Bottling Co 704 509-1812
5020 W W T Harris Blvd Charlotte (28269) *(G-1946)*

Coca-Cola, Arden *Also Called: Ccbcc Operations LLC (G-260)*

Coca-Cola, Boone *Also Called: Ccbcc Operations LLC (G-905)*

Coca-Cola, Bryson City *Also Called: Ccbcc Operations LLC (G-1009)*

Coca-Cola, Charlotte *Also Called: Ccbcc Operations LLC (G-1872)*

Coca-Cola, Charlotte *Also Called: Ccbcc Operations LLC (G-1873)*

Coca-Cola, Charlotte *Also Called: Ccbcc Operations LLC (G-1874)*

Coca-Cola, Charlotte *Also Called: Ccbcc Operations LLC (G-1875)*

Coca-Cola, Charlotte *Also Called: Ccbcc Operations LLC (G-1876)*

Coca-Cola, Charlotte *Also Called: Coca-Cola Consolidated Inc (G-1947)*

Coca-Cola, Charlotte *Also Called: Coca-Cola Consolidated Inc (G-1948)*

Coca-Cola, Charlotte *Also Called: Coca-Cola Consolidated Inc (G-1949)*

Coca-Cola, Clayton *Also Called: Ccbcc Operations LLC (G-3138)*

Coca-Cola, Clayton *Also Called: Coca-Cola Consolidated Inc (G-3141)*

Coca-Cola, Elizabeth City *Also Called: Coca-Cola Consolidated Inc (G-4382)*

Coca-Cola, Fayetteville *Also Called: Ccbcc Operations LLC (G-4572)*

Coca-Cola, Greensboro *Also Called: Ccbcc Operations LLC (G-5434)*

Coca-Cola, Greenville *Also Called: Ccbcc Operations LLC (G-5953)*

Coca-Cola, Halifax *Also Called: Ccbcc Operations LLC (G-6046)*

Coca-Cola, Hamlet *Also Called: Ccbcc Operations LLC (G-6053)*

Coca-Cola, Hickory *Also Called: Ccbcc Operations LLC (G-6292)*

Coca-Cola, Kinston *Also Called: Coca-Cola Consolidated Inc (G-7402)*

Coca-Cola, Leland *Also Called: Coca-Cola Consolidated Inc (G-7539)*

Coca-Cola, Monroe *Also Called: Ccbcc Operations LLC (G-8455)*

Coca-Cola, Mount Airy *Also Called: Ccbcc Operations LLC (G-9112)*

Coca-Cola, New Bern *Also Called: Ccbcc Operations LLC (G-9352)*

Coca-Cola, Newton *Also Called: Coca-Cola Consolidated Inc (G-9455)*

Coca-Cola, Raleigh *Also Called: Durham Coca-Cola Bottling Co (G-10066)*

Coca-Cola, Sanford *Also Called: Sanford Coca-Cola Bottling Co (G-11229)*

Coca-Cola, Statesville *Also Called: Ccbcc Operations LLC (G-11676)*

Coca-Cola, Whiteville *Also Called: Ccbcc Operations LLC (G-12579)*

Coca-Cola Consolidated Inc 704 398-2252
801 Black Satchel Rd Charlotte (28216) *(G-1947)*

Coca-Cola Consolidated Inc 980 321-3001
5001 Chesapeake Dr Charlotte (28216) *(G-1948)*

Coca-Cola Consolidated Inc (PA) 980 392-8298
4100 Coca Cola Plz Ste 100 Charlotte (28211) *(G-1949)*

Coca-Cola Consolidated Inc 919 550-0611
977 Shotwell Rd Ste 104 Clayton (27520) *(G-3141)*

Coca-Cola Consolidated Inc 252 334-1820
1210 George Wood Dr Elizabeth City (27909) *(G-4382)*

Coca-Cola Consolidated Inc 704 551-4500
4194 W Vernon Ave Kinston (28504) *(G-7402)*

Coca-Cola Consolidated Inc 919 763-3172
2210 Mercantile Dr Leland (28451) *(G-7539)*

Coca-Cola Consolidated Inc 828 322-5096
820 E 1st St Newton (28658) *(G-9455)*

Cochrane Steel, Monroe *Also Called: Cochrane Steel Industries Inc (G-8462)*

Cochrane Steel Industries Inc 704 291-9330
5529 Cannon Dr Monroe (28110) *(G-8462)*

Coco Lumber Company LLC 336 906-3754
2101 Sardis Rd N Ste 201 Charlotte (28227) *(G-1950)*

Cocoa Botanics Corporation 980 565-7739
2217 Matthews Township Pkwy Ste D-113 Matthews (28105) *(G-8108)*

Coconut Paradise Inc 704 662-3443
803 Performance Rd Mooresville (28115) *(G-8641)*

Code LLC 828 328-6004
2013 1st St Se Hickory (28602) *(G-6304)*

Coder Foundry 704 910-3077
8430 University Exec Park Dr Charlotte (28262) *(G-1951)*

Coding Institute LLC 239 280-2300
2222 Sedwick Rd Ste 1 Durham (27713) *(G-3980)*

Coeur Inc 252 946-1963
209 Creekside Dr Washington (27889) *(G-12382)*

Cog Glbal Media/Consulting LLC 980 239-8042
738 Ablow Dr Matthews (28105) *(G-8109)*

Cogent Dynamics Inc 828 628-9025
33 Meadow Brook Dr Fletcher (28732) *(G-4730)*

Cognito Promo, Raleigh *Also Called: Tannis Root Productions Inc (G-10533)*

Coil Innovation Usa Inc 919 659-0300
125 Edinburgh South Dr Ste 201 Cary (27511) *(G-1330)*

Coker Feed Mill Inc 919 778-3491
1439 Hood Swamp Rd Goldsboro (27534) *(G-5207)*

Col-Eve Metal Products Co 336 472-7039
702 Bryant Rd Lexington (27292) *(G-7667)*

Cold Mountain Capital LLC (PA) 828 210-8129
2 Town Square Blvd Asheville (28803) *(G-479)*

Cold Off Press LLC 984 444-9006
416 W South St Ste 100 Raleigh (27601) *(G-10003)*

Cold Water No Bleach LLC 336 505-9584
914 Corona St Durham (27707) *(G-3981)*

Cole Machine Inc 336 222-8381
6144 Patterson Rd Snow Camp (27349) *(G-11474)*

A
L
P
H
A
B
E
T
I
C

Colefields Publishing Inc.................................704 661-1599
2626 Hampton Ave Charlotte (28207) *(G-1952)*

Coleman Cable LLC......................................828 389-8013
788 Tusquittee Rd Hayesville (28904) *(G-6139)*

Colfax Pump Group.......................................704 289-6511
1710 Airport Rd Monroe (28110) *(G-8463)*

Colfax Trailer & Repair LLC............................336 993-8511
8426a Norcross Rd Colfax (27235) *(G-3275)*

Collegate Clors Christn Colors.........................919 536-8179
4204 Destrier Dr Durham (27703) *(G-3982)*

College Sun Do...910 521-9189
701 W 3rd St Pembroke (28372) *(G-9657)*

Colliers Welding LLC....................................910 818-5728
773 Mary Jordan Ln Fayetteville (28311) *(G-4576)*

Collin Mfg Inc...919 917-6264
99 Pelican Cir Oriental (28571) *(G-9599)*

Collins & Aikman Europe Inc............................704 548-2350
701 Mccullough Dr Charlotte (28262) *(G-1953)*

Collins & Aikman Interiors.............................704 548-2350
701 Mccullough Dr Charlotte (28262) *(G-1954)*

Collins & Aikman International..........................704 548-2350
701 Mccullough Dr Charlotte (28262) *(G-1955)*

Collins & Aikman Prpts Inc.............................704 548-2350
701 Mccullough Dr Charlotte (28262) *(G-1956)*

Collins Aerospace.......................................704 423-7000
2730 W Tyvola Rd Charlotte (28217) *(G-1957)*

Collins Aerospace, Charlotte *Also Called: Goodrich Corporation (G-2227)*

Collins Aerospace, Winston Salem *Also Called: B/E Aerospace Inc (G-13094)*

Collins Aerospace, Winston Salem *Also Called: B/E Aerospace Inc (G-13098)*

Collins Aerospace, Winston Salem *Also Called: B/E Aerospace Inc (G-13099)*

Collins Aerospace, Winston Salem *Also Called: Rockwell Collins Inc (G-13320)*

Collins Aerospace, Winston Salem *Also Called: Rockwell Collins Inc (G-13322)*

Collins Akman Canada Dom Holdg.......................704 548-2350
701 Mccullough Dr Charlotte (28262) *(G-1958)*

Collins Banks Investments Inc..........................252 439-1200
311 Staton Rd Greenville (27834) *(G-5956)*

Collins Fabrication & Wldg LLC.........................704 861-9326
1204 N Chester St Gastonia (28052) *(G-5024)*

Colonial LLC (PA).......................................336 434-5600
536 Townsend Ave High Point (27263) *(G-6572)*

Colonial Cabinets LLC...................................910 579-2954
259 Koolabrew Dr Nw Calabash (28467) *(G-1209)*

Colonial Tin Works Inc..................................336 668-4126
7609 Canoe Rd Greensboro (27409) *(G-5453)*

Colony Gums LLC..704 226-9666
2626 Executive Point Dr Monroe (28110) *(G-8464)*

Colony Tire Corporation.................................252 973-0004
1463 N Wesleyan Blvd Rocky Mount (27804) *(G-10829)*

Colored Metal Products Inc.............................704 482-1407
103 Cameron St Shelby (28152) *(G-11322)*

Colowrap LLC...888 815-3376
3333 Durham Chapel Hill Blvd Ste A200 Durham (27707) *(G-3983)*

Colquimica Adhesives Inc...............................704 318-4750
2205 Beltway Blvd Ste 200 Charlotte (28214) *(G-1959)*

Colsenkeane Leather LLC................................704 750-9887
1707 E 7th St Charlotte (28204) *(G-1960)*

Coltec Industries Inc...................................704 731-1500
5605 Carnegie Blvd Ste 500 Charlotte (28209) *(G-1961)*

Columbia Carolina Division, Old Fort *Also Called: Columbia Plywood Corporation (G-9592)*

Columbia Forest Products Inc...........................336 605-0429
Centruty Drive Ste 200 Greensboro (27401) *(G-5454)*

Columbia Forest Products Inc (PA)......................336 605-0429
7900 Mccloud Rd Ste 200 Greensboro (27409) *(G-5455)*

Columbia Forest Products Inc...........................828 724-9495
369 Columbia Carolina Rd Old Fort (28762) *(G-9591)*

Columbia Panel Mfg Co Inc..............................336 861-4100
100 Giles St High Point (27263) *(G-6573)*

Columbia Plywood Corporation..........................828 724-4191
369 Columbia Carolina Rd Old Fort (28762) *(G-9592)*

Columbia Silica Sand LLC...............................803 755-1036
1410 Commonwealth Dr Ste 201 Wilmington (28403) *(G-12745)*

Columbia West Virginia Corp (HQ).......................336 605-0429
7820 Thorndike Rd Greensboro (27409) *(G-5456)*

Columbiana Hi Tech LLC.................................336 497-3600
1621 Old Greensboro Rd Kernersville (27284) *(G-7258)*

Columbus Industries LLC (PA)...........................910 872-1625
941 Cabbage Rd Bladenboro (28320) *(G-875)*

Columbus McKinnon, Charlotte *Also Called: Columbus McKinnon Corporation (G-1962)*

Columbus McKinnon, Wadesboro *Also Called: Columbus McKinnon Corporation (G-12240)*

Columbus McKinnon Corporation (PA)....................716 689-5400
13320 Ballantyne Corporate Pl Ste D Charlotte (28277) *(G-1962)*

Columbus McKinnon Corporation.........................704 694-2156
2020 Country Club Rd Wadesboro (28170) *(G-12240)*

Columbus Pallet Company Inc...........................910 655-4513
813 Lennon Rd Delco (28436) *(G-3735)*

Column & Post, Fuquay Varina *Also Called: Column & Post Inc (G-4874)*

Column & Post Inc......................................919 255-1533
8013 Purfoy Rd Fuquay Varina (27526) *(G-4874)*

Coman Publishing Co Inc (PA)...........................919 688-0218
324 Blackwell St Ste 560 Durham (27701) *(G-3984)*

Combat Medical Systems LLC............................704 705-1222
13359 Reese Blvd E Huntersville (28078) *(G-6977)*

Combat Support Products Inc............................919 552-0205
3738 Rawls Church Rd Fuquay Varina (27526) *(G-4875)*

Combilift USA LLC......................................336 378-8884
303 Concord St Greensboro (27406) *(G-5457)*

Combinations Embroidery, Thomasville *Also Called: Combintons Screen Prtg EMB Inc (G-12009)*

Combintons Screen Prtg EMB Inc........................336 472-4420
4 N Robbins St Thomasville (27360) *(G-12009)*

Comedycd...336 273-0077
400 Nottingham Rd Greensboro (27408) *(G-5458)*

Comer Sanitary Service Inc.............................336 629-8311
3039 Greensboro Street Ext Lexington (27295) *(G-7668)*

Comer Trucking, Lexington *Also Called: Comer Sanitary Service Inc (G-7668)*

Comfort Bay Home Fashions Inc.........................843 442-7477
2200 Main Ave Se Hickory (28602) *(G-6305)*

Comfort Bilt, Durham *Also Called: Smg Hearth and Home LLC (G-4240)*

Comfort Engineers Inc (PA).............................919 383-0158
4008 Comfort Ln Durham (27705) *(G-3985)*

Comfort Publishing Svcs LLC............................704 907-7848
8890 Brandon Cir Concord (28025) *(G-3338)*

Comfort Seals, Biscoe *Also Called: Comfort Tech Inc (G-851)*

Comfort Sleep LLC......................................336 267-5853
1100 National Hwy Ste L Thomasville (27360) *(G-12010)*

Comfort Tech Inc.......................................910 428-1779
Hgwy 2427 Biscoe (27209) *(G-851)*

Comfortland International LLC...........................866 277-3135
709 A O Smith Rd Mebane (27302) *(G-8236)*

Comm Scope Network, Claremont *Also Called: Commscope Inc North Carolina (G-3094)*

Comm Scope Network Cable Div, Newton *Also Called: Commscope Inc North Carolina (G-9457)*

Comm-Kab Inc...336 873-8787
1865 Spero Rd Asheboro (27205) *(G-340)*

Commdoor Inc...800 565-1851
5555 Yorke St Nw Concord (28027) *(G-3339)*

Commercial Cnstr Jantr Svcs, Raleigh *Also Called: Classic Cleaning LLC (G-9998)*

Commercial Enterprises NC Inc..........................910 592-8163
103 E Morisey Blvd Clinton (28328) *(G-3230)*

Commercial Fabricators Inc.............................828 465-1010
2045 Industrial Dr Newton (28658) *(G-9456)*

Commercial Flter Svc of Triad..........................336 272-1443
107 Creek Ridge Rd Ste F Greensboro (27406) *(G-5459)*

Commercial Lighting Services, Granite Falls *Also Called: AMP Services LLC (G-5294)*

Commercial Metals Company.............................336 584-0333
Park Road Burlington (27216) *(G-1073)*

Commercial Metals Company.............................704 375-5937
419 Atando Ave Charlotte (28206) *(G-1963)*

Commercial Metals Company.............................704 399-9020
301 Black Satchel Rd Charlotte (28216) *(G-1964)*

Commercial Metals Company.............................919 833-9737
2528 N Chester St Gastonia (28052) *(G-5025)*

Commercial Printing, Lincolnton *Also Called: Commercial Prtg Lincolnton NC (G-7822)*

Commercial Printing Company............................ 919 832-2828
3731 Centurion Dr Garner (27529) *(G-4922)*

Commercial Property LLC................................ 336 818-1078
209 Elkin Hwy North Wilkesboro (28659) *(G-9525)*

Commercial Prtg Co of Clinton........................ 910 592-8163
103 E Morisey Blvd Clinton (28328) *(G-3231)*

Commercial Prtg Lincolnton NC........................ 704 735-6831
523 N Aspen St Lincolnton (28092) *(G-7822)*

Commercial Ready Mix Pdts Inc........................ 252 332-3590
100 Hayes St E Ahoskie (27910) *(G-45)*

Commercial Ready Mix Pdts Inc........................ 252 335-9740
168 Knobbs Creek Dr Elizabeth City (27909) *(G-4383)*

Commercial Ready Mix Pdts Inc........................ 252 232-1250
115 Windchaser Way Moyock (27958) *(G-9278)*

Commercial Ready Mix Pdts Inc........................ 252 585-1777
1231 Vougemills Rd Pendleton (27862) *(G-9661)*

Commercial Seaming Co Inc............................ 252 492-6178
501 Walnut St Henderson (27536) *(G-6151)*

Commercial Spclty Trck Hldngs........................ 859 234-1100
1425 Brittney Ln Burlington (27215) *(G-1074)*

Commercial Vehicle Group Inc.......................... 704 886-6407
2845 Armentrout Dr Concord (28025) *(G-3340)*

Common Part Groupings LLC............................ 704 948-0097
11601 Hambright Rd Huntersville (28078) *(G-6978)*

Commonwealth Brands Inc.............................. 336 634-4200
714 Green Valley Rd Greensboro (27408) *(G-5460)*

Commonwealth Hosiery, Randleman *Also Called: Commonwealth Hosiery Mills Inc (G-10638)*

Commonwealth Hosiery Mills Inc...................... 336 498-2621
4964 Island Ford Rd Randleman (27317) *(G-10638)*

Commscope, Claremont *Also Called: Commscope Inc North Carolina (G-3096)*

Commscope, Claremont *Also Called: Commscope Holding Company Inc (G-3100)*

Commscope Inc North Carolina........................ 828 459-5000
3642 E Us Highway 70 Claremont (28610) *(G-3094)*

Commscope Inc North Carolina........................ 828 459-5001
3565 Centennial Blvd Claremont (28610) *(G-3095)*

Commscope Inc North Carolina (DH).................. 828 324-2200
3642 E Us Highway 70 Claremont (28610) *(G-3096)*

Commscope Inc North Carolina........................ 828 324-2200
2908 2nd Ave Nw Hickory (28601) *(G-6306)*

Commscope Inc North Carolina........................ 828 466-8600
1545 Saint James Church Rd Newton (28658) *(G-9457)*

Commscope LLC (HQ).................................. 828 324-2200
3642 E Us Highway 70 Claremont (28610) *(G-3097)*

Commscope Cnnctvity Sltons LLC...................... 828 324-2200
1100 Commscope Pl Se Hickory (28602) *(G-6307)*

Commscope Connectivity LLC (HQ).................... 828 324-2200
3642 E Us Highway 70 Claremont (28610) *(G-3098)*

Commscope Dsl Systems LLC.......................... 828 324-2200
3642 E Us Highway 70 Claremont (28610) *(G-3099)*

Commscope Holding Company Inc...................... 919 677-2422
101 Stamford Dr Cary (27513) *(G-1331)*

Commscope Holding Company Inc (PA)................ 828 459-5000
3642 E Us Highway 70 Claremont (28610) *(G-3100)*

Commscope Intl Holdings LLC.......................... 828 324-2200
3642 E Us Highway 70 Claremont (28610) *(G-3101)*

Commscope Solutions Intl Inc (HQ).................... 828 324-2200
3642 E Us Highway 70 Claremont (28610) *(G-3102)*

Commscope Technologies Fin LLC...................... 828 323-4970
3642 E Us Highway 70 Claremont (28610) *(G-3103)*

Commscope Technologies LLC (HQ).................... 828 324-2200
3642 E Us Highway 70 Claremont (28610) *(G-3104)*

Commscope Technologies LLC.......................... 919 329-8700
620 N Greenfield Pkwy Garner (27529) *(G-4923)*

Commscope Technologies LLC.......................... 336 665-6000
8420 Triad Dr Greensboro (27409) *(G-5461)*

Commscope Technologies LLC.......................... 828 324-2200
1100 Commscope Pl Se Hickory (28602) *(G-6308)*

Commscope Technologies LLC.......................... 919 934-9711
1315 Industrial Park Dr Smithfield (27577) *(G-11440)*

Communications & Pwr Inds LLC...................... 650 846-2900
1700 Cable Dr Ne Conover (28613) *(G-3505)*

Community Brewing Ventures LLC (PA)................ 800 579-6539
116 W A St Newton (28658) *(G-9458)*

Community First Media Inc............................ 704 482-4142
503 N Lafayette St Shelby (28150) *(G-11323)*

Community Newspapers Inc............................ 828 743-5101
426 Nc 107 S Cashiers (28717) *(G-1490)*

Community Newspapers Inc............................ 828 369-3430
690 Wayah St Franklin (28734) *(G-4822)*

Community Newspapers Inc............................ 828 389-8431
43 Main St Hayesville (28904) *(G-6140)*

Community Newspapers Inc............................ 828 479-3383
720 Tallulah Rd Robbinsville (28771) *(G-10758)*

Community Newspapers Inc............................ 828 765-7169
261 Locust St Spruce Pine (28777) *(G-11568)*

Communitys Kitchen L3c.............................. 828 817-2308
835 N Trade St Ste A Tryon (28782) *(G-12173)*

Comp-TAC Operations, Swansboro *Also Called: Hsg LLC (G-11886)*

Compagnie Parento Inc................................ 828 758-2525
340 Industrial Ct Lenoir (28645) *(G-7595)*

Compass Group Usa Inc................................ 704 398-6515
3112 Horseshoe Ln Charlotte (28208) *(G-1965)*

Compass Group Usa Inc................................ 919 381-9577
3300 Waterfield Dr Garner (27529) *(G-4924)*

Compass Group Usa Inc................................ 252 291-7733
2102 Industrial Park Dr Se Wilson (27893) *(G-12981)*

Compass Precision LLC (PA).......................... 704 790-6764
4600 Westinghouse Blvd Charlotte (28273) *(G-1966)*

Competition Tooling Inc.............................. 336 887-4414
219 Dublin Ave High Point (27260) *(G-6574)*

Competitive Solutions Inc (PA)........................ 919 851-0058
8340 Bandford Way Ste 103 Raleigh (27615) *(G-10004)*

Complete Comp St of Ralgh Inc........................ 919 828-5227
3016 Hillsborough St Ste 100 Raleigh (27607) *(G-10005)*

Compmillennia LLC.................................... 252 628-8065
706 Hackney Ave Washington (27889) *(G-12383)*

Component Sourcing Intl, Charlotte *Also Called: Remedios LLC (G-2706)*

Component Sourcing Intl LLC.......................... 704 843-9292
1301 Westinghouse Blvd Ste 1 Charlotte (28273) *(G-1967)*

Component Technology Intl Inc........................ 704 331-0888
1000 Upper Asbury Ave Charlotte (28206) *(G-1968)*

Composite Fabrics America LLC........................ 828 632-5220
105 Pierpoint Ln Taylorsville (28681) *(G-11954)*

Composite Factory LLC................................ 484 264-3306
255 Raceway Dr Mooresville (28117) *(G-8642)*

Composites.com, Beaufort *Also Called: Beaufort Composite Tech Inc (G-721)*

Compressed Gas Solutions, Raleigh *Also Called: American Welding & Gas Inc (G-9899)*

Compton Tape & Label Inc............................ 336 548-4400
3520 Us Highway 220 Madison (27025) *(G-7984)*

Compton Tape and Converting, Madison *Also Called: Compton Tape & Label Inc (G-7984)*

Computational Engrg Intl Inc (HQ).................... 919 363-0883
2166 N Salem St Ste 101 Apex (27523) *(G-148)*

Computer Task Group Inc.............................. 919 677-1313
8801 Fast Park Dr Ste 101 Raleigh (27617) *(G-10006)*

Computerway Food Systems Inc........................ 336 841-7289
2700 Westchester Dr High Point (27262) *(G-6575)*

Comset Management Group............................ 910 574-6007
3926 Gaithersburg Ln Hope Mills (28348) *(G-6926)*

Comtech Group Inc.................................... 919 313-4800
4819 Emperor Blvd Ste 400 Durham (27703) *(G-3986)*

Con Met, Canton *Also Called: Consolidated Metco Inc (G-1250)*

Con-Tab Inc.. 336 476-0104
4001 Ball Park Rd Thomasville (27360) *(G-12011)*

Concept Frames Inc.................................. 828 465-2015
2015 Industrial Dr Newton (28658) *(G-9459)*

Concept Fusion, Middlesex *Also Called: Concept Fusion LLC (G-8272)*

Concept Fusion LLC.................................. 252 406-7052
8200 Planer Mill Rd Middlesex (27557) *(G-8272)*

Concept Plastics Inc (PA)............................ 336 889-2001
1210 Hickory Chapel Rd High Point (27260) *(G-6576)*

Concept Steel Inc.................................... 704 874-0414
1801 Bradbury Ct Gastonia (28052) *(G-5026)*

ALPHABETIC

Concierge Consulting - Itsm, Charlotte *Also Called: Concierge Transit LLC (G-1969)*

Concierge Transit LLC.. 704 778-0755
  1623 Swan Dr Charlotte (28216) *(G-1969)*

Concise Manufacturing Inc... 704 796-8419
  630 Corporate Cir Salisbury (28147) *(G-11036)*

Concord Custom Cabinets.. 704 773-0081
  4530 Cochran Farm Rd Sw Concord (28027) *(G-3341)*

Concord Printing Company Inc..................................... 704 786-3717
  660 Abington Dr Ne Concord (28025) *(G-3342)*

Concord Trading Inc... 704 375-3333
  225 Wilshire Ave Sw Concord (28025) *(G-3343)*

Concrete Pipe & Precast LLC.. 910 892-6411
  452 Webb Rd Dunn (28334) *(G-3851)*

Concrete Pipe & Precast LLC.. 704 485-4614
  20047 Silver Rd Oakboro (28129) *(G-9576)*

Concrete Pumping By Macleod, Charlotte *Also Called: Macleod Construction Inc (G-2446)*

Concrete Service Co Inc (HQ)......................................910 483-0396
  130 Builders Blvd Fayetteville (28301) *(G-4577)*

Concrete Supply Co, Charlotte *Also Called: Concrete Supply Co LLC (G-1971)*

Concrete Supply Co LLC (HQ).....................................864 517-4055
  3823 Raleigh St Charlotte (28206) *(G-1970)*

Concrete Supply Co LLC (HQ).....................................704 372-2930
  3823 Raleigh St Charlotte (28206) *(G-1971)*

Concrete Supply Holdings Inc (PA).............................. 704 372-2930
  3823 Raleigh St Charlotte (28206) *(G-1972)*

Condar Company, Columbus *Also Called: Woodlane Envmtl Tech Inc (G-3305)*

Cone Denim LLC (DH).. 336 379-6165
  804 Green Valley Rd Ste 300 Greensboro (27408) *(G-5462)*

Cone Denim Mills, Greensboro *Also Called: Cone Denim LLC (G-5462)*

Conestoga Wood Spc Corp... 919 284-2258
  621 Johnston Pkwy Kenly (27542) *(G-7229)*

Conetoe Land & Timber LLC... 252 717-4648
  3820 Stevens Mill Rd Goldsboro (27530) *(G-5208)*

Confab Manufacturing Co LLC..................................... 704 366-7140
  6525 Morrison Blvd Ste 300 Charlotte (28211) *(G-1973)*

Conference Inc... 704 349-0203
  259 W Main Ave Gastonia (28052) *(G-5027)*

Conitex Sonoco Usa Inc... 704 864-5406
  1302 Industrial Pike Rd Gastonia (28052) *(G-5028)*

Conjet Inc... 636 485-4724
  3400 International Airport Dr Ste 100 Charlotte (28208) *(G-1974)*

Conmech Industries LLC.. 919 306-6228
  117 Beaver Creek Rd Apex (27502) *(G-149)*

Conmet, Monroe *Also Called: Consolidated Metco Inc (G-8468)*

Conn-Selmer Inc.. 704 289-6459
  2806 Mason St Monroe (28110) *(G-8465)*

Connected 2k LLC.. 910 321-7446
  1015 Robeson St Ste 103 Fayetteville (28305) *(G-4578)*

Connectivity Group LLC... 910 799-9023
  837 S Kerr Ave Wilmington (28403) *(G-12746)*

Connectmedia Ventures LLC.. 773 551-7446
  425 N Boylan Ave Raleigh (27603) *(G-10007)*

Conner Brothers Machine Co Inc.................................. 704 864-6084
  3200 Bessemer City Rd Bessemer City (28016) *(G-809)*

Connexion Technologies.. 919 674-0036
  111 Corning Rd Ste 250 Cary (27518) *(G-1332)*

Conopco Inc... 910 875-4121
  100 Faberge Blvd Raeford (28376) *(G-9834)*

Conover Lumber Company Inc...................................... 828 464-4591
  311 Conover Blvd E Conover (28613) *(G-3506)*

Conover Machine and Design Inc.................................. 828 328-6737
  231 33rd Street Dr Se Hickory (28602) *(G-6309)*

Conover Metal Products Inc... 828 464-9414
  315 S Mclin Creek Rd Conover (28613) *(G-3507)*

Conover Plastics, Conover *Also Called: Plastics Mlding Dsign Plus LLC (G-3546)*

Conrad Embroidery Company LLC................................ 828 645-3015
  22 A B Emblem Dr Weaverville (28787) *(G-12487)*

Conrad Industries Inc (PA)...828 645-3015
  22 A B Emblem Dr Weaverville (28787) *(G-12488)*

Conrad Tire & Automotive, Thomasville *Also Called: John Conrad Inc (G-12041)*

Conroll Corporation... 910 202-4292
  3302 Kitty Hawk Rd Ste 100 Wilmington (28405) *(G-12747)*

Conservation Station Inc.. 919 932-9201
  60 Sun Forest Way Chapel Hill (27517) *(G-1539)*

Consoldted Elctrnic Rsrces Inc.................................... 919 321-0004
  2933 S Miami Blvd Ste 124 Durham (27703) *(G-3987)*

Consolidated Diesel Inc... 252 437-6611
  9377 N Us Highway 301 Whitakers (27891) *(G-12574)*

Consolidated Elec Distrs Inc.. 828 433-4689
  208 W Fleming Dr Ste D Morganton (28655) *(G-8858)*

Consolidated Inspections Inc....................................... 919 658-5800
  526 Norwood Ezzell Rd Mount Olive (28365) *(G-9253)*

Consolidated Metco Inc... 360 828-2689
  90 Christ School Rd Arden (28704) *(G-263)*

Consolidated Metco Inc... 828 488-5126
  1821 Hwy 19 Bryson City (28713) *(G-1010)*

Consolidated Metco Inc... 828 488-5114
  171 Great Oak Dr Canton (28716) *(G-1250)*

Consolidated Metco Inc... 704 289-6492
  780 Patton Ave Monroe (28110) *(G-8466)*

Consolidated Metco Inc... 704 289-6491
  1700 N Charlotte Ave Monroe (28110) *(G-8467)*

Consolidated Metco Inc... 704 226-5246
  4220 Propel Way Monroe (28110) *(G-8468)*

Consolidated Mfg Intl LLC (PA).................................... 919 781-3411
  5816 Triangle Dr Raleigh (27617) *(G-10008)*

Consolidated Models Inc... 252 746-2171
  222 Pepsi Way Ayden (28513) *(G-656)*

Consolidated Pipe & Sup Co Inc................................... 336 294-8577
  2410 Binford St Greensboro (27407) *(G-5463)*

Consolidated Press Inc.. 704 372-6785
  3900 Greensboro St Charlotte (28206) *(G-1975)*

Consolidated Press Charlotte, Charlotte *Also Called: Consolidated Press Inc (G-1975)*

Consolidated Sciences Inc... 919 870-0344
  8390 Six Forks Rd Ste 101 Raleigh (27615) *(G-10009)*

Consolidated Truck Parts Inc....................................... 704 279-5543
  7665 Hwy 52 North Rockwell (28138) *(G-10794)*

Construction, Charlotte *Also Called: Self Made Clt (G-2785)*

Construction, Davidson *Also Called: Carolina Housing Solutions LLC (G-3699)*

Construction Attachments, Lenoir *Also Called: Construction Attachments Inc (G-7596)*

Construction Attachments Inc...................................... 828 758-2674
  1160 Cal Ct Lenoir (28645) *(G-7596)*

Construction Impts Depo Inc.. 336 859-2002
  1248 N Main St Denton (27239) *(G-3743)*

Construction Metal Pdts Inc... 704 871-8704
  2204 W Front St Statesville (28677) *(G-11678)*

Consuladated Media Group, Durham *Also Called: Triangle Tribune (G-4282)*

Consultants In Data Proc Inc....................................... 704 542-6339
  6911 Shannon Willow Rd Ste 100 Charlotte (28226) *(G-1976)*

Consulting & Management Svcs, Raleigh *Also Called: Volta Group Corporation LLC (G-10593)*

Consumer Concepts... 252 247-7000
  1506 Bridges St Morehead City (28557) *(G-8828)*

Contagious Graphics Inc.. 704 529-5600
  5901 Orr Rd Charlotte (28213) *(G-1977)*

Container Graphics Corp (PA).......................................919 481-4200
  114 Edinburgh South Dr Ste 104 Cary (27511) *(G-1333)*

Container Graphics Corp.. 704 588-7230
  10430 Southern Loop Blvd Pineville (28134) *(G-9720)*

Container Products Corporation (PA)............................ 910 392-6100
  112 N College Rd Wilmington (28405) *(G-12748)*

Container Systems Incorporated.................................. 919 496-6133
  6863 N Carolina 56 Hwy E Franklinton (27525) *(G-4847)*

Container Technology, Wilmington *Also Called: Container Technology Inc (G-12749)*

Container Technology Inc... 910 350-1303
  430 Raleigh St Wilmington (28412) *(G-12749)*

Contech Engnered Solutions LLC.................................. 704 596-4226
  4242 Raleigh St Charlotte (28213) *(G-1978)*

Contech Engnered Solutions LLC.................................. 919 858-7820
  4917 Waters Edge Dr Ste 271 Raleigh (27606) *(G-10010)*

Contech Engnered Solutions LLC.................................. 919 851-2880
  6115 Chapel Hill Rd Raleigh (27607) *(G-10011)*

Contego Medical Inc.. 919 606-3917
  3801 Lake Boone Trl Ste 100 Raleigh (27607) *(G-10012)*

Contempora Fabrics Inc 910 345-0150
351 Contempora Dr Lumberton (28358) *(G-7948)*

Contemporary Concepts Inc 704 864-9572
2940 Audrey Dr Gastonia (28054) *(G-5029)*

Contemporary Design Co LLC 704 375-6030
513 N Broad St Gastonia (28054) *(G-5030)*

Contemporary Furnishings Corp 336 857-2988
6550 Scarlet Oak Dr Denton (27239) *(G-3744)*

Contemporary Furnishings Corp (PA) 704 633-8000
1000 N Long St Salisbury (28144) *(G-11037)*

Contemporary Products Inc 919 779-4228
275 Hein Dr Garner (27529) *(G-4925)*

Contemporary Publishing Co 919 834-4432
1460 Diggs Dr Ste C Raleigh (27603) *(G-10013)*

Continental Auto Systems Inc 828 654-2000
1 Quality Way Fletcher (28732) *(G-4731)*

Continental Auto Systems Inc 828 584-4500
1103 Jamestown Rd Morganton (28655) *(G-8859)*

Continental Auto Systems Inc 828 584-4500
1103 Johnstown Rd Valdese (28690) *(G-12193)*

Continental Manufacturing Co 336 697-2591
814c Knox Rd Ste E Mc Leansville (27301) *(G-8220)*

Continental Stone Company 336 951-2945
159 Harvest Rd Reidsville (27320) *(G-10680)*

Continental Teves, Morganton *Also Called: Continental Auto Systems Inc (G-8859)*

Continental Ticking Corp Amer (PA) 336 570-0091
4101 South Nc Hwy 62 Alamance (27201) *(G-55)*

Continental Tool Works Inc 828 692-2578
690 Shepherd St Hendersonville (28792) *(G-6198)*

Contour Enterprises LLC 828 328-1550
3345 Clarence Towery Cir Hildebran (28637) *(G-6847)*

Contract Furniture Restoration, Davidson *Also Called: Davidson House Inc (G-3701)*

Contract Manufacturing Div, Belmont *Also Called: Custom Industries Inc (G-744)*

Contract Printing & Graphics 919 832-7178
2417 Bertie Dr Raleigh (27610) *(G-10014)*

Contract Seating Inc 828 322-6662
796 20th St Ne 4 Hickory (28601) *(G-6310)*

Controlled Release Tech Inc 704 487-0878
1016 Industry Dr Shelby (28152) *(G-11324)*

Controls Group, Charlotte *Also Called: Clarios LLC (G-1926)*

Controls Instrumentation Inc 704 786-1700
272 International Dr Nw Concord (28027) *(G-3344)*

Controls Southeast Inc 704 644-5000
12201 Nations Ford Rd Pineville (28134) *(G-9721)*

Convatec Inc 336 297-3021
7815 National Service Rd Ste 600 Greensboro (27409) *(G-5464)*

Convatec Inc 336 855-5500
7815 National Service Rd Ste 600 Greensboro (27409) *(G-5465)*

Convergence Technologies, Burlington *Also Called: RG Convergence Tech LLC (G-1146)*

Convergent Integration Inc 704 516-5922
10205 Foxhall Dr Charlotte (28210) *(G-1979)*

Conversant Products Inc 919 465-3456
120 Preston Executive Dr Ste 200 Cary (27513) *(G-1334)*

Convert-A-Stair LLC 888 908-5657
3013 Hall Watters Dr Ste C Wilmington (28405) *(G-12750)*

Converting Division, Raleigh *Also Called: Pratt Industries Inc (G-10387)*

Converting Technology Inc 336 333-2386
514 Teague St Greensboro (27406) *(G-5466)*

Conveying Solutions LLC 704 636-4241
804 Julian Rd Salisbury (28147) *(G-11038)*

Conveying Solutions LLC NC, Salisbury *Also Called: Conveying Solutions LLC (G-11038)*

Conveyor Tech LLC 919 776-7227
751 S Church St Goldston (27252) *(G-5257)*

Conveyor Technologies, Goldston *Also Called: Conveyor Tech LLC (G-5257)*

Conveyor Technologies Inc 919 732-8291
1218 Blacksmith Rd Efland (27243) *(G-4375)*

Conveyor Technologies of Sanford NC Inc 919 776-7227
5313 Womack Rd Sanford (27330) *(G-11165)*

Conway Development Inc (PA) 252 756-2168
2218 Dickinson Ave Greenville (27834) *(G-5957)*

Conway Entps Carteret Cnty LLC 252 504-3518
313 Laurel Rd Beaufort (28516) *(G-724)*

Conxit Technology Group Inc 877 998-4227
9101 Southern Pine Blvd Ste 250 Charlotte (28273) *(G-1980)*

Cook & Boardman Group LLC (HQ) 336 768-8872
3064 Salem Industrial Dr Winston Salem (27127) *(G-13127)*

Cook & Boardman Nc LLC 336 768-8872
3916 Westpoint Blvd Winston Salem (27103) *(G-13128)*

COOK & BOARDMAN NC, LLC, Winston Salem *Also Called: Cook & Boardman Nc LLC (G-13128)*

Cook Endoscopy, Winston Salem *Also Called: Wilson-Cook Medical Inc (G-13396)*

Cook Group Inc 336 744-0157
5941 Grassy Creek Blvd Winston Salem (27105) *(G-13129)*

Cook Incorporated 336 744-0157
4900 Bethania Station Rd Winston Salem (27105) *(G-13130)*

Cook Medical Endoscopy Div, Winston Salem *Also Called: Cook Group Inc (G-13129)*

Cooke Communications NC LLC 252 329-9500
1150 Sugg Pkwy Greenville (27834) *(G-5958)*

Cooke Companies Intl 919 968-0848
105 York Pl Chapel Hill (27517) *(G-1540)*

Cooke Rentals Mt Airy NC Inc 336 789-5068
18518 Statesville Rd Cornelius (28031) *(G-3595)*

Cooke Training, Chapel Hill *Also Called: Cooke Companies Intl (G-1540)*

Cool Runnings Jamaican LLC (PA) 919 818-9220
2700 Hidden Glen Ln Raleigh (27606) *(G-10015)*

Coolant & Cleaning Tech Inc 704 753-1333
7421 Morgan Mill Rd Monroe (28110) *(G-8469)*

Cooling Technology Inc 704 596-4109
7102 Windaliere Dr Cornelius (28031) *(G-3596)*

Cooper, Goldsboro *Also Called: Cooper-Standard Automotive Inc (G-5209)*

Cooper B-Line Inc 704 522-6272
3810 Ayscough Rd Charlotte (28211) *(G-1981)*

Cooper Bussmann LLC 252 566-0278
4758 Washington St La Grange (28551) *(G-7465)*

Cooper Crouse-Hinds LLC 252 566-3014
4758 Washington St La Grange (28551) *(G-7466)*

Cooper Industries LLC 304 545-1482
3912 Battleground Ave Greensboro (27410) *(G-5467)*

Cooper Technical Services Inc 910 285-2925
4527 S Us Highway 117 Rose Hill (28458) *(G-10903)*

Cooper Thomas & Benton, Chapel Hill *Also Called: Quick Color Solutions Inc (G-1564)*

Cooper-Standard Automotive Inc 919 735-5394
308 Fedelon Trl Goldsboro (27530) *(G-5209)*

Copia Labs Inc 910 904-1000
2501 Hwy 401 Bus Raeford (28376) *(G-9835)*

Copland, Burlington *Also Called: Copland Fabrics Inc (G-1075)*

Copland Fabrics Inc 336 226-0272
1714 Carolina Mill Rd Burlington (27217) *(G-1075)*

Copland Industries Inc 336 226-0272
1714 Carolina Mill Rd Burlington (27217) *(G-1076)*

Copper Barrel Distillery LLC 336 262-6500
532 Main St North Wilkesboro (28659) *(G-9526)*

Copy Cat Instant Prtg Chrltte 704 529-6606
4612 South Blvd Ste B Charlotte (28209) *(G-1982)*

Copy Express Charlotte Inc 704 527-1750
4004 South Blvd Ste A Charlotte (28209) *(G-1983)*

Copy King Inc (PA) 336 333-9900
611 W Gate City Blvd Greensboro (27403) *(G-5468)*

Copy King Printing, Greensboro *Also Called: Copy King Inc (G-5468)*

Copy Works 828 698-7622
348 7th Ave E Hendersonville (28792) *(G-6199)*

Copycat Print Shop Inc 910 799-1500
637 S Kerr Ave Wilmington (28403) *(G-12751)*

Copymasters Printing Svcs Inc 828 324-0532
818 1st Ave Sw Hickory (28602) *(G-6311)*

Copymatic Document Solutions, Raleigh *Also Called: Easter Seals Ucp NC & VA Inc (G-10070)*

Copymatic of Greenville, Greenville *Also Called: Copymatic United Cerebral (G-5959)*

Copymatic United Cerebral 252 695-6155
200 W 4th St Greenville (27858) *(G-5959)*

Copyrite, Shelby *Also Called: Westmoreland Printers Inc (G-11391)*

Corbett Package Company 910 763-9991
1200 Castle Hayne Rd Wilmington (28401) *(G-12752)*

A
L
P
H
A
B
E
T
I
C

Cordex Instruments Inc.. 877 836-0764
  5309 Monroe Rd Charlotte (28205) *(G-1984)*

Cordset Designs Inc... 252 568-4001
  100 W New St Pink Hill (28572) *(G-9765)*

Core Sound Imaging Inc.. 919 277-0636
  5510 Six Forks Rd Ste 200 Raleigh (27609) *(G-10016)*

Core Technology Molding Corp (PA)............................ 336 294-2018
  2911 E Gate City Blvd Ste 201 Greensboro (27410) *(G-5469)*

Core Technology Molding Corp.................................... 336 294-2018
  5201 Hayward Dr Greensboro (27406) *(G-5470)*

Coregroup Displays, Mooresville Also Called: Coregrp LLC *(G-8643)*

Coregrp LLC.. 845 876-5109
  631 Brawley School Rd Mooresville (28117) *(G-8643)*

Corilam Fabricating Co.. 336 993-2371
  5211 Macy Grove Rd Kernersville (27284) *(G-7259)*

Cormark International LLC.. 828 658-8455
  179 Reems Creek Rd Weaverville (28787) *(G-12489)*

Cormetech, Charlotte Also Called: Steag SCR-Tech Inc *(G-2863)*

Cormetech Inc (HQ).. 704 827-8933
  11707 Steele Creek Rd Charlotte (28273) *(G-1985)*

Cornell & Ferencz Inc.. 919 736-7373
  301 S George St Goldsboro (27530) *(G-5210)*

Cornell Lab Publishing Gropu, Cary Also Called: Phoenix St Claire Pubg LLC *(G-1420)*

Cornell Zimmer Organ Builders, Denver Also Called: C A Zimmer Inc *(G-3776)*

Corner Stone Plastics Inc... 336 629-1828
  1027 Luck Rd Asheboro (27205) *(G-341)*

Cornerstone Biopharma Inc.. 919 678-6507
  175 Regency Woods Pl Ste 600 Cary (27518) *(G-1335)*

Cornerstone Bldg Brands Inc (HQ)............................. 281 897-7788
  5020 Weston Pkwy Cary (27513) *(G-1336)*

Cornerstone Building Brands, Cary Also Called: Cornerstone Bldg Brands Inc *(G-1336)*

Cornerstone Kitchens Inc... 919 510-4200
  6300 Westgate Rd Ste C Raleigh (27617) *(G-10017)*

Cornerstone Software, Oak Ridge Also Called: Oakbrook Solutions Inc *(G-9573)*

Corney Transportation Inc... 800 354-9111
  19214 Us Highway 301 N Saint Pauls (28384) *(G-11004)*

Corning, Charlotte Also Called: Corning Optcal Cmmncations LLC *(G-1987)*

Corning, Durham Also Called: Corning Incorporated *(G-3988)*

Corning, Hickory Also Called: Corning Optcal Cmmncations LLC *(G-6312)*

Corning, Midland Also Called: Corning Incorporated *(G-8284)*

Corning, Newton Also Called: Corning Incorporated *(G-9460)*

Corning, Tarboro Also Called: Corning Incorporated *(G-11924)*

Corning, Wilmington Also Called: Corning Incorporated *(G-12753)*

Corning, Winston Salem Also Called: Corning Incorporated *(G-13131)*

Corning, Winston Salem Also Called: Corning Optcal Cmmncations LLC *(G-13132)*

Corning Incorporated... 919 620-6200
  1 Becton Cir Durham (27712) *(G-3988)*

Corning Incorporated... 704 569-6000
  14556 S Us Hwy 601 Midland (28107) *(G-8284)*

Corning Incorporated... 828 465-0016
  1500 Prodelin Dr Newton (28658) *(G-9460)*

Corning Incorporated... 252 316-4500
  7708 Us Highway 64 Alternate W Tarboro (27886) *(G-11924)*

Corning Incorporated... 910 784-7200
  310 N College Rd Wilmington (28405) *(G-12753)*

Corning Incorporated... 336 771-8000
  3180 Centre Park Blvd Winston Salem (27107) *(G-13131)*

Corning Optcal Cmmncations LLC (HQ)...................... 828 901-5000
  4200 Corning Pl Charlotte (28216) *(G-1986)*

Corning Optcal Cmmncations LLC............................... 828 901-5000
  4200 Corning Pl Charlotte (28216) *(G-1987)*

Corning Optcal Cmmncations LLC............................... 828 327-5290
  1164 23rd St Se Hickory (28602) *(G-6312)*

Corning Optcal Cmmncations LLC............................... 336 771-8000
  3180 Centre Park Blvd Winston Salem (27107) *(G-13132)*

Corob North America Inc.. 704 588-8408
  4901 Gibbon Rd A Charlotte (28269) *(G-1988)*

Corporate Place LLC.. 704 808-3848
  13320 Ballantyne Corporate Pl Charlotte (28277) *(G-1989)*

Corporate Resources, Kinston Also Called: Kinston Office Supply Co Inc *(G-7419)*

Corrtrac Systems Corporation..................................... 252 232-3975
  126 E Canvasback Dr Currituck (27929) *(G-3663)*

Corsan LLC.. 704 765-9979
  13201 Reese Blvd W Ste 100 Huntersville (28078) *(G-6979)*

Cortical Metrics LLC.. 919 903-9943
  209 Lloyd St Ste 360 Carrboro (27510) *(G-1267)*

Cortina Systems.. 919 226-1800
  523 Davis Dr Ste 300 Morrisville (27560) *(G-8960)*

Cosaint Arms, East Flat Rock Also Called: Agile Ventures LLC *(G-4328)*

Cosatron.. 704 785-8145
  640 Church St N Concord (28025) *(G-3345)*

Cosette Pharmaceuticals Inc...................................... 704 735-5700
  1877 Kawai Rd Lincolnton (28092) *(G-7823)*

Cosette Phrmctcals NC Labs LLC............................... 908 753-2000
  1877 Kawai Rd Lincolnton (28092) *(G-7824)*

Cosmetic Creations Inc.. 828 298-4625
  107 W Buckeye Rd Swannanoa (28778) *(G-11869)*

Cosmopros.. 704 717-7420
  1001 E W T Harris Blvd Charlotte (28213) *(G-1990)*

Cotner Cabinet.. 336 672-1560
  3004 Old County Farm Rd Sophia (27350) *(G-11486)*

Cotton Belt Inc.. 252 689-6847
  310 Staton Rd Greenville (27834) *(G-5960)*

Cotton Creek Chip Co, Mount Gilead Also Called: Jordan Lumber & Supply Inc *(G-9200)*

Cotton Creek Chip Company, Star Also Called: Jordan Lumber & Supply Inc *(G-11629)*

Cotton Gin and Warehouse, Newton Grove Also Called: Sampson Gin Company Inc *(G-9517)*

Coty, Sanford Also Called: Coty US LLC *(G-11167)*

Coty Inc.. 919 895-5000
  1400 Broadway Rd Sanford (27332) *(G-11166)*

Coty Sanford Factory, Sanford Also Called: Coty Inc *(G-11166)*

Coty US LLC.. 919 895-5374
  1400 Broadway Rd Sanford (27332) *(G-11167)*

Cougar Run Winery.. 704 788-2746
  215 Union St S Concord (28025) *(G-3346)*

Council Tool Company Inc (PA).................................... 910 646-3011
  345 Pecan Ln Lake Waccamaw (28450) *(G-7471)*

Council Trnsp & Logistics LLC..................................... 910 322-7588
  6217 Rhemish Dr Fayetteville (28304) *(G-4579)*

Councill Company LLC.. 336 859-2155
  1156 N Main St Denton (27239) *(G-3745)*

Counter Effect... 252 636-0080
  115 Justin Dr New Bern (28562) *(G-9356)*

Country At Home Furniture Inc.................................... 828 464-7498
  2010 Log Barn Rd Newton (28658) *(G-9461)*

Country Corner.. 919 444-9663
  2193 Us 64 Business E Pittsboro (27312) *(G-9780)*

Country Heart Braiding... 828 245-0562
  955 Hopper Rd Rutherfordton (28139) *(G-10981)*

Country Lotus Soaps LLC... 786 384-4174
  2313 Ginger Ln Apt H Charlotte (28213) *(G-1991)*

Country Snacks Mfg Inc... 252 433-4644
  513 Commerce Dr Henderson (27537) *(G-6152)*

County Nws-Ntrprs-Maiden Times, Newton Also Called: Observer News Enterprise Inc *(G-9483)*

County of Alexander... 828 632-1101
  255 Liledoun Rd Taylorsville (28681) *(G-11955)*

County of Anson.. 704 848-4849
  567 Filtration Rd Lilesville (28091) *(G-7784)*

County of Dare.. 252 475-5990
  600 S Mustian St Kill Devil Hills (27948) *(G-7315)*

County Press Inc... 919 894-2112
  113 S Market St Benson (27504) *(G-787)*

Courtesy Ford Inc.. 252 338-4783
  1310 N Road St Elizabeth City (27909) *(G-4384)*

Courtesy Ford Lincoln-Mercury, Elizabeth City Also Called: Courtesy Ford Inc *(G-4384)*

Covation Biomaterials LLC.. 252 643-7000
  4693 Highway 11 N Grifton (28530) *(G-6034)*

Covenantmade LLC.. 336 434-4725
  2509 Surrett Dr Archdale (27263) *(G-218)*

Covia Holdings Corporation.. 828 688-2169
  2241 Nc 197 Bakersville (28705) *(G-676)*

(G-0000) Company's Geographic Section entry number

Covia Holdings Corporation.................................... 980 495-2092
9930 Kincey Ave # 200 Huntersville (28078) *(G-6980)*

Covia Holdings Corporation.................................... 828 765-4823
Rag Branch Rd Spruce Pine (28777) *(G-11569)*

COVIA HOLDINGS CORPORATION, Bakersville *Also Called: Covia Holdings Corporation* *(G-676)*

COVIA HOLDINGS CORPORATION, Huntersville *Also Called: Covia Holdings Corporation* *(G-6980)*

COVIA HOLDINGS CORPORATION, Spruce Pine *Also Called: Covia Holdings Corporation* *(G-11569)*

Covia Holdings LLC.. 828 688-2169
Red Hill Iota Plant Bakersville (28705) *(G-677)*

Covia Holdings LLC.. 828 765-1114
136 Crystal Dr Spruce Pine (28777) *(G-11570)*

Covia Holdings LLC.. 828 765-1215
7638 S 226 Hwy Spruce Pine (28777) *(G-11571)*

Covia Holdings LLC.. 828 765-4251
Us Hwy 19 E Spruce Pine (28777) *(G-11572)*

Covia Holdings LLC.. 828 765-4283
Bakersville Rd Spruce Pine (28777) *(G-11573)*

Covidien Holding Inc.. 919 878-2930
8800 Durant Rd Raleigh (27616) *(G-10018)*

Coville Inc (PA).. 336 759-0115
8065 N Point Blvd Ste O Winston Salem (27106) *(G-13133)*

Covington Barcoding Inc..................................... 336 996-5759
1800 Watmead Rd Kernersville (27284) *(G-7260)*

Cowee Mountain Ruby Mine................................... 828 369-5271
6771 Sylva Rd Franklin (28734) *(G-4823)*

Cox Machine Co Inc.. 704 296-0118
2336 Concord Hwy Monroe (28110) *(G-8470)*

Cox Manufacturing Company Inc............................... 828 397-4123
220 10th St Sw Hickory (28602) *(G-6313)*

Cox Nrth Crlina Pblcations Inc................................ 252 482-4418
421 S Broad St Edenton (27932) *(G-4364)*

Cox Nrth Crlina Pblcations Inc................................ 252 335-0841
215 S Water St Elizabeth City (27909) *(G-4385)*

Cox Nrth Crlina Pblcations Inc (DH).......................... 252 329-9643
1150 Sugg Pkwy Greenville (27834) *(G-5961)*

Cox Nrth Crlina Pblcations Inc................................ 910 296-0239
102 Front St Kenansville (28349) *(G-7225)*

Cox Nrth Crlina Pblcations Inc................................ 252 792-1181
106 W Main St Williamston (27892) *(G-12669)*

Cox Precision Springs Inc.................................... 336 629-8500
3162 Spoons Chapel Rd Asheboro (27205) *(G-342)*

Coxe-Lewis Corporation...................................... 252 357-0050
96 Lewis Mill Rd Gatesville (27938) *(G-5171)*

CP Liquidation Inc... 704 921-1100
5104 N Graham St Charlotte (28269) *(G-1992)*

Cpg, Huntersville *Also Called: Common Part Groupings LLC (G-6978)*

CPI, New Bern *Also Called: Chatsworth Products Inc (G-9354)*

CPI Satcom & Antenna Tech Inc.............................. 704 462-7330
1700 Cable Dr Ne Conover (28613) *(G-3508)*

CPI Satcom & Antenna Tech Inc (DH)......................... 704 462-7330
1700 Cable Dr Ne Conover (28613) *(G-3509)*

CPM Acquisition Corp.. 972 243-8070
121 Proctor Ln Lexington (27292) *(G-7669)*

CPM of Nc Inc.. 704 467-5819
4222 Barfield St Concord (28027) *(G-3347)*

CPM Wolverine Proctor LLC.................................. 336 479-2983
121 Proctor Ln Lexington (27292) *(G-7670)*

CPM Wolverine Proctor LLC.................................. 336 248-5181
121 Proctor Ln Lexington (27292) *(G-7671)*

Cpp Global, Asheboro *Also Called: Carolina Precision Plastics L (G-335)*

Cpp Global, Mocksville *Also Called: Carolina Precision Plas LLC (G-8355)*

CPS Resources Inc.. 704 628-7678
2000 Innovation Dr Indian Trail (28079) *(G-7075)*

Cpscolor, Charlotte *Also Called: Corob North America Inc (G-1988)*

Crackle Holdings LP... 704 927-7620
1800 Continental Blvd Ste 200c Charlotte (28273) *(G-1993)*

Craft Brew Alliance Inc...................................... 828 263-1111
163 Boone Creek Dr Boone (28607) *(G-908)*

Craft Doors Usa LLC.. 828 469-7029
1516 Mount Olive Church Rd Newton (28658) *(G-9462)*

Craft Revolution LLC (PA)................................... 347 924-7540
4001 Yancey Rd Ste A Charlotte (28217) *(G-1994)*

Craft Village, Morganton *Also Called: South Mountain Crafts (G-8899)*

Craft-Tex, High Point *Also Called: Concept Plastics Inc (G-6576)*

Craftmark, Kinston *Also Called: Wall-Lenk Corporation (G-7435)*

Craftmaster Furniture Inc (DH).............................. 828 632-9786
221 Craftmaster Rd Hiddenite (28636) *(G-6494)*

Craftmaster Furniture Inc................................... 828 632-8127
750 Sharpe Ln Hiddenite (28636) *(G-6495)*

Craftsman Crate, Smithfield *Also Called: Great Waters Company (G-11445)*

Craftsman Foam Fabricators Inc.............................. 336 476-5655
196 Mason Way Thomasville (27360) *(G-12012)*

Craftsmanship Unlimited, Franklinton *Also Called: Architectural Craftsman Ltd (G-4846)*

Craftwood Veneers Inc...................................... 336 434-2158
822 Herman Ct High Point (27263) *(G-6577)*

Craig & Sandra Blackwell Inc................................ 252 473-1803
932 Harbor Rd Wanchese (27981) *(G-12339)*

Cranberry Wood Works Inc................................... 336 877-8771
13830 Us Highway 221 S Fleetwood (28626) *(G-4715)*

Crane Creek Garden, Mooresville *Also Called: Earth-Kind Inc (G-8659)*

Crane Resistoflex, Marion *Also Called: McC Holdings Inc (G-8052)*

Crane South LLC... 980 422-5874
2905 Westinghouse Blvd Ste 300 Charlotte (28273) *(G-1995)*

Cranford Silk Screen Prcess In.............................. 336 434-6544
7066 Mendenhall Rd Archdale (27263) *(G-219)*

Cranial Technologies Inc.................................... 336 760-5530
1590 Westbrook Plaza Dr Winston Salem (27103) *(G-13134)*

Craters and Freighters Raleigh, Raleigh *Also Called: Lls Investments Inc (G-10258)*

Craven Sign Services Inc................................... 336 883-7306
508 Old Thomasville Rd High Point (27260) *(G-6578)*

Craven Tire Inc.. 252 633-0200
318 1st St New Bern (28560) *(G-9357)*

Crawford Composites LLC.................................... 704 483-4175
3501 Denver Dr Denver (28037) *(G-3778)*

Crawford Industries LLC..................................... 336 884-8822
108 Lane Ave High Point (27260) *(G-6579)*

Crawford Road Liquidating Co................................ 704 871-1830
174 Crawford Rd Ste A Statesville (28625) *(G-11679)*

Craymer McElwee Holdings Inc.............................. 828 326-6100
6429 Hildebran Shelby Rd Hickory (28602) *(G-6314)*

Crazie Tees.. 704 898-2272
177 Brookstone Dr Mount Holly (28120) *(G-9226)*

CRC.. 704 664-1242
2425 Statesville Hwy Mooresville (28115) *(G-8644)*

CRC Machine & Fabrication Inc.............................. 980 522-1361
4375 Dallas Cherryville Hwy Bessemer City (28016) *(G-810)*

CRC Powder Coating, Mooresville *Also Called: CRC (G-8644)*

CRC Printing Co Inc.. 704 875-1804
15700 Old Statesville Rd Huntersville (28078) *(G-6981)*

Creasman D C Mfrs Fine Jewe, Asheville *Also Called: D C Crsman Mfr Fine Jwly Inc (G-482)*

Creations By Taylor.. 410 269-6430
2892 Long Run Farm Rd Mount Pleasant (28124) *(G-9261)*

Creations Cabinetry Design LLC.............................. 919 865-5979
3825 Junction Blvd Raleigh (27603) *(G-10019)*

Creative Brewing Company LLC.............................. 919 297-8182
809 S 2nd St Smithfield (27577) *(G-11441)*

Creative Caps Inc.. 919 701-1175
214 E Broad St Dunn (28334) *(G-3852)*

Creative Clout Agency, Morehead City *Also Called: Christian Focus Magazine (G-8825)*

Creative Custom Woodworks Inc............................. 910 431-8544
1290 S 15th St B Wilmington (28401) *(G-12754)*

Creative Fabric Services LLC................................ 704 861-8383
1675 Garfield Dr Gastonia (28052) *(G-5031)*

Creative Images Inc.. 919 467-2188
226 E Chatham St Cary (27511) *(G-1337)*

Creative Liquid Coatings Inc................................ 336 415-6214
710 Piedmont Triad West Dr Mount Airy (27030) *(G-9116)*

Creative Metal and Wood Inc................................ 336 475-9400
8512 Blackstone Dr Colfax (27235) *(G-3276)*

Creative Outdoor Advertising, Shelby *Also Called: Headrick Otdoor Mdia of Crlnas (G-11343)*

Creative Printers, Andrews *Also Called: Creative Printers & Brks Inc (G-106)*

Creative Printers Inc.. 336 246-7746
4 N 6th Ave West Jefferson (28694) *(G-12563)*

Creative Printers & Brks Inc....................................... 828 321-4663
980 Main St Andrews (28901) *(G-106)*

Creative Printing Inc... 828 265-2800
1738 Nc Highway 105 Byp Boone (28607) *(G-909)*

Creative Printing Stanley Inc...................................... 704 732-6398
4147 Stoney Creek Dr Lincolnton (28092) *(G-7825)*

Creative Prosthetics and Ortho................................... 828 994-4808
3305 16th Ave Se Ste 101 Conover (28613) *(G-3510)*

Creative Prtg Intrnet Svcs LLC................................... 828 265-2800
1738 Nc Highway 105 Byp Boone (28607) *(G-910)*

Creative Screening.. 919 467-5081
303 E Durham Rd Ste C Cary (27513) *(G-1338)*

Creative Services Usa Inc... 336 887-1958
1231 Montlieu Ave High Point (27262) *(G-6580)*

Creative Sign Solutions Inc.. 704 978-8499
563 Rimrock Rd Statesville (28625) *(G-11680)*

Creative Signs Inc.. 910 395-0100
4305 Oleander Dr Wilmington (28403) *(G-12755)*

Creative Stone, Fayetteville *Also Called: Creative Stone Fyetteville Inc (G-4580)*

Creative Stone Fyetteville Inc (PA)..............................910 491-1225
918 Foxhunt Ln Fayetteville (28314) *(G-4580)*

Creative T-Shirts Imaging LLC.................................... 919 828-0204
2526 Hillsborough St Ste 101 Raleigh (27607) *(G-10020)*

Creative Textiles Inc... 919 693-4427
615 Hillsboro St Oxford (27565) *(G-9609)*

Creative Tooling Solutions Inc.................................... 704 504-5415
10809 Southern Loop Blvd Pineville (28134) *(G-9722)*

Creative Woodcrafters Inc.. 828 252-9663
42 West Rd Leicester (28748) *(G-7522)*

Creedmoor Forest Products... 919 529-1779
2128 Hoerner Warldorf Rd Creedmoor (27522) *(G-3646)*

Creek Industries Inc.. 828 319-7490
87 Island In The Sky Trl Weaverville (28787) *(G-12490)*

Creek Life LLC.. 910 892-9337
471 Cleveland Crossing Dr Ste 101 Garner (27529) *(G-4926)*

Creekraft Cultured Marble Inc..................................... 252 636-5488
3205 Old Cherry Point Rd New Bern (28560) *(G-9358)*

Creekside Creative Design Inc..................................... 252 243-6272
206 Goldsboro St Sw Wilson (27893) *(G-12982)*

Creeled Inc... 919 313-5330
4001 E Hwy 54 Ste 2000 Durham (27709) *(G-3989)*

Creighton Ab Inc.. 336 349-8275
205 Watlington Industrial Dr Reidsville (27320) *(G-10681)*

Cres Tobacco Company LLC... 336 983-7727
3000 Big Oaks Rd King (27021) *(G-7325)*

Crest Electronics Inc.. 336 855-6422
3703 Alliance Dr Ste A Greensboro (27407) *(G-5471)*

Crestview Trading Post, Rockingham *Also Called: Allen Brothers Timber Company (G-10770)*

Crete Solutions LLC.. 910 726-1686
2005 Eastwood Rd Ste 200 Wilmington (28403) *(G-12756)*

Crh Americas Inc.. 704 282-8443
1139 N Charlotte Ave Monroe (28110) *(G-8471)*

Cricket Forge LLC.. 919 680-3513
2314 Operations Dr Durham (27705) *(G-3990)*

Crisp Printers Inc.. 704 867-6663
2022 E Ozark Ave Gastonia (28054) *(G-5032)*

Cristal Dragon Candle Company................................... 336 997-4210
3271 Moir Farm Rd Sandy Ridge (27046) *(G-11142)*

Criticore Inc (PA)..704 542-6876
9525 Monroe Rd Ste 150 Charlotte (28270) *(G-1996)*

Crizaf Inc.. 919 251-7661
2, 1534 Cher Dr, Durham (27713) *(G-3991)*

Crizaf Srl, Durham *Also Called: Crizaf Inc (G-3991)*

Crm A LLC... 888 600-7567
8000 Weston Pkwy Ste 100 Cary (27513) *(G-1339)*

Crmnext Inc... 415 424-4644
702 Oberlin Rd Ofc Ofc Raleigh (27605) *(G-10021)*

Crmp, Ahoskie *Also Called: Commercial Ready Mix Pdts Inc (G-45)*

Crmp Inc... 252 358-5461
115 Hwy 158 W Winton (27986) *(G-13428)*

Crockers Inc... 336 366-2005
1821 Joe Layne Mill Rd Elkin (28621) *(G-4442)*

Croft Precision Tools Inc.. 704 399-4124
4424 Taggart Creek Rd Ste 108 Charlotte (28208) *(G-1997)*

Crompton Instruments.. 919 557-8698
8000 Purfoy Rd Fuquay Varina (27526) *(G-4876)*

Croscill Home LLC.. 919 735-7111
200 Ne Outer Loop Oxford (27565) *(G-9610)*

Cross & Crown, Ayden *Also Called: Free Will Bptst Press Fndtion (G-657)*

Cross Canvas Company Inc.. 828 252-0440
63 Glendale Ave Asheville (28803) *(G-480)*

Cross Hose and Fitting, Greensboro *Also Called: Cross Technologies Inc (G-5473)*

Cross Manufacturing LLC.. 336 269-6542
2505 Parrish St Burlington (27215) *(G-1077)*

Cross Precision Measurement, Greensboro *Also Called: Cross Technologies Inc (G-5472)*

Cross Technologies Inc (PA).. 800 327-7727
4400 Piedmont Pkwy Greensboro (27410) *(G-5472)*

Cross Technologies Inc.. 336 370-4673
3012 S Elm Eugene St Ste A Greensboro (27406) *(G-5473)*

Cross Technologies Inc.. 336 292-0511
6541c Franz Warner Pkwy Whitsett (27377) *(G-12603)*

Cross Technology Inc (PA)... 336 725-4700
101 Cross Tech Dr East Bend (27018) *(G-4322)*

Crossroads Coatings, Statesville *Also Called: Crossroads Coatings Inc (G-11681)*

Crossroads Coatings Inc... 704 873-2244
208 Bucks Industrial Rd Statesville (28625) *(G-11681)*

Crossroads Fuel Service Inc.. 252 426-5216
395 Ocean Hwy N Hertford (27944) *(G-6252)*

Crossroads Tire Store Inc... 704 888-2064
4430 Albemarle Rd Midland (28107) *(G-8285)*

Croswait Custom Composites Inc................................... 252 423-1245
90 Dusty Ln Wanchese (27981) *(G-12340)*

Crowder Trucking LLC.. 910 797-4163
6776 Saint Julian Way Fayetteville (28314) *(G-4581)*

Crowdguard Inc.. 919 605-1948
12218 Bradford Green Sq Ste 151 Cary (27519) *(G-1340)*

Crown Case Co... 704 453-1542
801 Atando Ave Ste C Charlotte (28206) *(G-1998)*

Crown Defense Ltd.. 202 800-8848
2320 N Nc 16 Business Hwy Denver (28037) *(G-3779)*

Crown Equipment Corporation....................................... 336 291-2500
8220 Tyner Rd Colfax (27235) *(G-3277)*

Crown Equipment Corporation....................................... 704 721-4000
8401 Westmoreland Dr Nw Concord (28027) *(G-3348)*

Crown Equipment Corporation....................................... 919 773-4160
1000 N Greenfield Pkwy Ste 1090 Garner (27529) *(G-4927)*

Crown Equipment Corporation....................................... 252 522-3088
2000 Dobbs Farm Rd Kinston (28504) *(G-7403)*

Crown Foam Products Inc.. 336 434-4024
921 Baker Rd Ste 3 High Point (27263) *(G-6581)*

Crown Heritage Inc... 336 835-1424
296 Gentry Rd Elkin (28621) *(G-4443)*

Crown Lift Trucks, Colfax *Also Called: Crown Equipment Corporation (G-3277)*

Crown Lift Trucks, Garner *Also Called: Crown Equipment Corporation (G-4927)*

Crown Lift Trucks, Kinston *Also Called: Crown Equipment Corporation (G-7403)*

Crown Town Industries LLC.. 704 579-0387
813 Hydrangea Cir Nw Concord (28027) *(G-3349)*

Crown Trophy Inc... 336 851-1011
201 Pomona Dr Ste C Greensboro (27407) *(G-5474)*

Crp Usa LLC... 704 660-0258
127 Goodwin Cir Mooresville (28115) *(G-8645)*

CRS Laboratories, Apex *Also Called: Sciepharm LLC (G-193)*

CRS Laboratories, Durham *Also Called: Sciepharm LLC (G-4225)*

CRS/Las Inc... 910 392-0883
120 Racine Dr Ste 3 Wilmington (28403) *(G-12757)*

Crude LLC... 919 391-8185
501 E Davie St Raleigh (27601) *(G-10022)*

(G-0000) Company's Geographic Section entry number

Cruise Industry News, Charlotte *Also Called: Mathisen Ventures Inc (G-2468)*

Crumble Cups LLC 919 520-7414
2161 S Wilmington St Raleigh (27603) *(G-10023)*

Crump Group USA Inc 936 465-5870
4626 Coleman Dr Nashville (27856) *(G-9317)*

Crumpler Plastic Pipe Inc 910 525-4046
852 Autry Hwy 24 Roseboro (28382) *(G-10912)*

Crww Specialty Composites Inc 828 548-5002
2678 Heart Dr Bldg B Claremont (28610) *(G-3105)*

Cryogen LLC 919 649-7027
2626 Glenwood Ave Ste 140 Raleigh (27608) *(G-10024)*

Cryovac LLC (HQ) 980 430-7000
2415 Cascade Pointe Blvd Charlotte (28208) *(G-1999)*

Cryovac Intl Holdings Inc (HQ) 980 430-7000
2415 Cascade Pointe Blvd Charlotte (28208) *(G-2000)*

Cryovac Leasing Corporation 980 430-7000
2415 Cascade Pointe Blvd Charlotte (28208) *(G-2001)*

Crypton Mills LLC 828 202-5875
3400 Hwy 221a Cliffside (28024) *(G-3225)*

Crystal Coast Machine LLC 252 876-3859
190 Aeronautical Way New Bern (28562) *(G-9359)*

Crystal Impressions Ltd 704 821-7678
14200 E Independence Blvd Indian Trail (28079) *(G-7076)*

Crystal Plant, Spruce Pine *Also Called: Covia Holdings LLC (G-11570)*

Cs Alloys 704 675-5810
2888 Colony Woods Dr Gastonia (28054) *(G-5033)*

Cs Carolina Inc 336 578-0110
1305 Graham St Burlington (27217) *(G-1078)*

Cs Ink, Madison *Also Called: Custom Screens Inc (G-7985)*

Cs Systems Company Inc 800 525-9878
1465 Sand Hill Rd Ste 2050 Candler (28715) *(G-1222)*

Csa Wireless, Conover *Also Called: Amphenol Antenna Solutions Inc (G-3489)*

CSC Awnings Inc 336 744-5006
3950 N Liberty St Winston Salem (27105) *(G-13135)*

CSC Bearing North America Inc 734 456-6206
1574 Startown Rd Lincolnton (28092) *(G-7826)*

CSC Family Holdings Inc 336 993-2680
9035 Us Hwy 421 Colfax (27235) *(G-3278)*

CSC Family Holdings Inc (PA) 336 275-9711
101 Centreport Dr Ste 400 Greensboro (27409) *(G-5475)*

CSC Family Holdings Inc 252 459-7116
341 Corbett Rd Nashville (27856) *(G-9318)*

CSC Sheet Metal Inc 919 544-8887
1310 E Cornwallis Rd Durham (27713) *(G-3992)*

Csi, Charlotte *Also Called: Component Sourcing Intl LLC (G-1967)*

Csi, Madison *Also Called: Deep South Holding Company Inc (G-7986)*

Csi, Newton *Also Called: Custom Socks Ink Inc (G-9463)*

Csi, Pineville *Also Called: Controls Southeast Inc (G-9721)*

Csi Armoring Inc 336 313-8561
425 Industrial Dr Lexington (27295) *(G-7672)*

Csit Group 828 233-5750
205 Newstock Rd Asheville (28804) *(G-481)*

CSM, Graham *Also Called: CSM Manufacturing Inc (G-5266)*

CSM Logistics LLC 980 800-2621
4835 Sirona Dr Ste 300 Charlotte (28273) *(G-2002)*

CSM Manufacturing, Graham *Also Called: Red Wolfe Industries LLC (G-5284)*

CSM Manufacturing Inc 336 570-2282
913 Washington St Graham (27253) *(G-5266)*

CSS, Greensboro *Also Called: Ddp Spclty Elctrnic Mtls US 9 (G-5490)*

Cstruct, Raleigh *Also Called: Starta Development Inc (G-10505)*

CT Commercial Paper LLC 704 485-3212
349 S Main St Oakboro (28129) *(G-9577)*

CT Nassau Mat Tape & Ticking, Alamance *Also Called: Continental Ticking Corp Amer (G-55)*

Ct-Nassau Tape LLC 336 570-0091
4101 S N Carolina Hwy 62 Alamance (27201) *(G-56)*

Ct-Nassau Ticking LLC 336 570-0091
1504 Anthony Rd Burlington (27215) *(G-1079)*

Ctc, Gastonia *Also Called: Champion Thread Company (G-5018)*

Ctc Holdings LLC (PA) 704 867-6611
165 Bluedevil Dr Gastonia (28056) *(G-5034)*

Cth-Shrrill Occsional Furn Div, Hickory *Also Called: Sherrill Furniture Company (G-6440)*

CTI, Wilmington *Also Called: Ceres Turf Inc (G-12741)*

CTI Property Services Inc 919 787-3789
5450 Old Wake Forest Rd Raleigh (27609) *(G-10025)*

CTI Systems, Sanford *Also Called: Conveyor Technologies of Sanford NC Inc (G-11165)*

CTS, Rocky Point *Also Called: Cincinnati Thermal Spray Inc (G-10878)*

CTS Cleaning Systems Inc 910 483-5349
2185 Angelia M St Fayetteville (28312) *(G-4582)*

CTX Builders Supply 704 983-6748
2100 Sterling Dr Albemarle (28001) *(G-66)*

Cub Creek Kitchens & Baths Inc 336 651-8983
309 Wilkesboro Ave North Wilkesboro (28659) *(G-9527)*

Culp Inc 662 844-7144
2742 Tucker St # A Burlington (27215) *(G-1080)*

Culp Inc (PA) 336 889-5161
1823 Eastchester Dr High Point (27265) *(G-6582)*

Culp Inc 336 885-2800
7209 Us Highway 158 Stokesdale (27357) *(G-11810)*

Culp Inc 336 643-7751
7209 Us Highway 158 Stokesdale (27357) *(G-11811)*

Culp of Mississippi, Burlington *Also Called: Culp Inc (G-1080)*

Culp Ticking, Stokesdale *Also Called: Culp Inc (G-11811)*

Culpeper Roanoke Rapids LLC 252 678-3804
2262 W 10th St Roanoke Rapids (27870) *(G-10736)*

Cultivated Cocktails, Asheville *Also Called: H&H Distillery LLC (G-514)*

Culture Shock Toys, Huntersville *Also Called: PCS Collectibles LLC (G-7030)*

Cumberland Grav & Sand Min Co (PA) 828 686-3844
Old Us Highway 70 Swannanoa (28778) *(G-11870)*

Cumberland Gravel, Marion *Also Called: B V Hedrick Gravel & Sand Co (G-8032)*

Cumberland Gravel & Sand Co 704 633-4241
Salisbury (28145) *(G-11039)*

Cumberland Sand and Gravel 704 474-3165
12423 Old Aquadale Rd Norwood (28128) *(G-9555)*

Cumins Machinery Corp 336 622-1000
312 W Luther Ave Liberty (27298) *(G-7762)*

Cummins, Charlotte *Also Called: Cummins Inc (G-2003)*

Cummins, Charlotte *Also Called: Pcai Inc (G-2622)*

Cummins, Greensboro *Also Called: Cummins Inc (G-5476)*

Cummins, Kenly *Also Called: Cummins Inc (G-7230)*

Cummins Inc 704 596-7690
3700 Jeff Adams Dr Charlotte (28206) *(G-2003)*

Cummins Inc 336 275-4531
513 Preddy Blvd Greensboro (27406) *(G-5476)*

Cummins Inc 919 284-9111
350 Cummins Dr Kenly (27542) *(G-7230)*

Cummins Inc 919 284-9111
350 Cummins Dr Kenly (27542) *(G-7231)*

Cummins Inc 704 588-1240
11101 Nations Ford Rd Pineville (28134) *(G-9723)*

Cumulus - Statesville West, Statesville *Also Called: Fibrix LLC (G-11696)*

Cumulus Fibres - Charlotte, Charlotte *Also Called: Fibrix LLC (G-2150)*

Cumulus Fibres - Statesville, Statesville *Also Called: Fibrix LLC (G-11697)*

Cumulus Fibres Inc 704 394-2111
1101 Tar Heel Rd Charlotte (28208) *(G-2004)*

Cunningham Brick Company 336 248-8541
701 N Main St Lexington (27292) *(G-7673)*

Cupcake Bar 919 816-2905
315 Monmouth Ave Durham (27701) *(G-3993)*

Cupcake Stop Shop LLC 919 457-7900
6902 Cameron Crest Cir Apt 118 Raleigh (27613) *(G-10026)*

Curious Discoveries Inc 336 643-0432
7911 Windspray Dr Summerfield (27358) *(G-11837)*

Curlee Machinery Company 919 467-9311
412 Field St Cary (27513) *(G-1341)*

Current Enterprises Inc 919 469-1227
125 International Dr Ste J Morrisville (27560) *(G-8961)*

Currie Motorsports Inc 910 580-1765
611 College Dr Raeford (28376) *(G-9836)*

Currier Woodworks Inc 252 725-4233
1622 Live Oak St Beaufort (28516) *(G-725)*

Cursed Society LLC..702 445-5601
27 Covey Ln Apt G Greensboro (27406) *(G-5477)*

Curti USA Corporation.................................910 769-1977
161 Poole Rd Belville (28451) *(G-779)*

Curtis L Maclean L C....................................704 940-5531
227 Manufacturers Blvd Mooresville (28115) *(G-8646)*

Curtis Packing Company (PA).......................336 275-7684
2416 Randolph Ave Greensboro (27406) *(G-5478)*

Curtiss-Wright Controls Inc (HQ)................704 869-4600
15801 Brixham Hill Ave Ste 200 Charlotte (27277) *(G-2005)*

Curtiss-Wright Controls Inc.......................704 869-2320
3120 Northwest Blvd Gastonia (28052) *(G-5035)*

Curtiss-Wright Controls Inc.......................704 869-2300
201 Old Boiling Springs Rd Shelby (28152) *(G-11325)*

Curtiss-Wright Controls Inc.......................704 481-1150
201 Old Boiling Springs Rd Shelby (28152) *(G-11326)*

Curtiss-Wright Corporation........................973 541-3700
13925 Ballantyne Corporate Pl Charlotte (28277) *(G-2006)*

Curtiss-Wright Corporation........................704 869-4675
500 Springbrook Rd Charlotte (28217) *(G-2007)*

Curtiss-Wright Corporation (PA).................704 869-4600
130 Harbour Place Dr Ste 300 Davidson (28036) *(G-3700)*

Curtiss-Wright Corporation........................704 481-1150
201 Old Boiling Springs Rd Shelby (28152) *(G-11327)*

Curved Plywood Inc....................................336 249-6901
111 E 7th Ave Lexington (27292) *(G-7674)*

Curvemakers Inc...919 690-1121
115 Corporation Dr Oxford (27565) *(G-9611)*

Curvemakers Inc (PA).................................919 821-5792
703 W Johnson St Raleigh (27603) *(G-10027)*

Cushion Manufacturing Inc........................828 324-9555
1343 9th Ave Ne Hickory (28601) *(G-6315)*

Custom Air Trays Inc (PA)...........................336 889-8729
2112 S Elm St High Point (27260) *(G-6583)*

Custom Armor Group Inc............................336 617-4667
4270 Piedmont Pkwy Ste 102 Greensboro (27410) *(G-5479)*

Custom Assemblies Inc..............................919 202-4533
330 E Main St Pine Level (27568) *(G-9678)*

Custom Automated Machines Inc................704 289-7038
509 E Windsor St Monroe (28112) *(G-8472)*

Custom Brick and Supplied Co., Raleigh *Also Called: Custom Brick Company Inc (G-10028)*

Custom Brick Company Inc.........................919 832-2804
1833 Capital Blvd Raleigh (27604) *(G-10028)*

Custom Cabinet Works...............................828 396-6348
180 N Main St Granite Falls (28630) *(G-5301)*

Custom Cabinets By Livengood..................704 279-3031
490 Parks Rd Salisbury (28146) *(G-11040)*

Custom Canvas Works Inc..........................919 662-4800
540 Dynamic Dr Garner (27529) *(G-4928)*

Custom Cnc LLC...828 734-8293
6989 Carolina Blvd Clyde (28721) *(G-3257)*

Custom Cnverting Solutions Inc..................336 292-2616
1207 Boston Rd Greensboro (27407) *(G-5480)*

Custom Controls Unlimited LLC..................919 812-6553
2600 Garner Station Blvd Raleigh (27603) *(G-10029)*

Custom Corrugated Cntrs Inc......................704 588-0371
5024 Westinghouse Blvd Charlotte (28273) *(G-2008)*

Custom Design Inc......................................704 637-7110
2001 S Main St Salisbury (28144) *(G-11041)*

Custom Designs and Upholstery..................336 882-1516
1372 Unity St # B Thomasville (27360) *(G-12013)*

Custom Doors Incorporated........................704 982-2885
800 Laton Rd Albemarle (28001) *(G-67)*

Custom Educational Furn LLC.....................800 255-9189
2696 Nc Highway 16 S Taylorsville (28681) *(G-11956)*

Custom Electric Mfg LLC............................248 305-7700
180 International Dr Nw Concord (28027) *(G-3350)*

Custom Enterprises Inc..............................336 226-8296
129 E Ruffin St Burlington (27217) *(G-1081)*

Custom Extrusion Inc.................................336 495-7070
2971 Taylor Dr Asheboro (27203) *(G-343)*

Custom Fabric Samples Inc.........................336 472-1854
261 Sunset Dr Thomasville (27360) *(G-12014)*

Custom Finishers Inc (PA)..........................336 431-7141
2213 Shore St High Point (27263) *(G-6584)*

Custom Gears Inc.......................................704 735-6883
3565 Hwy 155 S Lincolnton (28092) *(G-7827)*

Custom Glass Works Inc.............................704 597-0290
2000 W Morehead St Ste F Charlotte (28208) *(G-2009)*

Custom Golf Car Supply Inc........................704 855-1130
1735 Heilig Rd Salisbury (28146) *(G-11042)*

Custom Hydraulics & Design (PA)...............704 347-0023
242 Dick Beam Rd Cherryville (28021) *(G-3061)*

Custom Industries Inc................................704 825-3346
111 Hubbard St Belmont (28012) *(G-744)*

Custom Industries Inc (PA).........................336 299-2885
215 Aloe Rd Greensboro (27409) *(G-5481)*

Custom Light and Sound Inc.......................919 286-1122
2506 Guess Rd Durham (27705) *(G-3994)*

Custom Machine Company Inc....................704 629-5326
221 White Jenkins Rd Bessemer City (28016) *(G-811)*

Custom Machining Inc................................336 996-0855
121 Majestic Way Ct Ste D Kernersville (27284) *(G-7261)*

Custom Marble Corporation (PA)................910 215-0679
150 Safford Dr Pinehurst (28374) *(G-9690)*

Custom Marine Fabrication Inc...................252 638-5422
2401 Us Highway 70 E New Bern (28560) *(G-9360)*

Custom Marking & Printing Inc...................704 866-8245
907 Bessemer City Rd Gastonia (28052) *(G-5036)*

Custom Medical Specialties Inc...................919 202-8462
330 E Main St Pine Level (27568) *(G-9679)*

Custom Metal Finishing.............................704 445-1710
617 E Main St # B Cherryville (28021) *(G-3062)*

Custom Metal Products, Wilmington *Also Called: Metal-Cad Stl Frmng Systems In (G-12852)*

Custom Neon & Graphics Inc......................704 344-1715
1722 Toal St Charlotte (28206) *(G-2010)*

Custom Packaging Inc................................828 684-5060
20 Beale Rd Arden (28704) *(G-264)*

Custom Packaging of Asheville, Arden *Also Called: Custom Packaging Inc (G-264)*

Custom Patch Hats LLC..............................919 424-7723
1505 Capital Blvd Ste 14b Raleigh (27603) *(G-10030)*

Custom Plastic Forming, Salisbury *Also Called: Custom Golf Car Supply Inc (G-11042)*

Custom Polymers, Charlotte *Also Called: Custom Polymers Inc (G-2011)*

Custom Polymers Inc (PA)...........................704 332-6070
831 E Morehead St Ste 840 Charlotte (28202) *(G-2011)*

Custom Polymers Pet LLC (PA)....................866 717-0716
831 E Morehead St Ste 840 Charlotte (28202) *(G-2012)*

Custom Printing Solutions Inc....................336 992-1161
1355 S Park Dr Kernersville (27284) *(G-7262)*

Custom Products Inc..................................704 663-4159
1618 Landis Hwy Mooresville (28115) *(G-8647)*

Custom Rehabilitation Spc Inc....................910 471-2962
7225 Anaca Point Rd Wilmington (28411) *(G-12758)*

Custom Screens Inc....................................336 427-0265
2216 Us Highway 311 Madison (27025) *(G-7985)*

Custom Seatings..828 879-1964
3011 High Peak Rd Valdese (28690) *(G-12194)*

Custom Sgns - Dsign Mnfcture I, Apex *Also Called: Mercury Signs Inc (G-180)*

Custom Sheetmetal Services Inc.................919 282-1088
5109 Neal Rd Durham (27705) *(G-3995)*

Custom Smiles Inc......................................919 331-2090
123 Fish Dr Ste 101 Angier (27501) *(G-118)*

Custom Socks Ink Inc.................................828 695-9869
2011 N Main Ave Newton (28658) *(G-9463)*

Custom Steel Incorporated.........................919 383-9170
3161 Hillsborough Rd Durham (27705) *(G-3996)*

Custom Steel Boats Inc..............................252 745-7447
102 Yacht Dr Merritt (28556) *(G-8267)*

Custom Steel Fabricators Inc......................336 498-5099
362 Providence Church Rd Randleman (27317) *(G-10639)*

Custom Surfaces Corporation.....................252 638-3800
115 Justin Dr New Bern (28562) *(G-9361)*

Custom Veneers Inc 828 758-7001
1790 Cedar Dr Lenoir (28645) *(G-7597)*

Custom Win Trtments Dctr Items, Boone *Also Called: Bettys Drapery Design Workroom*
(G-897)

Custom Wood Products, Monroe *Also Called: Robert Hamms LLC (G-8552)*

Customer Service Center Repair, Monroe *Also Called: Goodrich Corporation (G-8494)*

Customer Service Department, Cary *Also Called: Oxford University Press LLC (G-1413)*

Customer Service Spare, Monroe *Also Called: Goodrich Corporation (G-8493)*

Cut Above Construction 828 758-8557
3815 Charles White Ln Lenoir (28645) *(G-7598)*

Cutting Edge Stoneworks, Mooresville *Also Called: Cutting Edge Stoneworks Inc (G-8648)*

Cutting Edge Stoneworks Inc 704 799-1227
161 Mckenzie Rd Mooresville (28115) *(G-8648)*

Cutting Systems Inc 704 592-2451
774 Zeb Rd Union Grove (28689) *(G-12184)*

Cv Industries Inc (PA) 828 328-1851
401 11th St Nw Hickory (28601) *(G-6316)*

Cvc & Equipment, Cherryville *Also Called: CVC Equipment Company (G-3063)*

CVC Equipment Company 704 300-6242
316 Old Stubbs Rd Ste 1 Cherryville (28021) *(G-3063)*

Cvmr (usa) Inc 828 288-3768
2702 Centennial Rd Union Mills (28167) *(G-12188)*

Cw Landscapes, Efland *Also Called: Chapman Welding LLC (G-4374)*

CWC Fabricating 704 360-8264
2530 Graham Rd Mount Ulla (28125) *(G-9268)*

Cwi Services LLC 704 560-9755
3382 Willow Cir Se Southport (28461) *(G-11518)*

Cyber Defense Advisors 336 899-6072
3336 Wall Rd Greensboro (27407) *(G-5482)*

Cyber Imaging Systems Inc 919 872-5179
8300 Falls Of Neuse Rd Raleigh (27615) *(G-10031)*

Cyberlux Corporation (PA) 984 363-6894
800 Park Offices Dr Ste 3209 Research Triangle Pa (27709) *(G-10707)*

Cycle Pro LLC 704 662-6682
261 Rolling Hill Rd Ste 1a Mooresville (28117) *(G-8649)*

Cycra Racing, Thomasville *Also Called: Sv Plastics LLC (G-12077)*

Cycra Racing Systems, Thomasville *Also Called: Next World Design Inc (G-12054)*

Cygany Inc 773 293-2999
2712 Denise Dr Greensboro (27407) *(G-5483)*

Cymbal LLC 877 365-9622
2500 Regency Pkwy Cary (27518) *(G-1342)*

Cynthia Saar 910 480-2523
5139 Front St Stedman (28391) *(G-11806)*

Cyp, Tryon *Also Called: Carolina Yarn Processors Inc (G-12172)*

Cypress Bend Vineyards Inc 910 369-0411
21904 Riverton Rd Wagram (28396) *(G-12255)*

Cypress Mountain Company (HQ) 252 758-2179
107 Staton Ct Greenville (27834) *(G-5962)*

Cyrco Inc 336 668-0977
120 N Chimney Rock Rd Greensboro (27409) *(G-5484)*

Cyril Bath Company (PA) 704 289-8531
1610 Airport Rd Monroe (28110) *(G-8473)*

Cytonet LLC
801 Capitola Dr Ste 8 Durham (27713) *(G-3997)*

Czechmate Enterprises LLC 704 784-6547
6101 Zion Church Rd Concord (28025) *(G-3351)*

D & B Concepts Inc 336 885-8292
613 Prospect St High Point (27260) *(G-6585)*

D & B Printing Co 919 876-3530
3000 Trawick Rd Raleigh (27604) *(G-10032)*

D & D Displays Inc 336 667-8765
126 Shaver St North Wilkesboro (28659) *(G-9528)*

D & D Entps Greensboro Inc 336 495-3407
1337 Burnetts Chapel Rd Greensboro (27406) *(G-5485)*

D & D Entps Greensboro Inc 336 495-3407
10458 Us Highway 220 Bus N Randleman (27317) *(G-10640)*

D & D Machine Works Inc 704 878-0117
111 Dealwood Dr Statesville (28625) *(G-11682)*

D & D Precision Tool, Greensboro *Also Called: D & D Entps Greensboro Inc (G-5485)*

D & F Consolidated Inc 704 664-6660
2205 Mocaro Dr Statesville (28677) *(G-11683)*

D & L Cabinets Inc 336 376-6009
1010 Rolling Oaks Dr Graham (27253) *(G-5267)*

D & M Logging of Wnc LLC 828 648-4366
1936 Beaverdam Rd Canton (28716) *(G-1251)*

D & M Packing Company 704 982-3716
687 Morgan Rd Albemarle (28001) *(G-68)*

D & S International Inc 336 578-3800
700 Trollingwood Hawflds Rd Mebane (27302) *(G-8237)*

D & T Soy Candles 704 320-2804
152 Hawk Rd Polkton (28135) *(G-9814)*

D & W Logging Inc 919 820-0826
1771 Stricklands Crossroads Rd Four Oaks (27524) *(G-4810)*

D A C, Rural Hall *Also Called: Dac Products Inc (G-10958)*

D A Moore, Concord *Also Called: K&H Acquisition Company LLC (G-3388)*

D Block Metals LLC (PA) 704 705-5895
1111 Jenkins Rd Gastonia (28052) *(G-5037)*

D Block Metals LLC 980 238-2600
1808 Indian Creek Rd Lincolnton (28092) *(G-7828)*

D C Crsman Mfr Fine Jwly Inc 828 252-9891
269 Tunnel Rd Asheville (28805) *(G-482)*

D C Thomas Group Inc (PA) 336 299-6263
6540 W Market St Greensboro (27409) *(G-5486)*

D C Thomas Group Inc 252 433-0132
860 Commerce Dr Henderson (27537) *(G-6153)*

D J Enviro Solutions 828 495-7448
334 Riverview Rd Taylorsville (28681) *(G-11957)*

D M & E Corporation 704 482-8876
833 S Post Rd Shelby (28152) *(G-11328)*

D R Burton Healthcare LLC 252 228-7038
3936 South Fields St Farmville (27828) *(G-4526)*

D R Kincaid Chair Co Inc 828 754-0255
3122 Sheely Rd Lenoir (28645) *(G-7599)*

D T Bracy Logging Inc 252 332-8332
520 Kiwanis St Ahoskie (27910) *(G-46)*

D T M, Kings Mountain *Also Called: Diversified Textile Mchy Corp (G-7360)*

D&E Freight LLC 704 977-4847
4427 Knollcrest Dr Charlotte (28208) *(G-2013)*

D&S Company Inc 828 894-2778
265 Hugh Champion Rd Tryon (28782) *(G-12174)*

D2 Government Solutions LLC (PA) 662 655-4554
820 Aviation Dr Ste 1 New Bern (28562) *(G-9362)*

D3 Software Inc 336 870-9138
277 Creekside Dr High Point (27265) *(G-6586)*

Dac Products Inc 336 969-9786
625 Montroyal Rd Rural Hall (27045) *(G-10958)*

Dae Systems, Claremont *Also Called: Dynamic Air Engineering Inc (G-3112)*

Daedalus Composites LLC 252 368-9000
109 Anchors Way Dr Edenton (27932) *(G-4365)*

Daedalus Yachts, Edenton *Also Called: Daedalus Composites LLC (G-4365)*

Daetwyler Cstm Fbrction McHnin, Huntersville *Also Called: Max Daetwyler Corp (G-7012)*

Daewoo-Folger Automotive, Charlotte *Also Called: Subaru Folger Automotive (G-2877)*

Dagenhart Pallet Inc 828 241-2374
2088 Mathis Church Rd Catawba (28609) *(G-1511)*

Daikin Applied Americas Inc 704 588-0087
13504 S Point Blvd Ste G Charlotte (28273) *(G-2014)*

Dails Pallet & Produce Inc 252 717-1338
2884 Neuse Rd Kinston (28501) *(G-7404)*

Daily Courier 828 245-6431
162 N Main St Rutherfordton (28139) *(G-10982)*

Daily Dispatch, Henderson *Also Called: Henderson Newspapers Inc (G-6158)*

Daily Grind LLC 910 541-0471
114 N Topsail Dr Surf City (28445) *(G-11862)*

Daily Herald, Roanoke Rapids *Also Called: Wick Communications Co (G-10747)*

Daily Living Solutions Inc 704 614-0977
9711 Stewart Spring Ln Charlotte (28216) *(G-2015)*

Daily Manufacturing Inc 704 782-0700
4820 Pless Rd Rockwell (28138) *(G-10795)*

Daily Record The, Dunn *Also Called: Record Publishing Company (G-3866)*

Daily Reflector , The, Greenville *Also Called: Cox Nrth Crlina Pblcations Inc (G-5961)*

Daily Tarheel, Chapel Hill *Also Called: Dth Publishing Inc (G-1541)*

A
L
P
H
A
B
E
T
I
C

Daimler Truck North Amer LLC.................... 704 645-5000
  11550 Statesville Blvd Cleveland (27013) *(G-3213)*

Daimler Truck North Amer LLC.................... 704 868-5700
  1400 Tulip Dr Gastonia (28052) *(G-5038)*

Dairy Fresh, Winston Salem *Also Called: New Dairy Opco LLC (G-13263)*

Dairy Queen, Charlotte *Also Called: Lmb Corp (G-2429)*

Dairy Services.................... 919 303-2442
  100 Cordova Ct Raleigh (27606) *(G-10033)*

Daisy Pink Co.................... 704 907-3526
  10335 Worsley Ln Charlotte (28269) *(G-2016)*

Dak Americas, Fayetteville *Also Called: Alpek Polyester Usa LLC (G-4550)*

Dakota Fab & Welding Inc.................... 919 881-0027
  1420 W 3rd St Siler City (27344) *(G-11406)*

Dal Leather Inc.................... 828 302-1667
  2139 St Johns Church Rd Ne Conover (28613) *(G-3511)*

Dalco GF Technologies LLC.................... 828 459-2577
  2050 Evergreen Dr Ne Conover (28613) *(G-3512)*

Dalco Gft Nonwovens LLC.................... 828 459-2577
  2050 Evergreen Dr Ne Conover (28613) *(G-3513)*

Dale Advertising Inc.................... 704 484-0971
  2523 Taylor Rd Shelby (28152) *(G-11329)*

Dale Ray Fabrics LLC.................... 704 932-6411
  1121 N Main St Kannapolis (28081) *(G-7206)*

Dale Reynolds Cabinets Inc.................... 704 890-5962
  301 Kimmswick Rd Charlotte (28214) *(G-2017)*

Dales Welding Service.................... 919 872-6969
  7352 Berkshire Downs Dr Raleigh (27616) *(G-10034)*

Daliah Plastics Corp.................... 336 629-0551
  134 W Wainman Ave Asheboro (27203) *(G-344)*

Dallas Fabrication.................... 704 629-4000
  1346 Ramseur Rd Bessemer City (28016) *(G-812)*

Dallas L Pridgen Inc.................... 919 732-4422
  104 Morningside Dr Carrboro (27510) *(G-1268)*

Dallas L Pridgen Jewelry, Carrboro *Also Called: Dallas L Pridgen Inc (G-1268)*

Dallas Machine and.................... 704 629-5611
  1326 Ramseur Rd Bessemer City (28016) *(G-813)*

Dallas Machine Company, Bessemer City *Also Called: Dallas Machine and (G-813)*

Dallas Trans LLC.................... 704 965-6057
  4030 Wake Forest Rd Ste 349 Raleigh (27609) *(G-10035)*

Daltons Metal Works, Winston Salem *Also Called: Daltons Metal Works Inc (G-13136)*

Daltons Metal Works Inc.................... 336 731-1442
  2411 Gumtree Rd Winston Salem (27107) *(G-13136)*

Damco Inc.................... 252 633-1404
  1103 Us Highway 17 N New Bern (28560) *(G-9363)*

Dampp-Chaser, Hendersonville *Also Called: Dampp-Chaser Electronics Corp (G-6200)*

Dampp-Chaser Electronics Corp.................... 828 692-8271
  1410 Spartanburg Hwy Hendersonville (28792) *(G-6200)*

Damsel In Defense.................... 919 744-8776
  109 Lake Point Dr Clayton (27527) *(G-3142)*

Dan Moore Inc.................... 336 475-8350
  405 Albertson Rd Thomasville (27360) *(G-12015)*

Dan Morton Logging.................... 919 693-1898
  1671 Sunset Rd Oxford (27565) *(G-9612)*

Dana Fancy Foods.................... 828 685-2937
  101 Lytle Rd Hendersonville (28792) *(G-6201)*

Dana Industries.................... 919 496-3262
  Timberlake Rd Louisburg (27549) *(G-7913)*

Danaher Indus Sensors Contrls.................... 910 862-5426
  2100 W Broad St Elizabethtown (28337) *(G-4424)*

Danbartex LLC.................... 704 323-8728
  120 Commercial Dr Ste A Mooresville (28115) *(G-8650)*

Danby Barcoding LLC.................... 770 416-9845
  1800 Watmead Rd Kernersville (27284) *(G-7263)*

Dandy Light Traps Inc.................... 980 223-2744
  1256 N Barkley Rd Statesville (28677) *(G-11684)*

Dani Leather USA Inc.................... 973 598-0890
  635 Southwest St Ste A High Point (27260) *(G-6587)*

Daniel Carpenter Mustang, Concord *Also Called: Mustang Reproductions Inc (G-3408)*

Daniel Winkler Knifemaker LLC.................... 828 262-3691
  141 Leigh Ln Boone (28607) *(G-911)*

Daniel, Johnny Logging, Denton *Also Called: Johnny Daniel (G-3752)*

Daniels Boatworks Inc.................... 252 473-1400
  620 Harbor Rd Wanchese (27981) *(G-12341)*

Daniels Business Services Inc (PA).................... 828 277-8250
  131 Sweeten Creek Rd 25a Asheville (28803) *(G-483)*

Daniels Graphics, Asheville *Also Called: Daniels Business Services Inc (G-483)*

Daniels Lumber Sales Inc.................... 336 622-5486
  3224 Staley Store Rd Liberty (27298) *(G-7763)*

Daniels Woodcarving Co Inc.................... 828 632-7336
  2325 Nc Highway 90 E Taylorsville (28681) *(G-11958)*

Danisson Trading, Kernersville *Also Called: Danisson USA Trading Ltd LLC (G-7264)*

Danisson USA Trading Ltd LLC.................... 704 965-8317
  210 Serenity Pointe Dr Kernersville (27284) *(G-7264)*

Danley Sound Labs Inc.................... 877 419-5805
  204 Dogwood Rd Candler (28715) *(G-1223)*

Dannies Logging Inc.................... 919 528-2370
  2155 Tar River Rd Creedmoor (27522) *(G-3647)*

Dantherm Filtration Inc.................... 336 889-5599
  150 Transit Ave Thomasville (27360) *(G-12016)*

Dap Products Inc.................... 704 799-9640
  125 Infield Ct Mooresville (28117) *(G-8651)*

Daphne Lawson Espino.................... 910 290-2762
  413 N Railroad Ave Beulaville (28518) *(G-841)*

Dara Holsters & Gear Inc.................... 919 374-2170
  4120 Wendell Blvd Wendell (27591) *(G-12531)*

Daramic LLC (DH).................... 704 587-8599
  11430 N Community House Rd Ste 350 Charlotte (28277) *(G-2018)*

Darius All Access, Wilmington *Also Called: Darius All Access LLC (G-12759)*

Darius All Access LLC.................... 910 262-8567
  1013 Glenlea Dr Wilmington (28405) *(G-12759)*

Dark Moon Distileries LLC.................... 704 222-8063
  60 Deer Run, Banner Elk Banner Elk (28604) *(G-683)*

Darling Ingredients Inc.................... 910 483-0473
  1309 Industrial Dr Fayetteville (28301) *(G-4583)*

Darling Ingredients Inc.................... 704 864-9941
  5533 York Hwy Gastonia (28052) *(G-5039)*

Darling Ingredients Inc.................... 910 289-2083
  469 Yellowcut Rd Rose Hill (28458) *(G-10904)*

Darling Ingredients Inc.................... 704 694-3701
  656 Little Duncan Rd Wadesboro (28170) *(G-12241)*

Darnel Inc.................... 704 625-9869
  1809 Airport Rd Monroe (28110) *(G-8474)*

Darran Furniture, High Point *Also Called: Darran Furniture Inds Inc (G-6588)*

Darran Furniture Inds Inc.................... 336 861-2400
  2402 Shore St High Point (27263) *(G-6588)*

Darrell T Bracy.................... 252 358-1432
  520 Kiwanis St Ahoskie (27910) *(G-47)*

Dart Container Corp Georgia.................... 336 495-1101
  3219 Wesleyan Rd Randleman (27317) *(G-10641)*

Das Oil Werks LLC.................... 919 267-5781
  198 Hidden Field Ln New Hill (27562) *(G-9409)*

Data443 Risk Mitigation Inc.................... 919 858-6542
  4000 Sancar Way Ste 400 Durham (27709) *(G-3998)*

Database Incorporated.................... 202 684-6252
  3342 Rose Of Sharon Rd Durham (27712) *(G-3999)*

Dataforce, Charlotte *Also Called: Mjt Us Inc (G-2510)*

Datamark Graphics Inc.................... 336 629-0267
  603 W Bailey St Asheboro (27203) *(G-345)*

Datar Cancer Genetics Inc.................... 919 377-2119
  500 Perimeter Park Dr Unit A Morrisville (27560) *(G-8962)*

Datascope North America Inc.................... 980 819-5244
  4427 Wilgrove Mint Hill Rd Mint Hill (28227) *(G-8336)*

Dataspectrum.................... 919 341-3300
  4700 Falls Of Neuse Rd Raleigh (27609) *(G-10036)*

Datawise LLC.................... 704 293-1482
  9111 Kristen Lake Ct Charlotte (28270) *(G-2019)*

Daughters & Ryan Inc.................... 919 284-0153
  207 Johnston Pkwy Kenly (27542) *(G-7232)*

Daughtridge Enterprises Inc.................... 252 977-7775
  1200 East St Rocky Mount (27801) *(G-10809)*

Dauntless Discovery LLC.................... 610 909-7383
  4141 Parklake Ave Ste 130 Raleigh (27612) *(G-10037)*

2025 Harris North Carolina
Manufacturers Directory

(G-0000) Company's Geographic Section entry number

Davcom Enterprises Inc.. 919 872-9522
2621 Spring Forest Rd Ste 105 Raleigh (27616) *(G-10038)*

Dave Steel Company Inc (PA)....................................828 252-2771
40 Meadow Rd Asheville (28803) *(G-484)*

David Allen Company Inc (PA)....................................919 821-7100
150 Rush St Raleigh (27603) *(G-10039)*

David Bennett..919 798-3424
80 H H Mckoy Ln Fuquay Varina (27526) *(G-4877)*

David Oreck Candle...336 375-8411
3500 N Ohenry Blvd Greensboro (27405) *(G-5487)*

David Presnell...336 372-5989
1397 Us Highway 21 S Sparta (28675) *(G-11537)*

David R Webb Company Inc.......................................336 605-3355
300 Standard Dr Greensboro (27409) *(G-5488)*

David Raynor Logging Inc..910 980-0129
4718 Long St Linden (28356) *(G-7873)*

David Rothschild Co Inc...336 342-0035
618 Grooms Rd Reidsville (27320) *(G-10682)*

David Vizard Motortec Features..................................865 850-0666
109 Mistywood Dr Mount Holly (28120) *(G-9227)*

David West..910 271-0757
9090 Us Hwy 117 N Willard (28478) *(G-12665)*

David Yurman Enterprises LLC..................................704 366-7259
4400 Sharon Rd Ste 177 Charlotte (28211) *(G-2020)*

Davidson Daily, Kinston Also Called: Magic Mile Media Inc *(G-7421)*

Davidson House Inc..704 791-0171
643 Portside Dr Davidson (28036) *(G-3701)*

Davidson Printing Inc..336 357-0555
223 S Main St Ste D Lexington (27292) *(G-7675)*

Davidson Steel Services LLC.....................................336 775-1234
11075 Old Us Highway 52 # 100 Winston Salem (27107) *(G-13137)*

Davidson Wine Co LLC..614 738-0051
10930 Zac Hill Rd Davidson (28036) *(G-3702)*

Davidsonspeed Printing, Lexington Also Called: Davidson Printing Inc *(G-7675)*

Davie County Publishing Co (HQ)...............................336 751-2120
171 S Main St Mocksville (27028) *(G-8357)*

Davis Brothers Roofing..828 578-8561
2404 N Center St Unit B Hickory (28601) *(G-6317)*

Davis Cabinet Co Wilson Inc......................................252 291-9052
6116 Green Pond Rd Sims (27880) *(G-11429)*

Davis Davis Mch & Wldg Co Inc.................................252 443-2652
4956 Community Dr Rocky Mount (27804) *(G-10830)*

Davis Equipment Handlers Inc...................................704 792-9176
3860 Abiliene Rd Charlotte (28205) *(G-2021)*

Davis Furniture Industries Inc (PA).............................336 889-2009
2401 College Dr High Point (27260) *(G-6589)*

Davis Machine Co Inc..704 865-2863
158 Superior Stainless Rd Gastonia (28052) *(G-5040)*

Davis Mechanical Inc..704 272-9366
4368 Nc 218 Peachland (28133) *(G-9651)*

Davis Newell Company Inc...910 762-3500
2962 N Kerr Ave Wilmington (28405) *(G-12760)*

Davis Rug, Shelby Also Called: Davis Rug Company *(G-11330)*

Davis Rug Company...704 434-7231
3938 Barclay Rd Shelby (28152) *(G-11330)*

Davis Sign Company Inc..336 765-2990
208 Regent Dr Winston Salem (27103) *(G-13138)*

Davis Steel and Iron Co Inc.......................................704 821-7676
1035 Commercial Dr Matthews (28104) *(G-8165)*

Davis Vogler Enterprises LLC.....................................402 257-7188
5316 Camilla Dr Charlotte (28226) *(G-2022)*

Day 3 Lwncare Ldscpg Prfctnist..................................910 574-8422
1637 Woodfield Rd Fayetteville (28303) *(G-4584)*

Day International Prtg Pdts, Arden Also Called: Flint Group US LLC *(G-272)*

Dayco Manufacturing Inc...919 989-1820
6116 Us 70 W Clayton (27520) *(G-3143)*

Daydream Education LLC...800 591-6150
21 Listening Cv Clyde (28721) *(G-3258)*

Daystar Machining Tech Inc.......................................828 684-1316
356 Cane Creek Rd Fletcher (28732) *(G-4732)*

Daystar Materials Inc..919 734-0460
200 W Dewey St Goldsboro (27530) *(G-5211)*

Daytech Solutions LLC...336 918-4122
101 N Chestnut St Ste 211 Winston Salem (27101) *(G-13139)*

Dayton Bag & Burlap Co..704 873-7271
233 Commerce Blvd Statesville (28625) *(G-11685)*

Daztech Inc..800 862-6360
214 Walnut St Wilmington (28401) *(G-12761)*

Daztech Promotions, Wilmington Also Called: Daztech Inc *(G-12761)*

DB CUSTOM CRAFTS LLC..336 867-4107
267 Kendall Farms Ct Winston Salem (27107) *(G-13140)*

Db North Carolina Holdings Inc (HQ)..........................910 323-4848
458 Whitfield St Fayetteville (28306) *(G-4585)*

Db Power Sports..828 324-1500
2830 Springs Rd Ne Hickory (28601) *(G-6318)*

Dbf Inc..910 548-6725
100 Fall Creek Dr Ste A Jacksonville (28540) *(G-7122)*

Dbt Coatings LLC..336 834-9700
3625 N Elm St Ste 100a Greensboro (27455) *(G-5489)*

Dbt Holdings LLC..704 900-6606
6030 Airport Dr Charlotte (28208) *(G-2023)*

Dbw Print & Promo..704 906-8551
6012 Bayfield Pkwy Concord (28027) *(G-3352)*

Dce Inc..704 230-4649
138 Cayuga Dr Ste C Mooresville (28117) *(G-8652)*

Dcli, Charlotte Also Called: Direct Chassislink Inc *(G-2050)*

DCS USA Corporation..919 535-8000
3000 Bear Cat Way Ste 118 Morrisville (27560) *(G-8963)*

Ddi, Raleigh Also Called: Ddi Print *(G-10040)*

Ddi Print..919 829-8810
5210 Western Blvd Raleigh (27606) *(G-10040)*

Ddm Inc...910 686-1481
210 Sea Shell Ln Wilmington (28411) *(G-12762)*

Ddp Spclty Elctrnic Mtls US 9....................................336 547-7112
2914 Patterson St Greensboro (27407) *(G-5490)*

De Feet, Hildebran Also Called: De Feet International Inc *(G-6848)*

De Feet International Inc..828 397-7025
371 I40 Access Rd Hildebran (28637) *(G-6848)*

Deal Machine Shop Inc..704 872-7618
400 Beulah Rd Statesville (28625) *(G-11686)*

Deal-Rite Feeds Inc...704 873-8646
109 Anna Dr Statesville (28625) *(G-11687)*

Dean S Ready Mixed Inc..704 982-5520
517 Old Charlotte Rd Albemarle (28001) *(G-69)*

Dean St Processing LLC...252 235-0401
5645 Deans St Bailey (27807) *(G-669)*

DEB Manufacturing Inc...704 703-6618
4040 Dearborn Pl Nw Concord (28027) *(G-3353)*

Deb SBS Inc...704 263-4240
1100 S Highway 27 Stanley (28164) *(G-11613)*

Debbing Inspirations, Greensboro Also Called: Tapestries Ltd *(G-5851)*

Deberry Land & Timber Inc...910 572-2698
112 Leslie St Troy (27371) *(G-12159)*

Debmed Usa LLC..704 263-4240
2815 Coliseum Centre Dr # 6 Charlotte (28217) *(G-2024)*

Debotech Inc..704 664-1361
130 Infield Ct Mooresville (28117) *(G-8653)*

Decal Source Inc...336 574-3141
804 Knox Rd Mc Leansville (27301) *(G-8221)*

December Diamonds Inc...828 926-3308
3425 Dellwood Rd Waynesville (28786) *(G-12455)*

Decima Corporation LLC..734 516-1535
2201 South Blvd Charlotte (28203) *(G-2025)*

Decker Advanced Fabrication, Charlotte Also Called: Joseph F Decker *(G-2379)*

Deckle Paperboard Sales Inc......................................910 686-9145
256 Osprey Pl Wilmington (28411) *(G-12763)*

Decolux USA..704 340-3532
6024 Shining Oak Ln Charlotte (28269) *(G-2026)*

Decor Glass, Sylva Also Called: Decor Glass Specialties Inc *(G-11891)*

Decor Glass Specialties Inc.......................................828 586-8180
61 Timber Creek Cir Sylva (28779) *(G-11891)*

Decorative Def Con Coatings, Aberdeen Also Called: Tfam Solutions LLC *(G-26)*

Decore-Ative Spc NC LLC...704 291-9669
701 Industrial Dr Monroe (28110) *(G-8475)*

A
L
P
H
A
B
E
T
I
C

Dedon Inc (DH)...336 790-1070
  657 Brigham Rd Ste C Greensboro (27409) *(G-5491)*

Deep Creek Timber, Wadesboro *Also Called: James L Johnson (G-12246)*

Deep River Fabricators Inc.................................336 824-8881
  240 E Main St Franklinville (27248) *(G-4856)*

Deep River Printing, Greensboro *Also Called: Deep Rver Mlls Ctd Fabrics Inc (G-5492)*

Deep Rver Mlls Ctd Fabrics Inc (PA)....................910 464-3135
  1904 Lendew St Greensboro (27408) *(G-5492)*

Deep South Holding Company Inc.........................336 427-0265
  2216 Us Highway 311 Madison (27025) *(G-7986)*

Deere & Company...919 567-6400
  6501 S Nc 55 Hwy Fuquay Varina (27526) *(G-4878)*

Deere & Company...336 996-8100
  1000 John Deere Rd Kernersville (27284) *(G-7265)*

Deere-Hitachi Cnstr McHy, Kernersville *Also Called: Deere & Company (G-7265)*

Deerhunter Tree Stands Inc................................704 462-1116
  5944 Leil Rd Hickory (28602) *(G-6319)*

Deetag USA Inc (DH)..828 465-2644
  1232 Fedex Dr Sw Conover (28613) *(G-3514)*

Defense Logistics Services LLC..........................703 449-1620
  231 Meed Ct Ste 104 Fayetteville (28303) *(G-4586)*

Definitive Media Corp (PA).................................714 730-4958
  2000 Centre Green Way Ste 300 Cary (27513) *(G-1343)*

Degesch America Inc..800 548-2778
  1810 Firestone Pkwy Ne Wilson (27893) *(G-12983)*

Dehn Inc (HQ)...772 460-9315
  500 S Main St Ste 115 Mooresville (28115) *(G-8654)*

Dehydration LLC...252 747-8200
  963 Hwy 258 S Snow Hill (28580) *(G-11479)*

Dej Holdings LLC (PA)......................................704 799-4800
  349 Cayuga Dr Mooresville (28117) *(G-8655)*

Deka Batteries & Cables, Winston Salem *Also Called: East Penn Manufacturing Co (G-13152)*

Del-Mark Inc...828 322-6180
  1225 Main Ave Sw Hickory (28602) *(G-6320)*

Delaby Brace and Limb Co.................................910 484-2509
  405 Owen Dr Fayetteville (28304) *(G-4587)*

Delaney Holdings Co..704 808-3848
  13320 Ballantyne Corporate Pl Charlotte (28277) *(G-2027)*

Delbert White Logging Inc..................................252 209-4779
  452 White Oak Rd Windsor (27983) *(G-13051)*

Delcor Polymers Inc..704 847-0640
  2536 Winterbrooke Dr Matthews (28105) *(G-8110)*

Deliveright Logistics Inc...................................862 279-7332
  176 L F I Complex Ln Lexington (27295) *(G-7676)*

Delizza LLC..252 442-0270
  6610 Corporation Pkwy Battleboro (27809) *(G-696)*

Delkote Machine Finishing Inc............................828 253-1023
  69 Bingham Rd Asheville (28806) *(G-485)*

Dellinger Enterprises Ltd..................................704 825-9687
  759 Cason St Belmont (28012) *(G-745)*

Dellner Inc...704 527-2121
  4016 Shutterfly Rd Ste 100 Charlotte (28217) *(G-2028)*

Dellner Brakes, Charlotte *Also Called: Dellner Inc (G-2028)*

Delta Contractors Inc.......................................817 410-9481
  6309 Castlebrooke Ln Linden (28356) *(G-7874)*

Delta Mold Inc...704 588-6600
  9415 Stockport Pl Charlotte (28273) *(G-2029)*

Delta Msrment Cmbstn Cntrls LL.........................919 623-7133
  207 Kettlebridge Dr Cary (27511) *(G-1344)*

Delta Phoenix Inc...336 621-3960
  4820 Us Hwy 29 N Greensboro (27405) *(G-5493)*

Deltec Homes Inc (PA).....................................828 253-0483
  69 Bingham Rd Asheville (28806) *(G-486)*

Deluxe Corporation...336 851-4600
  3703 Farmington Dr Greensboro (27407) *(G-5494)*

Deluxe Printing Co Inc.....................................828 322-1329
  10 9th St Nw Hickory (28601) *(G-6321)*

Deluxe Printing Group, Hickory *Also Called: Deluxe Printing Co Inc (G-6321)*

Delve Interiors LLC...336 274-4661
  7820 Thorndike Rd Greensboro (27409) *(G-5495)*

Delzer Construction...919 625-0755
  632 Northwoods Dr Cary (27513) *(G-1345)*

Demilo Bros NC LLC..704 771-0762
  1807 Palazzo Dr Waxhaw (28173) *(G-12428)*

Demilo Bros., Waxhaw *Also Called: Demilo Bros NC LLC (G-12428)*

Demmel Inc...828 585-6600
  100 Old World Cir East Flat Rock (28726) *(G-4329)*

Dennis Vineyards Inc.......................................704 982-6090
  24043 Endy Rd Albemarle (28001) *(G-70)*

Denso Manufacturing NC Inc..............................252 754-1000
  1125 Sugg Pkwy Greenville (27834) *(G-5963)*

Denso Manufacturing NC Inc (DH)........................704 878-6663
  470 Crawford Rd Statesville (28625) *(G-11688)*

Dental Equipment LLC......................................704 588-2126
  11727 Fruehauf Dr Charlotte (28273) *(G-2030)*

Denton Orator..336 859-3131
  26 N Main St Denton (27239) *(G-3746)*

Dentonics Inc..704 238-0245
  2833 Top Hill Rd Monroe (28110) *(G-8476)*

Dentsply North America LLC...............................844 848-0137
  13320 Ballantyne Corporate Pl Charlotte (28277) *(G-2031)*

DENTSPLY SIRONA, Charlotte *Also Called: Dentsply Sirona Inc (G-2032)*

Dentsply Sirona Inc (PA)...................................844 848-0137
  13320 Ballantyne Corporate Pl Charlotte (28277) *(G-2032)*

Denver Global Products Inc................................704 665-1800
  6420 Rea Rd Ste A1 Charlotte (28277) *(G-2033)*

Denver Waterjet LLC..980 222-7447
  3865 N Nc 16 Business Hwy Denver (28037) *(G-3780)*

Depalo Foods Inc..704 827-0245
  2010 Oaks Pkwy Belmont (28012) *(G-746)*

Department of Solid Waste, Taylorsville *Also Called: County of Alexander (G-11955)*

Deringer-Ney Inc..828 649-3232
  155 Deringer Dr Marshall (28753) *(G-8079)*

Derita Precision Mch Co Inc...............................704 392-7285
  605 Toddville Rd Charlotte (28214) *(G-2034)*

Derrow Enterprises Inc.....................................252 635-3375
  7001 Us Highway 70 E New Bern (28562) *(G-9364)*

Descher Automation, Raleigh *Also Called: Descher LLC (G-10041)*

Descher LLC...919 828-7708
  1613 Old Louisburg Rd Raleigh (27604) *(G-10041)*

Desco Equipment Company Inc...........................704 873-2844
  1031 S Meeting St Statesville (28677) *(G-11689)*

Desco Industries Inc..919 718-0000
  920 J R Industrial Dr Sanford (27332) *(G-11168)*

Desco Industries Inc..919 718-0000
  926 J R Industrial Dr Sanford (27332) *(G-11169)*

Desco Industries Inc..919 718-0000
  914 J R Industrial Dr Sanford (27332) *(G-11170)*

Desco Industries Inc..919 718-0000
  917 J R Industrial Dr Sanford (27332) *(G-11171)*

Design Concepts Incorporated............................336 887-1932
  341 South Rd High Point (27262) *(G-6590)*

Design Engred Fbrications Inc.............................336 768-8260
  2461 Spaugh Industrial Dr Winston Salem (27103) *(G-13141)*

Design Master Displays, High Point *Also Called: Master Displays Inc (G-6706)*

Design Printing Inc...336 472-3333
  1107 Trinity St Thomasville (27360) *(G-12017)*

Design Specialties Inc......................................919 772-6955
  3640 Banks Rd Raleigh (27603) *(G-10042)*

Design Surfaces Inc...919 781-0310
  1212 Front St Raleigh (27609) *(G-10043)*

Design Surfaces of Raleigh, Raleigh *Also Called: Design Surfaces Inc (G-10043)*

Design Theory LLC..336 912-0155
  1020 Surrett Dr High Point (27260) *(G-6591)*

Design Tool Inc..828 328-6414
  1607 Norfolk Pl Sw Conover (28613) *(G-3515)*

Design Workshop Incorporated............................910 293-7329
  1696 Nc 24 And 50 Hwy Warsaw (28398) *(G-12359)*

Design Workshop, The, Wilmington *Also Called: Diane Britt (G-12764)*

Designed For Joy..919 395-2884
  2408 Merion Creek Dr Apex (27539) *(G-150)*

Designelement...919 383-5561
  972 Trinity Rd Raleigh (27607) *(G-10044)*

Designer Fabrics Inc..704 305-4144
412 Action Dr Nw Concord (28027) *(G-3354)*

Designer Woodwork..910 521-1252
1616 Hiawatha Rd Pembroke (28372) *(G-9658)*

Designline Corporation.....................................704 494-7800
2309 Nevada Blvd Charlotte (28273) *(G-2035)*

Designline Intl Holdings, Charlotte Also Called: Designline Corporation *(G-2035)*

Designline Usa LLC...704 494-7800
2309 Nevada Blvd Charlotte (28273) *(G-2036)*

Designmaster Furniture Inc...............................828 324-7992
1283 23rd St Se Hickory (28602) *(G-6322)*

Designs By Rachel...828 783-0698
220 Reservoir Rd Spruce Pine (28777) *(G-11574)*

Designs In Wood..336 372-8995
122 E Doughton St Sparta (28675) *(G-11538)*

Designtek Fabrication Inc..................................910 359-0130
16824 A Hwy 211 Red Springs (28377) *(G-10666)*

Deurotech America Inc.......................................980 272-6827
4526 Westinghouse Blvd Ste A Charlotte (28273) *(G-2037)*

Deutsche Beverage, Charlotte Also Called: Dbt Holdings LLC *(G-2023)*

Devada, Research Triangle Pa Also Called: Dzone Inc *(G-10708)*

Deverger Systems Inc...919 201-5146
87 Downing St Asheville (28806) *(G-487)*

Devil Dog Manufacturing Co Inc........................919 269-7485
400 E Gannon Ave Zebulon (27597) *(G-13507)*

Devils Kindred MC...336 712-7689
310 S Chestnut St Swansboro (28584) *(G-11884)*

Deviney Lumber & Salvage, Casar Also Called: M O Deviney Lumber Co Inc *(G-1489)*

Devmir Legwear Inc...919 545-5500
136 Fayetteville St Pittsboro (27312) *(G-9781)*

Devora Designs Inc..336 782-0964
1315 Creekshire Way Apt 312 Winston Salem (27103) *(G-13142)*

Dew Group Enterprises Inc................................919 585-0100
501 Atkinson St Clayton (27520) *(G-3144)*

Dewalt Industrial Tool, Greensboro Also Called: Black & Decker (us) Inc *(G-5391)*

Dewey S Bakery Inc (PA)....................................336 748-0230
3840 Kimwell Dr Winston Salem (27103) *(G-13143)*

Dewill Inc..919 426-9550
951 High House Rd Cary (27513) *(G-1346)*

Dewoolfson Down, Banner Elk Also Called: Dewoolfson Down Intl Inc *(G-684)*

Dewoolfson Down Intl Inc (PA)..........................828 963-2750
9452 Nc Highway 105 S Banner Elk (28604) *(G-684)*

Dex Media East LLC...919 297-1600
1001 Winstead Dr Ste 1 Cary (27513) *(G-1347)*

Dex n Dox..910 576-4644
225 Basswood Rd Troy (27371) *(G-12160)*

Dex One Corporation...919 297-1600
1001 Winstead Dr Cary (27513) *(G-1348)*

Dexco McHining Fabrication LLC.........................336 584-0260
326 Macarthur Ln Burlington (27217) *(G-1082)*

Dexios Services LLC..704 946-5101
10308 Bailey Rd Ste 430 Cornelius (28031) *(G-3597)*

Dexter Inc..828 459-7904
5718 Oxford School Rd Claremont (28610) *(G-3106)*

Dexter Inc (PA)..919 510-5050
8411 Glenwood Ave Ste 101 Raleigh (27612) *(G-10045)*

Dexter Furniture, Raleigh Also Called: Dexter Inc *(G-10045)*

Dexterity LLC...919 524-7732
104 Azalea Dr Greenville (27858) *(G-5964)*

Df Framing LLC..919 368-7903
510 N Garden Ave Siler City (27344) *(G-11407)*

Dfa Dairy Brands Fluid LLC................................704 341-2794
3540 Toringdon Way Ste 200 Charlotte (28277) *(G-2038)*

Dfa Dairy Brands Fluid LLC................................336 714-9032
1079 W Saint James St Tarboro (27886) *(G-11925)*

Dfa US Inc...336 756-0590
300 Bethel Church Rd Mocksville (27028) *(G-8358)*

Dfp Inc (PA)..336 841-3028
685 Southwest St High Point (27260) *(G-6592)*

Dg Matrix Inc..724 877-7773
809 Montvale Ridge Dr Cary (27519) *(G-1349)*

Dhollandia Us Llc (HQ)......................................909 251-7979
270 Southridge Pkwy Bessemer City (28016) *(G-814)*

Diabetic Sock Club..800 214-0218
109 Crowders Creek Rd Gastonia (28052) *(G-5041)*

Diagnostic Devices..704 599-5908
2701 Hutchison Mcdonald Rd Ste A Charlotte (28269) *(G-2039)*

Diagnostic Shop Inc...704 933-3435
723 Fairview St Kannapolis (28083) *(G-7207)*

Diagnostic Shop and Repair, Kannapolis Also Called: Diagnostic Shop Inc *(G-7207)*

Diamond Apparel, Mocksville Also Called: Carolina Square Inc *(G-8356)*

Diamond Brand Canvas Products, Fletcher Also Called: WC&r Interests LLC *(G-4777)*

Diamond Dog Tools Inc......................................828 687-3686
75 Old Shoals Rd Arden (28704) *(G-265)*

Diamond Enterprises..828 495-4448
5171 Icard Ridge Rd Hickory (28601) *(G-6323)*

Diamond Finish Car Wash, Charlotte Also Called: G & E Investments Inc *(G-2183)*

Diamond Orthopedic LLC....................................704 585-8258
1669 Federal St Gastonia (28052) *(G-5042)*

Diamond Outdoor Entps Inc................................336 857-1450
9035 Nc Highway 49 S Denton (27239) *(G-3747)*

Diamond Power Intl LLC.....................................704 625-4900
13024 Ballantyne Corporate Pl Ste 700 Charlotte (28277) *(G-2040)*

Diamond Pwr Eqity Invstmnts In.........................704 625-4900
13024 Ballantyne Corporate Pl Ste 700 Charlotte (28277) *(G-2041)*

Diamond Research and Dev, Hickory Also Called: Diamond Enterprises *(G-6323)*

Diamondback Industries LLC...............................336 956-8871
4683 Old Salisbury Rd Lexington (27295) *(G-7677)*

Diamondback Products Inc..................................336 236-9800
40 W 12th Ave Lexington (27292) *(G-7678)*

Diane Britt...910 763-9600
3205 Kitty Hawk Rd Ste 1 Wilmington (28405) *(G-12764)*

Diarkis LLC..704 888-5244
142 Cara Ct Locust (28097) *(G-7891)*

Diazit Company Inc..919 556-5188
8120 Diazit Dr Wake Forest (27587) *(G-12272)*

Dicey Fabrics, Shelby Also Called: Dicey Mills Inc *(G-11331)*

Dicey Mills Inc...704 487-6324
430 Neisler St (Off Hwy 74 W) Shelby (28152) *(G-11331)*

Dickerson Group Inc (PA)...................................704 289-3111
1111 Metropolitan Ave Ste 1090 Charlotte (28204) *(G-2042)*

Dickie CD & Associates Inc.................................704 527-9102
4612 South Blvd Ste A Charlotte (28209) *(G-2043)*

Dickie Jones..828 733-5084
883 Whitaker Branch Rd Newland (28657) *(G-9428)*

Dicks Store..336 548-9358
547 Mccollum Rd Madison (27025) *(G-7987)*

Dickson Elberton Mill Inc...................................336 226-3556
1831 N Park Ave Burlington (27217) *(G-1083)*

Die-Tech Inc..336 475-9186
4 Stanley Ave Thomasville (27360) *(G-12018)*

Diebold Nixdorf Incorporated.............................704 599-3100
5900 Northwoods Business Pkwy Ste K Charlotte (28269) *(G-2044)*

Dienes Apparatus Inc...704 525-3770
9220 Rodney St Pineville (28134) *(G-9724)*

Digger Specialties Inc..919 255-2533
8013 Purfoy Rd Fuquay Varina (27526) *(G-4879)*

Digger Specialties Inc..336 495-1517
4256 Heath Dairy Rd Randleman (27317) *(G-10642)*

Digital AP Prtg DBA F4mily Mtt............................980 939-8066
3623 Latrobe Dr Charlotte (28211) *(G-2045)*

Digital Audio Corporation...................................919 572-6767
116 Brightwater Heights Dr Hendersonville (28791) *(G-6202)*

Digital Design & Modeling LLC............................336 766-2155
6201 Hacker Bend Ct Winston Salem (27103) *(G-13144)*

Digital Designs Inc...704 790-7100
3540 Toringdon Way Ste 200 Charlotte (28277) *(G-2046)*

Digital High Point, Hickory Also Called: Carolina Container LLC *(G-6284)*

Digital High Point, High Point Also Called: Carolina Container Company *(G-6558)*

Digital Highpoint LLC...336 883-7146
401 Model Farm Rd Ste 101 High Point (27263) *(G-6593)*

Digital Print & Imaging Inc.................................910 341-3005
115 Red Banks Rd Ste A Greenville (27858) *(G-5965)*

A
L
P
H
A
B
E
T
I
C

Digital Printing Systems Inc (PA).................. 704 525-0190
606 E Hebron St Charlotte (28273) *(G-2047)*

Digital Progressions Inc....................... 336 676-6570
5101 W Market St Greensboro (27409) *(G-5496)*

Digital Recorders Inc......................... 919 361-2155
598 Airport Blvd Ste 300 Morrisville (27560) *(G-8964)*

Digital Turbine Media Inc (HQ)...............866 254-2453
410 Blackwell St Durham (27701) *(G-4000)*

Digitalchalk, Asheville *Also Called: Sciolytix Inc (G-597)*

Digitaurus Inc.............................. 910 794-9243
4605 Wrightsville Ave Wilmington (28403) *(G-12765)*

Digitome Corporation........................ 860 651-5560
210 Delburg St Davidson (28036) *(G-3703)*

Digits....................................... 336 721-0209
306 S Stratford Rd Winston Salem (27103) *(G-13145)*

Digitz, Raleigh *Also Called: Complete Comp St of Ralgh Inc (G-10005)*

Dignify Therapeutics LLC.................... 919 371-8138
2 Davis Dr Durham (27709) *(G-4001)*

Dilisym Services Inc........................ 919 558-1323
6 Davis Dr Durham (27709) *(G-4002)*

Dill Air Controls Products LLC (PA)...........919 692-2300
1145 Se Industry Dr Oxford (27565) *(G-9613)*

Dilworth Custom Framing..................... 704 370-7660
125 Remount Rd Ste C2 Charlotte (28203) *(G-2048)*

Dilworth Mattress Company Inc (PA)...........704 333-6564
211 W Worthington Ave Charlotte (28203) *(G-2049)*

Dime EMB LLC................................ 336 765-0910
3929 Westpoint Blvd Ste A Winston Salem (27103) *(G-13146)*

Dimension Milling Co Inc..................... 336 983-2820
12885 Nc Highway 47 Denton (27239) *(G-3748)*

Dimension Wood Products Inc................ 828 459-9891
2885 Kelly Blvd Claremont (28610) *(G-3107)*

Dimensional Metals Inc..................... 704 279-9691
819 S Salisbury Ave Salisbury (28146) *(G-11043)*

Dimill Enterprises LLC...................... 919 629-2011
531 Pylon Dr Raleigh (27606) *(G-10046)*

Dine America, Chapel Hill *Also Called: Journalistic Inc (G-1550)*

Direct Chassislink Inc (PA).................. 704 594-3800
3525 Whitehall Park Dr Ste 400 Charlotte (28273) *(G-2050)*

Direct Diagnostic Services, Morganton *Also Called: Direct Diagnostic Services LLC (G-8860)*

Direct Diagnostic Services LLC............... 843 708-3891
125 Wamsutta Mill Rd Ste A Morganton (28655) *(G-8860)*

Direct Digital LLC (PA)..................... 704 557-0987
615 S College St Ste 1300 Charlotte (28202) *(G-2051)*

Direct Distribution Inds Inc................. 910 217-0000
24581 Main St Wagram (28396) *(G-12256)*

Direct Legal Mail LLC........................ 919 353-9158
8800 Westgate Park Dr Ste 110 Raleigh (27617) *(G-10047)*

Direct Pack East LLC....................... 910 331-0071
612 Airport Rd Rockingham (28379) *(G-10774)*

Direct Promotional, Greensboro *Also Called: Web 4 Half LLC (G-5914)*

Direct South Logistics, Sanford *Also Called: Southern Elc & Automtn Corp (G-11235)*

Direct Wholesale Signs LLC.................. 704 750-2842
711 York Rd Kings Mountain (28086) *(G-7359)*

Direct Wood Products........................ 336 238-2516
808 Grimes Blvd Lexington (27292) *(G-7679)*

DIRECT WOOD PRODUCTS, Lexington *Also Called: Direct Wood Products (G-7679)*

Directional, Thomasville *Also Called: Directional Buying Group Inc (G-12019)*

Directional Buying Group Inc................ 336 472-6187
201 E Holly Hill Rd Thomasville (27360) *(G-12019)*

Directus Holdings LLC (PA)..................919 510-8410
6016 Triangle Dr Raleigh (27617) *(G-10048)*

Disco Hi-TEC America Inc................... 919 468-6003
3000 Aerial Center Pkwy Ste 140 Morrisville (27560) *(G-8965)*

Discount Box & Pallet Inc (PA)..............336 272-2220
3174 Weeden St Staley (27355) *(G-11594)*

Discount Pallet Services LLC................ 910 892-3760
319 Ira B Tart Rd Dunn (28334) *(G-3853)*

Discount Printing Inc...................... 704 365-3665
2914 Crosby Rd Charlotte (28211) *(G-2052)*

Discount Tires & Auto Repair................ 336 788-0057
812 Waughtown St Winston Salem (27107) *(G-13147)*

Discover Night LLC.......................... 888 825-6282
4030 Wake Forest Rd Ste 349 Raleigh (27609) *(G-10049)*

Discovery Insurance Company................ 800 876-1492
604 N Queen St Kinston (28501) *(G-7405)*

Disher Packing Co, Yadkinville *Also Called: If Disher Meat Processing (G-13444)*

Display Options Woodwork Inc................ 704 599-6525
205 Colonial Dr Belmont (28012) *(G-747)*

Disruptive Enterprises LLC (PA)............. 336 567-0104
1452 Industry Dr Burlington (27215) *(G-1084)*

Distinction Hospitality Inc................. 336 875-3043
4100 Mendenhall Oaks Pkwy Ste 200 High Point (27265) *(G-6594)*

Distinction Leather Company
210 Lap Rd Ne Conover (28613) *(G-3516)*

Distinctive Bldg & Design Inc................ 828 456-4730
24 Chloe Ln Waynesville (28786) *(G-12456)*

Distinctive Cabinets Inc..................... 704 529-6234
319 Old Hebron Rd Ste A Charlotte (28273) *(G-2053)*

Distinctive Furniture Inc (PA).............. 828 754-3947
1750 Taylorsville Rd Se Lenoir (28645) *(G-7600)*

Distinctive Soul Creations LLC............... 704 299-3269
214 Oakton Glen Ct Charlotte (28262) *(G-2054)*

Distributor, Youngsville *Also Called: Tar River Trading Post LLC (G-13490)*

Diverse Corporate Tech Inc.................. 828 245-3717
289 Shiloh Rd Forest City (28043) *(G-4787)*

Diverse Security Systems Inc............... 919 848-9599
8831 Westgate Park Dr Ste 100 Raleigh (27617) *(G-10050)*

Diversfied Holdings Dallas Inc............... 704 922-5293
124 W Catawba Ave Mount Holly (28120) *(G-9228)*

Diversfied McHning Cncepts Inc.............. 828 665-2465
5 Sagefield Dr Candler (28715) *(G-1224)*

Diversfied Prtg Techniques Inc............... 704 583-9433
13336 S Ridge Dr Charlotte (28273) *(G-2055)*

Diversified Disposables Mfg, Wilmington *Also Called: Ddm Inc (G-12762)*

Diversified Energy LLC..................... 828 266-9800
148 Highway 105 Ext Ste 202 Boone (28607) *(G-912)*

Diversified Foam Inc (PA).................. 336 463-5512
1813 Us 601 Hwy Yadkinville (27055) *(G-13440)*

Diversified Intl Holdings Inc................. 910 777-7122
107 Potomac Ct Winnabow (28479) *(G-13064)*

Diversified Signs Graphics Inc............... 704 392-8165
5245 Old Dowd Rd Charlotte (28208) *(G-2056)*

Diversified Specialties Inc................. 704 825-3671
10 Airline Ave Belmont (28012) *(G-748)*

Diversified Technologies, Jamestown *Also Called: SBS Diversified Tech Inc (G-7179)*

Diversified Textile Mchy Corp................ 704 739-2121
133 Kings Rd Kings Mountain (28086) *(G-7360)*

Diversified Welding and Steel................ 704 504-1111
10801 Nations Ford Rd Pineville (28134) *(G-9725)*

Diversified Wood Products Inc............... 252 793-6600
111 W Water St Ste 1 Plymouth (27962) *(G-9801)*

Divine Creations........................... 704 364-5844
216 Glenn Abby Dr Morehead City (28557) *(G-8829)*

Divine Llama Vineyards LLC................. 336 699-2525
4126 Divine Llama Ln East Bend (27018) *(G-4323)*

Divine South Baking Co LLC................. 828 421-2042
2254 Dillard Rd Highlands (28741) *(G-6845)*

Division 5 LLC.............................. 336 725-0521
1725 Vargrave St Winston Salem (27107) *(G-13148)*

Division Eight Inc......................... 336 852-1275
2206 N Church St Greensboro (27405) *(G-5497)*

Division II, Hickory *Also Called: Unifour Finishers Inc (G-6478)*

Division of Leggett Platt, Statesville *Also Called: Iredell Fiber Inc (G-11717)*

Division One, Hickory *Also Called: Unifour Finishers Inc (G-6477)*

Division Six Incorporated.................... 910 420-3305
115 Justin Dr New Bern (28562) *(G-9365)*

DIVORCECARE, Wake Forest *Also Called: Church Initiative Inc (G-12269)*

Dix Enterprises Inc......................... 336 558-9512
2436 Lake Oak High Point (27265) *(G-6595)*

Dixie Electro Mech Svcs Inc................. 704 332-1116
2115 Freedom Dr Charlotte (28208) *(G-2057)*

Dixie Reel & Box Co, Charlotte *Also Called: Lone Star Container Sales Corp (G-2433)*

Dixon Custom Cabinetry LLC.............................. 336 992-3306
129 Furlong Industrial Dr Kernersville (27284) *(G-7266)*

Dixon Quick Coupling, Dallas *Also Called: Dixon Valve & Coupling Co LLC (G-3668)*

Dixon Valve & Coupling Co LLC........................... 704 334-9175
2925 Chief Ct Dallas (28034) *(G-3668)*

Dize Awning and Tent Company, Winston Salem *Also Called: Dize Company (G-13149)*

Dize Company... 336 722-5181
1512 S Main St Winston Salem (27127) *(G-13149)*

Dj Powder Coating, Kernersville *Also Called: Dj Powdercoating Ironwork LLC (G-7267)*

Dj Powdercoating Ironwork LLC............................ 336 310-4725
232 Industrial Way Dr Ste A Kernersville (27284) *(G-7267)*

DL Hopper & Associates Inc................................ 252 838-1062
402 Sea Gate Dr Newport (28570) *(G-9440)*

DLM Sales Inc.. 704 399-2776
5901 N Hill Cir Charlotte (28213) *(G-2058)*

Dlss Manufacturing LLC..................................... 919 619-7594
697 Hillsboro St Pittsboro (27312) *(G-9782)*

Dma Inc.. 704 527-0992
3123 May St Charlotte (28217) *(G-2059)*

Dmarcian (PA).. 828 767-7588
43 S Broad St Ste 203 Brevard (28712) *(G-969)*

DMC LLC (PA).. 980 352-9806
1319 Lily Green Ct Nw Concord (28027) *(G-3355)*

Dmnc Greenville Plant, Greenville *Also Called: Denso Manufacturing NC Inc (G-5963)*

Dna Group Inc (PA)... 919 881-0889
2841 Plaza Pl Ste 200 Raleigh (27612) *(G-10051)*

Dna Services Inc.. 910 279-2775
770 Settlers Ln Kure Beach (28449) *(G-7464)*

DNB Humidifier Mfg Inc...................................... 336 764-2076
175 Dixie Club Rd Winston Salem (27107) *(G-13150)*

Dnj Engine Comp Onents.................................... 704 855-5505
1450 N Main St China Grove (28023) *(G-3073)*

Dnl Services LLC.. 910 689-8759
64 Blue Heron Dr Harrells (28444) *(G-6100)*

Dnp Imagingcomm America Corp (DH).................... 704 784-8100
4524 Enterprise Dr Nw Concord (28027) *(G-3356)*

Dnp Photo Imaging, Concord *Also Called: Dnp Imagingcomm America Corp (G-3356)*

Do It Best, Garner *Also Called: Hudson S Hardware Inc (G-4933)*

Do It Best, Raleigh *Also Called: Capitol City Lumber Company (G-9970)*

Doble Engineering Company................................ 919 380-7461
2200 Gateway Centre Blvd Ste 207 Morrisville (27560) *(G-8966)*

Doc Porters Distillery LLC.................................. 704 266-1399
1010 Lexington Ave Charlotte (28203) *(G-2060)*

Docmagnet Inc... 919 788-7999
6220 Angus Dr Ste 100 Raleigh (27617) *(G-10052)*

Docu Source of NC... 919 459-5900
951 Aviation Pkwy Ste 600 Morrisville (27560) *(G-8967)*

Document Comm Solutions Inc............................. 336 856-1300
205 Aloe Rd Greensboro (27409) *(G-5498)*

Document Directs Inc.. 919 829-8810
5210 Western Blvd Raleigh (27606) *(G-10053)*

Document Imaging Systems Inc............................ 919 460-9440
8709 Stage Ford Rd Raleigh (27615) *(G-10054)*

Docusource North Carolina LLC........................... 919 459-5900
2800 Slater Rd Morrisville (27560) *(G-8968)*

Dodson Defense LLC... 336 421-9649
4756 Blanchard Rd Burlington (27217) *(G-1085)*

DOE & Ingalls Investors Inc (HQ)......................... 919 598-1986
4813 Emperor Blvd Ste 300 Durham (27703) *(G-4003)*

DOE & Ingalls Management LLC (DH)..................... 919 598-1986
4813 Emperor Blvd Ste 300 Durham (27703) *(G-4004)*

DOE & Inglls Nrth Crlina Opti.............................. 919 282-1792
4063 Stirrup Creek Dr Durham (27703) *(G-4005)*

Doggies r US... 336 455-1113
2940 E Market St Greensboro (27405) *(G-5499)*

Dogwood Print... 919 906-0617
400 Big Branch Ln Wendell (27591) *(G-12532)*

Dokja Inc (PA)... 336 852-5190
602 S Edwardia Dr Greensboro (27409) *(G-5500)*

Dolan LLC... 919 829-9333
107 Fayetteville St 3rd Fl Raleigh (27601) *(G-10055)*

Dole Food, Charlotte *Also Called: Dole Food Company Inc (G-2061)*

Dole Food Company Inc (DH)............................... 818 874-4000
200 S Tryon St Ste 600 Charlotte (28202) *(G-2061)*

Domco Technology LLC...................................... 888 834-8541
1342 Barnardsville Hwy Ste A Barnardsville (28709) *(G-691)*

Domenicks Furniture Mfr LLC.............................. 336 442-3348
1107 Tate St High Point (27260) *(G-6596)*

Domestic Fabrics Blankets Corp........................... 252 523-7948
2002 W Vernon Ave Kinston (28504) *(G-7406)*

Domino's, Fayetteville *Also Called: Dominos Pizza LLC (G-4588)*

Dominos Pizza LLC... 910 424-4884
5133 Raeford Rd Fayetteville (28304) *(G-4588)*

Domtar Paper Company LLC................................ 252 752-1100
1029 Old Creek Rd Greenville (27834) *(G-5966)*

Domtar Paper Company LLC................................ 252 793-8111
1375 Nc Hwy 149 N Plymouth (27962) *(G-9802)*

Donald Auton.. 704 872-7528
841 Reynolds Rd Statesville (28677) *(G-11690)*

Donald Haack Diamonds Inc................................ 704 365-4400
3900 Colony Rd Ste E Charlotte (28211) *(G-2062)*

Donald Hack Diamonds Fine Gems, Charlotte *Also Called: Donald Haack Diamonds Inc (G-2062)*

Donald Henley & Sons Sawmill............................. 336 625-5665
2351 Old Cedar Falls Rd Asheboro (27203) *(G-346)*

Donald R Young Logging Inc................................ 910 934-6769
165 Buie Farm Ln Lillington (27546) *(G-7795)*

Donalds Welding Inc.. 910 298-5234
1806 S Nc 111 Hwy Chinquapin (28521) *(G-3082)*

Done-Gone Adios Inc... 336 993-7300
1318 Shields Rd Kernersville (27284) *(G-7268)*

Dons Fine Jewelry Inc.. 336 724-7826
2503 Lewisville Clemmons Rd Clemmons (27012) *(G-3181)*

Donut Shop... 910 640-3317
1602 S Madison St Whiteville (28472) *(G-12580)*

Donzi Marine LLC... 252 975-2000
1653 Whichards Beach Rd Washington (27889) *(G-12384)*

Door Store of America Inc.................................. 919 781-3200
10681 World Trade Blvd Raleigh (27617) *(G-10056)*

Door Works Huntersville LLC............................... 704 947-1900
11701 Mccord Rd Bldg 11 Huntersville (28078) *(G-6982)*

Doosan Bobcat North Amer Inc............................ 704 883-3500
1293 Glenway Dr Statesville (28625) *(G-11691)*

Dorel Ecommerce Inc.. 828 378-0092
37 Haywood St Ste 300 Asheville (28801) *(G-488)*

Dorian Corporation... 910 352-6939
901 Martin St Wilmington (28401) *(G-12766)*

Dormer Pramet LLC.. 800 877-3745
1483 Dogwood Way Mebane (27302) *(G-8238)*

Dorsett Printing Company................................... 910 895-3520
1203 Rockingham Rd Rockingham (28379) *(G-10775)*

Dorsett Technologies Inc (PA)............................. 855 387-2232
100 Woodlyn Dr Yadkinville (27055) *(G-13441)*

DOT Blue Readi-Mix LLC.................................... 704 391-3000
1022 Exchange St Charlotte (28208) *(G-2063)*

DOT Blue Readi-Mix LLC.................................... 704 247-2778
7406 Millbrook Rd Harrisburg (28075) *(G-6107)*

DOT Blue Readi-Mix LLC.................................... 704 247-2777
1703 Morgan Mill Rd Monroe (28110) *(G-8477)*

DOT Blue Readi-Mix LLC.................................... 704 978-2331
158 Intercraft Dr Statesville (28625) *(G-11692)*

DOT Blue Services Inc....................................... 704 342-2970
11819 Reames Rd Charlotte (28269) *(G-2064)*

DOT Master, Lexington *Also Called: Draft DOT International LLC (G-7680)*

Dotson Metal Finishing Inc.................................. 828 298-9844
16 Old Charlotte Hwy Asheville (28803) *(G-489)*

Double Hung LLC... 888 235-8956
2801 Patterson St Greensboro (27407) *(G-5501)*

Double O Plastics Inc.. 704 788-8517
981 Biscayne Dr Concord (28027) *(G-3357)*

Douglas Battery Mfg Co...................................... 336 650-7000
500 Battery Dr Winston Salem (27107) *(G-13151)*

Douglas Fabrication & Mch Inc............ 919 365-7553
430 Industrial Dr Wendell (27591) *(G-12533)*

Douglas Temple & Son Inc.............. 252 771-5676
1273 Lynchs Corner Rd Elizabeth City (27909) *(G-4386)*

Dova Pharmaceuticals, Morrisville *Also Called: Dova Pharmaceuticals Inc (G-8969)*

Dova Pharmaceuticals Inc (HQ).............. 919 748-5975
3015 Carrington Mill Blvd Morrisville (27560) *(G-8969)*

Dove Communications Inc.............. 336 855-5491
7 Wendy Ct Ste B Greensboro (27409) *(G-5502)*

Dove Medical Supply LLC.............. 336 643-9367
8164 Mabe Marshall Rd Bldg 2 Summerfield (27358) *(G-11838)*

Dover Foods Inc.............. 800 348-7416
353 Banner Farm Rd Mills River (28759) *(G-8313)*

Dow Silicones Corporation.............. 336 547-7100
2914 Patterson St Greensboro (27407) *(G-5503)*

Down East Molding Company, Ahoskie *Also Called: H T Jones Lumber Company (G-50)*

Down East Offroad Inc.............. 252 246-9440
1425 Thorne Ave S Wilson (27893) *(G-12984)*

Down East Printing, Morehead City *Also Called: Coastal Press Inc (G-8827)*

Down South Logging LLC.............. 843 333-1649
121 Lake Tabor Dr Tabor City (28463) *(G-11909)*

Downtown Graphics Network Inc.............. 704 637-0855
1409 S Fulton St Salisbury (28144) *(G-11044)*

Downtown Raleigh.............. 919 821-7897
402 Glenwood Ave Raleigh (27603) *(G-10057)*

Downtown Raleigh Publishing, Raleigh *Also Called: Raleigh Downtowner (G-10422)*

Downtown Tire, Hendersonville *Also Called: Downtown Tire Center Inc (G-6203)*

Downtown Tire Center Inc.............. 828 693-1676
108 S King St Hendersonville (28792) *(G-6203)*

Doyle Enterprises, High Point *Also Called: W V Doyle Enterprises Inc (G-6831)*

Dozier Industrial Electric Inc.............. 252 451-0020
1151 Atlantic Ave Rocky Mount (27801) *(G-10810)*

DP Hill Inc.............. 252 568-4282
1439 Hwy 258 Richlands (28574) *(G-10720)*

Dp Hill Manufacturing, Richlands *Also Called: DP Hill Inc (G-10720)*

Dp Solutions Inc (HQ)..............336 854-7700
1801 Stanley Rd Ste 301 Greensboro (27407) *(G-5504)*

Dpi, Greenville *Also Called: DSM Pharmaceuticals Inc (G-5970)*

Dpi Newco LLC.............. 252 758-3436
5900 Martin Luther King Jr Hwy Greenville (27834) *(G-5967)*

Dps Molding Inc.............. 732 763-4811
276 Bailey Ln Vanceboro (28586) *(G-12215)*

Dpsi, Greensboro *Also Called: Dp Solutions Inc (G-5504)*

Dr Logging LLC.............. 910 417-9643
506 Bauersfeld St Hamlet (28345) *(G-6054)*

Dr Pepper, West Jefferson *Also Called: Dr Ppper Btlg W Jffrson NC In (G-12564)*

Dr Pepper, Wilmington *Also Called: Dr Pepper Co of Wilmington (G-12767)*

Dr Pepper Co of Wilmington.............. 910 792-5400
415 Landmark Dr Wilmington (28412) *(G-12767)*

Dr Pepper/Seven-Up Bottling.............. 828 322-8090
2401 14th Avenue Cir Nw Hickory (28601) *(G-6324)*

Dr Ppper Btlg W Jffrson NC In.............. 336 846-2433
109 W 3rd St West Jefferson (28694) *(G-12564)*

Dracor Water Systems, Durham *Also Called: Drch Inc (G-4007)*

Dradura USA Corp.............. 252 637-9660
197 Bosch Blvd New Bern (28562) *(G-9366)*

Draft DOT International LLC.............. 336 775-0525
5450 N Nc Highway 150 Lexington (27295) *(G-7680)*

Draka Communication, Claremont *Also Called: Draka Communications Americas Inc (G-3108)*

Draka Communications Americas Inc.............. 828 459-8456
2512 Penny Rd Claremont (28610) *(G-3108)*

Draka Elevator Products Inc (DH).............. 252 446-8113
2151 N Church St Rocky Mount (27804) *(G-10831)*

Draka Holdings Usa Inc.............. 828 383-0020
2512 Penny Rd Claremont (28610) *(G-3109)*

Draka Transport USA LLC.............. 828 459-8895
2512 Penny Rd Claremont (28610) *(G-3110)*

Draka Usa Inc.............. 828 459-9787
2512 Penny Rd Claremont (28610) *(G-3111)*

Drake Enterprises Ltd.............. 828 524-7045
219 E Palmer St Franklin (28734) *(G-4824)*

Drake S Fresh Pasta Company.............. 336 861-5454
636 Southwest St High Point (27260) *(G-6597)*

Drake Software LLC.............. 828 524-2922
235 E Palmer St Franklin (28734) *(G-4825)*

Dramar Machine Devices Inc.............. 704 866-0904
108 Chickasaw Rd Gastonia (28056) *(G-5043)*

Drapery Hardware, Huntersville *Also Called: Nova Wildcat Drapery Hdwr LLC (G-7023)*

Draxlor Industries Inc.............. 757 274-6771
228 S Riverdale Dr Durham (27712) *(G-4006)*

Drch Inc.............. 919 383-9421
3518 Medford Rd Durham (27705) *(G-4007)*

Dream Kreams LLC.............. 919 491-1984
549 Arbor Hill Rd Apt 5a Kernersville (27284) *(G-7269)*

Dreamship Inc.............. 908 601-8152
12212 Kyle Abbey Ln Raleigh (27613) *(G-10058)*

Dreamshipper, Raleigh *Also Called: Dreamship Inc (G-10058)*

Dreamstone Gran MBL & Quartz, Garner *Also Called: USA Dreamstone LLC (G-4970)*

Dreamweavers Brewery LLC.............. 704 507-7773
115 E North Main St Waxhaw (28173) *(G-12429)*

Drew Roberts LLC.............. 336 497-1679
6627 Barton Creek Dr Whitsett (27377) *(G-12604)*

Drews Cabinets and Cases.............. 919 796-3985
8100 Nc Highway 42 E Selma (27576) *(G-11286)*

Drexel Heritage Furnishings.............. 828 391-6400
825 Visionary St Lenoir (28645) *(G-7601)*

Drexel Heritage Home Furnsngs.............. 336 812-4430
741 W Ward Ave High Point (27260) *(G-6598)*

Drill & Fill Mfg LLC.............. 252 937-4555
5484 S Old Carriage Rd Rocky Mount (27803) *(G-10832)*

Drink A Bull LLC.............. 919 818-3321
921 Holloway St Ste 103 Durham (27701) *(G-4008)*

Driveco Inc.............. 704 615-2111
13519 Norlington Ct Charlotte (28273) *(G-2065)*

Driver Distribution Inc.............. 984 204-2929
9413 Owls Nest Dr Raleigh (27613) *(G-10059)*

Driver License, Salisbury *Also Called: North Carolina Dept Trnsp (G-11098)*

Drnc, Conover *Also Called: Blue Inc Usa LLC (G-3494)*

Dromma Bed, Hickory *Also Called: Comfort Bay Home Fashions Inc (G-6305)*

Dronescape Pllc.............. 704 953-3798
9716 Rea Rd Ste B Charlotte (28277) *(G-2066)*

Drs Consulting, Raleigh *Also Called: Drs Transportation Inc (G-10060)*

Drs Transportation Inc.............. 919 215-2770
10820 Oliver Rd Apt 101 Raleigh (27614) *(G-10060)*

Drum Filter Media Inc.............. 336 434-4195
901 W Fairfield Rd High Point (27263) *(G-6599)*

Drydog Barriers LLC.............. 704 334-8222
2034 Van Buren Ave Ste C Indian Trail (28079) *(G-7077)*

Ds Smith Packaging, Asheboro *Also Called: Southcorr LLC (G-396)*

Ds Smith Packaging and Paper.............. 336 668-0871
4328 Federal Dr Ste 105 Greensboro (27410) *(G-5505)*

Ds Smith PLC.............. 919 557-3148
301 Thomas Mill Rd Holly Springs (27540) *(G-6898)*

DSA Master Crafted Doors, Raleigh *Also Called: Door Store of America Inc (G-10056)*

Dse, Mooresville *Also Called: Kgt Enterprises Inc (G-8704)*

Dse Express LLC.............. 540 686-0981
10 Valley View Ct Sanford (27332) *(G-11172)*

DSI Blackpages, Asheville *Also Called: Deverger Systems Inc (G-487)*

DSI Innovations LLC.............. 336 893-8385
42 High Tech Blvd Thomasville (27360) *(G-12020)*

DSM.............. 408 582-2610
202 Crestline Blvd Greenville (27834) *(G-5968)*

Dsm Inc.............. 919 876-2802
266 W Millbrook Rd Raleigh (27609) *(G-10061)*

DSM Desotech Inc.............. 704 862-5000
1101 N Carolina 27 Stanley (28164) *(G-11614)*

DSM Hpf, Greenville *Also Called: Avient Protective Mtls LLC (G-5943)*

DSM Pharmaceuticals Inc.............. 252 758-3436
5900 Martin Luther King Jr Hwy Greenville (27834) *(G-5969)*

DSM Pharmaceuticals Inc.............. 252 758-3436
5900 Martin Luther King Jr Hwy Greenville (27834) *(G-5970)*

(G-0000) Company's Geographic Section entry number

Dst Manufacturing LLC.. 336 676-6096
166 Regal Dr Randleman (27317) *(G-10643)*

Dtbtla Inc.. 336 769-0000
4301 Waterleaf Ct Greensboro (27410) *(G-5506)*

Dth Publishing Inc... 919 962-1163
151 E Rosemary St Ste 101 Chapel Hill (27514) *(G-1541)*

Dtp Inc... 336 272-5122
1 Wendy Ct Ste E Greensboro (27409) *(G-5507)*

Dublin Woodwork Shop... 910 862-2289
N S Hwy 87 E Dublin (28332) *(G-3831)*

Dubose National Enrgy Svcs Inc... 704 295-1060
103 Waxhaw Professional Park Dr Ste D Waxhaw (28173) *(G-12430)*

Dubose Strapping Inc (PA)... 910 590-1020
906 Industrial Dr Clinton (28328) *(G-3232)*

Ducduc LLC... 212 226-1868
3200 Wake Forest Rd Ste 204 Raleigh (27609) *(G-10062)*

Ducduc Nyc, Raleigh *Also Called: Ducduc LLC (G-10062)*

Duck Head LLC.. 855 457-1865
816 S Elm St Greensboro (27406) *(G-5508)*

Duck-Rabbit Craft Brewery Inc.. 252 753-7745
4519 West Pine St Farmville (27828) *(G-4527)*

Duco-SCI Inc... 704 289-9502
6004 Stitt St Monroe (28110) *(G-8478)*

Dudley Inc... 704 636-8850
475 Majolica Rd Salisbury (28147) *(G-11045)*

Dudleys Fence Company... 252 566-5759
4126 Fields Station Rd La Grange (28551) *(G-7467)*

Due Process Stable Trdg Co LLC... 910 608-0284
4111 W 5th St Lumberton (28358) *(G-7949)*

Duff-Norton Company, Inc., Charlotte *Also Called: Yale Industrial Products Inc (G-3038)*

Duke Athletic Products, Yanceyville *Also Called: Royal Textile Mills Inc (G-13460)*

Duke Energy Center.. 919 464-0960
2 E South St Raleigh (27601) *(G-10063)*

Duke Human Vaccine Institute.. 919 684-5384
2 Genome Ct Durham (27710) *(G-4009)*

Duke Student Publishing Co Inc.. 919 684-3811
101 Union Dr Durham (27708) *(G-4010)*

Duke University.. 919 687-3600
905 W Main St Ste 19 Durham (27701) *(G-4011)*

Duke University Press, Durham *Also Called: Duke University (G-4011)*

Dukester Productions Entrmt Co, Goldsboro *Also Called: Monk Lekeisha (G-5230)*

Dunavants Welding & Steel Inc.. 252 338-6533
207 Us Highway 158 E Camden (27921) *(G-1211)*

Dunbar Foods Corporation.. 910 892-3175
1000 S Fayetteville Ave Dunn (28334) *(G-3854)*

Duncan Design Ltd... 919 834-7713
2308 Wake Forest Rd Ste E Raleigh (27608) *(G-10064)*

Duncan Junior D.. 336 871-3599
1165 Troy Brown Rd Sandy Ridge (27046) *(G-11143)*

Duncan-Parnell Inc.. 252 977-7832
2741 N Wesleyan Blvd Rocky Mount (27804) *(G-10833)*

Duncan, JD Logging, Sandy Ridge *Also Called: Duncan Junior D (G-11143)*

Dunlop Aircraft Tyres Inc.. 336 283-0979
205 Enterprise Way Mocksville (27028) *(G-8359)*

Dunn Manufacturing Corp (PA)... 704 283-2147
1400 Goldmine Rd Monroe (28110) *(G-8479)*

Duocraft Cabinets & Dist Co (PA).. 252 240-1476
1306 Bridges St Morehead City (28557) *(G-8830)*

Duotech Services LLC... 828 369-5111
245 Industrial Park Rd Franklin (28734) *(G-4826)*

Duplin Forest Products Inc.. 910 285-5381
312 Jack Dale Rd Wallace (28466) *(G-12320)*

Duplin Times, Kenansville *Also Called: Cox Nrth Crlina Pblcations Inc (G-7225)*

Duplin Wine Cellars Inc (PA)... 910 289-3888
505 N Sycamore St Rose Hill (28458) *(G-10905)*

Dupont.. 919 414-0089
5816 Raddington St Raleigh (27613) *(G-10065)*

Dupont, Durham *Also Called: Dupont Specialty Pdts USA LLC (G-4013)*

Dupont, Fayetteville *Also Called: Eidp Inc (G-4595)*

Dupont, Grifton *Also Called: Eidp Inc (G-6035)*

Dupont, Kinston *Also Called: Eidp Inc (G-7408)*

Dupont, Kinston *Also Called: Eidp Inc (G-7409)*

Dupont, Leland *Also Called: Eidp Inc (G-7540)*

Dupont Electronic Polymers L P (HQ)................................... 919 248-5135
14 Tw Alexander Dr Durham (27709) *(G-4012)*

Dupont Specialty Pdts USA LLC.. 919 248-5109
4020 Stirrup Creek Dr Durham (27703) *(G-4013)*

Dupont Teijin Films... 910 433-8200
3216 Cedar Creek Rd Fayetteville (28312) *(G-4589)*

Dura-Craft Die Inc.. 828 632-1944
1442 Liledoun Rd Taylorsville (28681) *(G-11959)*

Durabar Metals Services Div, Salisbury *Also Called: Charter Dura-Bar Inc (G-11032)*

Durable Wood Preservers Inc... 704 537-3113
7901 Pence Rd Charlotte (28215) *(G-2067)*

Durafiber Technologies... 704 912-3700
13620 Reese Blvd E # 400 Huntersville (28078) *(G-6983)*

Durafiber Technologies (dft) Inc.. 704 912-3700
13620 Reese Blvd E Ste 400 Huntersville (28078) *(G-6984)*

Durafiber Technologies (dft) Operations LLC........................ 704 912-3770
13620 Reese Blvd E Ste 400 Huntersville (28078) *(G-6985)*

Durafiber Technologies DFT Inc.. 704 639-2722
7401 Statesville Blvd Salisbury (28147) *(G-11046)*

Durafiber Technologies DFT Inc.. 919 356-3824
672 Douglas Farm Rd Sanford (27332) *(G-11173)*

Duraline Imaging Inc.. 828 692-1301
580 Upward Rd Ste 1 Flat Rock (28731) *(G-4707)*

Duramax Holdings LLC.. 704 588-9191
12700 General Dr Charlotte (28273) *(G-2068)*

Durham Bookcases, Durham *Also Called: Bookcase Shop (G-3938)*

Durham Coca-Cola Bottling Co.. 919 510-0574
1 Floretta Pl Raleigh (27613) *(G-10066)*

Durham Coca-Cola Bottling Company (PA)............................ 919 383-1531
3214 Hillsborough Rd Durham (27705) *(G-4014)*

Durham Distillery Llc.. 919 937-2121
711 Washington St Durham (27701) *(G-4015)*

Duro, Charlotte *Also Called: Duro Hilex Poly LLC (G-2069)*

Duro Hilex Poly LLC (DH).. 800 845-6051
3436 Toringdon Way Ste 100 Charlotte (28277) *(G-2069)*

Dustcontrol Inc.. 910 395-1808
6720 Amsterdam Way Ste 400 Wilmington (28405) *(G-12768)*

Dustin Ellis Logging... 704 732-6027
1186 Confederate Rd Lincolnton (28092) *(G-7829)*

Dusty Rhoads Hvac Inc... 252 261-5892
3822 Elijah Baum Dr Kitty Hawk (27949) *(G-7444)*

Dutch Kettle LLC.. 336 468-8422
5016 Hunting Creek Church Rd Hamptonville (27020) *(G-6083)*

Dutch Kettle, The, Hamptonville *Also Called: Dutch Kettle LLC (G-6083)*

Dutch Miller Auto Group, Charlotte *Also Called: Dutch Miller Charlotte Inc (G-2070)*

Dutch Miller Charlotte Inc.. 704 522-8422
7725 South Blvd Charlotte (28273) *(G-2070)*

Dutchman Creek Self-Storage.. 919 363-8878
8712 Holly Springs Rd Apex (27539) *(G-151)*

Duty Tire and Service Center, Raleigh *Also Called: Village Tire Center Inc (G-10588)*

DVine Foods... 910 862-2576
1585 Hwy 107 South Elizabethtown (28337) *(G-4425)*

Dwd Industries LLC.. 336 498-6327
151 Southern Dr Randleman (27317) *(G-10644)*

Dwiggins Metal Masters Inc.. 336 751-2379
122 Wilkesboro St Mocksville (27028) *(G-8360)*

DWM INTERNATIONAL INC... 646 290-7448
2151 Hawkins St Ste 1225 Charlotte (28203) *(G-2071)*

Dwp, Plymouth *Also Called: Diversified Wood Products Inc (G-9801)*

Dxterity Solutions, Mooresville *Also Called: 27 Software US Inc (G-8589)*

Dymetrol Company Inc (PA).. 866 964-8632
1305 W Seaboard St Bladenboro (28320) *(G-876)*

Dyna-Tech Manufacturing Inc... 704 839-0203
5639 Cannon Dr Monroe (28110) *(G-8480)*

Dynacast, Charlotte *Also Called: Dynacast LLC (G-2072)*

Dynacast, Charlotte *Also Called: Dynacast US Holdings Inc (G-2075)*

Dynacast LLC (DH).. 704 927-2790
11325 N Community House Rd Ste 300 Charlotte (28277) *(G-2072)*

Dynacast International LLC (HQ)................ 704 927-2790
  14045 Ballantyne Corporate Pl Charlotte (28277) *(G-2073)*

Dynacast US Holdings Inc................ 704 927-2786
  14045 Ballantyne Corporate Pl Ste 300 Charlotte (28277) *(G-2074)*

Dynacast US Holdings Inc (DH)................ 704 927-2790
  14045 Ballantyne Corporate Pl Ste 400 Charlotte (28277) *(G-2075)*

Dynagraphics Screenprintng................ 919 212-2898
  125 Quantum St Holly Springs (27540) *(G-6899)*

Dynamac Corporation................ 919 544-6428
  1910 Sedwick Rd Ste 300a Durham (27713) *(G-4016)*

Dynamic Air Engineering Inc................ 714 540-1000
  2421 Bga Dr Claremont (28610) *(G-3112)*

Dynamic Machine Works LLC................ 336 462-7370
  2655 Knob Hill Dr Clemmons (27012) *(G-3182)*

Dynamic Machining X Mfg LLC................ 336 362-3425
  157 Industrial Dr King (27021) *(G-7326)*

Dynamic Mounting................ 704 978-8723
  120b Pitt Rd Mooresville (28115) *(G-8656)*

Dynamic Nutraceuticals LLC (PA)................ 704 380-2324
  1441 Wilkesboro Hwy Statesville (28625) *(G-11693)*

Dynamic Stampings NC Inc................ 704 509-2501
  1412 Castle Ct Gastonia (28052) *(G-5044)*

Dynamic Systems Inc................ 828 683-3523
  104 Morrow Branch Rd Leicester (28748) *(G-7523)*

Dynapar Corporation (HQ)................ 800 873-8731
  2100 W Broad St Elizabethtown (28337) *(G-4426)*

Dynea, Moncure *Also Called: Arclin USA LLC (G-8400)*

Dynisco Bearing, Hickory *Also Called: Dynisco Instruments LLC (G-6325)*

Dynisco Instruments LLC................ 828 326-9888
  1291 19th Street Ln Nw Hickory (28601) *(G-6325)*

Dystar Americas Holding Corp (PA)................ 704 561-3000
  9844 Southern Pine Blvd Ste A Charlotte (28273) *(G-2076)*

Dystar Carolina Chemical Corp................ 704 391-6322
  8309 Wilkinson Blvd Charlotte (28214) *(G-2077)*

Dystar LP (DH)................ 704 561-3000
  9844 Southern Pine Blvd Ste A Charlotte (28273) *(G-2078)*

Dystar LP................ 336 342-6631
  209 Watlington Industrial Dr Reidsville (27320) *(G-10683)*

Dzone Inc................ 919 678-0300
  600 Park Offices Dr Ste 150 Research Triangle Pa (27709) *(G-10708)*

E & M Concrete Inc................ 919 235-7221
  7505 Troy Stone Dr Fuquay Varina (27526) *(G-4880)*

E A Duncan Cnstr Co Inc................ 910 653-3535
  1475 Savannah Rd Tabor City (28463) *(G-11910)*

E and J Publishing LLC................ 877 882-2138
  3502 Lukes Dr Charlotte (28216) *(G-2079)*

E By Design LLC................ 980 231-5483
  20823 N Main St Ste 115 Cornelius (28031) *(G-3598)*

E C P, Middlesex *Also Called: Eastcoast Packaging Inc (G-8274)*

E C U Univ Prtg & Graphics................ 252 737-1301
  2612 E 10th St Greenville (27858) *(G-5971)*

E Cache & Co LLC................ 919 590-0779
  6316 Old Sugar Creek Rd Ste E Charlotte (28269) *(G-2080)*

E F P Inc................ 336 498-4134
  8013 Adams Farm Rd Randleman (27317) *(G-10645)*

E Feibusch Company Inc................ 336 434-5095
  516 Townsend Ave High Point (27263) *(G-6600)*

E G A Products Inc................ 704 664-1221
  208 Mckenzie Rd Mooresville (28115) *(G-8657)*

E Gads Screen Printing & EMB, Elizabeth City *Also Called: Marvin Bailey Screen Printing (G-4397)*

E J Victor Inc (PA)................ 828 437-1991
  110 Wamsutta Mill Rd Morganton (28655) *(G-8861)*

E J Victor Furniture, Morganton *Also Called: E J Victor Inc (G-8861)*

E P D, Wendell *Also Called: Electronic Products Design Inc (G-12535)*

E T Sales Inc................ 704 888-4010
  13570 Broadway Ave Midland (28107) *(G-8286)*

E W Godwin S Sons Inc (PA)................ 910 762-7747
  1207 Castle Hayne Rd Wilmington (28401) *(G-12769)*

E Z Stop Number Two................ 828 627-9081
  8721 Carolina Blvd Clyde (28721) *(G-3259)*

E- Stitch.com, Snow Hill *Also Called: Happy Jack Incorporated (G-11480)*

E-Liquid Brands LLC................ 828 385-5090
  120 Commercial Dr Mooresville (28115) *(G-8658)*

E-N-G Mobile Systems LLC (HQ)................ 925 798-4060
  810 Tom Starling Rd Fayetteville (28306) *(G-4590)*

E-Z Dumper Products LLC................ 717 762-8432
  150 Vardon Ct Southern Pines (28387) *(G-11497)*

E&C Medical Intelligence Inc................ 609 228-7898
  100 Regency Forest Dr Ste 200 Cary (27518) *(G-1350)*

E2m Kitchen LLC................ 704 731-5070
  1907 Gateway Blvd Charlotte (28208) *(G-2081)*

Eagle Assembly Unlimited Inc................ 252 462-0408
  8928 Main St Castalia (27816) *(G-1492)*

Eagle Carports Inc (PA)................ 800 579-8589
  210 Airport Rd Mount Airy (27030) *(G-9117)*

Eagle Compressors, Greensboro *Also Called: Eagle Compressors Inc (G-5509)*

Eagle Compressors Inc (PA)................ 336 370-4159
  3003 Thurston Ave Greensboro (27406) *(G-5509)*

Eagle Laser, High Point *Also Called: Custom Finishers Inc (G-6584)*

Eagle Machining Usa Inc................ 717 235-9383
  13728 Statesville Rd Huntersville (28078) *(G-6986)*

Eagle Products Inc................ 336 886-5688
  1200 Surrett Dr High Point (27260) *(G-6601)*

Eagle Rock Concrete LLC................ 919 596-7077
  500 Pristine Water Dr Apex (27539) *(G-152)*

Eagle Rock Concrete LLC (PA)................ 919 781-3744
  8310 Bandford Way Raleigh (27615) *(G-10067)*

Eagle Rock Concrete LLC................ 919 281-0120
  8311 Bandford Way Ste 7 Raleigh (27615) *(G-10068)*

Eagle Sportswear LLC................ 919 365-9805
  4251 Wendell Blvd Wendell (27591) *(G-12534)*

Eagle Sportswear LLC................ 252 235-4082
  10447 S Nash St Middlesex (27557) *(G-8273)*

Eagle Superabrasives Inc................ 828 261-7281
  141 33rd Street Dr Se Hickory (28602) *(G-6326)*

Eagle USA, Wendell *Also Called: Eagle Sportswear LLC (G-12534)*

Eaglestone Technology Inc................ 336 476-0244
  1401 Kensington Dr High Point (27262) *(G-6602)*

Earls Precision Machining................ 919 542-1869
  365 Taylors Chapel Rd Sanford (27330) *(G-11174)*

Early Bird Hosiery Mills Inc................ 828 324-6745
  1011 10th Street Blvd Nw Hickory (28601) *(G-6327)*

Earnmoore, High Point *Also Called: Cartridge World (G-6562)*

Earth Edge LLC................ 828 624-0252
  940 23rd St Sw Hickory (28602) *(G-6328)*

Earth Guild, Asheville *Also Called: Grateful Union Family Inc (G-510)*

Earth Matters Inc................ 410 747-4400
  4943 Looking Glass Trl Denver (28037) *(G-3781)*

Earth-Kind Inc................ 701 751-4456
  346 E Plaza Dr Ste D Mooresville (28115) *(G-8659)*

Earthknit, Liberty *Also Called: Supertex Inc (G-7781)*

Eas Incorporated................ 704 734-4945
  420 Canterbury Rd Kings Mountain (28086) *(G-7361)*

East Carolina Brace Limb Inc................ 252 726-8068
  209 N 35th St Ste 1 Morehead City (28557) *(G-8831)*

East Carolina Trucks, Garner *Also Called: Carroll Co (G-4920)*

East Cast Emrgncy Response Svc, Beulaville *Also Called: Daphne Lawson Espino (G-841)*

East Coast Biologics................ 717 919-9980
  311 Wagoner Dr Fayetteville (28303) *(G-4591)*

East Coast Designs LLC................ 910 865-1070
  781 Tobermory Rd Fayetteville (28306) *(G-4592)*

East Coast Digital Inc................ 919 304-1142
  100 E Ruffin St Mebane (27302) *(G-8239)*

East Coast Door & Hardware Inc................ 704 791-4128
  464 Action Dr Nw Concord (28027) *(G-3358)*

East Coast Fab LLC................ 336 285-7444
  195 Labrador Dr Randleman (27317) *(G-10646)*

East Coast Firewood LLC................ 919 542-0792
  840 Moncure Pittsboro Rd Moncure (27559) *(G-8403)*

East Coast Log & Timber Inc................ 252 568-4344
  305 Kator Dunn Rd Albertson (28508) *(G-99)*

(G-0000) Company's Geographic Section entry number

East Coast Logging Inc.. 252 794-4054
128 Mizelle Ln Windsor (27983) *(G-13052)*

East Coast Mouldings, North Wilkesboro Also Called: Ecmd Inc *(G-9529)*

East Coast Oxygen Inc.. 828 252-7770
310 Elk Park Dr Asheville (28804) *(G-490)*

East Coast Stl Fabrication Inc....................................... 757 351-2601
116 N Granby St Hertford (27944) *(G-6253)*

East Coast Umbrella Inc... 910 462-2500
6321 Andrew Jackson Hwy Laurel Hill (28351) *(G-7482)*

East Crlina Metal Treating Inc (PA).............................. 919 834-2100
1117 Capital Blvd Raleigh (27603) *(G-10069)*

East Crlina Olseed Prcssors LL.................................... 252 935-5553
2015 Nc Highway 45 N Pantego (27860) *(G-9643)*

East Crlina Orthtics Prsthtics, Elizabeth City Also Called: Albemrle Orthotics Prosthetics
(G-4378)

East Fork, Asheville Also Called: East Fork Pottery LLC *(G-492)*

East Fork Pottery LLC.. 828 237-7200
144 Caribou Rd Ste 70 Asheville (28803) *(G-491)*

East Fork Pottery LLC (PA)... 828 237-7200
531 Short Mcdowell St Asheville (28803) *(G-492)*

East Fork Pottery LLC.. 828 575-2150
15 W Walnut St # A Asheville (28801) *(G-493)*

East Industries Inc... 252 442-9662
1114 Instrument Dr Rocky Mount (27804) *(G-10834)*

East Penn Manufacturing Co... 336 771-1380
3117 Starlight Dr Ste 200 Winston Salem (27107) *(G-13152)*

Eastcoast Packaging Inc... 919 562-6060
10235 E Finch Ave Middlesex (27557) *(G-8274)*

Easter Seals Ucp NC & VA Inc...................................... 919 856-0250
2533 Atlantic Ave Raleigh (27604) *(G-10070)*

Eastern Band Cherokee Indians..................................... 828 497-6824
2000 Old #4 Rd Cherokee (28719) *(G-3053)*

Eastern Bikes, Raleigh Also Called: Driver Distribution Inc *(G-10059)*

Eastern Cabinet Company Inc.. 252 237-5245
3100 Meteor Dr Wilson (27893) *(G-12985)*

Eastern Cabinet Installers Inc...................................... 336 774-2966
4735 Kester Mill Rd Winston Salem (27103) *(G-13153)*

Eastern Carolina Vault Co Inc....................................... 252 243-5614
1214 Queen St E Wilson (27893) *(G-12986)*

Eastern Compost LLC.. 252 446-3636
8487 Battleboro-Leggett Rd Elm City (27822) *(G-4465)*

Eastern Crlina Agrculture Svcs, Robersonville Also Called: Carolina Eastern Inc *(G-10766)*

Eastern Crlina Vctonal Ctr Inc (PA)............................... 252 758-4188
2100 N Greene St Greenville (27834) *(G-5972)*

Eastern Elevator Inc... 877 840-2638
176 Mine Lake Ct Raleigh (27615) *(G-10071)*

Eastern Hydraulic & Pwr Transm, Rocky Mount Also Called: Wilson Iron Works Incorporated
(G-10820)

Eastern Offset Printing Co... 252 247-6791
410 W Fort Macon Rd Atlantic Beach (28512) *(G-639)*

Eastern Plastics Company.. 704 542-7786
10724 Carmel Commons Blvd Ste 580 Charlotte (28226) *(G-2082)*

Eastern Ready Mix LLC.. 919 207-2722
3170 Federal Rd Benson (27504) *(G-788)*

Eastern Sun Communications Inc................................... 704 408-7668
4019 Sheridan Dr Charlotte (28205) *(G-2083)*

Eastern Wholesale Fence LLC....................................... 631 698-0975
7401 Statesville Blvd Salisbury (28147) *(G-11047)*

Easth20 Holdings Llc.. 919 313-2100
4224 Tudor Ln Ste 101 Greensboro (27410) *(G-5510)*

Eastonsweb Multimedia... 704 607-0941
4111 Nicole Eileen Ln Charlotte (28216) *(G-2084)*

Easy Mask, Cary Also Called: Loparex LLC *(G-1392)*

Easy Stones Corp.. 980 201-9506
1440 Westinghouse Blvd Ste A Charlotte (28273) *(G-2085)*

Easyglass Inc... 336 786-1800
1 Andrew Pearson Dr Mount Airy (27030) *(G-9118)*

Easykeyscom Inc.. 877 839-5397
11407 Granite St Charlotte (28273) *(G-2086)*

Eatclub Inc.. 609 578-7942
114 Saint Ayers Way Chapel Hill (27517) *(G-1542)*

Eaton Corporation... 828 684-2381
221 Heywood Rd Arden (28704) *(G-266)*

Eaton Corporation... 910 677-5375
2900 Doc Bennett Rd Fayetteville (28306) *(G-4593)*

Eaton Corporation... 828 286-4157
240 Daniel Rd Forest City (28043) *(G-4788)*

Eaton Corporation... 704 937-7411
744 S Battleground Ave Kings Mountain (28086) *(G-7362)*

Eaton Corporation... 910 695-2900
15 Centennial Blvd Pinehurst (28374) *(G-9691)*

Eaton Corporation... 919 870-3000
8609 Six Forks Rd Raleigh (27615) *(G-10072)*

Eaton Corporation... 864 433-1603
8380 Capital Blvd Raleigh (27616) *(G-10073)*

Eaton Corporation... 919 872-3020
3301 Spring Forest Rd Raleigh (27616) *(G-10074)*

Eaton Corporation... 336 322-0696
2564 Durham Rd Roxboro (27573) *(G-10924)*

Eaton Corporation... 919 965-2341
1100 E Preston St Selma (27576) *(G-11287)*

Eaton Power Quality Corp.. 919 872-3020
8609 Six Forks Rd Raleigh (27615) *(G-10075)*

Eaton Power Quality Group Inc (DH).............................. 919 872-3020
8609 Six Forks Rd Raleigh (27615) *(G-10076)*

Eaton US Raleigh, Raleigh Also Called: Eaton Corporation *(G-10073)*

Eaton-Schultz Inc... 704 331-8004
3800 Woodpark Blvd Ste I Charlotte (28206) *(G-2087)*

Eatumup Lure Company Inc.. 336 218-0896
116 S Walnut Cir Greensboro (27409) *(G-5511)*

Ebert Sign Company Inc.. 336 768-2867
7815 N Nc Highway 150 Lexington (27295) *(G-7681)*

Ecii, Whitsett Also Called: Engineered Controls Intl LLC *(G-12605)*

Eclipse Composite Engrg Inc.. 801 601-8559
138 Cedar Pointe Dr Mooresville (28117) *(G-8660)*

Eclipse Composites Engineering, Mooresville Also Called: Eclipse Composite Engrg Inc
(G-8660)

Ecmd Inc... 336 835-1182
541 Gentry Rd Elkin (28621) *(G-4444)*

Ecmd Inc (PA).. 336 667-5976
2 Grandview St North Wilkesboro (28659) *(G-9529)*

Eco Building Corporation... 910 736-1540
16824 A Nc-211 Red Springs (28377) *(G-10667)*

Eco-Kids LLC... 207 899-2752
6316 J Richard Dr Ste C Raleigh (27617) *(G-10077)*

Ecoatm LLC... 858 324-4111
200 Village Dr Boone (28607) *(G-913)*

Ecodyst, Apex Also Called: Ecodyst Inc *(G-153)*

Ecodyst Inc... 919 599-4963
1010 Goodworth Dr Apex (27539) *(G-153)*

Ecolab, Greensboro Also Called: Kay Chemical Company *(G-5642)*

Ecolab Inc... 704 527-5912
9335 Harris Corners Pkwy Ste 100 Charlotte (28269) *(G-2088)*

Ecolab Inc... 336 931-2289
8300 Capital Dr Greensboro (27409) *(G-5512)*

Ecolab Inc... 336 931-3423
1101 Gallimore Dairy Rd High Point (27265) *(G-6603)*

Ecolab Inc... 336 931-2237
90 Piedmont Industrial Dr Ste 400 Winston Salem (27107) *(G-13154)*

Ecolab Kay Chemical Company, Greensboro Also Called: Ecolab Inc *(G-5512)*

Economy Clrs Lillington LLC... 910 893-3927
235 Skeet Range Rd Coats (27521) *(G-3261)*

Economy Grinding, Charlotte Also Called: Economy Grinding Straightening *(G-2089)*

Economy Grinding Straightening..................................... 704 400-2500
432 Springbrook Rd Charlotte (28217) *(G-2089)*

Ecovehicle Enterprises Inc... 704 544-9907
15022 Ballantyne Country Club Dr Charlotte (28277) *(G-2090)*

ECR Software Corporation (PA)...................................... 828 265-2907
277 Howard St Boone (28607) *(G-914)*

Ecrs, Boone Also Called: ECR Software Corporation *(G-914)*

Ecs Group-NC LLC... 919 830-1171
6424 Zebulon Rd Wake Forest (27587) *(G-12273)*

Ecu Print Shop, Greenville *Also Called: E C U Univ Prtg & Graphics (G-5971)*

Ecvc, Greenville *Also Called: Eastern Crlina Vctonal Ctr Inc (G-5972)*

Ed Kemp Associates, High Point *Also Called: Ed Kemp Associates Inc (G-6604)*

Ed Kemp Associates Inc 336 869-2155
3001 N Main St High Point (27265) *(G-6604)*

Ed S Tire Laurinburg Inc 910 277-0565
300 Biggs St Laurinburg (28352) *(G-7498)*

ED&d, Cary *Also Called: Educated Design & Development Incorporated (G-1351)*

Edc Inc (PA) 336 993-0468
950 Old Winston Rd Kernersville (27284) *(G-7270)*

Edco Products Inc 828 264-1490
643 Greenway Rd Ste J5 Boone (28607) *(G-915)*

Eddie Hsr S Prcsion McHning In 704 750-4244
613 Slater St Kings Mountain (28086) *(G-7363)*

Eddie S Mountain Machine Inc 828 685-0733
2011 Pilot Mountain Rd Hendersonville (28792) *(G-6204)*

Eddies Welding Inc 704 585-2024
213 Halyburton Rd Stony Point (28678) *(G-11833)*

Edelbrock LLC 919 718-9737
5715 Clyde Rhyne Dr Sanford (27330) *(G-11175)*

Eden Brothers, Arden *Also Called: Vista Horticultural Group Inc (G-317)*

Eden Dry Cleaners, Charlotte *Also Called: M and R Inc (G-2444)*

Edenton Boatworks LLC 252 482-7600
140 Midway Dr Edenton (27932) *(G-4366)*

Edge Broadband Solutions LLC 828 785-1420
244 Lea Plant Rd Waynesville (28786) *(G-12457)*

Edge of The Carolinas Magazine, Wilmington *Also Called: Quinlan Publishing Company (G-12894)*

Edge Promo Team LLC 919 946-4218
7868 Us 70 Bus Hwy W Ste B Clayton (27520) *(G-3145)*

Edge Welding Supply, Mooresville *Also Called: M 5 Scentific Glassblowing Inc (G-8716)*

Edge-Works Manufacturing Co 910 455-9834
272 W Stag Park Service Rd Burgaw (28425) *(G-1022)*

Edgewell Per Care Brands LLC 336 672-4500
2331 Carl Dr Asheboro (27203) *(G-347)*

Edgewell Per Care Brands LLC 336 629-1581
800 Albemarle Rd Asheboro (27203) *(G-348)*

Edgewell Per Care Brands LLC 336 672-4500
419 Art Bryan Dr Asheboro (27203) *(G-349)*

Edgeworks, Burgaw *Also Called: Edge-Works Manufacturing Co (G-1022)*

EDM Technology Inc., High Point *Also Called: Paragon ID High Point Us Inc (G-6726)*

Edmac, Charlotte *Also Called: Edmac Compressor Parts (G-2091)*

Edmac Compressor Parts 800 866-2959
2101 Westinghouse Blvd Ste D Charlotte (28273) *(G-2091)*

Edmiston Hydrlic Swmill Eqp In 336 921-2304
8540 W Nc Highway 268 Boomer (28606) *(G-890)*

Eds Pallet World Inc 828 453-8986
559 Race Path Church Rd Ellenboro (28040) *(G-4457)*

Edsel G Barnes Jr Inc 252 793-4170
1458 Morrattock Rd Plymouth (27962) *(G-9803)*

Edtech Systems LLC 919 341-0613
6115 Corporate Ridge Rd Raleigh (27607) *(G-10078)*

Educated Design & Development Incorporated 919 469-9434
901 Sheldon Dr Cary (27513) *(G-1351)*

Education Center LLC 336 854-0309
8886 Rymack Dr Oak Ridge (27310) *(G-9571)*

Educatrx Inc 980 328-0013
504 Kintyre Dr Monroe (28112) *(G-8481)*

Edward Ferrell Lewis Mittman, High Point *Also Called: Dfp Inc (G-6592)*

Edward Heil Screw Products 828 345-6140
1114 1st St W Conover (28613) *(G-3517)*

Edwards Electronic Systems Inc (HQ) 919 359-2239
3821 Powhatan Rd Clayton (27520) *(G-3146)*

Edwards Timber Company Inc (PA) 704 624-5098
2215 Old Lawyers Rd Marshville (28103) *(G-8087)*

Edwards Transportation, Marshville *Also Called: Edwards Wood Products Inc (G-8088)*

Edwards Unlimited Inc 252 226-4583
3355 Raleigh Rd Henderson (27537) *(G-6154)*

Edwards Wood Pdts Inc/Woodlawn 828 756-4758
8482 Us 221 N Marion (28752) *(G-8041)*

Edwards Wood Products Inc 704 624-5098
9979 Old Liberty Rd Liberty (27298) *(G-7764)*

Edwards Wood Products Inc 336 622-7537
3231 Staley Store Rd Liberty (27298) *(G-7765)*

Edwards Wood Products Inc (PA) 704 624-3624
2215 Old Lawyers Rd Marshville (28103) *(G-8088)*

Edwards Wood Products Inc 910 276-6870
19500 Old Lumberton Rd Laurinburg (28352) *(G-7499)*

Edwin Reaves 901 326-6382
1630 Flintshire Rd Fayetteville (28304) *(G-4594)*

Eekkohart Floors & Lbr Co Inc 336 409-2672
1133 N Main St Mocksville (27028) *(G-8361)*

Efa Inc 336 378-2603
3112 Pleasant Garden Rd Greensboro (27406) *(G-5513)*

Efa Inc (DH) 336 275-9401
3112 Pleasant Garden Rd Greensboro (27406) *(G-5514)*

Efco USA Inc 800 332-6872
11600 Goodrich Dr Charlotte (28273) *(G-2092)*

Effikal LLC 252 522-3031
2630 Airport Rd Kinston (28504) *(G-7407)*

Effipharma Inc 919 338-2628
2018 N Lakeshore Dr Chapel Hill (27514) *(G-1543)*

Eg-Gilero, Durham *Also Called: Gilero LLC (G-4047)*

Ega Southeast, Mooresville *Also Called: E G A Products Inc (G-8657)*

Egger, Linwood *Also Called: Egger Wood Products LLC (G-7876)*

Egger Wood Products LLC 336 843-7000
300 Egger Pkwy Linwood (27299) *(G-7876)*

Egi Associates Inc 704 561-3337
417 Minuet Ln Ste A Charlotte (28217) *(G-2093)*

Ei LLC 704 857-0707
380 Knollwood St Ste 700 Winston Salem (27103) *(G-13155)*

Ei Solution Works, Winston Salem *Also Called: Ei LLC (G-13155)*

Eidolon Designs, Raleigh *Also Called: Michael Parker Cabinetry (G-10298)*

Eidp Inc 910 483-4681
22828 Nc Highway 87 W Fayetteville (28306) *(G-4595)*

Eidp Inc 252 522-6111
4693 Highway 11 N Grifton (28530) *(G-6035)*

Eidp Inc 252 522-6896
2204 Pink Hill Rd Kinston (28504) *(G-7408)*

Eidp Inc 252 522-6286
4693 Hwy 11 N Kinston (28502) *(G-7409)*

Eidp Inc 910 371-4000
3500 Daniels Rd Ne Leland (28451) *(G-7540)*

Eisai Inc 919 941-6920
4130 Parklake Ave Ste 500 Raleigh (27612) *(G-10079)*

Eizi Group Llc 919 397-3638
9008 Riverview Park Dr Raleigh (27613) *(G-10080)*

Ej, Apex *Also Called: Ej Usa Inc (G-154)*

Ej Usa Inc 919 362-7744
1006 Investment Blvd Apex (27502) *(G-154)*

Ekc Advanced Elec USA 4 LLC 302 774-1000
1209 Orange St Wilmington (28401) *(G-12770)*

El Comal Inc 336 788-8110
2390 E Sprague St Winston Salem (27107) *(G-13156)*

Elan Trading Inc 704 342-1696
3826 Raleigh St Charlotte (28206) *(G-2094)*

Elanco US Inc 812 230-2745
3200 Northline Ave Ste 300 Greensboro (27408) *(G-5515)*

Eland Industries Inc 910 304-5353
353 Washington Acres Rd Hampstead (28443) *(G-6071)*

Elastic Fabric of America, Greensboro *Also Called: Efa Inc (G-5514)*

Elastic Fabrics of America, Greensboro *Also Called: Efa Inc (G-5513)*

ELASTIC PRODUCTS, Andrews *Also Called: Industrial Opportunities Inc (G-107)*

Elastic Therapy LLC 336 625-0529
718 Industrial Park Ave Asheboro (27205) *(G-350)*

Elberta Crate & Box Co 252 257-4659
619 N Main St Warrenton (27589) *(G-12352)*

Elborn Holdings LLC 919 917-1419
17408 Lynx Den Ct Davidson (28036) *(G-3704)*

Elder Hosiery Mills Inc 336 226-0673
139 Homewood Ave Burlington (27217) *(G-1086)*

(G-0000) Company's Geographic Section entry number

Electric Fshing Reel Systems I............................336 273-9101
1700 Sullivan St Greensboro (27405) *(G-5516)*

Electric Glass Fiber Amer LLC.............................336 357-8151
473 New Jersey Church Rd Lexington (27292) *(G-7682)*

Electric Glass Fiber Amer LLC (DH).....................704 434-2261
940 Washburn Switch Rd Shelby (28150) *(G-11332)*

Electric Meter Division, Raleigh Also Called: Elster Solutions LLC *(G-10084)*

Electric Motor Rewinding Inc..............................252 338-8856
407 N Poindexter St Elizabeth City (27909) *(G-4387)*

Electric Motor Service of Shelby Inc.................704 482-9979
1143 Airport Rd Shelby (28150) *(G-11333)*

Electric Motor Shop, Rocky Mount Also Called: Electric Mtr Sp Wake Frest Inc *(G-10835)*

Electric Motor Svc Ahoskie Inc.........................252 332-4364
2103 Us Highway 13 S Ahoskie (27910) *(G-48)*

Electric Mtr Sls Svc Pitt Cnty...........................252 752-3170
202 Hooker Rd Greenville (27834) *(G-5973)*

Electric Mtr Sp Wake Frest Inc...........................252 446-4173
2421 W Raleigh Blvd Rocky Mount (27803) *(G-10835)*

Electric Mtr Sp Wake Frest Inc (PA)...................919 556-3229
1225 N White St Wake Forest (27587) *(G-12274)*

Electrical, Raeford Also Called: Bennett Elec Maint & Cnstr LLC *(G-9832)*

Electrical Apparatus & Mch Co...........................704 333-2987
5619 Gallagher Dr Gastonia (28052) *(G-5045)*

Electrical Equipment Company...........................910 276-2141
226 N Wilkinson Dr Laurinburg (28352) *(G-7500)*

Electrical Panel & Contrls Inc............................336 434-4445
645 Mcway Dr High Point (27263) *(G-6605)*

Electro Magnetic Research Inc............................919 365-3723
9576 Covered Bridge Rd Zebulon (27597) *(G-13508)*

Electro Switch Corp...919 833-0707
2010 Yonkers Rd Raleigh (27604) *(G-10081)*

Electro-Motion Agency, Charlotte Also Called: Alan R Williams Inc *(G-1636)*

Electrolux Home Products Inc.............................252 527-5100
4850 W Vernon Ave Kinston (28504) *(G-7410)*

Electronic Imaging Svcs Inc...............................704 587-3323
1500 Continental Blvd Charlotte (28273) *(G-2095)*

Electronic Products Design Inc...........................919 365-9199
2554 Lake Wendell Rd Wendell (27591) *(G-12535)*

Electronic Services, Farmville Also Called: Esco Electronic Services Inc *(G-4528)*

Electropin Technologies LLC..............................919 288-1203
110 Centura Dr Goldsboro (27530) *(G-5212)*

Electroswitch, Raleigh Also Called: Electro Switch Corp *(G-10081)*

Electrotek, Fayetteville Also Called: Energetics Inc *(G-4597)*

Elektran Inc..910 997-6640
220 River Rd Rockingham (28379) *(G-10776)*

Elektrikredd LLC..704 805-0110
2123 Stevens Mill Rd Matthews (28104) *(G-8166)*

Element Designs, Charlotte Also Called: Element Designs Inc *(G-2096)*

Element Designs Inc...704 332-3114
235 Crompton St Charlotte (28273) *(G-2096)*

Element West LLC...336 853-6118
266 Haywood Rd Lexington (27295) *(G-7683)*

Elements Brands, Charlotte Also Called: Elements Brands LLC *(G-2097)*

Elements Brands LLC..503 230-8008
1515 Mockingbird Ln Ste 400 Charlotte (28209) *(G-2097)*

Elevate Cleaning Service..................................347 928-4030
2120 Fort Bragg Rd Fayetteville (28303) *(G-4596)*

Elevate Textiles Inc..336 379-6220
906 N Anthony St Burlington (27217) *(G-1087)*

Elevate Textiles Inc (HQ)..................................336 379-6220
121 W Trade St Ste 1700 Charlotte (28202) *(G-2098)*

Elevate Textiles Inc..910 997-5001
740 Old Cheraw Hwy Cordova (28330) *(G-3580)*

Elevate Textiles Holding Corp (PA)....................336 379-6220
121 W Trade St Ste 1700 Charlotte (28202) *(G-2099)*

Elevator & Amusement DVC Bur, Raleigh Also Called: North Carolina Dept Labor *(G-10335)*

Elevator Controls and Security, Wake Forest Also Called: Ecs Group-NC LLC *(G-12273)*

Elevators & Conveyors, Charlotte Also Called: Citilift Company *(G-1919)*

Elgi Compressors USA Inc (HQ)........................704 943-7966
4610 Entrance Dr Ste A Charlotte (28273) *(G-2100)*

Eli Lilly and Company.......................................317 296-1226
59 Moore Dr Durham (27709) *(G-4017)*

Eli Research It Journals, Durham Also Called: Academy Association Inc *(G-3877)*

Elite Auto Lights, Inc., Flat Rock Also Called: Three GS Enterprises Inc *(G-4714)*

Elite Comfort Solutions LLC..............................828 328-2201
1115 Farrington St Sw Bldg 1 Conover (28613) *(G-3518)*

Elite Cushion Company, Conover Also Called: Richard Shew *(G-3554)*

Elite Custom Coatings, Raleigh Also Called: Cast Iron Elegance Inc *(G-9987)*

Elite Displays & Design Inc...............................336 472-8200
6771 Pikeview Dr Thomasville (27360) *(G-12021)*

Elite Furniture Mfg Inc......................................336 882-0406
928 Millis St High Point (27260) *(G-6606)*

Elite Graphics Inc..336 887-2923
1305 N Main St High Point (27262) *(G-6607)*

Elite Marine LLC..919 495-6388
554 Old Roberts Rd Benson (27504) *(G-789)*

Elite Metal Performance LLC.............................704 660-0006
132 Conifer Dr Statesville (28625) *(G-11694)*

Elite Mountain Business LLC.............................828 349-0403
21 Sanderstown Rd Franklin (28734) *(G-4827)*

Elite Textiles Fabrication Inc.............................888 337-0977
1124 Roberts Ln Ste 101 High Point (27260) *(G-6608)*

Elite Wood Classics Inc....................................910 454-8745
4392 Long Beach Rd Se Oak Island (28461) *(G-9565)*

Elizabeth Carbide Die Co, Lexington Also Called: Elizabeth Carbide NC Inc *(G-7684)*

Elizabeth Carbide NC Inc..................................336 472-5555
5801 E Us Highway 64 Lexington (27292) *(G-7684)*

Elizabeth City Yard, Elizabeth City Also Called: Legacy Vulcan LLC *(G-4396)*

Elizabeth Logistic LLC......................................803 920-3931
1000 Loudoun Rd Indian Trail (28079) *(G-7078)*

Elizabeth S Java Express..................................919 777-5282
120 S Moore St Sanford (27330) *(G-11176)*

Elk Products Inc..828 397-4200
3266 Us Highway 70 Connelly Springs (28612) *(G-3476)*

Elkamet Inc..828 233-4001
201 Mills St East Flat Rock (28726) *(G-4330)*

Elkay Ohio Plumbing Pdts Co.............................910 739-8181
880 Caton Rd Lumberton (28360) *(G-7950)*

Elkay Plumbing Products Co..............................910 739-8181
880 Caton Rd Lumberton (28360) *(G-7951)*

Elkin Creek Vineyard LLC..................................336 526-5119
318 Elkin Creek Mill Rd Elkin (28621) *(G-4445)*

Elkin Furniture, Elkin Also Called: Vaughan-Bassett Furn Co Inc *(G-4453)*

Elkins Sawmill Inc..919 362-1235
670 King Rd Moncure (27559) *(G-8404)*

Ella B Candles LLC...980 339-8898
9517 Monroe Rd Ste C Charlotte (28270) *(G-2101)*

Elledge Family Inc...919 876-2300
2900 Spring Forest Rd Ste 101 Raleigh (27616) *(G-10082)*

Ellenburg Sheet Metal......................................704 872-2089
353 Stamey Farm Rd Statesville (28625) *(G-11695)*

Ellerre Tech Inc...704 524-9096
107 E Robinson St Dallas (28034) *(G-3669)*

Ellis Jewelers, Lexington Also Called: Jewel Masters Inc *(G-7701)*

Ellis Lumber Co and Logs, Shelby Also Called: Ellis Lumber Company Inc *(G-11334)*

Ellis Lumber Company Inc..................................704 482-1414
1681 S Lafayette St Shelby (28152) *(G-11334)*

Ellis Publishing Company Inc.............................252 444-1999
3200 Wellons Blvd New Bern (28562) *(G-9367)*

Ellison Company Inc...704 889-7518
13501 S Ridge Dr Charlotte (28273) *(G-2102)*

Ellison Technologies Inc....................................704 545-7362
9724 Southern Pine Blvd Charlotte (28273) *(G-2103)*

Elmarco Inc..919 334-6495
1101 Aviation Pkwy Ste E Morrisville (27560) *(G-8970)*

Elnik Systems LLC..973 239-6066
12004 Carolina Logistics Dr Ste A Pineville (28134) *(G-9726)*

Elomi Inc...904 591-0095
22 Carpenter Ct Nw Concord (28027) *(G-3359)*

Elsag North America LLC (PA)...........................336 379-7135
4221 Tudor Ln Greensboro (27410) *(G-5517)*

Elsco Inc (PA)..509 885-4525
  199 Crocker St Seaboard (27876) *(G-11271)*

Elster American Meter Company LLC (HQ)...........402 873-8200
  855 S Mint St Charlotte (28202) *(G-2104)*

Elster Electricity, Raleigh *Also Called: Elster Solutions LLC (G-10083)*

Elster Solutions LLC...............................919 212-4819
  201 S Rogers Ln Raleigh (27610) *(G-10083)*

Elster Solutions LLC (DH)...........................919 212-4800
  208 S Rogers Ln Raleigh (27610) *(G-10084)*

Elxr Health Inc....................................919 917-8484
  334 Blackwell St Ste B005 Durham (27701) *(G-4018)*

Elxsi Corporation..................................407 849-1090
  6325 Ardrey Kell Rd Ste 400 Charlotte (28277) *(G-2105)*

Em2 Machine Corp...................................336 297-4110
  7939 Highfill Rd Summerfield (27358) *(G-11839)*

Em2 Machine Corporation............................336 707-8409
  1030 Boulder Rd Greensboro (27409) *(G-5518)*

Emage Medical LLC..................................704 904-1873
  7515 Robin Crest Rd Charlotte (28226) *(G-2106)*

Emanuel Hoggard....................................252 794-3724
  837 Askewville Rd Windsor (27983) *(G-13053)*

Emanuel Hoggard Logging, Windsor *Also Called: Emanuel Hoggard (G-13053)*

Emath360 LLC.......................................919 744-4944
  302 Parish House Rd Cary (27513) *(G-1352)*

Emb Inc..336 945-0759
  4180 Mendenhall Oaks Pkwy Ste 100 High Point (27265) *(G-6609)*

Embrex LLC (HQ)....................................919 941-5185
  1040 Swabia Ct Durham (27703) *(G-4019)*

Embrex Poultry Health LLC..........................910 844-5566
  22300 Skyway Church Rd Maxton (28364) *(G-8200)*

Embroid It...704 617-0357
  16324 York Rd Charlotte (28278) *(G-2107)*

Embroidery 2, Pineville *Also Called: Blp Products and Services Inc (G-9716)*

Embroidery Authority, Burnsville *Also Called: Amy Smith (G-1182)*

Embroidery Store, The, Winston Salem *Also Called: Dime EMB LLC (G-13146)*

Embroidme...919 316-1538
  105 W Nc Highway 54 Ste 261 Durham (27713) *(G-4020)*

EMC Corporation....................................720 341-3274
  10815 David Taylor Dr Ste 200 Charlotte (28262) *(G-2108)*

EMC Corporation....................................919 767-0641
  4121 Surles Ct Durham (27703) *(G-4021)*

EMC Corporation....................................919 851-3241
  701 Corporate Center Dr Ste 425 Raleigh (27607) *(G-10085)*

Emco, Wilson *Also Called: Emco Wheaton Retail Corp (G-12987)*

Emco Wheaton Retail Corp...........................252 243-0150
  2300 Industrial Park Dr Se Wilson (27893) *(G-12987)*

Emerald Carolina Chemical LLC......................704 393-0089
  8309 Wilkinson Blvd Charlotte (28214) *(G-2109)*

Emerald Hollow Gems, Hiddenite *Also Called: Hiddenite Gems Inc (G-6499)*

Emerald Tool and Mold Inc..........................336 996-6445
  106 Furlong Industrial Dr Kernersville (27284) *(G-7271)*

Emerald Village Inc................................828 765-6463
  387 Mckinney Mine Rd Little Switzerland (28749) *(G-7882)*

Emergency Responder Systems, Charlotte *Also Called: Rf Das Systems Inc (G-2722)*

Emerging Technology Institute, Red Springs *Also Called: Eco Building Corporation (G-10667)*

Emergo Therapeutics Inc............................919 649-5544
  6208 Fayetteville Rd Ste 104 Durham (27713) *(G-4022)*

Emerson, Shelby *Also Called: Emerson Electric Co (G-11335)*

Emerson Electric Co................................704 480-8519
  Plant 4I-32 4401 East Dix Shelby (28150) *(G-11335)*

Emerson Prcess MGT Pwr Wtr Slt.....................704 357-0294
  6135 Lakeview Rd Charlotte (28269) *(G-2110)*

Emery Corporation..................................828 433-1536
  1523 N Green St Morganton (28655) *(G-8862)*

Emf Industries, Dallas *Also Called: Erecto Mch & Fabrication Inc (G-3670)*

EMI, Columbus *Also Called: Energy Management Insulation (G-3301)*

Eminess Technologies Inc...........................704 283-2600
  1412 Airport Rd Monroe (28110) *(G-8482)*

Emitbio Inc..919 321-1726
  615 Davis Dr Morrisville (27560) *(G-8971)*

Emp Services, Statesville *Also Called: Elite Metal Performance LLC (G-11694)*

Empire Carpet & Blinds Inc.........................704 541-3988
  10500 Mcmullen Creek Pkwy Charlotte (28226) *(G-2111)*

Employus Inc.......................................919 706-4008
  122 E Chatham St Ste 300 Cary (27511) *(G-1353)*

EMR Electric, Zebulon *Also Called: Electro Magnetic Research Inc (G-13508)*

Emrise Corporation.................................408 200-3040
  2530 Meridian Pkwy Durham (27713) *(G-4023)*

Emtelle USA Inc....................................828 707-9970
  101 Mills Gap Rd Unit A Fletcher (28732) *(G-4733)*

En Fleur Corporation...............................919 556-1623
  124 Fairview Rd Louisburg (27549) *(G-7914)*

Enc Conveyance, Rocky Mount *Also Called: Enc Conveyance LLC (G-10811)*

Enc Conveyance LLC.................................252 378-9990
  4314 Bulluck School Rd Rocky Mount (27801) *(G-10811)*

Encertec Inc.......................................336 288-7226
  415 Pisgah Church Rd Ste 302 Greensboro (27455) *(G-5519)*

Encore Group Inc...................................336 768-7859
  111 Cloverleaf Dr Winston Salem (27103) *(G-13157)*

Encore Label & Packaging, Charlotte *Also Called: Grand Encore Charlotte LLC (G-2231)*

Encube Ethicals Inc................................919 767-3292
  200 Meredith Dr Ste 202 Durham (27713) *(G-4024)*

End Camp North.....................................980 337-4600
  300 Camp Rd Charlotte (28206) *(G-2112)*

End of Days Distillery, Wilmington *Also Called: Eod Distillery LLC (G-12771)*

Endaxi Company Inc.................................919 467-8895
  137 Trans Air Dr Morrisville (27560) *(G-8972)*

Endeavor Fabrication Group, Durham *Also Called: Endeavour Fbrication Group Inc (G-4025)*

Endeavour Fbrication Group Inc.....................919 479-1453
  1534 Cher Dr Durham (27713) *(G-4025)*

Endgrain Woodworks LLC.............................980 237-2612
  301 Queens Rd Apt 302 Charlotte (28204) *(G-2113)*

Endless Plastics LLC...............................336 346-1839
  3704 Alliance Dr Ste B Greensboro (27407) *(G-5520)*

Endura Products LLC................................336 991-8818
  210 E Commerce Ave High Point (27260) *(G-6610)*

Endura Products LLC (DH)............................336 668-2472
  8817 W Market St Colfax (27235) *(G-3279)*

Eneco East Inc.....................................828 322-6008
  Hickory (28603) *(G-6329)*

Enepay Corporation.................................919 788-1454
  7226 Summit Waters Ln Raleigh (27613) *(G-10086)*

Energetics Inc.....................................910 483-2581
  455 Hillsboro St Fayetteville (28301) *(G-4597)*

Energizer Battery Mfg..............................336 736-7936
  419 Art Bryan Dr Asheboro (27203) *(G-351)*

Energizer Holdings Inc.............................336 672-3526
  800 Albemarle Rd Asheboro (27203) *(G-352)*

Energy and Entropy Inc.............................919 933-1365
  301 Palafox Dr Chapel Hill (27516) *(G-1544)*

Energy Conversion Syste............................910 892-8081
  10 Carlie Cs Dr Dunn (28334) *(G-3855)*

Energy Management Insulation.......................828 894-3635
  Columbus (28722) *(G-3301)*

Energy Solutions (us) LLC..........................919 786-4555
  9650 Strickland Rd Ste 103 Raleigh (27615) *(G-10087)*

Energy Solutions (US) LLC, Raleigh *Also Called: Energy Solutions (us) LLC (G-10087)*

Energy Svers Windows Doors Inc.....................252 758-8700
  1806 Dickinson Ave Greenville (27834) *(G-5974)*

Enertia Building Systems Inc.......................919 556-2391
  13312 Garffe Sherron Rd Wake Forest (27587) *(G-12275)*

Enfield Tire Service Inc...........................252 445-5016
  301 N Mcdaniel St Enfield (27823) *(G-4482)*

Enforge LLC..704 983-4146
  1600 Woodhurst Ln Albemarle (28001) *(G-71)*

Eng Solutions Inc..................................919 831-1830
  1109 Pinehurst Dr Chapel Hill (27517) *(G-1545)*

Engcon North America Inc...........................203 691-5920
  2827 Earlham Pl High Point (27263) *(G-6611)*

Engine Systems Inc (HQ)............................252 977-2720
  175 Freight Rd Rocky Mount (27804) *(G-10836)*

Engineered Attachments LLC.................................... 336 703-5266
200 Kapp St Winston Salem (27105) *(G-13158)*

Engineered Coated Fabrics, Rutherfordton *Also Called: Trelleborg Ctd Systems US Inc*
(G-10998)

Engineered Controls Intl LLC.................................... 336 226-3244
3181 Lear Dr Burlington (27215) *(G-1088)*

Engineered Controls Intl LLC.................................... 828 466-2153
911 Industrial Dr Sw Conover (28613) *(G-3519)*

Engineered Controls Intl LLC (HQ)........................... 336 449-7707
100 Rego Dr Elon (27244) *(G-4469)*

Engineered Controls Intl LLC.................................... 336 449-7706
1239 Rock Creek Dairy Rd Whitsett (27377) *(G-12605)*

Engineered Processing Eqp LLC............................... 919 321-6891
5036 Country Club Dr N Wilson (27896) *(G-12988)*

Engineered Recycling Company LLC......................... 704 358-6700
1011 Woodward Ave 1101 Charlotte (28206) *(G-2114)*

Engineered Software.. 336 299-4843
615 Guilford Ave Greensboro (27401) *(G-5521)*

Engineered Steel Products LLC................................. 336 495-5266
4977 Plainfield Rd Sophia (27350) *(G-11487)*

Engineered Steel Products Inc.................................. 336 495-5266
4977 Plainfield Rd Sophia (27350) *(G-11488)*

Engineering Consulting Svcs, Greensboro *Also Called: McLean Sbsrface Utlity Engrg L*
(G-5687)

Engineering Mfg Svcs Co... 704 821-7325
5634 Cannon Dr Monroe (28110) *(G-8483)*

Engineering Reprographics, Raleigh *Also Called: Document Imaging Systems Inc (G-10054)*

England Inc... 336 861-5266
222 S Main St High Point (27260) *(G-6612)*

Englishs All Wood Homes Inc................................... 252 524-5000
608 Queen St Grifton (28530) *(G-6036)*

Ennis-Flint, Thomasville *Also Called: Flint Trading Inc (G-12027)*

Ennis-Flint, Thomasville *Also Called: Road Infrstrcture Inv Hldngs I (G-12066)*

Ennis-Flint Inc (HQ).. 800 331-8118
4161 Piedmont Pkwy Ste 370 Greensboro (27410) *(G-5522)*

Ennis-Flint Inc.. 800 331-8118
4189 Eagle Hill Dr Ste 110 High Point (27265) *(G-6613)*

Ennis-Flint Inc.. 336 477-8439
505 County Line Rd Thomasville (27360) *(G-12022)*

Ennis-Flint Inc.. 800 331-8118
115 Todd Ct Thomasville (27360) *(G-12023)*

Eno Scientific LLC.. 910 778-2660
1606 Faucette Mill Rd Hillsborough (27278) *(G-6865)*

Enovis Corporation.. 704 289-6511
1710 Airport Rd Monroe (28110) *(G-8484)*

Enplas Life Tech Inc... 828 633-2250
230 Sardis Rd Asheville (28806) *(G-494)*

Enpoco, Spindale *Also Called: Watts Drainage Products Inc (G-11549)*

Enpro, Charlotte *Also Called: Enpro Inc (G-2115)*

Enpro Inc (PA).. 704 731-1500
5605 Carnegie Blvd Ste 500 Charlotte (28209) *(G-2115)*

Enrg Brand LLC.. 980 298-8519
1235 East Blvd Ste E2168 Charlotte (28203) *(G-2116)*

Enriched Abundance Entp LLC................................. 704 369-6363
15316 Trickling Water Ct Charlotte (28273) *(G-2117)*

Ensales Electrical Assoc Inc.................................... 910 298-3305
140 E Park Dr Unit B Beulaville (28518) *(G-842)*

Ensystex Inc (PA)... 888 398-3772
202 Fairway Dr Ste A Fayetteville (28305) *(G-4598)*

Enterprise Loggers Company Inc.............................. 252 586-4805
681 Enterprise Rd Littleton (27850) *(G-7885)*

Enterprise Metal Tag Plant, Raleigh *Also Called: North Crlina Dept Adult Crrcto (G-10337)*

Enterprise Rendering Company................................. 704 485-3018
28821 Bethlehem Church Rd Oakboro (28129) *(G-9578)*

Enterprise Twd... 704 822-6166
7482 Nc 73 Hwy Stanley (28164) *(G-11615)*

Enterprise, The, Williamston *Also Called: Cox Nrth Crlina Pblcations Inc (G-12669)*

Entex Technologies Inc.. 919 933-1380
1340 Environ Way Chapel Hill (27517) *(G-1546)*

Entropy, Rocky Point *Also Called: Sea Mark Boats Inc (G-10882)*

Entrust Services LLC... 336 274-5175
130 S Walnut Cir Greensboro (27409) *(G-5523)*

Enttec Americas LLC... 919 200-6468
3874 S Alston Ave Ste 103 Durham (27713) *(G-4026)*

Enviboats LLC.. 910 213-3200
104 Sparkling Brook Way Southport (28461) *(G-11519)*

Envicor Enterprises LLC.. 877 823-7231
207a Computer Dr Smithfield (27577) *(G-11442)*

Envirco Corporation (PA).. 919 775-2201
101 Mcneill Rd Sanford (27330) *(G-11177)*

Envirnmental Svcs of Charlotte, Charlotte *Also Called: DOT Blue Services Inc (G-2064)*

Envirnmental Win Solutions LLC.............................. 704 200-2001
1401 Morningside Dr Charlotte (28205) *(G-2118)*

Envirnmntal Cmfort Sltions Inc................................ 980 272-7327
1400 S Main St Kannapolis (28081) *(G-7208)*

Envirnmntal Prcess Systems Inc.............................. 704 827-0740
227 Lamplighter Ln Mount Holly (28120) *(G-9229)*

Envirnmntal Systems RES Inst I............................. 704 541-9810
3325 Springbank Ln Ste 200 Charlotte (28226) *(G-2119)*

Enviroclean Solutions, Durham *Also Called: Bottom Line Technologies Inc (G-3939)*

Environmental Inks, Morganton *Also Called: Siegwerk Eic LLC (G-8897)*

Environmental Inks and Coatings Canada Ltd........... 828 433-1922
1 Quality Products Rd Morganton (28655) *(G-8863)*

Environmental Science US LLC (HQ)........................ 800 331-2867
5000 Centre Green Way Ste 400 Cary (27513) *(G-1354)*

Environmental Specialties LLC (DH)......................... 919 829-9300
4412 Tryon Rd Raleigh (27606) *(G-10088)*

Environmental Supply Co Inc.................................... 919 956-9688
708 E Club Blvd Durham (27704) *(G-4027)*

Enviroserve Chemicals Inc....................................... 910 892-1791
603 S Wilson Ave Dunn (28334) *(G-3856)*

Envirotek Worldwide LLC... 704 285-6400
2701 Hutchison Mcdonald Rd Ste A Charlotte (28269) *(G-2120)*

Envisia Therapeutics Inc.. 919 973-1440
4301 Emperor Blvd Ste 200 Durham (27703) *(G-4028)*

Envision Glass Inc.. 336 283-9701
3950 N Liberty St Winston Salem (27105) *(G-13159)*

Envision Inc.. 919 832-8962
625 Hutton St Ste 102 Raleigh (27606) *(G-10089)*

Enviva Pellets Ahoskie LLC...................................... 301 657-5560
142 Nc Highway 561 W Ahoskie (27910) *(G-49)*

Enviva Pellets Sampson LLC.................................... 301 657-5560
5 Connector Rd Faison (28341) *(G-4516)*

Enwood Structures, Raleigh *Also Called: Zenecar LLC (G-10623)*

Enzyme Customs... 704 888-8278
515 Redah Ave Locust (28097) *(G-7892)*

Eod Distillery LLC.. 910 399-1133
1815 Castle St Wilmington (28403) *(G-12771)*

Eon Labs Inc.. 252 234-2222
4700 Sandoz Dr Wilson (27893) *(G-12989)*

Eoncoat LLC (PA)... 941 928-9401
3337 Air Park Rd Ste 6 Fuquay Varina (27526) *(G-4881)*

Eoncoat LLC... 941 928-9401
1333 Virginia St Sw Lenoir (28645) *(G-7602)*

Ep Custom Products Inc.. 704 483-8793
7823 Commerce Dr Denver (28037) *(G-3782)*

EP Nisbet Company.. 704 332-7755
1818 Baxter St Charlotte (28204) *(G-2121)*

Epi Centre Sundries... 704 650-9575
210 E Trade St Charlotte (28202) *(G-2122)*

Epi Group Llc (PA).. 843 577-7111
4020 Stirrup Creek Dr Durham (27703) *(G-4029)*

Epic Apparel... 980 335-0463
8118 Statesville Rd Charlotte (28269) *(G-2123)*

Epic Enterprises Inc (PA)... 910 692-5750
845 Valley View Rd Southern Pines (28387) *(G-11498)*

Epic Kites LLC.. 203 209-6831
508 Schooner Ct Kill Devil Hills (27948) *(G-7316)*

Epic Restorations LLC.. 866 597-2733
118 Commerce Dr Roxboro (27573) *(G-10925)*

Epicypher, Durham *Also Called: Epicypher Inc (G-4030)*

Epicypher Inc.. 855 374-2461
6 Davis Dr Durham (27709) *(G-4030)*

Epk LLC..980 643-4787
425 Klumac Rd Salisbury (28144) *(G-11048)*

Epk Industrial Solutions, Salisbury Also Called: Epk LLC *(G-11048)*

Epl, Wake Forest Also Called: Epl & Solar Corp *(G-12276)*

Epl & Solar Corp..201 577-8966
5517 Sedge Wren Dr Wake Forest (27587) *(G-12276)*

Epoch Solutions, Roxboro Also Called: P&A Indstrial Fabrications LLC *(G-10938)*

Epsilon Holdings LLC..336 763-6147
2103 E Town Blvd Ste 105 Greensboro (27455) *(G-5524)*

Epsiusa...704 827-0740
1124 W Charlotte Ave Mount Holly (28120) *(G-9230)*

Epv Corporation...704 494-7800
2309 Nevada Blvd Charlotte (28273) *(G-2124)*

Equagen Engineers, Raleigh Also Called: Equagen Engineers Pllc *(G-10090)*

Equagen Engineers Pllc..919 444-5442
8045 Arco Corporate Dr Ste 220 Raleigh (27617) *(G-10090)*

Equilibar LLC...828 650-6590
320 Rutledge Rd Fletcher (28732) *(G-4734)*

Equinom Enterprises LLC.......................................704 817-8489
16310 Magnolia Woods Ln Charlotte (28277) *(G-2125)*

Equipment & Supply Inc..704 289-6565
4507 W Highway 74 Monroe (28110) *(G-8485)*

Equipment Dsign Fbrication Inc................................704 372-4513
201 Davis Heights Dr Gastonia (28052) *(G-5046)*

Equipment Enterprises Division, Charlotte Also Called: Ward Vessel and Exchanger Corp
(G-3004)

Equipment Parts Inc (PA)......................................704 827-7545
795 Cason St Belmont (28012) *(G-749)*

Equipment Shop, Newland Also Called: North Carolina Dept Trnsp *(G-9433)*

ERA Polymers Corporation......................................704 931-3675
1101 S Highway 27 Stanley (28164) *(G-11616)*

ERC, Charlotte Also Called: Engineered Recycling Company LLC *(G-2114)*

Erdle Perforating Holdings Inc................................704 588-4380
1100 Culp Rd # A Charlotte (28241) *(G-2126)*

Erecto Mch & Fabrication Inc..................................704 922-8621
3653 Dallas Cherryville Hwy Dallas (28034) *(G-3670)*

Eric Arnold Klein...828 464-0001
504a W 25th St Newton (28658) *(G-9464)*

Eric Martin Jermey..704 692-0389
1815 Salem Church Rd Bostic (28018) *(G-962)*

Erico International Corp......................................910 944-3355
188 Carolina Rd Aberdeen (28315) *(G-4)*

Ericson Foods Inc...336 317-2199
4143 Wycliff Dr Winston Salem (27106) *(G-13160)*

Erleclair Inc..919 233-7710
301 Ashville Ave Ste 121 Cary (27518) *(G-1355)*

Esc Brands LLC (PA)...888 331-8332
664 Old Hargrave Rd Lexington (27295) *(G-7685)*

Escazu Artisan Chocolate LLC..................................919 832-3433
936 N Blount St Raleigh (27604) *(G-10091)*

Esco Electronic Services Inc..................................252 753-4433
268 Hwy 121 And 264 Alternate Farmville (27828) *(G-4528)*

Esco Group LLC..919 900-8226
3221 Durham Dr Ste 118 Raleigh (27603) *(G-10092)*

Esco Industries Inc...336 495-3772
4717 Island Ford Rd Randleman (27317) *(G-10647)*

Esher LLC..704 975-1463
9911 Rose Commons Dr Huntersville (28078) *(G-6987)*

Eskimo 7 Limited...252 726-8181
5317 Hwy 70 W Morehead City (28557) *(G-8832)*

Esri, Charlotte Also Called: Envirnmntal Systems RES Inst I *(G-2119)*

Essay Operations Inc (PA).....................................252 443-6010
3701 Winchester Rd Rocky Mount (27804) *(G-10837)*

Essay Polyfab, Rocky Mount Also Called: Essay Operations Inc *(G-10837)*

Essentra Packaging, Clayton Also Called: Mm Clayton LLC *(G-3160)*

Essex Group Inc..704 921-9605
3300 Woodpark Blvd Charlotte (28206) *(G-2127)*

Estate Mentors Inc...877 378-7567
3980 Premier Dr Ste 110 High Point (27265) *(G-6614)*

Esterline Defense Technologies, Lillington Also Called: Esterline Technologies Corp *(G-7796)*

Esterline Technologies Corp...................................910 814-1222
608 E Mcneill St Lillington (27546) *(G-7796)*

Estes Machine Co...336 786-7680
256 Snowhill Dr Mount Airy (27030) *(G-9119)*

Etbf LLC...937 543-2223
3863 Sweeten Creek Rd Arden (28704) *(G-267)*

Etc Division, Conover Also Called: CPI Satcom & Antenna Tech Inc *(G-3508)*

Ethan Allen Maiden Division, Maiden Also Called: Ethan Allen Retail Inc *(G-8012)*

Ethan Allen Retail Inc.......................................828 428-9361
700 S Main Ave Maiden (28650) *(G-8012)*

Etherngton Cnservation Ctr Inc...............................336 665-1317
1010 Arnold St Greensboro (27405) *(G-5525)*

Ethicon Endo - Surgery, Cary Also Called: Ethicon Inc *(G-1356)*

Ethicon Inc..919 234-2124
125 Edinburgh South Dr Ste 201 Cary (27511) *(G-1356)*

Ethics Archery LLC...980 429-2070
2664 Sam Houser Rd Vale (28168) *(G-12208)*

Ethics Bullets, Vale Also Called: Ethics Archery LLC *(G-12208)*

Ethnicraft Usa LLC...336 885-2055
101 Prospect St High Point (27260) *(G-6615)*

Etimex USA Inc...704 583-0002
9405 D Ducks Ln Ste A Charlotte (28273) *(G-2128)*

Etk International Inc..704 819-1541
1005 Andrea Pl Indian Trail (28079) *(G-7079)*

Euclid Chemical Company......................................704 283-2544
914 N Johnson St Monroe (28110) *(G-8486)*

Euclid Innovations Inc (PA)..................................877 382-5431
101 S Tryon St Ste 2410 Charlotte (28280) *(G-2129)*

Eudy's Cabinet Manufacturing, Stanfield Also Called: S Eudy Cabinet Shop Inc *(G-11608)*

Eudys Cabinet Manufacturing..................................704 888-4454
12303 Renee Ford Rd Stanfield (28163) *(G-11605)*

Eugenes Trucking Inc...910 267-0555
10422 Faison Hwy Faison (28341) *(G-4517)*

Euliss Oil Company Inc.......................................336 622-3055
122 S Foster St Liberty (27298) *(G-7766)*

Eurisko Beer Company, Asheville Also Called: Between Two Worlds LLC *(G-453)*

Eurodrawer, Mocksville Also Called: Olon Industries Inc (us) *(G-8383)*

Eurogold Art...336 989-6205
251 N Main St Kernersville (27284) *(G-7272)*

Eurohansa Inc..336 885-1010
1213 Dorris Ave High Point (27260) *(G-6616)*

Ev Fleet Inc...704 425-6272
11701 Mount Holly Rd Bldg 32 Charlotte (28214) *(G-2130)*

Evangelistic Press, Concord Also Called: Charlotte Printing Company Inc *(G-3334)*

Evans and McClain LLC..919 374-5578
555 Fayetteville St Ste 201 Raleigh (27601) *(G-10093)*

Evans Hosiery, Connelly Springs Also Called: R Evans Hosiery LLC *(G-3482)*

Evans Logging Inc..252 792-3865
1047 Fleming Cir Jamesville (27846) *(G-7183)*

Evans Machinery Inc..252 243-4006
5123 Ivy Ct Wilson (27893) *(G-12990)*

Evans, Bill Co, Laurinburg Also Called: M C C of Laurinburg Inc *(G-7506)*

Evelyn T Burney..336 473-9794
2551 N Church St Rocky Mount (27804) *(G-10838)*

Event 1 Software Inc...360 567-3752
8529 Six Forks Rd Ste 400 Raleigh (27615) *(G-10094)*

Event Extravaganza LLC.......................................252 679-7004
407 S Griffin St Ste E Elizabeth City (27909) *(G-4388)*

Ever Glo Sign Co Inc...704 633-3324
4975 S Main St Salisbury (28147) *(G-11049)*

Eveready Mix Concrete Co Inc.................................336 961-6688
421 Old Hwy E Yadkinville (27055) *(G-13442)*

Everest Textile Usa LLC......................................828 245-6755
1331 W Main St Forest City (28043) *(G-4789)*

Everettes Company Inc..336 956-2097
4805 Old Linwood Rd Linwood (27299) *(G-7877)*

Everettes Industrial Repr Svc................................252 527-4269
117 Dobbs Pl Goldsboro (27534) *(G-5213)*

Everglow Na Inc..704 841-2580
1122 Industrial Dr Ste 112 Matthews (28105) *(G-8111)*

Evergreen Forest Products Inc.. 910 762-9156
2605 Blue Clay Rd Wilmington (28405) *(G-12772)*

Evergreen Logging LLC... 910 654-1662
686 Homer Nance Rd Evergreen (28438) *(G-4498)*

Evergreen Packaging, Canton *Also Called: Blue Ridge Paper Products LLC (G-1244)*

Evergreen Packaging, Canton *Also Called: Blue Ridge Paper Products LLC (G-1245)*

Evergreen Packaging, Waynesville *Also Called: Blue Ridge Paper Products LLC (G-12451)*

Evergreen Packaging LLC... 828 454-0676
175 Main St Canton (28716) *(G-1252)*

Evergreen Packaging LLC... 919 828-9134
2215 S Wilmington St Raleigh (27603) *(G-10095)*

Evergreen Pallets LLC.. 828 313-0050
3815 N Main St Granite Falls (28630) *(G-5302)*

Evergreen Silks, Matthews *Also Called: Evergreen Silks NC Inc (G-8112)*

Evergreen Silks NC Inc... 704 845-5577
901 Sam Newell Rd Ste I Matthews (28105) *(G-8112)*

Everkem Diversified Pdts Inc... 336 661-7801
120 Regent Dr Winston Salem (27103) *(G-13161)*

Eversharp Saw & Tool Inc.. 828 345-1200
1241 13th St Ne Hickory (28601) *(G-6330)*

Everview.. 800 549-4722
201 Technology Ln Mount Airy (27030) *(G-9120)*

Every Day Carry LLc... 203 231-0256
4716 Black Pine Ct Winnabow (28479) *(G-13065)*

Everyday Edisons LLC.. 704 369-7333
520 Elliot St Ste 200 Charlotte (28202) *(G-2131)*

Everything Attachments.. 828 464-0161
1506 Emmanuel Church Rd Conover (28613) *(G-3520)*

Everything Industrial Supply.. 743 333-2222
164 N Hawthorne Rd Winston Salem (27104) *(G-13162)*

Eview Technology Inc.. 919 878-5199
4909 Green Rd Ste 133 Raleigh (27616) *(G-10096)*

Evolution of Style LLC.. 914 329-3078
2901 N Davidson St Unit 170 Charlotte (28205) *(G-2132)*

Evolution Technologies Inc.. 919 544-3777
1121 Situs Ct Ste 130 Raleigh (27606) *(G-10097)*

Evonik Corporation.. 336 333-3565
2401 Doyle St Greensboro (27406) *(G-5526)*

Evoqua Water Technologies LLC................................... 919 477-2161
1301 S Briggs Ave Ste 116 Durham (27703) *(G-4031)*

Ew Jackson Transportation LLC.................................... 919 586-2514
113 Gingerlilly Ct Holly Springs (27540) *(G-6900)*

Ew2 Environmental Inc (PA)... 704 542-2444
7245 Pineville Matthews Rd Ste 100 Charlotte (28226) *(G-2133)*

Exact Cut Inc... 336 207-4022
824 Winston St Greensboro (27405) *(G-5527)*

Excel Inc.. 704 735-6535
509 Lee Ave Lincolnton (28092) *(G-7830)*

Excelsior Sewing LLC.. 828 398-8056
125 Brickton Dr Fletcher (28732) *(G-4735)*

Executive Grooming LLC.. 919 706-5382
5910 Duraleigh Rd Ste 133 Raleigh (27612) *(G-10098)*

Executive Promotions Inc.. 704 663-4000
2987 Charlotte Hwy 21 Mooresville (28117) *(G-8661)*

Exela Drug Substance LLC.. 828 758-5474
1245 Blowing Rock Blvd Lenoir (28645) *(G-7603)*

Exela Pharma Sciences LLC (PA)................................ 828 758-5474
1245 Blowing Rock Blvd Lenoir (28645) *(G-7604)*

Exemplar Laboratories LLC.. 336 817-6794
405 E Center St Lexington (27292) *(G-7686)*

Exhibit World Inc.. 704 882-2272
13701 E Independence Blvd Indian Trail (28079) *(G-7080)*

Exide.. 704 357-9845
3308 Oak Lake Blvd Ste A Charlotte (28208) *(G-2134)*

Exide Battery, Charlotte *Also Called: Exide Technologies LLC (G-2135)*

Exide Technologies LLC.. 704 521-8016
648 Griffith Rd Ste G Charlotte (28217) *(G-2135)*

Exide Technologies LLC.. 919 553-3578
104 N Tech Dr Clayton (27520) *(G-3147)*

Exley Custom Woodwork Inc.. 910 763-5445
2921 Castle Hayne Rd Castle Hayne (28429) *(G-1498)*

Exlon Extrusion Inc.. 336 621-1295
2971 Taylor Dr Asheboro (27203) *(G-353)*

Exotics Power Coat.. 336 831-3865
745 Cinema Ct Kernersville (27284) *(G-7273)*

Expersis Software Inc... 919 874-0608
1060 Kennicott Ave Cary (27513) *(G-1357)*

Explosives Supply Company (PA)................................. 828 765-2762
167 Roan Rd Spruce Pine (28777) *(G-11575)*

Expogo Inc.. 910 452-3976
411 Landmark Dr Wilmington (28412) *(G-12773)*

Expogo Displays & Graphics, Wilmington *Also Called: Expogo Inc (G-12773)*

Exposure Software LLC... 919 832-4124
1111 Haynes St Ste 107 Raleigh (27604) *(G-10099)*

Express Graphics, Winston Salem *Also Called: Graphic Productions Inc (G-13184)*

Express Printing, Jacksonville *Also Called: Print Express Inc (G-7138)*

Express Wire Services Inc... 704 393-5156
2947 Interstate St Charlotte (28208) *(G-2136)*

Express, The, Wadesboro *Also Called: Anson Express (G-12233)*

Expressive Screen Printing... 910 739-3221
504 Peterson Dr Lumberton (28358) *(G-7952)*

Exquisite Granite and MBL Inc...................................... 336 851-8890
6207 Tri Port Ct Greensboro (27409) *(G-5528)*

Extensive Builders LLC.. 980 621-3793
2604 Old Wilkesboro Rd Salisbury (28144) *(G-11050)*

Exterior Vinyl Wholesale.. 336 838-7772
1808 Industrial Dr Wilkesboro (28697) *(G-12634)*

Exteriors Inc Ltd... 919 325-2251
650 W Manchester Rd Spring Lake (28390) *(G-11561)*

Extreme, Morrisville *Also Called: Extreme Networks Inc (G-8973)*

Extreme Networks Inc (PA).. 408 579-2800
2121 Rdu Center Dr Ste 300 Morrisville (27560) *(G-8973)*

Extron Electronics.. 919 850-1000
2500 N Raleigh Blvd Raleigh (27604) *(G-10100)*

Eye Dialogue.. 704 567-7789
412 N Crigler St Charlotte (28216) *(G-2137)*

Eye Glass Lady LLC.. 828 669-2154
411 Tomahawk Ave Black Mountain (28711) *(G-864)*

Eye Trax Inc... 800 594-4157
4200 Performance Rd Charlotte (28214) *(G-2138)*

EZ Beverage Company Wilmington, Wilmington *Also Called: Zeskp LLC (G-12958)*

EZ Custom Screen Printing.. 704 821-8488
600 Union West Blvd Ste B Matthews (28104) *(G-8167)*

EZ Custom Scrnprinting EMB Inc.................................. 704 821-9641
200 Foxton Rd Matthews (28104) *(G-8168)*

Ezbrew Inc... 833 233-2739
1006 Sw Maynard Rd Cary (27511) *(G-1358)*

Eztax, Durham *Also Called: Billsoft Inc (G-3927)*

F & C Repair and Sales LLC... 704 907-2461
4720 Brookshire Blvd Charlotte (28216) *(G-2139)*

F & H Print Sign Design LLC... 252 335-0181
1725 City Center Blvd Ste C Elizabeth City (27909) *(G-4389)*

F & M Steel Products Inc... 910 793-1345
3314 Enterprise Dr Wilmington (28405) *(G-12774)*

F B Publications, Fayetteville *Also Called: Up & Coming Magazine (G-4689)*

F B Publications Inc.. 910 484-6200
909 S Mcpherson Church Rd Fayetteville (28303) *(G-4599)*

F C C LLC.. 336 883-7314
4045 Premier Dr Ste 200 High Point (27265) *(G-6617)*

F L Turlington Lumber Co Inc.. 910 592-7197
229 E Railroad St Clinton (28328) *(G-3233)*

Fab Designs Incorporated.. 704 636-2349
2231 Old Wilkesboro Rd Salisbury (28144) *(G-11051)*

Fab-Con, Oakboro *Also Called: Fab-Con Machinery Dev Corp (G-9579)*

Fab-Con Machinery Dev Corp (PA)............................... 704 486-7120
201 E 10th St Oakboro (28129) *(G-9579)*

Fab-Tec Inc... 704 864-6872
3626 Dallas Hgh Shls Hwy Dallas (28034) *(G-3671)*

Fabco Industries... 919 481-3010
312 N Dixon Ave Cary (27513) *(G-1359)*

Fabric Services Hickory Inc.. 828 397-7331
130 Kline Industrial Park 3rd St Ne Hildebran (28637) *(G-6849)*

Fabricated Solutions LLC.................................... 704 982-7789
  1210 Poplar St Albemarle (28001) *(G-72)*

Fabrication Associates Inc.................................. 704 535-8050
  7950 Pence Rd Charlotte (28215) *(G-2140)*

Fabrication Automation LLC................................. 704 785-2120
  2772 Concord Pkwy S Concord (28027) *(G-3360)*

Fabrineering LLC... 704 999-9906
  8955 W Nc 152 Hwy Mooresville (28115) *(G-8662)*

Fabrix Inc... 704 953-1239
  231 Foster Ave Ste A Charlotte (28203) *(G-2141)*

Fabulous Figurez LLC... 336 894-6014
  7535 Old Warsaw Rd Turkey (28393) *(G-12181)*

Faces South Inc.. 336 883-0647
  1330 Lincoln Dr High Point (27260) *(G-6618)*

Facilitydudecom Inc... 919 459-6430
  11000 Regency Pkwy Ste 200 Cary (27518) *(G-1360)*

Factory Systems, Raleigh Also Called: Symbrium Inc *(G-10525)*

Fae Nectar, Asheville Also Called: Asheville Meadery LLC *(G-438)*

Fagus Grecon Inc.. 503 641-7731
  648 Griffith Rd Ste A Charlotte (28217) *(G-2142)*

Failure Free Reading, Concord Also Called: Jfl Enterprises Inc *(G-3385)*

Fain Enterprises Inc... 336 724-0417
  309 Deerglade Rd Winston Salem (27104) *(G-13163)*

Fainting Goat Spirits LLC.................................... 336 273-6221
  321 W Wendover Ave Greensboro (27408) *(G-5529)*

Fair Game Beverage Company............................. 919 245-5434
  220 Lorax Ln Unit 15 Pittsboro (27312) *(G-9783)*

Fair Products Inc... 919 467-1599
  806 Reedy Creek Rd Cary (27513) *(G-1361)*

Fairchild Industrial Pdts Co (DH).......................... 336 659-3400
  3920 Westpoint Blvd Winston Salem (27103) *(G-13164)*

Faircloth Machine Shop Inc.................................. 336 777-1529
  2355 Farrington Point Dr Winston Salem (27107) *(G-13165)*

Fairfield Chair Company...................................... 828 785-5571
  606 Kincaid Cir Lenoir (28645) *(G-7605)*

Fairfield Chair Company (PA)............................... 828 758-5571
  1331 Harper Ave Sw Lenoir (28645) *(G-7606)*

Fairgrove Furniture Co Inc................................... 828 322-8570
  1350 21st Street Dr Se Hickory (28602) *(G-6331)*

Fairmont Metal Finishing Inc................................ 336 434-4188
  1301 Corporation Dr Archdale (27263) *(G-220)*

Fairview Woodcarving Inc.................................... 828 428-9491
  2092 Anaconda Ln Maiden (28650) *(G-8013)*

FAIRWAY OUTDOOR ADVERTISING LLC, Wilmington Also Called: Fairway Outdoor Advg LLC *(G-12775)*

Fairway Outdoor Advg LLC.................................. 919 755-1900
  508 Capital Blvd Raleigh (27603) *(G-10101)*

Fairway Outdoor Advg LLC.................................. 910 343-1900
  1530 S College Rd Ste 600 Wilmington (28403) *(G-12775)*

Fairway Printing Inc.. 919 779-4797
  821 Purser Dr Ste A Raleigh (27603) *(G-10102)*

Faith Computer Repairs....................................... 910 730-1731
  3404 Nc Highway 211 W Lumberton (28360) *(G-7953)*

Faith Farm Inc... 704 431-4566
  585 W Ritchie Rd Ste A Salisbury (28147) *(G-11052)*

Faith Prsthtc-Rthotic Svcs Inc (DH)...................... 704 782-0908
  1025 Concord Pkwy N Concord (28026) *(G-3361)*

Faizon Global Inc... 704 774-1141
  2115 W Roosevelt Blvd # 70 Monroe (28110) *(G-8487)*

Falcon Industries LLC... 336 229-1048
  2834 Bedford St Burlington (27215) *(G-1089)*

Falls Automotive & Tire Svc, Winston Salem Also Called: Falls Automotive Service Inc *(G-13166)*

Falls Automotive Service Inc................................ 336 723-0521
  1548 S Main St Winston Salem (27127) *(G-13166)*

Falls of Neuse Management LLC........................... 919 573-2900
  4900 Falls Of Neuse Rd Ste 150 Raleigh (27609) *(G-10103)*

Family Industries Inc.. 919 875-4499
  631 Macon Pl Raleigh (27609) *(G-10104)*

Family Traditions, Gastonia Also Called: Fidelity Associates Inc *(G-5047)*

Fanuc America Corporation................................... 704 596-5121
  13245 Reese Blvd W Ste 140 Huntersville (28078) *(G-6988)*

Fanuc Robotics, Huntersville Also Called: Fanuc America Corporation *(G-6988)*

Farm Chemicals Inc (PA)..................................... 910 875-4277
  2274 Saint Pauls Dr Raeford (28376) *(G-9837)*

Farm Services Inc.. 336 226-7381
  125 E Elm St Graham (27253) *(G-5268)*

Farmer Machine Group LLC.................................. 704 629-5133
  308 White Jenkins Rd Bessemer City (28016) *(G-815)*

Farmers of The Foothills, Marion Also Called: McDowell Lfac *(G-8055)*

Farr Knitting Company Inc.................................... 336 625-5561
  171 Boyd Ave Asheboro (27205) *(G-354)*

Farrior Steel Works, Farmville Also Called: Jack A Farrior Inc *(G-4532)*

Farris Belt & Saw Company.................................. 704 527-6166
  235 Foster Ave Charlotte (28203) *(G-2143)*

Farris Fab & Machine Inc..................................... 704 629-4879
  1941 Bess Town Rd Bessemer City (28016) *(G-816)*

Farris Fab & Machine Inc..................................... 704 629-4879
  522 Bess Town Rd Bessemer City (28016) *(G-817)*

Farris Fab & Machine Inc (PA).............................. 704 629-4879
  1006 W Academy St Cherryville (28021) *(G-3064)*

Farris Fab. & Machine, Inc., Bessemer City Also Called: Farris Fab & Machine Inc *(G-816)*

FARRIS FAB. & MACHINE, INC., Bessemer City Also Called: Farris Fab & Machine Inc *(G-817)*

Farval Lubrication Systems.................................. 252 527-6001
  2685 Airport Rd Kinston (28504) *(G-7411)*

Farval Lubrication Systems (DH)........................... 252 527-6001
  808 Aviation Parkway Kinston (28504) *(G-7412)*

Fast Arch of Carolinas Inc................................... 336 431-2724
  617 Eden Ter Ste B Archdale (27263) *(G-221)*

Fast Pro Media LLC.. 704 799-8040
  10308 Bailey Rd Ste 422 Cornelius (28031) *(G-3599)*

Fast Pro Media LLC.. 704 799-8040
  10308 Bailey Rd Ste 422 Cornelius (28031) *(G-3600)*

Fastlife Transport LLC (PA).................................. 484 350-6754
  7710 Holliswood Ct Charlotte (28217) *(G-2144)*

Fastrack Publishing Co Inc.................................. 828 294-0544
  1602 Corral Dr Hickory (28602) *(G-6332)*

Fastsigns, Asheville Also Called: Playrace Inc *(G-577)*

Fastsigns, Charlotte Also Called: Beaty Corporation *(G-1765)*

Fastsigns, Charlotte Also Called: CD Dickie & Associates Inc *(G-1878)*

Fastsigns, Charlotte Also Called: Dickie CD & Associates Inc *(G-2043)*

Fastsigns, Charlotte Also Called: Qasioun LLC *(G-2678)*

Fastsigns, Durham Also Called: Meredith Media Co *(G-4130)*

Fastsigns, Fayetteville Also Called: Signify It Inc *(G-4669)*

Fastsigns, High Point Also Called: Elite Graphics Inc *(G-6607)*

Fastsigns, Monroe Also Called: Classic Sign Services LLC *(G-8461)*

Fastsigns, Raleigh Also Called: Davcom Enterprises Inc *(G-10038)*

Fastsigns, Wilmington Also Called: Creative Signs Inc *(G-12755)*

Fastsigns 111701, Raleigh Also Called: McKnight15 Inc *(G-10285)*

Fat Man Fabrications Inc...................................... 704 545-0369
  8621c Fairview Rd Mint Hill (28227) *(G-8337)*

Fathom Holdings Inc (PA).................................... 888 455-6040
  2000 Regency Pkwy Ste 300 Cary (27518) *(G-1362)*

Fathom Offshore, Wilmington Also Called: Fathom Offshore Holdings LLC *(G-12776)*

Fathom Offshore Holdings LLC............................. 910 399-6882
  3018 N Kerr Ave Ste A Wilmington (28405) *(G-12776)*

Fawn Industries Inc.. 252 462-4700
  100 Industry Ct Nashville (27856) *(G-9319)*

Fayblock Materials Inc.. 910 323-9198
  130 Builders Blvd Fayetteville (28301) *(G-4600)*

Fayetteville Observer, The, Fayetteville Also Called: Db North Carolina Holdings Inc *(G-4585)*

Fayetteville Observer, The, Fayetteville Also Called: Fayetteville Publishing Co *(G-4601)*

Fayetteville Publishing Co (DH)............................ 910 323-4848
  302 Worth St Fayetteville (28301) *(G-4601)*

Fayetteville Steel, Fayetteville Also Called: McCune Technology Inc *(G-4638)*

FCC, Laurinburg Also Called: FCC (north Carolina) LLC *(G-7501)*

FCC (north Carolina) LLC.................................... 910 462-4465
  18000 Fieldcrest Rd Laurinburg (28352) *(G-7501)*

FCC Butner... 919 575-3900
  Butner (27509) *(G-1201)*

(G-0000) Company's Geographic Section entry number

Fci-An Agricultural Service Co, Raeford *Also Called: Farm Chemicals Inc (G-9837)*

FEC Inc..828 765-4599
284 Roan Rd Spruce Pine (28777) *(G-11576)*

Federal Ridge, Greensboro *Also Called: Patheon Softgels Inc (G-5736)*

Fee Kees Wreaths LLC.....................................704 636-1008
1047 Landsdown Dr Salisbury (28147) *(G-11053)*

Feeder Innovations Corporation.......................910 276-3511
9781 Mccoll Rd Laurinburg (28352) *(G-7502)*

Feedtrail Incorporated.....................................757 618-7760
811 Handsworth Ln Apt 108 Raleigh (27607) *(G-10105)*

Feetures Company, Newton *Also Called: Flagship Brands LLC (G-9465)*

Feinberg Enterprises Inc..................................704 822-2400
3 Caldwell Dr Belmont (28012) *(G-750)*

Felice Hosiery Co Inc......................................336 996-2371
118 Burke St Kernersville (27284) *(G-7274)*

Feller LLC (DH)..910 383-6920
9100 Industrial Blvd Ne Leland (28451) *(G-7541)*

Felts Lumber Co Inc.......................................336 368-5667
1377 Perch Rd Pinnacle (27043) *(G-9768)*

Femco Radio Controls, Archdale *Also Called: Hubbell Industrial Contrls Inc (G-226)*

Fence Quarter LLC...800 205-0128
318 Burke Dr Morganton (28655) *(G-8864)*

Fennec Pharmaceuticals Inc (PA)...................919 636-4530
68 Tw Alexander Dr Research Triangle Pa (27709) *(G-10709)*

Fenwal Safety Systems, Wilson *Also Called: Kidde Technologies Inc (G-13000)*

Ferebee Asphalt, Charlotte *Also Called: Ferebee Corporation (G-2145)*

Ferebee Corporation (HQ)...............................704 509-2586
10045 Metromont Industrial Blvd Charlotte (28269) *(G-2145)*

Ferguson & Company LLC...............................704 332-4396
201 S Tryon St Charlotte (28202) *(G-2146)*

Ferguson Box..704 597-0310
10820 Quality Dr Charlotte (28278) *(G-2147)*

Ferguson Cabinet Works.................................828 433-8710
4188 Nc 181 Morganton (28655) *(G-8865)*

Ferguson Companies
1638 Clyde Fitzgerald Rd Linwood (27299) *(G-7878)*

Ferguson Design Inc.......................................704 394-0120
236 Hawthorne Park Ave Belmont (28012) *(G-751)*

Ferguson Fibers, Linwood *Also Called: Ferguson Companies (G-7878)*

Ferguson Highway Products Inc........................704 320-3087
212 Old Dutch Rd W Indian Trail (28079) *(G-7081)*

Ferguson Supply and Box Mfg Co (PA).............704 597-0310
10820 Quality Dr Charlotte (28278) *(G-2148)*

Ferguson Waterworks.....................................704 540-7225
10039 Industrial Dr Pineville (28134) *(G-9727)*

Ferncrest Fashions Inc...................................704 283-6422
4813 Starcrest Dr Monroe (28110) *(G-8488)*

Fernel Therapeutics Inc..................................919 614-2375
408 Gablefield Ln Apex (27502) *(G-155)*

Ferree Trailer, Liberty *Also Called: Vision Metals Inc (G-7783)*

Ferrofab Inc..910 557-5624
1416 Hylan Ave Hamlet (28345) *(G-6055)*

Fervent Pharmaceuticals LLC..........................252 558-9700
740 Greenville Blvd Ste 400-151 Greenville (27834) *(G-5975)*

Fex Straw Manufacturing Inc...........................910 671-4141
191 Magna Blvd Lumberton (28360) *(G-7954)*

Ffi Holdings III Corp (PA)...............................800 690-3650
3915 Shopton Rd Charlotte (28217) *(G-2149)*

Ffnc, High Point *Also Called: Future Foam Inc (G-6625)*

Ffnc Inc...336 885-4121
1300 Prospect St High Point (27260) *(G-6619)*

Ffr Electrics LLC..828 654-7555
400 Hickory Dr Unit 2 Mars Hill (28754) *(G-8077)*

Fiber Company..336 725-5277
8863 Belhaven Ct Lewisville (27023) *(G-7650)*

Fiber Composites LLC (HQ).............................704 463-7120
181 Random Dr New London (28127) *(G-9415)*

Fiber Composites LLC....................................704 463-7118
44017 Us 52 Hwy N New London (28127) *(G-9416)*

Fiber Cushioning Inc (PA)...............................336 629-8442
4454 Us Highway 220 Bus S Asheboro (27205) *(G-355)*

Fiber Cushioning Inc......................................336 887-4782
113 Motsinger St High Point (27260) *(G-6620)*

Fiber N C Div, Marion *Also Called: Jeld-Wen Inc (G-8045)*

Fiber-Line LLC..828 326-8700
280 Performance Dr Se Hickory (28602) *(G-6333)*

Fiberlink...901 826-8126
151 Flower House Loop Troutman (28166) *(G-12137)*

Fiberlink Inc..828 274-5629
122 Deerlake Dr Asheville (28803) *(G-495)*

Fiberon..704 463-2955
411 International Dr Nw Concord (28027) *(G-3362)*

Fiberon, New London *Also Called: Fiber Composites LLC (G-9415)*

Fiberon Recycling, New London *Also Called: Fiber Composites LLC (G-9416)*

Fibex LLC...336 358-5014
7109 Cessna Dr Greensboro (27409) *(G-5530)*

Fibrecrete Pprsrvtion Tech Inc.........................336 789-7259
131 Saint James Way Mount Airy (27030) *(G-9121)*

Fibreworks Composites LLC............................704 696-1084
143 Thunder Rd Mooresville (28115) *(G-8663)*

Fibrix LLC...704 394-2111
1101 Tar Heel Rd Charlotte (28208) *(G-2150)*

Fibrix LLC (HQ)...828 459-7064
1820 Evans St Ne Conover (28613) *(G-3521)*

Fibrix LLC...704 872-5223
166 Orbit Rd Statesville (28677) *(G-11696)*

Fibrix LLC...704 878-0027
1004 Bucks Industrial Rd Statesville (28625) *(G-11697)*

Fibrix Filtration, Mooresville *Also Called: Branford Filtration LLC (G-8620)*

Fics America Inc..704 329-7391
2815 Coliseum Centre Dr Ste 300 Charlotte (28217) *(G-2151)*

Fiddlin Fish Brewing Co..................................336 999-8945
772 N Trade St Winston Salem (27101) *(G-13167)*

Fiddlin' Fish Brewing Company, Winston Salem *Also Called: Fiddlin Fish Brewing Co (G-13167)*

Fidelity Associates Inc...................................704 864-3766
2936 Rousseau Ct Gastonia (28054) *(G-5047)*

Fidelity Pharmaceuticals LLC..........................704 274-3192
11957 Ramah Church Rd Huntersville (28078) *(G-6989)*

Field Controls LLC (DH).................................252 208-7300
2630 Airport Rd Kinston (28504) *(G-7413)*

Fieldco Machining Inc....................................828 891-4100
5164 Old Haywood Rd Fletcher (28732) *(G-4736)*

Fieldx Inc..919 926-7001
7504 Deer Track Dr Raleigh (27613) *(G-10106)*

Fiestic Inc...888 935-3999
555 Fayetteville St Ste 201 Raleigh (27601) *(G-10107)*

Fil-Chem Inc...919 878-1270
3808 Evander Way Raleigh (27613) *(G-10108)*

Filament Fabrics, Burnsville *Also Called: Glen Raven Mtl Solutions LLC (G-1185)*

Filer Micro Welding..828 248-1813
251 Terry Filer Rd Forest City (28043) *(G-4790)*

Filet of Chicken...336 751-4752
251 Eaton Rd Mocksville (27028) *(G-8362)*

Fill Pac LLC..828 322-1916
1140 Tate Blvd Se Hickory (28602) *(G-6334)*

Fillauer North Carolina Inc..............................828 658-8330
220 Merrimon Ave Ste A Weaverville (28787) *(G-12491)*

Filltech Inc..704 279-4300
228 W Main St Rockwell (28138) *(G-10796)*

Filltech USA LLC..704 279-4300
380 Palmer Cir Rockwell (28138) *(G-10797)*

Filmon Process Corp......................................828 684-1360
100 Baldwin Rd Arden (28704) *(G-268)*

Filspecusa, Ellerbe *Also Called: Richmond Specialty Yarns LLC (G-4462)*

Filtec Precise Inc...910 653-5200
218 N Us Highway 701 Byp Tabor City (28463) *(G-11911)*

Filter Shop LLC...704 860-4822
2403 Lowell Rd Gastonia (28054) *(G-5048)*

Filter Srvcng of Chrltte 135.............................704 619-3768
6608 Woodmont Pl Charlotte (28211) *(G-2152)*

Filtex Inc..828 874-2100
160 Fashion Ave Rutherford College (28671) *(G-10971)*

Filtration Technology, Greensboro *Also Called: Filtration Technology Inc (G-5532)*

Filtration Technology Inc (PA).................................... 336 294-5655
110 Pomona Dr Greensboro (27407) *(G-5531)*

Filtration Technology Inc... 336 509-9960
110 Pomona Dr Greensboro (27407) *(G-5532)*

Filtrona Filters Inc... 336 362-1333
303 Gallimore Dairy Rd Greensboro (27409) *(G-5533)*

Fimia Inc.. 828 697-8447
201 Arbutus Ln Hendersonville (28739) *(G-6205)*

Finch Industries Incorporated..................................... 336 472-4499
104 Williams St Thomasville (27360) *(G-12024)*

Finch's Print Shop, Louisburg *Also Called: Brodie-Jones Printing Co Inc (G-7910)*

Fine Art Tapestries, Tryon *Also Called: Pure Country Inc (G-12177)*

Fine Line Hosiery Inc... 336 498-8022
2012 Sunny Ln Asheboro (27205) *(G-356)*

Fine Sheer Industries Inc.. 704 375-3333
225 Wilshire Ave Sw Concord (28025) *(G-3363)*

Fineline Prototyping Inc.. 919 781-7702
3700 Pleasant Grove Church Rd Morrisville (27560) *(G-8974)*

Fines and Carriel Inc... 919 929-0702
1322 Fordham Blvd Ste 5 Chapel Hill (27514) *(G-1547)*

Finishing Partners Inc.. 704 583-7322
1301 Westinghouse Blvd Ste E Charlotte (28273) *(G-2153)*

Finishworks, Hickory *Also Called: RPM Indstrial Ctings Group Inc (G-6433)*

Finnord North America Corp.. 704 723-4913
14514 Sunset Walk Ln Huntersville (28078) *(G-6990)*

Fintronx LLC.. 919 324-3960
5995 Chapel Hill Rd Ste 119 Raleigh (27607) *(G-10109)*

Fire & Safety Outfitters, Charlotte *Also Called: Lightning X Products Inc (G-2421)*

Fire Fly Ballons 2006 LLC.. 704 878-9501
850 Meacham Rd Statesville (28677) *(G-11698)*

Fire Hose Direct, Mooresville *Also Called: Fireresq Incorporated (G-8664)*

Fire Retardant Chem Tech LLC..................................... 980 253-8880
3465 Gribble Rd Matthews (28104) *(G-8169)*

Firefly Balloons 2010 Inc.. 704 878-9501
850 Meacham Rd Statesville (28677) *(G-11699)*

Firefly Balloons Inc... 704 878-9501
810 Salisbury Rd Statesville (28677) *(G-11700)*

Firehouse Cabinets... 704 689-5243
715 Brook Forest Dr Belmont (28012) *(G-752)*

Fireline Shields Llc... 704 948-3680
15336 Old Statesville Rd Huntersville (28078) *(G-6991)*

Fireplace Guy, The, Kure Beach *Also Called: Dna Services Inc (G-7464)*

Fireproof Office Files, Asheville *Also Called: Blue-Hen Inc (G-458)*

Fireresq Incorporated.. 888 975-0858
115 Corporate Center Dr Ste J Mooresville (28117) *(G-8664)*

Firestone, Durham *Also Called: Bridgestone Ret Operations LLC (G-3941)*

Firestone, Fayetteville *Also Called: Bridgestone Ret Operations LLC (G-4562)*

Firestone, Gastonia *Also Called: Bridgestone Ret Operations LLC (G-5005)*

Firestone, Goldsboro *Also Called: Bridgestone Ret Operations LLC (G-5202)*

Firestone, Greensboro *Also Called: Bridgestone Ret Operations LLC (G-5399)*

Firestone, Greensboro *Also Called: Bridgestone Ret Operations LLC (G-5400)*

Firestone, Greensboro *Also Called: Bridgestone Ret Operations LLC (G-5401)*

Firestone, Kinston *Also Called: Bridgestone Ret Operations LLC (G-7397)*

Firestone, Raleigh *Also Called: Bridgestone Ret Operations LLC (G-9958)*

Firestone, Raleigh *Also Called: Bridgestone Ret Operations LLC (G-9959)*

Firestone, Wilson *Also Called: Bridgestone Ret Operations LLC (G-12973)*

Firestone, Winston Salem *Also Called: Bridgestone Ret Operations LLC (G-13110)*

Firestone Fibers Textiles LLC...................................... 704 734-2110
100 Firestone Ln Kings Mountain (28086) *(G-7364)*

Firestopping Products Inc.. 336 661-0102
120 Regent Dr Winston Salem (27103) *(G-13168)*

Firetech, Hendersonville *Also Called: Hiviz Lighting Inc (G-6217)*

Firm Ascend LLC... 704 464-3024
224 Westinghouse Blvd Ste 602 Charlotte (28273) *(G-2154)*

First Alance Logistics MGT LLC.................................... 704 522-0233
14120 Ballantyne Corporate Pl Charlotte (28277) *(G-2155)*

First Choice, Wilson *Also Called: Buy Smart Inc (G-12976)*

First Choice Properties, Shelby *Also Called: Joe Robin Darnell (G-11350)*

First Coast Energy LLP... 828 667-0625
301 Smokey Park Hwy Asheville (28806) *(G-496)*

First Impressions Ltd... 704 536-3622
8500 Monroe Rd Charlotte (28212) *(G-2156)*

First Leads Inc.. 919 672-5329
201 W Main St Ste 305 Durham (27701) *(G-4032)*

First Noodle Co Inc... 704 393-3238
333 Oakdale Rd Charlotte (28216) *(G-2157)*

First Prrity Emrgncy Vhcles In.................................... 908 645-0788
1208 School St Wilkesboro (28697) *(G-12635)*

First Rate Blinds.. 800 655-1080
19701 Bethel Church Rd # 178 Cornelius (28031) *(G-3601)*

Firstmark Aerospace Corp.. 919 956-4200
1176 Telecom Dr Creedmoor (27522) *(G-3648)*

Firstmark Controls, Creedmoor *Also Called: Firstmark Aerospace Corp (G-3648)*

Firstreport Software Inc.. 828 441-0404
369 London Rd Asheville (28803) *(G-497)*

Fish Getter Lure Co LLC.. 704 538-9863
254 Hull Rd Casar (28020) *(G-1488)*

Fish Hippie, Mount Airy *Also Called: Old North State Winery Inc (G-9161)*

Fishel Steel Company.. 336 788-2880
760 Palmer Ln Winston Salem (27107) *(G-13169)*

Fisher Athletic Equipment Inc..................................... 704 636-5713
2060 Cauble Rd Salisbury (28144) *(G-11054)*

Fisher Scientific Company LLC..................................... 800 252-7100
275 Aiken Rd Asheville (28804) *(G-498)*

Fisher Textiles Inc.. 800 554-8886
4211 Matthews Indian Trail Rd Matthews (28104) *(G-8170)*

Fisherman Creations Inc... 252 725-0138
1175 Hwy 70 Otway Beaufort (28516) *(G-726)*

Fiskars Brands Inc.. 336 292-6237
322 Edwardia Dr Ste D Greensboro (27409) *(G-5534)*

Fit1media LLC... 919 925-2200
8601 Six Forks Rd Ste 400 Raleigh (27615) *(G-10110)*

Fitch Sign Company Inc.. 704 482-2916
341 N Post Rd Shelby (28152) *(G-11336)*

Fitt Usa Inc.. 866 348-8872
136 Corporate Park Dr Ste I Mooresville (28117) *(G-8665)*

Fitzbradshaw Racing, Mooresville *Also Called: Highline Performance Group (G-8684)*

Five Star Bodies.. 262 325-9126
177 Houston Rd Troutman (28166) *(G-12138)*

Five Star Coffee Roasters LLC..................................... 919 671-0645
108 Thomas Mill Rd Ste 101 Holly Springs (27540) *(G-6901)*

Fixed-NC LLC... 252 751-1911
1830a Old Fire Tower Rd Greenville (27858) *(G-5976)*

Fixxus Indus Holdings Co LLC..................................... 336 674-3088
6116 Old Mendenhall Rd Archdale (27263) *(G-222)*

Fla Orthopedics Inc (DH)... 800 327-4110
5825 Carnegie Blvd Charlotte (28209) *(G-2158)*

Flagship Brands LLC (PA).. 888 801-7227
2084 Fairgrove Church Rd Newton (28658) *(G-9465)*

Flagstone Foods LLC... 252 795-6500
201 E 3rd St Robersonville (27871) *(G-10767)*

Flair Designs, Robbins *Also Called: Minhas Furniture House Inc (G-10754)*

Flame Tech Inc.. 336 661-7801
120 Regent Dr Winston Salem (27103) *(G-13170)*

Flame-Tec LLC.. 844 352-6383
136 Hillview Blvd Hendersonville (28792) *(G-6206)*

Flameoff Coatings Inc (PA).. 888 816-7468
3915 Beryl Rd Ste 130 Raleigh (27607) *(G-10111)*

Flanagan Printing Company Inc.................................... 828 693-7380
127 3rd Ave W Hendersonville (28792) *(G-6207)*

Flanders Corporation... 919 934-3020
2121 Wal Pat Rd Smithfield (27577) *(G-11443)*

Flanders Corporation (DH).. 252 946-8081
531 Flanders Filter Rd Washington (27889) *(G-12385)*

Flanders Filters Inc... 252 217-3978
1418 Wal Pat Rd Smithfield (27577) *(G-11444)*

Flanders Filters Inc (DH)... 252 946-8081
531 Flanders Filter Rd Washington (27889) *(G-12386)*

Flanders Precisionaire, Smithfield *Also Called: Flanders Corporation (G-11443)*

Flane Tech, Winston Salem *Also Called: Firestopping Products Inc (G-13168)*

Flash Printing Company Inc.. 704 375-2474
1003 Louise Ave Ste A Charlotte (28205) *(G-2159)*

Flash Technology LLC.. 980 474-3700
6325 Ardrey Kell Rd Ste 400 Charlotte (28277) *(G-2160)*

Flat Iron Mill Works LLC.. 828 768-7770
22 Pear Tree Ln Leicester (28748) *(G-7524)*

Flat Rock Tool & Mold Inc... 828 692-2578
690 Shepherd St Hendersonville (28792) *(G-6208)*

Flat Water Corp... 704 584-7764
800 Clanton Rd Ste R Charlotte (28217) *(G-2161)*

Flavor Sciences Inc... 828 758-2525
715 Houck Mountain Rd Taylorsville (28681) *(G-11960)*

Flavors Ice Cream, Raleigh *Also Called: Antkar LLC (G-9905)*

Flawless Touch Detailing LLC.. 910 987-8093
450 W Russell St Ste 102 Fayetteville (28301) *(G-4602)*

Flawtech Inc... 704 795-4401
4486 Raceway Dr Sw Concord (28027) *(G-3364)*

Fleet Fixers Inc.. 704 986-0066
927a Concord Rd Albemarle (28001) *(G-73)*

Fleet Readiness Center East, Cherry Point *Also Called: United States Dept of Navy (G-3057)*

Fleetgenius of Nc Inc.. 828 726-3001
1808 Norwood St Sw Lenoir (28645) *(G-7607)*

Fleetwood, Raleigh *Also Called: Udm Systems LLC (G-10571)*

Fletcher Industries Inc.. 910 692-7133
1485 Central Dr 22 Southern Pines (28387) *(G-11499)*

Fletcher Limestone Company Inc.. 828 684-6701
639 Fanning Bridge Rd Fletcher (28732) *(G-4737)*

Fletcher Machine Inds Inc.. 336 249-6101
4305 E Us Highway 64 Lexington (27292) *(G-7687)*

Flex Finishing Inc... 704 342-3600
4811 Worth Pl Charlotte (28216) *(G-2162)*

Flex Tram, Lexington *Also Called: Carter Millwork Inc (G-7661)*

Flexgen Power Systems Inc... 855 327-5674
2175 Presidential Dr Ste 100 Durham (27703) *(G-4033)*

Flexgen Power Systems Inc (PA).. 855 327-5674
280 S Mangum St Ste 150 Durham (27701) *(G-4034)*

Flexi North America LLC.. 704 588-0785
2405 Center Park Dr Charlotte (28217) *(G-2163)*

Flextrol Corporation.. 704 888-1120
192 Browns Hill Rd Locust (28097) *(G-7893)*

Flextronics Corporation... 704 598-3300
6800 Solectron Dr Charlotte (28262) *(G-2164)*

Flextronics Intl USA Inc.. 704 509-8700
6800 Solectron Dr Charlotte (28262) *(G-2165)*

Flextronics Intl USA Inc.. 919 998-4000
1000 Innovation Ave Morrisville (27560) *(G-8975)*

Flint Acquisition Corp... 336 475-6600
115 Todd Ct Thomasville (27360) *(G-12025)*

Flint Group Inc.. 828 687-4363
25 Old Shoals Rd Arden (28704) *(G-269)*

Flint Group Flexographic Pdts, Arden *Also Called: Flint Group Inc (G-269)*

Flint Group Print Media N Amer, Arden *Also Called: Flint Group US LLC (G-270)*

Flint Group US LLC... 828 687-4309
95 Glenn Bridge Rd Arden (28704) *(G-270)*

Flint Group US LLC... 828 687-4291
25 Old Shoals Rd Arden (28704) *(G-271)*

Flint Group US LLC... 828 687-2485
95 Glenn Bridge Rd Arden (28704) *(G-272)*

Flint Group US LLC... 704 504-2626
2915 Whitehall Park Dr Ste 600 Charlotte (28273) *(G-2166)*

Flint Hill Textiles Inc.. 704 434-9331
2240 Flint Hill Church Rd Shelby (28152) *(G-11337)*

Flint Spinning LLC.. 336 665-3000
7736 Mccloud Rd Ste 300 Greensboro (27409) *(G-5535)*

Flint Trading Inc.. 336 308-3770
505 County Line Rd Thomasville (27360) *(G-12026)*

Flint Trading Inc.. 336 475-6600
115 Todd Ct Thomasville (27360) *(G-12027)*

Flo-Tite Inc Valves & Contrls.. 910 738-8904
4815 W 5th St Lumberton (28358) *(G-7955)*

Float Lifts of Carolinas LLC.. 919 972-1082
8012 Yellow Daisy Dr Wilmington (28412) *(G-12777)*

Flologic Inc.. 919 878-1808
1015 Aviation Pkwy Ste 900 Morrisville (27560) *(G-8976)*

Floor Azzo, Siler City *Also Called: Floorazzo (G-11408)*

Floorazzo.. 919 663-1684
215 W 3rd St Siler City (27344) *(G-11408)*

Floorazzo Tile LLC... 919 663-1684
1217 Harold Andrews Rd Siler City (27344) *(G-11409)*

Flooring Manufacturing, Franklin *Also Called: Beasley Flooring Products Inc (G-4818)*

Flores Crane Services LLC.. 704 243-4347
8705 Kentucky Derby Dr Waxhaw (28173) *(G-12431)*

Flores Welding Inc... 919 838-1060
961 Palace Garden Way Raleigh (27603) *(G-10112)*

Florida Marine Tanks Inc (HQ).. 305 620-9030
120 Peter Gill Rd Henderson (27537) *(G-6155)*

Florida Progress Corporation (DH)..................................... 704 382-3853
410 S Wilmington St Raleigh (27601) *(G-10113)*

Flow Control Group, Charlotte *Also Called: Ffi Holdings III Corp (G-2149)*

Flow Dental, Battleboro *Also Called: Flow X Ray Corporation (G-697)*

Flow Rhythm Inc.. 704 737-2178
1520 Mockingbird Ln Charlotte (28209) *(G-2167)*

Flow Sciences Inc.. 910 763-1717
2025 Mercantile Dr Leland (28451) *(G-7542)*

Flow X Ray Corporation... 631 242-9729
133 Wolf Rd Battleboro (27809) *(G-697)*

Flowers Bakery, Goldsboro *Also Called: Franklin Baking Company LLC (G-5214)*

Flowers Bakery, Jamestown *Also Called: Flowers Bkg Co Jamestown LLC (G-7161)*

Flowers Bakery, Sanford *Also Called: Flowers Bkg Co Jamestown LLC (G-11178)*

Flowers Bakery of Winston-Salem LLC................................. 336 785-8700
315 Cassell St Winston Salem (27107) *(G-13171)*

Flowers Bakery Outlet, Winston Salem *Also Called: Flowers Bkg Co Jamestown LLC (G-13172)*

Flowers Baking Co Newton LLC... 336 903-1345
802 N Moravian St Wilkesboro (28697) *(G-12636)*

Flowers Baking Co. of Newton, LLC, Wilkesboro *Also Called: Flowers Baking Co Newton LLC (G-12636)*

Flowers Bkg Co Jamestown LLC.. 704 305-0766
2044 Kannapolis Hwy Concord (28027) *(G-3365)*

Flowers Bkg Co Jamestown LLC.. 704 305-0766
403 W Kings Hwy Ste C Eden (27288) *(G-4346)*

Flowers Bkg Co Jamestown LLC.. 252 492-1519
875 S Beckford Dr Henderson (27536) *(G-6156)*

Flowers Bkg Co Jamestown LLC (HQ)................................. 336 841-8840
801 W Main St Jamestown (27282) *(G-7161)*

Flowers Bkg Co Jamestown LLC.. 704 296-1000
5524 W Highway 74 Monroe (28110) *(G-8489)*

Flowers Bkg Co Jamestown LLC.. 919 776-8932
708 E Main St Sanford (27330) *(G-11178)*

Flowers Bkg Co Jamestown LLC.. 336 744-3525
5610 Shattalon Dr Winston Salem (27105) *(G-13172)*

Flowers Slaughterhouse LLC.. 252 235-4106
5154a Saint Rose Church Rd Sims (27880) *(G-11430)*

Flowserve Corporation.. 704 494-0497
2801 Hutchison Mcdonald Rd Ste T Charlotte (28269) *(G-2168)*

Flowserve Corporation.. 910 371-9011
2216 Mercantile Dr Leland (28451) *(G-7543)*

Flowserve US Inc... 972 443-6500
1900 S Saunders St Raleigh (27603) *(G-10114)*

Flowserve US Inc., Raleigh *Also Called: Flowserve US Inc (G-10114)*

Floyd S Braces and Limbs Inc... 910 763-0821
709 Parkway Blvd Wilmington (28412) *(G-12778)*

Fluid Power Technology, Charlotte *Also Called: Parmer International Inc (G-2613)*

Fluid Sealing Supply, Concord *Also Called: Michael Simmons (G-3401)*

Fluid Watercraft, Raleigh *Also Called: Sirocco Marine LLC (G-10483)*

Flynn Burner Corporation... 704 660-1500
225 Mooresville Blvd Mooresville (28115) *(G-8666)*

Flynt/Amtex Inc (PA)... 336 226-0621
2908 Alamance Rd Burlington (27215) *(G-1090)*

FMC Corporation... 704 868-5300
161 Kings Mtn Hwy Bessemer City (28016) *(G-818)*

FMC Corporation..704 426-5336
　1115 Bessemer City Kings Mtn Hwy Bessemer City (28016) *(G-819)*

FMC Lithium Division, Bessemer City *Also Called: FMC Corporation (G-819)*

Fmp Equipment Corp....336 621-2882
　6204 Technology Dr Browns Summit (27214) *(G-992)*

Fms Enterprises Usa Inc.......................................704 735-4249
　2001 Kawai Rd Lincolnton (28092) *(G-7831)*

Fmt, Henderson *Also Called: Florida Marine Tanks Inc (G-6155)*

Fmt Food and Beverage Systems, Greensboro *Also Called: Smart Machine Technologies Inc (G-5817)*

Focal Point Architectural Pdts, Tarboro *Also Called: Focal Point Products Inc (G-11926)*

Focal Point Products Inc.....................................252 824-0015
　3006 Anaconda Rd Tarboro (27886) *(G-11926)*

Focke & Co Inc..336 449-7200
　5730 Millstream Rd Whitsett (27377) *(G-12606)*

Focus Newspaper, Hickory *Also Called: Tucker Production Incorporated (G-6475)*

Focusales Inc..919 614-3076
　6113 Chowning Ct Raleigh (27612) *(G-10115)*

Foell Packing Company of NC................................919 776-0592
　2209 Boone Trail Rd Sanford (27330) *(G-11179)*

Fogle Computing Corporation................................828 697-9080
　131 Camellia Way Hendersonville (28739) *(G-6209)*

Fogleman and Partners, Hickory *Also Called: Inform Inc (G-6368)*

Foiled Agin Choclat Coins LLC..............................919 342-4601
　1488 Mcneill Rd # A Sanford (27330) *(G-11180)*

Fontaine Modification Company (DH).......................704 392-8502
　9827 Mount Holly Rd Charlotte (28214) *(G-2169)*

Fontem US LLC..888 207-4588
　628 Green Valley Rd Ste 500 Greensboro (27408) *(G-5536)*

Foo Machine & Tool Precision...............................919 258-5099
　311 W Harrington Ave Broadway (27505) *(G-986)*

Food Industry, Wendell *Also Called: Magnificent Concessions LLC (G-12538)*

Foot To Die For..704 577-2822
　2545 Valleyview Dr Charlotte (28212) *(G-2170)*

Foothills Brewing..336 997-9484
　3800 Kimwell Dr Winston Salem (27103) *(G-13173)*

Foothills Sug Cured Cntry Hams............................336 835-2411
　522 S Main St Jonesville (28642) *(G-7195)*

Foothold Publications Inc....................................770 891-3423
　2656 Garden Knoll Ln Raleigh (27614) *(G-10116)*

Forbes Custom Cabinets LLC................................919 362-4277
　2025 Production Dr Apex (27539) *(G-156)*

Forbes Fixtures, Apex *Also Called: Forbes Custom Cabinets LLC (G-156)*

Forbes Printing, Lenoir *Also Called: A Forbes Company (G-7565)*

Forbo Belting..704 948-0800
　12201 Vanstory Dr Huntersville (28078) *(G-6992)*

Forbo Movement Systems....................................704 334-5353
　10125 S Tryon St Charlotte (28273) *(G-2171)*

Forbo Siegling LLC...704 948-0800
　13245 Reese Blvd W Huntersville (28078) *(G-6993)*

Forbo Siegling LLC...704 948-0800
　12120 Herbert Wayne Ct Huntersville (28078) *(G-6994)*

Forbo Siegling LLC (HQ)......................................704 948-0800
　12201 Vanstory Dr Huntersville (28078) *(G-6995)*

Force Protection Inc...336 597-2381
　3300 Jim Thorpe Hwy Roxboro (27574) *(G-10926)*

Forest City Pallett Co Inc....................................828 652-8432
　5159 Harmony Grove Rd Nebo (28761) *(G-9328)*

Forest Millwork Inc...828 251-5264
　93 Thompson St Asheville (28803) *(G-499)*

Forever Outdoors, Marion *Also Called: Joseph Sotanski (G-8047)*

Forged Cstm Met Fbrication LLC...........................910 274-8300
　6804 Holly Shelter Rd Castle Hayne (28429) *(G-1499)*

Forklift Pro Inc..704 716-3636
　9801 Industrial Dr Pineville (28134) *(G-9728)*

Form Tech Concrete Forms Inc..............................704 395-9910
　1000 Thomasboro Dr Charlotte (28208) *(G-2172)*

Form Technologies Inc (PA).................................704 927-2790
　11325 N Community House Rd Ste 300 Charlotte (28277) *(G-2173)*

Forma-Fab Metals Inc...919 563-5630
　5816 Us 70 W Mebane (27302) *(G-8240)*

Formcut 3d, Cary *Also Called: Size Stream LLC (G-1459)*

Forsyth Family Magazine Inc................................336 782-0331
　6255 Towncenter Dr Clemmons (27012) *(G-3183)*

Forsyth Printing Company Inc...............................336 969-0383
　627 Forum Pkwy Rural Hall (27045) *(G-10959)*

Fortech Inc..704 333-0621
　2124 Wilkinson Blvd Charlotte (28208) *(G-2174)*

Fortem Genus Inc...910 574-5214
　427 Franklin St Fayetteville (28301) *(G-4603)*

Forterra Brick LLC...704 341-8750
　7400 Carmel Executive Park Dr Ste 200 Charlotte (28226) *(G-2175)*

Forterra Pipe & Precast LLC................................910 892-6411
　452 Webb Rd Dunn (28334) *(G-3857)*

Fortiline LLC (DH)..704 788-9800
　7025 Northwinds Dr Nw Concord (28027) *(G-3366)*

Fortiline Waterworks, Concord *Also Called: Fortiline LLC (G-3366)*

Fortis Track, Raleigh *Also Called: Smart Cast Group (G-10487)*

Fortner Lumber Inc...704 585-2383
　991 Liberty Church Rd Hiddenite (28636) *(G-6496)*

Fortovia Therapeutics Inc (PA).............................919 872-5578
　8540 Colonnade Center Dr Ste 101 Raleigh (27615) *(G-10117)*

Fortrans Inc..919 365-8004
　7400 Siemens Rd Ste B Wendell (27591) *(G-12536)*

FORTREA, Durham *Also Called: Fortrea Holdings Inc (G-4035)*

Fortrea Holdings Inc (PA)....................................480 295-7600
　8 Moore Dr Durham (27709) *(G-4035)*

Fortress Forest International, Conover *Also Called: Fortress International Corp NC (G-3522)*

Fortress International Corp NC..............................336 645-9365
　1808 Emmanuel Church Rd Conover (28613) *(G-3522)*

Fortress Wood Products Inc.................................336 854-5121
　3874 Bethel Drive Ext High Point (27260) *(G-6621)*

Forveson Corp...336 292-6237
　322 Edwardia Dr Ste D Greensboro (27409) *(G-5537)*

Forward Design & Print Co Inc..............................704 776-9304
　1903 Tom Williams Rd Monroe (28112) *(G-8490)*

Forward Dsptching Lgistics LLC............................252 907-9797
　3033 Clubway Dr Apt 124 Greenville (27834) *(G-5977)*

Foss Industrial Recycling LLC..............................336 342-4812
　7037 Us Highway 70 W La Grange (28551) *(G-7468)*

Foster Tire Sales Inc..336 248-6726
　1609 S Main St Lexington (27292) *(G-7688)*

Foundry Commercial...704 348-6875
　101 N Tryon St Ste 1000 Charlotte (28246) *(G-2176)*

Fountain Powerboats, Washington *Also Called: Pro-Line North Carolina Inc (G-12409)*

Four Corners Frmng Gallery Inc............................704 662-7154
　148 N Main St Mooresville (28115) *(G-8667)*

Four Corners Home Inc (PA).................................828 398-4187
　1 Page Ave Ste 112l Asheville (28801) *(G-500)*

Four Oks/Benson News In Review, Benson *Also Called: County Press Inc (G-787)*

Four Points Recycling LLC...................................910 333-5961
　309 King Rd Jacksonville (28540) *(G-7123)*

Fourshare LLC..336 714-0448
　6645 Holder Rd Clemmons (27012) *(G-3184)*

Fox Apparel Inc..336 629-7641
　100 Industrial Park Ave Asheboro (27205) *(G-357)*

Fox Factory Inc..828 633-6840
　1240 Brevard Rd Asheville (28806) *(G-501)*

Foxster Opco LLC...910 297-6996
　118 Circle Dr Hampstead (28443) *(G-6072)*

Fps Wind Down Inc...336 776-9165
　3820 N Liberty St Winston Salem (27105) *(G-13174)*

Fpt Infrastructure, Mount Airy *Also Called: Fibrecrete Pprsrvtion Tech Inc (G-9121)*

Fragrant Passage Candle Co LP............................336 375-8411
　3500 N Ohenry Blvd Greensboro (27405) *(G-5538)*

Framewright Inc...828 459-2284
　1824 Brian Dr Ne Conover (28613) *(G-3523)*

Frank Door Company, Newport *Also Called: TRf Manufacturing NC Inc (G-9445)*

Frankie York Logging Co......................................252 633-4825
　2250 Us Highway 17 N New Bern (28560) *(G-9368)*

Franklin Baking Company LLC (HQ).......................919 735-0344
　500 W Grantham St Goldsboro (27530) *(G-5214)*

(G-0000) Company's Geographic Section entry number

Franklin Baking Company LLC............................ 252 752-4600
1107 Myrtle St Greenville (27834) *(G-5978)*

Franklin Baking Company LLC............................ 252 752-4600
3350 Frog Level Rd Greenville (27834) *(G-5979)*

Franklin Baking Company LLC............................ 910 425-5090
217 Woodington Rd Hope Mills (28348) *(G-6927)*

Franklin Baking Company LLC............................ 919 832-7942
1404 S Bloodworth St Raleigh (27610) *(G-10118)*

Franklin Baking Company LLC............................ 252 410-0255
610 Julian R Allsbrook Hwy Roanoke Rapids (27870) *(G-10737)*

Franklin Baking Company LLC............................ 252 946-3340
5398 Us Highway 264 E Washington (27889) *(G-12387)*

Franklin County Newspapers Inc......................... 919 496-6503
109 S Bickett Blvd Louisburg (27549) *(G-7915)*

Franklin Investments, Charlotte *Also Called: Diversfied Prtg Techniques Inc (G-2055)*

Franklin Logistical Services Inc......................... 919 556-6711
112 Franklin Park Dr Youngsville (27596) *(G-13472)*

Franklin Machine Company LLC........................... 828 524-2313
231 Depot St Franklin (28734) *(G-4828)*

Franklin Partleboard, Moncure *Also Called: Aconcagua Timber Corp (G-8398)*

Franklin Sheet Metal, Franklin *Also Called: Franklin Sheet Metal Shop Inc (G-4829)*

Franklin Sheet Metal Shop Inc........................... 828 524-2821
791 Ulco Dr Ste A Franklin (28734) *(G-4829)*

Franklin Times, Louisburg *Also Called: Franklin County Newspapers Inc (G-7915)*

Franklin Veneers Inc...................................... 919 494-2284
5735 Nc Hwy 56 E Franklinton (27525) *(G-4848)*

Franklinton Concrete Plant, Franklinton *Also Called: S T Wooten Corporation (G-4853)*

Franks Millwright Services............................... 336 248-6692
1207 Ashland Dr Lexington (27295) *(G-7689)*

Fraser West Inc... 910 655-4106
361 Federal Rd Riegelwood (28456) *(G-10724)*

Frazier Holdings LLC...................................... 919 868-8651
2009 Pope Ct Clayton (27520) *(G-3148)*

Frct, Matthews *Also Called: Fire Retardant Chem Tech LLC (G-8169)*

Freakin Pekin.. 828 705-3313
D114 Morganton Heights Blvd Morganton (28655) *(G-8866)*

Fred L Brown.. 336 643-7523
2913 Pleasant Ridge Rd Summerfield (27358) *(G-11840)*

Fred Marvin and Associates Inc......................... 330 784-9211
496 Gallimore Dairy Rd Ste D Greensboro (27409) *(G-5539)*

Fred Marvin Associates, Greensboro *Also Called: Fred Marvin and Associates Inc (G-5539)*

Fred R Harrris Logging Inc............................... 919 853-2266
527 Schloss Rd Louisburg (27549) *(G-7916)*

Fred Smith Company, Raleigh *Also Called: Fsc II LLC (G-10122)*

Fred Winfield Lumber Co Inc............................. 828 648-3414
Dutch Cove Rd Canton (28716) *(G-1253)*

Frederick and Frederick Entp............................ 252 235-4849
8520 Hilliard Rd Middlesex (27557) *(G-8275)*

Free Press, The, Kinston *Also Called: Kinston Free Press Company (G-7417)*

Free Will Bptst Press Fndtion (PA)...................... 252 746-6128
3928 Lee St Ayden (28513) *(G-657)*

Freedom Beverage Company.............................. 336 316-1260
4319 Waterleaf Ct Ste 101 Greensboro (27410) *(G-5540)*

Freedom Creative Solutions, Winston Salem *Also Called: Freedom Mailing & Mktg Inc (G-13175)*

Freedom Enterprise LLC.................................. 502 510-7296
1235 East Blvd Ste E Pmb 2238 Charlotte (28203) *(G-2177)*

Freedom Industries Inc................................... 252 984-0007
4000 E Old Spring Hope Rd Rocky Mount (27804) *(G-10839)*

Freedom Mailing & Mktg Inc............................. 336 595-6300
427 W End Blvd Winston Salem (27101) *(G-13175)*

Freedom Metals Inc...................................... 704 333-1214
2014 Vanderbilt Rd Charlotte (28206) *(G-2178)*

Freeman Container Company Inc......................... 704 922-7972
121 Freeman Franklin Rd Dallas (28034) *(G-3672)*

Freeman Corrugated Containers, Dallas *Also Called: Freeman Container Company Inc (G-3672)*

Freeman Custom Welding Inc............................. 919 210-6267
2108 Langdon Rd Raleigh (27604) *(G-10119)*

Freeman Screen Printers Inc............................. 704 521-9148
4442 South Blvd Ste B Charlotte (28209) *(G-2179)*

Freight Company, Charlotte *Also Called: D&E Freight LLC (G-2013)*

Freightliner Parts Plant, Gastonia *Also Called: Daimler Truck North Amer LLC (G-5038)*

Freirich Foods Inc
815 W Kerr St Salisbury (28144) *(G-11055)*

French Apron Manufacturing Co.......................... 704 865-7666
1619 Madison St Gastonia (28052) *(G-5049)*

French Broad Chocolates LLC............................ 828 252-4181
821 Riverside Dr Asheville (28801) *(G-502)*

French Heritage Inc (PA)................................. 336 882-3565
1638 W English Rd High Point (27262) *(G-6622)*

Frenzelit Inc.. 336 814-4317
4165 Old Salisbury Rd Lexington (27295) *(G-7690)*

Fresenius Kabi Usa LLC.................................. 252 991-2692
5200 Corporate Pkwy Wilson (27893) *(G-12991)*

Fresh Air Technologies LLC.............................. 704 622-7877
2246 Stevens Mill Rd Ste B Matthews (28104) *(G-8171)*

Fresh As A Daisy, High Point *Also Called: Fresh As A Daisy Inc (G-6623)*

Fresh As A Daisy Inc..................................... 336 869-3002
3601 Huntingridge Dr High Point (27265) *(G-6623)*

Fresh Point LLC... 919 895-0790
237 Kenmont Dr Holly Springs (27540) *(G-6902)*

Fresh-N-Mobile LLC....................................... 704 251-4643
8640 University City Blvd Ste 135 Charlotte (28213) *(G-2180)*

Freud, High Point *Also Called: Freud America Inc (G-6624)*

Freud America Inc... 800 334-4107
218 Feld Ave High Point (27263) *(G-6624)*

Freudenberg Nonwoven, Durham *Also Called: Freudenberg Prfmce Mtls LP (G-4037)*

Freudenberg Nonwovens Limited Partnership........... 919 620-3900
3500 Industrial Dr Durham (27704) *(G-4036)*

Freudenberg Performance Materials L.P., Candler *Also Called: Freudenberg Prfmce Mtls LP (G-1225)*

FREUDENBERG PERFORMANCE MATERIALS L.P., Durham *Also Called: Freudenberg Prfmce Mtls LP (G-4038)*

Freudenberg Prfmce Mtls LP.............................. 828 665-5000
1301 Sand Hill Rd Candler (28715) *(G-1225)*

Freudenberg Prfmce Mtls LP (HQ)....................... 919 479-7443
3500 Industrial Dr Durham (27704) *(G-4037)*

Freudenberg Prfmce Mtls LP.............................. 919 620-3900
3440 Industrial Dr Durham (27704) *(G-4038)*

Freudnberg Rsdntial Fltrtion T (DH)..................... 828 328-1142
420 3rd Ave Nw Hickory (28601) *(G-6335)*

Friedrich Metal Pdts Co Inc.............................. 336 375-3067
6204 Technology Dr Browns Summit (27214) *(G-993)*

Friendship Upholstery Co Inc............................. 828 632-9836
6035 Church Rd Taylorsville (28681) *(G-11961)*

Frisby Aerospace Inc..................................... 336 712-8004
4520 Hampton Rd Clemmons (27012) *(G-3185)*

Frisby Technologies Inc (PA)............................. 336 998-6652
136 Medical Dr Advance (27006) *(G-32)*

Frit Car Inc... 252 638-2675
Hwy 17 N Ste 2012 Bridgeton (28519) *(G-984)*

Frito-Lay, Charlotte *Also Called: Frito-Lay North America Inc (G-2181)*

Frito-Lay North America Inc.............................. 704 588-4150
2911 Nevada Blvd Charlotte (28273) *(G-2181)*

Frito-Lay North America Inc.............................. 980 224-3730
3215 Kitty Hawk Rd Wilmington (28405) *(G-12779)*

Froehling & Robertson Inc................................ 804 264-2701
310 Hubert St Raleigh (27603) *(G-10120)*

Front Line Express LLC................................... 800 260-1357
4086 Clovelly Dr Greensboro (27406) *(G-5541)*

Front Porch Ice Cream, Mooresville *Also Called: Mooresville Ice Cream Company LLC (G-8725)*

Front Street Vlg Mstr Assn Inc.......................... 252 838-1524
2450 Lennoxville Rd Beaufort (28516) *(G-727)*

Frontier Meat Processing Inc............................ 704 843-3921
8303 Lancaster Hwy Waxhaw (28173) *(G-12432)*

Frontier Yarns Inc (HQ).................................. 919 776-9940
1823 Boone Trail Rd Sanford (27330) *(G-11181)*

Frontier Yarns Inc.. 919 776-9940
1823 Boone Trail Rd Sanford (27330) *(G-11182)*

Frostie Bottom At Doors, Claremont *Also Called: Frostie Bottom Tree Stand LLC (G-3113)*

A
L
P
H
A
B
E
T
I
C

Frostie Bottom Tree Stand LLC.................................... 828 466-1708
3280 Yount Rd Claremont (28610) *(G-3113)*

Frsteam By Sun Cleaners, Newton *Also Called: Sun Cleaners & Laundry Inc (G-9500)*

Fryeday Coffee Roasters LLC.................................... 704 879-9083
106 E 1st St Unit B Lowell (28098) *(G-7931)*

Fs LLC.................................... 919 309-9727
4122 Bennett Memorial Rd Ste 304 Durham (27705) *(G-4039)*

Fsc Holdings Inc.................................... 919 782-1247
6001 Westgate Rd Raleigh (27617) *(G-10121)*

Fsc II LLC (HQ).................................... 919 783-5700
701 Corporate Center Dr Ste 101 Raleigh (27607) *(G-10122)*

Fsc Therapeutics LLC.................................... 704 941-2500
6100 Fairview Rd Ste 300 Charlotte (28210) *(G-2182)*

Fsm Liquidation Corp.................................... 919 776-9940
1823 Boone Trail Rd Sanford (27330) *(G-11183)*

Ft Media Holdings LLC (HQ).................................... 336 605-0121
7025 Albert Pick Rd Ste 200 Greensboro (27409) *(G-5542)*

FTM Enterprises Inc.................................... 910 798-2045
301 N Green Meadows Dr Ste C Wilmington (28405) *(G-12780)*

Ftp Co, Greenville *Also Called: Modern Lightning Protection Co (G-6005)*

Fudgeboat Inc.................................... 910 617-9793
920 Riptide Ln Carolina Beach (28428) *(G-1261)*

Fueltec Systems LLC.................................... 828 212-1141
3821 N Main St Granite Falls (28630) *(G-5303)*

Fuji Foods Inc.................................... 336 897-3373
6205 Corporate Park Dr Browns Summit (27214) *(G-994)*

Fuji Foods Inc (DH).................................... 336 375-3111
6206 Corporate Park Dr Browns Summit (27214) *(G-995)*

Fuji Foods Inc.................................... 336 226-8817
363 W Old Glencoe Rd Burlington (27217) *(G-1091)*

Fuji Silysia Chemical Ltd.................................... 919 484-4158
1215 Sugg Pkwy Greenville (27834) *(G-5980)*

Fuji Silysia Chemical USA Ltd.................................... 252 413-0003
1215 Sugg Pkwy Greenville (27834) *(G-5981)*

Fujifilm Diosynth Biotechnolog.................................... 919 337-4400
6051 George Watts Hill Dr Durham (27709) *(G-4040)*

Fujifilm Dsynth Btchnlgies USA (DH).................................... 919 337-4400
101 J Morris Commons Ln Ste 300 Morrisville (27560) *(G-8977)*

Fulcher Elc Fayetteville Inc.................................... 910 483-7772
1744 Middle River Loop Fayetteville (28312) *(G-4604)*

Fulfords Restorations (PA).................................... 252 243-7727
320 Barnes St S Wilson (27893) *(G-12992)*

Full Throttle Fabrication LLC.................................... 910 770-1180
1047 Old Cribbtown Rd Chadbourn (28431) *(G-1519)*

Fuller Specialty Company Inc.................................... 336 226-3446
804 Bradley St Burlington (27215) *(G-1092)*

Fuller Wldg & Fabricators Inc.................................... 336 751-3712
980 Salisbury Rd Mocksville (27028) *(G-8363)*

Fulton Technology Corporation.................................... 828 657-1611
337 S Pea Ridge Rd Mooresboro (28114) *(G-8584)*

Fun Publications Inc.................................... 919 847-5263
12513 Birchfalls Dr Raleigh (27614) *(G-10123)*

Funball, Greensboro *Also Called: Intertech Corporation (G-5621)*

Funco Inc.................................... 704 788-3003
2583 Armentrout Dr Concord (28025) *(G-3367)*

Fundamental Playgrounds, Raleigh *Also Called: Brookhurst Associates (G-9961)*

Funder America Inc.................................... 336 751-3501
200 Funder Dr Mocksville (27028) *(G-8364)*

Funder America Inc (HQ).................................... 336 751-3501
200 Funder Dr Mocksville (27028) *(G-8365)*

Funny Bone EMB & Screening.................................... 704 663-4711
829 Plaza Ln Mooresville (28115) *(G-8668)*

Fuquay-Varina Baking Co Inc.................................... 919 557-2237
127 S Main St Fuquay Varina (27526) *(G-4882)*

Furiex Pharmaceuticals LLC.................................... 919 456-7800
3900 Paramount Pkwy Ste 150 Morrisville (27560) *(G-8978)*

Furnace Rebuilders Inc.................................... 704 483-4025
915 Dove Ct Denver (28037) *(G-3783)*

Furniture At Work.................................... 336 472-6619
6089 Kennedy Rd Trinity (27370) *(G-12114)*

Furniture City Color, High Point *Also Called: F C C LLC (G-6617)*

Furniture Company.................................... 910 686-1937
822 Santa Maria Ave Wilmington (28411) *(G-12781)*

Furniture Concepts.................................... 828 323-1590
909 10th St Ne Hickory (28601) *(G-6336)*

Furniture Fair Inc.................................... 910 455-4044
418 White St Jacksonville (28546) *(G-7124)*

Furniture Lab, Carrboro *Also Called: Rapp Productions Inc (G-1271)*

Furniture Tday Media Group LLC.................................... 336 605-0121
7025 Albert Pick Rd Ste 200 Greensboro (27409) *(G-5543)*

Furnlite, Fallston *Also Called: Furnlite Inc (G-4523)*

Furnlite Inc.................................... 704 538-3193
344 Wilson Rd Fallston (28042) *(G-4523)*

Fusion Incorporated.................................... 252 244-4300
276 Bailey Ln Vanceboro (28586) *(G-12216)*

Fusion Sport Inc.................................... 720 987-4403
122 E Parrish St Durham (27701) *(G-4041)*

Fusion Welding.................................... 508 320-3525
37 Brandon Ln Rocky Point (28457) *(G-10879)*

Futrell Precasting LLC.................................... 252 568-3481
3430 Old Pink Hill Rd Deep Run (28525) *(G-3732)*

Future Foam, High Point *Also Called: Ffnc Inc (G-6619)*

Future Foam Inc.................................... 336 861-8095
3803 Comanche Rd Archdale (27263) *(G-223)*

Future Foam Inc.................................... 336 885-4121
1300 Prospect St High Point (27260) *(G-6625)*

Fxi Inc.................................... 336 431-1171
2222 Surrett Dr High Point (27263) *(G-6626)*

G & E Investments Inc.................................... 704 395-2155
601 S Kings Dr Charlotte (28204) *(G-2183)*

G & E Software Inc.................................... 910 762-5608
1410 Commonwealth Dr Ste 102b Wilmington (28403) *(G-12782)*

G & G Enterprises.................................... 336 764-2493
210 Industrial Dr Ste 2 Clemmons (27012) *(G-3186)*

G & G Forest Products.................................... 704 539-5110
147 Lumber Dr Union Grove (28689) *(G-12185)*

G & G Lumber Company Inc.................................... 704 539-5110
179 Lumber Dr Harmony (28634) *(G-6098)*

G & G Management LLC.................................... 336 444-6271
1603 Battleground Ave Ste F Greensboro (27408) *(G-5544)*

G & G Moulding Inc.................................... 828 438-1112
801 N Green St Morganton (28655) *(G-8867)*

G & H Broadway Logging Inc.................................... 252 229-4594
145 Territorial Rd New Bern (28560) *(G-9369)*

G & J Machine Shop Inc (PA).................................... 336 668-0996
7800 Boeing Dr Greensboro (27409) *(G-5545)*

G & M Milling Co Inc.................................... 704 873-5758
4000 Taylorsville Hwy Statesville (28625) *(G-11701)*

G A Lankford Construction.................................... 828 254-2467
333 Old Nc 20 Hwy Alexander (28701) *(G-100)*

G and G Art and Frame, Morganton *Also Called: G & G Moulding Inc (G-8867)*

G Denver and Co LLC (HQ).................................... 704 896-4000
800 Beaty St Ste A Davidson (28036) *(G-3705)*

G Force South, Asheboro *Also Called: Longs Machine & Tool Inc (G-374)*

G M I, Pine Level *Also Called: General Metals Inc (G-9680)*

G P Kittrell & Son Inc.................................... 252 465-8929
1260 Nc Highway 32 N Corapeake (27926) *(G-3579)*

G R T Electronics, Raleigh *Also Called: Grt Electronics LLC (G-10150)*

G S I, Greensboro *Also Called: Graphic Systems Intl Inc (G-5574)*

G S Materials Inc.................................... 336 584-1745
1521 Huffman Mill Rd Burlington (27215) *(G-1093)*

G T Racing Heads Inc.................................... 336 905-7988
2735 Banner Whitehead Rd Sophia (27350) *(G-11489)*

G-4 Electric Inc.................................... 336 495-0500
4635 Us Highway 220 Bus N Asheboro (27203) *(G-358)*

G-Loc Brakes LLC.................................... 704 765-0213
503 Performance Rd Mooresville (28115) *(G-8669)*

G.T.a, Reidsville *Also Called: Global Textile Alliance Inc (G-10685)*

G1 Therapeutics, Durham *Also Called: G1 Therapeutics Inc (G-4042)*

G1 Therapeutics Inc.................................... 919 213-9835
700 Park Offices Dr Ste 200 Durham (27709) *(G-4042)*

2025 Harris North Carolina
Manufacturers Directory

(G-0000) Company's Geographic Section entry number

GA Communications Inc..704 360-1860
  136 Fairview Rd Ste 220 Mooresville (28117) *(G-8670)*

Gabden Entertainment, Statesville *Also Called: Gabden LLC (G-11702)*

Gabden LLC...704 451-8646
  232 N Center St Statesville (28677) *(G-11702)*

Gaines Motor Lines Inc (PA).....................................828 322-2000
  2349 13th Ave Sw Hickory (28602) *(G-6337)*

Gainsborough Baths LLC...336 357-0797
  41 Rogers Rd Lexington (27292) *(G-7691)*

Gainsbrough Specialist Bathing, Lexington *Also Called: Gainsborough Baths LLC (G-7691)*

Gainspan Corporation...408 627-6500
  3131 Rdu Center Dr Ste 135 Morrisville (27560) *(G-8979)*

Galaxy Electronics Inc...704 343-9881
  4233 Trailer Dr Charlotte (28269) *(G-2184)*

Galaxy Graphics Inc...704 724-9057
  1028 Brenham Ln Matthews (28105) *(G-8113)*

Galaxy Pressure Washing Inc....................................888 299-3129
  10810 Southern Loop Blvd Ste 12 Pineville (28134) *(G-9729)*

Gale Global Research Inc...910 795-8595
  7007 Robert Ruark Dr Leland (28451) *(G-7544)*

Gale Pacific, Charlotte *Also Called: Gale Pacific Usa Inc (G-2185)*

Gale Pacific Usa Inc (HQ)..407 772-7900
  5311 77 Center Dr Ste 150 Charlotte (28217) *(G-2185)*

Gallery G, Charlotte *Also Called: Artistic Images Inc (G-1699)*

Gallery of Cabinets, The, Winston Salem *Also Called: M T N of Pinellas Inc (G-13242)*

Gallimore Body Shop, Asheboro *Also Called: Gallimore Fmly Investments Inc (G-359)*

Gallimore Fmly Investments Inc................................336 625-5138
  1431 E Salisbury St Asheboro (27203) *(G-359)*

Gallo Lea Organics LLC..828 337-1037
  9 Inglewood Rd Asheville (28804) *(G-503)*

Gallolea Pizza Kits, Asheville *Also Called: Gallo Lea Organics LLC (G-503)*

Galloreecom..704 644-0978
  6211 Moss Bank Ct Charlotte (28262) *(G-2186)*

Galvan Industries Inc...704 455-5102
  7315 Galvan Way Harrisburg (28075) *(G-6108)*

Galvanizing Consultants Inc......................................336 603-4218
  687 Winners Pt Whitsett (27377) *(G-12607)*

Galvix Inc...925 434-6243
  1036 Canyon Shadows Ct Cary (27519) *(G-1363)*

Gamble Associates Inc..704 375-9301
  701 Johnson Rd Charlotte (28206) *(G-2187)*

Gamble Pallet & Whse Eqp Co, Charlotte *Also Called: Gamble Associates Inc (G-2187)*

Game Box Builders, Greensboro *Also Called: Game Box LLC (G-5546)*

Game Box LLC (PA)..866 241-1882
  143 Industrial Ave Greensboro (27406) *(G-5546)*

Gametime Imagewear, Lincolnton *Also Called: Jax Brothers Inc (G-7834)*

Gamma Js Inc...336 294-3838
  4101 Beechwood Dr Greensboro (27410) *(G-5547)*

Gamma Technologies Inc (PA)....................................919 319-5272
  125 International Dr Ste B Morrisville (27560) *(G-8980)*

Gannett Media Corp...828 649-1075
  58 Back St Marshall (28753) *(G-8080)*

Gannett Media Corp...919 467-1402
  107b Quail Fields Ct Morrisville (27560) *(G-8981)*

Garage Guys...704 494-8841
  4820 N Graham St Charlotte (28269) *(G-2188)*

Garage Shop LLC...980 500-0583
  4252 Burnwood Trl Denver (28037) *(G-3784)*

Garb Athletics, Statesville *Also Called: Badger Sportswear LLC (G-11666)*

Garden Metalwork...828 733-1077
  3640 Rd Newland (28657) *(G-9429)*

Gardner Asphalt Co..336 784-8924
  1664 S Martin Luther King Jr Dr Winston Salem (27107) *(G-13176)*

Gardner Gibson, Winston Salem *Also Called: Gardner Asphalt Co (G-13176)*

Gardner Glass Products, North Wilkesboro *Also Called: Gardner Glass Products Inc (G-9531)*

Gardner Glass Products Inc.......................................336 838-2151
  201 Elkin Hwy North Wilkesboro (28659) *(G-9530)*

Gardner Glass Products Inc (PA)...............................336 651-9300
  301 Elkin Hwy North Wilkesboro (28659) *(G-9531)*

Gardner Machinery Corporation................................704 372-3890
  700 N Summit Ave Charlotte (28216) *(G-2189)*

Garick LLC..704 455-6418
  8829 Rocky River Rd Harrisburg (28075) *(G-6109)*

Garland Apparel Group LLC.......................................646 647-2790
  120 S Church Ave Garland (28441) *(G-4908)*

Garland Farm Supply Inc (PA)...................................910 529-9731
  250 N Belgrade Ave Garland (28441) *(G-4909)*

Garland Heritage NC, Garland *Also Called: Garland Apparel Group LLC (G-4908)*

Garlock Bearings, Charlotte *Also Called: Coltec Industries Inc (G-1961)*

Garmin International Inc...919 337-0116
  100 Regency Forest Dr Cary (27518) *(G-1364)*

Garner Concrete Plant, Garner *Also Called: S T Wooten Corporation (G-4962)*

Garner Concrete Plant, Garner *Also Called: S T Wooten Corporation (G-4963)*

Garner Woodworks LLC..828 775-1790
  304 Patton Hill Rd Swannanoa (28778) *(G-11871)*

Garners Septic Tank Inc...919 718-5181
  8574 Turnpike Rd Raeford (28376) *(G-9838)*

Garnett Component Sales Inc....................................919 562-5158
  2824 Penfold Ln Wake Forest (27587) *(G-12277)*

Garrettcom Inc (HQ)..510 438-9071
  1113 N Main St Mooresville (28115) *(G-8671)*

Garris Grading and Paving Inc..................................252 749-1101
  5950 Gay Rd Farmville (27828) *(G-4529)*

Gary Forte Woodworking Inc.....................................704 780-0095
  1424 Forest Ln Monroe (28112) *(G-8491)*

Gary J Younts Machine Company..............................336 476-7930
  4786 Turnpike Ct Thomasville (27360) *(G-12028)*

Gary Tucker..919 837-5724
  12988 Nc 902 Hwy Bear Creek (27207) *(G-714)*

Gas Dept, Shelby *Also Called: City of Shelby (G-11318)*

Gas-Fired Products Inc (PA).......................................704 372-3485
  1700 Parker Dr Charlotte (28208) *(G-2190)*

Gasboy International Inc...336 547-5000
  7300 W Friendly Ave Greensboro (27410) *(G-5548)*

Gasp Inc...828 891-1628
  80 Emma Sharp Rd Ste 5 Fletcher (28732) *(G-4738)*

Gastex LLC...704 824-9861
  3051 Aberdeen Blvd Gastonia (28054) *(G-5050)*

Gaston County Dyeing Machine Company.................704 822-5000
  1310 Charles Raper Jonas Hwy Mount Holly (28120) *(G-9231)*

Gaston Fabrication, Mount Holly *Also Called: Gaston County Dyeing Machine Company (G-9231)*

Gaston Gazette LLP..704 869-1700
  1893 Remount Rd Gastonia (28056) *(G-5051)*

Gaston Indus Machining LLC.....................................704 825-3346
  125 Robinsons Park Dr Bessemer City (28016) *(G-820)*

Gaston Printing and Signs LLC..................................702 267-5633
  720 Wood Lily Dr Belmont (28012) *(G-753)*

Gaston Screen Printing Inc..704 399-0459
  8620 Wilkinson Blvd Charlotte (28214) *(G-2191)*

Gaston Systems Inc..704 263-6000
  200 S Main St Stanley (28164) *(G-11617)*

Gastonia...704 377-3687
  860 Summit Crossing Pl Gastonia (28054) *(G-5052)*

Gastonia Iron Works, Mount Holly *Also Called: Gastonia Ornamental Wldg Inc (G-9232)*

Gastonia Ornamental Wldg Inc..................................704 827-1146
  624 Legion Rd Mount Holly (28120) *(G-9232)*

Gate City Kitchens LLC...336 378-0870
  201 Creek Ridge Rd Ste D Greensboro (27406) *(G-5549)*

Gate Precast Company..919 603-1633
  3800 Oxford Loop Oxford (27565) *(G-9614)*

Gatehouse Media LLC...336 626-6103
  500 Sunset Ave Asheboro (27203) *(G-360)*

Gates County Index Shopper, Ahoskie *Also Called: Boone Newspapers Inc (G-43)*

Gates Custom Milling Inc...252 357-0116
  681 Nc Highway 37 S Gatesville (27938) *(G-5172)*

Gateway Campus..919 833-0096
  1306 Hillsborough St Raleigh (27605) *(G-10124)*

Gathering Place Pubg Co LLC....................................919 742-5850
  274 Lambert Chapel Rd Siler City (27344) *(G-11410)*

A
L
P
H
A
B
E
T
I
C

Gaylord Inc.. 704 694-2434
  4600 Lebanon Rd Ste K Charlotte (28227) *(G-2192)*

Gb Biosciences LLC (DH)............................ 336 632-6000
  410 S Swing Rd Greensboro (27409) *(G-5550)*

Gb Industries... 828 692-9163
  3005 Spartanburg Hwy East Flat Rock (28726) *(G-4331)*

Gb Labs LLC.. 919 606-7253
  794 American Way Lexington (27295) *(G-7692)*

Gbc Distribution LLC................................... 704 341-8473
  10123 Park Rd Charlotte (28210) *(G-2193)*

Gbf Inc.. 336 665-0205
  2427 Penny Rd High Point (27265) *(G-6627)*

Gc Valves, Charlotte *Also Called: General Control Equipment Co (G-2199)*

Gdais, Greensboro *Also Called: General Dynmics Mssion Systems (G-5553)*

GE, Charlotte *Also Called: GE Vernova International LLC (G-2194)*

GE, Charlotte *Also Called: General Electric Company (G-2200)*

GE, Durham *Also Called: GE Aircraft Engs Holdings Inc (G-4043)*

GE, Indian Trail *Also Called: General Electric Company (G-7082)*

GE, Mebane *Also Called: General Electric Company (G-8241)*

GE Aircraft Engs Holdings Inc..................... 919 361-4400
  3701 S Miami Blvd Durham (27703) *(G-4043)*

GE Aviation, Asheville *Also Called: GE Aviation Systems LLC (G-504)*

GE Aviation Systems LLC............................. 828 210-5076
  502 Sweeten Creek Industrial Park Asheville (28803) *(G-504)*

GE Vernova International LLC....................... 704 587-1300
  12037 Goodrich Dr Charlotte (28273) *(G-2194)*

Ge-Hitchi Nclear Enrgy Amrcas (HQ)............910 819-5000
  3901 Castle Hayne Rd Castle Hayne (28429) *(G-1500)*

Ge-Hitchi Nclear Enrgy Intl LL (HQ).............518 433-4338
  3901 Castle Hayne Rd Wilmington (28402) *(G-12783)*

Gea Intec LLC.. 919 433-0131
  4319 S Alston Ave Ste 105 Durham (27713) *(G-4044)*

Geami Ltd.. 919 654-7700
  3401 Gresham Lake Rd Ste 110 Raleigh (27615) *(G-10125)*

Gee-Lock, Mooresville *Also Called: G-Loc Brakes LLC (G-8669)*

Geecee, Smithfield *Also Called: Lampe & Malphrus Lumber Co (G-11453)*

Geeks On Call, Durham *Also Called: Comtech Group Inc (G-3986)*

Gefran Inc... 501 442-1521
  4209 Stuart Andrew Blvd Ste C Charlotte (28217) *(G-2195)*

Geiger International Inc................................ 828 324-6500
  218 Cline Park Dr Hildebran (28637) *(G-6850)*

Gelarto Inc.. 646 795-3505
  18 S Water St Wilmington (28401) *(G-12784)*

Gelder & Associates Inc.............................. 919 772-6895
  3901 Gelder Dr Raleigh (27603) *(G-10126)*

Gem Asset Acquisition LLC.......................... 919 851-0799
  200 Travis Park Cary (27511) *(G-1365)*

Gem Asset Acquisition LLC (PA)................... 704 225-3321
  1855 Lindbergh St Ste 500 Charlotte (28208) *(G-2196)*

Gem Asset Acquisition LLC.......................... 704 697-9577
  1955 Scott Futrell Dr Charlotte (28208) *(G-2197)*

Gem Asset Acquisition LLC.......................... 336 854-8200
  139 S Walnut Cir Greensboro (27409) *(G-5551)*

Gem Mountain, Spruce Pine *Also Called: Buchanan Gem Stone Mines Inc (G-11567)*

Gem-Dandy, Madison *Also Called: Madison Company Inc (G-7992)*

Gem-Dandy, Madison *Also Called: The Madison Company Inc (G-8001)*

Gems Frst Stop Med Sltions LLC.................. 336 965-9500
  5807 W Gate City Blvd Greensboro (27407) *(G-5552)*

Gemseal, Charlotte *Also Called: Gem Asset Acquisition LLC (G-2196)*

Gemseal Pavement Products (PA).................866 264-8273
  3700 Arco Corporate Dr Ste 425 Charlotte (28273) *(G-2198)*

Gemseal Pvments Pdts - Raleigh, Cary *Also Called: Gem Asset Acquisition LLC (G-1365)*

Gemseal Pvmnts Pdts - Chrlotte, Charlotte *Also Called: Gem Asset Acquisition LLC (G-2197)*

Gen Trak, Liberty *Also Called: Sfp Research Inc (G-7779)*

Genco... 919 963-4227
  130 Four Oaks Pkwy Four Oaks (27524) *(G-4811)*

Gene Franklin Brisson, Bladenboro *Also Called: Columbus Industries LLC (G-875)*

Genelect Services Inc.................................. 828 255-7999
  50 Glendale Ave Asheville (28803) *(G-505)*

Generac Distributors, Asheville *Also Called: Genelect Services Inc (G-505)*

General Contactor, Statesville *Also Called: Hillgray Innovations LLC (G-11712)*

General Contracting, Rocky Point *Also Called: Carlton Enterprizes LLC (G-10877)*

General Contractor, Greensboro *Also Called: Kcs Imprv & Cnstr Co Inc (G-5645)*

General Control Equipment Co....................... 704 588-0484
  456 Crompton St Charlotte (28273) *(G-2199)*

General Dynamics Corporation..................... 336 698-8571
  5440 Millstream Rd Ste W300 Mc Leansville (27301) *(G-8222)*

General Dynamics Worldwide, Fort Bragg *Also Called: General Dynmics Mssion Systems (G-4803)*

General Dynmics Mssion Systems................ 910 497-7900
  6812 Butner Rd And Letterman St Bldg 8 Fort Bragg (28310) *(G-4803)*

General Dynmics Mssion Systems................ 336 323-9752
  3801 Boren Dr Greensboro (27407) *(G-5553)*

General Dynmics Mssion Systems................ 336 698-8000
  5440 Millstream Rd Ste W300 Mc Leansville (27301) *(G-8223)*

General Electric Company............................. 704 561-5700
  4601 Park Rd Ste 400 Charlotte (28209) *(G-2200)*

General Electric Company............................. 704 821-8260
  171 Associate Ln Indian Trail (28079) *(G-7082)*

General Electric Company............................. 919 563-7445
  I-85 Buckhorn Rd Mebane (27302) *(G-8241)*

General Electric Company............................. 919 563-5561
  6801 Industrial Dr Mebane (27302) *(G-8242)*

General Electric Company............................. 910 675-5000
  3901 Castle Hayne Rd Wilmington (28401) *(G-12785)*

General Fertilizer Eqp Inc........................... 336 299-4711
  429 Edwardia Dr Greensboro (27409) *(G-5554)*

General Foam Plastics Corp.......................... 757 857-0153
  501 Daniel St Tarboro (27886) *(G-11927)*

General Glass International, Rockingham *Also Called: Ggi Glass Distributors Corp (G-10777)*

General Industries Inc................................. 919 751-1791
  3048 Thoroughfare Rd Goldsboro (27534) *(G-5215)*

General Machining Inc.................................. 336 342-2759
  37 W Plymouth Reidsville (27320) *(G-10684)*

General Mch Wldg of Burlington.................. 336 227-5400
  3304 Maple Ave Burlington (27215) *(G-1094)*

General Metals Inc....................................... 919 202-0100
  328 E Main St Pine Level (27568) *(G-9680)*

General Motor Repair & Svc Inc................... 336 292-1715
  2206 Westbrook St Greensboro (27407) *(G-5555)*

General Precision Svc.................................. 919 553-2604
  321 E Main St Clayton (27520) *(G-3149)*

General Refrigeration Company.................... 919 661-4727
  96 Shipwash Dr Garner (27529) *(G-4929)*

General Shale Brick, Wilmington *Also Called: General Shale Brick Inc (G-12786)*

General Shale Brick Inc............................... 704 937-7431
  1622 Longbranch Rd Grover (28073) *(G-6043)*

General Shale Brick Inc............................... 919 775-2121
  300 Brick Plant Rd Moncure (27559) *(G-8405)*

General Shale Brick Inc............................... 919 775-2121
  7101 Creedmoor Rd Raleigh (27613) *(G-10127)*

General Shale Brick Inc............................... 910 452-3498
  3750 Us Highway 421 N Wilmington (28401) *(G-12786)*

General Steel Drum LLC (PA)....................... 704 525-7160
  4500 South Blvd Charlotte (28209) *(G-2201)*

General Wood Preserving Co Inc.................. 910 371-3131
  1901 Wood Treatment Rd Ne Leland (28451) *(G-7545)*

Generations L LLC....................................... 336 835-3095
  220 Winston Rd Jonesville (28642) *(G-7196)*

Generics Bidco II LLC.................................. 980 389-2501
  3700 Woodpark Blvd Ste A Charlotte (28206) *(G-2202)*

Generics Bidco II LLC (DH)..........................704 612-8830
  3241 Woodpark Blvd Charlotte (28206) *(G-2203)*

Genesis Water Technologies Inc................... 704 360-5165
  10130 Perimeter Pkwy Ste 200 Charlotte (28216) *(G-2204)*

Genesys Cloud Services Inc......................... 317 872-3000
  4307 Emperor Blvd Ste 300 Durham (27703) *(G-4045)*

Genesys Technology Inc............................... 336 789-0763
  506 Bennett St Mount Airy (27030) *(G-9122)*

Genetic Medicine Building, Chapel Hill *Also Called: Viiv Healthcare Company (G-1590)*

Geneva Software Company Inc.......................... 336 275-8887
445 Dolley Madison Rd Ste 402 Greensboro (27410) *(G-5556)*

Genevieve M Brownlee.................................... 336 226-5260
2824 Anthony Rd Burlington (27215) *(G-1095)*

Genie Products, Brevard *Also Called: Grey Holdings Inc (G-970)*

Genixus, Concord *Also Called: Genixus Corp (G-3368)*

Genixus, Kannapolis *Also Called: Genixus Corp (G-7209)*

Genixus Corp... 877 436-4987
4715 Corporate Dr Nw Ste 100 Concord (28027) *(G-3368)*

Genixus Corp (PA).. 877 436-4987
150 N Research Campus Dr Kannapolis (28081) *(G-7209)*

Genpak, Charlotte *Also Called: Genpak LLC (G-2206)*

Genpak, Charlotte *Also Called: Great Pacific Entps US Inc (G-2235)*

Genpak Industries Inc................................... 518 798-9511
10601 Westlake Dr Charlotte (28273) *(G-2205)*

Genpak LLC (DH)... 800 626-6695
10601 Westlake Dr Charlotte (28273) *(G-2206)*

Genpak LLC.. 704 588-6202
1001 Westinghouse Blvd Charlotte (28273) *(G-2207)*

Gentle Machine and Tool Inc........................... 336 492-5055
2716 Us Highway 601 N Mocksville (27028) *(G-8366)*

Gentry Mills Inc... 704 983-5555
2035 Kingsley Dr Albemarle (28001) *(G-74)*

Gentry Plastics Inc...................................... 704 864-4300
1808 Bradbury Ct Gastonia (28052) *(G-5053)*

Gentrys Cabnt Doors..................................... 336 957-8787
2872 Austin Little Mtn Rd Roaring River (28669) *(G-10749)*

Geo Plastics... 704 588-8585
3801 Westinghouse Commons Dr Charlotte (28273) *(G-2208)*

Geo Specialty Chemicals Inc.......................... 252 793-2121
Main St Extension Plymouth (27962) *(G-9804)*

Geo-Lin Inc... 336 884-0648
107 Hillstone Dr Jamestown (27282) *(G-7162)*

Geographics Screenprinting Inc....................... 704 357-3300
3622 Green Park Cir Charlotte (28217) *(G-2209)*

George Clinical Inc....................................... 919 789-2022
120 Penmarc Dr Raleigh (27603) *(G-10128)*

George F Wlson Wldg Fbrication....................... 828 262-1668
1777 Nc Highway 194 N Boone (28607) *(G-916)*

George P Gatling Logging................................ 252 465-8983
223 Nc Highway 32 S Sunbury (27979) *(G-11847)*

George W Dahl Company Inc............................. 336 668-4444
8439 Triad Dr Greensboro (27409) *(G-5557)*

George's Bbq Sauce, Nashville *Also Called: Georges Sauces LLC (G-9320)*

Georges Sauces LLC...................................... 252 459-3084
1173 Womble Rd Nashville (27856) *(G-9320)*

Georgia Poultry Equipment Co, Newton Grove *Also Called: Hog Slat Incorporated (G-9514)*

Georgia Pratt Box Inc.................................... 919 872-3007
5620 Departure Dr Raleigh (27616) *(G-10129)*

Georgia-Carolina Quarries Inc (PA)................... 336 786-6978
1700 Fancy Gap Rd Mount Airy (27030) *(G-9123)*

Georgia-Pacific, Asheboro *Also Called: Georgia-Pacific LLC (G-361)*

Georgia-Pacific, Dudley *Also Called: Georgia-Pacific LLC (G-3836)*

Georgia-Pacific, Dudley *Also Called: Georgia-Pacific LLC (G-3837)*

Georgia-Pacific, Middleburg *Also Called: Georgia-Pacific LLC (G-8271)*

Georgia-Pacific LLC...................................... 336 629-2151
200 Mcdowell Rd Asheboro (27205) *(G-361)*

Georgia-Pacific LLC...................................... 919 580-1078
139 Brewington Dr Dudley (28333) *(G-3836)*

Georgia-Pacific LLC...................................... 919 736-2722
2457b Old Mt Olive Hwy Dudley (28333) *(G-3837)*

Georgia-Pacific LLC...................................... 252 438-2238
Hwy 158 And Interstate 85 Middleburg (27556) *(G-8271)*

Georgia-Pacific LLC...................................... 910 642-5041
1980 Georgia Pacific Rd Whiteville (28472) *(G-12581)*

Geosonics Inc.. 919 790-9500
5874 Faringdon Pl Ste 100 Raleigh (27609) *(G-10130)*

Geosurfaces Southeast Inc.............................. 704 660-3000
150 River Park Rd Mooresville (28117) *(G-8672)*

Geotrak Incorporated.................................... 919 303-1467
2521 Schieffelin Rd Ste 136 Apex (27502) *(G-157)*

Gerald Hartsoe... 336 498-3233
3109 Tom Brown Rd Randleman (27317) *(G-10648)*

Gerald's Yarns, Lincolnton *Also Called: Marilyn Cook (G-7842)*

Gerbing's Heated Clothing, Greensboro *Also Called: Gerbings LLC (G-5558)*

Gerbings LLC.. 800 646-5916
816 S Elm St Ste D Greensboro (27406) *(G-5558)*

Gerdau Ameristeel US Inc............................... 704 596-0361
6601 Lakeview Rd Charlotte (28269) *(G-2210)*

Gerdau Ameristeel US Inc............................... 919 833-9737
2126 Garner Rd Raleigh (27610) *(G-10131)*

Gerresheimer Glass Inc.................................. 828 433-5000
114 Wamsutta Mill Rd Morganton (28655) *(G-8868)*

Gerringer Enterprises.................................... 336 227-6535
180 Spoon Dr Burlington (27217) *(G-1096)*

Gersan Industries Incorporated....................... 336 886-5455
607 Blake Ave High Point (27260) *(G-6628)*

Gerson & Gerson Inc..................................... 252 235-2441
10601 E Finch Ave Middlesex (27557) *(G-8276)*

Ges Industries (PA)....................................... 252 430-8851
78 Walter Grissom Rd Kittrell (27544) *(G-7441)*

Gesipa Fasteners Usa Inc............................... 336 751-1555
126 Quality Dr Mocksville (27028) *(G-8367)*

Gesipa Fasteners Usa Inc (PA)......................... 609 208-1740
126 Quality Dr Mocksville (27028) *(G-8368)*

Get Custom Print.. 336 682-3891
504 Edgewood St Kernersville (27284) *(G-7275)*

Getbridge LLC... 919 645-2800
434 Fayetteville St Fl 9 Raleigh (27601) *(G-10132)*

Gfl Environmental Company, Raleigh *Also Called: Waste Industries Usa LLC (G-10598)*

Gfsi Holdings LLC (HQ)..................................336 519-8080
9700 Commerce Pkwy Winston Salem (27105) *(G-13177)*

Ggi Glass Distributors Corp............................ 910 895-2022
208 Silver Grove Church Rd Rockingham (28379) *(G-10777)*

Ggr, Leland *Also Called: Gale Global Research Inc (G-7544)*

Ghx Industrial LLC....................................... 336 996-7271
1295 S Park Dr Kernersville (27284) *(G-7276)*

Gibbs Machine Company Incorporated............... 336 856-1907
2012 Fairfax Rd Greensboro (27407) *(G-5559)*

Gibraltar Packaging Inc................................. 910 439-6137
6530 Franz Warner Pkwy Whitsett (27377) *(G-12608)*

Gibson Accumulator LLC................................. 336 449-4753
2208 Airpark Rd Burlington (27215) *(G-1097)*

Gibson Mill Ciderworks, Concord *Also Called: Cabarrus Brewing Company LLC (G-3326)*

Gifted Hands Styling Salon............................. 828 781-2781
1316 Us Highway 70 Sw Hickory (28602) *(G-6338)*

Gigabeam Corporation................................... 919 206-4426
4021 Stirrup Creek Dr Ste 400 Durham (27703) *(G-4046)*

Gik Inc.. 919 872-9498
1801 Saint Albans Dr Ste B Raleigh (27609) *(G-10133)*

Gilbarco Inc (HQ)... 336 547-5000
7300 W Friendly Ave Greensboro (27410) *(G-5560)*

Gilbarco Veeder-Root, Greensboro *Also Called: Gilbarco Inc (G-5560)*

Gildan Activewear (eden) Inc.......................... 336 623-9555
602 E Meadow Rd Eden (27288) *(G-4347)*

Gilead Sciences Inc...................................... 650 574-3000
305 Church At North Hills St Raleigh (27609) *(G-10134)*

Gilero LLC (PA).. 919 595-8220
4319 S Alston Ave Ste 100 Durham (27713) *(G-4047)*

Giles Chemical Corporation............................. 828 452-4784
75 Giles Pl Waynesville (28786) *(G-12458)*

Giles Chemical Corporation (HQ)......................828 452-4784
102 Commerce St Waynesville (28786) *(G-12459)*

Giles Chemical Industries, Waynesville *Also Called: Giles Chemical Corporation (G-12459)*

Gillam & Mason Inc....................................... 252 356-2874
1835 Nc 45 Highway N Cofield (27922) *(G-3266)*

Gillespies Fabrication Design, Salisbury *Also Called: Gillespies Fbrction Design Inc (G-11056)*

Gillespies Fbrction Design Inc......................... 704 636-2349
110 Hidden Creek Dr Salisbury (28147) *(G-11056)*

Gilley Printers Inc.. 910 295-6317
22 Rattlesnake Trl Pinehurst (28374) *(G-9692)*

Gillikin Marine Railways Inc................................252 726-7284
195 Morgan Rd Beaufort (28516) *(G-728)*

Gilmore Globl Lgstics Svcs Inc.............................919 277-2700
101 Southcenter Ct Ste 100-E Morrisville (27560) *(G-8982)*

Ginas Processing & Prtg Ctr..................................910 476-0037
114 Harris Ln Raeford (28376) *(G-9839)*

Ginger Supreme Inc...919 812-8986
4925 Lett Rd Apex (27539) *(G-158)*

Gingers Revenge LLC..828 505-2462
829 Riverside Dr Ste 100 Asheville (28801) *(G-506)*

Gingras Sleep Medicine PA..................................704 944-0562
6207 Park South Dr Ste 101 Charlotte (28210) *(G-2211)*

Ginkgo Print Studio LLC......................................828 275-6300
1 Grace Ave Asheville (28804) *(G-507)*

Ginkgo Stone LLC...704 451-8678
5340 Camilla Dr Charlotte (28226) *(G-2212)*

Ginny O s Inc..919 816-7276
946 Penny Branch Rd Warsaw (28398) *(G-12360)*

Gitsum Precision LLC..336 453-3998
390 Duggins Rd Stoneville (27048) *(G-11821)*

GK Software USA, Raleigh Also Called: GK Software Usa Inc *(G-10135)*

GK Software Usa Inc..984 255-7995
9121 Anson Way Ste 150 Raleigh (27615) *(G-10135)*

GKN Automotive, Newton Also Called: GKN Driveline Newton LLC *(G-9466)*

GKN Automotive, Newton Also Called: GKN Driveline Newton LLC *(G-9467)*

GKN Automotive Grinding Whee, Mebane Also Called: GKN Driveline North Amer Inc
(G-8244)

GKN Dna Inc...919 304-7378
1067 Trollingwood Hawflds Rd Mebane (27302) *(G-8243)*

GKN Driveline Newton LLC (HQ)............................828 428-3711
1848 Gkn Way Newton (28658) *(G-9466)*

GKN Driveline Newton LLC....................................828 428-5292
2900 S Us 321 Hwy Newton (28658) *(G-9467)*

GKN Driveline North Amer Inc...............................919 304-7200
1067 Trollingwood Hawflds Rd Mebane (27302) *(G-8244)*

GKN Driveline North Amer Inc...............................919 708-4500
4901 Womack Rd Sanford (27330) *(G-11184)*

GKN Driveline North Amer Inc...............................336 364-6200
6400 Durham Rd Timberlake (27583) *(G-12100)*

GKN Driveline Roxboro, Timberlake Also Called: GKN Driveline North Amer Inc *(G-12100)*

GKN Sinter Metals LLC...828 464-0642
407 Thornburg Dr Se Conover (28613) *(G-3524)*

GKN Sinter Metals - Conover, Conover Also Called: GKN Sinter Metals LLC *(G-3524)*

Glacier Forestry Inc..704 902-2594
135 Jocelyn Ln Apt 108 Mooresville (28117) *(G-8673)*

Gladiator Enterprises Inc.....................................336 944-6932
5505 Weslo Willow Dr Greensboro (27409) *(G-5561)*

Gladsons Logging LLC...252 670-8813
8902 Nc Highway 306 S Aurora (27806) *(G-642)*

Glam Gal, Castle Hayne Also Called: AC Valor Reyes LLC *(G-1493)*

Glaser Designs Inc...415 552-3188
2825 Seclusion Ct Apt A Raleigh (27612) *(G-10136)*

Glass & Window Warehouse, Siler City Also Called: Orare Inc *(G-11422)*

Glass Jug...919 818-6907
5410 Nc Highway 55 Ste V Durham (27713) *(G-4048)*

Glass Jug LLC..919 813-0135
5410 Nc Highway 55 Ste V Durham (27713) *(G-4049)*

Glass Unlimited, High Point Also Called: Glass Unlimited High Point Inc *(G-6629)*

Glass Unlimited High Point Inc.............................336 889-4551
2149 Brevard Rd High Point (27263) *(G-6629)*

Glass Works of Hickory Inc..................................828 322-2122
1040 Old Lenoir Rd Ste B Hickory (28601) *(G-6339)*

Glatfelter Composite Fibers NA, Pisgah Forest Also Called: Glatfelter Corporation *(G-9769)*

Glatfelter Corporation...828 877-2110
2795 King Rd Pisgah Forest (28768) *(G-9769)*

Glatfelter Inds Asheville Inc.................................828 670-0041
1265 Sand Hill Rd Candler (28715) *(G-1226)*

Glatfelter Mt Holly LLC..704 812-2299
100 Buckeye Dr Mount Holly (28120) *(G-9233)*

Glatflter Sntara Old Hckry Inc (DH).......................615 526-2100
4350 Congress St Ste 600 Charlotte (28209) *(G-2213)*

Glaxosmithkline, Durham Also Called: Glaxosmithkline LLC *(G-4051)*

Glaxosmithkline, Zebulon Also Called: Glaxosmithkline LLC *(G-13509)*

Glaxosmithkline LLC...704 962-5786
8625 Covedale Crossings Cir Cornelius (28031) *(G-3602)*

Glaxosmithkline LLC...919 483-5302
5 3313 Gsk Co Durham (27713) *(G-4050)*

Glaxosmithkline LLC...919 483-2100
410 Blackwell St Durham (27701) *(G-4051)*

Glaxosmithkline LLC...252 315-9774
406 Blackwell St Durham (27701) *(G-4052)*

Glaxosmithkline LLC...919 483-2100
2512 S Tricenter Blvd Durham (27713) *(G-4053)*

Glaxosmithkline LLC...336 392-3058
3408 Old Barn Rd Greensboro (27410) *(G-5562)*

Glaxosmithkline LLC...919 628-3630
7030 Kit Creek Rd Morrisville (27560) *(G-8983)*

Glaxosmithkline LLC...919 483-5006
52069 Five Moore Dr Research Triangle Pa (27709) *(G-10710)*

Glaxosmithkline LLC...919 269-5000
1011 N Arendell Ave Zebulon (27597) *(G-13509)*

Glaxosmithkline Services Inc................................919 483-2100
5 Moore Dr Durham (27709) *(G-4054)*

Glemco LLC...866 619-6707
1624 Northside Dr Statesville (28625) *(G-11703)*

Glemco Parts, Statesville Also Called: Glemco LLC *(G-11703)*

Glen Raven Inc...336 227-6211
3726 Altamahaw Union Ridge Rd Altamahaw (27202) *(G-103)*

Glen Raven Inc (PA)..336 227-6211
192 Glen Raven Rd Burlington (27217) *(G-1098)*

Glen Raven Mtl Solutions LLC...............................828 682-2142
73 E Us Highway 19e Burnsville (28714) *(G-1185)*

Glen Rven Tchnical Fabrics LLC (HQ).....................336 227-6211
1831 N Park Ave Burlington (27217) *(G-1099)*

Glen Rven Tchnical Fabrics LLC............................336 229-5576
1821 N Park Ave Burlington (27217) *(G-1100)*

Glen Touch Division, Altamahaw Also Called: Glen Raven Inc *(G-103)*

Glendon Pyrophllite Rock Quar, Sanford Also Called: Glendon Pyrophyllite Inc *(G-11185)*

Glendon Pyrophyllite Inc......................................919 464-5243
1789 Clarence Mckeithen Rd Sanford (27330) *(G-11185)*

Glenmark Phrmceuticals Inc USA...........................704 218-2600
4147 Goldmine Rd Monroe (28110) *(G-8492)*

Glenn Lumber Company Inc..................................704 434-7873
145 Rockford Rd Shelby (28152) *(G-11338)*

Glenn Mauser Company Inc..................................828 464-8996
3240 20th Ave Se Newton (28658) *(G-9468)*

Glenn Trexler & Sons Log Inc...............................704 694-5644
1095 Bethel Rd Wadesboro (28170) *(G-12242)*

Glenraven.com, Burlington Also Called: Glen Raven Inc *(G-1098)*

Glenraven.com, Burlington Also Called: Glen Rven Tchnical Fabrics LLC *(G-1099)*

Glenwood Village Exxon, Raleigh Also Called: Wmb of Wake County Inc *(G-10612)*

GLG Corporation (PA)..336 784-0396
3410 Thomasville Rd Winston Salem (27107) *(G-13178)*

Glh Systems & Controls Inc.................................980 581-1304
4667 Love Mill Rd Stanfield (28163) *(G-11606)*

Glia Beauty, Raleigh Also Called: Cryogen LLC *(G-10024)*

Glidden Professional Paint Ctr, Fayetteville Also Called: PPG Architectural Finishes Inc
(G-4655)

Glidden Professional Paint Ctr, Gastonia Also Called: PPG Architectural Finishes Inc
(G-5123)

Glidden Professional Paint Ctr, Greensboro Also Called: PPG Architectural Finishes Inc
(G-5754)

Glidden Professional Paint Ctr, Matthews Also Called: PPG Architectural Finishes Inc
(G-8141)

Glidden Professional Paint Ctr, Mooresville Also Called: PPG Architectural Finishes Inc
(G-8751)

Glidden Professional Paint Ctr, Morganton Also Called: PPG Architectural Finishes Inc
(G-8888)

Glidden Professional Paint Ctr, Raleigh Also Called: PPG Architectural Finishes Inc *(G-10383)*

Glidden Professional Paint Ctr, Raleigh Also Called: PPG Architectural Finishes Inc *(G-10384)*

Glidden Professional Paint Ctr, Salisbury Also Called: PPG Architectural Finishes Inc
(G-11105)

Glitzbybritt, Greensboro *Also Called: Brittany Smith (G-5407)*

Global Bioprotect LLC.. 336 861-0162
2714 Uwharrie Rd High Point (27263) *(G-6630)*

Global Dominion Enterprise, Charlotte *Also Called: Reginald DWayne Dillard (G-2704)*

Global Door Controls, Charlotte *Also Called: Imperial Usa Ltd (G-2316)*

Global Ecosciences Inc....................................... 252 631-6266
7723 Benthill Ct Wake Forest (27587) *(G-12278)*

Global Emssons Systems Inc-USA......................... 704 585-8490
158 Houston Rd Troutman (28166) *(G-12139)*

Global Filter Source LLC..................................... 919 571-4945
6212 Westgate Rd Ste A Raleigh (27617) *(G-10137)*

Global Forming Tech Ltd...................................... 919 234-1384
801 Cascade Pointe Ln Ste 102 Cary (27513) *(G-1366)*

Global Graphics Solution, Thomasville *Also Called: Wright of Thomasville Inc (G-12091)*

Global Laser Enrichment LLC................................ 910 819-7255
4110 Us Highway 421 N # 100 Wilmington (28401) *(G-12787)*

Global Nuclear Fuel LLC...................................... 910 819-6181
3901 Castle Hayne Rd Wilmington (28401) *(G-12788)*

Global Nuclear Fuel-Americas LLC (HQ).................. 910 819-5950
3901 Castle Hayne Rd Castle Hayne (28429) *(G-1501)*

Global Packaging Inc... 610 666-1608
106 Marks Creek Ln Hamlet (28345) *(G-6056)*

Global Plasma Solutions Inc................................. 980 279-5622
3101 Yorkmont Rd Ste 400 Charlotte (28208) *(G-2214)*

Global Products & Mfg Svcs Inc............................ 360 870-9876
6000 Fairview Rd Ste 1200 Charlotte (28210) *(G-2215)*

Global Products LLC.. 336 227-7327
144 Industrial Ave Greensboro (27406) *(G-5563)*

Global Resource Corporation................................ 919 972-7803
9400 Globe Center Dr Ste 101 Morrisville (27560) *(G-8984)*

Global Resource NC Inc.. 910 793-4770
1001 Broomsedge Ter Wilmington (28412) *(G-12789)*

Global Sensors LLC... 704 827-4331
63 Mcadenville Rd Belmont (28012) *(G-754)*

Global Skyware, Smithfield *Also Called: Raven Antenna Systems Inc (G-11461)*

Global Software LLC.. 919 872-7800
3200 Atlantic Ave Ste 200 Raleigh (27604) *(G-10138)*

GLOBAL SOFTWARE, LLC, Raleigh *Also Called: Global Software LLC (G-10138)*

Global Stone Impex LLC....................................... 336 609-1113
5088 Bartholomews Ln Greensboro (27407) *(G-5564)*

Global Synergy Group Inc..................................... 704 254-9886
13663 Providence Rd Ste 370 Matthews (28104) *(G-8172)*

Global Textile Alliance Inc (PA)............................. 336 347-7601
2361 Holiday Loop Reidsville (27320) *(G-10685)*

Global Veneer Sales Inc....................................... 336 885-5061
112 Hodgin St High Point (27262) *(G-6631)*

Glover Corporation Inc... 919 821-5535
2401 Atlantic Ave Raleigh (27604) *(G-10139)*

Glover Materials Inc (PA)...................................... 252 536-2660
4493 Us Highway 301 Pleasant Hill (27866) *(G-9797)*

Glover Printing Company, Raleigh *Also Called: Glover Corporation Inc (G-10139)*

Glovers Welding LLC.. 252 586-7692
638 Oak Grove Church Rd Littleton (27850) *(G-7886)*

Gloves-Online Inc... 919 468-4244
231 E Johnson St Ste K Cary (27513) *(G-1367)*

GLS Products LLC (PA)... 704 334-2425
1209 Lilac Rd Charlotte (28209) *(G-2216)*

Glycotech Inc... 910 371-2234
2271 Andrew Jackson Hwy Ne Leland (28451) *(G-7546)*

GM Defense LLC.. 800 462-8782
4280 Defender Way Nw Concord (28027) *(G-3369)*

GM Nameplate NC Division, Monroe *Also Called: Boyd Gmn Inc (G-8446)*

Gmd Logging Inc... 704 985-5460
44100 Dennis Rd Albemarle (28001) *(G-75)*

Gmg Group LLC... 252 441-8374
115 W Saint Clair St Kill Devil Hills (27948) *(G-7317)*

Gmg International Inc (DH).................................... 800 845-6051
3436 Toringdon Way Ste 100 Charlotte (28277) *(G-2217)*

GNB Ventures LLC... 704 488-4468
1800 Associates Ln Charlotte (28217) *(G-2218)*

GNH Pharmaceuticals USA LLC............................. 704 585-8769
1235 East Blvd Ste E499 Charlotte (28203) *(G-2219)*

GNT Usa LLC... 914 524-0600
One Exberry Dr Dallas (28034) *(G-3673)*

Go Ask Erin LLC.. 336 747-3777
328 Virgilina Rd Roxboro (27573) *(G-10927)*

Go Energies LLC.. 877 712-5999
1410 Commonwealth Dr Ste 102b Wilmington (28403) *(G-12790)*

Go Energies Holdings Inc (PA)............................... 910 762-5802
1410 Commonwealth Dr Ste 102b Wilmington (28403) *(G-12791)*

Go Ev and Go Green Corp..................................... 704 327-9040
9711 David Taylor Dr Apt 106 Charlotte (28262) *(G-2220)*

Go For Green Fleet Svcs LLC................................. 803 306-3683
1911 Greymouth Rd Apt 305 Charlotte (28262) *(G-2221)*

Go Gloves, Cary *Also Called: Gloves-Online Inc (G-1367)*

Go Green Miracle Balm... 630 209-0226
17810 Half Moon Ln Apt A Cornelius (28031) *(G-3603)*

Go Green Plumbing, Greensboro *Also Called: Go Green Services LLC (G-5565)*

Go Green Racing... 916 295-2621
409 Performance Rd Mooresville (28115) *(G-8674)*

Go Green Services LLC... 336 252-2999
300 Pomona Dr Greensboro (27407) *(G-5565)*

Go Postal In Boone Inc... 828 262-0027
207 New Market Ctr Boone (28607) *(G-917)*

Goaero LLC.. 815 713-1190
7680 Airline Rd Ste C Greensboro (27409) *(G-5566)*

Goals In Service LLC.. 919 440-2656
103 Richard Dupree Ln Seven Springs (28578) *(G-11297)*

Gocaissoncom.. 336 454-4610
3210 Dillon Rd Jamestown (27282) *(G-7163)*

God's Son Plumbing Repair, Wilson *Also Called: Gods Son Plumbing Inc (G-12993)*

Godfrey Group, Cary *Also Called: Portable Displays LLC (G-1424)*

Godfrey Lumber Company Inc (PA)......................... 704 872-6366
1715 Amity Hill Rd Statesville (28677) *(G-11704)*

Gods Son Plumbing Inc... 252 299-0983
1711 Roxbury Dr N Wilson (27893) *(G-12993)*

Godwin Manufacturing Co Inc (PA)......................... 910 897-4995
17666 Us 421 S Dunn (28334) *(G-3858)*

Goembel Inc... 919 303-0485
7303 Vanclaybon Rd Apex (27523) *(G-159)*

Goffstar Inc.. 704 895-3878
5015 W W T Harris Blvd Ste F Charlotte (28269) *(G-2222)*

Gogofiber, Waynesville *Also Called: Edge Broadband Solutions LLC (G-12457)*

Goins Signs Inc... 336 427-5783
1811 Victory Hill Church Rd Stoneville (27048) *(G-11822)*

Gold Bond Building Pdts LLC (HQ).......................... 704 365-7300
2001 Rexford Rd Charlotte (28211) *(G-2223)*

Gold Bond Building Pdts LLC................................. 910 799-3954
838 Sunnyvale Dr Wilmington (28412) *(G-12792)*

Gold Creek Inc.. 336 468-4495
3441 Lone Hickory Rd Hamptonville (27020) *(G-6084)*

Gold Leaf Publishers, Raleigh *Also Called: News and Observer Pubg Co (G-10331)*

Gold Medal North Carolina Il................................. 336 665-4997
410 Gallimore Dairy Rd Ste G Greensboro (27409) *(G-5567)*

Gold Medal Products Co.. 336 665-4997
410 Gallimore Dairy Rd Ste G Greensboro (27409) *(G-5568)*

Gold Medal Products-Carolina, Greensboro *Also Called: Gold Medal Products Co (G-5568)*

Gold Refinery... 336 501-2977
2177 Scott Rd Browns Summit (27214) *(G-996)*

Gold Refinery... 336 471-4817
3954 Huttons Lake Ct High Point (27265) *(G-6632)*

Gold Toe Stores Inc (DH)...................................... 828 464-0751
514 W 21st St Newton (28658) *(G-9469)*

Golden Grove Inc... 910 293-4209
364 W Park Dr Warsaw (28398) *(G-12361)*

Golden Grove USA, Mount Olive *Also Called: Carolina Nut Inc (G-9251)*

Golden Pop Shop LLC... 704 236-9455
9805 Statesville Rd Ste 6012 Charlotte (28269) *(G-2224)*

Golden Rctangle Enteprises Inc............................. 828 389-3336
2966 Nc 69 Hayesville (28904) *(G-6141)*

Golden Valley Mfg Plant Div, Bostic *Also Called: Milliken & Company (G-963)*

Golding Farms, Winston Salem *Also Called: Golding Farms Foods Inc (G-13179)*

Golding Farms Foods Inc (PA).. 336 766-6161
  6061 Gun Club Rd Winston Salem (27103) *(G-13179)*

Goldmine Software.. 704 944-3579
  10130 Mallard Creek Rd Ste 300 Charlotte (28262) *(G-2225)*

Goldsboro Milling Company.. 919 778-3130
  938 Millers Chapel Rd Goldsboro (27534) *(G-5216)*

Goldsboro Neon Sign Co Inc.. 919 735-2035
  712 N George St Goldsboro (27530) *(G-5217)*

Goldsboro News-Argus, Goldsboro *Also Called: Wayne Printing Company Inc (G-5252)*

Goldsboro Strter Altrntor Svc.. 919 735-6745
  105 E Oak St Goldsboro (27530) *(G-5218)*

Goldsmith By Rudi Ltd.. 828 693-1030
  434 N Main St Hendersonville (28792) *(G-6210)*

Goldtoemoretz LLC... 828 464-0751
  514 W 21st St Newton (28658) *(G-9470)*

Golf Associates, Asheville *Also Called: Pinkston Properties LLC (G-575)*

Golf Associates Advertising Co....................................... 828 252-6544
  91 Westside Dr Asheville (28806) *(G-508)*

Golf Associates Score Card Co, Asheville *Also Called: Golf Associates Advertising Co (G-508)*

Golf Pride, Pinehurst *Also Called: Eaton Corporation (G-9691)*

Golf Shop.. 704 636-7070
  747 Club Dr Salisbury (28144) *(G-11057)*

Golfstar Technology LLC.. 910 420-3122
  75 Lakewood Dr Pinehurst (28374) *(G-9693)*

Gonzalez Welding Inc.. 336 270-8179
  817 E Parker St Graham (27253) *(G-5269)*

Good Earth Ministries.. 828 287-9826
  156 River Ridge Pkwy Rutherfordton (28139) *(G-10983)*

Good Grief Marketing LLC.. 336 989-1984
  2609 E Market St Greensboro (27401) *(G-5569)*

Good Measure Graphics, Kill Devil Hills *Also Called: Gmg Group LLC (G-7317)*

Good Vibrationz LLC.. 919 820-3084
  1020 Red Banks Rd Ste 150 Greenville (27858) *(G-5982)*

Good Will Catholic Media LLC... 704 731-0651
  13315 Carowinds Blvd Ste 2 Charlotte (28273) *(G-2226)*

Good Will Publishers Inc (PA)... 704 853-3237
  1520 S York Rd Gastonia (28052) *(G-5054)*

Goodberry Creamery Inc (PA)... 919 878-8870
  305 Capcom Ave Wake Forest (27587) *(G-12279)*

Goodberrys Creamery Rest, Wake Forest *Also Called: Goodberry Creamery Inc (G-12279)*

Gooder Grafix Inc... 828 349-4097
  522 E Main St Franklin (28734) *(G-4830)*

Goodman Millwork Inc... 704 633-2421
  201 Lumber St Salisbury (28144) *(G-11058)*

Goodnight Brothers Prod Co Inc (PA).............................. 828 264-8892
  372 Industrial Park Dr Boone (28607) *(G-918)*

Goodrich Corporation (HQ).. 704 423-7000
  2730 W Tyvola Rd Charlotte (28217) *(G-2227)*

Goodrich Corporation.. 704 282-2500
  4115 Corporate Center Dr Monroe (28110) *(G-8493)*

Goodrich Corporation.. 704 282-2500
  4115 Corporate Center Dr Monroe (28110) *(G-8494)*

Goodrich Fuel Utility Systems, Charlotte *Also Called: Rtx Corporation (G-2740)*

Goodson S All Terrain Log Inc.. 910 347-7919
  173 Goodson Trl Jacksonville (28546) *(G-7125)*

Goodyear, Holly Springs *Also Called: Goodyear Tire & Rubber Company (G-6903)*

Goodyear, Mebane *Also Called: Goodyear Tire & Rubber Company (G-8245)*

Goodyear, Oxford *Also Called: Perry Brothers Tire Svc Inc (G-9623)*

Goodyear, Statesville *Also Called: Goodyear Tire & Rubber Company (G-11705)*

Goodyear, Winston Salem *Also Called: Goodyear Tire & Rubber Company (G-13180)*

Goodyear Tire & Rubber Company.................................. 910 488-9295
  6650 Ramsey St Fayetteville (28311) *(G-4605)*

Goodyear Tire & Rubber Company.................................. 919 552-9340
  932 N Main St Holly Springs (27540) *(G-6903)*

Goodyear Tire & Rubber Company.................................. 984 983-0161
  1352 Trollingwood Hawflds Rd Mebane (27302) *(G-8245)*

Goodyear Tire & Rubber Company.................................. 704 928-4500
  108 Business Park Dr Statesville (28677) *(G-11705)*

Goodyear Tire & Rubber Company.................................. 336 794-0035
  130 Country Club Ln Winston Salem (27104) *(G-13180)*

Goose and Monkey Brewhouse LLC................................ 336 239-0206
  401 S Railroad St Lexington (27292) *(G-7693)*

Goose and The Monkey Brewhouse, Lexington *Also Called: Goose and Monkey Brewhouse LLC (G-7693)*

Gordon Enterprises... 919 776-8784
  3125 Hawkins Ave Sanford (27330) *(G-11186)*

Gore S Mar Met Fabrication Inc...................................... 910 763-6066
  302 N Channel Haven Dr Wilmington (28409) *(G-12793)*

Gore S Trlr Manufacturer S Inc....................................... 910 642-2246
  305 Gores Trailer Rd Whiteville (28472) *(G-12582)*

Goshen Engineering Inc.. 919 429-9798
  439 Nc Highway 55 E Mount Olive (28365) *(G-9254)*

Goslen Printing Company.. 336 768-5775
  3250 Healy Dr Winston Salem (27103) *(G-13181)*

Gouge Logging... 828 675-9216
  360 Rock Creek Rd Burnsville (28714) *(G-1186)*

Gough Econ Inc.. 704 399-4501
  9400 N Lakebrook Rd Charlotte (28214) *(G-2228)*

Gould & Goodrich, Lillington *Also Called: Point Blank Enterprises Inc (G-7801)*

Goulston Technologies Inc (HQ)..................................... 704 289-6464
  700 N Johnson St Monroe (28110) *(G-8495)*

Gounmanned LLC... 919 835-2140
  533 Pylon Dr Raleigh (27606) *(G-10140)*

Gourmet Foods USA LLC... 704 248-1724
  10415 Bailey Rd Cornelius (28031) *(G-3604)*

Government Sales LLC... 252 726-6315
  4644 Arendell St Ste A Morehead City (28557) *(G-8833)*

GP Fabrication Inc.. 336 361-0410
  9968 Us 158 Reidsville (27320) *(G-10686)*

GP Foam Fabricators Inc... 336 434-3600
  220 Swathmore Ave High Point (27263) *(G-6633)*

GP Technology LLC.. 919 876-3666
  4807 Beryl Rd Raleigh (27606) *(G-10141)*

Gpi, Gastonia *Also Called: Gentry Plastics Inc (G-5053)*

Gpms, Charlotte *Also Called: Global Products & Mfg Svcs Inc (G-2215)*

Gpx Intelligence Inc.. 888 260-0706
  620a S Elm St Greensboro (27406) *(G-5570)*

Grace Apparel Company Inc... 828 242-8172
  19 Timber Park Dr Black Mountain (28711) *(G-865)*

Grace Communion International (PA)............................... 626 650-2300
  3120 Whitehall Park Dr Charlotte (28273) *(G-2229)*

Gracefully Broken LLC... 980 474-0309
  2131 Autumn Cyprus Ave Gastonia (28054) *(G-5055)*

Gracefully Gifted Hands LLC.. 845 248-8743
  8480 Honeycutt Rd Ste 200 Raleigh (27615) *(G-10142)*

Gracie & Lucas LLC.. 704 707-3207
  224 Wiredell Ave Mooresville (28115) *(G-8675)*

Gracie Goodness Inc.. 910 792-0800
  113 Portwatch Way Ste 101 Wilmington (28412) *(G-12794)*

Grady & Son Atkins Logging.. 919 934-7785
  1401 Devils Racetrack Rd Four Oaks (27524) *(G-4812)*

Grady Distributing Co Inc.. 919 556-5630
  640 Park Ave Youngsville (27596) *(G-13473)*

Grady-White Boats Inc.. 252 752-2111
  5121 Martin Luther King Jr Hwy Greenville (27834) *(G-5983)*

Graedon Enterprises Inc... 919 493-0448
  5900 Beech Bluff Ln Durham (27705) *(G-4055)*

Graham Cracker LLC... 336 288-4440
  514 Pisgah Church Rd Greensboro (27455) *(G-5571)*

Graham Dyeing & Finishing Inc...................................... 336 228-9981
  240 Hawkins St Burlington (27217) *(G-1101)*

Grahams Transportation LLC.. 910 627-6880
  6642 Keeler Dr Fayetteville (28303) *(G-4606)*

Grailgame Inc.. 804 517-3102
  301 N Scales St Reidsville (27320) *(G-10687)*

Gram Furniture.. 828 241-2836
  4513 Nc Highway 10 E Claremont (28610) *(G-3114)*

Grancreations Inc.. 704 332-7625
  3400 N Graham St Charlotte (28206) *(G-2230)*

Grand Encore Charlotte LLC.. 513 482-7500
  3700 Rose Lake Dr Charlotte (28217) *(G-2231)*

Grand Manor Furniture Inc.......... 828 758-5521
929 Harrisburg Dr Sw Lenoir (28645) *(G-7608)*

Grandeur Manufacturing Inc.......... 336 526-2468
2200 Nc Highway 67 Jonesville (28642) *(G-7197)*

Grandfather Vinyrd Winery LLC.......... 828 963-2400
225 Vineyard Ln Banner Elk (28604) *(G-685)*

Grandmas Sugar Shack.......... 336 760-8822
209 S Gordon Dr Winston Salem (27104) *(G-13182)*

Grandwell Industries Inc.......... 919 557-1221
6109 S Nc 55 Hwy Fuquay Varina (27526) *(G-4883)*

Granges Americas Inc.......... 704 633-6020
1709 Jake Alexander Blvd S Salisbury (28146) *(G-11059)*

Granite Falls Furnaces LLC.......... 828 324-4394
1230 Premier Rd Granite Falls (28630) *(G-5304)*

Granite Falls Plant, Granite Falls Also Called: Chase Corporation *(G-5300)*

Granite Knitwear Inc (PA).......... 704 279-5526
805 S Salisbury Ave Granite Quarry (28072) *(G-5326)*

Granite Memorials Inc.......... 336 786-6596
636 S Main St Mount Airy (27030) *(G-9124)*

Granite Tactical Vehicles Inc.......... 336 789-5555
915 Newsome St Mount Airy (27030) *(G-9125)*

Granite Tape Co.......... 828 396-5614
4 Cedar St Granite Falls (28630) *(G-5305)*

Granville Equipment LLC.......... 919 693-1425
4602a Watkins Rd Oxford (27565) *(G-9615)*

Granville Pallet Co Inc.......... 919 528-2347
3566 Us Highway 15 Oxford (27565) *(G-9616)*

Granville Publishing Co Inc.......... 919 528-2393
418 N Main St Creedmoor (27522) *(G-3649)*

Grapgic Design, Huntersville Also Called: Tudg Multimedia Firm *(G-7061)*

Graphic Attack Inc.......... 252 491-2174
Harbinger Commercial Park Ste 34 Harbinger (27941) *(G-6095)*

Graphic Components LLC.......... 336 542-2128
2800 Patterson St Greensboro (27407) *(G-5572)*

Graphic Design, Spruce Pine Also Called: Designs By Rachel *(G-11574)*

Graphic Finshg Solutions LLC.......... 336 255-7857
1207 Boston Rd Greensboro (27407) *(G-5573)*

Graphic Image, Wilmington Also Called: Graphic Image of Cape Fear Inc *(G-12795)*

Graphic Image of Cape Fear Inc.......... 910 313-6768
2840 S College Rd Wilmington (28412) *(G-12795)*

Graphic Impressions Inc.......... 704 596-4921
7910 District Dr Charlotte (28213) *(G-2232)*

Graphic Master, Youngsville Also Called: Via Prnting Graphic Design Inc *(G-13497)*

Graphic Packaging Intl LLC.......... 704 588-1750
8800 Crump Rd Pineville (28134) *(G-9730)*

Graphic Packaging Intl LLC.......... 336 744-1222
320 W Hanes Mill Rd Winston Salem (27105) *(G-13183)*

Graphic Printing, Elkin Also Called: Kathie S Mc Daniel *(G-4446)*

Graphic Productions Inc.......... 336 765-9335
301 N Main St Ste 2104 Winston Salem (27101) *(G-13184)*

Graphic Products Inc.......... 919 894-3661
105 S Wall St Benson (27504) *(G-790)*

Graphic Rewards Inc.......... 336 969-2733
130 Northstar Dr Ste B Rural Hall (27045) *(G-10960)*

Graphic Systems Intl Inc.......... 336 662-8686
7 Lockheed Ct Greensboro (27409) *(G-5574)*

Graphical Creations Inc.......... 704 888-8870
106 Conveyor Beltway Dr Stanfield (28163) *(G-11607)*

Graphik Dimensions Limited.......... 800 332-8884
2103 Brentwood St High Point (27263) *(G-6634)*

Graphix Solution Inc.......... 919 213-0371
1094 Classic Rd Apex (27539) *(G-160)*

Graphixx Screen Printing Inc.......... 919 736-3995
601 N James St Ste B Goldsboro (27530) *(G-5219)*

Grasche, Hickory Also Called: Grasche USA Inc *(G-6340)*

Grasche USA Inc.......... 828 322-1226
240 Performance Dr Se Hickory (28602) *(G-6340)*

Grass America Inc.......... 336 996-4041
1202 Nc Highway 66 S Kernersville (27284) *(G-7277)*

Grassy Creek Vineyard & Winery.......... 336 835-2458
235 Chatham Cottage Ln State Road (28676) *(G-11636)*

Grateful Steps Foundation.......... 828 277-0998
119 Buffalo Trl Asheville (28805) *(G-509)*

Grateful Union Family Inc (PA).......... 828 622-3258
33 Haywood St Asheville (28801) *(G-510)*

Graveoke Inc.......... 704 534-3480
1814 Bradenton Dr Charlotte (28206) *(G-2233)*

Graves Inc.......... 252 792-1191
1909 W Main St Williamston (27892) *(G-12670)*

Gray Flex Systems Inc (PA).......... 910 897-3539
232 N Ida St Coats (27521) *(G-3262)*

Gray Manufacturing Co.......... 615 841-3066
8548 Highland Glen Dr Charlotte (28269) *(G-2234)*

Gray Manufacturing Tech LLC.......... 704 489-2206
3570 Denver Dr Denver (28037) *(G-3785)*

Gray Metal South Inc (PA).......... 910 892-2119
600 N Powell Ave Dunn (28334) *(G-3859)*

Gray Ox Inc.......... 704 662-8247
155 Quiet Cove Rd Mooresville (28117) *(G-8676)*

Gray Wolf Log Homes Inc.......... 828 586-4662
538 Big Oak Springs Rd Sylva (28779) *(G-11892)*

Graybeard Distillery Inc.......... 919 361-9980
4625 Industry Ln Durham (27713) *(G-4056)*

Grayson Wireless, Garner Also Called: Commscope Technologies LLC *(G-4923)*

Great Eastern Sun, Asheville Also Called: Great Eastern Sun Trdg Co Inc *(G-511)*

Great Eastern Sun Trdg Co Inc.......... 828 665-7790
92 Mcintosh Rd Asheville (28806) *(G-511)*

Great Pacific Entps US Inc (DH).......... 980 256-7729
10601 Westlake Dr Charlotte (28273) *(G-2235)*

Great Products Inc.......... 910 944-2020
Us Hwy 15 501 Aberdeen (28315) *(G-5)*

Great Star Industrial Usa LLC (DH).......... 704 892-4965
9836 Northcross Center Ct Ste A Huntersville (28078) *(G-6996)*

Great Wagon Road Distlg Co LLC.......... 704 469-9330
227 Southside Dr Ste B Charlotte (28217) *(G-2236)*

Great Waters Company.......... 919 818-4081
1215 S Crescent Dr Smithfield (27577) *(G-11445)*

Greater Diversity News, Wilmington Also Called: Promiseland Media Inc *(G-12891)*

Greater Wilmington Business.......... 910 343-8600
101 N 3rd St Wilmington (28401) *(G-12796)*

Grecon Dimter Inc.......... 828 397-5139
8658 Huffman Ave Connelly Springs (28612) *(G-3477)*

Grecon Inc (HQ).......... 503 641-7731
648 Griffith Rd Ste A Charlotte (28217) *(G-2237)*

Grede II LLC.......... 910 428-2111
530 E Main St Biscoe (27209) *(G-852)*

Green Apple Studio.......... 919 377-2239
590 E Chatham St Cary (27511) *(G-1368)*

Green Bean Counters LLC.......... 919 545-2324
587 Old Farrington Rd Chapel Hill (27517) *(G-1548)*

Green Compass LLC (PA).......... 833 336-9223
305 Raleigh St Ste D Wilmington (28412) *(G-12797)*

Green Line Defense LLC.......... 828 707-5236
36 Renaissance Pl Leicester (28748) *(G-7525)*

Green Line Media Inc.......... 828 251-1333
2 Wall St Ste 214 Asheville (28801) *(G-512)*

Green Mountain Intl LLC.......... 800 942-5151
235 Pigeon St Waynesville (28786) *(G-12460)*

Green Pastures Lawn Care.......... 828 758-9265
5920 Hollow Springs Cir Boomer (28606) *(G-891)*

Green Power Producers.......... 704 844-8990
10600 Nations Ford Rd # 150 Charlotte (28273) *(G-2238)*

Green River Resource MGT.......... 828 697-0357
195 Blueberry Farm Rd Zirconia (28790) *(G-13530)*

Green State Landscape & Nrsry, Lumberton Also Called: Taylco Inc *(G-7974)*

Green Stream Technologies Inc.......... 844 499-8880
12339 Wake Union Church Rd Wake Forest (27587) *(G-12280)*

Green Waste Management LLC.......... 704 289-0720
101 N Tryon St Ste 112 Charlotte (28246) *(G-2239)*

Greenbrook Design Center, Shelby Also Called: Walker Woodworking Inc *(G-11390)*

Greencross Inc.......... 704 984-6700
241 W North St Albemarle (28001) *(G-76)*

Greene Imaging & Design Inc 919 787-3737
6320 Angus Dr Ste E Raleigh (27617) *(G-10143)*

Greene Logging 336 667-6960
9145 Boone Trl Purlear (28665) *(G-9831)*

Greene Mountain Outdoors LLC 336 670-2186
2321 Yellow Banks Rd North Wilkesboro (28659) *(G-9532)*

Greene Precision Products Inc 828 262-0116
4016 Nc Highway 194 N Boone (28607) *(G-919)*

Greenfield Energy LLC 910 509-1805
213 Seacrest Dr Wrightsville Beach (28480) *(G-13431)*

Greenheck Fan Co 336 852-5788
3816 Patterson St Greensboro (27407) *(G-5575)*

Greenheck Fan Corporation 704 476-3700
2000 Partnership Dr Shelby (28150) *(G-11339)*

Greenleaf Corporation 828 693-0461
761 Roper Rd East Flat Rock (28726) *(G-4332)*

Greenlights LLC 919 766-8900
1211 Walnut St Cary (27511) *(G-1369)*

Greenline Corporation 704 333-3377
200 Forsyth Hall Dr Ste E Charlotte (28273) *(G-2240)*

Greenology Products LLC 877 473-3650
7020 Cynrow Blvd Raleigh (27615) *(G-10144)*

Greens Machine & Tool Inc 828 654-0042
8 Park Ridge Dr Fletcher (28732) *(G-4739)*

Greensboro Distilling LLC 336 273-6221
321 W Wendover Ave Greensboro (27408) *(G-5576)*

Greensboro Industrial Platers, Greensboro *Also Called: Nb Corporation (G-5705)*

Greensboro Industrial Platers, Greensboro *Also Called: Nb Corporation (G-5706)*

Greensboro Metal Parts, Jamestown *Also Called: Hemco Wire Products Inc (G-7164)*

Greensboro News & Record LLC 336 373-7000
3001 S Elm Eugene St Greensboro (27406) *(G-5577)*

Greensboro Tire & Auto Service 336 294-9495
4615 W Market St Ste A Greensboro (27407) *(G-5578)*

Greensboro Tire 3, Greensboro *Also Called: Greensboro Tire & Auto Service (G-5578)*

Greensboro Voice 336 255-1006
407 E Washington St Greensboro (27401) *(G-5579)*

Greensboro Wilbert, Greensboro *Also Called: Wilbert Funeral Services Inc (G-5919)*

Greenstory Globl Gvrnment Mlta 828 446-9278
3811 Gordon St Terrell (28682) *(G-11989)*

Greenville Division, Greenville *Also Called: Robert Bosch Tool Corporation (G-6019)*

Greenville Marble & Gran Works, Greenville *Also Called: Conway Development Inc (G-5957)*

Greenville Rdymx Dpd Team Con, Winterville *Also Called: Greenville Ready Mix Concrete (G-13416)*

Greenville Ready Mix Concrete (PA) 252 756-0119
5039 Nc 11 S Winterville (28590) *(G-13416)*

Greenville Seamless Gutters, Greenville *Also Called: Team Gsg LLC (G-6026)*

Greenwich Bay Trading Co Inc 919 781-5008
5809 Triangle Dr Ste C Raleigh (27617) *(G-10145)*

Greenworks North America LLC (PA) 888 909-6757
500 S Main St Ste 450 Mooresville (28115) *(G-8677)*

Greenworks Tools, Mooresville *Also Called: Greenworks North America LLC (G-8677)*

Greer Laboratories Inc 828 758-2388
Hwy 90 Lenoir (28645) *(G-7609)*

Greer Laboratories Inc (DH) 828 754-5327
639 Nuway Cir Lenoir (28645) *(G-7610)*

Greg Price 847 778-4426
107 Patton Ln Hampstead (28443) *(G-6073)*

Gregory Hill Frame 828 428-0007
108 W Cemetery St Maiden (28650) *(G-8014)*

Gregory Poole Equipment Co 252 931-5100
5200 Martin Luther King Jr Hwy Greenville (27834) *(G-5984)*

Gregory Poole Equipment Co 919 872-2691
2620 Discovery Dr Raleigh (27616) *(G-10146)*

Gregory Vineyards 919 427-9409
275 Bowling Spring Dr Angier (27501) *(G-119)*

Greif Inc 704 588-3895
900 Westinghouse Blvd Charlotte (28273) *(G-2241)*

Greiner Bio-One North Amer Inc (DH) 704 261-7800
4238 Capital Dr Monroe (28110) *(G-8496)*

Greiner-Bio-One, Monroe *Also Called: Greiner Bio-One North Amer Inc (G-8496)*

Gresco Manufacturing Inc 336 475-8101
216 E Holly Hill Rd Thomasville (27360) *(G-12029)*

Gresham Lake Concrete Plant, Raleigh *Also Called: S T Wooten Corporation (G-10455)*

Grey Area News 919 637-6973
70 Harrison St Zebulon (27597) *(G-13510)*

Grey Holdings Inc 828 862-4772
283 Old Rosman Hwy Brevard (28712) *(G-970)*

Grey House Publishing, Concord *Also Called: Grey House Publishing Inc (G-3370)*

Grey House Publishing Inc 704 784-0051
624 Foxwood Dr Se Concord (28025) *(G-3370)*

Greybeard Printing Inc 828 252-3082
1304c Patton Ave Ste C Asheville (28806) *(G-513)*

Greystone Concrete Pdts Inc 252 438-5144
2100 Us 1/158 Hwy Henderson (27537) *(G-6157)*

Grice Showcase Display Mfg Inc 704 423-8888
5001 White Oak Rd Charlotte (28210) *(G-2242)*

Griffin Automotive Marine Inc 252 940-0714
450 Herring Club Rd Washington (27889) *(G-12388)*

Griffin Industries LLC 704 624-9140
5805 Highway 74 E Marshville (28103) *(G-8089)*

Griffin Marketing Group 336 558-5802
4608 Knightbridge Rd Greensboro (27455) *(G-5580)*

Griffin Motion LLC 919 577-6333
1040 Classic Rd Apex (27539) *(G-161)*

Griffin Printing Inc 919 832-6931
500 Uwharrie Ct Ste A Raleigh (27606) *(G-10147)*

Griffin Tubing Company Inc 336 449-4822
906 Burlington Ave Gibsonville (27249) *(G-5176)*

Griffiths Corporation 704 552-6793
10134 Industrial Dr Pineville (28134) *(G-9731)*

Griffiths Corporation 704 554-5657
10240 Industrial Dr Pineville (28134) *(G-9732)*

Grifols, Clayton *Also Called: Grifols Therapeutics LLC (G-3151)*

Grifols Inc 919 553-5011
8368 Us 70 Bus Hwy W Clayton (27520) *(G-3150)*

Grifols Therapeutics LLC 919 359-7069
9257 Us 70 Bus Hwy W Ste B-302 Clayton (27520) *(G-3151)*

Grifols Therapeutics LLC 919 553-0172
8368 Clayton Blvd Clayton (27520) *(G-3152)*

Grifols Therapeutics LLC 919 316-6214
85 Tw Alexander Dr Durham (27709) *(G-4057)*

Grifols Therapeutics LLC 919 316-6612
1017 Main Campus Dr Ste 2580 Raleigh (27606) *(G-10148)*

Grifols Therapeutics LLC (DH) 919 316-6300
79 Tw Alexander Dr Research Triangle Pa (27709) *(G-10711)*

Grindtec Enterprises Corp. 704 636-1825
3402 Mooresville Rd Salisbury (28147) *(G-11060)*

Grins Beverages, Winston Salem *Also Called: Grins Enterprises LLC (G-13185)*

Grins Enterprises LLC 336 831-0534
1051 Arbor Rd Winston Salem (27104) *(G-13185)*

Grip Pod Systems Intl LLC 239 233-3694
6321 Swallow Cove Ln Raleigh (27614) *(G-10149)*

Groninger USA LLC 704 588-3873
14045 S Lakes Dr Charlotte (28273) *(G-2243)*

Groupe Lacasse LLC 336 778-2098
2235 Lewisville Clemmons Rd Ste D Clemmons (27012) *(G-3187)*

Grove Stone & Sand, Swannanoa *Also Called: B V Hedrick Gravel & Sand Co (G-11866)*

Grove Stone & Sand Division, Salisbury *Also Called: B V Hedrick Gravel & Sand Co (G-11021)*

Grover Gaming Inc (PA) 252 329-7900
3506 Greenville Blvd Ne Greenville (27834) *(G-5985)*

Grover Industries Inc (PA) 828 859-9125
219 Laurel Ave Grover (28073) *(G-6044)*

Growler Manufacturing & Engrg, Robbins *Also Called: Carolina Growler Inc (G-10752)*

Grp Inc 919 776-9940
1823 Boone Trail Rd Sanford (27330) *(G-11187)*

Grt Electronics LLC 919 821-1996
3805 Beryl Rd Raleigh (27607) *(G-10150)*

Grubb & Son Sawmill Inc 336 241-2252
1498 Summey Town Rd Trinity (27370) *(G-12115)*

Gruma Corporation 919 778-5553
401 Gateway Dr Goldsboro (27534) *(G-5220)*

(G-0000) Company's Geographic Section entry number

Gryphon House Inc.. 800 638-0928
   1310 Lewisville Clemmons Rd Lewisville (27023) *(G-7651)*

GSM Services, Gastonia *Also Called: GSM Services Inc (G-5056)*

GSM Services Inc.. 704 864-0344
   1535 W May Ave Gastonia (28052) *(G-5056)*

Gso Printing.. 336 292-1601
   317 S Westgate Dr Ste A Greensboro (27407) *(G-5581)*

Gso Printing Inc.. 336 288-5778
   2 Hill Valley Ct Greensboro (27410) *(G-5582)*

Gt Rhyno Construction LLC.................................. 919 737-3620
   7061 Fox Meadow Ln Apt 911 Raleigh (27616) *(G-10151)*

Gtg Engineering, Clarendon *Also Called: Gtg Engineering Inc (G-3127)*

Gtg Engineering Inc (PA)...................................... 877 569-8572
   766 Furnie Hammond Rd Clarendon (28432) *(G-3127)*

Gtg Engineering Inc.. 910 457-0068
   4956 Long Beach Rd Se Ste 14 Southport (28461) *(G-11520)*

Guardian Strapping, Clinton *Also Called: Dubose Strapping Inc (G-3232)*

Guerbet, Raleigh *Also Called: Guerbet LLC (G-10152)*

Guerbet LLC.. 919 878-2930
   8800 Durant Rd Ste 800 Raleigh (27616) *(G-10152)*

Guerrero Enterprises Inc..................................... 828 286-4900
   1621 Poors Ford Rd Rutherfordton (28139) *(G-10984)*

Guerrilla Rf Inc... 336 510-7840
   2000 Pisgah Church Rd Greensboro (27455) *(G-5583)*

Guilford Business Forms, High Point *Also Called: Gbf Inc (G-6627)*

Guilford Fabricators Inc....................................... 336 434-3163
   5261 Glenola Industrial Dr High Point (27263) *(G-6635)*

Guilford Mills LLC... 910 794-5810
   1001 Military Cutoff Rd Ste 300 Wilmington (28405) *(G-12798)*

Guilford Orthtic Prothetic Inc.............................. 336 676-5394
   405 Parkway St Ste G Greensboro (27401) *(G-5584)*

Guilford Performance Textiles, Wilmington *Also Called: Lear Corporation (G-12831)*

Gulfstream Steel & Supply, Holly Ridge *Also Called: Gulfstream Steel & Supply Inc (G-6888)*

Gulfstream Steel & Supply Inc............................ 910 329-5100
   301 Us Highway 17 S Ste 1 Holly Ridge (28445) *(G-6888)*

Gullistan Carpet, Aberdeen *Also Called: Hampton Capital Partners LLC (G-6)*

Gum Drop Cases LLC.. 206 805-0818
   1515 W Green Dr High Point (27260) *(G-6636)*

Gunboat International Ltd..................................... 252 305-8700
   829 Harbor Rd Wanchese (27981) *(G-12342)*

Gunk, Indian Trail *Also Called: Radiator Specialty Company (G-7097)*

Gunmar Machine Corporation.............................. 910 738-6295
   310 Hines St Lumberton (28358) *(G-7956)*

Gusto Packing Company, Garner *Also Called: Butterball LLC (G-4918)*

Guy Chaddock and Company LLC........................ 828 584-0664
   100 Reep Dr Morganton (28655) *(G-8869)*

Guy N Langley... 252 972-9875
   2026 Leggett Rd Rocky Mount (27801) *(G-10812)*

Guyclee Millwork.. 919 202-5738
   1251 S Pollock St Selma (27576) *(G-11288)*

Gxs Wraps, Apex *Also Called: Graphix Solution Inc (G-160)*

Gym 30, Wake Forest *Also Called: Trickfit & Suepack Training (G-12309)*

H & B Tool & Die Supply Co................................. 704 376-8531
   5005 W Wt Harris Blvd Ste A Charlotte (28269) *(G-2244)*

H & H Farm Machine Co Inc.................................. 704 753-1555
   7916 Unionville Brief Rd Monroe (28110) *(G-8497)*

H & H Furniture Mfrs Inc...................................... 336 873-7245
   236 N Broad St Seagrove (27341) *(G-11274)*

H & H Polishing Inc.. 704 393-8728
   4256 Golf Acres Dr Charlotte (28208) *(G-2245)*

H & H Products Incorporated (PA)....................... 910 891-4276
   275 Carlie Cs Dr Dunn (28334) *(G-3860)*

H & H Representatives Inc................................... 704 596-6950
   University Parkway Charlotte (28229) *(G-2246)*

H & H REPRESENTATIVES, INC, Charlotte *Also Called: H & H Representatives Inc (G-2246)*

H & H Wood Products Inc..................................... 704 233-4148
   3349 Us Hwy 74 E Wingate (28174) *(G-13062)*

H & H Woodworking Inc.. 336 884-5848
   530 Gatewood Ave High Point (27262) *(G-6637)*

H & L Logging Inc.. 252 793-2778
   1166 Long Ridge Rd Plymouth (27962) *(G-9805)*

H & M Wood Preserving Inc.................................. 704 279-5188
   280 Zion Church Rd Gold Hill (28071) *(G-5192)*

H & P Wood Turnings Inc...................................... 910 675-2784
   9375 Us Hwy 117 S Rocky Point (28457) *(G-10880)*

H & R Mullis Machine Inc..................................... 704 791-4149
   151 Highway 24 27 E Midland (28107) *(G-8287)*

H & T Chair Co Inc... 828 264-7742
   1598 Meat Camp Rd Boone (28607) *(G-920)*

H & V Processing Inc.. 336 224-2985
   251 Primrose Drive Ext Lexington (27292) *(G-7694)*

H + M USA Management Co Inc............................ 704 599-9325
   3200 Woodpark Blvd Charlotte (28206) *(G-2247)*

H Brothers Fine Wdwkg LLC................................ 931 216-1955
   1512 Earpsboro Rd Zebulon (27597) *(G-13511)*

H C Production Co... 910 483-5267
   218 Tolar St Fayetteville (28306) *(G-4607)*

H Clyde Moore Jr.. 910 642-3507
   790 Honey Field Rd Whiteville (28472) *(G-12583)*

H D Technologies, Morganton *Also Called: Barefoot Cnc Inc (G-8852)*

H F I, Randleman *Also Called: Hughes Furniture Inds Inc (G-10650)*

H F Kinney Co Inc... 704 540-9367
   13852 Ballantyne Meadows Dr Charlotte (28277) *(G-2248)*

H Horseshoe... 336 853-5913
   194 Sandy Creek Ln Lexington (27295) *(G-7695)*

H M Elliott Inc.. 704 663-8226
   387 Pitt Rd Mooresville (28115) *(G-8678)*

H Parsons Incorporated.. 828 757-9191
   100 Parsons Park Dr Lenoir (28645) *(G-7611)*

H S G, Swansboro *Also Called: High Speed Gear Inc (G-11885)*

H T Jones Lumber Company................................. 252 332-4135
   204 Catherine Creek Rd N Ahoskie (27910) *(G-50)*

H T Wade Enterprises Inc.................................... 336 375-8900
   5838 Rudd Station Rd Browns Summit (27214) *(G-997)*

H V O, Waynesville *Also Called: Haywood Vctnal Opprtnities Inc (G-12461)*

H W Culp Lumber Company.................................. 704 463-7311
   491 Us Hwy 52 N New London (28127) *(G-9417)*

H W S Company Inc (HQ)...................................... 828 322-8624
   856 7th Ave Se Hickory (28602) *(G-6341)*

H-T-L Perma USA Ltd Partnr (PA)........................ 704 377-3100
   10333 Westlake Dr Charlotte (28273) *(G-2249)*

H.E.A.L. Marketplace, Rutherfordton *Also Called: Heal (G-10986)*

H&A Scientific Inc... 252 752-4315
   105 Regency Blvd Ste A Greenville (27834) *(G-5986)*

H&H Distillery LLC.. 828 338-9779
   204 Charlotte Hwy Ste D Asheville (28803) *(G-514)*

H&H Metal Fab... 828 757-3747
   3050 Mcmillan Pl Lenoir (28645) *(G-7612)*

H&M Woodpreserving, Gold Hill *Also Called: H & M Wood Preserving Inc (G-5192)*

H&M Woodworks Inc... 919 496-5993
   504 S Bickett Blvd Louisburg (27549) *(G-7917)*

H&S Autoshot LLC.. 847 662-8500
   302 Rolling Hill Rd Mooresville (28117) *(G-8679)*

H2h Blinds.. 704 628-5084
   13137 Bleinheim Ln Matthews (28105) *(G-8114)*

Haand Hospitality, Burlington *Also Called: Haand Inc (G-1102)*

Haand Inc.. 336 350-7597
   413 Tucker St Burlington (27215) *(G-1102)*

HackEDU Inc (PA)... 804 742-2533
   1235 East Blvd Ste E Pmb 5073 Charlotte (28203) *(G-2250)*

Hackner Home LLC... 980 552-9573
   806 W Warren St Shelby (28150) *(G-11340)*

Hackney, Washington *Also Called: Transportation Tech Inc (G-12416)*

Hackney & Sons Midwest Inc.............................. 252 946-6521
   911 W 5th St Washington (27889) *(G-12389)*

Hackney A Div VT Spclzed Vhcle, Washington *Also Called: VT Hackney Inc (G-12419)*

Haeco Americas, Greensboro *Also Called: Haeco Americas LLC (G-5585)*

Haeco Americas LLC (DH)..................................... 336 668-4410
   623 Radar Rd Greensboro (27410) *(G-5585)*

Haeco Americas Cabin Solutions, Greensboro *Also Called: Brice Manufacturing Co Inc (G-5398)*

Haeco Americas Cabin Solutions, Greensboro *Also Called: Zim Arcraft Cbin Solutions LLC (G-5932)*

Haeco Americas Cabin Solutions, Winston Salem *Also Called: Zim Arcraft Cbin Solutions LLC (G-13411)*

Hafele America Co (HQ)... 800 423-3531
　3901 Cheyenne Dr Archdale (27263) *(G-224)*

Haigler Electric & Cnstr, Monroe *Also Called: Trimworks Inc (G-8570)*

Hair Collection, The, Raleigh *Also Called: Magazine Nakia Lashawn (G-10266)*

Haircutters of Raleigh Inc.. 919 781-3465
　4024 Barrett Dr Ste 102 Raleigh (27609) *(G-10153)*

Hairfield Wilbert Burial Vlt.. 828 437-4319
　3098 Morganton Furniture Rd Morganton (28655) *(G-8870)*

Hais Kookies & More.. 980 819-8256
　600 Hartford Ave Charlotte (28209) *(G-2251)*

Halcore Group Inc... 336 982-9824
　101 Gates Ln Jefferson (28640) *(G-7188)*

Halcore Group Inc... 336 846-8010
　101 Gates Ln Jefferson (28640) *(G-7189)*

Haldex Inc.. 828 652-9308
　5334 Us Hwy 221 N Marion (28752) *(G-8042)*

Hale's Sample Shop, High Point *Also Called: Solid Frames Inc (G-6784)*

Hales Welding and Fabrication.. 252 907-5508
　900 Carr Farm Rd Macclesfield (27852) *(G-7980)*

Halifax EMC... 252 445-5111
　12867 Nc Highway 481 Enfield (27823) *(G-4483)*

Halifax Media Group.. 704 869-1700
　1893 Remount Rd Gastonia (28054) *(G-5057)*

Halifax Media Holdings LLC... 828 692-5763
　1717 Four Seasons Blvd Hendersonville (28792) *(G-6211)*

Hall Tire and Battery Co Inc.. 336 275-3812
　2222 Martin Luther King Jr Dr Greensboro (27406) *(G-5586)*

Ham Brothers Inc.. 704 827-1303
　205 Shamrock Rd Gastonia (28056) *(G-5058)*

Ham Wayco Company.. 919 735-3962
　506 N William St Goldsboro (27530) *(G-5221)*

Hamby Brother S Incorporated... 336 667-1154
　Us Hwy 421 North Wilkesboro (28659) *(G-9533)*

Hamby Brothers Concrete Inc... 828 754-2176
　2051 Morganton Blvd Sw Lenoir (28645) *(G-7613)*

Hamilton... 704 896-1427
　400 Avinger Ln Davidson (28036) *(G-3706)*

Hamilton Beach Brands Inc... 252 975-0444
　234 Springs Rd Washington (27889) *(G-12390)*

Hamilton Drywall Products, Monroe *Also Called: Mbp Acquisition LLC (G-8528)*

Hamilton Indus Grinding Inc... 828 253-6796
　273 Kimberly Ave Asheville (28804) *(G-515)*

Hamilton Machine Works LLC... 919 779-6892
　908 Withers Rd Raleigh (27603) *(G-10154)*

Hamilton Sundstrand Corp... 860 654-6000
　2730 W Tyvola Rd Charlotte (28217) *(G-2252)*

Hamlet Paper Packaging, Hamlet *Also Called: Hood Packaging Corporation (G-6057)*

Hamlin Sheet Metal Company Inc....................................... 919 894-2224
　200 N Walton Ave Benson (27504) *(G-791)*

Hamlin Sheet Metal Company Incorporated (PA)............. 919 772-8780
　1411 W Garner Rd Garner (27529) *(G-4930)*

Hammer Publications, Greensboro *Also Called: Rhinoceros Times (G-5787)*

Hammill Construction Co Inc.. 704 279-5309
　5051 St Stephens Church Rd Gold Hill (28071) *(G-5193)*

Hammock Consumer, Charlotte *Also Called: Hammock Pharmaceuticals Inc (G-2253)*

Hammock Pharmaceuticals Inc... 704 727-7926
　11922 General Dr Unit C Charlotte (28273) *(G-2253)*

Hammond Electric Motor Company...................................... 704 983-3178
　811 Concord Rd Albemarle (28001) *(G-77)*

Hampstead Publishing, Hampstead *Also Called: Topsail Voice LLC (G-6078)*

Hampton Art Inc.. 252 975-7207
　1481 W 2nd St Ste 109 Washington (27889) *(G-12391)*

Hampton Capital Partners LLC
　3140 Nc Highway 5 Aberdeen (28315) *(G-6)*

Hamrick Fence Company... 704 434-5011
　407 E College Ave Boiling Springs (28017) *(G-884)*

Hamrick Precast LLC.. 704 434-6551
　415 W College Ave Shelby (28152) *(G-11341)*

Hancock & Grandson Inc... 252 728-2416
　971 Harkers Island Rd Beaufort (28516) *(G-729)*

Hancock & Moore LLC (HQ).. 828 495-8235
　166 Hancock And Moore Ln Taylorsville (28681) *(G-11962)*

Hancock & Moore LLC.. 828 495-8235
　405 Rink Dam Rd Taylorsville (28681) *(G-11963)*

Hanes, Conover *Also Called: Hanes Companies - NJ LLC (G-3526)*

Hanes, Winston Salem *Also Called: Hanesbrands Inc (G-13188)*

Hanes Companies Inc.. 828 464-4673
　500 N Mclin Creek Rd Conover (28613) *(G-3525)*

Hanes Companies Inc (HQ)... 336 747-1600
　815 Buxton St Winston Salem (27101) *(G-13186)*

Hanes Companies - NJ LLC.. 828 464-4673
　500 N Mclin Creek Rd Conover (28613) *(G-3526)*

Hanes Inds A Div Hnes Cmpanies, Conover *Also Called: Hanes Companies Inc (G-3525)*

Hanes Industries, Winston Salem *Also Called: Hanes Companies Inc (G-13186)*

Hanes Industries-Newton.. 828 469-2000
　2042 Fairgrove Church Rd Newton (28658) *(G-9471)*

Hanesbrands Export Canada LLC.. 336 519-8080
　1000 E Hanes Mill Rd Winston Salem (27105) *(G-13187)*

Hanesbrands Inc.. 910 462-2001
　18400 Fieldcrest Rd Laurel Hill (28351) *(G-7483)*

Hanesbrands Inc.. 336 789-6118
　645 W Pine St Mount Airy (27030) *(G-9126)*

Hanesbrands Inc.. 336 519-8080
　710 Almondridge Dr Rural Hall (27045) *(G-10961)*

Hanesbrands Inc (PA)... 336 519-8080
　1000 E Hanes Mill Rd Winston Salem (27105) *(G-13188)*

Haney's Tire, Laurinburg *Also Called: Haneys Tire Recapping Svc LLC (G-7503)*

Haneys Tire Recapping Svc LLC.. 910 276-2636
　1663 S Main St Laurinburg (28352) *(G-7503)*

Hangcha America, Charlotte *Also Called: Hc Forklift America Corp (G-2266)*

Hanger Clinic, Greensboro *Also Called: Bio-Tech Prsthtics Orthtics In (G-5390)*

Hanging C Farms.. 704 239-6691
　709 China Grove Rd Kannapolis (28083) *(G-7210)*

Hanor Co Inc.. 252 977-0035
　6717 Nc 97 W Battleboro (27809) *(G-698)*

Hanover Electric Motor Svc Inc.. 910 762-3702
　602 Wellington Ave Wilmington (28401) *(G-12799)*

Hanover Electric Motors & Sups, Wilmington *Also Called: Hanover Electric Motor Svc Inc (G-12799)*

Hanover Iron Works Inc... 910 763-7318
　2602 Park Ave Wilmington (28403) *(G-12800)*

Hanover Iron Works Shtmtl Inc... 910 399-1146
　1861 Dawson St Wilmington (28403) *(G-12801)*

Hans Kissle Company LLC... 980 500-1630
　5118 Apple Creek Pkwy Dallas (28034) *(G-3674)*

Hans Krug.. 704 370-0809
　4310 Sharon Rd Ste U01 Charlotte (28211) *(G-2254)*

Hanson Brick, Charlotte *Also Called: Forterra Brick LLC (G-2175)*

Hanwha Advanced Mtls Amer LLC....................................... 704 434-2271
　925 Washburn Switch Rd Shelby (28150) *(G-11342)*

Hanwha Shelby, Shelby *Also Called: Hanwha Advanced Mtls Amer LLC (G-11342)*

Hao WEI Lai Inc.. 336 789-9969
　2021 Rockford St Mount Airy (27030) *(G-9127)*

Happy Jack Incorporated... 252 747-2911
　2122 Hwy 258 S Snow Hill (28580) *(G-11480)*

Harbisonwalker Intl Inc... 704 599-6540
　6600 Northpark Blvd Ste E Charlotte (28216) *(G-2255)*

Harbor Lines LLC.. 910 279-3796
　127 Northern Blvd Wilmington (28401) *(G-12802)*

Harbor Welding Inc... 252 473-3777
　935 Harbor Rd Wanchese (27981) *(G-12343)*

Harborlite, Youngsville *Also Called: Imerys Perlite Usa Inc (G-13475)*

Harco Air LLC.. 252 491-5220
　116 Ballast Rock Rd Unit L Powells Point (27966) *(G-9821)*

Harco Printing Incorporated... 336 771-0234
　130 Back Forty Dr Winston Salem (27127) *(G-13189)*

Hardcoatings, Charlotte *Also Called: Hardcoatings Inc (G-2256)*

Hardcoatings Inc.. 704 377-2996
　2601 Lucena St Charlotte (28206) *(G-2256)*

Harding Enterprise Inc......................................252 725-9785
1110 Spartina Dr Beaufort (28516) *(G-730)*

Hardison Tire Co Inc...252 745-4561
13504 Nc Highway 55 Bayboro (28515) *(G-711)*

Hardister Logging..336 857-2397
5571 Sandalwood Dr Denton (27239) *(G-3749)*

Hardwood Designs, Hillsborough *Also Called: Athol Arbor Corporation (G-6859)*

HARDWOOD DESIGNS, Hillsborough *Also Called: Kotek Holdings Inc (G-6870)*

Hardwood Publishing Co Inc...............................704 543-4408
6400 Bannington Rd Charlotte (28226) *(G-2257)*

Hardwood Review Export, Charlotte *Also Called: Hardwood Publishing Co Inc (G-2257)*

Hardwood Store of NC Inc..................................336 449-9627
106v E Railroad Ave Gibsonville (27249) *(G-5177)*

Hare Asian Trading Company LLC.........................910 524-4667
49 International Rd Burgaw (28425) *(G-1023)*

Hargenrader Cstm Woodcraft LLC.........................828 896-7182
2481 23rd St Ne Hickory (28601) *(G-6342)*

Hargrove Countertops & ACC Inc.........................919 981-0163
5250 Old Wake Forest Rd Ste 100 Raleigh (27609) *(G-10155)*

Hari Krupa Oil and Gas LLC................................860 805-1704
6031 Claudias Ln Apt 201 Winston Salem (27103) *(G-13190)*

Harley S Woodworks Inc....................................828 776-0120
917 N Fork Rd Barnardsville (28709) *(G-692)*

Harmony House Foods Inc..................................800 696-1395
277 Industrial Park Rd Franklin (28734) *(G-4831)*

Harmony Timberworks, Boone *Also Called: Soha Holdings LLC (G-942)*

Harper Companies Intl Inc..................................800 438-3111
11625 Steele Creek Rd Charlotte (28273) *(G-2258)*

Harper Corporation of America (PA)......................704 588-3371
11625 Steele Creek Rd Charlotte (28273) *(G-2259)*

Harper-Love Adhesives Corp (HQ).........................704 588-4395
11101 Westlake Dr Charlotte (28273) *(G-2260)*

Harrah Enterprise Ltd..336 253-3963
10308 Bailey Rd Ste 416 Cornelius (28031) *(G-3605)*

Harrell Proper Transport LLC...............................336 202-7135
205 Boling Springs Ct Whitsett (27377) *(G-12609)*

Harrins Sand & Gravel Inc...................................828 254-2744
195 Amboy Rd Asheville (28806) *(G-516)*

Harris House Furn Inds Inc..................................336 431-2802
104 Seminole Dr Archdale (27263) *(G-225)*

Harris Logging LLC..336 859-2786
7508 Brantley Gordon Rd Denton (27239) *(G-3750)*

Harris Lumber Company Inc.................................828 245-2664
1266 Big Island Rd Rutherfordton (28139) *(G-10985)*

Harris Products Group, The, Winston Salem *Also Called: J W Harris Co Inc (G-13213)*

Harris Rebar Inc..919 528-8333
803 S Market St Benson (27504) *(G-792)*

Harris Repair Service, Charlotte *Also Called: L3harris Technologies Inc (G-2405)*

Harris Solar Inc..704 490-8374
356 Belvedere Dr Nw Concord (28027) *(G-3371)*

Harris Teeter LLC..704 846-7117
1811 Matthews Township Pkwy Matthews (28105) *(G-8115)*

Harris Teeter LLC..919 859-0110
5563 Western Blvd Ste 38 Raleigh (27606) *(G-10156)*

Harris Teeter 038, Raleigh *Also Called: Harris Teeter LLC (G-10156)*

Harris Teeter 157, Matthews *Also Called: Harris Teeter LLC (G-8115)*

Harris Wood Products Inc...................................704 550-5494
40425 Tower Rd New London (28127) *(G-9418)*

Harris-Robinette Inc...252 813-5794
412 Harris Acre Ln Pinetops (27864) *(G-9706)*

Harrison Fence Inc..919 244-6908
1680 E Williams St Apex (27539) *(G-162)*

Harriss & Covington Hosiery, High Point *Also Called: Harriss Cvington Hsy Mills Inc (G-6639)*

Harriss & Covington Hsy Mills...............................336 882-6811
1232 Hickory Chapel Rd High Point (27260) *(G-6638)*

Harriss Cvington Hsy Mills Inc..............................336 882-6811
1250 Hickory Chapel Rd High Point (27260) *(G-6639)*

Harsco Metro Rail LLC.......................................980 960-2624
3440 Toringdon Way Ste 100 Charlotte (28277) *(G-2261)*

Harsco Rail LLC (HQ)...980 960-2624
3440 Toringdon Way Ste 100 Charlotte (28277) *(G-2262)*

Hartford Products Inc..919 471-5937
6224 Acorn Ridge Trl Hillsborough (27278) *(G-6866)*

Hartley Brothers Sawmill Inc................................336 921-2955
8507 West North Carolina Hwy 268 Boomer (28606) *(G-892)*

Hartley Loudspeakers Inc...................................910 392-1200
5732 Oleander Dr Wilmington (28403) *(G-12803)*

Hartley Ready Mix Con Mfg Inc.............................336 294-5995
1040 Boulder Rd Greensboro (27409) *(G-5587)*

Hartley Ready Mix Con Mfg Inc (PA)......................336 788-3928
3510 Rothrock St Winston Salem (27107) *(G-13191)*

Harts Striping, Archdale *Also Called: Steelcity LLC (G-244)*

Harvest Homes and Handi Houses (PA)...................336 243-2382
2100 S Main St Lexington (27292) *(G-7696)*

Harvest Homes and Handi Houses..........................704 637-3878
3711 Statesville Blvd Salisbury (28147) *(G-11061)*

Harvest Time Bread Company...............................910 436-9013
501 Piedmont Triad West Dr Mount Airy (27030) *(G-9128)*

Harvey & Sons Net & Twine..................................252 729-1731
804 Hwy 70 Davis Davis (28524) *(G-3726)*

Harvey Fertilizer and Gas Co................................252 753-2063
4419 West Pine St Farmville (27828) *(G-4530)*

Harvey Fertilizer and Gas Co................................919 731-2474
2937 N William St Goldsboro (27530) *(G-5222)*

Harvey Fertilizer and Gas Co................................252 523-9090
1291 Hwy 258 N Kinston (28504) *(G-7414)*

Harvey Fertilizer and Gas Co (PA)..........................252 526-4150
303 Bohannon Rd Kinston (28501) *(G-7415)*

Harvey Gin & Cotton, Kinston *Also Called: Harvey Fertilizer and Gas Co (G-7415)*

Harwood Signs..704 857-6203
112 Chippewa Trl China Grove (28023) *(G-3074)*

Hasco America Inc...828 650-2631
270 Rutledge Rd Unit B Fletcher (28732) *(G-4740)*

Hatleys Signs & Service Inc.................................704 723-4027
4495 Motorsports Dr Sw Ste 110 # 1 Concord (28027) *(G-3372)*

Hatrack River Enterprises Inc...............................336 282-9848
401 Willoughby Blvd Greensboro (27408) *(G-5588)*

Hatteras Canvas Products, Greenville *Also Called: Hatteras Hammocks Inc (G-5987)*

Hatteras Hammocks Inc.....................................252 758-0641
305 Industrial Blvd Greenville (27834) *(G-5987)*

Hatteras Networks Inc.......................................919 991-5440
637 Davis Dr Morrisville (27560) *(G-8985)*

Hatteras Yachts, New Bern *Also Called: White River Marine Group LLC (G-9406)*

Hatteras Yachts Inc..252 633-3101
110 N Glenburnie Rd New Bern (28560) *(G-9370)*

Hauser Hvac Installation.....................................336 416-2173
480 S Peace Haven Rd Winston Salem (27103) *(G-13192)*

Haw River Farmhouse Ales LLC.............................336 525-9270
1713 Sax-Beth Church Rd Saxapahaw (27340) *(G-11262)*

Hawaiian Shaved Ice, Clinton *Also Called: Mary Macks Inc (G-3234)*

Hawk Distributors Inc..888 334-1307
2980 Lee Ave Sanford (27332) *(G-11188)*

Haworth Inc..828 328-5600
1610 Deborah Herman Rd Sw Conover (28613) *(G-3527)*

Haworth Inc..336 885-4021
1673 W English Rd High Point (27262) *(G-6640)*

Haworth Conover Manufacturing, Conover *Also Called: Haworth Inc (G-3527)*

Haworth Health Environments LLC..........................828 328-5600
1610 Deborah Herman Rd Sw Conover (28613) *(G-3528)*

Hawthorne Services...910 436-9013
1 Fort Bragg Fayetteville (28307) *(G-4608)*

Haydon & Company..919 781-1293
1803 Oberlin Rd Raleigh (27608) *(G-10157)*

Hayes & Lunsford Elec Contrs, Asheville *Also Called: Presley Group Ltd (G-584)*

Hayes Print-Stamp Co Inc....................................336 667-1116
1150 Foster St Wilkesboro (28697) *(G-12637)*

Hayfield Auto Sales, Alexander *Also Called: G A Lankford Construction (G-100)*

Haynes International, Mountain Home *Also Called: Haynes Wire Company (G-9274)*

Haynes International Inc......................................765 456-6000
158 N Egerton Rd Hendersonville (28792) *(G-6212)*

Haynes Wire Company..828 692-5791
158 N Edgerton Rd Mountain Home (28758) *(G-9274)*

ALPHABETIC

Haynes Wire Company, Hendersonville *Also Called: Haynes International Inc (G-6212)*

Hayward, Charlotte *Also Called: Hayward Holdings Inc (G-2263)*

Hayward Holdings Inc (PA)..704 837-8002
1415 Vantage Park Dr Ste 400 Charlotte (28203) *(G-2263)*

Hayward Industrial Products (DH)..704 837-8002
1415 Vantage Park Dr Ste 400 Charlotte (28203) *(G-2264)*

Hayward Industries Inc (HQ)..704 837-8002
1415 Vantage Park Dr Ste 400 Charlotte (28203) *(G-2265)*

Hayward Industries Inc...336 712-9900
1 Hayward Industrial Dr Clemmons (27012) *(G-3188)*

Hayward Industries Inc...336 712-9900
1 Hayward Industrial Dr Clemmons (27012) *(G-3189)*

Hayward Plastic Products Div, Charlotte *Also Called: Hayward Industrial Products (G-2264)*

Haywood Pool Products, Charlotte *Also Called: Hayward Industries Inc (G-2265)*

Haywood Vctnal Opprtnities Inc...828 454-9682
172 Riverbend St Waynesville (28786) *(G-12461)*

Hazel Keller Cosmetics, Monroe *Also Called: Keller Cosmetics Inc (G-8512)*

HB Fuller Adhesives LLC..415 878-7202
523 Davis Dr Ste 400 Morrisville (27560) *(G-8986)*

HB Fuller Company...336 294-5939
2302 W Meadowview Rd Greensboro (27407) *(G-5589)*

Hbb Global LLC..615 306-1270
8324 Covington Hill Way Apex (27539) *(G-163)*

Hbf Textiles, Hickory *Also Called: Hickory Business Furniture LLC (G-6348)*

Hbi Wh Minority Holdings LLC...336 519-8080
1000 E Hanes Mill Rd Winston Salem (27105) *(G-13193)*

Hc Composites LLC..252 641-8000
1090 W Saint James St Tarboro (27886) *(G-11928)*

Hc Forklift America Corp...980 888-8335
1338 Hundred Oaks Dr Ste Dd Charlotte (28217) *(G-2266)*

Hdb Inc..800 403-2247
3901 Riverdale Dr Greensboro (27406) *(G-5590)*

Hdm Furniture Industries Inc...336 882-8135
37 9th Street Pl Se Hickory (28602) *(G-6343)*

Hdm Furniture Industries Inc...800 349-4579
37 9th Street Pl Se Hickory (28602) *(G-6344)*

Hdm Furniture Industries Inc...336 812-4434
741 W Ward Ave Plant37 High Point (27260) *(G-6641)*

Headbands of Hope LLC...919 323-4140
7498 Waterside Peak Dr Denver (28037) *(G-3786)*

Headrick Otdoor Mdia of Crlnas...704 487-5971
600 S Morgan St Shelby (28150) *(G-11343)*

Heal..828 287-8787
360 Carpenter Rd Rutherfordton (28139) *(G-10986)*

Healing Crafter..336 567-1620
4435 Garden Club St High Point (27265) *(G-6642)*

Healing Springs Farmacy...336 549-6159
812 Stoney Hill Cir Greensboro (27406) *(G-5591)*

Health At Home Inc..850 543-4482
1321 Cavendish Ct Charlotte (28211) *(G-2267)*

Health Choice Pharmacy..281 741-8358
2690 Hendersonville Rd Arden (28704) *(G-273)*

Health Educator Publications...919 243-1299
476 Shotwell Rd Ste 102 Clayton (27520) *(G-3153)*

Health Services, Charlotte *Also Called: Unity Hlthcare Lab Billing LLP (G-2964)*

Health Supply Us LLC..888 408-1694
205 Raceway Dr Ste 3 Mooresville (28117) *(G-8680)*

Healthline Info Systems Inc..704 655-0447
705 Northeast Dr Ste 17 Davidson (28036) *(G-3707)*

Healthlink Europe..919 368-2187
611 Creekside Dr Raleigh (27609) *(G-10158)*

Healthlink Europe..919 783-4142
3737 Glenwood Ave Ste 100 Raleigh (27612) *(G-10159)*

Healthlink Europe & Intl, Raleigh *Also Called: Healthlink International Inc (G-10160)*

Healthlink International Inc..877 324-2837
2235 Gateway Access Pt Raleigh (27607) *(G-10160)*

Healthspan Dx, Durham *Also Called: Sapere Bio Inc (G-4220)*

Hearn Graphic Finishing Inc...336 760-1467
209 Regent Dr Winston Salem (27103) *(G-13194)*

Hearsay Guides LLC...336 584-1440
5005 Windsor Ct Elon (27244) *(G-4470)*

Hearst Corporation..704 348-8000
3540 Toringdon Way Ste 700 # 7 Charlotte (28277) *(G-2268)*

Hearst Corporation..704 348-8000
3540 Toringdon Way Ste 700 # 7 Charlotte (28277) *(G-2269)*

Hearst Service Center, Charlotte *Also Called: Hearst Corporation (G-2268)*

Heart Electric, Bessemer City *Also Called: Heart Electric Motor Service (G-821)*

Heart Electric Motor Service..704 922-4720
Rt 1 Costner School Rd Bessemer City (28016) *(G-821)*

Hearth & Home Technologies LLC..336 274-1663
215 Industrial Ave Ste A Greensboro (27406) *(G-5592)*

HEARTH & HOME TECHNOLOGIES, LLC, Greensboro *Also Called: Hearth & Home Technologies LLC (G-5592)*

Heartwood Pine Floors Inc..919 542-4394
2722 Nc 87 S Moncure (27559) *(G-8406)*

Heartwood Refuge...828 513-5016
389 Courtland Blvd Hendersonville (28791) *(G-6213)*

Heat Transfer Sales, LLC, Greensboro *Also Called: Hoffman Hydronics LLC (G-5603)*

Heath and Sons Management, Rocky Point *Also Called: Heath and Sons MGT Svcs LLC (G-10881)*

Heath and Sons MGT Svcs LLC..910 679-6142
514 Complex Rd Rocky Point (28457) *(G-10881)*

Heatmaster LLC (PA)...919 639-4568
3625 Benson Rd Angier (27501) *(G-120)*

Heaven & Earth Works..845 797-0902
102 College Station Dr Brevard (28712) *(G-971)*

Heavenly Cheesecakes..336 577-9390
11040 Old Us Highway 52 Winston Salem (27107) *(G-13195)*

Heavy Duty Electric, Goldsboro *Also Called: Prolec-GE Waukesha Inc (G-5238)*

Heckler Brewing Company..910 748-0085
5780 Ramsey St Ste 110 Fayetteville (28311) *(G-4609)*

Hedgecock Racing Entps Inc...336 887-4221
1520 Horneytown Rd High Point (27265) *(G-6643)*

Hedrick B V Gravel & Sand Co..704 848-4165
403 Gravel Plant Rd Lilesville (28091) *(G-7785)*

Hedrick Brothers Lumber Co Inc...336 746-5885
6736 Nc Highway 47 Lexington (27292) *(G-7697)*

Hedrick Construction...336 362-3443
838 Crosscreek Rd Kernersville (27284) *(G-7278)*

Hedrick Industries, Stanley *Also Called: B V Hedrick Gravel & Sand Co (G-11611)*

Hefner Reels LLC...828 632-5717
34 Wittenburg Industrial Dr Taylorsville (28681) *(G-11964)*

Hefty Concrete Inc...910 483-1598
309 Ivan Dr Fayetteville (28306) *(G-4610)*

Heico Fasteners Inc (HQ)...828 261-0184
2377 8th Ave Nw Hickory (28601) *(G-6345)*

Heidelberg Materials Us Inc...252 235-4162
7225 Neverson Rd Sims (27880) *(G-11431)*

Heidelberg Mtls Sthast Agg LLC...252 235-4162
Bailey (27807) *(G-670)*

Heidelberg Mtls Sthast Agg LLC...910 893-8308
3155 Nc 210 S Bunnlevel (28323) *(G-1016)*

Heidelberg Mtls Sthast Agg LLC...910 893-2111
Sr 2016 Lillington (27546) *(G-7797)*

Heidelberg Mtls Sthast Agg LLC...252 222-0812
5101 Business Dr Morehead City (28557) *(G-8834)*

Heidelberg Mtls Sthast Agg LLC...919 936-4221
476 Edwards Rd Princeton (27569) *(G-9824)*

Heidelberg Mtls Sthast Agg LLC...919 787-0613
5001 Duraleigh Rd Raleigh (27612) *(G-10161)*

Heidelberg Mtls Sthast Agg LLC...919 556-4011
10501 Capital Blvd Wake Forest (27587) *(G-12281)*

Heidelberg Mtls US Cem LLC..919 682-5791
1031 Drew St Durham (27701) *(G-4058)*

Heintz Bros Automotives Inc..704 872-8081
1475 Old Mountain Rd Statesville (28677) *(G-11706)*

Heiq Chemtex Inc (HQ)..704 795-9322
2725 Armentrout Dr Concord (28025) *(G-3373)*

Heist Brewery, Charlotte *Also Called: Heist Brewing Company LLC (G-2270)*

Heist Brewing Company LLC...603 969-8012
525 Oakland Ave Apt 1 Charlotte (28204) *(G-2270)*

Helena Agri-Enterprises Inc..828 685-1182
3642 Chimney Rock Rd Hendersonville (28792) *(G-6214)*

Helena Agri-Enterprises LLC.................... 910 422-8901
13866 Hwy 301 S Rowland (28383) *(G-10915)*

Helium Agency LLC............................... 919 833-1358
2207 Alexander Rd Raleigh (27608) *(G-10162)*

Helium Brands LLC............................... 561 350-1328
109 Granby Ct Cary (27511) *(G-1370)*

Hell On Horsecreek Brewing, Madison *Also Called: Lichtenberg Inc (G-7991)*

Helms Machine Company.......................... 704 289-5571
216 N Bivens Rd Monroe (28110) *(G-8498)*

Helpmehelpu, Raleigh *Also Called: Holley Selinda (G-10171)*

Hema Online Indian Btq LLC..................... 919 771-4374
1954 Rothesay Dr Apex (27502) *(G-164)*

Hemco Wire Products Inc......................... 336 454-7280
301 Scientific St Jamestown (27282) *(G-7164)*

Hemispheres Magazine............................ 336 255-0195
1301 Carolina St Greensboro (27401) *(G-5593)*

Hemo Bioscience Inc............................. 919 313-2888
4022 Stirrup Creek Dr Ste 311 Durham (27703) *(G-4059)*

Hemosonics LLC.................................. 800 280-5589
4020 Stirrup Creek Dr Ste 105 Durham (27703) *(G-4060)*

Hemosonics LLC.................................. 800 280-5589
4020 Stirrup Creek Dr Durham (27703) *(G-4061)*

Hendersnvlle Affrdbl Hsing Cor.................. 828 692-6175
203 N Justice St Hendersonville (28739) *(G-6215)*

Henderson Newspapers Inc........................ 252 436-2700
420 S Garnett St Henderson (27536) *(G-6158)*

Hendrens Racg Engs Chassis Inc.................. 828 286-0780
1310 Us 221 Hwy N Rutherfordton (28139) *(G-10987)*

Hendrix Batting Company......................... 336 431-1181
2310 Surrett Dr High Point (27263) *(G-6644)*

Henkel Corporation.............................. 704 633-1731
485 Cedar Springs Rd Salisbury (28147) *(G-11062)*

Henkel Corporation, Salisbury *Also Called: Henkel Corporation (G-11062)*

Henkel Electronic Materials, Salisbury *Also Called: Henkel US Operations Corp (G-11063)*

Henkel US Operations Corp....................... 704 799-0385
150 Fairview Rd Ste 225 Mooresville (28117) *(G-8681)*

Henkel US Operations Corp....................... 704 647-3500
825 Cedar Springs Rd Salisbury (28147) *(G-11063)*

Henley Sawmill, Asheboro *Also Called: Donald Henley & Sons Sawmill (G-346)*

Henniges Automotive N Amer Inc (DH)............. 336 342-9300
226 Watlington Industrial Dr Reidsville (27320) *(G-10688)*

Henry & Rye Incorporated........................ 919 365-7045
485 Old Wilson Rd Ste 1 Wendell (27591) *(G-12537)*

Henry The Great, High Point *Also Called: Henry Williams Jr (G-6645)*

Henry Williams Jr (PA).......................... 336 897-8714
455 S Main St High Point (27260) *(G-6645)*

Hensel Phelps.................................... 828 585-4689
171 Wright Brothers Way Fletcher (28732) *(G-4741)*

Hensley Corporation............................. 828 230-9447
9 Madelyn Ln Fairview (28730) *(G-4507)*

Henson Family Investments LLC................... 910 817-9450
395 Ledbetter Rd Rockingham (28379) *(G-10778)*

Henson's Printing, Smithfield *Also Called: Hinsons Typing & Printing (G-11446)*

Hepsco, Charlotte *Also Called: Hydralic Engnered Pdts Svc Inc (G-2305)*

Heraeus Quartz North Amer LLC................... 910 799-6230
3016 Boundary St Wilmington (28405) *(G-12804)*

Herald Huntersville............................. 704 766-2100
200 S Old Statesville Rd Huntersville (28078) *(G-6997)*

Herald Printing Co Inc.......................... 252 537-2505
916 Roanoke Ave Roanoke Rapids (27870) *(G-10738)*

Herald Printing Inc............................. 252 726-3534
201 N 17th St Morehead City (28557) *(G-8835)*

Herald-Sun, The, Durham *Also Called: News and Observer Pubg Co (G-4148)*

Herbal Ingenuity, Wilkesboro *Also Called: Herbal Innovations LLC (G-12638)*

Herbal Innovations LLC.......................... 336 818-2332
151 Herbal Ingenuity Way Wilkesboro (28697) *(G-12638)*

Herbalife Manufacturing LLC..................... 336 970-6400
3200 Temple School Rd Winston Salem (27107) *(G-13196)*

Herbs Gaia Inc (PA)............................. 828 884-4242
101 Gaia Herbs Rd Brevard (28712) *(G-972)*

Hercules Steel Company Inc (PA)................. 910 488-5110
950 Country Club Dr Fayetteville (28301) *(G-4611)*

Herff Jones, Charlotte *Also Called: Herff Jones LLC (G-2272)*

Herff Jones LLC................................. 704 845-3355
9525 Monroe Rd Ste 150 Charlotte (28270) *(G-2271)*

Herff Jones LLC................................. 704 962-1483
14931 Santa Lucia Dr Charlotte (28277) *(G-2272)*

Herff Jones LLC................................. 704 873-5563
307 E Front St Statesville (28677) *(G-11707)*

Heritage Building Company LLC................... 704 431-4494
114 N Center St Ste 300 Statesville (28677) *(G-11708)*

Heritage Classic Wovens LLC..................... 828 247-6010
155 Westerly Hills Dr Forest City (28043) *(G-4791)*

Heritage Concrete, Sanford *Also Called: Heritage Concrete Service Corp (G-11189)*

Heritage Concrete Service Corp.................. 910 892-4445
1300 N Mckay Ave Dunn (28334) *(G-3861)*

Heritage Concrete Service Corp (PA)............. 919 775-5014
140 Deep River Rd Sanford (27330) *(G-11189)*

Heritage Custom Signs & Disp.................... 704 655-1465
2731 Interstate St Charlotte (28208) *(G-2273)*

Heritage Design & Supply LLC.................... 919 453-1622
6833 Mount Herman Rd Morrisville (27560) *(G-8987)*

Heritage Flag LLC............................... 910 725-1540
230 S Bennett St Southern Pines (28387) *(G-11500)*

Heritage Knitting Co LLC........................ 704 872-7653
240 Wilson Park Rd Statesville (28625) *(G-11709)*

Heritage Prtg & Graphics Inc.................... 704 551-0700
2739 Interstate St Charlotte (28208) *(G-2274)*

Heritage Steel LLC.............................. 704 431-4097
3870 Statesville Blvd Salisbury (28147) *(G-11064)*

Herman Reeves Sheet Metal, Gastonia *Also Called: Herman Reeves Tex Shtmtl Inc (G-5059)*

Herman Reeves Tex Shtmtl Inc.................... 704 865-2231
1617 E Ozark Ave Gastonia (28054) *(G-5059)*

Hermes Marine LLC (PA).......................... 252 368-9000
109 Anchors Way Dr Edenton (27932) *(G-4367)*

Hermes Medical Solutions Inc.................... 252 355-4373
710 Cromwell Dr Farmville (27828) *(G-4531)*

Heron Therapeutics, Cary *Also Called: Heron Therapeutics Inc (G-1371)*

Heron Therapeutics Inc (PA)..................... 858 251-4400
100 Regency Forest Dr Ste 300 Cary (27518) *(G-1371)*

Herrin Bros Coal & Ice Co....................... 704 332-2193
315 E 36th St Charlotte (28206) *(G-2275)*

Hersey Meters Co LLC............................ 704 278-2221
10210 Statesville Blvd Cleveland (27013) *(G-3214)*

Hersey Meters Division, Cleveland *Also Called: Mueller Systems LLC (G-3216)*

Hershey, Kenly *Also Called: Hershey Company (G-7233)*

Hershey Company................................. 919 284-0272
104 Hershey Dr Kenly (27542) *(G-7233)*

Hershey Group................................... 336 855-3888
2010 New Garden Rd Ste A Greensboro (27410) *(G-5594)*

Hertford ABC Board.............................. 252 426-5290
803 S Church St Hertford (27944) *(G-6254)*

Hertz Kompressoren USA Inc...................... 704 579-5900
11910 Mount Holly Hntrsvlle Rd Huntersville (28078) *(G-6998)*

Hess Manufacturing Inc.......................... 704 637-3300
185 Piper Ln Salisbury (28147) *(G-11065)*

Hester Enterprises Inc.......................... 704 865-4480
214 Superior Stainless Rd Gastonia (28052) *(G-5060)*

Heubach Colorants USA LLC....................... 408 686-2935
5500 77 Center Dr Charlotte (28217) *(G-2276)*

Hewlin Brothers Lumber Co....................... 252 586-6473
18555 Nc Highway 48 Enfield (27823) *(G-4484)*

Hexatech Inc.................................... 919 481-4412
991 Aviation Pkwy Ste 800 Morrisville (27560) *(G-8988)*

Hexatech Inc.................................... 919 633-0583
8311 Brier Creek Pkwy Raleigh (27617) *(G-10163)*

Hexion Inc...................................... 910 483-1311
1411 Industrial Dr Fayetteville (28301) *(G-4612)*

Hexion Inc...................................... 336 884-8918
1717 W Ward Ave High Point (27260) *(G-6646)*

Hexion Inc...................................... 828 584-3800
114 Industrial Blvd Morganton (28655) *(G-8871)*

A
L
P
H
A
B
E
T
I
C

Hexpol, Statesville *Also Called: Hexpol Compounding NC Inc (G-11710)*

Hexpol Compounding NC Inc..704 872-1585
   280 Crawford Rd Statesville (28625) *(G-11710)*

Heyco Werk USA Inc...434 634-8810
   5134 Apple Creek Pkwy Dallas (28034) *(G-3675)*

Heyel Custom Metal...919 957-8442
   1224 Home Ct Raleigh (27603) *(G-10164)*

Heyel Custom Metal Inc...919 957-8442
   1224 Home Ct Raleigh (27603) *(G-10165)*

Hf Group LLC...336 931-0800
   1010 Arnold St Greensboro (27405) *(G-5595)*

HFC Prestige Products Inc...919 895-5300
   1400 Broadway Rd Sanford (27332) *(G-11190)*

Hfi Wind Down Inc...828 438-5767
   109 E Fleming Dr 7 Morganton (28655) *(G-8872)*

Hfi Wind Down Inc...828 430-3355
   410 Hogan St Morganton (28655) *(G-8873)*

Hhh Tempering Resources Inc...................................336 201-5396
   5901 Gun Club Rd Winston Salem (27103) *(G-13197)*

HI & Dri Boat Lift Systems Inc...................................704 663-5438
   1277 River Hwy Mooresville (28117) *(G-8682)*

Hi-TEC Machine Corp...828 652-1060
   2082 Silvers Welch Rd Old Fort (28762) *(G-9593)*

Hi-TEC Plating Inc...704 872-8969
   1603 Salisbury Rd Statesville (28677) *(G-11711)*

Hi-Tech Fabrication Inc..919 781-6150
   222 Glenwood Ave Apt 503 Raleigh (27603) *(G-10166)*

Hi-Tech Screens Inc..828 452-5151
   188 Blossom Ridge Dr Mooresville (28117) *(G-8683)*

Hi-Tech Signs, Charlotte *Also Called: S Tri Inc (G-2745)*

Hiab, Cornelius *Also Called: Hiab USA Inc (G-3606)*

Hiab USA Inc...704 896-9089
   18627 Starcreek Dr Cornelius (28031) *(G-3606)*

Hiatus, Charlotte *Also Called: Hiatus Inc (G-2277)*

Hiatus Inc..844 572-6185
   1515 Mockingbird Ln Ste 400 Charlotte (28209) *(G-2277)*

Hibco Plastics Inc...336 463-2391
   1820 Us 601 Hwy Yadkinville (27055) *(G-13443)*

Hickman, Arden *Also Called: Wph Ventures Inc (G-319)*

Hickman Oil & Ice, Troy *Also Called: Hickman Oil & Ice Co Inc (G-12161)*

Hickman Oil & Ice Co Inc...910 576-2501
   165 Lemonds Drywall Rd Troy (27371) *(G-12161)*

Hickory Adchem Inc...828 327-0936
   123 23rd St Sw Hickory (28602) *(G-6346)*

Hickory Brands Inc..828 322-2600
   429 27th St Nw Hickory (28601) *(G-6347)*

Hickory Business Furniture LLC (HQ)........................828 328-2064
   900 12th Street Dr Nw Hickory (28601) *(G-6348)*

Hickory Chair, Hickory *Also Called: Hickory Chair Company (G-6349)*

Hickory Chair Company..800 225-0265
   37 9th Street Pl Se Hickory (28602) *(G-6349)*

Hickory Color & Chemical Co, High Point *Also Called: Marlowe-Van Loan Sales Co (G-6700)*

Hickory Daily Record, Hickory *Also Called: Hickory Publishing Co Inc (G-6352)*

Hickory Dyg & Winding Co Inc...................................828 322-1550
   1025 10th St Ne Hickory (28601) *(G-6350)*

Hickory Heritage of Falling Creek Inc
   3211b Falling Creek Rd Hickory (28601) *(G-6351)*

Hickory Leather Company, Vale *Also Called: Meghan Blake Industries Inc (G-12209)*

Hickory Mfg Division, Hickory *Also Called: Sherrill Furniture Company (G-6439)*

Hickory Printing Group Inc H.....................................828 465-3431
   725 Reese Dr Sw Conover (28613) *(G-3529)*

Hickory Printing Solutions LLC..................................828 465-3431
   725 Reese Dr Sw Conover (28613) *(G-3530)*

Hickory Publishing Co Inc...828 322-4510
   1100 Park Place 11th Ave Se Hickory (28601) *(G-6352)*

Hickory Saw & Tool Inc...828 324-5585
   406 9th St Se Hickory (28602) *(G-6353)*

Hickory Springs - Metal Plant, Hickory *Also Called: Hickory Springs Mfg Co (G-6358)*

Hickory Springs California LLC..................................828 328-2201
   235 2nd Ave Nw Hickory (28601) *(G-6354)*

Hickory Springs Manufacturing Company (PA)............828 328-2201
   235 2nd Ave Nw Hickory (28601) *(G-6355)*

Hickory Springs Mfg Co...828 322-7994
   871 Highland Ave Ne Hickory (28601) *(G-6356)*

Hickory Springs Mfg Co...828 328-2201
   2230 Main Ave Se Hickory (28602) *(G-6357)*

Hickory Springs Mfg Co...828 325-4757
   140 Mcdonald Pkwy Hickory (28603) *(G-6358)*

Hickory Springs Mfg Co...828 632-9733
   Sharpe Rd Hiddenite (28636) *(G-6497)*

Hickory Springs Mfg Co...336 861-4195
   1325 Baker Rd High Point (27263) *(G-6647)*

Hickory Springs Mfg Co...336 491-4131
   1905 Alleghany St High Point (27263) *(G-6648)*

Hickory Springs Mfg Co...828 728-9274
   2145 Norwood St Sw Lenoir (28645) *(G-7614)*

Hickory Springs Mfg Rubbr, Lenoir *Also Called: Hickory Springs Mfg Co (G-7614)*

Hickory Throwing Company..828 322-1158
   520 20th St Se Hickory (28602) *(G-6359)*

Hickory White Company, Hickory *Also Called: H W S Company Inc (G-6341)*

Hickory Wire Inc..828 322-9473
   1711 11th Ave Sw Hickory (28602) *(G-6360)*

Hickory Yarns, Hickory *Also Called: Hickory Dyg & Winding Co Inc (G-6350)*

Hicks Mechanical, Mount Airy *Also Called: Hicks Wterstoves Solar Systems (G-9129)*

Hicks Wterstoves Solar Systems................................336 789-4977
   2649 S Main St Mount Airy (27030) *(G-9129)*

Hiddenite Conference Ctr LLC....................................828 352-9200
   471 Sulphur Springs Rd Hiddenite (28636) *(G-6498)*

Hiddenite Gems Inc...828 632-3394
   484 Emerald Hollow Mine Dr Hiddenite (28636) *(G-6499)*

High and High Inc..252 257-2390
   268 Country Club Dr Henderson (27536) *(G-6159)*

High Cntry Cbnets Bnner Elk In..................................828 898-3435
   2850 Tynecastle Hwy Banner Elk (28604) *(G-686)*

High Cntry Tmbrframe Gllery WD................................828 264-8971
   689 George Wilson Rd Boone (28607) *(G-921)*

High Concepts LLC..704 377-3467
   7806 Creek Park Dr Denver (28037) *(G-3787)*

High Country Candles, Blowing Rock *Also Called: Wildflwers Btq of Blowing Rock (G-882)*

High Country Chair Weaving, Lansing *Also Called: Jerry Blevins (G-7477)*

High Country Electric Mtrs LLC..................................336 838-4808
   1268 Suncrest Orchard Rd North Wilkesboro (28659) *(G-9534)*

High Country Media LLC..828 733-2448
   428 Pineola St Newland (28657) *(G-9430)*

High Country News Inc..828 264-2262
   1600 Highway 105 Boone (28607) *(G-922)*

High Definition Tool Corp...828 397-2467
   7600 Carolina Tool Dr Connelly Springs (28612) *(G-3478)*

High Five Enterprises Inc...828 279-5962
   12 Strawberry Ln Weaverville (28787) *(G-12492)*

High Ground Incorporated..704 372-6620
   2209 Park Rd Ste 1 Charlotte (28203) *(G-2278)*

High Mobility Solutions Inc..704 849-8242
   648 Matthews Mint Hill Rd Ste D Matthews (28105) *(G-8116)*

High Performance Adaptive, Denver *Also Called: Crawford Composites LLC (G-3778)*

High Performance Marketing Inc................................919 870-9915
   158 Wind Chime Ct Raleigh (27615) *(G-10167)*

High Point Enterprise Inc...336 434-2716
   213 Woodbine St High Point (27260) *(G-6649)*

High Point Enterprise Inc...336 883-2839
   712 W Lexington Ave High Point (27262) *(G-6650)*

High Point Enterprise Inc...336 472-9500
   512 Turner St Thomasville (27360) *(G-12030)*

High Point Enterprise Llc (HQ)...................................336 888-3500
   213 Woodbine St High Point (27260) *(G-6651)*

High Point Enterprise, Inc., High Point *Also Called: High Point Enterprise Llc (G-6651)*

High Point Fibers Inc...336 887-8771
   601 Old Thomasville Rd High Point (27260) *(G-6652)*

High Point Furniture 0n64, High Point *Also Called: Leggett & Platt Incorporated (G-6691)*

High Point Furniture Inds Inc (PA)..............................336 431-7101
   1104 Bedford St High Point (27263) *(G-6653)*

High Point Pharmaceuticals LLC..................................336 841-0300
4170 Mendenhall Oaks Pkwy High Point (27265) *(G-6654)*

High Point Precast Pdts Inc.....................................336 434-1815
4130 W Us Highway 64 Lexington (27295) *(G-7698)*

High Point Quilting Inc...336 861-4180
1601 Blandwood Dr High Point (27260) *(G-6655)*

High Point Spring 1506, High Point Also Called: Leggett & Platt Incorporated *(G-6690)*

High Speed Gear Inc..910 325-1000
87 Old Hammock Rd Swansboro (28584) *(G-11885)*

High Speed Welding LLC...910 632-4427
1536 Castle Hayne Rd 6 Wilmington (28405) *(G-12805)*

High Temperature Tech Inc......................................704 375-2111
4324 Revolution Park Dr Ste 106 Charlotte (28203) *(G-2279)*

High Vacuum Electronics Inc....................................910 738-1219
2200 Cox Rd Lumberton (28358) *(G-7957)*

High-Tech Fabrications Inc......................................336 871-2990
3045 Nc 704 Hwy E Lawsonville (27022) *(G-7519)*

Highcorp Incorporated...910 642-4104
127 W Columbus St Whiteville (28472) *(G-12584)*

Highland, Asheville Also Called: Highland Brewing Company Inc *(G-517)*

Highland Brewing Company Inc.................................828 299-3370
12 Old Charlotte Hwy Ste H Asheville (28803) *(G-517)*

Highland Composites...704 924-3090
416 Gallimore Dairy Rd Ste N Greensboro (27409) *(G-5596)*

Highland Containers Inc (DH)...................................336 887-5400
100 Ragsdale Rd Jamestown (27282) *(G-7165)*

Highland Containers Inc....336 887-5400
3520 Dillon Rd Jamestown (27282) *(G-7166)*

Highland Craftsmen Inc....828 765-9010
534 Oak Ave Spruce Pine (28777) *(G-11577)*

Highland Foam Inc...828 327-0400
1560 Deborah Herman Rd Sw Conover (28613) *(G-3531)*

Highland House, Hickory Also Called: Century Furniture LLC *(G-6302)*

Highland Industries Inc..336 547-1600
629 Green Valley Rd Ste 300 Greensboro (27408) *(G-5597)*

Highland Industries Inc...336 855-0625
10 Northline Pl Greensboro (27410) *(G-5598)*

Highland International..828 265-2513
160b Den-Mac Dr Boone (28607) *(G-923)*

Highland International LLC.......................................828 265-2513
465 Industrial Park Dr Boone (28607) *(G-924)*

Highland Mills, Concord Also Called: Fine Sheer Industries Inc *(G-3363)*

Highland Paving Co LLC..910 482-0080
1351 Wilmington Hwy Fayetteville (28306) *(G-4613)*

Highland Tank NC Inc...336 218-0801
2700 Patterson St Greensboro (27407) *(G-5599)*

Highland Tool, Mills River Also Called: Highland Tool and Gauge Inc *(G-8314)*

Highland Tool and Gauge Inc....................................828 891-8557
5500 Old Haywood Rd Mills River (28759) *(G-8314)*

Highline Performance Group.....................................704 799-3500
114 Meadow Hill Cir Mooresville (28117) *(G-8684)*

Highpoint Century Showroom, High Point Also Called: Century Furniture LLC *(G-6566)*

Highs Welding Shop...704 624-5707
1027 Unarco Rd Marshville (28103) *(G-8090)*

Hightower Group LLC...816 286-1051
211 Fraley Rd High Point (27263) *(G-6656)*

Highway Patrol, Kinston Also Called: North Crlina Dept Crime Ctrl P *(G-7424)*

Hildreth Mechanical & Maint, Laurel Hill Also Called: Tony D Hildreth *(G-7488)*

Hildreth Ready Mix LLC..704 694-2034
518 W Us Highway 74 Rockingham (28379) *(G-10779)*

Hildreth Wood Products Inc......................................704 826-8326
825 Mount Vernon Rd Wadesboro (28170) *(G-12243)*

Hilex Poly Co LLC (DH)   3436 Toringdon Way Ste 100 Charlotte (28277) *(G-2280)*

Hill Country Woodworks, Chapel Hill Also Called: Nobscot Construction Co Inc *(G-1560)*

Hill Hosiery Mill Inc..336 472-7908
602 Davidson St Thomasville (27360) *(G-12031)*

Hill Spinning Division, Thomasville Also Called: Hill Hosiery Mill Inc *(G-12031)*

Hill-Pak Inc...336 431-3833
5453 Lilly Flower Rd High Point (27263) *(G-6657)*

Hill-Rom Inc....919 854-3600
1225 Crescent Green Ste 300 Cary (27518) *(G-1372)*

Hill's Tire & Auto, Goldsboro Also Called: Super Retread Center Inc *(G-5248)*

Hillgray Innovations LLC...704 923-6618
119 Galley Ln Statesville (28677) *(G-11712)*

Hilliard Fabricators LLC..336 861-8833
501 Carolina Ave Thomasville (27360) *(G-12032)*

Hills Machinery Company LLC...................................828 820-5265
5481 Old Haywood Rd Mills River (28759) *(G-8315)*

Hillshire Brands Company..336 519-8080
470 W Hanes Mill Rd Frnt Frnt Winston Salem (27105) *(G-13198)*

Hilton Vineyards LLC..704 776-9656
3310 Crow Rd Monroe (28112) *(G-8499)*

Him Inc..336 409-7795
King (27021) *(G-7327)*

Himcen Battery, Apex Also Called: Himcen Battery Inc *(G-165)*

Himcen Battery Inc....408 828-8744
2313 Blue Cedar Ct Apex (27523) *(G-165)*

Hinderer & Muehlich, Charlotte Also Called: H + M USA Management Co Inc *(G-2247)*

Hinnant Farms Vineyard LLC.....................................919 965-3350
826 Pine Level Micro Road Pine Level (27568) *(G-9681)*

Hinson Industries Inc...252 937-7171
109 Zebulon Ct Rocky Mount (27804) *(G-10840)*

Hinsons Typing & Printing.......................................919 934-9036
1294 W Market St Smithfield (27577) *(G-11446)*

Hip Labels, Greensboro Also Called: Lovejoy Corporation Inc *(G-5667)*

Hipra Scientific USA..919 605-8256
3835 Generosity Ct Ste 108 Garner (27529) *(G-4931)*

Hirsch Solutions LLC...631 701-2112
11515 Vanstory Dr Ste 145 Huntersville (28078) *(G-6999)*

Hirschfeld Industries, Greensboro Also Called: CSC Family Holdings Inc *(G-5475)*

Hirschfeld Industries Brdg LLC.................................336 271-8252
101 Centreport Dr Ste 400 Greensboro (27409) *(G-5600)*

Hirschfeld Industries-Bridge, Greensboro Also Called: Hirschfeld Industries Brdg LLC *(G-5600)*

His Company Inc..800 537-0351
2516 Independence Blvd Ste 201 Wilmington (28412) *(G-12806)*

His Glassworks Inc....828 254-2559
2000 Riverside Dr Ste 19 Asheville (28804) *(G-518)*

Hitachi ABB Power Grids, Raleigh Also Called: Hitachi Energy USA Inc *(G-10168)*

Hitachi Energy USA Inc...919 649-7022
901 Main Campus Dr Raleigh (27606) *(G-10168)*

Hitachi Energy USA Inc...919 324-5403
1345 Express Dr Raleigh (27603) *(G-10169)*

Hitachi Energy USA Inc (HQ)....................................919 856-2360
901 Main Campus Dr Raleigh (27606) *(G-10170)*

Hitachi Metals NC Ltd, China Grove Also Called: Proterial North Carolina Ltd *(G-3078)*

Hitch Crafters LLC....336 859-3257
853 Cid Rd Lexington (27292) *(G-7699)*

Hitech Circuits Inc....336 838-3420
7711 Idlewild Rd Indian Trail (28079) *(G-7083)*

Hitech Controls Inc...336 498-1534
1348 Plantation Ct Randleman (27317) *(G-10649)*

Hiviz Led Lighting LLC....703 662-3458
149 Twin Springs Rd Hendersonville (28792) *(G-6216)*

Hiviz Lighting Inc...703 382-5675
149 Twin Springs Rd Hendersonville (28792) *(G-6217)*

HL James LLC...516 398-3311
1911 W Club Blvd Durham (27705) *(G-4062)*

Hlm Legacy Group Inc..704 878-8823
129 Honeycutt Rd Troutman (28166) *(G-12140)*

Hlmf Logistics Inc...704 782-0356
11516 Downs Rd Pineville (28134) *(G-9733)*

HM Frame Company Inc....828 428-3354
1903 Gkn Way Newton (28658) *(G-9472)*

HM Liquidation Inc....828 495-8235
166 Hancock & Moore Ln Hickory (28601) *(G-6361)*

Hmf Inc...704 821-6765
3479 Gribble Rd Matthews (28104) *(G-8173)*

Hmi USA, High Point Also Called: Home Meridian Group LLC *(G-6660)*

Hobes Country Hams Inc (PA)....................................336 670-3401
389 Elledge Mill Rd North Wilkesboro (28659) *(G-9535)*

Hockmeyer Equipment Corp.....................................252 338-4705
6 Kitty Hawk Ln Elizabeth City (27909) *(G-4390)*

HOCKMEYER EQUIPMENT CORP., Elizabeth City Also Called: Hockmeyer Equipment Corp (G-4390)

Hodge Farms LLC.. 704 278-2684
11235 Nc Highway 801 Mount Ulla (28125) *(G-9269)*

Hodges Precision Machine................................... 336 366-3024
116 Tobe Hudson Rd Dobson (27017) *(G-3821)*

Hoffer Calibration Svcs LLC................................. 252 338-6379
1100 W Ehringhaus St Ste C Elizabeth City (27909) *(G-4391)*

Hoffer Flow Controls Inc...................................... 252 331-1997
107 Kitty Hawk Ln Elizabeth City (27909) *(G-4392)*

Hoffman Building Tech Inc (PA)............................ 336 292-8777
3816 Patterson St Greensboro (27407) *(G-5601)*

Hoffman Hydronics LLC....................................... 800 842-3328
4321 Piedmont Pkwy Greensboro (27410) *(G-5602)*

Hoffman Hydronics LLC (HQ)...............................336 294-3838
321 Piedmont Pkwy Greensboro (27410) *(G-5603)*

Hoffman Materials LLC... 717 243-2011
230 Timberbrook Ln Granite Falls (28630) *(G-5306)*

Hoffman Materials Inc.. 717 243-2011
230 Timberbrook Ln Granite Falls (28630) *(G-5307)*

Hoffman Plasti, High Point Also Called: Hoffman Plasti-Form Company (G-6658)

Hoffman Plasti-Form Company............................. 336 431-2934
5432 Edgar Rd High Point (27263) *(G-6658)*

Hofler H S & Sons Lumber Co............................. 252 465-8603
577 Nc Highway 32 N Sunbury (27979) *(G-11848)*

Hofler Logging Inc.. 252 465-8921
491 Nc Highway 32 S Sunbury (27979) *(G-11849)*

Hog Slat Incorporated... 252 209-0092
440 Nc Highway 561 W Aulander (27805) *(G-640)*

Hog Slat Incorporated... 910 862-7081
2229 Us Highway 701 N Elizabethtown (28337) *(G-4427)*

Hog Slat Incorporated (PA)................................. 800 949-4647
206 Fayetteville St Newton Grove (28366) *(G-9514)*

Hog Slat Incorporated... 800 949-4647
117 W Weeksdale Dr Newton Grove (28366) *(G-9515)*

Hog Slat Incorporated... 919 663-3321
17720 Us Highway 64 W Siler City (27344) *(G-11411)*

Hogan Cabinetry and Mllwk LLC.......................... 704 856-0425
1720 S Main St China Grove (28023) *(G-3075)*

Hogans Racing Manifolds Inc............................... 704 799-3424
115 Thunder Rd Mooresville (28115) *(G-8685)*

Hoh Corporation... 336 723-9274
1701 Vargrave St Winston Salem (27107) *(G-13199)*

Holder Backhoe & Hauling Inc............................. 336 622-7388
4660 Randolph Church Rd Liberty (27298) *(G-7767)*

Holder Machine & Mfg Co..................................... 828 479-8627
1483 Fontana Rd Robbinsville (28771) *(G-10759)*

Holders Restaurant Furniture............................... 828 754-8383
2310 Morganton Blvd Sw Lenoir (28645) *(G-7615)*

Holland Industrial, Henderson Also Called: Holland Supply Company (G-6160)

Holland Supply Company...................................... 252 492-7541
518 W Montgomery St Henderson (27536) *(G-6160)*

Holley Selinda.. 919 351-9466
700 Peterson St Raleigh (27610) *(G-10171)*

Hollingsworth & Vose Company........................... 704 708-5913
143 Sardis Pointe Rd Matthews (28105) *(G-8117)*

Hollingsworth Heating Air Cond........................... 252 824-0355
1893 Mcnair Rd Tarboro (27886) *(G-11929)*

Hollingswrth Cbnets Intrors LL............................ 910 251-1490
2913 Castle Hayne Rd Castle Hayne (28429) *(G-1502)*

Hollister Incorporated.. 919 792-2095
5959 Triangle Town Blvd Ste 1085 Raleigh (27616) *(G-10172)*

Holman & Moody Inc... 704 394-4141
9119 Forsyth Park Dr Charlotte (28273) *(G-2281)*

Holman Automotive Inc....................................... 704 583-2888
9119 Forsyth Park Dr Charlotte (28273) *(G-2282)*

Holmes Logging - Wallace LLC............................ 910 271-1216
2788 Lightwood Bridge Rd Wallace (28466) *(G-12321)*

Holt Group, High Point Also Called: Holt Group Inc (G-6659)

Holt Group Inc (PA)..336 668-2770
4198 Eagle Hill Dr Ste 105 High Point (27265) *(G-6659)*

Holt Hosiery Mills Inc.. 336 227-1431
733 Koury Dr Burlington (27215) *(G-1103)*

Holt Sublimation Printing & Products Inc............. 336 222-3600
2208 Airpark Rd Burlington (27215) *(G-1104)*

Holy Cow Publications LLC................................. 704 900-5779
811 Queens Rd Apt 1 Charlotte (28207) *(G-2283)*

Holz-Her Us Inc (DH)..704 587-3400
124 Crosslake Park Dr Mooresville (28117) *(G-8686)*

Home City Ltd (PA).. 910 428-2196
2086 Hwy 2427 W Biscoe (27209) *(G-853)*

Home Elevators & Lift, Sunset Beach Also Called: Home Elevators & Lift Pdts LLC (G-11850)

Home Elevators & Lift Pdts LLC........................... 910 427-0006
8311 Ocean Hwy W Sunset Beach (28468) *(G-11850)*

Home Fabrics, Goldsboro Also Called: Cloth Barn Inc (G-5206)

Home Impressions Inc... 828 328-1142
420 3rd Ave Nw Hickory (28601) *(G-6362)*

Home Meridian Group LLC (HQ).......................... 336 819-7200
2485 Penny Rd High Point (27265) *(G-6660)*

Home Meridian Holdings Inc................................. 336 887-1985
2485 Penny Rd High Point (27265) *(G-6661)*

Home Security Bars, Greenville Also Called: Energy Svers Windows Doors Inc (G-5974)

Home State Apparel, Greensboro Also Called: Mischief Makers Local 816 LLC (G-5694)

Home T LLC.. 646 797-4768
652 Griffith Rd Ste I Charlotte (28217) *(G-2284)*

Home Team Athletics Inc...................................... 910 938-0862
242 Wilmington Hwy 17 Jacksonville (28540) *(G-7126)*

Homeland Creamery LLC..................................... 336 685-6455
6506 Bowman Dairy Rd Julian (27283) *(G-7201)*

Homes & Land Mag of High S, Boone Also Called: Ty Brown (G-948)

Homeserve NC LLC... 740 552-8497
2225 Castle Rock Farm Rd Pittsboro (27312) *(G-9784)*

Homestead Country Built Furn (PA)...................... 910 799-6489
4942 Tanbark Dr Wilmington (28412) *(G-12807)*

Hometown Sports Embroidery, Hillsborough Also Called: Hometown Sports Inc (G-6867)

Hometown Sports Inc... 919 732-7090
3301 St Marys Rd Hillsborough (27278) *(G-6867)*

Homs, Pittsboro Also Called: Homs LLC (G-9785)

Homs LLC.. 919 533-4752
193 Lorax Ln Pittsboro (27312) *(G-9785)*

Honda Aero LLC (HQ)..336 226-2376
2989 Tucker Street Ext Burlington (27215) *(G-1105)*

Honda Aircraft Co Service Ctr, Greensboro Also Called: Honda Aircraft Company LLC (G-5604)

Honda Aircraft Company LLC.............................. 336 662-0246
6420 Ballinger Rd Bldg 400 Greensboro (27410) *(G-5604)*

Honda Aircraft Company LLC.............................. 336 662-0246
404 S Chimney Rock Rd Greensboro (27409) *(G-5605)*

Honda Aircraft Company LLC (HQ).......................336 662-0246
6430 Ballinger Rd Greensboro (27410) *(G-5606)*

Honeycutt Custom Cabinets Inc........................... 910 567-6766
1068 Baptist Chapel Rd Autryville (28318) *(G-648)*

Honeygirl Meadery LLC....................................... 919 399-3056
1604 Lathrop St Durham (27703) *(G-4063)*

Honeywell.. 734 942-5823
13509 S Point Blvd Ste 150 Charlotte (28273) *(G-2285)*

Honeywell, Charlotte Also Called: Honeywell International Inc (G-2286)

Honeywell, Fort Bragg Also Called: Honeywell International Inc (G-4804)

Honeywell, Raleigh Also Called: Honeywell International Inc (G-10173)

Honeywell Authorized Dealer, Charlotte Also Called: Carolina Products Inc (G-1854)

Honeywell Authorized Dealer, Kitty Hawk Also Called: Dusty Rhoads Hvac Inc (G-7444)

Honeywell Authorized Dealer, Littleton Also Called: Airboss Heating and Coolg Inc (G-7883)

Honeywell Authorized Dealer, Raleigh Also Called: Allen Kelly & Co Inc (G-9892)

Honeywell Authorized Dealer, Wilmington Also Called: Kenny Fowler Heating and A Inc (G-12827)

Honeywell International Inc (PA)........................... 704 627-6200
855 S Mint St Charlotte (28202) *(G-2286)*

Honeywell International Inc................................... 910 436-5144
1 Fort Bragg Fort Bragg (28307) *(G-4804)*

Honeywell International Inc................................... 919 662-7539
201 S Rogers Ln Raleigh (27610) *(G-10173)*

Honeywell International Inc.................... 252 977-2100
3475 N Wesleyan Blvd Rocky Mount (27804) *(G-10841)*

Honeywell SEC Americas LLC.................... 919 563-5911
1027 Corporate Park Dr Mebane (27302) *(G-8246)*

Hood Container Corporation.................... 336 887-5400
3520 Dillon Rd Jamestown (27282) *(G-7167)*

Hood Container Corporation.................... 336 784-0445
555 Aureole St Winston Salem (27107) *(G-13200)*

Hood Packaging Corporation.................... 910 582-1842
740 Cheraw Rd Hamlet (28345) *(G-6057)*

Hoodoo Honey LLC.................... 252 548-0697
3600 N Duke St Ste 1 Durham (27704) *(G-4064)*

Hooker Furnishings Corporation.................... 336 819-7200
2485 Penny Rd Fl 2 High Point (27265) *(G-6662)*

Hoover Treated Wood Pdts Inc.................... 866 587-8761
1772 Trueblood Rd Weldon (27890) *(G-12520)*

Hope Renovations.................... 919 960-1957
3 Bolin Hts Chapel Hill (27514) *(G-1549)*

Hope Tree Publishing LLC.................... 336 858-5301
916 Big Creek Ct High Point (27265) *(G-6663)*

Hopkins Poultry Company.................... 336 656-3361
7741 Doggett Rd Browns Summit (27214) *(G-998)*

Horballs Inc.................... 919 925-0483
1009 Lila Ln Raleigh (27614) *(G-10174)*

Horiba Instruments Inc.................... 828 676-2801
270 Rutledge Rd Unit D Fletcher (28732) *(G-4742)*

Horizon Forest Products, Raleigh *Also Called: Horizon Frest Pdts Wlmngton LP (G-10175)*

Horizon Forest Products Co LP.................... 336 993-9663
9050 W Market St Colfax (27235) *(G-3280)*

Horizon Frest Pdts Wlmngton LP.................... 919 424-8265
4115 Commodity Pkwy Raleigh (27610) *(G-10175)*

Horizon Home Imports Inc.................... 704 859-5133
6211 Clementine Dr Clemmons (27012) *(G-3190)*

Horizon Publications Inc.................... 828 464-0221
309 N College Ave Newton (28658) *(G-9473)*

Horizon Tool Inc.................... 336 299-4182
7918 Industrial Village Rd Greensboro (27409) *(G-5607)*

Horizon Vision Research Inc.................... 910 796-8600
1717 Shipyard Blvd Ste 140 Wilmington (28403) *(G-12808)*

Hormel, Charlotte *Also Called: Hormel Foods Corp Svcs LLC (G-2287)*

Hormel Foods Corp Svcs LLC.................... 704 527-1535
3420 Toringdon Way Charlotte (28277) *(G-2287)*

Hornet Capital LLC (PA).................... 252 641-8000
1090 W Saint James St Tarboro (27886) *(G-11930)*

Hornwood Inc (PA).................... 704 848-4121
766 Haileys Ferry Rd Lilesville (28091) *(G-7786)*

Hornwood Inc.................... 704 694-3009
204 E Wade St Wadesboro (28170) *(G-12244)*

Horseware Triple Crown Blanket.................... 252 208-0080
1030 N Rogers Ln Raleigh (27610) *(G-10176)*

Hortonworks Inc.................... 855 846-7866
312 Blackwell St Ste 100 Durham (27701) *(G-4065)*

Hose Products Division, Greensboro *Also Called: Parker-Hannifin Corporation (G-5734)*

Hoser Inc.................... 704 989-7151
1132 Curtis St Monroe (28112) *(G-8500)*

Hospira Inc.................... 252 977-5111
6551 N Us Highway 301 Battleboro (27809) *(G-699)*

Hospira Inc.................... 704 335-1300
2815 Coliseum Centre Dr Ste 250 Charlotte (28217) *(G-2288)*

Hospira Inc.................... 919 553-3831
8484 Us 70 Bus Hwy W Clayton (27520) *(G-3154)*

Hospira Inc.................... 252 977-5500
Highway 301 North Rocky Mount (27801) *(G-10813)*

Hospira Inc.................... 252 977-5111
4285 N Wesleyan Blvd Rocky Mount (27804) *(G-10842)*

Hospitality Mints LLC.................... 828 262-0950
996 George Wilson Rd Boone (28607) *(G-925)*

Hot Box Power Coating Inc.................... 704 398-8224
1033 Berryhill Rd Charlotte (28208) *(G-2289)*

Hot Chillys, Southern Pines *Also Called: Performance Apparel LLC (G-11503)*

Hot Shot Services LLC.................... 336 244-0331
2202 Us 21 State Road (28676) *(G-11637)*

Hotchkis Bryde Incorporated.................... 704 660-3060
118 Infield Ct Ste A Mooresville (28117) *(G-8687)*

Hotchkis Performance Mfg Inc.................... 704 660-3060
118 Infield Ct Ste A Mooresville (28117) *(G-8688)*

Houdiniesq, Durham *Also Called: Logicbit Software LLC (G-4108)*

House of Hops.................... 919 819-0704
6909 Glenwood Ave Raleigh (27612) *(G-10177)*

House of Raeford Farms Inc.................... 910 289-3191
1000 E Central Ave Raeford (28376) *(G-9840)*

House of Raeford Farms Inc (HQ).................... 912 222-4090
3333 S Us 117 Hwy Rose Hill (28458) *(G-10906)*

House of Raeford Farms Inc.................... 910 285-2349
253 Butterball Rd Teachey (28464) *(G-11987)*

House of Raeford Farms Inc.................... 910 763-0475
118 Cardinal Drive Ext Ste 102 Wilmington (28405) *(G-12809)*

House of Raeford Farms La LLC.................... 336 751-4752
251 Eaton Rd Mocksville (27028) *(G-8369)*

House Staffer, Durham *Also Called: First Leads Inc (G-4032)*

House-Autry Mills Inc (PA).................... 919 963-6200
7000 Us Highway 301 S Four Oaks (27524) *(G-4813)*

How Great Thou Art Publication.................... 704 851-3117
Hwy 52 Sr 1003 Ste 357 Mc Farlan (28102) *(G-8216)*

Howard Brothers Mfg LLC.................... 919 772-4800
1321 Bobbitt Dr Garner (27529) *(G-4932)*

Howell & Sons Canvas Repairs.................... 704 892-7913
29015 North Main St Cornelius (28031) *(G-3607)*

Howling Moon Distillery Inc.................... 828 208-1469
361 Bradford Rd Burnsville (28714) *(G-1187)*

Howmet Aerospace Inc.................... 704 334-7276
301 N Smith St Charlotte (28202) *(G-2290)*

Howmet Aerospace Inc, Charlotte *Also Called: Howmet Aerospace Inc (G-2290)*

HP, Charlotte *Also Called: HP Inc (G-2291)*

HP Inc.................... 704 523-3548
4035 South Blvd Charlotte (28209) *(G-2291)*

HP Textile, Winston Salem *Also Called: Hpfabrics Inc (G-13201)*

Hpc NC.................... 704 978-0103
280 Crawford Rd Statesville (28625) *(G-11713)*

Hpfabrics Inc.................... 336 231-0278
3821 Kimwell Dr Winston Salem (27103) *(G-13201)*

Hpfi, High Point *Also Called: High Point Furniture Inds Inc (G-6653)*

Hrtms Incorporated.................... 919 741-5099
801 Corporate Center Dr Ste 130 Raleigh (27607) *(G-10178)*

Hs Hyosung Usa Inc.................... 336 495-2202
890 Pineview Rd Asheboro (27203) *(G-362)*

Hs Hyosung Usa Inc (DH).................... 704 790-6100
15801 Brixham Hill Ave Ste 575 Charlotte (28277) *(G-2292)*

Hs Hyosung USA Holdings Inc (HQ).................... 704 790-6134
15801 Brixham Hill Ave Ste 575 Charlotte (28277) *(G-2293)*

Hsg LLC (PA).................... 910 325-1000
87 Old Hammock Rd Swansboro (28584) *(G-11886)*

Hsi Legacy Inc.................... 704 376-9631
3528 N Graham St Charlotte (28206) *(G-2294)*

Hsm, Matthews *Also Called: High Mobility Solutions Inc (G-8116)*

Hsm Solutions, Hickory *Also Called: Hickory Springs Manufacturing Company (G-6355)*

Htc Logging Inc.................... 828 625-1601
1055 Cooper Gap Rd Mill Spring (28756) *(G-8301)*

Htm Concepts Inc.................... 252 794-2122
118 County Farm Rd Windsor (27983) *(G-13054)*

Htx Imaging, Carrboro *Also Called: Htx Technologies LLC (G-1269)*

Htx Technologies LLC.................... 919 928-5688
610 Jones Ferry Rd Ste 207 Carrboro (27510) *(G-1269)*

Hubbell Incorporated.................... 828 687-8505
20 Glenn Bridge Rd Arden (28704) *(G-274)*

Hubbell Industrial Contrls Inc (HQ).................... 336 434-2800
4301 Cheyenne Dr Archdale (27263) *(G-226)*

Hubbell Premise Wiring, Arden *Also Called: Hubbell Incorporated (G-274)*

Huber + Suhner Inc (DH).................... 704 790-7300
3540 Toringdon Way Ste 560 Charlotte (28277) *(G-2295)*

Huber + Suhner North Amer Corp (HQ).................... 704 790-7300
3540 Toringdon Way Charlotte (28277) *(G-2296)*

A
L
P
H
A
B
E
T
I
C

Huber Engineered Woods LLC (HQ)........................800 933-9220
10925 David Taylor Dr Ste 300 Charlotte (28262) *(G-2297)*

Huber Technology Inc (DH)................................704 949-1010
1009 Airlie Pkwy Denver (28037) *(G-3788)*

Huber Usa Inc...919 674-4266
1101 Nowell Rd # 110 Raleigh (27607) *(G-10179)*

Hubergroup USA Inc..336 292-5501
651 Brigham Rd Ste C Greensboro (27409) *(G-5608)*

Hubersuhner, Charlotte *Also Called: Huber + Suhner North Amer Corp* *(G-2296)*

Huck Cycles Corporation..................................704 275-1735
11020 Bailey Rd Ste D Cornelius (28031) *(G-3608)*

Huddle Furniture Inc (PA)................................828 874-8888
1801 Main St E Valdese (28690) *(G-12195)*

Hudson Industries LLC.....................................704 480-0014
439 Neisler St Shelby (28152) *(G-11344)*

Hudson Overall Company Inc............................336 314-5024
527 S Elm St Greensboro (27406) *(G-5609)*

Hudson Paving Inc...910 895-5910
120 Yates Hill Rd Rockingham (28379) *(G-10780)*

Hudson S Hardware Inc (PA).............................919 553-3030
305 Benson Rd Garner (27529) *(G-4933)*

Hudson's Hardware, Castle Hayne *Also Called: Castle Hayne Hardware LLC* *(G-1497)*

Hudson's Hill, Greensboro *Also Called: Hudson Overall Company Inc* *(G-5609)*

Huff Mj LLC..910 313-3133
5617 Carolina Beach Rd Wilmington (28412) *(G-12810)*

Huffman Finishing Company Inc........................828 396-1741
4919 Hickory Blvd Granite Falls (28630) *(G-5308)*

Huffman Sales and Service LLC.........................828 234-0693
326 Macarthur Ln Burlington (27217) *(G-1106)*

Hugger Inc...704 735-7422
1443 E Gaston St Lincolnton (28092) *(G-7832)*

Hugger Mugger LLC...910 585-2749
229 Wicker St Sanford (27330) *(G-11191)*

Hugh's Sheet Metal, Statesville *Also Called: Hughs Sheet Mtal Sttsvlle LLC* *(G-11714)*

Hughes Furniture Inds Inc (PA).........................336 498-8700
952 S Stout Rd Randleman (27317) *(G-10650)*

Hughes Metal Works, Greensboro *Also Called: Hughes Metal Works LLC* *(G-5610)*

Hughes Metal Works LLC..................................336 297-0808
1914 Fairfax Rd Greensboro (27407) *(G-5610)*

Hughes Products Co Inc....................................336 769-3788
241 Emily Ann Dr Winston Salem (27107) *(G-13202)*

Hughes Sup of Thomasville Inc..........................336 475-8146
175 Kanoy Rd Thomasville (27360) *(G-12033)*

Hughs Sheet Mtal Sttsvlle LLC...........................704 872-4621
1312 N Barkley Rd Statesville (28677) *(G-11714)*

Huitt Mills Inc (PA)..828 322-8628
115 10th St Ne Hildebran (28637) *(G-6851)*

Hull Brothers Lumber Co Inc.............................336 789-5252
579 Maple Hollow Rd Mount Airy (27030) *(G-9130)*

Hull's Wall Covering, Bessemer City *Also Called: Patricia Hall* *(G-829)*

Humber Street Facility Inc................................919 775-3628
105 E Humber St Sanford (27330) *(G-11192)*

Humboldt Mfg Co Inc.......................................919 832-6509
2525 Atlantic Ave Raleigh (27604) *(G-10180)*

Hunckler Fabrication LLC..................................336 753-0905
123 S Park Pl Mocksville (27028) *(G-8370)*

Huneywood Inc...704 385-9785
7123 Sugar And Wine Rd Monroe (28110) *(G-8501)*

Huneywood Frames, Monroe *Also Called: Huneywood Inc* *(G-8501)*

Hunsucker Printing Co Inc.................................336 629-9125
522 N Fayetteville St Asheboro (27203) *(G-363)*

Hunt Country Component LLC............................336 475-7000
1120 Trinity St Thomasville (27360) *(G-12034)*

Hunt Logging Co....919 853-2850
2233 Person Rd Louisburg (27549) *(G-7918)*

Hunter Douglas Inc..704 629-6500
201 Southridge Pkwy Bessemer City (28016) *(G-822)*

Hunter Fan Company..704 896-9250
20464 Chartwell Center Dr Ste H Cornelius (28031) *(G-3609)*

Hunter Farms...336 822-2300
1900 N Main St High Point (27262) *(G-6664)*

Hunter Farms, High Point *Also Called: Hunter Farms* *(G-6664)*

Hunter Innovations Ltd.....................................919 848-8814
1201 Corporation Pkwy Raleigh (27610) *(G-10181)*

Hunter Liver Mush Inc......................................828 652-7902
98 Poteat Rd Marion (28752) *(G-8043)*

Hunter Millwork Inc...704 821-0144
422 Seaboard Dr Matthews (28104) *(G-8174)*

Huntington House Inc.......................................828 495-4400
210 Bethlehem Park Ln Taylorsville (28681) *(G-11965)*

Huntington House Inc (PA)................................828 495-4400
661 Rink Dam Rd Hickory (28601) *(G-6363)*

Huntpack Inc..704 986-0684
320 Anderson Rd Albemarle (28001) *(G-78)*

Huntsman Corporation......................................706 272-4020
3400 Westinghouse Blvd Charlotte (28273) *(G-2298)*

Huntsman International LLC...............................704 588-6082
3400 Westinghouse Blvd Charlotte (28273) *(G-2299)*

Huntsman Textile Effects..................................704 587-5000
3400 Westinghouse Blvd Charlotte (28273) *(G-2300)*

Hurleys Ornamental Iron..................................910 576-4731
2179 Love Joy Rd Troy (27371) *(G-12162)*

Hurricane Aqua Sports Inc................................910 293-2941
170 Water Tank Rd Warsaw (28398) *(G-12362)*

Hurricane Kayaks, Warsaw *Also Called: Hurricane Aqua Sports Inc* *(G-12362)*

Hurst Jaws of Life Inc (HQ)...............................704 487-6961
711 N Post Rd Shelby (28150) *(G-11345)*

Husky Rack and Wire, Denver *Also Called: Wireway/Husky Corp* *(G-3817)*

Huso Inc..845 553-0100
6 Mountain Farm Ln Black Mountain (28711) *(G-866)*

Husqvarna Forest & Garden, Charlotte *Also Called: Husqvrna Cnsmr Otdoor Pdts NA* *(G-2301)*

Husqvarna Prof Outdoor Pdts, Charlotte *Also Called: Husqvrna Cnsmr Otdoor Pdts NA* *(G-2302)*

Husqvrna Cnsmr Otdoor Pdts NA (HQ)................704 597-5000
9335 Harris Corners Pkwy Ste 500 Charlotte (28269) *(G-2301)*

Husqvrna Cnsmr Otdoor Pdts NA.......................704 597-5000
7349 Statesville Rd Charlotte (28269) *(G-2302)*

Husqvrna Cnsmr Otdoor Pdts NA.......................704 494-4810
8825 Statesville Rd Charlotte (28269) *(G-2303)*

Hutton Vineyards LLC.......................................336 374-2321
103 Buck Fork Rd Dobson (27017) *(G-3822)*

Huvepharma Inc..910 506-4649
22300 Skyway Church Rd Maxton (28364) *(G-8201)*

Hvte Inc...919 274-8899
90 Mosswood Blvd Ste 100 Youngsville (27596) *(G-13474)*

Hydac Technology Corp.....................................610 266-0100
1051 Airlie Pkwy Denver (28037) *(G-3789)*

Hyde Park Partners Inc (PA)..............................704 587-4819
11529 Wilmar Blvd Charlotte (28273) *(G-2304)*

Hydralic Engnered Pdts Svc Inc.........................704 374-1306
803 Pressley Rd Ste 101 Charlotte (28217) *(G-2305)*

Hydraulic Hose Depot Inc.................................252 356-1862
1520c River Rd Cofield (27922) *(G-3267)*

Hydraulic Valve Division, Forest City *Also Called: Parker-Hannifin Corporation* *(G-4795)*

Hydraulics Express..828 251-2500
40 Interstate Blvd Asheville (28806) *(G-519)*

Hydreco Inc..704 295-7575
1500 Continental Blvd Ste Z Charlotte (28273) *(G-2306)*

Hydro Conduit LLC...336 475-1371
208 Randolph St Thomasville (27360) *(G-12035)*

Hydro Conduit LLC...252 243-6153
1600 Thorne Ave S Wilson (27893) *(G-12994)*

Hydro Extrusion Usa LLC..................................336 227-8826
1512 Industry Dr Burlington (27215) *(G-1107)*

Hydro Service & Supplies Inc (PA)......................919 544-3744
513 United Dr Durham (27713) *(G-4066)*

Hydro Tube Enterprises Inc...............................919 258-3070
2645 Mount Pisgah Church Rd Sanford (27332) *(G-11193)*

Hydro Tube South LLC......................................919 258-3070
2645 Mount Pisgah Church Rd Sanford (27332) *(G-11194)*

Hydrohoist of North Carolina.............................704 799-1910
1258 River Hwy Mooresville (28117) *(G-8689)*

(G-0000) Company's Geographic Section entry number

Hydrohoist of The Carolinas, Mooresville *Also Called: Hydrohoist of North Carolina (G-8689)*

Hydromer Inc (PA).. 908 526-2828
4715 Corporate Dr Nw Ste 200 Concord (28027) *(G-3374)*

Hygeia Marketing Corporation................................ 704 933-5190
729 S Main St Kannapolis (28081) *(G-7211)*

Hygiene Systems Inc.. 910 462-2661
10442 Old Wire Rd Laurel Hill (28351) *(G-7484)*

Hylite Led, Charlotte *Also Called: Arva LLC (G-1701)*

Hype World Inc... 336 588-8666
2817 Summergrove Ct Matthews (28105) *(G-8118)*

Hyper Networks LLC.. 704 837-8411
12249 Nations Ford Rd Pineville (28134) *(G-9734)*

Hyperbranch, Durham *Also Called: Stryker Corporation (G-4253)*

Hyperbranch Medical Tech Inc................................ 919 433-3325
800 Capitola Dr Ste 12 Durham (27713) *(G-4067)*

Hypernova Inc... 704 360-0096
1228 Archdale Dr Apt E Charlotte (28217) *(G-2307)*

Hypernova Solutions, Charlotte *Also Called: Hypernova Inc (G-2307)*

Hyster-Yale Group Inc... 252 931-5100
1400 Sullivan Dr Greenville (27834) *(G-5988)*

Hyster-Yale Group Inc... 252 931-5100
5200 Martin Luther King Jr Hwy Greenville (27834) *(G-5989)*

HYSTER-YALE GROUP, INC., Greenville *Also Called: Hyster-Yale Group Inc (G-5989)*

Hyster-Yale Materials Hdlg Inc (HQ)........................ 252 931-5100
1400 Sullivan Dr Greenville (27834) *(G-5990)*

Hzo, Morrisville *Also Called: Hzo Inc (G-8989)*

Hzo Inc (PA).. 919 439-0505
5151 Mccrimmon Pkwy Ste 208 Morrisville (27560) *(G-8989)*

I & I Sling Inc... 336 323-1532
3824 Patterson St Greensboro (27407) *(G-5611)*

I A C, Red Springs *Also Called: Industrial and Agricultural Chemicals Incorporated (G-10668)*

I C E A, Raleigh *Also Called: Interntnal Chldbrth Edcatn Ass (G-10208)*

I C E S Gaston County Inc...................................... 704 263-1418
102 Mariposa Rd Stanley (28164) *(G-11618)*

I G M, Charlotte *Also Called: IGM Resins USA Inc (G-2311)*

I G P.. 828 728-5338
1477 Connelly Springs Rd Lenoir (28645) *(G-7616)*

I Must Garden LLC... 919 929-2299
1500 Garner Rd Ste D Raleigh (27610) *(G-10182)*

I N I, Morrisville *Also Called: Ini Power Systems Inc (G-8993)*

I R C, Boone *Also Called: Tresco (G-946)*

I S A, Research Triangle Pa *Also Called: International Society Automtn (G-10713)*

I S G, Raleigh *Also Called: Insurance Systems Group Inc (G-10203)*

I T G, Greensboro *Also Called: Itg Holdings Inc (G-5628)*

I T G Raeford... 910 875-3736
1001 Turnpike Rd Raeford (28376) *(G-9841)*

I W S, High Point *Also Called: Interior Wood Specialties Inc (G-6675)*

I-40 Machine and Tool Inc.................................... 704 881-0242
223 Commerce Blvd Statesville (28625) *(G-11715)*

I-Leadr Inc.. 910 431-5252
2220 Lazy Ln Sherrills Ford (28673) *(G-11392)*

I-Lumenate LLC.. 336 448-0356
353 Jonestown Rd Winston Salem (27104) *(G-13203)*

I2e Group LLC.. 336 884-2014
2108 S Elm St High Point (27260) *(G-6665)*

IAMS, Henderson *Also Called: Mars Petcare Us Inc (G-6166)*

Ibd Outdoor Rooms, Concord *Also Called: Mystic Lifestyle Inc (G-3409)*

IBM, Durham *Also Called: International Bus Mchs Corp (G-4080)*

Ibx Lumber LLC.. 252 935-4050
405 Mainstem Rd Pantego (27860) *(G-9644)*

Ica Mid-Atlantic Inc.. 336 447-4546
6532 Judge Adams Rd Whitsett (27377) *(G-12610)*

Icagen LLC.. 919 941-5206
1035 Swabia Ct Ste 110 Durham (27703) *(G-4068)*

Ican Clothes Company.. 910 670-1494
1617 Owen Dr Fayetteville (28304) *(G-4614)*

Icare Tonomoter, Raleigh *Also Called: Icare Usa Inc (G-10183)*

Icare Usa Inc... 919 877-9607
809 Faulkner Pl Raleigh (27609) *(G-10183)*

ICC, High Point *Also Called: Industrial Container Corp (G-6670)*

Ice, Matthews *Also Called: International Cnstr Eqp Inc (G-8175)*

Ice Companies Inc (PA)... 910 791-1970
2820 Carolina Beach Rd Wilmington (28412) *(G-12811)*

Ice Cube Recording Studios.................................... 910 260-7616
801 Greenfield St Wilmington (28401) *(G-12812)*

Ice River Springs Usa Inc (HQ)............................... 519 925-2929
601 E Union St Morganton (28655) *(G-8874)*

Ice River Springs Water, Morganton *Also Called: Ice River Springs Usa Inc (G-8874)*

ICEE Company... 704 357-6865
1901 Associates Ln Ste A Charlotte (28217) *(G-2308)*

ICEE Company... 910 346-3937
13 E Doris Ave Ste H Jacksonville (28540) *(G-7127)*

ICI Copy Forms & Printing, Charlotte *Also Called: Insta Copy Shop Ltd (G-2339)*

Ickler Manufacturing LLC....................................... 704 658-1195
229 Pitt Rd Mooresville (28115) *(G-8690)*

Icon Boiler Inc... 844 562-4266
2025 16th St Greensboro (27405) *(G-5612)*

Icon Coolers LLC.. 855 525-4266
7213 Ogden Business Ln Wilmington (28411) *(G-12813)*

Icon Sign Systems Inc... 828 253-4266
23 Villemagne Dr Asheville (28804) *(G-520)*

Iconic Marine Group LLC....................................... 252 975-2000
1653 Whichards Beach Rd Chocowinity (27817) *(G-3083)*

Icons America LLC.. 704 922-0041
1055 Gastonia Technology Pkwy Dallas (28034) *(G-3676)*

Icontact LLC... 919 957-6150
2450 Perimeter Park Dr Ste 105 Morrisville (27560) *(G-8990)*

ICP, Winston Salem *Also Called: Industrial Control Panels Inc (G-13206)*

Ics North America Corp... 704 794-6620
323 Corban Ave Sw Ste 504 Concord (28025) *(G-3375)*

ID Images LLC... 704 494-0444
2311 Distribution Center Dr Ste A Charlotte (28269) *(G-2309)*

Idaho Timber NC LLC.. 910 654-5555
1844 Joe Brown Hwy S Chadbourn (28431) *(G-1520)*

Idaho Timber NC LLC (HQ)..................................... 252 430-0030
1431 Nicholas St Henderson (27536) *(G-6161)*

Idaho Wood Inc.. 208 263-9521
114 Southgate Dr Oxford (27565) *(G-9617)*

Idea Oven LLC.. 910 343-5280
3507 Marathon Ave Castle Hayne (28429) *(G-1503)*

Idea People Inc.. 704 398-4437
14311 Reese Blvd W Huntersville (28078) *(G-7000)*

Idea Software Inc.. 407 453-3883
10814 Greater Hills St Raleigh (27614) *(G-10184)*

Ideablock LLC... 919 551-5054
212 W Main St Ste 302 Durham (27701) *(G-4069)*

Ideacode Inc... 919 341-5170
11010 W Northwood St Greensboro (27408) *(G-5613)*

Ideaitlia Cntmporary Furn Corp............................... 828 464-1000
1902 Emmanuel Church Rd Conover (28613) *(G-3532)*

Ideal Accessories, Oxford *Also Called: Ideal Fastener Corporation (G-9618)*

Ideal Fastener Corporation (PA).............................. 919 693-3115
603 W Industry Dr Oxford (27565) *(G-9618)*

Ideal Precast Inc.. 919 801-8287
7020 Mount Hermon Church Rd Durham (27705) *(G-4070)*

Ideal Precision Meter Inc...................................... 919 571-2000
5816 Creedmoor Rd Ste 103 Raleigh (27612) *(G-10185)*

Ideal Printing Services Inc.................................... 336 784-0074
4240 Kernersville Rd Ste D Kernersville (27284) *(G-7279)*

Ideas Aesthetech, Wendell *Also Called: Modern Tool Service (G-12539)*

Identify Yourself LLC... 252 202-1452
6146 N Croatan Hwy Unit C Kitty Hawk (27949) *(G-7445)*

Identigraph Signs & Awnings.................................. 704 635-7911
1132 Curtis St Monroe (28112) *(G-8502)*

Identity Custom Signage Inc.................................. 336 882-7446
324 Burton Ave High Point (27262) *(G-6666)*

Idexx Pharmaceuticals Inc.................................... 336 834-6500
7009 Albert Pick Rd Greensboro (27409) *(G-5614)*

Idustrial Burkett Services...................................... 252 244-0143
2050 Nc Highway 43 Vanceboro (28586) *(G-12217)*

Idx Corporation..252 948-2048
  234 Springs Rd Washington (27889) *(G-12392)*

Idx Impressions LLC (DH)..703 550-6902
  234 Springs Rd Washington (27889) *(G-12393)*

Idx North Carolina, Washington *Also Called: Idx Corporation (G-12392)*

Ie Furniture Inc (PA)...336 475-5050
  1121 Corporation Dr Archdale (27263) *(G-227)*

Ientertainment Network Inc (PA).............................919 238-4090
  100 Club Dr Ste 203 Burnsville (28714) *(G-1188)*

If Armor International LLC...704 482-1399
  2501 W Dixon Blvd Shelby (28152) *(G-11346)*

If Disher Meat Processing..336 463-2907
  1437 Old Stage Rd Yadkinville (27055) *(G-13444)*

Ifab Corp (HQ)..704 864-3032
  2408 Forbes Rd Gastonia (28056) *(G-5061)*

Ifanatic LLC (PA)..919 387-6062
  105 Shalon Ct Apex (27502) *(G-166)*

Ifb Solutions, Winston Salem *Also Called: Winstn-Slem Inds For Blind Inc (G-13398)*

Ifpo - Ifmo/American Image Inc..................................336 945-9867
  5043 Highland Grove Pl Hamptonville (27020) *(G-6085)*

Ifs Industries, Morrisville *Also Called: Ifs Industries Inc (G-8991)*

Ifs Industries Inc..919 234-1397
  100 Southcenter Ct Ste 300 Morrisville (27560) *(G-8991)*

Ifta Usa Inc...919 659-8393
  4819 Emperor Blvd Ste 400 Durham (27703) *(G-4071)*

Igh Enterprises Inc..704 372-6744
  2001 W Morehead St Charlotte (28208) *(G-2310)*

IGM Resins USA Inc (DH)..704 588-2500
  8700 Red Oak Blvd Ste M Charlotte (28217) *(G-2311)*

Igm Specialties Holding Inc (DH)..............................704 945-8702
  3300 Westinghouse Blvd Charlotte (28273) *(G-2312)*

Ika, Wilmington *Also Called: Ika-Works Inc (G-12814)*

Ika-Works Inc (HQ)..910 452-7059
  2635 Northchase Pkwy Se Wilmington (28405) *(G-12814)*

Ilco Unican Holding Corp...252 446-3321
  400 Jeffreys Rd Rocky Mount (27804) *(G-10843)*

Illinois Tool Works Inc...336 996-7046
  1210 S Park Dr Kernersville (27284) *(G-7280)*

Ilmor Marine LLC...704 360-1901
  186 Penske Way Mooresville (28115) *(G-8691)*

Ilsemann Corp...610 323-4143
  2555 Westinghouse Blvd Charlotte (28273) *(G-2313)*

Iluka Resources Inc...904 284-9832
  4208 Six Forks Rd Ste 1000 Raleigh (27609) *(G-10186)*

Iluma Alliance, Durham *Also Called: Premex Inc (G-4196)*

Ilumivu Inc..410 570-8846
  1200 Ridgefield Blvd Ste 170 Asheville (28806) *(G-521)*

Im8 (us) LLC..862 485-8325
  11401 Granite St Charlotte (28273) *(G-2314)*

Imaflex Usa Inc...336 885-8131
  7137 Prospect Church Rd Thomasville (27360) *(G-12036)*

Imaflex Usa Inc (HQ)...336 474-1190
  1200 Unity St Thomasville (27360) *(G-12037)*

Image 360, Raleigh-Rtp, Raleigh *Also Called: Greene Imaging & Design Inc (G-10143)*

Image Design...910 862-8988
  113 W Broad St Elizabethtown (28337) *(G-4428)*

Image Designs Ink LLC..252 235-1964
  12687 Sanford St Bailey (27807) *(G-671)*

Image Industries NC Inc..828 464-8882
  1848 Saint Pauls Church Rd Newton (28658) *(G-9474)*

Image Innovation Group, High Point *Also Called: Image Innovation Group Inc (G-6667)*

Image Innovation Group Inc......................................336 883-6010
  3301 N Main St High Point (27265) *(G-6667)*

Image Matters Inc..336 940-3000
  1808 Ramhurst Dr Clemmons (27012) *(G-3191)*

Image Works Inc..336 668-3338
  120 Wade St Ste A Jamestown (27282) *(G-7168)*

Imagemark, Gastonia *Also Called: Imagemark Business Svcs Inc (G-5062)*

Imagemark Business Svcs Inc (PA)............................704 865-4912
  3145 Northwest Blvd Gastonia (28052) *(G-5062)*

Images of America Inc...336 475-7106
  829 Blair St Thomasville (27360) *(G-12038)*

Imagesmith, Arden *Also Called: Smith & Fox Inc (G-307)*

Imagination Fabrication...919 280-4430
  810 Center St Apex (27502) *(G-167)*

Imagine One LLC..828 324-6454
  420 3rd Ave Nw Hickory (28601) *(G-6364)*

Imagine One Resources LLC.......................................828 328-1142
  420 3rd Ave Nw Hickory (28601) *(G-6365)*

Imagine That Creations LLC.......................................480 528-6775
  104 Eastside Dr Black Mountain (28711) *(G-867)*

Imagineoptix Corporation..919 757-4945
  20 Tw Alexander Dr Ste 100 Durham (27709) *(G-4072)*

Imaginesoftware, Charlotte *Also Called: Technology Partners LLC (G-2904)*

Imbrium Therapeutics LP...984 439-1075
  400 Park Offices Dr Ste Ll 102 Morrisville (27560) *(G-8992)*

IMC, Shelby *Also Called: Imc-Metalsamerica LLC (G-11347)*

Imc-Metalsamerica LLC (HQ)......................................704 482-8200
  135 Old Boiling Springs Rd Shelby (28152) *(G-11347)*

Imerys Clays Inc..828 648-2668
  125 N Main St Canton (28716) *(G-1254)*

Imerys Mica Kings Mountain Inc................................704 739-3616
  1469 S Battleground Ave Kings Mountain (28086) *(G-7365)*

Imerys Perlite Usa Inc...919 562-0031
  100 Robert Blunt Dr Youngsville (27596) *(G-13475)*

Imleagues, Wake Forest *Also Called: Imleagues LLC (G-12282)*

Imleagues LLC..919 617-1113
  1728 Talbot Ridge St Wake Forest (27587) *(G-12282)*

Immedia Print, Winston Salem *Also Called: Baicy Communications Inc (G-13101)*

Immi Safeguard, High Point *Also Called: Indiana Mills & Manufacturing (G-6669)*

Immixt LLC...336 207-8679
  9743 Silk Hope Liberty Rd Siler City (27344) *(G-11412)*

Immunotek Bio Centers LLC.......................................828 569-6264
  1040 2nd St Ne Hickory (28601) *(G-6366)*

Immunotek Bio Centers LLC.......................................336 781-4901
  1628 S Main St Ste 105 High Point (27260) *(G-6668)*

IMO Industries Inc (HQ)...301 323-9000
  420 National Business Pkwy Fl 5 Monroe (28110) *(G-8503)*

IMO Industries Inc...704 289-6511
  1710 Airport Rd Monroe (28110) *(G-8504)*

IMO Pump, Monroe *Also Called: Colfax Pump Group (G-8463)*

Impact Plastics Inc..910 205-1493
  1057 County Home Rd Hamlet (28345) *(G-6058)*

Impact Technologies LLC...704 400-5364
  4171 Deerfield Dr Nw Concord (28027) *(G-3376)*

Impeccable Improvements NC, Salisbury *Also Called: Shield & Steel Enterprises LLC (G-11116)*

Imperial Falcon Group Inc...646 717-1128
  3440 Toringdon Way Ste 205 Charlotte (28277) *(G-2315)*

Imperial Machine Co, Bessemer City *Also Called: Imperial Machine Company Inc (G-823)*

Imperial Machine Company Inc..................................704 739-8038
  4429 Kings Mountain Hwy Bessemer City (28016) *(G-823)*

Imperial Printing Pdts Co Inc....................................704 554-1188
  141 Robins St Lowell (28098) *(G-7932)*

Imperial Usa Ltd..704 596-2444
  1535 Elizabeth Ave Ste 201 Charlotte (28204) *(G-2316)*

Imperial Vault Company...336 983-6343
  1 Sun Dr King (27021) *(G-7328)*

Implus LLC...828 485-3318
  1279 19th Street Ln Nw Hickory (28601) *(G-6367)*

Implus Footcare LLC (DH)..800 446-7587
  2001 Tw Alexander Dr Durham (27709) *(G-4073)*

Imprinting Systems Spcalty Inc.................................704 527-4545
  803 Pressley Rd Ste 104 Charlotte (28217) *(G-2317)*

Improved Nature LLC..919 588-2299
  101 Vandora Springs Rd Garner (27529) *(G-4934)*

Impulse NC, Mount Olive *Also Called: AFL Network Services Inc (G-9246)*

Impulse NC LLC...919 658-2311
  100 Impulse Way Mount Olive (28365) *(G-9255)*

IMR Holdings LLC..980 287-8139
  10028 Highlands Crossing Dr Charlotte (28277) *(G-2318)*

IMS, Winston Salem *Also Called: International McHy Sls Inc (G-13210)*

(G-0000) Company's Geographic Section entry number

IMS Fabrication Inc......................................704 216-0255
150 Summit Park Dr Salisbury (28146) *(G-11066)*

IMS Usa LLC...910 796-2040
110 Portwatch Way Ste 103 Wilmington (28412) *(G-12815)*

In Blue Handmade Inc.................................828 774-5094
20 Westside Dr Asheville (28806) *(G-522)*

In Greensboro..336 621-0279
2722 N Church St Ste P Greensboro (27405) *(G-5615)*

In Pink..919 380-1487
112 Swiss Stone Ct Cary (27513) *(G-1373)*

In Style Kitchen Cabinetry..........................336 769-9605
8570 N Nc Highway 109 Winston Salem (27107) *(G-13204)*

Incantare Art By Marilyn LLC......................704 713-8846
15701 Pedlar Mills Rd Charlotte (28278) *(G-2319)*

Indaux Usa Inc...336 861-0740
548 Nc Highway 801 N Advance (27006) *(G-33)*

Independence Lumber Inc...........................276 773-3744
18900 Riverwind Ln Davidson (28036) *(G-3708)*

Independence Printing................................336 771-0234
130 Back Forty Dr Winston Salem (27127) *(G-13205)*

Independent Beverage Co LLC (PA).............704 399-2504
3936 Corporation Cir Charlotte (28216) *(G-2320)*

Indian Head Industries Inc (PA)..................704 547-7411
6200 Harris Technology Blvd Charlotte (28269) *(G-2321)*

Indian Head Industries Inc.........................704 547-7411
229 Park Ave Murphy (28906) *(G-9290)*

Indian Health Spring Water, Murphy Also Called: CHI Resources *(G-9289)*

Indian Motorcycle Charlotte, Lowell Also Called: Indian Motorcycle Company *(G-7933)*

Indian Motorcycle Company.........................704 879-4560
110 Indian Walk Lowell (28098) *(G-7933)*

Indian Tff-Tank Greensboro Inc...................336 625-2629
2491 Mountain Lake Rd Asheboro (27205) *(G-364)*

Indiana Chair Frame 3200, Liberty Also Called: Indiana Chair Frame Company *(G-7768)*

Indiana Chair Frame Company......................574 825-9355
330 N Greensboro St Liberty (27298) *(G-7768)*

Indiana Mills & Manufacturing....................336 862-7519
200 Swathmore Ave High Point (27263) *(G-6669)*

Indie Services..336 524-6966
205 E Davis St Burlington (27215) *(G-1108)*

Indivior Manufacturing LLC.........................804 594-0974
8900 Capital Blvd Raleigh (27616) *(G-10187)*

Indramat Div, Charlotte Also Called: Bosch Rexroth Corporation *(G-1801)*

Indtool Inc...336 226-4923
766 Koury Dr Burlington (27215) *(G-1109)*

Induction Food Systems Inc........................919 907-0179
2609 Discovery Dr Ste 115 Raleigh (27616) *(G-10188)*

Indulor America LP......................................336 578-6855
932 E Elm St Graham (27253) *(G-5270)*

Industrial Air Inc.......................................336 292-1030
428 Edwardia Dr Greensboro (27409) *(G-5616)*

Industrial Alloys Inc...................................704 882-2887
3013 Eaton Ave Indian Trail (28079) *(G-7084)*

Industrial and Agricultural Chemicals Incorporated.........910 843-2121
2042 Buie Philadelphus Rd Red Springs (28377) *(G-10668)*

Industrial Anodizing...................................336 434-2110
112 School Rd Trinity (27370) *(G-12116)*

Industrial Automation Company...................877 727-8757
544 Pylon Dr Raleigh (27606) *(G-10189)*

Industrial Cleaning Eqp Co, Wilmington Also Called: Ice Companies Inc *(G-12811)*

Industrial Cnnctons Sltons LLC (DH)...........203 229-3932
305 Gregson Dr Cary (27511) *(G-1374)*

Industrial Coatings, Greensboro Also Called: PPG Industries Inc *(G-5756)*

Industrial Construction, Sylva Also Called: Wnc White Corporation *(G-11905)*

Industrial Container Corp............................336 886-7031
107 Motsinger St High Point (27260) *(G-6670)*

Industrial Container Inc..............................336 882-1310
107 Motsinger St High Point (27260) *(G-6671)*

Industrial Control Panels Inc.......................336 661-3037
152 Capp St Ste A Winston Salem (27105) *(G-13206)*

Industrial Ctd Fabrics Group, Rutherfordton Also Called: Trelleborg Ctd Systems US Inc *(G-10996)*

Industrial Elcpltg Co Inc.............................704 867-4547
1401 Gaston Ave Gastonia (28052) *(G-5063)*

Industrial Elcpltg Co Inc (PA).....................704 867-4547
307 Linwood Rd Gastonia (28052) *(G-5064)*

Industrial Glass Tech LLC...........................704 853-2429
112 Superior Stainless Rd Gastonia (28052) *(G-5065)*

Industrial Glass Technologies, Gastonia Also Called: Industrial Glass Tech LLC *(G-5065)*

Industrial Hard Carbon LLC.........................704 489-1488
771 Crosspoint Dr Denver (28037) *(G-3790)*

Industrial Heat LLC....................................919 743-5727
1017 Main Campus Dr Ste 3800 Raleigh (27606) *(G-10190)*

Industrial Lubricants Inc.............................336 767-0013
1110 Fairchild Rd Winston Salem (27105) *(G-13207)*

Industrial Machine & Wldg Inc....................910 251-1393
1918 Castle Hayne Rd Wilmington (28401) *(G-12816)*

Industrial Machine Company........................704 922-9750
103 Nelda St Dallas (28034) *(G-3677)*

Industrial Mch Solutions Inc........................919 872-0016
3734 Overlook Rd Raleigh (27616) *(G-10191)*

Industrial Mechanical Services....................828 397-3231
2354 Us Hwy 70 Hildebran (28637) *(G-6852)*

Industrial Mechatronics Inc........................704 900-2407
117 Freeland Ln Charlotte (28217) *(G-2322)*

Industrial Metal Craft Inc...........................704 864-3416
901 Tulip Dr Gastonia (28052) *(G-5066)*

Industrial Metal Maint Inc...........................910 285-3240
164 John Deere Rd Teachey (28464) *(G-11988)*

Industrial Motions Inc................................734 284-8944
1401 Boxwood Ln Apex (27502) *(G-168)*

Industrial Mtal Flame Spryers.....................919 596-9381
419 Salem St Durham (27703) *(G-4074)*

Industrial Mtal Pdts Abrdeen I....................910 944-8110
461 Carolina Rd Aberdeen (28315) *(G-7)*

Industrial Opportunities Inc........................828 321-4754
2586 Business 19 Andrews (28901) *(G-107)*

Industrial Piping Inc...................................704 588-1100
212 S Tryon St Ste 1050 Charlotte (28281) *(G-2323)*

Industrial Power Inc (PA)............................910 483-4230
703 Whitfield St Fayetteville (28306) *(G-4615)*

Industrial Prcess Slutions Inc......................336 926-1511
915 Germantown Rd Wilkesboro (28697) *(G-12639)*

Industrial Recycling Services......................704 462-1882
2815 Woodtech Dr Newton (28658) *(G-9475)*

Industrial Sheet Metal Works.....................828 654-9655
149 Old Shoals Rd Arden (28704) *(G-275)*

Industrial Sign & Graphics Inc (PA).............704 371-4985
4227 N Graham St Charlotte (28206) *(G-2324)*

Industrial Sup Solutions Inc (PA)................704 636-4241
804 Julian Rd Salisbury (28147) *(G-11067)*

Industrial Tech Svcs Amrcas In (DH)...........704 808-3848
13320 Ballantyne Corporate Pl Charlotte (28277) *(G-2325)*

Industrial Timber LLC (PA).........................704 919-1215
6441 Hendry Rd Ste B Charlotte (28269) *(G-2326)*

Industrial Timber LLC................................704 919-1215
330 White Plains Rd Hiddenite (28636) *(G-6500)*

Industrial Tling Svcs Ashvlle......................828 683-4168
1259 Alexander Rd Leicester (28748) *(G-7526)*

Industrial Welding &..................................910 309-8540
5936 Tabor Church Rd Fayetteville (28312) *(G-4616)*

Industrial Wood Products Inc (PA)...............336 333-5959
9205 Hwy 22 S Climax (27233) *(G-3226)*

Industries of Blind Inc (PA)........................336 274-1591
920 W Gate City Blvd Greensboro (27403) *(G-5617)*

Industry Choice Solutions LLC.....................828 628-1991
98 Bishop Cove Rd Fairview (28730) *(G-4508)*

Industry Nine LLC......................................828 210-5113
21 Old County Home Rd Asheville (28806) *(G-523)*

Indy Week...919 832-8774
709 W Jones St Raleigh (27603) *(G-10192)*

Ineos Automotive Americas LLC..................404 513-8577
2020 Progress Ct Ste 100-112 Raleigh (27608) *(G-10193)*

ALPHABETIC

Inferensys Inc.. 910 398-1200
112 Dare Pines Way Durham (27703) *(G-4075)*

Infinite Blue Inc... 919 744-7704
8913 Brandon Station Rd Ste A Raleigh (27613) *(G-10194)*

Infinite Software Resorces LLC (PA)............ 704 509-0031
3020 Prosperity Church Rd 1 Charlotte (28269) *(G-2327)*

Infinity Communications LLC (PA)................ 919 797-2334
5201 International Dr Durham (27712) *(G-4076)*

Infinity Custom Cabinets, Leland *Also Called: Boone Enterprises LLC (G-7534)*

Infinity S End Inc (PA).................................. 704 900-8355
7804 Fairview Rd Ste C Charlotte (28226) *(G-2328)*

Infinity Signs and Screen Prtg, Charlotte *Also Called: Infinity S End Inc (G-2328)*

Infinity Stingray Products, Otto *Also Called: J Culpepper & Co (G-9606)*

Infisoft Software... 704 307-2619
7422 Carmel Executive Park Dr Charlotte (28226) *(G-2329)*

Info-Gel LLC (PA)... 704 599-5770
2311 Distribution Center Dr Ste F Charlotte (28269) *(G-2330)*

Infobelt LLC (PA).. 980 223-4000
4100 Beresford Rd Charlotte (28211) *(G-2331)*

Inform Inc.. 828 322-7766
415 1st Ave Nw Hickory (28601) *(G-6368)*

Information Age Publishing Inc..................... 704 752-9125
11600 N Community House Rd # R Charlotte (28277) *(G-2332)*

Information Tech Works LLC (HQ)................. 919 232-5332
4809 Little Falls Dr Raleigh (27609) *(G-10195)*

Informtion Rtrrval Cmpanies Inc.................. 919 460-7447
3500 Regency Pkwy Ste 140 Cary (27511) *(G-1375)*

Infosense Inc... 704 644-1164
2102 Cambridge Beltway Dr Ste D1 Charlotte (28273) *(G-2333)*

Infosense Inc (PA).. 704 644-1164
8116 S Tryon St Ste B3-203 Charlotte (28273) *(G-2334)*

Infrastrcture Sltons Group Inc..................... 704 833-8048
505 E Plaza Dr Mooresville (28115) *(G-8692)*

Ing Source LLC... 828 855-0481
1340 14th Avenue Ct Sw Hickory (28602) *(G-6369)*

Ingalls Alton... 252 975-2056
115 N Respess St Washington (27889) *(G-12394)*

Ingalls and Associates, Washington *Also Called: Ingalls Alton (G-12394)*

Ingersoll Rand Inc....................................... 704 774-4290
6000 General Commerce Dr Charlotte (28213) *(G-2335)*

INGERSOLL RAND INC (PA)........................ 704 896-4000
525 Harbour Place Dr Ste 600 Davidson (28036) *(G-3709)*

Ingersoll Rand Inc....................................... 828 375-8240
501 Sanford Ave Mocksville (27028) *(G-8371)*

Ingersoll-Rand, Charlotte *Also Called: Ingersoll-Rand Company (G-2336)*

Ingersoll-Rand, Southern Pines *Also Called: Trane Technologies Company LLC (G-11512)*

Ingersoll-Rand Company............................. 704 655-4836
10000 Twin Lakes Pkwy Charlotte (28269) *(G-2336)*

Ingersoll-Rand Indus US Inc (HQ)............... 704 896-4000
525 Harbour Place Dr Ste 600 Davidson (28036) *(G-3710)*

Ingersoll-Rand Intl Holdg............................ 704 655-4000
800 Beaty St Davidson (28036) *(G-3711)*

Ingersoll-Rand US Holdco Inc (PA).............. 704 655-4000
800 Beaty St Ste E Davidson (28036) *(G-3712)*

Ingle Protective Systems Inc....................... 704 788-3327
231 Pounds Ave Sw Concord (28025) *(G-3377)*

Ingles, Boiling Springs *Also Called: Ingles Markets Incorporated (G-885)*

Ingles Markets Incorporated....................... 704 434-0096
214 N Main St Boiling Springs (28017) *(G-885)*

Ingram Machine & Balancing....................... 828 254-3420
48 Ben Lippen Rd Asheville (28806) *(G-524)*

Ingram Racing Engines, Asheville *Also Called: Ingram Machine & Balancing (G-524)*

Ingram Woodyards Inc................................. 910 556-1250
1925 Jefferson Davis Hwy Sanford (27330) *(G-11195)*

Ingredion Incorporated................................ 336 785-0100
4501 Overdale Rd Winston Salem (27107) *(G-13208)*

Inhalon Biopharma Inc................................ 650 439-0110
104 Tw Alexander Dr Rm 2021rtp Durham (27709) *(G-4077)*

Ini Power Systems Inc.................................. 919 677-7112
137 Trans Air Dr Morrisville (27560) *(G-8993)*

Injection Technology Corporation................ 828 684-1362
199 Airport Rd Arden (28704) *(G-276)*

Ink n Stitches LLC....................................... 336 633-3898
2739 Us Highway 220 Bus S Asheboro (27205) *(G-365)*

Ink Tec Inc.. 828 465-6411
1838 Saint Pauls Church Rd Newton (28658) *(G-9476)*

Ink Well.. 336 727-9750
1650 Hutton St Winston Salem (27127) *(G-13209)*

Ink Well, Durham *Also Called: Ink Well Inc (G-4078)*

Ink Well, Winston Salem *Also Called: Ink Well (G-13209)*

Ink Well Inc.. 919 682-8279
3112 N Roxboro St Durham (27704) *(G-4078)*

Inkwell... 919 433-7539
2823 Bragg Blvd Fayetteville (28303) *(G-4617)*

Inman Septic Tank Service Inc..................... 910 763-1146
2631 Blue Clay Rd Wilmington (28405) *(G-12817)*

Inn-Flow LLC.. 919 277-9027
5640 Dillard Dr Ste 300 Cary (27518) *(G-1376)*

Inn-Flow Hotel Software, Cary *Also Called: Inn-Flow LLC (G-1376)*

Innait, Charlotte *Also Called: Innait Inc (G-2337)*

Innait Inc... 406 241-5245
5524 Joyce Dr Charlotte (28215) *(G-2337)*

Innavasc Medical Inc................................... 813 902-2228
110 Swift Ave Durham (27705) *(G-4079)*

Inneroptic Technology Inc........................... 919 732-2090
3421 Carriage Trl Hillsborough (27278) *(G-6868)*

Inniah Production Incorporated................... 828 765-6800
152 Summit Ave Spruce Pine (28777) *(G-11578)*

Innisbrook Wraps, Greensboro *Also Called: Shamrock Corporation (G-5809)*

Innobioactives LLC..................................... 336 235-0838
7325 W Friendly Ave Ste H Greensboro (27410) *(G-5618)*

Innocrin Pharmaceuticals Inc...................... 919 467-8539
701 Wagstaff Rd Fuquay Varina (27526) *(G-4884)*

Innofa Usa LLC... 336 635-2900
716 Commerce Dr Eden (27288) *(G-4348)*

Innospec, High Point *Also Called: Innospec Active Chemicals LLC (G-6672)*

Innospec Active Chemicals LLC (HQ)........... 336 882-3308
510 W Grimes Ave High Point (27260) *(G-6672)*

Innospec Active Chemicals LLC.................... 704 633-8028
500 Hinkle Ln Salisbury (28144) *(G-11068)*

Innospec Inc... 704 633-8028
500 Hinkle Ln Salisbury (28144) *(G-11069)*

Innospec Inc... 704 633-8028
500 Hinkle Ln Salisbury (28144) *(G-11070)*

Innospec Performance Chemicals, Salisbury *Also Called: Innospec Active Chemicals LLC (G-11068)*

Innospec Performance Chemicals, Salisbury *Also Called: Innospec Inc (G-11069)*

Innospec Performance Chemicals, Salisbury *Also Called: Innospec Inc (G-11070)*

Innova-Con Incorporated............................. 919 303-1467
2521 Schieffelin Rd Ste 136 Apex (27502) *(G-169)*

Innovaknits LLC.. 828 536-9348
350 5th Ave Se Conover (28613) *(G-3533)*

Innovasource LLC....................................... 704 584-0072
11515 Vanstory Dr Ste 110 Huntersville (28078) *(G-7001)*

Innovation Brewing LLC.............................. 828 586-9678
414 W Main St Sylva (28779) *(G-11893)*

Innovative Awngs & Screens LLC................. 833 337-4233
19825 North Cove Rd Ste B Cornelius (28031) *(G-3610)*

Innovative Business Growth LLC.................. 888 334-4367
1157 S Cox St Asheboro (27203) *(G-366)*

Innovative Cushions LLC............................. 336 861-2060
4010 Cheyenne Dr Archdale (27263) *(G-228)*

Innovative Custom Cabinets Inc.................. 813 748-0655
1018 Robinhood Ln Kannapolis (28081) *(G-7212)*

Innovative Design Tech LLC........................ 919 331-0204
475 S Raleigh St Angier (27501) *(G-121)*

Innovative Fabrication Inc........................... 919 544-0254
1730 Round Rock Dr Raleigh (27615) *(G-10196)*

Innovative Kitchens Baths Inc..................... 336 279-1188
2912 Manufacturers Rd Greensboro (27406) *(G-5619)*

Innovative Knitting LLC............................... 336 350-8122
3720 S Church St Burlington (27215) *(G-1110)*

Innovative Laminations Company................. 252 745-8133
51a Halls Creek Rd New Bern (28560) *(G-9371)*

Innovative Mfg Solutions Inc..919 219-2424
    675 Wooded Lake Dr Apex (27523) *(G-170)*

Innovative Technology Mfg LLC...980 248-3731
    136 Lugnut Ln Ste C Mooresville (28117) *(G-8693)*

Innovtors In McRwave Technolgy, Matthews *Also Called: Cem Corporation (G-8162)*

Innowera Ltd Liability Company..214 295-9508
    8529 Six Forks Rd Ste 400 Raleigh (27615) *(G-10197)*

Inotec AMD Inc...888 354-9772
    1350 4th St Nw Hickory (28601) *(G-6370)*

Inovaetion Inc...919 651-1628
    8601 Six Forks Rd Ste 400 Raleigh (27615) *(G-10198)*

Inovative Vapes of Boone...828 386-1041
    244 Shadowline Dr Boone (28607) *(G-926)*

Inplac North America Inc...704 587-1151
    10926 S Tryon St Ste F Charlotte (28273) *(G-2338)*

Inprimo Solutions Inc..919 390-7776
    7925 Vandemere Ct Raleigh (27615) *(G-10199)*

Inquire Journal, The, Monroe *Also Called: Paxton Media Group (G-8540)*

Insect Shield LLC (PA)...336 272-4157
    814 W Market St Greensboro (27401) *(G-5620)*

Inshore Technology Associates, Castle Hayne *Also Called: Idea Oven LLC (G-1503)*

Insightsoftware, Raleigh *Also Called: Insightsoftware LLC (G-10200)*

Insightsoftware LLC (PA)...919 872-7800
    8529 Six Forks Rd Ste 300 Raleigh (27615) *(G-10200)*

Insource Sftwr Solutions Inc...704 895-1052
    19421 Liverpool Pkwy Ste A Cornelius (28031) *(G-3611)*

Inspectionxpert Corporation..919 249-6442
    1 Glenwood Ave Ste 500 Raleigh (27603) *(G-10201)*

Inspiration Leather Design Inc...336 420-2265
    4713 Barrington Place Ct Jamestown (27282) *(G-7169)*

Inspire Creative Studios Inc...910 395-0200
    720 N 3rd St Ste 101 Wilmington (28401) *(G-12818)*

Insta Copy Shop Ltd..704 376-1350
    4311 South Blvd Ste D Charlotte (28209) *(G-2339)*

Instant Imprints...704 864-1510
    2258 Helen Dr Gastonia (28054) *(G-5067)*

Instant Imprints, Raleigh *Also Called: Nine Thirteen LLC (G-10332)*

Instantiations Inc...855 476-2558
    4917 Waters Edge Dr Ste 268 Raleigh (27606) *(G-10202)*

Insteel, Mount Airy *Also Called: Insteel Industries Inc (G-9131)*

Insteel Industries Inc (PA)..336 786-2141
    1373 Boggs Dr Mount Airy (27030) *(G-9131)*

Insteel Wire Products Company (HQ).....................................336 719-9000
    1373 Boggs Dr Mount Airy (27030) *(G-9132)*

Institute For Resch Biotecnoly...252 689-2205
    2905 S Memorial Dr Greenville (27834) *(G-5991)*

Instrotek Inc (PA)...919 875-8371
    1 Triangle Dr Research Triangle Pa (27709) *(G-10712)*

Insty-Prints, Raleigh *Also Called: Pamela A Adams (G-10355)*

Insul Kor, Greensboro *Also Called: Quality Housing Corporation (G-5778)*

Insulsure, Mooresville *Also Called: Attic Tent Inc (G-8601)*

Insurance Systems Group Inc..919 834-4907
    827 N Bloodworth St Raleigh (27604) *(G-10203)*

Intas Pharmaceuticals Limited..919 941-7878
    8041 Arco Corporate Dr Ste 200 Raleigh (27617) *(G-10204)*

Integra Foods LLC..910 984-2007
    476 Industrial Dr Bladenboro (28320) *(G-877)*

Integrated Info Systems Inc..919 488-5000
    460 Boardwalk Dr Youngsville (27596) *(G-13476)*

Integrity Envmtl Solutions LLC (PA)....................................704 283-9765
    1127 Curtis St Ste 110 Monroe (28112) *(G-8505)*

Integrity Medical Solutions, Shelby *Also Called: Tube Enterprises Incorporated (G-11386)*

Integrted Cble Assmbly Hldings, Whitsett *Also Called: Ica Mid-Atlantic Inc (G-12610)*

Intelliagent, Cary *Also Called: Fathom Holdings Inc (G-1362)*

Intellicoat Technologies, Matthews *Also Called: Transcontinental AC US LLC (G-8154)*

Intelligent Apps LLC...919 628-6256
    12113 Oakwood View Dr Apt 202 Raleigh (27614) *(G-10205)*

Intelligent Endoscopy LLC..336 608-4375
    4740 Commercial Park Ct Ste 1 Clemmons (27012) *(G-3192)*

Intelligent Tool Corp..704 799-0449
    1151 Biscayne Dr Concord (28027) *(G-3378)*

Intensa Inc..336 884-4096
    1810 S Elm St High Point (27260) *(G-6673)*

Intensa Inc..336 884-4003
    1810 S Elm St High Point (27260) *(G-6674)*

Inteplast Group Corporation..704 504-3200
    10701 S Commerce Blvd Ste A Charlotte (28273) *(G-2340)*

Inter-Continental Corporation..828 464-8250
    2575 N Ashe Ave Newton (28658) *(G-9477)*

Inter-Continental Gear & Brake (PA)....................................704 599-3420
    6431 Reames Rd Charlotte (28216) *(G-2341)*

Interactive Intelligence, Durham *Also Called: Genesys Cloud Services Inc (G-4045)*

Interactive Safety Pdts Inc..704 664-7377
    9825 Northcross Center Ct Ste A Huntersville (28078) *(G-7002)*

Interconnect Products and Services Inc (PA)............................336 667-3356
    1206 Industrial Park Rd Wilkesboro (28697) *(G-12640)*

Intercontinental Metals Corp...336 786-2141
    1373 Boggs Dr Mount Airy (27030) *(G-9133)*

Intereco USA Belt Filter Press...919 349-6041
    7474 Creedmoor Rd Raleigh (27613) *(G-10206)*

Interflex Acquisition Co LLC (HQ)......................................336 921-3505
    3200 W Nc Highway 268 Wilkesboro (28697) *(G-12641)*

Interflex Acquisition Co LLC...336 921-3505
    3200 W Nc Highway 268 Wilkesboro (28697) *(G-12642)*

Interflex Group, Wilkesboro *Also Called: Interflex Acquisition Co LLC (G-12641)*

Interior Trim Creations, Matthews *Also Called: Itc Millwork LLC (G-8176)*

Interior Trim Creations Inc..704 821-1470
    11912 Erwin Ridge Ave Charlotte (28213) *(G-2342)*

Interior Wood Specialties Inc..336 431-0068
    1130 Bedford St High Point (27263) *(G-6675)*

Interlam Corporation...336 786-6254
    391 Hickory St Mount Airy (27030) *(G-9134)*

Intermarket Technology Inc...252 623-2199
    932 Page Rd Washington (27889) *(G-12395)*

International, Charlotte *Also Called: Notepad Enterprises LLC (G-2576)*

International Bus Mchs Corp..919 543-6919
    3039 Cornwallis Rd Durham (27709) *(G-4080)*

International Cnstr Eqp Inc (PA)..704 821-8200
    301 Warehouse Dr Matthews (28104) *(G-8175)*

International Embroidery..704 792-0641
    2890 Highway 49 N Concord (28025) *(G-3379)*

International Foam Pdts Inc (PA)..704 588-0080
    10530 Westlake Dr Charlotte (28273) *(G-2343)*

International Furnishings Inc...336 472-8422
    1506 Lexington Ave Thomasville (27360) *(G-12039)*

International Instrumentation...919 496-4208
    382 N Carolina 98 Hwy W Bunn (27508) *(G-1014)*

International McHy Sls Inc..336 759-9548
    8065 N Point Blvd Ste J Winston Salem (27106) *(G-13210)*

International Minute Press..919 762-0054
    316 Angier Rd Fuquay Varina (27526) *(G-4885)*

International Minute Press, Clinton *Also Called: Commercial Enterprises NC Inc (G-3230)*

International Minute Press, Fayetteville *Also Called: Os Press LLC (G-4649)*

International Minute Press, Gastonia *Also Called: Better Business Printing Inc (G-4998)*

International Minute Press, High Point *Also Called: James G Gouge (G-6677)*

International Minute Press, Raleigh *Also Called: Js Printing LLC (G-10224)*

International Minute Press, Raleigh *Also Called: Welloyt Enterprises Inc (G-10604)*

International Motors LLC..704 596-3860
    3325 Rotary Dr Charlotte (28269) *(G-2344)*

International Moulding NC, Morganton *Also Called: T Distribution NC Inc (G-8903)*

International Paper, Burgaw *Also Called: International Paper Company (G-1024)*

International Paper, Charlotte *Also Called: International Paper Company (G-2345)*

International Paper, Charlotte *Also Called: International Paper Company (G-2347)*

International Paper, Charlotte *Also Called: International Paper Company (G-2348)*

International Paper, Charlotte *Also Called: International Paper Company (G-2349)*

International Paper, Lumberton *Also Called: International Paper Company (G-7959)*

International Paper, Manson *Also Called: International Paper Company (G-8022)*

International Paper, New Bern *Also Called: International Paper Company (G-9372)*

International Paper, Raleigh *Also Called: International Paper Company (G-10207)*

International Paper, Riegelwood *Also Called: International Paper Company (G-10725)*

ALPHABETIC

International Paper, Riegelwood *Also Called: International Paper Company (G-10726)*

International Paper, Vanceboro *Also Called: International Paper Company (G-12218)*

International Paper Company..................................... 910 259-1723
3870 Highsmith Rd Burgaw (28425) *(G-1024)*

International Paper Company..................................... 704 393-8210
11020 David Taylor Dr Charlotte (28262) *(G-2345)*

International Paper Company..................................... 704 588-8522
10601 Westlake Dr Charlotte (28273) *(G-2346)*

International Paper Company..................................... 704 398-8354
5419 Hovis Rd Charlotte (28208) *(G-2347)*

International Paper Company..................................... 704 334-5222
201 E 28th St Charlotte (28206) *(G-2348)*

International Paper Company..................................... 704 588-8522
3700 Display Dr Charlotte (28273) *(G-2349)*

International Paper Company..................................... 910 738-6214
820 Caton Rd Lumberton (28360) *(G-7958)*

International Paper Company..................................... 910 738-8930
2060 W 5th St Lumberton (28358) *(G-7959)*

International Paper Company..................................... 252 456-3111
967 Us Highway 1 S Manson (27553) *(G-8022)*

International Paper Company..................................... 252 633-7407
1785 Weyerhaeuser Rd New Bern (28563) *(G-9372)*

International Paper Company..................................... 828 464-3841
1525 Mount Olive Church Rd Newton (28658) *(G-9478)*

International Paper Company..................................... 919 831-4764
5 W Hargett St Rm 914 Raleigh (27601) *(G-10207)*

International Paper Company..................................... 910 655-2211
1865 John Riegel Rd Riegelwood (28456) *(G-10725)*

International Paper Company..................................... 910 362-4900
865 John L Regel Rd Riegelwood (28456) *(G-10726)*

International Paper Company..................................... 252 633-7509
1785 Weyerhaeuser Rd Vanceboro (28586) *(G-12218)*

International Precast Inc.. 919 742-4241
2469 Old Us 421 N Siler City (27344) *(G-11413)*

International Society Automtn (PA)........................... 919 206-4176
67 T W Alexander Dr Research Triangle Pa (27709) *(G-10713)*

International Tela-Com Inc...................................... 828 651-9801
103 Underwood Rd Unit C Fletcher (28732) *(G-4743)*

International Thermodyne Inc.................................. 704 579-8218
3120 Latrobe Dr Ste 110 Charlotte (28211) *(G-2350)*

Interntnal Agrclture Group LLC.............................. 908 323-3246
106 Langtree Village Dr Ste 301 Mooresville (28117) *(G-8694)*

Interntnal Chldbrth Edcatn Ass.............................. 919 863-9487
1500 Sunday Dr Ste 102 Raleigh (27607) *(G-10208)*

Interntnal Instltion Group LL.................................. 704 231-1868
312 Riverside Dr Sparta (28675) *(G-11539)*

Interntnal Tray Pads Packg Inc............................... 910 944-1800
3299 Nc Highway 5 Aberdeen (28315) *(G-8)*

Interntonal Specialty Pdts Inc................................ 828 326-9053
1720 Tate Blvd Se Hickory (28602) *(G-6371)*

Interpace Pharma Solutions Inc.............................. 919 678-7024
133 Southcenter Ct Ste 400 Morrisville (27560) *(G-8994)*

Interroll Corporation.. 910 799-1100
3000 Corporate Dr Wilmington (28405) *(G-12819)*

Interroll USA Holding LLC..................................... 910 799-1100
3000 Corporate Dr Wilmington (28405) *(G-12820)*

Interrs-Exteriors Asheboro Inc............................... 336 629-2148
2013 S Fayetteville St Asheboro (27203) *(G-367)*

Intersport Group Inc.. 814 968-3085
336 Willowdale Church Rd Vilas (28692) *(G-12230)*

Interstate All Batteries Ctr.................................... 704 979-3430
8605 Concord Mills Blvd Concord (28027) *(G-3380)*

Interstate Foam & Supply Inc................................ 828 459-9700
306 Comfort Dr Ne Conover (28613) *(G-3534)*

Interstate Narrow Fabrics Inc................................ 336 578-1037
1101 Porter Ave Haw River (27258) *(G-6132)*

Interstate Sign Company Inc................................. 336 789-3069
1990 Rockford St Mount Airy (27030) *(G-9135)*

Intertape Polymer Corp.. 252 792-2083
1622 Twin Bridges Rd Everetts (27825) *(G-4497)*

Intertape Polymer Corp.. 980 907-4871
13722 Bill Mcgee Rd Midland (28107) *(G-8288)*

Intertape Polymer Group, Midland *Also Called: Intertape Polymer Corp (G-8288)*

Intertech Corporation... 336 621-1891
3240 N Ohenry Blvd Greensboro (27405) *(G-5621)*

Intrinsic Advanced Mtls LLC.................................. 704 874-5000
531 Cotton Blossom Cir Gastonia (28054) *(G-5068)*

Intuitive Surgical Inc... 408 523-2100
1650 Tw Alexander Dr Durham (27703) *(G-4081)*

Inventive Graphics Inc... 704 814-4900
9129 Monroe Rd Ste 160 Charlotte (28270) *(G-2351)*

Invictus Lighting LLC... 828 855-9324
1401 Main Ave Sw Hickory (28602) *(G-6372)*

Invisible Fencing of Mtn Reg................................. 828 667-8847
176 Pete Luther Rd Candler (28715) *(G-1227)*

Invista Capital Management LLC............................. 704 636-6000
Hwy 70 W Salisbury (28145) *(G-11071)*

INX International, Charlotte *Also Called: INX International Ink Co (G-2352)*

INX International Ink Co... 704 372-2080
10820 Withers Cove Park Dr Charlotte (28278) *(G-2352)*

INX International Ink Co... 910 371-3184
1901 Popular St Leland (28451) *(G-7547)*

INX International Ink Co... 704 414-6428
75 Coral St Rockwell (28138) *(G-10798)*

INX INTERNATIONAL INK CO, Rockwell *Also Called: INX International Ink Co (G-10798)*

INX Intrntnal Ctings Adhesives.............................. 910 371-3184
1901 Popular St Leland (28451) *(G-7548)*

Ioa Healthcare Furniture, Thomasville *Also Called: Images of America Inc (G-12038)*

Iomax USA LLC.. 704 662-1840
133 River Park Rd Mooresville (28117) *(G-8695)*

Ioto Usa LLC... 252 413-7343
1997 N Greene St Greenville (27834) *(G-5992)*

Ipas... 919 967-7052
4711 Hope Valley Rd Durham (27707) *(G-4082)*

Iperionx Critical Minerals LLC................................ 980 237-8900
129 W Trade St Ste 1405 Charlotte (28202) *(G-2353)*

Iperionx Limited... 980 237-8900
129 W Trade St Ste 1405 Charlotte (28202) *(G-2354)*

Iperionx Technology LLC...................................... 980 237-8900
129 W Trade St Ste 1405 Charlotte (28202) *(G-2355)*

Ipex USA LLC (DH)... 704 889-2431
10100 Rodney St Pineville (28134) *(G-9735)*

Ipex USA LLC... 704 889-2431
10100 Rodney St Pineville (28134) *(G-9736)*

Ipi Acquisition LLC... 704 588-1100
13504 S Point Blvd Ste M Charlotte (28273) *(G-2356)*

Ips.. 704 788-3327
338 Webb Rd Concord (28025) *(G-3381)*

Ips Corporation.. 919 598-2400
600 Ellis Rd Durham (27703) *(G-4083)*

Ips Perforating Inc.. 704 881-0050
1821 Weinig St Statesville (28677) *(G-11716)*

Iq Brands Inc (HQ).. 336 751-0040
129 Nc Highway 801 S Advance (27006) *(G-34)*

Iqe Inc... 610 861-6930
494 Gallimore Dairy Rd Ste A Greensboro (27409) *(G-5622)*

Iqe North Carolina LLC... 336 609-6270
494 Gallimore Dairy Rd Greensboro (27409) *(G-5623)*

Iqe PA, Greensboro *Also Called: Iqe Inc (G-5622)*

Iqe Rf LLC... 732 271-5990
494 Gallimore Dairy Rd Ste A Greensboro (27409) *(G-5624)*

Iqe Usa Inc... 610 861-6930
494 Gallimore Dairy Rd Greensboro (27409) *(G-5625)*

Iqmetrix USA Inc.. 704 987-9903
184 Longboat Rd Mooresville (28117) *(G-8696)*

Iqvia Pharma Inc (HQ)... 919 998-2000
4820 Emperor Blvd Durham (27703) *(G-4084)*

Irc, Cary *Also Called: Informtion Rtrval Cmpanies Inc (G-1375)*

Iredell Fiber Inc... 704 878-0884
124 Fanjoy Rd Statesville (28625) *(G-11717)*

Iron Box, Raleigh *Also Called: Iron Box LLC (G-10209)*

Iron Box LLC... 919 890-0025
1349 Express Dr Raleigh (27603) *(G-10209)*

Ironbound Waste Management, Wilmington Also Called: Secured Traffic Control LLC **(G-12915)**

Irsi Automation Inc..336 303-5320
3703 Hines Chapel Rd Mc Leansville (27301) **(G-8224)**

Irvan-Smith Inc..704 788-2554
1027 Central Dr Nw Concord (28027) **(G-3382)**

Irwin...704 987-4339
8936 N Pointe Executive P Huntersville (28078) **(G-7003)**

Irwin Construction Accessories, Huntersville Also Called: Irwin Industrial Tool Company **(G-7004)**

Irwin Industrial Tool Company (HQ).................................704 987-4555
8935 N Pointe Executive Park Dr Huntersville (28078) **(G-7004)**

ISA...919 549-8411
67 Alexander Dr Durham (27709) **(G-4085)**

Isenhour Furniture Company (PA)......................................828 632-8849
486 S Center St Taylorsville (28681) **(G-11966)**

Island Gazette Newspaper, The, Carolina Beach Also Called: Seaside Press Co Inc **(G-1264)**

Island Machining LLC..704 278-3553
265 Pitt Rd Mooresville (28115) **(G-8697)**

Island Wood Crafts Ltd...252 473-5363
776 Old Wharf Rd Wanchese (27981) **(G-12344)**

Island Xpertees, Nags Head Also Called: Island Xprtees of Oter Bnks In **(G-9298)**

Island Xprtees of Oter Bnks In...252 480-3990
2224 S Lark Ave Nags Head (27959) **(G-9298)**

Ism Inc..828 684-277
149 Old Shoals Rd Arden (28704) **(G-277)**

Isometrics Inc (PA)...336 349-2329
1266 N Scales St Reidsville (27320) **(G-10689)**

Isometrics Inc...336 342-4150
7537 Nc Highway 87 Reidsville (27320) **(G-10690)**

Ison Furniture Mfg Inc...336 476-4700
801 Trinity St Ste 3a Thomasville (27360) **(G-12040)**

Issi, Salisbury Also Called: Industrial Sup Solutions Inc **(G-11067)**

Issuer Direct, Raleigh Also Called: Access Newswire Inc **(G-9872)**

Itc Millwork LLC (PA)...704 821-1470
3619 Gribble Rd Matthews (28104) **(G-8176)**

Itech, Arden Also Called: Injection Technology Corporation **(G-276)**

Itek Graphics LLC...704 357-6002
7075 Aviation Blvd Nw Ste B Concord (28027) **(G-3383)**

Itg Brands..336 335-6600
420 N English St Greensboro (27405) **(G-5626)**

Itg Brands..919 366-0220
900 E Six Forks Rd Unit 210 Raleigh (27604) **(G-10210)**

Itg Brands LLC (HQ)..336 335-6669
628 Green Valley Rd Ste 500 Greensboro (27408) **(G-5627)**

Itg Holdings Inc..336 379-6220
804 Green Valley Rd Ste 300 Greensboro (27408) **(G-5628)**

Itg Holdings USA Inc..954 772-9000
714 Green Valley Rd Greensboro (27408) **(G-5629)**

Itl Corp...828 659-9663
203 College Dr Marion (28752) **(G-8044)**

Itm Ltd South..336 883-2400
1903 Brassfield Rd Greensboro (27410) **(G-5630)**

Itron Inc..919 876-2600
8529 Six Forks Rd Ste 100 Raleigh (27615) **(G-10211)**

Its A Snap..828 254-3456
66 Asheland Ave Asheville (28801) **(G-525)**

Its Your Time Business Center..336 754-4456
2735 Old Hollow Rd Walkertown (27051) **(G-12316)**

ITT LLC..704 716-7600
4828 Parkway Plaza Blvd # 200 Charlotte (28217) **(G-2357)**

ITT LLC..336 662-0113
8511 Norcross Rd Colfax (27235) **(G-3281)**

Iv-S Metal Stamping Inc..336 861-2100
2400 Shore St Archdale (27263) **(G-229)**

Ivars Display..909 923-2761
2001 Partnership Dr Shelby (28150) **(G-11348)**

Ivars Sportswear Inc...336 227-9683
408 W Interstate Service Rd Graham (27253) **(G-5271)**

Ivey Fixture & Design Inc...704 283-4398
2814 N Rocky River Rd Monroe (28110) **(G-8506)**

Ivey Icenhour DBA...704 786-0676
5690 Barrier Georgeville Rd Mount Pleasant (28124) **(G-9262)**

Ivey Lane, Greensboro Also Called: Ivey Ln Inc **(G-5631)**

Ivey Ln Inc..336 230-0062
103 Ward Rd Greensboro (27405) **(G-5631)**

Ivm Chemicals Inc..407 506-4913
301 Mccullough Dr Fl 4 Charlotte (28262) **(G-2358)**

Ivp Forest Products LLC..252 241-8126
125 Horton Dr Morehead City (28557) **(G-8836)**

Ivy Brand LLC...980 225-7866
106 Foster Ave Charlotte (28203) **(G-2359)**

Ixc Discovery Inc (PA)...919 941-5206
4222 Emperor Blvd Ste 350 Durham (27703) **(G-4086)**

Izitleather, Mount Airy Also Called: Willow Tex LLC **(G-9195)**

J & B Logging and Timber Co..919 934-4115
524 Brogden Rd Smithfield (27577) **(G-11447)**

J & B Tool Making Inc..704 827-4805
14522 Lucia Riverbend Hwy Mount Holly (28120) **(G-9234)**

J & D Managements LLC...910 321-7373
605 German St Fayetteville (28301) **(G-4618)**

J & D Thorpe Enterprises Inc..919 553-0918
116 Shady Meadow Ln Clayton (27520) **(G-3155)**

J & D Wood Inc...910 628-9000
4940 Centerville Church Rd Fairmont (28340) **(G-4502)**

J & J Logging Inc..252 430-1110
255 J P Taylor Rd Henderson (27537) **(G-6162)**

J & J Machine Works Inc...336 434-4081
1300 Corporation Dr Archdale (27263) **(G-230)**

J & K Tools LLC...828 299-0589
490 Upper Grassy Br Rd Asheville (28805) **(G-526)**

J & L Bckh/Nvrnmental Svcs Inc.......................................910 237-7351
3043 Tom Geddie Rd Eastover (28312) **(G-4337)**

J & M Woodworking Inc...828 728-3253
432 Pine Mountain Rd Hudson (28638) **(G-6950)**

J & P Entrprses of Crlinas Inc...704 861-1867
5640 Gallagher Dr Gastonia (28052) **(G-5069)**

J & P Machine Works Inc..252 758-1719
4291 Us Highway 264 E Greenville (27834) **(G-5993)**

J & P Wood Works Inc..336 788-1881
780 Megahertz Dr Winston Salem (27107) **(G-13211)**

J & S Fab Inc..704 528-4251
354 S Eastway Dr Troutman (28166) **(G-12141)**

J & W Service Incorporated...336 449-4584
7471 Danford Rd Whitsett (27377) **(G-12611)**

J &D Contractor Service Inc...919 427-0218
246 Scotts Ln Angier (27501) **(G-122)**

J A King..800 327-7727
7239 Acc Blvd Ste 101 Raleigh (27617) **(G-10212)**

J C Custom Sewing Inc..336 449-4586
106 E Railroad Ave Gibsonville (27249) **(G-5178)**

J C Enterprises...336 986-1688
936 Washington Ave Winston Salem (27101) **(G-13212)**

J C I, Selma Also Called: Johnston County Industries Inc **(G-11289)**

J C Lawrence Co...919 553-3044
9526 Connie Cove Rd Oriental (28571) **(G-9600)**

J Charles Saunders Co Inc...704 866-9156
1004 E Long Ave Gastonia (28054) **(G-5070)**

J Culpepper & Co...828 524-6842
8285 Georgia Rd Otto (28763) **(G-9606)**

J E Carpenter Logging Co Inc..252 633-0037
4911 Hermitage Rd Trent Woods (28562) **(G-12107)**

J E Herndon Company (HQ)..704 739-4711
1020 Je Herndon Access Rd Kings Mountain (28086) **(G-7366)**

J E Jones Lumber Company...336 472-3478
7255 E Us Highway 64 Lexington (27292) **(G-7700)**

J E Kerr Timber Co Corp...252 537-0544
1005 Old Halifax Rd Roanoke Rapids (27870) **(G-10739)**

J F Fabricators LLC (PA)...704 454-7224
7315 Millbrook Rd Harrisburg (28075) **(G-6110)**

J F Heat Treating Inc...704 864-0998
409 Airport Rd Gastonia (28056) **(G-5071)**

A
L
P
H
A
B
E
T
I
C

J J Jenkins Incorporated..704 821-6648
  3380 Smith Farm Rd Matthews (28104) *(G-8177)*

J L Anderson Co Inc..704 289-9599
  4812 W Highway 74 Monroe (28110) *(G-8507)*

J L Frame Shop Inc..828 256-6290
  1310 Houston Mill Rd Conover (28613) *(G-3535)*

J L Powell & Co Inc (PA)...910 642-8989
  135 E Main St Whiteville (28472) *(G-12585)*

J L Smith & Co Inc (PA)..704 521-1088
  901 Blairhill Rd Ste 400 Charlotte (28217) *(G-2360)*

J M C Tool and Machine, Sanford *Also Called: Bnp Inc (G-11157)*

J Massey Inc..704 821-7084
  3330 Smith Farm Rd Stallings (28104) *(G-11600)*

J Morgan Signs Inc...336 274-6509
  4421 S Elm Eugene St Greensboro (27406) *(G-5632)*

J R B and J Knitting Inc..910 439-4242
  4543 Nc Highway 109 S Mount Gilead (27306) *(G-9199)*

J R Cole Industries Inc (PA)....................................704 523-6622
  435 Minuet Ln Charlotte (28217) *(G-2361)*

J R Cole Industries Inc..704 523-6622
  10708 Granite St Charlotte (28273) *(G-2362)*

J R Craver & Associates Inc.....................................336 769-3330
  265 Ashbourne Lake Ct Clemmons (27012) *(G-3193)*

J R Nixon Welding...252 221-4574
  212 Center Hill Rd Tyner (27980) *(G-12183)*

J Signs and Graphics LLC.......................................910 315-2657
  1345 N Sandhills Blvd Ste 1 Aberdeen (28315) *(G-9)*

J Stahl Sales & Sourcing Inc (PA)............................828 645-3005
  81 Monticello Rd Weaverville (28787) *(G-12493)*

J W Harris Co Inc...336 831-8601
  1690 Lowery St Winston Salem (27101) *(G-13213)*

J W Jones Lumber Company Inc (PA).......................252 771-2497
  1443 Northside Rd Elizabeth City (27909) *(G-4393)*

J Wise Inc...828 202-5563
  313a Motz Ave Lincolnton (28092) *(G-7833)*

J-M Manufacturing Company Inc...............................919 575-6515
  2602 W Lyon Station Rd Creedmoor (27522) *(G-3650)*

J&J Outdoor Accessories...910 742-1969
  26955 Andrew Jackson Hwy E Delco (28436) *(G-3736)*

J&L Machine & Fabrication Inc.................................704 755-5552
  201 S Buckoak St Stanley (28164) *(G-11619)*

J&L Manufacturing Inc...919 801-3219
  192 Jarco Dr Fuquay Varina (27526) *(G-4886)*

J&R Cohoon Logging & Tidewater............................252 943-6300
  25912 Us Highway 264 E Pantego (27860) *(G-9645)*

J&R Precision Heating and Air.................................910 480-8322
  1625 Cumberland Dr Fayetteville (28311) *(G-4619)*

J&R SERvices/J&r Lumber Co..................................956 778-7005
  1319 Military Cutoff Rd Ste Cc Pmb 173 Wilmington (28405) *(G-12821)*

J4 Construction LLC..704 550-7970
  2634 W Hwy 74 W Wadesboro (28170) *(G-12245)*

J6 & Company LLC..336 997-4497
  5077 Bismark St Winston Salem (27105) *(G-13214)*

JA Smith Inc..704 860-4910
  305 Plainsview Church Rd Lawndale (28090) *(G-7517)*

Jabb of Carolinas Inc...919 965-9007
  302 E Brown St Pine Level (27568) *(G-9682)*

Jabec Enterprise Inc (PA)..336 655-8441
  5224 Mountain View Rd Winston Salem (27104) *(G-13215)*

Jabil Inc...828 684-3141
  100 Vista Blvd Arden (28704) *(G-278)*

Jabil Inc...828 209-4202
  724 Broadpointe Dr Mills River (28759) *(G-8316)*

Jack A Farrior Inc...252 753-2020
  9585 Us Highway 264a Farmville (27828) *(G-4532)*

Jack Cartwright Incorporated.................................336 889-9400
  2014 Chestnut Street Ext High Point (27262) *(G-6676)*

Jacks Motor Parts Inc..910 642-4077
  Hwy 701 Whiteville (28472) *(G-12586)*

Jackson Logging..919 658-2757
  2936 Summerlins Crossroad Rd Mount Olive (28365) *(G-9256)*

Jackson Paper Manufacturing Co (PA).....................828 586-5534
  152 W Main St Sylva (28779) *(G-11894)*

Jackson Products Inc...704 598-4949
  1109 Monterey Bay Dr Wake Forest (27587) *(G-12283)*

Jackson Wine..828 508-9292
  183 King St Brevard (28712) *(G-973)*

Jacksonville Metal Mfg Inc.......................................910 938-7635
  181 Piney Green Rd Jacksonville (28546) *(G-7128)*

Jacob Holtz Company LLC.......................................828 328-1003
  747 22nd Street Pl Se Hickory (28602) *(G-6373)*

Jacobs Creek Stone Company Inc............................336 857-2602
  2081 W Slate Mine Rd Denton (27239) *(G-3751)*

Jaeco Precision Inc...336 633-1025
  721 Jaeco Caudill Dr Asheboro (27205) *(G-368)*

Jag Graphics Inc..828 259-9020
  231 Biltmore Ave Asheville (28801) *(G-527)*

Jag Industries LLC...704 655-2507
  10408 Remembrance Trl Huntersville (28078) *(G-7005)*

Jaggaer, Durham *Also Called: Jaggaer LLC (G-4087)*

Jaggaer LLC (HQ)...919 659-2100
  700 Park Offices Dr Durham (27713) *(G-4087)*

Jaguar Gene Therapy LLC..919 465-6400
  203 Mackenan Dr Cary (27511) *(G-1377)*

Jak Moulding & Supply Inc......................................252 753-5546
  1565 Strickland Rd Walstonburg (27888) *(G-12332)*

James Bunn...252 293-4867
  4167 Black Creek Rd S Wilson (27893) *(G-12995)*

James Cotter Ironworks..919 644-2664
  5102 Eno Cemetery Rd Cedar Grove (27231) *(G-1517)*

James Fods Frnchise Corp Amer..............................336 437-0393
  611 E Gilbreath St Graham (27253) *(G-5272)*

James Foods Inc...336 437-0393
  611 E Gilbreath St Graham (27253) *(G-5273)*

James G Gouge...336 854-1551
  1001 Phillips Ave High Point (27262) *(G-6677)*

James Iron & Steel Inc...704 283-2299
  2819 Top Hill Rd Monroe (28110) *(G-8508)*

James Keith Nations...828 421-5391
  69 Thomas Valley Rd Whittier (28789) *(G-12624)*

James King...910 308-8818
  9998 Fayetteville Rd Fayetteville (28304) *(G-4620)*

James L Johnson..704 694-0103
  2151 Beaver Rd Wadesboro (28170) *(G-12246)*

James Lammers..252 491-2303
  7715 Caratoke Hwy Powells Point (27966) *(G-9822)*

James M Pleasants Company Inc (PA).....................800 365-9010
  603 Diamond Hill Ct Greensboro (27406) *(G-5633)*

James M Pleasants Company Inc.............................888 902-8324
  206 E Seneca Rd Greensboro (27406) *(G-5634)*

James Moore & Son Logging....................................336 656-9858
  7435 Friendship Church Rd Browns Summit (27214) *(G-999)*

James O 2, Hickory *Also Called: James Oxygen and Supply Co (G-6374)*

James Oxygen and Supply Co (PA)..........................704 322-5438
  30 Us Highway 321 Nw Hickory (28601) *(G-6374)*

James Ricks, Fayetteville *Also Called: Rk Enterprises LLC (G-4663)*

James River Equipment..704 821-7399
  2112 Morgan Mill Rd Monroe (28110) *(G-8509)*

JAMES TOOL COMPANY, Morganton *Also Called: James Tool Machine & Engrg Inc (G-8875)*

James Tool Machine & Engrg Inc (PA).....................828 584-8722
  130 Reep Dr Morganton (28655) *(G-8875)*

James W McManus Inc...828 688-2560
  2419 Beans Creek Rd Bakersville (28705) *(G-678)*

Jamestown News...336 841-4933
  206 E Main St Ste 1a Jamestown (27282) *(G-7170)*

Janesville LLC...828 668-9251
  157 Lackey Town Rd Old Fort (28762) *(G-9594)*

Jantec Sign Group LLC..336 429-5010
  196 Sexton Rd Mount Airy (27030) *(G-9136)*

Janus Development Group Inc.................................252 551-9042
  218 E Arlington Blvd Greenville (27858) *(G-5994)*

Jared Munday Electric Inc..828 355-9024
  123 Tarheel Ln Boone (28607) *(G-927)*

2025 Harris North Carolina
Manufacturers Directory

(G-0000) Company's Geographic Section entry number

Jared Sasnett Logging Co Inc 252 939-6289
1976 Neuse Rd Kinston (28501) *(G-7416)*

Jarrett Bay Offshore 919 803-1990
4209 Lassiter Mill Rd Ste 126 Raleigh (27609) *(G-10213)*

Jarrett Brothers 828 433-8036
200 Carbondale Ln Morganton (28655) *(G-8876)*

Jasie Blanks LLC 910 485-0016
3725 Ramsey St Ste 103c Fayetteville (28311) *(G-4621)*

Jason Case Corp 212 786-2288
4809 Hillsborough Rd Durham (27705) *(G-4088)*

Jasper Engine Exchange Inc 704 664-2300
200 Penske Way Mooresville (28115) *(G-8698)*

Jasper Library Furniture, Troutman *Also Called: Jasper Seating Company Inc (G-12142)*

Jasper Library Furniture, Troutman *Also Called: Liat LLC (G-12144)*

Jasper Motor Sports, Mooresville *Also Called: Jasper Engine Exchange Inc (G-8698)*

Jasper Penske Engines 704 788-8996
4361 Motorsports Dr Sw Concord (28027) *(G-3384)*

Jasper Seating Company Inc 704 528-4506
694 N Main St Troutman (28166) *(G-12142)*

Jax Brothers Inc 704 732-3351
536 N Generals Blvd Lincolnton (28092) *(G-7834)*

Jax Specialty Welding LLC 704 380-3548
621 Bristol Dr Statesville (28677) *(G-11718)*

Jaxonsigns 910 467-3409
874 E Ocean Hwy Holly Ridge (28445) *(G-6889)*

Jayson Concepts Inc 828 654-8900
115 Vista Blvd Arden (28704) *(G-279)*

JB II Printing LLC 336 222-0717
825 S Main St Burlington (27215) *(G-1111)*

Jb-Isecurity LLC 910 824-7601
505 Toxaway Ct Fayetteville (28314) *(G-4622)*

Jbb Packaging LLC 201 470-8501
100 Grace Dr Weldon (27890) *(G-12521)*

Jbm Manufacturing, Morehead City *Also Called: Jones Brothers Marine Mfg Inc (G-8837)*

Jbr Properties of Greenville Inc 252 355-9353
133 Forlines Rd Winterville (28590) *(G-13417)*

Jbs Case Ready, Lenoir *Also Called: Jbs USA LLC (G-7617)*

Jbs USA LLC 828 855-9571
1207 25th Street Pl Se Hickory (28602) *(G-6375)*

Jbs USA LLC 828 725-7000
1450 Homegrown Ct Lenoir (28645) *(G-7617)*

Jbs2 Inc 828 236-1300
875 Warren Wilson Rd Swannanoa (28778) *(G-11872)*

Jbt Aerotech Services 336 740-3737
6035 Old Oak Ridge Rd Greensboro (27410) *(G-5635)*

Jbt Marel Corporation 919 362-8811
2000 Lufkin Rd Apex (27539) *(G-171)*

JC Print 910 556-9663
321 N Front St Wilmington (28401) *(G-12822)*

Jci Jones Chemicals Inc 704 392-9767
1500 Tar Heel Rd Charlotte (28208) *(G-2363)*

Jctm, Charlotte *Also Called: Jctm LLC (G-2364)*

Jctm LLC 252 571-8678
16710 Tulloch Rd Charlotte (28278) *(G-2364)*

JD Apparel Inc 704 289-5600
1680 Williams Rd Monroe (28110) *(G-8510)*

Jd2 Company LLC 800 811-6441
3527 Governors Island Dr Denver (28037) *(G-3791)*

Jdh Capital LLC (PA) 704 357-1220
3735 Beam Rd Unit B Charlotte (28217) *(G-2365)*

Jebco Inc 919 557-2001
121 Thomas Mill Rd Holly Springs (27540) *(G-6904)*

Jefferies Socks LLC 336 226-7316
2203 Tucker St Burlington (27215) *(G-1112)*

Jeffers Logging Inc 919 708-2193
279 Garner Rd Sanford (27330) *(G-11196)*

Jefferson Group Inc 252 752-6195
225 Martin St Greenville (27834) *(G-5995)*

Jeffrey Sheffer 919 861-9126
3901 Commerce Park Dr Raleigh (27610) *(G-10214)*

Jeffreys Division, Colfax *Also Called: Phillips Corporation (G-3286)*

Jeld Wen International Supply, Charlotte *Also Called: Jeld-Wen Inc (G-2366)*

JELD-WEN, Charlotte *Also Called: Jeld-Wen Holding Inc (G-2367)*

Jeld-Wen Inc (HQ) 800 535-3936
2645 Silver Crescent Dr Charlotte (28273) *(G-2366)*

Jeld-Wen Inc 828 724-9511
100 Henry Mccall Rd Marion (28752) *(G-8045)*

Jeld-Wen Inc 336 838-0292
205 Lanes Dr North Wilkesboro (28659) *(G-9536)*

Jeld-Wen Composite, North Wilkesboro *Also Called: Jeld-Wen Inc (G-9536)*

Jeld-Wen Holding Inc (PA) 704 378-5700
2645 Silver Crescent Dr Charlotte (28273) *(G-2367)*

Jenesis Software Inc 828 245-1171
307 Georgetowne Dr Elon (27244) *(G-4471)*

Jenkins, Charlotte *Also Called: Jenkins Electric Company (G-2368)*

Jenkins Electric Company 800 438-3003
5933 Brookshire Blvd Charlotte (28216) *(G-2368)*

Jenkins Electric II LLC 704 392-7371
5933 Brookshire Blvd Charlotte (28216) *(G-2369)*

Jenkins Foods Inc 704 434-2347
2119 New House Rd Shelby (28150) *(G-11349)*

Jenkins Interiors, North Wilkesboro *Also Called: Jenkins Properties Inc (G-9537)*

Jenkins Millwork LLC 336 667-3344
1603 Industrial Dr Wilkesboro (28697) *(G-12643)*

Jenkins Properties Inc 336 667-4282
102 Chestnut St Ste 101 North Wilkesboro (28659) *(G-9537)*

Jenkins Services Group LLC 704 881-3210
5577 Little Mountain Rd Catawba (28609) *(G-1512)*

Jenni K Jewelry, Greenville *Also Called: Jkl Inc (G-5996)*

Jennifer Mowrer 336 714-6462
150 Kimel Park Dr Ste 100 Winston Salem (27103) *(G-13216)*

Jeremy Weitzel 919 878-4474
1228 United Dr Raleigh (27603) *(G-10215)*

Jerry Blevins 336 384-3726
1162 Deep Ford Rd Lansing (28643) *(G-7477)*

Jerry G Williams & Sons Inc 919 934-4115
524 Brogden Rd Smithfield (27577) *(G-11448)*

Jerry Huffman Sawmill 336 973-3606
287 Cactus Ln Wilkesboro (28697) *(G-12644)*

Jerry Huffman Sawmill & Log, Wilkesboro *Also Called: Jerry Huffman Sawmill (G-12644)*

Jerry Williams & Son Inc 919 934-4115
524 Brogden Rd Smithfield (27577) *(G-11449)*

Jeskri Associates Inc 704 291-9991
1821 N Rocky River Rd Monroe (28110) *(G-8511)*

Jessica Charles LLC 336 434-2124
535 Townsend Ave High Point (27263) *(G-6678)*

Jester-Crown Inc 919 872-1070
4721 Atlantic Ave Ste 119 Raleigh (27604) *(G-10216)*

Jestines Jewels Inc 704 904-0191
512 Klumac Rd Ste 4 Salisbury (28144) *(G-11072)*

Jewel Masters Inc (PA) 336 243-2711
221 W Us Highway 64 Lexington (27295) *(G-7701)*

Jewelry By Gail Inc 252 441-5387
207 E Driftwood St Nags Head (27959) *(G-9299)*

Jewers Doors Us Inc 888 510-5331
3714 Alliance Dr Ste 305 Greensboro (27407) *(G-5636)*

JFK Conferences LLC 980 255-3336
322 Ridgeway Ct Fayetteville (28311) *(G-4623)*

Jfl Enterprises Inc 704 786-7838
82 Spring St Sw Concord (28025) *(G-3385)*

Jfl LLC 919 440-3517
4353 West Perry St Farmville (27828) *(G-4533)*

Jgi Inc (PA) 704 522-8860
10108 Industrial Dr Pineville (28134) *(G-9737)*

Jh Logging 336 599-0278
1300 Virgilina Rd Roxboro (27573) *(G-10928)*

Jhd Enterprise LLC 919 612-1787
1102 Lake Ridge Dr Creedmoor (27522) *(G-3651)*

Jhrg Manufacturing LLC 252 478-4977
303 S Pine St Spring Hope (27882) *(G-11556)*

Jif Logging Inc 252 398-2249
411 E Woodrow School Rd Murfreesboro (27855) *(G-9282)*

Jiffy Division, High Point *Also Called: Sealed Air Corporation (G-6764)*

Jim Allred Taxidermy Supply..................................... 828 749-5900
   1309 Ozone Dr Saluda (28773) *(G-11139)*

Jim Fab of North Carolina Inc..................................... 704 278-1000
   10230 Statesville Blvd Cleveland (27013) *(G-3215)*

Jim Myers & Sons Inc.. 704 554-8397
   5120 Westinghouse Blvd Charlotte (28273) *(G-2370)*

Jimbuilt, Connelly Springs *Also Called: Jimbuilt Machines Inc (G-3479)*

Jimbuilt Machines Inc.. 828 874-3530
   2555 Israel Chapel Rd Connelly Springs (28612) *(G-3479)*

Jimmie Nelms Trucking, Louisburg *Also Called: Jimmy D Nelms Logging Inc (G-7919)*

Jimmy D Nelms Logging Inc.. 919 853-2597
   4021 Nc 561 Hwy Louisburg (27549) *(G-7919)*

Jimmys Coating Unlimited Inc..................................... 704 915-2420
   420 N Morehead St Gastonia (28054) *(G-5072)*

Jj Electronic Solutions Div, Sanford *Also Called: Desco Industries Inc (G-11168)*

Jka Idustries.. 980 225-5350
   353 Grayson Dr Salisbury (28147) *(G-11073)*

Jkl Inc (PA).. 252 355-6714
   727 Red Banks Rd Greenville (27858) *(G-5996)*

JKS Incorporated, Winston Salem *Also Called: JKS Motorsports Inc (G-13217)*

JKS Motorsports Inc (PA)... 336 722-4129
   876 N Liberty St Winston Salem (27101) *(G-13217)*

Jl Hosiery LLC.. 910 974-7156
   130 S Main St Candor (27229) *(G-1237)*

Jlmade LLC.. 252 515-2195
   2226 Jasper Forest Trl Winnabow (28479) *(G-13066)*

Jly Invstmnts Inc Fka Nwman Mc (HQ)......................... 336 273-8261
   2949 Lees Chapel Rd Browns Summit (27214) *(G-1000)*

JM Graphics Inc.. 704 375-1147
   3400 International Airport Dr Ste 950 Charlotte (28208) *(G-2371)*

JM Williams Timber Company...................................... 919 362-1333
   4525 Green Level West Rd Apex (27523) *(G-172)*

Jmc Tool & Machine Co.. 919 775-7070
   5910 Elwin Buchanan Dr Sanford (27330) *(G-11197)*

Jmk Tool & Die Inc.. 910 897-6373
   3482 Nc 27 E Coats (27521) *(G-3263)*

JMP Statistical Discovery Llc...................................... 877 594-6567
   920 Sas Campus Dr Cary (27513) *(G-1378)*

JMS Rebar Inc.. 336 273-9084
   1211 Rotherwood Rd Greensboro (27406) *(G-5637)*

JMS Southeast Inc.. 704 873-1835
   105 Temperature Ln Statesville (28677) *(G-11719)*

Jna, Mooresville *Also Called: Bucher Municipal N Amer Inc (G-8624)*

Jo-Mar Group LLC
   701 Plum St Belmont (28012) *(G-755)*

Jo-Mar Spinning, Belmont *Also Called: Jo-Mar Group LLC (G-755)*

Jo-Natta Transportation LLC....................................... 888 424-8789
   348 Foothill Ln Fayetteville (28311) *(G-4624)*

Joanna Co, Charlotte *Also Called: Chf Industries Inc (G-1911)*

Job Finder USA, Cary *Also Called: Prism Publishing Inc (G-1428)*

Job Shop Fabricators Inc.. 336 427-7300
   3522 Us Highway 220 Madison (27025) *(G-7988)*

Jobs Magazine LLC.. 919 319-6816
   1240 Se Maynard Rd Ste 104 Cary (27511) *(G-1379)*

Jocephus Originals Inc... 336 229-9600
   1003 W Main St Ste A4 Haw River (27258) *(G-6133)*

Jochum Industries... 336 288-7975
   710 Freemasons Dr Greensboro (27407) *(G-5638)*

Jody Stowe.. 704 519-6560
   2848 Lakeview Cir Matthews (28105) *(G-8119)*

Joe and Kitty Brown Inc... 704 629-4327
   1312 Ramseur Rd Bessemer City (28016) *(G-824)*

Joe and La Inc.. 336 585-0313
   326 Macarthur Ln Burlington (27217) *(G-1113)*

Joe Robin Darnell... 704 482-1186
   2115 Chatfield Rd Shelby (28150) *(G-11350)*

Joerns Healthcare Parent LLC (PA).............................. 800 966-6662
   2430 Whitehall Park Dr Ste 100 Charlotte (28273) *(G-2372)*

Joesigns Inc... 252 638-1622
   2617 Trent Rd New Bern (28562) *(G-9373)*

Jofra Graphics Inc... 910 259-1717
   401 Us Highway 117 S Burgaw (28425) *(G-1025)*

John Conrad Inc... 336 475-8144
   1028 Johnsontown Rd Thomasville (27360) *(G-12041)*

John Deere, Cary *Also Called: John Deere Consumer Pdts Inc (G-1380)*

John Deere, Fuquay Varina *Also Called: Revels Turf and Tractor LLC (G-4896)*

John Deere Authorized Dealer, Monroe *Also Called: James River Equipment (G-8509)*

John Deere Consumer Pdts Inc (HQ)............................ 919 804-2000
   2000 John Deere Run Cary (27513) *(G-1380)*

John Deere Kernersville LLC.. 336 996-8100
   1000 John Deere Rd Kernersville (27284) *(G-7281)*

John Deere Turf Care, Fuquay Varina *Also Called: Deere & Company (G-4878)*

John J Morton Company Inc (PA)................................. 704 332-6633
   2211 W Morehead St Charlotte (28208) *(G-2373)*

John Jenkins Company... 336 375-3717
   5949 Summit Ave Browns Summit (27214) *(G-1001)*

John Laughter Jewelry Inc.. 828 456-4772
   146 N Main St Waynesville (28786) *(G-12462)*

John Lindenberger.. 919 337-6741
   6429 Grassy Knoll Ln Raleigh (27616) *(G-10217)*

John W Foster Sales Inc... 704 821-3822
   3491 Gribble Rd Matthews (28104) *(G-8178)*

John West Auto Service Inc... 919 250-0825
   3216 Lake Woodard Dr Raleigh (27604) *(G-10218)*

Johnie Gregory Trck Bodies Inc................................... 252 264-2626
   337 Old Us Highway 17 Hertford (27944) *(G-6255)*

Johnny Daniel.. 336 859-2480
   230 Bringle Ferry Rd Denton (27239) *(G-3752)*

Johnny Slicks Inc.. 910 803-2159
   624 Us Highway 17 S Unit 1 Holly Ridge (28445) *(G-6890)*

Johnnys Tire Sales and Svc Inc................................... 252 353-8473
   2400 S Memorial Dr Ste 3a Greenville (27834) *(G-5997)*

Johnson Cnc LLC.. 910 428-1245
   133 S Main St Star (27356) *(G-11628)*

Johnson Concrete Company.. 704 786-4204
   106 Old Davidson Pl Nw Concord (28027) *(G-3386)*

Johnson Concrete Company.. 336 248-2918
   514 Burgin Dr Lexington (27292) *(G-7702)*

Johnson Concrete Company (PA)................................. 704 636-5231
   217 Klumac Rd Salisbury (28144) *(G-11074)*

Johnson Concrete Company.. 704 636-5231
   1401 Nc 42 Hwy Willow Spring (27592) *(G-12679)*

Johnson Concrete Products, Concord *Also Called: Johnson Concrete Company (G-3386)*

Johnson Concrete Products, Salisbury *Also Called: Johnson Concrete Company (G-11074)*

Johnson Controls.. 704 501-0500
   9826 Southern Pine Blvd Charlotte (28273) *(G-2374)*

Johnson Controls, Asheville *Also Called: Johnson Controls Inc (G-528)*

Johnson Controls, Charlotte *Also Called: Johnson Controls Inc (G-2375)*

Johnson Controls, Charlotte *Also Called: Johnson Controls Inc (G-2376)*

Johnson Controls, Durham *Also Called: Johnson Controls Inc (G-4089)*

Johnson Controls, High Point *Also Called: Clarios LLC (G-6569)*

Johnson Controls, Kernersville *Also Called: Clarios LLC (G-7257)*

Johnson Controls, Raleigh *Also Called: Johnson Controls Inc (G-10219)*

Johnson Controls, Wilmington *Also Called: Johnson Controls Inc (G-12823)*

Johnson Controls, Winterville *Also Called: Clarios LLC (G-13415)*

Johnson Controls Inc... 828 225-3200
   905 Riverside Dr Asheville (28804) *(G-528)*

Johnson Controls Inc... 704 521-8889
   9844 Southern Pine Blvd Ste B Charlotte (28273) *(G-2375)*

Johnson Controls Inc... 919 905-5745
   5 Moore Dr Durham (27709) *(G-4089)*

Johnson Controls Inc... 866 285-8345
   2700 Perimeter Park Dr Morrisville (27560) *(G-8995)*

Johnson Controls Inc... 919 743-3500
   633 Hutton St Ste 104 Raleigh (27606) *(G-10219)*

Johnson Controls Inc... 910 392-2372
   395 N Green Meadows Dr Wilmington (28405) *(G-12823)*

Johnson Controls Inc... 704 521-8889
   9844 Southern Pine Blvd Charlotte (28273) *(G-2376)*

Johnson Custom Boats Inc.. 910 232-4594
   6820a Market St Wilmington (28405) *(G-12824)*

Johnson Global Cmplnce Contrls.................... 704 552-1119
13950 Ballantyne Corporate Pl Charlotte (28277) *(G-2377)*

Johnson Harn Vngar Gee GL Pllc.................... 919 213-6163
434 Fayetteville St Ste 2200 Raleigh (27601) *(G-10220)*

Johnson Industrial Mchy Svcs........................ 252 239-1944
7160 Us Highway 117 Lucama (27851) *(G-7937)*

Johnson Lumber Products Inc......................... 910 532-4201
911 Eddie L Jones Rd Ivanhoe (28447) *(G-7111)*

Johnson Machine Co Inc............................... 252 638-2620
8 Batts Hill Rd New Bern (28562) *(G-9374)*

Johnson Nash & Sons Farms Inc (PA)................ 910 289-3113
3385 S Us 117 Hwy Rose Hill (28458) *(G-10907)*

Johnson Paving Company Inc......................... 828 652-4911
3101 Us 221 North Marion (28752) *(G-8046)*

Johnson's Industrial Coatings, Clemmons *Also Called: Paint Company of NC (G-3198)*

Johnston Casuals Furniture Inc...................... 336 838-5178
121 Shaver St North Wilkesboro (28659) *(G-9538)*

Johnston County Industries Inc...................... 919 743-8700
1100 E Preston St Selma (27576) *(G-11289)*

Joie of Seating Inc.................................... 704 795-7474
4537 Orphanage Rd Concord (28027) *(G-3387)*

Jolo Winery & Vineyards LLC......................... 954 816-5649
219 Jolo Winery Ln Pilot Mountain (27041) *(G-9671)*

Jon Kuhn Inc.. 336 722-2369
701 N Liberty St Winston Salem (27101) *(G-13218)*

Jones Brothers Marine Mfg Inc...................... 252 240-1995
100 Bateau Blvd Morehead City (28557) *(G-8837)*

Jones Doors & Windows Inc.......................... 336 998-8624
533 Joe Rd Mocksville (27028) *(G-8372)*

Jones Fabricare Inc (PA)............................. 336 272-7261
502 E Cornwallis Dr Greensboro (27405) *(G-5639)*

Jones Frame Inc...................................... 336 434-2531
5456 Uwharrie Rd High Point (27263) *(G-6679)*

Jones Furs, Greensboro *Also Called: Jones Fabricare Inc (G-5639)*

Jones Marine Inc..................................... 704 639-0173
10285 Bringle Ferry Rd Salisbury (28146) *(G-11075)*

Jones Media.. 828 264-3612
474 Industrial Park Dr Boone (28607) *(G-928)*

Jones Printing Company Inc......................... 919 774-9442
104 Hawkins Ave Sanford (27330) *(G-11198)*

Jones Vndrhle Vineyards Winery, Thurmond *Also Called: Jones Vondrehle Vineyards LLC (G-12097)*

Jones Vondrehle Vineyards LLC...................... 336 874-2800
964 Old Railroad Grade Rd Thurmond (28683) *(G-12097)*

Jonesville Water Plant, Jonesville *Also Called: Town of Jonesville (G-7199)*

Jordan Electric Motors Inc.......................... 919 708-7010
1303 Stockyard Rd Staley (27355) *(G-11595)*

Jordan Group Corporation........................... 803 309-9988
7007 Berolina Ln Apt 1613 Charlotte (28226) *(G-2378)*

Jordan Innvtive Fbrication LLC...................... 910 428-2368
275 Sedberry Rd Biscoe (27209) *(G-854)*

Jordan Lumber & Supply Inc......................... 910 439-6121
1939 Nc Highway 109 S Mount Gilead (27306) *(G-9200)*

Jordan Lumber & Supply Inc (PA).................... 910 439-6121
1939 Nc Highway 109 S Mount Gilead (27306) *(G-9201)*

Jordan Lumber & Supply Inc......................... 910 428-9048
4483 Spies Rd Star (27356) *(G-11629)*

Jordan Piping Inc.................................... 336 818-9252
300 8th St North Wilkesboro (28659) *(G-9539)*

Jordan-Holman Lumber Co Inc....................... 828 396-3101
650 N Main St Granite Falls (28630) *(G-5309)*

Jorlink Usa Inc...................................... 336 288-1613
3714 Alliance Dr Ste 100 Greensboro (27407) *(G-5640)*

Jorlink.com, Greensboro *Also Called: Jorlink Usa Inc (G-5640)*

Joseph C Woodard Prtg Co Inc...................... 919 829-0634
2815 S Saunders St Raleigh (27603) *(G-10221)*

Joseph F Decker..................................... 704 335-0021
341 Dalton Ave Charlotte (28206) *(G-2379)*

Joseph Halker.. 336 769-4734
481 Shady Grove Church Rd Winston Salem (27107) *(G-13219)*

Joseph Sotanski..................................... 407 324-6187
632 College Dr Marion (28752) *(G-8047)*

Josey Lumber Company Inc.......................... 252 826-5614
476 Lees Meadow Rd Scotland Neck (27874) *(G-11264)*

Josh Allred.. 336 873-1006
335 N Broad St Seagrove (27341) *(G-11275)*

Jostens, Winston Salem *Also Called: Jostens Inc (G-13220)*

Jostens Inc.. 336 765-0070
2505 Empire Dr Winston Salem (27103) *(G-13220)*

Joulin, Hickory *Also Called: Vacuum Handling North Amer LLC (G-6485)*

Journal Vacuum Science & Tech..................... 919 361-2787
51 Kilmayne Dr Ste 104 Cary (27511) *(G-1381)*

Journalbooks, Charlotte *Also Called: Timeplanner Calendars Inc (G-2920)*

Journalistic Inc..................................... 919 945-0700
101 Europa Dr Ste 150 Chapel Hill (27517) *(G-1550)*

Jowat Adhesives, Archdale *Also Called: Jowat Corporation (G-233)*

Jowat Corporation................................... 336 434-9356
5637 Evelyn View Dr Archdale (27263) *(G-231)*

Jowat Corporation................................... 336 442-5834
5265 Surrett Dr Archdale (27263) *(G-232)*

Jowat Corporation (HQ)............................. 336 434-9000
5608 Uwharrie Rd Archdale (27263) *(G-233)*

Jowat International Corp............................ 336 434-9000
5608 Uwharrie Rd Archdale (27263) *(G-234)*

Jowat Properties Corp.............................. 336 434-9000
5608 Uwharrie Rd Archdale (27263) *(G-235)*

Joy Dental Lab, Angier *Also Called: Custom Smiles Inc (G-118)*

JP Leather Arcona Division, Hudson *Also Called: Arcona Leather Company LLC (G-6941)*

JP Leather Company Inc............................. 828 396-7728
2615 Mission Rd Hudson (28638) *(G-6951)*

Jpi Coastal.. 704 310-5867
1114 Old Concord Rd Salisbury (28146) *(G-11076)*

Jpm, Greensboro *Also Called: James M Pleasants Company Inc (G-5633)*

JPS Communications Inc............................. 919 534-1168
5800 Departure Dr Raleigh (27616) *(G-10222)*

JPS Composite Materials Corp...................... 704 872-9831
535 Connor St Statesville (28677) *(G-11720)*

Jps Cupcakery LLC.................................. 919 894-5000
111 S Railroad St Benson (27504) *(G-793)*

JPS Elstmerics Westfield Plant...................... 336 351-0938
1535 Elastic Plant Rd Westfield (27053) *(G-12573)*

JPS Intrprbility Solutions Inc....................... 919 332-5009
5800 Departure Dr Raleigh (27616) *(G-10223)*

Jrg Technologies Corp.............................. 850 362-4310
9300 Harris Corners Pkwy Ste 450 Charlotte (28269) *(G-2380)*

Jri Development Group LLC......................... 704 660-8346
136 Knob Hill Rd Mooresville (28117) *(G-8699)*

Jri Shocks LLC...................................... 704 660-8346
116 Infield Ct Mooresville (28117) *(G-8700)*

Jrm Inc.. 888 576-7007
8491 N Nc Hwy 150 Clemmons (27012) *(G-3194)*

JRs Custom Framing................................. 704 449-2830
7604 Waterford Lakes Dr Charlotte (28210) *(G-2381)*

Js Fiber Co Inc (PA)................................ 704 871-1582
290 Marble Rd Statesville (28625) *(G-11721)*

Js Linens and Curtain Outlet (PA).................. 704 871-1582
290 Marble Rd Statesville (28625) *(G-11722)*

Js Printing LLC..................................... 919 773-1103
1824 Garner Station Blvd Raleigh (27603) *(G-10224)*

Js Royal Home Usa Inc............................. 704 542-2304
13451 S Point Blvd Charlotte (28273) *(G-2382)*

Jt International USA Inc............................. 201 871-1210
4000 Center At North Hills St Raleigh (27609) *(G-10225)*

Juan J Hernandez................................... 919 742-3381
4272 Piney Grove Church Rd Siler City (27344) *(G-11414)*

Juan Pino Signs Inc................................. 336 764-4422
2041 Gumtree Rd Winston Salem (27107) *(G-13221)*

Jubilee Screen Printing Inc......................... 910 673-4240
314 Grant St Ste F West End (27376) *(G-12555)*

Jugtown Pottery..................................... 910 464-3266
330 Jugtown Rd Seagrove (27341) *(G-11276)*

Julia's Pantry, Raleigh *Also Called: Julias Southern Foods LLC (G-10226)*

Julian Freirich Co, Salisbury *Also Called: Julian Freirich Food Products (G-11078)*

A
L
P
H
A
B
E
T
I
C

Julian Freirich Company Inc................................... 704 636-2621
815 W Kerr St Salisbury (28144) *(G-11077)*

Julian Freirich Food Products.............................. 704 636-2621
815 W Kerr St Salisbury (28144) *(G-11078)*

Julias Southern Foods LLC................................. 919 609-6745
5608 Primavera Ct Ste G Raleigh (27616) *(G-10226)*

Junaluska Mill Engineering.................................. 828 321-3693
181 Gipp Creek Rd Andrews (28901) *(G-108)*

Junior Johnson Country Hams, Wilkesboro Also Called: Suncrest Farms Cntry Hams Inc
(G-12654)

Juniper Networks Inc....................................... 888 586-4737
1730 Varsity Dr Ste 10 Raleigh (27606) *(G-10227)*

Jupiter Bathware Inc....................................... 800 343-8295
510 Jones St S Wilson (27893) *(G-12996)*

Just n Tyme Trucking LLC.................................. 704 804-9519
6015 Lake Forest Rd E Charlotte (28227) *(G-2383)*

Just Shrimp Holdings US Inc.............................. 805 832-1828
2820 Selwyn Ave Ste 420 Charlotte (28209) *(G-2384)*

Just Suspension, Denver Also Called: Suspensions LLC *(G-3808)*

Justenough Software Corp Inc........................... 800 949-3432
1009 Slater Rd Ste 420 Durham (27703) *(G-4090)*

Justi LLC... 919 434-5002
109 Oxyard Way Cary (27519) *(G-1382)*

Justice.. 910 392-1581
3500 Oleander Dr Ste 1054 Wilmington (28403) *(G-12825)*

Justice Bearing LLC....................................... 800 355-2500
243 Overhill Dr Ste D Mooresville (28117) *(G-8701)*

Justice Bearings, Mooresville Also Called: Justice Bearing LLC *(G-8701)*

Justneem LLC.. 919 414-8826
2416 Maxton Crest Dr Apex (27539) *(G-173)*

Justneem Body Care, Apex Also Called: Justneem LLC *(G-173)*

Jvst, Cary Also Called: Journal Vacuum Science & Tech *(G-1381)*

JW Metal Products, Monroe Also Called: Stainless Supply Inc *(G-8563)*

K & C Machine Co Inc...................................... 336 373-0745
601 Industrial Ave Greensboro (27406) *(G-5641)*

K & D Signs LLC... 336 786-1111
1078 S Main St Mount Airy (27030) *(G-9137)*

K & J Ashworth Logging LLC.............................. 336 879-2388
8797 Erect Rd Seagrove (27341) *(G-11277)*

K & K Stitch & Screen..................................... 336 246-5477
240 Helen Blevins Rd Unit 1 West Jefferson (28694) *(G-12565)*

K & L Resources... 910 494-3736
7809 Gallant Ridge Dr Fayetteville (28314) *(G-4625)*

K & M Products of NC Inc.................................. 828 524-5905
3248 Patton Rd Franklin (28734) *(G-4832)*

K & S Tool & Manufacturing Co........................... 336 410-7260
1247 Elon Pl High Point (27263) *(G-6680)*

K & S Tool & Manufacturing Co (PA)..................... 336 410-7260
614 Hendrix St High Point (27260) *(G-6681)*

K & W Welding LLC.. 910 895-9220
180 Old 74 Hwy Rockingham (28379) *(G-10781)*

K B I Biopharma, Durham Also Called: Kbi Biopharma Inc *(G-4094)*

K D S, Etowah Also Called: Kiln Drying Systems Cmpnnts In *(G-4496)*

K Formula Enterprises Inc................................. 910 323-3315
829 Gillespie St Ste A Fayetteville (28306) *(G-4626)*

K L Butler Logging Inc.................................... 910 648-6016
12237 Nc 41 Hwy W Bladenboro (28320) *(G-878)*

K W, Charlotte Also Called: Kem-Wove Inc *(G-2392)*

K-Flex USA LLC... 919 556-3475
100 K Flex Way Youngsville (27596) *(G-13477)*

K-M Machine Company Inc................................. 910 428-2368
275 Sedberry Rd Biscoe (27209) *(G-855)*

K-Tek Crlina Prcsion Spclty Mf, Pineville Also Called: Griffiths Corporation *(G-9732)*

K&B Galleries, Raleigh Also Called: Kitchen Bath Gllries N Hlls LL *(G-10237)*

K&H Acquisition Company LLC............................ 704 788-1128
36 Oak Dr Sw Concord (28027) *(G-3388)*

K&K Holdings Inc.. 704 341-5567
1310 S Church St Charlotte (28203) *(G-2385)*

K&M Sheet Metal LLC..................................... 919 544-8887
1310 E Cornwallis Rd Durham (27713) *(G-4091)*

K12 Computers... 336 754-6111
1203 Winston Rd Lexington (27295) *(G-7703)*

K2 Canine, Inc., Southern Pines Also Called: K2 Solutions Inc *(G-11501)*

K2 Scientific LLC.. 800 218-7613
3029 Horseshoe Ln Ste D Charlotte (28208) *(G-2386)*

K2 Solutions Inc.. 910 692-6898
5735 Us Hwy 1 N Southern Pines (28387) *(G-11501)*

K9 Installs Inc.. 743 207-1507
6255 Towncenter Dr Ste 875 Clemmons (27012) *(G-3195)*

Ka-Ex LLC... 704 343-5143
125 Remount Rd Ste C1 Pmb 2002 Charlotte (28203) *(G-2387)*

Kaba Access Control, Winston Salem Also Called: Kaba Ilco Corp *(G-13222)*

Kaba Ilco Corp (HQ)...................................... 252 446-3321
400 Jeffreys Rd Rocky Mount (27804) *(G-10844)*

Kaba Ilco Corp... 336 725-1331
2941 Indiana Ave Winston Salem (27105) *(G-13222)*

Kalajdzic Inc.. 855 465-4225
1415 River Ridge Dr Clemmons (27012) *(G-3196)*

Kaleida Systems Inc....................................... 704 814-4429
2530 Plantation Center Dr Ste A Matthews (28105) *(G-8120)*

Kaleido Inc.. 984 205-9436
16 W Martin St Fl 7 Raleigh (27601) *(G-10228)*

Kalinka Arms, Southport Also Called: Aboard Trade LLC *(G-11515)*

Kalo Foods, Stokesdale Also Called: Kalo Foods LLC *(G-11812)*

Kalo Foods LLC... 336 949-4802
119 Carlton Park Dr Stokesdale (27357) *(G-11812)*

KAM Tool & Die Inc....................................... 919 269-5099
530 N Industrial Dr Zebulon (27597) *(G-13512)*

Kamlar Corporation (PA).................................. 252 443-2576
444 Kamlar Rd Rocky Mount (27804) *(G-10845)*

Kamp Usa Inc... 336 668-1169
2321 E Martin Luther King Jr Dr High Point (27260) *(G-6682)*

Kannapolis Awards and Graphics......................... 704 224-3695
1103 Central Dr Kannapolis (28083) *(G-7213)*

Kansas City Sausage Co LLC.............................. 910 567-5604
1600 Martin Rd Godwin (28344) *(G-5189)*

Kanthal, Concord Also Called: Custom Electric Mfg LLC *(G-3350)*

Kanthal Thermal Process Inc............................. 704 784-3001
180 International Dr Nw Ste A Concord (28027) *(G-3389)*

KAO Specialties Americas LLC (HQ)...................... 336 884-2214
243 Woodbine St High Point (27260) *(G-6683)*

Kaotic Parts LLC.. 919 766-6040
4114 Pearl Rd Raleigh (27610) *(G-10229)*

Kapstone Kraft Paper, Roanoke Rapids Also Called: Westrock Paper and Packg LLC
(G-10745)

Kapstone Paper Packaging, Morrisville Also Called: Westrock Paper and Packg LLC *(G-9090)*

Karamedica Inc.. 919 302-1325
509 W North St Raleigh (27603) *(G-10230)*

Karastan.. 336 627-7200
335 Summit Rd Eden (27288) *(G-4349)*

Karl Ogden Enterprises Inc............................... 704 845-2785
1320 Industrial Dr Matthews (28105) *(G-8121)*

Karl RI Manufacturing..................................... 919 846-3801
11937 Appaloosa Run E Raleigh (27613) *(G-10231)*

Kart Precision Barrel Corp................................ 910 754-5212
3975 Garner St Sw Shallotte (28470) *(G-11303)*

Kashif Mazhar... 919 314-2891
68 Tw Alexander Dr Durham (27709) *(G-4092)*

Kask America Inc.. 704 960-4851
301 W Summit Ave Charlotte (28203) *(G-2388)*

Kat Designs Inc... 336 789-7288
280 Hickory St Mount Airy (27030) *(G-9138)*

Katchi Tees Incorporated................................. 252 315-4691
1108 Gold St N Wilson (27893) *(G-12997)*

Katesville Pallet Mill Inc................................. 919 496-3162
7119 Nc 56 Hwy Franklinton (27525) *(G-4849)*

Kathie S Mc Daniel....................................... 336 835-1544
765 Oakland Dr Elkin (28621) *(G-4446)*

Kattermann Ventures Inc.................................. 828 651-8737
282 Cane Creek Rd Fletcher (28732) *(G-4744)*

Kaufman Trailers Inc...................................... 336 790-6800
702 N Silver St Lexington (27292) *(G-7704)*

(G-0000) Company's Geographic Section entry number

Kavo Kerr Group.. 704 927-0617
  11727 Fruehauf Dr Charlotte (28273) *(G-2389)*

Kay & Sons Woodworks Inc............................... 919 556-1060
  2040 Forestville Rd Wake Forest (27587) *(G-12284)*

Kay Chemical Company...................................... 336 668-7290
  8300 Capital Dr Greensboro (27409) *(G-5642)*

Kaye Products Inc.. 919 732-6444
  535 Dimmocks Mill Rd Hillsborough (27278) *(G-6869)*

Kayla Jonise Bernhardt Crutch........................ 252 457-5367
  115 Carver St Elizabeth City (27909) *(G-4394)*

Kayne & Son Custom Hdwr Inc......................... 828 665-1988
  100 Daniel Ridge Rd Candler (28715) *(G-1228)*

Kayne & Son Hardware, Candler *Also Called: Kayne & Son Custom Hdwr Inc (G-1228)*

Kayser-Roth Corporation (DH)........................... 336 852-2030
  102 Corporate Center Blvd Greensboro (27408) *(G-5643)*

Kayser-Roth Hosiery Inc................................... 336 229-2269
  714 W Interstate Service Rd Graham (27253) *(G-5274)*

Kayser-Roth Hosiery Inc................................... 336 852-2030
  102 Corporate Center Blvd Greensboro (27408) *(G-5644)*

KB Socks Inc... 336 719-8000
  661 Linville Rd Mount Airy (27030) *(G-9139)*

Kbc of Nc LLC... 704 589-3711
  4114 Western Union School Rd Waxhaw (28173) *(G-12433)*

Kbi Biopharma Inc.. 919 479-9898
  2 Triangle Dr Durham (27709) *(G-4093)*

Kbi Biopharma Inc (DH)..................................... 919 479-9898
  1101 Hamlin Rd Durham (27704) *(G-4094)*

KBK Cstom Dsgns Essntial Oils........................ 252 886-3315
  1384 Northridge Dr Rocky Mount (27804) *(G-10846)*

Kbs Sales Co, Stanfield *Also Called: Eudys Cabinet Manufacturing (G-11605)*

Kc Stone Enterprise Inc.................................... 704 907-1361
  3006 Sardis Dr Indian Trail (28079) *(G-7085)*

Kch Engineered Systems, Forest City *Also Called: Kch Services Inc (G-4792)*

Kch Services Inc... 828 245-9836
  144 Industrial Dr Forest City (28043) *(G-4792)*

Kci, Charlotte *Also Called: Kincol Industries Incorporated (G-2397)*

Kci, Harrisburg *Also Called: Kci LLC (G-6111)*

Kci LLC.. 843 675-2626
  5924 Caldwell Park Dr Harrisburg (28075) *(G-6111)*

Kck Holding Corp.. 336 513-0002
  2215 Airpark Rd Burlington (27215) *(G-1114)*

Kcs Imprv & Cnstr Co Inc................................. 336 288-3865
  510 N Church St Ste C Greensboro (27401) *(G-5645)*

Kdh Defense Systems, Eden *Also Called: Kdh Defense Systems Inc (G-4350)*

Kdh Defense Systems Inc................................. 336 635-4158
  750a W Fieldcrest Rd Eden (27288) *(G-4350)*

Kds Fabricating and Mch Sp LLC....................... 828 632-5091
  4838 Nc Highway 90 E Hiddenite (28636) *(G-6501)*

Kdy Automation Solutions Inc........................... 888 219-0049
  150 Dominion Dr Ste E Morrisville (27560) *(G-8996)*

Keani Furniture Inc... 336 303-5484
  1546 N Fayetteville St Asheboro (27203) *(G-369)*

Kearfott Corporation... 828 350-5300
  2858 Us 70 Hwy Black Mountain (28711) *(G-868)*

Keck Logging Company...................................... 336 538-6903
  576 Browns Chapel Rd Gibsonville (27249) *(G-5179)*

Kee Auto Top Manufacturing Co........................ 704 332-8213
  3018 Stewart Creek Blvd Charlotte (28216) *(G-2390)*

Keebler, Sanford *Also Called: Keebler Company (G-11199)*

Keebler Company.. 919 774-6431
  5801 Mockingbird Ln Sanford (27332) *(G-11199)*

Keel Labs Inc.. 917 848-9066
  1015 Aviation Pkwy Ste 400 Morrisville (27560) *(G-8997)*

Keener Lumber Company Inc (PA)...................... 919 934-1087
  1209 W Market St Smithfield (27577) *(G-11450)*

Keener Wood Products Inc................................. 828 428-1562
  4274 Providence Mill Rd Maiden (28650) *(G-8015)*

Keglers Woodworks LLC.................................... 919 608-7220
  330 Dupont Cir Raleigh (27603) *(G-10232)*

Keiger Inc... 336 760-0099
  3735 Kimwell Dr Winston Salem (27103) *(G-13223)*

Keiger Printing Direct, Winston Salem *Also Called: Keiger Inc (G-13223)*

Keim Mineral Coatings Amer Inc........................ 704 588-4811
  3935 Perimeter West Dr Ste 100 Charlotte (28214) *(G-2391)*

Keith Call Logging LLC...................................... 336 262-3681
  Millers Creek (28651) *(G-8305)*

Keith Laws.. 336 973-7220
  1001 N Marley Ford Rd Wilkesboro (28697) *(G-12645)*

Keith Nations Log Company, Whittier *Also Called: James Keith Nations (G-12624)*

Kelhorn Corporation.. 828 837-5833
  199 Waldroup Rd Brasstown (28902) *(G-964)*

Kelishek Workshop, Brasstown *Also Called: Kelhorn Corporation (G-964)*

Kelken Enterprises LLC..................................... 910 890-7211
  12 Caco Dr Lillington (27546) *(G-7798)*

Kellanova... 704 370-1658
  13801 Reese Blvd W Huntersville (28078) *(G-7006)*

Keller Companies Inc.. 919 776-4641
  1600 Colon Rd Sanford (27330) *(G-11200)*

Keller Cosmetics Inc.. 704 399-2226
  2620 Stitt St Monroe (28110) *(G-8512)*

Keller Cres U To Be Phrmgraphi........................ 336 851-1150
  1072 Boulder Rd Greensboro (27409) *(G-5646)*

Keller Technology Corporation.......................... 704 875-1605
  11905 Vanstory Dr Huntersville (28078) *(G-7007)*

Kellex Corp... 828 874-0389
  501 Hoyle St Sw Valdese (28690) *(G-12196)*

Kelleys Sports and Awards Inc.......................... 828 728-4600
  2636 Hickory Blvd Hudson (28638) *(G-6952)*

Kellog, Huntersville *Also Called: Kellanova (G-7006)*

Kelly Hosiery Mill Inc.. 828 324-6456
  6450 Applehill Dr Hickory (28602) *(G-6376)*

Kem-Wove Inc (PA)... 704 588-0080
  10530 Westlake Dr Charlotte (28273) *(G-2392)*

Kemet Electronics Corporation.......................... 864 963-6300
  2501 W Dixon Blvd Shelby (28152) *(G-11351)*

Kemmler Products Inc....................................... 704 663-5678
  250 Canvasback Rd Mooresville (28117) *(G-8702)*

Ken Garner Mfg, Rural Hall *Also Called: Ken Garner Mfg - RHO Inc (G-10962)*

Ken Garner Mfg - RHO Inc................................. 336 969-0416
  8610 Chipboard Rd Rural Hall (27045) *(G-10962)*

Ken Horton Logging LLC.................................... 336 789-2849
  120 W Elm St Mount Airy (27030) *(G-9140)*

Ken Staley Co Inc.. 336 685-4294
  4675 Us Highway 64 E Bldg 16 Franklinville (27248) *(G-4857)*

Ken Wood Corp.. 252 792-6481
  1660 Arthur Corey Rd Williamston (27892) *(G-12671)*

Kencraft Manufacturing Inc............................... 252 291-0271
  4078 Us Highway 117 Wilson (27893) *(G-12998)*

Kendall Johnson Customs Inc............................ 336 748-3833
  3645 Indiana Ave Winston Salem (27105) *(G-13224)*

Kenly News, Kenly *Also Called: Richard D Stewart (G-7236)*

Kenmar Inc... 336 884-8722
  2531 Willard Dairy Rd High Point (27265) *(G-6684)*

Kenn M LLC... 678 755-6607
  6046 Inona Pl Raleigh (27606) *(G-10233)*

Kennametal Inc... 336 672-3313
  201 Yzex St Asheboro (27203) *(G-370)*

Kennametal Inc... 704 588-4777
  8910 Lenox Pointe Dr Ste F Charlotte (28273) *(G-2393)*

Kennametal Inc... 252 492-4163
  139 Warehouse Rd Henderson (27537) *(G-6163)*

Kennametal Inc... 252 536-5209
  100 Kennametal Dr Weldon (27890) *(G-12522)*

Kennelpro, Concord *Also Called: Sunbelt Enterprises Inc (G-3450)*

Kenneth Moore Signs... 910 458-6428
  6220 Riverwoods Dr Apt 103 Wilmington (28412) *(G-12826)*

Kenny Fowler Heating and A Inc (PA).................. 910 508-4553
  711 Wellington Ave Wilmington (28401) *(G-12827)*

Kenny Robinson S Wldg Svc Inc......................... 760 213-6454
  8975 Moody Rd Liberty (27298) *(G-7769)*

Kennys Components Inc..................................... 704 662-0777
  112 Loma Hill Dr Ste 101 Mooresville (28117) *(G-8703)*

Kenson Parenting Solutions...... 919 637-1499
1404 Wall Rd Ste 200 Wake Forest (27587) *(G-12285)*

Kenzie Layne Company...... 704 485-2282
506 Running Creek Church Rd Locust (28097) *(G-7894)*

Keowee Publishing Co Inc...... 828 877-4742
96 Merle Farm Ln Pisgah Forest (28768) *(G-9770)*

Kepley-Frank Hardwood Co Inc...... 336 746-5419
975 Conrad Hill Mine Rd Lexington (27292) *(G-7705)*

Keranetics LLC...... 336 725-0621
200 E 1st St Box 4 Winston Salem (27101) *(G-13225)*

Kerdea Technologies Inc...... 971 900-1113
1800 N Greene St Greenville (27834) *(G-5998)*

Kern-Liebers, Matthews *Also Called: Kern-Liebers USA Textile Inc (G-8122)*

Kern-Liebers USA Textile Inc...... 704 329-7153
921 Matthews Mint Hill Rd Ste C-D Matthews (28105) *(G-8122)*

Kernersville Adhesives Plant, Kernersville *Also Called: Caraustar Indus Cnsmr Pdts Gro (G-7249)*

Kernersville News, Kernersville *Also Called: Carter Publishing Company Inc (G-7253)*

Kernsville Tube Plant, Kernersville *Also Called: Caraustar Indus Cnsmr Pdts Gro (G-7250)*

Kerr's H R M Concrete, Hickory *Also Called: Kerrs Hickry Ready-Mixed Con (G-6377)*

Kerrs Hickry Ready-Mixed Con (PA)...... 828 322-3157
1126 1st Ave Sw Hickory (28602) *(G-6377)*

Keselowski Advanced Mfg LLC...... 704 799-0206
258 Aviation Dr Statesville (28677) *(G-11723)*

Kessebohmer USA Inc...... 910 338-5080
4301 Us Highway 421 N Wilmington (28401) *(G-12828)*

Kestrel I Acquisition Corporation...... 919 990-7500
1035 Swabia Ct Durham (27703) *(G-4095)*

Ketchie-Houston, Concord *Also Called: Ketchie-Houston Inc (G-3390)*

Ketchie-Houston Inc...... 704 786-5101
201 Winecoff School Rd Concord (28027) *(G-3390)*

Keter Us Inc...... 704 263-1967
2369 Charles Raper Jonas Hwy Stanley (28164) *(G-11620)*

Kewaunee Scientific Corp (PA)...... 704 873-7202
2700 W Front St Statesville (28677) *(G-11724)*

Key City Furniture Company Inc...... 336 818-1161
1804 River St Wilkesboro (28697) *(G-12646)*

Key Gas Components Inc (PA)...... 828 655-1700
160 Clay St Marion (28752) *(G-8048)*

Key Packing Company Inc...... 910 464-5054
596 Maness Rd Robbins (27325) *(G-10753)*

Key Printing Inc...... 252 459-4783
1036 E Washington St Nashville (27856) *(G-9321)*

Keya USA, High Point *Also Called: Kamp Usa Inc (G-6682)*

Keymac USA LLC...... 704 877-5137
8301 Arrowridge Blvd Ste I Charlotte (28273) *(G-2394)*

Keyper Systems, Harrisburg *Also Called: Marcon International Inc (G-6113)*

Keypoint LLC...... 704 962-8110
8002 New Town Rd Waxhaw (28173) *(G-12434)*

Keypoint Fabrication, Waxhaw *Also Called: Keypoint LLC (G-12434)*

Keystone Foods LLC...... 336 342-6601
227 Equity Dr Reidsville (27320) *(G-10691)*

Keystone Powdered Metal Co...... 704 435-4036
100 Commerce Dr Cherryville (28021) *(G-3065)*

Keystone Powdered Metal Co...... 704 730-8805
779 Sunnyside Shady Rest Rd Kings Mountain (28086) *(G-7367)*

Kfh, Lexington *Also Called: Kepley-Frank Hardwood Co Inc (G-7705)*

Kgi Trading NC, Charlotte *Also Called: Moon N Sea Nc LLC (G-2518)*

Kgt Enterprises Inc...... 704 662-3272
185 Mckenzie Rd Mooresville (28115) *(G-8704)*

Ki Agency LLC...... 919 977-7075
5812 Triangle Dr Raleigh (27617) *(G-10234)*

Kidde Safety, Mebane *Also Called: Walter Kidde Portable Eqp Inc (G-8263)*

Kidde Technologies Inc...... 252 237-7004
4200 Airport Dr Nw Wilson (27896) *(G-12999)*

Kidde Technologies Inc (HQ)...... 252 237-7004
4200 Airport Dr Nw Wilson (27896) *(G-13000)*

Kidde Technologies Inc...... 252 237-7004
4200 Airport Dr Nw Wilson (27896) *(G-13001)*

Kidkusion Inc...... 252 946-7162
623 River Rd Washington (27889) *(G-12396)*

Kids Playhouse LLC...... 704 299-4449
10823 John Price Rd Charlotte (28273) *(G-2395)*

Kidsvidz Productions...... 704 663-4487
694 Big Indian Loop Mooresville (28117) *(G-8705)*

Kieffer Starlite Company...... 800 659-2493
609 Junction St Mount Airy (27030) *(G-9141)*

Kiln Drying Systems Cmpnnts In...... 828 891-8115
234 Industrial Dr Etowah (28729) *(G-4496)*

Kiln-Directcom...... 910 259-9794
200a Progress Dr Burgaw (28425) *(G-1026)*

Kilwins Chocolate & Ice Cream, Blowing Rock *Also Called: Bilcat Inc (G-880)*

Kimballs Screen Print Inc...... 704 636-0488
1315 Union Church Rd Salisbury (28146) *(G-11079)*

Kimbees Inc...... 336 323-8773
317 Martin Luthe Greensboro (27406) *(G-5647)*

Kimberly Gordon Studios Inc...... 980 287-6420
525 N Tryon St Charlotte (28202) *(G-2396)*

Kimberly-Clark Corporation...... 828 698-5230
32 Smyth Ave Hendersonville (28792) *(G-6218)*

Kincaid Furniture Company Inc (HQ)...... 828 728-3261
240 Pleasant Hill Rd Hudson (28638) *(G-6953)*

Kincol Industries Incorporated...... 704 372-8435
1721 Toal St Charlotte (28206) *(G-2397)*

Kindermusik, Greensboro *Also Called: Kindermusik International Inc (G-5648)*

Kindermusik International Inc...... 800 628-5687
237 Burgess Rd Ste C Greensboro (27409) *(G-5648)*

Kindled Provisions LLC...... 919 542-0792
840 Moncure Pittsboro Rd Moncure (27559) *(G-8407)*

Kindred Rolling Doors LLC...... 704 905-3806
3420 Country Club Dr Gastonia (28056) *(G-5073)*

Kinetic Systems Inc...... 919 322-7200
4900 Prospectus Dr Ste 500 Durham (27713) *(G-4096)*

King Aerospace and Tech, New Bern *Also Called: Accuking Inc (G-9330)*

King Bio Inc...... 828 398-6058
150 Westside Dr Asheville (28806) *(G-529)*

King Bio Inc (PA)...... 828 255-0201
3 Westside Dr Asheville (28806) *(G-530)*

King Business Service Inc...... 910 610-1030
1680 S Main St Laurinburg (28352) *(G-7504)*

King Charles Industries LLC...... 704 848-4121
766 Haileys Ferry Rd Lilesville (28091) *(G-7787)*

King Features Syndicate, Charlotte *Also Called: Hearst Corporation (G-2269)*

King Hickory Furniture Company...... 828 324-0472
728 Highland Ave Ne Hickory (28601) *(G-6378)*

King Hickory Furniture Company (PA)...... 828 322-6025
1820 Main Ave Se Hickory (28602) *(G-6379)*

King Hickory Furniture Company...... 336 841-6140
2016 W Green Dr High Point (27260) *(G-6685)*

King International Corporation...... 336 983-5171
275 S Main St King (27021) *(G-7329)*

King Pharmaceutical R & D, Cary *Also Called: King Phrmceuticals RES Dev LLC (G-1383)*

King Phrmceuticals RES Dev LLC...... 919 653-7001
4000 Centre Green Way Ste 300 Cary (27513) *(G-1383)*

King Signs, Fayetteville *Also Called: Mass Connection Inc (G-4636)*

King Splash, Kings Mountain *Also Called: Specialty Textiles Inc (G-7387)*

King Stone Innovation LLC...... 704 352-1134
7313 Mossborough Ct Charlotte (28227) *(G-2398)*

King Textiles LLC...... 336 861-3257
400 Interstate Dr Archdale (27263) *(G-236)*

King Tutt Graphics LLC...... 877 546-4888
1113 Transport Dr Raleigh (27603) *(G-10235)*

Kingdom Woodworks Inc...... 704 678-8134
405 Margrace Rd Kings Mountain (28086) *(G-7368)*

Kings Chandelier Company...... 336 623-6188
1023 Friendly Rd Eden (27288) *(G-4351)*

Kings Mountain Intl Inc...... 704 739-4227
1755 S Battleground Ave Kings Mountain (28086) *(G-7369)*

Kings Plush Inc...... 704 739-9931
515 Marie St Kings Mountain (28086) *(G-7370)*

Kings Prtble Wldg Fbrction LLC...... 336 789-2372
832 W Lebanon St Mount Airy (27030) *(G-9142)*

Kingsdown Incorporated (HQ)..................................919 563-3531
110 S Fourth St Mebane (27302) *(G-8247)*

Kingsdown Acquisition Corp.....................................919 563-3531
126 W Holt St Mebane (27302) *(G-8248)*

Kinneys Stamp & Engraving, Charlotte Also Called: H F Kinney Co Inc *(G-2248)*

Kinston Free Press Company....................................252 527-3191
2103 N Queen St Kinston (28501) *(G-7417)*

Kinston Neuse Corporation.......................................252 522-3088
2000 Dobbs Farm Rd Kinston (28504) *(G-7418)*

Kinston Office Supply Co Inc (PA)..............................252 523-7654
704 Plaza Blvd Ste B Kinston (28501) *(G-7419)*

Kinston Plant, Grifton Also Called: Covation Biomaterials LLC *(G-6034)*

Kirk & Blum Manufacturing Co....................................801 728-6533
8735 W Market St Greensboro (27409) *(G-5649)*

Kisner Corporation..919 510-8410
6016 Triangle Dr Raleigh (27617) *(G-10236)*

Kitchen Art, Greensboro Also Called: Marsh Furniture Company *(G-5676)*

Kitchen Bath Gllries N Hlls LL....................................919 600-6200
4209 Lassiter Mill Rd Ste 130 Raleigh (27609) *(G-10237)*

Kitchen Cabinet Designers LLC...................................919 833-6532
431 Milburnie Lake Dr Raleigh (27610) *(G-10238)*

Kitchen Cabinet Distributors, Raleigh Also Called: Kitchen Cabinet Designers LLC *(G-10238)*

Kitchen Distributors of South, Matthews Also Called: Mid Carolina Cabinets Inc *(G-8134)*

Kitchen Man Inc...910 408-1322
6361 Ocean Hwy E Ste 1 Winnabow (28479) *(G-13067)*

Kitchen Masters Charlotte LLC...................................704 375-3320
504 Sarazen Way Salisbury (28144) *(G-11080)*

Kitchen Tune-Up...833 259-1838
10810 Independence Pointe Pkwy Ste H Matthews (28105) *(G-8123)*

Kitchens Unlimited Asheville, Asheville Also Called: Sjr Incorporated *(G-601)*

Kitchens.com, Cornelius Also Called: White Picket Media Inc *(G-3630)*

Kitty Hawk Kites Inc..252 441-4124
3933 S Croatan Hwy Nags Head (27959) *(G-9300)*

Kjc, Winston Salem Also Called: Kendall Johnson Customs Inc *(G-13224)*

Kkb Biltmore Inc...828 274-6711
479 Hendersonville Rd Asheville (28803) *(G-531)*

Klazzy Magazine Inc..704 293-8321
100 N Tryon St Ste B220-127 Charlotte (28202) *(G-2399)*

Klazzy.com The Magazine, Charlotte Also Called: Klazzy Magazine Inc *(G-2399)*

KLb Enterprises Incorporated....................................336 605-0773
209 Citation Ct Greensboro (27409) *(G-5650)*

Klearoptics Inc...760 224-6770
150 N Reasearch Campus Dr Ste 3505 Lattimore (28089) *(G-7480)*

Kleiberit Adhesives USA Inc......................................704 843-3339
109b Howie Mine Rd Waxhaw (28173) *(G-12435)*

Kliersolutions...919 806-1287
4041 Brook Cross Dr Apex (27539) *(G-174)*

Klingspor, Hickory Also Called: Klingspor Abrasives Inc *(G-6380)*

Klingspor Abrasives Inc (HQ).....................................828 322-3030
2555 Tate Blvd Se Hickory (28602) *(G-6380)*

Kloud Hemp Co...336 740-2528
2701 S Elm Eugene St Ste E Greensboro (27406) *(G-5651)*

Kme Consolidated Inc...704 847-9888
529 Crestdale Rd Matthews (28105) *(G-8124)*

Kn Furniture Inc..336 953-3259
244 Nc Highway 22 N Ramseur (27316) *(G-10626)*

Kna..704 847-4280
9535 Monroe Rd Ste 150 Charlotte (28270) *(G-2400)*

Knapheide Trck Eqp Co Midsouth................................910 484-0558
3572 Fieldstone Trce Midland (28107) *(G-8289)*

Knapheide Truck Equipment Ctrs, Midland Also Called: Knapheide Trck Eqp Co Midsouth *(G-8289)*

Knight Communications Inc.......................................704 568-7804
6301 Creft Cir Indian Trail (28079) *(G-7086)*

Knight Safety Coatings Co Inc...................................910 458-3145
201 Beval Rd Wilmington (28401) *(G-12829)*

Knit-Wear Fabrics Inc..336 226-4342
145 N Cobb Ave Burlington (27217) *(G-1115)*

Knitwear America Inc...704 396-1193
5740 Rocky Mount Rd Granite Falls (28630) *(G-5310)*

Knorr Brake Truck Systems Co...................................888 836-6922
115 Summit Park Dr Salisbury (28146) *(G-11081)*

Knowledge Management Assoc LLC..............................781 250-2001
8529 Six Forks Rd Ste 400 Raleigh (27615) *(G-10239)*

Kodak...919 559-7232
1100 Perimeter Park Dr Ste 108 Morrisville (27560) *(G-8998)*

Kohnle Cabinetry..828 640-2498
250 Rocky Acres Rd Hickory (28601) *(G-6381)*

Koi Pond Brewing Company LLC..................................252 231-1660
1107 Falls Rd Rocky Mount (27804) *(G-10847)*

Kol Incorporated..919 872-2340
5700 Buffaloe Rd Raleigh (27616) *(G-10240)*

Kolb Boyette & Assoc Inc...919 544-7839
514 United Dr Ste A Durham (27713) *(G-4097)*

Kolcraft Enterprises Inc..910 944-9345
10832 Nc 211 Hwy Aberdeen (28315) *(G-10)*

Konami Digital Entrmt Inc..310 220-8100
1953 Tw Alexander Dr Durham (27703) *(G-4098)*

Konica Mnlta Hlthcare Amrcas I..................................919 792-6420
2217 Us 70 Hwy E Garner (27529) *(G-4935)*

Kontane Logistics Inc (PA)..828 397-5501
3876 Martin Fish Pond St Hickory (28603) *(G-6382)*

Kontek Industries Inc...704 273-5040
805 Mccombs Ave Kannapolis (28083) *(G-7214)*

Kontoor, Greensboro Also Called: Kontoor Brands Inc *(G-5653)*

Kontoor Brands Inc...336 332-3586
400 N Elm St Greensboro (27401) *(G-5652)*

Kontoor Brands Inc (PA)...336 332-3400
400 N Elm St Greensboro (27401) *(G-5653)*

Kontoor Brands Inc...336 332-3577
1421 S Elm Eugene St Greensboro (27406) *(G-5654)*

Kooks Custom Headers...704 838-1110
2333 Salisbury Hwy Statesville (28677) *(G-11725)*

Kooks Custom Headers Inc..704 768-2288
141 Advantage Pl Statesville (28677) *(G-11726)*

Korber Medipak Systems N Amer, Morrisville Also Called: Korber Pharma Inc *(G-8999)*

Korber Pharma Inc (DH)..727 538-4644
2243 Energy Dr Apex (27502) *(G-175)*

Korber Pharma Inc..727 538-4644
8000 Regency Pkwy Ste 403 Cary (27518) *(G-1384)*

Korber Pharma Inc..727 538-4644
1001 Aviation Pkwy Ste 200 Morrisville (27560) *(G-8999)*

Kordsa Inc..910 462-2051
17780 Armstrong Rd Laurel Hill (28351) *(G-7485)*

Kosa, Wilmington Also Called: Stepan Company *(G-12930)*

Kotek Holdings Inc..919 643-1100
511 Valley Forge Rd Hillsborough (27278) *(G-6870)*

Kotohira...336 667-0150
1206 River St Wilkesboro (28697) *(G-12647)*

Kowa Research Institute Inc.....................................919 433-1600
430 Davis Dr Ste 200 Morrisville (27560) *(G-9000)*

Kr Publications...910 852-1525
4100 Nelson Way Lumberton (28360) *(G-7960)*

Kraft Foods, Charlotte Also Called: Kraft Heinz Foods Company *(G-2401)*

Kraft Heinz Foods Company.......................................704 565-5500
2815 Coliseum Centre Dr Ste 100 Charlotte (28217) *(G-2401)*

Kraftsman Inc..336 824-1114
10051 Us Highway 64 E Ramseur (27316) *(G-10627)*

Kraftsman Tactical Inc..336 465-3576
1650 Woodhurst Ln Albemarle (28001) *(G-79)*

Kraken-Skulls...910 500-9100
822 Shannon Dr Fayetteville (28303) *(G-4627)*

Kral USA Inc...704 814-6164
901a Matthews Mint Hill Rd Matthews (28105) *(G-8125)*

Kranken Signs Vehicle Wraps....................................704 339-0059
310 N Polk St Pineville (28134) *(G-9738)*

Kratos Antenna Solutions Corp...................................919 934-9711
1315 Industrial Park Dr Smithfield (27577) *(G-11451)*

Kraze Custom Prints, Monroe Also Called: Faizon Global Inc *(G-8487)*

Kreber...336 861-2700
221 Swathmore Ave High Point (27263) *(G-6686)*

A
L
P
H
A
B
E
T
I
C

Kreber Enterprises, High Point Also Called: Kreber (G-6686)

Krebs Corporation.. 336 548-3250
703 W Decatur St Madison (27025) (G-7989)

Krenitsky Pharmaceuticals Inc................................ 919 493-4631
2516 Homestead Rd Chapel Hill (27516) (G-1551)

Krieger Cabinets Dewayne.. 704 630-0609
415 Sailboat Dr Salisbury (28146) (G-11082)

Krigen Pharmaceuticals LLC.................................... 919 523-7530
800 Edwards Dr Lillington (27546) (G-7799)

Krispy Kreme, Gastonia Also Called: Krispy Kreme Doughnut Corp (G-5074)

Krispy Kreme, Greensboro Also Called: Krispy Kreme Doughnut Corp (G-5655)

Krispy Kreme, Winston Salem Also Called: Krispy Kreme Doughnut Corp (G-13226)

Krispy Kreme, Winston Salem Also Called: Krispy Kreme Doughnuts Inc (G-13228)

Krispy Kreme Doughnut Corp (DH).......................... 980 270-7117
2116 Hawkins St Ste 102 Charlotte (28203) (G-2402)

Krispy Kreme Doughnut Corp................................... 919 669-6151
2990 E Franklin Sq Gastonia (28052) (G-5074)

Krispy Kreme Doughnut Corp................................... 336 854-8275
3704 W Gate City Blvd Greensboro (27407) (G-5655)

Krispy Kreme Doughnut Corp................................... 336 733-3780
259 S Stratford Rd Winston Salem (27103) (G-13226)

Krispy Kreme Doughnut Corp................................... 336 726-8908
3190 Centre Park Blvd Winston Salem (27107) (G-13227)

Krispy Kreme Doughnuts Inc (HQ)........................... 336 725-2981
370 Knollwood St Winston Salem (27103) (G-13228)

Krodsa USA Inc... 910 462-2041
17780 Armstrong Rd Laurel Hill (28351) (G-7486)

Kronos Carolinas, Greensboro Also Called: Ukg Kronos Systems LLC (G-5885)

Kroops Brands LLC.. 704 635-7963
2913 Chamber Dr Monroe (28110) (G-8513)

Kroy Building Products, Cary Also Called: Mastic Home Exteriors Inc (G-1399)

Krs Plastics Inc.. 910 653-3602
26 Tabor Industrial Park Rd Tabor City (28463) (G-11912)

Krueger International Inc... 336 434-5011
217 Feld Ave High Point (27263) (G-6687)

Krw Packaging Machinery Inc.................................... 828 658-0912
81 Monticello Rd Weaverville (28787) (G-12494)

KS Custom Woodworks Inc.. 252 714-3957
3205 Fire Tower Rd Walstonburg (27888) (G-12333)

KS Precious Metals LLC... 910 687-0244
Pinehurst (28374) (G-9694)

KSA, High Point Also Called: KAO Specialties Americas LLC (G-6683)

Ksep Systems LLC.. 919 339-1850
598 Airport Blvd Ste 600 Morrisville (27560) (G-9001)

Ksm, Shelby Also Called: Ksm Castings USA Inc (G-11352)

Ksm Castings USA Inc (DH)...................................... 704 751-0559
120 Blue Brook Dr Shelby (28150) (G-11352)

Kuebler Inc... 704 705-4711
10430 Harris Oak Blvd Ste J Charlotte (28269) (G-2403)

Kuenz America Inc.. 984 255-1018
9321 Focal Pt Ste 8 Raleigh (27617) (G-10241)

Kuntrys Soul-Food & Bbq LLC................................... 910 797-0766
418 Minnow Ct Fayetteville (28312) (G-4628)

Kurz Transfer Products LP (HQ)................................ 704 927-3700
11836 Patterson Rd Huntersville (28078) (G-7008)

Kurz Transfer Products LP.. 336 764-4128
4939 N Nc Highway 150 Lexington (27295) (G-7706)

Kustom Kraft Wdwrks Mt Airy In............................... 336 786-2831
3096 Westfield Rd Mount Airy (27030) (G-9143)

Kwik Elc Mtr Sls & Svc Inc (PA)................................ 252 335-2524
511 Witherspoon St Elizabeth City (27909) (G-4395)

Kwik Kopy Printing, Asheville Also Called: Pope Printing & Design Inc (G-580)

Kyma Technologies Inc.. 919 789-8880
8829 Midway West Rd Raleigh (27617) (G-10242)

Kymera International LLC (PA)................................... 919 544-8090
2601 Weck Dr Durham (27709) (G-4099)

Kyocera Precision Tools Inc (DH).............................. 800 823-7284
1 Quality Way Fletcher (28732) (G-4745)

L & B Jandrew Enterprises.. 828 687-8927
1927 Spartanburg Hwy Hendersonville (28792) (G-6219)

L & K Machining Inc.. 336 222-9444
1312 Whitsett St Burlington (27215) (G-1116)

L & R Installations Inc.. 336 547-8998
2303 Adams Farm Pkwy Greensboro (27407) (G-5656)

L & R Knitting Inc... 828 874-2960
6350 Claude Brittain Rd Hickory (28602) (G-6383)

L & R Specialties Inc.. 704 853-3296
2757 W Franklin Blvd Gastonia (28052) (G-5075)

L & S Automotive Inc.. 704 391-7657
1214 Caldwell Williams Rd Charlotte (28216) (G-2404)

L & S Custom Trailer Service, Charlotte Also Called: L & S Automotive Inc (G-2404)

L and L Machine Co Inc... 704 864-5521
158 Superior Stainless Rd Gastonia (28052) (G-5076)

L B Plastics LLC.. 704 663-1543
482 E Plaza Dr Mooresville (28115) (G-8706)

L C B of Mount Airy, Mount Airy Also Called: Travis L Bunker (G-9187)

L C Industries Inc (PA).. 919 596-8277
4500 Emperor Blvd Durham (27703) (G-4100)

L C Industries Inc.. 919 596-8277
4525 Campground Rd Fayetteville (28314) (G-4629)

L D Davis, Monroe Also Called: LD Davis Industries Inc (G-8514)

L F Delp Lumber Co Inc... 336 359-8202
2601 Nc Highway 113 Laurel Springs (28644) (G-7489)

L F I Services Inc.. 215 343-0411
1136 Broadway Rd Sanford (27332) (G-11201)

L F T Inc.. 828 253-6830
123 Lyman St Asheville (28801) (G-532)

L G M, Maiden Also Called: C O Jelliff Corporation (G-8008)

L G Sourcing Inc (HQ)... 704 758-1000
1000 Lowes Blvd Mooresville (28117) (G-8707)

L L C Batteries of N C.. 919 331-0241
101 Medical Dr Angier (27501) (G-123)

L P, North Wilkesboro Also Called: Louisiana-Pacific Corporation (G-9543)

L Rancho Investments Inc.. 336 431-1004
5740 Hopewell Church Rd Trinity (27370) (G-12117)

L T Welding, Gibsonville Also Called: Larry D Troxler (G-5180)

L TS Gas and Snaks.. 910 762-7130
2461 Carolina Beach Rd Wilmington (28401) (G-12830)

L'Eggs - Hanes - Bali, Mount Airy Also Called: Hanesbrands Inc (G-9126)

L&P Dstribution Ctr Furn 8814, Conover Also Called: Leggett & Platt Incorporated (G-3538)

L3harris Technologies Inc.. 704 588-7126
8406 Mcalpine Dr Charlotte (28217) (G-2405)

La Barge Inc... 336 812-2400
1925 Eastchester Dr High Point (27265) (G-6688)

La Estrella Inc... 919 639-6559
61 W Williams St Angier (27501) (G-124)

La Farm Inc.. 919 657-0657
220 W Chatham St Cary (27511) (G-1385)

La Farm Bakery, Cary Also Called: La Farm Inc (G-1385)

La Noticia Inc... 704 568-6966
5936 Monroe Rd Charlotte (28212) (G-2406)

La Noticia Foundation, Charlotte Also Called: La Noticia Inc (G-2406)

La Tortilleria, Winston Salem Also Called: La Tortilleria LLC (G-13229)

La Tortilleria LLC.. 336 773-0010
2900 Lowery St Winston Salem (27101) (G-13229)

Lab Designs LLC (PA).. 336 429-4114
391 Hickory St Mount Airy (27030) (G-9144)

Lab Dsgns Archtctural Laminate, Mount Airy Also Called: Lab Designs LLC (G-9144)

Label & Printing Solutions Inc.................................. 919 782-1242
201 Buncombe St Raleigh (27609) (G-10243)

Label Line Ltd.. 336 857-3115
5356 Nc Highway 49 S Asheboro (27205) (G-371)

Label Printing Systems Inc....................................... 336 760-3271
3937 Westpoint Blvd Winston Salem (27103) (G-13230)

Label Store, The, Charlotte Also Called: Rapid Response Inc (G-2689)

Labels Tags & Inserts Inc.. 336 227-8485
2302 Airpark Rd Burlington (27215) (G-1117)

Laborie Sons Cstm Wodworks LLC........................... 910 769-2524
301 Chesterfield Rd Castle Hayne (28429) (G-1504)

Laceys Tree Service.. 910 330-2868
221 Jenkins Rd Jacksonville (28540) (G-7129)

Lacquer Craft Hospitality Inc (DH)................................336 822-8086
2575 Penny Rd High Point (27265) *(G-6689)*

Lacy J Miller Machine..336 764-0518
7987 Old Us Highway 52 Lexington (27295) *(G-7707)*

Lady May Swets Confections Inc...........................704 749-9258
14301 S Lakes Dr Ste C Charlotte (28273) *(G-2407)*

Lafauci...919 244-5912
5001 Sunset Forest Cir Holly Springs (27540) *(G-6905)*

Laird Thermal Systems Inc....................................919 597-7300
629 Davis Dr Ste 200 Morrisville (27560) *(G-9002)*

Lake City Electric Motor Repr................................336 248-2377
915 S Talbert Blvd Lexington (27292) *(G-7708)*

Lake Creek Logging & Trckg Inc............................910 532-2041
3744 Nc Highway 210 E Harrells (28444) *(G-6101)*

Lake Gaston Gazette, Littleton Also Called: Womack Publishing Co Inc *(G-7888)*

Lake Norman EMB & Monogramming.....................704 892-8450
21228 Catawba Ave Cornelius (28031) *(G-3612)*

Lake Norman Times, Mooresville Also Called: Womack Publishing Company Inc *(G-8800)*

Lake Printing & Design, Charlotte Also Called: Goffstar Inc *(G-2222)*

Lake Shore Radiator Inc...336 271-2626
211c Creek Ridge Rd Greensboro (27406) *(G-5657)*

Lakebrook Corporation...207 947-4051
3506 E Yacht Dr Oak Island (28465) *(G-9566)*

Lakeside Cstm Tees & Embroider...........................704 274-3730
9216 Westmoreland Rd Ste B Cornelius (28031) *(G-3613)*

Lakeside Mills Inc (PA)...828 286-4866
398 W Main St Spindale (28160) *(G-11547)*

Lam Factory, The, Canton Also Called: Coast Lamp Manufacturing Inc *(G-1249)*

Lambda Technologies Inc..919 462-1919
2200 Gateway Centre Blvd Morrisville (27560) *(G-9003)*

Lambeth Dimension Inc...336 629-3838
443 Mount Shepherd Road Ext Asheboro (27205) *(G-372)*

Lamco Machine Tool Inc..252 247-4360
135 Industrial Dr Morehead City (28557) *(G-8838)*

Lamination Services Inc..336 643-7369
6919 Us Highway 158 Stokesdale (27357) *(G-11813)*

Lammers Glass & Design, Powells Point Also Called: James Lammers *(G-9822)*

Lampe & Malphrus Lumber Co................................919 934-6152
37 E Peedin Rd Smithfield (27577) *(G-11452)*

Lampe & Malphrus Lumber Co (PA)........................919 934-6152
37 E Peedin Rd Smithfield (27577) *(G-11453)*

Lampe & Malphrus Lumber Co................................919 934-1124
210 N 10th St Smithfield (27577) *(G-11454)*

Lanart International Inc...704 875-1972
10325 Hambright Rd Huntersville (28078) *(G-7009)*

Lancer Incorporated...910 428-2181
135 S Lancer Rd Star (27356) *(G-11630)*

Land and Loft LLC...315 560-7060
701 Georgetown Rd Raleigh (27608) *(G-10244)*

Lander Tubular Pdts USA Inc..................................828 369-6682
66 Van Raalte St Franklin (28734) *(G-4833)*

Landfill Gas Producers...704 844-8990
10600 Nations Ford Rd # 150 Charlotte (28273) *(G-2408)*

Landmark Coatings, Mocksville Also Called: Landmark Coatings LLC *(G-8373)*

Landmark Coatings LLC...336 492-2492
933 Danner Rd Mocksville (27028) *(G-8373)*

Landmark Printing Inc...919 833-5151
901 W Hodges St Raleigh (27608) *(G-10245)*

Landmark Printing Co Inc..919 833-5151
901 W Hodges St Raleigh (27608) *(G-10246)*

Landscape Design & Lawn Maint, Charlotte Also Called: Carolina Lawnscape Inc *(G-1849)*

Landsdown Mining Corporation...............................704 753-5400
3949 Blue Banks Loop Rd Ne Leland (28451) *(G-7549)*

Lane Construction Corporation...............................919 876-4550
3010 Gresham Lake Rd Raleigh (27615) *(G-10247)*

Lane Land & Timber Inc...252 443-1151
5631 Hart Farm Rd Battleboro (27809) *(G-700)*

Langley Indus McHning Fbrction, Sharpsburg Also Called: Scoggins Industrial Inc *(G-11307)*

Laniers Screen Printing...336 857-2699
6271 Bombay School Rd Denton (27239) *(G-3753)*

Lantal Textiles Inc (HQ)..336 969-9551
1300 Langenthal Dr Rural Hall (27045) *(G-10963)*

Lantern of Hendersonville LLC...............................828 513-5033
755 N Main St Hendersonville (28792) *(G-6220)*

Lanxess Corporation...704 923-0121
1225 Gastonia Technology Pkwy Dallas (28034) *(G-3678)*

Lanxess Corporation...704 868-7200
214 W Ruby Ave Gastonia (28054) *(G-5077)*

Large & Small Graphics, Wallace Also Called: Lsg LLC *(G-12322)*

Larger Than Life Inflatables, Oriental Also Called: Russo Mike DBA Lrger Than Lf I *(G-9602)*

Larlin Cushion Company..828 465-5599
1950 Fairgrove Church Rd Hickory (28602) *(G-6384)*

Larry Bissette Inc...919 773-2140
8012 Dirt Rd Apex (27539) *(G-176)*

Larry D Troxler...336 585-1141
6170 Nc Highway 87 N Gibsonville (27249) *(G-5180)*

Larry S Cabinet Shop Inc..252 442-4330
4217 S Church St Rocky Mount (27803) *(G-10848)*

Larry S Sausage Company.......................................910 483-5148
1624 Middle River Loop Fayetteville (28312) *(G-4630)*

Larry Shackelford...919 467-8817
309 Dunhagan Pl Cary (27511) *(G-1386)*

Larrys Beans Inc...919 828-1234
1507 Gavin St Raleigh (27608) *(G-10248)*

Laru Industries Inc...704 821-7503
115 Business Park Dr Indian Trail (28079) *(G-7087)*

Laser Dynamics Inc...704 658-9769
104 Performance Rd Mooresville (28115) *(G-8708)*

Laser Image Printing & Mktg, Durham Also Called: Laser Ink Corporation *(G-4101)*

Laser Ink Corporation...919 361-5822
4018 Patriot Dr Ste 200 Durham (27703) *(G-4101)*

Laser Precision Cutting Inc.....................................828 658-0644
181 Reems Creek Rd Ste 3 Weaverville (28787) *(G-12495)*

Laser Recharge Carolina Inc...................................919 467-5902
2474 Walnut St Cary (27518) *(G-1387)*

Lash Out Inc...919 342-0221
117 Georgetowne Dr Clayton (27520) *(G-3156)*

Late Model Digest, Murphy Also Called: McLoud Media *(G-9292)*

Latham Inc..336 857-3702
6509 Scarlet Oak Dr Denton (27239) *(G-3754)*

Latham-Hall Corporation...336 475-9723
5003 Ball Park Rd Thomasville (27360) *(G-12042)*

Laticrete International Inc.......................................910 582-2252
299 Industry Dr Hamlet (28345) *(G-6059)*

Latino Communications Inc.....................................704 319-5044
7508 E Independence Blvd Ste 109 Charlotte (28227) *(G-2409)*

Latino Communications Inc.....................................919 645-1680
150 Fayetteville St Ste 110 Raleigh (27601) *(G-10249)*

Latino Communications Inc (PA).............................336 714-2823
3067 Waughtown St Winston Salem (27107) *(G-13231)*

Launchmagiccom Inc...845 234-4440
500 Westover Dr Pmb 13081 Sanford (27330) *(G-11202)*

Laundry Svc Tech Ltd Lblty Co................................908 327-1997
2217 Matthews Township Pkwy Ste D Matthews (28105) *(G-8126)*

Laura Gaskin...828 628-5891
922 Garren Creek Rd Fairview (28730) *(G-4509)*

Laurel Gray Vineyards Inc.......................................336 468-9463
5726 W Old Us 421 Hwy Hamptonville (27020) *(G-6086)*

Laurel Hill Paper Co...910 997-4526
126 1st St Cordova (28330) *(G-3581)*

Laurel of Asheville LLC...828 670-7503
110 Executive Park Asheville (28801) *(G-533)*

Laurel of Asheville, The, Asheville Also Called: Laurel of Asheville LLC *(G-533)*

Laurinburg Exchange, Laurinburg Also Called: Champion Media LLC *(G-7496)*

Laurinburg Feed Mill, Laurinburg Also Called: Murphy-Brown LLC *(G-7510)*

Laurinburg Machine Company..................................910 276-0360
715 Park Cir Laurinburg (28352) *(G-7505)*

Lava Cable, Fayetteville Also Called: Mark Stoddard *(G-4634)*

Lawing Marble Co Inc..704 732-0360
2523 E Highway 150 Lincolnton (28092) *(G-7835)*

Lawrence Williams...910 462-2332
10200 Andrew Jackson Hwy Laurel Hill (28351) *(G-7487)*

Layer27...919 909-9088
205 Blue Heron Dr Youngsville (27596) *(G-13478)*

Layton Optics, Greensboro *Also Called: Optics Inc (G-5726)*

Laytons Custom Boatworks LLC.. 252 482-1504
103 Anchors Way Dr Edenton (27932) *(G-4368)*

Lazar Industries LLC (PA).. 919 742-9303
3025 Hamp Stone Rd Siler City (27344) *(G-11415)*

Lazar Industries East Inc.. 919 742-9303
3025 Hamp Stone Rd Siler City (27344) *(G-11416)*

Lazeredge LLC.. 336 480-7934
244 Brunswick Ln Mount Airy (27030) *(G-9145)*

Lba Group Inc (PA).. 252 329-9243
3400 Tupper Dr Greenville (27834) *(G-5999)*

Lba Technology Inc.. 252 757-0279
3400 Tupper Dr Greenville (27834) *(G-6000)*

Lbm Industries Inc.. 828 966-4270
17668 Rosman Hwy Sapphire (28774) *(G-11258)*

Lbm Industries Inc (PA).. 828 966-4270
2000 Whitewater Rd Sapphire (28774) *(G-11259)*

Lbm Industries Inc.. 828 631-1227
21 E Hall Hts Sylva (28779) *(G-11895)*

Lc America Inc.. 336 676-5129
8221 Tyner Rd Colfax (27235) *(G-3282)*

Lc Foods LLC.. 919 510-6688
3809 Frazier Dr Ste 101 Raleigh (27610) *(G-10250)*

Lcf Enterprise (PA).. 208 415-4300
719 6th Ave Nw Hickory (28601) *(G-6385)*

LCI, Charlotte *Also Called: LCI Corporation International (G-2411)*

LCI, Sanford *Also Called: Lee County Industries Inc (G-11205)*

LCI Corporation International.. 704 399-7441
4404b Chesapeake Dr Charlotte (28216) *(G-2410)*

LCI Corporation International.. 704 399-7441
4433 Chesapeake Dr Charlotte (28216) *(G-2411)*

LD Davis Industries Inc.. 704 289-4551
2031 E Roosevelt Blvd Monroe (28112) *(G-8514)*

LDR Designs.. 252 375-4484
3113 Cleere Ct Greenville (27858) *(G-6001)*

Le Bleu Corporation.. 828 254-5105
212 Baldwin Rd Arden (28704) *(G-280)*

Lea Aid, Spring Hope *Also Called: Lea Aid Acquisition Company (G-11557)*

Lea Aid Acquisition Company.. 919 872-6210
117 N Ash St Spring Hope (27882) *(G-11557)*

Lea Industries Inc.. 336 294-5233
240 Pleasant Hill Rd Hudson (28638) *(G-6954)*

Lea R N, Raleigh *Also Called: R N Lea Inc (G-10418)*

Leading Edge Safety Systems, New Bern *Also Called: Pucuda Inc (G-9389)*

Leanders, Concord *Also Called: Tameka Burros (G-3451)*

Leapfrog Document Services Inc.. 704 372-1078
4651 Charlotte Park Dr Ste 230 Charlotte (28217) *(G-2412)*

Lear Corporation.. 910 296-8671
1754 N Nc 11 903 Hwy Kenansville (28349) *(G-7226)*

Lear Corporation.. 910 794-5810
1001 Military Cutoff Rd Ste 300 Wilmington (28405) *(G-12831)*

Lear Enterprises Inc.. 704 321-0027
8145 Ardrey Kell Rd Charlotte (28277) *(G-2413)*

Learningstationcom Inc (PA).. 704 926-5400
8022 Providence Rd Ste 500 Charlotte (28277) *(G-2414)*

Leaseaccelerator, Raleigh *Also Called: Leaseaccelerator Inc (G-10251)*

Leaseaccelerator Inc (PA).. 866 446-0980
8529 Six Forks Rd Raleigh (27615) *(G-10251)*

Leather Magic Inc.. 704 283-5078
1104 Leewood Dr Monroe (28112) *(G-8515)*

Leather Miracles LLC.. 828 464-7448
3350 20th Ave Se Hickory (28602) *(G-6386)*

Leathercraft Inc.. 828 322-3305
102 Section House Rd Conover (28613) *(G-3536)*

Lebos Shoe Store Inc.. 704 987-6540
20605 Torrence Chapel Rd Cornelius (28031) *(G-3614)*

Ledford Logging Co Inc.. 828 644-5410
1737 Sunny Point Rd Murphy (28906) *(G-9291)*

Ledford Upholstery.. 704 732-0233
202 W Pine St Lincolnton (28092) *(G-7836)*

Ledford Upholstery & Fabrics, Lincolnton *Also Called: Ledford Upholstery (G-7836)*

Ledger Hardware Inc.. 828 688-4798
5489 S 226 Hwy Bakersville (28705) *(G-679)*

Ledger Publishing Company.. 919 693-2646
200 W Spring St Oxford (27565) *(G-9619)*

Lee, Greensboro *Also Called: Lee Apparel Company Inc (G-5658)*

Lee Apparel Company Inc (DH).. 336 332-3400
400 N Elm St Greensboro (27401) *(G-5658)*

Lee Brick & Tile Company.. 919 774-4800
3704 Hawkins Ave Sanford (27330) *(G-11203)*

Lee Builder Mart Inc
1000 N Horner Blvd Sanford (27330) *(G-11204)*

Lee Controls LLC.. 732 752-5200
8250 River Rd Southport (28461) *(G-11521)*

Lee County Industries Inc.. 919 775-3439
2711 Tramway Rd Sanford (27332) *(G-11205)*

Lee Industries LLC (PA).. 828 464-8318
210 4th St Sw Conover (28613) *(G-3537)*

Lee Industries LLC.. 828 464-8318
402 W 25th St Newton (28658) *(G-9479)*

Lee Industries LLC.. 828 464-8318
1620 Fisher Ct Newton (28658) *(G-9480)*

Lee Linear.. 800 221-0811
8250 River Rd Southport (28461) *(G-11522)*

Lee Marks (PA).. 919 493-2208
4304 Amesbury Ln Durham (27707) *(G-4102)*

Lee Spring Company LLC.. 336 275-3631
104 Industrial Ave Greensboro (27406) *(G-5659)*

Leeboy, Lincolnton *Also Called: St Engineering Leeboy Inc (G-7856)*

Leeboy, Lincolnton *Also Called: VT Leeboy Inc (G-7869)*

Lees Press and Pubg Co LLC.. 833 440-0770
3515 David Cox Rd Charlotte (28269) *(G-2415)*

Lees Tackle Inc.. 910 386-5100
5316 Us Highway 421 N Wilmington (28401) *(G-12832)*

Leesona Corp.. 336 226-5511
2050b Willow Spring Ln Burlington (27215) *(G-1118)*

Legacy Aerospace & Defense, Arden *Also Called: Legacy Aerospace and Def LLC (G-281)*

Legacy Aerospace and Def LLC (PA).. 828 398-0981
150 Glenn Bridge Rd Arden (28704) *(G-281)*

Legacy Biogas, Goldsboro *Also Called: Legacy Biogas LLC (G-5223)*

Legacy Biogas LLC.. 713 253-9013
107 Cassedale Dr Goldsboro (27534) *(G-5223)*

Legacy Commercial Service LLC.. 757 831-5291
13921 Allison Forest Trl Charlotte (28278) *(G-2416)*

Legacy Graphics Inc.. 919 741-6262
191 Technology Dr Garner (27529) *(G-4936)*

Legacy Knitting LLC.. 844 762-2678
3310 Kitty Hawk Rd Ste 100 Wilmington (28405) *(G-12833)*

Legacy Manufacturing LLC.. 704 525-0498
537 Scholtz Rd Charlotte (28217) *(G-2417)*

Legacy Mechanical.. 704 225-8558
2715 Gray Fox Rd Monroe (28110) *(G-8516)*

Legacy Paddlesports LLC.. 828 684-1933
210 Old Airport Rd Fletcher (28732) *(G-4746)*

Legacy Pre-Finishing Inc.. 704 528-7136
450 S Eastway Dr Troutman (28166) *(G-12143)*

Legacy Vulcan LLC.. 828 963-7100
3869 Hwy 105 S Boone (28607) *(G-929)*

Legacy Vulcan LLC.. 704 788-7833
7680 Poplar Tent Rd Concord (28027) *(G-3391)*

Legacy Vulcan LLC.. 252 338-2201
174 Knobbs Creek Dr Elizabeth City (27909) *(G-4396)*

Legacy Vulcan LLC.. 336 835-1439
12362 Nc 268 Elkin (28621) *(G-4447)*

Legacy Vulcan LLC.. 828 255-8561
Hwy 19 & 23 S Enka (28728) *(G-4487)*

Legacy Vulcan LLC.. 704 279-5566
16745 Old Beatty Ford Rd Gold Hill (28071) *(G-5194)*

Legacy Vulcan LLC.. 252 438-3161
696 Greystone Rd Henderson (27537) *(G-6164)*

Legacy Vulcan LLC.. 828 692-0254
2960 Clear Creek Rd Hendersonville (28792) *(G-6221)*

2025 Harris North Carolina
Manufacturers Directory

(G-0000) Company's Geographic Section entry number

Legacy Vulcan LLC.. 828 754-5348
  2008 Wilkesboro Blvd Lenoir (28645) *(G-7618)*

Legacy Vulcan LLC.. 828 437-2616
  Causby Quarry Rd Morganton (28655) *(G-8877)*

Legacy Vulcan LLC.. 336 838-8072
  776 Quarry Rd # 115 North Wilkesboro (28659) *(G-9540)*

Legacy Vulcan LLC.. 910 895-2415
  353 Galestown Rd Rockingham (28379) *(G-10782)*

Legacy Vulcan LLC.. 336 767-0911
  4401 N Patterson Ave Winston Salem (27105) *(G-13232)*

Legalis Dms LLC.. 919 741-8260
  1315 Oakwood Ave Raleigh (27610) *(G-10252)*

Legend-Tees... 828 585-2066
  37 Loop Rd Arden (28704) *(G-282)*

Legends Countertops LLC.. 980 230-4501
  138 Buffalo Ave Nw Unit 3 Concord (28025) *(G-3392)*

Leggett & Platt Incorporated.................................... 336 379-7777
  911 Northridge St Greensboro (27403) *(G-5660)*

Leggett & Platt Incorporated.................................... 336 884-4306
  1629 Blandwood Dr High Point (27260) *(G-6690)*

Leggett & Platt Incorporated.................................... 855 853-3539
  161 Proctor Ln Lexington (27292) *(G-7709)*

Leggett & Platt Incorporated.................................... 336 622-0121
  330 N Greensboro St Liberty (27298) *(G-7770)*

Leggett & Platt Incorporated.................................... 704 380-6208
  178 Orbit Rd Statesville (28677) *(G-11727)*

Leggett & Platt Incorporated..................................... 828 322-6855
  1401 Deborah Herman Rd Sw Conover (28613) *(G-3538)*

Leggett & Platt Incorporated..................................... 336 889-2600
  1430 Sherman Ct High Point (27260) *(G-6691)*

Leggett & Platt Incorporated..................................... 336 889-2600
  1430 Sherman Ct High Point (27260) *(G-6692)*

Lehr LLC... 704 827-9368
  12703 Commerce Station Dr Huntersville (28078) *(G-7010)*

Leica Microsystems Nc Inc...................................... 919 428-9661
  4222 Emperor Blvd Ste 390 Durham (27703) *(G-4103)*

Leighdeux LLC... 704 965-4889
  355 Eastover Rd Charlotte (28207) *(G-2418)*

Leistriz Advanced Turbine Components Inc................. 336 969-1352
  3050 Westinghouse Rd Ste 190 Rural Hall (27045) *(G-10964)*

Leisure Craft Holdings LLC....................................... 828 693-8241
  940 Upward Rd Flat Rock (28731) *(G-4708)*

Leisure Craft Inc.. 828 693-8241
  940 Upward Rd Flat Rock (28731) *(G-4709)*

Leitz Tooling Demp's Div., Archdale *Also Called: Leitz Tooling Systems LP (G-237)*

Leitz Tooling Systems LP.. 336 861-3367
  401 Interstate Dr Archdale (27263) *(G-237)*

Leke LLC.. 704 523-1452
  10800 Nations Ford Rd Pineville (28134) *(G-9739)*

Leland Machine Shop Inc... 910 371-0360
  767 Village Rd Ne Leland (28451) *(G-7550)*

Lelantos Group Inc... 704 780-4127
  132 Joe Knox Ave Ste 100 Mooresville (28117) *(G-8709)*

Lely Manufacturing Inc... 252 291-7050
  4608 Lely Rd Wilson (27893) *(G-13002)*

Len Corporation.. 919 876-2964
  525 Hinton Oaks Blvd Knightdale (27545) *(G-7452)*

Lennox International Inc... 828 633-4805
  1251 Sand Hill Rd Candler (28715) *(G-1229)*

Lennox Store Asheville, Candler *Also Called: Lennox International Inc (G-1229)*

Lenoir Concrete Cnstr Co... 828 759-0449
  562 Abington Rd Lenoir (28645) *(G-7619)*

Lenoir Mirror Company... 828 728-3271
  401 Kincaid St Lenoir (28645) *(G-7620)*

Lenoir Printing Inc... 828 758-7260
  401 Harper Ave Sw Lenoir (28645) *(G-7621)*

Lenoir Printing Solutions, Lenoir *Also Called: Lenoir Printing Inc (G-7621)*

Lenovo (united States) Inc....................................... 919 486-9627
  5241 Paramount Pkwy Morrisville (27560) *(G-9004)*

Lenovo (united States) Inc....................................... 919 237-8389
  7001 Development Dr Bldg 7 Morrisville (27560) *(G-9005)*

Lenovo (united States) Inc (HQ)................................ 855 253-6686
  8001 Development Dr Morrisville (27560) *(G-9006)*

Lenovo Global Tech US Inc (HQ)............................... 855 253-6686
  8001 Development Dr Morrisville (27560) *(G-9007)*

Lenovo Holding Company Inc (HQ)............................ 855 253-6686
  8001 Development Dr Morrisville (27560) *(G-9008)*

Lenovo International, Morrisville *Also Called: Lenovo (united States) Inc (G-9006)*

Lenovo US Fulfillment Ctr LLC................................... 855 253-6686
  1009 Think Pl Morrisville (27560) *(G-9009)*

Lenscrafters, Fayetteville *Also Called: Luxottica of America Inc (G-4631)*

Lenscrafters, Goldsboro *Also Called: Luxottica of America Inc (G-5226)*

Leo Gaev Metalworks Inc... 919 883-4666
  616 Nc Highway 54 W Chapel Hill (27516) *(G-1552)*

Leoforce LLC... 919 539-5434
  500 W Peace St Raleigh (27603) *(G-10253)*

Leonard Alum Utlity Bldngs Inc................................. 336 226-9410
  2602 Alamance Rd Burlington (27215) *(G-1119)*

Leonard Alum Utlity Bldngs Inc (PA)......................... 336 789-5018
  630 W Independence Blvd Ste 3 Mount Airy (27030) *(G-9146)*

Leonard Alum Utlity Bldngs Inc................................. 919 872-4442
  4239 Capital Blvd Raleigh (27604) *(G-10254)*

Leonard Alum Utlity Bldngs Inc................................. 910 392-4921
  5705 Market St Wilmington (28405) *(G-12834)*

Leonard Automatics Inc... 704 483-9316
  5894 Balsom Ridge Rd Denver (28037) *(G-3792)*

Leonard Block Company.. 336 764-0607
  2390 Midway School Rd Winston Salem (27107) *(G-13233)*

Leonard Building & Trck Cover, Wilmington *Also Called: Leonard Alum Utlity Bldngs Inc (G-12834)*

Leonard Building & Trck Covers, Mount Airy *Also Called: Leonard Alum Utlity Bldngs Inc (G-9146)*

Leonard Building & Truck ACC, Raleigh *Also Called: Leonard Alum Utlity Bldngs Inc (G-10254)*

Leonard Building and Truck ACC, Burlington *Also Called: Leonard Alum Utlity Bldngs Inc (G-1119)*

Leonard Electric Mtr Repr Inc.................................... 336 625-2375
  531 N Fayetteville St Asheboro (27203) *(G-373)*

Leonard Frabrication & Design, Denver *Also Called: Leonard Automatics Inc (G-3792)*

Leonard Logging Co... 336 857-2776
  4057 Salem Church Rd Denton (27239) *(G-3755)*

Leonard McSwain Sptic Tank Svc.............................. 704 482-1380
  3020 Ramseur Church Rd Shelby (28150) *(G-11353)*

Leonard Products, Oak Island *Also Called: Lakebrook Corporation (G-9566)*

Leonardo, Greensboro *Also Called: Leonardo US Cyber SEC Sltons L (G-5661)*

Leonardo US Cyber SEC Sltons L (PA)........................ 336 379-7135
  4221 Tudor Ln Greensboro (27410) *(G-5661)*

Leonine Protection Systems LLC................................ 704 296-2675
  309 Dutchmans Meadow Dr Mount Holly (28120) *(G-9235)*

Lets Talk Some Shit.. 704 264-6212
  7400 Old Mount Holly Rd Paw Creek (28130) *(G-9649)*

Level 4 Designs Corp.. 336 235-3450
  7027 Albert Pick Rd Ste 103 Greensboro (27409) *(G-5662)*

Levi Innovations Inc... 828 684-6640
  122 Continuum Dr Fletcher (28732) *(G-4747)*

Levi Strauss International.. 828 665-2417
  800 Brevard Rd Asheville (28806) *(G-534)*

Leviosa Motor Shades, Mooresville *Also Called: Penrock LLC (G-8745)*

Leviton Manufacturing Co Inc................................... 828 584-1611
  113 Industrial Blvd Morganton (28655) *(G-8878)*

Leviton Manufacturing Co Inc................................... 336 846-3246
  618 S Jefferson Ave West Jefferson (28694) *(G-12566)*

Lewis Brothers Tire & Algnmt.................................. 919 359-9050
  451 E Main St Clayton (27520) *(G-3157)*

Lewis Frank Specialty Products, Salisbury *Also Called: Carolina Print Works Inc (G-11027)*

Lewis Machine Company Inc.................................... 828 668-7752
  712 Catawba River Rd Old Fort (28762) *(G-9595)*

Lewis Moore Prtg & Graphics, Raleigh *Also Called: Moore Printing & Graphics Inc (G-10314)*

Lewtak Pipe Organ Builders Inc................................ 336 554-2251
  211 Parsley Ln Mocksville (27028) *(G-8374)*

Lexington Electric Motor Repr, Lexington *Also Called: Lake City Electric Motor Repr (G-7708)*

A
L
P
H
A
B
E
T
I
C

Lexington Furniture Inds Inc (PA)............... 336 474-5300
 1300 National Hwy Thomasville (27360) *(G-12043)*

Lexington Gas Dept, City of, Lexington *Also Called: City of Lexington (G-7666)*

Lexington Home Brands, Thomasville *Also Called: Lexington Furniture Inds Inc (G-12043)*

Lexington Plant Nippon Elc GL, Lexington *Also Called: Nippon Electric Glass Co Ltd*
(G-7722)

Lexington Road Properties Inc............... 336 650-7209
 500 Battery Dr Winston Salem (27107) *(G-13234)*

Lexitas Pharma Services Inc (PA)............... 919 205-0012
 5425 Page Rd Ste 410 Durham (27703) *(G-4104)*

Lgc Consulting Inc............... 704 216-0171
 1217 Speedway Blvd Salisbury (28146) *(G-11083)*

Li-Ion Motors Corp............... 704 662-0827
 158 Rolling Hill Rd Mooresville (28117) *(G-8710)*

Liat LLC............... 704 528-4506
 694 N Main St Troutman (28166) *(G-12144)*

Libasci Woodworks Inc............... 828 524-7073
 401 Dobson Mountain Rd R Franklin (28734) *(G-4834)*

Liberty Dry Kiln Corp............... 336 622-5490
 3246 Staley Store Rd Liberty (27298) *(G-7771)*

Liberty Embroidery Inc............... 336 548-1802
 301 K Fork Rd Madison (27025) *(G-7990)*

Liberty Hse Utility Buildings............... 828 209-3390
 65 Dalton Rd Horse Shoe (28742) *(G-6929)*

Liberty Investment & MGT Corp............... 919 544-0344
 455 Kitty Hawk Dr Morrisville (27560) *(G-9010)*

Liberty Lumber Company............... 336 622-4901
 9979 Old Liberty Rd Liberty (27298) *(G-7772)*

Liberty Press, Rutherfordton *Also Called: S Ruppe Inc (G-10992)*

Liberty Sign and Lighting LLC............... 336 703-7465
 375 Ridge Rd Lexington (27295) *(G-7710)*

Liberty Street Baggage, Asheville *Also Called: Saundra D Hall (G-595)*

Liberty Trailers LLC............... 219 866-7141
 5806 York Martin Rd Liberty (27298) *(G-7773)*

Liberty Wood Products Inc............... 828 524-7958
 874 Iotla Church Rd Franklin (28734) *(G-4835)*

Libra Life Group Llc............... 910 550-8664
 9371 Cassadine Ct Leland (28451) *(G-7551)*

Libra Logistics/Escort, Leland *Also Called: Libra Life Group Llc (G-7551)*

Liburdi, Mooresville *Also Called: Liburdi Dimetrics Corporation (G-8711)*

Liburdi Dimetrics Corporation............... 704 230-2510
 2599 Charlotte Hwy Mooresville (28117) *(G-8711)*

Liburdi Turbine Services LLC............... 704 230-2510
 2599 Charlotte Hwy Mooresville (28117) *(G-8712)*

License Plate Agency............... 910 763-7076
 2390 Carolina Beach Rd Wilmington (28401) *(G-12835)*

Lichtenberg Inc............... 336 949-9438
 107 E Murphy St Madison (27025) *(G-7991)*

Lidseen North Carolina Inc............... 828 389-8082
 6382 Old Hwy 64 W Hayesville (28904) *(G-6142)*

Lie Loft, Raleigh *Also Called: Land and Loft LLC (G-10244)*

Liebel-Flarsheim Company LLC............... 919 878-2930
 8800 Durant Rd Raleigh (27616) *(G-10255)*

Liechti America............... 704 948-1277
 13245 Reese Blvd W Ste 100 Huntersville (28078) *(G-7011)*

Life, Cary *Also Called: Living Intntionally For Excell (G-1391)*

Lifespan Incorporated (PA)............... 704 944-5100
 1511 Shopton Rd Ste A Charlotte (28217) *(G-2419)*

Lifespan Incorporated............... 336 838-2614
 2070 River Rd Liberty Grove Rd North Wilkesboro (28659) *(G-9541)*

Lift Bodies Inc............... 336 667-2588
 1675 Elkin Hwy 268 North Wilkesboro (28659) *(G-9542)*

Liftavator Inc............... 252 634-1717
 4430 Us Highway 70 E New Bern (28560) *(G-9375)*

Liggett Group LLC (DH)............... 919 304-7700
 100 Maple Ln Mebane (27302) *(G-8249)*

Light Source Usa Inc............... 704 504-8399
 3935 Westinghouse Blvd Charlotte (28273) *(G-2420)*

Light-Beams Publishing............... 603 659-1300
 111 Island Palms Dr Carolina Beach (28428) *(G-1262)*

Lightcreed Labs, Durham *Also Called: Wolfspeed Inc (G-4307)*

Lightform Inc............... 908 281-9098
 403 Shelwood Cir Apt H Asheville (28804) *(G-535)*

Lighthouse of Wayne County Inc............... 919 736-1313
 405 E Walnut St Goldsboro (27530) *(G-5224)*

Lighthouse Press Inc............... 919 371-8640
 102 Eagle Meadow Ct Cary (27519) *(G-1388)*

Lightjunction............... 919 607-9717
 400 Innovation Ave # 150 Morrisville (27560) *(G-9011)*

Lightjunction, Morrisville *Also Called: Busiapp Corporation (G-8947)*

Lightning Bolt Ink LLC............... 828 281-1274
 100 N Lexington Ave Asheville (28801) *(G-536)*

Lightning Protection, Waynesville *Also Called: Alp Systems Inc (G-12450)*

Lightning Prtction Systems LLC............... 252 213-9900
 5901 Triangle Dr Raleigh (27617) *(G-10256)*

Lightning X Products Inc............... 704 295-0299
 2365 Tipton Dr Charlotte (28206) *(G-2421)*

Lights-Lights LLC............... 919 798-2317
 1206 Bill Avery Rd Coats (27521) *(G-3264)*

Ligna Machinery Inc............... 336 584-0030
 315 Macarthur Ln Burlington (27217) *(G-1120)*

Lignaterra Global LLC............... 970 481-6952
 6000 Fairview Rd Ste 1200 Charlotte (28210) *(G-2422)*

Likeable Press LLC............... 844 882-8340
 227 W 4th St Charlotte (28202) *(G-2423)*

Lilas Trunk............... 919 548-0784
 145 Cc Routh Rd Bear Creek (27207) *(G-715)*

Lillies Intriors Cstm Quilting, Thomasville *Also Called: Lillys Interiors Cstm Quilting (G-12044)*

Lillys Interiors Cstm Quilting............... 336 475-1421
 1165 Hillside Dr Thomasville (27360) *(G-12044)*

Lime-Chem Inc............... 910 843-2121
 8135 Red Rd Rockwell (28138) *(G-10799)*

Limestone Products Inc (PA)............... 704 283-9492
 3302 W Highway 74 B Monroe (28110) *(G-8517)*

Limitless Wldg Fabrication LLC............... 252 753-0660
 3543 South Fields St Farmville (27828) *(G-4534)*

Linamar Forgings Carolina Inc............... 252 237-8181
 2401 Old Stantonsburg Rd Wilson (27894) *(G-13003)*

Linamar Light Metal S-Mr LLC............... 828 348-4010
 490 Ferncliff Park Dr Fletcher (28732) *(G-4748)*

Linamar North Carolina Inc............... 828 348-5343
 2169 Hendersonville Rd Arden (28704) *(G-283)*

Lincoln County Fabricators Inc............... 704 735-1398
 513 Jason Rd Lincolnton (28092) *(G-7837)*

Lincoln Financial, Greensboro *Also Called: Abe Entercom Holdings LLC (G-5337)*

Lincoln Herald LLC............... 704 735-3620
 611 N Laurel St Lincolnton (28092) *(G-7838)*

Lincotek Surface Solutions, Hickory *Also Called: Turbocoating Corp (G-6476)*

Linde Advanced Mtl Tech Inc............... 828 862-4772
 283 Old Rosman Hwy Brevard (28712) *(G-974)*

Linde Gas & Equipment Inc............... 919 380-7411
 1120 W Chatham St Cary (27511) *(G-1389)*

Linde Gas & Equipment Inc............... 704 587-7096
 3810 Shutterfly Rd Ste 100 Charlotte (28217) *(G-2424)*

Linde Gas & Equipment Inc............... 919 549-0633
 11 Triangle Dr Durham (27709) *(G-4105)*

Linde Gas & Equipment Inc............... 866 543-3427
 1304 Roosevelt Ct Whitsett (27377) *(G-12612)*

Linde Gas North America, Cary *Also Called: Linde Gas & Equipment Inc (G-1389)*

Linde Gas North America, Charlotte *Also Called: Linde Gas & Equipment Inc (G-2424)*

Linde Gas North America, Durham *Also Called: Linde Gas & Equipment Inc (G-4105)*

Linde Gas North America, Whitsett *Also Called: Linde Gas & Equipment Inc (G-12612)*

Linde Inc............... 910 343-0241
 Hwy 421 N Wilmington (28405) *(G-12836)*

Linden St Holdings Inc............... 336 472-5555
 5801 E Us Highway 64 Lexington (27292) *(G-7711)*

Linder Industrial Machinery Co............... 980 777-8345
 5733 Davidson Hwy Concord (28027) *(G-3393)*

Lindley Laboratories Inc (PA)............... 336 449-7521
 106 E Railroad Ave Gibsonville (27249) *(G-5181)*

Lindley Mills Inc............... 336 376-6190
 7763 Lindley Mill Rd Graham (27253) *(G-5275)*

Lindsay Precast Inc.................................... 919 494-7600
2675 Us 1 Hwy Franklinton (27525) *(G-4850)*

LINDSAY PRECAST, INC., Franklinton Also Called: Lindsay Precast Inc *(G-4850)*

Line Drive Sports Center Inc...................... 336 824-1692
161 Crestwick Rd Ramseur (27316) *(G-10628)*

Lingle Electric Repair Inc........................... 704 636-5591
600 N Main St Salisbury (28144) *(G-11084)*

Linkone Src LLC.. 252 206-0960
2018 Beeler Rd S Wilson (27893) *(G-13004)*

Linor Technology Inc.................................. 336 485-6199
4741 S Main St Winston Salem (27127) *(G-13235)*

Linprint Company.. 910 763-5103
3405 Market St Unit 2 Wilmington (28403) *(G-12837)*

Linter North America Corp (DH)................. 828 645-4261
48 Patton Ave Asheville (28801) *(G-537)*

Linville Falls Winery.................................. 828 733-9021
9557 Linville Falls Hwy Newland (28657) *(G-9431)*

Linwood Inc.. 336 300-8307
3979 Old Linwood Rd Lexington (27292) *(G-7712)*

Lionel LLC (PA).. 704 454-4371
6301 Performance Dr Sw Concord (28027) *(G-3394)*

Lions Services Inc..................................... 704 921-1527
4600 N Tryon St Ste A Charlotte (28213) *(G-2425)*

Lionstar Transport LLC.............................. 336 448-0166
2597 Landmark Dr Winston Salem (27103) *(G-13236)*

Liposcience, Morrisville Also Called: Liposcience Inc *(G-9012)*

Liposcience Inc.. 919 212-1999
100 Perimeter Park Dr Ste C Morrisville (27560) *(G-9012)*

Liqui-Box Corporation (HQ)....................... 804 325-1400
2415 Cascade Pointe Blvd Charlotte (28208) *(G-2426)*

Liquid Ice Corporation............................... 704 882-3505
500 Union West Blvd Ste C Matthews (28104) *(G-8179)*

Liquid Moly, Salisbury Also Called: Lockrey Company LLC *(G-11085)*

Liquid Process Systems Inc..................... 704 821-1115
1025 Technology Dr Ste A Indian Trail (28079) *(G-7088)*

Liquidating Reichhold Inc......................... 919 990-7500
1035 Swabia Ct Durham (27703) *(G-4106)*

Liquidehr Inc.. 866 618-1531
1939 High House Rd Ste 107 Cary (27519) *(G-1390)*

Litex Industries Inc................................... 704 799-3758
120 N Commercial Dr Mooresville (28115) *(G-8713)*

Litho Priting Inc... 919 755-9542
1501 S Blount St Raleigh (27603) *(G-10257)*

Lithography Design, Raleigh Also Called: Litho Priting Inc *(G-10257)*

Little Beekeeper LLC.................................. 704 215-9690
3978 Stoney Creek Dr Lincolnton (28092) *(G-7839)*

Little Logging Inc...................................... 704 201-8185
1513 N Main St Oakboro (28129) *(G-9580)*

Little Red Wagon Granola, Durham Also Called: Lrw Holdings Inc *(G-4110)*

Little River Furniture, Ether Also Called: Blackstone Furniture Inds Inc *(G-4494)*

Little River Metalworks LLC...................... 919 920-0292
132 Blueberry Rd Goldsboro (27530) *(G-5225)*

Little River Naturals LLC........................... 919 760-3708
7408 Riley Hill Rd Zebulon (27597) *(G-13513)*

Little River Yachts Inc............................... 828 323-4955
1100 Commscope Pl Se Hickory (28602) *(G-6387)*

Live It Boutique LLC.................................. 704 492-2402
509 Old Vine Ct Charlotte (28214) *(G-2427)*

Livedo Usa Inc... 252 237-1373
4925 Livedo Dr Wilson (27893) *(G-13005)*

Livengood Innovations LLC....................... 336 925-7604
12068 S Nc Highway 150 Linwood (27299) *(G-7879)*

Livin' Rooms, Claremont Also Called: Dexter Inc *(G-3106)*

Living Intntionally For Excell.................... 810 600-3425
200 Commonwealth Ct Ste 200 Cary (27511) *(G-1391)*

Living Wise, High Point Also Called: Wise Living Inc *(G-6838)*

Livingston & Haven, Charlotte Also Called: Hyde Park Partners Inc *(G-2304)*

Livingston & Haven LLC (HQ).................... 704 588-3670
11529 Wilmar Blvd Charlotte (28273) *(G-2428)*

Lizmere Cavaliers....................................... 704 418-2543
403 S Washington St Shelby (28150) *(G-11354)*

Lizzys Logos Inc.. 704 321-2588
3118 Savannah Hills Dr Matthews (28105) *(G-8127)*

Ljm Machine Co Inc.................................... 336 764-0518
7987 Old Us Highway 52 Lexington (27295) *(G-7713)*

LL Cultured Marble Inc.............................. 336 789-3908
1184 Maple Grove Church Rd Mount Airy (27030) *(G-9147)*

LLC Ferguson Copeland (HQ)................... 828 584-0664
100 Reep Dr Morganton (28655) *(G-8879)*

Llewellyn Mtal Fabricators Inc................. 704 283-4816
4816 Persimmon Ct Monroe (28110) *(G-8518)*

Liflex LLC.. 336 777-5000
220 Polo Rd Winston Salem (27105) *(G-13237)*

Lloyds Chatham Ltd Partnership.............. 919 742-4692
511 Dorado Dr High Point (27265) *(G-6693)*

Lloyds Fabricating Solutions.................... 336 250-0154
5896 Denton Rd Thomasville (27360) *(G-12045)*

Lloyds Oyster House Inc........................... 910 754-6958
1642 Village Point Rd Sw Shallotte (28470) *(G-11304)*

Lls Investments Inc (PA)........................... 919 662-7283
3400 Lake Woodard Dr Raleigh (27604) *(G-10258)*

Lm, Granite Falls Also Called: Lubrimetal Corporation *(G-5311)*

Lm Shea LLC... 919 608-1901
8201 Candelaria Dr Raleigh (27616) *(G-10259)*

Lmb Corp... 704 547-8886
3020 Prosperity Church Rd Ste D Charlotte (28269) *(G-2429)*

Lmg Holdings Inc....................................... 919 653-0910
4920 S Alston Ave Durham (27713) *(G-4107)*

Lns Turbo Inc (DH)..................................... 704 739-7111
203 Turbo Dr Kings Mountain (28086) *(G-7371)*

Lns Turbo North America.......................... 704 435-6376
242 Dick Beam Rd Cherryville (28021) *(G-3066)*

Loading Republic Inc................................. 704 561-1077
191 Crowell Dr Nw Concord (28025) *(G-3395)*

Loba-Wakol LLC.. 704 527-5919
2732 Us Highway 74 W Wadesboro (28170) *(G-12247)*

Lobbyguard Solutions LLC........................ 919 785-3301
4700 Six Forks Rd Ste 300 Raleigh (27609) *(G-10260)*

Lock Drives Inc.. 704 588-1844
11198 Downs Rd Pineville (28134) *(G-9740)*

Locklear Cabinet and Woodworks, Rowland Also Called: Locklear Cabinets Wdwrk Sp Inc *(G-10916)*

Locklear Cabinets Wdwrk Sp Inc............. 910 521-4463
4659 Cabinet Shop Rd Rowland (28383) *(G-10916)*

Lockrey Company LLC (PA)....................... 856 665-4794
614 Emerald Bay Dr Salisbury (28146) *(G-11085)*

Locktite Log Systems, Salisbury Also Called: Log Home Builders Inc *(G-11087)*

Lockwood Identity Inc............................... 704 597-9801
6225 Old Concord Rd Charlotte (28213) *(G-2430)*

Locust Monument LLC................................ 704 888-5600
713 Main St W Locust (28097) *(G-7895)*

Locust Plastics Inc.................................... 704 636-2742
630 Industrial Ave Salisbury (28144) *(G-11086)*

Lodging By Liberty Inc.............................. 336 622-2201
50 Industrial Park Dr Siler City (27344) *(G-11417)*

Loflin Concrete Co Inc.............................. 336 904-2788
2105 Pisgah Church Rd Kernersville (27284) *(G-7282)*

Loflin Fabrication, Denton Also Called: Loflin Fabrication LLC *(G-3756)*

Loflin Fabrication LLC............................... 336 859-4333
1379 Cranford Rd Denton (27239) *(G-3756)*

Loflin Handle Co Inc.................................. 336 463-2422
2837 Courtney Huntsville Rd Yadkinville (27055) *(G-13445)*

Loftin & Company Inc................................ 704 393-9393
1908 Gateway Blvd Charlotte (28208) *(G-2431)*

Loftin & Company Printers, Charlotte Also Called: Loftin & Company Inc *(G-2431)*

Log Cabin Homes Ltd................................. 252 454-1548
7677 N Halifax Rd Battleboro (27809) *(G-701)*

Log Cabin Homes Ltd (PA)........................ 252 454-1500
513 Keen St # 515 Rocky Mount (27804) *(G-10849)*

Log Home Builders Inc.............................. 704 638-0677
470 B Leazer Rd Salisbury (28147) *(G-11087)*

Log Home Cooperative America, Jefferson Also Called: Log Homes of America Inc *(G-7190)*

Log Homes of America Inc......................... 336 982-8989
2999 Us Highway 221 N Jefferson (28640) *(G-7190)*

Logan Text Fabrics, Greensboro *Also Called: Oakhurst Textiles Inc (G-5718)*

Logangate Homes Timber Homes, Asheville *Also Called: Rclgh Inc (G-588)*

Logic Hydraulic Controls Inc...................... 910 791-9293
6616 Windmill Way Wilmington (28405) *(G-12838)*

Logic Manufacturing Inc........................... 704 821-0535
4009 Fawnbrooke Dr Indian Trail (28079) *(G-7089)*

Logicbit Software LLC............................. 888 366-2280
2530 Meridian Pkwy Ste 300 Durham (27713) *(G-4108)*

Logicom Computer Systems Inc.................... 910 256-5916
1121 Military Cutoff Rd Ste C Wilmington (28405) *(G-12839)*

Logiksavvy Solutions LLC......................... 336 392-6149
2204 Flora Vista Ct Greensboro (27406) *(G-5663)*

Logistimatics, Greensboro *Also Called: Gpx Intelligence Inc (G-5570)*

Logo Dogz... 888 827-8866
4808 Persimmon Ct Monroe (28110) *(G-8519)*

Logo Label Printing Company...................... 919 309-0007
4416 Bennett Memorial Rd Ste 101 Durham (27705) *(G-4109)*

Logo Wear Graphics LLC........................... 336 382-0455
300 Norman Farm Rd Summerfield (27358) *(G-11841)*

Logodogz, Monroe *Also Called: Reliance Management Group Inc (G-8551)*

Logonation Inc.................................... 704 799-0612
128 Overhill Dr Ste 102 Mooresville (28117) *(G-8714)*

Logosdirect LLC................................... 866 273-2335
6303 Oleander Dr Ste 102b Wilmington (28403) *(G-12840)*

Lollipop Cenral................................... 704 934-0015
3111 Mocking Bird Ln Kannapolis (28083) *(G-7215)*

Lomar Specialty Advg Inc......................... 704 788-4380
7148 Weddington Rd Nw Ste 110 Concord (28027) *(G-3396)*

London Luxury LLC................................ 980 819-1966
3540 Toringdon Way Ste 200 Charlotte (28277) *(G-2432)*

Lone Star Container Sales Corp.................... 704 588-1737
10901 Carpet St Charlotte (28273) *(G-2433)*

Long Asp Pav Trckg of Grnsburg................... 336 643-4121
4349 Us Highway 220 N Summerfield (27358) *(G-11842)*

Long Branch Partners LLC......................... 828 837-1400
1960 Brasstown Rd Brasstown (28902) *(G-965)*

Long J E & Sons Grading Inc (PA)................. 336 228-9706
3218 Foy Jane Trl Burlington (27217) *(G-1121)*

Long Trailer Co Inc.............................. 252 823-8828
313 Bass Ln Tarboro (27886) *(G-11931)*

Long, J E Sand & Stone, Burlington *Also Called: Long J E & Sons Grading Inc (G-1121)*

Longhorn Roofing Inc............................. 704 774-1080
1302 Walkup Ave Monroe (28110) *(G-8520)*

Longleaf Services Inc............................ 800 848-6224
116 S Boundary St Chapel Hill (27514) *(G-1553)*

Longleaf Truss Company........................... 910 673-4711
4476 Nc Highway 211 West End (27376) *(G-12556)*

Longs Machine & Tool Inc......................... 336 625-3844
2224 S Fayetteville St Asheboro (27205) *(G-374)*

Longwood Industries Inc (DH)..................... 336 272-3710
706 Green Valley Rd Ste 212 Greensboro (27408) *(G-5664)*

Longworth Industries Inc......................... 910 673-5290
3140 Nc 5 Hwy Aberdeen (28315) *(G-11)*

Longworth Industries Inc......................... 910 974-3068
480 E Main St Candor (27229) *(G-1238)*

Longworth Industries Inc (DH)................... 910 673-5290
565 Air Tool Dr Ste K Southern Pines (28387) *(G-11502)*

Lonza Rtp.. 800 748-8979
523 Davis Dr Ste 400 Morrisville (27560) *(G-9013)*

Looking Glass Creamery LLC....................... 828 458-0088
115 Harmon Dairy Ln Columbus (28722) *(G-3302)*

Lookwhatqmade LLC................................ 980 330-1995
101 N Tryon St Ste 112 Charlotte (28246) *(G-2434)*

Loparex LLC (DH)................................. 919 678-7700
1255 Crescent Green Ste 400 Cary (27518) *(G-1392)*

Loparex LLC...................................... 336 635-0192
816 W Fieldcrest Rd Eden (27288) *(G-4352)*

Lord Corporation................................. 919 342-3380
406 Gregson Dr Cary (27511) *(G-1393)*

Lord Corporation (HQ)............................ 919 468-5979
111 Lord Dr Cary (27511) *(G-1394)*

Lord Corporation................................. 919 469-2500
110 Lord Dr Cary (27511) *(G-1395)*

Lord Corporation................................. 877 275-5673
200 Lord Dr Nc Cary (27511) *(G-1396)*

Lord Far East Inc................................ 919 468-5979
111 Lord Dr Cary (27511) *(G-1397)*

Lorillard LLC (DH)............................... 336 741-2000
401 N Main St Winston Salem (27101) *(G-13238)*

Lorillard Tobacco Company LLC.................... 336 335-6600
714 Green Valley Rd Greensboro (27408) *(G-5665)*

Los Vientos Windpower Ib LLC..................... 704 594-6200
526 S Church St Charlotte (28202) *(G-2435)*

Lotus Bakeries Us LLC............................ 415 956-8956
2010 Park Center Dr Mebane (27302) *(G-8250)*

Loud Lemon Beverage LLC.......................... 919 949-7649
8512 Meadow View Ln Bahama (27503) *(G-666)*

Louisiana-Pacific Corporation.................... 336 696-2751
1068 Abtco Rd North Wilkesboro (28659) *(G-9543)*

Louisiana-Pacific Corporation.................... 336 696-2751
1151 Abtco Rd Roaring River (28669) *(G-10750)*

Louisiana-Pacific Corporation.................... 336 599-8080
10475 Boston Rd Roxboro (27574) *(G-10929)*

Louisiana-Pacific Southern Div, Roxboro *Also Called: Louisiana-Pacific Corporation* *(G-10929)*

Love Knot Candles................................ 336 456-1619
4603 Barn Owl Ct Greensboro (27406) *(G-5666)*

Lovegrass Kitchen Inc............................ 919 205-8426
300 S Main St Ste 108 Holly Springs (27540) *(G-6906)*

Lovejoy Corporation Inc.......................... 336 472-0674
2207 Granville Rd Greensboro (27408) *(G-5667)*

Lovekin & Young PC............................... 828 322-5435
110 N Center St Hickory (28601) *(G-6388)*

Loven Ready Mix LLC.............................. 828 265-4671
1996 Us Highway 421 N Boone (28607) *(G-930)*

Low Country Steel SC LLC (PA)................... 336 283-9611
2529 Viceroy Dr Winston Salem (27103) *(G-13239)*

Low Impact Tech USA Inc.......................... 828 428-6310
269 Cane Creek Rd Fletcher (28732) *(G-4749)*

Lowder Steel Inc................................. 336 431-9000
2450 Coltrane Mill Rd Archdale (27263) *(G-238)*

Lowes Global Sourcing, Mooresville *Also Called: L G Sourcing Inc (G-8707)*

Loy & Loy Inc.................................... 919 942-6356
205 Travora St Graham (27253) *(G-5276)*

Lpm Inc.. 704 922-6137
2703 Ashbourne Dr Gastonia (28056) *(G-5078)*

Lpmylan Specialty, Greensboro *Also Called: Mylan Pharmaceuticals Inc (G-5703)*

Lps Tag & Label, Winston Salem *Also Called: Label Printing Systems Inc (G-13230)*

Lq3 Pharmaceuticals, Morrisville *Also Called: Lq3 Pharmaceuticals Inc (G-9014)*

Lq3 Pharmaceuticals Inc.......................... 919 794-7391
419 Davis Dr Ste 100 Morrisville (27560) *(G-9014)*

Lr Manufacturing Inc............................. 910 399-1410
60 Dream Ave Delco (28436) *(G-3737)*

Lrc, Cary *Also Called: Laser Recharge Carolina Inc (G-1387)*

Lrw Holdings Inc................................. 919 609-4172
2310 Sparger Rd Ste B Durham (27705) *(G-4110)*

Ls Cable & System USA Inc........................ 252 824-3553
2801 Anaconda Rd Tarboro (27886) *(G-11932)*

LS Starrett Company.............................. 336 789-5141
1372 Boggs Dr Mount Airy (27030) *(G-9148)*

Ls Woodworks, Castle Hayne *Also Called: Laborie Sons Cstm Wodworks LLC (G-1504)*

Lsa, Concord *Also Called: Lomar Specialty Advg Inc (G-3396)*

Lsc Communications Inc........................... 704 889-5800
10519 Industrial Dr Pineville (28134) *(G-9741)*

Lsg LLC.. 919 878-5500
268 Hc Powers Rd Wallace (28466) *(G-12322)*

Lsrwm Corp....................................... 704 866-8533
1225 Isley Rd Gastonia (28052) *(G-5079)*

Ltd Industries LLC (PA).......................... 704 897-2182
5509 David Cox Rd Charlotte (28269) *(G-2436)*

(G-0000) Company's Geographic Section entry number

Ltlb Holding Company (PA)............ 828 624-1460
1350 4th Street Dr Nw Hickory (28601) *(G-6389)*

Ltlb Holding Company............ 704 585-2908
1095 Mcclain Rd Hiddenite (28636) *(G-6502)*

Lubrimetal Corporation............ 828 212-1083
2889 Countryside Dr Granite Falls (28630) *(G-5311)*

Lubrizol Advanced Mtls Inc............ 704 587-5583
11425 Granite St Charlotte (28273) *(G-2437)*

Lubrizol Global Management Inc............ 704 865-7451
207 Telegraph Dr Gastonia (28056) *(G-5080)*

Lucas Concrete Products Inc............ 704 525-9622
401 Rountree Rd Charlotte (28217) *(G-2438)*

Lucerno Dynamics LLC............ 317 294-1395
140 Towerview Ct Cary (27513) *(G-1398)*

Lucid Innovative Tech LLC............ 910 233-5214
9244 Industrial Blvd Ne Leland (28451) *(G-7552)*

Luck Stone - Pittsboro, Moncure *Also Called: Luck Stone Corporation (G-8408)*

Luck Stone Corporation............ 919 545-0027
4189 Nc Highway 87 S Moncure (27559) *(G-8408)*

Luck Stone Corporation............ 336 786-4693
525 Quarry Rd Mount Airy (27030) *(G-9149)*

Lucky Country USA LLC............ 828 428-8313
3333 Finger Mill Rd Lincolnton (28092) *(G-7840)*

Lucky Landports............ 704 399-9880
6510 Rozzelles Ferry Rd Charlotte (28214) *(G-2439)*

Lucky Man Inc (HQ)............ 828 251-0090
160 Broadway St Asheville (28801) *(G-538)*

Lucy In Rye LLC............ 828 586-4601
612 W Main St Sylva (28779) *(G-11896)*

Ludwig Industries, Monroe *Also Called: Conn-Selmer Inc (G-8465)*

Lullicoin LLC............ 336 955-1159
3540 Toringdon Way Charlotte (28277) *(G-2440)*

Lulu Press Inc............ 919 447-3290
700 Park Offices Dr Ste 250 Durham (27709) *(G-4111)*

Lulu Technology Circus Inc............ 919 459-5858
860 Aviation Pkwy Ste 300 Morrisville (27560) *(G-9015)*

Lulu.com, Morrisville *Also Called: Lulu Technology Circus Inc (G-9015)*

Lululemon............ 336 723-3002
312 S Stratford Rd Winston Salem (27103) *(G-13240)*

Lumberton Overhead Doors Inc............ 910 739-6426
1519 Carthage Rd Ste C Lumberton (28358) *(G-7961)*

Lumedica Inc............ 919 886-1863
404 Hunt St Ste 520 Durham (27701) *(G-4112)*

Lumenfocus, Henderson *Also Called: Lumenfocus LLC (G-6165)*

Lumenfocus LLC............ 252 430-6970
880 Facet Rd Henderson (27537) *(G-6165)*

Lumenlux LLC............ 704 222-7787
8037 Fairview Rd Ste J-3 Mint Hill (28227) *(G-8338)*

Lumeova Inc............ 908 229-4651
3801 Lake Boone Trl Ste 260 Raleigh (27607) *(G-10261)*

Lumina News............ 910 256-6569
7232 Wrightsville Ave Wilmington (28403) *(G-12841)*

Lumsden Steel, Wilmington *Also Called: Lumsden Welding Company (G-12842)*

Lumsden Welding Company............ 910 791-6336
6736 Carolina Beach Rd Wilmington (28412) *(G-12842)*

Lunar International Tech LLC............ 800 975-7153
338 S Sharon Amity Rd Charlotte (28211) *(G-2441)*

Luray Textiles Inc............ 336 670-3725
300 Luray Rd North Wilkesboro (28659) *(G-9544)*

Luray Textiles & Knitting, North Wilkesboro *Also Called: Luray Textiles Inc (G-9544)*

Lustar Dyeing and Finshg Inc............ 828 274-2440
144 Caribou Rd Asheville (28803) *(G-539)*

Lusty Monk LLC............ 828 645-5056
29 Canoe Ln Asheville (28804) *(G-540)*

Lutheran Svcs For The Aging............ 910 457-5604
4843 Southport Supply Rd Se Southport (28461) *(G-11523)*

Luthiers Workshop LLC............ 919 241-4578
2207 Leah Dr Ste 102 Hillsborough (27278) *(G-6871)*

Lutze Inc............ 704 504-0222
13330 S Ridge Dr Charlotte (28273) *(G-2442)*

Luxemark Company............ 919 863-0101
6909 Glenwood Ave Ste 106 Raleigh (27612) *(G-10262)*

Luxfer, Graham *Also Called: Metal Impact East LLC (G-5278)*

Luxor Hydration LLC............ 919 568-5047
3600 N Duke St Durham (27704) *(G-4113)*

Luxottica of America Inc............ 910 867-0200
302 Cross Creek Mall Fayetteville (28303) *(G-4631)*

Luxottica of America Inc............ 919 778-5692
611 N Berkeley Blvd Ste B Goldsboro (27534) *(G-5226)*

Luxuriously Natural Soaps LLC............ 910 378-9064
3620 Wilmington Hwy Jacksonville (28540) *(G-7130)*

Lxd Research & Display LLC............ 919 600-6440
7516 Precision Dr Ste 100 Raleigh (27617) *(G-10263)*

Lydall Inc............ 336 468-8522
1241 Buck Shoals Rd Hamptonville (27020) *(G-6087)*

Lydall Inc............ 336 468-1323
2029 Anna Dr Yadkinville (27055) *(G-13446)*

Lydech Thermal Acoustical Inc (HQ)............ 248 277-4900
1245 Buck Shoals Rd Hamptonville (27020) *(G-6088)*

Lydech Thermal Acoustical Inc............ 336 468-8522
1241 Buck Shoals Rd Hamptonville (27020) *(G-6089)*

Lyerlys Wldg & Fabrication Inc............ 704 680-2317
215 Woodson Rd Gold Hill (28071) *(G-5195)*

Lyf-Tym Building Products, Charlotte *Also Called: Beacon Roofing Supply Inc (G-1763)*

Lynchs Office Supply Co Inc (PA)............ 252 537-6041
921 Roanoke Ave Roanoke Rapids (27870) *(G-10740)*

Lyndon Steel Company LLC (DH)............ 336 785-0848
1947 Union Cross Rd Winston Salem (27107) *(G-13241)*

Lynn Electronics Corporation............ 704 369-0093
5409 Shoreview Dr Concord (28025) *(G-3397)*

Lynn Jones Race Cars............ 252 522-0705
1168 Woodington Rd Kinston (28504) *(G-7420)*

Lynn Ladder Scaffolding Co Inc............ 301 336-4700
3801 Corporation Cir Charlotte (28216) *(G-2443)*

Lyon Apartments, Wadesboro *Also Called: Lyon Company (G-12248)*

Lyon Company............ 919 787-0024
208 S Rutherford St Wadesboro (28170) *(G-12248)*

Lyon Logging............ 336 957-3131
3256 S Center Church Rd Thurmond (28683) *(G-12098)*

Lyon Metal & Supply, Hildebran *Also Called: Lyon Roofing Inc (G-6853)*

Lyon Roofing Inc............ 828 397-2301
323 S Center St Hildebran (28637) *(G-6853)*

Lyons Hosiery Inc............ 336 789-2651
719 S South St Mount Airy (27030) *(G-9150)*

M & A Equipment Inc (PA)............ 704 703-9400
156 Exmore Rd Ste 100 Mooresville (28117) *(G-8715)*

M & G Polymers Usa LLC............ 910 509-4414
1979 Eastwood Rd Wilmington (28403) *(G-12843)*

M & G Screen Service, Sanford *Also Called: Ralph B Hall (G-11223)*

M & J Marine LLC............ 252 249-0522
1218 Lupton Dr Oriental (28571) *(G-9601)*

M & J Stucco LLC............ 704 634-2249
Monroe (28111) *(G-8521)*

M & K Logging LLC............ 252 349-8975
310 Parker Rd New Bern (28562) *(G-9376)*

M & M Electric Service Inc............ 704 867-0221
1680 Garfield Dr Gastonia (28052) *(G-5081)*

M & M Electric Service NC, Gastonia *Also Called: M & M Electric Service Inc (G-5081)*

M & M Frame Company Inc............ 336 859-8166
18847 S Nc Highway 109 Denton (27239) *(G-3757)*

M & M Graphics, Charlotte *Also Called: S&A Marketing Inc (G-2746)*

M & M Signs and Awnings Inc............ 336 352-4300
1465 Ladonia Church Rd Mount Airy (27030) *(G-9151)*

M & M Stone Sculpting & Engrv............ 336 877-3842
498 Carter Miller Rd Todd (28684) *(G-12104)*

M & M Technology Inc............ 704 882-9432
7711 Idlewild Rd Indian Trail (28079) *(G-7090)*

M & M Tire and Auto Inc............ 336 643-7877
5570 Spotswood Cir Summerfield (27358) *(G-11843)*

M & N Equipment Rental, Colfax *Also Called: M&N Construction Supply Inc (G-3283)*

M & P Polymers Inc............ 910 246-6585
135 Applecross Rd Pinehurst (28374) *(G-9695)*

M & R Forestry Service Inc............ 980 439-1261
24062 Sam Rd Albemarle (28001) *(G-80)*

M & R Retreading & Oil Co Inc.................... 704 474-4101
  337 W Whitley St Norwood (28128) *(G-9556)*

M & S Manufacturing, Lenoir *Also Called: M & S Warehouse Inc (G-7622)*

M & S Systems, Kernersville *Also Called: M & S Systems Inc (G-7283)*

M & S Systems Inc.. 336 996-7118
  951 Nc Highway 66 S Ste 6b Kernersville (27284) *(G-7283)*

M & S Warehouse Inc (PA)......................... 828 728-3733
  1712 Hickory Blvd Sw Lenoir (28645) *(G-7622)*

M & W Fab, Smithfield *Also Called: Ace Fabrication Inc (G-11433)*

M 5 Scentific Glassblowing Inc.................. 704 663-0101
  706c Performance Rd Mooresville (28115) *(G-8716)*

M A I N, Asheville *Also Called: Mountain Area Info Netwrk (G-552)*

M and M Docks LLC..................................... 336 537-0092
  10235 Nc Highway 8 Lexington (27292) *(G-7714)*

M and R Inc.. 704 332-5999
  820 E 7th St Ste C Charlotte (28202) *(G-2444)*

M B C I, Cary *Also Called: Nci Group Inc (G-1405)*

M C B Displays, Greensboro *Also Called: Quality Prtg Cartridge Fctry (G-5779)*

M C C of Laurinburg Inc............................. 910 276-0519
  200 Johns Rd Laurinburg (28352) *(G-7506)*

M C H, Concord *Also Called: Moores Cylinder Heads LLC (G-3404)*

M D I, Shelby *Also Called: Modern Densifying Inc (G-11363)*

M D N Cabinets, Garner *Also Called: MDN Cabinets Inc (G-4940)*

M D Prevatt Inc.. 919 796-4944
  338 Winding Oak Way Clayton (27520) *(G-3158)*

M F C Inc.. 252 322-5004
  Hwy 33 Aurora (27806) *(G-643)*

M G Newell Corporation (PA)..................... 336 393-0100
  301 Citation Ct Greensboro (27409) *(G-5668)*

M Grill, Charlotte *Also Called: 3nine USA Inc (G-1602)*

M H Investments, Fayetteville *Also Called: Muriel Harris Investments Inc (G-4644)*

M I, Durham *Also Called: Measurement Incorporated (G-4122)*

M I Connection... 704 662-3255
  435 S Broad St Mooresville (28115) *(G-8717)*

M M & D Harvesting Inc.............................. 252 793-4074
  385 Roxie Reese Rd Plymouth (27962) *(G-9806)*

M M M Inc (PA)... 252 527-0229
  501 W Railroad St La Grange (28551) *(G-7469)*

M O Deviney Lumber Co Inc (PA)............... 704 538-9071
  838 Moriah School Rd Casar (28020) *(G-1489)*

M P I Lable Systems Carolina, Charlotte *Also Called: Miller Products Inc (G-2505)*

M S I Precision Machine Inc....................... 704 629-9375
  725 E Maine Ave Bessemer City (28016) *(G-825)*

M T I, Mills River *Also Called: Medical Cable Specialists Inc (G-8317)*

M T Industries Inc...................................... 828 697-2864
  1584 Airport Rd Hendersonville (28792) *(G-6222)*

M T N of Pinellas Inc.................................. 727 823-1650
  135 Crowne Chase Dr Apt 16 Winston Salem (27104) *(G-13242)*

M-B Industries Inc...................................... 828 862-4201
  9205 Rosman Hwy Rosman (28772) *(G-10913)*

M-M Components, Denton *Also Called: M & M Frame Company Inc (G-3757)*

M-Prints Inc... 828 265-4929
  713 W King St Boone (28607) *(G-931)*

M.C. Exteriors, Fuquay Varina *Also Called: E & M Concrete Inc (G-4880)*

M&J Oldco Inc.. 336 854-0309
  3515 W Market St Ste 200 Greensboro (27403) *(G-5669)*

M&N Construction Supply Inc..................... 336 996-7740
  8431 Norcross Rd Colfax (27235) *(G-3283)*

M&N Construction Supply Inc..................... 910 791-0908
  323 Eastwood Rd Ste A Wilmington (28403) *(G-12844)*

M&S Enterprises Inc................................... 910 259-1763
  784 New Rd Burgaw (28425) *(G-1027)*

M2 Optics Inc... 919 342-5619
  5621 Departure Dr Ste 117 Raleigh (27616) *(G-10264)*

M3 Products Com....................................... 631 938-1245
  1537 Golden Rain Dr Matthews (28104) *(G-8180)*

Maa Umiya Inc... 410 818-6811
  1141 Lenoir Rhyne Blvd Se Hickory (28602) *(G-6390)*

Maag Reduction Inc (HQ)........................... 704 716-9000
  9401 Southern Pine Blvd Ste Q Charlotte (28273) *(G-2445)*

Mables Headstone & Monu Co LLP (PA)..... 919 724-8705
  206 West Wilton Ave Creedmoor (27522) *(G-3652)*

Mabry Industries Inc.................................. 336 584-1311
  2903 Gibsonville Ossipee Rd Elon College (27244) *(G-4474)*

MAC Grading Co... 910 531-4642
  971 Leroy Autry Rd Autryville (28318) *(G-649)*

Mac Panel, High Point *Also Called: Mac Panel Company LLC (G-6694)*

Mac Panel Company LLC (PA)..................... 336 861-3100
  551 W Fairfield Rd High Point (27263) *(G-6694)*

Mac-Vann Inc... 919 577-0746
  1650 Colon Rd Sanford (27330) *(G-11206)*

Mac/Fab Company Inc................................ 704 822-1103
  913 W Catawba Ave Mount Holly (28120) *(G-9236)*

Machine Builders & Design Inc.................. 704 482-3456
  806 N Post Rd Shelby (28150) *(G-11355)*

Machine Consulting Svcs Inc..................... 919 596-3033
  1545 Cooper St Durham (27703) *(G-4114)*

Machine Control Company Inc.................... 704 708-5782
  1030 Industrial Dr Matthews (28105) *(G-8128)*

Machine Shop, Mooresville *Also Called: Island Machining LLC (G-8697)*

Machine Shop, Wilmington *Also Called: Penco Precision LLC (G-12873)*

Machine Shop of Charlotte, The, Mount Holly *Also Called: Modern Mold & Tool Company (G-9238)*

Machine Shop, Job Shop, Burlington *Also Called: L & K Machining Inc (G-1116)*

Machine Specialties LLC............................ 336 603-1919
  6511 Franz Warner Pkwy Whitsett (27377) *(G-12613)*

Machinery Sales... 704 822-0110
  7659 Old Plank Rd Stanley (28164) *(G-11621)*

Machinery Sales and Service, Stanley *Also Called: Machinery Sales (G-11621)*

Machinex.. 336 665-5030
  716 Gallimore Dairy Rd High Point (27265) *(G-6695)*

Machinex Technologies Inc........................ 773 867-8801
  716 Gallimore Dairy Rd High Point (27265) *(G-6696)*

Machining, Statesville *Also Called: D & D Machine Works Inc (G-11682)*

Machining Solutions Inc............................. 704 528-5436
  102 Corporate Dr Troutman (28166) *(G-12145)*

Machining Technology Services.................. 704 282-1071
  1817 N Rocky River Rd Monroe (28110) *(G-8522)*

Mack Molding Company Inc........................ 704 878-9641
  149 Water Tank Rd Statesville (28677) *(G-11728)*

Mack S Liver Mush Inc............................... 704 434-6188
  6126 Mckee Rd Shelby (28150) *(G-11356)*

Mack Trucks Inc (HQ)................................ 336 291-9001
  7900 National Service Rd Greensboro (27409) *(G-5670)*

Mack's Livermush & Meats, Shelby *Also Called: Mack S Liver Mush Inc (G-11356)*

Macleod Construction Inc (PA)................... 704 483-3580
  4304 Northpointe Industrial Blvd Charlotte (28216) *(G-2446)*

Maco Inc.. 704 434-6800
  521 Plato Lee Rd Shelby (28150) *(G-11357)*

Macom Technology Solutions Inc............... 919 407-4768
  3028 Cornwallis Rd Ste 200 Durham (27709) *(G-4115)*

Macom Technology Solutions Inc............... 919 807-9100
  523 Davis Dr Ste 500 Morrisville (27560) *(G-9016)*

Macon Printing, Franklin *Also Called: Drake Enterprises Ltd (G-4824)*

Macs Farms Sausage Co Inc....................... 910 594-0095
  209 Raleigh St Newton Grove (28366) *(G-9516)*

Made By Custom LLC.................................. 704 980-9840
  3206 N Davidson St Charlotte (28205) *(G-2447)*

Madem-Moorecraft Reels USA Inc.............. 252 823-2510
  3006 Anaconda Rd Tarboro (27886) *(G-11933)*

Madern Usa Inc.. 919 363-4248
  1010 Burma Dr Apex (27539) *(G-177)*

Madison Ave, Concord *Also Called: Minka Lighting Inc (G-3403)*

Madison Company Inc (PA)......................... 336 548-9624
  200 W Academy St Madison (27025) *(G-7992)*

Madison Manufacturing Company............... 828 622-7500
  172 S Andrews Ave Hot Springs (28743) *(G-6933)*

Madix.. 804 456-3007
  2326 Hales Rd Raleigh (27608) *(G-10265)*

Mafic USA LLC.. 704 967-8006
  119 Metrolina Plz Shelby (28150) *(G-11358)*

Magazine Nakia Lashawn..919 875-1156
   2833 Roundleaf Ct Raleigh (27604) *(G-10266)*

Maggie Valley Sanitary Dst, Maggie Valley *Also Called: Town of Maggie Valley Inc (G-8006)*

Magic Factory LLC..919 585-5644
   3818 Somerset Dr Durham (27707) *(G-4116)*

Magic Mile Media Inc...252 572-1330
   105 W Blount St Kinston (28501) *(G-7421)*

Magna Composites LLC..704 797-8744
   6701 Statesville Blvd Salisbury (28147) *(G-11088)*

Magna Machining Inc...704 463-9904
   111 3rd Park Dr Richfield (28137) *(G-10719)*

Magnera Corporation (PA)......................................866 744-7380
   9335 Harris Corners Pkwy Ste 300 Charlotte (28269) *(G-2448)*

Magnet America, King *Also Called: Magnet America Intl Inc (G-7330)*

Magnet America Intl Inc...336 985-0320
   512 Newsome Rd King (27021) *(G-7330)*

Magnet Guys..855 624-4897
   720 Industrial Park Ave Asheboro (27205) *(G-375)*

Magnevolt Inc...919 553-2202
   5335 Us 70 Bus Hwy W Clayton (27520) *(G-3159)*

Magnificent Concessions LLC................................919 413-1558
   106 Northwinds North Dr Wendell (27591) *(G-12538)*

Magnolia Linen Inc..336 449-0447
   106 E Railroad Ave Gibsonville (27249) *(G-5182)*

Magnum Enterprize Inc..252 524-5391
   525 Country Acres Rd Grifton (28530) *(G-6037)*

Magnum Manufacturing LLC...................................704 983-1340
   40867 Airport Rd New London (28127) *(G-9419)*

Magnum Telemetry, Grifton *Also Called: Magnum Enterprize Inc (G-6037)*

Magnussen, Greensboro *Also Called: Magnussen Home Furnishings Inc (G-5671)*

Magnussen Home Furnishings Inc (HQ)..................336 841-4424
   4523 Green Point Dr Ste 109 Greensboro (27410) *(G-5671)*

Mahle Motorsports Inc...888 255-1942
   270 Rutledge Rd Unit C Fletcher (28732) *(G-4750)*

Mail Box Book Company, The, Greensboro *Also Called: M&J Oldco Inc (G-5669)*

Mail Management Services LLC..............................828 236-0076
   88 Roberts St Asheville (28801) *(G-541)*

Mailbox, The, Oak Ridge *Also Called: Education Center LLC (G-9571)*

Mailing Solutions Plus, Mooresville *Also Called: Executive Promotions Inc (G-8661)*

Main Filter LLC..704 735-0009
   1443 E Gaston St Lincolnton (28092) *(G-7841)*

Main Street Rag Publishing Co...............................704 573-2516
   4614 Wilgrove Mint Hill Rd Ste G3 Mint Hill (28227) *(G-8339)*

Mainetti Usa Inc..828 844-0105
   101 Mills Gap Rd Fletcher (28732) *(G-4751)*

Majestic Xpress Handwash Inc..............................919 440-7611
   103 N John St Ste D Goldsboro (27530) *(G-5227)*

Major Display Inc (PA)...800 260-1067
   131 Franklin Plaza Dr Ste 363 Franklin (28734) *(G-4836)*

Majorpower Corporation...919 563-6610
   7011 Industrial Dr Mebane (27302) *(G-8251)*

Make An Impression Inc...919 557-7400
   202 Premier Dr Holly Springs (27540) *(G-6907)*

Make Solutions Inc..623 444-0098
   23 Tacoma St Asheville (28801) *(G-542)*

Makemine Inc...704 906-7164
   805 Pressley Rd Ste 109 Charlotte (28217) *(G-2449)*

Makhteshim Agan North Amer Inc (DH)...................919 256-9300
   8601 Six Forks Rd Ste 300 Raleigh (27615) *(G-10267)*

Mallard Creek Polymers, Charlotte *Also Called: Mallard Creek Polymers LLC (G-2451)*

Mallard Creek Polymers LLC..................................704 547-0622
   14800 Mallard Creek Rd Charlotte (28262) *(G-2450)*

Mallard Creek Polymers LLC (PA)...........................704 547-0622
   8901 Research Dr Charlotte (28262) *(G-2451)*

Mallard Creek Polymers LLC..................................877 240-0171
   2800 Morehead Rd Charlotte (28262) *(G-2452)*

Mallard Creek Polymers LLC..................................704 547-0622
   2388 Speedrail Dr Harrisburg (28075) *(G-6112)*

Mallinckrodt LLC..919 878-2800
   8801 Capital Blvd Raleigh (27616) *(G-10268)*

Mallinckrodt LLC..919 878-2900
   8800 Durant Rd Raleigh (27616) *(G-10269)*

Mammoth Machine and Design LLC........................704 727-3330
   197 Pitt Rd Mooresville (28115) *(G-8718)*

Man Lift, Shelby *Also Called: If Armor International LLC (G-11346)*

Man Lift Mfg Co...414 486-1760
   2501 W Dixon Blvd Shelby (28152) *(G-11359)*

Mana Nutrition, Matthews *Also Called: Mana Nutritive Aid Pdts Inc (G-8129)*

Mana Nutritive Aid Pdts Inc (PA)............................855 438-6262
   130 Library Ln Ste A Matthews (28105) *(G-8129)*

Mang Systems Inc..704 292-1041
   500 Union West Blvd Ste B Matthews (28104) *(G-8181)*

Manhattan Amrcn Terrazzo Strip.............................336 622-4247
   2433 Us Hwy 421 Staley (27355) *(G-11596)*

Mann Custom Boats Inc...252 473-1716
   6300 Us Highway 64 # 264 Manns Harbor (27953) *(G-8020)*

Mann Media Inc..336 286-0600
   800 Green Valley Rd Ste 106 Greensboro (27408) *(G-5672)*

Mann+hmmel Fltrtion Tech Group (DH)....................704 869-3300
   1 Wix Way Gastonia (28053) *(G-5082)*

Mann+hmmel Fltrtion Tech Intrm (DH).....................704 869-3300
   1 Wix Way Gastonia (28054) *(G-5083)*

Mann+hmmel Fltrtion Tech US LL............................704 869-3700
   1 Wix Way Gastonia (28054) *(G-5084)*

Mann+hmmel Fltrtion Tech US LL (DH).....................704 869-3300
   1 Wix Way Gastonia (28054) *(G-5085)*

Mann+hmmel Prlator Filters LLC (DH).....................910 425-4181
   3200 Natal St Ste 64069 Fayetteville (28306) *(G-4632)*

Mann+hmmel Prlator Filters LLC.............................910 425-4181
   3200 Natal St Fayetteville (28306) *(G-4633)*

Mann+hmmel Prlator Filters LLC.............................704 869-3441
   1 Wix Way Gastonia (28054) *(G-5086)*

Mann+hummel Filtration Technol..............................704 869-3500
   2900 Northwest Blvd Gastonia (28052) *(G-5087)*

Mann+hummel Filtration Technol..............................704 869-3952
   1551 Mount Olive Church Rd Gastonia (28052) *(G-5088)*

Mann+hummel Filtration Technol..............................704 869-3501
   2900 Northwest Blvd Gastonia (28052) *(G-5089)*

Mann+hummel Filtration Technology Holdings Inc......704 869-3300
   1 Wix Way Gastonia (28054) *(G-5090)*

Manna Corp North Carolina (PA).............................828 696-3642
   508 N Main St Hendersonville (28792) *(G-6223)*

Manna Designs, Hendersonville *Also Called: Manna Corp North Carolina (G-6223)*

Mannhmmel Fltration Tech Group, Gastonia *Also Called: Mann+hmmel Fltrtion Tech US LL (G-5085)*

Manning and Co., Pinehurst *Also Called: Manning Fabrics Inc (G-9696)*

Manning Building Products LLC...............................919 662-9894
   108 Professional Ct Ste A Garner (27529) *(G-4937)*

Manning Fabrics Inc...910 295-1970
   42028 Us 1 Hwy Pinebluff (28373) *(G-9687)*

Manning Fabrics Inc (PA)..910 295-1970
   650a Page St Pinehurst (28374) *(G-9696)*

Mannington Mills Inc..336 884-5600
   210 N Pendleton St High Point (27260) *(G-6697)*

Mannington Mills Inc..704 824-3551
   200 Saxony Dr Mc Adenville (28101) *(G-8214)*

Manroy Defense Systems, Spindale *Also Called: Manroy Usa LLC (G-11548)*

Manroy Usa LLC...828 286-9274
   159 Yelton St Spindale (28160) *(G-11548)*

Mantissa Corporation...704 525-1749
   616 Pressley Rd Charlotte (28217) *(G-2453)*

Mantissa Material Handling, Charlotte *Also Called: Mantissa Corporation (G-2453)*

Manual Woodworkers Weavers Inc (PA)...................828 692-7333
   3737 Howard Gap Rd Hendersonville (28792) *(G-6224)*

Manufactur LLC..919 937-2090
   201 W Main St Durham (27701) *(G-4117)*

Manufacturer, Hickory *Also Called: Purthermal LLC (G-6422)*

Manufacturer, Indian Trail *Also Called: Sunseeker North America Inc (G-7101)*

Manufacturing, Fuquay Varina *Also Called: Boehrnger Inglheim Anmal Hlth (G-4871)*

Manufacturing, Raleigh *Also Called: Progress Solar Solutions LLC (G-10401)*

Manufacturing, Sanford *Also Called: Black Collection Apparel LLC (G-11156)*

Manufacturing Methods LLC...................................910 371-1700
   9244 Industrial Blvd Ne Leland (28451) *(G-7553)*

Manufacturing Services Inc................................704 629-4163
725 E Maine Ave Bessemer City (28016) *(G-826)*

Manufacturing Systems Eqp Inc......................704 283-2086
2812 Chamber Dr Monroe (28110) *(G-8523)*

Maola Milk and Ice Cream Co..........................252 756-3160
107 Hungate Dr Greenville (27858) *(G-6002)*

Maola Milk and Ice Cream Co..........................844 287-1970
307 N First Ave New Bern (28560) *(G-9377)*

MAOLA MILK AND ICE CREAM COMPANY, Greenville *Also Called: Maola Milk and Ice Cream Co (G-6002)*

Map Shop LLC..704 332-5557
3421 St Vardell Ln Ste H Charlotte (28217) *(G-2454)*

Map Supply Inc..336 731-3230
132 Poplar Loop Dr Flat Rock (28731) *(G-4710)*

Mapjoy LLC...919 450-8360
4501 Marena Pl Durham (27707) *(G-4118)*

Maple View Ice Cream.....................................919 960-5535
6900 Rocky Ridge Rd Hillsborough (27278) *(G-6872)*

Maplewood Imaging Ctr...................................336 397-6000
3155 Maplewood Ave Winston Salem (27103) *(G-13243)*

Maranz Inc...336 996-7776
2860 Lowery St Winston Salem (27101) *(G-13244)*

Marbach America Inc..704 644-4900
100 Forsyth Hall Dr Ste B Charlotte (28273) *(G-2455)*

Marc Machine Works Inc.................................704 865-3625
5042 York Hwy Gastonia (28052) *(G-5091)*

Marcal Paper Mills LLC...................................828 322-1805
612 3rd Ave Ne Hickory (28601) *(G-6391)*

March Furniture Manufacturing Inc..................336 824-4413
447 Reed Creek Rd Ramseur (27316) *(G-10629)*

Marco Pproducts, New Bern *Also Called: Marco Products Inc (G-9378)*

Marco Products Inc...215 956-0313
214 Kale Rd New Bern (28562) *(G-9378)*

Marcon International Inc..................................704 455-9400
5679 Harrisburg Ind Pk Dr Harrisburg (28075) *(G-6113)*

Marian Manufacturing Plant, Marion *Also Called: ABB Motors and Mechanical Inc (G-8029)*

Marietta Martin Materials Inc...........................704 525-7740
8701 Red Oak Blvd Ste 540 Charlotte (28217) *(G-2456)*

Marietta Martin Materials Inc...........................252 749-2641
5368 Allen Gay Rd Fountain (27829) *(G-4806)*

Marietta Martin Materials Inc...........................919 772-3563
1111 E Garner Rd Garner (27529) *(G-4938)*

Marietta Martin Materials Inc...........................336 668-3253
413 S Chimney Rock Rd Greensboro (27409) *(G-5673)*

Marietta Martin Materials Inc...........................828 322-8386
1989 11th Ave Se Hickory (28602) *(G-6392)*

Marietta Martin Materials Inc...........................336 886-5015
5725 Riverdale Dr Jamestown (27282) *(G-7171)*

Marietta Martin Materials Inc...........................336 769-3803
4572 High Point Rd Kernersville (27284) *(G-7284)*

Marietta Martin Materials Inc...........................704 739-4761
181 Quarry Rd Kings Mountain (28086) *(G-7372)*

Marietta Martin Materials Inc...........................910 743-6471
2998 Belgrade Swansboro Rd Maysville (28555) *(G-8211)*

Marietta Martin Materials Inc...........................704 283-4915
2111 N Rocky River Rd Monroe (28110) *(G-8524)*

Marietta Martin Materials Inc...........................919 788-4392
6028 Triangle Dr Raleigh (27617) *(G-10270)*

Marietta Martin Materials Inc...........................336 349-3333
7639 Nc Highway 87 Reidsville (27320) *(G-10692)*

Marietta Martin Materials Inc...........................704 636-6372
3825 Trexler St Salisbury (28147) *(G-11089)*

Marietta Martin Materials Inc...........................704 873-8191
220 Quarry Rd Statesville (28677) *(G-11729)*

Marietta Martin Materials Inc...........................704 278-2218
720 Quarry Rd Woodleaf (27054) *(G-13429)*

Marilyn Cook..704 735-4414
2628 Buffalo Forest Rd Lincolnton (28092) *(G-7842)*

Marine & Industrial Plastics............................252 224-1000
Hwy 17 Sermon Lane Pollocksville (28573) *(G-9817)*

Marine Fabrications LLC.................................252 473-4767
31 Beverly Dr Wanchese (27981) *(G-12345)*

Marine Systems Inc..828 254-5354
7 Westside Dr Asheville (28806) *(G-543)*

Marine Tooling Technology Inc........................336 887-9577
2100 E Martin Luther King Jr Dr Ste 106 High Point (27260) *(G-6698)*

Marinemax, Wrightsville Beach *Also Called: Marinemax of North Carolina (G-13432)*

Marinemax of North Carolina..........................910 256-8100
130 Short St Wrightsville Beach (28480) *(G-13432)*

Marion Cultured Marble Inc.............................828 724-4782
4805 Us 70 W Marion (28752) *(G-8049)*

Marion Machine Div, Marion *Also Called: Superior Machine Co SC Inc (G-8068)*

Marion Machine LLC..800 627-1639
169 Machine Shop Rd Marion (28752) *(G-8050)*

Marius Pharmaceuticals LLC..........................919 374-1913
2301 Sugar Bush Rd Ste 510 Raleigh (27612) *(G-10271)*

Mark III Logging Inc...910 862-4820
16324 Nc Highway 87 W Tar Heel (28392) *(G-11917)*

Mark Stoddard...910 797-7214
1935 Brawley Ave Fayetteville (28314) *(G-4634)*

Mark Trece, Greensboro *Also Called: Mark/Trece Inc (G-5674)*

Mark/Trece Inc..973 884-1005
902 Norwalk St Greensboro (27407) *(G-5674)*

Mark/Trece Inc..336 292-3424
6799 Leaf Crest Dr Apt 2c Whitsett (27377) *(G-12614)*

Markell Printing and Prom Pdts, Burlington *Also Called: Markell Publishing Company Inc (G-1122)*

Markell Publishing Company Inc......................336 226-7148
718 E Davis St Burlington (27215) *(G-1122)*

Market Depot USA Nc Inc...............................888 417-8685
4501 Green Point Dr Ste 500 Greensboro (27410) *(G-5675)*

Market of Raleigh LLC.....................................919 212-2100
4111 New Bern Ave Raleigh (27610) *(G-10272)*

Marketing One Sportswear Inc.......................704 334-9333
3101 Yorkmont Rd Ste 1100 Charlotte (28208) *(G-2457)*

Markraft Cabinets Direct Sales........................910 762-1986
2705 Castle Creek Ln Wilmington (28401) *(G-12845)*

Marlatex Corporation.......................................704 829-7797
8425 Winged Bourne Charlotte (28210) *(G-2458)*

Marley Company LLC (DH)..............................704 752-4400
13515 Ballantyne Corporate Pl Charlotte (28277) *(G-2459)*

Marlin Company Inc..828 758-9999
1211 Underdown Ave Sw Lenoir (28645) *(G-7623)*

Marlin Company Inc (HQ)...............................828 754-0980
1333 Virginia St Sw Lenoir (28645) *(G-7624)*

Marlinwoodworks LLC.....................................919 343-2605
50 Otto Rd Lillington (27546) *(G-7800)*

Marlowe Loans Sales, High Point *Also Called: Marlowe-Van Loan Corporation (G-6699)*

Marlowe-Van Loan Corporation.......................336 886-7126
1224 W Ward Ave High Point (27260) *(G-6699)*

Marlowe-Van Loan Sales Co...........................336 882-3351
1224 W Ward Ave High Point (27260) *(G-6700)*

Marmon Engine Controls LLC.........................843 701-5145
2519 Dana Dr Laurinburg (28352) *(G-7507)*

Marmon Holdings Inc......................................910 291-2571
2519 Dana Dr Laurinburg (28352) *(G-7508)*

Marmon Powertrain Controls, Aberdeen *Also Called: Rostra Precision Controls Inc (G-23)*

Marmonpowertrain, Laurinburg *Also Called: Marmon Engine Controls LLC (G-7507)*

Marpac LLC (PA)..910 602-1421
3870 Us Highway 421 N Wilmington (28401) *(G-12846)*

Marquis Contract Corporation (PA)..................336 884-8200
231 South Rd High Point (27262) *(G-6701)*

Marquis Seating, High Point *Also Called: Marquis Contract Corporation (G-6701)*

Mars Petcare Us Inc.......................................252 438-1600
845 Commerce Dr Henderson (27537) *(G-6166)*

Marsh Furniture Company................................336 229-5122
605 W Harden St Graham (27253) *(G-5277)*

Marsh Furniture Company................................336 273-8196
2503 Greengate Dr Greensboro (27406) *(G-5676)*

Marsh Furniture Company................................336 884-7393
1015 S Centennial St High Point (27260) *(G-6702)*

Marsh Furniture Company (PA).......................336 884-7363
1001 S Centennial St High Point (27260) *(G-6703)*

Marsh Kitchens, High Point *Also Called: Marsh Furniture Company (G-6703)*

Marsh Kitchens of High Point, High Point *Also Called: Marsh Furniture Company (G-6702)*

Marsh-Armfield Incorporated... 336 882-4175
1237 Hickory Chapel Rd High Point (27260) *(G-6704)*

Marshall Air Systems Inc.. 704 525-6230
419 Peachtree Dr S Charlotte (28217) *(G-2460)*

Marshall Group of NC Inc... 252 638-8585
2400 Trent Rd New Bern (28562) *(G-9379)*

Marshall Middleby Inc... 919 762-1000
1100 Old Honeycutt Rd Fuquay Varina (27526) *(G-4887)*

Marshall USA LLC.. 301 481-1241
7130 Bentley Rd Greensboro (27409) *(G-5677)*

Marties Miniatures... 336 869-5952
392 Northbridge Dr High Point (27265) *(G-6705)*

Martin Industries, Albemarle *Also Called: Ram Industries Inc (G-87)*

Martin Innovations, Rocky Mount *Also Called: Martin Manufacturing Co LLC (G-10850)*

Martin Logging, Bostic *Also Called: Eric Martin Jermey (G-962)*

Martin Lumber & Mulch LLC.. 252 935-5294
301 Mainstem Rd Pantego (27860) *(G-9646)*

Martin Manufacturing Co LLC.. 919 741-5439
2585 Eastern Ave Rocky Mount (27804) *(G-10850)*

Martin Marietta, Garner *Also Called: Marietta Martin Materials Inc (G-4938)*

Martin Marietta, Raleigh *Also Called: Martin Marietta Magnesia Specialties LLC (G-10273)*

Martin Marietta, Raleigh *Also Called: Martin Marietta Materials Inc (G-10277)*

Martin Marietta, Randleman *Also Called: Martin Marietta Materials Inc (G-10652)*

Martin Marietta Aggregates, Benson *Also Called: Martin Marietta Materials Inc (G-794)*

Martin Marietta Aggregates, Burlington *Also Called: Martin Marietta Materials Inc (G-1123)*

Martin Marietta Aggregates, Castle Hayne *Also Called: Martin Marietta Materials Inc (G-1505)*

Martin Marietta Aggregates, Charlotte *Also Called: Marietta Martin Materials Inc (G-2456)*

Martin Marietta Aggregates, Charlotte *Also Called: Martin Marietta Materials Inc (G-2461)*

Martin Marietta Aggregates, Charlotte *Also Called: Martin Marietta Materials Inc (G-2462)*

Martin Marietta Aggregates, Charlotte *Also Called: Martin Marietta Materials Inc (G-2463)*

Martin Marietta Aggregates, China Grove *Also Called: Martin Marietta Materials Inc (G-3076)*

Martin Marietta Aggregates, Concord *Also Called: Martin Marietta Materials Inc (G-3398)*

Martin Marietta Aggregates, Fountain *Also Called: Marietta Martin Materials Inc (G-4806)*

Martin Marietta Aggregates, Fuquay Varina *Also Called: Martin Marietta Materials Inc (G-4888)*

Martin Marietta Aggregates, Greensboro *Also Called: Marietta Martin Materials Inc (G-5673)*

Martin Marietta Aggregates, Greensboro *Also Called: Martin Marietta Materials Inc (G-5678)*

Martin Marietta Aggregates, Greensboro *Also Called: Martin Marietta Materials Inc (G-5679)*

Martin Marietta Aggregates, Hickory *Also Called: Marietta Martin Materials Inc (G-6392)*

Martin Marietta Aggregates, Kings Mountain *Also Called: Marietta Martin Materials Inc (G-7372)*

Martin Marietta Aggregates, Landis *Also Called: Martin Marietta Materials Inc (G-7474)*

Martin Marietta Aggregates, Leland *Also Called: Martin Marietta Materials Inc (G-7554)*

Martin Marietta Aggregates, Lenoir *Also Called: Martin Marietta Materials Inc (G-7625)*

Martin Marietta Aggregates, Maysville *Also Called: Marietta Martin Materials Inc (G-8211)*

Martin Marietta Aggregates, Monroe *Also Called: Marietta Martin Materials Inc (G-8524)*

Martin Marietta Aggregates, New Bern *Also Called: Martin Marietta Materials Inc (G-9380)*

Martin Marietta Aggregates, Raleigh *Also Called: Marietta Martin Materials Inc (G-10270)*

Martin Marietta Aggregates, Raleigh *Also Called: Marietta Martin Materials Inc (G-10276)*

Martin Marietta Aggregates, Randleman *Also Called: Martin Marietta Materials Inc (G-10651)*

Martin Marietta Aggregates, Reidsville *Also Called: Marietta Martin Materials Inc (G-10692)*

Martin Marietta Aggregates, Richlands *Also Called: Martin Marietta Materials Inc (G-10721)*

Martin Marietta Aggregates, Salisbury *Also Called: Marietta Martin Materials Inc (G-11089)*

Martin Marietta Aggregates, Sanford *Also Called: Martin Marietta Materials Inc (G-11207)*

Martin Marietta Aggregates, Statesville *Also Called: Marietta Martin Materials Inc (G-11729)*

Martin Marietta Aggregates, Woodleaf *Also Called: Marietta Martin Materials Inc (G-13429)*

Martin Marietta Magnesia Specialties LLC (HQ)................... 800 648-7400
4123 Parklake Ave Raleigh (27612) *(G-10273)*

Martin Marietta Materials Inc.. 919 894-2003
13661 Raleigh Rd Benson (27504) *(G-794)*

Martin Marietta Materials Inc.. 336 584-8875
1671 Huffman Mill Rd Burlington (27215) *(G-1123)*

Martin Marietta Materials Inc.. 910 675-2283
5408 Holly Shelter Rd Castle Hayne (28429) *(G-1505)*

Martin Marietta Materials Inc.. 910 602-6058
5635 Holly Shelter Rd Castle Hayne (28429) *(G-1506)*

Martin Marietta Materials Inc.. 919 929-7131
1807 Hwy 54 W Chapel Hill (27516) *(G-1554)*

Martin Marietta Materials Inc.. 704 547-9775
575 E Mallard Creek Church Rd Charlotte (28262) *(G-2461)*

Martin Marietta Materials Inc.. 704 588-1471
11325 Texland Blvd Charlotte (28273) *(G-2462)*

Martin Marietta Materials Inc.. 704 392-1333
4551 Beatties Ford Rd Charlotte (28216) *(G-2463)*

Martin Marietta Materials Inc.. 704 932-4377
2270 China Grove Rd China Grove (28023) *(G-3076)*

Martin Marietta Materials Inc.. 704 786-8415
7219 Weddington Rd Nw Concord (28027) *(G-3398)*

Martin Marietta Materials Inc.. 919 557-7412
7400 Buckhorn Duncan Road Fuquay Varina (27526) *(G-4888)*

Martin Marietta Materials Inc.. 336 375-7584
5800 Eckerson Rd Greensboro (27405) *(G-5678)*

Martin Marietta Materials Inc.. 336 674-0836
3957 Liberty Rd Greensboro (27406) *(G-5679)*

Martin Marietta Materials Inc.. 704 932-4379
Landis (28088) *(G-7474)*

Martin Marietta Materials Inc.. 910 371-3848
1635 Malmo Loop Rd Ne Leland (28451) *(G-7554)*

Martin Marietta Materials Inc.. 828 754-3077
1325 Bradford Mountain Rd Lenoir (28645) *(G-7625)*

Martin Marietta Materials Inc.. 252 633-5308
1315 Old Us 70 W New Bern (28560) *(G-9380)*

Martin Marietta Materials Inc.. 919 664-1700
2235 Gateway Access Pt Ste 400 Raleigh (27607) *(G-10274)*

Martin Marietta Materials Inc.. 360 424-3441
4123 Parklake Ave Raleigh (27612) *(G-10275)*

Martin Marietta Materials Inc.. 919 863-4305
2501 Blue Ridge Rd Raleigh (27607) *(G-10276)*

Martin Marietta Materials Inc (PA)....................................... 919 781-4550
4123 Parklake Ave Raleigh (27612) *(G-10277)*

Martin Marietta Materials Inc.. 336 672-1501
2757 Hopewood Rd Randleman (27317) *(G-10651)*

Martin Marietta Materials Inc.. 336 672-1501
2757 Hopewood Rd Randleman (27317) *(G-10652)*

Martin Marietta Materials Inc.. 910 324-7430
131 Duffy Field Rd Richlands (28574) *(G-10721)*

Martin Marietta Materials Inc.. 919 788-4391
1227 Willett Rd Sanford (27332) *(G-11207)*

Martin Materials Inc... 336 697-1800
4801 Burlington Rd Greensboro (27405) *(G-5680)*

Martin Meats, Godwin *Also Called: Coastal Protein Products Inc (G-5188)*

Martin Obrien Cabinetmaker.. 336 773-1334
1940 Brantley St Winston Salem (27103) *(G-13245)*

Martin Sprocket & Gear Inc... 817 258-3000
306 Bethany Rd Albemarle (28001) *(G-81)*

Martin Sprocket & Gear Inc... 704 394-9111
3901 Scott Futrell Dr Charlotte (28208) *(G-2464)*

Martin Welding Inc... 919 436-8805
816 Old Crowder Dr Garner (27529) *(G-4939)*

Martin Wood Products Inc... 336 548-3470
680 Bald Hill Loop Madison (27025) *(G-7993)*

Martinez Wldg Fabrication Corp... 919 957-8904
2901 Carpenter Pond Rd Raleigh (27613) *(G-10278)*

Martins Fmous Pstry Shoppe Inc.. 800 548-1200
1933 Scott Futrell Dr Charlotte (28208) *(G-2465)*

Martins Fmous Pstry Shoppe Inc.. 800 548-1200
2320 Southern Ave Fayetteville (28306) *(G-4635)*

Martins Fmous Pstry Shoppe Inc.. 800 548-1200
1031 E Mountain St Bldg 314 Kernersville (27284) *(G-7285)*

Martins Woodworking, Lattimore *Also Called: Martins Woodworking LLC (G-7481)*

Martins Woodworking LLC.. 704 473-7617
100 Martin St Lattimore (28089) *(G-7481)*

Marus Dental, Charlotte *Also Called: Dental Equipment LLC (G-2030)*

Marvel-Schbler Arcft Crbrtors... 336 446-0002
2208 Airpark Rd Burlington (27215) *(G-1124)*

Marvell Semiconductor Inc.. 408 222-2500
3015 Carrington Mill Blvd Morrisville (27560) *(G-9017)*

Marves Industries Inc.. 828 397-4400
  205 Cline Park Dr Hildebran (28637) *(G-6854)*

Marvin Bailey Screen Printing.................................. 252 335-1554
  1403 N Road St Elizabeth City (27909) *(G-4397)*

Marx LLC.. 828 396-6700
  4276 Helena St Granite Falls (28630) *(G-5312)*

Marx Industries, Hudson *Also Called: Marx Industries Incorporated (G-6955)*

Marx Industries Incorporated................................. 828 396-6700
  4276 Helena St Hudson (28638) *(G-6955)*

Mary Kay Inc... 336 998-1663
  685 Redland Rd Advance (27006) *(G-35)*

Mary Macks Inc.. 770 234-6333
  214 Armory Dr Clinton (28328) *(G-3234)*

Mas Acme USA... 336 625-2161
  159 North St Asheboro (27203) *(G-376)*

Masco, Mooresville *Also Called: Masco Corporation (G-8719)*

Masco Corporation... 704 658-9646
  344 E Plaza Dr Mooresville (28115) *(G-8719)*

Mason Inlet Distillery LLC..................................... 910 200-4584
  611 Everbreeze Ln Wilmington (28411) *(G-12847)*

Masonboro Sound Machinery Inc............................ 910 452-5090
  4628 Northchase Pkwy Ne Wilmington (28405) *(G-12848)*

Masonite Corporation... 704 599-0235
  7300 Reames Rd Charlotte (28216) *(G-2466)*

Masonite International Corp..................................... 919 575-3700
  1712 E D St Butner (27509) *(G-1202)*

Masonry Reinforcing Corp Amer (PA)...................... 704 525-5554
  400 Rountree Rd Charlotte (28217) *(G-2467)*

Mass Connection Inc.. 910 424-0940
  2828 Enterprise Ave Fayetteville (28306) *(G-4636)*

Mass Enterprises LLC.. 443 585-0732
  4310 Us Highway 70 E New Bern (28560) *(G-9381)*

Massey Ready-Mix Concrete Inc.............................. 336 221-8100
  1421 Railroad St Burlington (27217) *(G-1125)*

Mast General Store Inc.. 423 895-1632
  996 George Wilson Rd Boone (28607) *(G-932)*

Mast General Store CPC, Boone *Also Called: Mast General Store Inc (G-932)*

Mast Woodworks.. 336 468-1194
  5328 Saint Paul Church Rd Hamptonville (27020) *(G-6090)*

Master Displays Inc... 336 884-5575
  5657 Prospect St High Point (27263) *(G-6706)*

Master Form Inc... 704 292-1041
  500 Union West Blvd Ste B Matthews (28104) *(G-8182)*

Master Hatchery, Siler City *Also Called: Mountaire Farms LLC (G-11418)*

Master Kraft Inc... 704 234-2673
  3350 Smith Farm Rd Matthews (28104) *(G-8183)*

Master Machining Inc... 910 675-3660
  410 Hermitage Rd Castle Hayne (28429) *(G-1507)*

Master Marketing Group LLC (PA)........................... 870 932-4491
  4801 Glenwood Ave Ste 310 Raleigh (27612) *(G-10279)*

Master Screens South LLC...................................... 704 226-9600
  600 Broome St Monroe (28110) *(G-8525)*

Master Tesh Stone Works.. 828 898-8333
  1921 Tynecastle Hwy Banner Elk (28604) *(G-687)*

Master Tesh Stone Works The, Banner Elk *Also Called: Master Tesh Stone Works (G-687)*

Master Tow Inc... 910 630-2000
  783 Slocomb Rd Fayetteville (28311) *(G-4637)*

Masterbrand Cabinets Inc.. 765 491-2385
  632 Dixon St Lexington (27292) *(G-7715)*

Masterbrand Cabinets LLC...................................... 252 523-4131
  651 Collier Loftin Rd Kinston (28504) *(G-7422)*

Mastercraft, Raleigh *Also Called: National Mastercraft Inds Inc (G-10324)*

Masterfield Furniture Co Inc.................................... 828 632-8535
  6463 Church Rd Taylorsville (28681) *(G-11967)*

Masters Hand Print Works Inc.................................. 828 652-5833
  5 Old Greenlee Rd W Marion (28752) *(G-8051)*

Masters Moving Services Inc.................................... 919 523-9836
  4220 Gallatree Ln Raleigh (27616) *(G-10280)*

Mastertent, Charlotte *Also Called: Zingerle Group Usa Inc (G-3048)*

Masterwrap Inc... 336 243-4515
  969 American Way Lexington (27295) *(G-7716)*

Mastic Home Exteriors Inc (DH)............................. 816 426-8200
  5020 Weston Pkwy Ste 400 Cary (27513) *(G-1399)*

Matchem Inc... 336 886-5000
  1115 Clinton Ave High Point (27260) *(G-6707)*

Matcor Mtal Fbrction Wlcome In.............................. 336 731-5700
  835 Salem Rd Lexington (27295) *(G-7717)*

Mateenbar USA Inc.. 704 662-2005
  2011 Highway 49 S Concord (28027) *(G-3399)*

Material Handling, Mount Airy *Also Called: T P Supply Co Inc (G-9183)*

Material Handling Tech - NC, Morrisville *Also Called: Material Handling Technologies Inc (G-9018)*

Material Handling Technologies Inc (PA).................. 919 388-0050
  113 International Dr Morrisville (27560) *(G-9018)*

Material Return LLC.. 828 234-5368
  647 Hopewell Rd Morganton (28655) *(G-8880)*

Materials Division, Cary *Also Called: Lord Corporation (G-1393)*

Matheson Tri-Gas Inc... 919 556-6461
  326 Forestville Rd Wake Forest (27587) *(G-12286)*

Mathis Elec Sls & Svc Inc....................................... 828 274-5925
  102a Caribou Rd Asheville (28803) *(G-544)*

Mathis Electronics, Asheville *Also Called: Mathis Elec Sls & Svc Inc (G-544)*

Mathis Quarries Inc.. 336 984-4010
  873 Cove Creek Dr North Wilkesboro (28659) *(G-9545)*

Mathisen Ventures Inc.. 212 986-1025
  17343 Meadow Bottom Rd Charlotte (28277) *(G-2468)*

Matlab Inc (PA).. 336 629-4161
  1112 Nc Highway 49 S Asheboro (27205) *(G-377)*

Matsusada Precision Inc... 704 496-2644
  5960 Fairview Rd Ste 400 Charlotte (28210) *(G-2469)*

Matt Bieneman Enterprises LLC.............................. 704 856-0200
  1375 Deal Rd Mooresville (28115) *(G-8720)*

Matt's Auto Shop, Raleigh *Also Called: Scattered Wrenches Inc (G-10460)*

Mattamuskeet Seafood Inc...................................... 252 926-2431
  24694 Us Highway 264 Swanquarter (27885) *(G-11880)*

Matthew Johnson Logging....................................... 919 291-0197
  536 Farrell Rd Sanford (27330) *(G-11208)*

Matthew Warren Inc (PA) 3426 Toringdon Way Ste 400 Charlotte (28277) *(G-2470)*

Matthews Building Supply Co.................................. 704 847-2106
  325 W Matthews St Matthews (28105) *(G-8130)*

Matthews Millwork Inc.. 704 821-4499
  1105 Jim Cir Monroe (28110) *(G-8526)*

Matthews Mobile Media LLC.................................... 336 303-4982
  6343 Burnt Poplar Rd Greensboro (27409) *(G-5681)*

Matthews Spcialty Vehicles Inc................................ 336 297-9600
  211 American Ave Greensboro (27409) *(G-5682)*

Mattress Firm... 252 443-1259
  794 Sutters Creek Blvd Rocky Mount (27804) *(G-10851)*

Mauser Usa LLC... 704 398-2325
  1209 Tar Heel Rd Charlotte (28208) *(G-2471)*

Mauser Usa LLC... 704 625-0737
  701 Lawton Rd Charlotte (28216) *(G-2472)*

Mauser Usa LLC... 704 455-2111
  12180 University Cy Blvd Harrisburg (28075) *(G-6114)*

Maverick Biofeuls.. 919 749-8717
  104 Tw Alexander Dr Bldg 4a Durham (27709) *(G-4119)*

Maverick Biofuels... 919 931-1434
  104 Tw Alexander Dr Durham (27709) *(G-4120)*

Maverick Enterprises, Monroe *Also Called: Maverick Enterprises Intl Inc (G-8527)*

Maverick Enterprises Intl Inc................................... 704 291-9474
  818 Circle Trace Rd Monroe (28110) *(G-8527)*

Mavidon, Flat Rock *Also Called: Carroll-Baccari Inc (G-4705)*

Max B Smith Jr... 828 434-0238
  1055 Blowing Rock Rd Boone (28607) *(G-933)*

Max Daetwyler Corp (DH).. 704 875-1200
  13420 Reese Blvd W Huntersville (28078) *(G-7012)*

Max Solutions Inc (PA).. 215 458-7050
  700 Derita Rd Bldg B Concord (28027) *(G-3400)*

Max Solutions USA, Concord *Also Called: Max Solutions Inc (G-3400)*

Maxam North America Inc (PA)................................ 214 736-8100
  106 Langtree Village Dr Ste 301 Mooresville (28117) *(G-8721)*

Maxim Label Packg High Pt Inc (PA)....................... 336 861-1666
  506 Townsend Ave High Point (27263) *(G-6708)*

2025 Harris North Carolina
Manufacturers Directory

(G-0000) Company's Geographic Section entry number

Maxime Knitting International..803 627-2768
  4925 Sirona Dr Ste 200 Charlotte (28273) *(G-2473)*

Maximizer Systems Inc..828 345-6036
  1010 21st Street Dr Se Hickory (28602) *(G-6393)*

Maximum Asp...919 544-7900
  9221 Globe Center Dr Ste 120 Morrisville (27560) *(G-9019)*

Maxpro Manufacturing LLC..910 640-5505
  31 Industrial Blvd Whiteville (28472) *(G-12587)*

Maxson & Associates..336 632-0524
  2618 Battleground Ave Greensboro (27408) *(G-5683)*

Maxson and Assoc Greensboro, Greensboro *Also Called: Maxson & Associates (G-5683)*

Maxtronic Technologies LLC...704 756-5354
  9545 Greyson Ridge Dr Charlotte (28277) *(G-2474)*

Maxxdrive LLC...704 600-8684
  1847 E Dixon Blvd Shelby (28152) *(G-11360)*

May-Craft Fiberglass Pdts Inc.......................................919 934-3000
  96 Hillsboro Rd Four Oaks (27524) *(G-4814)*

Mayberry Distillery..336 719-6860
  461 N South St Mount Airy (27030) *(G-9152)*

Maybin Emergency Power Inc..828 697-1195
  197 Mountain Valley Cemetery Rd Zirconia (28790) *(G-13531)*

Maynard Frame Shop Inc...910 428-2033
  306 Mcbride Lumber Rd Star (27356) *(G-11631)*

Maynard S Fabricators Inc...336 230-1048
  2227 W Lee St Ste A Greensboro (27403) *(G-5684)*

Mayne Pharma, Raleigh *Also Called: Mayne Pharma Commercial LLC (G-10281)*

Mayne Pharma Commercial LLC.......................................984 242-1400
  3301 Benson Dr Ste 401 Raleigh (27609) *(G-10281)*

Mayne Pharma LLC...252 752-3800
  3301 Benson Dr Ste 401 Raleigh (27609) *(G-10282)*

Mayne Pharma Ventures LLC...252 752-3800
  3301 Benson Dr Ste 401 Raleigh (27609) *(G-10283)*

Mayo, Tarboro *Also Called: Mayo Knitting Mill Inc (G-11934)*

Mayo Knitting Mill Inc (PA)...252 823-3101
  2204 W Austin St Tarboro (27886) *(G-11934)*

Mayo Resources Inc..336 996-7776
  2860 Lowery St Winston Salem (27101) *(G-13246)*

Mayse Manufacturing Co Inc (PA)....................................828 245-1891
  2201 Us Highway 221 S Forest City (28043) *(G-4793)*

Maysteel Porters LLC..704 864-1313
  469 Hospital Dr Ste A Gastonia (28054) *(G-5092)*

MB Marketing & Mfg Inc..828 285-0882
  128 Bingham Rd Ste 400 Asheville (28806) *(G-545)*

Mb-F Inc (PA)..336 379-9352
  620 Industrial Ave Greensboro (27406) *(G-5685)*

Mbm, Asheville *Also Called: MB Marketing & Mfg Inc (G-545)*

Mbp Acquisition LLC...704 349-5055
  6090 Willis Way Monroe (28110) *(G-8528)*

Mc Clatchy Interactive USA..919 861-1200
  1101 Haynes St Raleigh (27604) *(G-10284)*

Mc Cullough Auto Elc & Assoc.......................................704 376-5388
  3219 N Davidson St Charlotte (28205) *(G-2475)*

Mc Farland & Company Inc...336 246-4460
  960 Nc Highway 88 W Jefferson (28640) *(G-7191)*

Mc Gees Crating Inc...828 758-4660
  1640 Wilkesboro Blvd Lenoir (28645) *(G-7626)*

Mc Kenzie Taxidermy Supply, Salisbury *Also Called: McKenzie Sports Products LLC (G-11091)*

Mc Neely's Store Rental & Eqpt, Sylva *Also Called: Lbm Industries Inc (G-11895)*

MC Precast Concrete Inc...919 367-3636
  520 Pristine Water Dr Apex (27539) *(G-178)*

McAd Inc..336 299-3030
  100 Landmark Dr Greensboro (27409) *(G-5686)*

McBride Lumber Co Partnr LLC.......................................910 428-2747
  668 Mcbride Lumber Rd Star (27356) *(G-11632)*

McC Holdings Inc..828 724-4000
  1 Quality Way Marion (28752) *(G-8052)*

McCabes Indus Mllwrght Mfg Inc.....................................910 843-8699
  9502 Nc Highway 71 N Red Springs (28377) *(G-10669)*

McCarthy Tire Service Company.......................................910 791-0132
  118 Portwatch Way Wilmington (28412) *(G-12849)*

McComb Industries Lllp..336 229-9139
  1311 Industry Dr Burlington (27215) *(G-1126)*

McCombs Steel Company Inc (PA)....................................704 873-7563
  117 Slingshot Rd Statesville (28677) *(G-11730)*

McCorkle Sign Company Inc...919 687-7080
  1107 E Geer St Durham (27704) *(G-4121)*

McCotter Industries Inc..704 282-2102
  108 S Hayne St Monroe (28112) *(G-8529)*

McCreary Modern Inc (PA)..828 464-6465
  2564 S Us 321 Hwy Newton (28658) *(G-9481)*

McCrorie Group LLC (PA)...828 328-4538
  330 19th St Se Hickory (28602) *(G-6394)*

McCrorie Wood Products, Hickory *Also Called: McCrorie Group LLC (G-6394)*

McCune Technology Inc..910 424-2978
  4801 Research Dr Fayetteville (28306) *(G-4638)*

McDaniel Delmar (PA)..336 284-6377
  144 Whetstone Dr Mocksville (27028) *(G-8375)*

McDaniel Awning Co..704 636-8503
  225 White Farm Rd Salisbury (28147) *(G-11090)*

McDaniel Awning Manufacturing, Salisbury *Also Called: McDaniel Awning Co (G-11090)*

McDonald Services Inc...704 597-0590
  1734 University Commercial Pl Charlotte (28213) *(G-2476)*

McDonald Services Inc (PA)..704 753-9669
  7427 Price Tucker Rd Monroe (28110) *(G-8530)*

McDonalds...910 295-1112
  260 Ivey Ln Pinehurst (28374) *(G-9697)*

McDowell Cement Products Co (HQ)..................................828 652-5721
  S Garden St Marion (28752) *(G-8053)*

McDowell Cement Products Co...828 765-2762
  167 Roan Rd Spruce Pine (28777) *(G-11579)*

McDowell County Millwork LLC..828 682-6215
  4 Old West Henderson St Marion (28752) *(G-8054)*

McDowell Lfac..828 289-5553
  263 Barnes Rd Ste J Marion (28752) *(G-8055)*

McDowells Mch Fabrication Inc.......................................336 720-9944
  2312a Cragmore Rd Winston Salem (27107) *(G-13247)*

McF Operating LLC...828 685-8821
  352 Jet St Hendersonville (28792) *(G-6225)*

McGee Brothers Machine & Wldg......................................828 766-9122
  2585 Halltown Rd Spruce Pine (28777) *(G-11580)*

McGee Brothers Mch & Wldg Co, Spruce Pine *Also Called: McGee Brothers Machine & Wldg (G-11580)*

McGee Corporation...704 882-1500
  12100 Stallings Commerce Dr Matthews (28105) *(G-8131)*

McGill Advsory Pblications Inc.......................................866 727-6100
  8816 Red Oak Blvd Ste 240 Charlotte (28217) *(G-2477)*

McGill Corporation...919 467-1993
  1220 Se Maynard Rd Cary (27511) *(G-1400)*

McGill Environmental Gp LLC...919 362-1161
  634 Christian Chapel Church Rd New Hill (27562) *(G-9410)*

McGrann Digital Imaging, Charlotte *Also Called: McGrann Paper Corporation (G-2478)*

McGrann Paper Corporation (PA)......................................800 240-9455
  13400 Sage Thrasher Ln Charlotte (28278) *(G-2478)*

McIntyre Manufacturing Group Inc....................................336 476-3646
  310 Kendall Mill Rd Thomasville (27360) *(G-12046)*

McJast Inc...828 884-4809
  6497 Old Hendersonville Hwy Pisgah Forest (28768) *(G-9771)*

McKeel & Sons Logging Inc...252 244-3903
  170 Spruill Town Rd Vanceboro (28586) *(G-12219)*

McKelvey Fulks..704 357-1550
  1432 Center Park Dr Charlotte (28217) *(G-2479)*

McKenzie Sports Products LLC (PA)...................................704 279-7985
  1910 Saint Luke Church Rd Salisbury (28146) *(G-11091)*

McKenzie Supply Company..910 276-1691
  1600 Us Highway 401 Byp S Laurinburg (28352) *(G-7509)*

McKinley Leather Hickory Inc...828 459-2884
  3131 W Main St Claremont (28610) *(G-3115)*

McKinney Electric & Mch Co Inc......................................828 765-7910
  12923 S 226 Hwy Spruce Pine (28777) *(G-11581)*

McKinney Garbage Service, Spruce Pine *Also Called: McKinney Lwncare Grbage Svc LL (G-11582)*

McKinney Lwncare Grbage Svc LL................................. 828 766-9490
  1113 Dale Rd Spruce Pine (28777) *(G-11582)*

McKinnon Enterprise LLC.. 919 408-6365
  1449 Aultroy Dr Fayetteville (28306) *(G-4639)*

McKnight15 Inc.. 919 326-6488
  3912 Bluffwind Dr Raleigh (27603) *(G-10285)*

McKoys Logging Company Inc...................................... 910 862-2706
  3006 W Broad St Elizabethtown (28337) *(G-4429)*

McLamb Group Inc.. 704 333-1171
  1003 Louise Ave Apt B Charlotte (28205) *(G-2480)*

McLean Lighting Works, Greensboro *Also Called: A M Moore and Company Inc (G-5332)*

McLean Precision Cabinetry Inc.................................... 910 327-9217
  2507 Nc Highway 172 Sneads Ferry (28460) *(G-11472)*

McLean Sbsrface Utlity Engrg L................................... 336 340-0024
  3015 E Bessemer Ave Greensboro (27405) *(G-5687)*

McLendon Logging Incorporated................................... 910 439-6223
  671 Nc Highway 731 W Mount Gilead (27306) *(G-9202)*

McLoud Media.. 828 837-9539
  1192 Andrews Rd Ste H Murphy (28906) *(G-9292)*

McLoud Trucking & Rigging, Yadkinville *Also Called: Advantage Machinery Svcs Inc (G-13435)*

McManus Microwave, Bakersville *Also Called: James W McManus Inc (G-678)*

McMichael Mills Inc.. 336 584-0134
  2050 Willow Spring Ln Burlington (27215) *(G-1127)*

McMichael Mills Inc (PA).. 336 548-4242
  130 Shakey Rd Mayodan (27027) *(G-8207)*

McMurray Fabrics Inc (PA).. 910 944-2128
  105 Vann Pl (Sandhills Industrial Park) Aberdeen (28315) *(G-12)*

McMurray Fabrics Inc... 704 732-9613
  1140 N Flint St Lincolnton (28092) *(G-7843)*

McNamara & Company, Kernersville *Also Called: Chichibone Inc (G-7256)*

McNaughton-Mckay Southeast Inc................................ 910 392-0940
  6719 Amsterdam Way Wilmington (28405) *(G-12850)*

McNeely Motorsports Inc.. 704 426-7430
  340 Seaboard Dr Matthews (28104) *(G-8184)*

McNeely Trucking Co... 828 966-4270
  17692 Rosman Hwy Sapphire (28774) *(G-11260)*

McNeelys Store Rental & Eqp, Sapphire *Also Called: Lbm Industries Inc (G-11259)*

McNeill Frame Inc.. 336 873-7934
  3631 Alternate Rd Seagrove (27341) *(G-11278)*

McNeilly Champion Furniture, Lawndale *Also Called: McNeillys Inc (G-7518)*

McNeillys Inc.. 704 300-1712
  229 Carpenters Grove Church Rd Lawndale (28090) *(G-7518)*

McPherson Beverages Inc... 252 537-3571
  1330 Stancell St Roanoke Rapids (27870) *(G-10741)*

McRae Industries Inc.. 910 439-6149
  125 Wadeville Fire Station Rd Mount Gilead (27306) *(G-9203)*

McRae Industries Inc (PA)... 910 439-6147
  400 N Main St Mount Gilead (27306) *(G-9204)*

MCS, Durham *Also Called: Machine Consulting Svcs Inc (G-4114)*

McShan Inc... 980 355-9790
  16607 Riverstone Way Ste 200 Charlotte (28277) *(G-2481)*

McW Custom Doors, Madison *Also Called: Martin Wood Products Inc (G-7993)*

Mdb Investors LLC... 704 507-6850
  4000 Sam Wilson Rd Charlotte (28214) *(G-2482)*

Mdi Solutions LLC... 845 721-6758
  760 Choate Rd Salisbury (28146) *(G-11092)*

Mdkscrubs LLC... 980 250-4708
  8401 Parkland Cir Apt 102 Charlotte (28227) *(G-2483)*

Mdm Mfg LLC... 919 908-6574
  206 Stockbridge Pl Hillsborough (27278) *(G-6873)*

MDN Cabinets Inc.. 919 662-1090
  3411 Integrity Dr Ste 100 Garner (27529) *(G-4940)*

Mdsi Inc.. 919 783-8730
  3505 Lake Herman Dr Bldg A Browns Summit (27214) *(G-1002)*

Mdt Bromley LLC... 828 651-8737
  282 Cane Creek Rd Fletcher (28732) *(G-4752)*

Meadow Burke Products, Charlotte *Also Called: Merchants Metals Inc (G-2491)*

Meadows Mills Inc... 336 838-2282
  1352 W D St North Wilkesboro (28659) *(G-9546)*

Meadwestvaco Research Center, Raleigh *Also Called: Westrock Mwv LLC (G-10606)*

Measurement Controls Inc... 704 921-1101
  6131 Old Concord Rd Charlotte (28213) *(G-2484)*

Measurement Incorporated (PA).................................... 919 683-2413
  423 Morris St Durham (27701) *(G-4122)*

Meat Farm, Pinetown *Also Called: Acre Station Meat Farm Inc (G-9707)*

Meatinternational LLC.. 910 628-8267
  266 Bethesda Church Rd Fairmont (28340) *(G-4503)*

Mebane Enterprise, Mebane *Also Called: Womack Publishing Co Inc (G-8265)*

Mecha Inc.. 919 858-0372
  6204 Daimler Way Ste 107 Raleigh (27607) *(G-10286)*

Mechanical Maintenance Inc.. 336 676-7133
  6028 Liberty Rd Climax (27233) *(G-3227)*

Mechanical Spc Contrs Inc.. 919 829-9300
  4412 Tryon Rd Raleigh (27606) *(G-10287)*

Mechanical Specialty Inc... 336 272-5606
  1901 E Wendover Ave Greensboro (27405) *(G-5688)*

Mechlanburg Newspaper Group, Huntersville *Also Called: Herald Huntersville (G-6997)*

Meco Inc.. 919 557-7330
  501 Community Dr Fuquay Varina (27526) *(G-4889)*

Med Express/Medical Spc Inc....................................... 919 572-2568
  3874 S Alston Ave Ste 103 Durham (27713) *(G-4123)*

Medaccess Inc.. 828 264-4085
  1236 Gladdens Creek Rd Robbinsville (28771) *(G-10760)*

Medallion Athletic Products, Mooresville *Also Called: Geosurfaces Southeast Inc (G-8672)*

Medallion Company Inc (HQ).. 919 990-3500
  250 Crown Blvd Timberlake (27583) *(G-12101)*

Medaloni Cellars LLC... 305 509-2004
  470 Yadkin Valley Trl Lewisville (27023) *(G-7652)*

Medals To Honor Inc.. 910 326-4275
  176 Oyster Ln Hubert (28539) *(G-6935)*

Medaptus Inc.. 617 896-4000
  4917 Waters Edge Dr Ste 135 Raleigh (27606) *(G-10288)*

Medcor Inc... 888 579-1050
  550 Scout Rd Lexington (27292) *(G-7718)*

Medi Mall Inc... 877 501-6334
  189 Continuum Dr Ste A Fletcher (28732) *(G-4753)*

Medi Manufacturing Inc.. 336 449-4440
  6481 Franz Warner Pkwy Whitsett (27377) *(G-12615)*

Media Wilimington Co.. 910 791-0688
  6700 Netherlands Dr Unit A Wilmington (28405) *(G-12851)*

Medical Action, Arden *Also Called: Medical Action Industries Inc (G-284)*

Medical Action Industries Inc (HQ)................................ 631 404-3700
  25 Heywood Rd Arden (28704) *(G-284)*

Medical Cable Specialists Inc....................................... 828 890-2888
  2133 Old Fanning Bridge Rd Mills River (28759) *(G-8317)*

Medical Device Bus Svcs Inc.. 704 423-0033
  900 Center Park Dr Ste Bc Charlotte (28217) *(G-2485)*

Medical Engineering Labs.. 704 487-0166
  3039 Longwood Dr Shelby (28152) *(G-11361)*

Medical Missionary Press.. 828 649-3976
  491 Blue Hill Rd Marshall (28753) *(G-8081)*

Medical Murray, Charlotte *Also Called: Murray Inc (G-2535)*

Medical Spclties of Crlnas Inc...................................... 910 575-4542
  565 Meadow Ridge Sunset Beach (28468) *(G-11851)*

Medical Specialist Mfg, Charlotte *Also Called: Gaylord Inc (G-2192)*

Medical Specialties Inc... 704 694-2434
  308 Parson St Wadesboro (28170) *(G-12249)*

Medicor Imaging Inc... 704 332-5532
  1927 S Tryon St Ste 200 Charlotte (28203) *(G-2486)*

Medkoo Inc.. 919 636-5577
  2224 Sedwick Rd Ste 102 Durham (27713) *(G-4124)*

Medkoo Biosciences, Durham *Also Called: Medkoo Inc (G-4124)*

Medley S Garage Welding.. 336 674-0422
  5879 Cherokee Trl Pleasant Garden (27313) *(G-9792)*

Medlin Office Supply, Oriental *Also Called: J C Lawrence Co (G-9600)*

Medlio, Durham *Also Called: Medlio Inc (G-4125)*

Medlio Inc.. 919 599-4870
  3313 Old Chapel Hill Rd Durham (27707) *(G-4125)*

Medlit Solutions... 919 878-6789
  191 Technology Dr Garner (27529) *(G-4941)*

Medlit Solutions LLC (HQ)................................919 878-6789
191 Technology Dr Garner (27529) *(G-4942)*

Medmassager, Fletcher *Also Called: Medi Mall Inc (G-4753)*

Medtrnic Sofamor Danek USA Inc.....................919 457-9982
2000 Regency Pkwy Ste 270 Cary (27518) *(G-1401)*

Medtronic, Cary *Also Called: Medtrnic Sofamor Danek USA Inc (G-1401)*

Medvertical LLC..919 867-4268
3725 National Dr Ste 160 Raleigh (27612) *(G-10289)*

Mega Machine Shop Inc.................................336 492-2728
130 Macy Langston Ln Mocksville (27028) *(G-8376)*

Mega Media Concepts Ltd Lblty........................973 919-5661
101 Old Hendersonville Hwy Brevard (28712) *(G-975)*

Megawood Inc...910 572-3796
670 W Allenton St Mount Gilead (27306) *(G-9205)*

Megawood Holdings Inc.................................910 439-2124
610 W Allenton St Mount Gilead (27306) *(G-9206)*

Meghan Blake Industries Inc...........................704 462-2988
7514 W Nc 10 Hwy Vale (28168) *(G-12209)*

Megtec India Holdings LLC.............................704 625-4900
13024 Ballantyne Corporate Pl Ste 700 Charlotte (28277) *(G-2487)*

Megtec Turbosonic Tech Inc............................704 625-4900
13024 Ballantyne Corporate Pl Ste 700 Charlotte (28277) *(G-2488)*

Meherrin River Forest Pdts Inc........................252 558-4238
1478 Trueblood Rd Weldon (27890) *(G-12523)*

Meherrin River International, Weldon *Also Called: Meherrin River Forest Pdts Inc (G-12523)*

Mel, Shelby *Also Called: Medical Engineering Labs (G-11361)*

Mel Schlesinger...336 525-6357
1001 S Marshall St Ste 290 Winston Salem (27101) *(G-13248)*

Melatex Incorporated...................................704 332-5046
3818 Northmore St Charlotte (28205) *(G-2489)*

Melinta Therapeutics LLC..............................919 313-6601
6340 Quadrangle Dr Ste 36 Chapel Hill (27517) *(G-1555)*

Mellineum Printing......................................919 267-5752
2015 Production Dr Apex (27539) *(G-179)*

Melltronics Industrial Inc (PA)........................704 821-6651
3479 Gribble Rd Matthews (28104) *(G-8185)*

Melt ME, Charlotte *Also Called: Patrice Brent (G-2615)*

Melt Your Heart, Leicester *Also Called: Melt Your Heart LLC (G-7527)*

Melt Your Heart LLC....................................828 989-6749
162 Brookshire Rd Leicester (28748) *(G-7527)*

Memios LLC...336 664-5256
7609 Business Park Dr # B Greensboro (27409) *(G-5689)*

Memories, Mooresville *Also Called: Memories of Orangeburg Inc (G-8722)*

Memories of Orangeburg Inc...........................803 533-0035
126 Foxfield Park Dr Mooresville (28115) *(G-8722)*

Memscap Inc (HQ)......................................919 248-4102
3021 E Cornwallis Rd Research Triangle Pk Durham (27709) *(G-4126)*

Memscap Inc..919 248-1441
3026 Cornwallis Rd Durham (27709) *(G-4127)*

Mepla-Alfit Incorporated...............................336 289-2300
1202 Nc Highway 66 S Kernersville (27284) *(G-7286)*

Merch Connect Studios Inc.............................336 501-6722
1724 Holbrook St Greensboro (27403) *(G-5690)*

Merch Unlimited, Garner *Also Called: Creek Life LLC (G-4926)*

Merchant 1 Manufacturing LLC........................336 617-3008
200 Starview Ln Summerfield (27358) *(G-11844)*

Merchant 1 Marketing LLC.............................888 853-9992
2900 Pacific Ave Greensboro (27406) *(G-5691)*

Merchant Cash Systems LLC..........................336 499-9937
301 S Mcdowell St Ste 125 Charlotte (28204) *(G-2490)*

Merchants, Havelock *Also Called: Merchants Inc (G-6123)*

Merchants Inc...252 447-2121
174 Us Highway 70 W Havelock (28532) *(G-6123)*

Merchants Metals, Raleigh *Also Called: Merchants Metals LLC (G-10290)*

Merchants Metals, Statesville *Also Called: Merchants Metals LLC (G-11731)*

Merchants Metals Inc...................................704 921-9192
3401 Woodpark Blvd Ste A Charlotte (28206) *(G-2491)*

Merchants Metals LLC..................................919 598-8471
6512 Mount Herman Rd Raleigh (27617) *(G-10290)*

Merchants Metals LLC..................................704 878-8706
165 Fanjoy Rd Statesville (28625) *(G-11731)*

Merck, Charlotte *Also Called: Merck & Co Inc (G-2492)*

Merck, Durham *Also Called: Merck Sharp & Dohme LLC (G-4128)*

Merck & Co Inc..908 423-3000
10301 David Taylor Dr Charlotte (28262) *(G-2492)*

Merck Sharp & Dohme LLC.............................919 425-4000
5325 Old Oxford Rd Durham (27712) *(G-4128)*

Merck Sharp & Dohme LLC.............................252 243-2011
4633 Merck Rd W Wilson (27893) *(G-13006)*

Merck Teknika LLC......................................919 620-7200
100 Rodolphe St Bldg 1300 Durham (27712) *(G-4129)*

Mercury Signs Inc......................................919 808-1205
7306 Vanclaybon Rd Apex (27523) *(G-180)*

Meredith - Webb Prtg Co Inc...........................336 228-8378
334 N Main St Burlington (27217) *(G-1128)*

Meredith Media Co......................................919 748-4808
4015 University Dr Ste 2d Durham (27707) *(G-4130)*

Merfin Systems LLC....................................800 874-6373
105 Industrial Dr King (27021) *(G-7331)*

Merge LLC..919 832-3924
1410 Hillsborough St Raleigh (27605) *(G-10291)*

Merge Media Ltd..919 688-9969
104 S Christopher Rd Chapel Hill (27514) *(G-1556)*

Merge Records, Chapel Hill *Also Called: Merge Media Ltd (G-1556)*

Merge Scientific Solutions LLC........................919 346-0999
208 Technology Park Ln Ste 108 Fuquay Varina (27526) *(G-4890)*

Meridian Brick LLC.....................................704 636-0131
700 S Long St Salisbury (28144) *(G-11093)*

Meridian Dyed Yarn Group, Gastonia *Also Called: Meridian Industries Inc (G-5093)*

Meridian Granite Company..............................919 781-4550
2710 Wycliff Rd Raleigh (27607) *(G-10292)*

Meridian Industries Inc.................................704 824-7880
40 Rex Ave Gastonia (28054) *(G-5093)*

Meridian Kiosks, Aberdeen *Also Called: Meridian Zero Degrees LLC (G-13)*

Meridian Prfmce Systems Inc...........................706 905-5637
2018 Dilworth Rd E Charlotte (28203) *(G-2493)*

Meridian Spcalty Yrn Group Inc (HQ)..................828 874-2151
312 Colombo St Sw Valdese (28690) *(G-12197)*

Meridian Zero Degrees LLC (PA).......................866 454-6757
312 S Pine St Aberdeen (28315) *(G-13)*

Meritor Inc..910 425-4181
3200 Natal St Fayetteville (28306) *(G-4640)*

Meritor Inc..828 687-2000
1000 Rockwell Dr Fletcher (28732) *(G-4754)*

Meritor Inc..828 687-2000
1000 Rockwell Dr Fletcher (28732) *(G-4755)*

Meritor Inc..828 247-0440
160 Ash Dr Forest City (28043) *(G-4794)*

Meritor Inc..910 844-9401
22021 Skyway Church Rd Ste B Maxton (28364) *(G-8202)*

Meritor Inc..910 844-9401
22021 Skyway Church Rd Ste A Maxton (28364) *(G-8203)*

Meritor Inc..828 433-4600
105 Wamsutta Mill Rd Morganton (28655) *(G-8881)*

Merrill Resources Inc...................................828 877-4450
99 Cascade Lake Rd Penrose (28766) *(G-9662)*

Merritt Logging & Chipping Co.........................910 862-4905
1109 W Swanzy St Elizabethtown (28337) *(G-4430)*

Mertek Solutions Inc...................................919 774-7827
3913 Hawkins Ave Sanford (27330) *(G-11209)*

Merz, Raleigh *Also Called: Merz Incorporated (G-10293)*

Merz Incorporated......................................919 582-8196
6501 Six Forks Rd Raleigh (27615) *(G-10293)*

Merz North America Inc (DH)...........................919 582-8000
6501 Six Forks Rd Raleigh (27615) *(G-10294)*

Merz Pharmaceuticals LLC.............................919 582-8000
6601 Six Forks Rd Raleigh (27615) *(G-10295)*

Mesa Quality, Hendersonville *Also Called: Mesa Quality Fenestration Inc (G-6226)*

Mesa Quality Fenestration Inc.........................828 393-0132
968 Crab Creek Rd Hendersonville (28739) *(G-6226)*

Messer LLC...704 583-0313
2820 Nevada Blvd Charlotte (28273) *(G-2494)*

A
L
P
H
A
B
E
T
I
C

Messer LLC..908 464-8100
375 Nc Hwy 24 Midland (28107) *(G-8290)*

Mestek Inc..252 753-5323
3576 South Fields St Farmville (27828) *(G-4535)*

Metal & Materials Proc LLC...........................260 438-8901
3250 Nc Highway 5 Aberdeen (28315) *(G-14)*

Metal ARC..910 770-1180
5547 James B White Hwy S Whiteville (28472) *(G-12588)*

Metal Crafters of Goldsboro NC....................919 778-7200
855 Nc 111 Hwy S Goldsboro (27534) *(G-5228)*

Metal Creations, Fletcher *Also Called: Welding Solutions LLC (G-4778)*

Metal Depots, Raleigh *Also Called: Nci Group Inc (G-10328)*

Metal Fabrication, Henderson *Also Called: Edwards Unlimited Inc (G-6154)*

Metal Graphic, Raleigh *Also Called: Knowledge Management Assoc LLC (G-10239)*

Metal Impact East LLC...................................336 578-4515
235 Riverbend Rd Graham (27253) *(G-5278)*

Metal Impact East LLC...................................743 205-1900
1200 Jay Ln Graham (27253) *(G-5279)*

Metal Improvement Company LLC..................704 525-3818
500 Springbrook Rd Charlotte (28217) *(G-2495)*

Metal Improvement Company LLC..................414 536-1573
1931 Jordache Ct Gastonia (28052) *(G-5094)*

Metal Roofing Systems LLC...........................704 820-3110
7687 Mikron Dr Stanley (28164) *(G-11622)*

Metal Sales Manufacturing Corp....................704 859-0550
188 Quality Dr Mocksville (27028) *(G-8377)*

Metal Stamping Solutions, Sanford *Also Called: Wolverine Mtal Stmping Sltons (G-11253)*

Metal Structures Plus LLC.............................704 896-7155
561 Oak Tree Rd Mooresville (28117) *(G-8723)*

Metal Tech Murfreesboro Inc (PA)..................252 398-4041
314 W Broad St Murfreesboro (27855) *(G-9283)*

Metal Tech of Murfreesboro, Murfreesboro *Also Called: Metal Tech Murfreesboro Inc (G-9283)*

Metal Treating Div, Gastonia *Also Called: Mik All Machine Co Inc (G-5097)*

Metal Works High Point Inc............................336 886-4612
918 W Kivett Dr High Point (27262) *(G-6709)*

Metal Works Mfg Co.......................................704 482-1399
2501 W Dixon Blvd Shelby (28152) *(G-11362)*

Metal-Cad Stl Frmng Systems In.....................910 343-3338
150 Division Dr Wilmington (28401) *(G-12852)*

Metalcraft & Mech Svc Inc.............................919 736-1029
147 Aycock Dr Goldsboro (27530) *(G-5229)*

Metalcraft Air Filtration, Washington *Also Called: Camfil Usa Inc (G-12376)*

Metalcraft Fabricating Company.....................919 477-2117
1316 Old Oxford Rd Durham (27704) *(G-4131)*

Metalfab of North Carolina LLC......................704 841-1090
11145 Monroe Rd Matthews (28105) *(G-8132)*

Metallix Refining Inc......................................252 413-0346
251 Industrial Blvd Greenville (27834) *(G-6003)*

Metallus Inc..330 471-6293
205 Industrial Park Dr Columbus (28722) *(G-3303)*

Metaltek, Morrisville *Also Called: Liberty Investment & MGT Corp (G-9010)*

Metchem Inc..910 944-1405
106 Jordan Pl Aberdeen (28315) *(G-15)*

Metro Fire Lifesafety LLC...............................704 529-7348
2714 Forbes Rd Gastonia (28056) *(G-5095)*

Metro Print Inc...704 827-3796
800 W Central Ave Mount Holly (28120) *(G-9237)*

Metro Productions Inc....................................919 851-6420
6005 Chapel Hill Rd Raleigh (27607) *(G-10296)*

Metro Woodcrafter, Charlotte *Also Called: Metro Woodcrafter of Nc Inc (G-2496)*

Metro Woodcrafter of Nc Inc..........................704 394-9622
3710 Performance Rd Charlotte (28214) *(G-2496)*

Metrographics Printing, Charlotte *Also Called: Flash Printing Company Inc (G-2159)*

Metrohose Incorporated.................................252 329-9891
2009 N Greene St Greenville (27834) *(G-6004)*

Metrolina Woodworks Inc...............................704 821-9095
3475 Gribble Rd Stallings (28104) *(G-11601)*

Metrotech Chemicals Inc................................704 343-9315
2101 Wilkinson Blvd Charlotte (28208) *(G-2497)*

Metso Power USA, Charlotte *Also Called: Valmet Inc (G-2972)*

Metso USA Inc...877 677-2005
3200 Bessemer City Rd Bessemer City (28016) *(G-827)*

Mettech Inc (PA)..919 833-9460
105 S Wilmington St Raleigh (27601) *(G-10297)*

Metyx USA Inc...704 824-1030
2504 Lowell Rd Gastonia (28054) *(G-5096)*

Metzgers Burl Wood Gallery..........................828 452-2550
101 N Main St Waynesville (28786) *(G-12463)*

Meusburger Us Inc...704 526-0330
4600 Lebanon Rd Ste A-1 Mint Hill (28227) *(G-8340)*

Mexichem Spcalty Compounds Inc..................704 889-7821
9635 Industrial Dr Pineville (28134) *(G-9742)*

Mey Corporation (PA).....................................919 932-5800
121 S Estes Dr Ste 101 Chapel Hill (27514) *(G-1557)*

Mfi Products Inc (HQ).....................................910 944-2128
105 Vann Pl Aberdeen (28315) *(G-16)*

Mg Foods Inc...336 724-6327
3195 Centre Park Blvd Winston Salem (27107) *(G-13249)*

Mg12 LP...828 440-1144
874 S Trade St Tryon (28782) *(G-12175)*

MGM Brakes, Charlotte *Also Called: Indian Head Industries Inc (G-2321)*

MGM Brakes, Murphy *Also Called: Indian Head Industries Inc (G-9290)*

Mh Libman Woodturning.................................828 360-5530
191 Lyman St Asheville (28801) *(G-546)*

MHS Ltd...336 767-2641
4961 Home Rd Ste A Winston Salem (27106) *(G-13250)*

MHS Ltd (PA)...336 767-2641
4959 Home Rd Winston Salem (27106) *(G-13251)*

Mi-, Durham *Also Called: Advanced Digital Systems Inc (G-3881)*

Mias Inc..704 665-1098
14240 S Lakes Dr Charlotte (28273) *(G-2498)*

Mias Group, Charlotte *Also Called: Mias Inc (G-2498)*

Mic Equip Rebuild, Gastonia *Also Called: Metal Improvement Company LLC (G-5094)*

Micell Technologies Inc..................................919 313-2102
801 Capitola Dr Ste 1 Durham (27713) *(G-4132)*

Michael H Branch Inc......................................252 532-0930
1621 Old Emporia Rd Gaston (27832) *(G-4979)*

Michael L Goodson Logging Inc.......................910 346-8399
171 Goodson Trl Jacksonville (28546) *(G-7131)*

Michael Parker Cabinetry................................919 833-5117
414 Dupont Cir Ste 4 Raleigh (27603) *(G-10298)*

Michael S North Wilkesboro Inc.......................336 838-5964
900 Main St North Wilkesboro (28659) *(G-9547)*

Michael Simmons...704 298-1103
6012 Bayfield Pkwy Ste 302 Concord (28027) *(G-3401)*

Michael Tate..336 374-4695
1455 Simpson Mill Rd Mount Airy (27030) *(G-9153)*

Michaelian & Kohlberg Inc (PA).......................828 891-8511
5216 Brevard Rd Horse Shoe (28742) *(G-6930)*

Michaels Creamery Inc...................................910 292-4172
439 Westwood Shopping Ctr Ste 148 Fayetteville (28314) *(G-4641)*

Michaels Jewelry, North Wilkesboro *Also Called: Michael S North Wilkesboro Inc (G-9547)*

Micheal Langdon Logging Inc.........................910 890-5295
7249 Ross Rd Erwin (28339) *(G-4491)*

Michelson Enterprises Inc..............................828 693-5500
701 Oriole Dr Hendersonville (28792) *(G-6227)*

Michigan Packaging Company........................704 455-4206
2215 Mulberry Rd Concord (28025) *(G-3402)*

Mickey Truck Bodies Inc.................................336 882-6806
1425 Bethel Dr High Point (27260) *(G-6710)*

Mickey Truck Bodies Inc (PA).........................336 882-6806
1305 Trinity Ave High Point (27261) *(G-6711)*

Mickey Truck Bodies Inc.................................336 882-6806
Hwy 29-70 Thomasville (27360) *(G-12047)*

Micro Epsilon Amer Ltd Partnr (PA).................919 787-9707
8120 Brownleigh Dr Raleigh (27617) *(G-10299)*

Micro Epsilon America, Raleigh *Also Called: Micro Epsilon Amer Ltd Partnr (G-10299)*

Micro Lens Technology Inc..............................704 893-2109
2001 Van Buren Ave Indian Trail (28079) *(G-7091)*

Micro Lens Technology Inc (PA)......................704 847-9234
3308 Mikelynn Dr Matthews (28105) *(G-8133)*

Micro Measurements, Wendell *Also Called: Vishay Measurements Group Inc* **(G-12552)**

Micro Scribe Publishing Inc.................................... 919 848-0388
732 Lanham Pl Raleigh (27615) **(G-10300)**

Micro Technology Unlimited, Raleigh *Also Called: Consolidated Sciences Inc* **(G-10009)**

Micro-OHM Corporation.. 800 845-5167
14460 Falls Of Neuse Rd Ste 149-273 Raleigh (27614) **(G-10301)**

Microban, Huntersville *Also Called: Microban Products Company* **(G-7013)**

Microban Products Company (DH)............................ 704 766-4267
11400 Vanstory Dr Huntersville (28078) **(G-7013)**

Microbrush International, Monroe *Also Called: Dentonics Inc* **(G-8476)**

Microchip Technology Inc.. 919 844-7510
7901 Strickland Rd Ste 101 Raleigh (27615) **(G-10302)**

Microfine Inc... 336 768-1480
100 Cloverleaf Dr Winston Salem (27103) **(G-13252)**

Micronova Systems Inc... 910 202-0564
2038 Oleander Dr Wilmington (28403) **(G-12853)**

Micropore Technologies Inc.................................... 984 344-7499
2121 Tw Alexander Dr Ste 124-8 Morrisville (27560) **(G-9020)**

Microsoft, Charlotte *Also Called: Microsoft Corporation* **(G-2499)**

Microsoft Corporation... 704 527-2987
8055 Microsoft Way Charlotte (28273) **(G-2499)**

Microsolv Technology Corp..................................... 720 949-1302
9158 Industrial Blvd Ne Leland (28451) **(G-7555)**

Micross Advnced Intrcnnect TEC........................... 919 248-1872
3021 Cornwallis Rd Research Triangle Pa (27709) **(G-10714)**

Micross Components, Research Triangle Pa *Also Called: Micross Advnced Intrcnnect TEC* **(G-10714)**

Microtech, Mills River *Also Called: Microtech Knives Inc* **(G-8318)**

Microtech Defense Inds Inc.................................... 828 684-4355
15a National Ave Fletcher (28732) **(G-4756)**

Microtech Knives Inc (PA)...................................... 828 684-4355
321 Fanning Fields Rd Mills River (28759) **(G-8318)**

Microthermics Inc.. 919 878-8045
3216 Wellington Ct Ste 102 Raleigh (27615) **(G-10303)**

Microtronic Us LLC.. 336 869-0429
401 Dorado Dr High Point (27265) **(G-6712)**

Mid Atlantic Book Bindery, Greensboro *Also Called: Hf Group LLC* **(G-5595)**

Mid Atlantic Hydraulics & Mch, Washington *Also Called: Mid-Atlantic Tool and Die Inc* **(G-12397)**

Mid Carolina Cabinets Inc...................................... 704 358-9950
1418 Industrial Dr Matthews (28105) **(G-8134)**

Mid Town Dixie Express Fuel.................................. 336 318-1200
455 W Salisbury St Asheboro (27203) **(G-378)**

Mid-Atlantic Concrete Pdts Inc............................... 336 774-6544
2460 Armstrong Dr Winston Salem (27103) **(G-13253)**

Mid-Atlantic Crane and Eqp Co.............................. 919 790-3535
3224 Northside Dr Raleigh (27615) **(G-10304)**

Mid-Atlantic Drainage Inc (PA).............................. 828 324-0808
105 Ge Plant Rd Sw Conover (28613) **(G-3539)**

Mid-Atlantic Specialties Inc.................................... 919 212-1939
5200 Trademark Dr Ste 102 Raleigh (27610) **(G-10305)**

Mid-Atlantic Tool and Die Inc................................ 252 946-2598
5324 Us Highway 264 W Washington (27889) **(G-12397)**

Midcoastal Development Corp................................. 336 622-3091
2435 Old 421 Rd Staley (27355) **(G-11597)**

Middle of Nowhere Music LLC................................ 301 237-7290
112 Nc 54 Apt B8 Carrboro (27510) **(G-1270)**

Middleby Marshall Inc (HQ).................................... 919 762-1000
1100 Old Honeycutt Rd Fuquay Varina (27526) **(G-4891)**

Middlesex Plant... 252 235-2121
8171 Planer Mill Rd Middlesex (27557) **(G-8277)**

Mideast Division, Concord *Also Called: Legacy Vulcan LLC* **(G-3391)**

Midland Bottling LLC.. 919 865-2300
4141 Parklake Ave Ste 600 Raleigh (27612) **(G-10306)**

Midnight Machining, Marion *Also Called: New World Technologies Inc* **(G-8058)**

Midsouth Power Eqp Co Inc................................... 336 389-0515
518 Corliss St Greensboro (27406) **(G-5692)**

Midstate Mills Inc.. 828 464-1611
11 N Brady Ave Newton (28658) **(G-9482)**

Midway Blind & Awning Co Inc............................... 336 226-4532
1836 E Webb Ave Burlington (27217) **(G-1129)**

Midwest Modular Services Ltd................................ 847 417-0010
216 Tarheel Dr Moyock (27958) **(G-9279)**

Mign Inc.. 609 304-1617
301 Camp Rd Ste 105 Charlotte (28206) **(G-2500)**

Mijo Enterprises Inc.. 252 442-6806
2220 N Wesleyan Blvd Rocky Mount (27804) **(G-10852)**

Mik All Machine Co Inc (PA).................................. 704 866-4302
905 Hanover St Gastonia (28054) **(G-5097)**

Mike Atkins & Son Logging Inc.............................. 919 965-8002
4336 Browns Pond Rd Selma (27576) **(G-11290)**

Mike DS Bbq LLC.. 866 960-8652
455 S Driver St Durham (27703) **(G-4133)**

Mike Luszcz.. 252 717-6282
3424 Sagewood Ct Winterville (28590) **(G-13418)**

Mike Powell Inc... 910 792-6152
3407a Enterprise Dr Wilmington (28405) **(G-12854)**

Mike S Custom Cabinets Inc.................................. 252 224-5351
587 Island Creek Rd Pollocksville (28573) **(G-9818)**

Mike's Hosiery, Mount Airy *Also Called: Michael Tate* **(G-9153)**

Mikes Welding & Fabricating.................................. 336 472-5804
2871 Old Highway 29 Thomasville (27360) **(G-12048)**

Mikron Industries.. 253 398-1382
2505 Meridian Pkwy # 250 Durham (27713) **(G-4134)**

Mikropor America Inc..
10512 Kilmory Ter Charlotte (28210) **(G-2501)**

Mikropul LLC... 704 998-2600
4500 Chesapeake Dr Charlotte (28216) **(G-2502)**

Mil3 Inc.. 919 362-1217
500 Upchurch St Apex (27502) **(G-181)**

Milesi Wood Coatings, Charlotte *Also Called: Ivm Chemicals Inc* **(G-2358)**

Military Products Inc.. 910 637-0315
5425 Nc Highway 211 West End (27376) **(G-12557)**

Military Wraps Inc... 910 671-0008
3400a David St Lumberton (28358) **(G-7962)**

Milkco, Asheville *Also Called: Milkco Inc* **(G-547)**

Milkco Inc... 828 254-8428
220 Deaverview Rd Asheville (28806) **(G-547)**

Mill Art Wood.. 919 828-7376
1500 Capital Blvd Raleigh (27603) **(G-10307)**

Mill-Chem Manufacturing Inc................................. 336 889-8038
650 Bassett Dr Thomasville (27360) **(G-12049)**

Millar Industries Inc.. 828 687-0639
20 Loop Rd Arden (28704) **(G-285)**

Millenia Usa LLC
3211c Falling Creek Rd Hickory (28601) **(G-6395)**

Millenium Print Group (PA).................................... 919 818-1229
4301 Waterleaf Ct Greensboro (27410) **(G-5693)**

Millenium Print Group, Raleigh *Also Called: Park Communications LLC* **(G-10358)**

Millennium Buildings Inc.. 866 216-8499
317 W Atkins St Dobson (27017) **(G-3823)**

Millennium Landscaping, High Point *Also Called: True Portion Inc* **(G-6813)**

Millennium Mfg or US Chem, Boone *Also Called: US Buildings LLC* **(G-949)**

Millennium Mfg Structures LLC.............................. 828 265-3737
353 Industrial Park Dr Boone (28607) **(G-934)**

Millennium Packaging Svc LLC............................... 775 353-5127
1953 Tw Alexander Dr Ste A Durham (27703) **(G-4135)**

Millennium Pharmaceuticals Inc............................. 866 466-7779
10430 Harris Oak Blvd Ste 1 Charlotte (28269) **(G-2503)**

Millennium Print Group, Greensboro *Also Called: Park Communications LLC* **(G-5732)**

Millennium Print Group, Morrisville *Also Called: Unlimted Potential Sanford Inc* **(G-9083)**

Miller Bee Supply Inc.. 336 670-2249
496 Yellow Banks Rd North Wilkesboro (28659) **(G-9548)**

Miller Brothers Lumber Co, Elkin *Also Called: Miller Brothers Lumber Co Inc* **(G-4448)**

Miller Brothers Lumber Co Inc............................... 336 366-3400
350 Elkin Wildlife Rd Elkin (28621) **(G-4448)**

Miller Ctrl Mfg Inc Clinton NC............................... 910 592-5112
1008 Southwest Blvd Clinton (28328) **(G-3235)**

Miller Dumpster Service LLC................................. 704 504-9300
16450 Shallow Pond Rd Charlotte (28278) **(G-2504)**

Miller Glass... 828 681-8083
72 Bradley Branch Rd Arden (28704) **(G-286)**

A
L
P
H
A
B
E
T
I
C

Miller Logging Co Inc.. 252 229-9860
7901 Main St Vanceboro (28586) *(G-12220)*

Miller Products Inc.. 704 587-1870
4100 Turtle Creek Ln Charlotte (28273) *(G-2505)*

Miller Products Co, Greensboro Also Called: Easth20 Holdings Llc *(G-5510)*

Miller S Utility MGT Inc.. 910 298-3847
163 Jackson Store Rd Beulaville (28518) *(G-843)*

Miller Saws & Supplies Inc... 252 636-3347
115 Ridgewood Trl New Bern (28560) *(G-9382)*

Miller Sheet Metal Co Inc.. 336 751-2304
2038 Us Highway 601 S Mocksville (27028) *(G-8378)*

Millers Sports and Trophies....................................... 252 792-2050
101 Washington St Williamston (27892) *(G-12672)*

Milligan House Movers Inc (PA).................................. 910 653-2272
2115 Swamp Fox Hwy E Tabor City (28463) *(G-11913)*

Milliken & Company.. 828 247-4300
2080 Nc Highway 226 Bostic (28018) *(G-963)*

Milliken & Company.. 336 548-5680
109 Turner Rd Mayodan (27027) *(G-8208)*

Milliken Calabash Seafood, Shallotte Also Called: Lloyds Oyster House Inc *(G-11304)*

Mills Manufacturing Corp (PA).................................... 828 645-3061
22 Mills Pl Asheville (28804) *(G-548)*

Millstreet Design, Forest City Also Called: Heritage Classic Wovens LLC *(G-4791)*

Millwood, Charlotte Also Called: Millwood Inc *(G-2506)*

Millwood Inc.. 704 817-7541
5950 Fairview Rd Ste 250 Charlotte (28210) *(G-2506)*

Millys Jamaican Jerk Seasoning, Raleigh Also Called: Cool Runnings Jamaican LLC *(G-10015)*

Milpak Graphics Inc... 336 347-8772
2880 Big Oaks Dr King (27021) *(G-7332)*

Milspec Plastics, Candler Also Called: Cs Systems Company Inc *(G-1222)*

Milwaukee Instruments Inc.. 252 443-3630
2950 Business Park Dr Rocky Mount (27804) *(G-10853)*

Minas Equity Partners LLC... 336 724-5152
2710 Boulder Park Ct Winston Salem (27101) *(G-13254)*

Mincar Group Inc.. 919 772-7170
215 Tryon Rd Raleigh (27603) *(G-10308)*

Minda North America LLC.. 828 313-0092
10 N Summit Ave Granite Falls (28630) *(G-5313)*

Mindfully Made Brands, Winston Salem Also Called: Mindfully Made Usa LLC *(G-13255)*

Mindfully Made Usa LLC.. 336 701-0377
1976 Runnymede Rd Winston Salem (27104) *(G-13255)*

Minelli Usa LLC.. 828 578-6734
1245 26th St Se Hickory (28602) *(G-6396)*

Mineral Research & Development, Harrisburg Also Called: Venator Chemicals LLC *(G-6120)*

Mineral Springs Fertilizer Inc.................................... 704 843-2683
5901 Eubanks Mineral Springs (28108) *(G-8327)*

Minges Bottling Group.. 252 636-5898
256 Middle St New Bern (28560) *(G-9383)*

Minges Printing & Advg Co.. 704 867-6791
323 S Chestnut St Gastonia (28054) *(G-5098)*

Minges Printing Company, Gastonia Also Called: Minges Printing & Advg Co *(G-5098)*

Minhas Furniture House Inc.. 910 898-0808
6844 Nc 705 Hwy Robbins (27325) *(G-10754)*

Mini Storage of North Carolina, Statesville Also Called: Betco Inc *(G-11670)*

Miningstore, Cary Also Called: Aurum Capital Ventures Inc *(G-1300)*

Minipro LLC.. 844 517-4776
1289 Fordham Blvd Ste 263 Chapel Hill (27514) *(G-1558)*

Minka Lighting Inc... 704 785-9200
435 Business Blvd Nw Concord (28027) *(G-3403)*

Minky Botique The, Concord Also Called: Designer Fabrics Inc *(G-3354)*

Minnewawa Inc... 865 522-8103
130 Sunrise Center Dr Thomasville (27360) *(G-12050)*

Minnewawa Inc... 865 522-8103
10612 Providence Rd Ste D Charlotte (28277) *(G-2507)*

Mint Hill Cabinet Shop, Monroe Also Called: Mint Hill Cabinet Shop Inc *(G-8531)*

Mint Hill Cabinet Shop Inc... 704 821-9373
5519 Cannon Dr Monroe (28110) *(G-8531)*

Mint Hill Industries... 704 545-8852
7313 Old Oak Ln Mint Hill (28227) *(G-8341)*

Minute Man Anchors, East Flat Rock Also Called: Mma Manufacturing Inc *(G-4334)*

Minute-Man Products Inc... 828 692-0256
305 W King St East Flat Rock (28726) *(G-4333)*

Minuteman Press, Charlotte Also Called: Babusci Crtive Prtg Imging LLC *(G-1735)*

Minuteman Press, Clinton Also Called: Commercial Prtg Co of Clinton *(G-3231)*

Minuteman Press, Gastonia Also Called: Minuteman Press of Gastonia *(G-5099)*

Minuteman Press of Gastonia..................................... 704 867-3366
495 E Long Ave Gastonia (28054) *(G-5099)*

Minuteman Quick Copy Svc Inc.................................. 910 455-5353
207 W Bayshore Blvd Jacksonville (28540) *(G-7132)*

Miracle Recreation Eqp Co... 704 875-6550
11515 Vanstory Dr Ste 100 Huntersville (28078) *(G-7014)*

Mirchandani Inc.. 919 872-8871
3904 Peppertree Pl Raleigh (27604) *(G-10309)*

Mirror Tech Inc... 336 342-6041
1011 Freeway Dr Reidsville (27320) *(G-10693)*

Mirrormate LLC... 704 390-7377
9317 Monroe Rd Ste A Charlotte (28270) *(G-2508)*

Mischief Makers Local 816 LLC.................................. 336 763-2003
1504 Rainbow Dr Greensboro (27403) *(G-5694)*

Misonix, Durham Also Called: Misonix LLC *(G-4136)*

Misonix LLC (HQ).. 631 694-9555
4721 Emperor Blvd Durham (27703) *(G-4136)*

Misonix Opco Inc (DH).. 631 694-9555
4721 Emperor Blvd Durham (27703) *(G-4137)*

Miss Tortillas Inc.. 919 598-8646
3801 Wake Forest Rd Ste 106 Durham (27703) *(G-4138)*

Mission Foods, Goldsboro Also Called: Gruma Corporation *(G-5220)*

Mission Srgcal Innovations LLC.................................. 678 699-6057
7424 Acc Blvd Ste 104 Raleigh (27617) *(G-10310)*

Mitchell Concrete Products Inc................................... 919 934-4333
490 W Market St Smithfield (27577) *(G-11455)*

Mitchell Meat Processing, Walnut Cove Also Called: Mitchells Meat Processing *(G-12328)*

Mitchell Medlin Machine Shop.................................... 704 289-2840
1394 Walkup Ave Ste C Monroe (28110) *(G-8532)*

Mitchell Water/Filtering Plant, Greensboro Also Called: City of Greensboro *(G-5446)*

Mitchell Welding Inc.. 828 765-2620
7080 Us 19e Spruce Pine (28777) *(G-11583)*

Mitchells Meat Processing... 336 591-7420
401 Mitchell St Walnut Cove (27052) *(G-12328)*

Mitchum Quality Snack, Charlotte Also Called: Igh Enterprises Inc *(G-2310)*

Miters Touch, Banner Elk Also Called: Miters Touch Inc *(G-688)*

Miters Touch Inc... 828 963-4445
591 Old Hartley Rd Banner Elk (28604) *(G-688)*

Mitsubishi Chem Methacrylates, Charlotte Also Called: Mitsubishi Chemical Amer Inc *(G-2509)*

Mitsubishi Chemical Amer Inc (DH)............................ 980 580-2839
9115 Harris Corners Pkwy Ste 300 Charlotte (28269) *(G-2509)*

Mitsubishi Materials USA Corp................................... 980 312-3100
105 Corporate Center Dr Ste A Mooresville (28117) *(G-8724)*

Mitt S Nitts Inc... 919 596-6793
1014 S Hoover Rd Durham (27703) *(G-4139)*

Mixon Mills Inc... 828 297-5431
4965 Us Highway 421 N Vilas (28692) *(G-12231)*

Mixx Pt 5, Swannanoa Also Called: Mixx-Point 5 Project LLC *(G-11873)*

Mixx-Point 5 Project LLC... 858 298-4625
107 W Buckeye Rd Swannanoa (28778) *(G-11873)*

Mjt Us Inc.. 704 826-7828
6801 Northpark Blvd Ste A Charlotte (28216) *(G-2510)*

Mk Global Holdings LLC (DH)..................................... 704 334-1904
5101 Terminal St Charlotte (28208) *(G-2511)*

Mk Pro Logistics LLC... 980 420-8156
7001 Sweetfield Dr Huntersville (28078) *(G-7015)*

Mkc85 Inc (PA).. 910 762-1986
2705 Castle Creek Ln Wilmington (28401) *(G-12855)*

Mlb Screen Printing... 704 363-6124
12008 Regal Lily Ln Huntersville (28078) *(G-7016)*

Mlf Company LLC.. 919 231-9401
3248 Lake Woodard Dr Raleigh (27604) *(G-10311)*

Mlg Trmscndent Trckg Trnsp Svc................................ 336 905-1192
3495 Hickswood Forest Dr High Point (27265) *(G-6713)*

(G-0000) Company's Geographic Section entry number

Mm Clayton LLC.. 919 553-4113
1000 Ccc Dr Clayton (27520) (G-3160)

Mma Manufacturing Inc.. 828 692-0256
305 W King St East Flat Rock (28726) (G-4334)

Mmb One Inc (PA)... 704 523-8163
4629 Dwight Evans Rd Charlotte (28217) (G-2512)

Mmdi Inc.. 704 882-4550
200 Beltway Blvd Matthews (28104) (G-8186)

Mmj Machining and Fabg Inc.................................... 336 495-1029
1332 Gene Allred Dr Randleman (27317) (G-10653)

MMS Logistics Incorporated..................................... 336 214-3552
1509 Guinness Dr Mc Leansville (27301) (G-8225)

Mobius Imaging, Charlotte Also Called: Mobius Imaging LLC (G-2513)

Mobius Imaging LLC.. 704 773-7652
1723 Beverly Dr Charlotte (28207) (G-2513)

Mocaro Dyeing & Finishing, Monroe Also Called: Sdfc LLC (G-8556)

Mocaro Dyeing & Finishing Inc................................. 704 878-6645
2201 Mocaro Dr Statesville (28677) (G-11732)

Mocaro Industries Inc... 704 878-6645
2201 Mocaro Dr Statesville (28677) (G-11733)

Mocha Memoir Press.. 336 404-7445
931 S Main St Kernersville (27284) (G-7287)

Mock Tire & Automotive Inc...................................... 336 753-8473
132 Interstate Dr Mocksville (27028) (G-8379)

Mock Tire & Automotive Inc...................................... 336 774-0081
834 S Stratford Rd Winston Salem (27103) (G-13256)

Mock Tire & Automotive Inc (PA).............................. 336 768-1010
4752 Country Club Rd Winston Salem (27104) (G-13257)

Modacam Incorporated.. 704 489-8500
3762 Deer Run Denver (28037) (G-3793)

Modena Southern Dyeing Corp................................. 704 866-9156
1010 E Ozark Ave Gastonia (28054) (G-5100)

Modern Densifying Inc.. 704 434-8335
662 Plato Lee Rd Shelby (28150) (G-11363)

Modern Information Svcs Inc.................................... 704 872-1020
436 S Center St Statesville (28677) (G-11734)

Modern Lightning Protection Co.............................. 252 756-3006
302 Queen Annes Rd Greenville (27858) (G-6005)

Modern Machine and Metal Fabricators Inc............. 336 993-4808
3201 Centre Park Blvd Winston Salem (27107) (G-13258)

Modern Machining Inc.. 919 775-7332
115 Brady Rd Sanford (27330) (G-11210)

Modern Mold & Tool Company.................................. 704 377-2300
1050 Ironwood Dr Mount Holly (28120) (G-9238)

Modern Polymers Inc.. 704 435-5825
901 W Academy St Cherryville (28021) (G-3067)

Modern Recreational Tech Inc.................................. 847 272-2278
7625 Thorndike Rd Greensboro (27409) (G-5695)

Modern Recreational Tech Inc.................................. 800 221-4466
7625 Thorndike Rd Greensboro (27409) (G-5696)

Modern Tool Service.. 919 365-7470
100 Walnut St Wendell (27591) (G-12539)

Modlins Anonized Aluminum Wldg............................ 252 753-7274
4551 Nc Highway 121 Farmville (27828) (G-4536)

Modoral Brands Inc.. 336 741-7230
401 N Main St Winston Salem (27101) (G-13259)

Moduslink Corporation... 781 663-5000
990 N Greenfield Pkwy Garner (27529) (G-4943)

Moe Jt Enterprises Inc... 423 512-1427
130 Back Forty Dr Winston Salem (27127) (G-13260)

Moehring-Group, Beaufort Also Called: Atlantic Veneer Company LLC (G-719)

Moen, New Bern Also Called: Moen Incorporated (G-9384)

Moen Incorporated.. 252 638-3300
101 Industrial Dr New Bern (28562) (G-9384)

Moes Hndy Svcs Fnce Instl Mno.............................. 910 712-1402
185 Desert Orchid Cir Raeford (28376) (G-9842)

Moffitt Machine Company Inc................................... 910 485-2159
232 Winslow St Fayetteville (28301) (G-4642)

Mohawk Industries, Garner Also Called: Mohawk Industries Inc (G-4944)

Mohawk Industries Inc.. 919 661-5590
2000 Pergo Pkwy Garner (27529) (G-4944)

Mohawk Industries Inc.. 919 609-4759
800 N Greenfield Pkwy Garner (27529) (G-4945)

Mohawk Industries Inc.. 910 439-6959
149 Homanit Usa Rd Mount Gilead (27306) (G-9207)

Mohawk Industries Inc.. 336 313-4156
550 Cloniger Dr Thomasville (27360) (G-12051)

Mohawk Laminate & Hardwood, Thomasville Also Called: Mohawk Industries Inc (G-12051)

Mohican Mills Inc.. 704 735-3343
1419 E Gaston St Lincolnton (28092) (G-7844)

Moire Creations America LLC (PA).......................... 704 482-9860
1808 Country Garden Dr Shelby (28150) (G-11364)

Moissanite.com, LLC, Morrisville Also Called: Charlesandcolvardcom LLC (G-8956)

Mojo Sportswear Inc.. 252 758-4176
1016 Myrtle St Greenville (27834) (G-6006)

Mojo Sportwear, Greenville Also Called: Mojo Sportswear Inc (G-6006)

Molded Fiber Glass, Morganton Also Called: Molded Fibr GL Cmpny/Nrth Crli (G-8882)

Molded Fibr GL Cmpny/Nrth Crli.............................. 828 584-4974
213 Reep Dr Morganton (28655) (G-8882)

Molds of Bethlehem, Hickory Also Called: Bethlehem Manufacturing Co (G-6270)

Molecular Toxicology Inc... 828 264-9099
157 Industrial Park Dr Boone (28607) (G-935)

Molley Chomper LLC.. 404 769-1439
1124 Jerd Branch Rd Lansing (28643) (G-7478)

Moltox, Boone Also Called: Molecular Toxicology Inc (G-935)

Momentive Performance Mtls Inc............................. 704 805-6252
9129 Southern Pine Blvd Charlotte (28273) (G-2514)

Momentive Performance Mtls Inc............................. 704 805-6200
13620 Reese Blvd E Ste 310 Huntersville (28078) (G-7017)

Momentive Performance Mtls USA, Huntersville Also Called: Momentive Performance Mtls Inc (G-7017)

Mon Macaron LLC... 984 200-1387
111 Seaboard Ave Ste 118 Raleigh (27604) (G-10312)

Mona Lisa Foods, Hendersonville Also Called: Barry Callebaut USA LLC (G-6185)

Monarch Color Corporation (PA).............................. 704 394-4626
5327 Brookshire Blvd Charlotte (28216) (G-2515)

Monarch Knitting McHy Corp.................................... 704 283-8171
601 Mcarthur Cir Monroe (28110) (G-8533)

Monarch Knitting McHy Corp (PA)............................ 704 291-3300
115 N Secrest Ave Monroe (28110) (G-8534)

Monarch Manufacturing, Monroe Also Called: Monarch Knitting McHy Corp (G-8534)

Monarch Manufacturing Corp................................... 704 283-8171
115 N Secrest Ave Monroe (28110) (G-8535)

Monarch Medical Tech LLC....................................... 704 335-1300
112 S Tryon St Ste 800 Charlotte (28284) (G-2516)

Monarch Printers.. 704 376-1533
3900 Greensboro St Charlotte (28206) (G-2517)

Mongoose LLC.. 919 400-0772
423 Lakeside Ave Burlington (27217) (G-1130)

Monitor Roller Mill Inc.. 336 591-4126
109 E 4th St Walnut Cove (27052) (G-12329)

Monk Lekeisha... 910 385-0361
Goldsboro (27533) (G-5230)

Mono Plate Inc.. 631 643-3100
2404 Pilsley Rd Apex (27539) (G-182)

Monogram Asheville.. 828 707-8110
800 Brevard Rd Ste 812 Asheville (28806) (G-549)

Monroe Metal Manufacturing, Monroe Also Called: Monroe Metal Manufacturing Inc (G-8536)

Monroe Metal Manufacturing Inc............................. 800 366-1391
6025 Stitt St Monroe (28110) (G-8536)

Monsanto Company... 252 212-5421
5746 Pearsall St Battleboro (27809) (G-702)

MONSANTO COMPANY, Battleboro Also Called: Monsanto Company (G-702)

Monster Brewing Company LLC................................ 828 883-2337
342 Mountain Industrial Dr Brevard (28712) (G-976)

Monte Enterprises Inc... 252 637-5803
3204 Neuse Blvd New Bern (28560) (G-9385)

Monte Printing Co, New Bern Also Called: Monte Enterprises Inc (G-9385)

Montgomery Logging Inc.. 910 572-2806
207 Atkins Dairy Rd Troy (27371) (G-12163)

Month9 Books LLC (PA).. 919 645-5786
4208 Six Forks Rd Ste 1000 Raleigh (27609) (G-10313)

Montrose Hanger Co, Wilson *Also Called: Swofford Inc (G-13034)*

Montys Welding & Fabrication.................................. 919 337-7859
157 Creek Commons Ave Garner (27529) *(G-4946)*

Monumental Contractors Inc..................................... 762 352-0564
4111 Field Crossing Dr Winston Salem (27107) *(G-13261)*

Moog Components Group, Murphy *Also Called: Moog Inc (G-9293)*

Moog Inc.. 828 837-5115
1995 Nc Highway 141 Murphy (28906) *(G-9293)*

Moon Audio... 919 649-5018
1157 Executive Cir Ste 101 Cary (27511) *(G-1402)*

Moon N Sea Nc LLC.. 704 588-1963
12810 Virkler Dr Charlotte (28273) *(G-2518)*

Moondance Soaps & More, Raleigh *Also Called: Rachel Dubois (G-10419)*

Moonshine Press.. 828 371-8519
162 Riverwood Dr Franklin (28734) *(G-4837)*

Moore Machine Products Inc..................................... 910 592-2718
919 Rowan Rd Clinton (28328) *(G-3236)*

Moore Printing & Graphics Inc................................... 919 821-3293
5320 Departure Dr Raleigh (27616) *(G-10314)*

Moore S Welding Service Inc..................................... 919 837-5769
142 Elmer Moore Rd Bear Creek (27207) *(G-716)*

Moore Signs, Wilmington *Also Called: Kenneth Moore Signs (G-12826)*

Moorecraft Reels Inc... 252 823-2510
101 Royster St Tarboro (27886) *(G-11935)*

Moorecraft Wood Proucts Inc.................................... 252 823-2510
101 Royster St Tarboro (27886) *(G-11936)*

Moores Cylinder Heads LLC (PA)................................ 704 786-8412
323 Corban Ave Sw Ste 515 Concord (28025) *(G-3404)*

Moores Fiberglass Inc.. 252 753-2583
926 Howell Swamp Church Rd Walstonburg (27888) *(G-12334)*

Moores Mch Co Fayetteville Inc (PA)............................ 919 837-5354
13120 Nc 902 Hwy Bear Creek (27207) *(G-717)*

Moores Upholstering Interiors................................... 704 240-8393
308 S Poplar St Lincolnton (28092) *(G-7845)*

Mooresville Ice Cream Company LLC............................. 704 664-5456
172 N Brd St Mooresville (28115) *(G-8725)*

Mooresville NC.. 704 909-6459
174 Mandarin Dr Mooresville (28117) *(G-8726)*

Mooresvlle Pub Wrks Snttion De................................. 704 664-4278
2523 Charlotte Hwy Mooresville (28117) *(G-8727)*

Morbern LLC.. 336 883-4332
401 Fraley Rd High Point (27263) *(G-6714)*

Morbern USA Inc (HQ)... 336 883-4332
401 Fraley Rd High Point (27263) *(G-6715)*

More Than Billboards Inc... 336 723-1018
2737 W Mountain St Kernersville (27284) *(G-7288)*

More Than Just Art Inc... 910 864-7797
6441 Yadkin Rd Ste E Fayetteville (28303) *(G-4643)*

Moretz & Sipe Inc.. 828 327-8661
3261 Highland Ave Ne Hickory (28601) *(G-6397)*

Moretz Signs Inc.. 828 387-4600
125 Staghorn Hollow Rd Beech Mountain (28604) *(G-738)*

Morgan Advanced Mtls Tech Inc................................. 910 892-9677
504 N Ashe Ave Dunn (28334) *(G-3862)*

Morgan Creek Seafood, Beaufort *Also Called: Gillikin Marine Railways Inc (G-728)*

Morgan Fertilizer, Farmville *Also Called: Harvey Fertilizer and Gas Co (G-4530)*

Morgan Printers Inc... 252 355-5588
4120 Bayswater Rd Winterville (28590) *(G-13419)*

Morgans Cabinets Inc.. 704 485-8693
8056 Rocky River Rd Oakboro (28129) *(G-9581)*

Morganton Pressure Vessels LLC, Marion *Also Called: Mpv Mrgnton Prssure Vssels NC (G-8057)*

Morinaga America, Mebane *Also Called: Morinaga America Foods Inc (G-8252)*

Morinaga America Foods Inc..................................... 919 643-2439
4391 Wilson Rd Mebane (27302) *(G-8252)*

Morningstar Signs and Banners.................................. 704 861-0020
307 E Franklin Blvd Gastonia (28054) *(G-5101)*

Moroil Corp... 704 795-9595
6867 Belt Rd Concord (28027) *(G-3405)*

Moroil Technologies, Concord *Also Called: Moroil Corp (G-3405)*

Morris & Associates Inc.. 919 582-9200
803 Morris Dr Garner (27529) *(G-4947)*

Morris East, Charlotte *Also Called: Morris Family Theatrical Inc (G-2519)*

Morris Family Theatrical Inc (PA)................................ 704 332-3304
6900 Morris Estate Dr Charlotte (28262) *(G-2519)*

Morris Machine Company Inc..................................... 704 824-4242
122 Stroupe Rd Gastonia (28056) *(G-5102)*

Morris Machine Sales, Gastonia *Also Called: Morris Machine Company Inc (G-5102)*

Morris South LLC... 704 523-6008
8530 Steele Creek Place Dr Ste H Charlotte (28273) *(G-2520)*

Morris South M T S, Charlotte *Also Called: Morris South LLC (G-2520)*

Morrisette Paper Company Inc................................... 336 342-5570
105 E Harrison St Reidsville (27320) *(G-10694)*

Morrison Mill Work... 828 774-5415
51 Thompson St Asheville (28803) *(G-550)*

Morton Buildings Inc... 252 291-1300
3042 Forest Hills Rd Sw Ste C Wilson (27893) *(G-13007)*

Morton Metalcraft Company N.................................... 336 731-5700
Welcome (27374) *(G-12512)*

Morven Partners LP... 252 482-2193
185 Peanut Dr Edenton (27932) *(G-4369)*

Morven Partners LP... 252 794-3435
406 Spring St Windsor (27983) *(G-13055)*

Mosack Group LLC.. 888 229-2874
11210 Allen Station Dr Mint Hill (28227) *(G-8342)*

Moss Brothers Tires & Svc Inc................................... 910 895-4572
190 W Us Highway 74 Rockingham (28379) *(G-10783)*

Moss Sign Company Inc.. 828 299-7766
526 Swannanoa River Rd Asheville (28805) *(G-551)*

Moss Supply Company (PA)...................................... 704 596-8717
5001 N Graham St Charlotte (28269) *(G-2521)*

Mother Earth Brewing LLC.. 252 208-2437
311 N Herritage St Kinston (28501) *(G-7423)*

Mother Murphys Labs Inc... 336 273-1737
300 Dougherty St Greensboro (27406) *(G-5697)*

Mother Murphys Labs Inc (PA)................................... 336 273-1737
2826 S Elm Eugene St Greensboro (27406) *(G-5698)*

Motion-Eaze, Randleman *Also Called: North Carolina Lumber Company (G-10654)*

Motioncraft By Sherrill Div, Morganton *Also Called: Sherrill Furniture Company (G-8896)*

Motivo Furniture, High Point *Also Called: Ariston Hospitality Inc (G-6528)*

Moto Group LLC.. 828 350-7653
40 Cane Creek Industrial Park Rd Fletcher (28732) *(G-4757)*

Motor Rite Inc.. 919 625-3653
1001 Corporation Pkwy Ste 100 Raleigh (27610) *(G-10315)*

Motor Shop Inc... 704 867-8488
5001 York Hwy Gastonia (28052) *(G-5103)*

Motor Vhcles Lcense Plate Agcy................................. 252 338-6965
1545 N Road St Ste E Elizabeth City (27909) *(G-4398)*

Motoring Inc.. 704 809-1265
139 Golden Pond Ln Mooresville (28117) *(G-8728)*

Motorola Mobility LLC.. 919 294-1289
7001 Development Dr Morrisville (27560) *(G-9021)*

Motorsport Innovations Inc....................................... 704 728-7837
19220 Callaway Hills Ln Davidson (28036) *(G-3713)*

Motorsports Designs Inc.. 336 454-1181
300 Old Thomasville Rd High Point (27260) *(G-6716)*

Motorsports Machining Tech LLC................................. 336 475-3742
37 High Tech Blvd Thomasville (27360) *(G-12052)*

Motsinger Block Plant Inc.. 336 764-0350
199 Disher Rd Winston Salem (27107) *(G-13262)*

Moulding Millwork LLC... 704 504-9880
11445 Granite St Unit C Charlotte (28273) *(G-2522)*

Moulding Source Incorporated................................... 704 658-1111
184 Azalea Rd Mooresville (28115) *(G-8729)*

Mount Airy Signs & Letters Inc.................................. 336 786-5777
1543 Fancy Gap Rd Mount Airy (27030) *(G-9154)*

Mount Holly West Plant, Mount Holly *Also Called: Clariant Corporation (G-9224)*

Mount Hope Machinery Co
2000 Donald Ross Rd Charlotte (28208) *(G-2523)*

Mount Olive Pickle Company...................................... 704 867-5585
1534 Union Rd Ste A Gastonia (28054) *(G-5104)*

Mount Olive Pickle Company Inc................................. 704 867-5585
1534 Union Rd Ste A Gastonia (28054) *(G-5105)*

Mount Olive Pickle Company Inc (PA)............................919 658-2535
  1 Cucumber Blvd Mount Olive (28365) *(G-9257)*

Mount Olive Tribune, Mount Olive *Also Called: Benmot Publishing Company Inc (G-9247)*

Mount Vernon Chemicals LLC.......................................336 226-1161
  2001 Willow Spring Ln Burlington (27215) *(G-1131)*

Mount Vernon Mills Inc...336 226-1161
  2001 Willow Spring Ln Burlington (27215) *(G-1132)*

Mountain Area Info Netwrk..828 255-0182
  34 Wall St Ste 407 Asheville (28801) *(G-552)*

Mountain Bear & Co Inc..828 631-0156
  28 Church St Dillsboro (28725) *(G-3819)*

Mountain Cabinetry Closets LLC....................................828 966-9000
  309 S Country Club Rd Brevard (28712) *(G-977)*

Mountain Graphics, Asheville *Also Called: Art Enterprises Inc (G-431)*

Mountain Homes of Wnc LLC...828 216-2546
  12 White Walnut Dr Weaverville (28787) *(G-12496)*

Mountain International LLC...828 606-0194
  1345 Old Hendersonville Hwy Brevard (28712) *(G-978)*

Mountain Khakis, Charlotte *Also Called: Mk Global Holdings LLC (G-2511)*

Mountain Leisure Hot Tubs LLC.....................................828 649-7727
  40 Business Park Cir Ste 60 Arden (28704) *(G-287)*

Mountain Machine, Hendersonville *Also Called: Eddie S Mountain Machine Inc (G-6204)*

Mountain Manner Exotic Jellies, Marble *Also Called: Pamela Stoeppelwerth (G-8027)*

Mountain Rcrtion Log Cbins LLC....................................828 387-6688
  8007 Linville Falls Hwy Newland (28657) *(G-9432)*

Mountain Showcase, Hendersonville *Also Called: Mountain Showcase Group Inc (G-6228)*

Mountain Showcase Group Inc.......................................828 692-9494
  211 Sugarloaf Rd Hendersonville (28792) *(G-6228)*

Mountain Times Inc...336 246-6397
  7 W Main St West Jefferson (28694) *(G-12567)*

Mountain Top Woodworking...336 982-4059
  816 Old Obids Rd West Jefferson (28694) *(G-12568)*

Mountain Xpress, Asheville *Also Called: Green Line Media Inc (G-512)*

Mountaineer Inc...828 452-0661
  220 N Main St Waynesville (28786) *(G-12464)*

Mountaineer Yellowpages...866 758-0123
  16126 Glen Miro Dr Huntersville (28078) *(G-7018)*

Mountaintop Cheesecakes LLC.......................................336 391-9127
  209 Sunburst Ln Mocksville (27028) *(G-8380)*

Mountaire Farms LLC...910 974-3232
  203 Morris Farm Rd Candor (27229) *(G-1239)*

Mountaire Farms LLC...910 843-3332
  17269 Nc 71 Hwy N Lumber Bridge (28357) *(G-7939)*

Mountaire Farms LLC...910 843-5942
  17269 N Carolina Hwy 71 Lumber Bridge (28357) *(G-7940)*

Mountaire Farms LLC...919 663-1768
  4555 Old Us Hwy 421 N Siler City (27344) *(G-11418)*

Mountaire Farms Inc..910 843-5942
  17269 Hwy 71 Lumber Bridge (28357) *(G-7941)*

Mountaire Farms Inc..910 844-3126
  10800 Pell Dr Maxton (28364) *(G-8204)*

Mountaire Farms Inc..919 663-0848
  1101 E 3rd St Siler City (27344) *(G-11419)*

Mountaire Farms Inc..704 978-3055
  2206 W Front St Statesville (28677) *(G-11735)*

Mountaire Farms Inc..704 978-3055
  2206 W Front St Statesville (28677) *(G-11736)*

Mountaire Farms North Carolina, Candor *Also Called: Mountaire Farms LLC (G-1239)*

Mountaire Farms, L.L.C., Lumber Bridge *Also Called: Mountaire Farms LLC (G-7940)*

Movers and Shakers LLC...980 771-0505
  1016 W Craighead Rd Charlotte (28206) *(G-2524)*

Moving Screens Incorporated..336 364-9259
  7807 Helena Moriah Rd Rougemont (27572) *(G-10914)*

Mpe Usa Inc..704 340-4910
  10424 Rodney St Pineville (28134) *(G-9743)*

MPS Greensboro, Greensboro *Also Called: Multi Packaging Solutions (G-5699)*

Mpv Morganton Pressu..828 652-3704
  1 Alfredo Baglioni Dr Marion (28752) *(G-8056)*

Mpv Mrgnton Prssure Vssels NC......................................828 652-3704
  1 Alfredo Baglioni Dr Marion (28752) *(G-8057)*

Mpx Manufacturing Inc...704 762-9207
  1531 S Main St Salisbury (28144) *(G-11094)*

Mr Bs Fun Foods Inc (PA)..828 879-1901
  2616 Israel Chapel Rd Connelly Springs (28612) *(G-3480)*

Mr Tire Inc...828 262-3555
  1563 Blowing Rock Rd Boone (28607) *(G-936)*

Mr Tire Inc...704 483-1500
  357 N Nc 16 Business Hwy Denver (28037) *(G-3794)*

Mr Tire Inc...828 322-8130
  2105 N Center St Hickory (28601) *(G-6398)*

Mr Tire Inc...704 739-6456
  407 S Battleground Ave Kings Mountain (28086) *(G-7373)*

Mr Tire Inc...828 758-0047
  1306 Morganton Blvd Sw Lenoir (28645) *(G-7627)*

Mr Tire Inc...704 735-8024
  609 E Main St Lincolnton (28092) *(G-7846)*

Mr Tire Inc...704 484-0816
  315 S Dekalb St Shelby (28150) *(G-11365)*

Mr Tire Inc...704 872-4127
  149 E Front St Statesville (28677) *(G-11737)*

Mr Tobacco..919 747-9052
  4011 Capital Blvd Ste 125 Raleigh (27604) *(G-10316)*

Mra Services Inc..704 933-4300
  2500 S Cannon Blvd Kannapolis (28083) *(G-7216)*

Mrr Southern LLC..919 436-3571
  5842 Faringdon Pl Ste 1 Raleigh (27609) *(G-10317)*

Mrrefinish LLC..336 625-2400
  1804 Winchester Heights Dr Asheboro (27205) *(G-379)*

Ms Whlchair N CA AM State Coor....................................828 230-1129
  61 Cheek Rd Weaverville (28787) *(G-12497)*

MSA Safety Sales LLC...910 353-1540
  352 White St Jacksonville (28546) *(G-7133)*

MSI, Bessemer City *Also Called: Manufacturing Services Inc (G-826)*

MSI, Mooresville *Also Called: MSI Defense Solutions LLC (G-8730)*

MSI Defense Solutions LLC..704 660-8348
  136 Knob Hill Rd Mooresville (28117) *(G-8730)*

Mt Airy Meat Center Inc...336 786-2023
  133 Old Buck Shoals Rd Mount Airy (27030) *(G-9155)*

Mt Gilead Cut & Sew Inc..910 439-9909
  112 N Main St Mount Gilead (27306) *(G-9208)*

Mt Holly Plant, Charlotte *Also Called: Clariant Corporation (G-1924)*

MTI Medical Cables LLC...828 890-2888
  2133 Old Fanning Bridge Rd Fletcher (28732) *(G-4758)*

MTS Communication Products, Clayton *Also Called: Multi Technical Services Inc (G-3161)*

MTS Holdings Corp Inc..336 227-0151
  2900 Tucker St Burlington (27215) *(G-1133)*

MTS Sensors Division, Cary *Also Called: MTS Systems Corporation (G-1403)*

MTS Systems Corporation..919 677-2352
  3001 Sheldon Dr Cary (27513) *(G-1403)*

MTS Systems Roehrig, Greensboro *Also Called: Roehrig Engineering Inc (G-5793)*

Mud Duck Construction, Bolivia *Also Called: Mud Duck Operations (G-886)*

Mud Duck Operations..910 253-7669
  1470 Old Lennon Rd Se Bolivia (28422) *(G-886)*

Muddy Dog LLC...919 371-2818
  5196 Beaver Creek Rd New Hill (27562) *(G-9411)*

Muddy Dog Roasting Co, New Hill *Also Called: Muddy Dog LLC (G-9411)*

Muddy River Distillery LLC..336 516-4190
  250 N Main St Mount Holly (28120) *(G-9239)*

Mudgear LLC..347 674-9102
  2522 Handley Pl Charlotte (28226) *(G-2525)*

Mueller Die Cut Solutions Inc (HQ).................................704 588-3900
  10415 Westlake Dr Charlotte (28273) *(G-2526)*

Mueller Steam Specialty (DH).......................................910 865-8241
  1491 Nc Highway 20 W Saint Pauls (28384) *(G-11005)*

Mueller Steam Specialty, Saint Pauls *Also Called: Mueller Steam Specialty (G-11005)*

Mueller Systems LLC..704 278-2221
  10210 Statesville Blvd Cleveland (27013) *(G-3216)*

Mugo Gravel & Grading Inc (PA).....................................704 782-3478
  2600 Concord Pkwy S Concord (28027) *(G-3406)*

Mulch Magicians, Waxhaw *Also Called: Pressure Washing Near Me LLC (G-12437)*

A
L
P
H
A
B
E
T
I
C

Mulch Masters, Raleigh *Also Called: Mulch Masters of NC Inc (G-10318)*

Mulch Masters of NC Inc... 919 676-0031
  10200 Durant Rd Raleigh (27614) *(G-10318)*

Mulch Solutions LLC... 704 956-2343
  900 Warren Coleman Blvd Concord (28025) *(G-3407)*

Mull's Concrete & Septic Tanks, Morganton *Also Called: Mulls Con & Septic Tanks Inc (G-8883)*

Mullen Publications Inc... 704 527-5111
  9301 Forsyth Park Dr Ste A Charlotte (28273) *(G-2527)*

Mulls Con & Septic Tanks Inc.. 828 437-0959
  2416 Mount Home Church Rd Morganton (28655) *(G-8883)*

Multi Form, Wilmington *Also Called: Micronova Systems Inc (G-12853)*

Multi Packaging Solutions.. 336 855-7142
  7915 Industrial Village Rd Greensboro (27409) *(G-5699)*

Multi Technical Services Inc... 919 553-2995
  950 Nc Highway 42 W Clayton (27520) *(G-3161)*

Multi-Color Corporation... 828 658-6800
  15 Conrad Industrial Dr Weaverville (28787) *(G-12498)*

Multi-Shifter Inc.. 704 588-9611
  11110 Park Charlotte Blvd Charlotte (28273) *(G-2528)*

Multidrain Systems, Inc., Statesville *Also Called: ABT Foam Inc (G-11643)*

Multigen Diagnostics LLC... 336 510-1120
  1100 Revolution Mill Dr Ste 1 Greensboro (27405) *(G-5700)*

Multisite Led LLC.. 650 823-7247
  6715 Fairview Rd Charlotte (28210) *(G-2529)*

Multitrode Inc.. 561 994-8090
  14125 S Bridge Cir Charlotte (28273) *(G-2530)*

Muncy Winds, Vilas *Also Called: MW Enterprises Inc (G-12232)*

Mundo Uniformes LLC.. 704 287-1527
  10806 Reames Rd Ste W Charlotte (28269) *(G-2531)*

Mundy Machine & Fabricating Co, Dallas *Also Called: Mundy Machine Co Inc (G-3679)*

Mundy Machine Co Inc.. 704 922-8663
  3934 Puetts Chapel Rd Dallas (28034) *(G-3679)*

Munibilling.. 800 259-7020
  3300 Battleground Ave Ste 402 Greensboro (27410) *(G-5701)*

Murano Corporation.. 919 294-8233
  68 Tw Alexander Dr Ste 207 Durham (27709) *(G-4140)*

Murata Machinery Usa Inc (DH)...................................... 704 875-9280
  2120 Queen City Dr Charlotte (28208) *(G-2532)*

Murata McHy USA Holdings Inc (HQ)............................... 704 394-8331
  2120 Queen City Dr Charlotte (28266) *(G-2533)*

Muratatec, Charlotte *Also Called: Murata McHy USA Holdings Inc (G-2533)*

Muratec, Charlotte *Also Called: Murata Machinery Usa Inc (G-2532)*

Murdock Webbing Company Inc.. 252 823-1131
  1052 W Saint James St Tarboro (27886) *(G-11937)*

Muriel Harris Investments Inc... 800 932-3191
  3900 Murchison Rd Fayetteville (28311) *(G-4644)*

Murphy Printing & Vinyl LLC... 828 835-4848
  180 Beulah Ln Murphy (28906) *(G-9294)*

Murphy S Custom Cabinetry Inc....................................... 828 891-3050
  351 Hidden Woods Ln Hendersonville (28791) *(G-6229)*

Murphy USA, Lenoir *Also Called: Murphy USA Inc (G-7628)*

Murphy USA Inc.. 828 758-7055
  915 Blowing Rock Blvd Lenoir (28645) *(G-7628)*

Murphy-Brown LLC... 252 221-4463
  4033 Virginia Rd Hobbsville (27946) *(G-6884)*

Murphy-Brown LLC... 910 277-8999
  19600 Andrew Jackson Hwy Laurinburg (28352) *(G-7510)*

Murphy-Brown LLC... 910 293-3434
  210 Chief Ln Rose Hill (28458) *(G-10908)*

Murphy-Brown LLC... 910 282-4264
  152 Farrow To Finish Ln Rose Hill (28458) *(G-10909)*

Murphy-Brown LLC (DH).. 910 293-3434
  2822 W Nc 24 Hwy Warsaw (28398) *(G-12363)*

Murray Inc... 704 329-0400
  4508 Westinghouse Blvd Ste B Charlotte (28273) *(G-2534)*

Murray Inc... 847 620-7990
  8531 Steele Creek Place Dr Unit D Charlotte (28273) *(G-2535)*

Musa Gold LLC.. 704 579-7894
  8425 Cleve Brown Rd Charlotte (28269) *(G-2536)*

Muscadine Naturals Inc.. 888 628-5898
  6332 Cephis Dr Clemmons (27012) *(G-3197)*

Music & Arts.. 919 329-6069
  2566 Timber Dr Garner (27529) *(G-4948)*

Music Garden, Greensboro *Also Called: Music Matters Inc (G-5702)*

Music Matters Inc... 336 272-5303
  507 Arlington St Greensboro (27406) *(G-5702)*

Musicland Express.. 828 627-9431
  500 Jones Cove Rd Clyde (28721) *(G-3260)*

Musicmedic.com, Wilmington *Also Called: Dorian Corporation (G-12766)*

Mustang Reproductions Inc.. 704 786-0990
  4310 Concord Pkwy S Concord (28027) *(G-3408)*

Mutual Dropcloth, Monroe *Also Called: Dunn Manufacturing Corp (G-8479)*

Muviq Usa LLC.. 910 843-1024
  16824 Nc Highway 211 W Red Springs (28377) *(G-10670)*

Mva Leatherwood LLC.. 704 519-4200
  4530 Park Rd Charlotte (28209) *(G-2537)*

Mvi Productions, Charlotte *Also Called: Palmer Senn (G-2606)*

Mvp Group International Inc (HQ)..................................... 843 216-8380
  430 Gentry Rd Elkin (28621) *(G-4449)*

Mvp Group International.. 336 527-2238
  830 Fowler Rd Mount Airy (27030) *(G-9156)*

Mw Components, Charlotte *Also Called: Mw Industries Inc (G-2538)*

Mw Defense Systems, Lumberton *Also Called: Military Wraps Inc (G-7962)*

MW Enterprises Inc... 828 963-7083
  5014 Nc Highway 105 S Vilas (28692) *(G-12232)*

Mw Industries Inc (PA)... 704 837-0331
  3426 Toringdon Way Ste 100 Charlotte (28277) *(G-2538)*

Mw Manufacturers Inc.. 919 677-3900
  5020 Weston Pkwy Ste 400 Cary (27513) *(G-1404)*

Mww On Demand, Hendersonville *Also Called: Manual Woodworkers Weavers Inc (G-6224)*

My Alabaster Box LLC.. 919 873-1442
  5412 Cahaba Way Raleigh (27616) *(G-10319)*

My Kolors, Clemmons *Also Called: Kalajdzic Inc (G-3196)*

My Threesons Gourmet... 336 324-5638
  2138 Wentworth St Reidsville (27320) *(G-10695)*

Myers Forest Products Inc... 704 278-4532
  355 Barber Junction Rd Cleveland (27013) *(G-3217)*

Myers Tool and Machine Co Inc....................................... 336 956-1324
  156 Dixon St Lexington (27292) *(G-7719)*

Myfuturenc Inc.. 919 649-7834
  311 New Bern Ave Unit 26246 Raleigh (27611) *(G-10320)*

Mylan Pharmaceuticals Inc.. 336 271-6571
  2898 Manufacturers Rd Greensboro (27406) *(G-5703)*

Myricks Cabinet Shop Inc.. 919 266-3720
  2329 Hodge Rd Knightdale (27545) *(G-7453)*

Myricks Custom Fab Inc.. 828 645-5800
  181 Reems Creek Rd Ste 2 Weaverville (28787) *(G-12499)*

Mystic Farm & Distillery, Durham *Also Called: Barrister and Brewer LLC (G-3913)*

Mystic Lifestyle Inc... 704 960-4530
  184 Academy Ave Nw Concord (28025) *(G-3409)*

N C Coil Inc... 336 983-4440
  529b S Main St King (27021) *(G-7333)*

N C Mtor Vhcl Lcnse Plate Agcy, Burlington *Also Called: NC Motor Vhcl Lcnse Plate Agcy (G-1136)*

N C Sock, Hickory *Also Called: North Carolina Sock Inc (G-6403)*

N W L Capacitors, Snow Hill *Also Called: Nwl Inc (G-11481)*

N2 Company Inc... 910 202-0917
  5051 New Centre Dr Ste 210 Wilmington (28403) *(G-12856)*

N2 Franchising Inc.. 844 353-5378
  160 Mine Lake Ct Ste 200 Raleigh (27615) *(G-10321)*

N2 Publishing... 336 293-3845
  161 Shallowbrook Dr Advance (27006) *(G-36)*

N3xt Inc.. 704 905-2209
  8022 Providence Rd Ste 500-130 Charlotte (28277) *(G-2539)*

Naarva.. 704 333-3070
  614 Chipley Ave Charlotte (28205) *(G-2540)*

Nabell USA Corporation.. 704 986-2455
  208 Charter St Albemarle (28001) *(G-82)*

Nacho Industries Inc.. 919 937-9471
  8 Heath Pl Durham (27705) *(G-4141)*

Nachos & Beer LLC... 828 298-2280
  230 Charlotte Hwy Asheville (28803) *(G-553)*

(G-0000) Company's Geographic Section entry number

Naes-Oms.. 252 536-4525
   1200 Julian R Allsbrook Hwy Weldon (27890) *(G-12524)*

Nafshi Enterprises LLC................................. 910 986-9888
   14796 Us Highway 15 501 Aberdeen (28315) *(G-17)*

Nags Head Hammock Co, Nags Head *Also Called: Nags Head Hammocks LLC (G-9301)*

Nags Head Hammocks LLC (PA)................... 252 441-6115
   1801 Croatan Hwy Nags Head (27959) *(G-9301)*

Nakos Paper Products Inc............................ 704 238-0717
   2020 Starita Rd Ste G Charlotte (28206) *(G-2541)*

Nala Membranes Inc..................................... 540 230-5606
   2 Davis Dr # 113 Durham (27709) *(G-4142)*

Nano-Purification Solutions, Charlotte *Also Called: Air & Gas Solutions LLC (G-1631)*

Nantahala Talc & Limestone Co.................... 828 321-4239
   720 Hewitts Rd Topton (28781) *(G-12105)*

NANTAHALA TALC & LIMESTONE CO, Topton *Also Called: Nantahala Talc & Limestone Co (G-12105)*

NAPA Auto Parts, Four Oaks *Also Called: Roy Dunn (G-4815)*

NAPA Filters... 704 864-6748
   1 Wix Way Gastonia (28054) *(G-5106)*

Napco, Sparta *Also Called: Napco Inc (G-11540)*

Napco Inc (DH)... 336 372-5214
   120 Trojan Ave Sparta (28675) *(G-11540)*

Napoleon James.. 413 331-9560
   6113 Delta Landing Rd Charlotte (28227) *(G-2542)*

Narayana Inc... 828 708-0954
   247 Old Weaverville Rd Asheville (28804) *(G-554)*

Nascent, Charlotte *Also Called: Nascent Technology LLC (G-2543)*

Nascent Technology LLC.............................. 704 654-3035
   2744 Yorkmont Rd Charlotte (28208) *(G-2543)*

Nash Brick Company.................................... 252 443-4965
   532 Nash Brick Rd Enfield (27823) *(G-4485)*

Nash Building Systems Inc.......................... 252 823-1905
   1803 Anaconda Rd Tarboro (27886) *(G-11938)*

Nash County Newspapers Inc....................... 252 459-7101
   203 W Washington St Nashville (27856) *(G-9322)*

Nashville Graphic, Nashville *Also Called: Nash County Newspapers Inc (G-9322)*

Nashville Wldg & Mch Works Inc.................. 252 243-0113
   2356 Firestone Pkwy Ne Wilson (27893) *(G-13008)*

Nassau Tape, Alamance *Also Called: Ct-Nassau Tape LLC (G-56)*

Nat, Fletcher *Also Called: North American Trade LLC (G-4759)*

Nat Black Logging Inc.................................. 704 826-8834
   Mcbride Rd Ansonville (28007) *(G-130)*

Natel Inc... 336 227-1227
   1257 S Church St Burlington (27215) *(G-1134)*

Nathan Beiler.. 252 935-5141
   2685 Nc Highway 45 N Pantego (27860) *(G-9647)*

National Air Filters Inc................................. 919 231-8596
   1109 N New Hope Rd Raleigh (27610) *(G-10322)*

National Coatings & Supplies, Raleigh *Also Called: Falls of Neuse Management LLC (G-10103)*

National Color Graphics Inc......................... 704 263-3187
   98 Rutledge Rd Mount Holly (28120) *(G-9240)*

National Container Group LLC...................... 704 393-9050
   1209c Tar Heel Rd Charlotte (28208) *(G-2544)*

National Conveyors Company Inc.................. 860 325-4011
   4404a Chesapeake Dr Charlotte (28216) *(G-2545)*

National Ctr For Social Impact..................... 984 212-2285
   1053 E Whitaker Mill Rd Ste 115 Raleigh (27604) *(G-10323)*

National Foam Inc... 919 639-6151
   141 Junny Rd Angier (27501) *(G-125)*

National Foam Inc (PA)................................. 919 639-6100
   141 Junny Rd Angier (27501) *(G-126)*

National Gyps Receivables LLC.................... 704 365-7300
   2001 Rexford Rd Charlotte (28211) *(G-2546)*

National Gypsum, Charlotte *Also Called: Gold Bond Building Pdts LLC (G-2223)*

National Gypsum Comp, Wilmington *Also Called: Proform Finishing Products LLC (G-12890)*

National Gypsum Company, Charlotte *Also Called: Proform Finishing Products LLC (G-2674)*

National Gypsum Services Co....................... 704 365-7300
   2001 Rexford Rd Charlotte (28211) *(G-2547)*

National Marble Products Inc....................... 910 326-3005
   404 Channel Dr Emerald Isle (28594) *(G-4478)*

National Mastercraft Inds Inc...................... 919 896-8858
   14 Glenwood Ave Ste 22 Raleigh (27603) *(G-10324)*

National Peening Inc (DH)............................ 704 872-0113
   1902 Weinig St Statesville (28677) *(G-11738)*

National Pipe & Plastics Inc........................ 336 996-2711
   9609 W Market St Colfax (27235) *(G-3284)*

National Print Services Inc.......................... 704 892-9209
   678 Big Indian Loop Mooresville (28117) *(G-8731)*

National Reconition, Greensboro *Also Called: Crown Trophy Inc (G-5474)*

National Roller Supply Inc........................... 704 853-1174
   811 Grover St Gastonia (28054) *(G-5107)*

National Salvage & Svc Corp....................... 919 739-5633
   430 Old Mt Olive Hwy Dudley (28333) *(G-3838)*

National Sign & Decal Inc............................ 828 478-2123
   2199 Lynmore Dr Sherrills Ford (28673) *(G-11393)*

National Spinning Co Inc............................. 910 298-3131
   326 Lyman Rd Beulaville (28518) *(G-844)*

National Spinning Co Inc............................. 336 226-0141
   226 Glen Raven Rd Burlington (27217) *(G-1135)*

National Spinning Co Inc (PA)...................... 252 975-7111
   1481 W 2nd St Ste 103 Washington (27889) *(G-12398)*

National Spinning Co Inc............................. 910 642-4181
   Hwy 130 240 Spinning Rd Whiteville (28472) *(G-12589)*

National Spnning Oprations LLC.................. 252 975-7111
   1481 W 2nd St Ste 103 Washington (27889) *(G-12399)*

National Tank Monitor Inc............................ 704 335-8265
   9801 Ferguson Rd Charlotte (28227) *(G-2548)*

National Textile Engravers, Charlotte *Also Called: Graveoke Inc (G-2233)*

National Textile Supply, Charlotte *Also Called: W M Plastics Inc (G-2996)*

National Voctnl Tech Honor Soc.................... 828 698-8011
   1011 Airport Rd Flat Rock (28731) *(G-4711)*

National Wden Pllet Cont Assoc.................... 919 837-2105
   2340 Ike Brooks Rd Siler City (27344) *(G-11420)*

National Wiper Alliance, Swannanoa *Also Called: Jbs2 Inc (G-11872)*

National Wood Product, Mills River *Also Called: Woodpecker Sawmill (G-8325)*

National Wood Products, Mills River *Also Called: Alan Kimzey (G-8310)*

Nationwide Analgesics LLC.......................... 704 651-5551
   3116 Weddington Rd Ste 900 Matthews (28105) *(G-8135)*

Native Amercn Collections Xii, Cherokee *Also Called: Cherokee Publications (G-3051)*

Native Naturalz Inc....................................... 336 334-2984
   805 Stoney Hill Cir Greensboro (27406) *(G-5704)*

Natrx Inc.. 919 263-0667
   6220 Angus Dr Ste 101 Raleigh (27617) *(G-10325)*

Natural Bath and Body Products, Jacksonville *Also Called: Luxuriously Natural Soaps LLC (G-7130)*

Natural Granite & Marble Inc........................ 919 872-1508
   3100 Stony Brook Dr Ste N1 Raleigh (27604) *(G-10326)*

Naturally ME Boutique Inc............................ 919 519-0783
   3231 Shannon Rd Apt 31c Durham (27707) *(G-4143)*

Natures Cup LLC... 910 795-2700
   1930 Club Pond Rd Raeford (28376) *(G-9843)*

Natures Own Gallery, Rocky Mount *Also Called: Mijo Enterprises Inc (G-10852)*

Natures Pharmacy Inc................................... 828 251-0094
   752 Biltmore Ave Asheville (28803) *(G-555)*

Naturesrules Inc... 336 427-2526
   2094 Ellisboro Rd Madison (27025) *(G-7994)*

Natvar, Clayton *Also Called: Tekni-Plex Inc (G-3174)*

Naval Air Warfare, Cherry Point *Also Called: United States Dept of Navy (G-3055)*

Navelite LLC.. 336 509-9924
   3220 Peninsula Dr Jamestown (27282) *(G-7172)*

Navex Global Inc.. 866 297-0224
   13950 Ballantyne Corporate Pl Ste 300 Charlotte (28277) *(G-2549)*

Nb Corporation... 336 852-8786
   123 S Edwardia Dr Greensboro (27409) *(G-5705)*

Nb Corporation (PA)...................................... 336 274-7654
   725 Kenilworth St Greensboro (27403) *(G-5706)*

NC Custom Leather Inc................................. 828 404-2973
   1118 1st St W Conover (28613) *(G-3540)*

NC Diesel Performance LLC.......................... 704 431-3257
   5213 Mooresville Rd Salisbury (28147) *(G-11095)*

NC Filtration of Florida LLC..................704 822-4444
1 Miller St Belmont (28012) *(G-756)*

NC Graphic Pros LLC..................252 492-7326
2232 Rocky Ford Rd Kittrell (27544) *(G-7442)*

NC Imprints Inc..................336 790-4546
3199 E Holly Grove Rd Lexington (27292) *(G-7720)*

NC License Plate Agency..................910 347-1000
521 Yopp Rd Jacksonville (28540) *(G-7134)*

NC Motor Vhcl Lcnse Plate Agcy..................336 228-7152
2668 Ramada Rd Burlington (27215) *(G-1136)*

NC Moulding Acquisition LLC..................336 249-7309
808 Martin Luther King Jr Blvd Lexington (27292) *(G-7721)*

NC Printing LLC..................828 393-4615
1524 Haywood Rd Hendersonville (28791) *(G-6230)*

NC Products, Raleigh *Also Called: Oldcastle Infrastructure Inc (G-10344)*

NC Quality Sales LLC..................336 786-7211
136 Greyhound Rd Mount Airy (27030) *(G-9157)*

NC Sand and Rock Inc..................919 538-9001
9520 Kennebec Rd Willow Spring (27592) *(G-12680)*

NC Sign and Lighting Svc LLC..................586 764-0563
213 Hillstone Pl Jamestown (27282) *(G-7173)*

NC Softball Sales..................704 663-2134
117 E Statesville Ave Mooresville (28115) *(G-8732)*

NC Solar, Raleigh *Also Called: NC Solar Now Inc (G-10327)*

NC Solar Now Inc..................919 833-9096
2517 Atlantic Ave Raleigh (27604) *(G-10327)*

NC Steel Services Inc..................252 393-7888
141 Seth Thomas Ln Swansboro (28584) *(G-11887)*

Ncd Hickory, Hickory *Also Called: New Carbon Company LLC (G-6401)*

Ncfi, Mount Airy *Also Called: Ncfi Polyurethanes (G-9158)*

Ncfi Polyurethanes..................336 789-9161
1515 Carter St Mount Airy (27030) *(G-9158)*

Ncfi Polyurethanes, Mount Airy *Also Called: Barnhardt Manufacturing Co (G-9101)*

Nci Group Inc (DH)..................281 897-7788
5020 Weston Pkwy Cary (27513) *(G-1405)*

Nci Group Inc..................919 926-4800
5115 New Bern Ave Raleigh (27610) *(G-10328)*

Ncino, Wilmington *Also Called: Ncino Inc (G-12857)*

Ncino Inc (PA)..................888 676-2466
6770 Parker Farm Dr Ste 100 Wilmington (28405) *(G-12857)*

Ncino Opco Inc (HQ)..................888 676-2466
6770 Parker Farm Dr Ste 200 Wilmington (28405) *(G-12858)*

NCM, Goldsboro *Also Called: North Carolina Mfg Inc (G-5231)*

Ncoast Communications (PA)..................252 247-7442
201 N 17th St Morehead City (28557) *(G-8839)*

Ncontact Surgical LLC
1001 Aviation Pkwy Ste 400 Morrisville (27560) *(G-9022)*

NCR, Cary *Also Called: NCR Voyix Corporation (G-1406)*

NCR Voyix Corporation..................937 445-5000
115 Centrewest Ct Cary (27513) *(G-1406)*

NCSMJ Inc..................704 544-1118
9433 Pineville Matthews Rd Pineville (28134) *(G-9744)*

ND Southeastern Fastener..................704 329-0033
2220 Center Park Dr Ste C Charlotte (28217) *(G-2550)*

Ndsl Inc..................919 790-7877
1000 Parliament Ct Durham (27703) *(G-4144)*

Neal S Pallet Company Inc..................704 393-8568
8808 Wilkinson Blvd Charlotte (28214) *(G-2551)*

Neals Carpentry & Cnstr..................910 346-6154
153 White Oak Blvd Jacksonville (28546) *(G-7135)*

Neat Feet Hosiery Inc..................336 573-2177
304 Main St Stoneville (27048) *(G-11823)*

Neco Division, Salisbury *Also Called: Pyrotek Incorporated (G-11108)*

Nederman Inc..................336 821-0827
150 Transit Ave Thomasville (27360) *(G-12053)*

Nederman Manufacturing..................704 898-7945
4500 Chesapeake Dr Charlotte (28216) *(G-2552)*

Nederman Mikropul LLC (DH)..................704 998-2600
4404a Chesapeake Dr Charlotte (28216) *(G-2553)*

Nederman Mikropul Canada Inc (DH)..................704 998-2606
4404a Chesapeake Dr Charlotte (28216) *(G-2554)*

Neighborhood Smoothie LLC..................919 845-5513
10115 Second Star Ct Raleigh (27613) *(G-10329)*

Neil Allen Industries Inc..................336 887-6500
2101 E Martin Luther King Jr Dr High Point (27260) *(G-6717)*

Nelson Holdings Nc Inc..................828 322-9226
5 20th St Sw Hickory (28602) *(G-6399)*

Nelson Logging Company Inc..................919 849-2547
9557 Nc Highway 96 Oxford (27565) *(G-9620)*

Nelson Oil Company, Hickory *Also Called: Nelson Holdings Nc Inc (G-6399)*

Nelson Rodriguez..................828 433-1223
341 E Parker Rd Morganton (28655) *(G-8884)*

Neocase, Clemmons *Also Called: Groupe Lacasse LLC (G-3187)*

Neocutis, Raleigh *Also Called: Merz North America Inc (G-10294)*

Neomonde Bakery, Morrisville *Also Called: Neomonde Baking Company (G-9023)*

Neomonde Baking Company (PA)..................919 469-8009
220 Dominion Dr Ste A Morrisville (27560) *(G-9023)*

Neopac Us Inc..................908 342-0990
4940 Lamm Rd Wilson (27893) *(G-13009)*

Neptco, Lenoir *Also Called: Neptco Incorporated (G-7629)*

Neptco Incorporated..................828 313-0149
3908 Hickory Blvd Granite Falls (28630) *(G-5314)*

Neptco Incorporated..................828 728-5951
2012 Hickory Blvd Sw Lenoir (28645) *(G-7629)*

Neptune Hlth Wllness Innvtion..................888 664-9166
408 S Mclin Creek Rd Conover (28613) *(G-3541)*

Nester Hosiery, Mount Airy *Also Called: Nester Hosiery LLC (G-9160)*

Nester Hosiery Inc..................336 789-0026
1400 Carter St Mount Airy (27030) *(G-9159)*

Nester Hosiery LLC (PA)..................336 789-0026
1546 Carter St Mount Airy (27030) *(G-9160)*

NESTER HOSIERY, INC., Mount Airy *Also Called: Nester Hosiery Inc (G-9159)*

Nestle Purina Petcare Company..................314 982-1000
863 E Meadow Rd Eden (27288) *(G-4353)*

Netapp Inc..................919 476-4571
7301 Kit Creek Rd Durham (27709) *(G-4145)*

Netceed, Winston Salem *Also Called: Walker and Associates Inc (G-13386)*

Netqem LLC..................919 544-4122
1012 Park Glen Pl Durham (27713) *(G-4146)*

Network Integrity Systems, Hickory *Also Called: Network Integrity Systems Inc (G-6400)*

Network Integrity Systems Inc..................828 322-2181
1937 Tate Blvd Se Hickory (28602) *(G-6400)*

Neu Spice and Seasonings Llc..................252 378-7912
4571 Us Highway 264 W Washington (27889) *(G-12400)*

Neurametrix Inc..................408 507-2366
18 Lookout Rd Asheville (28804) *(G-556)*

Neuronex Inc..................919 460-9500
9001 Aerial Center Pkwy Ste 110 Morrisville (27560) *(G-9024)*

Neurotronik Inc..................919 883-4155
4021 Stirrup Creek Dr Ste 210 Durham (27703) *(G-4147)*

Neverson Quarry, Sims *Also Called: Heidelberg Materials Us Inc (G-11431)*

New Anthem LLC (PA)..................910 319-7430
110 Greenfield St Wilmington (28401) *(G-12859)*

New Beginnings Trnsp LLC..................704 293-0493
5904 Johnnette Dr Charlotte (28212) *(G-2555)*

New Bern Asphalt Plant, New Bern *Also Called: S T Wooten Corporation (G-9393)*

New Boston Fruit Slice & Confe..................919 775-2471
2627 Watson Ave Sanford (27332) *(G-11211)*

New Can Company Inc..................704 853-3711
121 Crowders Creek Rd Gastonia (28052) *(G-5108)*

New Carbon Company LLC..................574 247-2270
1040 Old Lenoir Rd Unit 1040 Hickory (28601) *(G-6401)*

New Dairy Opco LLC..................336 725-8141
800 E 21st St Winston Salem (27105) *(G-13263)*

New Drections Screen Prtrs Inc..................704 393-1769
241 I K Beatty St Charlotte (28214) *(G-2556)*

New East Cartridge Inc..................252 329-0837
1809 Dickinson Ave Greenville (27834) *(G-6007)*

New Element..................704 890-7292
1021 Polk St Charlotte (28206) *(G-2557)*

New Finish Inc..................704 474-4116
8353 Us 52 Hwy S Norwood (28128) *(G-9557)*

New Generation Yarn Corp..................................... 336 449-5607
 1248 Springwood Church Rd Gibsonville (27249) *(G-5183)*

New Growth Press LLC.. 336 378-7775
 1301 Carolina St Ste 124 Greensboro (27401) *(G-5707)*

New Hanover Printing, Wilmington *Also Called: New Hanover Printing and Pubg (G-12860)*

New Hanover Printing & Pubg, Wilmington *Also Called: Aztech Products Inc (G-12717)*

New Hanover Printing and Pubg.............................. 910 520-7173
 2145 Wrightsville Ave Wilmington (28403) *(G-12860)*

New Innovative Products Inc.................................. 919 631-6759
 2180 Hwy 70 E Pine Level (27568) *(G-9683)*

New Market, Greenville *Also Called: Grover Gaming Inc (G-5985)*

New Paradigm Therapeutics Inc.............................. 919 259-0026
 8024 Burnette Womack 100 Dental Cir Chapel Hill (27599) *(G-1559)*

New Peco Inc.. 828 684-1234
 10 Walden Dr Arden (28704) *(G-288)*

New Phoenix Aerospace Inc.................................... 919 380-8500
 6008 Triangle Dr Ste 101 Raleigh (27617) *(G-10330)*

New River Distilling Co LLC.................................... 732 673-4852
 180 W Yuma Ln Deep Gap (28618) *(G-3728)*

New Sarum Brewing Co LLC.................................... 704 310-5048
 109 N Lee St Salisbury (28144) *(G-11096)*

New South Fabricator LLC...................................... 704 922-2072
 930 Ashebrook Park Rd Dallas (28034) *(G-3680)*

New South Lumber Company Inc............................. 336 376-3130
 4408 Mount Hermon Rock Crk Rd Graham (27253) *(G-5280)*

New Standard Corporation...................................... 252 446-5481
 3883 S Church St Rocky Mount (27803) *(G-10854)*

New Vision Investments Inc.................................... 336 757-1120
 4310 Enterprise Dr Ste I Winston Salem (27106) *(G-13264)*

New Vision Momentum Entp LLC............................. 800 575-1244
 4456 The Plaza Ste E Charlotte (28215) *(G-2558)*

New Wave Acrylics, Charlotte *Also Called: TFS Management Group LLC (G-2910)*

New World Technologies Inc................................... 828 652-8662
 78 W Marion Business Park Marion (28752) *(G-8058)*

New York Air Brake LLC.. 315 786-5200
 985 Whitney Dr Salisbury (28147) *(G-11097)*

Newco, Greenville *Also Called: Dpi Newco LLC (G-5967)*

Newcomb Spring Corp... 704 588-2043
 2633 Plastics Dr Gastonia (28054) *(G-5109)*

Newcomb Spring of Carolina, Gastonia *Also Called: Newcomb Spring Corp (G-5109)*

Newell, Roxboro *Also Called: Newell & Sons Inc (G-10930)*

Newell & Sons Inc.. 336 597-2248
 211 Clayton Ave Roxboro (27573) *(G-10930)*

Newell Brands Distribution LLC.............................. 770 418-7000
 3211 Aberdeen Blvd Gastonia (28054) *(G-5110)*

Newell Brands Inc.. 336 812-8181
 4110 Premier Dr High Point (27265) *(G-6718)*

Newell Brands Inc.. 704 987-4760
 9815 Northcross Center Ct Ste 8 Huntersville (28078) *(G-7019)*

Newell Brands Inc.. 704 895-8082
 8935 N Pointe Executive Park Dr Huntersville (28078) *(G-7020)*

Newell Novelty Co Inc... 336 597-2246
 25 Weeks Dr Roxboro (27573) *(G-10931)*

Newfound Tire & Quick Lube Inc............................ 828 683-3232
 642 Newfound Rd Leicester (28748) *(G-7528)*

Newgrass Brewing Company LLC............................. 704 477-2795
 101 Columns Cir Shelby (28150) *(G-11366)*

Newman-Whitney, Browns Summit *Also Called: Jly Invstmnts Inc Fka Nwman Mc (G-1000)*

Newport/Morehead Cy Con Plant, Garner *Also Called: S T Wooten Corporation (G-4961)*

Newriverwelding... 336 413-3040
 271 Merrells Lake Rd Mocksville (27028) *(G-8381)*

News & Observer Recycling Ctr, Garner *Also Called: News and Observer Pubg Co (G-4949)*

News & Record... 336 627-1781
 1921 Vance St Reidsville (27320) *(G-10696)*

News & Record Commercial Prtg.............................. 336 373-7300
 200 E Market St Greensboro (27401) *(G-5708)*

News 14 Carolina.. 704 973-5700
 316 E Morehead St Ste 316 Charlotte (28202) *(G-2559)*

News and Observer Pubg Co................................... 919 894-4170
 611 Chicopee Rd Benson (27504) *(G-795)*

News and Observer Pubg Co................................... 919 419-6500
 2530 Meridian Pkwy Ste 300 Durham (27713) *(G-4148)*

News and Observer Pubg Co................................... 919 829-8903
 1402 Mechanical Blvd Garner (27529) *(G-4949)*

News and Observer Pubg Co (DH)............................ 919 829-4500
 421 Fayetteville St Ste 104 Raleigh (27601) *(G-10331)*

News of Orange County, Hillsborough *Also Called: Womack Publishing Co Inc (G-6882)*

News Reporter, Whiteville *Also Called: Highcorp Incorporated (G-12584)*

Newton Instrument Company (PA)............................ 919 575-6426
 111 E A St Butner (27509) *(G-1203)*

Newton Machine Co Inc... 704 394-2099
 1120 N Hoskins Rd Charlotte (28216) *(G-2560)*

Newton Sign Co Inc... 910 347-1661
 310 Preston Rd Jacksonville (28540) *(G-7136)*

Nexjen Systems LLC... 704 969-7070
 5933 Brookshire Blvd Charlotte (28216) *(G-2561)*

Next Generation Plastics Inc.................................. 828 453-0221
 161 Bugger Hollow Rd Ellenboro (28040) *(G-4458)*

Next Magazine.. 910 609-0638
 458 Whitfield St Fayetteville (28306) *(G-4645)*

Next Safety Inc... 336 246-7700
 676 S Main St Jefferson (28640) *(G-7192)*

Next World Design Inc... 800 448-1223
 42 High Tech Blvd Thomasville (27360) *(G-12054)*

Nexxt Level Trucking LLC...................................... 980 205-4425
 627 Minuet Ln Charlotte (28217) *(G-2562)*

Nexxus Lighting Inc.. 704 405-0416
 124 Floyd Smith Office Park Dr Ste 300 Charlotte (28262) *(G-2563)*

Ng Corporate LLC.. 704 365-7300
 2001 Rexford Rd Charlotte (28211) *(G-2564)*

Ng Operations LLC (PA).. 704 365-7300
 2001 Rexford Rd Charlotte (28211) *(G-2565)*

Ng Operations LLC.. 704 916-2082
 5901 Carnegie Blvd Charlotte (28209) *(G-2566)*

NG OPERATIONS, LLC, Charlotte *Also Called: Ng Operations LLC (G-2566)*

Ngc Receivables, Charlotte *Also Called: National Gyps Receivables LLC (G-2546)*

NGK Ceramics Usa Inc (HQ).................................... 704 664-7000
 119 Mazeppa Rd Mooresville (28115) *(G-8733)*

Ngx... 866 782-7749
 3002 Anaconda Rd Tarboro (27886) *(G-11939)*

Nhanced Semiconductors Inc.................................. 630 561-6813
 800 Perimeter Park Dr Ste B Morrisville (27560) *(G-9025)*

Ni4l Antennas and Elec LLC.................................... 828 738-6445
 3861 Mount Olive Church Rd Moravian Falls (28654) *(G-8810)*

Niagara Bottling LLC... 909 815-6310
 178 Mooresville Blvd Mooresville (28115) *(G-8734)*

Nic Nac Welding Co... 704 502-5178
 550 W 32nd St Charlotte (28206) *(G-2567)*

Nice Blends Corp.. 910 640-1000
 222 Industrial Blvd Whiteville (28472) *(G-12590)*

Nichols Spdmtr & Instr Co Inc................................ 336 273-2881
 1336 Oakland Ave Greensboro (27403) *(G-5709)*

Nichols Speedometer & Instr Co, Greensboro *Also Called: Nichols Spdmtr & Instr Co Inc (G-5709)*

Niels Jorgensen Company Inc................................. 910 259-1624
 200 Progress Dr Burgaw (28425) *(G-1028)*

Night, Raleigh *Also Called: Discover Night LLC (G-10049)*

Nine Thirteen LLC... 919 876-8070
 5300 Atlantic Ave Ste 105 Raleigh (27609) *(G-10332)*

Nine-Ai Inc.. 781 825-3267
 359 Armour St Davidson (28036) *(G-3714)*

Ninos Wldg & Cnstr Svcs LLC................................. 980 214-5804
 11901 Everett Keith Rd Huntersville (28078) *(G-7021)*

Nippon Electric Glass, Shelby *Also Called: Electric Glass Fiber Amer LLC (G-11332)*

Nippon Electric Glass Co Ltd.................................. 336 357-8151
 473 New Jersey Church Rd Lexington (27292) *(G-7722)*

Niras Inc... 919 439-4562
 1000 Centre Green Way Ste 200 Cary (27513) *(G-1407)*

Nissens Cooling Solutions Inc................................ 704 696-8575
 110 Oakpark Dr Ste 105 Mooresville (28115) *(G-8735)*

Nite Crawlers LLC... 980 229-8706
 301 S Mcdowell St Ste 125-1898 Charlotte (28204) *(G-2568)*

Nitro Manufacturing Inc..704 663-3155
510 Performance Rd Mooresville (28115) *(G-8736)*

Nitronex LLC...919 807-9100
523 Davis Dr Ste 500 Morrisville (27560) *(G-9026)*

Nitta Gelatin Holdings Inc (HQ)......................919 238-3300
598 Airport Blvd Ste 900 Morrisville (27560) *(G-9027)*

Nitta Gelatin Usa Inc.....................................910 484-0457
598 Airport Blvd Morrisville (27560) *(G-9028)*

Nkt Cables, Cary *Also Called: Nkt Inc (G-1408)*

Nkt Inc..919 601-1970
1255 Crescent Green Cary (27518) *(G-1408)*

Nls, Lexington *Also Called: Nutraceutical Lf Sciences Inc (G-7727)*

NN, Charlotte *Also Called: Nn Inc (G-2569)*

Nn Inc (PA)..980 264-4300
6210 Ardrey Kell Rd Ste 120 Charlotte (28277) *(G-2569)*

No Evil Foods LLC..828 367-1536
108 Monticello Rd Ste 2000 Weaverville (28787) *(G-12500)*

No Nonsense, Greensboro *Also Called: Kayser-Roth Corporation (G-5643)*

No Sweat Specialties, Pilot Mountain *Also Called: Sports Solutions Inc (G-9674)*

Noa, Swannanoa *Also Called: Nonwovens of America Inc (G-11874)*

Noa Living, Burlington *Also Called: Mongoose LLC (G-1130)*

Noahs Inc..704 718-2354
7289 Meeting St Charlotte (28210) *(G-2570)*

Noble Bros Cabinets Mllwk LLC (PA)...............252 482-9100
107 Marine Dr Edenton (27932) *(G-4370)*

Noble Bros Cabinets Mllwk LLC......................252 335-1213
505 E Church St Apt 2 Elizabeth City (27909) *(G-4399)*

Noble Brothers Logging Company...................252 355-2587
237 W Meath Dr Winterville (28590) *(G-13420)*

Noble Oil Services Inc...................................919 774-8180
5617 Clyde Rhyne Dr Sanford (27330) *(G-11212)*

Noble Wholesalers Inc...................................409 739-3803
356 Trenburg Pl Clayton (27520) *(G-3162)*

Nobscot Construction Co Inc..........................919 929-2075
2113 Old Greensboro Rd Chapel Hill (27516) *(G-1560)*

Nocturnal Product Dev LLC............................919 321-1331
8128 Renaissance Pkwy Ste 210 Durham (27713) *(G-4149)*

Noel Group LLC (PA)......................................919 269-6500
501 Innovative Way Zebulon (27597) *(G-13514)*

Nokia of America Corporation........................919 850-6000
2301 Sugar Bush Rd Ste 300 Raleigh (27601) *(G-10333)*

Nolan Manufacturing LLC...............................336 490-0086
18868 S Nc Highway 109 Denton (27239) *(G-3758)*

Nolarec, Carthage *Also Called: Stevens Lighting Inc (G-1281)*

Nolen Machine Co Inc....................................704 867-7851
119 Bob Nolen Rd Gastonia (28056) *(G-5111)*

Noles Cabinets Inc..919 552-4257
2290 N Grassland Dr Fuquay Varina (27526) *(G-4892)*

Nomaco Inc (HQ)...919 269-6500
501 Innovative Way Zebulon (27597) *(G-13515)*

Nomacorc Holdings LLC.................................919 460-2200
400 Vintage Park Dr Zebulon (27597) *(G-13516)*

Nomad Houseboats Inc...................................252 288-5670
208 Outrigger Rd New Bern (28562) *(G-9386)*

Nomadic Display, Greensboro *Also Called: Nomadic North America LLC (G-5711)*

Nomadic Display LLC.....................................800 336-5019
7602 Business Park Dr Greensboro (27409) *(G-5710)*

Nomadic North America LLC (HQ)...................703 866-9200
7602 Business Park Dr Greensboro (27409) *(G-5711)*

Nomadic State of Mind, Fayetteville *Also Called: CBA Productions Inc (G-4571)*

None...336 408-6008
1411 Plaza West Rd Winston Salem (27103) *(G-13265)*

Noni Bacca Winery...910 397-7617
420 Eastwood Rd Wilmington (28403) *(G-12861)*

Nontoxic Pthgen Erdction Cons......................800 308-1094
1258 Mann Dr Ste 200 Matthews (28105) *(G-8136)*

Nonwovens of America Inc.............................828 236-1300
875 Warren Wilson Rd Swannanoa (28778) *(G-11874)*

Norag Technology LLC (PA)............................336 316-0417
1214 Nc Highway 700 Pelham (27311) *(G-9655)*

Noralex Inc (PA)..252 974-1253
215 Wilmar Rd Vanceboro (28586) *(G-12221)*

Noralex Timber, Vanceboro *Also Called: Noralex Inc (G-12221)*

Norca Engineered Products LLC......................919 846-2010
7201 Creedmoor Rd Ste 150 Raleigh (27613) *(G-10334)*

Norcor Technologies Corp..............................704 309-4101
4291 Harbor Ridge Dr Greensboro (27406) *(G-5712)*

Norcraft Companies LP...................................336 622-4281
6163 Old 421 Rd Liberty (27298) *(G-7774)*

Nord Gear Corporation...................................888 314-6673
300 Forsyth Hall Dr Charlotte (28273) *(G-2571)*

Nordfab, Thomasville *Also Called: Dantherm Filtration Inc (G-12016)*

Nordfab Ducting..336 821-0840
4404 Chesapeake Dr Charlotte (28216) *(G-2572)*

Nordfab LLC..336 821-0829
150 Transit Ave Thomasville (27360) *(G-12055)*

Nordson Corporation......................................724 656-5600
1291 19th Street Ln Nw Hickory (28601) *(G-6402)*

Nordson Xaloy, Hickory *Also Called: Nordson Corporation (G-6402)*

Nordson Xaloy, Hickory *Also Called: Xaloy Extrusion LLC (G-6492)*

Noregon Systems Inc.....................................336 615-8555
7823 National Service Rd Ste 100 Greensboro (27409) *(G-5713)*

Norell Inc..828 584-2600
1001 Innovation Dr Morganton (28655) *(G-8885)*

Normac, Hendersonville *Also Called: Normac Incorporated (G-6231)*

Normac Incorporated (PA)..............................828 209-9000
93 Industrial Dr Hendersonville (28739) *(G-6231)*

Normac Kitchens Inc......................................704 485-1911
607 N Central Ave Locust (28097) *(G-7896)*

Normac Kitchens Inc (HQ)..............................704 485-1911
226 S Main St Oakboro (28129) *(G-9582)*

Norman E Clark..336 573-9629
251 Duck Rd Stoneville (27048) *(G-11824)*

Norman Lake Graphics Inc.............................704 896-8444
9735 Northcross Center Ct Ste L Huntersville (28078) *(G-7022)*

Normandie Bakery Inc....................................910 686-1372
7316 Market St Wilmington (28411) *(G-12862)*

Normtex Incorporated....................................828 428-3363
1700 Verrazzano Pl Wilmington (28405) *(G-12863)*

Norsan Media LLC..704 494-7181
8655 Crown Crescent Ct Charlotte (28227) *(G-2573)*

North Amercn Aerodynamics Inc (PA).............336 599-9266
1803 N Main St Roxboro (27573) *(G-10932)*

North American Attachments, Winston Salem *Also Called: Engineered Attachments LLC (G-13158)*

North American Implements............................336 476-2904
12608 E Old Us Highway 64 Lexington (27292) *(G-7723)*

North American Implements Inc......................336 476-2904
215 Washboard Rd Thomasville (27360) *(G-12056)*

North American Trade LLC..............................828 712-3004
388 Cane Creek Rd Ste 22 Fletcher (28732) *(G-4759)*

North Buncombe Quarry, Weaverville *Also Called: B V Hedrick Gravel & Sand Co (G-12482)*

North Cape Fear Logging LLC.........................910 876-3197
125 Charlie Smith Dr Harrells (28444) *(G-6102)*

North Carolina Converting LLC.......................704 871-2912
1001 Bucks Industrial Rd Statesville (28625) *(G-11739)*

North Carolina Department of A......................828 684-8188
785 Airport Rd Arden (28704) *(G-289)*

North Carolina Dept Labor.............................919 807-2770
1101 Mail Service Ctr Raleigh (27699) *(G-10335)*

North Carolina Dept Trnsp..............................828 733-9002
North Carolina Hwy 181 Newland (28657) *(G-9433)*

North Carolina Dept Trnsp..............................704 633-5873
5780 S Main St Salisbury (28147) *(G-11098)*

North Carolina Lawyers Weekly, Raleigh *Also Called: Dolan LLC (G-10055)*

North Carolina Lumber Company.....................336 498-6600
1 Parrish Dr Randleman (27317) *(G-10654)*

North Carolina McGee, Matthews *Also Called: McGee Corporation (G-8131)*

North Carolina Mfg Inc...................................919 734-1115
100 Industry Ct Goldsboro (27530) *(G-5231)*

North Carolina Moulding Co, Lexington *Also Called: NC Moulding Acquisition LLC (G-7721)*

(G-0000) Company's Geographic Section entry number

North Carolina Mulch Inc.................................. 252 478-4609
3277 Prong Creek Rd Middlesex (27557) *(G-8278)*

North Carolina Plywood LLC.............................. 850 948-2211
512 E Main St Whiteville (28472) *(G-12591)*

North Carolina Sock Inc................................... 828 327-4664
5521 Suttlemyre Ln Hickory (28601) *(G-6403)*

North Carolina State Dar Plant, Raleigh *Also Called: North Carolina State Univ (G-10336)*

North Carolina State Univ.................................. 919 515-2760
Food Science Bldg Rm 12 Raleigh (27695) *(G-10336)*

North Carolina Tobacco Mfg LLC.......................... 252 238-6514
7427 N. Carolina Way Stantonsburg (27883) *(G-11626)*

North Carolina Warehouse, Troy *Also Called: Precision Textiles LLC (G-12164)*

North Coast Container, Charlotte *Also Called: General Steel Drum LLC (G-2201)*

North Crlina Dept Adult Crrcto........................... 919 733-0867
1150 Martin Luther King Jr Blvd Raleigh (27601) *(G-10337)*

North Crlina Dept Crime Ctrl P........................... 252 522-1511
2214 W Vernon Ave Kinston (28504) *(G-7424)*

North Crlina Dept Crime Ctrl P........................... 336 599-9233
3434 Burlington Rd Roxboro (27574) *(G-10933)*

North Crlina Lcense Plate Agcy........................... 910 485-1590
815 Elm St Fayetteville (28303) *(G-4646)*

North Crlina Orthtics Prsthtic............................ 919 210-0906
2717 Leighton Ridge Dr Wake Forest (27587) *(G-12287)*

North Crlina Rnwable Prpts LLC........................... 407 536-5346
176 Mine Lake Ct Ste 100 Raleigh (27615) *(G-10338)*

North Crlina Spnning Mills Inc............................ 704 732-1171
104 Industrial Park Rd Lincolnton (28092) *(G-7847)*

North Crolina Tortilla Mfg LLC............................ 270 861-5956
3181 Progress Dr Lincolnton (28092) *(G-7848)*

North Fork Electric Inc.................................... 336 982-4020
1309 Willie Brown Rd Crumpler (28617) *(G-3661)*

North Sports Inc... 252 995-4970
Waterside Shops Hwy 45 Avon (27915) *(G-651)*

North Star Fbrication Repr Inc............................ 704 393-5243
124 Carothers St Charlotte (28216) *(G-2574)*

North State Flexibles, Greensboro *Also Called: St Johns Packaging Usa LLC (G-5833)*

North State Machine Inc.................................. 336 956-1441
1775 Tyro Rd Lexington (27295) *(G-7724)*

North State Millwork...................................... 252 442-9090
2950 Raleigh Rd Rocky Mount (27803) *(G-10855)*

North State Signs Inc.................................... 919 977-7053
553 Pylon Dr Ste D Raleigh (27606) *(G-10339)*

North State Steel Inc.................................... 919 496-2506
1801 Nc 98 Hwy W Louisburg (27549) *(G-7920)*

North State Steel At Louisburg, Louisbrg *Also Called: North State Steel Inc (G-7920)*

North State Steel Inc (PA)................................ 252 830-8884
1010 W Gum Rd Greenville (27834) *(G-6008)*

Northampton Peanut Company............................. 252 585-0916
413 Main St Severn (27877) *(G-11298)*

Northeast Foods Inc..................................... 919 585-5178
68 Harvest Mill Ln Clayton (27520) *(G-3163)*

Northeast Textiles.. 704 799-2235
105 Oakpark Dr Ste A Mooresville (28115) *(G-8737)*

Northeast Tool and Mfg Company.......................... 704 882-1187
15200 Idlewild Rd Matthews (28104) *(G-8187)*

Northeastern Ready Mix................................... 252 335-1931
183 Knobbs Creek Dr Elizabeth City (27909) *(G-4400)*

Northern Star Technologies Inc........................... 516 353-3333
1712 Price Rd Indian Trail (28079) *(G-7092)*

Northline Nc LLC.. 336 283-4811
262 Northstar Dr Ste 122 Rural Hall (27045) *(G-10965)*

Northrop Grmman Gdnce Elec Inc.......................... 704 588-2340
1201 Continental Blvd Charlotte (28273) *(G-2575)*

Northrop Grmman Tchncal Svcs I.......................... 252 447-7575
4280 6th Ave Cherry Point Air Station Havelock (28532) *(G-6124)*

Northrop Grmman Technical Svcs, Atlantic *Also Called: Northrop Grumman Systems Corp (G-638)*

Northrop Grumman Info Systems, Morrisville *Also Called: Northrop Grumman Systems Corp (G-9029)*

Northrop Grumman Systems Corp.......................... 252 225-0911
Bldg 7029 Atlantic (28511) *(G-638)*

Northrop Grumman Systems Corp.......................... 252 447-7557
Bldg 4280 Cherry Point (28533) *(G-3054)*

Northrop Grumman Systems Corp.......................... 919 465-5020
3005 Carrington Mill Blvd Morrisville (27560) *(G-9029)*

Northside Millwork Inc.................................... 919 732-6100
301 Millstone Dr Hillsborough (27278) *(G-6874)*

Northstar Computer Tech Inc.............................. 980 272-1969
5014 Hampton Meadows Rd Monroe (28110) *(G-8537)*

Northstar Travel Media.................................... 336 714-3328
331 High St Winston Salem (27101) *(G-13266)*

Northwest AG Product..................................... 509 547-8234
1001 Winstead Dr Ste 480 Cary (27513) *(G-1409)*

Northwest Coatings Systems Inc........................... 336 924-1459
5640 Clinedale Ct Pfafftown (27040) *(G-9664)*

Northwest Machine and Supply............................ 336 526-2029
204 3rd St Ronda (28670) *(G-10895)*

Norton Door Controls..................................... 704 233-4011
3000 E Highway 74 Monroe (28112) *(G-8538)*

Norton Door Controls Yale SEC, Monroe *Also Called: Assa Abloy Accessories and (G-8433)*

Nortria Inc.. 919 440-3253
8801 Fast Park Dr Ste 301 Raleigh (27617) *(G-10340)*

Norwood Manufacturing Inc............................... 704 474-0505
680 Lanier Rd Norwood (28128) *(G-9558)*

Not Just Archery.. 828 294-7727
2201 Moss Farm Rd Hickory (28602) *(G-6404)*

Notemeal Inc.. 312 550-2049
122 E Parrish St Durham (27701) *(G-4150)*

Notepad Enterprises LLC................................. 704 377-3467
901 N Tryon St Ste G Charlotte (28206) *(G-2576)*

Nouveau Verre Holdings Inc (DH)......................... 336 545-0011
3802 Robert Porcher Way Greensboro (27410) *(G-5714)*

Nova Enterprises Inc (PA)............................... 828 687-8770
305 Airport Rd Arden (28704) *(G-290)*

Nova Kitchen & Bath, Arden *Also Called: Nova Enterprises Inc (G-290)*

Nova Mobility Systems Inc................................ 800 797-9861
8604 Cliff Cameron Dr Ste 152 Charlotte (28269) *(G-2577)*

Nova Wildcat Drapery Hdwr LLC........................... 704 696-5110
10115 Kincey Ave Ste 210 Huntersville (28078) *(G-7023)*

Novabus, Greensboro *Also Called: Prevost Car (us) Inc (G-5763)*

Novaerus US Inc (PA)..................................... 813 304-2468
3540 Toringdon Way Ste 200 Charlotte (28277) *(G-2578)*

Novaflex Hose Inc.. 336 578-2161
449 Trollingwood Rd Haw River (27258) *(G-6134)*

Novalent Ltd.. 336 375-7555
2319 Joe Brown Dr Greensboro (27405) *(G-5715)*

Novartis Vccnes Dagnostics Inc (HQ)...................... 617 871-7000
475 Green Oaks Pkwy Holly Springs (27540) *(G-6908)*

Novas Bakery Inc (PA)................................... 704 333-5566
1800 Odessa Ln Charlotte (28216) *(G-2579)*

Novem Industries Inc.................................... 704 660-6460
1801 Cottonwood St Charlotte (28206) *(G-2580)*

Novex Innovations LLC................................... 336 231-6693
101 N Chestnut St Ste 303 Winston Salem (27101) *(G-13267)*

Novisystems Inc.. 919 205-5005
1315 Ileagnes Rd Raleigh (27603) *(G-10341)*

Novo Nordisk Phrm Inds LP................................ 919 820-9985
646 Glp Oneway Clayton (27527) *(G-3164)*

Novo Nordisk Phrm Inds LP................................ 919 820-9985
3611 Powhatan Rd Clayton (27527) *(G-3165)*

Novo Nordisk Phrm Inds LP................................ 919 550-2200
5235 International Dr Durham (27712) *(G-4151)*

Novoclem, Morrisville *Also Called: Vast Therapeutics Inc (G-9085)*

Novolex, Charlotte *Also Called: Clydesdle Acq Hld Inc (G-1935)*

Novolex, Charlotte *Also Called: Hilex Poly Co LLC (G-2280)*

Novolex, Charlotte *Also Called: Novolex Heritage Bag LLC (G-2582)*

Novolex, Charlotte *Also Called: Novolex Holdings LLC (G-2583)*

Novolex Bagcraft Inc (DH)................................ 800 845-6051
3436 Toringdon Way Ste 100 Charlotte (28227) *(G-2581)*

Novolex Covington, Charlotte *Also Called: Waddington North America Inc (G-2998)*

Novolex Heritage Bag LLC (DH)............................ 800 845-6051
3436 Toringdon Way Ste 100 Charlotte (28277) *(G-2582)*

Novolex Holdings LLC (DH)..............................800 845-6051
  3436 Toringdon Way Ste 100 Charlotte (28277) *(G-2583)*

Novolex Shields LLC (DH)..............................800 845-6051
  3436 Toringdon Way Ste 100 Charlotte (28277) *(G-2584)*

Novozymes, Franklinton *Also Called: Novozymes North America Inc (G-4851)*

Novozymes North America Inc (HQ)...................919 494-2014
  77 Perrys Chapel Church Rd Franklinton (27525) *(G-4851)*

Novozymes North America Inc..........................919 494-3220
  9000 Development Dr Morrisville (27560) *(G-9030)*

Noxon Automation USA LLC.............................919 390-1560
  150 Dominion Dr Ste B Morrisville (27560) *(G-9031)*

NPC Corporation...336 998-2386
  140 Theodore Dr Mocksville (27028) *(G-8382)*

NPS Holdings LLC..828 757-7501
  1427 Yadkin River Rd Lenoir (28645) *(G-7630)*

Npx One LLC..910 997-2217
  112 Sonoco Paper Mill Rd Rockingham (28379) *(G-10784)*

Nrfp Logging LLC..919 738-0989
  206 Connie Cir Goldsboro (27530) *(G-5232)*

Nsi Industries...800 321-5847
  9730 Northcross Center Ct Huntersville (28078) *(G-7024)*

Nsi Lab Solutions Inc....................................919 789-3000
  7212 Acc Blvd Raleigh (27617) *(G-10342)*

Ntb, Greensboro *Also Called: Tbc Retail Group Inc (G-5854)*

Nterline, Morrisville *Also Called: Xschem Inc (G-9091)*

NTI Systems, High Point *Also Called: I2e Group LLC (G-6665)*

Nu Expression, Clemmons *Also Called: Print Express Enterprises Inc (G-3199)*

Nu-Tech, East Bend *Also Called: Cross Technology Inc (G-4322)*

Nu-Tech Enterprises Inc.................................336 725-1691
  340 E Nc 67 Highway Byp East Bend (27018) *(G-4324)*

Nuclamp, Oak Ridge *Also Called: Nuclamp System LLC (G-9572)*

Nuclamp System LLC......................................336 643-1766
  8585 Benbow Merrill Rd Oak Ridge (27310) *(G-9572)*

Nuclear Energy Ne US, Wilmington *Also Called: Ge-Hitchi Nclear Enrgy Intl LL (G-12783)*

Nucleus Radiopharma Inc................................980 483-1766
  130 Harbour Place Dr Ste 340 Davidson (28036) *(G-3715)*

NUCOR, Charlotte *Also Called: Nucor Corporation (G-2586)*

Nucor Castrip Arkansas LLC............................704 366-7000
  1915 Rexford Rd Charlotte (28211) *(G-2585)*

Nucor Corporation (PA)...................................704 366-7000
  1915 Rexford Rd Ste 400 Charlotte (28211) *(G-2586)*

Nucor Corporation...252 356-3700
  1505 River Rd Cofield (27922) *(G-3268)*

Nucor Corporation...336 481-7924
  6776 E Us Highway 64 Lexington (27292) *(G-7725)*

Nucor Energy Holdings Inc..............................704 366-7000
  1915 Rexford Rd Charlotte (28211) *(G-2587)*

Nucor Rebar Fabrication NC Inc.......................910 739-9747
  2790 Kenny Biggs Rd Lumberton (28358) *(G-7963)*

Nucor Steel Lexington, Lexington *Also Called: Nucor Corporation (G-7725)*

Nucor Steel Sales Corporation.........................302 622-4066
  1915 Rexford Rd Charlotte (28211) *(G-2588)*

Nufabrx LLC..888 683-2279
  1515 Mockingbird Ln Ste 400 Charlotte (28209) *(G-2589)*

Nunn Probst Installations Inc..........................704 822-9443
  6428 W Wilkinson Blvd Belmont (28012) *(G-757)*

Nunnery-Freeman Inc.....................................252 438-3149
  2117 Coleman Pl Henderson (27536) *(G-6167)*

Nunnery-Freeman Mfg Co, Henderson *Also Called: Nunnery-Freeman Inc (G-6167)*

Nussbaum Auto Solutions LP (PA).....................704 864-2470
  1932 Jorache Ct Gastonia (28052) *(G-5112)*

Nutec Inc..877 318-2430
  11830 Mount Holly Hntrsvlle Rd Huntersville (28078) *(G-7025)*

Nutex Concepts NC Corp.................................828 726-8801
  2424 Norwood St Sw Lenoir (28645) *(G-7631)*

Nutkao USA Inc..252 595-1000
  7044 Nc 48 Battleboro (27809) *(G-703)*

Nutra-Pharma Mfg Corp NC.............................631 846-2500
  130 Lexington Pkwy Lexington (27295) *(G-7726)*

Nutraceutical Lf Sciences Inc..........................336 956-0800
  130 Lexington Pkwy Lexington (27295) *(G-7727)*

Nutrien AG Solutions Inc.................................252 322-4111
  1530 Nc Highway 306 S Aurora (27806) *(G-644)*

Nutrien AG Solutions Inc.................................252 235-4161
  9702 Global Rd Bailey (27807) *(G-672)*

Nutrien AG Solutions Inc.................................252 585-0282
  Ampac Rd Conway (27820) *(G-3578)*

Nutrien AG Solutions Inc.................................252 977-2025
  1160 Brake Rd Rocky Mount (27801) *(G-10814)*

Nutrien Phosphate, Aurora *Also Called: Nutrien AG Solutions Inc (G-644)*

Nutrotonic LLC...855 948-0008
  5031 W W T Harris Blvd Ste H Charlotte (28269) *(G-2590)*

Nuvasive Inc...336 430-3169
  1250 Revolution Mill Dr Greensboro (27405) *(G-5716)*

Nuvotronics Inc (DH).....................................434 298-6940
  2305 Presidential Dr Durham (27703) *(G-4152)*

Nv-Ths, Flat Rock *Also Called: National Voctnl Tech Honor Soc (G-4711)*

Nvent Thermal LLC..919 552-3811
  8000 Purfoy Rd Fuquay Varina (27526) *(G-4893)*

Nvh Inc (DH)...336 545-0011
  3802 Robert Porcher Way Greensboro (27410) *(G-5717)*

Nvidia Corporation..408 486-2000
  2600 Meridian Pkwy Durham (27713) *(G-4153)*

Nvizion Inc...336 985-3862
  129 Charles Rd King (27021) *(G-7334)*

Nvn Liquidation Inc (PA).................................212 765-9100
  4020 Stirrup Creek Dr Ste 110 Durham (27703) *(G-4154)*

Nvr Inc..704 484-7170
  132 Riverside Ct Kings Mountain (28086) *(G-7374)*

NVR Building Products, Kings Mountain *Also Called: Nvr Inc (G-7374)*

Nwl Inc..252 747-5943
  204 Carolina Dr Snow Hill (28580) *(G-11481)*

Nwl Capacitors, Snow Hill *Also Called: CD Snow Hill LLC (G-11478)*

Nxp Usa Inc..919 468-3251
  113 Fieldbrook Ct Cary (27519) *(G-1410)*

Nyp Corp Frmrly New Yrkr-Pters.......................910 739-4403
  299 Osterneck Robetex Dr Lumberton (28358) *(G-7964)*

Nypro, Arden *Also Called: Nypro Asheville Inc (G-291)*

Nypro Asheville Inc.......................................828 684-3141
  100 Vista Blvd Arden (28704) *(G-291)*

Nypro Inc...919 304-1400
  1018 Corporate Park Dr Mebane (27302) *(G-8253)*

Nypro Mebane, Mebane *Also Called: Nypro Inc (G-8253)*

Nypro Oregon Inc...541 753-4700
  100 Vista Blvd Arden (28704) *(G-292)*

O D Eyecarecenter P A...................................252 443-7011
  3044 Sunset Ave Rocky Mount (27804) *(G-10856)*

O Grayson Company.......................................704 932-6195
  6509 Grayson Ln Kannapolis (28081) *(G-7217)*

O Henry House Ltd..336 431-5350
  308 Greenoak Dr Archdale (27263) *(G-239)*

O R Prdgen Sons Sptic Tank I..........................252 442-3338
  4824 S Halifax Rd Rocky Mount (27803) *(G-10857)*

O-Taste-N-c LLC...919 696-9547
  19 Gainey Rd Dunn (28334) *(G-3863)*

Oak & Grist Distilling Co LLC...........................914 450-0589
  40 West St Asheville (28801) *(G-557)*

Oak & Grist Distilling Co LLC...........................828 357-5750
  1556 Grovestone Rd Black Mountain (28711) *(G-869)*

Oak City Customs LLC....................................919 995-5561
  501 Mack Todd Rd Ste 109 Zebulon (27597) *(G-13517)*

Oak City Metal LLC..919 375-4535
  700 Pony Rd Ste C Zebulon (27597) *(G-13518)*

Oak Ridge Industries LLC................................252 833-4061
  1228 Page Rd Washington (27889) *(G-12401)*

Oak-Bark Corporation....................................910 655-2263
  1507 Cronly Dr Riegelwood (28456) *(G-10727)*

Oak-Bark Corporation (PA) 514 Wayne Dr Wilmington (28403) *(G-12864)*

Oakbrook Solutions Inc..................................336 714-0321
  5930 Tarleton Dr Oak Ridge (27310) *(G-9573)*

Oakdale Cotton Mills......................................336 454-1144
  710 Oakdale Rd Jamestown (27282) *(G-7174)*

(G-0000) Company's Geographic Section entry number

Oakhurst Company Inc (PA).. 336 474-4600
2016 Van Buren St # 101 High Point (27260) *(G-6719)*

Oakhurst Textiles Inc.. 336 668-0733
203 Citation Ct Greensboro (27409) *(G-5718)*

Oakie S Tire & Recapping Inc.. 704 482-5629
800 W Warren St Shelby (28150) *(G-11367)*

Oaks Unlimited Inc (PA).. 828 926-1621
3530 Jonathan Creek Rd Waynesville (28785) *(G-12465)*

Oakstone Associates LLC... 704 946-5101
10308 Bailey Rd Ste 430 Cornelius (28031) *(G-3615)*

Oakwood Homes, Fletcher *Also Called: Clayton Homes Inc (G-4729)*

Oasis Akhal-Tekes.. 704 843-3139
6528 Rehobeth Rd Waxhaw (28173) *(G-12436)*

Oasys Mobile Inc.. 919 807-5600
8000 Regency Pkwy Ste 285 Cary (27518) *(G-1411)*

Obbc Inc.. 252 261-0612
75 E Dogwood Trl Kitty Hawk (27949) *(G-7446)*

Obi Machine & Tool Inc... 252 946-1580
411 Patrick Ln Chocowinity (27817) *(G-3084)*

Objective Security Corporation.. 415 997-9967
555 Fayetteville St Ste 201 Raleigh (27601) *(G-10343)*

OBrian Tarping Systems Inc.. 252 291-6710
110 Beacon St W Wilson (27893) *(G-13010)*

OBrian Tarping Systems Inc (PA)..................................... 252 291-2141
2330 Womble Brooks Rd E Wilson (27893) *(G-13011)*

OBrien Logging Co.. 910 655-3830
988 Livingston Chapel Rd Delco (28436) *(G-3738)*

Observer News Enterprise, Newton *Also Called: Horizon Publications Inc (G-9473)*

Observer News Enterprise Inc.. 828 464-0221
309 N College Ave Newton (28658) *(G-9483)*

Obx Boatworks LLC.. 336 878-9490
2100 E Martin Luther King Jr Dr Ste 121 High Point (27260) *(G-6720)*

Occasions Group Inc.. 919 751-2400
305 N Spence Ave Goldsboro (27534) *(G-5233)*

Occasions Group Inc... 252 321-5805
1055 Greenville Blvd Sw Greenville (27834) *(G-6009)*

Occidental Chemical Corp... 910 675-7200
5408 Holly Shelter Rd Castle Hayne (28429) *(G-1508)*

Ocean 10 Security LLC... 828 484-1481
329 Gashes Creek Rd Asheville (28803) *(G-558)*

Ocean Woodworking Inc.. 910 579-2233
6863 Beach Dr Sw Ocean Isle Beach (28469) *(G-9588)*

Oceania Hardwoods LLC... 910 862-4447
474 Sweet Home Church Rd Elizabethtown (28337) *(G-4431)*

Ocufii Incorporated.. 804 874-4036
11211 James Coy Rd Huntersville (28078) *(G-7026)*

Ocutech Inc.. 919 967-6460
105 Conner Dr Ste 2105 Chapel Hill (27514) *(G-1561)*

Odigia Inc... 336 462-8056
300 S Liberty St Ste 210 Winston Salem (27101) *(G-13268)*

Odin Technologies LLC... 408 309-1925
4810 Ashley Park Ln Unit C1-1307 Charlotte (28210) *(G-2591)*

Oe Filters, Fayetteville *Also Called: Mann+hmmel Prlator Filters LLC (G-4632)*

Oerlikon AM US Inc.. 980 260-2827
12012 Vanstory Dr Huntersville (28078) *(G-7027)*

Oerlikon Metco (us) Inc.. 713 715-6300
12012 Vanstory Dr Huntersville (28078) *(G-7028)*

Ofc Fabricators, Statesville *Also Called: Ohio Foam Corporation (G-11740)*

Office Furniture Marketing, Holly Springs *Also Called: Ofm LLC (G-6909)*

Office of Printing, Boone *Also Called: Appalachian State University (G-896)*

Office Sup Svcs Inc Charlotte (PA)................................... 704 786-4677
4490 Artdale Rd Sw Concord (28027) *(G-3410)*

Office Supply Services, Concord *Also Called: Office Sup Svcs Inc Charlotte (G-3410)*

Offshore Marine Elec LLC... 252 504-2624
1381 Old Winberry Rd Newport (28570) *(G-9441)*

Ofm LLC.. 919 303-6389
161 Tradition Trl Holly Springs (27540) *(G-6909)*

Ogburn Village Solutions, Winston Salem *Also Called: Village Produce & Cntry Str In (G-13381)*

Ogden Enterprises, Matthews *Also Called: Karl Ogden Enterprises Inc (G-8121)*

Ogden Group, Matthews *Also Called: Ogden Sales Group LLC (G-8137)*

Ogden Sales Group LLC.. 704 845-2785
1320 Industrial Dr Matthews (28105) *(G-8137)*

OHerns Welding Inc... 910 484-2087
5379 Butler Nursery Rd Fayetteville (28306) *(G-4647)*

Ohio Electric Motors Inc... 828 626-2901
30 Paint Fork Rd Barnardsville (28709) *(G-693)*

Ohio Foam Corporation.. 704 883-8402
2185 Salisbury Hwy Statesville (28677) *(G-11740)*

Ohio Mat Lcnsing Cmpnnts Group (DH)............................336 861-3500
1 Office Parkway Rd Trinity (27370) *(G-12118)*

Ohio-Sealy Mattress Mfg Co.. 336 861-3500
1 Office Parkway Rd Trinity (27370) *(G-12119)*

Ohlins Usa Inc.. 828 692-4525
703 S Grove St Hendersonville (28792) *(G-6232)*

Oil Mill Salvage Recyclers Inc.. 910 268-2111
13840 Oil Mill Rd Gibson (28343) *(G-5175)*

Oiles America Corporation (HQ)... 704 784-4500
4510 Enterprise Dr Nw Concord (28027) *(G-3411)*

Okaya Shinnichi Corp America... 704 588-3131
300 Crompton St Charlotte (28273) *(G-2592)*

Oklawaha Brewing Company LLC....................................... 828 595-9956
147 1st Ave E Hendersonville (28792) *(G-6233)*

Okuma America Corporation... 704 588-7000
11900 Westhall Dr Charlotte (28278) *(G-2593)*

Old Belt Extracts LLC.. 336 530-5784
317 Lucy Garrett Rd Roxboro (27574) *(G-10934)*

Old Castle Apg South Inc.. 919 383-2521
106 S Lasalle St Durham (27705) *(G-4155)*

Old Castle Service Inc... 336 992-1601
920 Old Winston Rd Kernersville (27284) *(G-7289)*

Old Dominion Win Door Hanover, Charlotte *Also Called: Moss Supply Company (G-2521)*

Old Growth Riverwood Inc... 910 762-4077
1407b Castle Hayne Rd Wilmington (28401) *(G-12865)*

Old Hickory Log Homes Inc... 704 489-8989
4279 Burnwood Trl Denver (28037) *(G-3795)*

Old Hickory Tannery Inc (PA).. 828 465-6599
970 Locust St Newton (28658) *(G-9484)*

Old Master Cabinets, Greensboro *Also Called: Burlington Distributing Co (G-5411)*

Old Mill Precision Gun Works &... 704 284-2832
323 Old Mill Rd Bessemer City (28016) *(G-828)*

Old North State Winery Inc.. 336 789-9463
308 N Main St Mount Airy (27030) *(G-9161)*

Old Rm Co LLC.. 919 217-0222
512 Three Sisters Rd Knightdale (27545) *(G-7454)*

Old Salem Incorporated... 336 721-7305
730 S Poplar St Winston Salem (27101) *(G-13269)*

Old Salem Town Merchant, Winston Salem *Also Called: Old Salem Incorporated (G-13269)*

Old Saratoga Inc... 252 238-2175
6351 Nc Hwy 222 Saratoga (27873) *(G-11261)*

Old School Crushing Co Inc.. 919 661-0011
250 Old Mechanical Ct Garner (27529) *(G-4950)*

Old School Mill Inc.. 704 781-5451
28113 Nc 24 27 Hwy Albemarle (28001) *(G-83)*

Old Style Printing... 828 452-1122
1046 Sulphur Springs Rd Waynesville (28786) *(G-12466)*

Old Town Soap Co.. 704 796-8775
104 S Main St China Grove (28023) *(G-3077)*

Old Wood Co, Asheville *Also Called: Old Wood Company (G-559)*

Old Wood Company.. 828 259-9663
99 Riverside Dr Asheville (28801) *(G-559)*

Oldcastle Adams.. 336 310-0542
3415 Sandy Ridge Rd Colfax (27235) *(G-3285)*

Oldcastle Apg, Cornelius *Also Called: Oldcastle Retail Inc (G-3616)*

Oldcastle Apg South Inc.. 336 854-8200
139 S Walnut Cir Greensboro (27409) *(G-5719)*

Oldcastle Infrastructure Inc... 704 788-4050
4905 Stough Rd Sw Concord (28027) *(G-3412)*

Oldcastle Infrastructure Inc... 910 433-2931
3960 Cedar Creek Rd Fayetteville (28312) *(G-4648)*

Oldcastle Infrastructure Inc... 919 552-2252
1431 Products Rd Fuquay Varina (27526) *(G-4894)*

Oldcastle Infrastructure Inc........................ 919 772-6269
  920 Withers Rd Raleigh (27603) *(G-10344)*

Oldcastle Retail Inc (DH)........................ 704 525-1621
  625 Griffith Rd Ste 100 Charlotte (28217) *(G-2594)*

Oldcastle Retail Inc........................ 704 799-8083
  18637 Northline Dr Ste S Cornelius (28031) *(G-3616)*

Olde Lexington Products Inc........................ 336 956-2355
  480 Cedarwood Dr Linwood (27299) *(G-7880)*

Olde Raleigh Distillery LLC........................ 919 208-0044
  209 N Arendell Ave Zebulon (27597) *(G-13519)*

Ole Mexican Foods Inc........................ 704 587-1763
  11001a S Commerce Blvd Charlotte (28273) *(G-2595)*

Ole-Charlotte Distribution Ctr, Charlotte Also Called: Ole Mexican Foods Inc *(G-2595)*

Oleksynprannyk LLC........................ 704 450-0182
  149 Cayuga Dr Ste A3 Mooresville (28117) *(G-8738)*

Olens B Enterprises, Greensboro Also Called: Spring Repair Service Inc *(G-5832)*

Olive Beaufort Oil Company........................ 252 504-2474
  300 Front St Ste 4 Beaufort (28516) *(G-731)*

Olive Euro Oil LLC........................ 336 310-4624
  1369 S Park Dr Kernersville (27284) *(G-7290)*

Olive Hill Wldg & Fabrication, Roxboro Also Called: Olive Hl Wldg Fabrication Inc *(G-10935)*

Olive Hl Wldg Fabrication Inc........................ 336 597-0737
  1940 Semora Rd Roxboro (27574) *(G-10935)*

Oliventures Inc (PA)........................800 231-2619
  6325 Falls Of Neuse Rd Ste 35-122 Raleigh (27615) *(G-10345)*

Oliver Rubber Company LLC........................ 336 629-1436
  408 Telephone Ave Asheboro (27205) *(G-380)*

Olivia Machine & Tool Inc........................ 919 499-6021
  815 Seawell Rosser Rd Sanford (27332) *(G-11213)*

Ollis Enterprises Inc........................ 828 265-0004
  1613 Industrial Dr Wilkesboro (28697) *(G-12648)*

Olon Industries Inc (us)........................ 630 232-4705
  279 Bethel Church Rd Mocksville (27028) *(G-8383)*

Olpr.leather Goods Co., Mooresville Also Called: Oleksynprannyk LLC *(G-8738)*

OLT Logging Inc........................ 919 894-4506
  451 Marshall Ln Smithfield (27577) *(G-11456)*

Olympic Products LLC (PA)........................336 378-9620
  4100 Pleasant Garden Rd Greensboro (27406) *(G-5720)*

Olympic Products LLC........................ 336 378-9620
  4100 Pleasant Garden Rd Greensboro (27406) *(G-5721)*

Omega Manufacturing Corp........................ 704 597-0418
  1800 Industrial Center Cir Charlotte (28213) *(G-2596)*

Omega Precious Metals........................ 269 903-9330
  40 Shorrey Pl Youngsville (27596) *(G-13479)*

Omega Studios Inc........................ 704 889-5800
  10519 Industrial Dr Pineville (28134) *(G-9745)*

Omni Group LLC........................ 828 404-3104
  1140 Tate Blvd Se Hickory (28602) *(G-6405)*

Omni Mold & Die LLC........................ 336 724-5152
  2710 Boulder Park Ct Winston Salem (27101) *(G-13270)*

Omni Systems, Laurel Hill Also Called: Hygiene Systems Inc *(G-7484)*

Omnia Industries LLC........................ 704 707-6062
  1430 Industrial Dr Ste A Matthews (28105) *(G-8138)*

Omnia LLC........................ 919 696-2193
  115 Certainteed Dr Oxford (27565) *(G-9621)*

Omnia Products, Oxford Also Called: Omnia LLC *(G-9621)*

Omnia Products LLC........................ 919 514-3977
  115 Certainteed Dr Oxford (27565) *(G-9622)*

Omtex, Rutherford College Also Called: Aquafil OMara Inc *(G-10970)*

On Demand Printing & Desi........................ 828 252-0965
  200 Patton Ave Asheville (28801) *(G-560)*

On Demand Screen Printing LLC........................ 704 661-0788
  2242 Roberta Rd Concord (28027) *(G-3413)*

On Point Mobile Detailing LLC........................ 404 593-8882
  10906 Featherbrook Rd Apt 1b Charlotte (28262) *(G-2597)*

On Time Metal LLC........................ 828 635-1001
  31 Wayfound Church Rd Hiddenite (28636) *(G-6503)*

On-Site Hose Inc........................ 919 303-3840
  1001 Goodworth Dr Apex (27539) *(G-183)*

Oncoceutics Inc........................ 678 897-0563
  2505 Meridian Pkwy Ste 100 Durham (27713) *(G-4156)*

One Furniture Group Corp........................ 336 235-0221
  6520 Airport Center Dr Ste 204 Greensboro (27409) *(G-5722)*

One Hundred Ten Percent Screen........................ 252 728-3848
  150 Lake Rd Beaufort (28516) *(G-732)*

One Library At A Time Inc........................ 704 578-1812
  4107 Crossgate Rd Charlotte (28226) *(G-2598)*

One On One Press LLC........................ 910 228-8821
  616 Princess St Wilmington (28401) *(G-12866)*

One Source Document Solutions........................ 336 482-2360
  311 Pomona Dr Ste D Greensboro (27407) *(G-5723)*

One Source SEC & Sound Inc........................ 281 850-9487
  122 Summerville Dr Ste 101 Mooresville (28115) *(G-8739)*

One Srce Dcument Solutions Inc........................ 800 401-9544
  4355 Federal Dr Ste 140 Greensboro (27410) *(G-5724)*

Oneaka Dance Company........................ 704 299-7432
  4430 The Plaza # 13 Charlotte (28215) *(G-2599)*

Oneh2 Inc........................ 844 996-6342
  620 23rd St Nw Hickory (28601) *(G-6406)*

Oneida Molded Plastics LLC........................ 919 663-3141
  920 E Raleigh St Siler City (27344) *(G-11421)*

Onion Peel Software Inc........................ 919 460-1789
  1 Copley Pkwy Ste 480 Morrisville (27560) *(G-9032)*

Onixx Manufacturing LLC........................ 828 298-4625
  107 W Buckeye Rd Swannanoa (28778) *(G-11875)*

Onsat Magazine, Shelby Also Called: Triple D Publishing Inc *(G-11385)*

Onsite Woodwork Corporation........................ 704 523-1380
  645 Pressley Rd Ste E Charlotte (28217) *(G-2600)*

Onslow Bay Boatworks & Marine........................ 910 270-3703
  175 Sloop Point Loop Rd Hampstead (28443) *(G-6074)*

OnTarget Labs Inc (PA)........................ 919 846-3877
  8605 Bell Grove Way Raleigh (27615) *(G-10346)*

Ontex North America, Stokesdale Also Called: Ontex Operations Usa LLC *(G-11814)*

Ontex Operations Usa LLC (HQ)........................ 770 346-9250
  9300 Nc Highway 65 Stokesdale (27357) *(G-11814)*

Ontex Stokesdale, Stokesdale Also Called: Valor Brands LLC *(G-11817)*

Ontic Engineering and Mfg Inc........................ 919 395-3908
  1176 Telecom Dr Creedmoor (27522) *(G-3653)*

Onyx, Stanley Also Called: Onyx Environmental Solutions Inc *(G-11623)*

Onyx Environmental Solutions Inc........................ 800 858-3533
  7781 S Little Egypt Rd Stanley (28164) *(G-11623)*

Oowee Incorporated........................ 828 633-0289
  2194 Smoky Park Hwy Ste 100 Candler (28715) *(G-1230)*

Open Book Extracts, Roxboro Also Called: Old Belt Extracts LLC *(G-10934)*

Open South Imports, Hillsborough Also Called: Sommerville Enterprises LLC *(G-6878)*

Openfire Systems........................ 336 251-3991
  5450 Boone Trl Millers Creek (28651) *(G-8306)*

Operable Inc........................ 757 617-0935
  1209 Winkworth Way Wake Forest (27587) *(G-12288)*

Operating, Wilmington Also Called: Ekc Advanced Elec USA 4 LLC *(G-12770)*

Operating Shelby LLC Tag........................ 704 482-1399
  2501 W Dixon Blvd Shelby (28152) *(G-11368)*

Optical Place Inc (PA)........................336 274-1300
  2633 Randleman Rd Greensboro (27406) *(G-5725)*

Optical Wholesale, Greensboro Also Called: Optical Place Inc *(G-5725)*

Opticare, Rocky Mount Also Called: O D Eyecarecenter P A *(G-10856)*

Opticoncepts Inc........................ 828 320-0138
  911 W Union St Morganton (28655) *(G-8886)*

Optics Inc........................ 336 288-9504
  1607 Westover Ter Ste B Greensboro (27408) *(G-5726)*

Optics Inc (PA)........................ 336 884-5677
  1105 N Lindsay St Side Side High Point (27262) *(G-6721)*

Optimum Lighting, Henderson Also Called: Optimum Lighting LLC *(G-6168)*

Optimum Lighting LLC........................ 508 646-3324
  880 Facet Rd Henderson (27537) *(G-6168)*

Opto Alignment Technology Inc........................ 704 893-0399
  1034 Van Buren Ave Ste A Indian Trail (28079) *(G-7093)*

Optometric Eyecare Center Inc........................ 910 326-3050
  775 W Corbett Ave Swansboro (28584) *(G-11888)*

Optomill Solutions LLC........................ 704 560-4037
  1223 Clover Ln Matthews (28104) *(G-8188)*

Optopol Usa Inc.. 833 678-6765
  3915 Beryl Rd Ste 130 Raleigh (27607) *(G-10347)*

Opulence of Southern Pine.............................. 919 467-1781
  400 Daniels St Raleigh (27605) *(G-10348)*

Opw Feling Containment Systems, Smithfield *Also Called: Opw Fueling Components Inc*
(G-11458)

Opw Fling Cntnment Systems Inc (DH).............919 209-2280
  3250 Us Highway 70 Bus W Smithfield (27577) *(G-11457)*

Opw Fueling Components Inc.......................... 919 464-4569
  3250 Us Highway 70 Bus W Smithfield (27577) *(G-11458)*

Ora Inc... 540 903-7177
  315 Baldwin Ave Marion (28752) *(G-8059)*

Oracle, Matthews *Also Called: Oracle Systems Corporation (G-8139)*

Oracle, Morrisville *Also Called: Oracle Corporation (G-9033)*

Oracle, Raleigh *Also Called: Oracle of God Ministries Nc (G-10349)*

Oracle, Raleigh *Also Called: Oracle Systems Corporation (G-10350)*

Oracle Corporation.. 919 595-2500
  5200 Paramount Pkwy Ste 100 Morrisville (27560) *(G-9033)*

Oracle Flexible Packaging Inc........................ 336 777-5000
  220 Polo Rd Winston Salem (27105) *(G-13271)*

Oracle Hearing Group.................................... 732 349-6804
  1016 Striking Island Dr Wilmington (28403) *(G-12867)*

Oracle of God Ministries Nc........................... 919 522-2113
  5731 New Bern Ave Raleigh (27610) *(G-10349)*

Oracle Packaging, Winston Salem *Also Called: Llflex LLC (G-13237)*

Oracle Systems Corporation.......................... 704 423-1426
  1608 Nightshade Pl Matthews (28105) *(G-8139)*

Oracle Systems Corporation.......................... 919 257-2300
  8081 Arco Corporate Dr Ste 270 Raleigh (27617) *(G-10350)*

Oramental Post... 704 376-8111
  10108 Industrial Dr Pineville (28134) *(G-9746)*

Orange Bakery Inc.. 704 875-3003
  13400 Reese Blvd W Huntersville (28078) *(G-7029)*

Orange Steel Roofing Products, Fayetteville *Also Called: Union Corrugating Company*
(G-4685)

Orare Inc... 919 742-1003
  812 E 3rd St Siler City (27344) *(G-11422)*

Orbita Corporation... 910 256-5300
  6740 Netherlands Dr Ste D Wilmington (28405) *(G-12868)*

Orca Tactical, Norlina *Also Called: Claypro LLC (G-9520)*

Organizer Llc.. 336 391-7591
  274 Glen Eagles Dr Winston Salem (27104) *(G-13272)*

Orgbook Inc.. 615 483-5410
  4307 Emperor Blvd Ste 300 Durham (27703) *(G-4157)*

Orgspan Inc.. 855 674-7726
  4307 Emperor Blvd Ste 300 Durham (27703) *(G-4158)*

Oriel Therapeutics Inc.................................... 919 313-1290
  630 Davis Dr Ste 120 Durham (27713) *(G-4159)*

Origami Ink LLC.. 828 225-2300
  6 Boston Way Ste 10 Asheville (28803) *(G-561)*

Origin Food Group LLC................................... 704 768-9000
  306 Stamey Farm Rd Statesville (28677) *(G-11741)*

Original New York Seltzer LLC (HQ)................ 323 500-0757
  19109 W Catawba Ave Ste 200 Cornelius (28031) *(G-3617)*

Original Nuthouse Brand, Edenton *Also Called: Morven Partners LP (G-4369)*

Oriole Mill, The, Hendersonville *Also Called: Michelson Enterprises Inc (G-6227)*

Orlandos Cstm Design T-Shirts...................... 919 220-5515
  2824 N Roxboro St Durham (27704) *(G-4160)*

Ornamental, Archdale *Also Called: Ornamental Mouldings LLC (G-240)*

Ornamental Mouldings LLC (DH).................... 336 431-9120
  3804 Comanche Rd Archdale (27263) *(G-240)*

Ornamental Specialties Inc............................. 704 821-9154
  3488 Gribble Rd Matthews (28104) *(G-8189)*

Oro Manufacturing Company.......................... 704 283-2186
  5000 Stitt St Monroe (28110) *(G-8539)*

Orpak Usa Inc... 201 441-9820
  7300 W Friendly Ave Greensboro (27410) *(G-5727)*

Orthopedic Appliance Company...................... 828 254-6305
  75 Victoria Rd Asheville (28801) *(G-562)*

Orthopedic Appliance Company...................... 828 348-1960
  910 Tate Blvd Se Hickory (28602) *(G-6407)*

Orthopedic Services....................................... 336 716-3349
  3303 Healy Dr Winston Salem (27103) *(G-13273)*

Orthorx Inc... 919 929-5550
  400 Meadowmont Village Cir # 425 Chapel Hill (27517) *(G-1562)*

Oryx Systems Inc... 704 519-8803
  3056 Eaton Ave Indian Trail (28079) *(G-7094)*

Os Press LLC.. 910 485-7955
  1005 Arsenal Ave Fayetteville (28305) *(G-4649)*

Osa, Charlotte *Also Called: Okaya Shinnichi Corp America (G-2592)*

Osage Pecan Company................................... 660 679-6137
  713 Claybank Rd West Jefferson (28694) *(G-12569)*

Oslo Press Inc.. 919 606-2028
  2316 Foxtrot Rd Raleigh (27610) *(G-10351)*

Osprea Logistics USA, Charlotte *Also Called: Osprea Logistics Usa LLC (G-2601)*

Osprea Logistics Usa LLC.............................. 704 504-1677
  11108 Quality Dr Charlotte (28273) *(G-2601)*

Ossid LLC (DH)... 252 446-6177
  4000 College Rd Battleboro (27809) *(G-704)*

Ossiriand Inc.. 336 385-1100
  106 Hidden Valley Rd Creston (28615) *(G-3658)*

Ostec Industries Corp.................................... 704 488-3841
  4103 Sinclair St Denver (28037) *(G-3796)*

OSteel Buildings Inc (PA)...............................704 824-6061
  1180 Old Redbud Dr Gastonia (28056) *(G-5113)*

Ostwalt Leasing Co Inc.................................. 704 528-4528
  867 S Main St Troutman (28166) *(G-12146)*

Ostwalt Machine Company Inc........................ 704 528-5730
  140 Apple Hill Rd Troutman (28166) *(G-12147)*

Ostwalt-Vault Co, Troutman *Also Called: Carolina Cemetery Park Corp (G-12132)*

Otb Machinery Inc.. 336 323-1035
  51 Proctor Rd Thomasville (27360) *(G-12057)*

Otis Elevator Company................................... 828 251-1248
  203 Elk Park Dr Asheville (28804) *(G-563)*

Otis Elevator Company................................... 704 519-0100
  9625 Southern Pine Blvd Ste G Charlotte (28273) *(G-2602)*

Ottenweller Co Inc... 336 783-6959
  401 Technology Ln Mount Airy (27030) *(G-9162)*

Ottis' Fish Market, Morehead City *Also Called: Carolina ATL Seafood Entps (G-8822)*

Otto & Moore Furn Designers, High Point *Also Called: Otto and Moore Inc (G-6722)*

Otto and Moore Inc... 336 887-0017
  701 Eastchester Dr High Point (27262) *(G-6722)*

Otto Environmental Systems, Charlotte *Also Called: Duramax Holdings LLC (G-2068)*

Otto Envmtl Systems NC LLC.......................... 800 227-5885
  12700 Gen Dr Charlotte (28273) *(G-2603)*

Our Home - Lincolnton, Lincolnton *Also Called: North Crolina Tortilla Mfg LLC (G-7848)*

Our Pride Foods, Roxboro *Also Called: Our Pride Foods Roxboro Inc (G-10936)*

Our Pride Foods Roxboro Inc.......................... 336 597-4978
  1128 N Main St Roxboro (27573) *(G-10936)*

Our State Magazine, Greensboro *Also Called: Mann Media Inc (G-5672)*

Outdura, Hudson *Also Called: Sattler Corp (G-6958)*

Outer Banks Centinel, Nags Head *Also Called: Slam Publications LLC (G-9303)*

Outer Banks Hammocks Inc............................ 910 256-4001
  7228 Wrightsville Ave Wilmington (28403) *(G-12869)*

Outer Banks Internet Inc................................ 252 441-6698
  3116 N Croatan Hwy Ste 104 Kill Devil Hills (27948) *(G-7318)*

Outer Banks Press, Kitty Hawk *Also Called: Obbc Inc (G-7446)*

Outlaw Step Co... 252 568-4384
  2491 Burncoat Rd Deep Run (28525) *(G-3733)*

Output Services Group Inc............................. 336 783-5948
  201 Technology Ln Mount Airy (27030) *(G-9163)*

Outrider USA, Mars Hill *Also Called: Ffr Electrics LLC (G-8077)*

Over Rainbow Inc.. 704 332-5521
  1431 Bryant St Charlotte (28208) *(G-2604)*

Overnight Sofa Corporation........................... 828 324-2271
  3043 1st Ave Sw Hickory (28602) *(G-6408)*

Overstreet Sign Contrs Inc............................ 919 596-7300
  2210 Page Rd Ste 101 Durham (27703) *(G-4161)*

Overwith Inc... 704 866-8148
  1220 Industrial Ave Gastonia (28054) *(G-5114)*

Owen G Dunn Co Inc (PA)................................252 633-3197
  3731 Trent Rd New Bern (28562) *(G-9387)*

Owens Corning Gastonia Plant, Dallas *Also Called: Owens Crning Nn-Woven Tech LLC* *(G-3681)*

Owens Corning Glass Metal Svcs.......................................704 721-2000
4535 Enterprise Dr Nw Concord (28027) *(G-3414)*

Owens Corning Sales LLC..419 248-8000
3321 Durham Rd Roxboro (27573) *(G-10937)*

Owens Crning Nn-Woven Tech LLC......................................740 321-6131
1230 Gastonia Technology Pkwy Dallas (28034) *(G-3681)*

Owens Quilting Inc...828 695-1495
101 E 11th St Ste 13 Newton (28658) *(G-9485)*

Oxford Public Ledger, Oxford *Also Called: Ledger Publishing Company (G-9619)*

Oxford University Press LLC...919 677-0977
4000 Centre Green Way Cary (27513) *(G-1412)*

Oxford University Press LLC...919 677-0977
4000 Centre Green Way Cary (27513) *(G-1413)*

Oyama Cabinet Inc..828 327-2668
115 Ge Plant Rd Sw Conover (28613) *(G-3542)*

Oyster Merger Sub II LLC..919 474-6700
4721 Emperor Blvd Ste 100 Durham (27703) *(G-4162)*

P & D Archtectural Precast Inc..252 566-9811
323 E Railroad St La Grange (28551) *(G-7470)*

P & G Manufacturing Wash Inc..252 946-9110
339 Old Bath Hwy Washington (27889) *(G-12402)*

P & P Distributing Company...910 582-1968
307 Industry Dr Hamlet (28345) *(G-6060)*

P & S Welding Inc..910 285-3126
8414 Us Hwy 117 N Willard (28478) *(G-12666)*

P C S, Winston Salem *Also Called: Personal Communication Systems Inc (G-13285)*

P P Kiln Erectors...980 825-2263
5351 Faith Rd Salisbury (28146) *(G-11099)*

P P M Cycle and Custom..336 434-5243
112 School Rd Trinity (27370) *(G-12120)*

P R Sparks Enterprises Inc..336 272-7200
1333 Headquarters Dr Greensboro (27405) *(G-5728)*

P S G, Greensboro *Also Called: Printing Svcs Greensboro Inc (G-5765)*

P T I, Conover *Also Called: Plastic Technology Inc (G-3545)*

P W I Computer Accessories, Winston Salem *Also Called: Panel Wholesalers Incorporated* *(G-13275)*

P&A Indstrial Fabrications LLC (HQ)....................................336 322-1766
1841 N Main St Roxboro (27573) *(G-10938)*

P&S Machining Fabrication LLC...336 227-0151
2900 Tucker St Burlington (27215) *(G-1137)*

P1 Catawba Development Co LLC..704 462-1882
2815 Woodtech Dr Newton (28658) *(G-9486)*

P4rts LLC...561 717-7580
106 Langtree Village Dr Ste 301 Mooresville (28117) *(G-8740)*

Pace Incorporated (PA)...910 695-7223
346 Grant Rd Vass (28394) *(G-12228)*

Pace Communications Inc (PA)..336 378-6065
1301 Carolina St Ste 200 Greensboro (27401) *(G-5729)*

Pace Scientific Inc..704 799-0688
112 Paul Critcher Dr Boone (28607) *(G-937)*

Pace Worldwide, Vass *Also Called: Pace Incorporated (G-12228)*

Paceline, Monroe *Also Called: Spt Technology Inc (G-8562)*

Paceline Inc (PA)..704 290-5007
10737 Independence Pointe Pkwy Ste 103 Matthews (28105) *(G-8140)*

Pacific Coast Feather LLC...252 492-0051
100 Comfort Dr Henderson (27537) *(G-6169)*

Pacific Seacraft LLC...252 948-1421
1481 W 2nd St Washington (27889) *(G-12403)*

Pack Brothers Log & Grading, Mill Spring *Also Called: Pack Brothers Logging (G-8302)*

Pack Brothers Logging...828 894-2191
1559 Highway 9 S Mill Spring (28756) *(G-8302)*

Pack Your Wings, Black Mountain *Also Called: Eye Glass Lady LLC (G-864)*

Package Craft LLC (DH)...252 825-0111
146 Package Craft Rd Bethel (27812) *(G-840)*

Package Crafters Incorporated..336 431-9700
1040 E Springfield Rd High Point (27263) *(G-6723)*

Packaging and Supply Solutions, Wilmington *Also Called: Atlantic Corporation (G-12713)*

Packaging Corporation America...252 753-8450
9156 West Marlboro Rd Farmville (27828) *(G-4537)*

Packaging Corporation America...336 434-0600
801 N William St Goldsboro (27530) *(G-5234)*

Packaging Corporation America...704 664-5010
307 Oates Rd Ste B Mooresville (28117) *(G-8741)*

Packaging Corporation America...828 584-1511
114 Dixie Blvd Morganton (28655) *(G-8887)*

Packaging Corporation America...828 286-9156
321 Industrial Park Rd Rutherfordton (28139) *(G-10988)*

Packaging Corporation America...704 633-3611
1302 N Salisbury Ave Salisbury (28144) *(G-11100)*

Packaging Corporation America...336 434-0600
212 Roelee St Trinity (27370) *(G-12121)*

Packaging Plus North Carolina..336 643-4097
8301 Sangor Dr Summerfield (27358) *(G-11845)*

Packaging Services..919 630-4145
4112 Willow Oak Rd Raleigh (27604) *(G-10352)*

Packet Pushers Interactive LLC...928 793-2450
500 Westover Dr Ste 16993 Sanford (27330) *(G-11214)*

Packiq, Fayetteville *Also Called: Packiq LLC (G-4650)*

Packiq LLC...910 964-4331
800 Technology Dr Ste 110 Fayetteville (28306) *(G-4650)*

Packo Bottling Inc...919 496-4286
42 Golden Leaf Dr Louisburg (27549) *(G-7921)*

Pacon Manufacturing Co LLC..910 239-3001
100 Quality Dr Leland (28451) *(G-7556)*

Pactiv LLC...910 944-1800
3299 Nc Hwy 5 Aberdeen (28315) *(G-18)*

Pactiv LLC...828 396-2373
3825 N Main St Granite Falls (28630) *(G-5315)*

Pactiv LLC...336 292-2796
520 Radar Rd Greensboro (27410) *(G-5730)*

Pactiv LLC...252 527-6300
1447 Enterprise Blvd Kinston (28504) *(G-7425)*

Pactiv LLC...828 758-7580
303 Advantage Ct Lenoir (28645) *(G-7632)*

Pag Asb LLC..336 883-4187
2410 Schirra Pl High Point (27263) *(G-6724)*

Page Plantation Shuttering Co, Hamlet *Also Called: P & P Distributing Company (G-6060)*

Pages Hydro Dipping Coatings...910 322-2077
7455 Lane Rd Linden (28356) *(G-7875)*

Pages Screen Printing LLC...336 759-7979
4110 Cherry St Winston Salem (27105) *(G-13274)*

Pai Services LLC..856 231-4667
11215 N Community House Rd Ste 800 Charlotte (28277) *(G-2605)*

Painpathways Magazine, Winston Salem *Also Called: Jennifer Mowrer (G-13216)*

Paint Company of NC...336 764-1648
10436 N Nc Hwy 150 Clemmons (27012) *(G-3198)*

Painting By Bill, Fayetteville *Also Called: Peaches Enterprises Inc (G-4653)*

Painting By Colors LLC..919 963-2300
562 Rock Pillar Rd Clayton (27520) *(G-3166)*

Pair Cutoms Boats, Washington *Also Called: Pair Marine Inc (G-12404)*

Pair Marine Inc..252 717-7009
106 Tarheel Dr Washington (27889) *(G-12404)*

Pak-Lite Inc...919 563-1097
6508 E Washington Street Ext Mebane (27302) *(G-8254)*

Palace Green, Raleigh *Also Called: Palace Green LLC (G-10353)*

Palace Green LLC..919 827-7950
4701 Violet Fields Way Raleigh (27612) *(G-10353)*

Paladin Custom Works...336 996-2796
230 Perry Rd Kernersville (27284) *(G-7291)*

Paladin Furniture, Hiddenite *Also Called: Paladin Industries Inc (G-6504)*

Paladin Industries Inc...828 635-0448
5270 Nc Highway 90 E Hiddenite (28636) *(G-6504)*

Paletria La Mnrca McHacana LLC..919 803-0636
3901 Capital Blvd Ste 155 Raleigh (27604) *(G-10354)*

Pallet Alliance Inc...919 442-1400
318 Blackwell St Ste 260 Durham (27701) *(G-4163)*

Pallet Express Inc...336 621-2266
6306 Old 421 Rd Liberty (27298) *(G-7775)*

Pallet Plus Inc...336 887-1810
12990 Trinity Rd Trinity (27370) *(G-12122)*

Pallet Resource of NC Inc.................... 336 731-8338
4572 N Nc Highway 150 Lexington (27295) *(G-7728)*

Pallet World.................... 919 800-1113
670 John Lee Rd Dunn (28334) *(G-3864)*

Pallet World USA Inc.................... 828 298-7270
124 Sondley Pkwy Asheville (28805) *(G-564)*

Palletone, Siler City Also Called: Palletone North Carolina Inc *(G-11423)*

Palletone North Carolina Inc.................... 919 575-6491
10 26th St Butner (27509) *(G-1204)*

Palletone North Carolina Inc.................... 336 492-5565
165 Turkey Foot Rd Mocksville (27028) *(G-8384)*

Palletone North Carolina Inc (HQ).................... 704 462-1882
2340 Ike Brooks Rd Siler City (27344) *(G-11423)*

Pallets & Such, Bessemer City Also Called: Ross Woodworking Inc *(G-832)*

Pallets & Such, Bessemer City Also Called: Ross Woodworking Inc *(G-833)*

Pallets and More.................... 919 815-6134
119 N Cheatham St Franklinton (27525) *(G-4852)*

Palmer Instruments Inc.................... 828 658-3131
234 Old Weaverville Rd Asheville (28804) *(G-565)*

Palmer Senn.................... 704 451-3971
3113 Airlie St Charlotte (28205) *(G-2606)*

Palmer Wahl Instrmnttion Group, Asheville Also Called: Palmer Instruments Inc *(G-565)*

Palmer Wahl Instrmnttion Group, Asheville Also Called: Palmer Wahl Instruments Inc *(G-566)*

Palmer Wahl Instruments Inc.................... 828 658-3131
234 Old Weaverville Rd Asheville (28804) *(G-566)*

Palmetto and Associate LLC.................... 336 382-7432
223 S Elm St Greensboro (27401) *(G-5731)*

Palmetto Brick-Florence, Monroe Also Called: J L Anderson Co Inc *(G-8507)*

Palziv North America, Louisburg Also Called: Palziv North America Inc *(G-7922)*

Palziv North America Inc.................... 919 497-0010
7966 Nc 56 Hwy Louisburg (27549) *(G-7922)*

Pam Trading Corporation.................... 336 668-0901
1135 Snow Bridge Ln Kernersville (27284) *(G-7292)*

Pamela A Adams.................... 919 876-5949
3812 Tarheel Dr Ste D Raleigh (27609) *(G-10355)*

Pamela Stoeppelwerth.................... 828 837-7293
929 Coalville Rd Marble (28905) *(G-8027)*

Pamela Taylor.................... 828 692-8599
101 1st Ave W Hendersonville (28792) *(G-6234)*

Pamlico Air, Washington Also Called: Cleanaire Inc *(G-12381)*

Pamlico Air Inc (DH).................... 252 995-6267
112 S Respess St Washington (27889) *(G-12405)*

Pamlico Packing Co Inc (PA).................... 252 745-3688
66 Cross Rd S Grantsboro (28529) *(G-5331)*

Pamlico Packing Co Inc.................... 252 745-3688
28 N First St Vandemere (28587) *(G-12226)*

Pamlico Screen Printing Inc.................... 252 944-6001
7669 Broad Creek Rd Washington (27889) *(G-12406)*

Pamlico Shores Inc.................... 252 926-0011
14166 Us Highway 264 Swanquarter (27885) *(G-11881)*

Pamor Fine Print.................... 919 559-2846
5924 Crepe Myrtle Ct Raleigh (27609) *(G-10356)*

Pan American Screw LLC (HQ).................... 828 466-0060
630 Reese Dr Sw Conover (28613) *(G-3543)*

Pan Glo, Charlotte, Charlotte Also Called: Russell T Bundy Associates Inc *(G-2743)*

Panaceutics Nutrition Inc.................... 919 797-9623
6 Davis Dr Durham (27709) *(G-4164)*

Panel Wholesalers Incorporated.................... 336 765-4040
3841 Kimwell Dr Winston Salem (27103) *(G-13275)*

Panels By Paith Inc.................... 336 599-3437
2728 Allensville Rd Roxboro (27574) *(G-10939)*

Panenergy Corp (DH).................... 704 594-6200
526 S Church St Charlotte (28202) *(G-2607)*

Papa Lonnies Inc.................... 336 573-9313
154 Dogwood Rd Stoneville (27048) *(G-11825)*

Papa Parusos Foods Inc.................... 910 484-8999
3426 Clinton Rd Fayetteville (28312) *(G-4651)*

Paper Development, Reidsville Also Called: Morrisette Paper Company Inc *(G-10694)*

Paper Perfector LLC.................... 910 695-1092
125 Brookfield Dr Pinehurst (28374) *(G-9698)*

Paper Specialties Inc.................... 919 431-0028
2708 Discovery Dr Ste J Raleigh (27616) *(G-10357)*

Paperfoam Packaging Usa LLC.................... 910 371-0480
4220 Us Highway 421 N Wilmington (28401) *(G-12870)*

Papersassy Boutique, Winston Salem Also Called: Devora Designs Inc *(G-13142)*

Paperworks.................... 704 548-9057
3040 Parker Green Trl Charlotte (28269) *(G-2608)*

Paperworks Industries Inc.................... 910 439-6137
5465 Nc Highway 73 W Mount Gilead (27306) *(G-9209)*

Paperworks Industries Inc.................... 336 447-7278
6530 Franz Warner Pkwy Whitsett (27377) *(G-12616)*

Paraclete Xp Sky Venture LLC.................... 910 848-2600
190 Paraclete Dr Raeford (28376) *(G-9844)*

Paraclete Xp Skyventure LLC.................... 910 904-0027
925 Doc Brown Rd Raeford (28376) *(G-9845)*

Paradigm Solutions Inc.................... 910 392-2611
1213 Culbreth Dr Wilmington (28405) *(G-12871)*

Paradise Printers.................... 336 570-2922
3651 Alamance Rd Burlington (27215) *(G-1138)*

Paragon Films Inc.................... 828 632-5552
255 We Baab Industrial Dr Taylorsville (28681) *(G-11968)*

Paragon Global LLC.................... 336 899-8525
2415 W English Rd High Point (27262) *(G-6725)*

Paragon ID High Point Us Inc.................... 336 882-8115
210 Old Thomasville Rd High Point (27260) *(G-6726)*

Paragon Medical - Southington, Charlotte Also Called: Matthew Warren Inc *(G-2470)*

Paramason, Louisburg Also Called: En Fleur Corporation *(G-7914)*

Parameter Generation Ctrl Inc.................... 828 669-8717
1054 Old Us Hwy 70 W Black Mountain (28711) *(G-870)*

Parata Systems LLC (HQ).................... 888 727-2821
106 Roche Dr Durham (27703) *(G-4165)*

Parchment Press, Hiddenite Also Called: Hiddenite Conference Ctr LLC *(G-6498)*

Parhelion Incorporated.................... 866 409-1839
126 N Salem St Ste 200 Apex (27502) *(G-184)*

Parish Sign & Service Inc.................... 910 875-6121
627 Laurinburg Rd Raeford (28376) *(G-9846)*

Park Ave Division, Burlington Also Called: Glen Rven Tchnical Fabrics LLC *(G-1100)*

Park Communications LLC.................... 336 292-4000
4301 Waterleaf Ct Greensboro (27410) *(G-5732)*

Park Communications LLC (HQ).................... 919 852-1117
10900 World Trade Blvd Raleigh (27617) *(G-10358)*

Park Court Properties RE Inc.................... 919 304-3110
1404 Dogwood Way Unit C Mebane (27302) *(G-8255)*

Park Elevator Co, Gastonia Also Called: Park Manufacturing Company *(G-5115)*

Park Manufacturing Company (PA).................... 704 869-6128
3112 Northwest Blvd Gastonia (28052) *(G-5115)*

Park Shirt Company.................... 931 879-5894
321 E Russell St Fayetteville (28301) *(G-4652)*

Parkdale Incorporated (PA).................... 704 874-5000
531 Cotton Blossom Cir Gastonia (28054) *(G-5116)*

Parkdale Mills Incorporated.................... 704 825-5324
103 E Woodrow Ave Belmont (28012) *(G-758)*

Parkdale Mills Incorporated.................... 704 913-3917
1000 Parkdale Dr Belmont (28012) *(G-759)*

Parkdale Mills Incorporated.................... 704 825-2529
501 10th St Belmont (28012) *(G-760)*

Parkdale Mills Incorporated (HQ).................... 704 874-5000
531 Cotton Blossom Cir Gastonia (28054) *(G-5117)*

Parkdale Mills Incorporated.................... 704 739-7411
500 S Railroad Ave Kings Mountain (28086) *(G-7375)*

Parkdale Mills Incorporated.................... 704 855-3164
100 S Main St Landis (28088) *(G-7475)*

Parkdale Mills Incorporated.................... 336 243-2141
100 Mill St Lexington (27295) *(G-7729)*

Parkdale Mills Incorporated.................... 704 292-1255
Hwy 75 Mineral Springs (28108) *(G-8328)*

Parkdale Mills Incorporated.................... 704 822-0778
101 Mill St Mount Holly (28120) *(G-9241)*

Parkdale Mills Incorporated.................... 336 476-3181
400 Carmalt St Thomasville (27360) *(G-12058)*

Parkdale Mills Incorporated.................... 336 591-4644
1660 Us 311 Hwy N Walnut Cove (27052) *(G-12330)*

Parkdale Mills Inc.. 704 857-3456
414 N Meriah St Landis (28088) *(G-7476)*

Parkdale Plant 23, Landis *Also Called: Parkdale Mills Incorporated (G-7475)*

Parkdale Plant 24, Landis *Also Called: Parkdale Mills Inc (G-7476)*

Parkdale Plant 26, Walnut Cove *Also Called: Parkdale Mills Incorporated (G-12330)*

Parkdale Plant 5, Kings Mountain *Also Called: Parkdale Mills Incorporated (G-7375)*

Parkdale Plant 68, Mount Holly *Also Called: Parkdale Mills Incorporated (G-9241)*

Parkdale Plants 3 & 4, Lexington *Also Called: Parkdale Mills Incorporated (G-7729)*

Parker Athletic Products LLC................................ 704 370-0400
2401 Distribution St Charlotte (28203) *(G-2609)*

Parker Brothers Incorporated.............................. 910 564-4132
825 Kitty Fork Rd Clinton (28328) *(G-3237)*

Parker Gas Company Inc (PA)................................ 800 354-7250
1504 Sunset Ave Clinton (28328) *(G-3238)*

Parker Hosiery Company Inc................................. 828 668-7628
78 Catawba Ave Old Fort (28762) *(G-9596)*

Parker Hydraulics, Kings Mountain *Also Called: Parker-Hannifin Corporation (G-7376)*

Parker Industries Inc... 828 437-7779
4867 Rhoney Rd Connelly Springs (28612) *(G-3481)*

Parker Legwear, Old Fort *Also Called: Parker Hosiery Company Inc (G-9596)*

Parker Marine Enterprises Inc.............................. 252 728-5621
2570 Nc Highway 101 Beaufort (28516) *(G-733)*

Parker Medical Associates LLC............................ 704 344-9998
2400 Distribution St Charlotte (28203) *(G-2610)*

Parker Medical Associates LLC (PA)..................... 704 344-9998
2400 Distribution St Charlotte (28203) *(G-2611)*

Parker Metal Finishing Company........................... 336 275-9657
719 W Gate City Blvd Ste D Greensboro (27403) *(G-5733)*

Parker Oil Inc... 828 253-7265
290 Depot St Asheville (28801) *(G-567)*

Parker Service Center, Mooresville *Also Called: Parker-Hannifin Corporation (G-8742)*

Parker Southern Inc.. 828 428-3506
15 W Holly St Maiden (28650) *(G-8016)*

Parker-Hannifin Corporation................................ 704 588-3246
9225 Forsyth Park Dr Charlotte (28273) *(G-2612)*

Parker-Hannifin Corporation................................ 828 245-3233
203 Pine St Forest City (28043) *(G-4795)*

Parker-Hannifin Corporation................................ 336 373-1761
125 E Meadowview Rd Greensboro (27406) *(G-5734)*

Parker-Hannifin Corporation................................ 252 652-6592
245 Belltown Rd Havelock (28532) *(G-6125)*

Parker-Hannifin Corporation................................ 704 739-9781
101 Canterbury Rd Kings Mountain (28086) *(G-7376)*

Parker-Hannifin Corporation................................ 704 664-1922
2559 Charlotte Hwy Mooresville (28117) *(G-8742)*

Parker-Hannifin Corporation................................ 704 662-3500
149 Crawford Rd Statesville (28625) *(G-11742)*

Parker-Hannifin Corporation................................ 252 237-6171
2600 Wilco Blvd S Wilson (27893) *(G-13012)*

Parker-Lord, Cary *Also Called: Lord Corporation (G-1394)*

Parkers Equipment Company............................... 252 560-0088
3204 Hwy 258 S Snow Hill (28580) *(G-11482)*

Parks Family Meats LLC..................................... 217 446-4600
1618 Nc 24 And 50 Hwy Warsaw (28398) *(G-12364)*

Parkway Asheville, Arden *Also Called: Parkway Products LLC (G-293)*

Parkway Products LLC....................................... 828 684-1362
199 Airport Rd Arden (28704) *(G-293)*

Parkway Products LLC....................................... 828 684-1362
199 Airport Rd Arden (28704) *(G-294)*

Parkwood Corporation....................................... 910 815-4300
3506 E Yacht Dr Oak Island (28465) *(G-9567)*

Parmer International Inc..................................... 704 374-0066
1225 Graphic Ct Ste D Charlotte (28206) *(G-2613)*

Parrish Contracting LLC..................................... 828 524-9100
3370 Bryson City Rd Franklin (28734) *(G-4838)*

Parrish Tire Company.. 704 372-2013
300 E 36th St Charlotte (28206) *(G-2614)*

Parrish Tire Company.. 336 334-9979
2809 Thurston Ave Greensboro (27406) *(G-5735)*

Parrish Tire Company.. 704 872-6565
547 Winston Rd Jonesville (28642) *(G-7198)*

Parrish Tire Company (PA)................................... 800 849-8473
5130 Indiana Ave Winston Salem (27106) *(G-13276)*

Parsons Metal Fabricators Inc.............................. 828 758-7521
265 Wildwood Rd Lenoir (28645) *(G-7633)*

Parton Export, Rutherfordton *Also Called: Parton Lumber Company Inc (G-10990)*

Parton Forest Products Inc.................................. 828 287-4257
251 Parton Rd Rutherfordton (28139) *(G-10989)*

Parton Lumber Company Inc (PA).......................... 828 287-4257
251 Parton Rd Rutherfordton (28139) *(G-10990)*

Parts and Systems Company Inc........................... 828 684-7070
44 Buck Shoals Rd Ste D2 Arden (28704) *(G-295)*

Party Tables Land Co LLC................................... 919 596-3521
2455 S Alston Ave Durham (27713) *(G-4166)*

Party Time Inc... 910 454-4577
1658 N Howe St Ste 1 Southport (28461) *(G-11524)*

Pas USA Inc.. 252 974-5500
2010 W 15th St Washington (27889) *(G-12407)*

Pasb Inc.. 704 490-2556
303 N Cannon Blvd Kannapolis (28083) *(G-7218)*

Paschal Associates Ltd...................................... 336 625-2535
324 S Wilmington St Raleigh (27601) *(G-10359)*

Pasco, Arden *Also Called: Parts and Systems Company Inc (G-295)*

Pashes LLC.. 704 682-6535
328 E Broad St Statesville (28677) *(G-11743)*

Pass & Seymour Inc.. 315 468-6211
4515 Enterprise Dr Nw Concord (28027) *(G-3415)*

Pass & Seymour Legrand, Concord *Also Called: Pass & Seymour Inc (G-3415)*

Passport Health Triangle..................................... 919 781-0053
8450 Chapel Hill Rd Ste 205 Cary (27513) *(G-1414)*

Pasture Management Systems Inc......................... 704 436-6401
10325 Nc Highway 49 N Mount Pleasant (28124) *(G-9263)*

Patch Rubber Company...................................... 252 536-2574
100 Patch Rubber Rd Weldon (27890) *(G-12525)*

Patel Deepal... 704 634-5141
4898 Aldridge Pl Nw Concord (28027) *(G-3416)*

Patheon, Greenville *Also Called: Patheon Manufacturing Svcs LLC (G-6010)*

Patheon, Morrisville *Also Called: Patheon Pharmaceuticals Inc (G-9035)*

Patheon, Morrisville *Also Called: Patheon Phrmceuticals Svcs Inc (G-9036)*

Patheon Calculus Merger LLC.............................. 919 226-3200
3900 Paramount Pkwy Morrisville (27560) *(G-9034)*

Patheon Inc.. 919 226-3200
4815 Emperor Blvd Ste 100 Durham (27703) *(G-4167)*

Patheon Inc.. 919 226-3200
4815 Emperor Blvd Ste 100 Durham (27703) *(G-4168)*

Patheon Manufacturing Svcs LLC.......................... 252 758-3436
5900 Martin Luther King Jr Hwy Greenville (27834) *(G-6010)*

Patheon Pharmaceuticals Inc............................... 866 728-4366
4125 Premier Dr High Point (27265) *(G-6727)*

Patheon Pharmaceuticals Inc (DH)........................ 919 226-3200
3900 Paramount Pkwy Morrisville (27560) *(G-9035)*

Patheon Phrmceuticals Svcs Inc (DH)..................... 919 226-3200
3900 Paramount Pkwy Morrisville (27560) *(G-9036)*

Patheon Softgels Inc... 336 812-8700
7902 Indlea Point Ste 112 Greensboro (27409) *(G-5736)*

Patheon Softgels Inc (DH)................................... 336 812-8700
4125 Premier Dr High Point (27265) *(G-6728)*

Patholdco Inc (HQ)... 919 212-1300
108 Nova Dr Morrisville (27560) *(G-9037)*

Patholdco Inc.. 919 369-0345
5217 Blue Stem Ct Raleigh (27606) *(G-10360)*

Pathway Technologies Inc (PA)............................. 919 847-2680
8400 Six Forks Rd Ste 202 Raleigh (27615) *(G-10361)*

Patrice Brent.. 980 999-7217
8606 Panglemont Dr Charlotte (28269) *(G-2615)*

Patricia Hall.. 704 729-6133
128 Terrace Dr Bessemer City (28016) *(G-829)*

Patrick Yarn Mill Inc.. 704 739-4119
501 York Rd Kings Mountain (28086) *(G-7377)*

Patrick Yarns, Kings Mountain *Also Called: Patrick Yarn Mill Inc (G-7377)*

Patriot Blinds & More, Jacksonville *Also Called: Dbf Inc (G-7122)*

Patriot Clean Fuel LLC....................................... 704 896-3600
214 Mazeppa Rd Mooresville (28115) *(G-8743)*

Pattern Box..704 535-8743
8325 Nathanael Greene Ln Charlotte (28227) *(G-2616)*

Patterson Custom Drapery............................910 791-4332
4315 Deer Creek Ln Wilmington (28405) *(G-12872)*

Pattons Medical, Charlotte Also Called: Pattons Medical LLC *(G-2617)*

Pattons Medical LLC....................................704 529-5442
4610 Entrance Dr Ste H Charlotte (28273) *(G-2617)*

Patty Cakes..828 696-8240
5 Star Ln Hendersonville (28791) *(G-6235)*

Patty Knio..919 995-2670
3008 Campbell Rd Raleigh (27606) *(G-10362)*

Paul Casper Inc...919 269-5362
3533 Rosinburg Rd Zebulon (27597) *(G-13520)*

Paul Charles Englert....................................704 824-2102
1820 Spencer Mountain Rd Gastonia (28054) *(G-5118)*

Paul Davis Restoration, Winston Salem Also Called: Moe Jt Enterprises Inc *(G-13260)*

Paul Hoge Creations Inc...............................704 624-6860
7105 E Marshville Blvd Marshville (28103) *(G-8091)*

Paul James O'Brian, Delco Also Called: Preferred Logging *(G-3739)*

Paul Norman Company Inc.............................704 399-4221
8700 Wilkinson Blvd Charlotte (28214) *(G-2618)*

Paul Robert, Taylorsville Also Called: Paul Robert Chair Inc *(G-11969)*

Paul Robert Chair Inc (PA)............................828 632-7021
266 Martin Luther King Dr Taylorsville (28681) *(G-11969)*

Pauls Cstm Fbrication Mch LLC......................757 746-2743
166 Us Highway 158 W Camden (27921) *(G-1212)*

Pauls Water Treatment LLC...........................336 886-5600
1224 W Ward Ave High Point (27260) *(G-6729)*

Pavco Inc...704 496-6800
9401 Nations Ford Rd Charlotte (28273) *(G-2619)*

Paxton Media Group...................................704 289-1541
1508 Skyway Dr Monroe (28110) *(G-8540)*

Payload Media Inc......................................919 367-2969
129 Parkcrest Dr Cary (27519) *(G-1415)*

Payment Collect LLC...................................828 214-5550
70 Charlotte St Asheville (28801) *(G-568)*

Payzer LLC...866 488-6525
11111 Carmel Commons Blvd Ste 400 Charlotte (28226) *(G-2620)*

Pb & J Industries Inc....................................919 661-2738
8805 Running Oak Dr Raleigh (27617) *(G-10363)*

Pbc of Aberdeen, Aberdeen Also Called: Builders Frstsrce - Sthast Gro *(G-2)*

Pbi Performance Products Inc (PA)..................704 554-3378
9800 Southern Pine Blvd Ste D Charlotte (28273) *(G-2621)*

PBM Graphics Inc.......................................919 544-6222
4102 S Miami Blvd Durham (27703) *(G-4169)*

PBM Graphics Inc (DH)................................919 544-6222
3700 S Miami Blvd Durham (27703) *(G-4170)*

PBM Graphics Inc.......................................336 664-5800
415 Westcliff Rd Greensboro (27409) *(G-5737)*

Pbs Ventures Inc..252 235-2001
5469 Us Highway 264a Bailey (27807) *(G-673)*

PC Satellite Solutions..................................252 217-7237
325 Jones White Rd Roper (27970) *(G-10899)*

PC Signs & Graphics LLC..............................919 661-5801
180 Hein Dr Garner (27529) *(G-4951)*

PCA, Farmville Also Called: Packaging Corporation America *(G-4537)*

PCA, Goldsboro Also Called: Packaging Corporation America *(G-5234)*

PCA, Lenoir Also Called: Polychem Alloy Inc *(G-7635)*

PCA/High Point 334, Trinity Also Called: Packaging Corporation America *(G-12121)*

Pca/Morganton 354, Morganton Also Called: Packaging Corporation America *(G-8887)*

Pca/Regional Design Center, Mooresville Also Called: Packaging Corporation America *(G-8741)*

Pca/Salisbury 375, Salisbury Also Called: Packaging Corporation America *(G-11100)*

Pcai Inc...704 588-1240
11101 Nations Ford Rd Charlotte (28206) *(G-2622)*

PCC Airfoils LLC..919 774-4300
5105 Rex Mcleod Dr Sanford (27330) *(G-11215)*

PCI of North Carolina LLC............................919 467-5151
100 Falcone Pkwy Cary (27511) *(G-1416)*

Pcore..919 734-0460
200 W Dewey St Goldsboro (27530) *(G-5235)*

PCS Collectibles LLC (PA)............................805 306-1140
9825 Northcross Center Ct Huntersville (28078) *(G-7030)*

Pcs Phosphate Company Inc..........................252 322-4111
Aurora (27806) *(G-645)*

Pcsi, Gastonia Also Called: Powder Coating Services Inc *(G-5122)*

Pcx Holding LLC..919 550-2800
370 Spectrum Dr Knightdale (27545) *(G-7455)*

Pdf and Associates.....................................252 332-7749
116 Luther Brown Rd Colerain (27924) *(G-3271)*

PDM Lighting LLC.......................................919 771-3230
3737 Glenwood Ave Ste 100 Raleigh (27612) *(G-10364)*

Pea Creek Mine LLC....................................252 814-1388
4747 Us Highway 264 E Greenville (27834) *(G-6011)*

Peaberry, Asheville Also Called: Peaberry Press LLC *(G-569)*

Peaberry Press LLC.....................................828 773-1489
802 Fairview Rd Ste 800 Asheville (28803) *(G-569)*

Peace of Mind Publications...........................919 308-5137
1321 Shiley Dr Durham (27704) *(G-4171)*

Peaches 'n Cream, Burlington Also Called: Bonaventure Co LLC *(G-1053)*

Peaches Enterprises Inc................................910 868-5800
1014 Cain Rd Fayetteville (28303) *(G-4653)*

Peachland Dsign Fbrication LLC......................704 272-9296
3129 Deep Springs Church Rd Peachland (28133) *(G-9652)*

Peachtree Lumber Company Inc......................828 837-0118
6926 Highway 64 W Brasstown (28902) *(G-966)*

Peacoat Media LLC.....................................336 298-1133
101 N Chestnut St Ste 203 Winston Salem (27101) *(G-13277)*

Peak Clean Energy LLC...............................303 588-2789
11330 Vanstory Dr Huntersville (28078) *(G-7031)*

Peak Demand Inc.......................................252 360-2777
605 Tarboro Street Anx Sw Wilson (27893) *(G-13013)*

Peak Steel LLC..919 362-5955
1610 N Salem St Apex (27523) *(G-185)*

Peak Truss Builders LLC...............................919 552-5933
1220 N Main St Holly Springs (27540) *(G-6910)*

Peanut, Dublin Also Called: Peanut Processors Inc *(G-3832)*

Peanut Processors Inc (PA)...........................910 862-2136
7329 Albert St Dublin (28332) *(G-3832)*

Peanut Processors Sherman Inc......................910 862-2136
7329 Albert St Dublin (28332) *(G-3833)*

Pearl River Group LLC.................................704 283-4667
6027 Stitt St Monroe (28110) *(G-8541)*

Pearson Company, Hickory Also Called: Hdm Furniture Industries Inc *(G-6343)*

Pearson Textiles Inc....................................919 776-8730
7975 Villanow Dr Sanford (27332) *(G-11216)*

Peco, Arden Also Called: Peco Inc *(G-296)*

Peco Inc...828 684-1234
100 Airport Rd Arden (28704) *(G-296)*

Pedmark, Research Triangle Pa Also Called: Fennec Pharmaceuticals Inc *(G-10709)*

Peelle Company...631 231-6000
115 N Secrest Ave Monroe (28110) *(G-8542)*

Peerless Blowers, Hot Springs Also Called: Madison Manufacturing Company *(G-6933)*

Pegasus Builders Supply LLC.........................919 244-1586
2228 Page Rd Ste 108 Durham (27703) *(G-4172)*

Peggs Recreation Inc...................................704 660-0007
408 N Main St Mooresville (28115) *(G-8744)*

Pelican Ventures LLC..................................919 518-8203
5924 Wild Orchid Trl Raleigh (27613) *(G-10365)*

Pelton & Crane Company.............................704 588-2126
11727 Fruehauf Dr Charlotte (28273) *(G-2623)*

Pemmco Manufacturing Inc..........................336 625-1122
631 Veterans Loop Rd Asheboro (27205) *(G-381)*

Pen-Cell Plastics Inc...................................252 467-2210
546 English Rd Rocky Mount (27804) *(G-10858)*

Pencco Inc..252 235-5300
10143 Us 264a Middlesex (27557) *(G-8279)*

Penco Precision LLC....................................910 292-6542
1901 Blue Clay Rd Ste I Wilmington (28405) *(G-12873)*

Penco Products Inc (DH)..............................252 917-5287
1820 Stonehenge Dr Greenville (27858) *(G-6012)*

Penco Products Inc.....................................252 798-4000
1301 Penco Dr Hwy 125 Hamilton (27840) *(G-6049)*

**A
L
P
H
A
B
E
T
I
C**

Pendulum Inc..704 491-6320
  6128 Brookshire Blvd Ste A Charlotte (28216) *(G-2624)*

Penn, Smithfield *Also Called: Penn Compression Moulding Inc (G-11459)*

Penn Compression Moulding Inc (PA)................919 934-5144
  309 Components Dr Smithfield (27577) *(G-11459)*

Penn Engineering & Mfg Corp...........................336 631-8741
  2400 Lowery St Winston Salem (27101) *(G-13278)*

Pennsylvania Trans Tech Inc.............................910 875-7600
  201 Carolina Dr Raeford (28376) *(G-9847)*

Pennsylvania Transformer Co, Raeford *Also Called: Pennsylvania Trans Tech Inc (G-9847)*

Penrock LLC...704 800-6722
  251 Knoxview Ln Mooresville (28117) *(G-8745)*

Penske Racing South Inc (DH)...........................704 664-2300
  200 Penske Way Mooresville (28115) *(G-8746)*

Pentair Pool Products, Sanford *Also Called: Pentair Water Pool and Spa Inc (G-11217)*

Pentair Water Pool and Spa Inc.........................919 463-4640
  400 Regency Forest Dr Ste 300 Cary (27518) *(G-1417)*

Pentair Water Pool and Spa Inc (DH).................919 566-8000
  1620 Hawkins Ave Sanford (27330) *(G-11217)*

People's Pharmacy, The, Durham *Also Called: Graedon Enterprises Inc (G-4055)*

Pep Filters, Mooresville *Also Called: Pep Filters Inc (G-8747)*

Pep Filters Inc..704 662-3133
  120 Talbert Rd Ste J Mooresville (28117) *(G-8747)*

Pepsi Bottling Group Inc...................................704 507-4031
  5047 Highway 24 27 E Midland (28107) *(G-8291)*

Pepsi Bottling Ventures LLC...............................800 879-8884
  500 Gregson Dr Cary (27511) *(G-1418)*

Pepsi Bottling Ventures LLC...............................828 264-7702
  7467 Old 421 S Deep Gap (28618) *(G-3729)*

Pepsi Bottling Ventures LLC...............................252 335-4355
  109 Corporate Dr Elizabeth City (27909) *(G-4401)*

Pepsi Bottling Ventures LLC...............................919 865-2388
  1900 Treygan Rd Garner (27529) *(G-4952)*

Pepsi Bottling Ventures LLC...............................919 863-4000
  1900 Pepsi Way Fl 1 Garner (27529) *(G-4953)*

Pepsi Bottling Ventures LLC...............................919 778-8300
  2707 N Park Dr Goldsboro (27534) *(G-5236)*

Pepsi Bottling Ventures LLC...............................704 455-0800
  22 Pepsi Way Harrisburg (28075) *(G-6115)*

Pepsi Bottling Ventures LLC (DH)........................919 865-2300
  4141 Parklake Ave Raleigh (27612) *(G-10366)*

Pepsi Bottling Ventures LLC...............................252 451-1811
  620 Health Dr Rocky Mount (27804) *(G-10859)*

Pepsi Bottling Ventures LLC...............................910 865-1600
  137 Pepsi Way Saint Pauls (28384) *(G-11006)*

Pepsi Bottling Ventures LLC...............................704 873-0249
  1703 Gregory Rd Statesville (28677) *(G-11744)*

Pepsi Bottling Ventures LLC...............................910 792-5400
  415 Landmark Dr Wilmington (28412) *(G-12874)*

Pepsi Bottling Ventures LLC...............................336 464-9227
  295 Business Park Dr Winston Salem (27107) *(G-13279)*

Pepsi Bottling Ventures LLC...............................336 464-9227
  390 Business Park Dr Winston Salem (27107) *(G-13280)*

Pepsi Bottling Ventures LLC...............................336 724-4800
  3425 Myer Lee Dr Winston Salem (27101) *(G-13281)*

Pepsi Cola Bottling Co.......................................828 650-7800
  200 Fanning Field Fletcher (28732) *(G-4760)*

Pepsi Cola Co..704 357-9166
  3530 Toringdon Way Ste 400 Charlotte (28277) *(G-2625)*

Pepsi-Cola, Cherryville *Also Called: Pepsi-Cola Metro Btlg Co Inc (G-3068)*

Pepsi-Cola, Deep Gap *Also Called: Pepsi Bottling Ventures LLC (G-3729)*

Pepsi-Cola, Garner *Also Called: Pepsi Bottling Ventures LLC (G-4953)*

Pepsi-Cola, Goldsboro *Also Called: Pepsi Bottling Ventures LLC (G-5236)*

Pepsi-Cola, Granite Falls *Also Called: Pepsi-Cola Btlg Hickry NC Inc (G-5316)*

Pepsi-Cola, Harrisburg *Also Called: Pepsi Bottling Ventures LLC (G-6115)*

Pepsi-Cola, Hickory *Also Called: Pepsi-Cola Btlg Hickry NC Inc (G-6409)*

Pepsi-Cola, Hickory *Also Called: Pepsi-Cola Btlg Hickry NC Inc (G-6410)*

Pepsi-Cola, Raleigh *Also Called: Pepsi Bottling Ventures LLC (G-10366)*

Pepsi-Cola, Rocky Mount *Also Called: Pepsi Bottling Ventures LLC (G-10859)*

Pepsi-Cola, Rocky Mount *Also Called: Pepsi-Cola Metro Btlg Co Inc (G-10860)*

Pepsi-Cola, Statesville *Also Called: Pepsi Bottling Ventures LLC (G-11744)*

Pepsi-Cola, Whittier *Also Called: Pepsi-Cola Btlg Hickry NC Inc (G-12625)*

Pepsi-Cola, Wilmington *Also Called: Pepsi Bottling Ventures LLC (G-12874)*

Pepsi-Cola, Winston Salem *Also Called: Pepsi Bottling Ventures LLC (G-13279)*

Pepsi-Cola, Winston Salem *Also Called: Pepsi Bottling Ventures LLC (G-13281)*

Pepsi-Cola, Winston Salem *Also Called: Pepsi-Cola Metro Btlg Co Inc (G-13282)*

Pepsi-Cola Bottler, Winston Salem *Also Called: Pepsi Bottling Ventures LLC (G-13280)*

Pepsi-Cola Btlg Hickry NC Inc...........................828 322-8090
  47 Duke St Granite Falls (28630) *(G-5316)*

Pepsi-Cola Btlg Hickry NC Inc...........................828 322-8090
  2640 Main Ave Nw Hickory (28601) *(G-6409)*

Pepsi-Cola Btlg Hickry NC Inc (PA).....................828 322-8090
  2401 14th Avenue Cir Nw Hickory (28601) *(G-6410)*

Pepsi-Cola Btlg Hickry NC Inc...........................828 497-1235
  1060 Gateway Rd Whittier (28789) *(G-12625)*

Pepsi-Cola Metro Btlg Co Inc.............................980 581-1099
  2820 South Blvd Charlotte (28209) *(G-2626)*

Pepsi-Cola Metro Btlg Co Inc.............................704 736-2640
  152 Commerce Dr Cherryville (28021) *(G-3068)*

Pepsi-Cola Metro Btlg Co Inc.............................252 446-7181
  620 Health Dr Rocky Mount (27804) *(G-10860)*

Pepsi-Cola Metro Btlg Co Inc.............................336 896-4000
  1100 Reynolds Blvd Winston Salem (27105) *(G-13282)*

Pepsico, Charlotte *Also Called: Pepsi Cola Co (G-2625)*

Pepsico, Charlotte *Also Called: Pepsi-Cola Metro Btlg Co Inc (G-2626)*

Pepsico, Marion *Also Called: Pepsico Inc (G-8060)*

Pepsico, Midland *Also Called: Pepsi Bottling Group Inc (G-8291)*

Pepsico, Roanoke Rapids *Also Called: McPherson Beverages Inc (G-10741)*

Pepsico, Saint Pauls *Also Called: Pepsi Bottling Ventures LLC (G-11006)*

Pepsico, Winston Salem *Also Called: Pepsico Inc (G-13283)*

Pepsico Inc..828 756-4662
  8337 Us 221 N Marion (28752) *(G-8060)*

Pepsico Inc...914 253-2000
  Winston Salem (27105) *(G-13283)*

Perdue Agribusiness, Cofield *Also Called: Perdue Farms Inc (G-3269)*

Perdue Ecop Crushing, Pantego *Also Called: East Crlina Olseed Prcssors LL (G-9643)*

Perdue Farms, Candor *Also Called: Perdue Farms Inc (G-1240)*

Perdue Farms, Elkin *Also Called: Perdue Farms Inc (G-4450)*

Perdue Farms, Halifax *Also Called: Perdue Farms Inc (G-6047)*

Perdue Farms, Kenly *Also Called: Perdue Farms Inc (G-7234)*

Perdue Farms, Murfreesboro *Also Called: Perdue Farms Inc (G-9284)*

Perdue Farms, Nashville *Also Called: Perdue Farms Inc (G-9323)*

Perdue Farms, Winston Salem *Also Called: Perdue Farms Inc (G-13284)*

Perdue Farms, Yadkinville *Also Called: Perdue Farms Inc (G-13447)*

Perdue Farms Inc...252 348-4287
  2108 Us Highway 13 S Ahoskie (27910) *(G-51)*

Perdue Farms Inc...910 673-4148
  Hwy 211 S Candor (27229) *(G-1240)*

Perdue Farms Inc...704 278-2228
  9150 Statesville Blvd Cleveland (27013) *(G-3218)*

Perdue Farms Inc...252 358-8245
  242 Perdue Rd Cofield (27922) *(G-3269)*

Perdue Farms Inc...704 789-2400
  862 Harris St Nw Concord (28025) *(G-3417)*

Perdue Farms Inc...252 338-1543
  1268 Us Highway 17 S Elizabeth City (27909) *(G-4402)*

Perdue Farms Inc...336 366-2591
  105 Greenwood Cir Elkin (28621) *(G-4450)*

Perdue Farms Inc...252 758-2141
  1623 N Greene St Greenville (27834) *(G-6013)*

Perdue Farms Inc...252 583-5731
  1201 State Rd Halifax (27839) *(G-6047)*

Perdue Farms Inc...919 284-2033
  9266 Revell Rd Kenly (27542) *(G-7234)*

Perdue Farms Inc...252 348-4200
  3539 Governors Rd Lewiston Woodville (27849) *(G-7647)*

Perdue Farms Inc...910 738-8581
  1801 Godwin Ave Lumberton (28358) *(G-7965)*

Perdue Farms Inc..252 398-5112
Hwy 158 W Murfreesboro (27855) *(G-9284)*

Perdue Farms Inc..252 459-9763
1835 Us Highway 64a Nashville (27856) *(G-9323)*

Perdue Farms Inc..336 896-9121
7996 N Point Blvd Winston Salem (27106) *(G-13284)*

Perdue Farms Inc..336 679-7733
806 W Main St Yadkinville (27055) *(G-13447)*

PERDUE FARMS INC., Ahoskie *Also Called: Perdue Farms Inc (G-51)*

PERDUE FARMS INC., Elizabeth City *Also Called: Perdue Farms Inc (G-4402)*

PERDUE FARMS INC., Lewiston Woodville *Also Called: Perdue Farms Inc (G-7647)*

PERDUE FARMS INC., Lumberton *Also Called: Perdue Farms Inc (G-7965)*

Perdue Farms Incorporated...910 997-8600
416 S Long Dr Rockingham (28379) *(G-10785)*

Perdue Farms Warehouse, Greenville *Also Called: Perdue Farms Inc (G-6013)*

Perdue Grain Market, Cleveland *Also Called: Perdue Farms Inc (G-3218)*

Perfect 10 Brands LLC..702 738-0183
129 Glenmore Rd Cary (27519) *(G-1419)*

Perfect Fit Industries LLC...800 864-7618
8501 Tower Point Dr Ste C Charlotte (28227) *(G-2627)*

Perfection Fabrics Inc...828 328-3322
841a F Avenue Dr Se Hickory (28602) *(G-6411)*

Perfection Gear Inc (DH)...828 253-0000
9 N Bear Creek Rd Asheville (28806) *(G-570)*

Perfection Products Co, Greensboro *Also Called: P R Sparks Enterprises Inc (G-5728)*

Performance Additives LLC...215 321-4388
222 Central Park Ave Pinehurst (28374) *(G-9699)*

Performance Apparel LLC...805 541-0989
565 Air Tool Dr Ste K Southern Pines (28387) *(G-11503)*

Performance Center, Mooresville *Also Called: Performance Racing Whse Inc (G-8749)*

Performance Entps & Parts Inc...................................336 621-6572
4104 Burlington Rd Greensboro (27405) *(G-5738)*

Performance Fibers..704 947-7193
12721 Longstock Ct Huntersville (28078) *(G-7032)*

Performance Goods LLC..704 361-8600
5825 Mctaggart Ln Charlotte (28269) *(G-2628)*

Performance Machine & Fab Inc.................................336 983-0414
1050 Denny Rd King (27021) *(G-7335)*

Performance Parts Intl LLC..704 660-1084
104 Blue Ridge Trl Mooresville (28117) *(G-8748)*

Performance Plastics Pdts Inc....................................336 454-0350
126 Wade St Ste D Jamestown (27282) *(G-7175)*

Performance Print Services LLC..................................919 957-9995
1 Tw Alexander Dr Ste 130 Durham (27709) *(G-4173)*

Performance Racing Whse Inc....................................704 838-1400
145 Blossom Ridge Dr Mooresville (28117) *(G-8749)*

Perfusio Corp...252 656-0404
102a Hungate Dr Greenville (27858) *(G-6014)*

Perigen, Cary *Also Called: E&C Medical Intelligence Inc (G-1350)*

Perkem Technology, Stanley *Also Called: DSM Desotech Inc (G-11614)*

Perkins Fabrications Inc..828 688-3157
5632 Nc 261 Bakersville (28705) *(G-680)*

Perlman Inc...704 332-1164
5312 Wingedfoot Rd Charlotte (28226) *(G-2629)*

Perma Flex Rller Tchnlgy-Rgnge, Salisbury *Also Called: Perma-Flex Rollers Inc (G-11102)*

Perma Flex Roller Technology (PA)............................704 633-1201
1415 Jake Alexander Blvd S Salisbury (28146) *(G-11101)*

Perma-Flex Rollers Inc..704 633-1201
1415 Jake Alexander Blvd S Salisbury (28146) *(G-11102)*

Permatech, LLC, Graham *Also Called: Vesuvius Nc LLC (G-5288)*

Perry Brothers Tire Svc Inc..919 693-2128
606 Lewis St Oxford (27565) *(G-9623)*

Perry Brothers Tire Svc Inc (PA)................................919 775-7225
610 Wicker St Sanford (27330) *(G-11218)*

Perry Glass Co, Henderson *Also Called: A R Perry Corporation (G-6146)*

Perrycraft Inc...336 372-2545
1549 Us Highway 21 S Sparta (28675) *(G-11541)*

Perrys Frame Inc..828 327-4681
3785 Thompson St Newton (28658) *(G-9487)*

Perseus Intermediate Inc..919 474-6700
4721 Emperor Blvd Ste 100 Durham (27703) *(G-4174)*

Person Printing Company Inc.....................................336 599-2146
115 Clayton Ave Roxboro (27573) *(G-10940)*

Personal Communication Systems Inc.........................336 722-4917
301 N Main St Winston Salem (27101) *(G-13285)*

Petco, Kenly *Also Called: Petroleum Tank Corporation (G-7235)*

Peter J Hamann...910 484-7877
337 Mcmillan St Fayetteville (28301) *(G-4654)*

Petnet Solutions Inc...919 572-5544
2310 Presidential Dr Ste 108 Durham (27703) *(G-4175)*

Petnet Solutions Inc...865 218-2000
3908 Westpoint Blvd Ste E Winston Salem (27103) *(G-13286)*

Petra Precision Machining...919 751-3461
3413 Central Heights Rd Goldsboro (27534) *(G-5237)*

Petroleum Tank Corporation......................................919 284-2418
600 N Gardner Ave Kenly (27542) *(G-7235)*

Petroliance LLC...336 472-3000
814 Lexington Ave Thomasville (27360) *(G-12059)*

Petteway Body Shop Inc..910 455-3272
1362 Old Maplehurst Rd Jacksonville (28540) *(G-7137)*

Petteway Rentals, Jacksonville *Also Called: Petteway Body Shop Inc (G-7137)*

Petty Machine Company Inc.......................................704 864-3254
2403 Forbes Rd Gastonia (28056) *(G-5119)*

Pevo Sports Co..910 397-9388
212 Transcom Ct Wilmington (28401) *(G-12875)*

Pexco LLC...336 493-7500
2971 Taylor Dr Asheboro (27203) *(G-382)*

Pf2 Eis LLC...704 549-6931
10735 David Taylor Dr Ste 100 Charlotte (28262) *(G-2630)*

Pfaff Molds Ltd Partnership..704 423-9484
11825 Westhall Dr Charlotte (28278) *(G-2631)*

PFC Group LLC...704 393-4040
5900 Old Mount Holly Rd Charlotte (28208) *(G-2632)*

Pfi, Graham *Also Called: Pure Flow Inc (G-5283)*

Pfizer, Durham *Also Called: Pfizer Inc (G-4176)*

Pfizer Inc...252 382-3309
6563 N Us Highway 301 Battleboro (27809) *(G-705)*

Pfizer Inc...919 941-5185
1040 Swabia Ct Durham (27703) *(G-4176)*

Pfizer Inc...252 977-5111
4285 N Wesleyan Blvd Rocky Mount (27804) *(G-10861)*

Pfizer Inc...919 775-7100
4300 Oak Park Rd Sanford (27330) *(G-11219)*

Pfizer Poultry Health Embrex, Durham *Also Called: Embrex LLC (G-4019)*

Pgi Nonwovens, Charlotte *Also Called: Chicopee Inc (G-1914)*

Pgi Polymer Inc..704 697-5100
9335 Harris Corners Pkwy Ste 300 Charlotte (28269) *(G-2633)*

Pgw, Elkin *Also Called: Pgw Auto Glass LLC (G-4451)*

Pgw Auto Glass LLC..336 258-4950
300 Pgw Dr Elkin (28621) *(G-4451)*

Pharmaceutic Litho Label Inc.....................................336 785-4000
3360 Old Lexington Rd Winston Salem (27107) *(G-13287)*

Pharmaceutical Dimensions..336 297-4851
7353 W Friendly Ave # A Greensboro (27410) *(G-5739)*

Pharmaceutical Equipment Svcs.................................239 699-9120
15 Magnolia Hill Ct Asheville (28806) *(G-571)*

Pharmagra Holding Company LLC.............................828 884-8656
158 Mclean Rd Brevard (28712) *(G-979)*

Pharmasone LLC...910 679-8364
1800 Sir Tyler Dr Wilmington (28405) *(G-12876)*

Pharmgate Animal Health LLC....................................910 679-8364
1800 Sir Tyler Dr Wilmington (28405) *(G-12877)*

Pharmgate Inc (HQ)..910 679-8364
1800 Sir Tyler Dr Wilmington (28405) *(G-12878)*

Pharr Fibers and Yarns, Mc Adenville *Also Called: Mannington Mills Inc (G-8214)*

Pharr McAdenville Corporation (PA)............................704 824-3551
100 Main St Mc Adenville (28101) *(G-8215)*

Pharr Ph/Crescent Plant, Mc Adenville *Also Called: Coats HP Inc (G-8213)*

Phase II Creations Inc..336 249-0673
109 E 7th Ave Lexington (27292) *(G-7730)*

Phelps Wood Products LLC.......................................336 284-2149
12010 Statesville Blvd Cleveland (27013) *(G-3219)*

ALPHABETIC

Phil Barker's Refinishing, Greensboro *Also Called: Barker and Martin Inc (G-5385)*

Phil Parkey & Associates, Candler *Also Called: Southern Organ Services Ltd (G-1233)*

Phil S Tire Service Inc.. 828 682-2421
617 W Main St Burnsville (28714) *(G-1189)*

Philip Brady.. 336 581-3999
185 Charlie Garner Rd Bennett (27208) *(G-782)*

Philip Morris, Winston Salem *Also Called: Philip Morris USA Inc (G-13288)*

Philip Morris USA Inc... 336 744-4401
4338 Grove Ave Winston Salem (27105) *(G-13288)*

Philip Products, Asheville *Also Called: Tompkins Industries Inc (G-620)*

Philips Semiconductors, Cary *Also Called: Nxp Usa Inc (G-1410)*

Phillip Dunn Logging Co Inc..................................... 252 633-4577
508 Madam Moores Ln New Bern (28562) *(G-9388)*

Phillips Corporation... 336 665-1080
8500 Triad Dr Colfax (27235) *(G-3286)*

Phillips Iron Works, Raleigh *Also Called: Canalta Enterprises LLC (G-9965)*

Phillips Plating Co Inc.. 252 637-2695
1617 Hwy 17 N Ste 1617 Bridgeton (28519) *(G-985)*

Philosophy Inc (HQ).. 602 794-8701
1400 Broadway Rd Sanford (27332) *(G-11220)*

Philpott Motors Ltd.. 704 566-2400
5401 E Independence Blvd Charlotte (28212) *(G-2634)*

Phitonex Inc... 855 874-4866
701 W Main St Ste 200 Durham (27701) *(G-4177)*

Phoenix Aluminum, Winston Salem *Also Called: Alpha Aluminum LLC (G-13082)*

Phoenix Assembly NC LLC.. 252 801-4250
7101 N Us Highway 301 Battleboro (27809) *(G-706)*

Phoenix Home Furnishings Inc
2485 Penny Rd High Point (27265) *(G-6730)*

Phoenix Packaging Inc... 336 724-1978
111 E 10th St Winston Salem (27101) *(G-13289)*

Phoenix Sign Pros Inc.. 252 756-5685
4409 Corey Rd Winterville (28590) *(G-13421)*

Phoenix St Claire Pubg LLC..................................... 919 303-3223
321 Glen Echo Ln Apt C Cary (27518) *(G-1420)*

Phoenix Tapes Usa LLC... 704 588-3090
10900 S Commerce Blvd Charlotte (28273) *(G-2635)*

Phoenix Technology Ltd... 910 259-6804
2 Progress Dr Burgaw (28425) *(G-1029)*

Phoenix Trimming, Tarboro *Also Called: Murdock Webbing Company Inc (G-11937)*

Phononic Inc (PA).. 919 908-6300
801 Capitola Dr Durham (27713) *(G-4178)*

Photo Emblem Incorporated.................................... 336 784-4000
5010 S Main St Winston Salem (27107) *(G-13290)*

Photolynx LLC.. 760 787-1177
2020 Progress Ct Raleigh (27608) *(G-10367)*

Photon Energy Corp... 888 336-8128
1095 Hendersonville Rd Asheville (28803) *(G-572)*

Photonicare Inc.. 866 411-3277
2800 Meridian Pkwy Ste 175 Durham (27713) *(G-4179)*

Phynix Pc Inc... 503 890-1444
51 Abba Cir Middlesex (27557) *(G-8280)*

Picassomoesllc.. 216 703-4547
513 Patriots Pointe Dr Hillsborough (27278) *(G-6875)*

Piccione Vinyards.. 312 342-0181
2364 Cedar Forest Rd Ronda (28670) *(G-10896)*

Pickett Hosiery Mills Inc.. 336 227-2716
707 S Main St Burlington (27215) *(G-1139)*

Pickles Manufacturing LLC....................................... 910 267-4711
354 N Faison Ave Faison (28341) *(G-4518)*

Pictureframes.com, High Point *Also Called: Graphik Dimensions Limited (G-6634)*

Pie Pushers... 919 901-0743
625 Hugo St Durham (27704) *(G-4180)*

Piece of Pie LLC.. 919 286-7421
904 9th St Durham (27705) *(G-4181)*

Piedmont Animal Health Inc..................................... 336 544-0320
204 Muirs Chapel Rd Ste 200 Greensboro (27410) *(G-5740)*

Piedmont AVI Cmponent Svcs LLC........................... 336 423-5100
7102 Cessna Dr Greensboro (27409) *(G-5741)*

Piedmont Block, Lexington *Also Called: Johnson Concrete Company (G-7702)*

Piedmont Business Forms Inc................................... 828 464-0010
703 W C St Newton (28658) *(G-9488)*

Piedmont Candy Company.. 336 248-2477
305 E Us Highway 64 Lexington (27292) *(G-7731)*

Piedmont Candy Company (PA)................................ 336 248-2477
404 Market St Lexington (27292) *(G-7732)*

Piedmont Cheerwine Bottling, Colfax *Also Called: Piedmont Cheerwine Bottling Co (G-3287)*

Piedmont Cheerwine Bottling Co.............................. 336 993-7733
2913 Sandy Ridge Rd Colfax (27235) *(G-3287)*

Piedmont Chemical Inds I LLC.................................. 336 885-5131
331 Burton Ave High Point (27261) *(G-6731)*

Piedmont Cmposites Tooling LLC............................. 828 632-8883
33 Lewittes Rd Taylorsville (28681) *(G-11970)*

Piedmont Components, Mount Gilead *Also Called: Capitol Funds Inc (G-9198)*

Piedmont Components Division, Shelby *Also Called: Capitol Funds Inc (G-11315)*

Piedmont Components Division, Shelby *Also Called: Capitol Funds Inc (G-11316)*

Piedmont Corrugated, Valdese *Also Called: Piedmont Corrugated Specialty (G-12198)*

Piedmont Corrugated Specialty................................ 828 874-1153
340 Morgan St Se Valdese (28690) *(G-12198)*

Piedmont Custom Meats Inc..................................... 336 628-4949
430 Nc Highway 49 S Asheboro (27205) *(G-383)*

Piedmont Distillers Inc... 336 445-0055
3960 Us Highway 220 Madison (27025) *(G-7995)*

Piedmont Fiberglass Inc... 828 632-8883
1166 Bunch Dr Statesville (28677) *(G-11745)*

Piedmont First Aid, Statesville *Also Called: Tmgcr Inc (G-11791)*

Piedmont Flight Inc.. 336 776-6070
3789 N Liberty St Winston Salem (27105) *(G-13291)*

Piedmont Flight Training, Winston Salem *Also Called: Piedmont Flight Inc (G-13291)*

Piedmont Graphics Inc... 336 230-0040
6903 International Dr Greensboro (27409) *(G-5742)*

Piedmont Hardware Brands, Huntersville *Also Called: Amerock LLC (G-6965)*

Piedmont Hardwood Lbr Co Inc................................ 704 436-9311
9000 Nc Highway 49 N Mount Pleasant (28124) *(G-9264)*

Piedmont Indus Coatings Inc.................................... 336 377-3399
160 University Center Dr Winston Salem (27105) *(G-13292)*

Piedmont Joinery Inc... 919 632-3703
2322 Glendale Ave Durham (27704) *(G-4182)*

Piedmont Lithium Carolinas Inc (HQ)....................... 434 664-7643
42 E Catawba St Belmont (28012) *(G-761)*

Piedmont Lithium Inc (PA)....................................... 704 461-8000
42 E Catawba St Belmont (28012) *(G-762)*

Piedmont Lminating Coating Inc............................... 336 272-1600
1812 Sullivan St Greensboro (27405) *(G-5743)*

Piedmont Logging LLC... 919 562-1861
870 Park Ave Youngsville (27596) *(G-13480)*

Piedmont Machine & Mfg, Concord *Also Called: Elomi Inc (G-3359)*

Piedmont Marble Inc.. 336 274-1800
5014 Robdot Dr Oak Ridge (27310) *(G-9574)*

Piedmont Mediaworks Inc.. 828 575-2250
5a Hedgerose Ct Asheville (28805) *(G-573)*

Piedmont Metals Burlington Inc................................ 336 584-7742
215 Macarthur Ln Burlington (27217) *(G-1140)*

Piedmont Metalworks LLC.. 919 598-6500
5902 Us 70 W Mebane (27302) *(G-8256)*

Piedmont Office Products, Newton *Also Called: Piedmont Business Forms Inc (G-9488)*

Piedmont Packaging Inc (PA)................................... 336 886-5043
1141 Foust Ave High Point (27260) *(G-6732)*

Piedmont Pallet & Cont Inc...................................... 336 284-6302
667 Hendrix Farm Circle Ln Woodleaf (27054) *(G-13430)*

Piedmont Paper Stock Inc.. 336 285-8592
3909 Riverdale Dr Greensboro (27406) *(G-5744)*

Piedmont Parachute Inc... 336 597-2225
2712 Durham Rd Roxboro (27573) *(G-10941)*

Piedmont Pipe Mfg LLC.. 704 489-0911
7871 Commerce Dr Denver (28037) *(G-3797)*

Piedmont Plastics Inc (PA)....................................... 704 597-8200
5010 W W T Harris Blvd Charlotte (28269) *(G-2636)*

Piedmont Plating Corporation................................... 336 272-2311
3005 Holts Chapel Rd Greensboro (27401) *(G-5745)*

2025 Harris North Carolina
Manufacturers Directory

(G-0000) Company's Geographic Section entry number

Piedmont Poultry, Lumber Bridge *Also Called: Mountaire Farms LLC (G-7939)*

Piedmont Precision Products 828 304-0791
347 Highland Ave Se Hickory (28602) *(G-6412)*

Piedmont Printing, Asheboro *Also Called: Trejo Soccer Academy LLC (G-410)*

Piedmont Publishing 336 727-4099
418 N Marshall St Winston Salem (27101) *(G-13293)*

Piedmont Sales, Sanford *Also Called: Piedmont Sales & Rentals LLC (G-11221)*

Piedmont Sales & Rentals LLC 919 499-9888
5074 Nc 87 N Sanford (27332) *(G-11221)*

Piedmont Sand, Swannanoa *Also Called: Cumberland Grav & Sand Min Co (G-11870)*

Piedmont Springs Company Inc 828 322-5347
118 11th Street Pl Sw Hickory (28602) *(G-6413)*

Piedmont Stairworks LLC (PA) 704 697-0259
2246 Old Steele Creek Rd Charlotte (28208) *(G-2637)*

Piedmont Stairworks LLC 704 483-3721
8135 Mallard Rd Denver (28037) *(G-3798)*

Piedmont Steel Company LLC 336 875-5133
3480 Friendship Ledford Rd Winston Salem (27107) *(G-13294)*

Piedmont Surfaces of Triad LLC 336 627-7790
615 Monroe St Eden (27288) *(G-4354)*

Piedmont Technical Services 770 530-8313
9127 Arbor Glen Ln Charlotte (28210) *(G-2638)*

Piedmont Truck Tires Inc 828 277-1549
125 Sweeten Creek Rd Asheville (28803) *(G-574)*

Piedmont Truck Tires Inc 828 202-5337
1317 Emmanuel Church Rd Conover (28613) *(G-3544)*

Piedmont Truck Tires Inc 336 223-9412
704 Myrtle Dr Graham (27253) *(G-5281)*

Piedmont Truck Tires Inc (HQ) 336 668-0091
312 S Regional Rd Greensboro (27409) *(G-5746)*

Piedmont Turning & Wdwkg Co 336 475-7161
328 Jarrett Rd Thomasville (27360) *(G-12060)*

Piedmont Weld & Pipe Inc 704 782-7774
172 Buffalo Ave Nw Concord (28025) *(G-3418)*

Piedmont Well Covers Inc 704 664-8488
1135 Mazeppa Rd Mount Ulla (28125) *(G-9270)*

Piedmont Wood Products Inc 828 632-4077
1924 Black Oak Ridge Rd Taylorsville (28681) *(G-11971)*

Pierce Farrier Supply Inc 704 753-4358
9705 Pierce Rd Indian Trail (28079) *(G-7095)*

Pierre Foods, Claremont *Also Called: Advancepierre Foods Inc (G-3087)*

Pig Pounder LLC 336 255-1306
1107 Grecade St Greensboro (27408) *(G-5747)*

Pig Pounder Brewery, Greensboro *Also Called: Pig Pounder LLC (G-5747)*

Pike Electric, Greensboro *Also Called: Pike Electric LLC (G-5748)*

Pike Electric LLC 336 316-7068
3511 W Market St Greensboro (27403) *(G-5748)*

Pilgrim Tract Society Inc 336 495-1241
105 Depot St Randleman (27317) *(G-10655)*

Pilgrims Pride Chkn Oprtons Di, Concord *Also Called: Pilgrims Pride Corporation (G-3419)*

Pilgrims Pride Corporation 704 721-3585
2925 Armentrout Dr Concord (28025) *(G-3419)*

Pilgrims Pride Corporation 704 624-2171
5901 Hwy 74 E Marshville (28103) *(G-8092)*

Pilgrims Pride Corporation 919 774-7333
484 Zimmerman Rd Sanford (27330) *(G-11222)*

Pilgrims Pride Corporation 336 622-4251
2607 Old 421 Rd Staley (27355) *(G-11598)*

Pilgrims Pride Corporation 704 233-4047
205 Edgewood Dr Wingate (28174) *(G-13063)*

Pilkington North America Inc 910 276-5630
13121 S Rocky Ford Rd Laurinburg (28352) *(G-7511)*

Pilot LLC 864 430-6337
375 E Connecticut Ave Southern Pines (28387) *(G-11504)*

Pilot LLC (PA) 910 692-7271
145 W Pennsylvania Ave Southern Pines (28387) *(G-11505)*

Pilot Press LLC 910 692-8366
175 Davis St Southern Pines (28387) *(G-11506)*

Pilot View Wood Works, High Point *Also Called: Pilot View Wood Works Inc (G-6733)*

Pilot View Wood Works Inc 336 883-2511
412 Berkley St High Point (27260) *(G-6733)*

Pinco Usa Inc 704 895-5766
10620 Bailey Rd Ste A Cornelius (28031) *(G-3618)*

Pine Creek Products LLC 336 399-8806
2856 Country Club Rd Winston Salem (27104) *(G-13295)*

Pine Glo Products Inc 919 556-7787
115 Legacy Crest Ct Zebulon (27597) *(G-13521)*

Pine Hall Brick Co Inc 336 721-7500
634 Lindsey Bridge Rd Madison (27025) *(G-7996)*

Pine Hall Brick Co Inc (PA) 336 721-7500
2701 Shorefair Dr Winston Salem (27105) *(G-13296)*

Pine Island Sportswear, Monroe *Also Called: JD Apparel Inc (G-8510)*

Pine Log 118 Trdtnal Living Rd, State Road *Also Called: Pine Log Co Inc (G-11638)*

Pine Log Co Inc 336 366-2770
118 Traditional Living Rd State Road (28676) *(G-11638)*

Pine RES Instrumentation Inc 919 782-8320
2741 Campus Walk Ave Bldg 100 Durham (27705) *(G-4183)*

Pine State Corporate AP LLC 336 789-9437
219 Frederick St Mount Airy (27030) *(G-9164)*

Pine State Corporative Apparel, Mount Airy *Also Called: Pine State Corporate AP LLC (G-9164)*

Pine View Buildings LLC 704 876-1501
933 Tomlin Mill Rd Statesville (28625) *(G-11746)*

Pink Hill Wellness Edu Center 252 568-2425
301 S Pine St Pink Hill (28572) *(G-9766)*

Pink Zebra Moving Charlotte NC, Charlotte *Also Called: Movers and Shakers LLC (G-2524)*

Pinkston Properties LLC 828 252-9867
91 Westside Dr Asheville (28806) *(G-575)*

Pinnacle Converting Eqp & Svcs 704 376-3855
11325 Nations Ford Rd Ste A Pineville (28134) *(G-9747)*

Pinnacle Converting Eqp Inc (PA) 704 376-3855
11325 Nations Ford Rd Ste A Pineville (28134) *(G-9748)*

Pinnacle Furnishings 910 944-0908
10570 Nc Highway 211 E Ste G Aberdeen (28315) *(G-19)*

Pioneer, Sparta *Also Called: Amano Pioneer Eclipse Corp (G-11534)*

Pioneer Diversities, Newton *Also Called: Eric Arnold Klein (G-9464)*

Pioneer Machine Works Inc 704 864-5528
1221 W 2nd Ave Gastonia (28052) *(G-5120)*

Pioneer Printing Company Inc 336 789-4011
203 N South St Mount Airy (27030) *(G-9165)*

Pioneer Square Brands Inc (PA) 360 733-5608
1515 W Green Dr High Point (27260) *(G-6734)*

Pioneer Srgcal Orthblogics Inc (DH) 252 355-4405
1800 N Greene St Ste A Greenville (27834) *(G-6015)*

Pioneer Srgical Orthobiologics, Greenville *Also Called: Angstrom Medica Inc (G-5936)*

PIP Printing, Burlington *Also Called: JB II Printing LLC (G-1111)*

PIP Printing, Burlington *Also Called: PIP Printing & Document Servic (G-1141)*

PIP Printing, Burlington *Also Called: Postal Instant Press (G-1142)*

PIP Printing, Cary *Also Called: Triangle Solutions Inc (G-1473)*

PIP Printing, Greenville *Also Called: Renascence Inc (G-6018)*

PIP Printing, Rocky Mount *Also Called: C D J & P Inc (G-10826)*

PIP Printing, Sanford *Also Called: Sillaman & Sons Inc (G-11233)*

PIP Printing, Winston Salem *Also Called: Rite Instant Printing Inc (G-13319)*

PIP Printing & Document Servic 336 222-0717
717 Chapel Hill Rd Burlington (27215) *(G-1141)*

Pipe Bridge Products Inc 919 786-4499
5208 Rembert Dr Raleigh (27612) *(G-10368)*

Pipeline Enterprises LLC 804 593-6999
1543 Barnes St Reidsville (27320) *(G-10697)*

Pipeline Plastics LLC 817 693-4100
15159 Andrew Jackson Hwy Sw Fair Bluff (28439) *(G-4499)*

Piranha, Greensboro *Also Called: Piranha Nail and Staple Inc (G-5749)*

Piranha Industries Inc 704 248-7843
2515 Allen Rd S Charlotte (28269) *(G-2639)*

Piranha Nail and Staple Inc 336 852-8358
901 Norwalk St Ste E Greensboro (27407) *(G-5749)*

Pisgah Laboratories Inc 828 884-2789
3222 Old Hendersonville Hwy Pisgah Forest (28768) *(G-9772)*

Pitman Knits Inc 704 276-3262
7625 Palm Tree Church Rd Vale (28168) *(G-12210)*

Pitney Bowes, Greensboro *Also Called: Pitney Bowes Inc (G-5750)*

Pitney Bowes, Raleigh *Also Called: Pitney Bowes Inc (G-10369)*

Pitney Bowes Inc.. 336 805-3320
4161 Piedmont Pkwy Greensboro (27410) *(G-5750)*

Pitney Bowes Inc.. 919 785-3480
3150 Spring Forest Rd Ste 122 Raleigh (27616) *(G-10369)*

Pitt Road Ex Lube & Car Wash, Elizabeth City *Also Called: Pitt Road LLC (G-4403)*

Pitt Road LLC.. 252 331-5818
711 N Hughes Blvd Elizabeth City (27909) *(G-4403)*

Plan B Enterprises LLC... 919 387-4856
3217 Hinsley Rd New Hill (27562) *(G-9412)*

Plan Nine Publishing Inc... 336 454-7766
1237 Elon Pl High Point (27263) *(G-6735)*

Plane Defense Ltd.. 828 254-6061
175 N Mason Way Hendersonville (28792) *(G-6236)*

Planet Logo Inc... 910 763-2554
23 N Front St # 3 Wilmington (28401) *(G-12879)*

Planet Smoothie, Mooresville *Also Called: Yummy Tummy Ga LLC (G-8804)*

Plant 12, Sanford *Also Called: GKN Driveline North Amer Inc (G-11184)*

Plant 15, Belmont *Also Called: Parkdale Mills Incorporated (G-758)*

Plant 17, Belmont *Also Called: Parkdale Mills Incorporated (G-759)*

Plant 21, Mineral Springs *Also Called: Parkdale Mills Incorporated (G-8328)*

Plant 6, Lenoir *Also Called: Bernhardt Furniture Company (G-7581)*

Plant 6 & 7, Thomasville *Also Called: Parkdale Mills Incorporated (G-12058)*

Plantation House Foods Inc...................................... 919 381-5495
3316 Stoneybrook Dr Durham (27705) *(G-4184)*

Plantd Inc... 434 906-3445
3220 Knotts Grove Rd Oxford (27565) *(G-9624)*

Plasgad Usa LLC... 980 223-2197
933 Meacham Rd Statesville (28677) *(G-11747)*

Plaskolite LLC... 704 588-3800
1100 Bond St Charlotte (28208) *(G-2640)*

Plaskolite North Carolina LLC (HQ)........................... 704 588-3800
1100 Bond St Charlotte (28208) *(G-2641)*

Plasma Games... 252 721-3294
208 Bracken Ct Raleigh (27615) *(G-10370)*

Plasma Games Inc.. 919 627-1252
112 Wind Chime Ct Raleigh (27615) *(G-10371)*

Plastek Group.. 910 895-2089
206 Enterprise Dr Rockingham (28379) *(G-10786)*

Plastex Fabricators, Charlotte *Also Called: PFC Group LLC (G-2632)*

Plasti-Form, Asheville *Also Called: Braiform Enterprises Inc (G-461)*

Plastic Art Design Inc... 919 878-1672
5811 Mchines Pl Raleigh (27616) *(G-10372)*

Plastic Ingenuity Inc.. 919 693-2009
113 Certainteed Dr Oxford (27565) *(G-9625)*

Plastic Oddities, Forest City *Also Called: Diverse Corporate Tech Inc (G-4787)*

Plastic Oddities Inc.. 704 484-1830
1701 Burke Rd Shelby (28152) *(G-11369)*

Plastic Products Inc (PA)... 704 739-7463
1413 Bessemer City Kings Mtn Hwy Bessemer City (28016) *(G-830)*

Plastic Products Inc... 704 739-7463
1051 York Rd Kings Mountain (28086) *(G-7378)*

Plastic Solutions Inc.. 678 353-2100
324 Tiney Rd Ellenboro (28040) *(G-4459)*

Plastic Technology Inc.. 828 328-8570
1101 Farrington St Sw # 3 Conover (28613) *(G-3545)*

Plastic Technology Inc (HQ)..................................... 828 328-2201
235 2nd Ave Nw Hickory (28601) *(G-6414)*

Plasticard Products Inc... 828 665-7774
99 Pond Rd Asheville (28806) *(G-576)*

Plastics Color, Asheboro *Also Called: Chroma Color Corporation (G-339)*

Plastics Family Holdings Inc.................................... 704 597-8555
3000 Crosspoint Center Ln Ste A Charlotte (28269) *(G-2642)*

Plastics Mlding Dsgn Plus LLC................................. 828 459-7853
1803 Conover Blvd E Conover (28613) *(G-3546)*

Plastiexports TN LLC.. 423 735-2207
9405 D Ducks Ln Ste A Charlotte (28273) *(G-2643)*

Plastiflex North Carolina LLC................................... 704 871-8448
2101 Sherrill Dr Statesville (28625) *(G-11748)*

Plat LLC.. 828 358-4564
5740 Rocky Mount Rd Granite Falls (28630) *(G-5317)*

Plataine Inc.. 336 883-7657
319 Ardmore Cir High Point (27262) *(G-6736)*

Platesetterscom.. 888 380-7483
114 Industrial Ave Greensboro (27406) *(G-5751)*

Playerz Haul, Charlotte *Also Called: Brown Mitchell Hodges LLC (G-1813)*

Playpower Inc (DH).. 704 949-1600
11515 Vanstory Dr Ste 100 Huntersville (28078) *(G-7033)*

Playrace Inc... 828 251-2211
1202 Patton Ave Asheville (28806) *(G-577)*

Playtex Dorado LLC.. 336 519-8080
1000 E Hanes Mill Rd Winston Salem (27105) *(G-13297)*

Plazit-Polygal, Charlotte *Also Called: Plaskolite LLC (G-2640)*

Pleasant Garden Dry Kiln... 336 674-2863
1221 Briarcrest Dr Pleasant Garden (27313) *(G-9793)*

Pleasant Gardens Machine Inc.................................. 828 724-4173
2708 Us 70 W Marion (28752) *(G-8061)*

Pleb Urban Winery... 828 767-6445
289 Lyman St Asheville (28801) *(G-578)*

Plexus Corp.. 919 807-8000
5511 Capital Center Dr Ste 600 Raleigh (27606) *(G-10373)*

Plm Inc.. 336 788-7529
2371 Farrington Point Dr Winston Salem (27107) *(G-13298)*

Plott Bakery Products, Rocky Mount *Also Called: Evelyn T Burney (G-10838)*

Plum Print Inc... 828 633-5535
45 S French Broad Ave Ste 100 Asheville (28801) *(G-579)*

Plush Comforts.. 336 882-9185
508 Ashe St High Point (27262) *(G-6737)*

Plushh LLC... 919 647-7911
3633 Top Of The Pines Ct Raleigh (27604) *(G-10374)*

Ply Gem, Cary *Also Called: Ply Gem Holdings Inc (G-1421)*

Ply Gem Holdings Inc (DH)....................................... 919 677-3900
5020 Weston Pkwy Ste 400 Cary (27513) *(G-1421)*

Ply Gem Industries, Cary *Also Called: Ply Gem Industries Inc (G-1422)*

Ply Gem Industries Inc (DH)..................................... 919 677-3900
5020 Weston Pkwy Ste 400 Cary (27513) *(G-1422)*

Plycem USA LLC.. 336 696-2007
1149 Abtco Rd North Wilkesboro (28659) *(G-9549)*

Plymouth Mill, Plymouth *Also Called: Domtar Paper Company LLC (G-9802)*

Plywood Plant, Whiteville *Also Called: Georgia-Pacific LLC (G-12581)*

Pma Products Inc... 800 762-0844
6120 Smithwood Rd Liberty (27298) *(G-7776)*

Pmb Industries Inc... 336 453-3121
632 Dixon St Lexington (27292) *(G-7733)*

PME, Mooresville *Also Called: Pro-Motor Engines Inc (G-8755)*

PMG Acquisition Corp... 828 758-7381
123 Pennton Ave Nw Lenoir (28645) *(G-7634)*

PMG Acquisitions Group Div, Lenoir *Also Called: PMG Acquisition Corp (G-7634)*

PMG SM Holdings LLC... 336 548-3250
703 W Decatur St Madison (27025) *(G-7997)*

PMG-DH Company.. 919 419-6500
1530 N Gregson St Ste 2a Durham (27701) *(G-4185)*

Pmt, Fayetteville *Also Called: Precision Machine Tech Inc (G-4656)*

Pnb Manufacturing.. 336 883-0021
2315 E Martin Luther King Jr Dr Ste A High Point (27260) *(G-6738)*

Pocket Yacht Company, New Bern *Also Called: Mass Enterprises LLC (G-9381)*

Pocono Coated Products LLC.................................... 704 445-7891
100 Sweetree St Cherryville (28021) *(G-3069)*

Poehler Enterprises Inc... 704 239-1166
10515 Jim Sossoman Rd Midland (28107) *(G-8292)*

Pogo, Raleigh *Also Called: Pogo Software Inc (G-10375)*

Pogo Software Inc.. 407 267-4864
8212 Oak Leaf Ct Raleigh (27615) *(G-10375)*

Pogomaxy Inc.. 919 623-0118
3737 Benson Dr Raleigh (27609) *(G-10376)*

Point Blank Enterprises Inc...................................... 910 893-2071
709 E Mcneill St Lillington (27546) *(G-7801)*

Polarean Inc... 919 206-7900
2500 Meridian Pkwy Ste 175 Durham (27713) *(G-4186)*

Polarmax/Xgo, Southern Pines *Also Called: Longworth Industries Inc (G-11502)*

Polk Sawmill LLC... 828 863-0436
206 Will Green Rd Tryon (28782) *(G-12176)*

Polli Garment, Raleigh *Also Called: Caromed International Inc (G-9981)*

Polly and Associates LLC..910 319-7564
7426 Janice Ln Wilmington (28411) *(G-12880)*

Poly One Distribution...704 872-8168
114 Morehead Rd Statesville (28677) *(G-11749)*

Poly Packaging Systems Inc....................................336 889-8334
2150 Brevard Rd High Point (27263) *(G-6739)*

Poly Plastic Products NC Inc...................................704 624-2555
1206 Traywick Rd Marshville (28103) *(G-8093)*

Poly-Tech Industrial Inc..704 992-8100
11330 Vanstory Dr Huntersville (28078) *(G-7034)*

Poly-Tech Industrial Inc..704 948-8055
13728 Statesville Rd Huntersville (28078) *(G-7035)*

Polychem Alloy Inc..828 754-7570
240 Polychem Ct Lenoir (28645) *(G-7635)*

Polycor Holdings Inc (PA).......................................828 459-7064
1820 Evans St Ne Conover (28613) *(G-3547)*

Polyhose Incorporated...732 512-9141
353 Acme Way Wilmington (28401) *(G-12881)*

Polymer Concepts Inc..336 495-7713
124 Regal Dr Randleman (27317) *(G-10656)*

Polymer Group, Benson *Also Called: Chicopee Inc (G-786)*

Polyone Corporation...704 838-0457
114 Morehead Rd Statesville (28677) *(G-11750)*

Polyone Distribution...919 413-4547
118 Brandi Dr Rolesville (27571) *(G-10889)*

Polypore Inc..704 587-8409
11430 N Community House Rd Ste 350 Charlotte (28277) *(G-2644)*

Polypore International LP (HQ).................................704 587-8409
13800 S Lakes Dr Charlotte (28273) *(G-2645)*

Polyprint Usa Inc...888 389-8618
1704 East Blvd Charlotte (28203) *(G-2646)*

Polyquest Incorporated (PA)....................................910 342-9554
1979 Eastwood Rd Ste 201 Wilmington (28403) *(G-12882)*

Polystone Columns, Wilmington *Also Called: Chadsworth Incorporated (G-12742)*

Polytec Inc (PA)..704 277-3960
191 Barley Park Ln Mooresville (28115) *(G-8750)*

Polyvlies Usa Inc...336 769-0206
260 Business Park Dr Winston Salem (27107) *(G-13299)*

Polyvnyl Fnce By Digger Spc In, Randleman *Also Called: Digger Specialties Inc (G-10642)*

Polyzen LLC...919 319-9599
1041 Classic Rd Apex (27539) *(G-186)*

Polyzen Inc..919 319-9599
115 Woodwinds Industrial Ct Cary (27511) *(G-1423)*

Polyzen, Inc., Apex *Also Called: Polyzen LLC (G-186)*

Pomdevices LLC..919 200-6538
178 Colvard Park Dr Durham (27713) *(G-4187)*

Ponysaurus Brewing LLC...919 455-3737
219 Hood St Durham (27701) *(G-4188)*

Poochpad Products, Winston Salem *Also Called: Microfine Inc (G-13252)*

Poole Printing Company, Raleigh *Also Called: Readable Communications Inc (G-10434)*

Poole Printing Company Inc.....................................919 876-5260
1400 Mapleside Ct Raleigh (27609) *(G-10377)*

Pop Designs Mktg Solutions LLC............................336 444-4033
1153 Holly Springs Rd Mount Airy (27030) *(G-9166)*

Pope Printing & Design Inc......................................828 274-5945
485 Hendersonville Rd Ste 7 Asheville (28803) *(G-580)*

Popes Signature Gallery..828 396-9494
3965 Us Highway 321a Hudson (28638) *(G-6956)*

Poplin & Sons Machine Co Inc.................................704 289-2079
2118 Stafford Street Ext Monroe (28110) *(G-8543)*

Poppe Inc..828 345-6036
313 Main Ave Ne Hickory (28601) *(G-6415)*

Poppelmann Plastics USA LLC.................................828 466-9500
2180 Heart Dr Claremont (28610) *(G-3116)*

Poppelmann Properties USA LLC.............................828 466-9500
2180 Heart Dr Claremont (28610) *(G-3117)*

Poppies International I Inc..252 442-4016
6610 Corporation Pkwy Battleboro (27809) *(G-707)*

Poppy Handcrafted Popcorn Inc (PA)......................828 552-3149
12 Gerber Rd Asheville (28803) *(G-581)*

Poppy Handcrafted Popcorn Inc..............................828 552-3149
78 Catawba Ave Ste A Old Fort (28762) *(G-9597)*

Pork Company..910 293-2157
139 Carter Best Rd Warsaw (28398) *(G-12365)*

Port City Elevator Inc..910 790-9300
5704 Nixon Ln Castle Hayne (28429) *(G-1509)*

Port City Films, Wilmington *Also Called: Inspire Creative Studios Inc (G-12818)*

Port City Signs & Graphics Inc................................910 350-8242
4011 Oleander Dr Wilmington (28403) *(G-12883)*

Portable Displays LLC...919 544-6504
5640 Dillard Dr Ste 301 Cary (27518) *(G-1424)*

Portable Outdoor Equipment, Durham *Also Called: Bolton Investors Inc (G-3937)*

Porter's Fabrications, Gastonia *Also Called: Porters Group LLC (G-5121)*

Porters Group LLC...704 864-1313
469 Hospital Dr Ste A Gastonia (28054) *(G-5121)*

Posh Pad...910 988-4800
700 Mill Bay Dr Stedman (28391) *(G-11807)*

Positive Prints Prof Svcs LLC..................................336 701-2330
1821 Hillandale Rd Ste 1b Pmb 256 Durham (27705) *(G-4189)*

Post & Courier, The, Durham *Also Called: Epi Group Llc (G-4029)*

Post Consumer Brands LLC.....................................336 672-0124
2525 Bank St Asheboro (27203) *(G-384)*

Post EC Holdings Inc..919 989-0175
207a Computer Dr Smithfield (27577) *(G-11460)*

Post Publishing Company...704 633-8950
131 W Innes St Salisbury (28144) *(G-11103)*

Postal Instant Press..336 222-0717
825 S Main St Burlington (27215) *(G-1142)*

Postal Liquidation Inc
3791 S Alston Ave Durham (27713) *(G-4190)*

Postmark, Kernersville *Also Called: Salem One Inc (G-7299)*

Potash Corp Saskatchewan Inc...............................252 322-4111
1530 Hwy 306 S Aurora (27806) *(G-646)*

Poteet Printing Systems LLC...................................704 588-0005
9103 Forsyth Park Dr Charlotte (28273) *(G-2647)*

Potter Logging...704 483-2738
2037 Cameron Heights Cir Denver (28037) *(G-3799)*

Potter's Lumber, Creston *Also Called: Ossiriand Inc (G-3658)*

Potts Logging Inc..704 463-7549
39342 Holly Ridge Rd New London (28127) *(G-9420)*

Powder Coat USA...919 954-7170
4200 Atlantic Ave Ste 130 Raleigh (27604) *(G-10378)*

Powder Coating By 3 S X...704 784-3724
4317 Triple Crown Dr Sw Concord (28027) *(G-3420)*

Powder Coating Services Inc....................................704 349-4100
1260 Shannon Bradley Rd Gastonia (28052) *(G-5122)*

Powder River Technologies Inc................................828 465-2894
1987 Industrial Dr Newton (28658) *(G-9489)*

Powder Works Inc..336 475-7715
6698 Pikeview Dr Thomasville (27360) *(G-12061)*

Powdertek..828 225-3250
6 Bagwell Mill Rd Arden (28704) *(G-297)*

Powell & Stokes Inc...252 794-2138
217 Us Highway 13 N Windsor (27983) *(G-13056)*

Powell Industries Inc (PA).......................................828 926-9114
4595 Jonathan Creek Rd Waynesville (28785) *(G-12467)*

Powell Ink Inc...828 253-6886
191 Charlotte St Asheville (28801) *(G-582)*

Powell Welding Inc..828 433-0831
3156 Hwy 70 Drexel (28619) *(G-3830)*

Powell Wholesale Lumber, Waynesville *Also Called: Powell Industries Inc (G-12467)*

Powell's Ready-Mix, Roanoke Rapids *Also Called: Allie M Powell III (G-10729)*

Power Adhesives, Charlotte *Also Called: GLS Products LLC (G-2216)*

Power Adhesives Ltd..704 578-9984
1209 Lilac Rd Charlotte (28209) *(G-2648)*

Power and Ctrl Solutions LLC..................................704 609-9623
6205 Boykin Spaniel Rd Charlotte (28277) *(G-2649)*

Power Chem Inc...919 365-3400
7316b Siemens Rd Wendell (27591) *(G-12540)*

Power Clean Chem, Concord *Also Called: Patel Deepal (G-3416)*

Power Components Inc.. 704 321-9481
  10837 Coachman Cir Charlotte (28277) *(G-2650)*

Power Curbers Inc (PA)...704 636-5871
  727 Bendix Dr Salisbury (28146) *(G-11104)*

Power Generation Mfg Oper Div, Rural Hall *Also Called: Siemens Energy Inc (G-10967)*

Power Integrity Corp... 336 379-9773
  2109 Patterson St Greensboro (27407) *(G-5752)*

Power Pros, Zebulon *Also Called: Asp Holdings Inc (G-13504)*

Power Support Engineering Inc..................................... 813 909-1199
  653 Barlow Fields Dr Hayesville (28904) *(G-6143)*

Power Tech Engines, Concord *Also Called: Jasper Penske Engines (G-3384)*

Power Technologies, Raleigh *Also Called: ABB Enterprise Software Inc (G-9862)*

Power-Utility Products Company (PA).......................704 375-0776
  8710 Air Park West Dr Ste 100 Charlotte (28214) *(G-2651)*

Poweramerica Institute.. 919 515-6013
  930 Main Campus Dr Ste 20 Raleigh (27606) *(G-10379)*

Powercat Group, Tarboro *Also Called: Hc Composites LLC (G-11928)*

Powergpu LLC.. 919 702-6757
  762 Park Ave Youngsville (27596) *(G-13481)*

Powerhouse Resources Intl LLC.................................. 919 291-1783
  2710 Wycliff Rd Ste 105 Raleigh (27607) *(G-10380)*

Powerlab Inc... 336 650-0706
  3352 Old Lexington Rd Bldg 43 Winston Salem (27107) *(G-13300)*

Powerlyte Paintball Game Pdts................................... 919 713-4317
  5811 Mchines Pl Ste 105 Raleigh (27616) *(G-10381)*

Powers Boatworks... 910 762-3636
  2725 Old Wrightsboro Rd Unit 8a Wilmington (28405) *(G-12884)*

Powersecure, Wake Forest *Also Called: Powersecure International Inc (G-12289)*

Powersecure Inc.. 919 818-8700
  6137 Princeton Kenly Rd Princeton (27569) *(G-9825)*

Powersecure International Inc..................................... 919 556-3056
  1609 Heritage Commerce Ct Wake Forest (27587) *(G-12289)*

Powersecure Solar, Durham *Also Called: Powersecure Solar LLC (G-4191)*

Powersecure Solar LLC.. 919 213-0798
  4068 Stirrup Creek Dr Durham (27703) *(G-4191)*

Powersigns Inc.. 910 343-1789
  3617 1/2 Market St Wilmington (28403) *(G-12885)*

Powersolve Corporation LLC...................................... 919 662-8515
  117b Pierce Rd Garner (27529) *(G-4954)*

Powertac Usa Inc.. 919 239-4470
  3702 Alliance Dr Ste C Greensboro (27407) *(G-5753)*

Powertec Industrial Motors Inc.................................. 704 227-1580
  13509 S Point Blvd Ste 190 Charlotte (28273) *(G-2652)*

Pozen Inc.. 919 913-1030
  8310 Bandford Way Raleigh (27615) *(G-10382)*

PPCS, Garner *Also Called: Proven Prof Cnstr Svcs LLC (G-4956)*

Ppd, Wilmington *Also Called: Ppd Inc (G-12886)*

Ppd Inc (HQ)... 910 251-0081
  929 N Front St Wilmington (28401) *(G-12886)*

Ppd Clinical Research, Morrisville *Also Called: Thermo Fisher Scientific Inc (G-9070)*

Ppd International Holdings LLC (DH)........................... 910 251-0081
  929 N Front St Wilmington (28401) *(G-12887)*

PPG 4434, Wilmington *Also Called: PPG Industries Inc (G-12888)*

PPG 4650, Cary *Also Called: PPG Industries Inc (G-1425)*

PPG 4655, Kill Devil Hills *Also Called: PPG Industries Inc (G-7319)*

PPG 4668, Charlotte *Also Called: PPG Industries Inc (G-2654)*

PPG 4669, Raleigh *Also Called: PPG Industries Inc (G-10385)*

PPG 4670, Charlotte *Also Called: PPG Industries Inc (G-2653)*

PPG 4685, Durham *Also Called: PPG Industries Inc (G-4192)*

PPG 9490, Winston Salem *Also Called: PPG Industries Inc (G-13301)*

PPG Architectural Finishes Inc.................................... 910 484-5161
  894 Elm St Ste A Fayetteville (28303) *(G-4655)*

PPG Architectural Finishes Inc.................................... 704 864-6783
  729 E Franklin Blvd Gastonia (28054) *(G-5123)*

PPG Architectural Finishes Inc.................................... 336 273-9761
  5103 W Market St Greensboro (27409) *(G-5754)*

PPG Architectural Finishes Inc.................................... 704 847-7251
  1600 Matthews Mint Hill Rd Ste B Matthews (28105) *(G-8141)*

PPG Architectural Finishes Inc.................................... 704 658-9250
  142 S Cardigan Way Mooresville (28117) *(G-8751)*

PPG Architectural Finishes Inc.................................... 828 438-9210
  511 Burkemont Ave Morganton (28655) *(G-8888)*

PPG Architectural Finishes Inc.................................... 919 872-6500
  2205 Westinghouse Blvd 11 Raleigh (27604) *(G-10383)*

PPG Architectural Finishes Inc.................................... 919 779-5400
  1458 Garner Station Blvd Raleigh (27603) *(G-10384)*

PPG Architectural Finishes Inc.................................... 704 633-0673
  1333 Klumac Rd Salisbury (28147) *(G-11105)*

PPG Industries Inc.. 919 319-0113
  210 Nottingham Dr Cary (27511) *(G-1425)*

PPG Industries Inc.. 704 542-8880
  10701 Park Rd Charlotte (28210) *(G-2653)*

PPG Industries Inc.. 704 523-0888
  3022 Griffith St Charlotte (28203) *(G-2654)*

PPG Industries Inc.. 919 382-3100
  3161 Hillsborough Rd Durham (27705) *(G-4192)*

PPG Industries Inc.. 919 772-3093
  4347 Baylor St Greensboro (27455) *(G-5755)*

PPG Industries Inc.. 336 856-9280
  109 P P G Rd Greensboro (27409) *(G-5756)*

PPG Industries Inc.. 252 480-1970
  2800 N Croatan Hwy Kill Devil Hills (27948) *(G-7319)*

PPG Industries Inc.. 704 658-9250
  128 Overhill Dr Ste 104 Mooresville (28117) *(G-8752)*

PPG Industries Inc.. 919 981-0600
  5500 Atlantic Springs Rd Raleigh (27616) *(G-10385)*

PPG Industries Inc.. 910 452-3289
  4125 Oleander Dr Wilmington (28403) *(G-12888)*

PPG Industries Inc.. 336 771-8878
  1455 Trademart Blvd Winston Salem (27127) *(G-13301)*

PPG Traffic Solutions, Greensboro *Also Called: Ennis-Flint Inc (G-5522)*

PPG-Devold LLC.. 704 434-2261
  940 Washburn Switch Rd Shelby (28150) *(G-11370)*

Ppi, Mooresville *Also Called: Performance Parts Intl LLC (G-8748)*

PQ Recycling LLC (HQ)...910 342-9554
  1979 Eastwood Rd Ste 201 Wilmington (28403) *(G-12889)*

Practice Fusion Inc (DH)... 415 346-7700
  305 Church At North Hills St Ste 100 Raleigh (27609) *(G-10386)*

Practicepro Sftwr Systems Inc.................................... 212 244-2100
  14225 Plantation Park Blvd Charlotte (28277) *(G-2655)*

Practichem, Morrisville *Also Called: Practichem LLC (G-9038)*

Practichem LLC... 919 714-8430
  10404 Chapel Hill Rd Ste 112 Morrisville (27560) *(G-9038)*

Praetego Inc... 919 237-7969
  68 Tw Alexander Dr Durham (27709) *(G-4193)*

Pramana LLC... 910 233-5118
  709 Dennison Ln Cary (27519) *(G-1426)*

Pratt (jet Corr) Inc.. 704 878-6615
  185 Deer Ridge Dr Statesville (28625) *(G-11751)*

Pratt & Whitney, Mooresville *Also Called: Pratt & Whitney Eng Svcs Inc (G-8753)*

Pratt & Whitney Eng Svcs Inc..................................... 860 565-4321
  330 Pratt And Whitney Blvd Asheville (28806) *(G-583)*

Pratt & Whitney Eng Svcs Inc..................................... 704 660-9999
  169 Stumpy Creek Rd Mooresville (28117) *(G-8753)*

Pratt Industries... 704 864-4022
  975 Tulip Dr Gastonia (28052) *(G-5124)*

Pratt Industries Inc.. 919 334-7400
  5620 Departure Dr Raleigh (27616) *(G-10387)*

Pratt Industries Inc.. 704 878-6615
  185 Deer Ridge Dr Statesville (28625) *(G-11752)*

Pratt Industries USA, Statesville *Also Called: Pratt (jet Corr) Inc (G-11751)*

Pratt Mller Engrg Fbrction LLC.................................... 704 977-0642
  9801 Kincey Ave Ste 175 Huntersville (28078) *(G-7036)*

Praxair, Wilmington *Also Called: Linde Inc (G-12836)*

Pre - War Guitars Co., Hillsborough *Also Called: Luthiers Workshop LLC (G-6871)*

Pre Flight Inc... 828 758-1138
  1035 Harper Ave Sw Lenoir (28645) *(G-7636)*

Precast Solutions Inc.. 336 656-7991
  7121 Choctaw Ct Browns Summit (27214) *(G-1003)*

Precast Terrazzo Entps Inc... 919 231-6200
  1107 N New Hope Rd Raleigh (27610) *(G-10388)*

Precedent Furniture, High Point *Also Called: Sherrill Furniture Company (G-6768)*

Precedent Furniture, Newton *Also Called: Sherrill Furniture Company (G-9494)*

Precept, Arden *Also Called: Precept Medical Products Inc (G-298)*

Precept Medical Products Inc (DH)................................828 681-0209
370 Airport Rd Arden (28704) *(G-298)*

Precious Oils Up On The Hill, Troutman *Also Called: Up On Hill (G-12155)*

Precise Sheet Metal Mech LLC.....................................336 693-3246
124 Winterfield Dr Raeford (28376) *(G-9848)*

Precise Technology Inc..704 576-9527
4201 Congress St Ste 340 Charlotte (28209) *(G-2656)*

Precision, Durham *Also Called: Precision Biosciences Inc (G-4194)*

Precision Alloys Inc..919 231-6329
1040 Corporation Pkwy Ste T Raleigh (27610) *(G-10389)*

Precision Biosciences Inc (PA).....................................919 314-5512
302 E Pettigrew St Ste A100 Durham (27701) *(G-4194)*

Precision Boat Mfg..336 395-8795
808 Carraway Dr Graham (27253) *(G-5282)*

Precision Cabinets Inc..828 262-5080
1324 Old 421 S Boone (28607) *(G-938)*

Precision Comb Works Inc..704 864-2761
2524 N Chester St Gastonia (28052) *(G-5125)*

Precision Concepts Intl LLC (PA)..................................704 360-8923
16810 Kenton Dr Huntersville (28078) *(G-7037)*

Precision Concepts Mebane LLC (DH)............................919 563-9292
1403a S Third Street Ext Mebane (27302) *(G-8257)*

Precision Design Machinery..336 889-8157
1509 Bethel Dr High Point (27260) *(G-6740)*

Precision Drive Systems LLC (PA).................................704 922-1206
4367 Dallas Cherryville Hwy Bessemer City (28016) *(G-831)*

Precision Enterprises, Randleman *Also Called: Gerald Hartsoe (G-10648)*

Precision Fabrication Inc...336 885-6091
2000 Nuggett Rd High Point (27263) *(G-6741)*

Precision Fabricators Inc (PA).....................................336 835-4763
Hwy 268 Ronda (28670) *(G-10897)*

Precision Fabrics Group Inc (PA)..................................336 281-3049
333 N Greene St Ste 100 Greensboro (27401) *(G-5757)*

Precision Fermentations Inc.......................................919 717-3983
2810 Meridian Pkwy Durham (27713) *(G-4195)*

Precision Industries Inc..828 465-3418
305 N Mclin Creek Rd Conover (28613) *(G-3548)*

Precision Machine Products Inc...................................704 865-7490
2347 N Chester St Gastonia (28052) *(G-5126)*

Precision Machine Tech Inc..910 678-8665
230 S Eastern Blvd Fayetteville (28301) *(G-4656)*

Precision Machine Tools Corp......................................704 882-3700
500 Union West Blvd Ste A Matthews (28104) *(G-8190)*

Precision Materials LLC (PA).......................................828 632-8851
6246 Nc Highway 16 S Taylorsville (28681) *(G-11972)*

Precision Mch Components Inc....................................704 201-8482
8075 Pine Lake Rd Denver (28037) *(G-3800)*

Precision Mch Fabrication Inc.....................................919 231-8648
1100 N New Hope Rd Raleigh (27610) *(G-10390)*

Precision McHning Eddie Husers, Kings Mountain *Also Called: Eddie Hsr S Prcsion McHning In (G-7363)*

Precision Metal Finishing Inc......................................704 799-0250
962 N Main St Mooresville (28115) *(G-8754)*

Precision Metals LLC..919 762-7481
589 Old Roberts Rd Benson (27504) *(G-796)*

Precision Mindset Pllc..704 508-1314
130 April Showers Ln Statesville (28677) *(G-11753)*

Precision Pallet LLC...252 935-5355
405 Mainstem Rd Pantego (27860) *(G-9648)*

Precision Part Systems, Winston Salem *Also Called: Precision Part Systems Wnstn-S (G-13302)*

Precision Part Systems Wnstn-S...................................336 723-5210
1035 W Northwest Blvd Winston Salem (27101) *(G-13302)*

Precision Partners LLC..704 560-6442
1830 Statesville Ave Charlotte (28206) *(G-2657)*

Precision Partners LLC..800 545-3121
1830 Statesville Ave Ste C Charlotte (28206) *(G-2658)*

Precision Pdts Asheville Inc (PA)..................................828 684-4207
118 Glenn Bridge Rd Arden (28704) *(G-299)*

Precision Pdts Prfmce Ctr Inc......................................828 684-8569
191 Airport Rd Arden (28704) *(G-300)*

Precision Printing..252 338-2450
307 S Road St Elizabeth City (27909) *(G-4404)*

Precision Printing..336 273-5794
2832 Randleman Rd Ste D Greensboro (27406) *(G-5758)*

Precision Printing, Wilkesboro *Also Called: Ollis Enterprises Inc (G-12648)*

Precision Processing System, Statesville *Also Called: Southern Prestige Industries Inc (G-11770)*

Precision Signs Inc..919 615-0979
5455 Raynor Rd Garner (27529) *(G-4955)*

Precision Stampers Inc...919 366-3333
480 Old Wilson Rd Wendell (27591) *(G-12541)*

Precision Textiles, High Point *Also Called: Precision Textiles LLC (G-6742)*

Precision Textiles LLC...336 861-0168
5522 Uwharrie Rd High Point (27263) *(G-6742)*

Precision Textiles LLC...910 515-6696
163 Glen Rd Troy (27371) *(G-12164)*

Precision Time Systems Inc..910 253-9850
959 Little Macedonia Rd Nw Supply (28462) *(G-11857)*

Precision Tool & Stamping Inc.....................................910 592-0174
800 Warsaw Rd Clinton (28328) *(G-3239)*

Precision Tool Dye and Mold.......................................828 687-2990
69 Bagwell Mill Rd Arden (28704) *(G-301)*

Precision Walls Inc..336 852-7710
7215 Cessna Dr Greensboro (27409) *(G-5759)*

Precision Wldg Mch Charlotte......................................704 357-1288
4701 Beam Rd Charlotte (28217) *(G-2659)*

Precisionaire Inc (DH)..252 946-8081
531 Flanders Filter Rd Washington (27889) *(G-12408)*

Precisionaire of Smithfield, Washington *Also Called: Precisionaire Inc (G-12408)*

Precor Incorporated...336 603-1000
1818 Youngs Mill Rd Greensboro (27406) *(G-5760)*

Predatar Inc..919 827-4516
4208 Six Forks Rd Ste 1000 Raleigh (27609) *(G-10391)*

Preferred Communication Inc......................................919 575-4600
410 Central Ave Butner (27509) *(G-1205)*

Preferred Data Corporation..336 886-3282
1208 Eastchester Dr High Point (27265) *(G-6743)*

Preferred Logging..910 471-4011
969 Livingston Chapel Rd Delco (28436) *(G-3739)*

Preformed Line Products Co..704 983-6161
1700 Woodhurst Ln Albemarle (28001) *(G-84)*

Preformed Line Products Co..336 461-3513
446 Glenbrook Spg New London (28127) *(G-9421)*

Preformed Line Products Co, New London *Also Called: Preformed Line Products Co (G-9421)*

Pregel America, Concord *Also Called: Pregel America Inc (G-3421)*

Pregel America Inc (DH)...704 707-0300
4450 Fortune Ave Nw Concord (28027) *(G-3421)*

Pregis Innovative Packg LLC (DH).................................847 597-2200
3825 N Main St Granite Falls (28630) *(G-5318)*

Pregis LLC..828 465-9197
500 Thornburg Dr Se Conover (28613) *(G-3549)*

Pregis LLC..828 396-2373
3825 N Main St Granite Falls (28630) *(G-5319)*

Pregnancy Support Services.......................................919 490-0203
1777 Fordham Blvd Ste 203 Chapel Hill (27514) *(G-1563)*

Prem Corp..704 921-1799
2901 Stewart Creek Blvd Charlotte (28216) *(G-2660)*

Premedia Group LLC...336 274-2421
7605 Business Park Dr Ste F Greensboro (27409) *(G-5761)*

Premex Inc...561 962-4128
1307 Person St Durham (27703) *(G-4196)*

Premier Body Armor LLC...704 750-3118
1552 Union Rd Ste E Gastonia (28054) *(G-5127)*

Premier Cakes, Raleigh *Also Called: Premier Cakes LLC (G-10392)*

Premier Cakes LLC..919 274-8511
6617 Falls Of Neuse Rd Ste 105 Raleigh (27615) *(G-10392)*

Premier Magnesia LLC (PA)..828 452-4784
75 Giles Pl Waynesville (28786) *(G-12468)*

Premier Mfg Co...704 781-4001
3520 Fieldstone Trce Midland (28107) *(G-8293)*

A
L
P
H
A
B
E
T
I
C

Premier Powder Coating Inc..........336 672-3828
  1948 N Fayetteville St Asheboro (27203) *(G-385)*

Premier Quilting Corporation..........919 693-1151
  720 W Industry Dr Oxford (27565) *(G-9626)*

Premier Tool LLC..........704 895-8223
  20409 Zion Ave Cornelius (28031) *(G-3619)*

Premiere Fibers LLC..........704 826-8321
  10056 Hwy 52 N Ansonville (28007) *(G-131)*

Premium Cushion Inc..........828 464-4783
  1009 1st St W Conover (28613) *(G-3550)*

Premium Fabricators LLC..........828 464-3818
  419 4th St Sw Conover (28613) *(G-3551)*

Premix North Carolina LLC..........704 412-7922
  5119 Apple Creek Pkwy Dallas (28034) *(G-3682)*

Prepac Manufacturing US LLC..........800 665-1266
  3031 Hendren Rd Whitsett (27377) *(G-12617)*

Presicion Wall, Raleigh Also Called: Design Specialties Inc *(G-10042)*

Presley Group Ltd (DH)..........828 254-9971
  739 Dogwood Rd Asheville (28806) *(G-584)*

Presnells Prtg & Photography, Sparta Also Called: David Presnell *(G-11537)*

Press Ganey Associates Inc..........800 232-8032
  700 E Morehead St Ste 100 Charlotte (28202) *(G-2661)*

Press Glass Inc (HQ)..........336 573-2393
  8901 Us Highway 220 Stoneville (27048) *(G-11826)*

Pressure Power Systems, Kernersville Also Called: Spartan Manufacturing Corp *(G-7302)*

Pressure Washing Near Me LLC..........704 280-0351
  10002 King George Ln Waxhaw (28173) *(G-12437)*

Prestage Foods Inc..........910 865-6611
  4470 Nc Hwy 20 E Saint Pauls (28384) *(G-11007)*

Prestige Cleaning Incorporated..........704 752-7747
  13903 Ballantyne Meadows Dr Charlotte (28277) *(G-2662)*

Prestige Fabricators Inc..........336 626-4595
  905 Nc Highway 49 S Asheboro (27205) *(G-386)*

Prestige Farms Inc..........919 861-8867
  2414 Crabtree Blvd Raleigh (27604) *(G-10393)*

Prestige Label, Burgaw Also Called: Atlantic Corp Wilmington Inc *(G-1019)*

Prestige Millwork Inc..........910 428-2360
  671 Spies Rd Star (27356) *(G-11633)*

Prestress of Carolinas LLC..........704 587-4273
  11630 Texland Blvd Charlotte (28273) *(G-2663)*

Pretium Packaging, Greensboro Also Called: Pretium Packaging LLC *(G-5762)*

Pretium Packaging LLC..........336 621-1891
  3240 N Ohenry Blvd Greensboro (27405) *(G-5762)*

Pretoria Transit Interiors Inc..........615 867-8515
  13501 S Ridge Dr Charlotte (28273) *(G-2664)*

Pretty Baby Herbal Soaps..........704 209-0669
  1050 Winding Brook Ln Salisbury (28146) *(G-11106)*

Pretty Paid LLC..........980 443-3876
  608 York Rd Kings Mountain (28086) *(G-7379)*

Preventech, Indian Trail Also Called: Preventive Technologies Inc *(G-7096)*

Preventive Technologies Inc..........704 684-1211
  4330 Matthews Indian Trail Rd Indian Trail (28079) *(G-7096)*

Prevost Car (us) Inc (DH)..........908 222-7211
  7817 National Service Rd Greensboro (27409) *(G-5763)*

Prevost Car (us) Inc..........336 812-3504
  1951 Eastchester Dr Unit E High Point (27265) *(G-6744)*

Prezioso Ventures LLC..........704 793-1602
  5410 Powerhouse Ct Concord (28027) *(G-3422)*

Price Logging Inc..........252 792-5687
  1901 Mill Rd Jamesville (27846) *(G-7184)*

Price Metal Spinning Inc..........704 922-3195
  3202 Puetts Chapel Rd Dallas (28034) *(G-3683)*

Pricely Inc..........336 431-2055
  7210 Suits Rd High Point (27263) *(G-6745)*

Pride Communications Inc..........704 375-9553
  8401 University Exec Park Dr Ste 122 Charlotte (28262) *(G-2665)*

Pride Magazine, Charlotte Also Called: Pride Communications Inc *(G-2665)*

Pride Publishing & Typsg Inc..........704 531-9988
  920 Central Ave Charlotte (28204) *(G-2666)*

Pridgen Woodwork Inc..........910 642-7175
  910 Jefferson St Whiteville (28472) *(G-12592)*

Prima Elements LLC..........910 483-8406
  124 Anderson St Fayetteville (28301) *(G-4657)*

Primaforce, Burlington Also Called: Disruptive Enterprises LLC *(G-1084)*

Primax Pumps, Charlotte Also Called: Primax Usa Inc *(G-2667)*

Primax Usa Inc..........704 587-3377
  11000 S Commerce Blvd Ste A Charlotte (28273) *(G-2667)*

Prime Beverage Group LLC..........704 385-5451
  215 International Dr Nw Ste B Concord (28027) *(G-3423)*

Prime Beverage Group LLC (PA)..........704 385-5450
  12800 Jamesburg Dr Huntersville (28078) *(G-7038)*

Prime Coatings LLC..........828 855-1136
  442 Highland Ave Se Hickory (28602) *(G-6416)*

Prime Mill LLC..........336 819-4300
  1946 W Green Dr High Point (27260) *(G-6746)*

Prime Source Opc LLC..........336 661-3300
  320 Perimeter Point Blvd Winston Salem (27105) *(G-13303)*

Prime Syntex LLC..........828 324-5496
  6980 Pikeview Dr Thomasville (27360) *(G-12062)*

Prime Water Services Inc..........919 504-1020
  9400 Ransdell Rd Ste 9 Raleigh (27603) *(G-10394)*

Primesource Corporation..........336 661-3300
  320a Perimeter Point Blvd Winston Salem (27105) *(G-13304)*

Primevigilance Inc..........781 703-5540
  5430 Wade Park Blvd Ste 208 Raleigh (27607) *(G-10395)*

Primo Inc..........888 822-5815
  19009 Peninsula Point Dr Cornelius (28031) *(G-3620)*

Primo Print, Cornelius Also Called: Primo Inc *(G-3620)*

Prince Group LLC..........828 681-8860
  209 Broadpointe Dr Mills River (28759) *(G-8319)*

Prince Manufacturing Corp..........828 681-8860
  209 Broadpointe Dr Mills River (28759) *(G-8320)*

Prince Mfg - Asheville, Mills River Also Called: Prince Manufacturing Corp *(G-8320)*

Prince Mfg - Greenville, Mills River Also Called: Prince Group LLC *(G-8319)*

Princeton Asphalt Plant, Princeton Also Called: S T Wooten Corporation *(G-9827)*

Princeton Information..........980 224-7114
  201 S College St Charlotte (28244) *(G-2668)*

Prinston Laboratories, Charlotte Also Called: Generics Bidco II LLC *(G-2202)*

Prinston Laboratories, Charlotte Also Called: Generics Bidco II LLC *(G-2203)*

Print Doc Pack and..........910 454-9104
  114 E Nash St Southport (28461) *(G-11525)*

Print Express Enterprises Inc..........336 765-5505
  6255 Towncenter Dr Clemmons (27012) *(G-3199)*

Print Express Inc..........910 455-4554
  117 N Marine Blvd Jacksonville (28540) *(G-7138)*

Print Haus Inc..........828 456-8622
  641 N Main St Waynesville (28786) *(G-12469)*

Print Management Group LLC..........704 821-0114
  425 E Arrowhead Dr Charlotte (28213) *(G-2669)*

Print Marks Screen Prtg & EMB, Durham Also Called: Lee Marks *(G-4102)*

Print Media Associates Inc..........704 529-0555
  834 Tyvola Rd Ste 110 Charlotte (28217) *(G-2670)*

Print Path LLC..........828 855-9966
  1215 15th Street Dr Ne Hickory (28601) *(G-6417)*

Print Professionals..........607 279-3335
  280 Oakmont Cir Pinehurst (28374) *(G-9700)*

Print Shoppe of Rocky Mt Inc..........252 442-9912
  140 S Business Ct Rocky Mount (27804) *(G-10862)*

Print Social..........980 430-4483
  403 Gilead Rd Ste A Huntersville (28078) *(G-7039)*

Print Usa Inc..........910 485-2254
  505 S Eastern Blvd Fayetteville (28301) *(G-4658)*

Print Works Fayetteville Inc..........910 864-8100
  3724 Sycamore Dairy Rd Ste 100 Fayetteville (28303) *(G-4659)*

Printcraft Company Inc..........336 248-2544
  259 City Lake Rd Lexington (27295) *(G-7734)*

Printcrafters Incorporated..........704 873-7387
  115 W Water St Statesville (28677) *(G-11754)*

Printech, Charlotte Also Called: Ceramco Incorporated *(G-1889)*

Printery..........336 852-9774
  2100 Fairfax Rd Ste 101a Greensboro (27407) *(G-5764)*

Printful Inc (PA)..818 351-7181
11025 Westlake Dr Charlotte (28273) *(G-2671)*

Printing & Packaging Inc..........................704 482-3866
1015 Buffalo St Shelby (28150) *(G-11371)*

Printing Partners Inc..................................336 996-2268
365 W Bodenhamer St Kernersville (27284) *(G-7293)*

Printing Press...828 299-1234
16 Pleasant Ridge Dr Asheville (28805) *(G-585)*

Printing Pro...704 748-9396
1310 L R Schronce Ln Iron Station (28080) *(G-7106)*

Printing Svcs Greensboro Inc...................336 274-7663
2206 N Church St Greensboro (27405) *(G-5765)*

Printlogic Inc...336 626-6b80
2753 Us Highway 220 Bus S Asheboro (27205) *(G-387)*

Printmarketing LLC......................................828 261-0063
320 19th St Se Hickory (28602) *(G-6418)*

Printology Signs Graphics LLC...................843 473-4984
10931 Zac Hill Rd Davidson (28036) *(G-3716)*

Printpack Inc..828 693-1723
3510 Asheville Hwy Hendersonville (28791) *(G-6237)*

Printpack Inc..828 649-3800
100 Kenpak Ln Marshall (28753) *(G-8082)*

Printpack Medical Store, Marshall Also Called: Printpack Inc *(G-8082)*

Printsurge Incorporated..............................919 854-4376
2308 Beaver Oaks Ct Raleigh (27606) *(G-10396)*

Printworld, Monroe Also Called: Synthomer Inc *(G-8567)*

Priority Backgrounds LLC...........................919 557-3247
118 N Johnson St Fuquay Varina (27526) *(G-4895)*

Priscllas Crystal Cast Wnes In....................252 422-8336
187 Hibbs Road Ext Newport (28570) *(G-9442)*

Prism Printing & Design Inc.........................919 706-5977
109 Loch Haven Ln Cary (27518) *(G-1427)*

Prism Publishing Inc (PA)............................919 319-6816
1240 Se Maynard Rd Ste 104 Cary (27511) *(G-1428)*

Prism Research Glass Inc............................919 571-0078
6004 Triangle Dr Ste B Raleigh (27617) *(G-10397)*

Prism Specialties NC, Raleigh Also Called: Dimill Enterprises LLC *(G-10046)*

Private Label Manufacturing, Winston Salem Also Called: Plm Inc *(G-13298)*

Privette Enterprises Inc...............................704 634-3291
2751 Old Charlotte Hwy Monroe (28110) *(G-8544)*

Prize Management LLC.................................252 532-1939
8287 Nc Highway 46 Garysburg (27831) *(G-4977)*

Pro Cal Prof Decals Inc (PA).......................704 795-6090
4366 Triple Crown Dr Sw Concord (28027) *(G-3424)*

Pro Choice Contractors Corp.......................919 696-7383
2405 Churchill Rd Raleigh (27608) *(G-10398)*

Pro Feet, Burlington Also Called: Wilson Brown Inc *(G-1180)*

Pro Laundry Equipment, Matthews Also Called: Laundry Svc Tech Ltd Lblty Co *(G-8126)*

Pro Pallet South Inc.....................................910 576-4902
105 Poole Rd Troy (27371) *(G-12165)*

Pro Refrigeration Inc....................................336 283-7281
319 Farmington Rd Mocksville (27028) *(G-8385)*

Pro Tool Company Inc..................................336 998-9212
1765 Peoples Creek Rd Advance (27006) *(G-37)*

Pro Tronics, Knightdale Also Called: Protronics Inc *(G-7457)*

Pro Ultrasonics Inc......................................828 584-1005
3076 Hwy 18 N / Us 64 Morganton (28655) *(G-8889)*

Pro-Blend Chemical Co, Winston Salem Also Called: Industrial Lubricants Inc *(G-13207)*

Pro-Fabrication Inc......................................704 795-7563
4328 Triple Crown Dr Sw Concord (28027) *(G-3425)*

Pro-Face America LLC (HQ).........................734 477-0600
235 Burgess Rd Ste D Greensboro (27409) *(G-5766)*

Pro-Kay Supply Inc.....................................910 628-0882
5032 Atkinson Rd Orrum (28369) *(G-9604)*

Pro-Line North Carolina Inc.........................252 975-2000
1653 Whichards Beach Rd Washington (27889) *(G-12409)*

Pro-Motor Engines Inc.................................704 664-6800
102 S Iredell Industrial Park Rd Mooresville (28115) *(G-8755)*

Pro-System Inc..704 799-8100
121 Oakpark Dr Mooresville (28115) *(G-8756)*

Pro-Tech Inc..704 872-6227
1256 N Barkley Rd Statesville (28677) *(G-11755)*

Proash LLC (HQ)..336 597-8734
1514 Dunnaway Rd Semora (27343) *(G-11295)*

Problem Solver Inc......................................919 596-5555
1053 E Whitaker Mill Rd Ste 115 Raleigh (27604) *(G-10399)*

Process Automation Tech Inc.......................828 298-1055
3113 Sweeten Creek Rd Asheville (28803) *(G-586)*

Process Electronics Corp............................704 827-9019
100 Brickyard Rd Mount Holly (28120) *(G-9242)*

Procoaters Inc...336 992-0012
216 Industrial Way Dr Kernersville (27284) *(G-7294)*

Procter & Gamble, Browns Summit Also Called: Procter & Gamble Mfg Co *(G-1004)*

Procter & Gamble, Greensboro Also Called: Procter & Gamble Mfg Co *(G-5767)*

Procter & Gamble Mfg Co............................336 954-0000
6200 Bryan Park Rd Browns Summit (27214) *(G-1004)*

Procter & Gamble Mfg Co............................336 954-0000
100 S Swing Rd Greensboro (27409) *(G-5767)*

Proctorfree Inc...704 759-6569
210 Delburg St Davidson (28036) *(G-3717)*

Producers Gin Murfreesboro LLC................252 398-3762
336 Benthall Bridge Rd Murfreesboro (27855) *(G-9285)*

Product Identification Inc............................919 544-4136
1725 Carpenter Fletcher Rd Ste 201 Durham (27713) *(G-4197)*

Product Quest Manufacturing Inc................386 239-8787
380 Knollwood St Ste 700 Winston Salem (27103) *(G-13305)*

Product Quest Manufacturing LLC..............386 239-8787
380 Knollwood St Ste 700 Winston Salem (27103) *(G-13306)*

Production Division, Kinston Also Called: Sanderson Farms Inc *(G-7427)*

Production Media Inc...................................919 325-0120
2501 Blue Ridge Rd Ste 250 Raleigh (27607) *(G-10400)*

Production Systems Inc...............................336 886-7161
1500 Trinity Ave High Point (27260) *(G-6747)*

Production Tool and Die, Charlotte Also Called: Legacy Manufacturing LLC *(G-2417)*

Production Tool and Die Co Inc....................704 525-0498
537 Scholtz Rd Charlotte (28217) *(G-2672)*

Production Wldg Fbrication Inc.....................828 687-7466
1791 Brevard Rd Arden (28704) *(G-302)*

Productive Tool, Dallas Also Called: Brooks of Dallas Inc *(G-3666)*

Proedge Precision LLC.................................704 872-3393
113 Hatfield Rd Statesville (28625) *(G-11756)*

Proface America, Greensboro Also Called: Pro-Face America LLC *(G-5766)*

Profection Embroidery, Concord Also Called: Tef Inc *(G-3455)*

Professinal Sales Associates......................336 210-2756
2783 Nc Highway 68 S Ste 116 High Point (27265) *(G-6748)*

Professional Bus Systems Inc.....................704 333-2444
201 E Cama St Charlotte (28217) *(G-2673)*

Professional Laminating, Cary Also Called: Professional Laminating LLC *(G-1430)*

Professional Laminating LLC.......................919 465-0400
107 Turnberry Ln Cary (27518) *(G-1429)*

Professional Laminating LLC.......................919 465-0400
233 E Johnson St Ste M Cary (27513) *(G-1430)*

Professnal Alterations EMB Inc....................910 577-8484
2113 Lejeune Blvd Jacksonville (28546) *(G-7139)*

Professnal Prprty Prservations, Raeford Also Called: William Brantley *(G-9856)*

Profile Products LLC....................................828 327-4165
219 Simpson St Sw Conover (28613) *(G-3552)*

Profilform Us Inc..252 430-0392
101 Eastern Minerals Rd Henderson (27537) *(G-6170)*

Proform Finishing Products LLC (DH)..........704 365-7300
2001 Rexford Rd Charlotte (28211) *(G-2674)*

Proform Finishing Products LLC..................704 398-3900
1725 Wester Rd Mount Holly (28120) *(G-9243)*

Proform Finishing Products LLC..................910 799-3954
838 Sunnyvale Dr Wilmington (28412) *(G-12890)*

Proforma Hanson Branding..........................210 437-3061
4257 Wallburg High Point Rd High Point (27265) *(G-6749)*

Proforma Print Source..................................919 383-2070
3600 N Duke St Durham (27704) *(G-4198)*

Proforma Promographix, Carolina Beach Also Called: Promographix Inc *(G-1263)*

Progress Energy Florida, Raleigh Also Called: Florida Progress Corporation *(G-10113)*

Progress Software Corp...............................919 461-4200
3005 Carrington Mill Blvd Morrisville (27560) *(G-9039)*

Progress Solar Solutions LLC................................ 919 363-3738
1108 N New Hope Rd Raleigh (27610) *(G-10401)*

Progressive Business Media, Greensboro *Also Called: Ft Media Holdings LLC (G-5542)*

Progressive Elc Greenville LLC............................. 252 413-6957
8606 Canal Dr Emerald Isle (28594) *(G-4479)*

Progressive Furniture Inc...................................... 828 459-2151
2555 Penny Rd Claremont (28610) *(G-3118)*

Progressive Graphics Inc....................................... 919 821-3223
3707 Hillsborough St Raleigh (27607) *(G-10402)*

Progressive Industries Inc..................................... 919 267-6948
1020 Goodworth Dr Apex (27539) *(G-187)*

Progressive Intl Elec Inc....................................... 919 266-4442
1106 Great Falls Ct Knightdale (27545) *(G-7456)*

Progressive Service Die Co................................... 910 353-4836
226 White St Jacksonville (28546) *(G-7140)*

Progressive Tool & Mfg Inc................................... 336 664-1130
245 Standard Dr Greensboro (27409) *(G-5768)*

Project Bean LLC... 201 438-1598
13359 Reese Blvd E Huntersville (28078) *(G-7040)*

Prokidney LLC... 336 448-2857
3929 Westpoint Blvd Ste G Winston Salem (27103) *(G-13307)*

Prokidney Corp (PA).. 336 999-7019
2000 Frontis Plaza Blvd Ste 250 Winston Salem (27103) *(G-13308)*

Prolec-GE Waukesha LLC...................................... 919 734-8900
2701 Us Highway 117 S Goldsboro (27530) *(G-5238)*

Promatic Automation Inc....................................... 828 684-1700
9a National Ave Fletcher (28732) *(G-4761)*

Prometals Inc.. 919 693-8884
510 1/2 Hillsboro St Oxford (27565) *(G-9627)*

Promethera Biosciences LLC................................. 919 354-1930
6 Davis Dr Durham (27709) *(G-4199)*

Promethera Biosciences LLC (PA).......................... 919 354-1933
4700 Falls Of Neuse Rd Ste 400 Raleigh (27609) *(G-10403)*

Prometheus Group Holdings LLC........................... 919 835-0810
4601 Six Forks Rd Ste 220 Raleigh (27609) *(G-10404)*

Prominence Furniture Inc...................................... 336 475-6505
415 Commercial Park Dr Thomasville (27360) *(G-12063)*

Promiseland Media Inc.. 910 762-1337
272 N Front St Ste 406 Wilmington (28401) *(G-12891)*

Promographix Inc... 919 846-1379
406 Fayetteville Ave Carolina Beach (28428) *(G-1263)*

Promothreads Inc.. 704 248-0942
19824 W Catawba Ave Ste C Cornelius (28031) *(G-3621)*

Promotional Products Plus, Newport *Also Called: Carolina Tailors Inc (G-9439)*

Propane Trucks & Tanks Inc (PA).......................... 919 362-5000
1600 E Williams St Apex (27539) *(G-188)*

Propella Therapeutics Inc..................................... 703 631-7523
120 Mosaic Blvd Ste 120-3 Pittsboro (27312) *(G-9786)*

Propharma Group LLC (HQ)................................... 888 242-0559
107 W Hargett St Raleigh (27601) *(G-10405)*

Prophysics Innovations Inc................................... 919 245-0406
1911 Evans Rd Cary (27513) *(G-1431)*

Proplastic Designs Inc.. 866 649-8665
2900 Westinghouse Blvd Ste 118 Charlotte (28273) *(G-2675)*

Prosapient, Raleigh *Also Called: Prosapient Inc (G-10406)*

Prosapient Inc.. 984 282-2823
555 Fayetteville St Ste 700 Raleigh (27601) *(G-10406)*

Prospective Communications LLC........................... 336 287-5535
1959 N Peace Haven Rd Winston Salem (27106) *(G-13309)*

Protech Fabrication Inc... 704 663-1721
575 Edmiston Rd Mount Ulla (28125) *(G-9271)*

Protech Metals LLC.. 910 295-6905
3619 Murdocksville Rd Pinehurst (28374) *(G-9701)*

Protechnologies Inc... 336 368-1375
331 Shellybrook Dr Pilot Mountain (27041) *(G-9672)*

Protect Plus Air, Hickory *Also Called: Freudnberg Rsdntial Fltrtion T (G-6335)*

Protect Plus Pro LLC.. 828 328-1142
420 3rd Ave Nw Ste A Hickory (28601) *(G-6419)*

Protection Products Inc... 828 324-2173
1010 3rd Ave Nw Hickory (28601) *(G-6420)*

Protein For Pets Opco LLC.................................... 252 206-0960
2018 Beeler Rd S Wilson (27893) *(G-13014)*

Protek Services LLC... 910 556-4121
905 Cranes Creek Rd Cameron (28326) *(G-1215)*

Proterial North Carolina Ltd.................................. 704 855-2800
1 Hitachi Metals Dr China Grove (28023) *(G-3078)*

Protex Sport Products Inc...................................... 336 956-2419
1029 S Main St Salisbury (28144) *(G-11107)*

Proto Labs Inc... 833 245-8827
3700 Pleasant Grove Church Rd Morrisville (27560) *(G-9040)*

Protocase Mfg Usa Inc.. 866 849-3911
929 N Front St Ste 403 Wilmington (28401) *(G-12892)*

Prototech Manufacturing Inc................................. 508 646-8849
715 Page Rd Washington (27889) *(G-12410)*

Prototype Tooling Co.. 704 864-7777
1811 W Franklin Blvd Gastonia (28052) *(G-5128)*

Protronics Inc.. 919 217-0007
861 Old Knight Rd Ste 102 Knightdale (27545) *(G-7457)*

Proven Prof Cnstr Svcs LLC.................................. 919 821-2696
463 Cleveland Crossing Dr Ste 101 Garner (27529) *(G-4956)*

Provizion Led, Charlotte *Also Called: Carolina Signs and Wonders Inc (G-1856)*

Proximal Design Labs LLC.................................... 919 599-5742
1421 Carolina Pines Ave Raleigh (27603) *(G-10407)*

Proximity Bakery, Greensboro *Also Called: Proximity Foods Corporation (G-5769)*

Proximity Foods Corporation................................. 336 691-1700
1117 W Cornwallis Dr Greensboro (27408) *(G-5769)*

Prysmian Cables & Systems USA, Claremont *Also Called: Draka Holdings Usa Inc (G-3109)*

Prysmian Cbles Systems USA LLC.......................... 828 322-9473
1711 11th Ave Sw Hickory (28602) *(G-6421)*

PS Cisco, Statesville *Also Called: Tube Specialties Co Inc (G-11795)*

Psa Incorporated.. 910 371-1115
150 Backhoe Rd Ne Belville (28451) *(G-780)*

PSI Control Solutions LLC (PA)............................. 704 596-5617
9900 Twin Lakes Pkwy Charlotte (28269) *(G-2676)*

PSI Liquidating Inc.. 704 888-9930
605 N Central Ave Ste A Locust (28097) *(G-7897)*

PSI Pharma Support America Inc............................ 919 249-2660
10 Laboratory Dr Durham (27709) *(G-4200)*

PSI Power & Controls, Charlotte *Also Called: PSI Control Solutions LLC (G-2676)*

Psi-Polymer Systems Inc...................................... 828 468-2600
1703 Pineview St Se Conover (28613) *(G-3553)*

PSM Enterprises Inc... 336 789-8888
219 Frederick St Mount Airy (27030) *(G-9167)*

Psnc Energy... 919 367-2735
2451 Schieffelin Rd Apex (27502) *(G-189)*

Pt Marketing Incorporated..................................... 412 471-8995
8360 Six Forks Rd Ste 204 Raleigh (27615) *(G-10408)*

PT&D, Charlotte *Also Called: Production Tool and Die Co Inc (G-2672)*

Ptc, Winston Salem *Also Called: Parrish Tire Company (G-13276)*

Pti, Hickory *Also Called: Plastic Technology Inc (G-6414)*

Pti, Pilot Mountain *Also Called: Protechnologies Inc (G-9672)*

Public Health Corps Inc.. 336 545-2999
3300 Battleground Ave Ste 270 Greensboro (27410) *(G-5770)*

Publishing Group Inc.. 704 847-7150
211 W Matthews St Ste 105 Matthews (28105) *(G-8142)*

Publishing Group, The, Matthews *Also Called: Publishing Group Inc (G-8142)*

Publishing/Education, Shelby *Also Called: Silver Ink Publishing Inc (G-11378)*

Pucuda Inc... 860 526-8004
3100 Oaks Rd New Bern (28560) *(G-9389)*

Puett Trucking & Logging...................................... 919 853-2071
1796 Person Rd Louisburg (27549) *(G-7923)*

Puffing Monkey... 919 556-7779
2115 S Main St Wake Forest (27587) *(G-12290)*

Pulaski Furniture, High Point *Also Called: Home Meridian Holdings Inc (G-6661)*

Pulp Mill, Vanceboro *Also Called: Weyerhaeuser Company (G-12223)*

Pumpkin Pacific LLC... 704 226-4176
10206 Pineshadow Dr Apt 107 Charlotte (28262) *(G-2677)*

Pumps Blowers & Elc Mtrs LLC.............................. 919 286-4975
2712 Edmund St Durham (27705) *(G-4201)*

Pungo River Timber Company, Pantego *Also Called: Nathan Beiler (G-9647)*

Punker LLC.. 828 322-1951
1112 Lincoln County Pkwy Lincolnton (28092) *(G-7849)*

Puny Human LLC.. 919 420-4538
6278 Glenwood Ave Raleigh (27612) *(G-10409)*

Pupco, Charlotte *Also Called: Power-Utility Products Company (G-2651)*

Purdue Pharmaceuticals LP..................................... 252 265-1900
4701 International Blvd Wilson (27893) *(G-13015)*

Pure Country Inc... 828 871-2890
81 Skylar Dr Tryon (28782) *(G-12177)*

Pure Flow Inc (PA)... 336 532-0300
1241 Jay Ln Graham (27253) *(G-5283)*

Pure Water Innovations Inc.................................... 919 301-8189
272 Williams Rd Spring Hope (27882) *(G-11558)*

Pureon Inc.. 480 505-3409
1412 Airport Rd Monroe (28110) *(G-8545)*

Purilum LLC.. 252 931-8020
967 Woodridge Park Rd Greenville (27834) *(G-6016)*

Purina Mills, Statesville *Also Called: Purina Mills LLC (G-11757)*

Purina Mills LLC.. 704 872-0456
173 Mcness Rd Statesville (28677) *(G-11757)*

Purolator Advanced Filtration, Greensboro *Also Called: Purolator Facet Inc (G-5771)*

Purolator Facet Inc (HQ)... 336 668-4444
8439 Triad Dr Greensboro (27409) *(G-5771)*

Purple Star Graphics Inc... 704 723-4020
32 Union St S Concord (28025) *(G-3426)*

Purser Centl Rewinding Co Inc (PA)........................ 704 786-3131
865 Concord Pkwy N Concord (28027) *(G-3427)*

Purthermal LLC... 828 855-0108
1720 Tate Blvd Se Hickory (28602) *(G-6422)*

Putsch, Fletcher *Also Called: Putsch & Company Inc (G-4762)*

Putsch & Company Inc (HQ).................................... 828 684-0671
352 Cane Creek Rd Fletcher (28732) *(G-4762)*

Puzzle Piece LLC... 910 688-7119
2287 Underwood Rd Carthage (28327) *(G-1278)*

Pyrotek Incorporated.. 704 642-1993
970 Grace Church Rd Salisbury (28147) *(G-11108)*

Pyxus International Inc... 252 753-8000
8958 West Marlboro Rd Farmville (27828) *(G-4538)*

Q C Apparel Inc... 828 586-5663
330 Scotts Creek Rd Sylva (28779) *(G-11897)*

Q M S, Candler *Also Called: Quality Musical Systems Inc (G-1231)*

Q T Corporation... 252 399-7600
2700 Forest Hills Rd Sw Wilson (27893) *(G-13016)*

Qasioun LLC... 704 531-8000
4845 E Independence Blvd Unit B Charlotte (28212) *(G-2678)*

Qc LLC (DH).. 800 883-0010
1001 Winstead Dr Ste 480 Cary (27513) *(G-1432)*

Qcs Acquisition Corporation.................................... 252 446-5000
130 N Business Ct Rocky Mount (27804) *(G-10863)*

QMAX Industries, Charlotte *Also Called: QMAX Industries LLC (G-2679)*

QMAX Industries LLC... 704 643-7299
11000 S Commerce Blvd Charlotte (28273) *(G-2679)*

QMF Mtal Elctrnic Slutions Inc................................ 336 992-8002
324 Berry Garden Rd Kernersville (27284) *(G-7295)*

Qni, Raleigh *Also Called: Qualia Networks Inc (G-10413)*

QORVO, Greensboro *Also Called: Qorvo Inc (G-5773)*

Qorvo Inc.. 336 664-1233
7908 Piedmont Triad Pkwy Bldg D Greensboro (27409) *(G-5772)*

Qorvo Inc (PA)... 336 664-1233
7628 Thorndike Rd Greensboro (27409) *(G-5773)*

Qorvo International Holdg Inc (DH).......................... 336 664-1233
7628 Thorndike Rd Greensboro (27409) *(G-5774)*

Qorvo International Svcs Inc..................................... 336 664-1233
7628 Thorndike Rd Greensboro (27409) *(G-5775)*

Qorvo Us Inc.. 336 662-1150
7907 Piedmont Triad Pkwy Greensboro (27409) *(G-5776)*

Qorvo Us Inc.. 336 931-8298
7914 Piedmont Triad Pkwy Greensboro (27409) *(G-5777)*

Qorvo Us Inc.. 503 615-9000
4113 Devondale Ct Jamestown (27282) *(G-7176)*

Qplot Corporation.. 949 302-7928
3245 Lewis Farm Rd Raleigh (27607) *(G-10410)*

Qrmc Ltd... 828 696-2000
11 S Egerton Rd Hendersonville (28792) *(G-6238)*

Qspac Industries Inc... 704 635-7815
506 Miller St Monroe (28110) *(G-8546)*

Qst Industries Inc... 336 751-1000
140 Lionheart Dr Mocksville (27028) *(G-8386)*

Quad City High Prfmce Coatings.............................. 937 623-2282
1427 Green Hill Rd Ne Leland (28451) *(G-7557)*

Quad/Graphics Inc... 706 648-5456
10911 Granite St Charlotte (28273) *(G-2680)*

QUAD/GRAPHICS INC., Charlotte *Also Called: Quad/Graphics Inc (G-2680)*

Quadron Holdings Inc.. 919 523-5376
4105 Glen Laurel Dr Raleigh (27612) *(G-10411)*

Quail Dry Cleaning... 704 947-7335
5818 Prosperity Church Rd Charlotte (28269) *(G-2681)*

Qualcomm, Clemmons *Also Called: Qualcomm Incorporated (G-3200)*

Qualcomm Datacenter Tech Inc................................ 858 567-1121
8045 Arco Corporate Dr Raleigh (27617) *(G-10412)*

Qualcomm Incorporated.. 336 323-3300
6209 Ramada Dr Ste A Clemmons (27012) *(G-3200)*

Qualia Networks Inc... 805 637-2083
3732 Westbury Lake Dr Raleigh (27603) *(G-10413)*

Qualicaps Inc.. 336 449-3900
6505 Franz Warner Pkwy Whitsett (27377) *(G-12618)*

Qualiseal Technology LLC.. 704 731-1522
5605 Carnegie Blvd Ste 500 Charlotte (28209) *(G-2682)*

Qualitrol Company LLC.. 704 587-9267
3030 Whitehall Park Dr Charlotte (28273) *(G-2683)*

Quality Beverage LLC... 910 371-3596
157 Poole Rd Belville (28451) *(G-781)*

Quality Beverage LLC (PA)....................................... 704 637-5881
1413 Jake Alexander Blvd S Salisbury (28146) *(G-11109)*

Quality Beverage Brands, Salisbury *Also Called: Quality Beverage LLC (G-11109)*

Quality Cleaning Services LLC.................................. 919 638-4969
3639 Guess Rd Durham (27705) *(G-4202)*

Quality Concrete Co Inc... 910 483-7155
1587 Wilmington Hwy Fayetteville (28306) *(G-4660)*

Quality Contemporary Furniture.............................. 919 758-7277
2517 Floyd Dr # B Raleigh (27610) *(G-10414)*

Quality Conveyor Solutions, Rocky Mount *Also Called: Qcs Acquisition Corporation (G-10863)*

Quality Custom Woodworks Inc................................ 704 843-1584
5019 Pleasant Springs Rd Waxhaw (28173) *(G-12438)*

Quality Equipment LLC... 919 493-3545
3821 Durham Chapel Hill Blvd Durham (27707) *(G-4203)*

Quality Fabricators.. 336 622-3402
1151 Langley Rd Staley (27355) *(G-11599)*

Quality Foods From Sea Inc..................................... 252 338-5455
173 Knobbs Creek Dr Elizabeth City (27909) *(G-4405)*

Quality Home Fashions Inc....................................... 704 983-5906
28569 Flint Ridge Rd Albemarle (28001) *(G-85)*

Quality Housing Corporation.................................... 336 274-2622
1400 Battleground Ave Ste 205 Greensboro (27408) *(G-5778)*

Quality Insulation Company...................................... 252 438-3711
132 Carey Chapel Rd Henderson (27537) *(G-6171)*

Quality Investments Inc.. 252 492-8777
1902 N Garnett St Henderson (27536) *(G-6172)*

Quality Lghtning Prtection Inc (PA).......................... 919 832-9399
743 Pershing Rd Raleigh (27608) *(G-10415)*

Quality Lightning Protection, Raleigh *Also Called: Capital Lghtning Prtection Inc (G-9968)*

Quality Machine & Tool.. 336 769-9131
1793 Union Cross Rd Kernersville (27284) *(G-7296)*

Quality Marble.. 336 472-1000
416 Julian Ave Thomasville (27360) *(G-12064)*

Quality Mch & Fabrication Inc.................................. 252 435-6041
444 Guinea Mill Rd Moyock (27958) *(G-9280)*

Quality Mechanical Contrs LLC................................ 336 228-0638
3032a Rock Hill Rd Burlington (27215) *(G-1143)*

Quality Musical Systems Inc.................................... 828 667-5719
204 Dogwood Rd Candler (28715) *(G-1231)*

Quality Packaging Corp (PA).................................... 336 881-5300
255 Swathmore Ave High Point (27263) *(G-6750)*

Quality Precast Inc.. 919 497-0660
100 Gayline Dr Louisburg (27549) *(G-7924)*

A
L
P
H
A
B
E
T
I
C

Quality Products & Machine LLC............................704 504-3330
4600 Westinghouse Blvd Charlotte (28273) *(G-2684)*

Quality Prtg Cartridge Fctry.................................336 852-2505
6700 W Market St Greensboro (27409) *(G-5779)*

Quality Saw Shop Inc..336 882-1722
1208 Elon Pl High Point (27263) *(G-6751)*

Quality Seafood Co Inc...252 338-2800
177 Knobbs Creek Dr Elizabeth City (27909) *(G-4406)*

Quality Steel Fabrication Inc...............................336 961-2670
1301 Union Cross Church Rd Yadkinville (27055) *(G-13448)*

Quality Trck Bodies & Repr Inc...........................252 245-5100
5316 Rock Quarry Rd Elm City (27822) *(G-4466)*

Qualpak LLC...910 610-1213
16000 Joy St Laurinburg (28352) *(G-7512)*

Qualtech Industries Inc..704 734-0345
311 Industrial Dr Kings Mountain (28086) *(G-7380)*

Quantex Inc...919 219-9604
280 W Haywood St Wendell (27591) *(G-12542)*

Quantico Tactical Incorporated............................910 944-5800
9796 Aberdeen Rd Aberdeen (28315) *(G-20)*

Quantum Machinery Group, Mooresville *Also Called: M & A Equipment Inc (G-8715)*

Quantum Materials LLC (HQ)................................336 605-9002
5280 National Center Dr Colfax (27235) *(G-3288)*

Quantum Newswire...919 439-8800
150 Fayetteville St 2800d108 Raleigh (27601) *(G-10416)*

Quantum Plastics Raleigh, Kenly *Also Called: Rpp Acquisition LLC (G-7237)*

Quantum Solutions...828 615-7500
365 Main Ave Sw Hickory (28602) *(G-6423)*

Quantum Usa LLP...919 799-7171
1405 E 11th St Siler City (27344) *(G-11424)*

Quarries Petroleum..919 387-0986
2540 Schieffelin Rd Apex (27502) *(G-190)*

Quarry & Kiln LLC..704 888-0775
1334 Nc-24 W Midland (28107) *(G-8294)*

Quarter Turn LLC...336 712-0811
8340 Holler Farm Rd Clemmons (27012) *(G-3201)*

Quartz, Spruce Pine *Also Called: Quartz Corp USA (G-11584)*

Quartz Corp USA (DH)..828 766-2104
8342 S 226 Bypass Spruce Pine (28777) *(G-11584)*

Quartz Matrix LLC..828 631-3207
283 Winding Ridge Dr Sylva (28779) *(G-11898)*

Quatrobio LLC..919 460-9500
3000 Rdu Center Dr Morrisville (27560) *(G-9041)*

Que Pasa, Winston Salem *Also Called: Latino Communications Inc (G-13231)*

Que Pasa Charlotte, Charlotte *Also Called: Latino Communications Inc (G-2409)*

Queen City Engrg & Design Pllc...........................704 918-5851
51 Carpenter Ct Nw Ste A Concord (28027) *(G-3428)*

Queen City Pastry Llc..704 660-5706
137 Speedway Ln Mooresville (28117) *(G-8757)*

Queen City Screen Printers.................................980 335-2334
1907 Bobolink Ln Charlotte (28226) *(G-2685)*

Queen of Wines LLC...919 348-6630
122 Wright Hill Dr Durham (27712) *(G-4204)*

Queens Creek Seafood...910 326-4801
105 Huffman Ln Hubert (28539) *(G-6936)*

Queensboro Industries Inc...................................910 251-1251
1400 Marstellar St Wilmington (28401) *(G-12893)*

Queensboro Shirt Company, Wilmington *Also Called: Queensboro Industries Inc (G-12893)*

Quest Software Inc...919 337-4719
133 Southcenter Ct Morrisville (27560) *(G-9042)*

QUEST SOFTWARE, INC., Morrisville *Also Called: Quest Software Inc (G-9042)*

Quick Color Solutions..336 698-0951
829 Knox Rd Mc Leansville (27301) *(G-8226)*

Quick Color Solutions Inc....................................336 282-3900
1801 E Franklin St Ste 208b Chapel Hill (27514) *(G-1564)*

Quick Copy Print Shop, Salisbury *Also Called: Baileys Quick Copy Shop Inc (G-11022)*

Quick N Easy 12 Nc739...336 824-3832
8112 Us Highway 64 E Ramseur (27316) *(G-10630)*

Quick Practice, Charlotte *Also Called: Practicepro Sftwr Systems Inc (G-2655)*

Quick Print, Brevard *Also Called: Blue Ridge Quick Print Inc (G-968)*

Quick Print, Fletcher *Also Called: Asheville Quickprint (G-4720)*

Quick Print, Salisbury *Also Called: Quick Print of Concord (G-11110)*

Quick Print Henderson Inc...................................252 492-8905
416 Dabney Dr Henderson (27536) *(G-6173)*

Quick Print of Concord...704 782-6634
700 N Long St Ste C Salisbury (28144) *(G-11110)*

Quick-Deck Inc..704 888-0327
137 Pine Forest Rd Locust (28097) *(G-7898)*

Quickie Manufacturing Corp................................910 737-6500
2880 Kenny Biggs Rd Lumberton (28358) *(G-7966)*

Quickshipkeys.com, Charlotte *Also Called: Easykeyscom Inc (G-2086)*

Quik Print Inc..910 738-6775
232 E 4th St Lumberton (28358) *(G-7967)*

Quiknit Crafting Inc..704 861-1030
1916 S York Rd Gastonia (28052) *(G-5129)*

Quikrete Companies LLC......................................704 272-7677
13471 Us Highway 74 W Peachland (28133) *(G-9653)*

Quikrete Peachland, Peachland *Also Called: Quikrete Companies LLC (G-9653)*

Quiktron Inc..828 327-6009
925 Old Lenoir Rd Hickory (28601) *(G-6424)*

Quillen Welding Services LLC..............................252 269-4908
110 Bonner Ave Morehead City (28557) *(G-8840)*

Quilt Lizzy...252 257-3800
4260 Lee St Ayden (28513) *(G-658)*

Quinlan Publishing Company...............................229 886-7995
2102 Pender Ave Wilmington (28403) *(G-12894)*

Quinsite LLC Fka Mile 5 Anlyti.............................317 313-5152
1818 Martin Luther King Jr Blvd Pmb 185 Chapel Hill (27514) *(G-1565)*

Quintiles Pharma, Inc., Durham *Also Called: Iqvia Pharma Inc (G-4084)*

Quo Vademus LLC...910 296-1632
277 Faison W Mcgowan Rd Kenansville (28349) *(G-7227)*

Qws LLC..252 723-2106
110 Bonner Ave Morehead City (28557) *(G-8841)*

R & D Label LLC..336 889-2900
117 Wade St Jamestown (27282) *(G-7177)*

R & D Plastics Inc...828 684-2692
526 Crest Rd Flat Rock (28731) *(G-4712)*

R & D Weaving Inc...828 248-1910
376 Pinehurst Rd Ellenboro (28040) *(G-4460)*

R & H Welding LLC..919 763-7955
3020 Cornwallis Rd Garner (27529) *(G-4957)*

R & J Mechanical & Welding LLC..........................919 362-6630
554 E Williams St Apex (27502) *(G-191)*

R & J Road Service Inc...252 239-1404
5014 Saint Marys Church Rd Lucama (27851) *(G-7938)*

R & L, Kings Mountain *Also Called: R and L Collision Center Inc (G-7381)*

R & R Ironworks Inc..828 448-0524
501 Salem Rd Morganton (28655) *(G-8890)*

R & R Logging Inc...704 483-5733
1040 N Ingleside Farm Rd Iron Station (28080) *(G-7107)*

R & R Powder Coating Inc....................................704 853-0727
190 Gibson Ct Dallas (28034) *(G-3684)*

R & S Logging Inc...252 426-5880
771 Lake Rd Hertford (27944) *(G-6256)*

R & S Precision Customs LLC...............................704 984-3480
338 E Main St Albemarle (28001) *(G-86)*

R & S Sporting Goods Ctr Inc...............................336 599-0248
515 S Morgan St Roxboro (27573) *(G-10942)*

R A G S, Wilmington *Also Called: Ruth Arnold Graphics & Signs (G-12907)*

R A Serafini Inc...704 864-6763
111 Lagrande St Gastonia (28056) *(G-5130)*

R and L Collision Center Inc.................................704 739-2500
1207 S Battleground Ave Kings Mountain (28086) *(G-7381)*

R and R Auto Repr & Tires Inc..............................336 784-6893
2704 Old Lexington Rd Winston Salem (27107) *(G-13310)*

R D Jones Packing Co Inc.....................................910 267-2846
192 N Nc Hwy 50 Faison (28341) *(G-4519)*

R D Tillson & Associates Inc.................................336 454-1410
105 Cottonwood Dr Jamestown (27282) *(G-7178)*

R E B B Industries, Yadkinville *Also Called: Viewriver Machine Corporation (G-13457)*

R E Bengel Sheet Metal Co...................................252 637-3404
1311 N Craven St New Bern (28560) *(G-9390)*

2025 Harris North Carolina
Manufacturers Directory

(G-0000) Company's Geographic Section entry number

R E Mason Enterprises Inc (PA)................910 483-5016
515 Person St Fayetteville (28301) *(G-4661)*

R E R Services................818 993-1826
55 N High Point Rd Southport (28461) *(G-11526)*

R Evans Hosiery LLC................828 397-3715
8177 Grover Evans Sr Rd Connelly Springs (28612) *(G-3482)*

R Gregory Jewelers Inc (PA)................704 872-6669
122 W Broad St Statesville (28677) *(G-11758)*

R H Bolick & Company Inc................828 322-7847
1210 9th Ave Ne Hickory (28601) *(G-6425)*

R J Reynolds Tobacco Company................336 741-0400
100 Moore-Rjr Dr Tobaccoville (27050) *(G-12102)*

R J Reynolds Tobacco Company................919 366-0220
7408 Siemens Rd Ste D Wendell (27591) *(G-12543)*

R J Reynolds Tobacco Company................252 291-4700
1500 Charleston St Se Wilson (27893) *(G-13017)*

R J Reynolds Tobacco Company (DH)................336 741-5000
401 N Main St Winston Salem (27101) *(G-13311)*

R J Reynolds Tobacco Company................336 741-2132
950 Reynolds Blvd Bldg 605-12 Winston Salem (27105) *(G-13312)*

R J Rynolds Tob Holdings Inc (DH)................336 741-5000
401 N Main St Winston Salem (27102) *(G-13313)*

R J Yeller Distribution Inc................800 944-2589
1835 Lindbergh St Charlotte (28208) *(G-2686)*

R Jacobs Fine Plbg & Hdwr Inc................919 720-4202
8613 Glenwood Ave Ste 103 Raleigh (27617) *(G-10417)*

R L Lasater Printing................919 639-6662
32 E Depot St Angier (27501) *(G-127)*

R L Roten Woodworking LLC................336 982-3830
1312 Howard Colvard Rd Crumpler (28617) *(G-3662)*

R N Lea Inc................919 247-5998
707 N West St Ste 104 Raleigh (27603) *(G-10418)*

R O Givens Signs Inc................252 338-6578
1145 Parsonage St Elizabeth City (27909) *(G-4407)*

R R Donnelley, Gastonia *Also Called: R R Donnelley & Sons Company (G-5131)*

R R Donnelley, Wilson *Also Called: R R Donnelley & Sons Company (G-13018)*

R R Donnelley & Sons Company................919 596-8942
1 Litho Way Durham (27703) *(G-4205)*

R R Donnelley & Sons Company................704 864-5717
1205 Isley Rd Gastonia (28052) *(G-5131)*

R R Donnelley & Sons Company................252 243-0337
1900 Charleston St Se Wilson (27893) *(G-13018)*

R R Mickey Logging Inc................910 205-0525
1014 Boyd Lake Rd Hamlet (28345) *(G-6061)*

R S Integrators Inc................704 588-8288
11172 Downs Rd Pineville (28134) *(G-9749)*

R S Skillen................828 433-5353
2080 Us 70 E Morganton (28655) *(G-8891)*

R T Barbee Company Inc................704 375-4421
724 Montana Dr Ste F Charlotte (28216) *(G-2687)*

R W Britt Logging Inc................252 799-7682
7281 Long Ridge Rd Pinetown (27865) *(G-9709)*

R W Garcia Co Inc................828 428-0115
3181 Progress Dr Lincolnton (28092) *(G-7850)*

R-Anell Custom Homes Inc................704 483-5511
3549 N Nc 16 Business Hwy Denver (28037) *(G-3801)*

R-Anell Housing Group LLC................704 445-9610
235 Anthony Grove Rd Crouse (28033) *(G-3659)*

R. R. Donnelley & Sons, Durham *Also Called: PBM Graphics Inc (G-4170)*

R/W Connection Inc................252 446-0114
136 S Business Ct Rocky Mount (27804) *(G-10864)*

R&D Plastics of Hickory Ltd................828 431-4660
345 26th Street Dr Se Hickory (28602) *(G-6426)*

R&H Machining Fabrication Inc................828 253-8930
329 Emma Rd Asheville (28806) *(G-587)*

R&J Custom Exhaust, Apex *Also Called: R & J Mechanical & Welding LLC (G-191)*

R&R Iron Works, Morganton *Also Called: R & R Ironworks Inc (G-8890)*

R65 Labs Inc................919 219-1983
108.5 E Parrish St Durham (27701) *(G-4206)*

R82 Inc................704 882-0668
13137 Bleinheim Ln Matthews (28105) *(G-8143)*

Rabbit Bottom Logging Co, Warrenton *Also Called: Rabbit Bottom Logging Co Inc (G-12353)*

Rabbit Bottom Logging Co Inc................252 257-3585
Hc 151 Warrenton (27589) *(G-12353)*

Rabuns Trlr Repr Tire Svc Inc................704 764-7841
4519 Old Pageland Monroe Rd Monroe (28112) *(G-8547)*

Race Tech Race Cars Cmpnnts In................336 538-4941
403 Macarthur Ln Burlington (27217) *(G-1144)*

Race Technologies Concord NC................704 799-0530
7275 Westwinds Blvd Nw Concord (28027) *(G-3429)*

Raceway 6739, Hickory *Also Called: Maa Umiya Inc (G-6390)*

Rachel Dubois................919 870-8063
6013 Old Horseman Trl Raleigh (27613) *(G-10419)*

Rack Works Inc................336 368-1302
207 Premier Ln Pilot Mountain (27041) *(G-9673)*

Rackwise, Raleigh *Also Called: Rackwise Inc (G-10420)*

Rackwise Inc................919 533-5533
4020 Westchase Blvd Ste 470 Raleigh (27607) *(G-10420)*

Radel Inc................336 245-8078
209 Mercantile Dr Winston Salem (27105) *(G-13314)*

Radford Quarries Inc (PA)................828 264-7008
5605 Bamboo Rd Boone (28607) *(G-939)*

Radiator Specialty Company (PA)................704 688-2302
600 Radiator Rd Indian Trail (28079) *(G-7097)*

Radon Control Inc................828 265-9534
Boone (28607) *(G-940)*

Raffaldini Vneyards Winery LLC................336 835-9463
450 Groce Rd Ronda (28670) *(G-10898)*

Rafters and Walls LLC................980 404-0209
2312 W Randolph Rd Shelby (28150) *(G-11372)*

Ragg Co Inc................336 838-4895
627 Elkin Hwy North Wilkesboro (28659) *(G-9550)*

Rai Services Company................336 741-6774
401 N Main St Winston Salem (27101) *(G-13315)*

Railroad Friction Pdts Corp................910 844-9709
13601 Airport Rd Maxton (28364) *(G-8205)*

Rainbow Upholstery & Furniture, Wake Forest *Also Called: Rufco Inc (G-12294)*

Rainey and Wilson Logistics................910 736-8540
1308 Checker Dr Raeford (28376) *(G-9849)*

Rainforest Nutritionals Inc................919 847-2221
9201 Leesville Rd Ste 120c Raleigh (27613) *(G-10421)*

Raleigh Denim, Raleigh *Also Called: Raleigh Workshop Inc (G-10431)*

Raleigh Downtowner................919 821-9000
12 E Hargett St Raleigh (27601) *(G-10422)*

Raleigh Engraving Co................919 832-5557
806 N West St Raleigh (27603) *(G-10423)*

Raleigh Engraving Press, Raleigh *Also Called: Raleigh Engraving Co (G-10423)*

Raleigh Facility, Raleigh *Also Called: Evergreen Packaging LLC (G-10095)*

Raleigh Magazine................919 307-3047
6511 Creedmoor Rd Ste 207 Raleigh (27613) *(G-10424)*

Raleigh Mechanical & Mtls Inc................919 598-4601
7405 Acc Blvd Raleigh (27617) *(G-10425)*

Raleigh Plant, Raleigh *Also Called: Eagle Rock Concrete LLC (G-10068)*

Raleigh Powder Coating Co................919 301-8065
2100 Garner Rd Raleigh (27610) *(G-10426)*

Raleigh Printing, Raleigh *Also Called: Raleigh Printing & Typing Inc (G-10427)*

Raleigh Printing & Typing Inc................919 662-8001
5415 Fayetteville Rd Raleigh (27603) *(G-10427)*

Raleigh Ringers................919 847-7574
2200 E Millbrook Rd Ste 113 Raleigh (27604) *(G-10428)*

Raleigh Road Box Corporation................252 438-7401
Rr 9 Box 403 Henderson (27536) *(G-6174)*

Raleigh Saw Co Inc................919 832-2248
5805 Departure Dr Ste C Raleigh (27616) *(G-10429)*

Raleigh Tees, Raleigh *Also Called: Raleigh Tees LLC (G-10430)*

Raleigh Tees LLC................919 850-3378
4909 Alpinis Dr Ste 113 Raleigh (27616) *(G-10430)*

Raleigh Ventures Inc................910 350-0036
6725 Amsterdam Way Wilmington (28405) *(G-12895)*

Raleigh Workshop Inc................919 917-8969
319 W Martin St Raleigh (27601) *(G-10431)*

Ralph B Hall............919 258-3634
804 Cox Maddox Rd Sanford (27332) *(G-11223)*

Ralph Harris Leather Inc............336 874-2100
219 Pat Nixon Rd State Road (28676) *(G-11639)*

Ralph Lauren Corporation............336 632-5000
4100 Beechwood Dr Greensboro (27425) *(G-5780)*

Ralph Lauren Corporation............336 632-5000
4190 Eagle Hill Dr High Point (27265) *(G-6752)*

Ralph S Frame Works Inc............336 431-2168
2231 Shore St High Point (27263) *(G-6753)*

Ram Industries Inc............704 982-4015
1135 Montgomery Ave Albemarle (28001) *(G-87)*

Ram Jack Foundation Repair, Durham Also Called: Fs LLC *(G-4039)*

Rambus Inc............919 960-6600
512 E Franklin St Ste 200 Chapel Hill (27514) *(G-1566)*

Ramco............704 794-6620
323 Corban Ave Sw Concord (28025) *(G-3430)*

Ramco Fabricators LLC............336 996-6073
9501 W Market St Colfax (27235) *(G-3289)*

Ramco Machine & Pump Svc Inc............910 371-3388
1054 Thistle Downs St Se Leland (28451) *(G-7558)*

Ramseur Inter-Lock Knitting Co............336 824-2427
2409 Old Lexington Rd Asheboro (27205) *(G-388)*

Ramsey Industries Inc............704 827-3560
816 Woodlawn St Belmont (28012) *(G-763)*

Ramsey Products Corporation............704 394-0322
135 Performance Dr Belmont (28012) *(G-764)*

Rancho Park Publishing Inc............919 942-9493
8 Matchwood Pittsboro (27312) *(G-9787)*

Rand Ange Enterprises Inc............336 472-7313
800 Bryan Rd Thomasville (27360) *(G-12065)*

Randall Printing Inc............336 272-3333
1029 Huffman St Greensboro (27405) *(G-5781)*

Randall Supply Inc (PA)............704 289-6479
2409 Walkup Ave Monroe (28110) *(G-8548)*

Randall-Reilly LLC............704 814-1390
1509 Orchard Lake Dr Ste E Charlotte (28270) *(G-2688)*

Randleman Carton Plant, Randleman Also Called: Caraustar Cstm Packg Group Inc *(G-10636)*

Randolph Goodson Logging Inc............910 347-5117
170 Jenkins Rd Jacksonville (28540) *(G-7141)*

Randolph Machine Inc (PA)............336 625-0411
1206 Uwharrie St Asheboro (27203) *(G-389)*

Randolph Machine Inc............336 799-1039
498 Pointe South Dr Randleman (27317) *(G-10657)*

Randolph Packing Company............336 672-1470
403 W Balfour Ave Asheboro (27203) *(G-390)*

Randolph Street - Pipe, Thomasville Also Called: Hydro Conduit LLC *(G-12035)*

Random & Kind LLC............919 249-8809
1348 Scholar Dr Durham (27703) *(G-4207)*

Random Rues Botanical LLC............252 214-2759
1290 E Arlington Blvd Greenville (27858) *(G-6017)*

Randy D Miller Lumber Co Inc............336 973-7515
538 Hwy 16 N Wilkesboro (28697) *(G-12649)*

Ranpak Corp............919 790-8225
3401 Gresham Lake Rd Raleigh (27615) *(G-10432)*

Rapid Cut, Wilmington Also Called: US Prototype Inc *(G-12943)*

Rapid Exchange, Clinton Also Called: Parker Gas Company Inc *(G-3238)*

Rapid Response Inc............704 588-8890
218 Westinghouse Blvd Charlotte (28273) *(G-2689)*

Rapid Response Technology LLC............910 763-3856
1900 Eastwood Rd Ste 27 Wilmington (28403) *(G-12896)*

Rapid Run Transport LLC............704 615-3458
12430 Clackwyck Ln Charlotte (28262) *(G-2690)*

Rapidform Inc............408 856-6200
1001 Winstead Dr Ste 400 Cary (27513) *(G-1433)*

Rapp Productions Inc............919 913-0270
103 W Weaver St Carrboro (27510) *(G-1271)*

Raptor Attachments, Archdale Also Called: US Metal Crafters LLC *(G-245)*

Rasin Haitian Restaurant LLC............704 780-5129
10104 Bellhaven Blvd Charlotte (28214) *(G-2691)*

Ratoon Agroprocessing LLC............828 273-9114
5290 Nc 226 S Marion (28752) *(G-8062)*

Raven Antenna Systems Inc............919 934-9711
1315 Outlet Center Dr Smithfield (27577) *(G-11461)*

Raven Rock Manufacturing Inc............910 308-8430
803 E Broad St Dunn (28334) *(G-3865)*

Ravenox Rope, Burlington Also Called: Genevieve M Brownlee *(G-1095)*

Rawco LLC............908 832-7700
18435 Train Station Dr Cornelius (28031) *(G-3622)*

Rawco Precision Manufacturing, Cornelius Also Called: Rawco LLC *(G-3622)*

Ray Houses Machine Shop............919 553-1249
110 N Tech Dr Clayton (27520) *(G-3167)*

Ray Roofing Company Inc............704 372-0100
2921 N Tryon St Charlotte (28206) *(G-2692)*

Raybow Usa Inc............828 884-8656
158 Mclean Rd Brevard (28712) *(G-980)*

Raylabcon, Burgaw Also Called: WR Rayson Co Inc *(G-1041)*

Raylen Vineyards Inc............336 998-3100
3055 Heather Meadow Dr Winston Salem (27106) *(G-13316)*

Raymond Brown Well Company Inc............336 374-4999
1109 N Main St Danbury (27016) *(G-3695)*

Rays Classic Vinyl Repair Inc............910 520-1626
440 Crooked Creek Rd Hampstead (28443) *(G-6075)*

Rb3 Digital Graphics, Wake Forest Also Called: Rb3 Enterprises Inc *(G-12291)*

Rb3 Enterprises Inc............919 795-5822
4701 Rogers Rd Wake Forest (27587) *(G-12291)*

Rbc Inc............336 889-7573
310 S Elm St High Point (27260) *(G-6754)*

Rbc Inc (PA)............336 861-5800
7310 Us Highway 311 Sophia (27350) *(G-11490)*

Rbi Manufacturing Inc............252 977-6764
4642 S Us Highway 301 Rocky Mount (27803) *(G-10865)*

Rbi Precision, Rocky Mount Also Called: Rbi Manufacturing Inc *(G-10865)*

Rbw LLC............919 319-1289
105 Graywick Way Cary (27513) *(G-1434)*

RC Boldt Publishing LLC (PA)............904 624-0033
804 Ocean Dr Oak Island (28465) *(G-9568)*

Rclgh Inc............828 707-4383
69 Bingham Rd Asheville (28806) *(G-588)*

RCM Industries Inc............828 286-4003
401 Aallied Dr Rutherfordton (28139) *(G-10991)*

Rcws Inc (PA)............919 680-2655
421 W Corporation St Durham (27701) *(G-4208)*

RDc Debris Removal Cnstr LLC............323 614-2353
149 Rainbow Ln Smithfield (27577) *(G-11462)*

Rdd Pharma Inc............302 319-9970
8480 Honeycutt Rd Ste 120 Raleigh (27615) *(G-10433)*

RDh Tire and Retread Company............980 368-4576
1315 Redmon Rd Cleveland (27013) *(G-3220)*

RDM Industrial Electronics Inc (PA)............828 652-8346
850 Harmony Grove Rd Nebo (28761) *(G-9329)*

RE Shads Group LLC............704 299-8972
5819 Creola Rd Charlotte (28270) *(G-2693)*

Reacredence It Solutions Inc............980 399-4071
8936 N Pointe Executive Park Dr Ste 240 Huntersville (28078) *(G-7041)*

React Innovations LLC............704 773-1276
1809 Browning Ave Charlotte (28205) *(G-2694)*

Readable Communications Inc............919 876-5260
2609 Spring Forest Rd Raleigh (27616) *(G-10434)*

Readilite & Barricade Inc (PA)............919 231-8309
708 Freedom Dr Raleigh (27610) *(G-10435)*

Ready Mix, Charlotte Also Called: Redi-Mix LP *(G-2699)*

Ready Mix Concrete, Durham Also Called: Chandler Concrete Inc *(G-3969)*

Ready Mix Concrete, Washington Also Called: Argos USA LLC *(G-12373)*

Ready Mix Concrete Co, Sims Also Called: Argos USA LLC *(G-11428)*

Ready Mix Concrete of Sanford, Raleigh Also Called: Argos USA LLC *(G-9914)*

Ready Mix of Carolinas Inc............704 888-3027
364 Browns Hill Rd Locust (28097) *(G-7899)*

Ready Mixed Concrete............252 758-1181
3928 Jolly Rd Ayden (28513) *(G-659)*

(G-0000) Company's Geographic Section entry number

Ready Mixed Concrete, Clinton *Also Called: Argos USA LLC (G-3228)*

Ready Mixed Concrete, New Bern *Also Called: Smyrna Ready Mix Concrete LLC (G-9397)*

Ready Mixed Concrete, Williamston *Also Called: Argos USA LLC (G-12667)*

Ready Mixed Concrete Co, Dunn *Also Called: Argos USA LLC (G-3845)*

Ready Mixed Concrete Co, Raleigh *Also Called: Argos USA LLC (G-9913)*

Ready Mixed Concrete Co, Roanoke Rapids *Also Called: Argos USA LLC (G-10730)*

Ready Mixed Concrete Co Fuquay, Fuquay Varina *Also Called: Argos USA LLC (G-4866)*

Ready Mixed Concrete Company, Raleigh *Also Called: Argos Ready Mix (carolinas) Corp (G-9912)*

Ready Solutions Inc.. 704 534-9221
112 Eden St Davidson (28036) *(G-3718)*

Readymixed, Newport *Also Called: Argos USA LLC (G-9437)*

Reagents Holdings LLC (HQ)................................. 800 732-8484
3825 Parrott Dr Charlotte (28214) *(G-2695)*

Real Estate Book, The, Charlotte *Also Called: Colefields Publishing Inc (G-1952)*

Real Producers, Mooresville *Also Called: Roosterfish Media LLC (G-8761)*

Real Time Content, Charlotte *Also Called: Randall-Reilly LLC (G-2688)*

Reality Check Sports, Concord *Also Called: Ics North America Corp (G-3375)*

Realxperience LLC.. 512 775-4386
5109 Sweet Clover Ct Durham (27703) *(G-4209)*

Rebb Industries Inc... 336 463-2311
1617 Fern Valley Rd Yadkinville (27055) *(G-13449)*

Rebecca Kaye International, Raeford *Also Called: Rebecca Trickey (G-9850)*

Rebecca Trickey.. 910 584-5549
389 Gibson Dr Raeford (28376) *(G-9850)*

Rec Plus Inc... 704 375-9098
1101 Central Ave Charlotte (28204) *(G-2696)*

Reclaim, Wake Forest *Also Called: Reclaim Filters and Systems (G-12292)*

Reclaim Filters and Systems (PA)......................... 919 528-1787
1129 Hidden Hills Dr Wake Forest (27587) *(G-12292)*

Recon Usa LLC.. 252 206-1391
4744 Potato House Ct Wilson (27893) *(G-13019)*

Reconditioning Dept, Thomasville *Also Called: Mickey Truck Bodies Inc (G-12047)*

Record Publishing Company.................................. 910 230-1948
99 W Broad St Dunn (28334) *(G-3866)*

Record Stor Depot-Shred Depo, Greensboro *Also Called: Piedmont Paper Stock LLC (G-5744)*

Record Usa Inc (PA).. 704 289-9212
4324 Phil Hargett Ct Monroe (28110) *(G-8549)*

Recoupl Inc.. 704 544-0202
16430 Redstone Mountain Ln Charlotte (28277) *(G-2697)*

Red 5 Printing Inc.. 704 996-3848
18631 Northline Dr Cornelius (28031) *(G-3623)*

Red Adept Publishing LLC.................................... 919 798-7410
104 Bugenfield Ct Garner (27529) *(G-4958)*

Red Bull Distribution Co Inc................................. 910 500-1566
95 Outer Banks Dr Havelock (28532) *(G-6126)*

Red Gremlin Design Studio, Boone *Also Called: Max B Smith Jr (G-933)*

Red Hand Media LLC (PA).................................... 704 523-6987
1230 W Morehead St Ste 308 Charlotte (28208) *(G-2698)*

Red Hat Inc (HQ)... 919 754-3700
100 E Davie St Raleigh (27601) *(G-10436)*

Red House Cabinets LLC...................................... 919 201-2101
9660 Falls Of Neuse Rd Raleigh (27615) *(G-10437)*

Red Maple Logging Company Inc.......................... 704 279-6379
10007 Meismer Ln Rockwell (28138) *(G-10800)*

Red Oak Sales Company (PA)................................ 704 483-8464
7912 Commerce Dr Denver (28037) *(G-3802)*

Red Shed Woodworks Inc...................................... 828 768-3854
200 Carl Bowman Rd Marshall (28753) *(G-8083)*

Red Sky Shelters LLC... 828 258-8417
2002 Riverside Dr Ste 42h Asheville (28804) *(G-589)*

Red Springs Distribution Ctr, Red Springs *Also Called: Muviq Usa LLC (G-10670)*

Red Wolfe Industries LLC..................................... 336 570-2282
913 Washington St Graham (27253) *(G-5284)*

Redbird Screen Printing LLC................................. 919 946-0005
8711 Owl Roost Pl Raleigh (27617) *(G-10438)*

Reddy Ice LLC... 704 824-4611
2306 Lowell Rd Gastonia (28054) *(G-5132)*

Reddy Ice LLC... 910 738-9930
903 E Elizabethtown Rd Lumberton (28358) *(G-7968)*

Reddy Ice LLC... 919 782-9358
8700 Ice Dr Raleigh (27613) *(G-10439)*

Redhill Biopharma Inc.. 984 444-7010
8045 Arco Corporate Dr Raleigh (27617) *(G-10440)*

Redi-Frame Inc.. 828 322-4227
207 20th St Se Hickory (28602) *(G-6427)*

Redi-Mix Concrete, Castle Hayne *Also Called: Argos USA LLC (G-1495)*

Redi-Mix Concrete, Denver *Also Called: Argos USA LLC (G-3772)*

Redi-Mix Concrete, Garner *Also Called: Argos USA LLC (G-4916)*

Redi-Mix Concrete, Hickory *Also Called: Argos USA LLC (G-6267)*

Redi-Mix Concrete, Mooresville *Also Called: Argos USA LLC (G-8600)*

Redi-Mix Concrete, Winston Salem *Also Called: Argos USA LLC (G-13089)*

Redi-Mix LP.. 704 596-6511
11509 Reames Rd Charlotte (28269) *(G-2699)*

Redrum Press... 866 374-7881
414 S 5th Ave Wilmington (28401) *(G-12897)*

Redtail Group LLC... 828 539-4700
2131 Us 70 Hwy Unit C Swannanoa (28778) *(G-11876)*

Redtruc LLC.. 704 968-7888
5131 Gorham Dr Charlotte (28226) *(G-2700)*

Redux Beverages LLC... 951 304-1144
2318 Oakhurst Trl Hillsborough (27278) *(G-6876)*

Redy Mix of Carolinas Inc.................................... 704 888-2224
364 Browns Hill Rd Locust (28097) *(G-7900)*

Reeb Millwork Corporation................................... 336 751-4650
346 Bethel Church Rd Mocksville (27028) *(G-8387)*

Reeder Pallet Company Inc................................... 336 879-3095
435 Reeder Rd Seagrove (27341) *(G-11279)*

Reedy Chem Foam Spclty Addtves, Charlotte *Also Called: Reedy International Corp (G-2701)*

Reedy International Corp (PA)............................... 980 819-6930
9301 Forsyth Park Dr Ste A Charlotte (28273) *(G-2701)*

Reel Solutions Inc.. 910 947-3117
1341 Red Branch Rd Carthage (28327) *(G-1279)*

Reel-Scout Inc... 704 348-1484
1900 Abbott St Ste 100 Charlotte (28203) *(G-2702)*

Reel-Tex Inc.. 704 868-4419
4905 Sparrow Dairy Rd Gastonia (28056) *(G-5133)*

Reese Sign Service, Goldsboro *Also Called: Reese Sign Service Inc (G-5239)*

Reese Sign Service Inc... 919 580-0705
3271 Us Highway 117 N Goldsboro (27530) *(G-5239)*

Refractory Construction, Salisbury *Also Called: Virginia Carolina Refr Inc (G-11133)*

Refresco Beverages US Inc................................... 252 234-0493
4843 International Blvd Wilson (27893) *(G-13020)*

Refresco Beverages US Inc................................... 252 234-0493
1805 Purina Cir S Wilson (27893) *(G-13021)*

Refresco Wilson, Wilson *Also Called: Refresco Beverages US Inc (G-13020)*

Regal Rexnord Corporation................................... 800 825-6544
701 Carrier Dr Charlotte (28216) *(G-2703)*

Regency Fibers LLC.. 828 459-7645
2788 S Oxford St Claremont (28610) *(G-3119)*

Regimental Flag & T Shirts.................................. 919 496-2888
29 Secession Ln Louisburg (27549) *(G-7925)*

Reginald DWayne Dillard....................................... 980 254-5505
13026 Planters Row Dr Charlotte (28278) *(G-2704)*

Region 3 Tasc Services, High Point *Also Called: High Point Enterprise Inc (G-6650)*

Rego, Burlington *Also Called: Engineered Controls Intl LLC (G-1088)*

Regulator Marine Inc.. 252 482-3837
187 Peanut Dr Edenton (27932) *(G-4371)*

Rehab Solutions Inc... 800 273-3418
3029 Senna Dr Matthews (28105) *(G-8144)*

Reich LLC.. 828 651-9019
140 Vista Blvd Arden (28704) *(G-303)*

Reichhold Holdings Us Inc.................................... 919 990-7500
1035 Swabia Ct Durham (27703) *(G-4210)*

Reichhold Liquidation, Inc., Durham *Also Called: Liquidating Reichhold Inc (G-4106)*

Relentless Wldg & Fabrication............................... 336 402-3749
903 Londonderry Dr High Point (27265) *(G-6755)*

Reliable Bedding Company.................................... 336 883-0648
7147 Mendenhall Rd Archdale (27263) *(G-241)*

Reliable Construction Co Inc............................ 704 289-1501
   100 N Sutherland Ave Ste A Monroe (28110) *(G-8550)*

Reliable Hauling and Grading, Concord *Also Called: Reliable Woodworks Inc (G-3431)*

Reliable Quilting Company............................ 336 886-7036
   414 South Rd High Point (27262) *(G-6756)*

Reliable Woodworks Inc............................ 704 785-9663
   2989 Old Salisbury Concord Rd Concord (28025) *(G-3431)*

Reliance Management Group Inc............................ 704 282-2255
   4910 Starcrest Dr Monroe (28110) *(G-8551)*

Reliance Packaging LLC............................ 910 944-2561
   175 Anderson St Aberdeen (28315) *(G-21)*

Relyus, Hope Mills *Also Called: William George Printing LLC (G-6928)*

Reman Technologies Inc............................ 704 921-2293
   11421 Reames Rd Charlotte (28269) *(G-2705)*

Remedios LLC............................ 203 453-6000
   1301 Westinghouse Blvd Ste I Charlotte (28273) *(G-2706)*

Remington 1816 Foundation............................ 866 686-7778
   1435 W Morehead St Ste 120 Charlotte (28208) *(G-2707)*

Remington Arms Company LLC............................ 800 544-8892
   870 Remington Dr Madison (27025) *(G-7998)*

Remington Arms Company LLC............................ 800 544-8892
   870 Remington Dr Madison (27025) *(G-7999)*

Remodeez LLC............................ 704 428-9050
   1920 Abbott St Ste 303 Charlotte (28203) *(G-2708)*

Rempac LLC............................ 910 737-6557
   2005 Starlite Dr Lumberton (28358) *(G-7969)*

Renaissance Fiber LLC............................ 860 857-5987
   500 W 5th St Ste 400 Winston Salem (27101) *(G-13317)*

Renaissance Innovations LLC............................ 774 901-4642
   2534 Whilden Dr Durham (27713) *(G-4211)*

RENAISSANCE INNOVATIONS, LLC, Durham *Also Called: Renaissance Innovations LLC (G-4211)*

Renascence Inc............................ 252 355-1636
   3185 Moseley Dr Greenville (27858) *(G-6018)*

Renew Life Cleansing Co, Durham *Also Called: Renew Life Formulas LLC (G-4212)*

Renew Life Formulas LLC (HQ)............................ 727 450-1061
   210 W Pettigrew St Durham (27701) *(G-4212)*

Renew Recycling LLC............................ 919 550-8012
   440 S Tech Park Ln Clayton (27520) *(G-3168)*

Renewable Power Producers LLC............................ 704 844-8990
   10600 Nations Ford Rd # 150 Charlotte (28273) *(G-2709)*

Renewble Enrgy Intgrtion Group............................ 704 596-6186
   9115 Old Statesville Rd Ste A Charlotte (28269) *(G-2710)*

Renewco-Meadow Branch LLC............................ 404 584-3552
   1609 Heritage Commerce Ct Wake Forest (27587) *(G-12293)*

Renfro Brands, Mount Airy *Also Called: Renfro LLC (G-9170)*

Renfro LLC............................ 336 786-3000
   304 Willow St Mount Airy (27030) *(G-9168)*

Renfro LLC............................ 336 719-8290
   801 W Lebanon St Mount Airy (27030) *(G-9169)*

Renfro LLC (HQ)............................ 336 719-8000
   661 Linville Rd Mount Airy (27030) *(G-9170)*

Renfro Mexico Holdings LLC............................ 336 786-3501
   661 Linville Rd Mount Airy (27030) *(G-9171)*

Rennasentient Inc............................ 919 233-7710
   301 Ashville Ave Cary (27518) *(G-1435)*

Renner Usa Corp............................ 704 527-9261
   651 Michael Wylie Dr Charlotte (28217) *(G-2711)*

Renner Wood Companies............................ 704 527-9261
   651 Michael Wylie Dr Charlotte (28217) *(G-2712)*

Renwood Mills, Newton *Also Called: Renwood Mills LLC (G-9490)*

Renwood Mills LLC............................ 828 465-0302
   11 N Brady Ave Newton (28658) *(G-9490)*

Repair Services, Mills River *Also Called: Western Crlina TI Mold Corp In (G-8324)*

Repi LLC............................ 704 648-0252
   2825 Repi Ct Dallas (28034) *(G-3685)*

Resco Products Inc............................ 336 299-1441
   3600 W Wendover Ave Greensboro (27407) *(G-5782)*

Resco Products Inc............................ 336 299-1441
   3600 W Wendover Ave Greensboro (27407) *(G-5783)*

Research Triangle Software Inc............................ 919 233-8796
   109 Lochview Dr Cary (27518) *(G-1436)*

Research Trngle Edtrial Sltons............................ 919 808-2719
   9 Amador Pl Durham (27712) *(G-4213)*

Reservoir Group LLC............................ 610 764-0269
   9219 Heritage Woods Pl Charlotte (28269) *(G-2713)*

Resident Culture Brewing LLC............................ 704 333-1862
   2101 Central Ave Charlotte (28205) *(G-2714)*

Residential/Commercial Cnstr, Polkton *Also Called: AMP Agency (G-9812)*

Resideo LLC............................ 704 525-8899
   800 Clanton Rd Ste F Charlotte (28217) *(G-2715)*

Resideo LLC............................ 336 668-3644
   4500 Green Point Dr Ste 103 Greensboro (27409) *(G-5784)*

Resideo LLC............................ 919 872-5556
   2741 Noblin Rd Ste 101 Raleigh (27604) *(G-10441)*

Resinall Corp............................ 252 585-1445
   302 Water St Severn (27877) *(G-11299)*

Resinart East Inc............................ 828 687-0215
   201 Old Airport Rd Fletcher (28732) *(G-4763)*

Resolute Elevator LLC............................ 919 903-0189
   2309 Airpark Rd Burlington (27215) *(G-1145)*

Resource Recovery Company, Hickory *Also Called: Poppe Inc (G-6415)*

Restaurant Furniture Inc............................ 828 459-9992
   2688 E Us Highway 70 Claremont (28610) *(G-3120)*

Retail, Charlotte *Also Called: Live It Boutique LLC (G-2427)*

Retail Installation Svcs LLC............................ 336 818-1333
   142 Lexi Dr Millers Creek (28651) *(G-8307)*

Retail Market Place............................ 984 201-1948
   950 W Market St Smithfield (27577) *(G-11463)*

Retrofix Screws LLC............................ 980 432-8412
   710 Mitchell Ave Salisbury (28144) *(G-11111)*

Retroject Inc............................ 919 619-3042
   1125 Pinehurst Dr Chapel Hill (27517) *(G-1567)*

Reuben James Auto Electric............................ 910 980-1056
   7386 N West St Falcon (28342) *(G-4521)*

Reuel, Goldsboro *Also Called: Pcore (G-5235)*

Reuel Inc............................ 919 734-0460
   200 W Dewey St Goldsboro (27530) *(G-5240)*

Revels Turf and Tractor LLC (PA)............................ 919 552-5697
   2217 N Main St Fuquay Varina (27526) *(G-4896)*

Revi Technical Wear, Greensboro *Also Called: Eatumup Lure Company Inc (G-5511)*

Revloc Reclamation Service Inc............................ 704 625-4900
   13024 Ballantyne Corporate Pl Ste 700 Charlotte (28277) *(G-2716)*

Revlon Inc............................ 919 603-2782
   1501 Williamsboro St Oxford (27565) *(G-9628)*

Revlon Inc............................ 919 603-2000
   1501 Williamsboro St Oxford (27565) *(G-9629)*

Revlon Accounts Payable, Oxford *Also Called: Revlon Inc (G-9628)*

Revlon Consumer Products Corp............................ 919 603-2000
   1501 Williamsboro St Oxford (27565) *(G-9630)*

Revmax Performance LLC............................ 877 780-4334
   4400 Westinghouse Blvd 2 Charlotte (28273) *(G-2717)*

Revolution Pd LLC............................ 919 949-0241
   379 White Smith Rd Pittsboro (27312) *(G-9788)*

Revoultion Oil Inc............................ 704 577-2546
   291 Cayuga Dr Mooresville (28117) *(G-8758)*

Revware Inc............................ 919 790-0000
   1645 Old Louisburg Rd Raleigh (27604) *(G-10442)*

Rex Oil Company, Thomasville *Also Called: Petroliance LLC (G-12059)*

Rexam Beauty and Closures Inc............................ 704 551-1500
   4201 Congress St Ste 340 Charlotte (28209) *(G-2718)*

Rexam Cosmetic Packaging, Charlotte *Also Called: Rexam Beauty and Closures Inc (G-2718)*

Reyes Prdctos Mxcnos Reyes LLC............................ 704 777-5805
   2905 Benjamin Hill Cir Raleigh (27610) *(G-10443)*

Reynaers Inc............................ 480 272-9688
   9347 D Ducks Ln Charlotte (28273) *(G-2719)*

Reynolda Mfg Solutions Inc............................ 336 699-4204
   1200 Flint Hill Rd East Bend (27018) *(G-4325)*

Reynolda Mfg Solutions Inc............................ 336 699-4204
   1200 Flint Hill Rd East Bend (27018) *(G-4326)*

Reynolds & Reynolds, Charlotte *Also Called: Reynolds and Reynolds Company (G-2721)*

Reynolds Advanced Mtls Inc............................ 704 357-0600
   10725a John Price Rd Charlotte (28273) *(G-2720)*

(G-0000) Company's Geographic Section entry number

Reynolds American Inc (HQ)................................ 336 741-2000
401 N Main St Winston Salem (27101) *(G-13318)*

Reynolds and Reynolds Company.......................... 321 287-3939
6000 Monroe Rd Ste 340 Charlotte (28212) *(G-2721)*

Reynolds Consumer Products, Huntersville *Also Called: Reynolds Consumer Products Inc*
(G-7042)

Reynolds Consumer Products Inc............................ 704 371-5550
14201 Meacham Farm Dr Huntersville (28078) *(G-7042)*

Rf Das Systems Inc.. 980 279-2388
8230 Trail View Dr Charlotte (28226) *(G-2722)*

Rf Micro Devices Inc.. 336 664-1233
7628 Thorndike Rd Greensboro (27409) *(G-5785)*

RFH Tactical Mobility Inc....................................... 910 916-0284
748 Dotmond Rd Milton (27305) *(G-8326)*

Rfhic US Corporation.. 919 677-8780
920 Morrisville Pkwy Morrisville (27560) *(G-9043)*

Rfmd, Greensboro *Also Called: Rf Micro Devices Inc (G-5785)*

Rfmd LLC... 336 664-1233
7628 Thorndike Rd Greensboro (27409) *(G-5786)*

Rfmd Infrstrcture PDT Group In............................. 704 996-2997
327 Hillsborough St Raleigh (27603) *(G-10444)*

Rfr, Oxford *Also Called: Rfr Metal Fabrication Inc (G-9631)*

Rfr Metal Fabrication Inc...................................... 919 693-1354
3204 Knotts Grove Rd Oxford (27565) *(G-9631)*

Rfsprotech LLC.. 704 845-2785
1320 Industrial Dr Matthews (28105) *(G-8145)*

RG Convergence Tech LLC................................... 336 953-2796
1325 N Church St B Burlington (27217) *(G-1146)*

Rga Enterprises Inc (PA)...................................... 704 398-0487
4001 Performance Rd Charlotte (28214) *(G-2723)*

Rgees LLC.. 828 708-7178
170 Bradley Branch Rd Ste 6&7 Arden (28704) *(G-304)*

Rhd Service LLC... 919 297-1600
1001 Winstead Dr Ste 1 Cary (27513) *(G-1437)*

Rheem Manufacturing Company............................. 336 495-6800
4744 Island Ford Rd Randleman (27317) *(G-10658)*

Rheem Sales Company, Randleman *Also Called: Rheem Manufacturing Company (G-10658)*

Rhf Investments Inc (PA)...................................... 828 326-8350
401 11th St Nw Hickory (28601) *(G-6428)*

Rhf Investments Inc.. 828 632-7070
165 Matheson Park Ave Taylorsville (28681) *(G-11973)*

Rhino Networks LLC.. 855 462-9434
1025 Brevard Rd Ste 8 Asheville (28806) *(G-590)*

Rhino Times, Greensboro *Also Called: Snap Publications LLC (G-5819)*

Rhinoceros Times.. 336 763-4170
216 W Market St Greensboro (27401) *(G-5787)*

Rhinoshelf.com, Angier *Also Called: Innovative Design Tech LLC (G-121)*

Rhyno Enterprises.. 252 291-6700
709 Tarboro St Sw Wilson (27893) *(G-13022)*

Ribbon Enterprises Inc.. 828 264-6444
1640 Old 421 S Boone (28607) *(G-941)*

Ribometrix.. 919 744-9634
701 W Main St Ste 200 Durham (27701) *(G-4214)*

Rice S Glass Company Inc.................................... 919 967-9214
107 Lloyd St Carrboro (27510) *(G-1272)*

Ricewrap Foods Corporation................................. 919 614-1179
300 Business Park Dr Butner (27509) *(G-1206)*

Richa Inc.. 704 944-0230
231 E Tremont Ave Charlotte (28203) *(G-2724)*

Richa Inc (PA)... 704 331-9744
800 N College St Charlotte (28206) *(G-2725)*

RICHA GRAPHICS, Charlotte *Also Called: Richa Inc (G-2725)*

Richard C Jones... 919 853-2096
7823 Nc 561 Hwy Louisburg (27549) *(G-7926)*

Richard Chldress Racg Entps In............................ 336 731-3334
236 Industrial Dr Welcome (27374) *(G-12513)*

Richard Chldress Racg Entps In (PA)...................... 336 731-3334
425 Industrial Dr Welcome (27374) *(G-12514)*

Richard D Stewart.. 919 284-2295
201 W 2nd St Kenly (27542) *(G-7236)*

Richard E Page.. 704 988-7090
8500 Andrew Carnegie Blvd Charlotte (28262) *(G-2726)*

Richard Lewis Von.. 910 628-9292
1928 Indian Swamp Rd Orrum (28369) *(G-9605)*

Richard Scarborough Boat Works........................... 252 473-3646
Ficket Lump Rd Wanchese (27981) *(G-12346)*

Richard Schwartz... 914 358-4518
322 S College Rd Wilmington (28403) *(G-12898)*

Richard Shew.. 828 781-3294
6202 N Nc 16 Hwy Conover (28613) *(G-3554)*

Richard West Co Inc.. 252 793-4440
1174 Us Highway 64 W Plymouth (27962) *(G-9807)*

Richard Wilcox.. 919 218-5907
1400 Struble Cir Willow Spring (27592) *(G-12681)*

Richards Welding and Repr Inc.............................. 828 396-8705
3080 Dry Ponds Rd Granite Falls (28630) *(G-5320)*

Richards Wldg Met Fbrction LLC............................ 919 626-0134
7324 Siemens Rd Wendell (27591) *(G-12544)*

Richardson Racing Products Inc............................. 704 784-2602
1028 Central Dr Nw Unit C Concord (28027) *(G-3432)*

Richmond County Gmrs Inc.................................. 910 461-0260
109 George Dawkins Dr Hamlet (28345) *(G-6062)*

Richmond Dental and Medical, Charlotte *Also Called: Barnhardt Manufacturing Company*
(G-1755)

Richmond Investment (PA).................................... 910 410-8200
611 Airport Rd Rockingham (28379) *(G-10787)*

Richmond Millwork LLC....................................... 910 331-1009
707 Haywood St Rockingham (28379) *(G-10788)*

Richmond Observer LLP....................................... 910 817-3169
505 Rockingham Rd Rockingham (28379) *(G-10789)*

Richmond Specialty Yarns LLC.............................. 910 652-5554
1748 N Us Highway 220 Ellerbe (28338) *(G-4462)*

Richmond Steel Welding...................................... 910 582-4026
895 Airport Rd Rockingham (28379) *(G-10790)*

Rickys Welding Inc... 252 336-4437
899 S Sandy Hook Rd Shiloh (27974) *(G-11394)*

Ricura Corporation... 704 875-0366
11515 Vanstory Dr Ste 110 Huntersville (28078) *(G-7043)*

Riddle & Company LLC.. 336 229-1856
1214 Turrentine St Burlington (27215) *(G-1147)*

Riddle Home & Gift, Burlington *Also Called: Riddle & Company LLC (G-1147)*

Riddley Metals Inc.. 704 435-8829
639 Washburn Switch Rd Shelby (28150) *(G-11373)*

Riddley Retail Fixtures Inc.................................... 704 435-8829
119 Bess Rd Kings Mountain (28086) *(G-7382)*

Ride Best LLC.. 252 489-2959
24267 Hwy 12 Rodanthe (27968) *(G-10888)*

Ridge Line Homes, Franklin *Also Called: Elite Mountain Business LLC (G-4827)*

Ridgewood Management LLC................................. 336 644-0006
808 James Doak Pkwy Greensboro (27455) *(G-5788)*

Rifled Air Conditioning Inc................................... 800 627-1707
2810 Earlham Pl High Point (27263) *(G-6757)*

Rigem Right... 252 726-9508
173 Hankison Dr Newport (28570) *(G-9443)*

Rikki Tikki Tees.. 828 454-0515
546 Hazelwood Ave Waynesville (28786) *(G-12470)*

Riley Defense Inc... 704 507-9224
25 18th St Nw Hickory (28601) *(G-6429)*

Riley Technologies LLC.. 704 663-6319
170 Overhill Dr Mooresville (28117) *(G-8759)*

Rinehart Racing Inc.. 828 350-7653
40 Cane Creek Industrial Park Rd Fletcher (28732) *(G-4764)*

Ringadoc, Raleigh *Also Called: Practice Fusion Inc (G-10386)*

Rings True LLC.. 919 265-7600
200 N Greensboro St Ste B9 Carrboro (27510) *(G-1273)*

Rinker Materials... 704 455-1100
2268 Speedrail Dr Harrisburg (28075) *(G-6116)*

Rinker Materials... 704 827-8175
1725 Drywall Dr Mount Holly (28120) *(G-9244)*

Ripari Automotive LLC... 585 267-0228
2910 Patishall Ln Charlotte (28214) *(G-2727)*

Ripoff Holsters, Wilmington *Also Called: Arma Co LLC (G-12709)*

Ripstop By Roll LLC.. 877 525-7210
1023 S Miami Blvd Durham (27703) *(G-4215)*

Riptide Publishing LLC................................908 295-4517
  128 Academy St Burnsville (28714) *(G-1190)*

Rise Over Run Inc (PA)................................303 819-1566
  2131 Us 70 Hwy Unit C Swannanoa (28778) *(G-11877)*

Ritas One Inc..919 650-2415
  208 Dowington Ln Cary (27519) *(G-1438)*

Ritch Face Veneer Company...........................336 883-4184
  1330 Lincoln Dr High Point (27260) *(G-6758)*

Ritchie Foam Company Inc.............................704 663-2533
  214 E Waterlynn Rd Mooresville (28117) *(G-8760)*

Rite Instant Printing Inc...............................336 768-5061
  1011 Burke St Winston Salem (27101) *(G-13319)*

Riteway Express Inc of NC.............................828 966-4822
  1106 Rosman Hwy Brevard (28712) *(G-981)*

Riverbed Technology LLC..............................415 247-8800
  5425 Page Rd Ste 200 Durham (27703) *(G-4216)*

Riverbend Frameworks, Claremont *Also Called: Carolina House Furniture Inc (G-3090)*

Riverside, Wilmington *Also Called: Riverside Adventure Company (G-12899)*

Riverside Adventure Company.........................910 457-4944
  5 S Water St Wilmington (28401) *(G-12899)*

Riverside Brick & Supply, Winston Salem *Also Called: Pine Hall Brick Co Inc (G-13296)*

Riverside Mattress Co Inc.............................910 483-0461
  225 Dunn Rd Fayetteville (28312) *(G-4662)*

Riverview Cabinet & Supply Inc.......................336 228-1486
  1111 N Riverview Dr Burlington (27217) *(G-1148)*

Riverwood Casual, Lexington *Also Called: Riverwood Inc (G-7735)*

Riverwood Inc..336 956-3034
  632 Dixon St Lexington (27292) *(G-7735)*

Rivet Solutions Inc....................................888 487-3849
  308 Wheatberry Hill Dr Matthews (28104) *(G-8191)*

Rk Enterprises LLC....................................910 481-0777
  121 N Racepath St Fayetteville (28301) *(G-4663)*

RLM/Universal Packaging Inc..........................336 644-6161
  8607 Cedar Hollow Rd Greensboro (27455) *(G-5789)*

Rls Commercial Interiors Inc..........................919 365-4086
  7212 Siemens Rd Wendell (27591) *(G-12545)*

Rm Liquidation Inc (PA)...............................828 274-7996
  81 Thompson St Asheville (28803) *(G-591)*

RMC Advanced Technologies Inc......................704 325-7100
  1400 Burris Rd Newton (28658) *(G-9491)*

Rmg Leather Usa LLC.................................828 466-5489
  1226 Fedex Dr Sw Conover (28613) *(G-3555)*

RNS International Inc..................................704 329-0444
  5001 Sirus Ln Charlotte (28208) *(G-2728)*

Road Infrstrcture Inv Hldngs I (HQ)..................336 475-6600
  115 Todd Ct Thomasville (27360) *(G-12066)*

Road King Trailers Inc................................828 670-8012
  2240 Smoky Park Hwy Candler (28715) *(G-1232)*

Roadactive Suspension Inc...........................704 523-2646
  2705 Whitehall Park Dr Charlotte (28273) *(G-2729)*

Roadmaster Truck Company, Grifton *Also Called: Roadmster Trck Conversions Inc (G-6038)*

Roadmster Trck Conversions Inc.....................252 412-3980
  6482 N Highland Blvd Grifton (28530) *(G-6038)*

Roadrnner Mtrcycle Turing Trvl.......................336 765-7780
  2245 Lewisville Clemmons Rd Ste D Clemmons (27012) *(G-3202)*

Roadsafe Traffic Systems Inc.........................919 772-9401
  913 Finch Ave High Point (27263) *(G-6759)*

Roanoke Chowan Ready Mix Inc.......................252 332-7995
  108 Williford Rd Ahoskie (27910) *(G-52)*

Roanoke Truss Inc....................................252 537-0012
  711 E 15th St Roanoke Rapids (27870) *(G-10742)*

Roanoke Valley Steel Corp............................252 538-4137
  101 Kennametal Dr Weldon (27890) *(G-12526)*

Roaring Lion Publishing...............................828 350-1454
  47 Stone River Dr Asheville (28804) *(G-592)*

Robbinsville Cstm Molding Inc........................828 479-2317
  1450 Old Hwy 129 Robbinsville (28771) *(G-10761)*

Robbinsville Plant, Charlotte *Also Called: CCL Label Inc (G-1877)*

Robco Manufacturing Inc..............................252 438-7399
  651 Bearpond Rd Henderson (27536) *(G-6175)*

Robert Abbey Inc (PA).................................828 322-3480
  3166 Main Ave Se Hickory (28602) *(G-6430)*

Robert Bergelin Company (PA).........................828 437-6409
  120 S Sterling St Morganton (28655) *(G-8892)*

Robert Blake..704 720-9341
  1522 La Forest Ln Concord (28027) *(G-3433)*

Robert Bosch Tool Corporation........................252 551-7512
  310 Staton Rd Greenville (27834) *(G-6019)*

Robert Bosch Tool Corporation........................704 735-7464
  1980 Indian Creek Rd Lincolnton (28092) *(G-7851)*

Robert Citrano...910 264-7746
  1710 Dawson St Ste C Wilmington (28403) *(G-12900)*

Robert D Starr..336 697-0286
  1211 Youngs Mill Rd Greensboro (27405) *(G-5790)*

Robert H Wager Company Inc.........................336 969-6909
  570 Montroyal Rd Rural Hall (27045) *(G-10966)*

Robert Hamms LLC....................................704 605-8057
  3028 Proverbs Ct Monroe (28110) *(G-8552)*

Robert L Rich Tmber Hrvstg Inc.......................910 529-7321
  360 Rich Rd Garland (28441) *(G-4910)*

Robert Laskowski.....................................203 732-0846
  232 Stony Branch Rd New Bern (28562) *(G-9391)*

Robert Raper Welding Inc.............................252 399-0598
  5326 Evansdale Rd Wilson (27893) *(G-13023)*

Robert S Concrete Service Inc........................910 391-3973
  508 Lamon St Fayetteville (28301) *(G-4664)*

Robert St Clair Co Inc................................919 847-8611
  7701 Leesville Rd Raleigh (27613) *(G-10445)*

Roberts Company, The, Winterville *Also Called: Jbr Properties of Greenville Inc (G-13417)*

Roberts Family Enterprises LLP........................919 785-3111
  7101 Ebenezer Church Rd Raleigh (27612) *(G-10446)*

Roberts Polypro Inc...................................704 588-1794
  5416 Wyoming Ave Charlotte (28273) *(G-2730)*

Robertson-Ceco II Corporation (DH)...................281 897-7788
  5020 Weston Pkwy Cary (27513) *(G-1439)*

Robesonion, Mooresville *Also Called: Champion Media LLC (G-8637)*

Robetex Inc (PA)......................................910 671-8787
  2504 Fayetteville Rd Lumberton (28358) *(G-7970)*

Robins Lane Press, Lewisville *Also Called: Gryphon House Inc (G-7651)*

Robinson & Son Machine Inc..........................910 592-4779
  446 Faison Hwy Clinton (28328) *(G-3240)*

Robinson Hosiery Mill Inc.............................828 874-2228
  113 Robinson St Se Valdese (28690) *(G-12199)*

Robinsons Welding Service............................336 622-3150
  3465 Staley Store Rd Liberty (27298) *(G-7777)*

Robix America Inc.....................................336 668-9555
  7104 Cessna Dr Greensboro (27409) *(G-5791)*

Robling Medical, Youngsville *Also Called: Robling Medical LLC (G-13482)*

Robling Medical LLC...................................919 570-9605
  90 Weathers Ct Youngsville (27596) *(G-13482)*

Roblon US Inc...828 396-2121
  3908 Hickory Blvd Granite Falls (28630) *(G-5321)*

ROC-N-Soc Inc.......................................828 452-1736
  151 Kelly Park Ln Waynesville (28786) *(G-12471)*

Rocas Welding LLC....................................252 290-2233
  923 E Trinity Ave Ste F Durham (27704) *(G-4217)*

Rochling Engineering, Dallas *Also Called: Roechling Indus Gastonia LP (G-3686)*

Rock Industrial Services Inc...........................910 652-6267
  157 S Railroad St Ellerbe (28338) *(G-4463)*

Rock of Ages, Salisbury *Also Called: Carolina Quarries Inc (G-11028)*

Rock-Tenn Converting, Winston Salem *Also Called: Westrock Converting LLC (G-13392)*

Rock-Weld Industries Inc..............................336 375-6862
  3515 Associate Dr Greensboro (27405) *(G-5792)*

Rocket Installation LLC................................704 657-9492
  329 Talley St Troutman (28166) *(G-12148)*

Rocketprint Software LLC..............................336 267-7272
  211 Hb Newsome Pl Denton (27239) *(G-3759)*

Rockfish Creek Winery LLC............................910 729-0648
  1709 Arabia Rd Raeford (28376) *(G-9851)*

Rockgeist LLC...518 461-2009
  2000 Riverside Dr Ste 33 Asheville (28804) *(G-593)*

Rockingham Plant, Rockingham *Also Called: Perdue Farms Incorporated (G-10785)*

Rocktenn In-Store Solutions Inc.......................828 245-9871
  376 Pine St Forest City (28043) *(G-4796)*

(G-0000) Company's Geographic Section entry number

Rockwell Automation Inc.................................. 919 804-0200
113 Edinburgh South Dr Ste 200 Cary (27511) *(G-1440)*

Rockwell Automation Inc.................................. 704 665-6000
9401 Southern Pine Blvd Ste E Charlotte (28273) *(G-2731)*

Rockwell Automation Inc.................................. 828 652-0074
510 Rockwell Dr Marion (28752) *(G-8063)*

Rockwell Automation Inc.................................. 828 645-4235
70 Reems Creek Rd Weaverville (28787) *(G-12501)*

Rockwell Collins, Charlotte *Also Called: B/E Aerospace Inc (G-1731)*

Rockwell Collins Inc....................................... 336 744-3288
190 Oak Plaza Blvd Winston Salem (27105) *(G-13320)*

Rockwell Collins Inc....................................... 336 776-3444
2599 Empire Dr Winston Salem (27103) *(G-13321)*

Rockwell Collins Inc....................................... 336 744-1097
1455 Fairchild Rd Winston Salem (27105) *(G-13322)*

Rockwood Lithium... 704 739-2501
348 Holiday Inn Dr Kings Mountain (28086) *(G-7383)*

Rocky Mount Awning & Tent Co........................ 252 442-0184
602 N Church St Rocky Mount (27804) *(G-10866)*

Rocky Mount Cord Company............................. 252 977-9130
381 N Grace St Rocky Mount (27804) *(G-10867)*

Rocky Mount Electric Motor LLC....................... 252 446-1510
3870 S Church St Rocky Mount (27803) *(G-10868)*

Rocky Mount Mill LLC..................................... 919 890-6000
2619 Western Blvd Raleigh (27606) *(G-10447)*

Rocky River Vineyards LLC.............................. 704 781-5035
11685 Reed Mine Rd Midland (28107) *(G-8295)*

Roctool Inc... 888 364-6321
5900 Westover Dr #15609 Sanford (27330) *(G-11224)*

Rod Jahner... 919 435-7580
157 Crooked Gulley Cir Sunset Beach (28468) *(G-11852)*

Rodeco Company.. 919 775-7149
5811 Elwin Buchanan Dr Sanford (27330) *(G-11225)*

Roderick Mch Erectors Wldg Inc....................... 910 343-0381
2701 Blue Clay Rd Wilmington (28405) *(G-12901)*

Rodney S Cstm Cut Sign Co Inc........................ 919 362-9669
600 Irving Pkwy Holly Springs (27540) *(G-6911)*

Rodney Tyler... 336 629-0951
530 Albemarle Rd Asheboro (27203) *(G-391)*

Rodney's Sign Company, Holly Springs *Also Called: Rodney S Cstm Cut Sign Co Inc (G-6911)*

Roechling Indus Gastonia LP (DH)..................... 704 922-7814
903 Gastonia Technology Pkwy Dallas (28034) *(G-3686)*

Roehrig Engineering Inc.................................. 336 956-3800
603 Woodland Dr Greensboro (27408) *(G-5793)*

Roger D Thomas... 919 258-3148
8313 Hillcrest Farm Rd Sanford (27330) *(G-11226)*

Rogers Express Lube LLC................................ 828 648-7772
167 Pisgah Dr Canton (28716) *(G-1255)*

Rogers Group Inc... 828 657-9331
1385 Ferry Rd Mooresboro (28114) *(G-8585)*

Rogers Knitting Inc....................................... 336 789-4155
181 Beasley Rd Mount Airy (27030) *(G-9172)*

Rogers Manufacturing Company (PA)................. 910 259-9898
505 W Wilmington St Burgaw (28425) *(G-1030)*

Rogers Portable Buildings, Burgaw *Also Called: Rogers Manufacturing Company (G-1030)*

Rogers Screenprinting EMB Inc (PA).................. 910 628-1983
10306 Nc Highway 41 S Fairmont (28340) *(G-4504)*

Rogers Screenprinting EMB Inc........................ 910 738-6208
1988 N Roberts Ave Lumberton (28358) *(G-7971)*

Roi Industries Group Inc................................. 919 788-7728
700a E Club Blvd Durham (27704) *(G-4218)*

Roi Machinery & Automation, Durham *Also Called: Roi Industries Group Inc (G-4218)*

Rol-Mol Inc... 828 328-1210
2205 Us Highway 70 Sw Hickory (28602) *(G-6431)*

Rolf Koerner, Charlotte *Also Called: Rolf Koerner LLC (G-2732)*

Rolf Koerner LLC.. 704 714-8866
514 Springbrook Rd Ste B Charlotte (28217) *(G-2732)*

Roll-Tech, Hickory *Also Called: Roll-Tech Molding Products LLC (G-6432)*

Roll-Tech Molding Products LLC........................ 828 431-4515
243 Performance Dr Se Hickory (28602) *(G-6432)*

Rollease Acmeda Inc..................................... 800 552-5100
375 Workman St Sw Conover (28613) *(G-3556)*

Rollease Acmeda Dist Ctr, Conover *Also Called: Rollease Acmeda Inc (G-3556)*

Rollforming LLC... 336 468-4317
4708 Hunting Creek Church Rd Hamptonville (27020) *(G-6091)*

Rolling Umbrellas Inc.................................... 828 754-4200
1932 Valway Rd Lenoir (28645) *(G-7637)*

Rolls Enterprises Inc..................................... 919 545-9401
2277 Otis Johnson Rd Pittsboro (27312) *(G-9789)*

Romac Industries Inc.................................... 704 922-9595
114 Eason Rd Dallas (28034) *(G-3687)*

Romac Industries Inc.................................... 704 915-3317
400 E Fields St Dallas (28034) *(G-3688)*

Romanos Pizza.. 704 782-5020
349 Copperfield Blvd Ne Ste A Concord (28025) *(G-3434)*

Romanos Pizza Italian Rest, Concord *Also Called: Romanos Pizza (G-3434)*

Romeo Six LLC.. 919 589-7150
260 Premier Dr Holly Springs (27540) *(G-6912)*

Romoco, Rocky Mount *Also Called: Rocky Mount Cord Company (G-10867)*

Ronak LLC.. 781 589-1973
2302 Skye Ln Cary (27518) *(G-1441)*

Rondol Cordon Logging Inc............................. 252 944-9220
101 Raccoon Run Washington (27889) *(G-12411)*

Ronnie Andrews... 336 921-4017
5077 Beaver Creek Rd Boomer (28606) *(G-893)*

Ronnie Andrews Logging, Boomer *Also Called: Ronnie Andrews (G-893)*

Ronnie Boyds Logging LLC.............................. 336 613-0229
153 Nance St Eden (27288) *(G-4355)*

Ronnie Garrett Logging.................................. 828 894-8413
4625 Landrum Rd Columbus (28722) *(G-3304)*

Ronnie L Poole.. 336 657-3956
14596 Nc Highway 18 N Ennice (28623) *(G-4489)*

Ronny D Phelps... 828 206-6339
12 E Lawson Rd Hot Springs (28743) *(G-6934)*

Roobrik Inc.. 919 667-7750
301 S Elm St Ste 421 Greensboro (27401) *(G-5794)*

Roofing Supply.. 919 779-6223
3609 Jones Sausage Rd Garner (27529) *(G-4959)*

Roofing Tools and Eqp Inc (PA)........................ 252 291-1800
3710 Weaver Rd Wilson (27893) *(G-13024)*

Roosterfish Media LLC................................... 980 722-7454
129 Ashford Hollow Ln Mooresville (28117) *(G-8761)*

Root Spring Scraper Co.................................. 269 382-2025
1 York Pl Pinehurst (28374) *(G-9702)*

Roots Food, Fairview *Also Called: Roots Organic Gourmet LLC (G-4510)*

Roots Organic Gourmet LLC............................ 828 232-2828
125 Winding Rdg Fairview (28730) *(G-4510)*

Roots Run Deep LLC..................................... 919 909-9117
90 Oak Leaf Trl Youngsville (27596) *(G-13483)*

Rose Ice & Coal Company............................... 910 762-2464
1202 Market St Wilmington (28401) *(G-12902)*

Rose Media Inc.. 919 736-1154
200 N Cottonwood Dr Goldsboro (27530) *(G-5241)*

Rose Reprographics....................................... 336 222-0727
2030 S Church St Burlington (27215) *(G-1149)*

Rose Welding & Crane Service I........................ 252 796-9171
1060 S Gum Neck Rd Columbia (27925) *(G-3296)*

Rositas Tortillas Inc..................................... 910 944-0577
1317 N Sandhills Blvd Aberdeen (28315) *(G-22)*

Ross Phelps Logging Co Inc............................ 252 356-2560
1548 Wakelon Rd Colerain (27924) *(G-3272)*

Ross Skid Products Inc.................................. 828 652-7450
7 Landis Rd Marion (28752) *(G-8064)*

Ross Woodworking Inc................................... 704 629-4551
125 L E Perry Rd Bessemer City (28016) *(G-832)*

Ross Woodworking Inc (PA)............................. 704 629-4551
1004 Dameron Rd Bessemer City (28016) *(G-833)*

Rosti Cary NC, Cary *Also Called: Spnc Associates Inc (G-1466)*

Rostra Powertrain Controls, Laurinburg *Also Called: Marmon Holdings Inc (G-7508)*

Rostra Precision Controls Inc........................... 910 291-2502
3056 Nc Hwy 5 Aberdeen (28315) *(G-23)*

ALPHABETIC

Rotary Club Statesville..............704 872-6851
318 N Center St Statesville (28677) *(G-11759)*

Roto-Plate Inc..............336 226-4965
2025 Cesnna Dr Burlington (27215) *(G-1150)*

Rotork-Fairchild Indus Pdts Co..............336 659-3400
3920 Westpoint Blvd Winston Salem (27103) *(G-13323)*

Rotron Incorporated..............336 449-3400
1210 Nc Highway 61 Whitsett (27377) *(G-12619)*

Round Peak Vineyards LLC..............336 352-5595
765 Round Peak Church Rd Mount Airy (27030) *(G-9173)*

Roush & Yates Racing Engs LLC..............704 799-6216
112 Byers Creek Rd Mooresville (28117) *(G-8762)*

Roush & Yates Racing Engs LLC (PA)..............704 799-6216
297 Rolling Hill Rd Mooresville (28117) *(G-8763)*

Roush Yates Mfg Solutions, Mooresville *Also Called: Roush & Yates Racing Engs LLC* *(G-8762)*

Roush's Racing, Concord *Also Called: Rp Motor Sports Inc* *(G-3435)*

Router Bit Service Company Inc..............336 431-5535
7018 Tomball Rd High Point (27263) *(G-6760)*

Routh Sign Service..............336 272-0895
318 Creek Ridge Rd Ste B Greensboro (27406) *(G-5795)*

Rovertym..............704 635-7305
3308 Westwood Industrial Dr Ste E Monroe (28110) *(G-8553)*

Rowan Custom Cabinets Inc..............704 855-4778
2515 S Us 29 Hwy China Grove (28023) *(G-3079)*

Rowan Precision Machining Inc..............704 279-6092
707 N Salisbury Ave Granite Quarry (28072) *(G-5327)*

Rowdy Manufacturing, Mooresville *Also Called: Rowdy Manufacturing LLC (G-8764)*

Rowdy Manufacturing LLC..............704 662-0000
161 Byers Creek Rd Mooresville (28117) *(G-8764)*

Rowes..............828 241-2609
7546 Long Island Rd Catawba (28609) *(G-1513)*

Rowland Woodworking Inc..............336 887-0700
111 E Market Center Dr High Point (27260) *(G-6761)*

Rowmark LLC..............252 448-9900
182 Industrial Park Dr Trenton (28585) *(G-12110)*

Roxboro Broom Works, Roxboro *Also Called: Newell Novelty Co Inc (G-10931)*

Roxboro Ewp Mill, Roxboro *Also Called: Boise Cascade Wood Pdts LLC (G-10920)*

Roxboro Welding..............336 364-2307
3735 Cates Mill Rd Roxboro (27574) *(G-10943)*

Roy Bridgmohan..............804 426-9652
596 Industry Dr Henderson (27537) *(G-6176)*

Roy Dunn..............919 963-3700
101 Dunn St Four Oaks (27524) *(G-4815)*

Royal Appliance Manufacturing, Charlotte *Also Called: TTI Floor Care North Amer Inc (G-2951)*

Royal Baths Manufacturing Co..............704 837-1701
4525 Reagan Dr # A Charlotte (28206) *(G-2733)*

Royal Blunts Connections Inc..............919 961-4910
4900 Thornton Rd Ste 109 Raleigh (27616) *(G-10448)*

Royal Carolina Corporation..............336 292-8845
7305 Old Friendly Rd Greensboro (27410) *(G-5796)*

Royal Colony Furniture Inc..............336 472-8833
20 Carolina Ave Thomasville (27360) *(G-12067)*

Royal Cup Inc..............704 597-5756
3010 Hutchison Mcdonald Rd Ste F Charlotte (28269) *(G-2734)*

Royal Faires Inc (PA)..............704 896-5555
16445 Poplar Tent Rd Huntersville (28078) *(G-7044)*

Royal Hosiery Company Inc (PA)..............828 496-2200
10 N Summit Ave Granite Falls (28630) *(G-5322)*

Royal Manufacturing, Charlotte *Also Called: Royal Baths Manufacturing Co (G-2733)*

Royal Oak Stairs Inc..............919 855-8988
3201 Wellington Ct Ste 104 Raleigh (27615) *(G-10449)*

Royal Park Uniforms Inc..............336 562-3345
14139 Nc Highway 86 S Prospect Hill (27314) *(G-9829)*

Royal Textile Mills Inc..............336 694-4121
929 Firetower Rd Yanceyville (27379) *(G-13460)*

Royal Textile Products Sw LLC..............602 276-4598
2918 Caldwell Ridge Pkwy Charlotte (28213) *(G-2735)*

Royal Welding LLC..............704 750-9353
413 N Polk St Unit H Pineville (28134) *(G-9750)*

Royal Wire Products Inc..............704 596-2110
7500 Grier Rd Charlotte (28213) *(G-2736)*

Royale Comfort Seating Inc..............828 352-9021
140 Alspaugh Dam Rd Taylorsville (28681) *(G-11974)*

Royale Komfort Bedding Inc..............828 632-5631
2320 All Healing Springs Rd Taylorsville (28681) *(G-11975)*

Royalkind LLC..............252 355-7484
2131 Jubilee Ln Winterville (28590) *(G-13422)*

Royall Development Co Inc..............336 889-2569
325 Kettering Rd High Point (27263) *(G-6762)*

Royce Apparel Inc..............704 933-6000
408 Long Meadow Dr Salisbury (28147) *(G-11112)*

Royce Company, Knightdale *Also Called: Len Corporation (G-7452)*

Royce Company LLC..............910 395-0046
6500 Windmill Way Wilmington (28405) *(G-12903)*

Royce Too LLC (HQ)..............212 356-1627
3330 Healy Dr Ste 200 Winston Salem (27103) *(G-13324)*

Rp Fletcher Machine Co Inc..............336 249-6101
4305 E Us Highway 64 Lexington (27292) *(G-7736)*

Rp Motor Sports Inc..............704 720-4200
4202 Roush Pl Nw Concord (28027) *(G-3435)*

RPM Indstrial Ctings Group Inc (HQ)..............828 261-0325
2220 Us Highway 70 Se Ste 100 Hickory (28602) *(G-6433)*

RPM Indstrial Ctings Group Inc..............828 261-0325
22 S Center St Hickory (28602) *(G-6434)*

RPM Indstrial Ctings Group Inc..............828 261-0325
22 S Center St Hickory (28602) *(G-6435)*

RPM Indstrial Ctings Group Inc..............828 728-8266
3190 Hickory Blvd Hudson (28638) *(G-6957)*

RPM Installions Inc..............704 907-0868
19843 Henderson Rd Cornelius (28031) *(G-3624)*

RPM Plastics, Conover *Also Called: RPM Plastics Inc (G-3557)*

RPM Plastics Inc..............704 871-0518
2041 S Mclin Creek Rd Conover (28613) *(G-3557)*

RPM Plastics LLC..............704 871-0518
933 Meacham Rd Statesville (28677) *(G-11760)*

RPM Products Inc..............704 871-0518
2301 Speedball Rd Statesville (28677) *(G-11761)*

Rpoc Inc (PA)..............910 371-3184
5900b Oleander Dr Wilmington (28403) *(G-12904)*

Rpp Acquisition LLC..............919 248-9001
131 Johnston Pkwy Kenly (27542) *(G-7237)*

Rq Industries Inc..............704 701-1071
19 Franklin Ave Nw Concord (28025) *(G-3436)*

RR Donnelley, Durham *Also Called: R R Donnelley & Sons Company (G-4205)*

Rrd Packaging Solutions, Greensboro *Also Called: PBM Graphics Inc (G-5737)*

Rs Industries Inc..............704 289-2734
17776 Kings Point Dr Cornelius (28031) *(G-3625)*

Rsa Security LLC..............704 847-4725
250 N Trade St Matthews (28105) *(G-8146)*

RSC Bio Solutions LLC (HQ)..............800 661-3558
2318 Arty Ave Charlotte (28208) *(G-2737)*

RSC Chemical Solutions LLC..............704 821-7643
600 Radiator Rd Indian Trail (28079) *(G-7098)*

RSI Home Products Inc..............828 428-6300
838 Lincoln County Pkwy Lincolnton (28092) *(G-7852)*

RSI Leasing Inc NS Tbt..............704 587-9300
2820 Nevada Blvd Charlotte (28273) *(G-2738)*

RSR Fitness Inc..............919 255-1233
1207 N New Hope Rd Raleigh (27610) *(G-10450)*

Rssbus Inc..............919 969-7675
490 Sun Forest Way Chapel Hill (27517) *(G-1568)*

Rstack Solutions LLC..............980 337-1295
3540 Toringdon Way Ste 200 Charlotte (28277) *(G-2739)*

Rt Cardiac Systems Inc..............954 908-1074
5420 Deer Forest Trl Raleigh (27614) *(G-10451)*

Rtt Machine & Welding Svc Inc..............919 269-6863
12671 W Nc 97 Zebulon (27597) *(G-13522)*

Rtx Corporation..............704 423-7000
2730 W Tyvola Rd Charlotte (28217) *(G-2740)*

Rubber Mill, Liberty *Also Called: Rubber Mill Inc (G-7778)*

(G-0000) Company's Geographic Section entry number

Rubber Mill Inc... 336 622-1680
9897 Old Liberty Rd Liberty (27298) **(G-7778)**

Rubbermaid, Huntersville *Also Called: Rubbermaid Commercial Pdts LLC* **(G-7045)**

Rubbermaid, Huntersville *Also Called: Rubbermaid Incorporated* **(G-7046)**

Rubbermaid, Huntersville *Also Called: Rubbermaid Incorporated* **(G-7047)**

Rubbermaid Commercial Pdts LLC (DH)..................540 667-8700
8900 N Pointe Executive Park Dr Huntersville (28078) **(G-7045)**

Rubbermaid Incorporated.. 704 987-4339
8936 N Pointe Executive Park Dr Huntersville (28078) **(G-7046)**

Rubbermaid Incorporated.. 888 859-8294
16905 Northcross Dr Ste 120 Huntersville (28078) **(G-7047)**

Rucker Intrgrted Logistics LLC................................ 704 352-2018
15519 Rathangan Dr Charlotte (28273) **(G-2741)**

Ruckus Wireless LLC.. 919 677-0571
101 Stamford Dr Cary (27513) **(G-1442)**

Ruckus Wireless LLC.. 503 495-9240
3642 E Us Highway 70 Claremont (28610) **(G-3121)**

Ruddick Operating Company LLC............................ 704 372-5404
301 S Tryon St Ste 1800 Charlotte (28282) **(G-2742)**

Rudisill Frame Shop Inc... 828 464-7020
780 Buchanan Pl Newton (28658) **(G-9492)**

Rufco Inc (PA).. 919 829-1332
5101 Unicon Dr Wake Forest (27587) **(G-12294)**

Rufus N Ivie III... 704 482-2559
4007 Hillview Dr Shelby (28152) **(G-11374)**

Rug & Home, Asheville *Also Called: Rug & Home Inc* **(G-594)**

Rug & Home Inc... 828 785-4480
5 Rocky Ridge Rd Asheville (28806) **(G-594)**

Rugby Acquisition LLC... 336 993-8686
637 Graves St Kernersville (27284) **(G-7297)**

Rugged Metal Designs Inc..................................... 336 352-5150
1004 Red Hill Creek Rd Dobson (27017) **(G-3824)**

Ruhl Inc.. 910 497-3172
26 Mockingbird Ln Spring Lake (28390) **(G-11562)**

Ruhl Tech Engineering, Spring Lake *Also Called: Ruhl Inc* **(G-11562)**

Rulmeca Corporation... 910 794-9294
3200 Corporate Dr Ste D Wilmington (28405) **(G-12905)**

Rusco Fixture, Norwood *Also Called: Rusco Fixture Company Inc* **(G-9559)**

Rusco Fixture Company Inc..................................... 704 474-3184
11635 Nc 138 Hwy Norwood (28128) **(G-9559)**

Rush Masonry Management LLC.............................. 910 787-9100
234 Clayton James Rd Jacksonville (28540) **(G-7142)**

Rushfurnitiure.com, High Point *Also Called: Vrush Industries Inc* **(G-6829)**

Ruskin Inc.. 828 324-6500
1189 27th Street Dr Se Hickory (28602) **(G-6436)**

Ruskin LLC... 919 583-5444
166 Nc 581 Hwy S Goldsboro (27530) **(G-5242)**

Russ Knits Inc... 910 974-4114
520 E Main St Candor (27229) **(G-1241)**

Russ Simmons... 910 686-1656
414 Biscayne Dr Wilmington (28411) **(G-12906)**

Russell Finex Inc.. 704 588-9808
625 Eagleton Downs Dr Pineville (28134) **(G-9751)**

Russell Loudermilk Logging................................... 828 632-4968
330 Dee Loudermelk Ln Taylorsville (28681) **(G-11976)**

Russell Printing Inc.. 404 366-0552
2589 Deep Creek Church Rd Burlington (27217) **(G-1151)**

Russell Standard, Greensboro *Also Called: Russell Standard Nc LLC* **(G-5798)**

Russell Standard Corporation................................. 336 292-6875
1124 S Holden Rd Greensboro (27407) **(G-5797)**

Russell Standard Nc LLC....................................... 336 292-6875
1124 S Holden Rd Greensboro (27407) **(G-5798)**

Russell T Bundy Associates Inc.............................. 704 523-6132
3400 Pelton St Charlotte (28217) **(G-2743)**

Russell-Fshion Foot Hsy Mlls I............................... 336 299-0741
3804 Buncombe Dr Greensboro (27407) **(G-5799)**

Russo Mike DBA Lrger Than Lf I............................. 760 942-0289
1109 Yardarm Dr Oriental (28571) **(G-9602)**

Rust-Oleum, Mooresville *Also Called: Rust-Oleum Corporation* **(G-8765)**

Rust-Oleum Corporation... 704 662-7730
157 Cedar Pointe Dr Ste A Mooresville (28117) **(G-8765)**

Rust911 Inc.. 607 425-2882
1206 8th Ave Sw Hickory (28602) **(G-6437)**

Ruth Arnold Graphics & Signs................................ 910 793-9087
102 Portwatch Way Ste C Wilmington (28412) **(G-12907)**

Ruth Hicks Enterprise Inc...................................... 704 469-4741
9417 Marvin School Rd Waxhaw (28173) **(G-12439)**

Rutland Fire Clay Company.................................... 802 775-5519
1430 Environ Way Chapel Hill (27517) **(G-1569)**

Rutland Group Inc.. 704 553-0046
13827 Carowinds Blvd Ste A Charlotte (28273) **(G-2744)**

Rutland Group Inc (HQ)... 704 553-0046
10021 Rodney St Pineville (28134) **(G-9752)**

Rutland Holdings LLC (PA)..................................... 704 553-0046
10021 Rodney St Pineville (28134) **(G-9753)**

Rutland Plastic Technologies, Pineville *Also Called: Rutland Holdings LLC* **(G-9753)**

Rv One Superstores Charlotte, Concord *Also Called: Axle Holdings LLC* **(G-3316)**

Rvb Systems Group Inc... 919 362-5211
5504 Quails Call Ct Garner (27529) **(G-4960)**

Rwm Casters, Gastonia *Also Called: Lsrwm Corp* **(G-5079)**

Rwm Casters, Greensboro *Also Called: Staunton Capital Inc* **(G-5838)**

Rx Textiles, Matthews *Also Called: Paceline Inc* **(G-8140)**

Ryder Integrated Logistics Inc................................ 336 227-1130
1603 Anthony Rd Burlington (27215) **(G-1152)**

Ryder Integrated Logistics Inc................................ 336 227-1130
1361 Anthony Rd Burlington (27215) **(G-1153)**

Ryjak Enterprises LLC.. 910 638-0716
1050 N May St Southern Pines (28387) **(G-11507)**

S & A Cherokee LLC... 919 674-6020
301 Cascade Pointe Ln Ste 101 Cary (27513) **(G-1443)**

S & A Cherokee Publishing, Cary *Also Called: S & A Cherokee LLC* **(G-1443)**

S & D Coffee Inc (HQ).. 704 782-3121
300 Concord Pkwy S Concord (28027) **(G-3437)**

S & D Coffee and Tea, Concord *Also Called: S & D Coffee Inc* **(G-3437)**

S & D Machine & Tool Inc....................................... 919 479-8433
1404 Old Oxford Rd Durham (27704) **(G-4219)**

S & K Logging Inc.. 252 794-2045
1408 S King St Windsor (27983) **(G-13057)**

S & L Creations Inc.. 704 824-1930
120 E 1st St Lowell (28098) **(G-7934)**

S & L Sawmill Inc.. 704 483-3264
3044 N Nc 16 Business Hwy Denver (28037) **(G-3803)**

S & S Repair Service Inc.. 252 756-5989
1196 Pocosin Rd Winterville (28590) **(G-13423)**

S & S Samples Inc.. 336 472-0402
880 Whitehart School Rd Thomasville (27360) **(G-12068)**

S & S Trawl Shop Inc.. 910 842-9197
896 Stanbury Rd Sw Supply (28462) **(G-11858)**

S & W Metal Works Inc.. 252 641-0912
1813 Anaconda Rd Tarboro (27886) **(G-11940)**

S & W Ready Mix Con Co LLC.................................. 910 592-2191
1395 Turkey Hwy Clinton (28328) **(G-3241)**

S & W Ready Mix Con Co LLC (DH)........................... 910 592-1733
217 Lisbon St Clinton (28329) **(G-3242)**

S & W Ready Mix Con Co LLC.................................. 910 645-6868
1460 Mercer Mill Rd Elizabethtown (28337) **(G-4432)**

S & W Ready Mix Con Co LLC.................................. 910 864-0939
1309 S Reilly Rd Fayetteville (28314) **(G-4665)**

S & W Ready Mix Con Co LLC.................................. 919 751-1796
624 Powell Rd Goldsboro (27534) **(G-5243)**

S & W Ready Mix Con Co LLC.................................. 910 329-1201
307 W Ocean Rd Holly Ridge (28445) **(G-6891)**

S & W Ready Mix Con Co LLC.................................. 252 527-1881
604 E New Bern Rd Kinston (28504) **(G-7426)**

S & W Ready Mix Con Co LLC.................................. 252 726-2566
5161 Business Dr Morehead City (28557) **(G-8842)**

S & W Ready Mix Con Co LLC.................................. 252 633-2115
1300 Us Highway 17 N New Bern (28560) **(G-9392)**

S & W Ready Mix Con Co LLC.................................. 910 496-3232
545 W Manchester Rd Spring Lake (28390) **(G-11563)**

S & W Ready Mix Con Co LLC.................................. 910 285-2191
768 Sw Railroad St Wallace (28466) **(G-12323)**

S & W Ready Mix Concrete, Elizabethtown *Also Called: S & W Ready Mix Con Co LLC* *(G-4432)*

S & W Ready Mix Concrete, Holly Ridge *Also Called: S & W Ready Mix Con Co LLC* *(G-6891)*

S and R Sheet Metal Inc..336 476-1069
521 Broad St Thomasville (27360) *(G-12069)*

S Banner Cabinets Incorporated................................828 733-2031
299 Watauga St Newland (28657) *(G-9434)*

S C C, Reidsville *Also Called: Smith-Carolina Corporation* *(G-10698)*

S C I A Inc...919 387-7000
204 Dundalk Way Cary (27511) *(G-1444)*

S Chamblee Incorporated...919 833-7561
1300 Hodges St Raleigh (27604) *(G-10452)*

S Choice Baker Inc...919 556-1188
343 S White St Ste B Wake Forest (27587) *(G-12295)*

S Dorsett Upholstery Inc...336 472-7076
406 Aycock St Thomasville (27360) *(G-12070)*

S Duff Fabricating Inc...910 298-3060
228 N Nc 41 Hwy Beulaville (28518) *(G-845)*

S E Lab Group Inc..707 253-8852
5565 Icard Ridge Rd Hickory (28601) *(G-6438)*

S Eudy Cabinet Shop Inc..704 888-4454
12303 Renee Ford Rd Stanfield (28163) *(G-11608)*

S F M, Lexington *Also Called: Special Fab & Machine Inc* *(G-7745)*

S Foil Incorporated...704 455-5134
2283 Nc Highway 49 S Harrisburg (28075) *(G-6117)*

S G L Carbon, Morganton *Also Called: Sgl Carbon LLC* *(G-8895)*

S H Woodworking..336 463-2885
1316 Travis Rd Yadkinville (27055) *(G-13450)*

S K Bowling Inc..252 243-1803
1068 Fieldsboro Rd Walstonburg (27888) *(G-12335)*

S Kivett Inc..910 592-0161
711 Southwest Blvd Clinton (28328) *(G-3243)*

S Loflin Enterprises Inc...704 633-1159
133 S Main St Salisbury (28144) *(G-11113)*

S Oakley Machine Shop Inc.......................................336 599-6105
126 W Gordon St Roxboro (27573) *(G-10944)*

S P Co Inc..919 848-3599
200 W Millbrook Rd Raleigh (27609) *(G-10453)*

S P X, Charlotte *Also Called: Marley Company LLC* *(G-2459)*

S Ruppe Inc...828 287-4936
137 Taylor St Rutherfordton (28139) *(G-10992)*

S S C 7516-7, Asheboro *Also Called: Southern States Coop Inc* *(G-397)*

S S C 7579 7, Creedmoor *Also Called: Southern States Coop Inc* *(G-3655)*

S S C 7793-7, Mount Airy *Also Called: Southern States Coop Inc* *(G-9178)*

S S C 7795-7, Mount Olive *Also Called: Southern States Coop Inc* *(G-9259)*

S S C 7883-7, Roxboro *Also Called: Southern States Coop Inc* *(G-10945)*

S S C 7912-7, Statesville *Also Called: Southern States Coop Inc* *(G-11772)*

S S C Oxford Svc, Oxford *Also Called: Southern States Coop Inc* *(G-9636)*

S S I, Brevard *Also Called: Smith Systems Inc* *(G-982)*

S S I, Charlotte *Also Called: Schaefer Systems International Inc* *(G-2763)*

S Strickland Diesel Svc Inc.......................................252 291-6999
5451 Old Raleigh Rd Wilson (27893) *(G-13025)*

S T I, Winston Salem *Also Called: Salem Technologies Inc* *(G-13327)*

S T Wooten Corporation..919 363-3141
51 Red Cedar Way Apex (27523) *(G-192)*

S T Wooten Corporation..919 562-1851
255 Material Rd Franklinton (27525) *(G-4853)*

S T Wooten Corporation..919 772-7991
3625 Banks Rd Fuquay Varina (27526) *(G-4897)*

S T Wooten Corporation..252 393-2206
12200 Cleveland Rd Garner (27529) *(G-4961)*

S T Wooten Corporation..919 779-6089
925 E Garner Rd Garner (27529) *(G-4962)*

S T Wooten Corporation..919 779-7589
12204 Cleveland Rd Garner (27529) *(G-4963)*

S T Wooten Corporation..252 636-2568
245 Parker Rd New Bern (28562) *(G-9393)*

S T Wooten Corporation..919 965-9880
6401 Us Highway 70 E Princeton (27569) *(G-9826)*

S T Wooten Corporation..919 965-7176
6401 Us Highway 70 E Princeton (27569) *(G-9827)*

S T Wooten Corporation..919 783-5507
9001 Fortune Way Raleigh (27613) *(G-10454)*

S T Wooten Corporation..252 291-5165
6937 Capital Blvd Raleigh (27616) *(G-10455)*

S T Wooten Corporation..919 776-2736
966 Rocky Fork Church Rd Sanford (27332) *(G-11227)*

S T Wooten Corporation..910 762-1940
220 Sutton Lake Rd Wilmington (28401) *(G-12908)*

S T Wooten Corporation..252 291-5165
2710 Commerce Rd S Wilson (27893) *(G-13026)*

S T Wooten Corporation (PA).....................................252 291-5165
3801 Black Creek Rd Se Wilson (27894) *(G-13027)*

S Tri Inc..704 542-8186
10110 Johnston Rd Ste 12 Charlotte (28210) *(G-2745)*

S W G, Durham *Also Called: Smart Wires Inc* *(G-4239)*

S Y Shop Inc..704 545-7710
4475 Morris Park Dr Ste G Mint Hill (28227) *(G-8343)*

S Zaytoun Custom Cabinets Inc.................................252 638-8390
1206 Pollock St New Bern (28560) *(G-9394)*

S-L Snacks National LLC (DH)...................................704 554-1421
13024 Balntyn Corp Pl Charlotte (28277) *(G-2747)*

S-L Snacks Pa LLC...704 554-1421
13024 Balntyn Corp Pl Charlotte (28277) *(G-2748)*

S. T. Wooten, Wilson *Also Called: S T Wooten Corporation* *(G-13027)*

S&A Marketing Inc..704 376-0938
2526 S Tyron St Charlotte (28203) *(G-2746)*

S&F Products...714 412-1298
6112 N Deer Ridge Dr Holly Springs (27540) *(G-6913)*

Saab Barracuda LLC...910 814-3088
608 E Mcneill St Lillington (27546) *(G-7802)*

Sachs Peanuts LLC...910 647-4711
9323 Hwy 70 Clarkton (28433) *(G-3128)*

Sack-UPS Corporation..828 584-4579
1611 Jamestown Rd Morganton (28655) *(G-8893)*

Sackner Products Inc..704 380-6204
178 Orbit Rd Statesville (28677) *(G-11762)*

Saertex Multicom LP (DH)..704 946-9229
12200 Mount Holly Hntrsvlle Rd Huntersville (28078) *(G-7048)*

Saertex Multicom LP...704 946-9229
12200 Mount Holly Hntrsvlle Rd Ste A Huntersville (28078) *(G-7049)*

Saertex Usa LLC...704 464-5998
12200 Mount Holly Hntrsvlle Rd Huntersville (28078) *(G-7050)*

Saf-Holland Inc..336 310-4595
952 Kensal Green Dr Kernersville (27284) *(G-7298)*

Safe Air Systems Inc...336 674-0749
210 Labrador Dr Randleman (27317) *(G-10659)*

Safe Care Rx, Asheville *Also Called: King Bio Inc* *(G-530)*

Safe Fire Detection Inc...704 821-7920
5915 Stockbridge Dr Monroe (28110) *(G-8554)*

Safe Home Pro Inc...704 662-2299
18635 Starcreek Dr Ste B Cornelius (28031) *(G-3626)*

Safe Tire & Auto Services, Clinton *Also Called: Safe Tire & Autos LLC* *(G-3244)*

Safe Tire & Autos LLC...910 590-3101
1308 Hobbton Hwy Clinton (28328) *(G-3244)*

Safe Waze, Concord *Also Called: VH Industries Inc* *(G-3464)*

Safeguard America, Huntersville *Also Called: Combat Medical Systems LLC* *(G-6977)*

Safeguard Medical..855 428-6074
13359 Reese Blvd E Huntersville (28078) *(G-7051)*

Safeguard Medical Alarms Inc (PA)............................312 506-2900
13359 Reese Blvd E Huntersville (28078) *(G-7052)*

Safety & Security Intl Inc...336 285-8673
4270 Piedmont Pkwy Ste 102 Greensboro (27410) *(G-5800)*

Safewaze LLC..704 262-7893
225 Wilshire Ave Sw Concord (28025) *(G-3438)*

Saft America Inc...828 874-4111
313 Crescent St Ne Valdese (28690) *(G-12200)*

Sag Harbor Industries Inc...252 753-7175
3595 Mandarin Dr Farmville (27828) *(G-4539)*

Sage Mule...336 209-9183
608 Battleground Ave Greensboro (27401) *(G-5801)*

Sage Payroll Services, Charlotte *Also Called: Pai Services LLC* *(G-2605)*

Sailcraft Service, Oriental *Also Called: M & J Marine LLC (G-9601)*

Saint Benedict Press, LLC, Charlotte *Also Called: Good Will Catholic Media LLC (G-2226)*

Saint Paul Mountain Vineyards... 828 685-4002
588 Chestnut Gap Rd Hendersonville (28792) *(G-6239)*

Saint-Gobain Vetrotex Amer Inc.. 704 895-5906
8936 N Pointe Executive Park Dr Ste 165 Huntersville (28078) *(G-7053)*

Salazar Custom Framing LLC.. 919 349-0830
111 Raynor Sands Dr Dunn (28334) *(G-3867)*

Salem Baking Company, Winston Salem *Also Called: Dewey S Bakery Inc (G-13143)*

Salem Carpet Mills, Charlotte *Also Called: Shaw Industries Group Inc (G-2795)*

Salem Collection, The, Clemmons *Also Called: J R Craver & Associates Inc (G-3193)*

Salem One Inc.. 336 722-2886
1155 Distribution Ct Kernersville (27284) *(G-7299)*

Salem One Inc (PA)... 336 744-9990
5670 Shattalon Dr Winston Salem (27105) *(G-13325)*

Salem Printing, Winston Salem *Also Called: Salem One Inc (G-13325)*

Salem Professional Anesthesia.. 336 998-3396
128 Peachtree Ln Ste B Advance (27006) *(G-38)*

Salem Sports Inc (PA)... 336 722-2444
1519 S Martin Luther King Jr Dr Winston Salem (27107) *(G-13326)*

Salem Stone Quarry, Kernersville *Also Called: Marietta Martin Materials Inc (G-7284)*

Salem Technologies Inc.. 336 777-3652
2580 Salem Point Ct Winston Salem (27103) *(G-13327)*

Salem Woodworking Company.. 336 768-7443
4849 Kester Mill Rd Winston Salem (27103) *(G-13328)*

Salice, Charlotte *Also Called: Salice America Inc (G-2749)*

Salice America Inc (DH)... 704 841-7810
2123 Crown Centre Dr Charlotte (28227) *(G-2749)*

Salient Sciences, Hendersonville *Also Called: Digital Audio Corporation (G-6202)*

Salisbury Mtal Fabrication LLC.. 704 278-0785
565 Trexler Loop Salisbury (28144) *(G-11114)*

Salisbury Operations, Salisbury *Also Called: Teijin Automotive Tech Inc (G-11123)*

Salisbury Post, Salisbury *Also Called: Post Publishing Company (G-11103)*

Salon & Spa Design Services... 919 556-6380
7208 Ledford Grove Ln Wake Forest (27587) *(G-12296)*

Salon Couture.. 910 693-1611
180 Council Way Southern Pines (28387) *(G-11508)*

Salonexclusive Beauty LLC... 704 488-3909
3015 Kraus Glen Dr Charlotte (28214) *(G-2750)*

Salt Marsh Home, Jarvisburg *Also Called: Carolina Csual Otdoor Furn Inc (G-7185)*

Salt Water Lite, Jonesville *Also Called: Grandeur Manufacturing Inc (G-7197)*

Salt Wood Products Inc (PA).. 252 830-8875
3016 Jones Park Rd Greenville (27834) *(G-6020)*

Salt Wood Products 2, Greenville *Also Called: Salt Wood Products Inc (G-6020)*

Saltwater Signworks Inc.. 910 212-5020
3013 Hall Watters Dr Ste B Wilmington (28405) *(G-12909)*

Salty Turtle Beer Company... 910 803-2019
103 Triton Ln Surf City (28445) *(G-11863)*

Salubrent Phrma Solutions Corp... 301 980-7224
150 N Research Campus Dr Ste 3700 Kannapolis (28081) *(G-7219)*

Salud LLC.. 980 495-6612
3306 N Davidson St Charlotte (28205) *(G-2751)*

Saluda Mountain Products Inc... 828 696-2296
561 S Allen Rd Flat Rock (28731) *(G-4713)*

Saluda Yarn Co Inc... 828 749-2861
Greenville & Walnut Streets Saluda (28773) *(G-11140)*

Salute Industries Inc... 844 937-2588
105 Apache Dr Archdale (27263) *(G-242)*

Salvin Dental Specialties LLC... 704 442-5400
3450 Latrobe Dr Charlotte (28211) *(G-2752)*

Sam M Butler Inc... 704 364-8647
447 S Sharon Amity Rd Ste 125 Charlotte (28211) *(G-2753)*

Sam M Butler Inc... 910 276-2360
504 S King St Laurinburg (28352) *(G-7513)*

Sam M Butler Inc (PA)... 910 277-7456
17900 Dana Dr Laurinburg (28352) *(G-7514)*

Sam Software Corp.. 910 233-9924
103 Oxmoor Pl Wilmington (28403) *(G-12910)*

Samoa Corporation.. 828 645-2290
90 Monticello Rd Weaverville (28787) *(G-12502)*

Sample Group Inc (PA).. 828 658-9040
179 Merrimon Ave Ste 100 Weaverville (28787) *(G-12503)*

Sampletech Inc.. 336 882-1717
2101 W Green Dr High Point (27260) *(G-6763)*

Sampson Gin Company Inc.. 910 567-5111
5625 Newton Grove Hwy Newton Grove (28366) *(G-9517)*

Sams Motor Rewinding, Jacksonville *Also Called: Stone Cllins Mtr Rewinding Inc (G-7155)*

Samson Marketing, High Point *Also Called: Lacquer Craft Hospitality Inc (G-6689)*

Samsung Semiconductor Inc.. 919 380-8483
8000 Regency Pkwy Ste 585 Cary (27518) *(G-1445)*

Sanctuary Systems LLC.. 305 989-0953
701 S Wilson St Fremont (27830) *(G-4860)*

Sand Hammer Forging Inc... 919 554-9554
594 Bert Winston Rd Youngsville (27596) *(G-13484)*

Sanders Company Inc.. 252 338-3995
410 N Poindexter St Elizabeth City (27909) *(G-4408)*

Sanders Electric Motor Svc, Lenoir *Also Called: Sanders Electric Motor Svc Inc (G-7638)*

Sanders Electric Motor Svc Inc... 828 754-0513
285 Wildwood Rd Lenoir (28645) *(G-7638)*

Sanders Industries Inc.. 410 277-8565
559 Bow And Arrow Cv Waynesville (28785) *(G-12472)*

Sanders Ridge Inc (PA)... 336 677-1700
3200 Round Hill Rd Boonville (27011) *(G-958)*

Sanders Ridge Vinyrd & Winery, Boonville *Also Called: Sanders Ridge Inc (G-958)*

Sanderson Farms Inc... 252 208-0036
1536 Smithfield Way Kinston (28504) *(G-7427)*

Sanderson Farms Inc... 910 274-0220
2076 Nc Highway 20 W Saint Pauls (28384) *(G-11008)*

Sanderson Farms LLC... 910 887-2284
6762 Nc Highway 41 N Lumberton (28358) *(G-7972)*

Sanderson Farms LLC Proc Div.. 910 274-0220
2076 Nc Highway 20 W Saint Pauls (28384) *(G-11009)*

Sanderson Farms, Inc., Saint Pauls *Also Called: Sanderson Farms Inc (G-11008)*

Sandhills Cnsld Svcs Inc... 919 718-7909
200 E Williams St Sanford (27332) *(G-11228)*

Sandhlls Fbrctors Crane Svcs I.. 910 673-4573
6536 7 Lakes Vlg West End (27376) *(G-12558)*

Sandoz Inc.. 252 234-2222
4700 Sandoz Dr Wilson (27893) *(G-13028)*

Sandvik Inc (HQ)... 919 563-5008
1483 Dogwood Way Mebane (27302) *(G-8258)*

Sandvik Coromant, Mebane *Also Called: Sandvik Inc (G-8258)*

Sandvik McHning Sltons USA LLC... 919 563-5008
295 Maple Ln Mebane (27302) *(G-8259)*

Sandvik Tooling.. 919 563-5008
1483 Dogwood Way Mebane (27302) *(G-8260)*

Sandviper, Morganton *Also Called: Sack-UPS Corporation (G-8893)*

Sandy Land Peanut Company Inc.. 252 356-2679
229 Swains Mill Rd Harrellsville (27942) *(G-6104)*

Sandy Ridge Pork... 919 989-8878
2080 Wilsons Mills Rd Smithfield (27577) *(G-11464)*

Sanford Asphalt Plant, Sanford *Also Called: S T Wooten Corporation (G-11227)*

Sanford Coca-Cola Bottling Co.. 919 774-4111
1605 Hawkins Ave Sanford (27330) *(G-11229)*

Sanford S Atv Repair LLC.. 252 438-2730
887 Weldon Rd Henderson (27537) *(G-6177)*

Sanford Steel Corporation... 919 898-4799
375 Claude Hash Rd Goldston (27252) *(G-5258)*

Sanford Transition Company Inc... 919 775-4989
5108 Rex Mcleod Dr Sanford (27330) *(G-11230)*

Sanher Stucco & Lather Inc.. 704 241-8517
1101 Tyvola Rd Ste 110 Charlotte (28217) *(G-2754)*

Sanicap, Greensboro *Also Called: Public Health Corps Inc (G-5770)*

Sans, Gastonia *Also Called: Sans Technical Fibers LLC (G-5134)*

Sans Technical Fibers LLC... 704 869-8311
2020 Remount Rd Gastonia (28054) *(G-5134)*

Santa Fe Natural Tob Co Inc.. 919 690-1905
104 Enterprise Ct Oxford (27565) *(G-9632)*

Santa Fe Natural Tobacco, Winston Salem *Also Called: Santa Fe Natural Tobacco Company Foundation (G-13329)*

Santa Fe Natural Tobacco Company Foundation (DH)..................... 800 332-5595
401 N Main St Winston Salem (27101) *(G-13329)*

Santa Fe Ntural Tob Foundation.. 919 690-0880
3220 Knotts Grove Rd Oxford (27565) *(G-9633)*

Santarus Inc.. 919 862-1000
8510 Colonnade Center Dr Raleigh (27615) *(G-10456)*

Santronics, Sanford Also Called: Santronics Inc *(G-11231)*

Santronics Inc... 919 775-1223
3010 Lee Ave Sanford (27332) *(G-11231)*

Sapere Bio Inc... 919 260-2565
400 Park Offices Dr Ste 113 Durham (27709) *(G-4220)*

Sapona Manufacturing Co Inc... 336 873-8700
7039 Us Highway 220 S Asheboro (27205) *(G-392)*

Sapona Manufacturing Co Inc... 336 625-2161
159 North St Asheboro (27203) *(G-393)*

Sapona Manufacturing Co Inc (PA).. 336 625-2727
2478 Cedar Falls Rd Cedar Falls (27230) *(G-1515)*

Sapona Plastic LLC... 336 873-7201
798 Nc Highway 705 Seagrove (27341) *(G-11280)*

Sapona Plastics, Asheboro Also Called: Sapona Manufacturing Co Inc *(G-392)*

Sapona Plastics LLC... 336 873-8700
7039 Us Highway 220 S Asheboro (27205) *(G-394)*

Sapphire Tchncal Solutions LLC... 704 561-3100
10230 Rodney St Pineville (28134) *(G-9754)*

Saputo Cheese USA Inc... 910 569-7070
116 Industrial Park Biscoe (27209) *(G-856)*

Saputo Cheese USA Inc... 847 267-1100
131 Wright Way Troy (27371) *(G-12166)*

Sara Lee, Winston Salem Also Called: Hillshire Brands Company *(G-13198)*

Sara Lee Bakery Outlet, Tarboro Also Called: Bimbo Bakeries Usa Inc *(G-11923)*

Sara Lee Socks.. 336 789-6118
100 Woltz St Mount Airy (27030) *(G-9174)*

Sarahs Salsa Inc.. 336 508-3033
622 Myers Ln Greensboro (27408) *(G-5802)*

Sarda Technologies Inc... 919 757-6825
100 Capitola Dr Ste 308 Durham (27713) *(G-4221)*

Sare Granite & Tile.. 828 676-2666
128 Greene Rd Arden (28704) *(G-305)*

Sare Kitchen and Bed, Arden Also Called: Sare Granite & Tile *(G-305)*

Sarstedt Inc (PA).. 828 465-4000
1025 Saint James Church Rd Newton (28658) *(G-9493)*

Sas Federal LLC... 919 531-7505
100 Sas Campus Dr Cary (27513) *(G-1446)*

SAS Industries Inc... 631 727-1441
100 Corporate Dr Elizabeth City (27909) *(G-4409)*

Sas Institute Inc.. 954 494-8189
940 Nw Cary Pkwy Cary (27513) *(G-1447)*

Sas Institute Inc.. 919 677-8000
Cary (27512) *(G-1448)*

Sas Institute Inc.. 919 531-4153
820 Sas Campus Dr # C Cary (27513) *(G-1449)*

Sas Institute Inc (PA).. 919 677-8000
100 Sas Campus Dr Cary (27513) *(G-1450)*

Sas Institute Inc.. 704 831-5595
2200 Interstate North Dr Charlotte (28280) *(G-2755)*

Sas Institute Inc.. 704 331-3956
525 N Tryon St Ste 1600 Charlotte (28202) *(G-2756)*

Sash and Saber Castings... 919 870-5513
119 Dublin Rd Raleigh (27609) *(G-10457)*

Satco Truck Equipment Inc.. 919 383-5547
2007 Cheek Rd Durham (27704) *(G-4222)*

Satellite & Cellular, Waynesville Also Called: Sbg Digital Inc *(G-12473)*

Sato America, Charlotte Also Called: Sato America LLC *(G-2757)*

Sato America LLC (HQ)... 704 644-1650
14125 S Bridge Cir Charlotte (28273) *(G-2757)*

Sato Global Solutions Inc.. 954 261-3279
10350 Nations Ford Rd Ste A Charlotte (28273) *(G-2758)*

Satsuma, Durham Also Called: Satsuma Pharmaceuticals Inc *(G-4223)*

Satsuma Pharmaceuticals Inc.. 650 410-3200
4819 Emperor Blvd Ste 340 Durham (27703) *(G-4223)*

Sattler Corp.. 828 759-2100
447 Main St Hudson (28638) *(G-6958)*

Sauder Woodworking Co.. 704 799-6782
119 Magnolia Park Dr Mooresville (28117) *(G-8766)*

Saueressig North America Inc... 336 395-6200
2056 Willow Spring Ln Burlington (27215) *(G-1154)*

Sauers & Co Processed Veneers, Lexington Also Called: Sauers & Company Inc *(G-7737)*

Sauers & Company Inc.. 336 956-1200
363 Dixon St Lexington (27292) *(G-7737)*

Saunders Phrad, Gastonia Also Called: Modena Southern Dyeing Corp *(G-5100)*

Saunders Thread Company, Gastonia Also Called: J Charles Saunders Co Inc *(G-5070)*

Saundra D Hall.. 828 251-9859
237 S Liberty St Asheville (28801) *(G-595)*

Savannah Boats, Benson Also Called: Elite Marine LLC *(G-789)*

Savatech Corp... 386 760-0706
715 Railroad Ave Rutherfordton (28139) *(G-10993)*

Save-A-Load Inc... 704 650-4947
327 W Tremont Ave Ste A Charlotte (28203) *(G-2759)*

Savoye Solutions Inc.. 919 466-9784
5408 Von Hoyt Dr Raleigh (27613) *(G-10458)*

Savvy - Discountscom News Ltr.. 252 729-8691
195 Old Nassau Road Williston Smyrna (28579) *(G-11471)*

Sawmill Catering LLC... 910 769-7455
2528 Castle Hayne Rd Wilmington (28401) *(G-12911)*

Sawyers Sign Service Inc
608 Allred Mill Rd Mount Airy (27030) *(G-9175)*

Saybolt LP.. 910 763-8444
2321 Burnett Blvd Wilmington (28401) *(G-12912)*

Sbfi-North America Inc (DH).. 828 236-3993
123 Lyman St Asheville (28801) *(G-596)*

Sbg Digital Inc.. 828 476-0030
1562 S Main St Waynesville (28786) *(G-12473)*

Sbm Industries LLC.. 919 625-3672
3948 Browning Pl Ste 208 Raleigh (27609) *(G-10459)*

SBS Diversified Tech Inc... 336 884-5564
125 Wade St Jamestown (27282) *(G-7179)*

SC Johnson Prof USA Inc (DH)... 443 521-1606
2815 Coliseum Centre Dr Ste 600 Charlotte (28217) *(G-2760)*

SC Johnson Prof USA Inc.. 704 263-4240
2408 Doyle St Greensboro (27406) *(G-5803)*

SC Johnson Prof USA Inc.. 704 263-4240
1100 S Highway 27 Stanley (28164) *(G-11624)*

SC Johnson Professional... 704 263-4240
1100 S Hwy Stanley (28164) *(G-11625)*

Scalawag... 917 671-7240
318 Blackwell St Durham (27701) *(G-4224)*

Scaltrol Inc.. 678 990-0858
2010 Sterling Rd Charlotte (28209) *(G-2761)*

Scattered Wrenches Inc.. 919 480-1605
130 Annaron Ct Raleigh (27603) *(G-10460)*

Scenery Solutions, Erwin Also Called: Vegherb LLC *(G-4493)*

Scenic Scape, Lexington Also Called: Cunningham Brick Company *(G-7673)*

Scentair Technologies LLC (PA).. 704 504-2320
3810 Shutterfly Rd Ste 900 Charlotte (28217) *(G-2762)*

Schaefer Shelving, Charlotte Also Called: Schaefer Systems Intl Inc *(G-2764)*

Schaefer Systems International Inc (HQ)...................................... 704 944-4500
5032 Sirona Dr Ste 100 Charlotte (28273) *(G-2763)*

Schaefer Systems Intl Inc... 704 944-4500
10125 Westlake Dr Bldg 3 Charlotte (28273) *(G-2764)*

Schaefer Systems Intl Inc... 704 944-4550
10124 Westlake Dr Charlotte (28273) *(G-2765)*

Schafer Manufacturing Co LLC... 704 528-5321
551 N Main St Troutman (28166) *(G-12149)*

Schelling America Inc... 919 544-0430
301 Kitty Hawk Dr Morrisville (27560) *(G-9044)*

Schenck USA Corp.. 704 529-5300
1232 Commerce St Sw Conover (28613) *(G-3558)*

Schindler 9749, Clinton Also Called: Schindler Elevator Corporation *(G-3245)*

Schindler Elevator Corporation.. 910 590-5590
821 Industrial Dr Clinton (28328) *(G-3245)*

Schlaadt Plastics Limited, New Bern Also Called: Schlaadt USA Limited *(G-9395)*

Schlaadt USA Limited... 252 634-9494
198 Bosch Blvd New Bern (28562) *(G-9395)*

(G-0000) Company's Geographic Section entry number

Schleich USA Inc.. 704 659-7997
10000 Twin Lakes Pkwy Ste A Charlotte (28269) *(G-2766)*

Schletter NA Inc... 704 595-4200
11529 Wilmar Blvd Charlotte (28273) *(G-2767)*

Schmalz Inc.. 919 713-0880
5850 Oak Forest Dr Raleigh (27616) *(G-10461)*

Schneider Automation Inc..................................... 919 855-1262
2641 Sumner Blvd Raleigh (27616) *(G-10462)*

Schneider Electric, Knightdale *Also Called: Schneider Electric Usa Inc (G-7458)*

Schneider Electric, Morrisville *Also Called: Schneider Electric Usa Inc (G-9045)*

Schneider Electric Usa Inc.................................. 919 266-3671
Hwy 64 East Knightdale (27545) *(G-7458)*

Schneider Electric Usa Inc.................................. 888 778-2733
1101 Shiloh Glenn Dr # 100 Morrisville (27560) *(G-9045)*

Schneider Mills Inc (PA)..................................... 828 632-8181
1170 Nc Highway 16 N Taylorsville (28681) *(G-11977)*

Schoenberg Salt Co... 336 766-0600
4927 Home Rd Winston Salem (27106) *(G-13330)*

School Directorease LLC...................................... 240 206-6273
1213 W Morehead St Charlotte (28208) *(G-2768)*

Schooldude.com, Cary *Also Called: Brightly Software Inc (G-1315)*

Schunk, Morrisville *Also Called: Schunk Intec Inc (G-9046)*

Schunk Intec Inc... 919 572-2705
211 Kitty Hawk Dr Morrisville (27560) *(G-9046)*

Schutz Container Systems Inc.............................. 336 249-6816
138 Walser Rd Lexington (27295) *(G-7738)*

Schwartz Steel Service Inc................................... 704 865-9576
525 N Broad St Gastonia (28054) *(G-5135)*

Schweitzer-Mauduit Intl Inc.................................. 252 360-4666
2711 Commerce Rd S Wilson (27893) *(G-13029)*

SCI Sharp Controls Inc....................................... 704 394-1395
11331 Downs Rd Pineville (28134) *(G-9755)*

Science Applications Intl Corp.............................. 910 822-2100
4317 Ramsey St Ste 303 Fayetteville (28311) *(G-4666)*

Scienscope Products, Matthews *Also Called: M3 Products Com (G-8180)*

Scientigo Inc (PA).. 704 837-0500
6701 Carmel Rd Ste 205 Charlotte (28226) *(G-2769)*

Sciepharm LLC (PA)... 307 352-9559
2201 Candun Dr Ste 102 Apex (27523) *(G-193)*

Sciepharm LLC... 307 352-9559
5441 Lumley Rd Ste 103 Durham (27703) *(G-4225)*

Scinovia Corp... 703 957-0396
8801 Fast Park Dr Ste 301 Raleigh (27617) *(G-10463)*

Sciolytix Inc... 877 321-2451
2 Town Square Blvd Ste 330 Asheville (28803) *(G-597)*

Scion International US.. 919 570-9303
2520 Laurelford Ln Wake Forest (27587) *(G-12297)*

Scipher Medicine Corporation............................... 781 755-2063
4134 S Alston Ave Ste 104 Durham (27713) *(G-4226)*

Sciquest, Morrisville *Also Called: Biosupplynet Inc (G-8941)*

Sciquest Holdings Inc.. 919 659-2100
5151 Mccrimmon Pkwy Ste 216 Morrisville (27560) *(G-9047)*

Sciquest Parent LLC (PA).................................... 919 659-2100
3020 Carrington Mill Blvd Ste 100 Morrisville (27560) *(G-9048)*

Sciteck Diagnostics Inc....................................... 828 650-0409
317 Rutledge Rd Fletcher (28732) *(G-4765)*

Scivolutions Inc.. 704 853-0100
811 Floyd St Kings Mountain (28086) *(G-7384)*

Scoggins Industrial Inc.. 252 977-9222
4842 Us-301 Sharpsburg (27878) *(G-11307)*

Scootatrailertm.. 336 671-0444
1370 Payne Rd Lexington (27295) *(G-7739)*

Scorpio Acquisition Corp...................................... 704 697-5100
9335 Harris Corners Pkwy Ste 300 Charlotte (28269) *(G-2770)*

Scorpion Products Inc.. 336 813-3241
741 Spainhour Rd King (27021) *(G-7336)*

Scorpius, Morrisville *Also Called: Scorpius Holdings Inc (G-9049)*

Scorpius Holdings Inc (PA).................................. 919 240-7133
627 Davis Dr Ste 400 Morrisville (27560) *(G-9049)*

Scotland Neck Heart Pine Inc............................... 252 826-2755
25574 Hwy 125 Scotland Neck (27874) *(G-11265)*

Scott Automation, Charlotte *Also Called: Scott Systems Intl Inc (G-2771)*

Scott Bader Inc... 330 920-4410
212 Quality Dr Mocksville (27028) *(G-8388)*

Scott Safety, Monroe *Also Called: Scott Technologies Inc (G-8555)*

Scott Systems Intl Inc (DH).................................. 704 362-1115
2205 Beltway Blvd Ste 100 Charlotte (28214) *(G-2771)*

Scott Technologies Inc (HQ)................................. 704 291-8300
4320 Goldmine Rd Monroe (28110) *(G-8555)*

Scotts & Associates Inc....................................... 336 581-3141
1699 Hoyt Scott Rd Bear Creek (27207) *(G-718)*

Scotts Company LLC... 704 663-6088
319 Oates Rd Ste A Mooresville (28117) *(G-8767)*

SCR Controls Inc.. 704 821-6651
3479 Gribble Rd Matthews (28104) *(G-8192)*

SCR-Tech LLC.. 704 504-0191
11707 Steele Creek Rd Charlotte (28273) *(G-2772)*

SCR/ Melltronics, Matthews *Also Called: SCR Controls Inc (G-8192)*

Scrappy's Metal Recycling, Gastonia *Also Called: Paul Charles Englert (G-5118)*

Screen Master.. 252 492-8407
904 Buckhorn St Henderson (27536) *(G-6178)*

Screen Printers Unlimited LLC.............................. 336 667-8737
331 E Main St Ste 1 Wilkesboro (28697) *(G-12650)*

Screen Specialty Shop Inc.................................... 336 982-4135
8406 Nc Highway 163 West Jefferson (28694) *(G-12570)*

Scribbles Software LLC.. 704 390-5690
10617 Southern Loop Blvd Pineville (28134) *(G-9756)*

Scriptorium Pubg Svcs Inc................................... 919 481-2701
4220 Apex Hwy Ste 340 Durham (27713) *(G-4227)*

Scs Wood Products, Sanford *Also Called: Sandhills Cnsld Svcs Inc (G-11228)*

Sdfc LLC... 704 878-6645
3511 Essex Pointe Dr Monroe (28110) *(G-8556)*

Sdv Medical Services, Fletcher *Also Called: Sdv Office Systems LLC (G-4766)*

Sdv Office Systems LLC....................................... 844 968-9500
34 Redmond Dr Apt C Fletcher (28732) *(G-4766)*

SE Co-Brand Ventures LLC.................................. 704 598-9322
6801 Northlake Mall Dr Ste 188 Charlotte (28216) *(G-2773)*

Sea Food Express, Elizabeth City *Also Called: Quality Foods From Sea Inc (G-4405)*

Sea Mark Boats Inc... 910 675-1877
13991 Nc Hwy 210 Rocky Point (28457) *(G-10882)*

Sea Striker Inc... 252 247-4113
158 Little Nine Rd Morehead City (28557) *(G-8843)*

Sea Supreme Inc... 919 556-1188
343 S White St Ste B Wake Forest (27587) *(G-12298)*

Seabrook Ingredients, Edenton *Also Called: Universal Blanchers LLC (G-4372)*

Seacon Corp... 704 331-3920
525 N Tryon St Ste 1600 Charlotte (28202) *(G-2774)*

Seacon Corporation (PA)...................................... 704 333-6000
1917 John Crosland Jr Dr Charlotte (28208) *(G-2775)*

Seafarer LLC (PA)... 704 624-3200
220 E Main St Marshville (28103) *(G-8094)*

Seagate Technology LLC...................................... 910 821-8310
7211 Ogden Business Ln Ste 201 Wilmington (28411) *(G-12913)*

Seagoing Uniform, Marshville *Also Called: Seafarer LLC (G-8094)*

Seagrove Lumber LLC.. 910 428-9663
558 Little River Golf Dr Seagrove (27341) *(G-11281)*

Seal Innovation Inc... 919 302-7870
2520 Kenmore Dr Raleigh (27608) *(G-10464)*

Seal It Services Inc... 919 777-0374
3301 Industrial Dr Sanford (27332) *(G-11232)*

Seal Master, Madison *Also Called: Krebs Corporation (G-7989)*

Seal Master, Madison *Also Called: PMG SM Holdings LLC (G-7997)*

Seal Seasons Inc.. 919 245-3535
4426 S Miami Blvd Ste 105 Durham (27703) *(G-4228)*

Sealed Air, Charlotte *Also Called: Sealed Air Corporation (G-2776)*

Sealed Air Corporation (PA)................................. 980 221-3235
2415 Cascade Pointe Blvd Charlotte (28208) *(G-2776)*

Sealed Air Corporation.. 336 883-9184
2150 Brevard Rd High Point (27263) *(G-6764)*

Sealed Air Corporation.. 828 728-6610
2001 International Blvd Hudson (28638) *(G-6959)*

Sealed Air Corporation.. 828 726-2100
  2075 Valway Rd Lenoir (28645) *(G-7639)*

Sealed Air Corporation (us).. 201 791-7600
  2415 Cascade Pointe Blvd Charlotte (28208) *(G-2777)*

Sealed Air Intl Holdings LLC....................................... 980 221-3235
  2415 Cascade Pointe Blvd Charlotte (28208) *(G-2778)*

Sealed Air LLC.. 980 430-7000
  2415 Cascade Pointe Blvd Charlotte (28208) *(G-2779)*

Sealmaster, Raleigh *Also Called: Thorworks Industries Inc (G-10547)*

Sealy & Company, Trinity *Also Called: Sealy Corporation (G-12123)*

Sealy Corporation (HQ)..336 861-3500
  1 Office Parkway Rd Trinity (27370) *(G-12123)*

Sealy Mattress, Trinity *Also Called: Sealy Mattress Mfg Co LLC (G-12125)*

Sealy Mattress Company (DH).....................................336 861-3500
  1 Office Parkway Rd Trinity (27370) *(G-12124)*

Sealy Mattress Mfg Co LLC.. 336 861-2900
  239 Sealy Dr Trinity (27370) *(G-12125)*

Seam-Craft Inc... 336 861-4156
  702 Prospect St High Point (27260) *(G-6765)*

Seam-Craft Inc... 336 861-4156
  1501 Potts Ave High Point (27260) *(G-6766)*

Seans Transportation LLC... 646 603-8128
  6826 Centerline Dr Charlotte (28278) *(G-2780)*

Seaport Crane, Wilmington *Also Called: Roderick Mch Erectors Wldg Inc (G-12901)*

Seas Publications.. 919 266-0035
  3608 Ladywood Ct Raleigh (27616) *(G-10465)*

Seashore Builders Inc.. 910 259-3404
  5930 Nc Hwy 50 Maple Hill (28454) *(G-8026)*

Seaside Press Co Inc... 910 458-8156
  1003 Bennet Ln Ste F Carolina Beach (28428) *(G-1264)*

Seaward Action Inc.. 252 671-1684
  219 Oakcrest Dr Wilmington (28403) *(G-12914)*

Seaway Printing & Mailing, Southport *Also Called: Seaway Printing Company (G-11527)*

Seaway Printing Company... 910 457-6158
  4130 Long Beach Rd Se Southport (28461) *(G-11527)*

Second Earth Inc.. 336 740-9333
  3716 Alliance Dr Ste C Greensboro (27407) *(G-5804)*

Second Green Holdings Inc.. 336 996-6073
  9501 W Market St Colfax (27235) *(G-3290)*

Second Main Phase Slutions LLC................................. 704 303-0090
  407 Clairview Ln Matthews (28105) *(G-8147)*

Second Nature, New Bern *Also Called: Test ME Out Inc (G-9399)*

Secret Chocolatier LLC... 704 323-8178
  2935 Providence Rd Ste 104 Charlotte (28211) *(G-2781)*

Secret Spot Inc... 252 441-4030
  2815 S Croatan Hwy Nags Head (27959) *(G-9302)*

Secret Spot Surf Shop, Nags Head *Also Called: Secret Spot Inc (G-9302)*

Secure Canopy LLC.. 980 322-0590
  1215 Pineview St Albemarle (28001) *(G-88)*

SECURE RESTORATION, Arden *Also Called: Etbf LLC (G-267)*

Secured Shred.. 443 288-6375
  3901 Barrett Dr Ste 306 Raleigh (27609) *(G-10466)*

Secured Traffic Control LLC.. 910 233-8148
  2801 Bloomfield Ln Wilmington (28412) *(G-12915)*

Security 101 Raleigh, Durham *Also Called: A&B Integrators LLC (G-3876)*

Security Consult Inc... 704 531-8399
  1318 Beechdale Dr Charlotte (28212) *(G-2782)*

Security Journey, Charlotte *Also Called: HackEDU Inc (G-2250)*

Security Self Storage... 919 544-3969
  1945 E Cornwallis Rd Durham (27713) *(G-4229)*

Security Ultraviolet, Cary *Also Called: S C I A Inc (G-1444)*

Sedgefield By Adams, High Point *Also Called: Adams Wood Turning Inc (G-6509)*

Sedgewick Industries, High Point *Also Called: Whitewood Contracts LLC (G-6834)*

Sedia Systems Inc.. 336 887-3818
  335 Commerce Pl Asheboro (27203) *(G-395)*

See Clearly Inc.. 929 464-6887
  207 S Westgate Dr Ste B Greensboro (27407) *(G-5805)*

Seeco, Indian Trail *Also Called: Southern Electrical Eqp Co Inc (G-7099)*

Seema Intl Custom Cabinetry....................................... 917 703-0820
  1012 Lightfoot Ct Wake Forest (27587) *(G-12299)*

Seg Systems LLC... 704 579-5800
  10701 Hambright Rd Huntersville (28078) *(G-7054)*

SEI Technologies, Hickory *Also Called: Solomon Engineering Inc (G-6452)*

Seiren North America LLC (HQ).....................................828 430-3456
  1500 E Union St Morganton (28655) *(G-8894)*

Selbach Machinery LLC... 910 794-9350
  314 N Green Meadows Dr Ste 400 Wilmington (28405) *(G-12916)*

Select Air Systems, Monroe *Also Called: Select Air Systems Usa Inc (G-8557)*

Select Air Systems Usa Inc... 704 289-1122
  2716 Chamber Dr Monroe (28110) *(G-8557)*

Select Frame Shop Inc.. 910 428-1225
  138 Coggins Rd Biscoe (27209) *(G-857)*

Select Furniture Company Inc...................................... 336 886-3572
  408 South Rd High Point (27262) *(G-6767)*

Select Hardwoods Div, Millers Creek *Also Called: Church & Church Lumber LLC (G-8304)*

Select Mold Service Inc.. 910 323-1287
  419 Glidden St Fayetteville (28301) *(G-4667)*

Select Stainless, Matthews *Also Called: Metalfab of North Carolina LLC (G-8132)*

Select Stainless Products LLC..................................... 888 843-2345
  7621 Little Ave Ste 212 Charlotte (28226) *(G-2783)*

Selectbuild Construction Inc....................................... 208 331-4300
  4800 Falls Of Neuse Rd Ste 400 Raleigh (27609) *(G-10467)*

Selective Enterprises Inc (PA)..................................... 704 588-3310
  10701 Texland Blvd Charlotte (28273) *(G-2784)*

Selee Corporation (DH)... 828 697-2411
  700 Shepherd St Hendersonville (28792) *(G-6240)*

Self Made Clt.. 704 249-5263
  9111 Olmsted Dr Charlotte (28262) *(G-2785)*

Selina Naturally, Arden *Also Called: Celtic Ocean International Inc (G-261)*

Selpro LLC.. 336 513-0550
  408 Gallimore Dairy Rd Ste C Greensboro (27409) *(G-5806)*

Semper FI Water LLC.. 910 381-3569
  508 Cozy Crow Trl Jacksonville (28540) *(G-7143)*

Seneca Devices Inc.. 301 412-3576
  2 Davis Dr Durham (27709) *(G-4230)*

Sennett Security Products LLC..................................... 336 375-1134
  6109 Corporate Park Dr Browns Summit (27214) *(G-1005)*

Sennett Security Products LLC (PA)..............................336 404-3284
  21 Beech Ridge Ct Greensboro (27455) *(G-5807)*

Senox Corporation... 704 371-5043
  3500 Woodpark Blvd Charlotte (28206) *(G-2786)*

Sensational Signs.. 704 358-1099
  2100 N Davidson St Charlotte (28205) *(G-2787)*

Sensory Analytics LLC.. 336 315-6090
  405b Pomona Dr Greensboro (27407) *(G-5808)*

Sensus.. 919 376-2617
  113 Gorecki Pl Cary (27513) *(G-1451)*

Sensus, Morrisville *Also Called: Sensus USA Inc (G-9051)*

Sensus Metering Systems, Morrisville *Also Called: Sensus USA Inc (G-9052)*

Sensus USA Inc.. 919 879-3200
  639 Davis Dr Morrisville (27560) *(G-9050)*

Sensus USA Inc (HQ).. 919 845-4000
  637 Davis Dr Morrisville (27560) *(G-9051)*

Sensus USA Inc.. 919 576-6185
  400 Perimeter Park Dr Ste K Morrisville (27560) *(G-9052)*

Sentinel Door Controls Inc.. 704 921-4627
  3020 Hutchison Mcdonald Rd Ste D Charlotte (28269) *(G-2788)*

Sentinel Newspapers (PA)... 828 389-8338
  23 Riverwalk Cir Hayesville (28904) *(G-6144)*

Sentry Vault Service Inc... 252 243-2241
  6905 Shallingtons Mill Rd Elm City (27822) *(G-4467)*

Separation Technologies LLC....................................... 336 597-9814
  1514 Dunnaway Rd Semora (27343) *(G-11296)*

September Signs & Graphics LLC.................................. 910 791-9084
  6731 Amsterdam Way Ste 4 Wilmington (28405) *(G-12917)*

Seqirus Inc (DH)..919 577-5000
  475 Green Oaks Pkwy Holly Springs (27540) *(G-6914)*

Serenity Home Services LLC.. 910 233-8733
  767 Morrison Farm Rd Troutman (28166) *(G-12150)*

Serra Wireless Inc... 980 318-0873
  2431 Tallet Trce Charlotte (28216) *(G-2789)*

Serum Source International Inc................................ 704 588-6607
406 Belvedere Ln Waxhaw (28173) *(G-12440)*

Service Electric and Control.................................... 704 888-5100
703 Redah Ave Locust (28097) *(G-7901)*

Service Rofg Shtmtl Wlmngton I................................ 910 343-9860
4838 Us Highway 421 N Wilmington (28401) *(G-12918)*

Service Roofing and Shtmtl Co.................................. 252 758-2179
107 Staton Ct Greenville (27834) *(G-6021)*

Service Thread Co, Charlotte *Also Called: Sam M Butler Inc (G-2753)*

Service Thread Manufacturing, Laurinburg *Also Called: Sam M Butler Inc (G-7513)*

Service Thread Manufacturing, Laurinburg *Also Called: Sam M Butler Inc (G-7514)*

SES Integration
7575 Westwinds Blvd Nw Ste B Concord (28027) *(G-3439)*

Sesame Technologies Inc....................................... 252 964-2205
3718 River Rd Washington (27889) *(G-12412)*

Sesmfg LLC... 803 917-3248
1705 Orr Industrial Ct Ste C Charlotte (28213) *(G-2790)*

Seven Cast... 704 335-0692
901 N Church St Charlotte (28206) *(G-2791)*

Seven Lakes News Corporation................................. 910 685-0320
2033 7 Lks S West End (27376) *(G-12559)*

Seymour Advanced Tech LLC.................................... 704 709-9070
3593 Denver Dr Unit 964 Denver (28037) *(G-3804)*

Sfp Research Inc... 336 622-5266
121 W Swannanoa Ave Liberty (27298) *(G-7779)*

Sg-Clw Inc... 336 865-4980
1700 N Liberty St Winston Salem (27105) *(G-13331)*

Sgl Carbon LLC.. 828 437-3221
307 Jamestown Rd Morganton (28655) *(G-8895)*

Sgl Carbon LLC (DH).. 704 593-5100
10715 David Taylor Dr Ste 460 Charlotte (28262) *(G-2792)*

Sgl Composites Inc.. 704 593-5100
10715 David Taylor Dr Ste 460 Charlotte (28262) *(G-2793)*

Sgl Technologies LLC... 704 593-5100
10715 David Taylor Dr Ste 460 Charlotte (28262) *(G-2794)*

Sgrtex LLC... 336 635-9420
335 Summit Rd Eden (27288) *(G-4356)*

Shadow Creek Consulting Inc.................................. 716 860-7397
124 Commerce Blvd Statesville (28625) *(G-11763)*

Shadowtrack 24/7, Fletcher *Also Called: Shadowtrack 247 LLC (G-4767)*

Shadowtrack 247 LLC... 828 398-0980
45 Park Ridge Dr Fletcher (28732) *(G-4767)*

Shalag Nonwovens, Oxford *Also Called: Shalag US Inc (G-9634)*

Shalag US Inc
917 Se Industry Dr Oxford (27565) *(G-9634)*

Shallco Inc... 919 934-3135
308 Components Dr Smithfield (27577) *(G-11465)*

Shallowford Farms Popcorn, Yadkinville *Also Called: Shallowford Farms Popcorn Inc (G-13451)*

Shallowford Farms Popcorn Inc................................ 336 463-5938
3732 Hartman Rd Yadkinville (27055) *(G-13451)*

Shamrock Corporation (PA)..................................... 336 574-4200
422 N Chimney Rock Rd Greensboro (27410) *(G-5809)*

Shannon Media Inc.. 919 933-1551
1777 Fordham Blvd Ste 105 Chapel Hill (27514) *(G-1570)*

Sharp Stone Supply Inc... 336 659-7777
126 Griffith Plaza Dr Winston Salem (27103) *(G-13332)*

Sharpe Co (PA).. 336 724-2871
230 Charlois Blvd Winston Salem (27103) *(G-13333)*

Sharpe Images, Winston Salem *Also Called: Sharpe Images Properties Inc (G-13334)*

Sharpe Images Properties Inc (PA)............................ 336 724-2871
230 Charlois Blvd Winston Salem (27103) *(G-13334)*

Shat-R-Shield Lighting Inc...................................... 800 223-0853
116 Ryan Patrick Dr Salisbury (28147) *(G-11115)*

Shaver Wood Products Inc...................................... 704 278-1482
14440 Statesville Blvd Cleveland (27013) *(G-3221)*

Shaw Industries Inc... 828 369-1701
301 Depot St Franklin (28734) *(G-4839)*

Shaw Industries Group Inc...................................... 877 996-5942
10901 Texland Blvd Charlotte (28273) *(G-2795)*

Shaw Industries Group Inc...................................... 877 996-5942
10901 Texland Blvd Charlotte (28273) *(G-2796)*

Shawmut Corporation... 336 229-5576
1821 N Park Ave Burlington (27217) *(G-1155)*

Shawmut Corporation, Burlington *Also Called: Shawmut Corporation (G-1155)*

Shawn Trucking and Towing, Charlotte *Also Called: Seans Transportation LLC (G-2780)*

Shearline Boatworks LLC.. 252 726-6916
127 Hestron Dr Morehead City (28557) *(G-8844)*

Shed Brand Inc (PA).. 704 523-0096
216 Iverson Way Ste A Charlotte (28203) *(G-2797)*

Sheet Metal Duct Suppliers LLC............................... 919 732-4362
214 Millstone Dr Hillsborough (27278) *(G-6877)*

Sheet Metal Products Inc....................................... 919 954-9950
3728 Overlook Rd Raleigh (27616) *(G-10468)*

Sheets Laundry Club Inc.. 704 662-8696
211 Mckenzie Rd Mooresville (28115) *(G-8768)*

Sheets Smith Wealth MGT Inc.................................. 336 765-2020
120 Club Oaks Ct Ste 200 Winston Salem (27104) *(G-13335)*

Shelby Business Cards.. 704 481-8341
2020 E Dixon Blvd Shelby (28152) *(G-11375)*

Shelby Elastics, Shelby *Also Called: Shelby Elastics of North Carolina LLC (G-11376)*

Shelby Elastics of North Carolina LLC........................ 704 487-4301
639 N Post Rd Shelby (28150) *(G-11376)*

Shelby Freedom Star Inc....................................... 704 484-7000
315 E Graham St Shelby (28150) *(G-11377)*

Shelby Star The, Shelby *Also Called: Shelby Freedom Star Inc (G-11377)*

Shelton Logging & Chipping Inc............................... 336 548-3860
2861 Anglin Mill Rd Stoneville (27048) *(G-11827)*

Shelton Vineyards Inc.. 336 366-4818
286 Cabernet Ln Dobson (27017) *(G-3825)*

Shenandoah Wood Preservers Inc............................. 252 826-4151
301 E 16th St Scotland Neck (27874) *(G-11266)*

Shep Berryhill Woodworking.................................... 828 242-3227
197 Deaverview Rd Asheville (28806) *(G-598)*

Shepherd Family Logging LLC................................. 910 572-4098
138 Ivey St Troy (27371) *(G-12167)*

Sherri Gossett.. 910 367-0099
801 Bragg Dr Wilmington (28409) *(G-12919)*

Sherrill Contract Mfg Inc (PA).................................. 704 922-7871
110 Durkee Ln Dallas (28034) *(G-3689)*

Sherrill Furniture, Hickory *Also Called: Sherrill Furniture Company (G-6441)*

Sherrill Furniture Company..................................... 828 322-8624
856 7th Ave Se Hickory (28602) *(G-6439)*

Sherrill Furniture Company..................................... 828 328-5241
2425 Highland Ave Ne Hickory (28601) *(G-6440)*

Sherrill Furniture Company (PA)............................... 828 322-2640
2405 Highland Ave Ne Hickory (28601) *(G-6441)*

Sherrill Furniture Company..................................... 336 884-0974
301 Steele St Ste 4 High Point (27260) *(G-6768)*

Sherrill Furniture Company..................................... 828 437-2256
516 Drexel Rd Morganton (28655) *(G-8896)*

Sherrill Furniture Company..................................... 828 465-0844
1425 Smyre Farm Rd Newton (28658) *(G-9494)*

Sherwin-Williams, Charlotte *Also Called: Sherwin-Williams Company (G-2798)*

Sherwin-Williams, Greensboro *Also Called: Sherwin-Williams Company (G-5810)*

Sherwin-Williams, Raleigh *Also Called: Sherwin-Williams Company (G-10469)*

Sherwin-Williams, Statesville *Also Called: Sherwin-Williams Company (G-11764)*

Sherwin-Williams Company.................................... 704 548-2820
10300 Claude Freeman Dr Charlotte (28262) *(G-2798)*

Sherwin-Williams Company.................................... 336 292-3000
113 Stage Coach Trl Greensboro (27409) *(G-5810)*

Sherwin-Williams Company.................................... 919 436-2460
5301 Capital Blvd Raleigh (27616) *(G-10469)*

Sherwin-Williams Company.................................... 704 881-0245
188 Side Track Dr Statesville (28625) *(G-11764)*

Sherwood Refractores, Sanford *Also Called: PCC Airfoils LLC (G-11215)*

Shibumi Shade Inc... 336 816-9903
4039 Atlantic Ave Raleigh (27604) *(G-10470)*

Shield & Steel Enterprises LLC................................ 704 607-0869
417b Peach Orchard Rd Salisbury (28147) *(G-11116)*

Shiftwizard Inc... 866 828-3318
909 Aviation Pkwy Ste 700 Morrisville (27560) *(G-9053)*

Shimadzu Scientific Instrs Inc.................................. 919 425-1010
    4022 Stirrup Creek Dr Ste 312 Durham (27703) *(G-4231)*

Shipman Technologies Inc.................................. 919 294-8405
    2933 S Miami Blvd Ste 122 Durham (27703) *(G-4232)*

Shirleys Prof Alterations EMB, Jacksonville *Also Called: Professnal Alterations EMB Inc* *(G-7139)*

Shoaf Precast Septic Tank Inc.................................. 336 787-5826
    4130 W Us Highway 64 Lexington (27295) *(G-7740)*

Shoaf Precasting, Lexington *Also Called: Shoaf Precast Septic Tank Inc (G-7740)*

Shock Absorber Division, Mooresville *Also Called: Thyssenkrupp Bilstein Amer Inc (G-8786)*

Shodja Textiles Inc.................................. 910 914-0456
    68 Industrial Dr Whiteville (28472) *(G-12593)*

Shoffner Industries Inc.................................. 336 226-9356
    5631 S Nc Highway 62 Burlington (27215) *(G-1156)*

Shop Dawg Signs LLC.................................. 919 556-2672
    4154 Shearon Farms Ave Ste 109 Wake Forest (27587) *(G-12300)*

Shopbot Tools Inc.................................. 919 680-4800
    3333b Industrial Dr Durham (27704) *(G-4233)*

Shopper.................................. 252 633-1153
    3200 Wellons Blvd New Bern (28562) *(G-9396)*

Shopper The, New Bern *Also Called: Shopper (G-9396)*

Short Run Pro LLC.................................. 704 825-1599
    710 E Catawba St Ste A Belmont (28012) *(G-765)*

Shortway Brewing Company LLC (PA).................................. 252 777-3065
    228 Chatham St Newport (28570) *(G-9444)*

Shower ME With Love LLC.................................. 704 302-1555
    4845 Ashley Park Ln Ste H Charlotte (28210) *(G-2799)*

Showline Inc (PA).................................. 919 255-9160
    2114 Atlantic Ave Ste 160 Raleigh (27604) *(G-10471)*

Showline Automotive Pdts Inc (PA).................................. 919 255-9160
    1108 N New Hope Rd Raleigh (27610) *(G-10472)*

Showroom, High Point *Also Called: King Hickory Furniture Company (G-6685)*

Shred Instead, Raleigh *Also Called: Secured Shred (G-10466)*

Shred-Tech Usa LLC.................................. 919 387-8220
    4701 Trademark Dr Raleigh (27610) *(G-10473)*

Shuford Mills LLC (HQ).................................. 828 324-4265
    1985 Tate Blvd Se Ste 54 Hickory (28602) *(G-6442)*

Shuford Yarns, Hickory *Also Called: Shuford Mills LLC (G-6442)*

Shuford Yarns LLC.................................. 828 396-2342
    5100 Burns Rd Granite Falls (28630) *(G-5323)*

Shuford Yarns LLC (PA).................................. 828 324-4265
    1985 Tate Blvd Se Ste 54 Hickory (28602) *(G-6443)*

Shuford Yarns Management Inc.................................. 828 324-4265
    1985 Tate Blvd Se Ste 54 Hickory (28602) *(G-6444)*

Shur Line Inc.................................. 317 442-8850
    116 Exmore Rd Mooresville (28117) *(G-8769)*

Shurtape Technologies LLC.................................. 704 553-9441
    4725 Piedmont Row Dr Ste 210 Charlotte (28210) *(G-2800)*

Shurtape Technologies LLC.................................. 828 304-8302
    1985 Tate Blvd Se Hickory (28603) *(G-6445)*

Shurtech Brands, Hickory *Also Called: Stm Industries Inc (G-6459)*

Shurtech Brands LLC.................................. 704 799-0779
    150 Fairview Rd Mooresville (28117) *(G-8770)*

Shutter Factory Inc.................................. 252 974-2795
    6139w Us Highway 264 W Washington (27889) *(G-12413)*

Shutter Production Inc.................................. 910 289-2620
    227 First St Rose Hill (28458) *(G-10910)*

Shutter Works, The, Middlesex *Also Called: Frederick and Frederick Entp (G-8275)*

Shutterbug Grafix & Signs.................................. 910 315-1556
    300 Kelly Rd Ste B3 Pinehurst (28374) *(G-9703)*

Shuttercraft Inc.................................. 704 708-9079
    921 Matthews Mint Hill Rd Ste D Matthews (28105) *(G-8148)*

Sia Abrasives Inc USA.................................. 704 587-7355
    1980 Indian Creek Rd Lincolnton (28092) *(G-7853)*

Sibelco.................................. 828 765-1114
    107 Harris Mining Company Rd Spruce Pine (28777) *(G-11585)*

Sibelco North America Inc.................................. 828 766-6050
    74 Harris Mining Company Rd Spruce Pine (28777) *(G-11586)*

Sibelco North America Inc.................................. 828 766-6050
    136 Crystal Dr Spruce Pine (28777) *(G-11587)*

Sicel Technologies Inc.................................. 919 465-2236
    3800 Gateway Centre Blvd Morrisville (27560) *(G-9054)*

Sid Jenkins Inc.................................. 336 632-0707
    3004 Harnett Dr Greensboro (27407) *(G-5811)*

Sideboard.................................. 910 612-4398
    4107 Oleander Dr Ste C Wilmington (28403) *(G-12920)*

Sides Custom Furniture, High Point *Also Called: Sides Furniture Inc (G-6769)*

Sides Furniture Inc.................................. 336 869-5509
    1812 Horneytown Rd High Point (27265) *(G-6769)*

Sidney Perry Cooper III.................................. 252 257-3886
    445 Nc Highway 58 Warrenton (27589) *(G-12354)*

Sieber Industrial Inc.................................. 252 746-2003
    221 Pepsi Way Ayden (28513) *(G-660)*

Siegwerk Eic LLC (DH).................................. 800 368-4657
    1 Quality Products Rd Morganton (28655) *(G-8897)*

Siemens Airport.................................. 704 359-5551
    5601 Wilkinson Blvd Charlotte (28208) *(G-2801)*

Siemens Corporation.................................. 919 465-1287
    3333 Regency Pkwy Cary (27518) *(G-1452)*

Siemens Energy Inc.................................. 704 551-5100
    5101 Westinghouse Blvd Charlotte (28273) *(G-2802)*

Siemens Energy Inc.................................. 336 969-1351
    3050 Westinghouse Rd Rural Hall (27045) *(G-10967)*

Siemens Energy Inc.................................. 919 365-2200
    7000 Siemens Rd Wendell (27591) *(G-12546)*

Siemens Industry Inc.................................. 919 365-2200
    7000 Siemens Rd Wendell (27591) *(G-12547)*

Siemens Industry Software Inc.................................. 704 227-6600
    13024 Ballantyne Corporate Pl Charlotte (28277) *(G-2803)*

Siemens Med Solutions USA Inc.................................. 919 468-7400
    221 Gregson Dr Cary (27511) *(G-1453)*

Siemens PLM Software, Charlotte *Also Called: Siemens Industry Software Inc (G-2803)*

Siemens Power Transmission & Distribution Inc.................................. 919 463-8702
    110 Macalyson Ct Cary (27511) *(G-1454)*

Siena Plastics LLC.................................. 704 323-5252
    839 Exchange St Charlotte (28208) *(G-2804)*

Sierra Nevada Corporation.................................. 919 595-8551
    1030 Swabia Ct Ste 100 Durham (27703) *(G-4234)*

Sierra Nevada Corporation.................................. 910 307-0362
    3139 Doc Bennett Rd Fayetteville (28306) *(G-4668)*

Sierra Nevada Corporation.................................. 775 331-0222
    795 Sw Broad St Southern Pines (28387) *(G-11509)*

SIERRA NEVADA CORPORATION, Durham *Also Called: Sierra Nevada Corporation (G-4234)*

SIERRA NEVADA CORPORATION, Fayetteville *Also Called: Sierra Nevada Corporation* *(G-4668)*

SIERRA NEVADA CORPORATION, Southern Pines *Also Called: Sierra Nevada Corporation* *(G-11509)*

Sierra Software LLC.................................. 877 285-2867
    143 Industrial Ave Greensboro (27406) *(G-5812)*

Sighttech LLC.................................. 855 997-4448
    9421 Perimeter Station Dr Apt 101 Charlotte (28216) *(G-2805)*

Sigma Engineered Solutions PC (PA).................................. 919 773-0011
    120 Sigma Dr Garner (27529) *(G-4964)*

Sigma Plastics Group.................................. 336 885-8091
    2319 W English Rd High Point (27262) *(G-6770)*

Sigma Xi Scntfic RES Hnor Soc.................................. 919 549-4691
    3200 Chapel Hill Nelson Hwy Ste 300 Durham (27709) *(G-4235)*

Sign & Awning Systems Inc.................................. 919 892-5900
    2785 Us 301 N Dunn (28334) *(G-3868)*

Sign A Rama, Raleigh *Also Called: Sign-A-Rama (G-10474)*

Sign A Rama Inc.................................. 336 893-8042
    5054 Styers Ferry Rd Lewisville (27023) *(G-7653)*

Sign and Graphics, Roxboro *Also Called: R & S Sporting Goods Ctr Inc (G-10942)*

Sign Art, Charlotte *Also Called: Lockwood Identity Inc (G-2430)*

Sign Company of Wilmington Inc.................................. 910 392-1414
    428 Landmark Dr Wilmington (28412) *(G-12921)*

Sign Connection Inc.................................. 704 868-4500
    1660 Pacolet Dr Gastonia (28052) *(G-5136)*

Sign Here, Denver *Also Called: Sign Here of Lake Norman Inc (G-3805)*

Sign Here of Lake Norman Inc.................................. 704 483-6454
    422 N Nc 16 Business Hwy Denver (28037) *(G-3805)*

Sign Manufacturing, Fayetteville *Also Called: Connected 2k LLC (G-4578)*

Sign Medic Inc.................................. 336 789-5972
    1410 Boggs Dr Mount Airy (27030) *(G-9176)*

Sign Mine Inc.. 336 884-5780
2211 Eastchester Dr High Point (27265) *(G-6771)*

Sign Resources of NC.. 336 310-4611
673 Gralin St Ste B Kernersville (27284) *(G-7300)*

Sign Shop of The Triangle Inc.......................... 919 363-3930
4001 Midstream Ct Apex (27539) *(G-194)*

Sign Shoppe Inc.. 910 754-5144
782 Ocean Hwy W Supply (28462) *(G-11859)*

Sign Systems Inc... 828 322-5622
315 9th St Se Hickory (28602) *(G-6446)*

Sign Technology Inc... 336 887-3211
311 Berkley St High Point (27260) *(G-6772)*

Sign World Inc... 704 529-4440
200 Foster Ave Charlotte (28203) *(G-2806)*

Sign Worxpress... 336 437-9889
2529 S Church St Burlington (27215) *(G-1157)*

Sign-A-Rama... 919 383-5561
972 Trinity Rd Raleigh (27607) *(G-10474)*

Sign-A-Rama, Asheville *Also Called: Piedmont Mediaworks Inc (G-573)*

Sign-A-Rama, Bolivia *Also Called: Thats A Good Sign Inc (G-887)*

Sign-A-Rama, Charlotte *Also Called: Baac Business Solutions Inc (G-1732)*

Sign-A-Rama, Clayton *Also Called: J & D Thorpe Enterprises Inc (G-3155)*

Sign-A-Rama, Fayetteville *Also Called: Buzz Saw Inc (G-4564)*

Sign-A-Rama, Greensboro *Also Called: Vic Inc (G-5903)*

Sign-A-Rama, Lewisville *Also Called: Sign A Rama Inc (G-7653)*

Sign-A-Rama, Raleigh *Also Called: Jester-Crown Inc (G-10216)*

Sign-A-Rama, Wilmington *Also Called: Global Resource NC Inc (G-12789)*

Signal Signs of Ga Inc...................................... 828 494-4913
15 Running Bear Rd Murphy (28906) *(G-9295)*

Signalscape Inc... 919 859-4565
200 Regency Forest Dr Ste 310 Cary (27518) *(G-1455)*

Signature Custom Cabinets LLC....................... 704 753-4874
2106 E Highway 218 Monroe (28110) *(G-8558)*

Signature Custom Wdwkg Inc............................ 336 983-9905
1050 Denny Rd King (27021) *(G-7337)*

Signature Flight Air Inc..................................... 919 840-4400
1725 E International Dr Morrisville (27560) *(G-9055)*

Signature Gallery, Hudson *Also Called: Popes Signature Gallery (G-6956)*

Signature Seasonings LLC................................ 252 746-1001
3254 Nc 102 E Ayden (28513) *(G-661)*

Signature Seating Inc.. 828 325-0174
1718 9th Ave Nw Hickory (28601) *(G-6447)*

Signature Signs Inc... 336 431-2072
211 Berkley St High Point (27260) *(G-6773)*

Signcaster Corporation...................................... 336 712-2525
6210 Hacker Bend Ct Ste B Winston Salem (27103) *(G-13336)*

Signcraft Solutions, Wake Forest *Also Called: Shop Dawg Signs LLC (G-12300)*

Signfactory Direct Inc.. 336 903-0300
1202 Industrial Park Rd Wilkesboro (28697) *(G-12651)*

Signify It Inc... 910 678-8111
700 Ramsey St Fayetteville (28301) *(G-4669)*

Signlite Services Inc... 336 751-9543
151 Industrial Blvd Mocksville (27028) *(G-8389)*

Signlogic Inc... 910 862-8965
174 S Poplar St Elizabethtown (28337) *(G-4433)*

Signs By Tomorrow.. 704 527-6100
2440 Whitehall Park Dr Ste 100 Charlotte (28273) *(G-2807)*

Signs By Tomorrow, Beech Mountain *Also Called: Moretz Signs Inc (G-738)*

Signs Etc... 336 722-9341
2432 Cherokee Ln Winston Salem (27103) *(G-13337)*

Signs Etc, Charlotte *Also Called: Signs Etc of Charlotte (G-2809)*

Signs Etc, Pineville *Also Called: Jgi Inc (G-9737)*

Signs Etc of Charlotte (PA)............................... 704 522-8860
4941 Chastain Ave Charlotte (28217) *(G-2808)*

Signs Etc of Charlotte....................................... 704 522-8860
4044 South Blvd Charlotte (28209) *(G-2809)*

Signs Now.. 919 546-0006
2424 Atlantic Ave Raleigh (27604) *(G-10475)*

Signs Now, Chapel Hill *Also Called: Fines and Carriel Inc (G-1547)*

Signs Now, Charlotte *Also Called: K&K Holdings Inc (G-2385)*

Signs Now, Gastonia *Also Called: Signz Inc (G-5137)*

Signs Now, Greenville *Also Called: Signs Now 103 LLC (G-6022)*

Signs Now, Morrisville *Also Called: AAA Mobile Signs LLC (G-8915)*

Signs Now, Pineville *Also Called: Signs Now Charlotte (G-9757)*

Signs Now 103 LLC... 252 355-0768
118b Greenville Blvd Se Greenville (27858) *(G-6022)*

Signs Now Charlotte.. 704 844-0552
600 Towne Centre Blvd Ste 404 Pineville (28134) *(G-9757)*

Signs Sealed Delivered..................................... 919 213-1280
6409 Fayetteville Rd Durham (27713) *(G-4236)*

Signs Unlimited Inc... 919 596-7612
6801 Mount Hermon Church Rd Unit C Durham (27705) *(G-4237)*

Signsations Ltd... 571 340-3330
104 Concord Dr Chapel Hill (27516) *(G-1571)*

Signsmith Custom Signs & Awnin..................... 252 752-4321
1709 Evans St Greenville (27834) *(G-6023)*

Signworks North Carolina Inc............................ 336 956-7446
373 Marco Blvd Lexington (27295) *(G-7741)*

Signz Inc.. 704 824-7446
3608 S New Hope Rd Gastonia (28056) *(G-5137)*

Sii Dry Kilns, Lexington *Also Called: Southeastern Installation Inc (G-7744)*

Sika Corporation (DH)....................................... 704 810-0500
1909 Kyle Ct Gastonia (28052) *(G-5138)*

Silanna Semicdtr N Amer Inc............................ 984 444-6500
1130 Situs Ct Ste 100 Raleigh (27606) *(G-10476)*

Silar LLC (DH).. 910 655-4212
333 Neils Eddy Rd Riegelwood (28456) *(G-10728)*

Silar Laboratories, Riegelwood *Also Called: Silar LLC (G-10728)*

Silicones Inc.. 336 886-5018
211 Woodbine St High Point (27260) *(G-6774)*

Silkscreen Specialists....................................... 910 353-8859
2239 Lejeune Blvd Jacksonville (28546) *(G-7144)*

Sillaman & Sons Inc.. 919 774-6324
356 Wilson Rd Sanford (27332) *(G-11233)*

Silver Dollar Gun Pawn Sp Inc.......................... 336 824-8989
6787 Jordan Rd Ramseur (27316) *(G-10631)*

Silver Ink Publishing Inc................................... 704 473-0192
917 Beau Rd Shelby (28152) *(G-11378)*

Silver Knight Pcs LLC....................................... 910 824-2054
1324 Bragg Blvd Fayetteville (28311) *(G-4670)*

Silver Moon Nutraceuticals LLC........................ 828 698-5795
111 Fletcher Commercial Dr Ste B Fletcher (28732) *(G-4768)*

Silver-Line Plastics LLC (DH)............................ 828 252-8755
900 Riverside Dr Asheville (28804) *(G-599)*

Silverlining Screen Prtrs Inc............................. 919 554-0340
90 Mosswood Blvd Ste 600 Youngsville (27596) *(G-13485)*

Simmie Bullard... 910 600-3191
787 Goins Rd Pembroke (28372) *(G-9659)*

Simmie Bullard Construction, Pembroke *Also Called: Simmie Bullard (G-9659)*

Simmons, Charlotte *Also Called: Ssb Manufacturing Company (G-2853)*

Simmons Hosiery Mill Inc (PA).......................... 828 327-4890
3715 9th Street Cir Ne Hickory (28601) *(G-6448)*

Simmons Logging & Trucking Inc....................... 910 287-6344
5923 Simmons Rd Nw Ash (28420) *(G-322)*

Simmons Scientific Products, Wilmington *Also Called: Russ Simmons (G-12906)*

Simon Industries Inc... 919 469-2004
2910 Industrial Dr Raleigh (27609) *(G-10477)*

Simontic Composite Inc..................................... 336 897-9885
2901 E Gate City Blvd Ste 2500 Greensboro (27401) *(G-5813)*

Simonton Windows & Doors Inc......................... 919 677-3938
5020 Weston Pkwy Ste 300 Cary (27513) *(G-1456)*

Simple & Sentimental LLC................................. 252 320-9458
6248 Nc 11 S Ayden (28513) *(G-662)*

Simplecertifiedmailcom LLC.............................. 888 462-1750
111 Commonwealth Ct Ste 103 Cary (27511) *(G-1457)*

Simpleshot.. 888 202-7475
2000 Riverside Dr Ste 5a Asheville (28804) *(G-600)*

Simplicity Sofas Inc.. 800 813-2889
414 Grayson St High Point (27260) *(G-6775)*

Simplicti, Cary *Also Called: Simplicti Sftwr Solutions Inc (G-1458)*

Simplicti Sftwr Solutions Inc.. 919 858-8898
 1255 Crescent Green Ste 145 Cary (27518) *(G-1458)*

Simplifyber Inc... 919 396-8355
 625 Hutton St Ste 106 Raleigh (27606) *(G-10478)*

Simply Btiful Events Decor LLC... 252 375-3839
 1263 Windsong Dr Greenville (27858) *(G-6024)*

Simply Natural Creamery LLC.. 252 746-3334
 1265 Carson Edwards Rd Ayden (28513) *(G-663)*

Simply Stitching, Advance *Also Called: Twg Inc (G-40)*

Simplyhome LLC... 828 684-8441
 48 Fisk Dr Arden (28704) *(G-306)*

Simpson Strong-Tie Company Inc....................................... 336 841-1338
 4485 Premier Dr Ste 101 High Point (27265) *(G-6776)*

Sincere Scents Co LLC.. 910 616-4697
 7300 River Rd Se Trlr 84 Southport (28461) *(G-11528)*

Singer Equipment Company Inc... 910 484-1128
 933 Robeson St Fayetteville (28305) *(G-4671)*

Singer T&L, Fayetteville *Also Called: Singer Equipment Company Inc (G-4671)*

Single Temperature Contrls Inc... 704 504-4800
 14201 S Lakes Dr Ste B Charlotte (28273) *(G-2810)*

Singley Specialty Co Inc... 336 852-8581
 1025 Willowbrook Dr Greensboro (27403) *(G-5814)*

Singsa... 336 882-9160
 2401 Penny Rd High Point (27265) *(G-6777)*

Sinnovatek Inc.. 919 694-0974
 2609 Discovery Dr Ste 115 Raleigh (27616) *(G-10479)*

Sinnovita Inc... 919 694-0974
 2609 Discovery Dr Ste 115 Raleigh (27616) *(G-10480)*

Sinowest Mfg LLC... 919 289-9337
 5915 Oak Forest Dr Ste 103 Raleigh (27616) *(G-10481)*

Sipe Lumber Company Inc... 828 632-4679
 2750 Us Highway 64 90 W Taylorsville (28681) *(G-11978)*

Sipes Carving Shop Inc... 828 327-3077
 1450 10th Ave Sw Hickory (28602) *(G-6449)*

Sippin Snax Cft Beer Wine Snck, Greensboro *Also Called: See Clearly Inc (G-5805)*

Siqnarama Pinevillw... 704 835-1123
 10615 Industrial Dr Ste 200 Pineville (28134) *(G-9758)*

Sir Speedy, Asheville *Also Called: Jag Graphics Inc (G-527)*

Sir Speedy, Burlington *Also Called: Natel Inc (G-1134)*

Sir Speedy, Durham *Also Called: Bennett & Associates Inc (G-3925)*

Sir Speedy, Greensboro *Also Called: Dokja Inc (G-5500)*

Sir Speedy, High Point *Also Called: Weber and Weber Inc (G-6833)*

Sir Speedy, Mooresville *Also Called: Sir Speedy Printing (G-8771)*

Sir Speedy, Raleigh *Also Called: Cascadas Nye Corporation (G-9985)*

Sir Speedy, Raleigh *Also Called: Gik Inc (G-10133)*

Sir Speedy, Statesville *Also Called: Modern Information Svcs Inc (G-11734)*

Sir Speedy, Winston Salem *Also Called: Weber and Weber Inc (G-13387)*

Sir Speedy Printing.. 704 664-1911
 124 E Plaza Dr Ste C Mooresville (28115) *(G-8771)*

Sirchie Acquisition Co LLC (PA)... 800 356-7311
 100 Hunter Pl Youngsville (27596) *(G-13486)*

Sirchie Finger Print Labs, Youngsville *Also Called: Sirchie Acquisition Co LLC (G-13486)*

Sire Tees.. 919 787-6843
 6104 Westgate Rd Ste 115 Raleigh (27617) *(G-10482)*

Sirius Energies Corporation (PA).. 704 425-6272
 545 Hamberton Ct Nw Concord (28027) *(G-3440)*

Sirius Tactical Entps LLC.. 704 256-3660
 679 Brandy Ct Waxhaw (28173) *(G-12441)*

Sirocco Marine LLC.. 954 692-8333
 5100 N Glen Dr Raleigh (27609) *(G-10483)*

Sisco Safety, Charlotte *Also Called: GNB Ventures LLC (G-2218)*

Sitech Precision, Raleigh *Also Called: GP Technology LLC (G-10141)*

Sitelink Software LLC.. 919 865-0789
 3301 Atlantic Ave Raleigh (27604) *(G-10484)*

Sitzer & Spuria Inc.. 919 929-0299
 601 W Rosemary St Unit 111 Chapel Hill (27516) *(G-1572)*

Sitzer Spuria Studios, Chapel Hill *Also Called: Sitzer & Spuria Inc (G-1572)*

Size Stream LLC... 919 355-5708
 223 Commonwealth Ct Cary (27511) *(G-1459)*

Sjr Incorporated... 828 254-8966
 120 New Leicester Hwy Asheville (28806) *(G-601)*

Skan US Inc... 919 354-6380
 7409 Acc Blvd Ste 200 Raleigh (27617) *(G-10485)*

Skatells Mfg Jewelers, Pineville *Also Called: NCSMJ Inc (G-9744)*

Skeen Decorative Fabrics Inc.. 336 884-4044
 1220 W Market Center Dr High Point (27260) *(G-6778)*

Skeen Textiles Inc... 336 884-4044
 1900 S Elm St High Point (27260) *(G-6779)*

Skeen Txtiles Auto Fabrics Inc... 336 884-4044
 1900 S Elm St High Point (27260) *(G-6780)*

Skelly Inc... 828 433-7070
 628 E Meeting St Morganton (28655) *(G-8898)*

Skettis Woodworks.. 336 671-9866
 2225 Sedgemont Dr Winston Salem (27103) *(G-13338)*

Skidril Industries LLC.. 800 843-3745
 235 Labrador Dr Randleman (27317) *(G-10660)*

Skifam LLC... 336 722-6111
 119 S Stratford Rd Winston Salem (27104) *(G-13339)*

Skin Boys LLC.. 910 259-2232
 140 Industrial Dr Burgaw (28425) *(G-1031)*

Skin So Soft Spa Inc... 800 674-7554
 4456 The Plaza Ste 5e Charlotte (28215) *(G-2811)*

Skinner Company.. 336 580-4716
 414 E Montcastle Dr Greensboro (27406) *(G-5815)*

Skipper Graphics... 910 754-8729
 209 Village Rd Sw Shallotte (28470) *(G-11305)*

Sklar Bov Solutions Inc.. 704 872-7277
 1105 E Garner Bagnal Blvd Statesville (28677) *(G-11765)*

Skybien Press LLC.. 919 544-1777
 1920 E Nc Highway 54 Ste 30 Durham (27713) *(G-4238)*

Skyland Prsthtics Orthtics Inc.. 828 684-1644
 3845 Hendersonville Rd Fletcher (28732) *(G-4769)*

Skyline Plastic Systems Inc... 828 891-2515
 2220 Jeffress Rd Mills River (28759) *(G-8321)*

Skyview Commercial Cleaning... 704 858-0134
 5725 Carnegie Blvd Charlotte (28209) *(G-2812)*

Skyworks Solutions Inc.. 336 291-4200
 406 Gallimore Dairy Rd Greensboro (27409) *(G-5816)*

SL - Laser Systems LLC.. 704 561-9990
 4920 Larkmoore Ct Charlotte (28208) *(G-2813)*

SL Laser Systems LP... 704 561-9990
 8107 Arrowridge Blvd Ste Q Charlotte (28273) *(G-2814)*

SL Liquidation LLC... 910 353-3666
 408 White St Jacksonville (28546) *(G-7145)*

SL Liquidation LLC (DH).. 860 525-0821
 405 White St Jacksonville (28546) *(G-7146)*

SL Liquidation LLC... 910 353-3666
 405 White St Jacksonville (28546) *(G-7147)*

Slack & Parr International (HQ)... 704 527-2975
 Hwy 321 Dallas (28034) *(G-3690)*

Slade, Statesville *Also Called: Slade Operating Company LLC (G-11766)*

Slade Operating Company LLC... 704 873-1366
 2030 Simonton Rd Statesville (28625) *(G-11766)*

Slam Publications LLC.. 252 480-2234
 2910 S Croatan Hwy Unit 19 Nags Head (27959) *(G-9303)*

Slane Hosiery Mills Inc.. 336 883-4136
 313 S Centennial St High Point (27260) *(G-6781)*

Sleepworthy, Greenville *Also Called: Cotton Belt Inc (G-5960)*

Sleepy Creek Turkeys LLC... 919 778-3130
 938 Millers Chapel Rd Goldsboro (27534) *(G-5244)*

Sleepy Creek Turkeys, Inc., Goldsboro *Also Called: Sleepy Creek Turkeys LLC (G-5244)*

Slickedit Inc.. 919 473-0070
 408 Bathgate Ln Cary (27513) *(G-1460)*

Sloans Machine Shop.. 919 499-5655
 1186 Walker Rd Sanford (27332) *(G-11234)*

Sls Baking Company.. 704 421-2763
 15720 Brixham Hill Ave Charlotte (28277) *(G-2815)*

Slum Dog Head Gear LLC.. 704 713-8125
 9912 Jeanette Cir Charlotte (28213) *(G-2816)*

Small Brothers Tire Co Inc... 704 289-3531
 1725 Concord Ave Monroe (28110) *(G-8559)*

(G-0000) Company's Geographic Section entry number

Small Business Software LLC.................................... 919 400-8298
5117 Wickham Rd Raleigh (27606) *(G-10486)*

Small Tire Company, Monroe *Also Called: Small Brothers Tire Co Inc (G-8559)*

Smallhd LLC (DH).. 919 439-2166
301 Gregson Dr Cary (27511) *(G-1461)*

Smart Cast Group.. 855 971-2287
5540 Centerview Dr Ste 204 Raleigh (27606) *(G-10487)*

Smart Desks, Mooresville *Also Called: Cbt Supply (G-8636)*

Smart Electric North Amer LLC.................................. 828 323-1200
1550 Deborah Herman Rd Sw Conover (28613) *(G-3559)*

Smart Machine Technologies Inc................................ 276 632-9853
2105 Mimosa Dr Greensboro (27403) *(G-5817)*

Smart Way, Charlotte *Also Called: Smartway of Carolinas LLC (G-2817)*

Smart Wires Inc (PA).. 919 294-3999
1035 Swabia Ct Ste 130 Durham (27703) *(G-4239)*

Smartlink Mobile Systems LLC.................................. 919 674-8400
1000 Centre Green Way Ste 250 Cary (27513) *(G-1462)*

Smartrac Tech Fletcher Inc... 828 651-6051
267 Cane Creek Rd Fletcher (28732) *(G-4770)*

Smartrac Technology, Fletcher *Also Called: Upm Raflatac Inc (G-4776)*

Smartware Group Inc... 866 858-7800
11000 Regency Pkwy Ste 110 Cary (27518) *(G-1463)*

Smartway of Carolinas LLC.. 704 900-7877
3304 Eastway Dr Charlotte (28205) *(G-2817)*

SMC Corporation of America...................................... 704 947-7556
9801 Kincey Ave Ste 150 Huntersville (28078) *(G-7055)*

SMC Holdco Inc.. 910 844-3956
22261 Skyway Church Rd Laurinburg (28353) *(G-7515)*

Smg Hearth and Home LLC....................................... 919 973-4079
3871 S Alston Ave Durham (27713) *(G-4240)*

SMI, Charlotte *Also Called: Specialty Manufacturing Inc (G-2841)*

Smiling Hara LLC.. 828 545-4150
735 N Fork Rd Barnardsville (28709) *(G-694)*

Smiling Hara Tempeh, Barnardsville *Also Called: Smiling Hara LLC (G-694)*

Smissons Inc.. 660 537-3219
425 Swann Trl Clayton (27527) *(G-3169)*

Smith & Associates, Cary *Also Called: Cherokee Publishing Co Inc (G-1326)*

Smith & Fox Inc... 828 684-4512
19 Walden Dr Arden (28704) *(G-307)*

Smith Architectural Metals LLC.................................. 336 273-1970
4536 S Holden Rd Greensboro (27406) *(G-5818)*

Smith Brothers Logging.. 828 265-1506
136 Clyde Ln Deep Gap (28618) *(G-3730)*

Smith Companies Lexington Inc (PA).......................... 336 249-4941
720 W Center St Lexington (27292) *(G-7742)*

Smith Draperies Inc... 336 226-2183
2347 W Hanford Rd Burlington (27215) *(G-1158)*

Smith Electric Co, Lawndale *Also Called: JA Smith Inc (G-7517)*

Smith Fabrication Inc... 704 660-5170
2136 Coddle Creek Hwy Mooresville (28115) *(G-8772)*

Smith Family Screen Printing..................................... 336 317-4849
5311 Appomattox Rd Pleasant Garden (27313) *(G-9794)*

Smith Millwork Inc... 800 222-8498
920 Robbins Cir Lexington (27292) *(G-7743)*

Smith Novelty Company Inc....................................... 704 982-7413
2120 W Main St Albemarle (28001) *(G-89)*

Smith Setzer and Sons Inc.. 828 241-3161
4708 E Nc 10 Hwy Catawba (28609) *(G-1514)*

Smith Systems Inc.. 828 884-3490
6 Mill Creek Ctr Brevard (28712) *(G-982)*

Smith Utility Buildings.. 336 957-8211
13721 Longbottom Rd Traphill (28685) *(G-12106)*

Smith Woodturning Inc... 828 464-2230
2427 Claremont Rd Newton (28658) *(G-9495)*

Smith-Carolina Corporation.. 336 349-2905
654 Freeway Dr Reidsville (27320) *(G-10698)*

Smithfeld Fresh Meats Sls Corp................................. 910 862-7675
15855 Hwy 87 W Tar Heel (28392) *(G-11918)*

Smithfield Foods Inc.. 910 299-3009
424 E Railroad St Clinton (28328) *(G-3246)*

Smithfield Foods Inc.. 704 298-0936
2975 Dale Earnhardt Blvd Kannapolis (28083) *(G-7220)*

Smithfield Foods Inc.. 252 208-4700
1780 Smithfield Way Kinston (28504) *(G-7428)*

Smithfield Foods Inc.. 910 241-2022
16261 Nc Highway 87 W Tar Heel (28392) *(G-11919)*

Smithfield Foods Inc.. 910 862-7675
15855 Nc Highway 87 W Tar Heel (28392) *(G-11920)*

Smithfield Grain, Hobbsville *Also Called: Murphy-Brown LLC (G-6884)*

Smithfield Grain, Warsaw *Also Called: Murphy-Brown LLC (G-12363)*

Smithfield Packing Company Inc................................. 910 592-2104
424 E Railroad St Clinton (28328) *(G-3247)*

Smithgroup, Winston Salem *Also Called: Sg-Clw Inc (G-13331)*

Smiths Custom Kitchen Inc... 828 652-9033
58 Butterfly Dr Marion (28752) *(G-8065)*

Smiths Logging... 910 653-4422
13169 Swamp Fox Hwy E Tabor City (28463) *(G-11914)*

Smithway Inc.. 828 628-1756
20 Smith Farm Rd Fairview (28730) *(G-4511)*

Smithway Inc.. 828 628-1756
Us Highway 74 A E Fairview (28730) *(G-4512)*

Sml Raleigh LLC.. 919 585-0100
501 Atkinson St Clayton (27520) *(G-3170)*

Smoke House Lumber Company................................. 252 257-3303
2711 Nc Highway 58 Warrenton (27589) *(G-12355)*

Smokey Mountain Amusements.................................. 828 479-2814
5660 Tallulah Rd Robbinsville (28771) *(G-10762)*

Smokey Mountain Lumber Inc (PA)............................ 828 298-3958
19 Lower Grassy Branch Rd Asheville (28805) *(G-602)*

Smoky Mountain Jet Boats LLC................................ 828 488-0522
414 Black Hill Rd Bryson City (28713) *(G-1011)*

Smoky Mountain Machining Inc................................. 828 665-1193
80 Mcintosh Rd Asheville (28806) *(G-603)*

Smoky Mountain News Inc (PA)................................. 828 452-4251
144 Montgomery St Waynesville (28786) *(G-12474)*

Smoky Mtn Nativ Plant Assn...................................... 828 479-8788
546 Upper Tuskeegee Rd Robbinsville (28771) *(G-10763)*

Smt Inc.. 919 782-4804
7300 Acc Blvd Raleigh (27617) *(G-10488)*

Smw, Gastonia *Also Called: Speedwell Machine Works Inc (G-5140)*

Smyrna Ready Mix Concrete LLC............................... 252 447-5356
417 Miller Blvd Havelock (28532) *(G-6127)*

Smyrna Ready Mix Concrete LLC.............................. 252 637-4155
1715 Race Track Rd New Bern (28562) *(G-9397)*

Snap One, Charlotte *Also Called: Snap One Holdings Corp (G-2819)*

Snap One LLC (DH)... 704 927-7620
1800 Continental Blvd Ste 200 Charlotte (28273) *(G-2818)*

Snap One Holdings Corp (HQ)................................... 704 927-7620
1800 Continental Blvd Ste 200 Charlotte (28273) *(G-2819)*

Snap Publications LLC... 336 274-8531
216 W Market St Ste A Greensboro (27401) *(G-5819)*

Snap Rite Manufacturing Inc (PA).............................. 910 897-4080
232 N Ida St Coats (27521) *(G-3265)*

Snap-On Power Tools Inc... 828 835-4400
250 Snap On Dr Murphy (28906) *(G-9296)*

Snap-On Tools, Murphy *Also Called: Snap-On Power Tools Inc (G-9296)*

Snapav, Charlotte *Also Called: Snap One LLC (G-2818)*

Snider Tire Inc... 704 373-2910
900 Atando Ave Charlotte (28206) *(G-2820)*

Snider Tire Inc... 336 691-5480
330 E Lindsay St Greensboro (27401) *(G-5820)*

Snider Tire Inc... 828 324-9955
1226 21st Street Dr Se Hickory (28602) *(G-6450)*

Sniders Machine Shop Inc.. 704 279-6129
8025 Highway 52 Rockwell (28138) *(G-10801)*

Snowbird Logging LLC... 828 479-6635
270 Dick Branch Rd Robbinsville (28771) *(G-10764)*

Snp Inc... 919 598-0400
1301 S Briggs Ave Ste 110 Durham (27703) *(G-4241)*

Snyder Packaging, Concord *Also Called: Snyder Packaging Inc (G-3441)*

Snyder Packaging Inc... 704 786-3111
788 Harris St Nw Concord (28025) *(G-3441)*

Snyder Paper, Newton *Also Called: Snyder Paper Corporation (G-9496)*

Snyder Paper Corporation.................................... 800 222-8562
85 Thompson St Asheville (28803) *(G-604)*

Snyder Paper Corporation.................................... 336 884-1172
1104 W Ward Ave High Point (27260) *(G-6782)*

Snyder Paper Corporation.................................... 828 464-1189
1813 Mount Olive Church Rd Newton (28658) *(G-9496)*

Snyders-Lance Inc... 704 557-8013
1900 Continental Blvd Charlotte (28273) *(G-2821)*

Sobi Inc... 844 506-3682
3015 Carrington Mill Blvd Ste 410 Morrisville (27560) *(G-9056)*

Socialtopias LLC.. 704 910-1713
1415 S Church St Ste C Charlotte (28203) *(G-2822)*

Society Awards, Charlotte *Also Called: DWM INTERNATIONAL INC (G-2071)*

Sock Factory Inc.. 828 328-5207
1371 13th St Sw Hickory (28602) *(G-6451)*

Sock Inc.. 561 254-2223
1908 Belvedere Ave Charlotte (28205) *(G-2823)*

Socks and Other Things LLC.............................. 704 904-2472
4413 Mickleton Rd Charlotte (28226) *(G-2824)*

Sofidel Shelby LLC... 704 476-3802
671 Washburn Switch Rd Shelby (28150) *(G-11379)*

Software Goldsmith Inc..................................... 919 346-0403
5305 Lake Edge Dr Holly Springs (27540) *(G-6915)*

Software Professionals Inc................................. 503 860-4507
8529 Six Forks Rd Ste 400 Raleigh (27615) *(G-10489)*

Sofware, Hendersonville *Also Called: Sofware LLC (G-6241)*

Sofware LLC (PA)... 828 820-2810
217 Covington Cove Ln Hendersonville (28739) *(G-6241)*

Soha Holdings LLC... 828 264-2314
645 Roby Greene Rd Boone (28607) *(G-942)*

Soisa Inc... 336 940-4006
111 Dalton Business Ct Ste 101 Mocksville (27028) *(G-8390)*

Sol-Rex Miniature Lamp Works............................ 845 292-1510
802 Mulberry St Beaufort (28516) *(G-734)*

Sola Publishing.. 336 226-8240
1074 W Main St Graham (27253) *(G-5285)*

Solace Healthcare Furn LLC............................... 336 884-0046
815 W Ward Ave High Point (27260) *(G-6783)*

Solar Hot Limited.. 919 439-2387
1105 Transport Dr Raleigh (27603) *(G-10490)*

Solar Hot USA, Raleigh *Also Called: Solar Hot Limited (G-10490)*

Solar Pack.. 919 515-2194
1791 Varsity Dr Raleigh (27606) *(G-10491)*

Solara Automation, Morrisville *Also Called: Aae North America LLC (G-8916)*

Solarbrook Water and Pwr Corp (PA)..................... 919 231-3205
1220 Corporation Pkwy Ste 103 Raleigh (27610) *(G-10492)*

Solarh2ot Ltd... 919 439-2387
1105 Transport Dr Raleigh (27603) *(G-10493)*

Solarhot, Raleigh *Also Called: Solarh2ot Ltd (G-10493)*

Solarpack, Raleigh *Also Called: Solar Pack (G-10491)*

Solero Technologies Shelby LLC.......................... 704 482-9582
1100 Airport Rd Shelby (28150) *(G-11380)*

Solid Frames Inc.. 336 882-5082
501 Garrison St High Point (27260) *(G-6784)*

Solid Holdings LLC.. 704 423-0260
3820 Rose Lake Dr Charlotte (28217) *(G-2825)*

Solo Foods LLC... 910 259-9407
201w Progress Dr Burgaw (28425) *(G-1032)*

Solomon Engineering Inc.................................. 828 855-1652
340 9th St Se Hickory (28602) *(G-6452)*

Solvekta LLC.. 336 944-4677
2110 Rockglen Ln Greensboro (27410) *(G-5821)*

Solvere LLC... 704 829-1015
69 Mcadenville Rd Belmont (28012) *(G-766)*

Somers Lumber and Mfg Inc............................... 704 539-4751
126 Oakleaf Rd Harmony (28634) *(G-6099)*

Something For Youth... 252 799-8837
503 E Main St Williamston (27892) *(G-12673)*

Sommerville Enterprises LLC.............................. 919 924-1594
202 Holiday Park Rd Hillsborough (27278) *(G-6878)*

Somnigroup International Inc.............................. 336 861-2900
1 Office Parkway Rd Trinity (27370) *(G-12126)*

Sona Autocomp USA LLC.................................... 919 965-5555
500 Oak Tree Dr Selma (27576) *(G-11291)*

Sona Blw Precision Forge Inc............................. 919 828-3375
500 Oak Tree Dr Selma (27576) *(G-11292)*

Sonablate Corp (PA)... 888 874-4384
10130 Perimeter Pkwy Ste 410 Charlotte (28216) *(G-2826)*

Sonaron LLC... 808 232-6168
7790 Cottonwood Ave Fayetteville (28314) *(G-4672)*

Sonaspection International................................. 704 262-3384
6851 Belt Rd Concord (28027) *(G-3442)*

Song of Wood Ltd.. 828 669-7675
203 W State St Black Mountain (28711) *(G-871)*

Sonicaire Inc.. 336 712-2437
3831 Kimwell Dr Winston Salem (27103) *(G-13340)*

Sonoco, Elon College *Also Called: Sonoco Products Company (G-4475)*

Sonoco, Forest City *Also Called: Sonoco Products Company (G-4797)*

Sonoco Hickory Inc (HQ).................................... 828 328-2466
1246 Main Ave Se Hickory (28602) *(G-6453)*

Sonoco Products Company................................. 828 648-1987
6175 Pigeon Rd Canton (28716) *(G-1256)*

Sonoco Products Company................................. 704 875-2685
12000 Vance Davis Dr Charlotte (28269) *(G-2827)*

Sonoco Products Company................................. 336 449-7731
212 Cook Rd Elon College (27244) *(G-4475)*

Sonoco Products Company................................. 828 245-0118
323 Pine St Forest City (28043) *(G-4797)*

Sonoco Products Company................................. 828 322-8844
1214 Highland Ave Ne Hickory (28601) *(G-6454)*

Sonoco Products Company................................. 910 455-6903
417 Meadowview Rd Jacksonville (28540) *(G-7148)*

Sonoco Recycling, Jacksonville *Also Called: Sonoco Products Company (G-7148)*

Sonshine Promises, Waynesville *Also Called: Cedar Hill Studio & Gallery (G-12453)*

Sony Music Holdings Inc.................................... 336 886-1807
921 Eastchester Dr High Point (27262) *(G-6785)*

Sorbe Ltd... 704 562-2991
111 Cupped Oak Dr Ste A Matthews (28104) *(G-8193)*

Sorrells Cabinet Co Inc................................... 919 639-4320
490 Chesterfield Lake Rd Lillington (27546) *(G-7803)*

Sorrells Sheree White (PA)................................. 828 452-4864
1834 Cove Creek Rd Waynesville (28785) *(G-12475)*

Sostram Corporation.. 919 226-1195
2525 Meridian Pkwy Ste 350 Durham (27713) *(G-4242)*

Sota Vision Inc... 800 807-7187
1325 Aj Tucker Loop Midland (28107) *(G-8296)*

Soto Industries LLC... 706 643-5011
6201 Fairview Rd Ste 200 Charlotte (28210) *(G-2828)*

Soulku LLC (PA)... 828 273-4278
45 S French Broad Ave Ste 180 Asheville (28801) *(G-605)*

Sound Heavy Machinery Inc (PA)........................ 910 782-2477
1809 Blue Clay Rd Wilmington (28405) *(G-12922)*

Sound Parts & Service, Wilmington *Also Called: Sound Heavy Machinery Inc (G-12922)*

Sound Trees, Davis *Also Called: Harvey & Sons Net & Twine (G-3726)*

Soundside Orthtics Prsthtics L........................... 910 238-2026
1715 Country Club Rd Ste B Jacksonville (28546) *(G-7149)*

Soundside Recycling & Mtls Inc.......................... 252 491-8666
7565 Caratoke Hwy Jarvisburg (27947) *(G-7186)*

Soup Maven LLC... 727 919-5242
825 Merrimon Ave Ste C Asheville (28804) *(G-606)*

Source Technolgies Holdings, Charlotte *Also Called: St Investors Inc (G-2856)*

South / Win LLC (DH)....................................... 336 398-5650
112 Maxfield Rd Greensboro (27405) *(G-5822)*

South Atlantic LLC.. 336 376-0410
3025 Steelway Dr Graham (27253) *(G-5286)*

South Atlantic LLC (DH).................................... 910 332-1900
1907 S 17th St Ste 2 Wilmington (28401) *(G-12923)*

South Atlantic Galvanizing, Graham *Also Called: South Atlantic LLC (G-5286)*

South Atlantic Galvanizing, Wilmington *Also Called: South Atlantic LLC (G-12923)*

South Boulevard Associates Inc.......................... 704 525-7160
186 Cherokee Rd Charlotte (28207) *(G-2829)*

South Central Oil and Prpn Inc........................... 704 982-2173
2121 W Main St Albemarle (28001) *(G-90)*

South City Print, Charlotte *Also Called: Print Media Associates Inc (G-2670)*

South East Manufacturing Co..................... 252 291-0925
113 Walnut St W Wilson (27893) *(G-13030)*

South Florida Business Journal, Charlotte *Also Called: American City Bus Journals Inc (G-1664)*

South Fork Industries Inc.......................... 828 428-9921
100 W Pine St Maiden (28650) *(G-8017)*

South Mountain Crafts............................. 828 433-2607
300 Enola Rd Morganton (28655) *(G-8899)*

South Point Hospitality Inc........................ 704 542-2304
13451 S Point Blvd Charlotte (28273) *(G-2830)*

South Side Bargain Center, Winston Salem *Also Called: GLG Corporation (G-13178)*

South-East Lumber Company...................... 336 996-5322
1896 W Mountain St Kernersville (27284) *(G-7301)*

South-Tek Systems LLC............................ 910 332-4173
3700 Us Highway 421 N Wilmington (28401) *(G-12924)*

Southag Mfg Inc.................................... 919 365-5111
2023 Wendell Blvd Wendell (27591) *(G-12548)*

Southandenglish LLC.............................. 336 888-8333
1314 Starr Dr High Point (27260) *(G-6786)*

Southbend, Fuquay Varina *Also Called: Middleby Marshall Inc (G-4891)*

Southbridge Inc.................................... 828 350-9112
2000 Riverside Dr Ste 5 Asheville (28804) *(G-607)*

Southco Industries Inc............................. 704 482-1477
1840 E Dixon Blvd Shelby (28152) *(G-11381)*

Southcorr LLC...................................... 336 498-1700
3021 Taylor Dr Asheboro (27203) *(G-396)*

Southeast Leather, High Point *Also Called: Coast To Coast Lea & Vinyl Inc (G-6571)*

Southeast Tubular Products Inc................... 704 883-8883
1308 Industrial Dr Statesville (28625) *(G-11767)*

Southeast Wood Products Inc..................... 910 285-4359
444 Jack Dale Rd Wallace (28466) *(G-12324)*

Southeaster Plastic Inc............................ 336 275-6616
605 Diamond Hill Ct Greensboro (27406) *(G-5823)*

Southeastern Concrete Pdts Co................... 704 873-2226
2325 Salisbury Hwy Statesville (28677) *(G-11768)*

Southeastern Container Inc (PA)...................828 350-7200
1250 Sand Hill Rd Enka (28728) *(G-4488)*

Southeastern Container Inc........................ 704 710-4200
293 Industrial Dr Kings Mountain (28086) *(G-7385)*

Southeastern Corrugated LLC (PA)............... 980 224-9551
10901 Carpet St Charlotte (28273) *(G-2831)*

Southeastern Die of NC............................ 336 275-5212
510 Corliss St Greensboro (27406) *(G-5824)*

Southeastern Elevator LLC........................ 252 726-9983
143 Industrial Dr Morehead City (28557) *(G-8845)*

Southeastern Enterprises (HQ)................... 704 373-1750
3545 Asbury Ave Charlotte (28206) *(G-2832)*

Southeastern Hardwoods Inc...................... 828 581-0197
734 Bee Tree Rd Swannanoa (28778) *(G-11878)*

Southeastern Installation Inc (PA)............... 704 352-7146
207 Cedar Lane Dr Lexington (27292) *(G-7744)*

Southeastern Mch & Wldg Co Inc................. 910 791-6661
142 Shipyard Blvd Wilmington (28412) *(G-12925)*

Southeastern Minerals Inc........................ 252 492-0831
170 Eastern Minerals Rd Henderson (27537) *(G-6179)*

SOUTHEASTERN MINERALS, INC., Henderson *Also Called: Southeastern Minerals Inc (G-6179)*

Southeastern Packg Plant 2, Concord *Also Called: Michigan Packaging Company (G-3402)*

Southeastern Plastics, Greensboro *Also Called: Southeaster Plastic Inc (G-5823)*

Southeastern Sign Works Inc...................... 336 789-5516
609 Junction St Mount Airy (27030) *(G-9177)*

Southeastern Steel Cnstr Inc...................... 910 346-4462
225 Ellis Blvd Jacksonville (28540) *(G-7150)*

Southeastern Tool & Die Inc....................... 910 944-7677
105 Taylor St Aberdeen (28315) *(G-24)*

Southeastern Transformer Co, Dunn *Also Called: Trans East Inc (G-3869)*

Souther Signs Company, Wilmington *Also Called: Cbr Signs LLC (G-12737)*

Southern AG Insecticides, Boone *Also Called: Southern AG Insecticides Inc (G-943)*

Southern AG Insecticides Inc...................... 828 264-8843
395 Brook Hollow Rd Boone (28607) *(G-943)*

Southern AG Insecticides Inc...................... 828 692-2233
511 Maple St Hendersonville (28792) *(G-6242)*

Southern Aggregates, Staley *Also Called: Midcoastal Development Corp (G-11597)*

Southern ATL Spring Mfg Sls LL................... 704 279-1331
127 Rowan St Granite Quarry (28072) *(G-5328)*

Southern Baptist Church, Weaverville *Also Called: Brookstone Baptist Church (G-12485)*

Southern Block Company........................... 910 293-7844
510 W Hill St Warsaw (28398) *(G-12366)*

Southern Cabinet Co Inc........................... 704 373-2299
1418 Industrial Dr Matthews (28105) *(G-8149)*

Southern Cast Inc.................................. 704 335-0692
901 N Church St Charlotte (28206) *(G-2833)*

Southern Classic Seating LLC..................... 336 498-3130
7064 Us Highway 311 Sophia (27350) *(G-11491)*

Southern Classic Stairs Inc........................ 828 285-9828
24 Carl Roberts Rd Alexander (28701) *(G-101)*

Southern Concrete Incorporated.................. 919 906-4069
3560 Mcarthur Rd Broadway (27505) *(G-987)*

Southern Concrete Materials...................... 704 641-9604
2807 Armentrout Dr Concord (28025) *(G-3443)*

Southern Concrete Materials Inc (HQ).............828 253-6421
35 Meadow Rd Asheville (28803) *(G-608)*

Southern Concrete Mtls Inc........................ 828 684-3636
Hendersonville Rd Arden (28704) *(G-308)*

Southern Concrete Mtls Inc........................ 828 670-6450
80 Pond Rd Asheville (28806) *(G-609)*

Southern Concrete Mtls Inc........................ 828 682-2298
129 Depot St Burnsville (28714) *(G-1191)*

Southern Concrete Mtls Inc........................ 704 394-2346
11609 Texland Blvd Charlotte (28273) *(G-2834)*

Southern Concrete Mtls Inc........................ 704 394-2344
715 State St Charlotte (28208) *(G-2835)*

Southern Concrete Mtls Inc........................ 828 681-5178
250 Old Hendersonville Rd Fletcher (28732) *(G-4771)*

Southern Concrete Mtls Inc........................ 828 524-3555
493 Wells Grove Rd Franklin (28734) *(G-4840)*

Southern Concrete Mtls Inc........................ 828 692-6517
715 Shepherd St Hendersonville (28792) *(G-6243)*

Southern Concrete Mtls Inc........................ 877 788-3001
1155 Chuck Taylor Ln Salisbury (28147) *(G-11117)*

Southern Concrete Mtls Inc........................ 828 586-5280
1362 W Main St Sylva (28779) *(G-11899)*

Southern Concrete Mtls Inc........................ 828 456-9048
201 Boundary St Waynesville (28786) *(G-12476)*

Southern Data Systems Inc........................ 919 781-7603
7758 Nc Highway 96 Oxford (27565) *(G-9635)*

Southern Design Cabinetry LLC................... 919 263-9414
740 Merritt Capital Dr Ste 120 Wake Forest (27587) *(G-12301)*

Southern Devices Inc............................... 828 584-1611
113 Industrial Blvd Morganton (28655) *(G-8900)*

Southern Digital Watch Repair.................... 336 299-6718
4009 Groometown Rd Greensboro (27407) *(G-5825)*

Southern Distilling Co LLC........................ 704 677-4069
211 Jennings Rd Statesville (28625) *(G-11769)*

Southern Distilling Company, Statesville *Also Called: Southern Distilling Co LLC (G-11769)*

Southern Elc & Automtn Corp..................... 919 718-0122
800 Hawkins Ave Sanford (27330) *(G-11235)*

Southern Electric Motor Co........................ 919 688-7879
2121 Front St # 25 Durham (27705) *(G-4243)*

Southern Electrical Eqp Co Inc (PA).............. 704 392-1396
4045 Hargrove Ave Charlotte (28208) *(G-2836)*

Southern Electrical Eqp Co Inc.................... 704 392-1396
1015 Van Buren Ave Indian Trail (28079) *(G-7099)*

Southern Engraving Company..................... 336 656-0084
3008 Windchase Ct High Point (27265) *(G-6787)*

Southern Environmental Cons, Raleigh *Also Called: Tower Engrg Professionals Inc (G-10554)*

Southern Equipment Company, Ayden *Also Called: Ready Mixed Concrete (G-659)*

Southern Estates Metal Roofing................... 704 245-2023
614 Maple St Locust (28097) *(G-7902)*

Southern Fabricators Inc........................... 704 272-7615
8188 Us Highway 74 W Polkton (28135) *(G-9815)*

Southern Fiber Inc (PA)...............................704 736-0011
1041 S Grove Extension Lincolnton (28093) *(G-7854)*

Southern Film Extruders, High Point *Also Called: Sigma Plastics Group (G-6770)*

Southern Film Extruders Inc......................336 885-8091
2319 W English Rd High Point (27262) *(G-6788)*

Southern Finishing Company Inc (PA)............336 573-3741
100 W Main St Stoneville (27048) *(G-11828)*

Southern Flow Companies, Princeton *Also Called: Powersecure Inc (G-9825)*

Southern Glove Inc.................................828 464-4884
749 Ac Little Dr Newton (28658) *(G-9497)*

Southern Hldings Goldsboro Inc...................919 920-6998
501 Patetown Rd Ste 4 Goldsboro (27530) *(G-5245)*

Southern Home Spa & Water Pdts, Greensboro *Also Called: Southern Home Spa and Wtr Pdts (G-5826)*

Southern Home Spa and Wtr Pdts..................336 286-3564
105 Edwardia Dr Greensboro (27409) *(G-5826)*

Southern Leisure Builders Inc...................910 381-0426
2444 Commerce Rd Jacksonville (28546) *(G-7151)*

Southern Lithoplate Inc (PA)....................919 556-9400
105 Jeffrey Way Youngsville (27596) *(G-13487)*

Southern Logging Inc..............................336 859-5057
250 Piedmont School Rd Denton (27239) *(G-3760)*

Southern Machine Services........................919 658-9300
300 Waller Rd Mount Olive (28365) *(G-9258)*

Southern Machining, Shelby *Also Called: Rufus N Ivie III (G-11374)*

Southern Marble Co LLC...........................704 982-4142
2033 W Main St Albemarle (28001) *(G-91)*

Southern Metals Company..........................704 394-3161
2200 Donald Ross Rd Charlotte (28208) *(G-2837)*

Southern Organ Services Ltd......................828 667-8230
3 English Pl Candler (28715) *(G-1233)*

Southern Pdmont Pping Fbrction..................704 272-7936
2798 Lower White Store Rd Peachland (28133) *(G-9654)*

Southern Pipe Inc.................................704 550-5935
445 N 4th St Albemarle (28001) *(G-92)*

Southern Pipe Inc (PA)...........................704 463-5202
135 Random Dr New London (28127) *(G-9422)*

Southern Precision Spring Inc....................704 392-4393
2200 Old Steele Creek Rd Charlotte (28208) *(G-2838)*

Southern Prestige Industries Inc.................704 872-9524
113 Hatfield Rd Statesville (28625) *(G-11770)*

Southern Prestige Intl LLC.......................704 872-9524
113 Hatfield Rd Statesville (28625) *(G-11771)*

Southern Printing Company Inc....................910 259-4807
203 S Dudley St Burgaw (28425) *(G-1033)*

Southern Products Company Inc....................910 281-3189
4303 Us Hwy 1 N Hoffman (28347) *(G-6885)*

Southern Quilters, Henderson *Also Called: Pacific Coast Feather LLC (G-6169)*

Southern Range Brewing LLC.......................704 289-4049
151 S Stewart St Monroe (28112) *(G-8560)*

Southern Resin Inc................................336 475-1348
3440 Denton Rd Thomasville (27360) *(G-12071)*

Southern Resources, Charlotte *Also Called: Elan Trading Inc (G-2094)*

Southern Roots Monogramming......................706 599-5383
148 Cotton Wood Rd Cleveland (27013) *(G-3222)*

Southern Rubber Company Inc......................336 299-2456
2209 Patterson St Greensboro (27407) *(G-5827)*

Southern Signworks................................828 683-8726
45 Single Tree Gap Rd Leicester (28748) *(G-7529)*

Southern Software Inc.............................336 879-3350
150 Perry Dr Southern Pines (28387) *(G-11510)*

Southern Software Inc.............................910 638-8700
7231 Cayman Dr Fayetteville (28306) *(G-4673)*

Southern Spring & Stamping.......................336 548-3520
2089 Us Highway 220 Stokesdale (27357) *(G-11815)*

Southern Staircase, Charlotte *Also Called: Artistic Southern Inc (G-1700)*

Southern Staircase, Charlotte *Also Called: Southern Staircase Inc (G-2839)*

Southern Staircase Inc............................704 357-1221
1108 Continental Blvd Ste O Charlotte (28273) *(G-2839)*

Southern Staircase Inc............................704 363-2123
1108 Continental Blvd Ste O Charlotte (28273) *(G-2840)*

Southern States Chemical Inc.....................910 762-5054
4600 Us Highway 421 N Wilmington (28401) *(G-12926)*

Southern States Coop Inc.........................336 629-3977
504 E Dixie Dr Asheboro (27203) *(G-397)*

Southern States Coop Inc.........................336 246-3201
2089 Sam Moss Hayes Rd Creedmoor (27522) *(G-3654)*

Southern States Coop Inc.........................919 528-1516
301 N Main St Creedmoor (27522) *(G-3655)*

Southern States Coop Inc.........................336 786-7545
202 Snowhill Dr Mount Airy (27030) *(G-9178)*

Southern States Coop Inc.........................919 658-5061
301 N Chestnut St Mount Olive (28365) *(G-9259)*

Southern States Coop Inc.........................919 693-6136
607 Hillsboro St Oxford (27565) *(G-9636)*

Southern States Coop Inc.........................252 823-2520
142 Commercial Rd Princeville (27886) *(G-9828)*

Southern States Coop Inc.........................336 599-2185
1112 N Main St Roxboro (27573) *(G-10945)*

Southern States Coop Inc.........................704 872-6364
2504 Davie Ave Statesville (28625) *(G-11772)*

Southern States Coop Inc.........................910 285-8213
939 Nw Railroad St Wallace (28466) *(G-12325)*

Southern Steel and Wire Inc......................336 548-9611
100 Minich Rd Madison (27025) *(G-8000)*

Southern Style Logging LLC.......................910 259-9897
3595 Little Kelly Rd Rocky Point (28457) *(G-10883)*

Southern Supreme Fruit Cakes, Bear Creek *Also Called: Scotts & Associates Inc (G-718)*

Southern Trade Publications Co (PA).............336 454-3516
6520 Airport Center Dr Ste 204 Greensboro (27409) *(G-5828)*

Southern Traditions Two Inc......................919 742-4692
55 Industrial Park Dr Siler City (27344) *(G-11425)*

Southern Trucking & Backhoe......................919 548-9723
165 Riverside Rd Siler City (27344) *(G-11426)*

Southern Vinyl Mfg Inc............................252 523-2520
2010 Smithfield Way Kinston (28504) *(G-7429)*

Southern Vneer Spclty Pdts LLC...................919 642-7004
306 Corinth Rd Moncure (27559) *(G-8409)*

Southern Wicked Distillery Inc...................919 539-1620
3211 Imperial Oaks Dr Raleigh (27614) *(G-10494)*

Southern Woodcraft Design LLC....................919 693-8995
114 Southgate Dr Oxford (27565) *(G-9637)*

Southern Woods Lumber Inc........................919 963-2233
3872 Old School Rd Four Oaks (27524) *(G-4816)*

Southern Woodworking Inc.........................336 693-5892
418 Hawthorne Ln Burlington (27215) *(G-1159)*

Southfield Ltd....................................336 434-6220
2224 Shore St High Point (27263) *(G-6789)*

Southfield Upholstered Furn, High Point *Also Called: Southfield Ltd (G-6789)*

Southill Industrial Carving......................336 472-5311
1861 N Nc Highway 109 Thomasville (27360) *(G-12072)*

Southland Amusements Vend Inc (PA)..............910 343-1809
1611 Castle Hayne Rd Ste D3 Wilmington (28401) *(G-12927)*

Southland Electrical Sup LLC.....................336 227-1486
147 N Main St Burlington (27217) *(G-1160)*

Southland Log Homes Inc..........................336 449-5388
5692 Millstream Rd Whitsett (27377) *(G-12620)*

Southline Converting LLC.........................828 781-6414
639 4th Street Pl Sw Conover (28613) *(G-3560)*

Southport Graphics LLC............................919 650-3822
9400 Globe Center Dr Ste 101 Morrisville (27560) *(G-9057)*

Southport NC......................................910 524-7425
5105 Bent Oak Ln Southport (28461) *(G-11529)*

Southstern Archtctural Systems, Charlotte *Also Called: Tom Rochester & Associates Inc (G-2928)*

Southstern Prcess Eqp Cntrls I...................704 483-1141
7558 Townsend Dr Denver (28037) *(G-3806)*

Southwire, Huntersville *Also Called: Southwire Company LLC (G-7056)*

Southwire Company LLC.............................704 379-9600
12331 Commerce Station Dr Huntersville (28078) *(G-7056)*

Southwood Doors LLC...............................704 625-2578
1222 Emmanuel Church Rd Ste 6 Conover (28613) *(G-3561)*

Sovereign Technologies LLC 828 358-5355
3908 Pinecrest Dr Ne Hickory (28601) *(G-6455)*

Spa and Salon, Fayetteville *Also Called: Brandy Thompson (G-4561)*

Space-Ray, Charlotte *Also Called: Gas-Fired Products Inc (G-2190)*

Spake Concrete Products Inc 704 482-2881
1110 N Post Rd Shelby (28150) *(G-11382)*

Spanglercv Inc 910 794-5547
3111 Kitty Hawk Rd Ste 2 Wilmington (28405) *(G-12928)*

Spanset Inc (HQ) 919 774-6316
3125 Industrial Dr Sanford (27332) *(G-11236)*

Spantek Expanded Metal Inc 704 479-6210
352 N Generals Blvd Lincolnton (28092) *(G-7855)*

Sparta Plastics, High Point *Also Called: Prime Mill LLC (G-6746)*

Spartacraft Inc 828 397-4630
7690 Sparta Craft Dr Connelly Springs (28612) *(G-3483)*

Spartan Blades LLC 910 757-0035
625 Se Service Rd Southern Pines (28387) *(G-11511)*

Spartan Dyers Inc 704 829-0467
217 Sterling St Belmont (28012) *(G-767)*

Spartan Manufacturing Corp (PA) 336 996-5585
1536 Brookford Industrial Dr Kernersville (27284) *(G-7302)*

Spartan Systems LLC 336 946-1244
106 York Way Ste 101 Advance (27006) *(G-39)*

Spartan Tower, Advance *Also Called: Spartan Systems LLC (G-39)*

Spatial Light LLC 617 213-0314
1017 Pueblo Ridge Pl Cary (27519) *(G-1464)*

Spc Heating & Cooling, Wendell *Also Called: Spc Mechanical Corporation (G-12549)*

Spc Mechanical Corporation (PA) 252 237-9035
1500 Wendell Rd Wendell (27591) *(G-12549)*

Spc-Usa Inc 910 875-9002
404 W Edinborough Ave Raeford (28376) *(G-9852)*

Spco., Raleigh *Also Called: S P Co Inc (G-10453)*

Spec, Denver *Also Called: Southstern Prcess Eqp Cntrls I (G-3806)*

Specgx LLC 919 878-4706
8801 Capital Blvd Raleigh (27616) *(G-10495)*

Special Fab & Machine Inc 336 956-2121
4133 Old Salisbury Rd Lexington (27295) *(G-7745)*

Special Service Plastic, Charlotte *Also Called: Baily Enterprises LLC (G-1742)*

Special T Hosiery Mills Inc 336 227-2858
1102 N Anthony St Burlington (27217) *(G-1161)*

Speciality Cox Mfg LLC 828 684-5762
25 Commerce Way Arden (28704) *(G-309)*

Specialized Packaging Flexo, Greensboro *Also Called: Specialized Packaging Radisson LLC (G-5829)*

Specialized Packaging Radisson LLC 336 574-1513
600 Industrial Ave Greensboro (27406) *(G-5829)*

Specialized Retail Svcs LLC 727 639-0804
115 Callisto Way Garner (27529) *(G-4965)*

Specialty Fabricators Inc 336 838-7704
1806 Industrial Dr Wilkesboro (28697) *(G-12652)*

Specialty Lighting LLC 704 538-6522
4203 Fallston Rd Fallston (28042) *(G-4524)*

Specialty Machine Co Inc 704 853-2102
1669 Federal St Gastonia (28052) *(G-5139)*

Specialty Manufacturing, Charlotte *Also Called: Pretoria Transit Interiors Inc (G-2664)*

Specialty Manufacturing Inc (HQ) 704 247-9300
13501 S Ridge Dr Charlotte (28273) *(G-2841)*

Specialty Nails Company 336 883-0135
5050 Prospect St High Point (27263) *(G-6790)*

Specialty National Inc 336 996-8783
119 Furlong Industrial Dr Ste E Kernersville (27284) *(G-7303)*

Specialty Perf LLC 704 872-9980
228 Crawford Rd Statesville (28625) *(G-11773)*

Specialty Products Intl Ltd 910 897-4706
820 N 14th St Erwin (28339) *(G-4492)*

Specialty Textiles Inc 704 710-8657
822 Floyd St Kings Mountain (28086) *(G-7386)*

Specialty Textiles Inc (PA) 704 739-4503
515 Marie St Kings Mountain (28086) *(G-7387)*

Specialty Transportation, Newton *Also Called: Specialty Trnsp Systems Inc (G-9498)*

Specialty Trnsp Systems Inc 828 464-9738
2720 N Main Ave Newton (28658) *(G-9498)*

Specialty Welding & Mch Inc 828 464-1104
505 E 16th St Newton (28658) *(G-9499)*

Specified Metals Inc 336 786-6254
391 Hickory St Mount Airy (27030) *(G-9179)*

Spectacular Publishing Inc 919 672-0289
3333 Durham Chapel Hill Blvd Ste A101 Durham (27707) *(G-4244)*

Spectra Integrated Systems Inc 919 876-3666
4805 Green Rd Ste 110 Raleigh (27616) *(G-10496)*

Spectrasite Communications LLC (HQ) 919 468-0112
400 Regency Forest Dr Ste 300 Cary (27518) *(G-1465)*

Spectrum Adhesives Inc 828 396-4200
3815 N Main St Granite Falls (28630) *(G-5324)*

Spectrum Brands Inc 800 854-3151
15040 Choate Cir Charlotte (28273) *(G-2842)*

Spectrum Brands Inc 704 658-2060
307 Oates Rd Ste F Mooresville (28117) *(G-8773)*

Spectrum News 919 882-4009
2505 Atlantic Ave Ste 102 Raleigh (27604) *(G-10497)*

Spectrum Products Inc 919 556-7797
153 Mosswood Blvd Youngsville (27596) *(G-13488)*

Spectrum Screen Prtg Svc Inc 919 481-9905
1232 Open Field Dr Garner (27529) *(G-4966)*

Spee Dee Que Instant Prtg Inc 919 683-1307
301 E Chapel Hill St Durham (27701) *(G-4245)*

Speed Brite Inc 704 639-9771
1810 W Innes St Salisbury (28144) *(G-11118)*

Speed Energy Drink LLC 704 949-1255
7100 Weddington Rd Nw Concord (28027) *(G-3444)*

Speed King Manufacturing Inc 910 457-1995
8128 River Rd Southport (28461) *(G-11530)*

Speed Pro Imaging N Charlotte, Cornelius *Also Called: Fast Pro Media LLC (G-3599)*

Speed Pro Imaging N Charlotte, Cornelius *Also Called: Fast Pro Media LLC (G-3600)*

Speed Utv, Concord *Also Called: Speed Utv LLC (G-3445)*

Speed Utv LLC 704 949-1255
7100 Weddington Rd Nw Concord (28027) *(G-3445)*

Speedball Art Products, Statesville *Also Called: Speedball Art Products Co LLC (G-11774)*

Speedball Art Products Co LLC 800 898-7224
2301 Speedball Rd Statesville (28677) *(G-11774)*

Speediprint Inc 910 483-2553
164 Westwood Shopping Ctr Fayetteville (28314) *(G-4674)*

Speedpro Imaging 704 321-1200
2301 Crownpoint Executive Dr Charlotte (28227) *(G-2843)*

Speedpro Imaging 919 578-4338
2400 Sumner Blvd Ste 110 Raleigh (27616) *(G-10498)*

Speedpro Imaging Durham 919 278-7964
1055 Stillwell Dr Unit 1141 Durham (27707) *(G-4246)*

Speedpro of Northwest Raleigh, Morrisville *Also Called: Triangle Inner Vision Company (G-9076)*

Speedway Link Inc 704 338-2028
3727 Weddington Ridge Ln Matthews (28105) *(G-8150)*

Speedwell Machine Works Inc 704 866-7418
1301 Crowders Creek Rd Gastonia (28052) *(G-5140)*

Speedy Spread, Greensboro *Also Called: General Fertilizer Eqp Inc (G-5554)*

Speer Concrete Inc 910 947-3144
4221 Us 15 501 Hwy Carthage (28327) *(G-1280)*

Speer Operational Tech LLC 864 631-2512
315 Baldwin Ave Marion (28752) *(G-8066)*

Spencer Bowman Customs, Oak Ridge *Also Called: B & B Welding Inc (G-9569)*

Spencer Health Solutions Inc 866 971-8564
2501 Aerial Center Pkwy Ste 100 Morrisville (27560) *(G-9058)*

Spencer Yachts Inc 252 473-2660
5698 Us Highway 64 # 264 Manns Harbor (27953) *(G-8021)*

Spencer-Pettus Machine Co, Bessemer City *Also Called: Tim Conner Enterprises Inc (G-835)*

Spenco Medical Corporation 919 544-7900
2001 Tw Alexander Dr Durham (27709) *(G-4247)*

Spevco Inc 336 924-8100
8118 Reynolda Rd Pfafftown (27040) *(G-9665)*

Spg Prints, Charlotte *Also Called: Spgprints America Inc (G-2844)*

Spgprints America Inc (DH) 704 598-7171
2121 Distribution Center Dr Ste E Charlotte (28269) *(G-2844)*

A
L
P
H
A
B
E
T
I
C

Sphenodon Tool Co Inc.. 252 757-3460
3530 Tupper Dr Greenville (27834) *(G-6025)*

SPI Express, Monroe *Also Called: Stegall Petroleum Inc (G-8564)*

Spinrite Yarns LP.. 252 833-4970
190 Plymouth St Washington (27889) *(G-12414)*

Spintech LLC.. 704 885-4758
159 Walker Rd Statesville (28625) *(G-11775)*

Spiral Graphics Inc... 919 571-3371
8821 Gulf Ct Ste A Raleigh (27617) *(G-10499)*

Spirit Aerosystems NC Inc....................................... 252 208-4645
2600 Aerosystems Blvd Kinston (28504) *(G-7430)*

Spiritus Systems, Aberdeen *Also Called: Spiritus Systems Company (G-25)*

Spiritus Systems Company....................................... 910 637-0196
112 Bud Pl Aberdeen (28315) *(G-25)*

Splawn Belting Inc... 336 227-4277
1758 Anthony Rd Burlington (27215) *(G-1162)*

Splendidcrm Software Inc....................................... 919 604-1258
705 Laurel Bay Ln Holly Springs (27540) *(G-6916)*

Spm Machine Works Inc.. 252 321-2134
4721 Old Nc 11 Ayden (28513) *(G-664)*

Spnc Associates Inc.. 919 467-5151
100 Falcone Pkwy Cary (27511) *(G-1466)*

Spod Inc... 910 477-6297
316 Cedar Rd Southport (28461) *(G-11531)*

Spoonflower, Durham *Also Called: Spoonflower Inc (G-4248)*

Spoonflower Inc (DH)... 919 886-7885
3871 S Alston Ave Durham (27713) *(G-4248)*

Sporting Goods, Winnabow *Also Called: Every Day Carry Llc (G-13065)*

Sports Products LLC.. 919 723-7470
1608 Heritage Commerce Ct Ste 100 Wake Forest (27587) *(G-12302)*

Sports Solutions Inc.. 336 368-1100
614 E Main St Pilot Mountain (27041) *(G-9674)*

Sports To You, Monroe *Also Called: McCotter Industries Inc (G-8529)*

Sportsedge Inc.. 704 528-0188
3425 Derby Pl Greensboro (27405) *(G-5830)*

Sportsfield Specialties, Mocksville *Also Called: Sportsfield Specialties Inc (G-8391)*

Sportsfield Specialties Inc...................................... 704 637-2140
155 Boyce Dr Mocksville (27028) *(G-8391)*

Spota LLC... 919 569-6765
1505 Basley St Wake Forest (27587) *(G-12303)*

Spranto America Inc.. 919 741-5095
1870 Lazio Ln Apex (27502) *(G-195)*

Spraying Systems Co.. 704 357-6499
5727 Westpark Dr Ste 204 Charlotte (28217) *(G-2845)*

Spring Air Mattress Corp.. 336 272-1141
401 N Raleigh St Greensboro (27401) *(G-5831)*

Spring Hope Enterprise Inc....................................... 252 478-3651
113 N Ash St Spring Hope (27882) *(G-11559)*

Spring Repair Service Inc.. 336 299-5660
5800 W Gate City Blvd Greensboro (27407) *(G-5832)*

Springmill Products Inc... 336 406-9050
1147 Walter Mabe Rd Lawsonville (27022) *(G-7520)*

Sprinkle of Sugar LLC... 336 474-8620
11 E Main St Thomasville (27360) *(G-12073)*

Sprout Pharmaceuticals Inc..................................... 919 882-0850
4350 Lassiter At North Hills Ave Ste 260 Raleigh (27609) *(G-10500)*

Spruce Pine Batch Inc... 828 765-9876
2490 Us 19e Spruce Pine (28777) *(G-11588)*

Spruce Pine Mica Company...................................... 828 765-4241
132 Mountain Laurel Dr Spruce Pine (28777) *(G-11589)*

Spt Technology Inc.. 612 332-1880
3107 Chamber Dr Monroe (28110) *(G-8561)*

Spt Technology Inc... 704 290-5007
4808 Persimmon Ct Monroe (28110) *(G-8562)*

Spuntech Industries Inc... 336 330-9000
555 N Park Dr Roxboro (27573) *(G-10946)*

SPX, Charlotte *Also Called: Clydeunion Pumps Inc (G-1936)*

SPX Cooling Tech LLC... 630 881-9777
13515 Ballantyne Corporate Pl Charlotte (28277) *(G-2846)*

SPX Cooling Tech, LLC, Charlotte *Also Called: SPX Cooling Tech LLC (G-2846)*

SPX Corporation... 336 627-6020
523 S New St Eden (27288) *(G-4357)*

SPX CORPORATION, Eden *Also Called: SPX Corporation (G-4357)*

SPX Flow, Charlotte *Also Called: SPX Flow Inc (G-2847)*

SPX Flow Inc (HQ).. 704 752-4400
13320 Ballantyne Corporate Pl Charlotte (28277) *(G-2847)*

SPX Flow Holdings Inc... 704 808-3848
13320 Ballantyne Corporate Pl Charlotte (28277) *(G-2848)*

SPX Flow Tech Systems Inc...................................... 704 752-4400
13320 Ballantyne Corporate Pl Charlotte (28277) *(G-2849)*

SPX Flow Technology Usa, Inc., Charlotte *Also Called: Industrial Tech Svcs Amrcas In (G-2325)*

SPX Flow Us LLC.. 919 735-4570
2719 Graves Dr Ste 10 Goldsboro (27534) *(G-5246)*

SPX Latin America Corporation................................. 704 808-3848
13320 Ballantyne Corporate Pl Charlotte (28277) *(G-2850)*

SPX Technologies Inc (PA)....................................... 980 474-3700
6325 Ardrey Kell Rd Ste 400 Charlotte (28277) *(G-2851)*

Square One Machine LLC... 704 600-6296
658 Washburn Switch Rd Shelby (28150) *(G-11383)*

Square Peg Construction Inc.................................... 828 277-5164
28 London Rd Asheville (28803) *(G-610)*

Squarehead Technology LLC..................................... 571 299-4849
200 1st Ave Nw Hickory (28601) *(G-6456)*

Squeaks Logging Inc... 252 794-1531
139 Republican Rd Windsor (27983) *(G-13058)*

Squeegee Tees & More Inc...................................... 704 888-0336
12410 Grey Commercial Rd Midland (28107) *(G-8297)*

Srb Technologies Inc (PA).. 336 659-2610
2580 Landmark Dr Winston Salem (27103) *(G-13341)*

SRI Performance LLC... 704 662-6982
122 Knob Hill Rd Mooresville (28117) *(G-8774)*

SRI Ventures Inc.. 919 427-1681
3415 Hawkins Ave Sanford (27330) *(G-11237)*

SRNg-T&w LLC... 704 271-9889
1942 E 7th St Charlotte (28204) *(G-2852)*

Ss Handcrafted Art LLC.. 704 664-2544
107 Glade Valley Ave Mooresville (28117) *(G-8775)*

Ssb Manufacturing Company.................................... 704 596-4935
5100r E W T Harris Blvd Charlotte (28269) *(G-2853)*

Ssd Designs LLC (PA).. 980 245-2988
9935d Rea Rd # 433 Charlotte (28277) *(G-2854)*

Ssi, Belmont *Also Called: Steel Specialty Co Belmont Inc (G-768)*

Ssi Services Inc... 919 867-1450
7231 Acc Blvd Ste 107 Raleigh (27617) *(G-10501)*

Ssnc LLC Pba NC Filtration, Belmont *Also Called: NC Filtration of Florida LLC (G-756)*

Sspc Inc
12016 Steele Creek Rd Charlotte (28273) *(G-2855)*

SSS Logging Inc.. 828 467-1155
29 Liberty Dr Marion (28752) *(G-8067)*

St Engineering Leeboy.. 704 966-3300
500 Lincoln County Parkway Ext Lincolnton (28092) *(G-7856)*

St Investors Inc.. 704 969-7500
4064 Colony Rd Ste 150 Charlotte (28211) *(G-2856)*

St Johns Museum of Art.. 910 763-0281
114 Orange St Wilmington (28401) *(G-12929)*

St Johns Packaging Usa LLC.................................... 336 292-9911
2619 Phoenix Dr Greensboro (27406) *(G-5833)*

St Pauls, NC Processing Plant, Saint Pauls *Also Called: Sanderson Farms LLC Proc Div (G-11009)*

St Timothy Chair Co Division, Conover *Also Called: Classic Leather Inc (G-3504)*

St. Pauls Hatchery, Lumberton *Also Called: Sanderson Farms LLC (G-7972)*

St.clair Coatings, Monroe *Also Called: As Inc (G-8430)*

Stabilus, Gastonia *Also Called: Stabilus Inc (G-5141)*

Stabilus Inc (DH).. 704 865-7444
1201 Tulip Dr Gastonia (28052) *(G-5141)*

Stable Holdco Inc.. 704 866-7140
1201 Tulip Dr Gastonia (28052) *(G-5142)*

Stackhouse Publishing Inc....................................... 203 699-6571
299 Blackberry Rd Boone (28607) *(G-944)*

Stacks Kitchen Matthews.. 704 243-2024
1315 N Broome St Waxhaw (28173) *(G-12442)*

Staclean Diffuser, Salisbury *Also Called: Staclean Diffuser Company LLC (G-11119)*

Staclean Diffuser Company LLC (PA)..............704 636-8697
2205 Executive Dr Salisbury (28147) *(G-11119)*

Staclear Inc...919 838-2844
7250 Acc Blvd Raleigh (27617) *(G-10502)*

Stafford Cutting Dies Inc.........................704 821-6330
131 Business Park Dr Indian Trail (28079) *(G-7100)*

Stage Dec, Greensboro Also Called: Stage Decoration and Sups Inc *(G-5834)*

Stage Decoration and Sups Inc..................336 621-5454
3519 Associate Dr Greensboro (27405) *(G-5834)*

Stainless & Nickel Alloys LLC....................704 201-2898
1700 W Pointe Dr Ste E Charlotte (28214) *(G-2857)*

Stainless Steel Spc Inc.............................919 779-4290
2025 Carr Pur Dr Raleigh (27603) *(G-10503)*

Stainless Stl Fabricators Inc......................919 833-3520
5325 Departure Dr Raleigh (27616) *(G-10504)*

Stainless Supply Inc..................................704 635-2064
307 N Secrest Ave Monroe (28110) *(G-8563)*

Stainless Valve Co, Monroe Also Called: B+e Manufacturing Co Inc *(G-8438)*

Stair Tamer Cargo Lifts, Shiloh Also Called: Stair Tamer LLC *(G-11395)*

Stair Tamer LLC..252 336-4437
899 S Sandy Hook Rd Shiloh (27974) *(G-11395)*

Staley Feed Mill, Staley Also Called: Pilgrims Pride Corporation *(G-11598)*

Staley Logging & Grading, Millers Creek Also Called: William Shawn Staley *(G-8308)*

Stallergenes Greer, Lenoir Also Called: Albion Medical Holdings Inc *(G-7570)*

Stallergenes Greer, Lenoir Also Called: Greer Laboratories Inc *(G-7610)*

Stallings Cabinets Inc...............................252 338-6747
508 N Hughes Blvd Elizabeth City (27909) *(G-4410)*

Stamp-Tech, Wendell Also Called: Precision Stampers Inc *(G-12541)*

Stampco Metal Products Inc.......................828 645-4271
108 Herron Cove Rd Weaverville (28787) *(G-12504)*

Stamper Sheet Metal Inc............................336 476-5145
357 Bud Kanoy Rd Archdale (27263) *(G-243)*

Stamping & Scrapbooking Rm Inc...............336 389-9538
2806 Randleman Rd Greensboro (27406) *(G-5835)*

Stampsource, Charlotte Also Called: Precision Partners LLC *(G-2657)*

Stampsource, Charlotte Also Called: Precision Partners LLC *(G-2658)*

Stanadyne Diesel Systems, Jacksonville Also Called: SL Liquidation LLC *(G-7147)*

Stanadyne Intrmdate Hldngs LLC (HQ)........860 525-0821
405 White St Jacksonville (28546) *(G-7152)*

Stanadyne Jacksonville LLC.......................860 683-4553
405 White St Jacksonville (28546) *(G-7153)*

Stanadyne Operating Co LLC (DH)..............910 353-3666
405 White St Jacksonville (28546) *(G-7154)*

Standard Mineral Division, Robbins Also Called: Vanderbilt Minerals LLC *(G-10755)*

Standard Tools and Eqp Co........................336 697-7177
4810 Clover Rd Greensboro (27405) *(G-5836)*

Standard Tytape Company Inc.....................828 693-6594
1495 N Main St Hendersonville (28792) *(G-6244)*

Stanford Manufacturing LLC.......................336 999-8799
3720 Stanford Way Clemmons (27012) *(G-3203)*

Stanley Black & Decker.............................704 987-2271
9829 Northcross Center Ct Huntersville (28078) *(G-7057)*

Stanley Black & Decker Inc........................704 509-0844
9115 Old Statesville Rd Ste E Charlotte (28269) *(G-2858)*

Stanley Black & Decker Inc........................704 789-7000
1000 Stanley Dr Concord (28027) *(G-3446)*

Stanley Black & Decker Inc........................704 293-9392
9930 Kincey Ave Huntersville (28078) *(G-7058)*

Stanley Customer Support Divis..................704 789-7000
1000 Stanley Dr Concord (28027) *(G-3447)*

Stanley E Dixon Jr Inc...............................252 332-5004
113 Rail Road St Ahoskie (27910) *(G-53)*

Stanley Engineered Fastening, Stanfield Also Called: Avdel USA LLC *(G-11603)*

Stanley Furniture Company LLC...................336 884-7700
200 N Hamilton St No 200 High Point (27260) *(G-6791)*

Stanley Works The, Concord Also Called: Stanley Black & Decker Inc *(G-3446)*

Stanly Fixs Acquisition LLC........................704 474-3184
11635 Nc 138 Hwy Norwood (28128) *(G-9560)*

Stanly Fixtures, Norwood Also Called: Stanly Fixs Acquisition LLC *(G-9560)*

Stanly Fixtures Company Inc.......................704 474-3184
11635 Nc 138 Hwy Norwood (28128) *(G-9561)*

Stans Quality Foods Inc.............................336 570-2572
1503 N Graham Hopedale Rd Burlington (27217) *(G-1163)*

Stanza Machinery Inc.................................704 599-0623
6801 Northpark Blvd Ste B Charlotte (28216) *(G-2859)*

Star America Inc (PA)................................704 788-4700
190 Cabarrus Ave W Concord (28025) *(G-3448)*

Star Fleet Communications Inc....................828 252-6565
224 Broadway St Asheville (28801) *(G-611)*

Star Food Products Inc (PA).......................336 227-4079
727 S Spring St Burlington (27215) *(G-1164)*

Star Milling Company.................................704 873-9561
247 Commerce Blvd Unit F Statesville (28625) *(G-11776)*

Star Ready-Mix Inc....................................336 725-9401
2865 Lowery St Winston Salem (27101) *(G-13342)*

Star Snax LLC...828 261-0255
103b Somerset Dr Nw Conover (28613) *(G-3562)*

Star Tickets Plus, Morrisville Also Called: Tickets Plus Inc *(G-9072)*

Star Wipers Inc...888 511-2656
2260 Raeford Ct Gastonia (28052) *(G-5143)*

Starcke Abrasives Usa Inc.........................704 583-3338
9109 Forsyth Park Dr Charlotte (28273) *(G-2860)*

Starcraft Diamonds Inc..............................252 717-2548
444 Stewart Pkwy Washington (27889) *(G-12415)*

Stardust Cellars, Winston Salem Also Called: Stardust Cellars LLC *(G-13343)*

Stardust Cellars LLC (PA)..........................336 466-4454
1764 Camden Rd Winston Salem (27103) *(G-13343)*

Starflite Companies Inc (PA)......................252 728-2690
530 Sensation Weigh Beaufort (28516) *(G-735)*

Starhgen Arospc Components LLC...............704 660-1001
333 Oates Rd Mooresville (28117) *(G-8776)*

Starlight Cases, Pine Level Also Called: New Innovative Products Inc *(G-9683)*

Starnes Pallet Service Inc (PA)...................704 596-9006
4000 Jeff Adams Dr Charlotte (28206) *(G-2861)*

Starpet Inc...336 672-0101
801 Pineview Rd Asheboro (27203) *(G-398)*

Starr's Party Ice, Greensboro Also Called: Robert D Starr *(G-5790)*

Starta Development Inc..............................919 865-7700
2610 Wycliff Rd Ste 19 Raleigh (27607) *(G-10505)*

State Electric Supply Company...................336 855-8200
2709 Patterson St Greensboro (27407) *(G-5837)*

State Hwy Patrol-Troop D, Roxboro Also Called: North Crlina Dept Crime Ctrl P *(G-10933)*

State Industries Inc...................................704 597-8910
4302 Raleigh St Charlotte (28213) *(G-2862)*

State Port Pilot...910 457-4568
114 E Moore St Southport (28461) *(G-11532)*

Statesville Breeder Feedmill, Statesville Also Called: Mountaire Farms Inc *(G-11736)*

Statesville Brick Company..........................704 872-4123
391 Brick Yard Rd Statesville (28677) *(G-11777)*

Statesville High..704 873-3491
474 N Center St Statesville (28677) *(G-11778)*

Statesville LLC...704 872-3303
151 Walker Rd Statesville (28625) *(G-11779)*

Statesville Med MGT Svcs LLC....................704 996-6748
1503 E Broad St Statesville (28625) *(G-11780)*

Statesville Pallet Company Inc....................828 632-0268
351 Old Mountain Rd Hiddenite (28636) *(G-6505)*

Static Control, Sanford Also Called: Static Control Components Inc *(G-11238)*

Static Control Components Inc (HQ).............919 774-3808
3010 Lee Ave Sanford (27332) *(G-11238)*

Static Control Ic-Disc Inc..........................919 774-3808
3010 Lee Ave Sanford (27332) *(G-11239)*

Staunton Capital Inc (PA)...........................704 866-8533
3406 W Wendover Ave Ste E Greensboro (27407) *(G-5838)*

Stay Alert Safety Services LLC....................919 828-5399
1240 Kirkland Rd Raleigh (27603) *(G-10506)*

Stay Online LLC (PA).................................888 346-4688
1506 Ivac Way Creedmoor (27522) *(G-3656)*

Stay-Right Pre-Cast Concrete Inc................919 494-7600
2675 Us1 Hwy Franklinton (27525) *(G-4854)*

STC Precision Cutting Tools, Greenville Also Called: Sphenodon Tool Co Inc *(G-6025)*

Steag SCR-Tech Inc (PA)............................704 827-8933
11707 Steele Creek Rd Charlotte (28273) *(G-2863)*

A L P H A B E T I C

Steel and Pipe Corporation......................... 919 776-0751
3709 Hawkins Ave Sanford (27330) *(G-11240)*

Steel City Services LLC............................... 919 698-2407
1129 E Geer St Durham (27704) *(G-4249)*

Steel Construct Systems LLC....................... 704 781-5575
118 Pine Forest Rd Locust (28097) *(G-7903)*

Steel Smart Incorporated............................. 919 736-0681
1042 Airport Rd Ne Pikeville (27863) *(G-9668)*

Steel Specialty Co Belmont Inc (PA)..............704 825-4745
5907 W Wilkinson Blvd Belmont (28012) *(G-768)*

Steel Supply and Erection Co........................ 336 625-4830
1237 N Fayetteville St Asheboro (27203) *(G-399)*

Steel Tech, Charlotte *Also Called: Waldenwood Group Inc (G-2999)*

Steel Tech, Charlotte *Also Called: Waldenwood Group LLC (G-3000)*

Steel Technologies Carolinas, Clinton *Also Called: Steel Technologies LLC (G-3248)*

Steel Technologies LLC............................... 910 592-1266
112 Sycamore St Clinton (28328) *(G-3248)*

Steel Technology Inc (PA)............................ 252 937-7122
2620 Business Park Dr Rocky Mount (27804) *(G-10869)*

Steelcity LLC (PA)...................................... 336 434-7000
505 Aztec Dr Archdale (27263) *(G-244)*

Steelco Inc.. 704 896-1207
1020 Commercial Dr Matthews (28104) *(G-8194)*

Steelcraft Structures LLC............................. 980 434-5400
1841 Amity Hill Rd Statesville (28677) *(G-11781)*

Steele Rubber Products Inc.......................... 704 483-9343
6180 Highway 150 E Denver (28037) *(G-3807)*

Steelfab Inc (PA)....................................... 704 394-5376
3025 Westport Rd Charlotte (28208) *(G-2864)*

Steelfab of Virginia Inc (HQ)........................ 919 828-9545
4909 Western Blvd Ste 100 Raleigh (27606) *(G-10507)*

Steelman Lumber & Pallet LLC...................... 336 468-2757
4744 Us 21 Hwy Hamptonville (27020) *(G-6092)*

Steelman Milling Company Inc....................... 336 463-5586
1517 Us 601 Hwy Yadkinville (27055) *(G-13452)*

Steelpoint, Matthews *Also Called: Mmdi Inc (G-8186)*

Stefano Foods Inc...................................... 704 399-3935
4825 Hovis Rd Charlotte (28208) *(G-2865)*

Stegall Petroleum Inc.................................. 704 283-5058
1907 Old Charlotte Hwy Monroe (28110) *(G-8564)*

Stein Fibers Ltd.. 704 599-2804
10130 Mallard Creek Rd Charlotte (28262) *(G-2866)*

Stein Fibers, Ltd., Charlotte *Also Called: Stein Fibers Ltd (G-2866)*

Stepan Company.. 316 828-1000
4600 Us Highway 421 N Wilmington (28402) *(G-12930)*

Stephanie Baxter....................................... 803 203-8467
1089 Peach Tree St Lincolnton (28092) *(G-7857)*

Stephanies Mattress LLC............................. 704 763-0705
5920 N Tryon St Charlotte (28213) *(G-2867)*

Stephen J McCusker................................... 336 884-1916
1705 Heathgate Pt High Point (27262) *(G-6792)*

Stephens Mechanical.................................. 336 998-2141
714 Cherry Hill Rd Mocksville (27028) *(G-8392)*

Stephenson Millwork Co Inc......................... 252 237-1141
210 Harper St Ne Wilson (27893) *(G-13031)*

Steri-Air LLC.. 336 434-1166
2109 Brevard Rd High Point (27263) *(G-6793)*

Sterimed, Charlotte *Also Called: Envirotek Worldwide LLC (G-2120)*

Sterling Cleora Corporation.......................... 919 563-5800
3115 Buckingham Rd Durham (27707) *(G-4250)*

Sterling Pharma USA, Cary *Also Called: Sterling Pharma Usa LLC (G-1467)*

Sterling Pharma Usa LLC............................. 919 678-0702
1001 Sheldon Dr Ste 101 Cary (27513) *(G-1467)*

Sterling Products Corporation....................... 646 423-3175
3924 S Holden Rd Greensboro (27406) *(G-5839)*

Sterling Rack Inc....................................... 704 866-9131
176 Tarheel Dr Gastonia (28056) *(G-5144)*

Sterling Sign, Greensboro *Also Called: Sterling Products Corporation (G-5839)*

Steve & Ray Banks Logging Inc..................... 910 743-3051
7625 New Bern Hwy Maysville (28555) *(G-8212)*

Steve Evans Logging Inc.............................. 252 792-1836
7096 Us Highway 17 Williamston (27892) *(G-12674)*

Steve Henry Woodcraft LLC.......................... 919 489-7325
4 Pine Tree Ln Chapel Hill (27514) *(G-1573)*

Steven C Haddock DBA Haddock.................... 252 714-2431
4122 Leary Mills Rd Vanceboro (28586) *(G-12222)*

Steven Smoakes....................................... 910 352-4287
595 Sharease Cir Wilmington (28405) *(G-12931)*

Steven-Robert Original Dessert, Pembroke *Also Called: Steven-Robert Originals LLC (G-9660)*

Steven-Robert Originals LLC......................... 910 521-0199
701 S Jones St Pembroke (28372) *(G-9660)*

Stevens Foodservice................................... 919 322-5470
8392 Six Forks Rd Ste 202 Raleigh (27615) *(G-10508)*

Stevens Lighting Inc (PA)............................. 910 944-7187
488 Bibey Rd Carthage (28327) *(G-1281)*

Stevens Packing Inc................................... 336 274-6033
3023 Randleman Rd Greensboro (27406) *(G-5840)*

Stevens Sausage Company Inc....................... 919 934-3159
3411 Stevens Sausage Rd Smithfield (27577) *(G-11466)*

Stevenso Vestal, Burlington *Also Called: Smith Draperies Inc (G-1158)*

Stevenson Woodworking............................... 919 362-9121
300 Hickory View Ln Apex (27502) *(G-196)*

Steves TS & Uniforms Inc............................. 919 554-4221
3129 Heritage Trade Dr Ste 108 Wake Forest (27587) *(G-12304)*

Stewart Gear Manufacturing, Gastonia *Also Called: Textile Parts and Mch Co Inc (G-5152)*

Stewart Superabsorbents LLC........................ 828 855-9316
1954 Main Ave Se Hickory (28602) *(G-6457)*

Stewarts Garage and Welding Co.................... 336 983-5563
6544 Doral Dr Tobaccoville (27050) *(G-12103)*

Stf Precision, Arden *Also Called: Diamond Dog Tools Inc (G-265)*

STI, Kings Mountain *Also Called: Kings Plush Inc (G-7370)*

STI, Kings Mountain *Also Called: Specialty Textiles Inc (G-7386)*

STI Polymer Inc... 800 874-5878
5618 Clyde Rhyne Dr Sanford (27330) *(G-11241)*

STI Turf Equipment LLC............................... 704 393-8873
4355 Golf Acres Dr Charlotte (28208) *(G-2868)*

Sticky Life.. 910 817-4531
321 Goldsboro St Newton Grove (28366) *(G-9518)*

Stiefel Laboratories Inc............................... 888 784-3335
410 Blackwell St Durham (27701) *(G-4251)*

Stiefel Laboratories Inc (DH)........................ 888 784-3335
5 Moore Dr Research Triangle Pa (27709) *(G-10715)*

Stikeleather Inc.. 828 352-9095
146 Windsor Dr Taylorsville (28681) *(G-11979)*

Stiletto Manufacturing Inc............................ 252 564-4877
107 S Water St Columbia (27925) *(G-3297)*

Stillwood, Burlington *Also Called: Stillwood Ammun Systems LLC (G-1165)*

Stillwood Ammun Systems LLC...................... 919 721-9096
642 E Webb Ave Burlington (27217) *(G-1165)*

Stine Gear & Machine Company...................... 704 445-1245
2015 Hephzibah Church Rd Bessemer City (28016) *(G-834)*

Stitch 98 Inc.. 704 235-5783
154 Talbert Pointe Dr Ste 101 Mooresville (28117) *(G-8777)*

Stitch Count, Ahoskie *Also Called: Stanley E Dixon Jr Inc (G-53)*

Stitch In Time Inc...................................... 910 497-4171
412 S Main St Spring Lake (28390) *(G-11564)*

Stitch-A-Doozy... 336 573-2339
140 Salems Ln Stoneville (27048) *(G-11829)*

Stitchcrafters Incorporated........................... 828 397-7656
7923 Houston Ave Hickory (28602) *(G-6458)*

Stitchery Inc.. 336 248-5604
134 Elk St Lexington (27292) *(G-7746)*

Stitches On Critter Pond.............................. 919 624-5886
7333 Critter Pond Rd Wake Forest (27587) *(G-12305)*

Stitchmaster, Greensboro *Also Called: Stitchmaster LLC (G-5841)*

Stitchmaster LLC....................................... 336 852-6448
309 S Regional Rd Greensboro (27409) *(G-5841)*

Stitchworks Embroidery, Washington *Also Called: Uniforms Galore (G-12417)*

Stm Industries Inc (PA)............................... 828 322-2700
1712 8th Street Dr Se Hickory (28602) *(G-6459)*

Stn Cushion Company.................................. 336 476-9100
3 Regency Industrial Blvd Thomasville (27360) *(G-12074)*

2025 Harris North Carolina
Manufacturers Directory

(G-0000) Company's Geographic Section entry number

Stock Building Supply Holdings LLC................................. 919 431-1000
8020 Arco Corporate Dr Ste 400 Raleigh (27617) *(G-10509)*

Stockhausen Superabsorber LLC (DH)............................. 336 333-7540
2401 Doyle St Greensboro (27406) *(G-5842)*

Stockholm Corporation... 704 552-9314
4729 Stockholm Ct Charlotte (28273) *(G-2869)*

Stokes Mfg LLC.. 336 270-8746
140 Somerset Church Rd Roxboro (27573) *(G-10947)*

Stoltz Automotive Inc... 336 595-4218
4861 New Walkertown Rd Walkertown (27051) *(G-12317)*

Stone & Leigh LLC.. 919 971-2096
1020 N Green St Morganton (28655) *(G-8901)*

Stone & Leigh Furniture, Morganton Also Called: Vlr LLC *(G-8909)*

Stone Cllins Mtr Rewinding Inc.. 910 347-2775
111 Ramsey Rd Jacksonville (28546) *(G-7155)*

Stone House Creek Logging.. 252 586-4477
615 Fleming Dairy Rd Littleton (27850) *(G-7887)*

Stone International USA, Thomasville Also Called: Stone Marble Co Inc *(G-12075)*

Stone Marble Co Inc.. 773 227-1161
7004 Pikeview Dr Thomasville (27360) *(G-12075)*

Stone Resource Inc.. 336 889-7800
2101 E Martin Luther King Jr Dr High Point (27260) *(G-6794)*

Stone Supply Inc.. 828 678-9966
159 Depot St Burnsville (28714) *(G-1192)*

Stonefield Cellars LLC... 336 632-2391
8220 Nc Highway 68 N Stokesdale (27357) *(G-11816)*

Stonefield Homes, Greensboro Also Called: Ridgewood Management LLC *(G-5788)*

Stonehaven Jewelry Gallery Ltd.. 919 462-8888
111 Adams St Cary (27513) *(G-1468)*

Stonemaster Inc... 704 333-0353
2949 S Ridge Ave Concord (28025) *(G-3449)*

Stonery LLC.. 704 662-8702
1077 Mecklenburg Hwy Mooresville (28115) *(G-8778)*

Stonetree Signs.. 336 625-0938
5321 New Hope Rd Denton (27239) *(G-3761)*

Stoneville Lumber Company Inc.. 336 623-4311
3442 Nc Highway 135 Stoneville (27048) *(G-11830)*

Stoneworx Inc... 252 937-8080
7015 Stanley Park Dr Rocky Mount (27804) *(G-10870)*

Stony Gap Wholesale Co Inc... 704 982-5360
40616c Stony Gap Rd Ste C Albemarle (28001) *(G-93)*

Stony Knoll Forge... 704 507-0179
1309 Hamiltons Cross Rd Marshville (28103) *(G-8095)*

Stop N Go LLC.. 919 523-7355
2916 Homebrook Ln Morrisville (27560) *(G-9059)*

Stop-Painting.com, Wake Forest Also Called: Spota LLC *(G-12303)*

Storagemotion Inc.. 704 746-3700
216 Overhill Dr Ste 104 Mooresville (28117) *(G-8779)*

Store 72, Greensboro Also Called: Consolidated Pipe & Sup Co Inc *(G-5463)*

Stork News, Fayetteville Also Called: Stork News Tm of America *(G-4675)*

Stork News Tm of America (PA)... 910 868-3065
5075 Morganton Rd 12a Fayetteville (28314) *(G-4675)*

Stork United Corporation.. 704 598-7171
3201 Rotary Dr Charlotte (28269) *(G-2870)*

Stormberg Foods LLC... 919 947-6011
1002b Sunburst Dr Goldsboro (27534) *(G-5247)*

Storopack Inc.. 800 827-7225
2598 Empire Dr Ste G Winston Salem (27103) *(G-13344)*

Storybook Farm Metal Shop Inc.. 919 967-9491
231 Storybook Farm Ln Chapel Hill (27516) *(G-1574)*

Storybook Metal Shop, Chapel Hill Also Called: Storybook Farm Metal Shop Inc *(G-1574)*

Stout Beverages LLC (PA)... 704 293-7640
518 N Sims St Kings Mountain (28086) *(G-7388)*

Stout Brands LLC... 704 293-7640
518 N Sims St Kings Mountain (28086) *(G-7389)*

Stove-Woodward Co, Youngsville Also Called: Stowe Woodward LLC *(G-13489)*

Stovers Precision Tooling Inc.. 704 876-3673
239 Treebark Rd Statesville (28625) *(G-11782)*

Stowe Enterprises Inc.. 800 315-6751
140 Royal Oak Dr Troutman (28166) *(G-12151)*

Stowe Woodward Licensco LLC... 919 526-1400
8537 Six Forks Rd Ste 300 Raleigh (27615) *(G-10510)*

Stowe Woodward LLC... 919 556-7235
8521 Six Forks Rd Raleigh (27615) *(G-10511)*

Stowe Woodward LLC... 360 636-0330
14101 Capital Blvd Ste 101 Youngsville (27596) *(G-13489)*

Stpi, Statesville Also Called: Southeast Tubular Products Inc *(G-11767)*

Strandberg Engrg Labs Inc... 336 274-3775
1302 N Ohenry Blvd Greensboro (27405) *(G-5843)*

Strategic 3d Solutions Inc... 919 451-5963
4805 Green Rd Ste 114 Raleigh (27616) *(G-10512)*

Strategic3dsolutions, Raleigh Also Called: Strategic 3d Solutions Inc *(G-10512)*

Strategy... 704 331-6521
525 N Tryon St Ste 1705 Charlotte (28202) *(G-2871)*

Stratford Die Casting Inc.. 336 784-0100
1665 S Martin Luther King Jr Dr Ste A Winston Salem (27107) *(G-13345)*

Stratford Metalfinishing Inc... 336 723-7946
1681 S Martin Luther King Jr Dr Winston Salem (27107) *(G-13346)*

Stratford Tool & Die Co Inc... 336 765-2030
3841 Kimwell Dr Winston Salem (27103) *(G-13347)*

Stratton Publishing & Mktg Inc... 703 914-9200
1457 Quadrant Cir Wilmington (28405) *(G-12932)*

Strawbridge Studios Inc (PA).. 919 286-9512
3616 Hillsborough Rd Ste D Durham (27705) *(G-4252)*

Streets Auto Sales & Four WD.. 704 888-8686
814 Main St W Locust (28097) *(G-7904)*

Stress-Tek, Wendell Also Called: Vishay Transducers Ltd *(G-12553)*

Strickland Backhoe... 910 893-5274
3216 Nc 210 S Bunnlevel (28323) *(G-1017)*

Strickland Bros Entps Inc.. 252 478-3058
3622 Wiggins Rd Spring Hope (27882) *(G-11560)*

Stripelight, Apex Also Called: Parhelion Incorporated *(G-184)*

Strobels Supply Inc.. 607 324-1721
1638 Clyde Fitzgerald Rd Linwood (27299) *(G-7881)*

Stromasys Corporation.. 617 500-4556
2840 Plaza Pl Ste 450 Raleigh (27612) *(G-10513)*

Strong Global Entrmt Inc (PA).. 704 994-8279
5960 Fairview Rd Ste 275 Charlotte (28210) *(G-2872)*

Strong Manufacturers, Pineville Also Called: Strong Medical Partners LLC *(G-9759)*

Strong Manufacturers, Pineville Also Called: Strong Medical Partners LLC *(G-9760)*

Strong Medical Partners LLC (PA)....................................... 716 626-9400
11519 Nations Ford Rd Ste 200 Pineville (28134) *(G-9759)*

Strong Medical Partners LLC... 716 507-4476
11515 Nations Ford Rd Pineville (28134) *(G-9760)*

Stronger By Science Tech LLC.. 336 391-9377
514 Daniels St 101 Raleigh (27605) *(G-10514)*

Stronghaven Incorporated... 770 739-6080
11135 Monroe Rd Matthews (28105) *(G-8151)*

Stroudcraft Marine LLC.. 910 623-4055
13991 Nc Hwy 210 Rocky Point (28457) *(G-10884)*

Stroup Machine & Mfg Inc.. 704 394-0023
2019 W Laporte Dr Charlotte (28216) *(G-2873)*

Stroupe Mirror Co.. 336 475-2181
2661 Reynolds Dr Winston Salem (27104) *(G-13348)*

Structral Catings Hertford LLC... 919 553-3034
930 River Rd Cofield (27922) *(G-3270)*

Structural 0201 LLC.. 240 288-8607
300 Roelee St Trinity (27370) *(G-12127)*

Structural Materials Inc... 828 754-6413
802 Old North Rd Nw Lenoir (28645) *(G-7640)*

Structural Planners Inc.. 919 848-8964
312 Dalton Dr Raleigh (27615) *(G-10515)*

Structural Steel of Carolina, Winston Salem Also Called: Division 5 LLC *(G-13148)*

Structural Steel Products Corp... 919 359-2811
8027 Us 70 Bus Hwy W Clayton (27520) *(G-3171)*

Structure Medical LLC... 704 799-3450
123 Cayuga Dr Mooresville (28117) *(G-8780)*

Structure Medical LLC... 256 461-0900
123 Cayuga Dr Mooresville (28117) *(G-8781)*

Strutmasters, Roxboro Also Called: Suspension Experts LLC *(G-10948)*

Stryker Corp... 919 455-6755
525 Pylon Dr Raleigh (27606) *(G-10516)*

Stryker Corporation.. 919 433-3325
800 Capitola Dr Ste 12 Durham (27713) *(G-4253)*

ALPHABETIC

STS Packaging Charlotte LLC.................... 980 259-2290
  1201 Westinghouse Blvd Charlotte (28273) *(G-2874)*

STS Screen Printing Inc........................... 704 821-8488
  107 Industrial Dr Matthews (28104) *(G-8195)*

Studio Displays Inc............................... 704 588-6590
  11150 Rivers Edge Rd Pineville (28134) *(G-9761)*

Studio Tk LLC.................................... 919 464-2920
  3940 Us 70 Hwy Business Clayton (27520) *(G-3172)*

Stump and Grind LLC.............................. 704 488-2271
  7420 Ponders End Ln Charlotte (28213) *(G-2875)*

Stump Logging................................... 910 620-7000
  61 Supply St Se Supply (28462) *(G-11860)*

Stump Printing Co Inc............................ 260 723-5171
  525 Lumina Ave S Wrightsville Beach (28480) *(G-13433)*

Stump's, Wrightsville Beach *Also Called: Stump Printing Co Inc (G-13433)*

Sturdy Control Div, Wilmington *Also Called: Sturdy Corporation (G-12933)*

Sturdy Corporation............................... 910 763-2500
  1822 Carolina Beach Rd Wilmington (28401) *(G-12933)*

Sturm Ruger & Company Inc....................... 336 427-0286
  700 S Ayersville Rd Mayodan (27027) *(G-8209)*

Style Upholstering Inc............................ 828 322-4882
  33 23rd Ave Ne Hickory (28601) *(G-6460)*

Suarez Bakery Inc................................ 704 525-0145
  4245 Park Rd Charlotte (28209) *(G-2876)*

Sub-Aquatics Inc................................. 336 674-0749
  210 Labrador Dr Randleman (27317) *(G-10661)*

Subaru Folger Automotive......................... 704 531-8888
  5701 E Independence Blvd Charlotte (28212) *(G-2877)*

Subsea Video Systems Inc......................... 252 338-1001
  611 Hull Dr Elizabeth City (27909) *(G-4411)*

Substance Incorporated........................... 800 985-9485
  3000 Frazier Dr Claremont (28610) *(G-3122)*

Subtle Impressions Inc
  1200 Industrial Ave Gastonia (28054) *(G-5145)*

Success Magazine, Raleigh *Also Called: Success Publishing Inc (G-10517)*

Success Publishing Inc............................ 919 807-1100
  150 Fayetteville St M Raleigh (27601) *(G-10517)*

Sue-Lynn Textiles Inc (PA)........................ 336 578-0871
  302 Roxboro St Haw River (27258) *(G-6135)*

Sugar Creek Brewing Co LLC....................... 704 521-3333
  215 Southside Dr Charlotte (28217) *(G-2878)*

Sugar Mountain Woodworks Inc..................... 423 292-6245
  3030 Sugar Mountain 2 Rd Newland (28657) *(G-9435)*

Sugar Pops...................................... 704 799-0959
  248 N Main St Mooresville (28115) *(G-8782)*

Sugarshack Bakery and EMB....................... 803 920-3311
  275 Sugar Loaf Rd Troy (27371) *(G-12168)*

Suits US, Mount Airy *Also Called: Suits Usa Inc (G-9180)*

Suits Usa Inc.................................... 336 786-8808
  1219a W Lebanon St Mount Airy (27030) *(G-9180)*

Sukkah Project, The, Chapel Hill *Also Called: Steve Henry Woodcraft LLC (G-1573)*

Sumitomo Elc Lightwave Corp (HQ)................. 919 541-8100
  201 S Rogers Ln Ste 100 Raleigh (27610) *(G-10518)*

Summer Industries, Welcome *Also Called: Summer Industries LLC (G-12515)*

Summer Industries LLC........................... 336 731-9217
  262 Welcome Center Court Welcome (27374) *(G-12515)*

Summit Agro Usa LLC............................. 984 260-0407
  240 Leigh Farm Rd Ste 415 Durham (27707) *(G-4254)*

Summit Aviation Inc.............................. 302 834-5400
  243 Burgess Rd Ste A Greensboro (27409) *(G-5844)*

Summit Logging LLC.............................. 910 734-8787
  1485 Beulah Church Rd Lumberton (28358) *(G-7973)*

Summit Materials, Wilmington *Also Called: American Materials Company LLC (G-12703)*

Summit Peak Pens and WD Works................... 336 404-8312
  412 E Starmount Ave Liberty (27298) *(G-7780)*

Summit Yarn LLC................................. 704 874-5000
  531 Cotton Blossom Cir Gastonia (28054) *(G-5146)*

Summus, Cary *Also Called: Oasys Mobile Inc (G-1411)*

Sumpters Jwly & Collectibles....................... 704 399-5348
  3501 Wilkinson Blvd Charlotte (28208) *(G-2879)*

Sumter Packaging Corporation..................... 704 873-0583
  844 Meacham Rd Statesville (28677) *(G-11783)*

Sun & Surf Containers Inc........................ 910 754-9600
  2589 Sun And Surf Ln Nw Shallotte (28470) *(G-11306)*

Sun Chemical Corporation......................... 704 587-4531
  1701 Westinghouse Blvd Charlotte (28273) *(G-2880)*

Sun Cleaners & Laundry Inc....................... 704 325-3722
  2306 N Main Ave Newton (28658) *(G-9500)*

Sun Drop Bottling, Rocky Mount *Also Called: Sun-Drop Btlg Rocky Mt NC Inc (G-10871)*

Sun Drop Bottling Co, Shelby *Also Called: Choice USA Beverage Inc (G-11317)*

Sun Fabricators Inc.............................. 336 885-0095
  701 W Ward Ave High Point (27260) *(G-6795)*

Sun Oven, Wilkesboro *Also Called: Sun Ovens International Inc (G-12653)*

Sun Ovens International Inc....................... 630 208-7273
  418 Wilkesboro Blvd Unit 1 Wilkesboro (28697) *(G-12653)*

Sun Path Contracting, Raeford *Also Called: Spc-Usa Inc (G-9852)*

Sun Path Products Inc............................ 910 875-9002
  404 W Edinborough Ave Raeford (28376) *(G-9853)*

Sun Publishing Company.......................... 919 942-5282
  107 N Roberson St Chapel Hill (27516) *(G-1575)*

Sun River Service Company, Wilson *Also Called: Protein For Pets Opco LLC (G-13014)*

Sun Valley Stl Fabrication Inc..................... 704 289-5830
  1810 Tower Industrial Dr Monroe (28110) *(G-8565)*

Sun-Drop Bottling Co, Lowell *Also Called: Choice USA Beverage Inc (G-7930)*

Sun-Drop Btlg Rocky Mt NC Inc.................... 252 977-4586
  2406 W Raleigh Blvd Rocky Mount (27803) *(G-10871)*

Sun-Journal Incorporated......................... 252 638-8101
  4901 Us Highway 17 S New Bern (28562) *(G-9398)*

Sunbelt Abrasives Inc............................ 336 882-6837
  1507 Bethel Dr High Point (27260) *(G-6796)*

Sunbelt Enterprises Inc........................... 704 788-4749
  263 Litaker Ln Concord (28025) *(G-3450)*

Sunbelt Spring & Stamping, Rosman *Also Called: M-B Industries Inc (G-10913)*

Suncast Corporation.............................. 704 274-5394
  9801 Kincey Ave Huntersville (28078) *(G-7059)*

Sunco Powder Systems Inc........................ 704 545-3922
  3230 Valentine Ln Charlotte (28270) *(G-2881)*

Suncrest Farms Cntry Hams Inc.................... 336 667-4441
  1148 Foster St Wilkesboro (28697) *(G-12654)*

Sunday Drive Holdings Inc......................... 919 825-5613
  421 Fayetteville St Ste 1100 Raleigh (27601) *(G-10519)*

Sundown Times, West Jefferson *Also Called: Mountain Times Inc (G-12567)*

Sundrop Printing................................. 704 960-1592
  700 N Cannon Blvd Kannapolis (28083) *(G-7221)*

Sunhs Warehouse LLC............................ 919 908-1523
  607 Ellis Rd Bldg 42a Durham (27703) *(G-4255)*

Sunnex, Charlotte *Also Called: Sunnex Inc (G-2882)*

Sunnex Inc...................................... 800 445-7869
  8001 Tower Point Dr Charlotte (28227) *(G-2882)*

Sunny View Pallet Company....................... 828 625-9907
  3057 Big Level Rd Mill Spring (28756) *(G-8303)*

Sunqest Inc (PA)................................ 828 325-4910
  1555 N Rankin Ave Newton (28658) *(G-9501)*

Sunray Inc...................................... 828 287-7030
  4761 Us 64 74a Hwy Rutherfordton (28139) *(G-10994)*

Sunrise Development LLC.......................... 828 453-0590
  650 Nc 120 Hwy Mooresboro (28114) *(G-8586)*

Sunrise Development USA, Mooresboro *Also Called: Sunrise Development LLC (G-8586)*

Sunrise Sawmill Inc.............................. 828 277-0120
  68 W Chapel Rd Asheville (28803) *(G-612)*

Sunrock Group Holdings Corp (PA)................. 919 747-6400
  200 Horizon Dr Ste 100 Raleigh (27615) *(G-10520)*

Sunseeker North America Inc...................... 704 684-5709
  4330 Matthews Indian Trail Rd Ste A Indian Trail (28079) *(G-7101)*

Sunseeker US Inc................................ 443 253-1546
  4330 Matthews Indian Trail Rd Indian Trail (28079) *(G-7102)*

Sunshine Mnfctred Strctres Inc.................... 704 279-6600
  850 Gold Hill Ave Rockwell (28138) *(G-10802)*

Sunshine Prosthetics Inc.......................... 833 266-9781
  118 Nash St Sw Ste E Wilson (27893) *(G-13032)*

Sunstar Heating Products Inc...................... 704 372-3486
  305 Doggett St Charlotte (28203) *(G-2883)*

(G-0000) Company's Geographic Section entry number

Suntech Medical Inc..919 654-2300
5827 S Miami Blvd Ste 100 Morrisville (27560) *(G-9060)*

Suntex Industries...336 784-1000
5000 S Main St Winston Salem (27107) *(G-13349)*

Suntory International (DH)..............................917 756-2747
4141 Parklake Ave Ste 600 Raleigh (27612) *(G-10521)*

Super Retread Center Inc (PA).....................919 734-0073
1213 S George St Goldsboro (27530) *(G-5248)*

Super Sagless, Statesville *Also Called: Leggett & Platt Incorporated (G-11727)*

Super Shred, Greenville *Also Called: Collins Banks Investments Inc (G-5956)*

Super-Net, Fuquay Varina *Also Called: American Netting Corp (G-4864)*

Superior Dry Kilns Inc...................................828 754-7001
2601 Withers Dr Hudson (28638) *(G-6960)*

Superior Essex Inc..252 823-5111
2801 Anaconda Rd Tarboro (27886) *(G-11941)*

Superior Essex Intl Inc..................................252 823-5111
2801 Anaconda Rd Tarboro (27886) *(G-11942)*

Superior Finishing Systems LLC...................336 956-2000
2132 Beckner Rd Lexington (27292) *(G-7747)*

Superior Fire Hose Corp...............................704 643-5888
10000 Industrial Dr Ste B Pineville (28134) *(G-9762)*

Superior Machine Co SC Inc.........................828 652-6141
169 Machine Shop Rd Marion (28752) *(G-8068)*

Superior Machine Shop Inc...........................910 675-1336
354 Sawdust Rd Rocky Point (28457) *(G-10885)*

Superior Manufacturing Company..................336 661-1200
4102 Indiana Ave Winston Salem (27105) *(G-13350)*

Superior Plastics Inc...................................704 864-5472
533 N Broad St Gastonia (28054) *(G-5147)*

Superior Powder Coating LLC.......................704 869-0004
123 Shannon Bradley Rd Gastonia (28052) *(G-5148)*

Superior Tooling Inc.....................................919 570-9762
2800 Superior Dr Wake Forest (27587) *(G-12306)*

Superior Walls, Salisbury *Also Called: Superior Walls Systems LLC (G-11120)*

Superior Walls, Salisbury *Also Called: Superior Walls Systems LLC (G-11121)*

Superior Walls Systems LLC.........................704 636-6200
3570 S Main St Salisbury (28147) *(G-11120)*

Superior Walls Systems LLC (PA)..................704 636-6200
3570 S Main St Salisbury (28147) *(G-11121)*

Superior Wood Products Inc..........................336 472-2237
10190 E Us Highway 64 Thomasville (27360) *(G-12076)*

Superskinsystems Inc...................................336 601-6005
3329 N Rockingham Rd Greensboro (27407) *(G-5845)*

Supertex Inc..336 622-1000
312 W Luther Ave Liberty (27298) *(G-7781)*

Suppliers To Wholesalers Inc......................704 375-7406
1816 W Pointe Dr Ste A Charlotte (28214) *(G-2884)*

Supplyone Rockwell Inc...............................704 279-5650
729 Palmer Rd Rockwell (28138) *(G-10803)*

Supreme Elastic Corporation.........................828 302-3836
325 Spencer Rd Ne Conover (28613) *(G-3563)*

Supreme Murphy Trck Bodies Inc..................252 291-2191
4000 Airport Dr Nw Wilson (27896) *(G-13033)*

Supreme Sweepers LLC.................................888 698-9996
6135 Park South Dr Ste 510 Charlotte (28210) *(G-2885)*

Supreme T-Shirts & Apparel..........................919 772-9040
2813 Banks Rd Raleigh (27603) *(G-10522)*

Sure Trip Inc (PA)...704 983-4651
703a Concord Rd Albemarle (28001) *(G-94)*

Sure Wood Products Inc...............................828 261-0004
980 3rd Ave Se Hickory (28602) *(G-6461)*

Surelift Inc...828 963-6899
151 H O Aldridge Rd Unit B Boone (28607) *(G-945)*

Surface Buff LLC..919 341-2873
9013 Duval Hill St Raleigh (27603) *(G-10523)*

Surfline Inc...252 715-1630
3335 S Virginia Dare Trl Nags Head (27959) *(G-9304)*

Surgical Center of Morehea..........................252 247-0314
3714 Guardian Ave Ste W Morehead City (28557) *(G-8846)*

Surgilum LLC...910 202-2202
2 N Front St Ste 5 Wilmington (28401) *(G-12934)*

Surratt Hosiery Mill Inc................................336 859-4583
22872 Nc Highway 8 Denton (27239) *(G-3762)*

Surry Chemicals Incorporated......................336 786-4607
241 Hickory St Mount Airy (27030) *(G-9181)*

Surry Collection, Mount Airy *Also Called: Kustom Kraft Wdwrks Mt Airy In (G-9143)*

Surteco SE, Greensboro *Also Called: Surteco USA Inc (G-5846)*

Surteco USA Inc..336 668-9555
7104 Cessna Dr Greensboro (27409) *(G-5846)*

Surtronics Inc..919 834-8027
4001 Beryl Rd Raleigh (27606) *(G-10524)*

Suspension Experts LLC..............................855 419-3072
118 Commerce Dr Roxboro (27573) *(G-10948)*

Suspensions LLC..704 809-1269
4723 Mountain Creek Ave Denver (28037) *(G-3808)*

Sustain Rng, Charlotte *Also Called: SRNg-T&w LLC (G-2852)*

Sustainable Corrugated LLC.........................828 608-0990
1000 Chain Dr Morganton (28655) *(G-8902)*

Sutherland Products Inc...............................800 854-3541
301 S Henry St Stoneville (27048) *(G-11831)*

Sutton Scientifics Inc..................................910 428-1600
246 W College St Star (27356) *(G-11634)*

Sv Plastics LLC..336 472-2242
42 High Tech Blvd Thomasville (27360) *(G-12077)*

Svcm...305 767-3595
536 N Generals Blvd Lincolnton (28092) *(G-7858)*

Svcm International, Lincolnton *Also Called: Svcm (G-7858)*

Swaim Inc (PA)..336 885-6131
1801 S University Pkwy High Point (27260) *(G-6797)*

Swaim Ornamental Iron Works.......................336 765-5271
2570 Landmark Dr Winston Salem (27103) *(G-13351)*

Swain & Temple Inc.....................................252 771-8147
149 Lilly Rd South Mills (27976) *(G-11493)*

Swanson Sheetmetal Inc..............................704 283-3955
320 Broome St Monroe (28110) *(G-8566)*

Swatch Works Inc.......................................336 626-9971
453 Oakhurst Rd Asheboro (27205) *(G-400)*

Swatchcraft, High Point *Also Called: E Feibusch Company Inc (G-6600)*

Swatchcraft LLC..336 434-5095
516 Townsend Ave High Point (27263) *(G-6798)*

Swatchworks Inc...336 626-9971
730 Industrial Park Ave Asheboro (27205) *(G-401)*

SWB Logging LLC.......................................704 485-3411
213 Glenwood Dr Oakboro (28129) *(G-9583)*

Sweatnet LLC...847 331-7287
310 Arlington Ave Unit 229 Charlotte (28203) *(G-2886)*

Sweep 24 LLC..980 428-5624
301 S Mcdowell St Charlotte (28204) *(G-2887)*

Sweet Room LLC..336 567-1620
4435 Garden Club St High Point (27265) *(G-6799)*

Swell Home Solutions Inc............................919 440-4692
109 Barfield St Mount Olive (28365) *(G-9260)*

Swimways...252 563-1101
3002 Anaconda Rd Tarboro (27886) *(G-11943)*

Swing Kurve Logistic Trckg LLC.....................704 506-7371
2428 Freedom Dr Charlotte (28208) *(G-2888)*

Swir Vision Systems Inc...............................919 248-0032
3021 Cornwallis Rd Durham (27709) *(G-4256)*

Swirl Oakhurst LLC......................................704 258-1209
1640 Oakhurst Commons Dr Ste 103 Charlotte (28205) *(G-2889)*

Swiss Diamond, Charlotte *Also Called: Swiss Made Brands USA Inc (G-2890)*

Swiss Made Brands USA Inc..........................704 900-6622
200 Forsyth Hall Dr Ste H Charlotte (28273) *(G-2890)*

Swk Technologies Inc..................................336 230-0200
2309 W Cone Blvd Ste 220 Greensboro (27408) *(G-5847)*

Swm Intl, Wilson *Also Called: Schweitzer-Mauduit Intl Inc (G-13029)*

Swofford Inc...252 478-5969
301 Railroad St S Wilson (27893) *(G-13034)*

Sword Conservatory Inc...............................919 557-4465
112 Tonks Trl Holly Springs (27540) *(G-6917)*

Sycamore Brewing LLC................................704 910-3821
401 W 24th St Charlotte (28206) *(G-2891)*

A L P H A B E T I C

Sycamore Cabinetry Inc.................................... 704 375-1617
  644 Dallas Bessemer City Hwy Dallas (28034) *(G-3691)*

Syd Inc.. 336 294-8807
  5223c W Market St Ste C Greensboro (27409) *(G-5848)*

Sylva Herald and Ruralite.................................. 828 586-2611
  539 W Main St Sylva (28779) *(G-11900)*

Sylva Herald Pubg Co Incthe............................. 828 586-2611
  539 W Main St Sylva (28779) *(G-11901)*

Sylva Herald, The, Sylva *Also Called: Sylva Herald and Ruralite (G-11900)*

Symbrium Inc (PA)..919 879-2470
  6021 Triangle Dr Raleigh (27617) *(G-10525)*

Synchrono Group Inc... 888 389-0439
  8601 Six Forks Rd Ste 400 Raleigh (27615) *(G-10526)*

Syncot Plastics LLC... 704 967-0010
  350 Eastwood Dr Belmont (28012) *(G-769)*

Syneos Health Consulting Inc............................ 919 876-9300
  1030 Sync St Morrisville (27560) *(G-9061)*

Synereca, Chapel Hill *Also Called: Synereca Pharmaceuticals Inc (G-1576)*

Synereca Pharmaceuticals Inc............................ 919 966-3929
  39519 Glenn Glade Chapel Hill (27517) *(G-1576)*

Synergem Technologies Inc............................... 866 859-0911
  371 Windrush Ln Mount Airy (27030) *(G-9182)*

Synnovator Inc.. 919 360-0518
  104 Tw Alexander Dr # 1 Durham (27709) *(G-4257)*

Synopsys Inc.. 919 941-6600
  710 Slater Rd Morrisville (27560) *(G-9062)*

Synoptix Companies LLC.................................. 910 790-3630
  130 Cinema Dr Wilmington (28403) *(G-12935)*

Synq Marketing Group LLC............................... 800 380-6360
  338 S Sharon Amity Rd Charlotte (28211) *(G-2892)*

Syntec Inc.. 336 861-9023
  200 Swathmore Ave High Point (27263) *(G-6800)*

Syntech Abrasives Inc....................................... 704 525-8030
  8325 Arrowridge Blvd Ste H Charlotte (28273) *(G-2893)*

Syntech of Burlington Inc................................. 336 570-2035
  1825 Frank Holt Dr Burlington (27215) *(G-1166)*

Syntegon Technology Svcs LLC (PA)..................919 877-0886
  2440 Sumner Blvd Raleigh (27616) *(G-10527)*

Syntha Group Inc (PA)......................................336 885-5131
  331 Burton Ave High Point (27262) *(G-6801)*

Synthetic Finishing, Hickory *Also Called: Tsg Finishing LLC (G-6473)*

Synthetic Finishing Co, Hickory *Also Called: Tsg Finishing LLC (G-6474)*

Synthetics Finishing, Hickory *Also Called: Tsg Finishing LLC (G-6471)*

Synthomer Inc.. 704 225-1872
  2011 N Rocky River Rd Monroe (28110) *(G-8567)*

Synthon, Durham *Also Called: Synthon Pharmaceuticals Inc (G-4258)*

Synthon Pharmaceuticals Inc............................ 919 493-6006
  1007 Slater Rd Ste 150 Durham (27703) *(G-4258)*

Synthonix Inc... 919 875-9277
  2713 Connector Dr Wake Forest (27587) *(G-12307)*

Syracuse Plastics, Cary *Also Called: PCI of North Carolina LLC (G-1416)*

Sysmetric USA.. 704 522-8778
  107 Infield Ct Mooresville (28117) *(G-8783)*

Systel Business Eqp Co Inc............................... 336 808-8000
  3517 W Wendover Ave Greensboro (27407) *(G-5849)*

Systel Office Automation, Greensboro *Also Called: Systel Business Eqp Co Inc (G-5849)*

T - Square Enterprises Inc................................. 704 846-8233
  8318 Pineville Matthews Rd Charlotte (28226) *(G-2894)*

T & J Panel Systems Inc................................... 704 924-8600
  269 Marble Rd Statesville (28625) *(G-11784)*

T & R Signs... 919 779-1185
  110 E Main St Garner (27529) *(G-4967)*

T & R Signs & Screen Printing, Garner *Also Called: T & R Signs (G-4967)*

T & S Hardwoods Inc.. 828 586-4044
  3635 Skyland Dr Sylva (28779) *(G-11902)*

T 2 E, Rocky Mount *Also Called: Trans-Tech Energy Inc (G-10817)*

T Air Inc (PA)... 980 595-2840
  11020 David Taylor Dr Ste 350 Charlotte (28262) *(G-2895)*

T C I, Charlotte *Also Called: Triple Crown International LLC (G-2946)*

T Cs Services Inc... 910 655-2796
  286 Jacobs Rd Bolton (28423) *(G-889)*

T D M Corporation
  333 White Pine Dr Fletcher (28732) *(G-4772)*

T Distribution NC Inc... 828 438-1112
  801 N Green St Morganton (28655) *(G-8903)*

T E Johnson Building and Rentl, Four Oaks *Also Called: T E Johnson Lumber Co Inc (G-4817)*

T E Johnson Lumber Co Inc.............................. 919 963-2233
  3872 Old School Rd Four Oaks (27524) *(G-4817)*

T E M A, Raleigh *Also Called: The Tarheel Electric Membership Association Incorporated (G-10544)*

T H Blue Inc... 910 673-3033
  226 Flowers Rd Eagle Springs (27242) *(G-4319)*

T Hoff Manufacturing Corp (PA)..........................919 833-8671
  4500 Preslyn Dr D Raleigh (27603) *(G-10528)*

T L V, Charlotte *Also Called: Tlv Corporation (G-2922)*

T M S, Raleigh *Also Called: Triangle Microsystems Inc (G-10558)*

T P Supply Co Inc.. 336 789-2337
  483 Belvue Dr Mount Airy (27030) *(G-9183)*

T Precision Machining Inc................................. 828 250-0993
  123 Lyman St Asheville (28801) *(G-613)*

T R P, Wilson *Also Called: Tobacco Rag Processors Inc (G-13035)*

T R P, Wilson *Also Called: Tobacco Rag Processors Inc (G-13037)*

T S Designs Incorporated................................. 336 226-5694
  2053 Willow Spring Ln Burlington (27215) *(G-1167)*

T S E, Fayetteville *Also Called: Tactical Support Equipment Inc (G-4676)*

T T S D Productions LLC................................... 704 829-6666
  27 E Woodrow Ave Belmont (28012) *(G-770)*

T Toppers, Belmont *Also Called: T T S D Productions LLC (G-770)*

T V S, Brevard *Also Called: Transylvnia Vcational Svcs Inc (G-983)*

T W Garner Food Company.................................. 336 661-1550
  600 Northgate Park Dr Winston Salem (27106) *(G-13352)*

T W Garner Food Company (PA)..........................336 661-1550
  614 W 4th St Winston Salem (27101) *(G-13353)*

T W Garner Food Company.................................. 336 661-1550
  4045 Indiana Ave Winston Salem (27105) *(G-13354)*

T W Hathcock Logging Inc................................ 704 485-9457
  25341 Millingport Rd Locust (28097) *(G-7905)*

T W Signs & Graphics, Mount Airy *Also Called: Kat Designs Inc (G-9138)*

T-Fab Precision Machining, Asheville *Also Called: T Precision Machining Inc (G-613)*

T-Metrics Inc... 704 523-9583
  4430 Stuart Andrew Blvd Charlotte (28217) *(G-2896)*

T-N-T Carports Inc.. 336 789-3818
  1050 Worth St Mount Airy (27030) *(G-9184)*

T-N-T Carports Inc (PA)..................................... 336 789-3818
  170 Holly Springs Rd Mount Airy (27030) *(G-9185)*

T. H. Blue Mulch, Eagle Springs *Also Called: T H Blue Inc (G-4319)*

T.L.g Atelier, Greenville *Also Called: Timothy L Griffin (G-6028)*

T&J Sales, Lincolnton *Also Called: Walter Reynolds (G-7870)*

Ta Lost Pines Woodwork..................................... 828 367-7517
  24 Rose Hill Rd Asheville (28803) *(G-614)*

Tab Index Inc... 919 876-8988
  2708 Discovery Dr Ste J Raleigh (27616) *(G-10529)*

Tab Steel & Fabricating Inc.............................. 828 323-8300
  3345 Clarence Towery Cir Hildebran (28637) *(G-6855)*

Table Rock Printers LLC................................... 828 433-1377
  205 N Sterling St Morganton (28655) *(G-8904)*

Tabor City Lumber Company (PA)........................910 653-3162
  510 N Main St Tabor City (28463) *(G-11915)*

Tabur Services.. 704 483-1650
  7845 Commerce Dr Denver (28037) *(G-3809)*

Tabur Services LLC... 704 483-1650
  7845 Commerce Dr Unit D Denver (28037) *(G-3810)*

TAC Air, Morrisville *Also Called: Signature Flight Air Inc (G-9055)*

TAC Shield, West End *Also Called: Military Products Inc (G-12557)*

Tactical Coatings Inc....................................... 704 692-4511
  1028 Railroad Ave Shelby (28152) *(G-11384)*

Tactical Mobility Training, Fayetteville *Also Called: James King (G-4620)*

Tactical Support Equipment Inc.......................... 910 425-3360
  4039 Barefoot Rd Fayetteville (28306) *(G-4676)*

Tactile Workshop LLC.. 919 738-9924
  1001 S Saunders St Raleigh (27603) *(G-10530)*

Tafford, Charlotte *Also Called: Tafford Uniforms LLC (G-2897)*

Tafford Uniforms LLC.. 888 823-3673
2121 Distribution Center Dr Ste E Charlotte (28269) *(G-2897)*

Tagoio Inc.. 984 263-4376
1017 Main Campus Dr Ste 2300 Raleigh (27606) *(G-10531)*

Taiji Medical Supplies Inc... 888 667-6658
3211 Progress Dr Lincolnton (28092) *(G-7859)*

Tailor Cut Wood Products Inc....................................... 828 632-2808
35 Wittenburg Industrial Dr Taylorsville (28681) *(G-11980)*

Tailored Chemical, Hickory *Also Called: Tailored Chemical Products Inc (G-6462)*

Tailored Chemical Products Inc (PA)............................... 828 322-6512
700 12th Street Dr Nw Ste B Hickory (28601) *(G-6462)*

Talladega Mchy & Sup Co NC (PA)................................ 256 362-4124
3510 Gillespie St Fayetteville (28306) *(G-4677)*

Tallahassee Democrat.. 919 832-9430
4600 Trinity Rd Raleigh (27607) *(G-10532)*

Talledega Machinery & Supply, Fayetteville *Also Called: Talladega Mchy & Sup Co NC (G-4677)*

Tallent Wood Works.. 704 592-2013
113 Kammerer Dr Statesville (28625) *(G-11785)*

Talley Machinery Corporation (HQ)............................... 336 664-0012
7009 Cessna Dr Greensboro (27409) *(G-5850)*

Tameka Burros... 330 338-8941
979 Ramsgate Dr Sw Concord (28025) *(G-3451)*

Tampco Inc.. 336 835-1895
316 Stainless Way Elkin (28621) *(G-4452)*

Tan Books and Publishers Inc (PA)................................ 704 731-0651
13315 Carowinds Blvd Ste Q Charlotte (28273) *(G-2898)*

Tandemloc Inc.. 252 447-7155
824 Nc Highway 101 Fontana Blvd Havelock (28532) *(G-6128)*

Tangles Knitting On Main LLC...................................... 704 243-7150
200 W North Main St Waxhaw (28173) *(G-12443)*

Tank Fab Inc.. 910 675-8999
8787 Us Hwy 117 S Rocky Point (28457) *(G-10886)*

Tannis Root Productions Inc.. 919 832-8552
1720 Capital Blvd Raleigh (27604) *(G-10533)*

Tapestries Ltd.. 336 883-9864
6 Westmount Ct Greensboro (27410) *(G-5851)*

Tapped Tees LLC... 919 943-9692
600 W Main St Apt 613 Durham (27701) *(G-4259)*

Tar Heel Bark, Harrisburg *Also Called: Garick LLC (G-6109)*

Tar Heel Credit Counciling.. 336 254-0348
2223 N Church St Greensboro (27405) *(G-5852)*

Tar Heel Cuisine Inc... 704 435-6979
1009 N Mountain St Cherryville (28021) *(G-3070)*

Tar Heel Fence & Vinyl.. 336 465-1297
5279 Branson Davis Rd Sophia (27350) *(G-11492)*

Tar Heel Grnd Cmmndery Order K................................ 910 867-6764
1940 Caviness St Fayetteville (28314) *(G-4678)*

Tar Heel Landworks LLC.. 336 941-3009
6858 Nc Highway 801 S Mocksville (27028) *(G-8393)*

Tar Heel Materials & Hdlg LLC..................................... 704 659-5143
725 Kesler Rd Cleveland (27013) *(G-3223)*

Tar Heel Mini Motoring Club.. 336 391-8084
380 Knollwood St Ste H129 Winston Salem (27103) *(G-13355)*

Tar Heel Tling Prcsion McHning.................................... 919 965-6160
3290 Us Highway 70 E Smithfield (27577) *(G-11467)*

Tar River Thinning Inc... 919 497-1647
176 Paul Sledge Rd Louisburg (27549) *(G-7927)*

Tar River Trading Post LLC.. 919 589-3618
385 Fleming Rd Youngsville (27596) *(G-13490)*

Tarboro Serv, Princeville *Also Called: Southern States Coop Inc (G-9828)*

Tarheel Enviromental LLC... 910 425-4939
633 Fred Hall Rd Stedman (28391) *(G-11808)*

Tarheel Mats Inc... 252 325-1903
654 Nc Highway 343 N Camden (27921) *(G-1213)*

Tarheel Monitoring LLC... 910 763-1490
709 Princess St Wilmington (28401) *(G-12936)*

Tarheel Oil, Boone *Also Called: BP Oil Corp Distributors (G-902)*

Tarheel Pavement Clg Svcs Inc.................................... 704 895-8015
18636 Starcreek Dr Ste G Cornelius (28031) *(G-3627)*

Tarheel Plastics LLC
2018 E Us Highway 64 Lexington (27292) *(G-7748)*

Tarheel Publishing Co... 919 553-9042
120 N Tech Dr Ste 102 Clayton (27520) *(G-3173)*

Tarheel Sand & Stone Inc... 336 468-4003
1108 Tuckda Way Hamptonville (27020) *(G-6093)*

Tarheel Solid Surfaces, Wilmington *Also Called: Tarheel Wood Designs Inc (G-12937)*

Tarheel Solutions LLC... 336 420-9265
6463 Walter Wright Rd Pleasant Garden (27313) *(G-9795)*

Tarheel Tool & Gauge LLC.. 704 213-6924
4665 Miller Rd Salisbury (28147) *(G-11122)*

Tarheel Wood Designs Inc.. 910 395-2226
6609b Windmill Way Wilmington (28405) *(G-12937)*

Tarheel Wood Treating Company................................... 919 467-9176
10309 Chapel Hill Rd Morrisville (27560) *(G-9063)*

Tarheel Woodcrafters Inc... 252 432-3035
1570 Hicksboro Rd Henderson (27537) *(G-6180)*

Tasman Industries Inc... 502 587-0701
1011 Porter St Ste 103 High Point (27263) *(G-6802)*

Tastebuds LLC.. 704 461-8755
208 N Main St Belmont (28012) *(G-771)*

Tastebuds Popcorn, Belmont *Also Called: Tastebuds LLC (G-771)*

Tat Piedmont, Greensboro *Also Called: Piedmont AVI Cmponent Svcs LLC (G-5741)*

Tat Technologies, Charlotte *Also Called: Tat Technologies Group (G-2899)*

Tat Technologies Group... 704 910-2215
9335 Harris Corners Pkwy Ste 26 Charlotte (28269) *(G-2899)*

Tate & Lyle Solutions USA LLC..................................... 252 482-0402
841 Avoca Farm Rd Ste 2 Merry Hill (27957) *(G-8269)*

Tatum Galleries Inc.. 828 963-6466
5320 Nc Highway 105 S Banner Elk (28604) *(G-689)*

Taurus Textiles, Statesville *Also Called: Badger Sportswear LLC (G-11665)*

Tavros Therapeutics Inc... 919 602-2631
8 Davis Dr Ste 100 Durham (27709) *(G-4260)*

Tawnico LLC.. 704 606-2345
11612 James Jack Ln Charlotte (28277) *(G-2900)*

Taxation Station LLC.. 336 209-3933
800 W Smith St Ste 209 Greensboro (27401) *(G-5853)*

Taylco Inc... 910 739-0405
2643 W Carthage Rd Lumberton (28360) *(G-7974)*

Taylor Boat Works... 252 726-6374
200 Pensacola Ave Morehead City (28557) *(G-8847)*

Taylor Communications Inc... 336 841-7700
4189 Eagle Hill Dr Ste 101 High Point (27265) *(G-6803)*

Taylor Communications Inc... 704 282-0989
1803 N Rocky River Rd Monroe (28110) *(G-8568)*

Taylor Interiors LLC... 980 207-3160
2818 Queen City Dr Charlotte (28208) *(G-2901)*

Taylor King Furniture Inc.. 828 632-7731
286 County Home Rd Taylorsville (28681) *(G-11981)*

Taylor Made Cases Inc.. 919 209-0555
107 Last Cast Dr Benson (27504) *(G-797)*

Taylor Manufacturing Inc... 910 862-2576
1585 Us Hwy 701 S Elizabethtown (28337) *(G-4434)*

Taylor Prime Labels & Packg, Goldsboro *Also Called: Occasions Group Inc (G-5233)*

Taylor Prime Labels & Packg, Greenville *Also Called: Occasions Group Inc (G-6009)*

Taylor Printing & Office Sup, Roxboro *Also Called: Person Printing Company Inc (G-10940)*

Taylor Products Inc.. 910 862-2576
1585 Us Hwy 701 S Elizabethtown (28337) *(G-4435)*

Taylor Timber Transport Inc.. 252 943-1550
1977 Old New Bern Rd Chocowinity (27817) *(G-3085)*

Taylorsville Precast Molds Inc...................................... 828 632-4608
128 Taylorsville Mfg Rd Taylorsville (28681) *(G-11982)*

Taylorsville Times.. 828 632-2532
24 E Main Ave Taylorsville (28681) *(G-11983)*

Tb Arhaus LLC... 828 465-6953
1211 Keisler Rd Se Conover (28613) *(G-3564)*

Tb Woods Incorporated... 704 588-5610
701 Carrier Dr Charlotte (28216) *(G-2902)*

Tbc Retail Group Inc.. 336 540-8066
2514 Battleground Ave Ste B Greensboro (27408) *(G-5854)*

Tc2 Labs LLC... 919 380-2171
3948 Browning Pl Ste 334 Raleigh (27609) *(G-10534)*

Tc2000.com, Wilmington *Also Called: Worden Brothers Inc (G-12954)*

TCBY, Lenoir *Also Called: Carolina Yogurt Inc (G-7591)*

Tce Manufacturing LLC.. 252 330-9919
1287 Salem Church Rd Elizabeth City (27909) *(G-4412)*

Tcgrx, Durham *Also Called: Chudy Group LLC (G-3975)*

Tcgrx, Durham *Also Called: Parata Systems LLC (G-4165)*

TCI, Ramseur *Also Called: Tower Components Inc (G-10632)*

TCI Mobility Inc.. 704 867-8331
1720 Industrial Pike Rd Gastonia (28052) *(G-5149)*

Tcom, Elizabeth City *Also Called: Tcom Ground Systems LP (G-4414)*

Tcom Limited Partnership... 252 330-5555
190 T Com Dr Elizabeth City (27909) *(G-4413)*

Tcom Ground Systems LP.. 252 338-3200
190 T Com Dr Elizabeth City (27909) *(G-4414)*

TCOM, LIMITED PARTNERSHIP, Elizabeth City *Also Called: Tcom Limited Partnership
(G-4413)*

Tcprst LLC... 910 791-9767
3534 S College Rd Ste I Wilmington (28412) *(G-12938)*

TCS Designs Inc... 828 324-9944
1851 9th Ave Ne Hickory (28601) *(G-6463)*

Tcsc, Winston Salem *Also Called: The Computer Solution Company (G-13362)*

Td Cloud, Raleigh *Also Called: Td Cloud Services (G-10535)*

Td Cloud Services... 518 258-6788
3129 Oaklyn Springs Dr Raleigh (27606) *(G-10535)*

Td Fiber, High Point *Also Called: Thomasville-Dexel Incorporated (G-6808)*

Tdc International LLC.. 704 875-1198
980 Derita Rd # B Concord (28027) *(G-3452)*

Te Connectivity.. 336 727-5295
3700 Reidsville Rd Winston Salem (27101) *(G-13356)*

Te Connectivity, Greensboro *Also Called: Commscope Technologies LLC (G-5461)*

Te Connectivity Corporation.. 828 338-1000
1396 Charlotte Hwy Fairview (28730) *(G-4513)*

Te Connectivity Corporation.. 828 338-1000
1396 Charlotte Hwy Fairview (28730) *(G-4514)*

Te Connectivity Corporation.. 919 552-3811
8000 Purfoy Rd Fuquay Varina (27526) *(G-4898)*

Te Connectivity Corporation.. 919 557-8425
8009 Purfoy Rd Fuquay Varina (27526) *(G-4899)*

Te Connectivity Corporation.. 919 552-3811
8000 Purfoy Rd Fuquay Varina (27526) *(G-4900)*

Te Connectivity Corporation.. 336 428-7200
8300 Triad Dr Greensboro (27409) *(G-5855)*

Te Connectivity Corporation.. 336 664-7000
8000 Piedmont Triad Pkwy Greensboro (27409) *(G-5856)*

Te Connectivity Corporation.. 336 665-4400
719 Pegg Rd Bldg 253 Greensboro (27409) *(G-5857)*

Te Connectivity Corporation.. 336 664-7000
3900 Reidsville Rd Winston Salem (27101) *(G-13357)*

Te Connectivity Corporation.. 336 727-5122
3800 Reidsville Rd Winston Salem (27101) *(G-13358)*

Tea and Honey Blends LLC... 919 673-4273
444 S Blount St Ste 115b Raleigh (27601) *(G-10536)*

Tea Rex Teahouse, Charlotte *Also Called: Brewitt & Dreenkupp Inc (G-1811)*

Teabar Publishing Inc... 252 764-2453
201n James Dr Emerald Isle (28594) *(G-4480)*

Team 21st... 910 826-3676
6316 Yadkin Rd Fayetteville (28303) *(G-4679)*

Team Connection.. 336 287-3892
2508 Griffith Meadows Dr Winston Salem (27103) *(G-13359)*

Team Gsg LLC.. 252 830-1032
851 Black Jack Simpson Rd Greenville (27858) *(G-6026)*

Team Industries Inc.. 828 837-5377
3750 Airport Rd Andrews (28901) *(G-109)*

Team Manufacturing - E W LLC.................................... 919 554-2442
35 Weathers Ct Youngsville (27596) *(G-13491)*

Team Penske, Mooresville *Also Called: Penske Racing South Inc (G-8746)*

Team X-Treme LLC.. 919 562-8100
600 S Main St Ste C Rolesville (27571) *(G-10890)*

Teamwork Inc.. 336 578-3456
1000 Georgetowne Dr Elon (27244) *(G-4472)*

Tearscience Inc.. 919 459-4880
5151 Mccrimmon Pkwy Ste 250 Morrisville (27560) *(G-9064)*

Tebo Displays LLC.. 919 832-8525
2609 Discovery Dr Ste 105 Raleigh (27616) *(G-10537)*

TEC Coat... 412 215-0152
14030 S Lakes Dr Charlotte (28273) *(G-2903)*

TEC Graphics Inc.. 919 567-2077
101 Technology Park Ln Fuquay Varina (27526) *(G-4901)*

TEC Tran Brake, Burlington *Also Called: Kck Holding Corp (G-1114)*

TEC-Ops, Hickory *Also Called: Blue Lagoon Inc (G-6273)*

Tecgrachem Inc.. 336 993-6785
1957 Nc Highway 66 S Kernersville (27284) *(G-7304)*

Tech Marketing, Raleigh *Also Called: Pt Marketing Incorporated (G-10408)*

Tech Medical Plastics Inc.. 919 563-9272
1403 Dogwood Way Mebane (27302) *(G-8261)*

Tech-Tool Inc... 919 906-6229
2561 Country Club Dr Hampstead (28443) *(G-6076)*

Techmet, Hickory *Also Called: Techmet Carbides Inc (G-6464)*

Techmet Carbides Inc... 828 624-0222
730 21st Street Dr Se Hickory (28602) *(G-6464)*

Technibilt Ltd (DH)... 828 464-7388
700 Technibilt Dr Newton (28658) *(G-9502)*

Technica Editorial Services.. 919 918-3991
205 W Main St Ste 206 Carrboro (27510) *(G-1274)*

Technical Center, Hickory *Also Called: Century Furniture LLC (G-6297)*

Technical Coating Intl Inc.. 910 371-0860
150 Backhoe Rd Ne Leland (28451) *(G-7559)*

Technical Development, Concord *Also Called: Tdc International LLC (G-3452)*

Technicon Acoustics, Concord *Also Called: Technicon Industries Inc (G-3453)*

Technicon Industries Inc... 704 788-1131
4412 Republic Ct Nw Concord (28027) *(G-3453)*

Technimark.. 336 736-9366
208 Nc Highway 62 W Randleman (27317) *(G-10662)*

Technimark LLC.. 336 498-4171
4509 Us Highway 220 Bus N Asheboro (27203) *(G-402)*

Technimark LLC.. 336 498-4171
2536 Bank St Asheboro (27203) *(G-403)*

Technimark LLC (HQ).. 336 498-4171
180 Commerce Pl Asheboro (27203) *(G-404)*

Technimark Reynosa LLC... 336 498-4171
2510 Bank St Asheboro (27203) *(G-405)*

Technimark Reynosa LLC (DH)..................................... 336 498-4171
180 Commerce Pl Asheboro (27203) *(G-406)*

Technique Chassis LLC.. 517 819-3579
4101 Roush Pl Nw Concord (28027) *(G-3454)*

Technology Partners LLC (PA)...................................... 704 553-1004
8757 Red Oak Blvd 2f Charlotte (28217) *(G-2904)*

Techseal Division, Wilson *Also Called: Parker-Hannifin Corporation (G-13012)*

Techsouth Inc.. 704 334-1100
601 Union West Blvd Matthews (28104) *(G-8196)*

Techtronic Industries, Charlotte *Also Called: TTI Floor Care North Amer Inc (G-2950)*

Tecnofirma America Inc.. 704 674-1296
2030 Airport Flex Dr Charlotte (28208) *(G-2905)*

Tecworks Inc... 704 829-9700
4041 S Cove Ln Belmont (28012) *(G-772)*

Ted Wheeler... 252 438-0820
2651 Hwy 158 Oxford (27565) *(G-9638)*

Ted's Service Company, Oxford *Also Called: Ted Wheeler (G-9638)*

Teddy Soft Paper Products Inc..................................... 336 784-5887
535 E Clemmonsville Rd Ste A Winston Salem (27107) *(G-13360)*

Tef Inc.. 704 786-9577
3650 Zion Church Rd Concord (28025) *(G-3455)*

Tegna, Asheville *Also Called: Asheville Citizen-Times (G-434)*

Teguar Computers, Charlotte *Also Called: Teguar Corporation (G-2906)*

Teguar Corporation (PA).. 704 960-1761
2920 Whitehall Park Dr Charlotte (28273) *(G-2906)*

Tehan Company Inc.. 800 283-7290
2620 Stag Park Rd Burgaw (28425) *(G-1034)*

Tehan Distributing, Burgaw *Also Called: Tehan Company Inc (G-1034)*

Teijin Automotive Tech Inc.. 828 757-8313
2424 Norwood St Sw Unit 300 Lenoir (28645) *(G-7641)*

Teijin Automotive Tech Inc.................................. 828 754-8441
601 Hibriten Dr Sw Lenoir (28645) *(G-7642)*

Teijin Automotive Tech Inc.................................. 828 466-7000
1400 Burris Rd Newton (28658) *(G-9503)*

Teijin Automotive Tech Inc.................................. 704 797-8744
6701 Statesville Blvd Salisbury (28147) *(G-11123)*

Tekelec, Morrisville *Also Called: Tekelec Global Inc (G-9066)*

Tekelec Inc
5200 Paramount Pkwy Morrisville (27560) *(G-9065)*

Tekelec Global Inc.. 919 460-5500
5200 Paramount Pkwy Morrisville (27560) *(G-9066)*

Tekni-Plex Inc.. 919 553-4151
8720 Us 70 Bus Hwy W Clayton (27520) *(G-3174)*

Teknor Apex Company.. 401 642-3598
3518 Dillon Rd Jamestown (27282) *(G-7180)*

Tektone Sound & Signal Mfg Inc........................ 828 524-9967
324 Industrial Park Rd Franklin (28734) *(G-4841)*

Tektronix, Charlotte *Also Called: Tektronix Inc (G-2907)*

Tektronix, Raleigh *Also Called: Tektronix Inc (G-10538)*

Tektronix Inc.. 704 527-5000
4400 Stuart Andrew Blvd Ste O Charlotte (28217) *(G-2907)*

Tektronix Inc.. 919 233-9490
5608 Pine Dr Raleigh (27606) *(G-10538)*

Telair US Cargo Systems, Goldsboro *Also Called: Telair US LLC (G-5249)*

Telair US LLC.. 919 705-2400
500a Gateway Dr Goldsboro (27534) *(G-5249)*

Telecmmnctons Resource MGT Inc.................... 919 779-0776
156 Annaron Ct Raleigh (27603) *(G-10539)*

Telecommunications Tech Inc............................ 919 556-7100
14101 Capital Blvd Ste 201 Youngsville (27596) *(G-13492)*

Teleflex, Durham *Also Called: Teleflex Incorporated (G-4261)*

Teleflex, Durham *Also Called: Teleflex Incorporated (G-4262)*

Teleflex, Morrisville *Also Called: Teleflex Incorporated (G-9067)*

Teleflex Incorporated.. 919 433-2575
2917 Weck Dr Research Triangle Park Durham (27709) *(G-4261)*

Teleflex Incorporated.. 919 433-2575
1805a Tw Alexander Dr Durham (27703) *(G-4262)*

Teleflex Incorporated.. 919 544-8000
3015 Carrington Mill Blvd Morrisville (27560) *(G-9067)*

Teleflex Medical Incorporated............................ 336 498-4153
312 Commerce Pl Asheboro (27203) *(G-407)*

Teleflex Medical Incorporated............................ 919 544-8000
4024 Stirrup Creek Dr Ste 270 Durham (27703) *(G-4263)*

Teleflex Medical Incorporated (HQ).................... 919 544-8000
3015 Carrington Mill Blvd Morrisville (27560) *(G-9068)*

Telepathic Graphics Inc (PA)............................ 919 342-4603
6001 Chapel Hill Rd Ste 106 Raleigh (27607) *(G-10540)*

Telepathic Graphics Inc.................................... 919 342-4603
1131 Atlantic Ave Rocky Mount (27801) *(G-10815)*

Telephonics Corporation.................................... 631 755-7446
1014 Consolidated Rd Elizabeth City (27909) *(G-4415)*

Telephys Inc.. 312 625-9128
610 Jetton St Ste 120 Davidson (28036) *(G-3719)*

Teletec Corporation.. 919 954-7300
5617 Departure Dr Ste 107 Raleigh (27616) *(G-10541)*

Telewire Supply, Cary *Also Called: Ruckus Wireless LLC (G-1442)*

Telit Wireless Solutions Inc (PA)...................... 919 439-7977
5425 Page Rd Ste 120 Durham (27703) *(G-4264)*

Tempest Aero Group.. 336 449-5054
1240 Springwood Church Rd Gibsonville (27249) *(G-5184)*

Tempest Environmental, Durham *Also Called: Tempest Envmtl Systems Inc (G-4266)*

Tempest Environmental Corp.............................. 919 973-1609
7 Al Acqua Dr Durham (27707) *(G-4265)*

Tempest Envmtl Systems Inc.............................. 919 973-1609
7 Al Acqua Dr Durham (27707) *(G-4266)*

Tempest Plus Marketing Group, Gibsonville *Also Called: Tempest Aero Group (G-5184)*

Temple Inc (PA).. 828 428-8031
102 S 7th Avenue Ext Maiden (28650) *(G-8018)*

Temple Furniture, Maiden *Also Called: Temple Inc (G-8018)*

Templex Inc.. 336 472-5933
3 Stanley Ave Thomasville (27360) *(G-12078)*

Tempo Products LLC.. 336 434-8649
2130 Brevard Rd High Point (27263) *(G-6804)*

Temposonics LLC.. 470 380-5103
3001 Sheldon Dr Cary (27513) *(G-1469)*

Temprano Techvestors Inc................................ 877 545-1509
2105 Northwest Blvd Newton (28658) *(G-9504)*

Tencarva Machinery Company LLC...................... 336 665-1435
1800 Sullivan St Greensboro (27405) *(G-5858)*

Tenda Bake, Newton *Also Called: Midstate Mills Inc (G-9482)*

Tengion, Winston Salem *Also Called: Tengion Inc (G-13361)*

Tengion Inc.. 336 722-5855
3929 Westpoint Blvd Ste G Winston Salem (27103) *(G-13361)*

Tenn-Tex Plastics Inc.. 336 931-1100
8011 National Service Rd Colfax (27235) *(G-3291)*

Tennessee Nedgraphics Inc................................ 704 414-4224
1809 Cross Beam Dr Ste E Charlotte (28217) *(G-2908)*

Tenowo Inc (DH).. 704 732-3525
1968 Kawai Rd Lincolnton (28092) *(G-7860)*

Tenowo Inc.. 704 732-3525
1582 Startown Rd Lincolnton (28092) *(G-7861)*

Teradata Corporation.. 919 816-1900
5565 Centerview Dr Ste 300 Raleigh (27606) *(G-10542)*

Terarecon Inc (PA).. 650 372-1100
4309 Emperor Blvd Ste 310 Durham (27703) *(G-4267)*

Tergus Pharma LLC (PA).................................... 919 549-9700
4018 Stirrup Creek Dr Durham (27703) *(G-4268)*

Terida LLC.. 910 693-1633
40 Augusta National Dr Pinehurst (28374) *(G-9704)*

Terra Tech Inc.. 906 399-0863
965 Derita Rd Concord (28027) *(G-3456)*

Terresolve, Charlotte *Also Called: RSC Bio Solutions LLC (G-2737)*

Terry Leggett Logging Co Inc............................ 252 927-4671
4403 Long Ridge Rd Pinetown (27865) *(G-9710)*

Terry Logging Company...................................... 919 477-9170
7917 S Lowell Rd Bahama (27503) *(G-667)*

Test ME Out Inc.. 252 635-6770
3262 Wellons Blvd New Bern (28562) *(G-9399)*

Testing Facility, Huntersville *Also Called: Newell Brands Inc (G-7019)*

Tethis Inc.. 919 808-2866
3401 Spring Forest Rd Raleigh (27616) *(G-10543)*

Teva Pharmaceuticals Usa Inc.......................... 336 316-4132
100 S Swing Rd Greensboro (27409) *(G-5859)*

Tex Care Medical, Burlington *Also Called: Flynt/Amtex Inc (G-1090)*

Tex Tech Industries, Kernersville *Also Called: Tex-Tech Industries Inc (G-7307)*

Tex-Tech Coatings LLC...................................... 336 992-7500
215 Drummond St Kernersville (27284) *(G-7305)*

Tex-Tech Coatings LLC (HQ).............................. 336 992-7500
1350 Bridgeport Dr Ste 1 Kernersville (27284) *(G-7306)*

Tex-Tech Industries Inc (PA)............................ 207 756-8605
1350 Bridgeport Dr Ste 1 Kernersville (27284) *(G-7307)*

Texdel, Conover *Also Called: Textile-Based Delivery Inc (G-3565)*

Texinnovate Inc.. 336 279-7800
7109 Cessna Dr Greensboro (27409) *(G-5860)*

Texlon Plastics Corp.. 704 866-8785
135 Wolfpack Rd Gastonia (28053) *(G-5150)*

Texpack USA Inc.. 704 864-5406
1302 Industrial Pike Rd Gastonia (28052) *(G-5151)*

Textile Designed Machine Co.............................. 704 664-1374
1320 Shearers Rd Mooresville (28115) *(G-8784)*

Textile Parts and Mch Co Inc............................ 704 865-5003
1502 W May Ave Gastonia (28052) *(G-5152)*

Textile Piece Dyeing Co Inc.............................. 704 732-4200
319 N Generals Blvd Lincolnton (28092) *(G-7862)*

Textile Printing Inc.. 704 521-8099
2431 Thornridge Rd Charlotte (28226) *(G-2909)*

Textile Products Inc.. 704 636-6221
119 121 N Main St Salisbury (28144) *(G-11124)*

Textile Rubber and Chem Co Inc........................ 704 376-3582
1020 Forsyth Ave Ste 100 Indian Trail (28079) *(G-7103)*

Textile Sales Intl Inc.. 704 483-7966
8172 Malibu Pointe Ln Denver (28037) *(G-3811)*

A
L
P
H
A
B
E
T
I
C

Textile Trends, Siler City *Also Called: Lazar Industries East Inc (G-11416)*

Textile-Based Delivery Inc.................................... 866 256-8420
350 5th Ave Se Conover (28613) *(G-3565)*

Textrol Laboratories Inc.................................... 704 764-3400
111 W Sandy Ridge Rd Monroe (28112) *(G-8569)*

Textron Aviation Inc.................................... 336 605-7000
615 Service Center Rd Greensboro (27410) *(G-5861)*

Textum Opco LLC.................................... 704 822-2400
3 Caldwell Dr Belmont (28012) *(G-773)*

Texture Plus Inc.................................... 631 218-9200
1477 Roseland Dr Lincolnton (28092) *(G-7863)*

Tfam Solutions LLC.................................... 910 637-0266
134 Aqua Shed Ct Aberdeen (28315) *(G-26)*

TFS Management Group LLC.................................... 704 399-3999
4331 Chesapeake Dr Charlotte (28216) *(G-2910)*

Tg Therapeutics, Morrisville *Also Called: Tg Therapeutics Inc (G-9069)*

Tg Therapeutics Inc (PA).................................... 877 575-8489
3020 Carrington Mill Blvd Ste 475 Morrisville (27560) *(G-9069)*

Tgr Enterprises Incorporated.................................... 828 665-4427
26 Charity Ln Candler (28715) *(G-1234)*

Th Mills, Statesville *Also Called: Thorneburg Hosiery Mills Inc (G-11787)*

Thanet Inc.................................... 704 483-4175
3501 Denver Dr Denver (28037) *(G-3812)*

Tharrington Parts, Rocky Mount *Also Called: Daughtridge Enterprises Inc (G-10809)*

That's Picklicious, Mount Olive *Also Called: Mount Olive Pickle Company Inc (G-9257)*

Thats A Good Sign Inc.................................... 301 870-0299
1802 Urchin Ln Se Bolivia (28422) *(G-887)*

Thayer Coggin, High Point *Also Called: Thayer Coggin Inc (G-6805)*

Thayer Coggin Inc.................................... 336 841-6000
230 South Rd High Point (27262) *(G-6805)*

The Audio Lab, Wilmington *Also Called: Hartley Loudspeakers Inc (G-12803)*

THE CHRONICLE, Durham *Also Called: Duke Student Publishing Co Inc (G-4010)*

The Computer Solution Company.................................... 336 409-0782
102 W 3rd St Ste 750 Winston Salem (27101) *(G-13362)*

The Design Center, Apex *Also Called: Goembel Inc (G-159)*

The Graham Star, Robbinsville *Also Called: Community Newspapers Inc (G-10758)*

The Havelock News, New Bern *Also Called: Ellis Publishing Company Inc (G-9367)*

The Interflex Group Inc.................................... 336 921-3505
3200 W Nc Highway 268 Wilkesboro (28697) *(G-12655)*

The Madison Company Inc.................................... 336 548-9624
200 W Academy St Madison (27025) *(G-8001)*

The McQuackins Company LLC.................................... 980 254-2309
2335 Jenkins Dairy Rd Gastonia (28052) *(G-5153)*

The Physics Teacher Magazine, Boone *Also Called: Appalachian State University (G-895)*

The Rolling Door Company, Gastonia *Also Called: Kindred Rolling Doors LLC (G-5073)*

The Southwood Furniture Corporation.................................... 828 465-1776
2860 Nathan St Hickory (28601) *(G-6465)*

The Summer House, Highlands *Also Called: Tiger Mountain Woodworks Inc (G-6846)*

The Tarheel Electric Membership Association Incorporated.................................... 919 876-4603
8730 Wadford Dr Raleigh (27616) *(G-10544)*

The Wheelchair Place LLC.................................... 828 855-9099
920 Tate Blvd Se Ste 104 Hickory (28602) *(G-6466)*

The Wynsum Gardener, Salisbury *Also Called: Bosmere Inc (G-11023)*

THEM International Inc.................................... 336 855-7880
1005 N Eugene St Greensboro (27401) *(G-5862)*

Theo Davis Printing, Zebulon *Also Called: Theo Davis Sons Incorporated (G-13523)*

Theo Davis Sons Incorporated.................................... 919 269-7401
1415 W Gannon Ave Zebulon (27597) *(G-13523)*

Thermaco Incorporated.................................... 336 629-4651
646 Greensboro St Asheboro (27203) *(G-408)*

Thermal Acoustical Group, Hamptonville *Also Called: Lydech Thermal Acoustical Inc (G-6088)*

Thermal Control Products Inc.................................... 704 454-7605
6324 Performance Dr Sw Concord (28027) *(G-3457)*

Thermal Metal Treating Inc.................................... 910 944-3636
9546 Hwy 211 East Aberdeen (28315) *(G-27)*

Thermal Pane Inc.................................... 336 722-9977
200 S Main St Lexington (27292) *(G-7749)*

Thermatec, Greensboro *Also Called: Hoffman Building Tech Inc (G-5601)*

Thermcraft Holding Co LLC.................................... 336 784-4800
3950 Overdale Rd Winston Salem (27107) *(G-13363)*

Thermik Corporation.................................... 252 636-5720
3498a Martin Dr New Bern (28562) *(G-9400)*

Thermo Elctron Scntfic Instrs.................................... 828 281-2651
501 Elk Park Dr Asheville (28804) *(G-615)*

Thermo Electron, Asheville *Also Called: Thermo Elctron Scntfic Instrs (G-615)*

Thermo Fisher Scientific, Asheville *Also Called: Thermo Fsher Scntfic Ashvle L (G-616)*

Thermo Fisher Scientific Inc.................................... 800 955-6288
4063 Stirrup Creek Dr Durham (27703) *(G-4269)*

Thermo Fisher Scientific Inc.................................... 800 955-6288
4125 Premier Dr High Point (27265) *(G-6806)*

Thermo Fisher Scientific Inc.................................... 919 380-2000
3900 Paramount Pkwy Morrisville (27560) *(G-9070)*

Thermo Fisher Scientific Inc.................................... 919 876-2352
3315 Atlantic Ave Raleigh (27604) *(G-10545)*

Thermo Fsher Scntfic Ashvlle L (HQ).................................... 828 658-2711
275 Aiken Rd Asheville (28804) *(G-616)*

Thermo Fsher Scntfic Ashvlle L.................................... 828 658-2711
220 Merrimon Ave Ste A Weaverville (28787) *(G-12505)*

Thermo King Corporation.................................... 732 652-6774
800 Beaty St Davidson (28036) *(G-3720)*

Thermo King Svc, Davidson *Also Called: Thermo King Corporation (G-3720)*

Thermo Products LLC (HQ).................................... 800 348-5130
92 W Fourth St Denton (27239) *(G-3763)*

Thermochem Recovery Intl.................................... 919 606-3282
5201 International Dr Durham (27712) *(G-4270)*

Thermodynamx, Waxhaw *Also Called: Thermodynamx LLC (G-12444)*

Thermodynamx LLC.................................... 704 622-1086
514 King St Waxhaw (28173) *(G-12444)*

Thieman Manufacturing Tech LLC.................................... 828 453-1866
531 Webb Rd Ellenboro (28040) *(G-4461)*

Thieman Technology, Ellenboro *Also Called: Thieman Manufacturing Tech LLC (G-4461)*

Thin Line Saddle Pads Inc.................................... 919 680-6803
2945 S Miami Blvd Ste 120-120 Durham (27703) *(G-4271)*

Thinking Maps Inc (PA).................................... 919 678-8778
401 Cascade Pointe Ln Cary (27513) *(G-1470)*

Third Street Screen Print Inc.................................... 919 365-2725
115 E Third St Wendell (27591) *(G-12550)*

This Week Magazine, Morehead City *Also Called: Carteret Publishing Company (G-8823)*

Thistle Meadow Winery Inc.................................... 800 233-1505
102 Thistle Mdw Laurel Springs (28644) *(G-7490)*

Thomas & Gray, Denton *Also Called: Councill Company LLC (G-3745)*

Thomas Brothers Foods LLC.................................... 336 672-0337
1852 Gold Hill Rd Asheboro (27203) *(G-409)*

Thomas Brothers Ham Company, Asheboro *Also Called: Thomas Brothers Foods LLC (G-409)*

Thomas Brothers Meat Proc, North Wilkesboro *Also Called: Thomas Brothers Slaughter Hse (G-9551)*

Thomas Brothers Slaughter Hse.................................... 336 667-1346
347 Thomas St North Wilkesboro (28659) *(G-9551)*

Thomas Built Buses Inc (DH).................................... 336 889-4871
1408 Courtesy Rd High Point (27260) *(G-6807)*

Thomas Buses, High Point *Also Called: Thomas Built Buses Inc (G-6807)*

Thomas Concrete Carolina Inc.................................... 704 333-0390
3701 N Graham St Charlotte (28206) *(G-2911)*

Thomas Concrete Carolina Inc.................................... 919 557-3144
140 Pamela Ct Fuquay Varina (27526) *(G-4902)*

Thomas Concrete Carolina Inc.................................... 919 460-5317
220 International Dr Morrisville (27560) *(G-9071)*

Thomas Concrete Carolina Inc (DH).................................... 919 832-0451
1131 Nw Street Raleigh (27603) *(G-10546)*

Thomas Concrete SC Inc.................................... 704 868-4545
5614 Union Rd Gastonia (28056) *(G-5154)*

Thomas Concrete South Carolina, Gastonia *Also Called: Thomas Concrete SC Inc (G-5154)*

Thomas Enterprises, Waynesville *Also Called: Rikki Tikki Tees (G-12470)*

Thomas Foods, Greensboro *Also Called: D C Thomas Group Inc (G-5486)*

Thomas Golf Inc.................................... 704 461-1342
9716 Rea Rd Ste B # 170 Charlotte (28277) *(G-2912)*

Thomas Lcklars Cbnets Lrnburg.................................... 910 369-2094
21720 Wagram Rd Laurinburg (28352) *(G-7516)*

Thomas Lee Fortner Sawmill.. 828 632-9525
  70 Mount Olive Church Rd Taylorsville (28681) *(G-11984)*

Thomas M Brown Inc... 704 597-0246
  1311 Amble Dr Charlotte (28206) *(G-2913)*

Thomas Mendolia MD.. 336 835-5688
  146 Reids Cove Dr Mooresville (28117) *(G-8785)*

Thomas Timber Inc... 910 532-4542
  3344 Nc Highway 210 E Harrells (28444) *(G-6103)*

Thomas Welding Service Inc... 919 471-6852
  1002 Communications Dr Durham (27704) *(G-4272)*

Thomasville Upholstery Inc.. 828 345-6225
  890 F Avenue Dr Se Hickory (28602) *(G-6467)*

Thomasville-Dexel Incorporated... 336 819-5550
  420 Fraley Rd High Point (27263) *(G-6808)*

Thomasvlle Mtal Fbricators Inc (PA)..................................... 336 248-4992
  200 Prospect Dr Lexington (27292) *(G-7750)*

Thomco Inc.. 336 292-3300
  2005 Boulevard St Ste F Greensboro (27407) *(G-5863)*

Thompson & Little Inc... 910 484-1128
  933 Robeson St Fayetteville (28305) *(G-4680)*

Thompson Printing & Packg Inc... 704 313-7323
  2457 Mccraw Rd Mooresboro (28114) *(G-8587)*

Thompson Screen Prints Inc.. 704 209-6161
  712 Palmer Rd Rockwell (28138) *(G-10804)*

Thompson Sunny Acres Inc.. 910 206-1801
  150 Thompson Farm Rd Rockingham (28379) *(G-10791)*

Thompson Traders Inc... 336 272-3003
  2024 E Market St Greensboro (27401) *(G-5864)*

Thomson Plastics Inc.. 336 843-4255
  2018 E Us Highway 64 Lexington (27292) *(G-7751)*

Thor.lo, Rockwell *Also Called: Thorneburg Hosiery Mills Inc (G-10805)*

Thorco LLC.. 919 363-6234
  301 Birdwood Ct Cary (27519) *(G-1471)*

Thornburg Machine & Sup Co Inc.. 704 735-5421
  1699 Smith Farm Rd Lincolnton (28092) *(G-7864)*

Thorneburg Hosiery Mills Inc.. 704 279-7247
  319 Link St Rockwell (28138) *(G-10805)*

Thorneburg Hosiery Mills Inc.. 704 872-6522
  1515 W Front St Statesville (28677) *(G-11786)*

Thorneburg Hosiery Mills Inc (PA)....................................... 704 872-6522
  2210 Newton Dr Statesville (28677) *(G-11787)*

Thorneburg Hosiery Mills Inc.. 704 838-6329
  1519 W Front St Statesville (28677) *(G-11788)*

Thorworks Industries Inc.. 919 852-3714
  550 Corporate Center Dr Raleigh (27607) *(G-10547)*

Thread, Cary *Also Called: Definitive Media Corp (G-1343)*

Thread Shed Clothing Company, Salisbury *Also Called: S Loflin Enterprises Inc (G-11113)*

Threadline Products Inc.. 704 527-9052
  3346 Pelton St Charlotte (28217) *(G-2914)*

Threatswitch Inc.. 877 449-3220
  300 W Summit Ave Ste 110 Charlotte (28203) *(G-2915)*

Three GS Enterprises Inc.. 828 696-2060
  100 Tabor Road Ext Flat Rock (28731) *(G-4714)*

Three Ladies and A Male LLC.. 704 287-1584
  3515 Arsenal Ct Apt 103 Charlotte (28273) *(G-2916)*

Three Sisters Ready Mix LLC... 919 217-0222
  512 Three Sisters Rd Knightdale (27545) *(G-7459)*

Three Stacks Distilling Co LLC... 252 468-0779
  906 Atlantic Ave Kinston (28501) *(G-7431)*

Three Stacks Distilling Co., Kinston *Also Called: Three Stacks Distilling Co LLC (G-7431)*

Three Trees Bindery... 704 724-9409
  1600 Burtonwood Cir Charlotte (28212) *(G-2917)*

Three Wishes Monogramming.. 980 298-2981
  8200 Blackjack Oak Ct Harrisburg (28075) *(G-6118)*

Thrift-Tents, Walnut Cove *Also Called: Agricltral-Industrial Fabr Inc (G-12326)*

Thrifty Tire.. 919 220-7800
  2903 N Roxboro St Durham (27704) *(G-4273)*

Thrills Hauling LLC.. 407 383-3483
  173 New Rockwood Rd Arden (28704) *(G-310)*

Throwin Stones LLC.. 828 280-7870
  825c Merrimon Ave Ste 123 Asheville (28804) *(G-617)*

Thuasne LLC.. 910 557-5378
  167 Marks Creek Ln Hamlet (28345) *(G-6063)*

Thunder Alley Enterprises.. 910 371-0119
  1224 Magnolia Village Way Leland (28451) *(G-7560)*

Thunder Eagle Enterprises Inc.. 828 242-0267
  165 Coleman Ave Apt 15d Asheville (28801) *(G-618)*

Thunderbird Metals East, Graham *Also Called: Metal Impact East LLC (G-5279)*

Thunderbird Technologies Inc.. 919 481-3239
  5540 Centerview Dr Ste 200 Raleigh (27606) *(G-10548)*

Thundrbird Mlding Grnsboro LLC... 336 668-3636
  7205 Cessna Dr Greensboro (27409) *(G-5865)*

Thundrbird Mlding Grnsboro LLC (DH)................................. 336 668-3636
  4833 W Gate City Blvd Greensboro (27407) *(G-5866)*

Thurman Toler... 252 758-4082
  1229 Sheppard Mill Rd Greenville (27834) *(G-6027)*

Thurston Genomics LLC.. 980 237-7547
  7806 Springs Village Ln Charlotte (28226) *(G-2918)*

Thyssenkrupp Bilstein Amer Inc.. 704 663-7563
  293 Timber Rd Mooresville (28115) *(G-8786)*

Tiara Inc.. 828 484-8236
  2002 Riverside Dr Ste 42k Asheville (28804) *(G-619)*

Tice Kitchens & Interiors LLC.. 919 366-4117
  1504 Capital Blvd Raleigh (27603) *(G-10549)*

Tickets Plus Inc (PA).. 616 222-4000
  909 Aviation Pkwy Ste 900 Morrisville (27560) *(G-9072)*

Tico Polishing... 704 788-2466
  2044 Wilshire Ct Sw Concord (28025) *(G-3458)*

Tideland News, Swansboro *Also Called: Carteret Publishing Company (G-11883)*

Tiedmont Printing, Asheboro *Also Called: Printlogic Inc (G-387)*

Tier 1 Graphics LLC... 704 625-6880
  18525 Statesville Rd Ste D10 Cornelius (28031) *(G-3628)*

Tier 1 Heating and Air LLC... 910 556-1444
  3459 Us Hwy 1 Vass (28394) *(G-12229)*

Tiffany Marble Company, Greensboro *Also Called: Sid Jenkins Inc (G-5811)*

Tiger Mountain Woodworks Inc.. 828 526-5577
  2089 Dillard Rd Highlands (28741) *(G-6846)*

Tiger Products, Elizabethtown *Also Called: Cape Fear Chemicals Inc (G-4420)*

Tiger Steel Inc.. 336 624-4481
  998 W Pine St Mount Airy (27030) *(G-9186)*

Tigerswan LLC... 919 439-7110
  3453 Apex Peakway Apex (27502) *(G-197)*

Tigertek Industrial Services, Stoneville *Also Called: Tigertek Industrial Svcs LLC (G-11832)*

Tigertek Industrial Svcs LLC... 336 623-1717
  2741 Nc Highway 135 Stoneville (27048) *(G-11832)*

Tigra Usa Inc.. 828 324-8227
  1106 8th Street Ct Se Hickory (28602) *(G-6468)*

Tileware, Hickory *Also Called: Tileware Global LLC (G-6469)*

Tileware Global LLC... 828 322-9273
  1021 16th St Ne Hickory (28601) *(G-6469)*

Tillery Accessories Inc... 704 474-3013
  7041 Riverview Rd Norwood (28128) *(G-9562)*

Tillson Engineering Laboratory, Jamestown *Also Called: R D Tillson & Associates Inc (G-7178)*

Tilson Machine Inc (PA).. 828 668-4416
  632 College Dr Marion (28752) *(G-8069)*

Tim Con Wood Products Inc... 252 793-4819
  1438 Cross Rd Roper (27970) *(G-10900)*

Tim Conner Enterprises Inc.. 704 629-4327
  1312 Ramseur Rd Bessemer City (28016) *(G-835)*

Tima Capital Inc.. 910 769-3273
  800 Sunnyvale Dr Wilmington (28412) *(G-12939)*

Timber Harvester Inc (PA).. 910 346-9754
  3862 Richlands Hwy Jacksonville (28540) *(G-7156)*

Timber Specialists Inc... 704 902-5146
  2123 Shelton Ave Statesville (28677) *(G-11789)*

Timber Specialists LLC... 704 873-5756
  2511 Heritage Cir Statesville (28625) *(G-11790)*

Timber Stand Improvements Inc.. 910 439-6121
  1939 Nc Highway 109 S Mount Gilead (27306) *(G-9210)*

Timber Wolf Forest Products... 828 728-7500
  3189 Freezer Locker Rd Hudson (28638) *(G-6961)*

ALPHABETIC

Timber Wolf Wood Creations Inc.............................. 704 309-5118
  2008 Starbrook Dr Charlotte (28210) *(G-2919)*

Timberlake Cabinet Company, Huntersville *Also Called: American Woodmark Corporation* *(G-6964)*

Timberlake Ventures Inc...................................... 704 896-7499
  1908 Eastwood Rd Ste 327 Wilmington (28403) *(G-12940)*

Timberline, Henderson *Also Called: Timberline Acquisition LLC (G-6181)*

Timberline Acquisition LLC.................................. 252 492-6144
  235 Warehouse Rd Henderson (27537) *(G-6181)*

Timeless Bedding Inc.. 336 472-6603
  306 Beech Retreat Dr Lexington (27292) *(G-7752)*

Timeplanner Calendars Inc.................................. 704 377-0024
  1010 Timeplanner Dr Charlotte (28206) *(G-2920)*

Times Journal Inc.. 828 682-4067
  22 N Main St Burnsville (28714) *(G-1193)*

Times News Publishing Company........................... 336 226-4414
  707 S Main St Burlington (27215) *(G-1168)*

Times Printing Company (PA)................................ 252 473-2105
  501 Budleigh St Manteo (27954) *(G-8024)*

Times Printing Company Inc................................. 252 441-2223
  1500 S Croatan Hwy Kill Devil Hills (27948) *(G-7320)*

Times-News, Burlington *Also Called: Times News Publishing Company (G-1168)*

Timken Company.. 704 736-2700
  1000 Timken Pl Iron Station (28080) *(G-7108)*

Timmerman Manufacturing Inc............................. 828 464-1778
  102 S Mclin Creek Rd Conover (28613) *(G-3566)*

Timmons Fabrications Inc.................................... 919 688-8998
  2818 Pervis Rd Durham (27704) *(G-4274)*

Timothy L Griffin.. 336 317-8314
  477 Huntingridge Rd Apt B Greenville (27834) *(G-6028)*

Timothy Lee Blacjmon.. 336 481-9038
  2658 Johnsontown Rd Thomasville (27360) *(G-12079)*

Tin Can Ventures LLC... 919 732-9078
  2207 Carr Store Rd Cedar Grove (27231) *(G-1518)*

Tin Cans LLC.. 910 322-2626
  906 S 8th St Lillington (27546) *(G-7804)*

Tint Plus.. 910 229-5303
  2850 Owen Dr Fayetteville (28306) *(G-4681)*

Tinypilot LLC... 336 422-6525
  5335 Robinhood Village Dr Winston Salem (27106) *(G-13364)*

Tipper Tie Inc (HQ)... 919 362-8811
  2000 Lufkin Rd Apex (27539) *(G-198)*

Tire Pros, Elon College *Also Called: Wilson Tire and Automotive Inc (G-4476)*

Tire Sls Svc Inc Fytteville NC (PA)........................ 910 485-1121
  400 Person St Fayetteville (28301) *(G-4682)*

Tires Incorporated of Clinton............................... 910 592-4741
  317 Southeast Blvd Clinton (28328) *(G-3249)*

Titan America LLC... 336 754-0143
  3193 Pine Hall Rd Belews Creek (27009) *(G-739)*

Titan Flow Control Inc (PA).................................. 910 735-0000
  290 Corporate Dr Lumberton (28358) *(G-7975)*

Titeflex Corporation.. 647 638-7160
  Charlotte (28265) *(G-2921)*

Titus, Tarboro *Also Called: Air System Components Inc (G-11922)*

Tivoli Woodworks Inc.. 336 602-3512
  4850 Bringle Ferry Rd Salisbury (28146) *(G-11125)*

Tk Elevator Corporation...................................... 336 272-4563
  22 Oak Branch Dr Ste C Greensboro (27407) *(G-5867)*

Tkm Global LLC.. 732 694-0311
  8041 Brier Creek Pkwy Raleigh (27617) *(G-10550)*

TLC, Elkin *Also Called: Mvp Group International Inc (G-4449)*

Tlv Corporation.. 704 597-9070
  13901 S Lakes Dr Charlotte (28273) *(G-2922)*

Tmb Cranes, Charlotte *Also Called: Thomas M Brown Inc (G-2913)*

Tmgcr Inc... 704 872-4461
  1002 Winston Ave Statesville (28677) *(G-11791)*

Tmp of Nc Inc.. 336 463-3225
  1201 Old Stage Rd Yadkinville (27055) *(G-13453)*

Tms International LLC... 704 604-0287
  6601 Lakeview Rd Charlotte (28269) *(G-2923)*

TNT Services Inc... 252 261-3073
  3908 Poor Ridge Rd Kitty Hawk (27949) *(G-7447)*

TNT Web & Grafix LLC.. 252 289-8846
  619 Western Ave Nashville (27856) *(G-9324)*

Tnw Ventures Inc.. 828 216-4089
  60 Bishop Ln Pisgah Forest (28768) *(G-9773)*

To The Point Inc... 336 725-5303
  130 Stratford Ct Ste E Winston Salem (27103) *(G-13365)*

To The Top Tires and Svc LLC............................... 252 886-3286
  327 E Raleigh Blvd Ste 943 Rocky Mount (27801) *(G-10816)*

Tobacco Merchants Association of The United States Inc., Raleigh *Also Called: Tobacco Mrchnts Assn of US Inc (G-10551)*

Tobacco Mrchnts Assn of US Inc........................... 919 872-5040
  901 Jones Franklin Rd Ste 102 Raleigh (27606) *(G-10551)*

Tobacco Outlet Products, Charlotte *Also Called: Tobacco Outlet Products LLC (G-2924)*

Tobacco Outlet Products LLC................................ 704 341-9388
  6401 Carmel Rd Ste 204 Charlotte (28226) *(G-2924)*

Tobacco Rag Processors Inc................................. 252 265-0081
  4744 Potato House Ct Wilson (27893) *(G-13035)*

Tobacco Rag Processors Inc................................. 252 237-8180
  2105 Black Creek Rd Se Bldg 6 Wilson (27893) *(G-13036)*

Tobacco Rag Processors Inc (PA)........................... 252 265-0081
  4737 Yank Rd Wilson (27893) *(G-13037)*

Tobe Manufacturing Inc...................................... 910 439-6203
  603 W Allenton St Mount Gilead (27306) *(G-9211)*

Today's Photographer Magazine, Hamptonville *Also Called: Ifpo - Ifmo/American Image Inc (G-6085)*

Todays Charlotte Woman..................................... 704 521-6872
  5200 Park Rd Ste 126 Charlotte (28209) *(G-2925)*

Todaytec LLC... 704 790-2440
  6701 Northpark Blvd Ste K Charlotte (28216) *(G-2926)*

Todco Inc.. 336 248-2001
  1123 Roy Lopp Rd Lexington (27292) *(G-7753)*

Toddler Tables, Raleigh *Also Called: Vaughan Enterprises Inc (G-10584)*

Todds Rv & Marine Inc.. 828 651-0007
  130 Lyndale Rd Hendersonville (28739) *(G-6245)*

Toe River Service Station LLC............................... 828 688-6385
  4928 S 226 Hwy Bakersville (28705) *(G-681)*

Tokai Carbon GE LLC (DH).................................. 980 260-1130
  6210 Ardrey Kell Rd Ste 270 Charlotte (28277) *(G-2927)*

Toler Welding & Repair, Greenville *Also Called: Thurman Toler (G-6027)*

Tom Burgiss... 336 359-2995
  294 Elk Knob Rd Laurel Springs (28644) *(G-7491)*

Tom Rochester & Associates Inc (PA)...................... 704 896-5805
  9325 Forsyth Park Dr Charlotte (28273) *(G-2928)*

Tom's Coin Laundry, Kings Mountain *Also Called: B & D Enterprises Inc (G-7348)*

Tomlinson of Orlando Inc.................................... 336 475-8000
  201 E Holly Hill Rd Thomasville (27360) *(G-12080)*

Tomlinson/Erwin-Lambeth Inc.............................. 336 472-5005
  201 E Holly Hill Rd Thomasville (27360) *(G-12081)*

Tommy Signs.. 704 877-1234
  8716 Maggie Robinson Rd Waxhaw (28173) *(G-12445)*

Tommy W Smith Inc.. 704 436-6616
  9825 Bowman Barrier Rd Mount Pleasant (28124) *(G-9265)*

Tommys Tubing & Stockenettes............................. 336 449-6461
  628 Wood St Gibsonville (27249) *(G-5185)*

Tomorrowmed Pharma LLC................................... 832 615-2880
  1101 Shiloh Glenn Dr Unit 1108 Morrisville (27560) *(G-9073)*

Tompkins Industries Inc...................................... 828 254-2351
  150 Westside Dr Asheville (28806) *(G-620)*

Toms Knit Fabrics... 704 867-4236
  699 Carlton Dr Apt A Gastonia (28054) *(G-5155)*

Toner Machining Tech Inc.................................... 828 432-8007
  1523 N Green St Morganton (28655) *(G-8905)*

Toner Machining Technologies.............................. 828 432-8007
  212 E Fleming Dr Morganton (28655) *(G-8906)*

Toney Lumber Company Inc.................................. 919 496-5711
  309 Bunn Rd Louisburg (27549) *(G-7928)*

Tony D Hildreth.. 910 276-1803
  22945 Broadwell Rd Laurel Hill (28351) *(G-7488)*

Tony S Ice Cream Company Inc (PA)........................ 704 867-7085
  604 E Franklin Blvd Gastonia (28054) *(G-5156)*

Tony's Custom Cabinets, Clinton *Also Called: Tonys Cabinets (G-3250)*

(G-0000) Company's Geographic Section entry number

TONY'S ICE CREAM CO INC, Gastonia *Also Called: Tonys Ice Cream Co Inc (G-5157)*

Tonyas Crocheted Creations.. 704 421-2143
7535 Marlbrook Dr Charlotte (28212) *(G-2929)*

Tonys Cabinets.. 910 592-2028
671 Cartertown Rd Clinton (28328) *(G-3250)*

Tonys Ice Cream Co Inc... 704 853-0018
520 E Franklin Blvd Gastonia (28054) *(G-5157)*

Too Hott Customs LLC.. 336 722-4919
1249 W Academy St Winston Salem (27103) *(G-13366)*

Tool Rental Depot LLC... 704 636-6400
2001 S Main St Salisbury (28144) *(G-11126)*

Tool-Weld LLC.. 843 986-4931
180 Cross Ridge Dr Rutherfordton (28139) *(G-10995)*

Toolcraft Inc North Carolina (PA).. 828 659-7379
1877 Rutherford Rd Marion (28752) *(G-8070)*

Tooling Division, Mocksville *Also Called: Gesipa Fasteners Usa Inc (G-8367)*

Toolmarx LLC... 919 725-0122
408 Ricks Dr Winston Salem (27103) *(G-13367)*

Tools USA, Greensboro *Also Called: Standard Tools and Eqp Co (G-5836)*

Top Dawg Landscape Inc... 336 877-7519
605 S Jefferson Ave # 1 West Jefferson (28694) *(G-12571)*

Top Notch Log Homes Inc.. 828 926-4300
3517 Jonathan Creek Rd Waynesville (28785) *(G-12477)*

Top Tier Paper Products Inc (PA)... 828 994-2222
409 Thornburg Dr Se Conover (28613) *(G-3567)*

Top Tobacco LP.. 910 646-3014
204 Top Tobacco Rd Lake Waccamaw (28450) *(G-7472)*

Topgolf... 704 612-4745
8024 Savoy Corporate Dr Charlotte (28273) *(G-2930)*

Toplink Publishing.. 888 375-9818
2227 Natmore Rd Kelly (28448) *(G-7223)*

Topquadrant Inc... 919 300-7945
930 Main Campus Dr Ste 300 Raleigh (27606) *(G-10552)*

Topsail Sportswear Inc.. 910 270-4903
15530 Us Highway 17 Hampstead (28443) *(G-6077)*

Topsail Voice LLC... 910 270-2944
14886 Us Highway 17 Hampstead (28443) *(G-6078)*

Topsider Building Systems Inc... 336 766-9300
3710 Dillon Industrial Dr Clemmons (27012) *(G-3204)*

Torpedo Specialty Wire Inc.. 252 977-3900
1115 Instrument Dr Rocky Mount (27804) *(G-10872)*

Tortilleria Duvy LLC.. 336 497-1510
1261 Nc Highway 66 S Kernersville (27284) *(G-7308)*

Tosaf Inc.. 704 396-7097
132 W Virginia Ave Bessemer City (28016) *(G-836)*

Tosaf Inc (DH).. 980 533-3000
330 Southridge Pkwy Bessemer City (28016) *(G-837)*

Tosaf Aw Inc... 980 533-3000
330 Southridge Pkwy Bessemer City (28016) *(G-838)*

Tosaf USA, Bessemer City *Also Called: Tosaf Inc (G-837)*

Toshiba, Durham *Also Called: Toshiba Globl Cmmrce Sltons In (G-4275)*

Toshiba Globl Cmmrce Sltons In (DH).................................. 919 544-8427
3901 S Miami Blvd Durham (27703) *(G-4275)*

Total Controls Inc... 704 821-6341
4420 Friendship Dr Ste A Matthews (28105) *(G-8152)*

Total Fire Systems Inc... 919 556-9161
30 Weathers Ct Youngsville (27596) *(G-13493)*

Total Sports Enterprises.. 704 237-3930
9624 Belloak Ln Waxhaw (28173) *(G-12446)*

Toter LLC.. 704 936-5610
6525 Morrison Blvd Ste 300 Charlotte (28211) *(G-2931)*

Toter LLC (DH).. 800 424-0422
841 Meacham Rd Statesville (28677) *(G-11792)*

Touch Tone Tees LLC.. 919 358-5536
3316c Capital Blvd Ste 8 Raleigh (27604) *(G-10553)*

Touch Up Solutions Inc... 828 428-9094
4372 Providence Mill Rd Maiden (28650) *(G-8019)*

Touchamerica Inc... 919 732-6968
437 Dimmocks Mill Rd Hillsborough (27278) *(G-6879)*

Touchstone Fine Cabinetry, Rutherfordton *Also Called: US Precision Cabinetry LLC (G-11002)*

Tourist Baseball Inc.. 828 258-0428
30 Buchanan Pl Asheville (28801) *(G-621)*

Towel City Tire & Wheel LLC.. 704 933-2143
1601 N Ridge Ave Kannapolis (28083) *(G-7222)*

Tower Components Inc... 336 824-2102
5960 Us Highway 64 E Ramseur (27316) *(G-10632)*

Tower Engrg Professionals Inc (PA)..................................... 919 661-6351
326 Tryon Rd Raleigh (27603) *(G-10554)*

Towerco LLC... 919 653-5700
5000 Valleystone Dr Ste 200 Cary (27519) *(G-1472)*

Town of Ahoskie... 252 332-3840
208 Johnny Mitchell Rd Ahoskie (27910) *(G-54)*

Town of Jonesville.. 336 835-2250
399 Shaw St Jonesville (28642) *(G-7199)*

Town of Maggie Valley Inc... 828 926-0145
45 Water Plant Rd Maggie Valley (28751) *(G-8006)*

Town of Tarboro.. 252 641-4284
600 Albemarle Ave Tarboro (27886) *(G-11944)*

Town of Waynesville.. 828 456-8497
341 Rocky Branch Rd Waynesville (28786) *(G-12478)*

Toxaway Concrete, Sapphire *Also Called: Lbm Industries Inc (G-11258)*

Toxaway Concrete Inc.. 828 966-4270
Hwy 64 E Cashiers (28717) *(G-1491)*

Toxplanet, Wilmington *Also Called: Timberlake Ventures Inc (G-12940)*

Toymakerz LLC.. 843 267-3477
2358 Holiday Loop Reidsville (27320) *(G-10699)*

Toyota Battery Mfg Inc... 469 292-6094
5938 Julian Airport Rd Liberty (27298) *(G-7782)*

Tpt Coating Inc.. 919 479-0758
150 Providence Rd Chapel Hill (27514) *(G-1577)*

Trac Plastics Inc... 704 864-9140
140 Superior Stainless Rd Gastonia (28052) *(G-5158)*

Trackx Technology LLC.. 888 787-2259
437 Dimmocks Mill Rd Ste 28 Hillsborough (27278) *(G-6880)*

Tractor Country Inc... 252 523-3007
5763 Hwy 70 Dover (28526) *(G-3829)*

Tracy's Gourmet, Asheville *Also Called: Tracys Gourmet LLC (G-622)*

Tracys Gourmet LLC.. 919 672-1731
315 Old Haw Creek Rd Asheville (28805) *(G-622)*

Trade Venture Stones LLC.. 919 803-3923
365 Spectrum Dr Ste 100 Knightdale (27545) *(G-7460)*

Trademark Landscape Group Inc.. 910 253-0560
360 Ocean Hwy E Supply (28462) *(G-11861)*

Trademark Ldscp Cntg Trdmark O, Supply *Also Called: Trademark Landscape Group Inc (G-11861)*

Tradewinds Coffee Co Inc.. 919 556-1835
6308 Mitchell Mill Rd Zebulon (27597) *(G-13524)*

Trafag Inc... 704 343-6339
8848 Red Oak Blvd Ste I Charlotte (28217) *(G-2932)*

Trailer Plus, New Bern *Also Called: Derrow Enterprises Inc (G-9364)*

Trailmate Inc.. 941 739-5743
912 Pinehurst Dr Chapel Hill (27517) *(G-1578)*

Training Industry Inc... 919 653-4990
110 Horizon Dr Ste 110 Raleigh (27615) *(G-10555)*

TRAININGINDUSTRY.COM, Raleigh *Also Called: Training Industry Inc (G-10555)*

Trajan Inc.. 919 435-1105
2942 Imperial Oaks Dr Raleigh (27614) *(G-10556)*

Tramway Veneers Inc... 919 776-7606
2603 Tramway Rd Sanford (27332) *(G-11242)*

Trane, Asheville *Also Called: Trane US Inc (G-623)*

Trane, Charlotte *Also Called: Trane US Inc (G-2934)*

Trane, Charlotte *Also Called: Trane US Inc (G-2935)*

Trane, Davidson *Also Called: Trane US Inc (G-3723)*

Trane, Greensboro *Also Called: Trane US Inc (G-5868)*

Trane, Greensboro *Also Called: Trane US Inc (G-5869)*

Trane, Greensboro *Also Called: Trane US Inc (G-5870)*

Trane, Morrisville *Also Called: Trane US Inc (G-9074)*

Trane Company (DH)... 704 398-4600
4500 Morris Field Dr Charlotte (28208) *(G-2933)*

Trane Technologies Company LLC (HQ)................................ 704 655-4000
800 Beaty St Ste E Davidson (28036) *(G-3721)*

Trane Technologies Company LLC................................ 336 751-3561
  501 Sanford Ave Mocksville (27028) *(G-8394)*

Trane Technologies Company LLC................................ 910 692-8700
  1725 Us 1 Hwy N Southern Pines (28387) *(G-11512)*

Trane Technologies Mfg LLC...................................... 704 655-4000
  800 Beaty St Davidson (28036) *(G-3722)*

Trane US Inc... 828 277-8664
  168 Sweeten Creek Rd Asheville (28803) *(G-623)*

Trane US Inc... 704 525-9600
  4501 S Tryon St Charlotte (28217) *(G-2934)*

Trane US Inc... 704 697-9006
  8610 Air Park West Dr Ste C Charlotte (28214) *(G-2935)*

Trane US Inc (DH)... 704 655-4000
  800 Beaty St Ste E Davidson (28036) *(G-3723)*

Trane US Inc... 336 273-6353
  3101 S Elm Eugene St # 100 Greensboro (27406) *(G-5868)*

Trane US Inc... 336 378-0670
  1915 N Church St Greensboro (27405) *(G-5869)*

Trane US Inc... 336 387-1735
  8408 Triad Dr Greensboro (27409) *(G-5870)*

Trane US Inc... 919 781-0458
  401 Kitty Hawk Dr Morrisville (27560) *(G-9074)*

Trans East Inc.. 910 892-1081
  405 E Edgerton St Dunn (28334) *(G-3869)*

Trans-Tech Energy Inc (PA)....................................... 252 446-4357
  14527 Us Highway 64 Alt W Rocky Mount (27801) *(G-10817)*

Trans-Tech Energy LLC... 254 840-3355
  14527 Us Highway 64 Alt W Rocky Mount (27801) *(G-10818)*

Transarctic, High Point *Also Called: Transarctic North Carolina Inc (G-6809)*

Transarctic North Carolina Inc.................................. 336 861-6116
  5270 Glenola Industrial Dr High Point (27263) *(G-6809)*

Transbotics Corporation.. 704 362-1115
  3400 Latrobe Dr Charlotte (28211) *(G-2936)*

Transcontinental AC US LLC (HQ)............................. 704 847-9171
  700 Crestdale Rd Matthews (28105) *(G-8153)*

Transcontinental AC US LLC...................................... 704 847-9171
  700 Crestdale Rd Matthews (28105) *(G-8154)*

Transcontinental Tvl LLC... 336 476-3131
  1308 Blair St Thomasville (27360) *(G-12082)*

Transdata Solutions Inc.. 919 770-9329
  221 N Horner Blvd Sanford (27330) *(G-11243)*

Transeco Energy Corporation.................................... 828 684-6400
  101 Fair Oaks Rd Arden (28704) *(G-311)*

Transenterix Surgical Inc.. 919 765-8400
  1 Tw Alexander Dr Ste 160 Durham (27703) *(G-4276)*

Transformer Sales & Service..................................... 910 594-1495
  1392 Massey Rd Newton Grove (28366) *(G-9519)*

Transit & Level Clinic, Cary *Also Called: C W Lawley Incorporated (G-1318)*

Transmission Div, Maxton *Also Called: Meritor Inc (G-8203)*

Transmission Unlimited, Mooresville *Also Called: Gracie & Lucas LLC (G-8675)*

TransMontaigne, Selma *Also Called: TransMontaigne Terminaling Inc (G-11293)*

TransMontaigne Terminaling Inc............................... 303 626-8200
  2600 W Oak St Selma (27576) *(G-11293)*

Transportation Tech Inc (DH).................................... 252 946-6521
  911 W 5th St Washington (27889) *(G-12416)*

Transtech Pharma LLC (PA)....................................... 336 841-0300
  3980 Premier Dr Ste 310 High Point (27265) *(G-6810)*

Transtex Belting... 704 334-5353
  10125 S Tryon St Charlotte (28273) *(G-2937)*

Transtex Belting, Charlotte *Also Called: Forbo Movement Systems (G-2171)*

Transylvnia Vcational Svcs Inc (PA).......................... 828 884-3195
  11 Mountain Industrial Dr Brevard (28712) *(G-983)*

Transylvnia Vcational Svcs Inc.................................. 828 884-1548
  1 Quality Way Fletcher (28732) *(G-4773)*

Trash Masher LLC... 786 357-2697
  1045 Burke St Winston Salem (27101) *(G-13368)*

Traumtic Drect Trnsfsion Dvcs................................. 423 364-5828
  1007 Woodbriar St Apex (27502) *(G-199)*

Travis Alfrey Woodworking Inc.................................. 910 639-3553
  9988 Aberdeen Rd Aberdeen (28315) *(G-28)*

Travis L Bunker.. 336 352-3289
  6198 W Pine St Mount Airy (27030) *(G-9187)*

Trawler Incorporated.. 252 745-3751
  569 Kelly Watson Rd Lowland (28552) *(G-7936)*

Traxon Technologies LLC... 201 508-1570
  2915 Whitehall Park Dr Charlotte (28273) *(G-2938)*

TRC Acquisition LLC.. 252 355-9353
  133 Forlines Rd Winterville (28590) *(G-13424)*

Treadz LLC... 704 664-0995
  2118 Charlotte Hwy Mooresville (28117) *(G-8787)*

Tree Brand Packaging Inc (PA)................................. 704 483-0719
  2800 Woodtech Dr Newton (28658) *(G-9505)*

Tree Craft Log Homes Inc.. 828 689-2240
  43 Back Hollow Rd Mars Hill (28754) *(G-8078)*

Tree Frog Industries LLC... 919 986-2229
  246 Dogwood Trl Wendell (27591) *(G-12551)*

Tree Masters Inc.. 828 464-9443
  101 E 11th St Ste 1 Newton (28658) *(G-9506)*

Treeforms Inc... 336 292-8998
  4242 Regency Dr Greensboro (27410) *(G-5871)*

Treeforms Lockers, Greensboro *Also Called: Treeforms Inc (G-5871)*

Trefena Welds.. 203 551-1370
  8408 Exmoor Trce Browns Summit (27214) *(G-1006)*

Treg Tool Inc.. 828 676-0035
  10 Summer Meadow Rd Arden (28704) *(G-312)*

Trego Innovations LLC... 919 374-0089
  2301 Wilco Blvd S Wilson (27893) *(G-13038)*

Trejo Soccer Academy LLC....................................... 336 899-7910
  2753 Us Highway 220 Bus S Asheboro (27205) *(G-410)*

Treklite Inc... 919 610-1788
  904 Dorothea Dr Raleigh (27603) *(G-10557)*

Trelleborg Ctd Systems US Inc................................. 828 286-9126
  715 Railroad Ave Rutherfordton (28139) *(G-10996)*

Trelleborg Ctd Systems US Inc................................. 864 576-1210
  715 Railroad Ave Rutherfordton (28139) *(G-10997)*

Trelleborg Ctd Systems US Inc................................. 828 286-9126
  631 Rock Rd Rutherfordton (28139) *(G-10998)*

Trelleborg Ctd Systems US Inc (PA)......................... 828 286-9126
  715 Railroad Ave Rutherfordton (28139) *(G-10999)*

Trelleborg Salisbury Inc... 704 797-8030
  510 Long Meadow Dr Salisbury (28147) *(G-11127)*

Trend Performance Products.................................... 828 862-8290
  114 Lime Kiln Ln Pisgah Forest (28768) *(G-9774)*

Trendy Nails, Creedmoor *Also Called: Jhd Enterprise LLC (G-3651)*

Trenton Emergency Med Svcs Inc............................. 252 448-2646
  105 Cherry St Trenton (28585) *(G-12111)*

Trenton Ems, Trenton *Also Called: Trenton Emergency Med Svcs Inc (G-12111)*

Tresata Inc (PA)... 980 224-2097
  1616 Candem Rd Ste 300 Charlotte (28203) *(G-2939)*

Tresco.. 361 985-3154
  736 Greenway Rd Boone (28607) *(G-946)*

Tresmc LLC... 919 900-0868
  2509 Ferdinand Dr Knightdale (27545) *(G-7461)*

Trexler Logging Inc.. 704 694-5272
  2292 Bethel Rd Wadesboro (28170) *(G-12250)*

TRf Manufacturing NC Inc.. 252 223-1112
  413 Howard Blvd Newport (28570) *(G-9445)*

Tri City Concrete Co LLC... 828 245-2011
  158 Withrow Rd Forest City (28043) *(G-4798)*

Tri County Gastroenterology, Mooresville *Also Called: Thomas Mendolia MD (G-8785)*

Tri State Componenets, Sparta *Also Called: Truss Shop Inc (G-11542)*

Tri State Plastics Inc... 704 865-7431
  507 E Davidson Ave Gastonia (28054) *(G-5159)*

Tri Tech Forensics National La, Leland *Also Called: Tri-Tech Forensics Inc (G-7561)*

Tri-City Concrete LLC... 704 372-2930
  3823 Raleigh St Charlotte (28206) *(G-2940)*

Tri-City Mechanical Contrs Inc.................................. 336 272-9495
  706 Utility St Greensboro (27405) *(G-5872)*

Tri-City Tire Service, Spindale *Also Called: Burnett Darrill Stephen (G-11545)*

Tri-County Industries Inc... 252 977-3800
  1250 Atlantic Ave Rocky Mount (27801) *(G-10819)*

Tri-H Molding Co... 252 491-8530
  135 W Side Ln Harbinger (27941) *(G-6096)*

(G-0000) Company's Geographic Section entry number

Tri-Star Plastics Corp... 704 598-2800
1387 N Nc 16 Business Hwy Denver (28037) *(G-3813)*

Tri-State Carports Inc (PA)....................................... 276 755-2081
304 Franklin St Mount Airy (27030) *(G-9188)*

Tri-Steel Fabricators Inc... 252 291-7900
6864 Wagon Wheel Rd Sims (27880) *(G-11432)*

Tri-TEC Ind Inc.. 704 424-5995
200 Peachtree Dr S Charlotte (28217) *(G-2941)*

Tri-Tech Forensics Inc (PA)....................................... 910 457-6600
3811 International Blvd Ne Ste 100 Leland (28451) *(G-7561)*

Tri-W Farms Inc... 910 533-3596
4671 Faison Hwy Clinton (28328) *(G-3251)*

Triac Corporation... 336 297-1130
611 Norwalk St Greensboro (27407) *(G-5873)*

Triad Anodizing & Plating Inc................................... 336 292-7028
3502 Spring Garden St Greensboro (27407) *(G-5874)*

Triad Automation Group, Winston Salem *Also Called: Triad Automation Group Inc (G-13369)*

Triad Automation Group Inc....................................... 336 767-1379
4994 Indiana Ave Ste F Winston Salem (27106) *(G-13369)*

Triad Business Card Assoc... 336 706-2729
3201 Summit Ave Greensboro (27405) *(G-5875)*

Triad Business Journal, Greensboro *Also Called: American City Bus Journals Inc (G-5354)*

Triad Corrugated Metal, Sanford *Also Called: Triad Corrugated Metal Inc (G-11244)*

Triad Corrugated Metal Inc (PA)............................... 336 625-9727
208 Luck Rd Asheboro (27205) *(G-411)*

Triad Corrugated Metal Inc....................................... 919 775-1663
109 Mcneill Rd Sanford (27330) *(G-11244)*

Triad Cutting Tools Inc.. 336 873-8708
5527 Us Highway 220 S Asheboro (27205) *(G-412)*

Triad Engines Parts & Svcs Inc................................. 800 334-6437
3439 S Aviation Dr Burlington (27215) *(G-1169)*

Triad Fabrication and Mch Inc................................... 336 993-6042
1080 Industrial Park Dr Kernersville (27284) *(G-7309)*

Triad Marine Center Inc.. 252 634-1880
4316 Us Highway 70 E New Bern (28560) *(G-9401)*

Triad Meats, Greensboro *Also Called: Stevens Packing Inc (G-5840)*

Triad Power & Controls Inc....................................... 336 375-9780
215 Industrial Ave Ste G Greensboro (27406) *(G-5876)*

Triad Precision Products Inc..................................... 336 474-0980
128 Sunrise Center Dr Thomasville (27360) *(G-12083)*

Triad Prefinish & Lbr Sls Inc..................................... 336 375-4849
3514 Associate Dr Greensboro (27405) *(G-5877)*

Triad Printing NC, Greensboro *Also Called: Triad Printing NC Inc (G-5878)*

Triad Printing NC Inc... 336 422-8752
1306 E Wendover Ave Greensboro (27405) *(G-5878)*

Triad Semiconductor Inc.. 336 774-2150
1760 Jonestown Rd Ste 100 Winston Salem (27103) *(G-13370)*

Triad Sheet Metal & Mech Inc................................... 336 379-9891
300 Lowdermilk St Greensboro (27401) *(G-5879)*

Triad Specialty Products, Greensboro *Also Called: Piedmont Animal Health Inc (G-5740)*

Triad Welding Contractors Inc................................... 336 882-3902
146 Silkwind Ct Clemmons (27012) *(G-3205)*

Triaga Inc.. 919 412-6019
1900 Stantonsburg Rd Se Wilson (27893) *(G-13039)*

Triangel Quarry, Cary *Also Called: Wake Stone Corporation (G-1481)*

Triangle Body Works Inc.. 336 788-0631
2014 Waughtown St Winston Salem (27107) *(G-13371)*

Triangle Brick Company (PA)..................................... 919 544-1796
6523 Nc Highway 55 Durham (27713) *(G-4277)*

Triangle Brick Company... 919 387-9257
294 King Rd Moncure (27559) *(G-8410)*

Triangle Brick Company... 704 695-1420
2960 Us Highway 52 N Wadesboro (28170) *(G-12251)*

Triangle Brick Merryoaks Plant, Moncure *Also Called: Triangle Brick Company (G-8410)*

Triangle Cabinet Company... 336 869-6401
809 Aberdeen Rd High Point (27265) *(G-6811)*

Triangle Chemical Company...................................... 919 942-3237
7100 Old Greensboro Rd Chapel Hill (27516) *(G-1579)*

Triangle Coatings Inc.. 919 781-6108
6721 Mount Herman Rd Morrisville (27560) *(G-9075)*

Triangle Converting Corp... 919 596-6656
2021 S Briggs Ave Durham (27703) *(G-4278)*

Triangle Custom Cabinets Inc................................... 919 387-1133
807 Center St Apex (27502) *(G-200)*

Triangle Custom Woodworks LLC (PA).................... 919 637-8857
526 Victoria Hills Dr S Fuquay Varina (27526) *(G-4903)*

Triangle Glass Service Inc... 919 477-9508
1320 Old Oxford Rd Ste 12 Durham (27704) *(G-4279)*

Triangle Indus Sup Hldings LLC (PA)....................... 704 395-0600
228 Westinghouse Blvd Ste 104 Charlotte (28273) *(G-2942)*

Triangle Inner Vision Company................................. 919 460-6013
100 Dominion Dr Ste 110 Morrisville (27560) *(G-9076)*

Triangle Installation Svc Inc..................................... 919 363-7637
2445 Reliance Ave Apex (27539) *(G-201)*

Triangle Kitchen Supply.. 919 562-3888
336 Bert Winston Rd Youngsville (27596) *(G-13494)*

Triangle Metalworks Inc.. 919 556-7786
100 Moores Pond Rd Youngsville (27596) *(G-13495)*

Triangle Microsystems Inc... 919 878-1880
1807 Garner Station Blvd Raleigh (27603) *(G-10558)*

Triangle Microworks Inc.. 919 870-5101
2840 Plaza Pl Ste 205 Raleigh (27612) *(G-10559)*

Triangle Plastics Inc.. 919 598-8839
6435 Mount Herman Rd Raleigh (27617) *(G-10560)*

Triangle Pointer Inc... 919 968-4801
88 Vilcom Center Dr Chapel Hill (27514) *(G-1580)*

Triangle Pointer Magazine, Chapel Hill *Also Called: Triangle Pointer Inc (G-1580)*

Triangle Prcsion Dgnostics Inc................................. 919 345-0110
2 Davis Dr Rm 203 Durham (27709) *(G-4280)*

Triangle Ready Mix LLC.. 919 859-4190
241 International Dr Morrisville (27560) *(G-9077)*

Triangle Regulatory Pubg LLC................................... 919 886-4587
7780 Brier Creek Pkwy Raleigh (27617) *(G-10561)*

Triangle Solutions Inc... 919 481-1235
1074 W Chatham St Cary (27511) *(G-1473)*

Triangle Stainless Inc.. 919 596-1335
200 20th St Butner (27509) *(G-1207)*

Triangle Steel Systems LLC....................................... 919 615-0282
133 Us 70 Hwy W Garner (27529) *(G-4968)*

Triangle Systems Inc (PA).. 919 544-0090
882 Pinehurst Dr Chapel Hill (27517) *(G-1581)*

Triangle Systems Inc... 919 544-0090
4364 S Alston Ave Durham (27713) *(G-4281)*

Triangle Trggr-Pint Thrapy Inc................................... 919 845-1818
184 Wind Chime Ct Ste 202 Raleigh (27615) *(G-10562)*

Triangle Tribune... 704 376-0496
115 Market St Ste 211 Durham (27701) *(G-4282)*

Triangle Web Printing, Durham *Also Called: Kolb Boyette & Assoc Inc (G-4097)*

Triangle Woodworks Inc.. 919 570-0337
7608 Fullard Dr Wake Forest (27587) *(G-12308)*

Tribodyn Technologies Inc... 859 750-6299
124 Tulip Dr Mooresville (28117) *(G-8788)*

Tribofilm Research Inc... 919 838-2844
7250 Acc Blvd Raleigh (27617) *(G-10563)*

Tribune Papers Inc... 828 606-5050
Asheville (28813) *(G-624)*

Trick Karts Inc.. 704 883-0089
935 Shelton Ave Statesville (28677) *(G-11793)*

Trick Tank Inc... 980 406-3200
2250 Toomey Ave Charlotte (28203) *(G-2943)*

Trickfit & Suepack Training.. 919 737-2231
918 Gateway Commons Cir Wake Forest (27587) *(G-12309)*

Tricorn Usa, Inc., Franklin *Also Called: Lander Tubular Pdts USA Inc (G-4833)*

Trident Fibers Inc.. 336 605-9002
7109 Cessna Dr Greensboro (27409) *(G-5880)*

Trident Lure... 910 520-4659
2153 Harrison St Wilmington (28401) *(G-12941)*

Triggermesh Inc... 919 228-8049
109 Harmony Hill Ln Cary (27513) *(G-1474)*

Trim Inc.. 336 751-3591
351 Bethel Church Rd Mocksville (27028) *(G-8395)*

Trimaco, Morrisville *Also Called: Cdv LLC (G-8953)*

Trimaco Inc (PA)... 919 674-3460
2300 Gateway Centre Blvd Ste 200 Morrisville (27560) *(G-9078)*

A
L
P
H
A
B
E
T
I
C

Trimantec.. 336 767-1379
4994 Indiana Ave Winston Salem (27106) *(G-13372)*

Trimech Solutions LLC.............................. 704 503-6644
201 Mccullough Dr Ste 300 Charlotte (28262) *(G-2944)*

Trimed LLC.. 919 615-2784
7429 Acc Blvd Ste 105 Raleigh (27617) *(G-10564)*

Trimfit Inc.. 336 476-6154
605 Pineywood Rd Thomasville (27360) *(G-12084)*

Trimm, Youngsville *Also Called: Trimm International Inc (G-13496)*

Trimm International Inc............................. 847 362-3700
112 Franklin Park Dr Youngsville (27596) *(G-13496)*

Trims Unlimited, Durham *Also Called: West & Associates of NC (G-4303)*

Trimsters Inc.. 919 639-3126
150 West Rd Angier (27501) *(G-128)*

Trimworks Inc... 704 753-4149
4705 Carriker Rd Monroe (28110) *(G-8570)*

Trinity Manufacturing Inc......................... 910 582-5650
11 Ev Hogan Dr Hamlet (28345) *(G-6064)*

Trio Labs Inc.. 919 818-9646
133 Southcenter Ct Ste 900 Morrisville (27560) *(G-9079)*

Trion Iaq, Sanford *Also Called: Air System Components Inc (G-11147)*

Tripath Imaging Inc (HQ)......................... 336 222-9707
780 Plantation Dr Burlington (27215) *(G-1170)*

Tripharm Services Inc.............................. 984 243-0800
627 Davis Dr Ste 100 Morrisville (27560) *(G-9080)*

Triple C Brewing Co, Charlotte *Also Called: Triple C Brewing Company LLC (G-2945)*

Triple C Brewing Company LLC............... 704 372-3212
2900 Griffith St Charlotte (28203) *(G-2945)*

Triple C Companies LLC........................... 704 966-1999
7911 Commerce Dr Denver (28037) *(G-3814)*

Triple Crown International LLC................. 704 846-4983
12205 Parks Farm Ln Charlotte (28277) *(G-2946)*

Triple D Publishing Inc............................ 704 482-9673
1300 S Dekalb St Shelby (28152) *(G-11385)*

Triple E Equipment LLC............................ 252 448-1002
3899 Nc Highway 58 N Trenton (28585) *(G-12112)*

Triple R MBL Cigr Lounge LLC................. 252 281-7738
163 S Winstead Ave Ste A Rocky Mount (27804) *(G-10873)*

Triplett & Coffey Inc................................. 828 263-0561
204 Jefferson Rd Boone (28607) *(G-947)*

Triplette Competition Arms, Mount Airy *Also Called: Triplette Fencing Supply Inc (G-9189)*

Triplette Fencing Supply Inc.................... 336 835-1205
786 W Lebanon St Mount Airy (27030) *(G-9189)*

Tristitch, Raleigh *Also Called: Progressive Graphics Inc (G-10402)*

Triton Glass LLC.. 704 982-4333
232 S 1st St Albemarle (28001) *(G-95)*

Triton Industries LLC................................ 336 816-3794
830 Fowler Rd Mount Airy (27030) *(G-9190)*

Triton International Woods LLC................. 252 823-6675
600 W James St Tarboro (27886) *(G-11945)*

Triton Marine Services Inc....................... 252 728-9958
1050 Sensation Weigh Beaufort (28516) *(G-736)*

Triton Water, Burlington *Also Called: Alamance Foods Inc (G-1043)*

Triumph Acttion Systms-Clmmons, Clemmons *Also Called: Triumph Actuation Systems LLC (G-3206)*

Triumph Actuation Systems LLC (HQ)..... 336 766-9036
4520 Hampton Rd Clemmons (27012) *(G-3206)*

Triumph Tool Nc Inc.................................. 828 676-3677
44 Buck Shoals Rd Ste B3 Arden (28704) *(G-313)*

Triune Business Furniture Inc.................. 336 884-8341
1101 Roberts Ln High Point (27260) *(G-6812)*

Trivantage LLC (HQ)................................. 800 786-1876
1831 N Park Ave Burlington (27217) *(G-1171)*

Trivium Packaging USA Inc...................... 336 785-8500
4000 Old Milwaukee Ln Winston Salem (27107) *(G-13373)*

TRM, Raleigh *Also Called: Telecmmnctons Resource MGT Inc (G-10539)*

Trojan Defense, Fletcher *Also Called: Moto Group LLC (G-4757)*

Trophy House Inc (PA)............................. 910 323-1791
3006 Bragg Blvd Fayetteville (28303) *(G-4683)*

Trophy On Maywood LLC.......................... 919 803-1333
656 Maywood Ave Raleigh (27603) *(G-10565)*

Tropical Nut & Fruit Co (PA).................... 800 438-4470
1100 Continental Blvd Charlotte (28273) *(G-2947)*

Trotters Sewing Company Inc.................. 336 629-4550
321 Industrial Park Ave Asheboro (27205) *(G-413)*

Troutman Careconnect Corp..................... 704 838-9389
191 Timber Lake Dr Troutman (28166) *(G-12152)*

Troutman Chair Company LLC.................. 704 872-7625
134 Rocker Ln Troutman (28166) *(G-12153)*

Troxler Electronic Labs Inc (PA).............. 919 549-8661
3008 Cornwallis Rd Research Triangle Pa (27709) *(G-10716)*

Troy Ready - Mix Inc................................. 910 572-1011
1739 Nc Highway 24 27 109 W Troy (27371) *(G-12169)*

Trs-Sesco LLC... 336 996-2220
721 Park Centre Dr Ste A Kernersville (27284) *(G-7310)*

Trtl Inc... 844 811-5816
120 Penmarc Dr Ste 118 Raleigh (27603) *(G-10566)*

Tru-Cast Inc... 336 294-2370
1208 Rail St Greensboro (27407) *(G-5881)*

Tru-Contour Inc... 704 455-8700
165 Brumley Ave Ne Concord (28025) *(G-3459)*

Tru-Contour Precast Division, Concord *Also Called: Tru-Contour Inc (G-3459)*

Truck Parts Inc.. 704 332-7909
707 Kennedy St Charlotte (28206) *(G-2948)*

Truck Shop, Graham *Also Called: Chandler Concrete Inc (G-5263)*

Trucking, Fayetteville *Also Called: Grahams Transportation LLC (G-4606)*

True Cabinet LLC....................................... 828 855-9200
2401 Us Highway 70 Sw Hickory (28602) *(G-6470)*

True Machine LLC...................................... 919 270-2552
6575 Huntsboro Rd Oxford (27565) *(G-9639)*

True Portion Inc... 336 362-6326
5220 High Point Rd High Point (27265) *(G-6813)*

Truefab LLC.. 919 620-8158
3401 Industrial Dr Durham (27704) *(G-4283)*

Truelook Inc... 833 878-3566
575 E 4th St Winston Salem (27101) *(G-13374)*

Truesteel Structures LLC.......................... 336 789-3818
1050 Worth St Mount Airy (27030) *(G-9191)*

Truflo Pumps Inc....................................... 336 664-9225
7105 Cessna Dr Greensboro (27409) *(G-5882)*

Trugreen Chemlawn, Candler *Also Called: Charles Hill Enterprises (G-1220)*

Truly Good Foods, Charlotte *Also Called: Tropical Nut & Fruit Co (G-2947)*

Trunorth Wrmty Plans N Amer L............... 800 903-7489
16740 Birkdale Commons Pkwy Huntersville (28078) *(G-7060)*

Trupoint Backyards, Hamptonville *Also Called: Vinyl Structures LLC (G-6094)*

Truss Buildings LLC.................................. 919 377-0217
1512 Wackena Rd Cary (27519) *(G-1475)*

Truss Shop Inc... 336 372-6260
84 Buffalo Rd S Sparta (28675) *(G-11542)*

Trussway, Whitsett *Also Called: Trussway Manufacturing Inc (G-12621)*

Trussway Manufacturing Inc.................... 336 883-6966
940 Golf House Rd W Ste 201 Whitsett (27377) *(G-12621)*

Truswood Inc (PA)..................................... 800 473-8787
8816 Running Oak Dr Raleigh (27617) *(G-10567)*

Truventure Logistics, Charlotte *Also Called: Firm Ascend LLC (G-2154)*

Trve-Avl LLC.. 303 909-1956
255 Short Coxe Ave Asheville (28801) *(G-625)*

Tryhard Infinity LLC.................................. 252 269-0985
3019 Brunswick Ave New Bern (28562) *(G-9402)*

Tryon Finishing Corporation..................... 828 859-5891
250 Screvens Rd Tryon (28782) *(G-12178)*

Tryon Newsmedia LLC.............................. 828 859-9151
16 N Trade St Tryon (28782) *(G-12179)*

Tryton Medical Inc.................................... 919 226-1490
1 Floretta Pl Rm 208 Raleigh (27676) *(G-10568)*

TS Krupa LLC... 336 782-1515
194 Briarcreek Dr Winston Salem (27107) *(G-13375)*

TS Woodworks & RAD Design Inc............. 704 238-1015
3213 Westwood Industrial Dr Monroe (28110) *(G-8571)*

TSA Griddle System, Lexington *Also Called: CPM Acquisition Corp (G-7669)*

Tsai Winddown Inc.................................... 704 873-3106
607 Meacham Rd Statesville (28677) *(G-11794)*

Tseng Information Systems Inc.................................. 919 682-9197
  813 Watts St Durham (27701) *(G-4284)*

Tsg Finishing LLC.. 828 328-5522
  2246 Us Highway 70 Se Hickory (28602) *(G-6471)*

Tsg Finishing LLC.. 828 328-5541
  515 23rd St Sw Hickory (28602) *(G-6472)*

Tsg Finishing LLC.. 828 328-5522
  515 23rd St Sw Hickory (28602) *(G-6473)*

Tsg Finishing LLC.. 828 328-5535
  1006 19th St Ne Hickory (28601) *(G-6474)*

Tsg2 Inc... 704 347-4484
  1235 East Blvd Ste E Charlotte (28203) *(G-2949)*

Tshirtskings, Charlotte *Also Called: Napoleon James (G-2542)*

Tsi, Denver *Also Called: Textile Sales Intl Inc (G-3811)*

Tsquared Cabinets... 336 655-0208
  118 Griffith Plaza Dr Winston Salem (27103) *(G-13376)*

TTI Floor Care North Amer Inc.................................. 440 996-2000
  8405 Ibm Dr Charlotte (28262) *(G-2950)*

TTI Floor Care North Amer Inc (DH)........................... 888 321-1134
  8405 Ibm Dr Charlotte (28262) *(G-2951)*

TTI Wireless, Youngsville *Also Called: Telecommunications Tech Inc (G-13492)*

Tube Enterprises Incorporated................................. 941 629-9267
  1028 Railroad Ave Shelby (28152) *(G-11386)*

Tube Specialties Co Inc.. 704 818-8933
  1401 Industrial Dr Statesville (28625) *(G-11795)*

Tube-Tech Solar, Raleigh *Also Called: Patty Knio (G-10362)*

Tubs-Usa LLC... 336 884-5737
  322 Fraley Rd High Point (27263) *(G-6814)*

Tubular Resources, Statesville *Also Called: Trick Karts Inc (G-11793)*

Tubular Textile LLC... 336 731-2860
  4157 Old Highway 52 Welcome (27374) *(G-12516)*

Tubular Textile Machinery....................................... 336 956-6444
  85 Hargrave Rd Lexington (27293) *(G-7754)*

Tuckaway Pines Inc... 704 979-3443
  8609 Concord Mills Blvd Concord (28027) *(G-3460)*

Tucker Logging... 336 857-2674
  6957 Gravel Hill Rd Denton (27239) *(G-3764)*

Tucker Production Incorporated................................ 828 322-1036
  264 1st Ave Nw Hickory (28601) *(G-6475)*

Tucker Welding, Bear Creek *Also Called: Gary Tucker (G-714)*

Tuckers Farm Inc.. 704 375-8199
  201 W 31st St Charlotte (28206) *(G-2952)*

Tudg Multimedia Firm.. 704 916-9819
  12523 Surreykirt Ln Huntersville (28078) *(G-7061)*

Tuff Shed Inc... 919 413-2494
  409 Airport Blvd Morrisville (27560) *(G-9081)*

Tumi Store - Chrltte Dglas Int.................................. 704 359-8771
  5501 Josh Birmingham Pkwy Unit 21a Charlotte (28208) *(G-2953)*

Turbocoating Corp... 828 328-8726
  1928 Main Ave Se Hickory (28602) *(G-6476)*

Turbomed LLC.. 973 527-5299
  1830 Owen Dr Ste 9 Fayetteville (28304) *(G-4684)*

Turkington, Clayton *Also Called: Baker Thermal Solutions LLC (G-3133)*

Turmar, Charlotte *Also Called: Turmar Marble Inc (G-2954)*

Turmar Marble Inc.. 704 391-1800
  914 Richland Dr Charlotte (28211) *(G-2954)*

Turn Bull Lumber Company (PA)............................... 910 862-4447
  474 Sweet Home Church Rd Elizabethtown (28337) *(G-4436)*

Turn Bull Lumber Company....................................... 336 272-5200
  1027 Arnold St Greensboro (27405) *(G-5883)*

Turnamics Inc.. 828 254-1059
  25 Old County Home Rd Asheville (28806) *(G-626)*

Turnberry Press.. 860 670-4892
  150 Crest Rd Southern Pines (28387) *(G-11513)*

Turner & Reeves Fence Co LLC................................ 910 671-8851
  2016 Pope Ct Clayton (27520) *(G-3175)*

Turner Boys Carrier Svc LLC................................... 919 946-7553
  1012 Southern Living Dr Raleigh (27610) *(G-10569)*

Turner Equipment Company Inc................................ 919 734-8328
  1502 Us Highway 117 S Goldsboro (27530) *(G-5250)*

Turner Greenhouses, Goldsboro *Also Called: Turner Equipment Company Inc (G-5250)*

Turnkey Technologies Inc....................................... 704 245-6437
  402 Bringle Ferry Rd Salisbury (28144) *(G-11128)*

Turnsmith LLC... 919 667-9804
  710 Market St Chapel Hill (27516) *(G-1582)*

Tuscarora Yarns Inc.. 704 436-6527
  8760 Franklin St E Mount Pleasant (28124) *(G-9266)*

Tutco Inc... 828 654-1665
  30 Legend Dr Arden (28704) *(G-314)*

Tutcu-Farnam Custom Products............................... 828 684-3766
  30 Legend Dr Arden (28704) *(G-315)*

Tvl International LLC.. 704 814-0930
  165 S Trade St Matthews (28105) *(G-8155)*

Tvs, Knightdale *Also Called: Trade Venture Stones LLC (G-7460)*

Twe Nonwovens Us Inc (HQ).................................. 336 431-7187
  2215 Shore St High Point (27263) *(G-6815)*

Twg Inc.. 336 998-9731
  652 Nc Highway 801 S Advance (27006) *(G-40)*

Twigs Screen Printing.. 910 770-1605
  5474 Sidney Cherry Grove Rd Tabor City (28463) *(G-11916)*

Twin Attic Publishing Hse Inc.................................. 919 426-0322
  1415 Cedar Branch Ct Wake Forest (27587) *(G-12310)*

Twin Carports LLC.. 336 790-8284
  1014 Melrose Ct East Bend (27018) *(G-4327)*

Twin City Custom Cabinets..................................... 336 773-7200
  1310 N Liberty St Winston Salem (27105) *(G-13377)*

Twin Cy Kwnis Fndtion Wnstn-SL.............................. 336 784-1649
  1 W 4th St Winston Salem (27101) *(G-13378)*

Twin Oaks Service South Inc................................... 704 914-7142
  1320 Stony Point Rd Shelby (28150) *(G-11387)*

Twin Troller Boats Inc.. 919 207-2622
  501 S Wall St Ste A Benson (27504) *(G-798)*

Twinvision North America Inc................................... 919 361-2155
  4018 Patriot Dr Ste 100 Durham (27703) *(G-4285)*

Twisted Paper Products Inc..................................... 336 393-0273
  7100 Cessna Dr Greensboro (27409) *(G-5884)*

Two Brothers NC LLC.. 336 516-5181
  1601 Anthony Rd Burlington (27215) *(G-1172)*

Two Fifty Cleaners.. 910 397-0071
  5601 Carolina Beach Rd Ste C Wilmington (28412) *(G-12942)*

Two of A Kind Publishing LLC.................................. 704 497-2879
  8239 Romana Red Ln Charlotte (28213) *(G-2955)*

Two Percent LLC.. 301 401-2750
  204 N Laurel St Lincolnton (28092) *(G-7865)*

Two Rivers Plant, Mayodan *Also Called: Milliken & Company (G-8208)*

Two Trees Distilling Co LLC..................................... 803 767-1322
  17 Continuum Dr Fletcher (28732) *(G-4774)*

Twork Technology Inc.. 704 218-9675
  3536 N Davidson St Charlotte (28205) *(G-2956)*

Twyford Printing Company Inc.................................. 910 892-3271
  200 E Canary St Dunn (28334) *(G-3870)*

Ty Brown.. 828 264-6865
  126 Iris Ln Apt 4 Boone (28607) *(G-948)*

Tyco Electronics, Greensboro *Also Called: Te Connectivity Corporation (G-5856)*

Tylerias Closet LLC... 252 325-6639
  1250 Jones White Rd Roper (27970) *(G-10901)*

Tyndall Machine Technologies, Pittsboro *Also Called: Tyndall Machine Tool Inc (G-9790)*

Tyndall Machine Tool Inc.. 919 542-4014
  154 Dogwood Ln Pittsboro (27312) *(G-9790)*

Tyrata Inc... 919 210-8992
  101 W Chapel Hill St Ste 200 Durham (27701) *(G-4286)*

Tyratech Inc.. 919 415-4275
  5151 Mccrimmon Pkwy Ste 275 Morrisville (27560) *(G-9082)*

Tyrell Ready Mix Inc.. 252 796-0265
  1280 Hwy 94 North Columbia (27925) *(G-3298)*

Tysinger Hosiery Mill Inc.. 336 472-2148
  1294 Old Nc Highway 109 Lexington (27292) *(G-7755)*

Tyson, Eastover *Also Called: Tyson Foods Inc (G-4338)*

Tyson, Monroe *Also Called: Tyson Foods Inc (G-8572)*

Tyson, Wilkesboro *Also Called: Tyson Foods Inc (G-12657)*

Tyson, Wilkesboro *Also Called: Tyson Foods Inc (G-12659)*

Tyson, Wilkesboro *Also Called: Tyson Foods Inc (G-12660)*

A L P H A B E T I C

Tyson Foods Inc...910 483-3282
3281 Baywood Rd Eastover (28312) *(G-4338)*

Tyson Foods Inc...704 283-7571
2023 Hasty St Monroe (28112) *(G-8572)*

Tyson Foods Inc...704 201-8654
2715 Cureton St Monroe (28112) *(G-8573)*

Tyson Foods Inc...919 774-7925
800 E Main St Sanford (27332) *(G-11245)*

Tyson Foods Inc...336 651-2866
1000 Spring St Wilkesboro (28697) *(G-12656)*

Tyson Foods Inc...336 838-2171
901 Wilkes St Wilkesboro (28697) *(G-12657)*

Tyson Foods Inc...336 838-2171
706 Factory St Wilkesboro (28697) *(G-12658)*

Tyson Foods Inc...336 838-0083
1600 River St Wilkesboro (28697) *(G-12659)*

Tyson Foods Inc...336 838-2171
115 Factory St Wilkesboro (28697) *(G-12660)*

Tyson Mexican Original Inc...............................919 777-9428
800 E Main St Sanford (27332) *(G-11246)*

Tyton NC Biofuels LLC.....................................910 878-7820
800 Pate Rd Raeford (28376) *(G-9854)*

U C S, Lincolnton *Also Called: Ucs Inc (G-7866)*

U C S, Lincolnton *Also Called: United Canvas & Sling Inc (G-7868)*

U F P, New London *Also Called: Ufp New London LLC (G-9423)*

U F P, Salisbury *Also Called: Ufp Salisbury LLC (G-11129)*

U K I Supreme, Conover *Also Called: Supreme Elastic Corporation (G-3563)*

U S A T, Chapel Hill *Also Called: Usat LLC (G-1587)*

U S Alloy Co..888 522-8296
825 Groves St Lowell (28098) *(G-7935)*

U S Bottlers McHy Co Inc.................................704 588-4750
11911 Steele Creek Rd Charlotte (28273) *(G-2957)*

U S Propeller Service Inc.................................704 528-9515
844 S Main St Troutman (28166) *(G-12154)*

U-Teck, Fayetteville *Also Called: R E Mason Enterprises Inc (G-4661)*

Uai Technology Inc..919 541-9339
68 Tw Alexander Dr Durham (27709) *(G-4287)*

Uchiyama Mfg Amer LLC (HQ)...........................919 731-2364
494 Arrington Bridge Rd Goldsboro (27530) *(G-5251)*

Ucs Inc...704 732-9922
511 Hoffman Rd Lincolnton (28092) *(G-7866)*

Udm Systems LLC...919 789-0777
6621 Fleetwood Dr Raleigh (27612) *(G-10570)*

Udm Systems LLC (PA).....................................919 789-0777
8311 Brier Creek Pkwy Ste 105-159 Raleigh (27617) *(G-10571)*

Udp, Trent Woods *Also Called: United Decorative Plas NC Inc (G-12108)*

Ufp Biscoe LLC..910 294-8179
402 Capel St Biscoe (27209) *(G-858)*

Ufp Mid-Atlantic, Clinton *Also Called: Ufp Site Built LLC (G-3252)*

Ufp Mid-Atlantic, Locust *Also Called: Ufp Site Built LLC (G-7906)*

Ufp New London LLC.......................................704 463-1400
174 Random Dr New London (28127) *(G-9423)*

Ufp Rockwell, Rockwell *Also Called: Ufp Rockwell LLC (G-10806)*

Ufp Rockwell LLC..704 279-0744
175 Old Mail Rd Rockwell (28138) *(G-10806)*

Ufp Salisbury LLC (DH).....................................704 855-1600
358 Woodmill Rd Salisbury (28147) *(G-11129)*

Ufp Salisbury LLC..704 855-1600
520 Grace Church Rd Salisbury (28147) *(G-11130)*

Ufp Site Built LLC...910 590-3220
254 Superior Dr Clinton (28328) *(G-3252)*

Ufp Site Built LLC...704 781-2520
147 Locust Level Dr Locust (28097) *(G-7906)*

UGLy Essentials LLC..910 319-9945
8601 Six Forks Rd Ste 400 Raleigh (27615) *(G-10572)*

Ukg Kronos Systems LLC.................................800 225-1561
8801 J M Keynes Dr Ste 240 Charlotte (28262) *(G-2958)*

Ukg Kronos Systems LLC.................................800 225-1561
101 Centreport Dr Ste 340 Greensboro (27409) *(G-5885)*

Ullman Group LLC...704 246-7333
10925 Westlake Dr Charlotte (28273) *(G-2959)*

Ullmanique Inc...336 885-5111
323 Old Thomasville Rd High Point (27260) *(G-6816)*

Ultimate Floor Cleaning...................................704 912-8978
9625 Commons East Dr Apt L Charlotte (28277) *(G-2960)*

Ultimate Products Inc (PA)...............................919 836-1627
3201 Wellington Ct Ste 115 Raleigh (27615) *(G-10573)*

Ultimate Textile Inc..828 286-8880
1437 Us 221 Hwy S Rutherfordton (28139) *(G-11000)*

Ultimix Records..336 288-7566
3404 W Wendover Ave Ste E Greensboro (27407) *(G-5886)*

Ultra, Shelby *Also Called: Ultra Machine & Fabrication Inc (G-11388)*

Ultra Coatings Incorporated.............................336 883-8853
3509 Jamac Rd High Point (27260) *(G-6817)*

Ultra Craft Companies, Liberty *Also Called: Norcraft Companies LP (G-7774)*

Ultra Elec Ocean Systems Inc..........................781 848-3400
204 Capcom Ave Wake Forest (27587) *(G-12311)*

Ultra Flex, High Point *Also Called: Hickory Springs Mfg Co (G-6648)*

Ultra Machine & Fabrication Inc........................704 482-1399
2501 W Dixon Blvd Shelby (28152) *(G-11388)*

Ultra Precision Machining, New Bern *Also Called: Bannister Inc (G-9339)*

Ultra Violet Systems Division, Charlotte *Also Called: Xylem Lnc (G-3035)*

Ultra-Mek Inc...336 859-4552
487 Bombay Rd Denton (27239) *(G-3765)*

Ultraloop Technologies Inc...............................919 636-2842
1289 Fordham Blvd Chapel Hill (27514) *(G-1583)*

Ultrascope, Charlotte *Also Called: Parker Medical Associates LLC (G-2611)*

Ultratech Industries Inc...................................919 779-2004
200 Hamlin Rd Benson (27504) *(G-799)*

Umethod Health Inc..984 232-6699
9660 Falls Of Neuse Rd Ste 138-146 Raleigh (27615) *(G-10574)*

Umi Company Inc...704 479-6210
352 N Generals Blvd Lincolnton (28092) *(G-7867)*

Umicore USA Inc (HQ)......................................919 874-7171
3600 Glenwood Ave Ste 250 Raleigh (27612) *(G-10575)*

Unadilla Antenna Mfg Co, Moravian Falls *Also Called: Ni4I Antennas and Elec LLC (G-8810)*

UNC Campus Health Services............................919 966-2281
320 Emergency Room Dr Chapel Hill (27599) *(G-1584)*

Under Covers Publishing...................................704 965-8744
703 Glendale Dr W Wilson (27893) *(G-13040)*

Underbrinks LLC...866 495-4465
705 Hedrick St Salisbury (28144) *(G-11131)*

Underground Baking Co LLC.............................828 674-7494
304 Yon Hill Rd Hendersonville (28792) *(G-6246)*

Uniboard USA LLC...919 542-2128
985 Corinth Rd Moncure (27559) *(G-8411)*

Unichem IV Ltd (PA)...336 578-5476
916 W Main St Haw River (27258) *(G-6136)*

Unicon Concrete, Statesville *Also Called: Argos USA LLC (G-11659)*

Unicon Concrete, Wake Forest *Also Called: Argos USA LLC (G-12261)*

Unifi, Greensboro *Also Called: Unifi Inc (G-5887)*

Unifi Inc (PA)...336 294-4410
7201 W Friendly Ave Greensboro (27410) *(G-5887)*

Unifi Inc...336 427-1890
805 Island Dr Madison (27025) *(G-8002)*

Unifi Inc...336 348-6539
2920 Vance Street Ext Reidsville (27320) *(G-10700)*

Unifi Inc...919 774-7401
1921 Boone Trail Rd Sanford (27330) *(G-11247)*

Unifi Inc...336 679-3830
1032 Unifi Industrial Rd Yadkinville (27055) *(G-13454)*

Unifi Kinston LLC..252 522-6518
4693 Hwy 11 Kinston (28504) *(G-7432)*

Unifi Manufacturing Inc (HQ)............................336 294-4410
7201 W Friendly Ave Greensboro (27410) *(G-5888)*

Unifi Manufacturing Inc....................................336 427-1515
601 E Main St Yadkinville (27055) *(G-13455)*

Unifi Manufacturing Inc....................................336 679-8891
1032 Unifi Industrial Rd Yadkinville (27055) *(G-13456)*

Unifi Plant 2, Reidsville *Also Called: Unifi Inc (G-10700)*

Unifi Plant 3, Madison *Also Called: Unifi Inc (G-8002)*

Unified Logistics NC, Moyock *Also Called: Andrea L Grizzle (G-9275)*

Unified Scrning Crshing - NC I (PA) 336 824-2151
136 Crestwick Rd Ramseur (27316) *(G-10633)*

Unified2 Globl Packg Group LLC 774 696-3643
3829 S Miami Blvd Ste 300 Durham (27703) *(G-4288)*

Uniform Express, Mocksville *Also Called: McDaniel Delmar (G-8375)*

Uniforms Galore 252 975-5878
628 River Rd Washington (27889) *(G-12417)*

Unifour Finishers Inc (PA) 828 322-9435
120 21st St Nw Hickory (28601) *(G-6477)*

Unifour Finishers Inc 828 322-9435
54 29th St Nw Hickory (28601) *(G-6478)*

Unifour Tech Inc 828 256-4962
2845 Robinson Rd Newton (28658) *(G-9507)*

Unigel Inc 828 228-2095
1027 19th St Sw Hickory (28602) *(G-6479)*

Unilever 910 988-1054
4152 Turnpike Rd Raeford (28376) *(G-9855)*

Unilever, Raeford *Also Called: Conopco Inc (G-9834)*

Union Concrete, Hillsborough *Also Called: Argos USA LLC (G-6858)*

Union Corrugating Company (DH) 910 483-0479
701 S King St Fayetteville (28301) *(G-4685)*

Union Grove Saw & Knife Inc 704 539-4442
157 Sawtooth Lane Union Grove (28689) *(G-12186)*

Union Masonry Inc 919 217-7806
4708 Forestville Rd Raleigh (27616) *(G-10576)*

Union Plastics Company 704 624-2112
132 E Union St Marshville (28103) *(G-8096)*

Union Sentinal, Hayesville *Also Called: Sentinel Newspapers (G-6144)*

Unique Background Solutions, Mount Airy *Also Called: Carolina Connections Inc (G-9107)*

Unique Body Blends Inc 910 302-5484
1108 Strathdon Ave Fayetteville (28304) *(G-4686)*

Unique Collating & Bindery Svc 336 664-0960
237 Burgess Rd Ste A Greensboro (27409) *(G-5889)*

Unique Concepts 919 366-2001
310 Shipwash Dr Ste 101 Garner (27529) *(G-4969)*

Unique Concepts, Wendell *Also Called: Yukon Inc (G-12554)*

Unique Home Theater Inc 704 787-3239
135 Scalybark Trl Concord (28027) *(G-3461)*

Unique Office Solutions Inc 336 854-0900
408 Gallimore Dairy Rd Ste E Greensboro (27409) *(G-5890)*

Unique Stone, Rockingham *Also Called: Henson Family Investments LLC (G-10778)*

Unique Stone Incorporated 910 817-9450
222 Lakeshore Dr Rockingham (28379) *(G-10792)*

Unique Tool and Mfg Co 336 498-2614
2054 Bruce Pugh Rd Franklinville (27248) *(G-4858)*

Uniquetex LLC 704 457-3003
700 S Battleground Ave Grover (28073) *(G-6045)*

Unison Engine Components Inc 828 274-4540
401 Sweeten Creek Industrial Park Asheville (28803) *(G-627)*

Unitape (usa) Inc 828 464-5695
620 Reese Dr Sw Conover (28613) *(G-3568)*

United Air Filter Company Corp 704 334-5311
1000 W Palmer St Charlotte (28208) *(G-2961)*

United Brass Works, Randleman *Also Called: United Brass Works Inc (G-10663)*

United Brass Works Inc (HQ) 336 498-2661
714 S Main St Randleman (27317) *(G-10663)*

United Canvas & Sling Inc 704 732-9922
511 Hoffman Rd Lincolnton (28092) *(G-7868)*

United Chemi-Con Inc 336 384-6903
185 Mcneil Rd Lansing (28643) *(G-7479)*

United Decorative Plas NC Inc 252 637-1803
812 Llewellyn Dr Trent Woods (28562) *(G-12108)*

United Finishers Intl Inc 336 883-3901
1950 W Green Dr High Point (27260) *(G-6818)*

United Finishing Systems LLC 704 873-2475
201 United Dr Statesville (28625) *(G-11796)*

United Glove Inc 828 464-2510
2017 N Stewart Ave Newton (28658) *(G-9508)*

United House Publishing 248 605-3787
4671 Garrison Inn Ct Nw Concord (28027) *(G-3462)*

United Lumber Inc 919 575-6491
10 26th St Butner (27509) *(G-1208)*

United Machine & Metal Fab Inc 828 464-5167
1220 Fedex Dr Sw Conover (28613) *(G-3569)*

United Machine Works Inc 252 752-7434
1716 Nc Highway 903 N Greenville (27834) *(G-6029)*

United Metal Finishing, Greensboro *Also Called: United Mtal Fnshg Inc Grnsboro (G-5891)*

United Mobile Imaging Inc 800 983-9840
2554 Lewisville Clemmons Rd Ste 201 Clemmons (27012) *(G-3207)*

United Mtal Fnshg Inc Grnsboro 336 272-8107
133 Blue Bell Rd Greensboro (27406) *(G-5891)*

United Packaging, Charlotte *Also Called: Apex Packaging Corporation LLC (G-1682)*

United Plastics Corporation 336 786-2127
511 Hay St Mount Airy (27030) *(G-9192)*

United Printing Company, Charlotte *Also Called: AEL Services LLC (G-1626)*

United Protective Tech LLC 704 888-2470
142 Cara Ct Locust (28097) *(G-7907)*

United Services Group LLC (PA) 980 237-1335
2505 Hutchison Mcdonald Rd Charlotte (28269) *(G-2962)*

United Southern Industries Inc (DH) 866 273-1810
486 Vance St Forest City (28043) *(G-4799)*

United States Dept of Navy 252 466-4514
Av 8b Psc Box 8019 Cherry Point (28533) *(G-3055)*

United States Dept of Navy 252 464-7228
Bldg 137 A St Cherry Point (28533) *(G-3056)*

United States Dept of Navy 252 466-4415
Cunningham Bldg 159 Cherry Point (28533) *(G-3057)*

United Supply Company, Charlotte *Also Called: Selective Enterprises Inc (G-2784)*

United Technical Services LLC 980 237-1335
2505 Hutchison Mcdonald Rd Charlotte (28269) *(G-2963)*

United Therapeatics, Research Triangle Pa *Also Called: United Therapeutics Corp (G-10717)*

United Therapeutics Corp 919 246-9389
2 Maughan Dr Durham (27709) *(G-4289)*

United Therapeutics Corp 919 485-8350
55 Tw Alexander Dr Research Triangle Pa (27709) *(G-10717)*

United TI & Stamping Co NC Inc 910 323-8588
2817 Enterprise Ave Fayetteville (28306) *(G-4687)*

United Visions Corp 704 953-4555
428 S Main St Ste B Pmb 135 Davidson (28036) *(G-3724)*

United Wood Products Inc 336 626-2281
451 Railroad St Asheboro (27203) *(G-414)*

Unitex Chemical Corp 336 378-0965
520 Broome Rd Greensboro (27406) *(G-5892)*

Unity Hlthcare Lab Billing LLP 980 209-0402
7508 E Independence Blvd Ste 109 Charlotte (28227) *(G-2964)*

Universal Air Products Corp 704 374-0600
4715 Stockholm Ct Charlotte (28273) *(G-2965)*

Universal Bedroom Furniture, High Point *Also Called: Universal Furniture Limited (G-6819)*

Universal Black Oxide Inc 704 867-1772
205 Oxford St Gastonia (28054) *(G-5160)*

Universal Blanchers LLC 252 482-2112
115 Peanut Dr Edenton (27932) *(G-4372)*

Universal Fibers Inc 336 672-2600
749 Pineview Rd Asheboro (27203) *(G-415)*

Universal Forest Products, Elizabeth City *Also Called: Universal Forest Products Inc (G-4416)*

Universal Forest Products Inc 252 338-0319
141 Knobbs Creek Dr Elizabeth City (27909) *(G-4416)*

Universal Furniture Intl Inc 828 241-3191
4436 Old Catawba Rd Claremont (28610) *(G-3123)*

Universal Furniture Intl Inc 828 464-0311
1099 2nd Avenue Pl Se Conover (28613) *(G-3570)*

Universal Furniture Limited (PA) 336 822-8888
2575 Penny Rd High Point (27265) *(G-6819)*

Universal Machine and Tool Inc 828 659-2002
1114 W Marion Business Park Marion (28752) *(G-8071)*

Universal Mania Inc 866 903-0852
1031 Robeson St Ste A Fayetteville (28305) *(G-4688)*

Universal Packaging, Greensboro *Also Called: RLM/Universal Packaging Inc (G-5789)*

Universal Plastic Products Inc 336 856-0882
3220 Peninsula Dr Jamestown (27282) *(G-7181)*

Universal Preservachem Inc 732 568-1266
2390 Park Center Dr Mebane (27302) *(G-8262)*

A L P H A B E T I C

Universal Printing & Pubg, Durham *Also Called: Atlantis Graphics Inc (G-3904)*

Universal Rubber Products Inc 704 483-1249
7780 Forest Oak Dr Denver (28037) *(G-3815)*

Universal Steel NC LLC 336 476-3105
630 Bassett Dr Thomasville (27360) *(G-12085)*

Universal Tire Service Inc 919 779-8798
4608 Fayetteville Rd Raleigh (27603) *(G-10577)*

University Directories LLC 800 743-5556
2520 Meridian Pkwy Ste 470 Durham (27713) *(G-4290)*

University NC At Chapel HI 919 962-0369
116 S Boundary St Chapel Hill (27514) *(G-1585)*

University NC Press, Chapel Hill *Also Called: University NC At Chapel HI (G-1585)*

University NC Press Inc 919 966-3561
116 S Boundary St Chapel Hill (27514) *(G-1586)*

UNIVERSITY OF NORTH CAROLINA P, Chapel Hill *Also Called: University NC Press Inc (G-1586)*

Unix Packaging LLC 310 877-7979
100 Ceramic Tile Dr Morganton (28655) *(G-8907)*

Unlimted Potential Sanford Inc 919 852-1117
9301 Globe Center Dr Ste 120 Morrisville (27560) *(G-9083)*

Unspecified Inc 919 907-2726
65 Tw Alexander Dr Unit 110324 Durham (27709) *(G-4291)*

Unx-Christeyns LLC (PA) 252 756-8616
707 E Arlington Blvd Greenville (27858) *(G-6030)*

Unx-Christeyns LLC 252 355-8433
1704 E Arlington Blvd Ste A Greenville (27858) *(G-6031)*

Unx-Christeyns LLC 252 756-8616
201 W 9th St Greenville (27835) *(G-6032)*

Up & Coming Magazine 910 391-3859
208 Rowan St Fayetteville (28301) *(G-4689)*

Up On Hill 704 664-7971
129 Fesperman Cir Troutman (28166) *(G-12155)*

Upchurch Machine Co Inc 704 588-2895
11633 Fruehauf Dr Charlotte (28273) *(G-2966)*

Upel Inc 336 519-8080
1000 E Hanes Mill Rd Winston Salem (27105) *(G-13379)*

Upholstery Design, Hickory *Also Called: Upholstery Designs Hickory Inc (G-6480)*

Upholstery Designs Hickory Inc 828 324-2002
1251 19th St Ne Hickory (28601) *(G-6480)*

Upi, Cary *Also Called: Upl NA Inc (G-1476)*

Upi Chem Distribution Center, Mebane *Also Called: Universal Preservachem Inc (G-8262)*

Upl NA Inc (HQ) 800 358-7642
15401 Weston Pkwy Ste 170 Cary (27513) *(G-1476)*

Upm Raflatac Inc 828 335-3289
535 Cane Creek Rd Fletcher (28732) *(G-4775)*

Upm Raflatac Inc 828 651-4800
267 Cane Creek Rd Fletcher (28732) *(G-4776)*

Upm Raflatac Inc (HQ) 828 651-4800
400 Broadpointe Dr Mills River (28759) *(G-8322)*

Upm Raflatac At Fletcher Bus, Fletcher *Also Called: Upm Raflatac Inc (G-4775)*

Upper Coastl Plain Bus Dev Ctr 252 234-5900
121 Nash St W Wilson (27893) *(G-13041)*

Upper Deck Company 760 496-9149
1750 Tw Alexander Dr Durham (27703) *(G-4292)*

Upper South Studio Inc 336 724-5480
330 S Main St Winston Salem (27101) *(G-13380)*

UPS, High Point *Also Called: Bryan Austin (G-6551)*

UPS Stores 2922, The, Laurinburg *Also Called: King Business Service Inc (G-7504)*

Upshinemedical, Charlotte *Also Called: Aj & Raine Scrubs & More LLC (G-1634)*

Uptown Catering Company, The, Charlotte *Also Called: Over Rainbow Inc (G-2604)*

Uptown Publishing Inc 704 543-0690
8037 Corporate Center Dr Charlotte (28226) *(G-2967)*

Urban Industries Corp 980 209-9471
12245 Nations Ford Rd Ste 505 Pineville (28134) *(G-9763)*

Urban Orchard Cider Company 252 904-5135
24 Buxton Ave Asheville (28801) *(G-628)*

Urban Skin Rx, Charlotte *Also Called: Usrx LLC (G-2969)*

Urban Spiced LLC 704 741-1174
15720 Brixham Hill Ave Ste 300 Charlotte (28277) *(G-2968)*

Urban Tactical and Cstm Armory 252 686-0122
643 Tyree Rd Kinston (28504) *(G-7433)*

Uretek LLC 203 468-0342
715 Railroad Ave Rutherfordton (28139) *(G-11001)*

Urethane Innovators Inc 252 637-7110
403 Industrial Dr New Bern (28562) *(G-9403)*

Urovant Sciences Inc 919 323-8528
324 Blackwell St Bay 11 Durham (27701) *(G-4293)*

US Arms & Ammunition LLC 252 652-7400
119 Mellen Rd New Bern (28562) *(G-9404)*

US Buildings LLC (PA) 828 264-6198
355 Industrial Park Dr Boone (28607) *(G-949)*

US Chemical Storage LLC 828 264-6032
1806 River St Wilkesboro (28697) *(G-12661)*

US Conec Ltd 828 323-8883
830 21st Street Dr Se Hickory (28602) *(G-6481)*

US Conec Ltd (HQ) 828 323-8883
1138 25th St Se Hickory (28602) *(G-6482)*

US Cotton LLC 704 874-5000
1000 Parkdale Dr Ste 1 Belmont (28012) *(G-774)*

US Cotton LLC (DH) 216 676-6400
531 Cotton Blossom Cir Gastonia (28054) *(G-5161)*

US Custom Socks Co LLC 336 549-1088
2522 Brandt Forest Ct Greensboro (27455) *(G-5893)*

US Drainage Systems LLC 828 855-1906
26 5th St Se Hickory (28602) *(G-6483)*

US Filter 828 274-8282
1129 Sweeten Creek Rd Asheville (28803) *(G-629)*

US Industrial Piping Inc 336 993-9505
105 Woodland Trl Kernersville (27284) *(G-7311)*

US Label Corporation 336 332-7000
2118 Enterprise Rd Greensboro (27408) *(G-5894)*

US Lbm Operating Co 2009 LLC 910 864-8787
1001 S Reilly Rd Ste 639 Fayetteville (28314) *(G-4690)*

US Legend Cars Intl Inc 704 455-3896
5245 Nc Highway 49 S Harrisburg (28075) *(G-6119)*

US Logoworks, Fayetteville *Also Called: US Logoworks LLC (G-4691)*

US Logoworks LLC 910 307-0312
4200 Morganton Rd Ste 105 Fayetteville (28314) *(G-4691)*

US Metal Crafters LLC 336 861-2100
2400 Shore St Archdale (27263) *(G-245)*

US Microwave Inc 520 891-2444
164 Fearrington Post Pittsboro (27312) *(G-9791)*

US Optics 828 874-2242
100 Beiersdorf Dr Connelly Springs (28612) *(G-3484)*

US Patriot LLC 803 787-9398
Bldg Z 3252 - 1017 Canopy Lane Fort Bragg (28307) *(G-4805)*

US Precision Cabinetry LLC 828 351-2020
160 Executive Dr Rutherfordton (28139) *(G-11002)*

US Print Inc 919 878-0981
1665 N Market Dr Raleigh (27609) *(G-10578)*

US Prototype Inc 866 239-2848
341 S College Rd Ste 11 Pmb 3004 Wilmington (28403) *(G-12943)*

US Soaps Manufacturing Co, Raleigh *Also Called: Showline Inc (G-10471)*

US Specialty Color Corp 704 292-1476
5624 Cannon Dr Monroe (28110) *(G-8574)*

US Tobacco Cooperative Inc (PA) 919 821-4560
1304 Annapolis Dr Raleigh (27608) *(G-10579)*

US Valve Corporation 910 799-9913
3111 Kitty Hawk Rd Wilmington (28405) *(G-12944)*

USA Attachments Inc 336 983-0763
105 Industrial Dr King (27021) *(G-7338)*

USA Display, Flat Rock *Also Called: Leisure Craft Inc (G-4709)*

USA Dreamstone LLC 919 615-4329
128 Yeargan Rd Ste C Garner (27529) *(G-4970)*

USA Dutch Inc (PA) 919 732-6956
3604 Southern Dr Efland (27243) *(G-4376)*

USA Dutch Inc 336 227-8600
778 Woody Dr Graham (27253) *(G-5287)*

USA Metal Structure LLP 336 717-2884
507 W Kapp St Dobson (27017) *(G-3826)*

USA Tire Sales and Storage LLC 910 424-5330
3696 Gillespie St Fayetteville (28306) *(G-4692)*

USa Wholesale and Distrg Inc........................ 888 484-6872
  500 Blount St Fayetteville (28301) *(G-4693)*

Usat LLC.. 919 942-4214
  104 S Estes Dr Ste 204 Chapel Hill (27514) *(G-1587)*

Usrx LLC.. 980 221-1200
  8604 Cliff Cameron Dr Ste 175 Charlotte (28269) *(G-2969)*

Usw-Menard Inc... 910 371-1899
  3600 Andrew Jackson Hwy Ne Leland (28451) *(G-7562)*

UTC Aerospace Systems, Charlotte *Also Called: Hamilton Sundstrand Corp (G-2252)*

Utd Technology Corp....................................... 704 612-0121
  4455 Morris Park Dr Ste J Mint Hill (28227) *(G-8344)*

Uteck.. 910 483-5016
  159 Rock Hill Rd Fayetteville (28312) *(G-4694)*

Utility Metering Solutions Inc........................... 910 270-2885
  231 Sloop Point Loop Rd Hampstead (28443) *(G-6079)*

Utility Precast Inc... 704 721-0106
  1420 Ivey Cline Rd Concord (28027) *(G-3463)*

Utility Solutions Inc....................................... 828 323-8914
  101 33rd S Dr Se Hickory (28602) *(G-6484)*

Utsey Duskie & Associates............................... 704 663-0036
  243 Overhill Dr Ste B Mooresville (28117) *(G-8789)*

Uwharrie Chair Company LLC............................ 336 431-2055
  5873 Parker St High Point (27263) *(G-6820)*

Uwharrie Frames Mfg LLC................................ 336 626-6649
  247 Leo Cranford Rd Asheboro (27205) *(G-416)*

Uwharrie Knits Inc.. 704 474-4123
  957 N Main St Norwood (28128) *(G-9563)*

Uwharrie Lumber Co....................................... 910 572-3731
  335 Page St Troy (27371) *(G-12170)*

V & B Construction Svcs Inc............................. 704 641-9936
  8413 Walkup Rd Waxhaw (28173) *(G-12447)*

V and E Components Inc (PA)............................ 336 884-0088
  720 W Fairfield Rd High Point (27263) *(G-6821)*

V I P, Henderson *Also Called: Quality Investments Inc (G-6172)*

V M Trucking Inc... 984 239-4853
  4915 Arendell St Morehead City (28557) *(G-8848)*

V1 Pharma, Raleigh *Also Called: V1 Pharma LLC (G-10580)*

V1 Pharma LLC (PA)....................................... 919 338-5744
  353 E Six Forks Rd Ste 220 Raleigh (27609) *(G-10580)*

VA Composites Inc... 844 474-2387
  707 S Pinehurst St Ste D Aberdeen (28315) *(G-29)*

Vacs America Inc... 910 259-9854
  3490 Stag Park Rd Burgaw (28425) *(G-1035)*

Vacuum Handling North Amer LLC...................... 828 327-2290
  2551 Us Highway 70 Sw Hickory (28602) *(G-6485)*

Val-U-King Group Inc...................................... 980 306-5342
  2312 Rufus Ratchford Rd Gastonia (28056) *(G-5162)*

Valassis Communications Inc............................ 919 544-4511
  4918 Prospectus Dr Durham (27713) *(G-4294)*

Valassis Communications Inc............................ 919 361-7900
  4918 Prospectus Dr Durham (27713) *(G-4295)*

Valassis Durham Printing Div, Durham *Also Called: Valassis Communications Inc (G-4294)*

Valassis Wichita Printing, Durham *Also Called: Valassis Communications Inc (G-4295)*

Vald Group Inc... 704 345-5145
  2108 South Blvd Ste 115 Charlotte (28203) *(G-2970)*

Valdese Packaging & Label Inc (PA).................... 828 879-9772
  302 Saint Germain Ave Se Valdese (28690) *(G-12201)*

Valdese Packaging & Label Inc.......................... 828 879-9772
  302 Saint Germain Ave Sw Valdese (28690) *(G-12202)*

Valdese Textiles Inc....................................... 828 874-4216
  1901 Main St E Valdese (28690) *(G-12203)*

Valdese Weavers, Valdese *Also Called: Valdese Weavers LLC (G-12206)*

Valdese Weavers LLC...................................... 828 874-2181
  705 Lovelady Rd Ne Valdese (28690) *(G-12204)*

Valdese Weavers LLC...................................... 828 874-2181
  280 Crescent St Ne Valdese (28690) *(G-12205)*

Valdese Weavers LLC (PA)................................ 828 874-2181
  1000 Perkins Rd Se Valdese (28690) *(G-12206)*

Valencell Inc... 919 747-3668
  4601 Six Forks Rd Ste 103 Raleigh (27609) *(G-10581)*

Valendrawers, Lexington *Also Called: Valendrawers Inc (G-7756)*

Valendrawers Inc.. 336 956-2118
  555 Dixon St Sapona Business Park Lexington (27293) *(G-7756)*

Valley Proteins... 252 348-4200
  3539 Governors Rd Lewiston Woodville (27849) *(G-7648)*

Valley Proteins (de) Inc................................. 336 333-3030
  2410 Randolph Ave Greensboro (27406) *(G-5895)*

Valley Proteins (de) Inc................................. 540 877-2533
  28844 Bethlehem Church Rd Oakboro (28129) *(G-9584)*

Valley Proteins (de), Inc., Oakboro *Also Called: Valley Proteins (de) Inc (G-9584)*

Valmet Inc... 803 289-4900
  3440 Toringdon Way Ste 300 Charlotte (28277) *(G-2971)*

Valmet Inc... 704 541-1453
  3430 Toringdon Way Charlotte (28277) *(G-2972)*

Valor Brands LLC.. 678 602-9268
  9300 Nc Highway 65 Stokesdale (27357) *(G-11817)*

Valspar Corporation....................................... 704 897-5700
  721 Jetton St Davidson (28036) *(G-3725)*

Value Clothing, Salisbury *Also Called: Value Clothing Inc (G-11132)*

Value Clothing Inc (PA).................................. 704 638-6111
  1310 Richard St Salisbury (28144) *(G-11132)*

Value Printing Inc... 919 380-9883
  604 E Chatham St Ste D Cary (27511) *(G-1477)*

Valwood Corporation...................................... 828 321-4717
  35 Coalville Rd Marble (28905) *(G-8028)*

Van Blake Dixon... 336 282-1861
  378 Air Harbor Rd Greensboro (27455) *(G-5896)*

Van Products Inc (PA)..................................... 919 878-7110
  2521 Noblin Rd Raleigh (27604) *(G-10582)*

Van Wingerden Grnhse Co Inc........................... 828 891-7389
  4078 Haywood Rd Mills River (28759) *(G-8323)*

Vance Industrial Elec Inc................................. 336 570-1992
  1208 Belmont St Burlington (27215) *(G-1173)*

Vanderbilt Minerals LLC.................................. 910 948-2266
  400 Spies Rd Robbins (27325) *(G-10755)*

Vandor Corporation....................................... 980 392-8107
  2301 Speedball Rd Statesville (28677) *(G-11797)*

Vanguard Culinary Group Ltd............................ 910 484-8999
  716 Whitfield St Fayetteville (28306) *(G-4695)*

Vanguard Furniture, Conover *Also Called: Vanguard Furniture Co Inc (G-3571)*

Vanguard Furniture Co Inc (PA)......................... 828 328-5601
  109 Simpson St Sw Conover (28613) *(G-3571)*

Vanguard Pai Lung LLC................................... 704 283-8171
  601 Mcarthur Cir Monroe (28110) *(G-8575)*

Vanguard Pailung, Monroe *Also Called: Vanguard Pai Lung LLC (G-8575)*

Vanguard Supreme, Monroe *Also Called: Monarch Manufacturing Corp (G-8535)*

Vanguard Supreme Div, Monroe *Also Called: Monarch Knitting McHy Corp (G-8533)*

Vann S Wldg & Orna Works Inc.......................... 704 289-6056
  709 Sikes Mill Rd Monroe (28110) *(G-8576)*

Vannoy Construction Arcft LLC.......................... 336 846-7191
  1608 Us Highway 221 N Jefferson (28640) *(G-7193)*

Vans Inc... 704 364-3811
  4400 Sharon Rd Ste 159 Charlotte (28211) *(G-2973)*

Vans Inc... 919 792-2555
  5959 Triangle Town Blvd Ste 1152 Raleigh (27616) *(G-10583)*

Vapor Honing Technologies, Lincolnton *Also Called: J Wise Inc (G-7833)*

Varco Pruden Buildings, Greensboro *Also Called: Bluescope Buildings N Amer Inc (G-5394)*

Variety Consult LLC....................................... 704 978-8108
  3735 Robert Riding Rd Shelby (28150) *(G-11389)*

Variform Inc... 828 277-6420
  12 Gerber Rd Ste A Asheville (28803) *(G-630)*

Vascular Pharmaceuticals Inc............................ 919 345-7933
  116 Manning Dr Chapel Hill (27599) *(G-1588)*

Vasiliy Yavdoshnyak....................................... 919 995-9469
  3517 Trawden Dr Wake Forest (27587) *(G-12312)*

Vasonova Inc.. 650 327-1412
  3015 Carrington Mill Blvd 3 Morrisville (27560) *(G-9084)*

Vast Therapeutics Inc..................................... 919 321-1403
  615 Davis Dr Ste 800 Morrisville (27560) *(G-9085)*

Vaughan Enterprises Inc.................................. 919 772-4765
  834 Purser Dr Ste 102 Raleigh (27603) *(G-10584)*

Vaughan Logging, Wake Forest *Also Called: Cjc Enterprises (G-12270)*

Vaughan-Bassett Furn Co Inc...336 835-2670
4109 Poplar Springs Rd Elkin (28621) *(G-4453)*

Vaughan-Bassett Furn Co Inc...336 889-9111
210 E Commerce Ave High Point (27260) *(G-6822)*

Vaughn Woodworking Inc...828 963-6858
442 Aldridge Rd Banner Elk (28604) *(G-690)*

Vault Enclosures, High Point *Also Called: Vault LLC (G-6823)*

Vault LLC..336 698-3796
1515 W Green Dr High Point (27260) *(G-6823)*

Vav Plastics Nc LLC..704 325-9332
8710 Air Park West Dr Ste 200 Charlotte (28214) *(G-2974)*

Vecoplan, Greensboro *Also Called: Vecoplan LLC (G-5897)*

Vecoplan LLC...336 861-6070
501 Gallimore Dairy Rd Greensboro (27409) *(G-5897)*

Vega Construction Company Inc..336 756-3477
137 W Main St Unit 8 Pilot Mountain (27041) *(G-9675)*

Vegherb LLC...800 914-9835
200 N 13th St Ste 3b Erwin (28339) *(G-4493)*

Veka East Inc...800 654-5589
90 Ceramic Tile Dr Morganton (28655) *(G-8908)*

Velocita Inc..336 764-8513
383 Grant Rd Clemmons (27012) *(G-3208)*

Venator Chemicals LLC...704 454-4811
5910 Pharr Mill Rd Harrisburg (28075) *(G-6120)*

Veneer Technologies Inc (PA)...252 223-5600
611 Verdun St Newport (28570) *(G-9446)*

Ventilation Direct..919 573-1522
14460 Falls Of Neuse Rd # 14 Raleigh (27614) *(G-10585)*

Ventura Inc...252 291-7125
7061 Pennwright Rd Fremont (27830) *(G-4861)*

Ventura Systems Inc...704 712-8630
160 Gibson Ct Dallas (28034) *(G-3692)*

Venture Cabinets..252 299-0051
7061 Pennwright Rd Fremont (27830) *(G-4862)*

Venture Products, Asheville *Also Called: Venture Products Intl Inc (G-631)*

Venture Products Intl Inc...828 285-0495
27 Mulvaney St Asheville (28803) *(G-631)*

Veon Inc...252 623-2102
601 W 5th St Washington (27889) *(G-12418)*

Veradigm, Raleigh *Also Called: Veradigm LLC (G-10586)*

Veradigm LLC (HQ)...919 847-8102
305 Church At North Hills Ste 100 Raleigh (27609) *(G-10586)*

Verbatim Americas LLC..704 547-6551
7300 Reames Rd Charlotte (28216) *(G-2975)*

Verbatim Americas LLC (PA)...704 547-6500
8210 University Exec Park Dr Ste 300 Charlotte (28262) *(G-2976)*

Verbatim Corporation...704 547-6500
8210 University Exec Park Dr Ste 300 Charlotte (28262) *(G-2977)*

Verdante, Lenoir *Also Called: Verdante Bioenergy Svcs LLC (G-7643)*

Verdante Bioenergy Svcs LLC..828 394-1246
628 Harper Ave Nw # D Lenoir (28645) *(G-7643)*

Verdesian Life Science US LLC (DH).....................................919 825-1901
1001 Winstead Dr Ste 480 Cary (27513) *(G-1478)*

Verdesian Life Sciences, Cary *Also Called: Verdesian Life Science US LLC (G-1478)*

Verellen Inc...336 889-7379
5297 Prospect St High Point (27263) *(G-6824)*

Verena Designs Inc (PA)...336 869-8235
812 W Green Dr High Point (27260) *(G-6825)*

Verinetics Inc..919 354-1029
2 Davis Dr Rtp (27709) *(G-10950)*

Veritiv Operating Company...336 834-3488
3 Centerview Dr Ste 100 Greensboro (27407) *(G-5898)*

Verity America LLC..347 960-4198
1340 Environ Way Chapel Hill (27517) *(G-1589)*

Vermeer Manufacturing Company...410 285-0200
10900 Carpet St Charlotte (28273) *(G-2978)*

Verona Cabinets & Surfaces LLC..704 755-5259
6700 South Blvd Charlotte (28217) *(G-2979)*

Vertical Access LLC...800 325-1116
900 Hwy 258 S Snow Hill (28580) *(G-11483)*

Vertical Solutions of NC Inc...919 285-2251
5040 Kinderston Dr Holly Springs (27540) *(G-6918)*

Verticalfx Inc...704 594-5000
107 Mcneil Ln Mooresville (28117) *(G-8790)*

Verve, Hendersonville *Also Called: Carolina Home Garden (G-6195)*

Vescom America Inc..252 431-6200
2289 Ross Mill Rd Henderson (27537) *(G-6182)*

Vestal Buick Gmc Inc..336 310-0261
900 Hwy 66 South Kernersville (27284) *(G-7312)*

Vestal Pontiac Buick GMC Truck, Kernersville *Also Called: Vestal Buick Gmc Inc (G-7312)*

Vestaron Corporation (PA)...919 694-1022
4025 Stirrup Creek Dr Ste 400 Durham (27703) *(G-4296)*

Vestcom Retail Solutions, Charlotte *Also Called: Electronic Imaging Svcs Inc (G-2095)*

Vestige Group LLC...704 321-4960
2459 Wilkinson Blvd Ste 205 Charlotte (28208) *(G-2980)*

Vesuvius Nc LLC...336 578-7728
911 E Elm St Graham (27253) *(G-5288)*

Vesuvius Penn Corporation (HQ)...724 535-4374
5510 77 Center Dr Ste 100 Charlotte (28217) *(G-2981)*

Vesuvius USA Corporation..412 429-1800
5510 77 Center Dr # 100 Charlotte (28217) *(G-2982)*

Vexea Mx LLC..910 787-9391
205 America Ct Jacksonville (28540) *(G-7157)*

Vf, Greensboro *Also Called: Kontoor Brands Inc (G-5652)*

Vf, Greensboro *Also Called: Workwear Outfitters LLC (G-5924)*

VF Corporation..336 424-6000
105 Corporate Center Blvd Greensboro (27408) *(G-5899)*

VF Corporation..336 424-6000
105 Corp Ctr Blvd Greensboro (27408) *(G-5900)*

Vf Jeanswear Inc (PA)...336 332-3400
105 Corporate Center Blvd Greensboro (27408) *(G-5901)*

Vf Receivables LP...336 424-6000
105 Corporate Center Blvd Greensboro (27408) *(G-5902)*

VFC Lightning Protection, Raleigh *Also Called: Lightning Prtction Systems LLC (G-10256)*

VH Industries Inc..704 743-2400
4451 Raceway Dr Sw Concord (28027) *(G-3464)*

Via Prnting Graphic Design Inc..919 872-8688
5841 Gentle Wind Dr Youngsville (27596) *(G-13497)*

Viasic Inc...336 774-2150
5015 Southpark Dr Ste 240 Durham (27713) *(G-4297)*

Viaticus Inc...252 258-4679
4104 Sterling Trace Dr Winterville (28590) *(G-13425)*

Viavi Solutions Inc...919 388-5100
1100 Perimeter Park Dr Ste 101 Morrisville (27560) *(G-9086)*

Vibration Solutions LLC..704 896-7535
5900 Harris Technology Blvd Ste G Charlotte (28269) *(G-2983)*

Vic Inc...336 545-1124
3410 W Wendover Ave Ste C Greensboro (27407) *(G-5903)*

Victaulic Company...910 371-5588
2010 Enterprise Dr Ne Leland (28451) *(G-7563)*

Victaulic Leland Facility, Leland *Also Called: Victaulic Company (G-7563)*

Victory 1 Performance Inc..704 799-1955
159 Lugnut Ln Mooresville (28117) *(G-8791)*

Victory Press LLC...704 660-0348
114 Eastbend Ct Ste 4 Mooresville (28117) *(G-8792)*

Victory Signs LLC...919 642-3091
2908 N Main St Fuquay Varina (27526) *(G-4904)*

Vida Wood Us Inc...919 934-9904
219 Peedin Rd Ste 102 Smithfield (27577) *(G-11468)*

Videndum Prod Solutions Inc..919 244-0760
215 Trimble Ave Cary (27511) *(G-1479)*

Video Fuel..919 676-9940
6417 Lakeland Dr Raleigh (27612) *(G-10587)*

Videri Chocolate Factory, Raleigh *Also Called: Beech Street Ventures LLC (G-9938)*

Viewriver Machine Corporation (PA)......................................336 463-2311
1617 Fern Valley Rd Yadkinville (27055) *(G-13457)*

Vigor LLC..980 474-1124
1209 S College St Apt 1130 Charlotte (28203) *(G-2984)*

Viiv Healthcare Company..919 445-2770
120 Mason Farm Rd Chapel Hill (27514) *(G-1590)*

Viiv Healthcare Company..919 483-2100
410 Blackwell St Durham (27701) *(G-4298)*

Viiv Healthcare US, Durham *Also Called: Viiv Healthcare Company (G-4298)*

Viking Steel Structures LLC.................................... 877 623-7549
   113 W Main St Nc Boonville (27011) *(G-959)*

Viking Truss Inc... 252 792-1051
   424 Railroad St Williamston (27892) *(G-12675)*

Viktors Gran MBL Kit Cnter Top............................ 828 681-0713
   28 Beale Rd Arden (28704) *(G-316)*

Villabona Iron Works Inc...................................... 252 522-4005
   1415 W New Bern Rd Kinston (28504) *(G-7434)*

Village Ceramics Inc.. 828 685-9491
   320 Q P Ln Hendersonville (28792) *(G-6247)*

Village Graphics... 252 745-4600
   204 Freemason St Oriental (28571) *(G-9603)*

Village Instant Printing Inc.................................. 919 968-0000
   2204 Damascus Church Rd Chapel Hill (27516) *(G-1591)*

Village Printers, Pinehurst *Also Called: Gilley Printers Inc (G-9692)*

Village Printing Co.. 336 629-0951
   530 Albemarle Rd Asheboro (27203) *(G-417)*

Village Produce & Cntry Str In.............................. 336 661-8685
   4219 N Liberty St Winston Salem (27105) *(G-13381)*

Village Tire Center Inc.. 919 862-8500
   5220 Atlantic Ave Raleigh (27616) *(G-10588)*

Villari Bros Foods LLC.. 910 293-2157
   135 Carter Best Rd Warsaw (28398) *(G-12367)*

Villari Food Group LLC (PA)................................. 910 293-2157
   1015 Ashes Dr Ste 102 Wilmington (28405) *(G-12945)*

Vim Products Inc.. 919 277-0267
   5060 Trademark Dr Raleigh (27610) *(G-10589)*

Vinatoru Enterprises Inc...................................... 336 227-4300
   209 W Hanover Rd Graham (27253) *(G-5289)*

Vincent L Taylor... 252 792-2987
   3930 Bear Grass Rd Williamston (27892) *(G-12676)*

Vine & Branch Woodworks LLC............................. 704 663-0077
   388 E Plaza Dr Mooresville (28115) *(G-8793)*

Vineyard Bluffton LLC.. 704 307-2737
   1001 Morehead Square Dr Ste 320 Charlotte (28203) *(G-2985)*

Vineyards On Scuppernong LLC............................ 252 796-4727
   1894 Nc Highway 94 N Columbia (27925) *(G-3299)*

Vintage Editions Inc.. 828 632-4185
   88 Buff Ln Taylorsville (28681) *(G-11985)*

Vintage South Inc.. 919 362-4079
   1100 Chimney Hill Dr Apex (27502) *(G-202)*

Vinventions Usa LLC.. 919 460-2200
   505 Innovative Way Zebulon (27597) *(G-13525)*

Vinyl Structures LLC.. 336 468-4311
   4708 Hunting Creek Church Rd Hamptonville (27020) *(G-6094)*

Vinyl Windows & Doors Corp................................ 910 944-2100
   165 Taylor St Aberdeen (28315) *(G-30)*

Violet Sanford Holdings LLC................................. 919 775-5931
   2209 Boone Trail Rd Sanford (27330) *(G-11248)*

Violino USA Ltd.. 336 889-6623
   123 S Hamilton St High Point (27260) *(G-6826)*

VIP Printing and Signs Express, Chapel Hill *Also Called: Village Instant Printing Inc (G-1591)*

Virginia Carolina Belting, Rocky Mount *Also Called: R/W Connection Inc (G-10864)*

Virginia Carolina Refr Inc (PA).............................. 704 216-0223
   1123 Speedway Blvd Salisbury (28146) *(G-11133)*

Virginia Mtal Trting Lynchburg, Raleigh *Also Called: East Crlina Metal Treating Inc (G-10069)*

Virginn-Plot Mdia Cmpanies LLC.......................... 252 441-3628
   2224 S Croatan Hwy Nags Head (27959) *(G-9305)*

Virtue Labs LLC (PA)... 844 782-4247
   426 S Dawson St Raleigh (27601) *(G-10590)*

Virtue Labs LLC... 781 316-5437
   95 W 32nd St Winston Salem (27105) *(G-13382)*

Virtus Entertainment Inc...................................... 919 467-9700
   114 Mackenan Dr Ste 100 Cary (27511) *(G-1480)*

Vise & Co LLC... 336 354-3702
   5063 Ramillie Run Winston Salem (27106) *(G-13383)*

Vishay Measurements Group Inc (HQ)................... 919 365-3800
   951 Wendell Blvd Wendell (27591) *(G-12552)*

Vishay Precision Group Inc................................... 919 374-5555
   Micro-Measurements Raleigh (27611) *(G-10591)*

Vishay Transducers Ltd (HQ)................................ 919 365-3800
   951 Wendell Blvd Wendell (27591) *(G-12553)*

Visigraphix Inc.. 336 882-1935
   8911 Cedar Spring Dr Colfax (27235) *(G-3292)*

Vision Contract Mfg LLC...................................... 336 405-8784
   1327 Lincoln Dr High Point (27260) *(G-6827)*

Vision Directional Drilling.................................... 336 570-4621
   3462 Nc Highway 62 E Burlington (27215) *(G-1174)*

Vision Envelope Inc... 704 392-9090
   2451 Executive St Charlotte (28208) *(G-2986)*

Vision Metals Inc... 336 622-7300
   5806 York Martin Rd Liberty (27298) *(G-7783)*

Vision Motor Cars Inc (PA)................................... 704 425-6271
   545 Hamberton Ct Nw Concord (28027) *(G-3465)*

Vision Print Solutions, Charlotte *Also Called: Vision Envelope Inc (G-2986)*

Vision Stairways & Mllwk LLC............................... 919 878-5622
   2200 Westinghouse Blvd Ste 108 Raleigh (27604) *(G-10592)*

Vision Technologies Inc.. 919 387-7878
   8509 Smith Rd Apex (27539) *(G-203)*

Visionair Inc.. 910 675-9117
   5601 Barbados Blvd Castle Hayne (28429) *(G-1510)*

Visions Interior Designs, Davidson *Also Called: United Visions Corp (G-3724)*

Visitech Systems Inc.. 919 387-0524
   1012 Napa Pl Apex (27502) *(G-204)*

Vista Horticultural Group Inc................................ 828 633-6338
   2099 Brevard Rd Arden (28704) *(G-317)*

Vista Products Inc... 910 582-0130
   10 Ev Hogan Dr Hamlet (28345) *(G-6065)*

Vista Tranquila Publishers LLC............................ 828 586-8401
   53 Lands End Dr Sylva (28779) *(G-11903)*

Visual Comfort... 980 666-4120
   2137 South Blvd Ste 100 Charlotte (28203) *(G-2987)*

Visual Impact Prfmce Systems L........................... 704 278-3552
   2720 Amity Hill Rd Cleveland (27013) *(G-3224)*

Visual Impressions, Charlotte *Also Called: Digital Printing Systems Inc (G-2047)*

Visual Products Inc.. 336 883-0156
   1019 Porter St High Point (27263) *(G-6828)*

Vita Foam, Greensboro *Also Called: Olympic Products LLC (G-5721)*

Vita Nonwovens, High Point *Also Called: Twe Nonwovens Us Inc (G-6815)*

Vitaflex LLC.. 888 616-8848
   1305 Graham St Burlington (27217) *(G-1175)*

Vitaflex USA, Burlington *Also Called: Vitaflex LLC (G-1175)*

Vittro Sign Studio.. 917 698-1594
   1106 Cameron Woods Dr Apex (27523) *(G-205)*

Vivet Home Brands, Greensboro *Also Called: Vivet Inc (G-5904)*

Vivet Inc (PA).. 909 390-1039
   1150 Pleasant Ridge Rd Ste A Greensboro (27409) *(G-5904)*

Viztek LLC... 919 792-6420
   2217 Us 70 Hwy E Garner (27529) *(G-4971)*

Vlr LLC.. 252 355-4610
   1020 N Green St Morganton (28655) *(G-8909)*

Vmod Fiber LLC... 704 525-6851
   811 Pressley Rd Charlotte (28217) *(G-2988)*

Vna Holding Inc (HQ)... 336 393-4890
   7825 National Service Rd Greensboro (27409) *(G-5905)*

VOCATIONAL SOLUTONS, East Flat Rock *Also Called: Vocatnal Sltons Hndrson Cnty I (G-4335)*

Vocatnal Sltons Hndrson Cnty I............................ 828 692-9626
   2110 Spartanburg Hwy East Flat Rock (28726) *(G-4335)*

Voco America Inc... 917 923-7698
   1104 Real Quiet Ln Waxhaw (28173) *(G-12448)*

Vocollect Inc.. 980 279-4119
   855 S Mint St Charlotte (28202) *(G-2989)*

Vogenx Inc... 919 659-5677
   3920 S Alston Ave Durham (27713) *(G-4299)*

Voith Fabrics Inc.. 252 291-3800
   3040 Black Creek Rd S Wilson (27893) *(G-13042)*

Volex Inc... 828 485-4500
   915 Tate Blvd Se Ste 144 Hickory (28602) *(G-6486)*

Volex Inc... 828 485-4500
   915 Tate Blvd Se Hickory (28602) *(G-6487)*

Volta Group Corporation LLC................................ 919 637-0273
   300 Fayetteville St Unit 1344 Raleigh (27602) *(G-10593)*

A
L
P
H
A
B
E
T
I
C

Voltage LLC..919 391-9405
1450 Raleigh Rd Ste 208 Chapel Hill (27517) *(G-1592)*

Volumetrics Med Systems LLC................................800 472-0900
4711 Hope Valley Rd Ste 4f Durham (27707) *(G-4300)*

Volvo Group North America LLC (DH)........................336 393-2000
7900 National Service Rd Greensboro (27409) *(G-5906)*

Volvo Group North America LLC..............................336 393-2000
8003 Piedmont Triad Pkwy Greensboro (27409) *(G-5907)*

Volvo Group North America LLC..............................336 393-2000
8203 Piedmont Triad Pkwy Greensboro (27409) *(G-5908)*

Volvo Group North America LLC..............................731 968-0151
7821 National Service Rd 1 Greensboro (27409) *(G-5909)*

Volvo Logistics North America Inc.........................336 393-4746
7900 National Service Rd Greensboro (27409) *(G-5910)*

Volvo Motor Graders Inc....................................704 609-3604
8844 Mount Holly Rd Charlotte (28214) *(G-2990)*

Volvo Trucks North America, Greensboro *Also Called: Volvo Group North America LLC*
(G-5906)

Volvo Trucks North America Inc (DH)........................336 393-2000
7900 National Service Rd Greensboro (27409) *(G-5911)*

Volvo Trucks Uptime Center, Greensboro *Also Called: Volvo Group North America LLC*
(G-5907)

Vontier, Raleigh *Also Called: Vontier Corporation (G-10594)*

Vontier Corporation (PA)...................................984 275-6000
5438 Wade Park Blvd Ste 601 Raleigh (27607) *(G-10594)*

Vortant Technologies LLC...................................828 645-1026
88 High Country Rd Weaverville (28787) *(G-12506)*

Vortex, Raleigh *Also Called: Vortex-Cyclone Technologies (G-10595)*

Vortex Aquatic Structures USA, Cornelius *Also Called: Vortex USA Inc (G-3629)*

Vortex USA Inc...972 410-3619
11024 Bailey Rd Ste C Cornelius (28031) *(G-3629)*

Vortex-Cyclone Technologies................................919 225-1724
4400 Blossom Hill Ct Raleigh (27613) *(G-10595)*

Vote Owl LLC...919 264-1796
932 Stone Falls Trl Raleigh (27614) *(G-10596)*

Vpc Foam USA Inc...336 626-4595
2206 Dumont St Asheboro (27203) *(G-418)*

Vpc Foam USA Inc (PA)......................................704 622-0552
1820 Evans St Ne Conover (28613) *(G-3572)*

Vpm Liquidating Inc..336 292-1781
2110 W Gate City Blvd Greensboro (27403) *(G-5912)*

Vrg Components Inc...980 244-3862
2020 Independence Commerce Dr Ste G Matthews (28105) *(G-8156)*

Vrush Industries Inc.......................................336 886-7700
118 N Wrenn St High Point (27260) *(G-6829)*

VT Hackney Inc...252 946-6521
400 Hackney Ave Washington (27889) *(G-12419)*

VT Leeboy Inc..704 966-3300
500 Lincoln County Parkway Ext Lincolnton (28092) *(G-7869)*

Vtv Therapeutics, High Point *Also Called: Transtech Pharma LLC (G-6810)*

Vtv Therapeutics LLC.......................................336 841-0300
3980 Premier Dr Ste 310 High Point (27265) *(G-6830)*

Vulcan Construction Mtls LLC...............................336 767-1201
3651 Penn Ave Winston Salem (27105) *(G-13384)*

Vulcan Construction Mtls LLC...............................336 767-0911
4401 N Patterson Ave Winston Salem (27105) *(G-13385)*

Vulcan Materials Company...................................828 963-7100
3869 Nc Highway 105 S Boone (28607) *(G-950)*

Vulcan Materials Company...................................704 549-1540
11020 David Taylor Dr Ste 105 Charlotte (28262) *(G-2991)*

Vulcan Materials Company...................................704 545-5687
11435 Brooks Mill Rd Charlotte (28227) *(G-2992)*

Vulcan Materials Company...................................828 692-0039
2284 Clear Creek Rd Hendersonville (28792) *(G-6248)*

Vulcan Materials Company...................................336 869-2148
2874 Nc Highway 66 S Kernersville (27284) *(G-7313)*

Vulcraft Carrier Corp......................................704 367-8674
2100 Rexford Rd Charlotte (28211) *(G-2993)*

Vwgc, Mills River *Also Called: Van Wingerden Grnhse Co Inc (G-8323)*

Vx Aerospace Corporation...................................828 433-5353
2080 Us 70 E Morganton (28655) *(G-8910)*

Vx Aerospace Holdings Inc..................................828 433-5353
2080 Us 70 E Morganton (28655) *(G-8911)*

Vyse Gelatin LLC...919 238-3300
598 Airport Blvd Ste 900 Morrisville (27560) *(G-9087)*

W & S Frame Company Inc....................................828 728-6078
4833 J M Craig Rd Granite Falls (28630) *(G-5325)*

W & T Logging LLC..252 209-4351
118 Conner Ln Windsor (27983) *(G-13059)*

W & W Electric Motor Shop Inc..............................910 642-2369
5240 James B White Hwy N Whiteville (28472) *(G-12594)*

W A Brown & Son Incorporated (PA)..........................704 636-5131
209 Long Meadow Dr Salisbury (28147) *(G-11134)*

W and W Truss Builders Inc.................................252 792-1051
424 Railroad St Williamston (27892) *(G-12677)*

W B Mason Co Inc...888 926-2766
10800 Withers Cove Park Dr Charlotte (28278) *(G-2994)*

W D Lee & Company..704 864-0346
212 Trakas Blvd Gastonia (28052) *(G-5163)*

W E Nixons Wldg & Hdwr Inc.................................252 221-4348
3036 Rocky Hock Rd Edenton (27932) *(G-4373)*

W F Harris Lighting Inc....................................704 283-7477
4015 Airport Extension Rd Monroe (28110) *(G-8577)*

W F N Z Radio Station, Charlotte *Also Called: CBS Radio Holdings Inc (G-1870)*

W G Cannon Paint Co Inc (PA)...............................828 754-5376
1015 Zacks Fork Rd Lenoir (28645) *(G-7644)*

W G of Southwest Raleigh Inc...............................919 629-7327
413 Redhill Rd Holly Springs (27540) *(G-6919)*

W H Bunting Thinning.......................................252 826-4025
2305 Bynums Bridge Rd Scotland Neck (27874) *(G-11267)*

W H Rgers Shtmtl Ir Wrks Inc...............................704 394-2191
837 Toddville Rd Charlotte (28214) *(G-2995)*

W M Cramer Lumber Co (PA)..................................828 397-7481
3486 Texs Fish Camp Rd Connelly Springs (28612) *(G-3485)*

W M Plastics Inc...704 599-0511
5301 Terminal St Charlotte (28208) *(G-2996)*

W N C Pallet Forest Pdts Inc...............................828 667-5426
1414 Smoky Park Hwy Candler (28715) *(G-1235)*

W R Long Inc...252 823-4570
1607 Cedar St Tarboro (27886) *(G-11946)*

W R Rayson Export Ltd......................................910 686-5802
720 S Dickerson St Burgaw (28425) *(G-1036)*

W R White Inc..252 794-6577
152 W Askewville St Windsor (27983) *(G-13060)*

W T Humphrey Inc (PA)......................................910 455-3555
2423 N Marine Blvd Jacksonville (28546) *(G-7158)*

W T Mander & Son Inc.......................................336 562-5755
1587 Egypt Rd Prospect Hill (27314) *(G-9830)*

W V Doyle Enterprises Inc..................................336 885-2035
1816 Belmar St High Point (27260) *(G-6831)*

W&W-Afco Steel LLC...336 993-2680
9035 W Market St Colfax (27235) *(G-3293)*

W&W-Afco Steel LLC...336 275-9711
101 Centreport Dr Ste 400 Greensboro (27409) *(G-5913)*

W&W-Afco Steel LLC...252 459-7116
341 Corbett Rd Nashville (27856) *(G-9325)*

Waddington Group Inc (DH)..................................800 845-6051
3436 Toringdon Way Ste 100 Charlotte (28277) *(G-2997)*

Waddington North America Inc (DH)..........................800 845-6051
3436 Toringdon Way Ste 100 Charlotte (28277) *(G-2998)*

Wade Biggs Logging Inc.....................................252 927-4470
2173 Biggs Rd Pinetown (27865) *(G-9711)*

Wade Manufacturing Company (PA)............................704 694-2131
76 Mill St Wadesboro (28170) *(G-12252)*

Wager, Rural Hall *Also Called: Robert H Wager Company Inc (G-10966)*

Waggoner Manufacturing Co..................................704 278-2000
1065 Hall Rd Mount Ulla (28125) *(G-9272)*

Wainwright Warehouse.......................................252 237-5121
2427 Us Highway 301 S Wilson (27893) *(G-13043)*

Wake Cross Roads Express LLC...............................919 266-7966
3501 Forestville Rd Raleigh (27616) *(G-10597)*

Wake Forest Gazette..919 556-3409
1255 S Main St Wake Forest (27587) *(G-12313)*

Wake Monument Company Inc (PA)........................919 556-3422
213 N Main St Rolesville (27571) *(G-10891)*

Wake Stone Corp..252 985-4411
7379 N Halifax Rd Battleboro (27809) *(G-708)*

Wake Stone Corporation..919 677-0050
222 Star Ln Cary (27513) *(G-1481)*

Wake Stone Corporation (PA)...............................919 266-1100
6821 Knightdale Blvd Knightdale (27545) *(G-7462)*

Wake Stone Corporation..919 775-7349
9725 Stone Quarry Rd Moncure (27559) *(G-8412)*

Wake Supply Company..252 234-6012
3200 Turnage Rd Wilson (27893) *(G-13044)*

Wakefield Solutions, Raleigh *Also Called: Simon Industries Inc (G-10477)*

Walco International..704 624-2473
531 E Main St Ste B Marshville (28103) *(G-8097)*

Waldensian Style Wines, Durham *Also Called: Drink A Bull LLC (G-4008)*

Waldenwood Group Inc...704 313-8004
3800 Woodpark Blvd Ste I Charlotte (28206) *(G-2999)*

Waldenwood Group LLC.......................................704 331-8004
3800 Woodpark Blvd Ste I Charlotte (28206) *(G-3000)*

Walex Products Company Inc (PA).........................910 371-2242
1949 Popular St Leland (28451) *(G-7564)*

Walgreen Co...704 525-2628
2215 W Arrowood Rd Charlotte (28217) *(G-3001)*

Walgreens, Charlotte *Also Called: Walgreen Co (G-3001)*

Walker and Associates Inc (DH)............................336 731-6391
110 Business Park Dr Winston Salem (27107) *(G-13386)*

Walker Draperies Inc...919 220-1424
2503 Broad St Durham (27704) *(G-4301)*

Walker Pallet Company Inc....................................910 259-2235
3802 New Savannah Rd Burgaw (28425) *(G-1037)*

Walker Street LLC..919 880-3959
104 Birchland Dr Fuquay Varina (27526) *(G-4905)*

Walker Woodworking Inc (PA)...............................704 434-0823
112 N Lafayette St Shelby (28150) *(G-11390)*

Walker's, Durham *Also Called: Walker Draperies Inc (G-4301)*

Wall-Lenk Corporation...252 527-4186
1950 Dr Martin Luther King Jr Blvd Kinston (28501) *(G-7435)*

Wallace Printing Inc..828 466-3300
2032 Fairgrove Church Rd Newton (28658) *(G-9509)*

Wallace Welding Inc..919 934-2488
403 W Market St Smithfield (27577) *(G-11469)*

Wallingford Coffee Mills Inc (PA)..........................513 771-3131
300 Concord Pkwy S Concord (28027) *(G-3466)*

Walls Welding...919 201-7544
212 Oak St Creedmoor (27522) *(G-3657)*

Walnut Cove Furniture Inc.....................................336 591-8008
4730 Nc 89 Hwy E Walnut Cove (27052) *(G-12331)*

Walter Kidde Portable Eqp Inc (HQ).......................919 563-5911
1016 Corporate Park Dr Mebane (27302) *(G-8263)*

Walter Printing Company Inc.................................704 982-8899
130 Anderson Rd Albemarle (28001) *(G-96)*

Walter Reynolds (PA)...704 735-6050
216 Old Lincolnton Crouse Rd Lincolnton (28092) *(G-7870)*

Walter Tape & Label Co, Albemarle *Also Called: Walter Printing Company Inc (G-96)*

Walton Lumber Co...919 563-6565
302 Circle Dr Mebane (27302) *(G-8264)*

Waltons Distillery Inc..910 347-7770
261 Ben Williams Rd Jacksonville (28540) *(G-7159)*

Wambam Fence Inc..877 778-5733
6935 Reames Rd Ste K Charlotte (28216) *(G-3002)*

Wanchese Dock and Haul LLC...............................252 473-6424
593 Baumtown Rd Wanchese (27981) *(G-12347)*

Wanda Nickel..828 265-3246
6764 Old 421 S Deep Gap (28618) *(G-3731)*

Wandfluh of America Inc.......................................847 566-5700
8200 Arrowridge Blvd Charlotte (28273) *(G-3003)*

Wangs and Thangs LLC..980 925-7010
2309 Penny Park Dr Apt D Gastonia (28052) *(G-5164)*

Wanzl North America, Newton *Also Called: Technibilt Ltd (G-9502)*

War Horse News Inc..910 430-0868
8404 Richlands Hwy Richlands (28574) *(G-10722)*

War Sport LLC..910 948-2237
13117 Nc Highway 24 27 Eagle Springs (27242) *(G-4320)*

Ward Vessel and Exchanger Corp (PA)....................704 568-3001
6835 E W T Harris Blvd Charlotte (28215) *(G-3004)*

Ward's Grocery, Raleigh *Also Called: Kol Incorporated (G-10240)*

Warehouse Distillery LLC......................................828 464-5183
2628 Northwest Blvd Newton (28658) *(G-9510)*

Warehouse Facility, Gastonia *Also Called: Industrial Elcpltg Co Inc (G-5063)*

Warm Industrial Nonwovens, Hendersonville *Also Called: Warm Products Inc (G-6249)*

Warm Products Inc..425 248-2424
581 Old Sunset Hill Rd Hendersonville (28792) *(G-6249)*

Warmack Lumber Co Inc.......................................252 638-1435
321 E Sunset Blvd Cove City (28523) *(G-3632)*

Warp Technologies Inc...919 552-2311
601 Irving Pkwy Holly Springs (27540) *(G-6920)*

Warren Oil Company LLC (PA)..............................910 892-6456
2340 Us 301 N Dunn (28334) *(G-3871)*

Warren Plastics Inc...704 827-9887
511 Rankin Ave Mount Holly (28120) *(G-9245)*

Warren Record, The, Warrenton *Also Called: Womack Publishing Co Inc (G-12356)*

Warrior Boats...336 885-2628
2100 E Martin Luther King Jr Dr High Point (27260) *(G-6832)*

Warsaw Welding Service Inc..................................910 293-4261
824 N Pine St Warsaw (28398) *(G-12368)*

Washington Alloy, Lowell *Also Called: U S Alloy Co (G-7935)*

Washington Cabinet Company................................252 946-3457
4799 Voa Rd Washington (27889) *(G-12420)*

Washington Crab, Washington *Also Called: Carolina Catch Inc (G-12377)*

Washington Daily News, Washington *Also Called: Washington News Publishing Co (G-12421)*

Washington News Publishing Co............................252 946-2144
217 N Market St Washington (27889) *(G-12421)*

Waste Container Repair Svcs.................................910 257-4474
2405 Wilmington Hwy Fayetteville (28306) *(G-4696)*

Waste Container Services LLC...............................910 257-4474
705 W Mountain Dr Fayetteville (28306) *(G-4697)*

Waste Industries Usa LLC (DH).............................919 325-3000
3301 Benson Dr Ste 601 Raleigh (27609) *(G-10598)*

Waste Smasher, Winston Salem *Also Called: Trash Masher LLC (G-13368)*

Waste Water Treatment Plant, Cherokee *Also Called: Eastern Band Cherokee Indians (G-3053)*

Wastequip..800 255-4126
841 Meacham Rd Statesville (28677) *(G-11798)*

Wastequip, Charlotte *Also Called: Wastequip LLC (G-3005)*

Wastequip LLC (DH)..704 366-7140
6525 Carnegie Blvd Ste 300 Charlotte (28211) *(G-3005)*

Wastequip Manufacturing Co LLC (DH)....................704 366-7140
6525 Carnegie Blvd Ste 300 Charlotte (28211) *(G-3006)*

Wastezero Inc (PA)...919 322-1208
8396 Six Forks Rd Ste 103 Raleigh (27615) *(G-10599)*

Watauga County Country Hams, Boone *Also Called: Goodnight Brothers Prod Co Inc (G-918)*

Watauga Creek LLC...828 369-7881
25 Setser Branch Rd Franklin (28734) *(G-4842)*

Watauga Opportunities Inc (PA).............................828 264-5009
642 Greenway Rd Boone (28607) *(G-951)*

Watauga Ready Mix, Crumpler *Also Called: Chandler Concrete Inc (G-3660)*

Watauga Ready Mixed..336 246-6441
525 George Wilson Rd Boone (28607) *(G-952)*

Water Tech Solutions Inc......................................704 408-8391
178 Cayuga Dr Mooresville (28117) *(G-8794)*

Water Treatment Department, Waynesville *Also Called: Town of Waynesville (G-12478)*

Water-Gen Inc..888 492-8370
10709 Granite St Charlotte (28273) *(G-3007)*

Water-Jel Technologies, Huntersville *Also Called: Project Bean LLC (G-7040)*

Water-Revolution LLC..336 525-1015
2246 Nc Highway 62 N Blanch (27212) *(G-879)*

Watergen Americas, Charlotte *Also Called: Water-Gen Inc (G-3007)*

Waterline Systems Inc..910 708-1000
270 Hogans Rd Hubert (28539) *(G-6937)*

Waterplant, Tarboro *Also Called: Town of Tarboro (G-11944)*

Waters Brothers Contrs Inc...................................252 446-7141
511 Instrument Dr Rocky Mount (27804) *(G-10874)*

A
L
P
H
A
B
E
T
I
C

Waters Corporation.. 910 270-3137
15430 Us Highway 17 Hampstead (28443) *(G-6080)*

Waterwheel Factory.. 828 369-5928
320 Arbor Ln Franklin (28734) *(G-4843)*

Watkins Agency Inc.. 704 213-6997
721 N Long St Salisbury (28144) *(G-11135)*

Watkins Cabinets LLC.. 704 634-1724
1418 Industrial Dr Matthews (28105) *(G-8157)*

Watkins Fitness & Sports Eqp, Salisbury *Also Called: Watkins Agency Inc (G-11135)*

Watson Concrete Pipe Company............................. 828 754-6476
2532 Morganton Blvd Sw Lenoir (28645) *(G-7645)*

Watson Electrical Cnstr Co LLC............................ 252 756-4550
3121 Bismarck St Greenville (27834) *(G-6033)*

Watson Metals Co.. 336 366-4500
2693 Poplar Springs Rd State Road (28676) *(G-11640)*

Watson Party Tables Inc (PA).................................. 919 294-9153
2455 S Alston Ave Durham (27713) *(G-4302)*

Watson Steel & Iron Works LLC.............................. 704 821-7140
3624 Gribble Rd Matthews (28104) *(G-8197)*

Watson Wood Works, Winston Salem *Also Called: J & P Wood Works Inc (G-13211)*

Watts Bumgarner & Brown Inc................................ 828 632-4797
9541 Us Highway 64 90 W Taylorsville (28681) *(G-11986)*

Watts Drainage Products Inc.................................. 828 288-2179
100 Watts Rd Spindale (28160) *(G-11549)*

Watts Regulator Co.. 828 286-4151
100 Watts Rd Spindale (28160) *(G-11550)*

Wave Front Computers LLC...................................... 919 896-6121
8015 Creedmoor Rd Ste 201 Raleigh (27613) *(G-10600)*

Wave Front Studios, Raleigh *Also Called: Wave Front Computers LLC (G-10600)*

WaveTherm Corporation.. 919 307-8071
5995 Chapel Hill Rd Ste 119 Raleigh (27607) *(G-10601)*

Waxhaw Cabinet Company, Waxhaw *Also Called: Black Mountain Cnstr Group Inc (G-12424)*

Waxhaw Candle Company LLC.................................. 980 245-2827
9830 Rea Rd Ste G Charlotte (28277) *(G-3008)*

Waxhaw Creamery LLC.. 704 843-7927
109 E North Main St Waxhaw (28173) *(G-12449)*

Wayne Farms, Dobson *Also Called: Wayne Farms LLC (G-3827)*

Wayne Farms, Elkin *Also Called: Wayne Farms LLC (G-4454)*

Wayne Farms LLC.. 336 386-8151
802 E Atkins St Dobson (27017) *(G-3827)*

Wayne Farms LLC.. 336 366-4413
10949 Nc 268 Elkin (28621) *(G-4454)*

Wayne Farms LLC.. 770 538-2120
332 E A St Newton (28658) *(G-9511)*

Wayne Industries Inc.. 336 434-5017
4107 Cheyenne Dr Archdale (27263) *(G-246)*

Wayne Printing Company Inc.................................. 919 778-2211
310 N Berkeley Blvd Goldsboro (27534) *(G-5252)*

Wayne Trademark International, Asheboro *Also Called: Wayne Trademark Prtg Packg LLC (G-419)*

Wayne Trademark Prtg Packg LLC.......................... 800 327-1290
5346 Nc Highway 49 S Asheboro (27205) *(G-419)*

Waynesville Soda Jerks, Waynesville *Also Called: Waynesville Soda Jerks LLC (G-12479)*

Waynesville Soda Jerks LLC.................................... 828 278-8589
35 Bridges St Waynesville (28786) *(G-12479)*

WB Embroidery Inc.. 828 432-0076
3076 Nc 18 S Morganton (28655) *(G-8912)*

WB Frames Inc.. 828 459-2147
3771 Sandy Ford Rd Hickory (28602) *(G-6488)*

WC&r Interests LLC.. 828 684-9848
145 Cane Creek Industrial Park Rd Ste 100 Fletcher (28732) *(G-4777)*

Wcc Television, Charlotte *Also Called: Bahakel Communications Ltd LLC (G-1740)*

Wdm Inc.. 704 283-7508
608 Broome St Monroe (28110) *(G-8578)*

We Appit LLC.. 910 465-2722
1319 Military Cutoff Rd Ste 184 Wilmington (28405) *(G-12946)*

We Pharma Inc.. 919 389-1478
951 Aviation Pkwy Ste 200 Morrisville (27560) *(G-9088)*

We Print T-Shirts Inc.. 910 822-8337
2598 Raeford Rd Fayetteville (28305) *(G-4698)*

Weapon Works LLC (PA).. 800 556-9498
1110 Vaughn Rd Burlington (27217) *(G-1176)*

Weapon Works LLC.. 800 556-9498
1433 University Dr Ste 102 Burlington (27215) *(G-1177)*

Wear-Flex Slings, Winston Salem *Also Called: MHS Ltd (G-13250)*

Wear-Flex Slings, Winston Salem *Also Called: MHS Ltd (G-13251)*

Weathers Machine Mfg Inc...................................... 919 552-5945
9535 Us 401 N Fuquay Varina (27526) *(G-4906)*

Weathersby Guild Louisville, Charlotte *Also Called: Freedom Enterprise LLC (G-2177)*

Weathervane Winery Inc.. 336 793-3366
1452 Welcome Arcadia Rd Lexington (27295) *(G-7757)*

Weavexx LLC.. 919 556-7235
8521 Six Forks Rd Raleigh (27615) *(G-10602)*

Web 4 Half LLC.. 855 762-4638
1301 Carolina St Ste 125a Greensboro (27401) *(G-5914)*

Web-Don, Charlotte *Also Called: Web-Don Incorporated (G-3009)*

Web-Don Incorporated (PA).................................... 800 532-0434
1400 Ameron Dr Charlotte (28206) *(G-3009)*

Webassign, Raleigh *Also Called: Cengage Learning Inc (G-9990)*

Webb S Maint & Piping Inc...................................... 252 972-2616
217 Daniels Ave Battleboro (27809) *(G-709)*

Webbs Logistics LLC.. 919 591-4308
111 Saint Marys St Garner (27529) *(G-4972)*

Weber and Weber Inc.. 336 889-6322
117 W Lexington Ave High Point (27262) *(G-6833)*

Weber and Weber Inc (PA)...................................... 336 722-4109
1011 Burke St Winston Salem (27101) *(G-13387)*

Weber Screwdriving Systems Inc............................ 704 360-5820
149 Knob Hill Rd Mooresville (28117) *(G-8795)*

Weber Stephen Products LLC.................................. 704 662-0335
200 Overhill Dr Mooresville (28117) *(G-8796)*

Webster Entps Jackson Cnty Inc............................ 828 586-8981
140 Little Savannah Rd Sylva (28779) *(G-11904)*

Webster Fine Art Limited (PA)................................ 919 349-8455
2800 Perimeter Park Dr Ste A Morrisville (27560) *(G-9089)*

Wede Corporation.. 704 864-1313
133 Industrial Dr Kings Mountain (28086) *(G-7390)*

Wedeco, Charlotte *Also Called: Xylem Water Solutions USA Inc (G-3037)*

Wedeco Uv Technologies Inc.................................. 704 716-7600
4828 Parkway Plaza Blvd Ste 200 Charlotte (28217) *(G-3010)*

Wedge Brewing Co.. 828 505-2792
125b Roberts St Asheville (28801) *(G-632)*

Wedpics.. 919 699-5676
6413 Rushingbrook Dr Raleigh (27612) *(G-10603)*

Weener Plastics Inc.. 252 206-1400
2201 Stantonsburg Rd Se Wilson (27893) *(G-13045)*

Weeping Radish Farm Brewry LLC.......................... 252 491-5205
6810 Caratoke Hwy Grandy (27939) *(G-5291)*

Weidenmiller Co.. 630 250-2500
1010 Burma Dr Apex (27539) *(G-206)*

Weiss USA LLC.. 704 282-4496
2213 Stafford Street Ext Monroe (28110) *(G-8579)*

Weissmann Travel Reports, Winston Salem *Also Called: Northstar Travel Media (G-13266)*

Welbuilt Homes Inc.. 910 323-0098
2311 Clinton Rd Fayetteville (28312) *(G-4699)*

Welcome Industrial Corp.. 336 329-9640
717 N Park Ave Burlington (27217) *(G-1178)*

Welding Company.. 336 667-0265
646 Old Us 421 Rd Wilkesboro (28697) *(G-12662)*

Welding Shop LLC.. 252 982-6567
102 Cb Daniels Sr Rd Wanchese (27981) *(G-12348)*

Welding Solutions LLC.. 828 665-4363
3632 Butler Bridge Rd Fletcher (28732) *(G-4778)*

Welding Spc & Mech Svcs Inc................................ 919 662-7898
555 Dynamic Dr Garner (27529) *(G-4973)*

Welding Specialties & Mech Svc, Garner *Also Called: Welding Spc & Mech Svcs Inc (G-4973)*

Weldon Mills Distillery, Weldon *Also Called: Weldon Mills Distillery LLC (G-12527)*

Weldon Mills Distillery LLC (PA)............................ 252 220-4235
200 Rock Fish Dr Weldon (27890) *(G-12527)*

Weldon Steel Corporation.. 252 536-2113
101 Kennametal Dr Weldon (27890) *(G-12528)*

Well Doctor LLC.. 704 909-9258
9607 Autumn Applause Dr Charlotte (28277) *(G-3011)*

Well-Bean Coffee & Crumbs LLC......................... 833 777-2326
4154 Shearon Farms Ave Ste 106 Wake Forest (27587) *(G-12314)*

Well-Bean Coffee Company, Wake Forest Also Called: Well-Bean Coffee & Crumbs LLC *(G-12314)*

Wellco Two Inc.. 828 667-4662
1835 Old Haywood Rd Asheville (28806) *(G-633)*

Wellness Robotronic Industries, Nebo Also Called: RDM Industrial Electronics Inc *(G-9329)*

Welloyt Enterprises Inc................................... 919 821-7897
221 W Martin St Raleigh (27601) *(G-10604)*

Wells Hosiery Mills Inc (PA)........................... 336 633-4881
1758 S Fayetteville St Asheboro (27205) *(G-420)*

Wells Jnkins Wells Mt Proc Inc....................... 828 245-5544
145 Rollins Rd Forest City (28043) *(G-4800)*

Wells Mechanical Services LLC....................... 252 532-2632
628 Raleigh Dr Roanoke Rapids (27870) *(G-10743)*

Wells Pork and Beef Pdts Inc.......................... 910 259-2523
750 Croomsbridge Rd Burgaw (28425) *(G-1038)*

Welsh Cstm Sltting Rwnding LLC..................... 336 665-6481
200 Citation Ct Greensboro (27409) *(G-5915)*

Welsh Paper Company, Youngsville Also Called: Franklin Logistical Services Inc *(G-13472)*

Wen Bray Heating & AC.................................. 828 267-0635
6034 Norcross Ln Hickory (28601) *(G-6489)*

Wendy Bs Cstm EMB Screen Prtg, Morganton Also Called: WB Embroidery Inc *(G-8912)*

Wendys Embrdred Spc Screen Prt..................... 704 982-5978
308 Concord Rd Albemarle (28001) *(G-97)*

Wenker Inc (PA).. 704 333-7790
112 S Tryon St Ste 1130 Charlotte (28284) *(G-3012)*

Wentworth Corporation................................... 336 548-1802
301 K Fork Rd Madison (27025) *(G-8003)*

Wep Clinical, Morrisville Also Called: We Pharma Inc *(G-9088)*

Wepak Corporation... 704 334-5781
601 Gulf Dr Charlotte (28208) *(G-3013)*

Wersunsllc.. 857 209-8701
615 Saint George Square Ct Ste 300 Winston Salem (27103) *(G-13388)*

Weslacova Corp... 336 838-2614
2070 River Rd Liberty Grove Rd North Wilkesboro (28659) *(G-9552)*

Wesley Hall Inc... 828 324-7466
141 Fairgrove Church Rd Se Conover (28613) *(G-3573)*

West & Associates of NC................................ 919 479-5680
4502b Bennett Memorial Rd Durham (27705) *(G-4303)*

West Dynamics Us Inc.................................... 704 735-0009
1443 E Gaston St Lincolnton (28092) *(G-7871)*

West Express... 704 276-9001
4472 W Highway 27 Vale (28168) *(G-12211)*

West Fraser Inc... 252 589-2011
4400 Nc Hwy 186 Seaboard (27876) *(G-11272)*

West Hllcrest Dda Group HM LLC..................... 336 478-7444
925 S Church St Burlington (27215) *(G-1179)*

West Jefferson Service, Creedmoor Also Called: Southern States Coop Inc *(G-3654)*

West Pharmaceutical Svcs Inc.......................... 252 522-8956
1028 Innovation Way Kinston (28504) *(G-7436)*

West Side Industries LLC................................ 980 223-8665
124 Hatfield Rd Statesville (28625) *(G-11799)*

West Side Prcsion Mch Pdts Inc....................... 908 647-4903
124 Hatfield Rd Statesville (28625) *(G-11800)*

West Stanly Fabrication Inc............................. 704 254-2967
16431 Sr 24/27 Oakboro (28129) *(G-9585)*

West Stkes Wldcat Grdron CLB I...................... 336 985-6152
321 Logan Ct King (27021) *(G-7339)*

Westbend Vineyards Inc.................................. 336 768-7520
599 S Stratford Rd Winston Salem (27103) *(G-13389)*

Westek, Monroe Also Called: Safe Fire Detection Inc *(G-8554)*

Western Anmal Dsase Dgnstc Lab, Arden Also Called: North Carolina Department of A *(G-289)*

Western Crlina Cstm Cswork Inc....................... 828 669-0459
2952 Us 70 Hwy Black Mountain (28711) *(G-872)*

Western Crlina Tl Mold Corp In........................ 828 890-4448
3 Brandy Branch Rd Mills River (28759) *(G-8324)*

Western Roto Engravers Incorporated (PA).......... 336 275-9821
533 Banner Ave Greensboro (27401) *(G-5916)*

Westlift, Goldsboro Also Called: Westlift LLC *(G-5253)*

Westlift LLC.. 919 242-4379
186 Belfast Rd Goldsboro (27530) *(G-5253)*

Westmoreland Printers Inc............................... 704 482-9100
2020 E Dixon Blvd Shelby (28152) *(G-11391)*

Westpoint Home Inc....................................... 910 369-2231
19320 Airbase Rd Wagram (28396) *(G-12257)*

Westrock, Lexington Also Called: Wrkco Inc *(G-7758)*

Westrock - Southern Cont LLC......................... 704 662-8496
279 Mooresville Blvd Mooresville (28115) *(G-8797)*

Westrock Company... 470 484-1183
2690 Kelly Blvd Claremont (28610) *(G-3124)*

Westrock Company... 828 248-4815
376 Pine Street Ext Forest City (28043) *(G-4801)*

Westrock Company... 919 861-8760
7605b Welborn St Raleigh (27615) *(G-10605)*

Westrock Company... 770 448-2193
8080 N Point Blvd Winston Salem (27106) *(G-13390)*

Westrock Converting LLC................................ 828 245-9871
376 Pine St Forest City (28043) *(G-4802)*

Westrock Converting LLC................................ 336 661-6736
5950 Grassy Creek Blvd Winston Salem (27105) *(G-13391)*

Westrock Converting LLC................................ 336 661-1700
5900 Grassy Creek Blvd Winston Salem (27105) *(G-13392)*

Westrock Kraft Paper LLC............................... 252 533-6000
100 Gaston Rd Roanoke Rapids (27870) *(G-10744)*

Westrock Merchandising Disp, Winston Salem Also Called: Westrock Rkt LLC *(G-13393)*

Westrock Merchandising Display, Rural Hall Also Called: Westrock Shared Services LLC *(G-10968)*

Westrock Mwv LLC.. 919 334-3200
1021 Main Campus Dr Raleigh (27606) *(G-10606)*

Westrock Paper and Packg LLC........................ 919 463-3100
5150 Mccrimmon Pkwy Morrisville (27560) *(G-9090)*

Westrock Paper and Packg LLC........................ 252 533-6000
100 Gaston Rd Roanoke Rapids (27870) *(G-10745)*

Westrock Rkt LLC.. 828 459-8006
2690 Kelly Blvd Claremont (28610) *(G-3125)*

Westrock Rkt LLC.. 828 464-5560
214 Conover Blvd E Conover (28613) *(G-3574)*

Westrock Rkt LLC.. 828 655-1303
468 Carolina Ave Marion (28752) *(G-8072)*

Westrock Rkt LLC.. 770 448-2193
1659 E Court St Marion (28752) *(G-8073)*

Westrock Rkt LLC.. 704 662-8494
279 Mooresville Blvd Mooresville (28115) *(G-8798)*

Westrock Rkt LLC.. 336 661-1700
5930 Grassy Creek Blvd Winston Salem (27105) *(G-13393)*

Westrock Rkt LLC.. 336 661-7180
5900a Grassy Creek Blvd Winston Salem (27105) *(G-13394)*

Westrock Shared Services LLC......................... 336 642-4165
520 Northridge Park Dr Rural Hall (27045) *(G-10968)*

Weststar, Cary Also Called: Weststar Precision Inc *(G-1482)*

Weststar Precision Inc.................................... 919 557-2820
101 Fern Bluff Way Cary (27518) *(G-1482)*

Westwood Manufacturing Inc............................ 910 862-9992
370 Ben Green Industrial Park Rd Elizabethtown (28337) *(G-4437)*

Westwood Robotic Technology, Elizabethtown Also Called: Westwood Manufacturing Inc *(G-4437)*

Wet Dog Glass LLC.. 910 428-4111
100 Russell Dr Star (27356) *(G-11635)*

Wetherington Logging Inc................................ 252 393-8435
245 Walters Ln Stella (28582) *(G-11809)*

Wewoka Gas Producers LLC............................ 704 844-8990
10600 Nations Ford Rd Charlotte (28273) *(G-3014)*

Weyerhaeuser, Vanceboro Also Called: Weyerhaeuser New Bern *(G-12224)*

Weyerhaeuser Co.. 828 464-3841
1525 Mount Olive Church Rd Newton (28658) *(G-9512)*

Weyerhaeuser Company.................................. 253 924-2345
10601 Westlake Dr Charlotte (28273) *(G-3015)*

Weyerhaeuser Company.................................. 336 835-5100
184 Gentry Rd Elkin (28621) *(G-4455)*

Weyerhaeuser Company.................................. 252 746-7200
371 E Hanrahan Rd Grifton (28530) *(G-6039)*

A
L
P
H
A
B
E
T
I
C

Weyerhaeuser Company.. 252 791-3200
　1000 Nc Highway 149 N Plymouth (27962) *(G-9808)*

Weyerhaeuser Company.. 252 633-7100
　1785 Weyerhaeuser Rd Vanceboro (28586) *(G-12223)*

Weyerhaeuser New Bern.. 252 633-7100
　1785 Weyerhaeuser Rd Vanceboro (28586) *(G-12224)*

Weyerhaeuser Nr Company.. 252 633-7100
　1482 Weyerhaeuser Rd Vanceboro (28586) *(G-12225)*

Whaley Foodservice LLC.. 704 529-6242
　8334 Arrowridge Blvd Ste K Charlotte (28273) *(G-3016)*

Whatever You Need Screen Print...................................... 704 287-8603
　531 Brightleaf Pl Nw Concord (28027) *(G-3467)*

Whats Your Sign LLC.. 919 274-5703
　720 Sawmill Rd Raleigh (27615) *(G-10607)*

Whatz Cookin LLC.. 336 353-0227
　123 Old Brintle St Mount Airy (27030) *(G-9193)*

Wheaton Plastic Operations, Youngsville *Also Called: Amcor Phrm Packg USA LLC*
(G-13461)

Wheatstone Corporation (PA)...252 638-7000
　600 Indl Dr New Bern (28562) *(G-9405)*

Wheel Pros LLC.. 336 851-6705
　2606 Phoenix Dr Ste 804 Greensboro (27406) *(G-5917)*

Wheeler Industries, Pikeville *Also Called: Wheeler Industries Inc (G-9669)*

Wheeler Industries Inc.. 919 736-4256
　4573 Us Highway 117 N Pikeville (27863) *(G-9669)*

Whi Sand & Gravel, Fayetteville *Also Called: Welbuilt Homes Inc (G-4699)*

Whimsical Prints Paper & Gifts.. 919 544-8491
　5826 Fayetteville Rd Ste 105 Durham (27713) *(G-4304)*

Whippoorwill Hills Inc.. 252 537-2765
　1509 E 10th St Roanoke Rapids (27870) *(G-10746)*

Whisper Soft Mills, Hampstead *Also Called: Babine Lake Corporation (G-6069)*

Whispering Willow, Denver *Also Called: Whispering Willow Soap Co LLC (G-3816)*

Whispering Willow Soap Co LLC...................................... 828 455-0322
　5851 Balsom Ridge Rd Ste B Denver (28037) *(G-3816)*

Whistle Stop Press Inc.. 910 695-1403
　175 Davis St Southern Pines (28387) *(G-11514)*

Whitaker Mill Works LLC.. 919 772-3030
　3801 Beryl Rd Raleigh (27607) *(G-10608)*

Whitaker S Tire Service Inc.. 704 786-6174
　530 Concord Pkwy N Concord (28027) *(G-3468)*

Whitakers Tire & Wheel Service, Concord *Also Called: Whitaker S Tire Service Inc (G-3468)*

White Cap LP.. 704 921-4420
　5900 W Wt Harris Blvd Charlotte (28269) *(G-3017)*

White Knght Engneered Pdts Inc...................................... 828 687-0940
　9 Sw Pack Sq Ste 201 Asheville (28801) *(G-634)*

White Knight Engineered Products, Inc., Asheville *Also Called: White Knght Engneered Pdts Inc (G-634)*

White Oak, Spindale *Also Called: White Oak Carpet Mills Inc (G-11551)*

White Oak Carpet Mills Inc.. 828 287-8892
　1553 Old Ballpark Rd Spindale (28160) *(G-11551)*

White Packing Co Inc -Va.. 540 373-9883
　5404 Hillsborough St Ste A Raleigh (27606) *(G-10609)*

White Picket Media Inc.. 773 769-8400
　21313 Island Forest Dr Cornelius (28031) *(G-3630)*

White River Marine Group LLC.. 252 633-3101
　110 N Glenburnie Rd New Bern (28560) *(G-9406)*

White S Tire Svc Wilson Inc.. 252 237-0770
　501 Goldsboro St S Wilson (27893) *(G-13046)*

White S Tire Svc Wilson Inc (PA)......................................252 237-5426
　701 Hines St S Wilson (27893) *(G-13047)*

White Stone Labs Inc.. 704 775-5274
　178 Cayuga Dr Mooresville (28117) *(G-8799)*

White Street Brewing Co Inc.. 919 647-9439
　400 Park Ave Youngsville (27596) *(G-13498)*

White Tiger Btq & Candle Co.. 919 610-7244
　3206 Smokey Path Sanford (27330) *(G-11249)*

Whitecaps, Monroe *Also Called: A C S Enterprises NC Inc (G-8414)*

Whitehat Seed Farms Inc.. 252 264-2427
　102 Whitehat Rd Hertford (27944) *(G-6257)*

Whitener Sales Company.. 828 253-0518
　91 Carter Cove Rd Asheville (28804) *(G-635)*

Whites Tire Svc New Bern Inc.. 252 633-1170
　2813 Neuse Blvd New Bern (28562) *(G-9407)*

Whiteside Machine Co, Claremont *Also Called: Whiteside Mch & Repr Co Inc (G-3126)*

Whiteside Mch & Repr Co Inc.. 828 459-2141
　4506 Shook Rd Claremont (28610) *(G-3126)*

Whiteville AG.. 910 914-0007
　3654 James B White Hwy S Whiteville (28472) *(G-12595)*

Whiteville Fabrick, Whiteville *Also Called: Shodja Textiles Inc (G-12593)*

Whiteville Fabrics LLC (PA).. 910 914-0456
　68 Industrial Dr Whiteville (28472) *(G-12596)*

Whiteville Fabrics LLC.. 910 639-4444
　68 Industrial Blvd Whiteville (28472) *(G-12597)*

Whiteville Forklift & Eqp.. 910 642-6642
　344 Vinson Blvd Whiteville (28472) *(G-12598)*

Whiteville Rentals, Whiteville *Also Called: Whiteville Forklift & Eqp (G-12598)*

Whitewood, Thomasville *Also Called: Whitewood Industries Inc (G-12086)*

Whitewood Contracts LLC.. 336 885-9300
　667 W Ward Ave High Point (27260) *(G-6834)*

Whitewood Industries Inc (PA).. 336 472-0303
　100 Liberty Dr Thomasville (27360) *(G-12086)*

Whitewoven Handweaving Studio, Waynesville *Also Called: Sorrells Sheree White (G-12475)*

Whitley Holding Company (PA).. 704 888-2625
　3827 Whitley Rd Midland (28107) *(G-8298)*

Whitley Manufacturing, Midland *Also Called: Whitley Holding Company (G-8298)*

Whitley Metals Inc.. 919 894-3326
　769 Mount Pleasant Rd Willow Spring (27592) *(G-12682)*

Whitley/Monahan Handle LLC.. 704 888-2625
　3827 Whitley Rd Midland (28107) *(G-8299)*

Whitney Screen Printing.. 910 673-0309
　2244 Nc Highway 211 Eagle Springs (27242) *(G-4321)*

Whole Harvest, Warsaw *Also Called: Whole Harvest Foods LLC (G-12369)*

Whole Harvest Foods LLC.. 910 293-7917
　376 W Park Dr Warsaw (28398) *(G-12369)*

Whole Log Lumber, Zirconia *Also Called: Green River Resource MGT (G-13530)*

Whole Sale Printing Inks, Morganton *Also Called: Arpro M-Tec LLC (G-8851)*

Wholesale, Fayetteville *Also Called: Jasie Blanks LLC (G-4621)*

Wholesale Glass Fabricators, Wilmington *Also Called: Heraeus Quartz North Amer LLC (G-12804)*

Wholesale Kennel Supply Co.. 919 742-2515
　163 Stockyard Rd Siler City (27344) *(G-11427)*

Wholesale Monument Company.. 336 789-2031
　3539 W Pine St Mount Airy (27030) *(G-9194)*

Wick Communications Co.. 252 537-2505
　1025 Roanoke Ave Roanoke Rapids (27870) *(G-10747)*

Wicked Oceans.. 252 269-0488
　3431 S Buccaneer Dr Nags Head (27959) *(G-9306)*

Wickes Manufacturing Company...................................... 704 548-2350
　701 Mccullough Dr Charlotte (28262) *(G-3018)*

Wieland, Wilmington *Also Called: Wieland Electric Inc (G-12947)*

Wieland Copper Products LLC.. 336 445-4500
　3990 Us 311 Hwy N Pine Hall (27042) *(G-9677)*

Wieland Electric Inc (DH).. 910 259-5050
　8207 Market St Ste P10680 Wilmington (28404) *(G-12947)*

Wigal Wood Works.. 580 890-9723
　508 Anson Dr Fayetteville (28311) *(G-4700)*

Wiggins Design Fabrication Inc.. 252 826-5239
　140 Edwards Fork Rd Scotland Neck (27874) *(G-11268)*

Wiggins Kart Shop Inc.. 704 855-3165
　4010 Nc 152 W China Grove (28023) *(G-3080)*

Wiggins North State Co Inc (PA)...................................... 919 556-3231
　204 S Main St Rolesville (27571) *(G-10892)*

Wikoff Color, Charlotte *Also Called: Wikoff Color Corporation (G-3019)*

Wikoff Color Corporation.. 704 392-4657
　2828 Interstate St Charlotte (28208) *(G-3019)*

Wikoff Color Corporation.. 336 668-3423
　7212 Cessna Dr Greensboro (27409) *(G-5918)*

Wilbert Inc (HQ).. 704 247-3850
　100 N Main St Ste 200 Belmont (28012) *(G-775)*

Wilbert Burial Vault Company.. 910 739-7276
　1015 S Roberts Ave Lumberton (28358) *(G-7976)*

Wilbert Funeral Services Inc... 800 828-5879
108 Buchanan Church Rd Greensboro (27405) *(G-5919)*

Wilbert Plastic Services, Belmont *Also Called: Wilbert Inc (G-775)*

Wilbert Plastic Services, Belmont *Also Called: Wilbert Plstic Svcs Acqstion L (G-777)*

Wilbert Plastic Services Inc....................................... 866 273-1810
100 N Main St Ste 200 Belmont (28012) *(G-776)*

Wilbert Plstic Svcs Acqstion L (DH)........................... 704 822-1423
1000 Oaks Pkwy Belmont (28012) *(G-777)*

Wilbert Plstic Svcs Acqstion L.................................... 704 455-5191
7301 Caldwell Rd Harrisburg (28075) *(G-6121)*

Wilbert Yates Vault Co Inc.. 704 399-8453
2839 Rosemont St Charlotte (28208) *(G-3020)*

Wild Brds Unlimited Concord NC, Concord *Also Called: Tuckaway Pines Inc (G-3460)*

Wildcat Petroleum Service Inc..................................... 704 379-0132
326 Hawksnest Ct Matthews (28104) *(G-8198)*

Wildcat Territory Inc.. 718 361-6726
110 W Guilford St Thomasville (27360) *(G-12087)*

Wilder Tactical LLC... 704 750-7141
120 Wolfpack Rd Gastonia (28056) *(G-5165)*

Wildflwers Btq of Blowing Rock.................................. 828 295-9655
Old Martin House On Main Street Blowing Rock (28605) *(G-882)*

Wildwood Lamps & Accents Inc (PA)............................ 252 446-3266
516 Paul St Rocky Mount (27803) *(G-10875)*

Wildwood Studios Inc.. 828 299-8696
2163 Riceville Rd Asheville (28805) *(G-636)*

Wilkes Welding and Mch Co Inc................................... 336 670-2742
1018 Mulberry Rd Mc Grady (28649) *(G-8217)*

Willard Rodney White.. 252 794-3245
142 E Askewville St Windsor (27983) *(G-13061)*

William Barnet & Son LLC... 252 522-2418
1411 Hwy 258 S Kinston (28504) *(G-7437)*

William Bostic... 336 629-5243
3854 Us Highway 64 E Asheboro (27203) *(G-421)*

William Brantley.. 910 627-7286
637 Dunrobin Dr Raeford (28376) *(G-9856)*

William George Printing LLC.. 910 221-2700
3469 Black And Decker Rd Hope Mills (28348) *(G-6928)*

William Goodyear Co (PA)... 704 283-7824
2802 Gray Fox Rd Monroe (28110) *(G-8580)*

William Shawn Staley.. 336 838-9193
838 Green Acres Mill Rd Millers Creek (28651) *(G-8308)*

William Stone & Tile Inc.. 910 353-0914
1525 Freedom Way Hubert (28539) *(G-6938)*

William Travis Jewelry Ltd... 919 968-0011
1819 Fordham Blvd Chapel Hill (27514) *(G-1593)*

Williams Easy Hitch Inc.. 919 302-0062
2310 Old Oxford Rd Durham (27704) *(G-4305)*

Williams Electric Mtr Repr Inc..................................... 919 859-9790
2515 Cox Mill Rd Ste A Sanford (27332) *(G-11250)*

Williams Industries Inc (PA).. 919 604-1746
1128 Tyler Farms Dr Raleigh (27603) *(G-10610)*

Williams Logging Inc... 919 542-2740
2371 Charlie Brooks Rd Moncure (27559) *(G-8413)*

Williams Machine & Tool, Laurel Hill *Also Called: Lawrence Williams (G-7487)*

Williams Performance Inc.. 704 603-4431
3140 Corriher Grange Rd Mount Ulla (28125) *(G-9273)*

Williams Plating Company Inc..................................... 828 681-0301
6 Industrial Dr Arden (28704) *(G-318)*

Williams Printing LLC.. 336 969-2733
510 Northridge Park Dr Rural Hall (27045) *(G-10969)*

Williams Ready Mix Pdts Inc....................................... 704 283-1137
2465 Old Charlotte Hwy Monroe (28110) *(G-8581)*

Williams Seafood Arapahoe Inc.................................. 252 249-0594
2383 Don Lee Rd Arapahoe (28510) *(G-208)*

Williams Skin Co... 910 323-2628
1812 Sapona Rd Fayetteville (28312) *(G-4701)*

Williamsburg Woodcraft Inc.. 919 965-3363
4901 Nc Highway 96 N Selma (27576) *(G-11294)*

Williamson Greenhouses Inc....................................... 910 592-7072
1469 Beulah Rd Clinton (28328) *(G-3253)*

Willis Consulting, Charlotte *Also Called: Goldmine Software (G-2225)*

Willis Manufacturing, Conover *Also Called: Willis Manufacturing Inc (G-3575)*

Willis Manufacturing Inc... 828 244-0435
1924 Emmanuel Church Rd Conover (28613) *(G-3575)*

Willow Creek Furniture Inc.. 336 889-0076
1949 W Green Dr High Point (27260) *(G-6835)*

Willow Street Plant, Mount Airy *Also Called: Renfro LLC (G-9168)*

Willow Tex LLC... 336 789-1009
501 Piedmont Triad West Dr Mount Airy (27030) *(G-9195)*

Willowcroft... 704 540-0367
15301 Marvin Rd Charlotte (28277) *(G-3021)*

Wilmington Box Company.. 910 259-0402
101 Industrial Dr Burgaw (28425) *(G-1039)*

Wilmington Camera Service LLC.................................. 910 343-1089
905 N 23rd St Wilmington (28405) *(G-12948)*

Wilmington Concrete Plant, Wilmington *Also Called: S T Wooten Corporation (G-12908)*

Wilmington Funeral & Cremation, Wilmington *Also Called: Wilmington Mortuary Svc Inc (G-12951)*

Wilmington Journal Company...................................... 910 762-5502
412 S 7th St Wilmington (28401) *(G-12949)*

Wilmington Journal, The, Wilmington *Also Called: Wilmington Journal Company (G-12949)*

Wilmington Machine Works Inc.................................... 910 343-8111
3416 Enterprise Dr Wilmington (28405) *(G-12950)*

Wilmington Mortuary Svc Inc...................................... 910 791-9099
1535 41st St Wilmington (28403) *(G-12951)*

Wilmington National Peening, Statesville *Also Called: National Peening Inc (G-11738)*

Wilmington Rbr & Gasket Co Inc.................................. 910 762-4262
321 Raleigh St Wilmington (28412) *(G-12952)*

Wilmington Record Center, Wilmington *Also Called: Raleigh Ventures Inc (G-12895)*

Wilmington Today LLC... 910 509-7195
1213 Culbreth Dr Wilmington (28405) *(G-12953)*

Wilmore Electronics, Hillsborough *Also Called: Wilmore Electronics Company Inc (G-6881)*

Wilmore Electronics Company Inc (PA)........................ 919 732-9351
607 Us Highway 70a E Hillsborough (27278) *(G-6881)*

Wilo Incorporated (DH)... 336 679-4440
350 W Maple St Yadkinville (27055) *(G-13458)*

Wilson Billboard Advg Inc... 919 934-2421
212 Bridge St Smithfield (27577) *(G-11470)*

Wilson Bros Logging Inc.. 252 445-5317
72 Gennie Rd Enfield (27823) *(G-4486)*

Wilson Brown Inc.. 336 226-0237
2220 Anthony Rd Burlington (27215) *(G-1180)*

Wilson Concrete Plant, Wilson *Also Called: S T Wooten Corporation (G-13026)*

Wilson Daily Times Inc.. 252 243-5151
126 Nash St. W Wilson (27893) *(G-13048)*

Wilson Grading LLC... 919 778-1580
132 Blue Bird Ln Goldsboro (27534) *(G-5254)*

Wilson Iron Works Incorporated (PA).......................... 252 291-4465
600 S Washington St Rocky Mount (27801) *(G-10820)*

Wilson Machine & Tool Inc.. 919 776-0043
4956 Womack Rd Sanford (27330) *(G-11251)*

Wilson Machine Sho.. 910 673-3505
333 Hoffman Rd West End (27376) *(G-12560)*

Wilson Marble, Marion *Also Called: Marion Cultured Marble Inc (G-8049)*

Wilson Mold & Machine Corp....................................... 252 243-1831
2131 Nc Highway 42 E Wilson (27893) *(G-13049)*

Wilson Signs, Smithfield *Also Called: Wilson Billboard Advg Inc (G-11470)*

Wilson Tire and Automotive Inc (PA)............................ 336 584-9638
1807 N Nc Highway 87 Elon College (27244) *(G-4476)*

Wilson Trophy & Hayes EMB, Wilson *Also Called: Rhyno Enterprises (G-13022)*

Wilson Wood Works, Wilson *Also Called: Wilson Woodworks Inc (G-13050)*

Wilson Woodworks Inc... 252 237-3179
2807 Crabtree St S Wilson (27893) *(G-13050)*

Wilson-Cook Medical Inc... 336 744-0157
5941 Grassy Creek Blvd Winston Salem (27105) *(G-13395)*

Wilson-Cook Medical Inc... 336 744-0157
4900 Bethania Station Rd Winston Salem (27105) *(G-13396)*

Wilson-Cook Medical Inc., Winston Salem *Also Called: Cook Incorporated (G-13130)*

Wilsonart LLC... 866 267-7360
145 Cane Creek Industrial Park Rd Fletcher (28732) *(G-4779)*

Wilsonart LLC... 828 684-2351
80 La White Dr Fletcher (28732) *(G-4780)*

Wilsonart LLC.. 828 684-2351
  300 Cane Creek Industrial Park Rd Fletcher (28732) *(G-4781)*

Wilsons Planning & Consulting........................ 919 592-0935
  1402 Harth Dr Garner (27529) *(G-4974)*

Wind Solutions LLC... 919 292-2096
  111 Rand St Sanford (27332) *(G-11252)*

Windak Inc... 828 322-2292
  1661 4th St Sw Conover (28613) *(G-3576)*

Windco LLC... 704 846-6029
  1505 Turring Dr Ste B Indian Trail (28079) *(G-7104)*

WINDLIFT, Durham *Also Called: Windlift Inc (G-4306)*

Windlift Inc.. 919 490-8575
  2445 S Alston Ave Durham (27713) *(G-4306)*

Window Motor World Inc.................................. 800 252-2649
  779 Ball Branch Rd Boone (28607) *(G-953)*

Windows & More, Morehead City *Also Called: Eskimo 7 Limited (G-8832)*

Windsor Fiberglass Inc................................... 910 259-0057
  301 Progress Dr Burgaw (28425) *(G-1040)*

Windsor Gallery, Salisbury *Also Called: Speed Brite Inc (G-11118)*

Windsor Window Company................................ 704 283-7459
  1400 N Sutherland Ave Monroe (28110) *(G-8582)*

Windsors Cbnetry For Kit Baths....................... 336 275-0190
  1816 Pembroke Rd Ste 2 Greensboro (27408) *(G-5920)*

Windsurfing Hatteras, Avon *Also Called: North Sports Inc (G-651)*

Wine To Water... 828 355-9655
  689 George Wilson Rd Boone (28607) *(G-954)*

Winecoff Memorials, Statesville *Also Called: Winecoff Mmrals Sttesville Inc (G-11801)*

Winecoff Mmrals Sttesville Inc....................... 704 873-9661
  2120 Newton Dr Statesville (28677) *(G-11801)*

Winery At The Blueberry Farm, Banner Elk *Also Called: Banner Elk Winery Inc (G-682)*

Winkler Knives, Boone *Also Called: Daniel Winkler Knifemaker LLC (G-911)*

Wins Smokehouse Services Ltd........................ 828 884-7476
  45 S Ridge Rd Pisgah Forest (28768) *(G-9775)*

Winso Dsgns Screenprinting LLC..................... 704 967-5776
  7027 Orr Rd Ste F Charlotte (28213) *(G-3022)*

Winstn-Slem Chronicle Pubg Inc..................... 336 722-8624
  1300 E 5th St Winston Salem (27101) *(G-13397)*

Winstn-Slem Inds For Blind Inc (PA)................ 336 759-0551
  7730 N Point Blvd Winston Salem (27106) *(G-13398)*

Winston Concept Furniture............................... 336 472-7839
  1110 Lexington Ave Thomasville (27360) *(G-12088)*

Winston Packaging Division, Winston Salem *Also Called: Winston Printing Company (G-13399)*

Winston Printing Company (PA)........................ 336 896-7631
  8095 N Point Blvd Winston Salem (27106) *(G-13399)*

Winston Salem Engraving Co........................... 336 725-4268
  446 Brookstown Ave Winston Salem (27101) *(G-13400)*

Winston Salem Journal..................................... 336 727-7211
  418 N Marshall St Winston Salem (27101) *(G-13401)*

Winston Steel Stair Co..................................... 336 721-0020
  216 Junia Ave Winston Salem (27127) *(G-13402)*

Winston Tool Company Inc.............................. 336 983-3722
  1025 Gause Dr King (27021) *(G-7340)*

Winston-Salem Casket Company...................... 336 661-1695
  4340 Indiana Ave Winston Salem (27105) *(G-13403)*

Winstons Woodworks.. 919 693-4120
  600 Sunset Ave Oxford (27565) *(G-9640)*

Winter Bell Company (PA)................................ 336 887-2651
  2018 Brevard Rd High Point (27263) *(G-6836)*

Winter Custom Yachts Inc................................ 910 325-7583
  270 Hogans Rd Hubert (28539) *(G-6939)*

Winterville Machine Works Inc......................... 252 756-2130
  2672 Mill St Winterville (28590) *(G-13426)*

Winton Products Company................................ 704 399-5151
  2500 West Blvd Ste B Charlotte (28208) *(G-3023)*

Wiper Technologies, Greensboro *Also Called: Global Products LLC (G-5563)*

Wire Form, Aberdeen *Also Called: Industrial Mtal Pdts Abrdeen I (G-7)*

Wire-Bond, Charlotte *Also Called: Masonry Reinforcing Corp Amer (G-2467)*

Wireless Communications NC, Charlotte *Also Called: McShan Inc (G-2481)*

Wirenet Inc.. 513 774-7759
  16740 Birkdale Commons Pkwy Ste 306 Huntersville (28078) *(G-7062)*

Wireway/Husky Corp (PA)................................ 704 483-1135
  6146 Denver Industrial Park Rd Denver (28037) *(G-3817)*

Wirthwein New Bern Corp................................ 252 634-2871
  901 Industrial Dr New Bern (28562) *(G-9408)*

Wirtz Wire Edm LLC.. 828 696-0830
  65a Commercial Hill Dr Hendersonville (28792) *(G-6250)*

Wisdom For Heart.. 866 482-4253
  2703 Jones Franklin Rd Ste 105 Cary (27518) *(G-1483)*

Wisdom House Books Inc................................. 919 883-4669
  209 Kousa Trl Chapel Hill (27516) *(G-1594)*

Wise Living Inc (PA)....................................... 323 541-0410
  216 Woodbine St High Point (27260) *(G-6837)*

Wise Living Inc.. 336 991-5346
  216 Woodbine St High Point (27260) *(G-6838)*

Wise Storage Solutions LLC............................ 336 789-5141
  1372 Boggs Dr Mount Airy (27030) *(G-9196)*

Wiser Systems Inc.. 919 551-5566
  819 W Hargett St Raleigh (27603) *(G-10611)*

Wispry Inc.. 919 854-7500
  4001 Weston Pkwy St 200 Cary (27513) *(G-1484)*

Wit & Whistle... 919 609-5309
  929 Manchester Dr Cary (27511) *(G-1485)*

With Purpose Pressure Wshg LLC.................... 336 965-9473
  2702 Renee Dr Greensboro (27407) *(G-5921)*

Witten Vent Company, Gastonia *Also Called: WV Holdings Inc (G-5168)*

Wix Filters, Gastonia *Also Called: Mann+hummel Filtration Technol (G-5089)*

Wix Filtration Products, Gastonia *Also Called: Mann+hummel Filtration Technol (G-5088)*

Wizards Wood Werks.. 252 813-3929
  7114 Shallingtons Mill Rd Macclesfield (27852) *(G-7981)*

Wlc Forklift Services LLC............................... 336 345-2571
  2433 Freeway Dr Reidsville (27320) *(G-10701)*

Wlc LLC.. 336 852-6422
  5509b W Friendly Ave Ste 201 Greensboro (27410) *(G-5922)*

Wmb of Wake County Inc................................. 919 782-0419
  2601 Glenwood Ave Raleigh (27608) *(G-10612)*

Wmc, Thomasville *Also Called: Woempner Machine Company Inc (G-12089)*

Wmf Americas Inc.. 704 882-3898
  3521 Faith Church Rd Indian Trail (28079) *(G-7105)*

Wmf USA, Indian Trail *Also Called: Wmf Americas Inc (G-7105)*

Wmw Marine, Winterville *Also Called: Winterville Machine Works Inc (G-13426)*

Wmxf AM 1400.. 828 456-8661
  54 N Main St Waynesville (28786) *(G-12480)*

Wna, Charlotte *Also Called: Waddington Group Inc (G-2997)*

Wnc Blue Ridge Fd Ventures LLC..................... 828 348-0130
  1461 Sand Hill Rd Candler (28715) *(G-1236)*

Wnc Dry Kiln Inc (PA).................................... 828 652-0050
  65 Jacktown Rd Marion (28752) *(G-8074)*

Wnc Homes & Realstate, Weaverville *Also Called: High Five Enterprises Inc (G-12492)*

Wnc Material Sales.. 828 658-8368
  351 Flat Creek Church Rd Weaverville (28787) *(G-12507)*

Wnc Refab Inc... 828 658-8368
  125 Old Homestead Trl Weaverville (28787) *(G-12508)*

Wnc Starter, Asheville *Also Called: Blue Ridge Elc Mtr Repr Inc (G-455)*

Wnc White Corporation..................................... 828 477-4895
  3563 Skyland Dr Sylva (28779) *(G-11905)*

Wnyh LLC.. 716 853-1800
  155 Boyce Dr Mocksville (27028) *(G-8396)*

Woempner Machine Company Inc................... 336 475-2268
  385 Lloyd Murphy Rd Thomasville (27360) *(G-12089)*

Wolf X-Ray Corporation.................................. 631 242-9729
  133 Wolf Rd Battleboro (27809) *(G-710)*

Wolfspeed, Durham *Also Called: Wolfspeed Inc (G-4308)*

Wolfspeed Inc... 919 407-5300
  4601 Silicon Dr 3rd Fl Durham (27703) *(G-4307)*

Wolfspeed Inc (PA).. 919 407-5300
  4600 Silicon Dr Durham (27703) *(G-4308)*

Wolfspeed Employee Services Co..................... 919 313-5300
  4600 Silicon Dr Durham (27703) *(G-4309)*

Wolverine Mtal Stmping Sltons......................... 919 774-4729
  5720 Clyde Rhyne Dr Sanford (27330) *(G-11253)*

Wolverine Proctor, Lexington *Also Called: CPM Wolverine Proctor LLC (G-7671)*

Womack Newspaper Inc.. 336 316-1231
5500 Adams Farm Ln Ste 204 Greensboro (27407) *(G-5923)*

Womack Newspapers, Jamestown *Also Called: Jamestown News (G-7170)*

Womack Publishing Co Inc.. 919 732-2171
109 E King St Hillsborough (27278) *(G-6882)*

Womack Publishing Co Inc.. 252 586-2700
378 Lizard Creek Rd Littleton (27850) *(G-7888)*

Womack Publishing Co Inc.. 919 563-3555
106 N Fourth St Mebane (27302) *(G-8265)*

Womack Publishing Co Inc.. 252 480-2234
2910 S Croatan Hwy Ste 19 Nags Head (27959) *(G-9307)*

Womack Publishing Co Inc.. 252 257-3341
112 N Main St Warrenton (27589) *(G-12356)*

Womack Publishing Company Inc.................................... 704 660-5520
548 Williamson Rd Ste 3 Mooresville (28117) *(G-8800)*

Wood and Anvil, Hampstead *Also Called: Greg Price (G-6073)*

Wood Barn Inc (PA).. 919 496-6714
206 Clifton Ridge Ct Louisburg (27549) *(G-7929)*

Wood Creations NC Inc.. 704 865-1822
2223 Plastics Dr Gastonia (28054) *(G-5166)*

Wood Designs, Monroe *Also Called: Wdm Inc (G-8578)*

Wood Done Right Inc.. 919 623-4557
525 Colony Woods Dr Chapel Hill (27517) *(G-1595)*

Wood Logging.. 910 866-4018
361 Gum Spring Rd White Oak (28399) *(G-12575)*

Wood Machine Service Inc... 252 446-2142
2 Great State Ln Rocky Mount (27803) *(G-10876)*

Wood N Things.. 910 990-4448
139 Buckhorn Creek Ln Clinton (28328) *(G-3254)*

Wood Products Packg Intl Inc.. 704 279-3011
3725 Faith Rd Faith (28041) *(G-4520)*

Wood Right Lumber Company.. 910 576-4642
225 Basswood Rd Troy (27371) *(G-12171)*

Wood Surgeon... 252 728-5767
1403 Lennoxville Rd Beaufort (28516) *(G-737)*

Wood Technology Inc (PA)... 828 464-8049
1317 Emmanuel Church Rd Conover (28613) *(G-3577)*

Wood Tooling Shop, Wilmington *Also Called: IMS Usa LLC (G-12815)*

Wood Works.. 910 579-1487
9040 Forest Dr Sw Sunset Beach (28468) *(G-11853)*

Woodland Hosiery Inc.. 910 439-4843
118 Hudson Ln Mount Gilead (27306) *(G-9212)*

Woodlane Envmtl Tech Inc... 828 894-8383
111 Kangaroo Dr Columbus (28722) *(G-3305)*

Woodlawn Tire & Alignment, Marion *Also Called: Woodlawn Tire and Algnmt Inc (G-8075)*

Woodlawn Tire and Algnmt Inc...................................... 828 756-4212
8021 Us 221 N Marion (28752) *(G-8075)*

Woodline Inc.. 336 476-7100
4695 Turnpike Ct Thomasville (27360) *(G-12090)*

Woodmark Originals Inc... 336 841-6409
1920 Jarrell St High Point (27260) *(G-6839)*

Woodmaster Custom Cabinets Inc.................................. 919 554-3707
436 Park Ave Youngsville (27596) *(G-13499)*

Woodmaster Woodworking, King *Also Called: Woodmasters Woodworking Inc (G-7341)*

Woodmasters Woodworking Inc...................................... 336 985-4000
402 Newsome Rd King (27021) *(G-7341)*

Woodmill Winery Inc.. 704 276-9911
1350 Woodmill Winery Ln Vale (28168) *(G-12212)*

Woodpecker Sawmill.. 828 891-8720
52 Sawmill Rd Mills River (28759) *(G-8325)*

Woodplay, Raleigh *Also Called: Family Industries Inc (G-10104)*

Woodshed Software... 941 240-1780
925 Mainsail Rd Salisbury (28146) *(G-11136)*

Woodsmiths, Lenoir *Also Called: Woodsmiths Company (G-7646)*

Woodsmiths Company.. 406 626-3102
418 Prospect St Nw Lenoir (28645) *(G-7646)*

Woodtech/Interiors Inc... 704 332-7215
2228 N Brevard St Charlotte (28206) *(G-3024)*

Woodtreaters Inc... 910 675-0038
224 Sawdust Rd Rocky Point (28457) *(G-10887)*

Woodward Compressor Sales, Charlotte *Also Called: Atlas Copco Compressors LLC (G-1714)*

Woodwizards Inc... 336 427-7698
4214 Ellisboro Rd Stokesdale (27357) *(G-11818)*

Woodworking Unlimited.. 252 235-5285
6378 Vance St Bailey (27807) *(G-674)*

Woodworking Unlimited Inc.. 704 903-8080
675 Bussell Rd Olin (28660) *(G-9598)*

Woodwright Co, Elm City *Also Called: Woodwright of Wilson Co Inc (G-4468)*

Woodwright of Wilson Co Inc... 252 243-9663
5753 Nc 58 Elm City (27822) *(G-4468)*

Woodys Chair Shop... 828 765-9277
784 Dale Rd Spruce Pine (28777) *(G-11590)*

Wool Novelty, High Point *Also Called: Woolfoam Corporation (G-6840)*

Woolfoam Corporation... 336 886-4964
107 Whittier Ave High Point (27262) *(G-6840)*

Wooten Graphics Inc... 336 731-4650
172 Hinkle Ln Welcome (27374) *(G-12517)*

Wooten John... 828 322-4031
3763 1st Ave Sw Hickory (28602) *(G-6490)*

Worden Brothers Inc.. 919 202-8555
6315 Boathouse Rd Wilmington (28403) *(G-12954)*

Work Well Hydrtion Systems LLC................................... 704 853-7788
1680 Garfield Dr Gastonia (28052) *(G-5167)*

Workcom Inc... 310 586-4000
1001 Winstead Dr Cary (27513) *(G-1486)*

Workday Inc.. 919 703-2559
4801 Glenwood Ave Ste 300 Raleigh (27612) *(G-10613)*

Working Widget Technology LLC.................................... 704 684-6277
7920 Alexander Rd Charlotte (28270) *(G-3025)*

Workwear Outfitters LLC... 877 824-0613
No Physical Location Greensboro (27420) *(G-5924)*

World Art Gallery Incorporated...................................... 910 989-0203
1116 Gum Branch Rd Jacksonville (28540) *(G-7160)*

World By Wood, Charlotte *Also Called: Lignaterra Global LLC (G-2422)*

World Elastic Corporation (PA)...................................... 704 786-9508
338 Webb Rd Concord (28025) *(G-3469)*

World Fibers Inc (PA).. 704 786-9508
338 Webb Rd Concord (28025) *(G-3470)*

World Stone Fabricators Inc... 704 372-9968
4908 Hovis Rd Charlotte (28208) *(G-3026)*

World Stone of Sanford LLC.. 919 468-8450
3201 Industrial Dr Sanford (27332) *(G-11254)*

World Wood Company.. 252 523-0021
12045 Old Us Highway 70 Cove City (28523) *(G-3633)*

Worldgranite & Stoneart Inc... 919 871-0078
4600 Twisted Oaks Dr Apt 1505 Raleigh (27612) *(G-10614)*

Worldwide Entrmt Mltimedia LLC................................... 704 208-6113
11511 Sidney Crest Ave Charlotte (28213) *(G-3027)*

Worldwide Protective Pdts LLC (DH).............................. 877 678-4568
1409 World Wide Ln Wilkesboro (28697) *(G-12663)*

Worldwide Protective Pdts LLC...................................... 336 933-8035
1404 River St Wilkesboro (28697) *(G-12664)*

Worldwide Protective Products, Wilkesboro *Also Called: Worldwide Protective Pdts LLC (G-12663)*

Worth Products LLC.. 252 747-9994
856 Hwy 258 S Snow Hill (28580) *(G-11484)*

Worthington Cylinder Corp... 336 777-8600
1690 Lowery St Winston Salem (27101) *(G-13404)*

Wound-About Inc... 336 368-5001
309 Nelson St Pilot Mountain (27041) *(G-9676)*

Wovenart Inc... 828 859-6349
687 N Trade St Tryon (28782) *(G-12180)*

Wovern Art, Tryon *Also Called: Wovenart Inc (G-12180)*

Wp Reidsville LLC... 336 342-1200
109 Sands Rd Reidsville (27320) *(G-10702)*

Wph Ventures Inc.. 828 676-1700
4 Commerce Way Arden (28704) *(G-319)*

Wpmhj LLC... 919 601-5445
4216 Atlantic Ave Raleigh (27612) *(G-10615)*

WR Rayson Co Inc.. 910 259-8100
720 S Dickerson St Burgaw (28425) *(G-1041)*

ALPHABETIC

Wrangler, Greensboro *Also Called: Wrangler Apparel Corp (G-5925)*

Wrangler Apparel Corp.. 336 332-3400
400 N Elm St Greensboro (27401) *(G-5925)*

Wre/Colortech, Greensboro *Also Called: Western Roto Engravers Incorporated (G-5916)*

Wright, Riegelwood *Also Called: Oak-Bark Corporation (G-10727)*

Wright & Hobbs Inc... 252 537-5817
105 W Becker Dr Roanoke Rapids (27870) *(G-10748)*

Wright Business Concepts Inc.. 828 466-1044
1320 Fairgrove Church Rd Hickory (28603) *(G-6491)*

Wright Chemicals LLC... 919 296-1771
4804 Page Creek Ln Durham (27703) *(G-4310)*

Wright Electric Inc... 704 435-6988
3114 Tryon Courthouse Rd Cherryville (28021) *(G-3071)*

Wright Machine & Tool Co Inc.. 828 298-8440
101 Jims Branch Rd Swannanoa (28778) *(G-11879)*

Wright of Thomasville Inc (PA).. 336 472-4200
5115 Prospect St Thomasville (27360) *(G-12091)*

Wright Printing Service Inc... 336 427-4768
1510 W Academy St Madison (27025) *(G-8004)*

Wright Roller Company.. 336 852-8393
1800 Fairfax Rd Ste K Greensboro (27407) *(G-5926)*

Writ Press Inc... 815 988-7074
1308 N Duke St Durham (27701) *(G-4311)*

Writing Penn LLC... 301 529-5324
4400 Turnberry Cir Durham (27712) *(G-4312)*

Wrkco Inc... 828 692-6254
200 Tabor Rd East Flat Rock (28726) *(G-4336)*

Wrkco Inc... 336 956-6000
101 Lexington Pkwy Lexington (27295) *(G-7758)*

Wrkco Inc... 919 304-0300
7411 Oakwood Street Ext Mebane (27302) *(G-8266)*

Wrkco Inc... 828 287-9430
300 Broyhill Rd Rutherfordton (28139) *(G-11003)*

Wrkco Inc... 336 759-7501
8080 N Point Blvd Winston Salem (27106) *(G-13405)*

Wrkco Inc... 770 448-2193
5900 Grassy Creek Blvd Winston Salem (27105) *(G-13406)*

Wrkco Inc... 336 765-7004
3946 Westpoint Blvd Winston Salem (27103) *(G-13407)*

Wst Logging LLC... 336 857-0147
7324 Checkmark Rd Denton (27239) *(G-3766)*

Wto Inc.. 704 714-7765
9210 Porters View Dr Charlotte (28273) *(G-3028)*

Wtvd Television LLC... 919 683-1111
411 Liberty St Durham (27701) *(G-4313)*

Wuko Inc.. 980 938-0512
3505 Associate Dr Greensboro (27405) *(G-5927)*

Wurth Revcar Fasteners Inc.. 919 772-9930
800 N Greenfield Pkwy Ste 810 Garner (27529) *(G-4975)*

WURTH REVCAR FASTENERS, INC., Garner *Also Called: Wurth Revcar Fasteners Inc (G-4975)*

WV Holdings Inc.. 704 853-8338
404 E Long Ave Gastonia (28054) *(G-5168)*

WW&s Construction Inc... 217 620-4042
817 Dallas Spencer Mtn Rd Dallas (28034) *(G-3693)*

Wwh Systems LLC, Gastonia *Also Called: Work Well Hydrtion Systems LLC (G-5167)*

Wwj LLC (PA)... 704 871-8500
1002 Bucks Industrial Rd Statesville (28625) *(G-11802)*

Www 123 Precious Metal Com, Wilmington *Also Called: 123 Precious Metal Ref LLC (G-12685)*

Www.candlevision.com, Marshville *Also Called: Paul Hoge Creations Inc (G-8091)*

Wyda Packaging Corp.. 980 403-3346
3301 Woodpark Blvd Charlotte (28206) *(G-3029)*

Wyeth Holdings LLC... 919 775-7100
4300 Oak Park Rd Sanford (27330) *(G-11255)*

Wyeth Pharmaceutical Division, Sanford *Also Called: Wyeth Holdings LLC (G-11255)*

Wyrick Machine and Tool Co... 336 841-8261
1215 Kearns Hackett Rd Pleasant Garden (27313) *(G-9796)*

Wysong and Miles Company... 336 621-3960
4820 Us 29 N Greensboro (27405) *(G-5928)*

Wysong Parts & Service, Greensboro *Also Called: Wysong and Miles Company (G-5928)*

Wysong Parts and Service, Greensboro *Also Called: Delta Phoenix Inc (G-5493)*

X-Celeprint Inc... 919 248-0020
2 Davis Dr Durham (27709) *(G-4314)*

X-Jet Technologies Inc... 800 983-7467
146 Annaron Ct Raleigh (27603) *(G-10616)*

Xaloy Extrusion LLC... 828 326-9888
1291 19th Street Ln Nw Hickory (28601) *(G-6492)*

Xanderglasses Inc... 617 286-3012
1 Glenwood Ave Ste 500 Raleigh (27603) *(G-10617)*

Xavier Power Systems.. 910 734-7813
885 Shawn Rd Lumberton (28358) *(G-7977)*

XCEL Hrmetic Mtr Rewinding Inc.. 704 694-6001
2356 Bethel Rd Wadesboro (28170) *(G-12253)*

Xceldyne LLC.. 336 472-2242
37 High Tech Blvd Thomasville (27360) *(G-12092)*

Xceldyne Group LLC (PA)... 336 472-2242
37 High Tech Blvd Thomasville (27360) *(G-12093)*

Xceldyne Technologies LLC.. 336 475-0201
37 High Tech Blvd Thomasville (27360) *(G-12094)*

Xdri Inc... 919 361-2155
4018 Patriot Dr Ste 100 Durham (27703) *(G-4315)*

Xelaqua Inc.. 919 964-4181
404b Glenwood Ave Raleigh (27603) *(G-10618)*

Xelera Inc... 855 493-5372
10806 Reames Rd Ste Y Charlotte (28269) *(G-3030)*

Xelera Inc... 540 915-6181
137 Cross Center Rd Denver (28037) *(G-3818)*

Xerium, Raleigh *Also Called: Andritz Fabrics and Rolls Inc (G-9904)*

Xerox Corporation... 919 428-9718
11000 Weston Pkwy Cary (27513) *(G-1487)*

Xeroxdata Center... 704 329-7245
1400 Cross Beam Dr Charlotte (28217) *(G-3031)*

Xilinx Inc.. 919 846-3922
220 Horizon Dr Ste 114 Raleigh (27615) *(G-10619)*

Xinray Systems Inc.. 919 701-4100
312 Silver Creek Trl Chapel Hill (27514) *(G-1596)*

Xintek Inc... 919 449-5799
312 Silver Creek Trl Chapel Hill (27514) *(G-1597)*

Xona Microfluidics Inc... 951 553-6400
76 Tw Alexander Dr Research Triangle Pa (27709) *(G-10718)*

Xp Climate Control LLC.. 828 266-2006
643 Greenway Rd Ste P Boone (28607) *(G-955)*

Xpc Corporation... 919 210-1756
3070 Business Park Dr Ste 108 Raleigh (27610) *(G-10620)*

Xpc Corporation... 800 582-4524
7239 Acc Blvd Raleigh (27617) *(G-10621)*

Xpertees Prfmce Screen Prtg... 910 763-7703
1406 Castle Hayne Rd Ste 2 Wilmington (28401) *(G-12955)*

Xpres LLC... 336 245-1596
111 Cloverleaf Dr Winston Salem (27103) *(G-13408)*

Xpress Line, Winston Salem *Also Called: Encore Group Inc (G-13157)*

Xpress Powder Coat, Gastonia *Also Called: Overwith Inc (G-5114)*

Xschem Inc (PA)... 919 379-3500
1500 Perimeter Park Dr Ste 300 Morrisville (27560) *(G-9091)*

Xsport Global Inc.. 212 541-6222
1800 Camden Rd # 107-196 Charlotte (28203) *(G-3032)*

Xsys Global, Arden *Also Called: Xsys North America Corporation (G-320)*

Xsys North America Corporation.. 828 654-6805
95 Glenn Bridge Rd Arden (28704) *(G-320)*

Xsys North America Corporation.. 828 687-2485
25 Old Shoals Rd Arden (28704) *(G-321)*

Xsys North America Corporation (DH).................................. 704 504-2626
2915 Whitehall Park Dr Ste 600 Charlotte (28273) *(G-3033)*

Xterior Sales & Service, Raleigh *Also Called: B&C Xterior Cleaning Svc Inc (G-9928)*

Xtinguish LLC... 704 868-9500
3021 N Myers St Charlotte (28205) *(G-3034)*

Xtra Light Manufacturing... 919 422-7281
1301 Davis Dr Apex (27523) *(G-207)*

Xtreme Fabrication Ltd.. 336 472-4562
25b High Tech Blvd Thomasville (27360) *(G-12095)*

Xtreme Postcard Profits System... 919 894-8886
22 Boardwalk Ave Benson (27504) *(G-800)*

Xtreme Power Conversion, Raleigh *Also Called: Xpc Corporation (G-10621)*

Xxxtreme Motorsport...704 663-1500
292 Rolling Hill Rd Mooresville (28117) *(G-8801)*

Xylem, Charlotte *Also Called: Wedeco Uv Technologies Inc (G-3010)*

Xylem Inc..919 772-4126
1328 Bobbitt Dr Garner (27529) *(G-4976)*

Xylem Lnc (DH)..704 409-9700
4828 Parkway Plaza Blvd # 200 Charlotte (28217) *(G-3035)*

Xylem Water Solutions USA Inc (HQ)....................704 409-9700
4828 Parkway Plaza Blvd Ste 200 Charlotte (28217) *(G-3036)*

Xylem Water Solutions USA Inc.............................704 409-9700
14125 S Bridge Cir Charlotte (28273) *(G-3037)*

Yackety Yack Publishing Inc...................................919 843-5092
Chapel Hill (27514) *(G-1598)*

Yadkin Lumber Company Inc..................................336 679-2432
800 N State St Yadkinville (27055) *(G-13459)*

Yadkin Valley Cabinet Co Inc.................................336 786-9860
135 Red Laurel Ln Mount Airy (27030) *(G-9197)*

Yadkin Valley Paving, Winston Salem *Also Called: Cloverleaf Mixing Inc (G-13125)*

Yale Industrial Products Inc (HQ)..........................704 588-4610
13320 Ballantyne Corporate Pl Ste D Charlotte (28277) *(G-3038)*

Yale Material Handling, Greenville *Also Called: Gregory Poole Equipment Co (G-5984)*

Yale Materials Handling, Greenville *Also Called: Hyster-Yale Materials Hdlg Inc (G-5990)*

Yale Rope Technologies Inc.....................................704 630-0331
634 Industrial Ave Salisbury (28144) *(G-11137)*

Yamco LLC..252 747-9267
310 Kingold Blvd Snow Hill (28580) *(G-11485)*

Yancey Common Times Journal, Burnsville *Also Called: Times Journal Inc (G-1193)*

Yancey Stone Inc..828 682-2645
19 Crushing Rd Burnsville (28714) *(G-1194)*

Yancey Stone Inc..828 684-5522
5 Williams Rd Fletcher (28732) *(G-4782)*

Yancy Common Times Journal..............................828 682-2120
22 N Main St Burnsville (28714) *(G-1195)*

Yancy County Common Times, Burnsville *Also Called: Yancy Common Times Journal (G-1195)*

Yang Mine Lines, Charlotte *Also Called: Yang Ming America Corporation (G-3039)*

Yang Ming America Corporation.............................704 357-3817
11124 Ascoli Pl Charlotte (28277) *(G-3039)*

Yanjan USA LLC...704 380-6230
159 Walker Rd Statesville (28625) *(G-11803)*

Yard Pro Sales and Service LLC............................252 641-9776
105 W Howard Ave Tarboro (27886) *(G-11947)*

Yat Usa Inc..480 584-4096
10506 Bryton Corporate Center Dr Huntersville (28078) *(G-7063)*

Yates Precision Machining LLC..............................704 662-7165
133 Byers Creek Rd Unit D Mooresville (28117) *(G-8802)*

Yeeka LLC...919 308-9826
11 Yarmouth Pl Durham (27707) *(G-4316)*

Yellow Dog Design Inc...336 553-2172
112 Oconnor St Greensboro (27406) *(G-5929)*

Yelton Milling Co, Spindale *Also Called: Lakeside Mills Inc (G-11547)*

Yepzy Inc..855 461-2678
57 Union St S Pmb 1234 Concord (28025) *(G-3471)*

Yes Real Estate Cnstr Group In.............................919 389-4104
4805 Green Rd Ste 103 Raleigh (27616) *(G-10622)*

Yes Weekly, Greensboro *Also Called: Womack Newspaper Inc (G-5923)*

Yg-1 America Inc...980 318-5348
11001 Park Charlotte Blvd Charlotte (28273) *(G-3040)*

Yildiz Entegre Usa Inc...910 763-4733
1715 Woodbine St Wilmington (28401) *(G-12956)*

YKK AP America Inc..336 665-1963
4524 Green Point Dr Ste 106 Greensboro (27410) *(G-5930)*

Yogasleep, Wilmington *Also Called: Marpac LLC (G-12846)*

Yontz & Sons Painting Inc.......................................336 784-7099
3803 S Main St Winston Salem (27127) *(G-13409)*

Yorkshire House Inc...336 869-9714
1904 Alleghany St High Point (27263) *(G-6841)*

Young & McQueen Grading Co Inc.........................828 682-7714
25 Crest View Rd Burnsville (28714) *(G-1196)*

Young Logging Company Inc...................................919 552-9753
1517 Clayton Rd Willow Spring (27592) *(G-12683)*

Younger Furniture Inc..336 476-0444
110 Todd Ct Thomasville (27360) *(G-12096)*

Youngs Welding & Machine Svcs...........................910 488-1190
787 Mcarthur Rd Fayetteville (28311) *(G-4702)*

Your Cabinet Connection Inc.................................919 641-2877
10315 Chapel Hill Rd Morrisville (27560) *(G-9092)*

Your Choice Pregnancy Clinic................................919 577-9050
607 N Ennis St Fuquay Varina (27526) *(G-4907)*

Your Source For Printing...704 957-5922
8116 S Tryon St Charlotte (28273) *(G-3041)*

Yourlogowear...704 664-1290
18700 Statesville Rd Cornelius (28031) *(G-3631)*

Youshirt, Clayton *Also Called: Noble Wholesalers Inc (G-3162)*

Yp Advrtising Pubg LLC Not LLC...........................704 522-5500
9144 Arrowpoint Blvd Ste 150 Charlotte (28273) *(G-3042)*

Yp Advrtising Pubg LLC Not LLC...........................910 794-5151
2250 Shipyard Blvd Wilmington (28403) *(G-12957)*

Yukon Inc...919 366-2001
485 Old Wilson Rd Ste 8 Wendell (27591) *(G-12554)*

Yukon Medical LLC...919 595-8250
4021 Stirrup Creek Dr Ste 200 Durham (27703) *(G-4317)*

Yukon Packaging LLC (PA).....................................704 214-0579
122 Backstretch Ln Mooresville (28117) *(G-8803)*

Yumitos Corporation...786 952-6202
3540 Toringdon Way Ste 200 Charlotte (28277) *(G-3043)*

Yummi Factory Corporation.....................................980 248-1062
40 Concord Commons Pl Sw Concord (28027) *(G-3472)*

Yummi Muffin, Concord *Also Called: Yummi Factory Corporation (G-3472)*

Yummy Tummy Ga LLC...704 658-0445
2105 Brawley School Rd Mooresville (28117) *(G-8804)*

Z Collection LLC...919 247-1513
77 Gennessee Dr Zebulon (27597) *(G-13526)*

Zarges Inc...704 357-6285
1440 Center Park Dr Charlotte (28217) *(G-3044)*

Zeal Industries LLC...828 575-9894
101 Bee Ridge Rd Asheville (28803) *(G-637)*

Zebra Communications Inc (PA).............................919 314-3700
9401 Globe Center Dr Ste 130 Morrisville (27560) *(G-9093)*

Zebra Print Solutions, Morrisville *Also Called: Zebra Communications Inc (G-9093)*

Zebra Technologies, Charlotte *Also Called: Zebra Technologies Corporation (G-3045)*

Zebra Technologies Corporation.............................704 517-5271
9075 Meadowmont View Dr Charlotte (28269) *(G-3045)*

Zekelman Industries Inc..704 560-6768
111 Pin Oak Ln Mooresville (28117) *(G-8805)*

Zelaya Bros LLC..980 833-0099
3525 Ritch Ave Charlotte (28206) *(G-3046)*

Zemex Industrial Minerals Inc................................828 765-5500
797 Altapass Hwy Spruce Pine (28777) *(G-11591)*

Zenecar LLC...919 518-0464
10224 Durant Rd Ste 201 Raleigh (27614) *(G-10623)*

Zenith Pumps, Monroe *Also Called: IMO Industries Inc (G-8503)*

Zeon Technologies Inc...704 680-9160
425 Lash Dr Salisbury (28147) *(G-11138)*

Zepsa Industries Inc...704 583-9220
1501 Westinghouse Blvd Charlotte (28273) *(G-3047)*

Zepsa Stairs, Charlotte *Also Called: Zepsa Industries Inc (G-3047)*

Zeskp LLC...910 762-8300
2027 Capital Dr Wilmington (28405) *(G-12958)*

ZF Chassis Components LLC...................................828 468-3711
1570 E P Street Ext Newton (28658) *(G-9513)*

ZF Lemforder, Newton *Also Called: ZF Chassis Components LLC (G-9513)*

Zibra LLC (PA)...704 271-4503
172 Broad Sound Pl Mooresville (28117) *(G-8806)*

Zickgraf Enterprises Inc..828 524-2313
231 Depot St Franklin (28734) *(G-4844)*

Zickgraf Enterprises Inc..704 369-1200
301 Depot St Franklin (28734) *(G-4845)*

Ziehl-Abegg Inc (DH)...336 834-9339
719 N Regional Rd Greensboro (27419) *(G-5931)*

A
L
P
H
A
B
E
T
I
C

Ziehl-Abegg Inc.. 336 934-9339
  4971 Millennium Dr Winston Salem (27107) *(G-13410)*

Zim Arcraft Cbin Solutions LLC (DH).................. 336 862-1418
  8010 Piedmont Triad Pkwy Greensboro (27409) *(G-5932)*

Zim Arcraft Cbin Solutions LLC.......................... 336 464-0122
  5568 Gumtree Rd Winston Salem (27107) *(G-13411)*

Zimmermann - Dynayarn Usa LLC......................... 336 222-8129
  327 E Elm St Graham (27253) *(G-5290)*

Zingerle Group Usa Inc....................................... 704 312-1600
  6965 Northpark Blvd Charlotte (28216) *(G-3048)*

Zink, Whitsett *Also Called: Zink Imaging Inc (G-12623)*

Zink Holdings LLC... 336 449-8000
  6900 Konica Dr Whitsett (27377) *(G-12622)*

Zink Imaging Inc.. 336 449-8000
  6900 Konica Dr Whitsett (27377) *(G-12623)*

Zion Industries Inc.. 828 397-2701
  9480 Neuville Ave Hildebran (28637) *(G-6856)*

Zippy Ice Inc (PA)... 980 355-9851
  5701 N Graham St Charlotte (28269) *(G-3049)*

Ziptronix Inc... 919 459-2400
  800 Perimeter Park Dr Ste B Morrisville (27560) *(G-9094)*

Zndus Inc (DH).. 704 981-8660
  214 James Farm Rd Statesville (28625) *(G-11804)*

Zoes Kitchen Inc... 336 748-0587
  205 S Stratford Rd Winston Salem (27103) *(G-13412)*

Zoetis Inc... 919 941-5185
  1040 Swabia Ct Durham (27703) *(G-4318)*

Zoetis Products LLC.. 336 333-9356
  620 S Elm St Ste 363 Greensboro (27406) *(G-5933)*

Zoeys Btq Style Spclty Trats.............................. 910 808-1778
  896 Shawtown Rd Lillington (27546) *(G-7805)*

Zonkd LLC.. 919 977-6463
  2419 Atlantic Ave Raleigh (27604) *(G-10624)*

Zonnic, Winston Salem *Also Called: Modoral Brands Inc (G-13259)*

Zoom Apparel Inc (PA).. 336 993-9666
  303 S Broad St Winston Salem (27101) *(G-13413)*

Zumco Inc... 828 891-3300
  199 Forest Knolls Pl Horse Shoe (28742) *(G-6931)*

Zurn Elkay Wtr Solutions Corp............................ 910 501-1853
  102 Elkay Way Lumberton (28358) *(G-7978)*

Zurn Elkay Wtr Solutions Corp............................ 855 663-9876
  5900 Elwin Buchanan Dr Sanford (27330) *(G-11256)*

Zurn Industries LLC.. 919 775-2255
  5900 Elwin Buchanan Dr Sanford (27330) *(G-11257)*

Zwz Bearing USA, Lincolnton *Also Called: CSC Bearing North America Inc (G-7826)*

Zysense LLC.. 215 485-1955
  6701 Glen Forrest Dr Chapel Hill (27517) *(G-1599)*

PRODUCT INDEX

• Product categories are listed in alphabetical order.

A

ABRASIVE STONES, EXC GRINDING STONES: Ground Or Whole
ABRASIVES
ABRASIVES: Coated
ACCELERATION INDICATORS & SYSTEM COMPONENTS: Aerospace
ACCELEROMETERS
ACID RESIST: Etching
ACIDS: Sulfuric, Oleum
ACOUSTICAL BOARD & TILE
ACRYLIC RESINS
ACTUATORS: Indl, NEC
ADDITIVE BASED PLASTIC MATERIALS: Plasticizers
ADHESIVES
ADHESIVES & SEALANTS
ADHESIVES: Epoxy
ADVERTISING AGENCIES
ADVERTISING AGENCIES: Consultants
ADVERTISING CURTAINS
ADVERTISING DISPLAY PRDTS
ADVERTISING REPRESENTATIVES: Newspaper
ADVERTISING SPECIALTIES, WHOLESALE
ADVERTISING SVCS: Direct Mail
ADVERTISING SVCS: Display
ADVERTISING SVCS: Outdoor
AERIAL WORK PLATFORMS
AGENTS, BROKERS & BUREAUS: Personal Service
AGRICULTURAL DISINFECTANTS
AGRICULTURAL EQPT: BARN, SILO, POULTRY, DAIRY/ LIVESTOCK MACH
AGRICULTURAL EQPT: Fertilizing Machinery
AGRICULTURAL EQPT: Fertilizng, Sprayng, Dustng/Irrigatn Mach
AGRICULTURAL EQPT: Grounds Mowing Eqpt
AGRICULTURAL EQPT: Turf & Grounds Eqpt
AGRICULTURAL MACHINERY & EQPT: Wholesalers
AIR CLEANING SYSTEMS
AIR CONDITIONING & VENTILATION EQPT & SPLYS: Wholesales
AIR CONDITIONING EQPT
AIR CONDITIONING EQPT, WHOLE HOUSE: Wholesalers
AIR CONDITIONING REPAIR SVCS
AIR CONDITIONING UNITS: Complete, Domestic Or Indl
AIR MATTRESSES: Plastic
AIR POLLUTION MEASURING SVCS
AIR PURIFICATION EQPT
AIRCRAFT & AEROSPACE FLIGHT INSTRUMENTS & GUIDANCE SYSTEMS
AIRCRAFT & HEAVY EQPT REPAIR SVCS
AIRCRAFT ASSEMBLY PLANTS
AIRCRAFT ENGINES & ENGINE PARTS: Air Scoops
AIRCRAFT ENGINES & ENGINE PARTS: Airfoils
AIRCRAFT ENGINES & ENGINE PARTS: Mount Parts
AIRCRAFT ENGINES & ENGINE PARTS: Research & Development, Mfr
AIRCRAFT ENGINES & PARTS
AIRCRAFT EQPT & SPLYS WHOLESALERS
AIRCRAFT FLIGHT INSTRUMENT REPAIR SVCS
AIRCRAFT LIGHTING
AIRCRAFT MAINTENANCE & REPAIR SVCS
AIRCRAFT PARTS & AUXILIARY EQPT: Assemblies, Fuselage
AIRCRAFT PARTS & AUXILIARY EQPT: Assys, Subassemblies/Parts
AIRCRAFT PARTS & AUXILIARY EQPT: Bodies
AIRCRAFT PARTS & AUXILIARY EQPT: Body & Wing Assys & Parts
AIRCRAFT PARTS & AUXILIARY EQPT: Body Assemblies & Parts
AIRCRAFT PARTS & AUXILIARY EQPT: Military Eqpt & Armament
AIRCRAFT PARTS & AUXILIARY EQPT: Research & Development, Mfr
AIRCRAFT PARTS & AUXILIARY EQPT: Tanks, Fuel
AIRCRAFT PARTS & EQPT, NEC
AIRCRAFT PARTS WHOLESALERS

AIRCRAFT SEATS
AIRCRAFT SERVICING & REPAIRING
AIRCRAFT: Airplanes, Fixed Or Rotary Wing
AIRCRAFT: Research & Development, Manufacturer
AIRPORTS, FLYING FIELDS & SVCS
ALARMS: Burglar
ALARMS: Fire
ALCOHOL: Ethyl & Ethanol
ALKALIES & CHLORINE
ALTERNATORS & GENERATORS: Battery Charging
ALTERNATORS: Automotive
ALUMINUM
ALUMINUM PRDTS
ALUMINUM: Ingots & Slabs
ALUMINUM: Ingots, Primary
ALUMINUM: Rolling & Drawing
AMMUNITION: Components
AMMUNITION: Small Arms
AMPLIFIERS
AMPLIFIERS: RF & IF Power
AMUSEMENT & RECREATION SVCS: Art Gallery, Commercial
AMUSEMENT ARCADES
AMUSEMENT MACHINES: Coin Operated
AMUSEMENT PARK DEVICES & RIDES
ANALGESICS
ANALYZERS: Blood & Body Fluid
ANALYZERS: Moisture
ANALYZERS: Network
ANALYZERS: Respiratory
ANESTHESIA EQPT
ANIMAL FEED & SUPPLEMENTS: Livestock & Poultry
ANIMAL FEED: Wholesalers
ANIMAL FOOD & SUPPLEMENTS: Bird Food, Prepared
ANIMAL FOOD & SUPPLEMENTS: Chicken Feeds, Prepared
ANIMAL FOOD & SUPPLEMENTS: Dog
ANIMAL FOOD & SUPPLEMENTS: Dog & Cat
ANIMAL FOOD & SUPPLEMENTS: Feed Supplements
ANIMAL FOOD & SUPPLEMENTS: Livestock
ANIMAL FOOD & SUPPLEMENTS: Meat Meal & Tankage
ANIMAL FOOD & SUPPLEMENTS: Pet, Exc Dog & Cat, Canned
ANIMAL FOOD & SUPPLEMENTS: Pet, Exc Dog & Cat, Dry
ANIMAL FOOD & SUPPLEMENTS: Poultry
ANIMAL FOOD/SUPPLEMENTS: Feeds Fm Meat/Meat/Veg Combnd Meals
ANNEALING: Metal
ANODIZING EQPT
ANODIZING SVC
ANTENNAS: Receiving
ANTI-GLARE MATERIAL
ANTIFREEZE
ANTIQUE REPAIR & RESTORATION SVCS, EXC FURNITURE & AUTOS
ANTISEPTICS, MEDICINAL
APPAREL ACCESS STORES
APPAREL DESIGNERS: Commercial
APPAREL FILLING MATERIALS: Cotton Waste, Kapok/ Related Matl
APPLIANCE PARTS: Porcelain Enameled
APPLIANCES, HOUSEHOLD: Kitchen, Major, Exc Refrigs & Stoves
APPLIANCES: Household, Refrigerators & Freezers
APPLIANCES: Major, Cooking
APPLIANCES: Small, Electric
APPLICATIONS SOFTWARE PROGRAMMING
AQUARIUMS & ACCESS: Glass
ARCHITECTURAL SVCS
ARMATURE REPAIRING & REWINDING SVC
ARMATURES: Ind
ARMOR PLATES
AROMATIC CHEMICAL PRDTS
ART DEALERS & GALLERIES
ART GOODS, WHOLESALE
ART MARBLE: Concrete
ARTIFICIAL FLOWERS & TREES
ARTISTS' MATERIALS, WHOLESALE

ARTS & CRAFTS SCHOOL
ARTWORK: Framed
ASPHALT & ASPHALT PRDTS
ASPHALT COATINGS & SEALERS
ASPHALT MINING & BITUMINOUS STONE QUARRYING SVCS
ASPHALT MIXTURES WHOLESALERS
ASPHALT PLANTS INCLUDING GRAVEL MIX TYPE
ASSEMBLING SVC: Plumbing Fixture Fittings, Plastic
ASSOCIATIONS: Business
ASSOCIATIONS: Real Estate Management
ASSOCIATIONS: Scientists'
ATOMIZERS
ATTENUATORS
AUDIO & VIDEO EQPT, EXC COMMERCIAL
AUDIO COMPONENTS
AUDIO ELECTRONIC SYSTEMS
AUDIO-VISUAL PROGRAM PRODUCTION SVCS
AUTO & HOME SUPPLY STORES: Auto & Truck Eqpt & Parts
AUTO & HOME SUPPLY STORES: Automotive Access
AUTO & HOME SUPPLY STORES: Automotive parts
AUTO & HOME SUPPLY STORES: Batteries, Automotive & Truck
AUTO & HOME SUPPLY STORES: Speed Shops, Incl Race Car Splys
AUTO & HOME SUPPLY STORES: Trailer Hitches, Automotive
AUTO & HOME SUPPLY STORES: Truck Eqpt & Parts
AUTO SPLYS & PARTS, NEW, WHSLE: Exhaust Sys, Mufflers, Etc
AUTOMATIC REGULATING CONTROL: Building Svcs Monitoring, Auto
AUTOMATIC REGULATING CONTROLS: AC & Refrigeration
AUTOMATIC REGULATING CONTROLS: Appliance Regulators
AUTOMATIC REGULATING CONTROLS: Appliance, Exc AirCond/Refr
AUTOMATIC REGULATING CONTROLS: Hardware, Environmental Reg
AUTOMATIC REGULATING CONTROLS: Hydronic Pressure Or Temp
AUTOMATIC REGULATING CONTROLS: Pneumatic Relays, Air-Cond
AUTOMATIC REGULATING CONTROLS: Refrig/Air-Cond Defrost
AUTOMATIC REGULATING CTRLS: Damper, Pneumatic Or Electric
AUTOMATIC TELLER MACHINES
AUTOMOBILES & OTHER MOTOR VEHICLES WHOLESALERS
AUTOMOBILES: Off-Road, Exc Recreational Vehicles
AUTOMOTIVE & TRUCK GENERAL REPAIR SVC
AUTOMOTIVE CUSTOMIZING SVCS, NONFACTORY BASIS
AUTOMOTIVE GLASS REPLACEMENT SHOPS
AUTOMOTIVE PARTS, ACCESS & SPLYS
AUTOMOTIVE PARTS: Plastic
AUTOMOTIVE PRDTS: Rubber
AUTOMOTIVE REPAIR SHOPS: Diesel Engine Repair
AUTOMOTIVE REPAIR SHOPS: Electrical Svcs
AUTOMOTIVE REPAIR SHOPS: Engine Rebuilding
AUTOMOTIVE REPAIR SHOPS: Machine Shop
AUTOMOTIVE REPAIR SHOPS: Rebuilding & Retreading Tires
AUTOMOTIVE REPAIR SHOPS: Sound System Svc & Installation
AUTOMOTIVE REPAIR SHOPS: Tire Recapping
AUTOMOTIVE REPAIR SHOPS: Tire Repair Shop
AUTOMOTIVE REPAIR SHOPS: Trailer Repair
AUTOMOTIVE REPAIR SHOPS: Wheel Alignment
AUTOMOTIVE REPAIR SVC
AUTOMOTIVE SPLYS & PARTS, NEW, WHOLESALE: Hardware
AUTOMOTIVE SPLYS & PARTS, NEW, WHOLESALE: Testing Eqpt, Eng
AUTOMOTIVE SPLYS & PARTS, NEW, WHOLESALE: Trailer Parts

AUTOMOTIVE SPLYS & PARTS, NEW, WHOLESALE: Wheels
AUTOMOTIVE SPLYS & PARTS, WHOLESALE, NEC
AUTOMOTIVE SVCS, EXC REPAIR & CARWASHES: Insp & Diagnostic
AUTOMOTIVE SVCS, EXC REPAIR & CARWASHES: Lubrication
AUTOMOTIVE SVCS, EXC RPR/CARWASHES: High Perf Auto Rpr/Svc
AUTOMOTIVE TRANSMISSION REPAIR SVC
AUTOMOTIVE WELDING SVCS
AUTOMOTIVE: Bodies
AUTOMOTIVE: Seat Frames, Metal
AUTOMOTIVE: Seating
AWNINGS & CANOPIES
AWNINGS & CANOPIES: Awnings, Fabric, From Purchased Matls
AWNINGS & CANOPIES: Canopies, Fabric, From Purchased Matls
AWNINGS: Fiberglass
AWNINGS: Metal
AXLES
AXLES: Rolled Or Forged, Made In Steel Mills

B

BACKHOES
BAGS & BAGGING: Knit
BAGS & CONTAINERS: Textile, Exc Sleeping
BAGS & SACKS: Shipping & Shopping
BAGS: Canvas
BAGS: Duffle, Canvas, Made From Purchased Materials
BAGS: Food Storage & Frozen Food, Plastic
BAGS: Food Storage & Trash, Plastic
BAGS: Paper
BAGS: Paper, Made From Purchased Materials
BAGS: Plastic
BAGS: Plastic & Pliofilm
BAGS: Plastic, Made From Purchased Materials
BAGS: Shipping
BAGS: Shopping, Made From Purchased Materials
BAKERIES, COMMERCIAL: On Premises Baking Only
BAKERIES: On Premises Baking & Consumption
BAKERY MACHINERY
BAKERY PRDTS, FROZEN: Wholesalers
BAKERY PRDTS: Bagels, Fresh Or Frozen
BAKERY PRDTS: Biscuits, Dry
BAKERY PRDTS: Bread, All Types, Fresh Or Frozen
BAKERY PRDTS: Cakes, Bakery, Exc Frozen
BAKERY PRDTS: Cakes, Bakery, Frozen
BAKERY PRDTS: Cookies
BAKERY PRDTS: Cookies & crackers
BAKERY PRDTS: Doughnuts, Exc Frozen
BAKERY PRDTS: Dry
BAKERY PRDTS: Frozen
BAKERY PRDTS: Pastries, Exc Frozen
BAKERY PRDTS: Pretzels
BAKERY PRDTS: Rolls, Bread Type, Fresh Or Frozen
BAKERY PRDTS: Wholesalers
BAKERY: Wholesale Or Wholesale & Retail Combined
BALERS
BALLOONS: Hot Air
BALLOONS: Novelty & Toy
BALLOONS: Toy & Advertising, Rubber
BANKS: Mortgage & Loan
BANNERS: Fabric
BANQUET HALL FACILITIES
BAR FIXTURES: Wood
BAR JOISTS & CONCRETE REINFORCING BARS: Fabricated
BARBECUE EQPT
BARGES BUILDING & REPAIR
BARRICADES: Metal
BARS & BAR SHAPES: Steel, Cold-Finished, Own Hot-Rolled
BARS: Concrete Reinforcing, Fabricated Steel
BASALT: Crushed & Broken
BASEBOARDS: Metal
BASEMENT WINDOW AREAWAYS: Concrete
BASES, BEVERAGE
BASKETS: Steel Wire
BATH SALTS
BATHROOM ACCESS & FITTINGS: Vitreous China & Earthenware
BATTERIES, EXC AUTOMOTIVE: Wholesalers

BATTERIES: Alkaline, Cell Storage
BATTERIES: Lead Acid, Storage
BATTERIES: Rechargeable
BATTERIES: Storage
BATTERIES: Wet
BATTERY CASES: Plastic Or Plastics Combination
BATTERY CHARGERS
BATTS & BATTING: Cotton
BEARINGS & PARTS Ball
BEARINGS: Ball & Roller
BEARINGS: Plastic
BEARINGS: Roller & Parts
BEAUTY & BARBER SHOP EQPT
BEAUTY & BARBER SHOP EQPT & SPLYS WHOLESALERS
BEAUTY SALONS
BEDDING, BEDSPREADS, BLANKETS & SHEETS
BEDDING, FROM SILK OR MANMADE FIBER
BEDS & ACCESS STORES
BEDS: Institutional
BEDSPREADS & BED SETS, FROM PURCHASED MATERIALS
BEDSPREADS, COTTON
BEER & ALE WHOLESALERS
BEER, WINE & LIQUOR STORES: Beer, Packaged
BELLOWS
BELTING: Rubber
BELTS & BELT PRDTS
BELTS: Conveyor, Made From Purchased Wire
BELTS: Seat, Automotive & Aircraft
BEVERAGE BASES & SYRUPS
BEVERAGE PRDTS: Malt, Barley
BEVERAGES, ALCOHOLIC: Ale
BEVERAGES, ALCOHOLIC: Applejack
BEVERAGES, ALCOHOLIC: Beer
BEVERAGES, ALCOHOLIC: Beer & Ale
BEVERAGES, ALCOHOLIC: Bourbon Whiskey
BEVERAGES, ALCOHOLIC: Distilled Liquors
BEVERAGES, ALCOHOLIC: Rum
BEVERAGES, ALCOHOLIC: Wines
BEVERAGES, MALT
BEVERAGES, NONALCOHOLIC: Bottled & canned soft drinks
BEVERAGES, NONALCOHOLIC: Carbonated
BEVERAGES, NONALCOHOLIC: Carbonated, Canned & Bottled, Etc
BEVERAGES, NONALCOHOLIC: Flavoring extracts & syrups, nec
BEVERAGES, NONALCOHOLIC: Fruit Drnks, Under 100% Juice, Can
BEVERAGES, NONALCOHOLIC: Soft Drinks, Canned & Bottled, Etc
BEVERAGES, NONALCOHOLIC: Tea, Iced, Bottled & Canned, Etc
BEVERAGES, WINE & DISTILLED ALCOHOLIC, WHOLESALE: Wine
BICYCLES, PARTS & ACCESS
BILLIARD & POOL TABLES & SPLYS
BINDING SVC: Books & Manuals
BINDINGS: Bias, Made From Purchased Materials
BIOLOGICAL PRDTS: Agar Culture Media
BIOLOGICAL PRDTS: Blood Derivatives
BIOLOGICAL PRDTS: Exc Diagnostic
BIOLOGICAL PRDTS: Vaccines
BIOLOGICAL PRDTS: Vaccines & Immunizing
BIOLOGICAL PRDTS: Veterinary
BIRTH CONTROL DEVICES: Rubber
BLADES: Knife
BLADES: Saw, Hand Or Power
BLANKBOOKS & LOOSELEAF BINDERS
BLANKBOOKS: Checkbooks & Passbooks, Bank
BLANKETS & BLANKETING, COTTON
BLEACHING YARN & FABRICS: Wool Or Similar Fibers
BLINDS & SHADES: Vertical
BLINDS : Window
BLOCKS & BRICKS: Concrete
BLOCKS: Landscape Or Retaining Wall, Concrete
BLOCKS: Paving
BLOCKS: Standard, Concrete Or Cinder
BLOWERS & FANS
BLOWERS & FANS
BLUEPRINTING SVCS
BOAT & BARGE COMPONENTS: Metal, Prefabricated
BOAT BUILDING & REPAIR
BOAT BUILDING & REPAIRING: Fiberglass

BOAT BUILDING & REPAIRING: Motorboats, Inboard Or Outboard
BOAT BUILDING & REPAIRING: Motorized
BOAT BUILDING & REPAIRING: Yachts
BOAT BUILDING & RPRG: Fishing, Small, Lobster, Crab, Oyster
BOAT DEALERS
BOAT DEALERS: Motor
BOAT LIFTS
BOAT REPAIR SVCS
BOATS & OTHER MARINE EQPT: Plastic
BODIES: Truck & Bus
BODY PARTS: Automobile, Stamped Metal
BOILER REPAIR SHOP
BOILERS & BOILER SHOP WORK
BOILERS: Low-Pressure Heating, Steam Or Hot Water
BOLTS: Metal
BOOK STORES
BOOK STORES: Children's
BOOKS, WHOLESALE
BOOTHS: Spray, Sheet Metal, Prefabricated
BOOTS: Men's
BOTTLED GAS DEALERS: Liquefied Petro, Dlvrd To Customers
BOTTLED GAS DEALERS: Propane
BOTTLES: Plastic
BOX & CARTON MANUFACTURING EQPT
BOXES & CRATES: Rectangular, Wood
BOXES & SHOOK: Nailed Wood
BOXES: Cash & Stamp, Stamped Metal
BOXES: Corrugated
BOXES: Junction, Electric
BOXES: Paperboard, Folding
BOXES: Paperboard, Set-Up
BOXES: Plastic
BOXES: Wooden
BRAKES & BRAKE PARTS
BRAKES: Metal Forming
BRASS & BRONZE PRDTS: Die-casted
BRAZING: Metal
BRICK, STONE & RELATED PRDTS WHOLESALERS
BRICKS & BLOCKS: Structural
BRICKS : Paving, Clay
BRICKS: Clay
BROADCASTING & COMMS EQPT: Antennas, Transmitting/ Comms
BROADCASTING & COMMS EQPT: Trnsmttng TV Antennas/ Grndng Eqpt
BROADCASTING & COMMUNICATIONS EQPT: Cellular Radio Telephone
BROADCASTING & COMMUNICATIONS EQPT: Studio Eqpt, Radio & TV
BROADCASTING STATIONS, RADIO: News
BROKERS' SVCS
BROKERS: Food
BROKERS: Printing
BRONZE FOUNDRY, NEC
BROOMS
BROOMS & BRUSHES
BROOMS & BRUSHES: Household Or Indl
BROOMS & BRUSHES: Paint Rollers
BROOMS & BRUSHES: Street Sweeping, Hand Or Machine
BUCKETS: Plastic
BUCKLES & PARTS
BUILDING & STRUCTURAL WOOD MEMBERS
BUILDING CLEANING & MAINTENANCE SVCS
BUILDING COMPONENTS: Structural Steel
BUILDING ITEM REPAIR SVCS, MISCELLANEOUS
BUILDING MAINTENANCE SVCS, EXC REPAIRS
BUILDING PRDTS & MATERIALS DEALERS
BUILDING PRDTS: Concrete
BUILDING PRDTS: Stone
BUILDINGS & COMPONENTS: Prefabricated Metal
BUILDINGS: Mobile, For Commercial Use
BUILDINGS: Portable
BUILDINGS: Prefabricated, Metal
BUILDINGS: Prefabricated, Wood
BULLETPROOF VESTS
BURIAL VAULTS: Concrete Or Precast Terrazzo
BURNERS: Gas, Indl
BUS BARS: Electrical
BUSHINGS & BEARINGS
BUSINESS ACTIVITIES: Non-Commercial Site

BUSINESS FORMS WHOLESALERS
BUSINESS FORMS: Printed, Manifold
BUSINESS TRAINING SVCS

C

CABINETS & CASES: Show, Display & Storage, Exc Wood
CABINETS: Bathroom Vanities, Wood
CABINETS: Entertainment
CABINETS: Entertainment Units, Household, Wood
CABINETS: Factory
CABINETS: Kitchen, Metal
CABINETS: Kitchen, Wood
CABINETS: Office, Wood
CABINETS: Show, Display, Etc, Wood, Exc Refrigerated
CABLE & OTHER PAY TELEVISION DISTRIBUTION
CABLE TELEVISION
CABLE TELEVISION PRDTS
CABLE: Coaxial
CABLE: Fiber Optic
CABLE: Noninsulated
CABLE: Ropes & Fiber
CABLE: Steel, Insulated Or Armored
CACAO BEAN PROCESSING
CAFES
CALCULATING & ACCOUNTING EQPT
CALIBRATING SVCS, NEC
CAMPERS: Truck Mounted
CAMSHAFTS
CANDLE SHOPS
CANDLES
CANDLES: Wholesalers
CANDY & CONFECTIONS: Candy Bars, Including Chocolate
 Covered
CANDY & CONFECTIONS: Chocolate Candy, Exc Solid
 Chocolate
CANDY & CONFECTIONS: Licorice
CANDY & CONFECTIONS: Nuts, Candy Covered
CANDY & CONFECTIONS: Popcorn Balls/Other Trtd
 Popcorn Prdts
CANDY, NUT & CONFECTIONERY STORES: Candy
CANDY: Chocolate From Cacao Beans
CANDY: Soft
CANNED SPECIALTIES
CANS & TUBES: Ammunition, Board Laminated With Metal
 Foil
CANS: Aluminum
CANS: Metal
CANS: Tin
CANVAS PRDTS
CAPACITORS & CONDENSERS
CAPACITORS: NEC
CAR WASH EQPT
CARBIDES
CARBON & GRAPHITE PRDTS, NEC
CARBURETORS
CARDS: Color
CARDS: Greeting
CARDS: Jacquard, Made From Purchased Materials
CARPET & UPHOLSTERY CLEANING SVCS
CARPETS & RUGS: Tufted
CARPETS, RUGS & FLOOR COVERING
CARS: Electric
CARTS: Grocery
CASES: Carrying
CASES: Carrying, Clothing & Apparel
CASES: Plastic
CASES: Shipping, Nailed Or Lock Corner, Wood
CASINGS: Sheet Metal
CAST STONE: Concrete
CASTINGS GRINDING: For The Trade
CASTINGS: Aerospace Investment, Ferrous
CASTINGS: Aerospace, Aluminum
CASTINGS: Aluminum
CASTINGS: Bronze, NEC, Exc Die
CASTINGS: Die, Aluminum
CASTINGS: Die, Nonferrous
CASTINGS: Gray Iron
CASTINGS: Machinery, Aluminum
CASTINGS: Precision
CASTINGS: Steel
CATALOG & MAIL-ORDER HOUSES
CATALOG SALES
CATALYSTS: Chemical

CATERERS
CAULKING COMPOUNDS
CEMENT & CONCRETE RELATED PRDTS & EQPT:
 Bituminous
CEMENT ROCK: Crushed & Broken
CEMENT: Asbestos, Siding
CEMENT: Heat Resistant
CEMENT: Hydraulic
CEMENT: Masonry
CEMENT: Natural
CHAIN: Welded, Made From Purchased Wire
CHASSIS: Motor Vehicle
CHASSIS: Travel Trailer
CHEMICAL ELEMENTS
CHEMICAL PROCESSING MACHINERY & EQPT
CHEMICALS & ALLIED PRDTS WHOLESALERS, NEC
CHEMICALS & ALLIED PRDTS, WHOLESALE: Adhesives
CHEMICALS & ALLIED PRDTS, WHOLESALE: Chemical
 Additives
CHEMICALS & ALLIED PRDTS, WHOLESALE: Chemicals,
 Indl
CHEMICALS & ALLIED PRDTS, WHOLESALE: Chemicals,
 Indl & Heavy
CHEMICALS & ALLIED PRDTS, WHOLESALE: Detergent/
 Soap
CHEMICALS & ALLIED PRDTS, WHOLESALE: Detergents
CHEMICALS & ALLIED PRDTS, WHOLESALE: Indl Gases
CHEMICALS & ALLIED PRDTS, WHOLESALE: Oil Additives
CHEMICALS & ALLIED PRDTS, WHOLESALE: Plastics
 Materials, NEC
CHEMICALS & ALLIED PRDTS, WHOLESALE: Plastics
 Prdts, NEC
CHEMICALS & ALLIED PRDTS, WHOLESALE: Plastics
 Sheets & Rods
CHEMICALS & ALLIED PRDTS, WHOLESALE: Polyurethane
 Prdts
CHEMICALS & ALLIED PRDTS, WHOLESALE: Resins
CHEMICALS & ALLIED PRDTS, WHOLESALE: Spec Clean/
 Sanitation
CHEMICALS & ALLIED PRDTS, WHOLESALE: Waxes, Exc
 Petroleum
CHEMICALS & OTHER PRDTS DERIVED FROM COKING
CHEMICALS, AGRICULTURE: Wholesalers
CHEMICALS: Agricultural
CHEMICALS: Bromine, Elemental
CHEMICALS: Fire Retardant
CHEMICALS: High Purity Grade, Organic
CHEMICALS: High Purity, Refined From Technical Grade
CHEMICALS: Inorganic, NEC
CHEMICALS: Lithium Compounds, Inorganic
CHEMICALS: Magnesium Compounds Or Salts, Inorganic
CHEMICALS: NEC
CHEMICALS: Phosphates, Defluorinated/Ammoniated, Exc
 Fertlr
CHEMICALS: Reagent Grade, Refined From Technical Grade
CHEMICALS: Silica Compounds
CHEMICALS: Water Treatment
CHICKEN SLAUGHTERING & PROCESSING
CHILDREN'S & INFANTS' CLOTHING STORES
CHILDREN'S WEAR STORES
CHOCOLATE, EXC CANDY FROM BEANS: Chips, Powder,
 Block, Syrup
CHOCOLATE, EXC CANDY FROM PURCH CHOC: Chips,
 Powder, Block
CHRISTMAS TREE LIGHTING SETS: Electric
CHRISTMAS TREES: Artificial
CHROMATOGRAPHY EQPT
CHUCKS
CIGARETTE & CIGAR PRDTS & ACCESS
CIGARETTE FILTERS
CIRCUIT BOARD REPAIR SVCS
CIRCUIT BREAKERS
CIRCUITS, INTEGRATED: Hybrid
CIRCUITS: Electronic
CIRCULAR KNIT FABRICS DYEING & FINISHING
CLAMPS & COUPLINGS: Hose
CLAMPS: Metal
CLAY, PETROLEUM REFINING: Chemically Processed
CLAY: Filtering, Treated
CLEANING EQPT: Commercial
CLEANING EQPT: Floor Washing & Polishing, Commercial
CLEANING EQPT: High Pressure
CLEANING OR POLISHING PREPARATIONS, NEC

CLEANING PRDTS: Automobile Polish
CLEANING PRDTS: Bleaches, Household, Dry Or Liquid
CLEANING PRDTS: Deodorants, Nonpersonal
CLEANING PRDTS: Disinfectants, Household Or Indl Plant
CLEANING PRDTS: Drain Pipe Solvents Or Cleaners
CLEANING PRDTS: Laundry Preparations
CLEANING PRDTS: Sanitation Preparations
CLEANING PRDTS: Sanitation Preps, Disinfectants/
 Deodorants
CLEANING PRDTS: Shoe Polish Or Cleaner
CLEANING PRDTS: Specialty
CLEANING SVCS: Industrial Or Commercial
CLOTHING & ACCESS, WOMEN, CHILDREN & INFANT,
 WHOL: Access
CLOTHING & ACCESS, WOMEN, CHILDREN & INFANT,
 WHOL: Uniforms
CLOTHING & ACCESS, WOMEN, CHILDREN/INFANT,
 WHOL: Baby Goods
CLOTHING & ACCESS, WOMEN, CHILDREN/INFANT,
 WHOL: Nightwear
CLOTHING & ACCESS: Handicapped
CLOTHING & ACCESS: Hospital Gowns
CLOTHING & ACCESS: Men's Miscellaneous Access
CLOTHING & ACCESS: Suspenders
CLOTHING & APPAREL STORES: Custom
CLOTHING & FURNISHINGS, MEN'S & BOYS',
 WHOLESALE: Shirts
CLOTHING & FURNISHINGS, MEN'S & BOYS',
 WHOLESALE: Uniforms
CLOTHING & FURNISHINGS, MENS & BOYS, WHOL:
 Sportswear/Work
CLOTHING STORES: T-Shirts, Printed, Custom
CLOTHING STORES: Uniforms & Work
CLOTHING STORES: Unisex
CLOTHING STORES: Work
CLOTHING: Academic Vestments
CLOTHING: Access, Women's & Misses'
CLOTHING: Aprons, Exc Rubber/Plastic, Women, Misses,
 Junior
CLOTHING: Aprons, Waterproof, From Purchased Materials
CLOTHING: Athletic & Sportswear, Men's & Boys'
CLOTHING: Athletic & Sportswear, Women's & Girls'
CLOTHING: Baker, Barber, Lab/Svc Ind Apparel, Washable,
 Men
CLOTHING: Belts
CLOTHING: Blouses, Women's & Girls'
CLOTHING: Caps, Baseball
CLOTHING: Children & Infants'
CLOTHING: Coats & Jackets, Leather & Sheep-Lined
CLOTHING: Coats & Suits, Men's & Boys'
CLOTHING: Collar & Cuff Sets, Knit
CLOTHING: Costumes
CLOTHING: Disposable
CLOTHING: Dresses
CLOTHING: Dresses & Skirts
CLOTHING: Hats & Headwear, Knit
CLOTHING: Hosiery, Pantyhose & Knee Length, Sheer
CLOTHING: Hospital, Men's
CLOTHING: Jackets & Vests, Exc Fur & Leather, Women's
CLOTHING: Jeans, Men's & Boys'
CLOTHING: Leather
CLOTHING: Men's & boy's underwear & nightwear
CLOTHING: Mens & Boys Jackets, Sport, Suede, Leatherette
CLOTHING: Neckwear
CLOTHING: Outerwear, Knit
CLOTHING: Outerwear, Women's & Misses' NEC
CLOTHING: Panty Hose
CLOTHING: Robes & Dressing Gowns
CLOTHING: Robes & Housecoats, Children's
CLOTHING: Service Apparel, Women's
CLOTHING: Shirts
CLOTHING: Shirts, Knit
CLOTHING: Shirts, Women's & Juniors', From Purchased
 Mtrls
CLOTHING: Socks
CLOTHING: Sportswear, Women's
CLOTHING: Sweaters & Sweater Coats, Knit
CLOTHING: Sweaters, Men's & Boys'
CLOTHING: Sweatshirts & T-Shirts, Men's & Boys'
CLOTHING: T-Shirts & Tops, Knit
CLOTHING: T-Shirts & Tops, Women's & Girls'
CLOTHING: Tights, Exc Women's
CLOTHING: Trousers & Slacks, Men's & Boys'

CLOTHING: Underwear, Knit
CLOTHING: Underwear, Women's & Children's
CLOTHING: Uniforms & Vestments
CLOTHING: Uniforms, Ex Athletic, Women's, Misses' & Juniors'
CLOTHING: Uniforms, Firemen's, From Purchased Materials
CLOTHING: Uniforms, Men's & Boys'
CLOTHING: Uniforms, Military, Men/Youth, Purchased Materials
CLOTHING: Uniforms, Work
CLOTHING: Work Apparel, Exc Uniforms
COAL & OTHER MINERALS & ORES WHOLESALERS
COAL MINING SERVICES
COAL MINING: Bituminous Coal & Lignite-Surface Mining
COATING COMPOUNDS: Tar
COATING SVC: Metals, With Plastic Or Resins
COATINGS: Epoxy
COATINGS: Polyurethane
COILS & TRANSFORMERS
COILS: Electric Motors Or Generators
COLORS: Pigments, Inorganic
COMBINATION UTILITIES, NEC
COMFORTERS & QUILTS, FROM MANMADE FIBER OR SILK
COMMERCIAL & OFFICE BUILDINGS RENOVATION & REPAIR
COMMERCIAL ART & GRAPHIC DESIGN SVCS
COMMERCIAL ART & ILLUSTRATION SVCS
COMMERCIAL CONTAINERS WHOLESALERS
COMMERCIAL EQPT WHOLESALERS, NEC
COMMERCIAL EQPT, WHOLESALE: Restaurant, NEC
COMMERCIAL EQPT, WHOLESALE: Scales, Exc Laboratory
COMMERCIAL EQPT, WHOLESALE: Store Fixtures & Display Eqpt
COMMERCIAL LAUNDRY EQPT
COMMERCIAL PHOTOGRAPHIC STUDIO
COMMERCIAL PRINTING & NEWSPAPER PUBLISHING
COMMON SAND MINING
COMMUNICATIONS EQPT WHOLESALERS
COMMUNICATIONS EQPT: Microwave
COMMUNICATIONS EQPT: Radio, Marine
COMMUNICATIONS SVCS: Data
COMMUNICATIONS SVCS: Internet Connectivity Svcs
COMMUNICATIONS SVCS: Internet Host Svcs
COMMUNICATIONS SVCS: Online Svc Providers
COMMUNICATIONS SVCS: Signal Enhancement Network Svcs
COMMUTATORS: Electronic
COMPOSITION STONE: Plastic
COMPOST
COMPRESSORS: Air & Gas
COMPRESSORS: Air & Gas, Including Vacuum Pumps
COMPRESSORS: Refrigeration & Air Conditioning Eqpt
COMPUTER & COMPUTER SOFTWARE STORES
COMPUTER & COMPUTER SOFTWARE STORES: Peripheral Eqpt
COMPUTER & COMPUTER SOFTWARE STORES: Personal Computers
COMPUTER & COMPUTER SOFTWARE STORES: Software & Access
COMPUTER & COMPUTER SOFTWARE STORES: Software, Bus/Non-Game
COMPUTER & COMPUTER SOFTWARE STORES: Software, Computer Game
COMPUTER & DATA PROCESSING EQPT REPAIR & MAINTENANCE
COMPUTER & OFFICE MACHINE MAINTENANCE & REPAIR
COMPUTER FACILITIES MANAGEMENT SVCS
COMPUTER GRAPHICS SVCS
COMPUTER PERIPHERAL EQPT REPAIR & MAINTENANCE
COMPUTER PERIPHERAL EQPT, NEC
COMPUTER PERIPHERAL EQPT, WHOLESALE
COMPUTER PERIPHERAL EQPT: Encoders
COMPUTER PERIPHERAL EQPT: Input Or Output
COMPUTER PROCESSING SVCS
COMPUTER PROGRAMMING SVCS: Custom
COMPUTER RELATED MAINTENANCE SVCS
COMPUTER SERVICE BUREAU
COMPUTER SOFTWARE DEVELOPMENT
COMPUTER SOFTWARE DEVELOPMENT & APPLICATIONS

COMPUTER SOFTWARE SYSTEMS ANALYSIS & DESIGN: Custom
COMPUTER STORAGE DEVICES, NEC
COMPUTER SYSTEMS ANALYSIS & DESIGN
COMPUTER TERMINALS
COMPUTERS, NEC
COMPUTERS, NEC, WHOLESALE
COMPUTERS, PERIPHERALS & SOFTWARE, WHOLESALE: Printers
COMPUTERS, PERIPHERALS & SOFTWARE, WHOLESALE: Software
COMPUTERS: Personal
CONCENTRATES, DRINK
CONCENTRATES, FLAVORING, EXC DRINK
CONCRETE BUILDING PRDTS WHOLESALERS
CONCRETE CURING & HARDENING COMPOUNDS
CONCRETE PLANTS
CONCRETE PRDTS
CONCRETE PRDTS, PRECAST, NEC
CONCRETE: Dry Mixture
CONCRETE: Ready-Mixed
CONDENSERS & CONDENSING UNITS: Air Conditioner
CONNECTORS: Electronic
CONSTRUCTION & MINING MACHINERY WHOLESALERS
CONSTRUCTION & ROAD MAINTENANCE EQPT: Drags, Road
CONSTRUCTION EQPT REPAIR SVCS
CONSTRUCTION EQPT: Attachments, Snow Plow
CONSTRUCTION EQPT: Cranes
CONSTRUCTION EQPT: Graders, Road
CONSTRUCTION EQPT: Loaders, Shovel, Self-Propelled
CONSTRUCTION EQPT: Roofing Eqpt
CONSTRUCTION MATERIALS, WHOLESALE: Aggregate
CONSTRUCTION MATERIALS, WHOLESALE: Architectural Metalwork
CONSTRUCTION MATERIALS, WHOLESALE: Awnings
CONSTRUCTION MATERIALS, WHOLESALE: Brick, Exc Refractory
CONSTRUCTION MATERIALS, WHOLESALE: Building Stone, Marble
CONSTRUCTION MATERIALS, WHOLESALE: Building, Exterior
CONSTRUCTION MATERIALS, WHOLESALE: Building, Interior
CONSTRUCTION MATERIALS, WHOLESALE: Cement
CONSTRUCTION MATERIALS, WHOLESALE: Concrete Mixtures
CONSTRUCTION MATERIALS, WHOLESALE: Doors, Garage
CONSTRUCTION MATERIALS, WHOLESALE: Masons' Materials
CONSTRUCTION MATERIALS, WHOLESALE: Millwork
CONSTRUCTION MATERIALS, WHOLESALE: Molding, All Materials
CONSTRUCTION MATERIALS, WHOLESALE: Pallets, Wood
CONSTRUCTION MATERIALS, WHOLESALE: Paving Materials
CONSTRUCTION MATERIALS, WHOLESALE: Plywood
CONSTRUCTION MATERIALS, WHOLESALE: Prefabricated Structures
CONSTRUCTION MATERIALS, WHOLESALE: Roofing & Siding Material
CONSTRUCTION MATERIALS, WHOLESALE: Sand
CONSTRUCTION MATERIALS, WHOLESALE: Septic Tanks
CONSTRUCTION MATERIALS, WHOLESALE: Siding, Exc Wood
CONSTRUCTION MATERIALS, WHOLESALE: Stone, Crushed Or Broken
CONSTRUCTION MATERIALS, WHOLESALE: Veneer
CONSTRUCTION MATERIALS, WHOLESALE: Windows
CONSTRUCTION MATLS, WHOL: Doors, Combination, Screen-Storm
CONSTRUCTION SAND MINING
CONSTRUCTION: Agricultural Building
CONSTRUCTION: Athletic & Recreation Facilities
CONSTRUCTION: Bridge
CONSTRUCTION: Commercial & Office Building, New
CONSTRUCTION: Commercial & Office Buildings, Prefabricated
CONSTRUCTION: Dams, Waterways, Docks & Other Marine
CONSTRUCTION: Drainage System
CONSTRUCTION: Farm Building
CONSTRUCTION: Food Prdts Manufacturing or Packing Plant

CONSTRUCTION: Heavy Highway & Street
CONSTRUCTION: Indl Buildings, New, NEC
CONSTRUCTION: Indl Plant
CONSTRUCTION: Land Preparation
CONSTRUCTION: Marine
CONSTRUCTION: Oil & Gas Pipeline Construction
CONSTRUCTION: Parking Lot
CONSTRUCTION: Pipeline, NEC
CONSTRUCTION: Residential, Nec
CONSTRUCTION: Sewer Line
CONSTRUCTION: Single-Family Housing
CONSTRUCTION: Single-family Housing, New
CONSTRUCTION: Swimming Pools
CONSTRUCTION: Transmitting Tower, Telecommunication
CONSTRUCTION: Water & Sewer Line
CONSULTING SVC: Business, NEC
CONSULTING SVC: Educational
CONSULTING SVC: Human Resource
CONSULTING SVC: Management
CONSULTING SVCS, BUSINESS: Communications
CONSULTING SVCS, BUSINESS: Energy Conservation
CONSULTING SVCS, BUSINESS: Environmental
CONSULTING SVCS, BUSINESS: Safety Training Svcs
CONSULTING SVCS, BUSINESS: Sys Engnrg, Exc Computer/ Prof
CONSULTING SVCS, BUSINESS: Systems Analysis & Engineering
CONSULTING SVCS, BUSINESS: Testing, Educational Or Personnel
CONSULTING SVCS: Scientific
CONTACT LENSES
CONTACTS: Electrical
CONTAINERS, GLASS: Water Bottles
CONTAINERS: Food, Folding, Made From Purchased Materials
CONTAINERS: Food, Liquid Tight, Including Milk
CONTAINERS: Frozen Food & Ice Cream
CONTAINERS: Glass
CONTAINERS: Laminated Phenolic & Vulcanized Fiber
CONTAINERS: Metal
CONTAINERS: Plastic
CONTAINERS: Sanitary, Food
CONTAINERS: Shipping, Bombs, Metal Plate
CONTAINERS: Wood
CONTRACTOR: Dredging
CONTRACTOR: Framing
CONTRACTOR: Rigging & Scaffolding
CONTRACTORS: Acoustical & Insulation Work
CONTRACTORS: Asbestos Removal & Encapsulation
CONTRACTORS: Carpentry Work
CONTRACTORS: Carpentry, Cabinet & Finish Work
CONTRACTORS: Carpentry, Finish & Trim Work
CONTRACTORS: Closet Organizers, Installation & Design
CONTRACTORS: Commercial & Office Building
CONTRACTORS: Communications Svcs
CONTRACTORS: Decontamination Svcs
CONTRACTORS: Directional Oil & Gas Well Drilling Svc
CONTRACTORS: Drywall
CONTRACTORS: Electric Power Systems
CONTRACTORS: Electronic Controls Installation
CONTRACTORS: Energy Management Control
CONTRACTORS: Fence Construction
CONTRACTORS: Fiber Optic Cable Installation
CONTRACTORS: Fiberglass Work
CONTRACTORS: Floor Laying & Other Floor Work
CONTRACTORS: Gas Field Svcs, NEC
CONTRACTORS: General Electric
CONTRACTORS: Glass Tinting, Architectural & Automotive
CONTRACTORS: Heating & Air Conditioning
CONTRACTORS: Heating Systems Repair & Maintenance Svc
CONTRACTORS: Highway & Street Construction, General
CONTRACTORS: Highway & Street Paving
CONTRACTORS: Hydraulic Eqpt Installation & Svcs
CONTRACTORS: Kitchen Cabinet Installation
CONTRACTORS: Machine Rigging & Moving
CONTRACTORS: Machinery Installation
CONTRACTORS: Marble Installation, Interior
CONTRACTORS: Masonry & Stonework
CONTRACTORS: Office Furniture Installation
CONTRACTORS: Oil & Gas Wells Pumping Svcs
CONTRACTORS: Oil Field Pipe Testing Svcs
CONTRACTORS: Ornamental Metal Work

CONTRACTORS: Painting, Commercial
CONTRACTORS: Painting, Indl
CONTRACTORS: Petroleum Storage Tanks, Pumping & Draining
CONTRACTORS: Plumbing
CONTRACTORS: Power Generating Eqpt Installation
CONTRACTORS: Prefabricated Window & Door Installation
CONTRACTORS: Process Piping
CONTRACTORS: Roustabout Svcs
CONTRACTORS: Septic System
CONTRACTORS: Sheet Metal Work, NEC
CONTRACTORS: Siding
CONTRACTORS: Structural Iron Work, Structural
CONTRACTORS: Structural Steel Erection
CONTRACTORS: Textile Warping
CONTRACTORS: Tile Installation, Ceramic
CONTRACTORS: Underground Utilities
CONTRACTORS: Warm Air Heating & Air Conditioning
CONTRACTORS: Water Well Drilling
CONTRACTORS: Windows & Doors
CONTRACTORS: Wood Floor Installation & Refinishing
CONTROL EQPT: Electric
CONTROLS & ACCESS: Indl, Electric
CONTROLS & ACCESS: Motor
CONTROLS: Automatic Temperature
CONTROLS: Electric Motor
CONTROLS: Environmental
CONTROLS: Thermostats, Built-in
CONVENIENCE STORES
CONVERTERS: Frequency
CONVERTERS: Rotary, Electrical
CONVEYOR SYSTEMS: Belt, General Indl Use
CONVEYOR SYSTEMS: Bulk Handling
CONVEYOR SYSTEMS: Pneumatic Tube
CONVEYOR SYSTEMS: Robotic
CONVEYORS & CONVEYING EQPT
COOKING & FOODWARMING EQPT: Commercial
COOKING EQPT, HOUSEHOLD: Ranges, Electric
COOKWARE, STONEWARE: Coarse Earthenware & Pottery
COOKWARE: Fine Earthenware
COOLING TOWERS: Metal
COPPER ORE MINING
COPPER PRDTS: Smelter, Primary
COPPER: Rolling & Drawing
CORD & TWINE
CORK & CORK PRDTS: Bottle
COSMETIC PREPARATIONS
COSMETICS & TOILETRIES
COSMETICS WHOLESALERS
COSMETOLOGY & PERSONAL HYGIENE SALONS
COUGH MEDICINES
COUNTER & SINK TOPS
COUNTERS OR COUNTER DISPLAY CASES, EXC WOOD
COUNTERS OR COUNTER DISPLAY CASES, WOOD
COUNTING DEVICES: Controls, Revolution & Timing
COUNTING DEVICES: Speedometers
COUPLINGS, EXC PRESSURE & SOIL PIPE
COUPLINGS: Hose & Tube, Hydraulic Or Pneumatic
COVERS: Automobile Seat
COVERS: Automotive, Exc Seat & Tire
CRANE & AERIAL LIFT SVCS
CRANES: Indl Plant
CRANES: Overhead
CREDIT CARD SVCS
CROWNS & CLOSURES
CULTURE MEDIA
CUPS & PLATES: Foamed Plastics
CURBING: Granite Or Stone
CURTAIN & DRAPERY FIXTURES: Poles, Rods & Rollers
CURTAIN WALLS: Building, Steel
CURTAINS: Window, From Purchased Materials
CUSHIONS & PILLOWS
CUSHIONS & PILLOWS: Bed, From Purchased Materials
CUSHIONS: Carpet & Rug, Foamed Plastics
CUSTOM COMPOUNDING OF RUBBER MATERIALS
CUT STONE & STONE PRODUCTS
CUTLERY
CUTLERY WHOLESALERS
CYCLIC CRUDES & INTERMEDIATES
CYLINDER & ACTUATORS: Fluid Power
CYLINDERS: Pump

D

DAIRY EQPT
DAIRY PRDTS STORE: Ice Cream, Packaged
DAIRY PRDTS STORES
DAIRY PRDTS: Acidophilus Milk
DAIRY PRDTS: Butter
DAIRY PRDTS: Canned Milk, Whole
DAIRY PRDTS: Cheese
DAIRY PRDTS: Dairy Based Desserts, Frozen
DAIRY PRDTS: Dietary Supplements, Dairy & Non-Dairy Based
DAIRY PRDTS: Ice Cream & Ice Milk
DAIRY PRDTS: Ice Cream, Bulk
DAIRY PRDTS: Ice Cream, Packaged, Molded, On Sticks, Etc.
DAIRY PRDTS: Milk & Cream, Cultured & Flavored
DAIRY PRDTS: Milk, Fluid
DAIRY PRDTS: Natural Cheese
DAIRY PRDTS: Processed Cheese
DAIRY PRDTS: Yogurt, Frozen
DATA PROCESSING & PREPARATION SVCS
DATA PROCESSING SVCS
DECORATIVE WOOD & WOODWORK
DEFENSE SYSTEMS & EQPT
DEGREASING MACHINES
DENTAL EQPT
DENTAL EQPT & SPLYS
DENTAL EQPT & SPLYS: Enamels
DENTAL EQPT & SPLYS: Orthodontic Appliances
DENTISTS' OFFICES & CLINICS
DEODORANTS: Personal
DEPARTMENT STORES
DEPARTMENT STORES: Country General
DEPILATORIES, COSMETIC
DERMATOLOGICALS
DESIGN SVCS, NEC
DESIGN SVCS: Commercial & Indl
DESIGN SVCS: Computer Integrated Systems
DETECTIVE & ARMORED CAR SERVICES
DIAGNOSTIC SUBSTANCES
DIAGNOSTIC SUBSTANCES OR AGENTS: Cytology & Histology
DIAGNOSTIC SUBSTANCES OR AGENTS: In Vitro
DIAGNOSTIC SUBSTANCES OR AGENTS: Microbiology & Virology
DIAGNOSTIC SUBSTANCES OR AGENTS: Radioactive
DIAGNOSTIC SUBSTANCES OR AGENTS: Veterinary
DIE CUTTING SVC: Paper
DIE SETS: Presses, Metal Stamping
DIES & TOOLS: Special
DIES: Cutting, Exc Metal
DIES: Diamond, Metalworking
DIES: Extrusion
DIES: Plastic Forming
DIODES: Light Emitting
DIODES: Solid State, Germanium, Silicon, Etc
DIRECT SELLING ESTABLISHMENTS: Food Svcs
DISASTER SVCS
DISCOUNT DEPARTMENT STORES
DISPLAY FIXTURES: Wood
DISPLAY ITEMS: Corrugated, Made From Purchased Materials
DISTRIBUTORS: Motor Vehicle Engine
DOCUMENT STORAGE SVCS
DOOR FRAMES: Wood
DOORS & WINDOWS: Storm, Metal
DOORS: Garage, Overhead, Metal
DOORS: Garage, Overhead, Wood
DOORS: Glass
DOORS: Screen, Metal
DRAPERIES & CURTAINS
DRAPERIES: Plastic & Textile, From Purchased Materials
DRAPERY & UPHOLSTERY STORES: Draperies
DRILL BITS
DRILLS & DRILLING EQPT: Mining
DRINKING PLACES: Bars & Lounges
DRINKING PLACES: Beer Garden
DRINKING WATER COOLERS WHOLESALERS: Mechanical
DRUG STORES
DRUGS & DRUG PROPRIETARIES, WHOLESALE
DRUGS & DRUG PROPRIETARIES, WHOLESALE: Bandages
DRUGS & DRUG PROPRIETARIES, WHOLESALE: Pharmaceuticals

DRUGS & DRUG PROPRIETARIES, WHOLESALE: Vitamins & Minerals
DRUGS AFFECTING NEOPLASMS & ENDOCRINE SYSTEMS
DRUGS: Parasitic & Infective Disease Affecting
DRUMS: Fiber
DRUMS: Shipping, Metal
DUCTING: Metal Plate
DUCTS: Sheet Metal
DUMPSTERS: Garbage
DUST OR FUME COLLECTING EQPT: Indl
DYES & PIGMENTS: Organic

E

EATING PLACES
EDUCATIONAL SVCS
ELECTRIC & OTHER SERVICES COMBINED
ELECTRIC MOTOR & GENERATOR AUXILIARY PARTS
ELECTRIC MOTOR REPAIR SVCS
ELECTRIC SERVICES
ELECTRIC SVCS, NEC: Power Generation
ELECTRIC WATER HEATERS WHOLESALERS
ELECTRICAL APPARATUS & EQPT WHOLESALERS
ELECTRICAL DISCHARGE MACHINING, EDM
ELECTRICAL EQPT REPAIR SVCS
ELECTRICAL EQPT REPAIR SVCS: High Voltage
ELECTRICAL EQPT: Automotive, NEC
ELECTRICAL GOODS, WHOLESALE: Batteries, Dry Cell
ELECTRICAL GOODS, WHOLESALE: Electrical Appliances, Major
ELECTRICAL GOODS, WHOLESALE: Electronic Parts
ELECTRICAL GOODS, WHOLESALE: Fittings & Construction Mat
ELECTRICAL GOODS, WHOLESALE: Generators
ELECTRICAL GOODS, WHOLESALE: Light Bulbs & Related Splys
ELECTRICAL GOODS, WHOLESALE: Security Control Eqpt & Systems
ELECTRICAL GOODS, WHOLESALE: Semiconductor Devices
ELECTRICAL GOODS, WHOLESALE: Telephone & Telegraphic Eqpt
ELECTRICAL GOODS, WHOLESALE: Wire & Cable
ELECTRICAL GOODS, WHOLESALE: Wire & Cable, Electronic
ELECTRICAL SPLYS
ELECTRICAL SUPPLIES: Porcelain
ELECTROMEDICAL EQPT
ELECTROMEDICAL EQPT WHOLESALERS
ELECTRON TUBES
ELECTRONIC DEVICES: Solid State, NEC
ELECTRONIC EQPT REPAIR SVCS
ELECTRONIC LOADS & POWER SPLYS
ELECTRONIC PARTS & EQPT WHOLESALERS
ELECTRONIC SHOPPING
ELECTROPLATING & PLATING SVC
ELEVATORS & EQPT
ELEVATORS WHOLESALERS
ELEVATORS: Installation & Conversion
EMBLEMS: Embroidered
EMBROIDERY ADVERTISING SVCS
EMBROIDERY KITS
EMERGENCY ALARMS
ENCLOSURES: Electronic
ENCLOSURES: Screen
ENDOCRINE PRDTS
ENGINE REBUILDING: Diesel
ENGINE REBUILDING: Gas
ENGINEERING SVCS
ENGINEERING SVCS: Building Construction
ENGINEERING SVCS: Chemical
ENGINEERING SVCS: Construction & Civil
ENGINEERING SVCS: Electrical Or Electronic
ENGINEERING SVCS: Machine Tool Design
ENGINEERING SVCS: Marine
ENGINEERING SVCS: Mechanical
ENGINES: Internal Combustion, NEC
ENGINES: Jet Propulsion
ENGINES: Marine
ENGRAVING SVC, NEC
ENGRAVING SVCS
ENVELOPES
ENVELOPES WHOLESALERS

P
R
D
T

I
N
D
E
X

ENZYMES
EPOXY RESINS
EQUIPMENT & VEHICLE FINANCE LEASING COMPANIES
EQUIPMENT: Pedestrian Traffic Control
EQUIPMENT: Rental & Leasing, NEC
ETCHING & ENGRAVING SVC
ETHYLENE-PROPYLENE RUBBERS: EPDM Polymers
EXHAUST SYSTEMS: Eqpt & Parts
EXPANSION JOINTS: Rubber
EXPLOSIVES
EXTRACTS, FLAVORING

F

FABRIC STORES
FABRICS & CLOTH: Quilted
FABRICS & CLOTHING: Rubber Coated
FABRICS: Acetate, Broadwoven
FABRICS: Apparel & Outerwear, Broadwoven
FABRICS: Apparel & Outerwear, Cotton
FABRICS: Automotive, From Manmade Fiber
FABRICS: Basket Weave, Cotton
FABRICS: Bonded-Fiber, Exc Felt
FABRICS: Broad Woven, Goods, Cotton
FABRICS: Broadwoven, Wool
FABRICS: Chenilles, Tufted Textile
FABRICS: Cloth, Warp Knit
FABRICS: Cotton, Narrow
FABRICS: Denims
FABRICS: Dress, Cotton
FABRICS: Elastic, From Manmade Fiber Or Silk
FABRICS: Fiberglass, Broadwoven
FABRICS: Glass & Fiberglass, Broadwoven
FABRICS: Glass, Narrow
FABRICS: Lacings, Textile
FABRICS: Laundry, Cotton
FABRICS: Nonwoven
FABRICS: Nylon, Broadwoven
FABRICS: Pile, Circular Knit
FABRICS: Polyester, Broadwoven
FABRICS: Polypropylene, Broadwoven
FABRICS: Resin Or Plastic Coated
FABRICS: Rubber & Elastic Yarns & Fabrics
FABRICS: Rubberized
FABRICS: Scrub Cloths
FABRICS: Shoe Laces, Exc Leather
FABRICS: Specialty Including Twisted Weaves, Broadwoven
FABRICS: Spunbonded
FABRICS: Tickings
FABRICS: Trimmings, Textile
FABRICS: Upholstery, Cotton
FABRICS: Upholstery, Wool
FABRICS: Warp & Flat Knit Prdts
FABRICS: Weft Or Circular Knit
FABRICS: Wool, Broadwoven
FABRICS: Worsted fabrics, broadwoven
FAMILY CLOTHING STORES
FANS, BLOWING: Indl Or Commercial
FANS, VENTILATING: Indl Or Commercial
FANS: Ceiling
FARM & GARDEN MACHINERY WHOLESALERS
FARM PRDTS, RAW MATERIALS, WHOLESALE: Broomcorn
FARM SPLYS WHOLESALERS
FARM SPLYS, WHOLESALE: Fertilizers & Agricultural
   Chemicals
FARM SPLYS, WHOLESALE: Insecticides
FASTENERS WHOLESALERS
FASTENERS: Metal
FASTENERS: Metal
FASTENERS: Notions, Hooks & Eyes
FASTENERS: Wire, Made From Purchased Wire
FAUCETS & SPIGOTS: Metal & Plastic
FELDSPAR: Ground Or Otherwise Treated
FENCE POSTS: Iron & Steel
FENCES OR POSTS: Ornamental Iron Or Steel
FENCING MADE IN WIREDRAWING PLANTS
FENCING MATERIALS: Docks & Other Outdoor Prdts, Wood
FENCING: Chain Link
FERTILIZER MINERAL MINING
FERTILIZER, AGRICULTURAL: Wholesalers
FERTILIZERS: Nitrogen Solutions
FERTILIZERS: Nitrogenous
FERTILIZERS: Phosphatic
FIBER & FIBER PRDTS: Acrylic

FIBER & FIBER PRDTS: Polyester
FIBER & FIBER PRDTS: Vinyl
FIBER OPTICS
FIBER: Vulcanized
FIBERS: Carbon & Graphite
FILM BASE: Cellulose Acetate Or Nitrocellulose Plastics
FILTER CLEANING SVCS
FILTER ELEMENTS: Fluid & Hydraulic Line
FILTERING MEDIA: Pottery
FILTERS
FILTERS & SOFTENERS: Water, Household
FILTERS & STRAINERS: Pipeline
FILTERS: Air
FILTERS: Air Intake, Internal Combustion Engine, Exc Auto
FILTERS: General Line, Indl
FILTRATION DEVICES: Electronic
FINANCIAL SVCS
FINGERPRINT EQPT
FINISHING AGENTS
FINISHING AGENTS: Textile
FINISHING SVCS
FIRE ALARM MAINTENANCE & MONITORING SVCS
FIRE ARMS, SMALL: Guns Or Gun Parts, 30 mm & Below
FIRE ARMS, SMALL: Pistols Or Pistol Parts, 30 mm & below
FIRE ARMS, SMALL: Rifles Or Rifle Parts, 30 mm & below
FIRE CONTROL EQPT REPAIR SVCS, MILITARY
FIRE CONTROL OR BOMBING EQPT: Electronic
FIRE DETECTION SYSTEMS
FIRE EXTINGUISHERS, WHOLESALE
FIRE EXTINGUISHERS: Portable
FIRE OR BURGLARY RESISTIVE PRDTS
FIREARMS & AMMUNITION, EXC SPORTING, WHOLESALE
FIREFIGHTING APPARATUS
FIREPLACE EQPT & ACCESS
FIREPLACES: Concrete
FIRST AID SPLYS, WHOLESALE
FISH & SEAFOOD PROCESSORS: Canned Or Cured
FISH & SEAFOOD PROCESSORS: Fresh Or Frozen
FISH & SEAFOOD WHOLESALERS
FISHING EQPT: Lures
FITTINGS & ASSEMBLIES: Hose & Tube, Hydraulic Or
   Pneumatic
FITTINGS & SPECIALTIES: Steam
FITTINGS: Pipe
FIXTURES & EQPT: Kitchen, Metal, Exc Cast Aluminum
FIXTURES: Cut Stone
FLAGS: Fabric
FLAGSTONES
FLAT GLASS: Float
FLAT GLASS: Window, Clear & Colored
FLOOR COVERING STORES
FLOOR COVERING STORES: Carpets
FLOOR COVERINGS WHOLESALERS
FLOOR COVERINGS: Rubber
FLOOR COVERINGS: Textile Fiber
FLOORING & SIDING: Metal
FLOORING: Hardwood
FLOWERS, ARTIFICIAL, WHOLESALE
FLUID METERS & COUNTING DEVICES
FLUID POWER PUMPS & MOTORS
FLUID POWER VALVES & HOSE FITTINGS
FOAM RUBBER
FOAMS & RUBBER, WHOLESALE
FOIL & LEAF: Metal
FOIL: Aluminum
FOOD COLORINGS
FOOD PRDTS, BREAKFAST: Cereal, Oatmeal
FOOD PRDTS, CANNED OR FRESH PACK: Fruit Juices
FOOD PRDTS, CANNED: Baby Food
FOOD PRDTS, CANNED: Barbecue Sauce
FOOD PRDTS, CANNED: Fruit Juices, Fresh
FOOD PRDTS, CANNED: Fruits
FOOD PRDTS, CANNED: Fruits & Fruit Prdts
FOOD PRDTS, CANNED: Jams, Jellies & Preserves
FOOD PRDTS, CANNED: Mexican, NEC
FOOD PRDTS, CONFECTIONERY, WHOLESALE: Candy
FOOD PRDTS, CONFECTIONERY, WHOLESALE: Snack
   Foods
FOOD PRDTS, DAIRY, WHOLESALE: Frozen Dairy Desserts
FOOD PRDTS, FISH & SEAFOOD: Crabmeat, Frozen
FOOD PRDTS, FISH & SEAFOOD: Fish, Filleted
FOOD PRDTS, FROZEN: Ethnic Foods, NEC
FOOD PRDTS, FROZEN: Fruits, Juices & Vegetables

FOOD PRDTS, FRUITS & VEGETABLES, FRESH,
   WHOLESALE: Fruits
FOOD PRDTS, WHOLESALE: Beans, Field
FOOD PRDTS, WHOLESALE: Beverages, Exc Coffee & Tea
FOOD PRDTS, WHOLESALE: Chocolate
FOOD PRDTS, WHOLESALE: Coffee, Green Or Roasted
FOOD PRDTS, WHOLESALE: Condiments
FOOD PRDTS, WHOLESALE: Dried or Canned Foods
FOOD PRDTS, WHOLESALE: Flavorings & Fragrances
FOOD PRDTS, WHOLESALE: Flour
FOOD PRDTS, WHOLESALE: Grain Elevators
FOOD PRDTS, WHOLESALE: Grains
FOOD PRDTS, WHOLESALE: Natural & Organic
FOOD PRDTS, WHOLESALE: Salad Dressing
FOOD PRDTS, WHOLESALE: Specialty
FOOD PRDTS, WHOLESALE: Spices & Seasonings
FOOD PRDTS, WHOLESALE: Water, Distilled
FOOD PRDTS: Almond Pastes
FOOD PRDTS: Animal & marine fats & oils
FOOD PRDTS: Cheese Curls & Puffs
FOOD PRDTS: Chicken, Processed, Cooked
FOOD PRDTS: Chicken, Processed, Fresh
FOOD PRDTS: Chicken, Slaughtered & Dressed
FOOD PRDTS: Coffee
FOOD PRDTS: Coffee Extracts
FOOD PRDTS: Cooking Oils, Refined Vegetable, Exc Corn
FOOD PRDTS: Corn Chips & Other Corn-Based Snacks
FOOD PRDTS: Corn Meal
FOOD PRDTS: Dips, Exc Cheese & Sour Cream Based
FOOD PRDTS: Dough, Pizza, Prepared
FOOD PRDTS: Dried & Dehydrated Fruits, Vegetables &
   Soup Mix
FOOD PRDTS: Edible fats & oils
FOOD PRDTS: Edible Oil Prdts, Exc Corn Oil
FOOD PRDTS: Flour
FOOD PRDTS: Flour & Other Grain Mill Products
FOOD PRDTS: Flour Mixes & Doughs
FOOD PRDTS: Fruit Juices
FOOD PRDTS: Gelatin Dessert Preparations
FOOD PRDTS: Ice, Cubes
FOOD PRDTS: Mixes, Bread & Bread-Type Roll
FOOD PRDTS: Mixes, Gravy, Dry
FOOD PRDTS: Mixes, Pancake From Purchased Flour
FOOD PRDTS: Mixes, Sauces, Dry
FOOD PRDTS: Mixes, Seasonings, Dry
FOOD PRDTS: Mustard, Prepared
FOOD PRDTS: Oils & Fats, Marine
FOOD PRDTS: Olive Oil
FOOD PRDTS: Pasta, Uncooked, Packaged With Other
   Ingredients
FOOD PRDTS: Peanut Butter
FOOD PRDTS: Pickles, Vinegar
FOOD PRDTS: Pork Rinds
FOOD PRDTS: Potato Chips & Other Potato-Based Snacks
FOOD PRDTS: Poultry, Processed, Cooked
FOOD PRDTS: Poultry, Processed, Frozen
FOOD PRDTS: Poultry, Slaughtered & Dressed
FOOD PRDTS: Raw cane sugar
FOOD PRDTS: Sandwiches
FOOD PRDTS: Seasonings & Spices
FOOD PRDTS: Soup Mixes
FOOD PRDTS: Tea
FOOD PRDTS: Tortilla Chips
FOOD PRDTS: Turkey, Slaughtered & Dressed
FOOD PRDTS: Vinegar
FOOD PRDTS: Wheat Flour
FOOD PRODUCTS MACHINERY
FOOD STORES: Convenience, Independent
FOOD STORES: Cooperative
FOOD STORES: Grocery, Independent
FOOD STORES: Supermarkets, Chain
FOOTWEAR, WHOLESALE: Athletic
FOOTWEAR, WHOLESALE: Boots
FOOTWEAR: Cut Stock
FORGINGS: Aircraft, Ferrous
FORGINGS: Automotive & Internal Combustion Engine
FORGINGS: Construction Or Mining Eqpt, Ferrous
FORGINGS: Iron & Steel
FORGINGS: Nonferrous
FORGINGS: Nuclear Power Plant, Ferrous
FORGINGS: Plumbing Fixture, Nonferrous
FORMS: Concrete, Sheet Metal
FOUNDRIES: Aluminum

FOUNDRIES: Gray & Ductile Iron
FOUNDRIES: Nonferrous
FOUNDRIES: Steel
FRAMES & FRAMING WHOLESALE
FRAMES: Chair, Metal
FRANCHISES, SELLING OR LICENSING
FREIGHT FORWARDING ARRANGEMENTS
FRICTION MATERIAL, MADE FROM POWDERED METAL
FRUITS & VEGETABLES WHOLESALERS: Fresh
FUEL ADDITIVES
FUEL DEALERS: Coal
FUEL OIL DEALERS
FUEL TREATING
FUELS: Diesel
FUELS: Nuclear
FUELS: Nuclear, Uranium Slug, Radioactive
FULLER'S EARTH MINING
FUND RAISING ORGANIZATION, NON-FEE BASIS
FUNGICIDES OR HERBICIDES
FURNACES & OVENS: Indl
FURNACES: Warm Air, Electric
FURNITURE COMPONENTS: Porcelain Enameled
FURNITURE PARTS: Metal
FURNITURE REFINISHING SVCS
FURNITURE REPAIR & MAINTENANCE SVCS
FURNITURE STOCK & PARTS: Hardwood
FURNITURE STOCK & PARTS: Turnings, Wood
FURNITURE STORES
FURNITURE WHOLESALERS
FURNITURE, HOUSEHOLD: Wholesalers
FURNITURE, MATTRESSES: Wholesalers
FURNITURE, OFFICE: Wholesalers
FURNITURE, OUTDOOR & LAWN: Wholesalers
FURNITURE, WHOLESALE: Beds & Bedding
FURNITURE, WHOLESALE: Chairs
FURNITURE, WHOLESALE: Lockers
FURNITURE, WHOLESALE: Racks
FURNITURE: Assembly Hall
FURNITURE: Bedroom, Wood
FURNITURE: Bedsprings, Assembled
FURNITURE: Box Springs, Assembled
FURNITURE: Cabinets & Filing Drawers, Office, Exc Wood
FURNITURE: Chairs & Couches, Wood, Upholstered
FURNITURE: Chairs, Household Upholstered
FURNITURE: Chairs, Household Wood
FURNITURE: Chairs, Household, Metal
FURNITURE: Chairs, Office Wood
FURNITURE: Church
FURNITURE: Couches, Sofa/Davenport, Upholstered Wood
  Frames
FURNITURE: Dining Room, Wood
FURNITURE: Fiberglass & Plastic
FURNITURE: Garden, Exc Wood, Metal, Stone Or Concrete
FURNITURE: Hotel
FURNITURE: Household, Metal
FURNITURE: Household, Upholstered, Exc Wood Or Metal
FURNITURE: Juvenile, Upholstered On Wood Frames
FURNITURE: Laboratory
FURNITURE: Lawn, Exc Wood, Metal, Stone Or Concrete
FURNITURE: Living Room, Upholstered On Wood Frames
FURNITURE: Mattresses & Foundations
FURNITURE: Mattresses, Box & Bedsprings
FURNITURE: Mattresses, Innerspring Or Box Spring
FURNITURE: Novelty, Wood
FURNITURE: Office, Exc Wood
FURNITURE: Office, Wood
FURNITURE: Recliners, Upholstered On Wood Frames
FURNITURE: School
FURNITURE: Sleep
FURNITURE: Stadium
FURNITURE: Storage Chests, Household, Wood
FURNITURE: Table Tops, Marble
FURNITURE: Tables, Household, Metal
FURNITURE: Tables, Office, Exc Wood
FURNITURE: Tables, Office, Wood
FURNITURE: Upholstered
FURNITURE: Wicker & Rattan
FUSES: Electric

G

GAMES & TOYS: Board Games, Children's & Adults'
GAMES & TOYS: Craft & Hobby Kits & Sets
GAMES & TOYS: Electronic

GAMES & TOYS: Erector Sets
GARBAGE CONTAINERS: Plastic
GAS & OIL FIELD EXPLORATION SVCS
GAS & OIL FIELD SVCS, NEC
GASES: Acetylene
GASES: Indl
GASES: Nitrogen
GASES: Oxygen
GASKETS
GASKETS & SEALING DEVICES
GASOLINE FILLING STATIONS
GASOLINE WHOLESALERS
GEARS
GEARS & GEAR UNITS: Reduction, Exc Auto
GEARS: Power Transmission, Exc Auto
GENERATION EQPT: Electronic
GENERATOR REPAIR SVCS
GENERATORS SETS: Steam
GIFT SHOP
GIFT, NOVELTY & SOUVENIR STORES: Gifts & Novelties
GLASS PRDTS, FROM PURCHASED GLASS: Insulating
GLASS PRDTS, FROM PURCHASED GLASS: Mirrored
GLASS PRDTS, FROM PURCHASED GLASS: Windshields
GLASS PRDTS, FROM PURCHD GLASS: Strengthened Or
  Reinforced
GLASS PRDTS, PRESSED OR BLOWN: Furnishings &
  Access
GLASS PRDTS, PRESSED OR BLOWN: Scientific Glassware
GLASS PRDTS, PRESSED OR BLOWN: Yarn, Fiberglass
GLASS, AUTOMOTIVE: Wholesalers
GLASS: Broadwoven Fabrics
GLASS: Fiber
GLASS: Flat
GLASS: Leaded
GLASS: Optical
GLASS: Pressed & Blown, NEC
GLASS: Tempered
GLASSWARE: Laboratory
GLOVES: Safety
GLOVES: Work
GOLF EQPT
GOLF GOODS & EQPT
GOURMET FOOD STORES
GRADING SVCS
GRANITE: Crushed & Broken
GRANITE: Cut & Shaped
GRAPHIC ARTS & RELATED DESIGN SVCS
GRASSES: Artificial & Preserved
GRAVE VAULTS, METAL
GREENHOUSES: Prefabricated Metal
GRINDING SVC: Precision, Commercial Or Indl
GROCERIES, GENERAL LINE WHOLESALERS
GUIDANCE SYSTEMS & EQPT: Space Vehicle
GUIDED MISSILES & SPACE VEHICLES
GUM & WOOD CHEMICALS
GUTTERS: Sheet Metal
GYPSUM PRDTS

H

HAIR & HAIR BASED PRDTS
HAIR CARE PRDTS
HAIR DRESSING, FOR THE TRADE
HAMPERS: Solid Fiber, Made From Purchased Materials
HANDBAGS
HANDBAGS: Women's
HANDLES: Brush Or Tool, Plastic
HANDYMAN SVCS
HANG GLIDERS
HARDWARE
HARDWARE & BUILDING PRDTS: Plastic
HARDWARE & EQPT: Stage, Exc Lighting
HARDWARE STORES
HARDWARE STORES: Builders'
HARDWARE STORES: Pumps & Pumping Eqpt
HARDWARE STORES: Tools
HARDWARE WHOLESALERS
HARDWARE, WHOLESALE: Bolts
HARDWARE, WHOLESALE: Builders', NEC
HARDWARE, WHOLESALE: Furniture, NEC
HARDWARE, WHOLESALE: Power Tools & Access
HARDWARE, WHOLESALE: Security Devices, Locks
HARDWARE: Builders'
HARDWARE: Door Opening & Closing Devices, Exc Electrical

HARDWARE: Furniture
HARDWARE: Furniture, Builders' & Other Household
HARDWARE: Parachute
HARNESS ASSEMBLIES: Cable & Wire
HEALTH AIDS: Exercise Eqpt
HEARING AIDS
HEAT TREATING: Metal
HEATERS: Swimming Pool, Electric
HEATING & AIR CONDITIONING UNITS, COMBINATION
HEATING EQPT: Complete
HEATING UNITS & DEVICES: Indl, Electric
HELICOPTERS
HELMETS: Athletic
HELMETS: Steel
HIGH ENERGY PARTICLE PHYSICS EQPT
HOBBY, TOY & GAME STORES: Arts & Crafts & Splys
HOBBY, TOY & GAME STORES: Toys & Games
HOISTS
HOLDING COMPANIES: Investment, Exc Banks
HOLDING COMPANIES: Personal, Exc Banks
HOME ENTERTAINMENT EQPT: Electronic, NEC
HOME FOR THE MENTALLY HANDICAPPED
HOME HEALTH CARE SVCS
HOMEFURNISHING STORES: Beddings & Linens
HOMEFURNISHING STORES: Lighting Fixtures
HOMEFURNISHING STORES: Pottery
HOMEFURNISHING STORES: Venetian Blinds
HOMEFURNISHINGS, WHOLESALE: Blinds, Vertical
HOMEFURNISHINGS, WHOLESALE: Fireplace Eqpt &
  Access
HOMEFURNISHINGS, WHOLESALE: Floor Cushion &
  Padding
HOMEFURNISHINGS, WHOLESALE: Linens, Table
HOMEFURNISHINGS, WHOLESALE: Wood Flooring
HOMES: Log Cabins
HOODS: Door, Aluminum
HORSESHOES
HOSE: Automobile, Rubber
HOSE: Flexible Metal
HOSE: Plastic
HOSE: Rubber
HOSIERY DYEING & FINISHING
HOSPITALS: Medical & Surgical
HOT TUBS
HOT TUBS: Plastic & Fiberglass
HOUSEHOLD ARTICLES, EXC FURNITURE: Cut Stone
HOUSEHOLD ARTICLES: Metal
HOUSEHOLD FURNISHINGS, NEC
HOUSEHOLD SEWING MACHINES WHOLESALERS:
  Electric
HOUSEWARES, ELECTRIC: Air Purifiers, Portable
HOUSEWARES, ELECTRIC: Heating Units, Electric
  Appliances
HOUSEWARES: Food Dishes & Utensils, Pressed & Molded
  Pulp
HUMIDIFIERS & DEHUMIDIFIERS
HYDRAULIC EQPT REPAIR SVC

I

ICE
ICE CREAM & ICES WHOLESALERS
IGNITION SYSTEMS: High Frequency
INCUBATORS & BROODERS: Farm
INDL & PERSONAL SVC PAPER WHOLESALERS
INDL & PERSONAL SVC PAPER, WHOLESALE: Shipping
  Splys
INDL CONTRACTORS: Exhibit Construction
INDL EQPT SVCS
INDL GASES WHOLESALERS
INDL MACHINERY & EQPT WHOLESALERS
INDL PROCESS INSTRUMENTS: Control
INDL PROCESS INSTRUMENTS: Elements, Primary
INDL SPLYS WHOLESALERS
INDL SPLYS, WHOLESALE: Bearings
INDL SPLYS, WHOLESALE: Clean Room Splys
INDL SPLYS, WHOLESALE: Drums, New Or Reconditioned
INDL SPLYS, WHOLESALE: Gaskets
INDL SPLYS, WHOLESALE: Mill Splys
INDL SPLYS, WHOLESALE: Power Transmission, Eqpt &
  Apparatus
INDL SPLYS, WHOLESALE: Rubber Goods, Mechanical
INDL SPLYS, WHOLESALE: Tools
INDL SPLYS, WHOLESALE: Tools, NEC

INDL SPLYS, WHOLESALE: Valves & Fittings
INDL TRUCK REPAIR SVCS
INDUSTRIAL & COMMERCIAL EQPT INSPECTION SVCS
INFORMATION RETRIEVAL SERVICES
INFORMATION SVCS: Consumer
INFRARED OBJECT DETECTION EQPT
INK: Printing
INSECTICIDES
INSECTICIDES & PESTICIDES
INSPECTION & TESTING SVCS
INSTRUMENTS & METERS: Measuring, Electric
INSTRUMENTS, LABORATORY: Analyzers, Automatic
  Chemical
INSTRUMENTS, MEASURING & CNTRL: Geophysical &
  Meteorological
INSTRUMENTS, MEASURING & CNTRLG: Aircraft & Motor
  Vehicle
INSTRUMENTS, MEASURING & CONTROLLING: Ion
  Chambers
INSTRUMENTS, MEASURING & CONTROLLING: Transits,
  Surveyors'
INSTRUMENTS, OPTICAL: Mirrors
INSTRUMENTS, SURGICAL & MED: Needles & Syringes,
  Hypodermic
INSTRUMENTS, SURGICAL & MEDICAL: Blood & Bone
  Work
INSTRUMENTS, SURGICAL & MEDICAL: Blood Transfusion
INSTRUMENTS, SURGICAL & MEDICAL: Catheters
INSTRUMENTS, SURGICAL & MEDICAL: IV Transfusion
INSTRUMENTS, SURGICAL & MEDICAL: Muscle Exercise,
  Ophthalmic
INSTRUMENTS, SURGICAL & MEDICAL: Ophthalmic
INSTRUMENTS: Analytical
INSTRUMENTS: Combustion Control, Indl
INSTRUMENTS: Electrocardiographs
INSTRUMENTS: Endoscopic Eqpt, Electromedical
INSTRUMENTS: Flow, Indl Process
INSTRUMENTS: Indl Process Control
INSTRUMENTS: Infrared, Indl Process
INSTRUMENTS: Measurement, Indl Process
INSTRUMENTS: Measuring, Electrical Power
INSTRUMENTS: Medical & Surgical
INSTRUMENTS: Optical, Analytical
INSTRUMENTS: Power Measuring, Electrical
INSTRUMENTS: Pressure Measurement, Indl
INSTRUMENTS: Radio Frequency Measuring
INSTRUMENTS: Seismographs
INSTRUMENTS: Test, Electronic & Electric Measurement
INSTRUMENTS: Test, Electronic & Electrical Circuits
INSULATING COMPOUNDS
INSULATION & ROOFING MATERIALS: Wood, Reconstituted
INSULATION MATERIALS WHOLESALERS
INSULATION: Felt
INSULATION: Fiberglass
INSULATORS & INSULATION MATERIALS: Electrical
INSULATORS, PORCELAIN: Electrical
INSURANCE: Agents, Brokers & Service
INTEGRATED CIRCUITS, SEMICONDUCTOR NETWORKS,
  ETC
INTERIOR DESIGN SVCS, NEC
INVERTERS: Nonrotating Electrical
INVERTERS: Rotating Electrical
INVESTORS, NEC
INVESTORS: Real Estate, Exc Property Operators

J

JEWELRY & PRECIOUS STONES WHOLESALERS
JEWELRY REPAIR SVCS
JEWELRY STORES
JEWELRY STORES: Precious Stones & Precious Metals
JEWELRY, PRECIOUS METAL: Medals, Precious Or
  Semiprecious
JEWELRY, PRECIOUS METAL: Rings, Finger
JEWELRY, PRECIOUS METAL: Settings & Mountings
JEWELRY, WHOLESALE
JEWELRY: Precious Metal
JIGS & FIXTURES
JOB PRINTING & NEWSPAPER PUBLISHING COMBINED
JOISTS: Fabricated Bar
JOISTS: Long-Span Series, Open Web Steel

K

KITCHEN CABINETS WHOLESALERS

KITCHEN UTENSILS: Food Handling & Processing Prdts,
  Wood
KITCHENWARE STORES
KNIT OUTERWEAR DYEING & FINISHING, EXC HOSIERY
  & GLOVE

L

LABELS: Cotton, Printed
LABELS: Paper, Made From Purchased Materials
LABELS: Woven
LABORATORIES, TESTING: Pollution
LABORATORIES, TESTING: Product Testing
LABORATORIES, TESTING: Product Testing, Safety/
  Performance
LABORATORIES: Biological Research
LABORATORIES: Biotechnology
LABORATORIES: Electronic Research
LABORATORIES: Medical
LABORATORIES: Physical Research, Commercial
LABORATORIES: Testing
LABORATORIES: Testing
LABORATORY APPARATUS & FURNITURE
LABORATORY APPARATUS, EXC HEATING & MEASURING
LABORATORY APPARATUS: Heating
LABORATORY APPARATUS: Pipettes, Hemocytometer
LABORATORY EQPT, EXC MEDICAL: Wholesalers
LABORATORY EQPT: Clinical Instruments Exc Medical
LABORATORY EQPT: Incubators
LABORATORY EQPT: Measuring
LACE GOODS & WARP KNIT FABRIC DYEING & FINISHING
LAMINATED PLASTICS: Plate, Sheet, Rod & Tubes
LAMINATING SVCS
LAMP & LIGHT BULBS & TUBES
LAMP BULBS & TUBES, ELECTRIC: Health, Infrared/
  Ultraviolet
LAMP BULBS & TUBES, ELECTRIC: Light, Complete
LAMP BULBS & TUBES/PARTS, ELECTRIC: Generalized
  Applications
LAMP SHADES: Glass
LAMPS: Boudoir, Residential
LAMPS: Table, Residential
LAND SUBDIVIDERS & DEVELOPERS: Commercial
LASER SYSTEMS & EQPT
LASERS: Welding, Drilling & Cutting Eqpt
LATEX: Foamed
LAUNDRY EQPT: Commercial
LAUNDRY SVC: Work Clothing Sply
LAWN & GARDEN EQPT
LAWN & GARDEN EQPT: Blowers & Vacuums
LAWN & GARDEN EQPT: Grass Catchers, Lawn Mower
LAWN & GARDEN EQPT: Lawnmowers, Residential, Hand
  Or Power
LAWN & GARDEN EQPT: Tractors & Eqpt
LEAF TOBACCO WHOLESALERS
LEASING & RENTAL: Construction & Mining Eqpt
LEASING & RENTAL: Medical Machinery & Eqpt
LEASING & RENTAL: Trucks, Without Drivers
LEASING: Passenger Car
LEATHER & CUT STOCK WHOLESALERS
LEATHER GOODS, EXC FOOTWEAR, GLOVES,
  LUGGAGE/ BELTING, WHOL
LEATHER GOODS: Card Cases
LEATHER GOODS: Garments
LEATHER GOODS: Holsters
LEATHER GOODS: Personal
LEATHER GOODS: Safety Belts
LEATHER TANNING & FINISHING
LEATHER, LEATHER GOODS & FURS, WHOLESALE
LEATHER: Accessory Prdts
LEATHER: Processed
LICENSE TAGS: Automobile, Stamped Metal
LIFE SAVING & SURVIVAL EQPT REPAIR SVCS,
  NONMEDICAL
LIGHTING EQPT: Flashlights
LIGHTING EQPT: Motor Vehicle, NEC
LIGHTING FIXTURES WHOLESALERS
LIGHTING FIXTURES, NEC
LIGHTING FIXTURES: Arc
LIGHTING FIXTURES: Decorative Area
LIGHTING FIXTURES: Fluorescent, Commercial
LIGHTING FIXTURES: Fluorescent, Residential
LIGHTING FIXTURES: Indl & Commercial
LIGHTING FIXTURES: Motor Vehicle

LIGHTING FIXTURES: Residential, Electric
LIGHTING FIXTURES: Street
LIGHTING FIXTURES: Swimming Pool
LIGHTING FIXTURES: Underwater
LIME ROCK: Ground
LIMESTONE: Crushed & Broken
LIMESTONE: Dimension
LINENS: Tablecloths, From Purchased Materials
LINERS & COVERS: Fabric
LINERS: Indl, Metal Plate
LININGS: Fabric, Apparel & Other, Exc Millinery
LIQUID CRYSTAL DISPLAYS
LITHIUM MINERAL MINING
LITHOGRAPHIC PLATES
LOADS: Electronic
LOCKERS
LOCKERS: Wood, Exc Refrigerated
LOCKS
LOCKS & LOCK SETS, WHOLESALE
LOCKS: Safe & Vault, Metal
LOCKSMITHS
LOGGING
LOGGING CAMPS & CONTRACTORS
LOGGING: Timber, Cut At Logging Camp
LOGGING: Wooden Logs
LOGS: Gas, Fireplace
LOTIONS OR CREAMS: Face
LOTIONS: SHAVING
LOUDSPEAKERS
LOZENGES: Pharmaceutical
LUBRICATING OIL & GREASE WHOLESALERS
LUBRICATION SYSTEMS & EQPT
LUGGAGE & BRIEFCASES
LUMBER & BLDG MATLS DEALER, RET: Electric Constructn
  Matls
LUMBER & BLDG MATLS DEALER, RET: Garage Doors, Sell/
  Install
LUMBER & BLDG MATRLS DEALERS, RETAIL: Doors,
  Wood/Metal
LUMBER & BLDG MTRLS DEALERS, RET: Planing Mill Prdts/
  Lumber
LUMBER & BUILDING MATERIAL DEALERS, RETAIL:
  Roofing Material
LUMBER & BUILDING MATERIALS DEALER, RET: Door &
  Window Prdts
LUMBER & BUILDING MATERIALS DEALER, RET: Masonry
  Matls/Splys
LUMBER & BUILDING MATERIALS DEALERS, RETAIL: Brick
LUMBER & BUILDING MATERIALS DEALERS, RETAIL:
  Sand & Gravel
LUMBER & BUILDING MATERIALS DEALERS, RETAIL:
  Siding
LUMBER & BUILDING MATERIALS RET DEALERS: Millwork
  & Lumber
LUMBER & BUILDING MATLS DEALERS, RET: Screens,
  Door/Window
LUMBER: Dimension, Hardwood
LUMBER: Flooring, Dressed, Softwood
LUMBER: Hardboard
LUMBER: Hardwood Dimension
LUMBER: Hardwood Dimension & Flooring Mills
LUMBER: Kiln Dried
LUMBER: Plywood, Hardwood
LUMBER: Plywood, Hardwood or Hardwood Faced
LUMBER: Plywood, Prefinished, Hardwood
LUMBER: Plywood, Softwood
LUMBER: Rails, Fence, Round Or Split
LUMBER: Treated
LUMBER: Veneer, Softwood

M

MACHINE PARTS: Stamped Or Pressed Metal
MACHINE TOOL ACCESS: Drills
MACHINE TOOL ACCESS: Tools & Access
MACHINE TOOL ATTACHMENTS & ACCESS
MACHINE TOOLS & ACCESS
MACHINE TOOLS, METAL CUTTING: Drilling
MACHINE TOOLS, METAL CUTTING: Drilling & Boring
MACHINE TOOLS, METAL CUTTING: Home Workshop
MACHINE TOOLS, METAL CUTTING: Lathes
MACHINE TOOLS, METAL CUTTING: Numerically Controlled
MACHINE TOOLS, METAL FORMING: Headers

MACHINE TOOLS, METAL FORMING: Mechanical, Pneumatic Or Hyd
MACHINE TOOLS, METAL FORMING: Punching & Shearing
MACHINE TOOLS, METAL FORMING: Rebuilt
MACHINE TOOLS: Metal Cutting
MACHINE TOOLS: Metal Forming
MACHINERY & EQPT, AGRICULTURAL, WHOLESALE: Agricultural, NEC
MACHINERY & EQPT, AGRICULTURAL, WHOLESALE: Lawn & Garden
MACHINERY & EQPT, INDL, WHOLESALE: Chemical Process
MACHINERY & EQPT, INDL, WHOLESALE: Conveyor Systems
MACHINERY & EQPT, INDL, WHOLESALE: Cranes
MACHINERY & EQPT, INDL, WHOLESALE: Engines & Parts, Diesel
MACHINERY & EQPT, INDL, WHOLESALE: Engines, Gasoline
MACHINERY & EQPT, INDL, WHOLESALE: Fans
MACHINERY & EQPT, INDL, WHOLESALE: Food Product Manufacturng
MACHINERY & EQPT, INDL, WHOLESALE: Hydraulic Systems
MACHINERY & EQPT, INDL, WHOLESALE: Indl Machine Parts
MACHINERY & EQPT, INDL, WHOLESALE: Instruments & Cntrl Eqpt
MACHINERY & EQPT, INDL, WHOLESALE: Machine Tools & Access
MACHINERY & EQPT, INDL, WHOLESALE: Machine Tools & Metalwork
MACHINERY & EQPT, INDL, WHOLESALE: Packaging
MACHINERY & EQPT, INDL, WHOLESALE: Safety Eqpt
MACHINERY & EQPT, INDL, WHOLESALE: Sewing
MACHINERY & EQPT, INDL, WHOLESALE: Textile & Leather
MACHINERY & EQPT, INDL, WHOLESALE: Trailers, Indl
MACHINERY & EQPT, WHOLESALE: Construction, General
MACHINERY & EQPT: Farm
MACHINERY & EQPT: Liquid Automation
MACHINERY, EQPT & SUPPLIES: Parking Facility
MACHINERY, FOOD PRDTS: Beverage
MACHINERY, FOOD PRDTS: Dairy & Milk
MACHINERY, FOOD PRDTS: Food Processing, Smokers
MACHINERY, FOOD PRDTS: Oilseed Crushing & Extracting
MACHINERY, FOOD PRDTS: Ovens, Bakery
MACHINERY, FOOD PRDTS: Packing House
MACHINERY, FOOD PRDTS: Processing, Poultry
MACHINERY, MAILING: Postage Meters
MACHINERY, PACKAGING: Packing & Wrapping
MACHINERY, PAPER INDUSTRY: Pulp Mill
MACHINERY, PRINTING TRADES: Plates
MACHINERY, TEXTILE: Creels
MACHINERY, TEXTILE: Printing
MACHINERY, WOODWORKING: Sanding, Exc Portable Floor Sanders
MACHINERY: Ammunition & Explosives Loading
MACHINERY: Automotive Related
MACHINERY: Bridge Or Gate, Hydraulic
MACHINERY: Construction
MACHINERY: Cotton Ginning
MACHINERY: Custom
MACHINERY: Electronic Component Making
MACHINERY: Ice Making
MACHINERY: Kilns, Lumber
MACHINERY: Metalworking
MACHINERY: Mining
MACHINERY: Packaging
MACHINERY: Paint Making
MACHINERY: Plastic Working
MACHINERY: Printing Presses
MACHINERY: Recycling
MACHINERY: Road Construction & Maintenance
MACHINERY: Robots, Molding & Forming Plastics
MACHINERY: Rubber Working
MACHINERY: Semiconductor Manufacturing
MACHINERY: Textile
MACHINERY: Tobacco Prdts
MACHINERY: Wire Drawing
MACHINERY: Woodworking
MACHINISTS' TOOLS & MACHINES: Measuring, Metalworking Type
MACHINISTS' TOOLS: Measuring, Precision

MACHINISTS' TOOLS: Precision
MACHINISTS' TOOLS: Scales, Measuring, Precision
MAGAZINES, WHOLESALE
MAGNESIUM
MAGNETIC INK & OPTICAL SCANNING EQPT
MAGNETIC TAPE, AUDIO: Prerecorded
MAGNETS: Permanent
MAIL-ORDER HOUSE, NEC
MAIL-ORDER HOUSES: Jewelry
MAIL-ORDER HOUSES: Women's Apparel
MAILBOX RENTAL & RELATED SVCS
MAILING LIST: Compilers
MAILING MACHINES WHOLESALERS
MAILING SVCS, NEC
MANAGEMENT CONSULTING SVCS: Administrative
MANAGEMENT CONSULTING SVCS: Automation & Robotics
MANAGEMENT CONSULTING SVCS: Business
MANAGEMENT CONSULTING SVCS: Business Planning & Organizing
MANAGEMENT CONSULTING SVCS: Distribution Channels
MANAGEMENT CONSULTING SVCS: Food & Beverage
MANAGEMENT CONSULTING SVCS: General
MANAGEMENT CONSULTING SVCS: Hospital & Health
MANAGEMENT CONSULTING SVCS: Industrial
MANAGEMENT CONSULTING SVCS: Industrial & Labor
MANAGEMENT CONSULTING SVCS: Quality Assurance
MANAGEMENT CONSULTING SVCS: Training & Development
MANAGEMENT CONSULTING SVCS: Transportation
MANAGEMENT SERVICES
MANAGEMENT SVCS: Business
MANAGEMENT SVCS: Construction
MANUFACTURING INDUSTRIES, NEC
MARBLE, BUILDING: Cut & Shaped
MARINE HARDWARE
MARINE RELATED EQPT
MARINE SPLYS WHOLESALERS
MARKETS: Meat & fish
MARKING DEVICES
MARKING DEVICES: Embossing Seals & Hand Stamps
MATERNITY WEAR STORES
MATS OR MATTING, NEC: Rubber
MATS, MATTING & PADS: Varnished Glass
MATTRESS PROTECTORS, EXC RUBBER
MEAT MARKETS
MEAT PRDTS: Bacon, Side & Sliced, From Purchased Meat
MEAT PRDTS: Bacon, Slab & Sliced, From Slaughtered Meat
MEAT PRDTS: Boxed Beef, From Slaughtered Meat
MEAT PRDTS: Ham, Smoked, From Purchased Meat
MEAT PRDTS: Prepared Beef Prdts From Purchased Beef
MEAT PRDTS: Sausages, From Purchased Meat
MEAT PROCESSING MACHINERY
MEDIA: Magnetic & Optical Recording
MEDICAL & HOSPITAL EQPT WHOLESALERS
MEDICAL & SURGICAL SPLYS: Bandages & Dressings
MEDICAL & SURGICAL SPLYS: Clothing, Fire Resistant & Protect
MEDICAL & SURGICAL SPLYS: Cosmetic Restorations
MEDICAL & SURGICAL SPLYS: Gynecological Splys & Appliances
MEDICAL & SURGICAL SPLYS: Ligatures
MEDICAL & SURGICAL SPLYS: Limbs, Artificial
MEDICAL & SURGICAL SPLYS: Orthopedic Appliances
MEDICAL & SURGICAL SPLYS: Personal Safety Eqpt
MEDICAL & SURGICAL SPLYS: Prosthetic Appliances
MEDICAL CENTERS
MEDICAL EQPT REPAIR SVCS, NON-ELECTRIC
MEDICAL EQPT: CAT Scanner Or Computerized Axial Tomography
MEDICAL EQPT: Diagnostic
MEDICAL EQPT: Electromedical Apparatus
MEDICAL EQPT: Ultrasonic Scanning Devices
MEDICAL EQPT: Ultrasonic, Exc Cleaning
MEDICAL SVCS ORGANIZATION
MEMBERSHIP ORGANIZATIONS, BUSINESS: Contractors' Association
MEMBERSHIP ORGANIZATIONS, BUSINESS: Growers' Association
MEMBERSHIP ORGANIZATIONS, PROFESSIONAL: Health Association
MEMBERSHIP ORGANIZATIONS, RELIGIOUS: Baptist Church
MEN'S & BOYS' CLOTHING STORES

MEN'S & BOYS' CLOTHING WHOLESALERS, NEC
MEN'S & BOYS' HOSIERY WHOLESALERS
MERCHANDISING MACHINE OPERATORS: Vending
METAL & STEEL PRDTS: Abrasive
METAL COMPONENTS: Prefabricated
METAL FINISHING SVCS
METAL OXIDE SILICONE OR MOS DEVICES
METAL SERVICE CENTERS & OFFICES
METAL STAMPING, FOR THE TRADE
METAL STAMPINGS: Perforated
METAL: Battery
METALS SVC CENTERS & WHOLESALERS: Foundry Prdts
METALS SVC CENTERS & WHOLESALERS: Pipe & Tubing, Steel
METALS SVC CENTERS & WHOLESALERS: Steel
METALS: Precious NEC
METALS: Primary Nonferrous, NEC
METALWORK: Miscellaneous
METALWORK: Ornamental
METALWORKING MACHINERY WHOLESALERS
METERING DEVICES: Gasoline Dispensing
METERING DEVICES: Water Quality Monitoring & Control Systems
METERS: Turbine Flow, Indl Process
MICROCIRCUITS, INTEGRATED: Semiconductor
MICROWAVE COMPONENTS
MILITARY INSIGNIA, TEXTILE
MILLWORK
MINERAL WOOL
MINERAL WOOL INSULATION PRDTS
MINERALS: Ground or Treated
MINIATURES
MINING EXPLORATION & DEVELOPMENT SVCS
MINING MACHINERY & EQPT WHOLESALERS
MIXTURES & BLOCKS: Asphalt Paving
MOBILE COMMUNICATIONS EQPT
MOBILE HOMES
MOBILE HOMES, EXC RECREATIONAL
MODELS: General, Exc Toy
MODULES: Computer Logic
MODULES: Solid State
MOLDED RUBBER PRDTS
MOLDING COMPOUNDS
MOLDINGS & TRIM: Metal, Exc Automobile
MOLDINGS & TRIM: Wood
MOLDINGS OR TRIM: Automobile, Stamped Metal
MOLDS: Indl
MONUMENTS & GRAVE MARKERS, WHOLESALE
MOPS: Floor & Dust
MOTION PICTURE & VIDEO DISTRIBUTION
MOTION PICTURE & VIDEO PRODUCTION SVCS: Educational
MOTION PICTURE PRODUCTION & DISTRIBUTION
MOTOR & GENERATOR PARTS: Electric
MOTOR CONTROL CENTERS
MOTOR HOMES
MOTOR VEHICLE ASSEMBLY, COMPLETE: Ambulances
MOTOR VEHICLE ASSEMBLY, COMPLETE: Buses, All Types
MOTOR VEHICLE ASSEMBLY, COMPLETE: Fire Department Vehicles
MOTOR VEHICLE ASSEMBLY, COMPLETE: Military Motor Vehicle
MOTOR VEHICLE ASSEMBLY, COMPLETE: Motor Buses
MOTOR VEHICLE ASSEMBLY, COMPLETE: Universal Carriers, Mil
MOTOR VEHICLE ASSEMBLY, COMPLETE: Wreckers, Tow Truck
MOTOR VEHICLE DEALERS: Automobiles, New & Used
MOTOR VEHICLE PARTS & ACCESS: Acceleration Eqpt
MOTOR VEHICLE PARTS & ACCESS: Air Conditioner Parts
MOTOR VEHICLE PARTS & ACCESS: Ball Joints
MOTOR VEHICLE PARTS & ACCESS: Body Components & Frames
MOTOR VEHICLE PARTS & ACCESS: Brakes, Air
MOTOR VEHICLE PARTS & ACCESS: Clutches
MOTOR VEHICLE PARTS & ACCESS: Cylinder Heads
MOTOR VEHICLE PARTS & ACCESS: Electrical Eqpt
MOTOR VEHICLE PARTS & ACCESS: Engines & Parts
MOTOR VEHICLE PARTS & ACCESS: Engs & Trans,Factory, Rebuilt
MOTOR VEHICLE PARTS & ACCESS: Fuel Pumps
MOTOR VEHICLE PARTS & ACCESS: Fuel Systems & Parts
MOTOR VEHICLE PARTS & ACCESS: Gas Tanks

MOTOR VEHICLE PARTS & ACCESS: Gears
MOTOR VEHICLE PARTS & ACCESS: Lifting Mechanisms, Dump Truck
MOTOR VEHICLE PARTS & ACCESS: Manifolds
MOTOR VEHICLE PARTS & ACCESS: Mufflers, Exhaust
MOTOR VEHICLE PARTS & ACCESS: Power Steering Eqpt
MOTOR VEHICLE PARTS & ACCESS: Propane Conversion Eqpt
MOTOR VEHICLE PARTS & ACCESS: Tire Valve Cores
MOTOR VEHICLE PARTS & ACCESS: Tops
MOTOR VEHICLE PARTS & ACCESS: Transmissions
MOTOR VEHICLE PARTS & ACCESS: Universal Joints
MOTOR VEHICLE PARTS & ACCESS: Wiring Harness Sets
MOTOR VEHICLE RACING & DRIVER SVCS
MOTOR VEHICLE SPLYS & PARTS WHOLESALERS: New
MOTOR VEHICLE: Hardware
MOTOR VEHICLE: Radiators
MOTOR VEHICLE: Shock Absorbers
MOTOR VEHICLE: Steering Mechanisms
MOTOR VEHICLE: Wheels
MOTOR VEHICLES & CAR BODIES
MOTOR VEHICLES, WHOLESALE: Fire Trucks
MOTOR VEHICLES, WHOLESALE: Truck tractors
MOTORCYCLE ACCESS
MOTORCYCLE DEALERS
MOTORCYCLES & RELATED PARTS
MOTORS: Electric
MOTORS: Fluid Power
MOTORS: Generators
MOUNTING SVC: Swatches & Samples
MULTIPLEXERS: Telephone & Telegraph
MUSEUMS & ART GALLERIES
MUSIC DISTRIBUTION APPARATUS
MUSICAL INSTRUMENTS & ACCESS: Carrying Cases
MUSICAL INSTRUMENTS & ACCESS: NEC
MUSICAL INSTRUMENTS & SPLYS STORES: Pianos
MUSICAL INSTRUMENTS WHOLESALERS
MUSICAL INSTRUMENTS: Guitars & Parts, Electric & Acoustic

N

NAILS: Steel, Wire Or Cut
NAME PLATES: Engraved Or Etched
NATURAL GAS DISTRIBUTION TO CONSUMERS
NATURAL GAS LIQUIDS PRODUCTION
NATURAL GAS PRODUCTION
NATURAL PROPANE PRODUCTION
NAVIGATIONAL SYSTEMS & INSTRUMENTS
NEW & USED CAR DEALERS
NICKEL
NITRILE RUBBERS: Butadiene-Acrylonitrile
NONCURRENT CARRYING WIRING DEVICES
NONFERROUS: Rolling & Drawing, NEC
NOVELTIES
NOVELTIES, PAPER, WHOLESALE
NOVELTIES: Paper, Made From Purchased Materials
NOVELTIES: Plastic
NOZZLES: Fire Fighting
NOZZLES: Spray, Aerosol, Paint Or Insecticide
NUCLEAR SHIELDING: Metal Plate
NURSERIES & LAWN & GARDEN SPLY STORES, RETAIL: Fertilizer
NUTRITION SVCS
NYLON FIBERS

O

OFFICE EQPT WHOLESALERS
OFFICE FURNITURE REPAIR & MAINTENANCE SVCS
OFFICE SPLY & STATIONERY STORES: Office Forms & Splys
OFFICE SPLYS, NEC, WHOLESALE
OFFICES & CLINICS OF DOCTORS OF MEDICINE: Radiologist
OIL & GAS FIELD MACHINERY
OIL FIELD SVCS, NEC
OIL TREATING COMPOUNDS
OILS & ESSENTIAL OILS
OILS: Mineral, Natural
OPHTHALMIC GOODS
OPHTHALMIC GOODS: Frames, Lenses & Parts, Eyeglasses
OPTICAL GOODS STORES
OPTICAL GOODS STORES: Eyeglasses, Prescription
OPTICAL GOODS STORES: Opticians

OPTICAL INSTRUMENTS & APPARATUS
OPTICAL INSTRUMENTS & LENSES
ORGANIZATIONS: Biotechnical Research, Noncommercial
ORGANIZATIONS: Medical Research
ORGANIZATIONS: Professional
ORGANIZATIONS: Religious
ORGANIZATIONS: Research Institute
ORIENTED STRANDBOARD
OVENS: Paint Baking & Drying

P

PACKAGE DESIGN SVCS
PACKAGING & LABELING SVCS
PACKAGING MATERIALS, WHOLESALE
PACKAGING MATERIALS: Paper
PACKAGING MATERIALS: Paper, Coated Or Laminated
PACKAGING MATERIALS: Plastic Film, Coated Or Laminated
PACKING & CRATING SVC
PACKING MATERIALS: Mechanical
PADS: Mattress
PAINTS & ADDITIVES
PAINTS & ALLIED PRODUCTS
PAINTS, VARNISHES & SPLYS WHOLESALERS
PAINTS, VARNISHES & SPLYS, WHOLESALE: Paints
PAINTS: Oil Or Alkyd Vehicle Or Water Thinned
PALLET LOADERS & UNLOADERS
PALLET REPAIR SVCS
PALLETS & SKIDS: Wood
PALLETS: Wood & Metal Combination
PANELS: Building, Metal
PAPER & BOARD: Die-cut
PAPER & PAPER PRDTS: Crepe, Made From Purchased Materials
PAPER PRDTS: Cleansing Tissues, Made From Purchased Material
PAPER PRDTS: Infant & Baby Prdts
PAPER PRDTS: Napkin Stock
PAPER PRDTS: Pressed & Molded Pulp & Fiber Prdts
PAPER PRDTS: Sanitary
PAPER PRDTS: Sanitary Tissue Paper
PAPER PRDTS: Toilet Paper, Made From Purchased Materials
PAPER, WHOLESALE: Fine
PAPER, WHOLESALE: Printing
PAPER: Absorbent
PAPER: Adhesive
PAPER: Book
PAPER: Building Laminated, Made From Purchased Materials
PAPER: Building, Insulating & Packaging
PAPER: Cardboard
PAPER: Cigarette
PAPER: Coated & Laminated, NEC
PAPER: Coated, Exc Photographic, Carbon Or Abrasive
PAPER: Corrugated
PAPER: Fine
PAPER: Packaging
PAPER: Specialty
PAPER: Tissue
PAPER: Waxed, Made From Purchased Materials
PAPER: Wrapping & Packaging
PAPERBOARD PRDTS: Folding Boxboard
PAPERBOARD PRDTS: Setup Boxboard
PARACHUTES
PARTICLEBOARD
PARTICLEBOARD: Laminated, Plastic
PARTITIONS & FIXTURES: Except Wood
PARTITIONS: Wood & Fixtures
PARTS: Metal
PATTERNS: Indl
PAVERS
PERFUME: Perfumes, Natural Or Synthetic
PERFUMES
PERSONAL DOCUMENT & INFORMATION SVCS
PESTICIDES
PET SPLYS
PETROLEUM BULK STATIONS & TERMINALS
PHARMACEUTICAL PREPARATIONS: Adrenal
PHARMACEUTICAL PREPARATIONS: Druggists' Preparations
PHARMACEUTICAL PREPARATIONS: Pills
PHARMACEUTICAL PREPARATIONS: Proprietary Drug
PHARMACEUTICAL PREPARATIONS: Solutions
PHARMACEUTICAL PREPARATIONS: Tablets

PHARMACEUTICALS
PHONOGRAPH RECORDS WHOLESALERS
PHOSPHATE ROCK MINING
PHOSPHATES
PHOTOCOPYING & DUPLICATING SVCS
PHOTOGRAPHIC EQPT & SPLYS
PHOTOGRAPHIC EQPT & SPLYS: Film, Sensitized
PHOTOGRAPHIC EQPT & SPLYS: Printing Eqpt
PHOTOGRAPHY SVCS: Commercial
PHYSICIANS' OFFICES & CLINICS: Medical doctors
PICTURE FRAMES: Metal
PICTURE FRAMES: Wood
PIECE GOODS & NOTIONS WHOLESALERS
PIECE GOODS, NOTIONS & DRY GOODS, WHOL: Textiles, Woven
PIECE GOODS, NOTIONS & OTHER DRY GOODS, WHOLESALE: Cotton
PIECE GOODS, NOTIONS & OTHER DRY GOODS, WHOLESALE: Fabrics
PIECE GOODS, NOTIONS/DRY GOODS, WHOL: Fabrics, Synthetic
PIPE & FITTINGS: Cast Iron
PIPE & FITTINGS: Soil, Cast Iron
PIPE FITTINGS: Plastic
PIPE SECTIONS, FABRICATED FROM PURCHASED PIPE
PIPE, SEWER: Concrete
PIPE: Concrete
PIPE: Plastic
PIPE: Sheet Metal
PIPELINE & POWER LINE INSPECTION SVCS
PIPELINE TERMINAL FACILITIES: Independent
PIPELINES: Natural Gas
PIPELINES: Refined Petroleum
PIPES & TUBES
PIPES & TUBES: Steel
PIPES & TUBES: Welded
PIPES: Steel & Iron
PLAQUES: Picture, Laminated
PLASMAS
PLASTIC WOOD
PLASTICIZERS, ORGANIC: Cyclic & Acyclic
PLASTICS FILM & SHEET
PLASTICS FILM & SHEET: Polyethylene
PLASTICS FILM & SHEET: Polyvinyl
PLASTICS FILM & SHEET: Vinyl
PLASTICS FINISHED PRDTS: Laminated
PLASTICS MATERIAL & RESINS
PLASTICS MATERIALS, BASIC FORMS & SHAPES WHOLESALERS
PLASTICS PROCESSING
PLASTICS SHEET: Packing Materials
PLASTICS: Blow Molded
PLASTICS: Extruded
PLASTICS: Finished Injection Molded
PLASTICS: Molded
PLASTICS: Polystyrene Foam
PLASTICS: Thermoformed
PLATES: Steel
PLATFORMS: Cargo
PLATING & POLISHING SVC
PLATING SVC: Chromium, Metals Or Formed Prdts
PLAYGROUND EQPT
PLEATING & STITCHING SVC
PLUGS: Electric
PLUMBING FIXTURES
PLUMBING FIXTURES: Plastic
PLUMBING FIXTURES: Vitreous
POINT OF SALE DEVICES
POLE LINE HARDWARE
POLISHING SVC: Metals Or Formed Prdts
POLYESTERS
POLYETHYLENE RESINS
POLYMETHYL METHACRYLATE RESINS: Plexiglas
POLYSTYRENE RESINS
POLYTETRAFLUOROETHYLENE RESINS
POLYURETHANE RESINS
POLYVINYL CHLORIDE RESINS
POSTERS
POTASH MINING
POTPOURRI
POTTERY: Laboratory & Indl
POULTRY & SMALL GAME SLAUGHTERING & PROCESSING

POWDER: Aluminum Atomized
POWDER: Metal
POWER GENERATORS
POWER SUPPLIES: All Types, Static
POWER SWITCHING EQPT
POWER TOOLS, HAND: Chain Saws, Portable
PRECAST TERRAZZO OR CONCRETE PRDTS
PRECIOUS STONES & METALS, WHOLESALE
PRERECORDED TAPE, CD/RECORD STORES: Audio Tapes, Prerecorded
PRESSED FIBER & MOLDED PULP PRDTS, EXC FOOD
PRIMARY FINISHED OR SEMIFINISHED SHAPES
PRIMARY ROLLING MILL EQPT
PRINT CARTRIDGES: Laser & Other Computer Printers
PRINTED CIRCUIT BOARDS
PRINTERS & PLOTTERS
PRINTERS: Computer
PRINTERS: Magnetic Ink, Bar Code
PRINTING & BINDING: Books
PRINTING & ENGRAVING: Card, Exc Greeting
PRINTING & ENGRAVING: Financial Notes & Certificates
PRINTING & STAMPING: Fabric Articles
PRINTING & WRITING PAPER WHOLESALERS
PRINTING MACHINERY
PRINTING, COMMERCIAL: Business Forms, NEC
PRINTING, COMMERCIAL: Calendars, NEC
PRINTING, COMMERCIAL: Decals, NEC
PRINTING, COMMERCIAL: Envelopes, NEC
PRINTING, COMMERCIAL: Labels & Seals, NEC
PRINTING, COMMERCIAL: Letterpress & Screen
PRINTING, COMMERCIAL: Literature, Advertising, NEC
PRINTING, COMMERCIAL: Periodicals, NEC
PRINTING, COMMERCIAL: Promotional
PRINTING, COMMERCIAL: Screen
PRINTING, COMMERCIAL: Stationery, NEC
PRINTING, COMMERCIAL: Tags, NEC
PRINTING, LITHOGRAPHIC: Advertising Posters
PRINTING, LITHOGRAPHIC: Calendars
PRINTING, LITHOGRAPHIC: Forms, Business
PRINTING, LITHOGRAPHIC: Offset & photolithographic printing
PRINTING, LITHOGRAPHIC: Posters & Decals
PRINTING, LITHOGRAPHIC: Promotional
PRINTING, LITHOGRAPHIC: Tickets
PRINTING: Books
PRINTING: Broadwoven Fabrics. Cotton
PRINTING: Checkbooks
PRINTING: Commercial, NEC
PRINTING: Flexographic
PRINTING: Gravure, Labels
PRINTING: Gravure, Rotogravure
PRINTING: Laser
PRINTING: Letterpress
PRINTING: Lithographic
PRINTING: Manmade Fiber & Silk, Broadwoven Fabric
PRINTING: Offset
PRINTING: Photo-Offset
PRINTING: Photolithographic
PRINTING: Rotogravure
PRINTING: Screen, Broadwoven Fabrics, Cotton
PRINTING: Screen, Fabric
PRINTING: Screen, Manmade Fiber & Silk, Broadwoven Fabric
PRINTING: Thermography
PROFESSIONAL EQPT & SPLYS, WHOLESALE: Engineers', NEC
PROFESSIONAL EQPT & SPLYS, WHOLESALE: Optical Goods
PROFESSIONAL INSTRUMENT REPAIR SVCS
PROFILE SHAPES: Unsupported Plastics
PROMOTION SVCS
PROPERTY DAMAGE INSURANCE
PROTECTION EQPT: Lightning
PROTECTIVE FOOTWEAR: Rubber Or Plastic
PUBLIC RELATIONS & PUBLICITY SVCS
PUBLIC RELATIONS SVCS
PUBLISHERS: Art Copy & Poster
PUBLISHERS: Telephone & Other Directory
PUBLISHING & BROADCASTING: Internet Only
PUBLISHING & PRINTING: Art Copy
PUBLISHING & PRINTING: Books
PUBLISHING & PRINTING: Directories, NEC
PUBLISHING & PRINTING: Directories, Telephone

PUBLISHING & PRINTING: Magazines: publishing & printing
PUBLISHING & PRINTING: Music, Book
PUBLISHING & PRINTING: Newsletters, Business Svc
PUBLISHING & PRINTING: Newspapers
PUBLISHING & PRINTING: Pamphlets
PUBLISHING & PRINTING: Shopping News
PUBLISHING & PRINTING: Textbooks
PUBLISHING & PRINTING: Trade Journals
PUBLISHING & PRINTING: Yearbooks
PULLEYS: Power Transmission
PULP MILLS
PULP MILLS: Mechanical & Recycling Processing
PUMP JACKS & OTHER PUMPING EQPT: Indl
PUMPS & PARTS: Indl
PUMPS & PUMPING EQPT REPAIR SVCS
PUMPS & PUMPING EQPT WHOLESALERS
PUMPS: Domestic, Water Or Sump
PUMPS: Gasoline, Measuring Or Dispensing
PUMPS: Measuring & Dispensing
PUMPS: Oil, Measuring Or Dispensing
PURIFICATION & DUST COLLECTION EQPT

Q

QUILTING: Individuals

R

RACE CAR OWNERS
RACEWAYS
RADIO BROADCASTING & COMMUNICATIONS EQPT
RADIO BROADCASTING STATIONS
RADIO COMMUNICATIONS: Airborne Eqpt
RAILINGS: Prefabricated, Metal
RAILINGS: Wood
RAILROAD EQPT
RAILROAD EQPT & SPLYS WHOLESALERS
RAILROAD EQPT, EXC LOCOMOTIVES
RAILROAD EQPT: Brakes, Air & Vacuum
RAILROAD MAINTENANCE & REPAIR SVCS
RAILROAD RELATED EQPT
RAILROAD RELATED EQPT: Railway Track
RAILS: Steel Or Iron
RAMPS: Prefabricated Metal
RAZORS, RAZOR BLADES
REAL ESTATE AGENCIES & BROKERS
REAL ESTATE AGENTS & MANAGERS
REAL ESTATE INVESTMENT TRUSTS
REAL ESTATE LISTING SVCS
RECEIVERS: Radio Communications
RECORDS & TAPES: Prerecorded
RECREATIONAL VEHICLE PARTS & ACCESS STORES
REFINING: Petroleum
REFRACTORIES: Alumina Fused
REFRACTORIES: Clay
REFRACTORIES: Nonclay
REFRACTORY MATERIALS WHOLESALERS
REFRIGERATION & HEATING EQUIPMENT
REFRIGERATION EQPT & SPLYS WHOLESALERS
REFRIGERATION EQPT: Complete
REFRIGERATION SVC & REPAIR
REFUSE SYSTEMS
REGULATORS: Power
REHABILITATION CENTER, OUTPATIENT TREATMENT
REHABILITATION CTR, RESIDENTIAL WITH HEALTH CARE INCIDENTAL
RELAYS & SWITCHES: Indl, Electric
RELAYS: Control Circuit, Ind
REMOVERS & CLEANERS
REMOVERS: Paint
RENTAL SVCS: Electronic Eqpt, Exc Computers
RENTAL SVCS: Eqpt, Theatrical
RENTAL SVCS: Sign
RENTAL SVCS: Video Disk/Tape, To The General Public
RENTAL: Portable Toilet
REPRODUCTION SVCS: Video Tape Or Disk
RESEARCH & DEVELOPMENT SVCS, COMMERCIAL: Engineering Lab
RESEARCH, DEVELOPMENT & TESTING SVCS, COMMERCIAL: Business
RESEARCH, DEVELOPMENT & TESTING SVCS, COMMERCIAL: Medical
RESINS: Custom Compound Purchased
RESTAURANT EQPT: Carts

RESTAURANT EQPT: Sheet Metal
RESTAURANTS:Full Svc, American
RETAIL BAKERY: Cookies
RETAIL BAKERY: Doughnuts
RETAIL BAKERY: Pretzels
RETAIL STORES: Alcoholic Beverage Making Eqpt & Splys
RETAIL STORES: Audio-Visual Eqpt & Splys
RETAIL STORES: Business Machines & Eqpt
RETAIL STORES: Cleaning Eqpt & Splys
RETAIL STORES: Concrete Prdts, Precast
RETAIL STORES: Cosmetics
RETAIL STORES: Electronic Parts & Eqpt
RETAIL STORES: Flags
RETAIL STORES: Foam & Foam Prdts
RETAIL STORES: Ice
RETAIL STORES: Medical Apparatus & Splys
RETAIL STORES: Orthopedic & Prosthesis Applications
RETAIL STORES: Perfumes & Colognes
RETAIL STORES: Pet Food
RETAIL STORES: Religious Goods
RETAIL STORES: Tents
RETAIL STORES: Water Purification Eqpt
REUPHOLSTERY & FURNITURE REPAIR
RIVETS: Metal
ROAD CONSTRUCTION EQUIPMENT WHOLESALERS
ROBOTS: Assembly Line
ROLLING MILL MACHINERY
ROLLING MILL ROLLS: Cast Steel
ROLLS & BLANKETS, PRINTERS': Rubber Or Rubberized Fabric
ROOFING GRANULES
ROOFING MATERIALS: Asphalt
ROOFING MEMBRANE: Rubber
RUBBER PRDTS: Appliance, Mechanical
RUBBER PRDTS: Silicone
RUBBER PRDTS: Sponge
RUGS : Hand & Machine Made

S

SAFETY EQPT & SPLYS WHOLESALERS
SALES PROMOTION SVCS
SALT
SAMPLE BOOKS
SAND & GRAVEL
SAND MINING
SANDBLASTING EQPT
SANITARY SVC, NEC
SANITARY SVCS: Liquid Waste Collection & Disposal
SANITARY SVCS: Oil Spill Cleanup
SANITARY SVCS: Refuse Collection & Disposal Svcs
SANITARY SVCS: Rubbish Collection & Disposal
SANITARY SVCS: Waste Materials, Recycling
SASHES: Door Or Window, Metal
SATELLITES: Communications
SAWMILL MACHINES
SAWS & SAWING EQPT
SCALES & BALANCES, EXC LABORATORY
SCIENTIFIC EQPT REPAIR SVCS
SCIENTIFIC INSTRUMENTS WHOLESALERS
SCRAP & WASTE MATERIALS, WHOLESALE: Ferrous Metal
SCRAP & WASTE MATERIALS, WHOLESALE: Metal
SCRAP & WASTE MATERIALS, WHOLESALE: Paper
SCREENS: Woven Wire
SCREW MACHINE PRDTS
SCREWS: Metal
SEALANTS
SEALING COMPOUNDS: Sealing, synthetic rubber or plastic
SEARCH & NAVIGATION SYSTEMS
SEAT BELTS: Automobile & Aircraft
SEATING: Stadium
SECURE STORAGE SVC: Household & Furniture
SECURITY CONTROL EQPT & SYSTEMS
SECURITY DEVICES
SECURITY SYSTEMS SERVICES
SEMICONDUCTOR CIRCUIT NETWORKS
SEMICONDUCTOR DEVICES: Wafers
SEMICONDUCTORS & RELATED DEVICES
SENSORS: Infrared, Solid State
SEPTIC TANK CLEANING SVCS
SEPTIC TANKS: Concrete
SEWAGE & WATER TREATMENT EQPT
SEWING, NEEDLEWORK & PIECE GOODS STORES: Knitting Splys

PRDT INDEX

SHADES: Window
SHAPES & PILINGS, STRUCTURAL: Steel
SHEET METAL SPECIALTIES, EXC STAMPED
SHEETS: Fabric, From Purchased Materials
SHELVING: Office & Store, Exc Wood
SHIP BUILDING & REPAIRING: Cargo Vessels
SHOE STORES
SHOE STORES: Women's
SHOES: Canvas, Rubber Soled
SHOES: Men's
SHOES: Orthopedic, Children's
SHOES: Orthopedic, Men's
SHOES: Orthopedic, Women's
SHOES: Plastic Or Rubber
SHOES: Sandals, Rubber
SHOES: Women's
SHOT PEENING SVC
SHOWCASES & DISPLAY FIXTURES: Office & Store
SHOWER STALLS: Metal
SHOWER STALLS: Plastic & Fiberglass
SHREDDERS: Indl & Commercial
SHUTTERS, DOOR & WINDOW: Metal
SIDING MATERIALS
SIDING: Plastic
SIGN PAINTING & LETTERING SHOP
SIGNALING DEVICES: Sound, Electrical
SIGNALS: Traffic Control, Electric
SIGNS & ADVERTISING SPECIALTIES
SIGNS & ADVERTISING SPECIALTIES: Artwork, Advertising
SIGNS & ADVERTISING SPECIALTIES: Letters For Signs, Metal
SIGNS & ADVERTISING SPECIALTIES: Novelties
SIGNS & ADVERTISING SPECIALTIES: Scoreboards, Electric
SIGNS, ELECTRICAL: Wholesalers
SIGNS, EXC ELECTRIC, WHOLESALE
SIGNS: Electrical
SIGNS: Neon
SILICONES
SILK SCREEN DESIGN SVCS
SILO STAVES: Concrete Or Cast Stone
SINTER: Iron
SKILL TRAINING CENTER
SLINGS: Rope
SMOKE DETECTORS
SNIPS: Tinners'
SOFT DRINKS WHOLESALERS
SOFTWARE PUBLISHERS: Home Entertainment
SOFTWARE PUBLISHERS: Operating Systems
SOFTWARE TRAINING, COMPUTER
SOLAR CELLS
SOLAR HEATING EQPT
SOUND EQPT: Electric
SPACE PROPULSION UNITS & PARTS
SPAS
SPEAKER SYSTEMS
SPECIALTY FOOD STORES: Coffee
SPECIALTY FOOD STORES: Health & Dietetic Food
SPECIALTY FOOD STORES: Juices, Fruit Or Vegetable
SPECIALTY FOOD STORES: Vitamin
SPECIALTY OUTPATIENT CLINICS, NEC
SPORTING & ATHLETIC GOODS: Bowling Balls
SPORTING & ATHLETIC GOODS: Fishing Eqpt
SPORTING & ATHLETIC GOODS: Fishing Tackle, General
SPORTING & ATHLETIC GOODS: Gymnasium Eqpt
SPORTING & ATHLETIC GOODS: Hunting Eqpt
SPORTING & ATHLETIC GOODS: Racket Sports Eqpt
SPORTING & ATHLETIC GOODS: Rods & Rod Parts, Fishing
SPORTING & ATHLETIC GOODS: Shafts, Golf Club
SPORTING & ATHLETIC GOODS: Targets, Archery & Rifle Shooting
SPORTING & ATHLETIC GOODS: Team Sports Eqpt
SPORTING & ATHLETIC GOODS: Track & Field Athletic Eqpt
SPORTING & REC GOODS, WHOLESALE: Camping Eqpt & Splys
SPORTING & RECREATIONAL GOODS, WHOLESALE: Boat Access & Part
SPORTING FIREARMS WHOLESALERS
SPORTING GOODS STORES: Firearms
SPORTING GOODS STORES: Fishing Eqpt
SPORTING GOODS STORES: Specialty Sport Splys, NEC
SPORTING GOODS: Sleeping Bags
SPORTS APPAREL STORES

SPORTS CLUBS, MANAGERS & PROMOTERS
SPRINGS: Coiled Flat
SPRINGS: Furniture
SPRINGS: Mechanical, Precision
SPRINGS: Precision
SPRINGS: Steel
SPRINGS: Wire
STAINLESS STEEL
STAIRCASES & STAIRS, WOOD
STAMPINGS: Automotive
STAPLES: Steel, Wire Or Cut
STATIONARY & OFFICE SPLYS, WHOLESALE: Office Filing Splys
STATIONERY & OFFICE SPLYS WHOLESALERS
STATORS REWINDING SVCS
STATUARY & OTHER DECORATIVE PRDTS: Nonmetallic
STEEL & ALLOYS: Tool & Die
STEEL, COLD-ROLLED: Strip NEC, From Purchased HotRolled
STOKERS: Mechanical, Domestic Or Indl
STONE: Dimension, Metal
STONE: Quarrying & Processing, Own Stone Prdts
STONEWARE PRDTS: Pottery
STORE FIXTURES: Wood
STORES: Auto & Home Supply
STOVES: Wood & Coal Burning
STRAINERS: Line, Piping Systems
STRAPS: Braids, Textile
STRAPS: Webbing, Woven
STUDS & JOISTS: Sheet Metal
SUNDRIES & RELATED PRDTS: Medical & Laboratory, Rubber
SURFACE ACTIVE AGENTS
SURGICAL APPLIANCES & SPLYS
SURGICAL APPLIANCES & SPLYS
SURGICAL IMPLANTS
SUSPENSION SYSTEMS: Acoustical, Metal
SVC ESTABLISHMENT EQPT, WHOLESALE: Firefighting Eqpt
SVC ESTABLISHMENT EQPT, WHOLESALE: Laundry Eqpt & Splys
SVC ESTABLISHMENT EQPT, WHOLESALE: Taxidermist Tools & Eqpt
SWIMMING POOL ACCESS: Leaf Skimmers Or Pool Rakes
SWIMMING POOL EQPT: Filters & Water Conditioning Systems
SWITCHES: Electric Power, Exc Snap, Push Button, Etc
SWITCHES: Electronic
SWITCHES: Electronic Applications
SWITCHES: Time, Electrical Switchgear Apparatus
SWITCHGEAR & SWITCHBOARD APPARATUS
SWITCHGEAR & SWITCHGEAR ACCESS, NEC
SYNTHETIC RESIN FINISHED PRDTS, NEC
SYRUPS, DRINK
SYSTEMS ENGINEERING: Computer Related
SYSTEMS INTEGRATION SVCS
SYSTEMS INTEGRATION SVCS: Local Area Network
SYSTEMS SOFTWARE DEVELOPMENT SVCS

T

TABLE OR COUNTERTOPS, PLASTIC LAMINATED
TABLES: Lift, Hydraulic
TABLETS: Bronze Or Other Metal
TAGS & LABELS: Paper
TAGS: Paper, Blank, Made From Purchased Paper
TALLOW: Animal
TANK REPAIR & CLEANING SVCS
TANKS & OTHER TRACKED VEHICLE CMPNTS
TANKS: Lined, Metal
TANKS: Plastic & Fiberglass
TANKS: Standard Or Custom Fabricated, Metal Plate
TAPE DRIVES
TAPES, ADHESIVE: Masking, Made From Purchased Materials
TAPES: Fabric
TAPES: Pressure Sensitive
TAPES: Pressure Sensitive, Rubber
TARGET DRONES
TARPAULINS
TELECOMMUNICATION EQPT REPAIR SVCS, EXC TELEPHONES
TELEPHONE ANSWERING SVCS
TELEPHONE EQPT: NEC

TELEPHONE STATION EQPT & PARTS: Wire
TELEPHONE SVCS
TELEVISION BROADCASTING & COMMUNICATIONS EQPT
TELEVISION BROADCASTING STATIONS
TELEVISION: Closed Circuit Eqpt
TEMPERING: Metal
TEMPORARY HELP SVCS
TEST KITS: Pregnancy
TESTERS: Physical Property
TESTING SVCS
TEXTILE & APPAREL SVCS
TEXTILE CONVERTERS: Knit Goods
TEXTILE DESIGNERS
TEXTILE FINISHING: Dyeing, Manmade Fiber & Silk, Broadwoven
TEXTILE: Finishing, Raw Stock NEC
TEXTILES: Bagging, Jute
TEXTILES: Linen Fabrics
TEXTILES: Mill Waste & Remnant
THEATRICAL PRODUCERS & SVCS
THERMOPLASTIC MATERIALS
THIN FILM CIRCUITS
THREAD: Cotton
THREAD: Sewing
TILE: Brick & Structural, Clay
TIRE & INNER TUBE MATERIALS & RELATED PRDTS
TIRE CORD & FABRIC
TIRES & INNER TUBES
TIRES & TUBES WHOLESALERS
TIRES & TUBES, WHOLESALE: Automotive
TOBACCO: Chewing
TOBACCO: Chewing & Snuff
TOBACCO: Cigarettes
TOBACCO: Cigars
TOBACCO: Smoking
TOILET PREPARATIONS
TOILETRIES, WHOLESALE: Perfumes
TOILETRIES, WHOLESALE: Toilet Soap
TOILETRIES, WHOLESALE: Toiletries
TOOLS & EQPT: Taxidermist
TOOLS: Hand
TOOLS: Hand, Hammers
TOWELETTES: Premoistened
TOWERS, SECTIONS: Transmission, Radio & Television
TOYS: Dolls, Stuffed Animals & Parts
TOYS: Video Game Machines
TRAILER COACHES: Automobile
TRAILERS & PARTS: Boat
TRAILERS & PARTS: Horse
TRAILERS & TRAILER EQPT
TRAILERS: Camping, Tent-Type
TRAILERS: Truck, Chassis
TRANSDUCERS: Electrical Properties
TRANSFORMERS: Distribution
TRANSFORMERS: Distribution, Electric
TRANSFORMERS: Voltage Regulating
TRANSISTORS
TRANSMISSIONS: Motor Vehicle
TRANSPORTATION BROKERS: Truck
TRANSPORTATION EQPT & SPLYS WHOLESALERS, NEC
TRAP ROCK: Crushed & Broken
TRAVEL TRAILERS & CAMPERS
TRAYS: Plastic
TREAD RUBBER: Camelback For Tire Retreading
TROPHIES, NEC
TROPHIES, WHOLESALE
TROPHIES: Metal, Exc Silver
TRUCK & BUS BODIES: Beverage Truck
TRUCK & BUS BODIES: Bus Bodies
TRUCK & BUS BODIES: Garbage Or Refuse Truck
TRUCK & BUS BODIES: Motor Vehicle, Specialty
TRUCK & BUS BODIES: Truck Beds
TRUCK & BUS BODIES: Truck, Motor Vehicle
TRUCK & BUS BODIES: Utility Truck
TRUCK BODIES: Body Parts
TRUCK BODY SHOP
TRUCK GENERAL REPAIR SVC
TRUCK PARTS & ACCESSORIES: Wholesalers
TRUCKING & HAULING SVCS: Contract Basis
TRUCKING & HAULING SVCS: Heavy, NEC
TRUCKING & HAULING SVCS: Lumber & Log, Local
TRUCKING: Except Local
TRUCKING: Local, With Storage

TRUCKING: Local, Without Storage
TRUCKS & TRACTORS: Industrial
TRUCKS: Forklift
TRUCKS: Indl
TRUSSES: Wood, Floor
TUBES: Steel & Iron
TUBES: Vacuum
TUBING: Rubber
TUNGSTEN CARBIDE POWDER
TURBINES & TURBINE GENERATOR SET UNITS, COMPLETE
TURBINES & TURBINE GENERATOR SETS
TURBINES & TURBINE GENERATOR SETS & PARTS
TURNKEY VENDORS: Computer Systems
TWINE: Binder & Baler
TYPESETTING SVC

U

UMBRELLAS & CANES
UNIFORM STORES
UNIVERSITY
UPHOLSTERY FILLING MATERIALS
UPHOLSTERY MATERIALS, BROADWOVEN
UPHOLSTERY WORK SVCS
USED CAR DEALERS
USED MERCHANDISE STORES
UTENSILS: Household, Cooking & Kitchen, Metal
UTILITY TRAILER DEALERS

V

VACUUM CLEANERS: Indl Type
VACUUM SYSTEMS: Air Extraction, Indl
VALUE-ADDED RESELLERS: Computer Systems
VALVES
VALVES & PARTS: Gas, Indl
VALVES & PIPE FITTINGS
VALVES & REGULATORS: Pressure, Indl
VALVES: Aerosol, Metal
VALVES: Aircraft, Control, Hydraulic & Pneumatic
VALVES: Control, Automatic
VALVES: Fluid Power, Control, Hydraulic & pneumatic
VALVES: Indl
VALVES: Plumbing & Heating
VALVES: Regulating & Control, Automatic
VALVES: Regulating, Process Control
VALVES: Water Works
VAN CONVERSIONS
VARIETY STORES
VARNISHES, NEC
VEHICLES: Recreational
VENDING MACHINE OPERATORS: Sandwich & Hot Food
VENDING MACHINES & PARTS
VENTILATING EQPT: Metal
VETERINARY PHARMACEUTICAL PREPARATIONS
VIDEO & AUDIO EQPT, WHOLESALE
VIDEO PRODUCTION SVCS
VIDEO TAPE PRODUCTION SVCS

VISUAL COMMUNICATIONS SYSTEMS
VITAMINS: Natural Or Synthetic, Uncompounded, Bulk
VOCATIONAL REHABILITATION AGENCY
VOCATIONAL TRAINING AGENCY

W

WALLBOARD: Decorated, Made From Purchased Materials
WALLBOARD: Gypsum
WALLPAPER & WALL COVERINGS
WALLS: Curtain, Metal
WAREHOUSING & STORAGE FACILITIES, NEC
WAREHOUSING & STORAGE: Farm Prdts
WAREHOUSING & STORAGE: General
WAREHOUSING & STORAGE: Miniwarehouse
WAREHOUSING & STORAGE: Refrigerated
WARM AIR HEATING/AC EQPT/SPLYS, WHOL Warm Air Htg Eqpt/Splys
WASTE CLEANING SVCS
WATCH REPAIR SVCS
WATCHES
WATER HEATERS
WATER PURIFICATION EQPT: Household
WATER SUPPLY
WATER TREATMENT EQPT: Indl
WATER: Mineral, Carbonated, Canned & Bottled, Etc
WATER: Pasteurized & Mineral, Bottled & Canned
WATER: Pasteurized, Canned & Bottled, Etc
WATERPROOFING COMPOUNDS
WAVEGUIDES & FITTINGS
WAXES: Petroleum, Not Produced In Petroleum Refineries
WEATHER STRIP: Sponge Rubber
WEIGHING MACHINERY & APPARATUS
WELDING & CUTTING APPARATUS & ACCESS, NEC
WELDING EQPT & SPLYS WHOLESALERS
WELDING EQPT & SPLYS: Gas
WELDING EQPT REPAIR SVCS
WELDING EQPT: Electric
WELDING REPAIR SVC
WELDING SPLYS, EXC GASES: Wholesalers
WELDING TIPS: Heat Resistant, Metal
WHEELCHAIR LIFTS
WHEELCHAIRS
WHEELS & PARTS
WHEELS: Disc, Wheelbarrow, Stroller, Etc, Stamped Metal
WHIRLPOOL BATHS: Hydrotherapy
WINCHES
WINDINGS: Coil, Electronic
WINDMILLS: Electric Power Generation
WINDOW & DOOR FRAMES
WINDOW CLEANING SVCS
WINDOW FRAMES, MOLDING & TRIM: Vinyl
WINDOW SCREENING: Plastic
WINDOWS: Frames, Wood
WINDOWS: Wood
WINE & DISTILLED ALCOHOLIC BEVERAGES WHOLESALERS

WIRE
WIRE & CABLE: Aluminum
WIRE & CABLE: Nonferrous, Aircraft
WIRE & CABLE: Nonferrous, Automotive, Exc Ignition Sets
WIRE & CABLE: Nonferrous, Building
WIRE & WIRE PRDTS
WIRE FABRIC: Welded Steel
WIRE MATERIALS: Copper
WIRE MATERIALS: Steel
WIRE PRDTS: Ferrous Or Iron, Made In Wiredrawing Plants
WIRE PRDTS: Steel & Iron
WIRE: Communication
WIRE: Mesh
WIRE: Nonferrous
WIRE: Nonferrous, Appliance Fixture
WOMEN'S & CHILDREN'S CLOTHING WHOLESALERS, NEC
WOMEN'S & GIRLS' SPORTSWEAR WHOLESALERS
WOMEN'S CLOTHING STORES
WOMEN'S CLOTHING STORES: Ready-To-Wear
WOMEN'S FULL & KNEE LENGTH HOSIERY DYEING & FINISHING
WOOD & WOOD BY-PRDTS, WHOLESALE
WOOD CHIPS, PRODUCED AT THE MILL
WOOD PRDTS: Applicators
WOOD PRDTS: Battery Separators
WOOD PRDTS: Laundry
WOOD PRDTS: Moldings, Unfinished & Prefinished
WOOD PRDTS: Mulch Or Sawdust
WOOD PRDTS: Mulch, Wood & Bark
WOOD PRDTS: Outdoor, Structural
WOOD PRDTS: Panel Work
WOOD PRDTS: Signboards
WOOD PRODUCTS: Reconstituted
WOOD TREATING: Millwork
WOOD TREATING: Structural Lumber & Timber
WOODWORK & TRIM: Exterior & Ornamental
WOODWORK & TRIM: Interior & Ornamental
WOODWORK: Interior & Ornamental, NEC
WOVEN WIRE PRDTS, NEC

X

X-RAY EQPT & TUBES

Y

YARN & YARN SPINNING
YARN MILLS: Texturizing, Throwing & Twisting
YARN WHOLESALERS
YARN: Cotton, Spun
YARN: Knitting, Spun
YARN: Manmade & Synthetic Fiber, Spun
YARN: Needle & Handicraft, Spun
YARN: Nylon, Spun Staple
YARN: Plastic Coated, Made From Purchased Yarn
YARN: Polyester, Spun From Purchased Staple
YARN: Wool, Spun

PRODUCT SECTION

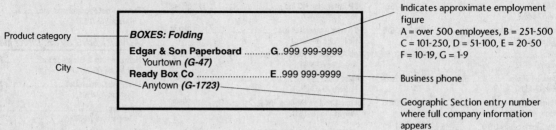

BOXES: Folding — *Product category*

Edgar & Son Paperboard ....G..999 999-9999
Yourtown *(G-47)* — *City*

Ready Box Co ....E..999 999-9999
Anytown *(G-1723)*

Indicates approximate employment figure
A = over 500 employees, B = 251-500
C = 101-250, D = 51-100, E = 20-50
F = 10-19, G = 1-9

Business phone

Geographic Section entry number where full company information appears

See footnotes for symbols and codes identification.
- Refer to the Industrial Product Index preceding this section to locate product headings.

ABRASIVE STONES, EXC GRINDING STONES: Ground Or Whole

His Glassworks Inc..................... G 828 254-2559
Asheville *(G-518)*

ABRASIVES

3M Company............................... G 704 588-4782
Charlotte *(G-1601)*

Advanced Superabrasives Inc............. E 828 689-3200
Mars Hill *(G-8076)*

Eagle Superabrasives Inc................. G 828 261-7281
Hickory *(G-6326)*

Farris Belt & Saw Company............... F 704 527-6166
Charlotte *(G-2143)*

Sia Abrasives Inc USA................... D 704 587-7355
Lincolnton *(G-7853)*

Starcke Abrasives Usa Inc............... E 704 583-3338
Charlotte *(G-2860)*

Sunbelt Abrasives Inc................... G 336 882-6837
High Point *(G-6796)*

Syntech Abrasives Inc................... F 704 525-8030
Charlotte *(G-2893)*

ABRASIVES: Coated

Klingspor Abrasives Inc................. C 828 322-3030
Hickory *(G-6380)*

ACCELERATION INDICATORS & SYSTEM COMPONENTS: Aerospace

Beyond Electronics Corp................. G 919 231-8000
Raleigh *(G-9940)*

Eco Building Corporation................ G 910 736-1540
Red Springs *(G-10667)*

New Phoenix Aerospace Inc............... F 919 380-8500
Raleigh *(G-10330)*

US Prototype Inc........................ E 866 239-2848
Wilmington *(G-12943)*

ACCELEROMETERS

Vinatoru Enterprises Inc................ G 336 227-4300
Graham *(G-5289)*

ACID RESIST: Etching

Chem-Tech Solutions Inc................. E 704 829-9202
Gastonia *(G-5019)*

Protek Services LLC..................... G 910 556-4121
Cameron *(G-1215)*

ACIDS: Sulfuric, Oleum

Southern States Chemical Inc............ E 910 762-5054
Wilmington *(G-12926)*

ACOUSTICAL BOARD & TILE

Mid-Atlantic Specialties Inc............ G 919 212-1939
Raleigh *(G-10305)*

ACRYLIC RESINS

Green Mountain Intl LLC................. G 800 942-5151
Waynesville *(G-12460)*

Phase II Creations Inc.................. G 336 249-0673
Lexington *(G-7730)*

Repi LLC................................ E 704 648-0252
Dallas *(G-3685)*

Stockhausen Superabsorber LLC........... E 336 333-7540
Greensboro *(G-5842)*

ACTUATORS: Indl, NEC

Aalberts Integrated Piping.............. E 704 841-6000
Charlotte *(G-1608)*

Shopbot Tools Inc....................... E 919 680-4800
Durham *(G-4233)*

Yale Industrial Products Inc............ E 704 588-4610
Charlotte *(G-3038)*

ADDITIVE BASED PLASTIC MATERIALS: Plasticizers

Tosaf Inc............................... F 980 533-3000
Bessemer City *(G-837)*

ADHESIVES

Beardowadams Inc........................ F 704 359-8443
Charlotte *(G-1764)*

Colquimica Adhesives Inc................ E 704 318-4750
Charlotte *(G-1959)*

Everkem Diversified Pdts Inc............ F 336 661-7801
Winston Salem *(G-13161)*

GLS Products LLC........................ G 704 334-2425
Charlotte *(G-2216)*

HB Fuller Adhesives LLC................. E 415 878-7202
Morrisville *(G-8986)*

HB Fuller Company....................... G 336 294-5939
Greensboro *(G-5589)*

Henkel US Operations Corp............... G 704 799-0385
Mooresville *(G-8681)*

Henkel US Operations Corp............... E 704 647-3500
Salisbury *(G-11063)*

Hexion Inc.............................. G 336 884-8918
High Point *(G-6646)*

Hickory Adchem Inc...................... G 828 327-0936
Hickory *(G-6346)*

INX Intrntnal Ctings Adhesives.......... C 910 371-3184
Leland *(G-7548)*

Ips Corporation......................... E 919 598-2400
Durham *(G-4083)*

Jowat Corporation....................... G 336 434-9356
Archdale *(G-231)*

Jowat Corporation....................... D 336 442-5834
Archdale *(G-232)*

Jowat Corporation....................... E 336 434-9000
Archdale *(G-233)*

Jowat International Corp................ E 336 434-9000
Archdale *(G-234)*

Jowat Properties Corp................... G 336 434-9000
Archdale *(G-235)*

Kestrel I Acquisition Corporation....... A 919 990-7500
Durham *(G-4095)*

Kleiberit Adhesives USA Inc............. F 704 843-3339
Waxhaw *(G-12435)*

LD Davis Industries Inc................. E 704 289-4551
Monroe *(G-8514)*

Liquidating Reichhold Inc............... A 919 990-7500
Durham *(G-4106)*

Lord Corporation........................ D 919 469-2500
Cary *(G-1395)*

Lord Corporation........................ B 919 468-5979
Cary *(G-1394)*

Lord Far East Inc....................... E 919 468-5979
Cary *(G-1397)*

Phoenix Tapes Usa LLC................... G 704 588-3090
Charlotte *(G-2635)*

Power Adhesives Ltd..................... G 704 578-9984
Charlotte *(G-2648)*

Pregis LLC.............................. E 828 465-9197
Conover *(G-3549)*

Psa Incorporated........................ G 910 371-1115
Belville *(G-780)*

Robix America Inc....................... C 336 668-9555
Greensboro *(G-5791)*

Rpoc Inc................................ C 910 371-3184
Wilmington *(G-12904)*

Rutland Fire Clay Company............... G 802 775-5519
Chapel Hill *(G-1569)*

Sika Corporation........................ E 704 810-0500
Gastonia *(G-5138)*

STI Polymer Inc......................... E 800 874-5878
Sanford *(G-11241)*

Textile Rubber and Chem Co Inc.......... G 704 376-3582
Indian Trail *(G-7103)*

Udm Systems LLC......................... G 919 789-0777
Raleigh *(G-10570)*

Udm Systems LLC......................... G 919 789-0777
Raleigh *(G-10571)*

Web-Don Incorporated.................... E 800 532-0434
Charlotte *(G-3009)*

Weiss USA LLC........................... G 704 282-4496
Monroe *(G-8579)*

PRODUCT

ADHESIVES & SEALANTS

Arclin USA LLC................................ G 919 542-2526
Moncure (G-8400)

Bio-Adhesive Alliance Inc..................... 336 285-3676
Mount Olive (G-9248)

Bostik Inc.. F 864 535-3759
Greenville (G-5948)

Carroll-Baccari Inc........................... G 561 585-2227
Flat Rock (G-4705)

Dbt Coatings LLC............................. G 336 834-9700
Greensboro (G-5489)

Ddp Spclty Elctrnic Mtls US 9............ E 336 547-7112
Greensboro (G-5490)

Hexpol Compounding NC Inc.............. A 704 872-1585
Statesville (G-11710)

His Company Inc.............................. G 800 537-0351
Wilmington (G-12806)

Knight Safety Coatings Co Inc............ F 910 458-3145
Wilmington (G-12829)

Loba-Wakol LLC.............................. E 704 527-5919
Wadesboro (G-12247)

Manning Fabrics Inc......................... G 910 295-1970
Pinehurst (G-9696)

Modern Recreational Tech Inc............. E 800 221-4466
Greensboro (G-5696)

Reichhold Holdings Us Inc.................. A 919 990-7500
Durham (G-4210)

Scott Bader Inc............................... E 330 920-4410
Mocksville (G-8388)

Slade Operating Company LLC........... E 704 873-1366
Statesville (G-11766)

Southern Resin Inc........................... E 336 475-1348
Thomasville (G-12071)

Tailored Chemical Products Inc........... D 828 322-6512
Hickory (G-6462)

ADHESIVES: Epoxy

Daystar Materials Inc........................ E 919 734-0460
Goldsboro (G-5211)

Laticrete International Inc................... F 910 582-2252
Hamlet (G-6059)

ADVERTISING AGENCIES

822tees Inc..................................... G 910 822-8337
Fayetteville (G-4541)

Advertising Design Systems Inc........... G 828 264-8060
Boone (G-894)

Clarks Printing Service Inc................. E 828 254-1432
Asheville (G-477)

Dale Advertising Inc.......................... G 704 484-0971
Shelby (G-11329)

Executive Promotions Inc................... F 704 663-4000
Mooresville (G-8661)

Fit1media LLC.................................. G 919 925-2200
Raleigh (G-10110)

Idea People Inc............................... G 704 398-4437
Huntersville (G-7000)

Ifpo - Ifmo/American Image Inc........... G 336 945-9867
Hamptonville (G-6085)

JB II Printing LLC............................. E 336 222-0717
Burlington (G-1111)

Lomar Specialty Advg Inc................... F 704 788-4380
Concord (G-3396)

Planet Logo Inc............................... G 910 763-2554
Wilmington (G-12879)

Shannon Media Inc........................... F 919 933-1551
Chapel Hill (G-1570)

Yp Advrtising Pubg LLC Not LLC......... C 704 522-5500
Charlotte (G-3042)

ADVERTISING AGENCIES: Consultants

B&P Enterprise NC Inc...................... G 727 669-6877
Hickory (G-6269)

Ed Kemp Associates Inc.................... G 336 869-2155
High Point (G-6604)

Golf Associates Advertising Co........... E 828 252-6544
Asheville (G-508)

Inform Inc....................................... F 828 322-7766
Hickory (G-6368)

Inspire Creative Studios Inc............... G 910 395-0200
Wilmington (G-12818)

ADVERTISING CURTAINS

Autoverters Inc................................ F 252 537-0426
Roanoke Rapids (G-10731)

Blur Development Group LLC.............. D 919 701-4213
Cary (G-1312)

Dorian Corporation........................... G 910 352-6939
Wilmington (G-12766)

Simontic Composite Inc..................... E 336 897-9885
Greensboro (G-5813)

ADVERTISING DISPLAY PRDTS

Ryder Integrated Logistics Inc............ G 336 227-1130
Burlington (G-1152)

Ryder Integrated Logistics Inc............ F 336 227-1130
Burlington (G-1153)

Web 4 Half LLC............................... E 855 762-4638
Greensboro (G-5914)

ADVERTISING REPRESENTATIVES:

Newspaper

Gatehouse Media LLC....................... E 336 626-6103
Asheboro (G-360)

Latino Communications Inc................ F 919 645-1680
Raleigh (G-10249)

ADVERTISING SPECIALTIES, WHOLESALE

B F I Industries Inc........................... G 919 229-4509
Wake Forest (G-12262)

C & M Enterprise Inc........................ G 704 545-1180
Mint Hill (G-8333)

Carroll Signs & Advertising................ G 336 983-3415
King (G-7324)

Causekeepers Inc............................ E 336 824-2518
Franklinville (G-4855)

Consumer Concepts.......................... F 252 247-7000
Morehead City (G-8828)

Dale Advertising Inc.......................... G 704 484-0971
Shelby (G-11329)

Daztech Inc..................................... G 800 862-6360
Wilmington (G-12761)

Dicks Store.................................... G 336 548-9358
Madison (G-7987)

Identify Yourself LLC........................ F 252 202-1452
Kitty Hawk (G-7445)

Ink n Stitches LLC........................... G 336 633-3898
Asheboro (G-365)

Markell Publishing Company Inc.......... G 336 226-7148
Burlington (G-1122)

Marketing One Sportswear Inc............ G 704 334-9333
Charlotte (G-2457)

Memories of Orangeburg Inc.............. G 803 533-0035
Mooresville (G-8722)

Office Sup Svcs Inc Charlotte............. E 704 786-4677
Concord (G-3410)

PSM Enterprises Inc......................... F 336 789-8888
Mount Airy (G-9167)

Silverlining Screen Prtrs Inc.............. G 919 554-0340
Youngsville (G-13485)

T & R Signs.................................... G 919 779-1185
Garner (G-4967)

Tannis Root Productions Inc............... G 919 832-8552
Raleigh (G-10533)

ADVERTISING SVCS: Direct Mail

Heritage Prtg & Graphics Inc.............. G 704 551-0700
Charlotte (G-2274)

Laser Ink Corporation....................... E 919 361-5822
Durham (G-4101)

Mb-F Inc.. D 336 379-9352
Greensboro (G-5685)

Meredith - Webb Prtg Co Inc.............. D 336 228-8378
Burlington (G-1128)

Professional Laminating LLC.............. G 919 465-0400
Cary (G-1430)

William George Printing LLC.............. E 910 221-2700
Hope Mills (G-6928)

Yp Advrtising Pubg LLC Not LLC......... C 704 522-5500
Charlotte (G-3042)

ADVERTISING SVCS: Display

Apple Rock Advg & Prom Inc.............. E 336 232-4800
Greensboro (G-5366)

RLM/Universal Packaging Inc............. F 336 644-6161
Greensboro (G-5789)

ADVERTISING SVCS: Outdoor

Signlite Services Inc......................... G 336 751-9543
Mocksville (G-8389)

Sweatnet LLC.................................. G 847 331-7287
Charlotte (G-2886)

AERIAL WORK PLATFORMS

Ken Garner Mfg - RHO Inc................. E 336 969-0416
Rural Hall (G-10962)

Man Lift Mfg Co............................... E 414 486-1760
Shelby (G-11359)

Mid-Atlantic Crane and Eqp Co........... E 919 790-3535
Raleigh (G-10304)

AGENTS, BROKERS & BUREAUS: Personal Service

Carolina Connections Inc................... G 336 786-7030
Mount Airy (G-9107)

Chicopee Inc................................... G 919 894-4111
Benson (G-786)

Garage Shop LLC............................ F 980 500-0583
Denver (G-3784)

Professnal Alterations EMB Inc........... G 910 577-8484
Jacksonville (G-7139)

AGRICULTURAL DISINFECTANTS

Degesch America Inc........................ E 800 548-2778
Wilson (G-12983)

I Must Garden LLC........................... G 919 929-2299
Raleigh (G-10182)

AGRICULTURAL EQPT: BARN, SILO, POULTRY, DAIRY/LIVESTOCK MACH

Lock Drives Inc............................... G 704 588-1844
Pineville (G-9740)

AGRICULTURAL EQPT: Fertilizing Machinery

General Fertilizer Eqp Inc.................. F 336 299-4711
Greensboro (G-5554)

AGRICULTURAL EQPT: Fertilizng, Sprayng, Dustng/Irrigatn Mach

Spectrum Products Inc.......................... G 919 556-7797
Youngsville (G-13488)

AGRICULTURAL EQPT: Grounds Mowing Eqpt

Befco Inc... E 252 977-9920
Rocky Mount (G-10824)

AGRICULTURAL EQPT: Turf & Grounds Eqpt

Carolina Golfco Inc............................. G 704 525-7846
Charlotte (G-1848)

Deere & Company................................. B 919 567-6400
Fuquay Varina (G-4878)

AGRICULTURAL MACHINERY & EQPT: Wholesalers

General Fertilizer Eqp Inc.................... F 336 299-4711
Greensboro (G-5554)

Griffin Industries LLC.......................... D 704 624-9140
Marshville (G-8089)

North American Implements Inc........... G 336 476-2904
Thomasville (G-12056)

AIR CLEANING SYSTEMS

3nine USA Inc...................................... F 512 210-4005
Charlotte (G-1602)

Acculabs Technologies Inc.................. G 919 468-8780
Morrisville (G-8917)

Cosatron... G 704 785-8145
Concord (G-3345)

D J Enviro Solutions............................ G 828 495-7448
Taylorsville (G-11957)

Eas Incorporated................................. G 704 734-4945
Kings Mountain (G-7361)

Nederman Mikropul LLC....................... E 704 998-2600
Charlotte (G-2553)

Novaerus US Inc.................................. G 813 304-2468
Charlotte (G-2578)

P & G Manufacturing Wash Inc............ G 252 946-9110
Washington (G-12402)

AIR CONDITIONING & VENTILATION EQPT & SPLYS: Wholesales

Filtration Technology Inc..................... G 336 294-5655
Greensboro (G-5531)

AIR CONDITIONING EQPT

Air System Components Inc.................. D 919 279-8868
Sanford (G-11146)

Air System Components Inc.................. D 919 775-2201
Sanford (G-11147)

Air System Components Inc.................. E 252 641-5900
Tarboro (G-11921)

Air System Components Inc.................. C 252 641-0875
Tarboro (G-11922)

Boles Holding Inc................................ G 828 264-4200
Boone (G-899)

Carrier Corporation............................. C 704 921-3800
Charlotte (G-1863)

Eneco East Inc.................................... G 828 322-6008
Hickory (G-6329)

Snap Rite Manufacturing Inc............... E 910 897-4080
Coats (G-3265)

Trane Company.................................... E 704 398-4600
Charlotte (G-2933)

Trane Technologies Company LLC........ A 704 655-4000
Davidson (G-3721)

Trane Technologies Mfg LLC................ G 704 655-4000
Davidson (G-3722)

Transarctic North Carolina Inc............. E 336 861-6116
High Point (G-6809)

AIR CONDITIONING EQPT, WHOLE HOUSE: Wholesalers

Boles Holding Inc................................ G 828 264-4200
Boone (G-899)

Gamma Js Inc...................................... F 336 294-3838
Greensboro (G-5547)

Roofing Tools and Eqp Inc................... G 252 291-1800
Wilson (G-13024)

AIR CONDITIONING REPAIR SVCS

Diagnostic Shop Inc............................ G 704 933-3435
Kannapolis (G-7207)

Johnson Controls Inc.......................... D 919 743-3500
Raleigh (G-10219)

AIR CONDITIONING UNITS: Complete, Domestic Or Indl

Airboss Heating and Coolg Inc............. G 252 586-0500
Littleton (G-7883)

Daikin Applied Americas Inc................. G 704 588-0087
Charlotte (G-2014)

Dynamic Air Engineering Inc................ E 714 540-1000
Claremont (G-3112)

Rifled Air Conditioning Inc.................... G 800 627-1707
High Point (G-6757)

Trane US Inc.. A 704 655-4000
Davidson (G-3723)

AIR MATTRESSES: Plastic

Ace Plastics Inc.................................. G 704 527-5752
Charlotte (G-1615)

Englishs All Wood Homes Inc.............. F 252 524-5000
Grifton (G-6036)

Fiber Composites LLC.......................... D 704 463-7118
New London (G-9416)

Global Packaging Inc........................... D 610 666-1608
Hamlet (G-6056)

Molded Fibr GL Cmpny/Nrth Crli.......... C 828 584-4974
Morganton (G-8882)

Poppelmann Properties USA LLC......... E 828 466-9500
Claremont (G-3117)

Pretium Packaging LLC........................ E 336 621-1891
Greensboro (G-5762)

Tri-Star Plastics Corp........................... E 704 598-2800
Denver (G-3813)

Vandor Corporation............................. E 980 392-8107
Statesville (G-11797)

AIR POLLUTION MEASURING SVCS

Environmental Supply Co Inc............... F 919 956-9688
Durham (G-4027)

AIR PURIFICATION EQPT

Absolent Inc.. F 919 570-2862
Raleigh (G-9870)

Air Control Inc..................................... E 252 492-2300
Henderson (G-6147)

Airbox Inc... E 855 927-1386
Statesville (G-11651)

Associated Metal Works Inc................. E 704 546-7002
Harmony (G-6097)

Ffi Holdings III Corp............................. E 800 690-3650
Charlotte (G-2149)

Flanders Filters Inc............................. C 252 946-8081
Washington (G-12386)

Global Plasma Solutions Inc................ E 980 279-5622
Charlotte (G-2214)

Kch Services Inc.................................. E 828 245-9836
Forest City (G-4792)

Mikropor America Inc........................... F
Charlotte (G-2501)

Schletter NA Inc.................................. F 704 595-4200
Charlotte (G-2767)

SCR-Tech LLC...................................... C 704 504-0191
Charlotte (G-2772)

Staclean Diffuser Company LLC........... F 704 636-8697
Salisbury (G-11119)

AIRCRAFT & AEROSPACE FLIGHT INSTRUMENTS & GUIDANCE SYSTEMS

United States Dept of Navy................... G 252 466-4514
Cherry Point (G-3055)

AIRCRAFT & HEAVY EQPT REPAIR SVCS

Brant & Lassiter Septic Tank............... G 252 587-4321
Potecasi (G-9819)

GE Aircraft Engs Holdings Inc.............. A 919 361-4400
Durham (G-4043)

AIRCRAFT ASSEMBLY PLANTS

Anuma Aerospace LLC......................... G 919 600-0142
Raleigh (G-9906)

BEC-Faye LLC...................................... G 252 714-8700
Grimesland (G-6040)

Boeing Arospc Operations Inc............. F 919 722-4351
Goldsboro (G-5201)

Boeing Company.................................. G 704 572-8280
Charlotte (G-1796)

CJ Partners LLC................................... G 336 838-3080
Wilkesboro (G-12633)

Cyberlux Corporation........................... F 984 363-6894
Research Triangle Pa (G-10707)

Hawthorne Services............................. G 910 436-9013
Fayetteville (G-4608)

Honda Aircraft Company LLC............... E 336 662-0246
Greensboro (G-5604)

Honda Aircraft Company LLC............... E 336 662-0246
Greensboro (G-5605)

Honda Aircraft Company LLC............... B 336 662-0246
Greensboro (G-5606)

Iomax USA LLC.................................... E 704 662-1840
Mooresville (G-8695)

Piedmont AVI Cmponent Svcs LLC....... C 336 423-5100
Greensboro (G-5741)

Signature Flight Air Inc........................ E 919 840-4400
Morrisville (G-9055)

Summit Aviation Inc............................. F 302 834-5400
Greensboro (G-5844)

United States Dept of Navy................... G 252 464-7228
Cherry Point (G-3056)

AIRCRAFT ENGINES & ENGINE PARTS: Air Scoops

GE Aircraft Engs Holdings Inc.............. A 919 361-4400
Durham (G-4043)

AIRCRAFT ENGINES & ENGINE PARTS: Airfoils

Pratt & Whitney Eng Svcs Inc.............. A 860 565-4321
Asheville (G-583)

AIRCRAFT ENGINES & ENGINE PARTS: Mount Parts

Hiab USA Inc....................................... F 704 896-9089
Cornelius (G-3606)

Lord Corporation................................. B 919 468-5979
Cary (G-1394)

Lord Far East Inc.................................G 919 468-5979
  Cary *(G-1397)*

AIRCRAFT ENGINES & ENGINE PARTS:
Research & Development, Mfr

Triad Engines Parts & Svcs Inc...........G 800 334-6437
  Burlington *(G-1169)*

AIRCRAFT ENGINES & PARTS

Carolina Precision Tech LLC..................E 215 675-4590
  Mooresville *(G-8633)*

Curtiss-Wright Controls Inc.................. E 704 869-2300
  Shelby *(G-11325)*

Fps Wind Down Inc............................F 336 776-9165
  Winston Salem *(G-13174)*

Glemco LLC..G 866 619-6707
  Statesville *(G-11703)*

Goodrich Corporation...........................C 704 423-7000
  Charlotte *(G-2227)*

Honda Aero LLC...................................D 336 226-2376
  Burlington *(G-1105)*

Honeywell...E 734 942-5823
  Charlotte *(G-2285)*

Honeywell International Inc....................G 910 436-5144
  Fort Bragg *(G-4804)*

Honeywell International Inc....................A 919 662-7539
  Raleigh *(G-10173)*

Honeywell International Inc....................A 704 627-6200
  Charlotte *(G-2286)*

James Tool Machine & Engrg Inc...........C 828 584-8722
  Morganton *(G-8875)*

Pratt & Whitney Eng Svcs Inc................B 704 660-9999
  Mooresville *(G-8753)*

Precision Metals LLC............................G 919 762-7481
  Benson *(G-796)*

Tat Technologies Group........................A 704 910-2215
  Charlotte *(G-2899)*

Thermal Pane Inc.................................G 336 722-9977
  Lexington *(G-7749)*

Unique Tool and Mfg Co........................E 336 498-2614
  Franklinville *(G-4858)*

AIRCRAFT EQPT & SPLYS WHOLESALERS

Ontic Engineering and Mfg Inc..............B 919 395-3908
  Creedmoor *(G-3653)*

AIRCRAFT FLIGHT INSTRUMENT REPAIR SVCS

T Air Inc...D 980 595-2840
  Charlotte *(G-2895)*

AIRCRAFT LIGHTING

B/E Aerospace Inc................................E 704 423-7000
  Charlotte *(G-1731)*

AIRCRAFT MAINTENANCE & REPAIR SVCS

D2 Government Solutions LLC...............E 662 655-4554
  New Bern *(G-9362)*

Piedmont AVI Cmponent Svcs LLC........C 336 423-5100
  Greensboro *(G-5741)*

Powerhouse Resources Intl LLC.............D 919 291-1783
  Raleigh *(G-10380)*

Zim Arcraft Cbin Solutions LLC.............F 336 862-1418
  Greensboro *(G-5932)*

AIRCRAFT PARTS & AUXILIARY EQPT:
Assemblies, Fuselage

Blue Force Technologies LLC.................D 919 443-1660
  Morrisville *(G-8942)*

AIRCRAFT PARTS & AUXILIARY EQPT:
Assys, Subassemblies/Parts

Blanket Aero LLC.................................G 704 591-2878
  Concord *(G-3321)*

Curtiss-Wright Controls Inc...................F 704 869-2320
  Gastonia *(G-5035)*

Curtiss-Wright Controls Inc...................E 704 869-4600
  Charlotte *(G-2005)*

Oro Manufacturing Company..................E 704 283-2186
  Monroe *(G-8539)*

AIRCRAFT PARTS & AUXILIARY EQPT:
Bodies

Collins Aerospace................................F 704 423-7000
  Charlotte *(G-1957)*

AIRCRAFT PARTS & AUXILIARY EQPT:
Body & Wing Assys & Parts

B/E Aerospace Inc................................E 704 423-7000
  Charlotte *(G-1731)*

AIRCRAFT PARTS & AUXILIARY EQPT:
Body Assemblies & Parts

AMF-NC Enterprise Company LLC...........F 704 489-2206
  Denver *(G-3769)*

Gray Manufacturing Tech LLC................F 704 489-2206
  Denver *(G-3785)*

AIRCRAFT PARTS & AUXILIARY EQPT:
Military Eqpt & Armament

Safety & Security Intl Inc......................G 336 285-8673
  Greensboro *(G-5800)*

Tigerswan LLC....................................C 919 439-7110
  Apex *(G-197)*

AIRCRAFT PARTS & AUXILIARY EQPT:
Research & Development, Mfr

Weststar Precision Inc..........................E 919 557-2820
  Cary *(G-1482)*

AIRCRAFT PARTS & AUXILIARY EQPT:
Tanks, Fuel

Isometrics Inc.....................................F 336 342-4150
  Reidsville *(G-10690)*

Isometrics Inc.....................................E 336 349-2329
  Reidsville *(G-10689)*

AIRCRAFT PARTS & EQPT, NEC

A & A Drone Service LLC.......................G 704 928-5054
  Statesville *(G-11642)*

Acme Aerofab LLC...............................G 704 806-3582
  Charlotte *(G-1618)*

Air-We-Go LLC.....................................E 704 289-6565
  Monroe *(G-8420)*

Aircraft Parts Solutions LLC...................G 843 300-1725
  Apex *(G-133)*

Ark Aviation Inc...................................G 336 379-0900
  Greensboro *(G-5369)*

B/E Aerospace Inc................................G 336 841-7698
  High Point *(G-6535)*

B/E Aerospace Inc................................G 336 293-1823
  Winston Salem *(G-13091)*

B/E Aerospace Inc................................G 336 293-1823
  Winston Salem *(G-13092)*

B/E Aerospace Inc................................E 336 744-6914
  Winston Salem *(G-13093)*

B/E Aerospace Inc................................E 336 767-2000
  Winston Salem *(G-13094)*

B/E Aerospace Inc................................C 520 733-1719
  Winston Salem *(G-13095)*

B/E Aerospace Inc................................C 336 776-3500
  Winston Salem *(G-13096)*

B/E Aerospace Inc................................C 336 767-2000
  Winston Salem *(G-13097)*

B/E Aerospace Inc................................F 336 692-8940
  Winston Salem *(G-13098)*

Ballistic Recovery Systems Inc..............E 651 457-7491
  Pinebluff *(G-9685)*

Beta Fueling Systems LLC.....................D 336 342-0306
  Reidsville *(G-10676)*

Brice Manufacturing Co Inc....................E 818 896-2938
  Greensboro *(G-5398)*

Carolina Ground Svc Eqp Inc..................F 252 565-0288
  New Bern *(G-9349)*

Carolina Metals Inc..............................F 828 667-0876
  Asheville *(G-470)*

Curtiss-Wright Controls Inc...................E 704 869-2300
  Shelby *(G-11325)*

D2 Government Solutions LLC...............E 662 655-4554
  New Bern *(G-9362)*

DEB Manufacturing Inc.........................G 704 703-6618
  Concord *(G-3353)*

Equipment & Supply Inc........................E 704 289-6565
  Monroe *(G-8485)*

Esterline Technologies Corp..................G 910 814-1222
  Lillington *(G-7796)*

Frisby Aerospace Inc............................G 336 712-8004
  Clemmons *(G-3185)*

GE Aviation Systems LLC......................C 828 210-5076
  Asheville *(G-504)*

General Electric Company......................A 910 675-5000
  Wilmington *(G-12785)*

Goaero LLC...G 815 713-1190
  Greensboro *(G-5566)*

Goodrich Corporation............................G 704 282-2500
  Monroe *(G-8493)*

Goodrich Corporation............................C 704 282-2500
  Monroe *(G-8494)*

Goodrich Corporation............................C 704 423-7000
  Charlotte *(G-2227)*

Gounmanned LLC.................................G 919 835-2140
  Raleigh *(G-10140)*

Honeywell International Inc....................E 252 977-2100
  Rocky Mount *(G-10841)*

James Tool Machine & Engrg Inc...........C 828 584-8722
  Morganton *(G-8875)*

Kearfott Corporation.............................B 828 350-5300
  Black Mountain *(G-868)*

Kidde Technologies Inc.........................D 252 237-7004
  Wilson *(G-13001)*

Legacy Aerospace and Def LLC.............G 828 398-0981
  Arden *(G-281)*

Logic Hydraulic Controls Inc..................E 910 791-9293
  Wilmington *(G-12838)*

Lord Corporation.................................B 919 468-5979
  Cary *(G-1394)*

Lord Far East Inc.................................G 919 468-5979
  Cary *(G-1397)*

PCC Airfoils LLC..................................B 919 774-4300
  Sanford *(G-11215)*

Pma Products Inc.................................G 800 762-0844
  Liberty *(G-7776)*

Proedge Precision LLC..........................E 704 872-3393
  Statesville *(G-11756)*

Purolator Facet Inc..............................E 336 668-4444
  Greensboro *(G-5771)*

R S Skillen..G 828 433-5353
  Morganton *(G-8891)*

Rockwell Collins Inc.............................. G 336 744-3288
Winston Salem (G-13320)

Rtx Corporation..................................... G 704 423-7000
Charlotte (G-2740)

Sierra Nevada Corporation.................... E 919 595-8551
Durham (G-4234)

Soisa Inc.. G 336 940-4006
Mocksville (G-8390)

Southern Prestige Intl LLC.................... F 704 872-9524
Statesville (G-11771)

Specialty Perf LLC................................ G 704 872-9980
Statesville (G-11773)

Spirit Aerosystems NC Inc..................... F 252 208-4645
Kinston (G-7430)

Starhgen Arospc Components LLC........ F 704 660-1001
Mooresville (G-8776)

T Air Inc... D 980 595-2840
Charlotte (G-2895)

Tcom Limited Partnership...................... B 252 330-5555
Elizabeth City (G-4413)

Telair US LLC....................................... C 919 705-2400
Goldsboro (G-5249)

Tempest Aero Group............................ E 336 449-5054
Gibsonville (G-5184)

Triumph Actuation Systems LLC........... C 336 766-9036
Clemmons (G-3206)

Unison Engine Components Inc............. B 828 274-4540
Asheville (G-627)

United States Dept of Navy................... E 252 466-4415
Cherry Point (G-3057)

Vannoy Construction Arcft LLC............. G 336 846-7191
Jefferson (G-7193)

Vx Aerospace Corporation.................... F 828 433-5353
Morganton (G-8910)

West Side Industries LLC...................... G 980 223-8665
Statesville (G-11799)

AIRCRAFT PARTS WHOLESALERS

Carolina Ground Svc Eqp Inc................ F 252 565-0288
New Bern (G-9349)

AIRCRAFT SEATS

B/E Aerospace Inc................................ F 704 423-7000
Winston Salem (G-13099)

B/E Aerospace Inc................................ E 704 423-7000
Charlotte (G-1731)

Custom Products Inc............................. D 704 663-4159
Mooresville (G-8647)

Zim Arcraft Cbin Solutions LLC............. B 336 464-0122
Winston Salem (G-13411)

Zim Arcraft Cbin Solutions LLC............. F 336 862-1418
Greensboro (G-5932)

AIRCRAFT SERVICING & REPAIRING

Haeco Americas LLC............................. A 336 668-4410
Greensboro (G-5585)

Textron Aviation Inc.............................. C 336 605-7000
Greensboro (G-5861)

AIRCRAFT: Airplanes, Fixed Or Rotary Wing

Charter Jet Transport Inc...................... G 704 359-8833
Charlotte (G-1907)

Marshall USA LLC................................. G 301 481-1241
Greensboro (G-5677)

Textron Aviation Inc.............................. C 336 605-7000
Greensboro (G-5861)

AIRCRAFT: Research & Development, Manufacturer

Vx Aerospace Corporation.................... F 828 433-5353
Morganton (G-8910)

Windlift Inc... G 919 490-8575
Durham (G-4306)

AIRPORTS, FLYING FIELDS & SVCS

Summit Aviation Inc.............................. F 302 834-5400
Greensboro (G-5844)

ALARMS: Burglar

Elk Products Inc.................................... E 828 397-4200
Connelly Springs (G-3476)

Honeywell SEC Americas LLC............... E 919 563-5911
Mebane (G-8246)

Tektone Sound & Signal Mfg Inc........... D 828 524-9967
Franklin (G-4841)

ALARMS: Fire

Kidde Technologies Inc......................... B 252 237-7004
Wilson (G-13000)

Safe Fire Detection Inc......................... F 704 821-7920
Monroe (G-8554)

ALCOHOL: Ethyl & Ethanol

Tyton NC Biofuels LLC.......................... E 910 878-7820
Raeford (G-9854)

ALKALIES & CHLORINE

Albemarle Corporation.......................... A 980 299-5700
Charlotte (G-1638)

Buckeye International Inc....................... G 704 523-9400
Charlotte (G-1817)

Global Ecosciences Inc......................... G 252 631-6266
Wake Forest (G-12278)

Occidental Chemical Corp..................... F 910 675-7200
Castle Hayne (G-1508)

Pavco Inc.. E 704 496-6800
Charlotte (G-2619)

PPG Industries Inc................................ G 919 772-3093
Greensboro (G-5755)

ALTERNATORS & GENERATORS: Battery Charging

Ziehl-Abegg Inc.................................... C 336 934-9339
Winston Salem (G-13410)

ALTERNATORS: Automotive

Goldsboro Strter Altrntor Svc................ G 919 735-6745
Goldsboro (G-5218)

ALUMINUM

3a Composites USA Inc......................... C 704 872-8974
Statesville (G-11641)

Alcoa Power Generating Inc.................. E 704 422-5691
Badin (G-665)

Essex Group Inc................................... G 704 921-9605
Charlotte (G-2127)

Muriel Harris Investments Inc............... F 800 932-3191
Fayetteville (G-4644)

ALUMINUM PRDTS

Alfiniti Inc... D 252 358-5811
Winton (G-13427)

Aviation Metals NC Inc.......................... F 704 264-1647
Charlotte (G-1721)

CCL Metal Science LLC......................... D 910 299-0911
Clinton (G-3229)

Container Products Corporation............. D 910 392-6100
Wilmington (G-12748)

Hydro Extrusion Usa LLC...................... D 336 227-8826
Burlington (G-1107)

J Massey Inc... F 704 821-7084
Stallings (G-11600)

Owens Corning Sales LLC..................... E 419 248-8000
Roxboro (G-10937)

Pexco LLC.. D 336 493-7500
Asheboro (G-382)

Seg Systems LLC................................. F 704 579-5800
Huntersville (G-7054)

ALUMINUM: Ingots & Slabs

AGM Carolina Inc.................................. G 336 431-4100
High Point (G-6511)

ALUMINUM: Ingots, Primary

Kymera International LLC....................... E 919 544-8090
Durham (G-4099)

ALUMINUM: Rolling & Drawing

Design Specialties Inc........................... G 919 772-6955
Raleigh (G-10042)

Mitsubishi Chemical Amer Inc............... D 980 580-2839
Charlotte (G-2509)

Southwire Company LLC....................... E 704 379-9600
Huntersville (G-7056)

AMMUNITION: Components

North American Trade LLC..................... G 828 712-3004
Fletcher (G-4759)

War Sport LLC...................................... G 910 948-2237
Eagle Springs (G-4320)

AMMUNITION: Small Arms

Every Day Carry LLc............................. F 203 231-0256
Winnabow (G-13065)

Global Synergy Group Inc..................... G 704 254-9886
Matthews (G-8172)

North American Trade LLC..................... G 828 712-3004
Fletcher (G-4759)

R & S Precision Customs LLC............... G 704 984-3480
Albemarle (G-86)

Riley Defense Inc.................................. G 704 507-9224
Hickory (G-6429)

Sirius Tactical Entps LLC....................... G 704 256-3660
Waxhaw (G-12441)

Stillwood Ammun Systems LLC............. G 919 721-9096
Burlington (G-1165)

AMPLIFIERS

Carr Amplifiers Inc................................ F 919 545-0747
Pittsboro (G-9778)

AMPLIFIERS: RF & IF Power

Akoustis Technologies Inc..................... G 704 997-5735
Huntersville (G-6963)

Lcf Enterprise....................................... G 208 415-4300
Hickory (G-6385)

AMUSEMENT & RECREATION SVCS: Art Gallery, Commercial

Clark Art Shop Inc................................ G 919 832-8319
Raleigh (G-9997)

AMUSEMENT ARCADES

Southland Amusements Vend Inc.......... E 910 343-1809
Wilmington (G-12927)

AMUSEMENT MACHINES: Coin Operated

Brian McGregor Enterprise.................... G 919 732-2317
Hillsborough (G-6861)

Southland Amusements Vend Inc.......... E 910 343-1809
Wilmington (G-12927)

AMUSEMENT PARK DEVICES & RIDES

PRODUCT

Buy Smart Inc........................G.... 252 293-4700
Wilson *(G-12976)*

Dynamic Machine Works LLC...............G..... 336 462-7370
Clemmons *(G-3182)*

North Carolina Dept Labor....................F..... 919 807-2770
Raleigh *(G-10335)*

Vortex USA Inc.....................F..... 972 410-3619
Cornelius *(G-3629)*

ANALGESICS

Nationwide Analgesics LLC...........G..... 704 651-5551
Matthews *(G-8135)*

Specgx LLC.............................C..... 919 878-4706
Raleigh *(G-10495)*

ANALYZERS: Blood & Body Fluid

Biomerieux Inc.........................B..... 919 620-2000
Durham *(G-3930)*

ANALYZERS: Moisture

Cem Corporation......................C..... 704 821-7015
Matthews *(G-8162)*

Cem Holdings Corporation................E..... 704 821-7015
Matthews *(G-8163)*

ANALYZERS: Network

Arris Technology Inc.................D..... 828 324-2200
Claremont *(G-3089)*

Comtech Group Inc...................G..... 919 313-4800
Durham *(G-3986)*

Infinity Communications LLC.........E..... 919 797-2334
Durham *(G-4076)*

Network Integrity Systems Inc............G..... 828 322-2181
Hickory *(G-6400)*

ANALYZERS: Respiratory

Polarean Inc...........................F..... 919 206-7900
Durham *(G-4186)*

ANESTHESIA EQPT

623 Medical LLC.....................F..... 877 455-0112
Morrisville *(G-8913)*

Cancer Diagnostics Inc..............E..... 877 846-5393
Durham *(G-3957)*

Carolina Lquid Chmistries Corp............E..... 336 722-8910
Greensboro *(G-5429)*

Salem Professional Anesthesia............G..... 336 998-3396
Advance *(G-38)*

Suntech Medical Inc..................D..... 919 654-2300
Morrisville *(G-9060)*

ANIMAL FEED & SUPPLEMENTS: Livestock & Poultry

Bartlett Milling Company LP...............D..... 704 872-9581
Statesville *(G-11667)*

Bay State Milling Company.................E..... 704 664-4873
Mooresville *(G-8606)*

Boggs Farm Center Inc...............G..... 704 538-7176
Fallston *(G-4522)*

Boonville Flour Feed Mill Inc............G..... 336 367-7541
Boonville *(G-957)*

Cargill Incorporated...................D..... 704 523-0414
Charlotte *(G-1841)*

Cargill Incorporated...................G..... 704 278-2941
Cleveland *(G-3210)*

Cargill Incorporated...................E..... 252 752-1879
Greenville *(G-5949)*

Coker Feed Mill Inc.................F..... 919 778-3491
Goldsboro *(G-5207)*

Darling Ingredients Inc..............F..... 704 864-9941
Gastonia *(G-5039)*

Garland Farm Supply Inc...............F..... 910 529-9731
Garland *(G-4909)*

Griffin Industries LLC..................D..... 704 624-9140
Marshville *(G-8089)*

Ifta Usa Inc...........................G..... 919 659-8393
Durham *(G-4071)*

Linkone Src LLC.....................G..... 252 206-0960
Wilson *(G-13004)*

Midstate Mills Inc..................C..... 828 464-1611
Newton *(G-9482)*

Monitor Roller Mill Inc..............G..... 336 591-4126
Walnut Cove *(G-12329)*

Mountaire Farms Inc................D..... 910 844-3126
Maxton *(G-8204)*

Murphy-Brown LLC...................D..... 910 277-8999
Laurinburg *(G-7510)*

Murphy-Brown LLC...................E..... 910 293-3434
Rose Hill *(G-10908)*

Murphy-Brown LLC...................C..... 910 282-4264
Rose Hill *(G-10909)*

Noahs Inc.............................F..... 704 718-2354
Charlotte *(G-2570)*

Nutrien AG Solutions Inc...............F..... 252 977-2025
Rocky Mount *(G-10814)*

Southeastern Minerals Inc................E..... 252 492-0831
Henderson *(G-6179)*

Southern States Coop Inc................G..... 336 629-3977
Asheboro *(G-397)*

Southern States Coop Inc................G..... 336 246-3201
Creedmoor *(G-3654)*

Southern States Coop Inc................E..... 919 528-1516
Creedmoor *(G-3655)*

Southern States Coop Inc................E..... 336 786-7545
Mount Airy *(G-9178)*

Southern States Coop Inc................E..... 919 658-5061
Mount Olive *(G-9259)*

Southern States Coop Inc................E..... 919 693-6136
Oxford *(G-9636)*

Southern States Coop Inc................G..... 252 823-2520
Princeville *(G-9828)*

Southern States Coop Inc................F..... 336 599-2185
Roxboro *(G-10945)*

Southern States Coop Inc................D..... 704 872-6364
Statesville *(G-11772)*

Southern States Coop Inc................F..... 910 285-8213
Wallace *(G-12325)*

Star Milling Company..................G..... 704 873-9561
Statesville *(G-11776)*

Steelman Milling Company Inc............G..... 336 463-5586
Yadkinville *(G-13452)*

Stevens Sausage Company Inc............D..... 919 934-3159
Smithfield *(G-11466)*

Valley Proteins (de) Inc................B..... 336 333-3030
Greensboro *(G-5895)*

ANIMAL FEED: Wholesalers

G & M Milling Co Inc................F..... 704 873-5758
Statesville *(G-11701)*

Mountaire Farms LLC..................B..... 910 974-3232
Candor *(G-1239)*

Mountaire Farms Inc................D..... 910 844-3126
Maxton *(G-8204)*

ANIMAL FOOD & SUPPLEMENTS: Bird Food, Prepared

Tuckaway Pines Inc...................G..... 704 979-3443
Concord *(G-3460)*

ANIMAL FOOD & SUPPLEMENTS: Chicken Feeds, Prepared

Braswell Milling Company.................E..... 252 459-2143
Nashville *(G-9311)*

Mountaire Farms LLC..................B..... 910 974-3232
Candor *(G-1239)*

ANIMAL FOOD & SUPPLEMENTS: Dog

Barbaras Canine Catering Inc................G..... 704 588-3647
Charlotte *(G-1749)*

Carolina Prime Pet Inc..............E..... 888 370-2360
Lenoir *(G-7590)*

Mars Petcare Us Inc................D..... 252 438-1600
Henderson *(G-6166)*

ANIMAL FOOD & SUPPLEMENTS: Dog & Cat

Braswell Milling Company.................E..... 252 459-2143
Nashville *(G-9311)*

Carolina By-Products Co..............G..... 336 333-3030
Greensboro *(G-5424)*

Crump Group USA Inc..................C..... 936 465-5870
Nashville *(G-9317)*

Nestle Purina Petcare Company............C..... 314 982-1000
Eden *(G-4353)*

Purina Mills LLC.....................D..... 704 872-0456
Statesville *(G-11757)*

ANIMAL FOOD & SUPPLEMENTS: Feed Supplements

Apc LLC................................E..... 919 965-2051
Selma *(G-11284)*

Darling Ingredients Inc..............F..... 704 694-3701
Wadesboro *(G-12241)*

Nutrotonic LLC.......................F..... 855 948-0008
Charlotte *(G-2590)*

S P Co Inc............................G..... 919 848-3599
Raleigh *(G-10453)*

ANIMAL FOOD & SUPPLEMENTS: Livestock

Mountaire Farms Inc..................C..... 704 978-3055
Statesville *(G-11736)*

ANIMAL FOOD & SUPPLEMENTS: Meat Meal & Tankage

Protein For Pets Opco LLC...................E..... 252 206-0960
Wilson *(G-13014)*

ANIMAL FOOD & SUPPLEMENTS: Pet, Exc Dog & Cat, Canned

Two Percent LLC.....................G..... 301 401-2750
Lincolnton *(G-7865)*

ANIMAL FOOD & SUPPLEMENTS: Pet, Exc Dog & Cat, Dry

Springmill Products Inc.................G..... 336 406-9050
Lawsonville *(G-7520)*

ANIMAL FOOD & SUPPLEMENTS: Poultry

G & M Milling Co Inc................F..... 704 873-5758
Statesville *(G-11701)*

Goldsboro Milling Company.................C..... 919 778-3130
Goldsboro *(G-5216)*

Johnson Nash & Sons Farms Inc............B..... 910 289-3113
Rose Hill *(G-10907)*

Pilgrims Pride Corporation.................B..... 704 624-2171
Marshville *(G-8092)*

ANIMAL FOOD/SUPPLEMENTS: Feeds Fm Meat/Meat/Veg Combnd Meals

Tyson Foods Inc.....................G..... 919 774-7925
Sanford *(G-11245)*

ANNEALING: Metal

By-Design Black Oxide & TI LLC........... F 828 874-0610
Valdese *(G-12190)*

ANODIZING EQPT

Hockmeyer Equipment Corp................. D 252 338-4705
Elizabeth City *(G-4390)*

ANODIZING SVC

Hardcoatings Inc.................................... F 704 377-2996
Charlotte *(G-2256)*

Industrial Anodizing.............................. G 336 434-2110
Trinity *(G-12116)*

Rodeco Company................................... F 919 775-7149
Sanford *(G-11225)*

ANTENNAS: Receiving

Eclipse Composite Engrg Inc................. E 801 601-8559
Mooresville *(G-8660)*

QMF Mtal Elctrnic Slutions Inc............. D 336 992-8002
Kernersville *(G-7295)*

Tecworks Inc... G 704 829-9700
Belmont *(G-772)*

ANTI-GLARE MATERIAL

Metal & Materials Proc LLC................... G 260 438-8901
Aberdeen *(G-14)*

ANTIFREEZE

Camco Manufacturing Inc...................... G 336 348-6609
Reidsville *(G-10678)*

ANTIQUE REPAIR & RESTORATION SVCS, EXC FURNITURE & AUTOS

Dimill Enterprises LLC.......................... G 919 629-2011
Raleigh *(G-10046)*

ANTISEPTICS, MEDICINAL

Esc Brands LLC..................................... G 888 331-8332
Lexington *(G-7685)*

APPAREL ACCESS STORES

Sweet Room LLC.................................... G 336 567-1620
High Point *(G-6799)*

Tafford Uniforms LLC............................ D 888 823-3673
Charlotte *(G-2897)*

APPAREL DESIGNERS: Commercial

LDR Designs.. G 252 375-4484
Greenville *(G-6001)*

APPAREL FILLING MATERIALS: Cotton Waste, Kapok/Related Matl

Cumulus Fibres Inc............................... B 704 394-2111
Charlotte *(G-2004)*

APPLIANCE PARTS: Porcelain Enameled

Acme Aerofab LLC................................. G 704 806-3582
Charlotte *(G-1618)*

Allied Tool and Machine Co................... G 336 993-2131
Kernersville *(G-7240)*

Custom Cnverting Solutions Inc............ E 336 292-2616
Greensboro *(G-5480)*

APPLIANCES, HOUSEHOLD: Kitchen, Major, Exc Refrigs & Stoves

Big Vac.. G 910 947-3654
Carthage *(G-1276)*

Crizaf Inc... G 919 251-7661
Durham *(G-3991)*

Psnc Energy.. G 919 367-2735
Apex *(G-189)*

Smartway of Carolinas LLC................... G 704 900-7877
Charlotte *(G-2817)*

APPLIANCES: Household, Refrigerators & Freezers

Bsh Home Appliances Corp................... B 252 672-9155
New Bern *(G-9343)*

K2 Scientific LLC................................... F 800 218-7613
Charlotte *(G-2386)*

APPLIANCES: Major, Cooking

Electrolux Home Products Inc............... B 252 527-5100
Kinston *(G-7410)*

Marshall Middleby Inc........................... D 919 762-1000
Fuquay Varina *(G-4887)*

Middleby Marshall Inc........................... C 919 762-1000
Fuquay Varina *(G-4891)*

Weber Stephen Products LLC................ F 704 662-0335
Mooresville *(G-8796)*

Whaley Foodservice LLC....................... D 704 529-6242
Charlotte *(G-3016)*

APPLIANCES: Small, Electric

Madison Manufacturing Company......... D 828 622-7500
Hot Springs *(G-6933)*

APPLICATIONS SOFTWARE PROGRAMMING

Able Softsystems Corp.......................... G 919 241-7907
Raleigh *(G-9868)*

Czechmate Enterprises LLC.................. G 704 784-6547
Concord *(G-3351)*

Fiestic Inc.. F 888 935-3999
Raleigh *(G-10107)*

Information Tech Works LLC.................. G 919 232-5332
Raleigh *(G-10195)*

Innait Inc... G 406 241-5245
Charlotte *(G-2337)*

Inneroptic Technology Inc..................... G 919 732-2090
Hillsborough *(G-6868)*

Natrx Inc.. E 919 263-0667
Raleigh *(G-10325)*

Sato Global Solutions Inc..................... G 954 261-3279
Charlotte *(G-2758)*

School Directorease LLC....................... G 240 206-6273
Charlotte *(G-2768)*

Splendidcrm Software Inc..................... G 919 604-1258
Holly Springs *(G-6916)*

Tc2 Labs LLC... G 919 380-2171
Raleigh *(G-10534)*

Telephys Inc.. G 312 625-9128
Davidson *(G-3719)*

AQUARIUMS & ACCESS: Glass

All Glass Inc.. G 828 324-8609
Hickory *(G-6262)*

Done-Gone Adios Inc............................ F 336 993-7300
Kernersville *(G-7268)*

Merge Scientific Solutions LLC............. G 919 346-0999
Fuquay Varina *(G-4890)*

ARCHITECTURAL SVCS

Carolina Timberworks LLC.................... F 828 266-9663
West Jefferson *(G-12561)*

Solid Holdings LLC................................ F 704 423-0260
Charlotte *(G-2825)*

Sterling Cleora Corporation.................. F 919 563-5800
Durham *(G-4250)*

ARMATURE REPAIRING & REWINDING SVC

Electrical Equipment Company.............. E 910 276-2141
Laurinburg *(G-7500)*

GE Vernova International LLC................. E 704 587-1300
Charlotte *(G-2194)*

Jenkins Electric II LLC.......................... E 704 392-7371
Charlotte *(G-2369)*

ARMATURES: Ind

Siemens Med Solutions USA Inc........... E 919 468-7400
Cary *(G-1453)*

ARMOR PLATES

Lelantos Group Inc............................... D 704 780-4127
Mooresville *(G-8709)*

AROMATIC CHEMICAL PRDTS

Balanced Health Plus LLC..................... F 704 604-9524
Charlotte *(G-1746)*

ART DEALERS & GALLERIES

World Art Gallery Incorporated............. G 910 989-0203
Jacksonville *(G-7160)*

ART GOODS, WHOLESALE

Cedar Hill Studio & Gallery................... G 828 456-6344
Waynesville *(G-12453)*

ART MARBLE: Concrete

Henson Family Investments LLC........... E 910 817-9450
Rockingham *(G-10778)*

ARTIFICIAL FLOWERS & TREES

Earth-Kind Inc....................................... G 701 751-4456
Mooresville *(G-8659)*

Evergreen Silks NC Inc.......................... F 704 845-5577
Matthews *(G-8112)*

Tree Masters Inc.................................... E 828 464-9443
Newton *(G-9506)*

ARTISTS' MATERIALS, WHOLESALE

Speedball Art Products Co LLC............. D 800 898-7224
Statesville *(G-11774)*

ARTS & CRAFTS SCHOOL

Stamping & Scrapbooking Rm Inc......... G 336 389-9538
Greensboro *(G-5835)*

ARTWORK: Framed

Laura Gaskin... G 828 628-5891
Fairview *(G-4509)*

ASPHALT & ASPHALT PRDTS

Barnhill Contracting Company............... F 336 584-1306
Burlington *(G-1051)*

Blythe Construction Inc......................... B 704 375-8474
Charlotte *(G-1793)*

Boggs Materials Inc............................... G 704 289-8482
Monroe *(G-8441)*

Boggs Transport Inc............................... G 704 289-8482
Monroe *(G-8442)*

Carolina Asphalt Maintenance.............. G 828 944-0425
Maggie Valley *(G-8005)*

Cloverleaf Mixing Inc............................ G 336 765-7900
Winston Salem *(G-13125)*

D&S Company Inc.................................. G 828 894-2778
Tryon *(G-12174)*

Garris Grading and Paving Inc.............. F 252 749-1101
Farmville *(G-4529)*

Highland Paving Co LLC........................ D 910 482-0080
Fayetteville *(G-4613)*

PRODUCT

ASPHALT COATINGS & SEALERS

Axalta Coating Systems USA LLC.......... F 336 802-5701
　High Point *(G-6533)*

Bridgestone Americas Inc...................... C 984 888-0413
　Durham *(G-3940)*

Carolina Solvents Inc............................ E 828 322-1920
　Hickory *(G-6287)*

Gemseal Pavement Products.................. G 866 264-8273
　Charlotte *(G-2198)*

ASPHALT MINING & BITUMINOUS STONE QUARRYING SVCS

Johnson Paving Company Inc................. F 828 652-4911
　Marion *(G-8046)*

ASPHALT MIXTURES WHOLESALERS

D&S Company Inc................................ G 828 894-2778
　Tryon *(G-12174)*

Fsc II LLC... F 919 783-5700
　Raleigh *(G-10122)*

ASPHALT PLANTS INCLUDING GRAVEL MIX TYPE

Apac-Atlantic Inc................................. D 336 412-6800
　Raleigh *(G-9907)*

Barnhill Contracting Company............... E 252 527-8021
　Kinston *(G-7395)*

Cardinal Stone Company Inc.................. G 336 846-7191
　Jefferson *(G-7187)*

Carolina Paving Hickory Inc.................. G 828 328-3909
　Hickory *(G-6285)*

Carolina Paving Hickory Inc.................. E 828 322-1706
　Hickory *(G-6286)*

Ferebee Corporation............................. C 704 509-2586
　Charlotte *(G-2145)*

S T Wooten Corporation........................ E 252 636-2568
　New Bern *(G-9393)*

S T Wooten Corporation........................ E 919 965-7176
　Princeton *(G-9827)*

S T Wooten Corporation........................ E 919 776-2736
　Sanford *(G-11227)*

ASSEMBLING SVC: Plumbing Fixture Fittings, Plastic

B & B Building Maintenance LLC........... G 910 494-2715
　Bunnlevel *(G-1015)*

Gods Son Plumbing Inc......................... G 252 299-0983
　Wilson *(G-12993)*

H & H Representatives Inc..................... G 704 596-6950
　Charlotte *(G-2246)*

Union Plastics Company....................... G 704 624-2112
　Marshville *(G-8096)*

ASSOCIATIONS: Business

Kidde Technologies Inc......................... B 252 237-7004
　Wilson *(G-12999)*

ASSOCIATIONS: Real Estate Management

Solarh2ot Ltd....................................... G 919 439-2387
　Raleigh *(G-10493)*

ASSOCIATIONS: Scientists'

International Society Automtn................. E 919 206-4176
　Research Triangle Pa *(G-10713)*

ATOMIZERS

Atlantic Group Usa Inc.......................... F 919 623-7824
　Raleigh *(G-9920)*

Biganodes LLC..................................... G 828 245-1115
　Forest City *(G-4784)*

Cambbro Manufacturing Company........ F 919 568-8506
　Mebane *(G-8234)*

Gallimore Fmly Investments Inc............. F 336 625-5138
　Asheboro *(G-359)*

Gentry Mills Inc................................... D 704 983-5555
　Albemarle *(G-74)*

Kerdea Technologies Inc....................... F 971 900-1113
　Greenville *(G-5998)*

Phillips Corporation.............................. E 336 665-1080
　Colfax *(G-3286)*

Qspac Industries Inc............................. E 704 635-7815
　Monroe *(G-8546)*

ATTENUATORS

M2 Optics Inc...................................... G 919 342-5619
　Raleigh *(G-10264)*

Shallco Inc.. E 919 934-3135
　Smithfield *(G-11465)*

AUDIO & VIDEO EQPT, EXC COMMERCIAL

Advanced Tech Systems Inc.................. F 336 299-6695
　Greensboro *(G-5343)*

Anthony Demaria Labs Inc.................... F 845 255-4695
　Cary *(G-1291)*

Cablenc LLC.. G 919 307-9065
　Zebulon *(G-13506)*

Cco Holdings LLC................................ C 828 414-4238
　Blowing Rock *(G-881)*

Cco Holdings LLC................................ C 828 355-4149
　Boone *(G-906)*

Cco Holdings LLC................................ C 910 292-4083
　Dunn *(G-3850)*

Cco Holdings LLC................................ B 828 270-7016
　Hickory *(G-6293)*

Cco Holdings LLC................................ C 919 502-4007
　Kenly *(G-7228)*

Cco Holdings LLC................................ C 828 394-0635
　Lenoir *(G-7592)*

Cco Holdings LLC................................ C 704 308-3361
　Lincolnton *(G-7820)*

Cco Holdings LLC................................ C 828 528-4004
　Newland *(G-9427)*

Cco Holdings LLC................................ C 919 200-6260
　Siler City *(G-11402)*

Cco Holdings LLC................................ C 828 368-4161
　Valdese *(G-12192)*

Evolution Technologies Inc.................... G 919 544-3777
　Raleigh *(G-10097)*

Integrated Info Systems Inc................... F 919 488-5000
　Youngsville *(G-13476)*

JPS Communications Inc....................... D 919 534-1168
　Raleigh *(G-10222)*

Multi Technical Services Inc.................. G 919 553-2995
　Clayton *(G-3161)*

Palmer Senn... G 704 451-3971
　Charlotte *(G-2606)*

PC Satellite Solutions........................... G 252 217-7237
　Roper *(G-10899)*

SES Integration.................................... G
　Concord *(G-3439)*

Wheatstone Corporation........................ D 252 638-7000
　New Bern *(G-9405)*

AUDIO COMPONENTS

Cary Audio Design LLC........................ E 919 355-0010
　Raleigh *(G-9983)*

East Coast Digital Inc........................... F 919 304-1142
　Mebane *(G-8239)*

AUDIO ELECTRONIC SYSTEMS

Eastern Sun Communications Inc........... G 704 408-7668
　Charlotte *(G-2083)*

Huso Inc.. G 845 553-0100
　Black Mountain *(G-866)*

Linor Technology Inc............................ F 336 485-6199
　Winston Salem *(G-13235)*

Moon Audio.. G 919 649-5018
　Cary *(G-1402)*

AUDIO-VISUAL PROGRAM PRODUCTION SVCS

Avcon Inc.. E 919 388-0203
　Cary *(G-1302)*

Cog Glbal Media/Consulting LLC........... E 980 239-8042
　Matthews *(G-8109)*

AUTO & HOME SUPPLY STORES: Auto & Truck Eqpt & Parts

Advance Stores Company Inc................. F 336 545-9091
　Greensboro *(G-5341)*

Prem Corp.. E 704 921-1799
　Charlotte *(G-2660)*

Satco Truck Equipment Inc.................... F 919 383-5547
　Durham *(G-4222)*

AUTO & HOME SUPPLY STORES: Automotive Access

Boondock S Manufacturing Inc............. G 828 891-4242
　Etowah *(G-4495)*

Down East Offroad Inc.......................... F 252 246-9440
　Wilson *(G-12984)*

Treadz LLC.. G 704 664-0995
　Mooresville *(G-8787)*

Van Products Inc.................................. E 919 878-7110
　Raleigh *(G-10582)*

AUTO & HOME SUPPLY STORES: Automotive parts

Carpenter Industries Inc....................... D 704 786-8139
　Concord *(G-3331)*

Heintz Bros Automotives Inc................. G 704 872-8081
　Statesville *(G-11706)*

Irvan-Smith Inc.................................... F 704 788-2554
　Concord *(G-3382)*

Kerdea Technologies Inc....................... F 971 900-1113
　Greenville *(G-5998)*

Kgt Enterprises Inc.............................. E 704 662-3272
　Mooresville *(G-8704)*

Roy Dunn.. G 919 963-3700
　Four Oaks *(G-4815)*

Sika Corporation.................................. E 704 810-0500
　Gastonia *(G-5138)*

AUTO & HOME SUPPLY STORES: Batteries, Automotive & Truck

Alk Investments LLC............................ G 984 233-5353
　Raleigh *(G-9891)*

Toyota Battery Mfg Inc.......................... E 469 292-6094
　Liberty *(G-7782)*

AUTO & HOME SUPPLY STORES: Speed Shops, Incl Race Car Splys

Garage Shop LLC................................. F 980 500-0583
　Denver *(G-3784)*

AUTO & HOME SUPPLY STORES: Trailer Hitches, Automotive

Leonard Alum Utlity Bldngs Inc............. G 919 872-4442
　Raleigh *(G-10254)*

AUTO & HOME SUPPLY STORES: Truck Eqpt & Parts

Consolidated Truck Parts Inc............... G 704 279-5543
Rockwell (G-10794)

Leonard Alum Utlity Bldngs Inc............ G 336 226-9410
Burlington (G-1119)

Leonard Alum Utlity Bldngs Inc............ D 336 789-5018
Mount Airy (G-9146)

AUTO SPLYS & PARTS, NEW, WHSLE: Exhaust Sys, Mufflers, Etc

Tri-City Mechanical Contrs Inc............... D 336 272-9495
Greensboro (G-5872)

AUTOMATIC REGULATING CONTROL: Building Svcs Monitoring, Auto

Delkote Machine Finishing Inc............... G 828 253-1023
Asheville (G-485)

Nascent Technology LLC...................... F 704 654-3035
Charlotte (G-2543)

AUTOMATIC REGULATING CONTROLS: AC & Refrigeration

Belham Management Ind LLC............... G 704 815-4246
Charlotte (G-1768)

Dorsett Technologies Inc...................... E 855 387-2232
Yadkinville (G-13441)

Thermik Corporation............................ E 252 636-5720
New Bern (G-9400)

Trane US Inc....................................... A 704 655-4000
Davidson (G-3723)

AUTOMATIC REGULATING CONTROLS: Appliance Regulators

Johnson Global Cmplnce Contrls.......... G 704 552-1119
Charlotte (G-2377)

AUTOMATIC REGULATING CONTROLS: Appliance, Exc AirCond/Refr

Pas USA Inc.. C 252 974-5500
Washington (G-12407)

AUTOMATIC REGULATING CONTROLS: Hardware, Environmental Reg

Green Stream Technologies Inc............. G 844 499-8880
Wake Forest (G-12280)

Layer27... G 919 909-9088
Youngsville (G-13478)

AUTOMATIC REGULATING CONTROLS: Hydronic Pressure Or Temp

Icare Usa Inc...................................... G 919 877-9607
Raleigh (G-10183)

AUTOMATIC REGULATING CONTROLS: Pneumatic Relays, Air-Cond

Ultratech Industries Inc........................ G 919 779-2004
Benson (G-799)

AUTOMATIC REGULATING CONTROLS: Refrig/Air-Cond Defrost

TRf Manufacturing NC Inc..................... E 252 223-1112
Newport (G-9445)

AUTOMATIC REGULATING CTRLS: Damper, Pneumatic Or Electric

Effikal LLC.. F 252 522-3031
Kinston (G-7407)

Salice America Inc............................... E 704 841-7810
Charlotte (G-2749)

AUTOMATIC TELLER MACHINES

Buvic LLC... G 910 302-7950
Fayetteville (G-4563)

Cisco Systems Inc............................... E 919 392-2000
Morrisville (G-8958)

Extron Electronics............................... G 919 850-1000
Raleigh (G-10100)

Noregon Systems Inc.......................... G 336 615-8555
Greensboro (G-5713)

AUTOMOBILES & OTHER MOTOR VEHICLES WHOLESALERS

Parker-Hannifin Corporation................. E 704 664-1922
Mooresville (G-8742)

Pro-System Inc.................................... F 704 799-8100
Mooresville (G-8756)

AUTOMOBILES: Off-Road, Exc Recreational Vehicles

American Growler Inc........................... E 352 671-5393
Robbins (G-10751)

Crown Defense Ltd.............................. G 202 800-8848
Denver (G-3779)

Down East Offroad Inc......................... F 252 246-9440
Wilson (G-12984)

AUTOMOTIVE & TRUCK GENERAL REPAIR SVC

Aiken-Black Tire Service Inc................. E 828 322-3736
Hickory (G-6261)

B & B Welding Inc............................... G 336 643-5702
Oak Ridge (G-9569)

Barnharts Tech Tire Repair Inc.............. G 336 337-1569
Lexington (G-7658)

Barrs Competition................................ F 704 482-5169
Shelby (G-11313)

Beamer Tire & Auto Repair Inc.............. F 336 882-7043
High Point (G-6541)

Bridgestone Ret Operations LLC........... G 336 282-4695
Greensboro (G-5401)

Courtesy Ford Inc................................ G 252 338-4783
Elizabeth City (G-4384)

Diagnostic Shop Inc............................ G 704 933-3435
Kannapolis (G-7207)

Discount Tires & Auto Repair................ G 336 788-0057
Winston Salem (G-13147)

F & C Repair and Sales LLC................. F 704 907-2461
Charlotte (G-2139)

Falls Automotive Service Inc................. G 336 723-0521
Winston Salem (G-13166)

Greensboro Tire & Auto Service............ G 336 294-9495
Greensboro (G-5578)

Haneys Tire Recapping Svc LLC........... G 910 276-2636
Laurinburg (G-7503)

John West Auto Service Inc.................. G 919 250-0825
Raleigh (G-10218)

L & S Automotive Inc........................... G 704 391-7657
Charlotte (G-2404)

Lewis Brothers Tire & Algnmt................ G 919 359-9050
Clayton (G-3157)

Mr Tire Inc.. G 828 262-3555
Boone (G-936)

Mr Tire Inc.. F 704 483-1500
Denver (G-3794)

Mr Tire Inc.. F 828 322-8130
Hickory (G-6398)

Mr Tire Inc.. G 704 739-6456
Kings Mountain (G-7373)

Mr Tire Inc.. G 828 758-0047
Lenoir (G-7627)

Mr Tire Inc.. G 704 735-8024
Lincolnton (G-7846)

Mr Tire Inc.. G 704 484-0816
Shelby (G-11365)

Mr Tire Inc.. G 704 872-4127
Statesville (G-11737)

NC Diesel Performance LLC................. G 704 431-3257
Salisbury (G-11095)

Quality Investments Inc........................ E 252 492-8777
Henderson (G-6172)

R & J Mechanical & Welding LLC.......... G 919 362-6630
Apex (G-191)

R and R Auto Repr & Tires Inc.............. G 336 784-6893
Winston Salem (G-13310)

Rabuns Trlr Repr Tire Svc Inc............... G 704 764-7841
Monroe (G-8547)

Snider Tire Inc.................................... F 336 691-5480
Greensboro (G-5820)

Spring Repair Service Inc..................... G 336 299-5660
Greensboro (G-5832)

Stoltz Automotive Inc........................... G 336 595-4218
Walkertown (G-12317)

Team X-Treme LLC.............................. G 919 562-8100
Rolesville (G-10890)

Universal Tire Service Inc..................... G 919 779-8798
Raleigh (G-10577)

Wooten John...................................... G 828 322-4031
Hickory (G-6490)

Zickgraf Enterprises Inc....................... G 828 524-2313
Franklin (G-4844)

AUTOMOTIVE CUSTOMIZING SVCS, NONFACTORY BASIS

Specialty Trnsp Systems Inc................. G 828 464-9738
Newton (G-9498)

AUTOMOTIVE GLASS REPLACEMENT SHOPS

A R Perry Corporation.......................... G 252 492-6181
Henderson (G-6146)

Orare Inc.. G 919 742-1003
Siler City (G-11422)

Rice S Glass Company Inc.................... E 919 967-9214
Carrboro (G-1272)

AUTOMOTIVE PARTS, ACCESS & SPLYS

Aerofabb LLC...................................... G 919 793-8487
Raleigh (G-9884)

American Racg Hders Exhust Inc.......... F 631 608-1986
Stanfield (G-11602)

Amsted Industries Incorporated............ G 704 226-5243
Monroe (G-8425)

Auria Albemarle LLC............................ B 704 983-5166
Albemarle (G-62)

Auria Old Fort LLC............................... C 828 668-7601
Old Fort (G-9589)

Auria Old Fort II LLC............................ D 828 668-3277
Old Fort (G-9590)

Auria Troy LLC.................................... D 910 572-3721
Troy (G-12157)

Ben Huffman Enterprises LLC............... G 704 724-4705
Mooresville (G-8607)

Billet Speed Inc................................ G 828 226-8127
Sylva (G-11890)

Borg-Warner Automotive Inc............. G 828 684-3501
Fletcher (G-4726)

Borgwarner Arden LLC...................... F 248 754-9200
Arden (G-256)

Brembo North America Inc................ G 704 799-0530
Concord (G-3324)

BT America Inc................................ G 704 434-8072
Boiling Springs (G-883)

Camco Manufacturing Inc................. G 336 348-6609
Reidsville (G-10678)

Carbotech USA Inc........................... G 704 481-8500
Concord (G-3330)

Carolina Cltch Brake Rbldrs In.......... G 828 327-9358
Hickory (G-6283)

Certification Services International LLC G 828 458-1573
Fletcher (G-4728)

City of Charlotte-Atando.................... G 704 336-2722
Charlotte (G-1922)

Classic Wood Manufacturing.............. G 336 691-1344
Greensboro (G-5448)

Coconut Paradise Inc........................ G 704 662-3443
Mooresville (G-8641)

Commercial Vehicle Group Inc........... E 704 886-6407
Concord (G-3340)

Consolidated Metco Inc.................... D 828 488-5126
Bryson City (G-1010)

Consolidated Metco Inc.................... C 828 488-5114
Canton (G-1250)

Consolidated Metco Inc.................... E 704 226-5246
Monroe (G-8468)

Continental Auto Systems Inc............. B 828 654-2000
Fletcher (G-4731)

Continental Auto Systems Inc............. E 828 584-4500
Valdese (G-12193)

Cooper-Standard Automotive Inc........ D 919 735-5394
Goldsboro (G-5209)

Cox Machine Co Inc.......................... G 704 296-0118
Monroe (G-8470)

Cummins Inc.................................... G 919 284-9111
Kenly (G-7231)

Cummins Inc.................................... G 704 588-1240
Pineville (G-9723)

Curtis L Maclean L C......................... C 704 940-5531
Mooresville (G-8646)

Cycle Pro LLC.................................. G 704 662-6682
Mooresville (G-8649)

Daimler Truck North Amer LLC........... A 704 868-5700
Gastonia (G-5038)

David Vizard Motortec Features.......... G 865 850-0666
Mount Holly (G-9227)

Dhollandia Us Llc............................. G 909 251-7979
Bessemer City (G-814)

Dnj Engine Comp Onents................... G 704 855-5505
China Grove (G-3073)

Doosan Bobcat North Amer Inc.......... C 704 883-3500
Statesville (G-11691)

Eaton Corporation............................ B 336 322-0696
Roxboro (G-10924)

Elite Metal Performance LLC.............. F 704 660-0006
Statesville (G-11694)

Epic Restorations LLC....................... G 866 597-2733
Roxboro (G-10925)

Five Star Bodies.............................. G 262 325-9126
Troutman (G-12138)

GKN Driveline Newton LLC................. E 828 428-5292
Newton (G-9467)

GKN Driveline North Amer Inc............ A 919 304-7200
Mebane (G-8244)

GKN Driveline North Amer Inc............ C 919 708-4500
Sanford (G-11184)

GKN Driveline North Amer Inc............ C 336 364-6200
Timberlake (G-12100)

Global Products LLC.......................... G 336 227-7327
Greensboro (G-5563)

GM Defense LLC............................... D 800 462-8782
Concord (G-3369)

Grede II LLC.................................... B 910 428-2111
Biscoe (G-852)

Hamilton Sundstrand Corp................. A 860 654-6000
Charlotte (G-2252)

Hanwha Advanced Mtls Amer LLC....... E 704 434-2271
Shelby (G-11342)

Hendrens Racg Engs Chassis Inc......... G 828 286-0780
Rutherfordton (G-10987)

Hickory Springs Mfg Co..................... F 336 491-4131
High Point (G-6648)

Holman & Moody Inc........................ G 704 394-4141
Charlotte (G-2281)

Hotchkis Bryde Incorporated.............. G 704 660-3060
Mooresville (G-8687)

Inter-Continental Gear & Brake.......... G 704 599-3420
Charlotte (G-2341)

Jri Development Group LLC................. F 704 660-8346
Mooresville (G-8699)

Jri Shocks LLC.................................. F 704 660-8346
Mooresville (G-8700)

Kck Holding Corp.............................. E 336 513-0002
Burlington (G-1114)

Kgt Enterprises Inc........................... E 704 662-3272
Mooresville (G-8704)

Kooks Custom Headers...................... G 704 838-1110
Statesville (G-11725)

Lear Enterprises Inc.......................... G 704 321-0027
Charlotte (G-2413)

Leonard Alum Utlity Bldngs Inc........... G 919 872-4442
Raleigh (G-10254)

Leonard Alum Utlity Bldngs Inc........... G 910 392-4921
Wilmington (G-12834)

Mack Trucks Inc............................... A 336 291-9001
Greensboro (G-5670)

Magna Composites LLC...................... B 704 797-8744
Salisbury (G-11088)

Mahle Motorsports Inc....................... F 888 255-1942
Fletcher (G-4750)

Mann+hmmel Prlator Filters LLC......... C 910 425-4181
Fayetteville (G-4633)

Mann+hmmel Prlator Filters LLC......... C 704 869-3441
Gastonia (G-5086)

Mann+hmmel Prlator Filters LLC......... E 910 425-4181
Fayetteville (G-4632)

Mann+hummel Filtration Technol......... D 704 869-3500
Gastonia (G-5087)

Mann+hummel Filtration Technol......... C 704 869-3501
Gastonia (G-5089)

Marmon Engine Controls LLC.............. E 843 701-5145
Laurinburg (G-7507)

MB Marketing & Mfg Inc.................... G 828 285-0882
Asheville (G-545)

Meritor Inc...................................... F 910 844-9401
Maxton (G-8202)

Meritor Inc...................................... D 910 844-9401
Maxton (G-8203)

Meritor Inc...................................... C 828 433-4600
Morganton (G-8881)

Metalcraft & Mech Svc Inc................. G 919 736-1029
Goldsboro (G-5229)

Moores Mch Co Fayetteville Inc.......... D 919 837-5354
Bear Creek (G-717)

Motoring Inc.................................... G 704 809-1265
Mooresville (G-8728)

Motorsport Innovations Inc................. G 704 728-7837
Davidson (G-3713)

Motorsports Machining Tech LLC......... G 336 475-3742
Thomasville (G-12052)

MSI Defense Solutions LLC................. D 704 660-8348
Mooresville (G-8730)

P4rts LLC.. E 561 717-7580
Mooresville (G-8740)

PCC Airfoils LLC............................... B 919 774-4300
Sanford (G-11215)

Precision Pdts Prfmce Ctr Inc............. F 828 684-8569
Arden (G-300)

Pro-Motor Engines Inc...................... G 704 664-6800
Mooresville (G-8755)

Race Technologies Concord NC........... G 704 799-0530
Concord (G-3429)

Reuben James Auto Electric............... G 910 980-1056
Falcon (G-4521)

Richardson Racing Products Inc........... G 704 784-2602
Concord (G-3432)

Ripari Automotive LLC....................... G 585 267-0228
Charlotte (G-2727)

Roadactive Suspension Inc................. G 704 523-2646
Charlotte (G-2729)

Rp Motor Sports Inc.......................... E 704 720-4200
Concord (G-3435)

Saf-Holland Inc................................ G 336 310-4595
Kernersville (G-7298)

Save-A-Load Inc............................... G 704 650-4947
Charlotte (G-2759)

Scorpion Products Inc....................... F 336 813-3241
King (G-7336)

SL Liquidation LLC............................ D 910 353-3666
Jacksonville (G-7145)

Spod Inc... G 910 477-6297
Southport (G-11531)

SRI Performance LLC......................... E 704 662-6982
Mooresville (G-8774)

Stanadyne Operating Co LLC.............. E 910 353-3666
Jacksonville (G-7154)

Teijin Automotive Tech Inc................. C 828 754-8441
Lenoir (G-7642)

Teijin Automotive Tech Inc................. C 828 466-7000
Newton (G-9503)

Tenowo Inc...................................... A 704 732-3525
Lincolnton (G-7861)

Thyssenkrupp Bilstein Amer Inc.......... F 704 663-7563
Mooresville (G-8786)

Trane Technologies Company LLC....... C 910 692-8700
Southern Pines (G-11512)

Trend Performance Products............... G 828 862-8290
Pisgah Forest (G-9774)

Uchiyama Mfg Amer LLC.................... F 919 731-2364
Goldsboro (G-5251)

US Legend Cars Intl Inc..................... E 704 455-3896
Harrisburg (G-6119)

Visual Impact Prfmce Systems L.......... G 704 278-3552
Cleveland (G-3224)

Wenker Inc...................................... G 704 333-7790
Charlotte (G-3012)

Xceldyne LLC................................... D 336 472-2242
Thomasville (G-12092)

AUTOMOTIVE PARTS: Plastic

Atlantic Automotive Entps LLC............ G 910 377-4108
Tabor City (G-11906)

Auto Parts Fayetteville LLC................ G 910 889-4026
Fayetteville (G-4555)

Borgwarner Turbo Systems LLC.......... D 828 684-4000
Arden (G-258)

Central Carolina Products Inc.............. C 336 226-1449
Burlington (G-1068)

Central Carolina Products Inc.............. D 336 226-0005
Burlington (G-1069)

Debotech Inc.................................C 704 664-1361
Mooresville (G-8653)

Heyco Werk USA Inc.....................E 434 634-8810
Dallas (G-3675)

Thanet Inc....................................G 704 483-4175
Denver (G-3812)

Trelleborg Salisbury Inc...............E 704 797-8030
Salisbury (G-11127)

AUTOMOTIVE PRDTS: Rubber

Hexpol Compounding NC Inc.........A 704 872-1585
Statesville (G-11710)

Lgc Consulting Inc.......................E 704 216-0171
Salisbury (G-11083)

Maranz Inc..................................D 336 996-7776
Winston Salem (G-13244)

AUTOMOTIVE REPAIR SHOPS: Diesel Engine Repair

Cummins Inc................................F 704 596-7690
Charlotte (G-2003)

S Strickland Diesel Svc Inc...........G 252 291-6999
Wilson (G-13025)

AUTOMOTIVE REPAIR SHOPS: Electrical Svcs

Goldsboro Strter Altrntor Svc........G 919 735-6745
Goldsboro (G-5218)

Mc Cullough Auto Elc & Assoc.......G 704 376-5388
Charlotte (G-2475)

R S Integrators Inc......................G 704 588-8288
Pineville (G-9749)

AUTOMOTIVE REPAIR SHOPS: Engine Rebuilding

Griffin Automotive Marine Inc........G 252 940-0714
Washington (G-12388)

Johnson Machine Co Inc...............G 252 638-2620
New Bern (G-9374)

AUTOMOTIVE REPAIR SHOPS: Machine Shop

Broadsight Systems Inc................G 336 837-1272
Mebane (G-8233)

Chiron America Inc.......................D 704 587-9526
Charlotte (G-1916)

G T Racing Heads Inc...................G 336 905-7988
Sophia (G-11489)

Performance Entps & Parts Inc......G 336 621-6572
Greensboro (G-5738)

Subaru Folger Automotive.............F 704 531-8888
Charlotte (G-2877)

AUTOMOTIVE REPAIR SHOPS: Rebuilding & Retreading Tires

Albemarle Tire Retreading Inc........G 704 982-4113
Albemarle (G-59)

Big Tire Outfitters........................G 919 568-9605
Mc Leansville (G-8218)

Bridgestone Ret Operations LLC.....G 919 471-4468
Durham (G-3941)

Bridgestone Ret Operations LLC.....G 910 864-4106
Fayetteville (G-4562)

Bridgestone Ret Operations LLC.....F 704 861-8146
Gastonia (G-5005)

Bridgestone Ret Operations LLC.....G 919 778-0230
Goldsboro (G-5202)

Bridgestone Ret Operations LLC.....G 336 282-6646
Greensboro (G-5399)

Bridgestone Ret Operations LLC.....F 336 852-8524
Greensboro (G-5400)

Bridgestone Ret Operations LLC.....G 252 522-5126
Kinston (G-7397)

Bridgestone Ret Operations LLC.....G 919 872-6402
Raleigh (G-9958)

Bridgestone Ret Operations LLC.....G 919 872-6566
Raleigh (G-9959)

Bridgestone Ret Operations LLC.....G 252 243-5189
Wilson (G-12973)

Bridgestone Ret Operations LLC.....G 336 725-1580
Winston Salem (G-13110)

Carolina Retread LLC...................G 910 642-4123
Whiteville (G-12578)

Dunlop Aircraft Tyres Inc..............E 336 283-0979
Mocksville (G-8359)

Piedmont Truck Tires Inc..............F 828 277-1549
Asheville (G-574)

Piedmont Truck Tires Inc..............F 336 223-9412
Graham (G-5281)

Piedmont Truck Tires Inc..............E 336 668-0091
Greensboro (G-5746)

RDh Tire and Retread Company......D 980 368-4576
Cleveland (G-3220)

Tire Sls Svc Inc Fytteville NC........E 910 485-1121
Fayetteville (G-4682)

AUTOMOTIVE REPAIR SHOPS: Sound System Svc & Installation

Sonaron LLC...............................G 808 232-6168
Fayetteville (G-4672)

AUTOMOTIVE REPAIR SHOPS: Tire Recapping

Accel Discount Tire......................G 704 636-0323
Salisbury (G-11012)

Aiken-Black Tire Service Inc..........E 828 322-3736
Hickory (G-6261)

Avery County Recapping Co Inc......G 828 733-0161
Newland (G-9424)

Bill Martin Inc.............................G 704 873-0241
Statesville (G-11671)

Bray S Recapping Service Inc........E 336 786-6182
Mount Airy (G-9105)

Cecil Budd Tire Company LLC........F 919 742-2322
Siler City (G-11403)

Claybrook Tire Inc.......................F 336 573-3135
Stoneville (G-11820)

Crossroads Tire Store Inc.............G 704 888-2064
Midland (G-8285)

Enfield Tire Service Inc................G 252 445-5016
Enfield (G-4482)

Foster Tire Sales Inc....................G 336 248-6726
Lexington (G-7688)

Greensboro Tire & Auto Service.....G 336 294-9495
Greensboro (G-5578)

Haneys Tire Recapping Svc LLC.....G 910 276-2636
Laurinburg (G-7503)

John Conrad Inc..........................G 336 475-8144
Thomasville (G-12041)

M & R Retreading & Oil Co Inc.......G 704 474-4101
Norwood (G-9556)

Merchants Inc.............................G 252 447-2121
Havelock (G-6123)

Mr Tire Inc.................................G 828 262-3555
Boone (G-936)

Mr Tire Inc.................................F 704 483-1500
Denver (G-3794)

Mr Tire Inc.................................F 828 322-8130
Hickory (G-6398)

Mr Tire Inc.................................G 704 739-6456
Kings Mountain (G-7373)

Mr Tire Inc.................................G 828 758-0047
Lenoir (G-7627)

Mr Tire Inc.................................G 704 735-8024
Lincolnton (G-7846)

Mr Tire Inc.................................G 704 484-0816
Shelby (G-11365)

Mr Tire Inc.................................G 704 872-4127
Statesville (G-11737)

Oakie S Tire & Recapping Inc........G 704 482-5629
Shelby (G-11367)

Parrish Tire Company...................E 704 872-6565
Jonesville (G-7198)

Parrish Tire Company...................D 800 849-8473
Winston Salem (G-13276)

Perry Brothers Tire Svc Inc...........F 919 693-2128
Oxford (G-9623)

Perry Brothers Tire Svc Inc...........E 919 775-7225
Sanford (G-11218)

Phil S Tire Service Inc..................G 828 682-2421
Burnsville (G-1189)

Richmond Investment....................E 910 410-8200
Rockingham (G-10787)

Small Brothers Tire Co Inc............G 704 289-3531
Monroe (G-8559)

Snider Tire Inc............................D 704 373-2910
Charlotte (G-2820)

Snider Tire Inc............................F 336 691-5480
Greensboro (G-5820)

Snider Tire Inc............................G 828 324-9955
Hickory (G-6450)

Super Retread Center Inc..............F 919 734-0073
Goldsboro (G-5248)

Tires Incorporated of Clinton.........F 910 592-4741
Clinton (G-3249)

Towel City Tire & Wheel LLC..........G 704 933-2143
Kannapolis (G-7222)

White S Tire Svc Wilson Inc...........G 252 237-0770
Wilson (G-13046)

White S Tire Svc Wilson Inc...........D 252 237-5426
Wilson (G-13047)

Whites Tire Svc New Bern Inc........G 252 633-1170
New Bern (G-9407)

AUTOMOTIVE REPAIR SHOPS: Tire Repair Shop

A 1 Tire Service Inc.....................G 828 684-1860
Fletcher (G-4716)

Autosmart Inc.............................G 919 210-7936
Apex (G-142)

Burnett Darrill Stephen.................G 828 287-8778
Spindale (G-11545)

Ed S Tire Laurinburg Inc...............G 910 277-0565
Laurinburg (G-7498)

Go Ev and Go Green Corp.............G 704 327-9040
Charlotte (G-2220)

Hall Tire and Battery Co Inc...........F 336 275-3812
Greensboro (G-5586)

Hardison Tire Co Inc....................F 252 745-4561
Bayboro (G-711)

Johnnys Tire Sales and Svc Inc......F 252 353-8473
Greenville (G-5997)

Lewis Brothers Tire & Algnmt.........G 919 359-9050
Clayton (G-3157)

Mock Tire & Automotive Inc...........E 336 753-8473
Mocksville (G-8379)

Mock Tire & Automotive Inc...........E 336 774-0081
Winston Salem (G-13256)

Mock Tire & Automotive Inc...........E 336 768-1010
Winston Salem (G-13257)

PRODUCT

Pumpkin Pacific LLC.............................. G 704 226-4176
Charlotte *(G-2677)*

Quality Investments Inc.......................... E 252 492-8777
Henderson *(G-6172)*

Safe Tire & Autos LLC........................... G 910 590-3101
Clinton *(G-3244)*

Stoltz Automotive Inc............................. G 336 595-4218
Walkertown *(G-12317)*

Tbc Retail Group Inc.............................. G 336 540-8066
Greensboro *(G-5854)*

Toe River Service Station LLC................ G 828 688-6385
Bakersville *(G-681)*

Treadz LLC.. G 704 664-0995
Mooresville *(G-8787)*

Vestal Buick Gmc Inc............................ D 336 310-0261
Kernersville *(G-7312)*

Village Tire Center Inc........................... G 919 862-8500
Raleigh *(G-10588)*

Wilson Tire and Automotive Inc.............. G 336 584-9638
Elon College *(G-4476)*

Woodlawn Tire and Algnmt Inc............... G 828 756-4212
Marion *(G-8075)*

AUTOMOTIVE REPAIR SHOPS: Trailer Repair

Colfax Trailer & Repair LLC.................... G 336 993-8511
Colfax *(G-3275)*

Spring Repair Service Inc....................... G 336 299-5660
Greensboro *(G-5832)*

AUTOMOTIVE REPAIR SHOPS: Wheel Alignment

Claybrook Tire Inc.................................. F 336 573-3135
Stoneville *(G-11820)*

Hall Tire and Battery Co Inc.................... F 336 275-3812
Greensboro *(G-5586)*

Whitaker S Tire Service Inc..................... G 704 786-6174
Concord *(G-3468)*

AUTOMOTIVE REPAIR SVC

Avery County Recapping Co Inc.............. G 828 733-0161
Newland *(G-9424)*

B S R-Hess Race Cars Inc..................... E 704 547-0901
Charlotte *(G-1730)*

Barnharts Tech Tire Repair Inc............... G 336 337-1569
Lexington *(G-7658)*

Beamer Tire & Auto Repair Inc............... F 336 882-7043
High Point *(G-6541)*

Carolina.. G 919 851-0906
Cary *(G-1321)*

Carolina Precision Mfg LLC.................... E 704 662-3480
Mooresville *(G-8632)*

Discount Tires & Auto Repair................. G 336 788-0057
Winston Salem *(G-13147)*

Nichols Spdmtr & Instr Co Inc................ G 336 273-2881
Greensboro *(G-5709)*

One Source SEC & Sound Inc................ G 281 850-9487
Mooresville *(G-8739)*

Prevost Car (us) Inc.............................. E 908 222-7211
Greensboro *(G-5763)*

Pumpkin Pacific LLC.............................. G 704 226-4176
Charlotte *(G-2677)*

R and R Auto Repr & Tires Inc............... G 336 784-6893
Winston Salem *(G-13310)*

Rabuns Trlr Repr Tire Svc Inc................ G 704 764-7841
Monroe *(G-8547)*

Scattered Wrenches Inc......................... G 919 480-1605
Raleigh *(G-10460)*

Treadz LLC.. G 704 664-0995
Mooresville *(G-8787)*

AUTOMOTIVE SPLYS & PARTS, NEW, WHOLESALE: Hardware

Mfi Products Inc..................................... F 910 944-2128
Aberdeen *(G-16)*

AUTOMOTIVE SPLYS & PARTS, NEW, WHOLESALE: Testing Eqpt, Eng

RNS International Inc.............................. E 704 329-0444
Charlotte *(G-2728)*

AUTOMOTIVE SPLYS & PARTS, NEW, WHOLESALE: Trailer Parts

A-1 Hitch & Trailors Sales Inc................. G 910 755-6025
Supply *(G-11854)*

AUTOMOTIVE SPLYS & PARTS, NEW, WHOLESALE: Wheels

Wheel Pros LLC..................................... G 336 851-6705
Greensboro *(G-5917)*

AUTOMOTIVE SPLYS & PARTS, WHOLESALE, NEC

Auto Machine Shop Inc.......................... G 910 483-6016
Fayetteville *(G-4554)*

Heintz Bros Automotives Inc................... G 704 872-8081
Statesville *(G-11706)*

Johnson Machine Co Inc......................... G 252 638-2620
New Bern *(G-9374)*

Lake Shore Radiator Inc......................... F 336 271-2626
Greensboro *(G-5657)*

Mann+hmmel Fltrtion Tech Group.......... G 704 869-3300
Gastonia *(G-5082)*

Mc Cullough Auto Elc & Assoc............... G 704 376-5388
Charlotte *(G-2475)*

Merchant 1 Marketing LLC..................... G 888 853-9992
Greensboro *(G-5691)*

Pfaff Molds Ltd Partnership.................... F 704 423-9484
Charlotte *(G-2631)*

Pgw Auto Glass LLC.............................. B 336 258-4950
Elkin *(G-4451)*

Pro-Motor Engines Inc........................... G 704 664-6800
Mooresville *(G-8755)*

Robert Blake... G 704 720-9341
Concord *(G-3433)*

AUTOMOTIVE SVCS, EXC REPAIR & CARWASHES: Insp & Diagnostic

Kaotic Parts LLC.................................... G 919 766-6040
Raleigh *(G-10229)*

AUTOMOTIVE SVCS, EXC REPAIR & CARWASHES: Lubrication

Newfound Tire & Quick Lube Inc............. G 828 683-3232
Leicester *(G-7528)*

AUTOMOTIVE SVCS, EXC RPR/ CARWASHES: High Perf Auto Rpr/Svc

Capital Value Center Sls & Svc............... G 910 799-4060
Wilmington *(G-12730)*

Pro-Motor Engines Inc........................... G 704 664-6800
Mooresville *(G-8755)*

Richard Chldress Racg Entps In.............. E 336 731-3334
Welcome *(G-12513)*

Richard Chldress Racg Entps In.............. B 336 731-3334
Welcome *(G-12514)*

AUTOMOTIVE TRANSMISSION REPAIR SVC

Bridgestone Ret Operations LLC............. G 336 282-4695
Greensboro *(G-5401)*

Parrish Tire Company............................. E 336 334-9979
Greensboro *(G-5735)*

AUTOMOTIVE WELDING SVCS

Donald Auton... G 704 872-7528
Statesville *(G-11690)*

Richards Welding and Repr Inc............... G 828 396-8705
Granite Falls *(G-5320)*

Technique Chassis LLC.......................... E 517 819-3579
Concord *(G-3454)*

United Services Group LLC..................... G 980 237-1335
Charlotte *(G-2962)*

AUTOMOTIVE: Bodies

Csi Armoring Inc.................................... G 336 313-8561
Lexington *(G-7672)*

AUTOMOTIVE: Seat Frames, Metal

Jeffrey Sheffer...................................... G 919 861-9126
Raleigh *(G-10214)*

AUTOMOTIVE: Seating

Clarios LLC.. E 866 589-8883
Charlotte *(G-1926)*

Clarios LLC.. E 336 884-5832
High Point *(G-6569)*

Clarios LLC.. C 336 761-1550
Kernersville *(G-7257)*

Clarios LLC.. E 252 754-0782
Winterville *(G-13415)*

Indiana Mills & Manufacturing................ C 336 862-7519
High Point *(G-6669)*

Johnson Controls Inc............................. F 828 225-3200
Asheville *(G-528)*

Johnson Controls Inc............................. F 919 905-5745
Durham *(G-4089)*

Johnson Controls Inc............................. D 919 743-3500
Raleigh *(G-10219)*

Johnson Controls Inc............................. E 910 392-2372
Wilmington *(G-12823)*

Johnson Controls Inc............................. E 704 521-8889
Charlotte *(G-2376)*

Joie of Seating Inc................................. G 704 795-7474
Concord *(G-3387)*

AWNINGS & CANOPIES

Hamlin Sheet Metal Company Inc........... D 919 894-2224
Benson *(G-791)*

Raleigh Mechanical & Mtls Inc............... F 919 598-4601
Raleigh *(G-10425)*

AWNINGS & CANOPIES: Awnings, Fabric, From Purchased Matls

Accent Awnings Inc................................ F 828 321-4517
Andrews *(G-104)*

Alpha Canvas and Awning Co Inc........... F 704 333-1581
Charlotte *(G-1650)*

Clark Art Shop Inc.................................. G 919 832-8319
Raleigh *(G-9997)*

Coastal Awnings Inc.............................. F 252 222-0707
Morehead City *(G-8826)*

Coastal Canvas Mfg Inc......................... G 252 728-4946
Beaufort *(G-723)*

Colored Metal Products Inc.................... F 704 482-1407
Shelby *(G-11322)*

CSC Awnings Inc................................... G 336 744-5006
Winston Salem *(G-13135)*

Custom Canvas Works Inc..................... G 919 662-4800
Garner *(G-4928)*

Rocky Mount Awning & Tent Co............ G 252 442-0184
Rocky Mount *(G-10866)*

Trivantage LLC.................................... D 800 786-1876
Burlington *(G-1171)*

AWNINGS & CANOPIES: Canopies, Fabric, From Purchased Matls

Custom Golf Car Supply Inc................. C 704 855-1130
Salisbury *(G-11042)*

AWNINGS: Fiberglass

Identigraph Signs & Awnings............... G 704 635-7911
Monroe *(G-8502)*

AWNINGS: Metal

Champion Win Co of Charlotte........... G 704 398-0085
Charlotte *(G-1891)*

Colored Metal Products Inc.................. F 704 482-1407
Shelby *(G-11322)*

Midway Blind & Awning Co Inc............. G 336 226-4532
Burlington *(G-1129)*

AXLES

Meritor Inc... F 828 687-2000
Fletcher *(G-4754)*

Meritor Inc... C 828 687-2000
Fletcher *(G-4755)*

Meritor Inc... C 828 247-0440
Forest City *(G-4794)*

AXLES: Rolled Or Forged, Made In Steel Mills

Meritor Inc... C 828 433-4600
Morganton *(G-8881)*

BACKHOES

Holder Backhoe & Hauling Inc............. G 336 622-7388
Liberty *(G-7767)*

Ronny D Phelps.................................... G 828 206-6339
Hot Springs *(G-6934)*

Southern Trucking & Backhoe............. G 919 548-9723
Siler City *(G-11426)*

Strickland Backhoe.............................. G 910 893-5274
Bunnlevel *(G-1017)*

BAGS & BAGGING: Knit

Adele Knits Inc.................................... C 336 499-6010
Winston Salem *(G-13072)*

Coville Inc.. F 336 759-0115
Winston Salem *(G-13133)*

Griffin Tubing Company Inc................. G 336 449-4822
Gibsonville *(G-5176)*

BAGS & CONTAINERS: Textile, Exc Sleeping

Hdb Inc.. G 800 403-2247
Greensboro *(G-5590)*

BAGS & SACKS: Shipping & Shopping

Tsg2 Inc... G 704 347-4484
Charlotte *(G-2949)*

BAGS: Canvas

J Stahl Sales & Sourcing Inc................ E 828 645-3005
Weaverville *(G-12493)*

BAGS: Duffle, Canvas, Made From Purchased Materials

Cross Canvas Company Inc.................. E 828 252-0440
Asheville *(G-480)*

BAGS: Food Storage & Frozen Food, Plastic

Bioselect Inc....................................... G 704 521-8585
Charlotte *(G-1784)*

BAGS: Food Storage & Trash, Plastic

Reynolds Consumer Products Inc........ A 704 371-5550
Huntersville *(G-7042)*

BAGS: Paper

Inplac North America Inc..................... G 704 587-1151
Charlotte *(G-2338)*

Westrock Rkt LLC................................ C 828 464-5560
Conover *(G-3574)*

BAGS: Paper, Made From Purchased Materials

Cardinal Bag & Envelope Co Inc........... E 704 225-9636
Monroe *(G-8450)*

Duro Hilex Poly LLC............................ D 800 845-6051
Charlotte *(G-2069)*

Hilex Poly Co LLC................................ D
Charlotte *(G-2280)*

BAGS: Plastic

Berry Global Films LLC....................... C 704 821-2316
Matthews *(G-8160)*

Bulk Sak International Inc.................... E 704 833-1361
Gastonia *(G-5006)*

Classic Packaging Company................ D 336 922-4224
Pfafftown *(G-9663)*

Cryovac Leasing Corporation.............. G 980 430-7000
Charlotte *(G-2001)*

Dayton Bag & Burlap Co...................... G 704 873-7271
Statesville *(G-11685)*

Hood Packaging Corporation............... C 910 582-1842
Hamlet *(G-6057)*

Printpack Inc.. C 828 693-1723
Hendersonville *(G-6237)*

Rgees LLC.. G 828 708-7178
Arden *(G-304)*

Rubbermaid Commercial Pdts LLC....... A 540 667-8700
Huntersville *(G-7045)*

Sealed Air Corporation........................ D 828 728-6610
Hudson *(G-6959)*

Transcontinental Tvl LLC..................... F 336 476-3131
Thomasville *(G-12082)*

Wastezero Inc...................................... E 919 322-1208
Raleigh *(G-10599)*

BAGS: Plastic & Pliofilm

Sealed Air Corporation (us).................. A 201 791-7600
Charlotte *(G-2777)*

Sealed Air LLC..................................... F 980 430-7000
Charlotte *(G-2779)*

BAGS: Plastic, Made From Purchased Materials

Hilex Poly Co LLC................................ D
Charlotte *(G-2280)*

Imaflex Usa Inc.................................... E 336 885-8131
Thomasville *(G-12036)*

Liqui-Box Corporation.......................... D 804 325-1400
Charlotte *(G-2426)*

Novolex Heritage Bag LLC................... C 800 845-6051
Charlotte *(G-2582)*

Poly Plastic Products NC Inc................ D 704 624-2555
Marshville *(G-8093)*

BAGS: Shipping

Automated Solutions LLC..................... F 828 396-9900
Granite Falls *(G-5296)*

Hood Packaging Corporation............... C 910 582-1842
Hamlet *(G-6057)*

Pro Choice Contractors Corp............... G 919 696-7383
Raleigh *(G-10398)*

BAGS: Shopping, Made From Purchased Materials

Downtown Graphics Network Inc.......... G 704 637-0855
Salisbury *(G-11044)*

BAKERIES, COMMERCIAL: On Premises Baking Only

Accidental Baker.................................. G 919 732-6777
Hillsborough *(G-6857)*

Apple Baking Company Inc................... E 704 637-6800
Salisbury *(G-11017)*

Bimbo Bakeries Usa Inc....................... A 252 641-2200
Tarboro *(G-11923)*

Bluebird Cupcakes............................... G 919 616-7347
Raleigh *(G-9950)*

Burney Sweets & More Inc.................. G 910 862-2099
Elizabethtown *(G-4419)*

Buttercreme Bakery Inc....................... G 336 722-1022
Winston Salem *(G-13113)*

Evelyn T Burney................................... G 336 473-9794
Rocky Mount *(G-10838)*

Event Extravaganza LLC...................... F 252 679-7004
Elizabeth City *(G-4388)*

Flowers Baking Co Newton LLC........... G 336 903-1345
Wilkesboro *(G-12636)*

Flowers Bkg Co Jamestown LLC.......... G 704 305-0766
Concord *(G-3365)*

Flowers Bkg Co Jamestown LLC.......... E 704 305-0766
Eden *(G-4346)*

Flowers Bkg Co Jamestown LLC.......... G 252 492-1519
Henderson *(G-6156)*

Flowers Bkg Co Jamestown LLC.......... G 704 296-1000
Monroe *(G-8489)*

Flowers Bkg Co Jamestown LLC.......... E 336 744-3525
Winston Salem *(G-13172)*

Franklin Baking Company LLC............. F 252 752-4600
Greenville *(G-5978)*

Franklin Baking Company LLC............. F 910 425-5090
Hope Mills *(G-6927)*

Franklin Baking Company LLC............. G 919 832-7942
Raleigh *(G-10118)*

Franklin Baking Company LLC............. G 252 946-3340
Washington *(G-12387)*

Fuquay-Varina Baking Co Inc............... G 919 557-2237
Fuquay Varina *(G-4882)*

Harris Teeter LLC................................ D 704 846-7117
Matthews *(G-8115)*

Harris Teeter LLC................................ D 919 859-0110
Raleigh *(G-10156)*

Ingles Markets Incorporated............... D 704 434-0096
Boiling Springs *(G-885)*

Jps Cupcakery LLC.............................. F 919 894-5000
Benson *(G-793)*

La Estrella Inc...................................... G 919 639-6559
Angier *(G-124)*

La Farm Inc.. E 919 657-0657
Cary *(G-1385)*

Lc Foods LLC....................................... G 919 510-6688
Raleigh *(G-10250)*

Martins Fmous Pstry Shoppe Inc........ G 800 548-1200
Charlotte *(G-2465)*

Novas Bakery Inc................................. F 704 333-5566
Charlotte *(G-2579)*

Employee Codes: A=Over 500 employees, B=251-500
C=101-250, D=51-100, E=20-50, F=10-19, G=1-9   2025 Harris North Carolina
Manufacturers Directory   1059

PRODUCT

Old Salem Incorporated............................G 336 721-7305
  Winston Salem (G-13269)

Orange Bakery Inc.....................................E 704 875-3003
  Huntersville (G-7029)

Sls Baking Company...................................G 704 421-2763
  Charlotte (G-2815)

BAKERIES: On Premises Baking & Consumption

Bakeboxx Company.....................................F 336 861-1212
  High Point (G-6536)

Dewey S Bakery Inc...................................F 336 748-0230
  Winston Salem (G-13143)

Ingles Markets Incorporated................D 704 434-0096
  Boiling Springs (G-885)

Normandie Bakery Inc...............................G 910 686-1372
  Wilmington (G-12862)

Novas Bakery Inc.......................................F 704 333-5566
  Charlotte (G-2579)

Sprinkle of Sugar LLC...............................G 336 474-8620
  Thomasville (G-12073)

Yummi Factory Corporation.....................E 980 248-1062
  Concord (G-3472)

BAKERY MACHINERY

Baker Thermal Solutions LLC...............E 919 674-3750
  Clayton (G-3133)

M G Newell Corporation............................D 336 393-0100
  Greensboro (G-5668)

Stanza Machinery Inc...............................E 704 599-0623
  Charlotte (G-2859)

BAKERY PRDTS, FROZEN: Wholesalers

Evelyn T Burney...G 336 473-9794
  Rocky Mount (G-10838)

BAKERY PRDTS: Bagels, Fresh Or Frozen

Dewey S Bakery Inc...................................F 336 748-0230
  Winston Salem (G-13143)

BAKERY PRDTS: Biscuits, Dry

Imperial Falcon Group Inc......................G 646 717-1128
  Charlotte (G-2315)

BAKERY PRDTS: Bread, All Types, Fresh Or Frozen

Bakkavor Foods Usa Inc..........................C 704 522-1977
  Charlotte (G-1745)

Flowers Bkg Co Jamestown LLC............E 919 776-8932
  Sanford (G-11178)

Flowers Bkg Co Jamestown LLC............D 336 841-8840
  Jamestown (G-7161)

Franklin Baking Company LLC.................F 252 752-4600
  Greenville (G-5979)

Franklin Baking Company LLC.................F 252 410-0255
  Roanoke Rapids (G-10737)

Franklin Baking Company LLC.................B 919 735-0344
  Goldsboro (G-5214)

BAKERY PRDTS: Cakes, Bakery, Exc Frozen

A Taste of Heavenly Sweetness.............G 336 825-7321
  Greensboro (G-5333)

Cupcake Stop Shop LLC...........................G 919 457-7900
  Raleigh (G-10026)

Flowers Bakery of Winston-Salem LLC. C 336 785-8700
  Winston Salem (G-13171)

Heavenly Cheesecakes.............................G 336 577-9390
  Winston Salem (G-13195)

Premier Cakes LLC....................................G 919 274-8511
  Raleigh (G-10392)

Scotts & Associates Inc............................F 336 581-3141
  Bear Creek (G-718)

Sweet Room LLC..G 336 567-1620
  High Point (G-6799)

BAKERY PRDTS: Cakes, Bakery, Frozen

Crumble Cups LLC......................................G 919 520-7414
  Raleigh (G-10023)

Hais Kookies & More...................................G 980 819-8256
  Charlotte (G-2251)

BAKERY PRDTS: Cookies

Gracie Goodness Inc.................................G 910 792-0800
  Wilmington (G-12794)

Kalo Foods LLC...G 336 949-4802
  Stokesdale (G-11812)

Keebler Company..C 919 774-6431
  Sanford (G-11199)

S-L Snacks National LLC...........................E 704 554-1421
  Charlotte (G-2747)

Scotts & Associates Inc............................F 336 581-3141
  Bear Creek (G-718)

Snyders-Lance Inc......................................G 704 557-8013
  Charlotte (G-2821)

Yummi Factory Corporation.....................E 980 248-1062
  Concord (G-3472)

BAKERY PRDTS: Cookies & crackers

B&G Foods Inc..E 336 849-7000
  Yadkinville (G-13437)

Burney Sweets & More Inc.......................G 910 862-2099
  Elizabethtown (G-4419)

Dewey S Bakery Inc...................................F 336 748-0230
  Winston Salem (G-13143)

Flowers Bakery of Winston-Salem LLC. C 336 785-8700
  Winston Salem (G-13171)

Grandmas Sugar Shack.............................G 336 760-8822
  Winston Salem (G-13182)

Old Salem Incorporated............................G 336 721-7305
  Winston Salem (G-13269)

S-L Snacks Pa LLC.....................................C 704 554-1421
  Charlotte (G-2748)

Steven-Robert Originals LLC....................C 910 521-0199
  Pembroke (G-9660)

BAKERY PRDTS: Doughnuts, Exc Frozen

Donut Shop..G 910 640-3317
  Whiteville (G-12580)

Krispy Kreme Doughnut Corp..................E 919 669-6151
  Gastonia (G-5074)

Krispy Kreme Doughnut Corp..................E 336 854-8275
  Greensboro (G-5655)

Krispy Kreme Doughnut Corp..................E 336 733-3780
  Winston Salem (G-13226)

Krispy Kreme Doughnut Corp..................C 980 270-7117
  Charlotte (G-2402)

Krispy Kreme Doughnuts Inc...................C 336 725-2981
  Winston Salem (G-13228)

BAKERY PRDTS: Dry

Divine South Baking Co LLC.....................G 828 421-2042
  Highlands (G-6845)

Evelyn T Burney...G 336 473-9794
  Rocky Mount (G-10838)

Lotus Bakeries Us LLC...............................G 415 956-8956
  Mebane (G-8250)

BAKERY PRDTS: Frozen

Bimbo Bakeries Usa Inc............................A 252 641-2200
  Tarboro (G-11923)

Kalo Foods LLC...G 336 949-4802
  Stokesdale (G-11812)

Orange Bakery Inc.....................................E 704 875-3003
  Huntersville (G-7029)

Stefano Foods Inc.......................................C 704 399-3935
  Charlotte (G-2865)

BAKERY PRDTS: Pastries, Exc Frozen

Carolina Foods LLC....................................B 704 333-9812
  Charlotte (G-1846)

BAKERY PRDTS: Pretzels

North Crolina Tortilla Mfg LLC...............D 270 861-5956
  Lincolnton (G-7848)

SE Co-Brand Ventures LLC........................G 704 598-9322
  Charlotte (G-2773)

BAKERY PRDTS: Rolls, Bread Type, Fresh Or Frozen

Martins Fmous Pstry Shoppe Inc...........G 800 548-1200
  Fayetteville (G-4635)

Martins Fmous Pstry Shoppe Inc...........G 800 548-1200
  Kernersville (G-7285)

BAKERY PRDTS: Wholesalers

Krispy Kreme Doughnuts Inc...................C 336 725-2981
  Winston Salem (G-13228)

Novas Bakery Inc.......................................F 704 333-5566
  Charlotte (G-2579)

BAKERY: Wholesale Or Wholesale & Retail Combined

All Baked Out Company.............................F 336 861-1212
  High Point (G-6516)

Bakemark USA LLC......................................D 336 848-9790
  Greensboro (G-5384)

Connectivity Group LLC.............................E 910 799-9023
  Wilmington (G-12746)

Depalo Foods Inc..E 704 827-0245
  Belmont (G-746)

Mon Macaron LLC.......................................G 984 200-1387
  Raleigh (G-10312)

Neomonde Baking Company......................E 919 469-8009
  Morrisville (G-9023)

Normandie Bakery Inc...............................G 910 686-1372
  Wilmington (G-12862)

Northeast Foods Inc..................................G 919 585-5178
  Clayton (G-3163)

Picassomoesllc...G 216 703-4547
  Hillsborough (G-6875)

Queen City Pastry Llc...............................E 704 660-5706
  Mooresville (G-8757)

Retail Market Place....................................G 984 201-1948
  Smithfield (G-11463)

Sprinkle of Sugar LLC...............................G 336 474-8620
  Thomasville (G-12073)

Suarez Bakery Inc......................................F 704 525-0145
  Charlotte (G-2876)

Tkm Global LLC...G 732 694-0311
  Raleigh (G-10550)

Underground Baking Co LLC.....................G 828 674-7494
  Hendersonville (G-6246)

BALERS

Airborn Industries Inc................................E 704 483-5000
  Lincolnton (G-7811)

Hog Slat Incorporated...............................F 800 949-4647
  Newton Grove (G-9515)

Jo-Mar Group LLC..E
  Belmont (G-755)

BALLOONS: Hot Air

Fire Fly Ballons 2006 LLC...................... G 704 878-9501
Statesville *(G-11698)*

Firefly Balloons 2010 Inc...................... G 704 878-9501
Statesville *(G-11699)*

BALLOONS: Novelty & Toy

A Stitch In Time....................................... G 828 274-5193
Asheville *(G-422)*

BALLOONS: Toy & Advertising, Rubber

Russo Mike DBA Lrger Than Lf l............ G 760 942-0289
Oriental *(G-9602)*

BANKS: Mortgage & Loan

GLG Corporation...................................... F 336 784-0396
Winston Salem *(G-13178)*

BANNERS: Fabric

Downtown Graphics Network Inc........... G 704 637-0855
Salisbury *(G-11044)*

BANQUET HALL FACILITIES

Communitys Kitchen L3c...................... G 828 817-2308
Tryon *(G-12173)*

BAR FIXTURES: Wood

Artisan Leaf LLC...................................... G 252 674-1223
Wilson *(G-12964)*

D & B Concepts Inc.................................. G 336 885-8292
High Point *(G-6585)*

Holt Group Inc... F 336 668-2770
High Point *(G-6659)*

Interlam Corporation.............................. E 336 786-6254
Mount Airy *(G-9134)*

BAR JOISTS & CONCRETE REINFORCING BARS: Fabricated

J F Fabricators LLC.................................. G 704 454-7224
Harrisburg *(G-6110)*

BARBECUE EQPT

Jebco Inc... E 919 557-2001
Holly Springs *(G-6904)*

BARGES BUILDING & REPAIR

Edenton Boatworks LLC.......................... E 252 482-7600
Edenton *(G-4366)*

BARRICADES: Metal

Barrier1 Systems Inc............................... F 336 617-8478
Greensboro *(G-5386)*

BARS & BAR SHAPES: Steel, Cold-Finished, Own Hot-Rolled

Muriel Harris Investments Inc................. F 800 932-3191
Fayetteville *(G-4644)*

BARS: Concrete Reinforcing, Fabricated Steel

Composite Factory LLC............................ F 484 264-3306
Mooresville *(G-8642)*

Freedom Industries Inc.......................... C 252 984-0007
Rocky Mount *(G-10839)*

Gastonia Ornamental Wldg Inc............... F 704 827-1146
Mount Holly *(G-9232)*

Gulfstream Steel & Supply Inc............... E 910 329-5100
Holly Ridge *(G-6888)*

Ifab Corp.. F 704 864-3032
Gastonia *(G-5061)*

Kontek Industries Inc.............................. F 704 273-5040
Kannapolis *(G-7214)*

Low Country Steel SC LLC...................... E 336 283-9611
Winston Salem *(G-13239)*

Lowder Steel Inc...................................... E 336 431-9000
Archdale *(G-238)*

Mechanical Spc Contrs Inc...................... D 919 829-9300
Raleigh *(G-10287)*

Underbrinks LLC...................................... G 866 495-4465
Salisbury *(G-11131)*

Universal Steel NC LLC............................ E 336 476-3105
Thomasville *(G-12085)*

BASALT: Crushed & Broken

Mafic USA LLC.. F 704 967-8006
Shelby *(G-11358)*

BASEBOARDS: Metal

Amarr Company.. G 336 936-0010
Mocksville *(G-8347)*

Building Envlope Erction Svcs................. F 252 747-2015
Snow Hill *(G-11476)*

Kindred Rolling Doors LLC...................... G 704 905-3806
Gastonia *(G-5073)*

BASEMENT WINDOW AREAWAYS: Concrete

David Allen Company Inc........................ C 919 821-7100
Raleigh *(G-10039)*

BASES, BEVERAGE

Prime Beverage Group LLC..................... C 704 385-5451
Concord *(G-3423)*

Prime Beverage Group LLC..................... D 704 385-5450
Huntersville *(G-7038)*

BASKETS: Steel Wire

Rack Works Inc.. E 336 368-1302
Pilot Mountain *(G-9673)*

BATH SALTS

Burts Bees Inc... B 919 998-5200
Durham *(G-3954)*

BATHROOM ACCESS & FITTINGS: Vitreous China & Earthenware

Custom Marble Corporation.................... G 910 215-0679
Pinehurst *(G-9690)*

Division Eight Inc.................................... F 336 852-1275
Greensboro *(G-5497)*

Tileware Global LLC................................. G 828 322-9273
Hickory *(G-6469)*

Welcome Industrial Corp......................... D 336 329-9640
Burlington *(G-1178)*

BATTERIES, EXC AUTOMOTIVE: Wholesalers

Exide Technologies LLC........................... G 919 553-3578
Clayton *(G-3147)*

L L C Batteries of N C.............................. G 919 331-0241
Angier *(G-123)*

BATTERIES: Alkaline, Cell Storage

Spectrum Brands Inc.............................. G 704 658-2060
Mooresville *(G-8773)*

BATTERIES: Lead Acid, Storage

Polypore International LP........................ D 704 587-8409
Charlotte *(G-2645)*

BATTERIES: Rechargeable

Saft America Inc...................................... B 828 874-4111
Valdese *(G-12200)*

BATTERIES: Storage

Associated Battery Company.................. G 704 821-8311
Matthews *(G-8158)*

Clarios LLC.. C 336 761-1550
Kernersville *(G-7257)*

East Penn Manufacturing Co.................. F 336 771-1380
Winston Salem *(G-13152)*

Energizer Holdings Inc........................... C 336 672-3526
Asheboro *(G-352)*

Exide.. G 704 357-9845
Charlotte *(G-2134)*

Infinite Blue Inc...................................... G 919 744-7704
Raleigh *(G-10194)*

Lexington Road Properties Inc............... C 336 650-7209
Winston Salem *(G-13234)*

Magnevolt Inc.. F 919 553-2202
Clayton *(G-3159)*

Smith Utility Buildings............................ G 336 957-8211
Traphill *(G-12106)*

Toyota Battery Mfg Inc........................... E 469 292-6094
Liberty *(G-7782)*

BATTERIES: Wet

Clarios LLC.. C 336 761-1550
Kernersville *(G-7257)*

Edgewell Per Care Brands LLC............... G 336 672-4500
Asheboro *(G-349)*

L L C Batteries of N C.............................. G 919 331-0241
Angier *(G-123)*

Lexington Road Properties Inc............... C 336 650-7209
Winston Salem *(G-13234)*

Saft America Inc...................................... B 828 874-4111
Valdese *(G-12200)*

Spectrum Brands Inc.............................. G 800 854-3151
Charlotte *(G-2842)*

BATTERY CASES: Plastic Or Plastics Combination

Fourshare LLC... F 336 714-0448
Clemmons *(G-3184)*

BATTERY CHARGERS

Exide Technologies LLC........................... G 704 521-8016
Charlotte *(G-2135)*

Exide Technologies LLC........................... G 919 553-3578
Clayton *(G-3147)*

Polypore Inc.. D 704 587-8409
Charlotte *(G-2644)*

BATTS & BATTING: Cotton

Kem-Wove Inc.. E 704 588-0080
Charlotte *(G-2392)*

BEARINGS & PARTS Ball

Baldor Dodge Reliance............................ E 828 652-0074
Marion *(G-8033)*

Ketchie-Houston Inc................................ E 704 786-5101
Concord *(G-3390)*

Linamar Forgings Carolina Inc............... D 252 237-8181
Wilson *(G-13003)*

Nn Inc.. G 980 264-4300
Charlotte *(G-2569)*

Reich LLC... C 828 651-9019
Arden *(G-303)*

BEARINGS: Ball & Roller

Atlantic Bearing Co Inc........................... G 252 243-0233
Wilson *(G-12965)*

Coc USA Inc.. G 888 706-0059
Matthews *(G-8107)*

Everything Industrial Supply................. G 743 333-2222
Winston Salem *(G-13162)*

Hpc NC... G 704 978-0103
Statesville *(G-11713)*

Justice Bearing LLC................................ G 800 355-2500
Mooresville *(G-8701)*

Ltlb Holding Company.............................. D 704 585-2908
Hiddenite *(G-6502)*

Ltlb Holding Company.............................. F 828 624-1460
Hickory *(G-6389)*

Timken Company..................................... C 704 736-2700
Iron Station *(G-7108)*

BEARINGS: Plastic

Enpro Inc.. C 704 731-1500
Charlotte *(G-2115)*

BEARINGS: Roller & Parts

American Roller Bearing Inc.................... C 828 624-1460
Hiddenite *(G-6493)*

American Roller Bearing Inc.................... F 828 624-1460
Morganton *(G-8850)*

Urethane Innovators Inc........................... E 252 637-7110
New Bern *(G-9403)*

BEAUTY & BARBER SHOP EQPT

American Eagle Mfg LLC.......................... G 252 633-0603
New Bern *(G-9331)*

Boyd Manufacturing Inc........................... F 336 301-6433
Siler City *(G-11400)*

Brandy Thompson.................................... F 321 252-2911
Fayetteville *(G-4561)*

Buddy Cut Inc.. G 888 608-4701
Pittsboro *(G-9777)*

Carolina Windows and Doors Inc........... F 252 756-2585
Greenville *(G-5951)*

Corsan LLC.. F 704 765-9979
Huntersville *(G-6979)*

Cosmopros... G 704 717-7420
Charlotte *(G-1990)*

Equagen Engineers Pllc........................... E 919 444-5442
Raleigh *(G-10090)*

Hanes Industries-Newton........................ G 828 469-2000
Newton *(G-9471)*

Mammoth Machine and Design LLC....... G 704 727-3330
Mooresville *(G-8718)*

Natrx Inc.. E 919 263-0667
Raleigh *(G-10325)*

Nederman Manufacturing......................... G 704 898-7945
Charlotte *(G-2552)*

Pmb Industries Inc.................................. G 336 453-3121
Lexington *(G-7733)*

Prezioso Ventures LLC............................ G 704 793-1602
Concord *(G-3422)*

Salon & Spa Design Services................. G 919 556-6380
Wake Forest *(G-12296)*

Skidril Industries LLC.............................. G 800 843-3745
Randleman *(G-10660)*

Sutton Scientifics Inc............................. G 910 428-1600
Star *(G-11634)*

Tribofilm Research Inc........................... G 919 838-2844
Raleigh *(G-10563)*

BEAUTY & BARBER SHOP EQPT & SPLYS WHOLESALERS

Cosmopros... G 704 717-7420
Charlotte *(G-1990)*

UGLy Essentials LLC............................... F 910 319-9945
Raleigh *(G-10572)*

BEAUTY SALONS

Gifted Hands Styling Salon..................... G 828 781-2781
Hickory *(G-6338)*

BEDDING, BEDSPREADS, BLANKETS & SHEETS

Js Royal Home Usa Inc.......................... E 704 542-2304
Charlotte *(G-2382)*

R & D Weaving Inc.................................. F 828 248-1910
Ellenboro *(G-4460)*

BEDDING, FROM SILK OR MANMADE FIBER

Sunrise Development LLC........................ F 828 453-0590
Mooresboro *(G-8586)*

BEDS & ACCESS STORES

Perfect Fit Industries LLC....................... C 800 864-7618
Charlotte *(G-2627)*

BEDS: Institutional

Kci LLC.. E 843 675-2626
Harrisburg *(G-6111)*

BEDSPREADS & BED SETS, FROM PURCHASED MATERIALS

Diane Britt.. G 910 763-9600
Wilmington *(G-12764)*

Pacific Coast Feather LLC....................... G 252 492-0051
Henderson *(G-6169)*

Smith Draperies Inc................................ F 336 226-2183
Burlington *(G-1158)*

BEDSPREADS, COTTON

Lillys Interiors Cstm Quilting.................. G 336 475-1421
Thomasville *(G-12044)*

BEER & ALE WHOLESALERS

Glass Jug... F 919 818-6907
Durham *(G-4048)*

Glass Jug LLC.. F 919 813-0135
Durham *(G-4049)*

Koi Pond Brewing Company LLC........... G 252 231-1660
Rocky Mount *(G-10847)*

Salty Turtle Beer Company..................... E 910 803-2019
Surf City *(G-11863)*

White Street Brewing Co Inc.................. F 919 647-9439
Youngsville *(G-13498)*

BEER, WINE & LIQUOR STORES: Beer, Packaged

Aviator Brewing Company Inc................ G 919 601-5497
Holly Springs *(G-6893)*

Koi Pond Brewing Company LLC........... G 252 231-1660
Rocky Mount *(G-10847)*

BELLOWS

Nabell USA Corporation........................... E 704 986-2455
Albemarle *(G-82)*

BELTING: Rubber

Beltservice Corporation........................... E 704 947-2264
Huntersville *(G-6973)*

Forbo Belting.. E 704 948-0800
Huntersville *(G-6992)*

Forbo Siegling LLC................................. F 704 948-0800
Huntersville *(G-6994)*

Forbo Siegling LLC................................. B 704 948-0800
Huntersville *(G-6995)*

BELTS & BELT PRDTS

All-State Industries Inc........................... G 704 588-4081
Charlotte *(G-1642)*

R/W Connection Inc................................. G 252 446-0114
Rocky Mount *(G-10864)*

BELTS: Conveyor, Made From Purchased Wire

Automated Solutions LLC........................ F 828 396-9900
Granite Falls *(G-5296)*

Belt Concepts America Inc...................... F 888 598-2358
Spring Hope *(G-11553)*

Belt Shop Inc.. F 704 865-3636
Gastonia *(G-4997)*

Everything Industrial Supply................... G 743 333-2222
Winston Salem *(G-13162)*

Forbo Movement Systems....................... E 704 334-5353
Charlotte *(G-2171)*

BELTS: Seat, Automotive & Aircraft

Aircraft Belts Inc.................................... E 919 956-4395
Creedmoor *(G-3635)*

BEVERAGE BASES & SYRUPS

Freedom Beverage Company.................. G 336 316-1260
Greensboro *(G-5540)*

Herbalife Manufacturing LLC.................. G 336 970-6400
Winston Salem *(G-13196)*

BEVERAGE PRDTS: Malt, Barley

Whitehat Seed Farms Inc........................ G 252 264-2427
Hertford *(G-6257)*

BEVERAGES, ALCOHOLIC: Ale

Creative Brewing Company LLC............. G 919 297-8182
Smithfield *(G-11441)*

Duck-Rabbit Craft Brewery Inc............... G 252 753-7745
Farmville *(G-4527)*

Foothills Brewing................................... G 336 997-9484
Winston Salem *(G-13173)*

Fresh Point LLC...................................... G 919 895-0790
Holly Springs *(G-6902)*

Goose and Monkey Brewhouse LLC...... F 336 239-0206
Lexington *(G-7693)*

Heist Brewing Company LLC.................. G 603 969-8012
Charlotte *(G-2270)*

Highland Brewing Company Inc............. F 828 299-3370
Asheville *(G-517)*

Innovation Brewing LLC.......................... G 828 586-9678
Sylva *(G-11893)*

White Street Brewing Co Inc.................. F 919 647-9439
Youngsville *(G-13498)*

BEVERAGES, ALCOHOLIC: Applejack

Bold Rock Partners LP............................. F 828 595-9940
Mills River *(G-8312)*

Warehouse Distillery LLC........................ G 828 464-5183
Newton *(G-9510)*

BEVERAGES, ALCOHOLIC: Beer

Anheuser-Busch LLC............................... F 704 321-9319
Charlotte *(G-1677)*

Aviator Brewing Company Inc................ G 919 601-5497
Holly Springs *(G-6893)*

Between Two Worlds LLC........................ G 828 774-5055
Asheville *(G-453)*

Beverage Innovation Corp...................... F 425 222-4900
Concord *(G-3320)*

Bombshell Beer Company LLC............... F 919 823-1933
Holly Springs *(G-6895)*

Bull Durham Beer Co LLC .... G 919 744-3568
  Durham (G-3951)

Cabarrus Brewing Company LLC .... E 704 490-4487
  Concord (G-3326)

Carolina Beverage Group LLC .... E 704 799-3627
  Mooresville (G-8629)

Craft Brew Alliance Inc .... G 828 263-1111
  Boone (G-908)

Dreamweavers Brewery LLC .... G 704 507-7773
  Waxhaw (G-12429)

Gingers Revenge LLC .... F 828 505-2462
  Asheville (G-506)

Glass Jug .... F 919 818-6907
  Durham (G-4048)

Glass Jug LLC .... F 919 813-0135
  Durham (G-4049)

Haw River Farmhouse Ales LLC .... G 336 525-9270
  Saxapahaw (G-11262)

Hugger Mugger LLC .... F 910 585-2749
  Sanford (G-11191)

Koi Pond Brewing Company LLC .... G 252 231-1660
  Rocky Mount (G-10847)

Monster Brewing Company LLC .... D 828 883-2337
  Brevard (G-976)

Mother Earth Brewing LLC .... G 252 208-2437
  Kinston (G-7423)

Nachos & Beer LLC .... G 828 298-2280
  Asheville (G-553)

New Anthem LLC .... G 910 319-7430
  Wilmington (G-12859)

New Sarum Brewing Co LLC .... G 704 310-5048
  Salisbury (G-11096)

Newgrass Brewing Company LLC .... G 704 477-2795
  Shelby (G-11366)

Ponysaurus Brewing LLC .... F 919 455-3737
  Durham (G-4188)

Resident Culture Brewing LLC .... E 704 333-1862
  Charlotte (G-2714)

Salty Turtle Beer Company .... E 910 803-2019
  Surf City (G-11863)

Salud LLC .... E 980 495-6612
  Charlotte (G-2751)

Southern Range Brewing LLC .... G 704 289-4049
  Monroe (G-8560)

Stout Beverages LLC .... E 704 293-7640
  Kings Mountain (G-7388)

Sugar Creek Brewing Co LLC .... E 704 521-3333
  Charlotte (G-2878)

Sycamore Brewing LLC .... E 704 910-3821
  Charlotte (G-2891)

Triple C Brewing Company LLC .... F 704 372-3212
  Charlotte (G-2945)

Trophy On Maywood LLC .... F 919 803-1333
  Raleigh (G-10565)

Wedge Brewing Co .... G 828 505-2792
  Asheville (G-632)

Weeping Radish Farm Brewry LLC .... G 252 491-5205
  Grandy (G-5291)

BEVERAGES, ALCOHOLIC: Beer & Ale

760 Craft Works LLC .... F 704 274-5216
  Huntersville (G-6962)

Bearwaters Brewing Company .... F 828 237-4200
  Canton (G-1242)

Brew Publik Incorporated .... G 704 231-2703
  Charlotte (G-1810)

Brewmasters Inc .... G 252 991-6035
  Wilson (G-12972)

Fiddlin Fish Brewing Co .... F 336 999-8945
  Winston Salem (G-13167)

Heckler Brewing Company .... G 910 748-0085
  Fayetteville (G-4609)

House of Hops .... G 919 819-0704
  Raleigh (G-10177)

Shortway Brewing Company LLC .... G 252 777-3065
  Newport (G-9444)

Southern Wicked Distillery Inc .... G 919 539-1620
  Raleigh (G-10494)

Trve-Avl LLC .... G 303 909-1956
  Asheville (G-625)

BEVERAGES, ALCOHOLIC: Bourbon Whiskey

Asheville Distilling Company .... G 828 575-2000
  Asheville (G-436)

BEVERAGES, ALCOHOLIC: Distilled Liquors

Barrister and Brewer LLC .... G 919 323-2777
  Durham (G-3913)

Bogue Sound Distillery Inc .... F 252 241-1606
  Newport (G-9438)

Broad Branch Distillery LLC .... G 336 207-7855
  Winston Salem (G-13111)

Buffalo City Distillery LLC .... G 252 256-1477
  Point Harbor (G-9809)

Call Family Distillers LLC .... G 336 990-0708
  Wilkesboro (G-12630)

Copper Barrel Distillery LLC .... G 336 262-6500
  North Wilkesboro (G-9526)

Dark Moon Distileries LLC .... G 704 222-8063
  Banner Elk (G-683)

Doc Porters Distillery LLC .... G 704 266-1399
  Charlotte (G-2060)

Durham Distillery Llc .... G 919 937-2121
  Durham (G-4015)

Eod Distillery LLC .... E 910 399-1133
  Wilmington (G-12771)

Fainting Goat Spirits LLC .... G 336 273-6221
  Greensboro (G-5529)

Fair Game Beverage Company .... G 919 245-5434
  Pittsboro (G-9783)

Graybeard Distillery Inc .... F 919 361-9980
  Durham (G-4056)

Great Wagon Road Distlg Co LLC .... F 704 469-9330
  Charlotte (G-2236)

Greensboro Distilling LLC .... G 336 273-6221
  Greensboro (G-5576)

H&H Distillery LLC .... G 828 338-9779
  Asheville (G-514)

Howling Moon Distillery Inc .... G 828 208-1469
  Burnsville (G-1187)

Mason Inlet Distillery LLC .... G 910 200-4584
  Wilmington (G-12847)

Mayberry Distillery .... G 336 719-6860
  Mount Airy (G-9152)

Muddy River Distillery LLC .... G 336 516-4190
  Mount Holly (G-9239)

New River Distilling Co LLC .... G 732 673-4852
  Deep Gap (G-3728)

Oak & Grist Distilling Co LLC .... G 914 450-0589
  Asheville (G-557)

Oak & Grist Distilling Co LLC .... G 828 357-5750
  Black Mountain (G-869)

Olde Raleigh Distillery LLC .... F 919 208-0044
  Zebulon (G-13519)

Southern Distilling Co LLC .... G 704 677-4069
  Statesville (G-11769)

Three Stacks Distilling Co LLC .... G 252 468-0779
  Kinston (G-7431)

Two Trees Distilling Co LLC .... G 803 767-1322
  Fletcher (G-4774)

Waltons Distillery Inc .... G 910 347-7770
  Jacksonville (G-7159)

Weldon Mills Distillery LLC .... G 252 220-4235
  Weldon (G-12527)

BEVERAGES, ALCOHOLIC: Rum

Azure Skye Beverages Inc .... G 704 909-7394
  Charlotte (G-1727)

BEVERAGES, ALCOHOLIC: Wines

American Alcohollery LLC .... G 704 960-7243
  Moravian Falls (G-8807)

Asheville Meadery LLC .... G 828 454-6188
  Asheville (G-438)

Autumn Creek Vineyards Inc .... G 336 548-9463
  Greensboro (G-5377)

Banner Elk Winery Inc .... G 828 898-9090
  Banner Elk (G-682)

Biltmore Estate Wine Co LLC .... C 828 225-6776
  Asheville (G-454)

Black Rock Landscaping LLC .... G 910 295-4470
  Carthage (G-1277)

Botanist and Barrel .... G 919 644-7777
  Cedar Grove (G-1516)

Burntshirt Vineyards LLC .... F 828 685-2402
  Hendersonville (G-6191)

Cape Fear Vineyard Winery LLC .... F 844 846-3386
  Elizabethtown (G-4421)

Cape Fear Vinyrd & Winery LLC .... G 910 645-4292
  Elizabethtown (G-4422)

Carolina Coast Vineyard .... G 910 707-1777
  Carolina Beach (G-1258)

Chateau Jourdain LLC .... G 786 273-2869
  Jonesville (G-7194)

Childress Vineyards LLC .... E 336 236-9463
  Lexington (G-7663)

Childress Winery LLC .... G 336 775-0522
  Lexington (G-7664)

Coastal Carolina Winery .... G 843 443-9463
  Cornelius (G-3594)

Cougar Run Winery .... G 704 788-2746
  Concord (G-3346)

Cypress Bend Vineyards Inc .... G 910 369-0411
  Wagram (G-12255)

Davidson Wine Co LLC .... F 614 738-0051
  Davidson (G-3702)

Dennis Vineyards Inc .... G 704 982-6090
  Albemarle (G-70)

Divine Llama Vineyards LLC .... G 336 699-2525
  East Bend (G-4323)

Drink A Bull LLC .... G 919 818-3321
  Durham (G-4008)

Duplin Wine Cellars Inc .... E 910 289-3888
  Rose Hill (G-10905)

Elkin Creek Vineyard LLC .... G 336 526-5119
  Elkin (G-4445)

Grandfather Vinyrd Winery LLC .... G 828 963-2400
  Banner Elk (G-685)

Grassy Creek Vineyard & Winery .... G 336 835-2458
  State Road (G-11636)

Gregory Vineyards .... G 919 427-9409
  Angier (G-119)

Hilton Vineyards LLC .... G 704 776-9656
  Monroe (G-8499)

Honeygirl Meadery LLC .... G 919 399-3056
  Durham (G-4063)

Hutton Vineyards LLC .... G 336 374-2321
  Dobson (G-3822)

Jackson Wine .... G 828 508-9292
  Brevard (G-973)

Jolo Winery & Vineyards LLC .... E 954 816-5649
  Pilot Mountain (G-9671)

Jones Vondrehle Vineyards LLC .... F 336 874-2800
  Thurmond (G-12097)

Laurel Gray Vineyards Inc...................... G 336 468-9463
Hamptonville (G-6086)

Linville Falls Winery.............................. G 828 733-9021
Newland (G-9431)

Medaloni Cellars LLC.............................. G 305 509-2004
Lewisville (G-7652)

Molley Chomper LLC.............................. G 404 769-1439
Lansing (G-7478)

Nomacorc Holdings LLC........................ E 919 460-2200
Zebulon (G-13516)

Noni Bacca Winery.................................. G 910 397-7617
Wilmington (G-12861)

Old North State Winery Inc.................... F 336 789-9463
Mount Airy (G-9161)

Piccione Vinyards.................................. G 312 342-0181
Ronda (G-10896)

Pig Pounder LLC.................................... G 336 255-1306
Greensboro (G-5747)

Pleb Urban Winery.................................. G 828 767-6445
Asheville (G-578)

Queen of Wines LLC.............................. F 919 348-6630
Durham (G-4204)

Raffaldini Vneyards Winery LLC............ F 336 835-9463
Ronda (G-10898)

Raylen Vineyards Inc.............................. G 336 998-3100
Winston Salem (G-13316)

Rise Over Run Inc.................................. G 303 819-1566
Swannanoa (G-11877)

Rockfish Creek Winery LLC.................... G 910 729-0648
Raeford (G-9851)

Rocky River Vineyards LLC.................... G 704 781-5035
Midland (G-8295)

Roots Run Deep LLC.............................. G 919 909-9117
Youngsville (G-13483)

Round Peak Vineyards LLC.................... G 336 352-5595
Mount Airy (G-9173)

Saint Paul Mountain Vineyards.............. F 828 685-4002
Hendersonville (G-6239)

Sanders Ridge Inc.................................. G 336 677-1700
Boonville (G-958)

Shelton Vineyards Inc............................ E 336 366-4818
Dobson (G-3825)

Sommerville Enterprises LLC................ F 919 924-1594
Hillsborough (G-6878)

Southern Range Brewing LLC................ G 704 289-4049
Monroe (G-8560)

Stardust Cellars LLC.............................. G 336 466-4454
Winston Salem (G-13343)

Stonefield Cellars LLC............................ G 336 632-2391
Stokesdale (G-11816)

Thistle Meadow Winery Inc.................... G 800 233-1505
Laurel Springs (G-7490)

Tom Burgiss.. G 336 359-2995
Laurel Springs (G-7491)

Vineyard Bluffton LLC............................ G 704 307-2737
Charlotte (G-2985)

Vineyards On Scuppernong LLC............ G 252 796-4727
Columbia (G-3299)

Weathervane Winery Inc........................ G 336 793-3366
Lexington (G-7757)

Willowcroft.. F 704 540-0367
Charlotte (G-3021)

Woodmill Winery Inc.............................. G 704 276-9911
Vale (G-12212)

BEVERAGES, MALT

Craft Revolution LLC.............................. F 347 924-7540
Charlotte (G-1994)

BEVERAGES, NONALCOHOLIC: Bottled & canned soft drinks

Aberdeen Coca-Cola Btlg Co Inc............ F 910 944-2305
Aberdeen (G-1)

Bebida Beverage Company.................... E 704 660-0226
Statesville (G-11668)

Carolina Beverage Corporation.............. E 704 636-2191
Salisbury (G-11024)

Carolina Bottling Company.................... D 704 637-5869
Salisbury (G-11025)

Ccbcc Inc.. B 704 557-4000
Charlotte (G-1871)

Ccbcc Operations LLC.......................... E 704 557-4038
Charlotte (G-1872)

Ccbcc Operations LLC.......................... E 252 752-2446
Greenville (G-5953)

Ccbcc Operations LLC.......................... E 252 536-3611
Halifax (G-6046)

Ccbcc Operations LLC.......................... E 910 582-3543
Hamlet (G-6053)

Ccbcc Operations LLC.......................... E 252 637-3157
New Bern (G-9352)

Ccbcc Operations LLC.......................... D 252 671-4515
New Bern (G-9353)

Ccbcc Operations LLC.......................... E 704 872-3634
Statesville (G-11676)

Ccbcc Operations LLC.......................... E 910 642-3002
Whiteville (G-12579)

Ccbcc Operations LLC.......................... D 828 687-1300
Arden (G-260)

Ccbcc Operations LLC.......................... E 828 297-2141
Boone (G-905)

Ccbcc Operations LLC.......................... E 828 488-2874
Bryson City (G-1009)

Ccbcc Operations LLC.......................... F 704 359-5600
Charlotte (G-1873)

Ccbcc Operations LLC.......................... E 704 399-6043
Charlotte (G-1875)

Ccbcc Operations LLC.......................... C 980 321-3226
Charlotte (G-1876)

Ccbcc Operations LLC.......................... D 919 359-2966
Clayton (G-3138)

Ccbcc Operations LLC.......................... E 910 483-6158
Fayetteville (G-4572)

Ccbcc Operations LLC.......................... D 336 664-1116
Greensboro (G-5434)

Ccbcc Operations LLC.......................... E 828 322-5097
Hickory (G-6292)

Ccbcc Operations LLC.......................... E 704 225-1973
Monroe (G-8455)

Ccbcc Operations LLC.......................... E 336 789-7111
Mount Airy (G-9112)

Ccbcc Operations LLC.......................... E 704 364-8728
Charlotte (G-1874)

Choice USA Beverage Inc...................... G 704 487-6951
Shelby (G-11317)

Coca Cola Bottling Co............................ G 704 509-1812
Charlotte (G-1946)

Coca-Cola Consolidated Inc.................. G 704 398-2252
Charlotte (G-1947)

Coca-Cola Consolidated Inc.................. D 980 321-3001
Charlotte (G-1948)

Coca-Cola Consolidated Inc.................. C 919 550-0611
Clayton (G-3141)

Coca-Cola Consolidated Inc.................. D 252 334-1820
Elizabeth City (G-4382)

Coca-Cola Consolidated Inc.................. E 704 551-4500
Kinston (G-7402)

Coca-Cola Consolidated Inc.................. G 919 763-3172
Leland (G-7539)

Coca-Cola Consolidated Inc.................. E 828 322-5096
Newton (G-9455)

Coca-Cola Consolidated Inc.................. A 980 392-8298
Charlotte (G-1949)

Durham Coca-Cola Bottling Co.............. G 919 510-0574
Raleigh (G-10066)

ICEE Company.. G 704 357-6865
Charlotte (G-2308)

Independent Beverage Co LLC.............. F 704 399-2504
Charlotte (G-2320)

McPherson Beverages Inc...................... E 252 537-3571
Roanoke Rapids (G-10741)

Old Saratoga Inc.................................... E 252 238-2175
Saratoga (G-11261)

Original New York Seltzer LLC.............. E 323 500-0757
Cornelius (G-3617)

Packo Bottling Inc.................................. E 919 496-4286
Louisburg (G-7921)

Pepsi-Cola Btlg Hickry NC Inc.............. G 828 322-8090
Granite Falls (G-5316)

Piedmont Cheerwine Bottling Co............ D 336 993-7733
Colfax (G-3287)

Quality Beverage LLC............................ G 704 637-5881
Salisbury (G-11109)

Sanford Coca-Cola Bottling Co.............. F 919 774-4111
Sanford (G-11229)

Suntory International.............................. F 917 756-2747
Raleigh (G-10521)

BEVERAGES, NONALCOHOLIC: Carbonated

Central Carolina Btlg Co Inc.................. G 919 542-3226
Bear Creek (G-713)

Frito-Lay North America Inc.................... G 980 224-3730
Wilmington (G-12779)

Midland Bottling LLC............................ G 919 865-2300
Raleigh (G-10306)

Pepsi Bottling Group Inc........................ G 704 507-4031
Midland (G-8291)

Pepsi Bottling Ventures LLC.................. E 800 879-8884
Cary (G-1418)

Pepsi Bottling Ventures LLC.................. E 252 335-4355
Elizabeth City (G-4401)

Pepsi Bottling Ventures LLC.................. D 919 865-2388
Garner (G-4952)

Pepsi Bottling Ventures LLC.................. C 919 863-4000
Garner (G-4953)

Pepsi Bottling Ventures LLC.................. E 919 778-8300
Goldsboro (G-5236)

Pepsi Bottling Ventures LLC.................. C 704 455-0800
Harrisburg (G-6115)

Pepsi Bottling Ventures LLC.................. E 252 451-1811
Rocky Mount (G-10859)

Pepsi Bottling Ventures LLC.................. D 910 865-1600
Saint Pauls (G-11006)

Pepsi Bottling Ventures LLC.................. E 704 873-0249
Statesville (G-11744)

Pepsi Bottling Ventures LLC.................. G 336 464-9227
Winston Salem (G-13279)

Pepsi Bottling Ventures LLC.................. E 336 464-9227
Winston Salem (G-13280)

Pepsi Bottling Ventures LLC.................. D 919 865-2300
Raleigh (G-10366)

Pepsi Cola Bottling Co............................ D 828 650-7800
Fletcher (G-4760)

Pepsi Cola Co.. G 704 357-9166
Charlotte (G-2625)

Pepsi-Cola Btlg Hickry NC Inc.............. D 828 497-1235
Whittier (G-12625)

Pepsi-Cola Btlg Hickry NC Inc.............. C 828 322-8090
Hickory (G-6410)

Pepsi-Cola Metro Btlg Co Inc................ G 980 581-1099
Charlotte (G-2626)

Pepsi-Cola Metro Btlg Co Inc................ A 336 896-4000
Winston Salem (G-13282)

Pepsico Inc.. G 828 756-4662
Marion (G-8060)

Pepsico Inc.................................... F 914 253-2000
Winston Salem *(G-13283)*

Raleigh Ventures Inc.................... G 910 350-0036
Wilmington *(G-12895)*

Red Bull Distribution Co Inc....... F 910 500-1566
Havelock *(G-6126)*

BEVERAGES, NONALCOHOLIC: Carbonated, Canned & Bottled, Etc

Choice USA Beverage Inc.............. D 704 823-1651
Lowell *(G-7930)*

Grins Enterprises LLC.................. G 336 831-0534
Winston Salem *(G-13185)*

Pepsi-Cola Metro Btlg Co Inc....... D 704 736-2640
Cherryville *(G-3068)*

Refresco Beverages US Inc........... E 252 234-0493
Wilson *(G-13020)*

Waynesville Soda Jerks LLC......... G 828 278-8589
Waynesville *(G-12479)*

BEVERAGES, NONALCOHOLIC: Flavoring extracts & syrups, nec

Bunge Oils Inc.............................. E 910 293-7917
Warsaw *(G-12358)*

Crude LLC.................................... G 919 391-8185
Raleigh *(G-10022)*

Fuji Foods Inc.............................. G 336 226-8817
Burlington *(G-1091)*

Great Eastern Sun Trdg Co Inc..... F 828 665-7790
Asheville *(G-511)*

Larrys Beans Inc.......................... G 919 828-1234
Raleigh *(G-10248)*

Mary Macks Inc............................ G 770 234-6333
Clinton *(G-3234)*

BEVERAGES, NONALCOHOLIC: Fruit Drnks, Under 100% Juice, Can

Alamance Foods Inc..................... C 336 226-6392
Burlington *(G-1043)*

BEVERAGES, NONALCOHOLIC: Soft Drinks, Canned & Bottled, Etc

Carolina Beverage Group LLC....... E 704 799-2337
Mooresville *(G-8630)*

Choice USA Beverage Inc.............. E 704 861-1029
Gastonia *(G-5020)*

Dr Pepper Co of Wilmington........ G 910 792-5400
Wilmington *(G-12767)*

Dr Pepper/Seven-Up Bottling....... G 828 322-8090
Hickory *(G-6324)*

Dr Ppper Btlg W Jffrson NC In...... E 336 846-2433
West Jefferson *(G-12564)*

Durham Coca-Cola Bottling Company... C 919 383-1531
Durham *(G-4014)*

Ginger Supreme Inc...................... G 919 812-8986
Apex *(G-158)*

Minges Bottling Group.................. F 252 636-5898
New Bern *(G-9383)*

Pepsi Bottling Ventures LLC......... E 828 264-7702
Deep Gap *(G-3729)*

Pepsi Bottling Ventures LLC......... D 910 792-5400
Wilmington *(G-12874)*

Pepsi Bottling Ventures LLC......... C 336 724-4800
Winston Salem *(G-13281)*

Pepsi-Cola Btlg Hickry NC Inc...... D 828 322-8090
Hickory *(G-6409)*

Pepsi-Cola Metro Btlg Co Inc....... G 252 446-7181
Rocky Mount *(G-10860)*

Quality Beverage LLC.................... E 910 371-3596
Belville *(G-781)*

Redux Beverages LLC.................... G 951 304-1144
Hillsborough *(G-6876)*

Refresco Beverages US Inc........... F 252 234-0493
Wilson *(G-13021)*

Sun-Drop Btlg Rocky Mt NC Inc.... G 252 977-4586
Rocky Mount *(G-10871)*

USa Wholesale and Distrg Inc...... F 888 484-6872
Fayetteville *(G-4693)*

BEVERAGES, NONALCOHOLIC: Tea, Iced, Bottled & Canned, Etc

Brewitt & Dreenkupp Inc.............. G 704 525-3366
Charlotte *(G-1811)*

S & D Coffee Inc........................... A 704 782-3121
Concord *(G-3437)*

BEVERAGES, WINE & DISTILLED ALCOHOLIC, WHOLESALE: Wine

Drink A Bull LLC.......................... G 919 818-3321
Durham *(G-4008)*

BICYCLES, PARTS & ACCESS

Huck Cycles Corporation.............. G 704 275-1735
Cornelius *(G-3608)*

Industry Nine LLC........................ G 828 210-5113
Asheville *(G-523)*

Rinehart Racing Inc..................... E 828 350-7653
Fletcher *(G-4764)*

Trailmate Inc............................... G 941 739-5743
Chapel Hill *(G-1578)*

BILLIARD & POOL TABLES & SPLYS

Mettech Inc.................................. G 919 833-9460
Raleigh *(G-10297)*

BINDING SVC: Books & Manuals

Adpress Printing Incorporated...... G 336 294-2244
Summerfield *(G-11835)*

American Multimedia Inc.............. D 336 229-7101
Burlington *(G-1045)*

Appalachian State University........ F 828 262-2047
Boone *(G-896)*

Arzberger Engravers Inc............... E 704 376-1151
Charlotte *(G-1702)*

Atlantis Graphics Inc................... E 919 361-5809
Durham *(G-3904)*

Bennett & Associates Inc............. G 919 477-7362
Durham *(G-3925)*

Boingo Graphics Inc..................... E 704 527-4963
Charlotte *(G-1797)*

BP Solutions Group Inc................ E 828 252-4476
Asheville *(G-460)*

Coastal Press Inc......................... G 252 726-1549
Morehead City *(G-8827)*

David Presnell............................. G 336 372-5989
Sparta *(G-11537)*

Docusource North Carolina LLC.... E 919 459-5900
Morrisville *(G-8968)*

Dokja Inc..................................... G 336 852-5190
Greensboro *(G-5500)*

Etherngton Cnservation Ctr Inc.... E 336 665-1317
Greensboro *(G-5525)*

Flash Printing Company Inc.......... E 704 375-2474
Charlotte *(G-2159)*

Free Will Bptst Press Fndtion....... F 252 746-6128
Ayden *(G-657)*

Gik Inc.. F 919 872-9498
Raleigh *(G-10133)*

Hickory Printing Solutions LLC..... B 828 465-3431
Conover *(G-3530)*

Holt Sublimation Printing &.......... G 336 222-3600
Burlington *(G-1104)*

Itek Graphics LLC........................ E 704 357-6002
Concord *(G-3383)*

Jag Graphics Inc.......................... G 828 259-9020
Asheville *(G-527)*

Joseph C Woodard Prtg Co Inc...... F 919 829-0634
Raleigh *(G-10221)*

Keiger Inc.................................... G 336 760-0099
Winston Salem *(G-13223)*

Lee County Industries Inc............. G 919 775-3439
Sanford *(G-11205)*

Loftin & Company Inc.................... E 704 393-9393
Charlotte *(G-2431)*

Measurement Incorporated........... D 919 683-2413
Durham *(G-4122)*

Medlit Solutions LLC.................... D 919 878-6789
Garner *(G-4942)*

Occasions Group Inc.................... E 252 321-5805
Greenville *(G-6009)*

Ollis Enterprises Inc.................... E 828 265-0004
Wilkesboro *(G-12648)*

Owen G Dunn Co Inc..................... G 252 633-3197
New Bern *(G-9387)*

Pamela A Adams........................... G 919 876-5949
Raleigh *(G-10355)*

Park Communications LLC............ D 336 292-4000
Greensboro *(G-5732)*

Person Printing Company Inc........ E 336 599-2146
Roxboro *(G-10940)*

Piedmont Business Forms Inc....... G 828 464-0010
Newton *(G-9488)*

Postal Instant Press..................... G 336 222-0717
Burlington *(G-1142)*

Powell Ink Inc.............................. F 828 253-6886
Asheville *(G-582)*

Printing Svcs Greensboro Inc........ G 336 274-7663
Greensboro *(G-5765)*

Quality Prtg Cartridge Fctry.......... G 336 852-2505
Greensboro *(G-5779)*

S Chamblee Incorporated............. E 919 833-7561
Raleigh *(G-10452)*

S Ruppe Inc.................................. G 828 287-4936
Rutherfordton *(G-10992)*

Subtle Impressions Inc................. E
Gastonia *(G-5145)*

Three Trees Bindery..................... G 704 724-9409
Charlotte *(G-2917)*

Trejo Soccer Academy LLC........... G 336 899-7910
Asheboro *(G-410)*

Weber and Weber Inc.................... F 336 722-4109
Winston Salem *(G-13387)*

BINDINGS: Bias, Made From Purchased Materials

International Foam Pdts Inc.......... G 704 588-0080
Charlotte *(G-2343)*

BIOLOGICAL PRDTS: Agar Culture Media

Duke Human Vaccine Institute...... G 919 684-5384
Durham *(G-4009)*

Grifols Therapeutics LLC.............. B 919 316-6300
Research Triangle Pa *(G-10711)*

BIOLOGICAL PRDTS: Blood Derivatives

Grifols Therapeutics LLC.............. F 919 316-6214
Durham *(G-4057)*

Grifols Therapeutics LLC.............. A 919 316-6612
Raleigh *(G-10148)*

Immunotek Bio Centers LLC......... E 828 569-6264
Hickory *(G-6366)*

PRODUCT

Immunotek Bio Centers LLC.................. E 336 781-4901
High Point *(G-6668)*

BIOLOGICAL PRDTS: Exc Diagnostic

Anatech Ltd................................ F 704 489-1488
Denver *(G-3770)*

Astellas Gene Therapies Inc.................. D 415 638-6561
Sanford *(G-11151)*

Biologix of The Triangle Inc................. G 919 696-4544
Cary *(G-1307)*

Boehrnger Inglheim Anmal Hlth............. D 919 577-9020
Fuquay Varina *(G-4871)*

Carolina Biological Supply Co.............. C 336 446-7600
Whitsett *(G-12601)*

Carolina Biological Supply Company.... C 336 584-0381
Burlington *(G-1060)*

Cedarlane Laboratories USA.................. E 336 513-5135
Burlington *(G-1067)*

Chelsea Therapeutics International Ltd. F 704 341-1516
Charlotte *(G-1908)*

Cytonet LLC.................................... F
Durham *(G-3997)*

Keranetics LLC................................. G 336 725-0621
Winston Salem *(G-13225)*

Microban Products Company............. E 704 766-4267
Huntersville *(G-7013)*

Molecular Toxicology Inc..................... F 828 264-9099
Boone *(G-935)*

Pfizer Inc... C 919 775-7100
Sanford *(G-11219)*

Precision Biosciences Inc.................. E 919 314-5512
Durham *(G-4194)*

Prokidney LLC.................................. E 336 448-2857
Winston Salem *(G-13307)*

Prokidney Corp................................. C 336 999-7019
Winston Salem *(G-13308)*

Serum Source International Inc............. F 704 588-6607
Waxhaw *(G-12440)*

Tengion Inc....................................... E 336 722-5855
Winston Salem *(G-13361)*

BIOLOGICAL PRDTS: Vaccines

Albion Medical Holdings Inc.................. F 800 378-3906
Lenoir *(G-7570)*

Greer Laboratories Inc......................... E 828 758-2388
Lenoir *(G-7609)*

Greer Laboratories Inc......................... C 828 754-5327
Lenoir *(G-7610)*

BIOLOGICAL PRDTS: Vaccines & Immunizing

Embrex LLC....................................... C 919 941-5185
Durham *(G-4019)*

Novartis Vccnes Dagnostics Inc........... B 617 871-7000
Holly Springs *(G-6908)*

Passport Health Triangle...................... G 919 781-0053
Cary *(G-1414)*

Seqirus Inc....................................... F 919 577-5000
Holly Springs *(G-6914)*

BIOLOGICAL PRDTS: Veterinary

Epicypher Inc..................................... F 855 374-2461
Durham *(G-4030)*

Quo Vademus LLC............................. G 910 296-1632
Kenansville *(G-7227)*

BIRTH CONTROL DEVICES: Rubber

Hygeia Marketing Corporation.............. G 704 933-5190
Kannapolis *(G-7211)*

BLADES: Knife

Daniel Winkler Knifemaker LLC............. G 828 262-3691
Boone *(G-911)*

BLADES: Saw, Hand Or Power

Raleigh Saw Co Inc............................. G 919 832-2248
Raleigh *(G-10429)*

BLANKBOOKS & LOOSELEAF BINDERS

American Sample House Inc.................. G 704 276-1970
Vale *(G-12207)*

Carolina Swatching Inc........................ F 828 327-9499
Hickory *(G-6288)*

E Feibusch Company Inc....................... E 336 434-5095
High Point *(G-6600)*

Swatchworks Inc................................. G 336 626-9971
Asheboro *(G-401)*

Visual Products Inc............................. F 336 883-0156
High Point *(G-6828)*

BLANKBOOKS: Checkbooks & Passbooks, Bank

Clarke Harland Corp............................ G 210 697-8888
High Point *(G-6570)*

BLANKETS & BLANKETING, COTTON

Designer Fabrics Inc............................ G 704 305-4144
Concord *(G-3354)*

Riddle & Company LLC......................... G 336 229-1856
Burlington *(G-1147)*

Westpoint Home Inc............................. F 910 369-2231
Wagram *(G-12257)*

BLEACHING YARN & FABRICS: Wool Or Similar Fibers

Burlington Industries LLC...................... C 336 379-6220
Greensboro *(G-5414)*

BLINDS & SHADES: Vertical

Carolina Blind Outlet Inc...................... G 828 697-8525
Hendersonville *(G-6194)*

Decolux USA...................................... G 704 340-3532
Charlotte *(G-2026)*

Raven Rock Manufacturing Inc.............. G 910 308-8430
Dunn *(G-3865)*

Shuttercraft Inc.................................. F 704 708-9079
Matthews *(G-8148)*

Vertical Solutions of NC Inc.................. G 919 285-2251
Holly Springs *(G-6918)*

Vista Products Inc.............................. D 910 582-0130
Hamlet *(G-6065)*

BLINDS : Window

Dbf Inc... G 910 548-6725
Jacksonville *(G-7122)*

Elite Textiles Fabrication Inc................. F 888 337-0977
High Point *(G-6608)*

Empire Carpet & Blinds Inc.................. G 704 541-3988
Charlotte *(G-2111)*

First Rate Blinds................................ G 800 655-1080
Cornelius *(G-3601)*

H2h Blinds.. G 704 628-5084
Matthews *(G-8114)*

Hunter Douglas Inc............................. C 704 629-6500
Bessemer City *(G-822)*

Mountaintop Cheesecakes LLC............. G 336 391-9127
Mocksville *(G-8380)*

Newell Brands Inc.............................. F 336 812-8181
High Point *(G-6718)*

Royal Textile Products Sw LLC............. G 602 276-4598
Charlotte *(G-2735)*

Selective Enterprises Inc...................... C 704 588-3310
Charlotte *(G-2784)*

Synoptix Companies LLC...................... F 910 790-3630
Wilmington *(G-12935)*

BLOCKS & BRICKS: Concrete

Custom Brick Company Inc.................... E 919 832-2804
Raleigh *(G-10028)*

East Fork Pottery LLC.......................... G 828 575-2150
Asheville *(G-493)*

Fayblock Materials Inc......................... D 910 323-9198
Fayetteville *(G-4600)*

General Shale Brick Inc........................ E 919 775-2121
Moncure *(G-8405)*

Hydro Conduit LLC.............................. G 252 243-6153
Wilson *(G-12994)*

Oldcastle Adams................................. G 336 310-0542
Colfax *(G-3285)*

Oldcastle Retail Inc............................ B 704 799-8083
Cornelius *(G-3616)*

Southeastern Concrete Pdts Co............. D 704 873-2226
Statesville *(G-11768)*

Southern Block Company...................... F 910 293-7844
Warsaw *(G-12366)*

BLOCKS: Landscape Or Retaining Wall, Concrete

Carolina Lawnscape Inc....................... G 803 230-5570
Charlotte *(G-1849)*

Dnl Services LLC............................... G 910 689-8759
Harrells *(G-6100)*

Global Stone Impex LLC....................... G 336 609-1113
Greensboro *(G-5564)*

Good Earth Ministries.......................... G 828 287-9826
Rutherfordton *(G-10983)*

Taylco Inc... E 910 739-0405
Lumberton *(G-7974)*

Top Dawg Landscape Inc...................... G 336 877-7519
West Jefferson *(G-12571)*

Trademark Landscape Group Inc........... F 910 253-0560
Supply *(G-11861)*

BLOCKS: Paving

Custom Brick Company Inc.................... E 919 832-2804
Raleigh *(G-10028)*

BLOCKS: Standard, Concrete Or Cinder

Adams Products Company...................... C 919 467-2218
Morrisville *(G-8919)*

Argos USA LLC................................... C 704 872-9566
Statesville *(G-11659)*

Greystone Concrete Pdts Inc................. E 252 438-5144
Henderson *(G-6157)*

Hefty Concrete Inc.............................. G 910 483-1598
Fayetteville *(G-4610)*

Johnson Concrete Company................... E 704 786-4204
Concord *(G-3386)*

Johnson Concrete Company................... E 336 248-2918
Lexington *(G-7702)*

Johnson Concrete Company................... E 704 636-5231
Willow Spring *(G-12679)*

Johnson Concrete Company................... E 704 636-5231
Salisbury *(G-11074)*

Leonard Block Company........................ G 336 764-0607
Winston Salem *(G-13233)*

Motsinger Block Plant Inc..................... G 336 764-0350
Winston Salem *(G-13262)*

Old Castle Apg South Inc...................... G 919 383-2521
Durham *(G-4155)*

Spake Concrete Products Inc................. F 704 482-2881
Shelby *(G-11382)*

Union Masonry Inc.................................... G 919 217-7806
Raleigh *(G-10576)*

BLOWERS & FANS

G Denver and Co LLC............................. E 704 896-4000
Davidson *(G-3705)*

Hunter Fan Company............................. G 704 896-9250
Cornelius *(G-3609)*

Rotron Incorporated.............................. C 336 449-3400
Whitsett *(G-12619)*

Air Purification Inc............................... F 919 783-6161
Raleigh *(G-9886)*

Bahnson Holdings Inc........................... D 336 760-3111
Clemmons *(G-3178)*

Breezer Holdings LLC............................ D 844 233-5673
Charlotte *(G-1809)*

Camfil Usa Inc...................................... E 828 465-2880
Conover *(G-3498)*

Camfil Usa Inc...................................... D 252 975-1141
Washington *(G-12376)*

Dynamic Air Engineering Inc.................. E 714 540-1000
Claremont *(G-3112)*

Environmental Specialties LLC............... D 919 829-9300
Raleigh *(G-10088)*

Field Controls LLC................................ D 252 208-7300
Kinston *(G-7413)*

Filter Shop LLC.................................... D 704 860-4822
Gastonia *(G-5048)*

Firefly Balloons Inc.............................. G 704 878-9501
Statesville *(G-11700)*

Greenheck Fan Corporation................... G 704 476-3700
Shelby *(G-11339)*

Hayward Industrial Products.................. C 704 837-8002
Charlotte *(G-2264)*

Hughs Sheet Mtal Sttsvlle LLC.............. F 704 872-4621
Statesville *(G-11714)*

Kirk & Blum Manufacturing Co.............. D 801 728-6533
Greensboro *(G-5649)*

Meadows Mills Inc................................ E 336 838-2282
North Wilkesboro *(G-9546)*

NC Filtration of Florida LLC................... D 704 822-4444
Belmont *(G-756)*

Nederman Inc....................................... D 336 821-0827
Thomasville *(G-12053)*

Pamlico Air Inc..................................... F 252 995-6267
Washington *(G-12405)*

Punker LLC.. F 828 322-1951
Lincolnton *(G-7849)*

Purolator Facet Inc............................... E 336 668-4444
Greensboro *(G-5771)*

Universal Air Products Corp.................. G 704 374-0600
Charlotte *(G-2965)*

WV Holdings Inc................................... G 704 853-8338
Gastonia *(G-5168)*

Ziehl-Abegg Inc.................................... E 336 834-9339
Greensboro *(G-5931)*

BLUEPRINTING SVCS

AEC Imaging & Graphics LLC................ G 910 693-1034
Hope Mills *(G-6922)*

Copy King Inc....................................... G 336 333-9900
Greensboro *(G-5468)*

Document Imaging Systems Inc............. G 919 460-9440
Raleigh *(G-10054)*

Occasions Group Inc............................. G 919 751-2400
Goldsboro *(G-5233)*

Richa Inc.. G 704 944-0230
Charlotte *(G-2724)*

Richa Inc.. F 704 331-9744
Charlotte *(G-2725)*

BOAT & BARGE COMPONENTS: Metal, Prefabricated

Gore S Mar Met Fabrication Inc............. G 910 763-6066
Wilmington *(G-12793)*

BOAT BUILDING & REPAIR

2topia Cycles Inc.................................. G 704 778-7849
Charlotte *(G-1600)*

33rd Strike Group LLC.......................... G 910 371-9688
Leland *(G-7530)*

A & J Canvas Inc.................................. E 252 244-1509
Vanceboro *(G-12213)*

Baja Marine Inc.................................... E 252 975-2000
Washington *(G-12374)*

Bilge Masters Inc.................................. G 704 995-4293
Charlotte *(G-1781)*

Blackbeards Boatworks.......................... G 252 726-6161
Morehead City *(G-8818)*

Brp US Inc.. G 828 766-1164
Spruce Pine *(G-11565)*

C E Hicks Enterprises Inc...................... F 919 772-5131
Garner *(G-4919)*

Cape Fear Boat Works Inc..................... F 910 371-3460
Navassa *(G-9326)*

Coastal Trimworks Inc........................... G 910 231-8532
Leland *(G-7538)*

Croswait Custom Composites Inc............ G 252 423-1245
Wanchese *(G-12340)*

Custom Marine Fabrication Inc............... G 252 638-5422
New Bern *(G-9360)*

Daniels Boatworks Inc........................... G 252 473-1400
Wanchese *(G-12341)*

Donzi Marine LLC.................................. G 252 975-2000
Washington *(G-12384)*

Elite Marine LLC.................................... E 919 495-6388
Benson *(G-789)*

Enviboats LLC....................................... G 910 213-3200
Southport *(G-11519)*

Gillikin Marine Railways Inc................... G 252 726-7284
Beaufort *(G-728)*

Gunboat International Ltd....................... F 252 305-8700
Wanchese *(G-12342)*

Harding Enterprise Inc........................... G 252 725-9785
Beaufort *(G-730)*

Hc Composites LLC............................... C 252 641-8000
Tarboro *(G-11928)*

Iconic Marine Group LLC....................... B 252 975-2000
Chocowinity *(G-3083)*

Jabec Enterprise Inc.............................. G 336 655-8441
Winston Salem *(G-13215)*

Jarrett Bay Offshore.............................. G 919 803-1990
Raleigh *(G-10213)*

Johnson Custom Boats Inc..................... G 910 232-4594
Wilmington *(G-12824)*

Laytons Custom Boatworks LLC............. G 252 482-1504
Edenton *(G-4368)*

Marinemax of North Carolina................. G 910 256-8100
Wrightsville Beach *(G-13432)*

Mike Luszcz... G 252 717-6282
Winterville *(G-13418)*

Nomad Houseboats Inc.......................... G 252 288-5670
New Bern *(G-9386)*

Obx Boatworks LLC............................... G 336 878-9490
High Point *(G-6720)*

Onslow Bay Boatworks & Marine............ G 910 270-3703
Hampstead *(G-6074)*

Pacific Seacraft LLC.............................. G 252 948-1421
Washington *(G-12403)*

Powers Boatworks................................. G 910 762-3636
Wilmington *(G-12884)*

Rings True LLC..................................... G 919 265-7600
Carrboro *(G-1273)*

Sea Mark Boats Inc.............................. G 910 675-1877
Rocky Point *(G-10882)*

Sirocco Marine LLC............................... G 954 692-8333
Raleigh *(G-10483)*

Starflite Companies Inc.......................... C 252 728-2690
Beaufort *(G-735)*

Stroudcraft Marine LLC.......................... F 910 623-4055
Rocky Point *(G-10884)*

Taylor Boat Works................................ G 252 726-6374
Morehead City *(G-8847)*

Taylor Manufacturing Inc....................... E 910 862-2576
Elizabethtown *(G-4434)*

Triad Marine Center Inc......................... G 252 634-1880
New Bern *(G-9401)*

U S Propeller Service Inc....................... G 704 528-9515
Troutman *(G-12154)*

Wanchese Dock and Haul LLC................ G 252 473-6424
Wanchese *(G-12347)*

Warrior Boats....................................... G 336 885-2628
High Point *(G-6832)*

Winterville Machine Works Inc............... D 252 756-2130
Winterville *(G-13426)*

BOAT BUILDING & REPAIRING: Fiberglass

Alb Boats... C 252 482-7600
Edenton *(G-4359)*

Bayliss Boatworks Inc........................... E 252 473-9797
Wanchese *(G-12336)*

Briggs Boat Works Incorporated............ G 252 473-2393
Wanchese *(G-12338)*

Budsin Wood Craft................................ G 252 729-1540
Marshallberg *(G-8084)*

Custom Steel Boats Inc......................... F 252 745-7447
Merritt *(G-8267)*

Grady-White Boats Inc.......................... C 252 752-2111
Greenville *(G-5983)*

Kencraft Manufacturing Inc.................... G 252 291-0271
Wilson *(G-12998)*

Mann Custom Boats Inc......................... E 252 473-1716
Manns Harbor *(G-8020)*

Marine Tooling Technology Inc............... G 336 887-9577
High Point *(G-6698)*

May-Craft Fiberglass Pdts Inc................ G 919 934-3000
Four Oaks *(G-4814)*

Pair Marine Inc..................................... F 252 717-7009
Washington *(G-12404)*

Parker Marine Enterprises Inc................ D 252 728-5621
Beaufort *(G-733)*

Richard Scarborough Boat Works........... G 252 473-3646
Wanchese *(G-12346)*

Shearline Boatworks LLC....................... G 252 726-6916
Morehead City *(G-8844)*

BOAT BUILDING & REPAIRING: Motorboats, Inboard Or Outboard

Barrs Competition.................................. F 704 482-5169
Shelby *(G-11313)*

Brp US Inc.. D 828 766-1100
Spruce Pine *(G-11566)*

CC Boats Inc.. G 252 482-3699
Edenton *(G-4363)*

Jones Marine Inc.................................. G 704 639-0173
Salisbury *(G-11075)*

Pro-Line North Carolina Inc................... D 252 975-2000
Washington *(G-12409)*

Rapid Response Technology LLC........... G 910 763-3856
Wilmington *(G-12896)*

Smoky Mountain Jet Boats LLC............. F 828 488-0522
Bryson City *(G-1011)*

P
R
O
D
U
C
T

BOAT BUILDING & REPAIRING: Motorized

Craig & Sandra Blackwell Inc................ G 252 473-1803
  Wanchese (G-12339)

Jones Brothers Marine Mfg Inc.............. G 252 240-1995
  Morehead City (G-8837)

M & J Marine LLC............................... F 252 249-0522
  Oriental (G-9601)

Todds Rv & Marine Inc........................ G 828 651-0007
  Hendersonville (G-6245)

BOAT BUILDING & REPAIRING: Yachts

Bennett Brothers Yachts Inc................. E 910 772-9277
  Wilmington (G-12719)

Caison Yachts Inc.............................. G 910 270-6394
  Hampstead (G-6070)

Daedalus Composites LLC.................... F 252 368-9000
  Edenton (G-4365)

Hatteras Yachts Inc............................ A 252 633-3101
  New Bern (G-9370)

Mass Enterprises LLC......................... F 443 585-0732
  New Bern (G-9381)

White River Marine Group LLC............... C 252 633-3101
  New Bern (G-9406)

BOAT BUILDING & RPRG: Fishing, Small, Lobster, Crab, Oyster

Bayliss Boatyard Inc........................... F 252 473-9797
  Wanchese (G-12337)

Regulator Marine Inc........................... D 252 482-3837
  Edenton (G-4371)

Spencer Yachts Inc............................ E 252 473-2660
  Manns Harbor (G-8021)

Trawler Incorporated.......................... G 252 745-3751
  Lowland (G-7936)

BOAT DEALERS

Cape Fear Yacht Works LLC.................. F 910 540-1685
  Wilmington (G-12729)

Kencraft Manufacturing Inc................... G 252 291-0271
  Wilson (G-12998)

M & J Marine LLC............................... F 252 249-0522
  Oriental (G-9601)

Mann Custom Boats Inc....................... E 252 473-1716
  Manns Harbor (G-8020)

BOAT DEALERS: Motor

Marinemax of North Carolina................. G 910 256-8100
  Wrightsville Beach (G-13432)

Nomad Houseboats Inc........................ G 252 288-5670
  New Bern (G-9386)

Todds Rv & Marine Inc........................ G 828 651-0007
  Hendersonville (G-6245)

Triad Marine Center Inc....................... G 252 634-1880
  New Bern (G-9401)

BOAT LIFTS

Boat Lift US Inc................................. G 239 283-9040
  Leland (G-7532)

Boat Lift Store Inc............................. G 252 586-5437
  Littleton (G-7884)

Boat Lift Warehouse LLC...................... G 877 468-5438
  Snow Hill (G-11475)

Float Lifts of Carolinas LLC.................. G 919 972-1082
  Wilmington (G-12777)

HI & Dri Boat Lift Systems Inc............... G 704 663-5438
  Mooresville (G-8682)

Hydrohoist of North Carolina................. G 704 799-1910
  Mooresville (G-8689)

Veon Inc.. F 252 623-2102
  Washington (G-12418)

BOAT REPAIR SVCS

Admiral Marine Pdts & Svcs Inc............. G 704 489-8771
  Denver (G-3767)

BOATS & OTHER MARINE EQPT: Plastic

Brunson Marine Group LLC.................... E 252 291-0271
  Wilson (G-12975)

Marine & Industrial Plastics................... G 252 224-1000
  Pollocksville (G-9817)

BODIES: Truck & Bus

Courtesy Ford Inc.............................. G 252 338-4783
  Elizabeth City (G-4384)

Daimler Truck North Amer LLC............... A 704 868-5700
  Gastonia (G-5038)

Designline Usa LLC............................ F 704 494-7800
  Charlotte (G-2036)

Epv Corporation................................ D 704 494-7800
  Charlotte (G-2124)

Immixt LLC....................................... G 336 207-8679
  Siler City (G-11412)

Laurinburg Machine Company................ G 910 276-0360
  Laurinburg (G-7505)

Matthews Spcialty Vehicles Inc.............. D 336 297-9600
  Greensboro (G-5682)

Mdb Investors LLC............................. F 704 507-6850
  Charlotte (G-2482)

Meritor Inc....................................... G 828 433-4600
  Morganton (G-8881)

Mickey Truck Bodies Inc...................... G 336 882-6806
  High Point (G-6710)

Mickey Truck Bodies Inc...................... G 336 882-6806
  Thomasville (G-12047)

Prevost Car (us) Inc........................... E 908 222-7211
  Greensboro (G-5763)

Smithway Inc.................................... G 828 628-1756
  Fairview (G-4511)

Volvo Logistics North America Inc.......... C 336 393-4746
  Greensboro (G-5910)

BODY PARTS: Automobile, Stamped Metal

AMF-NC Enterprise Company LLC.......... F 704 489-2206
  Denver (G-3769)

Borgwarner Turbo Systems LLC............. D 828 684-4000
  Arden (G-258)

Continental Auto Systems Inc................ B 828 654-2000
  Fletcher (G-4731)

Dutch Miller Charlotte Inc.................... F 704 522-8422
  Charlotte (G-2070)

Gray Manufacturing Tech LLC............... F 704 489-2206
  Denver (G-3785)

Harrah Enterprise Ltd......................... G 336 253-3963
  Cornelius (G-3605)

Irvan-Smith Inc................................. F 704 788-2554
  Concord (G-3382)

Performance Entps & Parts Inc.............. G 336 621-6572
  Greensboro (G-5738)

Revmax Performance LLC..................... F 877 780-4334
  Charlotte (G-2717)

BOILER REPAIR SHOP

Chicago Tube and Iron Company............ D 704 781-2060
  Locust (G-7890)

BOILERS & BOILER SHOP WORK

Icon Boiler Inc.................................. E 844 562-4266
  Greensboro (G-5612)

BOILERS: Low-Pressure Heating, Steam Or Hot Water

BOLTS: Metal

Canvas Mw LLC................................. C 336 627-6000
  Eden (G-4342)

BOLTS: Metal

Cardinal America Inc........................... G 704 810-1620
  Statesville (G-11675)

Derita Precision Mch Co Inc.................. F 704 392-7285
  Charlotte (G-2034)

Moore S Welding Service Inc................. G 919 837-5769
  Bear Creek (G-716)

BOOK STORES

Free Will Bptst Press Fndtion................ F 252 746-6128
  Ayden (G-657)

Good Will Publishers Inc...................... D 704 853-3237
  Gastonia (G-5054)

Grateful Steps Foundation.................... G 828 277-0998
  Asheville (G-509)

BOOK STORES: Children's

Idea People Inc................................. G 704 398-4437
  Huntersville (G-7000)

BOOKS, WHOLESALE

Book Lover Search............................. G 336 889-6127
  High Point (G-6549)

Cherokee Publications......................... G 828 627-2424
  Cherokee (G-3051)

Gryphon House Inc............................. F 800 638-0928
  Lewisville (G-7651)

Wisdom House Books Inc..................... G 919 883-4669
  Chapel Hill (G-1594)

BOOTHS: Spray, Sheet Metal, Prefabricated

Carolina Custom Booth Co LLC.............. E 336 886-3127
  High Point (G-6559)

Production Systems Inc........................ E 336 886-7161
  High Point (G-6747)

Standard Tools and Eqp Co................... E 336 697-7177
  Greensboro (G-5836)

Superior Finishing Systems LLC............. G 336 956-2000
  Lexington (G-7747)

Triad Welding Contractors Inc............... G 336 882-3902
  Clemmons (G-3205)

BOOTS: Men's

McRae Industries Inc.......................... E 910 439-6147
  Mount Gilead (G-9204)

BOTTLED GAS DEALERS: Liquefied Petro, Dlvrd To Customers

Euliss Oil Company Inc........................ G 336 622-3055
  Liberty (G-7766)

BOTTLED GAS DEALERS: Propane

Blossman Propane Gas & Appl............... F 828 396-0144
  Hickory (G-6272)

Parker Gas Company Inc...................... F 800 354-7250
  Clinton (G-3238)

BOTTLES: Plastic

Amcor Phrm Packg USA LLC................. D 919 556-9715
  Youngsville (G-13461)

CKS Packaging Inc............................. D 336 578-5800
  Graham (G-5265)

Intertech Corporation.......................... D 336 621-1891
  Greensboro (G-5621)

Precision Concepts Intl LLC.................. G 704 360-8923
  Huntersville (G-7037)

Sonoco Products Company.................... G 910 455-6903
  Jacksonville (G-7148)

Southeastern Container Inc.................... E 704 710-4200
Kings Mountain *(G-7385)*

Southeastern Container Inc.................... C 828 350-7200
Enka *(G-4488)*

Vav Plastics Nc LLC............................. G 704 325-9332
Charlotte *(G-2974)*

BOX & CARTON MANUFACTURING EQPT

W V Doyle Enterprises Inc.................... G 336 885-2035
High Point *(G-6831)*

BOXES & CRATES: Rectangular, Wood

M O Deviney Lumber Co Inc.................. G 704 538-9071
Casar *(G-1489)*

McBride Lumber Co Partnr LLC............ G 910 428-2747
Star *(G-11632)*

Moorecraft Wood Prpucts Inc............... G 252 823-2510
Tarboro *(G-11936)*

BOXES & SHOOK: Nailed Wood

Arcola Lumber Company Inc.................. E 252 257-4923
Warrenton *(G-12350)*

Carolina WD Pdts Mrshville Inc............ D 704 624-2119
Marshville *(G-8086)*

Clemmons Pallet Skid Works Inc.......... E 336 766-5462
Clemmons *(G-3180)*

Millennium Packaging Svc LLC............. G 775 353-5127
Durham *(G-4135)*

Spartacraft Inc...................................... E 828 397-4630
Connelly Springs *(G-3483)*

Timberline Acquisition LLC................... E 252 492-6144
Henderson *(G-6181)*

Universal Forest Products Inc............... F 252 338-0319
Elizabeth City *(G-4416)*

BOXES: Cash & Stamp, Stamped Metal

Umi Company Inc................................... G 704 479-6210
Lincolnton *(G-7867)*

BOXES: Corrugated

Axis Corrugated Container LLC............. F 919 575-0500
Butner *(G-1198)*

Carolina Container Company................. D 336 883-7146
High Point *(G-6558)*

Carolina Container LLC......................... E 828 322-3380
Hickory *(G-6284)*

Carolina Container LLC......................... E 910 277-0400
Laurinburg *(G-7494)*

Carolina Packaging & Sup Inc.............. D 919 201-5592
Raleigh *(G-9978)*

Corney Transportation Inc.................... E 800 354-9111
Saint Pauls *(G-11004)*

Custom Corrugated Cntrs Inc............... E 704 588-0371
Charlotte *(G-2008)*

Ds Smith PLC.. E 919 557-3148
Holly Springs *(G-6898)*

Ferguson & Company LLC.................... G 704 332-4396
Charlotte *(G-2146)*

Ferguson Box.. E 704 597-0310
Charlotte *(G-2147)*

Ferguson Supply and Box Mfg Co........ D 704 597-0310
Charlotte *(G-2148)*

Freeman Container Company Inc......... G 704 922-7972
Dallas *(G-3672)*

Georgia Pratt Box Inc........................... C 919 872-3007
Raleigh *(G-10129)*

Georgia-Pacific LLC............................. D 336 629-2151
Asheboro *(G-361)*

Highland Containers Inc....................... C 336 887-5400
Jamestown *(G-7166)*

Highland Containers Inc....................... C 336 887-5400
Jamestown *(G-7165)*

Hood Container Corporation.................. E 336 887-5400
Jamestown *(G-7167)*

Industrial Container Corp...................... F 336 886-7031
High Point *(G-6670)*

Inter-Continental Corporation............... D 828 464-8250
Newton *(G-9477)*

International Paper Company................. G 704 588-8522
Charlotte *(G-2349)*

International Paper Company................. D 910 738-6214
Lumberton *(G-7958)*

International Paper Company................. G 252 456-3111
Manson *(G-8022)*

International Paper Company................. G 252 633-7407
New Bern *(G-9372)*

Lone Star Container Sales Corp........... D 704 588-1737
Charlotte *(G-2433)*

Package Craft LLC................................ E 252 825-0111
Bethel *(G-840)*

Package Crafters Incorporated............. D 336 431-9700
High Point *(G-6723)*

Packaging Corporation America........... E 252 753-8450
Farmville *(G-4537)*

Packaging Corporation America........... D 336 434-0600
Goldsboro *(G-5234)*

Packaging Corporation America........... G 704 664-5010
Mooresville *(G-8741)*

Packaging Corporation America........... E 828 584-1511
Morganton *(G-8887)*

Packaging Corporation America........... E 828 286-9156
Rutherfordton *(G-10988)*

Packaging Corporation America........... D 704 633-3611
Salisbury *(G-11100)*

Packaging Corporation America........... E 336 434-0600
Trinity *(G-12121)*

Paperworks Industries Inc.................... C 910 439-6137
Mount Gilead *(G-9209)*

Paperworks Industries Inc.................... C 336 447-7278
Whitsett *(G-12616)*

Piedmont Corrugated Specialty............ D 828 874-1153
Valdese *(G-12198)*

Piedmont Packaging Inc....................... F 336 886-5043
High Point *(G-6732)*

Pratt (jet Corr) Inc............................... A 704 878-6615
Statesville *(G-11751)*

Pratt Industries................................... G 704 864-4022
Gastonia *(G-5124)*

Pratt Industries Inc.............................. D 919 334-7400
Raleigh *(G-10387)*

Pratt Industries Inc.............................. B 704 878-6615
Statesville *(G-11752)*

Stronghaven Incorporated.................... D 770 739-6080
Matthews *(G-8151)*

Sumter Packaging Corporation............ G 704 873-0583
Statesville *(G-11783)*

Sun & Surf Containers Inc................... G 910 754-9600
Shallotte *(G-11306)*

Sustainable Corrugated LLC................ D 828 608-0990
Morganton *(G-8902)*

Westrock - Southern Cont LLC............. E 704 662-8496
Mooresville *(G-8797)*

Westrock Company................................ F 470 484-1183
Claremont *(G-3124)*

Westrock Company................................ F 828 248-4815
Forest City *(G-4801)*

Westrock Converting LLC...................... B 828 245-9871
Forest City *(G-4802)*

Westrock Converting LLC...................... F 336 661-1700
Winston Salem *(G-13392)*

Westrock Paper and Packg LLC........... B 919 463-3100
Morrisville *(G-9090)*

Westrock Rkt LLC................................. E 828 655-1303
Marion *(G-8072)*

Westrock Rkt LLC................................. D 704 662-8494
Mooresville *(G-8798)*

Westrock Rkt LLC................................. D 336 661-1700
Winston Salem *(G-13393)*

Weyerhaeuser Company....................... G 253 924-2345
Charlotte *(G-3015)*

Wilmington Box Company..................... E 910 259-0402
Burgaw *(G-1039)*

Wrkco Inc... E 336 956-6000
Lexington *(G-7758)*

Wrkco Inc... E 828 287-9430
Rutherfordton *(G-11003)*

BOXES: Junction, Electric

Austin Company of Greensboro............ C 336 468-2851
Yadkinville *(G-13436)*

BOXES: Paperboard, Folding

A Klein & Co Inc................................... C 828 459-9261
Claremont *(G-3086)*

Caraustar Brlngton Rgid Box In........... G 336 226-1616
Burlington *(G-1059)*

Caraustar Cstm Packg Group Inc......... C 336 498-2631
Randleman *(G-10636)*

Container Systems Incorporated.......... D 919 496-6133
Franklinton *(G-4847)*

Graphic Packaging Intl LLC.................. C 704 588-1750
Pineville *(G-9730)*

Graphic Packaging Intl LLC.................. D 336 744-1222
Winston Salem *(G-13183)*

Kme Consolidated Inc.......................... E 704 847-9888
Matthews *(G-8124)*

Max Solutions Inc................................ E 215 458-7050
Concord *(G-3400)*

Pactiv LLC.. G 910 944-1800
Aberdeen *(G-18)*

Snyder Packaging Inc........................... D 704 786-3111
Concord *(G-3441)*

Specialized Packaging Radisson LLC.... D 336 574-1513
Greensboro *(G-5829)*

Thomco Inc... G 336 292-3300
Greensboro *(G-5863)*

Westrock Rkt LLC................................. D 828 459-8006
Claremont *(G-3125)*

Westrock Rkt LLC................................. C 828 464-5560
Conover *(G-3574)*

Westrock Rkt LLC................................. B 770 448-2193
Marion *(G-8073)*

BOXES: Paperboard, Set-Up

A Klein & Co Inc................................... C 828 459-9261
Claremont *(G-3086)*

Caraustar Cstm Packg Group Inc......... C 336 498-2631
Randleman *(G-10636)*

Caraustar Industries Inc....................... F 336 498-2631
Randleman *(G-10637)*

Eastcoast Packaging Inc....................... E 919 562-6060
Middlesex *(G-8274)*

Transylvnia Vcational Svcs Inc............. D 828 884-1548
Fletcher *(G-4773)*

Transylvnia Vcational Svcs Inc............. C 828 884-3195
Brevard *(G-983)*

Westrock Rkt LLC................................. D 828 459-8006
Claremont *(G-3125)*

Westrock Rkt LLC................................. D 704 662-8494
Mooresville *(G-8798)*

BOXES: Plastic

Amesbury Group Inc............................. D 704 978-2883
Statesville *(G-11655)*

PRODUCT

BOXES: Wooden

Carolina Crate & Pallet Inc...................... E 910 245-4001
Vass (G-12227)

BRAKES & BRAKE PARTS

Ceco Friction Products Inc..................... F 704 857-1156
Landis (G-7473)

Continental Auto Systems Inc............... B 828 584-4500
Morganton (G-8859)

Haldex Inc.. C 828 652-9308
Marion (G-8042)

Indian Head Industries Inc.................. D 704 547-7411
Murphy (G-9290)

Indian Head Industries Inc.................. E 704 547-7411
Charlotte (G-2321)

Mann+hmmel Fltrtion Tech Group......... E 704 869-3300
Gastonia (G-5082)

BRAKES: Metal Forming

Delta Phoenix Inc................................ E 336 621-3960
Greensboro (G-5493)

BRASS & BRONZE PRDTS: Die-casted

Carolina Foundry Inc............................ G 704 376-3145
Charlotte (G-1847)

BRAZING: Metal

Zion Industries Inc.............................. E 828 397-2701
Hildebran (G-6856)

BRICK, STONE & RELATED PRDTS WHOLESALERS

Custom Brick Company Inc.................... E 919 832-2804
Raleigh (G-10028)

Design Specialties Inc........................ G 919 772-6955
Raleigh (G-10042)

General Shale Brick Inc....................... E 919 775-2121
Raleigh (G-10127)

General Shale Brick Inc....................... G 910 452-3498
Wilmington (G-12786)

J&R SERvices/J&r Lumber Co............... G 956 778-7005
Wilmington (G-12821)

Sid Jenkins Inc................................... G 336 632-0707
Greensboro (G-5811)

Spake Concrete Products Inc................ F 704 482-2881
Shelby (G-11382)

BRICKS & BLOCKS: Structural

Forterra Brick LLC............................... C 704 341-8750
Charlotte (G-2175)

General Shale Brick Inc....................... F 704 937-7431
Grover (G-6043)

BRICKS : Paving, Clay

Demilo Bros NC LLC............................ G 704 771-0762
Waxhaw (G-12428)

BRICKS: Clay

Dudley Inc... G 704 636-8850
Salisbury (G-11045)

General Shale Brick Inc....................... E 919 775-2121
Moncure (G-8405)

General Shale Brick Inc....................... G 910 452-3498
Wilmington (G-12786)

J L Anderson Co Inc............................ G 704 289-9599
Monroe (G-8507)

Meridian Brick LLC.............................. D 704 636-0131
Salisbury (G-11093)

Nash Brick Company........................... F 252 443-4965
Enfield (G-4485)

Statesville Brick Company.................... D 704 872-4123
Statesville (G-11777)

BROADCASTING & COMMS EQPT: Antennas, Transmitting/Comms

CPI Satcom & Antenna Tech Inc............. C 704 462-7330
Conover (G-3508)

Lba Group Inc..................................... E 252 329-9243
Greenville (G-5999)

Lba Technology Inc.............................. E 252 757-0279
Greenville (G-6000)

Ni4l Antennas and Elec LLC................. G 828 738-6445
Moravian Falls (G-8810)

Qualia Networks Inc............................ G 805 637-2083
Raleigh (G-10413)

Rf Das Systems Inc............................. G 980 279-2388
Charlotte (G-2722)

BROADCASTING & COMMS EQPT: Trnsmttng TV Antennas/Grndng Eqpt

Raven Antenna Systems Inc.................. C 919 934-9711
Smithfield (G-11461)

BROADCASTING & COMMUNICATIONS EQPT: Cellular Radio Telephone

Serra Wireless Inc.............................. G 980 318-0873
Charlotte (G-2789)

BROADCASTING & COMMUNICATIONS EQPT: Studio Eqpt, Radio & TV

Audio Advice LLC................................ D 919 881-2005
Raleigh (G-9923)

BROADCASTING STATIONS, RADIO: News

Wtvd Television LLC............................. C 919 683-1111
Durham (G-4313)

BROKERS' SVCS

S P Co Inc... G 919 848-3599
Raleigh (G-10453)

BROKERS: Food

Alta Foods llc..................................... D 919 734-0233
Goldsboro (G-5197)

La Tortilleria LLC................................. C 336 773-0010
Winston Salem (G-13229)

Value Clothing Inc.............................. D 704 638-6111
Salisbury (G-11132)

BROKERS: Printing

Creative Printers & Brks Inc.................. G 828 321-4663
Andrews (G-106)

Fast Pro Media LLC............................. G 704 799-8040
Cornelius (G-3599)

Gilmore Globl Lgstics Svcs Inc............. D 919 277-2700
Morrisville (G-8982)

Mjt Us Inc.. G 704 826-7828
Charlotte (G-2510)

Randall Printing Inc............................ G 336 272-3333
Greensboro (G-5781)

BRONZE FOUNDRY, NEC

Saueressig North America Inc............... E 336 395-6200
Burlington (G-1154)

BROOMS

Newell Novelty Co Inc......................... G 336 597-2246
Roxboro (G-10931)

BROOMS & BRUSHES

Carolina Brush Company...................... E 704 867-0286
Gastonia (G-5011)

Quickie Manufacturing Corp.................. C 910 737-6500
Lumberton (G-7966)

Shur Line Inc..................................... E 317 442-8850
Mooresville (G-8769)

BROOMS & BRUSHES: Household Or Indl

Carolina Brush Mfg Co......................... E 704 867-0286
Gastonia (G-5012)

Zibra LLC... G 704 271-4503
Mooresville (G-8806)

BROOMS & BRUSHES: Paint Rollers

P&A Indstrial Fabrications LLC............... E 336 322-1766
Roxboro (G-10938)

BROOMS & BRUSHES: Street Sweeping, Hand Or Machine

Tarheel Pavement Clg Svcs Inc............. E 704 895-8015
Cornelius (G-3627)

BUCKETS: Plastic

Rubbermaid Incorporated..................... A 704 987-4339
Huntersville (G-7046)

Rubbermaid Incorporated..................... A 888 859-8294
Huntersville (G-7047)

BUCKLES & PARTS

Ideal Fastener Corporation................... C 919 693-3115
Oxford (G-9618)

BUILDING & STRUCTURAL WOOD MEMBERS

C & C Chipping Inc.............................. G 252 249-1617
Grantsboro (G-5330)

Capitol Funds Inc................................ F 910 439-5275
Mount Gilead (G-9198)

Capitol Funds Inc................................ E 704 487-8547
Shelby (G-11316)

Idaho Timber NC LLC.......................... E 252 430-0030
Henderson (G-6161)

Nvr Inc.. D 704 484-7170
Kings Mountain (G-7374)

Rafters and Walls LLC......................... E 980 404-0209
Shelby (G-11372)

Smokey Mountain Lumber Inc............... G 828 298-3958
Asheville (G-602)

Universal Forest Products Inc................ F 252 338-0319
Elizabeth City (G-4416)

BUILDING CLEANING & MAINTENANCE SVCS

A & B Chem-Dry.................................. F 919 878-0288
Raleigh (G-9859)

BUILDING COMPONENTS: Structural Steel

Asheville Maintenance and C................ E 828 687-8110
Arden (G-254)

Bet-Mac Wilson Steel Inc..................... G 919 528-1540
Creedmoor (G-3641)

Blacksand Metal Works LLC.................. F 703 489-8282
Fayetteville (G-4558)

C Tek Lean Solutions Inc...................... E 704 895-0090
Mooresville (G-8625)

H T Wade Enterprises Inc..................... F 336 375-8900
Browns Summit (G-997)

Hercules Steel Company Inc.................. E 910 488-5110
Fayetteville (G-4611)

Industrial Mtal Pdts Abrdeen I.............. F 910 944-8110
Aberdeen (G-7)

Maco Inc.. E 704 434-6800
Shelby (G-11357)

McCombs Steel Company Inc............... E 704 873-7563
Statesville (G-11730)

McCune Technology Inc....................... G 910 424-2978
Fayetteville (G-4638)

North State Steel Inc......................... F 919 496-2506
Louisburg (G-7920)

Nucor Corporation............................. C 704 366-7000
Charlotte (G-2586)

Peak Steel LLC................................. F 919 362-5955
Apex (G-185)

Sanford Steel Corporation.................... F 919 898-4799
Goldston (G-5258)

Southeastern Steel Cnstr Inc................ F 910 346-4462
Jacksonville (G-7150)

Specialty Manufacturing Inc................. D 704 247-9300
Charlotte (G-2841)

Steel Specialty Co Belmont Inc............. E 704 825-4745
Belmont (G-768)

Steelfab Inc..................................... B 704 394-5376
Charlotte (G-2864)

Structural Steel Products Corp.............. D 919 359-2811
Clayton (G-3171)

BUILDING ITEM REPAIR SVCS, MISCELLANEOUS

Western Crlina Tl Mold Corp In.............. F 828 890-4448
Mills River (G-8324)

BUILDING MAINTENANCE SVCS, EXC REPAIRS

Asheville Maintenance and C................ E 828 687-8110
Arden (G-254)

BUILDING PRDTS & MATERIALS DEALERS

Authentic Iron LLC............................ G 910 648-6989
Bladenboro (G-873)

Barber Furniture & Supply................... F 704 278-9367
Cleveland (G-3209)

Bfs Asset Holdings LLC...................... B 303 784-4288
Raleigh (G-9941)

Builders Firstsource Inc...................... F 336 884-5454
Greensboro (G-5409)

Builders Frstsrce - Rleigh LLC............. D 919 363-4956
Apex (G-147)

C & R Building Supply Inc.................. G 910 567-6293
Autryville (G-647)

Capitol City Lumber Company.............. F 919 832-6492
Raleigh (G-9970)

E W Godwin S Sons Inc..................... E 910 762-7747
Wilmington (G-12769)

GLG Corporation............................... F 336 784-0396
Winston Salem (G-13178)

Goodman Millwork Inc........................ F 704 633-2421
Salisbury (G-11058)

Interrs-Exteriors Asheboro Inc.............. G 336 629-2148
Asheboro (G-367)

Jak Moulding & Supply Inc.................. F 252 753-5546
Walstonburg (G-12332)

M O Deviney Lumber Co Inc................ G 704 538-9071
Casar (G-1489)

Robbinsville Cstm Molding Inc.............. F 828 479-2317
Robbinsville (G-10761)

Salt Wood Products Inc....................... G 252 830-8875
Greenville (G-6020)

Selectbuild Construction Inc................. F 208 331-4300
Raleigh (G-10467)

Sipe Lumber Company Inc.................... E 828 632-4679
Taylorsville (G-11978)

Smith Companies Lexington Inc............. G 336 249-4941
Lexington (G-7742)

Sorrells Cabinet Co Inc....................... G 919 639-4320
Lillington (G-7803)

Spake Concrete Products Inc................ F 704 482-2881
Shelby (G-11382)

T E Johnson Lumber Co Inc................. G 919 963-2233
Four Oaks (G-4817)

Thomas Concrete SC Inc..................... G 704 868-4545
Gastonia (G-5154)

Yadkin Lumber Company Inc................ G 336 679-2432
Yadkinville (G-13459)

BUILDING PRDTS: Concrete

Greystone Concrete Pdts Inc................ E 252 438-5144
Henderson (G-6157)

BUILDING PRDTS: Stone

Carolina North Granite Corp.................. D 336 719-2600
Mount Airy (G-9109)

BUILDINGS & COMPONENTS: Prefabricated Metal

American Carports Structures................ G 336 710-1091
Mount Airy (G-9098)

Amt/Bcu Inc..................................... E 336 622-6200
Liberty (G-7761)

Bluescope Buildings N Amer Inc............ G 336 996-4801
Greensboro (G-5394)

Carport Central Inc............................ E 336 673-6020
Mount Airy (G-9111)

Central States Mfg Inc........................ C 336 719-3280
Mount Airy (G-9113)

CF Steel LLC................................... G 704 516-1750
Midland (G-8283)

E A Duncan Cnstr Co Inc.................... G 910 653-3535
Tabor City (G-11910)

Friedrich Metal Pdts Co Inc.................. E 336 375-3067
Browns Summit (G-993)

Go Ask Erin LLC............................... G 336 747-3777
Roxboro (G-10927)

Heritage Steel LLC............................ F 704 431-4097
Salisbury (G-11064)

J&J Outdoor Accessories..................... G 910 742-1969
Delco (G-3736)

Mast Woodworks............................... F 336 468-1194
Hamptonville (G-6090)

McGee Corporation........................... D 704 882-1500
Matthews (G-8131)

Millennium Buildings Inc...................... G 866 216-8499
Dobson (G-3823)

Millennium Mfg Structures LLC.............. G 828 265-3737
Boone (G-934)

Milligan House Movers Inc................... G 910 653-2272
Tabor City (G-11913)

Morton Buildings Inc.......................... G 252 291-1300
Wilson (G-13007)

Nash Building Systems Inc................... E 252 823-1905
Tarboro (G-11938)

Neals Carpentry & Cnstr..................... G 910 346-6154
Jacksonville (G-7135)

Nucor Corporation............................. C 336 481-7924
Lexington (G-7725)

OSteel Buildings Inc.......................... F 704 824-6061
Gastonia (G-5113)

Pine View Buildings LLC..................... D 704 876-1501
Statesville (G-11746)

T-N-T Carports Inc............................ G 336 789-3818
Mount Airy (G-9184)

Triton Industries LLC.......................... F 336 816-3794
Mount Airy (G-9190)

Turner Equipment Company Inc............. E 919 734-8328
Goldsboro (G-5250)

Twin Carports LLC............................. G 336 790-8284
East Bend (G-4327)

Viking Steel Structures LLC.................. G 877 623-7549
Boonville (G-959)

BUILDINGS: Mobile, For Commercial Use

Conway Entps Carteret Cnty LLC.......... G 252 504-3518
Beaufort (G-724)

BUILDINGS: Portable

Alaska Structures Inc......................... D 910 323-0562
Fayetteville (G-4548)

Betco Inc.. D 704 872-2999
Statesville (G-11670)

Boxman Studios LLC.......................... G 704 333-3733
Mount Holly (G-9219)

Camelot Rturn Intrmdate Hldngs............ D 866 419-0042
Cary (G-1320)

Classic Steel Buildings Inc.................. G 252 465-4184
Sunbury (G-11846)

Cornerstone Bldg Brands Inc................ B 281 897-7788
Cary (G-1336)

Eagle Carports Inc............................ E 800 579-8589
Mount Airy (G-9117)

Harvest Homes and Handi Houses......... G 704 637-3878
Salisbury (G-11061)

Harvest Homes and Handi Houses......... G 336 243-2382
Lexington (G-7696)

Heritage Building Company LLC............ G 704 431-4494
Statesville (G-11708)

Mayse Manufacturing Co Inc................ G 828 245-1891
Forest City (G-4793)

Nci Group Inc................................... B 281 897-7788
Cary (G-1405)

Robertson-Ceco II Corporation.............. C 281 897-7788
Cary (G-1439)

Rogers Manufacturing Company............ G 910 259-9898
Burgaw (G-1030)

Simonton Windows & Doors Inc............ F 919 677-3938
Cary (G-1456)

Sunshine Mnfctred Strctres Inc.............. G 704 279-6600
Rockwell (G-10802)

US Chemical Storage LLC.................... E 828 264-6032
Wilkesboro (G-12661)

Vinyl Structures LLC.......................... G 336 468-4311
Hamptonville (G-6094)

BUILDINGS: Prefabricated, Metal

Coastal Machine & Welding Inc............. G 910 754-6476
Shallotte (G-11302)

Leonard Alum Utlity Bldngs Inc............. G 336 226-9410
Burlington (G-1119)

Leonard Alum Utlity Bldngs Inc............. G 919 872-4442
Raleigh (G-10254)

Leonard Alum Utlity Bldngs Inc............. G 910 392-4921
Wilmington (G-12834)

Leonard Alum Utlity Bldngs Inc............. D 336 789-5018
Mount Airy (G-9146)

Nci Group Inc................................... G 919 926-4800
Raleigh (G-10328)

Nucor Corporation............................. C 704 366-7000
Charlotte (G-2586)

BUILDINGS: Prefabricated, Wood

Deltec Homes Inc.............................. E 828 253-0483
Asheville (G-486)

PRODUCT

Johnston County Industries Inc.............. C 919 743-8700
   Selma *(G-11289)*

Outlaw Step Co.................................. G 252 568-4384
   Deep Run *(G-3733)*

Quality Housing Corporation................. F 336 274-2622
   Greensboro *(G-5778)*

Tuff Shed Inc.................................... G 919 413-2494
   Morrisville *(G-9081)*

Ufp New London LLC........................... F 704 463-1400
   New London *(G-9423)*

Wood Right Lumber Company............... G 910 576-4642
   Troy *(G-12171)*

BULLETPROOF VESTS

Arma Co LLC..................................... G 717 295-6805
   Wilmington *(G-12709)*

Greene Mountain Outdoors LLC............ F 336 670-2186
   North Wilkesboro *(G-9532)*

Premier Body Armor LLC...................... F 704 750-3118
   Gastonia *(G-5127)*

BURIAL VAULTS: Concrete Or Precast Terrazzo

Arnold-Wilbert Corporation.................. D 919 735-5008
   Goldsboro *(G-5200)*

Asheville Vault Service Inc.................. E 828 665-6799
   Candler *(G-1218)*

Best Workers Company........................ G 336 665-0076
   Riegelwood *(G-10723)*

Bryant Grant Mutual Burial Asn.............. G 828 524-2411
   Franklin *(G-4819)*

Carolina Cemetery Park Corp................ G 704 528-5543
   Troutman *(G-12132)*

Eastern Carolina Vault Co Inc.............. G 252 243-5614
   Wilson *(G-12986)*

Hairfield Wilbert Burial Vlt................. G 828 437-4319
   Morganton *(G-8870)*

Imperial Vault Company........................ F 336 983-6343
   King *(G-7328)*

Sentry Vault Service Inc...................... G 252 243-2241
   Elm City *(G-4467)*

Wilbert Burial Vault Company............... G 910 739-7276
   Lumberton *(G-7976)*

Wilbert Funeral Services Inc................ E 800 828-5879
   Greensboro *(G-5919)*

Wilbert Yates Vault Co Inc................... F 704 399-8453
   Charlotte *(G-3020)*

Wilmington Mortuary Svc Inc................ F 910 791-9099
   Wilmington *(G-12951)*

BURNERS: Gas, Indl

Flynn Burner Corporation..................... E 704 660-1500
   Mooresville *(G-8666)*

BUS BARS: Electrical

M & M Electric Service Inc.................. E 704 867-0221
   Gastonia *(G-5081)*

BUSHINGS & BEARINGS

ABB Motors and Mechanical Inc............. C 828 645-1706
   Weaverville *(G-12481)*

CSC Bearing North America Inc............. E 734 456-6206
   Lincolnton *(G-7826)*

BUSINESS ACTIVITIES: Non-Commercial Site

760 Craft Works LLC........................... F 704 274-5216
   Huntersville *(G-6962)*

Abercrombie Textiles Inc..................... G 704 487-0935
   Shelby *(G-11308)*

Allfuel Hst Inc.................................. F 919 868-9410
   Hampstead *(G-6066)*

Arisaka LLC...................................... F 919 601-5625
   Apex *(G-139)*

Bloom Ai Inc..................................... G 704 620-2886
   Cary *(G-1309)*

C&A Hockaday Transport LLC................ G 252 676-5956
   Roanoke Rapids *(G-10734)*

Charlies Heating & Cooling LLC............ G 336 260-1973
   Snow Camp *(G-11473)*

Classy Sassy 5 Jewels Boutique............ G 252 481-8144
   Greenville *(G-5954)*

Council Trnsp & Logistics LLC.............. G 910 322-7588
   Fayetteville *(G-4579)*

Covington Barcoding Inc...................... G 336 996-5759
   Kernersville *(G-7260)*

Creative Brewing Company LLC............ G 919 297-8182
   Smithfield *(G-11441)*

Crump Group USA Inc.......................... C 936 465-5870
   Nashville *(G-9317)*

DB CUSTOM CRAFTS LLC....................... F 336 867-4107
   Winston Salem *(G-13140)*

Dg Matrix Inc.................................... G 724 877-7773
   Cary *(G-1349)*

Drs Transportation Inc........................ G 919 215-2770
   Raleigh *(G-10060)*

Eatclub Inc....................................... G 609 578-7942
   Chapel Hill *(G-1542)*

Educatrx Inc..................................... G 980 328-0013
   Monroe *(G-8481)*

Envirnmntal Cmfort Sltions Inc............. E 980 272-7327
   Kannapolis *(G-7208)*

Every Day Carry LLc........................... F 203 231-0256
   Winnabow *(G-13065)*

Extensive Builders LLC....................... G 980 621-3793
   Salisbury *(G-11050)*

Exteriors Inc Ltd.............................. G 919 325-2251
   Spring Lake *(G-11561)*

Franks Millwright Services.................. G 336 248-6692
   Lexington *(G-7689)*

Fresh Point LLC................................ G 919 895-0790
   Holly Springs *(G-6902)*

Frostie Bottom Tree Stand LLC............ G 828 466-1708
   Claremont *(G-3113)*

Galaxy Pressure Washing Inc................ G 888 299-3129
   Pineville *(G-9729)*

Galvix Inc....................................... G 925 434-6243
   Cary *(G-1363)*

Gentrys Cabnt Doors........................... G 336 957-8787
   Roaring River *(G-10749)*

Georges Sauces LLC............................ G 252 459-3084
   Nashville *(G-9320)*

Go For Green Fleet Svcs LLC................ G 803 306-3683
   Charlotte *(G-2221)*

Gracefully Broken LLC........................ G 980 474-0309
   Gastonia *(G-5055)*

Hema Online Indian Btq LLC................ G 919 771-4374
   Apex *(G-164)*

High Five Enterprises Inc.................... G 828 279-5962
   Weaverville *(G-12492)*

Imperial Falcon Group Inc................... G 646 717-1128
   Charlotte *(G-2315)*

Implus Footcare LLC........................... B 800 446-7587
   Durham *(G-4073)*

IMR Holdings LLC.............................. G 980 287-8139
   Charlotte *(G-2318)*

Intelligent Apps LLC.......................... G 919 628-6256
   Raleigh *(G-10205)*

Intersport Group Inc.......................... G 814 968-3085
   Vilas *(G-12230)*

J &D Contractor Service Inc................ G 919 427-0218
   Angier *(G-122)*

J6 & Company LLC.............................. F 336 997-4497
   Winston Salem *(G-13214)*

Jenkins Services Group LLC................ G 704 881-3210
   Catawba *(G-1512)*

Jennifer Mowrer................................ G 336 714-6462
   Winston Salem *(G-13216)*

Jfl LLC.. G 919 440-3517
   Farmville *(G-4533)*

Justice Bearing LLC........................... G 800 355-2500
   Mooresville *(G-8701)*

Kaotic Parts LLC............................... G 919 766-6040
   Raleigh *(G-10229)*

Kenn M LLC...................................... G 678 755-6607
   Raleigh *(G-10233)*

Kindled Provisions LLC....................... F 919 542-0792
   Moncure *(G-8407)*

Klearoptics Inc................................. G 760 224-6770
   Lattimore *(G-7480)*

Livengood Innovations LLC.................. G 336 925-7604
   Linwood *(G-7879)*

Lucerno Dynamics LLC........................ G 317 294-1395
   Cary *(G-1398)*

Meridian Prfmce Systems Inc............... G 706 905-5637
   Charlotte *(G-2493)*

Mk Pro Logistics LLC.......................... G 980 420-8156
   Huntersville *(G-7015)*

Mountain Homes of Wnc LLC................ F 828 216-2546
   Weaverville *(G-12496)*

N3xt Inc.. G 704 905-2209
   Charlotte *(G-2539)*

Nafshi Enterprises LLC....................... G 910 986-9888
   Aberdeen *(G-17)*

NC Diesel Performance LLC.................. G 704 431-3257
   Salisbury *(G-11095)*

Ni4l Antennas and Elec LLC................ G 828 738-6445
   Moravian Falls *(G-8810)*

North American Trade LLC................... G 828 712-3004
   Fletcher *(G-4759)*

Northern Star Technologies Inc............ G 516 353-3333
   Indian Trail *(G-7092)*

Nucleus Radiopharma Inc..................... E 980 483-1766
   Davidson *(G-3715)*

Ocufii Inc.. G 804 874-4036
   Huntersville *(G-7026)*

Patrice Brent................................... G 980 999-7217
   Charlotte *(G-2615)*

PC Signs & Graphics LLC.................... G 919 661-5801
   Garner *(G-4951)*

Performance Parts Intl LLC.................. F 704 660-1084
   Mooresville *(G-8748)*

Phynix Pc Inc.................................... F 503 890-1444
   Middlesex *(G-8280)*

Power and Ctrl Solutions LLC.............. G 704 609-9623
   Charlotte *(G-2649)*

Prototech Manufacturing Inc................ F 508 646-8849
   Washington *(G-12410)*

Quadron Holdings Inc.......................... G 919 523-5376
   Raleigh *(G-10411)*

Random & Kind LLC............................ G 919 249-8809
   Durham *(G-4207)*

Rebecca Trickey................................ G 910 584-5549
   Raeford *(G-9850)*

Redtruc LLC..................................... G 704 968-7888
   Charlotte *(G-2700)*

Richmond County Gmrs Inc.................. G 910 461-0260
   Hamlet *(G-6062)*

Royal Textile Products Sw LLC............ G 602 276-4598
   Charlotte *(G-2735)*

Rucker Intrgrted Logistics LLC............ G 704 352-2018
   Charlotte *(G-2741)*

Scoggins Industrial Inc....................... F 252 977-9222
   Sharpsburg *(G-11307)*

Secured Shred.................................. G 443 288-6375
Raleigh *(G-10466)*

Serenity Home Services LLC.......... G 910 233-8733
Troutman *(G-12150)*

Sg-Clw Inc...................................... F 336 865-4980
Winston Salem *(G-13331)*

Sign Shop of The Triangle Inc........ G 919 363-3930
Apex *(G-194)*

Smissons Inc................................... G 660 537-3219
Clayton *(G-3169)*

Stephanie Baxter............................. G 803 203-8467
Lincolnton *(G-7857)*

Tawnico LLC................................... G 704 606-2345
Charlotte *(G-2900)*

Td Cloud Services........................... G 518 258-6788
Raleigh *(G-10535)*

The McQuackins Company LLC........ G 980 254-2309
Gastonia *(G-5153)*

Triangle Prcsion Dgnostics Inc....... G 919 345-0110
Durham *(G-4280)*

Triple Crown International LLC........ G 704 846-4983
Charlotte *(G-2946)*

Tryhard Infinity LLC........................ G 252 269-0985
New Bern *(G-9402)*

UGLy Essentials LLC....................... F 910 319-9945
Raleigh *(G-10572)*

Vote Owl LLC.................................. G 919 264-1796
Raleigh *(G-10596)*

Whatz Cookin LLC........................... G 336 353-0227
Mount Airy *(G-9193)*

WW&s Construction Inc.................. G 217 620-4042
Dallas *(G-3693)*

Z Collection LLC............................. G 919 247-1513
Zebulon *(G-13526)*

Zysense LLC................................... G 215 485-1955
Chapel Hill *(G-1599)*

BUSINESS FORMS WHOLESALERS

Austin Business Forms Inc.............. F 704 821-6165
Indian Trail *(G-7070)*

Consolidated Press Inc................... G 704 372-6785
Charlotte *(G-1975)*

Gbf Inc... D 336 665-0205
High Point *(G-6627)*

S Ruppe Inc.................................... G 828 287-4936
Rutherfordton *(G-10992)*

BUSINESS FORMS: Printed, Manifold

American Forms Mfg Inc.................. E 704 866-9139
Gastonia *(G-4991)*

Apperson Inc.................................. E 704 399-2571
Charlotte *(G-1685)*

Fain Enterprises Inc....................... G 336 724-0417
Winston Salem *(G-13163)*

Golf Associates Advertising Co....... E 828 252-6544
Asheville *(G-508)*

Holley Selinda................................ G 919 351-9466
Raleigh *(G-10171)*

Print Haus Inc................................ G 828 456-8622
Waynesville *(G-12469)*

R R Donnelley & Sons Company....... G 704 864-5717
Gastonia *(G-5131)*

Reynolds and Reynolds Company..... G 321 287-3939
Charlotte *(G-2721)*

S Ruppe Inc.................................... G 828 287-4936
Rutherfordton *(G-10992)*

Taylor Communications Inc............. F 336 841-7700
High Point *(G-6803)*

Taylor Communications Inc............. E 704 282-0989
Monroe *(G-8568)*

BUSINESS TRAINING SVCS

Training Industry Inc...................... D 919 653-4990
Raleigh *(G-10555)*

CABINETS & CASES: Show, Display & Storage, Exc Wood

Forbes Custom Cabinets LLC.......... E 919 362-4277
Apex *(G-156)*

Friedrich Metal Pdts Co Inc............ E 336 375-3067
Browns Summit *(G-993)*

CABINETS: Bathroom Vanities, Wood

Allen & Son S Cabinet Shop Inc....... G 919 963-2196
Four Oaks *(G-4807)*

American Woodmark Corporation...... F 540 665-9100
Stoneville *(G-11819)*

Designer Woodwork.......................... G 910 521-1252
Pembroke *(G-9658)*

Kitchen Cabinet Designers LLC........ C 919 833-6532
Raleigh *(G-10238)*

Mike Powell Inc............................... F 910 792-6152
Wilmington *(G-12854)*

Oyama Cabinet Inc.......................... G 828 327-2668
Conover *(G-3542)*

Riverview Cabinet & Supply Inc....... G 336 228-1486
Burlington *(G-1148)*

TS Woodworks & RAD Design Inc..... F 704 238-1015
Monroe *(G-8571)*

CABINETS: Entertainment

Distinctive Cabinets Inc.................. F 704 529-6234
Charlotte *(G-2053)*

Mountain Showcase Group Inc......... E 828 692-9494
Hendersonville *(G-6228)*

Quality Custom Woodworks Inc........ G 704 843-1584
Waxhaw *(G-12438)*

Quality Musical Systems Inc............ E 828 667-5719
Candler *(G-1231)*

Wood Technology Inc...................... E 828 464-8049
Conover *(G-3577)*

CABINETS: Entertainment Units, Household, Wood

Ocean Woodworking Inc.................. G 910 579-2233
Ocean Isle Beach *(G-9588)*

Philip Brady.................................... G 336 581-3999
Bennett *(G-782)*

CABINETS: Factory

Alligood Cabinet Shop..................... G 252 927-3201
Washington *(G-12372)*

AMG Casework LLC......................... F 919 462-9203
Morrisville *(G-8926)*

Contemporary Design Co LLC.......... F 704 375-6030
Gastonia *(G-5030)*

Drews Cabinets and Cases.............. G 919 796-3985
Selma *(G-11286)*

Tice Kitchens & Interiors LLC......... F 919 366-4117
Raleigh *(G-10549)*

Woodsmiths Company..................... G 406 626-3102
Lenoir *(G-7646)*

CABINETS: Kitchen, Metal

Conestoga Wood Spc Corp............... D 919 284-2258
Kenly *(G-7229)*

Greg Price...................................... G 847 778-4426
Hampstead *(G-6073)*

CABINETS: Kitchen, Wood

Advance Cabinetry Inc.................... F 828 676-3550
Fletcher *(G-4718)*

Alexanders Cbinets Countertops...... G 336 774-2966
Winston Salem *(G-13077)*

American Wood Reface of Triad....... G 336 345-2837
Kernersville *(G-7244)*

American Woodmark Corporation...... D 828 428-6300
Lincolnton *(G-7813)*

Artistic Kitchens & Baths LLC......... G 910 692-4000
Southern Pines *(G-11494)*

Ashleys Kit Bath Dsign Stdio L........ F 828 669-5281
Black Mountain *(G-860)*

Aspen Cabinetry Inc....................... G 828 466-0216
Conover *(G-3492)*

Atlantic Coast Cabinet Distrs.......... E 919 554-8165
Youngsville *(G-13462)*

Barber Furniture & Supply.............. F 704 278-9367
Cleveland *(G-3209)*

Bcac Holdings LLC.......................... G 910 754-5689
Supply *(G-11855)*

Bill Truitt Wood Works Inc.............. G 704 398-8499
Charlotte *(G-1782)*

Black Mountain Cnstr Group Inc...... F 704 243-5593
Waxhaw *(G-12424)*

Black Rock Granite & Cabinetry....... G 828 787-1100
Highlands *(G-6843)*

Blue Ridge Cab Connection LLC....... G 828 891-2281
Mills River *(G-8311)*

Brown Cabinet Co............................ G 704 933-2731
Kannapolis *(G-7205)*

Burlington Distributing Co............... G 336 292-1415
Greensboro *(G-5411)*

C & F Custom Cabinets Inc.............. E 910 424-7475
Hope Mills *(G-6923)*

Cabinet Creations Inc..................... G 919 542-3722
Moncure *(G-8401)*

Cabinet Door World LLC.................. F 877 929-2750
Hickory *(G-6279)*

Cabinet Makers Inc......................... G 704 876-2808
Statesville *(G-11674)*

Cabinet Shop Inc............................ G 252 726-6965
Morehead City *(G-8820)*

Cabinet Solutions Usa Inc............... E 828 358-2349
Hickory *(G-6280)*

Cabinet Transitions Inc................... G 336 382-7154
Greensboro *(G-5418)*

Cabinets and Things........................ G 828 652-1734
Union Mills *(G-12187)*

Cabinets Plus Inc............................ G 718 213-3300
Charlotte *(G-1828)*

Cabinetworks Group Mich LLC......... E 803 984-2285
Charlotte *(G-1829)*

Cabinetworks Group Mich LLC......... E 919 868-8174
Raleigh *(G-9964)*

Caldwell Cabinets NC LLC............... E 828 212-0000
Hudson *(G-6945)*

Cape Fear Cabinet Co Inc................ G 910 703-8760
Fayetteville *(G-4565)*

Cardinal Cabinetworks Inc............... G 919 829-3634
Raleigh *(G-9973)*

Carocraft Cabinets Inc.................... E 704 376-0022
Charlotte *(G-1843)*

Carolina Cab Specialist LLC............ G 919 818-4375
Cary *(G-1322)*

Carolina Cabinets of Cedar Pt......... G 252 393-6236
Swansboro *(G-11882)*

Carolina Custom Cabinetry.............. G 704 808-1225
Waxhaw *(G-12427)*

Carolina Custom Cabinets............... G 910 525-3096
Roseboro *(G-10911)*

Carolina Custom Cabinets Inc......... G 252 491-5475
Powells Point *(G-9820)*

Carolina Surfaces LLC............... G..... 910 874-1335 Elizabethtown *(G-4423)*	H Brothers Fine Wdwkg LLC.......... G.... 931 216-1955 Zebulon *(G-13511)*	Miters Touch Inc........................... G..... 828 963-4445 Banner Elk *(G-688)*
Carolnas Top Shelf Cstm Cbnets....... G.... 704 376-5844 Charlotte *(G-1862)*	Hans Krug.. F..... 704 370-0809 Charlotte *(G-2254)*	Morgans Cabinets Inc.................... F..... 704 485-8693 Oakboro *(G-9581)*
Casework Etc Inc........................ G..... 910 763-7119 Wilmington *(G-12735)*	Hargenrader Cstm Woodcraft LLC........ G.... 828 896-7182 Hickory *(G-6342)*	Mountain Cabinetry Closets LLC........... G.... 828 966-9000 Brevard *(G-977)*
Chesnick Corporation.................. F..... 919 231-2899 Raleigh *(G-9993)*	Heritage Design & Supply LLC........... E..... 919 453-1622 Morrisville *(G-8987)*	Mountain Showcase Group Inc........ E..... 828 692-9494 Hendersonville *(G-6228)*
Coastal Cabinetry Inc.................. G..... 910 367-8864 Shallotte *(G-11301)*	High Cntry Cbnets Bnner Elk In........... G.... 828 898-3435 Banner Elk *(G-686)*	Murphy S Custom Cabinetry Inc........ G.... 828 891-3050 Hendersonville *(G-6229)*
Colonial Cabinets LLC................. G..... 910 579-2954 Calabash *(G-1209)*	Hollingswrth Cbnets Intrors LL........... F..... 910 251-1490 Castle Hayne *(G-1502)*	Myricks Cabinet Shop Inc............. G..... 919 266-3720 Knightdale *(G-7453)*
Comm-Kab Inc............................. F..... 336 873-8787 Asheboro *(G-340)*	Honeycutt Custom Cabinets Inc........... E..... 910 567-6766 Autryville *(G-648)*	Noble Bros Cabinets Mllwk LLC........ G.... 252 335-1213 Elizabeth City *(G-4399)*
Commercial Property LLC............. E..... 336 818-1078 North Wilkesboro *(G-9525)*	Idx Impressions LLC.................... C..... 703 550-6902 Washington *(G-12393)*	Noble Bros Cabinets Mllwk LLC........ G.... 252 482-9100 Edenton *(G-4370)*
Concord Custom Cabinets............. G..... 704 773-0081 Concord *(G-3341)*	In Style Kitchen Cabinetry............. G..... 336 769-9605 Winston Salem *(G-13204)*	Noles Cabinets Inc...................... G..... 919 552-4257 Fuquay Varina *(G-4892)*
Conestoga Wood Spc Corp............ D..... 919 284-2258 Kenly *(G-7229)*	Innovative Custom Cabinets Inc........... G.... 813 748-0655 Kannapolis *(G-7212)*	Norcraft Companies LP.................. C..... 336 622-4281 Liberty *(G-7774)*
Corilam Fabricating Co................. E..... 336 993-2371 Kernersville *(G-7259)*	Innovative Kitchens Baths Inc........... G.... 336 279-1188 Greensboro *(G-5619)*	Normac Kitchens Inc..................... F..... 704 485-1911 Oakboro *(G-9582)*
Cornerstone Kitchens Inc............. G..... 919 510-4200 Raleigh *(G-10017)*	Island Wood Crafts Ltd................. G..... 252 473-5363 Wanchese *(G-12344)*	P R Sparks Enterprises Inc........... G..... 336 272-7200 Greensboro *(G-5728)*
Cotner Cabinet........................... G..... 336 672-1560 Sophia *(G-11486)*	Kay & Sons Woodworks Inc............. F..... 919 556-1060 Wake Forest *(G-12284)*	Pb & J Industries Inc.................... F..... 919 661-2738 Raleigh *(G-10363)*
Covenantmade LLC..................... G..... 336 434-4725 Archdale *(G-218)*	Kc Stone Enterprise Inc................. G..... 704 907-1361 Indian Trail *(G-7085)*	Precision Cabinets Inc.................. G..... 828 262-5080 Boone *(G-938)*
Creations Cabinetry Design LLC........... G.... 919 865-5979 Raleigh *(G-10019)*	Kitchen Masters Charlotte LLC........... G.... 704 375-3320 Salisbury *(G-11080)*	Prestige Millwork Inc................... G..... 910 428-2360 Star *(G-11633)*
Creative Woodcrafters Inc............. G..... 828 252-9663 Leicester *(G-7522)*	Kitchen Tune-Up.......................... G..... 833 259-1838 Matthews *(G-8123)*	Red House Cabinets LLC............... G..... 919 201-2101 Raleigh *(G-10437)*
Custom Cabinet Works.................. G..... 828 396-6348 Granite Falls *(G-5301)*	Kkb Biltmore Inc......................... G..... 828 274-6711 Asheville *(G-531)*	Robbinsville Cstm Molding Inc........... F..... 828 479-2317 Robbinsville *(G-10761)*
Custom Cabinets By Livengood........... G.... 704 279-3031 Salisbury *(G-11040)*	Kohnle Cabinetry........................ G..... 828 640-2498 Hickory *(G-6381)*	Rowan Custom Cabinets Inc........... G..... 704 855-4778 China Grove *(G-3079)*
Custom Marble Corporation............. G.... 910 215-0679 Pinehurst *(G-9690)*	Krieger Cabinets Dewayne.............. G..... 704 630-0609 Salisbury *(G-11082)*	Rugby Acquisition LLC.................. D..... 336 993-8686 Kernersville *(G-7297)*
Custom Surfaces Corporation........... G.... 252 638-3800 New Bern *(G-9361)*	Laborie Sons Cstm Wodworks LLC........ G.... 910 769-2524 Castle Hayne *(G-1504)*	S Banner Cabinets Incorporated........... E..... 828 733-2031 Newland *(G-9434)*
Cut Above Construction................. G.... 828 758-8557 Lenoir *(G-7598)*	Larry S Cabinet Shop Inc............... G..... 252 442-4330 Rocky Mount *(G-10848)*	S Eudy Cabinet Shop Inc............... G..... 704 888-4454 Stanfield *(G-11608)*
Cynthia Saar............................. G..... 910 480-2523 Stedman *(G-11806)*	Luxemark Company...................... G..... 919 863-0101 Raleigh *(G-10262)*	S Zaytoun Custom Cabinets Inc........... G.... 252 638-8390 New Bern *(G-9394)*
D & L Cabinets Inc...................... F..... 336 376-6009 Graham *(G-5267)*	Markraft Cabinets Direct Sales........... G.... 910 762-1986 Wilmington *(G-12845)*	Seema Intl Custom Cabinetry........... G.... 917 703-0820 Wake Forest *(G-12299)*
Davis Cabinet Co Wilson Inc........... G.... 252 291-9052 Sims *(G-11429)*	Marsh Furniture Company.............. G..... 336 229-5122 Graham *(G-5277)*	Selpro LLC................................. G..... 336 513-0550 Greensboro *(G-5806)*
Decima Corporation LLC................. E.... 734 516-1535 Charlotte *(G-2025)*	Marsh Furniture Company.............. F..... 336 273-8196 Greensboro *(G-5676)*	Signature Custom Cabinets LLC........... G.... 704 753-4874 Monroe *(G-8558)*
Distinctive Cabinets Inc................. F..... 704 529-6234 Charlotte *(G-2053)*	Marsh Furniture Company.............. F..... 336 884-7393 High Point *(G-6702)*	Sjr Incorporated......................... F..... 828 254-8966 Asheville *(G-601)*
Dublin Woodwork Shop.................. G.... 910 862-2289 Dublin *(G-3831)*	Marsh Furniture Company.............. B..... 336 884-7363 High Point *(G-6703)*	Smiths Custom Kitchen Inc............. G..... 828 652-9033 Marion *(G-8065)*
Duocraft Cabinets & Dist Co........... G.... 252 240-1476 Morehead City *(G-8830)*	Masterbrand Cabinets Inc.............. E..... 765 491-2385 Lexington *(G-7715)*	Sorrells Cabinet Co Inc................. G..... 919 639-4320 Lillington *(G-7803)*
Eastern Cabinet Company Inc........... G.... 252 237-5245 Wilson *(G-12985)*	Masterbrand Cabinets LLC............. D..... 252 523-4131 Kinston *(G-7422)*	Southern Cabinet Co Inc................. G.... 704 373-2299 Matthews *(G-8149)*
Eastern Cabinet Installers Inc........... G.... 336 774-2966 Winston Salem *(G-13153)*	McDowell County Millwork LLC........... G.... 828 682-6215 Marion *(G-8054)*	Southern Design Cabinetry LLC........... G.... 919 263-9414 Wake Forest *(G-12301)*
Eudys Cabinet Manufacturing........... F.... 704 888-4454 Stanfield *(G-11605)*	McLean Precision Cabinetry Inc........... G.... 910 327-9217 Sneads Ferry *(G-11472)*	Stallings Cabinets Inc.................... G.... 252 338-6747 Elizabeth City *(G-4410)*
Ferguson Cabinet Works................. G.... 828 433-8710 Morganton *(G-8865)*	MDN Cabinets Inc........................ G..... 919 662-1090 Garner *(G-4940)*	Sunhs Warehouse LLC................... G.... 919 908-1523 Durham *(G-4255)*
Firehouse Cabinets...................... G..... 704 689-5243 Belmont *(G-752)*	Metro Woodcrafter of Nc Inc........... E..... 704 394-9622 Charlotte *(G-2496)*	Sycamore Cabinetry Inc................. G.... 704 375-1617 Dallas *(G-3691)*
Gate City Kitchens LLC................. G..... 336 378-0870 Greensboro *(G-5549)*	Mid Carolina Cabinets Inc.............. G..... 704 358-9950 Matthews *(G-8134)*	Tarheel Wood Designs Inc.............. G.... 910 395-2226 Wilmington *(G-12937)*
Gentrys Cabnt Doors.................... G..... 336 957-8787 Roaring River *(G-10749)*	Mike S Custom Cabinets Inc........... G..... 252 224-5351 Pollocksville *(G-9818)*	Tarheel Woodcrafters Inc................. G.... 252 432-3035 Henderson *(G-6180)*
Goembel Inc.............................. F..... 919 303-0485 Apex *(G-159)*	Mint Hill Cabinet Shop Inc............. E..... 704 821-9373 Monroe *(G-8531)*	Thomas Lcklars Cbnets Lrnburg........... G.... 910 369-2094 Laurinburg *(G-7516)*

(G-0000) Company's Geographic Section entry number

Tice Kitchens & Interiors LLC............... F 919 366-4117
Raleigh *(G-10549)*

Tommy W Smith Inc................................ G 704 436-6616
Mount Pleasant *(G-9265)*

Tonys Cabinets.. G 910 592-2028
Clinton *(G-3250)*

Travis Alfrey Woodworking Inc............ G 910 639-3553
Aberdeen *(G-28)*

Triangle Cabinet Company..................... G 336 869-6401
High Point *(G-6811)*

Triangle Kitchen Supply........................ G 919 562-3888
Youngsville *(G-13494)*

True Cabinet LLC..................................... G 828 855-9200
Hickory *(G-6470)*

Tsquared Cabinets.................................. G 336 655-0208
Winston Salem *(G-13376)*

Twin City Custom Cabinets..................... G 336 773-7200
Winston Salem *(G-13377)*

US Precision Cabinetry LLC................... D 828 351-2020
Rutherfordton *(G-11002)*

Verona Cabinets & Surfaces LLC.......... G 704 755-5259
Charlotte *(G-2979)*

Vine & Branch Woodworks LLC............. G 704 663-0077
Mooresville *(G-8793)*

Walker Woodworking Inc........................ E 704 434-0823
Shelby *(G-11390)*

Watkins Cabinets LLC............................ G 704 634-1724
Matthews *(G-8157)*

Wilson Woodworks Inc............................ F 252 237-3179
Wilson *(G-13050)*

Windsors Cbnetry For Kit Baths............ G 336 275-0190
Greensboro *(G-5920)*

Winstons Woodworks............................. G 919 693-4120
Oxford *(G-9640)*

Wood Done Right Inc.............................. G 919 623-4557
Chapel Hill *(G-1595)*

Wood Technology Inc............................. E 828 464-8049
Conover *(G-3577)*

Woodmaster Custom Cabinets Inc......... F 919 554-3707
Youngsville *(G-13499)*

Woodmasters Woodworking Inc............. G 336 985-4000
King *(G-7341)*

Woodworking Unlimited........................ G 252 235-5285
Bailey *(G-674)*

Xylem Inc... G 919 772-4126
Garner *(G-4976)*

Yadkin Valley Cabinet Co Inc................. G 336 786-9860
Mount Airy *(G-9197)*

Your Cabinet Connection Inc................. G 919 641-2877
Morrisville *(G-9092)*

CABINETS: Office, Wood

3c Store Fixtures Inc............................. D 252 291-5181
Wilson *(G-12959)*

A R Byrd Company Inc........................... G 704 732-5675
Lincolnton *(G-7807)*

Appalachian Cabinet Inc........................ G 828 265-0830
Deep Gap *(G-3727)*

B&H Millwork and Fixtures Inc.............. E 336 431-0068
High Point *(G-6534)*

Boone Enterprises LLC.......................... G 910 859-8299
Leland *(G-7534)*

Custom Cabinets By Livengood............. G 704 279-3031
Salisbury *(G-11040)*

Element Designs Inc.............................. D 704 332-3114
Charlotte *(G-2096)*

M T N of Pinellas Inc............................. G 727 823-1650
Winston Salem *(G-13242)*

Ocean Woodworking Inc........................ G 910 579-2233
Ocean Isle Beach *(G-9588)*

Pridgen Woodwork Inc.......................... E 910 642-7175
Whiteville *(G-12592)*

Woodsmiths Company........................... G 406 626-3102
Lenoir *(G-7646)*

CABINETS: Show, Display, Etc, Wood, Exc Refrigerated

Ajs Dezigns Inc..................................... G 828 652-6304
Marion *(G-8030)*

Davis Cabinet Co Wilson Inc................. G 252 291-9052
Sims *(G-11429)*

Harris Wood Products Inc...................... G 704 550-5494
New London *(G-9418)*

Hollingswrth Cbnets Intrors LL............. F 910 251-1490
Castle Hayne *(G-1502)*

Rowland Woodworking Inc..................... E 336 887-0700
High Point *(G-6761)*

Washington Cabinet Company............... G 252 946-3457
Washington *(G-12420)*

CABLE & OTHER PAY TELEVISION DISTRIBUTION

M I Connection....................................... F 704 662-3255
Mooresville *(G-8717)*

CABLE TELEVISION

Cco Holdings LLC.................................. C 828 414-4238
Blowing Rock *(G-881)*

Cco Holdings LLC.................................. C 828 355-4149
Boone *(G-906)*

Cco Holdings LLC.................................. C 910 292-4083
Dunn *(G-3850)*

Cco Holdings LLC.................................. B 828 270-7016
Hickory *(G-6293)*

Cco Holdings LLC.................................. C 919 502-4007
Kenly *(G-7228)*

Cco Holdings LLC.................................. C 828 394-0635
Lenoir *(G-7592)*

Cco Holdings LLC.................................. C 704 308-3361
Lincolnton *(G-7820)*

Cco Holdings LLC.................................. C 828 528-4004
Newland *(G-9427)*

Cco Holdings LLC.................................. C 919 200-6260
Siler City *(G-11402)*

Cco Holdings LLC.................................. C 828 368-4161
Valdese *(G-12192)*

CABLE TELEVISION PRDTS

Edge Broadband Solutions LLC............. E 828 785-1420
Waynesville *(G-12457)*

CABLE: Coaxial

Commscope Technologies LLC.............. G 919 934-9711
Smithfield *(G-11440)*

Draka Communications Americas Inc.... B 828 459-8456
Claremont *(G-3108)*

CABLE: Fiber Optic

Arris Solutions LLC............................... A 678 473-2000
Claremont *(G-3088)*

Corning Incorporated............................ F 252 316-4500
Tarboro *(G-11924)*

Crww Specialty Composites Inc............. F 828 548-5002
Claremont *(G-3105)*

Emtelle USA Inc..................................... E 828 707-9970
Fletcher *(G-4733)*

Opticoncepts Inc................................... G 828 320-0138
Morganton *(G-8886)*

Sackner Products Inc............................ E 704 380-6204
Statesville *(G-11762)*

US Conec Ltd... G 828 323-8883
Hickory *(G-6481)*

US Conec Ltd... D 828 323-8883
Hickory *(G-6482)*

CABLE: Noninsulated

Coleman Cable LLC............................... D 828 389-8013
Hayesville *(G-6139)*

Voltage LLC... F 919 391-9405
Chapel Hill *(G-1592)*

CABLE: Ropes & Fiber

Jhrg Manufacturing LLC........................ G 252 478-4977
Spring Hope *(G-11556)*

Ls Cable & System USA Inc................... C 252 824-3553
Tarboro *(G-11932)*

Moon Audio.. G 919 649-5018
Cary *(G-1402)*

CABLE: Steel, Insulated Or Armored

Draka Elevator Products Inc.................. C 252 446-8113
Rocky Mount *(G-10831)*

CACAO BEAN PROCESSING

Beech Street Ventures LLC.................... E 919 755-5053
Raleigh *(G-9938)*

CAFES

Cabarrus Brewing Company LLC............ E 704 490-4487
Concord *(G-3326)*

Lovegrass Kitchen Inc........................... F 919 205-8426
Holly Springs *(G-6906)*

Sugar Creek Brewing Co LLC................ E 704 521-3333
Charlotte *(G-2878)*

CALCULATING & ACCOUNTING EQPT

Diebold Nixdorf Incorporated................ E 704 599-3100
Charlotte *(G-2044)*

One Source SEC & Sound Inc................ G 281 850-9487
Mooresville *(G-8739)*

CALIBRATING SVCS, NEC

Broadwind Indus Solutions LLC............ E 919 777-2907
Sanford *(G-11159)*

Cross Technologies Inc......................... E 800 327-7727
Greensboro *(G-5472)*

CAMPERS: Truck Mounted

Boondock S Manufacturing Inc.............. G 828 891-4242
Etowah *(G-4495)*

CAMSHAFTS

CAM Craft LLC....................................... G 828 681-5183
Arden *(G-259)*

CANDLE SHOPS

Wildflwers Btq of Blowing Rock............. G 828 295-9655
Blowing Rock *(G-882)*

CANDLES

Apollonias Candles Things LLC............. G 910 408-2508
Durham *(G-3896)*

Auralites Inc.. G 828 687-7990
Fletcher *(G-4722)*

Carolina Candle...................................... G 336 835-6020
Elkin *(G-4440)*

Cristal Dragon Candle Company............ G 336 997-4210
Sandy Ridge *(G-11142)*

D & T Soy Candles................................. G 704 320-2804
Polkton *(G-9814)*

Daisy Pink Co.. G 704 907-3526
Charlotte *(G-2016)*

David Oreck Candle............................... G 336 375-8411
Greensboro *(G-5487)*

PRODUCT

Ella B Candles LLC......................... E 980 339-8898
  Charlotte *(G-2101)*

Fragrant Passage Candle Co LP............. E 336 375-8411
  Greensboro *(G-5538)*

Love Knot Candles.......................... G 336 456-1619
  Greensboro *(G-5666)*

Luxuriously Natural Soaps LLC............. G 910 378-9064
  Jacksonville *(G-7130)*

Mvp Group International Inc................. E 336 527-2238
  Mount Airy *(G-9156)*

Mvp Group International Inc................. E 843 216-8380
  Elkin *(G-4449)*

Patrice Brent.............................. G 980 999-7217
  Charlotte *(G-2615)*

Paul Hoge Creations Inc.................... F 704 624-6860
  Marshville *(G-8091)*

Sincere Scents Co LLC...................... G 910 616-4697
  Southport *(G-11528)*

Tobacco Outlet Products LLC................ G 704 341-9388
  Charlotte *(G-2924)*

Waxhaw Candle Company LLC.................. G 980 245-2827
  Charlotte *(G-3008)*

White Tiger Btq & Candle Co................ G 919 610-7244
  Sanford *(G-11249)*

Wildflwers Btq of Blowing Rock............. G 828 295-9655
  Blowing Rock *(G-882)*

CANDLES: Wholesalers

Tobacco Outlet Products LLC................ G 704 341-9388
  Charlotte *(G-2924)*

CANDY & CONFECTIONS: Candy Bars, Including Chocolate Covered

French Broad Chocolates LLC................ G 828 252-4181
  Asheville *(G-502)*

CANDY & CONFECTIONS: Chocolate Candy, Exc Solid Chocolate

Carolina Chocolatiers Inc.................. G 828 652-4496
  Marion *(G-8038)*

Foiled Agin Choclat Coins LLC.............. G 919 342-4601
  Sanford *(G-11180)*

CANDY & CONFECTIONS: Licorice

Lucky Country USA LLC...................... E 828 428-8313
  Lincolnton *(G-7840)*

CANDY & CONFECTIONS: Nuts, Candy Covered

KLb Enterprises Incorporated............... F 336 605-0773
  Greensboro *(G-5650)*

CANDY & CONFECTIONS: Popcorn Balls/ Other Trtd Popcorn Prdts

Tastebuds LLC.............................. G 704 461-8755
  Belmont *(G-771)*

CANDY, NUT & CONFECTIONERY STORES: Candy

Beech Street Ventures LLC.................. E 919 755-5053
  Raleigh *(G-9938)*

Bilcat Inc................................. E 828 295-3088
  Blowing Rock *(G-880)*

Butterfields Candy LLC..................... G 252 459-2577
  Nashville *(G-9313)*

Chocolate Smiles Village LLC............... G 919 469-5282
  Cary *(G-1327)*

French Broad Chocolates LLC................ G 828 252-4181
  Asheville *(G-502)*

Secret Chocolatier LLC..................... G 704 323-8178
  Charlotte *(G-2781)*

Sugar Pops................................. G 704 799-0959
  Mooresville *(G-8782)*

CANDY: Chocolate From Cacao Beans

Chocolate Fetish LLC....................... G 828 258-2353
  Asheville *(G-475)*

Chocolate Smiles Village LLC............... G 919 469-5282
  Cary *(G-1327)*

CANDY: Soft

Morinaga America Foods Inc................. E 919 643-2439
  Mebane *(G-8252)*

CANNED SPECIALTIES

Ritas One Inc.............................. G 919 650-2415
  Cary *(G-1438)*

Stevens Foodservice........................ G 919 322-5470
  Raleigh *(G-10508)*

CANS & TUBES: Ammunition, Board Laminated With Metal Foil

C L Rabb Inc............................... E 704 865-0295
  Gastonia *(G-5010)*

Conitex Sonoco Usa Inc..................... C 704 864-5406
  Gastonia *(G-5028)*

Mm Clayton LLC............................. B 919 553-4113
  Clayton *(G-3160)*

CANS: Aluminum

Trivium Packaging USA Inc.................. B 336 785-8500
  Winston Salem *(G-13373)*

CANS: Metal

Container Products Corporation............. D 910 392-6100
  Wilmington *(G-12748)*

Fleetgenius of Nc Inc...................... C 828 726-3001
  Lenoir *(G-7607)*

Leisure Craft Holdings LLC................. D 828 693-8241
  Flat Rock *(G-4708)*

Leisure Craft Inc.......................... E 828 693-8241
  Flat Rock *(G-4709)*

Waste Container Services LLC............... G 910 257-4474
  Fayetteville *(G-4697)*

CANS: Tin

Tin Can Ventures LLC....................... G 919 732-9078
  Cedar Grove *(G-1518)*

Tin Cans LLC............................... G 910 322-2626
  Lillington *(G-7804)*

CANVAS PRDTS

A & J Canvas Inc........................... E 252 244-1509
  Vanceboro *(G-12213)*

Canvasmasters LLC.......................... G 828 369-0406
  Franklin *(G-4820)*

Cape Lookout Canvas & Customs.............. G 252 726-3751
  Morehead City *(G-8821)*

Cdv LLC.................................... F 919 674-3460
  Morrisville *(G-8953)*

Cross Canvas Company Inc................... E 828 252-0440
  Asheville *(G-480)*

DLM Sales Inc.............................. F 704 399-2776
  Charlotte *(G-2058)*

Dunn Manufacturing Corp.................... C 704 283-2147
  Monroe *(G-8479)*

Hatteras Hammocks Inc...................... C 252 758-0641
  Greenville *(G-5987)*

M & M Signs and Awnings Inc................ F 336 352-4300
  Mount Airy *(G-9151)*

OBrian Tarping Systems Inc................. F 252 291-6710
  Wilson *(G-13010)*

Prem Corp.................................. E 704 921-1799
  Charlotte *(G-2660)*

Sawyers Sign Service Inc................... F
  Mount Airy *(G-9175)*

WC&r Interests LLC......................... C 828 684-9848
  Fletcher *(G-4777)*

CAPACITORS & CONDENSERS

Nwl Inc.................................... E 252 747-5943
  Snow Hill *(G-11481)*

CAPACITORS: NEC

ABB Inc.................................... D 919 856-2360
  Raleigh *(G-9864)*

Hitachi Energy USA Inc..................... F 919 324-5403
  Raleigh *(G-10169)*

Hitachi Energy USA Inc..................... C 919 856-2360
  Raleigh *(G-10170)*

Kemet Electronics Corporation.............. E 864 963-6300
  Shelby *(G-11351)*

M2 Optics Inc.............................. G 919 342-5619
  Raleigh *(G-10264)*

Nwl Inc.................................... E 252 747-5943
  Snow Hill *(G-11481)*

Reuel Inc.................................. E 919 734-0460
  Goldsboro *(G-5240)*

United Chemi-Con Inc....................... B 336 384-6903
  Lansing *(G-7479)*

CAR WASH EQPT

Ferguson Companies......................... G
  Linwood *(G-7878)*

Majestic Xpress Handwash Inc............... G 919 440-7611
  Goldsboro *(G-5227)*

CARBIDES

Techmet Carbides Inc....................... D 828 624-0222
  Hickory *(G-6464)*

CARBON & GRAPHITE PRDTS, NEC

Asbury Graphite Mills...................... G 910 671-4141
  Lumberton *(G-7945)*

Debotech Inc............................... C 704 664-1361
  Mooresville *(G-8653)*

Energy Conversion Syste.................... G 910 892-8081
  Dunn *(G-3855)*

Morgan Advanced Mtls Tech Inc.............. C 910 892-9677
  Dunn *(G-3862)*

Pbi Performance Products Inc............... D 704 554-3378
  Charlotte *(G-2621)*

Sgl Carbon LLC............................. G 828 437-3221
  Morganton *(G-8895)*

Sgl Carbon LLC............................. E 704 593-5100
  Charlotte *(G-2792)*

Sgl Composites Inc......................... F 704 593-5100
  Charlotte *(G-2793)*

Slade Operating Company LLC................ E 704 873-1366
  Statesville *(G-11766)*

Thanet Inc................................. G 704 483-4175
  Denver *(G-3812)*

Tokai Carbon GE LLC........................ E 980 260-1130
  Charlotte *(G-2927)*

CARBURETORS

Bill Pink Carburetors LLC.................. G 704 575-1645
  Denver *(G-3774)*

Classic Carburetor Rebuilders.............. G 336 613-5715
  Eden *(G-4345)*

Marvel-Schbler Arcft Crbrtors.............. G 336 446-0002
  Burlington *(G-1124)*

(G-0000) Company's Geographic Section entry number

Robert Blake... G 704 720-9341
Concord *(G-3433)*

CARDS: Color

Copymatic United Cerebral...................... F 252 695-6155
Greenville *(G-5959)*

CARDS: Greeting

Walgreen Co.. G 704 525-2628
Charlotte *(G-3001)*

Wit & Whistle... G 919 609-5309
Cary *(G-1485)*

CARDS: Jacquard, Made From Purchased Materials

Valdese Weavers LLC............................. B 828 874-2181
Valdese *(G-12206)*

CARPET & UPHOLSTERY CLEANING SVCS

Bridgport Restoration Svcs Inc.............. G 336 996-1212
Kernersville *(G-7248)*

CARPETS & RUGS: Tufted

Karastan... G 336 627-7200
Eden *(G-4349)*

Mohawk Industries Inc........................... F 919 661-5590
Garner *(G-4944)*

CARPETS, RUGS & FLOOR COVERING

Bellaire Dynamik LLC.............................. G 704 779-3755
Charlotte *(G-1770)*

Burlington Industries LLC....................... C 336 379-6220
Greensboro *(G-5414)*

Columbia Forest Products Inc............... G 336 605-0429
Greensboro *(G-5454)*

Due Process Stable Trdg Co LLC.......... E 910 608-0284
Lumberton *(G-7949)*

Elevate Textiles Inc................................ F 336 379-6220
Charlotte *(G-2098)*

Elevate Textiles Holding Corp............... D 336 379-6220
Charlotte *(G-2099)*

Flint Hill Textiles Inc.............................. G 704 434-9331
Shelby *(G-11337)*

Furniture Fair Inc.................................... E 910 455-4044
Jacksonville *(G-7124)*

Hampton Capital Partners LLC.............. A
Aberdeen *(G-6)*

Horizon Home Imports Inc..................... G 704 859-5133
Clemmons *(G-3190)*

Itg Holdings Inc...................................... A 336 379-6220
Greensboro *(G-5628)*

Michaelian & Kohlberg Inc..................... G 828 891-8511
Horse Shoe *(G-6930)*

Mohawk Industries Inc........................... G 919 609-4759
Garner *(G-4945)*

Royal Textile Mills Inc............................ D 336 694-4121
Yanceyville *(G-13460)*

Shaw Industries Inc................................ B 828 369-1701
Franklin *(G-4839)*

Shaw Industries Group Inc..................... G 877 996-5942
Charlotte *(G-2795)*

Shaw Industries Group Inc..................... E 877 996-5942
Charlotte *(G-2796)*

White Oak Carpet Mills Inc.................... G 828 287-8892
Spindale *(G-11551)*

CARS: Electric

Ev Fleet Inc.. G 704 425-6272
Charlotte *(G-2130)*

Lynn Jones Race Cars............................ G 252 522-0705
Kinston *(G-7420)*

Performance Racing Whse Inc............... G 704 838-1400
Mooresville *(G-8749)*

Solar Pack.. E 919 515-2194
Raleigh *(G-10491)*

CARTS: Grocery

Technibilt Ltd.. E 828 464-7388
Newton *(G-9502)*

CASES: Carrying

Case Smith Inc....................................... F 336 969-9786
Rural Hall *(G-10955)*

CASES: Carrying, Clothing & Apparel

Cursed Society LLC................................ G 702 445-5601
Greensboro *(G-5477)*

Glaser Designs Inc................................ F 415 552-3188
Raleigh *(G-10136)*

Picassomoesllc....................................... G 216 703-4547
Hillsborough *(G-6875)*

Random & Kind LLC............................... G 919 249-8809
Durham *(G-4207)*

Tylerias Closet LLC................................ G 252 325-6639
Roper *(G-10901)*

CASES: Plastic

Dexterity LLC.. F 919 524-7732
Greenville *(G-5964)*

CASES: Shipping, Nailed Or Lock Corner, Wood

Carolina Crating Inc............................... E 910 276-7170
Laurinburg *(G-7495)*

Kontane Logistics Inc............................. E 828 397-5501
Hickory *(G-6382)*

Mc Gees Crating Inc............................... E 828 758-4660
Lenoir *(G-7626)*

CASINGS: Sheet Metal

Tfam Solutions LLC................................ G 910 637-0266
Aberdeen *(G-26)*

CAST STONE: Concrete

Custom Brick Company Inc.................... E 919 832-2804
Raleigh *(G-10028)*

Fletcher Limestone Company Inc.......... G 828 684-6701
Fletcher *(G-4737)*

CASTINGS GRINDING: For The Trade

Daily Grind LLC...................................... G 910 541-0471
Surf City *(G-11862)*

McJast Inc.. F 828 884-4809
Pisgah Forest *(G-9771)*

Petteway Body Shop Inc........................ G 910 455-3272
Jacksonville *(G-7137)*

Stump and Grind LLC............................. G 704 488-2271
Charlotte *(G-2875)*

CASTINGS: Aerospace Investment, Ferrous

Cold Mountain Capital LLC.................... F 828 210-8129
Asheville *(G-479)*

CASTINGS: Aerospace, Aluminum

CAT Logistics Inc................................... F 252 447-2490
New Bern *(G-9351)*

CASTINGS: Aluminum

Briggs-Shaffner Acquisition Co............. F 336 463-4272
Yadkinville *(G-13439)*

Consolidated Metco Inc......................... F 704 289-6492
Monroe *(G-8466)*

Consolidated Metco Inc......................... E 704 289-6491
Monroe *(G-8467)*

CASTINGS: Bronze, NEC, Exc Die

Kayne & Son Custom Hdwr Inc.............. G 828 665-1988
Candler *(G-1228)*

CASTINGS: Die, Aluminum

Carolina Foundry Inc.............................. G 704 376-3145
Charlotte *(G-1847)*

Cascade Die Casting Group Inc............ C 336 882-0186
High Point *(G-6564)*

Cs Alloys.. G 704 675-5810
Gastonia *(G-5033)*

Dynacast LLC... E 704 927-2790
Charlotte *(G-2072)*

Dynacast International LLC..................... G 704 927-2790
Charlotte *(G-2073)*

Ksm Castings USA Inc........................... E 704 751-0559
Shelby *(G-11352)*

Leggett & Platt Incorporated................. G 704 380-6208
Statesville *(G-11727)*

Linamar Light Metal S-Mr LLC.............. A 828 348-4010
Fletcher *(G-4748)*

RCM Industries Inc................................ C 828 286-4003
Rutherfordton *(G-10991)*

Sensus USA Inc..................................... C 919 576-6185
Morrisville *(G-9052)*

Sensus USA Inc..................................... E 919 845-4000
Morrisville *(G-9051)*

CASTINGS: Die, Nonferrous

Dynacast LLC... E 704 927-2790
Charlotte *(G-2072)*

Dynacast International LLC..................... G 704 927-2790
Charlotte *(G-2073)*

Dynacast US Holdings Inc...................... F 704 927-2786
Charlotte *(G-2074)*

CASTINGS: Gray Iron

Humber Street Facility Inc..................... G 919 775-3628
Sanford *(G-11192)*

Modacam Incorporated........................... G 704 489-8500
Denver *(G-3793)*

Southern Cast Inc.................................. E 704 335-0692
Charlotte *(G-2833)*

Venture Products Intl Inc....................... G 828 285-0495
Asheville *(G-631)*

CASTINGS: Machinery, Aluminum

Advanced Machine Services.................. G 910 410-0099
Rockingham *(G-10768)*

CASTINGS: Precision

PCC Airfoils LLC.................................... B 919 774-4300
Sanford *(G-11215)*

CASTINGS: Steel

Norca Engineered Products LLC........... E 919 846-2010
Raleigh *(G-10334)*

CATALOG & MAIL-ORDER HOUSES

Cbdmd Inc.. F 704 445-3060
Charlotte *(G-1869)*

Celtic Ocean International Inc................ E 828 299-9005
Arden *(G-261)*

Glen Raven Mtl Solutions LLC............... C 828 682-2142
Burnsville *(G-1185)*

Old Salem Incorporated......................... G 336 721-7305
Winston Salem *(G-13269)*

P
R
O
D
U
C
T

CATALOG SALES

Owen G Dunn Co Inc.................................. G 252 633-3197
New Bern *(G-9387)*

Stump Printing Co Inc............................... C 260 723-5171
Wrightsville Beach *(G-13433)*

Trophy House Inc..................................... F 910 323-1791
Fayetteville *(G-4683)*

CATALYSTS: Chemical

Advanced Marketing International Inc... F 910 392-0508
Wilmington *(G-12692)*

American Ripener LLC............................. G 704 527-8813
Charlotte *(G-1666)*

Clariant Corporation................................ D 704 331-7000
Charlotte *(G-1925)*

Coalogix Inc... C 704 827-8933
Charlotte *(G-1940)*

Cormetech Inc.. C 704 827-8933
Charlotte *(G-1985)*

Innospec Inc.. E 704 633-8028
Salisbury *(G-11069)*

Innospec Inc.. E 704 633-8028
Salisbury *(G-11070)*

CATERERS

Over Rainbow Inc.................................... G 704 332-5521
Charlotte *(G-2604)*

Sawmill Catering LLC.............................. F 910 769-7455
Wilmington *(G-12911)*

Sweet Room LLC..................................... G 336 567-1620
High Point *(G-6799)*

CAULKING COMPOUNDS

Dap Products Inc..................................... F 704 799-9640
Mooresville *(G-8651)*

Firestopping Products Inc...................... F 336 661-0102
Winston Salem *(G-13168)*

CEMENT & CONCRETE RELATED PRDTS & EQPT: Bituminous

John Deere Kernersville LLC................. A 336 996-8100
Kernersville *(G-7281)*

CEMENT ROCK: Crushed & Broken

Marietta Martin Materials Inc................. G 910 743-6471
Maysville *(G-8211)*

Martin Marietta Materials Inc................. F 360 424-3441
Raleigh *(G-10275)*

CEMENT: Asbestos, Siding

Plycem USA LLC...................................... C 336 696-2007
North Wilkesboro *(G-9549)*

CEMENT: Heat Resistant

3tex Inc.. E 919 481-2500
Rutherfordton *(G-10972)*

Martin Marietta Materials Inc................. C 919 781-4550
Raleigh *(G-10277)*

CEMENT: Hydraulic

Argos USA LLC.. G 919 942-0381
Carrboro *(G-1265)*

CEMENT: Masonry

Vega Construction Company Inc............ E 336 756-3477
Pilot Mountain *(G-9675)*

CEMENT: Natural

Beazer East Inc....................................... F 919 567-9512
Holly Springs *(G-6894)*

CHAIN: Welded, Made From Purchased Wire

Columbus McKinnon Corporation.......... C 716 689-5400
Charlotte *(G-1962)*

CHASSIS: Motor Vehicle

Direct Chassislink Inc............................ E 704 594-3800
Charlotte *(G-2050)*

Thomas Built Buses Inc.......................... A 336 889-4871
High Point *(G-6807)*

CHASSIS: Travel Trailer

Elite Metal Performance LLC.................. F 704 660-0006
Statesville *(G-11694)*

CHEMICAL ELEMENTS

New Element.. G 704 890-7292
Charlotte *(G-2557)*

Tutcu-Farnam Custom Products............ E 828 684-3766
Arden *(G-315)*

CHEMICAL PROCESSING MACHINERY & EQPT

CVC Equipment Company....................... G 704 300-6242
Cherryville *(G-3063)*

Envirotek Worldwide LLC....................... F 704 285-6400
Charlotte *(G-2120)*

Indian Tff-Tank Greensboro Inc............. G 336 625-2629
Asheboro *(G-364)*

CHEMICALS & ALLIED PRDTS WHOLESALERS, NEC

American Chrome & Chem NA Inc.......... F 910 675-7200
Castle Hayne *(G-1494)*

Arc3 Gases Inc.. G 336 275-3333
Greensboro *(G-5367)*

Arc3 Gases Inc.. G 704 220-1029
Monroe *(G-8429)*

Arc3 Gases Inc.. E 910 892-4016
Dunn *(G-3844)*

Chem-Tex Laboratories Inc.................... E 706 602-8600
Concord *(G-3335)*

Heiq Chemtex Inc.................................... G 704 795-9322
Concord *(G-3373)*

Jci Jones Chemicals Inc......................... F 704 392-9767
Charlotte *(G-2363)*

Newell Novelty Co Inc............................ G 336 597-2246
Roxboro *(G-10931)*

Pavco Inc... E 704 496-6800
Charlotte *(G-2619)*

Pencco Inc... F 252 235-5300
Middlesex *(G-8279)*

Reagents Holdings LLC.......................... E 800 732-8484
Charlotte *(G-2695)*

Reedy International Corp......................... F 980 819-6930
Charlotte *(G-2701)*

Reichhold Holdings Us Inc..................... A 919 990-7500
Durham *(G-4210)*

Rpoc Inc.. C 910 371-3184
Wilmington *(G-12904)*

Textile Rubber and Chem Co Inc........... G 704 376-3582
Indian Trail *(G-7103)*

Universal Preservachem Inc.................. D 732 568-1266
Mebane *(G-8262)*

CHEMICALS & ALLIED PRDTS, WHOLESALE: Adhesives

Jowat Corporation................................... E 336 434-9000
Archdale *(G-233)*

CHEMICALS & ALLIED PRDTS, WHOLESALE: Chemical Additives

Fil-Chem Inc.. G 919 878-1270
Raleigh *(G-10108)*

CHEMICALS & ALLIED PRDTS, WHOLESALE: Chemicals, Indl

Access Technologies LLC....................... G 574 286-1255
Mooresville *(G-8590)*

Fortrans Inc... G 919 365-8004
Wendell *(G-12536)*

Kymera International LLC....................... E 919 544-8090
Durham *(G-4099)*

Leke LLC.. G 704 523-1452
Pineville *(G-9739)*

Polytec Inc.. E 704 277-3960
Mooresville *(G-8750)*

Sostram Corporation.............................. G 919 226-1195
Durham *(G-4242)*

T - Square Enterprises Inc...................... G 704 846-8233
Charlotte *(G-2894)*

Umicore USA Inc..................................... E 919 874-7171
Raleigh *(G-10575)*

CHEMICALS & ALLIED PRDTS, WHOLESALE: Chemicals, Indl & Heavy

Advanced Marketing International Inc... F 910 392-0508
Wilmington *(G-12692)*

Kincol Industries Incorporated.............. G 704 372-8435
Charlotte *(G-2397)*

Marlowe-Van Loan Sales Co................... G 336 882-3351
High Point *(G-6700)*

CHEMICALS & ALLIED PRDTS, WHOLESALE: Detergent/Soap

Ada Marketing Inc................................... E 910 221-2189
Dunn *(G-3841)*

CHEMICALS & ALLIED PRDTS, WHOLESALE: Detergents

Greenology Products LLC....................... E 877 473-3650
Raleigh *(G-10144)*

South / Win LLC...................................... D 336 398-5650
Greensboro *(G-5822)*

CHEMICALS & ALLIED PRDTS, WHOLESALE: Indl Gases

Air & Gas Solutions LLC......................... E 704 897-2182
Charlotte *(G-1631)*

CHEMICALS & ALLIED PRDTS, WHOLESALE: Oil Additives

Carolina Bg... G 704 847-8840
Matthews *(G-8101)*

CHEMICALS & ALLIED PRDTS, WHOLESALE: Plastics Materials, NEC

Advanced Marketing International Inc... F 910 392-0508
Wilmington *(G-12692)*

CHEMICALS & ALLIED PRDTS, WHOLESALE: Plastics Prdts, NEC

Advanced Plastiform Inc........................ D 919 404-2080
Zebulon *(G-13500)*

Jowat International Corp......................... E 336 434-9000
Archdale *(G-234)*

Easth20 Holdings Llc.............................G 919 313-2100
  Greensboro (G-5510)

Mdsi Inc...G 919 783-8730
  Browns Summit (G-1002)

Repi LLC...E 704 648-0252
  Dallas (G-3685)

Tri-Star Plastics Corp...........................E 704 598-2800
  Denver (G-3813)

Wilbert Plstic Svcs Acqstion L.............E 704 455-5191
  Harrisburg (G-6121)

CHEMICALS & ALLIED PRDTS, WHOLESALE: Plastics Sheets & Rods

Custom Extrusion Inc............................G 336 495-7070
  Asheboro (G-343)

Endless Plastics LLC............................F 336 346-1839
  Greensboro (G-5520)

Piedmont Plastics Inc...........................D 704 597-8200
  Charlotte (G-2636)

United Plastics Corporation...................C 336 786-2127
  Mount Airy (G-9192)

CHEMICALS & ALLIED PRDTS, WHOLESALE: Polyurethane Prdts

Green Mountain Intl LLC........................G 800 942-5151
  Waynesville (G-12460)

CHEMICALS & ALLIED PRDTS, WHOLESALE: Resins

Reichhold Holdings Us Inc....................A 919 990-7500
  Durham (G-4210)

CHEMICALS & ALLIED PRDTS, WHOLESALE: Spec Clean/Sanitation

Desco Equipment Company Inc............G 704 873-2844
  Statesville (G-11689)

Sutherland Products Inc........................F 800 854-3541
  Stoneville (G-11831)

CHEMICALS & ALLIED PRDTS, WHOLESALE: Waxes, Exc Petroleum

Bonakemi Usa Incorporated.................D 704 220-6943
  Monroe (G-8445)

CHEMICALS & OTHER PRDTS DERIVED FROM COKING

Thermochem Recovery Intl.....................G 919 606-3282
  Durham (G-4270)

CHEMICALS, AGRICULTURE: Wholesalers

AG Provision LLC..................................E 910 296-0302
  Kenansville (G-7224)

Coastal Agrobusiness Inc......................G 828 697-2220
  Flat Rock (G-4706)

Coastal Agrobusiness Inc......................G 252 798-3481
  Hamilton (G-6048)

Coastal Agrobusiness Inc......................D 252 238-7391
  Greenville (G-5955)

Harvey Fertilizer and Gas Co................E 252 526-4150
  Kinston (G-7415)

Helena Agri-Enterprises LLC.................G 828 685-1182
  Hendersonville (G-6214)

Industrial and Agricultural....................E 910 843-2121
  Red Springs (G-10668)

Upl NA Inc...E 800 358-7642
  Cary (G-1476)

CHEMICALS: Agricultural

Aqua 10 Corporation.............................G 252 726-5421
  Morehead City (G-8813)

Arysta Lifescience Inc..........................E 919 678-4900
  Cary (G-1295)

Arysta Lifescience N Amer LLC............E 919 678-4900
  Cary (G-1296)

Atticus LLC...E 984 465-4754
  Cary (G-1299)

Chemours Company...............................G 910 483-4681
  Fayetteville (G-4573)

Chemours Company Fc LLC..................D 910 678-1314
  Fayetteville (G-4574)

Dupont..G 919 414-0089
  Raleigh (G-10065)

Fair Products Inc...................................G 919 467-1599
  Cary (G-1361)

Harvey Fertilizer and Gas Co................E 252 753-2063
  Farmville (G-4530)

Makhteshim Agan North Amer Inc.........E 919 256-9300
  Raleigh (G-10267)

Monsanto Company................................G 252 212-5421
  Battleboro (G-702)

Southeastern Minerals Inc.....................E 252 492-0831
  Henderson (G-6179)

Southern AG Insecticides Inc................E 828 264-8843
  Boone (G-943)

Southern AG Insecticides Inc................E 828 692-2233
  Hendersonville (G-6242)

Trinity Manufacturing Inc.......................D 910 582-5650
  Hamlet (G-6064)

Upl NA Inc...E 800 358-7642
  Cary (G-1476)

Vpm Liquidating Inc..............................F 336 292-1781
  Greensboro (G-5912)

CHEMICALS: Bromine, Elemental

Albemarle Amendments LLC..................F 800 535-3030
  Charlotte (G-1637)

Albemarle Corporation...........................A 980 299-5700
  Charlotte (G-1638)

CHEMICALS: Fire Retardant

Albemarle Corporation...........................A 980 299-5700
  Charlotte (G-1638)

Clariant Corporation..............................D 704 331-7000
  Charlotte (G-1925)

Fire Retardant Chem Tech LLC..............G 980 253-8880
  Matthews (G-8169)

CHEMICALS: High Purity Grade, Organic

Carbon Conversion Systems LLC..........G 919 883-4238
  Chapel Hill (G-1533)

Clariant Corporation..............................D 704 331-7000
  Charlotte (G-1925)

CHEMICALS: High Purity, Refined From Technical Grade

Cheltec Inc...G 941 355-1045
  Morganton (G-8855)

Sciepharm LLC.....................................G 307 352-9559
  Apex (G-193)

CHEMICALS: Inorganic, NEC

Access Technologies LLC......................G 574 286-1255
  Mooresville (G-8590)

Airgas Usa LLC.....................................G 704 394-1420
  Charlotte (G-1633)

Airgas Usa LLC.....................................G 919 544-3773
  Durham (G-3885)

Airgas Usa LLC.....................................G 919 735-5276
  Goldsboro (G-5196)

Akuratemp LLC......................................F 828 708-7178
  Arden (G-249)

Albemarle Corporation...........................C 704 739-2501
  Kings Mountain (G-7345)

Apollo Chemical Corp............................D 336 226-1161
  Burlington (G-1047)

Archroma US Inc...................................E 704 353-4100
  Charlotte (G-1692)

Arkema Inc..D 919 469-6700
  Cary (G-1294)

Baikowski International Corp..................F 704 587-7100
  Charlotte (G-1741)

Blue Nano Inc..F 888 508-6266
  Cornelius (G-3589)

Bluestone Metals & Chem LLC..............G 704 662-8632
  Cornelius (G-3590)

Bluestone Specialty Chem LLC.............F 704 662-8632
  Cornelius (G-3591)

Borden Chemical....................................G 828 584-3800
  Morganton (G-8853)

Bryson Industries Inc............................F 336 931-0026
  Thomasville (G-11999)

Carus LLC...E 704 822-1441
  Belmont (G-741)

Celanese...G 910 343-5000
  Wilmington (G-12740)

Chemol Company Inc.............................E 336 333-3050
  Greensboro (G-5443)

Chemtrade Logistics (us) Inc................G 773 646-2500
  Charlotte (G-1910)

Clift Industries Inc................................G 704 752-0031
  Mount Holly (G-9225)

Conference Inc......................................G 704 349-0203
  Gastonia (G-5027)

Corrtrac Systems Corporation................G 252 232-3975
  Currituck (G-3663)

Dupont Specialty Pdts USA LLC............E 919 248-5109
  Durham (G-4013)

Dystar LP..E 704 561-3000
  Charlotte (G-2078)

Eidp Inc..C 910 483-4681
  Fayetteville (G-4595)

Eidp Inc..D 252 522-6111
  Grifton (G-6035)

Eidp Inc..G 252 522-6896
  Kinston (G-7408)

Eidp Inc..G 910 371-4000
  Leland (G-7540)

Element West LLC.................................G 336 853-6118
  Lexington (G-7683)

Elements Brands LLC............................F 503 230-8008
  Charlotte (G-2097)

Energy Solutions (us) LLC.....................C 919 786-4555
  Raleigh (G-10087)

Fil-Chem Inc..G 919 878-1270
  Raleigh (G-10108)

Fortrans Inc..G 919 365-8004
  Wendell (G-12536)

Fuji Silysia Chemical USA Ltd...............E 252 413-0003
  Greenville (G-5981)

Geo Specialty Chemicals Inc................G 252 793-2121
  Plymouth (G-9804)

Gresco Manufacturing Inc......................G 336 475-8101
  Thomasville (G-12029)

Highland International.............................F 828 265-2513
  Boone (G-923)

Industrial and Agricultural....................E 910 843-2121
  Red Springs (G-10668)

Leke LLC...G 704 523-1452
  Pineville (G-9739)

M & G Polymers Usa LLC......................G 910 509-4414
  Wilmington (G-12843)

Marlowe-Van Loan Corporation............ G 336 886-7126
High Point *(G-6699)*

Metallix Refining Inc.......................... E 252 413-0346
Greenville *(G-6003)*

Microban Products Company.............. E 704 766-4267
Huntersville *(G-7013)*

Mount Vernon Chemicals LLC............ D 336 226-1161
Burlington *(G-1131)*

Mount Vernon Mills Inc.................... A 336 226-1161
Burlington *(G-1132)*

Netqem LLC................................... G 919 544-4122
Durham *(G-4146)*

Novalent Ltd................................... F 336 375-7555
Greensboro *(G-5715)*

Oneh2 Inc...................................... E 844 996-6342
Hickory *(G-6406)*

Pavco Inc....................................... E 704 496-6800
Charlotte *(G-2619)*

Pencco Inc..................................... F 252 235-5300
Middlesex *(G-8279)*

Piedmont Lithium Carolinas Inc........... F 434 664-7643
Belmont *(G-761)*

Rockwood Lithium........................... E 704 739-2501
Kings Mountain *(G-7383)*

Sciepharm LLC............................... F 307 352-9559
Durham *(G-4225)*

Sciteck Diagnostics Inc.................... G 828 650-0409
Fletcher *(G-4765)*

Sibelco... F 828 765-1114
Spruce Pine *(G-11585)*

Sostram Corporation........................ G 919 226-1195
Durham *(G-4242)*

Stepan Company............................. C 316 828-1000
Wilmington *(G-12930)*

Tecgrachem Inc............................... G 336 993-6785
Kernersville *(G-7304)*

Unichem IV Ltd............................... F 336 578-5476
Haw River *(G-6136)*

Venator Chemicals LLC.................... D 704 454-4811
Harrisburg *(G-6120)*

CHEMICALS: Lithium Compounds, Inorganic

Albemarle US Inc............................ C 704 739-2501
Kings Mountain *(G-7346)*

FMC Corporation............................. D 704 868-5300
Bessemer City *(G-818)*

FMC Corporation............................. B 704 426-5336
Bessemer City *(G-819)*

CHEMICALS: Magnesium Compounds Or Salts, Inorganic

Giles Chemical Corporation................ G 828 452-4784
Waynesville *(G-12458)*

Giles Chemical Corporation................ E 828 452-4784
Waynesville *(G-12459)*

CHEMICALS: NEC

Ae Technology Inc........................... F 704 528-2000
Troutman *(G-12130)*

Akuratemp LLC............................... F 828 708-7178
Arden *(G-249)*

American Chrome & Chem NA Inc......... F 910 675-7200
Castle Hayne *(G-1494)*

American Phoenix Inc....................... C 910 484-4007
Fayetteville *(G-4551)*

Attl Products Inc............................. G 336 475-8101
Thomasville *(G-11995)*

Blast Off Intl Chem & Mfg Co............... G 509 885-4525
Seaboard *(G-11269)*

Bnnano Inc..................................... F 844 926-6266
Burlington *(G-1052)*

Bonsal American Inc........................ D 704 525-1621
Charlotte *(G-1799)*

Buckeye International Inc................... G 704 523-9400
Charlotte *(G-1817)*

Burlington Chemical Co LLC................ G 336 584-0111
Greensboro *(G-5410)*

Camco Manufacturing LLC.................. C 336 668-7661
Greensboro *(G-5419)*

Championx LLC............................... G 704 506-4830
Belmont *(G-743)*

Chem-Tex Laboratories Inc................ E 706 602-8600
Concord *(G-3335)*

Chemtech North Carolina LLC............. E 910 514-9575
Lillington *(G-7794)*

Clariant Corporation........................ D 704 331-7000
Charlotte *(G-1923)*

Copia Labs Inc............................... G 910 904-1000
Raeford *(G-9835)*

Dst Manufacturing LLC...................... G 336 676-6096
Randleman *(G-10643)*

Emerald Carolina Chemical LLC........... F 704 393-0089
Charlotte *(G-2109)*

Enviroserve Chemicals Inc................. F 910 892-1791
Dunn *(G-3856)*

Eoncoat LLC................................... G 941 928-9401
Lenoir *(G-7602)*

Euclid Chemical Company.................. G 704 283-2544
Monroe *(G-8486)*

FMC Corporation............................. D 704 868-5300
Bessemer City *(G-818)*

FMC Corporation............................. B 704 426-5336
Bessemer City *(G-819)*

Freudenberg Prfmce Mtls LP............... C 828 665-5000
Candler *(G-1225)*

Gb Biosciences LLC......................... D 336 632-6000
Greensboro *(G-5550)*

Global Bioprotect LLC....................... F 336 861-0162
High Point *(G-6630)*

Gtg Engineering Inc.......................... G 910 457-0068
Southport *(G-11520)*

Hexion Inc...................................... E 910 483-1311
Fayetteville *(G-4612)*

Hospira Inc..................................... B 919 553-3831
Clayton *(G-3154)*

Ifs Industries Inc............................. E 919 234-1397
Morrisville *(G-8991)*

Ivm Chemicals Inc........................... E 407 506-4913
Charlotte *(G-2358)*

Jci Jones Chemicals Inc..................... F 704 392-9767
Charlotte *(G-2363)*

Laticrete International Inc................... F 910 582-2252
Hamlet *(G-6059)*

LCI Corporation International............... E 704 399-7441
Charlotte *(G-2411)*

Lime-Chem Inc................................ G 910 843-2121
Rockwell *(G-10799)*

Liquid Ice Corporation...................... F 704 882-3505
Matthews *(G-8179)*

Lubrizol Advanced Mtls Inc................. E 704 587-5583
Charlotte *(G-2437)*

Lubrizol Global Management Inc........... D 704 865-7451
Gastonia *(G-5080)*

Marlowe-Van Loan Sales Co............... G 336 882-3351
High Point *(G-6700)*

Microban Products Company.............. E 704 766-4267
Huntersville *(G-7013)*

Molecular Toxicology Inc................... F 828 264-9099
Boone *(G-935)*

Novalent Ltd................................... F 336 375-7555
Greensboro *(G-5715)*

Nsi Lab Solutions Inc....................... F 919 789-3000
Raleigh *(G-10342)*

Pavco Inc....................................... E 704 496-6800
Charlotte *(G-2619)*

Polytec Inc..................................... E 704 277-3960
Mooresville *(G-8750)*

Radiator Specialty Company............... D 704 688-2302
Indian Trail *(G-7097)*

RSC Bio Solutions LLC...................... G 800 661-3558
Charlotte *(G-2737)*

RSC Chemical Solutions LLC............... F 704 821-7643
Indian Trail *(G-7098)*

Rust911 Inc.................................... G 607 425-2882
Hickory *(G-6437)*

Seacon Corporation......................... F 704 333-6000
Charlotte *(G-2775)*

Sirchie Acquisition Co LLC................. C 800 356-7311
Youngsville *(G-13486)*

Soto Industries LLC......................... G 706 643-5011
Charlotte *(G-2828)*

Specgx LLC.................................... C 919 878-4706
Raleigh *(G-10495)*

Surry Chemicals Incorporated............. E 336 786-4607
Mount Airy *(G-9181)*

Tribodyn Technologies Inc.................. E 859 750-6299
Mooresville *(G-8788)*

Unitex Chemical Corp....................... E 336 378-0965
Greensboro *(G-5892)*

Venator Chemicals LLC.................... D 704 454-4811
Harrisburg *(G-6120)*

Vyse Gelatin Inc.............................. G 919 238-3300
Morrisville *(G-9087)*

Westrock Company........................... G 770 448-2193
Winston Salem *(G-13390)*

Winton Products Company.................. F 704 399-5151
Charlotte *(G-3023)*

Xelera Inc...................................... G 540 915-6181
Denver *(G-3818)*

CHEMICALS: Phosphates, Defluorinated/ Ammoniated, Exc Fertlr

Pcs Phosphate Company Inc............... E 252 322-4111
Aurora *(G-645)*

CHEMICALS: Reagent Grade, Refined From Technical Grade

Hemo Bioscience Inc........................ G 919 313-2888
Durham *(G-4059)*

Reagents Holdings LLC...................... E 800 732-8484
Charlotte *(G-2695)*

Synnovator Inc................................ G 919 360-0518
Durham *(G-4257)*

CHEMICALS: Silica Compounds

Fuji Silysia Chemical Ltd.................... F 919 484-4158
Greenville *(G-5980)*

CHEMICALS: Water Treatment

Loy & Loy Inc................................. G 919 942-6356
Graham *(G-5276)*

Matchem Inc................................... G 336 886-5000
High Point *(G-6707)*

Moe Jt Enterprises Inc....................... F 423 512-1427
Winston Salem *(G-13260)*

Pencco Inc..................................... F 252 235-5300
Middlesex *(G-8279)*

Second Earth Inc............................. G 336 740-9333
Greensboro *(G-5804)*

Xelera Inc...................................... G 855 493-5372
Charlotte *(G-3030)*

Xylem Water Solutions USA Inc........... D 704 409-9700
Charlotte *(G-3037)*

CHICKEN SLAUGHTERING & PROCESSING

Hopkins Poultry Company...... F 336 656-3361
Browns Summit *(G-998)*

Tyson Foods Inc...... G 704 201-8654
Monroe *(G-8573)*

Tyson Foods Inc...... G 919 774-7925
Sanford *(G-11245)*

CHILDREN'S & INFANTS' CLOTHING STORES

Cannon & Daughters Inc...... D 828 254-9236
Asheville *(G-466)*

Pashes LLC...... G 704 682-6535
Statesville *(G-11743)*

CHILDREN'S WEAR STORES

W E Nixons Wldg & Hdwr Inc...... G 252 221-4348
Edenton *(G-4373)*

CHOCOLATE, EXC CANDY FROM BEANS: Chips, Powder, Block, Syrup

Mountain Bear & Co Inc...... G 828 631-0156
Dillsboro *(G-3819)*

CHOCOLATE, EXC CANDY FROM PURCH CHOC: Chips, Powder, Block

Barry Callebaut USA LLC...... D 828 685-2443
Hendersonville *(G-6185)*

Escazu Artisan Chocolate LLC...... F 919 832-3433
Raleigh *(G-10091)*

Nutkao USA Inc...... E 252 595-1000
Battleboro *(G-703)*

CHRISTMAS TREE LIGHTING SETS: Electric

Posh Pad...... G 910 988-4800
Stedman *(G-11807)*

CHRISTMAS TREES: Artificial

Fisherman Creations Inc...... E 252 725-0138
Beaufort *(G-726)*

CHROMATOGRAPHY EQPT

Practichem LLC...... G 919 714-8430
Morrisville *(G-9038)*

Waters Corporation...... G 910 270-3137
Hampstead *(G-6080)*

CHUCKS

Tfam Solutions LLC...... G 910 637-0266
Aberdeen *(G-26)*

CIGARETTE & CIGAR PRDTS & ACCESS

E-Liquid Brands LLC...... E 828 385-5090
Mooresville *(G-8658)*

Medallion Company Inc...... C 919 990-3500
Timberlake *(G-12101)*

Purilum LLC...... E 252 931-8020
Greenville *(G-6016)*

USa Wholesale and Distrg Inc...... F 888 484-6872
Fayetteville *(G-4693)*

CIGARETTE FILTERS

Filtrona Filters Inc...... D 336 362-1333
Greensboro *(G-5533)*

CIRCUIT BOARD REPAIR SVCS

Esco Electronic Services Inc...... F 252 753-4433
Farmville *(G-4528)*

Protronics Inc...... F 919 217-0007
Knightdale *(G-7457)*

CIRCUIT BREAKERS

Dehn Inc...... F 772 460-9315
Mooresville *(G-8654)*

CIRCUITS, INTEGRATED: Hybrid

X-Celeprint Inc...... F 919 248-0020
Durham *(G-4314)*

CIRCUITS: Electronic

Acterna LLC...... F 919 388-5100
Morrisville *(G-8918)*

Advanced Substrate...... F 336 285-5955
Greensboro *(G-5342)*

Anuva Services Inc...... F 919 468-6441
Morrisville *(G-8928)*

Carolina Elctrnic Assmblers In...... E 919 938-1086
Smithfield *(G-11435)*

CMS Associates Inc...... G 919 365-0881
Wendell *(G-12530)*

Cnc-Ke Inc...... D 704 333-0145
Charlotte *(G-1939)*

Cooper Crouse-Hinds LLC...... D 252 566-3014
La Grange *(G-7466)*

Crackle Holdings LP...... A 704 927-7620
Charlotte *(G-1993)*

Diversified Intl Holdings Inc...... G 910 777-7122
Winnabow *(G-13064)*

Duotech Services LLC...... E 828 369-5111
Franklin *(G-4826)*

Edc Inc...... D 336 993-0468
Kernersville *(G-7270)*

Finnord North America Corp...... F 704 723-4913
Huntersville *(G-6990)*

Geotrak Incorporated...... F 919 303-1467
Apex *(G-157)*

Infosense Inc...... G 704 644-1164
Charlotte *(G-2333)*

Infosense Inc...... G 704 644-1164
Charlotte *(G-2334)*

Innova-Con Incorporated...... G 919 303-1467
Apex *(G-169)*

Iqe Rf Inc...... D 732 271-5990
Greensboro *(G-5624)*

Iqe Usa Inc...... G 610 861-6930
Greensboro *(G-5625)*

Pt Marketing Incorporated...... G 412 471-8995
Raleigh *(G-10408)*

Snap One LLC...... B 704 927-7620
Charlotte *(G-2818)*

Snap One Holdings Corp...... E 704 927-7620
Charlotte *(G-2819)*

Spruce Pine Mica Company...... F 828 765-4241
Spruce Pine *(G-11589)*

Tresco...... C 361 985-3154
Boone *(G-946)*

Wieland Electric Inc...... F 910 259-5050
Wilmington *(G-12947)*

CIRCULAR KNIT FABRICS DYEING & FINISHING

Carolina Mills Incorporated...... D 828 428-9911
Maiden *(G-8010)*

Century Textile Mfg Inc...... F 704 869-6660
Gastonia *(G-5016)*

Everest Textile Usa LLC...... C 828 245-6755
Forest City *(G-4789)*

Mocaro Dyeing & Finishing Inc...... D 704 878-6645
Statesville *(G-11732)*

Sdfc LLC...... F 704 878-6645
Monroe *(G-8556)*

South Fork Industries Inc...... D 828 428-9921
Maiden *(G-8017)*

Unifour Finishers Inc...... E 828 322-9435
Hickory *(G-6478)*

Unifour Finishers Inc...... E 828 322-9435
Hickory *(G-6477)*

CLAMPS & COUPLINGS: Hose

Parker-Hannifin Corporation...... E 704 664-1922
Mooresville *(G-8742)*

CLAMPS: Metal

Nuclamp System LLC...... G 336 643-1766
Oak Ridge *(G-9572)*

CLAY, PETROLEUM REFINING: Chemically Processed

Carolina Stalite Co Ltd Partnr...... E 704 279-2166
Gold Hill *(G-5191)*

CLAY: Filtering, Treated

Cormetech Inc...... C 704 827-8933
Charlotte *(G-1985)*

CLEANING EQPT: Commercial

Galaxy Pressure Washing Inc...... G 888 299-3129
Pineville *(G-9729)*

Green Waste Management LLC...... G 704 289-0720
Charlotte *(G-2239)*

Legacy Commercial Service LLC...... G 757 831-5291
Charlotte *(G-2416)*

Midsouth Power Eqp Co Inc...... F 336 389-0515
Greensboro *(G-5692)*

Quality Cleaning Services LLC...... F 919 638-4969
Durham *(G-4202)*

Skyview Commercial Cleaning...... G 704 858-0134
Charlotte *(G-2812)*

Supreme Sweepers LLC...... G 888 698-9996
Charlotte *(G-2885)*

Sweep 24 LLC...... F 980 428-5624
Charlotte *(G-2887)*

CLEANING EQPT: Floor Washing & Polishing, Commercial

Amano Pioneer Eclipse Corp...... D 336 372-8080
Sparta *(G-11534)*

Onyx Environmental Solutions Inc...... E 800 858-3533
Stanley *(G-11623)*

CLEANING EQPT: High Pressure

B&C Xterior Cleaning Svc Inc...... G 919 779-7905
Raleigh *(G-9928)*

Bk Seamless Gutters LLC...... G 252 955-5414
Spring Hope *(G-11554)*

Butler Trieu Inc...... G 910 346-4929
Jacksonville *(G-7118)*

Desco Equipment Company Inc...... G 704 873-2844
Statesville *(G-11689)*

Painting By Colors LLC...... G 919 963-2300
Clayton *(G-3166)*

CLEANING OR POLISHING PREPARATIONS, NEC

Ace Industries Inc...... G 336 427-5316
Madison *(G-7983)*

Amano Pioneer Eclipse Corp...... D 336 372-8080
Sparta *(G-11534)*

Employee Codes: A=Over 500 employees, B=251-500
C=101-250, D=51-100, E=20-50, F=10-19, G=1-9

2025 Harris North Carolina
Manufacturers Directory

1081

PRODUCT

Awesome Products Inc............................G 336 374-5900
Mount Airy *(G-9099)*

Busch Enterprises Inc............................G 704 878-2067
Statesville *(G-11673)*

Cherryville Distrg Co Inc........................G 704 435-9692
Cherryville *(G-3060)*

Elevate Cleaning Service........................G 347 928-4030
Fayetteville *(G-4596)*

Elsco Inc..G 509 885-4525
Seaboard *(G-11271)*

Eminess Technologies Inc......................E 704 283-2600
Monroe *(G-8482)*

Fresh As A Daisy Inc...............................G 336 869-3002
High Point *(G-6623)*

Harper Corporation of America...............C 704 588-3371
Charlotte *(G-2259)*

Ice Companies Inc.................................G 910 791-1970
Wilmington *(G-12811)*

Metrotech Chemicals Inc........................D 704 343-9315
Charlotte *(G-2497)*

Organizer Llc...G 336 391-7591
Winston Salem *(G-13272)*

Sutherland Products Inc..........................F 800 854-3541
Stoneville *(G-11831)*

CLEANING PRDTS: Automobile Polish

Unx-Christeyns LLC...............................G 252 355-8433
Greenville *(G-6031)*

CLEANING PRDTS: Bleaches, Household, Dry Or Liquid

Unx-Christeyns LLC...............................D 252 756-8616
Greenville *(G-6032)*

CLEANING PRDTS: Deodorants, Nonpersonal

Remodeez LLC.......................................F 704 428-9050
Charlotte *(G-2708)*

CLEANING PRDTS: Disinfectants, Household Or Indl Plant

Patel Deepal...G 704 634-5141
Concord *(G-3416)*

CLEANING PRDTS: Drain Pipe Solvents Or Cleaners

Entrust Services LLC.............................F 336 274-5175
Greensboro *(G-5523)*

CLEANING PRDTS: Laundry Preparations

A Cleaner Tomorrow Dry Clg LLC...........G 919 639-6396
Dunn *(G-3840)*

Dewill Inc..G 919 426-9550
Cary *(G-1346)*

Fresh-N-Mobile LLC...............................G 704 251-4643
Charlotte *(G-2180)*

M and R Inc...G 704 332-5999
Charlotte *(G-2444)*

Piece of Pie LLC....................................G 919 286-7421
Durham *(G-4181)*

Quail Dry Cleaning................................G 704 947-7335
Charlotte *(G-2681)*

CLEANING PRDTS: Sanitation Preparations

Mooresvlle Pub Wrks Snttion De............G 704 664-4278
Mooresville *(G-8727)*

CLEANING PRDTS: Sanitation Preps, Disinfectants/Deodorants

AEC Consumer Products LLC..............F 704 904-0578
Fayetteville *(G-4546)*

CLEANING PRDTS: Shoe Polish Or Cleaner

Hickory Brands Inc................................D 828 322-2600
Hickory *(G-6347)*

CLEANING PRDTS: Specialty

Autec Inc..E 704 871-9141
Statesville *(G-11663)*

Buckeye International Inc.......................G 704 523-9400
Charlotte *(G-1817)*

Ecolab Inc...E 336 931-2289
Greensboro *(G-5512)*

H & H Products Incorporated..................G 910 891-4276
Dunn *(G-3860)*

Illinois Tool Works Inc............................C 336 996-7046
Kernersville *(G-7280)*

Kay Chemical Company..........................A 336 668-7290
Greensboro *(G-5642)*

Microban Products Company...................E 704 766-4267
Huntersville *(G-7013)*

Mill-Chem Manufacturing Inc..................E 336 889-8038
Thomasville *(G-12049)*

Procter & Gamble Mfg Co.......................D 336 954-0000
Greensboro *(G-5767)*

Rga Enterprises Inc................................D 704 398-0487
Charlotte *(G-2723)*

Speed Brite Inc......................................G 704 639-9771
Salisbury *(G-11118)*

W G of Southwest Raleigh Inc.................G 919 629-7327
Holly Springs *(G-6919)*

CLEANING SVCS: Industrial Or Commercial

Darius All Access LLC............................E 910 262-8567
Wilmington *(G-12759)*

CLOTHING & ACCESS, WOMEN, CHILDREN & INFANT, WHOL: Access

AC Valor Reyes LLC...............................G 910 431-3256
Castle Hayne *(G-1493)*

CLOTHING & ACCESS, WOMEN, CHILDREN & INFANT, WHOL: Uniforms

Tresmc LLC..G 919 900-0868
Knightdale *(G-7461)*

CLOTHING & ACCESS, WOMEN, CHILDREN/ INFANT, WHOL: Baby Goods

Sunrise Development LLC........................F 828 453-0590
Mooresboro *(G-8586)*

CLOTHING & ACCESS, WOMEN, CHILDREN/ INFANT, WHOL: Nightwear

Sanders Industries Inc...........................G 410 277-8565
Waynesville *(G-12472)*

CLOTHING & ACCESS: Handicapped

Burlington Coat Fctry Whse Cor..............E 919 468-9312
Cary *(G-1317)*

Hinsons Typing & Printing.......................G 919 934-9036
Smithfield *(G-11446)*

CLOTHING & ACCESS: Hospital Gowns

Belvoir Manufacturing Corp.....................D 252 746-1274
Greenville *(G-5947)*

Health Supply Us LLC.............................F 888 408-1694
Mooresville *(G-8680)*

Whitewood Contracts LLC.......................E 336 885-9300
High Point *(G-6834)*

CLOTHING & ACCESS: Men's Miscellaneous Access

Apparel USA Inc.....................................E 212 869-5495
Fairmont *(G-4500)*

Duck Head LLC.......................................G 855 457-1865
Greensboro *(G-5508)*

Eagle Sportswear LLC.............................G 919 365-9805
Wendell *(G-12534)*

Hanesbrands Export Canada LLC............G 336 519-8080
Winston Salem *(G-13187)*

Jestines Jewels Inc.................................G 704 904-0191
Salisbury *(G-11072)*

Kayser-Roth Hosiery Inc.........................E 336 852-2030
Greensboro *(G-5644)*

Lebos Shoe Store Inc.............................F 704 987-6540
Cornelius *(G-3614)*

Military Products Inc...............................G 910 637-0315
West End *(G-12557)*

Mischief Makers Local 816 LLC..............E 336 763-2003
Greensboro *(G-5694)*

CLOTHING & ACCESS: Suspenders

Madison Company Inc.............................E 336 548-9624
Madison *(G-7992)*

The Madison Company Inc.......................E 336 548-9624
Madison *(G-8001)*

CLOTHING & APPAREL STORES: Custom

Global Products & Mfg Svcs Inc..............G 360 870-9876
Charlotte *(G-2215)*

Ics North America Corp...........................E 704 794-6620
Concord *(G-3375)*

Manna Corp North Carolina.....................G 828 696-3642
Hendersonville *(G-6223)*

CLOTHING & FURNISHINGS, MEN'S & BOYS', WHOLESALE: Shirts

Associated Distributors Inc......................G 910 895-5800
Hamlet *(G-6050)*

CLOTHING & FURNISHINGS, MEN'S & BOYS', WHOLESALE: Uniforms

Bob Barker Company Inc.........................C 800 334-9880
Fuquay Varina *(G-4870)*

Carolina Tailors Inc................................G 252 247-6469
Newport *(G-9439)*

CLOTHING & FURNISHINGS, MENS & BOYS, WHOL: Sportswear/Work

Flagship Brands LLC...............................E 888 801-7227
Newton *(G-9465)*

Ics North America Corp...........................E 704 794-6620
Concord *(G-3375)*

CLOTHING STORES: T-Shirts, Printed, Custom

K Formula Enterprises Inc........................G 910 323-3315
Fayetteville *(G-4626)*

Screen Master..G 252 492-8407
Henderson *(G-6178)*

CLOTHING STORES: Uniforms & Work

Gmg Group LLC......................................G 252 441-8374
Kill Devil Hills *(G-7317)*

McDaniel Delmar.....................................E 336 284-6377
Mocksville *(G-8375)*

CLOTHING STORES: Unisex

L Rancho Investments Inc.................. G 336 431-1004
Trinity *(G-12117)*

CLOTHING STORES: Work

Kontoor Brands Inc......................... A 336 332-3400
Greensboro *(G-5653)*

CLOTHING: Academic Vestments

Atlantic Trading LLC........................ F
Charlotte *(G-1711)*

CLOTHING: Access, Women's & Misses'

Apparel USA Inc............................. E 212 869-5495
Fairmont *(G-4500)*

Blacqueladi Styles LLC..................... G 877 977-7798
Cary *(G-1308)*

Centric Brands LLC......................... B 646 582-6000
Greensboro *(G-5438)*

Live It Boutique LLC........................ G 704 492-2402
Charlotte *(G-2427)*

Lm Shea LLC............................... G 919 608-1901
Raleigh *(G-10259)*

CLOTHING: Aprons, Exc Rubber/Plastic, Women, Misses, Junior

J C Custom Sewing Inc..................... G 336 449-4586
Gibsonville *(G-5178)*

CLOTHING: Aprons, Waterproof, From Purchased Materials

Drydog Barriers LLC........................ G 704 334-8222
Indian Trail *(G-7077)*

CLOTHING: Athletic & Sportswear, Men's & Boys'

Augusta Sportswear Inc.................... G 704 871-0990
Statesville *(G-11662)*

Badger Sportswear LLC.................... B 704 871-0990
Statesville *(G-11666)*

Gfsi Holdings LLC.......................... A 336 519-8080
Winston Salem *(G-13177)*

Ics North America Corp..................... E 704 794-6620
Concord *(G-3375)*

Levi Strauss International.................. E 828 665-2417
Asheville *(G-534)*

Mk Global Holdings LLC................... E 704 334-1904
Charlotte *(G-2511)*

Ramco..................................... G 704 794-6620
Concord *(G-3430)*

Walter Reynolds............................ G 704 735-6050
Lincolnton *(G-7870)*

CLOTHING: Athletic & Sportswear, Women's & Girls'

Alleson of Rochester Inc................... D 585 272-0606
Statesville *(G-11652)*

Ican Clothes Company...................... F 910 670-1494
Fayetteville *(G-4614)*

Kayla Jonise Bernhardt Crutch............ G 252 457-5367
Elizabeth City *(G-4394)*

Walter Reynolds............................ G 704 735-6050
Lincolnton *(G-7870)*

CLOTHING: Baker, Barber, Lab/Svc Ind Apparel, Washable, Men

Criticore Inc............................... F 704 542-6876
Charlotte *(G-1996)*

White Knght Engneered Pdts Inc........... E 828 687-0940
Asheville *(G-634)*

CLOTHING: Belts

Belt Shop Inc.............................. F 704 865-3636
Gastonia *(G-4997)*

Centric Brands LLC......................... B 646 582-6000
Greensboro *(G-5438)*

Hawk Distributors Inc...................... G 888 334-1307
Sanford *(G-11188)*

Madison Company Inc....................... E 336 548-9624
Madison *(G-7992)*

Military Products Inc....................... G 910 637-0315
West End *(G-12557)*

Point Blank Enterprises Inc................ D 910 893-2071
Lillington *(G-7801)*

The Madison Company Inc.................. E 336 548-9624
Madison *(G-8001)*

Wentworth Corporation..................... G 336 548-1802
Madison *(G-8003)*

CLOTHING: Blouses, Women's & Girls'

Grateful Union Family Inc.................. F 828 622-3258
Asheville *(G-510)*

CLOTHING: Caps, Baseball

Americap Co Inc............................ G 252 445-2388
Enfield *(G-4481)*

CLOTHING: Children & Infants'

Cannon & Daughters Inc.................... D 828 254-9236
Asheville *(G-466)*

Devil Dog Manufacturing Co Inc............ C 919 269-7485
Zebulon *(G-13507)*

Justice.................................... E 910 392-1581
Wilmington *(G-12825)*

Tiara Inc.................................. G 828 484-8236
Asheville *(G-619)*

CLOTHING: Coats & Jackets, Leather & Sheep-Lined

Gerbings LLC.............................. D 800 646-5916
Greensboro *(G-5558)*

CLOTHING: Coats & Suits, Men's & Boys'

American Safety Utility Corp............... E 704 482-0601
Shelby *(G-11311)*

Centric Brands LLC......................... B 646 582-6000
Greensboro *(G-5438)*

Trotters Sewing Company Inc.............. D 336 629-4550
Asheboro *(G-413)*

CLOTHING: Collar & Cuff Sets, Knit

C & L Manufacturing........................ G 336 957-8359
Hays *(G-6145)*

Charlotte Trimming Company Inc........... E 704 529-8427
Charlotte *(G-1905)*

CLOTHING: Costumes

Morris Family Theatrical Inc............... E 704 332-3304
Charlotte *(G-2519)*

CLOTHING: Disposable

Ddm Inc................................... G 910 686-1481
Wilmington *(G-12762)*

Pearl River Group LLC...................... G 704 283-4667
Monroe *(G-8541)*

Precept Medical Products Inc.............. F 828 681-0209
Arden *(G-298)*

CLOTHING: Dresses

Gerson & Gerson Inc....................... E 252 235-2441
Middlesex *(G-8276)*

Granite Knitwear Inc....................... E 704 279-5526
Granite Quarry *(G-5326)*

Hugger Inc................................ C 704 735-7422
Lincolnton *(G-7832)*

Jestines Jewels Inc........................ G 704 904-0191
Salisbury *(G-11072)*

CLOTHING: Dresses & Skirts

Contempora Fabrics Inc.................... C 910 345-0150
Lumberton *(G-7948)*

CLOTHING: Hats & Headwear, Knit

Slum Dog Head Gear LLC................... F 704 713-8125
Charlotte *(G-2816)*

CLOTHING: Hosiery, Pantyhose & Knee Length, Sheer

Acme - McCrary Corporation............... F 336 625-2161
Siler City *(G-11396)*

Acme-Mccrary Corporation................. C 336 625-2161
Asheboro *(G-323)*

Bossong Corporation....................... G 336 625-2175
Asheboro *(G-332)*

Cajah Corporation......................... C 828 728-7300
Hudson *(G-6944)*

Catawba Valley Finishing LLC............. E 828 464-2252
Newton *(G-9453)*

Central Carolina Hosiery Inc.............. E 910 428-9688
Biscoe *(G-849)*

De Feet International Inc.................. G 828 397-7025
Hildebran *(G-6848)*

Felice Hosiery Co Inc...................... E 336 996-2371
Kernersville *(G-7274)*

Fine Line Hosiery Inc...................... G 336 498-8022
Asheboro *(G-356)*

Glen Raven Inc............................ F 336 227-6211
Altamahaw *(G-103)*

Goldtoemoretz LLC........................ B 828 464-0751
Newton *(G-9470)*

Hanesbrands Inc........................... G 336 789-6118
Mount Airy *(G-9126)*

Huffman Finishing Company Inc............ C 828 396-1741
Granite Falls *(G-5308)*

Kayser-Roth Corporation................... C 336 852-2030
Greensboro *(G-5643)*

Mas Acme USA............................. G 336 625-2161
Asheboro *(G-376)*

Mayo Knitting Mill Inc..................... C 252 823-3101
Tarboro *(G-11934)*

Neat Feet Hosiery Inc...................... G 336 573-2177
Stoneville *(G-11823)*

North Carolina Sock Inc.................... G 828 327-4664
Hickory *(G-6403)*

Rogers Knitting Inc........................ G 336 789-4155
Mount Airy *(G-9172)*

Royal Hosiery Company Inc................ G 828 496-2200
Granite Falls *(G-5322)*

Simmons Hosiery Mill Inc.................. G 828 327-4890
Hickory *(G-6448)*

Slane Hosiery Mills Inc.................... C 336 883-4136
High Point *(G-6781)*

Special T Hosiery Mills Inc................ G 336 227-2858
Burlington *(G-1161)*

Surratt Hosiery Mill Inc................... G 336 859-4583
Denton *(G-3762)*

Teamwork Inc.............................. G 336 578-3456
Elon *(G-4472)*

Thorneburg Hosiery Mills Inc.............. E 704 279-7247
Rockwell *(G-10805)*

Thorneburg Hosiery Mills Inc.............. E 704 838-6329
Statesville *(G-11788)*

Zimmermann - Dynayarn Usa LLC......... E 336 222-8129
  Graham (G-5290)

CLOTHING: Hospital, Men's

Aj & Raine Scrubs & More LLC.............. G 646 374-5198
  Charlotte (G-1634)

Ics North America Corp...................... E 704 794-6620
  Concord (G-3375)

Keani Furniture Inc........................... E 336 303-5484
  Asheboro (G-369)

Smissons Inc.................................... G 660 537-3219
  Clayton (G-3169)

Tafford Uniforms LLC........................ D 888 823-3673
  Charlotte (G-2897)

West Hllcrest Dda Group HM LLC......... F 336 478-7444
  Burlington (G-1179)

CLOTHING: Jackets & Vests, Exc Fur & Leather, Women's

Fox Apparel Inc............................... C 336 629-7641
  Asheboro (G-357)

CLOTHING: Jeans, Men's & Boys'

Brilliant You LLC............................... G 336 343-5535
  Greensboro (G-5404)

CLOTHING: Leather

Inspiration Leather Design Inc............. G 336 420-2265
  Jamestown (G-7169)

Rmg Leather Usa LLC....................... G 828 466-5489
  Conover (G-3555)

CLOTHING: Men's & boy's underwear & nightwear

Carolina Apparel Group Inc................. D 704 694-6544
  Wadesboro (G-12239)

Wilo Incorporated............................. E 336 679-4440
  Yadkinville (G-13458)

CLOTHING: Mens & Boys Jackets, Sport, Suede, Leatherette

Fox Apparel Inc............................... C 336 629-7641
  Asheboro (G-357)

Wrangler Apparel Corp...................... B 336 332-3400
  Greensboro (G-5925)

CLOTHING: Neckwear

Angunique....................................... G 336 392-5866
  Greensboro (G-5364)

Brown & Church Neck Wear Co........... E 336 368-5502
  Pilot Mountain (G-9670)

Hbb Global LLC................................ G 615 306-1270
  Apex (G-163)

Hirsch Solutions LLC......................... G 631 701-2112
  Huntersville (G-6999)

HL James LLC................................. G 516 398-3311
  Durham (G-4062)

Lizzys Logos Inc.............................. G 704 321-2588
  Matthews (G-8127)

Mudgear LLC................................... G 347 674-9102
  Charlotte (G-2525)

Wicked Oceans................................ G 252 269-0488
  Nags Head (G-9306)

CLOTHING: Outerwear, Knit

Blue Lagoon Inc............................... G 828 324-2333
  Hickory (G-6273)

Hanesbrands Inc.............................. G 910 462-2001
  Laurel Hill (G-7483)

Hillshire Brands Company................... G 336 519-8080
  Winston Salem (G-13198)

Park Shirt Company.......................... G 931 879-5894
  Fayetteville (G-4652)

Pitman Knits Inc............................... G 704 276-3262
  Vale (G-12210)

Xtinguish LLC.................................. G 704 868-9500
  Charlotte (G-3034)

CLOTHING: Outerwear, Women's & Misses' NEC

Badger Sportswear LLC...................... D 704 871-0990
  Statesville (G-11665)

Belvoir Manufacturing Corp................. D 252 746-1274
  Greenville (G-5947)

Bennett Uniform Mfg Inc.................... F 336 232-5772
  Greensboro (G-5387)

Devil Dog Manufacturing Co Inc........... C 919 269-7485
  Zebulon (G-13507)

Divine Creations.............................. G 704 364-5844
  Morehead City (G-8829)

Eagle Sportswear LLC....................... G 252 235-4082
  Middlesex (G-8273)

Granite Knitwear Inc......................... E 704 279-5526
  Granite Quarry (G-5326)

Levi Strauss International................... G 828 665-2417
  Asheville (G-534)

McDaniel Delmar.............................. E 336 284-6377
  Mocksville (G-8375)

Mitt S Nitts Inc................................ E 919 596-6793
  Durham (G-4139)

Seafarer LLC................................... G 704 624-3200
  Marshville (G-8094)

CLOTHING: Panty Hose

Acme-Mccrary Corporation.................. C 919 663-2200
  Siler City (G-11397)

Acme-Mccrary Corporation.................. B 336 625-2161
  Asheboro (G-324)

Commonwealth Hosiery Mills Inc.......... D 336 498-2621
  Randleman (G-10638)

Concord Trading Inc.......................... E 704 375-3333
  Concord (G-3343)

Fine Sheer Industries Inc................... B 704 375-3333
  Concord (G-3363)

Hanesbrands Inc.............................. A 336 519-8080
  Winston Salem (G-13188)

Sue-Lynn Textiles Inc........................ E 336 578-0871
  Haw River (G-6135)

Upel Inc... G 336 519-8080
  Winston Salem (G-13379)

CLOTHING: Robes & Dressing Gowns

Sanders Industries Inc....................... G 410 277-8565
  Waynesville (G-12472)

CLOTHING: Robes & Housecoats, Children's

Sanders Industries Inc....................... G 410 277-8565
  Waynesville (G-12472)

CLOTHING: Service Apparel, Women's

Kontoor Brands Inc........................... A 336 332-3400
  Greensboro (G-5653)

CLOTHING: Shirts

Devil Dog Manufacturing Co Inc........... C 919 269-7485
  Zebulon (G-13507)

Funco Inc....................................... G 704 788-3003
  Concord (G-3367)

Royal Textile Mills Inc....................... D 336 694-4121
  Yanceyville (G-13460)

CLOTHING: Shirts, Knit

Associated Distributors Inc................. G 910 895-5800
  Hamlet (G-6050)

L C Industries Inc............................. C 919 596-8277
  Durham (G-4100)

Winstn-Slem Inds For Blind Inc........... B 336 759-0551
  Winston Salem (G-13398)

CLOTHING: Shirts, Women's & Juniors', From Purchased Mtrls

Kontoor Brands Inc........................... D 336 332-3586
  Greensboro (G-5652)

Wrangler Apparel Corp...................... B 336 332-3400
  Greensboro (G-5925)

CLOTHING: Socks

B & B Hosiery Mill............................ G 336 368-4849
  Pinnacle (G-9767)

B & M Wholesale Inc......................... G 336 789-3916
  Mount Airy (G-9100)

Beard Hosiery Co............................. D 828 758-1942
  Lenoir (G-7577)

Bossong Hosiery Mills Inc.................. C 336 625-2175
  Asheboro (G-333)

Cedar Valley Hosiery Mill Inc.............. G 828 396-1804
  Hudson (G-6949)

Commonwealth Hosiery Mills Inc.......... D 336 498-2621
  Randleman (G-10638)

Concord Trading Inc.......................... E 704 375-3333
  Concord (G-3343)

Custom Socks Ink Inc........................ E 828 695-9869
  Newton (G-9463)

De Feet International Inc.................... G 828 397-7025
  Hildebran (G-6848)

Diabetic Sock Club............................ G 800 214-0218
  Gastonia (G-5041)

Elder Hosiery Mills Inc....................... G 336 226-0673
  Burlington (G-1086)

Farr Knitting Company Inc.................. G 336 625-5561
  Asheboro (G-354)

Felice Hosiery Co Inc........................ E 336 996-2371
  Kernersville (G-7274)

Fine Sheer Industries Inc................... B 704 375-3333
  Concord (G-3363)

Goldtoemoretz LLC........................... B 828 464-0751
  Newton (G-9470)

Grady Distributing Co Inc................... F 919 556-5630
  Youngsville (G-13473)

Graham Dyeing & Finishing Inc............ D 336 228-9981
  Burlington (G-1101)

Hanesbrands Inc.............................. E 336 519-8080
  Rural Hall (G-10961)

Hanesbrands Inc.............................. A 336 519-8080
  Winston Salem (G-13188)

Harriss & Covington Hsy Mills............. G 336 882-6811
  High Point (G-6638)

Harriss Cvington Hsy Mills Inc............. C 336 882-6811
  High Point (G-6639)

Hill Hosiery Mill Inc.......................... G 336 472-7908
  Thomasville (G-12031)

Huitt Mills Inc................................. E 828 322-8628
  Hildebran (G-6851)

Implus LLC..................................... F 828 485-3318
  Hickory (G-6367)

J R B and J Knitting Inc.................... G 910 439-4242
  Mount Gilead (G-9199)

Jefferies Socks LLC.......................... F 336 226-7316
  Burlington (G-1112)

JI Hosiery LLC................................ F 910 974-7156
  Candor (G-1237)

Kayser-Roth Hosiery Inc...................F 336 229-2269
Graham *(G-5274)*

Kayser-Roth Hosiery Inc...................E 336 852-2030
Greensboro *(G-5644)*

KB Socks Inc...................G 336 719-8000
Mount Airy *(G-9139)*

Kelly Hosiery Mill Inc...................G 828 324-6456
Hickory *(G-6376)*

Legacy Knitting LLC...................G 844 762-2678
Wilmington *(G-12833)*

Lyons Hosiery Inc...................G 336 789-2651
Mount Airy *(G-9150)*

Mayo Knitting Mill Inc...................C 252 823-3101
Tarboro *(G-11934)*

NC Quality Sales LLC...................F 336 786-7211
Mount Airy *(G-9157)*

Neat Feet Hosiery Inc...................G 336 573-2177
Stoneville *(G-11823)*

Nester Hosiery Inc...................D 336 789-0026
Mount Airy *(G-9159)*

Nester Hosiery LLC...................E 336 789-0026
Mount Airy *(G-9160)*

North Carolina Sock Inc...................G 828 327-4664
Hickory *(G-6403)*

Peacoat Media LLC...................G 336 298-1133
Winston Salem *(G-13277)*

Pickett Hosiery Mills Inc...................E 336 227-2716
Burlington *(G-1139)*

R Evans Hosiery LLC...................E 828 397-8715
Connelly Springs *(G-3482)*

Renfro LLC...................D 336 719-8290
Mount Airy *(G-9169)*

Renfro LLC...................C 336 719-8000
Mount Airy *(G-9170)*

Renfro Mexico Holdings LLC...................G 336 786-3501
Mount Airy *(G-9171)*

Robinson Hosiery Mill Inc...................G 828 874-2228
Valdese *(G-12199)*

Royce Too LLC...................E 212 356-1627
Winston Salem *(G-13324)*

Russell-Fshion Foot Hsy Mlls I...................G 336 299-0741
Greensboro *(G-5799)*

Sara Lee Socks...................G 336 789-6118
Mount Airy *(G-9174)*

Sock Factory Inc...................E 828 328-5207
Hickory *(G-6451)*

Sock Inc...................G 561 254-2223
Charlotte *(G-2823)*

Socks and Other Things LLC...................G 704 904-2472
Charlotte *(G-2824)*

Special T Hosiery Mills Inc...................G 336 227-2858
Burlington *(G-1161)*

Sports Solutions Inc...................F 336 368-1100
Pilot Mountain *(G-9674)*

Surratt Hosiery Mill Inc...................G 336 859-4583
Denton *(G-3762)*

Teamwork Inc...................G 336 578-3456
Elon *(G-4472)*

Thorneburg Hosiery Mills Inc...................E 704 279-7247
Rockwell *(G-10805)*

Thorneburg Hosiery Mills Inc...................E 704 872-6522
Statesville *(G-11786)*

Thorneburg Hosiery Mills Inc...................E 704 838-6329
Statesville *(G-11788)*

Thorneburg Hosiery Mills Inc...................C 704 872-6522
Statesville *(G-11787)*

Trimfit Inc...................C 336 476-6154
Thomasville *(G-12084)*

Tysinger Hosiery Mill Inc...................F 336 472-2148
Lexington *(G-7755)*

Upel Inc...................G 336 519-8080
Winston Salem *(G-13379)*

US Custom Socks Co LLC...................G 336 549-1088
Greensboro *(G-5893)*

Wells Hosiery Mills Inc...................C 336 633-4881
Asheboro *(G-420)*

Wilson Brown Inc...................F 336 226-0237
Burlington *(G-1180)*

Woodland Hosiery Inc...................G 910 439-4843
Mount Gilead *(G-9212)*

CLOTHING: Sportswear, Women's

G & G Enterprises...................G 336 764-2493
Clemmons *(G-3186)*

Hanesbrands Inc...................G 910 462-2001
Laurel Hill *(G-7483)*

CLOTHING: Sweaters & Sweater Coats, Knit

Mitt S Nitts Inc...................E 919 596-6793
Durham *(G-4139)*

CLOTHING: Sweaters, Men's & Boys'

Home T LLC...................F 646 797-4768
Charlotte *(G-2284)*

CLOTHING: Sweatshirts & T-Shirts, Men's & Boys'

Wrangler Apparel Corp...................B 336 332-3400
Greensboro *(G-5925)*

CLOTHING: T-Shirts & Tops, Knit

Ba International LLC...................G 336 519-8080
Winston Salem *(G-13100)*

Blue Bay Distributing Inc...................G 919 957-1300
Durham *(G-3935)*

Hanesbrands Inc...................A 336 519-8080
Winston Salem *(G-13188)*

Hbi Wh Minority Holdings LLC...................G 336 519-8080
Winston Salem *(G-13193)*

Hugger Inc...................C 704 735-7422
Lincolnton *(G-7832)*

Kamp Usa Inc...................F 336 668-1169
High Point *(G-6682)*

Noble Wholesalers Inc...................G 409 739-3803
Clayton *(G-3162)*

Playtex Dorado LLC...................G 336 519-8080
Winston Salem *(G-13297)*

Royal Textile Mills Inc...................D 336 694-4121
Yanceyville *(G-13460)*

Upel Inc...................G 336 519-8080
Winston Salem *(G-13379)*

CLOTHING: T-Shirts & Tops, Women's & Girls'

Royce Apparel Inc...................E 704 933-6000
Salisbury *(G-11112)*

CLOTHING: Tights, Exc Women's

Central Carolina Hosiery Inc...................E 910 428-9688
Biscoe *(G-849)*

Star America Inc...................C 704 788-4700
Concord *(G-3448)*

CLOTHING: Trousers & Slacks, Men's & Boys'

Centric Brands LLC...................B 646 582-6000
Greensboro *(G-5438)*

Devil Dog Manufacturing Co Inc...................C 919 269-7485
Zebulon *(G-13507)*

Kontoor Brands Inc...................D 336 332-3586
Greensboro *(G-5652)*

Ralph Lauren Corporation...................G 336 632-5000
Greensboro *(G-5780)*

Wrangler Apparel Corp...................B 336 332-3400
Greensboro *(G-5925)*

CLOTHING: Underwear, Knit

Hillshire Brands Company...................G 336 519-8080
Winston Salem *(G-13198)*

CLOTHING: Underwear, Women's & Children's

Verena Designs Inc...................E 336 869-8235
High Point *(G-6825)*

CLOTHING: Uniforms & Vestments

Remington 1816 Foundation...................G 866 686-7778
Charlotte *(G-2707)*

Royal Park Uniforms Inc...................G 336 562-3345
Prospect Hill *(G-9829)*

Spiritus Systems Company...................E 910 637-0196
Aberdeen *(G-25)*

CLOTHING: Uniforms, Ex Athletic, Women's, Misses' & Juniors'

Bennett Uniform Mfg Inc...................F 336 232-5772
Greensboro *(G-5387)*

CLOTHING: Uniforms, Firemen's, From Purchased Materials

Salute Industries Inc...................G 844 937-2588
Archdale *(G-242)*

CLOTHING: Uniforms, Men's & Boys'

McDaniel Delmar...................E 336 284-6377
Mocksville *(G-8375)*

Tresmc LLC...................G 919 900-0868
Knightdale *(G-7461)*

CLOTHING: Uniforms, Military, Men/Youth, Purchased Materials

Lelantos Group Inc...................D 704 780-4127
Mooresville *(G-8709)*

Military Products Inc...................G 910 637-0315
West End *(G-12557)*

Safety & Security Intl Inc...................G 336 285-8673
Greensboro *(G-5800)*

US Patriot LLC...................F 803 787-9398
Fort Bragg *(G-4805)*

CLOTHING: Uniforms, Work

Bennett Uniform Mfg Inc...................F 336 232-5772
Greensboro *(G-5387)*

Intersport Group Inc...................G 814 968-3085
Vilas *(G-12230)*

Magnolia Linen Inc...................F 336 449-0447
Gibsonville *(G-5182)*

S Loflin Enterprises Inc...................F 704 633-1159
Salisbury *(G-11113)*

Tillery Accessories Inc...................G 704 474-3013
Norwood *(G-9562)*

CLOTHING: Work Apparel, Exc Uniforms

Causa LLC...................G 866 695-7022
Charlotte *(G-1868)*

Kontoor Brands Inc...................A 336 332-3400
Greensboro *(G-5653)*

COAL & OTHER MINERALS & ORES WHOLESALERS

Daystar Materials Inc..............................E 919 734-0460
Goldsboro *(G-5211)*

Norcor Technologies Corp.....................G 704 309-4101
Greensboro *(G-5712)*

COAL MINING SERVICES

Cowee Mountain Ruby Mine..................G 828 369-5271
Franklin *(G-4823)*

COAL MINING: Bituminous Coal & Lignite-Surface Mining

Florida Progress Corporation................C 704 382-3853
Raleigh *(G-10113)*

COATING COMPOUNDS: Tar

Actega North America Inc.....................G 704 736-9389
Kings Mountain *(G-7343)*

COATING SVC: Metals, With Plastic Or Resins

Coating Concepts Inc............................G 704 391-0499
Charlotte *(G-1941)*

COATINGS: Epoxy

New Finish Inc.....................................E 704 474-4116
Norwood *(G-9557)*

Renner Wood Companies.......................F 704 527-9261
Charlotte *(G-2712)*

COATINGS: Polyurethane

Axalta Coating Systems LLC...............G 855 629-2582
Concord *(G-3315)*

Lord Corporation.................................B 919 468-5979
Cary *(G-1394)*

Lord Far East Inc.................................G 919 468-5979
Cary *(G-1397)*

COILS & TRANSFORMERS

Carolina Metals Inc..............................F 828 667-0876
Asheville *(G-470)*

Coil Innovation Usa Inc.........................G 919 659-0300
Cary *(G-1330)*

Misonix Opco Inc..................................F 631 694-9555
Durham *(G-4137)*

Peak Demand Inc..................................F 252 360-2777
Wilson *(G-13013)*

Prolec-GE Waukesha Inc.......................B 919 734-8900
Goldsboro *(G-5238)*

Smart Wires Inc...................................D 919 294-3999
Durham *(G-4239)*

COILS: Electric Motors Or Generators

Lennox International Inc.........................C 828 633-4805
Candler *(G-1229)*

Sag Harbor Industries Inc.....................E 252 753-7175
Farmville *(G-4539)*

COLORS: Pigments, Inorganic

Americhem Inc.....................................E 704 782-6411
Concord *(G-3311)*

Avient Colorants USA LLC....................D 704 331-7000
Charlotte *(G-1723)*

Ultra Coatings Incorporated..................F 336 883-8853
High Point *(G-6817)*

COMBINATION UTILITIES, NEC

Noahs Inc..F 704 718-2354
Charlotte *(G-2570)*

COMFORTERS & QUILTS, FROM MANMADE FIBER OR SILK

Premier Quilting Corporation.................G 919 693-1151
Oxford *(G-9626)*

COMMERCIAL & OFFICE BUILDINGS RENOVATION & REPAIR

Exteriors Inc Ltd.................................G 919 325-2251
Spring Lake *(G-11561)*

International Tela-Com Inc....................G 828 651-9801
Fletcher *(G-4743)*

Lock Drives Inc...................................G 704 588-1844
Pineville *(G-9740)*

Seashore Builders Inc..........................E 910 259-3404
Maple Hill *(G-8026)*

COMMERCIAL ART & GRAPHIC DESIGN SVCS

Barron Legacy Mgmt Group LLC..........G 301 367-4735
Charlotte *(G-1757)*

Big Fish Dpi..G 704 545-8112
Mint Hill *(G-8331)*

Boundless Inc......................................G 919 622-9051
Four Oaks *(G-4809)*

CD Dickie & Associates Inc..................F 704 527-9102
Charlotte *(G-1878)*

Coastal Press Inc.................................G 252 726-1549
Morehead City *(G-8827)*

Cold Water No Bleach LLC....................G 336 505-9584
Durham *(G-3981)*

Contract Printing & Graphics................G 919 832-7178
Raleigh *(G-10014)*

Designs By Rachel...............................G 828 783-0698
Spruce Pine *(G-11574)*

Family Industries Inc...........................G 919 875-4499
Raleigh *(G-10104)*

Fast Pro Media LLC.............................G 704 799-8040
Cornelius *(G-3600)*

Fiestic Inc..F 888 935-3999
Raleigh *(G-10107)*

Gmg Group LLC...................................G 252 441-8374
Kill Devil Hills *(G-7317)*

Heritage Prtg & Graphics Inc................G 704 551-0700
Charlotte *(G-2274)*

High Performance Marketing Inc............G 919 870-9915
Raleigh *(G-10167)*

Merge LLC..G 919 832-3924
Raleigh *(G-10291)*

Metro Productions Inc..........................F 919 851-6420
Raleigh *(G-10296)*

Multi Packaging Solutions.....................A 336 855-7142
Greensboro *(G-5699)*

NC Graphic Pros LLC............................G 252 492-7326
Kittrell *(G-7442)*

Prism Publishing Inc............................F 919 319-6816
Cary *(G-1428)*

Triangle Solutions Inc..........................G 919 481-1235
Cary *(G-1473)*

COMMERCIAL ART & ILLUSTRATION SVCS

Skipper Graphics.................................G 910 754-8729
Shallotte *(G-11305)*

COMMERCIAL CONTAINERS WHOLESALERS

Boxman Studios LLC............................G 704 333-3733
Mount Holly *(G-9219)*

COMMERCIAL EQPT WHOLESALERS, NEC

Dandy Light Traps Inc..........................G 980 223-2744
Statesville *(G-11684)*

Satco Truck Equipment Inc...................F 919 383-5547
Durham *(G-4222)*

COMMERCIAL EQPT, WHOLESALE: Restaurant, NEC

Elxsi Corporation.................................B 407 849-1090
Charlotte *(G-2105)*

Government Sales LLC..........................G 252 726-6315
Morehead City *(G-8833)*

Singer Equipment Company Inc............E 910 484-1128
Fayetteville *(G-4671)*

Thompson & Little Inc..........................E 910 484-1128
Fayetteville *(G-4680)*

COMMERCIAL EQPT, WHOLESALE: Scales, Exc Laboratory

True Portion Inc..................................F 336 362-6326
High Point *(G-6813)*

COMMERCIAL EQPT, WHOLESALE: Store Fixtures & Display Eqpt

Riddley Retail Fixtures Inc....................E 704 435-8829
Kings Mountain *(G-7382)*

COMMERCIAL LAUNDRY EQPT

Leonard Automatics Inc........................E 704 483-9316
Denver *(G-3792)*

Talley Machinery Corporation................G 336 664-0012
Greensboro *(G-5850)*

COMMERCIAL PHOTOGRAPHIC STUDIO

Advertising Design Systems Inc............G 828 264-8060
Boone *(G-894)*

Timothy L Griffin................................G 336 317-8314
Greenville *(G-6028)*

COMMERCIAL PRINTING & NEWSPAPER PUBLISHING

Asian (korean) Herald Inc.....................G 704 332-5656
Charlotte *(G-1705)*

Automail LLC.......................................G 704 677-0152
Mooresville *(G-8602)*

Carter Publishing Company Inc.............F 336 993-2161
Kernersville *(G-7253)*

Carteret Publishing Company................G 910 326-5066
Swansboro *(G-11883)*

Charlotte Observer Pubg Co.................A 704 358-5000
Charlotte *(G-1899)*

Cooke Communications NC LLC............F 252 329-9500
Greenville *(G-5958)*

Dth Publishing Inc...............................G 919 962-1163
Chapel Hill *(G-1541)*

Duke Student Publishing Co Inc............G 919 684-3811
Durham *(G-4010)*

Fayetteville Publishing Co.....................E 910 323-4848
Fayetteville *(G-4601)*

Gaston Gazette LLP.............................A 704 869-1700
Gastonia *(G-5051)*

Halifax Media Holdings LLC..................G 828 692-5763
Hendersonville *(G-6211)*

High Country News Inc.........................G 828 264-2262
Boone *(G-922)*

High Point Enterprise Inc......................F 336 472-9500
Thomasville *(G-12030)*

High Point Enterprise Llc.....................C 336 888-3500
High Point *(G-6651)*

Nash County Newspapers Inc................ F 252 459-7101
Nashville *(G-9322)*

Rennasentient Inc.............................. G 919 233-7710
Cary *(G-1435)*

Skybien Press LLC............................. G 919 544-1777
Durham *(G-4238)*

Star Fleet Communications Inc............ G 828 252-6565
Asheville *(G-611)*

Sun-Journal Incorporated................... E 252 638-8101
New Bern *(G-9398)*

Taylorsville Times.............................. G 828 632-2532
Taylorsville *(G-11983)*

Times News Publishing Company........ F 336 226-4414
Burlington *(G-1168)*

Times Printing Company..................... E 252 473-2105
Manteo *(G-8024)*

Wilson Daily Times Inc...................... E 252 243-5151
Wilson *(G-13048)*

COMMON SAND MINING

Bulk Transport Service Inc................ G 910 329-0555
Holly Ridge *(G-6887)*

Columbia Silica Sand LLC................. G 803 755-1036
Wilmington *(G-12745)*

Cumberland Grav & Sand Min Co......... F 828 686-3844
Swannanoa *(G-11870)*

COMMUNICATIONS EQPT WHOLESALERS

Majorpower Corporation..................... E 919 563-6610
Mebane *(G-8251)*

US Microwave Inc............................ G 520 891-2444
Pittsboro *(G-9791)*

COMMUNICATIONS EQPT: Microwave

Commscope Inc North Carolina........... F 828 459-5001
Claremont *(G-3095)*

Commscope Inc North Carolina........... E 828 324-2200
Claremont *(G-3096)*

Commscope Cnnctvity Sltons LLC........ F 828 324-2200
Hickory *(G-6307)*

Commscope Technologies LLC............ G 919 934-9711
Smithfield *(G-11440)*

Commscope Technologies LLC............ A 828 324-2200
Claremont *(G-3104)*

COMMUNICATIONS EQPT: Radio, Marine

Triton Marine Services Inc................ G 252 728-9958
Beaufort *(G-736)*

COMMUNICATIONS SVCS: Data

Bluetick Inc.................................... F 336 294-4102
Greensboro *(G-5395)*

Gpx Intelligence Inc......................... E 888 260-0706
Greensboro *(G-5570)*

Spectrasite Communications LLC........ E 919 468-0112
Cary *(G-1465)*

COMMUNICATIONS SVCS: Internet Connectivity Svcs

Cengage Learning Inc....................... E 919 829-8181
Raleigh *(G-9990)*

Charlotte Observer Pubg Co............... A 704 358-5000
Charlotte *(G-1899)*

Telit Wireless Solutions Inc............... D 919 439-7977
Durham *(G-4264)*

COMMUNICATIONS SVCS: Internet Host Svcs

Mountain Area Info Netwrk................. F 828 255-0182
Asheville *(G-552)*

COMMUNICATIONS SVCS: Online Svc Providers

M I Connection................................ F 704 662-3255
Mooresville *(G-8717)*

COMMUNICATIONS SVCS: Signal Enhancement Network Svcs

Commscope LLC.............................. C 828 324-2200
Claremont *(G-3097)*

Commscope Holding Company Inc....... F 919 677-2422
Cary *(G-1331)*

Commscope Holding Company Inc....... A 828 459-5000
Claremont *(G-3100)*

COMMUTATORS: Electronic

Ashbran LLC................................... G 919 215-3567
Clayton *(G-3132)*

COMPOSITION STONE: Plastic

Fibreworks Composites LLC............... E 704 696-1084
Mooresville *(G-8663)*

COMPOST

Cmd Land Services LLC.................... G 919 554-2281
Wake Forest *(G-12271)*

Eastern Compost LLC....................... G 252 446-3636
Elm City *(G-4465)*

McGill Environmental Gp LLC............ F 919 362-1161
New Hill *(G-9410)*

Tarheel Enviromental LLC.................. G 910 425-4939
Stedman *(G-11808)*

COMPRESSORS: Air & Gas

Air & Gas Solutions LLC................... E 704 897-2182
Charlotte *(G-1631)*

Atlas Copco Compressors LLC........... F 704 525-0124
Charlotte *(G-1714)*

Eagle Compressors Inc..................... E 336 370-4159
Greensboro *(G-5509)*

Edmac Compressor Parts................... E 800 866-2959
Charlotte *(G-2091)*

Fresh Air Technologies LLC............... F 704 622-7877
Matthews *(G-8171)*

Hayward Industries Inc..................... A 336 712-9900
Clemmons *(G-3189)*

Hertz Kompressoren USA Inc............. G 704 579-5900
Huntersville *(G-6998)*

Ingersoll Rand Inc........................... E 704 774-4290
Charlotte *(G-2335)*

Metal Impact East LLC..................... G 743 205-1900
Graham *(G-5279)*

Nordson Corporation......................... F 724 656-5600
Hickory *(G-6402)*

Pattons Medical LLC......................... G 704 529-5442
Charlotte *(G-2617)*

Peco Inc.. E 828 684-1234
Arden *(G-296)*

Trane Technologies Company LLC........ B 336 751-3561
Mocksville *(G-8394)*

Universal Air Products Corp................ G 704 374-0600
Charlotte *(G-2965)*

COMPRESSORS: Air & Gas, Including Vacuum Pumps

Backyard Entps & Svcs LLC............... G 828 755-4960
Spindale *(G-11544)*

Elgi Compressors USA Inc................. G 704 943-7966
Charlotte *(G-2100)*

G Denver and Co LLC....................... E 704 896-4000
Davidson *(G-3705)*

INGERSOLL RAND INC...................... A 704 896-4000
Davidson *(G-3709)*

Ingersoll-Rand Indus US Inc............... D 704 896-4000
Davidson *(G-3710)*

Safe Air Systems Inc........................ E 336 674-0749
Randleman *(G-10659)*

Sub-Aquatics Inc............................. E 336 674-0749
Randleman *(G-10661)*

COMPRESSORS: Refrigeration & Air Conditioning Eqpt

City Compressor Rebuilders............... G 704 947-1811
Charlotte *(G-1921)*

COMPUTER & COMPUTER SOFTWARE STORES

Northstar Computer Tech Inc.............. G 980 272-1969
Monroe *(G-8537)*

Silver Knight Pcs LLC....................... G 910 824-2054
Fayetteville *(G-4670)*

COMPUTER & COMPUTER SOFTWARE STORES: Peripheral Eqpt

Global Products & Mfg Svcs Inc.......... G 360 870-9876
Charlotte *(G-2215)*

Preferred Data Corporation................ G 336 886-3282
High Point *(G-6743)*

Terarecon Inc................................. D 650 372-1100
Durham *(G-4267)*

COMPUTER & COMPUTER SOFTWARE STORES: Personal Computers

Complete Comp St of Ralgh Inc.......... E 919 828-5227
Raleigh *(G-10005)*

COMPUTER & COMPUTER SOFTWARE STORES: Software & Access

Infisoft Software............................. G 704 307-2619
Charlotte *(G-2329)*

Information Tech Works LLC............... G 919 232-5332
Raleigh *(G-10195)*

COMPUTER & COMPUTER SOFTWARE STORES: Software, Bus/Non-Game

Barefoot Cnc Inc............................. G 828 438-5038
Morganton *(G-8852)*

Payload Media Inc........................... G 919 367-2969
Cary *(G-1415)*

COMPUTER & COMPUTER SOFTWARE STORES: Software, Computer Game

Grover Gaming Inc........................... D 252 329-7900
Greenville *(G-5985)*

Ideacode Inc.................................. G 919 341-5170
Greensboro *(G-5613)*

COMPUTER & DATA PROCESSING EQPT REPAIR & MAINTENANCE

Artesian Future Technology LLC.......... G 919 904-4940
Chapel Hill *(G-1529)*

Complete Comp St of Ralgh Inc.......... E 919 828-5227
Raleigh *(G-10005)*

Innait Inc...................................... G 406 241-5245
Charlotte *(G-2337)*

P
R
O
D
U
C
T

COMPUTER & OFFICE MACHINE MAINTENANCE & REPAIR

Biz Technology Solutions LLC............... E 704 658-1707
Mooresville (G-8615)

Carolina Cartridge Systems Inc............. E 704 347-2447
Charlotte (G-1844)

Comtech Group Inc................................. G 919 313-4800
Durham (G-3986)

Northrop Grumman Systems Corp........ D 252 225-0911
Atlantic (G-638)

Silver Knight Pcs LLC............................. G 910 824-2054
Fayetteville (G-4670)

COMPUTER FACILITIES MANAGEMENT SVCS

Infobelt LLC.. F 980 223-4000
Charlotte (G-2331)

COMPUTER GRAPHICS SVCS

Big Fish Dpi.. G 704 545-8112
Mint Hill (G-8331)

Line Drive Sports Center Inc................. G 336 824-1692
Ramseur (G-10628)

Outer Banks Internet Inc....................... G 252 441-6698
Kill Devil Hills (G-7318)

Richa Inc... G 704 944-0230
Charlotte (G-2724)

Richa Inc... F 704 331-9744
Charlotte (G-2725)

S & A Cherokee LLC.............................. E 919 674-6020
Cary (G-1443)

Stitchmaster LLC................................... F 336 852-6448
Greensboro (G-5841)

Telepathic Graphics Inc........................ E 919 342-4603
Raleigh (G-10540)

COMPUTER PERIPHERAL EQPT REPAIR & MAINTENANCE

St Investors Inc..................................... D 704 969-7500
Charlotte (G-2856)

COMPUTER PERIPHERAL EQPT, NEC

Black Box Corporation........................... G 704 248-6430
Pineville (G-9715)

Brilliant Sole Inc.................................... G 339 222-8528
Wilmington (G-12723)

Cable Devices Incorporated.................. C 714 554-4370
Hickory (G-6281)

Carlisle Corporation.............................. A 704 501-1100
Charlotte (G-1842)

Commscope Technologies LLC.............. G 919 934-9711
Smithfield (G-11440)

Faith Computer Repairs......................... G 910 730-1731
Lumberton (G-7953)

H&A Scientific Inc.................................. G 252 752-4315
Greenville (G-5986)

Hema Online Indian Btq LLC................. G 919 771-4374
Apex (G-164)

Hermes Medical Solutions Inc.............. G 252 355-4373
Farmville (G-4531)

International Bus Mchs Corp.................. B 919 543-6919
Durham (G-4080)

JPS Communications Inc....................... D 919 534-1168
Raleigh (G-10222)

Pro-Face America LLC........................... E 734 477-0600
Greensboro (G-5766)

Revware Inc.. G 919 790-0000
Raleigh (G-10442)

Riverbed Technology LLC...................... E 415 247-8800
Durham (G-4216)

Rsa Security LLC................................... E 704 847-4725
Matthews (G-8146)

Savoye Solutions Inc............................ G 919 466-9784
Raleigh (G-10458)

Sighttech LLC.. G 855 997-4448
Charlotte (G-2805)

Southern Data Systems Inc.................. F 919 781-7603
Oxford (G-9635)

Technology Partners LLC...................... D 704 553-1004
Charlotte (G-2904)

Terarecon Inc... D 650 372-1100
Durham (G-4267)

Tinypilot LLC... G 336 422-6525
Winston Salem (G-13364)

Xerox Corporation................................. E 919 428-9718
Cary (G-1487)

Xeroxdata Center.................................. G 704 329-7245
Charlotte (G-3031)

COMPUTER PERIPHERAL EQPT, WHOLESALE

Vrush Industries Inc.............................. G 336 886-7700
High Point (G-6829)

COMPUTER PERIPHERAL EQPT: Encoders

Lea Aid Acquisition Company............... G 919 872-6210
Spring Hope (G-11557)

Lynn Electronics Corporation............... G 704 369-0093
Concord (G-3397)

Vocollect Inc... E 980 279-4119
Charlotte (G-2989)

COMPUTER PERIPHERAL EQPT: Input Or Output

Garrettcom Inc...................................... D 510 438-9071
Mooresville (G-8671)

Toshiba Globl Cmmrce Sltons In........... E 919 544-8427
Durham (G-4275)

COMPUTER PROCESSING SVCS

Northrop Grumman Systems Corp........ D 252 225-0911
Atlantic (G-638)

COMPUTER PROGRAMMING SVCS: Custom

Computer Task Group Inc...................... E 919 677-1313
Raleigh (G-10006)

Digital Designs Inc................................ E 704 790-7100
Charlotte (G-2046)

H&A Scientific Inc.................................. G 252 752-4315
Greenville (G-5986)

Predatar Inc... G 919 827-4516
Raleigh (G-10391)

COMPUTER RELATED MAINTENANCE SVCS

Champion Media LLC.............................. E 704 746-3955
Mooresville (G-8637)

NCR Voyix Corporation.......................... G 937 445-5000
Cary (G-1406)

Sighttech LLC.. G 855 997-4448
Charlotte (G-2805)

COMPUTER SERVICE BUREAU

Elxr Health Inc....................................... G 919 917-8484
Durham (G-4018)

COMPUTER SOFTWARE DEVELOPMENT

Add-On Technologies Inc....................... F 704 882-2227
Indian Trail (G-7066)

Advanced Digital Systems Inc.............. F 919 485-4819
Durham (G-3881)

Carolina Housing Solutions LLC........... G 704 995-7078
Davidson (G-3699)

Cmisolutions Inc.................................... E 704 759-9950
Charlotte (G-1937)

Ideacode Inc.. G 919 341-5170
Greensboro (G-5613)

Infisoft Software................................... G 704 307-2619
Charlotte (G-2329)

Insightsoftware LLC.............................. E 919 872-7800
Raleigh (G-10200)

Inspectionxpert Corporation................. F 919 249-6442
Raleigh (G-10201)

Kdy Automation Solutions Inc............... G 888 219-0049
Morrisville (G-8996)

Makemine LLC.. G 704 906-7164
Charlotte (G-2449)

Noregon Systems Inc............................ C 336 615-8555
Greensboro (G-5713)

Novisystems Inc.................................... G 919 205-5005
Raleigh (G-10341)

Pai Services LLC................................... E 856 231-4667
Charlotte (G-2605)

Pogo Software Inc................................. G 407 267-4864
Raleigh (G-10375)

Red Hat Inc.. A 919 754-3700
Raleigh (G-10436)

Rvb Systems Group Inc......................... G 919 362-5211
Garner (G-4960)

S C I A Inc... G 919 387-7000
Cary (G-1444)

USA Metal Structure LLP....................... G 336 717-2884
Dobson (G-3826)

Web 4 Half LLC...................................... E 855 762-4638
Greensboro (G-5914)

COMPUTER SOFTWARE DEVELOPMENT & APPLICATIONS

Aiken Development LLC......................... G 828 572-4040
Lenoir (G-7567)

Bae Systems Info Elctrnic Syst............. E 919 323-5800
Durham (G-3911)

Bluetick Inc... F 336 294-4102
Greensboro (G-5395)

Bravo Team LLC.................................... E 704 309-1918
Mooresville (G-8621)

Champion Media LLC.............................. E 704 746-3955
Mooresville (G-8637)

Computational Engrg Intl Inc................ E 919 363-0883
Apex (G-148)

Cyberlux Corporation............................ F 984 363-6894
Research Triangle Pa (G-10707)

Flameoff Coatings Inc........................... G 888 816-7468
Raleigh (G-10111)

Inspire Creative Studios Inc................. G 910 395-0200
Wilmington (G-12818)

Jasie Blanks LLC................................... F 910 485-0016
Fayetteville (G-4621)

Lenovo (united States) Inc.................... A 855 253-6686
Morrisville (G-9006)

Phononic Inc.. D 919 908-6300
Durham (G-4178)

Proctorfree Inc...................................... F 704 759-6569
Davidson (G-3717)

Tekelec Inc.. C
Morrisville (G-9065)

Tekelec Global Inc................................. A 919 460-5500
Morrisville (G-9066)

Vortant Technologies LLC..................... G 828 645-1026
Weaverville (G-12506)

COMPUTER SOFTWARE SYSTEMS ANALYSIS & DESIGN: Custom

27 Software US Inc...............................F 704 968-2879
Mooresville *(G-8589)*

Agingo Corporation.............................G 888 298-0777
Charlotte *(G-1629)*

Applied Strategies Inc.........................G 704 525-4478
Charlotte *(G-1688)*

Camelot Computers Inc.......................F 704 554-1670
Charlotte *(G-1832)*

Dynamac Corporation..........................E 919 544-6428
Durham *(G-4016)*

Intelligent Apps LLC.............................G 919 628-6256
Raleigh *(G-10205)*

International Bus Mchs Corp...............B 919 543-6919
Durham *(G-4080)*

Iqe North Carolina LLC........................F 336 609-6270
Greensboro *(G-5623)*

Jctm LLC..D 252 571-8678
Charlotte *(G-2364)*

Logicbit Software LLC..........................E 888 366-2280
Durham *(G-4108)*

Medicor Imaging Inc.............................G 704 332-5532
Charlotte *(G-2486)*

Openfire Systems.................................G 336 251-3991
Millers Creek *(G-8306)*

Terida LLC...F 910 693-1633
Pinehurst *(G-9704)*

Twork Technology Inc...........................G 704 218-9675
Charlotte *(G-2956)*

Xsport Global Inc.................................F 212 541-6222
Charlotte *(G-3032)*

COMPUTER STORAGE DEVICES, NEC

EMC Corporation..................................G 720 341-3274
Charlotte *(G-2108)*

EMC Corporation..................................G 919 851-3241
Raleigh *(G-10085)*

Halifax EMC..F 252 445-5111
Enfield *(G-4483)*

Netapp Inc..D 919 476-4571
Durham *(G-4145)*

Quantum Newswire..............................G 919 439-8800
Raleigh *(G-10416)*

Quantum Solutions...............................G 828 615-7500
Hickory *(G-6423)*

Quantum Usa LLP.................................G 919 799-7171
Siler City *(G-11424)*

Raleigh Ventures Inc............................G 910 350-0036
Wilmington *(G-12895)*

Seagate Technology LLC.......................G 910 821-8310
Wilmington *(G-12913)*

Verbatim Americas LLC.........................G 704 547-6551
Charlotte *(G-2975)*

Verbatim Americas LLC.........................D 704 547-6500
Charlotte *(G-2976)*

Verbatim Corporation...........................D 704 547-6500
Charlotte *(G-2977)*

Walker and Associates Inc...................C 336 731-6391
Winston Salem *(G-13386)*

COMPUTER SYSTEMS ANALYSIS & DESIGN

Innait Inc...G 406 241-5245
Charlotte *(G-2337)*

International Bus Mchs Corp.................B 919 543-6919
Durham *(G-4080)*

Meridian Zero Degrees LLC...................E 866 454-6757
Aberdeen *(G-13)*

COMPUTER TERMINALS

NCR Voyix Corporation..........................G 937 445-5000
Cary *(G-1406)*

Pro-Face America LLC...........................E 734 477-0600
Greensboro *(G-5766)*

COMPUTERS, NEC

Albert E Mann..G 919 497-0815
Louisburg *(G-7909)*

Axtra3d Inc..E 888 315-5103
Charlotte *(G-1726)*

Barcovvsion LLC...................................F 704 392-9371
Charlotte *(G-1751)*

Digital Audio Corporation.....................F 919 572-6767
Hendersonville *(G-6202)*

Dimill Enterprises LLC..........................G 919 629-2011
Raleigh *(G-10046)*

Fred L Brown...G 336 643-7523
Summerfield *(G-11840)*

General Dynmics Mssion Systems........F 910 497-7900
Fort Bragg *(G-4803)*

Green Apple Studio...............................G 919 377-2239
Cary *(G-1368)*

Hypernova Inc.......................................G 704 360-0096
Charlotte *(G-2307)*

International Bus Mchs Corp.................B 919 543-6919
Durham *(G-4080)*

Itron Inc..D 919 876-2600
Raleigh *(G-10211)*

K12 Computers......................................G 336 754-6111
Lexington *(G-7703)*

Lenovo (united States) Inc....................G 919 486-9627
Morrisville *(G-9004)*

Lenovo (united States) Inc....................C 919 237-8389
Morrisville *(G-9005)*

Lenovo (united States) Inc....................A 855 253-6686
Morrisville *(G-9006)*

Lenovo Global Tech US Inc....................A 855 253-6686
Morrisville *(G-9007)*

Lenovo US Fulfillment Ctr LLC..............F 855 253-6686
Morrisville *(G-9009)*

McKelvey Fulks.....................................G 704 357-1550
Charlotte *(G-2479)*

Salem Technologies Inc........................F 336 777-3652
Winston Salem *(G-13327)*

Serra Wireless Inc.................................G 980 318-0873
Charlotte *(G-2789)*

Shiftwizard Inc......................................F 866 828-3318
Morrisville *(G-9053)*

Silver Knight Pcs LLC............................G 910 824-2054
Fayetteville *(G-4670)*

Teguar Corporation...............................E 704 960-1761
Charlotte *(G-2906)*

Teradata Corporation............................F 919 816-1900
Raleigh *(G-10542)*

Usat LLC..E 919 942-4214
Chapel Hill *(G-1587)*

Utd Technology Corp.............................G 704 612-0121
Mint Hill *(G-8344)*

Walker and Associates Inc....................C 336 731-6391
Winston Salem *(G-13386)*

Zelaya Bros LLC....................................G 980 833-0099
Charlotte *(G-3046)*

COMPUTERS, NEC, WHOLESALE

Reynolds and Reynolds Company.........G 321 287-3939
Charlotte *(G-2721)*

Smartway of Carolinas LLC....................G 704 900-7877
Charlotte *(G-2817)*

COMPUTERS, PERIPHERALS & SOFTWARE, WHOLESALE: Printers

Amt Datasouth Corp.............................E 704 523-8500
Charlotte *(G-1675)*

Glover Corporation Inc..........................E 919 821-5535
Raleigh *(G-10139)*

Sato America LLC...................................C 704 644-1650
Charlotte *(G-2757)*

St Investors Inc.....................................D 704 969-7500
Charlotte *(G-2856)*

COMPUTERS, PERIPHERALS & SOFTWARE, WHOLESALE: Software

Envirnmntal Systems RES Inst I............E 704 541-9810
Charlotte *(G-2119)*

Iqe North Carolina LLC..........................F 336 609-6270
Greensboro *(G-5623)*

Medicor Imaging Inc..............................G 704 332-5532
Charlotte *(G-2486)*

COMPUTERS: Personal

HP Inc...G 704 523-3548
Charlotte *(G-2291)*

Lenovo Holding Company Inc................F 855 253-6686
Morrisville *(G-9008)*

CONCENTRATES, DRINK

Speed Energy Drink LLC........................G 704 949-1255
Concord *(G-3444)*

CONCENTRATES, FLAVORING, EXC DRINK

Alternative Ingredients Inc....................G 336 378-5368
Greensboro *(G-5351)*

CONCRETE BUILDING PRDTS WHOLESALERS

Adams Products Company......................C 919 467-2218
Morrisville *(G-8919)*

Merchants Metals Inc............................G 704 921-9192
Charlotte *(G-2491)*

Old Castle Apg South Inc......................G 919 383-2521
Durham *(G-4155)*

CONCRETE CURING & HARDENING COMPOUNDS

Continental Manufacturing Co...............G 336 697-2591
Mc Leansville *(G-8220)*

CONCRETE PLANTS

S T Wooten Corporation........................E 919 363-3141
Apex *(G-192)*

S T Wooten Corporation........................E 919 562-1851
Franklinton *(G-4853)*

S T Wooten Corporation........................E 919 772-7991
Fuquay Varina *(G-4897)*

S T Wooten Corporation........................E 252 393-2206
Garner *(G-4961)*

S T Wooten Corporation........................E 919 779-6089
Garner *(G-4962)*

S T Wooten Corporation........................E 919 779-7589
Garner *(G-4963)*

S T Wooten Corporation........................E 252 291-5165
Raleigh *(G-10455)*

S T Wooten Corporation........................E 910 762-1940
Wilmington *(G-12908)*

S T Wooten Corporation........................E 252 291-5165
Wilson *(G-13026)*

CONCRETE PRDTS

360 Ballistics LLC.................................G 919 883-8338
Cary *(G-1282)*

PRODUCT

Adams Products Company...................... C 919 467-2218
Morrisville (G-8919)

Beazer East Inc.. G 919 380-2610
Morrisville (G-8939)

Cast First Stone Ministry..................... G 704 437-1053
Troutman (G-12136)

Cast Stone Systems Inc......................... E 252 257-1599
Warrenton (G-12351)

Craven Tire Inc.. G 252 633-0200
New Bern (G-9357)

Fayblock Materials Inc......................... D 910 323-9198
Fayetteville (G-4600)

Gate Precast Company.......................... C 919 603-1633
Oxford (G-9614)

Imagine That Creations LLC............... G 480 528-6775
Black Mountain (G-867)

Merchants Metals Inc........................... G 704 921-9192
Charlotte (G-2491)

Mid-Atlantic Concrete Pdts Inc........... G 336 774-6544
Winston Salem (G-13253)

Mitchell Concrete Products Inc............. G 919 934-4333
Smithfield (G-11455)

Oldcastle Apg South Inc....................... G 336 854-8200
Greensboro (G-5719)

Oldcastle Infrastructure Inc................. F 910 433-2931
Fayetteville (G-4648)

Oldcastle Infrastructure Inc................. E 919 772-6269
Raleigh (G-10344)

Precast Solutions Inc............................ F 336 656-7991
Browns Summit (G-1003)

Precast Terrazzo Entps Inc.................. E 919 231-6200
Raleigh (G-10388)

Quikrete Companies LLC .... E 704 272-7677
Peachland (G-9653)

S T Wooten Corporation......................... F 919 783-5507
Raleigh (G-10454)

Speer Concrete Inc................................. E 910 947-3144
Carthage (G-1280)

Stay-Right Pre-Cast Concrete Inc.......... D 919 494-7600
Franklinton (G-4854)

Superior Walls Systems LLC................. E 704 636-6200
Salisbury (G-11120)

Superior Walls Systems LLC................. D 704 636-6200
Salisbury (G-11121)

Troy Ready - Mix Inc............................. G 910 572-1011
Troy (G-12169)

Tru-Contour Inc....................................... G 704 455-8700
Concord (G-3459)

CONCRETE PRDTS, PRECAST, NEC

A & D Precast Inc................................. G 704 735-3337
Lincolnton (G-7806)

Alcrete Pell City LLC............................ F 910 455-7040
Jacksonville (G-7113)

B & C Concrete Products Inc............... G 336 838-4201
North Wilkesboro (G-9522)

Ballistics Technology Intl Ltd............... G 252 360-1650
Wilson (G-12967)

Carolina Precast Concrete.................... G 910 230-0028
Dunn (G-3848)

Carr Precast Concrete Inc.................... F 910 892-1151
Dunn (G-3849)

Cherry Contracting Inc.......................... D 336 969-1825
Rural Hall (G-10957)

Coastal Precast Systems LLC.............. C 910 444-4682
Wilmington (G-12744)

Continental Stone Company.................. G 336 951-2945
Reidsville (G-10680)

Ideal Precast Inc.................................... G 919 801-8287
Durham (G-4070)

International Precast Inc........................ E 919 742-4241
Siler City (G-11413)

Lucas Concrete Products Inc................ E 704 525-9622
Charlotte (G-2438)

MC Precast Concrete Inc....................... G 919 367-3636
Apex (G-178)

Old Castle Apg South Inc..................... G 919 383-2521
Durham (G-4155)

Oldcastle Retail Inc................................ F 704 525-1621
Charlotte (G-2594)

P & D Archtectural Precast Inc............. F 252 566-9811
La Grange (G-7470)

Prestress of Carolinas LLC................... G 704 587-4273
Charlotte (G-2663)

Shoaf Precast Septic Tank Inc............. G 336 787-5826
Lexington (G-7740)

Smith-Carolina Corporation.................. E 336 349-2905
Reidsville (G-10698)

Utility Precast Inc................................... E 704 721-0106
Concord (G-3463)

CONCRETE: Dry Mixture

Bonsal American Inc.............................. D 704 525-1621
Charlotte (G-1799)

CONCRETE: Ready-Mixed

Abhw Concrete Co.................................. G 252 940-1002
Washington (G-12370)

Adams Oldcastle..................................... G 980 229-7678
Charlotte (G-1623)

Allen-Godwin Concrete Inc.................... G 910 686-4890
Wilmington (G-12702)

Allie M Powell III................................... G 252 535-9717
Roanoke Rapids (G-10729)

Argos Ready Mix (carolinas) Corp......... B 919 790-1520
Raleigh (G-9912)

Argos USA.. F 336 784-5181
Winston Salem (G-13088)

Argos USA LLC....................................... E 910 675-1262
Castle Hayne (G-1495)

Argos USA LLC....................................... G 704 679-9431
Charlotte (G-1695)

Argos USA LLC....................................... E 910 299-5046
Clinton (G-3228)

Argos USA LLC....................................... F 704 483-4013
Denver (G-3772)

Argos USA LLC....................................... G 910 892-3188
Dunn (G-3845)

Argos USA LLC....................................... G 919 552-2294
Fuquay Varina (G-4866)

Argos USA LLC....................................... E 919 772-4188
Garner (G-4916)

Argos USA LLC....................................... D 828 322-9325
Hickory (G-6267)

Argos USA LLC....................................... E 336 841-3379
High Point (G-6527)

Argos USA LLC....................................... G 919 732-7509
Hillsborough (G-6858)

Argos USA LLC....................................... E 252 527-8008
Kinston (G-7394)

Argos USA LLC....................................... G 704 872-9566
Mooresville (G-8600)

Argos USA LLC....................................... G 252 223-4348
Newport (G-9437)

Argos USA LLC....................................... F 919 828-3695
Raleigh (G-9913)

Argos USA LLC....................................... F 919 775-5441
Raleigh (G-9914)

Argos USA LLC....................................... E 919 790-1520
Raleigh (G-9915)

Argos USA LLC....................................... G 252 443-5046
Roanoke Rapids (G-10730)

Argos USA LLC....................................... G 252 291-8888
Sims (G-11428)

Argos USA LLC....................................... C 704 872-9566
Statesville (G-11659)

Argos USA LLC....................................... E 919 554-2087
Wake Forest (G-12261)

Argos USA LLC....................................... G 252 946-4704
Washington (G-12373)

Argos USA LLC....................................... G 252 792-3148
Williamston (G-12667)

Argos USA LLC....................................... G 910 686-4890
Wilmington (G-12707)

Argos USA LLC....................................... E 910 796-3469
Wilmington (G-12708)

Argos USA LLC....................................... D 336 784-4888
Winston Salem (G-13089)

Asheboro Ready-Mix Inc........................ G 336 672-0957
Asheboro (G-330)

B V Hedrick Gravel & Sand Co.............. E 704 633-5982
Salisbury (G-11021)

Black Concrete Inc................................. G 336 243-1388
Lexington (G-7659)

Blue DOT Readi-Mix LLC....................... F 704 971-7676
Mint Hill (G-8332)

Cabarrus Concrete Co........................... F 704 788-3000
Concord (G-3327)

Capital Rdymx Pittsboro LLC................. E 919 217-0222
Moncure (G-8402)

Capitol Funds Inc................................... F 910 439-5275
Mount Gilead (G-9198)

Capitol Funds Inc................................... E 704 487-8547
Shelby (G-11316)

Carolina Concrete Inc............................ F 704 596-6511
Charlotte (G-1845)

Carolina Concrete Inc............................ E 704 821-7645
Matthews (G-8102)

Carolina Concrete Materials.................. G 828 686-3040
Swannanoa (G-11867)

Carolina Ready Mix & Build.................... G 828 686-3041
Swannanoa (G-11868)

Carolina Ready-Mix LLC....................... G 704 225-1112
Monroe (G-8454)

Carolina Sunrock LLC........................... G 919 201-4201
Creedmoor (G-3644)

Carolina Sunrock LLC........................... E 252 433-4617
Kittrell (G-7440)

Carolina Sunrock LLC........................... E 919 861-1860
Raleigh (G-9979)

Carolina Sunrock LLC........................... E 919 554-0500
Wake Forest (G-12267)

Carolina Sunrock LLC........................... E 919 575-4502
Butner (G-1200)

Cemex Cnstr Mtls ATL LLC.................. G 704 873-3263
Statesville (G-11677)

Cemex Materials LLC............................ C 704 455-1100
Harrisburg (G-6106)

Cemex Materials LLC............................ D 800 627-2986
Thomasville (G-12008)

Cemex Materials LLC............................ C 252 243-6153
Wilson (G-12979)

Central Carolina Concrete LLC............. F 704 372-2930
Greensboro (G-5437)

CFI Ready Mix LLC................................ G 910 814-4238
Lillington (G-7792)

Chandler Con Pdts of Chrstnber............ G 336 226-1181
Burlington (G-1070)

Chandler Concrete Co Inc..................... G 910 974-4744
Biscoe (G-850)

Chandler Concrete Co Inc..................... G 336 635-0975
Eden (G-4343)

Chandler Concrete Co Inc..................... D 336 272-6127
Burlington (G-1071)

Chandler Concrete High Co.................... G 828 264-8694
Boone (G-907)

Chandler Concrete Inc................................ F 336 625-1070
Asheboro (G-337)

Chandler Concrete Inc................................ F 336 982-8760
Crumpler (G-3660)

Chandler Concrete Inc................................ F 919 598-1424
Durham (G-3969)

Chandler Concrete Inc............................... G 336 342-5771
Eden (G-4344)

Chandler Concrete Inc............................... G 336 222-9716
Graham (G-5263)

Chandler Concrete Inc................................ F 336 297-1179
Greensboro (G-5440)

Chandler Concrete Inc................................ E 919 644-1058
Hillsborough (G-6863)

Chandler Concrete Inc............................... G 919 542-4242
Pittsboro (G-9779)

Chandler Concrete Inc............................... G 336 599-8343
Roxboro (G-10923)

Chandler Concrete Inc............................... D 704 636-4711
Salisbury (G-11031)

Chandler Concrete Inc................................ F 336 372-4348
Sparta (G-11536)

Childers Concrete Company.................... F 336 841-3111
High Point (G-6568)

Commercial Ready Mix Pdts Inc............ G 252 332-3590
Ahoskie (G-45)

Commercial Ready Mix Pdts Inc............ F 252 335-9740
Elizabeth City (G-4383)

Commercial Ready Mix Pdts Inc............ G 252 232-1250
Moyock (G-9278)

Commercial Ready Mix Pdts Inc............ F 252 585-1777
Pendleton (G-9661)

Commercial Spclty Trck Hldngs............ C 859 234-1100
Burlington (G-1074)

Concrete Service Co Inc.......................... E 910 483-0396
Fayetteville (G-4577)

Concrete Supply Co LLC.......................... G 864 517-4055
Charlotte (G-1970)

Concrete Supply Co LLC.......................... E 704 372-2930
Charlotte (G-1971)

Concrete Supply Holdings Inc................ B 704 372-2930
Charlotte (G-1972)

Crete Solutions LLC.................................. E 910 726-1686
Wilmington (G-12756)

Crh Americas Inc....................................... C 704 282-8443
Monroe (G-8471)

Crmp Inc.. G 252 358-5461
Winton (G-13428)

Dean S Ready Mixed Inc.......................... G 704 982-5520
Albemarle (G-69)

DOT Blue Readi-Mix LLC.......................... G 704 391-3000
Charlotte (G-2063)

DOT Blue Readi-Mix LLC.......................... E 704 247-2778
Harrisburg (G-6107)

DOT Blue Readi-Mix LLC.......................... E 704 247-2777
Monroe (G-8477)

DOT Blue Readi-Mix LLC.......................... E 704 978-2331
Statesville (G-11692)

E & M Concrete Inc................................... G 919 235-7221
Fuquay Varina (G-4880)

Eagle Rock Concrete LLC......................... E 919 596-7077
Apex (G-152)

Eagle Rock Concrete LLC......................... E 919 281-0120
Raleigh (G-10068)

Eagle Rock Concrete LLC......................... E 919 781-3744
Raleigh (G-10067)

Eastern Ready Mix LLC............................. F 919 207-2722
Benson (G-788)

Eveready Mix Concrete Co Inc............... G 336 961-6688
Yadkinville (G-13442)

Explosives Supply Company................... F 828 765-2762
Spruce Pine (G-11575)

Greenville Ready Mix Concrete............... E 252 756-0119
Winterville (G-13416)

Greystone Concrete Pdts Inc.................. E 252 438-5144
Henderson (G-6157)

Hamby Brother S Incorporated............... F 336 667-1154
North Wilkesboro (G-9533)

Hamby Brothers Concrete Inc................. F 828 754-2176
Lenoir (G-7613)

Hamrick Precast LLC................................ G 704 434-6551
Shelby (G-11341)

Hartley Ready Mix Con Mfg Inc............. G 336 294-5995
Greensboro (G-5587)

Hartley Ready Mix Con Mfg Inc............. F 336 788-3928
Winston Salem (G-13191)

Heidelberg Materials Us Inc................... D 252 235-4162
Sims (G-11431)

Heidelberg Mtls Sthast Agg LLC........... E 919 556-4011
Wake Forest (G-12281)

Heidelberg Mtls US Cem LLC................. G 919 682-5791
Durham (G-4058)

Heritage Concrete Service Corp............ G 910 892-4445
Dunn (G-3861)

Heritage Concrete Service Corp............ G 919 775-5014
Sanford (G-11189)

Hildreth Ready Mix LLC........................... G 704 694-2034
Rockingham (G-10779)

Kerrs Hickry Ready-Mixed Con.............. E 828 322-3157
Hickory (G-6377)

Legacy Vulcan LLC................................... G 828 963-7100
Boone (G-929)

Legacy Vulcan LLC................................... G 704 788-7833
Concord (G-3391)

Legacy Vulcan LLC................................... G 252 338-2201
Elizabeth City (G-4396)

Legacy Vulcan LLC................................... G 336 835-1439
Elkin (G-4447)

Legacy Vulcan LLC................................... G 828 255-8561
Enka (G-4487)

Legacy Vulcan LLC................................... G 704 279-5566
Gold Hill (G-5194)

Legacy Vulcan LLC................................... G 252 438-3161
Henderson (G-6164)

Legacy Vulcan LLC................................... G 828 692-0254
Hendersonville (G-6221)

Legacy Vulcan LLC................................... G 828 754-5348
Lenoir (G-7618)

Legacy Vulcan LLC................................... G 828 437-2616
Morganton (G-8877)

Legacy Vulcan LLC................................... G 336 838-8072
North Wilkesboro (G-9540)

Legacy Vulcan LLC................................... G 910 895-2415
Rockingham (G-10782)

Legacy Vulcan LLC................................... D 336 767-0911
Winston Salem (G-13232)

Lenoir Concrete Cnstr Co....................... G 828 759-0449
Lenoir (G-7619)

Loflin Concrete Co Inc............................. E 336 904-2788
Kernersville (G-7282)

Loven Ready Mix LLC............................... G 828 265-4671
Boone (G-930)

Macleod Construction Inc....................... C 704 483-3580
Charlotte (G-2446)

Martin Marietta Materials Inc................. G 910 602-6058
Castle Hayne (G-1506)

Martin Marietta Materials Inc................. G 919 929-7131
Chapel Hill (G-1554)

Martin Marietta Materials Inc................. G 704 392-1333
Charlotte (G-2463)

Martin Marietta Materials Inc................. F 919 557-7412
Fuquay Varina (G-4888)

Martin Marietta Materials Inc................. F 704 932-4379
Landis (G-7474)

Martin Marietta Materials Inc................. G 919 664-1700
Raleigh (G-10274)

Martin Marietta Materials Inc................. G 910 324-7430
Richlands (G-10721)

Massey Ready-Mix Concrete Inc............ G 336 221-8100
Burlington (G-1125)

McDowell Cement Products Co.............. G 828 765-2762
Spruce Pine (G-11579)

McDowell Cement Products Co.............. F 828 652-5721
Marion (G-8053)

Mulls Con & Septic Tanks Inc................ G 828 437-0959
Morganton (G-8883)

Northeastern Ready Mix.......................... G 252 335-1931
Elizabeth City (G-4400)

Old Rm Co LLC... D 919 217-0222
Knightdale (G-7454)

Oldcastle Retail Inc................................. B 704 799-8083
Cornelius (G-3616)

Pea Creek Mine LLC................................. G 252 814-1388
Greenville (G-6011)

Quality Concrete Co Inc.......................... F 910 483-7155
Fayetteville (G-4660)

Quikrete Companies LLC......................... G 704 272-7677
Peachland (G-9653)

Ready Mix of Carolinas Inc..................... E 704 888-3027
Locust (G-7899)

Ready Mixed Concrete.............................. G 252 758-1181
Ayden (G-659)

Redy Mix of Carolinas Inc...................... G 704 888-2224
Locust (G-7900)

Rinker Materials....................................... F 704 455-1100
Harrisburg (G-6116)

Rinker Materials....................................... G 704 827-8175
Mount Holly (G-9244)

Roanoke Chowan Ready Mix Inc............ G 252 332-7995
Ahoskie (G-52)

Robert S Concrete Service Inc............... G 910 391-3973
Fayetteville (G-4664)

S & W Ready Mix Con Co LLC................. F 910 592-2191
Clinton (G-3241)

S & W Ready Mix Con Co LLC................. G 910 645-6868
Elizabethtown (G-4432)

S & W Ready Mix Con Co LLC................. F 910 864-0939
Fayetteville (G-4665)

S & W Ready Mix Con Co LLC................. F 919 751-1796
Goldsboro (G-5243)

S & W Ready Mix Con Co LLC................. F 910 329-1201
Holly Ridge (G-6891)

S & W Ready Mix Con Co LLC................. F 252 527-1881
Kinston (G-7426)

S & W Ready Mix Con Co LLC................. F 252 726-2566
Morehead City (G-8842)

S & W Ready Mix Con Co LLC................. F 252 633-2115
New Bern (G-9392)

S & W Ready Mix Con Co LLC................. F 910 496-3232
Spring Lake (G-11563)

S & W Ready Mix Con Co LLC................. F 910 285-2191
Wallace (G-12323)

S & W Ready Mix Con Co LLC................. F 910 592-1733
Clinton (G-3242)

S T Wooten Corporation........................... E 252 291-5165
Wilson (G-13027)

Smyrna Ready Mix Concrete LLC.......... G 252 447-5356
Havelock (G-6127)

Smyrna Ready Mix Concrete LLC.......... F 252 637-4155
New Bern (G-9397)

Southern Concrete Incorporated........... F 919 906-4069
Broadway (G-987)

Southern Concrete Materials.................. G 704 641-9604
Concord (G-3443)

Southern Concrete Materials Inc........... C 828 253-6421
Asheville (G-608)

PRODUCT

Southern Concrete Mtls Inc.............. E 828 684-3636
Arden (G-308)

Southern Concrete Mtls Inc.............. F 828 670-6450
Asheville (G-609)

Southern Concrete Mtls Inc.............. G 828 682-2298
Burnsville (G-1191)

Southern Concrete Mtls Inc.............. F 704 394-2346
Charlotte (G-2834)

Southern Concrete Mtls Inc.............. E 704 394-2344
Charlotte (G-2835)

Southern Concrete Mtls Inc.............. F 828 681-5178
Fletcher (G-4771)

Southern Concrete Mtls Inc.............. F 828 524-3555
Franklin (G-4840)

Southern Concrete Mtls Inc.............. E 828 692-6517
Hendersonville (G-6243)

Southern Concrete Mtls Inc.............. F 877 788-3001
Salisbury (G-11117)

Southern Concrete Mtls Inc.............. F 828 586-5280
Sylva (G-11899)

Southern Concrete Mtls Inc.............. F 828 456-9048
Waynesville (G-12476)

Southern Hldings Goldsboro Inc.......... G 919 920-6998
Goldsboro (G-5245)

Speer Concrete Inc.............. E 910 947-3144
Carthage (G-1280)

Star Ready-Mix Inc.............. G 336 725-9401
Winston Salem (G-13342)

Sunrock Group Holdings Corp.............. D 919 747-6400
Raleigh (G-10520)

Thomas Concrete Carolina Inc.............. F 704 333-0390
Charlotte (G-2911)

Thomas Concrete Carolina Inc.............. F 919 557-3144
Fuquay Varina (G-4902)

Thomas Concrete Carolina Inc.............. F 919 460-5317
Morrisville (G-9071)

Thomas Concrete Carolina Inc.............. F 919 832-0451
Raleigh (G-10546)

Thomas Concrete SC Inc.............. G 704 868-4545
Gastonia (G-5154)

Three Sisters Ready Mix LLC.............. G 919 217-0222
Knightdale (G-7459)

Titan America LLC.............. G 336 754-0143
Belews Creek (G-739)

TNT Services Inc.............. G 252 261-3073
Kitty Hawk (G-7447)

Toxaway Concrete Inc.............. F 828 966-4270
Cashiers (G-1491)

Tri City Concrete Co LLC.............. F 828 245-2011
Forest City (G-4798)

Tri-City Concrete LLC.............. G 704 372-2930
Charlotte (G-2940)

Triangle Ready Mix LLC.............. E 919 859-4190
Morrisville (G-9077)

Tyrrell Ready Mix Inc.............. G 252 796-0265
Columbia (G-3298)

Vulcan Construction Mtls LLC.............. G 336 767-1201
Winston Salem (G-13384)

Vulcan Construction Mtls LLC.............. E 336 767-0911
Winston Salem (G-13385)

Vulcan Materials Company.............. G 828 963-7100
Boone (G-950)

Vulcan Materials Company.............. G 704 549-1540
Charlotte (G-2991)

Vulcan Materials Company.............. G 704 545-5687
Charlotte (G-2992)

Vulcan Materials Company.............. G 828 692-0039
Hendersonville (G-6248)

Vulcan Materials Company.............. G 336 869-2148
Kernersville (G-7313)

Watauga Ready Mixed.............. G 336 246-6441
Boone (G-952)

White Cap LP.............. G 704 921-4420
Charlotte (G-3017)

Williams Ready Mix Pdts Inc.............. F 704 283-1137
Monroe (G-8581)

Wnc Material Sales.............. G 828 658-8368
Weaverville (G-12507)

CONDENSERS & CONDENSING UNITS: Air Conditioner

Bally Refrigerated Boxes Inc.............. C 252 240-2829
Morehead City (G-8815)

Rheem Manufacturing Company.............. C 336 495-6800
Randleman (G-10658)

CONNECTORS: Electronic

Vrg Components Inc.............. G 980 244-3862
Matthews (G-8156)

CONSTRUCTION & MINING MACHINERY WHOLESALERS

Gregory Poole Equipment Co.............. F 919 872-2691
Raleigh (G-10146)

James River Equipment.............. F 704 821-7399
Monroe (G-8509)

CONSTRUCTION & ROAD MAINTENANCE EQPT: Drags, Road

VT Leeboy Inc.............. B 704 966-3300
Lincolnton (G-7869)

CONSTRUCTION EQPT REPAIR SVCS

S & S Repair Service Inc.............. F 252 756-5989
Winterville (G-13423)

CONSTRUCTION EQPT: Attachments, Snow Plow

Root Spring Scraper Co.............. G 269 382-2025
Pinehurst (G-9702)

CONSTRUCTION EQPT: Cranes

Cavotec USA Inc.............. E 704 873-3009
Mooresville (G-8635)

CONSTRUCTION EQPT: Graders, Road

Champion LLC.............. F 704 392-1038
Charlotte (G-1890)

Four Points Recycling LLC.............. F 910 333-5961
Jacksonville (G-7123)

Stone Supply Inc.............. G 828 678-9966
Burnsville (G-1192)

CONSTRUCTION EQPT: Loaders, Shovel, Self-Propelled

Caterpillar Inc.............. D 919 550-1100
Clayton (G-3137)

CONSTRUCTION EQPT: Roofing Eqpt

Dimensional Metals Inc.............. G 704 279-9691
Salisbury (G-11043)

Metal Roofing Systems LLC.............. E 704 820-3110
Stanley (G-11622)

Roofing Tools and Eqp Inc.............. G 252 291-1800
Wilson (G-13024)

CONSTRUCTION MATERIALS, WHOLESALE: Aggregate

Concrete Service Co Inc.............. E 910 483-0396
Fayetteville (G-4577)

CONSTRUCTION MATERIALS, WHOLESALE: Architectural Metalwork

Design Specialties Inc.............. G 919 772-6955
Raleigh (G-10042)

CONSTRUCTION MATERIALS, WHOLESALE: Awnings

DLM Sales Inc.............. F 704 399-2776
Charlotte (G-2058)

Harvest Homes and Handi Houses.............. G 704 637-3878
Salisbury (G-11061)

Innovative Awngs & Screens LLC.............. F 833 337-4233
Cornelius (G-3610)

CONSTRUCTION MATERIALS, WHOLESALE: Brick, Exc Refractory

Pine Hall Brick Co Inc.............. E 336 721-7500
Winston Salem (G-13296)

CONSTRUCTION MATERIALS, WHOLESALE: Building Stone, Marble

Southern Marble Co LLC.............. G 704 982-4142
Albemarle (G-91)

CONSTRUCTION MATERIALS, WHOLESALE: Building, Exterior

Ace Marine Rigging & Supply Inc.............. F 252 726-6620
Morehead City (G-8811)

L G Sourcing Inc.............. E 704 758-1000
Mooresville (G-8707)

Sipe Lumber Company Inc.............. E 828 632-4679
Taylorsville (G-11978)

CONSTRUCTION MATERIALS, WHOLESALE: Building, Interior

Southern Staircase Inc.............. D 704 357-1221
Charlotte (G-2839)

West & Associates of NC.............. G 919 479-5680
Durham (G-4303)

CONSTRUCTION MATERIALS, WHOLESALE: Cement

Plycem USA LLC.............. C 336 696-2007
North Wilkesboro (G-9549)

CONSTRUCTION MATERIALS, WHOLESALE: Concrete Mixtures

Greenville Ready Mix Concrete.............. E 252 756-0119
Winterville (G-13416)

Speer Concrete Inc.............. E 910 947-3144
Carthage (G-1280)

Troy Ready - Mix Inc.............. G 910 572-1011
Troy (G-12169)

CONSTRUCTION MATERIALS, WHOLESALE: Doors, Garage

Amarr Company.............. C 336 744-5100
Winston Salem (G-13084)

Ultimate Products Inc.............. F 919 836-1627
Raleigh (G-10573)

CONSTRUCTION MATERIALS, WHOLESALE: Masons' Materials

Motsinger Block Plant Inc.............. G 336 764-0350
Winston Salem (G-13262)

CONSTRUCTION MATERIALS, WHOLESALE: Millwork

Ecmd Inc............................. D 336 667-5976
North Wilkesboro (G-9529)

Harris Wood Products Inc........................ G 704 550-5494
New London (G-9418)

Hunter Innovations Ltd........................... G 919 848-8814
Raleigh (G-10181)

Mesa Quality Fenestration Inc................. G 828 393-0132
Hendersonville (G-6226)

CONSTRUCTION MATERIALS, WHOLESALE: Molding, All Materials

Ornamental Mouldings LLC................... F 336 431-9120
Archdale (G-240)

Resinart East Inc................................ F 828 687-0215
Fletcher (G-4763)

CONSTRUCTION MATERIALS, WHOLESALE: Pallets, Wood

East Industries Inc.............................. D 252 442-9662
Rocky Mount (G-10834)

MAC Grading Co.................................. G 910 531-4642
Autryville (G-649)

Steelman Lumber & Pallet LLC.............. F 336 468-2757
Hamptonville (G-6092)

CONSTRUCTION MATERIALS, WHOLESALE: Paving Materials

Asphalt Emulsion Inds LLC..................... G 252 726-0653
Morehead City (G-8814)

CONSTRUCTION MATERIALS, WHOLESALE: Plywood

Weyerhaeuser Company......................... E 336 835-5100
Elkin (G-4455)

CONSTRUCTION MATERIALS, WHOLESALE: Prefabricated Structures

Outlaw Step Co..................................... G 252 568-4384
Deep Run (G-3733)

CONSTRUCTION MATERIALS, WHOLESALE: Roofing & Siding Material

Triad Corrugated Metal Inc..................... E 336 625-9727
Asheboro (G-411)

Union Corrugating Company................... E 910 483-0479
Fayetteville (G-4685)

CONSTRUCTION MATERIALS, WHOLESALE: Sand

Apac-Atlantic Inc................................. D 336 412-6800
Raleigh (G-9907)

Barnhill Contracting Company................ E 252 527-8021
Kinston (G-7395)

Welbuilt Homes Inc.............................. G 910 323-0098
Fayetteville (G-4699)

CONSTRUCTION MATERIALS, WHOLESALE: Septic Tanks

1st Choice Service Inc.......................... G 704 913-7685
Cherryville (G-3058)

Bobby Cahoon Construction Inc............. E 252 249-1617
Grantsboro (G-5329)

Explosives Supply Company................... F 828 765-2762
Spruce Pine (G-11575)

Southern Concrete Mtls Inc................... G 828 681-5178
Fletcher (G-4771)

Southern Concrete Mtls Inc................... E 828 692-6517
Hendersonville (G-6243)

CONSTRUCTION MATERIALS, WHOLESALE: Siding, Exc Wood

Carolina Home Exteriors LLC................. F 252 637-6599
New Bern (G-9350)

Vinyl Windows & Doors Corp.................. F 910 944-2100
Aberdeen (G-30)

Wake Supply Company.......................... G 252 234-6012
Wilson (G-13044)

CONSTRUCTION MATERIALS, WHOLESALE: Stone, Crushed Or Broken

Explosives Supply Company................... F 828 765-2762
Spruce Pine (G-11575)

Fletcher Limestone Company Inc........... G 828 684-6701
Fletcher (G-4737)

Heidelberg Mtls Sthast Agg LLC............. E 910 893-8308
Bunnlevel (G-1016)

Lbm Industries Inc.............................. F 828 966-4270
Sapphire (G-11258)

Martin Marietta Materials Inc................. G 336 674-0836
Greensboro (G-5679)

Radford Quarries Inc........................... F 828 264-7008
Boone (G-939)

Stone & Leigh LLC.............................. G 919 971-2096
Morganton (G-8901)

Surface Buff LLC................................ G 919 341-2873
Raleigh (G-10523)

Wake Stone Corporation....................... E 919 775-7349
Moncure (G-8412)

CONSTRUCTION MATERIALS, WHOLESALE: Veneer

Global Veneer Sales Inc........................ G 336 885-5061
High Point (G-6631)

Sauers & Company Inc......................... F 336 956-1200
Lexington (G-7737)

Southern Vneer Spclty Pdts LLC............ F 919 642-7004
Moncure (G-8409)

CONSTRUCTION MATERIALS, WHOLESALE: Windows

Double Hung LLC................................ E 888 235-8956
Greensboro (G-5501)

Tompkins Industries Inc........................ C 828 254-2351
Asheville (G-620)

Vinyl Windows & Doors Corp.................. F 910 944-2100
Aberdeen (G-30)

CONSTRUCTION MATLS, WHOL: Doors, Combination, Screen-Storm

Jeld-Wen Inc...................................... B 800 535-3936
Charlotte (G-2366)

CONSTRUCTION SAND MINING

American Materials Company LLC......... G 252 752-2124
Greenville (G-5935)

American Materials Company LLC......... E 910 532-6070
Ivanhoe (G-7109)

B V Hedrick Gravel & Sand Co.............. E 704 633-5982
Salisbury (G-11021)

Glover Materials Inc............................ G 252 536-2660
Pleasant Hill (G-9797)

Hedrick B V Gravel & Sand Co.............. G 704 848-4165
Lilesville (G-7785)

Welbuilt Homes Inc.............................. G 910 323-0098
Fayetteville (G-4699)

CONSTRUCTION: Agricultural Building

United Visions Corp.............................. G 704 953-4555
Davidson (G-3724)

CONSTRUCTION: Athletic & Recreation Facilities

Architectural Craftsman Ltd................... E 919 494-6911
Franklinton (G-4846)

Dimill Enterprises LLC.......................... G 919 629-2011
Raleigh (G-10046)

CONSTRUCTION: Bridge

Blythe Construction Inc........................ B 704 375-8474
Charlotte (G-1793)

CONSTRUCTION: Commercial & Office Building, New

Atlantic Group Usa Inc........................ F 919 623-7824
Raleigh (G-9920)

B V Hedrick Gravel & Sand Co.............. E 704 633-5982
Salisbury (G-11021)

M F C Inc... E 252 322-5004
Aurora (G-643)

Retail Installation Svcs LLC.................. G 336 818-1333
Millers Creek (G-8307)

W T Humphrey Inc............................... E 910 455-3555
Jacksonville (G-7158)

CONSTRUCTION: Commercial & Office Buildings, Prefabricated

Robinsons Welding Service.................... G 336 622-3150
Liberty (G-7777)

CONSTRUCTION: Dams, Waterways, Docks & Other Marine

Bobby Cahoon Construction Inc............. E 252 249-1617
Grantsboro (G-5329)

Component Sourcing Intl LLC................. E 704 843-9292
Charlotte (G-1967)

CONSTRUCTION: Drainage System

Barnhill Contracting Company............... D 910 488-1319
Fayetteville (G-4557)

Heath and Sons MGT Svcs LLC............. F 910 679-6142
Rocky Point (G-10881)

CONSTRUCTION: Farm Building

American Builders Anson Inc................. E 704 272-7655
Polkton (G-9811)

Hog Slat Incorporated.......................... B 800 949-4647
Newton Grove (G-9514)

CONSTRUCTION: Food Prdts Manufacturing or Packing Plant

Herbal Innovations LLC......................... E 336 818-2332
Wilkesboro (G-12638)

CONSTRUCTION: Heavy Highway & Street

Crowder Trucking LLC.......................... G 910 797-4163
Fayetteville (G-4581)

Dan Moore Inc.................................... G 336 475-8350
Thomasville (G-12015)

Long Asp Pav Trckg of Grnsburg.......... G 336 643-4121
Summerfield (G-11842)

S T Wooten Corporation....................... E 919 965-9880
Princeton (G-9826)

PRODUCT

CONSTRUCTION: Indl Buildings, New, NEC

Ansgar Industrial LLC............................ A 866 284-1931
Charlotte *(G-1679)*

B V Hedrick Gravel & Sand Co............... E 704 633-5982
Salisbury *(G-11021)*

Bwxt Investment Company...................... E 704 625-4900
Charlotte *(G-1824)*

Jbr Properties of Greenville Inc............. A 252 355-9353
Winterville *(G-13417)*

TRC Acquisition LLC............................... A 252 355-9353
Winterville *(G-13424)*

CONSTRUCTION: Indl Plant

Bwxt Investment Company...................... E 704 625-4900
Charlotte *(G-1824)*

Wnc White Corporation........................... E 828 477-4895
Sylva *(G-11905)*

CONSTRUCTION: Land Preparation

United Visions Corp................................ G 704 953-4555
Davidson *(G-3724)*

CONSTRUCTION: Marine

Triton Marine Services Inc..................... G 252 728-9958
Beaufort *(G-736)*

CONSTRUCTION: Oil & Gas Pipeline Construction

Integrity Envmtl Solutions LLC.............. D 704 283-9765
Monroe *(G-8505)*

CONSTRUCTION: Parking Lot

Apac-Atlantic Inc................................... D 336 412-6800
Raleigh *(G-9907)*

Barnhill Contracting Company................ E 252 527-8021
Kinston *(G-7395)*

Garris Grading and Paving Inc............... F 252 749-1101
Farmville *(G-4529)*

CONSTRUCTION: Pipeline, NEC

Pipeline Plastics LLC............................. G 817 693-4100
Fair Bluff *(G-4499)*

CONSTRUCTION: Residential, Nec

Atlantic Group Usa Inc........................... F 919 623-7824
Raleigh *(G-9920)*

Black Mountain Cnstr Group Inc............. F 704 243-5593
Waxhaw *(G-12424)*

Kitchen Tune-Up.................................... G 833 259-1838
Matthews *(G-8123)*

Seashore Builders Inc............................ E 910 259-3404
Maple Hill *(G-8026)*

United Visions Corp................................ G 704 953-4555
Davidson *(G-3724)*

CONSTRUCTION: Sewer Line

1st Choice Service Inc........................... G 704 913-7685
Cherryville *(G-3058)*

CONSTRUCTION: Single-Family Housing

Bennett Elec Maint & Cnstr LLC............. G 910 231-0300
Raeford *(G-9832)*

Brown Building Corporation.................... F 919 782-1800
Morrisville *(G-8944)*

Distinctive Bldg & Design Inc................. G 828 456-4730
Waynesville *(G-12456)*

Downtown Graphics Network Inc............ G 704 637-0855
Salisbury *(G-11044)*

GLG Corporation.................................... F 336 784-0396
Winston Salem *(G-13178)*

Heidelberg Mtls Sthast Agg LLC............. E 919 936-4221
Princeton *(G-9824)*

J &D Contractor Service Inc................... G 919 427-0218
Angier *(G-122)*

Kitchen Tune-Up.................................... G 833 259-1838
Matthews *(G-8123)*

RDc Debris Removal Cnstr LLC.............. E 323 614-2353
Smithfield *(G-11462)*

Safe Home Pro Inc................................. F 704 662-2299
Cornelius *(G-3626)*

Selectbuild Construction Inc.................. F 208 331-4300
Raleigh *(G-10467)*

Yes Real Estate Cnstr Group In.............. E 919 389-4104
Raleigh *(G-10622)*

CONSTRUCTION: Single-family Housing, New

Champion Home Builders Inc................. B 910 893-5713
Lillington *(G-7793)*

E A Duncan Cnstr Co Inc........................ G 910 653-3535
Tabor City *(G-11910)*

G A Lankford Construction..................... G 828 254-2467
Alexander *(G-100)*

High Cntry Tmbrframe Gllery WD........... G 828 264-8971
Boone *(G-921)*

Lewtak Pipe Organ Builders Inc............. G 336 554-2251
Mocksville *(G-8374)*

Lowder Steel Inc.................................... E 336 431-9000
Archdale *(G-238)*

Mike Powell Inc..................................... F 910 792-6152
Wilmington *(G-12854)*

Nobscot Construction Co Inc.................. G 919 929-2075
Chapel Hill *(G-1560)*

Nvr Inc... D 704 484-7170
Kings Mountain *(G-7374)*

Old Hickory Log Homes Inc.................... G 704 489-8989
Denver *(G-3795)*

Robbinsville Cstm Molding Inc............... F 828 479-2317
Robbinsville *(G-10761)*

W T Humphrey Inc.................................. E 910 455-3555
Jacksonville *(G-7158)*

CONSTRUCTION: Swimming Pools

Black Mountain Cnstr Group Inc............. F 704 243-5593
Waxhaw *(G-12424)*

Carolina Solar Structures Inc................. F 828 684-9900
Asheville *(G-471)*

CONSTRUCTION: Transmitting Tower, Telecommunication

Spectrasite Communications LLC........... E 919 468-0112
Cary *(G-1465)*

Wirenet Inc.. F 513 774-7759
Huntersville *(G-7062)*

CONSTRUCTION: Water & Sewer Line

Gillam & Mason Inc................................ G 252 356-2874
Cofield *(G-3266)*

Wnc White Corporation........................... E 828 477-4895
Sylva *(G-11905)*

CONSULTING SVC: Business, NEC

Alpha Theory LLC.................................. G 212 235-2180
Charlotte *(G-1652)*

Alpha Theory LLC.................................. G 212 235-2180
Charlotte *(G-1653)*

Atlantic Group Usa Inc........................... F 919 623-7824
Raleigh *(G-9920)*

Carolina Textile Services Inc.................. G 910 843-3033
Red Springs *(G-10665)*

Cleveland Compounding Inc.................... G 704 487-1971
Shelby *(G-11319)*

Competitive Solutions Inc...................... E 919 851-0058
Raleigh *(G-10004)*

Cycle Pro LLC.. G 704 662-6682
Mooresville *(G-8649)*

Environmental Supply Co Inc.................. F 919 956-9688
Durham *(G-4027)*

Noahs Inc.. F 704 718-2354
Charlotte *(G-2570)*

Piedmont Flight Inc................................ E 336 776-6070
Winston Salem *(G-13291)*

Security Consult Inc............................... G 704 531-8399
Charlotte *(G-2782)*

Spectrasite Communications LLC........... E 919 468-0112
Cary *(G-1465)*

Sutton Scientifcs Inc............................. G 910 428-1600
Star *(G-11634)*

CONSULTING SVC: Educational

Brightly Software Inc............................. C 919 816-8237
Cary *(G-1315)*

I-Leadr Inc... G 910 431-5252
Sherrills Ford *(G-11392)*

National Voctnl Tech Honor Soc............. G 828 698-8011
Flat Rock *(G-4711)*

Thinking Maps Inc.................................. G 919 678-8778
Cary *(G-1470)*

CONSULTING SVC: Human Resource

National Ctr For Social Impact............... G 984 212-2285
Raleigh *(G-10323)*

CONSULTING SVC: Management

Academy Association Inc........................ F 919 544-0835
Durham *(G-3877)*

Access Newswire Inc.............................. C 919 481-4000
Raleigh *(G-9872)*

Anew Look Homes LLC........................... G 800 796-5152
Hickory *(G-6264)*

Apex Analytix LLC.................................. C 336 272-4669
Greensboro *(G-5365)*

Carolina By-Products Co......................... G 336 333-3030
Greensboro *(G-5424)*

Eco Building Corporation........................ G 910 736-1540
Red Springs *(G-10667)*

Educatrx Inc.. G 980 328-0013
Monroe *(G-8481)*

Go Energies LLC.................................... F 877 712-5999
Wilmington *(G-12790)*

Go Energies Holdings Inc....................... G 910 762-5802
Wilmington *(G-12791)*

Intelligent Apps LLC.............................. G 919 628-6256
Raleigh *(G-10205)*

Jestines Jewels Inc................................ G 704 904-0191
Salisbury *(G-11072)*

Make Solutions Inc................................ F 623 444-0098
Asheville *(G-542)*

One Srce Dcument Solutions Inc............ E 800 401-9544
Greensboro *(G-5724)*

Red Oak Sales Company......................... G 704 483-8464
Denver *(G-3802)*

Sonaron LLC.. G 808 232-6168
Fayetteville *(G-4672)*

Wirenet Inc.. F 513 774-7759
Huntersville *(G-7062)*

CONSULTING SVCS, BUSINESS: Communications

Amplified Elctronic Design Inc............... F 336 223-4811
Greensboro *(G-5362)*

JPS Communications Inc....................... D 919 534-1168
Raleigh *(G-10222)*

Picassomoesllc............................ G 216 703-4547
Hillsborough *(G-6875)*

CONSULTING SVCS, BUSINESS: Energy Conservation

Envirnmntal Cmfort Sltions Inc.............. E 980 272-7327
Kannapolis *(G-7208)*

CONSULTING SVCS, BUSINESS: Environmental

Integrity Envmtl Solutions LLC.............. D 704 283-9765
Monroe *(G-8505)*

CONSULTING SVCS, BUSINESS: Safety Training Svcs

James King........................... G 910 308-8818
Fayetteville *(G-4620)*

CONSULTING SVCS, BUSINESS: Sys Engnrg, Exc Computer/ Prof

Aceyus Inc........................... E 704 443-7900
Charlotte *(G-1616)*

Bachstein Consulting LLC.................. G 410 322-4917
Youngsville *(G-13463)*

Camstar Systems Inc.................... C 704 227-6600
Charlotte *(G-1833)*

Ideacode Inc........................... G 919 341-5170
Greensboro *(G-5613)*

Qplot Corporation...................... G 949 302-7928
Raleigh *(G-10410)*

CONSULTING SVCS, BUSINESS: Systems Analysis & Engineering

Infinite Software Resorces LLC............. G 704 509-0031
Charlotte *(G-2327)*

CONSULTING SVCS, BUSINESS: Testing, Educational Or Personnel

Emath360 LLC........................ F 919 744-4944
Cary *(G-1352)*

Measurement Incorporated................. D 919 683-2413
Durham *(G-4122)*

CONSULTING SVCS: Scientific

Prophysics Innovations Inc................ G 919 245-0406
Cary *(G-1431)*

Qplot Corporation...................... G 949 302-7928
Raleigh *(G-10410)*

Tempest Environmental Corp............... G 919 973-1609
Durham *(G-4265)*

We Appit LLC.......................... G 910 465-2722
Wilmington *(G-12946)*

Xona Microfluidics Inc.................. G 951 553-6400
Research Triangle Pa *(G-10718)*

CONTACT LENSES

Chentech Corp......................... G 919 749-8765
Holly Springs *(G-6897)*

CONTACTS: Electrical

Deringer-Ney Inc...................... E 828 649-3232
Marshall *(G-8079)*

CONTAINERS, GLASS: Water Bottles

CHI Resources........................ G 828 835-7878
Murphy *(G-9289)*

CONTAINERS: Food, Folding, Made From Purchased Materials

Pactiv LLC............................ C 252 527-6300
Kinston *(G-7425)*

CONTAINERS: Food, Liquid Tight, Including Milk

Caraustar Industries Inc................ F 336 498-2631
Randleman *(G-10637)*

CONTAINERS: Frozen Food & Ice Cream

Candies Italian ICEE LLC................. G 980 475-7429
Charlotte *(G-1835)*

CONTAINERS: Glass

Gerresheimer Glass Inc.................. F 828 433-5000
Morganton *(G-8868)*

Precision Concepts Intl LLC............... G 704 360-8923
Huntersville *(G-7037)*

CONTAINERS: Laminated Phenolic & Vulcanized Fiber

Atlantic Custom Container Inc.............. G 336 437-9302
Graham *(G-5260)*

CONTAINERS: Metal

Carolina Expediters LLC................ G 888 537-5330
Mount Airy *(G-9108)*

CSM Logistics LLC...................... G 980 800-2621
Charlotte *(G-2002)*

Jhrg Manufacturing LLC.................. G 252 478-4977
Spring Hope *(G-11556)*

CONTAINERS: Plastic

Altium Packaging LLC.................... F 704 873-6729
Statesville *(G-11653)*

Altium Packaging LLC.................... D 336 472-1500
Thomasville *(G-11992)*

Altium Packaging LP.................... D 336 342-4749
Reidsville *(G-10673)*

Berry Global Inc...................... E 252 332-7270
Ahoskie *(G-42)*

Berry Global Inc...................... G 252 984-4100
Battleboro *(G-695)*

Berry Global Inc...................... C 704 664-3733
Mooresville *(G-8608)*

Berry Global Inc...................... D 252 984-4104
Rocky Mount *(G-10808)*

C&K Plastics Nc LLC................... G 833 232-4848
Mooresville *(G-8626)*

Cks Packaging......................... F 704 663-6510
Mooresville *(G-8638)*

CKS Packaging Inc.................... D 336 578-5800
Graham *(G-5265)*

CKS Packaging Inc.................... E 704 663-6510
Mooresville *(G-8639)*

Coltec Industries Inc.................... A 704 731-1500
Charlotte *(G-1961)*

Genpak Industries Inc................... E 518 798-9511
Charlotte *(G-2205)*

Genpak LLC........................... E 800 626-6695
Charlotte *(G-2206)*

Great Pacific Entps US Inc................ E 980 256-7729
Charlotte *(G-2235)*

Liqui-Box Corporation................... D 804 325-1400
Charlotte *(G-2426)*

New Innovative Products Inc............... G 919 631-6759
Pine Level *(G-9683)*

Plasgad Usa LLC...................... E 980 223-2197
Statesville *(G-11747)*

Plastic Ingenuity Inc.................. D 919 693-2009
Oxford *(G-9625)*

Proto Labs Inc....................... D 833 245-8827
Morrisville *(G-9040)*

Reynolds Consumer Products Inc.......... A 704 371-5550
Huntersville *(G-7042)*

Rubbermaid Commercial Pdts LLC........ A 540 667-8700
Huntersville *(G-7045)*

Sealed Air Corporation.................. D 828 728-6610
Hudson *(G-6959)*

Sonoco Products Company................ D 828 245-0118
Forest City *(G-4797)*

Sysmetric USA........................ G 704 522-8778
Mooresville *(G-8783)*

Technical Coating Intl Inc................ E 910 371-0860
Leland *(G-7559)*

THEM International Inc................. G 336 855-7880
Greensboro *(G-5862)*

Thomson Plastics Inc.................. D 336 843-4255
Lexington *(G-7751)*

Vault LLC............................. F 336 698-3796
High Point *(G-6823)*

CONTAINERS: Sanitary, Food

CKS Packaging Inc.................... E 704 663-6510
Mooresville *(G-8639)*

Thomco Inc........................... G 336 292-3300
Greensboro *(G-5863)*

Waddington Group Inc................... E 800 845-6051
Charlotte *(G-2997)*

CONTAINERS: Shipping, Bombs, Metal Plate

Crown Case Co......................... G 704 453-1542
Charlotte *(G-1998)*

Worthington Cylinder Corp............... C 336 777-8600
Winston Salem *(G-13404)*

CONTAINERS: Wood

Arcola Hardwood Company Inc............. G 252 257-4484
Warrenton *(G-12349)*

Arcola Lumber Company Inc.............. E 252 257-4923
Warrenton *(G-12350)*

Carolina Crate & Pallet Inc.............. E 910 245-4001
Vass *(G-12227)*

Carolina WD Pdts Mrshville Inc............ D 704 624-2119
Marshville *(G-8086)*

Dac Products Inc..................... E 336 969-9786
Rural Hall *(G-10958)*

Elberta Crate & Box Co................. C 252 257-4659
Warrenton *(G-12352)*

Kontane Logistics Inc................... G 828 397-5501
Hickory *(G-6382)*

Lee County Industries Inc.............. G 919 775-3439
Sanford *(G-11205)*

CONTRACTOR: Dredging

Stone Supply Inc..................... G 828 678-9966
Burnsville *(G-1192)*

CONTRACTOR: Framing

Seashore Builders Inc................. E 910 259-3404
Maple Hill *(G-8026)*

Selectbuild Construction Inc............ F 208 331-4300
Raleigh *(G-10467)*

CONTRACTOR: Rigging & Scaffolding

Advantage Machinery Svcs Inc............. E 336 463-4700
Yadkinville *(G-13435)*

Employee Codes: A=Over 500 employees, B=251-500
C=101-250, D=51-100, E=20-50, F=10-19, G=1-9

2025 Harris North Carolina
Manufacturers Directory

1095

PRODUCT

CONTRACTORS: Acoustical & Insulation Work

Delve Interiors LLC.................................. C 336 274-4661
  Greensboro (G-5495)

Sika Corporation....................................... E 704 810-0500
  Gastonia (G-5138)

CONTRACTORS: Asbestos Removal & Encapsulation

Carlton Enterprizes LLC........................... G 919 534-5424
  Rocky Point (G-10877)

CONTRACTORS: Carpentry Work

Architectural Craftsman Ltd.................. E 919 494-6911
  Franklinton (G-4846)

Artistic Southern Inc.............................. F 919 861-4695
  Charlotte (G-1700)

Athol Arbor Corporation....................... F 919 643-1100
  Hillsborough (G-6859)

Classic Cleaning LLC............................. E 800 220-7101
  Raleigh (G-9998)

Idx Impressions LLC.............................. C 703 550-6902
  Washington (G-12393)

Wildwood Studios Inc............................ G 828 299-8696
  Asheville (G-636)

CONTRACTORS: Carpentry, Cabinet & Finish Work

Cabinet Solutions Usa Inc...................... E 828 358-2349
  Hickory (G-6280)

Comm-Kab Inc.. F 336 873-8787
  Asheboro (G-340)

Marsh Furniture Company...................... F 336 273-8196
  Greensboro (G-5676)

Neals Carpentry & Cnstr....................... G 910 346-6154
  Jacksonville (G-7135)

Riddley Retail Fixtures Inc.................... E 704 435-8829
  Kings Mountain (G-7382)

Ullman Group LLC.................................. F 704 246-7333
  Charlotte (G-2959)

Vaughn Woodworking Inc....................... G 828 963-6858
  Banner Elk (G-690)

Washington Cabinet Company............... G 252 946-3457
  Washington (G-12420)

CONTRACTORS: Carpentry, Finish & Trim Work

Interior Trim Creations Inc..................... G 704 821-1470
  Charlotte (G-2342)

CONTRACTORS: Closet Organizers, Installation & Design

Closets By Design................................... D 704 361-6424
  Charlotte (G-1931)

CONTRACTORS: Commercial & Office Building

Black Mountain Cnstr Group Inc............ F 704 243-5593
  Waxhaw (G-12424)

J &D Contractor Service Inc.................. G 919 427-0218
  Angier (G-122)

Pro Choice Contractors Corp................ G 919 696-7383
  Raleigh (G-10398)

Stowe Enterprises Inc............................ G 800 315-6751
  Troutman (G-12151)

CONTRACTORS: Communications Svcs

Commscope Technologies LLC.............. A 828 324-2200
  Claremont (G-3104)

CONTRACTORS: Decontamination Svcs

Filtration Technology Inc....................... G 336 294-5655
  Greensboro (G-5531)

Noble Oil Services Inc........................... C 919 774-8180
  Sanford (G-11212)

CONTRACTORS: Directional Oil & Gas Well Drilling Svc

Vision Directional Drilling...................... G 336 570-4621
  Burlington (G-1174)

CONTRACTORS: Drywall

Precision Walls Inc................................. G 336 852-7710
  Greensboro (G-5759)

CONTRACTORS: Electric Power Systems

Power Integrity Corp.............................. E 336 379-9773
  Greensboro (G-5752)

CONTRACTORS: Electronic Controls Installation

Audio Vdeo Concepts Design Inc.......... G 704 821-2823
  Indian Trail (G-7069)

Custom Controls Unlimited LLC............ F 919 812-6553
  Raleigh (G-10029)

International Tela-Com Inc..................... G 828 651-9801
  Fletcher (G-4743)

Total Controls Inc.................................. G 704 821-6341
  Matthews (G-8152)

CONTRACTORS: Energy Management Control

Belham Management Ind LLC................ G 704 815-4246
  Charlotte (G-1768)

CONTRACTORS: Fence Construction

Afsc LLC... D 704 523-4936
  Charlotte (G-1627)

Asheville Contracting Co Inc.................. E 828 665-8900
  Candler (G-1217)

Automated Controls LLC........................ G 704 724-7625
  Huntersville (G-6970)

Digger Specialties Inc............................ G 336 495-1517
  Randleman (G-10642)

Englishs All Wood Homes Inc................ F 252 524-5000
  Grifton (G-6036)

Fence Quarter LLC................................. G 800 205-0128
  Morganton (G-8864)

Hamrick Fence Company........................ F 704 434-5011
  Boiling Springs (G-884)

Harrison Fence Inc................................. G 919 244-6908
  Apex (G-162)

Invisible Fencing of Mtn Reg................. G 828 667-8847
  Candler (G-1227)

CONTRACTORS: Fiber Optic Cable Installation

Nkt Inc... G 919 601-1970
  Cary (G-1408)

Telecmmnctons Resource MGT Inc....... F 919 779-0776
  Raleigh (G-10539)

Unitape (usa) Inc................................... G 828 464-5695
  Conover (G-3568)

CONTRACTORS: Fiberglass Work

Beacon Composites LLC........................ G 704 813-8408
  Creedmoor (G-3640)

Core Technology Molding Corp............. E 336 294-2018
  Greensboro (G-5469)

Gainsborough Baths LLC........................ F 336 357-0797
  Lexington (G-7691)

Moores Fiberglass Inc........................... F 252 753-2583
  Walstonburg (G-12334)

Piedmont Well Covers Inc..................... F 704 664-8488
  Mount Ulla (G-9270)

S Kivett Inc.. F 910 592-0161
  Clinton (G-3243)

CONTRACTORS: Floor Laying & Other Floor Work

Mrrefinish LLC....................................... F 336 625-2400
  Asheboro (G-379)

CONTRACTORS: Gas Field Svcs, NEC

Quick N Easy 12 Nc739.......................... G 336 824-3832
  Ramseur (G-10630)

Trans-Tech Energy Inc........................... G 252 446-4357
  Rocky Mount (G-10817)

TransMontaigne Terminaling Inc........... F 303 626-8200
  Selma (G-11293)

CONTRACTORS: General Electric

Cemco Electric Inc................................. F 704 504-0294
  Charlotte (G-1886)

Gillam & Mason Inc................................ G 252 356-2874
  Cofield (G-3266)

JA Smith Inc... G 704 860-4910
  Lawndale (G-7517)

M & M Electric Service Inc.................... E 704 867-0221
  Gastonia (G-5081)

Presley Group Ltd.................................. D 828 254-9971
  Asheville (G-584)

Southern Elc & Automtn Corp............... F 919 718-0122
  Sanford (G-11235)

Watson Electrical Cnstr Co LLC............ D 252 756-4550
  Greenville (G-6033)

CONTRACTORS: Glass Tinting, Architectural & Automotive

Dbf Inc... G 910 548-6725
  Jacksonville (G-7122)

Tint Plus... G 910 229-5303
  Fayetteville (G-4681)

CONTRACTORS: Heating & Air Conditioning

Chichibone Inc....................................... G 919 785-0090
  Morrisville (G-8957)

Commercial Flter Svc of Triad............... G 336 272-1443
  Greensboro (G-5459)

Envirnmntal Cmfort Sltions Inc............. E 980 272-7327
  Kannapolis (G-7208)

GSM Services Inc................................... D 704 864-0344
  Gastonia (G-5056)

Harco Air LLC.. G 252 491-5220
  Powells Point (G-9821)

Jenkins Services Group LLC.................. G 704 881-3210
  Catawba (G-1512)

CONTRACTORS: Heating Systems Repair & Maintenance Svc

Hollingsworth Heating Air Cond............ G 252 824-0355
  Tarboro (G-11929)

J & W Service Incorporated................... G 336 449-4584
  Whitsett (G-12611)

Kenny Fowler Heating and A Inc........... F 910 508-4553
  Wilmington (G-12827)

Saab Barracuda LLC...................................... E 910 814-3088
Lillington *(G-7802)*

CONTRACTORS: Highway & Street Construction, General

Brown Brothers Construction Co........... F 828 297-2131
Zionville *(G-13527)*

Brown Building Corporation.................. F 919 782-1800
Morrisville *(G-8944)*

Carlton Enterprizes LLC........................ G 919 534-5424
Rocky Point *(G-10877)*

Ferebee Corporation............................... C 704 509-2586
Charlotte *(G-2145)*

Heath and Sons MGT Svcs LLC............ F 910 679-6142
Rocky Point *(G-10881)*

Reliable Woodworks Inc........................ G 704 785-9663
Concord *(G-3431)*

S T Wooten Corporation......................... E 252 291-5165
Wilson *(G-13027)*

Stone Supply Inc.................................... G 828 678-9966
Burnsville *(G-1192)*

CONTRACTORS: Highway & Street Paving

Apac-Atlantic Inc................................... D 336 412-6800
Raleigh *(G-9907)*

Barnhill Contracting Company.............. G 704 721-7500
Concord *(G-3317)*

Barnhill Contracting Company.............. E 252 752-7608
Greenville *(G-5946)*

Barnhill Contracting Company.............. E 252 527-8021
Kinston *(G-7395)*

Blythe Construction Inc......................... E 336 854-9003
Greensboro *(G-5396)*

Blythe Construction Inc......................... B 704 375-8474
Charlotte *(G-1793)*

Dickerson Group Inc.............................. G 704 289-3111
Charlotte *(G-2042)*

Highland Paving Co LLC........................ D 910 482-0080
Fayetteville *(G-4613)*

Johnson Paving Company Inc............... F 828 652-4911
Marion *(G-8046)*

Lane Construction Corporation............. C 919 876-4550
Raleigh *(G-10247)*

Moretz & Sipe Inc................................... G 828 327-8661
Hickory *(G-6397)*

Russell Standard Corporation............... F 336 292-6875
Greensboro *(G-5797)*

Young & McQueen Grading Co Inc......... D 828 682-7714
Burnsville *(G-1196)*

CONTRACTORS: Hydraulic Eqpt Installation & Svcs

Atlantic Hydraulics Svcs LLC............... E 919 542-2985
Sanford *(G-11152)*

Limitless Wldg Fabrication LLC............ G 252 753-0660
Farmville *(G-4534)*

Satco Truck Equipment Inc................... F 919 383-5547
Durham *(G-4222)*

Wandfluh of America Inc....................... F 847 566-5700
Charlotte *(G-3003)*

CONTRACTORS: Kitchen Cabinet Installation

Cabinet Solutions Usa Inc.................... E 828 358-2349
Hickory *(G-6280)*

Sare Granite & Tile................................ G 828 676-2666
Arden *(G-305)*

Thomas Lcklars Cbnets Lrnburg........... G 910 369-2094
Laurinburg *(G-7516)*

CONTRACTORS: Machine Rigging & Moving

Advantage Machinery Svcs Inc............. E 336 463-4700
Yadkinville *(G-13435)*

RPM Plastics LLC.................................. E 704 871-0518
Statesville *(G-11760)*

CONTRACTORS: Machinery Installation

Alpha 3d LLC.. G 704 277-6300
Charlotte *(G-1649)*

Dustcontrol Inc...................................... F 910 395-1808
Wilmington *(G-12768)*

Johnson Industrial Mchy Svcs.............. E 252 239-1944
Lucama *(G-7937)*

Mantissa Corporation............................ E 704 525-1749
Charlotte *(G-2453)*

CONTRACTORS: Marble Installation, Interior

Apex Marble and Granite Inc................. E 919 462-9202
Morrisville *(G-8929)*

CONTRACTORS: Masonry & Stonework

Stonemaster Inc..................................... F 704 333-0353
Concord *(G-3449)*

Vega Construction Company Inc............ E 336 756-3477
Pilot Mountain *(G-9675)*

CONTRACTORS: Office Furniture Installation

Ie Furniture Inc..................................... E 336 475-5050
Archdale *(G-227)*

Retail Installation Svcs LLC.................. G 336 818-1333
Millers Creek *(G-8307)*

Unique Office Solutions Inc.................. F 336 854-0900
Greensboro *(G-5890)*

CONTRACTORS: Oil & Gas Wells Pumping Svcs

Well Doctor LLC..................................... G 704 909-9258
Charlotte *(G-3011)*

CONTRACTORS: Oil Field Pipe Testing Svcs

Doble Engineering Company.................. G 919 380-7461
Morrisville *(G-8966)*

CONTRACTORS: Ornamental Metal Work

Alamance Iron Works Inc...................... G 336 852-5940
Greensboro *(G-5346)*

Gastonia Ornamental Wldg Inc............. F 704 827-1146
Mount Holly *(G-9232)*

James Iron & Steel Inc.......................... G 704 283-2299
Monroe *(G-8508)*

CONTRACTORS: Painting, Commercial

Carlton Enterprizes LLC........................ G 919 534-5424
Rocky Point *(G-10877)*

Custom Steel Boats Inc......................... F 252 745-7447
Merritt *(G-8267)*

Yontz & Sons Painting Inc.................... G 336 784-7099
Winston Salem *(G-13409)*

CONTRACTORS: Painting, Indl

Auto Parts Fayetteville LLC.................. G 910 889-4026
Fayetteville *(G-4555)*

CONTRACTORS: Petroleum Storage Tanks, Pumping & Draining

Volta Group Corporation LLC................ E 919 637-0273
Raleigh *(G-10593)*

CONTRACTORS: Plumbing

Fixed-NC LLC... G 252 751-1911
Greenville *(G-5976)*

Go Green Services LLC.......................... D 336 252-2999
Greensboro *(G-5565)*

Heath and Sons MGT Svcs LLC............ F 910 679-6142
Rocky Point *(G-10881)*

Prestige Cleaning Incorporated............. F 704 752-7747
Charlotte *(G-2662)*

Prime Water Services Inc...................... G 919 504-1020
Raleigh *(G-10394)*

Proven Prof Cnstr Svcs LLC.................. F 919 821-2696
Garner *(G-4956)*

Spc Mechanical Corporation.................. C 252 237-9035
Wendell *(G-12549)*

CONTRACTORS: Power Generating Eqpt Installation

Power Support Engineering Inc.............. G 813 909-1199
Hayesville *(G-6143)*

CONTRACTORS: Prefabricated Window & Door Installation

Carolina Windows and Doors Inc.......... F 252 756-2585
Greenville *(G-5951)*

CONTRACTORS: Process Piping

Ansonville Piping & Fabg Inc................. G 704 826-8403
Ansonville *(G-129)*

Hicks Wterstoves Solar Systems........... F 336 789-4977
Mount Airy *(G-9129)*

Mechanical Spc Contrs Inc.................... D 919 829-9300
Raleigh *(G-10287)*

Southern Pdmont Pping Fbrction........... F 704 272-7936
Peachland *(G-9654)*

CONTRACTORS: Roustabout Svcs

Filter Srvcng of Chrltte 135.................. G 704 619-3768
Charlotte *(G-2152)*

CONTRACTORS: Septic System

Inman Septic Tank Service Inc.............. G 910 763-1146
Wilmington *(G-12817)*

Leonard McSwain Sptic Tank Svc........ G 704 482-1380
Shelby *(G-11353)*

O R Prdgen Sons Sptic Tank I............... G 252 442-3338
Rocky Mount *(G-10857)*

TNT Services Inc.................................... G 252 261-3073
Kitty Hawk *(G-7447)*

Trane US Inc... F 704 697-9006
Charlotte *(G-2935)*

CONTRACTORS: Sheet Metal Work, NEC

Carolina Machining Fabrication............ G 919 554-9700
Youngsville *(G-13469)*

Herman Reeves Tex Shtmtl Inc............. E 704 865-2231
Gastonia *(G-5059)*

Hughs Sheet Mtal Sttsvlle LLC............. F 704 872-4621
Statesville *(G-11714)*

Oak Ridge Industries LLC..................... E 252 833-4061
Washington *(G-12401)*

Protocase Mfg Usa Inc.......................... E 866 849-3911
Wilmington *(G-12892)*

R E Bengel Sheet Metal Co.................... G 252 637-3404
New Bern *(G-9390)*

Raleigh Mechanical & Mtls Inc............. F 919 598-4601
Raleigh *(G-10425)*

Taylorsville Precast Molds Inc.............. G 828 632-4608
Taylorsville *(G-11982)*

CONTRACTORS: Siding

Midway Blind & Awning Co Inc.............. G 336 226-4532
Burlington *(G-1129)*

Vinyl Windows & Doors Corp.................. F 910 944-2100
Aberdeen *(G-30)*

CONTRACTORS: Structural Iron Work, Structural

Apex Steel Corp....................................... E 919 362-6611
Raleigh *(G-9908)*

Garden Metalwork...................................... G 828 733-1077
Newland *(G-9429)*

Watson Steel & Iron Works LLC ..... E 704 821-7140
Matthews *(G-8197)*

CONTRACTORS: Structural Steel Erection

Ansonville Piping & Fabg Inc................ G 704 826-8403
Ansonville *(G-129)*

Asheville Maintenance and C................ E 828 687-8110
Arden *(G-254)*

Burton Steel Company............................ F 910 675-9241
Castle Hayne *(G-1496)*

Canalta Enterprises LLC......................... E 919 615-1570
Raleigh *(G-9965)*

King Stone Innovation LLC..................... G 704 352-1134
Charlotte *(G-2398)*

Roderick Mch Erectors Wldg Inc........... G 910 343-0381
Wilmington *(G-12901)*

Steel Supply and Erection Co................ F 336 625-4830
Asheboro *(G-399)*

Williams Industries Inc........................... C 919 604-1746
Raleigh *(G-10610)*

CONTRACTORS: Textile Warping

American Yarn LLC................................... G 919 614-1542
Burlington *(G-1046)*

CONTRACTORS: Tile Installation, Ceramic

David Allen Company Inc........................ C 919 821-7100
Raleigh *(G-10039)*

Precision Walls Inc.................................. G 336 852-7710
Greensboro *(G-5759)*

Sare Granite & Tile.................................. G 828 676-2666
Arden *(G-305)*

CONTRACTORS: Underground Utilities

Batista Grading Inc................................ F 919 359-3449
Clayton *(G-3134)*

McLean Sbsrface Utlity Engrg L............ F 336 340-0024
Greensboro *(G-5687)*

CONTRACTORS: Warm Air Heating & Air Conditioning

Envirnmntal Cmfort Sltions Inc.............. E 980 272-7327
Kannapolis *(G-7208)*

Freudnberg Rsdntial Fltrtion T............... E 828 328-1142
Hickory *(G-6335)*

James M Pleasants Company Inc.......... E 800 365-9010
Greensboro *(G-5633)*

Johnson Controls Inc.............................. D 704 521-8889
Charlotte *(G-2375)*

Kenny Fowler Heating and A Inc........... F 910 508-4553
Wilmington *(G-12827)*

Mestek Inc.. C 252 753-5323
Farmville *(G-4535)*

Spartan Systems LLC.............................. F 336 946-1244
Advance *(G-39)*

CONTRACTORS: Water Well Drilling

Merrill Resources Inc............................... G 828 877-4450
Penrose *(G-9662)*

CONTRACTORS: Windows & Doors

Jewers Doors Us Inc............................... E 888 510-5331
Greensboro *(G-5636)*

CONTRACTORS: Wood Floor Installation & Refinishing

Creative Stone Fyetteville Inc................ F 910 491-1225
Fayetteville *(G-4580)*

CONTROL EQPT: Electric

Abco Controls and Eqp Inc..................... G 704 394-2424
Charlotte *(G-1610)*

AC Corporation... B 336 273-4472
Greensboro *(G-5339)*

Fortech Inc... F 704 333-0621
Charlotte *(G-2174)*

ITT LLC... F 704 716-7600
Charlotte *(G-2357)*

ITT LLC... G 336 662-0113
Colfax *(G-3281)*

Masonite Corporation.............................. A 704 599-0235
Charlotte *(G-2466)*

Pro-Tech Inc... G 704 872-6227
Statesville *(G-11755)*

Rockwell Automation Inc........................ G 919 804-0200
Cary *(G-1440)*

Rockwell Automation Inc........................ E 704 665-6000
Charlotte *(G-2731)*

CONTROLS & ACCESS: Indl, Electric

Cross Technologies Inc........................... E 800 327-7727
Greensboro *(G-5472)*

Custom Controls Unlimited LLC............ F 919 812-6553
Raleigh *(G-10029)*

Eaton Corporation.................................... B 910 677-5375
Fayetteville *(G-4593)*

I C E S Gaston County Inc..................... G 704 263-1418
Stanley *(G-11618)*

Rockwell Automation Inc........................ F 828 652-0074
Marion *(G-8063)*

Textrol Laboratories Inc......................... E 704 764-3400
Monroe *(G-8569)*

CONTROLS & ACCESS: Motor

2391 Eatons Ferry Rd Assoc LLC.......... G 919 844-0565
Raleigh *(G-9857)*

Eaton Corporation.................................... C 919 870-3000
Raleigh *(G-10072)*

Griffin Motion LLC................................... F 919 577-6333
Apex *(G-161)*

Melltronics Industrial Inc....................... G 704 821-6651
Matthews *(G-8185)*

CONTROLS: Automatic Temperature

Hoffman Building Tech Inc..................... C 336 292-8777
Greensboro *(G-5601)*

JMS Southeast Inc................................. E 704 873-1835
Statesville *(G-11719)*

CONTROLS: Electric Motor

Eaton Corporation.................................... B 828 684-2381
Arden *(G-266)*

Hubbell Industrial Contrls Inc................ C 336 434-2800
Archdale *(G-226)*

CONTROLS: Environmental

AMR Systems LLC................................... G 704 980-9072
Charlotte *(G-1673)*

Building Automation Svcs LLC............... F 336 884-4026
High Point *(G-6552)*

Cooke Companies Intl.............................. F 919 968-0848
Chapel Hill *(G-1540)*

Dna Group Inc.. E 919 881-0889
Raleigh *(G-10051)*

Dynamac Corporation.............................. E 919 544-6428
Durham *(G-4016)*

Huber Usa Inc.. F 919 674-4266
Raleigh *(G-10179)*

Industrial Heat LLC................................. G 919 743-5727
Raleigh *(G-10190)*

Miller Ctrl Mfg Inc Clinton NC.............. G 910 592-5112
Clinton *(G-3235)*

Qualia Networks Inc................................ G 805 637-2083
Raleigh *(G-10413)*

Resideo LLC... G 919 872-5556
Raleigh *(G-10441)*

Ruskin LLC... G 919 583-5444
Goldsboro *(G-5242)*

Strandberg Engrg Labs Inc.................... F 336 274-3775
Greensboro *(G-5843)*

W A Brown & Son Incorporated............. E 704 636-5131
Salisbury *(G-11134)*

CONTROLS: Thermostats, Built-in

Solero Technologies Shelby LLC........... C 704 482-9582
Shelby *(G-11380)*

CONVENIENCE STORES

Coker Feed Mill Inc................................. F 919 778-3491
Goldsboro *(G-5207)*

J L Powell & Co Inc................................. G 910 642-8989
Whiteville *(G-12585)*

CONVERTERS: Frequency

Global Emssons Systems Inc-USA........ G 704 585-8490
Troutman *(G-12139)*

Greenfield Energy LLC............................ F 910 509-1805
Wrightsville Beach *(G-13431)*

CONVERTERS: Rotary, Electrical

DCS USA Corporation.............................. G 919 535-8000
Morrisville *(G-8963)*

CONVEYOR SYSTEMS: Belt, General Indl Use

Conveyor Technologies Inc..................... G 919 732-8291
Efland *(G-4375)*

Industrial Sup Solutions Inc.................. E 704 636-4241
Salisbury *(G-11067)*

Qcs Acquisition Corporation.................. G 252 446-5000
Rocky Mount *(G-10863)*

Rulmeca Corporation............................... G 910 794-9294
Wilmington *(G-12905)*

Smart Machine Technologies Inc........... D 276 632-9853
Greensboro *(G-5817)*

CONVEYOR SYSTEMS: Bulk Handling

RSI Leasing Inc NS Tbt.......................... G 704 587-9300
Charlotte *(G-2738)*

CONVEYOR SYSTEMS: Pneumatic Tube

Sunco Powder Systems Inc.................... E 704 545-3922
Charlotte *(G-2881)*

CONVEYOR SYSTEMS: Robotic

Westwood Manufacturing Inc.................. G 910 862-9992
Elizabethtown *(G-4437)*

CONVEYORS & CONVEYING EQPT

AC Corporation... B 336 273-4472
Greensboro *(G-5339)*

Advance Conveying Tech LLC................ E 704 710-4001
Kings Mountain *(G-7344)*

Advantage Conveyor Inc...................... F 919 781-0055
Raleigh (G-9881)

Altec Industries Inc............................... B 919 528-2535
Creedmoor (G-3637)

Automated Lumber Handling Inc........... G 828 754-4662
Lenoir (G-7574)

Basic Machinery Company Inc.............. D 919 663-2244
Siler City (G-11399)

Belt Concepts America Inc.................... F 888 598-2358
Spring Hope (G-11553)

Beltservice Corporation........................ E 704 947-2264
Huntersville (G-6973)

Columbus McKinnon Corporation........ C 716 689-5400
Charlotte (G-1962)

Conroll Corporation.............................. F 910 202-4292
Wilmington (G-12747)

Conveying Solutions LLC...................... F 704 636-4241
Salisbury (G-11038)

Conveyor Tech LLC............................... C 919 776-7227
Goldston (G-5257)

Conveyor Technologies of Sa............... D 919 776-7227
Sanford (G-11165)

Esco Group LLC................................... G 919 900-8226
Raleigh (G-10092)

Forbo Movement Systems..................... E 704 334-5353
Charlotte (G-2171)

Forbo Siegling LLC............................... B 704 948-0800
Huntersville (G-6995)

Gardner Machinery Corporation........... F 704 372-3890
Charlotte (G-2189)

Goals In Service LLC............................ G 919 440-2656
Seven Springs (G-11297)

Gough Econ Inc.................................... E 704 399-4501
Charlotte (G-2228)

Greenline Corporation.......................... G 704 333-3377
Charlotte (G-2240)

Interroll Corporation............................. C 910 799-1100
Wilmington (G-12819)

Interroll USA Holding LLC..................... D 910 799-1100
Wilmington (G-12820)

Ism Inc.. E
Arden (G-277)

Jack A Farrior Inc................................. D 252 753-2020
Farmville (G-4532)

Jayson Concepts Inc............................ G 828 654-8900
Arden (G-279)

Lns Turbo Inc....................................... D 704 739-7111
Kings Mountain (G-7371)

Machinex Technologies Inc................... F 773 867-8801
High Point (G-6696)

Mantissa Corporation........................... E 704 525-1749
Charlotte (G-2453)

Material Handling Technologies Inc....... D 919 388-0050
Morrisville (G-9018)

Memios LLC.. D 336 664-5256
Greensboro (G-5689)

National Conveyors Company Inc.......... G 860 325-4011
Charlotte (G-2545)

Niels Jorgensen Company Inc............... G 910 259-1624
Burgaw (G-1028)

Nunn Probst Installations Inc................ G 704 822-9443
Belmont (G-757)

Process Automation Tech Inc................ G 828 298-1055
Asheville (G-586)

Production Systems Inc......................... E 336 886-7161
High Point (G-6747)

Sherrill Contract Mfg Inc....................... F 704 922-7871
Dallas (G-3689)

Southco Industries Inc.......................... C 704 482-1477
Shelby (G-11381)

Superior Finishing Systems LLC........... G 336 956-2000
Lexington (G-7747)

Transbotics Corporation........................ E 704 362-1115
Charlotte (G-2936)

COOKING & FOODWARMING EQPT: Commercial

Ats Service Company LLC..................... G 512 905-9005
Godwin (G-5186)

Kuenz America Inc............................... F 984 255-1018
Raleigh (G-10241)

Marshall Air Systems Inc...................... D 704 525-6230
Charlotte (G-2460)

Sinnovatek Inc..................................... G 919 694-0974
Raleigh (G-10479)

COOKING EQPT, HOUSEHOLD: Ranges, Electric

The Tarheel Electric Member................ F 919 876-4603
Raleigh (G-10544)

COOKWARE, STONEWARE: Coarse Earthenware & Pottery

Haand Inc.. F 336 350-7597
Burlington (G-1102)

COOKWARE: Fine Earthenware

Swiss Made Brands USA Inc................. G 704 900-6622
Charlotte (G-2890)

COOLING TOWERS: Metal

Akg Nrth Amercn Operations Inc........... F 919 563-4286
Mebane (G-8229)

Marley Company LLC........................... C 704 752-4400
Charlotte (G-2459)

SPX Cooling Tech LLC.......................... F 630 881-9777
Charlotte (G-2846)

SPX Corporation.................................. F 336 627-6020
Eden (G-4357)

COPPER ORE MINING

Ames Copper Group LLC...................... E 860 622-7626
Shelby (G-11312)

COPPER PRDTS: Smelter, Primary

Imc-Metalsamerica LLC........................ F 704 482-8200
Shelby (G-11347)

COPPER: Rolling & Drawing

Essex Group Inc................................... G 704 921-9605
Charlotte (G-2127)

Manhattan Amrcn Terrazzo Strip........... C 336 622-4247
Staley (G-11596)

Torpedo Specialty Wire Inc................... D 252 977-3900
Rocky Mount (G-10872)

CORD & TWINE

All American Braids Inc........................ E 704 852-4380
Gastonia (G-4985)

Dayton Bag & Burlap Co....................... G 704 873-7271
Statesville (G-11685)

MHS Ltd... G 336 767-2641
Winston Salem (G-13250)

Standard Tytape Company Inc............... G 828 693-6594
Hendersonville (G-6244)

Yale Rope Technologies Inc.................. G 704 630-0331
Salisbury (G-11137)

CORK & CORK PRDTS: Bottle

Vinventions Usa LLC............................ C 919 460-2200
Zebulon (G-13525)

COSMETIC PREPARATIONS

A M P Laboratories Ltd......................... G 704 894-9721
Cornelius (G-3582)

Active Concepts LLC............................ G 704 276-7372
Lincolnton (G-7809)

Active Concepts LLC............................ E 704 276-7100
Lincolnton (G-7810)

Burts Bees Inc..................................... C 919 998-5200
Durham (G-3953)

Ei LLC.. B 704 857-0707
Winston Salem (G-13155)

Emage Medical LLC.............................. G 704 904-1873
Charlotte (G-2106)

Green Compass LLC............................ G 833 336-9223
Wilmington (G-12797)

Keller Cosmetics Inc............................ G 704 399-2226
Monroe (G-8512)

Litex Industries Inc.............................. G 704 799-3758
Mooresville (G-8713)

Narayana Inc....................................... G 828 708-0954
Asheville (G-554)

Onixx Manufacturing LLC..................... G 828 298-4625
Swannanoa (G-11875)

Revlon Inc... C 919 603-2782
Oxford (G-9628)

Revlon Inc... E 919 603-2000
Oxford (G-9629)

Revlon Consumer Products Corp.......... D 919 603-2000
Oxford (G-9630)

Usrx LLC.. E 980 221-1200
Charlotte (G-2969)

COSMETICS & TOILETRIES

Adoratherapy Inc................................. F 917 297-8904
Asheville (G-423)

Alywillow... G 919 454-4826
Raleigh (G-9894)

American Fiber & Finishing Inc............. E 704 984-9256
Albemarle (G-61)

Artisan Aromatics................................. G 800 456-6675
Burnsville (G-1183)

Body Shop Inc..................................... C 919 554-4900
Wake Forest (G-12265)

Burts Bees Inc..................................... C 919 238-6450
Morrisville (G-8946)

Cbdmd Inc... F 704 445-3060
Charlotte (G-1869)

Conopco Inc... B 910 875-4121
Raeford (G-9834)

Cosmetic Creations Inc........................ G 828 298-4625
Swannanoa (G-11869)

Coty Inc... D 919 895-5000
Sanford (G-11166)

Cryogen LLC.. F 919 649-7027
Raleigh (G-10024)

Deb SBS Inc.. G 704 263-4240
Stanley (G-11613)

Dexios Services LLC............................ G 704 946-5101
Cornelius (G-3597)

Filltech Inc... E 704 279-4300
Rockwell (G-10796)

Filltech USA LLC.................................. E 704 279-4300
Rockwell (G-10797)

Go Green Miracle Balm......................... G 630 209-0226
Cornelius (G-3603)

Greenwich Bay Trading Co Inc.............. E 919 781-5008
Raleigh (G-10145)

HFC Prestige Products Inc................... G 919 895-5300
Sanford (G-11190)

Little River Naturals LLC...................... G 919 760-3708
Zebulon (G-13513)

PRODUCT

Parkdale Mills Incorporated................... D 704 874-5000
Gastonia (G-5117)

Philosophy Inc................................... E 602 794-8701
Sanford (G-11220)

Plm Inc... G 336 788-7529
Winston Salem (G-13298)

Skin So Soft Spa Inc.......................... G 800 674-7554
Charlotte (G-2811)

Tea and Honey Blends LLC.................. G 919 673-4273
Raleigh (G-10536)

Unilever... F 910 988-1054
Raeford (G-9855)

Unique Body Blends Inc...................... G 910 302-5484
Fayetteville (G-4686)

Universal Preservachem Inc................ D 732 568-1266
Mebane (G-8262)

US Cotton LLC.................................. D 704 874-5000
Belmont (G-774)

US Cotton LLC.................................. C 216 676-6400
Gastonia (G-5161)

Virtue Labs LLC................................ E 781 316-5437
Winston Salem (G-13382)

Walex Products Company Inc.............. F 910 371-2242
Leland (G-7564)

COSMETICS WHOLESALERS

A M P Laboratories Ltd....................... G 704 894-9721
Cornelius (G-3582)

Cosmetic Creations Inc...................... G 828 298-4625
Swannanoa (G-11869)

Keller Cosmetics Inc.......................... G 704 399-2226
Monroe (G-8512)

Philosophy Inc.................................. E 602 794-8701
Sanford (G-11220)

Usrx LLC.. E 980 221-1200
Charlotte (G-2969)

COSMETOLOGY & PERSONAL HYGIENE SALONS

Katchi Tees Incorporated.................... G 252 315-4691
Wilson (G-12997)

COUGH MEDICINES

Generics Bidco II LLC......................... C 980 389-2501
Charlotte (G-2202)

Generics Bidco II LLC......................... D 704 612-8830
Charlotte (G-2203)

COUNTER & SINK TOPS

AP Granite Installation LLC.................. G 919 215-1795
Clayton (G-3131)

Cutting Edge Stoneworks Inc............... G 704 799-1227
Mooresville (G-8648)

Endeavour Fbrication Group Inc........... G 919 479-1453
Durham (G-4025)

Hargrove Countertops & ACC Inc......... E 919 981-0163
Raleigh (G-10155)

Old Castle Service Inc......................... G 336 992-1601
Kernersville (G-7289)

Sare Granite & Tile............................. G 828 676-2666
Arden (G-305)

Stonery LLC...................................... G 704 662-8702
Mooresville (G-8778)

William Stone & Tile Inc...................... G 910 353-0914
Hubert (G-6938)

COUNTERS OR COUNTER DISPLAY CASES, EXC WOOD

Mijo Enterprises Inc........................... G 252 442-6806
Rocky Mount (G-10852)

COUNTERS OR COUNTER DISPLAY CASES, WOOD

Carolina Countertops of Garner........... F 919 832-3335
Raleigh (G-9974)

COUNTING DEVICES: Controls, Revolution & Timing

Dynapar Corporation.......................... C 800 873-8731
Elizabethtown (G-4426)

COUNTING DEVICES: Speedometers

Nichols Spdmtr & Instr Co Inc.............. G 336 273-2881
Greensboro (G-5709)

COUPLINGS, EXC PRESSURE & SOIL PIPE

Victaulic Company............................. E 910 371-5588
Leland (G-7563)

COUPLINGS: Hose & Tube, Hydraulic Or Pneumatic

Anchor Coupling Inc........................... B 919 739-8000
Goldsboro (G-5198)

Bulldog Hose Company LLC................. E 919 639-6151
Angier (G-114)

Cross Technologies Inc....................... G 336 370-4673
Greensboro (G-5473)

On-Site Hose Inc............................... G 919 303-3840
Apex (G-183)

COVERS: Automobile Seat

Flint Hill Textiles Inc........................... G 704 434-9331
Shelby (G-11337)

COVERS: Automotive, Exc Seat & Tire

Guilford Mills LLC.............................. A 910 794-5810
Wilmington (G-12798)

Lear Corporation............................... A 910 794-5810
Wilmington (G-12831)

CRANE & AERIAL LIFT SVCS

CVC Equipment Company.................... G 704 300-6242
Cherryville (G-3063)

Flores Crane Services LLC.................. F 704 243-4347
Waxhaw (G-12431)

K-M Machine Company Inc.................. D 910 428-2368
Biscoe (G-855)

Moore S Welding Service Inc............... G 919 837-5769
Bear Creek (G-716)

Nashville Wldg & Mch Works Inc.......... E 252 243-0113
Wilson (G-13008)

Piedmont Fiberglass Inc...................... E 828 632-8883
Statesville (G-11745)

Steel Supply and Erection Co............... F 336 625-4830
Asheboro (G-399)

Tony D Hildreth................................. F 910 276-1803
Laurel Hill (G-7488)

Watson Steel & Iron Works LLC........... E 704 821-7140
Matthews (G-8197)

CRANES: Indl Plant

Kuenz America Inc............................. F 984 255-1018
Raleigh (G-10241)

CRANES: Overhead

Altec Industries Inc........................... B 919 528-2535
Creedmoor (G-3637)

Altec Northeast LLC.......................... E 508 320-9041
Creedmoor (G-3638)

CREDIT CARD SVCS

Atlantic Bankcard Center Inc............... G 336 855-9250
Greensboro (G-5374)

CROWNS & CLOSURES

Assa Abloy ACC Door Cntrls Gro......... C 877 974-2255
Monroe (G-8432)

CULTURE MEDIA

Business Mogul LLC........................... G 919 605-2165
Raleigh (G-9962)

CUPS & PLATES: Foamed Plastics

Unified2 Globl Packg Group LLC........... C 774 696-3643
Durham (G-4288)

CURBING: Granite Or Stone

Asp Distribution Inc........................... F 336 375-5672
Greensboro (G-5373)

Century Stone LLC............................. G 919 774-3334
Sanford (G-11161)

Georgia-Carolina Quarries Inc............. E 336 786-6978
Mount Airy (G-9123)

Grancreations Inc.............................. G 704 332-7625
Charlotte (G-2230)

CURTAIN & DRAPERY FIXTURES: Poles, Rods & Rollers

Locklear Cabinets Wdwrk Sp Inc.......... G 910 521-4463
Rowland (G-10916)

CURTAIN WALLS: Building, Steel

Central Steel Buildings Inc.................. F 336 789-7896
Mount Airy (G-9114)

Cornerstone Bldg Brands Inc............... B 281 897-7788
Cary (G-1336)

Eagle Carports Inc............................. E 800 579-8589
Mount Airy (G-9117)

Millennium Mfg Structures LLC............ G 828 265-3737
Boone (G-934)

Williams Industries Inc....................... C 919 604-1746
Raleigh (G-10610)

CURTAINS: Window, From Purchased Materials

National Mastercraft Inds Inc............... G 919 896-8858
Raleigh (G-10324)

CUSHIONS & PILLOWS

Arden Companies LLC......................... E 919 258-3081
Sanford (G-11149)

Carolina Fairway Cushions LLC............ G 336 434-4292
Thomasville (G-12003)

Dale Ray Fabrics LLC.......................... G 704 932-6411
Kannapolis (G-7206)

Fiber Cushioning Inc.......................... F 336 629-8442
Asheboro (G-355)

Hickory Springs Mfg Co...................... D 336 861-4195
High Point (G-6647)

Innovative Cushions LLC..................... G 336 861-2060
Archdale (G-228)

Js Fiber Co Inc.................................. E 704 871-1582
Statesville (G-11721)

North Carolina Lumber Company.......... G 336 498-6600
Randleman (G-10654)

Perfect Fit Industries LLC.................... C 800 864-7618
Charlotte (G-2627)

Royale Comfort Seating Inc................. D 828 352-9021
Taylorsville (G-11974)

Signature Seating Inc.............................. E 828 325-0174
Hickory *(G-6447)*

Snyder Paper Corporation...................... E 336 884-1172
High Point *(G-6782)*

Stn Cushion Company.......................... D 336 476-9100
Thomasville *(G-12074)*

Trtl Inc... G 844 811-5816
Raleigh *(G-10566)*

Wayne Industries Inc........................... E 336 434-5017
Archdale *(G-246)*

CUSHIONS & PILLOWS: Bed, From Purchased Materials

Creative Textiles Inc............................. G 919 693-4427
Oxford *(G-9609)*

Discover Night LLC................................ F 888 825-6282
Raleigh *(G-10049)*

Premium Cushion Inc........................... E 828 464-4783
Conover *(G-3550)*

Richard Shew...................................... F 828 781-3294
Conover *(G-3554)*

Somnigroup International Inc................ C 336 861-2900
Trinity *(G-12126)*

Sunrise Development LLC..................... F 828 453-0590
Mooresboro *(G-8586)*

Tempo Products LLC............................ E 336 434-8649
High Point *(G-6804)*

CUSHIONS: Carpet & Rug, Foamed Plastics

Fxi Inc... D 336 431-1171
High Point *(G-6626)*

Reedy International Corp....................... F 980 819-6930
Charlotte *(G-2701)*

Shaw Industries Group Inc................... E 877 996-5942
Charlotte *(G-2796)*

CUSTOM COMPOUNDING OF RUBBER MATERIALS

American Phoenix Inc........................... C 910 484-4007
Fayetteville *(G-4551)*

CUT STONE & STONE PRODUCTS

Buechel Stone Corp.............................. D 800 236-4474
Marion *(G-8037)*

Chadsworth Incorporated..................... G 910 763-7600
Wilmington *(G-12742)*

Clifford W Estes Co Inc........................ E 336 622-6410
Staley *(G-11593)*

Conway Development Inc...................... F 252 756-2168
Greenville *(G-5957)*

Custom Marble Corporation.................. G 910 215-0679
Pinehurst *(G-9690)*

E T Sales Inc....................................... F 704 888-4010
Midland *(G-8286)*

FTM Enterprises Inc............................. F 910 798-2045
Wilmington *(G-12780)*

Ginkgo Stone LLC................................ G 704 451-8678
Charlotte *(G-2212)*

Granite Memorials Inc.......................... G 336 786-6596
Mount Airy *(G-9124)*

Ivey Ln Inc.. F 336 230-0062
Greensboro *(G-5631)*

John J Morton Company Inc................. F 704 332-6633
Charlotte *(G-2373)*

M & M Stone Sculpting & Engrv............ G 336 877-3842
Todd *(G-12104)*

Meridian Granite Company................... G 919 781-4550
Raleigh *(G-10292)*

Quality Marble..................................... G 336 472-1000
Thomasville *(G-12064)*

Royal Baths Manufacturing Co.............. E 704 837-1701
Charlotte *(G-2733)*

RSI Home Products Inc........................ C 828 428-6300
Lincolnton *(G-7852)*

Sharp Stone Supply Inc....................... G 336 659-7777
Winston Salem *(G-13332)*

Sid Jenkins Inc.................................... G 336 632-0707
Greensboro *(G-5811)*

Wake Stone Corporatio......................... E 919 266-1100
Knightdale *(G-7462)*

World Stone Fabricators Inc.................. E 704 372-9968
Charlotte *(G-3026)*

World Stone of Sanford LLC.................. F 919 468-8450
Sanford *(G-11254)*

CUTLERY

Bic Corporation................................... D 704 598-7700
Charlotte *(G-1779)*

Butchers Best Inc................................ G 252 533-0961
Roanoke Rapids *(G-10733)*

Edge-Works Manufacturing Co.............. G 910 455-9834
Burgaw *(G-1022)*

Fred Marvin and Associates Inc............ G 330 784-9211
Greensboro *(G-5539)*

J Culpepper & Co................................ G 828 524-6842
Otto *(G-9606)*

Spartan Blades LLC............................. G 910 757-0035
Southern Pines *(G-11511)*

Sword Conservatory Inc....................... G 919 557-4465
Holly Springs *(G-6917)*

CUTLERY WHOLESALERS

Freud America Inc................................ C 800 334-4107
High Point *(G-6624)*

CYCLIC CRUDES & INTERMEDIATES

Burlington Chemical Co LLC................. G 336 584-0111
Greensboro *(G-5410)*

Dystar LP.. E 704 561-3000
Charlotte *(G-2078)*

Marlowe-Van Loan Corporation............ G 336 886-7126
High Point *(G-6699)*

Melatex Incorporated........................... F 704 332-5046
Charlotte *(G-2489)*

Tar Heel Landworks LLC...................... G 336 941-3009
Mocksville *(G-8393)*

Tar Heel Materials & Hdlg LLC............. G 704 659-5143
Cleveland *(G-3223)*

CYLINDER & ACTUATORS: Fluid Power

Atlantic Hydraulics Svcs LLC............... E 919 542-2985
Sanford *(G-11152)*

Curtiss-Wright Controls Inc.................. E 704 481-1150
Shelby *(G-11326)*

Indian Head Industries Inc................... E 704 547-7411
Charlotte *(G-2321)*

Solero Technologies Shelby LLC........... C 704 482-9582
Shelby *(G-11380)*

Triumph Actuation Systems LLC........... C 336 766-9036
Clemmons *(G-3206)*

Yale Industrial Products Inc................. E 704 588-4610
Charlotte *(G-3038)*

CYLINDERS: Pump

IMO Industries Inc............................... C 704 289-6511
Monroe *(G-8504)*

DAIRY EQPT

Dairy Services.................................... G 919 303-2442
Raleigh *(G-10033)*

DAIRY PRDTS STORE: Ice Cream, Packaged

Bilcat Inc.. E 828 295-3088
Blowing Rock *(G-880)*

Goodberry Creamery Inc...................... F 919 878-8870
Wake Forest *(G-12279)*

Mooresville Ice Cream Company LLC.... E 704 664-5456
Mooresville *(G-8725)*

Paletria La Mnrca McHacana LLC.......... G 919 803-0636
Raleigh *(G-10354)*

Tony S Ice Cream Company Inc............ F 704 867-7085
Gastonia *(G-5156)*

DAIRY PRDTS STORES

Buffalo Creek Farm & Crmry LLC........... G 336 969-5698
Germanton *(G-5174)*

Dewey S Bakery Inc............................. F 336 748-0230
Winston Salem *(G-13143)*

G & M Milling Co Inc............................ F 704 873-5758
Statesville *(G-11701)*

DAIRY PRDTS: Acidophilus Milk

Maola Milk and Ice Cream Co............... F 844 287-1970
New Bern *(G-9377)*

DAIRY PRDTS: Butter

Michaels Creamery Inc........................ G 910 292-4172
Fayetteville *(G-4641)*

Waxhaw Creamery LLC......................... F 704 843-7927
Waxhaw *(G-12449)*

DAIRY PRDTS: Canned Milk, Whole

Chef Martini LLC.................................. A 919 327-3183
Raleigh *(G-9992)*

DAIRY PRDTS: Cheese

Celebrity Dairy LLC............................. G 919 742-4931
Siler City *(G-11404)*

Old Salem Incorporated....................... G 336 721-7305
Winston Salem *(G-13269)*

Stans Quality Foods Inc....................... G 336 570-2572
Burlington *(G-1163)*

Tin Can Ventures LLC.......................... G 919 732-9078
Cedar Grove *(G-1518)*

DAIRY PRDTS: Dairy Based Desserts, Frozen

Antkar LLC.. G 919 322-4100
Raleigh *(G-9905)*

Delizza LLC... F 252 442-0270
Battleboro *(G-696)*

Hunter Farms...................................... C 336 822-2300
High Point *(G-6664)*

DAIRY PRDTS: Dietary Supplements, Dairy & Non-Dairy Based

Arms Race Nutrition LLC...................... G 888 978-2332
Statesville *(G-11660)*

Bestco LLC.. E 704 664-4300
Mooresville *(G-8610)*

Bionutra Life Sciences LLC.................. G 828 572-2838
Lenoir *(G-7587)*

Blue Ridge Silver Inc........................... G 828 729-8610
Boone *(G-898)*

Body Engineering Inc........................... G 704 650-3434
Matthews *(G-8099)*

Disruptive Enterprises LLC.................. G 336 567-0104
Burlington *(G-1084)*

Herbalife Manufacturing LLC................ G 336 970-6400
Winston Salem *(G-13196)*

Im8 (us) LLC....................................... G 862 485-8325
Charlotte *(G-2314)*

PRODUCT

Ka-Ex LLC.. G..... 704 343-5143
   Charlotte *(G-2387)*

Muscadine Naturals Inc........................ G..... 888 628-5898
   Clemmons *(G-3197)*

NPC Corporation.................................... G..... 336 998-2386
   Mocksville *(G-8382)*

Rainforest Nutritionals Inc................... G..... 919 847-2221
   Raleigh *(G-10421)*

DAIRY PRDTS: Ice Cream & Ice Milk

Goodberry Creamery Inc..................... F 919 878-8870
   Wake Forest *(G-12279)*

Mooresville Ice Cream Company LLC.... E 704 664-5456
   Mooresville *(G-8725)*

Simply Natural Creamery LLC............. E 252 746-3334
   Ayden *(G-663)*

DAIRY PRDTS: Ice Cream, Bulk

Homeland Creamery LLC....................... G..... 336 685-6455
   Julian *(G-7201)*

Maola Milk and Ice Cream Co................ E 252 756-3160
   Greenville *(G-6002)*

DAIRY PRDTS: Ice Cream, Packaged, Molded, On Sticks, Etc.

Good Vibrationz LLC.............................. G..... 919 820-3084
   Greenville *(G-5982)*

DAIRY PRDTS: Milk & Cream, Cultured & Flavored

Alamance Foods Inc.............................. C 336 226-6392
   Burlington *(G-1043)*

DAIRY PRDTS: Milk, Fluid

Carolina Yogurt Inc................................ G..... 828 754-9685
   Lenoir *(G-7591)*

Dfa Dairy Brands Fluid LLC.................. G..... 336 714-9032
   Tarboro *(G-11925)*

Maola Milk and Ice Cream Co................ E 252 756-3160
   Greenville *(G-6002)*

New Dairy Opco LLC............................. D 336 725-8141
   Winston Salem *(G-13263)*

DAIRY PRDTS: Natural Cheese

Looking Glass Creamery LLC................ G..... 828 458-0088
   Columbus *(G-3302)*

Saputo Cheese USA Inc.......................... C 847 267-1100
   Troy *(G-12166)*

DAIRY PRDTS: Processed Cheese

Ethnicraft Usa LLC............................... F 336 885-2055
   High Point *(G-6615)*

DAIRY PRDTS: Yogurt, Frozen

Carolina Yogurt Inc................................ G..... 828 754-9685
   Lenoir *(G-7591)*

DATA PROCESSING & PREPARATION SVCS

Computer Task Group Inc...................... E 919 677-1313
   Raleigh *(G-10006)*

Mjt Us Inc.. G..... 704 826-7828
   Charlotte *(G-2510)*

NCR Voyix Corporation.......................... G..... 937 445-5000
   Cary *(G-1406)*

DATA PROCESSING SVCS

Checkfree Services Corporation............. B 919 941-2640
   Durham *(G-3971)*

Consultants In Data Proc Inc................. G..... 704 542-6339
   Charlotte *(G-1976)*

Infobelt LLC.. F 980 223-4000
   Charlotte *(G-2331)*

Innait Inc... G..... 406 241-5245
   Charlotte *(G-2337)*

Quinsite LLC Fka Mile 5 Anlyti.............. F 317 313-5152
   Chapel Hill *(G-1565)*

Raleigh Ventures Inc............................. G..... 910 350-0036
   Wilmington *(G-12895)*

DECORATIVE WOOD & WOODWORK

A M Moore and Company Inc................ G..... 336 294-6994
   Greensboro *(G-5332)*

Archdale Millworks Inc......................... G..... 336 431-9019
   Archdale *(G-212)*

Blind Nail and Company Inc.................. G..... 919 967-0388
   Chapel Hill *(G-1530)*

Cormark International LLC.................... G..... 828 658-8455
   Weaverville *(G-12489)*

Cranberry Wood Works Inc.................. G..... 336 877-8771
   Fleetwood *(G-4715)*

Design Surfaces Inc.............................. G..... 919 781-0310
   Raleigh *(G-10043)*

G & G Management LLC........................ F 336 444-6271
   Greensboro *(G-5544)*

H & P Wood Turnings Inc..................... G..... 910 675-2784
   Rocky Point *(G-10880)*

Heritage Flag LLC................................ G..... 910 725-1540
   Southern Pines *(G-11500)*

Reliable Woodworks Inc........................ G..... 704 785-9663
   Concord *(G-3431)*

Renner Usa Corp................................... G..... 704 527-9261
   Charlotte *(G-2711)*

Saluda Mountain Products Inc............... F 828 696-2296
   Flat Rock *(G-4713)*

Square Peg Construction Inc................. G..... 828 277-5164
   Asheville *(G-610)*

Treeforms Inc.. E 336 292-8998
   Greensboro *(G-5871)*

Vintage Editions Inc............................. F 828 632-4185
   Taylorsville *(G-11985)*

DEFENSE SYSTEMS & EQPT

Blue Maiden Defense............................. G..... 678 292-8342
   Pinebluff *(G-9686)*

Blue Ridge Armor LLC.......................... G..... 844 556-6855
   Rutherfordton *(G-10977)*

Cyber Defense Advisors......................... G..... 336 899-6072
   Greensboro *(G-5482)*

Damsel In Defense................................ G..... 919 744-8776
   Clayton *(G-3142)*

Dodson Defense LLC............................. G..... 336 421-9649
   Burlington *(G-1085)*

Green Line Defense LLC........................ G..... 828 707-5236
   Leicester *(G-7525)*

Kdh Defense Systems Inc...................... C 336 635-4158
   Eden *(G-4350)*

Northstar Computer Tech Inc................. G..... 980 272-1969
   Monroe *(G-8537)*

Plane Defense Ltd................................. G..... 828 254-6061
   Hendersonville *(G-6236)*

Sash and Saber Castings....................... G..... 919 870-5513
   Raleigh *(G-10457)*

DEGREASING MACHINES

Cox Machine Co Inc.............................. G..... 704 296-0118
   Monroe *(G-8470)*

DENTAL EQPT

Anutra Medical Inc............................... E 919 648-1215
   Morrisville *(G-8927)*

Pelton & Crane Company....................... B 704 588-2126
   Charlotte *(G-2623)*

Preventive Technologies Inc.................. G..... 704 684-1211
   Indian Trail *(G-7096)*

DENTAL EQPT & SPLYS

Amann Girrbach North Amer LP............ F 704 837-1404
   Charlotte *(G-1660)*

Cefla Dental Group America.................. G..... 704 731-5293
   Charlotte *(G-1881)*

Custom Smiles Inc................................ F 919 331-2090
   Angier *(G-118)*

Dental Equipment LLC.......................... B 704 588-2126
   Charlotte *(G-2030)*

Dentonics Inc.. F 704 238-0245
   Monroe *(G-8476)*

Dentsply North America LLC................. G..... 844 848-0137
   Charlotte *(G-2031)*

Dentsply Sirona Inc.............................. A 844 848-0137
   Charlotte *(G-2032)*

Kavo Kerr Group................................... F 704 927-0617
   Charlotte *(G-2389)*

Salvin Dental Specialties LLC............... D 704 442-5400
   Charlotte *(G-2752)*

Voco America Inc.................................. G..... 917 923-7698
   Waxhaw *(G-12448)*

DENTAL EQPT & SPLYS: Enamels

Nelson Rodriguez.................................. G..... 828 433-1223
   Morganton *(G-8884)*

DENTAL EQPT & SPLYS: Orthodontic Appliances

Bioventus Inc.. D 919 474-6700
   Durham *(G-3932)*

Cdb Corporation................................... E 910 383-6464
   Leland *(G-7537)*

DENTISTS' OFFICES & CLINICS

Fidelity Associates Inc.......................... E 704 864-3766
   Gastonia *(G-5047)*

Preventive Technologies Inc.................. G..... 704 684-1211
   Indian Trail *(G-7096)*

DEODORANTS: Personal

Procter & Gamble Mfg Co...................... D 336 954-0000
   Greensboro *(G-5767)*

DEPARTMENT STORES

Belk Department Stores LP.................... E 704 357-4000
   Charlotte *(G-1769)*

Burlington Coat Fctry Whse Cor............ E 919 468-9312
   Cary *(G-1317)*

Gildan Activewear (eden) Inc................ C 336 623-9555
   Eden *(G-4347)*

DEPARTMENT STORES: Country General

Village Produce & Cntry Str In.............. G..... 336 661-8685
   Winston Salem *(G-13381)*

DEPILATORIES, COSMETIC

Beauty 4 Love LLC................................ G..... 704 802-2844
   Charlotte *(G-1766)*

Oakstone Associates LLC...................... F 704 946-5101
   Cornelius *(G-3615)*

DERMATOLOGICALS

Nvn Liquidation Inc.............................. E 212 765-9100
   Durham *(G-4154)*

DESIGN SVCS, NEC

Advanced Non-Lethal Tech Inc.............. G..... 847 812-6450
   Raleigh *(G-9880)*

(G-0000) Company's Geographic Section entry number

Ahlberg Cameras Inc...................... F 910 523-5876
Wilmington (G-12693)

Aria Designs LLC.......................... F 828 572-4303
Lenoir (G-7573)

Asheville Color & Imaging Inc.............. G 828 774-5040
Asheville (G-435)

By-Design Black Oxide & TI LLC.......... F 828 874-0610
Valdese (G-12190)

Designed For Joy............................ F 919 395-2884
Apex (G-150)

Evolution of Style LLC..................... G 914 329-3078
Charlotte (G-2132)

Keel Labs Inc............................... G 917 848-9066
Morrisville (G-8997)

Next World Design Inc...................... G 800 448-1223
Thomasville (G-12054)

Oak City Customs LLC..................... G 919 995-5561
Zebulon (G-13517)

Powerlyte Paintball Game Pdts.............. G 919 713-4317
Raleigh (G-10381)

Riley Technologies LLC..................... E 704 663-6319
Mooresville (G-8759)

Rockgeist LLC............................... G 518 461-2009
Asheville (G-593)

Salon & Spa Design Services................ G 919 556-6380
Wake Forest (G-12296)

Structural 0201 LLC........................ E 240 288-8607
Trinity (G-12127)

Sv Plastics LLC............................. G 336 472-2242
Thomasville (G-12077)

DESIGN SVCS: Commercial & Indl

AMP Agency................................. G 704 430-2313
Polkton (G-9812)

Bull City Designs LLC...................... E 919 908-6252
Durham (G-3949)

Distinctive Furniture Inc................... G 828 754-3947
Lenoir (G-7600)

Sitzer & Spuria Inc......................... G 919 929-0299
Chapel Hill (G-1572)

DESIGN SVCS: Computer Integrated Systems

057 Technology LLC........................ G 855 557-7057
Hickory (G-6258)

Cicero Inc.................................. G 919 380-5000
Cary (G-1328)

Computerway Food Systems Inc........... E 336 841-7289
High Point (G-6575)

Extreme Networks Inc....................... B 408 579-2800
Morrisville (G-8973)

General Dynmics Mssion Systems......... C 336 698-8000
Mc Leansville (G-8223)

Infobelt LLC................................ F 980 223-4000
Charlotte (G-2331)

Juniper Networks Inc....................... F 888 586-4737
Raleigh (G-10227)

Q T Corporation............................ G 252 399-7600
Wilson (G-13016)

S C I A Inc................................. G 919 387-7000
Cary (G-1444)

Silver Knight Pcs LLC...................... G 910 824-2054
Fayetteville (G-4670)

Sostram Corporation........................ G 919 226-1195
Durham (G-4242)

St Investors Inc............................ D 704 969-7500
Charlotte (G-2856)

Utd Technology Corp........................ G 704 612-0121
Mint Hill (G-8344)

DETECTIVE & ARMORED CAR SERVICES

A&B Integrators LLC....................... F 919 371-0750
Durham (G-3876)

Diebold Nixdorf Incorporated.............. E 704 599-3100
Charlotte (G-2044)

DIAGNOSTIC SUBSTANCES

Accugenomics Inc.......................... G 910 332-6522
Wilmington (G-12690)

AR Corp.................................... G 910 763-8530
Wilmington (G-12705)

Gbf Inc.................................... D 336 665-0205
High Point (G-6627)

Liebel-Flarsheim Company LLC............. C 919 878-2930
Raleigh (G-10255)

Liposcience Inc............................ G 919 212-1999
Morrisville (G-9012)

Molecular Toxicology Inc.................. F 828 264-9099
Boone (G-935)

Novartis Vccnes Dagnostics Inc............ B 617 871-7000
Holly Springs (G-6908)

Sapere Bio Inc............................. G 919 260-2565
Durham (G-4220)

Tripath Imaging Inc........................ D 336 222-9707
Burlington (G-1170)

DIAGNOSTIC SUBSTANCES OR AGENTS: Cytology & Histology

Multigen Diagnostics LLC.................. G 336 510-1120
Greensboro (G-5700)

DIAGNOSTIC SUBSTANCES OR AGENTS: In Vitro

Baebies Inc................................ D 919 891-0432
Durham (G-3912)

Datar Cancer Genetics Inc................. F 919 377-2119
Morrisville (G-8962)

Sciteck Diagnostics Inc.................... G 828 650-0409
Fletcher (G-4765)

DIAGNOSTIC SUBSTANCES OR AGENTS: Microbiology & Virology

Celplor LLC................................ G 919 961-1961
Cary (G-1324)

Thurston Genomics LLC.................... G 980 237-7547
Charlotte (G-2918)

DIAGNOSTIC SUBSTANCES OR AGENTS: Radioactive

Cardinal Health 414 LLC................... G 704 644-7989
Charlotte (G-1840)

Petnet Solutions Inc....................... G 919 572-5544
Durham (G-4175)

Petnet Solutions Inc....................... G 865 218-2000
Winston Salem (G-13286)

DIAGNOSTIC SUBSTANCES OR AGENTS: Veterinary

North Carolina Department of A............ G 828 684-8188
Arden (G-289)

DIE CUTTING SVC: Paper

Paper Specialties Inc...................... G 919 431-0028
Raleigh (G-10357)

DIE SETS: Presses, Metal Stamping

Parker Industries Inc...................... D 828 437-7779
Connelly Springs (G-3481)

DIES & TOOLS: Special

ABT Manufacturing LLC.................... E 704 847-9188
Statesville (G-11645)

Advance Machining Co Gastonia.......... G 704 866-7411
Gastonia (G-4984)

Ameritek Lasercut Dies Inc................ G 336 292-1165
Greensboro (G-5360)

Atlantic Tool & Die Co Inc................ G 910 270-2888
Hampstead (G-6068)

Brooks of Dallas Inc...................... E 704 922-5219
Dallas (G-3666)

Brothers Precision Tool Co................ G 704 982-5667
Albemarle (G-64)

Cascade Die Casting Group Inc........... E 336 882-0186
High Point (G-6563)

Container Graphics Corp................... F 919 481-4200
Cary (G-1333)

Continental Tool Works Inc................ G 828 692-2578
Hendersonville (G-6198)

Converting Technology Inc................. G 336 333-2386
Greensboro (G-5466)

Die-Tech Inc............................... G 336 475-9186
Thomasville (G-12018)

Dura-Craft Die Inc......................... G 828 632-1944
Taylorsville (G-11959)

Elizabeth Carbide NC Inc.................. G 336 472-5555
Lexington (G-7684)

Flat Rock Tool & Mold Inc................. G 828 692-2578
Hendersonville (G-6208)

Foot To Die For........................... G 704 577-2822
Charlotte (G-2170)

Gerald Hartsoe............................. G 336 498-3233
Randleman (G-10648)

H + M USA Management Co Inc............ G 704 599-9325
Charlotte (G-2247)

Its A Snap................................. G 828 254-3456
Asheville (G-525)

Jmk Tool & Die Inc........................ G 910 897-6373
Coats (G-3263)

KAM Tool & Die Inc........................ E 919 269-5099
Zebulon (G-13512)

Madern Usa Inc............................ E 919 363-4248
Apex (G-177)

Modern Mold & Tool Company.............. G 704 377-2300
Mount Holly (G-9238)

Northeast Tool and Mfg Company.......... E 704 882-1187
Matthews (G-8187)

Palmer Senn................................ G 704 451-3971
Charlotte (G-2606)

Precision Partners LLC..................... E 800 545-3121
Charlotte (G-2658)

Precision Tool & Stamping Inc............. E 910 592-0174
Clinton (G-3239)

Precision Tool Dye and Mold............... F 828 687-2990
Arden (G-301)

Progressive Service Die Co................. F 910 353-4836
Jacksonville (G-7140)

Progressive Tool & Mfg Inc................ F 336 664-1130
Greensboro (G-5768)

Prototype Tooling Co....................... G 704 864-7777
Gastonia (G-5128)

Southeastern Die of NC.................... G 336 275-5212
Greensboro (G-5824)

Specialty Machine Co Inc.................. G 704 853-2102
Gastonia (G-5139)

Stafford Cutting Dies Inc.................. D 704 821-6330
Indian Trail (G-7100)

Stampco Metal Products Inc................ G 828 645-4271
Weaverville (G-12504)

Stratford Tool & Die Co Inc................ G 336 765-2030
Winston Salem (G-13347)

Tgr Enterprises Incorporated.............. G 828 665-4427
Candler (G-1234)

PRODUCT

DIES & TOOLS: Special

Wirtz Wire Edm LLC............................... F 828 696-0830
Hendersonville (G-6250)

Wright Machine & Tool Co Inc................. E 828 298-8440
Swannanoa (G-11879)

DIES: Cutting, Exc Metal

DCS USA Corporation............................. G 919 535-8000
Morrisville (G-8963)

Marbach America Inc............................... E 704 644-4900
Charlotte (G-2455)

DIES: Diamond, Metalworking

Meusburger Us Inc................................ E 704 526-0330
Mint Hill (G-8340)

DIES: Extrusion

Industrial Mtal Flame Spryers................. G 919 596-9381
Durham (G-4074)

Qrmc Ltd... G 828 696-2000
Hendersonville (G-6238)

DIES: Plastic Forming

Alliance Precision Plas Corp................... E 828 286-8631
Spindale (G-11543)

Emerald Tool and Mold Inc.................... F 336 996-6445
Kernersville (G-7271)

Superior Tooling Inc............................... E 919 570-9762
Wake Forest (G-12306)

DIODES: Light Emitting

Creeled Inc... B 919 313-5330
Durham (G-3989)

Hiviz Led Lighting LLC.......................... F 703 662-3458
Hendersonville (G-6216)

Lumenlux LLC....................................... G 704 222-7787
Mint Hill (G-8338)

Multisite Led LLC................................. G 650 823-7247
Charlotte (G-2529)

DIODES: Solid State, Germanium, Silicon, Etc

Leviton Manufacturing Co Inc................. G 336 846-3246
West Jefferson (G-12566)

Lullicoin LLC... G 336 955-1159
Charlotte (G-2440)

Powersecure Solar LLC......................... C 919 213-0798
Durham (G-4191)

DIRECT SELLING ESTABLISHMENTS: Food Svcs

Lotus Bakeries Us LLC.......................... E 415 956-8956
Mebane (G-8250)

Over Rainbow Inc................................. G 704 332-5521
Charlotte (G-2604)

DISASTER SVCS

Fixed-NC LLC.. G 252 751-1911
Greenville (G-5976)

Infinity Communications LLC................. E 919 797-2334
Durham (G-4076)

DISCOUNT DEPARTMENT STORES

Val-U-King Group Inc.............................. G 980 306-5342
Gastonia (G-5162)

DISPLAY FIXTURES: Wood

D & D Displays Inc............................... E 336 667-8765
North Wilkesboro (G-9528)

Dac Products Inc.................................. E 336 969-9786
Rural Hall (G-10958)

Display Options Woodwork Inc.............. G 704 599-6525
Belmont (G-747)

Grice Showcase Display Mfg Inc............ G 704 423-8888
Charlotte (G-2242)

Spartacraft Inc.................................... E 828 397-4630
Connelly Springs (G-3483)

DISPLAY ITEMS: Corrugated, Made From Purchased Materials

Intermarket Technology Inc.................... E 252 623-2199
Washington (G-12395)

Rocktenn In-Store Solutions Inc............ B 828 245-9871
Forest City (G-4796)

Supplyone Rockwell Inc........................ C 704 279-5650
Rockwell (G-10803)

DISTRIBUTORS: Motor Vehicle Engine

Ineos Automotive Americas LLC............ G 404 513-8577
Raleigh (G-10193)

DOCUMENT STORAGE SVCS

Legalis Dms LLC.................................. F 919 741-8260
Raleigh (G-10252)

DOOR FRAMES: Wood

Cbg Acquisition Company...................... A 336 768-8872
Winston Salem (G-13121)

Cook & Boardman Group LLC............... D 336 768-8872
Winston Salem (G-13127)

Dac Products Inc.................................. E 336 969-9786
Rural Hall (G-10958)

Double Hung LLC.................................. E 888 235-8956
Greensboro (G-5501)

Jeld-Wen Inc....................................... C 336 838-0292
North Wilkesboro (G-9536)

DOORS & WINDOWS: Storm, Metal

Champion Win Co of Charlotte............... G 704 398-0085
Charlotte (G-1891)

Energy Svers Windows Doors Inc.......... G 252 758-8700
Greenville (G-5974)

Envirnmental Win Solutions LLC............ G 704 200-2001
Charlotte (G-2118)

Moss Supply Company........................... C 704 596-8717
Charlotte (G-2521)

Ramsey Industries Inc........................... F 704 827-3560
Belmont (G-763)

Vinyl Windows & Doors Corp................. F 910 944-2100
Aberdeen (G-30)

DOORS: Garage, Overhead, Metal

Amarr Company...................................... G 704 599-5858
Charlotte (G-1661)

Amarr Company...................................... C 336 744-5100
Winston Salem (G-13084)

DOORS: Garage, Overhead, Wood

Amarr Company...................................... G 704 599-5858
Charlotte (G-1661)

Amarr Company...................................... C 336 744-5100
Winston Salem (G-13084)

Craft Doors Usa LLC............................ F 828 469-7029
Newton (G-9462)

Custom Doors Incorporated.................... F 704 982-2885
Albemarle (G-67)

Lumberton Overhead Doors Inc............ G 910 739-6426
Lumberton (G-7961)

DOORS: Glass

Envision Glass Inc............................... G 336 283-9701
Winston Salem (G-13159)

DOORS: Screen, Metal

Owens Corning Sales LLC..................... E 419 248-8000
Roxboro (G-10937)

DRAPERIES & CURTAINS

Chf Industries Inc................................ E 212 951-7800
Charlotte (G-1912)

Ferncrest Fashions Inc......................... D 704 283-6422
Monroe (G-8488)

Lichtenberg Inc.................................... G 336 949-9438
Madison (G-7991)

Stage Decoration and Sups Inc............. G 336 621-5454
Greensboro (G-5834)

Textile Products Inc............................. E 704 636-6221
Salisbury (G-11124)

Wildcat Territory Inc............................ G 718 361-6726
Thomasville (G-12087)

DRAPERIES: Plastic & Textile, From Purchased Materials

Atlantic Window Coverings Inc............... E 704 392-0043
Charlotte (G-1712)

Carolina Custom Draperies Inc............... G 336 945-5190
Winston Salem (G-13116)

Diane Britt... G 910 763-9600
Wilmington (G-12764)

Patterson Custom Drapery...................... G 910 791-4332
Wilmington (G-12872)

Smith Draperies Inc............................. F 336 226-2183
Burlington (G-1158)

Walker Draperies Inc............................ F 919 220-1424
Durham (G-4301)

DRAPERY & UPHOLSTERY STORES: Draperies

Bettys Drapery Design Workroom........... G 828 264-2392
Boone (G-897)

Walker Draperies Inc............................ F 919 220-1424
Durham (G-4301)

DRILL BITS

Irwin Industrial Tool Company................. C 704 987-4555
Huntersville (G-7004)

DRILLS & DRILLING EQPT: Mining

Quantex Inc... G 919 219-9604
Wendell (G-12542)

DRINKING PLACES: Bars & Lounges

Bearwaters Brewing Company................. F 828 237-4200
Canton (G-1242)

Bold Rock Partners LP........................... F 828 595-9940
Mills River (G-8312)

Booneshine Brewing Co Inc................... G 828 263-4305
Boone (G-901)

Highland Brewing Company Inc............. F 828 299-3370
Asheville (G-517)

Innovation Brewing LLC........................ G 828 586-9678
Sylva (G-11893)

Koi Pond Brewing Company LLC........... G 252 231-1660
Rocky Mount (G-10847)

Oklawaha Brewing Company LLC........... F 828 595-9956
Hendersonville (G-6233)

Resident Culture Brewing LLC............... E 704 333-1862
Charlotte (G-2714)

Salty Turtle Beer Company.................... E 910 803-2019
Surf City (G-11863)

Shortway Brewing Company LLC........... G 252 777-3065
Newport (G-9444)

Sweet Room LLC.................................. G 336 567-1620
High Point *(G-6799)*

Triple C Brewing Company LLC............. F 704 372-3212
Charlotte *(G-2945)*

White Street Brewing Co Inc.................. F 919 647-9439
Youngsville *(G-13498)*

DRINKING PLACES: Beer Garden

Cabarrus Brewing Company LLC.......... E 704 490-4487
Concord *(G-3326)*

Glass Jug.. F 919 818-6907
Durham *(G-4048)*

Glass Jug LLC.................................... F 919 813-0135
Durham *(G-4049)*

Sugar Creek Brewing Co LLC.............. E 704 521-3333
Charlotte *(G-2878)*

Sycamore Brewing LLC...................... E 704 910-3821
Charlotte *(G-2891)*

DRINKING WATER COOLERS WHOLESALERS: Mechanical

Water-Gen Inc..................................... G 888 492-8370
Charlotte *(G-3007)*

DRUG STORES

Modoral Brands Inc.............................. G 336 741-7230
Winston Salem *(G-13259)*

Natures Pharmacy Inc.......................... G 828 251-0094
Asheville *(G-555)*

Walgreen Co.. G 704 525-2628
Charlotte *(G-3001)*

DRUGS & DRUG PROPRIETARIES, WHOLESALE

V1 Pharma LLC................................... G 919 338-5744
Raleigh *(G-10580)*

DRUGS & DRUG PROPRIETARIES, WHOLESALE: Bandages

Ambra Le Roy LLC............................. G 704 392-7080
Charlotte *(G-1662)*

DRUGS & DRUG PROPRIETARIES, WHOLESALE: Pharmaceuticals

Bioventus LLC.................................... D 800 396-4325
Durham *(G-3933)*

Glaxosmithkline LLC............................ G 252 315-9774
Durham *(G-4052)*

Glaxosmithkline LLC............................ F 919 483-2100
Durham *(G-4053)*

Glenmark Phrmceuticals Inc USA........ D 704 218-2600
Monroe *(G-8492)*

King Bio Inc....................................... D 828 255-0201
Asheville *(G-530)*

Purdue Pharmaceuticals LP................. F 252 265-1900
Wilson *(G-13015)*

Stiefel Laboratories Inc...................... C 888 784-3335
Durham *(G-4251)*

Stiefel Laboratories Inc...................... E 888 784-3335
Research Triangle Pa *(G-10715)*

DRUGS & DRUG PROPRIETARIES, WHOLESALE: Vitamins & Minerals

Interntnal Agrclture Group LLC............. F 908 323-3246
Mooresville *(G-8694)*

Premex Inc.. F 561 962-4128
Durham *(G-4196)*

DRUGS AFFECTING NEOPLASMS & ENDOCRINE SYSTEMS

Alcami Carolinas Corporation................ G 910 619-3952
Garner *(G-4913)*

Alcami Carolinas Corporation................ G 910 254-7000
Morrisville *(G-8923)*

Alcami Carolinas Corporation................ G 910 254-7000
Morrisville *(G-8924)*

Alcami Carolinas Corporation................ B 910 254-7000
Wilmington *(G-12698)*

DRUGS: Parasitic & Infective Disease Affecting

Novartis Vccnes Dagnostics Inc........... B 617 871-7000
Holly Springs *(G-6908)*

DRUMS: Fiber

Greif Inc.. D 704 588-3895
Charlotte *(G-2241)*

DRUMS: Shipping, Metal

General Steel Drum LLC...................... F 704 525-7160
Charlotte *(G-2201)*

Mauser Usa LLC................................ D 704 455-2111
Harrisburg *(G-6114)*

DUCTING: Metal Plate

Nordfab LLC....................................... C 336 821-0829
Thomasville *(G-12055)*

DUCTS: Sheet Metal

APT Industries Inc............................. F 704 598-9100
Charlotte *(G-1689)*

Dantherm Filtration Inc....................... F 336 889-5599
Thomasville *(G-12016)*

Gray Flex Systems Inc........................ D 910 897-3539
Coats *(G-3262)*

Hamlin Sheet Metal Company .... E :.... 919 772-8780
Garner *(G-4930)*

Harco Air LLC................................... G 252 491-5220
Powells Point *(G-9821)*

Jacksonville Metal Mfg Inc................... G 910 938-7635
Jacksonville *(G-7128)*

McGill Corporation.............................. F 919 467-1993
Cary *(G-1400)*

Monroe Metal Manufacturing Inc........... D 800 366-1391
Monroe *(G-8536)*

Suppliers To Wholesalers Inc............. G 704 375-7406
Charlotte *(G-2884)*

W T Humphrey Inc............................. E 910 455-3555
Jacksonville *(G-7158)*

DUMPSTERS: Garbage

Fleetgenius of Nc Inc......................... C 828 726-3001
Lenoir *(G-7607)*

J & L Bckh/Nvrnmental Svcs Inc........... G 910 237-7351
Eastover *(G-4337)*

Miller Dumpster Service LLC............... G 704 504-9300
Charlotte *(G-2504)*

Mrr Southern LLC.............................. G 919 436-3571
Raleigh *(G-10317)*

Waste Container Repair Svcs................ G 910 257-4474
Fayetteville *(G-4696)*

Waste Industries Usa LLC................... C 919 325-3000
Raleigh *(G-10598)*

Wastequip LLC.................................. F 704 366-7140
Charlotte *(G-3005)*

Wastequip Manufacturing Co LLC.......... G 704 366-7140
Charlotte *(G-3006)*

DUST OR FUME COLLECTING EQPT: Indl

Air Craftsmen Inc................................ F 336 248-5777
Statesville *(G-11650)*

Air Systems Mfg of Lenoir Inc............... E 828 757-3500
Lenoir *(G-7568)*

Bruning and Federle Mfg Co .... E 704 873-7237
Statesville *(G-11672)*

Dantherm Filtration Inc....................... F 336 889-5599
Thomasville *(G-12016)*

Jorlink Usa Inc.................................. F 336 288-1613
Greensboro *(G-5640)*

DYES & PIGMENTS: Organic

Clariant Corporation............................ D 704 331-7000
Charlotte *(G-1923)*

Dystar LP... C 336 342-6631
Reidsville *(G-10683)*

US Specialty Color Corp...................... G 704 292-1476
Monroe *(G-8574)*

EATING PLACES

Chatham News Publishing Co................ G 919 663-4042
Siler City *(G-11405)*

Cintoms Inc.. G 828 684-1317
Asheville *(G-476)*

Donut Shop.. G 910 640-3317
Whiteville *(G-12580)*

Emanuel Hoggard................................ F 252 794-3724
Windsor *(G-13053)*

Jebco Inc... E 919 557-2001
Holly Springs *(G-6904)*

McDonalds... F 910 295-1112
Pinehurst *(G-9697)*

Obbc Inc.. G 252 261-0612
Kitty Hawk *(G-7446)*

Stevens Sausage Company Inc............. D 919 934-3159
Smithfield *(G-11466)*

Tonys Ice Cream Co Inc....................... G 704 853-0018
Gastonia *(G-5157)*

EDUCATIONAL SVCS

Advanced Computer Lrng Co LLC......... E 910 779-2254
Fayetteville *(G-4544)*

Center for Creative Leadership.............. B 336 288-7210
Greensboro *(G-5436)*

Communitys Kitchen L3c..................... G 828 817-2308
Tryon *(G-12173)*

Lulu Technology Circus Inc................. E 919 459-5858
Morrisville *(G-9015)*

National Ctr For Social Impact.............. G 984 212-2285
Raleigh *(G-10323)*

ELECTRIC & OTHER SERVICES COMBINED

Flexgen Power Systems Inc................. G 855 327-5674
Durham *(G-4033)*

Flexgen Power Systems Inc................. F 855 327-5674
Durham *(G-4034)*

ELECTRIC MOTOR & GENERATOR AUXILIARY PARTS

ABB Motors and Mechanical Inc............ B 704 734-2500
Kings Mountain *(G-7342)*

ELECTRIC MOTOR REPAIR SVCS

A & W Electric Inc............................... E 704 333-4986
Charlotte *(G-1604)*

American Rewinding of NC Inc.............. E 704 589-1020
Monroe *(G-8423)*

Averitt Enterprises Inc........................ F 910 276-1294
Laurinburg *(G-7492)*

B & M Electric Motor Service................. G 828 267-0829
  Hickory (G-6268)

Blue Ridge Elc Mtr Repr Inc................... G 828 258-0800
  Asheville (G-455)

Bowden Electric Motor Svc Inc............. G 252 446-4203
  Rocky Mount (G-10825)

Brigman Electric Motors Inc.................... G 828 492-0568
  Canton (G-1246)

Brittenhams Rebuilding Service............ G 252 332-3181
  Ahoskie (G-44)

Canipe & Lynn Elc Mtr Repr Inc............. G 828 322-9052
  Hickory (G-6282)

Clayton Electric Mtr Repr Inc................. F 336 584-3756
  Elon College (G-4473)

Consolidated Truck Parts Inc................. G 704 279-5543
  Rockwell (G-10794)

Cornell & Ferencz Inc........................... G 919 736-7373
  Goldsboro (G-5210)

Custom Industries Inc........................... E 336 299-2885
  Greensboro (G-5481)

Dixie Electro Mech Svcs Inc................... F 704 332-1116
  Charlotte (G-2057)

Electric Motor Rewinding Inc................. G 252 338-8856
  Elizabeth City (G-4387)

Electric Motor Svc Ahoskie Inc............. G 252 332-4364
  Ahoskie (G-48)

Electric Mtr Sls Svc Pitt Cnty................. G 252 752-3170
  Greenville (G-5973)

Electric Mtr Sp Wake Frest Inc............. E 252 446-4173
  Rocky Mount (G-10835)

Electric Mtr Sp Wake Frest Inc............. E 919 556-3229
  Wake Forest (G-12274)

Elektran Inc.. G 910 997-6640
  Rockingham (G-10776)

Energetics Inc...................................... G 910 483-2581
  Fayetteville (G-4597)

Esco Electronic Services Inc................. F 252 753-4433
  Farmville (G-4528)

General Motor Repair & Svc Inc............. G 336 292-1715
  Greensboro (G-5555)

Hammond Electric Motor Company....... F 704 983-3178
  Albemarle (G-77)

Hanover Electric Motor Svc Inc............. G 910 762-3702
  Wilmington (G-12799)

High Country Electric Mtrs LLC............. G 336 838-4808
  North Wilkesboro (G-9534)

Jenkins Electric Company.................... D 800 438-3003
  Charlotte (G-2368)

Jordan Electric Motors Inc.................... F 919 708-7010
  Staley (G-11595)

Lake City Electric Motor Repr............... G 336 248-2377
  Lexington (G-7708)

Lingle Electric Repair Inc..................... F 704 636-5591
  Salisbury (G-11084)

Maybin Emergency Power Inc............... G 828 697-1195
  Zirconia (G-13531)

McKinney Electric & Mch Co Inc........... G 828 765-7910
  Spruce Pine (G-11581)

Motor Shop Inc.................................... G 704 867-8488
  Gastonia (G-5103)

Presley Group Ltd................................ D 828 254-9971
  Asheville (G-584)

Pumps Blowers & Elc Mtrs LLC............. G 919 286-4975
  Durham (G-4201)

Purser Centl Rewinding Co Inc............. F 704 786-3131
  Concord (G-3427)

Randall Supply Inc............................... E 704 289-6479
  Monroe (G-8548)

Rocky Mount Electric Motor LLC........... G 252 446-1510
  Rocky Mount (G-10868)

Sanders Electric Motor Svc Inc............. E 828 754-0513
  Lenoir (G-7638)

Southern Electric Motor Co.................. G 919 688-7879
  Durham (G-4243)

Stone Cllins Mtr Rewinding Inc............. G 910 347-2775
  Jacksonville (G-7155)

Tencarva Machinery Company LLC....... G 336 665-1435
  Greensboro (G-5858)

Tigertek Industrial Svcs LLC................. E 336 623-1717
  Stoneville (G-11832)

Watson Electrical Cnstr Co LLC........... D 252 756-4550
  Greenville (G-6033)

Williams Electric Mtr Repr Inc.............. G 919 859-9790
  Sanford (G-11250)

XCEL Hrmetic Mtr Rewinding Inc........... G 704 694-6001
  Wadesboro (G-12253)

ELECTRIC SERVICES

Pike Electric LLC................................. C 336 316-7068
  Greensboro (G-5748)

ELECTRIC SVCS, NEC: Power Generation

Florida Progress Corporation............... C 704 382-3853
  Raleigh (G-10113)

Panenergy Corp................................... F 704 594-6200
  Charlotte (G-2607)

ELECTRIC WATER HEATERS WHOLESALERS

McKenzie Supply Company.................. G 910 276-1691
  Laurinburg (G-7509)

ELECTRICAL APPARATUS & EQPT WHOLESALERS

ABB Inc.. E 704 587-1362
  Charlotte (G-1609)

ABB Inc.. C 919 856-2360
  Cary (G-1285)

Code LLC... E 828 328-6004
  Hickory (G-6304)

Dna Group Inc..................................... E 919 881-0889
  Raleigh (G-10051)

Envirnmntal Cmfort Sltions Inc............. E 980 272-7327
  Kannapolis (G-7208)

Exide Technologies LLC....................... G 704 521-8016
  Charlotte (G-2135)

His Company Inc.................................. G 800 537-0351
  Wilmington (G-12806)

Hubbell Industrial Contrls Inc............... C 336 434-2800
  Archdale (G-226)

JA Smith Inc.. G 704 860-4910
  Lawndale (G-7517)

Jenkins Electric Company.................... D 800 438-3003
  Charlotte (G-2368)

Johnson Controls Inc........................... D 704 521-8889
  Charlotte (G-2375)

Ls Cable & System USA Inc.................. C 252 824-3553
  Tarboro (G-11932)

Minka Lighting Inc............................... D 704 785-9200
  Concord (G-3403)

Resideo LLC....................................... G 704 525-8899
  Charlotte (G-2715)

Resideo LLC....................................... G 336 668-3644
  Greensboro (G-5784)

Resideo LLC....................................... G 919 872-5556
  Raleigh (G-10441)

Rotron Incorporated............................. C 336 449-3400
  Whitsett (G-12619)

Smart Electric North Amer LLC............. G 828 323-1200
  Conover (G-3559)

ELECTRICAL DISCHARGE MACHINING, EDM

Max Daetwyler Corp............................. E 704 875-1200
  Huntersville (G-7012)

Southern Prestige Intl LLC................... F 704 872-9524
  Statesville (G-11771)

Specialty Perf LLC............................... G 704 872-9980
  Statesville (G-11773)

ELECTRICAL EQPT REPAIR SVCS

Eaton Corporation............................... D 864 433-1603
  Raleigh (G-10073)

Eaton Corporation............................... C 919 872-3020
  Raleigh (G-10074)

Eaton Power Quality Corp.................... F 919 872-3020
  Raleigh (G-10075)

Eaton Power Quality Group Inc............. C 919 872-3020
  Raleigh (G-10076)

Electrical Equipment Company............. E 910 276-2141
  Laurinburg (G-7500)

ELECTRICAL EQPT REPAIR SVCS: High Voltage

Trans East Inc..................................... D 910 892-1081
  Dunn (G-3869)

Transformer Sales & Service................ G 910 594-1495
  Newton Grove (G-9519)

ELECTRICAL EQPT: Automotive, NEC

GKN Driveline North Amer Inc.............. A 919 304-7200
  Mebane (G-8244)

Mc Cullough Auto Elc & Assoc............. G 704 376-5388
  Charlotte (G-2475)

Radel Inc.. G 336 245-8078
  Winston Salem (G-13314)

Scattered Wrenches Inc....................... G 919 480-1605
  Raleigh (G-10460)

ELECTRICAL GOODS, WHOLESALE: Batteries, Dry Cell

Edgewell Per Care Brands LLC............. G 336 672-4500
  Asheboro (G-349)

ELECTRICAL GOODS, WHOLESALE: Electrical Appliances, Major

Psnc Energy.. G 919 367-2735
  Apex (G-189)

ELECTRICAL GOODS, WHOLESALE: Electronic Parts

Btc Electronic Components LLC........... E 919 229-2162
  Wake Forest (G-12266)

Huber + Suhner North Amer Corp......... D 704 790-7300
  Charlotte (G-2296)

Kuebler Inc... F 704 705-4711
  Charlotte (G-2403)

ELECTRICAL GOODS, WHOLESALE: Fittings & Construction Mat

Eizi Group Llc..................................... G 919 397-3638
  Raleigh (G-10080)

Sigma Engineered Solutions PC........... D 919 773-0011
  Garner (G-4964)

ELECTRICAL GOODS, WHOLESALE: Generators

Bolton Investors Inc............................. G 919 471-1197
  Durham (G-3937)

Cemco Electric Inc.............................. F 704 504-0294
  Charlotte (G-1886)

Cummins Inc..F 704 596-7690
Charlotte *(G-2003)*

Pcai Inc...D 704 588-1240
Charlotte *(G-2622)*

ELECTRICAL GOODS, WHOLESALE: Light Bulbs & Related Splys

Blue Sun Energy Inc...........................G 336 218-6707
Greensboro *(G-5393)*

Fintronx LLC.......................................F 919 324-3960
Raleigh *(G-10109)*

ELECTRICAL GOODS, WHOLESALE: Security Control Eqpt & Systems

A&B Integrators LLC...........................F 919 371-0750
Durham *(G-3876)*

Alert Protection Systems Inc................G 919 467-4357
Raleigh *(G-9890)*

Bright Light Technologies LLC..............G 910 212-6869
Lillington *(G-7790)*

Cargotec Port Security LLC.................G 919 620-1763
Durham *(G-3958)*

Edwards Electronic Systems Inc..........E 919 359-2239
Clayton *(G-3146)*

Lea Aid Acquisition Company..............G 919 872-6210
Spring Hope *(G-11557)*

Telecmmnctons Resource MGT Inc........F 919 779-0776
Raleigh *(G-10539)*

ELECTRICAL GOODS, WHOLESALE: Semiconductor Devices

Disco Hi-TEC America Inc....................G 919 468-6003
Morrisville *(G-8965)*

Synopsys Inc.....................................G 919 941-6600
Morrisville *(G-9062)*

ELECTRICAL GOODS, WHOLESALE: Telephone & Telegraphic Eqpt

Abacon Telecommunications LLC.........E 336 855-1179
Greensboro *(G-5335)*

ELECTRICAL GOODS, WHOLESALE: Wire & Cable

Abl Electronics Supply Inc...................G 704 784-4225
Concord *(G-3308)*

Iron Box LLC......................................E 919 890-0025
Raleigh *(G-10209)*

Wieland Electric Inc............................F 910 259-5050
Wilmington *(G-12947)*

ELECTRICAL GOODS, WHOLESALE: Wire & Cable, Electronic

Lutze Inc..E 704 504-0222
Charlotte *(G-2442)*

ELECTRICAL SPLYS

Electrical Equipment Company.............E 910 276-2141
Laurinburg *(G-7500)*

McKenzie Supply Company..................G 910 276-1691
Laurinburg *(G-7509)*

McNaughton-Mckay Southeast Inc........F 910 392-0940
Wilmington *(G-12850)*

Power-Utility Products Company...........F 704 375-0776
Charlotte *(G-2651)*

Southland Electrical Sup LLC................C 336 227-1486
Burlington *(G-1160)*

State Electric Supply Company............F 336 855-8200
Greensboro *(G-5837)*

ELECTRICAL SUPPLIES: Porcelain

Greenleaf Corporation.........................E 828 693-0461
East Flat Rock *(G-4332)*

Pyrotek Incorporated...........................E 704 642-1993
Salisbury *(G-11108)*

The Tarheel Electric Member................F 919 876-4603
Raleigh *(G-10544)*

ELECTROMEDICAL EQPT

Albemrle Orthotics Prosthetics.............G 252 332-4334
Ahoskie *(G-41)*

Automedx LLC....................................G 888 617-2904
Huntersville *(G-6971)*

Medi Mall Inc......................................G 877 501-6334
Fletcher *(G-4753)*

Misonix Opco Inc.................................F 631 694-9555
Durham *(G-4137)*

Odin Technologies LLC........................G 408 309-1925
Charlotte *(G-2591)*

Ribometrix..G 919 744-9634
Durham *(G-4214)*

Tearscience Inc...................................D 919 459-4880
Morrisville *(G-9064)*

United Mobile Imaging Inc...................G 800 983-9840
Clemmons *(G-3207)*

Volumetrics Med Systems LLC.............G 800 472-0900
Durham *(G-4300)*

ELECTROMEDICAL EQPT WHOLESALERS

Turbomed LLC.....................................F 973 527-5299
Fayetteville *(G-4684)*

ELECTRON TUBES

Ecoatm LLC..E 858 324-4111
Boone *(G-913)*

ELECTRONIC DEVICES: Solid State, NEC

Maxtronic Technologies LLC.................G 704 756-5354
Charlotte *(G-2474)*

ELECTRONIC EQPT REPAIR SVCS

Advanced Electronic Svcs Inc...............E 336 789-0792
Mount Airy *(G-9096)*

Anuva Services Inc..............................F 919 468-6441
Morrisville *(G-8928)*

Applied Drives Inc...............................G 704 573-2324
Charlotte *(G-1686)*

SCR Controls Inc.................................F 704 821-6651
Matthews *(G-8192)*

ELECTRONIC LOADS & POWER SPLYS

Emrise Corporation..............................C 408 200-3040
Durham *(G-4023)*

Parker-Hannifin Corporation.................C 704 588-3246
Charlotte *(G-2612)*

Santronics Inc.....................................A 919 775-1223
Sanford *(G-11231)*

US Prototype Inc.................................E 866 239-2848
Wilmington *(G-12943)*

Utility Solutions Inc.............................G 828 323-8914
Hickory *(G-6484)*

ELECTRONIC PARTS & EQPT WHOLESALERS

Acterna LLC.......................................F 919 388-5100
Morrisville *(G-8918)*

Commscope Technologies LLC..............G 919 329-8700
Garner *(G-4923)*

Dupont Specialty Pdts USA LLC............E 919 248-5109
Durham *(G-4013)*

His Company Inc.................................G 800 537-0351
Wilmington *(G-12806)*

Huber + Suhner Inc.............................E 704 790-7300
Charlotte *(G-2295)*

Interconnect Products and Services Inc E 336 667-3356
Wilkesboro *(G-12640)*

Lutze Inc..E 704 504-0222
Charlotte *(G-2442)*

Tactical Support Equipment Inc.............F 910 425-3360
Fayetteville *(G-4676)*

Vishay Measurements Group Inc............G 919 365-3800
Wendell *(G-12552)*

Walker and Associates Inc....................C 336 731-6391
Winston Salem *(G-13386)*

Wieland Electric Inc............................F 910 259-5050
Wilmington *(G-12947)*

Wiser Systems Inc...............................G 919 551-5566
Raleigh *(G-10611)*

ELECTRONIC SHOPPING

Buddy Cut Inc.....................................G 888 608-4701
Pittsboro *(G-9777)*

Fireresq Incorporated..........................F 888 975-0858
Mooresville *(G-8664)*

Grailgame Inc......................................G 804 517-3102
Reidsville *(G-10687)*

Nutrotonic LLC....................................F 855 948-0008
Charlotte *(G-2590)*

Simple & Sentimental LLC....................G 252 320-9458
Ayden *(G-662)*

Speed Utv LLC....................................G 704 949-1255
Concord *(G-3445)*

ELECTROPLATING & PLATING SVC

Amplate Inc..E 704 607-0191
Charlotte *(G-1672)*

Xceldyne Group LLC............................D 336 472-2242
Thomasville *(G-12093)*

ELEVATORS & EQPT

Crockers Inc.......................................F 336 366-2005
Elkin *(G-4442)*

Ecs Group-NC LLC..............................G 919 830-1171
Wake Forest *(G-12273)*

Home Elevators & Lift Pdts LLC.............E 910 427-0006
Sunset Beach *(G-11850)*

Otis Elevator Company.........................C 704 519-0100
Charlotte *(G-2602)*

Park Manufacturing Company................F 704 869-6128
Gastonia *(G-5115)*

Resolute Elevator LLC..........................E 919 903-0189
Burlington *(G-1145)*

Southeastern Elevator LLC....................G 252 726-9983
Morehead City *(G-8845)*

Vertical Access LLC.............................G 800 325-1116
Snow Hill *(G-11483)*

ELEVATORS WHOLESALERS

Otis Elevator Company.........................G 828 251-1248
Asheville *(G-563)*

Otis Elevator Company.........................C 704 519-0100
Charlotte *(G-2602)*

Port City Elevator Inc...........................E 910 790-9300
Castle Hayne *(G-1509)*

Tk Elevator Corporation.......................D 336 272-4563
Greensboro *(G-5867)*

ELEVATORS: Installation & Conversion

Home Elevators & Lift Pdts LLC.............E 910 427-0006
Sunset Beach *(G-11850)*

Park Manufacturing Company................F 704 869-6128
Gastonia *(G-5115)*

PRODUCT

Southeastern Elevator LLC...................... G 252 726-9983
Morehead City *(G-8845)*

EMBLEMS: Embroidered

Conrad Embroidery Company LLC....... E 828 645-3015
Weaverville *(G-12487)*

Conrad Industries Inc............................ D 828 645-3015
Weaverville *(G-12488)*

Lake Norman EMB & Monogramming.... G 704 892-8450
Cornelius *(G-3612)*

Mojo Sportswear Inc............................ G 252 758-4176
Greenville *(G-6006)*

Stitchery Inc.. G 336 248-5604
Lexington *(G-7746)*

EMBROIDERY ADVERTISING SVCS

Marketing One Sportswear Inc.............. G 704 334-9333
Charlotte *(G-2457)*

Orlandos Cstm Design T-Shirts.............. G 919 220-5515
Durham *(G-4160)*

Raleigh Tees LLC.................................. G 919 850-3378
Raleigh *(G-10430)*

Screen Printers Unlimited LLC.............. G 336 667-8737
Wilkesboro *(G-12650)*

US Logoworks LLC................................ F 910 307-0312
Fayetteville *(G-4691)*

EMBROIDERY KITS

Stitchmaster LLC.................................. F 336 852-6448
Greensboro *(G-5841)*

EMERGENCY ALARMS

C & S Antennas Inc.............................. F 828 324-2454
Conover *(G-3497)*

General Dynmics Mssion Systems........ C 336 698-8000
Mc Leansville *(G-8223)*

Johnson Controls................................. C 704 501-0500
Charlotte *(G-2374)*

New Innovative Products Inc................. G 919 631-6759
Pine Level *(G-9683)*

R & J Road Service Inc......................... G 252 239-1404
Lucama *(G-7938)*

Resideo LLC.. G 704 525-8899
Charlotte *(G-2715)*

Resideo LLC.. G 336 668-3644
Greensboro *(G-5784)*

Resideo LLC.. G 919 872-5556
Raleigh *(G-10441)*

Romeo Six LLC.................................... F 919 589-7150
Holly Springs *(G-6912)*

Safeguard Medical Alarms Inc.............. F 312 506-2900
Huntersville *(G-7052)*

Seal Innovation Inc.............................. G 919 302-7870
Raleigh *(G-10464)*

Squarehead Technology LLC................. G 571 299-4849
Hickory *(G-6456)*

ENCLOSURES: Electronic

Friedrich Metal Pdts Co Inc................. E 336 375-3067
Browns Summit *(G-993)*

Protocase Mfg Usa Inc......................... E 866 849-3911
Wilmington *(G-12892)*

Rfr Metal Fabrication Inc..................... D 919 693-1354
Oxford *(G-9631)*

ENCLOSURES: Screen

Carolina Solar Structures Inc............... F 828 684-9900
Asheville *(G-471)*

Innovative Awngs & Screens LLC.......... F 833 337-4233
Cornelius *(G-3610)*

ENDOCRINE PRDTS

Inneroptic Technology Inc.................... G 919 732-2090
Hillsborough *(G-6868)*

ENGINE REBUILDING: Diesel

Engine Systems Inc............................. D 252 977-2720
Rocky Mount *(G-10836)*

NC Diesel Performance LLC.................. G 704 431-3257
Salisbury *(G-11095)*

ENGINE REBUILDING: Gas

Holman Automotive Inc........................ G 704 583-2888
Charlotte *(G-2282)*

ENGINEERING SVCS

ABB Enterprise Software Inc................. C 919 582-3283
Raleigh *(G-9862)*

ABB Inc.. C 919 856-2360
Cary *(G-1285)*

Advanced Computer Lrng Co LLC.......... E 910 779-2254
Fayetteville *(G-4544)*

Belkoz Inc.. G 919 703-0694
Raleigh *(G-9939)*

Boeing Arospc Operations Inc............... F 919 722-4351
Goldsboro *(G-5201)*

Centrotherm Usa Inc........................... G 360 626-4445
Durham *(G-3968)*

Century Furniture LLC......................... D 828 326-8535
Hickory *(G-6297)*

Cross Technology Inc........................... E 336 725-4700
East Bend *(G-4322)*

Custom Controls Unlimited LLC............ F 919 812-6553
Raleigh *(G-10029)*

Dronescape Pllc.................................. G 704 953-3798
Charlotte *(G-2066)*

Duotech Services LLC........................... E 828 369-5111
Franklin *(G-4826)*

Electro Magnetic Research Inc.............. G 919 365-3723
Zebulon *(G-13508)*

Equagen Engineers Pllc....................... E 919 444-5442
Raleigh *(G-10090)*

Finnord North America Corp................. F 704 723-4913
Huntersville *(G-6990)*

Flextronics Intl USA Inc....................... C 919 998-4000
Morrisville *(G-8975)*

Froehling & Robertson Inc.................... E 804 264-2701
Raleigh *(G-10120)*

General Dynmics Mssion Systems........ C 336 698-8000
Mc Leansville *(G-8223)*

Global Products & Mfg Svcs Inc............. G 360 870-9876
Charlotte *(G-2215)*

Iomax USA LLC.................................... E 704 662-1840
Mooresville *(G-8695)*

JA Smith Inc.. G 704 860-4910
Lawndale *(G-7517)*

John Deere Consumer Pdts Inc.............. C 919 804-2000
Cary *(G-1380)*

Kdy Automation Solutions Inc............... G 888 219-0049
Morrisville *(G-8996)*

Keller Technology Corporation.............. E 704 875-1605
Huntersville *(G-7007)*

McLean Sbsrface Utlity Engrg L............. F 336 340-0024
Greensboro *(G-5687)*

MSI Defense Solutions LLC.................... D 704 660-8348
Mooresville *(G-8730)*

Multi Technical Services Inc.................. G 919 553-2995
Clayton *(G-3161)*

Penske Racing South Inc...................... C 704 664-2300
Mooresville *(G-8746)*

Pratt Mller Engrg Fbrction LLC.............. C 704 977-0642
Huntersville *(G-7036)*

Simon Industries Inc............................ E 919 469-2004
Raleigh *(G-10477)*

Ssi Services Inc.................................... G 919 867-1450
Raleigh *(G-10501)*

Sunqest Inc... G 828 325-4910
Newton *(G-9501)*

Team Industries Inc............................. D 828 837-5377
Andrews *(G-109)*

Volta Group Corporation LLC................ E 919 637-0273
Raleigh *(G-10593)*

Walker and Associates Inc.................... C 336 731-6391
Winston Salem *(G-13386)*

ENGINEERING SVCS: Building Construction

Queen City Engrg & Design Pllc............. G 704 918-5851
Concord *(G-3428)*

ENGINEERING SVCS: Chemical

ABB Inc.. E 704 587-1362
Charlotte *(G-1609)*

ENGINEERING SVCS: Construction & Civil

Young & McQueen Grading Co Inc......... D 828 682-7714
Burnsville *(G-1196)*

ENGINEERING SVCS: Electrical Or Electronic

Acroplis Cntrls Engineers Pllc................ F 919 275-3884
Raleigh *(G-9876)*

Doble Engineering Company.................. G 919 380-7461
Morrisville *(G-8966)*

Goshen Engineering Inc........................ G 919 429-9798
Mount Olive *(G-9254)*

SCR Controls Inc.................................. F 704 821-6651
Matthews *(G-8192)*

Subsea Video Systems Inc.................... G 252 338-1001
Elizabeth City *(G-4411)*

Vortant Technologies LLC..................... G 828 645-1026
Weaverville *(G-12506)*

ENGINEERING SVCS: Machine Tool Design

Descher LLC.. G 919 828-7708
Raleigh *(G-10041)*

Irsi Automation Inc.............................. G 336 303-5320
Mc Leansville *(G-8224)*

ENGINEERING SVCS: Marine

Big Rock Industries Inc......................... G 252 222-3618
Morehead City *(G-8816)*

ENGINEERING SVCS: Mechanical

Airspeed LLC....................................... E 919 644-1222
Mebane *(G-8227)*

Tdc International LLC........................... G 704 875-1198
Concord *(G-3452)*

ENGINES: Internal Combustion, NEC

Blue Gas Marine Inc............................ F 919 238-3427
Apex *(G-146)*

Caterpillar Inc..................................... E 919 777-2000
Sanford *(G-11160)*

Cummins Inc....................................... F 704 596-7690
Charlotte *(G-2003)*

Cummins Inc....................................... E 336 275-4531
Greensboro *(G-5476)*

Cummins Inc....................................... G 919 284-9111
Kenly *(G-7230)*

Cummins Inc....................................... G 704 588-1240
Pineville *(G-9723)*

Daimler Truck North Amer LLC............. A 704 645-5000
Cleveland *(G-3213)*

Holman & Moody Inc .... G 704 394-4141
Charlotte *(G-2281)*

Pcai Inc .... D 704 588-1240
Charlotte *(G-2622)*

Southport NC .... G 910 524-7425
Southport *(G-11529)*

ENGINES: Jet Propulsion

General Electric Company .... A 910 675-5000
Wilmington *(G-12785)*

ENGINES: Marine

Ilmor Marine LLC .... E 704 360-1901
Mooresville *(G-8691)*

Jones Marine Inc .... G 704 639-0173
Salisbury *(G-11075)*

Lehr LLC .... F 704 827-9368
Huntersville *(G-7010)*

ENGRAVING SVC, NEC

Anilox Roll Company Inc .... G 704 588-1809
Charlotte *(G-1678)*

Arden Engraving US Inc .... G 704 547-4581
Charlotte *(G-1694)*

More Than Just Art Inc .... G 910 864-7797
Fayetteville *(G-4643)*

Raleigh Engraving Co .... G 919 832-5557
Raleigh *(G-10423)*

Western Roto Engravers Incorporated .. E 336 275-9821
Greensboro *(G-5916)*

ENGRAVING SVCS

Fines and Carriel Inc .... G 919 929-0702
Chapel Hill *(G-1547)*

Signcaster Corporation .... G 336 712-2525
Winston Salem *(G-13336)*

ENVELOPES

S Ruppe Inc .... G 828 287-4936
Rutherfordton *(G-10992)*

Westrock Mwv LLC .... G 919 334-3200
Raleigh *(G-10606)*

ENVELOPES WHOLESALERS

Printing Press .... G 828 299-1234
Asheville *(G-585)*

ENZYMES

Alltech Inc .... E 336 635-5190
Eden *(G-4341)*

Enzyme Customs .... G 704 888-8278
Locust *(G-7892)*

Novozymes North America Inc ...... D 919 494-2014
Franklinton *(G-4851)*

EPOXY RESINS

Kestrel I Acquisition Corporation .... A 919 990-7500
Durham *(G-4095)*

EQUIPMENT & VEHICLE FINANCE LEASING COMPANIES

Vna Holding Inc .... A 336 393-4890
Greensboro *(G-5905)*

EQUIPMENT: Pedestrian Traffic Control

Pipeline Enterprises LLC .... D 804 593-6999
Reidsville *(G-10697)*

EQUIPMENT: Rental & Leasing, NEC

Arc3 Gases Inc .... G 336 275-3333
Greensboro *(G-5367)*

Arc3 Gases Inc .... G 704 220-1029
Monroe *(G-8429)*

Arc3 Gases Inc .... E 910 892-4016
Dunn *(G-3844)*

B V Hedrick Gravel & Sand Co .... E 704 633-5982
Salisbury *(G-11021)*

Cherokee Instruments Inc .... F 919 552-0554
Angier *(G-117)*

Classic Industrial Services .... G 919 209-0909
Smithfield *(G-11438)*

Lynn Ladder Scaffolding Co Inc .... G 301 336-4700
Charlotte *(G-2443)*

Medaccess Inc .... G 828 264-4085
Robbinsville *(G-10760)*

Sharpe Co .... E 336 724-2871
Winston Salem *(G-13333)*

ETCHING & ENGRAVING SVC

NC Graphic Pros LLC .... G 252 492-7326
Kittrell *(G-7442)*

Professional Laminating LLC .... G 919 465-0400
Cary *(G-1430)*

ETHYLENE-PROPYLENE RUBBERS: EPDM Polymers

Axchem Solutions Inc .... G 919 742-9810
Siler City *(G-11398)*

Custom Polymers Inc .... F 704 332-6070
Charlotte *(G-2011)*

Dupont Electronic Polymers L P .... F 919 248-5135
Durham *(G-4012)*

ERA Polymers Corporation .... E 704 931-3675
Stanley *(G-11616)*

Goulston Technologies Inc .... E 704 289-6464
Monroe *(G-8495)*

Indulor America LP .... D 336 578-6855
Graham *(G-5270)*

M & P Polymers Inc .... G 910 246-6585
Pinehurst *(G-9695)*

Tethis Inc .... E 919 808-2866
Raleigh *(G-10543)*

EXHAUST SYSTEMS: Eqpt & Parts

B & B Fabrication Inc .... F 623 581-7600
Mooresville *(G-8605)*

Cataler North America Corp .... C 828 970-0026
Lincolnton *(G-7819)*

EXPANSION JOINTS: Rubber

Frenzelit Inc .... E 336 814-4317
Lexington *(G-7690)*

EXPLOSIVES

Austin Powder Company .... E 828 645-4291
Denton *(G-3740)*

K2 Solutions Inc .... B 910 692-6898
Southern Pines *(G-11501)*

Maxam North America Inc .... F 214 736-8100
Mooresville *(G-8721)*

EXTRACTS, FLAVORING

Blue Mountain Enterprises Inc .... E 252 522-1544
Kinston *(G-7396)*

Flavor Sciences Inc .... E 828 758-2525
Taylorsville *(G-11960)*

Fuji Foods Inc .... E 336 897-3373
Browns Summit *(G-994)*

Fuji Foods Inc .... E 336 375-3111
Browns Summit *(G-995)*

Mother Murphys Labs Inc .... E 336 273-1737
Greensboro *(G-5697)*

Mother Murphys Labs Inc .... D 336 273-1737
Greensboro *(G-5698)*

Specialty Products Intl Ltd .... G 910 897-4706
Erwin *(G-4492)*

FABRIC STORES

Cloth Barn Inc .... F 919 735-3643
Goldsboro *(G-5206)*

Composite Fabrics America LLC .... G 828 632-5220
Taylorsville *(G-11954)*

Designer Fabrics Inc .... G 704 305-4144
Concord *(G-3354)*

Distinctive Furniture Inc .... G 828 754-3947
Lenoir *(G-7600)*

Ledford Upholstery .... G 704 732-0233
Lincolnton *(G-7836)*

McMurray Fabrics Inc .... D 704 732-9613
Lincolnton *(G-7843)*

FABRICS & CLOTH: Quilted

Fabric Services Hickory Inc .... G 828 397-7331
Hildebran *(G-6849)*

High Point Quilting Inc .... F 336 861-4180
High Point *(G-6655)*

FABRICS & CLOTHING: Rubber Coated

Trelleborg Ctd Systems US Inc .... C 828 286-9126
Rutherfordton *(G-10996)*

FABRICS: Acetate, Broadwoven

Composite Fabrics America LLC .... G 828 632-5220
Taylorsville *(G-11954)*

Crypton Mills LLC .... E 828 202-5875
Cliffside *(G-3225)*

David Rothschild Co Inc .... D 336 342-0035
Reidsville *(G-10682)*

Hanes Companies Inc .... B 828 464-4673
Conover *(G-3525)*

Kontoor Brands Inc .... E 336 332-3577
Greensboro *(G-5654)*

FABRICS: Apparel & Outerwear, Broadwoven

Ivy Brand LLC .... G 980 225-7866
Charlotte *(G-2359)*

FABRICS: Apparel & Outerwear, Cotton

Gracefully Broken LLC .... G 980 474-0309
Gastonia *(G-5055)*

Ivy Brand LLC .... G 980 225-7866
Charlotte *(G-2359)*

Makemine Inc .... G 704 906-7164
Charlotte *(G-2449)*

Mfi Products Inc .... F 910 944-2128
Aberdeen *(G-16)*

VF Corporation .... G 336 424-6000
Greensboro *(G-5899)*

VF Corporation .... F 336 424-6000
Greensboro *(G-5900)*

FABRICS: Automotive, From Manmade Fiber

Abercrombie Textiles I LLC .... F 704 487-1245
Shelby *(G-11309)*

Collins & Aikman Europe Inc .... E 704 548-2350
Charlotte *(G-1953)*

Collins & Aikman Interiors .... E 704 548-2350
Charlotte *(G-1954)*

Collins & Aikman International .... E 704 548-2350
Charlotte *(G-1955)*

Collins & Aikman Prpts Inc .... E 704 548-2350
Charlotte *(G-1956)*

Collins Akman Canada Dom Holdg .... E 704 548-2350
Charlotte *(G-1958)*

P
R
O
D
U
C
T

Highland Industries Inc................E 336 547-1600
Greensboro *(G-5597)*

Highland Industries Inc................E 336 855-0625
Greensboro *(G-5598)*

P&A Indstrial Fabrications LLC............E 336 322-1766
Roxboro *(G-10938)*

Seiren North America LLC............F 828 430-3456
Morganton *(G-8894)*

Wickes Manufacturing Company............E 704 548-2350
Charlotte *(G-3018)*

FABRICS: Basket Weave, Cotton

American Fiber & Finishing Inc............E 704 984-9256
Albemarle *(G-61)*

FABRICS: Bonded-Fiber, Exc Felt

Glatfelter Inds Asheville Inc............D 828 670-0041
Candler *(G-1226)*

FABRICS: Broad Woven, Goods, Cotton

American Silk Mills LLC............F 570 822-7147
High Point *(G-6522)*

Wade Manufacturing Company............E 704 694-2131
Wadesboro *(G-12252)*

FABRICS: Broadwoven, Wool

Barrday Corp............G 704 395-0311
Charlotte *(G-1756)*

Carlisle Finishing LLC............D 864 466-4173
Greensboro *(G-5423)*

Circa 1801............G 828 397-7003
Connelly Springs *(G-3475)*

I T G Raeford............G 910 875-3736
Raeford *(G-9841)*

Lustar Dyeing and Finshg Inc............G 828 274-2440
Asheville *(G-539)*

Milliken & Company............F 828 247-4300
Bostic *(G-963)*

Voith Fabrics Inc............B 252 291-3800
Wilson *(G-13042)*

Xtinguish LLC............G 704 868-9500
Charlotte *(G-3034)*

FABRICS: Chenilles, Tufted Textile

Paragon Global LLC............G 336 899-8525
High Point *(G-6725)*

FABRICS: Cloth, Warp Knit

Guilford Mills LLC............A 910 794-5810
Wilmington *(G-12798)*

Hornwood Inc............E 704 694-3009
Wadesboro *(G-12244)*

Hornwood Inc............B 704 848-4121
Lilesville *(G-7786)*

Lear Corporation............E 910 296-8671
Kenansville *(G-7226)*

Lear Corporation............A 910 794-5810
Wilmington *(G-12831)*

Mohican Mills Inc............B 704 735-3343
Lincolnton *(G-7844)*

FABRICS: Cotton, Narrow

Dunn Manufacturing Corp............C 704 283-2147
Monroe *(G-8479)*

Parkdale Mills Incorporated............D 704 874-5000
Gastonia *(G-5117)*

US Cotton LLC............D 704 874-5000
Belmont *(G-774)*

US Cotton LLC............C 216 676-6400
Gastonia *(G-5161)*

FABRICS: Denims

Burlington Industries LLC............C 336 379-6220
Greensboro *(G-5414)*

Cone Denim LLC............D 336 379-6165
Greensboro *(G-5462)*

Elevate Textiles Inc............F 336 379-6220
Charlotte *(G-2098)*

Elevate Textiles Holding Corp............D 336 379-6220
Charlotte *(G-2099)*

Itg Holdings Inc............A 336 379-6220
Greensboro *(G-5628)*

Raleigh Workshop Inc............E 919 917-8969
Raleigh *(G-10431)*

FABRICS: Dress, Cotton

Belk Department Stores LP............E 704 357-4000
Charlotte *(G-1769)*

Textile-Based Delivery Inc............E 866 256-8420
Conover *(G-3565)*

FABRICS: Elastic, From Manmade Fiber Or Silk

Efa Inc............C 336 275-9401
Greensboro *(G-5514)*

FABRICS: Fiberglass, Broadwoven

Admiral Marine Pdts & Svcs Inc............G 704 489-8771
Denver *(G-3767)*

Piedmont Cmposites Tooling LLC............D 828 632-8883
Taylorsville *(G-11970)*

Windsor Fiberglass Inc............G 910 259-0057
Burgaw *(G-1040)*

FABRICS: Glass & Fiberglass, Broadwoven

Feinberg Enterprises Inc............F 704 822-2400
Belmont *(G-750)*

FABRICS: Glass, Narrow

Nouveau Verre Holdings Inc............F 336 545-0011
Greensboro *(G-5714)*

Nvh Inc............G 336 545-0011
Greensboro *(G-5717)*

FABRICS: Lacings, Textile

Spuntech Industries Inc............C 336 330-9000
Roxboro *(G-10946)*

FABRICS: Laundry, Cotton

Trelleborg Ctd Systems US Inc............C 828 286-9126
Rutherfordton *(G-10999)*

FABRICS: Nonwoven

Advantage Nn-Wvens Cnvrting LL............G 828 635-1880
Taylorsville *(G-11948)*

Allyn International Trdg Corp............G 877 858-2482
Marshville *(G-8085)*

Avgol America Inc............C 336 936-2500
Mocksville *(G-8350)*

Avintiv Inc............E 704 697-5100
Charlotte *(G-1724)*

Avintiv Specialty Mtls Inc............C 704 660-6242
Mooresville *(G-8604)*

Avintiv Specialty Mtls Inc............A 704 697-5100
Charlotte *(G-1725)*

Carolina Nonwovens LLC............F 704 735-5600
Maiden *(G-8011)*

Chicopee Inc............G 919 894-4111
Benson *(G-786)*

Cumulus Fibres Inc............B 704 394-2111
Charlotte *(G-2004)*

Dalco GF Technologies LLC............D 828 459-2577
Conover *(G-3512)*

Dalco Gft Nonwovens LLC............D 828 459-2577
Conover *(G-3513)*

Fibrix LLC............E 704 394-2111
Charlotte *(G-2150)*

Fibrix LLC............E 704 872-5223
Statesville *(G-11696)*

Fibrix LLC............E 704 878-0027
Statesville *(G-11697)*

Freudenberg Nonwovens Limit............A 919 620-3900
Durham *(G-4036)*

Freudenberg Prfmce Mtls LP............C 828 665-5000
Candler *(G-1225)*

Freudenberg Prfmce Mtls LP............E 919 479-7443
Durham *(G-4037)*

Glatflter Sntara Old Hckry Inc............F 615 526-2100
Charlotte *(G-2213)*

Hanes Companies Inc............C 336 747-1600
Winston Salem *(G-13186)*

Hendrix Batting Company............C 336 431-1181
High Point *(G-6644)*

Kem-Wove Inc............E 704 588-0080
Charlotte *(G-2392)*

Lydall Inc............G 336 468-8522
Hamptonville *(G-6087)*

Lydall Inc............G 336 468-1323
Yadkinville *(G-13446)*

Mitt S Nitts Inc............E 919 596-6793
Durham *(G-4139)*

Mountain International LLC............E 828 606-0194
Brevard *(G-978)*

Nutex Concepts NC Corp............E 828 726-8801
Lenoir *(G-7631)*

Polyvlies Usa Inc............E 336 769-0206
Winston Salem *(G-13299)*

Saertex Usa LLC............C 704 464-5998
Huntersville *(G-7050)*

Scorpio Acquisition Corp............G 704 697-5100
Charlotte *(G-2770)*

Shalag US Inc............D
Oxford *(G-9634)*

Tenowo Inc............F 704 732-3525
Lincolnton *(G-7860)*

Twe Nonwovens Us Inc............E 336 431-7187
High Point *(G-6815)*

Vitaflex LLC............F 888 616-8848
Burlington *(G-1175)*

Warm Products Inc............F 425 248-2424
Hendersonville *(G-6249)*

Westpoint Home Inc............F 910 369-2231
Wagram *(G-12257)*

Yanjan USA LLC............C 704 380-6230
Statesville *(G-11803)*

FABRICS: Nylon, Broadwoven

Kings Plush Inc............C 704 739-9931
Kings Mountain *(G-7370)*

FABRICS: Pile, Circular Knit

Heritage Knitting Co LLC............E 704 872-7653
Statesville *(G-11709)*

Innofa Usa LLC............E 336 635-2900
Eden *(G-4348)*

Russ Knits Inc............F 910 974-4114
Candor *(G-1241)*

Toms Knit Fabrics............G 704 867-4236
Gastonia *(G-5155)*

FABRICS: Polyester, Broadwoven

Burlington Industries LLC............C 336 379-6220
Greensboro *(G-5414)*

Carriff Corporation Inc.............................. G 704 888-3330
Midland *(G-8282)*

Elevate Textiles Inc................................. F 336 379-6220
Charlotte *(G-2098)*

Elevate Textiles Holding Corp................. D 336 379-6220
Charlotte *(G-2099)*

Glen Raven Mtl Solutions LLC................ C 828 682-2142
Burnsville *(G-1185)*

Itg Holdings Inc....................................... A 336 379-6220
Greensboro *(G-5628)*

Performance Fibers.................................. F 704 947-7193
Huntersville *(G-7032)*

Wade Manufacturing Company................ E 704 694-2131
Wadesboro *(G-12252)*

FABRICS: Polypropylene, Broadwoven

Gale Pacific Usa Inc................................ F 407 772-7900
Charlotte *(G-2185)*

FABRICS: Resin Or Plastic Coated

Engineered Recycling Company LLC.... E 704 358-6700
Charlotte *(G-2114)*

Tosaf Aw Inc... D 980 533-3000
Bessemer City *(G-838)*

Uretek LLC.. G 203 468-0342
Rutherfordton *(G-11001)*

FABRICS: Rubber & Elastic Yarns & Fabrics

Efa Inc.. C 336 275-9401
Greensboro *(G-5514)*

McMichael Mills Inc................................. E 336 584-0134
Burlington *(G-1127)*

McMichael Mills Inc................................. C 336 548-4242
Mayodan *(G-8207)*

FABRICS: Rubberized

Contour Enterprises LLC........................ D 828 328-1550
Hildebran *(G-6847)*

FABRICS: Scrub Cloths

Mdkscrubs LLC....................................... G 980 250-4708
Charlotte *(G-2483)*

Star Wipers Inc....................................... E 888 511-2656
Gastonia *(G-5143)*

FABRICS: Shoe Laces, Exc Leather

Hickory Brands Inc.................................. D 828 322-2600
Hickory *(G-6347)*

FABRICS: Specialty Including Twisted Weaves, Broadwoven

Fiber Company.. G 336 725-5277
Lewisville *(G-7650)*

Weavexx LLC... A 919 556-7235
Raleigh *(G-10602)*

FABRICS: Spunbonded

Berry Global Inc...................................... A 704 697-5100
Charlotte *(G-1773)*

Chicopee Inc... E 704 697-5100
Charlotte *(G-1914)*

Pgi Polymer Inc....................................... A 704 697-5100
Charlotte *(G-2633)*

FABRICS: Tickings

Bekaertdeslee USA Inc........................... B 336 747-4900
Winston Salem *(G-13103)*

Ct-Nassau Ticking LLC............................ E 336 570-0091
Burlington *(G-1079)*

Culp Inc... C 336 643-7751
Stokesdale *(G-11811)*

FABRICS: Trimmings, Textile

Ramseur Inter-Lock Knitting Co............. G 336 824-2427
Asheboro *(G-388)*

West & Associates of NC......................... G 919 479-5680
Durham *(G-4303)*

FABRICS: Upholstery, Cotton

Carolina Mills Incorporated.................... D 828 428-9911
Maiden *(G-8010)*

Culp Inc... E 662 844-7144
Burlington *(G-1080)*

Cv Industries Inc..................................... G 828 328-1851
Hickory *(G-6316)*

Heritage Classic Wovens LLC................ G 828 247-6010
Forest City *(G-4791)*

Lantal Textiles Inc.................................. C 336 969-9551
Rural Hall *(G-10963)*

Marlatex Corporation.............................. E 704 829-7797
Charlotte *(G-2458)*

Swatchworks Inc..................................... G 336 626-9971
Asheboro *(G-401)*

Vlr LLC.. E 252 355-4610
Morganton *(G-8909)*

FABRICS: Upholstery, Wool

Lantal Textiles Inc.................................. C 336 969-9551
Rural Hall *(G-10963)*

FABRICS: Warp & Flat Knit Prdts

Innovaknits LLC....................................... G 828 536-9348
Conover *(G-3533)*

Whiteville Fabrics LLC............................ F 910 639-4444
Whiteville *(G-12597)*

Whiteville Fabrics LLC............................ F 910 914-0456
Whiteville *(G-12596)*

FABRICS: Weft Or Circular Knit

Contempora Fabrics Inc......................... C 910 345-0150
Lumberton *(G-7948)*

Early Bird Hosiery Mills Inc................... G 828 324-6745
Hickory *(G-6327)*

Flagship Brands LLC............................... E 888 801-7227
Newton *(G-9465)*

Heiq Chemtex Inc................................... G 704 795-9322
Concord *(G-3373)*

Innovaknits LLC....................................... G 828 536-9348
Conover *(G-3533)*

Innovative Knitting LLC.......................... E 336 350-8122
Burlington *(G-1110)*

Knit-Wear Fabrics Inc............................ E 336 226-4342
Burlington *(G-1115)*

McMurray Fabrics Inc............................. C 910 944-2128
Aberdeen *(G-12)*

Ramseur Inter-Lock Knitting Co............. G 336 824-2427
Asheboro *(G-388)*

Tommys Tubing & Stockenettes.............. F 336 449-6461
Gibsonville *(G-5185)*

FABRICS: Wool, Broadwoven

National Spinning Co Inc......................... C 910 298-3131
Beulaville *(G-844)*

FABRICS: Worsted fabrics, broadwoven

Burlington Industries III LLC.................. F 336 379-2000
Greensboro *(G-5413)*

Elevate Textiles Inc................................. F 336 379-6220
Charlotte *(G-2098)*

Elevate Textiles Holding Corp................. D 336 379-6220
Charlotte *(G-2099)*

Itg Holdings Inc....................................... A 336 379-6220
Greensboro *(G-5628)*

FAMILY CLOTHING STORES

Pdf and Associates.................................. G 252 332-7749
Colerain *(G-3271)*

Pretty Paid LLC....................................... G 980 443-3876
Kings Mountain *(G-7379)*

Raleigh Workshop Inc............................. E 919 917-8969
Raleigh *(G-10431)*

Ralph Lauren Corporation....................... G 336 632-5000
High Point *(G-6752)*

Secret Spot Inc....................................... G 252 441-4030
Nags Head *(G-9302)*

FANS, BLOWING: Indl Or Commercial

Greenheck Fan Co................................... G 336 852-5788
Greensboro *(G-5575)*

Sonicaire Inc... E 336 712-2437
Winston Salem *(G-13340)*

FANS, VENTILATING: Indl Or Commercial

Miller Ctrl Mfg Inc Clinton NC................ G 910 592-5112
Clinton *(G-3235)*

Select Air Systems Usa Inc.................... E 704 289-1122
Monroe *(G-8557)*

Trane US Inc.. A 704 655-4000
Davidson *(G-3723)*

FANS: Ceiling

Minka Lighting Inc.................................. D 704 785-9200
Concord *(G-3403)*

FARM & GARDEN MACHINERY WHOLESALERS

Tar River Trading Post LLC.................... G 919 589-3618
Youngsville *(G-13490)*

FARM PRDTS, RAW MATERIALS, WHOLESALE: Broomcorn

Barkleys Mill On Southern Cro............... G 828 626-3344
Weaverville *(G-12484)*

FARM SPLYS WHOLESALERS

C A Perry & Son Inc................................ G 252 330-2323
Elizabeth City *(G-4380)*

C A Perry & Son Inc................................ E 252 221-4463
Hobbsville *(G-6883)*

Southern States Coop Inc....................... D 704 872-6364
Statesville *(G-11772)*

Southern States Coop Inc....................... F 910 285-8213
Wallace *(G-12325)*

Thompson Sunny Acres Inc.................... G 910 206-1801
Rockingham *(G-10791)*

FARM SPLYS, WHOLESALE: Fertilizers & Agricultural Chemicals

Helena Agri-Enterprises LLC................. F 910 422-8901
Rowland *(G-10915)*

FARM SPLYS, WHOLESALE: Insecticides

Southern AG Insecticides Inc................ E 828 264-8843
Boone *(G-943)*

Southern AG Insecticides Inc................ E 828 692-2233
Hendersonville *(G-6242)*

FASTENERS WHOLESALERS

Dubose National Enrgy Svcs Inc............ G 704 295-1060
Waxhaw *(G-12430)*

Gesipa Fasteners Usa Inc...................... E 336 751-1555
Mocksville *(G-8367)*

Gesipa Fasteners Usa Inc...................... F 609 208-1740
Mocksville *(G-8368)*

PRODUCT

Heico Fasteners Inc................................. E 828 261-0184
Hickory *(G-6345)*

Magnum Manufacturing LLC................. F 704 983-1340
New London *(G-9419)*

ND Southeastern Fastener..................... G 704 329-0033
Charlotte *(G-2550)*

FASTENERS: Metal

Piranha Nail and Staple Inc................. G 336 852-8358
Greensboro *(G-5749)*

Wurth Revcar Fasteners Inc................. E 919 772-9930
Garner *(G-4975)*

Oak City Metal LLC................................. G 919 375-4535
Zebulon *(G-13518)*

Penn Engineering & Mfg Corp............. C 336 631-8741
Winston Salem *(G-13278)*

FASTENERS: Notions, Hooks & Eyes

Aplix Inc... B 704 588-1920
Charlotte *(G-1683)*

FASTENERS: Wire, Made From Purchased Wire

Eastern Wholesale Fence LLC............... D 631 698-0975
Salisbury *(G-11047)*

Redtail Group LLC................................... G 828 539-4700
Swannanoa *(G-11876)*

FAUCETS & SPIGOTS: Metal & Plastic

Masco Corporation................................. G 704 658-9646
Mooresville *(G-8719)*

FELDSPAR: Ground Or Otherwise Treated

Quartz Corp USA..................................... E 828 766-2104
Spruce Pine *(G-11584)*

FENCE POSTS: Iron & Steel

Moes Hndy Svcs Fnce Instl Mno............. G 910 712-1402
Raeford *(G-9842)*

FENCES OR POSTS: Ornamental Iron Or Steel

Alamance Iron Works Inc....................... G 336 852-5940
Greensboro *(G-5346)*

FENCING MADE IN WIREDRAWING PLANTS

Blue Ridge Metals Corporation............. C 828 687-2525
Fletcher *(G-4725)*

FENCING MATERIALS: Docks & Other Outdoor Prdts, Wood

1st Time Contracting.............................. G 774 289-3321
Clemmons *(G-3176)*

Phelps Wood Products LLC................... G 336 284-2149
Cleveland *(G-3219)*

Universal Forest Products Inc............... F 252 338-0319
Elizabeth City *(G-4416)*

FENCING: Chain Link

Classic Cleaning LLC............................. E 800 220-7101
Raleigh *(G-9998)*

Harrison Fence Inc................................. G 919 244-6908
Apex *(G-162)*

Merchants Metals LLC........................... C 704 878-8706
Statesville *(G-11731)*

Turner & Reeves Fence Co LLC............. G 910 671-8851
Clayton *(G-3175)*

FERTILIZER MINERAL MINING

Verdesian Life Science US LLC............. E 919 825-1901
Cary *(G-1478)*

FERTILIZER, AGRICULTURAL: Wholesalers

Boggs Farm Center Inc......................... G 704 538-7176
Fallston *(G-4522)*

Clapp Fertilizer and Trckg Inc............... G 336 449-6103
Whitsett *(G-12602)*

G P Kittrell & Son Inc............................. G 252 465-8929
Corapeake *(G-3579)*

Harvey Fertilizer and Gas Co................. E 252 753-2063
Farmville *(G-4530)*

Harvey Fertilizer and Gas Co................. F 252 523-9090
Kinston *(G-7414)*

Nutrien AG Solutions Inc....................... G 252 585-0282
Conway *(G-3578)*

FERTILIZERS: Nitrogen Solutions

Farm Chemicals Inc............................... F 910 875-4277
Raeford *(G-9837)*

FERTILIZERS: Nitrogenous

Carolina Eastern Inc............................. G 252 795-3128
Robersonville *(G-10766)*

Clapp Fertilizer and Trckg Inc............... G 336 449-6103
Whitsett *(G-12602)*

Harvey Fertilizer and Gas Co................. F 252 523-9090
Kinston *(G-7414)*

Harvey Fertilizer and Gas Co................. E 252 526-4150
Kinston *(G-7415)*

Kamlar Corporation............................... E 252 443-2576
Rocky Mount *(G-10845)*

Mineral Springs Fertilizer Inc............... G 704 843-2683
Mineral Springs *(G-8327)*

Nutrien AG Solutions Inc....................... G 252 235-4161
Bailey *(G-672)*

Southern States Coop Inc..................... G 336 246-3201
Creedmoor *(G-3654)*

Southern States Coop Inc..................... E 336 786-7545
Mount Airy *(G-9178)*

Southern States Coop Inc..................... E 919 658-5061
Mount Olive *(G-9259)*

Southern States Coop Inc..................... D 704 872-6364
Statesville *(G-11772)*

Southern States Coop Inc..................... F 910 285-8213
Wallace *(G-12325)*

FERTILIZERS: Phosphatic

Nutrien AG Solutions Inc....................... F 252 977-2025
Rocky Mount *(G-10814)*

Pcs Phosphate Company Inc................. E 252 322-4111
Aurora *(G-645)*

Southern States Coop Inc..................... G 336 246-3201
Creedmoor *(G-3654)*

Southern States Coop Inc..................... E 336 786-7545
Mount Airy *(G-9178)*

Southern States Coop Inc..................... E 919 658-5061
Mount Olive *(G-9259)*

Southern States Coop Inc..................... D 704 872-6364
Statesville *(G-11772)*

Southern States Coop Inc..................... F 910 285-8213
Wallace *(G-12325)*

FIBER & FIBER PRDTS: Acrylic

Coats HP Inc... B 704 824-9904
Mc Adenville *(G-8213)*

Coats HP Inc... E 704 329-5800
Charlotte *(G-1944)*

Mannington Mills Inc............................. D 704 824-3551
Mc Adenville *(G-8214)*

Pharr McAdenville Corporation............. D 704 824-3551
Mc Adenville *(G-8215)*

Snp Inc... F 919 598-0400
Durham *(G-4241)*

FIBER & FIBER PRDTS: Polyester

Auriga Polymers Inc............................... C 864 579-5570
Charlotte *(G-1717)*

Fibrix LLC.. E 828 459-7064
Conover *(G-3521)*

Polycor Holdings Inc............................. D 828 459-7064
Conover *(G-3547)*

Southern Fiber Inc................................. E 704 736-0011
Lincolnton *(G-7854)*

Stein Fibers Ltd..................................... D 704 599-2804
Charlotte *(G-2866)*

Warp Technologies Inc........................... C 919 552-2311
Holly Springs *(G-6920)*

FIBER & FIBER PRDTS: Vinyl

Military Wraps Inc................................... G 910 671-0008
Lumberton *(G-7962)*

Morbern LLC... F 336 883-4332
High Point *(G-6714)*

Trelleborg Ctd Systems US Inc............. C 828 286-9126
Rutherfordton *(G-10996)*

FIBER OPTICS

Connexion Technologies........................ F 919 674-0036
Cary *(G-1332)*

Corning Incorporated............................. D 910 784-7200
Wilmington *(G-12753)*

M2 Optics Inc... G 919 342-5619
Raleigh *(G-10264)*

Roblon US Inc... D 828 396-2121
Granite Falls *(G-5321)*

Royal Carolina Corporation................... E 336 292-8845
Greensboro *(G-5796)*

FIBER: Vulcanized

Royale Comfort Seating Inc................... D 828 352-9021
Taylorsville *(G-11974)*

FIBERS: Carbon & Graphite

Nouveau Verre Holdings Inc................. F 336 545-0011
Greensboro *(G-5714)*

Nvh Inc... G 336 545-0011
Greensboro *(G-5717)*

Sgl Technologies LLC............................. G 704 593-5100
Charlotte *(G-2794)*

FILM BASE: Cellulose Acetate Or Nitrocellulose Plastics

Icons America LLC................................. D 704 922-0041
Dallas *(G-3676)*

Printpack Inc... C 828 649-3800
Marshall *(G-8082)*

FILTER CLEANING SVCS

Hlmf Logistics Inc................................. G 704 782-0356
Pineville *(G-9733)*

FILTER ELEMENTS: Fluid & Hydraulic Line

Main Filter LLC....................................... E 704 735-0009
Lincolnton *(G-7841)*

FILTERING MEDIA: Pottery

Daramic LLC... D 704 587-8599
Charlotte *(G-2018)*

Selee Corporation................................. C 828 697-2411
Hendersonville *(G-6240)*

FILTERS

City of Morganton.................................F 828 584-1460
Morganton *(G-8857)*

Ddp Spclty Elctrnic Mtls US 9.............E 336 547-7112
Greensboro *(G-5490)*

Ffi Holdings III Corp............................E 800 690-3650
Charlotte *(G-2149)*

Flanders Corporation...........................D 919 934-3020
Smithfield *(G-11443)*

Flanders Filters Inc............................G 252 217-3978
Smithfield *(G-11444)*

Global Filter Source LLC......................G 919 571-4945
Raleigh *(G-10137)*

Liquid Process Systems Inc..................G 704 821-1115
Indian Trail *(G-7088)*

Ltd Industries LLC...............................E 704 897-2182
Charlotte *(G-2436)*

Mann+hummel Filtration Technol...........G 704 869-3952
Gastonia *(G-5088)*

NAPA Filters.......................................G 704 864-6748
Gastonia *(G-5106)*

Ralph B Hall..G 919 258-3634
Sanford *(G-11223)*

Rubber Mill Inc....................................E 336 622-1680
Liberty *(G-7778)*

Southern Products Company Inc...........E 910 281-3189
Hoffman *(G-6885)*

Textile Parts and Mch Co Inc...............G 704 865-5003
Gastonia *(G-5152)*

US Filter...G 828 274-8282
Asheville *(G-629)*

FILTERS & SOFTENERS: Water, Household

City of Greensboro..............................D 336 373-5855
Greensboro *(G-5446)*

Greenstory Globl Gvrnment Mlta...........F 828 446-9278
Terrell *(G-11989)*

Imagine One LLC.................................G 828 324-6454
Hickory *(G-6364)*

Water-Revolution LLC..........................G 336 525-1015
Blanch *(G-879)*

Wine To Water.....................................E 828 355-9655
Boone *(G-954)*

FILTERS & STRAINERS: Pipeline

Elxsi Corporation.................................B 407 849-1090
Charlotte *(G-2105)*

Hayward Industries Inc........................D 336 712-9900
Clemmons *(G-3188)*

Hayward Industries Inc........................B 704 837-8002
Charlotte *(G-2265)*

FILTERS: Air

Ffi Holdings III Corp............................E 800 690-3650
Charlotte *(G-2149)*

Nederman Mikropul LLC.......................E 704 998-2600
Charlotte *(G-2553)*

FILTERS: Air Intake, Internal Combustion Engine, Exc Auto

Canvas Sx LLC....................................C 980 474-3700
Charlotte *(G-1836)*

SPX Technologies Inc..........................D 980 474-3700
Charlotte *(G-2851)*

FILTERS: General Line, Indl

Beacon Industrial Mfg LLC...................A 704 399-7441
Charlotte *(G-1762)*

Drum Filter Media Inc..........................G 336 434-4195
High Point *(G-6599)*

Erdle Perforating Holdings Inc..............F 704 588-4380
Charlotte *(G-2126)*

John W Foster Sales Inc......................G 704 821-3822
Matthews *(G-8178)*

Mann+hmmel Fltrtion Tech US LL.........C 704 869-3300
Gastonia *(G-5085)*

Mann+hummel Filtration Technol...........C 704 869-3501
Gastonia *(G-5089)*

Reclaim Filters and Systems.................G 919 528-1787
Wake Forest *(G-12292)*

FILTRATION DEVICES: Electronic

Amiad Filtration Systems Ltd.................E 805 377-0288
Mooresville *(G-8598)*

Branford Filtration LLC.........................D 704 394-2111
Mooresville *(G-8620)*

Fueltec Systems LLC...........................G 828 212-1141
Granite Falls *(G-5303)*

Liquid Process Systems Inc..................G 704 821-1115
Indian Trail *(G-7088)*

Mann+hmmel Fltrtion Tech US LL.........C 704 869-3300
Gastonia *(G-5085)*

Nederman Mikropul Canada Inc............G 704 998-2606
Charlotte *(G-2554)*

Purolator Facet Inc..............................E 336 668-4444
Greensboro *(G-5771)*

FINANCIAL SVCS

Apex Analytix LLC...............................C 336 272-4669
Greensboro *(G-5365)*

Ats Service Company LLC.....................G 512 905-9005
Godwin *(G-5186)*

Katchi Tees Incorporated......................G 252 315-4691
Wilson *(G-12997)*

FINGERPRINT EQPT

Tri-Tech Forensics Inc..........................D 910 457-6600
Leland *(G-7561)*

FINISHING AGENTS

Fine Line Hosiery Inc...........................G 336 498-8022
Asheboro *(G-356)*

Lindley Laboratories Inc.......................F 336 449-7521
Gibsonville *(G-5181)*

FINISHING AGENTS: Textile

Cliffside Technologies Inc.....................G 828 657-4477
Mooresboro *(G-8583)*

Surry Chemicals Incorporated...............E 336 786-4607
Mount Airy *(G-9181)*

FINISHING SVCS

Blue Ridge Quick Print Inc....................G 828 883-2420
Brevard *(G-968)*

FIRE ALARM MAINTENANCE & MONITORING SVCS

Automated Controls LLC.......................G 704 724-7625
Huntersville *(G-6970)*

GNB Ventures LLC...............................F 704 488-4468
Charlotte *(G-2218)*

FIRE ARMS, SMALL: Guns Or Gun Parts, 30 mm & Below

Arisaka LLC...F 919 601-5625
Apex *(G-139)*

Bachstein Consulting LLC.....................G 410 322-4917
Youngsville *(G-13463)*

Grip Pod Systems Intl LLC....................G 239 233-3694
Raleigh *(G-10149)*

Remington Arms Company LLC.............C 800 544-8892
Madison *(G-7998)*

FIRE ARMS, SMALL: Pistols Or Pistol Parts, 30 mm & below

Microtech Defense Inds Inc...................G 828 684-4355
Fletcher *(G-4756)*

FIRE ARMS, SMALL: Rifles Or Rifle Parts, 30 mm & below

Remington Arms Company LLC.............C 800 544-8892
Madison *(G-7999)*

FIRE CONTROL EQPT REPAIR SVCS, MILITARY

Rk Enterprises LLC...............................G 910 481-0777
Fayetteville *(G-4663)*

FIRE CONTROL OR BOMBING EQPT: Electronic

Total Fire Systems Inc..........................E 919 556-9161
Youngsville *(G-13493)*

FIRE DETECTION SYSTEMS

Argus Fire CONtrol-Pf&s Inc.................E 704 372-1228
Charlotte *(G-1696)*

FIRE EXTINGUISHERS, WHOLESALE

Beco Holding Company Inc....................C 800 826-3473
Charlotte *(G-1767)*

GNB Ventures LLC...............................F 704 488-4468
Charlotte *(G-2218)*

Walter Kidde Portable Eqp Inc...............B 919 563-5911
Mebane *(G-8263)*

FIRE EXTINGUISHERS: Portable

Bonaventure Group Inc.........................F 919 781-6610
Raleigh *(G-9953)*

GNB Ventures LLC...............................F 704 488-4468
Charlotte *(G-2218)*

Speer Operational Tech LLC..................G 864 631-2512
Marion *(G-8066)*

FIRE OR BURGLARY RESISTIVE PRDTS

Airbox Inc..E 855 927-1386
Statesville *(G-11651)*

JMS Rebar Inc......................................G 336 273-9084
Greensboro *(G-5637)*

Mma Manufacturing Inc........................E 828 692-0256
East Flat Rock *(G-4334)*

North Star Fbrication Repr Inc...............G 704 393-5243
Charlotte *(G-2574)*

Sinnovatek Inc.....................................G 919 694-0974
Raleigh *(G-10479)*

West Side Industries LLC......................G 980 223-8665
Statesville *(G-11799)*

FIREARMS & AMMUNITION, EXC SPORTING, WHOLESALE

Consolidated Elec Distrs Inc..................G 828 433-4689
Morganton *(G-8858)*

FIREFIGHTING APPARATUS

Buckeye Fire Equipment Company........E 704 739-7415
Kings Mountain *(G-7351)*

Hurst Jaws of Life Inc..........................C 704 487-6961
Shelby *(G-11345)*

Kenmar Inc...F 336 884-8722
High Point *(G-6684)*

FIREPLACE EQPT & ACCESS

Hearth & Home Technologies LLC......... C 336 274-1663
Greensboro *(G-5592)*

Woodlane Envmtl Tech Inc...................... G 828 894-8383
Columbus *(G-3305)*

FIREPLACES: Concrete

Blue Rdge Elc Mmbers Fndtion I........... D 828 754-9071
Lenoir *(G-7588)*

FIRST AID SPLYS, WHOLESALE

Project Bean LLC................................... D 201 438-1598
Huntersville *(G-7040)*

FISH & SEAFOOD PROCESSORS: Canned Or Cured

Bay Breeze Seafood Rest Inc.................. F 828 697-7106
Hendersonville *(G-6186)*

Capt Neills Seafood Inc.......................... C 252 796-0795
Columbia *(G-3295)*

Carolina ATL Seafood Entps.................... G 252 728-2552
Morehead City *(G-8822)*

Lloyds Oyster House Inc......................... E 910 754-6958
Shallotte *(G-11304)*

Quality Foods From Sea Inc.................... D 252 338-5455
Elizabeth City *(G-4405)*

Quality Seafood Co Inc........................... G 252 338-2800
Elizabeth City *(G-4406)*

FISH & SEAFOOD PROCESSORS: Fresh Or Frozen

Bakkavor Foods Usa Inc......................... C 704 522-1977
Charlotte *(G-1745)*

Hare Asian Trading Company LLC......... E 910 524-4667
Burgaw *(G-1023)*

FISH & SEAFOOD WHOLESALERS

Atlantis Foods Inc.................................. E 336 768-6101
Clemmons *(G-3177)*

Bay Breeze Seafood Rest Inc.................. F 828 697-7106
Hendersonville *(G-6186)*

Pamlico Packing Co Inc.......................... F 252 745-3688
Vandemere *(G-12226)*

Pamlico Packing Co Inc.......................... F 252 745-3688
Grantsboro *(G-5331)*

FISHING EQPT: Lures

Fish Getter Lure Co LLC.......................... G 704 538-9863
Casar *(G-1488)*

FITTINGS & ASSEMBLIES: Hose & Tube, Hydraulic Or Pneumatic

Carolina Components Group Inc............ E 919 635-8438
Durham *(G-3960)*

Carolina Rubber & Spc Inc..................... G 336 744-5111
Winston Salem *(G-13118)*

Cross Technologies Inc.......................... E 800 327-7727
Greensboro *(G-5472)*

Custom Hydraulics & Design.................. F 704 347-0023
Cherryville *(G-3061)*

Deetag USA Inc...................................... G 828 465-2644
Conover *(G-3514)*

Dickie Jones.. G 828 733-5084
Newland *(G-9428)*

Eagle Assembly Unlimited Inc............... G 252 462-0408
Castalia *(G-1492)*

Eaton Corporation................................. D 828 286-4157
Forest City *(G-4788)*

Hydraulic Hose Depot Inc...................... G 252 356-1862
Cofield *(G-3267)*

Metrohose Incorporated........................ G 252 329-9891
Greenville *(G-6004)*

Talladega Mchy & Sup Co NC................. G 256 362-4124
Fayetteville *(G-4677)*

FITTINGS & SPECIALTIES: Steam

Tlv Corporation..................................... E 704 597-9070
Charlotte *(G-2922)*

FITTINGS: Pipe

Appalachian Pipe Distrs LLC................. G 704 688-5703
Charlotte *(G-1684)*

Atlantic Tube & Fitting LLC.................... G 704 545-6166
Mint Hill *(G-8330)*

General Refrigeration Company............. G 919 661-4727
Garner *(G-4929)*

FIXTURES & EQPT: Kitchen, Metal, Exc Cast Aluminum

Henry & Rye Incorporated..................... G 919 365-7045
Wendell *(G-12537)*

Metalfab of North Carolina LLC............. C 704 841-1090
Matthews *(G-8132)*

Select Stainless Products LLC............... G 888 843-2345
Charlotte *(G-2783)*

Singer Equipment Company Inc............ E 910 484-1128
Fayetteville *(G-4671)*

Thompson & Little Inc............................ E 910 484-1128
Fayetteville *(G-4680)*

FIXTURES: Cut Stone

Athena Marble Incorporated.................. G 704 636-7810
Salisbury *(G-11018)*

McAd Inc.. E 336 299-3030
Greensboro *(G-5686)*

FLAGS: Fabric

Dunn Manufacturing Corp...................... C 704 283-2147
Monroe *(G-8479)*

FLAGSTONES

Jacobs Creek Stone Company Inc......... F 336 857-2602
Denton *(G-3751)*

FLAT GLASS: Float

Cardinal Glass Industries Inc................. C 704 660-0900
Mooresville *(G-8628)*

FLAT GLASS: Window, Clear & Colored

Tint Plus... G 910 229-5303
Fayetteville *(G-4681)*

FLOOR COVERING STORES

Bfs Operations LLC............................... A 919 431-1000
Raleigh *(G-9942)*

Heartwood Pine Floors Inc.................... G 919 542-4394
Moncure *(G-8406)*

Stock Building Supply Holdings LLC..... A 919 431-1000
Raleigh *(G-10509)*

FLOOR COVERING STORES: Carpets

Interrs-Exteriors Asheboro Inc.............. G 336 629-2148
Asheboro *(G-367)*

FLOOR COVERINGS WHOLESALERS

Bonakemi Usa Incorporated.................. D 704 220-6943
Monroe *(G-8445)*

Freudenberg Nonwovens Limit.............. A 919 620-3900
Durham *(G-4036)*

FLOOR COVERINGS: Rubber

Core Technology Molding Corp.............. E 336 294-2018
Greensboro *(G-5469)*

Prototech Manufacturing Inc................. F 508 646-8849
Washington *(G-12410)*

FLOOR COVERINGS: Textile Fiber

Rug & Home Inc..................................... E 828 785-4480
Asheville *(G-594)*

FLOORING & SIDING: Metal

Centria Inc.. G 704 341-0202
Charlotte *(G-1887)*

FLOORING: Hardwood

Bona USA.. F 704 220-6943
Monroe *(G-8443)*

Eskimo 7 Limited................................... G 252 726-8181
Morehead City *(G-8832)*

Green River Resource MGT.................... F 828 697-0357
Zirconia *(G-13530)*

Horizon Forest Products Co LP.............. G 336 993-9663
Colfax *(G-3280)*

Horizon Frest Pdts Wlmngton LP........... D 919 424-8265
Raleigh *(G-10175)*

J L Powell & Co Inc................................ G 910 642-8989
Whiteville *(G-12585)*

Mannington Mills Inc.............................. E 336 884-5600
High Point *(G-6697)*

Old Growth Riverwood Inc..................... G 910 762-4077
Wilmington *(G-12865)*

Robert St Clair Co Inc............................ F 919 847-8611
Raleigh *(G-10445)*

Vivet Inc.. E 909 390-1039
Greensboro *(G-5904)*

FLOWERS, ARTIFICIAL, WHOLESALE

Government Sales LLC........................... G 252 726-6315
Morehead City *(G-8833)*

Jefferson Group Inc.............................. E 252 752-6195
Greenville *(G-5995)*

FLUID METERS & COUNTING DEVICES

Danaher Indus Sensors Contrls............. G 910 862-5426
Elizabethtown *(G-4424)*

Measurement Controls Inc..................... F 704 921-1101
Charlotte *(G-2484)*

Sensus.. E 919 376-2617
Cary *(G-1451)*

Vontier Corporation............................... C 984 275-6000
Raleigh *(G-10594)*

FLUID POWER PUMPS & MOTORS

Caterpillar Inc....................................... D 919 550-1100
Clayton *(G-3137)*

E-Z Dumper Products LLC...................... G 717 762-8432
Southern Pines *(G-11497)*

Hurst Jaws of Life Inc............................ C 704 487-6961
Shelby *(G-11345)*

Hyde Park Partners Inc.......................... D 704 587-4819
Charlotte *(G-2304)*

Hydralic Engnered Pdts Svc Inc............. G 704 374-1306
Charlotte *(G-2305)*

Livingston & Haven LLC.......................... C 704 588-3670
Charlotte *(G-2428)*

Logic Hydraulic Controls Inc................. E 910 791-9293
Wilmington *(G-12838)*

Parker-Hannifin Corporation.................. G 252 652-6592
Havelock *(G-6125)*

Parker-Hannifin Corporation.................. B 704 739-9781
Kings Mountain *(G-7376)*

Schunk Intec Inc.................................... D 919 572-2705
Morrisville *(G-9046)*

SCI Sharp Controls Inc.............................. G 704 394-1395
Pineville *(G-9755)*

FLUID POWER VALVES & HOSE FITTINGS

Cross Technologies Inc.......................... D 336 292-0511
Whitsett *(G-12603)*

Dixon Valve & Coupling Co LLC............. F 704 334-9175
Dallas *(G-3668)*

Engineered Controls Intl LLC.................. C 828 466-2153
Conover *(G-3519)*

George W Dahl Company Inc.................. E 336 668-4444
Greensboro *(G-5557)*

Hydac Technology Corp.......................... D 610 266-0100
Denver *(G-3789)*

Polyhose Incorporated............................ E 732 512-9141
Wilmington *(G-12881)*

Romac Industries Inc.............................. D 704 915-3317
Dallas *(G-3688)*

SCI Sharp Controls Inc........................... G 704 394-1395
Pineville *(G-9755)*

FOAM RUBBER

Bsci Inc.. G 704 664-3005
Mooresville *(G-8623)*

Carolina Custom Rubber Inc................... G 704 636-6989
Salisbury *(G-11026)*

Catawba Valley Fabrication Inc.............. F 828 459-1191
Conover *(G-3503)*

Craftsman Foam Fabricators Inc............ G 336 476-5655
Thomasville *(G-12012)*

Elite Comfort Solutions LLC................... C 828 328-2201
Conover *(G-3518)*

GP Foam Fabricators Inc........................ F 336 434-3600
High Point *(G-6633)*

Hickory Springs Manufacturi.................. D 828 328-2201
Hickory *(G-6355)*

Hickory Springs Mfg Co.......................... G 828 322-7994
Hickory *(G-6356)*

Hickory Springs Mfg Co.......................... D 828 728-9274
Lenoir *(G-7614)*

Highland Foam Inc.................................. G 828 327-0400
Conover *(G-3531)*

Hilliard Fabricators LLC.......................... F 336 861-8833
Thomasville *(G-12032)*

Interstate Foam & Supply Inc................ C 828 459-9700
Conover *(G-3534)*

Marx Industries Incorporated................. E 828 396-6700
Hudson *(G-6955)*

Ohio Foam Corporation.......................... F 704 883-8402
Statesville *(G-11740)*

Skelly Inc... F 828 433-7070
Morganton *(G-8898)*

FOAMS & RUBBER, WHOLESALE

Olympic Products LLC............................ D 336 378-9620
Greensboro *(G-5721)*

Snyder Paper Corporation...................... E 828 464-1189
Newton *(G-9496)*

FOIL & LEAF: Metal

Acme Liquidating Company LLC............. E 704 873-3731
Statesville *(G-11647)*

Granges Americas Inc............................ D 704 633-6020
Salisbury *(G-11059)*

Kurz Transfer Products LP...................... D 336 764-4128
Lexington *(G-7706)*

Kurz Transfer Products LP...................... D 704 927-3700
Huntersville *(G-7008)*

Reynolds Consumer Products Inc........... A 704 371-5550
Huntersville *(G-7042)*

FOIL: Aluminum

Granges Americas Inc............................ D 704 633-6020
Salisbury *(G-11059)*

Wyda Packaging Corp............................ F 980 403-3346
Charlotte *(G-3029)*

FOOD COLORINGS

GNT Usa LLC.. E 914 524-0600
Dallas *(G-3673)*

FOOD PRDTS, BREAKFAST: Cereal, Oatmeal

Post Consumer Brands LLC.................... F 336 672-0124
Asheboro *(G-384)*

FOOD PRDTS, CANNED OR FRESH PACK: Fruit Juices

Arcadia Beverage LLC............................ G 828 684-3556
Arden *(G-252)*

Arcadia Farms LLC................................ D 828 684-3556
Arden *(G-253)*

Clement Pappas Nc LLC......................... G 856 455-1000
Hendersonville *(G-6197)*

Dfa Dairy Brands Fluid LLC.................... G 704 341-2794
Charlotte *(G-2038)*

FOOD PRDTS, CANNED: Baby Food

Atlantic Natural Foods LLC..................... D 888 491-0524
Nashville *(G-9309)*

FOOD PRDTS, CANNED: Barbecue Sauce

Baileys Sauces Inc................................ G 252 756-7179
Greenville *(G-5944)*

Brookwood Farms Inc............................ D 919 663-3612
Siler City *(G-11401)*

Mike DS Bbq LLC................................... G 866 960-8652
Durham *(G-4133)*

Papa Lonnies Inc................................... G 336 573-9313
Stoneville *(G-11825)*

T W Garner Food Company..................... G 336 661-1550
Winston Salem *(G-13352)*

T W Garner Food Company..................... E 336 661-1550
Winston Salem *(G-13353)*

FOOD PRDTS, CANNED: Fruit Juices, Fresh

Cold Off Press LLC................................. G 984 444-9006
Raleigh *(G-10003)*

Dole Food Company Inc.......................... E 818 874-4000
Charlotte *(G-2061)*

McF Operating LLC................................ E 828 685-8821
Hendersonville *(G-6225)*

FOOD PRDTS, CANNED: Fruits

Blue Ridge Jams.................................... G 828 685-1783
Hendersonville *(G-6187)*

Carolina Canners Inc............................. D 843 537-5281
Southern Pines *(G-11496)*

Kraft Heinz Foods Company................... G 704 565-5500
Charlotte *(G-2401)*

Mindfully Made Usa LLC........................ E 336 701-0377
Winston Salem *(G-13255)*

FOOD PRDTS, CANNED: Fruits & Fruit Prdts

Lc Foods LLC... G 919 510-6688
Raleigh *(G-10250)*

FOOD PRDTS, CANNED: Jams, Jellies & Preserves

Dutch Kettle LLC................................... G 336 468-8422
Hamptonville *(G-6083)*

Palace Green LLC.................................. G 919 827-7950
Raleigh *(G-10353)*

Pamela Stoeppelwerth............................ G 828 837-7293
Marble *(G-8027)*

FOOD PRDTS, CANNED: Mexican, NEC

Plantation House Foods Inc.................... G 919 381-5495
Durham *(G-4184)*

Tyson Mexican Original Inc.................... E 919 777-9428
Sanford *(G-11246)*

FOOD PRDTS, CONFECTIONERY, WHOLESALE: Candy

Bilcat Inc... E 828 295-3088
Blowing Rock *(G-880)*

FOOD PRDTS, CONFECTIONERY, WHOLESALE: Snack Foods

Gold Medal Products Co.......................... G 336 665-4997
Greensboro *(G-5568)*

Lc America Inc....................................... F 336 676-5129
Colfax *(G-3282)*

Lotus Bakeries Us LLC........................... G 415 956-8956
Mebane *(G-8250)*

Lrw Holdings Inc.................................... G 919 609-4172
Durham *(G-4110)*

FOOD PRDTS, DAIRY, WHOLESALE: Frozen Dairy Desserts

Celebrity Dairy LLC............................... G 919 742-4931
Siler City *(G-11404)*

Queen City Pastry Llc............................ E 704 660-5706
Mooresville *(G-8757)*

FOOD PRDTS, FISH & SEAFOOD: Crabmeat, Frozen

Sea Supreme Inc................................... G 919 556-1188
Wake Forest *(G-12298)*

FOOD PRDTS, FISH & SEAFOOD: Fish, Filleted

Classic Seafood Group Inc..................... C 252 746-2818
Ayden *(G-654)*

FOOD PRDTS, FROZEN: Ethnic Foods, NEC

Ricewrap Foods Corporation.................. F 919 614-1179
Butner *(G-1206)*

FOOD PRDTS, FROZEN: Fruits, Juices & Vegetables

Alphin Brothers Inc................................ E 910 892-8751
Dunn *(G-3843)*

Caseiro International LLC....................... G 919 530-8333
Durham *(G-3964)*

Neighborhood Smoothie LLC.................. G 919 845-5513
Raleigh *(G-10329)*

Nice Blends Corp.................................... D 910 640-1000
Whiteville *(G-12590)*

Seal Seasons Inc................................... F 919 245-3535
Durham *(G-4228)*

FOOD PRDTS, FRUITS & VEGETABLES, FRESH, WHOLESALE: Fruits

Dole Food Company Inc.......................... E 818 874-4000
Charlotte *(G-2061)*

FOOD PRDTS, WHOLESALE: Beans, Field

PRODUCT

Catawba Farms Enterprises LLC............ F 828 464-5780
Newton (G-9452)

FOOD PRDTS, WHOLESALE: Beverages, Exc Coffee & Tea

Coca-Cola Consolidated Inc.................. C 919 550-0611
Clayton (G-3141)

FOOD PRDTS, WHOLESALE: Chocolate

Chocolate Fetish LLC............................ G 828 258-2353
Asheville (G-475)

Chocolate Smiles Village LLC................ G 919 469-5282
Cary (G-1327)

Escazu Artisan Chocolate LLC............ F 919 832-3433
Raleigh (G-10091)

FOOD PRDTS, WHOLESALE: Coffee, Green Or Roasted

Dfa Dairy Brands Fluid LLC .... G 704 341-2794
Charlotte (G-2038)

Larrys Beans Inc................................... G 919 828-1234
Raleigh (G-10248)

Royal Cup Inc....................................... F 704 597-5756
Charlotte (G-2734)

S & D Coffee Inc.................................. A 704 782-3121
Concord (G-3437)

Tradewinds Coffee Co Inc .... F 919 556-1835
Zebulon (G-13524)

FOOD PRDTS, WHOLESALE: Condiments

Mindfully Made Usa LLC....................... E 336 701-0377
Winston Salem (G-13255)

Vintage South Inc................................. G 919 362-4079
Apex (G-202)

FOOD PRDTS, WHOLESALE: Dried or Canned Foods

Clay County Food Pantry Inc................. G 828 389-1657
Hayesville (G-6138)

FOOD PRDTS, WHOLESALE: Flavorings & Fragrances

Azure Skye Beverages Inc..................... G 704 909-7394
Charlotte (G-1727)

FOOD PRDTS, WHOLESALE: Flour

Interntnal Agrclture Group LLC.............. F 908 323-3246
Mooresville (G-8694)

FOOD PRDTS, WHOLESALE: Grain Elevators

Murphy-Brown LLC................................ G 252 221-4463
Hobbsville (G-6884)

Murphy-Brown LLC................................ D 910 293-3434
Warsaw (G-12363)

FOOD PRDTS, WHOLESALE: Grains

C A Perry & Son Inc .... G 252 330-2323
Elizabeth City (G-4380)

C A Perry & Son Inc .... E 252 221-4463
Hobbsville (G-6883)

Celtic Ocean International Inc................. E 828 299-9005
Arden (G-261)

Clapp Fertilizer and Trckg Inc............... G 336 449-6103
Whitsett (G-12602)

Farm Chemicals Inc .... F 910 875-4277
Raeford (G-9837)

FOOD PRDTS, WHOLESALE: Natural & Organic

Celtic Ocean International Inc................. E 828 299-9005
Arden (G-261)

Chef Martini LLC.................................. A 919 327-3183
Raleigh (G-9992)

FOOD PRDTS, WHOLESALE: Salad Dressing

Tracys Gourmet LLC.............................. G 919 672-1731
Asheville (G-622)

FOOD PRDTS, WHOLESALE: Specialty

Tropical Nut & Fruit Co .... C 800 438-4470
Charlotte (G-2947)

FOOD PRDTS, WHOLESALE: Spices & Seasonings

Random Rues Botanical LLC.................. G 252 214-2759
Greenville (G-6017)

FOOD PRDTS, WHOLESALE: Water, Distilled

Alamance Foods Inc.............................. C 336 226-6392
Burlington (G-1043)

Carolina Bottle Mfr LLC......................... G 704 635-8759
Monroe (G-8451)

FOOD PRDTS: Almond Pastes

Herbal Innovations LLC......................... E 336 818-2332
Wilkesboro (G-12638)

FOOD PRDTS: Animal & marine fats & oils

Carolina By-Products Co .... G 336 333-3030
Greensboro (G-5424)

Coastal Protein Products Inc................. G 910 567-6102
Godwin (G-5188)

Darling Ingredients Inc.......................... G 910 289-2083
Rose Hill (G-10904)

Valley Proteins .... F 252 348-4200
Lewiston Woodville (G-7648)

Valley Proteins (de) Inc........................ B 336 333-3030
Greensboro (G-5895)

Valley Proteins (de) Inc........................ C 540 877-2533
Oakboro (G-9584)

FOOD PRDTS: Cheese Curls & Puffs

Bakers Southern Traditions Inc............. G 252 344-2120
Roxobel (G-10949)

Ginny O s Inc.. F 919 816-7276
Warsaw (G-12360)

Lc America Inc...................................... F 336 676-5129
Colfax (G-3282)

Stormberg Foods LLC............................ E 919 947-6011
Goldsboro (G-5247)

FOOD PRDTS: Chicken, Processed, Cooked

Filet of Chicken.................................... F 336 751-4752
Mocksville (G-8362)

FOOD PRDTS: Chicken, Processed, Fresh

Perdue Farms Inc................................. E 252 348-4287
Ahoskie (G-51)

Perdue Farms Inc................................. A 704 789-2400
Concord (G-3417)

Perdue Farms Inc................................. C 336 366-2591
Elkin (G-4450)

FOOD PRDTS: Chicken, Slaughtered & Dressed

Pilgrims Pride Corporation..................... E 704 721-3585
Concord (G-3419)

Pilgrims Pride Corporation..................... B 704 624-2171
Marshville (G-8092)

Pilgrims Pride Corporation..................... C 704 233-4047
Wingate (G-13063)

Sanderson Farms Inc............................ G 910 274-0220
Saint Pauls (G-11008)

Sanderson Farms LLC Proc Div............ A 910 274-0220
Saint Pauls (G-11009)

FOOD PRDTS: Coffee

Alamance Kaffee Werks LLC.................. G 662 617-4573
Burlington (G-1044)

Anchor Coffee Co Inc............................ G 336 265-7458
North Wilkesboro (G-9521)

Larrys Beans Inc................................... G 919 828-1234
Raleigh (G-10248)

Royal Cup Inc....................................... F 704 597-5756
Charlotte (G-2734)

FOOD PRDTS: Coffee Extracts

Muddy Dog LLC..................................... G 919 371-2818
New Hill (G-9411)

FOOD PRDTS: Cooking Oils, Refined Vegetable, Exc Corn

Whole Harvest Foods LLC...................... E 910 293-7917
Warsaw (G-12369)

FOOD PRDTS: Corn Chips & Other Corn-Based Snacks

Frito-Lay North America Inc................... C 704 588-4150
Charlotte (G-2181)

KLb Enterprises Incorporated................ F 336 605-0773
Greensboro (G-5650)

FOOD PRDTS: Corn Meal

Atkinson Milling Company...................... D 919 965-3547
Selma (G-11285)

House-Autry Mills Inc............................ E 919 963-6200
Four Oaks (G-4813)

Lakeside Mills Inc................................. F 828 286-4866
Spindale (G-11547)

FOOD PRDTS: Dips, Exc Cheese & Sour Cream Based

Apex Salsa Company............................ G 919 363-1486
Apex (G-137)

FOOD PRDTS: Dough, Pizza, Prepared

Boonville Flour Feed Mill Inc................. G 336 367-7541
Boonville (G-957)

Romanos Pizza...................................... G 704 782-5020
Concord (G-3434)

FOOD PRDTS: Dried & Dehydrated Fruits, Vegetables & Soup Mix

Dehydration LLC.................................... G 252 747-8200
Snow Hill (G-11479)

Naturesrules Inc................................... G 336 427-2526
Madison (G-7994)

Osage Pecan Company......................... F 660 679-6137
West Jefferson (G-12569)

FOOD PRDTS: Edible fats & oils

American Cltvtion Extrction Sv.............. G 336 544-1072
Greensboro (G-5355)

Bunge Oils Inc...................................... E 910 293-7917
Warsaw (G-12358)

FOOD PRDTS: Edible Oil Prdts, Exc Corn Oil

Herbs Gaia Inc...................................... D 828 884-4242
Brevard (G-972)

FOOD PRDTS: Flour

Lindley Mills Inc.. G 336 376-6190
Graham (G-5275)

FOOD PRDTS: Flour & Other Grain Mill Products

Archer-Daniels-Midland Company.......... E 704 332-3165
Charlotte (G-1691)

Archer-Daniels-Midland Company.......... C 910 457-5011
Southport (G-11516)

Murphy-Brown LLC................................... G 252 221-4463
Hobbsville (G-6884)

New Carbon Company LLC...................... G 574 247-2270
Hickory (G-6401)

FOOD PRDTS: Flour Mixes & Doughs

Dominos Pizza LLC................................... F 910 424-4884
Fayetteville (G-4588)

FOOD PRDTS: Fruit Juices

Milkco Inc... B 828 254-8428
Asheville (G-547)

FOOD PRDTS: Gelatin Dessert Preparations

Pregel America Inc................................... C 704 707-0300
Concord (G-3421)

FOOD PRDTS: Ice, Cubes

Ice Cube Recording Studios.................... G 910 260-7616
Wilmington (G-12812)

FOOD PRDTS: Mixes, Bread & Bread-Type Roll

Proximity Foods Corporation.................. G 336 691-1700
Greensboro (G-5769)

FOOD PRDTS: Mixes, Gravy, Dry

Bost Distributing Company Inc............... G 919 775-5931
Sanford (G-11158)

FOOD PRDTS: Mixes, Pancake From Purchased Flour

Julias Southern Foods LLC..................... G 919 609-6745
Raleigh (G-10226)

Lovegrass Kitchen Inc............................. F 919 205-8426
Holly Springs (G-6906)

FOOD PRDTS: Mixes, Sauces, Dry

American Miso Company Inc................... F 828 287-2940
Rutherfordton (G-10974)

FOOD PRDTS: Mixes, Seasonings, Dry

Julias Southern Foods LLC..................... G 919 609-6745
Raleigh (G-10226)

FOOD PRDTS: Mustard, Prepared

Lusty Monk LLC....................................... G 828 645-5056
Asheville (G-540)

FOOD PRDTS: Oils & Fats, Marine

Neptune Hlth Wllness Innvtion............... C 888 664-9166
Conover (G-3541)

FOOD PRDTS: Olive Oil

Olive Beaufort Oil Company.................... G 252 504-2474
Beaufort (G-731)

Olive Euro Oil LLC................................... G 336 310-4624
Kernersville (G-7290)

Oliventures Inc.. G 800 231-2619
Raleigh (G-10345)

FOOD PRDTS: Pasta, Uncooked, Packaged With Other Ingredients

Lc Foods LLC... G 919 510-6688
Raleigh (G-10250)

FOOD PRDTS: Peanut Butter

Morven Partners LP................................ E 252 482-2193
Edenton (G-4369)

Peanut Processors Inc........................... F 910 862-2136
Dublin (G-3832)

Peanut Processors Sherman Inc........... G 910 862-2136
Dublin (G-3833)

Universal Blanchers LLC......................... D 252 482-2112
Edenton (G-4372)

FOOD PRDTS: Pickles, Vinegar

Dana Fancy Foods................................... G 828 685-2937
Hendersonville (G-6201)

Mount Olive Pickle Company.................. G 704 867-5585
Gastonia (G-5104)

Mount Olive Pickle Company Inc........... E 704 867-5585
Gastonia (G-5105)

Mount Olive Pickle Company Inc........... C 919 658-2535
Mount Olive (G-9257)

FOOD PRDTS: Pork Rinds

American Skin Food Group LLC............. E 910 259-2232
Burgaw (G-1018)

Julias Southern Foods LLC..................... G 919 609-6745
Raleigh (G-10226)

Skin Boys LLC... F 910 259-2232
Burgaw (G-1031)

FOOD PRDTS: Potato Chips & Other Potato-Based Snacks

Golden Pop Shop LLC............................. G 704 236-9455
Charlotte (G-2224)

Igh Enterprises Inc................................. F 704 372-6744
Charlotte (G-2310)

FOOD PRDTS: Poultry, Processed, Cooked

Integra Foods LLC................................... F 910 984-2007
Bladenboro (G-877)

FOOD PRDTS: Poultry, Processed, Frozen

Advancepierre Foods Inc........................ A 828 459-7626
Claremont (G-3087)

FOOD PRDTS: Poultry, Slaughtered & Dressed

Johnson Nash & Sons Farms Inc........... B 910 289-3113
Rose Hill (G-10907)

Perdue Farms Incorporated................... A 910 997-8600
Rockingham (G-10785)

Tyson Foods Inc...................................... C 336 838-2171
Wilkesboro (G-12658)

FOOD PRDTS: Raw cane sugar

Golding Farms Foods Inc........................ D 336 766-6161
Winston Salem (G-13179)

FOOD PRDTS: Sandwiches

Advancepierre Foods Inc........................ A 828 459-7626
Claremont (G-3087)

FOOD PRDTS: Seasonings & Spices

Cool Runnings Jamaican LLC................. G 919 818-9220
Raleigh (G-10015)

Signature Seasonings LLC...................... G 252 746-1001
Ayden (G-661)

FOOD PRDTS: Soup Mixes

Anns House of Nuts................................ G 252 795-6500
Robersonville (G-10765)

FOOD PRDTS: Tea

Kimbees Inc... G 336 323-8773
Greensboro (G-5647)

Kloud Hemp Co.. G 336 740-2528
Greensboro (G-5651)

Natures Cup LLC..................................... G 910 795-2700
Raeford (G-9843)

Wallingford Coffee Mills Inc................... D 513 771-3131
Concord (G-3466)

FOOD PRDTS: Tortilla Chips

Gruma Corporation.................................. E 919 778-5553
Goldsboro (G-5220)

R W Garcia Co Inc................................... E 828 428-0115
Lincolnton (G-7850)

FOOD PRDTS: Turkey, Slaughtered & Dressed

House of Raeford Farms Inc................... A 912 222-4090
Rose Hill (G-10906)

FOOD PRDTS: Vinegar

Johnson Harn Vngar Gee GL Pllc.......... F 919 213-6163
Raleigh (G-10220)

FOOD PRDTS: Wheat Flour

Bartlett Milling Company LP................... D 704 872-9581
Statesville (G-11667)

Midstate Mills Inc................................... C 828 464-1611
Newton (G-9482)

FOOD PRODUCTS MACHINERY

AC Corporation....................................... B 336 273-4472
Greensboro (G-5339)

Are Management LLC.............................. E 336 855-7800
High Point (G-6526)

Babington Technology Inc...................... G 252 984-0349
Rocky Mount (G-10823)

Buhler Inc.. C 800 722-7483
Cary (G-1316)

Cates Mechanical Corporation............... G 704 458-5163
Charlotte (G-1866)

Designtek Fabrication Inc....................... F 910 359-0130
Red Springs (G-10666)

Flagstone Foods LLC.............................. B 252 795-6500
Robersonville (G-10767)

Fmp Equipment Corp............................. G 336 621-2882
Browns Summit (G-992)

Gea Intec LLC.. E 919 433-0131
Durham (G-4044)

Griffin Marketing Group.......................... G 336 558-5802
Greensboro (G-5580)

Induction Food Systems Inc................... G 919 907-0179
Raleigh (G-10188)

Jbt Aerotech Services............................. G 336 740-3737
Greensboro (G-5635)

Jbt Marel Corporation............................. G 919 362-8811
Apex (G-171)

Krispy Kreme Doughnut Corp................ E 336 726-8908
Winston Salem (G-13227)

Marshall Middleby Inc............................ D 919 762-1000
Fuquay Varina (G-4887)

Meadows Mills Inc................................... E 336 838-2282
North Wilkesboro (G-9546)

PRODUCT

Sinnovatek Inc...................................... G 919 694-0974
Raleigh *(G-10479)*

Smart Machine Technologies Inc............ D 276 632-9853
Greensboro *(G-5817)*

SPX Flow Inc.. C 704 752-4400
Charlotte *(G-2847)*

SPX Flow Tech Systems Inc................... A 704 752-4400
Charlotte *(G-2849)*

Utsey Duskie & Associates..................... G 704 663-0036
Mooresville *(G-8789)*

FOOD STORES: Convenience, Independent

B & D Enterprises Inc........................... G 704 739-2958
Kings Mountain *(G-7348)*

Rose Ice & Coal Company....................... G 910 762-2464
Wilmington *(G-12902)*

FOOD STORES: Cooperative

Communitys Kitchen L3c........................ G 828 817-2308
Tryon *(G-12173)*

Whole Harvest Foods LLC....................... E 910 293-7917
Warsaw *(G-12369)*

FOOD STORES: Grocery, Independent

Bluff Mountain Outfitters Inc.................. G 828 622-7162
Hot Springs *(G-6932)*

FOOD STORES: Supermarkets, Chain

Harris Teeter LLC................................ D 704 846-7117
Matthews *(G-8115)*

Harris Teeter LLC................................ D 919 859-0110
Raleigh *(G-10156)*

Ingles Markets Incorporated.................. D 704 434-0096
Boiling Springs *(G-885)*

Ruddick Operating Company LLC.......... A 704 372-5404
Charlotte *(G-2742)*

FOOTWEAR, WHOLESALE: Athletic

Implus Footcare LLC............................. B 800 446-7587
Durham *(G-4073)*

FOOTWEAR, WHOLESALE: Boots

McRae Industries Inc............................ C 910 439-6149
Mount Gilead *(G-9203)*

FOOTWEAR: Cut Stock

Quarter Turn LLC................................. G 336 712-0811
Clemmons *(G-3201)*

FORGINGS: Aircraft, Ferrous

Chatham Steel Corporation.................... E 912 233-4182
Durham *(G-3970)*

FORGINGS: Automotive & Internal Combustion Engine

Victory 1 Performance Inc...................... F 704 799-1955
Mooresville *(G-8791)*

FORGINGS: Construction Or Mining Eqpt, Ferrous

Volvo Motor Graders Inc........................ G 704 609-3604
Charlotte *(G-2990)*

FORGINGS: Iron & Steel

Component Sourcing Intl LLC.................. E 704 843-9292
Charlotte *(G-1967)*

FORGINGS: Nonferrous

GKN Driveline North Amer Inc................ C 919 708-4500
Sanford *(G-11184)*

FORGINGS: Nuclear Power Plant, Ferrous

Consolidated Pipe & Sup Co Inc............ F 336 294-8577
Greensboro *(G-5463)*

FORGINGS: Plumbing Fixture, Nonferrous

Entrust Services LLC........................... F 336 274-5175
Greensboro *(G-5523)*

FORMS: Concrete, Sheet Metal

Form Tech Concrete Forms Inc............... E 704 395-9910
Charlotte *(G-2172)*

M&N Construction Supply Inc................. G 336 996-7740
Colfax *(G-3283)*

FOUNDRIES: Aluminum

Cascade Die Casting Group Inc............. C 336 882-0186
High Point *(G-6564)*

Dynacast LLC...................................... E 704 927-2790
Charlotte *(G-2072)*

RCM Industries Inc.............................. C 828 286-4003
Rutherfordton *(G-10991)*

FOUNDRIES: Gray & Ductile Iron

Ej Usa Inc... G 919 362-7744
Apex *(G-154)*

FOUNDRIES: Nonferrous

Tru-Cast Inc.. E 336 294-2370
Greensboro *(G-5881)*

United Brass Works Inc......................... C 336 498-2661
Randleman *(G-10663)*

FOUNDRIES: Steel

Coder Foundry..................................... G 704 910-3077
Charlotte *(G-1951)*

Harris Rebar Inc.................................. G 919 528-8333
Benson *(G-792)*

Nucor Corporation............................... C 252 356-3700
Cofield *(G-3268)*

Seven Cast.. G 704 335-0692
Charlotte *(G-2791)*

FRAMES & FRAMING WHOLESALE

Four Corners Frmng Gallery Inc............. G 704 662-7154
Mooresville *(G-8667)*

T Distribution NC Inc............................ E 828 438-1112
Morganton *(G-8903)*

FRAMES: Chair, Metal

Precision Partners LLC.......................... G 704 560-6442
Charlotte *(G-2657)*

FRANCHISES, SELLING OR LICENSING

22nd Century Group Inc........................ F 716 270-1523
Mocksville *(G-8345)*

Body Shop Inc..................................... C 919 554-4900
Wake Forest *(G-12265)*

Ohio Mat Lcnsing Cmpnnts Group......... G 336 861-3500
Trinity *(G-12118)*

FREIGHT FORWARDING ARRANGEMENTS

Elizabeth Logistic LLC.......................... D 803 920-3931
Indian Trail *(G-7078)*

Rapid Run Transport LLC....................... F 704 615-3458
Charlotte *(G-2690)*

FRICTION MATERIAL, MADE FROM POWDERED METAL

Em2 Machine Corporation...................... G 336 707-8409
Greensboro *(G-5518)*

FRUITS & VEGETABLES WHOLESALERS: Fresh

Aseptia Inc.. C 678 373-6751
Raleigh *(G-9919)*

FUEL ADDITIVES

Carolina Bg.. G 704 847-8840
Matthews *(G-8101)*

FUEL DEALERS: Coal

Herrin Bros Coal & Ice Co...................... G 704 332-2193
Charlotte *(G-2275)*

FUEL OIL DEALERS

Euliss Oil Company Inc......................... G 336 622-3055
Liberty *(G-7766)*

Go Energies LLC.................................. F 877 712-5999
Wilmington *(G-12790)*

Go Energies Holdings Inc...................... G 910 762-5802
Wilmington *(G-12791)*

Herrin Bros Coal & Ice Co...................... G 704 332-2193
Charlotte *(G-2275)*

Hickman Oil & Ice Co Inc....................... G 910 576-2501
Troy *(G-12161)*

M & R Retreading & Oil Co Inc............... G 704 474-4101
Norwood *(G-9556)*

Parker Gas Company Inc........................ F 800 354-7250
Clinton *(G-3238)*

Starflite Companies Inc......................... C 252 728-2690
Beaufort *(G-735)*

FUEL TREATING

Opw Fueling Components Inc.................. E 919 464-4569
Smithfield *(G-11458)*

FUELS: Diesel

Sinowest Mfg LLC................................. G 919 289-9337
Raleigh *(G-10481)*

FUELS: Nuclear

Ge-Hitchi Nclear Enrgy Amrcas.............. A 910 819-5000
Castle Hayne *(G-1500)*

Ge-Hitchi Nclear Enrgy Intl LL............... E 518 433-4338
Wilmington *(G-12783)*

Global Laser Enrichment LLC................. D 910 819-7255
Wilmington *(G-12787)*

Global Nuclear Fuel LLC........................ F 910 819-6181
Wilmington *(G-12788)*

Global Nuclear Fuel-Americas LLC........ E 910 819-5950
Castle Hayne *(G-1501)*

FUELS: Nuclear, Uranium Slug, Radioactive

General Electric Company...................... A 910 675-5000
Wilmington *(G-12785)*

FULLER'S EARTH MINING

Profile Products LLC............................. D 828 327-4165
Conover *(G-3552)*

FUND RAISING ORGANIZATION, NON-FEE BASIS

Ipas.. C 919 967-7052
Durham *(G-4082)*

FUNGICIDES OR HERBICIDES

Scotts Company LLC............................. G 704 663-6088
Mooresville *(G-8767)*

Summit Agro Usa LLC........................... G 984 260-0407
Durham *(G-4254)*

FURNACES & OVENS: Indl

Buhler Inc..................................... C 800 722-7483
Cary *(G-1316)*

Industrial Prcess Slutions Inc..... G 336 926-1511
Wilkesboro *(G-12639)*

Southeastern Installation Inc....... E 704 352-7146
Lexington *(G-7744)*

FURNACES: Warm Air, Electric

Lennox International Inc................ C 828 633-4805
Candler *(G-1229)*

Thermo Products LLC.................... E 800 348-5130
Denton *(G-3763)*

FURNITURE COMPONENTS: Porcelain Enameled

Hunt Country Component LLC......... G 336 475-7000
Thomasville *(G-12034)*

Vrush Industries Inc..................... G 336 886-7700
High Point *(G-6829)*

FURNITURE PARTS: Metal

M & M Frame Company Inc............ G 336 859-8166
Denton *(G-3757)*

Problem Solver Inc...................... F 919 596-5555
Raleigh *(G-10399)*

Timmerman Manufacturing Inc....... F 828 464-1778
Conover *(G-3566)*

FURNITURE REFINISHING SVCS

Barker and Martin Inc................. G 336 275-5056
Greensboro *(G-5385)*

FURNITURE REPAIR & MAINTENANCE SVCS

Brice Manufacturing Co Inc.......... E 818 896-2938
Greensboro *(G-5398)*

Otto and Moore Inc..................... F 336 887-0017
High Point *(G-6722)*

Touch Up Solutions Inc............... E 828 428-9094
Maiden *(G-8019)*

FURNITURE STOCK & PARTS: Hardwood

A C Furniture Company Inc........... B 336 623-3430
Eden *(G-4339)*

Appalachian Lumber Company Inc...... E 336 973-7205
Wilkesboro *(G-12628)*

Ariston Hospitality Inc............... E 626 458-8668
High Point *(G-6528)*

Bruex Inc................................. E 828 754-1186
Lenoir *(G-7589)*

Carolina Leg Supply LLC.............. G 828 446-6838
Hudson *(G-6947)*

Curved Plywood Inc.................... G 336 249-6901
Lexington *(G-7674)*

Hughes Furniture Inds Inc........... C 336 498-8700
Randleman *(G-10650)*

Latham Inc............................... G 336 857-3702
Denton *(G-3754)*

M & S Warehouse Inc.................. E 828 728-3733
Lenoir *(G-7622)*

Mc Gees Crating Inc................... E 828 758-4660
Lenoir *(G-7626)*

Oak City Customs LLC................. G 919 995-5561
Zebulon *(G-13517)*

Pilot View Wood Works Inc........... G 336 883-2511
High Point *(G-6733)*

Quality Fabricators.................... G 336 622-3402
Staley *(G-11599)*

Rudisill Frame Shop Inc.............. E 828 464-7020
Newton *(G-9492)*

Ruskin Inc............................... G 828 324-6500
Hickory *(G-6436)*

Select Frame Shop Inc................ D 910 428-1225
Biscoe *(G-857)*

Sure Wood Products Inc.............. G 828 261-0004
Hickory *(G-6461)*

Valendrawers Inc....................... E 336 956-2118
Lexington *(G-7756)*

Woodline Inc............................. G 336 476-7100
Thomasville *(G-12090)*

Woodwright of Wilson Co Inc........ G 252 243-9663
Elm City *(G-4468)*

FURNITURE STOCK & PARTS: Turnings, Wood

Adams Wood Turning Inc............. G 336 882-0196
High Point *(G-6509)*

B & E Woodturning Inc................ G 828 758-2843
Lenoir *(G-7575)*

Ideaitlia Cntmporary Furn Corp...... C 828 464-1000
Conover *(G-3532)*

FURNITURE STORES

Aria Designs LLC....................... F 828 572-4303
Lenoir *(G-7573)*

Bassett Furniture Inds NC LLC...... A 828 465-7700
Newton *(G-9451)*

Bernhardt Furniture Company....... E 828 759-6205
Lenoir *(G-7584)*

Burrough Furniture.................... G 336 841-3129
Archdale *(G-215)*

Carolina Chair Inc..................... F 828 459-1330
Conover *(G-3499)*

Distinctive Furniture Inc............. G 828 754-3947
Lenoir *(G-7600)*

Ethan Allen Retail Inc................ E 828 428-9361
Maiden *(G-8012)*

Furniture Fair Inc...................... E 910 455-4044
Jacksonville *(G-7124)*

Hfi Wind Down Inc..................... C 828 438-5767
Morganton *(G-8872)*

Ideaitlia Cntmporary Furn Corp...... C 828 464-1000
Conover *(G-3532)*

Keani Furniture Inc.................... E 336 303-5484
Asheboro *(G-369)*

Lexington Furniture Inds Inc........ C 336 474-5300
Thomasville *(G-12043)*

M & S Warehouse Inc.................. E 828 728-3733
Lenoir *(G-7622)*

McNeillys Inc............................ E 704 300-1712
Lawndale *(G-7518)*

Miters Touch Inc....................... G 828 963-4445
Banner Elk *(G-688)*

Neil Allen Industries Inc............. G 336 887-6500
High Point *(G-6717)*

O Henry House Ltd..................... E 336 431-5350
Archdale *(G-239)*

Olde Lexington Products Inc......... G 336 956-2355
Linwood *(G-7880)*

Royal Colony Furniture Inc.......... G 336 472-8833
Thomasville *(G-12067)*

Sides Furniture Inc.................... G 336 869-5509
High Point *(G-6769)*

Smartway of Carolinas LLC........... G 704 900-7877
Charlotte *(G-2817)*

Tatum Galleries Inc.................... G 828 963-6466
Banner Elk *(G-689)*

Verellen Inc............................. E 336 889-7379
High Point *(G-6824)*

Woodwright of Wilson Co Inc........ G 252 243-9663
Elm City *(G-4468)*

World Art Gallery Incorporated...... G 910 989-0203
Jacksonville *(G-7160)*

Yukon Inc................................ F 919 366-2001
Wendell *(G-12554)*

FURNITURE WHOLESALERS

Apollo Designs LLC..................... E 336 886-0260
High Point *(G-6524)*

Ashley Furniture Inds LLC........... E 336 998-1066
Advance *(G-31)*

Brookline Furniture Co Inc........... D 336 841-8503
Archdale *(G-214)*

Funder America Inc.................... F 336 751-3501
Mocksville *(G-8364)*

Furniture At Work...................... G 336 472-6619
Trinity *(G-12114)*

Lexington Furniture Inds Inc........ C 336 474-5300
Thomasville *(G-12043)*

Lodging By Liberty Inc................ C 336 622-2201
Siler City *(G-11417)*

Minhas Furniture House Inc......... E 910 898-0808
Robbins *(G-10754)*

Prepac Manufacturing US LLC...... F 800 665-1266
Whitsett *(G-12617)*

Prime Mill LLC.......................... F 336 819-4300
High Point *(G-6746)*

Simplicity Sofas Inc................... G 800 813-2889
High Point *(G-6775)*

Stone Marble Co Inc................... G 773 227-1161
Thomasville *(G-12075)*

Vrush Industries Inc................... G 336 886-7700
High Point *(G-6829)*

Watauga Creek LLC..................... G 828 369-7881
Franklin *(G-4842)*

FURNITURE, HOUSEHOLD: Wholesalers

Carolina Csual Otdoor Furn Inc...... F 252 491-5171
Jarvisburg *(G-7185)*

Century Furniture LLC.................. C 828 267-8739
Hickory *(G-6302)*

Elite Furniture Mfg Inc................ G 336 882-0406
High Point *(G-6606)*

French Heritage Inc.................... F 336 882-3565
High Point *(G-6622)*

Ison Furniture Mfg Inc................ E 336 476-4700
Thomasville *(G-12040)*

Magnussen Home Furnishings Inc...... G 336 841-4424
Greensboro *(G-5671)*

Mongoose LLC........................... F 919 400-0772
Burlington *(G-1130)*

Rbc Inc................................... C 336 861-5800
Sophia *(G-11490)*

Southandenglish LLC................... G 336 888-8333
High Point *(G-6786)*

Woodwright of Wilson Co Inc........ G 252 243-9663
Elm City *(G-4468)*

FURNITURE, MATTRESSES: Wholesalers

Affordable Bedding Inc................ G 828 254-5555
Asheville *(G-424)*

Bekaertdeslee USA Inc................ B 336 747-4900
Winston Salem *(G-13103)*

Mattress Firm........................... G 252 443-1259
Rocky Mount *(G-10851)*

FURNITURE, OFFICE: Wholesalers

Artistic Frame Corp.................... B 212 289-2100
Kannapolis *(G-7202)*

Con-Tab Inc.............................. F 336 476-0104
Thomasville *(G-12011)*

Office Sup Svcs Inc Charlotte....... E 704 786-4677
Concord *(G-3410)*

Professinal Sales Associates................. G 336 210-2756
High Point *(G-6748)*

Unique Office Solutions Inc................. F 336 854-0900
Greensboro *(G-5890)*

FURNITURE, OUTDOOR & LAWN: Wholesalers

Outer Banks Hammocks Inc.................. F 910 256-4001
Wilmington *(G-12869)*

FURNITURE, WHOLESALE: Beds & Bedding

Amor Furniture and Bedding LLC......... F 336 795-0044
Liberty *(G-7760)*

Welcome Industrial Corp...................... D 336 329-9640
Burlington *(G-1178)*

FURNITURE, WHOLESALE: Chairs

Chateau DAx USA Ltd....................... G 336 885-9777
High Point *(G-6567)*

Jerry Blevins.................................... G 336 384-3726
Lansing *(G-7477)*

FURNITURE, WHOLESALE: Lockers

Penco Products Inc............................. C 252 798-4000
Hamilton *(G-6049)*

FURNITURE, WHOLESALE: Racks

Rack Works Inc................................. E 336 368-1302
Pilot Mountain *(G-9673)*

Wood Technology Inc......................... E 828 464-8049
Conover *(G-3577)*

FURNITURE: Assembly Hall

Beaufurn LLC................................... E 336 768-2544
High Point *(G-6543)*

FURNITURE: Bedroom, Wood

Gram Furniture.................................. G 828 241-2836
Claremont *(G-3114)*

Homestead Country Built Furn............. G 910 799-6489
Wilmington *(G-12807)*

Hooker Furnishings Corporation........... C 336 819-7200
High Point *(G-6662)*

Lea Industries Inc............................. C 336 294-5233
Hudson *(G-6954)*

Philip Brady.................................... G 336 581-3999
Bennett *(G-782)*

FURNITURE: Bedsprings, Assembled

Comfort Bay Home Fashions Inc.......... G 843 442-7477
Hickory *(G-6305)*

FURNITURE: Box Springs, Assembled

Cotton Belt Inc................................. D 252 689-6847
Greenville *(G-5960)*

Ohio Mat Lcnsing Cmpnnts Group........ G 336 861-3500
Trinity *(G-12118)*

FURNITURE: Cabinets & Filing Drawers, Office, Exc Wood

Blue-Hen Inc.................................... G 407 322-2262
Asheville *(G-458)*

L B Plastics LLC............................... D 704 663-1543
Mooresville *(G-8706)*

Sdv Office Systems LLC...................... F 844 968-9500
Fletcher *(G-4766)*

FURNITURE: Chairs & Couches, Wood, Upholstered

Dal Leather Inc................................. G 828 302-1667
Conover *(G-3511)*

Images of America Inc....................... D 336 475-7106
Thomasville *(G-12038)*

Southfield Ltd.................................. F 336 434-6220
High Point *(G-6789)*

Wise Living Inc................................. F 336 991-5346
High Point *(G-6838)*

FURNITURE: Chairs, Household Upholstered

Aria Designs LLC.............................. F 828 572-4303
Lenoir *(G-7573)*

Bradington-Young LLC........................ C 704 435-5881
Hickory *(G-6275)*

Brookline Furniture Co Inc.................. D 336 841-8503
Archdale *(G-214)*

C R Laine Furniture Co Inc.................. C 828 328-1831
Hickory *(G-6278)*

Century Furniture LLC........................ D 828 326-8458
Hickory *(G-6298)*

Century Furniture LLC........................ F 828 326-8495
Hickory *(G-6301)*

D R Kincaid Chair Co Inc.................... E 828 754-0255
Lenoir *(G-7599)*

Directional Buying Group Inc............... G 336 472-6187
Thomasville *(G-12019)*

Fairfield Chair Company..................... E 828 785-5571
Lenoir *(G-7605)*

Fairfield Chair Company..................... C 828 758-5571
Lenoir *(G-7606)*

Furniture Concepts............................ F 828 323-1590
Hickory *(G-6336)*

Grand Manor Furniture Inc.................. D 828 758-5521
Lenoir *(G-7608)*

Hdm Furniture Industries Inc............... A 800 349-4579
Hickory *(G-6344)*

International Furnishings Inc................ G 336 472-8422
Thomasville *(G-12039)*

Jack Cartwright Incorporated.............. E 336 889-9400
High Point *(G-6676)*

Jessica Charles LLC.......................... D 336 434-2124
High Point *(G-6678)*

Keani Furniture Inc............................ E 336 303-5484
Asheboro *(G-369)*

Kellex Corp..................................... C 828 874-0389
Valdese *(G-12196)*

Lee Industries LLC............................ C 828 464-8318
Newton *(G-9479)*

LLC Ferguson Copeland...................... C 828 584-0664
Morganton *(G-8879)*

McNeillys Inc................................... E 704 300-1712
Lawndale *(G-7518)*

Paul Robert Chair Inc........................ D 828 632-7021
Taylorsville *(G-11969)*

Prominence Furniture Inc.................... E 336 475-6505
Thomasville *(G-12063)*

Smith Novelty Company Inc................. G 704 982-7413
Albemarle *(G-89)*

Stone & Leigh LLC............................ G 919 971-2096
Morganton *(G-8901)*

Style Upholstering Inc........................ G 828 322-4882
Hickory *(G-6460)*

Verellen Inc.................................... E 336 889-7379
High Point *(G-6824)*

Whitewood Contracts LLC.................... E 336 885-9300
High Point *(G-6834)*

FURNITURE: Chairs, Household Wood

A C Furniture Company Inc.................. B 336 623-3430
Eden *(G-4339)*

A E Nesbitt Woodwork........................ G 828 625-2428
Black Mountain *(G-859)*

American of High Point Inc.................. F 336 431-1513
High Point *(G-6521)*

Baker Interiors Furniture Co................ G 336 431-9115
High Point *(G-6537)*

Baker Interiors Furniture Co................ D 336 431-9115
Connelly Springs *(G-3473)*

Barber Furniture & Supply................... F 704 278-9367
Cleveland *(G-3209)*

Barker and Martin Inc........................ G 336 275-5056
Greensboro *(G-5385)*

Bassett Furniture Direct Inc................ F 704 979-5700
Concord *(G-3318)*

Bernhardt Furniture Company.............. D 828 759-6652
Lenoir *(G-7580)*

Bernhardt Furniture Company.............. D 828 758-9811
Lenoir *(G-7581)*

Bernhardt Furniture Company.............. E 828 759-6205
Lenoir *(G-7584)*

Bernhardt Industries Inc..................... C 828 758-9811
Lenoir *(G-7585)*

Boggs Collective Inc.......................... G 828 398-9701
Asheville *(G-459)*

Bookcase Shop.................................. G 919 683-1922
Durham *(G-3938)*

Bradington-Young LLC........................ C 276 656-3335
Cherryville *(G-3059)*

Brown Cabinet Co.............................. G 704 933-2731
Kannapolis *(G-7205)*

Cabinet Makers Inc............................ G 704 876-2808
Statesville *(G-11674)*

Carolina Business Furn Inc.................. A 336 431-9400
High Point *(G-6556)*

Carroll Russell Mfg Inc....................... E 919 779-2273
Raleigh *(G-9982)*

Century Furniture LLC........................ D 828 326-8410
Hickory *(G-6295)*

Century Furniture LLC........................ C 828 326-8201
Hickory *(G-6296)*

Century Furniture LLC........................ D 828 326-8535
Hickory *(G-6297)*

Century Furniture LLC........................ G 336 889-8286
High Point *(G-6566)*

Chf Industries Inc............................. E 212 951-7800
Charlotte *(G-1912)*

Chris Isom Inc.................................. F 336 629-0240
Asheboro *(G-338)*

Classic Leather Inc............................ B 828 328-2046
Conover *(G-3504)*

Councill Company LLC........................ C 336 859-2155
Denton *(G-3745)*

Craftmaster Furniture Inc.................... A 828 632-8127
Hiddenite *(G-6495)*

Cv Industries Inc............................... G 828 328-1851
Hickory *(G-6316)*

Davis Furniture Industries Inc.............. C 336 889-2009
High Point *(G-6589)*

Design Workshop Incorporated............. F 910 293-7329
Warsaw *(G-12359)*

Drexel Heritage Furnishings................. G 828 391-6400
Lenoir *(G-7601)*

Easyglass Inc................................... G 336 786-1800
Mount Airy *(G-9118)*

Ethan Allen Retail Inc........................ E 828 428-9361
Maiden *(G-8012)*

Fairfield Chair Company..................... E 828 785-5571
Lenoir *(G-7605)*

Fairfield Chair Company..................... C 828 758-5571
Lenoir *(G-7606)*

Fulfords Restorations......................... G 252 243-7727
Wilson *(G-12992)*

Furniture Company............................ G 910 686-1937
Wilmington *(G-12781)*

G A Lankford Construction.................. G 828 254-2467
Alexander (G-100)

Guy Chaddock and Company LLC........ C 828 584-0664
Morganton (G-8869)

H & H Furniture Mfrs Inc.................... C 336 873-7245
Seagrove (G-11274)

Hancock & Moore LLC....................... C 828 495-8235
Taylorsville (G-11963)

Hdm Furniture Industries Inc.............. C 336 882-8135
Hickory (G-6343)

Hdm Furniture Industries Inc.............. A 800 349-4579
Hickory (G-6344)

Hfi Wind Down Inc............................ C 828 430-3355
Morganton (G-8873)

Hickory Chair Company...................... D 800 225-0265
Hickory (G-6349)

HM Frame Company Inc..................... E 828 428-3354
Newton (G-9472)

Hollingswrth Cbnets Intrors LL............ F 910 251-1490
Castle Hayne (G-1502)

Home Meridian Group LLC.................. D 336 819-7200
High Point (G-6660)

Home Meridian Holdings Inc............... C 336 887-1985
High Point (G-6661)

Ison Furniture Mfg Inc....................... E 336 476-4700
Thomasville (G-12040)

Johnston Casuals Furniture Inc........... D 336 838-5178
North Wilkesboro (G-9538)

Kenzie Layne Company...................... G 704 485-2282
Locust (G-7894)

Kincaid Furniture Company Inc........... D 828 728-3261
Hudson (G-6953)

Kolcraft Enterprises Inc..................... C 910 944-9345
Aberdeen (G-10)

Kustom Kraft Wdwrks Mt Airy In.......... G 336 786-2831
Mount Airy (G-9143)

Lacquer Craft Hospitality Inc.............. G 336 822-8086
High Point (G-6689)

Leathercraft Inc............................... C 828 322-3305
Conover (G-3536)

Leisure Craft Holdings LLC................. D 828 693-8241
Flat Rock (G-4708)

Leisure Craft Inc.............................. C 828 693-8241
Flat Rock (G-4709)

Linwood Inc..................................... G 336 300-8307
Lexington (G-7712)

Magnussen Home Furnishings Inc........ G 336 841-4424
Greensboro (G-5671)

Martin Obrien Cabinetmaker............... G 336 773-1334
Winston Salem (G-13245)

Michael Parker Cabinetry................... G 919 833-5117
Raleigh (G-10298)

Nobscot Construction Co Inc............... G 919 929-2075
Chapel Hill (G-1560)

Oak City Customs LLC....................... G 919 995-5561
Zebulon (G-13517)

Old Wood Company........................... G 828 259-9663
Asheville (G-559)

One Furniture Group Corp.................. G 336 235-0221
Greensboro (G-5722)

Phoenix Home Furnishings Inc............ C
High Point (G-6730)

Precast Terrazzo Entps Inc................. E 919 231-6200
Raleigh (G-10388)

Precision Materials LLC...................... F 828 632-8851
Taylorsville (G-11972)

Quality Contemporary Furniture.......... G 919 758-7277
Raleigh (G-10414)

Ralph S Frame Works Inc................... D 336 431-2168
High Point (G-6753)

Robert Bergelin Company................... E 828 437-6409
Morganton (G-8892)

Royal Colony Furniture Inc................. G 336 472-8833
Thomasville (G-12067)

Ruskin Inc...................................... G 828 324-6500
Hickory (G-6436)

Sherrill Furniture Company................ B 828 322-2640
Hickory (G-6441)

South Mountain Crafts....................... G 828 433-2607
Morganton (G-8899)

Southern Finishing Company Inc.......... F 336 573-3741
Stoneville (G-11828)

Stanley Furniture Company LLC........... C 336 884-7700
High Point (G-6791)

Stone Marble Co Inc......................... G 773 227-1161
Thomasville (G-12075)

Style Upholstering Inc...................... G 828 322-4882
Hickory (G-6460)

Superior Wood Products Inc............... G 336 472-2237
Thomasville (G-12076)

Tatum Galleries Inc.......................... G 828 963-6466
Banner Elk (G-689)

Thayer Coggin Inc............................ D 336 841-6000
High Point (G-6805)

The Southwood Furniture Corporation.. G 828 465-1776
Hickory (G-6465)

Tiger Mountain Woodworks Inc............ F 828 526-5577
Highlands (G-6846)

Treeforms Inc.................................. E 336 292-8998
Greensboro (G-5871)

Troutman Careconnect Corp............... F 704 838-9389
Troutman (G-12152)

Tsai Winddown Inc........................... E 704 873-3106
Statesville (G-11794)

Unigel Inc...................................... G 828 228-2095
Hickory (G-6479)

Universal Furniture Intl Inc................ G 828 241-3191
Claremont (G-3123)

Uwharrie Chair Company LLC.............. G 336 431-2055
High Point (G-6820)

Vaughan-Bassett Furn Co Inc.............. A 336 835-2670
Elkin (G-4453)

Vaughan-Bassett Furn Co Inc.............. A 336 889-9111
High Point (G-6822)

Wesley Hall Inc............................... E 828 324-7466
Conover (G-3573)

Willow Creek Furniture Inc................. G 828 889-0076
High Point (G-6835)

Winston Concept Furniture................. G 336 472-7839
Thomasville (G-12088)

Wise Living Inc................................ F 336 991-5346
High Point (G-6838)

Wood N Things................................ G 910 990-4448
Clinton (G-3254)

Woodsmiths Company........................ G 406 626-3102
Lenoir (G-7646)

Xylem Inc....................................... G 919 772-4126
Garner (G-4976)

Yorkshire House Inc......................... G 336 869-9714
High Point (G-6841)

Yukon Inc....................................... F 919 366-2001
Wendell (G-12554)

FURNITURE: Chairs, Household, Metal

Powder River Technologies Inc............ G 828 465-2894
Newton (G-9489)

FURNITURE: Chairs, Office Wood

Carolina House Furniture Inc.............. E 828 459-7400
Claremont (G-3090)

Davis Furniture Industries Inc............. C 336 889-2009
High Point (G-6589)

High Point Furniture Inds Inc.............. D 336 431-7101
High Point (G-6653)

Thomasville Upholstery Inc................. C 828 345-6225
Hickory (G-6467)

FURNITURE: Church

Gram Furniture................................ G 828 241-2836
Claremont (G-3114)

FURNITURE: Couches, Sofa/Davenport, Upholstered Wood Frames

Bernhardt Furniture Company............. C 828 758-9811
Lenoir (G-7582)

Contemporary Furnishings Corp........... D 704 633-8000
Salisbury (G-11037)

Craftmaster Furniture Inc.................. A 828 632-8127
Hiddenite (G-6495)

Craftmaster Furniture Inc.................. B 828 632-9786
Hiddenite (G-6494)

E J Victor Inc.................................. C 828 437-1991
Morganton (G-8861)

Framewright Inc.............................. G 828 459-2284
Conover (G-3523)

H W S Company Inc.......................... B 828 322-8624
Hickory (G-6341)

HM Liquidation Inc........................... G 828 495-8235
Hickory (G-6361)

Joseph Halker.................................. G 336 769-4734
Winston Salem (G-13219)

King Hickory Furniture Company.......... G 828 324-0472
Hickory (G-6378)

King Hickory Furniture Company.......... C 828 322-6025
Hickory (G-6379)

Lee Industries LLC........................... C 828 464-8318
Newton (G-9480)

Lee Industries LLC........................... B 828 464-8318
Conover (G-3537)

Sherrill Furniture Company................ B 828 322-2640
Hickory (G-6441)

Temple Inc..................................... D 828 428-8031
Maiden (G-8018)

The Southwood Furniture Corporation.. G 828 465-1776
Hickory (G-6465)

Thomasville Upholstery Inc................. C 828 345-6225
Hickory (G-6467)

Universal Furniture Limited................ D 336 822-8888
High Point (G-6819)

Vanguard Furniture Co Inc................. B 828 328-5601
Conover (G-3571)

FURNITURE: Dining Room, Wood

Bernhardt Furniture Company............. C 828 758-9811
Lenoir (G-7582)

Designmaster Furniture Inc................ E 828 324-7992
Hickory (G-6322)

E J Victor Inc.................................. C 828 437-1991
Morganton (G-8861)

Universal Furniture Limited................ D 336 822-8888
High Point (G-6819)

FURNITURE: Fiberglass & Plastic

Built To Last NC LLC......................... F 252 232-0055
Moyock (G-9277)

Carolina Casting Inc......................... G 336 884-7311
High Point (G-6557)

Keter Us Inc................................... D 704 263-1967
Stanley (G-11620)

FURNITURE: Garden, Exc Wood, Metal, Stone Or Concrete

Joseph Sotanski.............................. E 407 324-6187
Marion (G-8047)

PRODUCT

Riverwood Inc.. E 336 956-3034
Lexington *(G-7735)*

FURNITURE: Hotel

Contemporary Furnishings Corp........... D 704 633-8000
Salisbury *(G-11037)*

Distinction Hospitality Inc..................... F 336 875-3043
High Point *(G-6594)*

Iv-S Metal Stamping Inc......................... E 336 861-2100
Archdale *(G-229)*

Lee Industries LLC................................. B 828 464-8318
Conover *(G-3537)*

Neil Allen Industries Inc......................... G 336 887-6500
High Point *(G-6717)*

FURNITURE: Household, Metal

Biologics Inc... G 919 546-9810
Raleigh *(G-9945)*

Creative Metal and Wood Inc................. G 336 475-9400
Colfax *(G-3276)*

Hickory Springs Mfg Co......................... G 828 325-4757
Hickory *(G-6358)*

Leisure Craft Holdings LLC.................... D 828 693-8241
Flat Rock *(G-4708)*

Leisure Craft Inc.................................... C 828 693-8241
Flat Rock *(G-4709)*

Timmerman Manufacturing Inc............... F 828 464-1778
Conover *(G-3566)*

FURNITURE: Household, Upholstered, Exc Wood Or Metal

Bull City Designs LLC............................ E 919 908-6252
Durham *(G-3949)*

Creative Metal and Wood Inc................. G 336 475-9400
Colfax *(G-3276)*

French Heritage Inc............................... F 336 882-3565
High Point *(G-6622)*

Wise Living Inc....................................... F 323 541-0410
High Point *(G-6837)*

FURNITURE: Juvenile, Upholstered On Wood Frames

Kolcraft Enterprises Inc......................... C 910 944-9345
Aberdeen *(G-10)*

FURNITURE: Laboratory

Kewaunee Scientific Corp....................... A 704 873-7202
Statesville *(G-11724)*

FURNITURE: Lawn, Exc Wood, Metal, Stone Or Concrete

Suncast Corporation............................... E 704 274-5394
Huntersville *(G-7059)*

FURNITURE: Living Room, Upholstered On Wood Frames

Berkeley Home Furniture LLC................ G 336 882-0012
High Point *(G-6546)*

Cedar Rock Home Furnishings............... G 828 396-2361
Hudson *(G-6948)*

Century Furniture LLC............................ C 828 267-8739
Hickory *(G-6302)*

Cotton Belt Inc....................................... D 252 689-6847
Greenville *(G-5960)*

Hughes Furniture Inds Inc...................... C 336 498-8700
Randleman *(G-10650)*

Key City Furniture Company Inc............. C 336 818-1161
Wilkesboro *(G-12646)*

March Furniture Manufacturing Inc........ C 336 824-4413
Ramseur *(G-10629)*

Masterfield Furniture Co Inc................... E 828 632-8535
Taylorsville *(G-11967)*

McCreary Modern Inc............................. B 828 464-6465
Newton *(G-9481)*

Overnight Sofa Corporation.................... E 828 324-2271
Hickory *(G-6408)*

Select Furniture Company Inc................ F 336 886-3572
High Point *(G-6767)*

Swaim Inc... C 336 885-6131
High Point *(G-6797)*

Universal Furniture Intl Inc..................... C 828 464-0311
Conover *(G-3570)*

Violino USA Ltd...................................... E 336 889-6623
High Point *(G-6826)*

Younger Furniture Inc............................. D 336 476-0444
Thomasville *(G-12096)*

FURNITURE: Mattresses & Foundations

Comfort Sleep LLC................................ G 336 267-5853
Thomasville *(G-12010)*

L C Industries Inc.................................. C 919 596-8277
Fayetteville *(G-4629)*

L C Industries Inc.................................. C 919 596-8277
Durham *(G-4100)*

Somnigroup International Inc................... C 336 861-2900
Trinity *(G-12126)*

FURNITURE: Mattresses, Box & Bedsprings

Affordable Bedding Inc.......................... G 828 254-5555
Asheville *(G-424)*

Arden Companies LLC............................ D 919 258-3081
Sanford *(G-11150)*

Bjmf Inc.. E 704 554-6333
Charlotte *(G-1787)*

Carolina Mattress Guild Inc.................... D 336 841-8529
Thomasville *(G-12004)*

Culp Inc.. D 336 885-2800
Stokesdale *(G-11810)*

Iredell Fiber Inc..................................... F 704 878-0884
Statesville *(G-11717)*

Jones Frame Inc..................................... E 336 434-2531
High Point *(G-6679)*

Leggett & Platt Incorporated.................. C 336 379-7777
Greensboro *(G-5660)*

Leggett & Platt Incorporated.................. D 336 884-4306
High Point *(G-6690)*

Leggett & Platt Incorporated.................. G 855 853-3539
Lexington *(G-7709)*

Leggett & Platt Incorporated.................. F 336 622-0121
Liberty *(G-7770)*

Leggett & Platt Incorporated.................. E 828 322-6855
Conover *(G-3538)*

Leggett & Platt Incorporated.................. C 336 889-2600
High Point *(G-6691)*

Mattress Firm... G 252 443-1259
Rocky Mount *(G-10851)*

Reliable Quilting Company...................... G 336 886-7036
High Point *(G-6756)*

Stn Cushion Company............................ D 336 476-9100
Thomasville *(G-12074)*

Timeless Bedding Inc............................. G 336 472-6603
Lexington *(G-7752)*

Vaughan-Bassett Furn Co Inc................ A 336 835-2670
Elkin *(G-4453)*

FURNITURE: Mattresses, Innerspring Or Box Spring

Dilworth Mattress Company Inc............. G 704 333-6564
Charlotte *(G-2049)*

Kingsdown Incorporated......................... E 919 563-3531
Mebane *(G-8247)*

Kingsdown Acquisition Corp................... G 919 563-3531
Mebane *(G-8248)*

Ohio-Sealy Mattress Mfg Co................. C 336 861-3500
Trinity *(G-12119)*

Reliable Bedding Company..................... F 336 883-0648
Archdale *(G-241)*

Riverside Mattress Co Inc...................... E 910 483-0461
Fayetteville *(G-4662)*

Royale Komfort Bedding Inc................... G 828 632-5631
Taylorsville *(G-11975)*

Sealy Corporation................................... C 336 861-3500
Trinity *(G-12123)*

Sealy Mattress Company........................ C 336 861-3500
Trinity *(G-12124)*

Spring Air Mattress Corp....................... D 336 272-1141
Greensboro *(G-5831)*

Ssb Manufacturing Company................. C 704 596-4935
Charlotte *(G-2853)*

FURNITURE: Novelty, Wood

Artisans Guild Incorporated................... G 336 841-4140
High Point *(G-6530)*

Riverview Cabinet & Supply Inc............. G 336 228-1486
Burlington *(G-1148)*

FURNITURE: Office, Exc Wood

A C Furniture Company Inc.................... B 336 623-3430
Eden *(G-4339)*

Abercrombie Textiles I LLC.................... F 704 487-1245
Shelby *(G-11309)*

Advocacy To Allvate Hmlessness.......... G 919 810-3431
Raleigh *(G-9882)*

Bernhardt Furniture Company................ D 828 759-6245
Lenoir *(G-7579)*

Bernhardt Furniture Company................ E 828 759-6205
Lenoir *(G-7584)*

Bernhardt Industries Inc........................ C 828 758-9811
Lenoir *(G-7585)*

Buzzispace Inc....................................... G 336 821-3150
Winston Salem *(G-13114)*

Davidson House Inc............................... F 704 791-0171
Davidson *(G-3701)*

Davis Furniture Industries Inc................ C 336 889-2009
High Point *(G-6589)*

Delve Interiors LLC................................ C 336 274-4661
Greensboro *(G-5495)*

Frazier Holdings LLC............................. G 919 868-8651
Clayton *(G-3148)*

Haworth Inc.. E 828 328-5600
Conover *(G-3527)*

Images of America Inc........................... D 336 475-7106
Thomasville *(G-12038)*

Intensa Inc... G 336 884-4003
High Point *(G-6674)*

Kn Furniture Inc..................................... E 336 953-3259
Ramseur *(G-10626)*

Leathercraft Inc..................................... C 828 322-3305
Conover *(G-3536)*

Old Hickory Tannery Inc........................ E 828 465-6599
Newton *(G-9484)*

Sbfi-North America Inc.......................... F 828 236-3993
Asheville *(G-596)*

Studio Tk LLC.. E 919 464-2920
Clayton *(G-3172)*

Unique Office Solutions Inc................... F 336 854-0900
Greensboro *(G-5890)*

Wheatstone Corporation......................... D 252 638-7000
New Bern *(G-9405)*

FURNITURE: Office, Wood

A C Furniture Company Inc.................... B 336 623-3430
Eden *(G-4339)*

Amcase Inc.. E 336 784-5992
High Point *(G-6519)*

Bernhardt Furniture Company................ D 828 759-6245
Lenoir *(G-7579)*

Bernhardt Furniture Company................ D 828 758-9811
Lenoir *(G-7581)*

Bernhardt Furniture Company................ E 828 759-6205
Lenoir *(G-7584)*

Bernhardt Industries Inc........................ ..... 828 758-9811
Lenoir *(G-7585)*

Boss Design US Inc................................ G 844 353-7834
High Point *(G-6550)*

Bull City Designs LLC............................ E 919 908-6252
Durham *(G-3949)*

Cbt Supply.. G 803 617-8230
Mooresville *(G-8636)*

Classic Leather Inc................................ B 828 328-2046
Conover *(G-3504)*

Comm-Kab Inc.. F 336 873-8787
Asheboro *(G-340)*

Corilam Fabricating Co.......................... E 336 993-2371
Kernersville *(G-7259)*

Darran Furniture Inds Inc...................... C 336 861-2400
High Point *(G-6588)*

Delve Interiors LLC................................ C 336 274-4661
Greensboro *(G-5495)*

Geiger International Inc.......................... F 828 324-6500
Hildebran *(G-6850)*

Hancock & Moore LLC............................ C 828 495-8235
Taylorsville *(G-11963)*

Harris House Furn Inds Inc.................... E 336 431-2802
Archdale *(G-225)*

Haworth Inc.. E 828 328-5600
Conover *(G-3527)*

Hickory Business Furniture LLC............ B 828 328-2064
Hickory *(G-6348)*

Idx Impressions LLC.............................. C 703 550-6902
Washington *(G-12393)*

Ie Furniture Inc...................................... E 336 475-5050
Archdale *(G-227)*

Jasper Seating Company Inc................. C 704 528-4506
Troutman *(G-12142)*

Leathercraft Inc..................................... C 828 322-3305
Conover *(G-3536)*

Michael Parker Cabinetry...................... G 919 833-5117
Raleigh *(G-10298)*

Ofm LLC.. D 919 303-6389
Holly Springs *(G-6909)*

Parker Southern Inc.............................. F 828 428-3506
Maiden *(G-8016)*

Precision Materials LLC........................ F 828 632-8851
Taylorsville *(G-11972)*

Prestige Millwork Inc............................ G 910 428-2360
Star *(G-11633)*

Professinal Sales Associates............... G 336 210-2756
High Point *(G-6748)*

Sbfi-North America Inc.......................... F 828 236-3993
Asheville *(G-596)*

Sdv Office Systems LLC........................ F 844 968-9500
Fletcher *(G-4766)*

Triune Business Furniture Inc............... G 336 884-8341
High Point *(G-6812)*

Upholstery Designs Hickory Inc............ G 828 324-2002
Hickory *(G-6480)*

Xylem Inc... G 919 772-4126
Garner *(G-4976)*

FURNITURE: Recliners, Upholstered On Wood Frames

Joerns Healthcare Parent LLC.............. B 800 966-6662
Charlotte *(G-2372)*

FURNITURE: School

Artisans Guild Incorporated................. G 336 841-4140
High Point *(G-6530)*

Custom Educational Furn LLC............... F 800 255-9189
Taylorsville *(G-11956)*

Interior Wood Specialties Inc................ E 336 431-0068
High Point *(G-6675)*

Krueger International Inc....................... F 336 434-5011
High Point *(G-6687)*

Precision Materials LLC........................ F 828 632-8851
Taylorsville *(G-11972)*

FURNITURE: Sleep

Hill-Rom Inc... E 919 854-3600
Cary *(G-1372)*

Roadmster Trck Conversions Inc.......... G 252 412-3980
Grifton *(G-6038)*

FURNITURE: Stadium

Artisan LLC.. G 855 582-3539
Concord *(G-3313)*

Ken Staley Co Inc.................................. G 336 685-4294
Franklinville *(G-4857)*

FURNITURE: Storage Chests, Household, Wood

Liberty Hse Utility Buildings................. G 828 209-3390
Horse Shoe *(G-6929)*

FURNITURE: Table Tops, Marble

Nova Enterprises Inc............................. E 828 687-8770
Arden *(G-290)*

Trade Venture Stones LLC..................... G 919 803-3923
Knightdale *(G-7460)*

Web-Don Incorporated.......................... E 800 532-0434
Charlotte *(G-3009)*

Woodsmiths Company............................ G 406 626-3102
Lenoir *(G-7646)*

FURNITURE: Tables, Household, Metal

Swaim Inc... C 336 885-6131
High Point *(G-6797)*

FURNITURE: Tables, Office, Exc Wood

Con-Tab Inc.. F 336 476-0104
Thomasville *(G-12011)*

FURNITURE: Tables, Office, Wood

Evelyn T Burney..................................... G 336 473-9794
Rocky Mount *(G-10838)*

Ullmanique Inc....................................... G 336 885-5111
High Point *(G-6816)*

FURNITURE: Upholstered

A C Furniture Company Inc.................... B 336 623-3430
Eden *(G-4339)*

AB New Beginnings Inc......................... D 828 465-6953
Conover *(G-3487)*

Amor Furniture and Bedding LLC.......... F 336 795-0044
Liberty *(G-7760)*

Archdale Furniture Distributor.............. G 336 431-1081
Archdale *(G-211)*

Baker Interiors Furniture Co.................. G 336 431-9115
High Point *(G-6537)*

Bassett Furniture Inds NC LLC.............. A 828 465-7700
Newton *(G-9451)*

Bernhardt Furniture Company................ D 828 759-6652
Lenoir *(G-7580)*

Bernhardt Furniture Company................ D 828 758-9811
Lenoir *(G-7581)*

Bernhardt Furniture Company................ D 828 572-4664
Lenoir *(G-7583)*

Bernhardt Furniture Company................ E 828 759-6205
Lenoir *(G-7584)*

Bernhardt Industries Inc........................ C 828 758-9811
Lenoir *(G-7585)*

Blackstone Furniture Inds Inc............... F 910 428-2833
Ether *(G-4494)*

Bradington-Young LLC........................... C 276 656-3335
Cherryville *(G-3059)*

Burrough Furniture................................ G 336 841-3129
Archdale *(G-215)*

Cargill & Pendleton Inc......................... E 336 882-5510
High Point *(G-6555)*

Carolina Chair Inc.................................. F 828 459-1330
Conover *(G-3499)*

Carolina Mills Incorporated................... D 828 428-9911
Maiden *(G-8010)*

Carolina Tape & Supply Corp................ E 828 322-3991
Hickory *(G-6289)*

Century Furniture LLC........................... C 828 326-8201
Hickory *(G-6296)*

Century Furniture LLC........................... D 828 326-8410
Hickory *(G-6299)*

Century Furniture LLC........................... D 828 326-8650
Hickory *(G-6300)*

Chateau DAx USA Ltd............................ G 336 885-9777
High Point *(G-6567)*

Classic Leather Inc................................ B 828 328-2046
Conover *(G-3504)*

Contract Seating Inc.............................. G 828 322-6662
Hickory *(G-6310)*

Councill Company LLC........................... C 336 859-2155
Denton *(G-3745)*

Country At Home Furniture Inc.............. F 828 464-7498
Newton *(G-9461)*

Cox Manufacturing Company Inc........... E 828 397-4123
Hickory *(G-6313)*

Craymer McElwee Holdings Inc............ G 828 326-6100
Hickory *(G-6314)*

Creations By Taylor............................... G 410 269-6430
Mount Pleasant *(G-9261)*

Custom Designs and Upholstery............ F 336 882-1516
Thomasville *(G-12013)*

Cv Industries Inc.................................... G 828 328-1851
Hickory *(G-6316)*

Daniels Woodcarving Co Inc.................. F 828 632-7336
Taylorsville *(G-11958)*

Design Theory LLC................................. F 336 912-0155
High Point *(G-6591)*

Dexter Inc.. G 828 459-7904
Claremont *(G-3106)*

Dexter Inc.. G 919 510-5050
Raleigh *(G-10045)*

Dfp Inc... D 336 841-3028
High Point *(G-6592)*

Distinctive Furniture Inc....................... G 828 754-3947
Lenoir *(G-7600)*

Domenicks Furniture Mfr LLC............... E 336 442-3348
High Point *(G-6596)*

Elite Furniture Mfg Inc.......................... G 336 882-0406
High Point *(G-6606)*

England Inc.. D 336 861-5266
High Point *(G-6612)*

Friendship Upholstery Co Inc................ E 828 632-9836
Taylorsville *(G-11961)*

Geiger International Inc.......................... F 828 324-6500
Hildebran *(G-6850)*

Golden Rctangle Enteprises Inc............ G 828 389-3336
Hayesville *(G-6141)*

Hancock & Moore LLC............................ C 828 495-8235
Taylorsville *(G-11963)*

PRODUCT

Hancock & Moore LLC.................... D 828 495-8235
   Taylorsville *(G-11962)*

Hdm Furniture Industries Inc................ E 336 812-4434
   High Point *(G-6641)*

Hester Enterprises Inc.................... E 704 865-4480
   Gastonia *(G-5060)*

Hfi Wind Down Inc................. C 828 438-5767
   Morganton *(G-8872)*

HM Frame Company Inc................ E 828 428-3354
   Newton *(G-9472)*

Huddle Furniture Inc.................... E 828 874-8888
   Valdese *(G-12195)*

Huntington House Inc.................... E 828 495-4400
   Taylorsville *(G-11965)*

Huntington House Inc.................... C 828 495-4400
   Hickory *(G-6363)*

Indiana Chair Frame Company................ G 574 825-9355
   Liberty *(G-7768)*

Intensa Inc.................... G 336 884-4003
   High Point *(G-6674)*

Isenhour Furniture Company............... D 828 632-8849
   Taylorsville *(G-11966)*

Jarrett Brothers............... G 828 433-8036
   Morganton *(G-8876)*

Kincaid Furniture Company Inc........... D 828 728-3261
   Hudson *(G-6953)*

King Hickory Furniture Company........... G 336 841-6140
   High Point *(G-6685)*

Kn Furniture Inc.................... E 336 953-3259
   Ramseur *(G-10626)*

Lancer Incorporated.................... C 910 428-2181
   Star *(G-11630)*

Lazar Industries LLC.................... C 919 742-9303
   Siler City *(G-11415)*

Lazar Industries East Inc................ C 919 742-9303
   Siler City *(G-11416)*

Leathercraft Inc................... C 828 322-3305
   Conover *(G-3536)*

Level 4 Designs Corp................. G 336 235-3450
   Greensboro *(G-5662)*

Lexington Furniture Inds Inc................ C 336 474-5300
   Thomasville *(G-12043)*

Lloyds Chatham Ltd Partnership........... E 919 742-4692
   High Point *(G-6693)*

Lodging By Liberty Inc................ C 336 622-2201
   Siler City *(G-11417)*

M & M Frame Company Inc............... G 336 859-8166
   Denton *(G-3757)*

Marquis Contract Corporation............... E 336 884-8200
   High Point *(G-6701)*

McKinley Leather Hickory Inc............... E 828 459-2884
   Claremont *(G-3115)*

Minhas Furniture House Inc............... E 910 898-0808
   Robbins *(G-10754)*

Moores Upholstering Interiors............... G 704 240-8393
   Lincolnton *(G-7845)*

NC Custom Leather Inc................ F 828 404-2973
   Conover *(G-3540)*

Nobscot Construction Co Inc................ G 919 929-2075
   Chapel Hill *(G-1560)*

North Carolina Lumber Company........... G 336 498-6600
   Randleman *(G-10654)*

O Henry House Ltd................ E 336 431-5350
   Archdale *(G-239)*

Old Hickory Tannery Inc................ E 828 465-6599
   Newton *(G-9484)*

Paladin Industries Inc................ D 828 635-0448
   Hiddenite *(G-6504)*

Parker Southern Inc................... F 828 428-3506
   Maiden *(G-8016)*

Plat LLC................... F 828 358-4564
   Granite Falls *(G-5317)*

Popes Signature Gallery................ G 828 396-9494
   Hudson *(G-6956)*

R & D Weaving Inc................... F 828 248-1910
   Ellenboro *(G-4460)*

Rbc Inc.................... G 336 889-7573
   High Point *(G-6754)*

Rbc Inc.................... C 336 861-5800
   Sophia *(G-11490)*

Restaurant Furniture Inc................. F 828 459-9992
   Claremont *(G-3120)*

Rhf Investments Inc................ G 828 326-8350
   Hickory *(G-6428)*

Richard Shew.................... F 828 781-3294
   Conover *(G-3554)*

Rowes................... G 828 241-2609
   Catawba *(G-1513)*

Rufco Inc.................... G 919 829-1332
   Wake Forest *(G-12294)*

S Dorsett Upholstery Inc................ G 336 472-7076
   Thomasville *(G-12070)*

Seam-Craft Inc.................... G 336 861-4156
   High Point *(G-6765)*

Seam-Craft Inc.................... F 336 861-4156
   High Point *(G-6766)*

Sherrill Furniture Company................ F 828 322-8624
   Hickory *(G-6439)*

Sherrill Furniture Company................ F 828 328-5241
   Hickory *(G-6440)*

Sherrill Furniture Company................ F 336 884-0974
   High Point *(G-6768)*

Sherrill Furniture Company................ F 828 437-2256
   Morganton *(G-8896)*

Sherrill Furniture Company................ D 828 465-0844
   Newton *(G-9494)*

Sides Furniture Inc................ G 336 869-5509
   High Point *(G-6769)*

Simplicity Sofas Inc................ G 800 813-2889
   High Point *(G-6775)*

Southandenglish LLC................ G 336 888-8333
   High Point *(G-6786)*

Stone Marble Co Inc................ G 773 227-1161
   Thomasville *(G-12075)*

Superior Wood Products Inc................ G 336 472-2237
   Thomasville *(G-12076)*

Taylor King Furniture Inc................ C 828 632-7731
   Taylorsville *(G-11981)*

Tb Arhaus LLC.................... C 828 465-6953
   Conover *(G-3564)*

TCS Designs Inc.................... F 828 324-9944
   Hickory *(G-6463)*

Tomlinson/Erwin-Lambeth Inc................ D 336 472-5005
   Thomasville *(G-12081)*

Universal Furniture Intl Inc................ G 828 241-3191
   Claremont *(G-3123)*

Upholstery Designs Hickory Inc............ G 828 324-2002
   Hickory *(G-6480)*

Vaughan-Bassett Furn Co Inc................ A 336 835-2670
   Elkin *(G-4453)*

Watauga Creek LLC................ C 828 369-7881
   Franklin *(G-4842)*

Wesley Hall Inc.................... C 828 324-7466
   Conover *(G-3573)*

Woodmark Originals Inc................ C 336 841-6409
   High Point *(G-6839)*

FURNITURE: Wicker & Rattan

Acacia Home & Garden Inc................ F 828 465-1700
   Conover *(G-3488)*

Rbc Inc.................... C 336 861-5800
   Sophia *(G-11490)*

FUSES: Electric

Cooper Bussmann LLC.................... C 252 566-0278
   La Grange *(G-7465)*

GAMES & TOYS: Board Games, Children's & Adults'

Banilla Games Inc.................... G 252 329-7977
   Greenville *(G-5945)*

GAMES & TOYS: Craft & Hobby Kits & Sets

Bellalou Designs LLC.................... G 252 360-7866
   Wilson *(G-12970)*

Bougiejones................... G 704 492-3029
   Charlotte *(G-1804)*

Gracefully Gifted Hands LLC................ G 845 248-8743
   Raleigh *(G-10142)*

Jasie Blanks LLC.................... F 910 485-0016
   Fayetteville *(G-4621)*

Kenson Parenting Solutions................ G 919 637-1499
   Wake Forest *(G-12285)*

South Mountain Crafts................ G 828 433-2607
   Morganton *(G-8899)*

GAMES & TOYS: Electronic

Grailgame Inc.................... G 804 517-3102
   Reidsville *(G-10687)*

Wersunsllc.................... G 857 209-8701
   Winston Salem *(G-13388)*

GAMES & TOYS: Erector Sets

All Signs & Graphics LLC................ G 910 323-3115
   Fayetteville *(G-4549)*

GARBAGE CONTAINERS: Plastic

All Source Security Cont Cal................ G 704 504-9908
   Charlotte *(G-1641)*

County of Alexander.................... E 828 632-1101
   Taylorsville *(G-11955)*

Duramax Holdings LLC.................... C 704 588-9191
   Charlotte *(G-2068)*

Schaefer Systems International Inc........ C 704 944-4500
   Charlotte *(G-2763)*

Schaefer Systems Intl Inc................ G 704 944-4500
   Charlotte *(G-2764)*

Schaefer Systems Intl Inc................ G 704 944-4550
   Charlotte *(G-2765)*

Toter LLC.................... D 704 936-5610
   Charlotte *(G-2931)*

Toter LLC.................... E 800 424-0422
   Statesville *(G-11792)*

GAS & OIL FIELD EXPLORATION SVCS

BP Oil Corp Distributors.................... G 828 264-8516
   Boone *(G-902)*

Citi Energy LLC.................... G 336 379-0800
   Greensboro *(G-5445)*

Das Oil Werks LLC.................... G 919 267-5781
   New Hill *(G-9409)*

Energy and Entropy Inc.................... G 919 933-1365
   Chapel Hill *(G-1544)*

EP Nisbet Company.................... G 704 332-7755
   Charlotte *(G-2121)*

Maverick Biofuels.................... G 919 931-1434
   Durham *(G-4120)*

Mpv Morganton Pressu.................... F 828 652-3704
   Marion *(G-8056)*

GAS & OIL FIELD SVCS, NEC

Hari Krupa Oil and Gas LLC................ G 860 805-1704
   Winston Salem *(G-13190)*

Parker Oil Inc.............................. G 828 253-7265
Asheville *(G-567)*

GASES: Acetylene

Airgas Usa LLC........................... F 704 333-5475
Charlotte *(G-1632)*

Andy-OXY Co Inc......................... E 828 258-0271
Asheville *(G-426)*

GASES: Indl

Airgas Usa LLC........................... G 704 394-1420
Charlotte *(G-1633)*

Airgas Usa LLC........................... G 919 544-3773
Durham *(G-3885)*

Airgas Usa LLC........................... G 919 735-5276
Goldsboro *(G-5196)*

Airgas Usa LLC........................... G 910 392-2711
Wilmington *(G-12694)*

Arc3 Gases Inc........................... G 919 772-9500
Durham *(G-3897)*

Arc3 Gases Inc........................... G 336 275-3333
Greensboro *(G-5367)*

Arc3 Gases Inc........................... G 704 220-1029
Monroe *(G-8429)*

Arc3 Gases Inc........................... E 910 892-4016
Dunn *(G-3844)*

East Coast Oxygen Inc................. G 828 252-7770
Asheville *(G-490)*

James Oxygen and Supply Co........ E 704 322-5438
Hickory *(G-6374)*

Legacy Biogas LLC...................... G 713 253-9013
Goldsboro *(G-5223)*

Messer LLC................................ E 908 464-8100
Midland *(G-8290)*

Noahs Inc.................................. F 704 718-2354
Charlotte *(G-2570)*

GASES: Nitrogen

Linde Gas & Equipment Inc........... F 919 380-7411
Cary *(G-1389)*

Linde Gas & Equipment Inc........... F 704 587-7096
Charlotte *(G-2424)*

Linde Gas & Equipment Inc........... F 866 543-3427
Whitsett *(G-12612)*

Linde Inc.................................. G 910 343-0241
Wilmington *(G-12836)*

Matheson Tri-Gas Inc................... F 919 556-6461
Wake Forest *(G-12286)*

GASES: Oxygen

Linde Gas & Equipment Inc........... D 919 549-0633
Durham *(G-4105)*

Messer LLC................................ G 704 583-0313
Charlotte *(G-2494)*

GASKETS

Carolina Components Group Inc...... E 919 635-8438
Durham *(G-3960)*

CGR Products Inc........................ D 336 621-4568
Greensboro *(G-5439)*

Michael Simmons........................ G 704 298-1103
Concord *(G-3401)*

Mueller Die Cut Solutions Inc......... E 704 588-3900
Charlotte *(G-2526)*

SAS Industries Inc...................... F 631 727-1441
Elizabeth City *(G-4409)*

Southern Rubber Company Inc....... E 336 299-2456
Greensboro *(G-5827)*

Universal Rubber Products Inc........ G 704 483-1249
Denver *(G-3815)*

GASKETS & SEALING DEVICES

Coltec Industries Inc.................... A 704 731-1500
Charlotte *(G-1961)*

Enpro Inc.................................. C 704 731-1500
Charlotte *(G-2115)*

Henniges Automotive N Amer Inc.... C 336 342-9300
Reidsville *(G-10688)*

Pfaff Molds Ltd Partnership........... F 704 423-9484
Charlotte *(G-2631)*

GASOLINE FILLING STATIONS

College Sun Do............................ G 910 521-9189
Pembroke *(G-9657)*

Murphy USA Inc........................... E 828 758-7055
Lenoir *(G-7628)*

GASOLINE WHOLESALERS

Euliss Oil Company Inc................. G 336 622-3055
Liberty *(G-7766)*

Herrin Bros Coal & Ice Co.............. G 704 332-2193
Charlotte *(G-2275)*

GEARS

Ketchie-Houston Inc..................... E 704 786-5101
Concord *(G-3390)*

Tim Conner Enterprises Inc............ E 704 629-4327
Bessemer City *(G-835)*

GEARS & GEAR UNITS: Reduction, Exc Auto

Perfection Gear Inc...................... D 828 253-0000
Asheville *(G-570)*

GEARS: Power Transmission, Exc Auto

Carolina Keller LLC...................... C 252 237-8181
Wilson *(G-12978)*

Linamar Forgings Carolina Inc........ D 252 237-8181
Wilson *(G-13003)*

Martin Sprocket & Gear Inc............ F 817 258-3000
Albemarle *(G-81)*

Martin Sprocket & Gear Inc............ E 704 394-9111
Charlotte *(G-2464)*

Nord Gear Corporation.................. G 888 314-6673
Charlotte *(G-2571)*

GENERATION EQPT: Electronic

Ametek Electronics Systems........... F 800 645-9721
Knightdale *(G-7448)*

Ekc Advanced Elec USA 4 LLC........ G 302 774-1000
Wilmington *(G-12770)*

Equagen Engineers Pllc................ E 919 444-5442
Raleigh *(G-10090)*

Ifanatic LLC.............................. G 919 387-6062
Apex *(G-166)*

Laird Thermal Systems Inc............ E 919 597-7300
Morrisville *(G-9002)*

North Fork Electric Inc................. G 336 982-4020
Crumpler *(G-3661)*

Power Integrity Corp.................... E 336 379-9773
Greensboro *(G-5752)*

Powergpu LLC............................ F 919 702-6757
Youngsville *(G-13481)*

Powersecure International Inc......... A 919 556-3056
Wake Forest *(G-12289)*

Team Manufacturing - E W LLC....... D 919 554-2442
Youngsville *(G-13491)*

GENERATOR REPAIR SVCS

Allan Drth Sons Gnrtor Sls Svc....... G 828 526-9325
Highlands *(G-6842)*

Genelect Services Inc................... F 828 255-7999
Asheville *(G-505)*

GENERATORS SETS: Steam

Catamount Energy Corporation....... F 802 773-6684
Charlotte *(G-1865)*

GIFT SHOP

A Stitch In Time........................... G 828 274-5193
Asheville *(G-422)*

Burlington Outlet.......................... G 910 278-3442
Oak Island *(G-9564)*

Carolina Perfumer Inc................... G 910 295-5600
Pinehurst *(G-9688)*

James Lammers........................... G 252 491-2303
Powells Point *(G-9822)*

Jkl Inc...................................... F 252 355-6714
Greenville *(G-5996)*

Michael S North Wilkesboro Inc....... G 336 838-5964
North Wilkesboro *(G-9547)*

Oleksynprannyk LLC.................... F 704 450-0182
Mooresville *(G-8738)*

Starflite Companies Inc................. C 252 728-2690
Beaufort *(G-735)*

GIFT, NOVELTY & SOUVENIR STORES: Gifts & Novelties

Simple & Sentimental LLC............. G 252 320-9458
Ayden *(G-662)*

GLASS PRDTS, FROM PURCHASED GLASS: Insulating

Press Glass Inc........................... E 336 573-2393
Stoneville *(G-11826)*

GLASS PRDTS, FROM PURCHASED GLASS: Mirrored

Cgmi Acquisition Company LLC....... F 919 533-6123
Kernersville *(G-7255)*

Gardner Glass Products Inc........... F 336 838-2151
North Wilkesboro *(G-9530)*

Gardner Glass Products Inc........... C 336 651-9300
North Wilkesboro *(G-9531)*

Glass Works of Hickory Inc............ G 828 322-2122
Hickory *(G-6339)*

Lenoir Mirror Company.................. C 828 728-3271
Lenoir *(G-7620)*

GLASS PRDTS, FROM PURCHASED GLASS: Windshields

Florida Marine Tanks Inc............... F 305 620-9030
Henderson *(G-6155)*

GLASS PRDTS, FROM PURCHD GLASS: Strengthened Or Reinforced

PPG Industries Inc....................... G 919 772-3093
Greensboro *(G-5755)*

GLASS PRDTS, PRESSED OR BLOWN: Furnishings & Access

Decor Glass Specialties Inc........... G 828 586-8180
Sylva *(G-11891)*

GLASS PRDTS, PRESSED OR BLOWN: Scientific Glassware

M 5 Scentific Glassblowing Inc........ G 704 663-0101
Mooresville *(G-8716)*

GLASS PRDTS, PRESSED OR BLOWN: Yarn, Fiberglass

Employee Codes: A=Over 500 employees, B=251-500
C=101-250, D=51-100, E=20-50, F=10-19, G=1-9   2025 Harris North Carolina
Manufacturers Directory   1125

PRODUCT

Spt Technology Inc .... F 612 332-1880
Monroe (G-8561)

GLASS, AUTOMOTIVE: Wholesalers

Oldcastle Infrastructure Inc .... E 919 772-6269
Raleigh (G-10344)

GLASS: Broadwoven Fabrics

Nouveau Verre Holdings Inc .... F 336 545-0011
Greensboro (G-5714)

Nvh Inc .... G 336 545-0011
Greensboro (G-5717)

GLASS: Fiber

Corning Incorporated .... F 828 465-0016
Newton (G-9460)

Corning Incorporated .... F 252 316-4500
Tarboro (G-11924)

Corning Incorporated .... E 336 771-8000
Winston Salem (G-13131)

Mateenbar USA Inc .... E 704 662-2005
Concord (G-3399)

Piedmont Well Covers Inc .... F 704 664-8488
Mount Ulla (G-9270)

PPG Industries Inc .... G 919 772-3093
Greensboro (G-5755)

GLASS: Flat

A R Perry Corporation .... G 252 492-6181
Henderson (G-6146)

Corning Incorporated .... D 704 569-6000
Midland (G-8284)

Pgw Auto Glass LLC .... B 336 258-4950
Elkin (G-4451)

Pilkington North America Inc .... E 910 276-5630
Laurinburg (G-7511)

PPG Industries Inc .... G 919 772-3093
Greensboro (G-5755)

GLASS: Leaded

Custom Glass Works Inc .... G 704 597-0290
Charlotte (G-2009)

GLASS: Optical

Optometric Eyecare Center Inc .... G 910 326-3050
Swansboro (G-11888)

GLASS: Pressed & Blown, NEC

Bridgestone Americas Inc .... C 984 888-0413
Durham (G-3940)

Corning Optcal Cmmncations LLC .... B 336 771-8000
Winston Salem (G-13132)

Easyglass Inc .... G 336 786-1800
Mount Airy (G-9118)

Heraeus Quartz North Amer LLC .... E 910 799-6230
Wilmington (G-12804)

PPG-Devold LLC .... G 704 434-2261
Shelby (G-11370)

Preformed Line Products Co .... C 704 983-6161
Albemarle (G-84)

Spruce Pine Batch Inc .... G 828 765-9876
Spruce Pine (G-11588)

GLASS: Tempered

Cardinal CT Company .... E 336 719-6857
Mount Airy (G-9106)

GLASSWARE: Laboratory

Norell Inc .... G 828 584-2600
Morganton (G-8885)

Prism Research Glass Inc .... F 919 571-0078
Raleigh (G-10397)

GLOVES: Safety

Gloves-Online Inc .... G 919 468-4244
Cary (G-1367)

Ingle Protective Systems Inc .... G 704 788-3327
Concord (G-3377)

GLOVES: Work

American Made Products Inc .... F 252 747-2010
Hookerton (G-6921)

Carolina Glove Company .... E 828 464-1132
Conover (G-3500)

Southern Glove Inc .... B 828 464-4884
Newton (G-9497)

United Glove Inc .... E 828 464-2510
Newton (G-9508)

GOLF EQPT

Arnolds Welding Service Inc .... E 910 323-3822
Fayetteville (G-4553)

Custom Golf Car Supply Inc .... C 704 855-1130
Salisbury (G-11042)

Golf Shop .... G 704 636-7070
Salisbury (G-11057)

Revels Turf and Tractor LLC .... E 919 552-5697
Fuquay Varina (G-4896)

GOLF GOODS & EQPT

I Must Garden LLC .... G 919 929-2299
Raleigh (G-10182)

Land and Loft LLC .... G 315 560-7060
Raleigh (G-10244)

GOURMET FOOD STORES

Bakers Southern Traditions Inc .... G 252 344-2120
Roxobel (G-10949)

Blazing Foods LLC .... G 336 865-2933
Charlotte (G-1789)

Blue Ridge Jams .... G 828 685-1783
Hendersonville (G-6187)

Induction Food Systems Inc .... G 919 907-0179
Raleigh (G-10188)

Stormberg Foods LLC .... E 919 947-6011
Goldsboro (G-5247)

GRADING SVCS

Barnhill Contracting Company .... D 910 488-1319
Fayetteville (G-4557)

Carolina Paving Hickory Inc .... G 828 328-3909
Hickory (G-6285)

Carolina Paving Hickory Inc .... E 828 322-1706
Hickory (G-6286)

Cjc Enterprises .... E 919 266-3158
Wake Forest (G-12270)

Macleod Construction Inc .... C 704 483-3580
Charlotte (G-2446)

GRANITE: Crushed & Broken

Alamo North Texas Railroad Co .... G 919 787-9504
Raleigh (G-9888)

Blue Rock Materials LLC .... F 828 479-3581
Robbinsville (G-10757)

Charlotte Instyle Inc .... E 704 665-8880
Charlotte (G-1894)

Georgia-Carolina Quarries Inc .... E 336 786-6978
Mount Airy (G-9123)

Heidelberg Mtls Sthast Agg LLC .... E 910 893-8308
Bunnlevel (G-1016)

Heidelberg Mtls Sthast Agg LLC .... F 910 893-2111
Lillington (G-7797)

Heidelberg Mtls Sthast Agg LLC .... G 252 222-0812
Morehead City (G-8834)

Legacy Vulcan LLC .... G 704 788-7833
Concord (G-3391)

Legacy Vulcan LLC .... G 828 255-8561
Enka (G-4487)

Luck Stone Corporation .... E 336 786-4693
Mount Airy (G-9149)

Marietta Martin Materials Inc .... G 704 278-2218
Woodleaf (G-13429)

Martin Marietta Materials Inc .... G 336 584-8875
Burlington (G-1123)

Martin Marietta Materials Inc .... G 919 863-4305
Raleigh (G-10276)

Martin Marietta Materials Inc .... C 919 781-4550
Raleigh (G-10277)

Meridian Granite Company .... G 919 781-4550
Raleigh (G-10292)

Wake Stone Corp .... G 252 985-4411
Battleboro (G-708)

Wake Stone Corporation .... E 919 775-7349
Moncure (G-8412)

GRANITE: Cut & Shaped

Amanzi Marble & Granite LLC .... G 336 993-9998
Kernersville (G-7242)

Apex Marble and Granite Inc .... E 919 462-9202
Morrisville (G-8929)

Bloomday Granite & Marble Inc .... E 336 724-0300
Winston Salem (G-13108)

Carolina Quarries Inc .... D 704 633-0201
Salisbury (G-11028)

Creative Stone Fyetteville Inc .... F 910 491-1225
Fayetteville (G-4580)

King Stone Innovation LLC .... G 704 352-1134
Charlotte (G-2398)

Kitchen Man Inc .... F 910 408-1322
Winnabow (G-13067)

Mables Headstone & Monu Co LLP .... G 919 724-8705
Creedmoor (G-3652)

Master Tesh Stone Works .... G 828 898-8333
Banner Elk (G-687)

GRAPHIC ARTS & RELATED DESIGN SVCS

A Plus Graphics Inc .... G 252 243-0404
Wilson (G-12960)

Advertising Design Systems Inc .... G 828 264-8060
Boone (G-894)

Brandilly of Nc Inc .... G 919 278-7896
Raleigh (G-9957)

Connected 2k LLC .... G 910 321-7446
Fayetteville (G-4578)

Fast Pro Media LLC .... G 704 799-8040
Cornelius (G-3599)

Graphic Components LLC .... E 336 542-2128
Greensboro (G-5572)

Graphic Image of Cape Fear Inc .... G 910 313-6768
Wilmington (G-12795)

Idx Impressions LLC .... C 703 550-6902
Washington (G-12393)

JKS Motorsports Inc .... G 336 722-4129
Winston Salem (G-13217)

Kathie S Mc Daniel .... G 336 835-1544
Elkin (G-4446)

Kreber .... D 336 861-2700
High Point (G-6686)

Logo Wear Graphics LLC .... F 336 382-0455
Summerfield (G-11841)

Mark/Trece Inc .... E 336 292-3424
Whitsett (G-12614)

Signs Etc .... G 336 722-9341
Winston Salem (G-13337)

Studio Displays Inc .... F 704 588-6590
Pineville (G-9761)

Tannis Root Productions Inc .... G 919 832-8552
Raleigh *(G-10533)*

Timothy L Griffin .... G 336 317-8314
Greenville *(G-6028)*

Village Graphics .... G 252 745-4600
Oriental *(G-9603)*

Zebra Communications Inc .... E 919 314-3700
Morrisville *(G-9093)*

GRASSES: Artificial & Preserved

Plantd Inc .... D 434 906-3445
Oxford *(G-9624)*

GRAVE VAULTS, METAL

Winston-Salem Casket Company .... G 336 661-1695
Winston Salem *(G-13403)*

GREENHOUSES: Prefabricated Metal

Carolina Greenhouse Plants Inc .... G 252 523-9300
Kinston *(G-7398)*

Lock Drives Inc .... G 704 588-1844
Pineville *(G-9740)*

Van Wingerden Grnhse Co Inc .... E 828 891-7389
Mills River *(G-8323)*

Williamson Greenhouses Inc .... G 910 592-7072
Clinton *(G-3253)*

GRINDING SVC: Precision, Commercial Or Indl

Intelligent Tool Corp .... F 704 799-0449
Concord *(G-3378)*

GROCERIES, GENERAL LINE WHOLESALERS

USa Wholesale and Distrg Inc .... F 888 484-6872
Fayetteville *(G-4693)*

GUIDANCE SYSTEMS & EQPT: Space Vehicle

Firstmark Aerospace Corp .... D 919 956-4200
Creedmoor *(G-3648)*

GUIDED MISSILES & SPACE VEHICLES

End Camp North .... F 980 337-4600
Charlotte *(G-2112)*

GUM & WOOD CHEMICALS

Soto Industries LLC .... G 706 643-5011
Charlotte *(G-2828)*

Westrock Mwv LLC .... G 919 334-3200
Raleigh *(G-10606)*

GUTTERS: Sheet Metal

Beacon Roofing Supply Inc .... G 704 886-1555
Charlotte *(G-1763)*

Clt 2016 Inc .... D 704 886-1555
Charlotte *(G-1933)*

Triangle Installation Svc Inc .... G 919 363-7637
Apex *(G-201)*

GYPSUM PRDTS

Ng Operations LLC .... D 704 916-2082
Charlotte *(G-2566)*

Precision Walls Inc .... G 336 852-7710
Greensboro *(G-5759)*

Proform Finishing Products LLC .... E 704 398-3900
Mount Holly *(G-9243)*

Proform Finishing Products LLC .... B 704 365-7300
Charlotte *(G-2674)*

HAIR & HAIR BASED PRDTS

Brittany Smith .... G 912 313-0588
Greensboro *(G-5407)*

CCI Hair Boutique LLC .... F 407 216-9213
Hope Mills *(G-6925)*

E Cache & Co LLC .... F 919 590-0779
Charlotte *(G-2080)*

Gifted Hands Styling Salon .... G 828 781-2781
Hickory *(G-6338)*

Johnny Slicks Inc .... G 910 803-2159
Holly Ridge *(G-6890)*

Pashes LLC .... G 704 682-6535
Statesville *(G-11743)*

Z Collection LLC .... G 919 247-1513
Zebulon *(G-13526)*

HAIR CARE PRDTS

Blaq Beauty Naturalz Inc .... G 252 326-5621
Weldon *(G-12519)*

O Grayson Company .... E 704 932-6195
Kannapolis *(G-7217)*

Procter & Gamble Mfg Co .... B 336 954-0000
Browns Summit *(G-1004)*

Rebecca Trickey .... G 910 584-5549
Raeford *(G-9850)*

Salonexclusive Beauty LLC .... G 704 488-3909
Charlotte *(G-2750)*

Virtue Labs LLC .... G 844 782-4247
Raleigh *(G-10590)*

HAIR DRESSING, FOR THE TRADE

Ruth Hicks Enterprise Inc .... F 704 469-4741
Waxhaw *(G-12439)*

HAMPERS: Solid Fiber, Made From Purchased Materials

Westrock Rkt LLC .... C 336 661-7180
Winston Salem *(G-13394)*

HANDBAGS

Blacqueladi Styles LLC .... G 877 977-7798
Cary *(G-1308)*

HANDBAGS: Women's

Designed For Joy .... F 919 395-2884
Apex *(G-150)*

Glaser Designs Inc .... F 415 552-3188
Raleigh *(G-10136)*

HANDLES: Brush Or Tool, Plastic

Balcrank Corporation .... E 800 747-5300
Weaverville *(G-12483)*

HANDYMAN SVCS

Darius All Access LLC .... E 910 262-8567
Wilmington *(G-12759)*

HANG GLIDERS

Ride Best LLC .... G 252 489-2959
Rodanthe *(G-10888)*

HARDWARE

Alloy Fabricators Inc .... E 704 263-2281
Alexis *(G-102)*

Amesbury Acqstion Hldngs 2 Inc .... C 704 924-8586
Statesville *(G-11654)*

Amesbury Group Inc .... D 704 924-7694
Statesville *(G-11656)*

Appalchian Stove Fbrcators Inc .... G 828 253-0164
Asheville *(G-428)*

Balcrank Corporation .... E 800 747-5300
Weaverville *(G-12483)*

Blum Inc .... G 919 345-6214
Oak Ridge *(G-9570)*

CSC Family Holdings Inc .... G 336 993-2680
Colfax *(G-3278)*

Endura Products LLC .... E 336 991-8818
High Point *(G-6610)*

Industrial Mtal Pdts Abrdeen I .... F 910 944-8110
Aberdeen *(G-7)*

Kaba Ilco Corp .... B 336 725-1331
Winston Salem *(G-13222)*

Kdy Automation Solutions Inc .... G 888 219-0049
Morrisville *(G-8996)*

Kearfott Corporation .... B 828 350-5300
Black Mountain *(G-868)*

Ketchie-Houston Inc .... E 704 786-5101
Concord *(G-3390)*

Nova Mobility Systems Inc .... G 800 797-9861
Charlotte *(G-2577)*

Skinner Company .... G 336 580-4716
Greensboro *(G-5815)*

Sunray Inc .... E 828 287-7030
Rutherfordton *(G-10994)*

Village Produce & Cntry Str In .... G 336 661-8685
Winston Salem *(G-13381)*

WaveTherm Corporation .... E 919 307-8071
Raleigh *(G-10601)*

Wilmington Rbr & Gasket Co Inc .... F 910 762-4262
Wilmington *(G-12952)*

X-Jet Technologies Inc .... G 800 983-7467
Raleigh *(G-10616)*

HARDWARE & BUILDING PRDTS: Plastic

Ashland Products Inc .... C 815 266-0250
Huntersville *(G-6968)*

Caro-Polymers Inc .... F 704 629-5319
Bessemer City *(G-808)*

Chadsworth Incorporated .... G 910 763-7600
Wilmington *(G-12742)*

Corner Stone Plastics Inc .... G 336 629-1828
Asheboro *(G-341)*

Digger Specialties Inc .... F 919 255-2533
Fuquay Varina *(G-4879)*

Digger Specialties Inc .... G 336 495-1517
Randleman *(G-10642)*

Hayward Industrial Products .... C 704 837-8002
Charlotte *(G-2264)*

Hayward Industries Inc .... D 336 712-9900
Clemmons *(G-3188)*

Hayward Industries Inc .... B 704 837-8002
Charlotte *(G-2265)*

L B Plastics LLC .... D 704 663-1543
Mooresville *(G-8706)*

Manufacturing Services Inc .... E 704 629-4163
Bessemer City *(G-826)*

Performance Plastics Pdts Inc .... D 336 454-0350
Jamestown *(G-7175)*

Tenn-Tex Plastics Inc .... E 336 931-1100
Colfax *(G-3291)*

HARDWARE & EQPT: Stage, Exc Lighting

Stage Decoration and Sups Inc .... G 336 621-5454
Greensboro *(G-5834)*

HARDWARE STORES

Ace Marine Rigging & Supply Inc .... F 252 726-6620
Morehead City *(G-8811)*

AGM Carolina Inc .... G 336 431-4100
High Point *(G-6511)*

B&C Xterior Cleaning Svc Inc .... G 919 779-7905
Raleigh *(G-9928)*

C & M Industrial Supply Co .... G 704 483-4001
Mill Spring *(G-8300)*

P
R
O
D
U
C
T

Capitol Funds Inc.................................. F 910 439-5275
Mount Gilead *(G-9198)*

Capitol Funds Inc.................................. E 704 487-8547
Shelby *(G-11316)*

Discount Pallet Services LLC................. G 910 892-3760
Dunn *(G-3853)*

Hudson S Hardware Inc....................... E 919 553-3030
Garner *(G-4933)*

Ledger Hardware Inc........................... G 828 688-4798
Bakersville *(G-679)*

Matthews Building Supply Co............... E 704 847-2106
Matthews *(G-8130)*

W E Nixons Wldg & Hdwr Inc.............. G 252 221-4348
Edenton *(G-4373)*

HARDWARE STORES: Builders'

Bfs Operations LLC................................ A 919 431-1000
Raleigh *(G-9942)*

Castle Hayne Hardware LLC.................. G 910 675-9205
Castle Hayne *(G-1497)*

Gesipa Fasteners Usa Inc..................... F 609 208-1740
Mocksville *(G-8368)*

Stock Building Supply Holdings LLC..... A 919 431-1000
Raleigh *(G-10509)*

HARDWARE STORES: Pumps & Pumping Eqpt

Merrill Resources Inc........................... G 828 877-4450
Penrose *(G-9662)*

HARDWARE STORES: Tools

Shopbot Tools Inc................................ E 919 680-4800
Durham *(G-4233)*

Snap-On Power Tools Inc..................... C 828 835-4400
Murphy *(G-9296)*

Triad Cutting Tools Inc........................ G 336 873-8708
Asheboro *(G-412)*

HARDWARE WHOLESALERS

AGM Carolina Inc................................ G 336 431-4100
High Point *(G-6511)*

Allegion Access Tech LLC.................... E 704 789-7000
Concord *(G-3309)*

Belwith Products LLC........................... G 336 841-3899
High Point *(G-6545)*

Con-Tab Inc... F 336 476-0104
Thomasville *(G-12011)*

Grass America Inc............................... C 336 996-4041
Kernersville *(G-7277)*

Imperial Usa Ltd.................................. E 704 596-2444
Charlotte *(G-2316)*

Roots Organic Gourmet LLC................. F 828 232-2828
Fairview *(G-4510)*

Triangle Indus Sup Hldings LLC.......... G 704 395-0600
Charlotte *(G-2942)*

Vista Products Inc............................... D 910 582-0130
Hamlet *(G-6065)*

HARDWARE, WHOLESALE: Bolts

Bamal Corporation............................... F 980 225-7700
Charlotte *(G-1748)*

HARDWARE, WHOLESALE: Builders', NEC

Sentinel Door Controls LLC.................. F 704 921-4627
Charlotte *(G-2788)*

HARDWARE, WHOLESALE: Furniture, NEC

Hafele America Co............................... C 800 423-3531
Archdale *(G-224)*

Hickory Springs Manufacturi............... D 828 328-2201
Hickory *(G-6355)*

RPM Indstrial Ctings Group Inc............. C 828 261-0325
Hickory *(G-6435)*

Salice America Inc.............................. E 704 841-7810
Charlotte *(G-2749)*

HARDWARE, WHOLESALE: Power Tools & Access

Greenworks North America LLC............ D 888 909-6757
Mooresville *(G-8677)*

TTI Floor Care North Amer Inc.............. B 888 321-1134
Charlotte *(G-2951)*

Yat Usa Inc... G 480 584-4096
Huntersville *(G-7063)*

HARDWARE, WHOLESALE: Security Devices, Locks

A&B Integrators LLC............................ F 919 371-0750
Durham *(G-3876)*

HARDWARE: Builders'

Endura Products LLC........................... B 336 668-2472
Colfax *(G-3279)*

Masonite Corporation.......................... A 704 599-0235
Charlotte *(G-2466)*

Stanley Black & Decker Inc.................. G 704 509-0844
Charlotte *(G-2858)*

Stanley Black & Decker Inc.................. C 704 789-7000
Concord *(G-3446)*

HARDWARE: Door Opening & Closing Devices, Exc Electrical

Absolute Security & Lock Inc............... G 336 322-4598
Roxboro *(G-10917)*

Sentinel Door Controls LLC.................. F 704 921-4627
Charlotte *(G-2788)*

HARDWARE: Furniture

Acme Rental Company.......................... G 704 873-3731
Statesville *(G-11648)*

Belwith Products LLC........................... G 336 841-3899
High Point *(G-6545)*

Blum Inc.. B 704 827-1345
Stanley *(G-11612)*

Buie Manufacturing Company............... E 910 610-3504
Laurinburg *(G-7493)*

Division Eight Inc................................ F 336 852-1275
Greensboro *(G-5497)*

Fortress International Corp NC.............. G 336 645-9365
Conover *(G-3522)*

Hafele America Co............................... C 800 423-3531
Archdale *(G-224)*

Hickory Springs California LLC............. A 828 328-2201
Hickory *(G-6354)*

Hickory Springs Mfg Co....................... D 828 328-2201
Hickory *(G-6357)*

Imperial Usa Ltd.................................. E 704 596-2444
Charlotte *(G-2316)*

Jacob Holtz Company LLC.................... E 828 328-1003
Hickory *(G-6373)*

Mepla-Alfit Incorporated...................... E 336 289-2300
Kernersville *(G-7286)*

Ultra-Mek Inc...................................... D 336 859-4552
Denton *(G-3765)*

HARDWARE: Furniture, Builders' & Other Household

Custom Seatings.................................. G 828 879-1964
Valdese *(G-12194)*

Grass America Inc............................... C 336 996-4041
Kernersville *(G-7277)*

Ingersoll-Rand Indus US Inc................ D 704 896-4000
Davidson *(G-3710)*

HARDWARE: Parachute

Sun Path Products Inc......................... D 910 875-9002
Raeford *(G-9853)*

HARNESS ASSEMBLIES: Cable & Wire

Interconnect Products and Services Inc E 336 667-3356
Wilkesboro *(G-12640)*

Iron Box LLC.. E 919 890-0025
Raleigh *(G-10209)*

Lutze Inc... E 704 504-0222
Charlotte *(G-2442)*

Protechnologies Inc............................. E 336 368-1375
Pilot Mountain *(G-9672)*

HEALTH AIDS: Exercise Eqpt

ABC Fitness Products LLC.................... G 704 649-0000
Raleigh *(G-9867)*

Advantage Fitness Products Inc............ G 336 643-8810
Kernersville *(G-7239)*

RSR Fitness Inc................................... F 919 255-1233
Raleigh *(G-10450)*

Watkins Agency Inc.............................. G 704 213-6997
Salisbury *(G-11135)*

HEARING AIDS

Xanderglasses Inc............................... G 617 286-3012
Raleigh *(G-10617)*

HEAT TREATING: Metal

American Metallurgy Inc....................... G 336 889-3277
High Point *(G-6520)*

Bodycote Thermal Proc Inc.................. F 704 664-1808
Mooresville *(G-8618)*

East Crlina Metal Treating Inc.............. E 919 834-2100
Raleigh *(G-10069)*

Furnace Rebuilders Inc........................ F 704 483-4025
Denver *(G-3783)*

Industrial Prcess Slutions Inc.............. G 336 926-1511
Wilkesboro *(G-12639)*

J F Heat Treating Inc........................... G 704 864-0998
Gastonia *(G-5071)*

M-B Industries Inc............................... C 828 862-4201
Rosman *(G-10913)*

Thermal Metal Treating Inc.................. E 910 944-3636
Aberdeen *(G-27)*

United TI & Stamping Co NC Inc.......... D 910 323-8588
Fayetteville *(G-4687)*

HEATERS: Swimming Pool, Electric

Hayward Holdings Inc.......................... C 704 837-8002
Charlotte *(G-2263)*

Pentair Water Pool and Spa Inc........... D 919 463-4640
Cary *(G-1417)*

Pentair Water Pool and Spa Inc........... A 919 566-8000
Sanford *(G-11217)*

HEATING & AIR CONDITIONING UNITS, COMBINATION

American Coil Inc................................ G 310 515-1215
Bostic *(G-960)*

Charlies Heating & Cooling LLC........... G 336 260-1973
Snow Camp *(G-11473)*

Chichibone Inc.................................... F 919 785-0090
Kernersville *(G-7256)*

Freudnberg Rsdntial Fltrtion T............. E 828 328-1142
Hickory *(G-6335)*

Go Green Services LLC........................ D 336 252-2999
Greensboro *(G-5565)*

HEATING EQPT: Complete (continued)

J&R Precision Heating and Air.............. G 910 480-8322
  Fayetteville *(G-4619)*

Kenny Fowler Heating and A Inc.......... F 910 508-4553
  Wilmington *(G-12827)*

Tier 1 Heating and Air LLC.................. F 910 556-1444
  Vass *(G-12229)*

Trs-Sesco LLC.................................... D 336 996-2220
  Kernersville *(G-7310)*

Xp Climate Control LLC....................... G 828 266-2006
  Boone *(G-955)*

HEATING EQPT: Complete

Bahnson Holdings Inc........................... D 336 760-3111
  Clemmons *(G-3178)*

Jenkins Services Group LLC................ G 704 881-3210
  Catawba *(G-1512)*

Mestek Inc... C 252 753-5323
  Farmville *(G-4535)*

Trane US Inc...................................... G 336 387-1735
  Greensboro *(G-5870)*

HEATING UNITS & DEVICES: Indl, Electric

ABB Installation Products Inc................ E 828 322-1855
  Hickory *(G-6260)*

Custom Electric Mfg LLC...................... E 248 305-7700
  Concord *(G-3350)*

L F I Services Inc............................... G 215 343-0411
  Sanford *(G-11201)*

Lambda Technologies Inc..................... E 919 462-1919
  Morrisville *(G-9003)*

Nutec Inc.. E 877 318-2430
  Huntersville *(G-7025)*

Thermcraft Holding Co LLC.................. D 336 784-4800
  Winston Salem *(G-13363)*

Tutco Inc.. D 828 654-1665
  Arden *(G-314)*

HELICOPTERS

Vx Aerospace Holdings Inc................... F 828 433-5353
  Morganton *(G-8911)*

HELMETS: Athletic

Kask America Inc................................ E 704 960-4851
  Charlotte *(G-2388)*

HELMETS: Steel

Interactive Safety Pdts Inc................... G 704 664-7377
  Huntersville *(G-7002)*

HIGH ENERGY PARTICLE PHYSICS EQPT

Asco Power Technologies LP................ C 336 731-5009
  Welcome *(G-12509)*

Consolidated Elec Distrs Inc................. G 828 433-4689
  Morganton *(G-8858)*

HOBBY, TOY & GAME STORES: Arts & Crafts & Splys

Grateful Union Family Inc..................... F 828 622-3258
  Asheville *(G-510)*

HOBBY, TOY & GAME STORES: Toys & Games

Burlington Outlet................................. G 910 278-3442
  Oak Island *(G-9564)*

HOISTS

Columbus McKinnon Corporation.......... D 704 694-2156
  Wadesboro *(G-12240)*

Columbus McKinnon Corporation.......... C 716 689-5400
  Charlotte *(G-1962)*

Toter LLC.. E 800 424-0422
  Statesville *(G-11792)*

Yale Industrial Products Inc.................. E 704 588-4610
  Charlotte *(G-3038)*

HOLDING COMPANIES: Investment, Exc Banks

Alcami Holdings LLC............................ A 910 254-7000
  Wilmington *(G-12701)*

Atticus LLC.. E 984 465-4754
  Cary *(G-1299)*

Interroll USA Holding LLC.................... D 910 799-1100
  Wilmington *(G-12820)*

Ipi Acquisition LLC.............................. A 704 588-1100
  Charlotte *(G-2356)*

K&K Holdings Inc................................ G 704 341-5567
  Charlotte *(G-2385)*

Pharr McAdenville Corporation............. D 704 824-3551
  Mc Adenville *(G-8215)*

HOLDING COMPANIES: Personal, Exc Banks

Hlm Legacy Group Inc......................... C 704 878-8823
  Troutman *(G-12140)*

HOME ENTERTAINMENT EQPT: Electronic, NEC

Cymbal LLC.. G 877 365-9622
  Cary *(G-1342)*

Unique Home Theater Inc..................... G 704 787-3239
  Concord *(G-3461)*

HOME FOR THE MENTALLY HANDICAPPED

Watauga Opportunities Inc................... E 828 264-5009
  Boone *(G-951)*

HOME HEALTH CARE SVCS

Allotropica Technologies Inc................ G 919 522-4374
  Chapel Hill *(G-1524)*

Spencer Health Solutions Inc............... E 866 971-8564
  Morrisville *(G-9058)*

HOMEFURNISHING STORES: Beddings & Linens

Dewoolfson Down Intl Inc..................... G 828 963-2750
  Banner Elk *(G-684)*

Leighdeux LLC................................... G 704 965-4889
  Charlotte *(G-2418)*

HOMEFURNISHING STORES: Lighting Fixtures

Interrs-Exteriors Asheboro Inc.............. G 336 629-2148
  Asheboro *(G-367)*

HOMEFURNISHING STORES: Pottery

Ceder Creek Gallery & Pottery.............. G 919 528-1041
  Creedmoor *(G-3645)*

Jugtown Pottery.................................. G 910 464-3266
  Seagrove *(G-11276)*

HOMEFURNISHING STORES: Venetian Blinds

Dbf Inc.. G 910 548-6725
  Jacksonville *(G-7122)*

HOMEFURNISHINGS, WHOLESALE: Blinds, Vertical

Shutter Factory Inc............................. G 252 974-2795
  Washington *(G-12413)*

HOMEFURNISHINGS, WHOLESALE: Fireplace Eqpt & Access

Appalchian Stove Fbrcators Inc............. G 828 253-0164
  Asheville *(G-428)*

HOMEFURNISHINGS, WHOLESALE: Floor Cushion & Padding

Artisans Guild Incorporated.................. G 336 841-4140
  High Point *(G-6530)*

HOMEFURNISHINGS, WHOLESALE: Linens, Table

Sanders Industries Inc......................... G 410 277-8565
  Waynesville *(G-12472)*

HOMEFURNISHINGS, WHOLESALE: Wood Flooring

Green River Resource MGT.................. F 828 697-0357
  Zirconia *(G-13530)*

HOMES: Log Cabins

Bear Creek Log Tmber Homes LLC........ G 336 751-6180
  Mocksville *(G-8351)*

Braswell Realty.................................. G 828 733-5800
  Newland *(G-9426)*

Dex n Dox.. G 910 576-4644
  Troy *(G-12160)*

Distinctive Bldg & Design Inc................ G 828 456-4730
  Waynesville *(G-12456)*

Gray Wolf Log Homes Inc.................... G 828 586-4662
  Sylva *(G-11892)*

Log Cabin Homes Ltd.......................... G 252 454-1548
  Battleboro *(G-701)*

Log Cabin Homes Ltd.......................... D 252 454-1500
  Rocky Mount *(G-10849)*

Log Homes of America Inc................... G 336 982-8989
  Jefferson *(G-7190)*

Mast Woodworks................................. F 336 468-1194
  Hamptonville *(G-6090)*

Mountain Rcrtion Log Cbins LLC........... G 828 387-6688
  Newland *(G-9432)*

Old Hickory Log Homes Inc.................. G 704 489-8989
  Denver *(G-3795)*

South-East Lumber Company................ E 336 996-5322
  Kernersville *(G-7301)*

Southland Log Homes Inc.................... G 336 449-5388
  Whitsett *(G-12620)*

Tree Craft Log Homes Inc.................... G 828 689-2240
  Mars Hill *(G-8078)*

HOODS: Door, Aluminum

Envision Glass Inc.............................. G 336 283-9701
  Winston Salem *(G-13159)*

HORSESHOES

Blue Horseshoe.................................. G 980 312-8202
  Charlotte *(G-1790)*

H Horseshoe...................................... G 336 853-5913
  Lexington *(G-7695)*

Pierce Farrier Supply Inc..................... G 704 753-4358
  Indian Trail *(G-7095)*

HOSE: Automobile, Rubber

Mmb One Inc...................................... F 704 523-8163
  Charlotte *(G-2512)*

Steele Rubber Products Inc.................. D 704 483-9343
  Denver *(G-3807)*

PRODUCT

HOSE: Flexible Metal

Hoser Inc..............................G 704 989-7151
Monroe *(G-8500)*

Titeflex Corporation.........................D 647 638-7160
Charlotte *(G-2921)*

HOSE: Plastic

Titeflex Corporation.........................D 647 638-7160
Charlotte *(G-2921)*

HOSE: Rubber

Flextrol Corporation.........................F 704 888-1120
Locust *(G-7893)*

Industrial Power Inc.........................G 910 483-4230
Fayetteville *(G-4615)*

HOSIERY DYEING & FINISHING

Huffman Finishing Company Inc...........C 828 396-1741
Granite Falls *(G-5308)*

HOSPITALS: Medical & Surgical

Statesville Med MGT Svcs LLC...............G 704 996-6748
Statesville *(G-11780)*

HOT TUBS

Bradford Products LLC.........................D 910 791-2202
Leland *(G-7535)*

Mountain Leisure Hot Tubs LLC...........G 828 649-7727
Arden *(G-287)*

Southern Home Spa and Wtr Pdts.........G 336 286-3564
Greensboro *(G-5826)*

HOT TUBS: Plastic & Fiberglass

Creekraft Cultured Marble Inc.................G 252 636-5488
New Bern *(G-9358)*

HOUSEHOLD ARTICLES, EXC FURNITURE: Cut Stone

Capital Marble Creations Inc.................G 910 893-2462
Lillington *(G-7791)*

Piedmont Marble Inc.........................G 336 274-1800
Oak Ridge *(G-9574)*

HOUSEHOLD ARTICLES: Metal

ARC Steel Fabrication LLC.................F 980 533-8302
Bessemer City *(G-805)*

Artistic Ironworks LLC.........................G 919 908-6888
Durham *(G-3900)*

Gray Manufacturing Co.........................G 615 841-3066
Charlotte *(G-2234)*

Mecha Inc.........................F 919 858-0372
Raleigh *(G-10286)*

HOUSEHOLD FURNISHINGS, NEC

American Fiber & Finishing Inc...........E 704 984-9256
Albemarle *(G-61)*

Arden Companies LLC.........................D 919 258-3081
Sanford *(G-11150)*

Artisans Guild Incorporated.................G 336 841-4140
High Point *(G-6530)*

Blue Ridge Products Co Inc.................G 828 322-7990
Hickory *(G-6274)*

Bob Barker Company Inc.................C 800 334-9880
Fuquay Varina *(G-4870)*

Carpenter Co.........................E 828 632-7061
Taylorsville *(G-11952)*

Chf Industries Inc.........................E 212 951-7800
Charlotte *(G-1912)*

Deep River Fabricators Inc.................F 336 824-8881
Franklinville *(G-4856)*

Fiber Cushioning Inc.........................F 336 887-4782
High Point *(G-6620)*

Manual Woodworkers Weavers Inc........C 828 692-7333
Hendersonville *(G-6224)*

Party Tables Land Co LLC.................G 919 596-3521
Durham *(G-4166)*

Pure Country Inc.........................D 828 871-2890
Tryon *(G-12177)*

Q C Apparel Inc.........................G 828 586-5663
Sylva *(G-11897)*

Riddle & Company LLC.........................G 336 229-1856
Burlington *(G-1147)*

Snyder Paper Corporation.................E 828 464-1189
Newton *(G-9496)*

Textile Products Inc.........................E 704 636-6221
Salisbury *(G-11124)*

Westpoint Home Inc.........................F 910 369-2231
Wagram *(G-12257)*

Wildcat Territory Inc.........................G 718 361-6726
Thomasville *(G-12087)*

HOUSEHOLD SEWING MACHINES WHOLESALERS: Electric

Zibra LLC.........................G 704 271-4503
Mooresville *(G-8806)*

HOUSEWARES, ELECTRIC: Air Purifiers, Portable

Airbox Inc.........................E 855 927-1386
Statesville *(G-11651)*

Trick Tank Inc.........................G 980 406-3200
Charlotte *(G-2943)*

TTI Floor Care North Amer Inc...............D 440 996-2000
Charlotte *(G-2950)*

HOUSEWARES, ELECTRIC: Heating Units, Electric Appliances

Blossman Propane Gas & Appl.................F 828 396-0144
Hickory *(G-6272)*

HOUSEWARES: Food Dishes & Utensils, Pressed & Molded Pulp

Burrows Paper Corporation.................C 800 272-7122
Charlotte *(G-1819)*

HUMIDIFIERS & DEHUMIDIFIERS

American Moistening Co Inc.................F 704 889-7281
Pineville *(G-9712)*

HYDRAULIC EQPT REPAIR SVC

Atlantic Hydraulics Svcs LLC...............E 919 542-2985
Sanford *(G-11152)*

Auto Parts Fayetteville LLC.................G 910 889-4026
Fayetteville *(G-4555)*

ICE

Carolina Ice Inc.........................E 252 527-3178
Kinston *(G-7399)*

Dfa Dairy Brands Fluid LLC.................G 704 341-2794
Charlotte *(G-2038)*

Herrin Bros Coal & Ice Co.................G 704 332-2193
Charlotte *(G-2275)*

Hickman Oil & Ice Co Inc.................G 910 576-2501
Troy *(G-12161)*

Reddy Ice LLC.........................G 704 824-4611
Gastonia *(G-5132)*

Reddy Ice LLC.........................G 910 738-9930
Lumberton *(G-7968)*

Reddy Ice LLC.........................G 919 782-9358
Raleigh *(G-10439)*

Robert D Starr.........................G 336 697-0286
Greensboro *(G-5790)*

Rose Ice & Coal Company.................G 910 762-2464
Wilmington *(G-12902)*

Taylor Products Inc.........................G 910 862-2576
Elizabethtown *(G-4435)*

ICE CREAM & ICES WHOLESALERS

Dfa Dairy Brands Fluid LLC.................G 704 341-2794
Charlotte *(G-2038)*

Tonys Ice Cream Co Inc.................G 704 853-0018
Gastonia *(G-5157)*

IGNITION SYSTEMS: High Frequency

Lmg Holdings Inc.........................F 919 653-0910
Durham *(G-4107)*

INCUBATORS & BROODERS: Farm

Smoky Mtn Nativ Plant Assn.................G 828 479-8788
Robbinsville *(G-10763)*

Upper Coastl Plain Bus Dev Ctr...............G 252 234-5900
Wilson *(G-13041)*

INDL & PERSONAL SVC PAPER WHOLESALERS

Atlantic Corp Wilmington Inc.................E 910 259-3600
Burgaw *(G-1019)*

Atlantic Corp Wilmington Inc.................D 800 722-5841
Wilmington *(G-12712)*

C L Rabb Inc.........................E 704 865-0295
Gastonia *(G-5010)*

Gold Medal Products Co.................G 336 665-4997
Greensboro *(G-5568)*

Pactiv LLC.........................F 828 758-7580
Lenoir *(G-7632)*

Veritiv Operating Company.................G 336 834-3488
Greensboro *(G-5898)*

INDL & PERSONAL SVC PAPER, WHOLESALE: Shipping Splys

Lls Investments Inc.........................F 919 662-7283
Raleigh *(G-10258)*

INDL CONTRACTORS: Exhibit Construction

Exhibit World Inc.........................G 704 882-2272
Indian Trail *(G-7080)*

INDL EQPT SVCS

GE Vernova International LLC.................E 704 587-1300
Charlotte *(G-2194)*

Hydro Service & Supplies Inc...............E 919 544-3744
Durham *(G-4066)*

Jly Invstmnts Inc Fka Nwman Mc........E 336 273-8261
Browns Summit *(G-1000)*

Safe Air Systems Inc.........................E 336 674-0749
Randleman *(G-10659)*

Sub-Aquatics Inc.........................E 336 674-0749
Randleman *(G-10661)*

Waste Container Repair Svcs.................G 910 257-4474
Fayetteville *(G-4696)*

Westlift LLC.........................F 919 242-4379
Goldsboro *(G-5253)*

INDL GASES WHOLESALERS

Airgas Usa LLC.........................G 704 394-1420
Charlotte *(G-1633)*

Airgas Usa LLC.........................G 919 544-3773
Durham *(G-3885)*

Airgas Usa LLC.........................G 919 735-5276
Goldsboro *(G-5196)*

INDL MACHINERY & EQPT WHOLESALERS

3nine USA Inc..........................F 512 210-4005
Charlotte *(G-1602)*

American Linc Corporation.............E 704 861-9242
Gastonia *(G-4992)*

Arbon Equipment Corporation..........F 414 355-2600
Charlotte *(G-1690)*

Arc3 Gases Inc...........................G 704 220-1029
Monroe *(G-8429)*

Arc3 Gases Inc...........................E 910 892-4016
Dunn *(G-3844)*

Arnolds Welding Service Inc............E 910 323-3822
Fayetteville *(G-4553)*

Bear Pages...............................G 828 837-0785
Murphy *(G-9288)*

Birch Bros Southern Inc................E 704 843-2111
Waxhaw *(G-12423)*

Burris Machine Company Inc............G 828 322-6914
Hickory *(G-6277)*

C R Onsrud Inc..........................C 704 508-7000
Troutman *(G-12131)*

Carotek Inc..............................D 704 844-1100
Matthews *(G-8103)*

Cross Technologies Inc.................D 336 292-0511
Whitsett *(G-12603)*

Cummins Inc.............................F 704 596-7690
Charlotte *(G-2003)*

Deurotech America Inc.................G 980 272-6827
Charlotte *(G-2037)*

Drum Filter Media Inc..................G 336 434-4195
High Point *(G-6599)*

Dwd Industries LLC....................E 336 498-6327
Randleman *(G-10644)*

Encertec Inc.............................G 336 288-7226
Greensboro *(G-5519)*

Gamma Js Inc...........................F 336 294-3838
Greensboro *(G-5547)*

Gregory Poole Equipment Co...........F 919 872-2691
Raleigh *(G-10146)*

His Glassworks Inc.....................G 828 254-2559
Asheville *(G-518)*

Huber Technology Inc..................E 704 949-1010
Denver *(G-3788)*

Hunter Douglas Inc.....................C 704 629-6500
Bessemer City *(G-822)*

J & P Entrprses of Crlinas Inc..........E 704 861-1867
Gastonia *(G-5069)*

Ligna Machinery Inc....................G 336 584-0030
Burlington *(G-1120)*

Lock Drives Inc.........................G 704 588-1844
Pineville *(G-9740)*

Machinex................................G 336 665-5030
High Point *(G-6695)*

Mang Systems Inc.......................G 704 292-1041
Matthews *(G-8181)*

McDonald Services Inc.................G 704 753-9669
Monroe *(G-8530)*

Mixon Mills Inc.........................G 828 297-5431
Vilas *(G-12231)*

Morris Machine Company Inc...........G 704 824-4242
Gastonia *(G-5102)*

Northline Nc LLC.......................G 336 283-4811
Rural Hall *(G-10965)*

Oerlikon AM US Inc....................E 980 260-2827
Huntersville *(G-7027)*

Oerlikon Metco (us) Inc................F 713 715-6300
Huntersville *(G-7028)*

Palmer Wahl Instruments Inc...........E 828 658-3131
Asheville *(G-566)*

Pavco Inc...............................E 704 496-6800
Charlotte *(G-2619)*

Pharmaceutical Equipment Svcs........G 239 699-9120
Asheville *(G-571)*

Psi-Polymer Systems Inc...............E 828 468-2600
Conover *(G-3553)*

Roi Industries Group Inc...............G 919 788-7728
Durham *(G-4218)*

RPM Plastics LLC.......................E 704 871-0518
Statesville *(G-11760)*

Russell Finex Inc.......................F 704 588-9808
Pineville *(G-9751)*

Rvb Systems Group Inc.................G 919 362-5211
Garner *(G-4960)*

Schaefer Systems International Inc......C 704 944-4500
Charlotte *(G-2763)*

Schaefer Systems Intl Inc..............G 704 944-4550
Charlotte *(G-2765)*

Vrg Components Inc.....................G 980 244-3862
Matthews *(G-8156)*

West Dynamics Us Inc..................E 704 735-0009
Lincolnton *(G-7871)*

INDL PROCESS INSTRUMENTS: Control

Assembly Tech Components Inc..........G 919 773-0388
Garner *(G-4917)*

Electro Magnetic Research Inc..........G 919 365-3723
Zebulon *(G-13508)*

Hitech Controls Inc....................G 336 498-1534
Randleman *(G-10649)*

Sure Trip Inc............................F 704 983-4651
Albemarle *(G-94)*

INDL PROCESS INSTRUMENTS: Elements, Primary

Temposonics LLC.......................G 470 380-5103
Cary *(G-1469)*

INDL SPLYS WHOLESALERS

Allyn International Trdg Corp...........G 877 858-2482
Marshville *(G-8085)*

Automated Designs Inc.................F 828 696-9625
Flat Rock *(G-4703)*

Biganodes LLC..........................G 828 245-1115
Forest City *(G-4784)*

Carr Mill Supplies Inc..................G 336 883-0135
High Point *(G-6561)*

Custom Hydraulics & Design............F 704 347-0023
Cherryville *(G-3061)*

D M & E Corporation...................E 704 482-8876
Shelby *(G-11328)*

Genevieve M Brownlee.................G 336 226-5260
Burlington *(G-1095)*

H-T-L Perma USA Ltd Partnr...........E 704 377-3100
Charlotte *(G-2249)*

Holland Supply Company...............E 252 492-7541
Henderson *(G-6160)*

Industrial Sup Solutions Inc............E 704 636-4241
Salisbury *(G-11067)*

Ips Corporation.........................E 919 598-2400
Durham *(G-4083)*

Justice Bearing LLC.....................G 800 355-2500
Mooresville *(G-8701)*

Mount Hope Machinery Co...............F
Charlotte *(G-2523)*

Parker-Hannifin Corporation............D 336 373-1761
Greensboro *(G-5734)*

Person Printing Company Inc............E 336 599-2146
Roxboro *(G-10940)*

Purser Centl Rewinding Co Inc..........F 704 786-3131
Concord *(G-3427)*

Roots Organic Gourmet LLC.............F 828 232-2828
Fairview *(G-4510)*

Sanders Company Inc....................F 252 338-3995
Elizabeth City *(G-4408)*

SAS Industries Inc......................F 631 727-1441
Elizabeth City *(G-4409)*

Sherrill Contract Mfg Inc...............F 704 922-7871
Dallas *(G-3689)*

Strobels Supply Inc.....................F 607 324-1721
Linwood *(G-7881)*

Structural Materials Inc................G 828 754-6413
Lenoir *(G-7640)*

Triangle Indus Sup Hldings LLC.........G 704 395-0600
Charlotte *(G-2942)*

INDL SPLYS, WHOLESALE: Bearings

Oiles America Corporation..............F 704 784-4500
Concord *(G-3411)*

INDL SPLYS, WHOLESALE: Clean Room Splys

Murata Machinery Usa Inc..............C 704 875-9280
Charlotte *(G-2532)*

INDL SPLYS, WHOLESALE: Drums, New Or Reconditioned

National Container Group LLC...........G 704 393-9050
Charlotte *(G-2544)*

INDL SPLYS, WHOLESALE: Gaskets

Uchiyama Mfg Amer LLC.................F 919 731-2364
Goldsboro *(G-5251)*

INDL SPLYS, WHOLESALE: Mill Splys

Laurinburg Machine Company...........G 910 276-0360
Laurinburg *(G-7505)*

T P Supply Co Inc.......................E 336 789-2337
Mount Airy *(G-9183)*

Talladega Mchy & Sup Co NC............G 256 362-4124
Fayetteville *(G-4677)*

INDL SPLYS, WHOLESALE: Power Transmission, Eqpt & Apparatus

Alan R Williams Inc.....................E 704 372-8281
Charlotte *(G-1636)*

Altra Industrial Motion Corp............F 704 588-5610
Charlotte *(G-1658)*

Boston Gear LLC........................B 704 588-5610
Charlotte *(G-1802)*

INDL SPLYS, WHOLESALE: Rubber Goods, Mechanical

Carolina Custom Rubber Inc............G 704 636-6989
Salisbury *(G-11026)*

Cinters Inc..............................F 336 267-3051
Rocky Mount *(G-10828)*

Easth20 Holdings Llc...................G 919 313-2100
Greensboro *(G-5510)*

Novaflex Hose Inc......................D 336 578-2161
Haw River *(G-6134)*

Oliver Rubber Company LLC.............B 336 629-1436
Asheboro *(G-380)*

Parker-Hannifin Corporation............F 252 237-6171
Wilson *(G-13012)*

INDL SPLYS, WHOLESALE: Tools

B & M Wholesale Inc....................G 336 789-3916
Mount Airy *(G-9100)*

INDL SPLYS, WHOLESALE: Tools, NEC

Loflin Handle Co Inc....................G 336 463-2422
Yadkinville *(G-13445)*

Robert Bosch Tool Corporation............. E 704 735-7464
 Lincolnton (G-7851)

INDL SPLYS, WHOLESALE: Valves & Fittings

Bonomi North America Inc................... F 704 412-9031
 Charlotte (G-1798)

Consolidated Pipe & Sup Co Inc............. F 336 294-8577
 Greensboro (G-5463)

Flo-Tite Inc Valves & Contrls................. E 910 738-8904
 Lumberton (G-7955)

Fortiline LLC...................................... E 704 788-9800
 Concord (G-3366)

INDL TRUCK REPAIR SVCS

Whiteville Forklift & Eqp....................... G 910 642-6642
 Whiteville (G-12598)

INDUSTRIAL & COMMERCIAL EQPT INSPECTION SVCS

SCR-Tech LLC................................... C 704 504-0191
 Charlotte (G-2772)

INFORMATION RETRIEVAL SERVICES

Carolina Connections Inc..................... G 336 786-7030
 Mount Airy (G-9107)

Vrush Industries Inc............................ G 336 886-7700
 High Point (G-6829)

INFORMATION SVCS: Consumer

Telephys Inc..................................... G 312 625-9128
 Davidson (G-3719)

INFRARED OBJECT DETECTION EQPT

Spatial Light LLC............................... G 617 213-0314
 Cary (G-1464)

INK: Printing

Actega Wit Inc.................................. C 704 735-8282
 Lincolnton (G-7808)

Allied Pressroom Products Inc............... E 954 920-0909
 Monroe (G-8421)

American Water Graphics Inc................ G 828 247-0700
 Forest City (G-4783)

Archie Supply LLC.............................. G 336 987-0895
 Greensboro (G-5368)

Arpro M-Tec LLC................................ F 828 433-0699
 Morganton (G-8851)

Crossroads Fuel Service Inc.................. E 252 426-5216
 Hertford (G-6252)

DSM Desotech Inc.............................. G 704 862-5000
 Stanley (G-11614)

Environmental Inks and Coat................ C 828 433-1922
 Morganton (G-8863)

Flint Group Inc.................................. E 828 687-4363
 Arden (G-269)

Flint Group US LLC............................. G 828 687-4309
 Arden (G-270)

Flint Group US LLC............................. G 828 687-4291
 Arden (G-271)

Flint Group US LLC............................. G 704 504-2626
 Charlotte (G-2166)

Hubergroup USA Inc........................... F 336 292-5501
 Greensboro (G-5608)

Ink Tec Inc...................................... F 828 465-6411
 Newton (G-9476)

INX International Ink Co....................... E 704 372-2080
 Charlotte (G-2352)

INX International Ink Co....................... G 910 371-3184
 Leland (G-7547)

INX International Ink Co....................... F 704 414-6428
 Rockwell (G-10798)

Mirchandani Inc................................ G 919 872-8871
 Raleigh (G-10309)

Mitsubishi Chemical Amer Inc............... D 980 580-2839
 Charlotte (G-2509)

RPM Indstrial Ctings Group Inc............. C 828 261-0325
 Hickory (G-6434)

RPM Indstrial Ctings Group Inc............. C 828 728-8266
 Hudson (G-6957)

Rutland Group Inc.............................. G 704 553-0046
 Charlotte (G-2744)

Siegwerk Eic LLC............................... F 800 368-4657
 Morganton (G-8897)

Sun Chemical Corporation.................... D 704 587-4531
 Charlotte (G-2880)

Wikoff Color Corporation...................... E 704 392-4657
 Charlotte (G-3019)

Wikoff Color Corporation...................... E 336 668-3423
 Greensboro (G-5918)

Xsys North America Corporation............. E 828 687-2485
 Arden (G-321)

INSECTICIDES

Amika LLC....................................... G 984 664-9804
 Cary (G-1288)

Cape Fear Chemicals Inc..................... G 910 862-3139
 Elizabethtown (G-4420)

Jabb of Carolinas Inc.......................... G 919 965-9007
 Pine Level (G-9682)

Lanxess Corporation........................... E 704 868-7200
 Gastonia (G-5077)

Mey Corporation................................ G 919 932-5800
 Chapel Hill (G-1557)

Tyratech Inc..................................... E 919 415-4275
 Morrisville (G-9082)

INSECTICIDES & PESTICIDES

Vestaron Corporation.......................... G 919 694-1022
 Durham (G-4296)

INSPECTION & TESTING SVCS

Froehling & Robertson Inc.................... E 804 264-2701
 Raleigh (G-10120)

INSTRUMENTS & METERS: Measuring, Electric

International Instrumentation................. G 919 496-4208
 Bunn (G-1014)

INSTRUMENTS, LABORATORY: Analyzers, Automatic Chemical

Parata Systems LLC........................... C 888 727-2821
 Durham (G-4165)

Sciteck Diagnostics Inc....................... G 828 650-0409
 Fletcher (G-4765)

INSTRUMENTS, MEASURING & CNTRL: Geophysical & Meteorological

Russ Simmons.................................. G 910 686-1656
 Wilmington (G-12906)

INSTRUMENTS, MEASURING & CNTRLG: Aircraft & Motor Vehicle

Circor Pumps North America LLC.......... D 704 289-6511
 Monroe (G-8459)

Dynisco Instruments LLC..................... E 828 326-9888
 Hickory (G-6325)

IMO Industries Inc............................. D 301 323-9000
 Monroe (G-8503)

INSTRUMENTS, MEASURING & CONTROLLING: Ion Chambers

Biomerieux Inc.................................. G 800 682-2666
 Raleigh (G-9946)

INSTRUMENTS, MEASURING & CONTROLLING: Transits, Surveyors'

Pretoria Transit Interiors Inc................. D 615 867-8515
 Charlotte (G-2664)

INSTRUMENTS, OPTICAL: Mirrors

Glass Works of Hickory Inc................... G 828 322-2122
 Hickory (G-6339)

INSTRUMENTS, SURGICAL & MED: Needles & Syringes, Hypodermic

Becton Dickinson and Company........... B 201 847-6800
 Durham (G-3922)

INSTRUMENTS, SURGICAL & MEDICAL: Blood & Bone Work

Accumed Corp.................................. D 800 278-6796
 Raleigh (G-9874)

Acw Technology Inc............................ A
 Raleigh (G-9877)

Ascepi Medical Group LLC................... G 919 336-4246
 Raleigh (G-9918)

Healthlink Europe............................... F 919 783-4142
 Raleigh (G-10159)

MTI Medical Cables LLC...................... G 828 890-2888
 Fletcher (G-4758)

Sfp Research Inc............................... G 336 622-5266
 Liberty (G-7779)

Wnyh LLC.. C 716 853-1800
 Mocksville (G-8396)

INSTRUMENTS, SURGICAL & MEDICAL: Blood Transfusion

Charter Medical LLC........................... D 336 768-6447
 Winston Salem (G-13123)

INSTRUMENTS, SURGICAL & MEDICAL: Catheters

Cook Incorporated............................. A 336 744-0157
 Winston Salem (G-13130)

Mallinckrodt LLC............................... G 919 878-2900
 Raleigh (G-10269)

Robling Medical LLC........................... D 919 570-9605
 Youngsville (G-13482)

Teleflex Incorporated.......................... E 919 544-8000
 Morrisville (G-9067)

Zoes Kitchen Inc............................... E 336 748-0587
 Winston Salem (G-13412)

INSTRUMENTS, SURGICAL & MEDICAL: IV Transfusion

Luxor Hydration LLC........................... F 919 568-5047
 Durham (G-4113)

INSTRUMENTS, SURGICAL & MEDICAL: Muscle Exercise, Ophthalmic

Healthlink International Inc.................... G 877 324-2837
 Raleigh (G-10160)

INSTRUMENTS, SURGICAL & MEDICAL: Ophthalmic

Optopol Usa Inc.............................. G 833 678-6765
Raleigh *(G-10347)*

INSTRUMENTS: Analytical

Apex Waves LLC............................. G 919 809-5227
Cary *(G-1292)*

Biofluidica Inc................................ G 858 535-6493
Cary *(G-1306)*

Biomerieux Inc............................... B 919 620-2000
Durham *(G-3930)*

Bmg Labtech Inc............................ F 919 678-1633
Cary *(G-1313)*

Camag Scientific Inc..................... G 910 343-1830
Wilmington *(G-12727)*

Carolina Biological Supply Company..... C 336 584-0381
Burlington *(G-1060)*

DOE & Ingalls Investors Inc.......... E 919 598-1986
Durham *(G-4003)*

DOE & Ingalls Management LLC........... F 919 598-1986
Durham *(G-4004)*

DOE & Inglls Nrth Crlina Oprti........ E 919 282-1792
Durham *(G-4005)*

Environmental Supply Co Inc........ F 919 956-9688
Durham *(G-4027)*

Fisher Scientific Company LLC........ D 800 252-7100
Asheville *(G-498)*

Hamilton.. G 704 896-1427
Davidson *(G-3706)*

Horiba Instruments Inc.................. F 828 676-2801
Fletcher *(G-4742)*

Htx Technologies LLC.................... F 919 928-5688
Carrboro *(G-1269)*

Institute For Resch Biotecnoly......... G 252 689-2205
Greenville *(G-5991)*

Microsolv Technology Corp........... F 720 949-1302
Leland *(G-7555)*

Phitonex Inc.................................. G 855 874-4866
Durham *(G-4177)*

Sapphire Tchncal Solutions LLC........ G 704 561-3100
Pineville *(G-9754)*

Shimadzu Scientific Instrs Inc........ G 919 425-1010
Durham *(G-4231)*

Thermo Elctron Scntfic Instrs......... G 828 281-2651
Asheville *(G-615)*

Thermo Fisher Scientific Inc.......... F 800 955-6288
Durham *(G-4269)*

Thermo Fisher Scientific Inc.......... G 800 955-6288
High Point *(G-6806)*

Thermo Fisher Scientific Inc.......... G 919 380-2000
Morrisville *(G-9070)*

Thermo Fisher Scientific Inc.......... E 919 876-2352
Raleigh *(G-10545)*

Thermo Fsher Scntfic Ashvlle L........ B 828 658-2711
Weaverville *(G-12505)*

Thermo Fsher Scntfic Ashvlle L........ B 828 658-2711
Asheville *(G-616)*

Trajan Inc...................................... G 919 435-1105
Raleigh *(G-10556)*

Warren Oil Company LLC............... D 910 892-6456
Dunn *(G-3871)*

INSTRUMENTS: Combustion Control, Indl

Delta Msrment Cmbstn Cntrls LL........ E 919 623-7133
Cary *(G-1344)*

INSTRUMENTS: Electrocardiographs

US Prototype Inc........................... E 866 239-2848
Wilmington *(G-12943)*

INSTRUMENTS: Endoscopic Eqpt, Electromedical

Kyocera Precision Tools Inc............ G 800 823-7284
Fletcher *(G-4745)*

INSTRUMENTS: Flow, Indl Process

Hoffer Flow Controls Inc................. D 252 331-1997
Elizabeth City *(G-4392)*

INSTRUMENTS: Indl Process Control

AC Corporation.............................. B 336 273-4472
Greensboro *(G-5339)*

Acucal Inc..................................... G 252 337-9975
Elizabeth City *(G-4377)*

Eng Solutions Inc.......................... E 919 831-1830
Chapel Hill *(G-1545)*

Kdy Automation Solutions Inc........ G 888 219-0049
Morrisville *(G-8996)*

Strandberg Engrg Labs Inc........... F 336 274-3775
Greensboro *(G-5843)*

Thermaco Incorporated................. G 336 629-4651
Asheboro *(G-408)*

INSTRUMENTS: Infrared, Indl Process

Tc2 Labs LLC................................. G 919 380-2171
Raleigh *(G-10534)*

INSTRUMENTS: Measurement, Indl Process

QMAX Industries LLC.................... G 704 643-7299
Charlotte *(G-2679)*

Sapphire Tchncal Solutions LLC........ G 704 561-3100
Pineville *(G-9754)*

Southstern Prcess Eqp Cntrls I........ F 704 483-1141
Denver *(G-3806)*

Triad Automation Group Inc........... E 336 767-1379
Winston Salem *(G-13369)*

INSTRUMENTS: Measuring, Electrical Power

Hvte Inc.. G 919 274-8899
Youngsville *(G-13474)*

Ndsl Inc.. E 919 790-7877
Durham *(G-4144)*

INSTRUMENTS: Medical & Surgical

3M Company.................................. G 704 588-4782
Charlotte *(G-1601)*

Acme United Corporation............... E 252 822-5051
Rocky Mount *(G-10807)*

Adhezion Biomedical LLC.............. G 828 728-6116
Hudson *(G-6940)*

Alcon.. G 919 624-5868
Raleigh *(G-9889)*

Alveolus Inc.................................. E 704 921-2215
Charlotte *(G-1659)*

American Labor Inc....................... G 919 286-0726
Durham *(G-3891)*

Andersen Energy Inc..................... G 336 376-0107
Haw River *(G-6129)*

Andersen Products Inc.................. E 336 376-3000
Haw River *(G-6130)*

Andersen Sterilizers Inc................ E 336 376-8622
Haw River *(G-6131)*

Angstrom Medica Inc..................... F 781 933-6121
Greenville *(G-5936)*

Applied Catheter Tech Inc............. G 336 817-1005
Winston Salem *(G-13087)*

Bariatric Partners Inc.................... G 704 542-2256
Charlotte *(G-1752)*

Becton Dickinson and Company........ E 919 963-1307
Four Oaks *(G-4808)*

Biogeniv Inc.................................. G 828 850-1007
Lenoir *(G-7586)*

Biomedinnovations Inc.................. G 704 489-1290
Denver *(G-3775)*

Biomerieux Inc............................... B 919 620-2000
Durham *(G-3930)*

Bioventus Inc................................ D 919 474-6700
Durham *(G-3932)*

Birth Tissue Recovery LLC............. E 336 448-1910
Winston Salem *(G-13106)*

Brandel LLC.................................. G 704 525-4548
Charlotte *(G-1806)*

Carefusion 303 Inc........................ G 919 528-5253
Creedmoor *(G-3643)*

Carolina Precision Tech LLC.......... E 215 675-4590
Mooresville *(G-8633)*

Colowrap LLC............................... F 888 815-3376
Durham *(G-3983)*

Contego Medical Inc...................... E 919 606-3917
Raleigh *(G-10012)*

Convatec Inc................................. G 336 297-3021
Greensboro *(G-5464)*

Convatec Inc................................. C 336 855-5500
Greensboro *(G-5465)*

Cook Group Inc.............................. G 336 744-0157
Winston Salem *(G-13129)*

Core Sound Imaging Inc................. E 919 277-0636
Raleigh *(G-10016)*

Corning Incorporated.................... C 919 620-6200
Durham *(G-3988)*

Covidien Holding Inc..................... C 919 878-2930
Raleigh *(G-10018)*

Custom Assemblies Inc.................. E 919 202-4533
Pine Level *(G-9678)*

D R Burton Healthcare LLC............ F 252 228-7038
Farmville *(G-4526)*

Diamond Orthopedic LLC............... G 704 585-8258
Gastonia *(G-5042)*

Elite Metal Performance LLC.......... F 704 660-0006
Statesville *(G-11694)*

Emitbio Inc................................... G 919 321-1726
Morrisville *(G-8971)*

Genco... G 919 963-4227
Four Oaks *(G-4811)*

Gilero LLC.................................... B 919 595-8220
Durham *(G-4047)*

Greiner Bio-One North Amer Inc........ B 704 261-7800
Monroe *(G-8496)*

Health Supply Us LLC.................... F 888 408-1694
Mooresville *(G-8680)*

Healthlink Europe........................... F 919 368-2187
Raleigh *(G-10158)*

Horizon Vision Research Inc.......... G 910 796-8600
Wilmington *(G-12808)*

Hyperbranch Medical Tech Inc........ F 919 433-3325
Durham *(G-4067)*

Innavasc Medical Inc..................... F 813 902-2228
Durham *(G-4079)*

Intelligent Endoscopy LLC............. E 336 608-4375
Clemmons *(G-3192)*

Intuitive Surgical Inc..................... G 408 523-2100
Durham *(G-4081)*

Jaguar Gene Therapy LLC.............. F 919 465-6400
Cary *(G-1377)*

Janus Development Group Inc........ G 252 551-9042
Greenville *(G-5994)*

Karamedica Inc............................. G 919 302-1325
Raleigh *(G-10230)*

Kashif Mazhar............................... G 919 314-2891
Durham *(G-4092)*

Kyocera Precision Tools Inc............ G 800 823-7284
Fletcher *(G-4745)*

Logiksavvy Solutions LLC.............. G 336 392-6149
Greensboro *(G-5663)*

Lucerno Dynamics LLC.................. G 317 294-1395
Cary *(G-1398)*

Employee Codes: A=Over 500 employees, B=251-500
C=101-250, D=51-100, E=20-50, F=10-19, G=1-9

2025 Harris North Carolina
Manufacturers Directory

1133

PRODUCT

Martin Manufacturing Co LLC................ G 919 741-5439
Rocky Mount (G-10850)

Maximum Asp.. G 919 544-7900
Morrisville (G-9019)

Med Express/Medical Spc Inc................ F 919 572-2568
Durham (G-4123)

Medcor Inc.. G 888 579-1050
Lexington (G-7718)

Micell Technologies Inc......................... E 919 313-2102
Durham (G-4132)

Misonix Opco Inc.................................... F 631 694-9555
Durham (G-4137)

Mission Srgcal Innovations LLC............ G 678 699-6057
Raleigh (G-10310)

Murray Inc... E 704 329-0400
Charlotte (G-2534)

Murray Inc... E 847 620-7990
Charlotte (G-2535)

Ncontact Surgical LLC........................... F
Morrisville (G-9022)

Next Safety Inc....................................... F 336 246-7700
Jefferson (G-7192)

Nocturnal Product Dev LLC................... G 919 321-1331
Durham (G-4149)

Nuvasive Inc... G 336 430-3169
Greensboro (G-5716)

Oyster Merger Sub II LLC...................... C 919 474-6700
Durham (G-4162)

Pattons Medical LLC.............................. E 704 529-5442
Charlotte (G-2617)

Perseus Intermediate Inc....................... E 919 474-6700
Durham (G-4174)

Photonicare Inc...................................... E 866 411-3277
Durham (G-4179)

Pioneer Srgcal Orthblogics Inc............. F 252 355-4405
Greenville (G-6015)

Plexus Corp.. D 919 807-8000
Raleigh (G-10373)

Polyzen Inc... G 919 319-9599
Cary (G-1423)

Rdd Pharma Inc...................................... G 302 319-9970
Raleigh (G-10433)

React Innovations LLC........................... G 704 773-1276
Charlotte (G-2694)

Retrofix Screws LLC.............................. G 980 432-8412
Salisbury (G-11111)

Retroject Inc... G 919 619-3042
Chapel Hill (G-1567)

Rm Liquidation Inc................................. D 828 274-7996
Asheville (G-591)

Safeguard Medical.................................. D 855 428-6074
Huntersville (G-7051)

Sonablate Corp....................................... E 888 874-4384
Charlotte (G-2826)

Staclear Inc.. G 919 838-2844
Raleigh (G-10502)

Statesville Med MGT Svcs LLC.............. G 704 996-6748
Statesville (G-11780)

Strong Medical Partners LLC................. D 716 507-4476
Pineville (G-9760)

Strong Medical Partners LLC................. E 716 626-9400
Pineville (G-9759)

Stryker Corp.. G 919 455-6755
Raleigh (G-10516)

Stryker Corporation................................. F 919 433-3325
Durham (G-4253)

Surgilum LLC.. G 910 202-2202
Wilmington (G-12934)

Teleflex Incorporated.............................. G 919 433-2575
Durham (G-4261)

Teleflex Medical Incorporated................ G 336 498-4153
Asheboro (G-407)

Teleflex Medical Incorporated................ G 919 544-8000
Durham (G-4263)

Teleflex Medical Incorporated................ D 919 544-8000
Morrisville (G-9068)

Touchamerica Inc.................................... G 919 732-6968
Hillsborough (G-6879)

Transenterix Surgical Inc....................... D 919 765-8400
Durham (G-4276)

Traumtic Drect Trnsfsion Dvcs.............. G 423 364-5828
Apex (G-199)

Trimed LLC... G 919 615-2784
Raleigh (G-10564)

Tryton Medical Inc.................................. G 919 226-1490
Raleigh (G-10568)

Vasonova Inc.. F 650 327-1412
Morrisville (G-9084)

Visitech Systems Inc.............................. G 919 387-0524
Apex (G-204)

Webster Entps Jackson Cnty Inc........... G 828 586-8981
Sylva (G-11904)

Weslacova Corp...................................... G 336 838-2614
North Wilkesboro (G-9552)

Wilson-Cook Medical Inc....................... G 336 744-0157
Winston Salem (G-13395)

INSTRUMENTS: Optical, Analytical

Sensory Analytics LLC........................... E 336 315-6090
Greensboro (G-5808)

INSTRUMENTS: Power Measuring, Electrical

TTI Floor Care North Amer Inc............... B 888 321-1134
Charlotte (G-2951)

INSTRUMENTS: Pressure Measurement, Indl

Eno Scientific LLC.................................. G 910 778-2660
Hillsborough (G-6865)

Trafag Inc... G 704 343-6339
Charlotte (G-2932)

Vishay Precision Group Inc.................... F 919 374-5555
Raleigh (G-10591)

INSTRUMENTS: Radio Frequency Measuring

Clairvoyant Technology Inc.................... G 919 491-5062
Durham (G-3976)

INSTRUMENTS: Seismographs

Geosonics Inc... G 919 790-9500
Raleigh (G-10130)

INSTRUMENTS: Test, Electronic & Electric Measurement

Minipro LLC.. G 844 517-4776
Chapel Hill (G-1558)

MTS Systems Corporation...................... C 919 677-2352
Cary (G-1403)

Tektronix Inc... G 919 233-9490
Raleigh (G-10538)

Troxler Electronic Labs Inc.................... D 919 549-8661
Research Triangle Pa (G-10716)

INSTRUMENTS: Test, Electronic & Electrical Circuits

Konica Mnlta Hlthcare Amrcas I............ E 919 792-6420
Garner (G-4935)

Viztek LLC.. E 919 792-6420
Garner (G-4971)

INSULATING COMPOUNDS

Gtg Engineering Inc............................... G 877 569-8572
Clarendon (G-3127)

Tailored Chemical Products Inc.............. D 828 322-6512
Hickory (G-6462)

INSULATION & ROOFING MATERIALS: Wood, Reconstituted

Attic Tent Inc.. G 704 892-5399
Mooresville (G-8601)

INSULATION MATERIALS WHOLESALERS

Mid-Atlantic Specialties Inc................... G 919 212-1939
Raleigh (G-10305)

INSULATION: Felt

Performance Goods LLC......................... G 704 361-8600
Charlotte (G-2628)

INSULATION: Fiberglass

Owens Corning Glass Metal Svcs.......... D 704 721-2000
Concord (G-3414)

Wwj LLC.. E 704 871-8500
Statesville (G-11802)

INSULATORS & INSULATION MATERIALS: Electrical

Basalt Specialty Products Inc................ G 336 835-5153
Elkin (G-4439)

Chase Corporation.................................. G 828 396-2121
Granite Falls (G-5300)

Chase Corporation.................................. F 828 726-6023
Lenoir (G-7593)

Essex Group Inc...................................... G 704 921-9605
Charlotte (G-2127)

Penn Compression Moulding Inc........... G 919 934-5144
Smithfield (G-11459)

INSULATORS, PORCELAIN: Electrical

Duco-SCI Inc... F 704 289-9502
Monroe (G-8478)

Reuel Inc... E 919 734-0460
Goldsboro (G-5240)

INSURANCE: Agents, Brokers & Service

Hinson Industries Inc............................. G 252 937-7171
Rocky Mount (G-10840)

Katchi Tees Incorporated....................... G 252 315-4691
Wilson (G-12997)

Motor Vhcles Lcense Plate Agcy........... G 252 338-6965
Elizabeth City (G-4398)

INTEGRATED CIRCUITS, SEMICONDUCTOR NETWORKS, ETC

Advanced Micro Devices Inc.................. G 919 840-8080
Morrisville (G-8921)

Agile Microwave Technology Inc............ G 984 228-8001
Cary (G-1287)

Amkor Technology Inc............................ G 919 248-1800
Durham (G-3892)

Analog Devices Inc................................. F 336 202-6503
Durham (G-3895)

Analog Devices Inc................................. E 336 668-9511
Greensboro (G-5363)

Analog Devices Inc................................. F 919 831-2790
Raleigh (G-9902)

Broadcom Corporation............................ D 919 865-2954
Durham (G-3944)

Ekc Advanced Elec USA 4 LLC.............. G 302 774-1000
Wilmington (G-12770)

Galaxy Electronics Inc........................... F 704 343-9881
Charlotte (G-2184)

Kyma Technologies Inc............F.....919 789-8880
Raleigh *(G-10242)*

Nokia of America Corporation...............G.....919 850-6000
Raleigh *(G-10333)*

Qorvo Us Inc.............E.....336 931-8298
Greensboro *(G-5777)*

Qualcomm Datacenter Tech Inc.............D.....858 567-1121
Raleigh *(G-10412)*

Qualia Networks Inc.............G.....805 637-2083
Raleigh *(G-10413)*

Rfhic US Corporation.............G.....919 677-8780
Morrisville *(G-9043)*

Rhino Networks LLC.............E.....855 462-9434
Asheville *(G-590)*

Triad Semiconductor Inc.............D.....336 774-2150
Winston Salem *(G-13370)*

Vrg Components Inc.............G.....980 244-3862
Matthews *(G-8156)*

Wolfspeed Inc.............C.....919 407-5300
Durham *(G-4308)*

INTERIOR DESIGN SVCS, NEC

Delve Interiors LLC.............C.....336 274-4661
Greensboro *(G-5495)*

Tatum Galleries Inc.............G.....828 963-6466
Banner Elk *(G-689)*

Taylor Interiors LLC.............F.....980 207-3160
Charlotte *(G-2901)*

Textile Products Inc.............E.....704 636-6221
Salisbury *(G-11124)*

INVERTERS: Nonrotating Electrical

Majorpower Corporation.............E.....919 563-6610
Mebane *(G-8251)*

INVERTERS: Rotating Electrical

Everything Industrial Supply.............G.....743 333-2222
Winston Salem *(G-13162)*

INVESTORS, NEC

Atlantic Caribbean LLC.............G.....910 343-0624
Wilmington *(G-12711)*

Igm Specialties Holding Inc.............F.....704 945-8702
Charlotte *(G-2312)*

Rhf Investments Inc.............G.....828 326-8350
Hickory *(G-6428)*

Solarbrook Water and Pwr Corp.............G.....919 231-3205
Raleigh *(G-10492)*

INVESTORS: Real Estate, Exc Property Operators

Lm Shea LLC.............G.....919 608-1901
Raleigh *(G-10259)*

JEWELRY & PRECIOUS STONES WHOLESALERS

Made By Custom LLC.............G.....704 980-9840
Charlotte *(G-2447)*

NCSMJ Inc.............F.....704 544-1118
Pineville *(G-9744)*

JEWELRY REPAIR SVCS

D C Crsman Mfr Fine Jwly Inc.............G.....828 252-9891
Asheville *(G-482)*

Donald Haack Diamonds Inc.............G.....704 365-4400
Charlotte *(G-2062)*

Dons Fine Jewelry Inc.............G.....336 724-7826
Clemmons *(G-3181)*

John Laughter Jewelry Inc.............G.....828 456-4772
Waynesville *(G-12462)*

Made By Custom LLC.............G.....704 980-9840
Charlotte *(G-2447)*

R Gregory Jewelers Inc.............F.....704 872-6669
Statesville *(G-11758)*

Stonehaven Jewelry Gallery Ltd.............G.....919 462-8888
Cary *(G-1468)*

Sumpters Jwly & Collectibles.............G.....704 399-5348
Charlotte *(G-2879)*

JEWELRY STORES

Buchanan Gem Stone Mines Inc.............F.....828 765-6130
Spruce Pine *(G-11567)*

Byrd Designs Inc.............G.....828 628-0151
Fairview *(G-4506)*

Duncan Design Ltd.............G.....919 834-7713
Raleigh *(G-10064)*

Jewelry By Gail Inc.............G.....252 441-5387
Nags Head *(G-9299)*

Jkl Inc.............F.....252 355-6714
Greenville *(G-5996)*

Made By Custom LLC.............G.....704 980-9840
Charlotte *(G-2447)*

NCSMJ Inc.............F.....704 544-1118
Pineville *(G-9744)*

Speed Brite Inc.............G.....704 639-9771
Salisbury *(G-11118)*

William Travis Jewelry Ltd.............G.....919 968-0011
Chapel Hill *(G-1593)*

JEWELRY STORES: Precious Stones & Precious Metals

Barnes Dmnd Gllery Jwly Mfrs I.............G.....910 347-4300
Jacksonville *(G-7116)*

D C Crsman Mfr Fine Jwly Inc.............G.....828 252-9891
Asheville *(G-482)*

Donald Haack Diamonds Inc.............G.....704 365-4400
Charlotte *(G-2062)*

Dons Fine Jewelry Inc.............G.....336 724-7826
Clemmons *(G-3181)*

Haydon & Company.............G.....919 781-1293
Raleigh *(G-10157)*

Jewel Masters Inc.............F.....336 243-2711
Lexington *(G-7701)*

John Laughter Jewelry Inc.............G.....828 456-4772
Waynesville *(G-12462)*

Michael S North Wilkesboro Inc.............G.....336 838-5964
North Wilkesboro *(G-9547)*

R Gregory Jewelers Inc.............F.....704 872-6669
Statesville *(G-11758)*

Starcraft Diamonds Inc.............G.....252 717-2548
Washington *(G-12415)*

JEWELRY, PRECIOUS METAL: Medals, Precious Or Semiprecious

Diamond Outdoor Entps Inc.............G.....336 857-1450
Denton *(G-3747)*

JEWELRY, PRECIOUS METAL: Rings, Finger

Herff Jones LLC.............G.....704 962-1483
Charlotte *(G-2272)*

Herff Jones LLC.............G.....704 873-5563
Statesville *(G-11707)*

Jostens Inc.............B.....336 765-0070
Winston Salem *(G-13220)*

JEWELRY, PRECIOUS METAL: Settings & Mountings

D C Crsman Mfr Fine Jwly Inc.............G.....828 252-9891
Asheville *(G-482)*

Donald Haack Diamonds Inc.............G.....704 365-4400
Charlotte *(G-2062)*

JEWELRY, WHOLESALE

Duncan Design Ltd.............G.....919 834-7713
Raleigh *(G-10064)*

Soulku LLC.............F.....828 273-4278
Asheville *(G-605)*

JEWELRY: Precious Metal

123 Precious Metal Ref LLC.............G.....910 228-5403
Wilmington *(G-12685)*

Acme General Design Group LLC.............G.....843 466-6000
Benson *(G-783)*

Alex and Ani LLC.............G.....704 366-6029
Charlotte *(G-1640)*

Barnes Dmnd Gllery Jwly Mfrs I.............G.....910 347-4300
Jacksonville *(G-7116)*

Byrd Designs Inc.............G.....828 628-0151
Fairview *(G-4506)*

Charles & Colvard Ltd.............F.....919 468-0399
Morrisville *(G-8954)*

Classy Sassy 5 Jewels Boutique.............G.....252 481-8144
Greenville *(G-5954)*

Dallas L Pridgen Inc.............G.....919 732-4422
Carrboro *(G-1268)*

David Yurman Enterprises LLC.............G.....704 366-7259
Charlotte *(G-2020)*

Dons Fine Jewelry Inc.............G.....336 724-7826
Clemmons *(G-3181)*

Duncan Design Ltd.............G.....919 834-7713
Raleigh *(G-10064)*

Eurogold Art.............G.....336 989-6205
Kernersville *(G-7272)*

Goldsmith By Rudi Ltd.............G.....828 693-1030
Hendersonville *(G-6210)*

Haydon & Company.............G.....919 781-1293
Raleigh *(G-10157)*

Jewelry By Gail Inc.............G.....252 441-5387
Nags Head *(G-9299)*

Jkl Inc.............F.....252 355-6714
Greenville *(G-5996)*

John Laughter Jewelry Inc.............G.....828 456-4772
Waynesville *(G-12462)*

Michael S North Wilkesboro Inc.............G.....336 838-5964
North Wilkesboro *(G-9547)*

NCSMJ Inc.............F.....704 544-1118
Pineville *(G-9744)*

R Gregory Jewelers Inc.............F.....704 872-6669
Statesville *(G-11758)*

Soulku LLC.............F.....828 273-4278
Asheville *(G-605)*

Starcraft Diamonds Inc.............G.....252 717-2548
Washington *(G-12415)*

Sumpters Jwly & Collectibles.............G.....704 399-5348
Charlotte *(G-2879)*

William Travis Jewelry Ltd.............G.....919 968-0011
Chapel Hill *(G-1593)*

JIGS & FIXTURES

Cross Technology Inc.............E.....336 725-4700
East Bend *(G-4322)*

Worth Products LLC.............F.....252 747-9994
Snow Hill *(G-11484)*

JOB PRINTING & NEWSPAPER PUBLISHING COMBINED

Boone Newspapers Inc.............E.....252 332-2123
Ahoskie *(G-43)*

Spring Hope Enterprise Inc.............G.....252 478-3651
Spring Hope *(G-11559)*

Employee Codes: A=Over 500 employees, B=251-500
C=101-250, D=51-100, E=20-50, F=10-19, G=1-9

2025 Harris North Carolina
Manufacturers Directory

1135

PRODUCT

JOISTS: Fabricated Bar

Simpson Strong-Tie Company Inc.......... G 336 841-1338
High Point *(G-6776)*

JOISTS: Long-Span Series, Open Web Steel

Universal Steel NC LLC...................... E 336 476-3105
Thomasville *(G-12085)*

KITCHEN CABINETS WHOLESALERS

Dixon Custom Cabinetry LLC............... F 336 992-3306
Kernersville *(G-7266)*

Mint Hill Cabinet Shop Inc................. E 704 821-9373
Monroe *(G-8531)*

Murphy S Custom Cabinetry Inc............ G 828 891-3050
Hendersonville *(G-6229)*

Nova Enterprises Inc....................... E 828 687-8770
Arden *(G-290)*

United Finishers Intl Inc.................. G 336 883-3901
High Point *(G-6818)*

KITCHEN UTENSILS: Food Handling & Processing Prdts, Wood

Pamlico Shores Inc......................... E 252 926-0011
Swanquarter *(G-11881)*

KITCHENWARE STORES

Ashdan Enterprises......................... G 336 375-9698
Greensboro *(G-5372)*

KNIT OUTERWEAR DYEING & FINISHING, EXC HOSIERY & GLOVE

Textile Piece Dyeing Co Inc............... C 704 732-4200
Lincolnton *(G-7862)*

LABELS: Cotton, Printed

D & F Consolidated Inc..................... G 704 664-6660
Statesville *(G-11683)*

Minnewawa Inc.............................. F 865 522-8103
Thomasville *(G-12050)*

US Label Corporation....................... G 336 332-7000
Greensboro *(G-5894)*

LABELS: Paper, Made From Purchased Materials

Bay Tech Label Inc......................... G 828 296-8900
Asheville *(G-452)*

Grand Encore Charlotte LLC................. E 513 482-7500
Charlotte *(G-2231)*

J R Cole Industries Inc.................... D 704 523-6622
Charlotte *(G-2362)*

Label Line Ltd............................. D 336 857-3115
Asheboro *(G-371)*

Label Printing Systems Inc................. E 336 760-3271
Winston Salem *(G-13230)*

Lpm Inc.................................... G 704 922-6137
Gastonia *(G-5078)*

Milpak Graphics Inc........................ E 336 347-8772
King *(G-7332)*

Rapid Response Inc......................... G 704 588-8890
Charlotte *(G-2689)*

LABELS: Woven

Minnewawa Inc.............................. F 865 522-8103
Thomasville *(G-12050)*

LABORATORIES, TESTING: Pollution

Apex Instruments Incorporated............. E 919 557-7300
Fuquay Varina *(G-4865)*

LABORATORIES, TESTING: Product Testing

Alcami Carolinas Corporation.............. G 910 619-3952
Garner *(G-4913)*

Alcami Carolinas Corporation.............. B 910 254-7000
Wilmington *(G-12698)*

Bachstein Consulting LLC.................. G 410 322-4917
Youngsville *(G-13463)*

Catalent Pharma Solutions LLC............ F 919 481-4855
Morrisville *(G-8952)*

LABORATORIES, TESTING: Product Testing, Safety/Performance

Educated Design & Developme.............. E 919 469-9434
Cary *(G-1351)*

LABORATORIES: Biological Research

Alcami Carolinas Corporation.............. G 910 619-3952
Garner *(G-4913)*

Alcami Carolinas Corporation.............. G 910 254-7000
Morrisville *(G-8924)*

Alcami Carolinas Corporation.............. B 910 254-7000
Wilmington *(G-12698)*

LABORATORIES: Biotechnology

22nd Century Group Inc.................... F 716 270-1523
Mocksville *(G-8345)*

Cedarlane Laboratories USA............... E 336 513-5135
Burlington *(G-1067)*

Epicypher Inc............................. F 855 374-2461
Durham *(G-4030)*

Hydromer Inc.............................. E 908 526-2828
Concord *(G-3374)*

Neurametrix Inc........................... G 408 507-2366
Asheville *(G-556)*

Novex Innovations LLC..................... G 336 231-6693
Winston Salem *(G-13267)*

Praetego Inc.............................. G 919 237-7969
Durham *(G-4193)*

Precision Biosciences Inc................. E 919 314-5512
Durham *(G-4194)*

Tengion Inc............................... E 336 722-5855
Winston Salem *(G-13361)*

LABORATORIES: Electronic Research

Nuvotronics Inc........................... D 434 298-6940
Durham *(G-4152)*

LABORATORIES: Medical

Alcami Carolinas Corporation.............. G 910 254-7000
Wilmington *(G-12699)*

Biomerieux Inc............................ B 919 620-2000
Durham *(G-3930)*

LABORATORIES: Physical Research, Commercial

Case Farms LLC............................ D 919 735-5010
Dudley *(G-3835)*

Case Farms LLC............................ E 919 658-2252
Goldsboro *(G-5204)*

Case Farms LLC............................ F 704 528-4501
Troutman *(G-12133)*

Cisco Systems Inc......................... A 919 392-2000
Morrisville *(G-8959)*

Core Technology Molding Corp............. E 336 294-2018
Greensboro *(G-5469)*

Greer Laboratories Inc.................... E 828 758-2388
Lenoir *(G-7609)*

Health Supply Us LLC...................... F 888 408-1694
Mooresville *(G-8680)*

K2 Solutions Inc......................... B 910 692-6898
Southern Pines *(G-11501)*

King Phrmceuticals RES Dev LLC........... C 919 653-7001
Cary *(G-1383)*

Lexitas Pharma Services Inc.............. E 919 205-0012
Durham *(G-4104)*

Linde Gas & Equipment Inc................. D 919 549-0633
Durham *(G-4105)*

Lord Corporation.......................... D 919 469-2500
Cary *(G-1395)*

Penske Racing South Inc.................. C 704 664-2300
Mooresville *(G-8746)*

Pharmagra Holding Company LLC........... G 828 884-8656
Brevard *(G-979)*

Ppd Inc................................... C 910 251-0081
Wilmington *(G-12886)*

Propharma Group LLC....................... D 888 242-0559
Raleigh *(G-10405)*

Raybow Usa Inc............................ F 828 884-8656
Brevard *(G-980)*

Scentair Technologies LLC................. C 704 504-2320
Charlotte *(G-2762)*

Signalscape Inc........................... E 919 859-4565
Cary *(G-1455)*

Squarehead Technology LLC................. G 571 299-4849
Hickory *(G-6456)*

Transcontinental AC US LLC................ F 704 847-9171
Matthews *(G-8154)*

Tribofilm Research Inc.................... G 919 838-2844
Raleigh *(G-10563)*

Vacs America Inc.......................... G 910 259-9854
Burgaw *(G-1035)*

Venator Chemicals LLC..................... D 704 454-4811
Harrisburg *(G-6120)*

Walker and Associates Inc................. C 336 731-6391
Winston Salem *(G-13386)*

LABORATORIES: Testing

Acterna LLC............................... F 919 388-5100
Morrisville *(G-8918)*

Albion Medical Holdings Inc.............. F 800 378-3906
Lenoir *(G-7570)*

American Safety Utility Corp............. E 704 482-0601
Shelby *(G-11311)*

Avista Pharma Solutions Inc.............. E 919 544-8600
Durham *(G-3910)*

Dynisco Instruments LLC.................. E 828 326-9888
Hickory *(G-6325)*

Froehling & Robertson Inc................. E 804 264-2701
Raleigh *(G-10120)*

Greer Laboratories Inc.................... E 828 758-2388
Lenoir *(G-7609)*

Greer Laboratories Inc.................... C 828 754-5327
Lenoir *(G-7610)*

Sapphire Tchncal Solutions LLC........... G 704 561-3100
Pineville *(G-9754)*

SCR-Tech LLC.............................. C 704 504-0191
Charlotte *(G-2772)*

Tergus Pharma LLC......................... E 919 549-9700
Durham *(G-4268)*

Unity Hlthcare Lab Billing LLP........... G 980 209-0402
Charlotte *(G-2964)*

Liposcience Inc........................... C 919 212-1999
Morrisville *(G-9012)*

LABORATORY APPARATUS & FURNITURE

Air Control Inc........................... E 252 492-2300
Henderson *(G-6147)*

Carolina Biological Supply Company....... C 336 584-0381
Burlington *(G-1060)*

Corilam Fabricating Co.................... E 336 993-2371
Kernersville *(G-7259)*

Dove Medical Supply LLC...................... E 336 643-9367
Summerfield *(G-11838)*

Ika-Works Inc.. D 910 452-7059
Wilmington *(G-12814)*

Intensa Inc.. E 336 884-4096
High Point *(G-6673)*

Misonix LLC.. D 631 694-9555
Durham *(G-4136)*

Parameter Generation Ctrl Inc................ E 828 669-8717
Black Mountain *(G-870)*

S E Lab Group Inc.................................... G 707 253-8852
Hickory *(G-6438)*

Sarstedt Inc.. C 828 465-4000
Newton *(G-9493)*

Thermo Fsher Scntfic Ashvlle L.............. B 828 658-2711
Asheville *(G-616)*

LABORATORY APPARATUS, EXC HEATING & MEASURING

Biovind LLC... G 512 217-3077
Charlotte *(G-1786)*

Xona Microfluidics Inc.............................. G 951 553-6400
Research Triangle Pa *(G-10718)*

LABORATORY APPARATUS: Heating

Wall-Lenk Corporation.............................. E 252 527-4186
Kinston *(G-7435)*

LABORATORY APPARATUS: Pipettes, Hemocytometer

Corning Incorporated................................ C 919 620-6200
Durham *(G-3988)*

LABORATORY EQPT, EXC MEDICAL: Wholesalers

Carolina Biological Supply Co................. C 336 446-7600
Whitsett *(G-12601)*

Carolina Biological Supply Company....... C 336 584-0381
Burlington *(G-1060)*

Turbomed LLC... F 973 527-5299
Fayetteville *(G-4684)*

Wpmhj LLC.. G 919 601-5445
Raleigh *(G-10615)*

LABORATORY EQPT: Clinical Instruments Exc Medical

Clinicians Advocacy Group Inc............... G 704 751-9515
Charlotte *(G-1930)*

Fisher Scientific Company LLC............... D 800 252-7100
Asheville *(G-498)*

Gems Frst Stop Med Sltions LLC........... G 336 965-9500
Greensboro *(G-5552)*

Primevigilance Inc................................... G 781 703-5540
Raleigh *(G-10395)*

LABORATORY EQPT: Incubators

Pacon Manufacturing Co LLC.................. C 910 239-3001
Leland *(G-7556)*

LABORATORY EQPT: Measuring

Aisthesis Products Inc............................ G 828 627-6555
Clyde *(G-3255)*

LACE GOODS & WARP KNIT FABRIC DYEING & FINISHING

McComb Industries Lllp........................... D 336 229-9139
Burlington *(G-1126)*

LAMINATED PLASTICS: Plate, Sheet, Rod & Tubes

Bemis Manufacturing Company.............. C 828 754-1086
Lenoir *(G-7578)*

Clear Defense LLC................................... G 336 370-1699
Greensboro *(G-5450)*

Dynacast LLC.. E 704 927-2790
Charlotte *(G-2072)*

Manning Fabrics Inc................................ G 910 295-1970
Pinehurst *(G-9696)*

Rk Enterprises LLC.................................. G 910 481-0777
Fayetteville *(G-4663)*

Robetex Inc.. F 910 671-8787
Lumberton *(G-7970)*

Tech Medical Plastics Inc....................... G 919 563-9272
Mebane *(G-8261)*

Tekni-Plex Inc.. D 919 553-4151
Clayton *(G-3174)*

Templex Inc.. E 336 472-5933
Thomasville *(G-12078)*

Transcontinental AC US LLC................... F 704 847-9171
Matthews *(G-8154)*

Upm Raflatac Inc..................................... B 828 651-4800
Mills River *(G-8322)*

Wilsonart LLC... E 828 684-2351
Fletcher *(G-4781)*

LAMINATING SVCS

Esco Industries Inc................................. F 336 495-3772
Randleman *(G-10647)*

LAMP & LIGHT BULBS & TUBES

Adams Wood Turning Inc........................ G 336 882-0196
High Point *(G-6509)*

Greenlights LLC....................................... E 919 766-8900
Cary *(G-1369)*

Hiviz Lighting Inc..................................... G 703 382-5675
Hendersonville *(G-6217)*

Robert Abbey Inc..................................... C 828 322-3480
Hickory *(G-6430)*

Specialty Manufacturing Inc................... D 704 247-9300
Charlotte *(G-2841)*

Sunnex Inc... F 800 445-7869
Charlotte *(G-2882)*

Traxon Technologies LLC......................... G 201 508-1570
Charlotte *(G-2938)*

LAMP BULBS & TUBES, ELECTRIC: Health, Infrared/Ultraviolet

Variety Consult LLC................................. G 704 978-8108
Shelby *(G-11389)*

LAMP BULBS & TUBES, ELECTRIC: Light, Complete

Alk Investments LLC............................... G 984 233-5353
Raleigh *(G-9891)*

Fintronx LLC... F 919 324-3960
Raleigh *(G-10109)*

LAMP BULBS & TUBES/PARTS, ELECTRIC: Generalized Applications

Arva LLC... G 803 336-2230
Charlotte *(G-1701)*

Invictus Lighting LLC.............................. G 828 855-9324
Hickory *(G-6372)*

LAMP SHADES: Glass

Decor Glass Specialties Inc................... G 828 586-8180
Sylva *(G-11891)*

Done-Gone Adios Inc............................... F 336 993-7300
Kernersville *(G-7268)*

Industrial Glass Tech LLC....................... F 704 853-2429
Gastonia *(G-5065)*

Orare Inc.. G 919 742-1003
Siler City *(G-11422)*

Pgw Auto Glass LLC................................ B 336 258-4950
Elkin *(G-4451)*

Triangle Glass Service Inc...................... G 919 477-9508
Durham *(G-4279)*

LAMPS: Boudoir, Residential

Clarolux Inc.. E 336 378-6800
Greensboro *(G-5447)*

LAMPS: Table, Residential

Adams Wood Turning Inc........................ G 336 882-0196
High Point *(G-6509)*

Coast Lamp Manufacturing Inc.............. G 828 648-7876
Canton *(G-1249)*

Sunnex Inc... F 800 445-7869
Charlotte *(G-2882)*

Wildwood Lamps & Accents Inc............. E 252 446-3266
Rocky Mount *(G-10875)*

LAND SUBDIVIDERS & DEVELOPERS: Commercial

Capitol Funds Inc.................................... F 910 439-5275
Mount Gilead *(G-9198)*

Capitol Funds Inc.................................... E 704 487-8547
Shelby *(G-11316)*

LASER SYSTEMS & EQPT

SL Laser Systems LP............................... G 704 561-9990
Charlotte *(G-2814)*

Spectra Integrated Systems Inc............. G 919 876-3666
Raleigh *(G-10496)*

LASERS: Welding, Drilling & Cutting Eqpt

Sonaspection International...................... F 704 262-3384
Concord *(G-3442)*

LATEX: Foamed

Earth Edge LLC.. F 828 624-0252
Hickory *(G-6328)*

Sun Fabricators Inc................................. E 336 885-0095
High Point *(G-6795)*

LAUNDRY EQPT: Commercial

Hockmeyer Equipment Corp.................... D 252 338-4705
Elizabeth City *(G-4390)*

Laundry Svc Tech Ltd Lblty Co............... G 908 327-1997
Matthews *(G-8126)*

LAUNDRY SVC: Work Clothing Sply

Ican Clothes Company............................. F 910 670-1494
Fayetteville *(G-4614)*

LAWN & GARDEN EQPT

Befco Inc.. E 252 977-9920
Rocky Mount *(G-10824)*

Bosmere Inc... F 704 784-1608
Salisbury *(G-11023)*

Certified Lawnmower Inc......................... G 704 527-2765
Belmont *(G-742)*

Daphne Lawson Espino.......................... G 910 290-2762
Beulaville *(G-841)*

Deere & Company.................................... B 919 567-6400
Fuquay Varina *(G-4878)*

Green Pastures Lawn Care...................... G 828 758-9265
Boomer *(G-891)*

H & H Farm Machine Co Inc.................. F 704 753-1555
Monroe *(G-8497)*

Husqvrna Cnsmr Outdoor Pdts NA......... A 704 597-5000
Charlotte *(G-2302)*

Husqvrna Cnsmr Outdoor Pdts NA......... D 704 597-5000
Charlotte *(G-2301)*

John Deere Consumer Pdts Inc............. C 919 804-2000
Cary *(G-1380)*

Miller Saws & Supplies Inc.................. G 252 636-3347
New Bern *(G-9382)*

Root Spring Scraper Co........................ G 269 382-2025
Pinehurst *(G-9702)*

S Duff Fabricating Inc......................... G 910 298-3060
Beulaville *(G-845)*

Sunseeker North America Inc................ F 704 684-5709
Indian Trail *(G-7101)*

Swell Home Solutions Inc.................... G 919 440-4692
Mount Olive *(G-9260)*

United Southern Industries Inc............. D 866 273-1810
Forest City *(G-4799)*

Vegherb LLC...................................... F 800 914-9835
Erwin *(G-4493)*

LAWN & GARDEN EQPT: Blowers & Vacuums

Peco Inc... E 828 684-1234
Arden *(G-296)*

Sunseeker US Inc............................... G 443 253-1546
Indian Trail *(G-7102)*

LAWN & GARDEN EQPT: Grass Catchers, Lawn Mower

New Peco Inc..................................... E 828 684-1234
Arden *(G-288)*

LAWN & GARDEN EQPT: Lawnmowers, Residential, Hand Or Power

Darius All Access LLC......................... E 910 262-8567
Wilmington *(G-12759)*

Trailmate Inc...................................... G 941 739-5743
Chapel Hill *(G-1578)*

LAWN & GARDEN EQPT: Tractors & Eqpt

Husqvrna Cnsmr Outdoor Pdts NA......... A 704 494-4810
Charlotte *(G-2303)*

LEAF TOBACCO WHOLESALERS

Pyxus International Inc........................ C 252 753-8000
Farmville *(G-4538)*

LEASING & RENTAL: Construction & Mining Eqpt

International Cnstr Eqp Inc................... E 704 821-8200
Matthews *(G-8175)*

Sound Heavy Machinery Inc................. F 910 782-2477
Wilmington *(G-12922)*

LEASING & RENTAL: Medical Machinery & Eqpt

Medaccess Inc................................... G 828 264-4085
Robbinsville *(G-10760)*

Quick-Deck Inc................................... E 704 888-0327
Locust *(G-7898)*

LEASING & RENTAL: Trucks, Without Drivers

Dutchman Creek Self-Storage.............. G 919 363-8878
Apex *(G-151)*

Security Self Storage.......................... G 919 544-3969
Durham *(G-4229)*

LEASING: Passenger Car

Courtesy Ford Inc.............................. G 252 338-4783
Elizabeth City *(G-4384)*

LEATHER & CUT STOCK WHOLESALERS

Leather Miracles LLC.......................... E 828 464-7448
Hickory *(G-6386)*

LEATHER GOODS, EXC FOOTWEAR, GLOVES, LUGGAGE/ BELTING, WHOL

Carroll Companies Inc......................... E 828 264-2521
Boone *(G-904)*

LEATHER GOODS: Card Cases

Pioneer Square Brands Inc.................. G 360 733-5608
High Point *(G-6734)*

LEATHER GOODS: Garments

Coast To Coast Lea & Vinyl Inc............. G 336 886-5050
High Point *(G-6571)*

LEATHER GOODS: Holsters

Greene Mountain Outdoors LLC............ F 336 670-2186
North Wilkesboro *(G-9532)*

Point Blank Enterprises Inc.................. D 910 893-2071
Lillington *(G-7801)*

Taylor Made Cases Inc........................ F 919 209-0555
Benson *(G-797)*

LEATHER GOODS: Personal

Glaser Designs Inc............................ F 415 552-3188
Raleigh *(G-10136)*

McKinley Leather Hickory Inc............... E 828 459-2884
Claremont *(G-3115)*

Point Blank Enterprises Inc.................. D 910 893-2071
Lillington *(G-7801)*

LEATHER GOODS: Safety Belts

Ellison Company Inc........................... C 704 889-7518
Charlotte *(G-2102)*

VH Industries Inc............................... G 704 743-2400
Concord *(G-3464)*

LEATHER TANNING & FINISHING

Arcona Leather Company LLC............... G 828 396-7728
Hudson *(G-6941)*

Carolina Fur Dressing Company............ E 919 231-0086
Raleigh *(G-9976)*

Carroll Companies Inc......................... F 828 466-5489
Conover *(G-3502)*

Dani Leather USA Inc.......................... G 973 598-0890
High Point *(G-6587)*

Leather Miracles LLC.......................... E 828 464-7448
Hickory *(G-6386)*

LEATHER, LEATHER GOODS & FURS, WHOLESALE

Arcona Leather Company LLC............... G 828 396-7728
Hudson *(G-6941)*

Carroll Companies Inc......................... F 828 466-5489
Conover *(G-3502)*

Jenkins Properties Inc........................ E 336 667-4282
North Wilkesboro *(G-9537)*

LEATHER: Accessory Prdts

Oowee Incorporated........................... F 828 633-0289
Candler *(G-1230)*

Tasman Industries Inc......................... F 502 587-0701
High Point *(G-6802)*

LEATHER: Processed

Leather Magic Inc............................... G 704 283-5078
Monroe *(G-8515)*

LICENSE TAGS: Automobile, Stamped Metal

City of Graham................................... F 336 570-6811
Graham *(G-5264)*

License Plate Agency.......................... G 910 763-7076
Wilmington *(G-12835)*

NC License Plate Agency..................... G 910 347-1000
Jacksonville *(G-7134)*

NC Motor Vhcl Lcnse Plate Agcy.......... G 336 228-7152
Burlington *(G-1136)*

North Carolina Dept Trnsp................... E 704 633-5873
Salisbury *(G-11098)*

North Crlina Lcense Plate Agcy............ G 910 485-1590
Fayetteville *(G-4646)*

LIFE SAVING & SURVIVAL EQPT REPAIR SVCS, NONMEDICAL

Turbomed LLC.................................... F 973 527-5299
Fayetteville *(G-4684)*

LIGHTING EQPT: Flashlights

Energizer Holdings Inc........................ C 336 672-3526
Asheboro *(G-352)*

LIGHTING EQPT: Motor Vehicle, NEC

Three GS Enterprises Inc..................... F 828 696-2060
Flat Rock *(G-4714)*

LIGHTING FIXTURES WHOLESALERS

Clarolux Inc....................................... E 336 378-6800
Greensboro *(G-5447)*

Conservation Station Inc...................... G 919 932-9201
Chapel Hill *(G-1539)*

Egi Associates Inc.............................. F 704 561-3337
Charlotte *(G-2093)*

LIGHTING FIXTURES, NEC

Blue Sun Energy Inc........................... G 336 218-6707
Greensboro *(G-5393)*

Busiapp Corporation............................ G 877 558-2518
Morrisville *(G-8947)*

Dandy Light Traps Inc......................... G 980 223-2744
Statesville *(G-11684)*

Furnlite Inc.. E 704 538-3193
Fallston *(G-4523)*

Lightjunction..................................... G 919 607-9717
Morrisville *(G-9011)*

Nexxus Lighting Inc............................ F 704 405-0416
Charlotte *(G-2563)*

Parhelion Incorporated........................ F 866 409-1839
Apex *(G-184)*

PDM Lighting LLC............................... G 919 771-3230
Raleigh *(G-10364)*

Pelican Ventures LLC.......................... G 919 518-8203
Raleigh *(G-10365)*

Powertac Usa Inc............................... G 919 239-4470
Greensboro *(G-5753)*

Progress Solar Solutions LLC............... F 919 363-3738
Raleigh *(G-10401)*

S C I A Inc... G 919 387-7000
Cary *(G-1444)*

Specialty Manufacturing Inc................. D 704 247-9300
Charlotte *(G-2841)*

Srb Technologies Inc.......................... E 336 659-2610
Winston Salem *(G-13341)*

Sunnex Inc.. F 800 445-7869
Charlotte *(G-2882)*

W F Harris Lighting Inc............................ F 704 283-7477
Monroe *(G-8577)*

LIGHTING FIXTURES: Arc

Cyberlux Corporation............................. F 984 363-6894
Research Triangle Pa *(G-10707)*

LIGHTING FIXTURES: Decorative Area

Light Source Usa Inc............................. E 704 504-8399
Charlotte *(G-2420)*

LIGHTING FIXTURES: Fluorescent, Commercial

Optimum Lighting LLC........................... E 508 646-3324
Henderson *(G-6168)*

W F Harris Lighting Inc........................... F 704 283-7477
Monroe *(G-8577)*

LIGHTING FIXTURES: Fluorescent, Residential

W F Harris Lighting Inc........................... F 704 283-7477
Monroe *(G-8577)*

LIGHTING FIXTURES: Indl & Commercial

A M Moore and Company Inc................ G 336 294-6994
Greensboro *(G-5332)*

Arva LLC.. G 803 336-2230
Charlotte *(G-1701)*

Atlas Lighting Products Inc.................. C 336 222-9258
Burlington *(G-1049)*

Avcon Inc.. E 919 388-0203
Cary *(G-1302)*

Biologcal Innvtion Optmztion S........... F 321 260-2467
Wake Forest *(G-12264)*

Conservation Station Inc..................... G 919 932-9201
Chapel Hill *(G-1539)*

Enttec Americas LLC........................... F 919 200-6468
Durham *(G-4026)*

Idaho Wood Inc................................... F 208 263-9521
Oxford *(G-9617)*

Invictus Lighting LLC........................... G 828 855-9324
Hickory *(G-6372)*

Lumenfocus LLC................................. F 252 430-6970
Henderson *(G-6165)*

Progress Solar Solutions LLC.............. F 919 363-3738
Raleigh *(G-10401)*

Shat-R-Shield Lighting Inc.................. D 800 223-0853
Salisbury *(G-11115)*

Shield & Steel Enterprises LLC............ G 704 607-0869
Salisbury *(G-11116)*

Specialty Lighting LLC......................... F 704 538-6522
Fallston *(G-4524)*

Stevens Lighting Inc........................... F 910 944-7187
Carthage *(G-1281)*

LIGHTING FIXTURES: Motor Vehicle

B/E Aerospace Inc.............................. F 336 692-8940
Winston Salem *(G-13098)*

Go Ev and Go Green Corp.................... G 704 327-9040
Charlotte *(G-2220)*

LIGHTING FIXTURES: Residential, Electric

Epl & Solar Corp................................. G 201 577-8966
Wake Forest *(G-12276)*

LIGHTING FIXTURES: Street

Curlee Machinery Company.................. G 919 467-9311
Cary *(G-1341)*

M-B Industries Inc.............................. C 828 862-4201
Rosman *(G-10913)*

LIGHTING FIXTURES: Swimming Pool

Hayward Holdings Inc.......................... C 704 837-8002
Charlotte *(G-2263)*

LIGHTING FIXTURES: Underwater

Pentair Water Pool and Spa Inc........... D 919 463-4640
Cary *(G-1417)*

Pentair Water Pool and Spa Inc........... A 919 566-8000
Sanford *(G-11217)*

LIME ROCK: Ground

Limestone Products Inc....................... G 704 283-9492
Monroe *(G-8517)*

LIMESTONE: Crushed & Broken

Boyd Stone & Quarries......................... G 828 659-6862
Marion *(G-8036)*

Buffalo Crushed Stone Inc.................. F 919 688-6881
Durham *(G-3948)*

Bwi Etn LLC.. F 828 682-2645
Burnsville *(G-1184)*

Heidelberg Mtls Sthast Agg LLC........... E 919 936-4221
Princeton *(G-9824)*

Marietta Martin Materials Inc............... E 704 525-7740
Charlotte *(G-2456)*

Marietta Martin Materials Inc............... G 252 749-2641
Fountain *(G-4806)*

Marietta Martin Materials Inc............... G 919 772-3563
Garner *(G-4938)*

Marietta Martin Materials Inc............... G 336 668-3253
Greensboro *(G-5673)*

Marietta Martin Materials Inc............... G 828 322-8386
Hickory *(G-6392)*

Marietta Martin Materials Inc............... G 336 886-5015
Jamestown *(G-7171)*

Marietta Martin Materials Inc............... G 336 769-3803
Kernersville *(G-7284)*

Marietta Martin Materials Inc............... G 704 739-4761
Kings Mountain *(G-7372)*

Marietta Martin Materials Inc............... G 704 283-4915
Monroe *(G-8524)*

Marietta Martin Materials Inc............... F 919 788-4392
Raleigh *(G-10270)*

Marietta Martin Materials Inc............... G 336 349-3333
Reidsville *(G-10692)*

Marietta Martin Materials Inc............... F 704 636-6372
Salisbury *(G-11089)*

Marietta Martin Materials Inc............... G 704 873-8191
Statesville *(G-11729)*

Marietta Martin Materials Inc............... G 704 278-2218
Woodleaf *(G-13429)*

Martin Marietta Materials Inc............... G 919 894-2003
Benson *(G-794)*

Martin Marietta Materials Inc............... G 336 584-8875
Burlington *(G-1123)*

Martin Marietta Materials Inc............... G 910 675-2283
Castle Hayne *(G-1505)*

Martin Marietta Materials Inc............... G 704 547-9775
Charlotte *(G-2461)*

Martin Marietta Materials Inc............... G 704 588-1471
Charlotte *(G-2462)*

Martin Marietta Materials Inc............... G 704 932-4377
China Grove *(G-3076)*

Martin Marietta Materials Inc............... G 704 786-8415
Concord *(G-3398)*

Martin Marietta Materials Inc............... G 336 375-7584
Greensboro *(G-5678)*

Martin Marietta Materials Inc............... G 336 674-0836
Greensboro *(G-5679)*

Martin Marietta Materials Inc............... G 910 371-3848
Leland *(G-7554)*

Martin Marietta Materials Inc............... F 828 754-3077
Lenoir *(G-7625)*

Martin Marietta Materials Inc............... G 252 633-5308
New Bern *(G-9380)*

Martin Marietta Materials Inc............... G 336 672-1501
Randleman *(G-10651)*

Martin Marietta Materials Inc............... G 336 672-1501
Randleman *(G-10652)*

Martin Marietta Materials Inc............... G 919 788-4391
Sanford *(G-11207)*

Martin Marietta Materials Inc............... C 919 781-4550
Raleigh *(G-10277)*

Quarries Petroleum.............................. G 919 387-0986
Apex *(G-190)*

Radford Quarries Inc........................... F 828 264-7008
Boone *(G-939)*

LIMESTONE: Dimension

Nantahala Talc & Limestone Co............ F 828 321-4239
Topton *(G-12105)*

LINENS: Tablecloths, From Purchased Materials

Sanders Industries Inc......................... G 410 277-8565
Waynesville *(G-12472)*

Watson Party Tables Inc....................... F 919 294-9153
Durham *(G-4302)*

LINERS & COVERS: Fabric

Howell & Sons Canvas Repairs............. G 704 892-7913
Cornelius *(G-3607)*

Winstn-Slem Inds For Blind Inc............ B 336 759-0551
Winston Salem *(G-13398)*

LINERS: Indl, Metal Plate

B&B Cap Liners LLC............................. G 585 598-1828
Raleigh *(G-9927)*

LININGS: Fabric, Apparel & Other, Exc Millinery

Domestic Fabrics Blankets Corp........... E 252 523-7948
Kinston *(G-7406)*

LIQUID CRYSTAL DISPLAYS

Lxd Research & Display LLC.................. F 919 600-6440
Raleigh *(G-10263)*

Smallhd LLC....................................... F 919 439-2166
Cary *(G-1461)*

LITHIUM MINERAL MINING

Piedmont Lithium Inc........................... F 704 461-8000
Belmont *(G-762)*

LITHOGRAPHIC PLATES

F C C LLC.. G 336 883-7314
High Point *(G-6617)*

Southern Lithoplate Inc....................... C 919 556-9400
Youngsville *(G-13487)*

LOADS: Electronic

Vishay Transducers Ltd......................... E 919 365-3800
Wendell *(G-12553)*

LOCKERS

Penco Products Inc............................. E 252 917-5287
Greenville *(G-6012)*

LOCKERS: Wood, Exc Refrigerated

Treeforms Inc..................................... E 336 292-8998
Greensboro *(G-5871)*

P
R
O
D
U
C
T

LOCKS

Appalachian Technology LLC................ E 828 210-8888
Asheville *(G-427)*

Assa Abloy ACC Door Cntrls Gro.......... C 877 974-2255
Monroe *(G-8432)*

Norton Door Controls........................ F 704 233-4011
Monroe *(G-8538)*

LOCKS & LOCK SETS, WHOLESALE

Norton Door Controls........................ F 704 233-4011
Monroe *(G-8538)*

LOCKS: Safe & Vault, Metal

Kaba Ilco Corp.................................. B 336 725-1331
Winston Salem *(G-13222)*

LOCKSMITHS

ACS Advnced Clor Solutions Inc........... G 252 442-0098
Rocky Mount *(G-10821)*

Ilco Unican Holding Corp..................... G 252 446-3321
Rocky Mount *(G-10843)*

Kaba Ilco Corp.................................. A 252 446-3321
Rocky Mount *(G-10844)*

Omnia Industries LLC........................ G 704 707-6062
Matthews *(G-8138)*

LOGGING

Associated Artists Southport.............. G 910 457-5450
Southport *(G-11517)*

Autry Logging Inc.............................. G 910 303-4943
Stedman *(G-11805)*

Black River Logging Inc...................... G 910 669-2850
Ivanhoe *(G-7110)*

Bracey Bros Logging LLC.................... G 910 231-9543
Delco *(G-3734)*

Bradley Todd Baugus......................... G 252 665-4901
Maysville *(G-8210)*

Brett McHenry Logging LLC................. G 252 243-7285
Wilson *(G-12971)*

Buds Logging and Trucking................. G 704 465-8016
Wadesboro *(G-12238)*

Coastal Carolina Loggin..................... G 252 474-2165
Ernul *(G-4490)*

Conetoe Land & Timber LLC................ G 252 717-4648
Goldsboro *(G-5208)*

D & W Logging Inc............................. G 919 820-0826
Four Oaks *(G-4810)*

Dan Morton Logging.......................... G 919 693-1898
Oxford *(G-9612)*

Douglas Temple & Son Inc.................. G 252 771-5676
Elizabeth City *(G-4386)*

Dustin Ellis Logging.......................... G 704 732-6027
Lincolnton *(G-7829)*

East Coast Log & Timber Inc............... G 252 568-4344
Albertson *(G-99)*

Edsel G Barnes Jr Inc........................ F 252 793-4170
Plymouth *(G-9803)*

Emanuel Hoggard............................. F 252 794-3724
Windsor *(G-13053)*

Eric Martin Jermey........................... G 704 692-0389
Bostic *(G-962)*

General Wood Preserving Co Inc.......... G 910 371-3131
Leland *(G-7545)*

George P Gatling Logging................... G 252 465-8983
Sunbury *(G-11847)*

Gmd Logging Inc.............................. G 704 985-5460
Albemarle *(G-75)*

Hardister Logging............................. G 336 857-2397
Denton *(G-3749)*

Hunt Logging Co............................... G 919 853-2850
Louisburg *(G-7918)*

Ivey Icenhour DBA............................. G 704 786-0676
Mount Pleasant *(G-9262)*

J E Kerr Timber Co Corp..................... G 252 537-0544
Roanoke Rapids *(G-10739)*

James Keith Nations.......................... G 828 421-5391
Whittier *(G-12624)*

James L Johnson.............................. G 704 694-0103
Wadesboro *(G-12246)*

Juan J Hernandez............................. G 919 742-3381
Siler City *(G-11414)*

K & J Ashworth Logging LLC............... G 336 879-2388
Seagrove *(G-11277)*

Keith Laws...................................... G 336 973-7220
Wilkesboro *(G-12645)*

Laceys Tree Service........................... G 910 330-2868
Jacksonville *(G-7129)*

Lyon Logging................................... G 336 957-3131
Thurmond *(G-12098)*

M M & D Harvesting Inc...................... G 252 793-4074
Plymouth *(G-9806)*

Matthew Johnson Logging.................. G 919 291-0197
Sanford *(G-11208)*

McKoys Logging Company Inc.............. G 910 862-2706
Elizabethtown *(G-4429)*

Montgomery Logging Inc.................... G 910 572-2806
Troy *(G-12163)*

Nathan Beiler.................................. G 252 935-5141
Pantego *(G-9647)*

North Cape Fear Logging LLC.............. G 910 876-3197
Harrells *(G-6102)*

OBrien Logging Co............................ G 910 655-3830
Delco *(G-3738)*

Pack Brothers Logging....................... G 828 894-2191
Mill Spring *(G-8302)*

Piedmont Logging LLC....................... G 919 562-1861
Youngsville *(G-13480)*

Preferred Logging............................. G 910 471-4011
Delco *(G-3739)*

Richard Lewis Von............................ G 910 628-9292
Orrum *(G-9605)*

Ronnie L Poole................................. G 336 657-3956
Ennice *(G-4489)*

Shepherd Family Logging LLC............. G 910 572-4098
Troy *(G-12167)*

Southern Style Logging LLC................ G 910 259-9897
Rocky Point *(G-10883)*

SSS Logging Inc............................... G 828 467-1155
Marion *(G-8067)*

Steven C Haddock DBA Haddock.......... G 252 714-2431
Vanceboro *(G-12222)*

Stump Logging................................ G 910 620-7000
Supply *(G-11860)*

Summit Logging LLC.......................... G 910 734-8787
Lumberton *(G-7973)*

T W Hathcock Logging Inc................... G 704 485-9457
Locust *(G-7905)*

Top Notch Log Homes Inc................... G 828 926-4300
Waynesville *(G-12477)*

Triple E Equipment LLC...................... G 252 448-1002
Trenton *(G-12112)*

Vincent L Taylor............................... G 252 792-2987
Williamston *(G-12676)*

W H Bunting Thinning........................ G 252 826-4025
Scotland Neck *(G-11267)*

William Shawn Staley........................ G 336 838-9193
Millers Creek *(G-8308)*

Wst Logging LLC.............................. G 336 857-0147
Denton *(G-3766)*

Young Logging Company Inc............... G 919 552-9753
Willow Spring *(G-12683)*

LOGGING CAMPS & CONTRACTORS

360 Forest Products Inc...................... G 910 285-5838
Wallace *(G-12318)*

Alan Walsh Logging LLC..................... G 828 234-7500
Lenoir *(G-7569)*

Allen Brothers Timber Company........... G 910 997-6412
Rockingham *(G-10770)*

Allen R Goodson Logging Co............... G 910 455-4177
Jacksonville *(G-7115)*

Alligood Brothers Logging.................. G 252 927-2358
Washington *(G-12371)*

Anthony B Andrews Logging Inc........... G 252 448-8901
Trenton *(G-12109)*

Arcola Logging Co Inc........................ G 252 257-3205
Macon *(G-7982)*

Arrants Logging Inc........................... F 252 792-1889
Jamesville *(G-7182)*

Ashworth Logging............................. G 910 464-2136
Carthage *(G-1275)*

Atlantic Logging Inc........................... G 252 229-9997
New Bern *(G-9335)*

Backwoods Logging LLC.................... G 910 298-3786
Pink Hill *(G-9764)*

Barnes Logging Co Inc....................... F 252 799-6016
Plymouth *(G-9798)*

Bateman Logging Co Inc..................... F 252 482-8959
Edenton *(G-4362)*

Bill Ratliff Jr Logging I......................... G 704 694-5403
Wadesboro *(G-12235)*

Billy Harrell Logging Inc...................... G 252 221-4995
Tyner *(G-12182)*

Billy Harrell Logging Inc...................... G 252 426-1362
Hertford *(G-6251)*

Blankenship Logging......................... G 828 652-2250
Nebo *(G-9327)*

Bobby A Herring Logging.................... G 919 658-9768
Mount Olive *(G-9249)*

Boone Logging Company Inc............... G 252 443-7641
Elm City *(G-4464)*

Broadway Logging Co Inc................... E 252 633-2693
New Bern *(G-9341)*

Brown Brothers Lumber...................... G 828 632-6486
Taylorsville *(G-11951)*

Brown Creek Timber Company Inc........ G 704 694-3529
Wadesboro *(G-12237)*

Buck Lucas Logging Companies........... G 252 410-0160
Roanoke Rapids *(G-10732)*

Bundy Logging Company Inc............... G 252 357-0191
Gatesville *(G-5170)*

By Faith Logging Inc.......................... G 252 792-0019
Williamston *(G-12668)*

Cahoon Brothers Logging LLC............. F 252 943-9901
Pantego *(G-9641)*

Cahoon Logging Company Inc............. G 252 943-6805
Pinetown *(G-9708)*

Capps Noble Logging........................ G 828 696-9690
Zirconia *(G-13528)*

Caraway Logging Inc.......................... G 252 633-1230
New Bern *(G-9347)*

Carolina East Timber Inc.................... G 252 638-1914
New Bern *(G-9348)*

Cauley Construction Company............. G 252 522-1078
Kinston *(G-7401)*

Chapman Brothers Logging LLC.......... G 828 437-6498
Connelly Springs *(G-3474)*

Charles Ferguson Logging.................. G 336 921-3126
Moravian Falls *(G-8809)*

CJ Stallings Logging Inc..................... F 252 297-2272
Belvidere *(G-778)*

Claybourn Walters Log Co Inc............. F 910 628-7075
Fairmont *(G-4501)*

D & M Logging of Wnc LLC .... G 828 648-4366
  Canton (G-1251)

D T Bracy Logging Inc .... G 252 332-8332
  Ahoskie (G-46)

Dannies Logging Inc .... G 919 528-2370
  Creedmoor (G-3647)

Darrell T Bracy .... G 252 358-1432
  Ahoskie (G-47)

David Raynor Logging Inc .... E 910 980-0129
  Linden (G-7873)

Delbert White Logging Inc .... G 252 209-4779
  Windsor (G-13051)

Donald R Young Logging Inc .... G 910 934-6769
  Lillington (G-7795)

Down South Logging LLC .... G 843 333-1649
  Tabor City (G-11909)

Dr Logging LLC .... G 910 417-9643
  Hamlet (G-6054)

Duncan Junior D .... G 336 871-3599
  Sandy Ridge (G-11143)

Duplin Forest Products Inc .... G 910 285-5381
  Wallace (G-12320)

East Coast Logging Inc .... G 252 794-4054
  Windsor (G-13052)

Enterprise Loggers Company Inc .... F 252 586-4805
  Littleton (G-7885)

Evans Logging Inc .... F 252 792-3865
  Jamesville (G-7183)

Evergreen Forest Products Inc .... G 910 762-9156
  Wilmington (G-12772)

Evergreen Logging LLC .... G 910 654-1662
  Evergreen (G-4498)

Frankie York Logging Co .... G 252 633-4825
  New Bern (G-9368)

Fred R Harrris Logging Inc .... G 919 853-2266
  Louisburg (G-7916)

G & H Broadway Logging Inc .... G 252 229-4594
  New Bern (G-9369)

Glacier Forestry Inc .... G 704 902-2594
  Mooresville (G-8673)

Gladsons Logging LLC .... G 252 670-8813
  Aurora (G-642)

Glenn Trexler & Sons Log Inc .... G 704 694-5644
  Wadesboro (G-12242)

Gold Creek Inc .... G 336 468-4495
  Hamptonville (G-6084)

Goodson S All Terrain Log Inc .... G 910 347-7919
  Jacksonville (G-7125)

Gouge Logging .... G 828 675-9216
  Burnsville (G-1186)

Grady & Son Atkins Logging .... G 919 934-7785
  Four Oaks (G-4812)

Greene Logging .... G 336 667-6960
  Purlear (G-9831)

H & L Logging Inc .... F 252 793-2778
  Plymouth (G-9805)

H Clyde Moore Jr .... G 910 642-3507
  Whiteville (G-12583)

Harris Logging LLC .... G 336 859-2786
  Denton (G-3750)

Hofler Logging Inc .... G 252 465-8921
  Sunbury (G-11849)

Holmes Logging - Wallace LLC .... F 910 271-1216
  Wallace (G-12321)

Htc Logging Inc .... G 828 625-1601
  Mill Spring (G-8301)

J & J Logging Inc .... E 252 430-1110
  Henderson (G-6162)

J E Carpenter Logging Co Inc .... G 252 633-0037
  Trent Woods (G-12107)

J&R Cohoon Logging & Tidewater .... G 252 943-6300
  Pantego (G-9645)

Jackson Logging .... G 919 658-2757
  Mount Olive (G-9256)

James Moore & Son Logging .... G 336 656-9858
  Browns Summit (G-999)

Jared Sasnett Logging Co Inc .... G 252 939-6289
  Kinston (G-7416)

Jeffers Logging Inc .... G 919 708-2193
  Sanford (G-11196)

Jh Logging .... G 336 599-0278
  Roxboro (G-10928)

Jif Logging Inc .... G 252 398-2249
  Murfreesboro (G-9282)

Jimmy D Nelms Logging Inc .... G 919 853-2597
  Louisburg (G-7919)

Johnny Daniel .... G 336 859-2480
  Denton (G-3752)

K L Butler Logging Inc .... G 910 648-6016
  Bladenboro (G-878)

Keck Logging Company .... G 336 538-6903
  Gibsonville (G-5179)

Keith Call Logging LLC .... G 336 262-3681
  Millers Creek (G-8305)

Ken Horton Logging LLC .... G 336 789-2849
  Mount Airy (G-9140)

Ken Wood Corp .... G 252 792-6481
  Williamston (G-12671)

Lake Creek Logging & Trckg Inc .... F 910 532-2041
  Harrells (G-6101)

Lane Land & Timber Inc .... G 252 443-1151
  Battleboro (G-700)

Ledford Logging Co Inc .... G 828 644-5410
  Murphy (G-9291)

Leonard Logging Co .... G 336 857-2776
  Denton (G-3755)

Little Logging Inc .... F 704 201-8185
  Oakboro (G-9580)

M & K Logging LLC .... G 252 349-8975
  New Bern (G-9376)

Mark III Logging Inc .... G 910 862-4820
  Tar Heel (G-11917)

McKeel & Sons Logging Inc .... G 252 244-3903
  Vanceboro (G-12219)

McLendon Logging Incorporated .... G 910 439-6223
  Mount Gilead (G-9202)

Merritt Logging & Chipping Co .... G 910 862-4905
  Elizabethtown (G-4430)

Michael L Goodson Logging Inc .... G 910 346-8399
  Jacksonville (G-7131)

Micheal Langdon Logging Inc .... G 910 890-5295
  Erwin (G-4491)

Mike Atkins & Son Logging Inc .... G 919 965-8002
  Selma (G-11290)

Miller Logging Co Inc .... G 252 229-9860
  Vanceboro (G-12220)

Mud Duck Operations .... G 910 253-7669
  Bolivia (G-886)

Nat Black Logging Inc .... G 704 826-8834
  Ansonville (G-130)

Noble Brothers Logging Company .... G 252 355-2587
  Winterville (G-13420)

Nrfp Logging LLC .... G 919 738-0989
  Goldsboro (G-5232)

OLT Logging Inc .... G 919 894-4506
  Smithfield (G-11456)

Phillip Dunn Logging Co Inc .... G 252 633-4577
  New Bern (G-9388)

Potter Logging .... G 704 483-2738
  Denver (G-3799)

Potts Logging Inc .... G 704 463-7549
  New London (G-9420)

Price Logging Inc .... F 252 792-5687
  Jamesville (G-7184)

Puett Trucking & Logging .... G 919 853-2071
  Louisburg (G-7923)

R & R Logging Inc .... G 704 483-5733
  Iron Station (G-7107)

R & S Logging Inc .... G 252 426-5880
  Hertford (G-6256)

R R Mickey Logging Inc .... G 910 205-0525
  Hamlet (G-6061)

R W Britt Logging Inc .... G 252 799-7682
  Pinetown (G-9709)

Rabbit Bottom Logging Co Inc .... G 252 257-3585
  Warrenton (G-12353)

Randolph Goodson Logging Inc .... G 910 347-5117
  Jacksonville (G-7141)

Red Maple Logging Company Inc .... G 704 279-6379
  Rockwell (G-10800)

Richard C Jones .... G 919 853-2096
  Louisburg (G-7926)

Robert L Rich Tmber Hrvstg Inc .... G 910 529-7321
  Garland (G-4910)

Rondol Cordon Logging Inc .... G 252 944-9220
  Washington (G-12411)

Ronnie Andrews .... G 336 921-4017
  Boomer (G-893)

Ronnie Boyds Logging LLC .... G 336 613-0229
  Eden (G-4355)

Ronnie Garrett Logging .... G 828 894-8413
  Columbus (G-3304)

Ross Phelps Logging Co Inc .... F 252 356-2560
  Colerain (G-3272)

Russell Loudermilk Logging .... G 828 632-4968
  Taylorsville (G-11976)

S & K Logging Inc .... G 252 794-2045
  Windsor (G-13057)

Shelton Logging & Chipping Inc .... G 336 548-3860
  Stoneville (G-11827)

Simmons Logging & Trucking Inc .... G 910 287-6344
  Ash (G-322)

Smith Brothers Logging .... G 828 265-1506
  Deep Gap (G-3730)

Smiths Logging .... G 910 653-4422
  Tabor City (G-11914)

Snowbird Logging LLC .... G 828 479-6635
  Robbinsville (G-10764)

Southeast Wood Products Inc .... F 910 285-4359
  Wallace (G-12324)

Southern Logging Inc .... G 336 859-5057
  Denton (G-3760)

Squeaks Logging Inc .... G 252 794-1531
  Windsor (G-13058)

Steve Evans Logging Inc .... G 252 792-1836
  Williamston (G-12674)

Stone House Creek Logging .... G 252 586-4477
  Littleton (G-7887)

Swain & Temple Inc .... F 252 771-8147
  South Mills (G-11493)

SWB Logging LLC .... G 704 485-3411
  Oakboro (G-9583)

Tar River Thinning Inc .... G 919 497-1647
  Louisburg (G-7927)

Terry Leggett Logging Co Inc .... E 252 927-4671
  Pinetown (G-9710)

Terry Logging Company .... G 919 477-9170
  Bahama (G-667)

Thomas Timber Inc .... G 910 532-4542
  Harrells (G-6103)

Tim Con Wood Products Inc .... F 252 793-4819
  Roper (G-10900)

Timber Harvester Inc .... G 910 346-9754
  Jacksonville (G-7156)

Timber Specialists LLC .... F 704 873-5756
  Statesville (G-11790)

PRODUCT

Timber Stand Improvements Inc............ G 910 439-6121
Mount Gilead *(G-9210)*

Trexler Logging Inc................................. G 704 694-5272
Wadesboro *(G-12250)*

Tucker Logging...................................... G 336 857-2674
Denton *(G-3764)*

W & T Logging LLC............................... G 252 209-4351
Windsor *(G-13059)*

W R White Inc....................................... F 252 794-6577
Windsor *(G-13060)*

Wade Biggs Logging Inc........................ G 252 927-4470
Pinetown *(G-9711)*

Wetherington Logging Inc....................... G 252 393-8435
Stella *(G-11809)*

Williams Logging Inc............................. G 919 542-2740
Moncure *(G-8413)*

Wilson Bros Logging Inc........................ F 252 445-5317
Enfield *(G-4486)*

Wood Logging....................................... G 910 866-4018
White Oak *(G-12575)*

LOGGING: Timber, Cut At Logging Camp

Arauco - NA... G 910 569-7020
Biscoe *(G-846)*

Cjc Enterprises..................................... E 919 266-3158
Wake Forest *(G-12270)*

JM Williams Timber Company................ G 919 362-1333
Apex *(G-172)*

Log Home Builders Inc.......................... G 704 638-0677
Salisbury *(G-11087)*

Noralex Inc.. G 252 974-1253
Vanceboro *(G-12221)*

Timber Specialists Inc.......................... G 704 902-5146
Statesville *(G-11789)*

Turn Bull Lumber Company.................... F 336 272-5200
Greensboro *(G-5883)*

Wright & Hobbs Inc............................... E 252 537-5817
Roanoke Rapids *(G-10748)*

LOGGING: Wooden Logs

Ivp Forest Products LLC........................ F 252 241-8126
Morehead City *(G-8836)*

LOGS: Gas, Fireplace

Dna Services Inc................................... G 910 279-2775
Kure Beach *(G-7464)*

LOTIONS OR CREAMS: Face

3rd Phaze Bdy Oils Urban Lnks............. G 704 344-1138
Charlotte *(G-1603)*

Clutch Inc.. F 919 448-8654
Durham *(G-3979)*

Lash Out Inc.. G 919 342-0221
Clayton *(G-3156)*

Naturally ME Boutique Inc..................... G 919 519-0783
Durham *(G-4143)*

Product Quest Manufacturing Inc.......... C 386 239-8787
Winston Salem *(G-13305)*

Product Quest Manufacturing LLC......... B 386 239-8787
Winston Salem *(G-13306)*

SC Johnson Prof USA Inc...................... D 704 263-4240
Stanley *(G-11624)*

SC Johnson Prof USA Inc...................... C 443 521-1606
Charlotte *(G-2760)*

UGLy Essentials LLC............................ F 910 319-9945
Raleigh *(G-10572)*

LOTIONS: SHAVING

Johnny Slicks Inc.................................. G 910 803-2159
Holly Ridge *(G-6890)*

LOUDSPEAKERS

Quality Musical Systems Inc.................. E 828 667-5719
Candler *(G-1231)*

LOZENGES: Pharmaceutical

Bestco LLC.. C 704 664-4300
Mooresville *(G-8614)*

LUBRICATING OIL & GREASE WHOLESALERS

Moroil Corp.. F 704 795-9595
Concord *(G-3405)*

Warren Oil Company LLC....................... D 910 892-6456
Dunn *(G-3871)*

LUBRICATION SYSTEMS & EQPT

Balcrank Corporation............................. E 800 747-5300
Weaverville *(G-12483)*

Bijur Delimon Intl Inc............................ E 919 465-4448
Raleigh *(G-9944)*

Farval Lubrication Systems.................... E 252 527-6001
Kinston *(G-7411)*

Farval Lubrication Systems.................... E 252 527-6001
Kinston *(G-7412)*

Linter North America Corp...................... G 828 645-4261
Asheville *(G-537)*

Petroliance LLC..................................... C 336 472-3000
Thomasville *(G-12059)*

LUGGAGE & BRIEFCASES

Cross Canvas Company Inc.................... E 828 252-0440
Asheville *(G-480)*

Saundra D Hall...................................... G 828 251-9859
Asheville *(G-595)*

Tumi Store - Chrltte Dglas Int................ F 704 359-8771
Charlotte *(G-2953)*

LUMBER & BLDG MATLS DEALER, RET: Electric Constructn Matls

Southern Concrete Materials Inc............ C 828 253-6421
Asheville *(G-608)*

Southland Electrical Sup LLC................ C 336 227-1486
Burlington *(G-1160)*

LUMBER & BLDG MATLS DEALER, RET: Garage Doors, Sell/Install

Amarr Company...................................... C 336 744-5100
Winston Salem *(G-13084)*

LUMBER & BLDG MATRLS DEALERS, RETAIL: Doors, Wood/Metal

Carport Central Inc............................... E 336 673-6020
Mount Airy *(G-9111)*

LUMBER & BLDG MTRLS DEALERS, RET: Planing Mill Prdts/Lumber

Glenn Lumber Company Inc.................... E 704 434-7873
Shelby *(G-11338)*

Hewlin Brothers Lumber Co................... G 252 586-6473
Enfield *(G-4484)*

Walton Lumber Co................................. G 919 563-6565
Mebane *(G-8264)*

LUMBER & BUILDING MATERIAL DEALERS, RETAIL: Roofing Material

Triad Corrugated Metal Inc.................... E 336 625-9727
Asheboro *(G-411)*

LUMBER & BUILDING MATERIALS DEALER, RET: Door & Window Prdts

Hunter Millwork Inc............................... F 704 821-0144
Matthews *(G-8174)*

Maxson & Associates............................ G 336 632-0524
Greensboro *(G-5683)*

Shutter Production Inc.......................... G 910 289-2620
Rose Hill *(G-10910)*

TRf Manufacturing NC Inc..................... E 252 223-1112
Newport *(G-9445)*

LUMBER & BUILDING MATERIALS DEALER, RET: Masonry Matls/Splys

Glover Materials Inc.............................. G 252 536-2660
Pleasant Hill *(G-9797)*

Leonard Block Company........................ G 336 764-0607
Winston Salem *(G-13233)*

Superior Walls Systems LLC................. E 704 636-6200
Salisbury *(G-11120)*

LUMBER & BUILDING MATERIALS DEALERS, RETAIL: Brick

General Shale Brick Inc......................... F 704 937-7431
Grover *(G-6043)*

Pine Hall Brick Co Inc........................... F 336 721-7500
Madison *(G-7996)*

Triangle Brick Company......................... E 704 695-1420
Wadesboro *(G-12251)*

Triangle Brick Company......................... E 919 544-1796
Durham *(G-4277)*

LUMBER & BUILDING MATERIALS DEALERS, RETAIL: Sand & Gravel

Privette Enterprises Inc........................ E 704 634-3291
Monroe *(G-8544)*

LUMBER & BUILDING MATERIALS DEALERS, RETAIL: Siding

Carolina Windows and Doors Inc........... F 252 756-2585
Greenville *(G-5951)*

LUMBER & BUILDING MATERIALS RET DEALERS: Millwork & Lumber

Bfs Operations LLC.............................. A 919 431-1000
Raleigh *(G-9942)*

Builders Firstsource Inc........................ F 919 562-6601
Youngsville *(G-13465)*

Builders Firstsource - SE Grp............... G 910 313-3056
Wilmington *(G-12724)*

Smokey Mountain Lumber Inc................ G 828 298-3958
Asheville *(G-602)*

Stock Building Supply Holdings LLC..... A 919 431-1000
Raleigh *(G-10509)*

Triad Prefinish & Lbr Sls Inc................. G 336 375-4849
Greensboro *(G-5877)*

LUMBER & BUILDING MATLS DEALERS, RET: Screens, Door/Window

All Glass Inc... G 828 324-8609
Hickory *(G-6262)*

LUMBER: Dimension, Hardwood

Church & Church Lumber LLC................ D 336 973-5700
Wilkesboro *(G-12631)*

J & D Wood Inc...................................... F 910 628-9000
Fairmont *(G-4502)*

LUMBER: Flooring, Dressed, Softwood

Powell Industries Inc........................... D 828 926-9114
  Waynesville **(G-12467)**

Universal Forest Products Inc.............. F 252 338-0319
  Elizabeth City **(G-4416)**

LUMBER: Flooring, Dressed, Softwood

Beasley Flooring Products Inc............. E 828 524-3248
  Bryson City **(G-1008)**

LUMBER: Hardboard

Custom Finishers Inc........................... E 336 431-7141
  High Point **(G-6584)**

Louisiana-Pacific Corporation............. C 336 696-2751
  North Wilkesboro **(G-9543)**

LUMBER: Hardwood Dimension

Fortner Lumber Inc.............................. G 704 585-2383
  Hiddenite **(G-6496)**

North Carolina Lumber Company.......... G 336 498-6600
  Randleman **(G-10654)**

Parton Lumber Company Inc................. D 828 287-4257
  Rutherfordton **(G-10990)**

Tima Capital Inc................................... F 910 769-3273
  Wilmington **(G-12939)**

Turn Bull Lumber Company.................. E 910 862-4447
  Elizabethtown **(G-4436)**

W M Cramer Lumber Co........................ D 828 397-7481
  Connelly Springs **(G-3485)**

Walton Lumber Co............................... G 919 563-6565
  Mebane **(G-8264)**

LUMBER: Hardwood Dimension & Flooring Mills

Associated Hardwoods Inc.................... E 828 396-3321
  Granite Falls **(G-5295)**

Beasley Flooring Products Inc............. E 828 349-7000
  Franklin **(G-4818)**

Blue Ridge Lbr Log & Timber Co.......... G 336 961-5211
  Yadkinville **(G-13438)**

Blue Ridge Products Co Inc.................. G 828 322-7990
  Hickory **(G-6274)**

Cagle Sawmill Inc................................ G 336 857-2274
  Denton **(G-3741)**

Chris Isom Inc..................................... F 336 629-0240
  Asheboro **(G-338)**

Church & Church Lumber LLC.............. F 336 838-1256
  Millers Creek **(G-8304)**

Church & Church Lumber LLC.............. D 336 973-4297
  Wilkesboro **(G-12632)**

Clary Lumber Company......................... D 252 537-2558
  Gaston **(G-4978)**

Cleveland Lumber Company.................. E 704 487-5263
  Shelby **(G-11320)**

Columbia Forest Products Inc.............. G 336 605-0429
  Greensboro **(G-5454)**

Columbia Plywood Corporation............. B 828 724-4191
  Old Fort **(G-9592)**

Coxe-Lewis Corporation....................... G 252 357-0050
  Gatesville **(G-5171)**

Danbartex LLC..................................... G 704 323-8728
  Mooresville **(G-8650)**

David Raynor Logging Inc.................... E 910 980-0129
  Linden **(G-7873)**

Dimension Milling Co Inc..................... G 336 983-2820
  Denton **(G-3748)**

Edwards Wood Products Inc................. C 704 624-3624
  Marshville **(G-8088)**

Eekkohart Floors & Lbr Co Inc............. G 336 409-2672
  Mocksville **(G-8361)**

Ethan Allen Retail Inc.......................... E 828 428-9361
  Maiden **(G-8012)**

F L Turlington Lumber Co Inc............... E 910 592-7197
  Clinton **(G-3233)**

Framewright Inc.................................. G 828 459-2284
  Conover **(G-3523)**

Franklin Veneers Inc............................ G 919 494-2284
  Franklinton **(G-4848)**

Gates Custom Milling Inc..................... E 252 357-0116
  Gatesville **(G-5172)**

Glenn Lumber Company Inc.................. E 704 434-7873
  Shelby **(G-11338)**

H T Jones Lumber Company................. G 252 332-4135
  Ahoskie **(G-50)**

Hfi Wind Down Inc.............................. C 828 438-5767
  Morganton **(G-8872)**

HM Frame Company Inc....................... E 828 428-3354
  Newton **(G-9472)**

Hofler H S & Sons Lumber Co.............. G 252 465-8603
  Sunbury **(G-11848)**

Hull Brothers Lumber Co Inc............... G 336 789-5252
  Mount Airy **(G-9130)**

Jones Frame Inc.................................. E 336 434-2531
  High Point **(G-6679)**

Josey Lumber Company Inc.................. E 252 826-5614
  Scotland Neck **(G-11264)**

L F Delp Lumber Co Inc....................... G 336 359-8202
  Laurel Springs **(G-7489)**

Leisure Craft Holdings LLC.................. D 828 693-8241
  Flat Rock **(G-4708)**

Leisure Craft Inc................................. E 828 693-8241
  Flat Rock **(G-4709)**

Mac-Vann Inc....................................... G 919 577-0746
  Sanford **(G-11206)**

Maynard Frame Shop Inc..................... G 910 428-2033
  Star **(G-11631)**

Oceania Hardwoods LLC...................... G 910 862-4447
  Elizabethtown **(G-4431)**

Palletone North Carolina Inc............... D 704 462-1882
  Siler City **(G-11423)**

Piedmont Hardwood Lbr Co Inc............ F 704 436-9311
  Mount Pleasant **(G-9264)**

Price Logging Inc................................ F 252 792-5687
  Jamesville **(G-7184)**

Ritch Face Veneer Company................. G 336 883-4184
  High Point **(G-6758)**

Ross Phelps Logging Co Inc................. F 252 356-2560
  Colerain **(G-3272)**

Shaver Wood Products Inc................... D 704 278-1482
  Cleveland **(G-3221)**

T & S Hardwoods Inc........................... D 828 586-4044
  Sylva **(G-11902)**

Triton International Woods LLC............. D 252 823-6675
  Tarboro **(G-11945)**

United Finishers Intl Inc...................... G 336 883-3901
  High Point **(G-6818)**

Uwharrie Lumber Co............................ F 910 572-3731
  Troy **(G-12170)**

Veneer Technologies Inc...................... C 252 223-5600
  Newport **(G-9446)**

WB Frames Inc.................................... G 828 459-2147
  Hickory **(G-6488)**

Weyerhaeuser Company........................ F 252 746-7200
  Grifton **(G-6039)**

Wright & Hobbs Inc............................. E 252 537-5817
  Roanoke Rapids **(G-10748)**

Zickgraf Enterprises Inc...................... G 704 369-1200
  Franklin **(G-4845)**

LUMBER: Kiln Dried

Jordan-Holman Lumber Co Inc............. D 828 396-3101
  Granite Falls **(G-5309)**

McCreary Modern Inc.......................... B 828 464-6465
  Newton **(G-9481)**

Pleasant Garden Dry Kiln.................... G 336 674-2863
  Pleasant Garden **(G-9793)**

Southeastern Hardwoods Inc............... G 828 581-0197
  Swannanoa **(G-11878)**

World Wood Company........................... D 252 523-0021
  Cove City **(G-3633)**

LUMBER: Plywood, Hardwood

Adwood Corporation............................ E 336 884-1846
  High Point **(G-6510)**

Autumn House Inc............................... D 828 728-1121
  Granite Falls **(G-5297)**

Burke Veneers Inc............................... G 828 437-8510
  Morganton **(G-8854)**

Capitol Funds Inc................................ D 704 482-0645
  Shelby **(G-11315)**

Chesterfield Wood Products Inc........... F 828 433-0042
  Morganton **(G-8856)**

Columbia Panel Mfg Co Inc.................. D 336 861-4100
  High Point **(G-6573)**

Coxe-Lewis Corporation....................... G 252 357-0050
  Gatesville **(G-5171)**

Esco Industries Inc.............................. F 336 495-3772
  Randleman **(G-10647)**

Gates Custom Milling Inc..................... E 252 357-0116
  Gatesville **(G-5172)**

Georgia-Pacific LLC............................. D 919 580-1078
  Dudley **(G-3836)**

HM Frame Company Inc....................... E 828 428-3354
  Newton **(G-9472)**

Tramway Veneers Inc........................... G 919 776-7606
  Sanford **(G-11242)**

Ufp New London LLC........................... F 704 463-1400
  New London **(G-9423)**

LUMBER: Plywood, Hardwood or Hardwood Faced

Atlantic Veneer Company LLC.............. C 252 728-3169
  Beaufort **(G-719)**

Columbia Plywood Corporation............. B 828 724-4191
  Old Fort **(G-9592)**

Georgia-Pacific LLC............................. E 910 642-5041
  Whiteville **(G-12581)**

North Carolina Plywood LLC................. G 850 948-2211
  Whiteville **(G-12591)**

LUMBER: Plywood, Prefinished, Hardwood

Columbia Forest Products Inc.............. C 828 724-9495
  Old Fort **(G-9591)**

Columbia Forest Products Inc.............. D 336 605-0429
  Greensboro **(G-5455)**

G & G Lumber Company Inc.................. G 704 539-5110
  Harmony **(G-6098)**

Southern Vneer Spclty Pdts LLC.......... F 919 642-7004
  Moncure **(G-8409)**

LUMBER: Plywood, Softwood

Tima Capital Inc................................... F 910 769-3273
  Wilmington **(G-12939)**

LUMBER: Rails, Fence, Round Or Split

Afsc LLC... D 704 523-4936
  Charlotte **(G-1627)**

Asheville Contracting Co Inc................ E 828 665-8900
  Candler **(G-1217)**

LUMBER: Treated

Atlantic Wood & Timber LLC................ F 704 390-7479
  Charlotte **(G-1713)**

Coastal Treated Products LLC.............. F 252 410-0180
  Roanoke Rapids **(G-10735)**

Culpeper Roanoke Rapids LLC............ G 252 678-3804
  Roanoke Rapids (G-10736)
Durable Wood Preservers Inc............... G 704 537-3113
  Charlotte (G-2067)
Fiberon.. G 704 463-2955
  Concord (G-3362)
Fortress Wood Products Inc .... F 336 854-5121
  High Point (G-6621)
H & M Wood Preserving Inc .... E 704 279-5188
  Gold Hill (G-5192)
Shenandoah Wood Preservers Inc......... G 252 826-4151
  Scotland Neck (G-11266)
Ufp Salisbury LLC.................................. B 704 855-1600
  Salisbury (G-11130)
Ufp Salisbury LLC.................................. G 704 855-1600
  Salisbury (G-11129)
Universal Forest Products Inc............... F 252 338-0319
  Elizabeth City (G-4416)
Woodline Inc... G 336 476-7100
  Thomasville (G-12090)
Woodtreaters Inc................................... G 910 675-0038
  Rocky Point (G-10887)

LUMBER: Veneer, Softwood

A-1 Face Inc.. G 336 248-5555
  Lexington (G-7654)
David R Webb Company Inc.................... G 336 605-3355
  Greensboro (G-5488)

MACHINE PARTS: Stamped Or Pressed Metal

Bnp Inc... F 919 775-7070
  Sanford (G-11157)
Ceramco Incorporated........................... E 704 588-4814
  Charlotte (G-1889)
CMS Tool and Die Inc............................ F 910 458-3322
  Carolina Beach (G-1260)
Derita Precision Mch Co Inc................. G 704 392-7285
  Charlotte (G-2034)
Leesona Corp.. E 336 226-5511
  Burlington (G-1118)
Matt Bieneman Enterprises LLC........... G 704 856-0200
  Mooresville (G-8720)
Moores Mch Co Fayetteville Inc............ D 919 837-5354
  Bear Creek (G-717)
Spruce Pine Mica Company.................. F 828 765-4241
  Spruce Pine (G-11589)
Stroup Machine & Mfg Inc.................... G 704 394-0023
  Charlotte (G-2873)
Team 21st.. G 910 826-3676
  Fayetteville (G-4679)
Toner Machining Tech Inc..................... D 828 432-8007
  Morganton (G-8905)
Toolcraft Inc North Carolina................. F 828 659-7379
  Marion (G-8070)
Youngs Welding & Machine Svcs.......... G 910 488-1190
  Fayetteville (G-4702)

MACHINE TOOL ACCESS: Drills

Dormer Pramet LLC................................ C 800 877-3745
  Mebane (G-8238)
Robert Bosch Tool Corporation............. F 252 551-7512
  Greenville (G-6019)

MACHINE TOOL ACCESS: Tools & Access

21st Century Tech of Amer................... F 910 826-3676
  Fayetteville (G-4540)
Creative Tooling Solutions Inc.............. G 704 504-5415
  Pineville (G-9722)
Tar Heel Tling Prcsion McHning........... F 919 965-6160
  Smithfield (G-11467)
Toolcraft Inc North Carolina................. F 828 659-7379
  Marion (G-8070)

Yat Usa Inc... G 480 584-4096
  Huntersville (G-7063)

MACHINE TOOL ATTACHMENTS & ACCESS

Central Tool & Mfg Co Inc.................... G 828 328-2383
  Hickory (G-6294)
Eversharp Saw & Tool Inc.................... G 828 345-1200
  Hickory (G-6330)
Production Tool and Die Co Inc............ F 704 525-0498
  Charlotte (G-2672)
Selbach Machinery LLC......................... G 910 794-9350
  Wilmington (G-12916)

MACHINE TOOLS & ACCESS

C R Onsrud Inc...................................... C 704 508-7000
  Troutman (G-12131)
Calco Enterprises Inc........................... F 910 695-0089
  Aberdeen (G-3)
Canvas Sx LLC....................................... C 980 474-3700
  Charlotte (G-1836)
Carbo-Cut Inc... G 828 685-7890
  Hendersonville (G-6193)
Cooper Bussmann LLC.......................... C 252 566-0278
  La Grange (G-7465)
Em2 Machine Corp................................. G 336 297-4110
  Summerfield (G-11839)
Freud America Inc.................................. C 800 334-4107
  High Point (G-6624)
Kennametal Inc....................................... D 252 492-4163
  Henderson (G-6163)
Kyocera Precision Tools Inc.................. G 800 823-7284
  Fletcher (G-4745)
Lns Turbo North America...................... G 704 435-6376
  Cherryville (G-3066)
LS Starrett Company.............................. D 336 789-5141
  Mount Airy (G-9148)
North Carolina Mfg Inc......................... E 919 734-1115
  Goldsboro (G-5231)
Putsch & Company Inc.......................... E 828 684-0671
  Fletcher (G-4762)
Salice America Inc................................. E 704 841-7810
  Charlotte (G-2749)
Sandvik Inc... C 919 563-5008
  Mebane (G-8258)
Sandvik McHning Sltons USA LLC........ F 919 563-5008
  Mebane (G-8259)
Speedwell Machine Works Inc.............. E 704 866-7418
  Gastonia (G-5140)
SPX Technologies Inc............................ D 980 474-3700
  Charlotte (G-2851)
Stanley Black & Decker Inc.................. G 704 293-9392
  Huntersville (G-7058)
Toner Machining Tech Inc..................... D 828 432-8007
  Morganton (G-8905)
United Machine & Metal Fab Inc.......... E 828 464-5167
  Conover (G-3569)
W D Lee & Company.............................. G 704 864-0346
  Gastonia (G-5163)
W T Mander & Son Inc.......................... G 336 562-5755
  Prospect Hill (G-9830)
Wise Storage Solutions LLC................. E 336 789-5141
  Mount Airy (G-9196)

MACHINE TOOLS, METAL CUTTING: Drilling

Circor Precision Metering LLC.............. A 919 774-7667
  Sanford (G-11164)
J & B Tool Making Inc........................... G 704 827-4805
  Mount Holly (G-9234)
Sandvik Tooling...................................... G 919 563-5008
  Mebane (G-8260)

MACHINE TOOLS, METAL CUTTING: Drilling & Boring

Drill & Fill Mfg LLC............................... G 252 937-4555
  Rocky Mount (G-10832)
Grindtec Enterprises Corp..................... G 704 636-1825
  Salisbury (G-11060)

MACHINE TOOLS, METAL CUTTING: Home Workshop

Tactile Workshop LLC............................ G 919 738-9924
  Raleigh (G-10530)

MACHINE TOOLS, METAL CUTTING: Lathes

L & R Specialties Inc............................ F 704 853-3296
  Gastonia (G-5075)

MACHINE TOOLS, METAL CUTTING: Numerically Controlled

Casetec Precision Machine LLC........... G 704 663-6043
  Mooresville (G-8634)

MACHINE TOOLS, METAL FORMING: Headers

American Racg Hders Exhust Inc........... F 631 608-1986
  Stanfield (G-11602)

MACHINE TOOLS, METAL FORMING: Mechanical, Pneumatic Or Hyd

CPM Wolverine Proctor LLC.................. F 336 479-2983
  Lexington (G-7670)
CPM Wolverine Proctor LLC.................. D 336 248-5181
  Lexington (G-7671)

MACHINE TOOLS, METAL FORMING: Punching & Shearing

Murata Machinery Usa Inc..................... C 704 875-9280
  Charlotte (G-2532)
Murata McHy USA Holdings Inc............ F 704 394-8331
  Charlotte (G-2533)

MACHINE TOOLS, METAL FORMING: Rebuilt

Moores Mch Co Fayetteville Inc............ D 919 837-5354
  Bear Creek (G-717)

MACHINE TOOLS: Metal Cutting

Amada America Inc................................. G 877 262-3287
  High Point (G-6518)
Blue Inc Usa LLC................................... E 828 346-8660
  Conover (G-3494)
Brown Equipment and Capitl Inc.......... F 704 921-4644
  Monroe (G-8448)
C & J Machine Company Inc.................. G 704 922-5913
  Dallas (G-3667)
Central Tool & Mfg Co Inc.................... G 828 328-2383
  Hickory (G-6294)
Delta Phoenix Inc.................................. E 336 621-3960
  Greensboro (G-5493)
Exact Cut Inc.. G 336 207-4022
  Greensboro (G-5527)
Hamilton Indus Grinding Inc................. E 828 253-6796
  Asheville (G-515)
Industrial Mch Solutions Inc................ G 919 872-0016
  Raleigh (G-10191)
Kyocera Precision Tools Inc.................. G 800 823-7284
  Fletcher (G-4745)
Lynn Electronics Corporation................ G 704 369-0093
  Concord (G-3397)

Matcor Mtal Fbrction Wlcome In............ C 336 731-5700
Lexington *(G-7717)*

Okuma America Corporation................. C 704 588-7000
Charlotte *(G-2593)*

Protocase Mfg Usa Inc........................ E 866 849-3911
Wilmington *(G-12892)*

Putsch & Company Inc........................ E 828 684-0671
Fletcher *(G-4762)*

Schelling America Inc........................ E 919 544-0430
Morrisville *(G-9044)*

Schenck USA Corp............................ G 704 529-5300
Conover *(G-3558)*

Slack & Parr International.................. G 704 527-2975
Dallas *(G-3690)*

Superior Dry Kilns Inc...................... E 828 754-7001
Hudson *(G-6960)*

Tigra Usa Inc................................ G 828 324-8227
Hickory *(G-6468)*

Triad Cutting Tools Inc..................... G 336 873-8708
Asheboro *(G-412)*

Union Grove Saw & Knife Inc................ D 704 539-4442
Union Grove *(G-12186)*

Whiteside Mch & Repr Co Inc................ E 828 459-2141
Claremont *(G-3126)*

Wieland Electric Inc........................ F 910 259-5050
Wilmington *(G-12947)*

Windco LLC.................................. G 704 846-6029
Indian Trail *(G-7104)*

MACHINE TOOLS: Metal Forming

Arnolds Welding Service Inc................. E 910 323-3822
Fayetteville *(G-4553)*

Cyril Bath Company.......................... F 704 289-8531
Monroe *(G-8473)*

E G A Products Inc.......................... F 704 664-1221
Mooresville *(G-8657)*

Emery Corporation........................... D 828 433-1536
Morganton *(G-8862)*

Rollforming LLC............................. G 336 468-4317
Hamptonville *(G-6091)*

Schunk Intec Inc............................ D 919 572-2705
Morrisville *(G-9046)*

Sona Autocomp USA LLC....................... C 919 965-5555
Selma *(G-11291)*

Sona Blw Precision Forge Inc................ C 919 828-3375
Selma *(G-11292)*

Ultra Machine & Fabrication Inc............. C 704 482-1399
Shelby *(G-11388)*

Wuko Inc.................................... G 980 938-0512
Greensboro *(G-5927)*

Wysong and Miles Company.................... E 336 621-3960
Greensboro *(G-5928)*

MACHINERY & EQPT, AGRICULTURAL, WHOLESALE: Agricultural, NEC

Buy Smart Inc............................... G 252 293-4700
Wilson *(G-12976)*

MACHINERY & EQPT, AGRICULTURAL, WHOLESALE: Lawn & Garden

Southag Mfg Inc............................. G 919 365-5111
Wendell *(G-12548)*

MACHINERY & EQPT, INDL, WHOLESALE: Chemical Process

LCI Corporation International............... E 704 399-7441
Charlotte *(G-2411)*

MACHINERY & EQPT, INDL, WHOLESALE: Conveyor Systems

Machinex Technologies Inc................... F 773 867-8801
High Point *(G-6696)*

Mueller Die Cut Solutions Inc............... E 704 588-3900
Charlotte *(G-2526)*

MACHINERY & EQPT, INDL, WHOLESALE: Cranes

Hiab USA Inc................................ F 704 896-9089
Cornelius *(G-3606)*

Rose Welding & Crane Service I............. G 252 796-9171
Columbia *(G-3296)*

Thomas M Brown Inc.......................... F 704 597-0246
Charlotte *(G-2913)*

MACHINERY & EQPT, INDL, WHOLESALE: Engines & Parts, Diesel

Cummins Inc................................. E 336 275-4531
Greensboro *(G-5476)*

Cummins Inc................................. G 919 284-9111
Kenly *(G-7230)*

Engine Systems Inc.......................... D 252 977-2720
Rocky Mount *(G-10836)*

Pcai Inc.................................... D 704 588-1240
Charlotte *(G-2622)*

S Strickland Diesel Svc Inc................. G 252 291-6999
Wilson *(G-13025)*

MACHINERY & EQPT, INDL, WHOLESALE: Engines, Gasoline

Ledger Hardware Inc......................... G 828 688-4798
Bakersville *(G-679)*

MACHINERY & EQPT, INDL, WHOLESALE: Fans

Hunter Fan Company.......................... G 704 896-9250
Cornelius *(G-3609)*

MACHINERY & EQPT, INDL, WHOLESALE: Food Product Manufacturng

Babington Technology Inc.................... G 252 984-0349
Rocky Mount *(G-10823)*

Sinnovatek Inc.............................. G 919 694-0974
Raleigh *(G-10479)*

Smart Machine Technologies Inc.............. D 276 632-9853
Greensboro *(G-5817)*

Stork United Corporation.................... A 704 598-7171
Charlotte *(G-2870)*

MACHINERY & EQPT, INDL, WHOLESALE: Hydraulic Systems

AP&t North America Inc...................... F 704 292-2900
Monroe *(G-8427)*

Bosch Rexroth Corporation................... E 704 583-4338
Charlotte *(G-1801)*

Custom Hydraulics & Design.................. F 704 347-0023
Cherryville *(G-3061)*

Deetag USA Inc.............................. G 828 465-2644
Conover *(G-3514)*

Hyde Park Partners Inc...................... D 704 587-4819
Charlotte *(G-2304)*

Hydralic Engnered Pdts Svc Inc.............. G 704 374-1306
Charlotte *(G-2305)*

Industrial Sup Solutions Inc................ E 704 636-4241
Salisbury *(G-11067)*

Livingston & Haven LLC...................... C 704 588-3670
Charlotte *(G-2428)*

Parker-Hannifin Corporation................. D 828 245-3233
Forest City *(G-4795)*

Talladega Mchy & Sup Co NC.................. G 256 362-4124
Fayetteville *(G-4677)*

MACHINERY & EQPT, INDL, WHOLESALE: Indl Machine Parts

Cross Technologies Inc...................... E 800 327-7727
Greensboro *(G-5472)*

MACHINERY & EQPT, INDL, WHOLESALE: Instruments & Cntrl Eqpt

Grecon Inc.................................. F 503 641-7731
Charlotte *(G-2237)*

Linor Technology Inc........................ F 336 485-6199
Winston Salem *(G-13235)*

Weathers Machine Mfg Inc.................... F 919 552-5945
Fuquay Varina *(G-4906)*

MACHINERY & EQPT, INDL, WHOLESALE: Machine Tools & Access

Chiron America Inc.......................... D 704 587-9526
Charlotte *(G-1916)*

Container Graphics Corp..................... E 704 588-7230
Pineville *(G-9720)*

Okuma America Corporation................... C 704 588-7000
Charlotte *(G-2593)*

Phillips Corporation........................ E 336 665-1080
Colfax *(G-3286)*

Stanza Machinery Inc........................ E 704 599-0623
Charlotte *(G-2859)*

Triangle Glass Service Inc.................. G 919 477-9508
Durham *(G-4279)*

MACHINERY & EQPT, INDL, WHOLESALE: Machine Tools & Metalwork

Alamo Distribution LLC...................... C 704 398-5600
Belmont *(G-740)*

Schunk Intec Inc............................ D 919 572-2705
Morrisville *(G-9046)*

MACHINERY & EQPT, INDL, WHOLESALE: Packaging

Automated Machine Technologies.............. G 919 361-0121
Morrisville *(G-8936)*

Chase-Logeman Corporation................... F 336 665-0754
Greensboro *(G-5442)*

Glover Corporation Inc...................... E 919 821-5535
Raleigh *(G-10139)*

MACHINERY & EQPT, INDL, WHOLESALE: Safety Eqpt

Cintas Corporation No 2..................... E 336 632-4412
Greensboro *(G-5444)*

MACHINERY & EQPT, INDL, WHOLESALE: Sewing

Filter Shop LLC............................. D 704 860-4822
Gastonia *(G-5048)*

Hester Enterprises Inc...................... E 704 865-4480
Gastonia *(G-5060)*

MACHINERY & EQPT, INDL, WHOLESALE: Textile & Leather

Murata Machinery Usa Inc.................... C 704 875-9280
Charlotte *(G-2532)*

PRODUCT

Petroleum Tank Corporation.................. F 919 284-2418
  Kenly (G-7235)

MACHINERY & EQPT, INDL, WHOLESALE: Trailers, Indl

Kaufman Trailers Inc........................... E 336 790-6800
  Lexington (G-7704)

Southag Mfg Inc.................................. G 919 365-5111
  Wendell (G-12548)

MACHINERY & EQPT, WHOLESALE: Construction, General

Berco of America Inc........................... E 336 931-1415
  Greensboro (G-5388)

MACHINERY & EQPT: Farm

Case Basket Creations......................... G 828 381-4908
  Granite Falls (G-5299)

Case-Closed Investigations................... G 336 794-2274
  Morehead City (G-8824)

Deere & Company............................... G 336 996-8100
  Kernersville (G-7265)

Evans Machinery Inc........................... D 252 243-4006
  Wilson (G-12990)

Granville Equipment LLC...................... F 919 693-1425
  Oxford (G-9615)

Gum Drop Cases LLC........................... G 206 805-0818
  High Point (G-6636)

Hog Slat Incorporated......................... F 252 209-0092
  Aulander (G-640)

Hog Slat Incorporated......................... G 910 862-7081
  Elizabethtown (G-4427)

Hog Slat Incorporated......................... E 919 663-3321
  Siler City (G-11411)

Johnson Industrial Mchy Svcs.............. E 252 239-1944
  Lucama (G-7937)

North American Implements Inc............ G 336 476-2904
  Thomasville (G-12056)

Pasture Management Systems Inc......... F 704 436-6401
  Mount Pleasant (G-9263)

Sound Heavy Machinery Inc................. F 910 782-2477
  Wilmington (G-12922)

Strickland Bros Entps Inc.................... F 252 478-3058
  Spring Hope (G-11560)

MACHINERY & EQPT: Liquid Automation

Abco Automation Inc........................... C 336 375-6400
  Browns Summit (G-988)

Blueskye Automation LLC..................... E 404 998-1320
  Charlotte (G-1791)

Industrial Automation Company............ F 877 727-8757
  Raleigh (G-10189)

Irsi Automation Inc............................. G 336 303-5320
  Mc Leansville (G-8224)

MACHINERY, EQPT & SUPPLIES: Parking Facility

Autopark Logistics LLC........................ G 704 365-3544
  Charlotte (G-1718)

MACHINERY, FOOD PRDTS: Beverage

Community Brewing Ventures LLC......... G 800 579-6539
  Newton (G-9458)

Dbt Holdings LLC................................ D 704 900-6606
  Charlotte (G-2023)

Microthermics Inc............................... F 919 878-8045
  Raleigh (G-10303)

MACHINERY, FOOD PRDTS: Dairy & Milk

Corporate Place LLC........................... G 704 808-3848
  Charlotte (G-1989)

Delaney Holdings Co........................... G 704 808-3848
  Charlotte (G-2027)

Industrial Tech Svcs Amrcas In............ D 704 808-3848
  Charlotte (G-2325)

SPX Flow Holdings Inc......................... G 704 808-3848
  Charlotte (G-2848)

SPX Latin America Corporation............. G 704 808-3848
  Charlotte (G-2850)

MACHINERY, FOOD PRDTS: Food Processing, Smokers

Friedrich Metal Pdts Co Inc.................. E 336 375-3067
  Browns Summit (G-993)

Wins Smokehouse Services Ltd............. G 828 884-7476
  Pisgah Forest (G-9775)

MACHINERY, FOOD PRDTS: Oilseed Crushing & Extracting

East Crlina Olseed Prcssors LL.............. D 252 935-5553
  Pantego (G-9643)

MACHINERY, FOOD PRDTS: Ovens, Bakery

Middleby Marshall Inc.......................... C 919 762-1000
  Fuquay Varina (G-4891)

MACHINERY, FOOD PRDTS: Packing House

Carolina Packing House Sups............... G 910 653-3438
  Tabor City (G-11908)

Roi Industries Group Inc...................... G 919 788-7728
  Durham (G-4218)

MACHINERY, FOOD PRDTS: Processing, Poultry

Embrex LLC.. C 919 941-5185
  Durham (G-4019)

Stork United Corporation...................... A 704 598-7171
  Charlotte (G-2870)

MACHINERY, MAILING: Postage Meters

Pitney Bowes Inc................................ F 336 805-3320
  Greensboro (G-5750)

Pitney Bowes Inc................................ G 919 785-3480
  Raleigh (G-10369)

MACHINERY, PACKAGING: Packing & Wrapping

Roi Industries Group Inc...................... G 919 788-7728
  Durham (G-4218)

MACHINERY, PAPER INDUSTRY: Pulp Mill

Valmet Inc... G 803 289-4900
  Charlotte (G-2971)

MACHINERY, PRINTING TRADES: Plates

Container Graphics Corp...................... F 919 481-4200
  Cary (G-1333)

Digital Highpoint LLC........................... C 336 883-7146
  High Point (G-6593)

Mark/Trece Inc................................... E 336 292-3424
  Whitsett (G-12614)

MACHINERY, TEXTILE: Creels

Diversified Textile Mchy Corp............... G 704 739-2121
  Kings Mountain (G-7360)

MACHINERY, TEXTILE: Printing

Spgprints America Inc......................... D 704 598-7171
  Charlotte (G-2844)

Stork United Corporation...................... A 704 598-7171
  Charlotte (G-2870)

MACHINERY, WOODWORKING: Sanding, Exc Portable Floor Sanders

Singley Specialty Co Inc...................... G 336 852-8581
  Greensboro (G-5814)

MACHINERY: Ammunition & Explosives Loading

Advanced Plastiform Inc...................... D 919 404-2080
  Zebulon (G-13500)

Birch Bros Southern Inc....................... E 704 843-2111
  Waxhaw (G-12423)

MACHINERY: Automotive Related

Autec Inc.. E 704 871-9141
  Statesville (G-11663)

Canvas Sx LLC................................... C 980 474-3700
  Charlotte (G-1836)

Clean Green Inc................................. G 919 596-3500
  Durham (G-3977)

Enforge LLC....................................... E 704 983-4146
  Albemarle (G-71)

Global Resource Corporation................ G 919 972-7803
  Morrisville (G-8984)

NGK Ceramics Usa Inc......................... G 704 664-7000
  Mooresville (G-8733)

SPX Technologies Inc........................... D 980 474-3700
  Charlotte (G-2851)

Williams Performance Inc..................... G 704 603-4431
  Mount Ulla (G-9273)

MACHINERY: Bridge Or Gate, Hydraulic

Surelift Inc.. G 828 963-6899
  Boone (G-945)

MACHINERY: Construction

Altec Industries Inc............................ D 828 678-5500
  Burnsville (G-1181)

American Attachments Inc.................... G 336 859-2002
  Lexington (G-7655)

Arrow Equipment LLC.......................... G 803 765-2040
  Charlotte (G-1698)

Automated Designs Inc........................ F 828 696-9625
  Flat Rock (G-4703)

Beasley Contracting............................ G 828 479-3775
  Robbinsville (G-10756)

Berco of America Inc........................... E 336 931-1415
  Greensboro (G-5388)

Caterpillar Inc.................................... E 919 777-2000
  Sanford (G-11160)

Conjet Inc... G 636 485-4724
  Charlotte (G-1974)

Construction Attachments Inc.............. D 828 758-2674
  Lenoir (G-7596)

Construction Impts Depo Inc................ E 336 859-2002
  Denton (G-3743)

Cutting Systems Inc............................ D 704 592-2451
  Union Grove (G-12184)

Dan Moore Inc.................................... G 336 475-8350
  Thomasville (G-12015)

Design Engnred Fbrications Inc............. E 336 768-8260
  Winston Salem (G-13141)

Engcon North America Inc.................... F 203 691-5920
  High Point (G-6611)

Engineered Attachments LLC................ G 336 703-5266
  Winston Salem (G-13158)

Everything Attachments........................ F 828 464-0161
  Conover (G-3520)

Ferguson Highway Products Inc............ G..... 704 320-3087
   Indian Trail (G-7081)

General Fertilizer Eqp Inc...................... F 336 299-4711
   Greensboro (G-5554)

Hills Machinery Company LLC........... G..... 828 820-5265
   Mills River (G-8315)

Hockmeyer Equipment Corp.................. D 252 338-4705
   Elizabeth City (G-4390)

Infrastrcture Sltons Group Inc............. F 704 833-8048
   Mooresville (G-8692)

Ingersoll-Rand Intl Holdg...................... B 704 655-4000
   Davidson (G-3711)

Instrotek Inc.. E 919 875-8371
   Research Triangle Pa (G-10712)

Linder Industrial Machinery Co............. F 980 777-8345
   Concord (G-3393)

Loflin Fabrication LLC............................ E 336 859-4333
   Denton (G-3756)

North American Implements Inc............. G 336 476-2904
   Thomasville (G-12056)

Paladin Custom Works........................... G 336 996-2796
   Kernersville (G-7291)

Redi-Mix LP.. D 704 596-6511
   Charlotte (G-2699)

Roadsafe Traffic Systems Inc............... G.... 919 772-9401
   High Point (G-6759)

Roofing Supply...................................... G.... 919 779-6223
   Garner (G-4959)

Superior Dry Kilns Inc........................... E 828 754-7001
   Hudson (G-6960)

Tandemloc Inc.. D 252 447-7155
   Havelock (G-6128)

Tom Rochester & Associates Inc........... G.... 704 896-5805
   Charlotte (G-2928)

Vermeer Manufacturing Company........ F 410 285-0200
   Charlotte (G-2978)

MACHINERY: Cotton Ginning

Coastal Carolina Gin LLC...................... F 252 943-6990
   Pantego (G-9642)

MACHINERY: Custom

Angels Path Ventures Inc...................... G.... 828 654-9530
   Arden (G-251)

Appalachian Tool & Machine Inc........... E 828 669-0142
   Swannanoa (G-11864)

Automated Machine Technologies........ G.... 919 361-0121
   Morrisville (G-8936)

Axcellus LLC.. F 919 589-9800
   Apex (G-143)

Betech Inc.. G.... 828 687-9917
   Fletcher (G-4723)

Brock and Triplett Machine Sp............... G.... 336 667-6951
   Moravian Falls (G-8808)

Burlington Machine Service................... G.... 336 228-6758
   Burlington (G-1056)

Curti USA Corporation........................... G.... 910 769-1977
   Belville (G-779)

DSI Innovations LLC.............................. E 336 893-8385
   Thomasville (G-12020)

Erecto Mch & Fabrication Inc................. G.... 704 922-8621
   Dallas (G-3670)

General Machining Inc............................ G.... 336 342-2759
   Reidsville (G-10684)

Gordon Enterprises................................ G.... 919 776-8784
   Sanford (G-11186)

Goshen Engineering Inc......................... G.... 919 429-9798
   Mount Olive (G-9254)

Grandeur Manufacturing Inc.................. E 336 526-2468
   Jonesville (G-7197)

Holder Machine & Mfg Co...................... G.... 828 479-8627
   Robbinsville (G-10759)

I2e Group LLC.. G 336 884-2014
   High Point (G-6665)

Machine Builders & Design Inc.............. E 704 482-3456
   Shelby (G-11355)

Mecha Inc... F 919 858-0372
   Raleigh (G-10286)

Noxon Automation USA LLC.................. G 919 390-1560
   Morrisville (G-9031)

Ora Inc... G 540 903-7177
   Marion (G-8059)

Paul Norman Company Inc.................... G.... 704 399-4221
   Charlotte (G-2618)

Precision Fabricators Inc....................... G.... 336 835-4763
   Ronda (G-10897)

Production Wldg Fbrication Inc.............. G.... 828 687-7466
   Arden (G-302)

Tar Heel Tling Prcsion McHning............ F 919 965-6160
   Smithfield (G-11467)

Tdc International LLC............................. G.... 704 875-1198
   Concord (G-3452)

Turnamics Inc.. E 828 254-1059
   Asheville (G-626)

Turnkey Technologies Inc...................... G.... 704 245-6437
   Salisbury (G-11128)

Worth Products LLC............................... F 252 747-9994
   Snow Hill (G-11484)

MACHINERY: Electronic Component Making

Atmosphric Plsma Solutions Inc............ G..... 919 341-8325
   Cary (G-1298)

D M & E Corporation.............................. E 704 482-8876
   Shelby (G-11328)

Progressive Elc Greenville LLC............. G..... 252 413-6957
   Emerald Isle (G-4479)

Wispry Inc... G.... 919 854-7500
   Cary (G-1484)

MACHINERY: Ice Making

Work Well Hydrtion Systems LLC.......... G.... 704 853-7788
   Gastonia (G-5167)

MACHINERY: Kilns, Lumber

Kiln Drying Systems Cmpnnts In........... E 828 891-8115
   Etowah (G-4496)

Southeastern Installation Inc................. E 704 352-7146
   Lexington (G-7744)

Superior Dry Kilns Inc........................... E 828 754-7001
   Hudson (G-6960)

MACHINERY: Metalworking

Atlantic Hydraulics Svcs LLC................ E 919 542-2985
   Sanford (G-11152)

Efco USA Inc.. G.... 800 332-6872
   Charlotte (G-2092)

Feeder Innovations Corporation............ G.... 910 276-3511
   Laurinburg (G-7502)

G T Racing Heads Inc........................... G.... 336 905-7988
   Sophia (G-11489)

Gerringer Enterprises............................ G.... 336 227-6535
   Burlington (G-1096)

High Definition Tool Corp...................... E 828 397-2467
   Connelly Springs (G-3478)

IMS Fabrication Inc................................ E 704 216-0255
   Salisbury (G-11066)

Joe and La Inc....................................... F 336 585-0313
   Burlington (G-1113)

Manufacturing Methods LLC................. E 910 371-1700
   Leland (G-7553)

Mestek Inc.. C 252 753-5323
   Farmville (G-4535)

Obi Machine & Tool Inc......................... G.... 252 946-1580
   Chocowinity (G-3084)

Petty Machine Company Inc.................... E ... 704 864-3254
   Gastonia (G-5119)

Winston Steel Stair Co........................... G..... 336 721-0020
   Winston Salem (G-13402)

MACHINERY: Mining

80 Acres Urban Agriculture Inc.............. G..... 704 437-6115
   Granite Falls (G-5292)

Brunner & Lay Inc.................................. G 828 274-2770
   Flat Rock (G-4704)

Junaluska Mill Engineering..................... G.... 828 321-3693
   Andrews (G-108)

Paschal Associates Ltd.......................... F 336 625-2535
   Raleigh (G-10359)

MACHINERY: Packaging

Abco Automation Inc.............................. C 336 375-6400
   Browns Summit (G-988)

Alotech Inc... E 919 774-1297
   Goldston (G-5255)

Automated Machine Technologies......... G..... 919 361-0121
   Morrisville (G-8936)

Awcnc LLC.. G 252 633-5757
   New Bern (G-9336)

Axon LLC.. E 919 772-8383
   Raleigh (G-9926)

Aylward Enterprises LLC........................ E 252 639-9242
   New Bern (G-9337)

Cates Mechanical Corporation.............. G..... 704 458-5163
   Charlotte (G-1866)

Chase-Logeman Corporation................. F 336 665-0754
   Greensboro (G-5442)

Chudy Group LLC................................... D 262 279-5307
   Durham (G-3975)

Container Systems Incorporated............ D 919 496-6133
   Franklinton (G-4847)

Focke & Co Inc...................................... D 336 449-7200
   Whitsett (G-12606)

Groninger USA LLC................................ E 704 588-3873
   Charlotte (G-2243)

Keymac USA LLC................................... G.... 704 877-5137
   Charlotte (G-2394)

Korber Pharma Inc................................. E 727 538-4644
   Cary (G-1384)

Korber Pharma Inc................................. E 727 538-4644
   Morrisville (G-8999)

Korber Pharma Inc................................. D 727 538-4644
   Apex (G-175)

Krw Packaging Machinery Inc................. F 828 658-0912
   Weaverville (G-12494)

Ossid LLC... D 252 446-6177
   Battleboro (G-704)

Petty Machine Company Inc.................... E ... 704 864-3254
   Gastonia (G-5119)

R E R Services....................................... G.... 818 993-1826
   Southport (G-11526)

Roberts Polypro Inc............................... E 704 588-1794
   Charlotte (G-2730)

Syntegon Technology Svcs LLC............ E 919 877-0886
   Raleigh (G-10527)

Windak Inc.. F 828 322-2292
   Conover (G-3576)

MACHINERY: Paint Making

Corob North America Inc........................ F 704 588-8408
   Charlotte (G-1988)

MACHINERY: Plastic Working

Dymetrol Company Inc........................... F 866 964-8632
   Bladenboro (G-876)

Enplas Life Tech Inc............................... G.... 828 633-2250
   Asheville (G-494)

Employee Codes: A=Over 500 employees, B=251-500
C=101-250, D=51-100, E=20-50, F=10-19, G=1-9   2025 Harris North Carolina
Manufacturers Directory   1147

PRODUCT

Mdsi Inc.. G 919 783-8730
   Browns Summit *(G-1002)*

Petty Machine Company Inc........... E 704 864-3254
   Gastonia *(G-5119)*

Psi-Polymer Systems Inc................ E 828 468-2600
   Conover *(G-3553)*

Single Temperature Contrls Inc........... G 704 504-4800
   Charlotte *(G-2810)*

MACHINERY: Printing Presses

Coastal Press Inc............................ G 252 726-1549
   Morehead City *(G-8827)*

MACHINERY: Recycling

Apb Wrecker Service LLC................ G 704 400-0857
   Charlotte *(G-1681)*

McDonald Services Inc..................... E 704 597-0590
   Charlotte *(G-2476)*

McDonald Services Inc..................... G 704 753-9669
   Monroe *(G-8530)*

Shred-Tech Usa LLC....................... G 919 387-8220
   Raleigh *(G-10473)*

MACHINERY: Road Construction & Maintenance

Power Curbers Inc........................... D 704 636-5871
   Salisbury *(G-11104)*

MACHINERY: Robots, Molding & Forming Plastics

Ilsemann Corp................................... G 610 323-4143
   Charlotte *(G-2313)*

MACHINERY: Rubber Working

Mono Plate Inc................................. G 631 643-3100
   Apex *(G-182)*

MACHINERY: Semiconductor Manufacturing

Bayatronics LLC............................... E 980 432-0438
   Concord *(G-3319)*

Gladiator Enterprises Inc................. G 336 944-6932
   Greensboro *(G-5561)*

Industry Choice Solutions LLC........... G 828 628-1991
   Fairview *(G-4508)*

Kanthal Thermal Process Inc........... E 704 784-3001
   Concord *(G-3389)*

Power Components Inc..................... G 704 321-9481
   Charlotte *(G-2650)*

MACHINERY: Textile

A B Carter Inc.................................. D 704 865-1201
   Gastonia *(G-4982)*

Abercrombie Textiles Inc.................. G 704 487-0935
   Shelby *(G-11308)*

American Linc Corporation............... E 704 861-9242
   Gastonia *(G-4992)*

American Trutzschler Inc.................. D 704 399-4521
   Charlotte *(G-1670)*

Bowman-Hollis Manufacturing Co......... E 704 374-1500
   Charlotte *(G-1805)*

Briggs-Shaffner Acquisition Co......... F 336 463-4272
   Yadkinville *(G-13439)*

Burnett Machine Company Inc......... F 704 867-7786
   Gastonia *(G-5008)*

Carolina Loom Reed Company Inc........ G 336 274-7631
   Greensboro *(G-5428)*

Carolina Tex Sls Gastonia Inc......... G 704 739-1646
   Kings Mountain *(G-7357)*

Carolina Textile Services Inc............ G 910 843-3033
   Red Springs *(G-10665)*

Custom Enterprises Inc.................... G 336 226-8296
   Burlington *(G-1081)*

Custom Industries Inc....................... F 704 825-3346
   Belmont *(G-744)*

D & S International Inc...................... F 336 578-3800
   Mebane *(G-8237)*

D M & E Corporation........................ E 704 482-8876
   Shelby *(G-11328)*

Ellerre Tech Inc................................ G 704 524-9096
   Dallas *(G-3669)*

Elmarco Inc..................................... G 919 334-6495
   Morrisville *(G-8970)*

Excel Inc.. G 704 735-6535
   Lincolnton *(G-7830)*

Ferguson Companies........................ G
   Linwood *(G-7878)*

Fletcher Industries Inc..................... E 910 692-7133
   Southern Pines *(G-11499)*

French Apron Manufacturing Co........... G 704 865-7666
   Gastonia *(G-5049)*

Gastex LLC...................................... G 704 824-9861
   Gastonia *(G-5050)*

Imperial Machine Company Inc........... E 704 739-8038
   Bessemer City *(G-823)*

International McHy Sls Inc................ G 336 759-9548
   Winston Salem *(G-13210)*

Itm Ltd South................................... G 336 883-2400
   Greensboro *(G-5630)*

J & P Entrprses of Crlinas Inc........... E 704 861-1867
   Gastonia *(G-5069)*

J J Jenkins Incorporated.................. E 704 821-6648
   Matthews *(G-8177)*

Kern-Liebers USA Textile Inc............ E 704 329-7153
   Matthews *(G-8122)*

M-B Industries Inc........................... C 828 862-4201
   Rosman *(G-10913)*

Mount Hope Machinery Co............... F
   Charlotte *(G-2523)*

Murata McHy USA Holdings Inc........... F 704 394-8331
   Charlotte *(G-2533)*

Parts and Systems Company Inc........... F 828 684-7070
   Arden *(G-295)*

Pinco Usa Inc................................... G 704 895-5766
   Cornelius *(G-3618)*

Precision Comb Works Inc............... G 704 864-2761
   Gastonia *(G-5125)*

Precision Machine Products Inc........... D 704 865-7490
   Gastonia *(G-5126)*

Sam M Butler Inc............................. E 910 277-7456
   Laurinburg *(G-7514)*

Smart Machine Technologies Inc........... D 276 632-9853
   Greensboro *(G-5817)*

TCI Mobility Inc................................ F 704 867-8331
   Gastonia *(G-5149)*

Textrol Laboratories Inc................... E 704 764-3400
   Monroe *(G-8569)*

Tri State Plastics Inc........................ G 704 865-7431
   Gastonia *(G-5159)*

Tsg Finishing LLC............................ G 828 328-5522
   Hickory *(G-6471)*

Tsg Finishing LLC............................ E 828 328-5541
   Hickory *(G-6472)*

Tsg Finishing LLC............................ E 828 328-5522
   Hickory *(G-6473)*

Tubular Textile Machinery................ G 336 956-6444
   Lexington *(G-7754)*

MACHINERY: Tobacco Prdts

Jt International USA Inc..................... E 201 871-1210
   Raleigh *(G-10225)*

MACHINERY: Wire Drawing

Southern Steel and Wire Inc............ D 336 548-9611
   Madison *(G-8000)*

MACHINERY: Woodworking

Automated Lumber Handling Inc........... G 828 754-4662
   Lenoir *(G-7574)*

Carbide Saws Incorporated.............. G 336 882-6835
   High Point *(G-6554)*

Caterpillar Inc.................................. D 919 550-1100
   Clayton *(G-3137)*

Etk International Inc......................... G 704 819-1541
   Indian Trail *(G-7079)*

Eurohansa Inc.................................. G 336 885-1010
   High Point *(G-6616)*

Fletcher Machine Inds Inc................ D 336 249-6101
   Lexington *(G-7687)*

Grecon Dimter Inc............................ G 828 397-5139
   Connelly Springs *(G-3477)*

Jly Invstmnts Inc Fka Nwman Mc........... E 336 273-8261
   Browns Summit *(G-1000)*

Karl Ogden Enterprises Inc............... G 704 845-2785
   Matthews *(G-8121)*

Leitz Tooling Systems LP................. G 336 861-3367
   Archdale *(G-237)*

Mill Art Wood.................................. G 919 828-7376
   Raleigh *(G-10307)*

Ogden Sales Group LLC................... G 704 845-2785
   Matthews *(G-8137)*

Ostwalt Leasing Co Inc.................... D 704 528-4528
   Troutman *(G-12146)*

Otb Machinery Inc............................ G 336 323-1035
   Thomasville *(G-12057)*

Peco Inc... E 828 684-1234
   Arden *(G-296)*

Rfsprotech LLC................................ E 704 845-2785
   Matthews *(G-8145)*

Rp Fletcher Machine Co Inc............. D 336 249-6101
   Lexington *(G-7736)*

Smith Woodturning Inc..................... G 828 464-2230
   Newton *(G-9495)*

Venture Cabinets.............................. G 252 299-0051
   Fremont *(G-4862)*

MACHINISTS' TOOLS & MACHINES: Measuring, Metalworking Type

If Armor International LLC................ C 704 482-1399
   Shelby *(G-11346)*

Modern Tool Service......................... F 919 365-7470
   Wendell *(G-12539)*

MACHINISTS' TOOLS: Measuring, Precision

Linamar North Carolina Inc.............. F 828 348-5343
   Arden *(G-283)*

MACHINISTS' TOOLS: Precision

C & C Precision Machine Inc............ E 704 739-0505
   Kings Mountain *(G-7352)*

Cross Technology Inc....................... E 336 725-4700
   East Bend *(G-4322)*

Diamond Dog Tools Inc.................... D 828 687-3686
   Arden *(G-265)*

Kenmar Inc...................................... F 336 884-8722
   High Point *(G-6684)*

Penco Precision LLC........................ G 910 292-6542
   Wilmington *(G-12873)*

Unique Tool and Mfg Co.................. E 336 498-2614
   Franklinville *(G-4858)*

MACHINISTS' TOOLS: Scales, Measuring, Precision

Vishay Transducers Ltd................... E 919 365-3800
Wendell *(G-12553)*

MAGAZINES, WHOLESALE

Comfort Publishing Svcs LLC.............. G 704 907-7848
Concord *(G-3338)*

MAGNESIUM

Mg12 LP.. G 828 440-1144
Tryon *(G-12175)*

MAGNETIC INK & OPTICAL SCANNING EQPT

NCR Voyix Corporation...................... G 937 445-5000
Cary *(G-1406)*

MAGNETIC TAPE, AUDIO: Prerecorded

American Multimedia Inc.................... D 336 229-7101
Burlington *(G-1045)*

MAGNETS: Permanent

Docmagnet Inc................................. G 919 788-7999
Raleigh *(G-10052)*

MAIL-ORDER HOUSE, NEC

Grateful Union Family Inc.................. F 828 622-3258
Asheville *(G-510)*

MAIL-ORDER HOUSES: Jewelry

Dallas L Pridgen Inc.......................... G 919 732-4422
Carrboro *(G-1268)*

MAIL-ORDER HOUSES: Women's Apparel

Kayser-Roth Corporation.................... C 336 852-2030
Greensboro *(G-5643)*

MAILBOX RENTAL & RELATED SVCS

Bryan Austin................................... G 336 841-6573
High Point *(G-6551)*

King Business Service Inc.................. G 910 610-1030
Laurinburg *(G-7504)*

MAILING LIST: Compilers

Randall-Reilly LLC........................... C 704 814-1390
Charlotte *(G-2688)*

MAILING MACHINES WHOLESALERS

Bell and Howell LLC.......................... E 919 767-6400
Durham *(G-3924)*

MAILING SVCS, NEC

Alpha Mailing Service Inc.................. F 704 484-1711
Shelby *(G-11310)*

King Business Service Inc.................. G 910 610-1030
Laurinburg *(G-7504)*

Metro Productions Inc........................ F 919 851-6420
Raleigh *(G-10296)*

Mjt Us Inc....................................... G 704 826-7828
Charlotte *(G-2510)*

Salem One Inc.................................. F 336 722-2886
Kernersville *(G-7299)*

MANAGEMENT CONSULTING SVCS: Administrative

Reynolds Consumer Products Inc.......... A 704 371-5550
Huntersville *(G-7042)*

MANAGEMENT CONSULTING SVCS: Automation & Robotics

Design Tool Inc................................ E 828 328-6414
Conover *(G-3515)*

Goshen Engineering Inc...................... G 919 429-9798
Mount Olive *(G-9254)*

Irsi Automation Inc........................... G 336 303-5320
Mc Leansville *(G-8224)*

Scott Systems Intl Inc....................... F 704 362-1115
Charlotte *(G-2771)*

MANAGEMENT CONSULTING SVCS: Business

Competitive Solutions Inc.................. E 919 851-0058
Raleigh *(G-10004)*

J & D Managements LLC...................... G 910 321-7373
Fayetteville *(G-4618)*

MANAGEMENT CONSULTING SVCS: Business Planning & Organizing

Emath360 LLC.................................. F 919 744-4944
Cary *(G-1352)*

MANAGEMENT CONSULTING SVCS: Distribution Channels

Triple Crown International LLC.............. G 704 846-4983
Charlotte *(G-2946)*

MANAGEMENT CONSULTING SVCS: Food & Beverage

Microthermics Inc............................. F 919 878-8045
Raleigh *(G-10303)*

MANAGEMENT CONSULTING SVCS: General

K2 Solutions Inc............................... B 910 692-6898
Southern Pines *(G-11501)*

MANAGEMENT CONSULTING SVCS: Hospital & Health

UNC Campus Health Services................ D 919 966-2281
Chapel Hill *(G-1584)*

MANAGEMENT CONSULTING SVCS: Industrial

Q T Corporation................................ G 252 399-7600
Wilson *(G-13016)*

MANAGEMENT CONSULTING SVCS: Industrial & Labor

Archie Supply LLC............................. G 336 987-0895
Greensboro *(G-5368)*

MANAGEMENT CONSULTING SVCS: Quality Assurance

Propharma Group LLC........................ D 888 242-0559
Raleigh *(G-10405)*

MANAGEMENT CONSULTING SVCS: Training & Development

Camstar Systems Inc......................... C 704 227-6600
Charlotte *(G-1833)*

MANAGEMENT CONSULTING SVCS: Transportation

Nexxt Level Trucking LLC.................... G 980 205-4425
Charlotte *(G-2562)*

MANAGEMENT SERVICES

Allyn International Trdg Corp................ G 877 858-2482
Marshville *(G-8085)*

Drew Roberts LLC.............................. G 336 497-1679
Whitsett *(G-12604)*

J & D Managements LLC...................... G 910 321-7373
Fayetteville *(G-4618)*

Jebco Inc.. E 919 557-2001
Holly Springs *(G-6904)*

Kayser-Roth Corporation.................... C 336 852-2030
Greensboro *(G-5643)*

S & A Cherokee LLC........................... E 919 674-6020
Cary *(G-1443)*

Triangle Brick Company...................... E 919 544-1796
Durham *(G-4277)*

Volvo Logistics North America Inc......... C 336 393-4746
Greensboro *(G-5910)*

W T Humphrey Inc............................. E 910 455-3555
Jacksonville *(G-7158)*

MANAGEMENT SVCS: Business

Competitive Solutions Inc.................. E 919 851-0058
Raleigh *(G-10004)*

MANAGEMENT SVCS: Construction

Equagen Engineers Pllc...................... E 919 444-5442
Raleigh *(G-10090)*

Integrity Envmtl Solutions LLC............. D 704 283-9765
Monroe *(G-8505)*

Trademark Landscape Group Inc............ F 910 253-0560
Supply *(G-11861)*

MANUFACTURING INDUSTRIES, NEC

26 Industries Inc.............................. G 704 839-3218
Concord *(G-3306)*

A Plus Five Star Trnsp LLC.................. G 919 771-4820
Clayton *(G-3129)*

AIM Industries Inc............................. G 336 656-9990
Browns Summit *(G-989)*

Andy Maylish Fabrication Inc................ G 704 785-1491
Denver *(G-3771)*

Applied Components Mfg LLC................ G 828 323-8915
Hickory *(G-6265)*

Atlantic Manufacturing LLC.................. G 336 497-5500
Kernersville *(G-7246)*

Atlantic Mfg & Fabrication Inc.............. G 704 647-6200
Salisbury *(G-11019)*

Beast Chains................................... G 336 346-9081
High Point *(G-6542)*

Belev En U Water Mfg Co..................... G 704 458-9950
Huntersville *(G-6972)*

Blue Ridge Bracket Inc....................... G 828 808-3273
Fletcher *(G-4724)*

BR Lee Industries Inc......................... G 704 966-3317
Lincolnton *(G-7817)*

Brite Sky LLC................................... G 757 589-4676
Godwin *(G-5187)*

Brooks Manufacturing Solutions........... F 336 438-1280
Graham *(G-5261)*

Cambro... G 919 563-0761
Mebane *(G-8235)*

Carbon-Less Industries Inc.................. G 704 361-1231
Harrisburg *(G-6105)*

Carolina Gyps Reclamation LLC............. G 704 895-4506
Cornelius *(G-3593)*

Chatter Free Tling Sltions Inc............... G 828 659-7379
Marion *(G-8040)*

Clean Green Sustainable Lf LLC............. F 855 946-8785
Greensboro *(G-5449)*

PRODUCT

Collin Mfg Inc............................G..... 919 917-6264
Oriental *(G-9599)*

Commdoor Inc...........................G..... 800 565-1851
Concord *(G-3339)*

Concise Manufacturing Inc................G..... 704 796-8419
Salisbury *(G-11036)*

Conmech Industries LLC.................G..... 919 306-6228
Apex *(G-149)*

Continental Manufacturing Co.............336 697-2591
Mc Leansville *(G-8220)*

Cooper Industries LLC.................G..... 304 545-1482
Greensboro *(G-5467)*

Creek Industries Inc....................G..... 828 319-7490
Weaverville *(G-12490)*

Creek Life LLC..........................G..... 910 892-9337
Garner *(G-4926)*

Cross Manufacturing LLC.................G..... 336 269-6542
Burlington *(G-1077)*

Crown Town Industries LLC.............G..... 704 579-0387
Concord *(G-3349)*

Dale Reynolds Cabinets Inc..............G..... 704 890-5962
Charlotte *(G-2017)*

Dara Holsters & Gear Inc..............E..... 919 374-2170
Wendell *(G-12531)*

Direct Distribution Inds Inc.............G..... 910 217-0000
Wagram *(G-12256)*

Douglas Battery Mfg Co.................G..... 336 650-7000
Winston Salem *(G-13151)*

Draxlor Industries Inc...................757 274-6771
Durham *(G-4006)*

Dynamic Mounting.......................G..... 704 978-8723
Mooresville *(G-8656)*

Enepay Corporation.....................G..... 919 788-1454
Raleigh *(G-10086)*

Energizer Battery Mfg..................G..... 336 736-7936
Asheboro *(G-351)*

General Foam Plastics Corp..............G..... 757 857-0153
Tarboro *(G-11927)*

Health At Home Inc.....................F..... 850 543-4482
Charlotte *(G-2267)*

Hensley Corporation....................G..... 828 230-9447
Fairview *(G-4507)*

Hudson Industries LLC.................G..... 704 480-0014
Shelby *(G-11344)*

Humboldt Mfg Co Inc....................G..... 919 832-6509
Raleigh *(G-10180)*

Innovative Technology Mfg LLC...........G..... 980 248-3731
Mooresville *(G-8693)*

Jag Industries LLC......................G..... 704 655-2507
Huntersville *(G-7005)*

Jochum Industries.......................G..... 336 288-7975
Greensboro *(G-5638)*

Karl Rl Manufacturing...................G..... 919 846-3801
Raleigh *(G-10231)*

King Charles Industries LLC.............G..... 704 848-4121
Lilesville *(G-7787)*

Lee Linear.............................G..... 800 221-0811
Southport *(G-11522)*

Lr Manufacturing Inc....................G..... 910 399-1410
Delco *(G-3737)*

Manufactur LLC.........................G..... 919 937-2090
Durham *(G-4117)*

Maximizer Systems Inc.................G..... 828 345-6036
Hickory *(G-6393)*

Mdi Solutions LLC......................G..... 845 721-6758
Salisbury *(G-11092)*

Mikron Industries.......................G..... 253 398-1382
Durham *(G-4134)*

Minnewawa Inc.........................G..... 865 522-8103
Charlotte *(G-2507)*

Mint Hill Industries......................G..... 704 545-8852
Mint Hill *(G-8341)*

Mpx Manufacturing Inc.................G..... 704 762-9207
Salisbury *(G-11094)*

Nacho Industries Inc....................G..... 919 937-9471
Durham *(G-4141)*

Novem Industries Inc...................G..... 704 660-6460
Charlotte *(G-2580)*

Oleksynprannyk LLC...................F..... 704 450-0182
Mooresville *(G-8738)*

Optomill Solutions LLC.................G..... 704 560-4037
Matthews *(G-8188)*

Pag Asb LLC...........................G..... 336 883-4187
High Point *(G-6724)*

Pnb Manufacturing......................G..... 336 883-0021
High Point *(G-6738)*

Precision Boat Mfg......................G..... 336 395-8795
Graham *(G-5282)*

Producers Gin Murfreesboro LLC..........G..... 252 398-3762
Murfreesboro *(G-9285)*

Progressive Industries Inc...............G..... 919 267-6948
Apex *(G-187)*

Qualtech Industries Inc..................G..... 704 734-0345
Kings Mountain *(G-7380)*

Ratoon Agroprocessing LLC.............G..... 828 273-9114
Marion *(G-8062)*

Red Wolfe Industries LLC...............F..... 336 570-2282
Graham *(G-5284)*

Rockgeist LLC..........................G..... 518 461-2009
Asheville *(G-593)*

Rolling Umbrellas Inc...................G..... 828 754-4200
Lenoir *(G-7637)*

Rq Industries Inc.......................G..... 704 701-1071
Concord *(G-3436)*

Sapona Manufacturing Co Inc............G..... 336 625-2161
Asheboro *(G-393)*

Sbm Industries LLC....................G..... 919 625-3672
Raleigh *(G-10459)*

Seneca Devices Inc.....................F..... 301 412-3576
Durham *(G-4230)*

Sesmfg LLC...........................G..... 803 917-3248
Charlotte *(G-2790)*

Shoffner Industries Inc.................G..... 336 226-9356
Burlington *(G-1156)*

Speed King Manufacturing Inc...........G..... 910 457-1995
Southport *(G-11530)*

Steri-Air LLC..........................G..... 336 434-1166
High Point *(G-6793)*

Stokes Mfg LLC........................G..... 336 270-8746
Roxboro *(G-10947)*

Suntex Industries.......................F..... 336 784-1000
Winston Salem *(G-13349)*

Toolmarx LLC..........................G..... 919 725-0122
Winston Salem *(G-13367)*

Tree Frog Industries LLC................G..... 919 986-2229
Wendell *(G-12551)*

Urban Industries Corp...................G..... 980 209-9471
Pineville *(G-9763)*

Velocita Inc............................G..... 336 764-8513
Clemmons *(G-3208)*

Vision Contract Mfg LLC................E..... 336 405-8784
High Point *(G-6827)*

Xtra Light Manufacturing................G..... 919 422-7281
Apex *(G-207)*

Zeal Industries LLC.....................G..... 828 575-9894
Asheville *(G-637)*

MARBLE, BUILDING: Cut & Shaped

Beautimar Manufactured MBL Inc.........G..... 919 779-1181
Raleigh *(G-9937)*

Caesarstone Tech USA Inc...............G..... 818 779-0999
Charlotte *(G-1831)*

Exquisite Granite and MBL Inc............G..... 336 851-8890
Greensboro *(G-5528)*

Lawing Marble Co Inc...................G..... 704 732-0360
Lincolnton *(G-7835)*

Marion Cultured Marble Inc..............G..... 828 724-4782
Marion *(G-8049)*

National Marble Products Inc.............G..... 910 326-3005
Emerald Isle *(G-4478)*

Natural Granite & Marble Inc.............G..... 919 872-1508
Raleigh *(G-10326)*

Southern Marble Co LLC.................G..... 704 982-4142
Albemarle *(G-91)*

Stoneworx Inc..........................G..... 252 937-8080
Rocky Mount *(G-10870)*

Turmar Marble Inc......................G..... 704 391-1800
Charlotte *(G-2954)*

USA Dreamstone LLC...................G..... 919 615-4329
Garner *(G-4970)*

Wholesale Monument Company...........G..... 336 789-2031
Mount Airy *(G-9194)*

MARINE HARDWARE

Ace Marine Rigging & Supply Inc.........F..... 252 726-6620
Morehead City *(G-8811)*

Carolina North Mfg Inc...................G..... 336 992-0082
Kernersville *(G-7252)*

Custom Industries Inc...................E..... 336 299-2885
Greensboro *(G-5481)*

Marine Tooling Technology Inc............G..... 336 887-9577
High Point *(G-6698)*

Winterville Machine Works Inc............D..... 252 756-2130
Winterville *(G-13426)*

MARINE RELATED EQPT

Allied Marine Contractors LLC.............G..... 910 367-2159
Hampstead *(G-6067)*

Sturdy Corporation......................C..... 910 763-2500
Wilmington *(G-12933)*

Tcom Ground Systems LP................F..... 252 338-3200
Elizabeth City *(G-4414)*

MARINE SPLYS WHOLESALERS

Barbour S Marine Supply Co Inc..........G..... 252 728-2136
Beaufort *(G-720)*

Trivantage LLC.........................D..... 800 786-1876
Burlington *(G-1171)*

MARKETS: Meat & fish

Ashe Hams Inc.........................G..... 828 259-9426
Asheville *(G-432)*

Mitchells Meat Processing................F..... 336 591-7420
Walnut Cove *(G-12328)*

MARKING DEVICES

Ennis-Flint Inc..........................G..... 800 331-8118
Thomasville *(G-12023)*

Flint Trading Inc........................D..... 336 475-6600
Thomasville *(G-12027)*

MARKING DEVICES: Embossing Seals & Hand Stamps

Bear Pages............................G..... 828 837-0785
Murphy *(G-9288)*

MATERNITY WEAR STORES

Belevation LLC.........................F..... 803 517-9030
Biscoe *(G-847)*

MATS OR MATTING, NEC: Rubber

Blachford Rbr Acquisition Corp...........E..... 704 730-1005
Kings Mountain *(G-7350)*

L B Plastics LLC.......................D..... 704 663-1543
Mooresville *(G-8706)*

MATS, MATTING & PADS: Varnished Glass

Nouveau Verre Holdings Inc.................F 336 545-0011
Greensboro *(G-5714)*

Nvh Inc.......................................G 336 545-0011
Greensboro *(G-5717)*

MATTRESS PROTECTORS, EXC RUBBER

L C Industries Inc...............................C 919 596-8277
Durham *(G-4100)*

MEAT MARKETS

Acre Station Meat Farm Inc................F 252 927-3700
Pinetown *(G-9707)*

Hobes Country Hams Inc....................E 336 670-3401
North Wilkesboro *(G-9535)*

Mt Airy Meat Center Inc.....................G 336 786-2023
Mount Airy *(G-9155)*

Stevens Packing Inc...........................G 336 274-6033
Greensboro *(G-5840)*

Suncrest Farms Cntry Hams Inc.........E 336 667-4441
Wilkesboro *(G-12654)*

Wells Jnkins Wells Mt Proc Inc...........G 828 245-5544
Forest City *(G-4800)*

MEAT PRDTS: Bacon, Side & Sliced, From Purchased Meat

White Packing Co Inc -Va...................G 540 373-9883
Raleigh *(G-10609)*

MEAT PRDTS: Bacon, Slab & Sliced, From Slaughtered Meat

Murphy-Brown LLC.............................D 910 293-3434
Warsaw *(G-12363)*

MEAT PRDTS: Boxed Beef, From Slaughtered Meat

Smithfield Foods Inc...........................D 252 208-4700
Kinston *(G-7428)*

MEAT PRDTS: Ham, Smoked, From Purchased Meat

Ashe Hams Inc....................................G 828 259-9426
Asheville *(G-432)*

MEAT PRDTS: Prepared Beef Prdts From Purchased Beef

Harris-Robinette Inc...........................G 252 813-5794
Pinetops *(G-9706)*

Julian Freirich Company Inc...............E 704 636-2621
Salisbury *(G-11077)*

MEAT PRDTS: Sausages, From Purchased Meat

Carolina Packers Inc..........................D 919 934-2181
Smithfield *(G-11436)*

Jenkins Foods Inc...............................F 704 434-2347
Shelby *(G-11349)*

Larry S Sausage Company..................E 910 483-5148
Fayetteville *(G-4630)*

Stevens Sausage Company Inc...........D 919 934-3159
Smithfield *(G-11466)*

MEAT PROCESSING MACHINERY

Dean St Processing LLC......................G 252 235-0401
Bailey *(G-669)*

Tipper Tie Inc......................................C 919 362-8811
Apex *(G-198)*

MEDIA: Magnetic & Optical Recording

Assa Abloy AB.....................................E 704 283-2101
Monroe *(G-8431)*

Legalis Dms LLC.................................F 919 741-8260
Raleigh *(G-10252)*

MEDICAL & HOSPITAL EQPT WHOLESALERS

Albemrle Orthotics Prosthetics...........E 252 338-3002
Elizabeth City *(G-4378)*

Colowrap LLC......................................F 888 815-3376
Durham *(G-3983)*

Ddm Inc...G 910 686-1481
Wilmington *(G-12762)*

Dove Medical Supply LLC...................E 336 643-9367
Summerfield *(G-11838)*

Fidelity Pharmaceuticals LLC..............G 704 274-3192
Huntersville *(G-6989)*

Fla Orthopedics Inc............................D 800 327-4110
Charlotte *(G-2158)*

Janus Development Group Inc............G 252 551-9042
Greenville *(G-5994)*

RPM Products Inc................................G 704 871-0518
Statesville *(G-11761)*

Sg-Clw Inc..F 336 865-4980
Winston Salem *(G-13331)*

MEDICAL & SURGICAL SPLYS: Bandages & Dressings

Ambra Le Roy LLC..............................G 704 392-7080
Charlotte *(G-1662)*

Bar Squared Inc..................................F 919 878-0578
Raleigh *(G-9931)*

Caromed International Inc....................G 919 878-0578
Raleigh *(G-9981)*

Scivolutions Inc..................................G 704 853-0100
Kings Mountain *(G-7384)*

MEDICAL & SURGICAL SPLYS: Clothing, Fire Resistant & Protect

Precept Medical Products Inc.............F 828 681-0209
Arden *(G-298)*

United Protective Tech LLC.................E 704 888-2470
Locust *(G-7907)*

MEDICAL & SURGICAL SPLYS: Cosmetic Restorations

Random Rues Botanical LLC................G 252 214-2759
Greenville *(G-6017)*

MEDICAL & SURGICAL SPLYS: Gynecological Splys & Appliances

Ipas...C 919 967-7052
Durham *(G-4082)*

MEDICAL & SURGICAL SPLYS: Ligatures

Trimed LLC..G 919 615-2784
Raleigh *(G-10564)*

MEDICAL & SURGICAL SPLYS: Limbs, Artificial

Advanced Brace & Limb Inc................G 910 483-5737
Fayetteville *(G-4543)*

Albemrle Orthotics Prosthetics...........E 252 338-3002
Elizabeth City *(G-4378)*

Biotech Prsthtics Orthtics Drh.............G 919 471-4994
Durham *(G-3931)*

Center For Orthotic & Prosthet............D 919 585-4173
Clayton *(G-3139)*

Center For Orthtic Prsthtic CA.............E 919 797-1230
Durham *(G-3967)*

Delaby Brace and Limb Co..................G 910 484-2509
Fayetteville *(G-4587)*

East Carolina Brace Limb Inc..............G 252 726-8068
Morehead City *(G-8831)*

Faith Prsthtc-Rthotic Svcs Inc.............F 704 782-0908
Concord *(G-3361)*

Floyd S Braces and Limbs Inc............G 910 763-0821
Wilmington *(G-12778)*

Guilford Orthtic Prothetic Inc..............G 336 676-5394
Greensboro *(G-5584)*

Skyland Prsthtics Orthtics Inc.............E 828 684-1644
Fletcher *(G-4769)*

MEDICAL & SURGICAL SPLYS: Orthopedic Appliances

Ability Orthopedics..............................G 704 630-6789
Salisbury *(G-11011)*

Albemrle Orthotics Prosthetics...........G 252 332-4334
Ahoskie *(G-41)*

BSN Medical Inc..................................C 704 554-9933
Charlotte *(G-1815)*

Comfortland International LLC..............F 866 277-3135
Mebane *(G-8236)*

Custom Rehabilitation Spc Inc............G 910 471-2962
Wilmington *(G-12758)*

Fillauer North Carolina Inc..................E 828 658-8330
Weaverville *(G-12491)*

Ing Source LLC...................................F 828 855-0481
Hickory *(G-6369)*

Kaye Products Inc...............................E 919 732-6444
Hillsborough *(G-6869)*

Medical Specialties Inc.......................G 704 694-2434
Wadesboro *(G-12249)*

North Crlina Orthtics Prsthtic..............G 919 210-0906
Wake Forest *(G-12287)*

Orthopedic Appliance Company..........D 828 254-6305
Asheville *(G-562)*

Orthopedic Appliance Company..........G 828 348-1960
Hickory *(G-6407)*

Orthopedic Services............................G 336 716-3349
Winston Salem *(G-13273)*

Orthorx Inc..G 919 929-5550
Chapel Hill *(G-1562)*

R82 Inc..E 704 882-0668
Matthews *(G-8143)*

Spenco Medical Corporation...............E 919 544-7900
Durham *(G-4247)*

Structure Medical LLC.........................D 704 799-3450
Mooresville *(G-8780)*

Structure Medical LLC.........................D 256 461-0900
Mooresville *(G-8781)*

Thuasne LLC.......................................C 910 557-5378
Hamlet *(G-6063)*

MEDICAL & SURGICAL SPLYS: Personal Safety Eqpt

Health Supply Us LLC..........................F 888 408-1694
Mooresville *(G-8680)*

Jackson Products Inc...........................F 704 598-4949
Wake Forest *(G-12283)*

MSA Safety Sales LLC..........................D 910 353-1540
Jacksonville *(G-7133)*

Protection Products Inc........................E 828 324-2173
Hickory *(G-6420)*

Safewaze LLC......................................D 704 262-7893
Concord *(G-3438)*

PRODUCT

Spintech LLC.............................E 704 885-4758
Statesville (G-11775)

Taiji Medical Supplies Inc.....................G 888 667-6658
Lincolnton (G-7859)

Veon Inc..............................F 252 623-2102
Washington (G-12418)

MEDICAL & SURGICAL SPLYS: Prosthetic Appliances

Adaptive Technologies LLC..................G 919 231-6890
Raleigh (G-9878)

Alternative Care Group LLC..................G 336 499-5644
Kernersville (G-7241)

Atlantic Prosthetics Orthtcs..................G 919 806-3260
Durham (G-3903)

Bio-Tech Prsthtics Orthtics In.................336 768-3666
Winston Salem (G-13105)

Bio-Tech Prsthtics Orthtics In.................G 336 333-9081
Greensboro (G-5390)

Cape Fear Orthtics Prsthtics I................G 910 483-0933
Fayetteville (G-4566)

Creative Prosthetics and Ortho.............G 828 994-4808
Conover (G-3510)

Paceline Inc....................................D 704 290-5007
Matthews (G-8140)

Village Ceramics Inc........................G 828 685-9491
Hendersonville (G-6247)

MEDICAL CENTERS

Statesville Med MGT Svcs LLC...............G 704 996-6748
Statesville (G-11780)

MEDICAL EQPT REPAIR SVCS, NON-ELECTRIC

Trimed LLC......................................G 919 615-2784
Raleigh (G-10564)

MEDICAL EQPT: CAT Scanner Or Computerized Axial Tomography

Mobius Imaging LLC.........................E 704 773-7652
Charlotte (G-2513)

MEDICAL EQPT: Diagnostic

Direct Diagnostic Services LLC.............F 843 708-3891
Morganton (G-8860)

Mallinckrodt LLC..............................G 919 878-2900
Raleigh (G-10269)

MEDICAL EQPT: Electromedical Apparatus

Fernel Therapeutics Inc......................G 919 614-2375
Apex (G-155)

Vald Group Inc.................................G 704 345-5145
Charlotte (G-2970)

Vortant Technologies LLC....................G 828 645-1026
Weaverville (G-12506)

MEDICAL EQPT: Ultrasonic Scanning Devices

Hemosonics LLC..............................F 800 280-5589
Durham (G-4060)

Hemosonics LLC..............................E 800 280-5589
Durham (G-4061)

Size Stream LLC...............................G 919 355-5708
Cary (G-1459)

Trackx Technology LLC......................F 888 787-2259
Hillsborough (G-6880)

MEDICAL EQPT: Ultrasonic, Exc Cleaning

Bioventus LLC..................................D 800 396-4325
Durham (G-3933)

Inneroptic Technology Inc....................G 919 732-2090
Hillsborough (G-6868)

MEDICAL SVCS ORGANIZATION

Annihilare Medical Systems Inc.............F 855 545-5677
Lincolnton (G-7814)

Medaccess Inc.................................G 828 264-4085
Robbinsville (G-10760)

MEMBERSHIP ORGANIZATIONS, BUSINESS: Contractors' Association

High Temperature Tech Inc...................F 704 375-2111
Charlotte (G-2279)

MEMBERSHIP ORGANIZATIONS, BUSINESS: Growers' Association

US Tobacco Cooperative Inc.................D 919 821-4560
Raleigh (G-10579)

MEMBERSHIP ORGANIZATIONS, PROFESSIONAL: Health Association

Gems Frst Stop Med Sltions LLC...........G 336 965-9500
Greensboro (G-5552)

MEMBERSHIP ORGANIZATIONS, RELIGIOUS: Baptist Church

Brookstone Baptist Church...................E 828 658-9443
Weaverville (G-12485)

MEN'S & BOYS' CLOTHING STORES

Hudson Overall Company Inc...............G 336 314-5024
Greensboro (G-5609)

MEN'S & BOYS' CLOTHING WHOLESALERS, NEC

Apparel USA Inc...............................E 212 869-5495
Fairmont (G-4500)

Badger Sportswear LLC.......................D 704 871-0990
Statesville (G-11665)

Burlington Coat Fctry Whse Cor............E 919 468-9312
Cary (G-1317)

Gildan Activewear (eden) Inc.................C 336 623-9555
Eden (G-4347)

Gold Toe Stores Inc..........................G 828 464-0751
Newton (G-9469)

Madison Company Inc.......................E 336 548-9624
Madison (G-7992)

Raleigh Workshop Inc........................E 919 917-8969
Raleigh (G-10431)

Seafarer LLC...................................G 704 624-3200
Marshville (G-8094)

Walter Reynolds..............................G 704 735-6050
Lincolnton (G-7870)

MEN'S & BOYS' HOSIERY WHOLESALERS

Simmons Hosiery Mill Inc....................G 828 327-4890
Hickory (G-6448)

MERCHANDISING MACHINE OPERATORS: Vending

Coca-Cola Consolidated Inc.................C 919 550-0611
Clayton (G-3141)

Compass Group Usa Inc.....................A 704 398-6515
Charlotte (G-1965)

Compass Group Usa Inc.....................B 919 381-9577
Garner (G-4924)

METAL & STEEL PRDTS: Abrasive

Gulfstream Steel & Supply Inc...............E 910 329-5100
Holly Ridge (G-6888)

Keselowski Advanced Mfg LLC..............E 704 799-0206
Statesville (G-11723)

Tiger Steel Inc..................................G 336 624-4481
Mount Airy (G-9186)

METAL COMPONENTS: Prefabricated

Component Sourcing Intl LLC................E 704 843-9292
Charlotte (G-1967)

Norwood Manufacturing Inc..................E 704 474-0505
Norwood (G-9558)

Remedios LLC..................................G 203 453-6000
Charlotte (G-2706)

RMC Advanced Technologies Inc...........D 704 325-7100
Newton (G-9491)

METAL FINISHING SVCS

Fanuc America Corporation..................D 704 596-5121
Huntersville (G-6988)

Fil-Chem Inc....................................G 919 878-1270
Raleigh (G-10108)

METAL OXIDE SILICONE OR MOS DEVICES

Altera Corporation............................G 919 852-1004
Raleigh (G-9893)

METAL SERVICE CENTERS & OFFICES

Allens Gutter Service.........................G 910 738-9509
Lumberton (G-7944)

Biganodes LLC.................................G 828 245-1115
Forest City (G-4784)

Gulfstream Steel & Supply Inc...............E 910 329-5100
Holly Ridge (G-6888)

Iron Box LLC....................................E 919 890-0025
Raleigh (G-10209)

Pavco Inc..E 704 496-6800
Charlotte (G-2619)

METAL STAMPING, FOR THE TRADE

ABT Manufacturing LLC......................E 704 847-9188
Statesville (G-11645)

Allred Metal Stamping Works Inc...........E 336 886-5221
High Point (G-6517)

Carolina Stamping Company.................D 704 637-0260
Salisbury (G-11030)

Col-Eve Metal Products Co..................G 336 472-7039
Lexington (G-7667)

Component Sourcing Intl LLC................E 704 843-9292
Charlotte (G-1967)

Dynamic Stampings NC Inc..................G 704 509-2501
Gastonia (G-5044)

Griffiths Corporation.........................D 704 552-6793
Pineville (G-9731)

Griffiths Corporation.........................D 704 554-5657
Pineville (G-9732)

Hi-Tech Fabrication Inc.......................C 919 781-6150
Raleigh (G-10166)

Iv-S Metal Stamping Inc......................E 336 861-2100
Archdale (G-229)

K & S Tool & Manufacturing Co.............E 336 410-7260
High Point (G-6681)

M-B Industries Inc.............................C 828 862-4201
Rosman (G-10913)

New Standard Corporation...................C 252 446-5481
Rocky Mount (G-10854)

Parker Industries Inc.........................D 828 437-7779
Connelly Springs (G-3481)

Precision Partners LLC.......................E 800 545-3121
Charlotte (G-2658)

Precision Stampers Inc.......................G 919 366-3333
Wendell (G-12541)

SMC Holdco Inc......................................C 910 844-3956
Laurinburg *(G-7515)*

Southern Spring & Stamping...............F 336 548-3520
Stokesdale *(G-11815)*

United TI & Stamping Co NC Inc...........D 910 323-8588
Fayetteville *(G-4687)*

Wolverine Mtal Stmping Sltons............F 919 774-4729
Sanford *(G-11253)*

METAL STAMPINGS: Perforated

Erdle Perforating Holdings Inc..............F 704 588-4380
Charlotte *(G-2126)*

METAL: Battery

Aseptia Inc..C 678 373-6751
Raleigh *(G-9919)*

ATI Allvac..F 541 967-9000
Monroe *(G-8436)*

METALS SVC CENTERS & WHOLESALERS: Foundry Prdts

Sanders Company Inc............................F 252 338-3995
Elizabeth City *(G-4408)*

METALS SVC CENTERS & WHOLESALERS: Pipe & Tubing, Steel

Advanced Drainage Systems Inc............D 704 629-4151
Bessemer City *(G-803)*

Consolidated Pipe & Sup Co Inc............F 336 294-8577
Greensboro *(G-5463)*

METALS SVC CENTERS & WHOLESALERS: Steel

Alamo Distribution LLC.........................C 704 398-5600
Belmont *(G-740)*

Aviation Metals NC Inc..........................F 704 264-1647
Charlotte *(G-1721)*

Bessemer City Machine Shop Inc...........G 704 629-4111
Bessemer City *(G-806)*

C & B Salvage Company Inc...................G 336 374-3946
Ararat *(G-209)*

Charter Dura-Bar Inc............................F 704 637-1906
Salisbury *(G-11032)*

Chatham Steel Corporation...................E 912 233-4182
Durham *(G-3970)*

Chicago Tube and Iron Company...........D 704 781-2060
Locust *(G-7890)*

Dave Steel Company Inc........................D 828 252-2771
Asheville *(G-484)*

Dunavants Welding & Steel Inc..............G 252 338-6533
Camden *(G-1211)*

Freedom Metals Inc..............................F 704 333-1214
Charlotte *(G-2178)*

Harris Rebar Inc...................................G 919 528-8333
Benson *(G-792)*

Hercules Steel Company Inc..................E 910 488-5110
Fayetteville *(G-4611)*

Hsi Legacy Inc.....................................G 704 376-9631
Charlotte *(G-2294)*

McCombs Steel Company Inc.................E 704 873-7563
Statesville *(G-11730)*

McCune Technology Inc.........................G 910 424-2978
Fayetteville *(G-4638)*

Schwartz Steel Service Inc....................E 704 865-9576
Gastonia *(G-5135)*

Steel and Pipe Corporation...................E 919 776-0751
Sanford *(G-11240)*

Sun Valley Stl Fabrication Inc................F 704 289-5830
Monroe *(G-8565)*

METALS: Precious NEC

Alloyworks LLC....................................F 704 645-0511
Salisbury *(G-11015)*

KS Precious Metals LLC.........................G 910 687-0244
Pinehurst *(G-9694)*

Metallix Refining Inc............................E 252 413-0346
Greenville *(G-6003)*

Omega Precious Metals.........................G 269 903-9330
Youngsville *(G-13479)*

METALS: Primary Nonferrous, NEC

Cvmr (usa) Inc....................................C 828 288-3768
Union Mills *(G-12188)*

Parker-Hannifin Corporation.................E 704 662-3500
Statesville *(G-11742)*

METALWORK: Miscellaneous

Canalta Enterprises LLC.......................E 919 615-1570
Raleigh *(G-9965)*

Concept Steel Inc................................E 704 874-0414
Gastonia *(G-5026)*

Custom Design Inc...............................G 704 637-7110
Salisbury *(G-11041)*

Dave Steel Company Inc........................D 828 252-2771
Asheville *(G-484)*

Davis Steel and Iron Co Inc...................G 704 821-7676
Matthews *(G-8165)*

Dwiggins Metal Masters Inc...................G 336 751-2379
Mocksville *(G-8360)*

Eland Industries Inc.............................E 910 304-5353
Hampstead *(G-6071)*

Gerdau Ameristeel US Inc......................E 919 833-9737
Raleigh *(G-10131)*

Keypoint LLC.......................................F 704 962-8110
Waxhaw *(G-12434)*

Paul Charles Englert.............................G 704 824-2102
Gastonia *(G-5118)*

Protech Metals LLC...............................F 910 295-6905
Pinehurst *(G-9701)*

Steel Smart Incorporated......................E 919 736-0681
Pikeville *(G-9668)*

Steelfab Inc...B 704 394-5376
Charlotte *(G-2864)*

Steelfab of Virginia Inc.........................E 919 828-9545
Raleigh *(G-10507)*

Umi Company Inc.................................G 704 479-6210
Lincolnton *(G-7867)*

METALWORK: Ornamental

Apex Steel Corp...................................E 919 362-6611
Raleigh *(G-9908)*

Davis Steel and Iron Co Inc...................G 704 821-7676
Matthews *(G-8165)*

Esher LLC...G 704 975-1463
Huntersville *(G-6987)*

Ornamental Specialties Inc....................F 704 821-9154
Matthews *(G-8189)*

Vann S Wldg & Orna Works Inc..............F 704 289-6056
Monroe *(G-8576)*

METALWORKING MACHINERY WHOLESALERS

Amada America Inc...............................G 877 262-3287
High Point *(G-6518)*

Ellison Technologies Inc........................D 704 545-7362
Charlotte *(G-2103)*

Rodeco Company.................................F 919 775-7149
Sanford *(G-11225)*

METERING DEVICES: Gasoline Dispensing

Triangle Microsystems Inc.....................F 919 878-1880
Raleigh *(G-10558)*

METERING DEVICES: Water Quality Monitoring & Control Systems

Park Court Properties RE Inc.................F 919 304-3110
Mebane *(G-8255)*

METERS: Turbine Flow, Indl Process

Liburdi Turbine Services LLC.................F 704 230-2510
Mooresville *(G-8712)*

MICROCIRCUITS, INTEGRATED: Semiconductor

Cml Micro Circuit USA..........................E 336 744-5050
Winston Salem *(G-13126)*

Memscap Inc.......................................E 919 248-4102
Durham *(G-4126)*

Microchip Technology Inc......................F 919 844-7510
Raleigh *(G-10302)*

Micross Advnced Intrcnnect TEC...........E 919 248-1872
Research Triangle Pa *(G-10714)*

Northstar Computer Tech Inc.................G 980 272-1969
Monroe *(G-8537)*

Rt Cardiac Systems Inc.........................G 954 908-1074
Raleigh *(G-10451)*

Xilinx Inc...F 919 846-3922
Raleigh *(G-10619)*

MICROWAVE COMPONENTS

Cem Corporation..................................C 704 821-7015
Matthews *(G-8162)*

Communications & Pwr Inds LLC...........E 650 846-2900
Conover *(G-3505)*

Huber + Suhner Inc..............................E 704 790-7300
Charlotte *(G-2295)*

James W McManus Inc..........................G 828 688-2560
Bakersville *(G-678)*

Nuvotronics Inc...................................D 434 298-6940
Durham *(G-4152)*

US Microwave Inc................................G 520 891-2444
Pittsboro *(G-9791)*

MILITARY INSIGNIA, TEXTILE

Dickson Elberton Mill Inc.......................G 336 226-3556
Burlington *(G-1083)*

S Loflin Enterprises Inc.........................F 704 633-1159
Salisbury *(G-11113)*

MILLWORK

Acorn Woodworks NC LLC.....................G 828 361-9953
Murphy *(G-9286)*

Against Grain Woodworking Inc.............G 704 309-5750
Charlotte *(G-1628)*

Ajs Dezigns Inc....................................G 828 652-6304
Marion *(G-8030)*

American Woodmark Corporation...........E 704 947-3280
Huntersville *(G-6964)*

American Woodworkery Inc....................G 910 916-8098
Fayetteville *(G-4552)*

Archdale Millworks Inc..........................G 336 431-9019
Archdale *(G-212)*

Architectural Craftsman Ltd...................E 919 494-6911
Franklinton *(G-4846)*

Athol Arbor Corporation........................F 919 643-1100
Hillsborough *(G-6859)*

B&H Millwork and Fixtures Inc...............E 336 431-0068
High Point *(G-6534)*

Barewoodworking Inc...........................F 828 758-0694
Lenoir *(G-7576)*

PRODUCT

Bfs Asset Holdings LLC...................... B 303 784-4288
Raleigh *(G-9941)*

Bfs Operations LLC............................ A 919 431-1000
Raleigh *(G-9942)*

Black River Woodwork LLC.................. G 919 757-4559
Angier *(G-112)*

Bone Tred Beds Smmit Woodworks... G 910 319-7583
Wilmington *(G-12722)*

Brookshire Woodworking Inc.............. G 828 779-2119
Asheville *(G-462)*

Builders Firstsource Inc..................... F 919 562-6601
Youngsville *(G-13465)*

Building Center Inc............................ D 704 889-8182
Pineville *(G-9717)*

Built By Ben Woodworks LLC.............. G 336 438-1159
Burlington *(G-1055)*

Cardinal Millwork & Supply Inc.......... E 336 665-9811
Greensboro *(G-5422)*

Carolina Woodworks Trim of NC......... G 252 492-9259
Henderson *(G-6150)*

Carpathian Woodworks Inc................ G 919 669-7546
Clayton *(G-3136)*

Cleveland Lumber Company.............. E 704 487-5263
Shelby *(G-11320)*

Coastal Custom Wood Works LLC........ G 252 675-8732
New Bern *(G-9355)*

Coastal Millwork Supply Co............... E 910 763-3300
Wilmington *(G-12743)*

Contemporary Design Co LLC............ F 704 375-6030
Gastonia *(G-5030)*

Cook & Boardman Nc LLC.................. E 336 768-8872
Winston Salem *(G-13128)*

Creative Custom Woodworks Inc.......... G 910 431-8544
Wilmington *(G-12754)*

Crown Heritage Inc........................... G 336 835-1424
Elkin *(G-4443)*

Currier Woodworks Inc...................... G 252 725-4233
Beaufort *(G-725)*

Curvemakers Inc............................... G 919 690-1121
Oxford *(G-9611)*

Davis Cabinet Co Wilson Inc.............. G 252 291-9052
Sims *(G-11429)*

Davis Mechanical Inc......................... F 704 272-9366
Peachland *(G-9651)*

Division Six Incorporated.................. G 910 420-3305
New Bern *(G-9365)*

Ecmd Inc... C 336 835-1182
Elkin *(G-4444)*

Elite Wood Classics Inc..................... G 910 454-8745
Oak Island *(G-9565)*

Endgrain Woodworks LLC.................. G 980 237-2612
Charlotte *(G-2113)*

Flat Iron Mill Works LLC.................... G 828 768-7770
Leicester *(G-7524)*

Forest Millwork Inc............................ F 828 251-5264
Asheville *(G-499)*

Frederick and Frederick Entp............. F 252 235-4849
Middlesex *(G-8275)*

Funder America Inc............................ C 336 751-3501
Mocksville *(G-8365)*

Garner Woodworks LLC...................... G 828 775-1790
Swannanoa *(G-11871)*

Gary Forte Woodworking Inc.............. G 704 780-0095
Monroe *(G-8491)*

Gates Custom Milling Inc................... E 252 357-0116
Gatesville *(G-5172)*

GLG Corporation................................ F 336 784-0396
Winston Salem *(G-13178)*

Goodman Millwork Inc........................ F 704 633-2421
Salisbury *(G-11058)*

H & H Woodworking Inc...................... G 336 884-5848
High Point *(G-6637)*

H&M Woodworks Inc........................... F 919 496-5993
Louisburg *(G-7917)*

Harley S Woodworks Inc..................... G 828 776-0120
Barnardsville *(G-692)*

Hogan Cabinetry and Mllwk LLC......... G 704 856-0425
China Grove *(G-3075)*

Hunter Innovations Ltd....................... G 919 848-8814
Raleigh *(G-10181)*

Idx Impressions LLC.......................... C 703 550-6902
Washington *(G-12393)*

Interior Trim Creations Inc................. G 704 821-1470
Charlotte *(G-2342)*

J & M Woodworking Inc....................... F 828 728-3253
Hudson *(G-6950)*

J & P Wood Works Inc......................... E 336 788-1881
Winston Salem *(G-13211)*

Jeld-Wen Holding Inc......................... B 704 378-5700
Charlotte *(G-2367)*

Jenkins Millwork LLC.......................... E 336 667-3344
Wilkesboro *(G-12643)*

John Lindenberger............................. G 919 337-6741
Raleigh *(G-10217)*

Jones Doors & Windows Inc................ F 336 998-8624
Mocksville *(G-8372)*

Keglers Woodworks LLC...................... G 919 608-7220
Raleigh *(G-10232)*

Kingdom Woodworks Inc..................... G 704 678-8134
Kings Mountain *(G-7368)*

KS Custom Woodworks Inc................. G 252 714-3957
Walstonburg *(G-12333)*

Laborie Sons Cstm Wodworks LLC...... G 910 769-2524
Castle Hayne *(G-1504)*

Lee Builder Mart Inc.......................... E
Sanford *(G-11204)*

Libasci Woodworks Inc....................... G 828 524-7073
Franklin *(G-4834)*

Liberty Wood Products Inc.................. F 828 524-7958
Franklin *(G-4835)*

Louisiana-Pacific Corporation............ C 336 599-8080
Roxboro *(G-10929)*

Martins Woodworking LLC................... F 704 473-7617
Lattimore *(G-7481)*

Master Kraft Inc................................. E 704 234-2673
Matthews *(G-8183)*

Masterwrap Inc................................. E 336 243-4515
Lexington *(G-7716)*

Matthews Building Supply Co.............. E 704 847-2106
Matthews *(G-8130)*

Matthews Millwork Inc........................ G 704 821-4499
Monroe *(G-8526)*

Mesa Quality Fenestration Inc............ G 828 393-0132
Hendersonville *(G-6226)*

Metalfab of North Carolina LLC........... C 704 841-1090
Matthews *(G-8132)*

Metrolina Woodworks Inc.................... F 704 821-9095
Stallings *(G-11601)*

Metzgers Burl Wood Gallery................ G 828 452-2550
Waynesville *(G-12463)*

Mh Libman Woodturning..................... G 828 360-5530
Asheville *(G-546)*

Mike Powell Inc.................................. F 910 792-6152
Wilmington *(G-12854)*

Morrison Mill Work............................. G 828 774-5415
Asheville *(G-550)*

Moulding Millwork LLC........................ G 704 504-9880
Charlotte *(G-2522)*

Mountain Top Woodworking................ G 336 982-4059
West Jefferson *(G-12568)*

Normac Kitchens Inc.......................... F 704 485-1911
Oakboro *(G-9582)*

North State Millwork.......................... G 252 442-9090
Rocky Mount *(G-10855)*

Northside Millwork Inc........................ E 919 732-6100
Hillsborough *(G-6874)*

Old Mill Precision Gun Works &........... G 704 284-2832
Bessemer City *(G-828)*

Oyama Cabinet Inc............................ G 828 327-2668
Conover *(G-3542)*

Piedmont Joinery Inc......................... G 919 632-3703
Durham *(G-4182)*

Piedmont Stairworks LLC.................... G 704 483-3721
Denver *(G-3798)*

Piedmont Turning & Wdwkg Co........... G 336 475-7161
Thomasville *(G-12060)*

Piedmont Wood Products Inc.............. F 828 632-4077
Taylorsville *(G-11971)*

Pine Creek Products LLC.................... F 336 399-8806
Winston Salem *(G-13295)*

Ply Gem Holdings Inc......................... D 919 677-3900
Cary *(G-1421)*

Prestige Millwork Inc......................... G 910 428-2360
Star *(G-11633)*

Pro-Kay Supply Inc............................ G 910 628-0882
Orrum *(G-9604)*

R L Roten Woodworking LLC............... G 336 982-3830
Crumpler *(G-3662)*

Red Shed Woodworks Inc................... G 828 768-3854
Marshall *(G-8083)*

Reeb Millwork Corporation................. F 336 751-4650
Mocksville *(G-8387)*

Reliable Construction Co Inc.............. G 704 289-1501
Monroe *(G-8550)*

Richmond Millwork LLC....................... G 910 331-1009
Rockingham *(G-10788)*

Rowland Woodworking Inc.................. E 336 887-0700
High Point *(G-6761)*

S Banner Cabinets Incorporated......... E 828 733-2031
Newland *(G-9434)*

S H Woodworking................................ G 336 463-2885
Yadkinville *(G-13450)*

Salem Woodworking Company............ G 336 768-7443
Winston Salem *(G-13328)*

Sauder Woodworking Co..................... G 704 799-6782
Mooresville *(G-8766)*

Select Stainless Products LLC............ G 888 843-2345
Charlotte *(G-2783)*

Shep Berryhill Woodworking............... G 828 242-3227
Asheville *(G-598)*

Signature Custom Wdwkg Inc............. G 336 983-9905
King *(G-7337)*

Skettis Woodworks............................. G 336 671-9866
Winston Salem *(G-13338)*

Smith Companies Lexington Inc.......... G 336 249-4941
Lexington *(G-7742)*

Southern Staircase Inc....................... D 704 357-1221
Charlotte *(G-2839)*

Southern Woodcraft Design LLC......... G 919 693-8995
Oxford *(G-9637)*

Southern Woodworking Inc................. G 336 693-5892
Burlington *(G-1159)*

Spartacraft Inc.................................. E 828 397-4630
Connelly Springs *(G-3483)*

Stephenson Millwork Co Inc................ C 252 237-1141
Wilson *(G-13031)*

Stevenson Woodworking..................... G 919 362-9121
Apex *(G-196)*

Stock Building Supply Holdings LLC..... A 919 431-1000
Raleigh *(G-10509)*

Sugar Mountain Woodworks Inc.......... G 423 292-6245
Newland *(G-9435)*

Summit Peak Pens and WD Works........ G 336 404-8312
Liberty *(G-7780)*

Ta Lost Pines Woodwork..................... G 828 367-7517
Asheville *(G-614)*

Tallent Wood Works.................................. G 704 592-2013
Statesville (G-11785)

Tiger Mountain Woodworks Inc............ F 828 526-5577
Highlands (G-6846)

Timber Wolf Forest Products................. F 828 728-7500
Hudson (G-6961)

Timber Wolf Wood Creations Inc.......... G 704 309-5118
Charlotte (G-2919)

Tivoli Woodworks LLC............................ G 336 602-3512
Salisbury (G-11125)

Triangle Custom Woodworks LLC......... G 919 637-8857
Fuquay Varina (G-4903)

Triangle Woodworks Inc........................ G 919 570-0337
Wake Forest (G-12308)

TS Woodworks & RAD Design Inc........ F 704 238-1015
Monroe (G-8571)

Tuckers Farm Inc.................................... G 704 375-8199
Charlotte (G-2952)

United Finishers Intl Inc......................... G 336 883-3901
High Point (G-6818)

United Wood Products Inc...................... G 336 626-2281
Asheboro (G-414)

Vision Stairways & Mllwk LLC............... F 919 878-5622
Raleigh (G-10592)

Western Crlina Cstm Cswork Inc.......... F 828 669-0459
Black Mountain (G-872)

Whitaker Mill Works LLC........................ G 919 772-3030
Raleigh (G-10608)

Wigal Wood Works.................................. G 580 890-9723
Fayetteville (G-4700)

Windsor Window Company..................... D 704 283-7459
Monroe (G-8582)

Wizards Wood Werks.............................. G 252 813-3929
Macclesfield (G-7981)

Wood Surgeon... G 252 728-5767
Beaufort (G-737)

Wood Works.. G 910 579-1487
Sunset Beach (G-11853)

Woodmaster Custom Cabinets Inc........ F 919 554-3707
Youngsville (G-13499)

Woodtech/Interiors Inc........................... G 704 332-7215
Charlotte (G-3024)

Woodworking Unlimited Inc................... G 704 903-8080
Olin (G-9598)

Zepsa Industries Inc.............................. D 704 583-9220
Charlotte (G-3047)

MINERAL WOOL

Freudenberg Prfmce Mtls LP................ C 828 665-5000
Candler (G-1225)

JPS Communications Inc....................... D 919 534-1168
Raleigh (G-10222)

MINERAL WOOL INSULATION PRDTS

Dfa US Inc.. E 336 756-0590
Mocksville (G-8358)

MINERALS: Ground or Treated

Covia Holdings LLC................................ D 828 765-4283
Spruce Pine (G-11573)

Imerys Clays Inc..................................... G 828 648-2668
Canton (G-1254)

Imerys Mica Kings Mountain Inc........... F 704 739-3616
Kings Mountain (G-7365)

Iperionx Limited...................................... E 980 237-8900
Charlotte (G-2354)

Mathis Quarries Inc................................ G 336 984-4010
North Wilkesboro (G-9545)

Premier Magnesia LLC........................... E 828 452-4784
Waynesville (G-12468)

Southeastern Minerals Inc..................... E 252 492-0831
Henderson (G-6179)

Southern Products Company Inc........... E 910 281-3189
Hoffman (G-6885)

Vanderbilt Minerals LLC......................... E 910 948-2266
Robbins (G-10755)

MINIATURES

Marties Miniatures.................................. G 336 869-5952
High Point (G-6705)

MINING EXPLORATION & DEVELOPMENT SVCS

Charah LLC.. C 704 731-2300
Charlotte (G-1892)

Charah LLC.. C 502 873-6993
Mount Holly (G-9223)

Iperionx Critical Minerals LLC.............. E 980 237-8900
Charlotte (G-2353)

Iperionx Technology LLC...................... E 980 237-8900
Charlotte (G-2355)

RDc Debris Removal Cnstr LLC............ E 323 614-2353
Smithfield (G-11462)

MINING MACHINERY & EQPT WHOLESALERS

Component Sourcing Intl LLC................ E 704 843-9292
Charlotte (G-1967)

MIXTURES & BLOCKS: Asphalt Paving

Barnhill Contracting Company.............. G 704 721-7500
Concord (G-3317)

Barnhill Contracting Company.............. D 910 488-1319
Fayetteville (G-4557)

Barnhill Contracting Company.............. E 252 752-7608
Greenville (G-5946)

Blythe Construction Inc......................... G 704 788-9733
Concord (G-3322)

Blythe Construction Inc......................... E 336 854-9003
Greensboro (G-5396)

Brown Brothers Construction Co.......... F 828 297-2131
Zionville (G-13527)

Carolina Sunrock LLC............................ E 919 575-4502
Butner (G-1200)

Dickerson Group Inc.............................. G 704 289-3111
Charlotte (G-2042)

Fsc Holdings Inc.................................... G 919 782-1247
Raleigh (G-10121)

Gardner Asphalt Co................................ F 336 784-8924
Winston Salem (G-13176)

Gelder & Associates Inc....................... G 919 772-6895
Raleigh (G-10126)

Gem Asset Acquisition LLC.................. G 919 851-0799
Cary (G-1365)

Gem Asset Acquisition LLC.................. G 704 697-9577
Charlotte (G-2197)

Gem Asset Acquisition LLC.................. G 336 854-8200
Greensboro (G-5551)

Gem Asset Acquisition LLC.................. G 704 225-3321
Charlotte (G-2196)

Hudson Paving Inc................................. D 910 895-5910
Rockingham (G-10780)

Johnson Paving Company Inc............... F 828 652-4911
Marion (G-8046)

Krebs Corporation.................................. G 336 548-3250
Madison (G-7989)

Lane Construction Corporation............ G 919 876-4550
Raleigh (G-10247)

Long Asp Pav Trckg of Grnsburg......... G 336 643-4121
Summerfield (G-11842)

Russell Standard Corporation............... F 336 292-6875
Greensboro (G-5797)

Russell Standard Nc LLC...................... D 336 292-6875
Greensboro (G-5798)

S T Wooten Corporation........................ E 919 965-9880
Princeton (G-9826)

Sunrock Group Holdings Corp............. D 919 747-6400
Raleigh (G-10520)

Thorworks Industries Inc...................... G 919 852-3714
Raleigh (G-10547)

Vulcan Materials Company.................... G 704 545-5687
Charlotte (G-2992)

MOBILE COMMUNICATIONS EQPT

Dexterity LLC.. F 919 524-7732
Greenville (G-5964)

Motorola Mobility LLC............................ E 919 294-1289
Morrisville (G-9021)

MOBILE HOMES

Brig Homes NC.. G 252 459-7026
Nashville (G-9312)

Cavalier Home Builders LLC................. C 252 459-7026
Nashville (G-9316)

Clayton Homes Inc................................. G 828 667-8701
Candler (G-1221)

Clayton Homes Inc................................. G 828 684-1550
Fletcher (G-4729)

Elite Mountain Business LLC................ G 828 349-0403
Franklin (G-4827)

Esco Industries Inc................................ F 336 495-3772
Randleman (G-10647)

Home City Ltd.. G 910 428-2196
Biscoe (G-853)

Readilite & Barricade Inc....................... F 919 231-8309
Raleigh (G-10435)

Ridgewood Management LLC................. G 336 644-0006
Greensboro (G-5788)

Sunshine Mnfctred Strctres Inc........... G 704 279-6600
Rockwell (G-10802)

MOBILE HOMES, EXC RECREATIONAL

Champion Home Builders Inc............... B 910 893-5713
Lillington (G-7793)

CMH Manufacturing Inc......................... A 704 279-4659
Rockwell (G-10793)

R-Anell Custom Homes Inc................... G 704 483-5511
Denver (G-3801)

R-Anell Housing Group LLC.................. D 704 445-9610
Crouse (G-3659)

MODELS: General, Exc Toy

S Y Shop Inc.. G 704 545-7710
Mint Hill (G-8343)

MODULES: Computer Logic

Iqe North Carolina LLC.......................... F 336 609-6270
Greensboro (G-5623)

Pink Hill Wellness Edu Center.............. G 252 568-2425
Pink Hill (G-9766)

MODULES: Solid State

Telit Wireless Solutions Inc.................. D 919 439-7977
Durham (G-4264)

MOLDED RUBBER PRDTS

Flint Group US LLC................................ F 828 687-2485
Arden (G-272)

Longwood Industries Inc....................... F 336 272-3710
Greensboro (G-5664)

Nu-Tech Enterprises Inc........................ E 336 725-1691
East Bend (G-4324)

Patch Rubber Company.......................... C 252 536-2574
Weldon (G-12525)

PRODUCT

Qrmc Ltd.. G..... 828 696-2000
Hendersonville (G-6238)

Rp Fletcher Machine Co Inc.................... D..... 336 249-6101
Lexington (G-7736)

Rubber Mill Inc.. E..... 336 622-1680
Liberty (G-7778)

MOLDING COMPOUNDS

Parkway Products LLC........................... C..... 828 684-1362
Arden (G-294)

Plastiexports TN LLC............................. E..... 423 735-2207
Charlotte (G-2643)

Wp Reidsville LLC.................................. C..... 336 342-1200
Reidsville (G-10702)

MOLDINGS & TRIM: Metal, Exc Automobile

Airspeed LLC.. E..... 919 644-1222
Mebane (G-8227)

Kennys Components Inc......................... F..... 704 662-0777
Mooresville (G-8703)

Panels By Paith Inc................................ G..... 336 599-3437
Roxboro (G-10939)

MOLDINGS & TRIM: Wood

Chesnick Corporation............................ F..... 919 231-2899
Raleigh (G-9993)

Itc Millwork LLC..................................... D..... 704 821-1470
Matthews (G-8176)

Ornamental Mouldings LLC.................... F..... 336 431-9120
Archdale (G-240)

Trim Inc.. G..... 336 751-3591
Mocksville (G-8395)

Trimworks Inc... G..... 704 753-4149
Monroe (G-8570)

MOLDINGS OR TRIM: Automobile, Stamped Metal

Revolution Pd LLC.................................. G..... 919 949-0241
Pittsboro (G-9788)

MOLDS: Indl

Ameritech Die & Mold Inc...................... E..... 704 664-0801
Mooresville (G-8596)

Ameritech Die & Mold South Inc............ F..... 704 664-0801
Mooresville (G-8597)

Atlantic Mold Inc.................................... G..... 919 832-8151
Fuquay Varina (G-4868)

Bethlehem Manufacturing Co................. F..... 828 495-7731
Hickory (G-6270)

Brooks Tool Inc...................................... G..... 704 283-0112
Monroe (G-8447)

DEB Manufacturing Inc.......................... G..... 704 703-6618
Concord (G-3353)

Hasco America Inc................................. G..... 828 650-2631
Fletcher (G-4740)

R A Serafini Inc...................................... F..... 704 864-6763
Gastonia (G-5130)

Select Mold Service Inc......................... G..... 910 323-1287
Fayetteville (G-4667)

T D M Corporation.................................. E
Fletcher (G-4772)

MONUMENTS & GRAVE MARKERS, WHOLESALE

Conway Development Inc........................ F..... 252 756-2168
Greenville (G-5957)

MOPS: Floor & Dust

Lions Services Inc.................................. B..... 704 921-1527
Charlotte (G-2425)

Newell & Sons Inc.................................. G..... 336 597-2248
Roxboro (G-10930)

Quickie Manufacturing Corp................... C..... 910 737-6500
Lumberton (G-7966)

MOTION PICTURE & VIDEO DISTRIBUTION

AEC Consumer Products LLC................. F..... 704 904-0578
Fayetteville (G-4546)

MOTION PICTURE & VIDEO PRODUCTION SVCS: Educational

National Ctr For Social Impact............... G..... 984 212-2285
Raleigh (G-10323)

MOTION PICTURE PRODUCTION & DISTRIBUTION

Magic Factory LLC................................. E..... 919 585-5644
Durham (G-4116)

MOTOR & GENERATOR PARTS: Electric

ABB Motors and Mechanical Inc............. G..... 479 646-4711
Marion (G-8029)

Hlmf Logistics Inc.................................. G..... 704 782-0356
Pineville (G-9733)

Motor Rite Inc.. G..... 919 625-3653
Raleigh (G-10315)

SCR Controls Inc................................... F..... 704 821-6651
Matthews (G-8192)

Siemens Energy Inc............................... E..... 919 365-2200
Wendell (G-12546)

MOTOR CONTROL CENTERS

Siemens Industry Inc............................. C..... 919 365-2200
Wendell (G-12547)

MOTOR HOMES

Hunckler Fabrication LLC....................... F..... 336 753-0905
Mocksville (G-8370)

Van Products Inc.................................... E..... 919 878-7110
Raleigh (G-10582)

MOTOR VEHICLE ASSEMBLY, COMPLETE: Ambulances

First Prrity Emrgncy Vhcles In................ E..... 908 645-0788
Wilkesboro (G-12635)

Halcore Group Inc.................................. E..... 336 982-9824
Jefferson (G-7188)

Halcore Group Inc.................................. B..... 336 846-8010
Jefferson (G-7189)

Matthews Spcialty Vehicles Inc.............. D..... 336 297-9600
Greensboro (G-5682)

RFH Tactical Mobility Inc........................ F..... 910 916-0284
Milton (G-8326)

MOTOR VEHICLE ASSEMBLY, COMPLETE: Buses, All Types

Bus Safety Inc.. G..... 336 671-0838
Mocksville (G-8352)

Designline Corporation........................... C..... 704 494-7800
Charlotte (G-2035)

Prevost Car (us) Inc.............................. E..... 908 222-7211
Greensboro (G-5763)

Streets Auto Sales & Four WD................ G..... 704 888-8686
Locust (G-7904)

MOTOR VEHICLE ASSEMBLY, COMPLETE: Fire Department Vehicles

Trenton Emergency Med Svcs Inc.......... G..... 252 448-2646
Trenton (G-12111)

MOTOR VEHICLE ASSEMBLY, COMPLETE: Military Motor Vehicle

Fortem Genus Inc................................... G..... 910 574-5214
Fayetteville (G-4603)

James Tool Machine & Engrg Inc........... C..... 828 584-8722
Morganton (G-8875)

Operating Shelby LLC Tag...................... E..... 704 482-1399
Shelby (G-11368)

MOTOR VEHICLE ASSEMBLY, COMPLETE: Motor Buses

Epv Corporation..................................... D..... 704 494-7800
Charlotte (G-2124)

MOTOR VEHICLE ASSEMBLY, COMPLETE: Universal Carriers, Mil

Lelantos Group Inc................................. D..... 704 780-4127
Mooresville (G-8709)

MOTOR VEHICLE ASSEMBLY, COMPLETE: Wreckers, Tow Truck

Ashville Wrecker Service Inc.................. G..... 828 252-2388
Asheville (G-444)

MOTOR VEHICLE DEALERS: Automobiles, New & Used

ABB Motors and Mechanical Inc............. C..... 828 645-1706
Weaverville (G-12481)

Courtesy Ford Inc.................................. G..... 252 338-4783
Elizabeth City (G-4384)

Daimler Truck North Amer LLC............... A..... 704 645-5000
Cleveland (G-3213)

Dutch Miller Charlotte Inc...................... F..... 704 522-8422
Charlotte (G-2070)

Saab Barracuda LLC.............................. E..... 910 814-3088
Lillington (G-7802)

Subaru Folger Automotive...................... F..... 704 531-8888
Charlotte (G-2877)

Vestal Buick Gmc Inc............................. D..... 336 310-0261
Kernersville (G-7312)

Volvo Trucks North America Inc............. A..... 336 393-2000
Greensboro (G-5911)

MOTOR VEHICLE PARTS & ACCESS: Acceleration Eqpt

Axle Holdings LLC.................................. E..... 800 895-3276
Concord (G-3316)

Bosch Rexroth Corporation.................... E..... 704 583-4338
Charlotte (G-1801)

Carpenter Industries Inc........................ D..... 704 786-8139
Concord (G-3331)

Cleveland Yutaka Corporation................ D..... 704 480-9290
Shelby (G-11321)

Hitch Crafters LLC................................. G..... 336 859-3257
Lexington (G-7699)

Marmon Holdings Inc............................. G..... 910 291-2571
Laurinburg (G-7508)

Rostra Precision Controls Inc................. D..... 910 291-2502
Aberdeen (G-23)

MOTOR VEHICLE PARTS & ACCESS: Air Conditioner Parts

Longs Machine & Tool Inc...................... E..... 336 625-3844
Asheboro (G-374)

MOTOR VEHICLE PARTS & ACCESS: Ball Joints

Suspensions LLC.................................F 704 809-1269
Denver (G-3808)

MOTOR VEHICLE PARTS & ACCESS: Body Components & Frames

Can-AM Custom Trucks Inc....................G 704 334-0322
Charlotte (G-1834)

Jenkins Properties Inc............................E 336 667-4282
North Wilkesboro (G-9537)

MOTOR VEHICLE PARTS & ACCESS: Brakes, Air

Atkinson International Inc.......................E 704 865-7750
Gastonia (G-4995)

G-Loc Brakes LLC...................................G 704 765-0213
Mooresville (G-8669)

MOTOR VEHICLE PARTS & ACCESS: Clutches

FCC (north Carolina) LLC......................C 910 462-4465
Laurinburg (G-7501)

MOTOR VEHICLE PARTS & ACCESS: Cylinder Heads

Moores Cylinder Heads LLC..................E 704 786-8412
Concord (G-3404)

MOTOR VEHICLE PARTS & ACCESS: Electrical Eqpt

Autel New Energy US Inc.......................F 336 810-7083
Greensboro (G-5376)

MOTOR VEHICLE PARTS & ACCESS: Engines & Parts

Barrs Competition..................................F 704 482-5169
Shelby (G-11313)

Clarcor Eng MBL Solutions LLC............C 860 992-3496
Washington (G-12379)

Holman Automotive Inc..........................G 704 583-2888
Charlotte (G-2282)

Mann+hmmel Fltrtion Tech US LL........C 704 869-3700
Gastonia (G-5084)

Stanadyne Jacksonville LLC...................C 860 683-4553
Jacksonville (G-7153)

US Prototype Inc.....................................E 866 239-2848
Wilmington (G-12943)

Xceldyne Technologies LLC....................D 336 475-0201
Thomasville (G-12094)

MOTOR VEHICLE PARTS & ACCESS: Engs & Trans,Factory, Rebuilt

Jasper Engine Exchange Inc..................E 704 664-2300
Mooresville (G-8698)

Truck Parts Inc.......................................F 704 332-7909
Charlotte (G-2948)

MOTOR VEHICLE PARTS & ACCESS: Fuel Pumps

SL Liquidation LLC..................................E 860 525-0821
Jacksonville (G-7146)

Xtreme Fabrication Ltd...........................G 336 472-4562
Thomasville (G-12095)

MOTOR VEHICLE PARTS & ACCESS: Fuel Systems & Parts

SL Liquidation LLC..................................B 910 353-3666
Jacksonville (G-7147)

Stanadyne Intrmdate Hldngs LLC...........C 860 525-0821
Jacksonville (G-7152)

MOTOR VEHICLE PARTS & ACCESS: Gas Tanks

Edelbrock LLC..C 919 718-9737
Sanford (G-11175)

Isometrics Inc...F 336 342-4150
Reidsville (G-10690)

Isometrics Inc...E 336 349-2329
Reidsville (G-10689)

MOTOR VEHICLE PARTS & ACCESS: Gears

GKN Driveline Newton LLC.....................A 828 428-3711
Newton (G-9466)

MOTOR VEHICLE PARTS & ACCESS: Lifting Mechanisms, Dump Truck

Diamondback Products Inc.....................G 336 236-9800
Lexington (G-7678)

Godwin Manufacturing Co Inc................C 910 897-4995
Dunn (G-3858)

Satco Truck Equipment Inc.....................F 919 383-5547
Durham (G-4222)

MOTOR VEHICLE PARTS & ACCESS: Manifolds

Hogans Racing Manifolds Inc.................G 704 799-3424
Mooresville (G-8685)

MOTOR VEHICLE PARTS & ACCESS: Mufflers, Exhaust

AP Emissions Technologies LLC............A 919 580-2000
Goldsboro (G-5199)

Pro-Fabrication Inc.................................F 704 795-7563
Concord (G-3425)

MOTOR VEHICLE PARTS & ACCESS: Power Steering Eqpt

Cjr Products Inc......................................G 336 766-2710
Winston Salem (G-13124)

MOTOR VEHICLE PARTS & ACCESS: Propane Conversion Eqpt

Parker Gas Company Inc........................F 800 354-7250
Clinton (G-3238)

MOTOR VEHICLE PARTS & ACCESS: Tire Valve Cores

Dill Air Controls Products LLC................C 919 692-2300
Oxford (G-9613)

MOTOR VEHICLE PARTS & ACCESS: Tops

Kee Auto Top Manufacturing Co.............E 704 332-8213
Charlotte (G-2390)

MOTOR VEHICLE PARTS & ACCESS: Transmissions

Aisin North Carolina Corp.......................C 919 529-0951
Creedmoor (G-3636)

Aisin North Carolina Corp.......................A 919 479-6400
Durham (G-3886)

Borgwarner Inc.......................................E 828 684-4000
Arden (G-257)

Eaton Corporation..................................C 704 937-7411
Kings Mountain (G-7362)

MOTOR VEHICLE PARTS & ACCESS: Universal Joints

GKN Dna Inc...G 919 304-7378
Mebane (G-8243)

MOTOR VEHICLE PARTS & ACCESS: Wiring Harness Sets

Dce Inc...G 704 230-4649
Mooresville (G-8652)

Mr Tire Inc..F 828 322-8130
Hickory (G-6398)

MOTOR VEHICLE RACING & DRIVER SVCS

L Rancho Investments Inc......................G 336 431-1004
Trinity (G-12117)

Penske Racing South Inc.......................C 704 664-2300
Mooresville (G-8746)

MOTOR VEHICLE SPLYS & PARTS WHOLESALERS: New

Camco Manufacturing Inc......................G 336 348-6609
Reidsville (G-10678)

Capitol Bumper..G 919 772-7330
Fayetteville (G-4568)

Cummins Inc...E 336 275-4531
Greensboro (G-5476)

Nichols Spdmtr & Instr Co Inc................G 336 273-2881
Greensboro (G-5709)

Prevost Car (us) Inc...............................E 908 222-7211
Greensboro (G-5763)

Vna Holding Inc.......................................A 336 393-4890
Greensboro (G-5905)

Volvo Group North America LLC.............A 336 393-2000
Greensboro (G-5907)

Volvo Group North America LLC.............A 336 393-2000
Greensboro (G-5908)

Volvo Group North America LLC.............A 336 393-2000
Greensboro (G-5906)

Volvo Trucks North America Inc..............A 336 393-2000
Greensboro (G-5911)

Wind Solutions LLC.................................E 919 292-2096
Sanford (G-11252)

MOTOR VEHICLE: Hardware

Blue Ridge Global Inc.............................G 828 252-5225
Asheville (G-456)

Volvo Group North America LLC.............A 731 968-0151
Greensboro (G-5909)

MOTOR VEHICLE: Radiators

Lake Shore Radiator Inc.........................F 336 271-2626
Greensboro (G-5657)

MOTOR VEHICLE: Shock Absorbers

Fox Factory Inc.......................................G 828 633-6840
Asheville (G-501)

Lord Corporation....................................D 919 342-3380
Cary (G-1393)

Ohlins Usa Inc..E 828 692-4525
Hendersonville (G-6232)

MOTOR VEHICLE: Steering Mechanisms

Carolina Attachments LLC......................G 336 474-7309
Thomasville (G-12001)

PRODUCT

ZF Chassis Components LLC................ C 828 468-3711
Newton (G-9513)

MOTOR VEHICLE: Wheels

Gracie & Lucas LLC........................... G 704 707-3207
Mooresville (G-8675)

MOTOR VEHICLES & CAR BODIES

Bucher Municipal N Amer Inc............. E 704 658-1333
Mooresville (G-8624)

Carolina Movile Bus Systems............. G 336 475-0983
Thomasville (G-12005)

Daimler Truck North Amer LLC........... A 704 645-5000
Cleveland (G-3213)

Dej Holdings LLC.............................. E 704 799-4800
Mooresville (G-8655)

Ecovehicle Enterprises Inc................ G 704 544-9907
Charlotte (G-2090)

Epk LLC.. G 980 643-4787
Salisbury (G-11048)

Force Protection Inc......................... F 336 597-2381
Roxboro (G-10926)

GM Defense LLC............................... D 800 462-8782
Concord (G-3369)

Holman Automotive Inc..................... G 704 583-2888
Charlotte (G-2282)

International Motors LLC.................... G 704 596-3860
Charlotte (G-2344)

Jasper Engine Exchange Inc.............. E 704 664-2300
Mooresville (G-8698)

Jasper Penske Engines...................... F 704 788-8996
Concord (G-3384)

L Rancho Investments Inc.................. G 336 431-1004
Trinity (G-12117)

Maxxdrive LLC.................................. G 704 600-8684
Shelby (G-11360)

Mickey Truck Bodies Inc................... B 336 882-6806
High Point (G-6711)

Penske Racing South Inc................... C 704 664-2300
Mooresville (G-8746)

Prevost Car (us) Inc.......................... F 336 812-3504
High Point (G-6744)

Propane Trucks & Tanks Inc.............. F 919 362-5000
Apex (G-188)

Rp Motor Sports Inc......................... G 704 720-4200
Concord (G-3435)

Smith Fabrication Inc........................ G 704 660-5170
Mooresville (G-8772)

Southco Industries Inc...................... C 704 482-1477
Shelby (G-11381)

Subaru Folger Automotive.................. F 704 531-8888
Charlotte (G-2877)

Supreme Murphy Trck Bodies Inc....... C 252 291-2191
Wilson (G-13033)

Toymakerz LLC................................. F 843 267-3477
Reidsville (G-10699)

US Legend Cars Intl Inc..................... E 704 455-3896
Harrisburg (G-6119)

Vision Motor Cars Inc....................... G 704 425-6271
Concord (G-3465)

MOTOR VEHICLES, WHOLESALE: Fire Trucks

National Foam Inc............................. E 919 639-6100
Angier (G-126)

MOTOR VEHICLES, WHOLESALE: Truck tractors

Mack Trucks Inc............................... A 336 291-9001
Greensboro (G-5670)

MOTORCYCLE ACCESS

Capital Value Center Sls & Svc.......... G 910 799-4060
Wilmington (G-12730)

Edelbrock LLC.................................. C 919 718-9737
Sanford (G-11175)

P P M Cycle and Custom.................... G 336 434-5243
Trinity (G-12120)

MOTORCYCLE DEALERS

Barrs Competition............................. F 704 482-5169
Shelby (G-11313)

MOTORCYCLES & RELATED PARTS

B & B Welding Inc............................ G 336 643-5702
Oak Ridge (G-9569)

Barrs Competition............................. F 704 482-5169
Shelby (G-11313)

Driver Distribution Inc...................... G 984 204-2929
Raleigh (G-10059)

Indian Motorcycle Company............... G 704 879-4560
Lowell (G-7933)

Moto Group LLC............................... E 828 350-7653
Fletcher (G-4757)

Next World Design Inc....................... G 800 448-1223
Thomasville (G-12054)

Performance Parts Intl LLC................ F 704 660-1084
Mooresville (G-8748)

Suspension Experts LLC.................... E 855 419-3072
Roxboro (G-10948)

Sv Plastics LLC................................ G 336 472-2242
Thomasville (G-12077)

MOTORS: Electric

057 Technology LLC.......................... G 855 557-7057
Hickory (G-6258)

ABB Motors and Mechanical Inc......... G 336 272-6104
Greensboro (G-5336)

Asmo North America LLC................... A 704 872-2319
Statesville (G-11661)

Buehler Motor Inc............................. E 919 380-3333
Morrisville (G-8945)

Ohio Electric Motors Inc.................... D 828 626-2901
Barnardsville (G-693)

Petty Machine Company Inc............... E 704 864-3254
Gastonia (G-5119)

Powertec Industrial Motors Inc........... F 704 227-1580
Charlotte (G-2652)

Xavier Power Systems....................... F 910 734-7813
Lumberton (G-7977)

MOTORS: Fluid Power

Asmo Greenville of North Carolina Inc.. B 252 754-1000
Greenville (G-5939)

Denso Manufacturing NC Inc.............. B 252 754-1000
Greenville (G-5963)

MOTORS: Generators

Allan Drth Sons Gnrtor Sls Svc.......... G 828 526-9325
Highlands (G-6842)

Alternative Pwr Sls & Rent LLP.......... G 919 467-8001
Morrisville (G-8925)

Altom Fuel Cells LLC......................... G 828 231-6889
Leicester (G-7521)

Ao Smith Chatlotte........................... G 704 597-8910
Charlotte (G-1680)

Curtiss-Wright Corporation................ B 704 869-4600
Davidson (G-3700)

Denso Manufacturing NC Inc.............. B 704 878-6663
Statesville (G-11688)

Dna Group Inc.................................. E 919 881-0889
Raleigh (G-10051)

Eaton Corporation............................ B 828 684-2381
Arden (G-266)

Elnik Systems LLC............................ E 973 239-6066
Pineville (G-9726)

GE Vernova International LLC.............. E 704 587-1300
Charlotte (G-2194)

Genelect Services Inc....................... F 828 255-7999
Asheville (G-505)

Hitachi Energy USA Inc..................... C 919 856-2360
Raleigh (G-10170)

Ini Power Systems Inc....................... F 919 677-7112
Morrisville (G-8993)

Li-Ion Motors Corp............................ G 704 662-0827
Mooresville (G-8710)

Pinnacle Converting Eqp Inc.............. E 704 376-3855
Pineville (G-9748)

R D Tillson & Associates Inc.............. G 336 454-1410
Jamestown (G-7178)

Regal Rexnord Corporation................ G 800 825-6544
Charlotte (G-2703)

Rotron Incorporated.......................... C 336 449-3400
Whitsett (G-12619)

Siemens Energy Inc.......................... E 336 969-1351
Rural Hall (G-10967)

Trane Technologies Company LLC........ B 336 751-3561
Mocksville (G-8394)

MOUNTING SVC: Swatches & Samples

American Sample House Inc............... G 704 276-1970
Vale (G-12207)

Associated Printing & Svcs Inc........... G 828 286-9064
Rutherfordton (G-10975)

Carolina Swatching Inc...................... F 828 327-9499
Hickory (G-6288)

Creative Services Usa Inc.................. G 336 887-1958
High Point (G-6580)

E Feibusch Company Inc.................... E 336 434-5095
High Point (G-6600)

Kreber.. D 336 861-2700
High Point (G-6686)

Sampletech Inc................................ F 336 882-1717
High Point (G-6763)

MULTIPLEXERS: Telephone & Telegraph

Abacon Telecommunications LLC........ E 336 855-1179
Greensboro (G-5335)

Arris Solutions LLC........................... A 678 473-2000
Claremont (G-3088)

Avaya LLC.. B 919 425-8268
Research Triangle Pa (G-10705)

Conversant Products Inc.................... G 919 465-3456
Cary (G-1334)

Corning Incorporated........................ F 252 316-4500
Tarboro (G-11924)

Corning Optcal Cmmncations LLC........ A 828 901-5000
Charlotte (G-1986)

Emrise Corporation........................... C 408 200-3040
Durham (G-4023)

Extreme Networks Inc....................... B 408 579-2800
Morrisville (G-8973)

Hatteras Networks Inc....................... F 919 991-5440
Morrisville (G-8985)

JPS Communications Inc.................... D 919 534-1168
Raleigh (G-10222)

Newton Instrument Company.............. C 919 575-6426
Butner (G-1203)

Nvent Thermal LLC........................... B 919 552-3811
Fuquay Varina (G-4893)

Personal Communication Systems Inc.. D 336 722-4917
Winston Salem (G-13285)

R E Mason Enterprises Inc................. G 910 483-5016
Fayetteville (G-4661)

Siemens Corporation.................................F 919 465-1287
　Cary (G-1452)

Spectrasite Communications LLC...........E 919 468-0112
　Cary (G-1465)

Tabur Services LLC..................................G 704 483-1650
　Denver (G-3810)

Tekelec Inc..C
　Morrisville (G-9065)

Tekelec Global Inc.....................................A 919 460-5500
　Morrisville (G-9066)

Trimm International Inc..........................E 847 362-3700
　Youngsville (G-13496)

Usat LLC..E 919 942-4214
　Chapel Hill (G-1587)

Uteck..F 910 483-5016
　Fayetteville (G-4694)

MUSEUMS & ART GALLERIES

Mega Media Concepts Ltd Lblty.............G 973 919-5661
　Brevard (G-975)

MUSIC DISTRIBUTION APPARATUS

Worldwide Entrmt Mltimedia LLC...........G 704 208-6113
　Charlotte (G-3027)

MUSICAL INSTRUMENTS & ACCESS: Carrying Cases

Conn-Selmer Inc.......................................D 704 289-6459
　Monroe (G-8465)

MUSICAL INSTRUMENTS & ACCESS: NEC

Conn-Selmer Inc.......................................D 704 289-6459
　Monroe (G-8465)

Epi Centre Sundries.................................G 704 650-9575
　Charlotte (G-2122)

J L Smith & Co Inc....................................F 704 521-1088
　Charlotte (G-2360)

Lewtak Pipe Organ Builders Inc.............G 336 554-2251
　Mocksville (G-8374)

Lucky Man Inc...E 828 251-0090
　Asheville (G-538)

Luthiers Workshop LLC..........................G 919 241-4578
　Hillsborough (G-6871)

Music & Arts...G 919 329-6069
　Garner (G-4948)

MUSICAL INSTRUMENTS & SPLYS STORES: Pianos

MW Enterprises Inc.................................G 828 963-7083
　Vilas (G-12232)

MUSICAL INSTRUMENTS WHOLESALERS

J L Smith & Co Inc...................................F 704 521-1088
　Charlotte (G-2360)

MUSICAL INSTRUMENTS: Guitars & Parts, Electric & Acoustic

Kelhorn Corporation.................................G 828 837-5833
　Brasstown (G-964)

NAILS: Steel, Wire Or Cut

Masonite Corporation...............................A 704 599-0235
　Charlotte (G-2466)

Specialty Nails Company.........................G 336 883-0135
　High Point (G-6790)

NAME PLATES: Engraved Or Etched

Acme Nameplate & Mfg Inc.....................G 704 283-8175
　Monroe (G-8416)

Boyd Gmn Inc...C 206 284-2200
　Monroe (G-8446)

Product Identification Inc.......................E 919 544-4136
　Durham (G-4197)

NATURAL GAS DISTRIBUTION TO CONSUMERS

Blue Gas Marine Inc................................F 919 238-3427
　Apex (G-146)

Bolton Construction & Svc LLC...............D 919 861-1500
　Raleigh (G-9952)

NATURAL GAS LIQUIDS PRODUCTION

Bi County Gas Producers LLC................G 704 844-8990
　Charlotte (G-1778)

Green Power Producers...........................G 704 844-8990
　Charlotte (G-2238)

Landfill Gas Producers.............................G 704 844-8990
　Charlotte (G-2408)

Renewable Power Producers LLC.........G 704 844-8990
　Charlotte (G-2709)

NATURAL GAS PRODUCTION

City of Lexington......................................E 336 248-3945
　Lexington (G-7666)

City of Shelby...E 704 484-6840
　Shelby (G-11318)

Renewco-Meadow Branch LLC..............G 404 584-3552
　Wake Forest (G-12293)

SRNg-T&w LLC..G 704 271-9889
　Charlotte (G-2852)

Trans-Tech Energy LLC............................F 254 840-3355
　Rocky Mount (G-10818)

NATURAL PROPANE PRODUCTION

Diversified Energy LLC............................G 828 266-9800
　Boone (G-912)

Euliss Oil Company Inc...........................G 336 622-3055
　Liberty (G-7766)

South Central Oil and Prpn Inc...............G 704 982-2173
　Albemarle (G-90)

NAVIGATIONAL SYSTEMS & INSTRUMENTS

Garmin International Inc.........................A 919 337-0116
　Cary (G-1364)

NEW & USED CAR DEALERS

Streets Auto Sales & Four WD.................G 704 888-8686
　Locust (G-7904)

Window Motor World Inc..........................G 800 252-2649
　Boone (G-953)

NICKEL

Haynes International Inc.........................E 765 456-6000
　Hendersonville (G-6212)

Metal & Materials Proc LLC.....................G 260 438-8901
　Aberdeen (G-14)

Stainless & Nickel Alloys LLC.................G 704 201-2898
　Charlotte (G-2857)

Wanda Nickel...G 828 265-3246
　Deep Gap (G-3731)

NITRILE RUBBERS: Butadiene-Acrylonitrile

Kestrel I Acquisition Corporation............A 919 990-7500
　Durham (G-4095)

Liquidating Reichhold Inc........................A 919 990-7500
　Durham (G-4106)

NONCURRENT CARRYING WIRING DEVICES

Hydro Extrusion Usa LLC.......................D 336 227-8826
　Burlington (G-1107)

Pcore..F 919 734-0460
　Goldsboro (G-5235)

Preformed Line Products Co....................G 336 461-3513
　New London (G-9421)

Sigma Engineered Solutions PC.............D 919 773-0011
　Garner (G-4964)

NONFERROUS: Rolling & Drawing, NEC

Powerlab Inc..E 336 650-0706
　Winston Salem (G-13300)

Southern Metals Company.......................E 704 394-3161
　Charlotte (G-2837)

NOVELTIES

Encore Group Inc.....................................C 336 768-7859
　Winston Salem (G-13157)

NOVELTIES, PAPER, WHOLESALE

Stump Printing Co Inc..............................C 260 723-5171
　Wrightsville Beach (G-13433)

NOVELTIES: Paper, Made From Purchased Materials

Stump Printing Co Inc..............................C 260 723-5171
　Wrightsville Beach (G-13433)

NOVELTIES: Plastic

Carolina Print Works Inc.........................F 704 637-6902
　Salisbury (G-11027)

NOZZLES: Fire Fighting

Fireresq Incorporated..............................F 888 975-0858
　Mooresville (G-8664)

NOZZLES: Spray, Aerosol, Paint Or Insecticide

Merchant 1 Manufacturing LLC................G 336 617-3008
　Summerfield (G-11844)

Spraying Systems Co...............................G 704 357-6499
　Charlotte (G-2845)

NUCLEAR SHIELDING: Metal Plate

Columbiana Hi Tech LLC..........................G 336 497-3600
　Kernersville (G-7258)

NURSERIES & LAWN & GARDEN SPLY STORES, RETAIL: Fertilizer

Farm Services Inc....................................G 336 226-7381
　Graham (G-5268)

NUTRITION SVCS

Premex Inc...F 561 962-4128
　Durham (G-4196)

NYLON FIBERS

High Speed Gear Inc...............................F 910 325-1000
　Swansboro (G-11885)

OFFICE EQPT WHOLESALERS

Branch Office Solutions Inc.....................G 800 743-1047
　Indian Trail (G-7072)

Bryan Austin..G 336 841-6573
　High Point (G-6551)

Digital Print & Imaging Inc.....................G 910 341-3005
　Greenville (G-5965)

OFFICE FURNITURE REPAIR & MAINTENANCE SVCS

Freedom Enterprise LLC..........................G 502 510-7296
　Charlotte (G-2177)

PRODUCT

OFFICE SPLY & STATIONERY STORES: Office Forms & Splys

American Forms Mfg Inc.......................... E 704 866-9139
Gastonia *(G-4991)*

Carter Publishing Company Inc.............. F 336 993-2161
Kernersville *(G-7253)*

Jofra Graphics Inc.................................. G 910 259-1717
Burgaw *(G-1025)*

King Business Service Inc....................... G 910 610-1030
Laurinburg *(G-7504)*

L C Industries Inc.................................. C 919 596-8277
Fayetteville *(G-4629)*

L C Industries Inc.................................. C 919 596-8277
Durham *(G-4100)*

Lynchs Office Supply Co Inc.................... F 252 537-6041
Roanoke Rapids *(G-10740)*

M C C of Laurinburg Inc.......................... G 910 276-0519
Laurinburg *(G-7506)*

Office Sup Svcs Inc Charlotte.................. E 704 786-4677
Concord *(G-3410)*

Owen G Dunn Co Inc.............................. G 252 633-3197
New Bern *(G-9387)*

Print Management Group LLC.............. F 704 821-0114
Charlotte *(G-2669)*

Printing Press.. G 828 299-1234
Asheville *(G-585)*

Southern Printing Company Inc.............. G 910 259-4807
Burgaw *(G-1033)*

Times Printing Company.......................... E 252 473-2105
Manteo *(G-8024)*

Times Printing Company Inc.................... G 252 441-2223
Kill Devil Hills *(G-7320)*

W B Mason Co Inc.................................. E 888 926-2766
Charlotte *(G-2994)*

Westmoreland Printers Inc...................... F 704 482-9100
Shelby *(G-11391)*

Wright Printing Service Inc...................... G 336 427-4768
Madison *(G-8004)*

OFFICE SPLYS, NEC, WHOLESALE

Acme United Corporation......................... E 252 822-5051
Rocky Mount *(G-10807)*

Fain Enterprises Inc................................ G 336 724-0417
Winston Salem *(G-13163)*

OFFICES & CLINICS OF DOCTORS OF MEDICINE: Radiologist

Telephys Inc.. G 312 625-9128
Davidson *(G-3719)*

OIL & GAS FIELD MACHINERY

Patty Knio... G 919 995-2670
Raleigh *(G-10362)*

OIL FIELD SVCS, NEC

Duke Energy Center............................... F 919 464-0960
Raleigh *(G-10063)*

Jordan Piping Inc................................... G 336 818-9252
North Wilkesboro *(G-9539)*

Reservoir Group LLC.............................. G 610 764-0269
Charlotte *(G-2713)*

Saybolt LP.. G 910 763-8444
Wilmington *(G-12912)*

OIL TREATING COMPOUNDS

Thunder Eagle Enterprises Inc................ G 828 242-0267
Asheville *(G-618)*

OILS & ESSENTIAL OILS

Old Belt Extracts LLC............................. E 336 530-5784
Roxboro *(G-10934)*

Silver Moon Nutraceuticals LLC.............. G 828 698-5795
Fletcher *(G-4768)*

OILS: Mineral, Natural

Native Naturalz Inc................................. F 336 334-2984
Greensboro *(G-5704)*

OPHTHALMIC GOODS

Clarity Vision of Smithfield...................... G 919 938-6101
Smithfield *(G-11437)*

Luxottica of America Inc.......................... G 910 867-0200
Fayetteville *(G-4631)*

Luxottica of America Inc.......................... G 919 778-5692
Goldsboro *(G-5226)*

O D Eyecarecenter P A........................... G 252 443-7011
Rocky Mount *(G-10856)*

Ocutech Inc... G 919 967-6460
Chapel Hill *(G-1561)*

Optical Place Inc.................................... E 336 274-1300
Greensboro *(G-5725)*

OPHTHALMIC GOODS: Frames, Lenses & Parts, Eyeglasses

Eye Glass Lady LLC............................... F 828 669-2154
Black Mountain *(G-864)*

OPTICAL GOODS STORES

O D Eyecarecenter P A........................... G 252 443-7011
Rocky Mount *(G-10856)*

OPTICAL GOODS STORES: Eyeglasses, Prescription

Clarity Vision of Smithfield...................... G 919 938-6101
Smithfield *(G-11437)*

Luxottica of America Inc.......................... G 910 867-0200
Fayetteville *(G-4631)*

Luxottica of America Inc.......................... G 919 778-5692
Goldsboro *(G-5226)*

OPTICAL GOODS STORES: Opticians

Optical Place Inc.................................... E 336 274-1300
Greensboro *(G-5725)*

Optics Inc... G 336 288-9504
Greensboro *(G-5726)*

OPTICAL INSTRUMENTS & APPARATUS

Advanced Photonic Crystals LLC............ G 803 547-0881
Cornelius *(G-3583)*

ARW Optical Corp.................................. G 910 452-7373
Wilmington *(G-12710)*

Klearoptics Inc...................................... G 760 224-6770
Lattimore *(G-7480)*

Leica Microsystems Nc Inc...................... F 919 428-9661
Durham *(G-4103)*

Lightform Inc... G 908 281-9098
Asheville *(G-535)*

Rk Enterprises LLC................................ G 910 481-0777
Fayetteville *(G-4663)*

OPTICAL INSTRUMENTS & LENSES

C M M.. G 919 619-1716
Chapel Hill *(G-1532)*

Corning Incorporated.............................. D 910 784-7200
Wilmington *(G-12753)*

Imagineoptix Corporation........................ F 919 757-4945
Durham *(G-4072)*

M3 Products Com................................... G 631 938-1245
Matthews *(G-8180)*

New Vision Investments Inc..................... G 336 757-1120
Winston Salem *(G-13264)*

Optics Inc... G 336 288-9504
Greensboro *(G-5726)*

Optics Inc... G 336 884-5677
High Point *(G-6721)*

Opto Alignment Technology Inc.............. E 704 893-0399
Indian Trail *(G-7093)*

Roger D Thomas.................................... G 919 258-3148
Sanford *(G-11226)*

US Optics.. G 828 874-2242
Connelly Springs *(G-3484)*

ORGANIZATIONS: Biotechnical Research, Noncommercial

Kbi Biopharma Inc.................................. D 919 479-9898
Durham *(G-4094)*

ORGANIZATIONS: Medical Research

Biomedinnovations Inc............................ G 704 489-1290
Denver *(G-3775)*

Duke Human Vaccine Institute................ G 919 684-5384
Durham *(G-4009)*

King Phrmceuticals RES Dev LLC........... C 919 653-7001
Cary *(G-1383)*

ORGANIZATIONS: Professional

American Inst Crtif Pub Accntn................ B 919 402-0682
Durham *(G-3890)*

Assoction Intl Crtif Prof Accn.................. A 919 402-4500
Durham *(G-3901)*

ORGANIZATIONS: Religious

Church Initiative Inc................................ E 919 562-2112
Wake Forest *(G-12269)*

ORGANIZATIONS: Research Institute

Fire Retardant Chem Tech LLC............... G 980 253-8880
Matthews *(G-8169)*

Parata Systems LLC.............................. C 888 727-2821
Durham *(G-4165)*

ORIENTED STRANDBOARD

Louisiana-Pacific Corporation................. G 336 696-2751
Roaring River *(G-10750)*

OVENS: Paint Baking & Drying

Production Systems Inc........................... E 336 886-7161
High Point *(G-6747)*

Superior Finishing Systems LLC............. G 336 956-2000
Lexington *(G-7747)*

PACKAGE DESIGN SVCS

Piranha Industries Inc............................. G 704 248-7843
Charlotte *(G-2639)*

Precision Concepts Intl LLC.................... G 704 360-8923
Huntersville *(G-7037)*

St Johns Packaging Usa LLC.................. C 336 292-9911
Greensboro *(G-5833)*

PACKAGING & LABELING SVCS

Akuratemp LLC...................................... F 828 708-7178
Arden *(G-249)*

J R Cole Industries Inc............................ D 704 523-6622
Charlotte *(G-2362)*

Label & Printing Solutions Inc................. G 919 782-1242
Raleigh *(G-10243)*

Lions Services Inc.................................. B 704 921-1527
Charlotte *(G-2425)*

Piranha Industries Inc............................. G 704 248-7843
Charlotte *(G-2639)*

Royce Too LLC...................................... E 212 356-1627
Winston Salem *(G-13324)*

Salem One Inc.................................... C 336 744-9990
Winston Salem *(G-13325)*

Sanford Transition Company Inc............ E 919 775-4989
Sanford *(G-11230)*

Thompson Printing & Packg Inc............ G 704 313-7323
Mooresboro *(G-8587)*

PACKAGING MATERIALS, WHOLESALE

Aseptia Inc... C 678 373-6751
Raleigh *(G-9919)*

Atlantic Corp Wilmington Inc................. D 704 588-1400
Charlotte *(G-1710)*

Bagcraftpapercon III LLC...................... D 800 845-6051
Charlotte *(G-1739)*

Berlin Packaging LLC........................... G 704 612-4500
Charlotte *(G-1772)*

Blue Stone Industries Ltd..................... G 919 379-3986
Cary *(G-1310)*

Conitex Sonoco Usa Inc........................ C 704 864-5406
Gastonia *(G-5028)*

Geami Ltd... G 919 654-7700
Raleigh *(G-10125)*

Global Packaging Inc............................ D 610 666-1608
Hamlet *(G-6056)*

Interntnal Tray Pads Packg Inc.............. G 910 944-1800
Aberdeen *(G-8)*

Loparex LLC....................................... C 336 635-0192
Eden *(G-4352)*

Mm Clayton LLC.................................. B 919 553-4113
Clayton *(G-3160)*

Pactiv LLC.. G 910 944-1800
Aberdeen *(G-18)*

Paperfoam Packaging Usa LLC............. G 910 371-0480
Wilmington *(G-12870)*

Poly Packaging Systems Inc.................. D 336 889-8334
High Point *(G-6739)*

Pregis Innovative Packg LLC................. E 847 597-2200
Granite Falls *(G-5318)*

Pretium Packaging LLC......................... E 336 621-1891
Greensboro *(G-5762)*

Reliance Packaging LLC........................ E 910 944-2561
Aberdeen *(G-21)*

RLM/Universal Packaging Inc................ F 336 644-6161
Greensboro *(G-5789)*

Schutz Container Systems Inc............... D 336 249-6816
Lexington *(G-7738)*

Sonoco Hickory Inc.............................. D 828 328-2466
Hickory *(G-6453)*

Storopack Inc...................................... G 800 827-7225
Winston Salem *(G-13344)*

Thompson Printing & Packg Inc............ G 704 313-7323
Mooresboro *(G-8587)*

Unified2 Globl Packg Group LLC........... C 774 696-3643
Durham *(G-4288)*

PACKAGING MATERIALS: Paper

Abx Innvtive Pckg Slutions LLC............. D 980 443-1100
Charlotte *(G-1613)*

Box Board Products Inc......................... C 336 668-3347
Greensboro *(G-5397)*

Box Company of America LLC............... E 910 582-0100
Hamlet *(G-6051)*

Challnge Prtg of Crlnas Inc Th.............. G 919 777-2820
Sanford *(G-11163)*

Datamark Graphics Inc......................... E 336 629-0267
Asheboro *(G-345)*

Ds Smith PLC...................................... E 919 557-3148
Holly Springs *(G-6898)*

Dubose Strapping Inc........................... D 910 590-1020
Clinton *(G-3232)*

Eastcoast Packaging Inc....................... E 919 562-6060
Middlesex *(G-8274)*

Graphic Packaging Intl LLC................... C 704 588-1750
Pineville *(G-9730)*

Interntnal Tray Pads Packg Inc.............. G 910 944-1800
Aberdeen *(G-8)*

Label Line Ltd..................................... D 336 857-3115
Asheboro *(G-371)*

Multi Packaging Solutions..................... A 336 855-7142
Greensboro *(G-5699)*

Npx One LLC....................................... C 910 997-2217
Rockingham *(G-10784)*

Pactiv LLC.. C 252 527-6300
Kinston *(G-7425)*

Poly Packaging Systems Inc.................. D 336 889-8334
High Point *(G-6739)*

Pregis Innovative Packg LLC................. E 847 597-2200
Granite Falls *(G-5318)*

Quality Packaging Corp......................... G 336 881-5300
High Point *(G-6750)*

R R Donnelley & Sons Company............ D 252 243-0337
Wilson *(G-13018)*

Rgees Inc... G 828 708-7178
Arden *(G-304)*

Sealed Air Corporation (us).................. A 201 791-7600
Charlotte *(G-2777)*

St Johns Packaging Usa LLC................. C 336 292-9911
Greensboro *(G-5833)*

Storopack Inc...................................... G 800 827-7225
Winston Salem *(G-13344)*

Transcontinental AC US LLC................. F 704 847-9171
Matthews *(G-8154)*

Valdese Packaging & Label Inc............. E 828 879-9772
Valdese *(G-12201)*

Westrock Company............................... F 919 861-8760
Raleigh *(G-10605)*

Westrock Mwv LLC.............................. G 919 334-3200
Raleigh *(G-10606)*

PACKAGING MATERIALS: Paper, Coated Or Laminated

Atlantic Corporation............................. E 910 343-0624
Wilmington *(G-12713)*

Bagcraftpapercon III LLC...................... D 800 845-6051
Charlotte *(G-1739)*

PACKAGING MATERIALS: Plastic Film, Coated Or Laminated

Automated Solutions LLC...................... F 828 396-9900
Granite Falls *(G-5296)*

Goulston Technologies Inc.................... E 704 289-6464
Monroe *(G-8495)*

Jbb Packaging LLC.............................. G 201 470-8501
Weldon *(G-12521)*

Jd2 Company LLC................................ G 800 811-6441
Denver *(G-3791)*

Neopac Us Inc..................................... G 908 342-0990
Wilson *(G-13009)*

Paragon Films Inc............................... F 828 632-5552
Taylorsville *(G-11968)*

Shurtech Brands LLC........................... G 704 799-0779
Mooresville *(G-8770)*

PACKING & CRATING SVC

Broadwind Indus Solutions LLC............. E 919 777-2907
Sanford *(G-11159)*

Lls Investments Inc.............................. F 919 662-7283
Raleigh *(G-10258)*

PACKING MATERIALS: Mechanical

Interflex Acquisition Co LLC.................. C 336 921-3505
Wilkesboro *(G-12642)*

Packaging Plus North Carolina............... F 336 643-4097
Summerfield *(G-11845)*

The Interflex Group Inc......................... C 336 921-3505
Wilkesboro *(G-12655)*

PADS: Mattress

Bed In A Box....................................... E 800 588-5720
Mount Airy *(G-9102)*

Js Linens and Curtain Outlet.................. F 704 871-1582
Statesville *(G-11722)*

Leggett & Platt Incorporated................. G 704 380-6208
Statesville *(G-11727)*

PAINTS & ADDITIVES

Auto Parts Fayetteville LLC.................. G 910 889-4026
Fayetteville *(G-4555)*

Axalta Coating Systems Ltd................... E 336 802-4392
High Point *(G-6532)*

Crossroads Coatings Inc....................... F 704 873-2244
Statesville *(G-11681)*

Highland International LLC.................... F 828 265-2513
Boone *(G-924)*

Keim Mineral Coatings Amer Inc........... F 704 588-4811
Charlotte *(G-2391)*

Modern Recreational Tech Inc................ E 800 221-4466
Greensboro *(G-5696)*

Paint Company of NC........................... G 336 764-1648
Clemmons *(G-3198)*

Rack Works Inc.................................... E 336 368-1302
Pilot Mountain *(G-9673)*

Sherwin-Williams Company.................. D 704 548-2820
Charlotte *(G-2798)*

Sherwin-Williams Company.................. E 704 881-0245
Statesville *(G-11764)*

PAINTS & ALLIED PRODUCTS

Actega North America Inc..................... G 704 736-9389
Kings Mountain *(G-7343)*

Akzo Nobel Coatings Inc....................... E 336 841-5111
High Point *(G-6512)*

Americhem Inc..................................... E 704 782-6411
Concord *(G-3311)*

Axalta Coating Systems Ltd................... F 336 802-5701
High Point *(G-6531)*

Bay Painting Contractors...................... G 252 435-5374
Moyock *(G-9276)*

Bonakemi Usa Incorporated.................. D 704 220-6943
Monroe *(G-8445)*

Carolina Commercial Coatings.............. G 910 279-6045
Wilmington *(G-12733)*

Cdv LLC.. F 919 674-3460
Morrisville *(G-8953)*

Electric Glass Fiber Amer LLC............... B 704 434-2261
Shelby *(G-11332)*

Ennis-Flint Inc..................................... G 800 331-8118
High Point *(G-6613)*

Ennis-Flint Inc..................................... G 336 477-8439
Thomasville *(G-12022)*

Ennis-Flint Inc..................................... G 800 331-8118
Thomasville *(G-12023)*

Ennis-Flint Inc..................................... F 800 331-8118
Greensboro *(G-5522)*

Flint Acquisition Corp........................... D 336 475-6600
Thomasville *(G-12025)*

Flint Trading Inc................................... G 336 308-3770
Thomasville *(G-12026)*

Kestrel I Acquisition Corporation........... A 919 990-7500
Durham *(G-4095)*

Liquidating Reichhold Inc...................... A 919 990-7500
Durham *(G-4106)*

Lubrizol Global Management Inc............ D 704 865-7451
Gastonia *(G-5080)*

PRODUCT

Matlab Inc.. F 336 629-4161
  Asheboro *(G-377)*

Modern Recreational Tech Inc.............. D 847 272-2278
  Greensboro *(G-5695)*

Northwest Coatings Systems Inc........... G 336 924-1459
  Pfafftown *(G-9664)*

Piedmont Indus Coatings Inc.................. G 336 377-3399
  Winston Salem *(G-13292)*

PPG Architectural Finishes Inc.............. G 910 484-5161
  Fayetteville *(G-4655)*

PPG Architectural Finishes Inc.............. G 704 864-6783
  Gastonia *(G-5123)*

PPG Architectural Finishes Inc.............. G 336 273-9761
  Greensboro *(G-5754)*

PPG Architectural Finishes Inc.............. G 704 847-7251
  Matthews *(G-8141)*

PPG Architectural Finishes Inc.............. G 704 658-9250
  Mooresville *(G-8751)*

PPG Architectural Finishes Inc.............. G 828 438-9210
  Morganton *(G-8888)*

PPG Architectural Finishes Inc.............. G 919 872-6500
  Raleigh *(G-10383)*

PPG Architectural Finishes Inc.............. G 919 779-5400
  Raleigh *(G-10384)*

PPG Architectural Finishes Inc.............. G 704 633-0673
  Salisbury *(G-11105)*

PPG Industries Inc............................... G 919 319-0113
  Cary *(G-1425)*

PPG Industries Inc............................... G 704 542-8880
  Charlotte *(G-2653)*

PPG Industries Inc............................... G 704 523-0888
  Charlotte *(G-2654)*

PPG Industries Inc............................... G 919 382-3100
  Durham *(G-4192)*

PPG Industries Inc............................... G 919 772-3093
  Greensboro *(G-5755)*

PPG Industries Inc............................... G 252 480-1970
  Kill Devil Hills *(G-7319)*

PPG Industries Inc............................... G 704 658-9250
  Mooresville *(G-8752)*

PPG Industries Inc............................... G 919 981-0600
  Raleigh *(G-10385)*

PPG Industries Inc............................... G 910 452-3289
  Wilmington *(G-12888)*

PPG Industries Inc............................... G 336 771-8878
  Winston Salem *(G-13301)*

Renaissance Innovations LLC................ G 774 901-4642
  Durham *(G-4211)*

Road Infrstrcture Inv Hldngs I................ E 336 475-6600
  Thomasville *(G-12066)*

Rust-Oleum Corporation....................... G 704 662-7730
  Mooresville *(G-8765)*

S&F Products...................................... G 714 412-1298
  Holly Springs *(G-6913)*

Sherwin-Williams Company................... G 919 436-2460
  Raleigh *(G-10469)*

Sibelco North America Inc.................... D 828 766-6050
  Spruce Pine *(G-11586)*

Transcontinental AC US LLC.................. F 704 847-9171
  Matthews *(G-8154)*

PAINTS, VARNISHES & SPLYS WHOLESALERS

Keim Mineral Coatings Amer Inc............ F 704 588-4811
  Charlotte *(G-2391)*

PAINTS, VARNISHES & SPLYS, WHOLESALE: Paints

Akzo Nobel Coatings Inc....................... G 336 665-9897
  Greensboro *(G-5345)*

Controlled Release Tech Inc.................. G 704 487-0878
  Shelby *(G-11324)*

Highland International LLC..................... F 828 265-2513
  Boone *(G-924)*

Modern Recreational Tech Inc............... E 800 221-4466
  Greensboro *(G-5696)*

Sherwin-Williams Company................... E 336 292-3000
  Greensboro *(G-5810)*

PAINTS: Oil Or Alkyd Vehicle Or Water Thinned

Akzo Nobel Coatings Inc....................... F 704 366-8435
  Charlotte *(G-1635)*

Akzo Nobel Coatings Inc....................... G 336 665-9897
  Greensboro *(G-5345)*

Allied Pressroom Products Inc............... E 954 920-0909
  Monroe *(G-8421)*

PALLET LOADERS & UNLOADERS

Kinston Neuse Corporation.................... C 252 522-3088
  Kinston *(G-7418)*

PALLET REPAIR SVCS

Gamble Associates Inc......................... F 704 375-9301
  Charlotte *(G-2187)*

MAC Grading Co.................................. G 910 531-4642
  Autryville *(G-649)*

Neal S Pallet Company Inc.................... E 704 393-8568
  Charlotte *(G-2551)*

PALLETS & SKIDS: Wood

Alan Kimzey.. G 828 891-8720
  Mills River *(G-8310)*

Clary Lumber Company.......................... D 252 537-2558
  Gaston *(G-4978)*

Glenn Lumber Company Inc.................... E 704 434-7873
  Shelby *(G-11338)*

Johnston County Industries Inc.............. C 919 743-8700
  Selma *(G-11289)*

McBride Lumber Co Partnr LLC.............. G 910 428-2747
  Star *(G-11632)*

Pallets and More................................. G 919 815-6134
  Franklinton *(G-4852)*

Somers Lumber and Mfg Inc.................. F 704 539-4751
  Harmony *(G-6099)*

Steelman Lumber & Pallet LLC.............. F 336 468-2757
  Hamptonville *(G-6092)*

Tri-County Industries Inc....................... C 252 977-3800
  Rocky Mount *(G-10819)*

Triple C Companies LLC........................ E 704 966-1999
  Denver *(G-3814)*

Universal Forest Products Inc................ F 252 338-0319
  Elizabeth City *(G-4416)*

PALLETS: Wood & Metal Combination

T P Supply Co Inc................................ E 336 789-2337
  Mount Airy *(G-9183)*

PANELS: Building, Metal

Bonitz Inc... D 803 799-0181
  Concord *(G-3323)*

PAPER & BOARD: Die-cut

Boingo Graphics Inc............................. E 704 527-4963
  Charlotte *(G-1797)*

Box Company of America LLC................ E 910 582-0100
  Hamlet *(G-6051)*

Lakebrook Corporation.......................... G 207 947-4051
  Oak Island *(G-9566)*

Morrisette Paper Company Inc............... G 336 342-5570
  Reidsville *(G-10694)*

Mueller Die Cut Solutions Inc................ E 704 588-3900
  Charlotte *(G-2526)*

Subtle Impressions Inc......................... E
  Gastonia *(G-5145)*

Triangle Converting Corp....................... E 919 596-6656
  Durham *(G-4278)*

PAPER & PAPER PRDTS: Crepe, Made From Purchased Materials

Rgees LLC... G 828 708-7178
  Arden *(G-304)*

PAPER PRDTS: Cleansing Tissues, Made From Purchased Material

Cardinal Tissue LLC............................. D 815 503-2096
  Spindale *(G-11546)*

PAPER PRDTS: Infant & Baby Prdts

Shower ME With Love LLC..................... F 704 302-1555
  Charlotte *(G-2799)*

PAPER PRDTS: Napkin Stock

Nakos Paper Products Inc..................... G 704 238-0717
  Charlotte *(G-2541)*

PAPER PRDTS: Pressed & Molded Pulp & Fiber Prdts

Reynolds Consumer Products Inc........... A 704 371-5550
  Huntersville *(G-7042)*

PAPER PRDTS: Sanitary

Attends Healthcare Pdts Inc.................. G 252 752-1100
  Greenville *(G-5941)*

Attends Healthcare Products Inc............ B 800 428-8363
  Raleigh *(G-9921)*

Edtech Systems LLC............................. G 919 341-0613
  Raleigh *(G-10078)*

Hygiene Systems Inc............................ E 910 462-2661
  Laurel Hill *(G-7484)*

Kimberly-Clark Corporation.................... C 828 698-5230
  Hendersonville *(G-6218)*

Livedo Usa Inc.................................... D 252 237-1373
  Wilson *(G-13005)*

Pacon Manufacturing Co LLC................. C 910 239-3001
  Leland *(G-7556)*

Sealed Air Corporation.......................... D 828 728-6610
  Hudson *(G-6959)*

Valor Brands LLC................................. F 678 602-9268
  Stokesdale *(G-11817)*

PAPER PRDTS: Sanitary Tissue Paper

Kimberly-Clark Corporation.................... C 828 698-5230
  Hendersonville *(G-6218)*

PAPER PRDTS: Toilet Paper, Made From Purchased Materials

Cascades Tissue Group - NC Inc............ C 910 895-4033
  Rockingham *(G-10772)*

PAPER, WHOLESALE: Fine

McGrann Paper Corporation................... E 800 240-9455
  Charlotte *(G-2478)*

PAPER, WHOLESALE: Printing

Jasie Blanks LLC................................. F 910 485-0016
  Fayetteville *(G-4621)*

PAPER: Absorbent

Abzorbit Inc.. F 828 464-9944
  Newton *(G-9447)*

Encertec Inc... G 336 288-7226
Greensboro *(G-5519)*

Evergreen Packaging LLC......................... A 828 454-0676
Canton *(G-1252)*

PAPER: Adhesive

Avery Dennison Corporation................... G 336 553-2436
Greensboro *(G-5379)*

T - Square Enterprises Inc...................... G 704 846-8233
Charlotte *(G-2894)*

Tailored Chemical Products Inc............. D 828 322-6512
Hickory *(G-6462)*

PAPER: Book

Enriched Abundance Entp LLC............... F 704 369-6363
Charlotte *(G-2117)*

Magnera Corporation.................................. A 866 744-7380
Charlotte *(G-2448)*

PAPER: Building Laminated, Made From Purchased Materials

Acucote Inc.. C 336 578-1800
Graham *(G-5259)*

Cdv LLC... F 919 674-3460
Morrisville *(G-8953)*

PAPER: Building, Insulating & Packaging

Hibco Plastics Inc..................................... E 336 463-2391
Yadkinville *(G-13443)*

Technical Coating Intl Inc....................... E 910 371-0860
Leland *(G-7559)*

PAPER: Cardboard

Sonoco Products Company...................... G 910 455-6903
Jacksonville *(G-7148)*

PAPER: Cigarette

Filtrona Filters Inc.................................... D 336 362-1333
Greensboro *(G-5533)*

PAPER: Coated & Laminated, NEC

Avery Dennison Corporation................... D 336 621-2570
Greensboro *(G-5378)*

Avery Dennison Rfid Company............... G 626 304-2000
Greensboro *(G-5383)*

Datamark Graphics Inc........................... E 336 629-0267
Asheboro *(G-345)*

Intertape Polymer Corp........................... D 980 907-4871
Midland *(G-8288)*

J C Enterprises... G 336 986-1688
Winston Salem *(G-13212)*

Liflex LLC... C 336 777-5000
Winston Salem *(G-13237)*

Oracle Flexible Packaging Inc................ B 336 777-5000
Winston Salem *(G-13271)*

R T Barbee Company Inc........................ F 704 375-4421
Charlotte *(G-2687)*

TEC Graphics Inc...................................... F 919 567-2077
Fuquay Varina *(G-4901)*

Technical Coating Intl Inc....................... E 910 371-0860
Leland *(G-7559)*

Transcontinental AC US LLC................... F 704 847-9171
Matthews *(G-8154)*

Upm Raflatac Inc...................................... F 828 335-3289
Fletcher *(G-4775)*

Upm Raflatac Inc...................................... E 828 651-4800
Fletcher *(G-4776)*

PAPER: Coated, Exc Photographic, Carbon Or Abrasive

Avery Dennison Corporation................... G 864 938-1400
Greensboro *(G-5381)*

Avery Dennison Corporation................... F 336 665-6481
Greensboro *(G-5382)*

Blue Ridge Paper Products LLC............. C 828 452-0834
Waynesville *(G-12451)*

Loparex LLC... D 919 678-7700
Cary *(G-1392)*

PAPER: Corrugated

Atlantic Corp Wilmington Inc................. D 704 588-1400
Charlotte *(G-1710)*

Box Company of America LLC................ E 910 582-0100
Hamlet *(G-6051)*

Carolina Container Company.................. D 336 883-7146
High Point *(G-6558)*

Quality Packaging Corp........................... G 336 881-5300
High Point *(G-6750)*

PAPER: Fine

Blue Ridge Paper Products LLC............. C 828 235-3023
Canton *(G-1245)*

Blue Ridge Paper Products LLC............. D 828 454-0676
Canton *(G-1244)*

PAPER: Packaging

Ds Smith Packaging and Paper............. G 336 668-0871
Greensboro *(G-5505)*

Geami Ltd... E 919 654-7700
Raleigh *(G-10125)*

Ranpak Corp.. G 919 790-8225
Raleigh *(G-10432)*

Westrock Shared Services LLC.............. A 336 642-4165
Rural Hall *(G-10968)*

PAPER: Specialty

Glatfelter Corporation.............................. G 828 877-2110
Pisgah Forest *(G-9769)*

Westrock Kraft Paper LLC....................... G 252 533-6000
Roanoke Rapids *(G-10744)*

PAPER: Tissue

Burrows Paper Corporation..................... C 800 272-7122
Charlotte *(G-1819)*

Cascades Tissue Group - NC Inc........... C 910 895-4033
Rockingham *(G-10772)*

Laurel Hill Paper Co................................ G 910 997-4526
Cordova *(G-3581)*

PAPER: Waxed, Made From Purchased Materials

Burrows Paper Corporation..................... C 800 272-7122
Charlotte *(G-1819)*

PAPER: Wrapping & Packaging

Atlantic Corp Wilmington Inc................. D 704 588-1400
Charlotte *(G-1710)*

Pregis LLC... E 828 396-2373
Granite Falls *(G-5319)*

Transcontinental AC US LLC................... F 704 847-9171
Matthews *(G-8153)*

PAPERBOARD PRDTS: Folding Boxboard

Kme Consolidated Inc.............................. E 704 847-9888
Matthews *(G-8124)*

Printing & Packaging Inc......................... E 704 482-3866
Shelby *(G-11371)*

Westrock Converting LLC......................... F 336 661-6736
Winston Salem *(G-13391)*

PAPERBOARD PRDTS: Setup Boxboard

Napco Inc... C 336 372-5214
Sparta *(G-11540)*

PARACHUTES

Ballistic Recovery Systems Inc.............. E 651 457-7491
Pinebluff *(G-9685)*

Mills Manufacturing Corp........................ C 828 645-3061
Asheville *(G-548)*

North Amercn Aerodynamics Inc........... D 336 599-9266
Roxboro *(G-10932)*

Piedmont Parachute Inc.......................... G 336 597-2225
Roxboro *(G-10941)*

Saab Barracuda LLC................................. E 910 814-3088
Lillington *(G-7802)*

PARTICLEBOARD

Aconcagua Timber Corp.......................... B 919 542-2128
Moncure *(G-8398)*

Arauco - NA.. G 910 569-7020
Biscoe *(G-846)*

Olon Industries Inc (us).......................... F 630 232-4705
Mocksville *(G-8383)*

PARTICLEBOARD: Laminated, Plastic

Egger Wood Products LLC....................... B 336 843-7000
Linwood *(G-7876)*

Georgia-Pacific LLC.................................. D 919 580-1078
Dudley *(G-3836)*

PARTITIONS & FIXTURES: Except Wood

B&H Millwork and Fixtures Inc.............. E 336 431-0068
High Point *(G-6534)*

Chatsworth Products Inc......................... C 252 514-2779
New Bern *(G-9354)*

Coregrp LLC.. F 845 876-5109
Mooresville *(G-8643)*

Cub Creek Kitchens & Baths Inc.......... G 336 651-8983
North Wilkesboro *(G-9527)*

Ds Smith PLC.. E 919 557-3148
Holly Springs *(G-6898)*

E G A Products Inc.................................. F 704 664-1221
Mooresville *(G-8657)*

Hemco Wire Products Inc....................... G 336 454-7280
Jamestown *(G-7164)*

Idx Corporation... C 252 948-2048
Washington *(G-12392)*

Leisure Craft Holdings LLC.................... D 828 693-8241
Flat Rock *(G-4708)*

Leisure Craft Inc..................................... C 828 693-8241
Flat Rock *(G-4709)*

Madix... G 804 456-3007
Raleigh *(G-10265)*

Parker Brothers Incorporated................ G 910 564-4132
Clinton *(G-3237)*

Sid Jenkins Inc.. G 336 632-0707
Greensboro *(G-5811)*

Stanly Fixtures Company Inc.................. G 704 474-3184
Norwood *(G-9561)*

Technibilt Ltd.. E 828 464-7388
Newton *(G-9502)*

Thomasvlle Mtal Fbricators Inc............. E 336 248-4992
Lexington *(G-7750)*

Treeforms Inc.. E 336 292-8998
Greensboro *(G-5871)*

PARTITIONS: Wood & Fixtures

3c Store Fixtures Inc.............................. D 252 291-5181
Wilson *(G-12959)*

Amcase Inc.. E 336 784-5992
High Point *(G-6519)*

Corilam Fabricating Co............................ E 336 993-2371
Kernersville *(G-7259)*

Cub Creek Kitchens & Baths Inc............ G 336 651-8983
  North Wilkesboro (G-9527)

E T Sales Inc.. F 704 888-4010
  Midland (G-8286)

Hardwood Store of NC Inc...................... F 336 449-9627
  Gibsonville (G-5177)

Marsh Furniture Company........................ F 336 273-8196
  Greensboro (G-5676)

Michael Parker Cabinetry........................ G 919 833-5117
  Raleigh (G-10298)

Normac Kitchens Inc.............................. F 704 485-1911
  Oakboro (G-9582)

Reliable Construction Co Inc.................. G 704 289-1501
  Monroe (G-8550)

Rugby Acquisition LLC............................ D 336 993-8686
  Kernersville (G-7297)

Sheets Smith Wealth MGT Inc .... E 336 765-2020
  Winston Salem (G-13335)

Ullman Group LLC.................................. F 704 246-7333
  Charlotte (G-2959)

Wilsonart LLC.. G 866 267-7360
  Fletcher (G-4779)

PARTS: Metal

Alloy Fabricators Inc .... E 704 263-2281
  Alexis (G-102)

Royall Development Co Inc..................... C 336 889-2569
  High Point (G-6762)

PATTERNS: Indl

Lampe & Malphrus Lumber Co............... F 919 934-1124
  Smithfield (G-11454)

Pattern Box.. G 704 535-8743
  Charlotte (G-2616)

PAVERS

Young & McQueen Grading Co Inc......... D 828 682-7714
  Burnsville (G-1196)

PERFUME: Perfumes, Natural Or Synthetic

Coty US LLC.. A 919 895-5374
  Sanford (G-11167)

Scentair Technologies LLC..................... C 704 504-2320
  Charlotte (G-2762)

Up On Hill.. G 704 664-7971
  Troutman (G-12155)

PERFUMES

Carolina Perfumer Inc............................ G 910 295-5600
  Pinehurst (G-9688)

PERSONAL DOCUMENT & INFORMATION SVCS

Agingo Corporation................................ G 888 298-0777
  Charlotte (G-1629)

PESTICIDES

Nutrien AG Solutions Inc........................ F 252 977-2025
  Rocky Mount (G-10814)

PET SPLYS

Fill Pac LLC.. F 828 322-1916
  Hickory (G-6334)

Hudson S Hardware Inc.......................... E 919 553-3030
  Garner (G-4933)

L & B Jandrew Enterprises...................... G 828 687-8927
  Hendersonville (G-6219)

Lizmere Cavaliers.................................. G 704 418-2543
  Shelby (G-11354)

Microfine Inc.. G 336 768-1480
  Winston Salem (G-13252)

Walco International................................ G 704 624-2473
  Marshville (G-8097)

PETROLEUM BULK STATIONS & TERMINALS

Warren Oil Company LLC........................ D 910 892-6456
  Dunn (G-3871)

PHARMACEUTICAL PREPARATIONS: Adrenal

Cell Microsystems Inc............................ G 919 608-2035
  Durham (G-3966)

Daily Manufacturing Inc.......................... F 704 782-0700
  Rockwell (G-10795)

Glenmark Phrmceuticals Inc USA......... D 704 218-2600
  Monroe (G-8492)

PHARMACEUTICAL PREPARATIONS: Druggists' Preparations

Cardioxyl Pharmaceuticals Inc.............. G 919 869-8586
  Chapel Hill (G-1534)

Gale Global Research Inc....................... G 910 795-8595
  Leland (G-7544)

Hospira Inc.. F 704 335-1300
  Charlotte (G-2288)

Mylan Pharmaceuticals Inc.................... E 336 271-6571
  Greensboro (G-5703)

Natures Pharmacy Inc............................ G 828 251-0094
  Asheville (G-555)

New Paradigm Therapeutics Inc............. G 919 259-0026
  Chapel Hill (G-1559)

Niras Inc... G 919 439-4562
  Cary (G-1407)

Patheon Manufacturing Svcs LLC........... D 252 758-3436
  Greenville (G-6010)

Pharmagra Holding Company LLC......... G 828 884-8656
  Brevard (G-979)

Raybow Usa Inc.................................... F 828 884-8656
  Brevard (G-980)

Synthonix Inc.. F 919 875-9277
  Wake Forest (G-12307)

Tavros Therapeutics Inc......................... F 919 602-2631
  Durham (G-4260)

V1 Pharma LLC.................................... G 919 338-5744
  Raleigh (G-10580)

PHARMACEUTICAL PREPARATIONS: Pills

Bayer Corporation.................................. E 800 242-5897
  Durham (G-3919)

PHARMACEUTICAL PREPARATIONS: Proprietary Drug

Anelleo Inc.. G 919 448-4008
  Chapel Hill (G-1526)

Arrivo Management LLC......................... G 919 460-9500
  Morrisville (G-8932)

Avior Inc... G 919 234-0068
  Cary (G-1303)

Camargo Phrm Svcs LLC....................... G 513 618-0325
  Durham (G-3955)

Cornerstone Biopharma Inc.................... F 919 678-6507
  Cary (G-1335)

PHARMACEUTICAL PREPARATIONS: Solutions

Catalent Greenville Inc........................... D 252 752-3800
  Greenville (G-5952)

Fsc Therapeutics LLC............................ F 704 941-2500
  Charlotte (G-2182)

Tripharm Services Inc............................ F 984 243-0800
  Morrisville (G-9080)

PHARMACEUTICAL PREPARATIONS: Tablets

Nutraceutical Lf Sciences Inc................. C 336 956-0800
  Lexington (G-7727)

PHARMACEUTICALS

A1 Biochem Labs LLC............................ G 315 299-4775
  Wilmington (G-12687)

A2a Integrated Logistics Inc................... G 800 493-3736
  Fayetteville (G-4542)

Abbott Laboratories.............................. G 704 243-1832
  Waxhaw (G-12422)

Accord Healthcare Inc........................... E 919 941-7878
  Raleigh (G-9873)

Aceragen Inc.. F 919 271-1032
  Durham (G-3878)

Achelios Therapeutics LLC.................... G 919 354-6233
  Durham (G-3879)

Aer Therapeutics Inc............................. G 919 345-4256
  Raleigh (G-9883)

Aerami Therapeutics Inc........................ F 650 773-5926
  Durham (G-3882)

Aerie Pharmaceuticals Inc..................... G 919 237-5300
  Durham (G-3883)

Albemarle Corporation........................... A 980 299-5700
  Charlotte (G-1638)

Albion Medical Holdings Inc................... F 800 378-3906
  Lenoir (G-7570)

Alcami Carolinas Corporation................. E 919 957-5500
  Durham (G-3887)

Alcami Carolinas Corporation................. F 910 254-7000
  Morrisville (G-8922)

Alcami Carolinas Corporation................. G 910 254-7000
  Wilmington (G-12696)

Alcami Carolinas Corporation................. G 910 254-7000
  Wilmington (G-12697)

Alcami Carolinas Corporation................. G 910 254-7000
  Wilmington (G-12699)

Alcami Corporation................................ A 910 254-7000
  Wilmington (G-12700)

Alcami Holdings LLC.............................. A 910 254-7000
  Wilmington (G-12701)

AMO Pharma Services Corp.................. G 215 826-7420
  Durham (G-3893)

Amryt Pharmaceuticals Inc.................... F 877 764-3131
  Cary (G-1289)

Arbor Pharmaceuticals Inc..................... G 919 792-1700
  Raleigh (G-9910)

Areteia Therapeutics Inc........................ F 973 985-0597
  Chapel Hill (G-1527)

Array Biopharma Inc.............................. D 303 381-6600
  Morrisville (G-8931)

Asklepios Bopharmaceutical Inc............. C 919 561-6210
  Research Triangle Pa (G-10703)

Astrazeneca Pharmaceuticals LP........... C 919 647-4990
  Durham (G-3902)

Atsena Therapeutics Inc......................... F 352 273-9342
  Durham (G-3906)

Aurobindo Pharma USA Inc.................... E 732 839-9400
  Durham (G-3907)

Aurolife Pharma LLC.............................. E 732 839-9408
  Durham (G-3908)

Avadim Holdings Inc.............................. E 877 677-2723
  Asheville (G-447)

Avadim Holdings Inc.............................. E 877 677-2723
  Charlotte (G-1720)

Avient Protective Mtls LLC..................... D 704 862-5100
  Stanley (G-11609)

Avista Pharma Solutions Inc.................. E 919 544-8600
  Durham (G-3910)

Axitare Corporation	G	919 256-8196	
Raleigh (G-9925)			
B3 Bio Inc	G	919 226-3079	
Research Triangle Pa (G-10706)			
Balanced Pharma Incorporated	G	704 278-7054	
Cornelius (G-3588)			
Bausch Health Americas Inc	F	949 461-6000	
Durham (G-3918)			
Baxter Healthcare Corporation	F	828 756-6623	
Marion (G-8034)			
Baxter Healthcare Corporation	B	828 756-6600	
Marion (G-8035)			
Bayer Corp	F	704 373-0991	
Charlotte (G-1760)			
Bayer Cropscience Inc	E	412 777-2000	
Durham (G-3920)			
Bayer Healthcare LLC	F	919 461-6525	
Morrisville (G-8938)			
Bayer Hlthcare Pharmaceuticals	G	602 469-6846	
Raleigh (G-9934)			
Be Pharmaceuticals Inc	G	704 560-1444	
Cary (G-1305)			
Beaker Inc	F	919 803-7422	
Raleigh (G-9936)			
Bespak Laboratories Inc	E	919 884-2064	
Morrisville (G-8940)			
Bestco LLC	E	704 664-4300	
Mooresville (G-8611)			
Bestco LLC	C	704 664-4300	
Mooresville (G-8612)			
Bestco LLC	C	704 664-4300	
Mooresville (G-8613)			
Biocryst Pharmaceuticals Inc	B	919 859-1302	
Durham (G-3928)			
Biogen MA Inc	C	919 941-1100	
Durham (G-3929)			
Bioresource International Inc	G	919 267-3758	
Apex (G-145)			
Bpc Plasma Inc	F	910 463-2603	
Jacksonville (G-7117)			
Bright Holdings Usa Inc	C	919 327-5500	
Raleigh (G-9960)			
Bright Path Laboratories Inc	G	858 281-8121	
Kannapolis (G-7204)			
Brii Biosciences Inc	F	919 240-5605	
Durham (G-3943)			
Bristol-Myers Squibb Company	G	800 321-1335	
Charlotte (G-1812)			
Bristol-Myers Squibb Company	B	336 855-5500	
Greensboro (G-5406)			
Cambrex High Point Inc	D	336 841-5250	
High Point (G-6553)			
Capnostics LLC	G	610 442-1363	
Concord (G-3329)			
Cardinal Health 414 LLC	G	704 644-7989	
Charlotte (G-1840)			
Cardiopharma Inc	F	910 791-1361	
Wilmington (G-12732)			
Catalent Pharma Solutions LLC	G	919 481-4855	
Morrisville (G-8949)			
Catalent Pharma Solutions LLC	G	919 465-8101	
Morrisville (G-8950)			
Catalent Pharma Solutions Inc	F	919 465-8206	
Durham (G-3965)			
Catalent Pharma Solutions Inc	G	919 481-2614	
Morrisville (G-8951)			
Catalent Pharma Solutions LLC	F	919 481-4855	
Morrisville (G-8952)			
Cem-102 Pharmaceuticals Inc	F	919 576-2306	
Chapel Hill (G-1536)			
Cempra Pharmaceuticals Inc	F	919 803-6882	
Chapel Hill (G-1537)			
Cenerx Biopharma Inc	G	919 234-4072	
Cary (G-1325)			
Chemogenics Biopharma LLC	G	919 323-8133	
Durham (G-3972)			
Chimerix Inc	E	919 806-1074	
Durham (G-3973)			
Civentichem Usa LLC	G	919 672-8865	
Cary (G-1329)			
Cleveland Compounding Inc	G	704 487-1971	
Shelby (G-11319)			
Closure Medical Corporation	C	919 876-7800	
Raleigh (G-10001)			
Cloud Pharmaceuticals Inc	G	919 558-1254	
Durham (G-3978)			
Cmp Pharma Inc	E	252 753-7111	
Farmville (G-4525)			
Cosette Pharmaceuticals Inc	C	704 735-5700	
Lincolnton (G-7823)			
Cosette Phrmctcals NC Labs LLC	C	908 753-2000	
Lincolnton (G-7824)			
Dataspectrum	G	919 341-3300	
Raleigh (G-10036)			
Diagnostic Devices	G	704 599-5908	
Charlotte (G-2039)			
Dignify Therapeutics LLC	G	919 371-8138	
Durham (G-4001)			
Dova Pharmaceuticals Inc	E	919 748-5975	
Morrisville (G-8969)			
Dpi Newco LLC	A	252 758-3436	
Greenville (G-5967)			
DSM	F	408 582-2610	
Greenville (G-5968)			
Dsm Inc	G	919 876-2802	
Raleigh (G-10061)			
DSM Pharmaceuticals Inc	D	252 758-3436	
Greenville (G-5969)			
DSM Pharmaceuticals Inc	A	252 758-3436	
Greenville (G-5970)			
East Coast Biologics	G	717 919-9980	
Fayetteville (G-4591)			
Effipharma Inc	G	919 338-2628	
Chapel Hill (G-1543)			
Ei LLC	B	704 857-0707	
Winston Salem (G-13155)			
Eisai Inc	F	919 941-6920	
Raleigh (G-10079)			
Elanco US Inc	F	812 230-2745	
Greensboro (G-5515)			
Eli Lilly and Company	F	317 296-1226	
Durham (G-4017)			
Embrex Poultry Health LLC	G	910 844-5566	
Maxton (G-8200)			
Encube Ethicals Inc	G	919 767-3292	
Durham (G-4024)			
Engineered Processing Eqp LLC	G	919 321-6891	
Wilson (G-12988)			
Environmental Science US LLC	F	800 331-2867	
Cary (G-1354)			
Envisia Therapeutics Inc	E	919 973-1440	
Durham (G-4028)			
Eon Labs Inc	B	252 234-2222	
Wilson (G-12989)			
Exela Drug Substance LLC	G	828 758-5474	
Lenoir (G-7603)			
Exela Pharma Sciences LLC	G	828 758-5474	
Lenoir (G-7604)			
Exemplar Laboratories LLC	G	336 817-6794	
Lexington (G-7686)			
Fennec Pharmaceuticals Inc	E	919 636-4530	
Research Triangle Pa (G-10709)			
Fervent Pharmaceuticals LLC	G	252 558-9700	
Greenville (G-5975)			
Fidelity Pharmaceuticals LLC	G	704 274-3192	
Huntersville (G-6989)			
Fortovia Therapeutics Inc	G	919 872-5578	
Raleigh (G-10117)			
Fortrea Holdings Inc	E	480 295-7600	
Durham (G-4035)			
Fresenius Kabi Usa LLC	A	252 991-2692	
Wilson (G-12991)			
Fujifilm Diosynth Biotechnolog	G	919 337-4400	
Durham (G-4040)			
Fujifilm Dsynth Btchnlgies USA	D	919 337-4400	
Morrisville (G-8977)			
Furiex Pharmaceuticals LLC	F	919 456-7800	
Morrisville (G-8978)			
G1 Therapeutics Inc	C	919 213-9835	
Durham (G-4042)			
Gb Biosciences LLC	D	336 632-6000	
Greensboro (G-5550)			
Genixus Corp	G	877 436-4987	
Concord (G-3368)			
Genixus Corp	F	877 436-4987	
Kannapolis (G-7209)			
George Clinical Inc	G	919 789-2022	
Raleigh (G-10128)			
Gilead Sciences Inc	G	650 574-3000	
Raleigh (G-10134)			
Glaxosmithkline LLC	G	704 962-5786	
Cornelius (G-3602)			
Glaxosmithkline LLC	E	919 483-5302	
Durham (G-4050)			
Glaxosmithkline LLC	E	919 483-2100	
Durham (G-4051)			
Glaxosmithkline LLC	G	252 315-9774	
Durham (G-4052)			
Glaxosmithkline LLC	E	919 483-2100	
Durham (G-4053)			
Glaxosmithkline LLC	G	336 392-3058	
Greensboro (G-5562)			
Glaxosmithkline LLC	B	919 628-3630	
Morrisville (G-8983)			
Glaxosmithkline LLC	E	919 483-5006	
Research Triangle Pa (G-10710)			
Glaxosmithkline LLC	E	919 269-5000	
Zebulon (G-13509)			
Glaxosmithkline Services Inc	B	919 483-2100	
Durham (G-4054)			
GNH Pharmaceuticals USA LLC	G	704 585-8769	
Charlotte (G-2219)			
Greer Laboratories Inc	C	828 754-5327	
Lenoir (G-7610)			
Grifols Inc	E	919 553-5011	
Clayton (G-3150)			
Grifols Therapeutics LLC	D	919 359-7069	
Clayton (G-3151)			
Grifols Therapeutics LLC	C	919 553-0172	
Clayton (G-3152)			
Grifols Therapeutics LLC	B	919 316-6300	
Research Triangle Pa (G-10711)			
Hammock Pharmaceuticals Inc	G	704 727-7926	
Charlotte (G-2253)			
Health Choice Pharmacy	G	281 741-8358	
Arden (G-273)			
Heron Therapeutics Inc	C	858 251-4400	
Cary (G-1371)			
High Point Pharmaceuticals LLC	F	336 841-0300	
High Point (G-6654)			
Hipra Scientific USA	G	919 605-8256	
Garner (G-4931)			
Hospira Inc	E	252 977-5111	
Battleboro (G-699)			
Hospira Inc	B	919 553-3831	
Clayton (G-3154)			

PRODUCT

Hospira Inc...................................C 252 977-5500
Rocky Mount *(G-10813)*

Hospira Inc...................................A 252 977-5111
Rocky Mount *(G-10842)*

Icagen LLC...................................D 919 941-5206
Durham *(G-4068)*

Idexx Pharmaceuticals Inc..........G 336 834-6500
Greensboro *(G-5614)*

Imbrium Therapeutics LP...........F 984 439-1075
Morrisville *(G-8992)*

Indivior Manufacturing LLC.........D 804 594-0974
Raleigh *(G-10187)*

Inhalon Biopharma Inc.................G 650 439-0110
Durham *(G-4077)*

Innobioactives LLC.......................G 336 235-0838
Greensboro *(G-5618)*

Innocrin Pharmaceuticals Inc......G 919 467-8539
Fuquay Varina *(G-4884)*

Intas Pharmaceuticals Limited.....E 919 941-7878
Raleigh *(G-10204)*

Interpace Pharma Solutions Inc.....G 919 678-7024
Morrisville *(G-8994)*

Ioto Usa LLC..............................F 252 413-7343
Greenville *(G-5992)*

Iqvia Pharma Inc.........................D 919 998-2000
Durham *(G-4084)*

Ixc Discovery Inc.........................E 919 941-5206
Durham *(G-4086)*

Kbi Biopharma Inc.......................G 919 479-9898
Durham *(G-4093)*

Kbi Biopharma Inc.......................D 919 479-9898
Durham *(G-4094)*

Keranetics LLC............................G 336 725-0621
Winston Salem *(G-13225)*

King Bio Inc.................................D 828 255-0201
Asheville *(G-530)*

King Phrmceuticals RES Dev LLC.........C 919 653-7001
Cary *(G-1383)*

Kowa Research Institute Inc.........E 919 433-1600
Morrisville *(G-9000)*

Krenitsky Pharmaceuticals Inc.....G 919 493-4631
Chapel Hill *(G-1551)*

Krigen Pharmaceuticals LLC.........G 919 523-7530
Lillington *(G-7799)*

Ksep Systems LLC.......................G 919 339-1850
Morrisville *(G-9001)*

Lexitas Pharma Services Inc.........E 919 205-0012
Durham *(G-4104)*

Lonza Rtp....................................G 800 748-8979
Morrisville *(G-9013)*

Lq3 Pharmaceuticals Inc..............G 919 794-7391
Morrisville *(G-9014)*

Mallinckrodt LLC..........................D 919 878-2800
Raleigh *(G-10268)*

Mallinckrodt LLC..........................G 919 878-2900
Raleigh *(G-10269)*

Marius Pharmaceuticals LLC........G 919 374-1913
Raleigh *(G-10271)*

Mayne Pharma Commercial LLC.........B 984 242-1400
Raleigh *(G-10281)*

Mayne Pharma LLC......................C 252 752-3800
Raleigh *(G-10282)*

Mayne Pharma Ventures LLC........G 252 752-3800
Raleigh *(G-10283)*

Melinta Therapeutics LLC.............F 919 313-6601
Chapel Hill *(G-1555)*

Merck & Co Inc............................E 908 423-3000
Charlotte *(G-2492)*

Merck Sharp & Dohme LLC...........C 919 425-4000
Durham *(G-4128)*

Merck Sharp & Dohme LLC...........B 252 243-2011
Wilson *(G-13006)*

Merck Teknika LLC.......................E 919 620-7200
Durham *(G-4129)*

Merz Incorporated.......................C 919 582-8196
Raleigh *(G-10293)*

Merz North America Inc...............F 919 582-8000
Raleigh *(G-10294)*

Merz Pharmaceuticals LLC...........C 919 582-8000
Raleigh *(G-10295)*

Millennium Pharmaceuticals Inc.........D 866 466-7779
Charlotte *(G-2503)*

Mixx-Point 5 Project LLC..............G 858 298-4625
Swannanoa *(G-11873)*

Musa Gold LLC............................F 704 579-7894
Charlotte *(G-2536)*

Neuronex Inc...............................G 919 460-9500
Morrisville *(G-9024)*

Neurotronik Inc...........................E 919 883-4155
Durham *(G-4147)*

None..G 336 408-6008
Winston Salem *(G-13265)*

Nontoxic Pthgen Erdction Cons.........G 800 308-1094
Matthews *(G-8136)*

Nortria Inc...................................F 919 440-3253
Raleigh *(G-10340)*

Novo Nordisk Phrm Inds LP..........D 919 820-9985
Clayton *(G-3164)*

Novo Nordisk Phrm Inds LP..........C 919 820-9985
Clayton *(G-3165)*

Novo Nordisk Phrm Inds LP..........E 919 550-2200
Durham *(G-4151)*

Nucleus Radiopharma Inc.............E 980 483-1766
Davidson *(G-3715)*

Nutra-Pharma Mfg Corp NC..........D 631 846-2500
Lexington *(G-7726)*

Oncoceutics Inc...........................F 678 897-0563
Durham *(G-4156)*

OnTarget Labs Inc.......................G 919 846-3877
Raleigh *(G-10346)*

Oriel Therapeutics Inc..................G 919 313-1290
Durham *(G-4159)*

Patheon Calculus Merger LLC.........G 919 226-3200
Morrisville *(G-9034)*

Patheon Inc.................................G 919 226-3200
Durham *(G-4167)*

Patheon Inc.................................A 919 226-3200
Durham *(G-4168)*

Patheon Pharmaceuticals Inc.........A 866 728-4366
High Point *(G-6727)*

Patheon Pharmaceuticals Inc.........D 919 226-3200
Morrisville *(G-9035)*

Patheon Phrmceuticals Svcs Inc.........E 919 226-3200
Morrisville *(G-9036)*

Pfizer Inc....................................G 252 382-3309
Battleboro *(G-705)*

Pfizer Inc....................................F 919 941-5185
Durham *(G-4176)*

Pfizer Inc....................................D 252 977-5111
Rocky Mount *(G-10861)*

Pfizer Inc....................................C 919 775-7100
Sanford *(G-11219)*

Pharmaceutical Dimensions.........G 336 297-4851
Greensboro *(G-5739)*

Pharmaceutical Equipment Svcs.........G 239 699-9120
Asheville *(G-571)*

Pharmasone LLC..........................G 910 679-8364
Wilmington *(G-12876)*

Piedmont Animal Health Inc.........E 336 544-0320
Greensboro *(G-5740)*

Pozen Inc....................................F 919 913-1030
Raleigh *(G-10382)*

Ppd Inc.......................................C 910 251-0081
Wilmington *(G-12886)*

Ppd International Holdings LLC.........G 910 251-0081
Wilmington *(G-12887)*

Praetego Inc................................G 919 237-7969
Durham *(G-4193)*

Promethera Biosciences LLC.........F 919 354-1930
Durham *(G-4199)*

Promethera Biosciences LLC.........G 919 354-1933
Raleigh *(G-10403)*

Propella Therapeutics Inc.............G 703 631-7523
Pittsboro *(G-9786)*

PSI Pharma Support America Inc.........E 919 249-2660
Durham *(G-4200)*

Purdue Pharmaceuticals LP...........F 252 265-1900
Wilson *(G-13015)*

Qualicaps Inc..............................C 336 449-3900
Whitsett *(G-12618)*

Quatrobio LLC..............................G 919 460-9500
Morrisville *(G-9041)*

Rainforest Nutritionals Inc............G 919 847-2221
Raleigh *(G-10421)*

Redhill Biopharma Inc..................D 984 444-7010
Raleigh *(G-10440)*

Salubrent Phrma Solutions Corp.........G 301 980-7224
Kannapolis *(G-7219)*

Sandoz Inc..................................B 252 234-2222
Wilson *(G-13028)*

Santarus Inc................................B 919 862-1000
Raleigh *(G-10456)*

Satsuma Pharmaceuticals Inc.........F 650 410-3200
Durham *(G-4223)*

Scipher Medicine Corporation.........G 781 755-2063
Durham *(G-4226)*

Scorpius Holdings Inc...................E 919 240-7133
Morrisville *(G-9049)*

Sobi Inc.......................................G 844 506-3682
Morrisville *(G-9056)*

Solvekta LLC................................G 336 944-4677
Greensboro *(G-5821)*

Sprout Pharmaceuticals Inc.........F 919 882-0850
Raleigh *(G-10500)*

Sterling Pharma Usa LLC..............E 919 678-0702
Cary *(G-1467)*

Stiefel Laboratories Inc................C 888 784-3335
Durham *(G-4251)*

Stiefel Laboratories Inc................E 888 784-3335
Research Triangle Pa *(G-10715)*

Syneos Health Consulting Inc.........E 919 876-9300
Morrisville *(G-9061)*

Synereca Pharmaceuticals Inc.........G 919 966-3929
Chapel Hill *(G-1576)*

Synthon Pharmaceuticals Inc.........E 919 493-6006
Durham *(G-4258)*

Tarheel Solutions LLC...................G 336 420-9265
Pleasant Garden *(G-9795)*

Tergus Pharma LLC......................E 919 549-9700
Durham *(G-4268)*

Teva Pharmaceuticals Usa Inc.........D 336 316-4132
Greensboro *(G-5859)*

Tg Therapeutics Inc......................D 877 575-8489
Morrisville *(G-9069)*

Tomorrowmed Pharma LLC...........E 832 615-2880
Morrisville *(G-9073)*

Transtech Pharma LLC..................C 336 841-0300
High Point *(G-6810)*

Umethod Health Inc.....................F 984 232-6699
Raleigh *(G-10574)*

United Therapeutics Corp.............E 919 246-9389
Durham *(G-4289)*

United Therapeutics Corp.............D 919 485-8350
Research Triangle Pa *(G-10717)*

Universal Preservachem Inc.........D 732 568-1266
Mebane *(G-8262)*

2025 Harris North Carolina
Manufacturers Directory

(G-0000) Company's Geographic Section entry number

Urovant Sciences Inc.............................. F 919 323-8528
Durham *(G-4293)*

Vascular Pharmaceuticals Inc................. G 919 345-7933
Chapel Hill *(G-1588)*

Verinetics Inc... G 919 354-1029
Rtp *(G-10950)*

Viiv Healthcare Company........................ G 919 445-2770
Chapel Hill *(G-1590)*

Viiv Healthcare Company........................ A 919 483-2100
Durham *(G-4298)*

Vogenx Inc... G 919 659-5677
Durham *(G-4299)*

Vtv Therapeutics LLC............................. G 336 841-0300
High Point *(G-6830)*

We Pharma Inc....................................... D 919 389-1478
Morrisville *(G-9088)*

West Pharmaceutical Svcs Inc................ G 252 522-8956
Kinston *(G-7436)*

Wyeth Holdings LLC............................... A 919 775-7100
Sanford *(G-11255)*

Zoetis Inc.. C 919 941-5185
Durham *(G-4318)*

Zoetis Products LLC............................... G 336 333-9356
Greensboro *(G-5933)*

PHONOGRAPH RECORDS WHOLESALERS

Sony Music Holdings Inc......................... G 336 886-1807
High Point *(G-6785)*

PHOSPHATE ROCK MINING

Lbm Industries Inc.................................. F 828 966-4270
Sapphire *(G-11258)*

Pcs Phosphate Company Inc.................... E 252 322-4111
Aurora *(G-645)*

PHOSPHATES

Potash Corp Saskatchewan Inc................ E 252 322-4111
Aurora *(G-646)*

Scotts Company LLC.............................. G 704 663-6088
Mooresville *(G-8767)*

PHOTOCOPYING & DUPLICATING SVCS

Accelerated Press Inc............................. G 248 524-1850
Wilmington *(G-12689)*

Asheville Quickprint............................... G 828 252-7667
Fletcher *(G-4720)*

Better Business Printing Inc..................... G 704 867-3366
Gastonia *(G-4998)*

Branch Office Solutions Inc..................... G 800 743-1047
Indian Trail *(G-7072)*

Carolina Copy Services Inc...................... F 704 375-9099
Cornelius *(G-3592)*

Copycat Print Shop Inc........................... F 910 799-1500
Wilmington *(G-12751)*

Gik Inc.. F 919 872-9498
Raleigh *(G-10133)*

Kathie S Mc Daniel................................ G 336 835-1544
Elkin *(G-4446)*

Legalis Dms LLC................................... F 919 741-8260
Raleigh *(G-10252)*

Make An Impression Inc.......................... G 919 557-7400
Holly Springs *(G-6907)*

Moore Printing & Graphics Inc................. F 919 821-3293
Raleigh *(G-10314)*

Occasions Group Inc.............................. E 252 321-5805
Greenville *(G-6009)*

Print Express Inc.................................... F 910 455-4554
Jacksonville *(G-7138)*

Print Haus Inc....................................... G 828 456-8622
Waynesville *(G-12469)*

Printing Svcs Greensboro Inc.................. G 336 274-7663
Greensboro *(G-5765)*

Rite Instant Printing Inc.......................... G 336 768-5061
Winston Salem *(G-13319)*

Sharpe Images Properties Inc.................. E 336 724-2871
Winston Salem *(G-13334)*

Sillaman & Sons Inc............................... G 919 774-6324
Sanford *(G-11233)*

Triangle Solutions Inc............................. G 919 481-1235
Cary *(G-1473)*

Unlimted Potential Sanford Inc................. E 919 852-1117
Morrisville *(G-9083)*

Village Instant Printing Inc....................... G 919 968-0000
Chapel Hill *(G-1591)*

Weber and Weber Inc............................. F 336 722-4109
Winston Salem *(G-13387)*

Zebra Communications Inc....................... E 919 314-3700
Morrisville *(G-9093)*

PHOTOGRAPHIC EQPT & SPLYS

Applied Technologies Group..................... G 618 977-9872
Cornelius *(G-3584)*

Dmarcian.. E 828 767-7588
Brevard *(G-969)*

Jason Case Corp.................................... G 212 786-2288
Durham *(G-4088)*

Kliersolutions... G 919 806-1287
Apex *(G-174)*

Kodak.. G 919 559-7232
Morrisville *(G-8998)*

M T Industries Inc.................................. F 828 697-2864
Hendersonville *(G-6222)*

Strong Global Entrmt Inc......................... C 704 994-8279
Charlotte *(G-2872)*

Tehan Company Inc................................ G 800 283-7290
Burgaw *(G-1034)*

Zink Holdings LLC.................................. D 336 449-8000
Whitsett *(G-12622)*

Zink Imaging Inc..................................... E 336 449-8000
Whitsett *(G-12623)*

PHOTOGRAPHIC EQPT & SPLYS: Film, Sensitized

Nabell USA Corporation........................... E 704 986-2455
Albemarle *(G-82)*

PHOTOGRAPHIC EQPT & SPLYS: Printing Eqpt

Digital Progressions Inc.......................... G 336 676-6570
Greensboro *(G-5496)*

Rb3 Enterprises Inc................................ G 919 795-5822
Wake Forest *(G-12291)*

PHOTOGRAPHY SVCS: Commercial

Above Topsail LLC................................. G 910 803-1759
Holly Ridge *(G-6886)*

David Presnell.. G 336 372-5989
Sparta *(G-11537)*

PHYSICIANS' OFFICES & CLINICS: Medical doctors

Gems Frst Stop Med Sltions LLC............. G 336 965-9500
Greensboro *(G-5552)*

Herbs Gaia Inc....................................... D 828 884-4242
Brevard *(G-972)*

Orthopedic Services................................ G 336 716-3349
Winston Salem *(G-13273)*

PICTURE FRAMES: Metal

Four Corners Frmng Gallery Inc............... G 704 662-7154
Mooresville *(G-8667)*

Graphik Dimensions Limited..................... D 800 332-8884
High Point *(G-6634)*

PICTURE FRAMES: Wood

Four Corners Frmng Gallery Inc............... G 704 662-7154
Mooresville *(G-8667)*

G & G Moulding Inc................................ E 828 438-1112
Morganton *(G-8867)*

Graphik Dimensions Limited..................... D 800 332-8884
High Point *(G-6634)*

L G Sourcing Inc.................................... E 704 758-1000
Mooresville *(G-8707)*

Mirrormate LLC...................................... F 704 390-7377
Charlotte *(G-2508)*

Quantico Tactical Incorporated................. E 910 944-5800
Aberdeen *(G-20)*

World Art Gallery Incorporated................. G 910 989-0203
Jacksonville *(G-7160)*

PIECE GOODS & NOTIONS WHOLESALERS

Adele Knits Inc....................................... C 336 499-6010
Winston Salem *(G-13072)*

Continental Ticking Corp Amer................. D 336 570-0091
Alamance *(G-55)*

Culp Inc.. E 662 844-7144
Burlington *(G-1080)*

Domestic Fabrics Blankets Corp.............. E 252 523-7948
Kinston *(G-7406)*

Global Textile Alliance Inc....................... G 336 347-7601
Reidsville *(G-10685)*

Oakhurst Textiles Inc.............................. G 336 668-0733
Greensboro *(G-5718)*

Sam M Butler Inc................................... E 704 364-8647
Charlotte *(G-2753)*

Warm Products Inc................................. F 425 248-2424
Hendersonville *(G-6249)*

PIECE GOODS, NOTIONS & DRY GOODS, WHOL: Textiles, Woven

Gentry Mills Inc...................................... D 704 983-5555
Albemarle *(G-74)*

Pearson Textiles Inc............................... G 919 776-8730
Sanford *(G-11216)*

Svcm... G 305 767-3595
Lincolnton *(G-7858)*

PIECE GOODS, NOTIONS & OTHER DRY GOODS, WHOLESALE: Cotton

Barnhardt Manufacturing Co..................... C 704 331-0657
Charlotte *(G-1754)*

PIECE GOODS, NOTIONS & OTHER DRY GOODS, WHOLESALE: Fabrics

Cloth Barn Inc.. F 919 735-3643
Goldsboro *(G-5206)*

Copland Industries Inc............................. B 336 226-0272
Burlington *(G-1076)*

Freudenberg Prfmce Mtls LP.................... E 919 479-7443
Durham *(G-4037)*

Omnia LLC... G 919 696-2193
Oxford *(G-9621)*

Ripstop By Roll LLC................................ F 877 525-7210
Durham *(G-4215)*

PIECE GOODS, NOTIONS/DRY GOODS, WHOL: Fabrics, Synthetic

Polyvlies Usa Inc.................................... E 336 769-0206
Winston Salem *(G-13299)*

PIPE & FITTINGS: Cast Iron

ABT Foam Inc.. F 800 433-1119
Statesville *(G-11643)*

PIPE & FITTINGS: Soil, Cast Iron

Charlotte Pipe and Foundry Co........... C 800 438-6091
Charlotte *(G-1900)*

PIPE FITTINGS: Plastic

Charlotte Pipe and Foundry Co........... C 800 438-6091
Charlotte *(G-1900)*

Pipeline Plastics LLC........................... G 817 693-4100
Fair Bluff *(G-4499)*

PIPE SECTIONS, FABRICATED FROM PURCHASED PIPE

Ansgar Industrial LLC........................... A 866 284-1931
Charlotte *(G-1679)*

PIPE, SEWER: Concrete

Pipe Bridge Products Inc........................ G 919 786-4499
Raleigh *(G-10368)*

PIPE: Concrete

Advanced Drainage Systems Inc........... E 336 764-0341
Winston Salem *(G-13074)*

Autry Con Pdts & Bldrs Sup Co............. G 704 504-8830
Charlotte *(G-1719)*

Hydro Conduit LLC................................. G 336 475-1371
Thomasville *(G-12035)*

Johnson Concrete Company.................. E 704 636-5231
Willow Spring *(G-12679)*

Johnson Concrete Company.................. E 704 636-5231
Salisbury *(G-11074)*

Oldcastle Infrastructure Inc................... E 704 788-4050
Concord *(G-3412)*

Southeastern Concrete Pdts Co............. D 704 873-2226
Statesville *(G-11768)*

Watson Concrete Pipe Company........... G 828 754-6476
Lenoir *(G-7645)*

PIPE: Plastic

Advanced Drainage Systems Inc........... D 704 629-4151
Bessemer City *(G-803)*

Charlotte Pipe and Foundry Co............. B 704 348-5416
Charlotte *(G-1901)*

Charlotte Pipe and Foundry Co............. A 704 372-3650
Monroe *(G-8457)*

Charlotte Pipe and Foundry Co............. A 704 887-8015
Oakboro *(G-9575)*

Charlotte Pipe and Foundry Com.......... F 704 379-0700
Charlotte *(G-1902)*

Consolidated Pipe & Sup Co Inc............ F 336 294-8577
Greensboro *(G-5463)*

Crumpler Plastic Pipe Inc...................... D 910 525-4046
Roseboro *(G-10912)*

Fitt Usa Inc... F 866 348-8872
Mooresville *(G-8665)*

Ipex USA LLC... F 704 889-2431
Pineville *(G-9736)*

Ipex USA LLC... C 704 889-2431
Pineville *(G-9735)*

J-M Manufacturing Company Inc.......... D 919 575-6515
Creedmoor *(G-3650)*

National Pipe & Plastics Inc.................. C 336 996-2711
Colfax *(G-3284)*

Opw Fling Cntnment Systems Inc......... E 919 209-2280
Smithfield *(G-11457)*

Performance Plastics Pdts Inc............... D 336 454-0350
Jamestown *(G-7175)*

Silver-Line Plastics LLC........................ C 828 252-8755
Asheville *(G-599)*

Southern Pipe Inc.................................. F 704 550-5935
Albemarle *(G-92)*

Southern Pipe Inc.................................. E 704 463-5202
New London *(G-9422)*

Teknor Apex Company........................... D 401 642-3598
Jamestown *(G-7180)*

PIPE: Sheet Metal

Muriel Harris Investments Inc................ F 800 932-3191
Fayetteville *(G-4644)*

PIPELINE & POWER LINE INSPECTION SVCS

Appalachian Pipe Distrs LLC................. G 704 688-5703
Charlotte *(G-1684)*

Dronescape Pllc..................................... G 704 953-3798
Charlotte *(G-2066)*

PIPELINE TERMINAL FACILITIES: Independent

Speedway Link Inc................................. G 704 338-2028
Matthews *(G-8150)*

PIPELINES: Natural Gas

Panenergy Corp...................................... F 704 594-6200
Charlotte *(G-2607)*

PIPELINES: Refined Petroleum

Panenergy Corp...................................... F 704 594-6200
Charlotte *(G-2607)*

PIPES & TUBES

Charlotte Pipe and Foundry Co............. C 800 438-6091
Charlotte *(G-1900)*

Saertex Multicom LP.............................. E 704 946-9229
Huntersville *(G-7049)*

Saertex Multicom LP.............................. F 704 946-9229
Huntersville *(G-7048)*

PIPES & TUBES: Steel

Allrail Inc... G 828 287-3747
Rutherfordton *(G-10973)*

Appalachian Pipe Distrs LLC................. G 704 688-5703
Charlotte *(G-1684)*

Border Concepts Inc.............................. G 336 248-2419
Lexington *(G-7660)*

Border Concepts Inc.............................. G 704 541-5509
Charlotte *(G-1800)*

Fortiline LLC.. E 704 788-9800
Concord *(G-3366)*

Lander Tubular Pdts USA Inc................. C 828 369-6682
Franklin *(G-4833)*

Maysteel Porters LLC............................ B 704 864-1313
Gastonia *(G-5092)*

Piedmont Pipe Mfg LLC......................... G 704 489-0911
Denver *(G-3797)*

Porters Group LLC................................. B 704 864-1313
Gastonia *(G-5121)*

PIPES & TUBES: Welded

Blacksand Metal Works LLC.................. F 703 489-8282
Fayetteville *(G-4558)*

PIPES: Steel & Iron

Mechanical Spc Contrs Inc.................... D 919 829-9300
Raleigh *(G-10287)*

Okaya Shinnichi Corp America.............. E 704 588-3131
Charlotte *(G-2592)*

PLAQUES: Picture, Laminated

Coates Designers & Crafstmen.............. G 828 349-9700
Franklin *(G-4821)*

Professional Laminating LLC................. G 919 465-0400
Cary *(G-1430)*

PLASMAS

Plasma Games.. G 252 721-3294
Raleigh *(G-10370)*

Plasma Games Inc................................. E 919 627-1252
Raleigh *(G-10371)*

PLASTIC WOOD

Fiber Composites LLC............................ B 704 463-7120
New London *(G-9415)*

PLASTICIZERS, ORGANIC: Cyclic & Acyclic

Vpm Liquidating Inc............................... F 336 292-1781
Greensboro *(G-5912)*

PLASTICS FILM & SHEET

Abx Innvtive Pckg Slutions LLC............. D 980 443-1100
Charlotte *(G-1613)*

Bright View Technologies Corp.............. E 919 228-4370
Durham *(G-3942)*

Desco Industries Inc.............................. F 919 718-0000
Sanford *(G-11168)*

Liqui-Box Corporation........................... D 804 325-1400
Charlotte *(G-2426)*

Mastic Home Exteriors Inc..................... E 816 426-8200
Cary *(G-1399)*

Novolex Shields LLC............................. B 800 845-6051
Charlotte *(G-2584)*

Piedmont Plastics Inc............................ D 704 597-8200
Charlotte *(G-2636)*

Ready Solutions Inc............................... G 704 534-9221
Davidson *(G-3718)*

PLASTICS FILM & SHEET: Polyethylene

Berry Global Films LLC......................... C 704 821-2316
Matthews *(G-8160)*

Daliah Plastics Corp.............................. E 336 629-0551
Asheboro *(G-344)*

Inteplast Group Corporation.................. E 704 504-3200
Charlotte *(G-2340)*

Paragon Films Inc.................................. F 828 632-5552
Taylorsville *(G-11968)*

Southern Film Extruders Inc.................. C 336 885-8091
High Point *(G-6788)*

PLASTICS FILM & SHEET: Polyvinyl

Southern Prestige Intl LLC..................... F 704 872-9524
Statesville *(G-11771)*

Specialty Perf LLC................................. G 704 872-9980
Statesville *(G-11773)*

PLASTICS FILM & SHEET: Vinyl

Krs Plastics Inc...................................... F 910 653-3602
Tabor City *(G-11912)*

Rays Classic Vinyl Repair Inc................ G 910 520-1626
Hampstead *(G-6075)*

PLASTICS FINISHED PRDTS: Laminated

Ram Industries Inc................................. G 704 982-4015
Albemarle *(G-87)*

PLASTICS MATERIAL & RESINS

3a Composites Holding Inc.................... D 704 658-3527
Davidson *(G-3696)*

Abt Inc.. E 704 528-9806
Troutman *(G-12129)*

Albemarle Corporation........................... G 252 482-7423
Edenton *(G-4360)*

Albemarle Corporation.................... A 980 299-5700
　Charlotte (G-1638)

Allotropica Technologies Inc............. G 919 522-4374
　Chapel Hill (G-1524)

Alpek Polyester Miss Inc.................. C 228 533-4000
　Charlotte (G-1647)

American Durafilm Co Inc................ G 704 895-7701
　Mooresville (G-8595)

Arclin USA LLC.............................. G 919 542-2526
　Moncure (G-8400)

Auriga Polymers Inc....................... C 864 579-5570
　Charlotte (G-1717)

Aurora Plastics Inc......................... F 336 775-2640
　Welcome (G-12511)

Avient Protective Mtls LLC............... D 252 707-2547
　Greenville (G-5943)

Bluesky Polymers LLC..................... G 919 522-4374
　Cary (G-1311)

Canplast Usa Inc............................ G 336 668-9555
　Greensboro (G-5421)

Carpenter Co.................................. D 828 464-9470
　Conover (G-3501)

Carpenter Co.................................. E 828 322-6545
　Hickory (G-6290)

Carpenter Co.................................. D 336 861-5730
　High Point (G-6560)

Carpenter Co.................................. E 828 632-7061
　Taylorsville (G-11952)

Celanese Intl Corp.......................... G 704 480-5798
　Grover (G-6042)

Celgard LLC.................................. D 704 588-5310
　Charlotte (G-1884)

Celgard LLC.................................. D 800 235-4273
　Charlotte (G-1885)

Chase Corporation.......................... G 828 855-9316
　Hickory (G-6303)

Chroma Color Corporation............... D 336 629-9184
　Asheboro (G-339)

Chroma Color Corporation............... C 704 637-7000
　Salisbury (G-11033)

Cs Systems Company Inc................. F 800 525-9878
　Candler (G-1222)

Custom Polymers Inc...................... F 704 332-6070
　Charlotte (G-2011)

Custom Polymers Pet LLC............... D 866 717-0716
　Charlotte (G-2012)

Darnel Inc.................................... G 704 625-9869
　Monroe (G-8474)

Ddp Spclty Elctrnc Mtls US 9........... E 336 547-7112
　Greensboro (G-5490)

Delcor Polymers Inc....................... G 704 847-0640
　Matthews (G-8110)

Dow Silicones Corporation.............. C 336 547-7100
　Greensboro (G-5503)

Dupont Teijin Films........................ G 910 433-8200
　Fayetteville (G-4589)

Eastern Plastics Company................ G 704 542-7786
　Charlotte (G-2082)

Eidp Inc....................................... G 252 522-6286
　Kinston (G-7409)

Essay Operations Inc...................... G 252 443-6010
　Rocky Mount (G-10837)

Freudenberg Prfmce Mtls LP............ F 919 620-3900
　Durham (G-4038)

Future Foam Inc............................ D 336 885-4121
　High Point (G-6625)

Genpak LLC.................................. D 704 588-6202
　Charlotte (G-2207)

Gersan Industries Incorporated......... G 336 886-5455
　High Point (G-6628)

Hanwha Advanced Mtls Amer LLC..... E 704 434-2271
　Shelby (G-11342)

Hexion Inc.................................... E 910 483-1311
　Fayetteville (G-4612)

Hexion Inc.................................... G 336 884-8918
　High Point (G-6646)

Hexion Inc.................................... E 828 584-3800
　Morganton (G-8871)

Huntsman Textile Effects................. E 704 587-5000
　Charlotte (G-2300)

Imaflex Usa Inc............................ E 336 474-1190
　Thomasville (G-12037)

Intertape Polymer Corp................... D 252 792-2083
　Everetts (G-4497)

Jpi Coastal.................................. G 704 310-5867
　Salisbury (G-11076)

JPS Composite Materials Corp.......... C 704 872-9831
　Statesville (G-11720)

Kattermann Ventures Inc................. E 828 651-8737
　Fletcher (G-4744)

Lanxess Corporation....................... G 704 923-0121
　Dallas (G-3678)

Lanxess Corporation....................... E 704 868-7200
　Gastonia (G-5077)

Liquidating Reichhold Inc................. A 919 990-7500
　Durham (G-4106)

Mallard Creek Polymers LLC............ G 704 547-0622
　Charlotte (G-2450)

Mallard Creek Polymers LLC............ G 704 547-0622
　Harrisburg (G-6112)

Mallard Creek Polymers LLC............ G 704 547-0622
　Charlotte (G-2451)

Mdt Bromley LLC........................... E 828 651-8737
　Fletcher (G-4752)

Mexichem Spcalty Compounds Inc..... D 704 889-7821
　Pineville (G-9742)

Modern Densifying Inc.................... F 704 434-8335
　Shelby (G-11363)

Modern Polymers Inc...................... E 704 435-5825
　Cherryville (G-3067)

Olympic Products LLC..................... D 336 378-9620
　Greensboro (G-5721)

Olympic Products LLC..................... G 336 378-9620
　Greensboro (G-5720)

Performance Additives LLC.............. F 215 321-4388
　Pinehurst (G-9699)

Plaskolite LLC.............................. C 704 588-3800
　Charlotte (G-2640)

Plaskolite North Carolina LLC........... F 704 588-3800
　Charlotte (G-2641)

Plastic Products Inc....................... G 704 739-7463
　Bessemer City (G-830)

Plastic Solutions Inc...................... F 678 353-2100
　Ellenboro (G-4459)

Polychem Alloy Inc......................... E 828 754-7570
　Lenoir (G-7635)

Polyone Corporation....................... G 704 838-0457
　Statesville (G-11750)

Polyquest Incorporated................... F 910 342-9554
　Wilmington (G-12882)

Poppelmann Plastics USA LLC.......... E 828 466-9500
　Claremont (G-3116)

PPG Industries Inc......................... G 919 772-3093
　Greensboro (G-5755)

PQ Recycling LLC.......................... E 910 342-9554
　Wilmington (G-12889)

Pressure Washing Near Me LLC........ G 704 280-0351
　Waxhaw (G-12437)

Prototech Manufacturing Inc............ F 508 646-8849
　Washington (G-12410)

Reichhold Holdings Us Inc............... A 919 990-7500
　Durham (G-4210)

Resinall Corp............................... C 252 585-1445
　Severn (G-11299)

Rugby Acquisition LLC.................... D 336 993-8686
　Kernersville (G-7297)

Rutland Group Inc.......................... C 704 553-0046
　Pineville (G-9752)

Rutland Holdings LLC..................... E 704 553-0046
　Pineville (G-9753)

Sanctuary Systems LLC................... D 305 989-0953
　Fremont (G-4860)

Scentair Technologies LLC............... C 704 504-2320
　Charlotte (G-2762)

Schlaadt USA Limited..................... F 252 634-9494
　New Bern (G-9395)

Sealed Air Corporation.................... A 980 221-3235
　Charlotte (G-2776)

Spt Technology Inc......................... G 704 290-5007
　Monroe (G-8562)

Ssd Designs LLC........................... F 980 245-2988
　Charlotte (G-2854)

Stepan Company............................ C 316 828-1000
　Wilmington (G-12930)

Superskinsystems Inc..................... G 336 601-6005
　Greensboro (G-5845)

Syncot Plastics LLC....................... D 704 967-0010
　Belmont (G-769)

Tosaf Inc..................................... G 704 396-7097
　Bessemer City (G-836)

Toter LLC.................................... E 800 424-0422
　Statesville (G-11792)

Wilsonart LLC.............................. D 828 684-2351
　Fletcher (G-4780)

PLASTICS MATERIALS, BASIC FORMS & SHAPES WHOLESALERS

Ace Plastics Inc............................ G 704 527-5752
　Charlotte (G-1615)

Advanced Technology Inc................. E 336 668-0488
　Greensboro (G-5344)

Cardinal Plastics Inc....................... G 704 739-9420
　Kings Mountain (G-7354)

Interlam Corporation...................... E 336 786-6254
　Mount Airy (G-9134)

Mdt Bromley LLC........................... E 828 651-8737
　Fletcher (G-4752)

Mpe Usa Inc................................ E 704 340-4910
　Pineville (G-9743)

Poly-Tech Industrial Inc................... E 704 948-8055
　Huntersville (G-7035)

PLASTICS PROCESSING

Beacon Composites LLC.................. G 704 813-8408
　Creedmoor (G-3640)

Carolina Base - Pac Corp................. E 828 728-7304
　Hudson (G-6946)

Inplac North America Inc................. G 704 587-1151
　Charlotte (G-2338)

Lamination Services Inc.................. E 336 643-7369
　Stokesdale (G-11813)

Opw Fling Cntnment Systems Inc....... E 919 209-2280
　Smithfield (G-11457)

Salem Technologies Inc................... F 336 777-3652
　Winston Salem (G-13327)

Sealed Air Corporation (us).............. A 201 791-7600
　Charlotte (G-2777)

PLASTICS SHEET: Packing Materials

Bonset America Corporation............. C 336 375-0234
　Browns Summit (G-991)

Dymetrol Company Inc.................... F 866 964-8632
　Bladenboro (G-876)

Plastic Ingenuity Inc...................... D 919 693-2009
　Oxford (G-9625)

PRODUCT

PLASTICS: Blow Molded

Easth20 Holdings Llc...............................G..... 919 313-2100
Greensboro (G-5510)

Intertech Corporation..............................D..... 336 621-1891
Greensboro (G-5621)

PLASTICS: Extruded

Amesbury Group Inc................................D..... 704 924-7694
Statesville (G-11656)

Carolina Extruded Plastics Inc................E..... 336 272-1191
Greensboro (G-5426)

Manning Fabrics Inc..............................G..... 910 295-1970
Pinehurst (G-9696)

Rowmark LLC..G..... 252 448-9900
Trenton (G-12110)

PLASTICS: Finished Injection Molded

Alliance Precision Plas Corp...................E..... 828 286-8631
Spindale (G-11543)

Carlisle Corporation...............................A..... 704 501-1100
Charlotte (G-1842)

Cross Technology Inc............................E..... 336 725-4700
East Bend (G-4322)

Gentry Plastics Inc................................E..... 704 864-4300
Gastonia (G-5053)

Kennys Components Inc.........................F..... 704 662-0777
Mooresville (G-8703)

Medical Cable Specialists Inc.................E..... 828 890-2888
Mills River (G-8317)

Precise Technology Inc.........................G..... 704 576-9527
Charlotte (G-2656)

Rpp Acquisition LLC..............................E..... 919 248-9001
Kenly (G-7237)

Sonoco Hickory Inc...............................D..... 828 328-2466
Hickory (G-6453)

Tarheel Plastics LLC...............................E
Lexington (G-7748)

Tech Medical Plastics Inc......................G..... 919 563-9272
Mebane (G-8261)

Volex Inc..E..... 828 485-4500
Hickory (G-6486)

Volex Inc..E..... 828 485-4500
Hickory (G-6487)

PLASTICS: Molded

Accu-Form Polymers Inc........................E..... 910 293-6961
Warsaw (G-12357)

Aim Molding & Door LLC.........................G..... 704 913-7211
Charlotte (G-1630)

Amcor Tob Packg Americas Inc...............D..... 828 274-1611
Asheville (G-425)

Aqua Plastics Inc..................................F..... 828 324-6284
Hickory (G-6266)

Beaufort Composite Tech Inc..................G..... 252 728-1547
Beaufort (G-721)

Blue Ridge Molding LLC.........................D..... 828 485-2017
Conover (G-3496)

Bull Engineered Products Inc................E..... 704 504-0300
Charlotte (G-1818)

Centro Inc..D..... 319 626-3200
Claremont (G-3092)

Coats & Clark Inc....................................D..... 888 368-8401
Charlotte (G-1942)

Coats N Amer De Rpblica Dmncan...........C..... 800 242-8095
Charlotte (G-1945)

Dynacast LLC...E..... 704 927-2790
Charlotte (G-2072)

Hoffman Plasti-Form Company.................G..... 336 431-2934
High Point (G-6658)

Leonard Alum Utlity Bldngs Inc...............G..... 919 872-4442
Raleigh (G-10254)

Leonard Alum Utlity Bldngs Inc.............G..... 910 392-4921
Wilmington (G-12834)

Nypro Oregon Inc...................................B..... 541 753-4700
Arden (G-292)

Penn Compression Moulding Inc.............G..... 919 934-5144
Smithfield (G-11459)

Poly-Tech Industrial Inc..........................E..... 704 948-8055
Huntersville (G-7035)

Revolution Pd LLC..................................G..... 919 949-0241
Pittsboro (G-9788)

Sunray Inc...E..... 828 287-7030
Rutherfordton (G-10994)

PLASTICS: Polystyrene Foam

A Plus Service Inc...................................G..... 828 324-4397
Hickory (G-6259)

ABT Foam LLC...G..... 704 508-1010
Statesville (G-11644)

Amesbury Group Inc................................D..... 704 978-2883
Statesville (G-11655)

Amesbury Group Inc................................D..... 704 924-7694
Statesville (G-11656)

Armacell LLC...D..... 828 464-5880
Conover (G-3491)

Armacell LLC...C..... 919 913-0555
Chapel Hill (G-1528)

Armacell US Holdings LLC.......................C..... 919 304-3846
Mebane (G-8231)

Barnhardt Manufacturing Co....................C..... 704 331-0657
Charlotte (G-1754)

Barnhardt Manufacturing Co....................C..... 336 789-9161
Mount Airy (G-9101)

Barnhardt Manufacturing Company........C..... 800 277-0377
Charlotte (G-1755)

Bwh Foam and Fiber Inc.........................G..... 336 498-6949
Randleman (G-10635)

Carpenter Co...C..... 336 789-9161
Mount Airy (G-9110)

Crown Foam Products Inc......................F..... 336 434-4024
High Point (G-6581)

Dart Container Corp Georgia...................C..... 336 495-1101
Randleman (G-10641)

Deep River Fabricators Inc.....................F..... 336 824-8881
Franklinville (G-4856)

Ffnc Inc..D..... 336 885-4121
High Point (G-6619)

Frisby Technologies Inc.........................F..... 336 998-6652
Advance (G-32)

Future Foam Inc.....................................E..... 336 861-8095
Archdale (G-223)

Gaylord Inc...D..... 704 694-2434
Charlotte (G-2192)

Guilford Fabricators Inc.........................F..... 336 434-3163
High Point (G-6635)

Hickory Springs California LLC...............A..... 828 328-2201
Hickory (G-6354)

Kidkusion Inc...F..... 252 946-7162
Washington (G-12396)

Marx LLC..D..... 828 396-6700
Granite Falls (G-5312)

Marx Industries Incorporated..................E..... 828 396-6700
Hudson (G-6955)

Nomaco Inc..B..... 919 269-6500
Zebulon (G-13515)

Poly Packaging Systems Inc...................D..... 336 889-8334
High Point (G-6739)

Prototech Manufacturing Inc..................F..... 508 646-8849
Washington (G-12410)

Ritchie Foam Company Inc.....................G..... 704 663-2533
Mooresville (G-8760)

Sealed Air Corporation............................D..... 828 728-6610
Hudson (G-6959)

Sealed Air Corporation (us).....................A..... 201 791-7600
Charlotte (G-2777)

Swimways..F..... 252 563-1101
Tarboro (G-11943)

Trego Innovations LLC...........................G..... 919 374-0089
Wilson (G-13038)

Vpc Foam USA Inc....................................E..... 336 626-4595
Asheboro (G-418)

Vpc Foam USA Inc....................................E..... 704 622-0552
Conover (G-3572)

PLASTICS: Thermoformed

American Wick Drain Corp.......................E..... 704 296-5801
Monroe (G-8424)

Douglas Fabrication & Mch Inc...............F..... 919 365-7553
Wendell (G-12533)

Panel Wholesalers Incorporated.............F..... 336 765-4040
Winston Salem (G-13275)

Prime Mill LLC...F..... 336 819-4300
High Point (G-6746)

Thermodynamx LLC.................................G..... 704 622-1086
Waxhaw (G-12444)

US Drainage Systems LLC......................G..... 828 855-1906
Hickory (G-6483)

Wilbert Plstic Svcs Acqstion L.................E..... 704 455-5191
Harrisburg (G-6121)

PLATES: Steel

Cleveland-Cliffs Plate LLC.......................A..... 828 464-9214
Newton (G-9454)

PLATFORMS: Cargo

Quick-Deck Inc.......................................E..... 704 888-0327
Locust (G-7898)

PLATING & POLISHING SVC

Advanced Motor Sports Coatings...........G..... 336 472-5518
Thomasville (G-11990)

Advanced Plating Technologies...............G..... 704 291-9325
Monroe (G-8418)

Dave Steel Company Inc.........................D..... 828 252-2771
Asheville (G-484)

Prince Group LLC....................................D..... 828 681-8860
Mills River (G-8319)

Sterling Rack Inc.....................................G..... 704 866-9131
Gastonia (G-5144)

Te Connectivity Corporation...................C..... 336 665-4400
Greensboro (G-5857)

United TI & Stamping Co NC Inc..............D..... 910 323-8588
Fayetteville (G-4687)

Yontz & Sons Painting Inc......................G..... 336 784-7099
Winston Salem (G-13409)

PLATING SVC: Chromium, Metals Or Formed Prdts

C & R Hard Chrome Service Inc................G..... 704 861-8831
Gastonia (G-5009)

Hi-Tech Fabrication Inc............................C..... 919 781-6150
Raleigh (G-10166)

PLAYGROUND EQPT

Brookhurst Associates............................G..... 919 792-0987
Raleigh (G-9961)

Family Industries Inc...............................G..... 919 875-4499
Raleigh (G-10104)

Miracle Recreation Eqp Co......................C..... 704 875-6550
Huntersville (G-7014)

Peggs Recreation Inc.............................G..... 704 660-0007
Mooresville (G-8744)

Playpower Inc...E..... 704 949-1600
Huntersville (G-7033)

PLEATING & STITCHING SVC

Body Billboards Inc .... G 919 544-4540
Durham *(G-3936)*

Consumer Concepts .... F 252 247-7000
Morehead City *(G-8828)*

Freeman Screen Printers Inc .... G 704 521-9148
Charlotte *(G-2179)*

Gaston Screen Printing Inc .... G 704 399-0459
Charlotte *(G-2191)*

Pacific Coast Feather LLC .... G 252 492-0051
Henderson *(G-6169)*

Vocatnal Sltons Hndrson Cnty I ..... E 828 692-9626
East Flat Rock *(G-4335)*

PLUGS: Electric

Leviton Manufacturing Co Inc .... G 336 846-3246
West Jefferson *(G-12566)*

PLUMBING FIXTURES

Brasscraft Manufacturing Co .... E 336 475-2131
Thomasville *(G-11998)*

Flologic Inc .... G 919 878-1808
Morrisville *(G-8976)*

Key Gas Components Inc .... E 828 655-1700
Marion *(G-8048)*

Piedmont Well Covers Inc .... F 704 664-8488
Mount Ulla *(G-9270)*

Royal Baths Manufacturing Co ...... E 704 837-1701
Charlotte *(G-2733)*

SL Liquidation LLC .... B 910 353-3666
Jacksonville *(G-7147)*

Victaulic Company .... E 910 371-5588
Leland *(G-7563)*

Watts Drainage Products Inc .... F 828 288-2179
Spindale *(G-11549)*

PLUMBING FIXTURES: Plastic

Accent Comfort Services LLC .... E 704 509-1200
Charlotte *(G-1614)*

Custom Marble Corporation .... G 910 215-0679
Pinehurst *(G-9690)*

Jupiter Bathware Inc .... G 800 343-8295
Wilson *(G-12996)*

LL Cultured Marble Inc .... G 336 789-3908
Mount Airy *(G-9147)*

Marion Cultured Marble Inc .... G 828 724-4782
Marion *(G-8049)*

Moores Fiberglass Inc .... F 252 753-2583
Walstonburg *(G-12334)*

Plastic Oddities Inc .... G 704 484-1830
Shelby *(G-11369)*

PLUMBING FIXTURES: Vitreous

As America Inc .... F 704 398-4602
Charlotte *(G-1703)*

Athena Marble Incorporated .... G 704 636-7810
Salisbury *(G-11018)*

R Jacobs Fine Plbg & Hdwr Inc ..... G 919 720-4202
Raleigh *(G-10417)*

POINT OF SALE DEVICES

NCR Voyix Corporation .... G 937 445-5000
Cary *(G-1406)*

POLE LINE HARDWARE

Preformed Line Products Co .... C 704 983-6161
Albemarle *(G-84)*

POLISHING SVC: Metals Or Formed Prdts

Tico Polishing .... G 704 788-2466
Concord *(G-3458)*

POLYESTERS

Spt Technology Inc .... F 612 332-1880
Monroe *(G-8561)*

Unifi Kinston LLC .... G 252 522-6518
Kinston *(G-7432)*

POLYETHYLENE RESINS

Consolidated Pipe & Sup Co Inc ..... F 336 294-8577
Greensboro *(G-5463)*

Invista Capital Management LLC ..... C 704 636-6000
Salisbury *(G-11071)*

Starpet Inc .... C 336 672-0101
Asheboro *(G-398)*

POLYMETHYL METHACRYLATE RESINS: Plexiglas

Coates Designers & Crafstmen ...... G 828 349-9700
Franklin *(G-4821)*

Intrinsic Advanced Mtls LLC .... G 704 874-5000
Gastonia *(G-5068)*

POLYSTYRENE RESINS

Huntsman Corporation .... F 706 272-4020
Charlotte *(G-2298)*

Huntsman International LLC .... E 704 588-6082
Charlotte *(G-2299)*

POLYTETRAFLUOROETHYLENE RESINS

Alpek Polyester Usa LLC .... C 910 433-8200
Fayetteville *(G-4550)*

Norell Inc .... G 828 584-2600
Morganton *(G-8885)*

POLYURETHANE RESINS

Tailored Chemical Products Inc ...... D 828 322-6512
Hickory *(G-6462)*

POLYVINYL CHLORIDE RESINS

J-M Manufacturing Company Inc ..... D 919 575-6515
Creedmoor *(G-3650)*

Robix America Inc .... C 336 668-9555
Greensboro *(G-5791)*

W M Plastics Inc .... F 704 599-0511
Charlotte *(G-2996)*

POSTERS

Digital Printing Systems Inc .... E 704 525-0190
Charlotte *(G-2047)*

POTASH MINING

Pcs Phosphate Company Inc .... E 252 322-4111
Aurora *(G-645)*

POTPOURRI

Carolina Perfumer Inc .... G 910 295-5600
Pinehurst *(G-9688)*

POTTERY: Laboratory & Indl

Timothy L Griffin .... G 336 317-8314
Greenville *(G-6028)*

POULTRY & SMALL GAME SLAUGHTERING & PROCESSING

Broomes Poultry Inc .... G 704 983-0965
Albemarle *(G-63)*

Calvin C Mooney Poultry .... G 336 374-6690
Ararat *(G-210)*

Carolina Egg Companies Inc .... D 252 459-2143
Nashville *(G-9314)*

Case Farms LLC .... D 919 735-5010
Dudley *(G-3835)*

Case Farms LLC .... E 919 658-2252
Goldsboro *(G-5204)*

Case Farms LLC .... D 919 635-2390
Mount Olive *(G-9252)*

Case Farms LLC .... F 704 528-4501
Troutman *(G-12133)*

Case Farms Processing Inc .... E 704 528-4501
Troutman *(G-12134)*

Case Foods Inc .... A 919 736-4498
Goldsboro *(G-5205)*

House of Raeford Farms Inc .... A 910 289-3191
Raeford *(G-9840)*

House of Raeford Farms Inc .... A 910 285-2349
Teachey *(G-11987)*

House of Raeford Farms Inc .... B 910 763-0475
Wilmington *(G-12809)*

House of Raeford Farms La LLC ..... C 336 751-4752
Mocksville *(G-8369)*

Mountaire Farms LLC .... C 910 843-3332
Lumber Bridge *(G-7939)*

Mountaire Farms LLC .... B 910 843-5942
Lumber Bridge *(G-7940)*

Mountaire Farms LLC .... C 919 663-1768
Siler City *(G-11418)*

Mountaire Farms Inc .... A 910 843-5942
Lumber Bridge *(G-7941)*

Mountaire Farms Inc .... B 919 663-0848
Siler City *(G-11419)*

Mountaire Farms Inc .... G 704 978-3055
Statesville *(G-11735)*

Perdue Farms Inc .... C 910 673-4148
Candor *(G-1240)*

Perdue Farms Inc .... E 704 278-2228
Cleveland *(G-3218)*

Perdue Farms Inc .... A 252 358-8245
Cofield *(G-3269)*

Perdue Farms Inc .... E 252 338-1543
Elizabeth City *(G-4402)*

Perdue Farms Inc .... G 252 758-2141
Greenville *(G-6013)*

Perdue Farms Inc .... D 252 583-5731
Halifax *(G-6047)*

Perdue Farms Inc .... C 919 284-2033
Kenly *(G-7234)*

Perdue Farms Inc .... E 910 738-8581
Lumberton *(G-7965)*

Perdue Farms Inc .... C 252 398-5112
Murfreesboro *(G-9284)*

Perdue Farms Inc .... C 252 459-9763
Nashville *(G-9323)*

Perdue Farms Inc .... E 336 896-9121
Winston Salem *(G-13284)*

Perdue Farms Inc .... D 336 679-7733
Yadkinville *(G-13447)*

Pilgrims Pride Corporation .... E 919 774-7333
Sanford *(G-11222)*

Pilgrims Pride Corporation .... E 336 622-4251
Staley *(G-11598)*

Prestige Farms Inc .... G 919 861-8867
Raleigh *(G-10393)*

Sanderson Farms Inc .... F 252 208-0036
Kinston *(G-7427)*

Sanderson Farms LLC .... G 910 887-2284
Lumberton *(G-7972)*

Tyson Foods Inc .... F 910 483-3282
Eastover *(G-4338)*

Tyson Foods Inc .... E 704 283-7571
Monroe *(G-8572)*

Tyson Foods Inc .... G 336 651-2866
Wilkesboro *(G-12656)*

Tyson Foods Inc .... G 336 838-2171
Wilkesboro *(G-12657)*

Wayne Farms LLC.............................B 336 386-8151
Dobson *(G-3827)*

Wayne Farms LLC.............................F 770 538-2120
Newton *(G-9511)*

POWDER: Aluminum Atomized

Blue Ridge Metals Corporation...............C 828 687-2525
Fletcher *(G-4725)*

POWDER: Metal

D Block Metals LLC...........................G 980 238-2600
Lincolnton *(G-7828)*

D Block Metals LLC...........................F 704 705-5895
Gastonia *(G-5037)*

Oerlikon Metco (us) Inc......................F 713 715-6300
Huntersville *(G-7028)*

POWER GENERATORS

Bwx Technologies Inc.........................D 980 365-4000
Charlotte *(G-1823)*

Powersecure Inc..............................G 919 818-8700
Princeton *(G-9825)*

Xylem Lnc....................................E 704 409-9700
Charlotte *(G-3035)*

POWER SUPPLIES: All Types, Static

Asp Holdings Inc.............................G 888 330-2538
Zebulon *(G-13504)*

CD Snow Hill LLC.............................D 252 747-5943
Snow Hill *(G-11478)*

Matsusada Precision Inc......................G 704 496-2644
Charlotte *(G-2469)*

POWER SWITCHING EQPT

Dg Matrix Inc................................G 724 877-7773
Cary *(G-1349)*

Trimantec....................................E 336 767-1379
Winston Salem *(G-13372)*

POWER TOOLS, HAND: Chain Saws, Portable

Farm Services Inc............................G 336 226-7381
Graham *(G-5268)*

John Deere Consumer Pdts Inc.................C 919 804-2000
Cary *(G-1380)*

Yard Pro Sales and Service LLC...............G 252 641-9776
Tarboro *(G-11947)*

PRECAST TERRAZZO OR CONCRETE PRDTS

Concrete Pipe & Precast LLC..................F 910 892-6411
Dunn *(G-3851)*

Concrete Pipe & Precast LLC..................F 704 485-4614
Oakboro *(G-9576)*

Forterra Pipe & Precast LLC..................G 910 892-6411
Dunn *(G-3857)*

High Point Precast Pdts Inc..................G 336 434-1815
Lexington *(G-7698)*

Lindsay Precast Inc..........................E 919 494-7600
Franklinton *(G-4850)*

Quality Precast Inc..........................G 919 497-0660
Louisburg *(G-7924)*

PRECIOUS STONES & METALS, WHOLESALE

Sumpters Jwly & Collectibles.................G 704 399-5348
Charlotte *(G-2879)*

PRERECORDED TAPE, CD/RECORD STORES: Audio Tapes, Prerecorded

Song of Wood Ltd.............................G 828 669-7675
Black Mountain *(G-871)*

PRESSED FIBER & MOLDED PULP PRDTS, EXC FOOD

Tmgcr Inc....................................E 704 872-4461
Statesville *(G-11791)*

PRIMARY FINISHED OR SEMIFINISHED SHAPES

Industrial Alloys Inc........................F 704 882-2887
Indian Trail *(G-7084)*

Lee Controls LLC.............................G 732 752-5200
Southport *(G-11521)*

PRIMARY ROLLING MILL EQPT

Ew Jackson Transportation LLC................G 919 586-2514
Holly Springs *(G-6900)*

PRINT CARTRIDGES: Laser & Other Computer Printers

Ace Laser Recycling Inc......................G 919 775-5521
Sanford *(G-11145)*

Branch Office Solutions Inc..................G 800 743-1047
Indian Trail *(G-7072)*

Cartridge World..............................G 336 885-0989
High Point *(G-6562)*

Complete Comp St of Ralgh Inc................E 919 828-5227
Raleigh *(G-10005)*

Digital Highpoint LLC........................C 336 883-7146
High Point *(G-6593)*

Drew Roberts LLC.............................G 336 497-1679
Whitsett *(G-12604)*

New East Cartridge Inc.......................G 252 329-0837
Greenville *(G-6007)*

Sato Global Solutions Inc....................G 954 261-3279
Charlotte *(G-2758)*

Static Control Components Inc................A 919 774-3808
Sanford *(G-11238)*

PRINTED CIRCUIT BOARDS

615 Alton Place LLC..........................G 336 431-4487
High Point *(G-6506)*

Assembly Technologies Inc....................F 704 596-3903
Charlotte *(G-1706)*

Asteelflash USA Corp.........................C 919 882-5400
Morrisville *(G-8934)*

C-Tron Incorporated..........................G 919 494-7811
Youngsville *(G-13466)*

Circuit Board Assemblers Inc.................C 919 556-7881
Youngsville *(G-13471)*

Cml Micro Circuit USA........................E 336 744-5050
Winston Salem *(G-13126)*

Flextronics Corporation......................G 704 598-3300
Charlotte *(G-2164)*

Flextronics Intl USA Inc.....................B 704 509-8700
Charlotte *(G-2165)*

Flextronics Intl USA Inc.....................C 919 998-4000
Morrisville *(G-8975)*

Galaxy Electronics Inc.......................F 704 343-9881
Charlotte *(G-2184)*

Hitech Circuits Inc..........................G 336 838-3420
Indian Trail *(G-7083)*

Jabil Inc....................................E 828 684-3141
Arden *(G-278)*

Jabil Inc....................................G 828 209-4202
Mills River *(G-8316)*

M & M Technology Inc.........................E 704 882-9432
Indian Trail *(G-7090)*

Plexus Corp..................................D 919 807-8000
Raleigh *(G-10373)*

SBS Diversified Tech Inc.....................F 336 884-5564
Jamestown *(G-7179)*

Wolfspeed Inc................................C 919 407-5300
Durham *(G-4308)*

PRINTERS & PLOTTERS

Primesource Corporation......................F 336 661-3300
Winston Salem *(G-13304)*

Strategic 3d Solutions Inc...................G 919 451-5963
Raleigh *(G-10512)*

PRINTERS: Computer

Amt Datasouth Corp...........................E 704 523-8500
Charlotte *(G-1675)*

Branch Office Solutions Inc..................G 800 743-1047
Indian Trail *(G-7072)*

St Investors Inc.............................D 704 969-7500
Charlotte *(G-2856)*

PRINTERS: Magnetic Ink, Bar Code

Covington Barcoding Inc......................G 336 996-5759
Kernersville *(G-7260)*

Sato Global Solutions Inc....................G 954 261-3279
Charlotte *(G-2758)*

Thomco Inc...................................G 336 292-3300
Greensboro *(G-5863)*

Zebra Technologies Corporation...............G 704 517-5271
Charlotte *(G-3045)*

PRINTING & BINDING: Books

Hf Group LLC.................................E 336 931-0800
Greensboro *(G-5595)*

Tan Books and Publishers Inc.................G 704 731-0651
Charlotte *(G-2898)*

PRINTING & ENGRAVING: Card, Exc Greeting

Pinkston Properties LLC......................G 828 252-9867
Asheville *(G-575)*

PRINTING & ENGRAVING: Financial Notes & Certificates

Garage Shop LLC..............................F 980 500-0583
Denver *(G-3784)*

PRINTING & STAMPING: Fabric Articles

Broome Sign Company..........................G 704 782-0422
Concord *(G-3325)*

F & H Print Sign Design LLC..................G 252 335-0181
Elizabeth City *(G-4389)*

PSM Enterprises Inc..........................F 336 789-8888
Mount Airy *(G-9167)*

Simple & Sentimental LLC.....................G 252 320-9458
Ayden *(G-662)*

PRINTING & WRITING PAPER WHOLESALERS

Archie Supply LLC............................G 336 987-0895
Greensboro *(G-5368)*

PRINTING MACHINERY

Anilox Roll Company Inc......................G 704 588-1809
Charlotte *(G-1678)*

Cary Manufacturing Corporation...............G 704 527-4402
Charlotte *(G-1864)*

Cogent Dynamics Inc.................... G 828 628-9025
Fletcher (G-4730)

Creative Printing Inc.................... G 828 265-2800
Boone (G-909)

CTX Builders Supply..................... G 704 983-6748
Albemarle (G-66)

Diazit Company Inc........................ G 919 556-5188
Wake Forest (G-12272)

Diversfied Prtg Techniques Inc..... E 704 583-9433
Charlotte (G-2055)

Encore Group Inc............................ C 336 768-7859
Winston Salem (G-13157)

H F Kinney Co Inc........................... E 704 540-9367
Charlotte (G-2248)

Harper Companies Intl Inc............ G 800 438-3111
Charlotte (G-2258)

Harper Corporation of America........... C 704 588-3371
Charlotte (G-2259)

Mark/Trece Inc............................... F 973 884-1005
Greensboro (G-5674)

National Roller Supply Inc............. G 704 853-1174
Gastonia (G-5107)

Spgprints America Inc.................... D 704 598-7171
Charlotte (G-2844)

Trio Labs Inc.................................. F 919 818-9646
Morrisville (G-9079)

PRINTING, COMMERCIAL: Business Forms, NEC

Kalajdzic Inc.................................. F 855 465-4225
Clemmons (G-3196)

PRINTING, COMMERCIAL: Calendars, NEC

Timeplanner Calendars Inc........... C 704 377-0024
Charlotte (G-2920)

PRINTING, COMMERCIAL: Decals, NEC

Label & Printing Solutions Inc.............. G 919 782-1242
Raleigh (G-10243)

Magnet America Intl Inc................. E 336 985-0320
King (G-7330)

Pro Cal Prof Decals Inc.................. F 704 795-6090
Concord (G-3424)

PRINTING, COMMERCIAL: Envelopes, NEC

Vision Envelope Inc....................... F 704 392-9090
Charlotte (G-2986)

PRINTING, COMMERCIAL: Labels & Seals, NEC

All Stick Label LLC........................ G 336 659-4660
Winston Salem (G-13080)

American Label Tech LLC................ F 984 269-5078
Garner (G-4915)

CCL Label....................................... F 919 713-0388
Raleigh (G-9988)

CCL Label Inc................................. C 704 714-4800
Charlotte (G-1877)

CCL Label Inc................................. D 919 713-0388
Fuquay Varina (G-4872)

Datamark Graphics Inc.................. E 336 629-0267
Asheboro (G-345)

Draft DOT International LLC........... G 336 775-0525
Lexington (G-7680)

Hickory Printing Solutions LLC........ B 828 465-3431
Conover (G-3530)

Imprinting Systems Spcalty Inc............. G 704 527-4545
Charlotte (G-2317)

Miller Products Inc........................ E 704 587-1870
Charlotte (G-2505)

Multi Packaging Solutions................... A 336 855-7142
Greensboro (G-5699)

Multi-Color Corporation................. E 828 658-6800
Weaverville (G-12498)

Product Identification Inc.............. E 919 544-4136
Durham (G-4197)

Thomco Inc.................................... G 336 292-3300
Greensboro (G-5863)

PRINTING, COMMERCIAL: Letterpress & Screen

LDR Designs.................................. G 252 375-4484
Greenville (G-6001)

Logo Wear Graphics LLC................. F 336 382-0455
Summerfield (G-11841)

PRINTING, COMMERCIAL: Literature, Advertising, NEC

Carolina Classifiedscom LLC................ D 704 246-0900
Monroe (G-8452)

PRINTING, COMMERCIAL: Periodicals, NEC

Academy Association Inc................ F 919 544-0835
Durham (G-3877)

American City Bus Journals Inc............. G 704 973-1100
Charlotte (G-1665)

Duke University.............................. D 919 687-3600
Durham (G-4011)

Education Center LLC..................... E 336 854-0309
Oak Ridge (G-9571)

Jobs Magazine LLC........................ G 919 319-6816
Cary (G-1379)

Lafauci... G 919 244-5912
Holly Springs (G-6905)

Mb-F Inc.. D 336 379-9352
Greensboro (G-5685)

Scalawag....................................... F 917 671-7240
Durham (G-4224)

Spectrum News.............................. G 919 882-4009
Raleigh (G-10497)

Tourist Baseball Inc....................... E 828 258-0428
Asheville (G-621)

Up & Coming Magazine................... G 910 391-3859
Fayetteville (G-4689)

PRINTING, COMMERCIAL: Promotional

Acculink.. F 252 321-5805
Greenville (G-5934)

Black Collection Apparel LLC................ G 919 716-5183
Sanford (G-11156)

Identify Yourself LLC...................... F 252 202-1452
Kitty Hawk (G-7445)

Inspire Creative Studios Inc................. G 910 395-0200
Wilmington (G-12818)

Kraftsman Tactical Inc................... G 336 465-3576
Albemarle (G-79)

Magnet Guys.................................. G 855 624-4897
Asheboro (G-375)

Mass Connection Inc...................... G 910 424-0940
Fayetteville (G-4636)

McLamb Group Inc......................... G 704 333-1171
Charlotte (G-2480)

Valassis Communications Inc............... D 919 544-4511
Durham (G-4294)

Valassis Communications Inc............... D 919 361-7900
Durham (G-4295)

PRINTING, COMMERCIAL: Screen

1st Choice Activewear II LLC................ E 704 528-7814
Mooresville (G-8588)

822tees Inc.................................... G 910 822-8337
Fayetteville (G-4541)

A A Logo Gear................................ G 704 795-7100
Concord (G-3307)

A B C Screenprinting and EMB............. G 704 937-3452
Grover (G-6041)

Aardvark Screen Printing................ G 919 829-9058
Raleigh (G-9861)

AC Valor Reyes LLC........................ G 910 431-3256
Castle Hayne (G-1493)

Acorn Printing............................... G 704 868-4522
Bessemer City (G-801)

ADS N Art Screenprinting & EMB............ G 919 453-0400
Wake Forest (G-12258)

Advantage Marketing...................... G 919 872-8610
Louisburg (G-7908)

Amped Events LLC.......................... F 888 683-4386
Gastonia (G-4994)

Aquarius Designs & Logo Wear........... G 919 821-4646
Raleigh (G-9909)

Armac Inc....................................... F 919 878-9836
Raleigh (G-9916)

Art Enterprises Inc......................... G 828 277-1211
Asheville (G-431)

Art House....................................... G 919 552-7327
Fuquay Varina (G-4867)

Asheville Promo LLC...................... G 828 575-2767
Asheville (G-441)

Bender Apparel & Signs Inc................. G 252 636-8337
New Bern (G-9340)

Blp Products and Services Inc................ G 704 899-5505
Pineville (G-9716)

Body Billboards Inc........................ G 919 544-4540
Durham (G-3936)

Bradleys Inc.................................... E 704 484-2077
Shelby (G-11314)

Carolina Sgns Grphic Dsgns Inc............. G 919 383-3344
Durham (G-3962)

Carolina Tailors Inc........................ G 252 247-6469
Newport (G-9439)

Castle Shirt Company LLC............... G 336 992-7727
Kernersville (G-7254)

Causekeepers Inc........................... E 336 824-2518
Franklinville (G-4855)

Contagious Graphics Inc................. E 704 529-5600
Charlotte (G-1977)

Cranford Silk Screen Prcess In............. F 336 434-6544
Archdale (G-219)

Crazie Tees.................................... G 704 898-2272
Mount Holly (G-9226)

Creative Printers Inc...................... G 336 246-7746
West Jefferson (G-12563)

Creative Screening......................... G 919 467-5081
Cary (G-1338)

Creative T-Shirts Imaging LLC............. G 919 828-0204
Raleigh (G-10020)

Crystal Impressions Ltd.................. F 704 821-7678
Indian Trail (G-7076)

Dale Advertising Inc....................... G 704 484-0971
Shelby (G-11329)

Davis Vogler Enterprises LLC................ G 402 257-7188
Charlotte (G-2022)

DB CUSTOM CRAFTS LLC................ F 336 867-4107
Winston Salem (G-13140)

Deep South Holding Company Inc.......... D 336 427-0265
Madison (G-7986)

Digital Print & Imaging Inc............. G 910 341-3005
Greenville (G-5965)

Digitaurus Inc................................ G 910 794-9243
Wilmington (G-12765)

Dynagraphics Screenprintng.......... G 919 212-2898
Holly Springs (G-6899)

East Coast Designs LLC................. G..... 910 865-1070
  Fayetteville *(G-4592)*

Edge Promo Team LLC................... E..... 919 946-4218
  Clayton *(G-3145)*

Epic Apparel.................................. G..... 980 335-0463
  Charlotte *(G-2123)*

Expressive Screen Printing............ G..... 910 739-3221
  Lumberton *(G-7952)*

EZ Custom Screen Printing............ E..... 704 821-8488
  Matthews *(G-8167)*

EZ Custom Scrnprinting EMB Inc......... G..... 704 821-9641
  Matthews *(G-8168)*

Finch Industries Incorporated.......... D..... 336 472-4499
  Thomasville *(G-12024)*

First Impressions Ltd..................... F..... 704 536-3622
  Charlotte *(G-2156)*

Funny Bone EMB & Screening........ G..... 704 663-4711
  Mooresville *(G-8668)*

Galloreecom................................. G..... 704 644-0978
  Charlotte *(G-2186)*

Geographics Screenprinting Inc....... G..... 704 357-3300
  Charlotte *(G-2209)*

Graphixx Screen Printing Inc.......... G..... 919 736-3995
  Goldsboro *(G-5219)*

Home Team Athletics Inc............... G..... 910 938-0862
  Jacksonville *(G-7126)*

Image Designs Ink LLC.................. G..... 252 235-1964
  Bailey *(G-671)*

Infinity S End Inc.......................... F..... 704 900-8355
  Charlotte *(G-2328)*

Ink n Stitches LLC........................ G..... 336 633-3898
  Asheboro *(G-365)*

Jax Brothers Inc........................... G..... 704 732-3351
  Lincolnton *(G-7834)*

Jubilee Screen Printing Inc............ G..... 910 673-4240
  West End *(G-12555)*

K & K Stitch & Screen.................... G..... 336 246-5477
  West Jefferson *(G-12565)*

Kannapolis Awards and Graphics......... G..... 704 224-3695
  Kannapolis *(G-7213)*

Katchi Tees Incorporated............... G..... 252 315-4691
  Wilson *(G-12997)*

Kelleys Sports and Awards Inc....... G..... 828 728-4600
  Hudson *(G-6952)*

Kimballs Screen Print Inc.............. G..... 704 636-0488
  Salisbury *(G-11079)*

Kna... G..... 704 847-4280
  Charlotte *(G-2400)*

Kraken-Skulls.............................. F..... 910 500-9100
  Fayetteville *(G-4627)*

Lakeside Cstm Tees & Embroider......... G..... 704 274-3730
  Cornelius *(G-3613)*

Laniers Screen Printing................. G..... 336 857-2699
  Denton *(G-3753)*

Legend-Tees................................ G..... 828 585-2066
  Arden *(G-282)*

Logo Dogz................................... G..... 888 827-8866
  Monroe *(G-8519)*

Logo Label Printing Company......... G..... 919 309-0007
  Durham *(G-4109)*

Logonation Inc............................. E..... 704 799-0612
  Mooresville *(G-8714)*

Lsg LLC....................................... F..... 919 878-5500
  Wallace *(G-12322)*

Make An Impression Inc................ G..... 919 557-7400
  Holly Springs *(G-6907)*

Max B Smith Jr............................. G..... 828 434-0238
  Boone *(G-933)*

McCotter Industries Inc................. F..... 704 282-2102
  Monroe *(G-8529)*

Memories of Orangeburg Inc.......... G..... 803 533-0035
  Mooresville *(G-8722)*

Merch Connect Studios Inc............ G..... 336 501-6722
  Greensboro *(G-5690)*

Motorsports Designs Inc............... F..... 336 454-1181
  High Point *(G-6716)*

Moving Screens Incorporated........ G..... 336 364-9259
  Rougemont *(G-10914)*

Mundo Uniformes LLC................... G..... 704 287-1527
  Charlotte *(G-2531)*

National Sign & Decal Inc.............. G..... 828 478-2123
  Sherrills Ford *(G-11393)*

New Drections Screen Prtrs Inc...... G..... 704 393-1769
  Charlotte *(G-2556)*

Nvizion Inc.................................. G..... 336 985-3862
  King *(G-7334)*

Orlandos Cstm Design T-Shirts........... G..... 919 220-5515
  Durham *(G-4160)*

Pages Screen Printing LLC............ G..... 336 759-7979
  Winston Salem *(G-13274)*

Paraclete Xp Sky Venture LLC........ F..... 910 848-2600
  Raeford *(G-9844)*

Paraclete Xp Skyventure LLC......... E..... 910 904-0027
  Raeford *(G-9845)*

Paradigm Solutions Inc................. G..... 910 392-2611
  Wilmington *(G-12871)*

Paradise Printers.......................... G..... 336 570-2922
  Burlington *(G-1138)*

Pop Designs Mktg Solutions LLC......... G..... 336 444-4033
  Mount Airy *(G-9166)*

Poteet Printing Systems LLC.......... D..... 704 588-0005
  Charlotte *(G-2647)*

Progressive Graphics Inc.............. F..... 919 821-3223
  Raleigh *(G-10402)*

Promothreads Inc.......................... G..... 704 248-0942
  Cornelius *(G-3621)*

Queen City Screen Printers............ G..... 980 335-2334
  Charlotte *(G-2685)*

Queensboro Industries Inc............. C..... 910 251-1251
  Wilmington *(G-12893)*

R R Donnelley & Sons Company......... D..... 252 243-0337
  Wilson *(G-13018)*

Ragg Co Inc................................. G..... 336 838-4895
  North Wilkesboro *(G-9550)*

Reliance Management Group Inc......... F..... 704 282-2255
  Monroe *(G-8551)*

Rikki Tikki Tees........................... G..... 828 454-0515
  Waynesville *(G-12470)*

Rogers Screenprinting EMB Inc......... G..... 910 738-6208
  Lumberton *(G-7971)*

Screen Printers Unlimited LLC........ G..... 336 667-8737
  Wilkesboro *(G-12650)*

Screen Specialty Shop Inc............. G..... 336 982-4135
  West Jefferson *(G-12570)*

Silkscreen Specialists.................. G..... 910 353-8859
  Jacksonville *(G-7144)*

Silverlining Screen Prtrs Inc.......... G..... 919 554-0340
  Youngsville *(G-13485)*

Spectrum Screen Prtg Svc Inc......... F..... 919 481-9905
  Garner *(G-4966)*

Spiral Graphics Inc...................... G..... 919 571-3371
  Raleigh *(G-10499)*

Squeegee Tees & More Inc............ G..... 704 888-0336
  Midland *(G-8297)*

Steves TS & Uniforms Inc............. G..... 919 554-4221
  Wake Forest *(G-12304)*

STS Screen Printing Inc................ G..... 704 821-8488
  Matthews *(G-8195)*

Supreme T-Shirts & Apparel.......... E..... 919 772-9040
  Raleigh *(G-10522)*

T S Designs Incorporated.............. E..... 336 226-5694
  Burlington *(G-1167)*

T T S D Productions LLC................ G..... 704 829-6666
  Belmont *(G-770)*

Tannis Root Productions Inc........... G..... 919 832-8552
  Raleigh *(G-10533)*

Team Connection............................ G..... 336 287-3892
  Winston Salem *(G-13359)*

TEC Graphics Inc.......................... F..... 919 567-2077
  Fuquay Varina *(G-4901)*

Tef Inc.. G..... 704 786-9577
  Concord *(G-3455)*

Third Street Screen Print Inc.......... G..... 919 365-2725
  Wendell *(G-12550)*

Thompson Screen Prints Inc........... E..... 704 209-6161
  Rockwell *(G-10804)*

TNT Web & Grafix LLC................... G..... 252 289-8846
  Nashville *(G-9324)*

Touch Tone Tees LLC.................... G..... 919 358-5536
  Raleigh *(G-10553)*

We Print T-Shirts Inc.................... G..... 910 822-8337
  Fayetteville *(G-4698)*

Westmoreland Printers Inc............ F..... 704 482-9100
  Shelby *(G-11391)*

Winso Dsgns Screenprinting LLC......... G..... 704 967-5776
  Charlotte *(G-3022)*

Wooten Graphics Inc..................... G..... 336 731-4650
  Welcome *(G-12517)*

Xpertees Prfmce Screen Prtg.......... G..... 910 763-7703
  Wilmington *(G-12955)*

Yourlogowear............................... G..... 704 664-1290
  Cornelius *(G-3631)*

Zoom Apparel Inc.......................... G..... 336 993-9666
  Winston Salem *(G-13413)*

PRINTING, COMMERCIAL: Stationery, NEC

Devora Designs Inc...................... G..... 336 782-0964
  Winston Salem *(G-13142)*

Kimberly Gordon Studios Inc......... E..... 980 287-6420
  Charlotte *(G-2396)*

Texpack USA Inc.......................... G..... 704 864-5406
  Gastonia *(G-5151)*

Westrock Mwv LLC....................... G..... 919 334-3200
  Raleigh *(G-10606)*

PRINTING, COMMERCIAL: Tags, NEC

C & M Enterprise Inc.................... G..... 704 545-1180
  Mint Hill *(G-8333)*

Printcraft Company Inc.................. D..... 336 248-2544
  Lexington *(G-7734)*

PRINTING, LITHOGRAPHIC: Advertising Posters

McGrann Paper Corporation............. E..... 800 240-9455
  Charlotte *(G-2478)*

PRINTING, LITHOGRAPHIC: Calendars

Celestial Products Inc.................. G..... 540 338-4040
  Huntersville *(G-6975)*

PRINTING, LITHOGRAPHIC: Forms, Business

R T Barbee Company Inc................ F..... 704 375-4421
  Charlotte *(G-2687)*

PRINTING, LITHOGRAPHIC: Offset & photolithographic printing

Glover Corporation Inc.................. E..... 919 821-5535
  Raleigh *(G-10139)*

Readable Communications Inc........ G..... 919 876-5260
  Raleigh *(G-10434)*

Valdese Packaging & Label Inc........ F..... 828 879-9772
  Valdese *(G-12202)*

Valdese Packaging & Label Inc............ E 828 879-9772
Valdese *(G-12201)*

PRINTING, LITHOGRAPHIC: Posters & Decals

Heritage Prtg & Graphics Inc................ G 704 551-0700
Charlotte *(G-2274)*

PRINTING, LITHOGRAPHIC: Promotional

Ad Spice Marketing LLC...................... G 919 286-7110
Durham *(G-3880)*

B F I Industries Inc.............................. G 919 229-4509
Wake Forest *(G-12262)*

PRINTING, LITHOGRAPHIC: Tickets

Paragon ID High Point Us Inc............... E 336 882-8115
High Point *(G-6726)*

Tickets Plus Inc................................. E 616 222-4000
Morrisville *(G-9072)*

PRINTING: Books

Goslen Printing Company..................... F 336 768-5775
Winston Salem *(G-13181)*

Herff Jones LLC................................. G 704 845-3355
Charlotte *(G-2271)*

Lsc Communications Inc...................... F 704 889-5800
Pineville *(G-9741)*

Rose Reprographics........................... G 336 222-0727
Burlington *(G-1149)*

PRINTING: Broadwoven Fabrics. Cotton

Advanced Digital Textiles LLC.............. E 704 226-9600
Monroe *(G-8417)*

Holt Sublimation Printing &.................. G 336 222-3600
Burlington *(G-1104)*

PRINTING: Checkbooks

Deluxe Corporation............................ F 336 851-4600
Greensboro *(G-5494)*

Printing Press................................... G 828 299-1234
Asheville *(G-585)*

PRINTING: Commercial, NEC

Abe Entercom Holdings LLC................. G 336 691-4337
Greensboro *(G-5337)*

AEL Services LLC.............................. E 704 525-3710
Charlotte *(G-1626)*

Ambrose Signs Inc............................. G 252 338-8522
Camden *(G-1210)*

American Multimedia Inc...................... D 336 229-7101
Burlington *(G-1045)*

American Solutions For Bu................... G 919 848-2442
Raleigh *(G-9898)*

Appalachian State University................ F 828 262-2047
Boone *(G-896)*

Arzberger Engravers Inc...................... E 704 376-1151
Charlotte *(G-1702)*

Asheville Color & Imaging Inc.............. G 828 774-5040
Asheville *(G-435)*

Austin Business Forms Inc................... F 704 821-6165
Indian Trail *(G-7070)*

Brunswick Screen Prtg & EMB............. G 910 579-1234
Ocean Isle Beach *(G-9586)*

Bryan Austin..................................... G 336 841-6573
High Point *(G-6551)*

Circle Graphics Inc............................ C 919 864-4518
Raleigh *(G-9995)*

Comedycd.. G 336 273-0077
Greensboro *(G-5458)*

Consumer Concepts............................ F 252 247-7000
Morehead City *(G-8828)*

Contract Printing & Graphics................ G 919 832-7178
Raleigh *(G-10014)*

Daniels Business Services Inc.............. E 828 277-8250
Asheville *(G-483)*

David Presnell.................................. G 336 372-5989
Sparta *(G-11537)*

Dbt Coatings LLC............................... G 336 834-9700
Greensboro *(G-5489)*

Dime EMB LLC................................... F 336 765-0910
Winston Salem *(G-13146)*

Document Directs Inc.......................... G 919 829-8810
Raleigh *(G-10053)*

Dtbtla Inc.. F 336 769-0000
Greensboro *(G-5506)*

Easter Seals Ucp NC & VA Inc............. D 919 856-0250
Raleigh *(G-10070)*

Eatumup Lure Company Inc.................. G 336 218-0896
Greensboro *(G-5511)*

Electronic Imaging Svcs Inc................. F 704 587-3323
Charlotte *(G-2095)*

F C C LLC.. G 336 883-7314
High Point *(G-6617)*

Fabrix Inc.. G 704 953-1239
Charlotte *(G-2141)*

Fayetteville Publishing Co................... E 910 323-4848
Fayetteville *(G-4601)*

Flint Group US LLC............................ F 828 687-2485
Arden *(G-272)*

Gibraltar Packaging Inc....................... C 910 439-6137
Whitsett *(G-12608)*

Gilmore Globl Lgstics Svcs Inc............ D 919 277-2700
Morrisville *(G-8982)*

Gmg Group LLC................................. G 252 441-8374
Kill Devil Hills *(G-7317)*

Go Postal In Boone Inc........................ F 828 262-0027
Boone *(G-917)*

Golf Associates Advertising Co............. E 828 252-6544
Asheville *(G-508)*

Graphic Image of Cape Fear Inc............ G 910 313-6768
Wilmington *(G-12795)*

Herald Printing Inc............................. G 252 726-3534
Morehead City *(G-8835)*

High Performance Marketing Inc............ G 919 870-9915
Raleigh *(G-10167)*

ID Images LLC................................... G 704 494-0444
Charlotte *(G-2309)*

J C Lawrence Co............................... G 919 553-3044
Oriental *(G-9600)*

Kathie S Mc Daniel............................ G 336 835-1544
Elkin *(G-4446)*

Keiger Inc.. E 336 760-0099
Winston Salem *(G-13223)*

Label Printing Systems Inc.................. E 336 760-3271
Winston Salem *(G-13230)*

Labels Tags & Inserts Inc.................... F 336 227-8485
Burlington *(G-1117)*

Lake Norman EMB & Monogramming..... G 704 892-8450
Cornelius *(G-3612)*

M-Prints Inc..................................... G 828 265-4929
Boone *(G-931)*

Masters Hand Print Works Inc.............. G 828 652-5833
Marion *(G-8051)*

Maxim Label Packg High Pt Inc............ F 336 861-1666
High Point *(G-6708)*

Mb-F Inc.. D 336 379-9352
Greensboro *(G-5685)*

Measurement Incorporated................... D 919 683-2413
Durham *(G-4122)*

Medlit Solutions LLC.......................... G 919 878-6789
Garner *(G-4942)*

Mega Media Concepts Ltd Lblty............ G 973 919-5661
Brevard *(G-975)*

Millenium Print Group........................ G 919 818-1229
Greensboro *(G-5693)*

Napoleon James................................ G 413 331-9560
Charlotte *(G-2542)*

News & Record Commercial Prtg.......... F 336 373-7300
Greensboro *(G-5708)*

One Source Document Solutions........... G 336 482-2360
Greensboro *(G-5723)*

Owen G Dunn Co Inc.......................... G 252 633-3197
New Bern *(G-9387)*

Park Communications LLC................... D 336 292-4000
Greensboro *(G-5732)*

Park Communications LLC................... G 919 852-1117
Raleigh *(G-10358)*

Piedmont Business Forms Inc.............. G 828 464-0010
Newton *(G-9488)*

Plasticard Products Inc....................... F 828 665-7774
Asheville *(G-576)*

Prince Manufacturing Corp................... C 828 681-8860
Mills River *(G-8320)*

Print Express Inc............................... F 910 455-4554
Jacksonville *(G-7138)*

Print Haus Inc................................... G 828 456-8622
Waynesville *(G-12469)*

Printful Inc....................................... F 818 351-7181
Charlotte *(G-2671)*

Printing Press................................... G 828 299-1234
Asheville *(G-585)*

Printing Svcs Greensboro Inc.............. G 336 274-7663
Greensboro *(G-5765)*

Proforma Hanson Branding................... G 210 437-3061
High Point *(G-6749)*

Quik Print Inc................................... G 910 738-6775
Lumberton *(G-7967)*

R R Donnelley & Sons Company........... E 919 596-8942
Durham *(G-4205)*

Salem One Inc................................... C 336 744-9990
Winston Salem *(G-13325)*

Sharpe Images Properties Inc.............. E 336 724-2871
Winston Salem *(G-13334)*

Sml Raleigh LLC............................... G 919 585-0100
Clayton *(G-3170)*

St Johns Packaging Usa LLC............... C 336 292-9911
Greensboro *(G-5833)*

Stump Printing Co Inc......................... C 260 723-5171
Wrightsville Beach *(G-13433)*

Substance Incorporated...................... G 800 985-9485
Claremont *(G-3122)*

Tennessee Nedgraphics Inc................. F 704 414-4224
Charlotte *(G-2908)*

Times Printing Company Inc................. G 252 441-2223
Kill Devil Hills *(G-7320)*

Triad Printing NC Inc.......................... G 336 422-8752
Greensboro *(G-5878)*

Uniforms Galore................................. G 252 975-5878
Washington *(G-12417)*

Visigraphix Inc.................................. G 336 882-1935
Colfax *(G-3292)*

Walgreen Co..................................... G 704 525-2628
Charlotte *(G-3001)*

Winston Printing Company................... D 336 896-7631
Winston Salem *(G-13399)*

Wright of Thomasville Inc.................... F 336 472-4200
Thomasville *(G-12091)*

PRINTING: Flexographic

Valdese Packaging & Label Inc............ F 828 879-9772
Valdese *(G-12202)*

Valdese Packaging & Label Inc............ E 828 879-9772
Valdese *(G-12201)*

PRINTING: Gravure, Labels

Huntpack Inc......................................G 704 986-0684
  Albemarle *(G-78)*

PRINTING: Gravure, Rotogravure

Arzberger Engravers Inc.....................E 704 376-1151
  Charlotte *(G-1702)*

Big Fish Dpi.......................................G 704 545-8112
  Mint Hill *(G-8331)*

Business Wise Inc.............................G 704 554-4112
  Charlotte *(G-1822)*

Executive Promotions Inc..................F 704 663-4000
  Mooresville *(G-8661)*

Linprint Company...............................F 910 763-5103
  Wilmington *(G-12837)*

Sharpe Co..E 336 724-2871
  Winston Salem *(G-13333)*

Synthomer Inc....................................D 704 225-1872
  Monroe *(G-8567)*

PRINTING: Laser

Ics North America Corp......................E 704 794-6620
  Concord *(G-3375)*

Laser Ink Corporation.........................E 919 361-5822
  Durham *(G-4101)*

Theo Davis Sons Incorporated...........E 919 269-7401
  Zebulon *(G-13523)*

PRINTING: Letterpress

Arrowhead Graphics Inc......................G 336 274-2419
  Greensboro *(G-5370)*

Artcraft Press Inc...............................G 828 397-8612
  Icard *(G-7064)*

Carolina Printing Co............................G 919 834-0433
  Princeton *(G-9823)*

Carter Publishing Company Inc..........F 336 993-2161
  Kernersville *(G-7253)*

Concord Printing Company Inc...........G 704 786-3717
  Concord *(G-3342)*

Hunsucker Printing Co Inc..................G 336 629-9125
  Asheboro *(G-363)*

Imagemark Business Svcs Inc............G 704 865-4912
  Gastonia *(G-5062)*

Ingalls Alton......................................G 252 975-2056
  Washington *(G-12394)*

Pharmaceutic Litho Label Inc.............E 336 785-4000
  Winston Salem *(G-13287)*

Poole Printing Company Inc................G 919 876-5260
  Raleigh *(G-10377)*

Skipper Graphics...............................G 910 754-8729
  Shallotte *(G-11305)*

Twyford Printing Company Inc............G 910 892-3271
  Dunn *(G-3870)*

PRINTING: Lithographic

AEC Imaging & Graphics LLC.............G 910 693-1034
  Hope Mills *(G-6922)*

AEL Services LLC...............................E 704 525-3710
  Charlotte *(G-1626)*

Alexander Press Inc...........................G 336 884-8063
  High Point *(G-6514)*

All Occasion Printing..........................G 336 926-7766
  Winston Salem *(G-13079)*

AlphaGraphics....................................F 704 887-3430
  Charlotte *(G-1654)*

AlphaGraphics....................................G 336 759-8000
  Winston Salem *(G-13083)*

AlphaGraphics Downtown Raleigh.......G 919 832-2828
  Garner *(G-4914)*

AlphaGraphics Pineville......................G 704 541-3678
  Charlotte *(G-1655)*

Anav Yofi Inc......................................G 828 217-7746
  Charlotte *(G-1676)*

Appalachian State University..............F 828 262-2047
  Boone *(G-896)*

Artesian Future Technology LLC.........G 919 904-4940
  Chapel Hill *(G-1529)*

Arzberger Engravers Inc.....................E 704 376-1151
  Charlotte *(G-1702)*

Ballantyne One...................................G 704 926-7009
  Charlotte *(G-1747)*

Bennett & Associates Inc...................G 919 477-7362
  Durham *(G-3925)*

Boundless Inc.....................................G 919 622-9051
  Four Oaks *(G-4809)*

Brand Fuel Promotions.......................G 704 256-4057
  Waxhaw *(G-12425)*

Brandilly of Nc Inc.............................G 919 278-7896
  Raleigh *(G-9957)*

Brown Printing Inc..............................G 704 849-9292
  Charlotte *(G-1814)*

Canvas Giclee Printing........................G 910 458-4229
  Carolina Beach *(G-1257)*

Carden Printing Company....................G 336 364-2923
  Timberlake *(G-12099)*

Carolina Copy Services Inc.................F 704 375-9099
  Cornelius *(G-3592)*

Carolina Newspapers Inc....................G 336 274-7829
  Greensboro *(G-5431)*

Carolina Vinyl Printing........................G 910 603-3036
  Pinehurst *(G-9689)*

Carroll Signs & Advertising.................G 336 983-3415
  King *(G-7324)*

Cary Printing......................................G 919 266-9005
  Raleigh *(G-9984)*

Cascadas Nye Corporation..................F 919 834-8128
  Raleigh *(G-9985)*

Cavu Printing Inc................................G 336 818-9790
  Elkin *(G-4441)*

Chanmala Gallery Fine Art Prtg...........G 704 975-7695
  Wake Forest *(G-12268)*

City Prints LLC....................................G 404 273-5741
  Matthews *(G-8106)*

Clondalkin Pharma & Healthcare.........G 336 292-4555
  Greensboro *(G-5452)*

Coastal Press Inc...............................G 252 726-1549
  Morehead City *(G-8827)*

CPS Resources Inc.............................E 704 628-7678
  Indian Trail *(G-7075)*

Currie Motorsports Inc........................G 910 580-1765
  Raeford *(G-9836)*

Dbw Print & Promo.............................G 704 906-8551
  Concord *(G-3352)*

Digital AP Prtg DBA F4mily Mtt............G 980 939-8066
  Charlotte *(G-2045)*

Document Comm Solutions Inc............G 336 856-1300
  Greensboro *(G-5498)*

Dogwood Print....................................G 919 906-0617
  Wendell *(G-12532)*

Dokja Inc..G 336 852-5190
  Greensboro *(G-5500)*

Downtown Raleigh..............................G 919 821-7897
  Raleigh *(G-10057)*

E C U Univ Prtg & Graphics................F 252 737-1301
  Greenville *(G-5971)*

Ed Kemp Associates Inc.....................G 336 869-2155
  High Point *(G-6604)*

Erleclair Inc..E 919 233-7710
  Cary *(G-1355)*

Fast Pro Media LLC.............................G 704 799-8040
  Cornelius *(G-3599)*

Fast Pro Media LLC.............................G 704 799-8040
  Cornelius *(G-3600)*

Fayetteville Publishing Co...................E 910 323-4848
  Fayetteville *(G-4601)*

Free Will Bptst Press Fndtion...............F 252 746-6128
  Ayden *(G-657)*

Get Custom Print.................................G 336 682-3891
  Kernersville *(G-7275)*

Gik Inc..F 919 872-9498
  Raleigh *(G-10133)*

Gilmore Globl Lgstics Svcs Inc...........D 919 277-2700
  Morrisville *(G-8982)*

Ginas Processing & Prtg Ctr................G 910 476-0037
  Raeford *(G-9839)*

Ginkgo Print Studio LLC......................G 828 275-6300
  Asheville *(G-507)*

Greensboro News & Record LLC.........A 336 373-7000
  Greensboro *(G-5577)*

Gso Printing Inc..................................G 336 288-5778
  Greensboro *(G-5582)*

Hickory Printing Group Inc H...............F 828 465-3431
  Conover *(G-3529)*

High Concepts LLC.............................G 704 377-3467
  Denver *(G-3787)*

Industrial Motions Inc.........................G 734 284-8944
  Apex *(G-168)*

Industrial Sign & Graphics Inc.............E 704 371-4985
  Charlotte *(G-2324)*

Infinity S End Inc................................F 704 900-8355
  Charlotte *(G-2328)*

Instant Imprints..................................G 704 864-1510
  Gastonia *(G-5067)*

International Minute Press....................G 919 762-0054
  Fuquay Varina *(G-4885)*

Inventive Graphics Inc........................G 704 814-4900
  Charlotte *(G-2351)*

J R Cole Industries Inc........................F 704 523-6622
  Charlotte *(G-2361)*

Jag Graphics Inc................................G 828 259-9020
  Asheville *(G-527)*

Jones Media......................................G 828 264-3612
  Boone *(G-928)*

Keller Cres U To Be Phrmgraphi..........E 336 851-1150
  Greensboro *(G-5646)*

Kieffer Starlite Company.....................G 800 659-2493
  Mount Airy *(G-9141)*

Label & Printing Solutions Inc.............G 919 782-1242
  Raleigh *(G-10243)*

Laser Ink Corporation.........................E 919 361-5822
  Durham *(G-4101)*

M & S Systems Inc.............................G 336 996-7118
  Kernersville *(G-7283)*

Maxim Label Packg High Pt Inc............F 336 861-1666
  High Point *(G-6708)*

Mb-F Inc..D 336 379-9352
  Greensboro *(G-5685)*

Medlit Solutions.................................G 919 878-6789
  Garner *(G-4941)*

Meredith - Webb Prtg Co Inc..............D 336 228-8378
  Burlington *(G-1128)*

Minuteman Press of Gastonia..............G 704 867-3366
  Gastonia *(G-5099)*

Mjt Us Inc..G 704 826-7828
  Charlotte *(G-2510)*

Mlb Screen Printing............................G 704 363-6124
  Huntersville *(G-7016)*

Modern Information Svcs Inc...............G 704 872-1020
  Statesville *(G-11734)*

Monk Lekeisha...................................G 910 385-0361
  Goldsboro *(G-5230)*

More Than Billboards Inc....................E 336 723-1018
  Kernersville *(G-7288)*

Motorsports Designs Inc.....................F 336 454-1181
  High Point *(G-6716)*

Mountaineer Inc.......................................G 828 452-0661
Waynesville *(G-12464)*

Multi Packaging Solutions.....................A 336 855-7142
Greensboro *(G-5699)*

Natel Inc..G 336 227-1227
Burlington *(G-1134)*

NC Imprints Inc.....................................G 336 790-4546
Lexington *(G-7720)*

News and Observer Pubg Co.................A 919 829-4500
Raleigh *(G-10331)*

Nine Thirteen LLC.................................G 919 876-8070
Raleigh *(G-10332)*

Norman Lake Graphics Inc....................G 704 896-8444
Huntersville *(G-7022)*

Notepad Enterprises LLC......................G 704 377-3467
Charlotte *(G-2576)*

Observer News Enterprise Inc..............G 828 464-0221
Newton *(G-9483)*

Occasions Group Inc.............................G 919 751-2400
Goldsboro *(G-5233)*

Office Sup Svcs Inc Charlotte................E 704 786-4677
Concord *(G-3410)*

Omega Studios Inc...............................G 704 889-5800
Pineville *(G-9745)*

On Demand Screen Printing LLC..........G 704 661-0788
Concord *(G-3413)*

Os Press LLC..G 910 485-7955
Fayetteville *(G-4649)*

Owen G Dunn Co Inc............................G 252 633-3197
New Bern *(G-9387)*

Pamela A Adams...................................G 919 876-5949
Raleigh *(G-10355)*

Pamlico Screen Printing Inc.................G 252 944-6001
Washington *(G-12406)*

Park Communications LLC....................D 336 292-4000
Greensboro *(G-5732)*

Pharmaceutic Litho Label Inc...............E 336 785-4000
Winston Salem *(G-13287)*

Platesetterscom....................................G 888 380-7483
Greensboro *(G-5751)*

PMG Acquisition Corp...........................D 828 758-7381
Lenoir *(G-7634)*

Polly and Associates LLC......................G 910 319-7564
Wilmington *(G-12880)*

Polyprint Usa Inc...................................G 888 389-8618
Charlotte *(G-2646)*

Pretty Paid LLC.....................................G 980 443-3876
Kings Mountain *(G-7379)*

Print Doc Pack and...............................G 910 454-9104
Southport *(G-11525)*

Print Path LLC.......................................E 828 855-9966
Hickory *(G-6417)*

Printing Pro..G 704 748-9396
Iron Station *(G-7106)*

Pro Cal Prof Decals Inc.........................F 704 795-6090
Concord *(G-3424)*

Professional Bus Systems Inc...............G 704 333-2444
Charlotte *(G-2673)*

Professional Laminating LLC.................G 919 465-0400
Cary *(G-1429)*

Promographix Inc..................................F 919 846-1379
Carolina Beach *(G-1263)*

R & D Label LLC...................................G 336 889-2900
Jamestown *(G-7177)*

R L Lasater Printing..............................G 919 639-6662
Angier *(G-127)*

Rodney Tyler...G 336 629-0951
Asheboro *(G-391)*

Salem One Inc......................................F 336 722-2886
Kernersville *(G-7299)*

Salem One Inc......................................C 336 744-9990
Winston Salem *(G-13325)*

Scriptorium Pubg Svcs Inc....................G 919 481-2701
Durham *(G-4227)*

Sennett Security Products LLC..............D 336 375-1134
Browns Summit *(G-1005)*

Sennett Security Products LLC..............G 336 404-3284
Greensboro *(G-5807)*

Simple & Sentimental LLC....................G 252 320-9458
Ayden *(G-662)*

Sir Speedy Printing...............................G 704 664-1911
Mooresville *(G-8771)*

Smith Family Screen Printing...............G 336 317-4849
Pleasant Garden *(G-9794)*

Sundrop Printing...................................G 704 960-1592
Kannapolis *(G-7221)*

Swatchcraft LLC....................................G 336 434-5095
High Point *(G-6798)*

Sylva Herald and Ruralite.....................G 828 586-2611
Sylva *(G-11900)*

Thompson Printing & Packg Inc............G 704 313-7323
Mooresboro *(G-8587)*

Triangle Inner Vision Company.............G 919 460-6013
Morrisville *(G-9076)*

Tryon Newsmedia LLC..........................G 828 859-9151
Tryon *(G-12179)*

Twigs Screen Printing...........................G 910 770-1605
Tabor City *(G-11916)*

Valassis Communications Inc...............D 919 544-4511
Durham *(G-4294)*

Valassis Communications Inc...............G 919 361-7900
Durham *(G-4295)*

Verticalfx Inc..G 704 594-5000
Mooresville *(G-8790)*

Village Graphics...................................G 252 745-4600
Oriental *(G-9603)*

W B Mason Co Inc................................E 888 926-2766
Charlotte *(G-2994)*

Weber and Weber Inc...........................F 336 722-4109
Winston Salem *(G-13387)*

Westrock Rkt LLC.................................B 770 448-2193
Marion *(G-8073)*

Whatever You Need Screen Print..........G 704 287-8603
Concord *(G-3467)*

Whimsical Prints Paper & Gifts.............G 919 544-8491
Durham *(G-4304)*

Whitney Screen Printing.......................G 910 673-0309
Eagle Springs *(G-4321)*

Wick Communications Co......................E 252 537-2505
Roanoke Rapids *(G-10747)*

Wilsons Planning & Consulting.............G 919 592-0935
Garner *(G-4974)*

Xpres LLC...E 336 245-1596
Winston Salem *(G-13408)*

Xtreme Postcard Profits System...........G 919 894-8886
Benson *(G-800)*

Your Source For Printing.......................G 704 957-5922
Charlotte *(G-3041)*

PRINTING: Manmade Fiber & Silk, Broadwoven Fabric

Advanced Digital Textiles LLC..............E 704 226-9600
Monroe *(G-8417)*

Everest Textile Usa LLC........................C 828 245-6755
Forest City *(G-4789)*

Holt Sublimation Printing &..................G 336 222-3600
Burlington *(G-1104)*

Printology Signs Graphics LLC.............G 843 473-4984
Davidson *(G-3716)*

PRINTING: Offset

4 Over LLC..F 919 875-3187
Raleigh *(G-9858)*

A & M Paper and Printing.....................G 919 813-7852
Durham *(G-3874)*

A Better Image Printing Inc...................F 919 967-0319
Durham *(G-3875)*

A Forbes Company................................F
Lenoir *(G-7565)*

A Plus Graphics Inc..............................G 252 243-0404
Wilson *(G-12960)*

Able Graphics Company LLC.................G 336 753-1812
Mocksville *(G-8346)*

Abolder Image......................................F 336 856-1300
Greensboro *(G-5338)*

Accelerated Press Inc...........................G 248 524-1850
Wilmington *(G-12689)*

Acme Sample Books Inc........................E 336 883-4336
High Point *(G-6508)*

Adpress Printing Incorporated..............G 336 294-2244
Summerfield *(G-11835)*

Advanced Teo Corp...............................G 305 278-4474
Charlotte *(G-1625)*

Advantage Printing Inc..........................F 828 252-7667
Arden *(G-248)*

Advantage Printing & Design................G 252 523-8133
Kinston *(G-7392)*

American Indian Printing Inc.................G 336 230-1551
Greensboro *(G-5357)*

American Multimedia Inc.......................D 336 229-7101
Burlington *(G-1045)*

American Printers Inc............................G 252 977-7468
Rocky Mount *(G-10822)*

American Speedy Printing Ctrs..............G 828 322-3981
Hickory *(G-6263)*

Andrews Graphics LLC...........................G 252 633-3199
New Bern *(G-9334)*

Anitas Marketing Concepts Inc.............G 252 243-3993
Wilson *(G-12961)*

Apex Printing Company.........................G 919 362-9856
Apex *(G-136)*

Archdale Printing Company Inc.............G 336 884-5312
High Point *(G-6525)*

Arrowhead Graphics Inc........................G 336 274-2419
Greensboro *(G-5370)*

Artcraft Press Inc..................................G 828 397-8612
Icard *(G-7064)*

Artech Graphics Inc..............................G 704 545-9804
New London *(G-9413)*

Arthur Demarest..................................G 252 473-1449
Manteo *(G-8023)*

Asheville Print Shop.............................G 828 214-5286
Asheville *(G-440)*

Asheville Quickprint.............................G 828 252-7667
Fletcher *(G-4720)*

Associated Printing & Svcs Inc.............G 828 286-9064
Rutherfordton *(G-10975)*

Atlantis Graphics Inc............................E 919 361-5809
Durham *(G-3904)*

Austin Printing Company Inc.................G 704 289-1445
Monroe *(G-8437)*

Aztech Products Inc..............................G 910 763-5599
Wilmington *(G-12717)*

B P Printing and Copying Inc................G 704 821-8219
Matthews *(G-8159)*

Babusci Crtive Prtg Imging LLC............G 704 423-9864
Charlotte *(G-1735)*

Baicy Communications Inc....................G 336 722-7768
Winston Salem *(G-13101)*

Baileys Quick Copy Shop Inc................F 704 637-2020
Salisbury *(G-11022)*

Bakeshot Prtg & Graphics LLC.............G 704 532-9326
Charlotte *(G-1743)*

Barefoot Press Inc................................G 919 283-6396
Raleigh *(G-9933)*

Employee Codes: A=Over 500 employees, B=251-500
C=101-250, D=51-100, E=20-50, F=10-19, G=1-9

2025 Harris North Carolina
Manufacturers Directory

1177

PRODUCT

Barretts Printing House Inc	G	252 243-2820	Wilson (G-12968)
Bbf Printing Solutions	G	336 969-2323	Rural Hall (G-10952)
BEC-Car Printing Co Inc	F	704 873-1911	Statesville (G-11669)
Better Business Printing Inc	G	704 867-3366	Gastonia (G-4998)
Blackleys Printing Co	G	919 553-6813	Clayton (G-3135)
Blue Ridge Printing Co Inc	D	828 254-1000	Asheville (G-457)
Blue Ridge Quick Print Inc	G	828 883-2420	Brevard (G-968)
Boingo Graphics Inc	E	704 527-4963	Charlotte (G-1797)
BP Solutions Group Inc	E	828 252-4476	Asheville (G-460)
Brodie-Jones Printing Co Inc	G	252 438-7992	Louisburg (G-7910)
Buchanan Prtg & Graphics Inc	G	336 299-6868	Greensboro (G-5408)
Budget Printing Co	G	910 642-7306	Whiteville (G-12577)
Burco International Inc	G	828 252-4481	Asheville (G-463)
Burrow Family Corporation	E	336 887-3173	Asheboro (G-334)
C B C Printing	G	828 497-5510	Cherokee (G-3050)
C D J & P Inc	G	252 446-3611	Rocky Mount (G-10826)
Call Printing & Copying	G	704 821-6554	Indian Trail (G-7073)
Cardinal Graphics Inc	G	704 545-4144	Mint Hill (G-8334)
Carolina Print Mill	G	919 607-9452	Cary (G-1323)
Carolina Printing Co	G	919 834-0433	Princeton (G-9823)
Carolina Prtg Wilmington Inc	G	910 762-2453	Supply (G-11856)
Carter Printing	G	919 373-0531	Knightdale (G-7450)
Carter Printing & Graphics Inc	F	919 266-5280	Knightdale (G-7451)
Cashiers Printing Inc	G	828 787-1324	Highlands (G-6844)
Causekeepers Inc	E	336 824-2518	Franklinville (G-4855)
Central Carolina Printing LLC	G	910 572-3344	Asheboro (G-336)
Ceprint Solutions Inc	E	336 956-6327	Lexington (G-7662)
Charlotte Printing Company Inc	F	704 888-5181	Concord (G-3334)
Choice Printing LLC	G	919 790-0680	Raleigh (G-9994)
Clarks Printing Service Inc	E	828 254-1432	Asheville (G-477)
Cline Printing Inc	G	704 394-8144	Charlotte (G-1929)
Clinton Press Inc	F	336 275-8491	Greensboro (G-5451)
Coastal Impressions Inc	G	252 480-1717	Nags Head (G-9297)
Coble Printing Co Inc	G	919 693-4622	Oxford (G-9608)
Commercial Enterprises NC Inc	G	910 592-8163	Clinton (G-3230)
Commercial Printing Company	E	919 832-2828	Garner (G-4922)

Commercial Prtg Co of Clinton	G	910 592-8163	Clinton (G-3231)
Commercial Prtg Lincolnton NC	G	704 735-6831	Lincolnton (G-7822)
Concord Printing Company Inc	G	704 786-3717	Concord (G-3342)
Consolidated Press Inc	G	704 372-6785	Charlotte (G-1975)
Copy Cat Instant Prtg Chrltte	G	704 529-6606	Charlotte (G-1982)
Copy Express Charlotte Inc	G	704 527-1750	Charlotte (G-1983)
Copy King Inc	G	336 333-9900	Greensboro (G-5468)
Copy Works	G	828 698-7622	Hendersonville (G-6199)
Copycat Print Shop Inc	F	910 799-1500	Wilmington (G-12751)
Copymasters Printing Svcs Inc	G	828 324-0532	Hickory (G-6311)
CRC Printing Co Inc	G	704 875-1804	Huntersville (G-6981)
Creative Printers Inc	G	336 246-7746	West Jefferson (G-12563)
Creative Printers & Brks Inc	G	828 321-4663	Andrews (G-106)
Creative Printing Stanley Inc	G	704 732-6398	Lincolnton (G-7825)
Creative Prtg Intrnet Svcs LLC	G	828 265-2800	Boone (G-910)
Crisp Printers Inc	G	704 867-6663	Gastonia (G-5032)
CRS/Las Inc	F	910 392-0883	Wilmington (G-12757)
Custom Marking & Printing Inc	G	704 866-8245	Gastonia (G-5036)
Custom Printing Solutions Inc	G	336 992-1161	Kernersville (G-7262)
D & B Printing Co	G	919 876-3530	Raleigh (G-10032)
Daniels Business Services Inc	E	828 277-8250	Asheville (G-483)
Davidson Printing Inc	G	336 357-0555	Lexington (G-7675)
Ddi Print	F	919 829-8810	Raleigh (G-10040)
Deluxe Printing Co Inc	E	828 322-1329	Hickory (G-6321)
Design Printing Inc	G	336 472-3333	Thomasville (G-12017)
Dew Group Enterprises Inc	E	919 585-0100	Clayton (G-3144)
Discount Printing Inc	G	704 365-3665	Charlotte (G-2052)
Docu Source of NC	F	919 459-5900	Morrisville (G-8967)
Dorsett Printing Company	G	910 895-3520	Rockingham (G-10775)
Dove Communications Inc	G	336 855-5491	Greensboro (G-5502)
Dtbtla Inc	F	336 769-0000	Greensboro (G-5506)
Duncan-Parnell Inc	G	252 977-7832	Rocky Mount (G-10833)
Eastern Offset Printing Co	G	252 247-6791	Atlantic Beach (G-639)
Elledge Family Inc	F	919 876-2300	Raleigh (G-10082)
Fairway Printing Inc	G	919 779-4797	Raleigh (G-10102)
Flanagan Printing Company Inc	G	828 693-7380	Hendersonville (G-6207)

Flash Printing Company Inc	E	704 375-2474	Charlotte (G-2159)
Forsyth Printing Company Inc	G	336 969-0383	Rural Hall (G-10959)
Forward Design & Print Co Inc	G	704 776-9304	Monroe (G-8490)
Freedom Mailing & Mktg Inc	G	336 595-6300	Winston Salem (G-13175)
Galaxy Graphics Inc	G	704 724-9057	Matthews (G-8113)
Gaston Printing and Signs LLC	G	702 267-5633	Belmont (G-753)
Geo-Lin Inc	G	336 884-0648	Jamestown (G-7162)
Gibraltar Packaging Inc	C	910 439-6137	Whitsett (G-12608)
Gilley Printers Inc	G	910 295-6317	Pinehurst (G-9692)
Goffstar Inc	G	704 895-3878	Charlotte (G-2222)
Golf Associates Advertising Co	E	828 252-6544	Asheville (G-508)
Goslen Printing Company	F	336 768-5775	Winston Salem (G-13181)
Graphic Impressions Inc	E	704 596-4921	Charlotte (G-2232)
Graphic Products Inc	G	919 894-3661	Benson (G-790)
Greencross Inc	G	704 984-6700	Albemarle (G-76)
Greybeard Printing Inc	G	828 252-3082	Asheville (G-513)
Griffin Printing Inc	G	919 832-6931	Raleigh (G-10147)
Gso Printing	G	336 292-1601	Greensboro (G-5581)
Harco Printing Incorporated	G	336 771-0234	Winston Salem (G-13189)
Hayes Print-Stamp Co Inc	G	336 667-1116	Wilkesboro (G-12637)
Herald Printing Inc	G	252 726-3534	Morehead City (G-8835)
Heritage Prtg & Graphics Inc	G	704 551-0700	Charlotte (G-2274)
Hinson Industries Inc	G	252 937-7171	Rocky Mount (G-10840)
Hinsons Typing & Printing	G	919 934-9036	Smithfield (G-11446)
Htm Concepts Inc	F	252 794-2122	Windsor (G-13054)
Hunsucker Printing Co Inc	G	336 629-9125	Asheboro (G-363)
Ideal Printing Services Inc	G	336 784-0074	Kernersville (G-7279)
Image Works Inc	G	336 668-3338	Jamestown (G-7168)
Imagemark Business Svcs Inc	G	704 865-4912	Gastonia (G-5062)
Imperial Printing Pdts Co Inc	G	704 554-1188	Lowell (G-7932)
Independence Printing	G	336 771-0234	Winston Salem (G-13205)
Ingalls Alton	G	252 975-2056	Washington (G-12394)
Ink Well	G	336 727-9750	Winston Salem (G-13209)
Ink Well Inc	G	919 682-8279	Durham (G-4078)
Inkwell	G	919 433-7539	Fayetteville (G-4617)
Inprimo Solutions Inc	G	919 390-7776	Raleigh (G-10199)

Company	Code	Phone
Insta Copy Shop Ltd	F	704 376-1350
Charlotte (G-2339)		
Itek Graphics LLC	E	704 357-6002
Concord (G-3383)		
James G Gouge	G	336 854-1551
High Point (G-6677)		
JB II Printing LLC	E	336 222-0717
Burlington (G-1111)		
JC Print	G	910 556-9663
Wilmington (G-12822)		
JM Graphics Inc	G	704 375-1147
Charlotte (G-2371)		
Jofra Graphics Inc	G	910 259-1717
Burgaw (G-1025)		
Jones Printing Company Inc	G	919 774-9442
Sanford (G-11198)		
Joseph C Woodard Prtg Co Inc	F	919 829-0634
Raleigh (G-10221)		
Js Printing LLC	G	919 773-1103
Raleigh (G-10224)		
Kathie S Mc Daniel	G	336 835-1544
Elkin (G-4446)		
Keiger Inc	E	336 760-0099
Winston Salem (G-13223)		
Key Printing Inc	F	252 459-4783
Nashville (G-9321)		
Kinston Office Supply Co Inc	E	252 523-7654
Kinston (G-7419)		
Kolb Boyette & Assoc Inc	E	919 544-7839
Durham (G-4097)		
Landmark Printing Inc	G	919 833-5151
Raleigh (G-10245)		
Landmark Printing Co Inc	G	919 833-5151
Raleigh (G-10246)		
Legacy Graphics Inc	F	919 741-6262
Garner (G-4936)		
Lenoir Printing Inc	G	828 758-7260
Lenoir (G-7621)		
Litho Priting Inc	G	919 755-9542
Raleigh (G-10257)		
Loftin & Company Inc	E	704 393-9393
Charlotte (G-2431)		
Lynchs Office Supply Co Inc	F	252 537-6041
Roanoke Rapids (G-10740)		
M C C of Laurinburg Inc	G	910 276-0519
Laurinburg (G-7506)		
Mail Management Services LLC	F	828 236-0076
Asheville (G-541)		
Markell Publishing Company Inc	G	336 226-7148
Burlington (G-1122)		
Master Marketing Group LLC	G	870 932-4491
Raleigh (G-10279)		
Masters Hand Print Works Inc	G	828 652-5833
Marion (G-8051)		
Measurement Incorporated	D	919 683-2413
Durham (G-4122)		
Medlit Solutions LLC	D	919 878-6789
Garner (G-4942)		
Mellineum Printing	F	919 267-5752
Apex (G-179)		
Metro Productions Inc	F	919 851-6420
Raleigh (G-10296)		
Minges Printing & Advg Co	G	704 867-6791
Gastonia (G-5098)		
Minuteman Quick Copy Svc Inc	G	910 455-5353
Jacksonville (G-7132)		
Monarch Printers	G	704 376-1533
Charlotte (G-2517)		
Monte Enterprises Inc	G	252 637-5803
New Bern (G-9385)		
Moore Printing & Graphics Inc	F	919 821-3293
Raleigh (G-10314)		
Morgan Printers Inc	F	252 355-5588
Winterville (G-13419)		
Murphy Printing & Vinyl LLC	G	828 835-4848
Murphy (G-9294)		
NC Printing LLC	G	828 393-4615
Hendersonville (G-6230)		
New Hanover Printing and Pubg	G	910 520-7173
Wilmington (G-12860)		
Old Style Printing	G	828 452-1122
Waynesville (G-12466)		
Ollis Enterprises Inc	E	828 265-0004
Wilkesboro (G-12648)		
On Demand Printing & Desi	G	828 252-0965
Asheville (G-560)		
Pamela Taylor	G	828 692-8599
Hendersonville (G-6234)		
Pamor Fine Print	G	919 559-2846
Raleigh (G-10356)		
PBM Graphics Inc	C	919 544-6222
Durham (G-4169)		
PBM Graphics Inc	G	336 664-5800
Greensboro (G-5737)		
PBM Graphics Inc	C	919 544-6222
Durham (G-4170)		
Performance Print Services LLC	G	919 957-9995
Durham (G-4173)		
Perlman Inc	F	704 332-1164
Charlotte (G-2629)		
Person Printing Company Inc	E	336 599-2146
Roxboro (G-10940)		
Piedmont Business Forms Inc	G	828 464-0010
Newton (G-9488)		
Piedmont Graphics Inc	E	336 230-0040
Greensboro (G-5742)		
Pilgrim Tract Society Inc	G	336 495-1241
Randleman (G-10655)		
Pilot LLC	D	910 692-7271
Southern Pines (G-11505)		
Pioneer Printing Company Inc	G	336 789-4011
Mount Airy (G-9165)		
PIP Printing & Document Servic	G	336 222-0717
Burlington (G-1141)		
Plum Print Inc	F	828 633-5535
Asheville (G-579)		
Poole Printing Company Inc	G	919 876-5260
Raleigh (G-10377)		
Pope Printing & Design Inc	G	828 274-5945
Asheville (G-580)		
Postal Instant Press	G	336 222-0717
Burlington (G-1142)		
Powell Ink Inc	F	828 253-6886
Asheville (G-582)		
Precision Printing	G	252 338-2450
Elizabeth City (G-4404)		
Precision Printing	G	336 273-5794
Greensboro (G-5758)		
Prime Source Opc LLC	E	336 661-3300
Winston Salem (G-13303)		
Primo Inc	G	888 822-5815
Cornelius (G-3620)		
Print Express Enterprises Inc	G	336 765-5505
Clemmons (G-3199)		
Print Express Inc	F	910 455-4554
Jacksonville (G-7138)		
Print Haus Inc	G	828 456-8622
Waynesville (G-12469)		
Print Management Group LLC	F	704 821-0114
Charlotte (G-2669)		
Print Media Associates Inc	G	704 529-0555
Charlotte (G-2670)		
Print Professionals	G	607 279-3335
Pinehurst (G-9700)		
Print Shoppe of Rocky Mt Inc	G	252 442-9912
Rocky Mount (G-10862)		
Print Social	G	980 430-4483
Huntersville (G-7039)		
Print Usa Inc	G	910 485-2254
Fayetteville (G-4658)		
Print Works Fayetteville Inc	G	910 864-8100
Fayetteville (G-4659)		
Printcrafters Incorporated	G	704 873-7387
Statesville (G-11754)		
Printery	F	336 852-9774
Greensboro (G-5764)		
Printing & Packaging Inc	E	704 482-3866
Shelby (G-11371)		
Printing Partners Inc	G	336 996-2268
Kernersville (G-7293)		
Printing Press	G	828 299-1234
Asheville (G-585)		
Printing Svcs Greensboro Inc	G	336 274-7663
Greensboro (G-5765)		
Printlogic Inc	E	336 626-6680
Asheboro (G-387)		
Printmarketing LLC	G	828 261-0063
Hickory (G-6418)		
Printsurge Incorporated	G	919 854-4376
Raleigh (G-10396)		
Prism Printing & Design Inc	G	919 706-5977
Cary (G-1427)		
Proforma Print Source	G	919 383-2070
Durham (G-4198)		
Quad/Graphics Inc	E	706 648-5456
Charlotte (G-2680)		
Quality Prtg Cartridge Fctry	G	336 852-2505
Greensboro (G-5779)		
Quick Color Solutions	G	336 698-0951
Mc Leansville (G-8226)		
Quick Print Henderson Inc	G	252 492-8905
Henderson (G-6173)		
Quick Print of Concord	G	704 782-6634
Salisbury (G-11110)		
Quik Print Inc	G	910 738-6775
Lumberton (G-7967)		
Raleigh Printing & Typing Inc	G	919 662-8001
Raleigh (G-10427)		
Randall Printing Inc	G	336 272-3333
Greensboro (G-5781)		
Red 5 Printing LLC	G	704 996-3848
Cornelius (G-3623)		
Redbird Screen Printing LLC	G	919 946-0005
Raleigh (G-10438)		
Renascence Inc	G	252 355-1636
Greenville (G-6018)		
Richa Inc	G	704 944-0230
Charlotte (G-2724)		
Richa Inc	F	704 331-9744
Charlotte (G-2725)		
Rite Instant Printing Inc	G	336 768-5061
Winston Salem (G-13319)		
Russell Printing Inc	G	404 366-0552
Burlington (G-1151)		
S Chamblee Incorporated	E	919 833-7561
Raleigh (G-10452)		
S Ruppe Inc	G	828 287-4936
Rutherfordton (G-10992)		
S&A Marketing Inc	G	704 376-0938
Charlotte (G-2746)		
Seaside Press Co Inc	G	910 458-8156
Carolina Beach (G-1264)		
Seaway Printing Company	G	910 457-6158
Southport (G-11527)		
Shelby Business Cards	G	704 481-8341
Shelby (G-11375)		

PRODUCT

Silliman & Sons Inc.............................. G 919 774-6324
Sanford (G-11233)

Sire Tees.. G 919 787-6843
Raleigh (G-10482)

Smith & Fox Inc................................. F 828 684-4512
Arden (G-307)

Southern Printing Company Inc........... G 910 259-4807
Burgaw (G-1033)

Southport Graphics LLC..................... G 919 650-3822
Morrisville (G-9057)

Spee Dee Que Instant Prtg Inc............. G 919 683-1307
Durham (G-4245)

Speediprint Inc................................. F 910 483-2553
Fayetteville (G-4674)

T & R Signs..................................... G 919 779-1185
Garner (G-4967)

Table Rock Printers LLC..................... G 828 433-1377
Morganton (G-8904)

Tcprst LLC....................................... G 910 791-9767
Wilmington (G-12938)

Telepathic Graphics Inc...................... F 919 342-4603
Rocky Mount (G-10815)

Theo Davis Sons Incorporated............. E 919 269-7401
Zebulon (G-13523)

Trejo Soccer Academy LLC.................. G 336 899-7910
Asheboro (G-410)

Triangle Solutions Inc........................ G 919 481-1235
Cary (G-1473)

Twyford Printing Company Inc............. G 910 892-3271
Dunn (G-3870)

Unlimted Potential Sanford Inc............. E 919 852-1117
Morrisville (G-9083)

US Print Inc..................................... G 919 878-0981
Raleigh (G-10578)

Value Printing Inc.............................. G 919 380-9883
Cary (G-1477)

Via Prnting Graphic Design Inc............. G 919 872-8688
Youngsville (G-13497)

Victory Press LLC............................. G 704 660-0348
Mooresville (G-8792)

Village Instant Printing Inc.................. G 919 968-0000
Chapel Hill (G-1591)

Village Printing Co............................ F 336 629-0951
Asheboro (G-417)

Wallace Printing Inc.......................... F 828 466-3300
Newton (G-9509)

Walter Printing Company Inc............... G 704 982-8899
Albemarle (G-96)

Wayne Trademark Prtg Packg LLC........ E 800 327-1290
Asheboro (G-419)

Weber and Weber Inc......................... G 336 889-6322
High Point (G-6833)

Welloyt Enterprises Inc...................... G 919 821-7897
Raleigh (G-10604)

Whistle Stop Press Inc....................... F 910 695-1403
Southern Pines (G-11514)

William George Printing LLC............... E 910 221-2700
Hope Mills (G-6928)

Williams Printing LLC........................ E 336 969-2733
Rural Hall (G-10969)

Wright Printing Service Inc................. G 336 427-4768
Madison (G-8004)

Zebra Communications Inc................... E 919 314-3700
Morrisville (G-9093)

PRINTING: Photo-Offset

Occasions Group Inc.......................... E 252 321-5805
Greenville (G-6009)

PRINTING: Photolithographic

Interflex Acquisition Co LLC................ C 336 921-3505
Wilkesboro (G-12641)

PRINTING: Rotogravure

Master Screens South LLC................... G 704 226-9600
Monroe (G-8525)

Shamrock Corporation......................... C 336 574-4200
Greensboro (G-5809)

PRINTING: Screen, Broadwoven Fabrics, Cotton

Barron Legacy Mgmt Group LLC........... G 301 367-4735
Charlotte (G-1757)

Bread & Butter Custom Scrn Prt........... G 919 942-3198
Chapel Hill (G-1531)

Daztech Inc..................................... G 800 862-6360
Wilmington (G-12761)

Gaston Screen Printing Inc.................. G 704 399-0459
Charlotte (G-2191)

Graphic Attack Inc............................ G 252 491-2174
Harbinger (G-6095)

K Formula Enterprises Inc................... G 910 323-3315
Fayetteville (G-4626)

Mojo Sportswear Inc.......................... G 252 758-4176
Greenville (G-6006)

One Hundred Ten Percent Screen........... G 252 728-3848
Beaufort (G-732)

Raleigh Tees LLC.............................. G 919 850-3378
Raleigh (G-10430)

S & L Creations Inc.......................... G 704 824-1930
Lowell (G-7934)

Screen Master.................................. G 252 492-8407
Henderson (G-6178)

Silverlining Screen Prtrs Inc............... G 919 554-0340
Youngsville (G-13485)

T & R Signs..................................... G 919 779-1185
Garner (G-4967)

Tryon Finishing Corporation................. G 828 859-5891
Tryon (G-12178)

PRINTING: Screen, Fabric

A&M Screen Printing NC Inc................ G 910 792-1111
Wilmington (G-12686)

Amy Smith....................................... G 828 352-1001
Burnsville (G-1182)

Boardwalk Inc.................................. G 252 240-1095
Morehead City (G-8819)

Brandrpm LLC.................................. D 704 225-1800
Charlotte (G-1807)

Combintons Screen Prtg EMB Inc.......... G 336 472-4420
Thomasville (G-12009)

Dicks Store..................................... G 336 548-9358
Madison (G-7987)

Freeman Screen Printers Inc................ G 704 521-9148
Charlotte (G-2179)

G & G Enterprises............................. G 336 764-2493
Clemmons (G-3186)

Grace Apparel Company Inc................. G 828 242-8172
Black Mountain (G-865)

Hi-Tech Screens Inc.......................... G 828 452-5151
Mooresville (G-8683)

Htm Concepts Inc............................. F 252 794-2122
Windsor (G-13054)

Island Xprtees of Oter Bnks In............. E 252 480-3990
Nags Head (G-9298)

Lee Marks....................................... G 919 493-2208
Durham (G-4102)

Line Drive Sports Center Inc................ G 336 824-1692
Ramseur (G-10628)

M-Prints Inc.................................... G 828 265-4929
Boone (G-931)

Manna Corp North Carolina.................. G 828 696-3642
Hendersonville (G-6223)

Marketing One Sportswear Inc.............. G 704 334-9333
Charlotte (G-2457)

R & S Sporting Goods Ctr Inc.............. G 336 599-0248
Roxboro (G-10942)

Regimental Flag & T Shirts.................. G 919 496-2888
Louisburg (G-7925)

Rogers Screenprinting EMB Inc............. G 910 628-1983
Fairmont (G-4504)

Tapped Tees LLC.............................. G 919 943-9692
Durham (G-4259)

Textile Printing Inc........................... G 704 521-8099
Charlotte (G-2909)

PRINTING: Screen, Manmade Fiber & Silk, Broadwoven Fabric

Custom Screens Inc........................... G 336 427-0265
Madison (G-7985)

Gaston Screen Printing Inc.................. G 704 399-0459
Charlotte (G-2191)

Visigraphix Inc................................. G 336 882-1935
Colfax (G-3292)

PRINTING: Thermography

Endaxi Company Inc.......................... E 919 467-8895
Morrisville (G-8972)

Laru Industries Inc........................... G 704 821-7503
Indian Trail (G-7087)

PROFESSIONAL EQPT & SPLYS, WHOLESALE: Engineers', NEC

Sharpe Images Properties Inc.............. E 336 724-2871
Winston Salem (G-13334)

PROFESSIONAL EQPT & SPLYS, WHOLESALE: Optical Goods

Optical Place Inc.............................. E 336 274-1300
Greensboro (G-5725)

PROFESSIONAL INSTRUMENT REPAIR SVCS

Measurement Controls Inc................... F 704 921-1101
Charlotte (G-2484)

PROFILE SHAPES: Unsupported Plastics

American Extruded Plastics Inc............. E 336 274-1131
Greensboro (G-5356)

M2 Optics Inc.................................. G 919 342-5619
Raleigh (G-10264)

Plastic Technology Inc....................... E 828 328-8570
Conover (G-3545)

Plastic Technology Inc....................... F 828 328-2201
Hickory (G-6414)

Precise Technology Inc....................... G 704 576-9527
Charlotte (G-2656)

Robetex Inc..................................... F 910 671-8787
Lumberton (G-7970)

Roechling Indus Gastonia LP................ C 704 922-7814
Dallas (G-3686)

United Plastics Corporation................. C 336 786-2127
Mount Airy (G-9192)

Weener Plastics Inc........................... D 252 206-1400
Wilson (G-13045)

PROMOTION SVCS

822tees Inc..................................... G 910 822-8337
Fayetteville (G-4541)

Apple Rock Advg & Prom Inc................ E 336 232-4800
Greensboro (G-5366)

PROPERTY DAMAGE INSURANCE

Discovery Insurance Company.............. E 800 876-1492
Kinston *(G-7405)*

PROTECTION EQPT: Lightning

Capital Lghtning Prtection Inc................ G 919 832-5574
Raleigh *(G-9968)*

Dehn Inc... F 772 460-9315
Mooresville *(G-8654)*

Lightning Prtction Systems LLC............ D 252 213-9900
Raleigh *(G-10256)*

PROTECTIVE FOOTWEAR: Rubber Or Plastic

Winstn-Slem Inds For Blind Inc.............. B 336 759-0551
Winston Salem *(G-13398)*

PUBLIC RELATIONS & PUBLICITY SVCS

Ed Kemp Associates Inc........................ G 336 869-2155
High Point *(G-6604)*

Inform Inc.. F 828 322-7766
Hickory *(G-6368)*

PUBLIC RELATIONS SVCS

Inspire Creative Studios Inc.................. G 910 395-0200
Wilmington *(G-12818)*

S & A Cherokee LLC............................ E 919 674-6020
Cary *(G-1443)*

PUBLISHERS: Art Copy & Poster

Cedar Hill Studio & Gallery.................... G 828 456-6344
Waynesville *(G-12453)*

Klazzy Magazine Inc............................ G 704 293-8321
Charlotte *(G-2399)*

PUBLISHERS: Telephone & Other Directory

1 Click Web Solutions LLC.................... E 910 790-9330
Wilmington *(G-12684)*

Mountaineer Yellowpages...................... G 866 758-0123
Huntersville *(G-7018)*

School Directorease LLC...................... G 240 206-6273
Charlotte *(G-2768)*

SRI Ventures Inc................................. F 919 427-1681
Sanford *(G-11237)*

Tarheel Publishing Co.......................... F 919 553-9042
Clayton *(G-3173)*

PUBLISHING & BROADCASTING: Internet Only

Domco Technology LLC........................ G 888 834-8541
Barnardsville *(G-691)*

Fit1media LLC.................................... G 919 925-2200
Raleigh *(G-10110)*

Hearsay Guides LLC............................ G 336 584-1440
Elon *(G-4470)*

Imleagues LLC................................... F 919 617-1113
Wake Forest *(G-12282)*

Lookwhatqmade LLC............................ G 980 330-1995
Charlotte *(G-2434)*

Norsan Media LLC............................... E 704 494-7181
Charlotte *(G-2573)*

Outer Banks Internet Inc...................... G 252 441-6698
Kill Devil Hills *(G-7318)*

Timberlake Ventures Inc...................... G 704 896-7499
Wilmington *(G-12940)*

Training Industry Inc........................... D 919 653-4990
Raleigh *(G-10555)*

Yeeka LLC... G 919 308-9826
Durham *(G-4316)*

PUBLISHING & PRINTING: Art Copy

Document Imaging Systems Inc............ G 919 460-9440
Raleigh *(G-10054)*

Land and Loft LLC............................... G 315 560-7060
Raleigh *(G-10244)*

PUBLISHING & PRINTING: Books

International Society Automtn................ E 919 206-4176
Research Triangle Pa *(G-10713)*

Lulu Press Inc.................................... D 919 447-3290
Durham *(G-4111)*

Lulu Technology Circus Inc................... E 919 459-5858
Morrisville *(G-9015)*

Tan Books and Publishers Inc.............. G 704 731-0651
Charlotte *(G-2898)*

Two of A Kind Publishing LLC............... G 704 497-2879
Charlotte *(G-2955)*

PUBLISHING & PRINTING: Directories, NEC

Deverger Systems Inc.......................... G 919 201-5146
Asheville *(G-487)*

Strawbridge Studios Inc....................... D 919 286-9512
Durham *(G-4252)*

PUBLISHING & PRINTING: Directories, Telephone

University Directories LLC..................... D 800 743-5556
Durham *(G-4290)*

PUBLISHING & PRINTING: Magazines: publishing & printing

Greater Wilmington Business................ G 910 343-8600
Wilmington *(G-12796)*

Knight Communications Inc................... F 704 568-7804
Indian Trail *(G-7086)*

M&J Oldco Inc.................................... D 336 854-0309
Greensboro *(G-5669)*

Magazine Nakia Lashawn...................... G 919 875-1156
Raleigh *(G-10266)*

N2 Company Inc................................. E 910 202-0917
Wilmington *(G-12856)*

News and Observer Pubg Co................ A 919 829-4500
Raleigh *(G-10331)*

Obbc Inc... G 252 261-0612
Kitty Hawk *(G-7446)*

Randall-Reilly LLC.............................. C 704 814-1390
Charlotte *(G-2688)*

Red Hand Media LLC........................... F 704 523-6987
Charlotte *(G-2698)*

Rose Media Inc................................... F 919 736-1154
Goldsboro *(G-5241)*

Shannon Media Inc.............................. F 919 933-1551
Chapel Hill *(G-1570)*

Todays Charlotte Woman...................... G 704 521-6872
Charlotte *(G-2925)*

PUBLISHING & PRINTING: Music, Book

Kindermusik International Inc................ E 800 628-5687
Greensboro *(G-5648)*

Music Matters Inc............................... G 336 272-5303
Greensboro *(G-5702)*

PUBLISHING & PRINTING: Newsletters, Business Svc

Ft Media Holdings LLC......................... F 336 605-0121
Greensboro *(G-5542)*

Savvy - Discountscom News Ltr............ F 252 729-8691
Smyrna *(G-11471)*

PUBLISHING & PRINTING: Newspapers

ACC Sports Journal............................. G 919 846-7502
Raleigh *(G-9871)*

Advantage Newspaper.......................... E 910 323-0349
Fayetteville *(G-4545)*

Alameen A Haqq................................. G 336 965-8339
Greensboro *(G-5347)*

Anson Express................................... G 704 694-2480
Wadesboro *(G-12233)*

Apg/East LLC.................................... C 252 329-9500
Greenville *(G-5937)*

Asheville Citizen-Times........................ F 828 252-5611
Asheville *(G-434)*

Asheville Global Report........................ G 828 236-3103
Asheville *(G-437)*

Benmot Publishing Company Inc.......... G 919 658-9456
Mount Olive *(G-9247)*

Black Mountain News Inc...................... G 828 669-8727
Black Mountain *(G-861)*

Business Journals............................... G 704 371-3248
Charlotte *(G-1820)*

Camp Lejeune Globe............................ F 910 939-0705
Jacksonville *(G-7119)*

Cape Fear Newspapers Inc................... G 910 285-2178
Wallace *(G-12319)*

Carolinian Pubg Group LLC.................. G 919 834-5558
Raleigh *(G-9980)*

Carteret Publishing Company................ D 252 726-7081
Morehead City *(G-8823)*

Catawba Vly Youth Soccer Assoc.......... G 828 234-7082
Hickory *(G-6291)*

Catholic News and Herald.................... G 704 370-3333
Charlotte *(G-1867)*

Champion Media LLC........................... C 910 506-3021
Laurinburg *(G-7496)*

Charlotte Observer.............................. D 704 358-5000
Charlotte *(G-1896)*

Charlotte Observer Pubg Co................. E 704 987-3660
Charlotte *(G-1897)*

Charlotte Observer Pubg Co................. E 704 572-0747
Charlotte *(G-1898)*

Charlotte Observer Pubg Co................. E 704 358-6020
Matthews *(G-8105)*

Charlotte Post Pubg Co Inc.................. F 704 376-0496
Charlotte *(G-1904)*

Chatham News Publishing Co............... G 919 663-4042
Siler City *(G-11405)*

Chronicle Mill Land LLC....................... G 704 527-3227
Gastonia *(G-5021)*

Chronicles... G 252 617-1774
Jacksonville *(G-7121)*

Community First Media Inc................... G 704 482-4142
Shelby *(G-11323)*

Community Newspapers Inc.................. G 828 743-5101
Cashiers *(G-1490)*

Community Newspapers Inc.................. G 828 369-3430
Franklin *(G-4822)*

Community Newspapers Inc.................. G 828 389-8431
Hayesville *(G-6140)*

Community Newspapers Inc.................. G 828 479-3383
Robbinsville *(G-10758)*

Community Newspapers Inc.................. G 828 765-7169
Spruce Pine *(G-11568)*

County Press Inc................................. G 919 894-2112
Benson *(G-787)*

Cox Nrth Crlina Pblcations Inc.............. G 252 482-4418
Edenton *(G-4364)*

Cox Nrth Crlina Pblcations Inc.............. C 252 335-0841
Elizabeth City *(G-4385)*

Cox Nrth Crlina Pblcations Inc.............. D 252 792-1181
Williamston *(G-12669)*

Cox Nrth Crlina Pblcations Inc.............. C 252 329-9643
Greenville *(G-5961)*

PRODUCT

Daily Courier	G 828 245-6431	Lumina News	G 910 256-6569
Rutherfordton *(G-10982)*		Wilmington *(G-12841)*	
Daily Living Solutions Inc	G 704 614-0977	Mc Clatchy Interactive USA	G 919 861-1200
Charlotte *(G-2015)*		Raleigh *(G-10284)*	
Db North Carolina Holdings Inc	E 910 323-4848	McDowell Lfac	F 828 289-5553
Fayetteville *(G-4585)*		Marion *(G-8055)*	
Denton Orator	G 336 859-3131	Media Wilimington Co	G 910 791-0688
Denton *(G-3746)*		Wilmington *(G-12851)*	
Dolan LLC	F 919 829-9333	Mooresville NC	G 704 909-6459
Raleigh *(G-10055)*		Mooresville *(G-8726)*	
Ellis Publishing Company Inc	G 252 444-1999	Mountain Times Inc	G 336 246-6397
New Bern *(G-9367)*		West Jefferson *(G-12567)*	
Epi Group Llc	B 843 577-7111	Mullen Publications Inc	F 704 527-5111
Durham *(G-4029)*		Charlotte *(G-2527)*	
Franklin County Newspapers Inc	G 919 496-6503	News & Record	G 336 627-1781
Louisburg *(G-7915)*		Reidsville *(G-10696)*	
Gannett Media Corp	G 828 649-1075	News 14 Carolina	G 704 973-5700
Marshall *(G-8080)*		Charlotte *(G-2559)*	
Gannett Media Corp	F 919 467-1402	News and Observer Pubg Co	E 919 894-4170
Morrisville *(G-8981)*		Benson *(G-795)*	
Gastonia	G 704 377-3687	News and Observer Pubg Co	E 919 419-6500
Gastonia *(G-5052)*		Durham *(G-4148)*	
Granville Publishing Co Inc	G 919 528-2393	News and Observer Pubg Co	E 919 829-8903
Creedmoor *(G-3649)*		Garner *(G-4949)*	
Greensboro News & Record LLC	A 336 373-7000	News and Observer Pubg Co	A 919 829-4500
Greensboro *(G-5577)*		Raleigh *(G-10331)*	
Greensboro Voice	F 336 255-1006	Next Magazine	G 910 609-0638
Greensboro *(G-5579)*		Fayetteville *(G-4645)*	
Grey Area News	G 919 637-6973	Norman E Clark	G 336 573-9629
Zebulon *(G-13510)*		Stoneville *(G-11824)*	
Halifax Media Group	F 704 869-1700	Observer News Enterprise Inc	G 828 464-0221
Gastonia *(G-5057)*		Newton *(G-9483)*	
Hendersnvlle Affrdbl Hsing Cor	F 828 692-6175	Paxton Media Group	G 704 289-1541
Hendersonville *(G-6215)*		Monroe *(G-8540)*	
Henderson Newspapers Inc	F 252 436-2700	Pilot LLC	G 864 430-6337
Henderson *(G-6158)*		Southern Pines *(G-11504)*	
Herald Huntersville	G 704 766-2100	Pilot LLC	D 910 692-7271
Huntersville *(G-6997)*		Southern Pines *(G-11505)*	
Herald Printing Co Inc	G 252 537-2505	PMG-DH Company	C 919 419-6500
Roanoke Rapids *(G-10738)*		Durham *(G-4185)*	
Hickory Publishing Co Inc	E 828 322-4510	Post Publishing Company	D 704 633-8950
Hickory *(G-6352)*		Salisbury *(G-11103)*	
High Country Media LLC	G 828 733-2448	Pride Publishing & Typsg Inc	G 704 531-9988
Newland *(G-9430)*		Charlotte *(G-2666)*	
High Point Enterprise Inc	G 336 434-2716	Raleigh Downtowner	G 919 821-9000
High Point *(G-6649)*		Raleigh *(G-10422)*	
High Point Enterprise Inc	F 336 883-2839	Record Publishing Company	F 910 230-1948
High Point *(G-6650)*		Dunn *(G-3866)*	
Highcorp Incorporated	E 910 642-4104	Rhinoceros Times	G 336 763-4170
Whiteville *(G-12584)*		Greensboro *(G-5787)*	
Horizon Publications Inc	F 828 464-0221	Richard D Stewart	G 919 284-2295
Newton *(G-9473)*		Kenly *(G-7236)*	
In Greensboro	G 336 621-0279	Richmond Observer LLP	G 910 817-3169
Greensboro *(G-5615)*		Rockingham *(G-10789)*	
Indy Week	G 919 832-8774	Robert Laskowski	G 203 732-0846
Raleigh *(G-10192)*		New Bern *(G-9391)*	
Inform Inc	F 828 322-7766	Rotary Club Statesville	F 704 872-6851
Hickory *(G-6368)*		Statesville *(G-11759)*	
Jamestown News	G 336 841-4933	Ryjak Enterprises LLC	G 910 638-0716
Jamestown *(G-7170)*		Southern Pines *(G-11507)*	
Jones Media	G 828 264-3612	Seaside Press Co Inc	G 910 458-8156
Boone *(G-928)*		Carolina Beach *(G-1264)*	
Journal Vacuum Science & Tech	G 919 361-2787	Seven Lakes News Corporation	G 910 685-0320
Cary *(G-1381)*		West End *(G-12559)*	
Kinston Free Press Company	E 252 527-3191	Shelby Freedom Star Inc	D 704 484-7000
Kinston *(G-7417)*		Shelby *(G-11377)*	
La Noticia Inc	F 704 568-6966	Shopper	G 252 633-1153
Charlotte *(G-2406)*		New Bern *(G-9396)*	
Ledger Publishing Company	G 919 693-2646	Snap Publications LLC	G 336 274-8531
Oxford *(G-9619)*		Greensboro *(G-5819)*	
Lincoln Herald LLC	G 704 735-3620	Spectacular Publishing Inc	G 919 672-0289
Lincolnton *(G-7838)*		Durham *(G-4244)*	

Statesville High	G 704 873-3491
Statesville *(G-11778)*	
Statesville LLC	G 704 872-3303
Statesville *(G-11779)*	
Sylva Herald and Ruralite	G 828 586-2611
Sylva *(G-11900)*	
Sylva Herald Pubg Co Incthe	F 828 586-2611
Sylva *(G-11901)*	
Tallahassee Democrat	G 919 832-9430
Raleigh *(G-10532)*	
Times Journal Inc	G 828 682-4067
Burnsville *(G-1193)*	
Topsail Voice LLC	G 910 270-2944
Hampstead *(G-6078)*	
Triangle Tribune	G 704 376-0496
Durham *(G-4282)*	
Tribune Papers Inc	G 828 606-5050
Asheville *(G-624)*	
Tryon Newsmedia LLC	G 828 859-9151
Tryon *(G-12179)*	
Tucker Production Incorporated	G 828 322-1036
Hickory *(G-6475)*	
Twin Cy Kwnis Fndtion Wnstn-SL	G 336 784-1649
Winston Salem *(G-13378)*	
Up & Coming Magazine	G 910 391-3859
Fayetteville *(G-4689)*	
Virginn-Plot Mdia Cmpanies LLC	G 252 441-3628
Nags Head *(G-9305)*	
Wake Forest Gazette	G 919 556-3409
Wake Forest *(G-12313)*	
Washington News Publishing Co	F 252 946-2144
Washington *(G-12421)*	
Wayne Printing Company Inc	F 919 778-2211
Goldsboro *(G-5252)*	
West Stkes Wldcat Grdron CLB I	G 336 985-6152
King *(G-7339)*	
Wick Communications Co	E 252 537-2505
Roanoke Rapids *(G-10747)*	
Wilmington Journal Company	G 910 762-5502
Wilmington *(G-12949)*	
Winstn-Slem Chronicle Pubg Inc	G 336 722-8624
Winston Salem *(G-13397)*	
Winston Salem Journal	E 336 727-7211
Winston Salem *(G-13401)*	
Womack Newspaper Inc	G 336 316-1231
Greensboro *(G-5923)*	
Wtvd Television LLC	C 919 683-1111
Durham *(G-4313)*	
Yancy Common Times Journal	G 828 682-2120
Burnsville *(G-1195)*	

PUBLISHING & PRINTING: Pamphlets

Readable Communications Inc	G 919 876-5260
Raleigh *(G-10434)*	

PUBLISHING & PRINTING: Shopping News

News and Observer Pubg Co	A 919 829-4500
Raleigh *(G-10331)*	

PUBLISHING & PRINTING: Textbooks

Carson-Dellosa Publishing LLC	D 336 632-0084
Greensboro *(G-5433)*	

PUBLISHING & PRINTING: Trade Journals

Capre Omnimedia LLC	G 917 460-3572
Wilmington *(G-12731)*	
Ft Media Holdings LLC	F 336 605-0121
Greensboro *(G-5542)*	

PUBLISHING & PRINTING: Yearbooks

Herff Jones LLC	G 704 845-3355
Charlotte *(G-2271)*	

2025 Harris North Carolina
Manufacturers Directory

(G-0000) Company's Geographic Section entry number

PULLEYS: Power Transmission

Cavotec USA Inc..................................... E 704 873-3009
Mooresville *(G-8635)*

PULP MILLS

Arauco - NA... G 910 569-7020
Biscoe *(G-846)*

Broad River Forest Products................. G 828 287-8003
Rutherfordton *(G-10979)*

Buckeye Technologies Inc...................... C 704 822-6400
Mount Holly *(G-9220)*

Ingram Woodyards Inc............................ F 910 556-1250
Sanford *(G-11195)*

North Carolina Converting LLC............. G 704 871-2912
Statesville *(G-11739)*

Westrock Mwv LLC.................................. G 919 334-3200
Raleigh *(G-10606)*

Westrock Paper and Packg LLC............. B 252 533-6000
Roanoke Rapids *(G-10745)*

Weyerhaeuser Company.......................... E 252 633-7100
Vanceboro *(G-12223)*

PULP MILLS: Mechanical & Recycling Processing

Martin Materials Inc................................ G 336 697-1800
Greensboro *(G-5680)*

Old School Crushing Co Inc.................... G 919 661-0011
Garner *(G-4950)*

PUMP JACKS & OTHER PUMPING EQPT: Indl

Circor Precision Metering LLC.............. A 919 774-7667
Sanford *(G-11164)*

Enovis Corporation................................ F 704 289-6511
Monroe *(G-8484)*

Flowserve US Inc.................................... F 972 443-6500
Raleigh *(G-10114)*

PUMPS & PARTS: Indl

1st Choice Service Inc........................... G 704 913-7685
Cherryville *(G-3058)*

Allied/Carter Machining Inc.................... G 704 784-1253
Concord *(G-3310)*

Clyde Union (us) Inc............................... C 704 808-3000
Charlotte *(G-1934)*

Colfax Pump Group................................ C 704 289-6511
Monroe *(G-8463)*

G Denver and Co LLC............................ E 704 896-4000
Davidson *(G-3705)*

Hurst Jaws of Life Inc............................ C 704 487-6961
Shelby *(G-11345)*

Kral USA Inc... G 704 814-6164
Matthews *(G-8125)*

Primax Usa Inc....................................... G 704 587-3377
Charlotte *(G-2667)*

Stockholm Corporation.......................... E 704 552-9314
Charlotte *(G-2869)*

PUMPS & PUMPING EQPT REPAIR SVCS

McKinney Electric & Mch Co Inc............ G 828 765-7910
Spruce Pine *(G-11581)*

Motor Shop Inc....................................... G 704 867-8488
Gastonia *(G-5103)*

PUMPS & PUMPING EQPT WHOLESALERS

Air Control Inc.. E 252 492-2300
Henderson *(G-6147)*

Bfs Industries LLC.................................. E 919 575-6711
Butner *(G-1199)*

Bornemann Pumps Inc............................ G 704 849-8636
Matthews *(G-8100)*

Central East Services Inc....................... G 252 883-9629
Rocky Mount *(G-10827)*

Chichibone Inc.. G 919 785-0090
Morrisville *(G-8957)*

Chichibone Inc.. F 919 785-0090
Kernersville *(G-7256)*

Circor Precision Metering LLC.............. D 704 289-6511
Monroe *(G-8458)*

Circor Pumps North America LLC.......... D 704 289-6511
Monroe *(G-8459)*

Clydeunion Pumps Inc............................ E 704 808-3848
Charlotte *(G-1936)*

Dynisco Instruments LLC....................... E 828 326-9888
Hickory *(G-6325)*

Flowserve Corporation........................... E 704 494-0497
Charlotte *(G-2168)*

Flowserve Corporation........................... G 910 371-9011
Leland *(G-7543)*

Haldex Inc.. C 828 652-9308
Marion *(G-8042)*

Hayward Industries Inc........................... D 336 712-9900
Clemmons *(G-3188)*

Hayward Industries Inc........................... A 336 712-9900
Clemmons *(G-3189)*

Hayward Industries Inc........................... B 704 837-8002
Charlotte *(G-2265)*

IMO Industries Inc.................................. D 301 323-9000
Monroe *(G-8503)*

Ingersoll Rand Inc.................................. G 828 375-8240
Mocksville *(G-8371)*

INGERSOLL RAND INC............................ A 704 896-4000
Davidson *(G-3709)*

Ingersoll-Rand Company........................ D 704 655-4836
Charlotte *(G-2336)*

Ingersoll-Rand Indus US Inc.................. D 704 896-4000
Davidson *(G-3710)*

James M Pleasants Company Inc............ E 800 365-9010
Greensboro *(G-5633)*

Maag Reduction Inc................................ E 704 716-9000
Charlotte *(G-2445)*

Marley Company LLC.............................. C 704 752-4400
Charlotte *(G-2459)*

Merrill Resources Inc............................. G 828 877-4450
Penrose *(G-9662)*

Opw Fling Cntnment Systems Inc.......... E 919 209-2280
Smithfield *(G-11457)*

Raymond Brown Well Company Inc........ G 336 374-4999
Danbury *(G-3695)*

SL Liquidation LLC................................. B 910 353-3666
Jacksonville *(G-7147)*

SPX Flow Inc.. C 704 752-4400
Charlotte *(G-2847)*

Trs-Sesco LLC.. D 336 996-2220
Kernersville *(G-7310)*

Truflo Pumps Inc.................................... F 336 664-9225
Greensboro *(G-5882)*

Xaloy Extrusion LLC.............................. E 828 326-9888
Hickory *(G-6492)*

Xylem Water Solutions USA Inc............. D 704 409-9700
Charlotte *(G-3036)*

PUMPS: Domestic, Water Or Sump

Camp S Well and Pump Co Inc.............. G 828 453-7322
Ellenboro *(G-4456)*

Pentair Water Pool and Spa Inc............. D 919 463-4640
Cary *(G-1417)*

Pentair Water Pool and Spa Inc............. A 919 566-8000
Sanford *(G-11217)*

PUMPS: Gasoline, Measuring Or Dispensing

Balcrank Corporation............................. E 800 747-5300
Weaverville *(G-12483)*

Gilbarco Inc.. A 336 547-5000
Greensboro *(G-5560)*

PUMPS: Measuring & Dispensing

Aptargroup Inc.. C 828 970-6300
Lincolnton *(G-7815)*

Circor Precision Metering LLC.............. A 919 774-7667
Sanford *(G-11164)*

Gasboy International Inc.......................... F 336 547-5000
Greensboro *(G-5548)*

Marley Company LLC.............................. C 704 752-4400
Charlotte *(G-2459)*

Nelson Holdings Nc Inc.......................... F 828 322-9226
Hickory *(G-6399)*

PUMPS: Oil, Measuring Or Dispensing

Samoa Corporation................................ E 828 645-2290
Weaverville *(G-12502)*

PURIFICATION & DUST COLLECTION EQPT

Bwxt Investment Company..................... E 704 625-4900
Charlotte *(G-1824)*

Dustcontrol Inc....................................... F 910 395-1808
Wilmington *(G-12768)*

Envirco Corporation............................... G 919 775-2201
Sanford *(G-11177)*

Filtration Technology Inc........................ G 336 294-5655
Greensboro *(G-5531)*

Mikropul LLC.. G 704 998-2600
Charlotte *(G-2502)*

Ziehl-Abegg Inc...................................... C 336 934-9339
Winston Salem *(G-13410)*

QUILTING: Individuals

Owens Quilting Inc................................. G 828 695-1495
Newton *(G-9485)*

RACE CAR OWNERS

Garage Shop LLC................................... F 980 500-0583
Denver *(G-3784)*

RACEWAYS

Maa Umiya Inc.. G 410 818-6811
Hickory *(G-6390)*

RACKS: Pallet, Exc Wood

Wireway/Husky Corp............................... C 704 483-1135
Denver *(G-3817)*

RADIO BROADCASTING & COMMUNICATIONS EQPT

Ascom (us) Inc.. C 877 712-7266
Morrisville *(G-8933)*

CBS Radio Holdings Inc.......................... E 704 319-9369
Charlotte *(G-1870)*

Lea Aid Acquisition Company.................. G 919 872-6210
Spring Hope *(G-11557)*

Richmond County Gmrs Inc.................... G 910 461-0260
Hamlet *(G-6062)*

T-Metrics Inc.. E 704 523-9583
Charlotte *(G-2896)*

RADIO BROADCASTING STATIONS

Latino Communications Inc.................... F 704 319-5044
Charlotte *(G-2409)*

Latino Communications Inc.................... F 919 645-1680
Raleigh *(G-10249)*

Latino Communications Inc.................... D 336 714-2823
Winston Salem *(G-13231)*

Lyon Company.. F 919 787-0024
Wadesboro *(G-12248)*

PRODUCT

RADIO COMMUNICATIONS: Airborne Eqpt

Amphenol Antenna Solutions Inc............ E 828 324-6971
Conover *(G-3489)*

RAILINGS: Prefabricated, Metal

Alamance Steel Fabricators.................... G 336 887-3015
High Point *(G-6513)*

RAILINGS: Wood

Piedmont Stairworks LLC....................... G 704 697-0259
Charlotte *(G-2637)*

RAILROAD EQPT

Frit Car Inc... E 252 638-2675
Bridgeton *(G-984)*

Knorr Brake Truck Systems Co............. A 888 836-6922
Salisbury *(G-11081)*

Twin Oaks Service South Inc................. G 704 914-7142
Shelby *(G-11387)*

RAILROAD EQPT & SPLYS WHOLESALERS

Harsco Rail LLC..................................... G 980 960-2624
Charlotte *(G-2262)*

Kck Holding Corp.................................. E 336 513-0002
Burlington *(G-1114)*

RAILROAD EQPT, EXC LOCOMOTIVES

Railroad Friction Pdts Corp................... C 910 844-9709
Maxton *(G-8205)*

RAILROAD EQPT: Brakes, Air & Vacuum

Kck Holding Corp.................................. E 336 513-0002
Burlington *(G-1114)*

New York Air Brake LLC........................ D 315 786-5200
Salisbury *(G-11097)*

RAILROAD MAINTENANCE & REPAIR SVCS

Harsco Rail LLC..................................... G 980 960-2624
Charlotte *(G-2262)*

RAILROAD RELATED EQPT

Harsco Metro Rail LLC.......................... G 980 960-2624
Charlotte *(G-2261)*

RAILROAD RELATED EQPT: Railway Track

Harsco Rail LLC..................................... G 980 960-2624
Charlotte *(G-2262)*

St Engineering Leeboy Inc.................... B 704 966-3300
Lincolnton *(G-7856)*

RAILS: Steel Or Iron

Steel City Services LLC........................ F 919 698-2407
Durham *(G-4249)*

RAMPS: Prefabricated Metal

Quick-Deck Inc..................................... E 704 888-0327
Locust *(G-7898)*

Veon Inc... F 252 623-2102
Washington *(G-12418)*

RAZORS, RAZOR BLADES

Edgewell Per Care Brands LLC.............. E 336 672-4500
Asheboro *(G-347)*

Edgewell Per Care Brands LLC.............. E 336 629-1581
Asheboro *(G-348)*

Edgewell Per Care Brands LLC.............. G 336 672-4500
Asheboro *(G-349)*

Procter & Gamble Mfg Co..................... D 336 954-0000
Greensboro *(G-5767)*

REAL ESTATE AGENCIES & BROKERS

Green Waste Management LLC.............. G 704 289-0720
Charlotte *(G-2239)*

Joe Robin Darnell................................ G 704 482-1186
Shelby *(G-11350)*

Lyon Company....................................... F 919 787-0024
Wadesboro *(G-12248)*

REAL ESTATE AGENTS & MANAGERS

Brookhurst Associates.......................... G 919 792-0987
Raleigh *(G-9961)*

Brunswick Beacon Inc........................... G 910 754-6890
Shallotte *(G-11300)*

Jdh Capital LLC.................................... F 704 357-1220
Charlotte *(G-2365)*

Lindley Laboratories Inc........................ F 336 449-7521
Gibsonville *(G-5181)*

Town of Maggie Valley Inc..................... F 828 926-0145
Maggie Valley *(G-8006)*

REAL ESTATE INVESTMENT TRUSTS

Anew Look Homes LLC.......................... F 800 796-5152
Hickory *(G-6264)*

REAL ESTATE LISTING SVCS

Fathom Holdings Inc............................. E 888 455-6040
Cary *(G-1362)*

RECEIVERS: Radio Communications

JPS Intrprbility Solutions Inc................. E 919 332-5009
Raleigh *(G-10223)*

RECORDS & TAPES: Prerecorded

Cda Inc... C
Charlotte *(G-1879)*

Digital Recorders Inc............................ C 919 361-2155
Morrisville *(G-8964)*

Operable Inc... G 757 617-0935
Wake Forest *(G-12288)*

Puny Human LLC.................................. G 919 420-4538
Raleigh *(G-10409)*

Reel-Scout Inc...................................... F 704 348-1484
Charlotte *(G-2702)*

SMC Corporation of America................. F 704 947-7556
Huntersville *(G-7055)*

Sony Music Holdings Inc....................... G 336 886-1807
High Point *(G-6785)*

Turnsmith LLC...................................... G 919 667-9804
Chapel Hill *(G-1582)*

Xdri Inc.. G 919 361-2155
Durham *(G-4315)*

RECREATIONAL VEHICLE PARTS & ACCESS STORES

Derrow Enterprises Inc......................... G 252 635-3375
New Bern *(G-9364)*

REFINING: Petroleum

Harvey Fertilizer and Gas Co................ F 919 731-2474
Goldsboro *(G-5222)*

Murphy USA Inc.................................... E 828 758-7055
Lenoir *(G-7628)*

Norcor Technologies Corp..................... G 704 309-4101
Greensboro *(G-5712)*

Sg-Clw Inc... F 336 865-4980
Winston Salem *(G-13331)*

Stop N Go LLC...................................... G 919 523-7355
Morrisville *(G-9059)*

Volta Group Corporation LLC................ E 919 637-0273
Raleigh *(G-10593)*

Warren Oil Company LLC....................... D 910 892-6456
Dunn *(G-3871)*

REFRACTORIES: Alumina Fused

Vesuvius Nc LLC................................... D 336 578-7728
Graham *(G-5288)*

REFRACTORIES: Clay

Harbisonwalker Intl Inc......................... G 704 599-6540
Charlotte *(G-2255)*

Oldcastle Retail Inc.............................. B 704 799-8083
Cornelius *(G-3616)*

Pyrotek Incorporated............................ E 704 642-1993
Salisbury *(G-11108)*

Resco Products Inc............................... E 336 299-1441
Greensboro *(G-5782)*

REFRACTORIES: Nonclay

General Electric Company...................... A 910 675-5000
Wilmington *(G-12785)*

Vesuvius USA Corporation..................... D 412 429-1800
Charlotte *(G-2982)*

Virginia Carolina Refr Inc...................... G 704 216-0223
Salisbury *(G-11133)*

REFRACTORY MATERIALS WHOLESALERS

Harbisonwalker Intl Inc......................... G 704 599-6540
Charlotte *(G-2255)*

REFRIGERATION & HEATING EQUIPMENT

Aqua Logic Inc..................................... E 858 292-4773
Monroe *(G-8428)*

Beverage-Air Corporation...................... E 336 245-6400
Winston Salem *(G-13104)*

Buhler Inc.. C 800 722-7483
Cary *(G-1316)*

Carolina Products Inc............................ E 704 364-9029
Charlotte *(G-1854)*

Carrier Corporation.............................. G 704 494-2600
Morrisville *(G-8948)*

City Compressor Rebuilders.................. E 704 947-1811
Charlotte *(G-1920)*

Dienes Apparatus Inc............................ G 704 525-3770
Pineville *(G-9724)*

Hoffman Hydronics LLC........................ F 336 294-3838
Greensboro *(G-5603)*

James M Pleasants Company Inc........... E 800 365-9010
Greensboro *(G-5633)*

Morris & Associates Inc........................ D 919 582-9200
Garner *(G-4947)*

Parameter Generation Ctrl Inc.............. E 828 669-8717
Black Mountain *(G-870)*

Spartan Systems LLC........................... F 336 946-1244
Advance *(G-39)*

Supreme Murphy Trck Bodies Inc.......... C 252 291-2191
Wilson *(G-13033)*

Thermo King Corporation...................... E 732 652-6774
Davidson *(G-3720)*

Trane US Inc... G 828 277-8664
Asheville *(G-623)*

Trane US Inc... C 704 525-9600
Charlotte *(G-2934)*

Trane US Inc... F 704 697-9006
Charlotte *(G-2935)*

Trane US Inc... G 336 273-6353
Greensboro *(G-5868)*

Trane US Inc... F 336 378-0670
Greensboro *(G-5869)*

Trane US Inc... G 919 781-0458
Morrisville *(G-9074)*

United Air Filter Company Corp............. E 704 334-5311
Charlotte *(G-2961)*

Wen Bray Heating & AC............................ G 828 267-0635
Hickory *(G-6489)*

REFRIGERATION EQPT & SPLYS WHOLESALERS

Bally Refrigerated Boxes Inc................. C 252 240-2829
Morehead City *(G-8815)*

REFRIGERATION EQPT: Complete

Afe Victory Inc... C 856 428-4200
Winston Salem *(G-13075)*

Arneg LLC.. D 336 956-5300
Lexington *(G-7656)*

Cooling Technology Inc.......................... G 704 596-4109
Cornelius *(G-3596)*

Middleby Marshall Inc............................ C 919 762-1000
Fuquay Varina *(G-4891)*

Pro Refrigeration Inc.............................. E 336 283-7281
Mocksville *(G-8385)*

W A Brown & Son Incorporated............. E 704 636-5131
Salisbury *(G-11134)*

REFRIGERATION SVC & REPAIR

Chichibone Inc.. F 919 785-0090
Kernersville *(G-7256)*

Daikin Applied Americas Inc.................. G 704 588-0087
Charlotte *(G-2014)*

Environmental Specialties LLC.............. D 919 829-9300
Raleigh *(G-10088)*

Trs-Sesco LLC.. D 336 996-2220
Kernersville *(G-7310)*

REFUSE SYSTEMS

Eastern Crlina Vctonal Ctr Inc.............. D 252 758-4188
Greenville *(G-5972)*

Global Ecosciences Inc.......................... G 252 631-6266
Wake Forest *(G-12278)*

Parkdale Mills Incorporated................... F 704 825-2529
Belmont *(G-760)*

Wastezero Inc... E 919 322-1208
Raleigh *(G-10599)*

REGULATORS: Power

Elster American Meter Company LLC.... F 402 873-8200
Charlotte *(G-2104)*

REHABILITATION CENTER, OUTPATIENT TREATMENT

Transylvnia Vcational Svcs Inc.............. D 828 884-1548
Fletcher *(G-4773)*

Transylvnia Vcational Svcs Inc.............. C 828 884-3195
Brevard *(G-983)*

REHABILITATION CTR, RESIDENTIAL WITH HEALTH CARE INCIDENTAL

Gladiator Enterprises Inc....................... G 336 944-6932
Greensboro *(G-5561)*

RELAYS & SWITCHES: Indl, Electric

Dozier Industrial Electric Inc................. G 252 451-0020
Rocky Mount *(G-10810)*

Stay Online LLC...................................... E 888 346-4688
Creedmoor *(G-3656)*

Te Connectivity Corporation................... F 828 338-1000
Fairview *(G-4514)*

RELAYS: Control Circuit, Ind

Aiken Development LLC.......................... G 828 572-4040
Lenoir *(G-7567)*

General Electric Company....................... F 919 563-7445
Mebane *(G-8241)*

General Electric Company....................... B 919 563-5561
Mebane *(G-8242)*

REMOVERS & CLEANERS

Delta Contractors Inc............................. F 817 410-9481
Linden *(G-7874)*

REMOVERS: Paint

Electric Glass Fiber Amer LLC.............. C 336 357-8151
Lexington *(G-7682)*

RENTAL SVCS: Electronic Eqpt, Exc Computers

Tarheel Monitoring LLC.......................... G 910 763-1490
Wilmington *(G-12936)*

RENTAL SVCS: Eqpt, Theatrical

Stage Decoration and Sups Inc............. G 336 621-5454
Greensboro *(G-5834)*

RENTAL SVCS: Sign

R O Givens Signs Inc............................. G 252 338-6578
Elizabeth City *(G-4407)*

RENTAL SVCS: Video Disk/Tape, To The General Public

Wen Bray Heating & AC.......................... G 828 267-0635
Hickory *(G-6489)*

RENTAL: Portable Toilet

Comer Sanitary Service Inc................... G 336 629-8311
Lexington *(G-7668)*

Readilite & Barricade Inc....................... F 919 231-8309
Raleigh *(G-10435)*

REPRODUCTION SVCS: Video Tape Or Disk

American Multimedia Inc........................ D 336 229-7101
Burlington *(G-1045)*

RESEARCH & DEVELOPMENT SVCS, COMMERCIAL: Engineering Lab

Advanced Non-Lethal Tech Inc.............. G 847 812-6450
Raleigh *(G-9880)*

Vortant Technologies LLC...................... G 828 645-1026
Weaverville *(G-12506)*

RESEARCH, DEVELOPMENT & TESTING SVCS, COMMERCIAL: Business

Konica Mnlta Hlthcare Amrcas I............ E 919 792-6420
Garner *(G-4935)*

Viztek LLC... E 919 792-6420
Garner *(G-4971)*

RESEARCH, DEVELOPMENT & TESTING SVCS, COMMERCIAL: Medical

Alcami Carolinas Corporation................ G 910 254-7000
Wilmington *(G-12696)*

Alcami Carolinas Corporation................ G 910 254-7000
Wilmington *(G-12697)*

Birth Tissue Recovery LLC.................... E 336 448-1910
Winston Salem *(G-13106)*

Gale Global Research Inc....................... G 910 795-8595
Leland *(G-7544)*

RESINS: Custom Compound Purchased

Avient Colorants USA LLC..................... D 704 331-7000
Charlotte *(G-1723)*

Borealis Compounds Inc......................... E 908 798-7497
Taylorsville *(G-11950)*

Crp Usa LLC.. F 704 660-0258
Mooresville *(G-8645)*

Hexpol Compounding NC Inc.................. A 704 872-1585
Statesville *(G-11710)*

Lubrizol Global Management Inc............ D 704 865-7451
Gastonia *(G-5080)*

Premix North Carolina LLC..................... G 704 412-7922
Dallas *(G-3682)*

Rutland Group Inc................................... C 704 553-0046
Pineville *(G-9752)*

Rutland Holdings LLC............................. E 704 553-0046
Pineville *(G-9753)*

Sealed Air Corporation........................... D 828 728-6610
Hudson *(G-6959)*

Sealed Air Corporation (us)................... A 201 791-7600
Charlotte *(G-2777)*

Teknor Apex Company............................ D 401 642-3598
Jamestown *(G-7180)*

Tru-Contour Inc....................................... G 704 455-8700
Concord *(G-3459)*

Zeon Technologies Inc........................... G 704 680-9160
Salisbury *(G-11138)*

RESTAURANT EQPT: Carts

Holders Restaurant Furniture................. G 828 754-8383
Lenoir *(G-7615)*

RESTAURANT EQPT: Sheet Metal

Captive-Aire Systems Inc...................... G 704 843-7215
Waxhaw *(G-12426)*

Captive-Aire Systems Inc...................... C 919 887-2721
Youngsville *(G-13468)*

Captive-Aire Systems Inc...................... C 919 882-2410
Raleigh *(G-9972)*

Custom Industries Inc............................ E 336 299-2885
Greensboro *(G-5481)*

RESTAURANTS: Full Svc, American

Booneshine Brewing Co Inc.................... G 828 263-4305
Boone *(G-901)*

RETAIL BAKERY: Cookies

Swirl Oakhurst LLC................................. G 704 258-1209
Charlotte *(G-2889)*

RETAIL BAKERY: Doughnuts

Krispy Kreme Doughnut Corp................. E 919 669-6151
Gastonia *(G-5074)*

Krispy Kreme Doughnut Corp................. E 336 854-8275
Greensboro *(G-5655)*

Krispy Kreme Doughnut Corp................. E 336 733-3780
Winston Salem *(G-13226)*

Krispy Kreme Doughnut Corp................. E 336 726-8908
Winston Salem *(G-13227)*

Krispy Kreme Doughnut Corp................. C 980 270-7117
Charlotte *(G-2402)*

Krispy Kreme Doughnuts Inc................. C 336 725-2981
Winston Salem *(G-13228)*

RETAIL BAKERY: Pretzels

SE Co-Brand Ventures LLC.................... G 704 598-9322
Charlotte *(G-2773)*

RETAIL STORES: Alcoholic Beverage Making Eqpt & Splys

DNB Humidifier Mfg Inc.......................... F 336 764-2076
Winston Salem *(G-13150)*

Js Linens and Curtain Outlet.................. F 704 871-1582
Statesville *(G-11722)*

Employee Codes: A=Over 500 employees, B=251-500
C=101-250, D=51-100, E=20-50, F=10-19, G=1-9

2025 Harris North Carolina
Manufacturers Directory

1185

PRODUCT

RETAIL STORES: Audio-Visual Eqpt & Splys

Integrated Info Systems Inc.................. F 919 488-5000
Youngsville (G-13476)

Moon Audio.. G 919 649-5018
Cary (G-1402)

Utd Technology Corp............................... G 704 612-0121
Mint Hill (G-8344)

RETAIL STORES: Business Machines & Eqpt

Danbartex LLC.. G 704 323-8728
Mooresville (G-8650)

Lynchs Office Supply Co Inc.................. F 252 537-6041
Roanoke Rapids (G-10740)

RETAIL STORES: Cleaning Eqpt & Splys

Busch Enterprises Inc............................ G 704 878-2067
Statesville (G-11673)

RETAIL STORES: Concrete Prdts, Precast

Craven Tire Inc....................................... G 252 633-0200
New Bern (G-9357)

RETAIL STORES: Cosmetics

Usrx LLC... E 980 221-1200
Charlotte (G-2969)

RETAIL STORES: Electronic Parts & Eqpt

Applied Drives Inc.................................. G 704 573-2324
Charlotte (G-1686)

RETAIL STORES: Flags

Heritage Flag LLC................................. G 910 725-1540
Southern Pines (G-11500)

RETAIL STORES: Foam & Foam Prdts

Carpenter Co.. D 828 464-9470
Conover (G-3501)

Guilford Fabricators Inc.......................... F 336 434-3163
High Point (G-6635)

Pregis LLC.. E 828 396-2373
Granite Falls (G-5319)

RETAIL STORES: Ice

Airgas Usa LLC...................................... G 919 544-1056
Durham (G-3884)

Herrin Bros Coal & Ice Co..................... G 704 332-2193
Charlotte (G-2275)

RETAIL STORES: Medical Apparatus & Splys

All 4 U Home Medical LLC..................... G 828 437-0684
Morganton (G-8849)

Custom Rehabilitation Spc Inc.............. G 910 471-2962
Wilmington (G-12758)

Medi Mall Inc.. G 877 501-6334
Fletcher (G-4753)

Rm Liquidation Inc................................. D 828 274-7996
Asheville (G-591)

Safeguard Medical Alarms Inc.............. F 312 506-2900
Huntersville (G-7052)

Tekni-Plex Inc... D 919 553-4151
Clayton (G-3174)

United Mobile Imaging Inc..................... G 800 983-9840
Clemmons (G-3207)

RETAIL STORES: Orthopedic & Prosthesis Applications

Bio-Tech Prsthtics Orthtics In................ G 336 768-3666
Winston Salem (G-13105)

Bio-Tech Prsthtics Orthtics In................ G 336 333-9081
Greensboro (G-5390)

Cape Fear Orthtics Prsthtics I............... G 910 483-0933
Fayetteville (G-4566)

Faith Prsthtc-Rthotic Svcs Inc.............. F 704 782-0908
Concord (G-3361)

RETAIL STORES: Perfumes & Colognes

Body Shop Inc.. C 919 554-4900
Wake Forest (G-12265)

RETAIL STORES: Pet Food

Wholesale Kennel Supply Co................. G 919 742-2515
Siler City (G-11427)

RETAIL STORES: Religious Goods

Free Will Bptst Press Fndtion................. F 252 746-6128
Ayden (G-657)

RETAIL STORES: Tents

Zingerle Group Usa Inc.......................... E 704 312-1600
Charlotte (G-3048)

RETAIL STORES: Water Purification Eqpt

Evoqua Water Technologies LLC........... E 919 477-2161
Durham (G-4031)

Scaltrol Inc... G 678 990-0858
Charlotte (G-2761)

Second Earth Inc.................................... G 336 740-9333
Greensboro (G-5804)

Solarbrook Water and Pwr Corp............ G 919 231-3205
Raleigh (G-10492)

REUPHOLSTERY & FURNITURE REPAIR

Bedex LLC.. E 336 617-6755
High Point (G-6544)

S Dorsett Upholstery Inc........................ G 336 472-7076
Thomasville (G-12070)

S Kivett Inc... F 910 592-0161
Clinton (G-3243)

Stone Marble Co Inc.............................. G 773 227-1161
Thomasville (G-12075)

Unique Office Solutions Inc.................. F 336 854-0900
Greensboro (G-5890)

RIVETS: Metal

Gesipa Fasteners Usa Inc...................... E 336 751-1555
Mocksville (G-8367)

ROAD CONSTRUCTION EQUIPMENT WHOLESALERS

Carolina Traffic Devices Inc................... F 704 588-7055
Charlotte (G-1860)

ROBOTS: Assembly Line

Design Tool Inc....................................... E 828 328-6414
Conover (G-3515)

Fanuc America Corporation................... D 704 596-5121
Huntersville (G-6988)

Keller Technology Corporation.............. E 704 875-1605
Huntersville (G-7007)

Southern Machine Services.................... G 919 658-9300
Mount Olive (G-9258)

Verity America LLC................................. G 347 960-4198
Chapel Hill (G-1589)

ROLLING MILL MACHINERY

Tecnofirma America Inc.......................... G 704 674-1296
Charlotte (G-2905)

ROLLING MILL ROLLS: Cast Steel

American Builders Anson Inc................. E 704 272-7655
Polkton (G-9811)

ROLLS & BLANKETS, PRINTERS': Rubber Or Rubberized Fabric

Andritz Fabrics and Rolls Inc................ F 919 556-7235
Raleigh (G-9903)

Andritz Fabrics and Rolls Inc................ D 919 526-1400
Raleigh (G-9904)

Perma-Flex Rollers Inc.......................... D 704 633-1201
Salisbury (G-11102)

ROOFING GRANULES

3M Company... D 919 642-0006
Moncure (G-8397)

ROOFING MATERIALS: Asphalt

Exteriors Inc Ltd.................................... G 919 325-2251
Spring Lake (G-11561)

Longhorn Roofing Inc............................. F 704 774-1080
Monroe (G-8520)

Roofing Tools and Eqp Inc..................... G 252 291-1800
Wilson (G-13024)

ROOFING MEMBRANE: Rubber

Daramic LLC... D 704 587-8599
Charlotte (G-2018)

Longhorn Roofing Inc............................. F 704 774-1080
Monroe (G-8520)

RUBBER PRDTS: Appliance, Mechanical

Essay Operations Inc............................. G 252 443-6010
Rocky Mount (G-10837)

RUBBER PRDTS: Silicone

Seal It Services Inc................................ F 919 777-0374
Sanford (G-11232)

RUBBER PRDTS: Sponge

Rempac LLC.. E 910 737-6557
Lumberton (G-7969)

RUGS : Hand & Machine Made

Sorrells Sheree White............................ G 828 452-4864
Waynesville (G-12475)

SAFETY EQPT & SPLYS WHOLESALERS

American Safety Utility Corp.................. E 704 482-0601
Shelby (G-11311)

Speer Operational Tech LLC.................. G 864 631-2512
Marion (G-8066)

VH Industries Inc................................... G 704 743-2400
Concord (G-3464)

SALES PROMOTION SVCS

Rulmeca Corporation.............................. G 910 794-9294
Wilmington (G-12905)

UGLy Essentials LLC.............................. F 910 319-9945
Raleigh (G-10572)

SALT

Barker Industries Inc.............................. G 704 391-1023
Charlotte (G-1753)

Giles Chemical Corporation................... G 828 452-4784
Waynesville (G-12458)

Giles Chemical Corporation................... E 828 452-4784
Waynesville (G-12459)

Schoenberg Salt Co............................... G 336 766-0600
Winston Salem (G-13330)

SAMPLE BOOKS

Design Concepts Incorporated.............. F 336 887-1932
High Point (G-6590)

SAND & GRAVEL

American Materials Company LLC .... F 910 799-1411
Wilmington *(G-12703)*

Aquadale Query .... G 704 474-3165
Norwood *(G-9553)*

Atmax Engineering .... G 910 233-4881
Wilmington *(G-12715)*

B V Hedrick Gravel & Sand Co .... G 336 337-0706
Asheville *(G-450)*

B V Hedrick Gravel & Sand Co .... G 828 738-0332
Marion *(G-8032)*

B V Hedrick Gravel & Sand Co .... C 704 827-8114
Stanley *(G-11611)*

B V Hedrick Gravel & Sand Co .... C 828 686-3844
Swannanoa *(G-11866)*

B V Hedrick Gravel & Sand Co .... E 828 645-5560
Weaverville *(G-12482)*

Beazer East Inc .... F 919 567-9512
Holly Springs *(G-6894)*

Black Sand Company Inc .... G 336 788-6411
Winston Salem *(G-13107)*

Blue Rock Materials LLC .... F 828 479-3581
Robbinsville *(G-10757)*

Bobby Cahoon Construction Inc .... E 252 249-1617
Grantsboro *(G-5329)*

Bonsal American Inc .... D 704 525-1621
Charlotte *(G-1799)*

Carolina Stone LLC .... F 252 208-1633
Dover *(G-3828)*

Clifford W Estes Co Inc .... E 336 622-6410
Staley *(G-11593)*

Crowder Trucking LLC .... G 910 797-4163
Fayetteville *(G-4581)*

Cumberland Gravel & Sand Co .... G 704 633-4241
Salisbury *(G-11039)*

Cumberland Sand and Gravel .... G 704 474-3165
Norwood *(G-9555)*

Harrins Sand & Gravel Inc .... G 828 254-2744
Asheville *(G-516)*

Long Branch Partners LLC .... G 828 837-1400
Brasstown *(G-965)*

Long J E & Sons Grading Inc .... F 336 228-9706
Burlington *(G-1121)*

Martin Marietta Materials Inc .... F 360 424-3441
Raleigh *(G-10275)*

Martin Marietta Materials Inc .... C 919 781-4550
Raleigh *(G-10277)*

Mugo Gravel & Grading Inc .... E 704 782-3478
Concord *(G-3406)*

NC Sand and Rock Inc .... G 919 538-9001
Willow Spring *(G-12680)*

Parrish Contracting LLC .... G 828 524-9100
Franklin *(G-4838)*

Rogers Group Inc .... G 828 657-9331
Mooresboro *(G-8585)*

Soundside Recycling & Mtls Inc .... G 252 491-8666
Jarvisburg *(G-7186)*

Tarheel Sand & Stone Inc .... G 336 468-4003
Hamptonville *(G-6093)*

Thrills Hauling LLC .... F 407 383-3483
Arden *(G-310)*

SAND MINING

A-1 Sandrock Inc .... E 336 855-8195
Greensboro *(G-5334)*

G S Materials Inc .... E 336 584-1745
Burlington *(G-1093)*

Landsdown Mining Corporation .... F 704 753-5400
Leland *(G-7549)*

Prize Management LLC .... G 252 532-1939
Garysburg *(G-4977)*

SANDBLASTING EQPT

Hess Manufacturing Inc .... E 704 637-3300
Salisbury *(G-11065)*

SANITARY SVC, NEC

Integrity Envmtl Solutions LLC .... D 704 283-9765
Monroe *(G-8505)*

SANITARY SVCS: Liquid Waste Collection & Disposal

RDc Debris Removal Cnstr LLC .... E 323 614-2353
Smithfield *(G-11462)*

SANITARY SVCS: Oil Spill Cleanup

Global Ecosciences Inc .... G 252 631-6266
Wake Forest *(G-12278)*

Noble Oil Services Inc .... C 919 774-8180
Sanford *(G-11212)*

SANITARY SVCS: Refuse Collection & Disposal Svcs

Alleghany Garbage Service Inc .... G 336 372-4413
Sparta *(G-11533)*

National Container Group LLC .... G 704 393-9050
Charlotte *(G-2544)*

SANITARY SVCS: Rubbish Collection & Disposal

Waste Industries Usa LLC .... C 919 325-3000
Raleigh *(G-10598)*

SANITARY SVCS: Waste Materials, Recycling

A-1 Sandrock Inc .... E 336 855-8195
Greensboro *(G-5334)*

Clean Green Inc .... G 919 596-3500
Durham *(G-3977)*

Crizaf Inc .... G 919 251-7661
Durham *(G-3991)*

Custom Polymers Inc .... F 704 332-6070
Charlotte *(G-2011)*

Duramax Holdings LLC .... C 704 588-9191
Charlotte *(G-2068)*

Elan Trading Inc .... E 704 342-1696
Charlotte *(G-2094)*

Fiber Composites LLC .... D 704 463-7118
New London *(G-9416)*

Noble Oil Services Inc .... C 919 774-8180
Sanford *(G-11212)*

Soundside Recycling & Mtls Inc .... G 252 491-8666
Jarvisburg *(G-7186)*

Steelman Lumber & Pallet LLC .... F 336 468-2757
Hamptonville *(G-6092)*

SASHES: Door Or Window, Metal

Amesbury Group Inc .... D 704 978-2883
Statesville *(G-11655)*

Amesbury Group Inc .... D 704 924-7694
Statesville *(G-11656)*

Garden Metalwork .... G 828 733-1077
Newland *(G-9429)*

YKK AP America Inc .... F 336 665-1963
Greensboro *(G-5930)*

SATELLITES: Communications

Lunar International Tech LLC .... F 800 975-7153
Charlotte *(G-2441)*

McShan Inc .... G 980 355-9790
Charlotte *(G-2481)*

Sbg Digital Inc .... G 828 476-0030
Waynesville *(G-12473)*

Thompson Sunny Acres Inc .... G 910 206-1801
Rockingham *(G-10791)*

SAWMILL MACHINES

Bmi Wood Products Inc .... G 919 829-9505
Raleigh *(G-9951)*

Edmiston Hydrlic Swmill Eqp In .... G 336 921-2304
Boomer *(G-890)*

Ligna Machinery Inc .... G 336 584-0030
Burlington *(G-1120)*

Meadows Mills Inc .... E 336 838-2282
North Wilkesboro *(G-9546)*

SAWS & SAWING EQPT

Bolton Investors Inc .... G 919 471-1197
Durham *(G-3937)*

Ledger Hardware Inc .... G 828 688-4798
Bakersville *(G-679)*

Quality Equipment LLC .... G 919 493-3545
Durham *(G-4203)*

SCALES & BALANCES, EXC LABORATORY

Computerway Food Systems Inc .... E 336 841-7289
High Point *(G-6575)*

Vishay Transducers Ltd .... E 919 365-3800
Wendell *(G-12553)*

SCIENTIFIC EQPT REPAIR SVCS

Cherokee Instruments Inc .... F 919 552-0554
Angier *(G-117)*

SCIENTIFIC INSTRUMENTS WHOLESALERS

Fisher Scientific Company LLC .... D 800 252-7100
Asheville *(G-498)*

SCRAP & WASTE MATERIALS, WHOLESALE: Ferrous Metal

Allyn International Trdg Corp .... G 877 858-2482
Marshville *(G-8085)*

Elan Trading Inc .... E 704 342-1696
Charlotte *(G-2094)*

Renew Recycling LLC .... D 919 550-8012
Clayton *(G-3168)*

SCRAP & WASTE MATERIALS, WHOLESALE: Metal

S Foil Incorporated .... F 704 455-5134
Harrisburg *(G-6117)*

Umicore USA Inc .... E 919 874-7171
Raleigh *(G-10575)*

SCRAP & WASTE MATERIALS, WHOLESALE: Paper

Piedmont Paper Stock LLC .... F 336 285-8592
Greensboro *(G-5744)*

SCREENS: Woven Wire

Aluminum Screen Manufacturing .... G 336 605-8080
Greensboro *(G-5352)*

SCREW MACHINE PRDTS

Abbott Products Inc .... E 336 463-3135
Yadkinville *(G-13434)*

Accuking Inc .... G 252 649-2323
New Bern *(G-9330)*

Angels Path Ventures Inc .... G 828 654-9530
Arden *(G-251)*

B & Y Machining Co Inc .... G 252 235-2180
Bailey *(G-668)*

PRODUCT

Barefoot Cnc Inc..G 828 438-5038
Morganton *(G-8852)*

Black Mtn Mch Fabrication Inc.............E 828 669-9557
Black Mountain *(G-862)*

Bravo Team LLC.....................................E 704 309-1918
Mooresville *(G-8621)*

Carolina Screw Products.....................G 336 760-7400
Winston Salem *(G-13119)*

Conner Brothers Machine Co Inc..........D 704 864-6084
Bessemer City *(G-809)*

Curtis L Maclean L C............................C 704 940-5531
Mooresville *(G-8646)*

Edward Heil Screw Products................G 828 345-6140
Conover *(G-3517)*

Ellison Technologies Inc.......................D 704 545-7362
Charlotte *(G-2103)*

Gamma Technologies Inc......................G 919 319-5272
Morrisville *(G-8980)*

Gary J Younts Machine Company.........F 336 476-7930
Thomasville *(G-12028)*

Griffiths Corporation.............................D 704 554-5657
Pineville *(G-9732)*

IMS Usa LLC...G 910 796-2040
Wilmington *(G-12815)*

Manufacturing Services Inc..................E 704 629-4163
Bessemer City *(G-826)*

Mw Industries Inc.................................E 704 837-0331
Charlotte *(G-2538)*

West Side Industries LLC.....................G 980 223-8665
Statesville *(G-11799)*

SCREWS: Metal

C E Smith Co Inc...................................E 336 273-0166
Greensboro *(G-5416)*

Pan American Screw LLC......................D 828 466-0060
Conover *(G-3543)*

SEALANTS

Capital City Sealants LLC....................G 919 427-4077
Raleigh *(G-9967)*

Carolina Solvents Inc...........................E 828 322-1920
Hickory *(G-6287)*

Impact Technologies LLC.....................G 704 400-5364
Concord *(G-3376)*

Sensus USA Inc....................................C 919 576-6185
Morrisville *(G-9052)*

Sensus USA Inc....................................E 919 845-4000
Morrisville *(G-9051)*

SEALING COMPOUNDS: Sealing, synthetic rubber or plastic

Clesters Auto Rubber Seals LLC..........F 704 637-9979
Cleveland *(G-3211)*

Tosaf Inc...F 980 533-3000
Bessemer City *(G-837)*

SEARCH & NAVIGATION SYSTEMS

Assa Abloy Accessories and.................B 704 233-4011
Monroe *(G-8433)*

Bae Systems Inc...................................D 855 223-8363
Charlotte *(G-1738)*

Btc Electronic Components LLC............E 919 229-2162
Wake Forest *(G-12266)*

Commscope Inc North Carolina............E 828 324-2200
Claremont *(G-3096)*

Commscope Technologies LLC.............G 919 934-9711
Smithfield *(G-11440)*

Commscope Technologies LLC.............A 828 324-2200
Claremont *(G-3104)*

Curtiss-Wright Controls Inc.................E 704 869-2300
Shelby *(G-11325)*

Defense Logistics Services LLC...........D 703 449-1620
Fayetteville *(G-4586)*

Fil-Chem Inc...G 919 878-1270
Raleigh *(G-10108)*

General Dynmics Mssion Systems.......C 336 698-8000
Mc Leansville *(G-8223)*

General Electric Company.....................A 910 675-5000
Wilmington *(G-12785)*

Honeywell International Inc...................E 252 977-2100
Rocky Mount *(G-10841)*

Ickler Manufacturing LLC.....................G 704 658-1195
Mooresville *(G-8690)*

James W McManus Inc..........................G 828 688-2560
Bakersville *(G-678)*

JMS Southeast Inc...............................E 704 873-1835
Statesville *(G-11719)*

Kearfott Corporation.............................B 828 350-5300
Black Mountain *(G-868)*

Kidde Technologies Inc.........................B 252 237-7004
Wilson *(G-12999)*

Navelite LLC...G 336 509-9924
Jamestown *(G-7172)*

Northrop Grmman Gdnce Elec Inc.......E 704 588-2340
Charlotte *(G-2575)*

Northrop Grmman Tchncal Svcs I........E 252 447-7575
Havelock *(G-6124)*

Northrop Grumman Systems Corp.......D 252 225-0911
Atlantic *(G-638)*

Northrop Grumman Systems Corp.......D 252 447-7557
Cherry Point *(G-3054)*

Northrop Grumman Systems Corp.......C 919 465-5020
Morrisville *(G-9029)*

Rockwell Collins Inc.............................G 336 776-3444
Winston Salem *(G-13321)*

Rockwell Collins Inc.............................G 336 744-1097
Winston Salem *(G-13322)*

Roy Bridgmohan...................................G 804 426-9652
Henderson *(G-6176)*

Sierra Nevada Corporation...................E 919 595-8551
Durham *(G-4234)*

Sierra Nevada Corporation...................F 910 307-0362
Fayetteville *(G-4668)*

Sierra Nevada Corporation...................F 775 331-0222
Southern Pines *(G-11509)*

Tempest Aero Group.............................E 336 449-5054
Gibsonville *(G-5184)*

Ultra Elec Ocean Systems Inc..............F 781 848-3400
Wake Forest *(G-12311)*

Usat LLC...E 919 942-4214
Chapel Hill *(G-1587)*

SEAT BELTS: Automobile & Aircraft

Aircraft Belts Inc.................................E 919 956-4395
Creedmoor *(G-3635)*

SEATING: Stadium

4topps LLC...G 704 281-8451
Winston Salem *(G-13069)*

SECURE STORAGE SVC: Household & Furniture

Ideaitlia Cntmporary Furn Corp............C 828 464-1000
Conover *(G-3532)*

SECURITY CONTROL EQPT & SYSTEMS

A&B Integrators LLC.............................F 919 371-0750
Durham *(G-3876)*

American Physcl SEC Group LLC..........G 919 363-1894
Apex *(G-134)*

Audio Vdeo Concepts Design Inc..........G 704 821-2823
Indian Trail *(G-7069)*

Automated Controls LLC.......................G 704 724-7625
Huntersville *(G-6970)*

Cargotec Port Security LLC...................G 919 620-1763
Durham *(G-3958)*

Diverse Security Systems Inc...............G 919 848-9599
Raleigh *(G-10050)*

Leonine Protection Systems LLC..........G 704 296-2675
Mount Holly *(G-9235)*

Pathway Technologies Inc....................E 919 847-2680
Raleigh *(G-10361)*

Plan B Enterprises LLC.........................G 919 387-4856
New Hill *(G-9412)*

Security Consult Inc.............................G 704 531-8399
Charlotte *(G-2782)*

SECURITY DEVICES

Alert Protection Systems Inc...............G 919 467-4357
Raleigh *(G-9890)*

Campus Safety Products LLC...............G 919 321-1477
Durham *(G-3956)*

Carolina Growler Inc.............................E 910 948-2114
Robbins *(G-10752)*

Crowdguard Inc....................................G 919 605-1948
Cary *(G-1340)*

Edwards Electronic Systems Inc..........E 919 359-2239
Clayton *(G-3146)*

Hamrick Fence Company.......................F 704 434-5011
Boiling Springs *(G-884)*

Lea Aid Acquisition Company................G 919 872-6210
Spring Hope *(G-11557)*

Leonardo US Cyber SEC Sltons L.........D 336 379-7135
Greensboro *(G-5661)*

Stanley Black & Decker Inc..................C 704 789-7000
Concord *(G-3446)*

SECURITY SYSTEMS SERVICES

Advanced Detection Tech LLC..............E 704 663-1949
Mooresville *(G-8591)*

Diebold Nixdorf Incorporated...............E 704 599-3100
Charlotte *(G-2044)*

Integrated Info Systems Inc..................F 919 488-5000
Youngsville *(G-13476)*

Lunar International Tech LLC.................F 800 975-7153
Charlotte *(G-2441)*

One Source SEC & Sound Inc...............G 281 850-9487
Mooresville *(G-8739)*

Security Consult Inc.............................G 704 531-8399
Charlotte *(G-2782)*

Tektone Sound & Signal Mfg Inc...........D 828 524-9967
Franklin *(G-4841)*

Teletec Corporation..............................F 919 954-7300
Raleigh *(G-10541)*

SEMICONDUCTOR CIRCUIT NETWORKS

Silanna Semicdtr N Amer Inc................D 984 444-6500
Raleigh *(G-10476)*

SEMICONDUCTOR DEVICES: Wafers

Brumley/South Inc...............................G 704 664-9251
Mooresville *(G-8622)*

Hoffman Materials LLC.........................F 717 243-2011
Granite Falls *(G-5306)*

Iqe Inc..D 610 861-6930
Greensboro *(G-5622)*

SEMICONDUCTORS & RELATED DEVICES

Air Control Inc......................................E 252 492-2300
Henderson *(G-6147)*

Amalfi Semiconductor Inc.....................G 336 664-1233
Greensboro *(G-5353)*

Amkor Technology Inc...........................G 336 605-8009
Greensboro *(G-5361)*

Arva LLC... G 803 336-2230
Charlotte *(G-1701)*

ATI Industrial Automation Inc................ D 919 772-0115
Apex *(G-141)*

Convergent Integration Inc..................... G 704 516-5922
Charlotte *(G-1979)*

Corning Incorporated............................... F 252 316-4500
Tarboro *(G-11924)*

Cortina Systems...................................... G 919 226-1800
Morrisville *(G-8960)*

Disco Hi-TEC America Inc....................... G 919 468-6003
Morrisville *(G-8965)*

Flexgen Power Systems Inc.................... G 855 327-5674
Durham *(G-4033)*

Flexgen Power Systems Inc.................... F 855 327-5674
Durham *(G-4034)*

Gainspan Corporation.............................. D 408 627-6500
Morrisville *(G-8979)*

Harris Solar Inc....................................... G 704 490-8374
Concord *(G-3371)*

Hexatech Inc... F 919 481-4412
Morrisville *(G-8988)*

Hexatech Inc... G 919 633-0583
Raleigh *(G-10163)*

Kidde Technologies Inc........................... D 252 237-7004
Wilson *(G-13001)*

Kidsvidz Productions.............................. G 704 663-4487
Mooresville *(G-8705)*

Larry Shackelford.................................... G 919 467-8817
Cary *(G-1386)*

Macom Technology Solutions Inc......... D 919 807-9100
Morrisville *(G-9016)*

Marvell Semiconductor Inc..................... D 408 222-2500
Morrisville *(G-9017)*

Nhanced Semiconductors Inc................. E 630 561-6813
Morrisville *(G-9025)*

Nitronex LLC... E 919 807-9100
Morrisville *(G-9026)*

North Crlina Rnwable Prpts LLC............ G 407 536-5346
Raleigh *(G-10338)*

Nvidia Corporation.................................. F 408 486-2000
Durham *(G-4153)*

Nxp Usa Inc.. G 919 468-3251
Cary *(G-1410)*

Phononic Inc... D 919 908-6300
Durham *(G-4178)*

Poweramerica Institute........................... F 919 515-6013
Raleigh *(G-10379)*

Qorvo Inc.. C 336 664-1233
Greensboro *(G-5772)*

Qorvo Inc.. A 336 664-1233
Greensboro *(G-5773)*

Qorvo International Holdg Inc................. F 336 664-1233
Greensboro *(G-5774)*

Qorvo International Svcs Inc.................. G 336 664-1233
Greensboro *(G-5775)*

Qorvo Us Inc... G 336 662-1150
Greensboro *(G-5776)*

Qorvo Us Inc... G 503 615-9000
Jamestown *(G-7176)*

Rambus Inc... F 919 960-6600
Chapel Hill *(G-1566)*

Reuel Inc.. E 919 734-0460
Goldsboro *(G-5240)*

Rf Micro Devices Inc.............................. A 336 664-1233
Greensboro *(G-5785)*

Rfmd LLC.. C 336 664-1233
Greensboro *(G-5786)*

Rfmd Infrstrcture PDT Group In............. G 704 996-2997
Raleigh *(G-10444)*

Samsung Semiconductor Inc.................. G 919 380-8483
Cary *(G-1445)*

Sarda Technologies Inc........................... G 919 757-6825
Durham *(G-4221)*

Skan US Inc.. F 919 354-6380
Raleigh *(G-10485)*

Skyworks Solutions Inc.......................... E 336 291-4200
Greensboro *(G-5816)*

Thunderbird Technologies Inc................ G 919 481-3239
Raleigh *(G-10548)*

Viavi Solutions Inc................................. G 919 388-5100
Morrisville *(G-9086)*

Wolfspeed Inc... G 919 407-5300
Durham *(G-4307)*

Wolfspeed Employee Services Co.......... G 919 313-5300
Durham *(G-4309)*

Xylem Lnc... E 704 409-9700
Charlotte *(G-3035)*

Ziptronix Inc... F 919 459-2400
Morrisville *(G-9094)*

SENSORS: Infrared, Solid State

AMS USA Inc... G 919 755-2889
Raleigh *(G-9900)*

Northrop Grmman Gdnce Elec Inc......... E 704 588-2340
Charlotte *(G-2575)*

SEPTIC TANK CLEANING SVCS

Autry Con Pdts & Bldrs Sup Co.............. G 704 504-8830
Charlotte *(G-1719)*

Inman Septic Tank Service Inc............... G 910 763-1146
Wilmington *(G-12817)*

Mulls Con & Septic Tanks Inc................ G 828 437-0959
Morganton *(G-8883)*

SEPTIC TANKS: Concrete

Argos USA LLC.. C 704 872-9566
Statesville *(G-11659)*

Brant & Lassiter Septic Tank.................. G 252 587-4321
Potecasi *(G-9819)*

Futrell Precasting LLC............................ G 252 568-3481
Deep Run *(G-3732)*

Garners Septic Tank Inc......................... G 919 718-5181
Raeford *(G-9838)*

Inman Septic Tank Service Inc............... G 910 763-1146
Wilmington *(G-12817)*

Leonard McSwain Sptic Tank Svc......... G 704 482-1380
Shelby *(G-11353)*

Moretz & Sipe Inc.................................. G 828 327-8661
Hickory *(G-6397)*

Northeastern Ready Mix.......................... G 252 335-1931
Elizabeth City *(G-4400)*

O R Prdgen Sons Sptic Tank I................ G 252 442-3338
Rocky Mount *(G-10857)*

Southern Block Company......................... F 910 293-7844
Warsaw *(G-12366)*

TNT Services Inc..................................... G 252 261-3073
Kitty Hawk *(G-7447)*

SEWAGE & WATER TREATMENT EQPT

Allens Environmental Cnstr LLC............ G 407 774-7100
Brevard *(G-967)*

Amerochem Corporation.......................... E 252 634-9344
New Bern *(G-9333)*

Aqwa Inc... G 252 243-7693
Wilson *(G-12963)*

County of Dare.. C 252 475-5990
Kill Devil Hills *(G-7315)*

Lely Manufacturing Inc........................... F 252 291-7050
Wilson *(G-13002)*

Mann+hmmel Fltrtion Tech US LL......... C 704 869-3300
Gastonia *(G-5085)*

Town of Ahoskie...................................... G 252 332-3840
Ahoskie *(G-54)*

Xelaqua Inc... G 919 964-4181
Raleigh *(G-10618)*

SEWING, NEEDLEWORK & PIECE GOODS STORES: Knitting Splys

Innovaknits LLC...................................... G 828 536-9348
Conover *(G-3533)*

Meridian Spcalty Yrn Group Inc............. D 828 874-2151
Valdese *(G-12197)*

Uwharrie Knits Inc.................................. F 704 474-4123
Norwood *(G-9563)*

SHADES: Window

Penrock LLC.. E 704 800-6722
Mooresville *(G-8745)*

SHAPES & PILINGS, STRUCTURAL: Steel

ABB Installation Products Inc................. E 828 322-1855
Hickory *(G-6260)*

Jack A Farrior Inc................................... D 252 753-2020
Farmville *(G-4532)*

P & S Welding Inc................................... G 910 285-3126
Willard *(G-12666)*

Structural Materials Inc.......................... G 828 754-6413
Lenoir *(G-7640)*

SHEET METAL SPECIALTIES, EXC STAMPED

Able Metal Fabricators Inc..................... G 704 394-8972
Charlotte *(G-1611)*

Advanced Mfg Solutions NC Inc............. F 828 633-2633
Candler *(G-1216)*

Afi Capital Inc.. C 919 212-6400
Raleigh *(G-9885)*

Allied Sheet Metal Works Inc................ F 704 376-8469
Charlotte *(G-1645)*

Byers Prcision Fabricators Inc............... E 828 693-4088
Hendersonville *(G-6192)*

Gray Metal South Inc............................. D 910 892-2119
Dunn *(G-3859)*

Griffiths Corporation.............................. D 704 554-5657
Pineville *(G-9732)*

Kirk & Blum Manufacturing Co.............. D 801 728-6533
Greensboro *(G-5649)*

Len Corporation...................................... F 919 876-2964
Knightdale *(G-7452)*

Loflin Fabrication LLC............................ E 336 859-4333
Denton *(G-3756)*

New Peco Inc.. E 828 684-1234
Arden *(G-288)*

Oak Ridge Industries LLC...................... E 252 833-4061
Washington *(G-12401)*

QMF Mtal Elctrnic Slutions Inc............. D 336 992-8002
Kernersville *(G-7295)*

Rfr Metal Fabrication Inc....................... D 919 693-1354
Oxford *(G-9631)*

S and R Sheet Metal Inc........................ G 336 476-1069
Thomasville *(G-12069)*

S K Bowling Inc...................................... F 252 243-1803
Walstonburg *(G-12335)*

Swanson Sheetmetal Inc........................ F 704 283-3955
Monroe *(G-8566)*

Triangle Stainless Inc............................. G 919 596-1335
Butner *(G-1207)*

USA Dutch Inc... E 919 732-6956
Efland *(G-4376)*

SHEETS: Fabric, From Purchased Materials

Babine Lake Corporation......................... E 910 285-7955
Hampstead *(G-6069)*

Innovative Fabrication Inc....................... G 919 544-0254
Raleigh *(G-10196)*

P
R
O
D
U
C
T

Quality Home Fashions Inc...................... G 704 983-5906
   Albemarle *(G-85)*

SHELVING: Office & Store, Exc Wood

Innovative Design Tech LLC.................. G 919 331-0204
   Angier *(G-121)*

SHIP BUILDING & REPAIRING: Cargo Vessels

Yang Ming America Corporation............ G 704 357-3817
   Charlotte *(G-3039)*

SHOE STORES

Polyhose Incorporated.......................... E 732 512-9141
   Wilmington *(G-12881)*

SHOE STORES: Women's

W E Nixons Wldg & Hdwr Inc.................. G 252 221-4348
   Edenton *(G-4373)*

SHOES: Canvas, Rubber Soled

Vans Inc... G 704 364-3811
   Charlotte *(G-2973)*

SHOES: Men's

Allbirds Inc... F 980 296-0006
   Charlotte *(G-1643)*

SHOES: Orthopedic, Children's

Century Hosiery Inc................................ C 336 859-3806
   Denton *(G-3742)*

SHOES: Orthopedic, Men's

Century Hosiery Inc................................ C 336 859-3806
   Denton *(G-3742)*

SHOES: Orthopedic, Women's

Century Hosiery Inc................................ C 336 859-3806
   Denton *(G-3742)*

SHOES: Plastic Or Rubber

Vans Inc... G 919 792-2555
   Raleigh *(G-10583)*

SHOES: Sandals, Rubber

CBA Productions Inc.............................. G 703 568-4758
   Fayetteville *(G-4571)*

SHOES: Women's

McRae Industries Inc............................. E 910 439-6147
   Mount Gilead *(G-9204)*

SHOT PEENING SVC

Metal Improvement Company LLC........ D 704 525-3818
   Charlotte *(G-2495)*

Metal Improvement Company LLC........ G 414 536-1573
   Gastonia *(G-5094)*

National Peening Inc.............................. F 704 872-0113
   Statesville *(G-11738)*

SHOWCASES & DISPLAY FIXTURES: Office & Store

Amcase Inc... E 336 784-5992
   High Point *(G-6519)*

Grice Showcase Display Mfg Inc........... G 704 423-8888
   Charlotte *(G-2242)*

Master Displays Inc............................... D 336 884-5575
   High Point *(G-6706)*

SHOWER STALLS: Metal

Tubs-Usa LLC.. F 336 884-5737
   High Point *(G-6814)*

SHOWER STALLS: Plastic & Fiberglass

Moen Incorporated................................ D 252 638-3300
   New Bern *(G-9384)*

SHREDDERS: Indl & Commercial

Piedmont Paper Stock LLC.................... F 336 285-8592
   Greensboro *(G-5744)*

Secured Shred.. G 443 288-6375
   Raleigh *(G-10466)*

SHUTTERS, DOOR & WINDOW: Metal

Atlantic Coastal Shutters LLC............... G 252 441-4358
   Kill Devil Hills *(G-7314)*

Charlotte Shutter and Shades................ G 336 351-3391
   Westfield *(G-12572)*

Jeld-Wen Inc... B 800 535-3936
   Charlotte *(G-2366)*

Shutter Factory Inc............................... G 252 974-2795
   Washington *(G-12413)*

SIDING MATERIALS

Ply Gem Holdings Inc............................ D 919 677-3900
   Cary *(G-1421)*

Texture Plus Inc.................................... E 631 218-9200
   Lincolnton *(G-7863)*

Wake Supply Company.......................... G 252 234-6012
   Wilson *(G-13044)*

SIDING: Plastic

Certainteed LLC.................................... D 828 459-0556
   Claremont *(G-3093)*

Mastic Home Exteriors Inc.................... E 816 426-8200
   Cary *(G-1399)*

Variform Inc.. D 828 277-6420
   Asheville *(G-630)*

SIGN PAINTING & LETTERING SHOP

Broome Sign Company.......................... G 704 782-0422
   Concord *(G-3325)*

Creative Printers Inc............................. G 336 246-7746
   West Jefferson *(G-12563)*

Fitch Sign Company Inc......................... G 704 482-2916
   Shelby *(G-11336)*

Goldsboro Neon Sign Co Inc................. G 919 735-2035
   Goldsboro *(G-5217)*

JKS Motorsports Inc.............................. G 336 722-4129
   Winston Salem *(G-13217)*

Signs Etc.. G 336 722-9341
   Winston Salem *(G-13337)*

SIGNALING DEVICES: Sound, Electrical

Magnum Enterprize Inc.......................... G 252 524-5391
   Grifton *(G-6037)*

Marpac LLC... D 910 602-1421
   Wilmington *(G-12846)*

SIGNALS: Traffic Control, Electric

Carolina Pwr Signalization LLC.............. E 910 323-5589
   Fayetteville *(G-4570)*

Fulcher Elc Fayetteville Inc................... E 910 483-7772
   Fayetteville *(G-4604)*

SIGNS & ADVERTISING SPECIALTIES

310 Sign Company................................ G 704 910-2242
   Gastonia *(G-4981)*

910 Sign Co LLC................................... G 910 353-2298
   Jacksonville *(G-7112)*

AAA Mobile Signs LLC........................... G 919 463-9768
   Morrisville *(G-8915)*

ABC Signs... G 252 223-5900
   Newport *(G-9436)*

Acsm Inc... G 704 910-0243
   Charlotte *(G-1620)*

Action Graphics and Signs Inc.............. G 919 690-1260
   Bullock *(G-1012)*

Action Installs LLC............................... G 704 787-3828
   Wilkesboro *(G-12627)*

Ad Runner MBL Outdoor Advg Inc......... G 336 945-1190
   Lewisville *(G-7649)*

Advance Signs & Service Inc................. E 919 639-4666
   Angier *(G-110)*

American Sign Shop Inc........................ G 704 527-6100
   Charlotte *(G-1668)*

Ancient Mariner Inc.............................. F 704 635-7911
   Monroe *(G-8426)*

Andark Graphics Inc.............................. G 704 882-1400
   Indian Trail *(G-7067)*

Apple Rock Advg & Prom Inc................. E 336 232-4800
   Greensboro *(G-5366)*

Art Sign Co.. G 919 596-8681
   Durham *(G-3899)*

Artisan Direct LLC................................ G 704 655-9100
   Cornelius *(G-3586)*

Artistic Images Inc................................ G 704 332-6225
   Charlotte *(G-1699)*

Asi Signage North Carolina................... E 919 362-9669
   Holly Springs *(G-6892)*

Baac Business Solutions Inc................. G 704 333-4321
   Charlotte *(G-1732)*

Baldwin Sign & Awning.......................... G 910 642-8812
   Whiteville *(G-12576)*

Beane Signs Inc.................................... G 336 629-6748
   Asheboro *(G-331)*

Beaty Corporation................................ G 704 599-4949
   Charlotte *(G-1765)*

Blue Light Images Company Inc............ F 336 983-4986
   King *(G-7321)*

Boyd Gmn Inc.. C 206 284-2200
   Monroe *(G-8446)*

Boyles Sign Shop Inc............................ G 336 782-1189
   Germanton *(G-5173)*

Burchette Sign Company Inc................. F 336 996-6501
   Colfax *(G-3274)*

Buzz Saw Inc.. G 910 321-7446
   Fayetteville *(G-4564)*

Camco Manufacturing Inc...................... G 336 348-6609
   Reidsville *(G-10678)*

Capital Sign Solutions LLC................... E 919 789-1452
   Raleigh *(G-9969)*

Carolina Cstm Signs & Graphics........... G 336 681-4337
   Greensboro *(G-5425)*

Carolina Sgns Grphic Dsgns Inc........... G 919 383-3344
   Durham *(G-3962)*

Carolina Sign Co Inc............................. G 704 399-3995
   Charlotte *(G-1855)*

Carolina Sign Svc................................. G 919 247-0927
   Angier *(G-116)*

Carolina Signs & Lighting Inc................ G 336 399-1400
   King *(G-7323)*

Carolina Signs and Wonders Inc........... F 704 286-1343
   Charlotte *(G-1856)*

Casco Signs Inc.................................... E 704 788-9055
   Concord *(G-3333)*

Cbr Signs LLC....................................... G 910 794-8243
   Wilmington *(G-12737)*

Ccbs & Sign Shop Inc........................... G 252 728-4866
   Beaufort *(G-722)*

CD Dickie & Associates Inc................... F 704 527-9102
   Charlotte *(G-1878)*

Classic Sign Services LLC..................... G 704 401-1466
   Monroe *(G-8461)*

CMA Signs LLC .... F 919 245-8339
Hillsborough (G-6864)

Coates Designers & Crafstmen .... G 828 349-9700
Franklin (G-4821)

Cobb Sign Company Incorporated .... G 336 227-0181
Burlington (G-1072)

Connected 2k LLC .... G 910 321-7446
Fayetteville (G-4578)

Consumer Concepts .... F 252 247-7000
Morehead City (G-8828)

Contagious Graphics Inc .... E 704 529-5600
Charlotte (G-1977)

Creative Images Inc .... G 919 467-2188
Cary (G-1337)

Creative Sign Solutions Inc .... G 704 978-8499
Statesville (G-11680)

Creative Signs Inc .... G 910 395-0100
Wilmington (G-12755)

Davcom Enterprises Inc .... G 919 872-9522
Raleigh (G-10038)

Designelement .... F 919 383-5561
Raleigh (G-10044)

Dickie CD & Associates Inc .... F 704 527-9102
Charlotte (G-2043)

Digital Printing Systems Inc .... E 704 525-0190
Charlotte (G-2047)

Direct Wholesale Signs LLC .... G 704 750-2842
Kings Mountain (G-7359)

Diversified Signs Graphics Inc .... F 704 392-8165
Charlotte (G-2056)

Dize Company .... D 336 722-5181
Winston Salem (G-13149)

Elite Graphics Inc .... G 336 887-2923
High Point (G-6607)

Embroidme .... G 919 316-1538
Durham (G-4020)

Exhibit World Inc .... G 704 882-2272
Indian Trail (G-7080)

Expogo Inc .... F 910 452-3976
Wilmington (G-12773)

Fairway Outdoor Advg LLC .... G 919 755-1900
Raleigh (G-10101)

Fairway Outdoor Advg LLC .... G 910 343-1900
Wilmington (G-12775)

Ferguson Design Inc .... E 704 394-0120
Belmont (G-751)

Fines and Carriel Inc .... G 919 929-0702
Chapel Hill (G-1547)

Global Resource NC Inc .... G 910 793-4770
Wilmington (G-12789)

Gmg Group LLC .... G 252 441-8374
Kill Devil Hills (G-7317)

Goins Signs Inc .... G 336 427-5783
Stoneville (G-11822)

Graphic Productions Inc .... G 336 765-9335
Winston Salem (G-13184)

Graphix Solution Inc .... F 919 213-0371
Apex (G-160)

Greene Imaging & Design Inc .... G 919 787-3737
Raleigh (G-10143)

Guerrero Enterprises Inc .... G 828 286-4900
Rutherfordton (G-10984)

H F Kinney Co Inc .... E 704 540-9367
Charlotte (G-2248)

Hatleys Signs & Service Inc .... G 704 723-4027
Concord (G-3372)

Headrick Otdoor Mdia of Crlnas .... G 704 487-5971
Shelby (G-11343)

Heritage Custom Signs & Disp .... E 704 655-1465
Charlotte (G-2273)

Icon Sign Systems Inc .... G 828 253-4266
Asheville (G-520)

Identity Custom Signage Inc .... G 336 882-7446
High Point (G-6666)

Image Design .... F 910 862-8988
Elizabethtown (G-4428)

Industrial Sign & Graphics Inc .... E 704 371-4985
Charlotte (G-2324)

Infinity S End Inc .... F 704 900-8355
Charlotte (G-2328)

Island Xprtees of Oter Bnks In .... E 252 480-3990
Nags Head (G-9298)

J & D Thorpe Enterprises Inc .... G 919 553-0918
Clayton (G-3155)

J Morgan Signs Inc .... F 336 274-6509
Greensboro (G-5632)

J R Craver & Associates Inc .... G 336 769-3330
Clemmons (G-3193)

Jantec Sign Group LLC .... E 336 429-5010
Mount Airy (G-9136)

Jaxonsigns .... G 910 467-3409
Holly Ridge (G-6889)

JB II Printing LLC .... E 336 222-0717
Burlington (G-1111)

Jeremy Weitzel .... G 919 878-4474
Raleigh (G-10215)

Jester-Crown Inc .... G 919 872-1070
Raleigh (G-10216)

Jka Idustries .... G 980 225-5350
Salisbury (G-11073)

JKS Motorsports Inc .... G 336 722-4129
Winston Salem (G-13217)

K & D Signs LLC .... F 336 786-1111
Mount Airy (G-9137)

K&K Holdings Inc .... G 704 341-5567
Charlotte (G-2385)

Kenneth Moore Signs .... G 910 458-6428
Wilmington (G-12826)

Ki Agency LLC .... G 919 977-7075
Raleigh (G-10234)

King Tutt Graphics LLC .... E 877 546-4888
Raleigh (G-10235)

Kranken Signs Vehicle Wraps .... G 704 339-0059
Pineville (G-9738)

Leonardo US Cyber SEC Sltons L .... D 336 379-7135
Greensboro (G-5661)

Liberty Sign and Lighting LLC .... G 336 703-7465
Lexington (G-7710)

Lights-Lights LLC .... G 919 798-2317
Coats (G-3264)

Matthews Mobile Media LLC .... G 336 303-4982
Greensboro (G-5681)

McKnight15 Inc .... G 919 326-6488
Raleigh (G-10285)

Mega Media Concepts Ltd Lblty .... G 973 919-5661
Brevard (G-975)

Mercury Signs Inc .... G 919 808-1205
Apex (G-180)

Meredith Media Co .... G 919 748-4808
Durham (G-4130)

Metro Print Inc .... F 704 827-3796
Mount Holly (G-9237)

Moretz Signs Inc .... G 828 387-4600
Beech Mountain (G-738)

Morningstar Signs and Banners .... G 704 861-0020
Gastonia (G-5101)

Motorsports Designs Inc .... F 336 454-1181
High Point (G-6716)

NC Sign and Lighting Svc LLC .... F 586 764-0563
Jamestown (G-7173)

New Hanover Printing and Pubg .... G 910 520-7173
Wilmington (G-12860)

Newton Sign Co Inc .... G 910 347-1661
Jacksonville (G-7136)

Nomadic Display LLC .... G 800 336-5019
Greensboro (G-5710)

North State Signs Inc .... G 919 977-7053
Raleigh (G-10339)

Oramental Post .... G 704 376-8111
Pineville (G-9746)

PC Signs & Graphics LLC .... G 919 661-5801
Garner (G-4951)

Peaches Enterprises Inc .... G 910 868-5800
Fayetteville (G-4653)

Phoenix Sign Pros Inc .... G 252 756-5685
Winterville (G-13421)

Piedmont Mediaworks Inc .... F 828 575-2250
Asheville (G-573)

Planet Logo Inc .... G 910 763-2554
Wilmington (G-12879)

Playrace Inc .... E 828 251-2211
Asheville (G-577)

Port City Signs & Graphics Inc .... G 910 350-8242
Wilmington (G-12883)

Portable Displays LLC .... E 919 544-6504
Cary (G-1424)

Print Management Group LLC .... F 704 821-0114
Charlotte (G-2669)

Printology Signs Graphics LLC .... G 843 473-4984
Davidson (G-3716)

Professional Bus Systems Inc .... G 704 333-2444
Charlotte (G-2673)

Professional Laminating LLC .... G 919 465-0400
Cary (G-1430)

Purple Star Graphics Inc .... G 704 723-4020
Concord (G-3426)

Qasioun LLC .... F 704 531-8000
Charlotte (G-2678)

R and L Collision Center Inc .... F 704 739-2500
Kings Mountain (G-7381)

R O Givens Signs Inc .... G 252 338-6578
Elizabeth City (G-4407)

Readilite & Barricade Inc .... F 919 231-8309
Raleigh (G-10435)

Rec Plus Inc .... E 704 375-9098
Charlotte (G-2696)

Retail Installation Svcs LLC .... G 336 818-1333
Millers Creek (G-8307)

RLM/Universal Packaging Inc .... F 336 644-6161
Greensboro (G-5789)

Routh Sign Service .... G 336 272-0895
Greensboro (G-5795)

Salem Sports Inc .... G 336 722-2444
Winston Salem (G-13326)

Saltwater Signworks Inc .... G 910 212-5020
Wilmington (G-12909)

Sawyers Sign Service Inc .... F
Mount Airy (G-9175)

Seaward Action Inc .... G 252 671-1684
Wilmington (G-12914)

Shutterbug Grafix & Signs .... G 910 315-1556
Pinehurst (G-9703)

Sidney Perry Cooper III .... G 252 257-3886
Warrenton (G-12354)

Sign A Rama Inc .... G 336 893-8042
Lewisville (G-7653)

Sign Company of Wilmington Inc .... F 910 392-1414
Wilmington (G-12921)

Sign Resources of NC .... G 336 310-4611
Kernersville (G-7300)

Sign Shop of The Triangle Inc .... G 919 363-3930
Apex (G-194)

Sign Shoppe Inc .... G 910 754-5144
Supply (G-11859)

Sign Technology Inc .... G 336 887-3211
High Point (G-6772)

Employee Codes: A=Over 500 employees, B=251-500
C=101-250, D=51-100, E=20-50, F=10-19, G=1-9

2025 Harris North Carolina
Manufacturers Directory

1191

PRODUCT

Sign Worxpress............................ G 336 437-9889
Burlington *(G-1157)*

Sign-A-Rama............................... G 919 383-5561
Raleigh *(G-10474)*

Signfactory Direct Inc................. G 336 903-0300
Wilkesboro *(G-12651)*

Signify It Inc.............................. F 910 678-8111
Fayetteville *(G-4669)*

Signlogic Inc.............................. G 910 862-8965
Elizabethtown *(G-4433)*

Signs By Tomorrow..................... G 704 527-6100
Charlotte *(G-2807)*

Signs Etc................................... G 336 722-9341
Winston Salem *(G-13337)*

Signs Now.................................. G 919 546-0006
Raleigh *(G-10475)*

Signs Now 103 LLC..................... G 252 355-0768
Greenville *(G-6022)*

Signs Now Charlotte................... G 704 844-0552
Pineville *(G-9757)*

Signs Sealed Delivered.............. G 919 213-1280
Durham *(G-4236)*

Signsations Ltd.......................... G 571 340-3330
Chapel Hill *(G-1571)*

Signz Inc................................... G 704 824-7446
Gastonia *(G-5137)*

Siqnarama Pinevillw................... G 704 835-1123
Pineville *(G-9758)*

Southern Signworks.................... G 828 683-8726
Leicester *(G-7529)*

Speedpro Imaging....................... G 704 321-1200
Charlotte *(G-2843)*

Speedpro Imaging....................... G 919 578-4338
Raleigh *(G-10498)*

Speedpro Imaging Durham........... G 919 278-7964
Durham *(G-4246)*

Srb Technologies Inc.................. E 336 659-2610
Winston Salem *(G-13341)*

Stay Alert Safety Services LLC..... E 919 828-5399
Raleigh *(G-10506)*

Sterling Products Corporation...... G 646 423-3175
Greensboro *(G-5839)*

Sticky Life................................. G 910 817-4531
Newton Grove *(G-9518)*

Studio Displays Inc.................... F 704 588-6590
Pineville *(G-9761)*

Syd Inc..................................... G 336 294-8807
Greensboro *(G-5848)*

Tebo Displays LLC...................... G 919 832-8525
Raleigh *(G-10537)*

TEC Graphics Inc....................... F 919 567-2077
Fuquay Varina *(G-4901)*

Thats A Good Sign Inc................ G 301 870-0299
Bolivia *(G-887)*

Tommy Signs............................. G 704 877-1234
Waxhaw *(G-12445)*

Triangle Solutions Inc................ G 919 481-1235
Cary *(G-1473)*

Twinvision North America Inc....... C 919 361-2155
Durham *(G-4285)*

US Logoworks LLC...................... F 910 307-0312
Fayetteville *(G-4691)*

Vic Inc...................................... F 336 545-1124
Greensboro *(G-5903)*

Victory Signs LLC....................... G 919 642-3091
Fuquay Varina *(G-4904)*

Vintage Editions Inc................... F 828 632-4185
Taylorsville *(G-11985)*

Vittro Sign Studio....................... G 917 698-1594
Apex *(G-205)*

Web 4 Half LLC.......................... E 855 762-4638
Greensboro *(G-5914)*

Whats Your Sign LLC.................. G 919 274-5703
Raleigh *(G-10607)*

Wilson Billboard Advg Inc........... G 919 934-2421
Smithfield *(G-11470)*

SIGNS & ADVERTISING SPECIALTIES:
Artwork, Advertising

Awning Innovations..................... F 336 831-8996
Winston Salem *(G-13090)*

Graphic Components LLC............. E 336 542-2128
Greensboro *(G-5572)*

Merge LLC................................. G 919 832-3924
Raleigh *(G-10291)*

Ruth Arnold Graphics & Signs...... G 910 793-9087
Wilmington *(G-12907)*

Shop Dawg Signs LLC................. E 919 556-2672
Wake Forest *(G-12300)*

Signal Signs of Ga Inc................ G 828 494-4913
Murphy *(G-9295)*

Timothy L Griffin....................... G 336 317-8314
Greenville *(G-6028)*

SIGNS & ADVERTISING SPECIALTIES:
Letters For Signs, Metal

NC Graphic Pros LLC................... G 252 492-7326
Kittrell *(G-7442)*

Signworks North Carolina Inc...... G 336 956-7446
Lexington *(G-7741)*

SIGNS & ADVERTISING SPECIALTIES:
Novelties

Image Matters Inc...................... G 336 940-3000
Clemmons *(G-3191)*

Promographix Inc........................ F 919 846-1379
Carolina Beach *(G-1263)*

SIGNS & ADVERTISING SPECIALTIES:
Scoreboards, Electric

Major Display Inc....................... G 800 260-1067
Franklin *(G-4836)*

SIGNS, ELECTRICAL: Wholesalers

Kenneth Moore Signs................... G 910 458-6428
Wilmington *(G-12826)*

Southeastern Sign Works Inc........ G 336 789-5516
Mount Airy *(G-9177)*

SIGNS, EXC ELECTRIC, WHOLESALE

Signature Signs Inc.................... G 336 431-2072
High Point *(G-6773)*

Trivantage LLC........................... D 800 786-1876
Burlington *(G-1171)*

SIGNS: Electrical

ABC Signs and Graphics LLC....... G 252 652-6620
Havelock *(G-6122)*

Action Sign Company Lenoir Inc... G 828 754-4116
Lenoir *(G-7566)*

Ad-Art Signs Inc......................... G 704 377-5369
Charlotte *(G-1621)*

All Signs & Graphics LLC............ G 910 323-3115
Fayetteville *(G-4549)*

Allen Industries Inc.................... C 336 294-4777
Greensboro *(G-5350)*

Allen Industries Inc.................... D 336 668-2791
Greensboro *(G-5349)*

Anthem Displays LLC.................. F 910 746-8988
Elizabethtown *(G-4417)*

Anthem Displays LLC.................. G 910 862-3550
Elizabethtown *(G-4418)*

Aoa Signs Inc............................ G 336 679-3344
Wilson *(G-12962)*

B&P Enterprise NC Inc................ G 727 669-6877
Hickory *(G-6269)*

Beeson Sign Co Inc..................... G 336 993-5617
Kernersville *(G-7247)*

Blashfield Sign Company Inc........ G 910 485-7200
Fayetteville *(G-4559)*

Ebert Sign Company Inc.............. G 336 768-2867
Lexington *(G-7681)*

Ever Glo Sign Co Inc................... G 704 633-3324
Salisbury *(G-11049)*

Goldsboro Neon Sign Co Inc........ G 919 735-2035
Goldsboro *(G-5217)*

Grandwell Industries Inc............. E 919 557-1221
Fuquay Varina *(G-4883)*

Interstate Sign Company Inc........ E 336 789-3069
Mount Airy *(G-9135)*

Lockwood Identity Inc................. C 704 597-9801
Charlotte *(G-2430)*

McCorkle Sign Company Inc........ E 919 687-7080
Durham *(G-4121)*

Moss Sign Company Inc.............. F 828 299-7766
Asheville *(G-551)*

Parish Sign & Service Inc............ E 910 875-6121
Raeford *(G-9846)*

PFC Group LLC........................... D 704 393-4040
Charlotte *(G-2632)*

Powersigns Inc........................... G 910 343-1789
Wilmington *(G-12885)*

Reese Sign Service Inc............... G 919 580-0705
Goldsboro *(G-5239)*

Sensational Signs...................... G 704 358-1099
Charlotte *(G-2787)*

September Signs & Graphics LLC... G 910 791-9084
Wilmington *(G-12917)*

Sign & Awning Systems Inc......... G 919 892-5900
Dunn *(G-3868)*

Sign Connection Inc.................... F 704 868-4500
Gastonia *(G-5136)*

Sign Here of Lake Norman Inc...... G 704 483-6454
Denver *(G-3805)*

Sign Medic Inc........................... G 336 789-5972
Mount Airy *(G-9176)*

Sign World Inc............................ G 704 529-4440
Charlotte *(G-2806)*

Signature Signs Inc.................... G 336 431-2072
High Point *(G-6773)*

Signs Etc of Charlotte................ F 704 522-8860
Charlotte *(G-2808)*

Signs Unlimited Inc.................... F 919 596-7612
Durham *(G-4237)*

Southeastern Sign Works Inc........ G 336 789-5516
Mount Airy *(G-9177)*

Stonetree Signs......................... G 336 625-0938
Denton *(G-3761)*

SIGNS: Neon

Custom Neon & Graphics Inc....... G 704 344-1715
Charlotte *(G-2010)*

SILICONES

Momentive Performance Mtls Inc... C 704 805-6252
Charlotte *(G-2514)*

Momentive Performance Mtls Inc... E 704 805-6200
Huntersville *(G-7017)*

Xona Microfluidics Inc................ G 951 553-6400
Research Triangle Pa *(G-10718)*

SILK SCREEN DESIGN SVCS

Body Billboards Inc.................... G 919 544-4540
Durham *(G-3936)*

Moving Screens Incorporated............... G ... 336 364-9259
Rougemont (G-10914)

Rapp Productions Inc........................... F ... 919 913-0270
Carrboro (G-1271)

SILO STAVES: Concrete Or Cast Stone

Cava Di Pietra Inc............................... G ... 910 338-5024
Wilmington (G-12736)

SINTER: Iron

GKN Sinter Metals LLC....................... C ... 828 464-0642
Conover (G-3524)

SKILL TRAINING CENTER

Webster Entps Jackson Cnty Inc........... G ... 828 586-8981
Sylva (G-11904)

SLINGS: Rope

Ace Marine Rigging & Supply Inc........... F ... 252 726-6620
Morehead City (G-8811)

SMOKE DETECTORS

Walter Kidde Portable Eqp Inc.............. B ... 919 563-5911
Mebane (G-8263)

SNIPS: Tinners'

Irwin Industrial Tool Company............... C ... 704 987-4555
Huntersville (G-7004)

SOFT DRINKS WHOLESALERS

Choice USA Beverage Inc..................... G ... 704 487-6951
Shelby (G-11317)

Pepsi Bottling Ventures LLC.................. C ... 336 724-4800
Winston Salem (G-13281)

Pepsi-Cola Btlg Hickry NC Inc............... G ... 828 322-8090
Granite Falls (G-5316)

Pepsi-Cola Btlg Hickry NC Inc............... D ... 828 322-8090
Hickory (G-6409)

Pepsi-Cola Btlg Hickry NC Inc............... G ... 828 322-8090
Hickory (G-6410)

Zeskp LLC... G ... 910 762-8300
Wilmington (G-12958)

SOFTWARE PUBLISHERS: Home Entertainment

Boss Key Productions Inc..................... D ... 919 659-5704
Raleigh (G-9956)

Ientertainment Network Inc.................. G ... 919 238-4090
Burnsville (G-1188)

Konami Digital Entrmt Inc..................... E ... 310 220-8100
Durham (G-4098)

Micronova Systems Inc......................... G ... 910 202-0564
Wilmington (G-12853)

Utd Technology Corp............................ G ... 704 612-0121
Mint Hill (G-8344)

Wave Front Computers LLC................... G ... 919 896-6121
Raleigh (G-10600)

SOFTWARE PUBLISHERS: Operating Systems

Feedtrail Incorporated......................... F ... 757 618-7760
Raleigh (G-10105)

Innait Inc.. G ... 406 241-5245
Charlotte (G-2337)

JMP Statistical Discovery Llc................. F ... 877 594-6567
Cary (G-1378)

SOFTWARE TRAINING, COMPUTER

Academy Association Inc....................... F ... 919 544-0835
Durham (G-3877)

Camstar Systems Inc........................... C ... 704 227-6600
Charlotte (G-1833)

Ideacode Inc...................................... G ... 919 341-5170
Greensboro (G-5613)

SOLAR CELLS

510nano Inc....................................... F ... 919 521-5982
Durham (G-3873)

Centrotherm Usa Inc............................ G ... 360 626-4445
Durham (G-3968)

Micro-OHM Corporation....................... G ... 800 845-5167
Raleigh (G-10301)

SOLAR HEATING EQPT

Low Impact Tech USA Inc..................... G ... 828 428-6310
Fletcher (G-4749)

Solar Hot Limited................................ G ... 919 439-2387
Raleigh (G-10490)

Solarh2ot Ltd..................................... G ... 919 439-2387
Raleigh (G-10493)

Sunqest Inc....................................... G ... 828 325-4910
Newton (G-9501)

SOUND EQPT: Electric

Custom Light and Sound Inc................. E ... 919 286-1122
Durham (G-3994)

SPACE PROPULSION UNITS & PARTS

James Tool Machine & Engrg Inc........... C ... 828 584-8722
Morganton (G-8875)

SPAS

Southern Home Spa and Wtr Pdts......... G ... 336 286-3564
Greensboro (G-5826)

SPEAKER SYSTEMS

Danley Sound Labs Inc......................... G ... 877 419-5805
Candler (G-1223)

Hartley Loudspeakers Inc..................... G ... 910 392-1200
Wilmington (G-12803)

SPECIALTY FOOD STORES: Coffee

Tradewinds Coffee Co Inc..................... F ... 919 556-1835
Zebulon (G-13524)

Well-Bean Coffee & Crumbs LLC........... G ... 833 777-2326
Wake Forest (G-12314)

SPECIALTY FOOD STORES: Health & Dietetic Food

Nutrotonic LLC................................... F ... 855 948-0008
Charlotte (G-2590)

Suntory International............................ F ... 917 756-2747
Raleigh (G-10521)

SPECIALTY FOOD STORES: Juices, Fruit Or Vegetable

Cold Off Press LLC.............................. G ... 984 444-9006
Raleigh (G-10003)

SPECIALTY FOOD STORES: Vitamin

Daily Manufacturing Inc........................ F ... 704 782-0700
Rockwell (G-10795)

SPECIALTY OUTPATIENT CLINICS, NEC

Cape Fear Orthtics Prsthtics I............... G ... 910 483-0933
Fayetteville (G-4566)

SPORTING & ATHLETIC GOODS: Bowling Balls

Thunder Alley Enterprises..................... G ... 910 371-0119
Leland (G-7560)

SPORTING & ATHLETIC GOODS: Fishing Eqpt

Electric Fshing Reel Systems I.............. G ... 336 273-9101
Greensboro (G-5516)

Fathom Offshore Holdings LLC.............. G ... 910 399-6882
Wilmington (G-12776)

SPORTING & ATHLETIC GOODS: Fishing Tackle, General

Sea Striker Inc................................... G ... 252 247-4113
Morehead City (G-8843)

SPORTING & ATHLETIC GOODS: Gymnasium Eqpt

Carolina Gym Supply Corp..................... G ... 919 732-6999
Hillsborough (G-6862)

SPORTING & ATHLETIC GOODS: Hunting Eqpt

Deerhunter Tree Stands Inc................... G ... 704 462-1116
Hickory (G-6319)

Frostie Bottom Tree Stand LLC............. G ... 828 466-1708
Claremont (G-3113)

Hawk Distributors Inc........................... G ... 888 334-1307
Sanford (G-11188)

Hughes Products Co Inc....................... G ... 336 769-3788
Winston Salem (G-13202)

Kol Incorporated................................. G ... 919 872-2340
Raleigh (G-10240)

Rigem Right....................................... G ... 252 726-9508
Newport (G-9443)

Sports Products LLC............................ G ... 919 723-7470
Wake Forest (G-12302)

SPORTING & ATHLETIC GOODS: Racket Sports Eqpt

Syntech of Burlington Inc..................... F ... 336 570-2035
Burlington (G-1166)

SPORTING & ATHLETIC GOODS: Rods & Rod Parts, Fishing

Lees Tackle Inc.................................. G ... 910 386-5100
Wilmington (G-12832)

SPORTING & ATHLETIC GOODS: Shafts, Golf Club

Thomas Golf Inc................................. G ... 704 461-1342
Charlotte (G-2912)

VA Composites Inc.............................. G ... 844 474-2387
Aberdeen (G-29)

SPORTING & ATHLETIC GOODS: Targets, Archery & Rifle Shooting

McKenzie Sports Products LLC............. C ... 704 279-7985
Salisbury (G-11091)

SPORTING & ATHLETIC GOODS: Team Sports Eqpt

Parker Athletic Products LLC................ G ... 704 370-0400
Charlotte (G-2609)

SPORTING & ATHLETIC GOODS: Track & Field Athletic Eqpt

PRODUCT

Ucs Inc.................................D 704 732-9922
Lincolnton (G-7866)

United Canvas & Sling Inc.............E 704 732-9922
Lincolnton (G-7868)

SPORTING & REC GOODS, WHOLESALE: Camping Eqpt & Splys

Trivantage LLC.........................D 800 786-1876
Burlington (G-1171)

SPORTING & RECREATIONAL GOODS, WHOLESALE: Boat Access & Part

Custom Marine Fabrication Inc.........G 252 638-5422
New Bern (G-9360)

Iconic Marine Group LLC...............B 252 975-2000
Chocowinity (G-3083)

SPORTING FIREARMS WHOLESALERS

Every Day Carry LLc...................F 203 231-0256
Winnabow (G-13065)

North American Trade LLC..............G 828 712-3004
Fletcher (G-4759)

SPORTING GOODS STORES: Firearms

Bear Creek Arsenal LLC................C 919 292-6000
Sanford (G-11154)

Dara Holsters & Gear Inc..............E 919 374-2170
Wendell (G-12531)

Sturm Ruger & Company Inc.............B 336 427-0286
Mayodan (G-8209)

SPORTING GOODS STORES: Fishing Eqpt

Custom Marine Fabrication Inc.........G 252 638-5422
New Bern (G-9360)

Fathom Offshore Holdings LLC..........G 910 399-6882
Wilmington (G-12776)

SPORTING GOODS STORES: Specialty Sport Splys, NEC

Millers Sports and Trophies...........G 252 792-2050
Williamston (G-12672)

SPORTING GOODS: Sleeping Bags

Lomar Specialty Advg Inc..............F 704 788-4380
Concord (G-3396)

Treklite Inc..........................G 919 610-1788
Raleigh (G-10557)

SPORTS APPAREL STORES

Happy Jack Incorporated...............G 252 747-2911
Snow Hill (G-11480)

Rec Plus Inc..........................E 704 375-9098
Charlotte (G-2696)

SPORTS CLUBS, MANAGERS & PROMOTERS

Richard Chldress Racg Entps In........B 336 731-3334
Welcome (G-12514)

SPRINGS: Coiled Flat

Matthew Warren Inc....................E
Charlotte (G-2470)

SPRINGS: Furniture

Leggett & Platt Incorporated..........G 704 380-6208
Statesville (G-11727)

SPRINGS: Mechanical, Precision

Lee Spring Company LLC................E 336 275-3631
Greensboro (G-5659)

Northeast Tool and Mfg Company.........E 704 882-1187
Matthews (G-8187)

SPRINGS: Precision

Cox Precision Springs Inc.............F 336 629-8500
Asheboro (G-342)

SPRINGS: Steel

Bridgestone Americas Inc..............C 984 888-0413
Durham (G-3940)

Lee Spring Company LLC................E 336 275-3631
Greensboro (G-5659)

Southern ATL Spring Mfg Sls LL........E 704 279-1331
Granite Quarry (G-5328)

Stabilus Inc..........................D 704 865-7444
Gastonia (G-5141)

Stable Holdco Inc.....................B 704 866-7140
Gastonia (G-5142)

SPRINGS: Wire

Leggett & Platt Incorporated..........G 704 380-6208
Statesville (G-11727)

M-B Industries Inc....................C 828 862-4201
Rosman (G-10913)

N C Coil Inc..........................G 336 983-4440
King (G-7333)

Newcomb Spring Corp...................E 704 588-2043
Gastonia (G-5109)

Southern Precision Spring Inc.........E 704 392-4393
Charlotte (G-2838)

STAINLESS STEEL

Davis Equipment Handlers Inc..........G 704 792-9176
Charlotte (G-2021)

Gulfstream Steel & Supply Inc.........E 910 329-5100
Holly Ridge (G-6888)

Quality Mechanical Contrs LLC.........D 336 228-0638
Burlington (G-1143)

STAIRCASES & STAIRS, WOOD

Andronics Construction Inc............E 704 400-9562
Indian Trail (G-7068)

Carolina Stairs Inc...................F 704 664-5032
Mount Ulla (G-9267)

Convert-A-Stair LLC...................G 888 908-5657
Wilmington (G-12750)

Royal Oak Stairs Inc..................G 919 855-8988
Raleigh (G-10449)

Southern Staircase Inc................G 704 363-2123
Charlotte (G-2840)

Wood Barn Inc.........................E 919 496-6714
Louisburg (G-7929)

STAMPINGS: Automotive

Belwith Products LLC..................G 336 841-3899
High Point (G-6545)

Vibration Solutions LLC...............G 704 896-7535
Charlotte (G-2983)

STAPLES: Steel, Wire Or Cut

Schafer Manufacturing Co LLC..........G 704 528-5321
Troutman (G-12149)

STATIONARY & OFFICE SPLYS, WHOLESALE: Office Filing Splys

Cartridge World.......................G 336 885-0989
High Point (G-6562)

Sdv Office Systems LLC................F 844 968-9500
Fletcher (G-4766)

STATIONERY & OFFICE SPLYS WHOLESALERS

Archie Supply LLC.....................G 336 987-0895
Greensboro (G-5368)

Bic Corporation.......................D 704 598-7700
Charlotte (G-1779)

Digital Print & Imaging Inc...........G 910 341-3005
Greenville (G-5965)

Person Printing Company Inc...........E 336 599-2146
Roxboro (G-10940)

STATORS REWINDING SVCS

Leonard Electric Mtr Repr Inc.........G 336 625-2375
Asheboro (G-373)

W & W Electric Motor Shop Inc.........G 910 642-2369
Whiteville (G-12594)

STATUARY & OTHER DECORATIVE PRDTS: Nonmetallic

Cairn Studio Ltd......................G 704 892-3581
Davidson (G-3698)

STEEL & ALLOYS: Tool & Die

Greene Precision Products Inc.........G 828 262-0116
Boone (G-919)

STEEL, COLD-ROLLED: Strip NEC, From Purchased HotRolled

Sandvik Inc...........................C 919 563-5008
Mebane (G-8258)

STOKERS: Mechanical, Domestic Or Indl

Machining Technology Services.........G 704 282-1071
Monroe (G-8522)

STONE: Dimension, NEC

Carolina Quarries Inc.................D 704 633-0201
Salisbury (G-11028)

Carolina Sunrock LLC..................E 919 575-4502
Butner (G-1200)

Lbm Industries Inc....................G 828 631-1227
Sylva (G-11895)

Lbm Industries Inc....................F 828 966-4270
Sapphire (G-11259)

McNeely Trucking Co...................G 828 966-4270
Sapphire (G-11260)

Sunrock Group Holdings Corp...........D 919 747-6400
Raleigh (G-10520)

Tarheel Sand & Stone Inc..............G 336 468-4003
Hamptonville (G-6093)

STONE: Quarrying & Processing, Own Stone Prdts

American Stone Company................G 919 929-7131
Chapel Hill (G-1525)

B V Hedrick Gravel & Sand Co..........E 828 645-5560
Weaverville (G-12482)

Boone-Woody Mining Company Inc........B 828 675-5188
Micaville (G-8270)

Lbm Industries Inc....................F 828 966-4270
Sapphire (G-11258)

Midcoastal Development Corp............G 336 622-3091
Staley (G-11597)

Stonemaster Inc.......................F 704 333-0353
Concord (G-3449)

Wake Stone Corporation................E 919 677-0050
Cary (G-1481)

STONEWARE PRDTS: Pottery

East Fork Pottery LLC............................... G 828 237-7200
Asheville *(G-491)*

East Fork Pottery LLC............................... G 828 237-7200
Asheville *(G-492)*

STORE FIXTURES: Wood

Idx Impressions LLC.............................. C 703 550-6902
Washington *(G-12393)*

Ivey Fixture & Design Inc....................... G 704 283-4398
Monroe *(G-8506)*

Oyama Cabinet Inc................................. G 828 327-2668
Conover *(G-3542)*

Rusco Fixture Company Inc.................... E 704 474-3184
Norwood *(G-9559)*

Stanly Fixs Acquisition LLC.................... G 704 474-3184
Norwood *(G-9560)*

Sterling Cleora Corporation.................... F 919 563-5800
Durham *(G-4250)*

STORES: Auto & Home Supply

Courtesy Ford Inc.................................. G 252 338-4783
Elizabeth City *(G-4384)*

Cummins Inc.. E 336 275-4531
Greensboro *(G-5476)*

Dfa US Inc.. E 336 756-0590
Mocksville *(G-8358)*

L L C Batteries of N C............................ G 919 331-0241
Angier *(G-123)*

Piedmont Truck Tires Inc....................... F 828 277-1549
Asheville *(G-574)*

Piedmont Truck Tires Inc....................... F 336 223-9412
Graham *(G-5281)*

Piedmont Truck Tires Inc....................... F 336 668-0091
Greensboro *(G-5746)*

Trick Karts Inc....................................... G 704 883-0089
Statesville *(G-11793)*

Williams Electric Mtr Repr Inc............... G 919 859-9790
Sanford *(G-11250)*

STOVES: Wood & Coal Burning

Appalchian Stove Fbrcators Inc............. G 828 253-0164
Asheville *(G-428)*

Taylor Manufacturing Inc....................... E 910 862-2576
Elizabethtown *(G-4434)*

STRAINERS: Line, Piping Systems

Hayward Industrial Products.................. C 704 837-8002
Charlotte *(G-2264)*

STRAPS: Braids, Textile

All American Braids Inc.......................... E 704 852-4380
Gastonia *(G-4985)*

Standard Tytape Company Inc............... G 828 693-6594
Hendersonville *(G-6244)*

STRAPS: Webbing, Woven

Hickory Springs Mfg Co......................... F 336 491-4131
High Point *(G-6648)*

Murdock Webbing Company Inc........... E 252 823-1131
Tarboro *(G-11937)*

STUDS & JOISTS: Sheet Metal

H&S Autoshot LLC................................. E 847 662-8500
Mooresville *(G-8679)*

SUNDRIES & RELATED PRDTS: Medical & Laboratory, Rubber

Custom Assemblies Inc.......................... E 919 202-4533
Pine Level *(G-9678)*

Mount Hope Machinery Co...................... F
Charlotte *(G-2523)*

SURFACE ACTIVE AGENTS

Cht R Beitlich Corporation...................... E 704 523-4242
Charlotte *(G-1917)*

Diarkis LLC.. G 704 888-5244
Locust *(G-7891)*

Henkel Corporation................................ D 704 633-1731
Salisbury *(G-11062)*

Syntha Group Inc.................................. D 336 885-5131
High Point *(G-6801)*

SURGICAL APPLIANCES & SPLYS

Carolon Company.................................. D 336 969-6001
Rural Hall *(G-10954)*

Teleflex Incorporated............................ G 919 433-2575
Durham *(G-4261)*

Teleflex Incorporated............................ G 919 433-2575
Durham *(G-4262)*

410 Medical Inc..................................... F 919 241-7900
Durham *(G-3872)*

Allyn International Trdg Corp................. G 877 858-2482
Marshville *(G-8085)*

American Fiber & Finishing Inc.............. E 704 984-9256
Albemarle *(G-61)*

Amtai Medical Equipment Inc............... F 919 872-1803
Raleigh *(G-9901)*

Andersen Products Inc.......................... E 336 376-3000
Haw River *(G-6130)*

Andersen Sterilizers Inc........................ E 336 376-8622
Haw River *(G-6131)*

Beocare Inc... C 828 728-7300
Hudson *(G-6942)*

Biomedical Innovations Inc................... G 910 603-0267
Southern Pines *(G-11495)*

Coastal Machine & Welding Inc............ G 910 754-6476
Shallotte *(G-11302)*

Cranial Technologies Inc....................... G 336 760-5530
Winston Salem *(G-13134)*

Custom Medical Specialties Inc............ G 919 202-8462
Pine Level *(G-9679)*

Ethicon Inc.. F 919 234-2124
Cary *(G-1356)*

Hollister Incorporated........................... G 919 792-2095
Raleigh *(G-10172)*

Hyperbranch Medical Tech Inc.............. F 919 433-3325
Durham *(G-4067)*

Kayser-Roth Corporation...................... C 336 852-2030
Greensboro *(G-5643)*

Lifespan Incorporated........................... D 336 838-2614
North Wilkesboro *(G-9541)*

Lifespan Incorporated........................... E 704 944-5100
Charlotte *(G-2419)*

Medical Device Bus Svcs Inc................ F 704 423-0033
Charlotte *(G-2485)*

Medical Spclties of Crlnas Inc.............. G 910 575-4542
Sunset Beach *(G-11851)*

Mign Inc.. G 609 304-1617
Charlotte *(G-2500)*

Nufabrx LLC.. G 888 683-2279
Charlotte *(G-2589)*

Pacon Manufacturing Co LLC............... C 910 239-3001
Leland *(G-7556)*

Safe Home Pro Inc................................ F 704 662-2299
Cornelius *(G-3626)*

Soundside Orthtics Prsthtics L.............. G 910 238-2026
Jacksonville *(G-7149)*

Stryker Corporation............................... F 919 433-3325
Durham *(G-4253)*

Sunshine Prosthetics Inc....................... G 833 266-9781
Wilson *(G-13032)*

Test ME Out Inc.................................... G 252 635-6770
New Bern *(G-9399)*

VH Industries Inc.................................. G 704 743-2400
Concord *(G-3464)*

SURGICAL IMPLANTS

Medtrnic Sofamor Danek USA Inc.......... G 919 457-9982
Cary *(G-1401)*

Novex Innovations LLC.......................... G 336 231-6693
Winston Salem *(G-13267)*

SUSPENSION SYSTEMS: Acoustical, Metal

Hotchkis Performance Mfg Inc............... G 704 660-3060
Mooresville *(G-8688)*

Leo Gaev Metalworks Inc....................... G 919 883-4666
Chapel Hill *(G-1552)*

SVC ESTABLISHMENT EQPT, WHOLESALE: Firefighting Eqpt

Beco Holding Company Inc................... C 800 826-3473
Charlotte *(G-1767)*

Fireresq Incorporated............................ F 888 975-0858
Mooresville *(G-8664)*

Lightning X Products Inc........................ G 704 295-0299
Charlotte *(G-2421)*

SVC ESTABLISHMENT EQPT, WHOLESALE: Laundry Eqpt & Splys

Gardner Machinery Corporation............. F 704 372-3890
Charlotte *(G-2189)*

Laundry Svc Tech Ltd Lblty Co.............. G 908 327-1997
Matthews *(G-8126)*

Talley Machinery Corporation................ G 336 664-0012
Greensboro *(G-5850)*

SVC ESTABLISHMENT EQPT, WHOLESALE: Taxidermist Tools & Eqpt

Jim Allred Taxidermy Supply................. G 828 749-5900
Saluda *(G-11139)*

SWIMMING POOL ACCESS: Leaf Skimmers Or Pool Rakes

Hayward Industries Inc.......................... D 336 712-9900
Clemmons *(G-3188)*

Hayward Industries Inc.......................... B 704 837-8002
Charlotte *(G-2265)*

SWIMMING POOL EQPT: Filters & Water Conditioning Systems

Caldwells Water Conditioning................ G 828 253-6605
Asheville *(G-465)*

Hayward Holdings Inc............................ C 704 837-8002
Charlotte *(G-2263)*

Hayward Industries Inc.......................... D 336 712-9900
Clemmons *(G-3188)*

Hayward Industries Inc.......................... A 336 712-9900
Clemmons *(G-3189)*

Hayward Industries Inc.......................... B 704 837-8002
Charlotte *(G-2265)*

Pentair Water Pool and Spa Inc............. D 919 463-4640
Cary *(G-1417)*

Pentair Water Pool and Spa Inc............. A 919 566-8000
Sanford *(G-11217)*

SWITCHES: Electric Power, Exc Snap, Push Button, Etc

Electro Switch Corp............................... C 919 833-0707
Raleigh *(G-10081)*

P
R
O
D
U
C
T

Shallco Inc.................................... E 919 934-3135
Smithfield (G-11465)

Siemens Power Transmission .... A 919 463-8702
Cary (G-1454)

SWITCHES: Electronic

Applied Drives Inc............................ G 704 573-2324
Charlotte (G-1686)

High Vacuum Electronics Inc.................. G 910 738-1219
Lumberton (G-7957)

Silanna Semicdtr N Amer Inc.................. D 984 444-6500
Raleigh (G-10476)

SWITCHES: Electronic Applications

Silanna Semicdtr N Amer Inc.................. D 984 444-6500
Raleigh (G-10476)

SWITCHES: Time, Electrical Switchgear Apparatus

Precision Time Systems Inc................... G 910 253-9850
Supply (G-11857)

SWITCHGEAR & SWITCHBOARD APPARATUS

ABB Enterprise Software Inc................. C 919 582-3283
Raleigh (G-9862)

ABB Inc... E 704 587-1362
Charlotte (G-1609)

ABB Inc... C 252 827-2121
Pinetops (G-9705)

ABB Inc... D 919 856-2360
Raleigh (G-9864)

ABB Inc... C 919 856-2360
Cary (G-1285)

Carolina Elctrnic Assmblers In.............. E 919 938-1086
Smithfield (G-11435)

Carolina Products Inc........................ E 704 364-9029
Charlotte (G-1854)

Dna Group Inc................................. E 919 881-0889
Raleigh (G-10051)

General Electric Company..................... G 704 561-5700
Charlotte (G-2200)

General Electric Company..................... B 919 563-5561
Mebane (G-8242)

Grecon Inc...................................... F 503 641-7731
Charlotte (G-2237)

JA Smith Inc................................... G 704 860-4910
Lawndale (G-7517)

JMS Southeast Inc............................ E 704 873-1835
Statesville (G-11719)

Miller Ctrl Mfg Inc Clinton NC.............. G 910 592-5112
Clinton (G-3235)

Precision Mch Fabrication Inc............... D 919 231-8648
Raleigh (G-10390)

Reuel Inc....................................... E 919 734-0460
Goldsboro (G-5240)

Schneider Electric Usa Inc.................. B 919 266-3671
Knightdale (G-7458)

Schneider Electric Usa Inc.................. C 888 778-2733
Morrisville (G-9045)

Solero Technologies Shelby LLC............ C 704 482-9582
Shelby (G-11380)

SWITCHGEAR & SWITCHGEAR ACCESS, NEC

Eaton Corporation............................ B 828 684-2381
Arden (G-266)

Southern Electrical Eqp Co Inc.............. G 704 392-1396
Indian Trail (G-7099)

SYNTHETIC RESIN FINISHED PRDTS, NEC

Hornet Capital LLC........................... F 252 641-8000
Tarboro (G-11930)

SYRUPS, DRINK

Choice USA Beverage Inc.................... D 704 823-1651
Lowell (G-7930)

Little Beekeeper LLC......................... G 704 215-9690
Lincolnton (G-7839)

SYSTEMS ENGINEERING: Computer Related

Custom Controls Unlimited LLC........... F 919 812-6553
Raleigh (G-10029)

Qplot Corporation............................ G 949 302-7928
Raleigh (G-10410)

SYSTEMS INTEGRATION SVCS

Science Applications Intl Corp.............. G 910 822-2100
Fayetteville (G-4666)

SYSTEMS INTEGRATION SVCS: Local Area Network

Blue Wolf Technologies LLP................. G 919 810-1508
Raleigh (G-9949)

Romeo Six LLC................................ F 919 589-7150
Holly Springs (G-6912)

SYSTEMS SOFTWARE DEVELOPMENT SVCS

Billsoft Inc...................................... F 913 859-9674
Durham (G-3927)

Medicor Imaging Inc.......................... G 704 332-5532
Charlotte (G-2486)

Twork Technology Inc........................ G 704 218-9675
Charlotte (G-2956)

Worden Brothers Inc.......................... D 919 202-8555
Wilmington (G-12954)

TABLE OR COUNTERTOPS, PLASTIC LAMINATED

Custom Surfaces Corporation............... G 252 638-3800
New Bern (G-9361)

McAd Inc....................................... E 336 299-3030
Greensboro (G-5686)

Mkc85 Inc...................................... F 910 762-1986
Wilmington (G-12855)

TS Woodworks & RAD Design Inc......... F 704 238-1015
Monroe (G-8571)

TABLES: Lift, Hydraulic

Columbus McKinnon Corporation.......... C 716 689-5400
Charlotte (G-1962)

TABLETS: Bronze Or Other Metal

Penco Products Inc........................... C 252 798-4000
Hamilton (G-6049)

TAGS & LABELS: Paper

Abx Innvtive Pckg Slutions LLC........... D 980 443-1100
Charlotte (G-1613)

Graphic Finshg Solutions LLC.............. G 336 255-7857
Greensboro (G-5573)

Label & Printing Solutions Inc.............. G 919 782-1242
Raleigh (G-10243)

Tab Index Inc.................................. G 919 876-8988
Raleigh (G-10529)

US Print Inc.................................... G 919 878-0981
Raleigh (G-10578)

TAGS: Paper, Blank, Made From Purchased Paper

Wright of Thomasville Inc.................... F 336 472-4200
Thomasville (G-12091)

TALLOW: Animal

Darling Ingredients Inc....................... E 910 483-0473
Fayetteville (G-4583)

Darling Ingredients Inc....................... F 704 864-9941
Gastonia (G-5039)

TANK REPAIR & CLEANING SVCS

Noble Oil Services Inc....................... C 919 774-8180
Sanford (G-11212)

Petroleum Tank Corporation................. F 919 284-2418
Kenly (G-7235)

TANKS & OTHER TRACKED VEHICLE CMPNTS

Carolina Custom Tank LLC.................. G 980 406-3200
Gastonia (G-5013)

Parker Gas Company Inc..................... F 800 354-7250
Clinton (G-3238)

TANKS: Lined, Metal

Friedrich Metal Pdts Co Inc................. E 336 375-3067
Browns Summit (G-993)

M M M Inc..................................... G 252 527-0229
La Grange (G-7469)

TANKS: Plastic & Fiberglass

Asmo North America LLC..................... A 704 872-2319
Statesville (G-11661)

TANKS: Standard Or Custom Fabricated, Metal Plate

Adamson Global Technology Corp........ G 252 523-5200
Kinston (G-7391)

Bendel Tank Heat Exchanger LLC......... E 704 596-5112
Charlotte (G-1771)

Bthec Inc....................................... E 704 596-5112
Charlotte (G-1816)

Florida Marine Tanks Inc.................... F 305 620-9030
Henderson (G-6155)

Gaston County Dyeing Machin.............. D 704 822-5000
Mount Holly (G-9231)

General Industries Inc........................ E 919 751-1791
Goldsboro (G-5215)

Highland Tank NC Inc........................ C 336 218-0801
Greensboro (G-5599)

Industrial Air Inc.............................. C 336 292-1030
Greensboro (G-5616)

NC Diesel Performance LLC................. G 704 431-3257
Salisbury (G-11095)

Tank Fab Inc................................... F 910 675-8999
Rocky Point (G-10886)

Ward Vessel and Exchanger Corp......... D 704 568-3001
Charlotte (G-3004)

TAPE DRIVES

EMC Corporation.............................. F 919 767-0641
Durham (G-4021)

TAPES, ADHESIVE: Masking, Made From Purchased Materials

Cdv LLC.. F 919 674-3460
Morrisville (G-8953)

TAPES: Fabric

Carolina Narrow Fabric Company.......... C 336 631-3000
Winston Salem *(G-13117)*

Custom Fabric Samples Inc................... G 336 472-1854
Thomasville *(G-12014)*

Spanset Inc.. E 919 774-6316
Sanford *(G-11236)*

US Label Corporation.............................. G 336 332-7000
Greensboro *(G-5894)*

TAPES: Pressure Sensitive

Carolina Tape & Supply Corp.................. E 828 322-3991
Hickory *(G-6289)*

TAPES: Pressure Sensitive, Rubber

Achem Industry America Inc................... G 704 283-6144
Monroe *(G-8415)*

Carolina Tape & Supply Corp.................. E 828 322-3991
Hickory *(G-6289)*

Draft DOT International LLC.................... G 336 775-0525
Lexington *(G-7680)*

Granite Tape Co...................................... G 828 396-5614
Granite Falls *(G-5305)*

Lakebrook Corporation............................ G 207 947-4051
Oak Island *(G-9566)*

Neptco Incorporated............................... C 828 313-0149
Granite Falls *(G-5314)*

Neptco Incorporated............................... C 828 728-5951
Lenoir *(G-7629)*

Shurtape Technologies LLC.................... G 704 553-9441
Charlotte *(G-2800)*

Shurtape Technologies LLC.................... G 828 304-8302
Hickory *(G-6445)*

Stm Industries Inc.................................. E 828 322-2700
Hickory *(G-6459)*

TARGET DRONES

Cyberlux Corporation.............................. F 984 363-6894
Research Triangle Pa *(G-10707)*

Dronescape Pllc...................................... G 704 953-3798
Charlotte *(G-2066)*

TARPAULINS

Dize Company.. D 336 722-5181
Winston Salem *(G-13149)*

OBrian Tarping Systems Inc................... F 252 291-2141
Wilson *(G-13011)*

Trelleborg Ctd Systems US Inc.............. C 828 286-9126
Rutherfordton *(G-10999)*

TELECOMMUNICATION EQPT REPAIR SVCS, EXC TELEPHONES

Edge Broadband Solutions LLC.............. E 828 785-1420
Waynesville *(G-12457)*

TELEPHONE ANSWERING SVCS

Daniels Business Services Inc................ E 828 277-8250
Asheville *(G-483)*

TELEPHONE EQPT: NEC

Atcom Inc... F 704 357-7900
Charlotte *(G-1708)*

Lba Group Inc... E 252 329-9243
Greenville *(G-5999)*

Lba Technology Inc................................. E 252 757-0279
Greenville *(G-6000)*

Siemens Airport...................................... G 704 359-5551
Charlotte *(G-2801)*

TELEPHONE STATION EQPT & PARTS: Wire

Code LLC... E 828 328-6004
Hickory *(G-6304)*

TELEPHONE SVCS

M I Connection....................................... F 704 662-3255
Mooresville *(G-8717)*

TELEVISION BROADCASTING & COMMUNICATIONS EQPT

Bahakel Communications Ltd LLC.......... B 704 372-4434
Charlotte *(G-1740)*

Lets Talk Some Shit.............................. G 704 264-6212
Paw Creek *(G-9649)*

TELEVISION BROADCASTING STATIONS

News 14 Carolina................................... G 704 973-5700
Charlotte *(G-2559)*

Wtvd Television LLC............................... C 919 683-1111
Durham *(G-4313)*

TELEVISION: Closed Circuit Eqpt

Crest Electronics Inc.............................. G 336 855-6422
Greensboro *(G-5471)*

TEMPERING: Metal

Hhh Tempering Resources Inc............... F 336 201-5396
Winston Salem *(G-13197)*

Powerlyte Paintball Game Pdts.............. G 919 713-4317
Raleigh *(G-10381)*

TEMPORARY HELP SVCS

Delta Contractors Inc............................. F 817 410-9481
Linden *(G-7874)*

TEST KITS: Pregnancy

Gateway Campus.................................... G 919 833-0096
Raleigh *(G-10124)*

Pregnancy Support Services.................. G 919 490-0203
Chapel Hill *(G-1563)*

Your Choice Pregnancy Clinic............... G 919 577-9050
Fuquay Varina *(G-4907)*

TESTERS: Physical Property

Efco USA Inc.. G 800 332-6872
Charlotte *(G-2092)*

Roehrig Engineering Inc......................... G 336 956-3800
Greensboro *(G-5793)*

TESTING SVCS

Te Connectivity Corporation.................. C 336 727-5122
Winston Salem *(G-13358)*

TEXTILE & APPAREL SVCS

Crypton Mills LLC.................................. E 828 202-5875
Cliffside *(G-3225)*

Rogers Knitting Inc................................ G 336 789-4155
Mount Airy *(G-9172)*

TEXTILE CONVERTERS: Knit Goods

Badger Sportswear LLC.......................... D 704 871-0990
Statesville *(G-11665)*

Quiknit Crafting Inc............................... G 704 861-1030
Gastonia *(G-5129)*

TEXTILE DESIGNERS

Jubilee Screen Printing Inc.................... G 910 673-4240
West End *(G-12555)*

TEXTILE FINISHING: Dyeing, Manmade Fiber & Silk, Broadwoven

Hanes Companies Inc.............................. C 336 747-1600
Winston Salem *(G-13186)*

Upper South Studio Inc.......................... F 336 724-5480
Winston Salem *(G-13380)*

TEXTILE: Finishing, Raw Stock NEC

Carolina Yarn Processors Inc................. C 828 859-5891
Tryon *(G-12172)*

Unifi Inc... D 336 348-6539
Reidsville *(G-10700)*

TEXTILES: Bagging, Jute

Kids Playhouse LLC................................ G 704 299-4449
Charlotte *(G-2395)*

TEXTILES: Linen Fabrics

Leighdeux LLC....................................... G 704 965-4889
Charlotte *(G-2418)*

Opulence of Southern Pine.................... G 919 467-1781
Raleigh *(G-10348)*

TEXTILES: Mill Waste & Remnant

Firestone Fibers Textiles LLC................ A 704 734-2110
Kings Mountain *(G-7364)*

S & S Samples Inc................................. G 336 472-0402
Thomasville *(G-12068)*

William Barnet & Son LLC...................... C 252 522-2418
Kinston *(G-7437)*

THEATRICAL PRODUCERS & SVCS

Royal Faires Inc..................................... F 704 896-5555
Huntersville *(G-7044)*

THERMOPLASTIC MATERIALS

Alpek Polyester Usa LLC........................ D 704 940-7500
Charlotte *(G-1648)*

Aqua Plastics Inc................................... F 828 324-6284
Hickory *(G-6266)*

Microban Products Company................... E 704 766-4267
Huntersville *(G-7013)*

Poly One Distribution............................. G 704 872-8168
Statesville *(G-11749)*

Polyone Distribution.............................. G 919 413-4547
Rolesville *(G-10889)*

THIN FILM CIRCUITS

Industrial Hard Carbon LLC................... E 704 489-1488
Denver *(G-3790)*

THREAD: Cotton

Coats & Clark Inc................................... D 888 368-8401
Charlotte *(G-1942)*

Coats American Inc................................ C 800 242-8095
Charlotte *(G-1943)*

Coats N Amer De Rpblica Dmncan.......... C 800 242-8095
Charlotte *(G-1945)*

Ruddick Operating Company LLC........... A 704 372-5404
Charlotte *(G-2742)*

THREAD: Sewing

American & Efird LLC.............................. F 704 823-2501
Mount Holly *(G-9216)*

Ctc Holdings LLC................................... G 704 867-6611
Gastonia *(G-5034)*

Invista Capital Management LLC............ C 704 636-6000
Salisbury *(G-11071)*

J Charles Saunders Co Inc..................... E 704 866-9156
Gastonia *(G-5070)*

TILE: Brick & Structural, Clay

Clay Taylor Products Inc........................ D 704 636-2411
Salisbury *(G-11034)*

PRODUCT

Cunningham Brick Company................ C 336 248-8541
Lexington *(G-7673)*

General Shale Brick Inc...................... E 919 775-2121
Raleigh *(G-10127)*

Pine Hall Brick Co Inc........................ E 336 721-7500
Winston Salem *(G-13296)*

Triangle Brick Company...................... D 919 387-9257
Moncure *(G-8410)*

Triangle Brick Company...................... E 704 695-1420
Wadesboro *(G-12251)*

Triangle Brick Company...................... E 919 544-1796
Durham *(G-4277)*

TIRE & INNER TUBE MATERIALS & RELATED PRDTS

Mr Tire Inc.. G 704 735-8024
Lincolnton *(G-7846)*

TIRE CORD & FABRIC

Parker-Hannifin Corporation............... F 252 237-6171
Wilson *(G-13012)*

Tex-Tech Coatings LLC...................... D 336 992-7500
Kernersville *(G-7305)*

Tex-Tech Coatings LLC...................... F 336 992-7500
Kernersville *(G-7306)*

TIRES & INNER TUBES

Bestdrive LLC.................................... E 800 450-3187
Charlotte *(G-1774)*

Black Tire Service Inc........................ G 919 908-6347
Durham *(G-3934)*

Bridgestone Americas Inc.................. C 984 888-0413
Durham *(G-3940)*

Bridgestone Amrcas Tire Oprtons........... A 252 291-4275
Wilson *(G-12974)*

Carolina Giant Tires Inc..................... F 919 609-9077
Henderson *(G-6149)*

Derrow Enterprises Inc...................... G 252 635-3375
New Bern *(G-9364)*

Goodyear Tire & Rubber Company........ G 919 552-9340
Holly Springs *(G-6903)*

Oliver Rubber Company LLC............... B 336 629-1436
Asheboro *(G-380)*

Roll-Tech Molding Products LLC........... E 828 431-4515
Hickory *(G-6432)*

Too Hott Customs LLC...................... G 336 722-4919
Winston Salem *(G-13366)*

Wmb of Wake County Inc.................... G 919 782-0419
Raleigh *(G-10612)*

TIRES & TUBES WHOLESALERS

Bestdrive LLC.................................... E 800 450-3187
Charlotte *(G-1774)*

Derrow Enterprises Inc...................... G 252 635-3375
New Bern *(G-9364)*

Dunlop Aircraft Tyres Inc.................... E 336 283-0979
Mocksville *(G-8359)*

Mr Tire Inc.. F 704 483-1500
Denver *(G-3794)*

Mr Tire Inc.. F 828 322-8130
Hickory *(G-6398)*

Mr Tire Inc.. G 704 739-6456
Kings Mountain *(G-7373)*

Mr Tire Inc.. G 828 758-0047
Lenoir *(G-7627)*

Mr Tire Inc.. G 704 735-8024
Lincolnton *(G-7846)*

Mr Tire Inc.. G 704 484-0816
Shelby *(G-11365)*

Mr Tire Inc.. G 704 872-4127
Statesville *(G-11737)*

Parrish Tire Company........................ E 704 872-6565
Jonesville *(G-7198)*

Wmb of Wake County Inc.................... G 919 782-0419
Raleigh *(G-10612)*

TIRES & TUBES, WHOLESALE: Automotive

A 1 Tire Service Inc........................... G 828 684-1860
Fletcher *(G-4716)*

Accel Discount Tire........................... G 704 636-0323
Salisbury *(G-11012)*

Aiken-Black Tire Service Inc............... E 828 322-3736
Hickory *(G-6261)*

Albemarle Tire Retreading Inc............. G 704 982-4113
Albemarle *(G-59)*

Avery County Recapping Co Inc........... G 828 733-0161
Newland *(G-9424)*

Barnharts Tech Tire Repair Inc........... G 336 337-1569
Lexington *(G-7658)*

Beamer Tire & Auto Repair Inc........... F 336 882-7043
High Point *(G-6541)*

Bill Martin Inc................................... G 704 873-0241
Statesville *(G-11671)*

Bray S Recapping Service Inc............. E 336 786-6182
Mount Airy *(G-9105)*

Bridgestone Ret Operations LLC........... G 919 471-4468
Durham *(G-3941)*

Bridgestone Ret Operations LLC........... G 910 864-4106
Fayetteville *(G-4562)*

Bridgestone Ret Operations LLC........... F 704 861-8146
Gastonia *(G-5005)*

Bridgestone Ret Operations LLC........... G 919 778-0230
Goldsboro *(G-5202)*

Bridgestone Ret Operations LLC........... G 336 282-6646
Greensboro *(G-5399)*

Bridgestone Ret Operations LLC........... F 336 852-8524
Greensboro *(G-5400)*

Bridgestone Ret Operations LLC........... G 336 282-4695
Greensboro *(G-5401)*

Bridgestone Ret Operations LLC........... G 252 522-5126
Kinston *(G-7397)*

Bridgestone Ret Operations LLC........... G 919 872-6402
Raleigh *(G-9958)*

Bridgestone Ret Operations LLC........... G 919 872-6566
Raleigh *(G-9959)*

Bridgestone Ret Operations LLC........... G 252 243-5189
Wilson *(G-12973)*

Bridgestone Ret Operations LLC........... G 336 725-1580
Winston Salem *(G-13110)*

Bridgestone Amrcas Tire Oprtons........... A 252 291-4275
Wilson *(G-12974)*

Cecil Budd Tire Company LLC............. F 919 742-2322
Siler City *(G-11403)*

Claybrook Tire Inc............................. F 336 573-3135
Stoneville *(G-11820)*

Closed Tire Company Inc.................... F 704 864-5464
Gastonia *(G-5022)*

Colony Tire Corporation...................... G 252 973-0004
Rocky Mount *(G-10829)*

Crossroads Tire Store Inc.................... G 704 888-2064
Midland *(G-8285)*

Diagnostic Shop Inc........................... G 704 933-3435
Kannapolis *(G-7207)*

Discount Tires & Auto Repair............... G 336 788-0057
Winston Salem *(G-13147)*

Ed S Tire Laurinburg Inc.................... G 910 277-0565
Laurinburg *(G-7498)*

Enfield Tire Service Inc....................... G 252 445-5016
Enfield *(G-4482)*

Foster Tire Sales Inc.......................... G 336 248-6726
Lexington *(G-7688)*

Goodyear Tire & Rubber Company........ G 919 552-9340
Holly Springs *(G-6903)*

Goodyear Tire & Rubber Company........ G 984 983-0161
Mebane *(G-8245)*

Goodyear Tire & Rubber Company........ G 336 794-0035
Winston Salem *(G-13180)*

Greensboro Tire & Auto Service........... G 336 294-9495
Greensboro *(G-5578)*

Hall Tire and Battery Co Inc................ F 336 275-3812
Greensboro *(G-5586)*

Haneys Tire Recapping Svc LLC........... G 910 276-2636
Laurinburg *(G-7503)*

John Conrad Inc................................ G 336 475-8144
Thomasville *(G-12041)*

Johnnys Tire Sales and Svc Inc........... F 252 353-8473
Greenville *(G-5997)*

M & M Tire and Auto Inc.................... G 336 643-7877
Summerfield *(G-11843)*

M & R Retreading & Oil Co Inc........... G 704 474-4101
Norwood *(G-9556)*

McCarthy Tire Service Company........... F 910 791-0132
Wilmington *(G-12849)*

Merchants Inc................................... G 252 447-2121
Havelock *(G-6123)*

Mock Tire & Automotive Inc................ E 336 753-8473
Mocksville *(G-8379)*

Mock Tire & Automotive Inc................ E 336 774-0081
Winston Salem *(G-13256)*

Mock Tire & Automotive Inc................ E 336 768-1010
Winston Salem *(G-13257)*

Moss Brothers Tires & Svc Inc............. G 910 895-4572
Rockingham *(G-10783)*

Mr Tire Inc.. G 828 262-3555
Boone *(G-936)*

Mr Tire Inc.. F 704 483-1500
Denver *(G-3794)*

Mr Tire Inc.. F 828 322-8130
Hickory *(G-6398)*

Mr Tire Inc.. G 704 739-6456
Kings Mountain *(G-7373)*

Mr Tire Inc.. G 828 758-0047
Lenoir *(G-7627)*

Mr Tire Inc.. G 704 735-8024
Lincolnton *(G-7846)*

Mr Tire Inc.. G 704 484-0816
Shelby *(G-11365)*

Mr Tire Inc.. G 704 872-4127
Statesville *(G-11737)*

Oakie S Tire & Recapping Inc............. G 704 482-5629
Shelby *(G-11367)*

Parrish Tire Company........................ E 704 372-2013
Charlotte *(G-2614)*

Parrish Tire Company........................ E 336 334-9979
Greensboro *(G-5735)*

Parrish Tire Company........................ E 704 872-6565
Jonesville *(G-7198)*

Parrish Tire Company........................ D 800 849-8473
Winston Salem *(G-13276)*

Perry Brothers Tire Svc Inc................ F 919 693-2128
Oxford *(G-9623)*

Perry Brothers Tire Svc Inc................ E 919 775-7225
Sanford *(G-11218)*

Phil S Tire Service Inc....................... G 828 682-2421
Burnsville *(G-1189)*

Piedmont Truck Tires Inc.................... F 828 202-5337
Conover *(G-3544)*

Quality Investments Inc...................... E 252 492-8777
Henderson *(G-6172)*

R and R Auto Repr & Tires Inc........... G 336 784-6893
Winston Salem *(G-13310)*

Rabuns Trlr Repr Tire Svc Inc............. G 704 764-7841
Monroe *(G-8547)*

Richmond Investment......................... E 910 410-8200
Rockingham *(G-10787)*

Small Brothers Tire Co Inc .... G 704 289-3531
Monroe (G-8559)

Snider Tire Inc... D 704 373-2910
Charlotte (G-2820)

Snider Tire Inc... F 336 691-5480
Greensboro (G-5820)

Snider Tire Inc... G 828 324-9955
Hickory (G-6450)

Super Retread Center Inc........................... F 919 734-0073
Goldsboro (G-5248)

Team X-Treme LLC..................................... G 919 562-8100
Rolesville (G-10890)

Thrifty Tire... G 919 220-7800
Durham (G-4273)

Tire Sls Svc Inc Fytteville NC..................... E 910 485-1121
Fayetteville (G-4682)

Tires Incorporated of Clinton...................... F 910 592-4741
Clinton (G-3249)

Towel City Tire & Wheel LLC...................... G 704 933-2143
Kannapolis (G-7222)

Universal Tire Service Inc........................... G 919 779-8798
Raleigh (G-10577)

Village Tire Center Inc............................... G 919 862-8500
Raleigh (G-10588)

Whitaker S Tire Service Inc........................ G 704 786-6174
Concord (G-3468)

White S Tire Svc Wilson Inc....................... G 252 237-0770
Wilson (G-13046)

White S Tire Svc Wilson Inc....................... D 252 237-5426
Wilson (G-13047)

Whites Tire Svc New Bern Inc.................... G 252 633-1170
New Bern (G-9407)

Wilson Tire and Automotive Inc.................. G 336 584-9638
Elon College (G-4476)

TOBACCO: Chewing

American Snuff Company LLC..................... C 336 768-4630
Winston Salem (G-13085)

TOBACCO: Chewing & Snuff

Cres Tobacco Company LLC....................... E 336 983-7727
King (G-7325)

Ioto Usa LLC.. F 252 413-7343
Greenville (G-5992)

Itg Holdings USA Inc.................................. F 954 772-9000
Greensboro (G-5629)

Tobacco Rag Processors Inc...................... E 252 265-0081
Wilson (G-13035)

Tobacco Rag Processors Inc...................... E 252 237-8180
Wilson (G-13036)

Tobacco Rag Processors Inc...................... E 252 265-0081
Wilson (G-13037)

TOBACCO: Cigarettes

22nd Century Group Inc............................. F 716 270-1523
Mocksville (G-8345)

Commonwealth Brands Inc......................... C 336 634-4200
Greensboro (G-5460)

Fontem US LLC.. G 888 207-4588
Greensboro (G-5536)

Itg Brands... D 336 335-6600
Greensboro (G-5626)

Itg Brands... D 919 366-0220
Raleigh (G-10210)

Itg Brands LLC... E 336 335-6669
Greensboro (G-5627)

Liggett Group LLC...................................... B 919 304-7700
Mebane (G-8249)

Lorillard LLC.. D 336 741-2000
Winston Salem (G-13238)

Lorillard Tobacco Company LLC................. A 336 335-6600
Greensboro (G-5665)

Medallion Company Inc.............................. C 919 990-3500
Timberlake (G-12101)

Modoral Brands Inc.................................... G 336 741-7230
Winston Salem (G-13259)

Mr Tobacco.. G 919 747-9052
Raleigh (G-10316)

Philip Morris USA Inc................................. D 336 744-4401
Winston Salem (G-13288)

R J Reynolds Tobacco Company................ D 919 366-0220
Wendell (G-12543)

R J Reynolds Tobacco Company................ C 336 741-2132
Winston Salem (G-13312)

R J Rynolds Tob Holdings Inc.................... D 336 741-5000
Winston Salem (G-13313)

Rai Services Company............................... A 336 741-6774
Winston Salem (G-13315)

Reynolds American Inc............................... E 336 741-2000
Winston Salem (G-13318)

Santa Fe Ntural Tob Foundation................. C 919 690-0880
Oxford (G-9633)

Triaga Inc... G 919 412-6019
Wilson (G-13039)

US Tobacco Cooperative Inc...................... D 919 821-4560
Raleigh (G-10579)

Wainwright Warehouse............................... G 252 237-5121
Wilson (G-13043)

TOBACCO: Cigars

Modoral Brands Inc.................................... G 336 741-7230
Winston Salem (G-13259)

North Carolina Tobacco Mfg LLC............... F 252 238-6514
Stantonsburg (G-11626)

Reynolds American Inc............................... E 336 741-2000
Winston Salem (G-13318)

Santa Fe Natural Tob Co Inc...................... G 919 690-1905
Oxford (G-9632)

TOBACCO: Smoking

Modoral Brands Inc.................................... G 336 741-7230
Winston Salem (G-13259)

R J Reynolds Tobacco Company................ D 336 741-0400
Tobaccoville (G-12102)

R J Reynolds Tobacco Company................ C 336 741-2132
Winston Salem (G-13312)

R J Reynolds Tobacco Company................ D 336 741-5000
Winston Salem (G-13311)

Reynolds American Inc............................... E 336 741-2000
Winston Salem (G-13318)

Santa Fe Natural Tobacco Co.................... C 800 332-5595
Winston Salem (G-13329)

Top Tobacco LP... C 910 646-3014
Lake Waccamaw (G-7472)

TOILET PREPARATIONS

Cocoa Botanics Corporation...................... F 980 565-7739
Matthews (G-8108)

TOILETRIES, WHOLESALE: Perfumes

Mvp Group International Inc........................ E 843 216-8380
Elkin (G-4449)

TOILETRIES, WHOLESALE: Toilet Soap

Old Town Soap Co...................................... F 704 796-8775
China Grove (G-3077)

TOILETRIES, WHOLESALE: Toiletries

Bob Barker Company Inc............................ C 800 334-9880
Fuquay Varina (G-4870)

TOOLS & EQPT: Taxidermist

Jim Allred Taxidermy Supply...................... G 828 749-5900
Saluda (G-11139)

McKenzie Sports Products LLC.................. C 704 279-7985
Salisbury (G-11091)

TOOLS: Hand

Everkem Diversified Pdts Inc..................... F 336 661-7801
Winston Salem (G-13161)

TOOLS: Hand, Hammers

American Striking Tools Inc........................ G 910 769-1318
Wilmington (G-12704)

TOWELETTES: Premoistened

Albaad Usa Inc.. B 336 634-0091
Reidsville (G-10671)

TOWERS, SECTIONS: Transmission, Radio & Television

Towerco LLC.. F 919 653-5700
Cary (G-1472)

TOYS: Dolls, Stuffed Animals & Parts

PCS Collectibles LLC................................. G 805 306-1140
Huntersville (G-7030)

TOYS: Video Game Machines

Game Box LLC... G 866 241-1882
Greensboro (G-5546)

TRAILER COACHES: Automobile

Allison Globl Mnufacturing Inc................... G 704 392-7883
Charlotte (G-1646)

Southag Mfg Inc... G 919 365-5111
Wendell (G-12548)

TRAILERS & PARTS: Boat

Long Trailer Co Inc..................................... G 252 823-8828
Tarboro (G-11931)

TRAILERS & PARTS: Horse

Gore S Trlr Manufacturer S Inc.................. G 910 642-2246
Whiteville (G-12582)

TRAILERS & TRAILER EQPT

A-1 Hitch & Trailors Sales Inc................... G 910 755-6025
Supply (G-11854)

BOB Trailers Inc... E 208 375-5171
Charlotte (G-1795)

Colfax Trailer & Repair LLC....................... G 336 993-8511
Colfax (G-3275)

Faith Farm Inc.. G 704 431-4566
Salisbury (G-11052)

Kaufman Trailers Inc.................................. E 336 790-6800
Lexington (G-7704)

North Carolina Dept Trnsp......................... G 828 733-9002
Newland (G-9433)

TRAILERS: Camping, Tent-Type

Cold Mountain Capital LLC......................... F 828 210-8129
Asheville (G-479)

TRAILERS: Truck, Chassis

Ecovehicle Enterprises Inc......................... G 704 544-9907
Charlotte (G-2090)

TRANSDUCERS: Electrical Properties

MTS Systems Corporation.......................... C 919 677-2352
Cary (G-1403)

Smith Systems Inc...................................... E 828 884-3490
Brevard (G-982)

TRANSFORMERS: Distribution

PRODUCT

ABB Inc..D 919 856-2360
Raleigh *(G-9864)*

TRANSFORMERS: Distribution, Electric

ABB Power T & D Company Inc.............A 919 856-3806
Raleigh *(G-9866)*

Ced Incorporated..................................F 336 378-0044
Greensboro *(G-5435)*

Pennsylvania Trans Tech Inc.............. D 910 875-7600
Raeford *(G-9847)*

TRANSFORMERS: Voltage Regulating

Abundant Power Solutions LLC............G 704 271-9890
Charlotte *(G-1612)*

TRANSISTORS

Santronics Inc....................................A 919 775-1223
Sanford *(G-11231)*

TRANSMISSIONS: Motor Vehicle

Unique Tool and Mfg Co........................E 336 498-2614
Franklinville *(G-4858)*

TRANSPORTATION BROKERS: Truck

Deliveright Logistics Inc.....................C 862 279-7332
Lexington *(G-7676)*

TRANSPORTATION EQPT & SPLYS WHOLESALERS, NEC

At Your Service Express LLC..................E 704 270-9918
Charlotte *(G-1707)*

Foxster Opco LLC................................E 910 297-6996
Hampstead *(G-6072)*

Haeco Americas LLC............................A 336 668-4410
Greensboro *(G-5585)*

TRAP ROCK: Crushed & Broken

Carolina Sunrock LLC............................E 919 575-4502
Butner *(G-1200)*

Heidelberg Mtls Sthast Agg LLC............F 252 235-4162
Bailey *(G-670)*

Sunrock Group Holdings Corp.............. D 919 747-6400
Raleigh *(G-10520)*

TRAVEL TRAILERS & CAMPERS

Derrow Enterprises Inc..........................G 252 635-3375
New Bern *(G-9364)*

TRAYS: Plastic

Sherri Gossett.......................................G 910 367-0099
Wilmington *(G-12919)*

TREAD RUBBER: Camelback For Tire Retreading

White S Tire Svc Wilson Inc....................G 252 237-0770
Wilson *(G-13046)*

White S Tire Svc Wilson Inc................... D 252 237-5426
Wilson *(G-13047)*

TROPHIES, NEC

DWM INTERNATIONAL INC....................E 646 290-7448
Charlotte *(G-2071)*

TROPHIES, WHOLESALE

Trophy House Inc..................................F 910 323-1791
Fayetteville *(G-4683)*

TROPHIES: Metal, Exc Silver

Contemporary Products Inc....................G 919 779-4228
Garner *(G-4925)*

TRUCK & BUS BODIES: Beverage Truck

Mickey Truck Bodies Inc..........................B 336 882-6806
High Point *(G-6711)*

R J Yeller Distribution Inc........................G 800 944-2589
Charlotte *(G-2686)*

TRUCK & BUS BODIES: Bus Bodies

Thomas Built Buses Inc..........................A 336 889-4871
High Point *(G-6807)*

TRUCK & BUS BODIES: Garbage Or Refuse Truck

Waste Container Repair Svcs..................G 910 257-4474
Fayetteville *(G-4696)*

TRUCK & BUS BODIES: Motor Vehicle, Specialty

Anchor-Richey Emergency Vehicl..........E 828 495-8145
Taylorsville *(G-11949)*

Vna Holding Inc....................................A 336 393-4890
Greensboro *(G-5905)*

Volvo Group North America LLC............A 336 393-2000
Greensboro *(G-5907)*

Volvo Group North America LLC............A 336 393-2000
Greensboro *(G-5908)*

Volvo Group North America LLC............A 336 393-2000
Greensboro *(G-5906)*

TRUCK & BUS BODIES: Truck Beds

John Jenkins Company............................E 336 375-3717
Browns Summit *(G-1001)*

TRUCK & BUS BODIES: Truck, Motor Vehicle

American Scale Company LLC..............F 704 921-4556
Charlotte *(G-1667)*

TRUCK & BUS BODIES: Utility Truck

Adkins Truck Equipment Co....................E 704 596-2299
Charlotte *(G-1624)*

Satco Truck Equipment Inc......................F 919 383-5547
Durham *(G-4222)*

TRUCK BODIES: Body Parts

Cabarrus Plastics Inc............................C 704 784-2100
Concord *(G-3328)*

Can-AM Custom Trucks Inc....................G 704 334-0322
Charlotte *(G-1834)*

Carroll Co..F 919 779-1900
Garner *(G-4920)*

Fontaine Modification Company.............F 704 392-8502
Charlotte *(G-2169)*

Osprea Logistics Usa LLC....................E 704 504-1677
Charlotte *(G-2601)*

Volvo Trucks North America Inc.............A 336 393-2000
Greensboro *(G-5911)*

TRUCK BODY SHOP

Mickey Truck Bodies Inc..........................B 336 882-6806
High Point *(G-6711)*

Quality Trck Bodies & Repr Inc..............E 252 245-5100
Elm City *(G-4466)*

Triangle Body Works Inc.........................G 336 788-0631
Winston Salem *(G-13371)*

TRUCK GENERAL REPAIR SVC

Container Technology Inc......................G 910 350-1303
Wilmington *(G-12749)*

Mack Trucks Inc..................................A 336 291-9001
Greensboro *(G-5670)*

Satco Truck Equipment Inc......................F 919 383-5547
Durham *(G-4222)*

TRUCK PARTS & ACCESSORIES: Wholesalers

Consolidated Truck Parts Inc..................G 704 279-5543
Rockwell *(G-10794)*

Fontaine Modification Company.............F 704 392-8502
Charlotte *(G-2169)*

Truck Parts Inc....................................F 704 332-7909
Charlotte *(G-2948)*

Venture Products Intl Inc........................G 828 285-0495
Asheville *(G-631)*

TRUCKING & HAULING SVCS: Contract Basis

J & L Bckh/Nvrnmental Svcs Inc............G 910 237-7351
Eastover *(G-4337)*

Southeast Wood Products Inc................F 910 285-4359
Wallace *(G-12324)*

TRUCKING & HAULING SVCS: Heavy, NEC

Advantage Machinery Svcs Inc..............E 336 463-4700
Yadkinville *(G-13435)*

TRUCKING & HAULING SVCS: Lumber & Log, Local

Raleigh Road Box Corporation................G 252 438-7401
Henderson *(G-6174)*

TRUCKING: Except Local

Bundy Logging Company Inc..................G 252 357-0191
Gatesville *(G-5170)*

Firm Ascend LLC................................G 704 464-3024
Charlotte *(G-2154)*

RSI Leasing Inc NS Tbt............................G 704 587-9300
Charlotte *(G-2738)*

T H Blue Inc..E 910 673-3033
Eagle Springs *(G-4319)*

TRUCKING: Local, With Storage

Bundy Logging Company Inc..................G 252 357-0191
Gatesville *(G-5170)*

Comer Sanitary Service Inc..................G 336 629-8311
Lexington *(G-7668)*

Elizabeth Logistic LLC........................... D 803 920-3931
Indian Trail *(G-7078)*

Loflin Concrete Co Inc..........................E 336 904-2788
Kernersville *(G-7282)*

Lunar International Tech LLC....................F 800 975-7153
Charlotte *(G-2441)*

Wheeler Industries Inc..........................G 919 736-4256
Pikeville *(G-9669)*

TRUCKING: Local, Without Storage

Bobby Cahoon Construction Inc............E 252 249-1617
Grantsboro *(G-5329)*

Central Carolina Concrete LLC..............F 704 372-2930
Greensboro *(G-5437)*

Crowder Trucking LLC............................G 910 797-4163
Fayetteville *(G-4581)*

Fayblock Materials Inc.......................... D 910 323-9198
Fayetteville *(G-4600)*

H & M Wood Preserving Inc..................E 704 279-5188
Gold Hill *(G-5192)*

New Finish Inc.......................................E 704 474-4116
Norwood *(G-9557)*

Stone Supply Inc..................................G 828 678-9966
Burnsville *(G-1192)*

T H Blue Inc...E 910 673-3033
Eagle Springs *(G-4319)*

TRUCKS & TRACTORS: Industrial

Altec Industries Inc..................................B 919 528-2535
Creedmoor *(G-3637)*

Basic Machinery Company Inc.............D 919 663-2244
Siler City *(G-11399)*

Bromma Inc...E 919 620-8039
Durham *(G-3945)*

Caterpillar Inc..E 919 777-2000
Sanford *(G-11160)*

Cutting Systems Inc................................D 704 592-2451
Union Grove *(G-12184)*

Daimler Truck North Amer LLC.............A 704 645-5000
Cleveland *(G-3213)*

General Electric Company.......................F 919 563-7445
Mebane *(G-8241)*

General Electric Company.......................B 919 563-5561
Mebane *(G-8242)*

Gregory Poole Equipment Co................G 252 931-5100
Greenville *(G-5984)*

Hanging C Farms......................................F 704 239-6691
Kannapolis *(G-7210)*

Kaufman Trailers Inc...............................E 336 790-6800
Lexington *(G-7704)*

Master Tow Inc...E 910 630-2000
Fayetteville *(G-4637)*

McIntyre Manufacturing Group Inc.........D 336 476-3646
Thomasville *(G-12046)*

Nolan Manufacturing LLC.......................G 336 490-0086
Denton *(G-3758)*

Otto Envmtl Systems NC LLC.................B 800 227-5885
Charlotte *(G-2603)*

Propane Trucks & Tanks Inc...................F 919 362-5000
Apex *(G-188)*

Smithway Inc...G 828 628-1756
Fairview *(G-4511)*

Smithway Inc...E 828 628-1756
Fairview *(G-4512)*

Sterling Rack Inc......................................G 704 866-9131
Gastonia *(G-5144)*

Superior Dry Kilns Inc.............................E 828 754-7001
Hudson *(G-6960)*

TCI Mobility Inc..F 704 867-8331
Gastonia *(G-5149)*

Tcom Limited Partnership.......................B 252 330-5555
Elizabeth City *(G-4413)*

Wastequip LLC..F 704 366-7140
Charlotte *(G-3005)*

TRUCKS: Forklift

Combilift USA LLC....................................F 336 378-8884
Greensboro *(G-5457)*

Crown Equipment Corporation...............B 252 522-3088
Kinston *(G-7403)*

Forklift Pro Inc...F 704 716-3636
Pineville *(G-9728)*

Hc Forklift America Corp.........................F 980 888-8335
Charlotte *(G-2266)*

Hyster-Yale Group Inc.............................F 252 931-5100
Greenville *(G-5989)*

Hyster-Yale Materials Hdlg Inc...............D 252 931-5100
Greenville *(G-5990)*

Parkers Equipment Company..................G 252 560-0088
Snow Hill *(G-11482)*

Scootatrailertm...G 336 671-0444
Lexington *(G-7739)*

Westlift LLC...F 919 242-4379
Goldsboro *(G-5253)*

Whiteville Forklift & Eqp........................G 910 642-6642
Whiteville *(G-12598)*

Wlc Forklift Services LLC........................G 336 345-2571
Reidsville *(G-10701)*

TRUCKS: Indl

Bottomley Enterprises Inc......................D 336 657-6400
Mount Airy *(G-9104)*

Burton Global Logistics LLC...................E 336 663-6449
Burlington *(G-1057)*

C&A Hockaday Transport LLC.................G 252 676-5956
Roanoke Rapids *(G-10734)*

Cbj Transit LLC...D 252 417-9972
Garner *(G-4921)*

D&E Freight LLC..F 704 977-4847
Charlotte *(G-2013)*

Drs Transportation Inc............................G 919 215-2770
Raleigh *(G-10060)*

Dse Express LLC.......................................G 540 686-0981
Sanford *(G-11172)*

Elektrikredd LLC.......................................G 704 805-0110
Matthews *(G-8166)*

Forward Dsptching Lgistics LLC.............G 252 907-9797
Greenville *(G-5977)*

Go For Green Fleet Svcs LLC..................G 803 306-3683
Charlotte *(G-2221)*

Harrell Proper Transport LLC..................G 336 202-7135
Whitsett *(G-12609)*

Mlg Trnscndent Trckg Trnsp Svc...........G 336 905-1192
High Point *(G-6713)*

MMS Logistics Incorporated...................G 336 214-3552
Mc Leansville *(G-8225)*

Nexxt Level Trucking LLC........................G 980 205-4425
Charlotte *(G-2562)*

Rucker Intrgrted Logistics LLC...............G 704 352-2018
Charlotte *(G-2741)*

Swing Kurve Logistic Trckg LLC.............G 704 506-7371
Charlotte *(G-2888)*

Three Ladies and A Male LLC..................G 704 287-1584
Charlotte *(G-2916)*

V M Trucking Inc.......................................G 984 239-4853
Morehead City *(G-8848)*

TRUSSES: Wood, Floor

Ufp New London LLC................................F 704 463-1400
New London *(G-9423)*

Ufp Site Built LLC....................................E 704 781-2520
Locust *(G-7906)*

TUBES: Steel & Iron

Southeast Tubular Products Inc.............E 704 883-8883
Statesville *(G-11767)*

TUBES: Vacuum

Communications & Pwr Inds LLC...........E 650 846-2900
Conover *(G-3505)*

TUBING: Rubber

C & M Industrial Supply Co.....................G 704 483-4001
Mill Spring *(G-8300)*

Tekni-Plex Inc...D 919 553-4151
Clayton *(G-3174)*

TUNGSTEN CARBIDE POWDER

Betek Tools Inc...F 980 498-2523
Charlotte *(G-1775)*

TURBINES & TURBINE GENERATOR SET UNITS, COMPLETE

Bwxt Investment Company......................E 704 625-4900
Charlotte *(G-1824)*

Leistriz Advanced Turbine C...................C 336 969-1352
Rural Hall *(G-10964)*

TURBINES & TURBINE GENERATOR SETS

Babcock Wlcox Eqity Invstmnts.............G 704 625-4900
Charlotte *(G-1733)*

Babcock Wlcox Intl Sls Svc Cor.............G 704 625-4900
Charlotte *(G-1734)*

Caterpillar Inc..E 919 777-2000
Sanford *(G-11160)*

Diamond Power Intl LLC...........................G 704 625-4900
Charlotte *(G-2040)*

Diamond Pwr Eqity Invstmnts In.............G 704 625-4900
Charlotte *(G-2041)*

Megtec India Holdings LLC......................G 704 625-4900
Charlotte *(G-2487)*

Megtec Turbosonic Tech Inc....................G 704 625-4900
Charlotte *(G-2488)*

Revloc Reclamation Service Inc.............G 704 625-4900
Charlotte *(G-2716)*

Siemens Energy Inc.................................C 704 551-5100
Charlotte *(G-2802)*

Siemens Energy Inc.................................E 336 969-1351
Rural Hall *(G-10967)*

Windlift Inc...G 919 490-8575
Durham *(G-4306)*

Xylem Lnc...E 704 409-9700
Charlotte *(G-3035)*

TURBINES & TURBINE GENERATOR SETS & PARTS

Industrial Sup Solutions Inc....................E 704 636-4241
Salisbury *(G-11067)*

Wind Solutions LLC..................................E 919 292-2096
Sanford *(G-11252)*

TURNKEY VENDORS: Computer Systems

Acroplis Cntrls Engineers Pllc................F 919 275-3884
Raleigh *(G-9876)*

TWINE: Binder & Baler

Genevieve M Brownlee..............................G 336 226-5260
Burlington *(G-1095)*

TYPESETTING SVC

Advertising Design Systems Inc.............G 828 264-8060
Boone *(G-894)*

American Multimedia Inc..........................D 336 229-7101
Burlington *(G-1045)*

Appalachian State University....................F 828 262-2047
Boone *(G-896)*

Atlantis Graphics Inc...............................E 919 361-5809
Durham *(G-3904)*

Austin Printing Company Inc...................G 704 289-1445
Monroe *(G-8437)*

Bennett & Associates Inc........................G 919 477-7362
Durham *(G-3925)*

Boingo Graphics Inc................................E 704 527-4963
Charlotte *(G-1797)*

BP Solutions Group Inc...........................E 828 252-4476
Asheville *(G-460)*

Coastal Press Inc.....................................G 252 726-1549
Morehead City *(G-8827)*

CPS Resources Inc..................................E 704 628-7678
Indian Trail *(G-7075)*

Creative Printing Inc...............................G 828 265-2800
Boone *(G-909)*

Dokja Inc..G 336 852-5190
Greensboro *(G-5500)*

F C C LLC...G 336 883-7314
High Point *(G-6617)*

Fayetteville Publishing Co.......................E 910 323-4848
Fayetteville *(G-4601)*

PRODUCT

Flash Printing Company Inc................ E 704 375-2474
Charlotte *(G-2159)*

Free Will Bptst Press Fndtion............. F 252 746-6128
Ayden *(G-657)*

Gik Inc... F 919 872-9498
Raleigh *(G-10133)*

Greensboro News & Record LLC......... A 336 373-7000
Greensboro *(G-5577)*

Hickory Printing Solutions LLC............ B 828 465-3431
Conover *(G-3530)*

Ips... G 704 788-3327
Concord *(G-3381)*

Jag Graphics Inc................................. G 828 259-9020
Asheville *(G-527)*

Jones Media.. G 828 264-3612
Boone *(G-928)*

Joseph C Woodard Prtg Co Inc........... F 919 829-0634
Raleigh *(G-10221)*

Kathie S Mc Daniel.............................. G 336 835-1544
Elkin *(G-4446)*

Keiger Inc... E 336 760-0099
Winston Salem *(G-13223)*

Loftin & Company Inc.......................... E 704 393-9393
Charlotte *(G-2431)*

Measurement Incorporated................... D 919 683-2413
Durham *(G-4122)*

Medlit Solutions LLC............................ D 919 878-6789
Garner *(G-4942)*

Ollis Enterprises Inc............................ E 828 265-0004
Wilkesboro *(G-12648)*

Owen G Dunn Co Inc........................... G 252 633-3197
New Bern *(G-9387)*

Pamela A Adams................................. G 919 876-5949
Raleigh *(G-10355)*

Park Communications LLC................... D 336 292-4000
Greensboro *(G-5732)*

Person Printing Company Inc............... E 336 599-2146
Roxboro *(G-10940)*

Pilot LLC... D 910 692-7271
Southern Pines *(G-11505)*

Powell Ink Inc..................................... F 828 253-6886
Asheville *(G-582)*

Printery.. F 336 852-9774
Greensboro *(G-5764)*

Printing & Packaging Inc..................... E 704 482-3866
Shelby *(G-11371)*

Printing Partners Inc........................... G 336 996-2268
Kernersville *(G-7293)*

Printing Svcs Greensboro Inc............... G 336 274-7663
Greensboro *(G-5765)*

Quality Prtg Cartridge Fctry................. G 336 852-2505
Greensboro *(G-5779)*

Raleigh Engraving Co.......................... G 919 832-5557
Raleigh *(G-10423)*

Richard D Stewart............................... G 919 284-2295
Kenly *(G-7236)*

S Chamblee Incorporated.................... E 919 833-7561
Raleigh *(G-10452)*

S Ruppe Inc.. G 828 287-4936
Rutherfordton *(G-10992)*

Trejo Soccer Academy LLC.................. G 336 899-7910
Asheboro *(G-410)*

Tseng Information Systems Inc............. G 919 682-9197
Durham *(G-4284)*

Weber and Weber Inc.......................... F 336 722-4109
Winston Salem *(G-13387)*

UMBRELLAS & CANES

Arden Companies LLC......................... E 919 258-3081
Sanford *(G-11149)*

UNIFORM STORES

Tresmc LLC.. G 919 900-0868
Knightdale *(G-7461)*

UNIVERSITY

Appalachian State University................ G 828 262-7497
Boone *(G-895)*

Appalachian State University................ F 828 262-2047
Boone *(G-896)*

North Carolina State Univ.................... G 919 515-2760
Raleigh *(G-10336)*

University NC At Chapel Hl.................. G 919 962-0369
Chapel Hill *(G-1585)*

UPHOLSTERY FILLING MATERIALS

A Land of Furniture Inc....................... G 336 882-3866
High Point *(G-6507)*

Prime Syntex LLC................................ E 828 324-5496
Thomasville *(G-12062)*

Spuntech Industries Inc....................... C 336 330-9000
Roxboro *(G-10946)*

Zonkd LLC.. E 919 977-6463
Raleigh *(G-10624)*

UPHOLSTERY MATERIALS, BROADWOVEN

Carolina Mills Incorporated................. D 828 428-9911
Maiden *(G-8010)*

Culp Inc... C 336 889-5161
High Point *(G-6582)*

Dicey Mills Inc.................................... G 704 487-6324
Shelby *(G-11331)*

Hickory Heritage of Falling Creek Inc..... E
Hickory *(G-6351)*

Ledford Upholstery.............................. G 704 732-0233
Lincolnton *(G-7836)*

Valdese Weavers LLC.......................... B 828 874-2181
Valdese *(G-12206)*

UPHOLSTERY WORK SVCS

Davidson House Inc............................ F 704 791-0171
Davidson *(G-3701)*

Hughes Furniture Inds Inc................... C 336 498-8700
Randleman *(G-10650)*

Ledford Upholstery.............................. G 704 732-0233
Lincolnton *(G-7836)*

USED CAR DEALERS

Courtesy Ford Inc............................... G 252 338-4783
Elizabeth City *(G-4384)*

USED MERCHANDISE STORES

Etherngton Cnservation Ctr Inc............ E 336 665-1317
Greensboro *(G-5525)*

J C Lawrence Co.................................. G 919 553-3044
Oriental *(G-9600)*

Microtronic Us LLC.............................. G 336 869-0429
High Point *(G-6712)*

UTENSILS: Household, Cooking & Kitchen, Metal

Ashdan Enterprises.............................. G 336 375-9698
Greensboro *(G-5372)*

Kessebohmer USA Inc......................... F 910 338-5080
Wilmington *(G-12828)*

UTILITY TRAILER DEALERS

A-1 Hitch & Trailors Sales Inc.............. G 910 755-6025
Supply *(G-11854)*

Gore S Trlr Manufacturer S Inc............ G 910 642-2246
Whiteville *(G-12582)*

Kaufman Trailers Inc........................... E 336 790-6800
Lexington *(G-7704)*

Kraftsman Inc..................................... D 336 824-1114
Ramseur *(G-10627)*

Leonard Alum Utlity Bldngs Inc............ G 919 872-4442
Raleigh *(G-10254)*

Road King Trailers Inc......................... E 828 670-8012
Candler *(G-1232)*

VACUUM CLEANERS: Indl Type

Cary Manufacturing Corporation........... G 704 527-4402
Charlotte *(G-1864)*

Dustcontrol Inc.................................... F 910 395-1808
Wilmington *(G-12768)*

Vacs America Inc................................. G 910 259-9854
Burgaw *(G-1035)*

VACUUM SYSTEMS: Air Extraction, Indl

Schmalz Inc.. C 919 713-0880
Raleigh *(G-10461)*

Templex Inc.. E 336 472-5933
Thomasville *(G-12078)*

VALUE-ADDED RESELLERS: Computer Systems

Trimech Solutions LLC........................ G 704 503-6644
Charlotte *(G-2944)*

VALVES

US Valve Corporation........................... G 910 799-9913
Wilmington *(G-12944)*

VALVES & PARTS: Gas, Indl

Key Gas Components Inc..................... E 828 655-1700
Marion *(G-8048)*

VALVES & PIPE FITTINGS

Aalberts Integrated Piping................... E 704 841-6000
Charlotte *(G-1608)*

Controls Southeast Inc........................ C 704 644-5000
Pineville *(G-9721)*

Emco Wheaton Retail Corp.................. D 252 243-0150
Wilson *(G-12987)*

Engineered Controls Intl LLC............... C 336 226-3244
Burlington *(G-1088)*

Engineered Controls Intl LLC............... C 828 466-2153
Conover *(G-3519)*

Engineered Controls Intl LLC............... C 336 449-7706
Whitsett *(G-12605)*

Hayward Industries Inc........................ D 336 712-9900
Clemmons *(G-3188)*

Hayward Industries Inc........................ B 704 837-8002
Charlotte *(G-2265)*

James M Pleasants Company Inc.......... F 888 902-8324
Greensboro *(G-5634)*

James M Pleasants Company Inc.......... E 800 365-9010
Greensboro *(G-5633)*

Key Gas Components Inc..................... E 828 655-1700
Marion *(G-8048)*

Mosack Group LLC.............................. D 888 229-2874
Mint Hill *(G-8342)*

National Foam Inc............................... C 919 639-6151
Angier *(G-125)*

Romac Industries Inc........................... D 704 915-3317
Dallas *(G-3688)*

SCI Sharp Controls Inc........................ G 704 394-1395
Pineville *(G-9755)*

Spc Mechanical Corporation................ C 252 237-9035
Wendell *(G-12549)*

Titan Flow Control Inc......................... E 910 735-0000
Lumberton *(G-7975)*

United Brass Works Inc.......................... C 336 498-2661
Randleman (G-10663)

VALVES & REGULATORS: Pressure, Indl

Eizi Group Llc................................... G 919 397-3638
Raleigh (G-10080)

Engineered Controls Intl LLC.............. C 336 449-7707
Elon (G-4469)

Hayward Industrial Products............... C 704 837-8002
Charlotte (G-2264)

Mpv Mrgnton Prssure Vssels NC......... C 828 652-3704
Marion (G-8057)

Watts Regulator Co............................. A 828 286-4151
Spindale (G-11550)

VALVES: Aerosol, Metal

AP&t North America Inc...................... F 704 292-2900
Monroe (G-8427)

Cyrco Inc.. E 336 668-0977
Greensboro (G-5484)

Epic Enterprises Inc.......................... E 910 692-5750
Southern Pines (G-11498)

Ism Inc.. E
Arden (G-277)

Metal Works High Point Inc................. D 336 886-4612
High Point (G-6709)

Metal-Cad Stl Frmng Systems In.......... D 910 343-3338
Wilmington (G-12852)

Zurn Industries LLC.......................... E 919 775-2255
Sanford (G-11257)

VALVES: Aircraft, Control, Hydraulic & Pneumatic

Flo-Tite Inc Valves & Contrls............... E 910 738-8904
Lumberton (G-7955)

VALVES: Control, Automatic

ADC Industries Inc............................ G 919 550-9515
Clayton (G-3130)

Robert H Wager Company Inc.............. F 336 969-6909
Rural Hall (G-10966)

VALVES: Fluid Power, Control, Hydraulic & pneumatic

Hayward Industrial Products............... C 704 837-8002
Charlotte (G-2264)

Logic Hydraulic Controls Inc............... E 910 791-9293
Wilmington (G-12838)

McC Holdings Inc.............................. C 828 724-4000
Marion (G-8052)

Stanadyne Intrmdate Hldngs LLC........ C 860 525-0821
Jacksonville (G-7152)

Wandfluh of America Inc.................... F 847 566-5700
Charlotte (G-3003)

VALVES: Indl

Bonomi North America Inc.................. F 704 412-9031
Charlotte (G-1798)

Burkert USA Corporation.................... C 800 325-1405
Huntersville (G-6974)

Carolina Conveying Inc...................... G 828 235-1005
Canton (G-1248)

Celeros Flow Technology LLC.............. C 704 752-3100
Charlotte (G-1883)

Circor Pumps North America LLC......... C 877 853-7867
Monroe (G-8460)

Curtiss-Wright Corporation................. G 973 541-3700
Charlotte (G-2006)

Curtiss-Wright Corporation................. G 704 869-4675
Charlotte (G-2007)

Curtiss-Wright Corporation................. F 704 481-1150
Shelby (G-11327)

Curtiss-Wright Corporation................. B 704 869-4600
Davidson (G-3700)

Emco Wheaton Retail Corp................. D 252 243-0150
Wilson (G-12987)

Engineered Controls Intl LLC.............. C 336 226-3244
Burlington (G-1088)

Engineered Controls Intl LLC.............. C 336 449-7706
Whitsett (G-12605)

Engineering Mfg Svcs Co.................... F 704 821-7325
Monroe (G-8483)

Equilibar LLC.................................... E 828 650-6590
Fletcher (G-4734)

General Control Equipment Co............ F 704 588-0484
Charlotte (G-2199)

Hersey Meters Co LLC....................... G 704 278-2221
Cleveland (G-3214)

Mueller Steam Specialty..................... D 910 865-8241
Saint Pauls (G-11005)

Romac Industries Inc......................... D 704 922-9595
Dallas (G-3687)

Romac Industries Inc......................... D 704 915-3317
Dallas (G-3688)

Sensus USA Inc................................ C 919 576-6185
Morrisville (G-9052)

Sensus USA Inc................................ E 919 845-4000
Morrisville (G-9051)

Spanglercv Inc.................................. G 910 794-5547
Wilmington (G-12928)

SPX Flow Inc..................................... C 704 752-4400
Charlotte (G-2847)

United Brass Works Inc...................... C 336 498-2661
Randleman (G-10663)

Zurn Elkay Wtr Solutions Corp............ G 910 501-1853
Lumberton (G-7978)

VALVES: Plumbing & Heating

American Valve Inc............................ D 336 668-0554
Greensboro (G-5358)

Bonomi North America Inc.................. F 704 412-9031
Charlotte (G-1798)

Mid-Atlantic Drainage Inc................... F 828 324-0808
Conover (G-3539)

VALVES: Regulating & Control, Automatic

Brasscraft....................................... C 336 475-2131
Thomasville (G-11997)

Huber Technology Inc........................ E 704 949-1010
Denver (G-3788)

Parker-Hannifin Corporation............... D 828 245-3233
Forest City (G-4795)

US Valve Corporation........................ G 910 799-9913
Wilmington (G-12944)

VALVES: Regulating, Process Control

Tvl International LLC.......................... G 704 814-0930
Matthews (G-8155)

VALVES: Water Works

Zurn Elkay Wtr Solutions Corp............ F 855 663-9876
Sanford (G-11256)

VAN CONVERSIONS

Matthews Spcialty Vehicles Inc............ D 336 297-9600
Greensboro (G-5682)

VARIETY STORES

Atlantic Trading LLC.......................... F
Charlotte (G-1711)

Brasingtons Inc................................. G 704 694-5191
Wadesboro (G-12236)

Infinity S End Inc............................... F 704 900-8355
Charlotte (G-2328)

Shibumi Shade Inc............................ F 336 816-9903
Raleigh (G-10470)

VARNISHES, NEC

Valspar Corporation........................... G 704 897-5700
Davidson (G-3725)

VEHICLES: Recreational

Naarva... G 704 333-3070
Charlotte (G-2540)

Xxxtreme Motorsport......................... G 704 663-1500
Mooresville (G-8801)

VENDING MACHINE OPERATORS: Sandwich & Hot Food

Durham Coca-Cola Bottling Company... C 919 383-1531
Durham (G-4014)

VENDING MACHINES & PARTS

Country Corner................................. G 919 444-9663
Pittsboro (G-9780)

Jb-Isecurity LLC................................ G 910 824-7601
Fayetteville (G-4622)

Microtronic Us LLC............................ G 336 869-0429
High Point (G-6712)

VENTILATING EQPT: Metal

Northern Star Technologies Inc............ G 516 353-3333
Indian Trail (G-7092)

WV Holdings Inc............................... G 704 853-8338
Gastonia (G-5168)

VETERINARY PHARMACEUTICAL PREPARATIONS

Happy Jack Incorporated.................... G 252 747-2911
Snow Hill (G-11480)

Huvepharma Inc................................ F 910 506-4649
Maxton (G-8201)

Pharmgate Animal Health LLC............. G 910 679-8364
Wilmington (G-12877)

Pharmgate Inc.................................. F 910 679-8364
Wilmington (G-12878)

Wholesale Kennel Supply Co.............. G 919 742-2515
Siler City (G-11427)

VIDEO & AUDIO EQPT, WHOLESALE

Lea Aid Acquisition Company.............. G 919 872-6210
Spring Hope (G-11557)

VIDEO PRODUCTION SVCS

Inspire Creative Studios Inc................ G 910 395-0200
Wilmington (G-12818)

Metro Productions Inc........................ F 919 851-6420
Raleigh (G-10296)

VIDEO TAPE PRODUCTION SVCS

Palmer Senn.................................... G 704 451-3971
Charlotte (G-2606)

VISUAL COMMUNICATIONS SYSTEMS

Flat Water Corp................................ G 704 584-7764
Charlotte (G-2161)

Simplyhome LLC............................... F 828 684-8441
Arden (G-306)

VITAMINS: Natural Or Synthetic, Uncompounded, Bulk

PRODUCT

Interntnal Agrclture Group LLC............. F 908 323-3246
Mooresville **(G-8694)**

VOCATIONAL REHABILITATION AGENCY

Lee County Industries Inc.................... G 919 775-3439
Sanford **(G-11205)**

Tri-County Industries Inc..................... C 252 977-3800
Rocky Mount **(G-10819)**

Vocatnal Sltons Hndrson Cnty I........... E 828 692-9626
East Flat Rock **(G-4335)**

Watauga Opportunities Inc................ E 828 264-5009
Boone **(G-951)**

VOCATIONAL TRAINING AGENCY

Eastern Crlina Vctonal Ctr Inc.............. D 252 758-4188
Greenville **(G-5972)**

Hope Renovations........................... F 919 960-1957
Chapel Hill **(G-1549)**

WALLBOARD: Decorated, Made From Purchased Materials

National Gyps Receivables LLC........... G 704 365-7300
Charlotte **(G-2546)**

Ng Corporate LLC............................ E 704 365-7300
Charlotte **(G-2564)**

Ng Operations LLC.......................... G 704 365-7300
Charlotte **(G-2565)**

Proform Finishing Products LLC........... B 704 365-7300
Charlotte **(G-2674)**

WALLBOARD: Gypsum

Esco Industries Inc.......................... F 336 495-3772
Randleman **(G-10647)**

Proform Finishing Products LLC........... D 910 799-3954
Wilmington **(G-12890)**

WALLPAPER & WALL COVERINGS

Paperworks.................................. G 704 548-9057
Charlotte **(G-2608)**

WALLS: Curtain, Metal

3a Composites USA Inc...................... C 704 872-8974
Statesville **(G-11641)**

WAREHOUSING & STORAGE FACILITIES, NEC

Cairn Studio Ltd............................. E 704 664-7128
Mooresville **(G-8627)**

Trimfit Inc.................................... C 336 476-6154
Thomasville **(G-12084)**

WAREHOUSING & STORAGE: Farm Prdts

C A Perry & Son Inc......................... G 252 330-2323
Elizabeth City **(G-4380)**

C A Perry & Son Inc......................... E 252 221-4463
Hobbsville **(G-6883)**

WAREHOUSING & STORAGE: General

Ashley Furniture Inds LLC.................. E 336 998-1066
Advance **(G-31)**

Burton Global Logistics LLC............... E 336 663-6449
Burlington **(G-1057)**

Fishel Steel Company....................... G 336 788-2880
Winston Salem **(G-13169)**

Hafele America Co........................... C 800 423-3531
Archdale **(G-224)**

Metrohose Incorporated................... G 252 329-9891
Greenville **(G-6004)**

Pactiv LLC................................... F 828 396-2373
Granite Falls **(G-5315)**

Parkdale Mills Incorporated................. F 704 825-2529
Belmont **(G-760)**

Patheon Softgels Inc........................ F 336 812-8700
Greensboro **(G-5736)**

WAREHOUSING & STORAGE: Miniwarehouse

Warehouse Distillery LLC.................... G 828 464-5183
Newton **(G-9510)**

WAREHOUSING & STORAGE: Refrigerated

Smith Utility Buildings...................... G 336 957-8211
Traphill **(G-12106)**

WARM AIR HEATING/AC EQPT/SPLYS, WHOL Warm Air Htg Eqpt/Splys

Appalchian Stove Fbrcators Inc............ G 828 253-0164
Asheville **(G-428)**

Ultimate Products Inc....................... F 919 836-1627
Raleigh **(G-10573)**

WASTE CLEANING SVCS

Valley Proteins (de) Inc..................... B 336 333-3030
Greensboro **(G-5895)**

WATCH REPAIR SVCS

Southern Digital Watch Repair.............. G 336 299-6718
Greensboro **(G-5825)**

WATCHES

Orbita Corporation.......................... E 910 256-5300
Wilmington **(G-12868)**

WATER HEATERS

Prime Water Services Inc.................... G 919 504-1020
Raleigh **(G-10394)**

State Industries Inc......................... G 704 597-8910
Charlotte **(G-2862)**

WATER PURIFICATION EQPT: Household

Aquapro Solutions LLC...................... G 828 255-0772
Asheville **(G-430)**

Columbus Industries LLC.................... F 910 872-1625
Bladenboro **(G-875)**

Mikropor America Inc....................... F
Charlotte **(G-2501)**

Scaltrol Inc................................... G 678 990-0858
Charlotte **(G-2761)**

Tempest Envmtl Systems Inc................ G 919 973-1609
Durham **(G-4266)**

Water-Gen Inc............................... G 888 492-8370
Charlotte **(G-3007)**

WATER SUPPLY

Bolton Construction & Svc LLC............ D 919 861-1500
Raleigh **(G-9952)**

County of Anson............................ G 704 848-4849
Lilesville **(G-7784)**

Prime Water Services Inc.................... G 919 504-1020
Raleigh **(G-10394)**

Tempest Environmental Corp............... G 919 973-1609
Durham **(G-4265)**

WATER TREATMENT EQPT: Indl

A3-Usa Inc................................... G 724 871-7170
Chinquapin **(G-3081)**

Adr Hydro-Cut Inc........................... G 919 388-2251
Morrisville **(G-8920)**

Alpha-Advantage Inc........................ G 252 441-3766
Kitty Hawk **(G-7443)**

Amiad Filtration Systems Ltd............... E 805 377-0288
Mooresville **(G-8598)**

Amiad USA Inc.............................. F 704 662-3133
Mooresville **(G-8599)**

County of Anson............................ G 704 848-4849
Lilesville **(G-7784)**

Drch Inc..................................... G 919 383-9421
Durham **(G-4007)**

Eizi Group Llc............................... G 919 397-3638
Raleigh **(G-10080)**

Entex Technologies Inc...................... F 919 933-1380
Chapel Hill **(G-1546)**

Envirnmntal Prcess Systems Inc........... G 704 827-0740
Mount Holly **(G-9229)**

Ew2 Environmental Inc...................... G 704 542-2444
Charlotte **(G-2133)**

Hoh Corporation............................ F 336 723-9274
Winston Salem **(G-13199)**

Hydro Service & Supplies Inc............... E 919 544-3744
Durham **(G-4066)**

Imagine One Resources LLC................ G 828 328-1142
Hickory **(G-6365)**

Jim Myers & Sons Inc....................... D 704 554-8397
Charlotte **(G-2370)**

Meco Inc..................................... G 919 557-7330
Fuquay Varina **(G-4889)**

Miller S Utility MGT Inc...................... G 910 298-3847
Beulaville **(G-843)**

Nala Membranes Inc......................... G 540 230-5606
Durham **(G-4142)**

Pauls Water Treatment LLC................. G 336 886-5600
High Point **(G-6729)**

Pep Filters Inc............................... E 704 662-3133
Mooresville **(G-8747)**

Protect Plus Pro LLC........................ F 828 328-1142
Hickory **(G-6419)**

Pure Flow Inc................................ D 336 532-0300
Graham **(G-5283)**

Semper Fi Water LLC........................ G 910 381-3569
Jacksonville **(G-7143)**

Solarbrook Water and Pwr Corp............ G 919 231-3205
Raleigh **(G-10492)**

Tempest Environmental Corp............... G 919 973-1609
Durham **(G-4265)**

Town of Jonesville.......................... G 336 835-2250
Jonesville **(G-7199)**

Town of Maggie Valley Inc.................. F 828 926-0145
Maggie Valley **(G-8006)**

Town of Tarboro............................. E 252 641-4284
Tarboro **(G-11944)**

Town of Waynesville........................ G 828 456-8497
Waynesville **(G-12478)**

Wedeco Uv Technologies Inc............... D 704 716-7600
Charlotte **(G-3010)**

WATER: Mineral, Carbonated, Canned & Bottled, Etc

Milkco Inc................................... B 828 254-8428
Asheville **(G-547)**

Unix Packaging LLC......................... C 310 877-7979
Morganton **(G-8907)**

WATER: Pasteurized & Mineral, Bottled & Canned

Pure Water Innovations Inc................. G 919 301-8189
Spring Hope **(G-11558)**

WATER: Pasteurized, Canned & Bottled, Etc

Ice River Springs Usa Inc................... F 519 925-2929
Morganton **(G-8874)**

Le Bleu Corporation.................................G 828 254-5105
   Arden *(G-280)*

Niagara Bottling LLC................................G 909 815-6310
   Mooresville *(G-8734)*

Zeskp LLC..G 910 762-8300
   Wilmington *(G-12958)*

WATERPROOFING COMPOUNDS

Carlisle Corporation.................................A 704 501-1100
   Charlotte *(G-1842)*

Hzo Inc..E 919 439-0505
   Morrisville *(G-8989)*

WAVEGUIDES & FITTINGS

Commscope Inc North Carolina............E 828 324-2200
   Claremont *(G-3096)*

Commscope Technologies LLC...............G 919 934-9711
   Smithfield *(G-11440)*

Commscope Technologies LLC...............A 828 324-2200
   Claremont *(G-3104)*

WAXES: Petroleum, Not Produced In Petroleum Refineries

Carolina Golfco Inc.................................G 704 525-7846
   Charlotte *(G-1848)*

WEATHER STRIP: Sponge Rubber

Comfort Tech Inc....................................G 910 428-1779
   Biscoe *(G-851)*

Mustang Reproductions Inc....................F 704 786-0990
   Concord *(G-3408)*

WEIGHING MACHINERY & APPARATUS

True Portion Inc......................................F 336 362-6326
   High Point *(G-6813)*

Vision Metals Inc.....................................G 336 622-7300
   Liberty *(G-7783)*

WELDING & CUTTING APPARATUS & ACCESS, NEC

Flawtech Inc..E 704 795-4401
   Concord *(G-3364)*

Liburdi Dimetrics Corporation................E 704 230-2510
   Mooresville *(G-8711)*

Modlins Anonized Aluminum Wldg........G 252 753-7274
   Farmville *(G-4536)*

WELDING EQPT & SPLYS WHOLESALERS

Airgas Usa LLC.......................................F 704 333-5475
   Charlotte *(G-1632)*

Airgas Usa LLC.......................................G 704 394-1420
   Charlotte *(G-1633)*

Airgas Usa LLC.......................................G 919 544-3773
   Durham *(G-3885)*

Airgas Usa LLC.......................................G 919 735-5276
   Goldsboro *(G-5196)*

Airgas Usa LLC.......................................G 704 636-5049
   Salisbury *(G-11014)*

Airgas Usa LLC.......................................G 910 392-2711
   Wilmington *(G-12694)*

Andy-OXY Co Inc....................................E 828 258-0271
   Asheville *(G-426)*

James Oxygen and Supply Co...............E 704 322-5438
   Hickory *(G-6374)*

Matheson Tri-Gas Inc.............................F 919 556-6461
   Wake Forest *(G-12286)*

WELDING EQPT & SPLYS: Gas

American Welding & Gas Inc...................G 984 222-2600
   Raleigh *(G-9899)*

Kincol Industries Incorporated...............G 704 372-8435
   Charlotte *(G-2397)*

WELDING EQPT REPAIR SVCS

Spring Repair Service Inc.......................G 336 299-5660
   Greensboro *(G-5832)*

Techsouth Inc...G 704 334-1100
   Matthews *(G-8196)*

Timothy L Griffin....................................G 336 317-8314
   Greenville *(G-6028)*

WELDING EQPT: Electric

Fanuc America Corporation....................D 704 596-5121
   Huntersville *(G-6988)*

Qws LLC..E 252 723-2106
   Morehead City *(G-8841)*

WELDING REPAIR SVC

277 Metal Inc..G 704 372-4513
   Gastonia *(G-4980)*

A&W Welding Inc.....................................G 252 482-3233
   Edenton *(G-4358)*

Advanced Machine Services LLC...........G 910 410-0099
   Rockingham *(G-10769)*

Airgas Usa LLC.......................................G 704 636-5049
   Salisbury *(G-11014)*

Alloy Fabricators Inc..............................E 704 263-2281
   Alexis *(G-102)*

Ansonville Piping & Fabg Inc..................G 704 826-8403
   Ansonville *(G-129)*

Arc3 Gases Inc.......................................G 336 275-3333
   Greensboro *(G-5367)*

Arc3 Gases Inc.......................................G 704 220-1029
   Monroe *(G-8429)*

Arc3 Gases Inc.......................................E 910 892-4016
   Dunn *(G-3844)*

Archie S Steel Service Inc.......................G 252 355-5007
   Greenville *(G-5938)*

Asheville Prcsion Mch Rblding I.............G 828 254-0884
   Asheville *(G-442)*

Avery Machine & Welding Co..................G 828 733-4944
   Fayetteville *(G-4556)*

B & D Enterprises Inc.............................G 704 739-2958
   Kings Mountain *(G-7348)*

Badger Welding Incorporated.................G 828 863-2078
   Rutherfordton *(G-10976)*

Bentons Wldg Repr & Svcs Inc................G 910 343-8322
   Wilmington *(G-12720)*

Blacksand Metal Works LLC....................F 703 489-8282
   Fayetteville *(G-4558)*

Bladen Fabricators LLC...........................G 910 866-5225
   Bladenboro *(G-874)*

Blue Light Welding of Triad.....................G 336 442-9140
   Winston Salem *(G-13109)*

Boyd Welding and Mfg Inc......................F 828 247-0630
   Forest City *(G-4785)*

Brasingtons Inc.......................................G 704 694-5191
   Wadesboro *(G-12236)*

C & B Welding & Fab Inc.........................G 704 435-6942
   Bessemer City *(G-807)*

C & J Welding Inc....................................G 919 552-0275
   Holly Springs *(G-6896)*

Calhoun Welding Inc...............................G 252 281-1455
   Macclesfield *(G-7979)*

Carolina 1926 LLC...................................G 828 251-2500
   Asheville *(G-468)*

Carolina Welding & Cnstr.......................G 252 814-8740
   Kinston *(G-7400)*

Carotek Inc...D 704 844-1100
   Matthews *(G-8103)*

Chapman Welding LLC.............................G 919 951-8131
   Efland *(G-4374)*

Clayton Welding......................................G 252 717-5909
   Washington *(G-12380)*

Coastal Machine & Welding Inc...............G 910 754-6476
   Shallotte *(G-11302)*

Collins Fabrication & Wldg LLC...............G 704 861-9326
   Gastonia *(G-5024)*

Container Technology Inc........................G 910 350-1303
   Wilmington *(G-12749)*

Custom Enterprises Inc...........................G 336 226-8296
   Burlington *(G-1081)*

Custom Machine Company Inc................F 704 629-5326
   Bessemer City *(G-811)*

Cwi Services LLC.....................................G 704 560-9755
   Southport *(G-11518)*

Dales Welding Service.............................G 919 872-6969
   Raleigh *(G-10034)*

David Bennett...G 919 798-3424
   Fuquay Varina *(G-4877)*

David West..G 910 271-0757
   Willard *(G-12665)*

Davis Davis Mch & Wldg Co Inc..............F 252 443-2652
   Rocky Mount *(G-10830)*

Diversified Welding and Steel..................G 704 504-1111
   Pineville *(G-9725)*

Donalds Welding Inc...............................F 910 298-5234
   Chinquapin *(G-3082)*

Dunavants Welding & Steel Inc................G 252 338-6533
   Camden *(G-1211)*

Dutchman Creek Self-Storage.................G 919 363-8878
   Apex *(G-151)*

Eddies Welding Inc..................................G 704 585-2024
   Stony Point *(G-11833)*

Estes Machine Co....................................F 336 786-7680
   Mount Airy *(G-9119)*

Everettes Industrial Repr Svc..................F 252 527-4269
   Goldsboro *(G-5213)*

Fabrication Associates Inc......................D 704 535-8050
   Charlotte *(G-2140)*

Filer Micro Welding.................................G 828 248-1813
   Forest City *(G-4790)*

Flores Welding Inc..................................G 919 838-1060
   Raleigh *(G-10112)*

Franks Millwright Services.......................G 336 248-6692
   Lexington *(G-7689)*

Freeman Custom Welding Inc..................G 919 210-6267
   Raleigh *(G-10119)*

Full Throttle Fabrication LLC....................G 910 770-1180
   Chadbourn *(G-1519)*

Fusion Welding..G 508 320-3525
   Rocky Point *(G-10879)*

Gamma Js Inc...F 336 294-3838
   Greensboro *(G-5547)*

Gary Tucker..G 919 837-5724
   Bear Creek *(G-714)*

General Mch Wldg of Burlington..............G 336 227-5400
   Burlington *(G-1094)*

General Refrigeration Company...............G 919 661-4727
   Garner *(G-4929)*

George F Wlson Wldg Fbrication..............G 828 262-1668
   Boone *(G-916)*

Gibbs Machine Company Incorporated....E 336 856-1907
   Greensboro *(G-5559)*

Glovers Welding LLC...............................F 252 586-7692
   Littleton *(G-7886)*

Gonzalez Welding Inc..............................G 336 270-8179
   Graham *(G-5269)*

Gore S Mar Met Fabrication Inc...............G 910 763-6066
   Wilmington *(G-12793)*

Gunmar Machine Corporation..................F 910 738-6295
   Lumberton *(G-7956)*

Hales Welding and Fabrication.................G 252 907-5508
   Macclesfield *(G-7980)*

Employee Codes: A=Over 500 employees, B=251-500
C=101-250, D=51-100, E=20-50, F=10-19, G=1-9

2025 Harris North Carolina
Manufacturers Directory

1205

PRODUCT

Hancock & Grandson Inc.............................. G 252 728-2416
  Beaufort *(G-729)*

Harbor Welding Inc...................................... G 252 473-3777
  Wanchese *(G-12343)*

High Speed Welding LLC............................... F 910 632-4427
  Wilmington *(G-12805)*

Highs Welding Shop.................................... G 704 624-5707
  Marshville *(G-8090)*

Idustrial Burkett Services............................. G 252 244-0143
  Vanceboro *(G-12217)*

Imagination Fabrication................................ G 919 280-4430
  Apex *(G-167)*

Industrial Mch Solutions Inc......................... G 919 872-0016
  Raleigh *(G-10191)*

Industrial Metal Maint Inc............................. G 910 285-3240
  Teachey *(G-11988)*

Industrial Welding &................................... G 910 309-8540
  Fayetteville *(G-4616)*

Iv-S Metal Stamping Inc............................... E 336 861-2100
  Archdale *(G-229)*

J A King.. G 800 327-7727
  Raleigh *(G-10212)*

J R Nixon Welding...................................... G 252 221-4574
  Tyner *(G-12183)*

Jack A Farrior Inc....................................... D 252 753-2020
  Farmville *(G-4532)*

Jax Specialty Welding LLC............................ G 704 380-3548
  Statesville *(G-11718)*

Joe Robin Darnell....................................... G 704 482-1186
  Shelby *(G-11350)*

K & W Welding LLC..................................... G 910 895-9220
  Rockingham *(G-10781)*

Kenny Robinson S Wldg Svc Inc.............. G 760 213-6454
  Liberty *(G-7769)*

Kings Prtble Wldg Fbrction LLC................. G 336 789-2372
  Mount Airy *(G-9142)*

Larry D Troxler... G 336 585-1141
  Gibsonville *(G-5180)*

Limitless Wldg Fabrication LLC..................... G 252 753-0660
  Farmville *(G-4534)*

Lloyds Fabricating Solutions......................... F 336 250-0154
  Thomasville *(G-12045)*

Lumsden Welding Company.......................... G 910 791-6336
  Wilmington *(G-12842)*

Lyerlys Wldg & Fabrication Inc.................. G 704 680-2317
  Gold Hill *(G-5195)*

Marc Machine Works Inc.............................. F 704 865-3625
  Gastonia *(G-5091)*

Marine Fabrications LLC.............................. G 252 473-4767
  Wanchese *(G-12345)*

Martin Welding Inc..................................... G 919 436-8805
  Garner *(G-4939)*

Maynard S Fabricators Inc........................... G 336 230-1048
  Greensboro *(G-5684)*

Mechanical Maintenance Inc......................... F 336 676-7133
  Climax *(G-3227)*

Medley S Garage Welding............................ G 336 674-0422
  Pleasant Garden *(G-9792)*

Metal ARC... G 910 770-1180
  Whiteville *(G-12588)*

Mikes Welding & Fabricating........................ G 336 472-5804
  Thomasville *(G-12048)*

Miller Sheet Metal Co Inc............................ G 336 751-2304
  Mocksville *(G-8378)*

Mitchell Welding Inc................................... E 828 765-2620
  Spruce Pine *(G-11583)*

Modern Machine and Metal Fa...................... G 336 993-4808
  Winston Salem *(G-13258)*

Modlins Anonized Aluminum Wldg......... G 252 753-7274
  Farmville *(G-4536)*

Montys Welding & Fabrication....................... G 919 337-7859
  Garner *(G-4946)*

Moore S Welding Service Inc........................ G 919 837-5769
  Bear Creek *(G-716)*

Moores Mch Co Fayetteville Inc.................... D 919 837-5354
  Bear Creek *(G-717)*

MTS Holdings Corp Inc............................... E 336 227-0151
  Burlington *(G-1133)*

Nashville Wldg & Mch Works Inc.............. E 252 243-0113
  Wilson *(G-13008)*

Newriverwelding.. G 336 413-3040
  Mocksville *(G-8381)*

Nic Nac Welding Co.................................... G 704 502-5178
  Charlotte *(G-2567)*

Ninos Wldg & Cnstr Svcs LLC...................... G 980 214-5804
  Huntersville *(G-7021)*

OHerns Welding Inc.................................... G 910 484-2087
  Fayetteville *(G-4647)*

Olive HI Wldg Fabrication Inc....................... E 336 597-0737
  Roxboro *(G-10935)*

Paul Casper Inc... G 919 269-5362
  Zebulon *(G-13520)*

Perkins Fabrications Inc............................... G 828 688-3157
  Bakersville *(G-680)*

Peter J Hamann... G 910 484-7877
  Fayetteville *(G-4654)*

Piedmont Weld & Pipe Inc............................ G 704 782-7774
  Concord *(G-3418)*

Powell Welding Inc..................................... G 828 433-0831
  Drexel *(G-3830)*

Precision Fabricators Inc.............................. G 336 835-4763
  Ronda *(G-10897)*

Quillen Welding Services LLC....................... G 252 269-4908
  Morehead City *(G-8840)*

R & H Welding LLC..................................... G 919 763-7955
  Garner *(G-4957)*

R & J Mechanical & Welding LLC............. G 919 362-6630
  Apex *(G-191)*

Relentless Wldg & Fabrication....................... G 336 402-3749
  High Point *(G-6755)*

Richards Wldg Met Fbrction LLC................ F 919 626-0134
  Wendell *(G-12544)*

Rickys Welding Inc..................................... G 252 336-4437
  Shiloh *(G-11394)*

Robert Raper Welding Inc............................ G 252 399-0598
  Wilson *(G-13023)*

Robinsons Welding Service........................... G 336 622-3150
  Liberty *(G-7777)*

Rocas Welding LLC..................................... G 252 290-2233
  Durham *(G-4217)*

Roderick Mch Erectors Wldg Inc............. G 910 343-0381
  Wilmington *(G-12901)*

Rose Welding & Crane Service I............. G 252 796-9171
  Columbia *(G-3296)*

Roxboro Welding.. G 336 364-2307
  Roxboro *(G-10943)*

Royal Welding LLC..................................... G 704 750-9353
  Pineville *(G-9750)*

S Oakley Machine Shop Inc.......................... G 336 599-6105
  Roxboro *(G-10944)*

Southeastern Mch & Wldg Co Inc................ E 910 791-6661
  Wilmington *(G-12925)*

Steel Supply and Erection Co........................ F 336 625-4830
  Asheboro *(G-399)*

Stewarts Garage and Welding Co............. G 336 983-5563
  Tobaccoville *(G-12103)*

Storybook Farm Metal Shop Inc.................... G 919 967-9491
  Chapel Hill *(G-1574)*

Strickland Bros Entps Inc............................. F 252 478-3058
  Spring Hope *(G-11560)*

Thomas Welding Service Inc......................... G 919 471-6852
  Durham *(G-4272)*

Thornburg Machine & Sup Co Inc................. E 704 735-5421
  Lincolnton *(G-7864)*

Thurman Toler... G 252 758-4082
  Greenville *(G-6027)*

Tool-Weld LLC.. G 843 986-4931
  Rutherfordton *(G-10995)*

Trefena Welds... G 203 551-1370
  Browns Summit *(G-1006)*

Triplett & Coffey Inc................................... F 828 263-0561
  Boone *(G-947)*

United Technical Services LLC...................... F 980 237-1335
  Charlotte *(G-2963)*

United TI & Stamping Co NC Inc................... D 910 323-8588
  Fayetteville *(G-4687)*

Villabona Iron Works Inc.............................. F 252 522-4005
  Kinston *(G-7434)*

W D Lee & Company.................................. G 704 864-0346
  Gastonia *(G-5163)*

W E Nixons Wldg & Hdwr Inc....................... G 252 221-4348
  Edenton *(G-4373)*

Wallace Welding Inc.................................... F 919 934-2488
  Smithfield *(G-11469)*

Walls Welding.. G 919 201-7544
  Creedmoor *(G-3657)*

Warsaw Welding Service Inc......................... G 910 293-4261
  Warsaw *(G-12368)*

Waste Container Repair Svcs........................ G 910 257-4474
  Fayetteville *(G-4696)*

Webb S Maint & Piping Inc........................... F 252 972-2616
  Battleboro *(G-709)*

Welding Company....................................... G 336 667-0265
  Wilkesboro *(G-12662)*

Welding Shop LLC...................................... F 252 982-6567
  Wanchese *(G-12348)*

Welding Solutions LLC................................ E 828 665-4363
  Fletcher *(G-4778)*

Welding Spc & Mech Svcs Inc....................... G 919 662-7898
  Garner *(G-4973)*

Wells Mechanical Services LLC..................... G 252 532-2632
  Roanoke Rapids *(G-10743)*

West Stanly Fabrication Inc.......................... G 704 254-2967
  Oakboro *(G-9585)*

Wilkes Welding and Mch Co Inc.................... G 336 670-2742
  Mc Grady *(G-8217)*

Wilson Mold & Machine Corp........................ D 252 243-1831
  Wilson *(G-13049)*

Youngs Welding & Machine Svcs.............. G 910 488-1190
  Fayetteville *(G-4702)*

Zickgraf Enterprises Inc............................... G 828 524-2313
  Franklin *(G-4844)*

WELDING SPLYS, EXC GASES: Wholesalers

A R Perry Corporation................................. G 252 492-6181
  Henderson *(G-6146)*

Airgas Usa LLC... G 704 394-1420
  Charlotte *(G-1633)*

Airgas Usa LLC... G 919 544-3773
  Durham *(G-3885)*

Airgas Usa LLC... G 919 735-5276
  Goldsboro *(G-5196)*

WELDING TIPS: Heat Resistant, Metal

Babco Inc.. G 888 376-5083
  Ayden *(G-653)*

WHEELCHAIR LIFTS

Meghan Blake Industries Inc........................ E 704 462-2988
  Vale *(G-12209)*

Specialty Trnsp Systems Inc......................... G 828 464-9738
  Newton *(G-9498)*

Tk Elevator Corporation............................... D 336 272-4563
  Greensboro *(G-5867)*

Veon Inc.. F 252 623-2102
  Washington *(G-12418)*

WHEELCHAIRS

All 4 U Home Medical LLC..................... G 828 437-0684
Morganton *(G-8849)*

Ms Whlchair N CA AM State Coor.......... G 828 230-1129
Weaverville *(G-12497)*

The Wheelchair Place LLC..................... G 828 855-9099
Hickory *(G-6466)*

WHEELS & PARTS

Goodyear Tire & Rubber Company........ G 919 552-9340
Holly Springs *(G-6903)*

WHEELS: Disc, Wheelbarrow, Stroller, Etc, Stamped Metal

Oro Manufacturing Company................. E 704 283-2186
Monroe *(G-8539)*

WHIRLPOOL BATHS: Hydrotherapy

Royal Baths Manufacturing Co.............. E 704 837-1701
Charlotte *(G-2733)*

WINCHES

Ingersoll-Rand Indus US Inc................. D 704 896-4000
Davidson *(G-3710)*

WINDINGS: Coil, Electronic

Electronic Products Design Inc.............. G 919 365-9199
Wendell *(G-12535)*

Kwik Elc Mtr Sls & Svc Inc.................... G 252 335-2524
Elizabeth City *(G-4395)*

WINDMILLS: Electric Power Generation

Peak Clean Energy LLC........................ G 303 588-2789
Huntersville *(G-7031)*

WINDOW & DOOR FRAMES

Atrium Extrusion Systems Inc............... F 336 764-6400
Welcome *(G-12510)*

WINDOW CLEANING SVCS

W G of Southwest Raleigh Inc.............. G 919 629-7327
Holly Springs *(G-6919)*

WINDOW FRAMES, MOLDING & TRIM: Vinyl

Beacon Roofing Supply Inc................... G 704 886-1555
Charlotte *(G-1763)*

Clt 2016 Inc... D 704 886-1555
Charlotte *(G-1933)*

Jeld-Wen Inc.. C 336 838-0292
North Wilkesboro *(G-9536)*

Plastics Family Holdings Inc................. E 704 597-8555
Charlotte *(G-2642)*

Ramsey Industries Inc........................... F 704 827-3560
Belmont *(G-763)*

WINDOW SCREENING: Plastic

Carolina Home Exteriors LLC................ F 252 637-6599
New Bern *(G-9350)*

WINDOWS: Frames, Wood

Mw Manufacturers Inc........................... E 919 677-3900
Cary *(G-1404)*

WINDOWS: Wood

Ply Gem Industries Inc......................... D 919 677-3900
Cary *(G-1422)*

WINE & DISTILLED ALCOHOLIC BEVERAGES WHOLESALERS

Aviator Brewing Company Inc............... G 919 601-5497
Holly Springs *(G-6893)*

WIRE

Fishel Steel Company........................... G 336 788-2880
Winston Salem *(G-13169)*

Haynes Wire Company.......................... D 828 692-5791
Mountain Home *(G-9274)*

Lee Spring Company LLC...................... E 336 275-3631
Greensboro *(G-5659)*

Torpedo Specialty Wire Inc................... D 252 977-3900
Rocky Mount *(G-10872)*

WIRE & CABLE: Aluminum

Mark Stoddard...................................... G 910 797-7214
Fayetteville *(G-4634)*

Nkt Inc... G 919 601-1970
Cary *(G-1408)*

Trimantec... E 336 767-1379
Winston Salem *(G-13372)*

WIRE & CABLE: Nonferrous, Aircraft

Ls Cable & System USA Inc................. C 252 824-3553
Tarboro *(G-11932)*

Unitape (usa) Inc.................................. G 828 464-5695
Conover *(G-3568)*

WIRE & CABLE: Nonferrous, Automotive, Exc Ignition Sets

C O Jelliff Corporation.......................... G 828 428-3672
Maiden *(G-8008)*

Draka Transport USA LLC..................... G 828 459-8895
Claremont *(G-3110)*

Kaotic Parts LLC................................... G 919 766-6040
Raleigh *(G-10229)*

WIRE & CABLE: Nonferrous, Building

Abl Electronics Supply Inc................... G 704 784-4225
Concord *(G-3308)*

Essex Group Inc................................... G 704 921-9605
Charlotte *(G-2127)*

WIRE & WIRE PRDTS

American Fabricators............................ G 252 637-2600
New Bern *(G-9332)*

Cavert Wire Company Inc..................... E 800 969-2601
Rural Hall *(G-10956)*

Chatsworth Products Inc....................... C 252 514-2779
New Bern *(G-9354)*

Dradura USA Corp................................ D 252 637-9660
New Bern *(G-9366)*

Essex Group Inc................................... G 704 921-9605
Charlotte *(G-2127)*

Express Wire Services Inc.................... G 704 393-5156
Charlotte *(G-2136)*

Fuller Specialty Company Inc............... G 336 226-3446
Burlington *(G-1092)*

Hemco Wire Products Inc..................... G 336 454-7280
Jamestown *(G-7164)*

I & I Sling Inc....................................... G 336 323-1532
Greensboro *(G-5611)*

Ica Mid-Atlantic Inc.............................. G 336 447-4546
Whitsett *(G-12610)*

Leggett & Platt Incorporated................ D 336 889-2600
High Point *(G-6692)*

M-B Industries Inc................................ C 828 862-4201
Rosman *(G-10913)*

McIntyre Manufacturing Group Inc........ D 336 476-3646
Thomasville *(G-12046)*

McJast Inc.. F 828 884-4809
Pisgah Forest *(G-9771)*

Merchants Metals LLC.......................... G 919 598-8471
Raleigh *(G-10290)*

Merchants Metals LLC.......................... C 704 878-8706
Statesville *(G-11731)*

Preformed Line Products Co................. C 704 983-6161
Albemarle *(G-84)*

Prysmian Cbles Systems USA LLC...... E 828 322-9473
Hickory *(G-6421)*

Rack Works Inc..................................... E 336 368-1302
Pilot Mountain *(G-9673)*

Rolf Koerner LLC.................................. G 704 714-8866
Charlotte *(G-2732)*

Royal Wire Products Inc....................... E 704 596-2110
Charlotte *(G-2736)*

Sid Jenkins Inc..................................... G 336 632-0707
Greensboro *(G-5811)*

Unified Scrning Crshing - NC I.............. G 336 824-2151
Ramseur *(G-10633)*

Wieland Electric Inc.............................. F 910 259-5050
Wilmington *(G-12947)*

WIRE FABRIC: Welded Steel

A B Carter Inc....................................... D 704 865-1201
Gastonia *(G-4982)*

Insteel Wire Products Company............ E 336 719-9000
Mount Airy *(G-9132)*

Van Blake Dixon.................................... F 336 282-1861
Greensboro *(G-5896)*

Wireway/Husky Corp............................. C 704 483-1135
Denver *(G-3817)*

WIRE MATERIALS: Copper

Hickory Wire Inc................................... F 828 322-9473
Hickory *(G-6360)*

WIRE MATERIALS: Steel

Coleman Cable LLC.............................. D 828 389-8013
Hayesville *(G-6139)*

Granite Falls Furnaces LLC.................. E 828 324-4394
Granite Falls *(G-5304)*

Southern Steel and Wire Inc................. D 336 548-9611
Madison *(G-8000)*

Williams Industries Inc.......................... C 919 604-1746
Raleigh *(G-10610)*

WIRE PRDTS: Ferrous Or Iron, Made In Wiredrawing Plants

Cavert Wire Company Inc..................... E 800 969-2601
Rural Hall *(G-10956)*

Sandvik Inc.. C 919 563-5008
Mebane *(G-8258)*

WIRE PRDTS: Steel & Iron

Interntonal Specialty Pdts Inc............... G 828 326-9053
Hickory *(G-6371)*

WIRE: Communication

Commscope Inc North Carolina............ A 828 459-5000
Claremont *(G-3094)*

Commscope Inc North Carolina............ E 828 324-2200
Claremont *(G-3096)*

Commscope Technologies LLC............. A 828 324-2200
Claremont *(G-3104)*

Corning Optcal Cmmncations LLC....... A 828 327-5290
Hickory *(G-6312)*

Draka Holdings Usa Inc........................ A 828 383-0020
Claremont *(G-3109)*

Infinite Blue Inc.................................... G 919 744-7704
Raleigh *(G-10194)*

Sumitomo Elc Lightwave Corp.............. D 919 541-8100
Raleigh *(G-10518)*

Superior Essex Intl Inc.......................... C 252 823-5111
Tarboro *(G-11942)*

Employee Codes: A=Over 500 employees, B=251-500
C=101-250, D=51-100, E=20-50, F=10-19, G=1-9

2025 Harris North Carolina
Manufacturers Directory

PRODUCT

1207

WIRE: Mesh

Ashley Sling Inc............................. E 704 347-0071
Charlotte *(G-1704)*

WIRE: Nonferrous

AFL Network Services Inc .... E 704 289-5522
Mint Hill *(G-8329)*

AFL Network Services Inc .... E 919 658-2311
Mount Olive *(G-9246)*

Batt Fabricators Inc................... F 336 431-9334
Trinity *(G-12113)*

Coleman Cable LLC..................... D 828 389-8013
Hayesville *(G-6139)*

Corning Incorporated................. D 704 569-6000
Midland *(G-8284)*

Draka Elevator Products Inc......... C 252 446-8113
Rocky Mount *(G-10831)*

Draka Usa Inc............................ F 828 459-9787
Claremont *(G-3111)*

Frenzelit Inc............................ E 336 814-4317
Lexington *(G-7690)*

Huber + Suhner Inc.................... E 704 790-7300
Charlotte *(G-2295)*

Huber + Suhner North Amer Corp.......... D 704 790-7300
Charlotte *(G-2296)*

Leviton Manufacturing Co Inc .... E 828 584-1611
Morganton *(G-8878)*

Neptco Incorporated.................... C 828 728-5951
Lenoir *(G-7629)*

Ruckus Wireless LLC................... A 503 495-9240
Claremont *(G-3121)*

Superior Essex Inc..................... D 252 823-5111
Tarboro *(G-11941)*

WIRE: Nonferrous, Appliance Fixture

Cordset Designs Inc.................... G 252 568-4001
Pink Hill *(G-9765)*

WOMEN'S & CHILDREN'S CLOTHING WHOLESALERS, NEC

Apparel USA Inc......................... E 212 869-5495
Fairmont *(G-4500)*

Badger Sportswear LLC................ D 704 871-0990
Statesville *(G-11665)*

Burlington Coat Fctry Whse Cor.......... E 919 468-9312
Cary *(G-1317)*

Gerson & Gerson Inc................... E 252 235-2441
Middlesex *(G-8276)*

Raleigh Workshop Inc.................. E 919 917-8969
Raleigh *(G-10431)*

Seafarer LLC............................ G 704 624-3200
Marshville *(G-8094)*

Sorbe Ltd................................ G 704 562-2991
Matthews *(G-8193)*

Walter Reynolds........................ G 704 735-6050
Lincolnton *(G-7870)*

WOMEN'S & GIRLS' SPORTSWEAR WHOLESALERS

Ics North America Corp................ E 704 794-6620
Concord *(G-3375)*

Marketing One Sportswear Inc......... G 704 334-9333
Charlotte *(G-2457)*

WOMEN'S CLOTHING STORES

Live It Boutique LLC................... G 704 492-2402
Charlotte *(G-2427)*

Pine State Corporate AP LLC.......... F 336 789-9437
Mount Airy *(G-9164)*

W E Nixons Wldg & Hdwr Inc.......... G 252 221-4348
Edenton *(G-4373)*

WOMEN'S CLOTHING STORES: Ready-To-Wear

Bon Worth Inc........................... E 800 355-5131
Hendersonville *(G-6190)*

Grace Apparel Company Inc........... G 828 242-8172
Black Mountain *(G-865)*

WOMEN'S FULL & KNEE LENGTH HOSIERY DYEING & FINISHING

Star America Inc........................ C 704 788-4700
Concord *(G-3448)*

WOOD & WOOD BY-PRDTS, WHOLESALE

Decima Corporation LLC................ E 734 516-1535
Charlotte *(G-2025)*

WOOD CHIPS, PRODUCED AT THE MILL

Enviva Pellets Ahoskie LLC........... D 301 657-5560
Ahoskie *(G-49)*

Enviva Pellets Sampson LLC.......... D 301 657-5560
Faison *(G-4516)*

Godfrey Lumber Company Inc......... F 704 872-6366
Statesville *(G-11704)*

Jordan Lumber & Supply Inc.......... G 910 428-9048
Star *(G-11629)*

Keener Wood Products Inc............ G 828 428-1562
Maiden *(G-8015)*

Powell Industries Inc.................. D 828 926-9114
Waynesville *(G-12467)*

Valwood Corporation................... G 828 321-4717
Marble *(G-8028)*

Yildiz Entegre Usa Inc................. G 910 763-4733
Wilmington *(G-12956)*

WOOD PRDTS: Applicators

Alcorns Custom Woodworking Inc.......... G 336 342-0908
Reidsville *(G-10672)*

Fence Quarter LLC...................... G 800 205-0128
Morganton *(G-8864)*

Heartwood Pine Floors Inc............ G 919 542-4394
Moncure *(G-8406)*

National Salvage & Svc Corp.......... D 919 739-5633
Dudley *(G-3838)*

Robert Hamms LLC...................... G 704 605-8057
Monroe *(G-8552)*

WOOD PRDTS: Battery Separators

Daramic LLC.............................. D 704 587-8599
Charlotte *(G-2018)*

WOOD PRDTS: Laundry

C & D Woodworking Inc................ G 336 476-8722
Thomasville *(G-12000)*

Ges Industries.......................... E 252 430-8851
Kittrell *(G-7441)*

WOOD PRDTS: Moldings, Unfinished & Prefinished

Carter Millwork Inc.................... D 800 861-0734
Lexington *(G-7661)*

Ecmd Inc................................. D 336 667-5976
North Wilkesboro *(G-9529)*

Freedom Enterprise LLC................ G 502 510-7296
Charlotte *(G-2177)*

H & H Wood Products Inc............. G 704 233-4148
Wingate *(G-13062)*

H T Jones Lumber Company............ G 252 332-4135
Ahoskie *(G-50)*

Moulding Source Incorporated......... G 704 658-1111
Mooresville *(G-8729)*

Olde Lexington Products Inc.......... G 336 956-2355
Linwood *(G-7880)*

Profilform Us Inc....................... E 252 430-0392
Henderson *(G-6170)*

Robbinsville Cstm Molding Inc........ F 828 479-2317
Robbinsville *(G-10761)*

Smokey Mountain Lumber Inc.......... G 828 298-3958
Asheville *(G-602)*

WOOD PRDTS: Mulch Or Sawdust

Gates Custom Milling Inc.............. E 252 357-0116
Gatesville *(G-5172)*

Martin Lumber & Mulch LLC........... F 252 935-5294
Pantego *(G-9646)*

Mulch Solutions LLC.................... F 704 956-2343
Concord *(G-3407)*

Turn Bull Lumber Company............ E 910 862-4447
Elizabethtown *(G-4436)*

WOOD PRDTS: Mulch, Wood & Bark

A & J Pallets Inc....................... G 336 969-0265
Rural Hall *(G-10951)*

American Soil and Mulch Inc.......... G 919 460-1349
Raleigh *(G-9897)*

Carolina Bark Products LLC........... G 252 589-1324
Seaboard *(G-11270)*

Garick LLC............................... G 704 455-6418
Harrisburg *(G-6109)*

Highland Craftsmen Inc................ F 828 765-9010
Spruce Pine *(G-11577)*

Kamlar Corporation..................... E 252 443-2576
Rocky Mount *(G-10845)*

Mulch Masters of NC Inc.............. G 919 676-0031
Raleigh *(G-10318)*

North Carolina Mulch Inc............. G 252 478-4609
Middlesex *(G-8278)*

Privette Enterprises Inc.............. E 704 634-3291
Monroe *(G-8544)*

Soundside Recycling & Mtls Inc.......... G 252 491-8666
Jarvisburg *(G-7186)*

WOOD PRDTS: Outdoor, Structural

Vida Wood Us Inc....................... G 919 934-9904
Smithfield *(G-11468)*

WOOD PRDTS: Panel Work

Appalachian Lumber Company Inc.......... E 336 973-7205
Wilkesboro *(G-12628)*

Funder America Inc..................... F 336 751-3501
Mocksville *(G-8364)*

WOOD PRDTS: Signboards

Kenneth Moore Signs.................... G 910 458-6428
Wilmington *(G-12826)*

WOOD PRODUCTS: Reconstituted

Arauco North America Inc.............. D 919 542-2128
Moncure *(G-8399)*

Atc Panels Inc.......................... G 919 653-6053
Morrisville *(G-8935)*

Huber Engineered Woods LLC........... E 800 933-9220
Charlotte *(G-2297)*

Industrial Timber LLC................. D 704 919-1215
Hiddenite *(G-6500)*

Industrial Timber LLC................. D 704 919-1215
Charlotte *(G-2326)*

J R Craver & Associates Inc.......... G 336 769-3330
Clemmons *(G-3193)*

Louisiana-Pacific Corporation.............. C 336 599-8080
Roxboro (G-10929)

Uniboard USA LLC.............................. C 919 542-2128
Moncure (G-8411)

Weyerhaeuser Company...................... E 336 835-5100
Elkin (G-4455)

WOOD TREATING: Millwork

Jak Moulding & Supply Inc................ F 252 753-5546
Walstonburg (G-12332)

Ufp Biscoe LLC.................................. F 910 294-8179
Biscoe (G-858)

Ufp Rockwell LLC............................... G 704 279-0744
Rockwell (G-10806)

WOOD TREATING: Structural Lumber & Timber

Albemarle Wood Prsv Plant Inc............ G 704 982-2516
Albemarle (G-60)

Blue Ridge Lbr Log & Timber Co........... G 336 961-5211
Yadkinville (G-13438)

Boise Cascade Wood Pdts LLC............. E 336 598-3001
Roxboro (G-10920)

Carolina Square Inc............................ G 336 793-3222
Mocksville (G-8356)

Hoover Treated Wood Pdts Inc............. E 866 587-8761
Weldon (G-12520)

Soha Holdings LLC............................. E 828 264-2314
Boone (G-942)

Tarheel Wood Treating Company........... F 919 467-9176
Morrisville (G-9063)

Tri-H Molding Co................................ G 252 491-8530
Harbinger (G-6096)

WOODWORK & TRIM: Exterior & Ornamental

Triad Prefinish & Lbr Sls Inc................ G 336 375-4849
Greensboro (G-5877)

WOODWORK & TRIM: Interior & Ornamental

A and H Millwork Inc.......................... F 704 983-2402
Albemarle (G-57)

Bakers Quality Trim Inc...................... G 919 552-3621
Willow Spring (G-12678)

Chadsworth Incorporated.................... G 910 763-7600
Wilmington (G-12742)

Exley Custom Woodwork Inc................ G 910 763-5445
Castle Hayne (G-1498)

Hedrick Construction.......................... G 336 362-3443
Kernersville (G-7278)

Jody Stowe...................................... G 704 519-6560
Matthews (G-8119)

WOODWORK: Interior & Ornamental, NEC

Blumer & Stanton Entps Inc................ G 828 765-2800
Newland (G-9425)

Browns Woodworking LLC................... G 704 983-5917
Albemarle (G-65)

Idaho Wood Inc................................ F 208 263-9521
Oxford (G-9617)

Martin Wood Products Inc................... G 336 548-3470
Madison (G-7993)

Miters Touch Inc............................... G 828 963-4445
Banner Elk (G-688)

Onsite Woodwork Corporation.............. F 704 523-1380
Charlotte (G-2600)

Trimsters Inc.................................... G 919 639-3126
Angier (G-128)

Woodwizards Inc............................... G 336 427-7698
Stokesdale (G-11818)

WOVEN WIRE PRDTS, NEC

Ceramawire...................................... G 252 335-7411
Elizabeth City (G-4381)

Davis Newell Company Inc.................. F 910 762-3500
Wilmington (G-12760)

X-RAY EQPT & TUBES

Digitome Corporation......................... G 860 651-5560
Davidson (G-3703)

Flow X Ray Corporation...................... D 631 242-9729
Battleboro (G-697)

Wolf X-Ray Corporation...................... D 631 242-9729
Battleboro (G-710)

Xinray Systems Inc........................... F 919 701-4100
Chapel Hill (G-1596)

YARN & YARN SPINNING

American & Efird LLC......................... F 704 864-0977
Gastonia (G-4990)

American & Efird LLC......................... F 828 754-9066
Lenoir (G-7571)

Aquafil OMara Inc............................. C 828 874-2100
Rutherford College (G-10970)

Cs Carolina Inc................................ G 336 578-0110
Burlington (G-1078)

Cumins Machinery Corp...................... G 336 622-1000
Liberty (G-7762)

Filtec Precise Inc.............................. E 910 653-5200
Tabor City (G-11911)

Frontier Yarns Inc............................. D 919 776-9940
Sanford (G-11181)

Grateful Union Family Inc................... F 828 622-3258
Asheville (G-510)

Hampton Art Inc............................... C 252 975-7207
Washington (G-12391)

Hickory Dyg & Winding Co Inc............. F 828 322-1550
Hickory (G-6350)

Hickory Throwing Company.................. E 828 322-1158
Hickory (G-6359)

Invista Capital Management LLC........... C 704 636-6000
Salisbury (G-11071)

Krodsa USA Inc................................ G 910 462-2041
Laurel Hill (G-7486)

Marilyn Cook................................... G 704 735-4414
Lincolnton (G-7842)

Milliken & Company........................... F 828 247-4300
Bostic (G-963)

Milliken & Company........................... F 336 548-5680
Mayodan (G-8208)

National Spinning Co Inc.................... C 910 298-3131
Beulaville (G-844)

Normtex Incorporated........................ G 828 428-3363
Wilmington (G-12863)

North Crlina Spnning Mills Inc............. E 704 732-1171
Lincolnton (G-7847)

Oakdale Cotton Mills......................... G 336 454-1144
Jamestown (G-7174)

Parkdale Mills Incorporated................ F 704 825-2529
Belmont (G-760)

Parkdale Mills Incorporated................ E 704 739-7411
Kings Mountain (G-7375)

Parkdale Mills Incorporated................ E 704 855-3164
Landis (G-7475)

Parkdale Mills Incorporated................ E 704 292-1255
Mineral Springs (G-8328)

Parkdale Mills Incorporated................ C 336 476-3181
Thomasville (G-12058)

Parkdale Mills Incorporated................ C 336 591-4644
Walnut Cove (G-12330)

Patrick Yarn Mill Inc......................... C 704 739-4119
Kings Mountain (G-7377)

Richmond Specialty Yarns LLC............ C 910 652-5554
Ellerbe (G-4462)

Sgrtex LLC...................................... D 336 635-9420
Eden (G-4356)

Shuford Yarns LLC............................ D 828 324-4265
Hickory (G-6443)

Shuford Yarns Management Inc............ G 828 324-4265
Hickory (G-6444)

Spinrite Yarns LP.............................. G 252 833-4970
Washington (G-12414)

Supreme Elastic Corporation............... E 828 302-3836
Conover (G-3563)

Unifi Inc... D 336 348-6539
Reidsville (G-10700)

Unifi Inc... C 336 679-3830
Yadkinville (G-13454)

Unifi Manufacturing Inc...................... A 336 427-1515
Yadkinville (G-13455)

World Elastic Corporation................... E 704 786-9508
Concord (G-3469)

Zimmermann - Dynayarn Usa LLC........ E 336 222-8129
Graham (G-5290)

YARN MILLS: Texturizing, Throwing & Twisting

C S America Inc............................... D 336 578-0110
Burlington (G-1058)

Glen Raven Inc................................ F 336 227-6211
Altamahaw (G-103)

Hickory Dyg & Winding Co Inc............. F 828 322-1550
Hickory (G-6350)

Parkdale Mills Incorporated................ F 704 825-2529
Belmont (G-760)

Premiere Fibers LLC.......................... C 704 826-8321
Ansonville (G-131)

Sam M Butler Inc.............................. E 704 364-8647
Charlotte (G-2753)

Sam M Butler Inc.............................. E 910 276-2360
Laurinburg (G-7513)

Sapona Manufacturing Co Inc.............. C 336 873-8700
Asheboro (G-392)

Sapona Manufacturing Co Inc.............. E 336 625-2727
Cedar Falls (G-1515)

YARN WHOLESALERS

Freudenberg Prfmce Mtls LP............... C 828 665-5000
Candler (G-1225)

Normtex Incorporated........................ G 828 428-3363
Wilmington (G-12863)

YARN: Cotton, Spun

Coats & Clark Inc............................. D 888 368-8401
Charlotte (G-1942)

Coats N Amer De Rpblica Dmncan........ C 800 242-8095
Charlotte (G-1945)

Grp Inc... G 919 776-9940
Sanford (G-11187)

Parkdale Mills Incorporated................ E 704 825-5324
Belmont (G-758)

Parkdale Mills Incorporated................ D 704 913-3917
Belmont (G-759)

Parkdale Mills Incorporated................ E 704 822-0778
Mount Holly (G-9241)

Parkdale Mills Incorporated................ D 704 874-5000
Gastonia (G-5117)

Parkdale Mills Inc............................. E 704 857-3456
Landis (G-7476)

Rocky Mount Mill LLC........................ G 919 890-6000
Raleigh (G-10447)

Unifi Inc... G 919 774-7401
Sanford (G-11247)

YARN: Knitting, Spun

Carolina Mills Incorporated.................. D 828 428-9911
Maiden (G-8010)

National Spinning Co Inc.................. C 910 642-4181
Whiteville (G-12589)

Pearson Textiles Inc.................. G 919 776-8730
Sanford (G-11216)

Tuscarora Yarns Inc.................. B 704 436-6527
Mount Pleasant (G-9266)

YARN: Manmade & Synthetic Fiber, Spun

Charles Craft Inc.................. G 910 844-3521
Laurinburg (G-7497)

Coats HP Inc.................. B 704 824-9904
Mc Adenville (G-8213)

Coats HP Inc.................. E 704 329-5800
Charlotte (G-1944)

Fiber-Line LLC.................. D 828 326-8700
Hickory (G-6333)

Glen Raven Inc.................. C 336 227-6211
Burlington (G-1098)

Glen Rven Tchnical Fabrics LLC.......... C 336 229-5576
Burlington (G-1100)

Mannington Mills Inc.................. D 704 824-3551
Mc Adenville (G-8214)

Pharr McAdenville Corporation........... D 704 824-3551
Mc Adenville (G-8215)

Shuford Yarns LLC.................. C 828 396-2342
Granite Falls (G-5323)

Unifi Inc.................. C 336 427-1890
Madison (G-8002)

YARN: Needle & Handicraft, Spun

Summit Yarn LLC.................. G 704 874-5000
Gastonia (G-5146)

YARN: Nylon, Spun Staple

Kordsa Inc.................. C 910 462-2051
Laurel Hill (G-7485)

Unifi Inc.................. D 336 294-4410
Greensboro (G-5887)

Unifi Manufacturing Inc.................. A 336 679-8891
Yadkinville (G-13456)

Unifi Manufacturing Inc.................. C 336 294-4410
Greensboro (G-5888)

YARN: Plastic Coated, Made From Purchased Yarn

Sam M Butler Inc.................. E 910 277-7456
Laurinburg (G-7514)

YARN: Polyester, Spun From Purchased Staple

Parkdale Incorporated.................. D 704 874-5000
Gastonia (G-5116)

Parkdale Mills Incorporated.................. E 336 243-2141
Lexington (G-7729)

Universal Fibers Inc.................. C 336 672-2600
Asheboro (G-415)

YARN: Wool, Spun

National Spinning Co Inc.................. C 336 226-0141
Burlington (G-1135)

National Spinning Co Inc.................. C 252 975-7111
Washington (G-12398)

National Spnning Oprations LLC........... G 252 975-7111
Washington (G-12399)